LexisNexis® Electronic Books for Law Enforcement

Check criminal and traffic laws, research critical case notes, and study for promotion exams anywhere and in any way you want.

TABLET

SMARTPHONE

COMPUTER

BOOKS

After you download your new LexisNexis eBook you can access its content wherever, without the need to find Wi-Fi.

Covering over 40 states, LexisNexis print and eBook publications bring you:

- State Traffic and Criminal Laws
- Supreme Court Decisions
- Legal Guidelines
- Spanish Language Guides
- Case Notes
- Exam Prep Guides

SHOP
www.lexisnexis.com/lawenforcement

CALL
877.861.3389

FREE SAMPLE
lexisnexis.com/ebooks/le

WATCH VIDEO

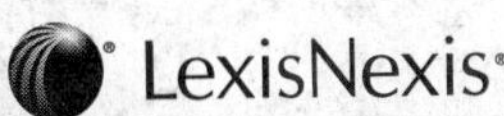

LexisNexis eBooks are available in both epub and mobi formats. The epub file format is compatible for use with e-reader software such as Adobe® Digital Editions and iBooks®, as well as devices like the Apple® iPad®. The mobi file format is compatible for use on Mobipocket e-reader software and devices like the Amazon® Kindle™ and BlackBerry®.

VIRGINIA CRIMINAL AND TRAFFIC LAW MANUAL

2016 EDITION

Prepared by the Editorial Staff of the Publisher

Reprinted from the Code of Virginia of 1950
and the 2016 Supplement

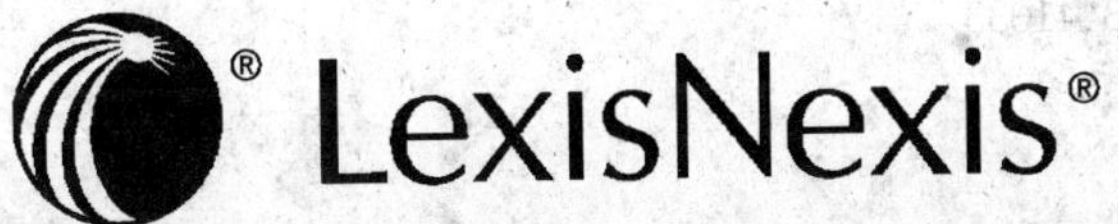

QUESTIONS ABOUT THIS PUBLICATION?

For CUSTOMER SERVICE ASSISTANCE concerning replacement pages, shipments, billing, reprint permission, or other matters,

please contact Customer Support at our self-service portal available 24/7 at *support.lexisnexis.com/print* or call us at 800-833-9844

For EDITORIAL **content questions** concerning this publication,

email: *LEpublications@lexisnexis.com*

For **information on other LEXISNEXIS MATTHEW BENDER publications,**

please call us at 877-461-8801
or visit our online bookstore at *www.lexisnexis.com/bookstore*

ISBN: 978-1-5221-1346-1

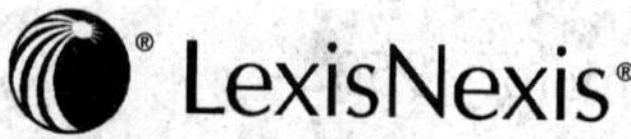

Matthew Bender & Company, Inc.
Editorial Offices
701 E. Water Street
Charlottesville, VA 22902
800-446-3410
www.lexisnexis.com

Product Number 3441033

(Pub. 34410)

Foreword

As publishers of the *Code of Virginia*, we are pleased to offer to the legal and law enforcement community the 2016 Edition of **Virginia Criminal and Traffic Law Manual**. This compilation of selected laws is fully up to date with statutes enacted through the 2016 Regular Session of the General Assembly. In addition to the handy listing of sections affected by recent legislation, this edition carries the "Highlights of the 2016 Virginia Legislative Session," which reflects the major changes in the year for criminal and traffic laws in Virginia; the "Supreme Court on Select Criminal and Traffic Issues" Appendix, which covers over fifty specific topics with multiple case summaries selected from the U.S. Supreme Court Reporter, Lawyer's Edition 2d, current through decisions filed July 12, 2016; and the "Virginia Legal Guidelines," which provides a dynamic overview of Criminal Procedure Law in the Commonwealth and is specifically crafted for the law enforcement officer.

We are committed to providing attorneys and law enforcement professionals with the most comprehensive, current and useful manuals possible. Accordingly, regular revisions of this book are planned, and we publish a host of other publications covering various topics of Virginia law.

We actively solicit your comments and suggestions. If you believe that there are statutes which should be included (or excluded), or if you have suggestions regarding index improvements, please write to us or call us toll-free at 1-800-833-9844; E-mail us at LEpublications@lexisnexis.com; or visit our website at www.lexisnexis.com\lawenforcement\. By providing us with your informed comments, you will be assured of having available a working tool which increases in value each year.

August 2016

Table of Contents

Comparable Sections Table

COMPARABLE SECTIONS OF TITLE 2.1

Former Section	Present Section
2.1-20.1	2.2-2818
2.1-20.1:2	51.1-1300
2.1-38	2.2-100
2.1-51.6	2.2-119
2.1-51.16	2.2-200, 2.2-221
2.1-51.17	2.2-200, 2.2-221, 2.2-222
2.1-51.17:01	2.2-223, 2.2-224
2.1-51.18	2.2-221
2.1-51.18:3	2.2-222
2.1-51.41	2.2-228
2.1-51.43	2.2-228
2.1-116.1	9.1-500
2.1-116.2	9.1-501
2.1-116.3	9.1-503
2.1-116.4	9.1-502
2.1-116.5	9.1-504 A, B, C
2.1-116.6	9.1-505
2.1-116.7	9.1-504 D
2.1-116.8	9.1-506
2.1-116.9	9.1-507
2.1-124	2.2-511
2.1-133.5	9.1-400 A
2.1-133.6	9.1-400 B
2.1-133.7	9.1-402
2.1-133.7:1	9.1-401
2.1-133.8	9.1-403
2.1-133.9	9.1-404
2.1-133.10	9.1-405
2.1-133.11	9.1-406
2.1-377	2.2-3800 A
2.1-378	2.2-3800 B, C
2.1-379	2.2-3801
2.1-380	2.2-3803 A, B
2.1-380.1	2.2-3804
2.1-381	2.2-3805
2.1-382	2.2-3806
2.1-383	2.2-3807
2.1-384	2.2-3802
2.1-384.1	2.2-3803 C
2.1-385	2.2-3808
2.1-385.1	2.2-3808.1
2.1-386	2.2-3809
2.1-394	2.2-1504
2.1-394.1	2.2-1505
2.1-394.2	Deleted
2.1-395	2.2-1506
2.1-396	Deleted
2.1-397	Deleted
2.1-402	2.2-1512
2.1-639.1	2.2-3100
2.1-639.2	2.2-3101
2.1-639.3	2.2-3102
2.1-639.4	2.2-3103
2.1-639.4:1	2.2-3104
2.1-639.4:2	2.2-3104.1
2.1-639.5	2.2-3105
2.1-639.6	2.2-3106
2.1-639.7	2.2-3107
2.1-639.7:1	2.2-3108
2.1-639.8	2.2-3109
2.1-639.9	2.2-3110
2.1-639.10	2.2-3111
2.1-639.11	2.2-3112
2.1-639.12	2.2-3113
2.1-639.13	2.2-3114
2.1-639.14	2.2-3115
2.1-639.14:1	2.2-3116
2.1-639.15	2.2-3117
2.1-639.15:1	2.2-3118
2.1-639.16	2.2-3119
2.1-639.17	2.2-3120
2.1-639.18	2.2-3121
2.1-639.19	2.2-3122
2.1-639.20	2.2-3123
2.1-639.21	2.2-3124
2.1-639.22	2.2-3125
2.1-639.23	2.2-3126
2.1-639.24	2.2-3127

COMPARABLE SECTIONS OF TITLE 3.1

Former Section	Present Section
3.1-796.66	3.2-5900, 3.2-6500
3.1-796.67	3.2-6501
3.1-796.67:1	3.2-5904
3.1-796.67:2	3.2-6502
3.1-796.68	3.2-6503
3.1-796.69	3.2-6508
3.1-796.70	3.2-6510
3.1-796.71	3.2-6511
3.1-796.72	3.2-6509
3.1-796.73	3.2-6504
3.1-796.74	3.2-6506
3.1-796.75	3.2-6520
3.1-796.76	3.2-6507
3.1-796.77	3.2-6505
3.1-796.78	3.2-6512
3.1-796.79	3.2-6513
3.1-796.80	3.2-6514
3.1-796.81	3.2-6515
3.1-796.82	3.2-6516
3.1-796.83	3.2-6517
3.1-796.83:1	3.2-6518
3.1-796.83:2	3.2-6519
3.1-796.84	3.2-6537
3.1-796.85	3.2-6524
3.1-796.86	3.2-6527
3.1-796.87	3.2-6528
3.1-796.87:1	3.2-6529
3.1-796.88	3.2-6530
3.1-796.89	3.2-6533
3.1-796.90	3.2-6526
3.1-796.91	3.2-6532
3.1-796.92	3.2-6531
3.1-796.93	3.2-6538
3.1-796.93:1	3.2-6540
3.1-796.93:2	3.2-6541
3.1-796.93:3	3.2-6542
3.1-796.94	3.2-6543
3.1-796.94:1	3.2-6544
3.1-796.94:2	3.2-6545
3.1-796.95	3.2-6539
3.1-796.96	3.2-6546
3.1-796.96:1	3.2-6547
3.1-796.96:2	3.2-6548
3.1-796.96:3, 3.1-796.96:4	Repealed
3.1-796.96:5	3.2-6549
3.1-796.96:6	3.2-6550
3.1-796.96:7	3.2-6551
3.1-796.97	3.2-6521 B, 3.2-6526 B
3.1-796.97:1	3.2-6521 A
3.1-796.98	3.2-6522
3.1-796.99	3.2-6523
3.1-796.100	3.2-6525
3.1-796.101	3.2-6434
3.1-796.102	3.2-6435
3.1-796.103	3.2-6436
3.1-796.104	3.2-6555
3.1-796.104:1	3.2-6556
3.1-796.105	3.2-6557
3.1-796.106	3.2-6558
3.1-796.106:1	3.2-6561
3.1-796.106:2	3.2-6559
3.1-796.107	3.2-6564
3.1-796.108	3.2-6565
3.1-796.109	Repealed
3.1-796.110	3.2-6560
3.1-796.111	3.2-6566
3.1-796.112	3.2-6567
3.1-796.113	3.2-6568
3.1-796.114	3.2-6563
3.1-796.115	3.2-6569
3.1-796.116	3.2-6552
3.1-796.117	Repealed

Former Section	Present Section
3.1-796.118	3.2-6553
3.1-796.119	3.2-6562
3.1-796.120	Deleted
3.1-796.121	3.2-6554
3.1-796.122	3.2-6570
3.1-796.123	Repealed
3.1-796.124	3.2-6571
3.1-796.125	3.2-6572
3.1-796.126	3.2-6573
3.1-796.126:1	3.2-6574
3.1-796.126:2	3.2-6575
3.1-796.126:3	3.2-6576
3.1-796.126:4	3.2-6577
3.1-796.126:5	3.2-6578
3.1-796.126:6	3.2-6579
3.1-796.126:7	3.2-6580
3.1-796.126:8	3.2-6581
3.1-796.126:9	3.2-6582
3.1-796.126:10	3.2-6583
3.1-796.126:11	3.2-6584
3.1-796.127	3.2-6585
3.1-796.127:1	3.2-6586
3.1-796.128	3.2-6587
3.1-796.128.1	3.2-6588
3.1-796.128.2	3.2-6589
3.1-796.129	3.2-6590

COMPARABLE SECTIONS OF TITLE 6.1

Former Section	Present Section
6.1-111	6.2-938 6.2-1039
6.1-112	6.2-939 6.2-1040
6.1-118.1	17.1-626.1
6.1-119	6.2-940 6.2-1042
6.1-120	6.2-942
6.1-122	6.2-943 6.2-1044 6.2-1062
6.1-123	6.2-944 6.2-1045 6.2-1063
6.1-124	6.2-945
6.1-125	6.2-946 6.2-1046 6.2-1064
6.1-194.93	6.2-1104
6.1-194.94	6.2-1107
6.1-225.62	6.2-1316
6.1-225.64	6.2-1305
6.1-444	6.2-1800
6.1-445	6.2-1801
6.1-468	6.2-1825

COMPARABLE SECTIONS OF TITLE 9

Former Section	Present Section
9-6.14:1	2.2-4000 A
9-6.14:2	Deleted
9-6.14:3	2.2-4000 B
9-6.14:4	2.2-4001
9-6.14:4.1	2.2-4002, 2.2-4005, 2.2-4006, 2.2-4011, 2.2-4018, 2.2-4025
9-6.14:5	2.2-4003
9-6.14:5.1	2.2-4004
9-6.14:7.1	2.2-4007
9-6.14:7.2	2.2-4008
9-6.14:8	2.2-4009
9-6.14:8.1	2.2-4010
9-6.14:9	2.2-4011 B, 2.2-4012
9-6.14:9.1	2.2-4013
9-6.14:9.2	2.2-4014
9-6.14:9.3	2.2-4015
9-6.14:9.4	2.2-4016
9-6.14:11	2.2-4019, 2.2-4021
9-6.14:12	2.2-4020, 2.2-4021
9-6.14:13	2.2-4022
9-6.14:14	2.2-4023
9-6.14:14.1	2.2-4024
9-6.14:15	2.2-4025
9-6.14:16	2.2-4025 C, 2.2-4026
9-6.14:17	2.2-4027
9-6.14:18	2.2-4028
9-6.14:19	2.2-4029
9-6.14:21	2.2-4030
9-6.14:22	2.2-4031
9-6.14:23	2.2-4032
9-6.14:24	2.2-4033
9-6.14:25	2.2-4017
9-183.1	9.1-138
9-183.2	9.1-140
9-183.3	9.1-139
9-183.4	9.1-142
9-183.5	9.1-143
9-183.6	9.1-144
9-183.7	9.1-145
9-183.8	9.1-146
9-183.9	9.1-149
9-183.10	9.1-148
9-183.11	9.1-147
9-183.12	9.1-150

COMPARABLE SECTIONS OF TITLE 23

Former Section	Present Section
23-9.2:4	23.1-602
23-9.2:15	23.1-806
23-9.2:16	23.1-807
23-9.2:17	23.1-808
23-50.16:4	23.1-2400
23-232	23.1-809
23-232.1	23.1-810
23-232.2	23.1-817
23-233	23.1-812
23-233.1	23.1-811
23-234	23.1-815
23-234.1	23.1-816
23-235	23.1-813
23-236	23.1-812
23-237	23.1-814
23-238	23.1-818

COMPARABLE SECTIONS OF TITLE 33.1

Former Section	Present Section
33.1-46.2	33.2-501
33.1-193	33.2-238
33.1-218	33.2-246
33.1-223.2:7	33.2-267
33.1-344	33.2-800
33.1-345	33.2-801

Former Section	Present Section
33.1-346	33.2-802
33.1-346.1	Repealed
33.1-347	33.2-803
33.1-379	33.2-1231
33.1-380	33.2-1232
33.1-381	33.2-1233

COMPARABLE SECTIONS OF TITLE 37.1

Former Section	Present Section
37.1-63	37.2-800
37.1-67.01	37.2-808
37.1-67.1	37.2-809 through 37.2-813
37.1-67.3	37.2-814 through 37.2-819
37.1-67.4	37.2-809, 37.2-820
37.1-67.5	37.2-802
37.1-67.5:01	37.2-802
37.1-67.6	37.2-821
37.1-70.1	37.2-900
37.1-70.2	37.2-901
37.1-70.3	37.2-902
37.1-70.4	37.2-903
37.1-70.5	37.2-904
37.1-70.6	37.2-905
37.1-70.7	37.2-906
37.1-70.8	37.2-907
37.1-70.9	37.2-908
37.1-70.10	37.2-909
37.1-70.11	37.2-910
37.1-70.12	37.2-911
37.1-70.13	37.2-912
37.1-70.14	37.2-913
37.1-70.15	37.2-914
37.1-70.16	37.2-915
37.1-70.17	37.2-916
37.1-70.18	37.2-917
37.1-70.19	37.2-918
37.1-71	37.2-829
37.1-72	37.2-830
37.1-73	37.2-831
37.1-74	37.2-832
37.1-75	37.2-833
37.1-76	37.2-834
37.1-77	37.2-835
37.1-78	37.2-836
37.1-103	37.2-844
37.1-104	37.2-845
37.1-104.1	37.2-846
37.1-104.2	37.2-847
37.1-148	37.2-426
37.1-150	37.2-427
37.1-151	37.2-428
37.1-152	37.2-429
37.1-153	37.2-430
37.1-154	37.2-431
37.1-155	DELETED
37.1-184	37.2-413
37.1-189	37.2-422

COMPARABLE SECTIONS OF TITLE 46.2, CHAPTER 19 TO TITLE 46.2, CHAPTER 15, ARTICLE 7.2

Former Section	Present Section
46.2-1973	46.2-1573.2
46.2-1974	46.2-1573.3
46.2-1975	46.2-1573.4
46.2-1976	46.2-1573.5
46.2-1977	46.2-1573.6
46.2-1978	46.2-1573.7
46.2-1979	46.2-1573.8
46.2-1980	46.2-1573.9
46.2-1981	46.2-1573.10
46.2-1982	46.2-1573.11
46.2-1983	46.2-1573.12

COMPARABLE SECTIONS OF TITLE 46.2, CHAPTER 19.1 TO TITLE 46.2, CHAPTER 15, ARTICLE 7.3

Former Section	Present Section
46.2-1992.66	46.2-1573.14
46.2-1992.67	46.2-1573.15
46.2-1992.68	46.2-1573.16
46.2-1992.69	46.2-1573.17
46.2-1992.70	46.2-1573.18
46.2-1992.71	46.2-1573.19
46.2-1992.72	46.2-1573.20
46.2-1992.73	46.2-1573.21
46.2-1992.74	46.2-1573.22
46.2-1992.75	46.2-1573.23
46.2-1992.76	46.2-1573.24

COMPARABLE SECTIONS OF TITLE 46.2 CHAPTER 19.2 TO TITLE 46.2, CHAPTER 15, ARTICLE 7.4

Former Section	Present Section
46.2-1993.64	46.2-1573.25.
46.2-1993.65	46.2-1573.26
46.2-1993.66	46.2-1573.27
46.2-1993.67	46.2-1573.28
46.2-1993.67:1	46.2-1573.29
46.2-1993.67:2	46.2-1573.30
46.2-1993.68	46.2-1573.31
46.2-1993.69	46.2-1573.32
46.2-1993.70	46.2-1573.33
46.2-1993.71	46.2-1573.34
46.2-1993.72	46.2-1573.35
46.2-1993.73	46.2-1573.36
46.2-1993.74	46.2-1573.37

COMPARABLE SECTIONS OF TITLE 63.1

Former Section	Present Section
63.1-171.3	46.2-932.1
63.1-248.1	63.2-1500
63.1-248.2	63.2-100
63.1-248.2	63.2-1501
63.1-248.2	63.2-1508
63.1-248.2:1	63.2-1504
63.1-248.3	63.2-1509
63.1-248.4	63.2-1510
63.1-248.4:1	63.2-1511
63.1-248.5	63.2-1512
63.1-248.5:1	63.2-1514
63.1-248.5:1.01	63.2-1513
63.1-248.6	63.2-1503
63.1-248.6:01	63.2-1505
63.1-248.6:02	63.2-1506
63.1-248.6:1	63.2-1526
63.1-248.6:2	63.2-1516
63.1-248.7	63.2-1502
63.1-248.7:1	63.2-1527
63.1-248.7:2	63.2-1726
63.1-248.8	63.2-1515

Former Section	Present Section	Former Section	Present Section	Former Section	Present Section
63.1-248.9	63.2-1517	63.1-248.13:1	63.2-1521	63.1-248.15	63.2-1525
63.1-248.10	63.2-1518	63.1-248.13:2	63.2-1522	63.1-248.16	63.2-1528
63.1-248.11	63.2-1519	63.1-248.13:3	63.2-1523	63.1-248.17	63.2-1507
63.1-248.13	63.2-1520	63.1-248.14	63.2-1524	63.1-248.19	63.2-1529

Sections Affected by 2016 Legislation

Code of Va. Section	Action	Chapter No.	Bill No.	Sec. No.
2.2-309	Amended	628	SB 294	1
3.2-6504.1	Enacted	679	SB 9	1
3.2-6549	Amended	678	HB 476	1
3.2-6552	Amended	757	HB 1231	1
3.2-6556	Amended	60	SB 651	1
3.2-6556	Amended	172	HB 1211	1
3.2-6557	Amended	678	HB 476	1
4.1-100	Amended	324	HB 562	1
4.1-100	Amended	710	HB 879	1
4.1-201	Amended	26	HB 706	1
8.01-225	Amended	144	HB 314	1
9.1-139	Amended	561	HB 434	1
9.1-400	Amended	677	HB 1345	1
9.1-400.1	Enacted	677	HB 1345	1
9.1-401	Amended	677	HB 1345	1
9.1-402	Amended	677	HB 1345	1
9.1-402.1	Amended	677	HB 1345	1
9.1-403	Amended	677	HB 1345	1
9.1-404	Amended	677	HB 1345	1
9.1-405	Amended	677	HB 1345	1
9.1-406	Repealed	677	HB 1345	2
9.1-407	Amended	677	HB 1345	1
9.1-902	Amended	586	HB 177	1
9.1-913	Amended	335	HB 628	1
9.1-914	Amended	424	HB 1101	1
9.1-1301	Amended	481	HB 1015	1
15.2-836.1	Enacted	498	HB 118	1
15.2-1716.1	Amended	213	SB 527	1
16.1-228	Amended	631	HB 600	1
16.1-247	Amended	626	SB 454	1
16.1-253.2	Amended	583	HB 610	1
16.1-253.2	Amended	585	HB 1087	1
16.1-253.2	Amended	638	SB 323	1
16.1-253.4	Amended	455	HB 588	1
16.1-260	Amended	704	SB 417	1
16.1-262	Amended	626	SB 454	1
16.1-263	Amended	626	SB 454	1
16.1-266.1	Amended	182	HB 671	1
16.1-266.1	Amended	509	SB 7	1
16.1-274.2	Enacted	726	HB 1213	1
16.1-279.1	Amended	102	HB 1056	1
16.1-284	Amended	626	SB 454	1
16.1-301	Amended	234	HB 541	1
18.2-57	Amended	420	HB 1226	1
18.2-57.3	Amended	422	HB 1334	1
18.2-57.3	Amended	742	HB 485	1
18.2-60.3	Amended	545	SB 339	1
18.2-60.3	Amended	696	HB 886	1
18.2-60.3	Amended	745	HB 752	1
18.2-60.4	Amended	583	HB 610	1
18.2-60.4	Amended	585	HB 1087	1
18.2-60.4	Amended	638	SB 323	1
18.2-132.1	Enacted	373	HB 1329	1
18.2-151.1	Enacted	687	HB 25	1
18.2-177.1	Enacted	236	HB 1319	1
18.2-287.01	Amended	257	SB 479	1
18.2-287.4	Amended	257	SB 479	1
18.2-308	Amended	257	SB 479	1
18.2-308	Amended	589	SB 544	1

Code of Va. Section	Action	Chapter No.	Bill No.	Sec. No.
18.2-308	Amended	672	HB 332	1
18.2-308.09	Amended	48	HB 1391	1
18.2-308.09	Amended	49	SB 49	1
18.2-308.09	Amended	337	HB 784	1
18.2-308.014	Amended	46	SB 610	1
18.2-308.014	Amended	47	HB 1163	1
18.2-308.016	Amended	209	SB 198	1
18.2-308.016	Enacted	257	SB 479	1
18.2-308.016	Amended	421	HB 1281	1
18.2-308.1	Amended	257	SB 479	1
18.2-308.1:4	Amended	48	HB 1391	1
18.2-308.1:4	Amended	49	SB 49	1
18.2-308.2	Amended	337	HB 784	1
18.2-308.2:2	Amended	697	HB 810	1
18.2-308.2:2	Amended	727	HB 206	1
18.2-308.2:3	Amended	48	HB 1391	1
18.2-308.2:3	Amended	49	SB 49	1
18.2-371.1	Amended	705	HB 1189	1
19.2-8	Amended	233	HB 510	1
19.2-8	Amended	253	SB 354	1
19.2-11.5	Enacted	332	SB 291	1
19.2-11.5	Enacted	698	HB 1160	1
19.2-11.6	Enacted	332	SB 291	1
19.2-11.6	Enacted	698	HB 1160	1
19.2-11.7	Enacted	332	SB 291	1
19.2-11.7	Enacted	698	HB 1160	1
19.2-11.8	Enacted	332	SB 291	1
19.2-11.8	Enacted	698	HB 1160	1
19.2-11.9	Enacted	332	SB 291	1
19.2-11.9	Enacted	698	HB 1160	1
19.2-11.10	Enacted	332	SB 291	1
19.2-11.10	Enacted	698	HB 1160	1
19.2-11.11	Enacted	332	SB 291	1
19.2-11.11	Enacted	698	HB 1160	1
19.2-13	Amended	551	SB 296	1
19.2-13.1	Enacted	416	HB 198	1
19.2-70.2	Amended	231	HB 176	1
19.2-70.3	Amended	549	HB 924	1
19.2-70.3	Amended	576	HB 875	1
19.2-70.3	Amended	616	HB 326	1
19.2-72	Amended	204	HB 1275	1
19.2-76.3	Amended	242	HB 1310	1
19.2-76.3	Amended	354	SB 707	1
19.2-124	Amended	621	SB 285	1
19.2-152.8	Amended	455	HB 588	1
19.2-163.04	Amended	164	SB 769	1
19.2-163.04	Amended	312	HB 65	1
19.2-168.1	Amended	445	HB 582	1
19.2-169.1	Amended	445	HB 582	1
19.2-169.5	Amended	445	HB 582	1
19.2-169.6	Amended	357	SB 566	1
19.2-169.6	Amended	599	HB 543	1
19.2-169.8	Enacted	446	HB 645	1
19.2-169.8	Enacted	449	SB 342	1
19.2-182	Amended	474	HB 364	1
19.2-215.9	Amended	262	HB 1294	1
19.2-268.3	Enacted	542	SB 358	1
19.2-268.3	Enacted	553	HB 227	1
19.2-303.5	Amended	201	HB 608	1
19.2-306	Amended	718	HB 605	1
19.2-353.5	Amended	282	HB 572	1
19.2-354	Amended	282	HB 572	1
19.2-368.5	Amended	456	HB 667	1
19.2-386.2	Amended	203	HB 771	1

Code of Va. Section	Action	Chapter No.	Bill No.	Sec. No.
19.2-386.2	Amended	423	SB 423	1
19.2-386.2:1	Amended	203	HB 771	1
19.2-386.2:1	Amended	423	SB 423	1
19.2-386.10	Amended	203	HB 771	1
19.2-386.10	Amended	423	SB 423	1
19.2-386.10	Amended	664	SB 457	1
19.2-386.14	Amended	203	HB 771	1
19.2-386.14	Amended	423	SB 423	1
19.2-389	Amended	454	HB 896	1
19.2-389	Amended	554	HB 1013	1
19.2-389	Amended	574	HB 536	1
19.2-389.1	Amended	554	HB 1013	1
19.2-392.2	Amended	617	HB 1149	1
22.1-176.1	Amended	57	SB 250	1
22.1-176.1	Amended	145	HB 353	1
22.1-277.07	Amended	257	SB 479	1
23-9.2:16	Amended	481	HB 1015	1
23-234	Amended	513	HB 1321	1
23-234	Amended	571	SB 83	1
23.1-602	Enacted	588	HB 209	1
23.1-806	Enacted	588	HB 209	1
23.1-807	Amended	481	HB 1015	1
23.1-807	Enacted	588	HB 209	1
23.1-808	Enacted	588	HB 209	1
23.1-809	Enacted	588	HB 209	1
23.1-810	Enacted	588	HB 209	1
23.1-811	Enacted	588	HB 209	1
23.1-812	Enacted	588	HB 209	1
23.1-813	Enacted	588	HB 209	1
23.1-814	Enacted	588	HB 209	1
23.1-815	Amended	513	HB 1321	1
23.1-815	Amended	571	SB 83	1
23.1-815	Enacted	588	HB 209	1
23.1-816	Enacted	588	HB 209	1
23.1-817	Enacted	588	HB 209	1
23.1-818	Enacted	588	HB 209	1
23.1-2400	Enacted	588	HB 209	1
29.1-301	Amended	63	SB 349	1
29.1-519	Amended	486	HB 1142	1
29.1-521	Amended	10	SB 344	1
29.1-521	Amended	62	SB 152	1
29.1-521	Amended	121	HB 262	1
29.1-521	Amended	372	HB 1311	1
29.1-527.2	Enacted	376	HB 584	1
29.1-528	Amended	64	SB 367	1
29.1-576.1	Enacted	540	HB 1115	1
33.2-500	Amended	753	HB 1069	1
33.2-501	Amended	699	HB 407	1
33.2-501	Amended	715	HB 715	1
33.2-503	Amended	753	HB 1069	1
33.2-504	Amended	753	HB 1069	1
37.2-809	Amended	569	HB 1110	1
37.2-809	Amended	693	SB 567	1
37.2-817	Amended	688	HB 616	1
37.2-837	Amended	688	HB 616	1
37.2-838	Amended	688	HB 616	1
43-32	Amended	397	HB 940	1
43-33	Amended	397	HB 940	1
43-34	Amended	397	HB 940	1
46.2-100	Amended	428	HB 869	1
46.2-100	Amended	500	SB 464	1
46.2-100	Amended	764	SB 375	1
46.2-205.2	Amended	368	HB 417	1
46.2-208	Amended	753	HB 1069	1

Code of Va. Section	Action	Chapter No.	Bill No.	Sec. No.
46.2-214	Amended	368	HB 417	1
46.2-214.4	Enacted	368	HB 417	1
46.2-320.1	Amended	29	HB 1026	1
46.2-323	Amended	488	SB 555	1
46.2-324.1	Amended	488	SB 555	1
46.2-325	Amended	381	HB 1287	1
46.2-328	Amended	368	HB 417	1
46.2-330	Amended	368	HB 417	1
46.2-334	Amended	488	SB 555	1
46.2-334.01	Amended	488	SB 555	1
46.2-335	Amended	488	SB 555	1
46.2-335.2	Amended	488	SB 555	1
46.2-341.4	Amended	429	HB 938	1
46.2-341.14	Amended	429	HB 938	1
46.2-341.14:1	Amended	429	HB 938	1
46.2-341.14:3	Amended	429	HB 938	1
46.2-341.14:9	Amended	429	HB 938	1
46.2-342	Amended	135	SB 176	1
46.2-342	Amended	743	HB 653	1
46.2-345	Amended	135	SB 176	1
46.2-345	Amended	743	HB 653	1
46.2-360	Amended	230	HB 172	1
46.2-391	Amended	230	HB 172	1
46.2-395	Amended	282	HB 572	1
46.2-600	Amended	428	HB 869	1
46.2-644.01	Amended	397	HB 940	1
46.2-644.02	Amended	397	HB 940	1
46.2-644.03	Amended	397	HB 940	1
46.2-649.1:1	Amended	125	HB 374	1
46.2-649.1:1	Amended	133	SB 91	1
46.2-653.1	Amended	349	SB 366	1
46.2-653.1	Amended	393	HB 1203	1
46.2-662	Amended	131	HB 1032	1
46.2-663	Amended	142	SB 658	1
46.2-664	Amended	142	SB 658	1
46.2-665	Amended	142	SB 658	1
46.2-666	Amended	142	SB 658	1
46.2-667	Amended	142	SB 658	1
46.2-668	Amended	142	SB 658	1
46.2-669	Amended	142	SB 658	1
46.2-670	Amended	142	SB 658	1
46.2-670.1	Enacted	379	HB 1269	1
46.2-671	Amended	142	SB 658	1
46.2-672	Amended	142	SB 658	1
46.2-673	Amended	142	SB 658	1
46.2-674	Amended	142	SB 658	1
46.2-675	Amended	142	SB 658	1
46.2-676	Amended	142	SB 658	1
46.2-677	Amended	142	SB 658	1
46.2-678	Amended	142	SB 658	1
46.2-679	Amended	142	SB 658	1
46.2-679.1	Amended	142	SB 658	1
46.2-679.2	Amended	142	SB 658	1
46.2-680	Amended	142	SB 658	1
46.2-707.1	Enacted	590	HB 388	1
46.2-711	Amended	125	HB 374	1
46.2-711	Amended	133	SB 91	1
46.2-725	Amended	143	SB 666	1
46.2-725	Amended	430	HB 1190	1
46.2-726	Amended	143	SB 666	1
46.2-726	Amended	430	HB 1190	1
46.2-750	Amended	302	SB 286	1
46.2-750	Amended	707	HB 454	1
46.2-800.3	Enacted	249	SB 163	1

Code of Va. Section	Action	Chapter No.	Bill No.	Sec. No.
46.2-810.1	Enacted	515	HB 1348	1
46.2-818.1	Enacted	607	SB 117	1
46.2-819	Amended	753	HB 1069	1
46.2-819.1	Amended	753	HB 1069	1
46.2-819.3	Amended	753	HB 1069	1
46.2-819.3:1	Amended	753	HB 1069	1
46.2-819.6	Amended	753	HB 1069	1
46.2-819.7	Repealed	753	HB 1069	3
46.2-819.8	Enacted	753	HB 1069	1
46.2-819.9	Enacted	753	HB 1069	1
46.2-819.10	Enacted	753	HB 1069	1
46.2-844	Amended	637	SB 120	1
46.2-844	Amended	700	HB 168	1
46.2-1005.1	Enacted	701	HB 939	1
46.2-1025	Amended	198	HB 329	1
46.2-1025	Amended	226	SB 299	1
46.2-1030	Amended	195	HB 10	1
46.2-1030	Amended	206	SB 25	1
46.2-1077	Amended	302	SB 286	1
46.2-1077	Amended	707	HB 454	1
46.2-1112	Amended	122	HB 267	1
46.2-1149.8	Enacted	115	HB 117	1
46.2-1149.8	Enacted	533	SB 719	1
46.2-1158.01	Amended	128	HB 507	1
46.2-1158.01	Amended	702	HB 213	1
46.2-1188	Amended	380	HB 1276	1
46.2-1219.2	Amended	708	HB 730	1
46.2-1233	Amended	476	HB 1060	1
46.2-1569	Amended	432	HB 1232	1
46.2-1569	Amended	534	SB 709	1
46.2-1571	Amended	432	HB 1232	1
46.2-1571	Amended	534	SB 709	1
46.2-1572.1	Amended	427	HB 747	1
46.2-1572.4	Amended	432	HB 1232	1
46.2-1572.4	Amended	534	SB 709	1
46.2-1700	Amended	437	HB 748	1
46.2-1701	Amended	437	HB 748	1
46.2-1701.4	Enacted	437	HB 748	1
46.2-1702	Amended	437	HB 748	1
46.2-2099.41	Amended	431	HB 1229	1
46.2-2099.42	Amended	431	HB 1229	1
51.5-44.1	Enacted	575	SB 363	1
52-25.1	Amended	214	SB 608	1
52-28.2	Enacted	333	HB 301	1
53.1-234	Amended	747	HB 815	1
54.1-3303	Amended	86	HB 498	1
54.1-3401	Amended	221	HB 528	1
54.1-3401	Amended	495	SB 463	1
54.1-3401.1	Repealed	221	HB 528	2
54.1-3408	Amended	144	HB 314	1
54.1-3410.2	Amended	221	HB 528	1
54.1-3411.2	Enacted	95	HB 629	1
54.1-3446	Amended	103	HB 1077	1
54.1-3446	Amended	112	SB 480	1
54.1-3452	Amended	499	HB 1292	1
54.1-3466	Amended	229	HB 170	1
54.1-4201.2	Enacted	44	SB 715	1
54.1-4201.2	Enacted	45	HB 1386	1
58.1-2259	Amended	34	HB 23	1
58.1-2290.1	Repealed	305	SB 372	2
58.1-4014	Amended	461	HB 1291	1
59.1-148.3	Amended	196	HB 51	1
59.1-148.3	Amended	210	SB 205	1
59.1-148.3	Amended	215	SB 615	1

Code of Va. Section	Action	Chapter No.	Bill No.	Sec. No.
63.2-100	Amended	631	HB 600	1
63.2-1502	Amended	631	HB 600	1
63.2-1515	Amended	454	HB 896	1
63.2-1726	Amended	580	HB 920	1

HIGHLIGHTS OF THE 2016 VIRGINIA LEGISLATIVE SESSION

ASSAULT & BATTERY

Law-Enforcement Officers

For assault and battery purposes, an employee of the Department of Corrections who has been designated by the Department to conduct internal investigations is a "law-enforcement officer." [§ 18.2-57]

CRIMINAL PROCEDURE

Bail

A district court must stay the imposition of its order granting bail in cases where there was a presumption against bail if the court receives notice that the Commonwealth is going to appeal the court's decision to the circuit court. The stay is limited to 5 days but can be waived if the defendant requests a hearing outside the 5 days. [§ 19.2-124]

Search & Seizure

An application for an ex parte order authorizing the installation and use of a pen register or trap and trace device may be filed in the jurisdiction where the ongoing criminal investigation is being conducted; where there is probable cause to believe that an offense was committed, is being committed, or will be committed; or where the person or persons who subscribe to the wire or electronic communication system live, work, or maintain an address or a post office box. [§ 19.2-70.2]

Summons

A summons for failure to appear on a mailed summons may be served by any person authorized to serve process. [§ 19.2-76.3]

DOMESTIC VIOLENCE

Prosecution

A person charged with first offense of assault and battery against a family or household member may have judgment deferred and be placed on local community-based probation. Upon completion, the proceeding may be dismissed. [§ 18.2-57.3]

Protective Orders

It is a Class 6 felony to stalk a party protected by a protective order or to commit an assault and battery resulting in any bodily injury upon a party protected by a protective order.
Any person who violates a protective order with which he has been served while knowingly armed with a firearm or other deadly weapon is guilty of a Class 6 felony. [§ 18.2-60.4]

It is a Class 6 felony for a person who is subject to a permanent protective order (i.e., a protective order with a maximum duration of 2 years) for family abuse to possess a firearm while the order is in effect. Such person may continue to possess and transport a firearm for 24 hours after being served with the order for the purposes of selling or transferring the firearm to another person. [§ 18.2-308.1:4]

An emergency protective order may prohibit the respondent from being in the physical presence of the petitioner or the petitioner's family or household members. "Physical presence" includes (i) intentionally maintaining direct visual contact with the petitioner or (ii) unreasonably being within 100 feet of the petitioner's residence or place of employment. [§ 19.2-152.8]

DRUGS

Paraphernalia

Possession or distribution of controlled paraphernalia is a Class 1 misdemeanor. [§ 54.1-3466]

FIREARMS

Judges

A judge or justice of the Commonwealth may carry a concealed handgun throughout the Commonwealth without a permit. [§ 18.2-308]

Possession

An individual who was adjudicated delinquent when 14 or older of a delinquent act that would be a felony if committed by an adult and has completed a term of enlistment of no less than 2 years in the U.S. Armed Forces and received an honorable discharge is not disqualified from obtaining a concealed handgun permit and may possess or transport any firearm or ammunition for a firearm, any stun weapon, or any explosive material. [§§ 18.2-308.09, 18.2-308.2]

The holder of an out-of-state concealed handgun permit who is at least 21 is authorized to carry a concealed handgun in Virginia if:

- the other state has a 24-hour-a-day means of verification of the validity of the permits issued in that state, if available;
- the person carries a government-issued photo identification and displays it upon demand of a law-enforcement officer; and
- the person has not previously had a Virginia concealed handgun permit revoked. [§ 18.2-308.014]

Stolen Firearms

Whenever a firearm is identified as stolen, the law-enforcement agency shall return such firearm to the rightful owner thereof, if known, provided the owner is not prohibited from possessing the firearm and the agency does not need to retain the firearm as evidence in a criminal prosecution. [§ 52-25.1]

FISH & GAME

Hunting on Sunday

Any person who hunts Rallidae, the family of birds that includes rails and other wetland birds, is exempt from the prohibition on hunting on Sunday. [§ 29.1-521]

FRAUD

Fraudulent Use of Hearing or Service Dog

Any person who knowingly and willfully fits a dog with a harness, collar, vest, sign, or identification card commonly used by a person with a disability in order to represent that the dog is a service dog or hearing dog to fraudulently gain public access for such dog in a public place is guilty of a Class 4 misdemeanor. [§ 51.5-44.1]

GAMBLING

Lottery

It is a Class 1 misdemeanor to operate a ticket courier service in the Commonwealth, i.e. a service operated for the purpose of purchasing Virginia Lottery tickets on behalf of individuals located within or outside the Commonwealth and delivering or transmitting such tickets, or electronic images thereof, to such individuals as a business-for-profit delivery service. [§ 58.1-4014]

RULES OF THE ROAD

Equipment

Motor vehicles may be equipped with visual displays of moving images if the equipment is factory-installed and has an interlock device that disables the equipment when the motor vehicle operator is performing a "driving task," i.e. a real-time function required to operate a vehicle in on-road traffic, excluding the selection of destinations and waypoints, and including steering, turning, lane keeping and lane changing, accelerating, and decelerating. [§ 46.2-1077]

Flooded Areas

The governing body of any locality may by ordinance prohibit any person from operating a motor vehicle or watercraft on a flooded highway, street, alley, or parking lot, regardless of whether such highway, street, alley, or parking lot is publicly or privately owned in such a manner as to increase the level of floodwaters to a level that causes or could reasonably be expected to cause damage to any real or personal property. Such ordinance shall not apply to any law-enforcement officer, firefighter, or emergency medical services personnel engaged in the performance of his duties nor to the operator of any vehicle owned or controlled by the Department of Transportation or a public utility company. Violation of such ordinance is a Class 4 misdemeanor. [§ 46.2-800.3]

Motorcycles

Motorcycles may be equipped with and use not more than five approved lights in order to provide general illumination ahead of the motorcycle. [§ 46.2-1030]

Opening Car Door

No operator shall open the door of a parked motor vehicle on the side adjacent to moving vehicular traffic unless it is reasonably safe to do so. Violation is a traffic infraction punishable by a fine up to $50. [§ 46.2-818.1]

Registration

A locality may impose a penalty of up to $250 upon the resident owner of a motor vehicle annually for as long as the motor vehicle remains unregistered in Virginia. [§ 46.2-662]

School Buses

A locality that has authorized by ordinance the installation and operation of a video-monitoring system on school buses for recording violations of unlawfully passing a stopped school bus may execute a summons for such violation by mailing a copy of the summons to the owner of a vehicle that unlawfully passed a stopped school bus. The summoned person has 30 business days from the mailing of the summons to inspect information collected by a video-monitoring system in connection with the violation. [§ 46.2-844]

Smoking

Any person who smokes in a motor vehicle, whether in motion or at rest, when a minor under the age of 8 is in the vehicle is subject to a $100 civil penalty. The offense may be charged on a uniform traffic summons form. This is a secondary offense. [§ 46.2-810.1]

Vehicle Length & Width

The Commissioner of the Department of Motor Vehicles may issue permits for vehicles transporting boats or other watercraft that exceed an outside width of 102 inches but do not exceed an outside width of 108 inches. [§ 46.2-1149.8]

SEX OFFENSES

Evidence

A health care provider that has collected a physical evidence recovery kit from a victim of sexual assault who has elected to report the offense shall forthwith notify the law-enforcement agency that such kit has been collected. The agency shall forthwith take possession of the physical evidence recovery kit. [§ 19.2-11.6]

Statute of Limitations

A prosecution of a misdemeanor under §§ 18.2-64.2 (carnal knowledge of inmate, parolee, probationer, detainee, or pretrial or posttrial offender), 18.2-67.4 (sexual battery), 18.2-67.4:1 (infected sexual battery), 18.2-67.4:2 (sexual abuse of child under 15), 18.2-67.5 (attempted rape or sexual battery), or 18.2-370.6 (penetration of mouth) where the victim is a minor at the time of the offense shall be commenced no later than 1 year after the victim reaches majority. [§ 19.2-8]

STALKING

Defined

Contacting or following or attempting to contact or follow the person at whom stalking conduct is directed after being given actual notice that the person does not want to be contacted or followed is prima facie evidence that the person intended to place the other person, or reasonably should have known that the other person was placed, in reasonable fear of death, criminal sexual assault, or bodily injury to himself or a family or household member.

A second offense of stalking committed within 5 years of a prior stalking conviction is punishable as a Class 6 felony. [§ 18.2-60.3]

TRESPASS

Hunting Dogs

Any person who intentionally releases hunting dogs on the lands of another which have been posted in accordance with the provisions of § 18.2-134.1 to hunt without the consent of the landowner or his agent is guilty of a Class 3 misdemeanor, first offense, or a Class 1 misdemeanor, second or subsequent offense. In addition, conviction, the court shall revoke such person's hunting or trapping license for 1 year. The fact that hunting dogs are present on the lands of another alone is not sufficient evidence to prove that the person acted intentionally. [§ 18.2-132.1]

VIRGINIA LEGAL GUIDELINES

Editor's Note: This is a general overview of criminal procedure law. It should be used to achieve understanding of basic principles but is not to be relied upon for guidance in a specific application. It is not to be used as a substitute for the opinion or advice of the appropriate legal counsel for the reader's department. To the extent possible, the information is current. However, very recent statutory and case law developments may not be covered.

I. INTRODUCTION

The Bill of Rights to the federal Constitution, and corresponding provisions in each state's constitution, provide citizens with certain fundamental safeguards from intrusive governmental conduct. Particularly relevant to situations involving a criminal suspect or defendant are the Fourth, Fifth, Sixth and, to a lesser extent, the Fourteenth Amendments. As a preliminary matter, the reader should note that the federal Bill of Rights, as ultimately interpreted by the Supreme Court, guarantees U.S. citizens enumerated fundamental freedoms and provides the constitutionally required minimum levels of protection. Under the principles of federalism, state courts are free, in interpreting their respective state constitutions, to afford greater protection to state citizens. In many instances, the language in a state constitution mirrors the federal provision, and state courts hold that the right granted by the state constitution is to be construed the same as that granted by the federal Constitution. See *Lowe v. Commonwealth*, 230 Va. 346, 321 S.E.2d 273 (1984), *cert. denied*, 475 U.S. 1084 (1986) (Article I, §10 of the Virginia Constitution provides "substantially the same" protections as the federal Fourth Amendment).

The Fourth Amendment guarantees the people the right to be secure in their persons, houses, papers and effects against unreasonable searches and seizures. This amendment also provides that no search or arrest warrants shall be issued except those based on probable cause and which particularly describe both the place to be searched and the person or things to be seized.

The equivalent to the Fourth Amendment in the Virginia Constitution is Article I, §10, "General Warrants of search or seizure prohibited." This section provides that general warrants "without any evidence of fact furnished previously to the issuance, or which do not designate any specific thing or person to be seized, or do not particularly describe the offense claimed to have been committed" are prohibited. As mentioned above, this section provides "substantially the same" protections as the federal Fourth Amendment.

The Fifth Amendment provides (in pertinent part) that no person shall be compelled to be a witness against oneself in a criminal case. The Supreme Court has also found that an integral part of an accused's right to be free from compelled incrimination is a judicially created right to have counsel present and a right to refuse to answer questions during a custodial interrogation, even though the Constitution does not specifically provide such a safeguard.

The Sixth Amendment provides that a defendant in a criminal case—and a suspect in a criminal investigation when the investigation has focused on him or her or has reached a critical stage—shall enjoy the right to counsel to aid in his or her defense.

The Fifth and Fourteenth Amendments provide that no person shall be deprived of life, liberty or property without the due process of law. In the context of the rights of a criminal suspect, this provision has been construed as offering protection against certain fundamentally unfair governmental conduct, particularly the use of suggestive, prejudicial or discriminatory identification procedures.

The ramifications of constitutional violations impact not only a law-enforcement officers' efforts to enforce the law and obtain the conviction of criminal offenders, but also may lead to monetary sanctions against individual officers and the particular department employing them. Evidence seized in violation of the foregoing principles (whether it is physical evidence, *e.g.*, contraband, or testimonial evidence, *e.g.*, a statement or confession) generally cannot be introduced into evidence in any subsequent trial. The evidence will be excluded by the operation of a doctrine known as the exclusionary rule. The mechanism by which the use of evidence is denied to prosecutors is called suppression. Moreover, officers who violate a person's constitutional rights may be civilly liable to that person in monetary damages. Officers, or the municipalities for which they work when they act in a

It is a Class 1 misdemeanor to falsely identify oneself to a law-enforcement officer with intent to deceive after being lawfully detained and asked one's identity. *Va. Code* §19.2-82.1.

e. **Justification for a Detention**.

(1) **Flight**. A suspect's flight, when confronted with police presence, may give the officer reasonable suspicion to pursue and detain the suspect. Note, however, that not all conduct that merely avoids contact with law-enforcement is considered flight from law-enforcement.

See, *e.g.*, *Illinois v. Wardlow*, 528 U.S. 119 (2000). Two uniformed officers were in the last car of a four-car police caravan that converged on an area of Chicago known for heavy narcotics trafficking, in order to investigate drug transactions. The officers observed defendant, who was standing next to a building holding an opaque bag, look at the police caravan, then run in the opposite direction. Given the character of the area and defendant's headlong flight ("the consummate act of evasion"), the officers had reasonable suspicion to stop him.

Compare with *Whitfield v. Commonwealth*, 265 Va. 358, 576 S.E.2d 463 (2003). At around 3:30 a.m., a Newport News officer was patrolling an area "notorious for crime problems," including illegal drug activity, burglaries, and prostitution. Although there had been no reports of specific criminal activity at that particular time, there had been several recent burglaries in the area. The officer saw defendant, dressed all in black, standing on private property about 15 feet from the roadway between a condemned house and an occupied dwelling. The officer knew this area was not "a common cut-through" to other property. Suspicious as to what defendant might be doing, the officer shined his spotlight on him. Defendant "took off running between the houses, going to the back of the house." Defendant then slowed to a fast-paced walk, looking back over his shoulder at the officer. Another officer arrived on the scene, and defendant ran away from him in "a zig-zag direction, back and forth" across the street. He then ran between houses and unsuccessfully tried to climb a 6-foot fence. When the officers found him at the fence, they had reasonable suspicion for an investigatory detention.

In *White v. Commonwealth*, 25 Va.App. 662, 492 S.E.2d 451 (1997), officers were patrolling in Lynchburg at around 9:15 p.m. on a mid-December night when they saw ten or fifteen males gathered in a semi-circle next to a Cadillac in a vacant lot. As the officers approached the group, they heard someone shout "5-0," a street term for police. The entire group of men ran, leaving the Cadillac with its engine running and a door wide open. The officers chased the men to the back of a nearby house, where they found defendant sitting on the back steps of the residence. Considering the time of year and late hour, it struck them as highly unusual that a man would be sitting on the back steps of a residence at that moment. Given that the officers had just seen a group of men flee, defendant's strange behavior justified an investigatory stop and frisk.

See also *Wallace v. Commonwealth*, 32 Va.App. 497, 528 S.E.2d 739 (2000). A state trooper was traveling along Route 47 just outside South Hill when he saw defendant traveling in the opposite direction, well below the speed limit. When defendant drifted over the fog line, the trooper decided to follow him to see if he could observe further signs of intoxication. After the trooper turned around, defendant accelerated, forcing the trooper to increase his speed. Defendant then made a right-hand turn without signaling and continued to accelerate through the turn, as evidenced by a "weight transfer" at the rear of his car. He then made another abrupt turn, again not signaling and again accelerating through it. However, he was not speeding, and because the trooper's was the only other car on the road, some 400 feet behind, defendant did not commit a traffic violation. Finally, defendant made a third abrupt, unsignaled turn into a driveway, where he turned off his lights. Even though defendant had not committed a traffic violation, his obvious attempt to elude the trooper established reasonable suspicion for an investigatory stop.

But see *Ewell v. Commonwealth*, 254 Va. 214, 491 S.E.2d 721 (1997). An off-duty Virginia Beach officer was working as a security guard at an apartment complex. Late one night, at around 12:30 a.m., he saw defendant's Oldsmobile parked next to an apartment which was a suspected site of narcotics activity. The officer was familiar with most of the complex's residents and their vehicles, but he did not recognize this car. When the officer approached in his marked vehicle, the Oldsmobile drove off. The officer saw defendant's face, but did not recognize him. Nevertheless, these observations alone were not enough to suggest criminal activity, so there was no reasonable suspicion for a stop.

(2) **High-Crime Area**. Presence in a high-crime area, when coupled with observations of suspicious activity, can create reasonable suspicion.

See, *e.g.*, *Parker v. Commonwealth*, 255 Va. 96, 496 S.E.2d 47 (1998). A Richmond officer was on patrol in the Creighton Court public housing development. The officer had made numerous drug arrests in and around the development and "personally considered that area to be an open-air drug market." On Creighton Road, he saw a group of young men (including defendant) standing around a Cadillac with its trunk open. As the marked patrol car drew near, the men immediately shut the trunk and dispersed. Defendant placed an item in the waistband of his shorts as he walked away down Creighton. The officer then began to drive down Creighton, staying parallel to defendant, who was about 20 feet away on the sidewalk. When defendant noticed the car following him, he turned around and began walking back the other way. The officer had reasonable suspicion to stop defendant for questioning.

Compare with *Buck v. Commonwealth*, 20 Va.App. 298, 456 S.E.2d 534 (1995). Plain-clothes Arlington County officers were patrolling a high-crime area where drug sales were known to frequently occur. They observed defendant standing on a corner talking with a "group of guys". When the officers' unmarked car passed, the group dispersed. The officers circled the block, and when they returned, defendant had moved down the block and was talking with another group. Once again, when the officers passed, this second group dispersed. The officers again drove around the block and, on their third pass through the area, they saw defendant sitting in the back seat of a car. As the officers neared, the car drove off. About three or four minutes later, the car returned and dropped defendant off about a block away from where he had been picked up. One of the officers would later testify that "smarter dealers" would only conduct drug transactions in cars, often driving around the block while doing so. After defendant got out of the car, an officer approached him on foot and identified himself. Defendant placed his closed fist to his mouth, then ran. The conduct the officers observed, when combined with the character of the surrounding neighborhood, established reasonable suspicion for a stop.

See also *U.S. v. McCoy*, 513 F.3d 405 (4th Cir. 2008). A Loudon County vice officer with over 10 years experience staked out a Safeway in Leesburg. He previously had observed controlled drug buys in the parking lot of this store, and later estimated that nearly half of all Loudon County drug deals occurred in grocery store or other retail store parking lots. Defendant and his girlfriend pulled into the lot in a Mitsubishi Eclipse, then parked in a space next to the officer's unmarked car. Neither exited the car. Two or three minutes later, a tow truck pulled up near the Eclipse, and the driver yelled to defendant, asking "where he wanted—where they wanted to meet." The officer could not hear defendant's response, but he saw defendant point south. The officer knew that it was common for drug dealers to change the location of a transaction at the last minute, as a form of counter-surveillance against police. The tow truck drove off, with the Eclipse following closely behind, to a Food Lion ¼-mile south of the Safeway along the same road; the officer had been involved in drug busts here, as well. The tow truck and Eclipse parked five to eight spaces apart in the far right corner of the lot, despite the availability of numerous empty spaces closer to the store. From two rows back, the officer watched as defendant exited the Eclipse and entered the passenger side of the tow truck. After about a minute, defendant got back out and walked back to his car. Given the officer's knowledge of drug deals in both store lots—as well as his expertise in how such deals are conducted—he had reasonable suspicion for an investigatory stop of defendant.

In *U.S. v. Edmonds*, 948 F. Supp. 562 (E.D.Va. 1996), *aff'd*, 149 F.3d 1171 (4th Cir.), *cert. denied*, 525 U.S. 912 (1998), an Arlington County officer was on patrol in Crystal City, an area which had experienced a recent rise in auto thefts. At about 10:30 p.m., he saw two men near a car parked on a grassy strip along South Eades Street, behind a parking garage. This was a clearly marked "No Parking" zone. One man was inside the car, while the other, the defendant, was standing just outside the open door. This was primarily a commercial area, so it was dark and deserted at that late hour. When defendant saw the officer's patrol car, he began to walk away, slinging a large duffel bag over his shoulder as he went. The officer recognized this as the kind of bag auto thieves often use to conceal their tools. As the officer drew closer, defendant began walking more quickly. The officer reasonably believed defendant was involved in auto theft or a related crime, so he lawfully stopped him.

But see *Goodwin v. Commonwealth*, 11 Va.App. 363, 398 S.E.2d 690 (1990). Defendant was walking down the 1100 block of St. James Street in Richmond, a high-crime area where the officers on patrol had made numerous arrests. It was a cold, late December night, and defendant had on a bulky winter coat. When defendant saw the officers' patrol car, he "jammed" his hand into a pocket of the coat. The officers did not see any item in defendant's hand or in his pocket. Defendant did not flee or attempt to avoid the officers, but continued to walk toward the patrol car until he walked right past it. The officers had not received a tip or other information suggesting defendant was involved in criminal activity, so, given all of the circumstances, the Court concluded that the officers did not have a reasonable suspicion to stop and frisk defendant; his behavior was equally consistent with innocent activity as with criminal.

Compare with *Riley v. Commonwealth*, 13 Va.App. 494, 412 S.E.2d 724 (1992). An officer saw defendant exit a vehicle along Dundee Street, near the corner of Midlothian Turnpike, another high-crime area of Richmond. Defendant turned his back to the officer and made a motion toward his waistband before closing the door to the vehicle. The officer never saw any illegal object. Defendant could have been tucking in his shirt or engaging in any number of other legitimate activities, and the officer had no prior knowledge of defendant or any possible criminal activities on his part. The general character of the neighborhood alone was not enough to establish reasonable suspicion.

(3) **Officer's Experience**. Officers are entitled to rely on their own knowledge and experience in forming reasonable suspicion.

See *e.g.*, *Harris v. Commonwealth*, 33 Va.App. 325, 533 S.E.2d 18 (2000). An anonymous tip reported that a black male named Mart Harris had a gun and was selling drugs near Davis Boulevard and a private road leading to the Cognic Square Apartments (a public housing complex). Officers arrived at this corner and saw three men, one of whom was defendant, seated on a bench near a sign reading "No trespassing. No loitering. No drinking." Defendant matched the description of Mart Harris given by the anonymous caller. Although the anonymous tip alone was not reliable enough to establish reasonable suspicion, one of the officers had worked in a drug elimination program at the apartment complex for 2½ years and was therefore quite familiar with its residents, but did not recognize defendant as a resident. This knowledge provided reasonable suspicion independent of the tip to stop and question defendant. (Note that once the stop was made on unrelated grounds, the information in the tip that defendant had a gun could be used to justify a pat-down, especially since he was wearing loose-fitting clothes that could have concealed a weapon.)

In *Shifflett v. Commonwealth*, 58 Va.App. 732, 716 S.E.2d 132 (2011), a state trooper saw a pick-up truck driving along Rockfish Valley Highway in Nelson County. It was nearly 10:00 p.m., very dark, with snow on the ground from a recent storm. There were three occupants in the truck's cab. The truck displayed a store-bought farm use tag, rather than an official license plate issued by the DMV for farm use vehicles. The trooper knew that unregulated vehicles can only be used under very limited statutory exemptions, all relating to agriculture. However, as he later testified, "It was late and night ... [a]nd in the wintertime, you'd don't see many farm use vehicles on the road." The trooper had reasonable suspicion to believe the truck was being operated in violation of state law.

In *Alston v. Commonwealth*, 40 Va.App. 728, 581 S.E.2d 245 (2003), three Richmond officers were on patrol in the Ruffin Road apartment complex, which was posted with "no trespassing" signs. The officers saw defendant driving inside the complex with three passengers. One of the officers recognized the front seat passenger as Pierre Stanberry; the officer knew Stanberry was banned from the complex because he had previously arrested him for trespass there at least twice. The officers could lawfully stop defendant's vehicle to investigate this apparent violation further.

Compare with *Raab v. Commonwealth*, 50 Va.App. 577, 652 S.E.2d 144 (2007). A Virginia Beach officer was on patrol along Ocean View Avenue at around 12:40 a.m. when he noticed defendant's vehicle in a restaurant parking lot, even though the restaurant had closed for the night and all the lights were off. The officer knew the lot was posted with signs restricting parking to "patrons only." Because the restaurant was closed, defendant could not have been a patron, so the officer has reasonable suspicion to believe he was trespassing, and grounds to make an investigatory stop.

In *Lowery v. Commonwealth*, 9 Va.App. 314, 388 S.E.2d 265 (1990), an officer saw defendant driving northbound on I-95 in a car with Florida license plates. A particular letter on the plates indicated that the car was a rental, so the officer checked DMV records and learned that the car was owned by Alpha Auto Leasing. Because the officer knew that local leasing agencies (unlike the larger national agencies) often prohibit lessees from taking vehicles out of state, he reasonably believed that defendant was involved in criminal activity and made a valid investigatory stop.

In *Shiflett v. Commonwealth*, 47 Va.App. 141, 622 S.E.2d 758 (2005), a game warden issued defendant a summons for a "spotlighting" violation. At that time, the warden learned that defendant's driving privileges were revoked because he had been adjudicated a habitual offender. Five months later, the warden saw defendant walk out of a market, get into a vehicle, and drive off. Because the warden knew that habitual offender status lasts at least 10 years, he had reasonable suspicion to believe that defendant was driving illegally, and made a valid stop.

See also *Ford v. Commonwealth*, 28 Va.App. 249, 503 S.E.2d 803 (1998). A detective saw defendant walking with two women in the parking lot of the Cloverleaf shopping mall. Defendant was carrying a white plastic bag. As the trio approached the wooded area on the east side of the lot, defendant looked over his shoulder several times, then separated from the women and entered the woods. He returned a minute or two later, without the bag, and the three entered the mall. The detective then entered the woods himself and, within 10 seconds, found a white plastic bag hidden beneath two old, discarded mattresses. It was the only bag in the area similar to the one defendant had been carrying. Inside were five "rolled up" pieces of women's clothing, with the store tags still attached. However, there was no receipt or sales slip in the bag. Thirty to forty-five minutes later, when defendant exited the mall, the detective had reasonable suspicion to stop and question him about his apparent shoplifting.

In *Jones v. Commonwealth*, 24 Va.App. 519, 484 S.E.2d 125 (1997), two Gloucester County officers were traveling in an unmarked Ford Bronco when a car driven by defendant pulled up alongside them. The front seat passenger motioned to the rear seat passengers, after which they all stared at the officers; one of the occupants gestured as if shooting a gun. The car then took position immediately behind and to the right of the Bronco. It remained in this position even as the officers sped up to 70 m.p.h., slowed back down to 50 m.p.h., and stopped at a red light. One of the officers would later testify that it seemed as if defendant was trying to ensure that his car "was always at an advantage to [their] vehicle." Three weeks earlier, a confidential-informant had told the officers that there was a "contract" out on them, in retaliation for a prior arrest. Several other informants had confirmed this story, and one even reported that money had been paid in advance for this purpose. One of the officers thought that defendant looked like one of the men arrested in that incident, so, when the officers entered York County, they obtained assistance from local officers. The York County officers had reasonable suspicion to stop defendant, based on the passengers' gestures, the prior reported threats on the officers' lives, and his own erratic driving.

Knowledge of an earlier crime in the area, coupled with observation of suspicious conduct, can justify a detention.

See, *e.g.*, *Brown v. Commonwealth*, 33 Va.App. 296, 553 S.E.2d 4 (2000). A 14-year-old girl was raped while selling subscriptions door to door along Lynn Street in Prince William County. Thirty minutes later, a bicycle officer who was looking for the suspect saw defendant talking on a public phone no more than three blocks from the scene of the crime. Defendant matched the victim's description of her attacker, and his pants and shoes were splattered with mud, suggesting he had recently walked through the boggy wooded area behind Lynn Street. When the officer rode his bike past defendant and looked at him without speaking to him, defendant turned and hurriedly walked away. The officer had reasonable suspicion to stop defendant in order to conduct a limited investigation to determine if he was the girl's assailant.

Compare with *Thomas v. Commonwealth*, 16 Va.App. 851, 434 S.E.2d 319 (1993), *on reh'g*, 18 Va.App. 454, 444 S.E.2d 275 (1994). A Norfolk officer received a call at around 5:00 a.m. reporting a stabbing at a nearby location. While checking the area, the officer saw defendant coming around from the back side of a motel less than a block from the crime scene, which was unusual given that there were "no rooms back there." Defendant matched the reported description of the assailant and was the only person the officer saw on the street. The officer had reasonable suspicion to detain defendant in order to question him regarding the stabbing.

In *Nelson v. Commonwealth*, 24 Va.App. 823, 485 S.E.2d 673 (1997), two Newport News officers were dispatched to investigate a possible burglary in progress at 210 Nina Court. When they arrived on the scene, they were met by a neighbor who told them she had observed a black female in a black skirt and multi-colored top leaving 210 Nina Court and walking down Colony Road. She added that she knew that the residents of that house were away and that she had never seen this person at the residence before. The officers drove down Colony Road and soon saw defendant, who was dressed as the neighbor had described. She was carrying an 8" straightened piece of coat hanger, which she laid on the curb as the officers approached. Defendant "was agitated and sweating profusely." When asked for identification, she said she had none. When asked her destination, she said she was walking to her home in Courthouse Green. However, as the officers pointed out, she had been walking in the opposite direction. After this, defendant's statements became "increasingly confusing and inconsistent, as she attempted to explain her actions to the officers." The officers had a particularized and objective basis for believing that defendant may have been involved in criminal activity, and therefore were justified in detaining her (in addition, because burglary is a felony that clearly has the potential for violence, a pat-down for weapons was also justified).

See also *Jackson v. Commonwealth*, 22 Va.App. 347, 470 S.E.2d 138 (1996). In the early morning hours, a Richmond officer working off-duty in a high-crime neighborhood saw "muzzle flash" and heard "several shots [fired] from handguns." He looked over to the area where the shots seemed to have originated and saw a group of seven or eight individuals. The officer had reasonable suspicion to stop and frisk each of them.

(4) **Tips**. Information provided by someone outside the circles of law-enforcement may provide sufficient justification for a stop if it carries with it sufficient indicia of reliability. Factors that bolster the reliability of information may include: the reliability and reputation of the person providing the tip; corroboration of the details contained in the tip by independent police work; and the extent to which any information provided by the informant has proved to be accurate or useful in the past.

See, *e.g.*, *O'Toole v. Commonwealth*, 20 Va.App. 540, 458 S.E.2d 595 (1995), *on reh'g*, 22 Va.App. 1, 467 S.E.2d 819 (1996). A reliable informant, whose previous tips had resulted in arrests and convictions for cocaine violations, told a Virginia Beach detective that he had been in defendant's apartment and that an unnamed person in the apartment told him that defendant was "making the rounds," delivering cocaine in a Ford Bronco with Virginia license plates "CHUXX." The informant added that defendant was being accompanied by a black male known as "Junie," who was about 5'5" and 150 pounds. The detective knew "Junie" was the nickname of Thomas Lee White, an individual he had previously arrested for a firearms violation. Thirty to forty minutes later, the detective saw the described Bronco, with White at the wheel. He had reasonable suspicion for an investigatory stop.

In *Giles v. Commonwealth*, 32 Va.App. 519, 529 S.E.2d 327 (2000), two women approached a Colonial Heights officer and told him that they had overheard a man say that he had a gun and was "looking to hurt someone" and that they then had seen him get into a car. The women identified the car, which was exiting a restaurant parking lot across the street with defendant as the driver and sole occupant. The officer stopped defendant and, although no weapon was found, eventually arrested him for DWI. The Court concluded this stop was supported by reasonable suspicion. Although the officer did not obtain the names or addresses of the two women, these were not anonymous tips. "[The officer] stood face to face with them and listened to their accounts. He was able to assess their credibility and the reliability of their information." Thus, he was in a better position to judge the reliability of the tips than if they had been called in to an anonymous phone line, so the women could be considered "identified" citizen-informants. Both women presented their reports "cogently" and were visibly frightened. In addition, the two reports corroborated one another (each woman based her report on what she had seen and heard). Moreover, the tips "suggested the imminence of serious and perhaps lethal danger." Because defendant was leaving the scene, the officer had to act without hesitation to prevent possible violence.

Compare with *U.S. v. Christmas*, 222 F.3d 141 (4th Cir. 2000). A woman approached an officer who was investigating an unrelated murder in a high-crime neighborhood and said, "You need to come and deal with the drugs and the guns that those guys have on the porch two doors down from me." Although the woman did not give her name, she did give her address (and the address of the alleged dealers), and insisted that police investigate her complaint immediately. The officer finally agreed to do so and went to the residence the woman had described. There he saw four people sitting on the porch, including defendant. He detained all four and patted them down. This seizure was supported by reasonable suspicion, because the officer had a "face-to-face" encounter with the woman who had incriminated them and was thus able to assess her credibility and demeanor first-hand. She lived only two houses away from the alleged dealers, so it was reasonable to conclude she would know of such criminal activity at the residence. Although she did not give her name, her address made her easy to identify and legally accountable for any false statements. Moreover, by giving her report in public, she exposed herself to a risk of reprisal by the dealers themselves. Finally, upon arriving at the house, the officer recognized defendant as a gang member who lived in another part of town. This corroborated the tip somewhat and suggested a possibility of violence. Under the totality of the circumstances, the woman's tip established reasonable suspicion.

In *Reed v. Commonwealth*, 36 Va.App. 260, 549 S.E.2d 616 (2001), a citizen called Richmond police on his cell phone and said that he had just seen someone break into a car at Allen and Main Streets. He gave a description of the perpetrator and began to follow him, remaining on the line with the dispatcher. An officer at Allen and Carey Streets soon saw a car that matched the description given by the caller. He also received confirmation from another unit that a burglarized car had been found at Allen and Main. The totality of the circumstances supported the reliability of the tip and justified a stop. The caller was clearly a disinterested citizen who had just witnessed a crime. Although the officer never spoke with him and it was not clear if he ever identified himself, he stayed on the phone with the dispatcher and continued to update the burglar's location, which added to his credibility. The fact that other officers found a burglarized car where the caller alleged they would also corroborated the tip.

See also *U.S. v. Martin*, 400 F. Supp.2d 871 (E.D.Va. 2005). A Richmond detective received a call from a confidential-informant (CI) who previously had provided him with information which always proved accurate. The CI had been a paid informant for three years, and his information had resulted in the issuance of five arrest warrants and at least twelve arrests. The CI stated that he had been in the Community Pride grocery store on Mechanicsville Turnpike when defendant lifted his T-shirt to surreptitiously show him the gun he was hiding in his pants pocket. The detective asked for a description of defendant and the CI responded that he was a light-skinned black male, wearing a long white T-shirt under a black or blue jacket, blue jeans, blue and yellow Nikes, a fitted baseball cap, and a black glove on one hand. Immediately after the call the detective and other officers set up surveillance outside the store. They saw the CI walk into the store. A short time later, the CI called the detective back to say defendant was no longer in the store, but might have gone to Maddox Street, his usual "hang out." The officers proceeded to Maddox, a block away from the store. They saw defendant, a light-skinned black male, standing in the street wearing a dark blue "hoodie" sweatshirt, a long white T-shirt, blue and yellow sneakers, and a baseball cap; his hand was in his pocket, so they could not see if he had on a glove. The Court ruled that the officers had reasonable suspicion to believe that defendant was the man described by the CI--the CI had a history of reliability, and police confirmed every aspect of the tip but the single glove. In addition, the Court found that under Virginia's "concealed carry" statute, the burden is on the person carrying a weapon to prove that he or she has a permit to do so (or that some other exception applies). Therefore, although possession of a concealed weapon is theoretically legal, the officers had reasonable suspicion to stop defendant to ensure that he had lawful possession of the gun.

But see *Beckner v. Commonwealth*, 15 Va.App. 533, 425 S.E.2d 530 (1993). A citizen pulled up behind a police cruiser and flashed his lights to get the officer's attention. When the officer pulled over, the driver pulled alongside and said that there was a white female driving a 1966 Chevy without a license at a nearby gas station. Although this face-to-face confrontation provided some indicia of the tipster's reliability, nothing he said established his basis of knowledge. He did not tell the officer *how* he knew that the woman's license was suspended. Therefore, the tip did not establish reasonable suspicion for a stop.

(5) **Anonymous Tips**. An anonymous tip, if corroborated by other observations and supported by indicia of reliability, can create reasonable suspicion.

See, *e.g.*, *Alabama v. White*, 496 U.S. 325 (1990). Montgomery police received an anonymous tip stating that defendant, carrying a brown briefcase filled with cocaine, would leave a specific unit of an apartment building and travel in her brown Plymouth station wagon, which had a broken taillight, to a specific motel. Police watched the apartment complex, and saw a brown Plymouth wagon with a broken taillight. They then watched defendant, empty-handed, exit the specified apartment, get into the car and drive directly toward the motel. Even though not every detail in the tip turned out to be totally correct, the partial corroboration by police alone provided reasonable suspicion for a stop.

See also *Navarette v. California*, 572 U.S. __ (2014). In Mendocino County, California, a driver called 911 to report that a silver Ford F-150 pickup truck with a specified license plate had just run her off the road, at mile marker 88 on southbound Highway 1. Roughly 18 minutes after the call, a California Highway Patrol officer spotted the same truck at mile marker 69, 19 miles south of the reported incident. The U.S Supreme Court ruled that, assuming the 911 call was anonymous, the officer nevertheless had reasonable suspicion to stop the truck. By reporting that she had been run off the road by a specific vehicle, the caller necessarily claimed eyewitness knowledge of the alleged dangerous driving—a driver's claim that another vehicle ran her off the road implies that the informant knows the other car was driven dangerously. That basis of knowledge lent significant support to the tip's reliability. In addition, the officer saw the truck in a location suggesting that the caller must have reported the incident soon after she was run off the road. The Court noted, "That sort of contemporaneous report has long been treated as especially reliable." In addition, 911 calls are recorded, which provides victims with an opportunity to identify the false tipster's voice and subject him to prosecution; a 911 caller's cell phone number can also be easily identified, further discouraging its use in giving false tips. Thus, the caller's use of the 911 system was another factor suggesting reliability. Finally, the Court noted that running another vehicle off a the road "suggests lane positioning problems, decreased vigilance, impaired judgment, or some combination of those recognized drunk driving cues." Thus there was reason to believe the driver of the truck might be intoxicated and therefore committing a crime. Under the totality of these circumstances, an investigatory stop was justified.

In *U.S. v. Perrin*, 45 F.3d 869 (4th Cir. 1995), *cert. denied*, 515 U.S. 1126 (1996), an anonymous call to York County police stated that "Charles Odell" (the defendant's first and middle names) was selling crack cocaine in the laundromat of the Yorktown Square Apartments, a known high-crime area. Three days later, the police received a second anonymous call alleging that "Charlie Red" (defendant's street name) was selling crack outside Building 4 of the same apartment complex. The officer was familiar with both the defendant and the character of the neighborhood where he was allegedly dealing. Within an hour of the second call, the officer drove by Building 4, where he saw defendant standing outside, drinking a beer. The fact that the officer received two calls within three days, both of which offered detailed descriptions of defendant's activities, combined with his own knowledge and observations, established reasonable suspicion for a stop.

In *Bulatko v. Commonwealth*, 16 Va.App. 135, 428 S.E.2d 306 (1993), an anonymous caller to the Chief of the Mount Jackson Police Department identified defendant by name, gave the color and license plate number of his Dodge, and stated that he was driving toward Mount Jackson without a license. A records check revealed that defendant was a habitual offender, and that the plate number the caller had given conformed to a car of the model and color he alleged. This sufficiently corroborated the tip, so that 45 minutes later, when the Chief saw defendant's Dodge driving into town, he had reasonable suspicion for a stop.

In *Sidney v. Commonwealth*, 280 Va. 517, 702 S.E.2d 124 (2010), a Petersburg officer received a radio dispatch reporting an anonymous tip called into police headquarters. The anonymous caller alleged that defendant was at 1300 Patterson Street, driving a tan Jeep Cherokee, with wood grain side paneling, and that there were outstanding warrants for his arrest. The officer quickly arrived at the Patterson Street address, and saw a Cherokee matching the caller's description with a male driver. He ran the license plate and learned the vehicle was registered to defendant's mother. Because the caller correctly predicted defendant's location and police were able to confirm other aspects of the tip—the Jeep was connected to defendant, the officer could presume that the dispatcher had confirmed warrants were outstanding for his arrest—reasonable suspicion existed for an investigatory stop.

See also *Gregory v. Commonwealth*, 22 Va.App. 100, 468 S.E.2d 117 (1996). At approximately 2:00 a.m., an anonymous tip to Richmond police stated that an individual "was standing out in the roadway" in the 1700 block of Carlyle Avenue, "flagging motorists down to ask them if they wanted to buy drugs." The tipster described this dealer as a black male dressed in dark jeans, tennis shoes, and a green sweat jacket with a green hooded jacket underneath, and provided the make and color of his vehicle. Two minutes after hearing a radio report regarding this tip, an officer approached the 1700 block of Carlyle. He knew this to be an area where police "always receive complaints of drug dealing." He saw defendant, a black male dressed as the tip had described and sitting in a matching vehicle. As the officer approached, defendant looked in his direction and became "slightly agitated". He then began to walk away from his vehicle, looking over his shoulder as he went. Defendant's furtive conduct and the officer's immediate verification of the many details the informant provided sufficiently corroborated the tip so that the officer was entitled to stop and frisk defendant.

But see *Florida v. J.L.*, 529 U.S. 266 (2000). An anonymous caller to Miami-Dade County police stated that a young black male dressed in a plaid shirt who was standing at a specified bus stop was carrying a gun. Officers arrived at the bus stop approximately six minutes later, and saw three black males, one of whom (defendant) was wearing a plaid shirt. Other than the tip, the officers had no reason to suspect any of the three of criminal activity. They saw no firearm, nor any threatening or unusual movements. However, the tip carried no indicia of reliability. It provided no predictive information, and, therefore, no means to test the caller's credibility. The caller neither explained how he knew defendant had a gun nor supplied any basis for believing that he had "inside information" about defendant. Therefore, the officers lacked reasonable suspicion, so that their stop of defendant was illegal.

Compare with *Jackson v. Commonwealth*, 267 Va. 666, 594 S.E.2d 595 (2004). Just after 2:00 a.m., the Newport News Police Department received an anonymous call complaining that three black makes were acting disorderly at 34th Street and Jefferson Avenue, and that "at least one of them had a firearm and was brandishing it." The caller also stated that the three "were getting into a car and leaving[,]" describing the car as a "white Honda." Three to five minutes later, officers arrived at the scene. They saw a white Honda leaving the area; there were no other white vehicles of any type. The Honda pulled out in front of one officer; the officer's headlights shined directly into the car and he could clearly see it was occupied by three black males. The Court concluded that the officer did not have reasonable suspicion. The facts provided by the caller were easily obtainable and provided no prediction of the future behavior of the three men. The caller never explained how he knew one of the men was brandishing a firearm nor furnished any basis to believe he had inside information regarding the men. He did not appear in person, so he was not liable for false information. He did not give a "first-person, present-tense" account, and provided no details about himself indicating that he was a concerned citizen rather than a prankster or person with a grudge against the three men. There was simply not enough information in the tip to justify a stop.

See also *Hardy v. Commonwealth*, 11 Va.App. 433, 399 S.E.2d 27 (1990). An anonymous caller to Richmond police stated that Kenneth Hardy (defendant) was walking north on Hull Street, dressed in a black coat with a white fur collar and a black fur hat. The unidentified caller went on the say that defendant was armed and had cocaine in his hat. Soon after receiving this tip, an officer who knew defendant saw him walking on Hull, wearing the described outfit. The Court found that the officer did not have reasonable suspicion for a stop. The anonymous tip provided nothing more than innocent details which any casual observer could have given. There were no predictions of defendant's future behavior, and no wealth of detail which would reveal the caller had an "inner-knowledge" of defendant's activities. Because of this, the reliability of the tip could not be established.

Contrast with *Scott v. Commonwealth*, 20 Va.App. 725, 560 S.E.2d 610 (1995). An anonymous tip stated that a light-complexioned black male in a white T-shirt, black shorts, and Nike tennis shoes with no socks was brandishing a gun in a laundromat. An officer was only one block away and arrived at the laundromat about one minute later. He saw defendant, who matched the description exactly, walking out. The Court found that, in this case, the officer's "immediate confirmation" of several details in the tip, when combined with the possibility of imminent danger to the public, justified a stop and frisk of defendant.

(6) **"Erratic" Driving**. Driving in an erratic manner in and of itself justifies a stop. An officer does not violate the Fourth Amendment by stopping and questioning someone who just committed a traffic violation in the officer's presence. Moreover, routine traffic infractions, even minor ones, can provide the requisite reasonable suspicion to stop a vehicle. For example, stops have been upheld when:

- the top of a truck's license plate was bent so that the issuing state could not be determined, and the bottom corner was bent so that the officer could not see if expiration stickers were present (*U.S. v. Greenwood*, 405 F. Supp.2d 673 (E.D.Va. 2005));
- a vehicle had an 8-inch crack in its windshield, because the crack possibly rendered the windshield defective (*U.S. v. Ellington*, 396 F. Supp.2d 695 (E.D.Va. 2005));
- a clump of air fresheners (*Freeman v. Commonwealth*, 65 Va.App. 407, 778 S.E.2d 519 (2015)) or a 3" x 5" opaque plastic parking pass (*Mason v. Commonwealth*, 2016 Va. LEXIS 59 (2016)) dangled from a rear-view mirror, potentially obstructed the driver's view;
- defendant swerved three to five times within his own lane markers, but at times did travel on top of the lane marker (*Commonwealth v. Johnson*, 90 Va. Cir. 127 (2015);
- a trailer appeared to be standard 8'6" width but was carrying a large prefabricated concrete wall that extended more than a foot over each side, making it exceed the statutory maximum width (*Morris v. City of Virginia Beach*, 707 S.E.2d 479 (Va. Ct. App. 2011));
- a license plate light was not functioning (*Harris v. Commonwealth*, 266 Va. 28, 581 S.E.2d 206 (2003));
- a vehicle displayed a pink rejection sticker (*Reel v. Commonwealth*, 31 Va.App. 262, 522 S.E.2d 881 (2000));
- a headlight was broken (*Reittinger v. Commonwealth*, 260 Va. 232, 532 S.E.2d 25 (2000));
- defendant was driving in the center lane of a freeway—10 to 15 m.p.h. below the posted speed limit—and weaved within his own lane three or four times over the course of two miles (*Freeman v. Commonwealth*, 20 Va.App. 658, 460 S.E.2d 261 (1995)).

See, *e.g.*, *U.S. v. Greenwood*, 405 F. Supp.2d 673 (E.D.Va. 2005) (lawful stop when the top of a truck's license plate was bent so that the issuing state could not be determined, and the bottom corner was bent so that the officer could not see if expiration stickers were present); *U.S. v. Ellington*, 396 F. Supp.2d 695 (E.D.Va. 2005) (reasonable suspicion when vehicle had an 8-inch crack in its windshield, because the crack possibly rendered the windshield defective); *Morris v. City of Virginia Beach*, 707 S.E.2d 479 (Va. Ct. App. 2011) (stop lawful when trailer appeared to be standard 8'6" width but was carrying a large prefabricated concrete wall that extended more than a foot over each side, making it exceed the statutory maximum width); *Harris v. Commonwealth*, 266 Va. 28, 581 S.E.2d 206 (2003) (valid stop for non-functioning license plate light); *Reel v. Commonwealth*, 31 Va.App. 262, 522 S.E.2d 881 (2000) (stop justified when vehicle displayed pink rejection sticker); *Reittinger v. Commonwealth*, 260 Va. 232, 532 S.E.2d 25 (2000) (valid stop for broken headlight); *Freeman v. Commonwealth*, 20 Va.App. 658, 460 S.E.2d 261 (1995) (reasonable suspicion for a stop when defendant was driving in the center lane of a freeway—10 to 15 m.p.h. below the posted speed limit—and weaved within his own lane three or four times over the course of two miles).

But see *Neal v. Commonwealth*, 27 Va.App. 233, 498 S.E.2d 422 (1998) ("An isolated instance of mild weaving within a lane is not sufficiently erratic to justify an investigatory stop[,]" although "repeated weaving within a lane provides sufficient reasonable and articulable suspicion to justify an investigatory stop."); *U.S. v. Wilson*, 205 F.3d 720 (4th Cir. 2000) (no reasonable suspicion to stop defendant when his vehicle displayed a temporary license tag, because the tag was legible, did not lack any necessary information, and was not concealed or improperly displayed).

Normally, once the officer issues a ticket or a warning for the traffic infraction, the reasonable suspicion ends and the driver can no longer be detained. However, if the officer uncovers additional facts that give rise to further reasonable suspicion, the scope of the detention may increase.

For example, in *Reittinger v. Commonwealth, supra*, defendant was stopped late at night on Route 11 in rural Rockbridge County for an inoperable headlight. Two armed deputies made the stop, and one stood on either side of the vehicle. After defendant produced a new headlight he said he planned to install the next day, the deputy on the driver's side gave him a verbal warning and told him that he was "free to go." However, immediately thereafter, the deputy asked if there were any illegal weapons or drugs in the car, and asked for defendant's consent to a search. He asked for consent two more times before defendant finally relented and agreed to a search. This was an illegal seizure. The purposes of the stop ended once the citation was issued, and the deputies had no specific, articulable facts which justified detaining defendant for further questioning.

See also *Harris v. Commonwealth, supra*. Defendant was stopped because his truck had a broken tag light. When first approached, defendant admitted that he knew the light was out. He had no driver's license, only a Social Security card, but the officer used this to confirm that he in fact had a valid license. The officer then returned defendant's Social Security card. He later testified that at this point he considered defendant free to go; however, he did not tell this to defendant. Instead, even though he later admitted he did not suspect defendant of any other criminal activity, he asked defendant for consent to search the truck. Defendant agreed. The Court concluded that this consent was the coerced product of an unlawful detention. At no time was defendant told he was free to leave or that he would not be charged with a traffic violation; defendant knew that he had committed a violation and failed to provide a license as required, but the officer did nothing to indicate that he was no longer subject to detention on these grounds. Nor did the officer turn off the flashing lights on his vehicle. The traffic stop was ongoing at the time the officer requested consent to search and this request was not supported by independent reasonable suspicion of other criminal activity. Therefore, the request expanded the scope of the stop beyond its initial justification, and was unlawful.

Contrast with *U.S. v. Brugal*, 209 F.3d 353 (4th Cir. 2000). Police set up a drug checkpoint off of exit 22 on I-95 (an isolated exit in Ridgeland) and placed two "decoy" signs stating "DRUG CHECKPOINT AHEAD," 1,000 and 500 feet before the exit in an attempt to lure drug couriers into leaving the highway. At around 3:30 a.m., defendant fell for this ruse, and pulled off at the exit. Once he was stopped, police learned defendant had a New York driver's license and address; however, his car had been rented in Miami 14 hours earlier and was scheduled to be returned in Miami in a few days. The officers knew I-95 is a major drug thoroughfare and that couriers often fly to Miami, purchase drugs there, and then drive back north in a rented car. Defendant claimed he had pulled off the highway to stop for gas. However, his tank was ¾-full; in addition, the previous exit had three clearly visible, well-lighted 24-hour gas stations, while there were no signs of activity at the checkpoint exit at such a late hour. Even though defendant's license and vehicle documentation were valid, the officers had reasonable suspicion to detain defendant further and ask for permission to search his car.

See also *Dickerson v. Commonwealth*, 266 Va. 14, 581 S.E.2d 195 (2003). Defendant was stopped for failure to yield to an emergency vehicle. The two deputies who made the stop asked defendant to perform sobriety tests, but ultimately decided not to arrest him for DWI. They told him he was free to go, but that he might be subpoenaed later for the failure-to-yield infraction. Defendant returned to his car, opened the door, and was beginning to get in when one of the deputies asked "if there was anything in the car [he] should know about," such as drugs. Defendant then admitted that there were marijuana "roaches" in the car's ashtray, which led to a warrantless search of the vehicle. The Court found that defendant was no longer seized when the deputy asked his question, so that the permissible scope of the traffic stop was not exceeded. The deputies did not threaten defendant or impede his ability to leave. In fact, defendant clearly believed he was free to leave, as evidenced by the fact he was already getting into his car to do so. The Court concluded that the mere presence of two uniformed deputies, standing alone, was not enough to turn the conversation into a "seizure."

Compare with *U.S. v. Meikle*, 407 F.3d 670 (4th Cir. 2005). Defendant was stopped on I-95 after drifting over the fog line onto the shoulder of the highway several times. After issuing a warning citation, the state trooper returned defendant's license and registration, shook his hand, and said he was free to leave. As defendant turned and began to walk back toward his vehicle, the trooper asked if he could talk to him again and defendant replied, "yes." The trooper asked if there were any drugs in the vehicle, then if he could search it. Because this was a purely consensual encounter, there was no violation of defendant's Fourth Amendment rights, even though the purpose of the stop had ended by the time the trooper made his request.

During a lawful traffic stop, an officer may always ask a passenger for identification; no separate showing is required. *U.S. v. Soriano-Jarquin*, 492 F.3d 495 (4th Cir. 2007), *cert denied*, 170 L.Ed.2d 76 (2008).

Note: **Drunk Drivers**. Research by the National Highway Transportation Safety Administration has identified the following indicators of drunk driving, in descending order of probability that the driver is intoxicated [percentages indicate the chances out of 100 that a driver exhibiting the behavior is intoxicated]:

- (i) Turning with a wide radius [65%]
- (ii) Straddling the center or a lane marker [65%]
- (iii) Appearing to be drunk (*e.g.* gripping the steering wheel tightly, driving with one's face close to the windshield, slouching in the seat, drinking in the vehicle, or staring straight ahead with eyes fixed) [60%]
- (iv) Almost striking an object or vehicle [60%]
- (v) Weaving [60%]
- (vi) Driving somewhere other than the designated roadway (*e.g.* on the shoulder or straight through a turn-only lane) [55%]
- (vii) Swerving [55%]
- (viii) Slow speed (10 m.p.h. or more below the speed limit) [50%]
- (ix) Stopping in lane without cause [50%]
- (x) Following too closely [50%]
- (xi) Drifting [50%]
- (xii) Tires on center or lane marker [45%]
- (xiii) Braking erratically [45%]
- (xiv) Driving into opposing or crossing traffic [45%]
- (xv) Signaling inconsistent with driving actions [40%]
- (xvi) Stopping inappropriately other than in lane [35%]
- (xvii) Slow response to traffic signals [40%]
- (xviii) Turning abruptly or illegally [35%]
- (xix) Accelerating or decelerating rapidly [35%]
- (xx) Headlights off at night [30%]

Of course, if more than one indicator is observed, it is even more likely that the driver is intoxicated (add 10% to the highest value among the indicators observed). Note that speeding is not an indicator of DWI; because of quicker judgment and reflexes, in some circumstances it may indicate sobriety. Once a stop is made, the officer should look for the following behaviors by the driver, as NHTSA has found them to be excellent predictors of DWI:

- (i) Difficulty with vehicle controls;
- (ii) Difficulty exiting vehicle;
- (iii) Fumbling with license or registration;
- (iv) Repeating questions or comments;
- (v) Swaying, unsteadiness or balance problems;
- (vi) Leaning on the vehicle (or other object);
- (vii) Slurred speech;
- (viii) Slowness in responding to questions, or asking officer to repeat questions;
- (ix) Providing incorrect information or changing answers;
- (x) Odor of alcohol.

(7) **Drug Courier Profiles**. Profiles of drug couriers are relied on by officers to identify potential suspects. Generally, a match to the profile alone does not create reasonable suspicion to detain the suspect. The officer must observe other conduct or circumstances that sufficiently heighten his suspicion. Often, undercover officers will survey airport or bus terminals for individuals matching a certain profile. Factors utilized in compiling this profile may include: (i) a journey that originated in a source city for narcotics, or a short round trip, with a brief stay in such a city; (ii) the suspect carrying a hard-sided suitcase; (iii) the suspect appearing nervous when questioned; (iv) tickets that were paid for in cash; (v) the suspect providing inconsistent or wavering answers to inquiries; (vi) furtive movements (*e.g.*, glancing over one's shoulder, not making eye contact, etc.). See *U.S. v. Sokolow*, 490 U.S. 1 (1989).

In *Williams v. Commonwealth*, 21 Va.App. 263, 463 S.E.2d 679 (1995), police surveillance revealed that defendant made same-day round-trips from Newport News to New York City twice in the course of a week. The officers knew New York to be a major source city for drugs. Defendant paid cash for his tickets—more specifically, he paid with $5, $10, and $20 bills. He also used a different name on each trip. When defendant returned from his second trip, officers approached him in the hope of initiating a consensual interview. When they asked if he would speak with them, he replied, "no," then gave a "head fake" and ran. Reasonable suspicion existed to stop defendant and detain him for questioning.

Compare with *Wechsler v. Commonwealth*, 20 Va.App. 162, 455 S.E.2d 744 (1995). A DEA agent assigned to the Dallas/Fort Worth airport notified agents at Washington National Airport to watch for an individual known as "Brian Wechsler" (defendant). Wechsler was flying to Washington National from Tucson, by way of Dallas, and had reserved a one-way ticket just one hour before take-off, then arrived mere minutes before take-off, paying for his ticket in cash. He had checked two bags, but was carrying another two bags, and a person matching his description had been seen walking around the Dallas airport "acting very nervous." Two agents waited at Washington National for Wechsler's scheduled flight to arrive. Defendant was on board, and, when he deplaned, he looked "right at" the agents then "put his head down very quickly." Defendant waited in the baggage claim area for about five minutes. However, he then made eye contact with the agents, after which he attempted to make a phone call before leaving to get a taxi without claiming any bags. The agents approached defendant outside by the cab stand and initiated a consensual interview. Defendant claimed that he threw his ticket away in Arizona and that he had not checked any bags nor just used the phone. He then consented to a search of his (carry-on) bags, where the agents found his ticket with two baggage check claim tickets attached, catching defendant in his lie. At this point, the agents had reasonable suspicion to detain defendant until the bags he checked (still circling the conveyor belt inside) could be sniffed by a drug dog.

In a typical scenario, a suspect matching the profile is approached by officers and asked a few questions. Often, a threshold issue in such cases is the nature of the questioning. If the encounter is consensual, then no Fourth Amendment concerns arise. If, however, the officers' suspicions are aroused and a more aggressive investigatory posture is assumed, the encounter may escalate into a *Terry* type detention, and the scope of the encounter must conform to constitutional guidelines. The method employed by investigating officers should be of the least intrusive means reasonably necessary to verify or dispel the officer's suspicion in a short period of time. Although the initial stop may be justified, it may become so protracted, exceeding a time limit that the officer would reasonably need to confirm or dispel his or her suspicions about possible trafficking activity, that it becomes unreasonable. To pass constitutional muster, a detention not only must be justified at its inception, but also must be reasonably related in scope to the circumstances that justified it in the first instance.

If, and when, such an encounter progresses into a full-blown detention, another frequently adjudicated question involves the seizure of a suspect's luggage, purse, handbag or other personal item. The general rule is that officers may effect a temporary seizure if they have reasonable suspicion that the luggage contains contraband. The seizure must be brief, and related in duration to dispelling any suspicion about what the luggage contains. *U.S. v. Place*, 462 U.S. 696 (1983). Frequently, the luggage is subjected to a sniff-test (by a dog trained to recognize, by smell, the presence of narcotics or other drugs) or officers try to obtain consent to search the luggage. In such cases, a distinction must be drawn between detaining and actually opening and searching a container. Although police may temporarily detain a container based upon reasonable suspicion, they generally may not open it without a warrant, or some recognized exception to the warrant requirement.

(8) **Roadblocks and Checkpoints**. Roadblocks and checkpoints are used to make temporary stops. Municipal, county and state law-enforcement divisions set up roadblocks and checkpoints for a variety of reasons: checking the validity of driver's license and registration; determining if the vehicle meets safety inspection minimums; deciding if the car has the necessary municipal parking permit; apprehending intoxicated drivers; etc.

What is at issue in these scenarios? Checkpoints involve a constitutional detention, a seizure of a person, without any level of particular, individualized doubt, *i.e.*, reasonable suspicion or probable cause. Since there is no focused suspicion on an individual, rather than assessing the existence or absence of probable cause or reasonable suspicion, when the use of a roadblock is challenged, courts will examine police conduct and the circumstances of the stop and determine if the checkpoint is a reasonable intrusion, and therefore justifiable, under the Fourth Amendment. In the context of sobriety checkpoints, this reasonableness determination involves an analysis of three factors: (i) the magnitude of a state's interest in preventing accidents caused by intoxicated drivers; (ii) the extent to which the checkpoint advances that goal; and (iii) the measure of intrusion on an individual's privacy, both objectively, as perceived by the reviewing court, and subjectively, as the motorist may perceive the intrusion.

The U.S. Supreme Court applied these factors to determine the constitutionality of a sobriety checkpoint in *Michigan Dep't of State Police v. Sitz*, 496 U.S. 444 (1990). Here, Michigan implemented a program where checkpoints would be set up at predetermined sites along state roads. All drivers passing through would be stopped and checked for obvious signs of intoxication. If such indications were detected, the motorist would be taken out of the flow of traffic and an officer would check his or her license and registration. If warranted, the officer would conduct field sobriety tests. All other motorists would continue unimpeded after the initial screening. The check lasted 75 minutes, during which 126 vehicles passed through. The average delay was 25 seconds. Three motorists were detained on suspicion of intoxication, and two were arrested. The Court held that this checkpoint passed constitutional muster. Citing the aforementioned factors, the Court found that:

> (i) Michigan had a substantial interest in eliminating drunken driving, noting that "no one can seriously dispute the magnitude of the drunken driving problem [or the] State's interest in eradicating it."
>
> (ii) This checkpoint advanced the State's interest in curbing the drunk driving problem, noting that the use of a permissible checkpoint is but one of many reasonable alternatives to remedying the problem, and "the choice among such reasonable alternatives remains with the governmental officials who have a unique understanding" of the problem and the resources available to combat it.
>
> (iii) The intrusion, both objective and subjective, was slight, pointing out the brevity (25 seconds) of the average encounter. The Court also noted that any subjective intrusion, such as making a motorist fearful or annoyed, was diminished by the fact that motorists could plainly see all vehicles were being stopped.

However, in *City of Indianapolis v. Edmond*, 531 U.S. 32 (2000), the U.S. Supreme Court found that roadblocks and checkpoints conducted for the "primary purpose" of "uncover[ing] evidence of ordinary criminal wrongdoing" violate the Fourth Amendment. Roadblocks should be directed toward administrative purposes, such as ensuring highway safety (for example, by removing the "immediate, vehicle-bound threat" caused by drunk drivers) or, where appropriate, policing the Nation's borders (by checking for illegal immigrants in areas reasonably close to the border); they must not be motivated by "the general interest in crime control." Thus, so-called "drug checkpoints," staffed with drug-sniffing dogs and conducted for the primary purpose of discovering and interdicting illegal narcotics, were unconstitutional. The Court did note that if exigent circumstances were present, an appropriately tailored roadblock whose primary purpose was crime-control would almost certainly be permitted (for example, to thwart an imminent terrorist attack or to catch a dangerous criminal likely to flee by a particular route). Of course, if police uncover evidence of criminal wrongdoing at a valid roadblock, they may seize the evidence and arrest its possessor.

Contrast with *Illinois v. Lidster*, 540 U.S. 419 (2004), where the Court upheld a highway checkpoint designed to obtain more information about a recent hit-and-run accident. The Court found that the primary purpose of this checkpoint was *not* to determine whether the motorists stopped had committed a crime, but to ask for their help as members of the public in providing information about a crime in all likelihood committed by others. The Court noted that because an information-seeking stop is brief and police do not ask questions designed to elicit self-incriminating information, such a stop is less likely to provoke anxiety or to prove intrusive than a stop to investigate criminal activity. In this case, the relevant public concern was grave - police were investigating a crime that resulted in a human death. Moreover, the checkpoint advanced this concern to a significant degree—it took place near the scene of the accident one week later at about the same time of night. It was reasonable to believe some of the drivers on the road at this time had also been in the area around the time of the accident (for example, workers leaving the night shift at a nearby industrial complex). Most importantly, the stops only minimally interfered with drivers. All vehicles were stopped systematically, and each stop lasted only a few seconds, during which time police requested information and distributed a flyer regarding the accident. Because the checkpoint was valid, defendant's arrest for DWI based on observations made while he was stopped at the checkpoint was valid.

Virginia courts have upheld checkpoints using reasoning similar to the U.S. Supreme Court. They have consistently ruled that Virginia has a substantial interest in protecting its motorists, passengers, and pedestrians from unsafe drivers. Therefore, the stops are reasonable. However, the checkpoint must be carried out pursuant to a plan embodying explicit, neutral limitations on the conduct of the officers. Checkpoints with the primary objective of enforcing safety requirements have been upheld under Virginia law. *Desposito v. Commonwealth*, 60 Va.App. 252, 726 S.E.2d 354 (2012).

For example, in *Simmons v. Commonwealth*, 238 Va. 200, 380 S.E.2d 656 (1989), a roadblock set up by two state troopers to check driver's licenses and equipment was unconstitutional, even though all vehicles passing through the checkpoint were stopped, when the decision to establish the roadblock and its location and duration were solely within the discretion of the troopers.

In *Brown v. Commonwealth*, 20 Va.App. 21, 454 S.E.2d 758 (1995), state troopers were operating a sobriety checkpoint in Saluda County pursuant to a memo issued by the Department of State Police. This memo explicitly stated that the checkpoint could be moved from its specified location to a second specified location only if "safety considerations prevent[ed] checkpoint operations at the intended location." However, the troopers chose to move the checkpoint solely because traffic was light at the original location and they were making few arrests. The checkpoint set up at the second location was unconstitutional, because the troopers failed to comply with the administrative guidelines.

Compare with *Hall v. Commonwealth*, 12 Va.App. 972, 406 S.E.2d 674 (1991). A memo issued by the Virginia State Police designated 54 locations in Accomack County where "checking details" could be set up. Troopers would be ordered by their supervisors to set up a checkpoint at the beginning of the week. However, the troopers themselves would choose the exact time during the week to conduct the checkpoint (subject to the 2-hour time limit set in the memo) and which of the 54 approved sites at which to locate it. The Court found that the discretion this method provided troopers was too broad and was thus likely to lead to abuse. Therefore, a checkpoint set up under these guidelines was unconstitutional.

Contrast with *Crouch v. Commonwealth*, 26 Va.App. 214, 494 S.E.2d 144 (1997). A state trooper received an assignment at the start of his work week to set up a traffic-checking detail some time during the week, though no date or time was specified. His supervisor directed him to set up the checkpoint at the intersection of Routes 29 and 211. Therefore, the trooper had no discretion as to the location. In addition, once he selected a time, the trooper was required to obtain approval from a supervisor who was not part of the detail before he began stopping vehicles, which further limited his discretion. The Court also noted the need to evaluate weather conditions and determine the availability of other officers provided a reasonable basis for this procedure. Furthermore, the trooper stopped all vehicles and operated the checkpoint for one hour, so it complied with State Police Guidelines. The trooper did not have "unbridled discretion" in deciding when and where to begin stopping cars, so the checkpoint he set up was valid.

See also *Price v. Commonwealth*, 24 Va.App. 785, 483 S.E.2d 496 (1997). At a roadblock, the driver of a car was ordered not to drive after police discovered that his driver's license had been suspended with notice. Defendant, the only passenger in the car, told the police that she was willing to drive the car. Because defendant did not have her license with her, the police contacted a dispatcher to check her DMV records from a computer to see if she was truly licensed to drive. While searching defendant's DMV records, the police computer also checked its database of outstanding warrants and discovered an outstanding warrant for her arrest. Defendant was arrested and heroin was found in her purse during a search incident to the arrest. The warrant check of defendant was performed in accordance with the roadblock plan, so that her arrest was proper and the heroin could be used as evidence against her.

A vehicle may be detained at a roadblock no longer than the brief period that is necessary to perform the activities authorized in the roadblock plan unless the officers develop reasonable suspicion that the motorist is unlicensed, the vehicle is not registered, or there is some other violation of the law. *Gilpin v. Commonwealth*, 26 Va.App. 105, 493 S.E.2d 393 (1997).

Evasive maneuvers seemingly intended to avoid a roadblock may also establish reasonable suspicion for a stop. However, merely avoiding a roadblock via completely legal maneuvers will not justify a stop; there must be some other factors which suggest that the motorist turned in order to evade the roadblock.

See *Bailey v. Commonwealth*, 28 Va.App. 724, 508 S.E.2d 889 (1999). State troopers were conducting a roadblock at the intersection of Routes 606 and 674 in Henry County. Traffic was "light." A knoll just north of the checkpoint blocked it from the view of southbound drivers, who could not see the roadblock until they reached the top of the knoll. When defendant's vehicle reached the top of the knoll, it stopped suddenly, then eased into the driveway of a private residence 50 to 75 yards before the roadblock. Defendant drove slowly—as if hesitant about stopping at the residence—and kept looking at the troopers the whole time. When defendant got out of his car, the troopers were justified in stopping him and asking to see his license.

Compare with *Commonwealth v. Eaves*, 13 Va.App. 162, 408 S.E.2d 925 (1991), where defendant made an "abrupt," "immediate" turn into a turn lane just 100 feet to $^{1}/_{10}$-mile before a traffic checkpoint, not activating his turn signal until the last moment. Defendant then made a U-turn and drove off in the opposite direction. Defendant's sudden reversal so soon before the roadblock justified an investigatory stop.

But see *Bass v. Commonwealth*, 259 Va. 470, 525 S.E.2d 921 (2000), where there was no reasonable suspicion to stop defendant when he turned into a gas station 500 feet before a roadblock, and then, without stopping, returned to the highway in the opposite direction. Defendant's driving maneuvers were completely legal, and there were many reasons why he may have made a U-turn. The officer who stopped defendant only had a hunch that he was trying to avoid the roadblock.

See also *Murphy v. Commonwealth*, 9 Va.App. 139, 384 S.E.2d 125 (1989), where there was no reasonable suspicion to stop when defendant made a "normal and legal" right-hand turn onto a dead-end street approximately 350 feet before a roadblock. Nothing distinguished defendant's operation of his vehicle from any other driver making a right turn.

(9) **"Pretext" Stops**. Pretext stop cases typically involve officers who have a hunch that the driver or passenger of a car is committing a given crime, *e.g.*, possession of narcotics. However, nothing they have observed rises to the level of reasonable suspicion necessary to stop the car. The police then observe the motorist commit a minor traffic violation, and use this infraction, "the claimed pretext," to stop the vehicle and pursue a more intrusive line of investigation. In the adjudicated cases, the pretext stop search typically leads to the discovery of contraband wholly unrelated to the reason for the stop. In *Whren v. U.S.*, 517 U.S. 806 (1996), the U.S. Supreme Court held that "Ulterior motives do not invalidate police conduct that is justified on the basis of probable cause to believe a violation of the law has occurred." The true motivating factor behind the stop is irrelevant. As long as there is probable cause to believe the rules of the road have been violated, a detention under such circumstances is lawful. A suspect may not claim that he or she was illegally detained merely because an officer had a hunch that a different, more serious crime was being committed, although the officer lacked proof for that proposition and intended to find evidence of that crime during the stop. If there is an objectively valid reason for the stop, even one involving a minor traffic infraction, subjective intentions are irrelevant. The Court did note that a stop motivated by an intent to single out members of a suspect class, such as race, would, however, be impermissible.

The *Whren* standard applies to arrests as well as investigatory stops—an arrest is valid as long as there was objective probable cause, even if the officer had a different subjective motivation for making the arrest. *Arkansas v. Sullivan*, 532 U.S. 769 (2001) (arrest for driving without registration or proof of insurance and carrying a weapon valid when supported by probable cause, even if the officer's "true" purpose for making the arrest was to search defendant's car for drugs). An arrest is valid even if the criminal offense for which probable cause actually exists is not "closely related" to the offense stated by the officer at the time of arrest. *Devenpeck v. Alford*, 543 U.S. 146 (2004).

2. **Search Incident to a Detention**. During an investigatory detention, an officer may come to reasonably believe that the persons with whom he is dealing may be armed and presently dangerous, and where nothing in the encounter serves to dispel his reasonable fear for his own or another's safety, he is entitled to conduct a carefully limited search of the

outer clothing to discover weapons which might be used to assault him. *Terry v. Ohio*, 392 U.S. 1 (1968); *Harrel v. Commonwealth*, 30 Va.App. 398, 517 S.E.2d 256 (1991).

See, *e.g.*, *Logan v. Commonwealth*, 29 Va.App. 353, 512 S.E.2d 160 (1999). An officer stopped a small, two-door car for lack of an inspection sticker. When he approached the car, he immediately saw a 9mm handgun in the middle of the dashboard. The car's four young passengers "all seemed kind of nervous." All four were ordered out of the vehicle. Once out, though, they kept putting their hands in their pockets, had a hard time remaining stationary, and continually made eye contact with one another. The officer had reasonable suspicion to pat-down all four young men.

Compare with *Bandy v. Commonwealth*, 52 Va.App. 510, 664 S.E.2d 519 (2008). A Newport News officer was on patrol around 5:00 a.m. in Harbor Homes, a Housing Authority property he knew to be a "high-drug, high-crime area" (the officer had personally made 20 narcotics arrests there in 3 years). After watching defendant knock on the door of a residence and receive no answer, the officer approached him and initiated a consensual encounter. Defendant was unable to give the officer the name or address of the person he was trying to visit, and gave "evasive, inconsistent answers" when asked where he was coming from. He also appeared nervous through the conversation, fidgeting, shifting his weight on his feet back and forth, and shifting his eyes looking around. The officer has to ask defendant to remove his hands from his pockets twice, and while he complied both times, he continued reaching toward his pockets as they spoke. Because defendant was in a high-crime area at such a late hour with no apparent justification, the officer had reasonable suspicion defendant was committing a crime (at the very least, trespassing); defendant's repeated motions toward his pocket made it reasonable for the officer to believe that he was armed and dangerous. Therefore, a pat-down was justified.

In *Commonwealth v. Smith*, 281 Va. 582, 709 S.E.2d 139 (2011), defendant was a passenger in a car stopped for a broken rear brake light. The officer asked for defendant's identification, as well as the driver's. When defendant's license was processed through PISTOL (Police Information System Totally On Line), the system returned an "alert" stating defendant was "probably armed and a narcotics seller/user." This provided the officer reasonable suspicion to frisk defendant.

In *Thompson v. Commonwealth*, 51 Va.App. 205, 656 S.E.2d 409 (2008), an officer was conducting surveillance in the Green Valley neighborhood of Arlington County, where police had made multiple arrests for narcotics and weapons. He saw defendant standing on a street corner known for drug sales, wandering around with no apparent purpose. Based on his 10 to 20 previous contacts with defendant (including an arrest), the officer knew him to use heroin and crack cocaine habitually. Defendant entered a van; the officer suspected he was relocating a different part of the neighborhood to use or purchase drugs, so he radioed his observations to other officers. Thos officers drove to defendant's house, and saw the van pull up nearby. One officer drove closer and saw defendant and two other men standing by the passenger side of the van, "huddled" together. One of the other men was looking around, "as if something was going on they didn't want people to see," while the third man used a lighter on an object he held up to (but not in) his mouth—the officer found this consistent with inhaling smoke from a crack pipe. As the officer approached, one of the men fled—the officer knew that when police converge on a group of individuals engaged in drug activity, one will often "rabbit away" to divert police attention while the others dispose of contraband, so this further suggested the men had been smoking crack. Because the officer could not see defendant's left hand, he frisked him. The Court upheld this pat-down, noting that this encounter took place in a high-crime neighborhood, and that crack users can be "unpredictable, combative [and] sometimes violent." Moreover, the officer testified that crack users often use their smoking devices and weapons, and the Court recognized that "guns often accompany drugs." The officer thus had a reasonable suspicion that defendant might be armed and dangerous.

See also *U.S. v. Mayo*, 361 F.3d 802 (4th Cir. 2004). Two officers were patrolling a "high-crime" neighborhood on the south side of Richmond. They saw defendant standing in the middle of the street, talking to someone on the side of the street. When defendant noticed the approaching marked police car, he put his hand into his left jacket pocket, did a 180° turn, and walked between two buildings of an apartment complex. The officers observed that defendant "either...has something heavy in [his] pocket or he was pushing his hand down into his pocket." This was consistent with an effort to maintain control of a weapon while walking. The officers drove around the corner to see if defendant would emerge from the other side of the apartment complex. He did, and when he saw the officers again, "he immediately stopped, just froze in his tracks for a split second, then started walking along the side of the building." The officers stopped defendant in order to ask him if he lived in the "No Trespassing" complex. He was unusually nervous—his eyes were extremely wide, his mouth was agape, and his shirt was "fluttering...as though he was shaking." The officers had reasonable suspicion to pat-down defendant.

In *El-Amin v. Commonwealth*, 269 Va. 15, 607 S.E.2d 115 (2005), Richmond police received an anonymous tip that six young black males were smoking marijuana at Front Street and Fifth Avenue. Two officers responded and saw four young black males walking about half a block from the intersection. Although there were no signs of drug activity, the officers called out to the group and asked to speak with them. Two of the young males approached, while defendant and the fourth individual stayed back, albeit separate from one another. Moments later, two more officers arrived on the scene. They saw the fourth individual turn away and shove his hands into his waistband. One of the back-up officers patted the young man down, found a pellet gun in his waistband, and yelled "gun." One of the first officers on the scene then frisked defendant, finding a .38 revolver. Even though the officers had no particularized safety concerns as to defendant prior to learning the fourth individual was armed, the Court concluded that the pat-down of defendant was supported by reasonable suspicion. All four young men were members of a group in a high-crime area during evening hours. Upon learning that one member of the group was armed, the officer was "warranted in inferring that the inherent tendency toward violence demonstrated by one group member carrying a gun raised reasonable and particularized safety concerns as to other members of the same group." Although the Court stressed that companionship with an armed person, standing alone, will not provide reasonable suspicion to frisk, it may when the time and place of the stop and activity of the group are also considered.

Officers must remember that there is no automatic right to conduct a pat-down search for weapons during a *Terry* stop, even when the stop takes place in a high-crime area; an officer may frisk only if there is reasonable suspicion to believe the suspect is armed and dangerous. *Baker v. Commonwealth*, 57 Va.App. 181, 700 S.E.2d 160 (2010).

See *Thompson v. Commonwealth*, 54 Va.App. 1, 675 S.E.2d 832 (2009). A Norfolk officer observed defendant and two other men "loitering" in front of a convenience store on Lafayette Boulevard. The officer had previously made arrests and undercover drug buys outside the store and knew the area to be an "open market for drug sales." Norfolk police were authorized to enforce the store's "no trespassing" signs. The officer watched defendant for about 15 minutes, and when his two companions left, began to approach him. Upon seeing the uniformed officer, defendant walked toward the store's front door, but turned around at the officer's request. The officer asked for defendant's identification, then patted him down, finding a handgun in his waistband. The Court ordered the gun suppressed because this pat-down was not supported by reasonable suspicion. The officer did not see defendant engage in any hand-to-hand transactions, contact with others, or maintenance of a "stash" that would suggest involvement in the drug trade. Defendant made no furtive gestures and did not conceal his hands from the officer. There were no bulges in his clothing which could have been a concealed weapon. The encounter occurred at 8:00 a.m., in broad daylight, and defendant cooperated with the officer. While the officer may have had a hunch that defendant was involved with drugs because of the neighborhood and the amount of time he spent outside the convenience store, a hunch does not create reasonable suspicion; no additional facts supported his conclusion that defendant might be armed and dangerous.

In *Stanley v. Commonwealth*, 16 Va.App. 873, 433 S.E.2d 512 (1993), a pat-down was not justified when defendant had a bulge in his front pants pocket caused by 28 folded bills and a small packet with a "tiny amount" of cocaine, as the officer could not reasonably have believed that this small bulge was a hidden weapon.

The scope of the search must be strictly limited, so that the officer seeks only items that could be used to harm him or her.

For example, in *Thompson v. Commonwealth*, 51 Va.App. 205, 656 S.E.2d 409 (2008), when the officer felt a "long, flat, hard object" in defendant's pants pocket, he lawfully removed what turned out to be a butterfly knife.

Compare with *James v. Commonwealth*, 22 Va.App. 740, 473 S.E.2d 90 (1996). Defendant was a passenger in a car, the driver of which was arrested on an outstanding felony warrant. After the driver was asked to step out of the vehicle, defendant began "making gestures" with his hands and leaned down to the right so that officers could only see one of his hands. When told to put his hands on the dashboard, he did so, but only for a few seconds. He was then told repeatedly to get out of the car. He finally did so, but appeared "jittery." The officers had reasonable suspicion to pat defendant down. The searching officer felt a hard object, about 3 inches long, in defendant's pocket. He reasonably believed this was a weapon, and validly removed what turned out to be a glass crack pipe.

But see *Harris v. Commonwealth*, 241 Va. 146, 400 S.E.2d 191 (1991). While lawfully frisking defendant, an officer found a film canister in his pocket. When he asked what was in it, defendant replied, "Film." The officer opened it anyway, and discovered cocaine. The Court suppressed this evidence, because the officer should have ended his search once he determined that defendant was unarmed. The film canister was too small to conceal a weapon, and the officer had only a hunch that it contained contraband.

If a weapon is found, the officer may seize the item, and retain it, if its possession is unlawful. If the officer determines that the suspect is not armed, the purpose of the frisk is satisfied and the probing can proceed no further. However, if in the frisking procedure an object is detected, in a pocket or under clothing, that is clearly not a weapon, but rather, and just as obviously, contraband, the item may be seized. The rule here is that officers conducting a *Terry* frisk are entitled to seize any item whose contour, shape or mass make its identity immediately apparent as contraband. The officer must be able to instantly tell the item is contraband, without resorting to further manipulation of the item. This corollary is sometimes called the "plain feel" doctrine. *Minnesota v. Dickerson*, 508 U.S. 366 (1993).

Minnesota v. Dickerson, *supra*, set out the three requirements for "plain feel." First, the officer must have some independent constitutional justification for placing his or her hands on the person. Second, the officer must have lawful reason to touch the area in question, *i.e.*, reasonable suspicion of finding a weapon there. Third, upon touching the area, the officer must, through the process of touching, garner probable cause to believe the object that he or she is touching constitutes evidence of crime, or contraband. The probable cause must be reasonably contemporaneous with the initial touching. Any evidence obtained as a result of an illegal pat-down or frisk is inadmissible under the "Exclusionary Rule."

See, *e.g.*, *U.S. v. Swann*, 149 F.3d 271 (4th Cir. 1998). An officer was investigating the recent theft of a wallet in an office building, when he encountered defendant and his companion stepping off an elevator, both men matching descriptions given by witnesses. The men seemed "edgy" and, when the officer said he needed to speak with them, one of the men tried to circle around and get behind him. This justified a frisk. The officer felt an object in defendant's left sock that he could not identify; it was "kind of abnormal, and it felt kind of hard." The officer then removed what turned out to be a stack of five stolen credit cards. Even though the officer did not know what the object was when he removed it, this seizure was justified. The object's hardness and shape suggested that it could have been a weapon. In addition, its location—in defendant's sock—also aroused the officer's suspicions. Defendant had pockets where he would normally be expected to store small items, implying that he was attempting to conceal the object in his sock.

But see *Murphy v. Commonwealth*, 264 Va. 568, 570 S.E.2d 836 (2002). An officer frisked defendant after finding him in a home being searched pursuant to a warrant for narcotics. Upon his first feel of a bulge in defendant's left front pants pocket, the officer knew it "to be a plastic baggy...which is the way I commonly know marijuana to be packaged." However, although the officer could hear plastic rattle and feel the object through the pants, this only allowed him to identify it as a plastic bag. From there, he only inferred that the bag contained marijuana. This conclusion was not drawn from his tactile perception, but was only an educated guess (albeit one that proved to be correct). Therefore, it was not immediately apparent that the bag contained marijuana until it was removed, and the officer's seizure of it was invalid.

See also *Cost v. Commonwealth*, 275 Va. 246, 657 S.E.2d 505 (2008). During a pat-down of defendant, an officer felt numerous capsules inside defendant's left front pants pocket. He reached into the pocket and pulled out a plastic bag with 20 capsules of heroin. The officer later admitted that although he had often seen heroin packaged in capsules, over-the-counter medications, such as Motrin or Tylenol, are often packaged in capsules as well. Therefore, when the officer felt the capsules, it was not readily apparent that they were contraband rather than some legal medicine. Therefore, this was not a valid plain feel seizure.

The safety concerns that underlie the *Terry* exception have relevance not only to detentions on the street or in a public place, but also to the detention of automobile drivers and passengers as well. The U.S. Supreme Court has noted that "roadside encounters between police and suspects are especially hazardous, and danger may arise from the possible presence of weapons in the area surrounding a suspect." Thus, the search of the passenger compartment of an automobile, limited to those areas in which a weapon may be placed or hidden, is permissible if the police officer possesses a reasonable belief based on specific and articulable facts which, taken together with the rational inferences from those facts, reasonably warrant the officer to believe that the suspect is dangerous and may gain immediate control of a weapon. *Michigan v. Long*, 463 U.S. 1032 (1983); *U.S. v. Sakyi*, 160 F.3d 164 (4th Cir. 1998). The search must be limited in scope to the area that the suspect can reach easily, sometimes called the "zone within the wingspan" or "grabbable area."

See *Jones v. Commonwealth*, 52 Va.App. 548, 665 S.E.2d 261 (2008). Late one evening, two Richmond officers began watching defendant's vehicle, which was parked outside a hotel known for drug trafficking. For the next 15 minutes, no one exited or approached the vehicle; defendant just looked down into his lap the entire time. The officers suspected that defendant was counting money, and that he was waiting to engage in a drug transaction but the other party was late. (The officer later testified, "Narcotics deals never go down on time. If you set up a narcotics deal using an informant or undercover officer to meet someone, or someone to meet a dealer or a buyer, it never goes down on time. Someone is always late.") After about 15 minutes, the officers walked over to the car and asked defendant what he was doing. Defendant started reaching toward the floorboard. The officers told him to keep his hands on the steering wheel, and while he initially complied, he reached down twice more during the stop. The third time, his hand came up holding a black bag, large enough to conceal a weapon. After defendant tossed the bag on the front seat and exited the car, per the officers' orders, a *Long* search of the vehicle for weapons was reasonable.

In *U.S. v. Sakyi*, *supra*, defendant was stopped for a non-functioning brake light. When he opened the glove compartment to retrieve his registration, the officer saw a box of Phillies Blunt cigars. The officer knew this brand of cigars was commonly employed by marijuana users to roll marijuana cigarettes. "Almost all the time" the officer had come into contact with Phillies Blunts—a total of several hundred cases—"there had also been evidence of marijuana." Therefore, the officer had a reasonable suspicion that there were drugs in the car and, given the "indisputable nexus between drugs and guns" and the lack of any evidence allaying his safety concerns, had reasonable suspicion to search the passenger compartment of defendant's car for weapons.

For safety reasons, following a lawful stop an officer may, as a matter of course, order the driver and any passengers to step out of the vehicle. *Pennsylvania v. Mimms*, 434 U.S. 106 (1977); *Maryland v. Wilson*,

519 U.S. 408 (1997); *Harris v. Commonwealth*, 27 Va.App. 554, 500 S.E.2d 257 (1998). An officer may also pat-down a driver or passenger during a traffic stop if there is reasonable suspicion to believe they may be armed and dangerous. *Arizona v. Johnson*, 555 U.S. 323 (2009).

3. **Reasonable Suspicion and Probable Cause**. The facts and observations divulged during an investigatory detention may lead to "probable cause" to arrest the person detained. However, the officer must possess facts sufficient to support crossing the threshold between mere reasonable suspicion to detain and question, and full probable cause to arrest, before the latter action may be taken. If the investigating officer does not yet possess facts sufficient to create probable cause to believe the detainee has committed a crime, yet restrains the liberty of the detainee in a manner consistent with a formal arrest, the detention, even if initially lawful, becomes illegal. For example, transporting a suspect involuntarily to a stationhouse for further questioning without probable cause to link him with a crime violates the detainee's Fourth Amendment rights. This more intrusive step in the investigatory process requires probable cause and cannot be justified on reasonable suspicion alone. Courts look to the extent of the restriction on an individual's freedom and movement, to determine if the restraint is more consistent with a detention, or a full-blown arrest. For example, although the use of handcuffs on a suspect is a "hallmark" of a formal arrest and is generally considered a watershed, where a temporary detention becomes an arrest, a suspect nonetheless may be handcuffed or similarly restrained during a temporary detention, if the circumstances warrant.

One of the most common pitfalls in the area of reasonable suspicions and probable cause is the timing of an officer's arrest. In his or her zeal, an officer frequently acts prematurely and, as a result, nullifies what might have been a valid arrest. Thus, an officer may have grounds to approach an individual to question him or her and may even have reason to stop a person in order to obtain information. Certain officers, based on a "hunch" or a "gut feeling" that the individual is "dirty," will search or arrest the individual before they legally have grounds to do so. Many officers feel that the results of the search will justify the police activity. However, the courts have made it quite clear that a bad arrest or a bad search cannot be salvaged or corrected by what the officer recovers from the suspect.

Therefore an officer must proceed with care when approaching an individual on the street or in a car. The officer may only intrude upon the individual's privacy to the extent permitted. The officer can only act in relation to the information he or she possesses at that time. If the information he or she possesses does not constitute probable cause to arrest, the officer must not act prematurely and cannot take the person into custody. A law-enforcement officer should proceed with questioning, surveillance, or other appropriate police work that can culminate in probable cause.

4. **Detention and Seizure of Property**. Persons and vehicles are not the only potential subjects of a temporary detention. Officers may temporarily seize and detain items of personal property when they possess a reasonable suspicion that the property is connected with criminal activity. The detention must last no longer than reasonably necessary for the purpose of determining if the item is in fact linked to a criminal endeavor. If a brief investigation reveals that it is not, then the property should be returned to the owner. The Fourth Amendment protects property as well as privacy. *Soldal v. Cook Co.*, 506 U.S. 538 (1992). Therefore, similar to the seizure of an individual, "seizures of property are subject to Fourth Amendment scrutiny." *Soldal, supra*. This is true even when no search within the meaning of the Amendment has taken place.

Property is detained most often when the police wish to detain luggage or a package to search it for drugs. Often there is a slight delay to obtain a drug-sniffing dog. Items also may be held to search for weapons, explosive material or other contraband. Although in many cases the police will not need full probable cause for the detention of the property, in all cases the police will need some type of objective justification.

A detention of property may be deemed more reasonable if the police allow the owner of the object to leave. The police should then arrange a way to get the detained item back to that individual if their suspicions turn out to be baseless.

A "seizure" of property occurs when "there is some meaningful interference with an individual's possessory interests in that property." *U.S. v. Jacobsen*, 466 U.S. 109 (1984).

In *U.S. v. Bond*, 529 U.S. 334 (2000), the U.S. Supreme Court held that warrantless "squeezing" or other physical manipulation by police of luggage in the overhead compartment of a vehicle or other publicly accessible space—as opposed to mere visual inspection—violates the Fourth Amendment. Although passengers must expect some "casual contact" with their bags by other passengers, they also have a reasonable expectation that their privacy will not be invaded by the other passengers feeling their bags in an exploratory manner.

D. Exclusionary Rule

1. **Judicially Created**. The exclusionary rule is a judicially created doctrine designed to protect those rights embodied in the Fourth Amendment. *Mapp v. Ohio*, 367 U.S. 643 (1961).

2. **Application**. The exclusionary rule is applicable only to constitutional violations by governmental actors. A violation of privacy by an individual who is not an agent of the government is not a constitutional violation; therefore, the exclusionary rule will not apply to such intrusions. See *U.S. v. Jacobsen*, 466 U.S. 109 (1984).

3. **Purpose**. The exclusionary rule serves as a deterrent to unlawful police conduct. *U.S. v. Leon*, 468

U.S. 897 (1984); *Colaw v. Commonwealth*, 32 Va.App. 806, 531 S.E.2d 31 (2000).

E. Probable Cause

1. **In General**. In a pre-trial, investigatory context, probable cause is the highest constitutional degree of suspicion (in a trial, or guilt phase context, the "beyond a reasonable doubt" standard would be an even higher level of skepticism, bordering on certainty of guilt). Probable cause does not mean that the arrestee actually committed the suspected crime, or that the officer possesses enough proof to convict the suspect at a trial, or even that the arrestee will go to trial for the alleged offense. It does mean that at the time of the arrest, a person of reasonable caution, in the position of the officer, taking into account his or her experience, knowledge, and observations, would believe that a crime has been or is being committed. *Taylor v. Commonwealth*, 222 Va. 816, 284 S.E.2d 833 (1981); *Yancey v. Commonwealth*, 30 Va.App. 510, 518 S.E.2d 325 (1999). When probable cause determinations, whether made by a magistrate or an officer in the field, are challenged, the outcome will often depend on the presence or absence of one seemingly insignificant factor. As with factors used in a reasonable suspicion analysis, when an isolated factor is viewed alone, it may seem trivial. When analyzed with all of the other circumstances surrounding the arrest, it may lead a reviewing court to conclude the conduct was reasonable, and that the challenged arrest was based on probable cause.

In a warrantless arrest situation a police officer will be making the initial probable cause determination. Since probable cause is a somewhat nebulous concept, courts have tried to provide guidance. The U.S. Supreme Court has stated that "[i]n determining probable cause, evidence required to establish guilt is not necessary, but on the other hand, good faith on the part of the arresting officers is not enough, and probable cause exists if the facts and circumstances known to the officer warrant a prudent man in believing that the offense has been committed." *Henry v. U.S.*, 361 U.S. 98 (1959).

2. **Legal Definition**. "Probable cause" (sometimes called "reasonable cause") is a standard of proof greater than that of reasonable suspicion needed for a detention. It does not rise to the level of proof needed to obtain a conviction. Probable cause to arrest may exist (as determined later by a reviewing court) even if the arresting officer subjectively did not believe he had sufficient facts to constitute probable cause, as long as the objective standard is met. An arrest may be effectuated pursuant to a validly executed warrant, or without, provided probable cause exists.

The highest (most invasive) level of contact a law-enforcement officer may have with a citizen is "probable cause to arrest." An officer may make a warrantless arrest if he or she has probable cause. Probable cause is the officer's knowledge of facts and circumstances based on reasonable, trustworthy information sufficient to warrant a reasonable person to believe that the suspect is committing or has committed an offense. *Jones v. Commonwealth*, 279 Va. 52, 688 S.E.2d 269 (2010).

"Probable cause" means that an officer need not have information which excludes every conceivable possibility of innocence. Probable cause depends upon probabilities, not certainties. Thus, it must appear to the officer that it is at least more probable than not that a crime has taken place, and that the one arrested is its perpetrator. Conduct equally compatible with guilt or innocence will not constitute probable cause.

The subsequent determination of the guilt or innocence of the person arrested does not determine the legality of the arrest. *Michigan v. DeFillippo*, 443 U.S. 31 (1979).

Because probable cause depends on the facts of each case, probable cause may or may not be found in certain instances.

3. **Cautions to Observe (Warrantless Arrest)**. As every officer knows, our society is overrun with drugs. Many people rely on the police to fight this "war" against drug activity. The police officer must resist the temptation to use whatever means possible in fighting this "war." Courts will not tolerate a violation of constitutional rights merely because it occurs in the fight against drugs.

Thus, while an exchange of money for a glassine envelope, tinfoil packet or small vial with white powder will constitute probable cause for an arrest in most cases, not every exchange will permit an arrest. An officer may feel that if he or she sees an exchange for any object, the courts will back him or her up should he or she make an arrest. This is not so. An officer must still have reason to believe that he or she is observing a sale of drugs. Should the officer observe an exchange of an object he or she cannot see, the officer should not move in to make an arrest unless there are other factors that make it probable that drugs are being transferred.

The officer cannot use the "high-crime area" factor as a crutch to make the arrest. Most geographical areas today can be considered high-crime areas, and that fact, in and of itself, will not turn an improper arrest for drugs into a valid arrest. An officer may feel that he or she knows from past experience that the individual has no other reason to be in this area than to buy or sell drugs. However, that fact by itself will not be enough probable cause to justify an arrest.

4. **Identification of Suspect Required**. An officer must be sure that the description of a suspect is sufficiently detailed before he or she can effectuate an arrest. If the description is too vague or general, the officer should refrain from making the mistake of arresting the suspect prematurely. Instead, he or she should ask the suspect certain questions or keep the suspect under surveillance. Obviously, if those procedures are not practical, the officer should use common sense and take reasonable steps to keep the suspect under observation.

The victim is the best source of identification of a suspect. The courts will assume that the victim is reliable and obviously knows what he or she is talking about. Unless a police officer has reason not to believe a victim (*i.e.*, if he or she exhibits emotional or mental problems), the officer can rely on the victim for sufficient identification and probable cause to make an arrest without having to verify the information.

A police officer can also rely on a citizen who is not the victim of a crime, to provide information which will constitute probable cause to make an arrest. While the courts have also found this type of citizen to be trustworthy, an officer must still verify that the citizen knows what he or she is talking about. This is known as the citizen's "basis of knowledge."

Occasionally a victim will tell a police officer that he or she is not absolutely certain of an identification or that a person only looks like the perpetrator of the crime. This information is usually insufficient to provide an officer with probable cause. However, probable cause will exist if the victim picks out a suspect's photograph.

5. **Informants**. When a police officer relies upon a confidential-informant for information, there are certain points that the officer must keep in mind. Before the courts will find probable cause based on the informant's information, the officer must be sure that the tip is reliable. Two important components of this determination include both the informant's "credibility" and "basis of knowledge."

In order to establish an informant's "credibility," an officer should determine the following: (i) whether the informant came forward in the past with accurate information; (ii) whether the informant is making a declaration against his or her penal interest; (iii) whether the officer can confirm details of the informant's story; (iv) whether the informant is an ordinary citizen who provides information solely to help solve a crime or prevent a future crime.

In order to establish an informant's "basis of knowledge," the officer must consider the following: (i) whether the informant spoke from personal knowledge; (ii) whether the officer observed conduct directly involving the criminal activity about which the informant gave information.

If, under the totality of the circumstances—including the informant's "credibility" and "basis of knowledge"—the reliability of the tip can be established by the officer, probable cause for an arrest will exist. *Russel v. Commonwealth*, 33 Va.App. 604, 535 S.E.2d 699 (2000).

See, *e.g.*, *Robinson v. Commonwealth*, 53 Va.App. 732, 675 S.E.2d 206 (2009). A Newport news officer received information at around 11:10 p.m. from a confidential-informant (CI) regarding an imminent drug transaction. This CI was registered with Newport News police and in the previous 4½ months, had given the officer information leading to three arrest; the officer also knew that before that, his tips had led other officers to at least five additional arrests. The CI stated that a black female named "Antionette" was in possession of cocaine and driving a gray Crown Victoria with specified license plates to the WaWa at Beechmont and Warwick. There should would meet a buyer for the drug. Officers set up surveillance around the WaWa by 11:25. Shortly after, a gray Crown Victoria driven by a black female (defendant) pulled into the store; its license plates matched those given by the CI. The car parked by a gas pump and defendant got out, looked left and right, then entered the store. She walked around for a minute, then met a man and walked with him to the back of the store, out of the officers' view. Defendant exited the store a minute later, returned to her car, and sat in it for a minute. The man then exited the store, walked past defendant's car, then turned around and walked back to it. He bent down, placed his left shoulder against the driver's side door, and placed his hand inside the door; after holding this position for 10 seconds, he walked away. Defendant then drove away without ever pumping gas, despite parking next to the pump. Police stopped defendant for a traffic violation, then arrested her for selling drugs. The Court upheld this arrest, even though the officer did not actually observe defendant engage in a drug transaction. The CI had a record of providing accurate information, having helped in at least eight arrests. In addition, the CI personally observed defendant in possession of narcotics ***and*** supported claim with detailed information **including** defendant's gender, race, and name; the color, make, model, and license plate number of her car; and her specific destination (the WaWa gas station). The CI correctly predicted that defendant was en route to the WaWa station and that she would meet a man there, which she indeed did under suspicious circumstances. An adequate basis of knowledge was established because the CI could not have made such accurate and detailed predictions of future events without personal or "inside" knowledge of the suspect's activities. The Court noted with favor that the officers did not arrest defendant as soon as she pulled into the WaWa, but waited and observed her suspicious movements, which corroborated the tip. These observations, when considered in the context of the reasonably trustworthy information provided by the CI, were sufficient to warrant a person of reasonable caution to believe that an offense had been committed.

In *Askew v. Commonwealth*, 38 Va.App. 718, 568 S.E.2d 403 (2002), the Newport News Vice and Narcotics Division received a telephone call from a known informant at around 10:45 p.m. The informant stated that he had just seen a "black male sitting on the steps" of 811 36th Street, Apartment number 1, with cocaine in his pocket; the informant went on to describe this man in detail (5'6", 145 pounds, medium brown complexion, medium length afro, in a gray T-shirt and black or dark blue pants). The informant had worked with the police as a paid informant for three years and, in that time, had given information leading to over 200 drug-related arrests. In fact, the informant had never given unreliable information. An officer near the scene was contacted, and he arrived at the specified address within six minutes of the call. He saw defendant, who matched the description given in the call, sitting on the steps of the apartment. The officer then had probable cause to arrest;

the informant's long history and the officer's own confirmation of several key details established the reliability of the tip.

Compare with *Jefferson v. Commonwealth*, 27 Va.App. 1, 497 S.E.2d 474 (1998). At around 6:00 p.m., a Henrico County officer received information from a known informant (who was seeking help on a misdemeanor charge by cooperating) stating that three people were selling drugs in front of 101 Virginia Avenue, "at the corner of Second and Virginia." The informant identified one of the men as Kenny "Boo" Jefferson (the defendant), a black male, 5'10" or 5'11", with a thin build, two gold teeth, and short, cropped hair, wearing a gray shirt, jeans, and gold chains. The informant went on to say that he had seen defendant exchange money for crack cocaine several times. After this call, the officer called a second informant whom he had known for approximately three or four months and worked with "maybe a dozen times." This second informant had provided information leading to several arrests although no convictions as of the date of this incident. Following the officer's instructions, this informant went by the corner "to see what was going on." At around 6:30 p.m., he reported back that there were indeed three individuals selling cocaine outside 101 Virginia Avenue, one of whom was defendant. The informant had directly seen defendant complete at least one drug sale, and his description of defendant matched the one given by the first informant. The officer then had probable cause for a warrantless arrest of defendant.

See also *McGuire v. Commonwealth*, 31 Va.App. 584, 525 S.E.2d 43 (2000). A Chesterfield detective was contacted by a confidential-informant who claimed to have recently purchased cocaine from defendant (the latest in what he said were approximately 100 buys from defendant). The informant described defendant as a thin black male in his early 20s with a brownish-silver Honda. Four days after this tip, the informant arranged a controlled buy of cocaine in a Wendy's parking lot. As the detective watched, the informant bought a substance (later proven to be cocaine) from a black male driving a brownish-silver Honda registered to defendant. When this car left the parking lot, police followed it to the Chesterfield Village Apartments, where defendant was known to reside. Although the detective could not see the dealer's face during the exchange, the surrounding circumstantial evidence clearly indicated that it was defendant (as the informant had alleged). Three days later, the informant called defendant once again and ordered two "8 balls" of cocaine, to be delivered to the same Wendy's. Five minutes after the call, police surveillance saw a black male (later identified as defendant) leave defendant's apartment, enter the brownish-silver Honda, and drive off in the general direction of the Wendy's. He was stopped and arrested. The previous controlled buy and defendant's conduct in leaving just after the informant's call established the informant's reliability, therefore, his tip provided the officers with probable cause to arrest.

In *Stephenson v. Commonwealth*, 18 Va.App. 247, 443 S.E.2d 173 (1994), a Newport News officer received a call from a citizen who lived in the 700 block of 32d Street. The citizen had previously complained of two black males "selling" on the 600 and 700 blocks, and the officer had told him to call back when the subjects returned. This citizen was not paid by or connected with the police, but had provided information which proved accurate in the past. In this call, the citizen stated that a black male in a white T-shirt, blue jeans, and a brown hat was selling cocaine out of a two-door gray Datsun with specified plates. As the officer approached the area, the citizen called him back on his cell phone and stated that the dealer had just gone from the 700 block of 32d Street to the 600 block. The officer hung up just as he was rounding the corner onto the 600 block, and his headlights shined right on defendant, who matched the caller's description. A man standing with defendant immediately ran. The officer had probable cause to arrest defendant.

But see *Byrd v. Commonwealth*, 50 Va.App. 542, 651 S.E.2d 414 (2007). A paid CI contacted a Portsmouth detective to say that defendant Shawn Byrd was selling heroin on the corner of Lincoln and Camden Streets, wearing a burgundy coat with fur hood and blue jeans. The detective did not ask, and the CI did not state, whether he had actually observed the sale or possession of narcotics by defendant. The detective had worked with this CI for about a year, receiving information from him six times—evidence was recovered on each occasion, and the information also led to one search warrant and three arrests. Moreover, the CI had never given information which proved false. Therefore, he was reliable. However, in this instance, he had no basis of knowledge to support his tip. There was no indication he had personally observed defendant dealing drugs. Nor could the deficiency of the CI's basis of knowledge be overcome by corroboration of the details in the tip—the CI did not predict any future activity on the part of defendant, or offer any details indicating personal or "inside" knowledge of his affairs. Every detail the CI provided and that police confirmed "was readily available to anyone passing that particular street corner on that particular afternoon." Therefore, this tip was not sufficient to establish probable cause to arrest defendant.

6. **Other Basis for Probable Cause**. When a police officer relies on information from fellow police officers or from official police sources, he or she is entitled to assume that the "sending" officer has "probable cause" and that the information is reliable and accurate. However, an officer should also realize that if he or she acts on information that has become stale or outdated before the arrest (*i.e.*, an outdated arrest warrant, parole warrant, stolen car report, etc.), the arrest will be voided by the courts. Note that a failure to make a diligent search for the defendant when acting on a warrant can invalidate an arrest.

"Probable cause" can come from a variety of sources. A police officer can obtain information from a defendant's accomplice. An officer can utilize fingerprints at the scene of a crime or even information from a conversation heard through a wall to obtain the necessary information for an arrest.

F. Arrest

1. **Defined**. The most invasive level of encounter a law-enforcement officer may have with a citizen is the formal arrest. Courts look to a variety of factors to determine whether an arrest has taken place, or whether a temporary detention has escalated into a formal arrest. Criteria employed in this evaluation include: (i) whether the initial encounter was consensual; (ii) the duration or scope of the encounter, not only regarding the length of the detention, but also with respect to the degree of intrusiveness; (iii) an officer's statement that an individual is not free to leave, and what a reasonable suspect in a similar situation would believe regarding his liberty; (iv) whether the officer in some way restrained the suspect, and the nature and extent of that restraint; (v) the level of physical force threatened or employed; (vi) whether weapons or dogs were used to restrain, coerce or intimidate the suspect; (vii) the number of officers conducting the stop, and the nature of their questioning; (viii) whether or not the individual was transported to another location; (ix) whether the encounter took place in public view, or in a private or secluded area.

Handcuffing alone does not render every seizure an arrest *U.S. v. Crittendon*, 883 F.2d 326 (4th Cir. 1989). Similarly, drawing a gun and frisking an individual does not necessarily make an encounter an arrest. *Wells v. Commonwealth*, 6 Va.App. 541, 371 S.E.2d 19 (1988).

For purposes of constitutional analysis, as with a *Terry* detention, when a suspect is formally arrested, he has been seized for Fourth Amendment purposes, thus calling constitutional protections into play. However, unlike the limited intrusion imposed during a *Terry* stop, an arrest imposes the greatest restraint on an individual's liberty short of incarceration, and a higher level of skepticism—probable cause—must be demonstrated.

2. **Warrantless Arrests**.

a. **In Public Places**. The common law rule, and the rule in Virginia, is that an officer is permitted to make a warrantless arrest in a public place for a misdemeanor or felony committed in his or her presence, as well as for a felony not committed in his or her presence, if the officer has probable cause to believe a felony has been committed and the arrestee committed it. *McGhee v. Commonwealth*, 280 Va. 620, 701 S.E.2d 58 (2010); *Armstrong v. Commonwealth*, 29 Va.App. 102, 510 S.E.2d 247 (1999).

A warrantless arrest for a misdemeanor is generally subject to the requirement that the offense be committed in the presence of the officer. *Smith v. Commonwealth*, 32 Va.App. 228, 527 S.E.2d 456 (2000). However, by statute, Virginia allows warrantless arrests to be made for certain specified misdemeanors, notably shoplifting, carrying a weapon onto school property, brandishing a firearm, assault and battery (including domestic violence), destruction of property, and theft of a vehicle. Also, the presence requirement is waived for a DWI arrest if both the officer and the person to be arrested are present at the scene of a vehicular accident or a medical facility where a person has been transported following an accident, as long as the arrest is made within three hours of the accident. Such an arrest must follow a "reasonable complaint" from an observer of the misdemeanor. *Va. Code* §19.2-81. Note that this section confers the power to make an arrest to all police officers, including those off-duty or privately employed. *Davis v. Commonwealth*, 44 Va.App. 562, 605 S.E.2d 790 (2004). Police may also arrest the "predominant physical aggressor" without a warrant following an assault and battery against a family or household member or a violation of a protective order. *Va. Code* §19.2-81.3. (See further discussion in **Domestic Violence**, below.)

Be aware that a third party report of a misdemeanor not committed in the arresting officer's presence, even if from a fellow officer, will not justify a warrantless arrest. *Penn v. Commonwealth*, 13 Va.App. 399, 412 S.E.2d 189 (1991), *aff'd*, 244 Va. 218, 420 S.E.2d 713 (1992). However, an arrest for a misdemeanor committed outside the presence of the officer will be valid if the officer received a radio message from his department or another law-enforcement agency within the Commonwealth stating that an arrest warrant for the offense is on file. *Archer v. Commonwealth*, 26 Va.App. 1, 492 S.E.2d 826 (1997).

Generally, rather than arrest a suspect for a misdemeanor for which the suspect cannot receive a jail sentence, the officer should take the suspect's name and address, issue a summons, and release the suspect from custody. *Va. Code* §19.2-74(A)(2) (note that there are exceptions for certain offenses under Title 46.2, relating to motor vehicles, including DWI, and public drunkenness). However, arrest is proper if the suspect fails or refuses to discontinue the unlawful act, or if the officer believes the suspect is likely to disregard a summons or cause harm to himself or others. *Va. Code* §19.2-74(A)(1)-(2).

See *Brown v. City of Danville*, 44 Va.App. 586, 605 S.E.2d 297 (2004), where a custodial arrest for obstruction of justice was proper when defendant continued "yelling and screaming" despite the officer's request that he stop.

See also *Fox v. Commonwealth*, 43 Va.App. 446, 598 S.E.2d 770 (2004). An officer made a valid custodial arrest of defendant for carrying a concealed weapon and removing the serial number from a handgun, even though both offenses are only misdemeanors, because defendant ran when the officer first approached him. This immediate flight suggested an "unwillingness to acquiesce in any proceeding[.]" In addition, the fact that defendant was carrying an untraceable gun was a strong indication that he intended to do harm to others.

As long as an officer has probable cause, he or she may make a warrantless arrest in a public place, even if he or she had time to first obtain a warrant. *U.S. v. Watson*, 423 U.S. 411 (1976).

Note: **Citizen's Arrest**. Any citizen—including an officer outside his or her territorial jurisdiction—can make an arrest for a felony or a misdemeanor constituting a breach of the peace committed within their presence, as long as the citizen only detains the offender until an authorized officer arrives and makes no attempt to gather evidence. *Hudson v. Commonwealth*, 266 Va. 371, 585 S.E.2d 583 (2003). In *Hudson*, a Petersburg officer was off-duty but still in uniform and driving a marked car outside the city limits when he saw defendant driving erratically. Defendant swerved so badly that he nearly ran the officer off the road. The officer activated his emergency lights and stopped defendant, ordering him to stay in his vehicle until a Chesterfield County officer arrived. The Court concluded that because defendant's erratic driving constituted a breach of the peace and the Petersburg officer did not use his position to interrogate defendant or ask him for identification, this was a valid citizen's arrest.

b. **Justification for a Warrantless Arrest**. Statements made by a co-offender or accomplice can lead to probable cause for the arrest of his or her partner, when such a statement is against the maker's penal interest, or is corroborated by the police through their own independent line of investigation. When the statement given implicates the maker in wrongdoing, courts may attach greater weight to it. It is sometimes said that statements against penal interest carry their own indicia of reliability because it is unlikely and unnatural for persons to falsely incriminate themselves.

Information that comes from a source outside of law-enforcement circles, from private citizens or police informers, may demonstrate facts sufficient to establish probable cause. To determine if an informant's tip supports a probable cause finding, courts will employ a totality of the circumstances analysis and examine all of the attendant factors, including the veracity and reliability of the informant, and the basis of the informant's knowledge. No one aspect of the tip or information, or the person giving it, is determinative on the issue of probable cause, but rather the sum of all the circumstances concerning the tip and the person making it must be examined (see discussion under **Informants**, above).

Police are entitled to rely on facts garnered by those with whom they work. When more than one officer is working on a particular case, a reviewing court will take into account all of the information known to all of the officers on the case (not just the information known to the one who made the arrest) to determine if there was probable cause to arrest. This is known as the "fellow officer rule." Probable cause may rest upon the collective knowledge of police where there is some degree of communication among them, rather than solely on the information possessed by the officer who made the arrest. If probable cause is possessed by one officer and the officer communicates with a second officer, then that second officer may arrest although he or she does not have independent probable cause.

See *Armstrong v. Commonwealth*, 29 Va.App. 102, 510 S.E.2d 247 (1999). An Alexandria officer was in a high-crime area watching for drug violations from a concealed location, 25 to 50 feet above street level; she had approximately 2,000 hours of experience and had seen crack cocaine at least 500 times. Using 20x80 binoculars, she saw defendant walking down the street with two women. When defendant was less than 100 feet away from her, he lifted his right hand in front of his body and opened his palm, exposing a "small, unpackaged, off-white, rock-like object, slightly smaller than a pencil eraser, which [the officer] believed to be a rock of crack cocaine." After looking at the rock for several seconds, defendant returned his hand to his side and got into a car with the two women. The officer radioed her observations to another officer on the ground, who then had probable cause to arrest defendant.

Flight, nervousness or evasive maneuvers when confronted with police presence, although not sufficient to create probable cause when standing alone, may create probable cause for arrest if coupled with a suspicion centering on the suspect.

See, *e.g.*, *Purdie v. Commonwealth*, 36 Va.App. 178, 549 S.E.2d 33 (2001). An Arlington officer tried to stop a vehicle because he believed its front window was too darkly tinted. Although he turned on his emergency lights and tapped on his siren several times, the car continued on for about 300 yards before finally pulling over. Upon approaching the car, the officer recognized defendant, the front seat passenger, as a "police runner" who was involved in drugs. The officer asked the vehicle's occupants to step out so he could test the windshield. As soon as he gave this order, defendant became very nervous; he was "hesitant" about getting out, "looking around a lot," and "hunched over slightly" as he did so. He remained in a bent position as he walked away from the car, suggesting that he had something hidden in his waistband area. Once he passed a back-up officer, he straightened up. Another officer on the scene began to pat defendant down. When this officer reached the waistband area, defendant lifted his leg and put his foot on the guardrail in a manner that concealed his groin area. This search found nothing, but the back-up officer felt that it had been inadequate. Defendant sat on the guardrail, looked at the officers, and then looked all around. He put his hands in his jacket pocket, as if "gathering something," then removed the hands with his fists clenched. However, after looking at the officers, he placed his hands back in his pockets. He repeated this conduct "a couple more times," prompting the back-up officer to order him to place his hands on the car and submit to another pat-down. Defendant walked to the car and began to put his hand toward it, but then "quickly brought his hand up to his mouth" and swallowed some unseen object he was carrying. Although the officer could not recognize this object by sight, given the surrounding circumstances (including defendant's evasive conduct), he could infer that it was an illegal substance, and therefore had probable cause to arrest.

In *Greene v. Commonwealth*, 17 Va.App. 606, 440 S.E.2d 138 (1994), defendant arrived at Norfolk International Airport from New York, a city considered "one of the primary sources for narcotics." He had an "unnatural bulge" in the crotch of his pants, "maybe the size of a tennis ball." A plain clothes Drug Interdiction Team agent approached defendant and initiated a consensual interview. In addition to repeated complaints that his rights were being violated, defendant stated that he had not just arrived from La Guardia, even though surveillance had seen him deplane. Defendant then stated that he wished to use the phone, and the agent stepped out of his way. Defendant walked to a phone about 10 to 15 feet away and picked up the receiver. However, when the agent was distracted by a conversation with a fellow agent, defendant slammed the phone down and ran for the restroom. The agent looked up and saw some type of white material hidden in the unzipped area of defendant's crotch. The agent caught up with defendant in a restroom stall, where defendant had dropped to his knees and was furiously trying to shove something into the commode with one hand, and flushing with the other. The agent had probable cause to arrest defendant (the cocaine defendant had flushed was later recovered from the sewer).

Compare with *U.S. v. Rabinowitz*, 991 F. Supp. 760 (W.D.Va. 1998). Police were conducting surveillance of several marijuana fields they had discovered in a wooded area of Albemarle County. Defendant arrived in this area, carrying a backpack, and began to make his way down a path leading to one of the fields. He kept looking around cautiously, as if he realized the local foliage had been disturbed. When he was within 30 yards of the field, officers revealed and identified themselves. Defendant turned, dropped his backpack, and ran. Police had probable cause to arrest him.

See also *Farmer v. Commonwealth*, 21 Va.App. 111, 462 S.E.2d 564 (1995). A Lynchburg officer received a dispatch relaying a tip from an unidentified citizen caller. The caller reported that she suspected a black male in a camouflage jacket and jeans was selling drugs in the 2800 block of Lorraine Street. She saw defendant flag down several cars, spend a short time talking with them, and then return to the sidewalk. The officer knew this area to be "one of the prime illicit drug distribution sites" in the city. He arrived at the 2800 block of Lorraine approximately five minutes after receiving the dispatch, and saw defendant, dressed as described, standing on the passenger side of a pick-up truck. When he looked up and saw the marked police cruiser, he turned away and began to walk down Front Street. When the officer called out to him, defendant turned and looked at the officer before he took off running. With the officer in pursuit, defendant jumped a fence and tried unsuccessfully to enter a locked house. At one point, defendant reached into his pockets as if trying to get rid of something. Finally, a back-up officer tackled defendant as he ran into a wooded area. Defendant's flight—in conjunction with the earlier tip and the high-crime area he was found in—established probable cause for his arrest.

A driver's refusal to perform field sobriety tests—when accompanied by evidence tending to show the driver has been drinking and that this has affected his mental or physical state—may be considered in determining whether there is probable cause to arrest the driver for DUI. *Jones v. Commonwealth*, 279 Va. 52, 688 S.E.2d 269 (2010).

Facts officers turn up through their own investigations, or by their own observations, can form the basis of probable cause.

See *Parker v. Commonwealth*, 255 Va. 96, 496 S.E.2d 47 (1998). An officer was patrolling near the Creighton Court housing development in Richmond, a high-drug area. Defendant was standing with a group of men around a Cadillac with an open trunk. When the men saw the marked patrol car, they shut the trunk and dispersed. As defendant walked away, he placed something in the waistband of his basketball shorts. After defendant switched directions in an apparent attempt to avoid the officer, he was stopped. Defendant's shorts were made of a thin, white, "mesh" material, and the officer could see a pink object between defendant's undergarments and his skin. The officer knew from his experience with drug arrests that dealers often hide their stash in their crotch area and that pink baggies are commonly used to package crack cocaine. He asked defendant whether there was anything in his shorts. Defendant said there was not and grabbed his basketball shorts and boxers "and started, in very exaggerated motions, pulling them to the side, up and down shaking them in and out[,]" in an apparent effort to keep the pink object from falling out. The officer had probable cause to arrest and validly seized the pink object (which, of course, proved to be crack) incident to that arrest.

In *Joyce v. Commonwealth*, 56 Va.App. 646, 696 S.E.2d 237 (2010), Norfolk police were conducting surveillance in the 600 block of Liberty Street, ,an area with a notorious reputation for being "infested with narcotics." Officers saw defendant standing directly under a "No Trespassing" sign posted on the side of a Shop 'N Go convenience store. (Store management had filed a letter with the police department requesting enforcement of its trespassing ban.) Defendant did not go in or out of the store, or attempt to do so. There were no doors on that side of the store, and thus no reason to loiter there. Police had probable cause to arrest defendant for trespassing.

See also *McCain v. Commonwealth*, 261 Va. 483, 545 S.E.2d 54 (2001). During a consensual encounter in a high-crime area of Danville, an officer asked to pat-down defendant. Defendant became "somewhat irate" and refused to consent to a search. He told the officer he was in the area to visit his brother and then walked to the front door of an apartment building (about 35 feet away) on which he began pounding. When no one answered, he walked to the right of the door, behind a staircase leading to the second floor. Through a decorative opening in the concrete wall that separated him from defendant, the officer "saw the shadow of an arm 'reach out' and heard the sound of a metal object making contact with another metal object." Defendant then began to walk back, while the officer re-approached him and again asked to frisk him. Defendant agreed, but the pat-down found nothing. The officer then retraced defendant's steps and, behind the stairs, found a shopping cart with a gun in it. He showed the gun to defendant and asked if it was his. Defendant responded by running away. The officer then, based on what he had seen and heard, had probable cause to arrest defendant for possession of a concealed weapon.

In *Moss v. Commonwealth*, 30 Va.App. 219, 516 S.E.2d 246 (1999), defendant was parked at a Lynchburg gas station when a police investigator walked up to his vehicle and initiated a consensual conversation. While talking with defendant, the investigator noticed a "brown, hand-rolled marijuana cigarette lying in the ashtray in plain view between the driver's seat and the front passenger seat of the vehicle." He recognized the illegal nature of the cigarette from his training and experience. This observation provided probable cause to arrest defendant.

Compare with *U.S. v. Humphries*, 372 F.3d 653 (4th Cir. 2004). Two Richmond officers were patrolling an area of the city known for drug trafficking. They saw five to fifteen persons just "hanging around" on one block. As the officers drew near in their marked police car, they saw defendant pat his waist area; they suspected that he was instinctively confirming the presence of a weapon there. The officers stopped about 20 feet away from the group and exited their car; they could already smell a strong odor of marijuana coming from the group. Defendant turned and quickly walked away. One officer began to follow him and asked him to stop, but defendant kept on walking. As the officer drew within 5 to 10 feet of defendant, he could smell the same strong odor of marijuana he had noticed before coming from defendant's person. Defendant ignored two more requests to stop before the officer finally caught up to him as he tried to enter a house. At this point, based on defendant's conduct and the smell of marijuana, the officer had probable cause to arrest.

But see *Brown v. Commonwealth*, 270 Va. 44, 620 S.E.2d 760 (2005). A Richmond officer was patrolling along Lakeview Avenue when he found defendant asleep in an illegally parked car, clenching a hand-rolled cigarette. The officer arrested defendant, because in his experience, hand-rolled cigarettes are commonly used to smoke marijuana. However, in this case, there was no other drug paraphernalia in the car, and the cigarette in question smelled like tobacco not marijuana (it contained tobacco laced with heroin and cocaine—obviously illegal, but the officer could not tell this based on smell). The officer also admitted at trial that some people do in fact roll their own *tobacco* cigarettes. The Court concluded that defendant's arrest was not supported by probable cause, because the officer had no reason to believe the cigarette contained marijuana rather than tobacco.

If the officer actually observes someone committing an offense, then there is probable cause to make an arrest. Even if the officer does not witness the actual acts that constitute the offense, circumstantial evidence may create probable cause to believe the crime has been committed.

See, *e.g.*, *Ross v. Commonwealth*, 35 Va.App. 103, 542 S.E.2d 819 (2001). An officer was sitting in his car at an intersection in a high-crime area of Richmond. The officer looked up and saw defendant approach the passenger side of another car that was stopped at the intersection. Defendant removed a plastic baggie from his waistband and handed the passenger in the car an unidentified object from the baggie in exchange for cash. The officer knew that baggies were often used to conceal drugs and that drug sales were common in this part of the city. Even though he could not see the object defendant sold, he nevertheless had probable cause to arrest him for possession of a controlled substance.

Compare with *Powell v. Commonwealth*, 27 Va.App. 173, 497 S.E.2d 899 (1998). Three Lynchburg officers were on patrol in an area known as an open air drug market. They observed defendant and two other men sitting on an 18"-high wall, facing the street with their backs to a parking lot. The men were seated about 3 feet apart from one another. Upon seeing the officers, defendant placed his left hand, which was clenched in a fist, behind his back, keeping it close to his body. When he returned the hand to his side, it was no longer clenched. Neither of the other two men made any hand motions. When the officers pulled over, defendant stood up and began to walk away. One of the officers looked behind the wall and found a brown paper bag of crack cocaine, 6 to 12 inches directly behind the place where defendant had been sitting. The officers then had probable cause to arrest defendant for possession of cocaine.

In *McGhee v. Commonwealth*, 280 Va. 620, 701 S.E.2d 58 (2010), an officer had probable cause to arrest defendant for public intoxication under §18.2-388 when defendant was sitting in the driver's seat of a parked car, there was a strong odor of alcohol coming from his breath, his eyes were bloodshot, and his speech was slurred.

In *Troncoso v. Commonwealth*, 12 Va.App. 942, 407 S.E.2d 349 (1991), an officer was on patrol when he saw a car with flashing lights stopped illegally in the roadway next to a parked Trans Am. He returned a short time later, and, while the illegally stopped car was now gone, the Trans Am remained. The car's three occupants quickly ducked down. When the officer pulled up behind the car, all three exited the vehicle in a "real hurry." The officer then activated his high-beams and spotlight. Defendant, who was by the driver's side door, stopped while the other two walked away quickly. Defendant became fidgety and began to sweat profusely, and the officer noticed a large bulge near his stomach area. At this point, the officer had reasonable suspicion for a stop. He also performed a pat-down, and felt that the bulge was caused by a soft substance in a plastic bag. However, since he could not be sure it was contraband, he did not seize it but instead went to his car to call for back-up. When he returned, he saw a bag of marijuana just under the Trans Am next to where defendant was standing. The officer knew that the bag had not been there when he went to his car just moments before. Therefore, he had probable cause to arrest defendant for possession of marijuana.

See also *Taylor v. Waters*, 81 F.3d 429 (4th Cir. 1996). Harold Duncan was arrested for selling cocaine base, and, after his arrest, he confessed to being a dealer. The informant who provided the information leading to Duncan's arrest also alleged that Duncan had used his apartment as a base of operations for several years, so police obtained a warrant to search it. When they arrived, they met Clarence Taylor, who revealed that he was Duncan's roommate. In the kitchen of the apartment, police found a metal pot and strainer with white residue (these utensils are often used to convert cocaine into cocaine base). When asked about them, Taylor did not deny knowledge of the items, but said that he used them to make tea. Police also found several plastic baggies with the corners torn off in the kitchen (these are commonly used to package cocaine), as well as a brown envelope with a white powdery substance in the trash in a common area of the apartment. Although Taylor said he had lived with Duncan for 12 years, he could not tell the officers what Duncan's occupation was. A search of Taylor's room found $5,500 in cash and records for bank accounts containing over $23,000. However, police also found four uncashed paychecks from Taylor's job as a waiter, which totaled only $1,907. The officers had probable cause to arrest Taylor for possession of and conspiracy to distribute cocaine.

In *Maryland v. Pringle*, 540 U.S. 366 (2003), a car with three male occupants was stopped for speeding in the early morning hours. When the driver retrieved his license from the glove compartment, an officer noticed a large amount of cash. Because he found this suspicious, the officer asked for and received consent to search the car. Police found $763 in the glove compartment and five glassine bags of cocaine between the back-seat armrest and the back-seat. All three men denied ownership of the drug. Because the cocaine was accessible to all the men, it was reasonable to infer all three had knowledge of, and exercised domain and control over, it. Police therefore had probable cause to arrest all three occupants, including defendant, the front-seat passenger.

But see *Whitehead v. Commonwealth*, 278 Va. 300, 683 S.E.2d 299 (2009). Defendant was one of two rear seat passengers in a car stopped for a traffic violation. During the stop, "Xantos," a drug dog, sniffed the car and alerted by sitting—a sign he had detected narcotics odors at his head height or above (had the odor been at ground level, Xantos would have lied down). Police searched the vehicle but found nothing. They then searched the driver and the other two passengers, but again found nothing. Finally, officers searched defendant and found two syringes in his pocket, as well as a bottle cap with burnt residue that proved to be heroin. The Court ruled this was not a valid search incident to arrest (the only possible justification for the search), because police did not have probable cause to arrest defendant. Probable cause must be particularized to the person arrested. Here, while Xantos' alert justified a search of the vehicle itself, there was no alert to defendant specifically. Xantos' handler admitted that sometimes the dog would react to an "old odor"—thus it was possible the odor came from drugs that had been removed from the car before defendant was ever in it. Although the fact that no drugs had been found in searches of the car and everyone else in it may have created a strong suspicion that defendant had drugs, probable cause requires more than a "strong suspicion." Defendant's arrest violated the Fourth Amendment.

c. **Warrantless Arrest at a Residence**. A distinction must be drawn between a warrantless arrest made in a public place, and one made in a residence. Historically, the home has enjoyed nearly sacrosanct status in American and English common law. Courts have long held that the home's threshold should not be crossed without significant justification. As a consequence of this long standing judicial respect for the integrity and privacy of the home, courts have held that in the absence of exigent circumstances or consent (see below), a law-enforcement official may not make a warrantless entry into a person's home (or the curtilage of the home) to effect his or her arrest. *Jefferson v. Commonwealth*, 27 Va.App. 1, 497 S.E.2d 474 (1998). Note, however, that a suspect cannot avoid a lawful warrantless public arrest already set in motion by retreating into his or her home. *U.S. v. Santana*, 427 U.S. 38 (1976).

The requirement of a warrant for an in-home arrest applies as well to the arrest of a suspect in a motel or hotel room where the suspect has set up a temporary residence. See *Archer v. Commonwealth*, 26 Va.App. 1, 492 S.E.2d 826 (1997). For similar reasons, if the police are to search in the home of a third party for a suspect for whose arrest they already have a warrant, they must obtain a search warrant before entering the third party's home, absent exigent circumstances or consent. *Steagald v. U.S.*, 451 U.S. 204 (1981).

The possession of an arrest warrant provides officers with the authority to arrest an individual within his or her own home, and limited authority to enter the dwelling for that purpose, if police have reason to believe that the subject of the warrant is inside at the time of entry. *Payton v. New York*, 445 U.S. 573 (1980). The result of these rules is that if a suspect is to be arrested in a residence, a warrant must be obtained first, or the Commonwealth will be forced to show that exigent circumstances or another applicable exception justified the otherwise illegal entry. If this burden is not met the arrest will be quashed. Any evidence the Commonwealth hopes to use as a result of the arrest may be suppressed.

The penalty for an unlawful arrest in a defendant's dwelling is the suppression of anything seized at the time of the arrest, either from the defendant or in the dwelling, and any statements made at the time of the arrest inside the home. However, if the officers in fact had probable cause to arrest, a confession obtained *after* the illegal warrantless entry to effect the arrest, or other evidence found outside the home, is not necessarily inadmissible at trial. *New York v. Harris*, 495 U.S. 14 (1990).

d. **Exceptions to the Warrant Requirement for Residence Arrest**.

(1) **Exigent Circumstances**. Generally, exigent circumstances are explained as those surrounding a fast moving, often tense series of events, which call for quick and decisive law-enforcement action. These are factors that allow law-enforcement agents to conduct a warrantless arrest, based on probable cause, when there exists an urgent need for official action and time to secure a warrant is not available. Factors considered in determining if exigent circumstances are present include (*Dorman v. U.S.*, 435 F.2d 385 (D.C. Cir. 1970)): (i) if the offense was violent in nature; (ii) a reasonable belief the suspect is armed; (iii) the level of certainty that the suspect committed the offense; (iv) the level of certainty that the suspect is in the building; (v) evidence indicating that the suspect is a flight risk; (vi) the time of day; (vii) the level of force officers need to obtain entry to the premises.

The police generally must be unable to obtain a warrant in the time necessary to meet and defuse the situation, or at the very least, contacting a magistrate must be extremely impractical (*e.g.*, late hour, remote location). In such situations, the requirement of a warrant may be excused. The presence of these extreme circumstances mandates the compelling need for quick activity and makes warrantless in-home arrests reasonable within the meaning of the Fourth Amendment. If such circumstances were not present, a warrant would be required. Often cited examples of the risks created when officers hesitate in making a warrantless in-home arrest and instead seek to obtain a warrant before acting include the following: (i) the risk of injury or death to officers or bystanders; (ii) the potential destruction or concealment of valuable evidence; or (iii) the possibility that the suspect may flee and elude capture.

A police officer can enter a premises without a warrant to protect individuals in distress, to assist victims of crimes that have just occurred, or to investigate suspicious signs of impending danger. In *People v. Mitchell*, 39 N.Y.2d 173, *cert. denied*, 426 U.S. 953 (1976), the Court held that there are three basic requirements for such action: (i) the police must have reasonable cause to believe that there is an emergency at hand and an immediate need for their assistance for the protection of life or property; (ii) the search must not be primarily motivated by an intent to arrest and seize evidence; and (iii) there must be some reasonable basis to associate the emergency with the area or property to be searched. Once the police respond and enter a premises pursuant to this exigency, they have the right to "restore or maintain the status quo during the emergency to control the dangerous or dynamic situation." This right enables the officer to take a number of intrusive actions ranging from a command to halt to a seizure of an individual. During the investigation of an emergency situation, the police may search for weapons to protect themselves and others and may look for injured or missing persons.

In *Brigham City v. Stuart*, 547 U.S. 398 (2006), four officers responded to a loud party at a residence at around 3:00 a.m. When they arrived, they heard sounds of an altercation occurring inside--"thumping and crashing" as well as people yelling "stop, stop" and "get off me." The officers looked in the front window but saw nothing; because the sounds seemed to be coming from the back of the house, they proceeded down the driveway to investigate further. From the end of the driveway, they could see two juveniles drinking beer in the back yard. When they entered the back yard, they saw an altercation taking place in the kitchen through a screen door and windows. "[F]our adults were attempting, with some difficulty, to restrain a juvenile." The juvenile, fists clenched, eventually "broke free, swung a fist and struck one of the adults in the face." That adult then spit blood into the sink. The other three adults continued to restrain the juvenile, pressing him against a refrigerator with such force that it slid across the floor. The officers called out, but were ignored. They then entered the residence and broke up the fight. The adults were arrested for contributing to the delinquency of a minor (because of the juveniles outside with beer), disorderly conduct and intoxication. The U.S. Supreme Court upheld this warrantless entry under the Fourth Amendment. The officers were confronted with ongoing violence. They had an objectively reasonable belief that "both the injured adult might need help and that the violence in the kitchen was just beginning." The Court noted that police are not required to wait until someone is unconscious (or semi-conscious) before entering: "The role of a peace officer includes preventing violence and restoring order, not simply rendering first aid to casualties; an officer is not like a boxing (or hockey) referee, poised to stop a bout only if it becomes too one-sided."

(2) **Hot Pursuit**. Hot pursuit can be thought of as a specific application of the general exigent circumstances exception. In *Warden v. Hayden*, 387 U.S. 294 (1967), the U.S. Supreme Court held that if police were in hot pursuit of a fleeing suspect, they were entitled to make a warrantless entry to effectuate the arrest if they had probable cause to believe the suspect committed a felony, and they believed he entered a specific dwelling. To justify a warrantless in-home arrest based on this exception, the Commonwealth must generally demonstrate that (i) the pursuit was undertaken immediately after the crime (*i.e.*, it was "hot"); and (ii) there was a continuity of pursuit from the crime to the place of arrest. Be aware, however, that this doctrine applies only to offenses punishable by incarceration; it does not apply when a suspect com-

mits only a nonjailable offense. *Welsh v. Wisconsin*, 466 U.S. 740 (1984); *Cherry v. Commonwealth*, 44 Va. App. 347, 605 S.E.2d 297 (2004).

See, e.g., *U.S. v. Jones*, 204 F.3d 541 (4th Cir. 2000). Officers noticed a group of men standing behind a car parked on a street corner in an area known for drug trafficking. One of the men, Claxton, had money in his hand and held it out to defendant, who had his hand out toward Claxton. Upon seeing the officers, Claxton placed a small plastic bag of white powder in his mouth, while defendant turned and walked away quickly, toward a residence. One of the officers ordered defendant to stop, but instead he ran up the porch stairs and entered the house, slamming the door behind him. Through a window, the officer saw defendant run up the interior stairs, clutching his pocket. Not only did the officer have probable cause to arrest defendant for the apparent drug transaction, he also could enter the house in hot pursuit in order to apprehend defendant (in addition, the Court noted that entry was further justified by the need to prevent defendant from destroying evidence, and, because the officer did not know whether or not defendant actually lived in the house, to ensure the safety of the possibly innocent inhabitants).

(3) **Consent**. A third exception to the warrant requirement for an in-home arrest comes into play when police officers are first given permission to enter the premises and then arrest a suspect inside. Valid consent to enter may be given by the owner, or one entitled to possession of the premises, or one with common control or joint access to the premises for most purposes. Valid consent is that which is given voluntarily (*i.e.*, in the absence of overbearing conduct on the part of the law-enforcement officials seeking permission). Consent may be either actually given, or implied from conduct or acts. The validity, or voluntariness, of consent is determined by examining all of the facts and circumstances surrounding the encounter.

(4) **Domestic Violence**. A law-enforcement officer may make a warrantless arrest for assault and battery or violation of a protective order against a family or household member even if the offense was not committed within the officer's presence. *Va. Code* §19.2-81.3(A). The officer must arrest the party whom the officer has probable cause to believe, based on the totality of the circumstances, was the predominant physical aggressor, unless there are special circumstances that would dictate a course of action other than arrest. In determining who was the predominant physical aggressor, the officer should consider:

- o who was the first aggressor;
- o the health and safety of family and household members;
- o prior complaints of abuse;
- o the relative severity of the injuries inflicted on each party;
- o whether any injuries were inflicted in self-defense;
- o witness statements;
- o any other observations.

Va. Code §19.2-81.3(B).

When investigating any complaint of domestic violence, upon request the officer must transport or arrange transportation of the alleged victim to a hospital, safe shelter, or magistrate. *Va. Code* §19.2-81.3(E).

Whenever an officer makes an arrest for domestic violence, the officer must petition for an emergency protective order (unless the arrestee is a minor). The officer must also petition for a protective order even when no arrest is made if the officer has probable cause to believe that a danger of domestic violence still exists (unless the suspected abuser is a minor). *Va. Code* §19.2-81.3(D). Regardless of whether or not an arrest is made, following a domestic violence incident the officer must file a written report stating the number of arrests made, or explaining why no arrest was made. Upon request, the officer's department must provide a copy of the report to the alleged victim. The officer must also provide the alleged victim with information regarding the legal and community resources available to victims of domestic violence, both orally and in writing. *Va. Code* §19.2-81.3(C).

3. **Arrests Pursuant to Warrant**. The essential difference between arrests with a warrant and those without involves where a person may be arrested. When acting pursuant to a warrant, police are entitled to arrest a suspect anywhere. This is not so, absent exigent circumstances, in the case of a warrantless arrest. Another distinction is that in a situation where an arrest is made with a warrant, the existence of probable cause is determined by a neutral and detached magistrate, who places his or her independent judgment between a perhaps overzealous law-enforcement official and the citizenry. In a situation where an arrest is made without a warrant, probable cause is determined by the officer in the field.

a. **Contents of the Arrest Warrant**. The arrest warrant must: (i) be directed to an appropriate officer or officers; (ii) name the accused (or, if his or her name is unknown, set forth a description by which he or she can be identified with reasonable certainty); (iii) describe the offense charged with reasonable certainty; (iv) command that the accused be arrested and brought before a court of appropriate jurisdiction in the county, city or town in which the offense was allegedly committed; and (v) be signed by the issuing officer. *Va. Code* §19.2-72.

b. **Delay in Making Arrest**. A criminal suspect has no constitutional right to be arrested. There is no requirement that once law-enforcement possesses probable cause to arrest, they do so immediately. However, a gap between the commission of the offense, or the time law-enforcement becomes aware of it, and the arrest may be so protracted that it violates the Due Process Clause of the Fourteenth Amendment. Although the Sixth Amendment guarantees a defendant the right to a speedy trial, it does not guarantee the right to a speedy arrest. However, an inordinate delay between the time a crime is committed and the time a defendant is arrested or indicted may violate

Due Process guarantees. To prevail on such a claim, a defendant must show that (i) the delay caused actual and substantial prejudice to the defendant; and (ii) the delay was the product of deliberate action or inaction by the prosecution in order to gain a tactical advantage. *Morrisette v. Commonwealth*, 264 Va. 386, 569 S.E.2d 47 (2002).

To demonstrate prejudice the defendant must show that real and tangible harm was done to his defense. The mere passage of time, and its effects, is not sufficient. The fact that "memories will dim, witnesses become inaccessible, and evidence will be lost" during the gap is inadequate to demonstrate the defendant cannot receive a fair trial and insufficient to show a Due Process violation. *U.S. v. Marion*, 404 U.S. 307 (1971).

c. **Who May Serve**. A law-enforcement officer may execute a warrant issued anywhere in the Commonwealth within his or her jurisdiction. When executing a warrant, the officer shall endorse the date of execution upon the warrant and return it to a judicial officer. *Va. Code* §19.2-76.

A "media ride-along," where a reporter and photographer accompanied police while an arrest warrant was served in a suspect's home, violated the Constitution. *Wilson v. Layne*, 526 U.S. 603 (1999).

An officer need not have physical possession of the arrest warrant prior to making an arrest. However, if the officer does not have possession of the warrant at the time of arrest, the officer must: (i) inform the arrestee of the offense charged and the fact that a warrant has been issued, and (ii) deliver a copy of the warrant to the arrestee as soon thereafter as practicable. *Va. Sup. Ct. R.* 3A:4.

d. **Knock-and-Announce Rule**. When executing an arrest warrant, law-enforcement officers should knock on the door of a residence or business, announce their purpose and authority, and give the occupants a reasonable opportunity to answer before forcing their way inside. *U.S. v. Grogins*, 163 F.3d 795 (4th Cir. 1998). However, there is no constitutional mandate that an officer knock and announce before entering a dwelling in every instance. In situations where exigent circumstances are present, an unannounced entry may be reasonable (*e.g.*, presence of weapons that may put officers at peril, the destruction of evidence, etc.). "A no-knock entry is justified when the police have a reasonable suspicion that knocking and announcing their presence, under the particular circumstances, would be dangerous or futile, or that it would inhibit the effective investigation of the crime." *Richards v. Wisconsin*, 520 U.S. 385 (1997). Police are not required to possess the higher standard of probable cause to believe that exigent circumstances exist, but only the less stringent standard of reasonable suspicion. *Henry v. Commonwealth*, 32 Va.App. 547, 529 S.E.2d 796 (2000). The failure to knock and announce is not a per se constitutional violation. There are no rigid rules to determine when an unannounced entry will be excused. The constitutionality of the entry will be judged on the particular facts and circumstances of each case. However, the failure to knock and announce may render an entry unreasonable, and therefore unconstitutional, when there is no showing of exigent circumstances that justify the failure to first knock.

e. **Protective Sweep**. In *Maryland v. Buie*, 494 U.S. 325 (1990), the U.S. Supreme Court held that when police make an arrest at a residence, they may conduct a warrantless search of the arrest scene, known as a "protective sweep." The extent of the sweep is limited to a brief cursory visual inspection of the premises. The Court reasoned that it is reasonable for officers to safeguard themselves by ensuring that no others are present who could injure them. It is important to note this is not a general crime scene exception to the warrant requirement but rather a doctrine that may be used to justify a warrantless search in particularized circumstances. A sweep is permissible only "when the searching officer possesses a reasonable belief based on specific and articulable facts that the area to be swept harbors an individual posing a danger to those on the arrest scene."

f. **Use of Force to Effect Arrest**. The general rule is that reasonable force may be used to place a suspect under arrest. The permissible quantum of force employed varies from situation to situation. A reasonable level of force in one context, may be unreasonable in another, and vice versa. Regardless, the essential principle remains that the force used must be reasonable under the particular circumstances surrounding the arrest. The analysis applied by courts to determine the reasonableness of an officer's actions, focuses on the police conduct, viewed objectively, in light of the circumstances confronting the officers at the time, without regard to their subjective intent or motivation. Factors a court will weigh include the severity of the crime at issue, whether the suspect posed an immediate threat to the officers or others, and whether the suspect was actively resisting arrest or attempting to evade arrest by flight. *Graham v. Connor*, 490 U.S. 386 (1989); *Turmon v. Jordan*, 405 F.3d 202 (4th Cir. 2005). The ultimate inquiry is whether a reasonable officer, confronted with the same circumstances, would have reacted in the same way.

In some situations, the use of deadly force is reasonable within the meaning of the Fourth Amendment. Deadly force does not mean force that necessarily results in the death of the suspect, but rather a level of force that is reasonably likely to cause death or serious bodily injury. The U.S. Supreme Court has described the circumstances under which the use of deadly force may be reasonable for purposes of Fourth Amendment analysis, and therefore permissible. In *Tennessee v. Garner*, 471 U.S. 1 (1985), the Court stated "Where the officer has probable cause to believe that the suspect poses a threat of serious physical harm, either to the officer or to others, it is not constitutionally unreasonable to prevent escape by using deadly force." Thus, if the suspect threatens the officer with a weapon or there is probable cause to believe that he has committed a crime involving the "infliction or threatened infliction of serious physical harm," the use of deadly force is permissible. If the officer does not have probable cause to believe the above, reasonable, non-deadly force must be used to effect the arrest.

The rule in *Garner* is not applicable to a situation involving an arrest by a private person because private citizens are not bound by the Fourth Amendment. Similar principles apply, however, to the use of force employed by a private individual to effect an arrest, although any potential excessive force claim would be premised on state law tort principles, rather than on a theory involving the deprivation of constitutional rights.

G. Procedure After Arrest

When an officer arrests the operator of a motor vehicle, and there is no legal cause to retain the vehicle, the officer must allow the arrestee to designate another person who is present at the scene of the arrest and a licensed driver to drive the motor vehicle from the scene to a place designated by the arrestee. If such a designation is not made, the officer may cause the vehicle to be taken to the nearest appropriate place for safekeeping. *Va. Code* §19.2-80.1.

When an individual is the subject of a warrantless arrest, he or she is entitled to a prompt judicial determination of probable cause to arrest (if he or she has been arrested pursuant to a warrant, a judge has already made a probable cause determination as a prerequisite to issuing the warrant). *Wilson v. Commonwealth*, 34 Va.App. 25, 527 S.E.2d 608 (2000). A prompt determination means that judicial hearing must be held as soon as is reasonably feasible. However, a finding must be made within 48 hours of the arrest. *County of Riverside v. McLaughlin*, 500 U.S. 44 (1991). A hearing provided within 48 hours may violate the promptness requirement if the arrested individual can prove that the probable cause determination was delayed in an unreasonable manner. Examples of unreasonable delays are ones for the purpose of gathering additional evidence against the defendant, or motivated by ill will toward the defendant. The judicial probable cause determination, may be combined with other proceedings, like an arraignment. If the Commonwealth fails to provide a determination within this 48-hour window, the burden of proof shifts to the government to demonstrate the existence of an emergency or other extraordinary circumstances justifying the delay.

The government cannot justify the failure to provide a determination within 48 hours on the basis of an intervening weekend (*e.g.*, a person arrested on Thursday not given a hearing until Monday).

When an officer makes an arrest pursuant to a warrant, the officer must endorse the date of execution on the warrant and return it to a judicial officer. *Va. Code* §19.2-76. After making an arrest based on a warrant, the arresting officer must bring the accused before a judicial officer. This should be done as quickly as possible. The judicial officer shall immediately conduct a bail hearing and either admit the accused to bail or commit him to jail. In misdemeanors, the judge may, with the consent of the accused and the Commonwealth, proceed to trial. The judge must be a judge of the court with proper jurisdiction. *Va. Code* §19.2-80. Whenever possible, the officer should obtain and provide the magistrate or court with the arrestee's criminal history information prior to the proceeding. *Va. Code* §19.2-80.2.

When officers make an arrest supported by probable cause to hold for a serious offense and bring the suspect to the station to be detained in custody, taking and analyzing a cheek swab of the arrestee's DNA is, like fingerprinting and photographing, a legitimate police booking procedure that is reasonable under the Fourth Amendment. *Maryland v. King*, 569 U.S. __ (2013).

When a public school teacher or other school employee is arrested for a felony or a Class 1 misdemeanor, a report must be filed with the employing superintendent as soon as practicable. A report must also be filed with the superintendent when a public school student age 18 or older is arrested for: a firearms offense; homicide; felonious assault and wounding; criminal sexual assault; manufacture, sale or possession of a Schedule I or II controlled substance or marijuana; arson; burglary; robbery; or street gang related activity. *Va. Code* §19.2-83.1.

III. CRIMINAL LIABILITY

In order for criminal liability to attach, a person must engage in a course of conduct during which two factors coincide: a voluntary act committed by the accused and a culpable mental state, existing at the time of the act, *e.g.*, negligently, recklessly, knowingly, or intentionally. Conduct is intentional when it is the actor's conscious objective to engage in that conduct. Conduct is knowing when the actor is aware that there is a high probability that he or she is engaging in that conduct. Conduct is reckless when the actor evinces a plain, conscious and unjustifiable disregard of harm, and that disregard involves a substantial deviation from acceptable standards. Conduct is criminally negligent when the actor's conduct shows a disregard for the safety of others under circumstances likely to cause injury or death. An act may, in some instances, be an omission to perform a duty that the law imposes. There are certain offenses that do not require a mental state coinciding with an act to create criminal liability; the act alone, regardless of the state of mind of the defendant when he committed the act, is sufficient to constitute the completed crime. These are called strict liability crimes.

IV. SEARCH & SEIZURE

The Fourth Amendment mandates that citizens shall be free from unreasonable searches and seizures. What type of governmental conduct is deemed unreasonable, and therefore unconstitutional, is determined by the particular facts and circumstances of each case. However, some hard and fast rules do provide guidance. First and foremost among these is the core principle that all searches, unless conducted pursuant to a warrant, are per se unreasonable, therefore unconstitutional. *McCary v. Commonwealth*,

228 Va. 219, 321 S.E.2d 637 (1984). There are, however, certain well-crafted exceptions to the warrant requirement, permitting warrantless searches when the requirements of the relevant exception are met. These are discussed below.

A. The Search Warrant

The Fourth Amendment requires that a search warrant be issued by a magistrate or judge who must, after receiving an oath or affirmation from the warrant applicant, make an independent, neutral and detached determination whether probable cause exists to believe that particularly described property will be found at a particular place. *Henderson v. Simms*, 223 F.3d 267 (4th Cir. 2000).

When applying for a warrant, an officer must present an affidavit that contains facts that support a finding of "probable cause." The affidavit may be filed via fax or other electronic means. *Va. Code* §19.2-54. The warrant and the affidavit or testimony on which it is based must be legally sufficient, *i.e.*, they must contain facts that show a crime was committed, and facts that indicate why evidence will be found in a given place. Cursory assertions and bare-bones allegations will not support a warrant. *Colaw v. Commonwealth*, 32 Va.App. 806, 531 S.E.2d 31 (2000).

A criminal defendant may challenge the validity of a warrant, or the sufficiency of an affidavit, on constitutional grounds, or may allege the warrant does not fulfill the requirements of the warrant statute. A constitutional challenge would, for example, involve assertions that the facts as alleged do not establish "probable cause," or that the warrant did not "particularly" describe the place to be searched, *et al.*, as required by the Fourth Amendment. A statutory challenge would involve allegations that the procedures did not comply with statutory requirements.

If the defendant shows that a search warrant contains false statements made by the affiant either knowingly or with reckless disregard for the truth, then the remaining information in the affidavit must independently establish probable cause, or else the warrant will be invalid. *Franks v. Delaware*, 438 U.S. 154 (1978); *Gregory v. Commonwealth*, 46 Va.App. 683, 621 S.E.2d 162 (2005); *Commonwealth v. Jennette*, 90 Va. Cir. 5 (2015).

There is no right to an adversarial hearing on the issue of obscenity prior to the issuance of a search warrant for allegedly obscene materials. However, there must be a prompt determination of obscenity following the seizure of such materials. *Heller v. New York*, 413 U.S. 483 (1973).

B. Neutral and Detached Magistrate

The warrant must be issued by a removed, impartial judge. This requirement is premised on the notion "that a warrant authorized by a neutral and detached judicial officer is a more reliable safeguard against improper searches than the hurried judgment of a law-enforcement officer engaged in the often competitive enterprise of ferreting out crime." *Lo-Ji Sales Inc. v. New York*, 442 U.S. 319 (1979). In *Lo-Ji*, the warrant was invalid when the magistrate who issued it went along on the raid he had authorized, and determined only when he saw certain materials what was obscene, and therefore what was to be seized. Similarly, where a warrant was issued by the state Attorney General, who was also actively involved in the investigation, and later prosecuted the case at trial, the initial probable cause determination was patently improper, for it was not made by an impartial and remote observer. *Coolidge v. New Hampshire*, 403 U.S. 443 (1971). To ensure the requisite neutrality, the issuing judge must not play a role in the investigation or the search itself.

Note: A search warrant for an attorney's office may only be issued by a circuit court judge. *Va. Code* §19.2-56.1.

C. Probable Cause Required—Justification for Issuance of a Search Warrant

The probable cause standard for issuance of a search warrant is essentially the same as that for arrest, the difference being that for a search warrant police must have probable cause to believe that a crime has been committed and that they can find certain evidence in a particular place. *Gregory v. Commonwealth*, 46 Va.App. 683, 621 S.E.2d 162 (2005); *Turner v. Commonwealth*, 14 Va.App. 737, 420 S.E.2d 235 (1992). When making a probable cause determination, the issuing magistrate is entitled to consider all the circumstances surrounding an alleged crime, *i.e.*, "the totality of the circumstances." There has to be, however, more than mere conjecture involved. Facts, real and demonstrable, must back up the allegations and assertions. Positive proof of an illegal endeavor and the location of incriminating evidence are not required, but rather a showing that there is a probability of criminal activity, and proof thereof in a specific location. The facts relied upon by the magistrate must be contained within the four corners of the affidavit. *Adams v. Commonwealth*, 48 Va.App. 737, 635 S.E. 20 (2006).

Three specific concepts, regarding sources of information, or the nature and quality of the information itself, pose special problems for courts when ascertaining the existence of probable cause: (i) the use of third party informants, rather than direct observation or personal knowledge; (ii) the facts relied upon may be too old or no longer accurate (staleness); (iii) the facts relied upon establish that a crime may take place, and evidence of that crime may be found in a certain place in the future, but not at present (anticipatory warrants).

1. **Informants**. Rarely do law-enforcement officers rely on their own direct observations to provide the underlying facts supporting a warrant. In many, if not most cases, a third party will provide documentation of a crime's commission, and detail where evidence or contraband can be found. To determine if an informant's tip supports a probable cause finding, courts will employ a totality of the circumstances analysis and examine all of the attendant factors, including the veracity and reliability of the informant, and the basis of the informant's knowledge, as well

as the extent to which that information can be or has been corroborated and verified. *Illinois v. Gates*, 462 U.S. 213 (1983); *Slace v. Commonwealth*, 43 Va.App. 61, 596 S.E.2d 90 (2004).

No one aspect of the tip or information, or the person giving it, is determinative on the issue of probable cause. A question regarding the informant's veracity may be compensated for by strong evidence confirming the way in which the informant obtained his or her information, or verification that the facts he or she relayed are accurate, or some other factors indicating the informant's reliability. *Polston v. Commonwealth*, 24 Va.App. 738, 485 S.E.2d 632 (1997), *aff'd*, 255 Va. 500, 498 S.E.2d 924 (1998). Even so, some broad generalizations may be made. Generally, the information provided by a non-confidential informant will be given greater deference than that provided by a confidential-informant, who asks that his or her identity be kept secret. Courts reason that if someone is willing to expose themselves to public scrutiny, then the information they pass on is likely more reliable than information given by someone who is reluctant to associate their identity with the tip.

Information given by a witness to or victim of a crime is likely to be perceived as more trustworthy than information given anonymously, or even by a known police informant. Generally, if other factors point to the conclusion that a witness's or victim's tip is reliable (*i.e.*, some corroboration), and there is no evidence that calls his or her motives for giving information into question, there will not be an inquiry into that informants credibility or veracity. *Lester v. Commonwealth*, 30 Va.App. 495, 518 S.E.2d 318 (1999). Moreover, witness and victim informers have not had the opportunity to build up a reputation for giving solid information to the authorities, as they have had no reason to do so. There is no past conduct by which to gauge their propensity for honesty. Witness and victim informers generally have nothing to gain by giving information to police, other than the satisfaction of knowing they may help solve a crime, or prevent the commission of another.

A distinction may also be drawn between an anonymous tip and a tip provided by an identified informant or one with whom police have previously worked. A court may give more credence to an informant known to police, especially if he or she has provided solid information in the past. When the identity of the informant is known, there may be some basis for determining how the tipster came about his or her information. Rarely will an anonymous, uncorroborated tip form the basis of probable cause or reasonable suspicion. However, independent corroboration on the part of officers working the case may bolster the tip and, if the information is sufficiently confirmed, create probable cause.

Statements against an informant's penal interest, *i.e.* which implicate him or herself in a crime, also carry a presumption of reliability, because courts reason it is unlikely and unnatural for persons to falsely incriminate themselves.

Regardless of who provides the information, the court will ultimately employ the same analysis, examining the totality of the circumstances; the informant's reputation for truthfulness, his or her dependability, and the circumstances under which he or she obtained the information.

See, *e.g.*, *Lester v. Commonwealth*, *supra*. A concerned citizen came forward to police and stated that defendant was a thief who sold stolen property and that defendant had offered to sell him jewelry and a rifle engraved with the name "Katharina Bergdoll." An officer checked police records and learned that Ms. Bergdoll had in fact reported a burglary four days earlier in which jewelry and a rifle had been taken. The officer who spoke with the informant knew him to be a long-time resident in the community, gainfully employed, who had never been arrested and who attended church on a regular basis. His only reason for remaining anonymous was fear of retribution. In addition, two other officers had received tips indicating that a white male known as "Paul" (defendant's first name) was selling stolen goods from the boarding house where defendant lived. Under the totality of circumstances, probable cause was established for a warrant to search defendant's residence.

Compare with *West v. Commonwealth*, 16 Va.App. 679, 432 S.E.2d 730 (1993). A confidential-informant (C-I) told a Gloucester County deputy that, a little over a week before, defendant had bragged to him about the 30 pounds of bacon and "boatload" of cigarettes he had stolen from stores he had broken into, saying that any time the C-I needed these things he should come by defendant's house and pick some up. The C-I also stated that defendant had mentioned taking a cash drawer as well. This C-I was a county resident and had given information to the deputy on two prior occasions resulting in two misdemeanor arrests. In addition, the deputy knew of two break-ins under investigation where large amounts of bacon and cigarettes had been taken. The deputy had probable cause for a warrant to search defendant's house.

In *Boyd v. Commonwealth*, 12 Va.App. 179, 402 S.E.2d 914 (1991), a C-I contacted Henrico County police and stated that, three days before, he had personally seen cocaine packaged for sale and scales for that purpose in defendant's Henrico residence at 1218 Wilkinson Road in Henrico. Although Henrico County police did not know this C-I's true name, an officer from another jurisdiction with whom the C-I had originally spoken did, and the affiant-officer from Henrico County was given a phone number and fictitious name with which he contacted the C-I. The affiant-officer averred that this C-I was a "concerned citizen" who had been a resident of Richmond for a year, held a substantial job, and had no criminal record. He also averred that the C-I was familiar with cocaine based on past personal use. Moreover, by checking DMV records, police records and a city street directory, police confirmed that defendant lived at the alleged address, that his house fit the description the C-I provided, and that he drove a Mercedes just as the C-I said he did. Probable cause was established for a search warrant.

If the informant appears in person before the magistrate, then the affidavit need not contain extrinsic corroboration of his or her reliability. *Polston v. Commonwealth, supra.*

2. **Staleness**. If there is an appreciable delay between the occurrence of the circumstances that create probable cause and the time a warrant is issued, the facts supporting the probable cause determination may become "stale," in that, although the alleged facts may have once supported a probable cause determination, presently, they may not. Courts reason that information demonstrating that evidence of a crime could once be found in a given location does not mean that evidence of a crime may necessarily be found there now. Stale information creates the mere suspicion crime has been committed, and does not rise to the level of probable cause.

Note that staleness is not judged solely by counting the number of days between the occurrence of the facts relied on in the affidavit and the issuance of the warrant (though that is a factor to consider). The Court must weigh all the facts and circumstances of the case, including the nature and length of the alleged illegal activity and the nature of the property to be seized and the place to be searched. *U.S. v. Rhynes*, 206 F.3d 349 (4th Cir. 1999); *Anzualda v. Commonwealth*, 44 Va.App. 764, 607 S.E.2d 749 (2005). In *Maye v. Commonwealth*, 44 Va.App. 463, 605 S.E.2d 353 (2004), the Court noted that selling drugs, by its very nature, is an ongoing activity.

3. **Anticipatory Warrants**. An "anticipatory warrant" is a warrant authorizing a search at some future time. When applying for an anticipatory warrant, the affiant-officer is, in essence, asserting that probable cause does not exist presently, but will exist following the occurrence of some "triggering event" (for example, controlled delivery of a package containing contraband). Anticipatory warrants are constitutional. To obtain such a warrant, the affidavit must provide facts establishing a fair probability that evidence of a crime or contraband will be found at the place to be searched *if* the triggering condition occurs, *and* probable cause to believe that the triggering condition *will occur. U.S. v. Grubbs*, 547 U.S. 90 (2006); see also *McNeill v. Commonwealth*, 20 Va.App. 674, 395 S.E.2d 460 (1990); *Commonwealth v. Vaughan*, 88 Va. Cir. 300 (2014).

In *Grubbs, supra*, defendant purchased a videotape of child pornography from a website operated by an undercover postal inspector. Authorities arranged a controlled delivery of the videotape, then obtained a search warrant for defendant's home; the affidavit in support of the warrant specifically provided that the warrant was not to be executed "unless and until the parcel has been delivered by a person(s) and has been physically taken into the residence." After defendant's wife signed for the videotape, the warrant was lawfully executed. The affidavit in this case clearly established that contraband would be present in defendant's home once the videotape was delivered--child porn is obviously illegal. In addition, there was probable cause to believe this condition would be satisfied; although it was possible defendant might have refused delivery, he was unlikely to do so after having ordered the videotape. Therefore, this was a valid anticipatory warrant.

The Fourth Amendment does not require that the triggering condition be set forth in the warrant itself, although that is the better practice. *U.S. v. Grubbs, supra.*

D. Particularity Requirement

The Fourth Amendment requires that a warrant specifically name both the places to be searched and the items to be seized. The purpose of this particularity requirement is to prevent general searches, *i.e.*, a rummaging for incriminating evidence without cause. The warrant must state the items and the places with distinctiveness, so that the officer executing the warrant will have no question, and no room for guesswork or discretionary choices, as to where he or she is to search, and for what they are looking. A valid warrant authorizes the executing officer to look for a particular item in any place it could logically be found (*e.g.*, narcotics may be reasonably expected to be found in a dresser drawer; a stolen Harley Davidson motorcycle, on the other hand, would not). However, the particularity requirement limits any arbitrary decisions as to what items may be seized. The warrant and the supporting affidavit may generally be read together to arrive at a sufficiently particular description.

The particularity requirement has two prongs: (i) a particularly described place, and (ii) particularly described items.

1. **Places to Be Searched**. The warrant must describe the location to be searched with sufficient particularity so that the executing officer can, with reasonable effort, ascertain and identify the place intended. *Jeffers v. Commonwealth*, 62 Va.App. 151, 743 S.E.2d 289 (2013). Generally, a description containing the address as it would appear on a mailing envelope, along with the name of the resident and a cursory listing of the physical appearance of the building itself, is sufficient for single unit dwellings. A problem arises, however, when the place to be searched is in a multi-unit structure, like an apartment in a complex or an office in a professional building. The general rule is that the description must describe the specific sub-unit to be searched, not the whole building. If the description merely lists the address of a building, which itself contains many residences or offices, and the law-enforcement agents executing the warrant have no means to determine which of the individual units is to be searched, the warrant may be invalid. See *Wilson v. Commonwealth, supra.*

2. **Items to Be Seized**. The search warrant must also describe the items to be seized with "reasonable specificity," limiting the discretion of the executing officers by directing them to seize only evidence of a specific crime. *Morke v. Commonwealth*, 14 Va.App. 496, 419 S.E.2d 410 (1992). The degree of particularity with which the items must be described will fluc-

tuate, depending on the nature and individual attributes of the subject items. *Moyer v. Commonwealth*, 33 Va.App. 8, 531 S.E.2d 580 (2000). However, a certain minimum level of specificity will always be required. For example, generic descriptions of contraband, such as "controlled and dangerous substances" or "all controlled substances" or "narcotic drugs," etc., are generally held to be sufficient descriptions, if the affidavit suggests the presence of more than one drug. Similarly, warrants directing officers to seize evidence of a specific crime have also consistently been held valid. *Moyer v. Commonwealth, supra.*

See, *e.g.*, *U.S. v. Dickerson*, 166 F.3d 667 (4th Cir. 1999), where a warrant for "Evidence of the crime of bank robbery" was upheld by the Court, which noted that bank robbery is a specific illegal act which generates "quite distinctive evidence" (*e.g.*, dye-stained money, bait bills and masks, all of which were seized by the officers).

However, in *Groh v. Ramirez*, 540 U.S. 551 (2004), a search warrant was plainly invalid when it provided no description of the type of evidence sought. The fact that the *application* for the warrant adequately described the "things to be seized" did not save it, because there were no words in the warrant incorporating other documents by reference and the application did not accompany the warrant (it had been sealed). Even though the search was conducted with restraint and only items listed in the application were seized, the search was unlawful.

E. Execution of the Search Warrant

1. **Time of Service**. A search warrant must be executed within 15 days of its issuance, or else be returned to the magistrate who issued it to be voided. *Va. Code* §19.2-56.

The search warrant must also be executed "forthwith." *Va. Code* §19.2-56. This has been held to mean "with reasonable dispatch and without undue delay." *Maye v. Commonwealth*, 44 Va.App. 463, 605 S.E.2d 353 (2004). See *Turner v. Commonwealth*, 14 Va.App. 737, 420 S.E.2d 235 (1992) (11-day delay before execution of a warrant valid when the warrant specified both a residence and an individual; the first six times officers went to the residence, nobody was home—the warrant was immediately served once police learned the subject had returned home); *Whitaker v. Commonwealth*, 37 Va.App. 21, 553 S.E.2d 539 (2001) (concern for officer safety may justify some delay in service—6-day delay reasonable when police waited for defendant, the sole resident, to return so he could control two attack dogs known to be on the premises). When any delay occurs, officers should make sure before executing the warrant that probable cause still exists.

A search warrant may be served at any time of the day or night. *Va. Code* §19.2-56.

2. **Knock or No-Knock**. As a matter of course, when executing a search warrant, law-enforcement officers should knock on the door of a residence or business, announce their purpose and authority, and give the occupants a reasonable opportunity to answer before forcing their way inside. *Park v. Commonwealth*, 32 Va.App. 407, 528 S.E.2d 172 (2000).

The amount of time police must wait to enter after knocking depends on the totality of the circumstances. *U.S. v. Banks*, 540 U.S. 31 (2003). In *Banks*, a 15 to 20 second delay between knocking and entry was held reasonable when police were searching for cocaine, which is easily disposable. The Court noted that police served the warrant during the middle of the day, when occupants would likely be up and around, and that a prudent dealer would keep cocaine near a commode or kitchen sink, meaning 15 to 20 seconds would likely be enough time for defendant to get in a position to rid his residence of cocaine.

Contrast with *Wynne v. Commonwealth*, 15 Va.App. 763, 427 S.E.2d 228 (1993) (5 seconds too short a wait to provide defendant with a reasonable opportunity to answer, particularly when officers could see him through a glass door and he made no furtive movements).

However, there is no constitutional mandate that an officer knock and announce before entering a dwelling in every instance. In situations where exigent circumstances are present, an unannounced entry may be reasonable (*e.g.*, presence of weapons that may put officers at peril, the destruction of evidence, etc.). "A no-knock entry is justified when the police have a reasonable suspicion that knocking and announcing their presence, under the particular circumstances, would be dangerous or futile, or that it would inhibit the effective investigation of the crime." *Richards v. Wisconsin*, 520 U.S. 385 (1997). See also *Wilson v. Arkansas*, 514 U.S. 927 (1995); *U.S. v. Ramirez*, 523 U.S. 65 (1998). Police are not required to possess the higher standard of probable cause to believe that exigent circumstances exist, but only the less stringent standard of reasonable suspicion. *Henry v. Commonwealth*, 32 Va.App. 547, 529 S.E.2d 796 (2000). The failure to knock and announce is not a per se constitutional violation, and there are no rigid rules to determine when an unannounced entry will be excused; rather, the constitutionality of the entry will be judged on the particular facts and circumstances of each case. Nevertheless, the failure to knock and announce may render an entry unreasonable, and therefore unconstitutional, where there is no showing of exigent circumstances that justify the failure to first knock.

In *Spivey v. Commonwealth*, 23 Va.App. 715, 479 S.E.2d 543 (1997), *overruled in part on other grounds*, *Henry v. Commonwealth*, *supra*, Portsmouth police used information from a reliable informant to obtain a warrant to search defendant's residence for cocaine. The informant told police that defendant was "known to have a .38 [handgun]." The informant also stated that defendant's son, Duane, was his supplier, and that Duane lived within one city block of defendant's residence and would frequently stay at the home of the defendant. Police knew Duane had been arrested just ten days before for discharging a firearm into an unoccupied vehicle. Because police reasonably feared that they might face two armed dealers, an unannounced entry was justified.

Generalizations about the common practices of drug dealers (for example, that they often use barricades and look-outs, or store drugs near the sink or bathroom for easy disposal) will not justify a no-knock entry. There must be specific evidence indicating that the persons in the residence to be searched have in fact taken such steps themselves or are otherwise likely to destroy evidence or pose a threat to officers before the knock-and-announce requirement will be waived. *Park v. Commonwealth, supra.*

Although officers should make every effort to comply with the knock-and-announce rule, in *Hudson v. Michigan*, 547 U.S. 586 (2006), the U.S. Supreme Court held that evidence seized pursuant to a valid search warrant is not subject to suppression under the Exclusionary Rule solely because the officers executing the warrant entered in violation of the knock-and-announce requirement. The Court did note that officers who violate the rule still face the threat of possible civil remedies (such as a lawsuit under 42 U.S.C. §1983) or internal discipline by their employer. See also *Perry v. Commonwealth*, 49 Va.App. 65, 636 S.E.2d 891 (2006).

The knock and announce requirement is waived if police gain entry by consent. This is true even if the officers use a ruse or stratagem to convince the suspect to open the door and invite them in. *Commonwealth v. Viar*, 15 Va.App. 490, 425 S.E.2d 86 (1992).

3. **Scope of the Search**. When executing a search warrant, officers are entitled to search the entire named premises for the items listed, and any closed containers, drawers, closets, etc., where they have probable cause to believe those items may be found. "A lawful search of fixed premises generally extends to the entire area in which the object of the search may be found and is not limited by the possibility that separate acts of entry or opening may be required to complete the search. Thus, a warrant that authorizes an officer to search a home for illegal weapons also provides authority to open closets, chests, drawers and containers in which the weapon might be found. A warrant to open a footlocker to search for marijuana would also authorize the opening of packages found inside." *U.S. v. Ross*, 456 U.S. 798 (1982).

Similarly, in *Dotson v. Commonwealth*, 47 Va.App. 237, 623 S.E.2d 414 (2005), a search warrant for drugs authorized the seizure and subsequent stationhouse search of a small locked fireproof safe found in the defendant's living room (a locksmith was required to open it so the search could not be done at the residence). Police had reason to expect they might find drugs or evidence of drug trafficking (*e.g.* cash or records) in the safe. In explaining the reasonableness of this belief, the Court noted, "the officers were not searching for an elephant in a matchbox."

Compare with *Beavers v. Commonwealth*, 245 Va. 268, 427 S.E.2d 411, *cert. denied*, 510 U.S. 859 (1993). Defendant broke into the victim's home and raped her. Police soon connected defendant to the crime and obtained both an arrest warrant and a search warrant for his home. One of the items listed in the search warrant was "bloodstained white medical gauze tape," which the victim reported defendant had wrapped around his hand after he cut himself while breaking in. Given the nature of gauze tape—which can easily be compressed to fit almost anywhere—one of the searching officers was authorized to search a small, multi-colored pouch he found in defendant's chest of drawers (although this pouch did not contain the gauze, it did contain jewelry which the officer recognized as having been taken from another rape-murder victim a year earlier; this jewelry was validly seized under the plain view doctrine).

See also *Moyer v. Commonwealth*, 33 Va.App. 8, 531 S.E.2d 580 (2000). When police had a warrant to search defendant's residence for pornographic photos of underage children, they could leaf through defendant's diaries, as such photos may have been held between the pages.

But see *Holloman v. Commonwealth*, 221 Va. 196, 275 S.E.2d 620 (1981). When ABC investigators were executing a search warrant for beer and whiskey at defendant's store, which did not have a liquor license, they could not lawfully search "five small [brown paper] bags" found behind the counter. The size of the bags, as well as their shape and weight when lifted, clearly indicated that they did not hold bottles or cans.

In addition, a valid warrant implicitly carries with it the limited authority to detain the occupants of the premises, or recall and similarly detain those seen leaving, while a proper search is conducted. *Michigan v. Summers*, 452 U.S. 692 (1981). Officers may detain anyone found in the residence, regardless of whether or not the occupant is a suspect named in the warrant, and may use reasonable force in detaining the occupants. *Muehler v. Mena*, 544 U.S. 93 (2005) (police justified in handcuffing woman for two to three hours while executing search warrant for weapons at the residence of a suspected gang member). See also *Illinois v. McArthur*, 531 U.S. 326 (2001), where the U.S. Supreme Court held that police could detain defendant on the front porch outside his home for two hours while they obtained a search warrant when they had probable cause to believe that marijuana was hidden inside the home, and that defendant would destroy this contraband if allowed to enter unescorted. (The Court noted with favor that this detention lasted only long enough for police, acting with diligence, to obtain a warrant.)

However, a person may not be detained incident to the execution of a search warrant unless the person is within the immediate vicinity of the premises to be searched—in other words, that area in which an occupant poses a real threat to the safe and efficient execution of the warrant. Courts can consider a number of number of factors to determine whether an occupant was detained within the immediate vicinity of the premises to be searched, including the lawful limits of the premises, whether the occupant was within the line of sight of his dwelling, and the ease of reentry from the occupant's location. *Bailey v. U.S.*, 568 U.S. __ (2013). In *Bailey*, defendant's detention was unlawful when he had left the house to be searched and driven a few hundred yards down the street before police seized him. See also *Whitaker v. Commonwealth*, 37 Va.App. 21, 553 S.E.2d 539 (2001), where defendant could not be detained when he was 1½ miles from his residence when the warrant was executed.

Remember that the authority to detain those present but not named in the warrant does not include the authority to search those persons, absent an independent justification for the search. *Ybarra v. Illinois*, 444 U.S. 85 (1979). For example, in *Ybarra*, a warrant issued to search a bar for narcotics gave the police authority to search the bartender named in the warrant, but not a patron who just happened to be there.

Compare with *Hayes v. Commonwealth*, 29 Va.App. 647, 514 S.E.2d 357 (1999) (police had no right to search defendant—who was seated on the porch outside a Petersburg residence where a search warrant for drugs was being executed—when the warrant did not list any specific persons to be searched or state that all persons at the residence were to be searched). But see *Murphy v. Commonwealth*, 37 Va.App. 556, 559 S.E.2d 890 (2002) (frisk of defendant justified when he was found in a private residence being searched for drugs and guns; it was reasonable to believe that people found inside the residence were involved in the illegal narcotics operation and were therefore likely to be armed).

The search warrant can itself authorize a search of "all persons present" at the time of execution, as long as a showing of probable cause is made in the supporting affidavit. *Morton v. Commonwealth*, 16 Va.App. 946, 434 S.E.2d 890 (1993) ("all persons present" warrant valid when the search was of a private residence. The object sought was crack cocaine, which could easily be hidden on the body, and surveillance had seen several known and convicted drug dealers enter the apartment over the past 60 days).

A search warrant for a dwelling also authorizes a search of any of the occupant's automobiles found within the curtilage of the dwelling, even if they were not specifically named in the warrant. *Glenn v. Commonwealth*, 10 Va.App. 150, 390 S.E.2d 505 (1990).

Any warrant issued for the search and seizure of a computer, computer network, or other device containing electronic or digital information shall be deemed to include the search and seizure of the physical components and the electronic or digital information contained in any such computer, computer network, or other device. Such search may be conducted in any location and is not limited to the location where the evidence was seized. *Va. Code* §19.2-53(B)-(C).

Police violate the Fourth Amendment when they allow members of the media to accompany them while executing a search warrant. *Hanlon v. Berger*, 526 U.S. 808 (1999).

When executing a warrant, officers may seize contraband or other evidence not listed in the warrant, in plain view, if the requirements of that doctrine are met. (See further discussion under **Plain View Doctrine**, below).

4. **Property Seized**. An officer who conducts a search pursuant to a warrant should note the date of execution on the warrant. If any property was seized as a result of the search, then the officer should fill out a list of such items. If no items were seized, this should be noted on the warrant. The warrant, the affidavit, and the list of property, if there is one, should then be filed in the court in which the warrant was obtained. *Va. Code* §19.2-57.

When law-enforcement agents seize property pursuant to a search warrant, Due Process requires that they give notice so that the owner can pursue any remedies available for return under state law; however, agents are not required to give owners notice of state law remedies established by published, generally available statutes and case law. *City of West Covina v. Perkins*, 525 U.S. 234 (1999).

F. Search of Containers

Regardless of whether the subject of a search is a container, like a briefcase, purse, suitcase or footlocker, instead of a house, car, office building or person, the general rule is the same; a warrant must be obtained before the container may be opened. The Fourth Amendment "proscribes—except in certain well defined circumstances—the search of that property unless accomplished pursuant to a judicial warrant issued on probable cause." *U.S. v. Ross*, 456 U.S. 798 (1982). These "well-defined circumstances," *e.g.*, a search incident to arrest or a booking search, are discussed under **Warrantless Searches**, below. The rationale advanced in this situation is similar to the reasoning behind the rule requiring warrants for the search of a home. When an individual manifests an expectation that certain items remain private by placing them in a closed container, it is unreasonable for the government to intrude on that expectation of privacy without the protections of a warrant based on a clear showing of probable cause. When dealing with items of personalty, the procedure prior to a search may be somewhat different, in that it is permissible to briefly detain personal property, based on a reasonable suspicion that it contains contraband.

A crucial, and often dispositive, distinction must be made between closed containers seized and detained from the possession of a person, and those containers taken from an automobile. If the container is found in an automobile, the police may almost always open and search the container without a warrant, if they have probable cause to think the container, or the car transporting it, contains contraband.

G. Exceptions to the Warrant Requirement (Warrantless Searches)

The general rule is that all searches and seizures conducted without a warrant are presumptively unreasonable and therefore unconstitutional. To justify a warrantless search, the Commonwealth must show that the search falls into one of the narrowly drawn exceptions to warrant requirement. Courts have, however, crafted a few specifically established and well-delineated exceptions to the general principle, and they are discussed in detail, below.

1. **Exigent Circumstances**. The situations that often fall under the exigent circumstances exception can be grouped into three general categories. An exigency exists if: (i) there is a good chance evidence—either contraband, instrumentalities used in the crime, or the fruits of the crime—is being or will be destroyed or concealed; (ii) it is likely a suspect will flee; (iii) there is a real danger to people. The rationale advanced for permitting warrantless searches under such circumstances is that extreme situations dictate that police act quickly, where there is no time to secure a warrant. The warrant requirement may be dispensed with when officers take actions that are necessary responses to an emergency situation. Courts permit warrantless searches where officers have probable cause and a qualifying set of circumstances.

2. **Destruction or Removal of Evidence**. Where police have a reasonable belief that evidence is being or about to be destroyed, a warrantless entry may be permitted under this exception. Where the police have an objectively reasonable fear that the evidence is being or about to be destroyed and a reasonable belief that there are people within the home presently capable of destroying or hiding the evidence, and the officer's fear is of an immediate or imminent destruction, the requirements of the exception are met. In order to invoke this exception, the prosecution must demonstrate that the seized evidence is of an "evanescent" nature (*i.e.*, an easily destructible item, like narcotics, which can be easily burned, secreted or flushed).

See, *e.g.*, *Smith v. Commonwealth*, 56 Va.App. 592, 696 S.E.2d 211 (2010). At around 2:00 a.m., a Portsmouth officer received an anonymous early morning call stating that "a white male named Jeremy Smith, and a black male named Bobby" were in Smith's residence, and that "Bobby" was Smith's drug dealer and was giving him narcotics. The officer immediately preceded to the residence, which turned out to be a basement apartment, arriving by 2:10. He knocked on the front door, and a voice inside asked, "Who is it?" The officer identified himself. A white male, later identified as defendant Jeremy Smith, partially opened the door. Through the doorway, the officer saw a black male "jump up from the couch and run towards the back of the apartment with something in his hand." The officer could not tell what the item was, but could see it was white. Because under the circumstances it was reasonable to believe that the black male was rushing to destroy drug evidence, a warrantless entry into the apartment was justified.

Compare with *Weathers v. Commonwealth*, 32 Va.App. 652, 529 S.E.2d 847 (2000). A Greenville County officer had a confidential-informant make a controlled buy of crack cocaine from Room 117 of the Dixie Motel. After the buy was completed, three officers immediately went to the door of the room and knocked. One of the occupants asked who was there and the officers identified themselves as police. Someone inside called out, "Wait a minute[,]" after which the officers heard "voices, movements and a commode being flushed." The officers reasonably believed persons inside the room were attempting to dispose of the remaining crack, and thus made a lawful warrantless entry to preserve evidence.

In *West v. Commonwealth*, 54 Va.App. 345, 678 S.E.2d 836 (2009), police arrived to investigate a burglary and attempted rape of a 94-year-old woman at around 6:15 a.m. The victim indicated that she had bitten her assailant when he attempted to kiss her, and also scratched him. When asked to describe her attacker, she said "Joe," the man who had lived in the house behind hers for 20 years, came to mind. Police knocked on defendant Joe West's front door at 7:38 that morning. He hid behind the door so that police could not see his whole body, but a detective did notice fresh scratches on his face, and also saw that his lip was cut but not yet scabbed over (consistent with being bitten recently). When the detective explained that they were investigating an incident in the neighborhood, defendant attempted to shut the door without asking any questions about that had happened. The detective stopped him, and officers then made a warrantless entry into the home. The Court ruled these police actions were justified by exigent circumstances. The victim's identification coupled with defendant's fresh injuries and odd behavior at the door established probable cause that defendant was the assailant they sought. A serious crime was under investigation, and blood and saliva was likely still on the attacker's body and clothing—"[t]his type of physical evidence is easily destroyed, by simply washing a pair of pants or taking a shower." Defendant could easily have destroyed the biological evidence of his guilt while the police sought a search or arrest warrant. Because defendant lived behind the victim's house, he could easily observe that the police were actively investigating the crime, which could have prompted him to destroy evidence or to flee. In addition, defendant was suspected of breaking into the home of an elderly woman and attempting to rape her—the danger to the community from this perpetrator continued if the police did not enter his house and quickly act to restrain the suspect. The warrantless police entry did not violate the Fourth Amendment.

See also *U.S. v. Cephas*, 254 F.3d 488 (4th Cir. 2001). A concerned citizen flagged an officer down and said that he had just been in an apartment where defendant was smoking marijuana with a 14-year-old girl. The officer went to the address indicated, which was only a block away, and, after entering the common area of an apartment building, knocked on the door of defendant's apartment. When defendant answered the door, the officer was met immediately by "a strong smell of marijuana coming from the apartment." The officer could also see a girl who appeared to be about 14 inside. The officer requested permission to enter, but defendant responded by trying to slam the door on him. The officer stuck his foot in the door to prevent this, and then made a warrantless entry. Upon review, the Court upheld this entry. Based on the tip and his own sense of smell, the officer had probable cause to believe that there was marijuana in the apartment; of course, this drug is readily destructible. Moreover, defendant now knew that there was an officer right outside his front door and had every reason to dispose of the contraband if the officer delayed his search to obtain a warrant.

Compare with *Cherry v. Commonwealth*, 44 Va.App. 347, 605 S.E.2d 297 (2004). An officer randomly chose to run the tags on a truck parked outside a residence; the check indicated that the tags were stolen. The officer approached the truck and saw that the ignition had been "popped." He then went to the front door of the residence "to figure out whose truck it was or if they even knew anything about the truck." A woman answered the door and as soon as she did, the officer could smell an odor of burning marijuana coming from inside the house. The woman "immediately yelled into the back, turned around and stated that police were at the door." There was a blanket hanging from the ceiling off to the right of the door; the officer could not see what was happening, but he could hear people begin to move around. This sudden movement indicated an effort to destroy the marijuana, which would almost certainly be gone by the time the officer could obtain a search warrant. Therefore, the officer made a lawful warrantless entry to prevent the destruction of this evidence.

The fact that the grounds for arrest involve narcotics, standing alone, does not create an exigent circumstance. The arrest of a narcotics suspect on his front doorstep, without any indication drugs are being hidden or destroyed, will not justify the arresting officers conducting a warrantless search of the arrestee's home for narcotics.

In *Evans v. Commonwealth*, 776 S.E.2d 760 (Va. 2015), three officers on bicycle patrol smelled an extremely strong odor of burn marijuana coming from an apartment window. The officers knocked on the apartment door three times—each time, defendant's mother answered. During the first encounter, the offic-ers asked "questions about someone smoking" and explained to her the "heavy odor of marijuana" that they smelled. During the second encounter, she appeared to be "shaking" and "nervous." She exclaimed, "Ain't nobody smoking weed in here," and then "slammed" the door in the "face" of one of the officers. During this brief episode, the officers smelled the odor of marijuana "like a gust of wind" coming from inside the apart-ment. When knocking on the door the third time, the officers "announced out loud it was the police." No one answered the door for about five minutes. During this period, the officers heard unspecified movement inside the apartment. After defendant's mother finally opened the door, she quickly tried to close it again. Another strong marijuana odor wafted through the doorway. One of officers put his hand on the door to prevent it from closing, then entered the apartment and observed in plain view "a burnt marijuana blunt" and marijuana residue. The Court upheld this warrantless entry. The officers had probable cause to believe there was contraband in the apartment based on the heavy odor of burnt marijuana. In addition, defendant's mother knew there were police officers at her front door, and her nervous conduct followed by her slamming the door implied that she knew the officers were aware that marijuana was present in the apartment, "which would naturally give her a potent incentive to destroy, discard, or hide the illegal drug (or ask others to do so) soon after she closed the door." Her conspicuously delayed response to the third knock, coupled with unspecific sounds of movement, contribute to the totality of facts demonstrating exigent circumstances. Because exigent circumstances supported this entry, the marijuana observed by the officers was lawfully seized.

The natural dissipation of alcohol in the blood does not automatically just a warrantless blood test of a drunk-driving suspect. In those drunk-driving investigations where police officers can reasonably obtain a warrant before a blood sample can be drawn without significantly undermining the efficacy of the search, the Fourth Amendment mandates that they do so. Exceptions to this requirement must be decided on a case to case basis, based on facts showing that securing a warrant would have been impractical. *Missouri v. McNeely*, 569 U.S. __ (2013).

3. **Flight of the Suspect**. If police have evidence demonstrating a suspect is an immediate flight risk, and has the present ability to flee the jurisdiction, a warrantless entry may be permitted to apprehend that suspect before flight.

4. **Safety of the Officer or Others**. If the officer believes that the suspect is armed and presents a real and immediate danger to the officers or other people, a warrantless entry is permitted.

See *Robinson v. Commonwealth*, 47 Va.App. 533, 625 S.E.2d 651 (2006), *aff'd*, 273 Va. 26, 639 S.E.2d 217, *cert. denied*, 550 U.S. 957 (2007). The Albemarle County Police Department received three separate calls regarding an alleged underage drinking party at defendants' residence. An officer arrived at the residence around 11:00 p.m. Ten to twenty cars were parked along the road outside the house, and two or three more were in the driveway. The officer pulled into the driveway and saw more cars, as well as some "activity" in the back yard. Before reaching the point where the walkway to the front door intersected the driveway, the officer saw two males holding clear beer bottles--both appeared to be underage. From about 7 or 8 yards away, they looked at the officer, yelled "cops," dropped the beer bottles, and ran toward the nearby woods. The officer pulled forward and saw a patio table covered in beer bottles, as well as bottles strewn through the back yard. He radioed other officers regarding the fleeing juveniles, then proceeded into the back yard "to look for the juvenile host." He walked up to the sliding glass back door of the residence, knocked, and saw two adults (the defendants) inside sitting at the kitchen table; the officer arrested both for contributing to the delinquency of minors. The Court upheld the officer's warrantless entry into the back yard (which was within the curtilage of the residence). Upon observing two apparent juveniles holding beer bottles, he had probable cause to believe a crime (specifically underage drinking) was being committed. Exigent circumstances were also present. Judging by the number of cars, beer bottles, and earlier reports of a party, it appeared many underage drinkers had driven to the residence. Pending the issuance of a search warrant for the premises, many of them may have attempted to drive home, placing themselves and the general public at great risk. There was also a risk that evidence would be lost--specifically the identities and blood alcohol levels of the fleeing young men--if the officer did not act quickly. In addition, the other party-goers, now aware that police were on the premises after the young men yelled out "cops," may also have fled or destroyed evidence to "cover up" the existence of the party.

In *Washington v. Commonwealth*, 60 Va.App. 427, 728 S.E.2d 521 (2012), a Mecklenburg County coupled called the sheriff's office to report the apparent burglary of their home. A deputy arrived to find a window had been broken out of one of the couple's vehicles, while a house window leading to the kitchen had been broken as well, and various items (including a toolbox) were missing. A single set of footprints led from the burglarized vehicle to the broken window. The deputy believed the prints to be fresh, as they were still sharp and it had only snowed that morning. He followed the prints, which ran in a continuous, uninterrupted path across the street to the front door of a residential trailer. When he knocked, the door swung open. The deputy called out, but no one answered. Fearing that the trailer was being burglarized at that moment, endangering anyone inside, the deputy entered. In plain view he saw the toolbox stolen from across the street as well as a pair of shoes with the same tread as the footprints. The Court ruled this entry was supported by exigent circumstances, so that the evidence found was admissible.

In *Ryburn v. Huff*, 556 U.S. __ (2012), two Burbank, California, officers responded to a call at a high school. There the principal informed them that a student, Vincent Huff, was rumored to have written a letter threatening to "shoot up" the school, and asked them to investigate. In interviewing Vincent's classmates, the officers learned he was a frequent target of bullying who had been absent from school for two days. The officers found this to be a cause for concern, as they had received training on targeted school violence and were aware that these characteristics are common among perpetrators of school shootings. The officers decided to continue their investigation by interviewing Vincent. At his house, the officers knocked on the door and announced several times they were with the Burbank Police Department. No one answered the door or otherwise responded to the knocks. One of the officers then called the home telephone. The officers could hear the phone ringing inside the house, but no one picked up. They next tried calling the cell phone of Vincent's mother, Mrs. Huff. When Mrs. Huff answered the phone, she indicated that both she and Vincent were inside the house; however, when the officers indicated they were outside and asked to speak with her, she hung up. One or two minutes later, Mrs. Huff and Vincent walked out of the house and stood on the front steps. The officers advised Vincent that they were there to discuss the threats. Vincent, apparently aware of the rumor that was circulating at his school, responded, "I can't believe you're here for that." An officer asked Mrs. Huff if they could continue the discussion inside the house, but she refused; in the officer's experience, it was "extremely unusual" for a parent to decline an officer's request to interview a juvenile inside. He also found it odd that Mrs. Huff never asked the officers the reason for their visit. The officer then asked if there were any guns in the house. Mrs. Huff responded by "immediately turn[ing] around and r[unning] into the house." The officers followed her in. There, after a brief argument with Vincent's father, the interview continued for 5 to 10 minutes; the officers concluded the rumor about Vincent was false and left. The Huffs brought an action claiming the police violated their rights by entering their home without a warrant. The U.S. Supreme Court disagreed, finding that Mrs. Huff's odd behavior, combined with the information the officers gathered at the school, could have led reasonable officers to believe "that there could be weapons inside the house, and that family members or the officers themselves were in danger."

When police come upon the scene of a homicide, they may make a "prompt warrantless search of the area to see if there are other victims or if a killer is still on the premises." *Mincey v. Arizona*, 437 U.S. 385 (1978). However, there is no general "murder scene" exception to the warrant requirement, and police may not continue to search for evidence once the crime scene has been secured. *Flippo v. West Virginia*, 528 U.S. 11 (1999).

See also *Hargraves v. Commonwealth*, 37 Va.App. 299, 557 S.E.2d 737 (2002), where police responded to an alarm at defendant's residence to find the doorjamb splintered and the rear bedroom ransacked. Although a brief sweep of the residence was justified to make sure there were no burglars or victims inside, the full-scale investigation undertaken by the officers (which included going through drawers and dusting for fingerprints) was not.

5. **Hot Pursuit**. This doctrine may be analyzed as a specific application of the exigent circumstance doctrine discussed above. A warrantless entry of a private dwelling will be allowed when police are in hot pursuit of a suspect who they have probable cause to believe committed a felony. The pursuing officers must also have probable cause to believe the suspect entered a specific dwelling. After following the suspect into a dwelling, the police may seize contraband, weapons, instrumentalities or fruits of crime that are in plain view.

See, *e.g.*, *Commonwealth v. Talbert*, 23 Va.App. 572, 478 S.E.2d 331 (1996). Alexandria police were conducting undercover surveillance at the corner of Alfred and Montgomery Streets. Officer William

Bunney watched as defendant, who was in a wheelchair, broke off a piece from a large rock of crack cocaine he had and gave it to another man. Defendant then wrapped plastic around his remaining crack and placed the rock by his side. After Officer Bunney radioed this information, other officers quickly moved in and apprehended the man who had just acquired the crack, who put up a struggle. When Officer Bunney looked again, he realized that he could no longer see defendant. He then saw a man backing a wheelchair into a house directly adjacent to the alley where the transaction had taken place; the man was lifting the wheelchair up the porch steps and backing into the house. Officer Bunney radioed his observations to his fellow officers and told them to hurry. When the other officers reached the house, they saw a man walking into the house with his back to the doorway. The inside door was completely open, while the outside door (which had an upper half made of glass) was still "open about a foot." One of the officers, who knew defendant, could see him in the living room through the glass portion of the exterior door. The Court found that the officers were in "hot pursuit" of defendant and could therefore enter the house without a warrant.

The "hot pursuit" doctrine applies only to offenses punishable by incarceration; it does not apply when a suspect commits only a non-jailable offense. *Welsh v. Wisconsin*, 466 U.S. 740 (1984); *Cherry v. Commonwealth*, 44 Va.App. 347, 605 S.E.2d 297 (2004). The burden is upon the Commonwealth to prove that the hot pursuit exception applies to specific facts.

6. **Search Incident to Arrest**. Upon the lawful arrest of a person, the arresting officer is entitled to search not only the person of the arrestee, but also the area that was in the immediate control of the suspect prior to the arrest. *Slayton v. Commonwealth*, 41 Va.App. 101, 582 S.E.2d 448 (2003). This exception is premised on the notion that the arrest of a suspect, when based on probable cause, is per se reasonable with respect to the Fourth Amendment. Since this intrusion on an individual's freedom is by definition lawful, a search incident to the arrest requires no additional justification. It is the fact of the arrest that establishes the authority to search. Notice that the arrest must be lawful, *i.e.*, based on probable cause. If the arrest is later deemed improper, all evidence seized incident to that arrest will be suppressed. Under this exception, a search of all effects in the suspect's possession is permissible. However, as mentioned, the scope of the search must be limited to the suspect's person, or what is in, or potentially could be in, the suspect's immediate control. Courts say that a region is within the immediate control of the suspect when he or she might immediately and easily gain possession of a weapon or destructible evidence from that area. *Chimel v. California*, 395 U.S. 752 (1969).

In *U.S. v. Currence*, 446 F.3d 554 (4th Cir. 2006), Richmond police received a tip that a man on a bicycle was selling drugs at a street corner. Two detectives found defendant on a bike at the alleged corner. They ordered defendant off the bike, then frisked him, finding cash but no drugs. Nevertheless, a radio check revealed an outstanding warrant, so defendant was arrested. Then, without using any tools, one of the detectives slid the end cap off the right handlebar of the bike and found plastic baggies of crack cocaine concealed inside it. The Court upheld this as a valid search incident to arrest. When the detectives first encountered defendant he was sitting on the bike, and was in close proximity to it throughout the stop, so it remained within his immediate control. Moreover, the detective was able to slide the cap off "with very minimal intrusion." The ready accessibility of the handlebar's interior made it searchable.

A search incident to arrest extends to the clothing worn by the arrestee. *U.S. v. Edwards*, 415 U.S. 800 (1974); *Williams v. Commonwealth*, 259 Va. 377, 527 S.E.2d 131 (2000). However, a strip search or search of the arrestee's body cavities is not justifiable as incident to arrest, unless there is a "clear indication" that evidence or a weapon is located within the suspect's body and exigent circumstances are present. *King v. Commonwealth*, 49 Va.App. 717, 644 S.E.2d 391 (2007).

Data on an suspect's cell phone—including texts, e-mails, photos and call logs—may not be searched incident to arrest. Officers must generally secure a warrant before conducting such a search, unless an exigency is present. However, officers may examine the physical aspects of a phone to ensure that it will not be used as a weapon—for example, to determine whether there is a razor blade hidden between the phone and its case. *Riley v. California*, 573 U.S. __ (2014).

A search incident to arrest is not allowed following a Class 3 or 4 misdemeanor where the officer issues a summons in lieu of custodial arrest, because the nature and duration of such encounters makes them different and less threatening than a full custodial arrest. *Lovelace v. Commonwealth*, 258 Va. 588, 522 S.E.2d 856 (1999) (no search when officer issues summons for drinking in public, a Class 4 misdemeanor). Some intrusion may be justified when a summons is issued, if necessary to preserve evidence or for safety concerns; however, this intrusion must be limited to what is necessary to answer those concerns, and cannot rise to the level of a full search. *Farrow v. Commonwealth*, 31 Va.App. 517, 525 S.E.2d 11 (2000).

The search may precede the arrest, as long as probable cause for the arrest exists independently of what is found during the search and probable cause to arrest exists before the search is conducted. In other words, an officer may not use the fruits of a search as the basis for the arrest of the suspect, and then seek to justify the search as one incident to the arrest. *Rawlings v. Kentucky*, 448 U.S. 98 (1980); *Purdie v. Commonwealth*, 36 Va.App. 178, 549 S.E.2d 33 (2001).

As long as probable cause to arrest the suspect for *some* offense existed at the time of arrest, then a search incident to arrest is valid, even if the officer subjectively believed he or she was arresting for another offense and even if the suspect was told that the arrest was for another offense. *Golden v. Commonwealth*, 30 Va.App. 618, 519 S.E.2d 378 (1999). In *Golden*, after Suffolk officers offered to give defendant a ride, she entered their car and offered to perform fellatio for $10. The officers arrested defendant for prostitution and searched her person incident to the arrest, finding two "crack stems." The Court found that probable cause did not exist to arrest defendant for prostitution, because there had been "no substantial act in furtherance" of the offense. Nevertheless, the officers did have probable cause to arrest defendant for solicitation; therefore the search incident to arrest was still valid. As long as there is probable cause to arrest for *a* crime at the time of the search, it does not matter that probable cause did not yet exist to establish the crime for which the defendant is ultimately arrested.

Compare with *Slayton v. Commonwealth*, *supra.* An officer had probable cause to arrest defendant for carrying a concealed weapon. Before formally arresting defendant, the officer searched his pocket and found cocaine. This search was not invalidated even though the actual ground on which defendant was arrested was possession of cocaine, not carrying a concealed weapon.

In *Virginia v. Moore*, 170 L. Ed. 2d 559 (2008), two Portsmouth officers stopped defendant following a tip he was driving with a suspended license. The officers determined that defendant's license was, in fact, suspended, and arrested him for the misdemeanor of driving on a suspended license. A subsequent search incident to that arrest found he was carrying 16 grams of crack cocaine and $516 in cash. However, the Supreme Court of Virginia determined that this was not a valid arrest, because none of the exceptions in §19.2-74 applied. Nevertheless, the U.S. Supreme Court upheld the search under the Fourth Amendment. Because the arrest was supported by probable cause, it was lawful under the U.S. Constitution, even if it was not lawful under the Virginia statute. Therefore, there was no constitutional requirement to suppress the evidence found on defendant's person.

A proper search incident to an arrest should be conducted contemporaneously with the arrest, *i.e.*, immediately preceding or succeeding that actual physical act of arrest. However, a search of articles in the possession of the defendant at the time of arrest may not only be conducted at the time of the arrest, but may instead be conducted later, and at a different location, if a reasonable explanation for the delay is put forth. *U.S. v. Edwards*, *supra* (delay of ten hours between arrest and station house search permissible).

When police arrest the driver of or a passenger in a vehicle, officers may search the passenger compartment of the vehicle incident to the arrest, but only if:

- the arrestee is within "reaching distance" of the passenger compartment at the time of the search, ***or***
- it is reasonable to believe the vehicle contains evidence of the offense of arrest.

Arizona v. Gant, 556 U.S. 332 (2009). If the arrestee has already been handcuffed and placed in the back of a patrol car, then a search of the vehicle is no longer justified because the arrestee is no longer capable of accessing any weapon potentially hidden inside, unless police reasonable expect to find evidence of the crime for which the arrest was made in the vehicle. While police can generally expect to find evidence following a drug arrest (*e.g.* more drugs, paraphernalia), a search is not allowed following a traffic violation (for example, driving with a suspended license) as no evidence of such offenses could be concealed inside the vehicle. Under *New York v. Belton*, 453 U.S. 454 (1981), the scope of a vehicle search incident to arrest includes the entire passenger compartment, and all containers located therein, locked or unlocked.

In *Armstead v. Commonwealth*, 56 Va.App. 569, 695 S.E.2d 561 (2010), a Newport News officer stopped defendant for violating a city noise ordinance. Defendant claimed he held a valid license, bit had no identification on him. Instead, he provided a name, date of birth, and Social Security number. The officer checked this information and concluded it was likely false. Defendant then claimed his license was actually in the District of Columbia—however the only license the officer found under the name given in D.C. was expired. The officer arrested defendant for giving false information under §18.2-186.3. The officer then searched defendant's car. He found a wallet with a Virginia identification, but in searching came across the remains of a marijuana cigar in an open ashtray and two clear bags of crack cocaine in the center console. The Court concluded this evidence was all lawfully seized as this was a valid search incident to arrest. The officer had reason to believe he might find evidence of defendant's true identity, evidence directly pertaining to the crime for which defendant was arrested.

As long as the above criteria are met, a search is allowed even when the arrestee is a "recent occupant" who has already stepped out of the vehicle when the officer first makes contact. *Thornton v. U.S.*, 541 U.S. 615 (2004). However, a search is not allowed during a routine traffic stop where only a traffic citation is issued and no formal arrest is made. *Knowles v. Iowa*, 525 U.S. 113 (1998).

Note: **The "Clothing Exception"**. If an arrestee has a substantial need for clothing, police may make a brief entry into the arrestee's residence in order to retrieve the appropriate garments. The burden is on the prosecution to demonstrate that the arrestee had a substantial need for the clothing sought, and that police conduct was limited strictly to meeting that need. *U.S. v. Gwinn*, 219 F.3d 326 (4th Cir. 2000). In *Gwinn*, defendant was arrested outside his trailer home while shirtless and shoeless. There was no Fourth Amendment violation when an officer made a warrantless entry into the trailer solely to retrieve clothing for defendant to wear. The Court noted with favor that this intrusion was slight, temporary, and strictly limited to obtaining shoes and a shirt for defendant, and that such clothing was necessary because defendant was arrested in a remote, rural area where he would have to walk over rough surfaces on his way to the patrol car. In addition, a chilly May evening was fast approaching at the time of arrest, so defendant would have been cold without a shirt.

7. **Emergency Aid**. Under this doctrine, a police officer can enter a premises without a warrant to protect individuals in distress, to assist victims of crimes that have just occurred or to investigate suspicious signs of impending danger. Warrantless entry is lawful if done to assist persons who are seriously injured or threatened with serious injury. *Brigham City v. Stuart*, 547 U.S. 398 (2006). This exigency, therefore, is based on the officer's obligation to protect life and property.

In *People v. Mitchell*, 39 N.Y.2d 173, *cert. denied*, 426 U.S. 953 (1976), the Court held that there are three basic requirements for the application of the emergency doctrine: (i) the police must have reasonable cause to believe that there is an emergency at hand and an immediate need for their assistance for the protection of life or property; (ii) the search must not be primarily motivated by an intent to arrest and seize evidence; and (iii) there must be some reasonable basis to associate the emergency with the area or property to be searched. Once the police respond and enter a premises pursuant to this exigency, they have the right to "restore or maintain the status quo during the emergency to control the dangerous or dynamic situation." This right enables the officer to take a number of intrusive actions ranging from a command to halt to a seizure of an individual. During the investigation of an emergency situation, the police may search for weapons to protect themselves and others and may look for injured or missing persons.

See, *e.g.*, *Michigan v. Fisher*, 558 U.S. 45 (2009), Brownstown, Michigan, officers responded to a complaint of a disturbance—a man was reportedly "going crazy" at a residence. Upon arrival, the officers found a household in considerable chaos: a pickup truck in the driveway with its front smashed, damaged fenceposts along the side of the property, and three broken house windows, the glass still on the ground outside. The officers also noticed blood on the hood of the pickup and on clothes inside of it, as well as on one of the doors to the house. Through a window, the officers could see defendant inside, screaming and throwing things. The back door was locked, and a couch had been placed to block the front door. The officers knocked, but defendant would not answer. They saw defendant had a cut on his hand and asked if he needed medical help, but defendant ignored these questions and demanded, with accompanying profanity, that they get a search warrant. One of the officers then pushed his way inside. The U.S. Supreme Court ruled that this warrantless entry was justified under the "Emergency Aid" doctrine because of defendant's violent behavior. Although the officers had not seen defendant hit anyone, they did see him throwing things, and it was objectively reasonable to believe that these projectiles might have a human target (perhaps a spouse or a child), or that defendant would hurt himself in the course of his rage.

See also *Reynolds v. Commonwealth*, 9 Va.App. 430, 388 S.E.2d 659 (1990). A Hanover County deputy stopped a car driven by Mark Fogg and discovered stolen items in his possession, including a television and two shotguns. When pressed, Fogg admitted that he had stolen the items from the defendants' residence about an hour earlier. Several officers went to the residence to investigate. Even though it was late at night, the front door was open, as defendant had left it. An investigator on the scene feared that the residents might be injured or dead, and entered to investigate. He found no persons, injured or otherwise, but did discover 29 marijuana plants in small paper cups in plain view. This was a valid entry, because the officer reasonably feared for the safety of the residents of the house, knowing that it had recently been burglarized by an armed man. Until the marijuana plants were discovered, police thought of defendant as a victim, not a suspect, so the search was not a pretext to discover evidence.

But see *Kyer v. Commonwealth*, 45 Va.App. 473, 612 S.E.2d 213 (2005). At around 4:00 a.m. on an August night, police saw that the door to defendant's apartment was open wide enough to "walk though it without touching the door." However, there were no signs of forced entry--no "pry marks, mangled locks, broken hinges, or disfigured door jams." In addition, "[n]o one called out for help. No sounds or observations suggested panic or danger within the apartment." None of the neighbors had reported any suspicious activity. In short, there was no other reason to believe a burglary or other crime was underway inside. The Court concluded that an open door on a Summer night--absent some other reason for concern--does not justify entry under the Emergency Aid Doctrine.

Note: **Firefighters**. Firefighters may make a warrantless entry into a burning building and seize any evidence of arson in plain view. They may also remain for a reasonable time after the blaze is extinguished to make sure it will not rekindle and to investigate its cause. However, additional entries to investigate must be made pursuant to the warrant proceedings governing administrative searches. *Michigan v. Tyler*, 436 U.S. 499 (1978); *Jones v. Commonwealth*, 29 Va.App. 363, 512 S.E.2d 165 (1999). See *Commonwealth v. Thornton*, 24 Va.App. 478, 483 S.E.2d 487 (1997). The Leesburg Volunteer Fire Department received a call regarding a possible fire at the Cavalier Arms Apartments. When the Captain arrived, he met a person who said he had smelled smoke and heard an alarm. While police, who had arrived on the scene in conjunction with the alarm, began to evacuate the building, the Captain knocked on the door of the apartment where the fire was reported, but received no answer. He did hear "what sounded like a smoke detector" inside. He then directed another firefighter to a rear window, who saw neither smoke nor flame but did hear the smoke detector. He removed the screen and entered through the window. Inside, on a table, he found an extremely loud pager which had been the source of the alarm-like noise. Next to the pager sat a marijuana cigarette. In addition, the firefighter saw a plastic bag with a green leafy substance in plain view on a coffee table. The firefighters handed this contraband over to the police officers as they left the scene. Because the firefighters reasonably believed that a fire was burning inside the apartment, their entry and seizure of the contraband was valid.

8. **Consent**. A tool often employed by law-enforcement officers is to simply ask a suspect for permission to search his or her person, car or residence. If the request is granted, the individual has in effect waived his or her privacy interest in the area searched. This being so, a lawful, warrantless search may be conducted pursuant to consent given by the suspect. *Kyer v. Commonwealth*, 45 Va.App. 473, 612 S.E.2d 213 (2005); *Elliot v. Commonwealth*, 61 Va.App. 48, 733 S.E.2d 146 (2012).

Valid consent to search may be rendered verbally (express consent) or inferred from the conduct or actions of the person from whom the police seek consent (implied consent). *Jean-Laurent v. Commonwealth*, 34 Va.App. 74, 538 S.E.2d 316 (2000) (noting that the burden of proving voluntariness is heavier when consent is based on an implication). Be aware that while consent need not be verbalized, mere acquiescence by the suspect to a search is not enough, especially when no explicit request to search has been made. *Lawrence v. Commonwealth*, 40 Va.App. 95, 578 S.E.2d 54 (2003).

In But see *Hawkins v. Commonwealth*, 65 Va.App. 101, 744 S.E.2d 492 (2015). Defendant was a passenger in a car stopped for a traffic infraction following a suspected hand-to-hand drug transaction. An officer asked defendant to step out of the car, then, after noticing a bulge under defendant's shirt, asked if he "could do him a favor" by raising his shirt "up a little bit." The officer's tone was congenial, even joking, and he did not instruct or command defendant to comply. Defendant responded by extending his arms completely out to his sides, raised halfway to his shoulders with his palms facing the officer; he did not say anything. The officer lifted defendant's shirt and saw a handgun in his waistband. The Court ruled that by assuming a common "frisk stance," defendant implicitly agreed to the officer's request to search. Therefore the handgun was lawfully found and seized.

But see *Lawrence v. Commonwealth*, supra. Defendant was stopped for a tag violation. After handcuffing defendant (which the Court found to be an unreasonable restraint on defendant's liberty under the circumstances), the officer asked him if he had his driver's license. Defendant replied that it was in his inner jacket pocket. Without first asking consent, the officer reached into the pocket and retrieved the license, as well as a bag of heroin he found with it. Under these circumstances, defendant merely acquiesced to the search; the officer's failure to obtain explicit consent therefore rendered the search and seizure unlawful.

Permission to search may also be obtained from a third party who possesses common authority over, or other sufficient relationship to, the premises or effects sought to be inspected. Moreover, even where the party granting permission does not in fact have legally sufficient control over the premises, the consent may nonetheless be valid if the officer reasonably believes that the party had common control. *Illinois v. Rodriguez*, 497 U.S. 177 (1990); *Glenn v. Commonwealth*, 275 Va. 123, 654 S.E.2d 910 (2008).

See, *e.g.*, *Jones v. Commonwealth*, 16 Va.App. 725, 432 S.E.2d 517 (1993). An officer responded to a call at Room 57 of the Richmond Motel, where a maid had found "suspected narcotics." There were no cars parked in the parking lot near the room, and the doors to Room 57 and several surrounding rooms were open as if the rooms were being cleaned. When the officer looked through the open doorway into Room 57, he saw no luggage or other personal effects. The maid met him at the doorway, and he followed her into the room where she showed him the drugs hidden in an air conditioner. The officer then went to the front office, where he learned that the room was still registered to defendant. Even though the maid did not actually have authority to consent to the officer's entry (as the room was still technically defendant's), the officer reasonably believed that she did based on the surrounding circumstances, so his entry was valid.

Compare with *Caldwell v. Commonwealth*, 15 Va.App. 540, 425 S.E.2d 534 (1993). Defendant's sister invited police to enter her mother's home in order to see items that her brother had stolen. The sister told police that, although she did not live there, her mother was in Texas and had left her in charge of the house. She did, in fact, have a key. Unbeknownst to police, defendant also lived at his mother's house, and he was present at the time of the search. However, he did not object to the search, and the police reasonably relied on the sister's representation of authority.

In *Vaughan v. Commonwealth*, 53 Va.App. 435, 672 S.E.2d 909 (2009), defendant was the back seat passenger in a car stopped for defective brake lights. The driver consented to a search of the car, and the officer asked defendant and the front seat passenger to get out because "it would be difficult to search with them in the car." Defendant exited, but left a book bag behind in the back seat area where he had been sitting. The officer found the book bag, removed it, and placed it on the trunk. None of the car's three occupants objected when he opened it and began to search. Inside, the officer found drug paraphernalia and a letter addressed to defendant. The Court upheld the officer's search. It was objectively reasonable to believe that the driver's unrestricted consent to search the car authorized a search of the book bag, a closed container, found inside the car. The bag had no identifying marks which would have connected it to defendant rather than the driver, and defendant left it in the car knowing the vehicle was about to be searched.

However, when one co-occupant of a residence consents to a search, but another co-occupant is also physically present and expressly objects to the search, then any subsequent search and seizure is unreasonable and invalid as to the objecting party. *Georgia v. Randolph*, 547 U.S. 103 (2006). In *Randolph*, defendant's wife called police regarding a domestic disturbance. When officers arrived, defendant was not home, but his wife alleged that he had a cocaine habit, and that he had drug paraphernalia in the house. While officers were speaking with defendant's wife, defendant returned home. He denied he had a drug habit, but also refused to consent to a search of the residence. Undeterred, the officer who asked defendant for consent then turned to defendant's wife and asked her; she readily agreed to let him search, leading the officer to a bedroom, where the officer saw a section of a drinking straw covered with a powdery residue. Because defendant had been present at the start of the search and objected to it, the contraband the officer observed could not be used against him. *Randolph* does not apply if the objecting occupant is not physically present at the residence—this is true even if police are the reason for the occupant's absence (*i.e.* if the occupant was lawfully detained or arrested prior to the request for consent to search being made). *Fernandez v. California*, 571 U.S.__ (2014).

Despite *Randolph*, a live-in guest of a homeowner cannot "veto the owner's right to invite anyone he may choose (whether police officers or anyone else) to accompany him into the common areas of his own home." When defendant occupied a bedroom in his stepfather's house but was not a co-owner or renter, he could not object when police entered a common hallway in the house and knocked on his bedroom door with his stepfather's permission. *Testa v. Commonwealth*, 55 Va.App. 275, 685 S.E.2d 213 (2009).

Generally a landlord cannot consent to a search of a tenant's residence, and a motel clerk cannot consent to a search of a guest's room. *Georgia v. Randolph, supra*; *McCary v. Commonwealth*, 36 Va.App. 27, 548 S.E.2d 239 (2001).

To be valid, consent must be given voluntarily. Courts will examine the circumstances under which the consent was given and ascertain if it was rendered intentionally and deliberately. Courts will inquire if the permission was the product of an essentially free and unconstrained choice by its maker. In making this determination, a court will consider the age, maturity, education, intelligence and experience of the individual giving permission, as well as the circumstances under which the consent was given, such as the number of officers present and their actions, and the duration, location and timing of the encounter. See *Weathers v. Commonwealth*, 32 Va.App. 652, 529 S.E.2d 847 (2000). The Commonwealth has the burden of proof to show by the preponderance of the evidence that the consent to search was freely and voluntarily given. *Anderson v. Commonwealth*, 256 Va. 580, 507 S.E.2d 339 (1998).

There is no requirement that officers tell an individual he or she has a right to refuse permission to search. While an individual's knowledge, or lack thereof, concerning his or her right to refuse permission, is a factor to be considered in assessing the voluntariness of any consent given, it is not dispositive. *U.S. v. Drayton*, 536 U.S. 194 (2002); *Elliot v. Commonwealth, supra*. Similarly, following a valid traffic stop, there is no requirement that an officer tell an individual that he or she is free to leave before asking for permission to search his or her vehicle. *Ohio v. Robinette*, 519 U.S. 33 (1996).

The search must be limited to those areas to which the defendant actually or implicitly gives permission to search. The scope of the search is generally determined with reference to that which the officer is seeking, *i.e.*, to areas or containers where the stated subject of the search could be located. In *Florida v. Jimeno*, 500 U.S. 248 (1991), the Court approved the search of a paper bag, found on the floor of a car, for narcotics, after the defendant had given consent to a general search of his car. The Court concluded that, based on these facts, it was reasonable for the searching officer to believe the scope of the consent given permitted him to open the bag. The defendant knew the purpose of the search was to look for drugs, and it was objectively reasonable to assume drugs could be found there.

In *Brooks v. Commonwealth*, 282 Va. 90, 712 S.E.2d 464 (2011), Petersburg officers responded to an anonymous report of shots fired in the same block as defendant's home. In a subsequent sweep, an officer found a casing on defendant's front stoop. The officer asked for permission to search the home for weapons, and defendant consented. In a bedroom, the officer found, inside a tote bag, a gift bag "with some weight in it." The bag was folded. Given the shape and weight of the bag, the officer could reasonably believe it held a gun, so it fell within the scope of defendant's consent.

Compare with *Bynum v. Commonwealth*, 23 Va.App. 412, 477 S.E.2d 750 (1996). Virginia Beach police were executing a search warrant for drugs on a motel room when defendant and two companions walked in. As soon as they saw the officers, they turned around and left. An officer followed and asked if he could help defendant. In the ensuing conversation, defendant denied possession of any drugs and consented to a search of his person for narcotics, specifically crack cocaine. Because the officer was searching for a "very small item," he "stuck [his] hands in [defendant's] pockets and removed the contents" without objection from defendant. What he found was a Toyota key, which struck the officer as unusual, as defendant previously claimed he had been dropped off at the motel because he did not have a car. Defendant said he had found the key and had no objection to the officer keeping it. Later, this key was connected to a stolen car, and defendant was arrested for the theft.

Defendant's pockets were a legitimate place where crack might have been stored, and defendant did not object to the officer's search of them. Therefore, the key was not outside the scope of defendant's consent and was validly seized.

See also *Edwards v. Commonwealth*, 38 Va.App. 823, 568 S.E.2d 454 (2002), holding that consent to a search of one's person generally extends to containers held by or closely associated with the person, unless explicitly excluded from the scope of the consent.

But see *Camden v. Commonwealth*, 17 Va.App. 725, 441 S.E.2d 38 (1994). An officer asked defendant if he could perform a pat-down search for weapons, and defendant agreed. However, the officer exceeded the scope of this consent when he searched defendant's wallet, as this went beyond a mere pat-down.

If, in an attempt to gain consent to search a residence, officers mislead a person by saying or implying they have a warrant and will search anyway, when in reality they do not, any permission given is invalid. *Bumper v. North Carolina*, 391 U.S. 543 (1968); *Crosby v. Commonwealth*, 6 Va.App. 193, 367 S.E.2d 730 (1988). However, the threat to obtain a warrant, while bearing on the voluntariness of consent, is not treated the same. Stating that a warrant can and will be obtained, if police in fact have the requisite grounds, will not automatically vitiate an ensuing consent. *U.S. v. Hummer*, 916 F.2d 186 (4th Cir. 1990), *cert. denied*, 499 U.S. 970 (1991); *Deer v. Commonwealth*, 17 Va.App. 730, 441 S.E.2d 33 (1994).

9. **Inventory and Booking**. As long as preexisting, standardized procedures are followed, police may conduct a warrantless search of a lawfully impounded automobile and its contents (*i.e.*, Inventory). Similarly, a lawful warrantless search of an arrestee and the containers in his or her possession may be made prior to incarceration (*i.e.*, Booking). These exceptions are premised on the notion that the police are, in addition to their other duties, fulfilling a caretaking role. They are protecting the property of the arrestee from loss or theft or vandalism and other fellow detainees from the possibility of assault if a weapon is smuggled in. They are also protecting themselves from possible charges of theft. See *Fauntleroy v. Commonwealth*, 62 Va.App. 238, 746 S.E.2d 65 (2013). Courts caution, however, that the extent of the search must be tailored to serve these objectives. An inventory or booking search must not be a ruse for a general rummaging in order to discover incriminating evidence.

With respect to the legitimacy of inventory searches, courts have found that reasonable departmental regulations relating to inventory procedures, when carried out in good faith, satisfy the Constitution. *South Dakota v. Opperman*, 428 U.S. 364 (1976); *Fauntleroy v. Commonwealth, supra*. The presence of preexisting and standardized procedures, as well as the absence of bad faith on the part of officers conducting the search, guards against the threat of using an inventory search as a pretext for looking for contraband or other evidence of crime without any individualized suspicion. Objects that are open to view in the vehicle are treated the same as objects that are hidden or otherwise concealed, so that when acting pursuant to the aforementioned criteria, officers conducting the search may open closed containers found in the vehicle and inventory their contents. *Colorado v. Bertine*, 479 U.S. 367 (1987).

In *Cantrell v. Commonwealth*, 65 Va.App. 53,774 S.E.2d 469 (2015), a search of a vehicle was not a valid inventory search—and evidence found was suppressed—when the officer who conducted the search admitted one of his purposes was to search for contraband.

The vehicle searched must lawfully be in police custody (*i.e.*, there are sufficient grounds for impoundment) at the time of the search. *Williams v. Commonwealth, supra*. Police may impound a vehicle in the possession of a person arrested away from their residence provided there are no immediate means to protect the vehicle and the police act pursuant to reasonable policies and procedures. *Butler v. Commonwealth*, 31 Va.App. 614, 525 S.E.2d 58 (2000). However, *Va. Code* §19.2-80.1 states that, if there is no legal cause for the retention of the motor vehicle, the arrestee must be allowed to designate a licensed driver present at the arrest scene to drive the vehicle away. Only if no such designation is made may the vehicle be impounded. In *Butler*, defendant was arrested while alone in his car, which was parked in the private, gated garage of an apartment complex. Because the car did not have a sticker authorizing it to park there and there were no other licensed drivers at the scene of the arrest, the car was lawfully impounded.

Once a vehicle is impounded, police do not require a warrant even when conducting a second or subsequent search. *Florida v. Myers*, 466 U.S. 380 (1984).

Similar to an inventory of a vehicle, the search of an arrestee and his or her personal effects, including closed containers, prior to incarceration is reasonable under the Fourth Amendment. "A stationhouse search of every item carried on or by the person who has lawfully been taken into custody by the police" is permissible. *Illinois v. Lafayette*, 462 U.S. 640 (1983). In *Lafayette*, police arrested the defendant and transported him to the precinct headquarters. At the time he was carrying a shoulder bag. The bag was opened, emptied, and found to contain contraband. The defendant argued that the search exceeded the scope of a permissible booking search. The Supreme Court disagreed, reasoning that the search served the important government interests of protecting the property of the arrestee, as well as protecting the police department from false claims. A routine booking and search is a reasonable way to promote these interests and thus is valid under the Fourth Amendment.

10. **Automobiles**. If police have probable cause to believe a moveable car contains contraband or evidence of a crime, they may lawfully conduct a search of the entire automobile, and any containers which could reasonably be expected to contain contraband, whether open or closed, without first se-

curing a warrant, whether the vehicle is located on public or private property. *U.S. v. Ford*, 88 F.3d 1350 (4th Cir.), *cert. denied*, 519 U.S. 599 (1996); *Taylor v. Commonwealth*, 222 Va. 816, 284 S.E.2d 833 (1981); *Commonwealth v. Martin*, 90 Va. Cir. 245 (2015).

See, *e.g.*, *Leeth v. Commonwealth*, 223 Va. 335, 288 S.E.2d 475 (1982). At around 10:25 p.m., a state trooper was stationed along Interstate 81 when he saw defendant driving toward him in excess of the speed limit. When defendant's car was within range, the trooper activated his police radar. The brake lights on defendant's car instantly came on, and the car "braked suddenly, almost to the point of skidding." The trooper proceeded to follow the car, and, with the use of his headlights, he could see "a small cord hanging down from the interior rear view mirror" and "the driver fumbling over the sun visor on the driver's side of the vehicle." Once defendant stopped, the trooper had probable cause to make a warrantless search of the car for a radar detector (which he found under the front seat).

In *Powell v. Commonwealth*, 57 Va.App. 329, 701 S.E.2d 831 (2010), a Danville officer was conducting surveillance of a suspected drug distribution hub in a home on Twin Oaks Lane. The residence was known as a "drug house," and numerous intelligence reports indicated that drug sales were ongoing there. The officer had participated in three warranted searches at the house, two of which found cocaine. The officer watched as defendant left the house, entered a car, and sped out of the driveway, almost hitting the officer's unmarked car. As the officer followed, defendant drove 80 mph, then pulled to the side of the road in an area near some dumpsters. Approximately 10 seconds later, another car pulled alongside defendant's. The driver of that car opened his door, so that it faced defendant's now open door. Through binoculars, the officer watched both drivers engage in a hand-to-hand transaction. Defendant gave the other driver a small item; based on the officer's training and experience, it was consistent with a "dime or twenty rock" of crack cocaine. Immediately after, defendant made a "wiping motion with his thumb across the other fingers," that the officer interpreted as an effort to wipe off "the crumbs of crack cocaine which is real tacky." The other vehicle then drove off. Based on what he had seen, the officer had probable cause both to arrest defendant and to search his car for drug evidence.

See also *Byrd v. Commonwealth*, 57 Va.App. 589, 704 S.E.2d 597 (2011). A Virginia Beach officer received a tip from a reliable informant at around 1:00 a.m. regarding an impending crack cocaine deal at a Harris Teeter store that was to take place in 30 minutes. The informant alleged that the sellers would be a black male and black female, who would arrive at the store in a green, four-door vehicle, with the female driving. The officer knew this store was in a high drug crime area, and had made numerous arrests there. Moreover, he had known this informant for 18 months, and worked with him for 6 months; in that time he had provided "very reliable information" regarding drug crimes which had resulted in 12 search warrants, the seizure of large quantities of drugs and money, and a number of arrests. Every tip provided by the informant had proven to be true. Police quickly set up surveillance of the Harris Teeter store. At 1:35, a green four-door car driven by a black female pulled into the parking lot. The car's passenger—defendant, a black male—went into the store, then returned 2 minutes later empty-handed. He got back into the car and it drove off. Because the informant had a long history of reliability, and provided significant details of the upcoming drug deal (when the vehicle would arrive, who would be driving) that were corroborated by police, officers had probable cause to stop and search the car.

This exception applies to all containers, whether owned by the driver or a passenger, and regardless of whether or not there is individualized probable cause to search a specific container. *Wyoming v. Houghton*, 526 U.S. 295 (1999) (after officer saw a syringe in plain view in the driver's pocket, he was entitled to search purse belonging to back seat passenger for narcotics). As long as there is probable cause to search the automobile, officers need not show facts establishing exigency. *Maryland v. Dyson*, 527 U.S. 465 (1999).

Historically, this exception to the warrant requirement was premised on the notion that a car is readily mobile. As such, there is a potential exigency, in that a vehicle containing contraband may be driven from the jurisdiction before officers have an opportunity to secure a warrant. More recently, courts have focused on the pervasive government regulation of automobiles. Because the state has a hand in so many facets of automobile ownership and use (*e.g.*, licensing, registration, emission and safety inspections, *et al.*), one's expectation of privacy in the solitude of his or her automobile and its contents is diminished. Automobiles, in our society, do not occupy the same sacrosanct position courts attribute to the home. With a lessened privacy interest, a greater intrusion becomes more reasonable, and permissible under the Fourth Amendment.

Stopping a car for a minor traffic violation, without more, will not create probable cause to believe the car contains contraband and justify a search of the vehicle. The officer must have a reasonable belief that a more serious crime has been committed, and probable cause to think that evidence of it can be found in the car.

Note: **Canine Searches**. The Fourth Amendment does not require that police have a reasonable, articulable suspicion of criminal activity before allowing a well-trained narcotics detection dog to sniff the exterior of a vehicle during a lawful traffic stop, as long as this does not prolong the duration of the stop. *Illinois v. Caballes*, 543 U.S. 405 (2005); *Thomas v. Commonwealth*, 57 Va. App. 267, 701 S.E.2d 87 (2010). Police may not extend an otherwise completed traffic stop in order to conduct a dog sniff, absent reasonable suspicion that there is contraband in the vehicle. *Rodriguez v. U.S.*, 575 U.S. __ (2015). An alert from a dog who performs reliably in detecting drugs will establish probable cause to search a vehicle. *Florida v. Harris*, 568 U.S. __ (2013). The narcotics detection dog's reliability can be established from its training and experience, as well as a proven track record of previous alerts to the existence of illegal narcotics. *Jones v. Commonwealth*, 277 Va. 171, 670 S.E.2d 727 (2009).

If probable cause exists for a warrantless search of a vehicle on the scene, the search may also be conducted later after the vehicle has been moved to the station house. *Texas v. White*, 423 U.S. 67 (1975), *reh'g denied*, 423 U.S. 1081 (1976).

Stated broadly, police have justification to conduct a warrantless search of a car, or an area or container within the car, in the following circumstances:

- the entire car, including the trunk and any closed containers, when it is readily mobile and police possess probable cause to believe it contains contraband or the fruits and instrumentalities of crime;
- the area within an occupant's immediate control, to ensure the officer's safety during a *Terry* stop;
- the entire passenger area of the car when they place an occupant of the car under arrest ***if*** the arrestee is within reaching distance of the passenger compartment at the time of the search ***or*** it is reasonable to believe the vehicle contains evidence of the offense of arrest;
- the entire car, and generally any closed containers within, as part of an inventory procedure when the car has been impounded;
- the entire car, when it has been abandoned;
- the entire car, when valid consent has been given, or specific areas or containers, when permission to search has been limited to those areas.

The effective officer should keep these principles in mind when making the decision to act without a warrant. Although the rule remains that warrantless searches are per se invalid, warrantless searches are permissible in a variety of situations. However, the justifications permitting warrantless searches differ. The thorough officer should make sure that the circumstances with which he or she is confronted fit within the aforementioned exceptions, before deciding on a course of action.

If there is probable cause to believe that a vehicle itself is forfeitable contraband, it may be seized from a public place without a warrant. *Florida v. White*, 526 U.S. 559 (1999); *U.S. v. Brookins*, 345 F.3d 231 (4th Cir. 2003).

Note: **GPS Tracking.** In *U.S. v. Jones*, 565 U.S. __ (2012), FBI agents installed a GPS tracking device on the undercarriage of defendant's Jeep while it was parked in a public parking lot. Over the next 28 days, the agents used the device to track the vehicle's movements (and once had to replace the device's battery when the Jeep was parked in a different public lot). By means of signals from multiple satellites, the device established the vehicle's location within 50 to 100 feet, and communicated that location by cellular phone to an FBI computer. It relayed more than 2,000 pages of data over the 4-week period. The U.S. Supreme Court found that installation of a GPS device, and the subsequent use of that device to monitor the vehicle's movements, constitutes a "search" within the meaning of the Fourth Amendment. The agents did more than conduct a visual inspection of the Jeep; by attaching the device to it, they encroached on a protected area. Because they did not first obtain a warrant, this search was illegal. Be aware that Virginia has enacted legislation allowing law-enforcement officers to apply for a search warrant from a judicial officer permitting the use of a GPS tracking device. *Va. Code* §19.2-56.2.

Note: **Other Vehicles.** Watercraft are considered similar to automobiles, and searches of watercraft may be conducted under the same circumstances that would justify a search of an automobile. *U.S. v. Villamonte-Marquez*, 462 U.S. 579 (1983). Upon a showing of probable cause, police can make a warrantless search of a mobile home in a public place, if it is being used for transportation rather than as a residence. In making this determination, officers should consider: the location of the mobile home; whether it is truly mobile (or, for example, on blocks); whether it is licensed; whether it is connected to utilities; and whether it has convenient access to a public road. *California v. Carney*, 471 U.S. 386 (1985). See also *Alvarez v. Commonwealth*, 24 Va.App. 768, 485 S.E.2d 646 (1997). Two New Orleans detectives were investigating a Greyhound bus at the New Orleans Union Passenger Terminal. The dog who accompanied them, "K-9 Robbie," "hit" on a box in one of the buses' cargo areas by biting it, indicating that it contained narcotics. The package was addressed to defendant's Martinsville residence. K-9 Robbie's "hit" established probable cause to believe that the package contained a controlled substance. Because the package was on a bus—a movable vehicle analogous to an automobile—the detectives could validly search it without first obtaining a warrant.

11. **Implied Consent (DWI Stops).** When an officer suspects a driver of DWI, the driver is entitled to have his or her breath analyzed by the officer to determine the probable alcohol content of his or her blood, if proper equipment is available. The driver has a right to refuse such tests, and the results of such tests are not admissible in a criminal trial. *Va. Code* §18.2-267.

Any driver who operates a motor vehicle upon any highway in the Commonwealth is deemed to have consented to have samples of his or her breath or blood taken for chemical testing to determine alcohol and/or drug content if the driver is arrested for DWI or a similar offense. The samples must be taken within 3 hours of the alleged offense. *Va. Code* §18.2-

268.2. There is no statutory requirement that an officer offer a driver a breath test rather than a blood test. *Patterson v. Commonwealth*, 62 Va.App. 488, 749 S.E.2d 538 (2013).

There must be a lawful arrest for consent to be implied. *Smith v. Commonwealth*, 32 Va.App. 228, 527 S.E.2d 456 (2000). Merely telling a driver that he or she is "under arrest," without more, does not constitute an arrest for implied consent purposes. *Bristol v. Commonwealth*, 272 Va. 568, 636 S.E.2d 460 (2006). In *Bristol*, following a motorcycle accident, an officer approached defendant in the emergency room, where he had been taken for his injuries. The officer told defendant he was under arrest and informed him of the implied consent provisions described above. Defendant agreed to blood tests, which the officer observed. The officer did not restrain defendant in any way before, during or after blood was drawn. After the blood work, the officer simply left the hospital and returned to the police station; he did not indicate that defendant had been arrested in his subsequent report of the incident. When defendant was released from the hospital later that day, he was not taken into police custody or before a magistrate (he would not be taken into custody for over 2 months). The Court concluded that defendant had not, in fact, been arrested, so the provisions §18.2-268.2 did not apply. Therefore, the results of the blood test taken at the officer's request were inadmissible.

In *Roseborough v. Commonwealth*, 281 Va. 233, 704 S.E.2d 44 (2011), an Alexandria officer found defendant standing near his crashed pick-up truck following a single-vehicle accident along an internal private road inside a gated community. Because defendant appeared intoxicated, the officer arrested him and requested he take a breath test; defendant agreed, and the test showed a result of .09 grams of blood alcohol . The Court ruled that because defendant was already out of the truck by the time the officer arrived on the scene, the DWI offense was not committed within the officer's presence—therefore, because it was a misdemeanor, the officer could not make a warrantless arrest. Moreover, because this accident occurred on a private road, not "the highways of the Commonwealth," a warrantless arrest was not justified under *Virginia Code* §19.2-81(C). As there was no lawful arrest, there was no implied consent and the results of the breath test were suppressed.

If the arrestee is suspected of driving under the influence of alcohol, a breath test must be given, unless such test is unavailable or the arrestee is physically unable to submit to such test. If the arrestee is suspected of driving under the influence of a controlled substance, a blood test should be given. *Va. Code* §18.2-268.2. A person arrested solely for driving under the influence of alcohol does not have a right to choose a blood test—a blood test will only be given if breath-testing equipment is unavailable or when the driver is physically unable to take a breath test. *Lamay v. Commonwealth*, 29 Va.App. 461, 513 S.E.2d 411 (1999). The burden of establishing a valid reason why a breath test was not available is on the Commonwealth. *Mason v. Commonwealth*, 15 Va.App. 583, 425 S.E.2d 544 (1993). However, the burden of proving physical inability to take a breath test is on the driver; if the driver cannot prove such physical inability, then the failure of the State to offer a blood test cannot be challenged. *Hudson v. Commonwealth*, 266 Va. 371, 585 S.E.2d 583 (2003).

The driver must be advised that he or she has a right to observe the process of analysis and to see the blood-alcohol reading on the equipment (if the testing device automatically produces a written print-out, a copy should be given to the driver). *Va. Code* §18.2-268.2.

It is unlawful for the arrested driver to refuse to submit to chemical tests. Following arrest, if the driver refuses to submit to chemical tests, the officer must advise the driver from a written form that:

- he or she is deemed to have consented to have breath or blood samples taken as a condition of driving;
- an unreasonable refusal to submit to such tests will be admissible as evidence at a criminal trial;
- an unreasonable refusal constitutes a separate offense punishable by suspension his or her driving privileges for one year;
- an unreasonable refusal within 10 years of a previous refusal or DWI conviction is a Class 2 misdemeanor; and
- an unreasonable refusal within 10 years of two previous refusals or DWI convictions is a Class 1 misdemeanor.

Va. Code §18.2-268.3(B). If the driver again refuses the tests, the officer must take the driver before a magistrate and certify under oath that the driver will not permit samples to be taken despite being read the implied consent warning. This sworn certification constitutes probable cause for the magistrate to issue a warrant or summons charging the person with the offense of unreasonable refusal. If the arrested driver has been taken to a medical facility, the arresting officer may issue a summons at the medical facility in lieu of securing a warrant or summons from the magistrate. *Va. Code* §18.2-268.3(C).

An arrested driver has no right to consult with an attorney prior to deciding whether or not submit to chemical tests, and cannot condition or qualify consent to tests upon having access to an attorney. *Bailey v. Commonwealth*, 215 Va. 130, 207 S.E.2d 828 (1974); *D'Amico v. Commonwealth*, 287 Va. 284, 754 S.E.2d 291 (2014). A refusal is "reasonable" only if it is supported by some factual basis, for example, if withdrawal of blood would endanger the driver's health. *Bailey v. Commonwealth, supra.*

The person who administers the breath test must possess a valid license to conduct such tests. *Va. Code* §18.2-268.9. However the person's training need only have been on "breath-test equipment" in general, not necessarily with the specific device used for the test. *Reynolds v. Commonwealth*, 30 Va.App. 153, 515

S.E.2d 808 (1999). Only a medical professional may withdraw a blood sample. *Va. Code* §18.2-268.5.

The implied consent law permits the taking of a blood sample from an incoherent or unconscious driver. *Va. Code* §18.2-268.2(C); *Oliver v. Commonwealth*, 40 Va.App. 20, 577 S.E.2d 514 (2003).

Following a refusal to submit to chemical tests and issuance of a warrant or summons by the magistrate, or if chemical tests are given and the results indicate an unlawful blood alcohol content, the arrested driver's license shall be suspended immediately. The suspension shall be for 7 days (or 60 days if charged with a second offense, or until trial if charged with a third or subsequent offense). The arresting officer must serve a notice of suspension personally on the driver, then promptly take possession of any Commonwealth-issued driver's license held by the person and deliver it to the magistrate. Promptly after arrest and service of the notice of suspension, the arresting officer must forward to the magistrate a sworn report of the arrest, including information which identifies the person arrested and sets forth the grounds for arrest. *Va. Code* §46.2-391.2. Note that this suspension is a civil sanction, designed to protect the public from intoxicated drivers, and is in addition to any suspension that may be imposed as punishment following conviction for DWI.

The procedures for testing following an arrest for boating while intoxicated are virtually identical to these. See *Va. Code* §29.1-738.2.

12. **Administrative Searches**. Searches and seizures may be undertaken by the Commonwealth and its agents wholly apart from those pursued by law-enforcement agencies. The constraints imposed by the Constitution apply to the state and federal governments and their subdivisions or agents. The U.S. Supreme Court has never limited the Amendment's prohibition on unreasonable searches and seizures to operations conducted by the police. Rather, the Court has long spoken of the Fourth Amendment's strictures as restraints imposed upon "governmental action"—that is, upon "the activities of sovereign authority." *New Jersey v. T.L.O.*, 469 U.S. 325 (1985).

If a search is conducted by a private person, or at the direction of a private sector entity, no constitutional concerns arise. The Constitution places limits on government, not private, action. *Buonocore v. Chesapeake & Potomac Telephone Co. of Virginia*, 254 Va. 469, 492 S.E.2d 439 (1997); *Debroux v. Commonwealth*, 32 Va.App. 364, 528 S.E.2d 151 (2000).

Detailed below are U.S. Supreme Court cases assessing the constitutionality of searches of an administrative character. In these instances, the Court has upheld searches in several situations where no law-enforcement officials were involved, but where those individuals conducting the search could be deemed agents of a state or political subdivision (*i.e.*, intermediaries acting at the state's behest or in some way advancing the state's agenda), and their actions thus subject to constitutional limitations.

These warrantless intrusions by state actors are justified by the rationale that particular situations may involve special needs of the government. The special needs doctrine concerns governmental objectives that go beyond the normal day to day needs of law-enforcement agencies. If special governmental needs are demonstrated, a reviewing court will balance the privacy interests of the individual against the magnitude of the state's need, to determine if a warrant, or at least some level of individualized suspicion (*i.e.*, probable cause or reasonable suspicion) is required to justify a search in each particular context.

The Court approved a warrantless search by school officials of schoolchildren, *New Jersey v. T.L.O., supra*; warrantless drug tests on student athletes, *Vernonia Sch. Dist. 47j v. Acton*, 515 U.S. 646 (1995), and students engaged in competitive extracurricular activities, *Bd. of Educ. of Indep. Sch. Dist. No. 92 of Pottawatomie Co. v. Earls*, 536 U.S. 822 (2002); a warrantless search by an employer of employees' desks, offices, or file cabinets, *O'Conner v. Ortega*, 480 U.S. 709 (1987); mandatory warrantless drug testing of both railway employees, *Skinner v. Railway Labor Executives Ass'n*, 489 U.S. 602 (1989), and customs officials, *Nat'l Treasury Employees Union v. Von Raab*, 489 U.S. 656 (1989).

However, in *Chandler v. Miller*, 520 U.S. 305 (1997), the Court struck down a Georgia statutory provision requiring that candidates for specified state political offices pass a urinalysis drug test within 30 days prior to qualifying for election. The Court reasoned that Georgia had failed to show a special need important enough to override the individual privacy interests of the candidates. The Court found that the "certification requirement is not well designed to identify candidates who violate anti-drug laws" and that the statute failed to show any concrete danger posed by a state official possibly using drugs. See also *Ferguson v. City of Charleston*, 532 U.S. 67 (2001), where the Court struck down a policy which required state hospital employees to perform drug tests on urine samples taken from pregnant women (without the informed consent of the women), then to report positive results to police, who arrested the women if they refused to enter a drug treatment program. The Court found that the "central and indispensable" purpose of this policy was to generate evidence for law-enforcement purposes, not to provide medical treatment, and noted that police were actively involved in the development of this policy as well as its day-to-day administration.

V. EXPECTATION OF PRIVACY

In *Katz v. U.S.*, 389 U.S. 347 (1967), the U.S. Supreme Court held that the Fourth Amendment safeguards against unreasonable searches and seizures only extend to those places or objects with respect to which a person has exhibited some expectation of privacy. This expectation is one which society is prepared to recognize as reasonable. There are three varieties of property to which courts have consistently held no reasonable privacy expectation applies, and to which no constitutioanal protections will attach. These are: objects in open fields, objects placed in plain view, and objects that have been abandoned. These places can be searched, and items in those areas seized, without first securing a warrant.

The Supreme Court has noted that "the touchstone" of any claimed Fourth Amendment violation is always the reasonableness of the government's intrusion upon a citizen's personal security. It is often said that the Fourth Amendment does not prohibit all searches and seizures, only unreasonable ones. The threshold question in determining if government conduct is reasonable, is inquiring whether a legitimate privacy interest has been invaded. In *Katz, supra*, the Court spelled out the analysis that will be used to determine when Fourth Amendment protections are implicated, and when they are not. The Constitution will protect people from government intrusion only with respect to those areas and items for which they subjectively have an expectation of privacy and only when that expectation is plainly one that society is prepared to recognize as reasonable. The Fourth Amendment protects "people—and not simply areas—against unreasonable searches and seizures." The Court noted that an expectation of privacy will vary from person to person, and place to place, reasoning that "objects, activities or statements that one exposes to outsiders may fall outside the protection of the Fourth Amendment because (one) has displayed them freely and has not shown an intention of keeping them private. One may also exhibit an expectation of privacy in an item, even though he or she takes it to a public place, if his or her acts manifest an intent to keep the item private." If no privacy violation occurred, the Fourth Amendment is not implicated, and there is no need to further examine government conduct. Likewise, if one person's privacy concerns have been trodden upon, other individuals whose interests were not interfered with do not have legal grounds, or standing, to challenge the government's conduct, and that conduct need not be analyzed.

If, however, a privacy violation has occurred, the courts will proceed to examine the conduct in question, and endeavor to determine if it was reasonable under the circumstances. If the actions are deemed reasonable, they are legal; if unreasonable, they are unconstitutional, bringing the specter of suppression and civil liability into the forefront. To aid in this reasonableness determination, courts employ a balancing analysis. On one side of the scale rests a person's privacy concerns regarding his home, body and possessions. On the other side of the scale rests the government's interest in advancing or promoting the law-enforcement conduct in question. If the privacy interest is weighty (*e.g.*, the inviolability of one's home), then intrusive government conduct is less likely to be reasonable under the circumstances. If, on the other hand, the government interest is significant (*e.g.*, curtailing the drug epidemic), and the individual's privacy interest is lessened (*e.g.*, items that may be carried about in one's car), then more intrusive government action is more likely to be deemed constitutionally reasonable under the circumstances.

Nonetheless, there remains a judicial preference for warrants, and the general rule remains that warrantless searches are per se unreasonable. The Supreme Court has provided some clear-cut guidelines in specific instances, the so-called "bright-line rules" (*e.g.*, requirement of a warrant for an in-home arrest, search of a passenger compartment when the occupant is arrested, etc.). Courts routinely state that they are hesitant to pronounce far-reaching rules of universal applicability. Rather, there is an increasing tendency to evaluate each case on its own facts, and resort to the balancing test to determine the reasonableness and hence the constitutionality of any given law-enforcement action. There are many circumstances to which no precedent applies. In cases that fall beyond the confines of these "bright-line" rules, where government conduct is in the periphery, or gray area of Fourth Amendment law, courts are increasingly likely to employ the balancing test. The outcome, obviously, will vary depending on the unique circumstances of each factual setting. In these cases, rather than employing a rule requiring a warrant for virtually all law-enforcement actions, subject to limited exceptions, courts will instead employ the above criteria to answer the question begged by the Fourth Amendment: was the conduct reasonable?

The following doctrines concern areas, objects within those areas and classes of property in which courts have consistently held individuals do not have a reasonable expectation of privacy. Because there is no privacy expectation, no search, within the meaning of the Constitution, can take place; *i.e.*, the Fourth Amendment is not implicated, there is no need to examine government acts, and no basis for suppression of evidence seized.

A. Plain View Doctrine

Under the plain view doctrine, the warrantless seizure of a piece of evidence that is in plain view is permissible when three criteria are met. First, the evidence must be seen from a lawful vantage point. Second, the seizing officer must have a right of lawful access to the object itself. Finally, it must be immediately apparent to the viewer that the object observed is incriminating evidence. In other words, the observing officer must have probable cause to believe the evidence in question is contraband or incriminating evidence. *U.S. v. Wells*, 98 F.3d 808 (4th Cir. 1996); *Cauls v. Commonwealth*, 55 Va.App. 90, 683 S.E.2d 847 (2009). Lawful vantage point means that the officer has a legal justification for his place of observation. Immediately apparent means that the officer needs to conduct no further investigation of the object or item in question to realize its evidentiary value.

See, *e.g.*, *Arnold v. Commonwealth*, 17 Va.App. 313, 437 S.E.2d 235 (1993). Defendant was a passenger in car stopped for not having a rear license plate. The officer noticed a Hecht's bag in the back seat next to defendant. Based on the way the bag was folded and the officer's experience in retail security, he suspected that the bag was lined with foil, a method often used by shoplifters to disable the anti-theft devices commonly placed on clothing. As the officer later explained, a plastic bag, after being folded down or rolled up, "will tend to open back up on its own". Foil-lined bags, however, stay rigid and keep their shape if rolled or folded. The officer also knew that possession of such a device is a misdemeanor, so he validly seized and searched the bag. Inside, he found six dresses on hangers with the store security tags still attached.

Compare with *Hogan v. Commonwealth*, 15 Va.App. 355, 423 S.E.2d 841 (1992). An officer stopped a car for running a red light. From outside the vehicle, he saw two white plastic bags which contained a powdery substance. These were lawfully seized under the plain view doctrine and later determined to be cocaine.

But see *Grandison v. Commonwealth*, 274 Va. 316, 645 S.E.2d 298 (2007). Defendant was a passenger in a stolen vehicle stopped in downtown Petersburg, an area known for drug activity. During a pat-down, an officer felt a hard object in the front watch pocket of defendant's jeans (which proved to be a cigarette lighter). The officer looked at the pocket, and saw a folded $1 bill protruding halfway out of it. He immediately recognized an "apothecary fold" (three times lengthwise, with the two ends folded toward the middle), which he knew to be a common way of storing drugs. Despite this, the folded dollar bill was legal material with a legitimate purpose. No other circumstances indicated criminal activity. Therefore, the officer did not have probable cause to retrieve the dollar bill, because it was not immediately apparent that it was contraband.

Compare with *Cauls v. Commonwealth*, *supra*. An officer saw the knotted, frayed end of a plastic bag protruding from the watch pocket of defendant's jeans—however, the officer could not see the bag's contents. Because the officer only had a hunch that the bag might contain drugs, there was no valid plain view seizure.

The theory behind the plain view doctrine is that when a police officer is conducting a lawful search and comes across an item or object that is not the object of a search, but is plainly incriminating, then the officer may seize that item. The justification for such a warrantless seizure is not a lack of privacy interest in the item (probable cause to believe that the object or item is contraband, evidence, or fruits or instrumentality of a crime is necessary), but that there is no intrusion beyond that which is already justified.

The importance of the plain view doctrine is that, technically, when conducting a search, an officer may seize only those objects or items described in a warrant or, in a warrantless search, those objects or items which the officer is lawfully authorized to seize under an exception to the warrant requirement. Thus, without the plain view doctrine, an officer searching an automobile for weapons would be forced to ignore evidence that was not a weapon. However, under the plain view doctrine, a seizure of other evidence is lawful.

Use of a flashlight to view an object does not make a plain view seizure unlawful. *Derr v. Commonwealth*, 6 Va.App. 215, 368 S.E.2d 916 (1988) (use of flashlight to look inside parked car upheld); *Gibson v. Commonwealth*, 50 Va.App. 744, 653 S.E.2d 626 (2007) (use of flashlight to look inside defendant's pocket at night did not change plain view nature discovery of marijuana in pocket). However, police cannot use a device which is not in general public use to explore details of the home that would previously have been unknowable without physical intrusion without first obtaining a warrant. *Kyllo v. U.S.*, 533 U.S. 27 (2001) (warrantless police use of a thermal imager, which measured the amount of heat emanating from different areas of defendant's house, violated the Fourth Amendment).

In *Redmond v. Commonwealth*, 57 Va.App. 254, 701 S.E.2d 81 (2010), evidence observed by an officer who entered defendant's residence as a prospective purchaser of the home (which was for sale) could be used to obtain a search warrant without violating the Fourth Amendment. The officer's actions did not violate defendant's reasonable expectation of privacy, as they did not exceed what one would expect of a prospective purchaser.

By analogy, the plain view doctrine has been expanded to include a "plain smell" corollary. "Probable cause may be supported by the detection of distinctive odors, as well as by sight." *Bunch v. Commonwealth*, 51 Va.App. 491, 658 S.E.2d 724 (2008). In *Bunch*, an officer had probable cause to arrest a driver and search a vehicle when he smelled a "heavy" odor of marijuana coming from the partially opened window of an illegally parked car, which got "noticeably stronger" when the driver stepped out and walked past the officer.

Similar to plain view is the theory of open view. However, in open view an officer needs no justification for his or her vantage point in that the object or item is in a place in which no person could have a reasonable expectation of privacy. Thus, there is no search being conducted when an officer finds an object or item in open view.

See *U.S. v. Taylor*, 90 F.3d 903 (4th Cir. 1996). Officers arrived at defendant's house to return a handgun seized during an earlier traffic stop. Through a picture window, about 8 feet to the left of the front door, they saw a large sum of currency and a bag of white powder on a table in the well-lit dining room. This evidence was visible from the street as well as from the front walkway and porch. The officers had the same right to view it as any other member of the public or guest would and were therefore justified in making a warrantless entry and seizure.

But see *Sheler v. Commonwealth*, 38 Va.App. 465, 566 S.E.2d 203 (2002) where a small piece of glass embedded in the sole of defendant's boot was not within open view. The Court noted that the officer could not see the glass shard until defendant had removed the boot and he had a chance to examine the crevices in the sole more closely. Moreover, because this took place during a consensual encounter, asking defendant to remove the boot constituted an illegal search. "Generally, people do not expect other persons will seize their shoes or other garments they wear and manipulate them to explore and expose unseen features." Therefore, the evidence found was suppressed.

Contrast with *Williams v. Commonwealth*, 259 Va. 377, 527 S.E.2d 131 (2000), where the Court upheld inspection of clothing *worn by an arrestee* which was lawfully seized and then examined sometime after the arrest. At that point, the defendant no longer had a reasonable expectation of privacy in the clothing.

"The seizure of property in plain view involves no invasion of privacy and is presumptively reasonable, assuming that there is probable cause to associate the property with criminal activity." *Payton v. New York*, 445 U.S. 573 (1980). This doctrine is premised on the notion that if an article is already in plain view, the owner of the property has not manifested any expectation of privacy in the object. Often, the critical factor in deciding the applicability of the doctrine to the admission of proffered evidence, involves a determination of whether or not the seizing officers are lawfully in the position from which they view the seized item. As long as law-enforcement officials have a proper justification for being where they conduct their observation, and have a right of access to the item seized, they may seize all contraband, fruits, and instrumentalities of crime, or those items that they have probable cause to believe are contraband, fruits, or instrumentalities of crime. Adequate justifications for being at a given vantage point would include being in a public area (*e.g.*, street, or business open to the public), working under the authority of a warrant, or where the intrusion that brings the police within plain view of the evidence is supported by one of the exceptions to the warrant requirement (*e.g.*, hot pursuit or exigent circumstances). A proper justification for the officers being where they are viewing from, in essence, means that the officer did not violate the defendant's constitutional rights in establishing his vantage point. To fall within the purview of this exception, the discovery of the incriminating items need not be inadvertent (*i.e.*, the seizing officer can be operating under the assumption that incriminating evidence will be found, or have an idea of what he or she will find), but the incriminating nature of the item must be immediately apparent. *Conway v. Commonwealth*, 12 Va.App. 711, 407 S.E.2d 310 (1991).

Courts sometimes draw a distinction between items seized in "plain" view and items seized in "open" view. Under this analysis, items in plain view are in a constitutionally protected area (*i.e.*, one in which there is a reasonable expectation of privacy). When these items are seized the question a reviewing court will ask is, once the item has been seen, is there a justification, like a warrant or an applicable exception, that will permit access? Or, if the item is seen from a constitutionally protected area, is there a justification for the law-enforcement personnel being in that protected area? For example, if contraband is seen in plain view, and the officer is justified in being at his vantage point, it does not always mean the contraband is subject to immediate seizure. If the contraband is in a home, or in the curtilage, and seen from without, a warrant must be procured, absent an applicable exception to the warrant requirement, before the home can be entered and the evidence seized. Items in open view, on the other hand, are items seen in an area that is not constitutionally protected (*i.e.*, where there is no reasonable expectation of privacy). Examples often cited are objects in open fields, on the body of a person, in a public building, or in a car. In this respect, the open view doctrine is essentially identical to the open fields concept, discussed below.

B. Areas and Items Surrounding the Home

The home is clearly a bastion of Fourth Amendment rights. The area around the home, often referred to as the "curtilage," also enjoys protection. This includes areas such as the garage, garden, or the immediate yard. However, courts have held that the area outside the curtilage is not worthy of the same protection.

1. **Curtilage**. The sanctity of one's home is at the core of Fourth Amendment rights. While objects in open areas do not receive the benefit of Fourth Amendment protections, courts have also ruled that constitutional safeguards will extend to zones immediately outside the home, an area called the curtilage. The extent of the curtilage is determined by factors that bear upon whether an individual reasonably may expect that the area in question should be treated as the home itself. Courts look to see if the area is used for the "intimate activity associated with the sanctity of a man's home and the privacies of life." The analysis employed by courts entails an examination of four factors: (i) the proximity of the area claimed to be curtilage to the home; (ii) whether the area is enclosed, for example, by a fence or hedge; (iii) the types of activities for which the homeowner uses the area; and (iv) the measures taken by the resident to guard the area from observation by people passing by. *U.S. v. Dunn*, 480 U.S. 294, *reh'g denied*, 481 U.S. 1024 (1987); *Jefferson v. Commonwealth*, 27 Va.App. 1, 497 S.E.2d 474 (1998).

As a consequence of the interplay between these two doctrines, the home and the curtilage are protected by the Constitution, and a warrant will generally be required to enter and search them. The open areas that surround those private protected zones do not occupy the same position of reverence and are not accorded the same protections.

In *Florida v. Jardines*, 569 U.S. __ (2013), the U.S. Supreme Court held that police use of a trained drug-sniffing dog in the curtilage of a residence—for example, around the front porch—is a "search" within the meaning of the Fourth Amendment, and therefore cannot be done without a warrant. But see *Sanders v. Commonwealth*, 64 Va.App. 734, 772 S.E.2d 15 (2015), finding no Fourth Amendment violation when a dog sniffed the area around defendant's motel room door on a second-floor open air walkway, as the walkway is a common area used by and accessible to all guests, motel employees and anyone else on the premises to access rooms.

Note: **The "Knock-and-Talk"**. Police with legitimate business may enter the curtilage, if there is an implicit invitation to do so. "[J]ust as private citizens may approach a home, absent contrary instructions from the owner, to knock on a door, so may the police approach without probable cause, a warrant, or exigency." Once within the curtilage, the officers may speak with anyone they find until asked to leave. This so-called "knock-and-talk" procedure does not violate the Fourth Amendment. *Rogers v. Pendleton*, 249 F.3d 279 (4th Cir. 2001). See also *Robinson v. Commonwealth*, 47 Va.App. 533, 625 S.E.2d 651 (2006),), *aff'd*, 639 S.E.2d 217 (Va.), *cert. denied*, 550 U.S. 957 (2007), where an officer did not conduct an illegal search by pulling into the defendants' driveway, where he could see into the back yard (the back yard was not visible from the street). There were no physical barriers or "No Trespassing" signs, and the officer did not drive past the walkway which connected the driveway to the front door. Therefore, he was still on a direct route to the front door when he observed juveniles drinking in the back yard. Although the Court noted that the officer made his approach somewhat late at night--around 11:00 p.m.--there were still lights on above the front door and along the walkway, and a number of cars were parked in the driveway and along the street outside the house. The officer could therefore reasonably infer that the residents had not gone to bed yet.

2. **Aerial Search**. Courts have found that it is unreasonable to have a privacy expectation in the aerial view of one's property. This is due to the fact that any private citizen may obtain such a view. Since there is no protected privacy interest in the view, police may conduct aerial searches without a warrant. *Dow Chemicals Co. v. U.S.*, 476 U.S. 227 (1986).

Per Virginia statute, no department of law enforcement of any county, city, or town may utilize an unmanned aircraft system except:

- during the execution of a search warrant issued pursuant to this chapter or an administrative or inspection warrant;
- when an Amber Alert is activated, Senior Alert, or Blue Alert is activated;
- where use of an unmanned aircraft system is determined to be necessary to alleviate an immediate danger to any person;
- for training exercises related to such uses; or
- if a person with legal authority consents to the warrantless search.

Va. Code § 19.2-60.1.

3. **Open Fields**. Courts have said that people cannot maintain a reasonable expectation of privacy as to items placed in open fields, or concerning activities conducted there. Because there is no intrusion on a constitutionally protected zone of privacy, the Fourth Amendment is not implicated when law-enforcement officials survey structures found, or activities conducted, in an open field. Because the Fourth Amendment does not protect open fields, the examination of objects therein does not constitute a search, and neither a warrant nor any exception to the warrant requirement need be shown to justify the seizure of articles in an open field. *Oliver v. U.S.*, 466 U.S. 170 (1984).

The type of land a court may deem an open field will depend on the unique circumstances of each parcel. A variety of circumstantial factors will be examined to determine if the area is treated as a non-private area, or if the owner has manifested a privacy interest, or has exhibited an intent to keep outsiders away. The presence or absence of "No Trespassing" signs, and the extent to which such a policy is enforced, is relevant in this determination, as is the presence or absence of a fence or hedge surrounding the field, and the extent to which the owner controls access to the field by use of a gate or chain across an entry lane.

Note that "open field" is a term of art and encompasses "any unoccupied or undeveloped area outside of the curtilage." Thus, land that is neither "open" nor a "field," as those terms are understood in common parlance, may still fall within this doctrine, *e.g.* a thickly wooded area. *Oliver v. U.S., supra.*

Courts have held that it is generally unreasonable to have an expectation of privacy in open areas of land. Even if the land shows evidence of an expectation of privacy, the courts will still only look at the reasonableness of that expectation.

4. **Abandoned Items or Garbage**. When property has been abandoned, it no longer falls within the area of protection afforded by the Fourth Amendment, and therefore can be searched or seized without a warrant or any other justification. *Hawley v. Commonwealth*, 206 Va. 479, 144 S.E.2d 314 (1985), *cert. denied*, 383 U.S. 910 (1986). When determining if property has been abandoned, courts will analyze the actions of the individual alleged to have discarded the article. The focus is not whether the defendant relinquished dominion and control of the property with respect to his or her possession, as would be the case if the ownership of the item were in dispute, but rather, whether the individual has relinquished any reasonable expectation of privacy in the article. When police conduct is lawful (*e.g.*, they have a lawful right to approach and question a person) and a suspect discards an item in a public place, then he or she can be said to have abandoned that item. Police may secure the item and, if incriminating, retain it for use later as evidence, without fear of the suspect claiming that the evidence was seized from him or her unlawfully.

Conversely, if officers do not have a justification for their initial actions (*e.g.*, detaining without reasonable suspicion), and the item is discarded in response to this unlawful activity, the evidence may be suppressed as the fruit of illegal law-enforcement activity. In this instance, courts say that the unlawful police action forced the abandonment. *U.S. v. Leshuk*,

65 F. 3d 1105 (4th Cir. 1995); *Moss v. Commonwealth*, 7 Va.App. 305, 373 S.E.2d 170 (1988).

See, *e.g.*, *Motley v. Commonwealth*, 17 Va.App. 439, 437 S.E.2d 232 (1993). An officer received a radio dispatch to be on the look-out for a "black male with a yellow hat and black Kings coat." No explanation was offered as to why this man was being sought by police. Nevertheless, when the officer saw defendant, who matched the description, he ordered him to stop. Upon hearing the officer, defendant dropped an object—later determined to be cocaine—to the ground. Because the officer had no reasonable suspicion to stop defendant, his abandonment of the cocaine was "forced" by an illegal stop, and the evidence was inadmissible.

Compare with *U.S. v. Wilson*, 953 F.2d 116 (4th Cir. 1991). When officers illegally and without reasonable suspicion detained defendant in an airport, defendant discarded his coat. The officers then searched the coat and found drugs. Defendant's abandonment of the coat was ruled involuntary, because it was prompted by the invalid stop. The evidence found in it was therefore suppressed.

When an individual abandons an item of personal property, he relinquishes a reasonable expectation of privacy in the discarded item. This is true whether an individual is putting trash to the curb or dropping evidence while fleeing from police. A showing of actual intent to abandon is not necessary. It is only necessary to show that the individual asserting a privacy interest in the property in question had relinquished sufficient control over the property so that he no longer had any reasonable expectation of privacy in the object or item. See *California v. Greenwood*, 486 U.S. 35 (1988) (renounce any expectation of privacy in garbage set out on the street); *U.S. v. Jackson*, 728 F.3d 367 (4th Cir. 2013) (no expectation of privacy in trash left for collection outside the curtilage of a home).

5. **Disclaimer of Ownership.** If a defendant disclaims ownership of property or any possessory interest, police may use such a denial as sufficient proof of either an intent to abandon the property or a lack of ownership of the property.

See, *e.g.*, *Wechsler v. Commonwealth*, 20 Va.App. 162, 455 S.E.2d 744 (1995). Defendant was stopped at Washington National Airport because he fit the profile of a drug courier (he had a one-way ticket from Tucson, bought with cash minutes before the flight). DEA agents learned from the airline that defendant had checked two bags. However, after making eye contact with the agents in the baggage claim area, defendant left without claiming them. During a consensual interview outside the airport, defendant denied that he had checked any bags. Even after a consensual search of defendant's carry-on bag found claim checks for two bags attached to his ticket, defendant continued his denials. By choosing to forego possession of the bags by leaving the airport without them and then repeatedly denying ownership of them, defendant abandoned the bags and could no longer object to the agents' warrantless search of them.

See also *U.S. v. Leshuk*, 65 F.3d 1105 (4th 1995). A hunter stumbled upon a marijuana patch in a rural, wooded area. After contacting the police, he led two officers back to the site, which was located about a mile off the road. The patch was surrounded by a chicken wire mesh enclosure, and contained 33 marijuana plants, all of which were wet around their bases, as if recently watered. Soon after arriving, the officers and the hunter heard a commotion nearby. They soon found the source of the noise—the defendants, who were stopped just 50 yards away from the marijuana grow. Defendants were standing next to a brown plastic garbage bags and two backpacks which had wire mesh attached, similar to the wire mesh used to enclose the marijuana plants; however, they denied ownership of these items. Therefore, they could not object when the officers searched the bag and backpacks, finding soil containers filled with marijuana, as well as fertilizer, containers of water, a machete, and other gardening implements.

C. The Caretaker Function

The "caretaker function" was first developed by the U.S. Supreme Court in *Cady v. Dombrowski*, 413 U.S. 433 (1973). The concept of the "caretaker function" is that the police are not always involved in the adversarial process of arresting criminals. Sometimes the police may act in other ways to help the public. This may be to render assistance to individuals in need or to provide protection for the rights and property of members of the general public. The "caretaker function" also applies to certain acts performed by police to secure a suspect's rights or property. The Courts will examine the reasonableness of any such act. However, probable cause is not necessary. Evidence that is found during such acts will be admissible.

See, *e.g.*, *Commonwealth v. Waters*, 20 Va.App. 285, 456 S.E.2d 527 (1995). A Leesburg officer was patrolling an apartment complex when he observed defendant swaying and walking unsteadily. Defendant appeared either intoxicated or ill. The officer approached him, tapped him on the shoulder, and said he wanted to make sure he could find his way home. The officer was reasonably concerned about defendant's safety. Therefore, this was not an illegal stop. When defendant began making threatening gestures and statements and the officer noticed a bulge on his left side, reasonable suspicion developed, so that a pat-down was justified.

Compare with *Commonwealth v. Parker*, 87 Va.Cir. 418 (2014). An officer saw defendant behind the wheel of a car in a restaurant parking lot. Defendant's keys were in the ignition, but the engine was not running. His eyes were closed and he did not appear to be moving. The officer tapped on the driver's side window for 10 to 15 seconds, but defendant did not respond. The officer then opened the car door, to see if defendant needed assistance—he was met with a strong odor of alcohol, which eventually led to defendant's arrest for being drunk in public. The Court ruled the officer acted reasonably in opening the car door—he did so to determine if defendant was safe and healthy.

In *U.S. v. Taylor*, 624 F.3d 626 (4th Cir. 2010), *cert. denied,* 179 L. Ed. 2d 786 (2011), a Richmond officer responded to a report of a lost 4 year-old girl found wandering along a busy street. A cab driver had found the girl and placed her in the back of his cab; her parents could not be found. When asked where she lived, the little girl pointed to a house. The officer walked her there and saw an interior door was open, although the exterior door was closed. The officer yelled "hello" but no one answered; the girl simply walked inside so the officer followed, continuing to yell "hello." He eventually found defendant, in bed in a back room. Defendant immediately identified the girl as his daughter. There was a bag of .22 bullets on a bureau next to defendant's bed, and the officer's observation of this ultimately led to defendant's conviction for being a felon in possession of ammunition. The Court ruled this observation was made lawfully under the caretaker doctrine—"the absence of responsible adult supervision of children is an exigent circumstance justifying a warrantless entry."

In *Commonwealth v. Mahon-Hall*, 87 Va.Cir. 115 (2013), a contractor working on a home in Radford contacted police late in the afternoon on December 22 to report that the house across the street from the one he was working on had its side door open. This struck him as odd, because he had observed no activity or occupants at the residence prior to that day. Officers arrived to find both the storm door and the interior solid door open—unusual given the time of year. In addition, the officers knew this area experienced a dramatic rise in burglaries around the holidays, when students in the nearby schools are away on break (to the point Radford police use special assignment undercover officers who work extra patrols during this time of year). The officers knocked and yelled but received no response. They then looked inside and saw the house was in disarray. Although there was no broken glass or sign of forced entry, one of the officers later testified this is common with burglaries, as victims simply do not lock their doors. The officers entered the house without first obtaining a warrant, and found drugs, drug paraphernalia, and child pornography in plain view. The Court upheld this entry—the officers were not investigating criminal activity, but instead were trying to determine if the homeowner was in need of medical assistance or the victim of a burglary. This was a valid police exercise of the caretaker function.

See also *Terry v. Commonwealth*, 23 Va.App. 87, 474 S.E.2d 172 (1996). A Henrico County officer was dispatched to Three Lakes Park in response to a medical emergency. When he arrived at the park, he was directed by park patrons to an area near one of the lakes where he found defendant in a semiconscious state. Defendant was blue in the face and around the lips, gasping for air and unable to talk. Nobody claimed to be his friend. The officer had received no information concerning any actual or suspected criminal activity in the area; in fact, there was a fishing pole and tackle box next to defendant, which led the officer to conclude defendant had simply been fishing in the lake. The officer initially assisted defendant until an EMS team arrived. The officer then searched defendant's fanny pack fanny pack hoping he could identify defendant, and also locate medical information and determine the cause of defendant's condition. He found an inhaler, but also found rolling papers. Cognizant of the fact that rolling papers are often used to smoke marijuana, he concluded that marijuana may have been the cause of defendant's attack. He therefore continued his search of the fanny pack, looking inside a pack of cigarettes; there he found a marijuana joint. He promptly relayed this information to the EMS workers, then seized the joint. Defendant was eventually arrested for possession of marijuana, some time after he had been taken to the hospital. The Court upheld the officer's search under the "caretaker" doctrine. At the time of the search, the officer had no information and no reason to suspect any criminal activity; his conduct at all times was consistent with rendering aid and assistance to defendant because of his medical condition. Even after he found the rolling papers, he continued his search solely to determine the cause of defendant's condition and to help render treatment, as evidenced by the fact that he immediately shared his discovery with the EMS workers. The seizure of the joint was therefore valid.

Note: **Emergency Custody of Mentally Ill Persons**. A law-enforcement officer who, based upon his or her own observation or the reliable reports of others, has probable cause to believe that a person (i) has mental illness, (ii) presents an imminent danger to himself or others as a result of mental illness or is so seriously mentally ill as to be substantially unable to care for himself, (iii) is in need of hospitalization or treatment, and (iv) is unwilling to volunteer or incapable of volunteering for hospitalization or treatment, may take that person into custody and transport the person to an appropriate location to assess the need for hospitalization or treatment without prior authorization. *Va. Code* §37.2-808.

D. Interception of Wire, Electronic or Oral Communications

Use of an electronic device to eavesdrop on a conversation constitutes a "search and seizure." *Katz v. U.S.*, 389 U.S. 347 (1967).

Any police officer who wishes to get authorization to conduct a wiretap must fill out an application. The application must state: (1) the identity of both the attorney for the Commonwealth and the police officer making the application; (2) "[a] full and complete statement of the facts and circumstance relied upon by the applicant to justify his belief that an order should be issued, including (i) details as to the particular offense that has been, is being, or is about to be committed (ii) a particular description of the nature and location of the facilities from which or the place where the communication is to be intercepted is to take place (iii) a particular description of the type of communication sought to be intercepted (iv) the identity of the person, if known, committing the offense and whose communications are to be intercepted" (*Va. Code* §19.2-68(2)); (3) the other investigative means that have failed, or why they would fail or be too dangerous; (4) the time period that the intercept will be needed, also any reasons why the intercept should continue after the information described has been obtained; (5) the facts concerning any past attempt to obtain an intercept on any of the suspects in the present application.

All applications must be made through the Attorney General or Deputy Attorney General. The Attorney General or Deputy Attorney General will review the application, verify it, and have it presented to a magistrate in the jurisdiction in which the communications will take place. The magistrate will then make a probable cause determination. *Va. Code* §§19.2-66 and 19.2-68. See *Va. Code* §§19.2-61 through 19.2-70.3 for further details.

Be aware that *Va. Code* §19.2-62 makes unlawful wiretaps a class 6 felony, while §19.2-69 provides for civil damages.

VI. THE EXCLUSIONARY RULE

The frequent result of unconstitutional actions by law-enforcement is the imposition of a judicially created remedy—banning the use of evidence gathered under such circumstances—called suppression. The exclusionary rule mandates that all evidence obtained by searches and seizures violative of the rights of an accused are inadmissible against that person in a subsequent trial. The rule is premised on the notion that if private, constitutionally protected areas can be searched, and items taken unlawfully are used to obtain a conviction, the protections of the Fourth Amendment are of little, if any, value. The exclusionary rule is in essence an enforcement mechanism, serving to give teeth to constitutional guarantees. The rule bars the use of all forms of illegally obtained evidence. Physical evidence as well as statements are subject to suppression, if they derive from an unconstitutional act, such as an unlawful arrest, illegal search or coercive interrogation. If law-enforcement officials come by evidence through exploitation of their illegal conduct, the evidence is said to be "tainted," and evidence tainted by illegal conduct on the part of law-enforcement is inadmissible against an accused.

The exclusionary rule applies not only to the illegally obtained evidence itself, but also bars the use of evidence derived from the initially obtained illegal evidence, because of the initial illegality. This derivative, or secondary evidence, including an officer's testimony based on knowledge garnered as a result of the illegal conduct, is often referred to as the "fruit of the poisonous tree." To invoke the protection of the "poisonous tree" principle, the defendant must first demonstrate there was a primary illegality (*i.e.*, an unconstitutional search or arrest, or a coerced confession), and secondly, a nexus, or connection, between the illegality and the derivative evidence. The nexus between the illegal act and the subject evidence must be so strong that police can be said to have obtained the evidence only by an exploitation of their illegal actions. If another event or outside factor weakens the connection between the illegality and the evidence, a principle referred to as attenuation, so that the evidence can no longer be said to be a by-product of the unlawful conduct, then suppression is not appropriate. The attenuating factor removes the stigma of the illegal law-enforcement action, so that denying the admission of the seized evidence does not serve the deterrent purposes of the exclusionary rule.

See *U.S. v. Sprinkle*, 106 F. 3d 613 (4th Cir. 1997). Officers conducted an unjustified *Terry* stop of the defendant. Because this initial stop was illegal, normally any evidence seized as a result of that stop would be inadmissible at trial. However, an independent act of the defendant constituted a new crime and gave the arresting officers a separate and constitutional basis for arrest. As officers told him they were going to pat him down for weapons, defendant pushed away and began to run. The officers gave chase, and, after about 100 feet, defendant pulled a handgun from his jacket and fired a shot in the general direction of one of the officers. Defendant then put the gun to his own head and said if the officer's did not leave, he would shoot himself. After a period of negotiation, defendant was persuaded to drop the weapon. The officers seized the gun and placed defendant under arrest. On appeal, the Court held that the gun was admissible, even though the initial detention was not justified. Defendant committed a new crime when he fired the gun at the officers. "At this point officer had probable cause to arrest defendant because the new crime purged the taint of the prior illegal stop. And the gun, which was in plain view at the scene of the new crime, could be legitimately seized."

The exclusionary rule is not mandated by the language of the Constitution. It is, rather, a judicially created remedy. Exclusion is appropriate where the underlying purposes of the Bill of Rights (*i.e.*, freedom from unbridled government intrusion) are best served. The rule prohibiting the use of illegally obtained evidence has its roots in the notion that we live in a society governed by the rule of law, not rule by law. If a government is not held to the standards found in the document that created it, then how can a government expect citizens to respect and abide by its pronouncements? Moreover, the rule is not designed to penalize officers for their mistakes or oversights, or to hamper their legitimate efforts. "The criminal does not go free because the constable blundered, but because the Constitution prohibits securing the evidence against" the defendant. *People v. Cahan*, 282 P.2d 905 (Cal. 1955). However, the rule does serve as a deterrent, in that it discourages officers from obtaining evidence in an illegal manner. If the evidence cannot be used to obtain a conviction, then the incentive to obtain it disappears. Put another way, law-enforcement is encouraged to respect constitutional guarantees in evidence gathering, for only evidence taken in accordance with those principles will be of any use.

The exclusionary rule is not applicable in a probation revocation proceeding absent a showing of bad faith on the part of the police. *Logan v. Commonwealth*, 276 Va. 533, 666 S.E.2d 346 (2008).

There are three well-recognized exceptions to the above rule: (i) the "independent source" and (ii) "inevitable discovery" doctrines, and (iii) the "good faith" exception. The first two are analogous to the attenuation concept, discussed above, where the connection between police misconduct and evidence of crime may be sufficiently protracted to permit the use of that evidence at trial. If an event or act is interposed between the initial illegality and the discovery of the evidence offered, then it may be argued that the evidence is not a byproduct or direct result of action tainted by illegal conduct. An attenuation argument may lead to the admission of evidence seized as a result of an illegal arrest or search in certain circumstances. For example, if a suspect's response to illegal police actions is itself a distinct and separate crime, then the suspect may be arrested or searched on the basis of that crime, even if the initial police conduct was illegal. The independent, intervening illegal act may be said to purge the seized evidence of the taint of the initial illegality. The relationship between any illegal conduct and the seizure is adequately attenuated, so that the effect is not the result of an illegality, and the admission of the seized item does not offend constitutional guarantees.

With respect to the independent source and inevitable discovery exceptions, the prosecution is, in effect, arguing that there is no nexus between the illegal conduct and the evidence, but rather the evidence was derived from other, constitutionally permissible sources. Attenuation analysis focuses on whether the proffered evidence has come to the attention of officers by an exploitation of illegal action or instead by means sufficiently distinguishable to be purged of the primary taint.

A. Independent Source

"The Fourth Amendment does not require the suppression of evidence initially discovered during police officer's illegal entry of private premises, if that evidence is also discovered during a later search pursuant to a valid warrant that is wholly independent of the initial illegal entry. The independent source doctrine permits the introduction of evidence initially discovered during, or as a consequence of, an unlawful search, but later obtained independently from lawful activities untainted by the initial illegality." *Murray v. U.S.*, 487 U.S. 533 (1988). The circumstances that justify the second lawful search must have no connection to the initial, unlawful conduct. The facts supporting the second search must arise wholly apart from those that purportedly justified the initial search (*e.g.*, a judicial finding of probable cause, and a warrant issued based on that finding, where the facts in the supporting affidavit derive completely from a source independent of facts garnered during an initial, illegal search).

In *Murray*, *supra*, officers conducting a narcotics investigation had probable cause to believe a large quantity of drugs was being stored in a warehouse. Before securing a warrant, they illegally entered the warehouse and confirmed their beliefs, finding several bales of marijuana. The officer subsequently applied for and obtained a search warrant, but made no mention of their entry to the issuing judge, basing their application only on facts they had accumulated prior to the unlawful entry. The Supreme Court held that if the earlier information in the affidavit in fact supported the probable cause determination, so that the later seizure of the marijuana was not a result of the illegal entry, but rather the result of a warrant executed pursuant to the independent probable cause finding, the evidence would not be suppressed.

B. Inevitable Discovery

"If the prosecution can establish by a preponderance of the evidence that the information ultimately or inevitably would have been discovered by lawful means then the deterrence rationale has so little basis that the evidence should be received." *Nix v. Williams*, 467 U.S. 431 (1984). Generally, courts will find evidence would have been inevitably discovered if the evidence would have been discovered, in the same condition, through an independent line of investigation, and where the independent investigation was already in progress at the time of the illegal search.

In *Nix*, *supra*, two officers illegally obtained from a suspect the location of the body of a child he had murdered. The defendant argued that testimony concerning the location and condition of the body should be suppressed as a result of this illegality. The Supreme Court disagreed, holding that if the prosecution could demonstrate that the child's body would have been discovered without the benefit of the defendant's statements, suppression was not appropriate. In this case, there was an extremely good chance that the state could demonstrate the body's location would have been inevitably discovered, as there was a 200-member search party combing the area, which in fact was scheduled to search the area where the body was found.

C. Good Faith Exception

This exception is a logical extension of the deterrent rationale behind the exclusionary rule. In effect, the exception represents a judicial recognition that an officer will not be encouraged to abide by constitutional rights, or discouraged from infringing upon them, where he or she objectively, reasonably and in good faith performs his or her duties, only to have a mistake, oversight or technical error by a third party hamper his or her efforts. Where an officer, operating in good faith, bases an arrest on a violation of a criminal statute or ordinance, and that statute is later deemed unconstitutional, retroactively rendering the arrest illegal, evidence discovered incident to that arrest will not be suppressed. *U.S. v. Leon*, 468 U.S. 897 (1984); *McCary v. Commonwealth*, 228 Va. 219, 321 S.E.2d 637 (1984). Similarly, suppression is inappropriate where an officer conducts a search or arrest in reasonable, good faith reliance on a warrant issued by a neutral and detached magistrate, and that warrant is later found defective or technically deficient. *Adams v. Commonwealth*, 275 Va. 260, 657 S.E.2d 87 (2008); *Colaw v. Commonwealth*, 32 Va.App. 806, 531 S.E.2d 31 (2000).

The U.S. Supreme Court has held that the exclusionary rule will not apply to evidence seized pursuant to a warrant executed in good faith, where the warrant is subsequently deemed defective because of clerical errors. *Arizona v. Evans*, 514 U.S. 1 (1995). In *Evans*, a motorist was pulled over for a routine traffic stop. The officer's in-dash computer indicated the motorist had an outstanding warrant for his arrest. He was placed under arrest, and a search of his car revealed a bag of marijuana. The officer did not know that the warrant under which he arrested the motorist had been quashed, and a clerk forgot to make the appropriate entry. The motorist sought to have the evidence suppressed as the fruit of an unlawful arrest. The Supreme Court denied suppression and held that "the exclusionary rule does not require suppression of evidence seized in violation of the Fourth Amendment where the erroneous information resulted from clerical errors of court employees."

The prosecution is not entitled to the benefit of the good faith exception in four circumstances: (i) when the warrant is based on an affidavit containing knowing or reckless falsity; (ii) when the magistrate simply acted as a rubber stamp for the police; (iii) when the supporting affidavit does not provide the magistrate with a substantial basis for determining the existence of probable cause; or (iv) when the warrant is so facially deficient that the officer could not reasonably rely on it. *Midkiff v. Commonwealth*, 54 Va.App. 323, 678 S.E.2d 287 (2009); *Commonwealth v. Vaughan*, 88 Va. Cir. 300 (2014).

VII. LIABILITY

A. Criminal Liability

Law-enforcement officers may be held criminally liable under both 18 U.S.C. §241 and 18 U.S.C. §242. However, neither section provides individual relief for the party whose rights were violated.

Under 18 U.S.C. §241, a law-enforcement officer is liable if he or she enters into a conspiracy to deprive any citizen of any right or privilege guaranteed by the Constitution. For this section, the only act that is necessary for a violation is an act in furtherance of the conspiracy. The penalty under this section is up to 10 years in prison and/or up to a $10,000 fine. If death results then the prison term may be for life.

18 U.S.C. §242 makes it an offense for a law-enforcement officer to act under color of law to willfully deprive any inhabitant of the United States of rights guaranteed by the Constitution or laws of the United States. Under color of law means under the pretense of law. The penalty under this section is up to 1 year in jail and/or up to a $1,000 fine.

B. Civil Liability

Under Title 42, Chapter 21, Subchapter 1, §1983 of the United States Code (commonly referred to as a "§1983" action), any person who, under pretense of law, deprives another of any constitutional right, "shall be liable to the party injured in an action at law, suit in equity, or other proper proceeding for redress."

Under this section the U.S. Supreme Court has held that an officer (and the department) may be sued for money damages by the victim of an unlawful arrest. *Malley v. Briggs*, 475 U.S. 335 (1986). Furthermore, the same civil liability for an objectively unreasonable arrest will apply to an objectively unreasonable search. *Anderson v. Creighton*, 483 U.S. 635 (1987).

It is important to note that a police officer's intent in making a false arrest is not material to an action for deprivation of civil rights brought under this statute. *Caballero v. City of Concord*, 956 F.2d 204 (9th Cir. 1992).

Once probable cause to arrest is established, a law-enforcement officer cannot be held liable for false arrest under state laws or for deprivation of civil rights under this statute. *Hunter v. Clardy*, 558 F.2d 290 (5th Cir. 1977). Any collateral bad motive or intent on the part of the arresting officer is immaterial.

Qualified immunity is an affirmative defense against §1983 claims. Its purpose is to shield public officials from undue interference with their duties and from potentially disabling threats of liability where the official acts objectively and reasonably in the good faith performance of his or her duties. The defense provides immunity from suit, not merely liability. *Saucier v. Katz*, 533 U.S. 194 (2001).

Some examples of the types of cases which have been brought under this statute are: (i) failure to advise grounds for arrest and detention, *Tilson v. Forrest City Police Dep't*, 28 F.3d 802 (8th Cir. 1994), *cert. denied*, 514 U.S. 1004 (1995); (ii) detaining the person arrested for too long a period, *Tilson v. Forrest City Police Dep't*, *supra*; (iii) use of unreasonable or excessive force during arrest or detention, *Elliott v. Leavitt*, 99 F.3d 640 (4th Cir. 1996); (iv) unlawful search and seizure by police, *Brouhard v. Lee*, 125 F.3d 656 (8th Cir. 1997); (v) interrogation in violation of a suspect's right to remain silent, *Cooper v. Dupink*, 963 F.2d 1220 (9th Cir.), *cert. denied*, 506 U.S. 953 (1992). But see *Scott v. Harris*, 550 U.S. 372 (2007) (actions undertaken by police to terminate a dangerous high-speed car chase that threatens the lives of innocent by-standers—such as bumping the fleeing vehicle—do not create liability under §1983 even when such actions place the fleeing motorist at risk of death or serious bodily injury); *Town of Castle Rock v. Gonzales*, 545 U.S. 748 (2005) (no liability under §1983 when police failed to arrest the plaintiff's husband for violation of a temporary restraining order).

Title 42 U.S.C. §1985(3) is the conspiracy counterpart of §1983. This section makes any person, who conspires with another to deprive a third person of any constitutional right, liable to that third person for damages. The violated individual may sue one or all of the conspirators.

Title 42 U.S.C. §1983 provides that every person who, under color of law, deprives another of any rights, privileges and immunities secured by the Constitution shall be liable to the party injured. Actions by a suspect, an arrestee or defendant may be premised, for example, on a claim of an unlawful arrest, the use of excessive force, a coerced confession, or an illegal search. See *Quinones v. Szorc*, 771 F.2d 289 (7th Cir. 1985); *Munson v. Friske*, 754 F.2d 683 (7th Cir. 1985); *Mass v. McClenahan*, 893 F. Supp. 225 (S.D.N.Y. 1995).

Individual officers and the municipality, but not the state, in which they work may be rendered liable under this section. See, *e.g.*, *Bd. of County Comm'rs of Bryan Co., Okl. v. Brown*, 520 U.S. 397 (1997), where the plaintiff sought to sue the county for alleged excessive force used by a deputy. The plaintiff's theory of recovery was that the county, and its agent, in this case the sheriff who hired the deputy, were negligent in hiring the deputy. She maintained that a brief background check would have revealed that there was a strong likelihood, based on the deputy's past behavior, that he would routinely use excessive force. The Supreme Court disagreed, reasoning that a county or municipality cannot be liable under §1983 merely because they employ a tort feasor. The plaintiff must show that there was a policy or custom of employing tort feasors. Moreover, the plaintiff must demonstrate a causal link between the municipality's conduct and the alleged injury. Here, the plaintiff did not prove any culpability on the part of the municipality. The Commonwealth itself cannot be a defendant in a §1983 action. The Court has ruled that a state, unlike a municipality, a county, or an individual officer, is not a person within the meaning of the statute, and therefore not amenable to suit.

Courts will, and routinely do, provide immunity from liability under this section. Immunity from suit "is the rule, not the exception." The doctrine of qualified immunity protects law-enforcement officers to the extent that their discretionary actions do not clearly violate a suspect's federal statutory or constitutional rights. To raise a triable "§1983" claim, the plaintiff must initially demonstrate that the rights allegedly transgressed were clearly established at the time of the alleged violation. *Wilson v. Layne*, 526 U.S. 603 (1999); *Trulock v. Freeh*, 275 F.3d 391 (4th Cir. 2001). In other words, in order for conduct to fall outside the scope of the qualified immunity doctrine and render an officer or his or her employer liable, the plaintiff must demonstrate it would be clear to a reasonable officer in that position that his or her actions are offending a well-settled constitutional or statutory right. Conversely, if the officer objectively, reasonably, and in good faith performs his or her duties, he or she will be shielded from a damage claim. An officer is immune for harm resulting from his or her actions, for example, if a reasonable officer could have believed a search to be lawful in light of clearly established law and the information the searching officers possessed, or if a reasonable officer would have believed there was probable cause to arrest. See *Anderson v. Creighton*, *supra*; *Gould v. Davis*, 165 F.3d 265 (4th Cir. 1998).

In addition to suits under §1983, officers may be liable for damages resulting from their unlawful actions in suits based on state law tort principles. See, *e.g.*, *Va. Code* §19.2-59.

VIII. FIFTH AMENDMENT RIGHTS AND PRIVILEGES

The Fifth Amendment of the U.S. Constitution contains numerous rights and privileges. However, two of particular importance in the area of police procedure are the privilege against self-incrimination and the right to an attorney during any custodial police interrogation. The privilege against self-incrimination may also be called the right to remain silent. The remedy for police violation of these rights is exclusion of all evidence obtained as a result of the violation. Also, individual officers may be liable in a civil or criminal context, or both, if found in violation of these rights.

The Fifth Amendment's prohibition against compelled self-incrimination requires that any custodial interrogation be preceded by advice to the suspect that he or she has the right to remain silent and also the right to the presence of an attorney. The Fifth Amendment itself does not mandate that *Miranda* warnings be given. Instead, the warnings, and the suppression of statements given by a custodial suspect in the absence of the warnings, are enforcement mechanisms, employed by the courts to preserve the essence of the right guaranteed by the amendment. The result of the rule is that custodial suspect, not given these warnings prior to an interrogation, may not have any statements he or she may make during that interrogation, used against him or her in a subsequent prosecution.

Moreover, if the suspect indicates that he or she wishes to remain silent, the interrogation must cease immediately, although the questioning generally may be resumed later. If the suspect requests counsel, the interrogation must cease until an attorney is present. Furthermore, if a suspect indicates he or she wants to deal with the police only through counsel, officers may not resume questioning unless the suspect initiates the contact and indicates he or she wishes to proceed without the benefit of counsel. To this extent, police conduct is determined by which right the suspect invokes. If the suspect invokes the right to counsel, an attorney must be provided, and the police cannot initiate further communications with the suspect without counsel present, unless the suspect approaches the officers and personally reinitiates the interrogation. If however, the suspect invokes the right to remain silent, police may generally reinitiate questioning after a break and after fresh warnings are administered, if the request that questioning cease is initially honored. New warnings at the resumption of questioning may not always be required.

If the court finds that the initial warnings are not too remote, and still sufficiently fresh to apprise the suspect of his or her rights, subsequent warnings may not be necessary.

Apart from these court created rules, the Fifth Amendment, by its terms, prohibits the State from forcing a criminal defendant into self-incrimination. Notice that the statements or evidence that a suspect is compelled to give must be testimonial or communicative in nature to fall under the Fifth Amendment's protection. The Fifth Amendment prohibits the State from marshaling evidence against a defendant only by "the cruel expedient of compelling it from his [or her] own mouth." Coercing a suspect into confessing, taking a statement prior to reading a custodial suspect *Miranda* warnings, or failing to honor a request for counsel or to remain silent, are methods by which courts have determined law-enforcement may offend the guarantees of the Fifth Amendment. However, even if potentially incriminating, the following statements are not considered testimonial: statements used for voice exemplars; answers to general on-the-scene questions during routine investigatory stops; answers to routine booking questions prior to incarceration. Moreover, the privilege does not prohibit the State from compelling a suspect to provide what may ultimately be used as evidence against him or her in another fashion. Therefore, a suspect does not have a privilege against revealing the color of his or her eyes, skin, the way his or her face looks, or the way he or she is dressed, his or her fingerprints or measurements, assuming a particular posture or stance, or making a specific gesture. These displays, which certainly may point to the suspect's identity and guilt, and in that regard be incriminating, nonetheless are real or physical evidence as opposed to testimonial, and a suspect may be compelled to show these physical attributes.

A. Miranda Rights

Suspects must be informed of their Fifth Amendment rights once they are in custody. Any statement made by a suspect in custody before he or she is apprised of these rights will be inadmissible. Suspects must be informed of the following:

- o You have the right to remain silent.
- o Anything you say can and will be used against you in court.
- o You have the right to consult with an attorney and have an attorney present during questioning.
- o If you cannot afford an attorney, one can be provided to you before questioning at no cost.

These rights must be presented to the suspect due to the fact that the U.S. Supreme Court has held that being interrogated while in custody is an inherently coercive situation. *Miranda v. Arizona*, 384 U.S. 436 (1966).

A suspect is entitled to the *Miranda* rights regardless of the nature or severity of the offense. *Berkemer v. McCarty*, 468 U.S. 420 (1984).

There is no requirement that an officer use the precise language of the *Miranda* decision. A warning is sufficient as long as it reasonably conveys the above rights to the suspect, regardless of whether or not the officer quotes the *Miranda* decision verbatim. *Duckworth v. Eagan*, 492 U.S. 195 (1989); *Williams v. Commonwealth*, 53 Va.App. 50, 669 S.E.2d 354 (2008).

B. Custody and Interrogation

A suspect is only accorded the *Miranda* protections during a custodial interrogation. Both elements (*i.e.*, custody and interrogation) must be present before the requirement that the warnings be given arises. *Burket v. Commonwealth*, 248 Va. 596, 450 S.E.2d 124 (1994), *cert. denied*, 514 U.S. 1053 (1995); *Watts v. Commonwealth*, 38 Va.App. 206, 562 S.E.2d 699 (2002); *Smith v. Commonwealth*, 65 Va.App. 288, 777 S.E.2d 235 (2015).

1. **Interrogation.** Interrogation is defined as questioning initiated by law-enforcement officers—either direct questioning or its functional equivalent. The term interrogation refers not only to express questioning, but also to any words or actions on the part of the police (other than those normally attendant to arrest and custody, *e.g.*, "routine booking questions") that the police should reasonably expect to elicit an incriminating response. *Rhode Island v. Innis*, 446 U.S. 291 (1980); *Commonwealth v. Quarles*, 283 Va. 214, 720 S.E.2d 84 (2012).

In *Emerson v. Commonwealth*, 43 Va.App. 263, 597 S.E.2d 242 (2004), police served a search warrant for weapons and drugs at defendant's Norfolk apartment. They found defendant, the sole occupant, in bed wearing only his boxer shorts. He was ordered to wait outside on the front porch, still clad only in his undershorts. The officers knew defendant would be transported to headquarters if any contraband were found and also knew that it was department policy to "dress the subject" before transporting him. Therefore, one of the officers asked defendant what he wanted to wear. Defendant described a specific shirt, a specific pair of shoes, and a pair of jean shorts on the floor beside his bed. A detective inside the apartment found these clothes and searched them for weapons and drugs. In the shorts he found a Newport cigarette pack which contained marijuana and cocaine. The detective handed the clothing to the detaining officer, who had not seen the search and was unaware anything had been removed. The officer asked if these were the shorts defendant wanted; defendant said yes and put them on. Defendant argued at trial that the officer's question constituted an un*Mirandized* interrogation, as the officer was essentially asking if he owned illegal narcotics by asking about the shorts. The Court disagreed, finding no interrogation. The officer's only purpose was to get defendant dressed, not to elicit incriminating information, as evidenced by the fact that he did not even know contraband had been found in the clothing and made no attempt to gain any information about the clothing or its contents.

In *Gates v. Commonwealth*, 30 Va.App. 352, 516 S.E.2d 731 (1999), defendant, who was already in custody on unrelated charges, was brought to an interview room where officers served him with an arrest warrant, told him he was being charged with murder, and began to read the warrant to him. Defendant interrupted, saying "Look, if y'all want to know the truth, I am going to tell you the truth." He then admitted to having been at the murder scene. The reading of the warrant to defendant was a routine part of the booking process and should not have been expected to elicit an incriminating response. Therefore, there was no interrogation, and defendant's statement was admissible.

Compare with *Giles v. Commonwealth*, 28 Va.App. 527, 507 S.E.2d 102 (1998). Defendant invoked his right to counsel, so the questioning investigator left him alone. Later, another officer approached defendant, and asked, "Did you speak with the investigator?" This was not a coercive question intended to elicit an incriminating statement, but simply a routine communication between police and the accused. The officer merely was inquiring about the status of the investigation. Therefore, the question did not constitute interrogation.

Contrast with *Timbers v. Commonwealth*, 28 Va.App. 187, 503 S.E.2d 233 (1998). After her arrest, defendant had signed her fingerprint card and Central Criminal Records Exchange form "Gwendolyn Timbers." Later that evening, a woman came into the police station with an item of clothing she said was for "Kelly Timbers." His suspicions raised, the officer who spoke to the woman went to the holding cell and called out, "Kelly Timbers?" Defendant looked over at him. The officer then said that if defendant's name was really "Kelly" that "she needed to come forward with that information." Even though officer did not directly ask defendant if she lied about her name, his statement nevertheless constituted interrogation because a reasonable observer would find that it was designed to elicit an incriminating response.

Spontaneous, volunteered statements are not subject to the *Miranda* requirement. *Blain v. Commonwealth*, 7 Va.App. 10, 371 S.E.2d 838 (1988).

See, *e.g.*, *Jenkins v. Commonwealth*, 244 Va. 445, 423 S.E.2d 360 (1992), *cert. denied*, 507 U.S. 1036 (1993). Two Warren County investigators were driving defendant from Washington County, where he had been arrested, back to Warren County, where he had committed a double murder. They did not question defendant regarding the crimes during the 7-hour trip. Defendant, however, was very "talkative," asking questions such as, "Did you all charge me with capital or what?" and, "When did you find the bodies?" In doing so, he related a number of incriminating facts about the crime. The investigators did not encourage defendant in any way, and, in fact, tried to stop him from talking by saying he could relate all the facts once they reached Warren County. Because defendant was in no way interrogated, his spontaneous statements were voluntary and therefore admissible.

As mentioned above, "routine booking questions" do not constitute interrogation, and need not be preceded by *Miranda* warnings. See *Pennsylvania v. Muñiz*, 496 U.S. 582 (1990) (questions regarding a suspect's name, address, height, weight, eye color, date of birth and current age do not qualify as custodial interrogation). Similarly, an officer's explaining to a suspect why he was arrested is not "interrogation." *U.S. v. Blake*, 571 F.3d 311 (4th Cir. 2009), *cert. denied*, 175 L.Ed.2d 919 (2010).

A request by police for consent to search does not constitute interrogation. *U.S. v. Tyson*, 360 F. Supp.2d 798 (E.D.Va. 2005).

Questioning by private citizens not directed or controlled by a law-enforcement agency need not be preceded by the *Miranda* warnings, even though their efforts may aid law-enforcement. See *Commonwealth v. J.D.*, 42 Va.App. 329, 591 S.E.2d 721 (2004) (high school student's un*Mirandized* responses to an associate principal's questions regarding stolen school property were admissible); *Mier v. Commonwealth*, 12 Va.App. 827, 407 S.E.2d 342 (1991) (private security officer's failure to *Mirandize* a shoplifting suspect did not render the suspect's statements inadmissible). But see *Estelle v. Smith*, 451 U.S. 454 (1981) (to be admissible, a defendant's statements to a court-appointed psychiatrist must be preceded by the *Miranda* warnings).

2. **Custody.** The warnings need only be read to suspects in custody. If statements are made in a noncustodial setting, no warnings are required. Hence a defendant cannot later attempt to bar the use of his or her statements at trial on the ground that they were elicited without the benefit of the *Miranda* warnings. Custody is a legal status during which the suspect has been formally arrested or deprived of his or her freedom of action in any significant way, *i.e.* to a degree normally associated with formal arrest. *Stansbury v. California*, 511 U.S. 318 (1994); *Brooks v. Commonwealth*, 282 Va. 90, 712 S.E.2d 464 (2011). Whether or not a suspect is in custody for purposes of *Miranda* warnings is an objective determination, based on all of the components of the setting, and determined on the basis of how a reasonable person in the suspect's situation would understand the circumstances. *Bynum v. Commonwealth*, 28 Va.App. 451, 506 S.E.2d 30 (1998). A custodial setting is not determined with reference to a suspect's belief that he or she is in police custody, or by a subjective belief on the part of the interrogating officers that they have placed the suspect in custody, unless that fact has been communicated to the suspect. *Bynum, supra.*

Factors a court will weigh in deciding whether a suspect was in custody include: (i) the manner in which the suspect was summoned by police; (ii) whether the surroundings were familiar or neutral to the suspect; (iii) the number of officers present; (iv) the degree of physical restraint imposed on the suspect (*e.g.* handcuffs); (v) the duration and character of the interrogation; and (vi) the extent to which the officers' beliefs regarding the suspect's potential culpability were manifested to the suspect. *Aldridge v. Commonwealth*, 44 Va.App. 618, 606 S.E.2d 539 (2004); *Harris v. Commonwealth*, 27 Va.App. 554, 500 S.E.2d 257 (1998). Note that a suspect's previous experience with law-enforcement is not relevant to the *Miranda* custody analysis. *Yarborough v. Alvarado*, 541 U.S. 652 (2004).

See, *e.g.*, *Ford v. Commonwealth*, 28 Va.App. 249, 503 S.E.2d 803 (1998). A detective saw defendant stash a bag in the woods outside a mall. When the detective checked the bag, he learned it contained clothing with the store tags still attached but no receipt or sales slip. Later, when the defendant left the mall, officers detained him for questioning. Although four officers approached defendant, only one detective actually questioned him. Defendant, who had two other people with him, was at no point surrounded by officers. This encounter took place in a public place in the middle of the afternoon and lasted less than a minute. Defendant was not handcuffed, searched, nor told that he was suspected of grand larceny. The detective only asked for his identification and whether he had been in the store from which the abandoned merchandise had been taken. Defendant was not in custody, so *Miranda* warnings were not required.

In *Brooks v. Commonwealth*, *supra*, Petersburg officers responded to an anonymous report of shots fired in the same block as defendant's home. In a subsequent sweep, an officer found a casing on defendant's front stoop. The officer asked for permission to search the home, and defendant consented. After finding a bag of cocaine and cash in a bedroom, the officer returned to defendant and asked "was this his money and drugs." Defendant admitted it was, which led to his arrest. At most, there were two officers present in the residence. This "interrogation" consisted of a single question. Defendant was not told he had to remain present during the search. The Court concluded that defendant was not in custody, so his answer to the officer's un*Mirandized* question was admissible.

But see *U.S. v. Colonna*, 511 F.3d 431 (4th Cir. 2007). After the FBI traced online child porn videos to an IP address registered to defendant's Chesapeake home, a 23-agent task force served a search warrant on the residence. The agents arrived at 6:29 a.m.; after learning from defendant's parents that he was still asleep, agents kicked open his bedroom door, then ordered him to get dressed and come downstairs at gunpoint. During the search, defendant's parents and little sister were told where to sit, and were also informed that if they went outside to smoke, they would not be allowed back into the house. Once downstairs, an agent asked defendant to speak in an FBI vehicle parked outside. Defendant agreed. He was told at the start of the interview that he was not under arrest; two agents then preceded to question him for 3 hours. Although he was allowed cigarette breaks during the interview, he was constantly guarded during these breaks. Twice during questioning the agents informed him that lying to an officer is a federal offense. During this interview, defendant made incriminating statements, including taking total responsibility for all material found on his computer. However he was not formally arrested until a year and 10 months later. Nevertheless, the Court concluded that defendant was in custody for *Miranda* purposes during this interview. Although defendant was ostensibly told he was not under arrest, the agents did everything short of actually physically restraining him to make him believe he was not free to leave. After 23 agents entered his home, he was held at gunpoint and under constant guard; he did not initiate police questioning and was never told that he was free to leave or that he did not have to respond to questions. Despite the initial assurance that he was not under arrest, a reasonable person in defendant's position would not have felt free to decline to speak. Because he was not *Mirandized*, his statements were suppressed.

A suspect not under formal arrest may nonetheless be in custody for *Miranda* purposes.

Similar to an arrest situation, in determining whether an individual was in custody for *Miranda* purposes, courts will not try to determine the subjective intent of the officers involved. Whether a person is in custody for *Miranda* purposes depends on whether the person is physically denied his or her freedom of action in any significant way or is placed in a situation in which he or she reasonably believes that his or her freedom of action or movement is restricted. Thus, police need not give *Miranda* warnings to an individual who is not restrained in any way and freely accompanies them to the police station. *California v. Beheler*, 463 U.S. 1121 (1983).

See, *e.g.*, *Bottenfield v. Commonwealth*, 25 Va.App. 316, 487 S.E.2d 883 (1997). A sergeant with the Augusta County Sheriff's Department asked defendant to come down to the Department building to discuss allegations of sexual abuse which had been made against him. Defendant agreed and came in the next day for a 35-minute interview. Defendant drove himself to the Sheriff's Department in his own vehicle. Once there, he was never told that he was under arrest or that he was going to be charged. The door to the sergeant's office remained open throughout the interview. The Court concluded that defendant was not in custody; therefore, his un*Mirandized* statements were admissible.

Compare with *Bynum v. Commonwealth*, *supra*. Defendant shot his wife while she was sitting in his truck in the driveway of their Portsmouth home. The wound was non-fatal, and the victim left the scene (apparently, defendant did not even realize he had hit her). The next morning, police asked defendant to come to the station for questioning and he agreed. He was given the option of driving himself, but chose to receive a ride from one of the officers. At the station, defendant was continually reassured that he was not under arrest and was free to leave at any time. He was never handcuffed during the interview, and when it ended, he was given a ride home. Even though defendant was the only suspect police had, he was not in custody during this interview, so *Miranda* warnings were not required.

In *Bailey v. Commonwealth*, 259 Va. 723, 529 S.E.2d 570, *cert. denied*, 531 U.S. 995 (2000), defendant's wife and son were found murdered in their home. Although defendant had killed them himself, he concocted a story for police claiming that his wife had been the recent target of threatening phone calls and notes. After the bodies were discovered, defendant accompanied officers to the police station "in an effort to continue the ruse[.]" He rode to the station in the front seat of a police vehicle. Once there, police offered him food and drink and he was allowed to step outside to smoke. On more than one occasion he was told that he was free to leave if he so desired. This was not a custodial situation.

Merely informing an individual of his or her *Miranda* rights does not necessarily create an in-custody situation. *Barkley v. Commonwealth*, 39 Va.App. 682, 576 S.E.2d 234 (2003).

A motorist stopped for an ordinary traffic violation is not in custody for *Miranda* purposes. *Pennsylvania v. Bruder*, 488 U.S. 9 (1988). See, *e.g.*, *Ramos v. Commonwealth*, 30 Va.App. 365, 516 S.E.2d 737 (1999) (defendant was not in custody when, following a stop for speeding, the officer detained him for 21 minutes and administered field sobriety tests, so an un*Mirandized* statement he made during those tests—that he "knew he was under the influence"—was admissible).

However, a motorist who is subsequently arrested, or otherwise placed in custody, must be given *Miranda* warnings prior to any questioning. Otherwise, any statements by the defendant may be inadmissible. *Berkemer v. McCarty*, 468 U.S. 420 (1984).

See *Dixon v. Commonwealth*, 270 Va. 34, 613 S.E.2d 398 (2005). A state trooper arrived at the scene of an accident along Interstate Route 64 in Norfolk around 2:40 a.m. Norfolk officers had already handcuffed defendant (one of the drivers) because he was acting "unruly" toward them. Defendant had a strong odor of alcohol emanating from his person. After the Norfolk officers removed their handcuffs, the trooper put his own on defendant, and placed defendant in the front seat of his patrol car, then locked and shut the door. The trooper told defendant that he was not under arrest but "was being detained for investigative reasons [and] for [police] safety." After asking some basic identification questions, the trooper asked defendant if he had been operating a vehicle, and if he had anything to drink that evening. The Court found that, despite the trooper's claim that this was merely a detention, this encounter went beyond a mere traffic stop and became a custodial situation. The Court stated that a person who has his hands cuffed behind his back and is placed in a locked patrol car at 3:00 a.m. would understand that his freedom was being restricted to a degree associated with formal arrest. Because defendant was not read his Miranda rights, his responses to the trooper's questions were suppressed.

Compare with *Hasan v. Commonwealth*, 276 Va. 674, 667 S.E.2d 568 (2008), where Newport News police stopped defendant because his vehicle matched a "Be-on-the-Lookout" concerning an armed robbery. There were initially 3 to 4 officers on the scene when the stop was initiated, and 2 to 4 more arrived during the stop, as well as a K-9 unit. At least some of the officers had handguns and shotguns drawn. Defendant was told through a P.A. system to drop his keys then exit the vehicle. As soon as he complied, an officer frisked and handcuffed him, with at least 5 other officers standing around him in a "cone" formation. Police then asked if there were any weapons in the car, and defendant admitted there was a gun under the front seat. Although defendant was ultimately exonerated of the robbery, police recovered a gun which led to concealed weapon and possession of a firearm by a felon convictions. However, the Court found this was not a routine traffic stop. Under the totality of the circumstances, defendant was in custody, so that the officer's question should have been preceded by *Miranda* warnings.

Note: Prisoners. The *Miranda* case does not hold that the inherently compelling pressures of custodial interrogation are always present when a prisoner is taken aside and questioned about events outside the prison walls. When a prisoner is questioned, the determination of custody should focus on all of the features of the interrogation. These include the language that is used in summoning the prisoner to the interview and the manner in which the interrogation is conducted. There was no "custody" when a prisoner in a Michigan jail was told at the outset of the interrogation, and was reminded again thereafter, that he could leave and go back to his cell whenever he wanted, and when was not physically restrained or threatened and was interviewed in a well-lit, average-sized conference room, where he was "not uncomfortable." *Howes v. Fields*, 565 U.S. __ (2012).

C. Invocation of Rights

After a suspect has been informed of his or her rights, the police may wish to ask the suspect questions. It is at this point that suspects must invoke their right to remain silent and/or their right to have counsel present. A suspect that does not invoke either right will be subject to further questioning. Note that if the suspect gives a response to questioning that is ambiguous but may be construed as invoking the right to counsel, the officers conducting the questioning are not required to clarify the response, and may continue questioning. Officers must stop all questioning only if there is an unambiguous, unequivocal request for counsel. *Davis v. U.S.*, 512 U.S. 452 (1994) ("Maybe I should talk to a lawyer" was not an unequivocal request for counsel, so continued questioning by police was upheld).

Compare with *Midkiff v. Commonwealth*, 250 Va. 262, 462 S.E.2d 112 (1995) (defendant's statements, "I'm scared to say anything without talking to a lawyer" and "I don't got to answer that...you know," merely showed a reservation on his part about continuing with the interrogation and were not an invocation of his right to an attorney); *Mueller v. Commonwealth*,

244 Va. 386, 422 S.E.2d 380 (1992) ("Do you think I need an attorney here?" is too ambiguous a statement to invoke the right to counsel).

However, in *McDaniel v. Commonwealth*, 30 Va.App. 602, 518 S.E.2d 851 (1999), defendant's statement "I think I would rather have an attorney speak for me" was a clear, unambiguous invocation of the right to counsel, so that all police questioning should have ceased. See also *Commonwealth v. Hilliard*, 270 Va. 42, 613 S.E.2d 579 (2005), where defendant's question, "Can I get a lawyer in here?"--followed by, "I already have a lawyer"--constituted an unequivocal request to meet with his attorney. Similarly, "I'd really like to talk to a lawyer now because this—oh my God, oh, my Jesus why?" also was held to be an unambiguous request. *Zektaw v. Commonwealth*, 278 Va. 127, 677 S.E.2d 49 (2009).

Similarly, any invocation of the right to remain silent must also be clear and unequivocal. *Green v. Commonwealth*, 27 Va.App. 646, 500 S.E.2d 835 (1998) (when defendant stated that he "didn't have anything more to say" there was no invocation of the right to remain silent, so continued questioning by police was proper). Compare with *Mitchell v. Commonwealth*, 30 Va.App. 520, 518 S.E.2d 330 (1999) (when, after being *Mirandized*, defendant responded, "I ain't got shit to say to y'all," but then began talking about the crime anyway, his statement was too ambiguous to serve as an invocation, especially when he immediately began to talk anyway); *Commonwealth v. Turner*, 87 Va.Cir. 132 (2013) (both "Do I have to talk about it now?" and "I don't think I should say anything" too ambiguous to invoke right to remain silent). See also *Connecticut v. Barrett*, 479 U.S. 523 (1987) (continued questioning proper when defendant said he would not give a *written* statement regarding a sexual assault without his attorney present, but added he had "no problem" talking about the incident).

1. **Right to Remain Silent**. When a suspect informs the police that he or she wishes not to speak then the police must "scrupulously honor" the suspect's right to remain silent. At this point all questioning must cease and the police are not allowed to say or do anything that is intended to elicit a response from the suspect or that is likely to elicit a response from the suspect. *Commonwealth v. Turner*, 87 Va.Cir. 132 (2013). If they do elicit a response, then such response will be inadmissible.

The police may start questioning again at a later time, as long as the suspect's first invocation of the right to remain silent is "scrupulously honored." Factors a court will consider in making this determination include: (i) whether, before questioning initially began, the suspect was "carefully advised" of the right to remain silent; (ii) whether questioning ceased immediately upon the suspect's invocation of the right, and no attempt was made by police to persuade the suspect to reconsider; (iii) whether a "significant period of time" has passed; (iv) whether fresh *Miranda* warnings have been given; (v) whether the new questioning concerns a different subject matter. *Weeks v. Commonwealth*, 248 Va. 460, 450 S.E.2d 379 (1994), *cert. denied*, 516 U.S. 829 (1995). Of course, the suspect may once again refuse to speak.

In *Weeks, supra*, defendant was initially advised of his right to silence, and police immediately ceased questioning when he invoked this right. Ten hours later, officers re-approached defendant, and although they did not re-read him the *Miranda* rights, they asked if he remembered them from "earlier today" and he said that he did. Even though defendant was questioned regarding the same crime as before, the officers had uncovered new facts, so they were not repeating the same questions from earlier in the day. This time around, defendant answered the questions freely and without hesitation. The Court concluded that this re-initiation of questioning was proper, and therefore, defendant's statements were admissible.

2. **Right to Counsel**. When a suspect invokes his or her right to counsel all questioning must cease immediately, and police may not initiate any new questioning until the suspect meets with an attorney. *Minnick v. Mississippi*, 498 U.S. 146 (1990); *Commonwealth v. Quarles*, 283 Va. 214, 720 S.E.2d 84 (2012). This is true whether the questioning is for the original offense or a different offense. *Arizona v. Roberson*, 486 U.S. 675 (1988). This prohibition even applies if the questioning officer is unaware that the suspect has already invoked his or her rights. *Giles v. Commonwealth*, 28 Va.App. 527, 507 S.E.2d 102 (1998). The only way that the police may then speak to the suspect without an attorney is if the suspect initiates the conversation. *Commonwealth v. Quarles, supra. Overbey v. Commonwealth*, 65 Va.App. 636, 779 S.E.2d 849 (2015). However, for any statement to be admissible, the police will still have to show that the suspect waived his or her rights. *Arizona v. Edwards*, 451 U.S. 477 (1981); *Zektaw v. Commonwealth*, 278 Va. 127, 677 S.E.2d 49 (2009).

Be aware that "initiates the conversation" is a term of art and does not necessarily mean the first person who speaks. Routine inquiries by a suspect, such as asking for a drink of water or to use the telephone, will not constitute an initiation of conversation justifying continued questioning by police. Instead, the suspect must convey a desire "to open up a general discussion relating directly or indirectly to the criminal investigation." *Oregon v. Bradshaw*, 462 U.S. 1039 (1983). In *Bradshaw*, after defendant invoked his right to counsel, he asked, "well what's going to happen to me now?" This question evidenced a desire to open up a generalized discussion about the investigation, so police could question him and obtain a valid waiver of his rights.

Compare with *Correll v. Commonwealth*, 232 Va. 454, 352 S.E.2d 352 (1987), where defendant, who had previously invoked his right to counsel, evinced a willingness and desire for a generalized discussion of the investigation when he told an investigator he wanted "to explain some things about the polygraph test" he had taken.

Similarly, routine inquiries by police do not violate a suspect's right to counsel. See *Giles v.*

Commonwealth, *supra*, where defendant was asked by an officer if he had already spoken to an investigator. This was a routine question inherent in the custodial process, not a question regarding the underlying crime, and thus did not infringe on defendant's right to counsel.

As long as the Sixth Amendment right to counsel has not yet attached, the failure of police to inform a suspect who is in custody that a third party (such as a relative) has retained counsel for him or her, or even that an attorney has made efforts to contact him or her, will not vitiate a waiver of *Miranda* rights by the suspect, because "[e]vents occurring outside the presence of the suspect and entirely unknown to him surely can have no bearing on the capacity to comprehend and relinquish a constitutional right." *Moran v. Burbine*, 475 U.S. 412 (1986).

The U.S. Supreme Court has ruled that when a suspect who has requested an attorney is released from pretrial custody for 14 days or more, then the *Edwards* rule no longer applies. After a 14-day break in custody, police may attempt to once again initiate questioning even though the suspect is not accompanied by an attorney. *Maryland v. Shatzer*, 559 U.S. 98 (2010).

3. **Waiver**. Once a custodial suspect has been given the *Miranda* warnings, he or she can, of course, waive his or her right to be silent or to counsel and decide to talk to the police. If the suspect voluntarily waives these rights, police may continue to question until the suspect requests an attorney or effectively renounces his or her waiver and relates that he or she wishes to remain silent. In *North Carolina v. Butler*, 441 U.S. 369 (1979), the U.S. Supreme Court held that courts may find a valid waiver even if the defendant only implicitly waives his or her *Miranda* rights. See also *Jackson v. Commonwealth*, 266 Va. 423, 587 S.E.2d 532 (2003) (waiver of *Miranda* rights need not be in writing to be valid). A suspect who has received and understood the *Miranda* warnings, and has not invoked his *Miranda* rights, waives the right to remain silent by making an uncoerced statement to the police. *Berghuis v. Thompkins*, 560 U.S. 370 (2010).

A suspect may waive his or her Fifth Amendment rights at any time. However, the prosecution will be asked to show not only that any such waiver was knowing and voluntary, but that the suspect understood the right that he or she was waiving. *Robinson v. Commonwealth*, 63 Va.App. 302, 756 S.E.2d 924 (2014). The Commonwealth bears the burden of proving the voluntariness of a statement by a preponderance of the evidence. *Colorado v. Connelly*, 479 U.S. 157 (1986); *Rashad v. Commonwealth*, 50 Va.App. 528, 651 S.E.2d 407 (2007). In checking to see that a waiver was legally sufficient, the courts will look to both the suspect's background (*e.g.* age, intelligence, prior experience with the criminal justice system), as well as the circumstances surrounding the interview (*e.g.*, length of detention, repeated or prolonged nature of questioning). See *Sellers v. Commonwealth*, 41 Va.App. 268, 584 S.E.2d 452 (2003); *Gwaltney v. Commonwealth*, 19 Va.App. 468, 452 S.E.2d 687 (1995). In addition, a suspect's repeated exposure to *Miranda* warnings may weigh in favor of concluding that the suspect knowingly and intelligently waived those rights. *Rodriguez v. Commonwealth*, 40 Va.App. 144, 578 S.E.2d 78 (2003). Suspects who are in pain, intoxicated or on drugs may be more susceptible to police coercion and therefore less able to give a voluntary waiver. *Commonwealth v. Peterson*, 15 Va.App. 486, 424 S.E.2d 722 (1992). Waivers obtained by improper means, such as suggesting that the suspect may receive some specific benefit by talking, are invalid.

Note: **Juveniles**. A juvenile can waive his or her Fifth Amendment rights. *Cary v. Commonwealth*, 40 Va.App. 480, 579 S.E.2d 691 (2003). While it is desirable to have a parent or guardian present when a waiver is made by a juvenile, the absence of a parent will not automatically invalidate the waiver; however, such absence is another factor the court will weigh in determining the voluntariness of the waiver. *Robinson v. Commonwealth*, *supra*; *Rodriguez v. Commonwealth*, *supra*.

A suspect may invoke or re-invoke either the right to remain silent or the right to counsel at any time and police must act accordingly.

Voluntariness and coercion are different sides of the same coin. If a confession or statement has been coerced or taken from a custodial suspect in the absence of *Miranda* warnings, there was no waiver. The statement is involuntary and therefore not the product of a free relinquishment of a known right, and hence not allowed in evidence at a trial. Conversely, if a confession or statement is voluntary, the suspect has either impliedly or expressly waived his rights and the statement or confession has not been coerced; therefore, the statement, and any other incriminating evidence deriving from it, is admissible.

One way in which a defendant may attempt to show his or her statement was involuntary is to show that actual physical or psychological force was used to coerce the confession (*e.g.*, actual or threatened bodily harm, or threats of adverse consequences).

See, *e.g.*, *Arizona v. Fulmiante*, 499 U.S. 279 (1991) (a "credible threat of physical violence" will render a subsequent statement involuntary); *Lynumm v. Illinois*, 372 U.S. 528 (1963) (defendant's confession involuntary when police told her that her state financial aid would be cut off and her six children taken from her unless she "cooperated" with them).

But see *Rose v. Lee*, 252 F.3d 676 (4th Cir. 2001) (statement that "things would go easier" on suspect if he confessed was not "a credible threat of physical violence" nor an unconstitutional coercion); *U.S. v. Braxton*, 112 F.3d 777 (4th Cir.), *cert. denied*, 522 U.S. 874 (1997) (officer's statement, "You're not coming clean...you can do five years because you're not coming clean," did not render defendant's subsequent statement involuntary, because it was a truthful statement regarding the penalty for giving a false statement to law-enforcement); *Bailey v.*

Commonwealth, 259 Va. 723, 529 S.E.2d 570, *cert. denied*, 531 U.S. 995 (2000) (defendant's will was not overborne when a detective suggested that he needed to get his "heart right with the Lord and that his soul would not rest until he did.").

A defendant may also attempt to show that the atmosphere surrounding the interrogation was so inherently coercive that his or her will was overborne, and the statement or confession was given involuntarily (*e.g.*, suspect was denied sleep, food and drink, use of restroom facilities, handcuffed, or left alone for extended periods).

Another way a defendant may demonstrate involuntariness is to show that a promise of leniency was made, and in return for his or her cooperation, the defendant was told that his or her punishment would be less severe. To prevail, the defendant must show not just that such a promise was made, but that he or she relied on it to such an extent that his or her will was overborne and the subsequent statement was therefore involuntary. The promise must cause the statement. Mere exhortations to tell the truth or promises to tell the prosecution of any cooperation will not render a subsequent statement involuntary.

The use of a ruse or deliberate falsehood by police will not necessarily render a subsequent statement involuntary. *Arthur v. Commonwealth*, 24 Va.App. 102, 480 S.E.2d 749 (1997). In *Arthur*, police prepared a "dummy" report indicating that defendant's fingerprints had been found at a murder scene (even though no fingerprints had in fact been recovered) and then confronted defendant with it at an interview. The Court found that this false report was not enough to overcome defendant's will or critically impair his capacity for self-determination, and his subsequent confession was therefore held to be voluntary. Similarly, a waiver of Fifth Amendment rights is not invalid solely because police do not inform the suspect of the potential subjects that might be covered in the interrogation before questioning begins. *Colorado v. Spring*, 479 U.S. 564 (1987).

As long as a suspect's initial un*Mirandized* statements were voluntary, statements voluntarily made by the suspect after the *Miranda* rights are read are admissible (even though the earlier unwarned statements must be suppressed). *Oregon v. Elstad*, 470 U.S. 298 (1985); *Aldridge v. Commonwealth*, 44 Va.App. 618, 606 S.E.2d 539 (2004). However, police may not use a "two-step" interview technique where they deliberately interview a suspect without reading the *Miranda* warnings until a confession is obtained, then, although that statement is inadmissible at trial, use facts gleaned from it to direct questioning during a successive post-*Miranda* interview. *Missouri v. Seibert*, 542 U.S. 600 (2004); *Kuhne v. Commonwealth*, 61 Va.App. 79, 733 S.E.2d 667 (2012).

D. Actions Not Protected by the Fifth Amendment

The Fifth Amendment only provides protection for suspects from being forced to give testimony that is self-incriminating. Suspects may still be forced to provide evidence that is not testimonial in nature. Thus suspects may be forced to provide answers to booking questions, such as name, address, and telephone number. Suspects may also be forced to allow the taking of physical evidence such as voice exemplars, handwriting samples, blood samples, hair samples, or evidence of physical characteristics. *Schmerber v. California*, 384 U.S. 757 (1966). Courts have also allowed videotaped dexterity tests, as well as other conduct on videotape as long as it is not testimonial evidence.

Although the Fifth Amendment allows the taking of such evidence, remember that the Fourth Amendment and its protections (*i.e.* the warrant requirement) may still be implicated. See *Hassell v. City of Chesapeake*, 64 F. Supp.2d 573 (E.D.Va. 1999) (urinalysis and blood test are both "searches" within the meaning of the Fourth Amendment); *Tipton v. Commonwealth*, 18 Va.App. 370, 444 S.E.2d 1 (1994) (blood test constitutes a "search" under the Fourth Amendment).

In *U.S. v. Patane*, 542 U.S. 630 (2004), the U.S. Supreme Court held that when a suspect's un*Mirandized* statements lead police to physical evidence, that evidence is admissible even though the underlying statements themselves are not.

E. Public Safety Exception

In certain limited circumstances, suspects may be questioned without first being *Mirandized* pursuant to the "Public Safety Exception." This doctrine was first announced by the U.S. Supreme Court in *New York v. Quarles*, 467 U.S. 649 (1984). In that case, an officer entered a supermarket in pursuit of defendant following a report that defendant had raped a woman. Upon seeing the officer, defendant turned and ran to the rear of the store. The officer followed, and although he lost sight of defendant for several seconds, he found him again and apprehended him. The victim had alleged defendant was carrying a gun, and when the officer frisked him, he discovered that defendant was wearing an empty shoulder holster. After handcuffing defendant, the officer asked him where the gun was. Defendant nodded in the direction of some empty cartons and responded, "the gun is over there." As other officers arrived, the first officer retrieved a loaded .38-caliber revolver from one of the cartons, then formally placed defendant under arrest and read him his *Miranda* rights.

There is no question but that defendant was in custody—he was in handcuffs surrounded by four police officers. And asking where a gun just used in a crime is located will likely elicit an incriminating response. Nevertheless, the Court held that there is a "public safety" exception to the requirement that *Miranda* warnings be given before a suspect's answers may be admitted into evidence. The Court noted that police were confronted with the immediate necessity of ascertaining the whereabouts of a gun they had every reason to believe defendant had just removed from his empty holster and discarded somewhere in the store. "So long as the gun was concealed somewhere in the supermarket, with its actual whereabouts unknown, it obviously posed more than one danger to the public safety: an accomplice might make use of it, a customer or employee might later come upon it." In such situations, if police were required to recite the *Miranda* warning before questioning, suspects in defendant's' position might well be deterred from responding. The Court concluded that "the need for answers to questions in a situation posing a threat to the public safety outweighs the need for the prophylactic rule protecting the Fifth Amendment's privilege against self-incrimination." The Court reasoned that "police officers can and will distinguish almost instinctively between questions necessary to secure their own safety or the safety of the public and questions designed solely to elicit testimonial evidence from a suspect." If the question is motivated primarily out of concern for the officer's safety, or that of the public at large, rather than a deliberate attempt to obtain an incriminating statement, there is no reason to bar the statement's subsequent use against its maker. Thus, the gun in the *Quarles* case was not suppressed, even though it was recovered as a direct result of defendant's un*Mirandized* statement.

See also *Anderson v. Commonwealth*, 279 Va. 85, 688 S.E.2d 605 (2010). At around 4:00 p.m., an off-duty Richmond officer was patrolling a private apartment complex enforcing its no trespass policy. He saw defendant standing beside a vehicle, talking to a woman sitting inside the car—he recognized neither of them, so he approached them to investigate the possible trespass. Defendant began to walk away, so the officer called out, "[S]ir, I need to talk t you." Defendant looked back, then took off running. As the officer gave chase, he saw defendant reach into his left pocket then throw away a "silverish, grayish object." The officer quickly caught up to defendant, and looked over to see that the object was, in fact, a handgun. As he handcuffed defendant, he asked, "Is it loaded?" Defendant replied, "[Y]eah, there can be one in it." This statement was later used at trial as evidence of defendant's knowing possession of the firearm as a felon. The Court ruled that even though it was not preceded by *Miranda* warnings, it was nevertheless admissible under the Public Safety Exception. The gun was lying unattended in a public space in the middle of the afternoon, and the officer had no back-up nearby. A loaded firearm could prove dangerous if someone, such as a child, happened upon it. The officer was justified in asking if the gun was loaded in order to learn how quickly he needed to retrieve it and "neutralize the volatile situation confronting" him.

IX. SIXTH AMENDMENT RIGHT TO COUNSEL

The Sixth Amendment right to counsel differs from the Fifth Amendment right to counsel in three principal ways. First, the right attaches when the criminal justice process has reached a critical stage, at the initiation of the prosecution, rather than during a custodial interrogation. A prosecution is initiated, for example, when:

- formal charges are filed,
- a preliminary hearing is held,
- an indictment or information is filed, or
- an arraignment is held.

Brewer v. Williams, 430 U.S. 387 (1977). So, for example, there is a right to have counsel present during a post arraignment line-up. But, the stage of the proceeding and the nature of the confrontation must be "trial-like" for the right to be implicated (*e.g.*, there is no Sixth Amendment right to counsel when police bring in a witness to examine a photo spread, because the accused is not being confronted).

Secondly, the Sixth Amendment right to counsel is offense specific. Once the right has attached for a given charge, the suspect cannot be questioned about that charge without counsel present. The suspect can, however, be questioned regarding other offenses for which the Sixth Amendment right has not yet attached without violating that provision. *McNeil v. Wisconsin*, 501 U.S. 171 (1991); *Alston v. Commonwealth*, 264 Va. 433, 570 S.E.2d 801 (2002). Suspects can even be questioned regarding an offense which is "factually related" to the offense for which this right has been invoked, as long as the offenses are not the same for Double Jeopardy purposes. *Texas v. Cobb*, 532 U.S. 162 (2001). On the other hand, the *Miranda* Fifth Amendment right to counsel is not offense specific. If a suspect has invoked his or her Fifth Amendment right to have counsel present during a custodial interrogation, that suspect cannot be questioned regarding *any* offense without counsel present. *Commonwealth v. Gregory*, 263 Va. 134, 557 S.E.2d 715 (2002). Of course, the suspect may waive his or her Sixth Amendment right to counsel, provided the waiver is knowing, intelligent and voluntary. This right to counsel is safeguarded by the exclusionary rule as well. If a statement is obtained in violation of the Sixth Amendment, it, and any other evidence that may come to light as a result of the statement, will be suppressed.

Finally, unlike the Fifth Amendment right, a waiver of the Sixth Amendment right to counsel is not valid if police fail to inform the suspect that an attorney is trying to reach him or her. *Patterson v. Illinois*, 487 U.S. 285 (1988).

X. SUSPECT IDENTIFICATION

Frequently, the Commonwealth will attempt to elicit at trial identification testimony from a witness to a crime who has made an out-of-court identification of the defendant. Typically, the testimony culminates in the witness pointing to the defendant in court and identifying him or her as the perpetrator. The defendant may challenge the admission of this testimony, claiming that the in-court identification was in fact the result of a suggestive, prior out-of-court identification, orchestrated by law-enforcement. The Fourteenth Amendment provides that no person shall lose his or her life, liberty or property without due process of law. The "Due Process Clause" protects a suspect from police identification procedures that are so impermissibly suggestive as to create a very significant likelihood of irreparable misidentification. *Simmons v. U.S.*, 390 U.S. 377 (1968); *Hodges v. Commonwealth*, 45 Va.App. 735, 613 S.E.2d 834 (2005).

See, *e.g.*, *U.S. v. Saunders*, 501 F.3d 384 (4th Cir. 2007), *cert. denied*, 169 L. Ed. 2d 836 (2008), where a six-photo array shown to a liquor store clerk following a robbery was impermissibly suggestive. Defendant's photo was set against a dark background and was taken without overhead lighting; in contrast, the other five "filler" photos were taken against light backgrounds with overhead lighting. The end result was that defendant's face appeared "significantly darker than the faces of the decoy suspects," distinguishing him from the other men pictured and giving him "a menacing countenance that was lacking in the men in the other five photos." The differences also suggested that defendant's photo was taken at a different time and place than the other photos, further making defendant stand out as a suspect. See also *U.S. v. Johnson*, 114 F.3d 435 (4th Cir. 1997), where an identification procedure was unduly suggestive when the victim was shown a single photo of defendant.

A suspect can challenge an identification by raising the issue of impermissible suggestiveness. If the requisite showing is made, a hearing will be held, after which the judge will make a ruling regarding the admissibility of testimony concerning the identification. To determine which practices are so unfairly suggestive as to deprive a suspect of Due Process, a court looks to the totality of the circumstances surrounding the out-of-court identification.

Even if an identification procedure is found to be unnecessarily suggestive, the resulting identification may still be admissible, if the reliability of the witness who made it can be independently established. Factors a court will consider in determining reliability include:

- the opportunity of the witness to view the defendant during the crime;
- the level of attention the witness was paying to the defendant;
- the accuracy of descriptions of the defendant made by the witness prior to the suggestive procedure;
- the witness' level of certainty in his or her identification; and
- the time between the crime and confrontation.

Neil v. Biggers, 409 U.S. 188 (1972); *Cuffee v. Commonwealth*, 61 Va.App. 353, 735 S.E.2d 693 (2013).

See, *e.g.*, *Bryant v. Commonwealth*, 10 Va.App. 421, 393 S.E.2d 216 (1990). The 8-year-old victim fell asleep watching television and then awoke to find herself being carried off out of her apartment by defendant. Once outside the apartment building, she managed to escape and sought help. Later that night, after defendant was arrested, police showed the victim three photographs, all of which depicted defendant, and told her that the photos were of a man who had just been arrested while prowling around her building. The victim then identified defendant as her abductor. The Court found that this "array" was impermissibly suggestive. Nevertheless, the Court concluded that the victim's identification of defendant was still reliable. The lighting in the apartment was adequate to see defendant's face, and, obviously, her attention "was riveted...on the person who was carrying her in his arms." The victim drew a picture of her abductor, and her description was remarkably accurate; she described defendant's "smooth" brown hair, blue jacket, jeans, and mustache, and noted that he used to work at the Farm Fresh store across the street from her apartment building. In fact, this description was accurate enough that officers relied on it in arresting defendant. The victim immediately identified defendant's photo as both the man who kidnapped her and the man who used to work in the Farm Fresh store. The fact that she was already familiar with defendant before the crime added to the reliability of her identification. Finally, the victim made her identification just two hours after the crime, so the events were fresh in her memory.

Compare with *Blevins v. Commonwealth*, 40 Va.App. 412, 579 S.E.2d 658 (2003). The victim was the subject of an attempted kidnapping in a parking garage. Defendant was detained as a suspect less than an hour later in a nearby park. Soon after, the victim was shown a single photo of defendant, and she identified him as her assailant. Although this procedure was suggestive, the Court, relying on the *Biggers* factors, found that the victim's identification was still reliable. She had ample opportunity to view her would-be kidnapper during the 25-minute attack. When he first approached, his "face was touching [hers]" and they "met eye to eye" just before he forced his way into her car. Although there was an initial struggle when the assailant first entered the car, he calmed down when the victim acquiesced to his demands, giving her a better view of him. The victim was parked next to a light in the garage, and the car had a "T-top" which allowed light in. Before even seeing the photo, the victim accurately described defendant as a short man, with short, "peppered gray" hair. Although her initial description of his clothing was inaccurate, she testified that she based her identification on defendant's "very distinctive facial appearance," not what he wore in the photo. She made her identification only an hour or so after the crime. Finally, she stated that she had "[a]bsolutely no" doubt that defendant was her attacker, adding the photo "was all I needed to be shown." The reliability of the witness's identification was thus independently established.

Note that the same constitutional safeguards apply to voice line-ups as to visual ones. See, *e.g.*, *Dance v. Commonwealth*, 32 Va.App. 466, 528 S.E.2d 723 (2000). A person called the Dollar General Corporation warehouse, said that there was a bomb in the building, and then hung up. The employee who took the call (Leslie Lavell) contacted police, who used "*57" to learn the origin of the call. Officers then went to the residence where the call was placed and interviewed the three people they found there; this interview was recorded. This recording was then played back for Lavell, approximately 1½ hours after the bomb threat. Before playing the tape, an officer told Lavell how it had been made and that the threatening caller was "probably" on the tape. Once it was played, Lavell was able to discount two of the people immediately: one was a woman, and the other was a man with a speech impediment whom she knew personally. However, she identified the third person (defendant) as the caller. The Court found that this identification procedure was impermissibly suggestive. It was akin to a show-up, in that defendant's was the only voice on the tape not known to Lavell, and the officer prejudiced the procedure by saying that the caller was "probably" on tape. However, Lavell's identification of defendant was nevertheless reliable. She testified that she clearly heard the caller's voice and was able to recall his words in their entirety. Before hearing the recording, Lavell identified the caller as African-American, based on his accent (defendant was African-American). Lavell selected defendant's voice less than two hours after the bomb threat and identified defendant as the caller as soon as he raised his voice on the tape. Moreover, she reiterated at trial that she was "a hundred percent sure" that the caller's voice and defendant's were the same.

XI. FOREIGN NATIONALS

Pursuant to Article 36 of the Vienna Convention, when a foreign national (including an illegal alien or alien with a "green card") is arrested or detained, he or she must be informed without delay of the right to have the consular officials of his or her home country notified and the right to communicate with those consular officials. This notice should be given in addition to, not instead of, the *Miranda* warnings.

Brief, routine detentions, such as for a traffic violation or accident investigation, do not trigger this requirement. However, if the foreign national is required to accompany a law-enforcement officer to a place of detention or is detained for a number of hours or overnight, the consular notification requirement will apply.

In addition, when a foreign national from one of the following countries is arrested or detained, the nearest consular officials must be notified without delay, *regardless* of the person's wishes. These countries include the following:

Algeria
Anguilla
Antigua and Barbuda
Armenia
Azerbaijan
Bahamas
Barbados
Belarus
Belize
Bermuda
British Virgin Islands
Brunei
Bulgaria
China (but not "Republic of China," *i.e.* Taiwan)
Costa Rica
Cyprus
Czech Republic
Dominica
Fiji
Gambia
Georgia
Ghana
Grenada
Guyana
Hong Kong
Hungary
Jamaica
Kazakhstan
Kiribati
Kuwait
Kyrgyzstan
Malaysia
Malta
Mauritius
Moldova
Mongolia
Montserrat
Nigeria
Philippines
Poland (nonpermanent residents only)
Romania
Russia
St. Kitts and Nevis
St. Lucia
St. Vincent and Grenadines
Seychelles
Sierra Leone
Singapore
Slovakia
Tajikistan
Tanzania
Tonga
Trinidad and Tobago
Tunisia
Turkmenistan
Turks and Caicos Islands
Tuvalu
Ukraine
United Kingdom
USSR (passports may still be in use)
Uzbekistan
Zambia
Zimbabwe

Note: Under no circumstances should any information indicating that a foreign national may have applied for asylum in the United States or elsewhere be disclosed to that person's government.

The following statement is suggested by the U.S. Department of State when consular notification is at the foreign national's option:

> As a non-U.S. citizen who is being arrested or detained, you are entitled to have us notify your country's consular representatives here in the United States. A consul-

> ar official from your country may be able to help you obtain legal counsel and may contact your family and visit you in detention, among other things. If you want us to notify your country's consular officials, you can request this notification now or at any time in the future. After your consular officials are notified, they may call or visit you. Do you want us to notify your country's consular officials?

The following statement is suggested by the U.S. Department of State when consular notification is mandatory:

> Because of your nationality, we are required to notify your country's consular representatives here in the United States that you have been arrested or detained. After your consular officials are notified, they may call or visit you. You are not required to accept their assistance, but they may be able to help you obtain legal counsel and may contact your family and visit you in detention, among other things. We will be notifying your country's consular officials as soon as possible.

Telephone and fax numbers of the foreign embassies and consulates in the United States and translations of the above statements into selected languages are available at the U.S. Department of State website http://travel.state.gov.

Although law-enforcement officers should make every effort to comply with these procedures, failure to do so is not a constitutional violation. Therefore, suppression of evidence is not an available remedy. *Sanchez-Llamas v. Oregon*, 548 U.S. 331 (2006); *Bell v. Commonwealth*, 264 Va. 172, 563 S.E.2d 695 (2002), *cert. denied*, 537 U.S. 1123 (2003).

XII. DIPLOMATIC IMMUNITY

The following information is provided for the guidance of the law-enforcement officer. Failure of the authorities of the United States to fully respect the privileges of foreign diplomatic and consular personnel may complicate diplomatic relations between the United States and the other State concerned. It also may lead to harsher treatment of U.S. personnel abroad, since the principle of reciprocity is integral to diplomatic and consular relations.

Diplomatic immunity does not exempt diplomatic officers from the obligation of conforming with national and local laws and regulations. Diplomatic immunity is not intended to serve as a license for such persons to flout the law and purposely avoid liability for their actions. The purpose of these privileges and immunities is not to benefit individuals but to ensure the efficient and effective performance of their official missions. This is a crucial point for law-enforcement officers to understand in their dealings with foreign diplomatic and consular personnel. While police officers are obliged under international customary and treaty law to recognize the immunity of the envoy, they must not ignore or condone the commission of crimes. The proper performance of police procedures in such cases is often essential in order for the United States to formulate appropriate measures through diplomatic channels to deal with such offenders.

A. Categories of Persons Entitled to Privileges and Immunities

1. **Staffs of Diplomatic Missions**. The categories of diplomatic mission personnel are defined primarily with reference to the functions performed.

"Diplomatic agent" is the term assigned to ambassadors and other diplomatic officers who generally have the function of dealing directly with the host country officials. This category enjoys the highest degree of immunity.

The next category is the "members of the administrative and technical staff" of the mission, which includes those persons who perform sophisticated and often sensitive duties but serve primarily in support of the activities of diplomatic agents. This category includes secretaries, certain clerical personnel, office managers and certain professional security personnel. Members of the administrative and technical staff also enjoy privileges and immunities, but ones that are in some respects less than those of diplomatic agents.

The last category is "members of the service staff" of the diplomatic mission who perform more menial tasks such as driving, cleaning, and building and grounds maintenance. These persons are afforded significantly less in the way of privileges and immunities.

It should be noted that the private servants of diplomatic personnel enjoy no jurisdictional immunity or inviolability in the United States.

Police officers usually do not have to deal with the distinctions given below. The U.S. Department of State will normally have issued identity documents. If no identity documents are available, telephone identification can be made as explained below.

a. **Diplomatic Agents**. Diplomatic agents enjoy the highest degree of privileges and immunities. They enjoy complete personal inviolability, which means that they may not be arrested or detained; they are owed a special measure of respect and protection; and neither their property nor residences may be entered or searched. Diplomatic agents also enjoy complete immunity from the criminal jurisdiction of the host State and thus cannot be prosecuted no matter how serious the offense. (Although it is not ordinarily of concern to police authorities, they also have immunity from civil suit except (i) in connection with real property transactions not conducted on behalf of the mission; (ii) in connection with any role they may play as executor for or as an heir to an estate being distributed in the host country; (iii) in connection with the performance of professional or commercial activities outside the scope of their official duties; or (iv) in respect of counter-claims in connection with activities outside the scope of their official duties when they have been the initiating party in a law suit.)

Diplomatic agents enjoy complete immunity from the obligation to provide evidence as witnesses and cannot be required to testify. This immunity is absolute and even extends to cases when they themselves have been the victim of a crime.

Family members forming part of the household of diplomatic agents enjoy precisely the same privileges and immunities as do the sponsoring diplomatic agents. The U.S. Department of State has held that family members enjoying this absolute immunity consist of the spouse, children under the age of 21, and children under the age of 23 who are full-time students at an institution of higher learning. Other persons than the above may be considered family members for the purpose of obtaining this absolute immunity if agreed to by the U.S. Department of State in extraordinary circumstances.

b. **Members of Administrative and Technical Staff**. Members of the administrative and technical staff of a diplomatic mission perform tasks critical to the inner workings of the embassy. Accordingly, they enjoy privileges and immunities identical to those of diplomatic agents regarding personal inviolability, immunity from criminal (and sometimes civil) jurisdiction, and immunity from the obligation to provide evidence as witnesses. Immunity from civil jurisdiction for members of the administrative and technical staff exists only for acts performed in connection with the performance of their official duties. This type of immunity is known as "official acts" or "functional" immunity. Like the family members of diplomatic agents, the recognized family members of administrative and technical staff enjoy the same privileges and immunities from the host country's criminal jurisdiction as their sponsors. Because these family members have no official duties to perform, they enjoy no immunity from civil jurisdiction.

c. **Members of Service Staff**. Members of the service staff of diplomatic missions perform more menial support tasks for the missions and are therefore accorded much less in the way of privileges and immunities than are those in the other categories. Service staff members have only official acts immunity in connection with all aspects of the host State jurisdiction, and they enjoy no personal inviolability or immunity from the obligation to provide evidence as witnesses. The families of service staff members enjoy no privileges or immunities.

d. **Nationals or Permanent Residents of the United States**. The general rules regarding immunity, as set forth above, assume that the staff members of a diplomatic mission are nationals of the sending country or some third country. Traditionally, countries are unwilling to surrender any jurisdiction over their own nationals. The United States, as a matter of policy, does not normally accept the accreditation of its own nationals or permanent residents as diplomatic agents. If it did so, such diplomatic agents would enjoy inviolability and jurisdictional immunity only in connection with the performance of official acts. The family members of diplomatic agents enjoy no privileges or immunities if they are "nationals" of the United States. If members of the administrative and technical staff (including their families) and members of the service staff are U.S. nationals or "permanent residents" of the United States, they enjoy no privileges or immunities.

e. **Special Bilateral Agreements**. There are some foreign countries in respect of which the categories set forth above are not applicable. These are countries with which the United States has concluded bilateral agreements that grant to all members of the staff of their respective embassies (provided that they are nationals of the sending country) the privileges and immunities to which only diplomatic agents are normally entitled. Although identity documents will normally clarify this situation, police officers should be aware of this distinction because they may have to confront situations where a chauffeur or mechanic from the embassy of one of these countries asserts a right to full diplomatic privileges and immunities.

f. **Waiver**. The privileges and immunities held by staffs of diplomatic missions are extended from one country to another in order to permit their respective representatives to effectively perform their duties. It may be said that the sending countries "own" these privileges and immunities. Although the individual enjoying such immunities may not effectively waive them, the sending State can, and occasionally does so. Police authorities should never address the commission of a serious crime by a person enjoying full criminal immunity with the belief that there is no possibility that a prosecution could result. The seeking of waiver of immunity is handled entirely via diplomatic channels. Effective and informed police work remains the foundation of a successful prosecution should the Department of State succeed in obtaining a waiver of immunity in a particular case.

2. **Members of Consular Posts (Normal and Special Bilateral)**. Consulates and their foreign personnel are often erroneously considered to be identical to foreign embassies and their staffs in the popular view of privileges and immunities. Traditionally, however, the function of consular posts is fundamentally different from that of the diplomatic missions. Consulates do not have the principal role of providing communication between the two countries but rather perform a variety of functions of principal interest to their respective sending countries (*e.g.*, issuance of travel documents, attending to the difficulties of their own countrymen who are present in the host country, and generally promoting the commerce of the sending country). Countries have long recognized the importance of consular functions to their overall relations but have been willing to grant only a significantly lower measure of privileges and immunities to the persons assigned to their countries at consular posts.

a. **Consular Officers**. Consular officers, generally speaking, are those members of consular posts who are recognized by both the sending and the host country as fully authorized to perform the broad array of formal consular functions. They have only official acts or functional immunity in respect of both criminal and civil matters (no civil immunity under any circumstances for actions arising from personal contracts or accidents caused by vehicles, vessels or aircraft which they are operating), and their personal inviolability is quite limited. Consular officers may be arrested pending trial provided that the underlying offense is a felony and that the arrest is made pursuant to a decision by a competent judicial authority (*e.g.*, a warrant issued by an appropriate court). Consular officers enjoy complete immunity from the obligation to provide evidence as witnesses in connection with matters involving their official duties, to produce official documents or to provide expert witness testimony on the laws of the sending country. Without a special bilateral agreement to the contrary, the family members of consular officers enjoy no personal inviolability and no jurisdictional immunity of any kind.

The concept of "official acts" immunity pertains in numerous different circumstances. It is very important that law-enforcement officers understand the nature of this protection. No law-enforcement (or State Department) officer is expected or authorized to determine whether a given set of circumstances constitutes an "official act." This is an issue which may only be resolved, as a matter of law, by the host country court with subject matter jurisdiction over the alleged crime. Thus a person enjoying official acts immunity from criminal jurisdiction may always be prosecuted if the responsible host government authorities believe that the criminal act is outside the scope of the individual's official duties, and may in this connection always be required to appear in court (in person or through counsel). At this point, however, such person may assert as an affirmative defense that the actions complained of arose in connection with the performance of official acts. If, upon examination of the circumstances complained of, the court agrees, then the court is without jurisdiction to proceed and the case must be dismissed. Although only a court may finally rule in such cases, it is reasonable for law-enforcement authorities to make decisions on whether or not to proceed with a case based on their own assessment of the court's likely decision on a particular fact situation.

b. **Consular Employees**. Consular employees perform the administrative and technical services for the consular post. They have no personal immunity, only official acts immunity. They enjoy immunity from the obligation to provide evidence as witnesses only in respect of official acts. Their family members enjoy no personal inviolability or jurisdictional immunities of any kind.

c. **Consular Service Staff**. Consular service staff do not enjoy personal inviolability or jurisdictional immunity of any kind. They do have immunity from the obligation to provide evidence as witnesses in respect of official acts. Their family members enjoy no personal immunity or jurisdictional immunity of any kind.

d. **Nationals or Permanent Residents of the United States**. As is the case with staff of diplomatic missions, members of consular posts have reduced privileges and immunities if they are U.S. nationals or permanent residents. In particular, consular officers who are U.S. nationals or permanent residents have personal inviolability only in respect of the performance of official acts; jurisdictional immunity only in connection with official acts; and immunity from the obligation to provide evidence as witnesses only in respect of official acts. Consular employees and consular service staff who are U.S. nationals or permanent residents enjoy no personal inviolability or jurisdictional immunity in the United States.

e. **Honorary Consuls**. Consular officers who are accredited as full-time practitioners of consular functions are referred to as "career" consular officers. These officers are normally nationals of the sending country who are sent to the United States to perform these functions for a specific period and then are transferred to a further assignment. Career consular officers are in fact prohibited by international law from engaging in professional or commercial activities outside the scope of their official consular functions.

Another category is that of "honorary" consular officers. These are generally part-time employees of the sending country who provide a degree of consular representation in places not covered by career consular officers. The privileges and immunities of honorary consular officers approximate those of career consular officers with limitations in certain respects. It is U.S. policy to recognize as honorary consular officers only those who are U.S. nationals or permanent residents. Accordingly, honorary consular officers in the United States have personal inviolability only in connection with official acts (arrest of honorary consuls is not limited only to felonies and does not require a warrant, as is the case with career consular officers), and enjoy only the more restricted form of official acts immunity accorded U.S. nationals or permanent residents, and immunity from the obligation to provide evidence as witnesses only in respect of official acts. Their family members enjoy no personal inviolability and no jurisdictional immunity of any kind.

3. **International Organization Personnel and National Missions to Such Organizations**. International organizations, such as the United Nations, are a relatively modern development. The privileges and immunities of the personnel of such organizations and the personnel of national missions to such organizations have a different basis than that of diplomatic and consular representatives. In the case of international organizations, the nations concerned have agreed that the important purposes of such organizations may only be accomplished if a certain measure of privileges and immunities are afforded to their participants. The nations concerned have concluded treaties embodying such grants of privileges and immunities and have also (*e.g.*, in the case of the United States) enacted domestic legislation granting certain minimal privileges and immunities to certain categories of persons not covered by the treaties. In determining the degree of inviolability or immunity, law-enforcement officers will be governed primarily

by the identity documents that have been issued to such persons.

a. **Personnel of International Organizations**. International organizations that have headquarters or other offices in the United States are staffed with the number of administrative and executive employees necessary to carry out their functions.

The vast majority of these employees enjoy only official acts immunity as provided for by U.S. domestic legislation (the International Organizations Immunities Act, 22 U.S.C. 288) and no personal inviolability. In certain cases, however, the most senior executives of such organizations have been accorded privileges and immunities equal to those afforded diplomatic agents. This is the case for the Secretary General and all assistant secretaries-general of the United Nations.

b. **Personnel of National Missions to International Organizations**. The United Nations and the Organization of American States are headquartered in the United States. Most of their member States maintain permanent missions in the United States. The persons staffing these missions are accredited to the international organization concerned (not to the United States). Their privileges and immunities are nonetheless often defined by reference to the status of diplomatic personnel who are accredited to the United States.

As is the case with diplomatic missions, the assignment of privileges and immunities is differentiated generally on the basis of the functions performed. Pursuant to international law, the most senior representatives in these missions to international organizations have privileges and immunities equivalent to those afforded diplomatic agents. The remainder of the staffs of these missions have only official acts immunity pursuant to the International Organizations Immunities Act and no personal inviolability.

Persons visiting in the United States on short-term official duty with diplomatic missions are ordinarily not recognized as enjoying any privileges and immunities (law-enforcement authorities should nonetheless always seek prompt verification from the Department of State in particular cases involving such individuals). In the case of the United Nations, however, a different legal situation exists. Short-term official visitors from other States to the United Nations or to international conferences convened by the United Nations may enjoy full diplomatic immunity equivalent to that afforded diplomatic agents. Owing to the temporary nature of their visit, such officials will normally not have the usual official identity documents recognizable in the United States. Law-enforcement officials should therefore be sensitive to the existence of this situation and always coordinate with the U.S. authorities indicated below if confronted with an apparent offender appearing to fall into this category.

B. Identification of Persons Entitled to Privileges and Immunities in the U.S.

1. **Foreign Diplomatic Passports and U.S. "Diplomatic" Visas: Not Conclusive**. Most foreigners in the United States who enjoy any degree of privileges and immunities possess a diplomatic passport issued by their country with a so-called "diplomatic" ("A" or "G") visa entered by U.S. authorities.* However, foreign diplomatic passports (even those which contain U.S. diplomatic visas) are not authoritative indications that their bearers enjoy any degree of privileges or immunities in the United States. This is the case because both foreign diplomatic passports and U.S. diplomatic-type visas are issued to a broad range of persons, including those who have no association with the categories of persons described and who therefore enjoy no privileges and immunities in the United States.

Law-enforcement officials should bear in mind, however, that the possession of these documents is an indication that the bearer might be entitled to privileges and immunities in the United States. For example, temporary duty visitors to the United Nations might have only such documents and might nonetheless be entitled to immunity in the United States. A similar situation could arise in connection with the foreign officer who has just joined a diplomatic mission or consular post and has not yet received the appropriate U.S. identity documents. In cases of doubt, police officers should always coordinate with U.S. authorities. (See **Telephonic Information/ Verification**, below.)

**All foreign personnel assigned to official duty at bilateral diplomatic or consular missions in the U.S. would have A-category visas. G-category visas are the equivalent, and are issued to foreigners assigned to duty at an international organization in the U.S. or at a foreign country's mission to such organization.*

2. **Tax Exemption Cards: Not Conclusive**. Under international law, most members of diplomatic missions and consular posts and certain people associated with international organizations would normally be entitled to exemption from sales taxation in the United States. However, significant numbers of these individuals do not enjoy this privilege owing to considerations based on reciprocity. The Department of State issues tax exemption cards to all those entitled to such exemptions, but this does not cover all persons in the United States who are entitled to privileges and immunities, nor do such tax cards give a definitive indication of the degree of immunity to which the bearer is entitled. Accordingly, tax exemption cards should not be relied upon for immunity purposes and should be considered only as an indication that the bearer may be entitled to some degree of immunity.

3. **Automobile Registration, License Plates, Drivers' Licenses: Not Conclusive**. The Department of State has recently taken over the registration of automobiles of persons entitled to privileges and immunities in the United States; the issuance of distinctive license plates for such vehicles; and the issuance of operator's permits for such persons to drive in the United States. As is the case with tax exemption cards, the purpose of these Federal registration documents and drivers' licenses is not

definitively to reflect the degree of privileges and immunities of the bearer. They should be relied upon only as an indication that the bearer is very likely entitled to at least some degree of immunity.

Vehicle license plates issued by the Department of State, in particular, must be properly understood by police authorities in order to avoid confusion. These plates are issued to persons entitled to privileges and immunities in the United States. The plates are coded to correspond generally with the degree of immunity to which the owner or principal operator is entitled (*e.g.*, the vehicle(s) of a diplomatic agent would have a "D" prefix; that of a member of the administrative and technical staff of a diplomatic mission would have an "S" prefix; and vehicles of consular personnel have a "C" prefix). These plates may be taken as a preliminary indication that the person operating the vehicle probably enjoys the degree of immunity indicated by the license code. It is ultimately only by determining the personal identity of the operator that his or her immunity may be established. Police officers should bear in mind that a car with "C" plates may in fact on occasion be operated by an ambassador (diplomatic agent) who is visiting a consulate. On the other hand, a diplomatic agent may not always be driving a vehicle with any kind of Federal plates; a rented or borrowed car may be in use at a particular time. The distinctive license plates are designed to provide helpful assistance in identifying vehicles that may be operated by persons enjoying diplomatic or consular immunity. However, they are not a definitive indication that such a person is operating the vehicle at any particular time.

Vehicle registration cards are issued by the Department of State to accompany diplomatic license plates. The card provides the vehicle description, name and address of the registered owner, and the license plate number assigned to the vehicle. Verification of the registered owner, vehicle or license plate can be made through standard access of "NLETS." Neither the registration cards nor the drivers licenses issued by the Department of State should be relied upon as conclusive indications of the status or immunity of the bearer.

4. **Formal Identity Documents Issued by the Department of State**. All of the forms of identity mentioned above provide an indication of possible immunity of a person possessing them. However, the only authoritative identity document is the identity card issued by the Department of State, Protocol Office.

There are three types of identification cards for diplomatic and consular personnel and to persons associated with international organizations who are entitled to privileges and immunities: "Diplomatic" (blue border for diplomats), "Official" (green border for employees), and "Consular" (red border for consular personnel). The cards are 3¾" x 2½" and contain a photograph of the bearer. The bearer's name, title, mission, city and state, date of birth, identification number, expiration date, and a U.S. Department of State seal appear on the front of the card. A brief statement of the bearer's immunity is printed on the reverse side. Space also is provided for the bearer's signature.

While this form of identification is generally to be relied upon, law-enforcement authorities are nonetheless urged immediately to seek verification as indicated below in connection with any serious incident or in any case where they have reason to doubt the validity of the card.

Police officers should be alert to the fact that newly arrived members of diplomatic and consular staffs may not yet have these official identity documents and should be prepared to contact the U.S. Department of State, Protocol Office, for verification if confronted with such situations.

5. **Telephonic Information/Verification**. Inquiry must be promptly made to the Department of State in any case where an individual claims immunity and cannot present satisfactory identification or in any case where the officer has reason to believe that invalid identification is being presented, or in any case where arrest or detention is made. The following telephone numbers are provided for use in this connection:

(202) 895-3521 during business hours; or

(866) 217-2089 after hours Diplomatic Security Command Center.

C. Incidents: Guidance for Police

1. **Generally**. The vast majority of the persons entitled to privileges and immunities in the United States are judicious in their actions and keenly aware of the significance attached to their actions as representatives of their sending country. On rare occasions, however, a member of this class or of his or her family may be involved in a criminal law violation. The more common violations involve traffic offenses such as illegal parking, speeding, and, less frequently, driving while intoxicated. Whatever the offense or circumstances of contact, police officers should keep in mind that such persons are official representatives of foreign governments who are to be accorded the maximum degree of respect possible under the circumstances. It is not an exaggeration to say that police handling incidents in this country may have a direct effect on the treatment of U.S. diplomatic or consular personnel abroad.

When, in the course of responding to or investigating an apparent violation of criminal law, a police officer is confronted with a person claiming immunity, official Department of State identification should immediately be requested in order to verify the person's status and immunity. Should the individual be unable to produce satisfactory identification, and the situation would normally warrant arrest or detention, the officer should inform the individual that he or she will be detained until proper identity can be confirmed. As described previously, this can be accomplished by contacting the appropriate Department of State office.

When proper identification is available, the individual's immunity should be fully respected to the degree to which the particular individual is entitled.

If it is established that the individual is entitled to the full inviolability and immunity of a diplomatic agent, he or she may not be arrested and should not, except in extraordinary circumstances (see **Personal Inviolability v. Public Safety**, below), be handcuffed or detained in any way. However, in an incident involving any person entitled to immunity, the officer should record all pertinent details from the identity card and fully record the details and circumstances of the incident in accordance with normal police procedures. Proper documentation of incidents is essential to permit the Department of State to take consequential steps, should they be considered appropriate.

2. **Personal Inviolability v. Public Safety**. Personal inviolability is enjoyed to some degree by a majority of foreign diplomatic or consular personnel. In its most extreme form, this inviolability precludes arrest or detention in any form and forbids U.S. authorities from intruding into their residences, automobiles, or other property. All such personal inviolability is, however, qualified by the understanding, well established in international law, that the host country does not give up its right to protect the safety and welfare of its populace and retains the right, in extraordinary circumstances, to prevent the commission of a crime. Thus, in circumstances where public safety is in imminent danger or it is apparent that a serious crime may otherwise be committed, police authorities may intervene to the extent necessary to halt such activity. This naturally includes the power of the police to defend themselves from personal harm.

3. **Traffic Enforcement**. Stopping a diplomatic or consular officer and issuing a traffic citation does not constitute arrest or detention and is permissible, although signature of the citation by such individual may not be required. Accordingly, a police officer should never hesitate to follow normal procedures to intervene in a traffic violation that he or she has observed—even if immunity ultimately bars any further action at the scene. The officer should always stop persons committing moving violations, issue a citation if appropriate, and report the incident in accordance with usual procedures. Sobriety tests may be offered in accordance with local procedures but may not be required or compelled. If the police officer judges the individual to be intoxicated, the officer should not (even in the case of diplomatic agents) permit the individual to continue to drive. The officer's primary concern in this connection should be the safety of the community and of the intoxicated individual. Depending on the circumstances, the following options are available: The officer may, with the individual's permission, take the individual to the police station or other location where he or she may recover sufficiently to drive; the officer may summon, or allow the individual to summon, a friend or relative to drive; or the police officer may call a taxi for the individual. If appropriate, the police may choose to provide the individual with transportation.

In any event, the police officer involved with the incident should fully document the facts of the incident and the identity of the individual, and a written report of the incident should be promptly forwarded to the Department of State. (In serious cases, report by telephone is also urged.) It is the Department of State's policy to suspend the operators license of foreign mission personnel not considered to be responsible drivers, and this policy may only be effectively enforced if all driving-related infractions (DUI, reckless driving, etc.) are fully reported to the Department of State.

The property of a person enjoying full immunity, including his or her vehicle, may not be searched or seized. Such vehicles may not be impounded or "booted" but may be towed the distance necessary to remove them from obstructing traffic or endangering public safety. If the vehicle is suspected of being stolen or used in the commission of a crime, occupants of the vehicle may be required to present vehicle documentation to permit police verification of the vehicle's status through standard access to "NLETS." Should the vehicle prove to have been stolen or to have been used by unauthorized persons in the commission of a crime, the inviolability to which the vehicle would normally be entitled must be considered temporarily suspended, and normal search of the vehicle and, if appropriate, its detention, are permissible.

4. **Correct Understanding of Immunity**. Frequently (and erroneously), immunity is understood to mean pardon, total exoneration or total release from the responsibility to comply with the law. In actuality, immunity is simply a legal barrier which precludes U.S. courts from exercising jurisdiction over cases against persons who enjoy it and in no way releases such persons from the duty, embodied in international law, to respect the laws and regulations of the United States. Even those who properly understand the concept of immunity sometimes believe that it is senseless to waste valuable police time in the investigation and paperwork essential to building a legal case, when there is no possibility that a conviction will result. This too is an incorrect perception. It can never be ascertained with certainty at the investigation stage that the person involved will continue to enjoy immunity when his or her government is confronted with the alleged criminal actions of such person and, in any event, there are diplomatic remedies available to deal with such persons even when immunity bars prosecution and conviction. As is explained in greater detail below, there are a number of important reasons for police authorities to give careful attention to the documentation of incidents involving persons enjoying privileges and immunities. Such incidents should always be promptly reported to the Department of State.

5. **Waiver of Immunity**. Even though individuals ultimately enjoy the protections afforded by diplomatic or consular privileges and immunities, it is for the benefit of the sending country that these protections are actually devised. This concept is well established in international law and explains the fact

that the individual concerned does not "own" the immunity. Such immunity may always be waived, in whole or in part, by the country that employs such person. While waiver of immunity in the face of criminal charges is not common, it is routinely sought and occasionally granted. The Department's ability to secure such waiver may depend to a large degree on the strength (and documentation) of the case at issue. Similarly, it is of little avail for the Department to secure waiver of immunity in a particular case, if the case has not been developed with sufficient care and completeness to permit a successful subsequent prosecution. Proper documentation and reporting by law-enforcement authorities plays a critical role in both of these respects.

6. **The *Persona Non Grata* (PNG) Procedure**. The criminal immunity which foreign diplomatic and consular personnel enjoy protects them, to the extent that it is not waived by their government, from the normal jurisdiction of the courts in respect of alleged criminal activity.

One of the oldest concepts of international diplomatic law, however, is that host countries may strip persons who become unacceptable to them of their privileges and immunities, allowing such persons only a reasonable time to remove themselves from the territory of the host country. This is known as the *persona non grata* (PNG) procedure. It may be employed by the host country at any time. There is no requirement, under international law, for such countries to justify their action.

For the United States, however, use of this procedure has inherent constraints. Even though their immunity may deprive such PNG persons of due process in the formal sense, it is felt that in most cases this remedy should be employed only when there is reasonable certainty that a criminal act has actually been committed. The United States' reputation for being a society governed by the rule of law is not served if it may be pointed to as having acted in an arbitrary, capricious or prejudiced manner in invoking the extreme diplomatic tool of declaring a foreign diplomat PNG. Similarly, any PNG action that the U.S. Government is not able to defend in appropriate detail may be understood by the other country involved as a political action and might thus result in the reciprocal PNG of an entirely innocent American diplomat abroad. A high standard of police investigation, records and reporting in diplomatic incident cases is therefore essential to permit the Department responsibly to exercise the diplomatic tools available to remove persons engaged in criminal activity from the United States.

7. **Official Acts Immunity**. Official acts immunity is not a prima facie bar to the exercise of jurisdiction by U.S. courts. Rather, it is an affirmative defense to be raised before the U.S. court with subject matter jurisdiction over the alleged crime. If such court, in the full light of all the relevant facts, determines that the action complained of was an official act, only at that point does international law preclude the further exercise of jurisdiction by the U.S. court. Because the judicial determination in a case of this type is very much dependent on the facts surrounding the incident, a full and complete police report may be critical in permitting the court to make a just decision.

8. **Termination of Immunity**. Criminal immunity, to the extent that it is enjoyed by a particular individual and to the extent that it is not waived by the sending State concerned, precludes the exercise by courts of the United States of jurisdiction over alleged criminal activity by such persons, whether such activity occurred during or prior to the period during which such person enjoys criminal immunity in the United States. This jurisdictional bar is, however, not a perpetual benefit for such person. With the exception of immunity for official acts (which subsists indefinitely), criminal immunity expires upon the termination of the diplomatic or consular tour of the individual enjoying such immunity, including a reasonable period of time for such person to depart the U.S. territory. Thereafter, if the law-enforcement authorities of the United States can obtain personal jurisdiction over a person alleged to have committed criminal acts in the United States, normal prosecution may go forward. This assumes, of course, that the case against such individual has been adequately developed at the time of the alleged action and that any applicable statute of limitations has not run. Obviously, careful and complete police work is required at the time of the alleged crime in order to lay the basis for such delayed prosecution, and it is important that the charges against such person be pushed as far as possible in the U.S. judicial system in order to lay the basis for such prosecution. Obtaining an indictment, information, or arrest warrant, even though they would be without immediate legal effect, would lay the basis for a prosecution at a later date.

The existence of an outstanding arrest warrant may be entered into the records of the U.S. immigration authorities and thus serve to bar the subsequent issuance of a U.S. visa permitting such person to enter the United States. It also should be kept in mind that persons who once resided in the United States in a status affording criminal immunity may later return for pleasure or otherwise under conditions affording them no criminal immunity. Additionally, in the case of serious crimes and with respect to foreign countries with which the United States enjoys an extradition relationship, it is not precluded under international law that international extradition may be effected.

D. Conclusion

It is important that the law-enforcement authorities of the United States always treat foreign diplomatic and consular personnel with respect and with due regard for the privileges and immunities to which they are entitled under international law. Any shortcomings have the potential of casting into doubt the commitment of the United States to carry out its international obligations or of negatively influencing larger foreign policy interests. Appropriate caution on the part of law-enforcement authorities should never escalate into a total "hands off" attitude in connection with criminal law-enforcement actions involving diplomats. Foreign diplomats who violate traffic laws should be cited. Allegations of serious crimes should be fully investigated, promptly reported to the Department of State, and procedurally developed to the maximum permissible extent. Local law-enforcement authorities should never be inhibited in their efforts to protect the public welfare in extreme situations. The U.S. Department of State should be advised promptly of any serious difficulties arising in connection with diplomatic or consular personnel. It has provided offices to assist police authorities in verifying individuals who may enjoy inviolability or immunity. Police departments should feel free to contact the Department of State for general advice in any matter bearing on diplomatic or consular personnel.

Appendix:
MISSING CHILDREN

When a child is abducted, a local law enforcement agency may request that the Virginia State Police issue an "Amber Alert," which provides notice of the abduction to the public via the media, including television and radio stations as well as wireless alerts to cell phones. For an Amber Alert to be activated:

- o the abducted child must be 17 or younger *or* currently enrolled in secondary school in the Commonwealth;
- o the law-enforcement agency must believe the abducted child is in imminent danger of serious bodily harm or death;
- o a law enforcement investigation must have verified the abduction or eliminated alternative explanations;
- o sufficient information must be available to disseminate to the public that could assist in locating the child, suspect and/or the suspect's vehicle; and
- o the child must be entered into the Virginia Criminal Information Network (VCIN) and the National Crime Information Center (NCIC) missing person files as soon as practical.

Amber Alerts may be local, regional or statewide; the initial decision to make a local or regional Amber Alert is at the discretion of the local or regional law-enforcement officials (after conferring with the State Police), while the initial decision to make a statewide Amber Alert is at the discretion of the State Police. Any local law-enforcement agency that locates a child who is the subject of an alert shall notify the Virginia State Police immediately that the child has been located. *Va. Code* §§52-34.1 – 52-34.3.

To activate an Amber Alert, contact:

Lt. William J. Reed, Jr.

P. O. Box 27472

Richmond, VA 23261-7472

804-674-6719

amber@vsp.virginia.gov

The following form should be completed when a missing child is reported:

SP-183 (Rev. 01-01-2006)

VIRGINIA MISSING CHILDREN INFORMATION CLEARINGHOUSE REPORT

INVESTIGATING OFFICER:

Date/Time Reported To Law Enforcement: ______

Date Entered VCIN/NCIC: ______

VIC No.: ______

PART 1

*Agency Submitting Report: | ORI No.:

*Last Name: | First Name: | Middle Name: | Suffix: | *Sex: | Race:

*Place of Birth: | *Date of Birth: * | Date of Emancipation if under 18 yoa**:

*Height: Ft. In. | *Weight Lbs. | *Eye Color: ☐ Maroon ☐ Gray ☐ Multicolor ☐ Black ☐ Green ☐ Hazel ☐ Pink ☐ Blue ☐ Brown ☐ Unknown | *Hair Color: ☐ Black ☐ Blond ☐ White ☐ Sandy ☐ Brown ☐ Gray ☐ Red ☐

Complexion: ☐ Fair/Light ☐ Albino ☐ Ruddy ☐ Lt. Brown ☐ Black ☐ Dark ☐ Sallow ☐ Med. Brown ☐ Medium ☐ Olive ☐ Yellow ☐ Dark Brown | Scars, Marks, Tattoos, Piercings and Other Characteristics:

Fingerprint Classification: | Social Security Number:

Operator's License Number: | O.L. State: | Date of Expiration: | DNA: ☐ Yes ☐ No Location of DNA:

*Date of Last Contact: | *Originating Agency Case Number:

*Fingerprints Available: ☐ Yes ☐ No Location of the Fingerprints: | *Photo Available: ☐ Yes ☐ No Photo Received: ☐ Yes ☐ No Photo sent to the State Police: ☐ Yes ☐ No | *Dental Records: ☐ Yes ☐ No Location of the Dental Records:

Blood Type: | Circumcision: ☐ C ☐ N ☐ U | Footprint Available: ☐ Yes ☐ No Location of the Footprints: | Body X-Rays Available: ☐ Full ☐ Partial ☐ No Location of the X-Rays:

*Medication Required: ☐ Yes ☐ No Medication Type: | *Name of School Last Attended: | *Code Number of School Last Attended: Code No.:

County/City Code of Birth: (Mandatory if POB is VA) | Mother's Maiden Name (if POB is VA): Last: First : Middle:

*Telephone # of investigating agency (accessible 24 hours) : Area Code (   ) - | *Authority for Release: ☐ Yes ☐ No (Part IV)

Last Seen in Company of: NAME(S):	Sex:	Race:
(1)		
(2)		

*Name of Child's Parents or Legal Guardian: Name:

Address/City/State/Zip: Phone:

MISCELLANEOUS DATA: (Information which may assist in identification: child's nickname, associates, direction of travel, hairstyle, clothing, etc.)

VEHICLE INFORMATION:

License Plate Number:	State:	Year of Exp. :	Lic. Type:	VIN:

Vehicle Year:	Make:	Model:	Style:	Color:

Corrective Vision Prescription:

Jewelry Type and Description:

*** MANDATORY DATA ELEMENTS**

****Date of Emancipation is individual's eighteenth birth date. NOT NEEDED FOR CHILD 18 OR OLDER**

CHECK APPLICABLE CONDITION:

1. ☐ DISABILITY:

   Child missing is under proven physical/mental disability thereby subjecting herself/himself or others to personal or immediate danger.

2. ☐ ENDANGERED:

   Child missing under circumstances indicating his/her physical safety is in danger.

3. ☐ INVOLUNTARY:

   Child missing under circumstances indicating the disappearance was not voluntary.

4. ☐ JUVENILE:

   Child under 18 years of age who is missing and does not meet entry criteria set forth in #1, 2, or 3. This category should not include children under the age of 12

5. ☐ MISSING CHILD:

   Child between the age of 18 and less than 21 years of age who is missing and does not meet the criteria set forth in #1, #2, or #3, Child entered as Missing Person Other (Message Key EMO)

PART III

I certify the person described in Part I is missing and that the information I have furnished is true and correct to the best of my knowledge and belief.

__________________	____________	______________
Signature	Date	Relationship

PART IV

I authorize any law-enforcement official to use photographs and/or any other identifying information I have provided in any manner they deem necessary in attempting to locate the person I am reporting missing.

I represent that I am the natural parent and/or legal guardian of the person named in this report, and have the legal right to sign this authorization and consent.

__________________	____________	______________
Signature	Date	Relationship

Virginia Missing Children Information Clearinghouse
Virginia State Police
Criminal Justice Information Services Division
P. O. Box 27472
Richmond, Virginia 23261-7472

Distribution:

	Mailed Original	Mailed "Located" copy
Virginia Missing Children Clearinghouse	Date __________	Date __________
Local School Division Superintendent – 1	Date __________	Date __________
Registrar of Vital Records – 1	Date __________	Date __________
P. O. Box 1000		
Richmond, Virginia 23208-1000	By __________	By __________

Cleared VCIN/NCIC Date __________

PLEASE ATTACH A CURRENT PHOTOGRAPH OF THE MISSING CHILD TO THIS FORM

Virginia Criminal and Traffic Law Manual

TITLE 2.1.
ADMINISTRATION OF THE GOVERNMENT GENERALLY.

[Repealed.]

TITLE 2.2.
ADMINISTRATION OF GOVERNMENT.

SUBTITLE I.
ORGANIZATION OF STATE GOVERNMENT.

CHAPTER 3.2.
OFFICE OF THE STATE INSPECTOR GENERAL.

Article 1.

General Provisions.

Article 2.

Behavioral Health and Developmental Services.

Article 3.

Corrections.

Article 4.

Juvenile Justice.

Article 5.

Transportation.

Article 6.

Tobacco Indemnification and Community Revitalization.

ARTICLE 1.
GENERAL PROVISIONS.

§ 2.2-307. Definitions.

As used in this chapter, unless the context requires a different meaning:

"Employee" means any person who is regularly employed full time on either a salaried or wage basis, whose tenure is not restricted as to temporary or provisional appointment, in the service of, and whose compensation is payable by, no more often than biweekly, in whole or in part, a state agency.

"Nonstate agency" means any public or private foundation, authority, institute, museum, corporation, or similar organization that is (i) not a unit of state government or a political subdivision of the Commonwealth as established by general law or special act and (ii) wholly or principally supported by state funds. "Nonstate agency" shall not include any such entity that receives state funds (a) as a subgrantee of a state agency, (b) through a state grant-in-aid program authorized by law, (c) as a result of an award of a competitive grant or a public contract for the procurement of goods, services, or construction, or (d) pursuant to a lease of real property as described in subdivision 5 of § 2.2-1149.

"Office" means the Office of the State Inspector General.

"Officer" means any person who is elected or appointed to a public office in a state agency.

"State agency" means any agency, institution, board, bureau, commission, council, or instrumentality of state government in the executive branch listed in the appropriation act.

History.
2011, cc. 798, 871.

§ 2.2-308. Office created; appointment of State Inspector General.

A. There is hereby created the Office of the State Inspector General, which shall be headed by a State Inspector General appointed by the Governor, subject to confirmation by the General Assembly. The

State Inspector General shall be appointed for a four-year term. The State Inspector General shall have at least five years of demonstrated experience or expertise in accounting, public administration, or audit investigations as a certified public accountant or a certified internal auditor. Vacancies shall be filled by appointment by the Governor for the unexpired term and shall be effective until 30 days after the next session of the ensuing General Assembly and, if confirmed, thereafter for the remainder of such term. The Governor may remove the State Inspector General from office for malfeasance, misfeasance, incompetence, misconduct, neglect of duty, absenteeism, conflict of interests, or failure to carry out the policies of the Commonwealth as established in the Constitution or by the General Assembly. The Governor shall set forth in a written public statement his reasons for removing the State Inspector General at the time the removal occurs.

B. The State Inspector General shall exercise the powers and perform the duties conferred or imposed upon him by law. The State Inspector General shall be responsible for the overall supervision of the Office.

C. Nothing in this chapter shall be construed to limit or prevent the General Assembly from reviewing the operations of any state agency or directing such review or audit by the Joint Legislative Audit and Review Commission or the Auditor of Public Accounts or to otherwise limit the statutory responsibilities of either the Joint Legislative Audit and Review Commission or the Auditor of Public Accounts.

History.
2011, cc. 798, 871.

§ 2.2-309. Powers and duties of State Inspector General.

A. The State Inspector General shall have power and duty to:

1. Operate and manage the Office and employ such personnel as may be required to carry out the provisions of this chapter;

2. Make and enter contracts and agreements as may be necessary and incidental to carry out the provisions of this chapter and apply for and accept grants from the United States government and agencies and instrumentalities thereof, and any other source, in furtherance of the provisions of this chapter;

3. Receive complaints from whatever source that allege fraud, waste, including task or program duplication, abuse, or corruption by a state agency or nonstate agency or by any officer or employee of the foregoing and determine whether the complaints give reasonable cause to investigate;

4. Receive complaints under § 2.2-2832 from persons alleging retaliation by an officer or employee of a state agency for providing testimony before a committee or subcommittee of the General Assembly and determine whether the complaints give reasonable cause to investigate;

5. Investigate the management and operations of state agencies, nonstate agencies, and independent contractors of state agencies to determine whether acts of fraud, waste, abuse, or corruption have been committed or are being committed by state officers or employees or independent contractors of a state agency or any officers or employees of a nonstate agency, including any allegations of criminal acts affecting the operations of state agencies or nonstate agencies. However, no investigation of an elected official of the Commonwealth to determine whether a criminal violation has occurred, is occurring, or is about to occur under the provisions of § 52-8.1 shall be initiated, undertaken, or continued except upon the request of the Governor, the Attorney General, or a grand jury;

6. Prepare a detailed report of each investigation stating whether fraud, waste, abuse, or corruption has been detected. If fraud, waste, abuse, or corruption is detected, the report shall (i) identify the person committing the wrongful act or omission, (ii) describe the wrongful act or omission, and (iii) describe any corrective measures taken by the state agency or nonstate agency in which the wrongful act or omission was committed to prevent recurrences of similar actions;

7. Provide timely notification to the appropriate attorney for the Commonwealth and law-enforcement agencies whenever the State Inspector General has reasonable grounds to believe there has been a violation of state criminal law;

8. Administer the Fraud and Abuse Whistle Blower Reward Fund created pursuant to § 2.2-3014;

9. Oversee the Fraud, Waste and Abuse Hotline;

10. Conduct performance reviews of state agencies to assess the efficiency, effectiveness, or economy of programs and to ascertain, among other things, that sums appropriated have been or are being expended for the purposes for which the appropriation was made and prepare a report for each performance review detailing any findings or recommendations for improving the efficiency, effectiveness, or economy of state agencies, including recommending changes in the law to the Governor and the General Assembly that are necessary to address such findings;

11. Coordinate and require standards for those internal audit programs in existence as of July 1, 2012, and for other internal audit programs in state agencies and nonstate agencies as needed in order to ensure that the Commonwealth's assets are subject to appropriate internal management controls;

12. As deemed necessary, assess the condition of the accounting, financial, and administrative controls of state agencies and nonstate agencies and make recommendations to protect the Commonwealth's assets;

13. Assist agency internal auditing programs with technical auditing issues and coordinate and

provide training to the Commonwealth's internal auditors;

14. Assist citizens in understanding their rights and the processes available to them to express concerns regarding the activities of a state agency or nonstate agency or any officer or employee of the foregoing;

15. Maintain data on inquiries received, the types of assistance requested, any actions taken, and the disposition of each such matter;

16. Upon request, assist citizens in using the procedures and processes available to express concerns regarding the activities of a state or nonstate agency or any officer or employee of the foregoing;

17. Ensure that citizens have access to the services provided by the State Inspector General and that citizens receive timely responses to their inquiries from the State Inspector General or his representatives; and

18. Do all acts necessary or convenient to carry out the purposes of this chapter.

B. If the State Inspector General receives a complaint from whatever source that alleges fraud, waste, abuse, or corruption by a public institution of higher education or any of its officers or employees, the State Inspector General shall, but for reasonable and articulable causes, refer the complaint to the internal audit department of the public institution of higher education for investigation. However, if the complaint concerns the president of the institution or its internal audit department, the investigation shall be conducted by the State Inspector General. The State Inspector General may provide assistance for investigations as may be requested by the public institution of higher education.

The public institution of higher education shall provide periodic updates on the status of any investigation and make the results of any such investigation available to the State Inspector General.

History.
2011, cc. 798, 871; 2013, cc. 717, 723; 2014, c. 788; 2016, c. 628.

§ 2.2-309.1. Additional powers and duties; behavioral health and developmental services.

A. The definitions found in § 37.2-100 shall apply mutatis mutandis to the terms used in this section.

B. In addition to the duties set forth in this chapter, the State Inspector General shall have the following powers and duties to:

1. Provide inspections of and make policy and operational recommendations for state facilities and for providers, including licensed mental health treatment units in state correctional facilities, in order to prevent problems, abuses, and deficiencies in and improve the effectiveness of their programs and services. The State Inspector General shall provide oversight and conduct announced and unannounced inspections of state facilities and of providers, including licensed mental health treatment units in state correctional facilities, on an ongoing basis in response to specific complaints of abuse, neglect, or inadequate care and as a result of monitoring serious incident reports and reports of abuse, neglect, or inadequate care or other information received. The State Inspector General shall conduct unannounced inspections at each state facility at least once annually;

2. Inspect, monitor, and review the quality of services provided in state facilities and by providers as defined in § 37.2-403, including licensed mental health treatment units in state correctional facilities;

3. Access any and all information, including confidential consumer information, related to the delivery of services to consumers in state facilities or served by providers, including licensed mental health treatment units in state correctional facilities. However, the State Inspector General shall not be given access to any proceedings, minutes, records, or reports of providers that are privileged under § 8.01-581.17, except that the State Inspector General shall be given access to any privileged information in state facilities and licensed mental health treatment units in state correctional facilities. All consumer information shall be maintained by the State Inspector General as confidential in the same manner as is required by the agency or provider from which the information was obtained;

4. Keep the General Assembly and the Joint Commission on Health Care fully and currently informed by means of reports required by § 2.2-313 concerning significant problems, abuses, and deficiencies relating to the administration of the programs and services of state facilities and of providers, including licensed mental health treatment units in state correctional facilities, to recommend corrective actions concerning the problems, abuses, and deficiencies, and report on the progress made in implementing the corrective actions;

5. Review, comment on, and make recommendations about, as appropriate, any reports prepared by the Department of Behavioral Health and Developmental Services and the critical incident data collected by the Department of Behavioral Health and Developmental Services in accordance with regulations adopted under § 37.2-400 to identify issues related to quality of care, seclusion and restraint, medication usage, abuse and neglect, staff recruitment and training, and other systemic issues;

6. As deemed necessary, monitor, review, and comment on regulations adopted by the Board of Behavioral Health and Developmental Services; and

7. Receive reports, information, and complaints from the Commonwealth's designated protection and advocacy system concerning issues related to quality of care provided in state facilities and by providers, including licensed mental health treatment units in state correctional facilities, and conduct independent reviews and investigations.

History.
2013, cc. 571, 717, 723; 2014, c. 788.

§ 2.2-309.2. Additional powers and duties; Tobacco Region Revitalization Commission.

The State Inspector General shall (i) review the condition of the Tobacco Region Revitalization Commission's accounting, financial, and administrative controls to ensure that the purposes set forth in Chapter 31 (§ 3.2-3100 et seq.) of Title 3.2 are lawfully achieved; (ii) investigate to resolve allegations of fraudulent, illegal, or inappropriate activities concerning (a) disbursements from the Tobacco Indemnification and Community Revitalization Endowment created pursuant to § 3.2-3104 and (b) distributions from the Tobacco Indemnification and Community Revitalization Fund created pursuant to § 3.2-3106; and (iii) detect fraud, waste, and abuse and take actions to prevent the same.

History.
2013, cc. 717, 723.

§ 2.2-309.3. Additional powers and duties; adult corrections.

A. The definitions found in § 53.1-1 shall apply mutatis mutandis to the terms used in this section.

B. In addition to the duties set forth in this chapter, the State Inspector General shall review, comment on, and make recommendations about, as appropriate, any reports prepared by the Department of Corrections and any critical incident data collected by the Department of Corrections in accordance with regulations adopted to identify issues related to quality of care, seclusion and restraint, medication usage, abuse and neglect, staff recruitment and training, and other systemic issues.

C. Nothing in this section shall be construed to grant the Office any authority over the operation and security of local jails that is not specified in other provisions of law.

History.
2013, cc. 717, 723; 2014, c. 788.

§ 2.2-309.4. Additional powers and duties; juvenile justice.

A. The definitions found in § 66-12 shall apply mutatis mutandis to the terms used in this section.

B. In addition to the duties set forth in this chapter, the State Inspector General shall review, comment on, and make recommendations about, as appropriate, any reports prepared by the Department of Juvenile Justice and any critical incident data collected by the Department of Juvenile Justice in accordance with regulations adopted to identify issues related to quality of care, seclusion and restraint, medication usage, abuse and neglect, staff recruitment and training, and other systemic issues.

C. Nothing in this section shall be construed to grant the Office any authority over the operation and security of detention homes that is not specified in other provisions of law.

History.
2013, cc. 717, 723; 2014, c. 788.

§ 2.2-310. Cooperation of state agencies and officers.

A. Each state agency and every officer and employee shall (i) promptly report any allegations of criminal acts or acts of fraud, waste, abuse, or corruption and (ii) cooperate with, and provide assistance to, the State Inspector General in the performance of any investigation. This reporting requirement shall be deemed satisfied for officers or employees of an agency once the agency head reports to the State Inspector General any allegations of criminal acts, fraud, waste, abuse, or corruption within the agency. Each state agency shall make its premises, equipment, personnel, books, records, and papers readily available to the State Inspector General upon request.

B. When a state agency head or officer discovers any unauthorized, illegal, irregular, or unsafe handling or expenditure of state funds, or if it comes to his attention that any unauthorized, illegal, or unsafe handling or expenditure of state funds is contemplated but not consummated, he shall promptly report the same to the State Inspector General.

C. The State Inspector General may enter upon the premises of any state agency at any time, without prior announcement, if necessary to the successful completion of an investigation. In the course of an investigation, the State Inspector General may question any officer or employee serving in, and any person transacting business with, the state agency and may inspect and copy any books, records, or papers in the possession of the state agency. The State Inspector General shall preserve the confidentiality of any information obtained from a state agency during the course of an investigation in accordance with applicable state and federal law.

History.
2011, cc. 798, 871; 2013, cc. 717, 723.

§ 2.2-311. Enforcement of laws by the State Inspector General or investigators; police power of the Office of State Inspector General; training.

A. The State Inspector General may designate himself and no more than 30 members of the investigations unit of the Office to have the same powers as a sheriff or a law-enforcement officer in the investigation of allegations of criminal behavior affecting the operations of a state agency or nonstate agency pursuant to his duties as set forth in this chapter. Such employees shall be subject to any minimum training standards established by the Department of Criminal Justice Services under

§ 9.1-102 for law-enforcement officers prior to exercising any law-enforcement power under this subsection.

The State Inspector General and the Superintendent of the Virginia State Police shall enter into a Memorandum of Understanding setting forth the respective roles and responsibilities of their agencies, including but not limited to the categories of investigations that will be overseen by each agency and how to avoid redundancy or operation conflicts. The Memorandum of Understanding will be approved by the Governor's chief of staff and will be reviewed periodically at the request of either agency, but not less than every four years, and revised as agreed to by the agencies and endorsed by the Governor's chief of staff.

B. The State Inspector General or investigators as may be designated by him also shall have the authority to issue summonses for violations of the statutes that the State Inspector General is required to enforce. In the event a person issued such a summons fails or refuses to discontinue the unlawful acts or refuses to give a written promise to appear at the time and place specified in the summons, the investigator may appear before a magistrate or other issuing authority having jurisdiction to obtain a criminal warrant pursuant to § 19.2-72.

C. All investigators appointed by the State Inspector General are vested with the authority to administer oaths or affirmations for the purpose of receiving complaints and conducting investigations of violations of the statutes and regulations that the State Inspector General is required to enforce. Such investigators are vested with the authority to obtain, serve, and execute any warrant, paper, or process issued by any court or magistrate or under the authority of the State Inspector General, and request and receive criminal history information under the provisions of § 19.2-389.

History.
2011, cc. 798, 871; 2013, cc. 717, 723.

§ 2.2-312. Subpoenas.

A. The State Inspector General or a designated subordinate may issue a subpoena for the appearance of an individual before any hearing conducted by the Office. The subpoena shall be served by the State Inspector General or a designated subordinate and enforced by the court of that jurisdiction.

B. The State Inspector General may make an ex parte application to the circuit court for the county or city wherein evidence sought is kept for the issuance of a subpoena duces tecum in furtherance of an investigation or to request production of any relevant records, documents, and physical or other evidence of any person, partnership, association, or corporation located in the Commonwealth. The court may issue and compel compliance with such a subpoena upon a showing of reasonable cause. Upon determining that reasonable cause exists to believe that evidence may be destroyed or altered, the court may issue a subpoena duces tecum requiring the immediate production of evidence.

History.
2011, cc. 798, 871.

§ 2.2-313. Reports.

A. The State Inspector General shall prepare an annual report to the Governor and the General Assembly summarizing the activities of the Office. Such report shall include, but need not be limited to: (i) a description of any significant problems, abuses, and deficiencies related to the management or operation of state agencies or nonstate agencies during the reporting period; (ii) a description of the recommendations for any corrective actions made by the Office during the reporting period with respect to significant problems, abuses, or deficiencies identified; (iii) a summary of matters referred to the attorneys for the Commonwealth and law-enforcement agencies and actions taken on them during the reporting period; (iv) information concerning the numbers of complaints received and types of investigations completed by the Office during the reporting period; (v) the development and maintenance of internal audit programs in state agencies and nonstate agencies; and (vi) the results of any state agency performance reviews, including a summary of any findings or recommendations for improving the efficiency of state agencies. The annual report shall cover the period July 1 until June 30 of the immediately preceding fiscal year. Notwithstanding any other provision of law, annual reports shall be transmitted directly to the Governor and the General Assembly.

B. The State Inspector General shall notify the Governor's chief of staff, the Speaker, Majority Leader, and Minority Leader of the House of Delegates, and the President pro tempore, Majority Leader, and Minority Leader of the Senate of problems, abuses, or deficiencies relating to the management or operation of a state agency or nonstate agency.

C. The State Inspector General shall keep the appropriate Secretaries advised of the Office's activities as they relate to each respective Secretary on at least a quarterly basis, and of any significant problems, abuses, or deficiencies relating to the management or operation of a state agency within each such Secretary's area of responsibility. However, when the State Inspector General becomes aware of significant problems, abuses, or deficiencies relating to the management or operation of a Secretary's office, the State Inspector General shall report the same immediately to the Governor's chief of staff.

D. The State Inspector General may conduct such additional investigations and make such reports relating to the management and operation of state agencies as are, in the judgment of the State Inspector General, necessary or desirable.

E. Notwithstanding any other provision of law, the reports, information, or documents required by or under this section shall be transmitted directly to the Governor's chief of staff and the General Assembly by the State Inspector General.

F. Records that are confidential under federal or state law shall be maintained as confidential by the State Inspector General and shall not be further disclosed, except as required by law.

History.
2011, cc. 798, 871; 2013, cc. 717, 723.

ARTICLE 2.
BEHAVIORAL HEALTH AND DEVELOPMENTAL SERVICES.

§§ 2.2-314 through 2.2-316: Repealed by Acts 2013, cc. 717 and 723, cl. 2.

Cross references.
For current provisions pertaining to additional duties of the Inspector General with respect to behavioral health and developmental services, see § 2.2-309.1.

ARTICLE 3.
CORRECTIONS.

§§ 2.2-317, 2.2-318: Repealed by Acts 2013, cc. 717 and 723, cl. 2.

Cross references.
For current provisions pertaining to additional duties of the Inspector General with respect to adult corrections, see § 2.2-309.3.

ARTICLE 4.
JUVENILE JUSTICE.

§§ 2.2-319, 2.2-320: Repealed by Acts 2013, cc. 717 and 723, cl. 2.

Cross references.
For current provisions pertaining to additional duties of the Inspector General with respect to juvenile justice, see § 2.2-309.4.

ARTICLE 5.
TRANSPORTATION.

§ 2.2-321: Repealed by Acts 2013, cc. 717 and 723, cl. 2.

ARTICLE 6.
TOBACCO INDEMNIFICATION AND COMMUNITY REVITALIZATION.

§ 2.2-322: Repealed by Acts 2013, cc. 717 and 723, cl. 2.

Cross references.
For current provisions pertaining to additional duties of the Inspector General with respect to the Tobacco Region Revitalization Commission, see § 2.2-309.2.

PART B.
DEPARTMENT OF LAW.

CHAPTER 5.
DEPARTMENT OF LAW.

Article 1.

General Provisions.

ARTICLE 1.
GENERAL PROVISIONS.

§ 2.2-511. Criminal cases.

A. Unless specifically requested by the Governor to do so, the Attorney General shall have no authority to institute or conduct criminal prosecutions in the circuit courts of the Commonwealth except in cases involving (i) violations of the Alcoholic Beverage Control Act (§ 4.1-100 et seq.), (ii) violation of laws relating to elections and the electoral process as provided in § 24.2-104, (iii) violation of laws relating to motor vehicles and their operation, (iv) the handling of funds by a state bureau, institution, commission or department, (v) the theft of state property, (vi) violation of the criminal laws involving child pornography and sexually explicit visual material involving children, (vii) the practice of law without being duly authorized or licensed or the illegal practice of law, (viii) violations of § 3.2-4212 or 58.1-1008.2, (ix) with the concurrence of the local attorney for the Commonwealth, violations of the Virginia Computer Crimes Act (§ 18.2-152.1 et seq.), (x) with the concurrence of the local attorney for the Commonwealth, violations of the Air Pollution Control Law (§ 10.1-1300 et seq.), the Virginia Waste Management Act (§ 10.1-1400 et seq.), and the State Water Control Law (§ 62.1-44.2 et seq.), (xi) with the concurrence of the local attorney for the Commonwealth, violations of Chapters 2 (§ 18.2-18 et seq.), 3 (§ 18.2-22 et seq.), and 10 (§ 18.2-434 et seq.) of Title 18.2, if such crimes relate to violations of law listed in clause (x) of this subsection, (xii) with the concurrence of the local attorney for the Commonwealth, criminal violations by Medicaid providers or their employees in the course of doing business, or violations of Chapter 13 (§ 18.2-512 et seq.) of Title 18.2, in which cases the Attorney General may leave the prosecution to the local attorney for the Commonwealth, or he may institute proceedings by information, presentment or indictment, as appropriate, and conduct the same, (xiii) with the concurrence of the local attorney for the Commonwealth, violations of Article 9 (§ 18.2-246.1 et seq.) of Chapter 6 of Title 18.2, (xiv) with the concurrence of the local attorney for the Commonwealth, assisting in the prosecution of violations of §§ 18.2-186.3 and 18.2-186.4, (xv) with the concurrence of the local attorney for the Commonwealth, assisting in the prosecution of violations of § 18.2-46.2, 18.2-46.3, or 18.2-46.5 when such violations are committed on the grounds of a state correctional facility, and (xvi) with the concurrence of the local attorney for the Commonwealth, assisting in the prosecution of violations of Article 10 (§ 18.2-246.6 et seq.) of Chapter 6 of Title 18.2.

In all other criminal cases in the circuit courts, except where the law provides otherwise, the authority of the Attorney General to appear or participate in the proceedings shall not attach unless and until a petition for appeal has been granted by the Court of Appeals or a writ of error has been granted by the Supreme Court. In all criminal cases before the Court of Appeals or the Supreme Court in which the Commonwealth is a party or is directly interested, the Attorney General shall appear and represent the Commonwealth. In any criminal case in which a petition for appeal has been granted by the Court of Appeals, the Attorney General shall continue to represent the Commonwealth in any further appeal of a case from the Court of Appeals to the Supreme Court.

B. The Attorney General shall, upon request of a person who was the victim of a crime and subject to such reasonable procedures as the Attorney General may require, ensure that such person is given notice of the filing, of the date, time and place and of the disposition of any appeal or habeas corpus proceeding involving the cases in which such person was a victim. For the purposes of this section, a victim is an individual who has suffered physical, psychological or economic harm as a direct result of the commission of a crime; a spouse, child, parent or legal guardian of a minor or incapacitated victim; or a spouse, child, parent or legal guardian of a victim of a homicide. Nothing in this subsection shall confer upon any person a right to appeal or modify any decision in a criminal, appellate or habeas corpus proceeding; abridge any right guaranteed by law; or create any cause of action for damages against the Commonwealth or any of its political subdivisions, the Attorney General or any of his employees or agents, any other officer, employee or agent of the Commonwealth or any of its political subdivisions, or any officer of the court.

History.

Code 1950, § 2-90; 1958, c. 235; 1966, c. 677, § 2.1-124; 1974, c. 490; 1975, c. 42; 1984, c. 703; 1993, c. 866; 1995, cc. 565, 839; 1997, c. 801; 1998, cc. 507, 510; 2000, c. 239; 2001, c. 844; 2002, cc. 588, 623; 2003, c. 103; 2004, cc. 450, 883, 996; 2007, c. 409; 2009, c. 847.

§ 2.2-515.2. Address confidentiality program established; victims of domestic violence or stalking; application; disclosure of records.

A. As used in this section:

"Address" means a residential street address, school address, or work address of a person as specified on the person's application to be a program participant.

"Applicant" means a person who is a victim of domestic violence or stalking or is a parent or guardian of a minor child or incapacitated person who is the victim of domestic violence or stalking.

"Domestic violence" means an act as defined in § 38.2-508 and includes threat of such acts committed against an individual in a domestic situation, regardless of whether these acts or threats have been reported to law-enforcement officers. Such threat must be a threat of force which would place any person in reasonable apprehension of death or bodily injury.

"Domestic violence programs" means public and not-for-profit agencies the primary mission of which is to provide services to victims of sexual or domestic violence or stalking.

"Program participant" means a person certified by the Office of the Attorney General as eligible to participate in the Address Confidentiality Program.

"Stalking" means conduct that is prohibited under § 18.2-60.3, regardless of whether the conduct has been reported to a law-enforcement officer or the assailant has been charged with or convicted for the alleged violation.

B. The Statewide Facilitator for Victims of Domestic Violence shall establish a program to be known as the "Address Confidentiality Program" to protect victims of domestic violence and stalking by authorizing the use of designated addresses for such victims. An individual who is at least 18 years of age, a parent or guardian acting on behalf of a minor, a guardian acting on behalf of an incapacitated person, or an emancipated minor may apply in person, at domestic violence programs that provide services where the role of the services provider is (i) to assist the eligible person in determining whether the address confidentiality program should be part of such person's overall safety plan; (ii) to explain the address confidentiality program services and limitations; (iii) to explain the program participant's responsibilities; and (iv) to assist the person eligible for participation with the completion of application materials. The Office of the Attorney General shall approve an application if it is filed in the manner and on the form prescribed by the Attorney General and if the application contains the following:

1. A sworn statement by the applicant declaring to be true and correct under penalty of perjury that the applicant has good reason to believe that:

a. The applicant, or the minor or incapacitated individual on whose behalf the application is made, is a victim of domestic violence or stalking;

b. The applicant fears further violent acts or acts of stalking from the applicant's assailant; and

c. The applicant is not on active parole or probation supervision requirements under federal, state, or local law.

2. A designation of the Office of the Attorney General as agent for the purpose of receiving mail on behalf of the applicant;

3. The applicant's actual address to which mail can be forwarded and a telephone number where the applicant can be called;

4. A listing of any minor children residing at the applicant's actual address, each minor child's date of birth, and each minor child's relationship to the applicant; and

5. The signature of the applicant and any person who assisted in the preparation of the application and the date.

C. Upon approval of a completed application, the Office of the Attorney General shall certify the applicant as a program participant. An applicant shall be certified for one year following the date of the approval, unless the certification is withdrawn or invalidated before that date. A program participant may apply to be recertified every year.

D. Upon receipt of first-class mail addressed to a program participant, the Attorney General or his designee shall forward the mail to the actual address of the program participant. The actual address of a program participant shall be available only to the Attorney General and to those employees involved in the operation of the Address Confidentiality Program and to law-enforcement officers. A program participant's actual address may be entered into the Virginia Criminal Information Network (VCIN) system so that it may be made known to law-enforcement officers accessing the VCIN system for law-enforcement purposes.

E. The Office of the Attorney General may cancel a program participant's certification if:

1. The program participant requests withdrawal from the program;

2. The program participant obtains a name change through an order of the court and does not provide notice and a copy of the order to the Office of the Attorney General within seven days after entry of the order;

3. The program participant changes his residence address and does not provide seven days' notice to the Office of the Attorney General prior to the change of address;

4. The mail forwarded by the Office of the Attorney General to the address provided by the program participant is returned as undeliverable;

5. Any information contained in the application is false;

6. The program participant has been placed on parole or probation while a participant in the address confidentiality program; or

7. The applicant is required to register as a sex offender pursuant to Chapter 9 (§ 9.1-900 et seq.) of Title 9.1.

For purposes of the address confidentiality program, residents of temporary housing for 30 days or less are not eligible to enroll in the address confidentiality program until a permanent residential address is obtained.

The application form shall contain a statement notifying each applicant of the provisions of this subsection.

F. A program participant may request that any state or local agency use the address designated by the Office of the Attorney General as the program participant's address, except when the program participant is purchasing a firearm from a dealer in firearms. The agency shall accept the address designated by the Office of the Attorney General as a program participant's address, unless the agency has received a written exemption from the Office of the Attorney General demonstrating to the satisfaction of the Attorney General that:

1. The agency has a bona fide statutory basis for requiring the program participant to disclose to it the actual location of the program participant; and

2. The disclosed confidential address of the program participant will be used only for that statutory purpose and will not be disclosed or made available in any way to any other person or agency.

A state agency may request an exemption by providing in writing to the Office of the Attorney General identification of the statute or administrative rule that demonstrates the agency's bona fide requirement and authority for the use of the actual address of an individual. A request for a waiver from an agency may be for an individual program participant, a class of program participants, or all program participants. The denial of an agency's exemption request shall be in writing and include a statement of the specific reasons for the denial. Acceptance or denial of an agency's exemption request shall constitute final agency action.

Any state or local agency that discloses the program participant's confidential address provided by the Office of the Attorney General shall be immune from civil liability unless the agency acted with gross negligence or willful misconduct.

A program participant's actual address shall be disclosed pursuant to a court order.

G. Records submitted to or provided by the Office of the Attorney General in accordance with this section shall be exempt from disclosure under the Virginia Freedom of Information Act (§ 2.2-3700 et seq.) to the extent such records contain information identifying a past or current program participant, including such person's name, actual and designated address, telephone number, and any email address. However, access shall not be denied to the person who is the subject thereof, or the parent or legal guardian of a program participant in cases where the program participant is a minor child or an incapacitated person, except when the parent or legal guardian is named as the program participant's assailant.

H. Neither the Office of the Attorney General, its officers or employees, or others who have a responsibility to a program participant under this section shall have any liability nor shall any cause of action arise against them in their official or personal capacity from the failure of a program participant to receive any first class mail forwarded to him by the Office of the Attorney General pursuant to this section. Nor shall any such liability or cause of action arise from the failure of a program participant to timely receive any first class mail forwarded by the Office of the Attorney General pursuant to this section.

History.

2007, c. 599; 2008, c. 649; 2011, cc. 97, 172; 2014, c. 439.

PART C.

STATE AGENCIES RELATED TO THE GENERAL OPERATION OF GOVERNMENT.

CHAPTER 6.

GENERAL PROVISIONS.

Article 1.

In General.

ARTICLE 1.

IN GENERAL.

§ 2.2-610. Furnishing copies of documents at no cost to law-enforcement officials.

All agencies and instrumentalities of the Commonwealth shall provide, at no cost, copies of documents requested by the Department of State Police or other law-enforcement officers as part of an active criminal investigation.

"Law-enforcement officer" means the same as that term is defined in § 9.1-101.

History.

1997, c. 44, § 2.1-2.2; 2001, c. 844.

CHAPTER 11.

DEPARTMENT OF GENERAL SERVICES.

Article 3.

Division Of Purchases And Supply.

ARTICLE 3.

DIVISION OF PURCHASES AND SUPPLY.

§ 2.2-1112. Standardization of materials, equipment and supplies.

A. So far as practicable, all materials, equipment and supplies, purchased by or for the officers, departments, agencies or institutions of the Commonwealth, shall be standardized by the Division, and no variation shall be allowed from any established standard without the written approval of the Division. The standard shall be determined upon the needs of all using agencies, so far as their needs are in common, and for groups of using agencies or single using agencies so far as their needs differ. When changes or alterations in equipment are necessary in order to permit the application of any standard, the changes and alterations shall be made as rapidly as possible.

B. The Division shall determine the proper equipment or electrical devices used to monitor the speed of any motor vehicle pursuant to § 46.2-882 and shall so advise the respective law-enforcement officials. Police chiefs and sheriffs shall ensure that all such equipment and devices meet or exceed the standards established by the Division. This subsection shall apply only to equipment and devices purchased on or after July 1, 1986.

C. The Division shall determine the proper equipment to be used to determine the decibel level of sound and shall so advise the respective law-enforcement officials. Police chiefs and sheriffs shall ensure that all such equipment and devices meet or exceed the standards established by the Division and shall maintain, inspect, calibrate, and test for accuracy all such equipment and devices on a schedule and in accordance with standards established by the Division.

History.

Code 1950, §§ 2-255, 2-256; 1958 c. 124; 1966, c. 677, §§ 2.1-279, 2.1-280; 1972, c. 494; 1977, c. 672, § 2.1-446; 1986, c. 530; 1991, c. 345; 2001, c. 844; 2010, c. 558.

TITLE 3.1.

AGRICULTURE, HORTICULTURE AND FOOD.

[Repealed.]

TITLE 3.2.
AGRICULTURE, ANIMAL CARE, AND FOOD.

SUBTITLE V.
DOMESTIC ANIMALS.

CHAPTER 65.
COMPREHENSIVE ANIMAL CARE.

Article 1.
General Provisions.

Article 2.
Animal Welfare.

Article 2.1.
Commercial Dog Breeding Operations.

Article 3.
Transportation and Sale of Animals.

Article 4.
Boarding Establishments and Groomers.

Article 5.
Rabies Control and Licensing of Dogs and Cats.

Article 6.
Authority of Local Governing Bodies.

ARTICLE 1.

GENERAL PROVISIONS.

§ 3.2-6500. Definitions.

As used in this chapter unless the context requires a different meaning:

"Abandon" means to desert, forsake, or absolutely give up an animal without having secured another owner or custodian for the animal or by failing to provide the elements of basic care as set forth in § 3.2-6503 for a period of five consecutive days.

"Adequate care" or *"care"* means the responsible practice of good animal husbandry, handling, production, management, confinement, feeding, watering, protection, shelter, transportation, treatment, and, when necessary, euthanasia, appropriate for the age, species, condition, size and type of the animal and the provision of veterinary care when needed to prevent suffering or impairment of health.

"Adequate exercise" or *"exercise"* means the opportunity for the animal to move sufficiently to maintain normal muscle tone and mass for the age, species, size, and condition of the animal.

"Adequate feed" means access to and the provision of food that is of sufficient quantity and nutritive value to maintain each animal in good health; is accessible to each animal; is prepared so as to permit ease of consumption for the age, species, condition, size and type of each animal; is provided in a clean and sanitary manner; is placed so as to minimize contamination by excrement and pests; and is provided at suitable intervals for the species, age, and condition of the animal, but at least once daily, except as prescribed by a veterinarian or as dictated by naturally occurring states of hibernation or fasting normal for the species.

"Adequate shelter" means provision of and access to shelter that is suitable for the species, age, condition, size, and type of each animal; provides adequate space for each animal; is safe and protects each animal from injury, rain, sleet, snow, hail, direct sunlight, the adverse effects of heat or cold, physical suffering, and impairment of health; is properly lighted; is properly cleaned; enables each animal to be clean and dry, except when detrimental to the species; and, for dogs and cats, provides a solid surface, resting platform, pad, floormat, or similar device that is large enough for the animal to lie on in a normal manner and can be maintained in a sanitary manner. Under this chapter, shelters whose wire, grid, or slat floors: (i) permit the animals' feet to pass through the openings; (ii) sag under the animals' weight; or (iii) otherwise do not protect the

animals' feet or toes from injury are not adequate shelter.

"Adequate space" means sufficient space to allow each animal to: (i) easily stand, sit, lie, turn about, and make all other normal body movements in a comfortable, normal position for the animal; and (ii) interact safely with other animals in the enclosure. When an animal is tethered, "adequate space" means a tether that permits the above actions and is appropriate to the age and size of the animal; is attached to the animal by a properly applied collar, halter, or harness configured so as to protect the animal from injury and prevent the animal or tether from becoming entangled with other objects or animals, or from extending over an object or edge that could result in the strangulation or injury of the animal; and is at least three times the length of the animal, as measured from the tip of its nose to the base of its tail, except when the animal is being walked on a leash or is attached by a tether to a lead line. When freedom of movement would endanger the animal, temporarily and appropriately restricting movement of the animal according to professionally accepted standards for the species is considered provision of adequate space.

"Adequate water" means provision of and access to clean, fresh, potable water of a drinkable temperature that is provided in a suitable manner, in sufficient volume, and at suitable intervals appropriate for the weather and temperature, to maintain normal hydration for the age, species, condition, size and type of each animal, except as prescribed by a veterinarian or as dictated by naturally occurring states of hibernation or fasting normal for the species; and is provided in clean, durable receptacles that are accessible to each animal and are placed so as to minimize contamination of the water by excrement and pests or an alternative source of hydration consistent with generally accepted husbandry practices.

"Adoption" means the transfer of ownership of a dog or a cat, or any other companion animal, from a releasing agency to an individual.

"Agricultural animals" means all livestock and poultry.

"Ambient temperature" means the temperature surrounding the animal.

"Animal" means any nonhuman vertebrate species except fish. For the purposes of § 3.2-6522, animal means any species susceptible to rabies. For the purposes of § 3.2-6570, animal means any nonhuman vertebrate species including fish except those fish captured and killed or disposed of in a reasonable and customary manner.

"Animal control officer" means a person appointed as an animal control officer or deputy animal control officer as provided in § 3.2-6555.

"Boarding establishment" means a place or establishment other than a public or private animal shelter where companion animals not owned by the proprietor are sheltered, fed, and watered in exchange for a fee.

"Collar" means a well-fitted device, appropriate to the age and size of the animal, attached to the animal's neck in such a way as to prevent trauma or injury to the animal.

"Commercial dog breeder" means any person who, during any 12-month period, maintains 30 or more adult female dogs for the primary purpose of the sale of their offspring as companion animals.

"Companion animal" means any domestic or feral dog, domestic or feral cat, nonhuman primate, guinea pig, hamster, rabbit not raised for human food or fiber, exotic or native animal, reptile, exotic or native bird, or any feral animal or any animal under the care, custody, or ownership of a person or any animal that is bought, sold, traded, or bartered by any person. Agricultural animals, game species, or any animals regulated under federal law as research animals shall not be considered companion animals for the purposes of this chapter.

"Consumer" means any natural person purchasing an animal from a dealer or pet shop or hiring the services of a boarding establishment. The term "consumer" shall not include a business or corporation engaged in sales or services.

"Dealer" means any person who in the regular course of business for compensation or profit buys, sells, transfers, exchanges, or barters companion animals. The following shall not be considered dealers: (i) any person who transports companion animals in the regular course of business as a common carrier or (ii) any person whose primary purpose is to find permanent adoptive homes for companion animals.

"Direct and immediate threat" means any clear and imminent danger to an animal's health, safety or life.

"Dump" means to knowingly desert, forsake, or absolutely give up without having secured another owner or custodian any dog, cat, or other companion animal in any public place including the right-of-way of any public highway, road or street or on the property of another.

"Emergency veterinary treatment" means veterinary treatment to stabilize a life-threatening condition, alleviate suffering, prevent further disease transmission, or prevent further disease progression.

"Enclosure" means a structure used to house or restrict animals from running at large.

"Euthanasia" means the humane destruction of an animal accomplished by a method that involves instantaneous unconsciousness and immediate death or by a method that involves anesthesia, produced by an agent that causes painless loss of consciousness, and death during such loss of consciousness.

"Exhibitor" means any person who has animals for or on public display, excluding an exhibitor licensed by the U.S. Department of Agriculture.

"Facility" means a building or portion thereof as designated by the State Veterinarian, other than a

private residential dwelling and its surrounding grounds, that is used to contain a primary enclosure or enclosures in which animals are housed or kept.

"Farming activity" means, consistent with standard animal husbandry practices, the raising, management, and use of agricultural animals to provide food, fiber, or transportation and the breeding, exhibition, lawful recreational use, marketing, transportation, and slaughter of agricultural animals pursuant to such purposes.

"Foster care provider" means a person who provides care or rehabilitation for companion animals through an affiliation with a public or private animal shelter, home-based rescue, releasing agency, or other animal welfare organization.

"Foster home" means a private residential dwelling and its surrounding grounds, or any facility other than a public or private animal shelter, at which site through an affiliation with a public or private animal shelter, home-based rescue, releasing agency, or other animal welfare organization care or rehabilitation is provided for companion animals.

"Groomer" means any person who, for a fee, cleans, trims, brushes, makes neat, manicures, or treats for external parasites any animal.

"Home-based rescue" means an animal welfare organization that takes custody of companion animals for the purpose of facilitating adoption and houses such companion animals in a foster home or a system of foster homes.

"Humane" means any action taken in consideration of and with the intent to provide for the animal's health and well-being.

"Humane investigator" means a person who has been appointed by a circuit court as a humane investigator as provided in § 3.2-6558.

"Humane society" means any incorporated, nonprofit organization that is organized for the purposes of preventing cruelty to animals and promoting humane care and treatment or adoptions of animals.

"Incorporated" means organized and maintained as a legal entity in the Commonwealth.

"Kennel" means any establishment in which five or more canines, felines, or hybrids of either are kept for the purpose of breeding, hunting, training, renting, buying, boarding, selling, or showing.

"Law-enforcement officer" means any person who is a full-time or part-time employee of a police department or sheriff's office that is part of or administered by the Commonwealth or any political subdivision thereof and who is responsible for the prevention and detection of crime and the enforcement of the penal, traffic or highway laws of the Commonwealth. Part-time employees are compensated officers who are not full-time employees as defined by the employing police department or sheriff's office.

"Livestock" includes all domestic or domesticated: bovine animals; equine animals; ovine animals; porcine animals; cervidae animals; capradae animals; animals of the genus Lama; ratites; fish or shellfish in aquaculture facilities, as defined in § 3.2-2600; enclosed domesticated rabbits or hares raised for human food or fiber; or any other individual animal specifically raised for food or fiber, except companion animals.

"New owner" means an individual who is legally competent to enter into a binding agreement pursuant to subdivision B 2 of § 3.2-6574, and who adopts or receives a dog or cat from a releasing agency.

"Ordinance" means any law, rule, regulation, or ordinance adopted by the governing body of any locality.

"Other officer" includes all other persons employed or elected by the people of Virginia, or by any locality, whose duty it is to preserve the peace, to make arrests, or to enforce the law.

"Owner" means any person who: (i) has a right of property in an animal; (ii) keeps or harbors an animal; (iii) has an animal in his care; or (iv) acts as a custodian of an animal.

"Pet shop" means an establishment where companion animals are bought, sold, exchanged, or offered for sale or exchange to the general public.

"Poultry" includes all domestic fowl and game birds raised in captivity.

"Primary enclosure" means any structure used to immediately restrict an animal or animals to a limited amount of space, such as a room, pen, cage, compartment, or hutch. For tethered animals, the term includes the shelter and the area within reach of the tether.

"Private animal shelter" means a facility operated for the purpose of finding permanent adoptive homes for animals that is used to house or contain animals and that is owned or operated by an incorporated, nonprofit, and nongovernmental entity, including a humane society, animal welfare organization, society for the prevention of cruelty to animals, or any other similar organization.

"Properly cleaned" means that carcasses, debris, food waste, and excrement are removed from the primary enclosure with sufficient frequency to minimize the animals' contact with the above-mentioned contaminants; the primary enclosure is sanitized with sufficient frequency to minimize odors and the hazards of disease; and the primary enclosure is cleaned so as to prevent the animals confined therein from being directly or indirectly sprayed with the stream of water, or directly or indirectly exposed to hazardous chemicals or disinfectants.

"Properly lighted" when referring to a facility means sufficient illumination to permit routine inspections, maintenance, cleaning, and housekeeping of the facility, and observation of the animals; to provide regular diurnal lighting cycles of either natural or artificial light, uniformly diffused throughout the facility; and to promote the well-being of the animals.

"Properly lighted" when referring to a private residential dwelling and its surrounding grounds means sufficient illumination to permit routine maintenance and cleaning thereof, and observation of the companion animals; and to provide regular diurnal lighting cycles of either natural or artificial light to promote the well-being of the animals.

"Public animal shelter" means a facility operated by the Commonwealth, or any locality, for the purpose of impounding or sheltering seized, stray, homeless, abandoned, unwanted, or surrendered animals or a facility operated for the same purpose under a contract with any locality.

"Releasing agency" means (i) a public animal shelter or (ii) a private animal shelter, humane society, animal welfare organization, society for the prevention of cruelty to animals, or other similar entity or home-based rescue that releases companion animals for adoption.

"Research facility" means any place, laboratory, or institution licensed by the U.S. Department of Agriculture at which scientific tests, experiments, or investigations involving the use of living animals are carried out, conducted, or attempted.

"Sanitize" means to make physically clean and to remove and destroy, to a practical minimum, agents injurious to health.

"Sore" means, when referring to an equine, that an irritating or blistering agent has been applied, internally or externally, by a person to any limb or foot of an equine; any burn, cut, or laceration that has been inflicted by a person to any limb or foot of an equine; any tack, nail, screw, or chemical agent that has been injected by a person into or used by a person on any limb or foot of an equine; any other substance or device that has been used by a person on any limb or foot of an equine; or a person has engaged in a practice involving an equine, and as a result of such application, infliction, injection, use, or practice, such equine suffers, or can reasonably be expected to suffer, physical pain or distress, inflammation, or lameness when walking, trotting, or otherwise moving, except that such term does not include such an application, infliction, injection, use, or practice in connection with the therapeutic treatment of an equine by or under the supervision of a licensed veterinarian. Notwithstanding anything contained herein to the contrary, nothing shall preclude the shoeing, use of pads, and use of action devices as permitted by 9 C.F.R. Part 11.2.

"Sterilize" or *"sterilization"* means a surgical or chemical procedure performed by a licensed veterinarian that renders a dog or cat permanently incapable of reproducing.

"Treasurer" includes the treasurer and his assistants of each county or city or other officer designated by law to collect taxes in such county or city.

"Treatment" or *"adequate treatment"* means the responsible handling or transportation of animals in the person's ownership, custody or charge, appropriate for the age, species, condition, size and type of the animal.

"Veterinary treatment" means treatment by or on the order of a duly licensed veterinarian.

"Weaned" means that an animal is capable of and physiologically accustomed to ingestion of solid food or food customary for the adult of the species and has ingested such food, without nursing, for a period of at least five days.

History.

1984, c. 492, § 29-213.36; 1987, c. 488, § 3.1-796.66; 1988, c. 538; 1991, c. 348; 1993, cc. 174, 959; 1995, c. 610; 1998, c. 817; 2002, cc. 351, 500, 787; 2003, c. 1007; 2008, cc. 9, 127, 852, 860; 2011, cc. 754, 886; 2014, c. 148; 2015, c. 492.

§ 3.2-6501. Regulations and guidelines.

The Board may adopt regulations and guidelines consistent with the objectives and intent of this chapter concerning the care and transportation of animals.

History.

1984, c. 492, § 29-213.37; 1987, c. 488, § 3.1-796.67; 2008, c. 860.

§ 3.2-6502. State Veterinarian's power to inspect premises where animals are kept; investigations and search warrants.

A. The State Veterinarian and each State Veterinarian's representative shall have the power to conduct inspections of public and private animal shelters, and inspect any business premises where animals are housed or kept, including any boarding establishment, kennel, pet shop, or the business premises of any dealer, exhibitor or groomer, at any reasonable time, for the purposes of determining if a violation of: (i) this chapter; (ii) any other state law governing the care, control or protection of animals; or (iii) any other state law governing property rights in animals has occurred.

B. Provisions for investigation of suspected violations of this chapter and other laws pertaining to animals are provided in § 3.2-6564. Provisions for obtaining a warrant and the power of search for violations of animal cruelty laws are provided in § 3.2-6568.

History.

1993, c. 601, § 3.1-796.67:2; 1998, c. 817; 2002, c. 787; 2003, c. 1007; 2008, c. 860; 2014, c. 148.

ARTICLE 2.

ANIMAL WELFARE.

§ 3.2-6503. Care of companion animals by owner; penalty.

A. Each owner shall provide for each of his companion animals:

1. Adequate feed;
2. Adequate water;
3. Adequate shelter that is properly cleaned;
4. Adequate space in the primary enclosure for the particular type of animal depending upon its age, size, species, and weight;

5. Adequate exercise;
6. Adequate care, treatment, and transportation; and
7. Veterinary care when needed to prevent suffering or disease transmission.

The provisions of this section shall also apply to every public or private animal shelter, or other releasing agency, and every foster care provider, dealer, pet shop, exhibitor, kennel, groomer, and boarding establishment. This section shall not require that animals used as food for other animals be euthanized.

B. Violation of this section is a Class 4 misdemeanor. A second or subsequent violation of subdivision A 1, 2, 3, or 7 is a Class 2 misdemeanor and a second or subsequent violation of subdivision A 4, 5, or 6 is a Class 3 misdemeanor.

History.
1984, c. 492, § 29-213.38; 1987, c. 488, § 3.1-796.68; 1991, c. 348; 1993, c. 174; 1996, c. 249; 1998, c. 817; 2002, c. 787; 2003, c. 1007; 2008, c. 860; 2010, c. 875; 2014, c. 148.

§ 3.2-6503.1. Care of agricultural animals by owner; penalty.

A. Each owner shall provide for each of his agricultural animals:
1. Feed to prevent malnourishment;
2. Water to prevent dehydration; and
3. Veterinary treatment as needed to address impairment of health or bodily function when such impairment cannot be otherwise addressed through animal husbandry, including humane destruction.

B. The provisions of this section shall not require an owner to provide feed or water when such is customarily withheld, restricted, or apportioned pursuant to a farming activity or if otherwise prescribed by a veterinarian.

C. There shall be a rebuttable presumption that there has been no violation of this section if an owner is unable to provide feed, water, or veterinary treatment due to an act of God.

D. The provisions of this section shall not apply to agricultural animals used for bona fide medical or scientific experimentation.

E. A violation of this section is a Class 4 misdemeanor.

History.
2011, cc. 754, 886.

§ 3.2-6504. Abandonment of animal; penalty.

No person shall abandon or dump any animal. Violation of this section is a Class 3 misdemeanor. Nothing in this section shall be construed to prohibit the release of an animal by its owner to a public or private animal shelter or other releasing agency.

History.
1984, c. 492, § 29-213.43; 1987, c. 488, § 3.1-796.73; 1993, c. 174; 2002, cc. 351, 787; 2003, c. 1007; 2008, c. 860; 2014, c. 148.

§ 3.2-6504.1. Civil immunity; forcible entry of motor vehicle to remove unattended companion animal.

No law-enforcement officer as defined in § 9.1-101, firefighter as defined in § 65.2-102, emergency medical services personnel as defined in § 32.1-111.1, or animal control officer who in good faith forcibly enters a motor vehicle in order to remove an unattended companion animal that is at risk of serious bodily injury or death shall be liable for any property damage to the vehicle entered or injury to the animal resulting from such forcible entry and removal of the animal, unless such property damage or injury results from gross negligence or willful or wanton misconduct.

History.
2016, c. 679.

§ 3.2-6505. Disposal of animals by means of decompression chamber and use of gas chamber for companion animals prohibited.

A. No animal shall be euthanized pursuant to the provisions of this chapter by means of a high altitude decompression chamber.

B. No companion animal shall be euthanized pursuant to the provisions of this chapter by means of a gas chamber.

History.
1984, c. 492, § 29-213.47; 1987, c. 488, § 3.1-796.77; 2008, cc. 8, 860.

§ 3.2-6506. Exceptions regarding veterinarians.

Sections 3.2-6503, 3.2-6504, 3.2-6508 through 3.2-6519, 3.2-6557, 3.2-6559, 3.2-6561, 3.2-6564, 3.2-6565, and 3.2-6574 through 3.2-6580 shall not apply to: (i) a place or establishment that is operated under the immediate supervision of a duly licensed veterinarian as a hospital or boarding establishment where animals are harbored, boarded and cared for incident to the treatment, prevention, or alleviation of disease processes during the routine practice of the profession of veterinary medicine; or (ii) animals boarded under the immediate supervision of a duly licensed veterinarian.

History.
1984, c. 492, § 29-213.44; 1987, c. 488, § 3.1-796.74; 1993, cc. 174, 959; 2008, c. 860.

§ 3.2-6507. Injured or sick animal; action by veterinarian.

A. If a licensed veterinarian is called or by his own action comes upon an animal that is sick or injured and the owner of such animal cannot be immediately located, then the licensed veterinarian, in his professional judgment, may treat, hospitalize or euthanize the animal without the permission of the owner. The veterinarian shall make such reports and keep such records of such sick or injured animals as may be prescribed by the Board of Veterinary Medicine, including the information required under subsection B of § 3.2-6557.

B. In no event shall a licensed veterinarian who has acted in good faith and properly exercised professional judgment regarding an animal be subject to liability for his actions in: (i) acting in accordance with subsection A; or (ii) reporting cases of suspected cruelty to animals.

History.
1984, c. 492, § 29-213.46; 1987, c. 488, § 3.1-796.76; 1999, c. 620; 2008, c. 860.

ARTICLE 2.1.

COMMERCIAL DOG BREEDING OPERATIONS.

§ 3.2-6507.1. Business license required.

No commercial dog breeder shall breed dogs in the Commonwealth without a valid business license issued by any locality, as applicable, where he maintains dogs for the purpose of commercial dog breeding.

History.
2008, c. 852, § 3.1-796.77:1.

§ 3.2-6507.2. Commercial dog breeding; requirements.

Commercial dog breeders shall:

1. Maintain no more than 50 dogs over the age of one year at any time for breeding purposes. However, a higher number of dogs may be allowed if approved by local ordinance after a public hearing. Any such ordinance may include additional requirements for commercial breeding operations;
2. Breed female dogs only: (i) after annual certification by a licensed veterinarian that the dog is in suitable health for breeding; (ii) after the dog has reached the age of 18 months; and (iii) if the dog has not yet reached the age of 8 years;
3. Dispose of dogs only by gift, sale, transfer, barter, or euthanasia by a licensed veterinarian;
4. Dispose of deceased dogs in accordance with § 3.2-6554;
5. Dispose of dog waste in accordance with state and federal laws and regulations; and
6. Maintain accurate records for at least five years including:

a. The date on which a dog enters the operation;

b. The person from whom the animal was purchased or obtained, including the address and phone number of such person;

c. A description of the animal, including the species, color, breed, sex, and approximate age and weight;

d. Any tattoo, microchip number, or other identification number carried by or appearing on the animal;

e. Each date that puppies were born to such animal and the number of puppies;

f. All medical care and vaccinations provided to the animal, including certifications required by a licensed veterinarian under this chapter; and

g. The disposition of each animal and the date.

History.
2008, c. 852, § 3.1-796.77:2.

§ 3.2-6507.3. Right of entry.

A. The Commissioner, the State Veterinarian or his assistant, any animal control officer, and any public health or safety official employed by the locality where a commercial dog breeder resides or maintains breeding operations may, upon receiving a complaint or upon his own motion, investigate any violation of the provisions of this chapter. Such investigation may include (i) the inspection of the books and records of any commercial dog breeder, (ii) the inspection of any companion animal owned by the commercial dog breeder, and (iii) the inspection of any place where animals are bred or maintained. In conducting the inspection, the Commissioner or animal control officer may enter any premises where animals may be bred or maintained during daytime hours.

B. Any commercial dog breeder who is the subject of an investigation by the Commissioner, the State Veterinarian, or an animal control officer shall, upon request, provide assistance to the Commissioner, the State Veterinarian, or the animal control officer in making any inspection authorized by this section.

History.
2008, c. 852, § 3.1-796.77:3.

§ 3.2-6507.4. Concurrent operation of releasing agency prohibited.

It is unlawful for a commercial dog breeder to operate or maintain a controlling interest in any releasing agency.

History.
2008, c. 852, § 3.1-796.77:4.

§ 3.2-6507.5. Penalty.

Any commercial dog breeder violating any provision of this article is guilty of a Class 1 misdemeanor.

History.
2008, c. 852, § 3.1-796.77:5.

§ 3.2-6507.6. Duty of attorneys for the Commonwealth.

It shall be the duty of each attorney for the Commonwealth to enforce this article.

History.
2008, c. 852, § 3.1-796.77:6.

ARTICLE 3.

TRANSPORTATION AND SALE OF ANIMALS.

§ 3.2-6508. Transporting animals; requirements; penalty.

A. No owner, railroad or other common carrier when transporting any animal shall allow that animal to be confined in any type of conveyance more than 24 consecutive hours without being exercised, properly rested, fed and watered as necessary for that particular type and species of animal. A reasonable extension of this time shall be permitted when an accident, storm or other act of God causes a delay. Adequate space in the primary enclosure within any type of conveyance shall be provided each animal depending upon the particular type and species of animal.

B. No person shall import into the Commonwealth, nor export from the Commonwealth, for the purpose of sale or offering for sale any dog or cat under the age of eight weeks without its dam.

C. Violation of this section is a Class 1 misdemeanor.

History.
1984, c. 492, § 29-213.39; 1987, c. 488, § 3.1-796.69; 1993, c. 174; 2008, c. 860.

§ 3.2-6508.1. Sale of dogs or cats prohibited in certain places.

A. It is unlawful for any person to sell, exchange, trade, barter, lease, or display for a commercial purpose any dog or cat on or in any roadside, public right-of-way, parkway, median, park, or recreation area; flea market or other outdoor market; or commercial parking lot, regardless of whether such act is authorized by the landowner.

B. This section shall not apply to:

1. The display of dogs or cats by or the adoption of dogs or cats from a humane society or private or public animal shelter as those terms are defined in § 3.2-6500;

2. The display of dogs or cats as part of a state or county fair exhibition, 4-H program, or similar exhibition or educational program;

3. The sale, exchange, or trade of dogs that are sold primarily for use in commonly-accepted hunting or livestock farming activities; or

4. A prearranged sale between a dog breeder and a specific individual purchaser. Such prearranged sale shall not take place at a regularly-occurring event such as a flea market or other organized trade venue.

History.
2015, c. 679.

§ 3.2-6509. Misrepresentation of animal's condition; penalties.

No person shall misrepresent the physical condition of any animal at the animal's sale, trade, delivery, or other method of transfer. For the purpose of this section, misrepresentation shall include selling, trading, delivering or otherwise transferring an animal to another person with the knowledge that the animal has an infection, communicable disease, parasitic infestation, abnormality or other physical defect that is not made known to the person receiving the animal. The sale of an agricultural animal that has external or internal parasites that are not made known to the person receiving the animal shall not be a violation of this section unless the animal is clinically ill or debilitated due to such parasites at the time of sale, trade, delivery or transfer of the animal. Violation of this section is a Class 3 misdemeanor.

History.
1984, c. 492, § 29-213.42; 1987, c. 488, § 3.1-796.72; 1998, c. 817; 2008, c. 860.

§ 3.2-6510. Sale of unweaned or certain immature animals prohibited, vaccinations required for dogs and cats; penalty.

A. No person shall sell, raffle, give away, or offer for sale as pets or novelties, or offer or give as a prize, premium, or advertising device any living chicks, ducklings, or other fowl under two months old in quantities of less than six or any unweaned mammalian companion animal or any dog or cat under the age of seven weeks without its dam or queen. Dealers may offer immature fowl, unweaned mammalian companion animals, dogs or cats under the age of seven weeks for sale as pets or novelties with the requirement that prospective owners take possession of the animals only after fowl have reached two months of age, mammalian companion animals have been weaned, and dogs and cats are at least seven weeks of age. Nothing in this section shall prohibit the sale, gift, or transfer of an unweaned animal: (i) as food for other animals; (ii) with the lactating dam or queen or a lactating surrogate dam or queen that has accepted the animal; (iii) due to a concern for the health or safety of the unweaned animal; or (iv) to animal control, a public or private animal shelter, or a veterinarian.

B. Dealers shall provide all dogs and cats with current vaccinations against contagious and infectious diseases, as recommended in writing and considered appropriate for the animal's age and breed by a licensed veterinarian, or pursuant to written recommendations provided by the manufacturer of such vaccines at least five days before any new owner takes possession of the animal. For dogs, the vaccinations required by this subsection shall include at a minimum canine distemper, adenovirus type II parainfluenza, and parvovirus. For cats, the vaccinations required by this subsection shall include at a minimum rhinotracheitis, calicivirus, and panleukopenia. Dealers shall provide the new owner with the dog's or cat's immunization history.

C. A violation of this section is a Class 3 misdemeanor.

History.
1984, c. 492, § 29-213.40; 1987, c. 488, § 3.1-796.70; 1993, c. 174; 1995, c. 625; 2006, c. 503; 2008, c. 860; 2014, c. 148.

§ 3.2-6511. Failure of dealer or pet shop to provide adequate care; penalty.

Any dealer or pet shop that fails to adequately house, feed, water, exercise or care for animals in his or its possession or custody as provided for under this chapter is guilty of a Class 3 misdemeanor. Such animals shall be subject to seizure and impoundment, and upon conviction of such person the animals may be sold, euthanized, or disposed of as provided by § 3.2-6546 for licensed, tagged, or tattooed animals. Such failure is also grounds for revocation of a permit or certificate of registration after public hearing. Any funds that result from such sale shall be used first to pay the costs of the local jurisdiction for the impoundment and disposition of the animals, and any funds remaining shall be paid to the owner, if known. If the owner is not found, the remaining funds shall be paid into the Literary Fund.

History.
1984, c. 492, § 29-213.41; 1987, c. 488, § 3.1-796.71; 1993, c. 174; 2008, c. 860.

§ 3.2-6511.1. Pet shops; procurement of dogs; penalty.

A. A pet shop shall sell or offer for adoption a dog procured only from a humane society or private or public animal shelter as those terms are defined in § 3.2-6500 or from a person who has not received from the U.S. Department of Agriculture, pursuant to enforcement of the federal Animal Welfare Act (7 U.S.C. § 2131 et seq.) or regulations adopted thereunder, (i) a citation for a direct violation or citations for three or more indirect violations for at least two years prior to the procurement of the dog or (ii) two consecutive citations for no access to the facility prior to the procurement of the dog.

B. It shall be unlawful for any commercial dog breeder who is not licensed by the U.S. Department of Agriculture pursuant to the federal Animal Welfare Act (7 U.S.C. § 2131 et seq.) or regulations adopted thereunder to sell any dog to a pet shop.

C. A pet shop shall retain records verifying compliance with this section for a minimum of two years after the disposition of any dog.

D. Any person violating any provision of this section is guilty of a Class 1 misdemeanor for each dog sold or offered for sale.

History.
2008, c. 852, § 3.1-796.71:1; 2015, c. 679.

§ 3.2-6512. Sale without pet dealer's animal history certificate violation of Consumer Protection Act; contents of certificate.

It shall be a violation of the Virginia Consumer Protection Act (§ 59.1-196 et seq.) for any pet dealer to sell a dog or cat within the Commonwealth stating, promising, or representing that the animal is registered or capable of being registered with any animal pedigree registry organization, without providing the consumer with a pet dealer's animal history certificate at the time the consumer takes possession of the dog or cat. The pet dealer's animal history certificate shall be signed by the pet dealer or his agent or employee and shall contain the following information:

1. The animal's breed, sex, age, color, and birth date;
2. The name and address of the person from whom the pet dealer purchased the animal;
3. The breeder's name and address;
4. The name and registration number of the animal's parents;
5. If the animal has been so examined, the date on which the animal has been examined by a licensed veterinarian, the name and address of such veterinarian, and a brief statement of any findings made; and
6. A statement of all vaccinations administered to the animal, including the identity and quantity of the vaccine, and the name and address of the person or licensed veterinarian administering or supervising the vaccinations.

The information contained in the pet dealer's animal history certificate required herein shall be informative only, and the pet dealer shall not be responsible in any manner for the accuracy of such information unless he knows or has reason to know that such information is erroneous.

A copy of the pet dealer's animal history certificate signed by the consumer shall be maintained by the pet dealer for a period of one year following the date of sale.

A pet shop operating in the Commonwealth shall post in a conspicuous place on or near the cage of any dog or cat available for sale the breeder's name, city, state, and USDA license number. A pet shop or a USDA licensed dealer who advertises any dog or cat for sale in the Commonwealth, including by Internet advertisement, shall provide prior to the time of sale the breeder's name, city, state, and USDA license number.

History.

1984, c. 492, § 29-213.48; 1987, c. 488, § 3.1-796.78; 2008, c. 860; 2014, c. 448.

§ 3.2-6513. Inclusion of false or misleading statements in certificate violation of Consumer Protection Act.

It shall be a violation of the Virginia Consumer Protection Act (§ 59.1-196 et seq.) for a pet dealer to include in the pet dealer's animal history certificate provided for in § 3.2-6512 any false or misleading statement regarding the information to be contained therein.

History.

1984, c. 492, § 29-213.49; 1987, c. 488, § 3.1-796.79; 2008, c. 860.

§ 3.2-6514. Consumer remedies for receipt of diseased animal upon certification by veterinarian.

A. If, at any time within 10 days following receipt of an animal, a licensed veterinarian certifies such animal to be unfit for purchase due to illness, a congenital defect deleterious to the health of the animal, or the presence of symptoms of a contagious or infectious disease other than parvovirus, or if at any time within 14 days following the receipt of an animal a licensed veterinarian certifies such animal to be unfit for purchase due to being infected with parvovirus, the pet dealer shall afford the consumer the right to choose one of the following options:

1. The right to return the animal or, in the case of an animal that has died, to present the veterinary certification, within three business days of certification and receive a refund of the purchase price including sales tax; or

2. The right to return the animal or, in the case of an animal that has died, to present the veterinary certification, within three business days of certification and to receive an exchange animal of equivalent value from the dealer, subject to the choice of the consumer; or

3. In the case of an animal purchased from a pet shop or a USDA licensed dealer, the right to retain the animal and to receive the reimbursement of veterinary fees in an amount up to the purchase price of the animal, including sales tax and the cost of the veterinary certification, incurred up to the time the consumer notifies the pet dealer of the intent to keep the animal. Such notification shall occur within three business days of certification. Veterinary costs incurred by the consumer after such notification shall be the responsibility of the consumer.

B. The refund or reimbursement required by subsection A shall be made by the pet dealer not later than 10 business days following receipt of a signed veterinary certification as provided in § 3.2-6515.

History.

1984, c. 492, § 29-213.50; 1987, c. 488, § 3.1-796.80; 2008, c. 860; 2014, c. 448.

§ 3.2-6515. Written notice of consumer remedies required to be supplied by pet dealers.

A pet dealer shall give the notice hereinafter set forth in writing to a consumer prior to the delivery of a dog or cat. Such notice shall be embodied in a written contract, the pet dealer's animal history certificate, or a separate document and shall state in ten-point boldface type the following:

NOTICE

The sale of dogs and cats is subject to the provisions of the Virginia Consumer Protection Act (§ 59.1-196 et seq.). In the event that a licensed veterinarian certifies your animal to be unfit for purchase within 10 days following receipt of your animal, or within 14 days following receipt if the animal is infected with parvovirus, you may choose: (i) to return your animal, or in the case of an animal that has died, the veterinary certification, and receive a refund of the purchase price including sales tax; or (ii) to return the animal and receive an exchange animal of your choice of equivalent value. In the case of an animal purchased from a pet shop or a USDA licensed dealer, you also may choose to retain the animal and receive reimbursement of the cost of veterinary certification and veterinary fees in an amount up to the purchase price of the animal.

In order to exercise these rights you must present a written veterinary certification that the animal is unfit to the pet dealer within three business days after receiving such certification.

If the pet dealer has promised to register your animal or to provide the papers necessary therefor and fails to do so within 120 days following the date of contract, you are entitled to return the animal and receive a refund of the purchase price or to retain the animal and receive a refund of an amount not to exceed 50 percent of the purchase price.

History.

1984, c. 492, § 29-213.51; 1987, c. 488, § 3.1-796.81; 2008, c. 860; 2014, c. 448.

§ 3.2-6516. Failure of pet dealer to effect registration after promise; violation of Consumer Protection Act; remedies; veterinary certification; finding of intestinal parasites; illness subsequent to sale.

A. It shall be a violation of the Virginia Consumer Protection Act (§ 59.1-196 et seq.) for a pet dealer to state, promise, or represent that a dog or cat is registered or capable of being registered with any animal pedigree registry organization if the pet dealer shall then fail to either effect such registration or provide the consumer with the documents necessary therefor within 120 days following the date of sale of such animal. In the event that a pet dealer fails to effect registration or to provide the necessary documents therefor within 120 days following the date of sale, the consumer shall be entitled to choose one of the following options:

1. To return the animal and to receive a refund of the purchase price plus sales tax; or
2. To retain the animal and to receive a refund of an amount not to exceed 50 percent of the purchase price and sales tax.

B. The veterinary certification and statement required herein shall be presented to the pet dealer not later than three business days following receipt thereof by the consumer and shall contain the following information:

1. The name of the owner;
2. The date or dates of the examination;
3. The breed, color, sex, and age of the animal;
4. A description of the veterinarian's findings;
5. A statement that the veterinarian certifies the animal to be unfit for purchase; and
6. The name and address of the certifying veterinarian and the date of the certification.

C. A veterinary finding of intestinal parasites shall not be grounds for declaring the animal unfit for purchase unless the animal is clinically ill due to such condition. An animal may not be found unfit for purchase on account of an injury sustained or illness contracted subsequent to the consumer taking possession thereof.

History.
1984, c. 492, § 29-213.52; 1987, c. 488, § 3.1-796.82; 2008, c. 860.

§ 3.2-6517. Remedies cumulative.

The remedies provided for pursuant to this article are cumulative and not exclusive and shall be in addition to any other remedy provided for by law.

History.
1984, c. 492, § 29-213.53; 1987, c. 488, § 3.1-796.83; 2008, c. 860.

ARTICLE 4.

BOARDING ESTABLISHMENTS AND GROOMERS.

§ 3.2-6518. Boarding establishments and groomers; veterinary care requirements; consumer notification; penalty.

A. When an animal is boarded at a boarding establishment, or under the care, custody or subject to the actions of a groomer, the boarding establishment or groomer shall be responsible for providing the animal care requirements for each animal as specified in § 3.2-6503.

B. If an animal becomes ill or injured while in the custody of the boarding establishment or groomer, the boarding establishment or groomer shall provide the animal with emergency veterinary treatment for the illness or injury. The consumer shall bear the reasonable and necessary costs of emergency veterinary treatment for any illness or injury occurring while the animal is in the custody of the boarding establishment or groomer. The boarding establishment or groomer shall pay for veterinary treatment of any injury that the animal sustains while at the establishment or under the care or custody of a groomer if the injury resulted from the establishment's or groomer's failure, whether accidental or intentional, to provide the care required by § 3.2-6503, or if the injury is a result of the actions of the boarding establishment or groomer. Boarding establishments and groomers shall not be required to bear the cost of veterinary treatment for injuries resulting from the animal's self-mutilation.

C. If an animal is seized from a boarding establishment or groomer because of the establishment's or groomer's failure to provide adequate food, water, shelter, exercise, and care as defined in § 3.2-6500 and required by § 3.2-6503 or because of any other violation of this chapter, the animal shall be returned to the rightful owner as soon as possible or, if the owner refuses to reclaim the animal, be impounded and disposition made pursuant to § 3.2-6569.

D. Violation of this section by a boarding establishment or groomer is a Class 1 misdemeanor.

History.
1993, c. 174, § 3.1-796.83:1; 1996, c. 249; 2008, c. 860.

§ 3.2-6519. Written notice of consumer remedies required to be supplied by boarding establishments; penalty.

A. A boarding establishment shall give the notice hereinafter set forth in writing to a consumer prior to the consumer's delivery of the animal to the boarding establishment. Such notice shall be embodied in a written document and shall state in ten-point boldfaced type the following:

NOTICE

The boarding of animals is subject to Article 4 (§ 3.2-6518 et seq.) of Chapter 65 of Title 3.2. If your animal becomes ill or injured while in the custody of the boarding establishment, the boarding establishment shall provide the animal with emergency veterinary treatment for the illness or injury.

The consumer shall bear the reasonable and necessary costs of emergency veterinary treatment for any illness or injury occurring while the animal is in the custody of the boarding establishment. The boarding establishment shall bear the expenses of veterinary treatment for any injury the animal sustains while at the boarding establishment if the injury resulted from the establishment's failure, whether accidental or intentional, to provide the care required by § 3.2-6503. Boarding establishments shall not be required to bear the cost of veterinary treatment for injuries resulting from the animal's self-mutilation.

B. In addition, the boarding establishment shall display the following notice, in ten-point boldfaced type, on a sign placed in a conspicuous location and manner at the boarding establishment's intake area:

PUBLIC NOTICE

THE BOARDING OF ANIMALS BY A BOARDING ESTABLISHMENT IS SUBJECT TO ARTICLE 4 (§ 3.2-6518 et seq.) OF CHAPTER 65 OF TITLE 3.2 OF THE CODE OF VIRGINIA. YOU HAVE SPECIFIC REMEDIES WHEN BOARDING ANIMALS IN THIS OR ANY OTHER BOARDING ESTABLISHMENT IN VIRGINIA. A COPY IS AVAILABLE IMMEDIATELY UPON REQUEST AND IS TO BE PRESENTED TO YOU AT THE TIME OF INTAKE IN THE FORM OF A WRITTEN DOCUMENT. IF YOU HAVE A COMPLAINT, YOU MAY CONTACT YOUR LOCAL LAW-ENFORCEMENT OFFICER OR THE VIRGINIA DEPARTMENT OF AGRICULTURE AND CONSUMER SERVICES, RICHMOND, VIRGINIA.

C. Failure to display or provide the consumer with the written notice as required by this section is a Class 3 misdemeanor.

History.

1993, c. 174, § 3.1-796.83:2; 1998, c. 817; 2008, c. 860.

§ 3.2-6520. Procedure for animals left unclaimed with veterinarian or boarding establishment after public notice; lien; sale.

Any animal not claimed by its owner from a licensed veterinarian or boarding establishment within 14 days after a letter of notice has been sent to the owner, by the veterinarian or boarding establishment, may be sold by the veterinarian or boarding establishment. The animal may be sold at public or private sale for fair compensation to a person capable of providing care consistent with this chapter. Any expense incurred by the veterinarian or boarding establishment becomes a lien on the animal and the proceeds of the sale shall first discharge this lien. Any balance of the proceeds shall be paid to the owner. If the owner cannot be found within the next ensuing 30 days, the balance shall be paid to the Literary Fund. If no purchaser is found, the animal may be offered for adoption or euthanized.

History.

1984, c. 492, § 29-213.45; 1987, c. 488, § 3.1-796.75; 1993, c. 174; 2008, c. 860.

ARTICLE 5.

RABIES CONTROL AND LICENSING OF DOGS AND CATS.

§ 3.2-6521. Rabies inoculation of companion animals; availability of certificate; rabies clinics.

A. The owner or custodian of all dogs and cats four months of age and older shall have such animal currently vaccinated for rabies by a licensed veterinarian or licensed veterinary technician who is under the immediate and direct supervision of a licensed veterinarian on the premises unless otherwise provided by regulations. The supervising veterinarian on the premises shall provide the owner or custodian of the dog or the cat with a rabies vaccination certificate or herd rabies vaccination certificate and shall keep a copy in his own files. The owner or custodian of the dog or the cat shall furnish within a reasonable period of time, upon the request of an animal control officer, humane investigator, law-enforcement officer, State Veterinarian's representative, or official of the Department of Health, the certificate of vaccination for such dog or cat. The vaccine used shall be licensed by the U.S. Department of Agriculture for use in that species. At the discretion of the local health director, a medical record from a licensed veterinary establishment reflecting a currently vaccinated status may serve as proof of vaccination.

B. All rabies clinics require the approval by the appropriate local health department and governing body. The licensed veterinarian who administers rabies vaccinations at the clinic shall (i) provide the owner or custodian a rabies vaccination certificate for each vaccinated animal and (ii) ensure that a licensed veterinary facility retains a copy of the rabies vaccination certificate. The sponsoring organization of a rabies clinic shall, upon the request of the owner or custodian, an animal control officer, a humane investigator, a law-enforcement officer, a State Veterinarian's representative, a licensed veterinarian, or an official of the Department of Health, provide the name and contact information of the licensed veterinary facility where a copy of the rabies vaccination certificate is retained. However, the county or city shall ensure that a clinic is conducted to serve its jurisdiction at least once every two years.

C. Vaccination subsequent to a summons to appear before a court for failure to do so shall not operate to relieve such owner from the penalties or court costs provided under § 16.1-69.48:1 or 17.1-275.7.

D. The Board of Health shall, by regulation, provide an exemption to the requirements of subsection A if an animal suffers from an underlying medical condition that is likely to result in a life-threatening condition in response to vaccination and such exemption would not risk public health and safety. For the purposes of § 3.2-6522, such exemption shall mean that the animal is considered not currently vaccinated for rabies. For the purposes of §§ 3.2-5902, 3.2-6526, and 3.2-6527, such exemption shall be considered in place of a current certificate of vaccination.

History.

1984, c. 492, § 29-213.67; 1987, c. 488, § 3.1-796.97; 1988, c. 538, § 3.1-796.97:1; 1992, c. 294; 1993, c. 817; 1994, c. 636; 1996, c. 351; 1998, c. 817; 2006, c. 836; 2008, c. 860; 2009, c. 756; 2010, cc. 182, 834; 2013, c. 286.

§ 3.2-6522. Rabid animals.

A. When there is sufficient reason to believe that the risk of exposure to rabies is elevated, the governing body of any locality may enact, and the local health director may recommend, an emergency ordinance that shall become effective immediately upon passage, requiring owners of all dogs and cats therein to keep the same confined on their premises unless leashed under restraint of the owner in such a manner that persons or animals will not be subject to the danger of being bitten by a rabid animal. Any such emergency ordinance enacted pursuant to the provisions of this section shall be operative for a period not to exceed 30 days unless renewed by the governing body of such locality in consultation with the local health director. The governing body of any locality shall also have the power and authority to pass ordinances restricting the running at large in their respective jurisdiction of dogs and cats that have not been inoculated or vaccinated against rabies and to provide penalties for the violation thereof.

B. Any dog or cat showing active signs of rabies or suspected of having rabies that is not known to have exposed a person, companion animal, or livestock to rabies shall be confined under competent observation for such a time as may be necessary to determine a diagnosis. If, in the discretion of the local health director, confinement is impossible or impracticable, such dog or cat shall be euthanized by one of the methods approved by the State Veterinarian as provided in § 3.2-6546. The disposition of other animals showing active signs of rabies shall be determined by the local health director and may include euthanasia and testing.

C. Every person having knowledge of the existence of an animal that is suspected to be rabid and that may have exposed a person, companion animal, or livestock to rabies shall report immediately to the local health department the existence of such animal, the place where seen, the owner's name, if known, and the signs suggesting rabies.

D. Any dog or cat for which no proof of current rabies vaccination is available and that may have been exposed to rabies through a bite, or through saliva or central nervous system tissue, in a fresh open wound or mucous membrane, by an animal suspected to be rabid shall be isolated in a public animal shelter, kennel, or enclosure approved by the local health department for a period not to exceed six months at the expense of the owner or custodian in a manner and by a date certain as determined by the local health director. A rabies vaccination shall be administered by a licensed veterinarian prior to release. Inactivated rabies vaccine may be administered at the beginning of isolation. Any dog or cat so bitten, or exposed to rabies through saliva or central nervous system tissue, in a fresh open wound or mucous membrane with proof of current vaccination, shall be revaccinated by a licensed veterinarian immediately following the exposure and shall be confined to the premises of the owner or custodian, or other site as may be approved by the local health department at the expense of the owner or custodian, for a period of 45 days. If the local health director determines that isolation is not feasible or maintained, such dog or cat shall be euthanized by one of the methods approved by the State Veterinarian as provided in § 3.2-6546. The disposition of such dogs or cats not so confined shall be at the discretion of the local health director.

E. At the discretion of the local health director, any animal that may have exposed a person shall be confined under competent observation for 10 days at the expense of the owner or custodian, unless the animal develops active signs of rabies, expires, or is euthanized before that time. A seriously injured or sick animal may be euthanized as provided in § 3.2-6546.

F. When any suspected rabid animal, other than a dog or cat, exposes or may have exposed a person to rabies through a bite, or through saliva or central nervous system tissue, in a fresh open wound or mucous membrane, decisions regarding the disposition of that animal shall be at the discretion of a local health director and may include euthanasia as provided in § 3.2-6546, or as directed by the state agency with jurisdiction over that species. When any animal, other than a dog or cat, is exposed or may have been exposed to rabies through a bite, or through saliva or central nervous system tissue, in a fresh open wound or mucous membrane, by an animal suspected to be rabid, decisions regarding the disposition of that newly exposed animal shall be at the discretion of a local health director.

G. When any animal may have exposed a person to rabies and subsequently expires due to illness or euthanasia, either within an observation period, where applicable, or as part of a public health investigation, its head or brain shall be sent to the Division of Consolidated Laboratory Services of the Department of General Services or be tested as directed by the local health department.

History.

1984, cc. 492, 527, § 29-213.68; 1987, c. 488, § 3.1-796.98; 1988, c. 538; 1991, c. 380; 2003, c. 479; 2008, c. 860; 2010, c. 834; 2014, c. 148.

§ 3.2-6523. Inoculation for rabies at public or private animal shelters.

Dogs and cats being adopted from a public or private animal shelter during the period an emergency ordinance is in force, as provided for in § 3.2-6522, may be inoculated for rabies by a certified animal technician at such shelter if the certified animal technician is under the immediate and direct supervision of a licensed veterinarian.

History.
1984, c. 384, § 29-213.68:1; 1987, c. 488, § 3.1-796.99; 2008, c. 860; 2014, c. 148.

§ 3.2-6524. Unlicensed dogs prohibited; ordinances for licensing cats.

A. It shall be unlawful for any person other than a releasing agency that has registered as such annually with local animal control to own a dog four months old or older in the Commonwealth unless such dog is licensed, as required by the provisions of this article.

B. The governing body of any locality may, by ordinance, prohibit any person other than a releasing agency that has registered as such annually with local animal control from owning a cat four months old or older within such locality unless such cat is licensed as provided by this article.

History.
1984, c. 492, § 29-213.55; 1987, c. 488, § 3.1-796.85; 1988, c. 538; 1993, c. 817; 2007, c. 640; 2008, c. 860.

§ 3.2-6525. Regulations to prevent spread of rabies.

A. The governing body of any locality may adopt such ordinances, regulations or other measures as may be deemed reasonably necessary to prevent the spread within its boundaries of the disease of rabies. Penalties may be provided for the violation of any such ordinances. If the ordinance declares the existence of an emergency, then the ordinance shall be in force upon passage.

B. The governing body of any locality may adopt an ordinance creating a program for the distribution of oral rabies vaccine within its boundaries to prevent the spread of rabies. An ordinance enacted pursuant to this subsection on or after July 1, 2010, shall be developed in consultation with the Department of Health and with written authorization from the Department of Game and Inland Fisheries in accordance with § 29.1-508.1 and shall contain the following provisions:

1. Notice shall be given to the owner or occupant of property prior to the entry upon the property for the purpose of the distribution of oral rabies vaccine or the use of any other methods to place oral rabies vaccine on the property. Notice shall be given by: (i) sending two letters by first-class mail, at successive intervals of not less than two weeks set forth in the ordinance; and (ii) printing a copy thereof, at least once, in a newspaper of general circulation in the locality concerned. Written notice shall be in a form approved by the governing body and shall include a description of the purpose for which entry upon the property is to be made, the time and method of rabies vaccine distribution at the property, and the submission deadline for requests by any owner or occupant of property who wishes to be excluded from the oral rabies vaccine distribution program.

2. The owner or occupant of property may refuse to allow the distribution of oral rabies vaccine upon such property. The ordinance shall establish procedures to be followed by any owner or occupant who wishes to be excluded from the oral rabies vaccine distribution program, including the time and method by which requests for nonparticipation must be received. If the governing body receives a request for nonparticipation by the owner or occupant of property for the distribution of oral rabies vaccine, no further action shall be taken to distribute oral vaccine, on such property for a period of one year.

Nothing in this subsection shall be construed to limit any authority for the distribution of oral rabies vaccine otherwise provided by law.

History.
1984, c. 492, § 29-213.69; 1987, c. 488, § 3.1-796.100; 2001, c. 674; 2008, c. 860; 2010, c. 834.

§ 3.2-6526. What dog or cat license shall consist of.

A. A dog or cat license shall consist of a license receipt and a metal tag. The tag shall be stamped or otherwise permanently marked to show the jurisdiction issuing the license and bear a serial number or other identifying information prescribed by the locality.

B. No license tag shall be issued for any dog or cat unless there is presented, to the treasurer or other officer of the locality, or other agent charged by law with the duty of issuing license tags for dogs and cats, satisfactory evidence that such dog or cat has been inoculated or vaccinated against rabies by a currently licensed veterinarian or currently licensed veterinary technician who was under the immediate and direct supervision of a licensed veterinarian on the premises.

History.
1984, c. 492, §§ 29-213.60, 29-213.67; 1987, c. 488, §§ 3.1-796.90, 3.1-796.97; 1993, c. 817; 1996, c. 351;1998, c. 394; 2006, c. 836; 2008, c. 860.

§ 3.2-6527. How to obtain license.

Any person may obtain a dog license or cat license if required by an ordinance adopted pursuant to subsection B of § 3.2-6524, by making oral or written application to the treasurer of the locality where such person resides, accompanied by the amount of license tax and current certificate of vaccination as required by this article or satisfactory evidence that such certificate has been obtained. The treasurer or other officer charged with the duty of issuing dog and cat licenses shall only have authority to license dogs and cats of resident owners or custodians who reside within the boundary limits of his county or city and may require information to this effect from any applicant. Upon receipt of proper application and current certificate of vaccination as required by this article or satisfactory evidence that such certificate has been obtained, the treasurer or other officer charged with the duty of issuing dog and cat licenses shall issue a license receipt for the amount on which he shall record the name and address of the owner or custodian, the date of payment, the year for which issued, the serial number of the tag, whether dog or cat, whether male or female, whether spayed or neutered, or whether a kennel, and deliver the metal license tags or plates provided for herein. The information thus received shall be retained by the treasurer, open to public inspection, during the period for which such license is valid. The treasurer may establish substations in convenient locations in the county or city and appoint agents for the collection of the license tax and issuance of such licenses.

History.

1984, c. 492, § 29-213.56; 1987, c. 488, § 3.1-796.86; 1991, c. 77; 1993, c. 817; 2006, c. 836; 2008, c. 860.

§ 3.2-6528. Amount of license tax.

The governing body of each county or city shall impose by ordinance a license tax on the ownership of dogs within its jurisdiction. The governing body of any locality that has adopted an ordinance pursuant to subsection B of § 3.2-6524 shall impose by ordinance a license tax on the ownership of cats within its jurisdiction. The governing body may establish different rates of taxation for ownership of female dogs, male dogs, spayed or neutered dogs, female cats, male cats, and spayed or neutered cats. The tax for each dog or cat shall not be less than $1 and not more than $10 for each year. If the dog or cat has been spayed, the tax shall not exceed the tax provided for a male dog or cat. Any ordinance may provide for a license tax for kennels of 10, 20, 30, 40, or 50 dogs or cats not to exceed $50 for any one such block of kennels.

No license tax shall be levied on any dog that is trained and serves as a guide dog for a blind person, that is trained and serves as a hearing dog for a deaf or hearing-impaired person, or that is trained and serves as a service dog for a mobility-impaired or otherwise disabled person.

As used in this section, "hearing dog," "mobility-impaired person," "otherwise disabled person," and "service dog" have the same meanings as assigned in § 51.5-40.1.

History.

1984, cc. 248, 492, § 29-213.57; 1986, c. 169; 1987, c. 488, § 3.1-796.87; 1993, c. 817; 1994, c. 108; 2006, c. 836; 2008, c. 860; 2014, c. 616.

§ 3.2-6529. Veterinarians to provide treasurer with rabies certificate information; civil penalty.

A. Each veterinarian who vaccinates a dog against rabies or directs a veterinary technician in his employ to vaccinate a dog against rabies shall provide the owner a copy of the rabies vaccination certificate. The veterinarian shall forward within 45 days a copy of the rabies vaccination certificate or the relevant information contained in such certificate to the treasurer of the locality where the vaccination occurs.

The rabies vaccination certificate shall include at a minimum the signature of the veterinarian, the animal owner's name and address, the species of the animal, the sex, the age, the color, the primary breed, whether or not the animal is spayed or neutered, the vaccination number, and expiration date. The rabies vaccination certificate shall indicate the locality where the animal resides.

B. It shall be the responsibility of the owner of each vaccinated animal that is not already licensed to apply for a license for the vaccinated dog. Beginning January 1, 2008, if the treasurer determines, from review of the rabies vaccination information provided by veterinarians, that the owner of an unlicensed dog has failed to apply for a license within 90 days of the date of vaccination, the treasurer shall transmit an application to the owner and request the owner to submit a completed application and pay the appropriate fee. Upon receipt of the completed application and payment of the license fee, the treasurer or other agent charged with the duty of issuing the dog licenses shall issue a license receipt and a permanent tag. The treasurer shall retain only the information that is required to be collected and open to public inspection pursuant to the provisions of this Chapter and shall forthwith destroy any rabies vaccination certificate or other similar record transmitted by a veterinarian to a treasurer pursuant to this section.

The treasurer shall remit any rabies vaccination certificate received for any animal owned by an individual residing in another locality to the local treasurer for the appropriate locality.

Any veterinarian that willfully fails to provide the treasurer of any locality with a copy of the rabies vaccination certificate or the information contained in such certificate may be subject to a civil penalty not to exceed $10 per certificate. Monies raised pursuant to this subsection shall be placed in the locality's general fund for the purpose of animal control activities including spay or neuter programs.

History.

2006, c. 836, § 3.1-796.87:1; 2007, c. 270; 2008, cc. 16, 860.

§ 3.2-6530. When license tax payable.

A. The license tax as prescribed in § 3.2-6528 is due not later than 30 days after a dog or cat has reached the age of four months, or not later than 30 days after an owner acquires a dog or cat four months of age or older and each year thereafter.

B. Licensing periods for individual dogs and cats may be equal to and may run concurrently with the rabies vaccination effective period. Any kennel license tax prescribed pursuant to § 3.2-6528 shall be due on January 1 and not later than January 31 of each year.

History.
1984, cc. 248, 492, § 29-213.58; 1986, c. 169; 1987, c. 488, § 3.1-796.88; 1990, c. 365; 1993, c. 817; 2006, c. 836; 2008, c. 860.

§ 3.2-6531. Displaying receipts; dogs to wear tags.

Dog and cat license receipts shall be carefully preserved by the licensees and exhibited promptly on request for inspection by any animal control officer or other officer. Dog license tags shall be securely fastened to a substantial collar by the owner or custodian and worn by such dog. It shall be unlawful for the owner to permit any licensed dog four months old or older to run or roam at large at any time without a license tag. The owner of the dog may remove the collar and license tag required by this section when: (i) the dog is engaged in lawful hunting; (ii) the dog is competing in a dog show; (iii) the dog has a skin condition that would be exacerbated by the wearing of a collar; (iv) the dog is confined; or (v) the dog is under the immediate control of its owner.

History.
1984, c. 492, § 29-213.62; 1987, c. 488, § 3.1-796.92; 1990, c. 365; 1993, c. 817; 1998, c. 817; 2008, c. 860.

§ 3.2-6532. Duplicate license tags.

If a dog or cat license tag is lost, destroyed or stolen, the owner or custodian shall at once apply to the treasurer or his agent who issued the original license for a duplicate license tag, presenting the original license receipt. Upon affidavit of the owner or custodian before the treasurer or his agent that the original license tag has been lost, destroyed or stolen, he shall issue a duplicate license tag that the owner or custodian shall immediately affix to the collar of the dog. The treasurer or his agent shall endorse the number of the duplicate and the date issued on the face of the original license receipt. The fee for a duplicate tag for any dog or cat shall be $1.

History.
1984, c. 492, § 29-213.61; 1987, c. 488, § 3.1-796.91; 1993, c. 817; 2008, c. 860.

§ 3.2-6533. Effect of dog or cat not wearing a license tag as evidence.

Any dog or cat not wearing a collar bearing a valid license tag shall prima facie be deemed to be unlicensed, and in any proceedings under this chapter the burden of proof of the fact that such dog or cat has been licensed, or is otherwise not required to bear a tag at the time, shall be on the owner of the dog or cat.

History.
1984, c. 492, § 29-213.59; 1987, c. 488, § 3.1-796.89; 1993, c. 817; 2006, c. 836; 2008, c. 860.

§ 3.2-6534. Disposition of funds.

Unless otherwise provided by ordinance of the local governing body, the treasurer of each locality shall keep all moneys collected by him for dog and cat license taxes in a separate account from all other funds collected by him. The locality shall use the funds for the following purposes:

1. The salary and expenses of the animal control officer and necessary staff;
2. The care and maintenance of a public animal shelter;
3. The maintenance of a rabies control program;
4. Payments as a bounty to any person neutering or spaying a dog up to the amount of one year of the license tax as provided by ordinance;
5. Payments for compensation as provided in § 3.2-6553; and
6. Efforts to promote sterilization of dogs and cats.

Any part or all of any surplus remaining in such account on December 31 of any year may be transferred by the governing body of such locality into the general fund of such locality.

History.
1984, c. 492, § 29-213.70; 1987, c. 488, § 3.1-796.101; 1993, c. 959; 1998, c. 817; 2008, c. 860; 2014, c. 148.

§ 3.2-6535. Supplemental funds.

Localities may supplement the dog and cat license tax fund with other funds as they consider appropriate. Localities shall supplement the dog and cat license tax fund to the extent necessary to provide for the salary and expenses of the animal control officer and staff and the care and maintenance of a public animal shelter as provided in subdivisions 1 and 2 of § 3.2-6534.

History.
1984, c. 492, § 29-213.71; 1987, c. 488, § 3.1-796.102; 1998, c. 817; 2008, c. 860; 2014, c. 148.

§ 3.2-6536. Payment of license tax subsequent to summons.

Payment of the license tax subsequent to a summons to appear before a court for failure to pay the license tax within the time required shall not operate to relieve such owner from the penalties or court costs provided under § 16.1-69.48:1 or 17.1-275.7.

History.
1984, c. 492, § 29-213.72; 1987, c. 488, § 3.1-796.103; 2008, c. 860; 2009, c. 756.

ARTICLE 6. AUTHORITY OF LOCAL GOVERNING BODIES.

§ 3.2-6537. Ordinances; penalties.

The governing body of any locality may, by ordinance, require a person operating a pet shop or operating as a dealer in companion animals to obtain a permit. Such local governing body may charge no more than $50 per year for such permit. The revenues derived therefrom shall be used for the administration and enforcement of such ordinance.

The aforementioned ordinance may provide: (i) that records be kept by the permittees as are deemed necessary; (ii) for public hearing prior to issuance, renewal or revocation of any such permit; or (iii) for the denial of issuance, denial of renewal or for the revocation of such permit for fraudulent practices or inhumane treatment of the animals dealt with by the permittee.

The ordinance may provide for either a criminal penalty not to exceed a Class 3 misdemeanor or a civil penalty not to exceed $500 for any violation of the ordinance. Any civil penalties collected shall be deposited by the local treasurer pursuant to § 3.2-6534.

History.
1984, c. 492, § 29-213.54; 1987, c. 488, § 3.1-796.84; 2005, c. 307; 2008, c. 860.

§ 3.2-6538. Governing body of any locality may prohibit dogs from running at large.

The governing body of any locality may prohibit the running at large of all or any category of dogs in all or any designated portion of such locality during such months as they may designate. Governing bodies may also require that dogs be confined, restricted or penned up during such periods. For the purpose of this section, a dog shall be deemed to run at large while roaming, running or self-hunting off the property of its owner or custodian and not under its owner's or custodian's immediate control. Any person who permits his dog to run at large, or remain unconfined, unrestricted or not penned up shall be deemed to have violated the provisions of this section.

History.
1984, c. 492, § 29-213.63; 1987, c. 488, § 3.1-796.93; 2008, c. 860.

§ 3.2-6539. Ordinance requiring dogs to be kept on leash.

The governing body of any locality may adopt ordinances requiring that dogs within any such locality be kept on a leash or otherwise restrained and may, by resolution directed to the circuit court, request the court to order a referendum as to whether any such ordinance so adopted shall become effective. Such referendum shall be held and conducted, and the results thereof ascertained and certified in accordance with § 24.2-684. The court shall require the governing body to give appropriate notice of the time, place and subject matter of such referendum.

The results of the referendum shall not be binding upon the governing body of the locality but may be used in ascertaining the sense of the voters.

History.
1984, c. 492, § 29-213.65; 1987, c. 488, § 3.1-796.95; 2008, c. 860.

§ 3.2-6540. Control of dangerous dogs; penalties.

A. As used in this section:

"Dangerous dog" means a canine or canine crossbreed that has bitten, attacked, or inflicted injury on a person or companion animal that is a dog or cat, or killed a companion animal that is a dog or cat. When a dog attacks or bites a companion animal that is a dog or cat, the attacking or biting dog shall not be deemed dangerous (i) if no serious physical injury as determined by a licensed veterinarian has occurred to the dog or cat as a result of the attack or bite; (ii) if both animals are owned by the same person; (iii) if such attack occurs on the property of the attacking or biting dog's owner or custodian; or (iv) for other good cause as determined by the court. No dog shall be found to be a dangerous dog as a result of biting, attacking, or inflicting injury on a dog or cat while engaged with an owner or custodian as part of lawful hunting or participating in an organized, lawful dog handling event. No dog that has bitten, attacked, or inflicted injury on a person shall be found to be a dangerous dog if the court determines, based on the totality of the evidence before it, that the dog is not dangerous or a threat to the community.

B. Any law-enforcement officer or animal control officer who has reason to believe that a canine or canine crossbreed within his jurisdiction is a dangerous dog shall apply to a magistrate serving the jurisdiction for the issuance of a summons requiring the owner or custodian, if known, to appear before a general district court at a specified time. The summons shall advise the owner of the nature of the proceeding and the matters at issue. If a law-enforcement officer successfully makes an application for the issuance of a summons, he shall contact the local animal control officer and inform him of the location of the dog and the relevant facts pertaining to his belief that the dog is dangerous. The animal control officer shall confine the animal until such time as evidence shall be heard and a verdict rendered. If the animal control officer determines that the owner or custodian can confine the animal in a manner that protects the public safety, he may permit the owner or custodian to confine the animal until such time as evidence shall be heard and a verdict rendered. The court, through its contempt powers, may compel the owner, custodian, or harborer of the animal to produce the animal. If, after hearing the evidence, the court finds that the animal is a dangerous dog, the court shall order the animal's owner to comply with the provisions of this section. The court, upon finding the animal to be a dangerous dog, may order the owner, custodian, or harborer thereof to pay restitution for actual damages to any person injured by the animal or whose companion animal was injured or killed by the animal. The court, in its discretion, may also order the owner to pay all reasonable expenses incurred in caring and providing for such dangerous dog from the time the animal is taken into custody until such time as the animal is disposed of or returned to the owner. The procedure for appeal and trial shall be the same as provided by law for misdemeanors. Trial by jury shall be as provided in Article 4 (§ 19.2-260 et seq.) of Chapter 15 of Title 19.2. The Commonwealth shall be required to prove its case beyond a reasonable doubt.

C. No canine or canine crossbreed shall be found to be a dangerous dog solely because it is a particular breed, nor is the ownership of a particular breed of canine or canine crossbreed prohibited. No animal shall be found to be a dangerous dog if the threat, injury, or damage was sustained by a person who was (i) committing, at the time, a crime upon the premises occupied by the animal's owner or custodian; (ii) committing, at the time, a willful trespass upon the premises occupied by the animal's owner or custodian; or (iii) provoking, tormenting, or physically abusing the animal, or can be shown to have repeatedly provoked, tormented, abused, or assaulted the animal at other times. No police dog that was engaged in the performance of its duties as such at the time of the acts complained of shall be found to be a dangerous dog. No animal that, at the time of the acts complained of, was responding to pain or injury, or was protecting itself, its kennel, its offspring, a person, or its owner's or custodian's property, shall be found to be a dangerous dog.

D. If the owner of an animal found to be a dangerous dog is a minor, the custodial parent or legal guardian shall be responsible for complying with all requirements of this section.

E. The owner of any animal found to be a dangerous dog shall, within 45 days of such finding, obtain a dangerous dog registration certificate from the local animal control officer or treasurer for a fee of $150, in addition to other fees that may be authorized by law. The local animal control officer or treasurer shall also provide the owner with a uniformly designed tag that identifies the animal as a dangerous dog. The owner shall affix the tag to the animal's collar and ensure that the animal wears the collar and tag at all times. By January 31 of each year, until such time as the dangerous dog is deceased, all certificates obtained pursuant to this subsection shall be updated and renewed for a fee of $85 and in the same manner as the initial certificate was obtained. The animal control officer shall post registration information on the Virginia Dangerous Dog Registry.

F. All dangerous dog registration certificates or renewals thereof required to be obtained under this section shall only be issued to persons 18 years of age or older who present satisfactory evidence (i) of the animal's current rabies vaccination, if applicable; (ii) that the animal has been neutered or spayed; and (iii) that the animal is and will be confined in a proper enclosure or is and will be confined inside the owner's residence or is and will be muzzled and confined in the owner's fenced-in yard until the proper enclosure is constructed. In addition, owners who apply for certificates or renewals thereof under this section shall not be issued a certificate or renewal thereof unless they present satisfactory evidence that (a) their residence is and will continue to be posted with clearly visible signs warning both minors and adults of the presence of a dangerous dog on the property and (b) the animal has been permanently identified by means of electronic implantation. All certificates or renewals thereof required to be obtained under this section shall only be issued to persons who present satisfactory evidence that the owner has liability insurance coverage, to the value of at least $100,000, that covers animal bites. The owner may obtain and maintain a bond in surety, in lieu of liability insurance, to the value of at least $100,000.

G. While on the property of its owner, an animal found to be a dangerous dog shall be confined indoors or in a securely enclosed and locked structure of sufficient height and design to prevent its escape or direct contact with or entry by minors, adults, or other animals. While so confined within the structure, the animal shall be provided for according to § 3.2-6503. When off its owner's property, an animal found to be a dangerous dog shall be kept on a leash and muzzled in such a manner as not to cause injury to the animal or interfere with the animal's vision or respiration, but so as to prevent it from biting a person or another animal.

H. The owner shall cause the local animal control officer to be promptly notified of (i) the names, addresses, and telephone numbers of all owners; (ii) all of the means necessary to locate the owner and the dog at any time; (iii) any complaints or incidents of attack by the dog upon any person or cat or dog; (iv) any claims made or lawsuits brought as a result of any attack; (v) chip identification information; (vi) proof of insurance or surety bond; and (vii) the death of the dog.

I. After an animal has been found to be a dangerous dog, the animal's owner shall immediately, upon learning of same, cause the local animal control authority to be notified if the animal (i) is loose or unconfined; (ii) bites a person or attacks another animal; or (iii) is sold, is given away, or dies. Any owner of a dangerous dog who relocates to a new address shall, within 10 days of relocating, provide written notice to the appropriate local animal control authority for the old address from which the animal has moved and the new address to which the animal has been moved.

J. Any owner or custodian of a canine or canine crossbreed or other animal is guilty of a:

1. Class 2 misdemeanor if the canine or canine crossbreed previously declared a dangerous dog pursuant to this section, when such declaration arose out of a separate and distinct incident, attacks and injures or kills a cat or dog that is a companion animal belonging to another person;

2. Class 1 misdemeanor if the canine or canine crossbreed previously declared a dangerous dog pursuant to this section, when such declaration arose out of a separate and distinct incident, bites a human being or attacks a human being causing bodily injury; or

3. Class 6 felony if any owner or custodian whose willful act or omission in the care, control, or containment of a canine, canine crossbreed, or other animal is so gross, wanton, and culpable as to show a reckless disregard for human life, and is the proximate cause of such dog or other animal attacking and causing serious bodily injury to any person.

The provisions of this subsection shall not apply to any animal that, at the time of the acts complained of, was responding to pain or injury, or was protecting itself, its kennel, its offspring, a person, or its owner's or custodian's property, or when the animal is a police dog that is engaged in the performance of its duties at the time of the attack.

K. The owner of any animal that has been found to be a dangerous dog who willfully fails to comply with the requirements of this section is guilty of a Class 1 misdemeanor.

Whenever an owner or custodian of an animal found to be a dangerous dog is charged with a violation of this section, the animal control officer shall confine the dangerous dog until such time as evidence shall be heard and a verdict rendered. The court, through its contempt powers, may compel the owner, custodian, or harborer of the animal to produce the animal.

Upon conviction, the court may (i) order the dangerous dog to be disposed of by a local governing body pursuant to § 3.2-6562 or (ii) grant the owner up to 45 days to comply with the requirements of this section, during which time the dangerous dog shall remain in the custody of the animal control officer until compliance has been verified. If the owner fails to achieve compliance within the time specified by the court, the court shall order the dangerous dog to be disposed of by a local governing body pursuant to § 3.2-6562. The court, in its discretion, may order the owner to pay all reasonable expenses incurred in caring and providing for such dangerous dog from the time the animal is taken into custody until such time that the animal is disposed of or returned to the owner.

L. All fees collected pursuant to this section, less the costs incurred by the animal control authority in producing and distributing the certificates and tags required by this section and fees due to the State Veterinarian for maintenance of the Virginia Dangerous Dog Registry, shall be paid into a special dedicated fund in the treasury of the locality for the purpose of paying the expenses of any training course required under § 3.2-6556.

M. The governing body of any locality may enact an ordinance parallel to this statute regulating dangerous dogs. No locality may impose a felony penalty for violation of such ordinances.

History.

1993, c. 977, § 3.1-796.93:1; 1994, c. 115; 1997, cc. 582, 892; 1998, c. 817; 2000, cc. 11, 727; 2003, cc. 785, 841; 2006, cc. 837, 864, 898; 2008, cc. 360, 551, 691, 860; 2009, c. 377; 2012, cc. 107, 236; 2013, cc. 58, 732.

§ 3.2-6540.1. Vicious dogs; penalties.

A. As used in this section:

"Serious injury" means an injury having a reasonable potential to cause death or any injury other than a sprain or strain, including serious disfigurement, serious impairment of health, or serious impairment of bodily function and requiring significant medical attention.

"Vicious dog" means a canine or canine crossbreed that has (i) killed a person, (ii) inflicted serious injury to a person, or (iii) continued to exhibit the behavior that resulted in a previous finding by a court or, on or before July 1, 2006, by an animal control officer as authorized by ordinance that it is a dangerous dog, provided that its owner has been given notice of that finding.

B. Any law-enforcement officer or animal control officer who has reason to believe that a canine or canine crossbreed within his jurisdiction is a vicious dog shall apply to a magistrate serving the jurisdiction for the issuance of a summons requiring the owner or custodian, if known, to appear before a general district court at a specified time. The summons shall advise the owner of the nature of the proceeding and the matters at issue. If a law-enforcement officer successfully makes an application for the issuance of a summons, he shall contact the local animal control officer and inform him of the location of the dog and the relevant facts pertaining to his belief that the dog is vicious. The animal control officer shall confine the animal until such time as evidence shall be heard and a verdict rendered. The court, through its contempt powers, may compel the owner, custodian, or harborer of the animal to produce the animal. If, after hearing the evidence, the court finds that the animal is a vicious dog, the court shall order the animal euthanized in accordance with the provisions of § 3.2-6562. The court, upon finding the animal to be a vicious dog, may order the owner, custodian, or harborer thereof to pay restitution for actual damages to any person injured by the animal or to the estate of any person killed by the animal. The court, in its discretion, may also order the owner to pay all reasonable expenses incurred in caring and providing for such vicious dog from the time the animal is taken into custody until such time as the animal is disposed of. The procedure for appeal and trial shall be the same as provided by law for misdemeanors. Trial by jury shall be as provided in Article 4 (§ 19.2-260 et seq.) of Chapter 15 of Title 19.2. The Commonwealth shall be required to prove its case beyond a reasonable doubt.

C. No canine or canine crossbreed shall be found to be a vicious dog solely because it is a particular breed, nor is the ownership of a particular breed of canine or canine crossbreed prohibited. No animal shall be found to be a vicious dog if the threat, injury, or damage was sustained by a person who was (i) committing, at the time, a crime upon the premises occupied by the animal's owner or custodian; (ii) committing, at the time, a willful trespass upon the premises occupied by the animal's owner or custodian; or (iii) provoking, tormenting, or physically abusing the animal, or can be shown to have repeatedly provoked, tormented, abused, or assaulted the animal at other times. No police dog that was engaged in the performance of its duties as such at the time of the acts complained of shall be found to be a vicious dog. No animal that, at the time of the acts complained of, was responding to pain or injury or was protecting itself, its kennel, its offspring, a person, or its owner's or custodian's property, shall be found to be a vicious dog.

D. Any owner or custodian of a canine or canine crossbreed or other animal whose willful act or omission in the care, control, or containment of a canine, canine crossbreed, or other animal is so gross, wanton, and culpable as to show a reckless disregard for human life and is the proximate cause of such dog or other animal attacking and causing serious injury to any person is guilty of a Class 6 felony. The provisions of this subsection shall not apply to any animal that, at the time of the acts complained of, was responding to pain or injury or was protecting itself, its kennel, its offspring, a person, or its owner's or custodian's property, or when the animal is a police dog that is engaged in the performance of its duties at the time of the attack.

E. The governing body of any locality may enact an ordinance parallel to this statute regulating vicious dogs. No locality may impose a felony penalty for violation of such ordinances.

History.
2013, cc. 58, 732.

§ 3.2-6541. Authority to prohibit training of attack dogs.

Fairfax County may enact an ordinance that prohibits persons from training dogs on residential property to attack. As used in this section, "attack" means to attack or respond aggressively, either with or without command. Any such ordinance shall exempt from its provisions the training of dogs owned by any person who resides on the property.

History.
1999, c. 848, § 3.1-796.93:2; 2008, c. 860.

§ 3.2-6542. Establishment of Dangerous Dog Registry.

The Commissioner shall establish the Virginia Dangerous Dog Registry to be maintained by the Department, Office of Animal Care and Health Policy. The State Veterinarian shall maintain information provided and posted by animal control officers or other such officials statewide on a website. All information collected for the Dangerous Dog Registry shall be available to animal control officers via the website. Registration information shall include the name of the animal, a photograph, sex, age, weight, primary breed, secondary breed, color and markings, whether spayed or neutered, the acts that resulted in the dog being designated as dangerous and associated trial docket information, microchip or tattoo number, address where the animal is maintained, name of the owner, address of the owner, telephone numbers of the owner, and a statement that the owner has complied with the provisions of the dangerous dog order. The address of the owner along with the name and breed of the dangerous dog, the acts that resulted in the dog being deemed dangerous, and information necessary to access court records of the adjudication shall be available to the general public. By January 31 of each year, until such time as the dangerous dog is deceased, the owner shall submit to an animal control officer or other designated local official of the county or city in which he currently resides a renewal registration that shall include all information contained in the original registration and any updates. The owner shall verify the information is accurate by annual resubmissions. The animal control officer or other such official shall post any updates on the website. In the event that the dangerous dog is moved to a different location, or contact information for the owner changes in any way at any time, the owner shall submit a renewal containing the address of the new location or other updated information within 10 days of such move or change to an animal control officer or other such official for the new location. There shall be no charge for any updated information provided between renewals. Each county and city shall submit to the

State Veterinarian by January 31 of each year $90 for each dangerous dog it initially registered and $25 for each dangerous dog for which it renewed registration within the previous calendar year. Any funds collected pursuant to this section shall be used by the State Veterinarian to maintain the registry and website. The website list shall be known as the Virginia Dangerous Dog Registry.

Actions of the Department relating to the establishment, operation, and maintenance of the Virginia Dangerous Dog Registry under this section shall be exempt from the provisions of the Administrative Process Act (§ 2.2-4000 et seq.).

Copies of all records, documents, and other papers pertaining to the Dangerous Dog Registry that are duly certified and authenticated in writing on the face of such documents to be true copies by the State Veterinarian or the Dangerous Dog Registry administrator shall be received as evidence with like effect as the original records, documents, or other papers in all courts of the Commonwealth.

History.

2006, cc. 837, 864, 898, § 3.1-796.93:3; 2008, c. 860; 2009, c. 354; 2012, cc. 107, 236.

§ 3.2-6543. Governing body of any locality may adopt certain ordinances.

A. The governing body of any locality of the Commonwealth may adopt, and make more stringent, ordinances that parallel §§ 3.2-6521 through 3.2-6539, 3.2-6546 through 3.2-6555, 3.2-6562, 3.2-6569, 3.2-6570, 3.2-6574 through 3.2-6580, and 3.2-6585 through 3.2-6590. Any town may choose to adopt by reference any ordinance of the surrounding county adopted under this section to be applied within its town limits, in lieu of adopting an ordinance of its own.

Any funds collected pursuant to the enforcement of ordinances adopted pursuant to the provisions of this section may be used for the purpose of defraying the costs of local animal control, including efforts to promote sterilization of cats and dogs.

B. Any locality may, by ordinance, establish uniform schedules of civil penalties for violations of specific provisions of ordinances adopted pursuant to this section. Civil penalties may not be imposed for violations of ordinances that parallel § 3.2-6570. Designation of a particular violation for a civil penalty shall be in lieu of criminal sanctions and preclude prosecution of such violation as a criminal misdemeanor. The schedule for civil penalties shall be uniform for each type of specified violation and the penalty for any one violation shall not be more than $150. Imposition of civil penalties shall not preclude an action for injunctive, declaratory or other equitable relief. Moneys raised pursuant to this subsection shall be placed in the locality's general fund.

An animal control officer or law-enforcement officer may issue a summons for a violation. Any person summoned or issued a ticket for a scheduled violation may make an appearance in person or in writing by mail to the department of finance or the treasurer of the locality issuing the summons or ticket prior to the date fixed for trial in court. Any person so appearing may enter a waiver of trial, admit liability, and pay the civil penalty established for the offense charged.

History.

1976, c. 182, § 15.1-29.1:1; 1984, c. 492, § 29-213.64; 1987, c. 488, § 3.1-796.94; 1993, c. 959; 1994, cc. 115, 630; 1995, c. 832; 1997, c. 587; 1998, c. 817; 2005, c. 304; 2008, c. 860; 2009, c. 107.

§ 3.2-6544. Regulation of keeping of animals and fowl.

A. Any locality may, for the preservation of public health, regulate by ordinance the keeping of animals or fowl, other than dogs and cats, within a certain distance of residences or other buildings or wells, springs, streams, creeks, or brooks, and provide that all or certain of such animals shall not be kept within certain areas.

B. Any locality may, by ordinance, prohibit cruelty to and abuse of animals and fowl; and may regulate or prohibit the running at large and the keeping of animals and fowl and provide for the impounding and confiscation of any such animal or fowl found at large or kept in violation of such regulations. Any such ordinance may require that owners of any exotic or poisonous animal found running at large pay a fee to cover the locality's actual cost in locating and capturing or otherwise disposing of the animal.

History.

Code 1950 §§ 15-20.1, 15-20.2; 1952, c. 694; 1954, c. 94; 1962, c. 623, §§ 15.1-517, 15.1-870; 1997, cc. 411, 587, § 3.1-796.94:1; 1999, c. 663; 2008, c. 860.

§ 3.2-6545. Regulation of sale of animals procured from animal shelters.

Any locality that maintains or supports, in whole or in part, a public or private animal shelter may by ordinance provide that no person who acquires an animal from such shelter shall be able to sell the animal within a period of six months from the time the animal is acquired from the shelter. Violation of the ordinance is a Class 1 misdemeanor.

History.

1972, c. 347, § 15.1-517.1; 1997, c. 587, § 3.1-796.94:2; 2008, c. 860; 2014, c. 148.

§ 3.2-6546. County or city public animal shelters; confinement and disposition of animals; affiliation with foster care providers; penalties; injunctive relief.

A. For purposes of this section:

"Animal" shall not include agricultural animals.

"Rightful owner" means a person with a right of property in the animal.

B. The governing body of each county or city shall maintain or cause to be maintained a public animal shelter and shall require dogs running at large without the tag required by § 3.2-6531 or in violation of an ordinance passed pursuant to § 3.2-6538 to be confined therein. Nothing in this section shall be construed to prohibit confinement of other companion animals in such a shelter. The governing body of any county or city need not own the facility required by this section but may contract for its establishment with a private group or in conjunction with one or more other local governing bodies. The governing body shall require that:

1. The public animal shelter shall be accessible to the public at reasonable hours during the week;

2. The public animal shelter shall obtain a signed statement from each of its directors, operators, staff, or animal caregivers specifying that each individual has never been convicted of animal cruelty, neglect, or abandonment, and each shelter shall update such statement as changes occur;

3. If a person contacts the public animal shelter inquiring about a lost companion animal, the shelter shall advise the person if the companion animal is confined at the shelter or if a companion animal of similar description is confined at the shelter;

4. The public animal shelter shall maintain a written record of the information on each companion animal submitted to the shelter by a private animal shelter in accordance with subsection D of § 3.2-6548 for a period of 30 days from the date the information is received by the shelter. If a person contacts the shelter inquiring about a lost companion animal, the shelter shall check its records and make available to such person any information submitted by a private animal shelter or allow such person inquiring about a lost animal to view the written records;

5. The public animal shelter shall maintain a written record of the information on each companion animal submitted to the shelter by a releasing agency other than a public or private animal shelter in accordance with subdivision F 2 of § 3.2-6549 for a period of 30 days from the date the information is received by the shelter. If a person contacts the shelter inquiring about a lost companion animal, the shelter shall check its records and make available to such person any information submitted by such releasing agency or allow such person inquiring about a lost companion animal to view the written records; and

6. The public animal shelter shall maintain a written record of the information on each companion animal submitted to the shelter by an individual in accordance with subdivision A 2 of § 3.2-6551 for a period of 30 days from the date the information is received by the shelter. If a person contacts the shelter inquiring about a lost companion animal, the shelter shall check its records and make available to such person any information submitted by the individual or allow such person inquiring about a lost companion animal to view the written records.

C. An animal confined pursuant to this section shall be kept for a period of not less than five days, such period to commence on the day immediately following the day the animal is initially confined in the facility, unless sooner claimed by the rightful owner thereof.

The operator or custodian of the public animal shelter shall make a reasonable effort to ascertain whether the animal has a collar, tag, license, tattoo, or other form of identification. If such identification is found on the animal, the animal shall be held for an additional five days, unless sooner claimed by the rightful owner. If the rightful owner of the animal can be readily identified, the operator or custodian of the shelter shall make a reasonable effort to notify the owner of the animal's confinement within the next 48 hours following its confinement.

If any animal confined pursuant to this section is claimed by its rightful owner, such owner may be charged with the actual expenses incurred in keeping the animal impounded. In addition to this and any other fees that might be levied, the locality may, after a public hearing, adopt an ordinance to charge the owner of an animal a fee for impoundment and increased fees for subsequent impoundments of the same animal.

D. If an animal confined pursuant to this section has not been claimed upon expiration of the appropriate holding period as provided by subsection C, it shall be deemed abandoned and become the property of the public animal shelter.

Such animal may be euthanized in accordance with the methods approved by the State Veterinarian or disposed of by the methods set forth in subdivisions 1 through 5. No shelter shall release more than two animals or a family of animals during any 30-day period to any one person under subdivisions 2, 3, or 4.

1. Release to any humane society, public or private animal shelter, or other releasing agency within the Commonwealth, provided that each humane society, animal shelter, or other releasing agency obtains a signed statement from each of its directors, operators, staff, or animal caregivers specifying that each individual has never been convicted of animal cruelty, neglect, or abandonment and updates such statements as changes occur;

2. Adoption by a resident of the county or city where the shelter is operated and who will pay the required license fee, if any, on such animal, provided that such resident has read and signed a statement specifying that he has never been convicted of animal cruelty, neglect, or abandonment;

3. Adoption by a resident of an adjacent political subdivision of the Commonwealth, if the resident has read and signed a statement specifying that he has never been convicted of animal cruelty, neglect, or abandonment;

4. Adoption by any other person, provided that such person has read and signed a statement specifying that he has never been convicted of animal cruelty, neglect, or abandonment and provided that no dog or cat may be adopted by any person who is not a resident of the county or city where the shelter is operated, or of an adjacent political subdivision, unless the dog or cat is first sterilized, and the shelter may require that the sterilization be done at the expense of the person adopting the dog or cat; or

5. Release for the purposes of adoption or euthanasia only, to an animal shelter, or any other releasing agency located in and lawfully operating under the laws of another state, provided that such animal shelter, or other releasing agency: (i) maintains records that would comply with § 3.2-6557; (ii) requires that adopted dogs and cats be sterilized; (iii) obtains a signed statement from each of its directors, operators, staff, and animal caregivers specifying that each individual has never been convicted of animal cruelty, neglect, or abandonment, and updates such statement as changes occur; and (iv) has provided to the public or private animal shelter or other releasing agency within the Commonwealth a statement signed by an authorized representative specifying the entity's compliance with clauses (i) through (iii), and the provisions of adequate care and performance of humane euthanasia, as necessary in accordance with the provisions of this chapter.

For purposes of recordkeeping, release of an animal by a public animal shelter to a public or private animal shelter or other releasing agency shall be considered a transfer and not an adoption. If the animal is not first sterilized, the responsibility for sterilizing the animal transfers to the receiving entity.

Any proceeds deriving from the gift, sale, or delivery of such animals shall be paid directly to the treasurer of the locality. Any proceeds deriving from the gift, sale, or delivery of such animals by a public or private animal shelter or other releasing agency shall be paid directly to the clerk or treasurer of the animal shelter or other releasing agency for the expenses of the society and expenses incident to any agreement concerning the disposing of such animal. No part of the proceeds shall accrue to any individual except for the aforementioned purposes.

E. Nothing in this section shall prohibit the immediate euthanasia of a critically injured, critically ill, or unweaned animal for humane purposes. Any animal euthanized pursuant to the provisions of this chapter shall be euthanized by one of the methods prescribed or approved by the State Veterinarian.

F. Nothing in this section shall prohibit the immediate euthanasia or disposal by the methods listed in subdivisions 1 through 5 of subsection D of an animal that has been released to a public or private animal shelter, other releasing agency, or animal control officer by the animal's rightful owner after the rightful owner has read and signed a statement: (i) surrendering all property rights in such animal; (ii) stating that no other person has a right of property in the animal; and (iii) acknowledging that the animal may be immediately euthanized or disposed of in accordance with subdivisions 1 through 5 of subsection D.

G. Nothing in this section shall prohibit any feral dog or feral cat not bearing a collar, tag, tattoo, or other form of identification that, based on the written statement of a disinterested person, exhibits behavior that poses a risk of physical injury to any person confining the animal, from being euthanized after being kept for a period of not less than three days, at least one of which shall be a full business day, such period to commence on the day the animal is initially confined in the facility, unless sooner claimed by the rightful owner. The statement of the disinterested person shall be kept with the animal as required by § 3.2-6557. For purposes of this subsection, a disinterested person shall not include a person releasing or reporting the animal.

H. No public animal shelter shall place a companion animal in a foster home with a foster care provider unless the foster care provider has read and signed a statement specifying that he has never been convicted of animal cruelty, neglect, or abandonment, and each shelter shall update such statement as changes occur. The shelter shall maintain the original statement and any updates to such statement in accordance with this chapter and for at least so long as the shelter has an affiliation with the foster care provider.

I. A public animal shelter that places a companion animal in a foster home with a foster care provider shall ensure that the foster care provider complies with § 3.2-6503.

J. If a public animal shelter finds a direct and immediate threat to a companion animal placed with a foster care provider, it shall report its findings to the animal control agency in the locality where the foster care provider is located.

K. The governing body shall require that the public animal shelter be operated in accordance with regulations issued by the Board. If this chapter or such regulations are violated, the locality may be assessed a civil penalty by the Board or its designee in an amount that does not exceed $1,000 per violation. Each day of the violation is a separate offense. In determining the amount of any civil penalty, the Board or its designee shall consider: (i) the history of previous violations at the shelter; (ii) whether the violation has caused injury to, death or suffering of, an animal; and (iii) the demonstrated good faith of the locality to achieve compliance after notification of the violation. All civil penalties assessed under this section shall be recovered in a civil action brought by the Attorney General in the name of the Commonwealth. Such civil penalties shall be paid into a special fund in the state treasury to the credit of the Department to be used in carrying out the purposes of this chapter.

L. If this chapter or any laws governing public animal shelters are violated, the Commissioner may bring an action to enjoin the violation or threatened violation of this chapter or the regulations pursuant thereto regarding public animal shelters, in the circuit court where the shelter is located. The Commissioner may request the Attorney General to bring such an action, when appropriate.

History.

1984, c. 492, §§ 29-213.36, 29-213.66; 1985, c. 21; 1987, c. 488, §§ 3.1-796.66, 3.1-796.96; 1988, c. 538; 1989, c. 344; 1991, c. 348; 1993, cc. 174, 817, 959; 1994, c. 936; 1995, c. 496; 1997, c. 159; 1998, c. 817; 1999, cc. 627, 672; 2000, c. 1010; 2002, cc. 53, 208, 787; 2003, c. 1007; 2008, cc. 345, 860; 2014, c. 148.

§ 3.2-6547. Acceptance of animals for research or experimentation; prohibition.

No person shall use or accept for the purpose of medical research or experimentation any animal bearing a tag, license, or tattooed identification, unless the individual who owns such animal consents thereto in writing.

History.

1990, c. 904, § 3.1-796.96:1; 2008, c. 860.

§ 3.2-6548. Private animal shelters; confinement and disposition of animals; affiliation with foster care providers; penalties; injunctive relief.

A. A private animal shelter may confine and dispose of animals in accordance with the provisions of subsections B through G of § 3.2-6546.

B. Each private animal shelter shall obtain a signed statement from each of its directors, operators, staff, and animal caregivers specifying that the individual has never been convicted of animal cruelty, neglect, or abandonment, and each shelter shall update such statement as changes occur.

C. The State Veterinarian or his representative shall inspect a private animal shelter prior to the shelter confining or disposing of animals pursuant to this section. The shelter shall meet the requirements of all laws with regard to confinement and disposition of animals before the shelter is approved to receive animals and provide a reasonable and comfortable climate appropriate for the age, species, condition, size, and type of animal.

D. A private animal shelter that confines an animal that has not been received from its owner shall, pursuant to this section, transmit a description of the animal including at least species, color, breed, size, sex, and other identification or markings and where the animal was found, and its contact information, including its name, address, and telephone number, to the public animal shelter in the county or city where the animal was found within 48 hours of the shelter receiving the animal. A shelter that confines and disposes of animals pursuant to this subsection shall be accessible to the public at reasonable hours, shall have its telephone number and address listed in a telephone directory, and shall post its contact information, including at least its name, address, and telephone number, in the public animal shelter in the locality where the shelter is located.

E. For purposes of recordkeeping, release of an animal by a private shelter to a public or private animal shelter or other releasing agency shall be considered a transfer and not an adoption. If the animal is not first sterilized, the responsibility for sterilizing the animal transfers to the receiving entity.

F. No private animal shelter shall place a companion animal in a foster home with a foster care provider unless the foster care provider has read and signed a statement specifying that he has never been convicted of animal cruelty, neglect, or abandonment, and the shelter shall update the statement as changes occur. The shelter shall maintain the original statement and any updates to such statement in accordance with this chapter and for at least so long as the shelter has an affiliation with the foster care provider.

G. A private animal shelter that places a companion animal in a foster home with a foster care provider shall ensure that the foster care provider complies with § 3.2-6503.

H. If a private animal shelter finds a direct and immediate threat to a companion animal placed with a foster care provider, it shall report its findings to the animal control agency in the locality where the foster care provider is located.

I. No private animal shelter shall be operated in violation of any local zoning ordinance.

J. A private animal shelter that confines and disposes of animals pursuant to this section shall be operated in accordance with this chapter. If this chapter is violated, the shelter may be assessed a civil penalty by the Board or its designee in an amount that does not exceed $1,000 per violation. Each day of the violation is a separate offense. In determining the amount of any civil penalty, the Board or its designee shall consider: (i) the history of previous violations at the shelter; (ii) whether the violation has caused injury to, death or suffering of, an animal; and (iii) the demonstrated good faith of the shelter to achieve compliance after notification of the violation. All civil penalties assessed under this section shall be recovered in a civil action brought by the Attorney General in the name of the Commonwealth. Such civil penalties shall be paid into a special fund in the state treasury to the credit of the Department to be used in carrying out the purposes of this chapter.

K. If this chapter or any laws governing private animal shelters are violated, the Commissioner may bring an action to enjoin the violation or threatened violation of this chapter or the regulations pursuant thereto regarding private animal shelters, in the circuit court where the shelter is located. The Commissioner may request the Attorney General to bring such an action, when appropriate.

History.

2001, c. 727, § 3.1-796.96:2; 2002, cc. 53, 208, 787; 2003, cc. 770, 1007; 2008, c. 860; 2014, c. 148.

§ 3.2-6549. Releasing agencies other than public or private animal shelters; confinement and disposition of companion animals; recordkeeping; affiliation with foster care providers; penalties.

A. A releasing agency other than a public or private animal shelter:

1. May confine and dispose of companion animals in accordance with subsections B through G of § 3.2-6546 if incorporated and not operated for profit;

2. Shall keep accurate records of each companion animal received for two years from the date of disposition of the companion animal. Records shall (i) include a description of the companion animal, including species, color, breed, sex, approximate weight, age, reason for release, owner's or finder's name, address, and telephone number, and license number or other identifying tags or markings, as well as disposition of the companion animal, and (ii) be made available upon request to the Department, animal control officers, and law-enforcement officers at mutually agreeable times. A releasing agency other than a public or private animal shelter shall annually submit a summary of such records to the State Veterinarian in a format prescribed by him, wherein a post office box may be substituted for a home address; and

3. Shall annually file with the State Veterinarian a copy of its intake policy.

For purposes of recordkeeping, release of a companion animal by a releasing agency to a public or private animal shelter or other releasing agency shall be considered a transfer and not an adoption. If the animal is not first sterilized, the responsibility for sterilizing the animal transfers to the receiving entity.

B. Each releasing agency other than a public or private animal shelter shall obtain a signed statement from each of its directors, operators, staff, or animal caregivers specifying that each individual has never been convicted of animal cruelty, neglect, or abandonment, and each such releasing agency shall update such statement as changes occur.

C. No releasing agency other than a public or private animal shelter shall place a companion animal in a foster home with a foster care provider unless the foster care provider has read and signed a statement specifying that the foster care provider has never been convicted of animal cruelty, neglect, or abandonment, and such releasing agency shall update the statement as changes occur. A releasing agency other than a public or private animal shelter shall maintain the original statement and any updates to such statement for so long as the releasing agency has an affiliation with the foster care provider.

D. A releasing agency other than a public or private animal shelter that places a companion animal in a foster home with a foster care provider shall ensure that the foster care provider complies with § 3.2-6503.

E. If a releasing agency other than a public or private animal shelter finds a direct and immediate threat to a companion animal placed with a foster care provider, it shall report its findings to the animal control agency in the area where the foster care provider is located.

F. Any releasing agency other than a public or private animal shelter that finds a companion animal or receives a companion animal that has not been released by its owner and (i) provides care or safekeeping or (ii) takes possession of such companion animal shall within 48 hours:

1. Make a reasonable attempt to notify the owner of the companion animal, if the owner can be ascertained from any tag, license, collar, tattoo, or other identification or markings, or if the owner of the companion animal is otherwise known to the releasing agency; and

2. Notify the public animal shelter that serves the locality where the companion animal was found and provide to the shelter contact information including at least a name and a contact telephone number, a description of the companion animal including at least species, breed, sex, size, color, information from any tag, license, collar, tattoo, or other identification or markings, and the location where the companion animal was found.

G. A releasing agency other than a public or private animal shelter shall comply with the provisions of § 3.2-6503.

H. No releasing agency other than a public or private animal shelter shall be operated in violation of any local zoning ordinance.

I. A releasing agency other than a public or private animal shelter that violates any provision of this section, other than subsection G, may be subject to a civil penalty not to exceed $250.

History.

2002, c. 787, § 3.1-796.96:5; 2003, cc. 770, 1007; 2008, c. 860; 2014, c. 148; 2016, c. 678.

§ 3.2-6550. Requirements for foster homes; penalty.

In addition to any other requirements of this chapter, foster homes shall be subject to the following:

1. No foster home shall be operated in violation of any local zoning ordinance; and

2. No private residential dwelling and its surrounding grounds that serves as a foster home shall

keep more than 50 companion animals on site at one time.

Any foster home found in violation of this section may be subject to a civil penalty not to exceed $250.

History.
2003, c. 1007, § 3.1-796.96:6; 2008, c. 860; 2014, c. 148.

§ 3.2-6551. Notification by individuals finding companion animals; penalty.

A. Any individual who finds a companion animal and (i) provides care or safekeeping or (ii) retains the companion animal in such a manner as to control its activities shall within 48 hours:

1. Make a reasonable attempt to notify the owner of the companion animal if the owner can be ascertained from any tag, license, collar, tattoo, or other form of identification or markings or if the owner of the animal is otherwise known to the individual; and

2. Notify the public animal shelter that serves the locality where the companion animal was found and provide to the shelter contact information, including at least a name and a contact telephone number, a description of the animal, including information from any tag, license, collar, tattoo, or other identification or markings, and the location where the companion animal was found.

B. If an individual finds a companion animal and (i) provides care or safekeeping or (ii) retains the companion animal in such a manner as to control its activities, the individual shall comply with the provisions of § 3.2-6503.

C. Any individual who violates this section may be subject to a civil penalty not to exceed $50 per companion animal.

History.
2003, c. 1007, § 3.1-796.96:7; 2008, c. 860; 2014, c. 148.

§ 3.2-6552. Dogs killing, injuring, or chasing livestock or poultry.

A. It shall be the duty of any animal control officer or other officer who may find a dog in the act of killing or injuring livestock or poultry to seize or kill such dog forthwith whether such dog bears a tag or not. Any person finding a dog committing any of the depredations mentioned in this section shall have the right to kill such dog on sight as shall any owner of livestock or his agent finding a dog chasing livestock on land utilized by the livestock when the circumstances show that such chasing is harmful to the livestock. Any court shall have the power to order the animal control officer or other officer to kill any dog known to be a confirmed livestock or poultry killer, and any dog killing poultry for the third time shall be considered a confirmed poultry killer. The court, through its contempt powers, may compel the owner, custodian, or harborer of the dog to produce the dog.

B. Any animal control officer who has reason to believe that any dog is killing livestock or poultry shall be empowered to seize such dog solely for the purpose of examining such dog in order to determine whether it committed any of the depredations mentioned herein. Any animal control officer or other person who has reason to believe that any dog is killing livestock, or committing any of the depredations mentioned in this section, shall apply to a magistrate serving the locality wherein the dog may be, who shall issue a warrant requiring the owner or custodian, if known, to appear before a general district court at a time and place named therein, at which time evidence shall be heard. If it shall appear that the dog is a livestock killer, or has committed any of the depredations mentioned in this section, the district court shall order that the dog be (i) killed or euthanized immediately by the animal control officer or other officer designated by the court or (ii) removed to another state that does not border on the Commonwealth and prohibited from returning to the Commonwealth. Any dog ordered removed from the Commonwealth that is later found in the Commonwealth shall be ordered by a court to be killed or euthanized immediately.

C. Notwithstanding the provisions of subsection B, if it is determined that the dog has killed or injured only poultry, the district court may, instead of ordering killing, euthanasia, or removal to another state pursuant to this section, order either (a) that the dog be transferred to another owner whom the court deems appropriate and permanently fitted with an identifying microchip registered to that owner or (b) that the dog be fitted with an identifying microchip registered to the owner and confined indoors or in a securely enclosed and locked structure of sufficient height and design to prevent the dog's escape; direct contact with the dog by minors, adults, or other animals; or entry by minors, adults, or other animals. The structure shall be designed to provide the dog with shelter from the elements of nature. When off its owner's property, any dog found to be a poultry killer shall be kept on a leash and muzzled in such a manner as not to cause injury to the dog or interfere with its vision or respiration, but so as to prevent it from biting a person or another animal.

History.
1984, c. 492, § 29-213.85; 1985, c. 385; 1987, c. 488, § 3.1-796.116; 1990, c. 222; 1993, c. 977; 1998, c. 817; 2008, cc. 551, 691, 860; 2014, c. 137; 2016, c. 757.

§ 3.2-6553. Compensation for livestock and poultry killed by dogs.

Any person who has any livestock or poultry killed or injured by any dog not his own shall be entitled to receive as compensation the fair market value of such livestock or poultry not to exceed $750 per animal or $10 per fowl if (i) the claimant has furnished evidence within 60 days of discovery of the quantity and value of the dead or injured livestock and the reasons the claimant believes that death or injury was caused by a dog; (ii) the animal control officer or other officer shall have been notified of the incident within 72 hours of its discovery; and (iii) the claimant first has exhausted his legal remedies against the owner, if known, of the dog doing the damage for which compensation under this section is sought. Exhaustion shall mean a judgment against the owner of the dog upon which an execution has been returned unsatisfied.

Local jurisdictions may by ordinance waive the requirements of clause (ii) or (iii) or both provided that the ordinance adopted requires that the animal control officer has conducted an investigation and that his investigation supports the claim. Upon payment under this section, the local governing body shall be subrogated to the extent of compensation paid to the right of action to the owner of the livestock or poultry against the owner of the dog and may enforce the same in an appropriate action at law.

History.

1984, c. 492, § 29-213.87; 1986, c. 108; 1987, c. 488, § 3.1-796.118; 1992, c. 461; 1998, c. 817; 2008, c. 860; 2014, cc. 116, 160.

§ 3.2-6554. Disposal of dead companion animals.

The owner of any companion animal shall forthwith cremate, bury, or sanitarily dispose of the animal upon its death. If, after notice, any owner fails to do so, the animal control officer or other officer shall bury or cremate the companion animal, and he may recover on behalf of the local jurisdiction from the owner his cost for this service.

History.

1984, c. 492, § 29-213.90; 1987, c. 488, § 3.1-796.121; 1993, c. 174; 1998, c. 817; 2008, c. 860.

ARTICLE 7.

ANIMAL CONTROL OFFICERS AND HUMANE INVESTIGATORS.

§ 3.2-6555. Position of animal control officer created.

The governing body of each county or city shall, or each town may, employ an officer to be known as the animal control officer who shall have the power to enforce this chapter, all ordinances enacted pursuant to this chapter and all laws for the protection of domestic animals. The governing body may also employ one or more deputy animal control officers to assist the animal control officer in the performance of his duties. Animal control officers and deputy animal control officers shall have knowledge of the animal control and protection laws of the Commonwealth that they are required to enforce. When in uniform or upon displaying a badge or other credentials of office, animal control officers and deputy animal control officers shall have the power to issue a summons or obtain a felony warrant as necessary, providing the execution of such warrant shall be carried out by any law-enforcement officer as defined in § 9.1-101, to any person found in the act of violating any such law or any ordinance enacted pursuant to such law of the locality where the animal control officer or deputy animal control officer is employed. Commercial dog breeding locations shall be subject to inspection by animal control at least twice annually and additionally upon receipt of a complaint or their own motion to ensure compliance with state animal care laws and regulations. The animal control officer and the deputy animal control officers shall be paid as the governing body of each locality shall prescribe.

Any locality where an animal control officer or deputy animal control officers have been employed may contract with one or more additional localities for enforcement of animal protection and control laws by the animal control officers or deputy animal control officers. Any such contract may provide that the locality employing the animal control officer or deputy animal control officers shall be reimbursed a portion of the salary and expenses of the animal control officer or deputy animal control officers.

Every locality employing an animal control officer shall submit to the State Veterinarian, on a form provided by him, information concerning the employment and training status of the animal control officers employed by the locality. The State Veterinarian may require that the locality notify him of any change in such information.

History.

1984, cc. 254, 492, § 29-213.73; 1987, c. 488, § 3.1-796.104; 1998, c. 817; 2003, c. 804; 2004, c. 181; 2008, cc. 852, 860.

§ 3.2-6556. Training of animal control officers.

A. Every locality employing animal control officers shall require that every animal control officer and deputy animal control officer completes the following training:

1. A basic animal control course that has been approved by the State Veterinarian. The basic animal control course shall include training in recognizing suspected child abuse and neglect and information on how complaints may be filed and shall be approved and implemented. Any animal control officer hired on or after July 1, 1998, and before July 1, 2017, shall complete the basic animal control course within two years from the date of hire. Any animal control officer hired on or after July 1, 2017, shall complete the basic animal control course within one year from the date of hire or within two years if the officer is attending a law-enforcement academy; and

2. Every three years, additional training approved by the State Veterinarian, 15 hours of which shall be training in animal control and protection.

The State Veterinarian shall develop criteria to be used in approving training courses and shall provide an opportunity for public comment on proposed criteria before the final criteria are adopted.

Subdivision 1 shall not apply to animal control officers or deputy animal control officers hired before July 1, 1998. The State Veterinarian may grant exemptions from the requirements of subdivision 1 to animal control officers hired on or after July 1, 1998, based on the animal control officer's previous training.

The State Veterinarian shall work to ensure the availability of these training courses through regional criminal justice training academies or other entities as approved by him. Based on information provided by authorized training entities, the State Veterinarian shall maintain the training records for all animal control officers for the purpose of documenting and ensuring that they are in compliance with this subsection.

B. Upon cause shown by a locality, the State Veterinarian may grant additional time during which the training required by subsection A may be completed by an animal control officer for the locality.

C. Any animal control officer that fails to complete the training required by subsection A shall be removed from office, unless the State Veterinarian has granted additional time as provided in subsection B.

History.

1998, c. 817, § 3.1-796.104:1; 2002, c. 418; 2004, c. 181; 2008, c. 860; 2016, cc. 60, 172.

§ 3.2-6557. Animal control officers and humane investigators; limitations; records; penalties.

A. No animal control officer, humane investigator, humane society, or custodian of any public or private animal shelter shall (i) obtain the release or transfer of an animal by the animal's owner to such animal control officer, humane investigator, humane society, or custodian for personal gain or (ii) give or sell or negotiate for the gift or sale to any individual, pet shop, dealer, or research facility of any animal that may come into his custody in the course of carrying out his official assignments. No animal control officer, humane investigator, or custodian of any public or private animal shelter shall be granted a dealer's license. Violation of this subsection is a Class 1 misdemeanor. Nothing in this section shall preclude any animal control officer or humane investigator from lawfully impounding any animal pursuant to § 3.2-6569.

B. An animal control officer, law-enforcement officer, humane investigator, or custodian of any public or private animal shelter, upon taking custody of any animal in the course of his official duties, or any representative of a humane society, upon obtaining custody of any animal on behalf of the society, shall immediately make a record of the matter. Such record shall include:

1. The date on which the animal was taken into custody;
2. The date of the making of the record;
3. A description of the animal, including the animal's species, color, breed, sex, approximate age, and approximate weight;
4. The reason for taking custody of the animal and the location where custody was taken;
5. The name and address of the animal's owner, if known;
6. Any license or rabies tag, tattoo, collar, or other identification number carried by or appearing on the animal; and
7. The disposition of the animal.

Records required by this subsection shall be maintained for at least five years and shall be available for public inspection upon request. A summary of such records shall be submitted annually to the State Veterinarian in a format prescribed by him.

C. Any animal control officer, law-enforcement officer, humane investigator, or custodian of any public or private animal shelter who takes custody of animals in the course of his official duties or representative of a humane society who takes custody of animals on behalf of the society shall annually file with the State Veterinarian a copy of his intake policy.

D. Any animal control officer or custodian of any public animal shelter who violates any provision of this chapter that relates to the seizure, impoundment, and custody of animals by an animal control officer may be subject to suspension or dismissal from his position.

E. Custodians and animal control officers engaged in the operation of a public animal shelter shall be required to have knowledge of the laws of the Commonwealth governing animals, including this chapter, as well as basic animal care.

History.

1984, c. 492, § 29-213.74; 1986, c. 315; 1987, c. 488, § 3.1-796.105; 1991, c. 65; 1993, c. 601; 1997, c. 286; 1998, c. 817; 2008, c. 860; 2014, c. 148; 2016, c. 678.

§ 3.2-6558. Humane investigators; qualifications; appointment; term.

A. A circuit court may reappoint any person as a humane investigator for any locality within its jurisdiction if the person:

1. Was appointed as a humane investigator prior to July 1, 2003; and
2. Has never been convicted of animal cruelty or neglect, any felony, or any crime of moral turpitude according to a criminal background check, which shall be performed by the attorney for the Commonwealth at the expense of the person seeking the appointment.

B. A circuit court may appoint a person to fill a vacancy in that jurisdiction created when a humane investigator who was appointed prior to July 1, 2003, is no longer willing or eligible to be a humane investigator, provided the person seeking appointment:

1. Has received a written recommendation from the administrative entity that oversees animal control in the locality where the humane investigator seeks appointment;

2. Has never been convicted of animal cruelty or neglect, any felony, or any crime of moral turpitude according to a criminal background check, which shall be performed by the attorney for the Commonwealth at the expense of the person seeking the appointment; and

3. Has completed a basic animal control course approved by the State Veterinarian pursuant to § 3.2-6556.

C. A person residing outside the Commonwealth may be appointed as a humane investigator only if he is employed by a humane society located within the locality where he is seeking appointment.

D. Reappointments of humane investigators shall be for terms of three years. Each humane investigator shall, during each term for which he is appointed, complete 15 hours of training in animal care and protection approved for animal control officers. If a humane investigator is appointed to a succeeding term before or within 30 days after his current term expires, a criminal background check shall not be required. If a humane investigator's term expires and he is not appointed to a succeeding term before or within 30 days after his current term expires, the humane investigator shall not be appointed to another term.

History.

1984, c. 492, § 29-213.75; 1987, c. 488, § 3.1-796.106; 1998, c. 817; 2003, c. 858; 2004, c. 181; 2008, c. 860.

§ 3.2-6559. Powers and duties of humane investigators.

A. Any humane investigator may, within the locality where he has been appointed, investigate violations of laws and ordinances regarding care and treatment of animals and disposal of dead animals.

B. Each humane investigator shall carry during the performance of his powers and duties under this chapter an identification card issued by the locality where the humane investigator is appointed. The identification card shall include the following information regarding the humane investigator:

1. His full name;
2. The locality where he has been appointed;
3. The name of the circuit court that appointed him;
4. The signature of the circuit court judge that appointed him;
5. A photograph of his face; and
6. The date of expiration of his appointment.

C. Each humane investigator shall record on a form approved by the administrative entity that oversees animal control every investigation he performs, maintain such record for five years, and make such record available upon request to any law-enforcement officer, animal control officer or State Veterinarian's representative. Each humane investigator shall file quarterly a report summarizing such records with the administrative agency that oversees animal control on an approved form. A humane investigator's appointment may be revoked as provided in § 3.2-6561 if he fails to file such report.

History.

1998, c. 817, § 3.1-796.106:2; 2003, c. 858; 2008, c. 860.

§ 3.2-6560. Expenses of humane investigators.

Neither the appointment of any humane investigator, nor the performance of any service or duty by him, shall require any locality or the Commonwealth to pay any cost or expense incurred by or on behalf of a humane investigator. Any locality may reimburse any humane investigator appointed for that locality for reasonable expenses incurred as the result of a specific request for services from the locality.

History.

1984, c. 492, § 29-213.79; 1986, c. 362; 1987, c. 488, § 3.1-796.110; 1998, c. 817; 2008, c. 860.

§ 3.2-6561. Revocation of appointment of humane investigators.

A. Upon a motion by the attorney for the Commonwealth, the circuit court that appointed a humane investigator may revoke his appointment if he is no longer able to perform the duties of a humane investigator; has been convicted of any felony, Class 1 misdemeanor, or a violation of any provision of this chapter or any other law regarding animals; or for good cause shown. The court shall notify the administrative entity that oversees animal control in the locality where the humane investigator was appointed of such revocation.

B. Any law-enforcement officer may investigate any allegation that a humane investigator has violated this chapter and report his findings and recommendations to the attorney for the Commonwealth.

History.

1998, c. 817, § 3.1-796.106:1; 1999, c. 376; 2003, c. 858; 2008, c. 860.

§ 3.2-6562. Capturing, confining, and euthanizing companion animals by animal control officers; approval of drugs used.

It shall be the duty of the animal control officer or any other officer to capture and confine any companion animal of unknown ownership found running at large on which the license fee has not been paid. Following the expiration of the holding period prescribed in § 3.2-6546, the animal control officer or other officer may deliver such companion animal to any person in his jurisdiction who will pay the required license fee on such companion animal. Prior to disposition by euthanasia or otherwise, all the provisions of § 3.2-6546 shall have been complied with. For all companion animals not otherwise disposed of as provided for in this chapter, it shall be the duty of the animal control officer or any other officer to euthanize such companion animals. Any person, animal control officer, or other officer euthanizing a companion animal under this chapter shall cremate, bury, or sanitarily dispose of the same.

All drugs and drug administering equipment used by animal control officers or other officers to capture companion animals pursuant to this chapter shall have been approved by the State Veterinarian.

History.
1984, c. 492, § 29-213.88; 1987, c. 488, § 3.1-796.119; 1991, c. 348; 1997, c. 159; 1998, c. 817; 2008, c. 860.

§ 3.2-6562.1. Rabies exposure; local authority and responsibility plan.

The local health director, in conjunction with the governing body of the locality, shall adopt a plan to control and respond to the risk of rabies exposure to persons and companion animals. Such plan shall set forth a procedure that promptly ensures the capture, confinement, isolation, or euthanasia of any animal that has exposed, or poses a risk of exposing, a person or companion animal to rabies. The plan shall identify the authority and responsibility of the local health department, law-enforcement officers, animal control officers, and any other persons with a duty to control or respond to a risk of rabies exposure. The plan shall provide for law-enforcement officers, animal control officers, and other persons to report to and be directed by the local health director for such purposes.

History.
2010, c. 834.

§ 3.2-6563. When animals to be euthanized; procedure.

Any humane investigator may lawfully cause to be euthanized any animal in his charge or found abandoned or not properly cared for when, in the judgment of the humane investigator and two reputable citizens called to view the same in his presence, and who shall give their written certificate, the animal appears to be injured, disabled or diseased, past recovery, or the injury, disease or disability is such that a reasonable owner would cause the animal to be euthanized.

Any humane investigator shall make every reasonable effort immediately to notify the owner of the animal that the humane investigator intends for the animal to be euthanized. The owner shall have a right to select one of the two reputable citizens called to view the animal and give written certificate of the animal's condition. In no event shall the determination as to disposition of the animal be delayed beyond 48 hours after such humane investigator first decides the animal should be euthanized. In the event that the two citizens called to give such certificate are unable to agree, they shall select a third reputable citizen and his decision shall be final.

History.
1984, c. 492, § 29-213.83; 1986, c. 362; 1987, c. 488, § 3.1-796.114; 1998, c. 817; 2008, c. 860.

ARTICLE 8.

SEARCH, SEIZURE, IMPOUNDING, AND ENFORCEMENT.

§ 3.2-6564. Complaint of suspected violation; investigation.

A. Upon receiving a complaint of a suspected violation of this chapter, any ordinance enacted pursuant to this chapter or any law for the protection of domestic animals, any animal control officer, law-enforcement officer, or State Veterinarian's representative may, for the purpose of investigating the allegations of the complaint, enter upon, during business hours, any business premises, including any place where animals or animal records are housed or kept, of any dealer, pet shop, groomer, or boarding establishment. Upon receiving a complaint of a suspected violation of any law or ordinance regarding care or treatment of animals or disposal of dead animals, any humane investigator may, for the purpose of investigating the allegations of the complaint, enter upon, during business hours, any business premises, including any place where animals or animal records are housed or kept, of any dealer, pet shop, groomer, or boarding establishment.

Upon obtaining a warrant as provided for in § 3.2-6568, the law-enforcement officer, animal control officer, State Veterinarian's representative, or humane investigator may enter upon any other premises where the animal or animals described in the complaint are housed or kept. Attorneys for the Commonwealth and law-enforcement officials shall provide such assistance as may be required in the conduct of such investigations.

B. If the investigation discloses that a violation of § 3.2-6503 has occurred, the investigating official shall notify the owner or custodian of the complaint and of what action is necessary to comply with this chapter.

History.
1984, c. 492, § 29-213.76; 1987, c. 488, § 3.1-796.107; 1991, c. 451; 1993, c. 174; 1998, c. 817; 2008, c. 860.

§ 3.2-6565. Impoundment; expenses; lien; disposition of animal.

When an animal control officer, humane investigator, law-enforcement officer or State Veterinarian's representative finds that an apparent violation of this chapter has rendered an animal in such a condition as to constitute a direct and immediate threat to its life, safety or health that the owner or custodian has failed to remedy, such animal control officer, humane investigator, law-enforcement officer or State Veterinarian's representative may impound the animal pursuant to § 3.2-6569 in a facility that will provide the elements of good care as set forth in § 3.2-6503 and shall then proceed to take such steps as are required to dispose of the animal pursuant to § 3.2-6569.

History.
1984, c. 492, § 29-213.77; 1987, c. 488, § 3.1-796.108; 1994, c. 387; 1998, c. 817; 2008, c. 860.

§ 3.2-6566. Preventing cruelty to animals; interference; penalty.

Each animal control officer, humane investigator or State Veterinarian's representative shall interfere to prevent the perpetration of any act of cruelty upon any animal in his presence. Any person who shall interfere with or obstruct or resist any humane investigator or State Veterinarian's representative in the discharge of his rights, powers, and duties as authorized and prescribed by law is guilty of a Class 4 misdemeanor.

History.
1984, c. 492, § 29-213.80; 1986, c. 362; 1987, c. 488, § 3.1-796.111; 1998, c. 817; 2008, c. 860; 2010, c. 240.

§ 3.2-6567. Enforcement authority.

All law-enforcement officers in the Commonwealth and State Veterinarian's representatives shall enforce the provisions of this chapter to the same extent other laws in the Commonwealth are enforced.

History.
1984, c. 492, § 29-213.81; 1987, c. 488, § 3.1-796.112; 1991, c. 121; 1998, c. 817; 2008, c. 860.

§ 3.2-6568. Power of search for violations of statutes against cruelty to animals.

When an affidavit is made under oath before a magistrate or court of competent jurisdiction by any animal control officer, humane investigator, law-enforcement officer, or State Veterinarian's representative that the complainant believes and has reasonable cause to believe that the laws in relation to cruelty to animals have been, are being, or are about to be violated in any particular building or place, such magistrate or judge, if satisfied that there is reasonable cause for such belief, shall issue a warrant authorizing any sheriff, deputy sheriff, or police officer to search the building or place. After issuing a warrant under this section, the magistrate or judge shall file the affidavit in the manner prescribed by § 19.2-54. After executing the warrant, the animal control officer, humane investigator, law-enforcement officer, or State Veterinarian's representative shall return the warrant to the clerk of the circuit court of the city or county wherein the search was made.

History.
1984, c. 492, § 29-213.82; 1986, c. 362; 1987, c. 488, § 3.1-796.113; 1994, c. 168; 1998, c. 817; 2008, cc. 543, 707, 860; 2014, c. 354.

§ 3.2-6569. Seizure and impoundment of animals; notice and hearing; disposition of animal; disposition of proceeds upon sale.

A. Any humane investigator, law-enforcement officer or animal control officer may lawfully seize and impound any animal that has been abandoned, has been cruelly treated, or is suffering from an apparent violation of this chapter that has rendered the animal in such a condition as to constitute a direct and immediate threat to its life, safety or health. The seizure or impoundment of an equine resulting from a violation of clause (iii) of subsection A or clause (ii) of subsection B of § 3.2-6570 may be undertaken only by the State Veterinarian or State Veterinarian's representative who has received training in the examination and detection of sore horses as required by 9 C.F.R. Part 11.7.

B. Before seizing or impounding any agricultural animal, the humane investigator, law-enforcement officer or animal control officer shall contact the State Veterinarian or State Veterinarian's representative, who shall recommend to the person the most appropriate action for effecting the seizure and impoundment. The humane investigator, law-enforcement officer or animal control officer shall notify the owner of the agricultural animal and the local attorney for the Commonwealth of the recommendation. The humane investigator, law-enforcement officer or animal control officer may impound the agricultural animal on the land where the agricultural animal is located if:

1. The owner or tenant of the land where the agricultural animal is located gives written permission;

2. A general district court so orders; or

3. The owner or tenant of the land where the agricultural animal is located cannot be immediately located, and it is in the best interest of the agricultural animal to be impounded on the land where it is located until the written permission of the owner or tenant of the land can be obtained.

If there is a direct and immediate threat to an agricultural animal, the humane investigator, law-enforcement officer or animal control officer may seize the animal, in which case the humane investigator, law-enforcement officer or animal control officer shall file within five business days on a form approved by the State Veterinarian a report on the condition of the animal at the time of the seizure, the location of impoundment, and any other information required by the State Veterinarian.

C. Upon seizing or impounding an animal, the humane investigator, law-enforcement officer or animal control officer shall petition the general district court in the city or county where the animal is seized for a hearing. The hearing shall be not more than 10 business days from the date of the seizure of the animal. The hearing shall be to determine whether the animal has been abandoned, has been cruelly treated, or has not been provided adequate care.

D. The humane investigator, law-enforcement officer, or animal control officer shall cause to be served upon the person with a right of property in the animal or the custodian of the animal notice of the hearing. If such person or the custodian is known and residing within the jurisdiction wherein the animal is seized, written notice shall be given at least five days prior to the hearing of the time and place of the hearing. If such person or the custodian is known but residing out of the jurisdiction where such animal is seized, written notice by any method or service of process as is provided by the Code of Virginia shall be given. If such person or the custodian is not known, the humane investigator, law-enforcement officer, or animal control officer shall cause to be published in a newspaper of general circulation in the jurisdiction wherein such animal is seized notice of the hearing at least one time prior to the hearing and shall further cause notice of the hearing to be posted at least five days prior to the hearing at the place provided for public notices at the city hall or courthouse wherein such hearing shall be held.

E. The procedure for appeal and trial shall be the same as provided by law for misdemeanors. Trial by jury shall be as provided in Article 4 (§ 19.2-260 et seq.) of Chapter 15 of Title 19.2. The Commonwealth shall be required to prove its case beyond a reasonable doubt.

F. The humane investigator, law-enforcement officer, or animal control officer shall provide for such animal until the court has concluded the hearing. Any locality may require the owner of any animal held pursuant to this subsection for more than thirty days to post a bond in surety with the locality for the amount of the cost of boarding the animal for a period of time set by ordinance, not to exceed nine months.

In any locality that has not adopted such an ordinance, a court may order the owner of an animal held pursuant to this subsection for more than 30 days to post a bond in surety with the locality for the amount of the cost of boarding the animal for a period of time not to exceed nine months. The bond shall not be forfeited if the owner is found to be not guilty of the violation.

If the court determines that the animal has been neither abandoned, cruelly treated, nor deprived of adequate care, the animal shall be returned to the owner. If the court determines that the animal has been (i) abandoned or cruelly treated, (ii) deprived of adequate care, as that term is defined in § 3.2-6500, or (iii) raised as a dog that has been, is, or is intended to be used in dogfighting in violation of § 3.2-6571, then the court shall order that the animal may be: (a) sold by a local governing body, if not a companion animal; (b) disposed of by a local governing body pursuant to subsection D of § 3.2-6546, whether such animal is a companion animal or an agricultural animal; or (c) delivered to the person with a right of property in the animal as provided in subsection G.

G. In no case shall the owner be allowed to purchase, adopt, or otherwise obtain the animal if the court determines that the animal has been abandoned, cruelly treated, or deprived of adequate care. The court shall direct that the animal be delivered to the person with a right of property in the animal, upon his request, if the court finds that the abandonment, cruel treatment, or deprivation of adequate care is not attributable to the actions or inactions of such person.

H. The court shall order the owner of any animal determined to have been abandoned, cruelly treated, or deprived of adequate care to pay all reasonable expenses incurred in caring and providing for such animal from the time the animal is seized until such time that the animal is disposed of in accordance with the provisions of this section, to the provider of such care.

I. The court may prohibit the possession or ownership of other companion animals by the owner of any companion animal found to have been abandoned, cruelly treated, or deprived of adequate care. In making a determination to prohibit the possession or ownership of companion animals, the court may take into consideration the owner's past record of convictions under this chapter or other laws prohibiting cruelty to animals or pertaining to the care or treatment of animals and the owner's mental and physical condition.

J. If the court finds that an agricultural animal has been abandoned or cruelly treated, the court may prohibit the possession or ownership of any other agricultural animal by the owner of the agricultural animal if the owner has exhibited a pattern of abandoning or cruelly treating agricultural animals as evidenced by previous convictions of violating § 3.2-6504 or 3.2-6570. In making a determination to prohibit the possession or ownership of agricultural animals, the court may take into consideration the owner's mental and physical condition.

K. Any person who is prohibited from owning or possessing animals pursuant to subsection I or J may petition the court to repeal the prohibition after two years have elapsed from the date of entry of the court's order. The court may, in its discretion, repeal the prohibition if the person can prove to the satisfaction of the court that the cause for the prohibition has ceased to exist.

L. When a sale occurs, the proceeds shall first be applied to the costs of the sale then next to the unreimbursed expenses for the care and provision of the animal, and the remaining proceeds, if any, shall be paid over to the owner of the animal. If the owner of the animal cannot be found, the proceeds remaining shall be paid into the Literary Fund.

M. Nothing in this section shall be construed to prohibit the humane destruction of a critically injured or ill animal for humane purposes by the impounding humane investigator, law-enforcement officer, animal control officer, or licensed veterinarian.

History.

1984, c. 492, § 29-213.84; 1986, c. 362; 1987, c. 488, § 3.1-796.115; 1990, c. 322; 1992, c. 123; 1993, c. 119; 1994, c. 387; 1998, c. 817; 1999, c. 113; 2002, c. 500; 2008, cc. 510, 860; 2011, cc. 754, 886.

ARTICLE 9.
CRUELTY TO ANIMALS.

§ 3.2-6570. Cruelty to animals; penalty.

A. Any person who: (i) overrides, overdrives, overloads, tortures, ill-treats, abandons, willfully inflicts inhumane injury or pain not connected with bona fide scientific or medical experimentation, or cruelly or unnecessarily beats, maims, mutilates, or kills any animal, whether belonging to himself or another; (ii) deprives any animal of necessary food, drink, shelter or emergency veterinary treatment; (iii) sores any equine for any purpose or administers drugs or medications to alter or mask such soring for the purpose of sale, show, or exhibition of any kind, unless such administration of drugs or medications is within the context of a veterinary client-patient relationship and solely for therapeutic purposes; (iv) ropes, lassoes, or otherwise obstructs or interferes with one or more legs of an equine in order to intentionally cause it to trip or fall for the purpose of engagement in a rodeo, contest, exhibition, entertainment, or sport unless such actions are in the practice of accepted animal husbandry or for the purpose of allowing veterinary care; (v) willfully sets on foot, instigates, engages in, or in any way furthers any act of cruelty to any animal; (vi) carries or causes to be carried by any vehicle, vessel or otherwise any animal in a cruel, brutal, or inhumane manner, so as to produce torture or unnecessary suffering; or (vii) causes any of the above things, or being the owner of such animal permits such acts to be done by another is guilty of a Class 1 misdemeanor.

In addition to the penalties provided in this subsection, the court may, in its discretion, require any person convicted of a violation of this subsection to attend an anger management or other appropriate treatment program or obtain psychiatric or psychological counseling. The court may impose the costs of such a program or counseling upon the person convicted.

B. Any person who: (i) tortures, willfully inflicts inhumane injury or pain not connected with bona fide scientific or medical experimentation, or cruelly and unnecessarily beats, maims, mutilates or kills any animal whether belonging to himself or another; (ii) sores any equine for any purpose or administers drugs or medications to alter or mask such soring for the purpose of sale, show, or exhibit of any kind, unless such administration of drugs or medications is under the supervision of a licensed veterinarian and solely for therapeutic purposes; (iii) ropes, lassoes, or otherwise obstructs or interferes with one or more legs of an equine in order to intentionally cause it to trip or fall for the purpose of engagement in a rodeo, contest, exhibition, entertainment, or sport unless such actions are in the practice of accepted animal husbandry or for the purpose of allowing veterinary care; (iv) maliciously deprives any companion animal of necessary food, drink, shelter or emergency veterinary treatment; (v) instigates, engages in, or in any way furthers any act of cruelty to any animal set forth in clauses (i) through (iv) or (vi) causes any of the actions described in clauses (i) through (v), or being the owner of such animal permits such acts to be done by another; and has been within five years convicted of a violation of this subsection or subsection A, is guilty of a Class 6 felony if the current violation or any previous violation of this subsection or subsection A resulted in the death of an animal or the euthanasia of an animal based on the recommendation of a licensed veterinarian upon determination that such euthanasia was necessary due to the condition of the animal, and such condition was a direct result of a violation of this subsection or subsection A.

C. Nothing in this section shall be construed to prohibit the dehorning of cattle conducted in a reasonable and customary manner.

D. This section shall not prohibit authorized wildlife management activities or hunting, fishing or trapping as regulated under other titles of the Code of Virginia, including Title 29.1, or to farming activities as provided under this title or regulations adopted hereunder.

E. It is unlawful for any person to kill a domestic dog or cat for the purpose of obtaining the hide, fur or pelt of the dog or cat. A violation of this subsection is a Class 1 misdemeanor. A second or subsequent violation of this subsection is a Class 6 felony.

F. Any person who: (i) tortures, willfully inflicts inhumane injury or pain not connected with bona fide scientific or medical experimentation or cruelly and unnecessarily beats, maims or mutilates any dog or cat that is a companion animal whether belonging to him or another; and (ii) as a direct result causes the death of such dog or cat that is a companion animal, or the euthanasia of such animal on the recommendation of a licensed veterinarian upon determination that such euthanasia was necessary due to the condition of the animal, is guilty of a Class 6 felony. If a dog or cat is attacked on its owner's property by a dog so as to cause injury or death, the owner of the injured dog or cat may use all reasonable and necessary force against the dog at the time of the attack to protect his dog or cat. Such owner may be presumed to have taken necessary and appropriate action to defend his dog or cat and shall therefore be presumed not to have violated this subsection. The provisions of this subsection shall not overrule § 3.2-6540, 3.2-6540.1, or 3.2-6552.

G. Any person convicted of violating this section may be prohibited by the court from possession or ownership of companion animals.

History.

1984, c. 492, § 29-213.91; 1987, c. 488, § 3.1-796.122; 1992, c. 177; 1998, c. 817; 1999, cc. 209, 620, 645; 2002, cc. 351, 500, 583, 613; 2003, cc. 787, 788; 2004, c. 217; 2007, c. 743; 2008, c. 860; 2013, cc. 58, 732; 2015, c. 491.

§ 3.2-6570.1. Sale of animals after cruelty or neglect conviction; penalty.

Any person who has been convicted of a violation of any law concerning abuse, neglect, or cruelty to animals that sells, offers for sale, or trades any companion animal is guilty of a Class 1 misdemeanor. However, a person may dispose of animals under the provisions of a court order.

History.

2008, c. 852, § 3.1-796.122:1.

§ 3.2-6571. Animal fighting; penalty.

A. No person shall knowingly:

1. Promote, prepare for, engage in, or be employed in, the fighting of animals for amusement, sport or gain;

2. Attend an exhibition of the fighting of animals;

3. Authorize or allow any person to undertake any act described in this section on any premises under his charge or control; or

4. Aid or abet any such acts.

Except as provided in subsection B, any person who violates any provision of this subsection is guilty of a Class 1 misdemeanor.

B. Any person who violates any provision of subsection A in combination with one or more of the following is guilty of a Class 6 felony:

1. When a dog is one of the animals;

2. When any device or substance intended to enhance an animal's ability to fight or to inflict injury upon another animal is used, or possessed with intent to use it for such purpose;

3. When money or anything of value is wagered on the result of such fighting;

4. When money or anything of value is paid or received for the admission of a person to a place for animal fighting;

5. When any animal is possessed, owned, trained, transported, or sold with the intent that the animal engage in an exhibition of fighting with another animal; or

6. When he permits or causes a minor to (i) attend an exhibition of the fighting of any animals or (ii) undertake or be involved in any act described in this subsection.

C. 1. Any animal control officer, as defined in § 3.2-6500, shall confiscate any animal that he determines has been, is, or is intended to be used in animal fighting and any equipment used in training such animal or used in animal fighting.

2. Upon confiscation of an animal, the animal control officer shall petition the appropriate court for a hearing for a determination of whether the animal has been, is, or is intended to be used in animal fighting. The hearing shall be not more than 10 business days from the date of the confiscation of the animal. If the court finds that the animal has not been used, is not used and is not intended to be used in animal fighting, it shall order the animal released to its owner. However, if the court finds probable cause to believe that the animal has been, is, or is intended to be used in animal fighting, the court shall order the animal forfeited to the locality unless the owner posts bond in surety with the locality in an amount sufficient to compensate the locality for its cost of caring for the animal for a period of nine months. He shall post additional bond for each successive nine-month period until a final determination by the trial court on any criminal charges brought pursuant to subsections A or B.

3. Upon a final determination of guilt by the trial court on criminal charges brought pursuant to subsections A or B, the court shall order that the animal be forfeited to the locality. Upon a final determination of not guilty by the trial court on the underlying criminal charges, a confiscated animal shall be returned to its owner and any bond shall be refunded to him.

D. Any person convicted of violating any provision of subsection A or B shall be prohibited by the court from possession or ownership of companion animals or cocks.

E. In addition to fines and costs, the court shall order any person who is convicted of a violation of this section to pay all reasonable costs incurred in housing, caring for, or euthanizing any confiscated animal. If the court finds that the actual costs are reasonable, it may order payment of actual costs.

F. The provisions of this section shall not apply to any law-enforcement officer in the performance of his duties. This section shall not prohibit (i) authorized wildlife management activities or hunting, fishing, or trapping authorized under any title of the

Code of Virginia or regulations promulgated thereto or (ii) farming activities authorized under Title 3.2 of the Code of Virginia or regulations promulgated thereto.

History.

1985, c. 408, § 29-213.92:1; 1987, c. 488, § 3.1-796.124; 1998, c. 817; 1999, c. 113; 2003, c. 857; 2008, cc. 543, 707, 860.

§ 3.2-6572: Reserved.

Editor's note.

Acts 2008, cc. 543 and 707 repealed former § 3.1-796.125, from which this section was derived. Pursuant to § 30-152, this section has been set out as reserved at the direction of the Virginia Code Commission.

§ 3.2-6573. Shooting birds for amusement, and renting premises for such purposes; penalty.

Live pigeons or other birds or fowl shall not be kept or used for the purpose of a target, or to be shot at either for amusement or as a test of skill in marksmanship. It is a Class 4 misdemeanor to shoot at a bird kept or used as aforesaid, or to be a party to such shooting. Any person who lets any building, room, field or premises, or knowingly permits the use thereof for the purpose of such shooting is guilty of a Class 4 misdemeanor.

Nothing contained herein shall apply to the shooting of wild game.

History.

1984, c. 492, § 29-213.94; 1987, c. 488, § 3.1-796.126; 2008, c. 860.

ARTICLE 10.

MANDATORY STERILIZATION OF DOGS AND CATS ADOPTED FROM RELEASING AGENCIES.

§ 3.2-6574. Sterilization of adopted dogs and cats; enforcement; civil penalty.

A. Every new owner of a dog or cat adopted from a releasing agency shall cause to be sterilized the dog or cat pursuant to the agreement required by subdivision 2 of subsection B of this article.

B. A dog or cat shall not be released for adoption from a releasing agency unless:

1. The animal has already been sterilized; or
2. The individual adopting the animal signs an agreement to have the animal sterilized by a licensed veterinarian: (i) within 30 days of the adoption, if the animal is sexually mature; or (ii) within 30 days after the animal reaches six months of age, if the animal is not sexually mature at the time of adoption.

C. A releasing agency may extend for 30 days the date by which a dog or cat must be sterilized on presentation of a written report from a veterinarian stating that the life or health of the adopted animal may be jeopardized by sterilization. In cases involving extenuating circumstances, the veterinarian and the releasing agency may negotiate the terms of an extension of the date by which the animal must be sterilized.

D. Nothing in this section shall preclude the sterilization of a sexually immature dog or cat upon the written agreement of the veterinarian, the releasing agency, and the new owner.

E. Upon the petition of an animal control officer, humane investigator, the State Veterinarian or a State Veterinarian's representative to the district court of the county or city where a violation of this article occurs, the court may order the new owner to take any steps necessary to comply with the requirements of this article. This remedy shall be exclusive of and in addition to any civil penalty that may be imposed under this article.

F. Any person who violates subsection A or B of this section shall be subject to a civil penalty not to exceed $250.

History.

1993, c. 959, § 3.1-796.126:1; 1998, c. 817; 2008, c. 860; 2010, c. 875.

§ 3.2-6575. Sterilization agreement.

Any agreement used by a releasing agency pursuant to subsection B of § 3.2-6574 shall contain:

1. The date of the agreement;
2. The names, addresses, and signatures of the releasing agency and the new owner;
3. A description of the dog or cat to be adopted;
4. The date by which the dog or cat is required to be sterilized; and
5. A statement printed in conspicuous, bold print, that sterilization of the dog or cat is required under this article; that a person who violates this article is subject to a civil penalty; and that the new owner may be compelled to comply with the provisions of this article.

History.

1993, c. 959, § 3.1-796.126:2; 2008, c. 860.

§ 3.2-6576. Sterilization confirmation; civil penalty.

Each new owner who signs a sterilization agreement shall, within seven days of the sterilization, cause to be delivered or mailed to the releasing agency written confirmation signed by the veterinarian who performed the sterilization. The confirmation shall briefly describe the dog or cat; include the new owner's name and address; certify that the sterilization was performed; and specify the date of the procedure. Any person who violates this section shall be subject to a civil penalty not to exceed $150.

History.

1993, c. 959, § 3.1-796.126:3; 1999, cc. 627, 672; 2008, c. 860.

§ 3.2-6577. Notification concerning lost, stolen or dead dogs or cats; civil penalty.

If an adopted dog or cat is lost or stolen or dies before the animal is sterilized and before the date by which the dog or cat is required to be sterilized, the new owner shall, within seven days of the animal's disappearance or death, notify the releasing agency of the animal's disappearance or death. Any person who violates this section shall be subject to a civil penalty not to exceed $25.

History.
1993, c. 959, § 3.1-796.126:4; 2008, c. 860.

§ 3.2-6578. Exemptions.

This article shall not apply to:

1. An owner reclaiming his dog or cat from a releasing agency;
2. A releasing agency within a locality that has adopted a more stringent mandatory sterilization ordinance; and
3. A local governing body that has disposed of an animal by sale or gift to a federal agency, state-supported institution, agency of the Commonwealth, agency of another state, or licensed federal dealer having its principal place of business located within the Commonwealth.

History.
1993, c. 959, § 3.1-796.126:5; 2008, c. 860.

§ 3.2-6579. Releasing agency; fees and deposits.

A local governing body or releasing agency may charge and collect from the new owner a fee or deposit before releasing a dog or cat for adoption to ensure sterilization.

History.
1993, c. 959, § 3.1-796.126:6; 2008, c. 860.

§ 3.2-6580. Civil penalties.

Any animal control officer, humane investigator, releasing agency, the State Veterinarian or State Veterinarian's representative shall be entitled to bring a civil action for any violation of this article that is subject to a civil penalty. Any civil penalty assessed pursuant to this article shall be paid into the treasury of the city or county where such civil action is brought and used for the purpose of defraying the costs of local animal control, including efforts to promote sterilization of cats and dogs.

History.
1993, c. 959, § 3.1-796.126:7; 1998, c. 817; 2002, c. 787; 2008, c. 860.

ARTICLE 11.
HYBRID CANINES.

§ 3.2-6581. Definitions.

As used in this article:

"Adequate confinement" means that, while on the property of its owner and not under the direct supervision and control of the owner or custodian, a hybrid canine shall be confined in a humane manner in a securely enclosed and locked structure of sufficient height and design to: (i) prevent the animal's escape; or if the hybrid canine is determined to be a dangerous dog pursuant to § 3.2-6540, the structure shall prevent direct contact with any person or animal not authorized by the owner to be in direct contact with the hybrid canine; and (ii) provide a minimum of 100 square feet of floor space for each adult animal. Tethering of a hybrid canine not under the direct supervision and control of the owner or custodian shall not be considered adequate confinement.

"Hybrid canine" means any animal that is or can be demonstrated to be a hybrid of the domestic dog and any other species of the Canidae family; that at any time has been permitted, registered, licensed, or advertised as such; or that at any time has been described, represented, or reported as such by its owner to a licensed veterinarian, law-enforcement officer, animal control officer, humane investigator, official of the Department of Health, or State Veterinarian's representative.

"Responsible ownership" means the ownership and humane care of a hybrid canine in such a manner as to comply with all laws and ordinances regarding hybrid canines and prevent endangerment by the animal to public health and safety.

History.
1997, c. 918, § 3.1-796.126:8; 1998, c. 817; 2008, c. 860; 2014, c. 461.

§ 3.2-6582. Hybrid canine ordinance; penalty.

A. Any locality may, by ordinance, establish a permit system to ensure the adequate confinement and responsible ownership of hybrid canines. Such ordinance may include requirements pertaining to (i) the term and expiration date of the permit; (ii) the number of hybrid canines that may be owned by a permittee; (iii) identification tags or tattooing of the animal; (iv) where the animal may be kept; (v) handling of the animal while not on the property of the owner; and (vi) information required to be provided when applying for a permit, such as the sex, color, height, vaccination records, length, or identifying marks of the hybrid canine. The ordinance shall not require that hybrid canines be disposed of by the owner unless the owner fails to obtain or renew any required permit or violates a provision of the ordinance or any other law pertaining to the responsible ownership of the hybrid canine. The locality may impose a permit fee to cover the cost of the permitting system.

B. Violation of an ordinance enacted pursuant to subsection A is a Class 3 misdemeanor for the first violation and a Class 1 misdemeanor for any subsequent violation. The ordinance may require a violator to surrender the hybrid canine for euthanasia in accordance with § 3.2-6562.

C. The provisions of subsections A and B shall not affect any ordinance adopted prior to July 1, 1997.

D. Any locality may, by ordinance, prohibit the keeping of hybrid canines.

History.

1997, c. 918, § 3.1-796.126:9; 2008, c. 860; 2014, c. 461.

§ 3.2-6583. Hybrid canines killing, injuring or chasing livestock.

It shall be the duty of any animal control officer or other officer who may find a hybrid canine in the act of killing or injuring livestock or poultry to kill such hybrid canine forthwith, whether such hybrid canine bears a tag or not. Any person finding a hybrid canine committing any of the depredations mentioned in this section may kill such hybrid canine on sight as may any owner of livestock or his agent finding a hybrid canine chasing livestock on land lawfully utilized by the livestock when the circumstances show that such chasing is harmful to the livestock. Any court may order the animal control officer or other officer to kill any hybrid canine known to be a confirmed livestock or poultry killer, and any hybrid canine that kills poultry for a third time shall be considered a confirmed poultry killer. The court, through its contempt powers, may compel the owner, custodian, or harborer of the hybrid canine to produce the hybrid canine.

Any animal control officer who has reason to believe that any hybrid canine is killing livestock or poultry shall be empowered to seize such hybrid canine solely for the purpose of examining such hybrid canine in order to determine whether it committed any of the depredations mentioned herein. Any animal control officer or other person who has reason to believe that any hybrid canine is killing livestock, or committing any of the depredations mentioned in this section, shall apply to a magistrate serving the locality where such hybrid canine may be, who shall issue a warrant requiring the owner or custodian, if known, to appear before a general district court, at which time evidence shall be heard. If it appears that the hybrid canine is a livestock killer, or has committed any of the depredations mentioned in this section, the district court shall order that the hybrid canine be: (i) killed immediately by the animal control officer or other officer designated by the court; or (ii) removed to another state that does not border on the Commonwealth and prohibited from returning to the Commonwealth. Any hybrid canine ordered removed from the Commonwealth that is later found in the Commonwealth shall be ordered by a court to be killed immediately.

History.

1997, c. 918, § 3.1-796.126:10; 1998, c. 817; 2008, cc. 551, 691, 860.

§ 3.2-6584. Compensation for livestock and poultry killed by hybrid canines.

Any person who has any livestock or poultry killed or injured by any hybrid canine not his own shall be entitled to receive as compensation the fair market value of such livestock or poultry not to exceed $750 per animal or $10 per fowl if (i) the claimant has furnished evidence within 60 days of discovery of the quantity and value of the dead or injured livestock and the reasons the claimant believes that death or injury was caused by a hybrid canine; (ii) the animal control officer or other officer shall have been notified of the incident within 72 hours of its discovery; and (iii) the claimant first has exhausted his legal remedies against the owner, if known, of the hybrid canine doing the damage for which compensation under this section is sought. Exhaustion shall mean a judgment against the owner of the hybrid canine upon which an execution has been returned unsatisfied.

Local jurisdictions may by ordinance waive the requirements of clause (ii) or (iii) or both provided that the ordinance adopted requires that the animal control officer has conducted an investigation and that his investigation supports the claim. Upon payment under this section the local governing body shall be subrogated to the extent of compensation paid to the right of action to the owner of the livestock or poultry against the owner of the hybrid canine and may enforce the same in an appropriate action at law.

History.

1997, c. 918, § 3.1-796.126:11; 1998, c. 817; 2008, c. 860; 2014, cc. 116, 160.

ARTICLE 12.

MISCELLANEOUS PROVISIONS.

§ 3.2-6585. Dogs and cats deemed personal property; rights relating thereto.

All dogs and cats shall be deemed personal property and may be the subject of larceny and malicious or unlawful trespass. Owners, as defined in § 3.2-6500, may maintain any action for the killing of any such animals, or injury thereto, or unlawful detention or use thereof as in the case of other personal property. The owner of any dog or cat that is injured or killed contrary to the provisions of this chapter by any person shall be entitled to recover the value thereof or the damage done thereto in an appropriate action at law from such person.

An animal control officer or other officer finding a stolen dog or cat, or a dog or cat held or detained contrary to law, shall have authority to seize and hold such animal pending action before a general district court or other court. If no such action is instituted within seven days, the animal control officer or other officer shall deliver the dog or cat to its owner.

The presence of a dog or cat on the premises of a person other than its legal owner shall raise no presumption of theft against the owner, and the animal control officer may take such animal and notify its legal owner. The legal owner of the animal shall pay a reasonable charge as the local governing body by ordinance shall establish for the keep of such animal while in the possession of the animal control officer.

History.
1984, c. 492, § 29-213.95; 1987, c. 488, § 3.1-796.127; 1988, c. 537; 1998, c. 817; 2008, c. 860.

§ 3.2-6586. Dog injuring or killing other companion animals.

The owner of any companion animal that is injured or killed by a dog shall be entitled to recover damages consistent with the provisions of § 3.2-6585 from the owner of such dog in an appropriate action at law if: (i) the injury occurred on the premises of the companion animal's owner; and (ii) the owner of the offending dog did not have the permission of the companion animal's owner for the dog to be on the premises at the time of the attack.

History.
2003, c. 841, § 3.1-796.127:1; 2008, c. 860.

§ 3.2-6587. Unlawful acts; penalties.

A. The following shall be unlawful acts and are Class 4 misdemeanors:

1. For any person to make a false statement in order to secure a dog or cat license to which he is not entitled.
2. For any dog or cat owner to fail to pay any license tax required by this chapter before February 1 for the year in which it is due. In addition, the court may order confiscation and the proper disposition of the dog or cat.
3. For any dog owner to allow a dog to run at large in violation of an ordinance passed pursuant to § 3.2-6539.
4. For any person to fail to obey an ordinance passed pursuant to §§ 3.2-6522 and 3.2-6525.
5. For any owner to fail to dispose of the body of his companion animals in accordance with § 3.2-6554.
6. For the owner of any dog or cat with a contagious or infectious disease to permit such dog or cat to stray from his premises if such disease is known to the owner.
7. For any person to conceal or harbor any dog or cat on which any required license tax has not been paid.
8. For any person, except the owner or custodian, to remove a legally acquired license tag from a dog or cat without the permission of the owner or custodian.
9. Any other violation of this chapter for which a specific penalty is not provided.

B. It is a Class 1 misdemeanor for any person to:

1. Present a false claim or to receive any money on a false claim under the provisions of § 3.2-6553; or
2. Impersonate a humane investigator.

History.
1984, c. 492, § 29-213.99; 1987, c. 488, § 3.1-796.128; 1993, cc. 174, 775, 817; 1998, c. 817; 2008, c. 860.

§ 3.2-6588. Intentional interference with a guide or leader dog; penalty.

A. It is unlawful for a person to, without just cause, willfully impede or interfere with the duties performed by a dog if the person knows or has reason to believe the dog is a guide or leader dog. A violation of this subsection is a Class 3 misdemeanor.

B. It is unlawful for a person to, without just cause, willfully injure a dog if the person knows or has reason to believe the dog is a guide or leader dog. A violation of this subsection is a Class 1 misdemeanor.

"Guide or leader dog" means a dog that: (i) serves as a dog guide for a blind person as defined in § 51.5-60 or for a person with a visual disability; (ii) serves as a listener for a deaf or hard-of-hearing person as defined in § 51.5-111; or (iii) provides support or assistance for a physically disabled or handicapped person.

History.
1995, c. 209, § 3.1-796.128:1; 2008, c. 860.

§ 3.2-6589. Selling garments containing dog or cat fur prohibited; penalty.

It is unlawful for any person to sell a garment containing the hide, fur, or pelt that he knows to be that of a domestic dog or cat. A violation of this section is punishable by a fine of not more than $10,000.

History.
1999, cc. 646, 678, § 3.1-796.128:2; 2008, c. 860.

§ 3.2-6590. Jurisdiction of general district courts; right of appeal.

Unless otherwise provided, the provisions of this article may be enforced by any general district court in cities or counties wherein the offense is committed or the offender or owner may be found. Every such offender shall have the right of appeal to the appropriate circuit court.

History.
1984, c. 492, § 29-213.100; 1987, c. 488, § 3.1-796.129; 2008, c. 860.

TITLE 4.1.

ALCOHOLIC BEVERAGE CONTROL ACT.

CHAPTER 1.

DEFINITIONS AND GENERAL PROVISIONS.

§ 4.1-100. (Effective until July 1, 2018) Definitions.

As used in this title unless the context requires a different meaning:

"Alcohol" means the product known as ethyl or grain alcohol obtained by distillation of any fermented liquor, rectified either once or more often, whatever the origin, and shall include synthetic ethyl alcohol, but shall not include methyl alcohol and alcohol completely denatured in accordance with formulas approved by the government of the United States.

"Alcohol vaporizing device" means any device, machine, or process that mixes any alcoholic beverages with pure oxygen or other gas to produce a vaporized product for the purpose of consumption by inhalation.

"Alcoholic beverages" includes alcohol, spirits, wine, and beer, and any one or more of such varieties containing one-half of one percent or more of alcohol by volume, including mixed alcoholic beverages, and every liquid or solid, powder or crystal, patented or not, containing alcohol, spirits, wine, or beer and capable of being consumed by a human being. Any liquid or solid containing more than one of the four varieties shall be considered as belonging to that variety which has the higher percentage of alcohol, however obtained, according to the order in which they are set forth in this definition; except that beer may be manufactured to include flavoring materials and other nonbeverage ingredients containing alcohol, as long as no more than 49 percent of the overall alcohol content of the finished product is derived from the addition of flavors and other nonbeverage ingredients containing alcohol for products with an alcohol content of no more than six percent by volume; or, in the case of products with an alcohol content of more than six percent by volume, as long as no more than one and one-half percent of the volume of the finished product consists of alcohol derived from added flavors and other nonbeverage ingredients containing alcohol.

"Art instruction studio" means any commercial establishment that provides to its customers all required supplies and step-by-step instruction in creating a painting or other work of art during a studio instructional session.

"Arts venue" means a commercial or nonprofit establishment that is open to the public and in which works of art are sold or displayed.

"Barrel" means any container or vessel having a capacity of more than 43 ounces.

"Bed and breakfast establishment" means any establishment (i) having no more than 15 bedrooms; (ii) offering to the public, for compensation, transitory lodging or sleeping accommodations; and (iii) offering at least one meal per day, which may but need not be breakfast, to each person to whom overnight lodging is provided.

"Beer" means any alcoholic beverage obtained by the fermentation of an infusion or decoction of barley, malt, and hops or of any similar products in drinkable water and containing one-half of one percent or more of alcohol by volume.

"Board" means the Virginia Alcoholic Beverage Control Board.

"Bottle" means any vessel intended to contain liquids and having a capacity of not more than 43 ounces.

"Canal boat operator" means any nonprofit organization that operates tourism-oriented canal boats for recreational purposes on waterways declared nonnavigable by the United States Congress pursuant to 33 U.S.C. § 59ii.

"Club" means any private nonprofit corporation or association which is the owner, lessee, or occupant of an establishment operated solely for a national, social, patriotic, political, athletic, or other like purpose, but not for pecuniary gain, the advantages of which belong to all of the members. It also means the establishment so operated. A corporation or association shall not lose its status as a club because of the conduct of charitable gaming conducted pursuant to Article 1.1:1 (§ 18.2-340.15 et seq.) of Chapter 8 of Title 18.2 in which nonmembers participate frequently or in large numbers, provided that no alcoholic beverages are served or consumed in the room where such charitable gaming is being conducted while such gaming is being conducted and that no alcoholic beverages are made available upon the premises to any person who is neither a member nor a bona fide guest of a member.

Any such corporation or association which has been declared exempt from federal and state income taxes as one which is not organized and operated for pecuniary gain or profit shall be deemed a nonprofit corporation or association.

"Container" means any barrel, bottle, carton, keg, vessel or other receptacle used for holding alcoholic beverages.

"Contract winemaking facility" means the premises of a licensed winery or farm winery that obtains grapes, fruits, and other agricultural products from a person holding a farm winery license and crushes, processes, ferments, bottles, or provides any combination of such services pursuant to an agreement with the farm winery licensee. For all purposes of this title, wine produced by a contract winemaking facility for a farm winery shall be considered to be wine owned and produced by the farm winery that supplied the grapes, fruits, or other agricultural products used in the production of the wine. The contract winemaking facility shall have no right to sell the wine so produced, unless the terms of payment have not been fulfilled in accordance with the contract. The contract winemaking facility may charge the farm winery for its services.

"Convenience grocery store" means an establishment which (i) has an enclosed room in a permanent structure where stock is displayed and offered for sale and (ii) maintains an inventory of edible items intended for human consumption consisting of a variety of such items of the types normally sold in grocery stores.

"Day spa" means any commercial establishment that offers to the public both massage therapy, performed by persons licensed in accordance with § 54.1-3029, and barbering or cosmetology services performed by persons licensed in accordance with Chapter 7 (§ 54.1-700 et seq.) of Title 54.1.

"Designated area" means a room or area approved by the Board for on-premises licensees.

"Dining area" means a public room or area in which meals are regularly served.

"Establishment" means any place where alcoholic beverages of one or more varieties are lawfully manufactured, sold, or used.

"Farm winery" means (i) an establishment (a) located on a farm in the Commonwealth on land zoned agricultural with a producing vineyard, orchard, or similar growing area and with facilities for fermenting and bottling wine on the premises where the owner or lessee manufactures wine that contains not more than 21 percent alcohol by volume or (b) located in the Commonwealth on land zoned agricultural with a producing vineyard, orchard, or similar growing area or agreements for purchasing grapes or other fruits from agricultural growers within the Commonwealth and with facilities for fermenting and bottling wine on the premises where the owner or lessee manufactures wine that contains not more than 21 percent alcohol by volume or (ii) an accredited public or private institution of higher education, provided that (a) no wine manufactured by the institution shall be sold, (b) the wine manufactured by the institution shall be used solely for research and educational purposes, (c) the wine manufactured by the institution shall be stored on the premises of such farm winery that shall be separate and apart from all other facilities of the institution, and (d) such farm winery is operated in strict conformance with the requirements of this clause (ii) and Board regulations. As used in this definition, the terms "owner" and "lessee" shall include a cooperative formed by an association of individuals for the purpose of manufacturing wine. In the event that such cooperative is licensed as a farm winery, the term "farm" as used in this definition includes all of the land owned or leased by the individual members of the cooperative as long as such land is located in the Commonwealth. For purposes of this definition, "land zoned agricultural" means (1) land zoned as an agricultural district or classification or (2) land otherwise permitted by a locality for farm winery use. For purposes of this definition, "land zoned agricultural" does not include land zoned "residential conservation." Except for the limitation on land zoned "residential conservation," nothing in the definition of "land zoned agricultural" shall otherwise limit or affect local zoning authority.

"Gift shop" means any bona fide retail store selling, predominantly, gifts, books, souvenirs, specialty items relating to history, original and handmade arts and products, collectibles, crafts, and floral arrangements, which is open to the public on a regular basis. Such shop shall be a permanent structure where stock is displayed and offered for sale and which has facilities to properly secure any stock of wine or beer. Such shop may be located (i) on the premises or grounds of a government registered national, state or local historic building or site or (ii) within the premises of a museum. The Board shall consider the purpose, characteristics, nature, and operation of the shop in determining whether it shall be considered a gift shop.

"Gourmet brewing shop" means an establishment which sells to persons to whom wine or beer may lawfully be sold, ingredients for making wine or brewing beer, including packaging, and rents to such persons facilities for manufacturing, fermenting and bottling such wine or beer.

"Gourmet shop" means an establishment provided with adequate inventory, shelving, and storage facilities, where, in consideration of payment, substantial amounts of domestic and imported wines and beers of various types and sizes and related products such as cheeses and gourmet foods are habitually furnished to persons.

"Government store" means a store established by the Board for the sale of alcoholic beverages.

"Hotel" means any duly licensed establishment, provided with special space and accommodation, where, in consideration of payment, food and lodging are habitually furnished to persons, and which has four or more bedrooms. It shall also mean the person who operates such hotel.

"Interdicted person" means a person to whom the sale of alcoholic beverages is prohibited by order pursuant to this title.

"Internet wine retailer" means a person who owns or operates an establishment with adequate inventory, shelving, and storage facilities, where, in consideration of payment, internet or telephone orders are taken and shipped directly to consumers and which establishment is not a retail store open to the public.

"Intoxicated" means a condition in which a person has drunk enough alcoholic beverages to observably affect his manner, disposition, speech, muscular movement, general appearance or behavior.

"Licensed" means the holding of a valid license issued by the Board.

"Licensee" means any person to whom a license has been granted by the Board.

"Liqueur" means any of a class of highly flavored alcoholic beverages that do not exceed an alcohol content of 25 percent by volume.

"Low alcohol beverage cooler" means a drink containing one-half of one percent or more of alcohol by volume, but not more than seven and one-half percent alcohol by volume, and consisting of spirits mixed with nonalcoholic beverages or flavoring or coloring materials; it may also contain water, fruit juices, fruit adjuncts, sugar, carbon dioxide, preservatives or other similar products manufactured by fermenting fruit or fruit juices. Low alcohol beverage coolers shall be treated as wine for all purposes of this title; except that low alcohol beverage coolers shall not be sold in localities that have not approved the sale of mixed beverages pursuant to § 4.1-124. In addition, low alcohol beverage coolers shall not be sold for on-premises consumption other than by mixed beverage licensees.

"Meal-assembly kitchen" means any commercial establishment that offers its customers, for off-premises consumption, ingredients for the preparation of meals and entrees in professional kitchen facilities located at the establishment.

"Meals" means, for a mixed beverage license, an assortment of foods commonly ordered in bona fide, full-service restaurants as principal meals of the day. Such restaurants shall include establishments specializing in full course meals with a single substantial entree.

"Member of a club" means (i) a person who maintains his membership in the club by the payment of monthly, quarterly, or annual dues in the manner established by the rules and regulations thereof or (ii) a person who is a member of a bona fide auxiliary, local chapter, or squadron composed of direct lineal descendants of a bona fide member, whether alive or deceased, of a national or international organization to which an individual lodge holding a club license is an authorized member in the same locality. It shall also mean a lifetime member whose financial contribution is not less than 10 times the annual dues of resident members of the club, the full amount of such contribution being paid in advance in a lump sum.

"Mixed beverage" or *"mixed alcoholic beverage"* means a drink composed in whole or in part of spirits.

"Mixer" means any prepackaged ingredients containing beverages or flavoring or coloring materials, and which may also contain water, fruit juices, fruit adjuncts, sugar, carbon dioxide, or preservatives which are not commonly consumed unless combined with alcoholic beverages, whether or not such ingredients contain alcohol. Such specialty beverage product shall be manufactured or distributed by a Virginia corporation.

"Place or premises" means the real estate, together with any buildings or other improvements thereon, designated in the application for a license as the place at which the manufacture, bottling, distribution, use or sale of alcoholic beverages shall be performed, except that portion of any such building or other improvement actually and exclusively used as a private residence.

"Public place" means any place, building, or conveyance to which the public has, or is permitted to have, access, including restaurants, soda fountains, hotel dining areas, lobbies and corridors of hotels, and any park, place of public resort or amusement, highway, street, lane, or sidewalk adjoining any highway, street, or lane.

The term shall not include (i) hotel or restaurant dining areas or ballrooms while in use for private meetings or private parties limited in attendance to members and guests of a particular group, association or organization; (ii) restaurants licensed by the Board in office buildings or industrial or similar facilities while such restaurant is closed to the public and in use for private meetings or parties limited in attendance to employees and nonpaying guests of the owner or a lessee of all or part of such building or facility; (iii) offices, office buildings or industrial facilities while closed to the public and in use for private meetings or parties limited in attendance to employees and nonpaying guests of the owner or a lessee of all or part of such building or facility; or (iv) private recreational or chartered boats which are not licensed by the Board and on which alcoholic beverages are not sold.

"Residence" means any building or part of a building or structure where a person resides, but does not include any part of a building which is not actually and exclusively used as a private residence, nor any part of a hotel or club other than a private guest room thereof.

"Resort complex" means a facility (i) with a hotel owning year-round sports and recreational facilities located contiguously on the same property or (ii) owned by a nonstock, nonprofit, taxable corporation with voluntary membership which, as its primary function, makes available golf, ski and other recreational facilities both to its members and the general public. The hotel or corporation shall have a mini-

mum of 140 private guest rooms or dwelling units contained on not less than 50 acres. The Board may consider the purpose, characteristics, and operation of the applicant establishment in determining whether it shall be considered as a resort complex. All other pertinent qualifications established by the Board for a hotel operation shall be observed by such licensee.

"Restaurant" means, for a beer, or wine and beer license or a limited mixed beverage restaurant license, any establishment provided with special space and accommodation, where, in consideration of payment, meals or other foods prepared on the premises are regularly sold.

"Restaurant" means, for a mixed beverage license other than a limited mixed beverage restaurant license, an established place of business (i) where meals with substantial entrees are regularly sold and (ii) which has adequate facilities and sufficient employees for cooking, preparing, and serving such meals for consumption at tables in dining areas on the premises, and includes establishments specializing in full course meals with a single substantial entree.

"Sale" and *"sell"* includes soliciting or receiving an order for; keeping, offering or exposing for sale; peddling, exchanging or bartering; or delivering otherwise than gratuitously, by any means, alcoholic beverages.

"Sangria" means a drink consisting of red or white wine mixed with some combination of sweeteners, fruit, fruit juice, soda, or soda water that may also be mixed with brandy, triple sec, or other similar spirits.

"Special agent" means an employee of the Department of Alcoholic Beverage Control whom the Board has designated as a law-enforcement officer pursuant to § 4.1-105.

"Special event" means an event sponsored by a duly organized nonprofit corporation or association and conducted for an athletic, charitable, civic, educational, political, or religious purpose.

"Spirits" means any beverage which contains alcohol obtained by distillation mixed with drinkable water and other substances, in solution, and includes, among other things, brandy, rum, whiskey, and gin, or any one or more of the last four named ingredients; but shall not include any such liquors completely denatured in accordance with formulas approved by the United States government.

"Wine" means any alcoholic beverage obtained by the fermentation of the natural sugar content of fruits or other agricultural products containing (i) sugar, including honey and milk, either with or without additional sugar; (ii) one-half of one percent or more of alcohol by volume; and (iii) no product of distillation. The term includes any wine to which wine spirits have been added, as provided in the Internal Revenue Code, to make products commonly known as "fortified wine" which do not exceed an alcohol content of 21 percent by volume.

"Wine cooler" means a drink containing one-half of one percent or more of alcohol by volume, and not more than three and two-tenths percent of alcohol by weight or four percent by volume consisting of wine mixed with nonalcoholic beverages or flavoring or coloring materials, and which may also contain water, fruit juices, fruit adjuncts, sugar, carbon dioxide, or preservatives and shall include other similar products manufactured by fermenting fruit or fruit juices. Wine coolers and similar fermented fruit juice beverages shall be treated as wine for all purposes except for taxation under § 4.1-236.

"With or without meals" means the selling and serving of alcoholic beverages by retail licensees for on-premises consumption whether or not accompanied by food so long as the total food-beverage ratio required by § 4.1-210, or the monthly food sale requirement established by Board regulation, is met by such retail licensee.

History.

Code 1950, §§ 4-2, 4-99; 1952, c. 496; 1954, c. 682; 1962, c. 533; 1968, c. 7, § 4-98.1; 1970, cc. 302, 309; 1974, cc. 460, 497; 1975, c. 408; 1976, cc. 64, 702; 1977, c. 280; 1980, cc. 324, 490; 1983, c. 340; 1984, c. 200; 1985, cc. 448, 457; 1988, c. 261, § 4-127; 1990, cc. 707, 932; 1991, c. 426; 1993, cc. 190, 866, 910; 1995, cc. 497, 518, 661; 1996, cc. 558, 604; 1997, cc. 124, 425; 1999, cc. 93, 171, 481; 2000, cc. 786, 1037, 1052; 2005, c. 911; 2006, c. 714; 2007, cc. 101, 295, 454, 558; 2008, cc. 198, 513, 875; 2013, cc. 107, 117; 2014, cc. 124, 510; 2015, cc. 25, 54, 288, 348, 735; 2016, cc. 324, 710.

§ 4.1-100. (Effective July 1, 2018) Definitions.

As used in this title unless the context requires a different meaning:

"Alcohol" means the product known as ethyl or grain alcohol obtained by distillation of any fermented liquor, rectified either once or more often, whatever the origin, and shall include synthetic ethyl alcohol, but shall not include methyl alcohol and alcohol completely denatured in accordance with formulas approved by the government of the United States.

"Alcohol vaporizing device" means any device, machine, or process that mixes any alcoholic beverages with pure oxygen or other gas to produce a vaporized product for the purpose of consumption by inhalation.

"Alcoholic beverages" includes alcohol, spirits, wine, and beer, and any one or more of such varieties containing one-half of one percent or more of alcohol by volume, including mixed alcoholic beverages, and every liquid or solid, powder or crystal, patented or not, containing alcohol, spirits, wine, or beer and capable of being consumed by a human being. Any liquid or solid containing more than one of the four varieties shall be considered as belonging to that variety which has the higher percentage of alcohol, however obtained, according to the order in which they are set forth in this definition; except that beer may be manufactured to include flavoring materials and other nonbeverage ingredients containing alcohol, as long as no more than 49 percent of the overall

alcohol content of the finished product is derived from the addition of flavors and other nonbeverage ingredients containing alcohol for products with an alcohol content of no more than six percent by volume; or, in the case of products with an alcohol content of more than six percent by volume, as long as no more than one and one-half percent of the volume of the finished product consists of alcohol derived from added flavors and other nonbeverage ingredients containing alcohol.

"Art instruction studio" means any commercial establishment that provides to its customers all required supplies and step-by-step instruction in creating a painting or other work of art during a studio instructional session.

"Arts venue" means a commercial or nonprofit establishment that is open to the public and in which works of art are sold or displayed.

"Authority" means the Virginia Alcoholic Beverage Control Authority created pursuant to this title.

"Barrel" means any container or vessel having a capacity of more than 43 ounces.

"Bed and breakfast establishment" means any establishment (i) having no more than 15 bedrooms; (ii) offering to the public, for compensation, transitory lodging or sleeping accommodations; and (iii) offering at least one meal per day, which may but need not be breakfast, to each person to whom overnight lodging is provided.

"Beer" means any alcoholic beverage obtained by the fermentation of an infusion or decoction of barley, malt, and hops or of any similar products in drinkable water and containing one-half of one percent or more of alcohol by volume.

"Board" means the Board of Directors of the Virginia Alcoholic Beverage Control Authority.

"Bottle" means any vessel intended to contain liquids and having a capacity of not more than 43 ounces.

"Canal boat operator" means any nonprofit organization that operates tourism-oriented canal boats for recreational purposes on waterways declared nonnavigable by the United States Congress pursuant to 33 U.S.C. § 59ii.

"Club" means any private nonprofit corporation or association which is the owner, lessee, or occupant of an establishment operated solely for a national, social, patriotic, political, athletic, or other like purpose, but not for pecuniary gain, the advantages of which belong to all of the members. It also means the establishment so operated. A corporation or association shall not lose its status as a club because of the conduct of charitable gaming conducted pursuant to Article 1.1:1 (§ 18.2-340.15 et seq.) of Chapter 8 of Title 18.2 in which nonmembers participate frequently or in large numbers, provided that no alcoholic beverages are served or consumed in the room where such charitable gaming is being conducted while such gaming is being conducted and that no alcoholic beverages are made available upon the premises to any person who is neither a member nor a bona fide guest of a member.

Any such corporation or association which has been declared exempt from federal and state income taxes as one which is not organized and operated for pecuniary gain or profit shall be deemed a nonprofit corporation or association.

"Container" means any barrel, bottle, carton, keg, vessel or other receptacle used for holding alcoholic beverages.

"Contract winemaking facility" means the premises of a licensed winery or farm winery that obtains grapes, fruits, and other agricultural products from a person holding a farm winery license and crushes, processes, ferments, bottles, or provides any combination of such services pursuant to an agreement with the farm winery licensee. For all purposes of this title, wine produced by a contract winemaking facility for a farm winery shall be considered to be wine owned and produced by the farm winery that supplied the grapes, fruits, or other agricultural products used in the production of the wine. The contract winemaking facility shall have no right to sell the wine so produced, unless the terms of payment have not been fulfilled in accordance with the contract. The contract winemaking facility may charge the farm winery for its services.

"Convenience grocery store" means an establishment which (i) has an enclosed room in a permanent structure where stock is displayed and offered for sale and (ii) maintains an inventory of edible items intended for human consumption consisting of a variety of such items of the types normally sold in grocery stores.

"Day spa" means any commercial establishment that offers to the public both massage therapy, performed by persons licensed in accordance with § 54.1-3029, and barbering or cosmetology services performed by persons licensed in accordance with Chapter 7 (§ 54.1-700 et seq.) of Title 54.1.

"Designated area" means a room or area approved by the Board for on-premises licensees.

"Dining area" means a public room or area in which meals are regularly served.

"Establishment" means any place where alcoholic beverages of one or more varieties are lawfully manufactured, sold, or used.

"Farm winery" means (i) an establishment (a) located on a farm in the Commonwealth on land zoned agricultural with a producing vineyard, orchard, or similar growing area and with facilities for fermenting and bottling wine on the premises where the owner or lessee manufactures wine that contains not more than 21 percent alcohol by volume or (b) located in the Commonwealth on land zoned agricultural with a producing vineyard, orchard, or similar growing area or agreements for purchasing grapes or other fruits from agricultural growers within the Commonwealth and with facilities for fermenting and bottling wine on the premises where the owner or lessee manufactures wine that contains not more than 21 percent alcohol by volume or (ii) an accredited public or private institution of higher education,

provided that (a) no wine manufactured by the institution shall be sold, (b) the wine manufactured by the institution shall be used solely for research and educational purposes, (c) the wine manufactured by the institution shall be stored on the premises of such farm winery that shall be separate and apart from all other facilities of the institution, and (d) such farm winery is operated in strict conformance with the requirements of this clause (ii) and Board regulations. As used in this definition, the terms "owner" and "lessee" shall include a cooperative formed by an association of individuals for the purpose of manufacturing wine. In the event that such cooperative is licensed as a farm winery, the term "farm" as used in this definition includes all of the land owned or leased by the individual members of the cooperative as long as such land is located in the Commonwealth. For purposes of this definition, "land zoned agricultural" means (1) land zoned as an agricultural district or classification or (2) land otherwise permitted by a locality for farm winery use. For purposes of this definition, "land zoned agricultural" does not include land zoned "residential conservation." Except for the limitation on land zoned "residential conservation," nothing in the definition of "land zoned agricultural" shall otherwise limit or affect local zoning authority.

"Gift shop" means any bona fide retail store selling, predominantly, gifts, books, souvenirs, specialty items relating to history, original and handmade arts and products, collectibles, crafts, and floral arrangements, which is open to the public on a regular basis. Such shop shall be a permanent structure where stock is displayed and offered for sale and which has facilities to properly secure any stock of wine or beer. Such shop may be located (i) on the premises or grounds of a government registered national, state or local historic building or site or (ii) within the premises of a museum. The Board shall consider the purpose, characteristics, nature, and operation of the shop in determining whether it shall be considered a gift shop.

"Gourmet brewing shop" means an establishment which sells to persons to whom wine or beer may lawfully be sold, ingredients for making wine or brewing beer, including packaging, and rents to such persons facilities for manufacturing, fermenting and bottling such wine or beer.

"Gourmet shop" means an establishment provided with adequate inventory, shelving, and storage facilities, where, in consideration of payment, substantial amounts of domestic and imported wines and beers of various types and sizes and related products such as cheeses and gourmet foods are habitually furnished to persons.

"Government store" means a store established by the Authority for the sale of alcoholic beverages.

"Hotel" means any duly licensed establishment, provided with special space and accommodation, where, in consideration of payment, food and lodging are habitually furnished to persons, and which has four or more bedrooms. It shall also mean the person who operates such hotel.

"Interdicted person" means a person to whom the sale of alcoholic beverages is prohibited by order pursuant to this title.

"Internet wine retailer" means a person who owns or operates an establishment with adequate inventory, shelving, and storage facilities, where, in consideration of payment, internet or telephone orders are taken and shipped directly to consumers and which establishment is not a retail store open to the public.

"Intoxicated" means a condition in which a person has drunk enough alcoholic beverages to observably affect his manner, disposition, speech, muscular movement, general appearance or behavior.

"Licensed" means the holding of a valid license granted by the Authority.

"Licensee" means any person to whom a license has been granted by the Authority.

"Liqueur" means any of a class of highly flavored alcoholic beverages that do not exceed an alcohol content of 25 percent by volume.

"Low alcohol beverage cooler" means a drink containing one-half of one percent or more of alcohol by volume, but not more than seven and one-half percent alcohol by volume, and consisting of spirits mixed with nonalcoholic beverages or flavoring or coloring materials; it may also contain water, fruit juices, fruit adjuncts, sugar, carbon dioxide, preservatives or other similar products manufactured by fermenting fruit or fruit juices. Low alcohol beverage coolers shall be treated as wine for all purposes of this title; except that low alcohol beverage coolers shall not be sold in localities that have not approved the sale of mixed beverages pursuant to § 4.1-124. In addition, low alcohol beverage coolers shall not be sold for on-premises consumption other than by mixed beverage licensees.

"Meal-assembly kitchen" means any commercial establishment that offers its customers, for off-premises consumption, ingredients for the preparation of meals and entrees in professional kitchen facilities located at the establishment.

"Meals" means, for a mixed beverage license, an assortment of foods commonly ordered in bona fide, full-service restaurants as principal meals of the day. Such restaurants shall include establishments specializing in full course meals with a single substantial entree.

"Member of a club" means (i) a person who maintains his membership in the club by the payment of monthly, quarterly, or annual dues in the manner established by the rules and regulations thereof or (ii) a person who is a member of a bona fide auxiliary, local chapter, or squadron composed of direct lineal descendants of a bona fide member, whether alive or deceased, of a national or international organization to which an individual lodge holding a club license is an authorized member in the same locality. It shall also mean a lifetime member whose

financial contribution is not less than 10 times the annual dues of resident members of the club, the full amount of such contribution being paid in advance in a lump sum.

"Mixed beverage" or *"mixed alcoholic beverage"* means a drink composed in whole or in part of spirits.

"Mixer" means any prepackaged ingredients containing beverages or flavoring or coloring materials, and which may also contain water, fruit juices, fruit adjuncts, sugar, carbon dioxide, or preservatives which are not commonly consumed unless combined with alcoholic beverages, whether or not such ingredients contain alcohol. Such specialty beverage product shall be manufactured or distributed by a Virginia corporation.

"Place or premises" means the real estate, together with any buildings or other improvements thereon, designated in the application for a license as the place at which the manufacture, bottling, distribution, use or sale of alcoholic beverages shall be performed, except that portion of any such building or other improvement actually and exclusively used as a private residence.

"Principal stockholder" means any person who individually or in concert with his spouse and immediate family members beneficially owns or controls, directly or indirectly, five percent or more of the equity ownership of any person that is a licensee of the Authority, or who in concert with his spouse and immediate family members has the power to vote or cause the vote of five percent or more of any such equity ownership. "Principal stockholder" does not include a broker-dealer registered under the Securities Exchange Act of 1934, as amended, that holds in inventory shares for sale on the financial markets for a publicly traded corporation holding, directly or indirectly, a license from the Authority.

"Public place" means any place, building, or conveyance to which the public has, or is permitted to have, access, including restaurants, soda fountains, hotel dining areas, lobbies and corridors of hotels, and any park, place of public resort or amusement, highway, street, lane, or sidewalk adjoining any highway, street, or lane.

The term shall not include (i) hotel or restaurant dining areas or ballrooms while in use for private meetings or private parties limited in attendance to members and guests of a particular group, association or organization; (ii) restaurants licensed by the Authority in office buildings or industrial or similar facilities while such restaurant is closed to the public and in use for private meetings or parties limited in attendance to employees and nonpaying guests of the owner or a lessee of all or part of such building or facility; (iii) offices, office buildings or industrial facilities while closed to the public and in use for private meetings or parties limited in attendance to employees and nonpaying guests of the owner or a lessee of all or part of such building or facility; or (iv) private recreational or chartered boats which are not licensed by the Board and on which alcoholic beverages are not sold.

"Residence" means any building or part of a building or structure where a person resides, but does not include any part of a building which is not actually and exclusively used as a private residence, nor any part of a hotel or club other than a private guest room thereof.

"Resort complex" means a facility (i) with a hotel owning year-round sports and recreational facilities located contiguously on the same property or (ii) owned by a nonstock, nonprofit, taxable corporation with voluntary membership which, as its primary function, makes available golf, ski and other recreational facilities both to its members and the general public. The hotel or corporation shall have a minimum of 140 private guest rooms or dwelling units contained on not less than 50 acres. The Authority may consider the purpose, characteristics, and operation of the applicant establishment in determining whether it shall be considered as a resort complex. All other pertinent qualifications established by the Board for a hotel operation shall be observed by such licensee.

"Restaurant" means, for a beer, or wine and beer license or a limited mixed beverage restaurant license, any establishment provided with special space and accommodation, where, in consideration of payment, meals or other foods prepared on the premises are regularly sold.

"Restaurant" means, for a mixed beverage license other than a limited mixed beverage restaurant license, an established place of business (i) where meals with substantial entrees are regularly sold and (ii) which has adequate facilities and sufficient employees for cooking, preparing, and serving such meals for consumption at tables in dining areas on the premises, and includes establishments specializing in full course meals with a single substantial entree.

"Sale" and *"sell"* includes soliciting or receiving an order for; keeping, offering or exposing for sale; peddling, exchanging or bartering; or delivering otherwise than gratuitously, by any means, alcoholic beverages.

"Sangria" means a drink consisting of red or white wine mixed with some combination of sweeteners, fruit, fruit juice, soda, or soda water that may also be mixed with brandy, triple sec, or other similar spirits.

"Special agent" means an employee of the Virginia Alcoholic Beverage Control Authority whom the Board has designated as a law-enforcement officer pursuant to § 4.1-105.

"Special event" means an event sponsored by a duly organized nonprofit corporation or association and conducted for an athletic, charitable, civic, educational, political, or religious purpose.

"Spirits" means any beverage which contains alcohol obtained by distillation mixed with drinkable water and other substances, in solution, and in-

cludes, among other things, brandy, rum, whiskey, and gin, or any one or more of the last four named ingredients; but shall not include any such liquors completely denatured in accordance with formulas approved by the United States government.

"Wine" means any alcoholic beverage obtained by the fermentation of the natural sugar content of fruits or other agricultural products containing (i) sugar, including honey and milk, either with or without additional sugar; (ii) one-half of one percent or more of alcohol by volume; and (iii) no product of distillation. The term includes any wine to which wine spirits have been added, as provided in the Internal Revenue Code, to make products commonly known as "fortified wine" which do not exceed an alcohol content of 21 percent by volume.

"Wine cooler" means a drink containing one-half of one percent or more of alcohol by volume, and not more than three and two-tenths percent of alcohol by weight or four percent by volume consisting of wine mixed with nonalcoholic beverages or flavoring or coloring materials, and which may also contain water, fruit juices, fruit adjuncts, sugar, carbon dioxide, or preservatives and shall include other similar products manufactured by fermenting fruit or fruit juices. Wine coolers and similar fermented fruit juice beverages shall be treated as wine for all purposes except for taxation under § 4.1-236.

"With or without meals" means the selling and serving of alcoholic beverages by retail licensees for on-premises consumption whether or not accompanied by food so long as the total food-beverage ratio required by § 4.1-210, or the monthly food sale requirement established by Board regulation, is met by such retail licensee.

History.

Code 1950, §§ 4-2, 4-99; 1952, c. 496; 1954, c. 682; 1962, c. 533; 1968, c. 7, § 4-98.1; 1970, cc. 302, 309; 1974, cc. 460, 497; 1975, c. 408; 1976, cc. 64, 702; 1977, c. 280; 1980, cc. 324, 490; 1983, c. 340; 1984, c. 200; 1985, cc. 448, 457; 1988, c. 261, § 4-127; 1990, cc. 707, 932; 1991, c. 426; 1993, cc. 190, 866, 910; 1995, cc. 497, 518, 661; 1996, cc. 558, 604; 1997, cc. 124, 425; 1999, cc. 93, 171, 481; 2000, cc. 786, 1037, 1052; 2005, c. 911; 2006, c. 714; 2007, cc. 101, 295, 454, 558; 2008, cc. 198, 513, 875; 2013, cc. 107, 117; 2014, cc. 124, 510; 2015, cc. 25, 38, 54, 288, 348, 730, 735; 2016, cc. 324, 710.

§ 4.1-103.01. Additional powers; access to certain tobacco sales records; inspections; penalty.

A. Notwithstanding the provisions of § 58.1-3 or any other provision of law, the Tax Commissioner shall provide to the Board the name, address, and other identifying information within his possession of all wholesale cigarette dealers.

B. All invoices, books, papers or other memoranda and records concerning the sale of cigarettes maintained by wholesale cigarette dealers pursuant to § 58.1-1007 shall be subject to inspection during normal business hours by special agents of the Board. Any person who, upon request by a special agent, unreasonably fails or refuses to allow an inspection of the records authorized by this subsection shall be guilty of a Class 2 misdemeanor.

C. The Board may use the information obtained from the Tax Commissioner or by the inspections authorized by subsection B only for the purpose of creating and maintaining a list of retail dealers to facilitate enforcement of the laws governing the sale of tobacco products to minors. Neither the Board nor any special agent shall divulge any information provided by the Tax Commissioner or obtained in the performance of the inspections authorized by subsection B to anyone other than to another special agent. Any person violating the provisions of this subsection shall be guilty of a Class 2 misdemeanor.

History.

1998, cc. 189, 364.

§ 4.1-105. Police power of members, agents and employees of Board.

Members of the Board are vested, and such agents and employees of the Board designated by it shall be vested, with like power to enforce the provisions of (i) this title and the criminal laws of the Commonwealth as is vested in the chief law-enforcement officer of a county, city, or town; (ii) § 3.2-4207; (iii) § 18.2-371.2; and (iv) § 58.1-1037.

History.

Code 1950, § 4-8; 1993, c. 866; 1997, cc. 812, 882; 2000, cc. 880, 901; 2006, c. 695.

CHAPTER 2.
ADMINISTRATION OF LICENSES.

Article 1.

General Provisions.

Section

ARTICLE 1.
GENERAL PROVISIONS.

§ 4.1-200. Exemptions from licensure.

The licensure requirements of this chapter shall not apply to:

1. A person in charge of an institution regularly conducted as a hospital or sanatorium for the care of persons in ill health, or as a home devoted exclusively to the care of aged people, who administers or causes to be administered alcoholic beverages to any bona fide patient or inmate of the institution who is in need of the same, either by way of external

application or otherwise for emergency medicinal purposes. Such person may charge for the alcoholic beverages so administered, and carry such stock as may be necessary for this purpose. No charge shall be made of any patient for the alcoholic beverages so administered to him where the same have been supplied to the institution by the Board free of charge.

2. The manufacture, sale and delivery or shipment by persons authorized under existing laws to engage in such business of any medicine containing sufficient medication to prevent it from being used as a beverage.

3. The manufacture, sale and delivery or shipment by persons authorized under existing laws to engage in such business of any medicinal preparations manufactured in accordance with formulas prescribed by the United States pharmacopoeia; national formulary, patent and proprietary preparations; and other bona fide medicinal and technical preparations; which contain no more alcohol than is necessary to extract the medicinal properties of the drugs contained in such preparations, and no more alcohol than is necessary to hold the medicinal agents in solution and to preserve the same, and which are manufactured and sold to be used exclusively as medicine and not as beverages.

4. The manufacture, sale and delivery or shipment of toilet, medicinal and antiseptic preparations and solutions not intended for internal human use nor to be sold as beverages.

5. The manufacture and sale of food products known as flavoring extracts which are manufactured and sold for cooking and culinary purposes only and not sold as beverages.

6. Any person who manufactures at his residence or at a gourmet brewing shop for domestic consumption at his residence, but not to be sold, dispensed or given away, except as hereinafter provided, wine or beer or both, in an amount not to exceed the limits permitted by federal law.

Any person who manufactures wine or beer in accordance with this subdivision may remove from his residence an amount not to exceed fifty liters of such wine or fifteen gallons of such beer on any one occasion for (i) personal or family use, provided such use does not violate the provisions of this title or Board regulations; (ii) giving to any person to whom wine or beer may be lawfully sold an amount not to exceed (a) one liter of wine per person per year or (b) seventy-two ounces of beer per person per year, provided such gift is for noncommercial purposes; or (iii) giving to any person to whom beer may lawfully be sold a sample of such wine or beer, not to exceed (a) one ounce of wine by volume or (b) two ounces of beer by volume for on-premises consumption at events organized for judging or exhibiting such wine or beer, including events held on the premises of a retail licensee. Nothing in this paragraph shall be construed to authorize the sale of such wine or beer.

The provision of this subdivision shall not apply to any person who resides on property on which a winery, farm winery, or brewery is located.

7. Any person who keeps and possesses lawfully acquired alcoholic beverages in his residence for his personal use or that of his family. However, such alcoholic beverages may be served or given to guests in such residence by such person, his family or servants when (i) such guests are 21 years of age or older or are accompanied by a parent, guardian, or spouse who is 21 years of age or older, (ii) the consumption or possession of such alcoholic beverages by family members or such guests occurs only in such residence where the alcoholic beverages are allowed to be served or given pursuant to this subdivision, and (iii) such service or gift is in no way a shift or device to evade the provisions of this title.

8. Any person who manufactures and sells cider to distillery licensees, or any person who manufactures wine from grapes grown by such person and sells it to winery licensees.

9. The sale of wine and beer in or through canteens or post exchanges on United States reservations when permitted by the proper authority of the United States.

10. The keeping and consumption of any lawfully acquired alcoholic beverages at a private meeting or private party limited in attendance to members and guests of a particular group, association or organization at a banquet or similar affair, or at a special event, if a banquet license has been granted. However, no banquet license shall be required for private meetings or private parties limited in attendance to the members of a common interest community as defined in § 54.1-2345 and their guests, provided (i) the alcoholic beverages shall not be sold or charged for in any way, (ii) the premises where the alcoholic beverages are consumed is limited to the common area regularly occupied and utilized for such private meetings or private parties, and (iii) such meetings or parties are not open to the public.

History.

Code 1950, §§ 4-50, 4-89, 4-90; 1954, c. 147; 1970, cc. 113, 541; 1972, cc. 75, 76, 741; 1973, c. 413; 1975, c. 408; 1976, c. 37; 1981, c. 410; 1984, c. 200; 1992, c. 349; 1993, c. 866; 1995, cc. 497, 518; 2001, c. 117; 2006, cc. 274, 740; 2010, c. 294; 2011, c. 8.

§ 4.1-201. Conduct not prohibited by this title; limitation.

A. Nothing in this title or any Board regulation adopted pursuant thereto shall prohibit:

1. Any club licensed under this chapter from keeping for consumption by its members any alcoholic beverages lawfully acquired by such members, provided the alcoholic beverages are not sold, dispensed or given away in violation of this title.

2. Any person from having grain, fruit or fruit products and any other substance, when grown or lawfully produced by him, distilled by any distillery licensee, and selling the distilled alcoholic beverages to the Board or selling or shipping them to any person outside of the Commonwealth in accordance with Board regulations. However, no alcoholic bev-

erages so distilled shall be withdrawn from the place where distilled except in accordance with Board regulations.

3. Any person licensed to manufacture and sell, or either, in the Commonwealth or elsewhere, alcoholic beverages other than wine or beer, from soliciting and taking orders from the Board for such alcoholic beverages.

4. The receipt by a person operating a licensed brewery of deliveries and shipments of beer in closed containers or the sale, delivery or shipment of such beer, in accordance with Board regulations to (i) persons licensed to sell beer at wholesale, (ii) persons licensed to sell beer at retail for the purpose of resale only as provided in subdivision B 4 of § 4.1-216, (iii) owners of boats registered under the laws of the United States sailing for ports of call of a foreign country or another state, and (iv) persons outside the Commonwealth for resale outside the Commonwealth.

5. The granting of any retail license to a brewery, distillery, or winery licensee, or to an applicant for such license, or to a lessee of such person, a wholly owned subsidiary of such person, or its lessee, provided the places of business or establishments for which the retail licenses are desired are located upon the premises occupied or to be occupied by such distillery, winery, or brewery, or upon property of such person contiguous to such premises, or in a development contiguous to such premises owned and operated by such person or a wholly owned subsidiary.

6. The receipt by a distillery licensee of deliveries and shipments of alcoholic beverages, other than wine and beer, in closed containers from other distilleries, or the sale, delivery or shipment of such alcoholic beverages, in accordance with Board regulations, to the Board and to persons outside the Commonwealth for resale outside the Commonwealth.

7. The receipt by a farm winery or winery licensee of deliveries and shipments of wine in closed containers from other wineries or farm wineries located inside or outside the Commonwealth, or the receipt by a winery licensee or farm winery licensee of deliveries and shipments of spirits distilled from fruit or fruit juices in closed containers from distilleries located inside or outside the Commonwealth to be used only for the fortification of wine produced by the licensee in accordance with Board regulations, or the sale, delivery or shipment of such wine, in accordance with Board regulations, to persons licensed to sell wine at wholesale for the purpose of resale, and to persons outside the Commonwealth for resale outside the Commonwealth.

8. The receipt by a fruit distillery licensee of deliveries and shipments of alcoholic beverages made from fruit or fruit juices in closed containers from other fruit distilleries owned by such licensee, or the sale, delivery or shipment of such alcoholic beverages, in accordance with Board regulations, to persons outside of the Commonwealth for resale outside of the Commonwealth.

9. Any farm winery or winery licensee from shipping or delivering its wine in closed containers to another farm winery or winery licensee for the purpose of additional bottling in accordance with Board regulations and the return of the wine so bottled to the manufacturing farm winery or winery licensee.

10. Any farm winery or winery licensee from selling and shipping or delivering its wine in closed containers to another farm winery or winery licensee, the wine so sold and shipped or delivered to be used by the receiving licensee in the manufacture of wine. Any wine received under this subsection shall be deemed an agricultural product produced in the Commonwealth for the purposes of § 4.1-219, to the extent it is produced from fresh fruits or agricultural products grown or produced in the Commonwealth. The selling licensee shall provide to the receiving licensee, and both shall maintain complete and accurate records of, the source of the fresh fruits or agricultural products used to produce the wine so transferred.

11. Any retail on-premises beer licensee, his agent or employee, from giving a sample of beer to persons to whom alcoholic beverages may be lawfully sold for on-premises consumption, or retail on-premises wine or beer licensee, his agent or employee, from giving a sample of wine or beer to persons to whom alcoholic beverages may be lawfully sold for on-premises consumption, or any mixed beverage licensee, his agent or employee, from giving a sample of wine, beer, or spirits to persons to whom alcoholic beverages may be lawfully sold for on-premises consumption. Samples of wine shall not exceed two ounces, samples of beer shall not exceed four ounces, and samples of spirits shall not exceed one-half ounce. No more than two product samples shall be given to any person per visit.

12. Any manufacturer, including any vendor authorized by any such manufacturer, whether or not licensed in the Commonwealth, from selling service items bearing alcoholic brand references to on-premises retail licensees or prohibit any such retail licensee from displaying the service items on the premises of his licensed establishment. Each such retail licensee purchasing such service items shall retain a copy of the evidence of his payment to the manufacturer or authorized vendor for a period of not less than two years from the date of each sale of the service items. As used in this subdivision, "service items" mean articles of tangible personal property normally used by the employees of on-premises retail licensees to serve alcoholic beverages to customers including, but not limited to, glasses, napkins, buckets, and coasters.

13. Any employee of an alcoholic beverage wholesaler or manufacturer, whether or not licensed in the Commonwealth, from distributing to retail licensees

and their employees novelties and specialties, including wearing apparel, having a wholesale value of $10 or less and that bear alcoholic beverage advertising. Such items may be distributed to retail licensees in quantities equal to the number of employees of the retail establishment present at the time the items are delivered. Thereafter, such employees may wear or display the items on the licensed premises.

14. Any (i) retail on-premises wine or beer licensee, his agent or employee from offering for sale or selling for one price to any person to whom alcoholic beverages may be lawfully sold a flight of wines or beers consisting of samples of not more than five different wines or beers and (ii) mixed beverage licensee, his agent or employee from offering for sale or selling for one price to any person to whom alcoholic beverages may be lawfully sold a flight of distilled spirits consisting of samples of not more than five different spirits products.

15. Any restaurant licensed under this chapter from permitting the consumption of lawfully acquired wine, beer, or cider by bona fide customers on the premises in all areas and locations covered by the license, provided that (i) all such wine, beer, or cider shall have been acquired by the customer from a retailer licensed to sell such alcoholic beverages and (ii) no such wine, beer, or cider shall be brought onto the licensed premises by the customer except in sealed, nonresealable bottles or cans. The licensee may charge a corkage fee to such customer for the wine, beer, or cider so consumed; however, the licensee shall not charge any other fee to such customer.

16. Any winery, farm winery, wine importer, or wine wholesaler licensee from providing to adult customers of licensed retail establishments information about wine being consumed on such premises.

B. No deliveries or shipments of alcoholic beverages to persons outside the Commonwealth for resale outside the Commonwealth shall be made into any state the laws of which prohibit the consignee from receiving or selling the same.

History.

Code 1950, § 4-89; 1954, c. 147; 1970, cc. 113, 541; 1972, cc. 75, 76; 1973, c. 413; 1975, c. 408; 1981, c. 410; 1984, c. 200; 1992, c. 349; 1993, c. 866; 1995, cc. 253, 317; 1997, c. 386; 2000, c. 786; 2003, c. 630; 2004, c. 379; 2006, cc. 106, 826; 2007, c. 820; 2011, c. 559; 2012, c. 376; 2013, c. 604; 2014, cc. 123, 455; 2015, cc. 404, 604; 2016, c. 26.

§ 4.1-201.1. Conduct not prohibited by this title; tastings conducted by manufacturers, wine or beer wholesalers, and authorized representatives.

A. Manufacturers of alcoholic beverages, whether or not licensed in the Commonwealth, and wine or beer wholesalers may conduct tastings of wine, beer, or spirits within hotels, restaurants, and clubs licensed for on-premises consumption provided:

1. The tastings are conducted only by (i) employees of such manufacturers or wholesalers or (ii) authorized representatives of such manufacturers or wholesalers, which authorized representatives have obtained a permit in accordance with subdivision A 15 of § 4.1-212;

2. Such employees or authorized representatives are present while the tastings are being conducted;

3. No category of alcoholic beverage products is offered to consumers unless the retail licensee on whose premises the tasting is conducted is licensed to sell that category of alcoholic beverage product;

4. All alcoholic beverage products used in the tasting are served to the consumer by employees of the retail licensee;

5. The quantity of wine, beer, or spirits provided to any person during the tasting does not exceed 12 ounces of beer, five ounces of wine, or one and one-half ounces of spirits; however, for any spirits tastings, no single sample shall exceed one-half ounce per spirits product offered and no more than three spirits products may be offered to any patron; and

6. All alcoholic beverage products used in the tasting are purchased from the retail licensee on whose premises the tasting is conducted; except that no more than $100 may be expended by or on behalf of any such manufacturer or wholesaler at any retail licensed premises during any 24-hour period. For the purposes of this subdivision, the $100 limitation shall be exclusive of taxes and gratuities, which gratuities may not exceed 20 percent of the cost of the alcoholic beverages, including taxes, for the alcoholic beverages purchased for the tasting.

B. Manufacturers, wholesalers, and their authorized representatives shall keep complete records of each tasting authorized by this section for a period of not less than two years, which records shall include the date and place of each tasting conducted and the dollar amount expended by the manufacturer, wholesaler, or his agent or representative in the purchase of the alcoholic beverages used in the tasting.

C. Manufacturers and wholesalers shall be held liable for any violation of this section committed by their employees or authorized representative in connection with their employment or representation at any tasting event.

History.

2006, c. 826; 2007, cc. 452, 722.

CHAPTER 3. PROHIBITED PRACTICES; PENALTIES; PROCEDURAL MATTERS.

Article 1. Prohibited Practices Generally.

Section

ARTICLE 1.

PROHIBITED PRACTICES GENERALLY.

§ 4.1-300. Illegal manufacture and bottling; penalty.

A. Except as otherwise provided in §§ 4.1-200 and 4.1-201, no person shall manufacture alcoholic beverages in the Commonwealth without being licensed under this title to manufacture such alcoholic beverages. Nor shall any person, other than a brewery licensee or bottler's licensee, bottle beer for sale.

B. The presence of mash at an unlicensed distillery shall constitute manufacturing within the meaning of this section.

C. Any person convicted of a violation of this section shall be guilty of a Class 6 felony.

History.

Code 1950, § 4-57; 1954, c. 484; 1974, c. 460; 1993, c. 866.

§ 4.1-301. Conspiracy to violate § 4.1-300; penalty.

If two or more persons conspire together to do any act which is in violation of § 4.1-300, and one or more of these persons does any act to effect the object of the conspiracy, each of the parties to such conspiracy shall be guilty of a Class 6 felony.

History.

1956, c. 70, § 4-57.1; 1993, c. 866.

§ 4.1-302. Illegal sale of alcoholic beverages in general; penalty.

If any person who is not licensed sells any alcoholic beverages except as permitted by this title, he shall be guilty of a Class 1 misdemeanor.

In the event of a second or subsequent conviction under this section, a jail sentence of no less than thirty days shall be imposed and in no case be suspended.

History.
Code 1950, § 4-58; 1952, c. 491; 1984, c. 603; 1993, c. 866.

§ 4.1-302.1. Use of alcohol vaporizing devices prohibited; penalty.

A. No person shall purchase, offer for sale or use, sell or use any vaporized form of an alcoholic beverage produced by an alcohol vaporizing device.

B. Any person convicted of a violation of this section shall be guilty of a Class 1 misdemeanor.

History.
2006, c. 714.

§ 4.1-302.2. Sale, purchase, use of powdered or crystalline alcohol prohibited; penalty.

A. No person shall purchase or possess, offer for sale or use, sell, or use any powdered or crystalline alcohol product.

B. As used in this section, "powdered or crystalline alcohol" means a product that is manufactured into a powdered or crystalline form and that contains any amount of alcohol.

C. A violation of this section is a Class 1 misdemeanor.

History.
2015, cc. 25, 735.

§ 4.1-303. Purchase of alcoholic beverages from person not authorized to sell; penalty.

If any person buys alcoholic beverages from any person other than the Board, a government store or a person authorized under this title to sell alcoholic beverages, he shall be guilty of a Class 1 misdemeanor.

History.
Code 1950, § 4-71; 1968, c. 7; 1993, c. 866.

§ 4.1-304. Persons to whom alcoholic beverages may not be sold; proof of legal age; penalty.

A. No person shall, except pursuant to subdivisions 1 through 5 of § 4.1-200, sell any alcoholic beverages to any individual when at the time of such sale he knows or has reason to believe that the individual to whom the sale is made is (i) less than 21 years of age, (ii) interdicted, or (iii) intoxicated. Any person convicted of a violation of this subsection is guilty of a Class 1 misdemeanor.

B. Any person who sells, except pursuant to subdivisions 1 through 5 of § 4.1-200, any alcoholic beverage to an individual who is less than 21 years of age and at the time of the sale does not require the individual to present bona fide evidence of legal age indicating that the individual is 21 years of age or older is guilty of a violation of this subsection. Bona fide evidence of legal age is limited to any evidence that is or reasonably appears to be an unexpired driver's license issued by any state of the United States or the District of Columbia, military identification card, United States passport or foreign government visa, unexpired special identification card issued by the Department of Motor Vehicles, or any other valid government-issued identification card bearing the individual's photograph, signature, height, weight, and date of birth, or which bears a photograph that reasonably appears to match the appearance of the purchaser. A student identification card shall not constitute bona fide evidence of legal age for purposes of this subsection. Any person convicted of a violation of this subsection is guilty of a Class 3 misdemeanor. Notwithstanding the provisions of § 4.1-202, the Board shall not take administrative action against a licensee for the conduct of his employee who violates this subsection.

C. No person shall be convicted of both subsections A and B for the same sale.

History.
Code 1950, § 4-62; 1970, c. 686; 1974, c. 460; 1979, c. 537; 1981, c. 24; 1982, c. 66; 1983, c. 608; 1985, c. 559; 1990, c. 771; 1993, c. 866; 2013, c. 562.

§ 4.1-305. Purchasing or possessing alcoholic beverages unlawful in certain cases; venue; exceptions; penalty; forfeiture; deferred proceedings; treatment and education programs and services.

A. No person to whom an alcoholic beverage may not lawfully be sold under § 4.1-304 shall consume, purchase or possess, or attempt to consume, purchase or possess, any alcoholic beverage, except (i) pursuant to subdivisions 1 through 7 of § 4.1-200; (ii) where possession of the alcoholic beverages by a person less than 21 years of age is due to such person's making a delivery of alcoholic beverages in pursuance of his employment or an order of his parent; or (iii) by any state, federal, or local law-enforcement officer or his agent when possession of an alcoholic beverage is necessary in the performance of his duties. Such person may be prosecuted either in the county or city in which the alcohol was possessed or consumed, or in the county or city in which the person exhibits evidence of physical indicia of consumption of alcohol. It shall be an affirmative defense to a charge of a violation of this subsection if the defendant shows that such consumption or possession was pursuant to subdivision 7 of § 4.1-200.

B. No person under the age of 21 years shall use or attempt to use any (i) altered, fictitious, facsimile or simulated license to operate a motor vehicle, (ii) altered, fictitious, facsimile or simulated document, including, but not limited to a birth certificate or student identification card, or (iii) motor vehicle operator's license, birth certificate or student identification card of another person in order to establish a false identification or false age for himself to consume, purchase or attempt to consume or purchase an alcoholic beverage.

C. Any person found guilty of a violation of this section shall be guilty of a Class 1 misdemeanor; and upon conviction, (i) such person shall be ordered to pay a mandatory minimum fine of $500 or ordered to perform a mandatory minimum of 50 hours of community service as a condition of probation supervision and (ii) the license to operate a motor vehicle in the Commonwealth of any such person age 18 or older shall be suspended for a period of not less than six months and not more than one year; the license to operate a motor vehicle in the Commonwealth of any juvenile shall be handled in accordance with the provisions of § 16.1-278.9. The court, in its discretion and upon a demonstration of hardship, may authorize an adult convicted of a violation of this section the use of a restricted permit to operate a motor vehicle in accordance with the provisions of subsection E of § 18.2-271.1 or when referred to a local community-based probation services agency established pursuant to Article 9 (§ 9.1-173 et seq.) of Chapter 1 of Title 9.1. During the period of license suspension, the court may require an adult who is issued a restricted permit under the provisions of this subsection to be (a) monitored by an alcohol safety action program, or (b) supervised by a local community-based probation services agency established pursuant to Article 9 (§ 9.1-173 et seq.) of Chapter 1 of Title 9.1, if one has been established for the locality. The alcohol safety action program or local community-based probation services agency shall report to the court any violation of the terms of the restricted permit, the required alcohol safety action program monitoring or local community-based probation services and any condition related thereto or any failure to remain alcohol-free during the suspension period.

D. Any alcoholic beverage purchased or possessed in violation of this section shall be deemed contraband and forfeited to the Commonwealth in accordance with § 4.1-338.

E. Any retail licensee who in good faith promptly notifies the Board or any state or local law-enforcement agency of a violation or suspected violation of this section shall be accorded immunity from an administrative penalty for a violation of § 4.1-304.

F. When any adult who has not previously been convicted of underaged consumption, purchase or possession of alcoholic beverages in Virginia or any other state or the United States is before the court, the court may, upon entry of a plea of guilty or not guilty, if the facts found by the court would justify a finding of guilt of a violation of subsection A, without entering a judgment of guilt and with the consent of the accused, defer further proceedings and place him on probation subject to appropriate conditions. Such conditions may include the imposition of the license suspension and restricted license provisions in subsection C. However, in all such deferred proceedings, the court shall require the accused to enter a treatment or education program or both, if available, that in the opinion of the court best suits the needs of the accused. If the accused is placed on local community-based probation, the program or services shall be located in any of the judicial districts served by the local community-based probation services agency or in any judicial district ordered by the court when the placement is with an alcohol safety action program. The services shall be provided by (i) a program licensed by the Department of Behavioral Health and Developmental Services, (ii) certified by the Commission on VASAP, or (iii) by a program or services made available through a community-based probation services agency established pursuant to Article 9 (§ 9.1-173 et seq.) of Chapter 1 of Title 9.1, if one has been established for the locality. When an offender is ordered to a local community-based probation services rather than the alcohol safety action program, the local community-based probation services agency shall be responsible for providing for services or referring the offender to education or treatment services as a condition of probation.

Upon violation of a condition, the court may enter an adjudication of guilt and proceed as otherwise provided. Upon fulfillment of the conditions, the court shall discharge the person and dismiss the proceedings against him without an adjudication of guilt. A discharge and dismissal hereunder shall be treated as a conviction for the purpose of applying this section in any subsequent proceedings.

When any juvenile is found to have committed a violation of subsection A, the disposition of the case shall be handled according to the provisions of Article 9 (§ 16.1-278 et seq.) of Chapter 11 of Title 16.1.

History.

Code 1950, § 4-62; 1970, c. 686; 1974, c. 460; 1979, c. 537; 1981, c. 24; 1982, c. 66; 1983, c. 608; 1985, c. 559; 1990, c. 771; 1993, c. 866; 1995, c. 374; 1996, cc. 626, 730; 2000, c. 325; 2002, c. 338; 2003, cc. 845, 849; 2004, cc. 322, 461; 2005, c. 895; 2006, c. 207; 2007, c. 133; 2009, cc. 248, 726, 813, 840; 2012, cc. 250, 260.

§ 4.1-306. Purchasing alcoholic beverages for one to whom they may not be sold; penalty; forfeiture.

A. Any person who purchases alcoholic beverages for another person, and at the time of such purchase knows or has reason to believe that the person for whom the alcoholic beverage was purchased was (i) interdicted, or (ii) intoxicated, is guilty of a Class 1 misdemeanor.

A1. Any person who purchases for, or otherwise gives, provides, or assists in the provision of alcoholic beverages to another person, when he knows or has reason to know that such person was less than 21 years of age, except (i) pursuant to subdivisions 1 through 7 of § 4.1-200; (ii) where possession of the alcoholic beverages by a person less than 21 years of age is due to such person's making a delivery of alcoholic beverages in pursuance of his employment or an order of his parent; or (iii) by any state, federal, or local law-enforcement officer when possession of an alcoholic beverage is necessary in the performance of his duties, is guilty of a Class 1 misdemeanor.

B. In addition to any other penalty authorized by law, any person found guilty of a violation of this section shall have his license to operate a motor vehicle suspended for a period of not more than one year. The court, in its discretion, may authorize any person convicted of a violation of this section the use of a restricted permit to operate a motor vehicle in accordance with the provisions of subsection D of § 16.1-278.9 or subsection E of § 18.2-271.1.

C. Any alcoholic beverages purchased in violation of this section shall be deemed contraband and forfeited to the Commonwealth in accordance with § 4.1-338.

History.

Code 1950, § 4-73; 1970, c. 686; 1993, c. 866; 2005, cc. 895, 898; 2006, c. 87; 2011, c. 31.

§ 4.1-307. Persons by whom alcoholic beverages may not be sold or served for on-premises consumption; penalty.

No person shall permit anyone employed by him under the age of (i) eighteen years to sell, serve or dispense in any manner alcoholic beverages for on-premises consumption, except pursuant to subdivisions 1 through 5 of § 4.1-200 or (ii) twenty-one years to prepare or mix alcoholic beverages in the capacity of bartender.

Any person convicted of a violation of this section shall be guilty of a Class 1 misdemeanor.

History.

Code 1950, § 4-63; 1974, c. 460; 1982, c. 66; 1983, c. 608; 1993, c. 866.

§ 4.1-308. Drinking alcoholic beverages, or offering to another, in public place; penalty; exceptions.

A. If any person takes a drink of alcoholic beverages or offers a drink thereof to another, whether accepted or not, at or in any public place, he shall be guilty of a Class 4 misdemeanor.

B. This section shall not prevent any person from drinking alcoholic beverages or offering a drink thereof to another in any rooms or areas approved by the Board in a licensed establishment, provided such establishment or the person who operates the same is licensed to sell alcoholic beverages at retail for on-premises consumption and the alcoholic beverages drunk or offered were purchased therein.

C. This section shall not prevent any person from drinking alcoholic beverages or offering a drink thereof to another in any room or area approved by the Board at an event for which a banquet license or mixed beverage special events license has been granted. Nor shall this section prevent, upon authorization of the licensee, any person from drinking his own lawfully acquired alcoholic beverages or offering a drink thereof to another in approved areas and locations at events for which a coliseum or stadium license has been granted.

D. This section shall not prevent any person from drinking alcoholic beverages or offering a drink thereof to another on a chartered boat being used for the transportation of passengers for compensation which is not licensed by the Board and which does not sell alcoholic beverages.

History.

Code 1950, § 4-78; 1956, c. 23; 1972, c. 143; 1977, c. 439; 1979, c. 622; 1986, c. 113; 1988, c. 893; 1989, c. 42; 1990, c. 932; 1993, c. 866.

§ 4.1-309. Drinking or possessing alcoholic beverages in or on public school grounds; penalty.

A. No person shall possess or drink any alcoholic beverage in or upon the grounds of any public elementary or secondary school during school hours or school or student activities.

B. In addition, no person shall drink and no organization shall serve any alcoholic beverage in or upon the grounds of any public elementary or secondary school after school hours or school or student activities, except for religious congregations using wine for sacramental purposes only.

C. Any person convicted of a violation of this section shall be guilty of a Class 2 misdemeanor.

D. This section shall not prohibit any person from possessing or drinking alcoholic beverages or any organization from serving alcoholic beverages in areas approved by the Board at a performing arts center owned by the City of Alexandria or the City of Portsmouth, provided the organization operating the performing arts center or its lessee has a license granted by the Board.

History.

1954, c. 651, § 4-78.1; 1982, c. 288; 1991, c. 710; 1993, c. 866; 1994, c. 844; 1997, cc. 784, 837; 2007, c. 813.

§ 4.1-309.1. Possessing or consuming alcoholic beverage while operating a school bus; penalty.

Any person who possesses or consumes an alcoholic beverage while operating a school bus and transporting children is guilty of a Class 1 misdemeanor. For purposes of this section, "school bus" shall have the same meaning as provided in § 46.2-100.

History.

2010, c. 169.

§ 4.1-310. Illegal importation, shipment and transportation of alcoholic beverages; penalty; exception.

A. No alcoholic beverages, other than wine or beer, shall be imported, shipped, transported or brought into the Commonwealth, other than to distillery licensees or winery licensees, unless consigned to the Board. However, the Board may permit such alcoholic beverages ordered by it from outside the Commonwealth for (i) persons, for industrial purposes, (ii) the manufacture of articles allowed to be manufactured under § 4.1-200, or (iii) hospitals, to be shipped or transported directly to such persons. On such orders or shipments of alcohol, the Board shall charge only a reasonable permit fee.

B. Except as otherwise provided in § 4.1-209.1 or 4.1-212.1, no wine shall be imported, shipped, transported or brought into the Commonwealth unless it is consigned to a wholesale wine licensee.

C. Except as otherwise provided in § 4.1-209.1 or 4.1-212.1, no beer shall be imported, shipped, transported or brought into the Commonwealth except to persons licensed to sell it.

D. Any person convicted of a violation of this section shall be guilty of a Class 1 misdemeanor.

E. The provisions of this chapter shall not prohibit (i) any person from bringing, in his personal possession, or through United States Customs in his accompanying baggage, into the Commonwealth not for resale, alcoholic beverages in an amount not to exceed one gallon or four liters if any part of the alcoholic beverages being transported is held in metric-sized containers, (ii) the shipment or transportation into the Commonwealth of a reasonable quantity of alcoholic beverages not for resale in the personal or household effects of a person relocating his place of residence to the Commonwealth, or (iii) the possession or storage of alcoholic beverages on passenger boats, dining cars, buffet cars and club cars, licensed under this title, or common carriers engaged in interstate or foreign commerce.

History.

Code 1950, § 4-84; 1970, c. 297; 1978, c. 436; 1983, c. 212; 1984, c. 200; 1993, c. 866; 1994, c. 826; 1995, cc. 253, 317; 2003, cc. 1029, 1030; 2007, cc. 99, 799.

§ 4.1-311. Limitations on transporting lawfully purchased alcoholic beverages; penalty.

A. The transportation of alcoholic beverages lawfully purchased in the Commonwealth in excess of the following limits is prohibited except in accordance with Board regulations:

1. Wine and beer, no limitation.

2. Alcoholic beverages other than wine and beer, three gallons, provided that not more than one gallon thereof shall be in containers holding less than one-fifth of a gallon. If any part of the alcoholic beverages being transported is held in metric-sized containers, the three-gallon limitation shall be construed to be 12 liters, and not more than 4 liters thereof shall be in containers smaller than 750 milliliters.

B. The transportation of alcoholic beverages lawfully purchased outside the Commonwealth, within, into or through the Commonwealth, in quantities in excess of one gallon or four liters if any part of the alcohol being transported is held in metric-sized containers, is prohibited except in accordance with Board regulations adopted pursuant to this section.

C. Any person transporting alcoholic beverages in violation of this section shall be guilty of a Class 1 misdemeanor.

History.

Code 1950, § 4-72; 1974, c. 460, § 4-72.1; 1975, c. 480; 1978, c. 436; 1993, c. 866.

§ 4.1-312. Limitation on carrying alcoholic beverages in motor vehicle transporting passengers for hire; penalty.

The transportation of alcoholic beverages in any motor vehicle which is being used, or is licensed, for the transportation of passengers for hire is prohibited, except when carried in the possession of a passenger who is being transported for compensation at the regular rate and fare charged other passengers.

Any person convicted of a violation of this section shall be guilty of a Class 1 misdemeanor.

History.

Code 1950, § 4-74; 1993, c. 866.

§ 4.1-313. Possessing, transporting, etc., alcoholic beverages illegally acquired; penalty.

A. No person, other than a common carrier, shall have, possess, keep, carry, ship or transport alcoholic beverages upon which the tax imposed by the laws of the United States has not been paid.

B. No person shall possess alcoholic beverages in amounts in excess of the limits provided in § 4.1-311 in containers not bearing evidence that they have been purchased from the Board or a person licensed to sell them, or other evidence that the tax due to the Commonwealth or the markup required by the Board has been paid, unless it can be proved that the alcoholic beverages were lawfully acquired by the possessor.

C. Any person convicted of a violation of this section shall be guilty of a Class 1 misdemeanor.

History.
Code 1950, § 4-75; 1954, c. 484; 1966, c. 408; 1974, c. 460; 1975, c. 481; 1976, c. 36; 1984, c. 603; 1993, c. 866.

§ 4.1-314. Keeping, possessing or storing still or distilling apparatus without a permit; penalty.

No person shall keep, store or have in his possession any still, or distilling apparatus, without a permit from the Board.

Any person convicted of a violation of this section shall be guilty of a Class 1 misdemeanor.

History.
Code 1950, § 4-77; 1993, c. 866.

§ 4.1-315. Possession without license to sell alcoholic beverages upon premises of restaurant; exceptions; penalty.

A. No alcoholic beverages shall be kept or allowed to be kept upon any premises or upon the person of any proprietor or person employed upon the premises of a restaurant or other place where food or refreshments of any kind are furnished for compensation, except such alcoholic beverages as such person owning or operating such place of business is licensed to purchase and to sell at such place of business.

B. This section shall not apply to (i) any residence; (ii) alcoholic beverages in the possession of a passenger being transported for compensation as provided in subsection D of § 4.1-308; (iii) dining areas in restaurants licensed by the Board while such areas are in use for private meetings or parties limited in attendance to members and guests of a particular group, association or organization; (iv) licensed restaurants in office buildings, industrial or similar facilities while such restaurant is closed to the public and is in use for private meetings or parties limited in attendance to employees and nonpaying guests of the owner or a lessee of all or part of such building or facility; or (v) any dining areas or private rooms of residents in an assisted living facility as defined in § 63.2-100 and licensed in accordance with Article 1 (§ 63.2-1800 et seq.) of Chapter 18 of Title 63.2.

C. Any person convicted of a violation of this section shall be guilty of a Class 1 misdemeanor.

History.
Code 1950, p. 876, § 4-61; 1954, c. 512; 1958, c. 270; 1968, c. 7; 1972, c. 168; 1974, c. 497; 1990, c. 932; 1993, c. 866; 2010, c. 114.

§ 4.1-316. Keeping or drinking alcoholic beverages upon premises of club; penalty.

No person operating a club for profit or otherwise, either public or private, shall (i) keep or allow to be kept any alcoholic beverages, either by himself or any other person, upon the premises or (ii) permit the drinking of any alcoholic beverages upon the premises, unless he is licensed to sell alcoholic beverages.

Any person convicted of a violation of this section shall be guilty of a Class 1 misdemeanor.

History.
Code 1950, § 4-61.1; 1954, c. 147; 1993, c. 866.

§ 4.1-317. Maintaining common nuisances; penalties.

A. All houses, boathouses, buildings, club or fraternity or lodge rooms, boats, cars and places of every description where alcoholic beverages are manufactured, stored, sold, dispensed, given away or used contrary to law, by any scheme or device whatever, shall be deemed common nuisances.

No person shall maintain, aid, abet or knowingly associate with others in maintaining a common nuisance.

Any person convicted of a violation of this subsection shall be guilty of a Class 1 misdemeanor.

B. In addition, after due notice and opportunity to be heard on the part of any owner or lessor not involved in the original offense, by a proceeding analogous to that provided in §§ 4.1-339 through 4.1-348 and upon proof of guilty knowledge, judgment may be given that such house, building, boathouse, car or other place, or any room or part thereof, be closed. The court may, upon the owner or lessor giving bond in the penalty of not less than $500 and with security to be approved by the court, conditioned that the premises shall not be used for unlawful purposes, or in violation of the provisions of this chapter for a period of five years, turn the same over to its owner or lessor; or proceeding may be had in equity as provided in § 4.1-335.

C. In a proceeding under this section, judgment shall not be entered against the owner, lessor, or lienholder of the property unless it is proved he (i) knew of the unlawful use of the property and (ii) had the right, because of such unlawful use, to enter and repossess the property.

History.
Code 1950, p. 877, § 4-81; 1954, c. 484; 1993, c. 866.

§ 4.1-318. Violations by armed person; penalty.

No person shall unlawfully manufacture, transport or sell any alcoholic beverages, and at the time of the unlawful manufacturing, transporting, or selling or aiding or assisting in any manner in such act, shall carry on or about his person, or have on or in any vehicle which he may be using to aid him in any such purpose, or have in his possession, actual or constructive, at or within 100 yards of any place where any such alcoholic beverages are being unlawfully manufactured, transported or sold, any dangerous weapon as described in § 18.2-308.

Any person convicted of a violation of this section shall be guilty of a Class 6 felony.

History.
Code 1950, § 4-83; 1993, c. 866.

§ 4.1-319. Disobeying subpoena; hindering conduct of hearing; penalty.

No person shall (i) fail or refuse to obey any subpoena issued by the Board, any Board member, or agent authorized by the Board to issue such subpoena or (ii) hinder the orderly conduct and decorum of any hearing held and conducted by the Board, any Board member, or agent authorized by the Board to hold and conduct such hearing.

Any person convicted of a violation of this section shall be guilty of a Class 1 misdemeanor.

History.
Code 1950, § 4-70; 1993, c. 866.

§ 4.1-320. Illegal advertising; penalty; exception.

A. Except in accordance with this title and Board regulations, no person shall advertise in or send any advertising matter into the Commonwealth about or concerning alcoholic beverages other than those which may legally be manufactured or sold without a license.

B. Manufacturers, wholesalers, and retailers may engage in the display of outdoor alcoholic beverage advertising on lawfully erected signs provided such display is done in accordance with § 4.1-112.2 and Board regulations.

C. Except as provided in subsection D, any person convicted of a violation of this section shall be guilty of a Class 1 misdemeanor.

D. For violations of § 4.1-112.2 relating to distance and zoning restrictions on outdoor advertising, the Board shall give the advertiser written notice to take corrective action to either bring the advertisement into compliance with this title and Board regulations or to remove such advertisement. If corrective action is not taken within 30 days, the advertiser shall be guilty of a Class 4 misdemeanor.

E. Neither this section nor any Board regulation shall prohibit (i) the awarding of watches of a wholesale value of less than $100 by a licensed distillery, winery or brewery, to participants in athletic contests; (ii) the exhibition or display of automobiles, boats, or aircraft regularly and normally used in racing or other competitive events and the sponsorship of an automobile, boat or aircraft racing team by a licensed distillery, winery or brewery and the display on the automobile, boat or aircraft and uniforms of the members of the racing team, the trademark or brand name of an alcoholic beverage manufactured by such distillery, winery or brewery; (iii) the sponsorship of a professional athletic event, including, but not limited to, golf, auto racing or tennis, by a licensed distillery, winery or brewery or the use of any trademark or brand name of any alcoholic beverage in connection with such sponsorship; (iv) the advertisement of beer by the display of such product's name on any airship, which advertising is paid for by the manufacturer of such product; (v) the advertisement of beer or any alcoholic beverage by the display of such product's name on any scale model, reproduction or replica of any motor vehicle, aircraft or watercraft offered for sale; (vi) the placement of billboard advertising within stadia, coliseums, or racetracks that are used primarily for professional or semiprofessional athletic or sporting events; or (vii) the sponsorship of an entertainment or cultural event.

History.
Code 1950, § 4-69; 1978, c. 630; 1979, c. 196; 1980, c. 407; 1993, c. 866; 1995, c. 222; 2009, c. 322; 2011, c. 728; 2012, cc. 760, 818.

§ 4.1-321. Delivery of alcoholic beverages to prisoners in jail prohibited; penalty.

No person shall deliver, or cause to be delivered, to any prisoner in any local correctional facility, any alcoholic beverage.

Any person convicted of a violation of this section shall be guilty of a Class 1 misdemeanor.

History.
Code 1950, § 4-93; 1993, c. 866.

§ 4.1-322. Possession or consumption of alcoholic beverages by interdicted persons; penalty.

No person who has been interdicted pursuant to § 4.1-333 or § 4.1-334 shall possess any alcoholic beverages, except those acquired in accordance with subdivisions 1 through 5 of § 4.1-200, nor be drunk in public in violation of § 18.2-388.

Any interdicted person found to be in violation of this section shall be guilty of a Class 1 misdemeanor.

History.
Code 1950, § 4-52; 1954, c. 484; 1982, c. 66; 1993, c. 866; 1996, c. 717.

§ 4.1-323. Attempts; aiding or abetting; penalty.

No person shall attempt to do any of the things prohibited by this title or to aid or abet another in doing, or attempting to do, any of the things prohibited by this title.

On an indictment, information or warrant for the violation of this title, the jury or the court may find the defendant guilty of an attempt, or being an accessory, and the punishment shall be the same as if the defendant were solely guilty of such violation.

History.
Code 1950, § 4-87; 1993, c. 866.

ARTICLE 2. PROHIBITED PRACTICES BY LICENSEES.

§ 4.1-324. Illegal sale or keeping of alcoholic beverages by licensees; penalty.

A. No licensee or any agent or employee of such licensee shall:

1. Sell any alcoholic beverages of a kind other than that which such license or this title authorizes him to sell;

2. Sell beer to which wine, spirits or alcohol has been added, except that a mixed beverage licensee may combine wine or spirits, or both, with beer pursuant to a patron's order;

3. Sell wine to which spirits or alcohol, or both, have been added, otherwise than as required in the manufacture thereof under Board regulations, except that a mixed beverage licensee may (i) make sangria that contains brandy, triple sec, or other similar spirits and (ii) combine beer or spirits, or both, with wine pursuant to a patron's order;

4. Sell alcoholic beverages of a kind which such license or this title authorizes him to sell, but to any person other than to those to whom such license or this title authorizes him to sell;

5. Sell alcoholic beverages which such license or this title authorizes him to sell, but in any place or in any manner other than such license or this title authorizes him to sell;

6. Sell any alcoholic beverages when forbidden by this title;

7. Keep or allow to be kept, other than in his residence and for his personal use, any alcoholic beverages other than that which he is authorized to sell by such license or by this title;

8. Sell any beer to a retail licensee, except for cash, if the seller holds a brewery, bottler's or wholesale beer license;

9. Sell any beer on draft and fail to display to customers the brand of beer sold or misrepresent the brand of any beer sold;

10. Sell any wine for delivery within the Commonwealth to a retail licensee, except for cash, if the seller holds a wholesale wine or farm winery license;

11. Keep or allow to be kept or sell any vaporized form of an alcoholic beverage produced by an alcohol vaporizing device;

12. Keep any alcoholic beverage other than in the bottle or container in which it was purchased by him except: (i) for a frozen alcoholic beverage; and (ii) in the case of wine, in containers of a type approved by the Board pending automatic dispensing and sale of such wine; or

13. Establish any normal or customary pricing of its alcoholic beverages that is intended as a shift or device to evade any "happy hour" regulations adopted by the Board; however, a licensee may increase the volume of an alcoholic beverage sold to a customer if there is a commensurate increase in the normal or customary price charged for the same alcoholic beverage.

B. Any person convicted of a violation of this section shall be guilty of a Class 1 misdemeanor.

C. Neither this section nor any Board regulation shall prohibit an on-premises restaurant licensee from using alcoholic beverages that the licensee otherwise is authorized to purchase and possess for the purposes of preparing and selling for on-premises consumption food products with a final alcohol content of more than one-half of one percent by volume, as long as such food products are sold to and consumed by persons who are 21 years of age or older.

History.
Code 1950, § 4-60; 1970, c. 360; 1974, c. 460; 1984, c. 603; 1993, c. 866; 1998, c. 238; 2006, c. 714; 2008, cc. 513, 629, 875.

§ 4.1-325. (Effective until July 1, 2018) Prohibited acts by mixed beverage licensees; penalty.

A. In addition to § 4.1-324, no mixed beverage licensee nor any agent or employee of such licensee shall:

1. Sell or serve any alcoholic beverage other than as authorized by law;

2. Sell any authorized alcoholic beverage to any person or at any place except as authorized by law;

3. Allow at the place described in his license the consumption of alcoholic beverages in violation of this title;

4. Keep at the place described in his license any alcoholic beverage other than that which he is licensed to sell;

5. Misrepresent the brand of any alcoholic beverage sold or offered for sale;

6. Keep any alcoholic beverage other than in the bottle or container in which it was purchased by him except (i) for a frozen alcoholic beverage, which may include alcoholic beverages in a frozen drink dispenser of a type approved by the Board; (ii) in the case of wine, in containers of a type approved by the Board pending automatic dispensing and sale of such wine; and (iii) as otherwise provided by Board regulation. Neither this subdivision nor any Board regulation shall prohibit any mixed beverage licensee from premixing containers of sangria, to which spirits may be added, to be served and sold for consumption on the licensed premises;

7. Refill or partly refill any bottle or container of alcoholic beverage or dilute or otherwise tamper with the contents of any bottle or container of alcoholic beverage, except as provided by Board regulation adopted pursuant to § 4.1-111 B 11;

8. Sell or serve any brand of alcoholic beverage which is not the same as that ordered by the purchaser without first advising such purchaser of the difference;

9. Remove or obliterate any label, mark or stamp affixed to any container of alcoholic beverages offered for sale;

10. Deliver or sell the contents of any container if the label, mark or stamp has been removed or obliterated;

11. Allow any obscene conduct, language, literature, pictures, performance or materials on the licensed premises;

12. Allow any striptease act on the licensed premises;

13. Allow persons connected with the licensed business to appear nude or partially nude;

14. Consume or allow the consumption by an employee of any alcoholic beverages while on duty and in a position that is involved in the selling or serving of alcoholic beverages to customers.

The provisions of this subdivision shall not prohibit any retail licensee or his designated employee from (i) consuming product samples or sample servings of (a) beer or wine provided by a representative of a licensed beer or wine wholesaler or manufacturer or (b) a distilled spirit provided by a permittee of the Board who represents a distiller, if such samples are provided in accordance with Board regulations and the retail licensee or his designated employee does not violate the provisions of subdivision 1 f of § 4.1-225 or (ii) tasting an alcoholic beverage that has been or will be delivered to a customer for quality control purposes;

15. Deliver to a consumer an original bottle of an alcoholic beverage purchased under such license whether the closure is broken or unbroken except in accordance with § 4.1-210.

The provisions of this subdivision shall not apply to the delivery of:

a. "Soju." For the purposes of this clause, "soju" means a traditional Korean alcoholic beverage distilled from rice, barley or sweet potatoes; or

b. Spirits, provided (i) the original container is no larger than 375 milliliters, (ii) the alcohol content is no greater than 15 percent by volume, and (iii) the contents of the container are carbonated and perishable;

16. Be intoxicated while on duty or employ an intoxicated person on the licensed premises;

17. Conceal any sale or consumption of any alcoholic beverages;

18. Fail or refuse to make samples of any alcoholic beverages available to the Board upon request or obstruct special agents of the Board in the discharge of their duties;

19. Store alcoholic beverages purchased under the license in any unauthorized place or remove any such alcoholic beverages from the premises;

20. Knowingly employ in the licensed business any person who has the general reputation as a prostitute, panderer, habitual law violator, person of ill repute, user or peddler of narcotics, or person who drinks to excess or engages in illegal gambling;

21. Keep on the licensed premises a slot machine or any prohibited gambling or gaming device, machine or apparatus;

22. Make any gift of an alcoholic beverage, other than as a gift made (i) to a personal friend, as a matter of normal social intercourse, so long as the gift is in no way a shift or device to evade the restriction set forth in this subdivision; (ii) to a person responsible for the planning, preparation or conduct on any conference, convention, trade show or event held or to be held on the premises of the licensee, when such gift is made in the course of usual and customary business entertainment and is in no way a shift or device to evade the restriction set forth in this subdivision; (iii) pursuant to subsection C of § 4.1-209; (iv) pursuant to subdivision A 11 of § 4.1-201; or (v) pursuant to any Board regulation. Any gift permitted by this subdivision shall be subject to the taxes imposed by this title on sales of alcoholic beverages. The licensee shall keep complete and accurate records of gifts given in accordance with this subdivision; or

23. Establish any normal or customary pricing of its alcoholic beverages that is intended as a shift or device to evade any "happy hour" regulations adopted by the Board; however, a licensee may increase the volume of an alcoholic beverage sold to a customer if there is a commensurate increase in the normal or customary price charged for the same alcoholic beverage.

B. Any person convicted of a violation of this section shall be guilty of a Class 1 misdemeanor.

C. The provisions of subdivisions A 12 and A 13 shall not apply to persons operating theaters, concert halls, art centers, museums, or similar establishments that are devoted primarily to the arts or theatrical performances, when the performances that are presented are expressing matters of serious literary, artistic, scientific, or political value.

History.

1968, c. 7, § 4-98.10; 1970, c. 120; 1974, c. 548; 1975, c. 483; 1976, cc. 750, 768; 1978, c. 69; 1979, c. 227; 1982, c. 316; 1983, c. 608; 1993, c. 866; 2000, c. 780; 2002, c. 105; 2003, c. 856; 2004, c. 913; 2006, cc. 256, 826; 2008, cc. 513, 629, 794, 875; 2009, cc. 20, 509; 2010, c. 481; 2013, c. 661; 2015, cc. 404, 604.

§ 4.1-325. (Effective July 1, 2018) Prohibited acts by mixed beverage licensees; penalty.

A. In addition to § 4.1-324, no mixed beverage licensee nor any agent or employee of such licensee shall:

1. Sell or serve any alcoholic beverage other than as authorized by law;

2. Sell any authorized alcoholic beverage to any person or at any place except as authorized by law;

3. Allow at the place described in his license the consumption of alcoholic beverages in violation of this title;

4. Keep at the place described in his license any alcoholic beverage other than that which he is licensed to sell;

5. Misrepresent the brand of any alcoholic beverage sold or offered for sale;

6. Keep any alcoholic beverage other than in the bottle or container in which it was purchased by him except (i) for a frozen alcoholic beverage, which may include alcoholic beverages in a frozen drink dispenser of a type approved by the Board; (ii) in the case of wine, in containers of a type approved by the Board pending automatic dispensing and sale of such wine; and (iii) as otherwise provided by Board regulation. Neither this subdivision nor any Board regulation shall prohibit any mixed beverage licensee from premixing containers of sangria, to which spirits may be added, to be served and sold for consumption on the licensed premises;

7. Refill or partly refill any bottle or container of alcoholic beverage or dilute or otherwise tamper with the contents of any bottle or container of alcoholic beverage, except as provided by Board regulation adopted pursuant to subdivision B 11 of § 4.1-111;

8. Sell or serve any brand of alcoholic beverage which is not the same as that ordered by the purchaser without first advising such purchaser of the difference;

9. Remove or obliterate any label, mark or stamp affixed to any container of alcoholic beverages offered for sale;

10. Deliver or sell the contents of any container if the label, mark or stamp has been removed or obliterated;

11. Allow any obscene conduct, language, literature, pictures, performance or materials on the licensed premises;

12. Allow any striptease act on the licensed premises;

13. Allow persons connected with the licensed business to appear nude or partially nude;

14. Consume or allow the consumption by an employee of any alcoholic beverages while on duty and in a position that is involved in the selling or serving of alcoholic beverages to customers.

The provisions of this subdivision shall not prohibit any retail licensee or his designated employee from (i) consuming product samples or sample servings of (a) beer or wine provided by a representative of a licensed beer or wine wholesaler or manufacturer or (b) a distilled spirit provided by a permittee of the Board who represents a distiller, if such samples are provided in accordance with Board regulations and the retail licensee or his designated employee does not violate the provisions of subdivision 1 f of § 4.1-225 or (ii) tasting an alcoholic beverage that has been or will be delivered to a customer for quality control purposes;

15. Deliver to a consumer an original bottle of an alcoholic beverage purchased under such license whether the closure is broken or unbroken except in accordance with § 4.1-210.

The provisions of this subdivision shall not apply to the delivery of:

a. "Soju." For the purposes of this subdivision, "soju" means a traditional Korean alcoholic beverage distilled from rice, barley or sweet potatoes; or

b. Spirits, provided (i) the original container is no larger than 375 milliliters, (ii) the alcohol content is no greater than 15 percent by volume, and (iii) the contents of the container are carbonated and perishable;

16. Be intoxicated while on duty or employ an intoxicated person on the licensed premises;

17. Conceal any sale or consumption of any alcoholic beverages;

18. Fail or refuse to make samples of any alcoholic beverages available to the Board upon request or obstruct special agents of the Board in the discharge of their duties;

19. Store alcoholic beverages purchased under the license in any unauthorized place or remove any such alcoholic beverages from the premises;

20. Knowingly employ in the licensed business any person who has the general reputation as a prostitute, panderer, habitual law violator, person of ill repute, user or peddler of narcotics, or person who drinks to excess or engages in illegal gambling;

21. Keep on the licensed premises a slot machine or any prohibited gambling or gaming device, machine or apparatus;

22. Make any gift of an alcoholic beverage, other than as a gift made (i) to a personal friend, as a matter of normal social intercourse, so long as the gift is in no way a shift or device to evade the restriction set forth in this subdivision; (ii) to a person responsible for the planning, preparation or conduct on any conference, convention, trade show or event held or to be held on the premises of the licensee, when such gift is made in the course of usual and customary business entertainment and is in no way a shift or device to evade the restriction set forth in this subdivision; (iii) pursuant to subsection C of § 4.1-209; (iv) pursuant to subdivision A 11 of § 4.1-201; or (v) pursuant to any Board regulation. Any gift permitted by this subdivision shall be subject to the taxes imposed by this title on sales of alcoholic beverages. The licensee shall keep complete and accurate records of gifts given in accordance with this subdivision; or

23. Establish any normal or customary pricing of its alcoholic beverages that is intended as a shift or device to evade any "happy hour" regulations adopted by the Board; however, a licensee may increase the volume of an alcoholic beverage sold to a

customer if there is a commensurate increase in the normal or customary price charged for the same alcoholic beverage.

B. Any person convicted of a violation of this section shall be guilty of a Class 1 misdemeanor.

C. The provisions of subdivisions A 12 and A 13 shall not apply to persons operating theaters, concert halls, art centers, museums, or similar establishments that are devoted primarily to the arts or theatrical performances, when the performances that are presented are expressing matters of serious literary, artistic, scientific, or political value.

History.
1968, c. 7, § 4-98.10; 1970, c. 120; 1974, c. 548; 1975, c. 483; 1976, cc. 750, 768; 1978, c. 69; 1979, c. 227; 1982, c. 316; 1983, c. 608; 1993, c. 866; 2000, c. 780; 2002, c. 105; 2003, c. 856; 2004, c. 913; 2006, cc. 256, 826; 2008, cc. 513, 629, 794, 875; 2009, cc. 20, 509; 2010, c. 481; 2013, c. 661; 2015, cc. 38, 404, 604, 730.

§ 4.1-325.01. Combined licenses for same premises.

On and after July 1, 2015, any licensee of the Alcoholic Beverage Control Board that holds both a mixed beverage restaurant license and a mixed beverage caterer's license for the same business premises may, upon request in writing to the Alcoholic Beverage Control Board, be granted a combined mixed beverage restaurant and caterer's license for the same business premises. The Alcoholic Beverage Control Board may require such licensee to surrender the previously granted mixed beverage restaurant license and mixed beverage caterer's license for the same licensed location. No additional license fee shall be assessed for this change.

History.
2015, c. 404.

§ 4.1-325.1. Falsifying application; penalty.

It shall be unlawful for any applicant for a banquet or special events license pursuant to § 4.1-209 or mixed beverage special events license pursuant to § 4.1-210 to knowingly make a false statement in order to secure a license or to alter, change, borrow, or lend or attempt to use, borrow, or lend a license. Any person violating this provision shall be guilty of a Class 3 misdemeanor.

History.
2002, c. 104.

§ 4.1-325.2. Prohibited acts by employees of wine or beer licensees; penalty.

A. In addition to the provisions of § 4.1-324, no retail wine or beer licensee or his agent or employee shall consume any alcoholic beverages while on duty and in a position that is involved in the selling or serving of alcoholic beverages to customers.

The provisions of this subsection shall not prohibit any retail licensee or his designated employee from (i) consuming product samples or sample servings of beer or wine provided by a representative of a licensed beer or wine wholesaler or manufacturer, if such samples are provided in accordance with Board regulations and the retail licensee or his designated employee does not violate the provisions of subdivision 1 f of § 4.1-225 or (ii) tasting an alcoholic beverage that has been or will be delivered to a customer for quality control purposes.

B. For the purposes of subsection A, a wine or beer wholesaler or farm winery licensee or its employees that participate in a wine or beer tasting sponsored by a retail wine or beer licensee shall not be deemed to be agents of the retail wine or beer licensee.

C. No retail wine or beer licensee, or his agent or employee shall make any gift of an alcoholic beverage, other than as a gift made (i) to a personal friend, as a matter of normal social intercourse, so long as the gift is in no way a shift or device to evade the restriction set forth in this subsection; (ii) to a person responsible for the planning, preparation or conduct on any conference, convention, trade show or event held or to be held on the premises of the licensee, when such gift is made in the course of usual and customary business entertainment and is in no way a shift or device to evade the restriction set forth in this subsection; (iii) pursuant to subsection C of § 4.1-209; (iv) pursuant to subdivision A 11 of § 4.1-201; or (v) pursuant to any Board regulation. Any gift permitted by this subsection shall be subject to the taxes imposed by this title on sales of alcoholic beverages. The licensee shall keep complete and accurate records of gifts given in accordance with this subsection.

D. Any person convicted of a violation of this section shall be subject to a civil penalty in an amount not to exceed $500.

History.
2002, c. 105; 2003, c. 856; 2006, cc. 256, 826; 2013, c. 661; 2015, cc. 404, 604.

§ 4.1-326. Sale of; purchase for resale; wine or beer from a person without a license; penalty.

No licensee, other than a common carrier operating in interstate or foreign commerce, licensed to sell wine or beer at retail shall purchase for resale or sell any wine or beer purchased from anyone other than a wholesale wine or wholesale beer licensee.

Nothing in this section shall prohibit the holder of a retail license issued pursuant to subdivision A 5 of § 4.1-201 from the purchase or sale of wine or beer from the winery or brewery located on or contiguous to the licensed retail premises.

Any person convicted of a violation of this section shall be guilty of a Class 1 misdemeanor.

History.
Code 1950, §§ 4-64, 4-66; 1984, c. 200; 1988, c. 261; 1993, c. 866; 2015, c. 412.

§ 4.1-327. Prohibiting transfer of wine or beer by licensees; penalty.

A. No retail licensee, except (i) a retail on-premises wine and beer licensee or (ii) a retail on-premises beer licensee, shall transfer any wine or beer from one licensed place of business to another licensed place of business whether such places of business are under the same ownership or not.

B. Any person convicted of a violation of this section shall be guilty of a Class 1 misdemeanor.

History.
1954, c. 338, § 4-34.1; 1993, c. 866.

§ 4.1-328. Prohibited trade practices; penalty.

A. No person subject to the jurisdiction of the Board shall violate, attempt to violate, solicit another person to violate or consent to any violation of § 4.1-216 or 4.1-216.1, or regulations adopted pursuant to subdivision B 3 of § 4.1-111.

B. Any person found by the Board to have committed a violation of this section shall be subject to a civil penalty as provided in § 4.1-227.

History.
1989, c. 528, § 4-79.1; 1992, c. 349; 1993, c. 866; 2007, c. 494.

§ 4.1-329. Illegal advertising materials; penalty.

No person subject to the jurisdiction of the Board shall induce, attempt to induce, or consent to, any manufacturer, as defined in § 4.1-216.1, or any wholesale licensee selling, renting, lending, buying for or giving to any person any advertising materials or decorations under circumstances prohibited by this title or Board regulations.

Any person found by the Board to have violated this section shall be subject to a civil penalty as provided in § 4.1-227.

History.
1981, c. 574, § 4-69.2; 1993, c. 866; 2007, c. 494.

§ 4.1-330. Solicitation by persons interested in manufacture, etc., of alcoholic beverages; penalty.

A. No person having any interest, direct or indirect, in the manufacture, distribution, or sale of spirits or other alcoholic beverages shall, without a permit granted by the Board and upon such conditions as the Board may prescribe, solicit either directly or indirectly (i) a mixed beverage licensee; (ii) any agent, servant, or employee of such licensee; or (iii) any person connected with the licensee in any capacity whatsoever in his licensed business, to sell or offer for sale the particular spirits or other alcoholic beverage in which such person may be so interested.

The Board, upon proof of any solicitation in violation of this subsection, may suspend or terminate the sale through government stores or its purchase of the brand of spirits or other alcoholic beverage which was the subject matter of the unlawful solicitation or promotion. In addition, the Board may suspend or terminate the sale through such stores or its purchase of all brands of spirits or other alcoholic beverages manufactured or distributed by either the employer or principal of such solicitor, the broker, or by the owner of the brand of spirits unlawfully solicited or promoted. The Board may impose a civil penalty not to exceed $250,000 in lieu of such suspension or termination of sales through government stores or purchases by the Board or portion thereof, or both.

Any person convicted of a violation of this subsection shall be guilty of a Class 1 misdemeanor.

B. No mixed beverage licensee or any agent, servant, or employee of such licensee, or any person connected with the licensee in any capacity whatsoever in his licensed business shall, either directly or indirectly, be a party to, consent to, solicit, or aid or abet another in a violation of subsection A.

The Board may suspend or revoke the license granted to such licensee, or may impose a civil penalty not to exceed $25,000 in lieu of such suspension or any portion thereof, or both.

Any person convicted of a violation of this subsection shall be guilty of a Class 1 misdemeanor.

History.
1968, c. 7, § 4-98.16; 1988, c. 786; 1990, c. 442; 1993, c. 866.

§ 4.1-331. Failure to pay tax or to deliver, keep and preserve records and accounts, or to allow examination and inspection; penalty.

No licensee shall fail or refuse to (i) pay any tax provided for in § 4.1-234 or § 4.1-236; (ii) deliver, keep and preserve such records, invoices and accounts as are required by § 4.1-204 or Board regulation; or (iii) allow such records, invoices and accounts or his place of business to be examined and inspected in accordance with § 4.1-204.

Any person convicted of a violation of this section shall be guilty of a Class 1 misdemeanor.

History.
Code 1950, § 4-65; 1988, c. 261, § 4-136; 1993, c. 866.

§ 4.1-332. Nonpayment of excise tax on beer and wine coolers; additional penalties.

A. No person shall sell beer or wine coolers to retailers or consumers without paying the excise tax imposed by § 4.1-236. No retailer shall purchase, receive, transport, store or sell any beer or wine coolers on which such retailer has reason to know such tax has not been paid and may not be paid.

Any person convicted of a violation of this subsection shall be guilty of a Class 1 misdemeanor.

B. In addition to subsection A, on each manufacturer, bottler or wholesaler who fails to make any return and pay the full amount of the tax required by § 4.1-236, there shall be imposed a civil penalty to be added to the tax in the amount of five percent of the proper tax due if the failure is for not more than thirty days, with an additional five percent for each additional thirty days, or fraction thereof, during which the failure continues. Such civil penalty shall not exceed twenty-five percent in the aggregate. In the case of a false or fraudulent return, where willful intent exists to defraud the Commonwealth of any excise tax due on beer and wine coolers, a civil penalty of fifty percent of the amount of the proper tax due shall be assessed. All penalties and interest shall be payable to the Board and if not so paid shall be collectible in the same manner as if they were a part of the tax imposed.

C. After reasonable notice to the manufacturer, bottler, wholesaler or retailer, the Board may suspend or revoke the license of the manufacturer, bottler, wholesaler or retailer who has failed to make any return or to pay the full amount of the excise tax.

History.
1988, c. 261, §§ 4-139, 4-140; 1993, c. 866.

ARTICLE 3.

PROCEDURAL MATTERS.

§ 4.1-333. Interdiction of intoxicated driver or habitual drunkard.

A. When after a hearing upon due notice it appears to the satisfaction of the circuit court of any county or city that any person, residing within such county or city, has been convicted of driving any automobile, truck, motorcycle, engine or train while intoxicated or has shown himself to be an habitual drunkard, the court may enter an order of interdiction prohibiting the sale of alcoholic beverages to such person until further ordered. The court entering any such order shall file a copy of the order with the Board.

B. The court entering any order of interdiction may alter, amend or cancel such order as it deems proper. A copy of any alteration, amendment or cancellation shall be filed with the Board.

History.
Code 1950, § 4-51; 1956, c. 53; 1982, c. 66; 1993, c. 866.

§ 4.1-334. Interdiction for illegal manufacture, possession, transportation or sale of alcoholic beverages.

When any person has been found guilty of the illegal manufacture, possession, transportation, or sale of alcoholic beverages or maintaining a common nuisance as defined in § 4.1-317, the court may without further notice or additional hearing enter an order of interdiction prohibiting the sale of alcoholic beverages to such person for one year from the date of the entry of the order, and thereafter if further ordered.

History.
Code 1950, § 4-52; 1954, c. 484; 1982, c. 66; 1993, c. 866.

§ 4.1-335. Enjoining nuisances.

A. In addition to the penalties imposed by § 4.1-317, the Board, its special agents, the attorney for the Commonwealth, or any citizen of the county, city, or town where a common nuisance as defined in § 4.1-317 exists may maintain a suit in equity in the name of the Commonwealth to enjoin the common nuisance.

B. The courts of equity shall have jurisdiction, and in every case where the bill charges, on the knowledge or belief of the complainant, and is sworn to by two reputable citizens, that alcoholic beverages are manufactured, stored, sold, dispensed, given away, or used in such house, building or other place described in § 4.1-317 contrary to the laws of the Commonwealth, an injunction shall be granted as soon as the bill is presented to the court. The injunction shall enjoin and restrain the owners, tenants, their agents, employees, servants, and any person connected with such house, building or other place, and all persons whomsoever from manufacturing, storing, selling, dispensing, giving away, or using alcoholic beverages on such premises. The injunction shall also restrain all persons from removing any alcoholic beverage then on such premises until the further order of the court. If the court is satisfied that the material allegations of the bill are true, although the premises complained of may not then be unlawfully used, it shall continue the injunction against such place for a period of time as the court deems proper. The injunction may be dissolved if a proper case is shown for dissolution.

History.
Code 1950, § 4-82; 1993, c. 866.

§ 4.1-336. Contraband beverages and other articles subject to forfeiture.

All stills and distilling apparatus and materials for the manufacture of alcoholic beverages, all alcoholic beverages and materials used in their manufacture, all containers in which alcoholic beverages may be found, which are kept, stored, possessed, or in any manner used in violation of the provisions of this title, and any dangerous weapons as described in § 18.2-308, which may be used, or which may be found upon the person or in any vehicle which such person is using, to aid such person in the unlawful manufacture, transportation or sale of alcoholic beverages, or found in the possession of such person, or any horse, mule or other beast of burden, any wagon, automobile, truck or vehicle of any nature whatsoever which is found in the immediate vicinity of any place where alcoholic beverages are being unlawfully manufactured and which such animal or vehicle is being used to aid in the unlawful manufacture, shall be deemed contraband and shall be forfeited to the Commonwealth.

Proceedings for the confiscation of the above property shall be in accordance with § 4.1-338 for all such property except motor vehicles which proceedings shall be in accordance with Chapter 22.1 (§ 19.2-386.1 et seq.) of Title 19.2.

History.

Code 1950, § 4-53; 1954, c. 484; 1993, c. 866; 2012, cc. 283, 756.

§ 4.1-337. Search warrants.

A. If complaint on oath is made that alcoholic beverages are being manufactured, sold, kept, stored, or in any manner held, used or concealed in a particular house, or other place, in violation of law, the judge, magistrate, or other person having authority to issue criminal warrants, to whom such complaint is made, if satisfied that there is a probable cause for such belief, shall issue a warrant to search such house or other place for alcoholic beverages. Such warrants, except as herein otherwise provided, shall be issued, directed and executed in accordance with the laws of the Commonwealth pertaining to search warrants.

B. Warrants issued under this title for the search of any automobile, boat, conveyance or vehicle, whether of like kind or not, or for the search of any article of baggage, whether of like kind or not, for alcoholic beverages, may be executed in any part of the Commonwealth where they are overtaken and shall be made returnable before any judge within whose jurisdiction such automobile, boat, conveyance, vehicle, truck, or article of baggage, or any of them, was transported or attempted to be transported contrary to law.

History.

Code 1950, § 4-54; 1993, c. 866.

§ 4.1-338. Confiscation proceedings; disposition of forfeited articles.

A. All proceedings for the confiscation of articles, except motor vehicles, declared contraband and forfeited to the Commonwealth under this chapter shall be as provided in this section.

B. Production of seized property. — Whenever any article declared contraband under the provisions of this title and required to be forfeited to the Commonwealth has been seized, with or without a warrant, by any officer charged with the enforcement of this title, he shall produce the contraband article and any person in whose possession it was found. In those cases where no person is found in possession of such articles the return shall so state and a copy of the warrant shall be posted on the door of the buildings or room where the articles were found, or if there is no door, then in any conspicuous place upon the premises.

In case of seizure of a still, doubler, worm, worm tub, mash tub, fermenting tub, or other distilling apparatus, for any offense involving their forfeiture, where it is impracticable to remove such distilling apparatus to a place of safe storage from the place where seized, the seizing officer may destroy such apparatus only as necessary to prevent use of all or any part thereof for the purpose of distilling. The destruction shall be in the presence of at least one credible witness, and such witness shall join the officer in a sworn report of the seizure and destruction, to be made to the Board. The report shall set forth the grounds of the claim of forfeiture, the reasons for seizure and destruction, an estimate of the fair cash value of the apparatus destroyed, and the materials remaining after such destruction. The report shall include a statement that, from facts within their own knowledge, the seizing officer and witness have no doubt whatever that the distilling apparatus was set up for use, or had been used in the unlawful distillation of spirits, and that it was impracticable to remove such apparatus to a place of safe storage.

In case of seizure of any quantity of mash, or of alcoholic beverages on which the tax imposed by the laws of the United States has not been paid, for any offense involving forfeiture of the same, the seizing officer may destroy them to prevent the use of all or any part thereof for the purpose of unlawful distillation of spirits or any other violation of this title. The destruction shall be in the presence of at least one credible witness, and such witness shall join the officer in a sworn report of the seizure and destruction, to be made to the Board. The report shall set forth the grounds of the claim of forfeiture, the reasons for seizure and destruction, and a statement that, from facts within their own knowledge, the seizing officer and witness have no doubt whatever that the mash was intended for use in the unlawful distillation of spirits, or that the alcoholic beverages were intended for use in violation of this title.

C. Hearing and determination. — Upon the return of the warrant as provided in this section, the court shall fix a time not less than ten days, unless waived by the accused in writing, and not more than thirty days thereafter, for the hearing on such return to determine whether or not the articles seized, or any part thereof, were used or in any manner kept, stored or possessed in violation of this title.

At such hearing if no claimant appears, the court shall declare the articles seized forfeited to the Commonwealth and, if such articles are not necessary as evidence in any pending prosecution, shall turn them over to the Board. Any person claiming an interest in any of the articles seized may appear at the hearing and file a written claim setting forth particularly the character and extent of his interest. The court shall certify the warrant and the articles seized along with any claim filed to the circuit court to hear and determine the validity of such claim.

If the evidence warrants, the court shall enter a judgment of forfeiture and order the articles seized to be turned over to the Board. Action under this section and the forfeiture of any articles hereunder shall not be a bar to any prosecution under any other provision of this title.

D. Disposition of forfeited beverages and other articles. — Any articles forfeited to the Commonwealth and turned over to the Board in accordance with this section shall be destroyed or sold by the Board as it deems proper. The net proceeds from such sales shall be paid into the Literary Fund. If the Board believes that any alcoholic beverages forfeited to the Commonwealth and turned over to the Board in accordance with this section cannot be sold and should not be destroyed, it may give such alcoholic beverages for medicinal purposes to any institution in the Commonwealth regularly conducted as a hospital, nursing home or sanatorium for the care of persons in ill health, or as a home devoted exclusively to the care of aged people, to supply the needs of such institution for alcoholic beverages for such purposes, provided that (i) the State Health Commissioner has issued a certificate stating that such institution has need for such alcoholic beverages and (ii) preference is accorded by the Board to institutions supported either in whole or in part by public funds. A record shall be made showing the amount issued in each case, to whom issued and the date when issued, and shall be kept in the offices of the State Health Commissioner and the Board. No charge shall be made to any patient for the alcoholic beverages supplied to him where they have been received from the Board pursuant to this section. Such alcoholic beverages shall be administered only upon approval of the patient's physician.

If the Board believes that any foodstuffs forfeited to the Commonwealth and turned over to the Board in accordance with this section are usable, should not be destroyed and cannot be sold or whose sale would be impractical, it may give such foodstuffs to any institution in the Commonwealth and shall prefer a gift to the local jail or other local correctional facility in the jurisdiction where seizure took place. A record shall be made showing the nature of the foodstuffs and amount given, to whom given and the date when given, and shall be kept in the offices of the Board.

History.

Code 1950, § 4-55; 1954, c. 484; 1958, c. 194; 1976, c. 37; 1993, c. 866; 1995, c. 196.

§ 4.1-339. Search and seizure of conveyances or vehicles used in violation of law; arrests.

A. When any officer charged with the enforcement of the alcoholic beverage control laws of the Commonwealth has reason to believe that alcoholic beverages illegally acquired, or being illegally transported, are in any conveyance or vehicle of any kind, either on land or on water (except a conveyance or vehicle owned or operated by a railroad, express, sleeping or parlor car or steamboat company, other than barges, tugs or small craft), he shall obtain a search warrant and search such conveyance or vehicle. If illegally acquired alcoholic beverages or alcoholic beverages being illegally transported in amounts in excess of one quart or one liter if in a metric-sized container are found, the officer shall seize the alcoholic beverages, seize and take possession of such conveyance or vehicle, and deliver them to the chief law-enforcement officer of the locality in which such seizure was made, taking his receipt therefor in duplicate.

B. The officer making such seizure shall also arrest all persons found in charge of such conveyance or vehicle and shall forthwith report in writing such seizure and arrest to the attorney for the Commonwealth for the county or city in which seizure and arrest were made.

History.

Code 1950, § 4-56; 1954, c. 504; 1968, c. 763; 1971, Ex. Sess., c. 155; 1973, c. 16; 1978, cc. 434, 436; 1981, c. 365; 1983, c. 271; 1984, c. 52; 1993, c. 866.

§§ 4.1-340 through 4.1-345: Repealed by Acts 2012, cc. 283 and 756, cl. 2.

Editor's note.

Former §§ 4.1-340 through 4.1-345, pertained to procedures involving forfeited property. For current procedures dealing with forfeiture see generally Chapters 22.1 (§ 19.2-386.1 et seq.) and Chapter 22.2 (§ 19.2-386.15 et seq.) of Title 19.2.

§ 4.1-346. Contraband beverages.

Alcoholic beverages seized pursuant to § 4.1-339 shall be deemed contraband as provided in § 4.1-336 and disposed of accordingly. Failure to maintain on a conveyance or vehicle a permit or other indicia of permission issued by the Board authorizing the transportation of alcoholic beverages within, into or through the Commonwealth when other Board regulations applicable to such transportation have been complied with shall not be cause for deeming such alcoholic beverages contraband.

History.

Code 1950, § 4-56; 1954, c. 504; 1968, c. 763; 1971, Ex. Sess., c. 155; 1973, c. 16; 1978, cc. 434, 436; 1981, c. 365; 1983, c. 271; 1984, c. 52; 1993, c. 866.

§ 4.1-347: Repealed by Acts 2012, cc. 283 and 756, cl. 2.

§ 4.1-348. Beverages not licensed under this title.

The provisions of §§ 4.1-339 through 4.1-348 shall not apply to alcoholic beverages which may be manufactured and sold without any license under the provisions of this title.

History.
Code 1950, § 4-56; 1954, c. 504; 1968, c. 763; 1971, Ex. Sess., c. 155; 1973, c. 16; 1978, cc. 434, 436; 1981, c. 365; 1983, c. 271; 1984, c. 52; 1993, c. 866.

§ 4.1-349. Punishment for violations of title or regulations; bond.

A. Any person convicted of a misdemeanor under the provisions of this title without specification as to the class of offense or penalty, or convicted of violating any other provision thereof, or convicted of violating any Board regulation, shall be guilty of a Class 1 misdemeanor.

B. In addition to the penalties imposed by this title for violations, any court before whom any person is convicted of a violation of any provision of this title may require such defendant to execute bond, with approved security, in the penalty of not more than $1,000, with the condition that the defendant will not violate any of the provisions of this title for the term of one year. If any such bond is required and is not given, the defendant shall be committed to jail until it is given, or until he is discharged by the court, provided he shall not be confined for a period longer than six months. If any such bond required by a court is not given during the term of the court by which conviction is had, it may be given before any judge or before the clerk of such court.

C. The provisions of this title shall not prevent the Board from suspending, revoking or refusing to continue the license of any person convicted of a violation of any provision of this title.

D. No court shall hear such a case unless the respective attorney for the Commonwealth or his assistant has been notified that such a case is pending.

History.
Code 1950, § 4-92; 1984, c. 603; 1993, c. 866.

§ 4.1-350. Witness not excused from testifying because of self-incrimination.

No person shall be excused from testifying for the Commonwealth as to any offense committed by another under this title by reason of his testimony tending to incriminate him. The testimony given by such person on behalf of the Commonwealth when called as a witness for the prosecution shall not be used against him and he shall not be prosecuted for the offense to which he testifies.

History.
Code 1950, § 4-94; 1993, c. 866.

§ 4.1-351. Previous convictions.

In any indictment, information or warrant charging any person with a violation of any provision of this title, it may be alleged and evidence may be introduced at the trial of such person to prove that such person has been previously convicted of a violation of this title.

History.
Code 1950, § 4-91; 1993, c. 866.

§ 4.1-352. Certificate of forensic scientist as evidence; requiring forensic scientist to appear.

The certificate of any forensic scientist employed by the Commonwealth on behalf of the Board or the Department of Forensic Science, when signed by him, shall be evidence in all prosecutions for violations of this title and all controversies in any judicial proceedings touching the mixture analyzed by him. On motion of the accused or any party in interest, the court may require the forensic scientist making the analysis to appear as a witness and be subject to cross-examination, provided such motion is made within a reasonable time prior to the day on which the case is set for trial.

History.
Code 1950, § 4-90; 1972, c. 741; 1981, c. 410; 1993, c. 866; 2003, c. 130; 2005, cc. 868, 881.

§ 4.1-353. Label on sealed container prima facie evidence of alcoholic content.

In any prosecution for violations of this title, where a sealed container is labeled as containing an alcoholic beverage as defined herein, such labeling shall be prima facie evidence of the alcoholic content of the container. Nothing shall preclude the introduction of other relevant evidence to establish the alcoholic content of a container, whether sealed or not.

History.
1962, c. 616, § 4-90.1; 1993, cc. 169, 866; 1997, c. 418.

§ 4.1-354. No recovery for alcoholic beverages illegally sold.

No action to recover the price of any alcoholic beverages sold in contravention of this title may be maintained.

History.
Code 1950, § 4-88; 1993, c. 866.

TITLE 5.1.
AVIATION.

CHAPTER 1.
AIRCRAFT, AIRMEN AND AIRPORTS GENERALLY.

Article 2.

Illegal Operation, etc.; Procedure; Penalties.

Article 3.

Structures Dangerous to Aircraft.

ARTICLE 2.
ILLEGAL OPERATION, ETC.; PROCEDURE; PENALTIES.

§ 5.1-13. Operation of aircraft while under influence of intoxicating liquors or drugs; reckless operation.

Any person who shall operate any aircraft within the airspace over, above or upon the lands or waters of this Commonwealth, while under the influence of intoxicating liquor or of any narcotic or any habit-forming drugs shall be guilty of a felony and shall be confined in a state correctional facility not less than one nor more than five years, or, in the discretion of the court or jury trying the case, be confined in jail not exceeding twelve months and fined not exceeding $500, or both such fine and imprisonment.

Any person who shall operate any aircraft within the airspace over, above or upon the lands or waters of this Commonwealth carelessly or heedlessly in willful or wanton disregard of the rights or safety of others, or without due caution and circumspection and in a manner so as to endanger any person or property, shall be guilty of a misdemeanor.

History.
Code 1950, § 5-10.1; 1964, c. 416; 1966, c. 576.

§ 5.1-14. Operation of unlicensed aircraft.

Any person who operates or causes to be operated any civil aircraft within the airspace over, above or upon the lands or waters of this Commonwealth, which aircraft has not been and is not at the time of such operation properly certificated under and in accordance with existing federal law and licensed under and in accordance with the existing laws of this Commonwealth and rules and regulations promulgated in pursuance thereof, shall be guilty of a misdemeanor.

History.
Code 1950, § 5-10.2; 1966, c. 576.

§ 5.1-15. Operation of aircraft by unlicensed persons.

Any person who operates any civil aircraft within the airspace over, above, or upon the lands or waters of this Commonwealth, without being, at the time of such operation, in possession of a valid airman's certificate for such operation, issued under and in accordance with existing federal law shall be deemed to be guilty of a Class 1 misdemeanor.

History.
Code 1950, § 5-10.3; 1966, c. 576; 1988, c. 45.

§ 5.1-16. Tampering with, etc., airplanes or markings of airports, landing fields or other aeronautical facilities.

It shall be unlawful for any person to tamper with, alter, destroy, remove, carry away, or cause to be carried away, an airplane or other flying device or instrumentality or any objects used for the marking of airports, landing fields, drop zones or other aeronautical facilities, or in any way change their position or location, except by and under the direction of the proper authorities charged with the maintenance and operation of such facilities. Any person violating any of the provisions of this section or who shall illegally have in his possession any objects or devices used for such markings, shall be guilty of a misdemeanor.

History.
Code 1950, § 5-10.4; 1966, c. 576.

§ 5.1-16.1. Misuse of licensed airports.

It shall be unlawful for any person or persons to use licensed airport runways, taxiways or ramp areas for other than aeronautical purposes without written approval of the controlling authority of such airport.

History.
1970, c. 717.

§ 5.1-17. Use of aircraft for hunting.

It shall be unlawful for any person to hunt, pursue or kill any wild waterfowl or other birds or animals by any means whatever during such time as such person is in flight in an aircraft in the airspace over the lands or waters of this Commonwealth. A violation of this section shall be deemed a misdemeanor.

History.
Code 1950, § 5-10.5; 1966, c. 576.

§§ 5.1-18, 5.1-19: Repealed by Acts 1988, c. 45.

§ 5.1-20. Pilot may restrain or arrest person interfering with operation of aircraft carrying passengers for hire.

The pilot of any aircraft carrying passengers for hire, or any person subject to his direction, may take such action as is reasonably necessary to restrain or arrest any person who interferes with, or threatens to interfere with, the operation of the aircraft in flight over the territory of this Commonwealth or to a destination within this Commonwealth.

History.
Code 1950, § 5-14.1; 1958, c. 561, § 1; 1966, c. 576.

§ 5.1-21. Powers of conservator of the peace conferred upon pilot.

The pilot of any aircraft carrying passengers for hire while actively engaged in the operation of such aircraft shall be a special policeman and have all the powers of a conservator of the peace in the enforcement of order on such aircraft and while in pursuit of persons for disorder upon such aircraft and until such persons as may be arrested by him shall have been placed in confinement or delivered to the custody of some other conservator of the peace or police officer.

History.
Code 1950, § 5-14.2; 1958, c. 561, § 2; 1966, c. 576.

§ 5.1-21.1. Powers of conservators of the peace conferred upon airport managers or designees.

The airport manager of any licensed Virginia airport or in his absence not more than two employees who are designated by him shall be special policemen and have all the powers of conservators of the peace in the enforcement of this title and its regulations as promulgated by the Board. Persons arrested by them shall be placed in confinement or delivered to the custody of some other conservator of the peace or police officer.

History.
1970, c. 717; 1979, c. 272; 1991, c. 339.

§ 5.1-22. Interference with operation of aircraft; penalties; venue.

Any person who interferes with or threatens to interfere with the operation of any aircraft, unless he is authorized by the Federal Aviation Administration or the armed forces of the United States, on or over the territory of the Commonwealth shall be guilty of a Class 1 misdemeanor. Where the act or acts of interference or threatened interference are of such a nature as to endanger the life of the aircraft's operator or the life of any other person, the person interfering or threatening to interfere shall be guilty of a Class 6 felony. Any person who knowingly and intentionally projects a point of light from a laser, laser gun sight, or any other device that simulates a laser at an aircraft is guilty of a Class 1 misdemeanor. Venue for the issuance of a warrant for the arrest and trial of any such person is hereby conferred upon any court having criminal jurisdiction in the political subdivision in the Commonwealth where the aircraft either took off prior to such offense, or where it lands or comes to rest subsequent to such offense, or in or over which the offense occurred.

History.
Code 1950, § 5-14.3; 1958, c. 561, § 3; 1966, c. 576; 1983, c. 560; 2012, c. 398.

§ 5.1-23. Jurisdiction of local and State Police.

The local police authorities of any city, incorporated town or county shall have jurisdiction on the premises of any airport, drop zone or landing field operated hereunder, either individually or jointly and the State Police shall have jurisdiction to investigate any aircraft accident. In the exercise of such jurisdiction the State Police and officers of the department of law enforcement of any city or county with an optional form of government may enter with immunity and without a warrant upon private property for the purpose of conducting such investigations. This section shall not repeal the provisions of any city charter in conflict herewith.

History.
Code 1950, § 5-37; 1966, c. 576; 1968, c. 737; 1979, c. 394; 1980, c. 721.

§ 5.1-24. Penalties.

Any person violating any of the provisions of this chapter, or violating any of the rules or regulations promulgated pursuant thereto by the Board, except as otherwise specifically provided, shall be deemed guilty of a misdemeanor and upon conviction shall be punished by a fine of not more than $100 or imprisonment in jail not exceeding one month, or both, in the discretion of the judge or jury trying the case; provided, that any person (excepting any government, political subdivision of the Commonwealth, or governmental subdivision or agency) establishing or operating an airport without first obtaining a permit as provided in § 5.1-8 shall, upon conviction, be fined not less than $100 nor more than $500 for each offense, and each day that the airport is operated without such permit shall be construed as a separate offense.

History.
Code 1950, § 5-11; 1966, c. 576; 1979, c. 272.

§ 5.1-25. Operation of aircraft by nonresident.

A nonresident of this Commonwealth may operate aircraft engaged in operations other than for hire or reward in accordance with regulations promulgated by the Board, provided such nonresident and the aircraft to be so operated shall have been certified under federal law and shall have complied with the laws of the state in which such nonresident resides relative to aircraft and the operation thereof. A nonresident-owned aircraft engaged in intrastate operation for hire or reward must be licensed with the Department in accordance with this title and the Board's regulations.

History.
Code 1950, § 5-12; 1966, c. 576; 1970, c. 717; 1979, c. 272; 1988, c. 45.

ARTICLE 3.

STRUCTURES DANGEROUS TO AIRCRAFT.

§ 5.1-25.1. Permit required for erection of certain structures.

It shall be unlawful for any person to erect any structure, any part of which penetrates into or through any licensed airport's or United States government or military air facility's clear zone, approach zone, imaginary surface, obstruction clearance surface, obstruction clearance zone, or surface or zone as described in regulations of the Department of Aviation or the Federal Aviation Administration, without securing a permit for its erection from the Board. This section shall not apply to any structure to be erected in a county, city or town which has an ordinance regulating the height of such structures to prevent the penetration of zones and surfaces provided for in Federal Aviation Regulation Part 77 and Rule 19 of the Department of Aviation.

For the purpose of this section, *"structure"* shall mean any object, including a mobile object, constructed or erected by man, including but not limited to buildings, towers, cranes, smokestacks, earth formations, overhead transmission lines, flag poles, and ship masts.

History.
1968, c. 744; 1979, c. 272; 1981, c. 326; 1989, cc. 202, 255; 1990, c. 384.

§ 5.1-25.2. Application for permit; notice and hearing.

Any person desiring to erect or cause to be erected any such structure shall make application to the Department for the issuance of a permit for such erection. Such application shall be forwarded immediately to the Board. The Department shall undertake an appropriate review of such application and submit its contents in writing to the Board as expeditiously as possible. The Board, after such notice to the public as it deems necessary, shall hold a public hearing not less than thirty days after the giving of such notice at which all interested parties shall be admitted to attend and state any objection which they may have to the erection of such structure.

History.
1968, c. 744; 1979, c. 272.

§ 5.1-25.3. When permit issued or denied; conditions to issuance.

The Board, if it finds that the erection of such structure will not be dangerous to aircraft using the airways of this Commission, shall issue the permit requested; but if it shall find that the erection of such structure will create a hazard to aircraft using such airways, it shall refuse the issuance of such a permit. The Board may, as a condition to the issuance of any permit, require the installation and maintenance of warning lights and any other devices which may be reasonably required to reduce the hazard which might be presented by the erection of such structure.

History.
1968, c. 744.

§ 5.1-25.4. Injunctions.

If any person commences the erection of a structure of the nature described in § 5.1-25.1 without securing the permit therein required, the Department shall have power to apply forthwith to the circuit court of the jurisdiction in which the structure is located or is to be located, for injunctive relief.

History.
1968, c. 744; 1979, c. 272.

Aviation

CHAPTER 9.
AIR CARRIERS.

Article 9.

Miscellaneous.

ARTICLE 9.
MISCELLANEOUS.

§ 5.1-140. Unlawful to disclose certain information.

It shall be unlawful for any air carrier or broker or any officer, receiver, trustee, lessee, agent, or employee of such carrier, broker, or person, or for any other person authorized by such carrier, broker, or person to receive information, knowingly to disclose to, or permit to be acquired by any person other than the shipper or consignee, without the consent of such shipper or consignee, any information concerning the nature, kind, quantity, destination, consignee, or routing of any property tendered or delivered to such air carrier or broker for such transportation, which information may be used to the detriment or prejudice of such shipper or consignee, or which may improperly disclose his business transactions to a competitor; and it shall also be unlawful for any person to solicit or receive knowingly any such information which may be so used.

Nothing in this chapter shall be construed to prevent the giving of such information in response to any legal process issued under the authority of any court, or to any officer or agent of the government of the United States or of any state, territory, or district thereof, in the exercise of his power, or to any officer or other duly authorized person seeking such information for the prosecution of persons charged with or suspected of crimes or to another carrier or broker, or its duly authorized agent, for the purpose of adjusting mutual traffic accounts in the ordinary course of business of such carriers or brokers.

History.
Code 1950, § 56-195; 1970, c. 708.

§ 5.1-141: Repealed by Acts 2001, c. 137.

§ 5.1-142. Reports, records, etc.

(a) The Commission is hereby authorized to require annual, periodic, or special reports from all air carriers except such as are exempted from the operation of the provisions of this chapter, to prescribe the manner and form in which such reports shall be made, and to require from such carriers specific answers to all questions upon which the Commission may deem information to be necessary. Such reports shall be under oath whenever the Commission so requires. The Commission may also require any air carrier to file with it a true copy of any contract, agreement, or arrangement between such carrier and any other carrier or person in relation to any traffic affected by the provisions of this chapter.

(b) The Commission may, in its discretion, prescribe the forms of any and all accounts, records, and memoranda to be kept by air carriers and the length of time such accounts, records and memoranda shall be preserved, including the accounts, records, and memoranda of the movement of traffic, as well as of the receipts and expenditures of money. The Commission or its employees shall at all times have access to all lands, buildings, and equipment of air carriers used in connection with their operation and also all accounts, records, and memoranda, including all documents, papers, and correspondence now existing, and kept, or required to be kept, by air carriers. The Commission and its employees shall have authority to inspect and examine any and all such lands, buildings, equipment, accounts, records, and memoranda, including all documents, papers, and correspondence now or hereafter existing and kept or required to be kept by such carriers. This provision shall apply to receivers of carriers and to operating trustees and, to the extent deemed necessary by the Commission, to persons having control, direct or indirect, over or affiliated with any air carrier.

(c) As used in this section the term "air carriers" includes brokers.

History.
Code 1950, § 56-197; 1970, c. 708.

§ 5.1-143. Reports of accidents.

It shall be the duty of the manager, agent or other proper officer of every air carrier doing business or operating in this Commonwealth to make to the Commission such report or reports as may be required by it, under oath, of all accidents in this Commonwealth resulting in injury to persons, equipment, or property of any kind, under such rules and regulations as may be prescribed by the Commission.

History.
Code 1950, § 56-198; 1970, c. 708.

§ 5.1-144. Certificate or permit holder not relieved of liability for negligence.

Nothing in this chapter shall relieve any holder of a certificate or permit by and under the authority of the Commission from any liability resulting from his negligence, whether or not he has complied with the requirements of this chapter.

History.
Code 1950, § 56-199; 1970, c. 708.

§ 5.1-145. Enforcement under Department of State Police or Commission; concurrent jurisdiction for investigations of accidents.

The enforcement of any provision of this chapter requiring the use of police officers shall be under the Department of State Police or under the Commission; except the department of law enforcement of any city or county with an optional form of government shall have concurrent jurisdiction for the investigations of aircraft accidents occurring within such city or county.

History.
Code 1950, § 56-200; 1964, c. 342; 1970, c. 708; 1979, c. 394; 1980, c. 721.

§ 5.1-146. Violations and penalties.

(a) Any person knowingly and willfully violating any provision of this chapter, or any rule, regulation, requirement, or order thereunder for which a penalty is not otherwise herein provided, shall, after proper proceeding before the Commission, and upon conviction thereof, be fined not more than $100 for the first offense and not more than $500 for any subsequent offense. Each day of such violation shall constitute a separate offense.

(b) Any person, whether carrier, shipper, consignee, or broker, or any officer, employee, agent, or representative thereof, who shall knowingly offer, grant, or give, or solicit, accept, or receive any rebate, concession, or discrimination in violation of any provision of this chapter, or who, by means of any false statement or representation, or by the use of any false or fictitious bill, bill of lading, receipt, voucher, roll, account, claim, certificate, affidavit, deposition, lease, or bill of sale or by any other means or device, shall knowingly and willfully assist, suffer or permit any person, natural or artificial, to obtain transportation of passengers or property subject to this chapter for less than the applicable rate, fare, or charge, or who shall knowingly and willfully by any such means or otherwise fraudulently seek to evade or defeat regulation as in this chapter provided for air carriers or brokers, shall be deemed guilty of a misdemeanor and upon conviction thereof be fined not more than $500 for the first offense and not more than $2,000 for any subsequent offense.

(c) Any air carrier, or broker, or any officer, agent, employee, or representative thereof who shall willfully fail or refuse to make a report to the Commission as required by this chapter, or to keep accounts, records and memoranda in the form and manner approved or prescribed by the Commission, or shall knowingly and willfully falsify, destroy, mutilate, or alter any such report, account, record, or memorandum, or shall knowingly and willfully file any false report, account, record, or memorandum, shall, after proper proceeding before the Commission and upon conviction thereof, be subject for each offense to a fine of not less than $100 and not more than $5,000.

History.
Code 1950, § 56-201; 1970, c. 708.

§ 5.1-147. Disposition of fees or sums collected.

All fees or sums collected by the Commission under the provisions of this chapter shall be deposited with the State Treasurer, and shall be set aside by him for the use of the Commission for the administration and enforcement of this chapter.

History.
Code 1950, § 56-202; 1970, c. 708.

§ 5.1-148. Employees of Commission not to have interest in carriers.

No employee of the Commission appointed or employed in the administration of this chapter shall in any manner have any pecuniary interest in, own any securities of, or hold any position with any air carrier, motor carrier, railroad, steamboat or canal company.

History.
Code 1950, § 56-203; 1970, c. 708.

§ 5.1-149. No property rights in airspace conferred by chapter.

Nothing in this chapter shall confer any proprietary or property rights in the use of the airspace of this Commonwealth.

History.
Code 1950, § 56-204; 1970, c. 708.

§ 5.1-150. Licenses, taxes, etc., not affected.

Nothing in this chapter shall be construed to relieve any person from the payment of any licenses, fees, taxes or levies now or hereafter imposed by law.

History.
Code 1950, § 56-205; 1970, c. 708.

§ 5.1-151. Right to amend, revoke, etc., rights, certificates or franchises.

The right and power of the General Assembly to amend, alter, revoke or repeal any and all rights, certificates, or franchises granted pursuant to the provisions of this chapter is hereby reserved.

History.
Code 1950, § 56-206; 1970, c. 708.

CHAPTER 10.
METROPOLITAN WASHINGTON AIRPORTS AUTHORITY.

§ 5.1-158. Police.

A. The Commonwealth hereby grants, accepts and agrees to concurrent police power authority over the Metropolitan Washington Airports as provided in Section 6009 (c) of the Metropolitan Washington Airports Act of 1986.

B. The Authority is authorized to establish and maintain a regular police force and to confer police powers to be exercised with respect to offenses occurring on the Authority Facilities upon its employees meeting the minimum requirements of the Department of Criminal Justice Services.

Such police officers shall have all powers vested in police officers under Chapter 17 of Title 15.2, Chapter 11 of Title 16.1, Title 18.2, Title 19.2, and Title 46.2 of the Code of Virginia as those titles may be amended from time to time and shall be responsible upon the Authority Facilities and within 300 yards of the Facilities for enforcing the laws of the Commonwealth, the Authority's rules and regulations and all other applicable ordinances, rules, and regulations.

Such police officers may issue summons to appear, or arrest on view or on information without warrant as permitted by law, and conduct before any judicial officer of competent jurisdiction any person violating, upon Authority Facilities, any rule or regulation of the Authority, any ordinance or regulation of any local political subdivision, or any other law of the Commonwealth.

C. The Department of State Police shall exercise the same powers upon Authority Facilities as elsewhere in the Commonwealth.

D. The Authority may enter into reciprocal or mutual aid agreements with the local political subdivisions in the National Capital Region as defined in § 2674(f)(2) of title 10 of the United States Code, those counties with a border abutting that area, and any municipalities therein; any agency of the Commonwealth, the District of Columbia, the State of Maryland; the federal government; or any combination of the foregoing for cooperation in the furnishing of services during a public service event, an emergency, or planned training, including law-enforcement, fire, rescue, emergency health, and medical services, transportation, communications, public works and engineering, mass care, and resource support. When responding to a request under such an agreement, Authority employees may go outside Authority facilities, and the Authority and its employees shall enjoy the same immunities from liability as localities and their employees do in responding under similar circumstances.

E. The police force of Arlington County shall have concurrent jurisdiction with the police force established herein at Ronald Reagan Washington National Airport. The Authority shall enter into an agreement with Arlington County regarding the exercise of police authority.

F. The sheriffs and police forces of Loudoun and Fairfax Counties shall continue to exercise concurrent jurisdiction with the police force established herein over the Authority Facilities situated within their respective counties.

History.
2001, c. 342; 2007, cc. 729, 742.

TITLE 6.1.
BANKING AND FINANCE.

[Repealed.]

§§ 6.1-1 through 6.1-479: Repealed by Acts 2010, c. 794, cl. 11, effective October 1, 2010.

Cross references.
For current title on Financial Institutions and Services, see Title 6.2 (§ 6.2-100 et seq.).

TITLE 6.2.
FINANCIAL INSTITUTIONS AND SERVICES.

CHAPTER 8.
BANKS.

Article 15.
Banking Offenses.

ARTICLE 15.
BANKING OFFENSES.

§ 6.2-938. Engaging in banking business without authority; Commission may examine accounts of suspected person; penalty.

A. Every person who trades or deals as a bank, or carries on banking, without authority of law, and their officers and agents, is guilty of a Class 6 felony.

B. The Commission shall have authority to examine the accounts, books, and papers of any person who it has reason to suspect is doing a banking business, in order to ascertain whether such person has violated, or is violating, any provision of this title. The refusal to submit such accounts, books, and papers shall be prima facie evidence of such violation.

History.
Code 1950, § 6-133; 1966, c. 584, § 6.1-111; 1992, c. 136; 1994, c. 7; 2010, c. 794.

§ 6.2-939. Unlawful use of terms indicating that business is bank; penalty.

A. A person not authorized to engage in the banking business in the Commonwealth by the provisions of this title or under the laws of the United States, shall not (i) use any office sign having thereon any name or other words indicating that any such office is the office of a bank; (ii) use or circulate any letterheads, billheads, blank notes, blank receipts, certificates, circulars, or any written or printed paper, having thereon any name or word indicating that such person is a bank; or (iii) use the word "bank," "banking," "banker," or "trust," or the equivalent thereof in any foreign language, or the plural thereof in connection with any business other than a banking business.

B. The foregoing prohibitions shall not apply to use by a bank holding company, as defined in § 6.2-800, of the word "bank," "banks," "banking," "banker," "trust," or the equivalent thereof in its name, or of a name similar to that of a subsidiary bank of such bank holding company.

C. The use of the above-mentioned words in the name of, or in connection with, any other business shall not be prohibited if the context or remaining words show clearly and definitely that the business is not a bank, and is not carrying on a banking business.

D. Any person violating the provisions of this section, either individually or as an interested party, is guilty of a Class 6 felony.

History.
Code 1950, § 6-134; 1966, c. 584, § 6.1-112; 1972, c. 187; 1992, cc. 24, 136; 2000, c. 56; 2003, c. 592; 2010, c. 794.

§ 6.2-940. Making derogatory statements affecting banks; penalty.

Any person who willfully and maliciously makes, circulates, or transmits to another any statement, rumor, or suggestion that is directly or by reference derogatory to the financial condition, or affects the solvency or financial standing of, any bank doing business in the Commonwealth, or who counsels, aids, procures, or induces another to start, transmit, or circulate any such statement or rumor, is guilty of a Class 1 misdemeanor.

History.
Code 1950, § 6-132; 1966, c. 584, § 6.1-119; 1991, c. 710; 2010, c. 794.

§ 6.2-941. Use of bank name, logo, or symbol for marketing purposes; penalty.

A. As used in this section, "name, logo, or symbol, or any combination thereof, of a bank" includes any name, logo, or symbol, or any combination thereof, that is deceptively similar to the name, logo, or symbol, or any combination thereof of a bank.

B. Except as provided in subsection C, no person shall use the name, logo, or symbol, or any combination thereof, of a bank in marketing material provided to or solicitation of another person in a manner such that a reasonable person may believe that the marketing material or solicitation originated from or is endorsed by the bank or that the bank is responsible for the marketing material or solicitation.

C. This section shall not apply to (i) an affiliate or agent of the bank or (ii) a person who uses the name, logo, or symbol of a bank with the consent of the bank.

D. Any person violating the provisions of this section, either individually or as an interested party, is guilty of a Class 1 misdemeanor. This section shall not affect the availability of any remedies otherwise available to a bank.

History.
2005, c. 240, § 6.1-119.1; 2010, c. 794.

§ 6.2-942. False certification of checks; penalty.

Any officer, employee, agent, or director of a bank who (i) certifies a check drawn on such bank and willfully fails forthwith to charge the amount thereof against the account of the drawer thereof or (ii) willfully certifies a check drawn on such bank when the drawer of such check does not have on deposit with the bank the amount of money subject to the payment of such check, is guilty of a Class 1 misdemeanor.

History.
Code 1950, § 6-136; 1966, c. 584, § 6.1-120; 2010, c. 794.

§ 6.2-943. Offenses by officer, director, agent, or employee of bank; penalties.

A. Any officer, director, agent, or employee of any bank who embezzles, abstracts, or willfully misapplies any of the moneys, funds, or credits of, or in the possession or control of, the bank is guilty of larceny and subject to the penalties provided in § 18.2-95 or 18.2-96.

B. Any officer, director, agent, or employee of any bank who (i) issues or puts forth any certificate of deposit, (ii) draws any order or bill of exchange, (iii) makes any acceptance, (iv) assigns any note, bond, draft, bill of exchange, mortgage, judgment, decree, or other instrument in writing, or (v) makes any false entry in any book, report, or statement of such bank, with intent in any case to injure or defraud the bank or any other individual or entity, or to deceive any officer of the bank or the Commission, or any agent or examiner authorized to examine the affairs of the bank, and any person, who, with the same intent, aids or abets any such officer, director, agent, or employee of such bank in any act described in clauses (i) through (v), is guilty of a Class 5 felony.

C. Any officer of a bank who knowingly makes a false statement of the condition of any bank is guilty of a Class 5 felony.

History.
Code 1950, §§ 6-128, 6-138; 1966, c. 584, § 6.1-122; 1974, c. 665; 2010, c. 794.

§ 6.2-944. Officers, directors, agents, and employees violating or causing bank to violate laws; civil liability not affected.

Any officer, director, agent, or employee of any bank who knowingly violates or who knowingly causes any bank to violate any provision of this chapter, or knowingly participates or knowingly acquiesces in any such violation, unless other punishment is provided for the offense of such officer, agent, or employee, is guilty of a Class 1 misdemeanor. The provisions of this section shall not affect the civil liability of any such officer, director, agent, or employee.

History.
Code 1950, § 6-139; 1966, c. 584, § 6.1-123; 1974, c. 665; 2010, c. 794.

§ 6.2-945. Receiving deposit knowing bank to be insolvent; penalty.

A. Any officer, director. or employee of any bank, or broker, who takes and receives, or permits to be received, a deposit from any person with the actual knowledge that the bank or broker is at the time insolvent, is guilty of embezzlement. Notwithstanding the provisions of § 18.2-111, an individual convicted of embezzlement pursuant to this section shall be fined double the amount so received and be subject to a term of imprisonment of not less than one nor more than three years, in the discretion of the jury, for each offense.

B. On the trial of any indictment under this section, it shall be the duty of the bank or broker, and its agent or officers, to produce in court, on demand of the attorney for the Commonwealth, all books and papers of the bank or broker, to be read as evidence on the trial of such indictment. In determining the question of the solvency of any bank, the capital stock thereof shall not be considered as a liability due by it.

History.
Code 1950, § 6-3; 1966, c. 584, § 6.1-124; 2010, c. 794.

§ 6.2-946. Civil penalties for violation of Commission's orders.

A. The Commission may impose, enter judgment for, and enforce by its process, a civil penalty not exceeding $10,000 upon any bank, or against any of its directors, officers, or employees, who it determines, in proceedings commenced in accordance with the Commission's Rules, has violated any lawful order of the Commission.

B. The Commission may remove from office any director or officer of a bank for a second or subsequent violation by him of any such order.

C. In all cases the defendant shall have an opportunity to be heard and to introduce evidence, and the right to appeal as provided by law.

History.
1968, c. 791, § 6.1-125; 1974, c. 665; 1976, c. 658; 2010, c. 794.

ARTICLE 16.

VOLUNTARY REGULATORY SELF-ASSESSMENTS.

§ 6.2-947. Definitions.

As used in this article, unless the context requires a different meaning:

"Bank" has the same meaning ascribed to the term in § 6.2-800 and includes any bank holding company, affiliates, and subsidiaries of a bank.

"Bank regulator" means any state, federal, or municipal governmental agency, bureau, commission, office, or other governmental entity charged with the regulation or supervision of a bank or the regulation or supervision of any activity in which a bank may be engaged. "Bank regulator" includes the Office of the Comptroller of the Currency, the Federal Reserve Board, the Federal Deposit Insurance Corporation, the Consumer Financial Protection Bureau, the Federal Trade Commission, and the Bureau.

"Self-assessment" means (i) a bank's voluntary, self-initiated internal assessment, audit, or review of the bank and its practices, policies, and procedures or (ii) a bank's voluntary, self-initiated assessment, audit, or review of the practices, policies, and procedures of a person acting under contract, directly or indirectly, as the bank's service provider, including mortgage servicers and sub-servicers, credit and debit card processors, and providers of loan document systems.

"Self-assessment report" means any document, including any audit, report, finding, communication, or opinion or any draft of an audit, report, finding, communication, or opinion, prepared by internal personnel or by outside attorneys, accountants, or consultants as a part of or in connection with a self-assessment that is made in good faith.

History.
2013, cc. 32, 148.

§ 6.2-948. Privilege for self-assessment reports.

Except as otherwise provided in this article:

1. A self-assessment report and any portion or contents thereof are privileged and are not admissible or subject to discovery in any civil or administrative litigation, action, proceeding, or investigation;

2. The self-assessment privilege shall be applicable regardless of whether a bank regulator or any other governmental authority in possession of a self-assessment report or any portion or contents thereof subsequently discloses it or any portion or contents thereof to a third party (i) in accordance with subsection B of § 6.2-101 or (ii) as required or permitted by any other state or federal law; and

3. Notwithstanding any state or federal law, a bank regulator or any other governmental authority in possession of a self-assessment report or any portion or contents thereof shall not disclose the report or any portion or contents thereof to a person in response to a request made pursuant to the Virginia Freedom of Information Act (§ 2.2-3700 et seq.) or any similar federal or state public records law.

History.
2013, cc. 32, 148.

§ 6.2-949. Exceptions from self-evaluation privilege.

The self-assessment privilege established by § 6.2-948 shall not apply:

1. If a bank expressly waives the protections of the self-assessment privilege established by § 6.2-948;

2. If a bank discloses a self-assessment report to any third party, provided that disclosure of a self-assessment report to a third party shall not void or waive the self-assessment privilege with respect to such self-assessment report if such third party (i) is a bank regulator, (ii) is subject to an agreement or obligation to preserve the confidentiality of the self-assessment report, which agreement or obligation to preserve confidentiality need not be in writing and may be evidenced by an indication of confidentiality on the face of any such self-assessment report, a verbal agreement regarding its confidentiality, an employment relationship, a principal-agent relationship, a fiduciary relationship, or an attorney-client relationship, or (iii) receives the self-assessment report from a person described in clause (i) or (ii);

3. If a court or hearing officer, after an in camera review, determines that (i) the privilege is being asserted for a fraudulent purpose, (ii) the self-assessment report was prepared to avoid disclosure of information in an investigative, administrative, or judicial proceeding that was underway at the time of its preparation or for which the bank had been provided written notification that an investigation into a specific violation had been initiated, or (iii) the self-assessment report addresses a matter reasonably expected to have an imminent and substantial harm to bank customers or consumers and the bank has not previously taken reasonable actions to correct the matter; or

4. To any self-assessment report requested by a bank regulator, provided that disclosure of a self-assessment report to a bank regulator shall not void or waive the self-assessment privilege with respect to such self-assessment report, and provided further that disclosure of a self-assessment report by a bank regulator to any third party shall not void or waive the self-assessment privilege with respect to such self-assessment report.

History.
2013, cc. 32, 148.

§ 6.2-950. Effect on other privileges.

Nothing in this article limits, waives, or abrogates the scope or nature of any statutory or common law privilege.

History.
2013, c. 32, 148.

ARTICLE 17.

BENEFITS CONSORTIUM.

§ 6.2-951. Definitions.

As used in this article:

"Benefits consortium" means a trust that complies with the conditions set forth in § 6.2-952.

"ERISA" means the federal Employee Retirement Income Security Act of 1974 (P.L. 93-406, 88 Stat. 829), as amended.

"Sponsoring association" means an association (i) the members of which are banks and employers that provide products and services to banks, (ii) that is incorporated under the Virginia Nonstock Corporation Act (§ 13.1-801 et seq.), (iii) that operates as a nonprofit entity under § 501(c)(6) of the Internal Revenue Code of 1986, (iv) that has been in existence for at least 20 years, and (v) that exists for purposes other than arranging for or providing health and welfare benefits to members. "Sponsoring association" includes any wholly owned subsidiary of a sponsoring association.

History.
2014, cc. 220, 296.

§ 6.2-952. Conditions for a benefits consortium.

A trust shall constitute a benefits consortium when all of the following conditions exist:

1. The trust is subject to (i) ERISA and U.S. Department of Labor regulations applicable to multiple employer welfare arrangements and (ii) the authority of the U.S. Department of Labor to enforce such law and regulations;

2. A Form M-1, Report for Multiple Employer Welfare Arrangements (MEWAs), for the applicable plan year shall be filed with the U.S. Department of Labor identifying the arrangement among the trust, sponsoring association, and benefit plans offered through the trust as a multiple employer welfare arrangement;

3. The trust operates as a nonprofit voluntary employee beneficiary association within the meaning of § 501(c)(9) of the Internal Revenue Code of 1986;

4. The trust's organizational documents:

a. Provide that the trust is sponsored by the sponsoring association;

b. State that its purpose is to provide medical, prescription drug, dental, and vision benefits to employees of the sponsoring association and its members and the dependents of those employees through benefits plans;

c. Provide that the funds of the trust are to be used for the benefit of the participating employees, and their dependents, through insurance, self-insurance, or a combination thereof as determined by the trustee and for defraying reasonable expenses of administering and operating the trust and the benefits plans offered through the trust;

d. Limit participation in the benefits plans offered through the trust to employers that are the sponsoring association, members of the sponsoring association, and their affiliates;

e. Limit the benefits plans offered through the trust to benefits plans sponsored by the sponsoring association;

f. Grant the sponsoring association the power to appoint the trustee of the trust;

g. Provide the trustee with powers for the control and management of the trust; and

h. Require the trustee to discharge its duties with respect to the trust in accordance with the fiduciary duties defined in ERISA;

5. Five or more employers participate in the benefits plans offered through the trust;

6. The trust establishes and maintains reserves determined in accordance with sound actuarial principles;

7. The trust has purchased and maintains policies of specific, aggregate, and terminal excess insurance with retention levels determined in accordance with sound actuarial principles from insurers licensed to transact the business of insurance in the Commonwealth;

8. The trust has secured one or more guarantees or standby letters of credit guaranteeing the payment of claims under the benefits plans offered through the trust in an aggregate amount not less than (i) the trust's annual aggregate excess insurance retention level, minus (ii) the annual premium assessments for the benefits plans offered through the trust, minus (iii) the trust's net assets, which net assets amount shall be net of the trust's reasonable estimate of incurred but not reported claims; and such guarantees or letters of credit have been issued by (a) banks participating in the benefits plans offered through the trust or (b) qualified United States financial institutions as such term is used in subdivision 2 c of § 38.2-1316.4;

9. The trust has purchased and maintains commercially reasonable fiduciary liability insurance;

10. The trust has purchased and maintains a bond that satisfies the requirements of ERISA;

11. The trust is audited annually by an independent certified public accountant;

12. The trust does not include in its name the words "insurance," "insurer," "underwriter," "mu-

tual," or any other word or term or combination of words or terms that is uniquely descriptive of an insurance company or insurance business unless the context of the remaining words or terms clearly indicates that the entity is not an insurance company and is not carrying on the business of insurance; and

13. The trust does not pay commissions or other remuneration to any person that is conditioned upon the enrollment of persons in any benefits plan offered by the trust.

History.
2014, cc. 220, 296.

§ 6.2-953. Benefits consortium and sponsoring association not subject to regulation or taxation as an insurance company.

A. A benefits consortium shall not be subject to:

1. The provisions of Title 38.2 and regulations adopted thereunder, including those provisions and regulations otherwise applicable to multiple employer welfare arrangements; or

2. The tax levied on insurance companies pursuant to § 58.1-2501.

B. The sponsoring association of a benefits consortium or any of its subsidiaries shall not, by virtue of its sponsorship of the benefits consortium or the benefits plans offered through the benefits consortium, be subject to any provisions or regulations described in subdivision A 1 or any tax described in subdivision A 2.

History.
2014, cc. 220, 296.

CHAPTER 10.
ENTITIES CONDUCTING TRUST BUSINESS.

Article 2.

Trust Companies.

Article 3.

Trust Subsidiaries.

ARTICLE 2.
TRUST COMPANIES.

§ 6.2-1039. Engaging in trust business without authority; Commission may examine accounts of suspected person; penalty.

A. Every person who trades or deals as a trust company, or conducts a trust business, without authority of law, and their officers and agents, is guilty of a Class 6 felony.

B. The Commission shall have authority to examine the accounts, books, and papers of any person who it has reason to suspect is doing a trust business, in order to ascertain whether such person has violated, or is violating, any provision of this title. The refusal to submit such accounts, books, and papers shall be prima facie evidence of such violation.

History.
Code 1950, § 6-133; 1966, c. 584, § 6.1-111; 1992, c. 136; 1994, c. 7; 2010, c. 794.

§ 6.2-1040. Unlawful use of terms indicating that business is trust company; penalty.

A. A person not authorized to engage in the trust business in the Commonwealth by the provisions of this title or under the laws of the United States, shall not (i) use any office sign having thereon any name or other words indicating that any such office is the office of a trust company; (ii) use or circulate any letterheads, billheads, blank notes, blank receipts, certificates, circulars or any written or printed paper, having thereon any name or word indicating that such person is a trust company; or (iii) use the word "trust" or the equivalent thereof in any foreign language, or the plural thereof in connection with any business other than a trust business.

B. The foregoing prohibitions shall not apply to use by a trust company holding company of the word "trust" or the equivalent thereof in its name, or of a name similar to that of a subsidiary trust company of such trust company holding company.

C. The use of the above-mentioned words in the name of, or in connection with, any other business shall not be prohibited if the context or remaining words show clearly and definitely that the business is not a trust company, and is not carrying on a trust business.

D. Any person violating the provisions of this section, either individually or as an interested party, is guilty of a Class 6 felony.

History.

Code 1950, § 6-134; 1966, c. 584, § 6.1-112; 1972, c. 187; 1992, cc. 24, 136; 2000, c. 56; 2003, c. 592; 2010, c. 794.

§ 6.2-1042. Making derogatory statements affecting trust companies; penalty.

Any person who willfully and maliciously makes, circulates or transmits to another, any statement, rumor or suggestion that is directly or by reference derogatory to the financial condition, or affects the solvency or financial standing of, any trust company doing business in the Commonwealth, or who counsels, aids, procures or induces another to start, transmit, or circulate any such statement or rumor, is guilty of a Class 1 misdemeanor.

History.

Code 1950, § 6-132; 1966, c. 584, § 6.1-119; 1991, c. 710; 2010, c. 794.

§ 6.2-1044. Offenses by officer, director, agent or employee of trust company; penalties.

A. Any officer, director, agent, or employee of any trust company who embezzles, abstracts, or willfully misapplies any of the moneys, funds or credits of, or in the possession or control of the trust company is guilty of larceny and subject to the penalties provided in § 18.2-95 or 18.2-96.

B. Any officer, director, agent or employee of any trust company who (i) issues or puts forth any certificate of deposit, (ii) draws any order or bill of exchange, (iii) makes any acceptance, (iv) assigns any note, bond, draft, bill of exchange, mortgage, judgment, decree or other instrument in writing, or (v) makes any false entry in any book, report or statement of such trust company with intent in any case to injure or defraud the trust company, or any other individual or entity, or to deceive any officer of the trust company or the Commission, or any agent or examiner authorized to examine the affairs of the trust company, and any person, who, with like intent, aids or abets any such officer, director, agent or employee of such trust company in any act described in clauses (i) through (v), is guilty of a Class 5 felony.

C. Any officer of a trust company who knowingly makes a false statement of the condition of any trust company is guilty of a Class 5 felony.

History.

Code 1950, §§ 6-128, 6-138; 1966, c. 584, § 6.1-122; 1974, c. 665; 2010, c. 794.

§ 6.2-1045. Officers, directors, agents and employees violating or causing trust company to violate laws; civil liability not affected.

Any officer, director, agent, or employee of any trust company who knowingly violates or who knowingly causes any trust company to violate any provision of this chapter, or knowingly participates or knowingly acquiesces in any such violation, unless other punishment is provided for the offense of such officer, agent, or employee, is guilty of a Class 1 misdemeanor. The provisions of this section shall not affect the civil liability of any such officer, director, agent or employee.

History.

Code 1950, § 6-139; 1966, c. 584, § 6.1-123; 1974, c. 665; 2010, c. 794.

§ 6.2-1046. Civil penalties for violation of Commission's orders.

A. The Commission may impose, enter judgment for, and enforce by its process, a civil penalty not exceeding $10,000 upon any trust company or against any of its directors, officers, or employees, who it determines, in proceedings commenced in accordance with the Commission's Rules, has violated any lawful order of the Commission.

B. The Commission may remove from office any director or officer of a trust company for a second or subsequent violation by him of any such order.

C. In all cases the defendant shall have an opportunity to be heard and to introduce evidence, and the right to appeal as provided by law.

History.

1968, c. 791, § 6.1-125; 1974, c. 665; 1976, c. 658; 2010, c. 794.

ARTICLE 3.

TRUST SUBSIDIARIES.

§ 6.2-1062. Offenses by officer, director, agent or employee of trust subsidiary; penalties.

A. Any officer, director, agent, or employee of any trust subsidiary who embezzles, abstracts, or willfully misapplies any of the moneys, funds or credits of, or in the possession or control of the trust subsidiary is guilty of larceny and subject to the penalties provided in § 18.2-95 or 18.2-96.

B. Any officer, director, agent or employee of any trust subsidiary who (i) issues or puts forth any certificate of deposit, (ii) draws any order or bill of exchange, (iii) makes any acceptance, (iv) assigns any note, bond, draft, bill of exchange, mortgage, judgment, decree or other instrument in writing, or (v) makes any false entry in any book, report or statement of such trust subsidiary with intent in any case to injure or defraud the trust subsidiary, or any other individual or entity, or to deceive any officer of the trust subsidiary or the Commission, or any agent or examiner authorized to examine the affairs of the trust subsidiary, and any person, who, with like intent, aids or abets any such officer, director, agent or employee of such trust subsidiary in any act described in clauses (i) through (v), is guilty of a Class 5 felony.

C. Any officer of a trust subsidiary who knowingly makes a false statement of the condition of any trust subsidiary is guilty of a Class 5 felony.

History.
Code 1950, §§ 6-128, 6-138; 1966, c. 584, § 6.1-122; 1974, c. 665; 2010, c. 794.

§ 6.2-1063. Officers, directors, agents and employees violating or causing trust subsidiary to violate laws; civil liability not affected.

Any officer, director, agent, or employee of any trust subsidiary who knowingly violates or who knowingly causes any trust subsidiary to violate any provision of this chapter, or knowingly participates or knowingly acquiesces in any such violation, unless other punishment is provided for the offense of such officer, agent, or employee, is guilty of a Class 1 misdemeanor. The provisions of this section shall not affect the civil liability of any such officer, director, agent or employee.

History.
Code 1950, § 6-139; 1966, c. 584, § 6.1-123; 1974, c. 665; 2010, c. 794.

§ 6.2-1064. Civil penalties for violation of Commission's orders.

A. The Commission may impose, enter judgment for, and enforce by its process, a civil penalty not exceeding $10,000 upon any trust subsidiary or against any of its directors, officers, or employees, who it determines, in proceedings commenced in accordance with the Commission's Rules, has violated any lawful order of the Commission.

B. The Commission may remove from office any director or officer of a trust subsidiary for a second or subsequent violation by him of any such order.

C. In all cases the defendant shall have an opportunity to be heard and to introduce evidence, and the right to appeal as provided by law.

History.
1968, c. 791, § 6.1-125; 1974, c. 665; 1976, c. 658; 2010, c. 794.

CHAPTER 11.
SAVINGS INSTITUTIONS.

Article 1.

General Provisions.

ARTICLE 1.
GENERAL PROVISIONS.

§ 6.2-1104. False statements and similar actions prohibited; penalty.

Any person who knowingly makes or causes to be made, directly or indirectly, or through any agency, any false statement or report, or willfully overvalues any land, property, or security, for the purpose of influencing in any way the action of any savings institution upon any application, advance, discount, purchase or repurchase agreement, commitment, or loan or any change or extension thereof, by renewal, deferment of action or otherwise, or the acceptance, release, or substitution of security therefor, is guilty of a Class 1 misdemeanor.

History.
1985, c. 425, § 6.1-194.93; 1986, c. 509; 2010, c. 794.

§ 6.2-1107. Defamation of savings institutions and certain federal agencies prohibited; penalty.

No person shall willfully and knowingly make, issue, circulate, or transmit, or cause or knowingly permit to be made, issued, circulated, or transmitted, any statement or rumor, written, printed, reproduced in any manner, or by word of mouth, that is untrue in fact and is (i) malicious, in that it is calculated to injure reputation or business, and (ii) derogatory to the financial condition or standing of any savings institution or Federal Home Loan Bank. Any person who violates this section is guilty of a Class 2 misdemeanor.

History.
Code 1950, § 6-201.52; 1960, c. 402; 1966, c. 584, § 6.1-182; 1972, c. 796, § 6.1-195.62; 1985, c. 425, § 6.1-194.94; 1990, c. 3; 2010, c. 794.

CHAPTER 13.
CREDIT UNIONS.

Article 1.

General Provisions.

Article 2.

Supervision and Regulation.

ARTICLE 1. GENERAL PROVISIONS.

§ 6.2-1305. Making or circulating derogatory statements affecting credit unions; penalty.

Any person who willfully and maliciously makes, circulates, or transmits to another any statement or rumor that is untrue in facts and is directly or by inference derogatory to the financial condition or affects the solvency or financial standing of any credit union doing business in the Commonwealth, or who knowingly counsels, aids, procures, or induces another to start, transmit, or circulate any such statement or rumor, is guilty of a Class 3 misdemeanor.

History.
1991, c. 170, § 6.1-225.64; 2010, c. 794.

ARTICLE 2. SUPERVISION AND REGULATION.

§ 6.2-1316. Offenses; penalty.

Any officer, director, employee, receiver, or agent of a credit union who willfully does any of the following is guilty of a Class 6 felony:

1. With the intent to deceive, falsifies any book of account, report, statement, record, or other document of a credit union, whether by alteration, false entry, omission, or otherwise;
2. Signs, issues, publishes, or transmits to a government agency any book of account, report, statement, record, or other document that he knows to be false;
3. By means of deceit, obtains a signature to a writing that is a subject of forgery;
4. With intent to deceive, destroys any credit union book of account, report, statement, record, or other document; or
5. With the intent to defraud, shares or receives directly or indirectly any money, property, or benefits through any transaction of the credit union.

History.
1985, c. 363, § 6.1-223.2; 1990, c. 373, § 6.1-225.62; 2010, c. 794.

CHAPTER 18. PAYDAY LENDERS.

Section

§ 6.2-1800. Definitions.

As used in this chapter, unless the context requires a different meaning:

"Check" means a draft drawn on the account of an individual at a depository institution.

"Depository institution" means a bank, savings institution, or credit union.

"Licensee" means a person to whom a license has been issued under this chapter.

"Payday loan" means a small, short-maturity loan on the security of (i) a check, (ii) any form of assignment of an interest in the account of an individual at a depository institution, or (iii) any form of assignment of income payable to an individual, other than loans based on income tax refunds.

"Principal" means any person who, directly or indirectly, owns or controls (i) 10 percent or more of the outstanding stock of a stock corporation or (ii) a 10 percent or greater interest in a nonstock corporation or a limited liability company.

History.
2002, c. 897, § 6.1-444; 2005, c. 571; 2010, c. 794.

§ 6.2-1801. License requirement.

A. No person shall engage in the business of making payday loans to any consumer residing in the Commonwealth, whether or not the person has an office or conducts business at a location in the Commonwealth, except in accordance with the provisions of this chapter and without having first obtained a license under this chapter from the Commission.

B. No person shall engage in the business of arranging or brokering payday loans for any consumer residing in the Commonwealth, whether or not the person has an office or conducts business at a location in the Commonwealth.

History.
2002, c. 897, § 6.1-445; 2005, c. 571; 2010, c. 794.

§ 6.2-1825. Criminal penalties.

Any person violating § 6.2-1801 is guilty of a Class 6 felony. For the purposes of this section, each violation shall constitute a separate offense.

History.
2002, c. 897, § 6.1-468; 2010, c. 794.

TITLE 8.01.
CIVIL REMEDIES AND PROCEDURE.

CHAPTER 3.
ACTIONS.

ARTICLE 3.
INJURY TO PERSON OR PROPERTY.

§ 8.01-40.3. Unauthorized dissemination, etc., of criminal history record information; civil action.

A. Any person who disseminates, publishes, or maintains or causes to be disseminated, published, or maintained the criminal history record information as defined in § 9.1-101 of an individual pertaining to that individual's charge or arrest for a criminal offense and solicits, requests, or accepts money or other thing of value for removing such criminal history record information shall be liable to the individual who is the subject of the information for actual damages or $500, whichever is greater, in addition to reasonable attorney fees and costs.

B. Nothing in this section shall be construed to impose liability on:

1. An interactive computer service, as defined in 47 U.S.C. § 230(f), for content provided by another person.
2. Any speech protected by Article I, Section 12 of the Constitution of Virginia.

C. As used in this section, *"criminal history record information"* means the same as that term is defined in § 9.1-101.

History.
2015, cc. 414, 415.

ARTICLE 7.
MOTOR VEHICLE ACCIDENTS.

§ 8.01-63. Liability for death or injury to guest in motor vehicle.

Any person transported by the owner or operator of any motor vehicle as a guest without payment for such transportation and any personal representative of any such guest so transported shall be entitled to recover damages against such owner or operator for death or injuries to the person or property of such guest resulting from the negligent operation of such motor vehicle. However, this statute does not limit any defense otherwise available to the owner or operator.

History.
Code 1950, § 8-646.1; 1974, c. 551; 1977, c. 617.

§ 8.01-64. Liability for negligence of minor.

Every owner of a motor vehicle causing or knowingly permitting a minor under the age of sixteen years who is not permitted under the provisions of § 46.2-335 to drive such a vehicle upon a highway, and any person who gives or furnishes a motor vehicle to such minor, shall be jointly or severally liable with such minor for any damages caused by the negligence of such minor in driving such vehicle.

History.
Code 1950, § 8-646.2; 1977, c. 617.

§ 8.01-65. Defense of lack of consent of owner.

It shall be a valid defense to any action brought for the negligent operation of a motor vehicle for the owner of such vehicle to prove that the same was being driven or used without his knowledge or consent, express or implied, but the burden of proof thereof shall be on such owner.

History.

Code 1950, § 8-646.8; 1977, c. 617.

§ 8.01-66. Recovery of damages for loss of use of vehicle.

A. Whenever any person is entitled to recover for damage to or destruction of a motor vehicle, he shall, in addition to any other damages to which he may be legally entitled, be entitled to recover the reasonable cost which was actually incurred in hiring a comparable substitute vehicle for the period of time during which such person is deprived of the use of his motor vehicle. However, such rental period shall not exceed a reasonable period of time for such repairs to be made or if the original vehicle is a total loss, a reasonable time to purchase a new vehicle. Nothing herein contained shall relieve the claimant of the duty to mitigate damages.

B. Whenever any insurance company licensed in this Commonwealth to write insurance as defined in § 38.2-124 or any self-insured company refuses or fails to provide a comparable temporary substitute vehicle to any person entitled to recover the actual cost of hiring a substitute vehicle as set forth in subsection A, and if the trial judge of a court of proper jurisdiction subsequently finds that such refusal or failure was not made in good faith, such company shall be liable to that person in the amount of $500 or double the amount of the rental cost he is entitled to recover under subsection A, whichever amount is greater. If the trial court finds that an action brought against an insurance company or any self-insured company under subsection B is frivolous, or not to have been brought in good faith, the court may in its discretion require the plaintiff to pay the reasonable attorney's fees, not to exceed $350, incurred by the defendant in defending the action. This section shall in no way preclude any party from seeking such additional common law remedies as might otherwise be available.

History.

Code 1950, § 8-646.9; 1975, c. 478; 1977, c. 617; 1979, c. 499; 1986, c. 296; 1987, c. 116; 1989, c. 348; 2010, c. 343.

§ 8.01-66.1. Remedy for arbitrary refusal of motor vehicle insurance claim.

A. Whenever any insurance company licensed in this Commonwealth to write insurance as defined in § 38.2-124 denies, refuses or fails to pay to its insured a claim of $3,500 or less in excess of the deductible, if any, under the provisions of a policy of motor vehicle insurance issued by such company to the insured and it is subsequently found by the judge of a court of proper jurisdiction that such denial, refusal or failure to pay was not made in good faith, the company shall be liable to the insured in an amount double the amount otherwise due and payable under the provisions of the insured's policy of motor vehicle insurance, together with reasonable attorney's fees and expenses.

The provisions of this subsection shall be construed to include an insurance company's refusal or failure to pay medical expenses to persons covered under the terms of any medical payments coverage extended under a policy of motor vehicle insurance, when the amount of the claim therefor is $3,500 or less and the refusal was not made in good faith.

B. Notwithstanding the provisions of subsection A, whenever any insurance company licensed in this Commonwealth to write insurance as defined in § 38.2-124 denies, refuses or fails to pay to a third party claimant, on behalf of an insured to whom such company has issued a policy of motor vehicle liability insurance, a claim of $3,500 or less made by such third party claimant and if the judge of a court of proper jurisdiction finds that the insured is liable for the claim, the third party claimant shall have a cause of action against the insurance company. If the judge finds that such denial, refusal or failure to pay was not made in good faith, the company, in addition to the liability assumed by the company under the provisions of the insured's policy of motor vehicle liability insurance, shall be liable to the third party claimant in an amount double the amount of the judgment awarded the third party claimant, together with reasonable attorney's fees and expenses.

C. Notwithstanding the provisions of subsections A and B whenever any person who has paid a fee to the Department of Motor Vehicles to register an uninsured motor vehicle pursuant to § 46.2-706 or any person who has furnished proof of financial responsibility in lieu of obtaining a policy or policies of motor vehicle liability insurance pursuant to the provisions of Title 46.2 or any person who is required and has failed either to pay such fee or to furnish such proof pursuant to the provisions of Title 46.2 denies, refuses or fails to pay to a claimant a claim of $3,500 or less made by such claimant as a result of a motor vehicle accident; and if the trial judge of a court of proper jurisdiction finds that such denial, refusal or failure to pay was not made in good faith, such person shall be liable to the claimant in an amount double the amount otherwise due and payable together with reasonable attorney's fees and expenses.

For the purposes of this subsection C "person" shall mean and include any natural person, firm, partnership, association or corporation.

D. 1. Whenever a court of proper jurisdiction finds that an insurance company licensed in this Commonwealth to write insurance as defined in § 38.2-124 denies, refuses or fails to pay to its insured a claim of more than $3,500 in excess of the deductible, if any, under the provisions of a policy of motor vehicle insurance issued by such company to the insured and it is subsequently found by the judge of a court of proper jurisdiction that such denial, refusal or failure to pay was not made in good faith, the company shall be liable to the insured in the amount otherwise due and payable under the provisions of the insured's policy of motor vehicle insurance, plus interest on the amount due at double the rate provided in § 6.2-301 from the date that the claim was submitted to the insurer or its authorized agent, together with reasonable attorney's fees and expenses.

2. The provisions of this subsection shall be construed to include an insurance company's refusal or failure to pay medical expenses to persons covered under the terms of any medical payments coverage extended under a policy of motor vehicle insurance when the refusal was not made in good faith.

History.

1977, c. 621; 1979, c. 521; 1980, c. 437; 1989, c. 698; 1991, c. 155; 1997, c. 401; 2002, c. 631.

ARTICLE 18.2.

COMPENSATION FOR WRONGFUL INCARCERATION FOR A FELONY CONVICTION.

§ 8.01-195.10. Purpose; action by the General Assembly required; definitions.

A. The purpose of this article is to provide directions and guidelines for the compensation of persons who have been wrongfully incarcerated in the Commonwealth. Compensation for wrongful incarceration is governed by Article IV, Section 14 of the Constitution of Virginia, which prohibits the General Assembly from granting relief in cases in which the courts or other tribunals may have jurisdiction and any individual seeking payment of state funds for wrongful incarceration shall be deemed to have waived all other claims. The payment and receipt of any compensation for wrongful incarceration shall be contingent upon the General Assembly appropriating funds for that purpose. This article shall not provide an entitlement to compensation for persons wrongfully incarcerated or require the General Assembly to appropriate funds for the payment of such compensation. No estate of or personal representative for a decedent shall be entitled to seek a claim for compensation for wrongful incarceration.

B. As used in this article:

"Incarceration" or *"incarcerated"* means confinement in a local or regional correctional facility, juvenile correctional center, state correctional facility, residential detention center, or facility operated pursuant to the Corrections Private Management Act (§ 53.1-261 et seq.).

"Wrongful incarceration" or *"wrongfully incarcerated"* means incarceration for a felony conviction for which (i) the conviction has been vacated pursuant to Chapter 19.2 (§ 19.2-327.2 et seq.) or 19.3 (§ 19.2-327.10 et seq.) of Title 19.2, or the person incarcerated has been granted an absolute pardon for the commission of a crime that he did not commit, (ii) the person incarcerated must have entered a final plea of not guilty, or regardless of the plea, any person sentenced to death, or convicted of a Class 1 felony, a Class 2 felony, or any felony for which the maximum penalty is imprisonment for life, and (iii) the person incarcerated did not by any act or omission on his part intentionally contribute to his conviction for the felony for which he was incarcerated.

History.

2004, cc. 818, 840; 2010, cc. 496, 557.

§ 8.01-195.11. Compensation for wrongful incarceration.

A. Any person who is convicted of a felony by a county or city circuit court of the Commonwealth and is wrongfully incarcerated for such felony may be awarded compensation in an amount equal to 90 percent of the inflation adjusted Virginia per capita personal income as reported by the Bureau of Economic Analysis of the United States Department of Commerce for each year of incarceration, or portion thereof.

B. Any compensation computed pursuant to subsection A and approved by the General Assembly shall be paid by the Comptroller by his warrant on the State Treasurer in favor of the person found to have been wrongfully incarcerated. The person wrongfully incarcerated shall be paid an initial lump sum equal to 20 percent of the compensation award with the remaining 80 percent of the principal of the compensation award to be used by the State Treasurer to purchase an annuity from any A+ rated company, including any A+ rated company from which the Virginia Lottery may purchase an annuity, to provide equal monthly payments to such person for a period certain of 25 years commencing no later than one year after the effective date of the appropriation. The annuity shall provide that it shall not be sold, discounted, or used as securitization for loans and mortgages by the person awarded compensation. The annuity shall, however, contain beneficiary provisions providing for the annuity's continued disbursement in the event of the death of the person awarded compensation. All payments or costs of annuities under this section shall be made by check issued by the State Treasurer on warrant of the Comptroller.

C. Any person who is convicted of a felony by a county or city circuit court of the Commonwealth and is wrongfully incarcerated for such felony shall receive a transition assistance grant of $15,000 to be paid from the Criminal Fund, which amount shall be deducted from any award received pursuant to subsection B. In addition, such person shall be entitled to receive reimbursement up to $10,000 for tuition for career and technical training within the Virginia community college system contingent upon successful completion of the training. Reimbursement for tuition shall be provided by the community college at which the career or technical training was completed.

History.
2004, cc. 818, 840; 2010, c. 557; 2012, c. 675; 2014, c. 225.

§ 8.01-195.12. Conditions for continued compensation.

A. Any person awarded compensation under this article who is subsequently convicted of a felony shall, immediately upon such conviction, not be eligible to receive any unpaid amounts from any compensation awarded and his beneficiaries shall not be eligible to receive any payments under an annuity purchased pursuant to subsection B of § 8.01-195.11. Any unpaid amounts remaining under any annuity shall become the property of the Commonwealth and shall be deposited into the general fund of the state treasury.

A1. Any person awarded compensation under this article who is subsequently incarcerated upon the revocation of parole or probation resulting from the commission of an act that constitutes a crime shall, during the period of such incarceration, forfeit any payments under an annuity purchased pursuant to subsection B of § 8.01-195.11. Any forfeited amounts under any annuity shall become the property of the Commonwealth and shall be deposited into the general fund of the state treasury.

B. As a condition of receiving any compensation under this article, a person shall execute a release and waiver forever releasing (i) the Commonwealth or any agency, instrumentality, officer, employee, or political subdivision thereof, (ii) any legal counsel appointed pursuant to § 19.2-159, and (iii) all other parties of interest, from any present or future claims the person receiving compensation may have against such enumerated parties and arising out of the factual situation in connection with the conviction for which compensation is being sought under this article. In addition, the person receiving compensation shall not have been awarded a finally adjudicated judgment in a court of law against or received any funds pursuant to a settlement agreement with any person or entity described in this subsection for compensation or damages arising out of the factual situation in connection with the conviction.

History.
2004, cc. 818, 840; 2010, c. 557.

ARTICLE 21.
MISCELLANEOUS PROVISIONS.

§ 8.01-225. Persons rendering emergency care, obstetrical services exempt from liability.

A. Any person who:

1. In good faith, renders emergency care or assistance, without compensation, to any ill or injured person (i) at the scene of an accident, fire, or any life-threatening emergency; (ii) at a location for screening or stabilization of an emergency medical condition arising from an accident, fire, or any life-threatening emergency; or (iii) en route to any hospital, medical clinic, or doctor's office, shall not be liable for any civil damages for acts or omissions resulting from the rendering of such care or assistance. For purposes of this subdivision, emergency care or assistance includes the forcible entry of a motor vehicle in order to remove an unattended minor at risk of serious bodily injury or death, provided the person has attempted to contact a law-enforcement officer, as defined in § 9.1-101, a firefighter, as defined in § 65.2-102, emergency medical services personnel, as defined in § 32.1-111.1, or an emergency 911 system, if feasible under the circumstances.

2. In the absence of gross negligence, renders emergency obstetrical care or assistance to a female in active labor who has not previously been cared for in connection with the pregnancy by such person or by another professionally associated with such person and whose medical records are not reasonably available to such person shall not be liable for any civil damages for acts or omissions resulting from the rendering of such emergency care or assistance. The immunity herein granted shall apply only to the emergency medical care provided.

3. In good faith and without compensation, including any emergency medical services provider who holds a valid certificate issued by the Commissioner of Health, administers epinephrine in an emergency to an individual shall not be liable for any civil damages for ordinary negligence in acts or omissions resulting from the rendering of such treatment if such person has reason to believe that the individual receiving the injection is suffering or is about to suffer a life-threatening anaphylactic reaction.

4. Provides assistance upon request of any police agency, fire department, emergency medical services agency, or governmental agency in the event of an accident or other emergency involving the use, handling, transportation, transmission, or storage of liquefied petroleum gas, liquefied natural gas, hazardous material, or hazardous waste as defined in § 10.1-1400 or regulations of the Virginia Waste Management Board shall not be liable for any civil damages resulting from any act of commission or omission on his part in the course of his rendering such assistance in good faith.

5. Is an emergency medical services provider possessing a valid certificate issued by authority of the State Board of Health who in good faith renders emergency care or assistance, whether in person or by telephone or other means of communication, without compensation, to any injured or ill person, whether at the scene of an accident, fire, or any

other place, or while transporting such injured or ill person to, from, or between any hospital, medical facility, medical clinic, doctor's office, or other similar or related medical facility, shall not be liable for any civil damages for acts or omissions resulting from the rendering of such emergency care, treatment, or assistance, including but in no way limited to acts or omissions which involve violations of State Department of Health regulations or any other state regulations in the rendering of such emergency care or assistance.

6. In good faith and without compensation, renders or administers emergency cardiopulmonary resuscitation (CPR); cardiac defibrillation, including, but not limited to, the use of an automated external defibrillator (AED); or other emergency life-sustaining or resuscitative treatments or procedures which have been approved by the State Board of Health to any sick or injured person, whether at the scene of a fire, an accident, or any other place, or while transporting such person to or from any hospital, clinic, doctor's office, or other medical facility, shall be deemed qualified to administer such emergency treatments and procedures and shall not be liable for acts or omissions resulting from the rendering of such emergency resuscitative treatments or procedures.

7. Operates an AED at the scene of an emergency, trains individuals to be operators of AEDs, or orders AEDs, shall be immune from civil liability for any personal injury that results from any act or omission in the use of an AED in an emergency where the person performing the defibrillation acts as an ordinary, reasonably prudent person would have acted under the same or similar circumstances, unless such personal injury results from gross negligence or willful or wanton misconduct of the person rendering such emergency care.

8. Maintains an AED located on real property owned or controlled by such person shall be immune from civil liability for any personal injury that results from any act or omission in the use in an emergency of an AED located on such property unless such personal injury results from gross negligence or willful or wanton misconduct of the person who maintains the AED or his agent or employee.

9. Is an employee of a school board or of a local health department approved by the local governing body to provide health services pursuant to § 22.1-274 who, while on school property or at a school-sponsored event, (i) renders emergency care or assistance to any sick or injured person; (ii) renders or administers emergency cardiopulmonary resuscitation (CPR); cardiac defibrillation, including, but not limited to, the use of an automated external defibrillator (AED); or other emergency life-sustaining or resuscitative treatments or procedures that have been approved by the State Board of Health to any sick or injured person; (iii) operates an AED, trains individuals to be operators of AEDs, or orders AEDs; or (iv) maintains an AED, shall not be liable for civil damages for ordinary negligence in acts or omissions on the part of such employee while engaged in the acts described in this subdivision.

10. Is a volunteer in good standing and certified to render emergency care by the National Ski Patrol System, Inc., who, in good faith and without compensation, renders emergency care or assistance to any injured or ill person, whether at the scene of a ski resort rescue, outdoor emergency rescue, or any other place or while transporting such injured or ill person to a place accessible for transfer to any available emergency medical system unit, or any resort owner voluntarily providing a ski patroller employed by him to engage in rescue or recovery work at a resort not owned or operated by him, shall not be liable for any civil damages for acts or omissions resulting from the rendering of such emergency care, treatment, or assistance, including but not limited to acts or omissions which involve violations of any state regulation or any standard of the National Ski Patrol System, Inc., in the rendering of such emergency care or assistance, unless such act or omission was the result of gross negligence or willful misconduct.

11. Is an employee of (i) a school board, (ii) a school for students with disabilities as defined in § 22.1-319 licensed by the Board of Education, or (iii) a private school accredited pursuant to § 22.1-19 as administered by the Virginia Council for Private Education and is authorized by a prescriber and trained in the administration of insulin and glucagon, who, upon the written request of the parents as defined in § 22.1-1, assists with the administration of insulin or administers glucagon to a student diagnosed as having diabetes who requires insulin injections during the school day or for whom glucagon has been prescribed for the emergency treatment of hypoglycemia shall not be liable for any civil damages for ordinary negligence in acts or omissions resulting from the rendering of such treatment if the insulin is administered according to the child's medication schedule or such employee has reason to believe that the individual receiving the glucagon is suffering or is about to suffer life-threatening hypoglycemia. Whenever any such employee is covered by the immunity granted herein, the school board or school employing him shall not be liable for any civil damages for ordinary negligence in acts or omissions resulting from the rendering of such insulin or glucagon treatment.

12. Is a school nurse, an employee of a school board, an employee of a local governing body, or an employee of a local health department who is authorized by a prescriber and trained in the administration of epinephrine and who provides, administers, or assists in the administration of epinephrine to a student believed in good faith to be having an anaphylactic reaction, or is the prescriber of the epinephrine, shall not be liable for any civil damages for ordinary negligence in acts or omissions resulting from the rendering of such treatment.

13. Is an employee of a school for students with disabilities, as defined in § 22.1-319 and licensed by the Board of Education, or an employee of a private school that is accredited pursuant to § 22.1-19 as administered by the Virginia Council for Private Education who is authorized by a prescriber and trained in the administration of epinephrine and who administers or assists in the administration of epinephrine to a student believed in good faith to be having an anaphylactic reaction, or is the prescriber of the epinephrine, shall not be liable for any civil damages for ordinary negligence in acts or omissions resulting from the rendering of such treatment. Whenever any employee is covered by the immunity granted in this subdivision, the school shall not be liable for any civil damages for ordinary negligence in acts or omissions resulting from such administration or assistance.

14. Is an employee of a provider licensed by the Department of Behavioral Health and Developmental Services, or provides services pursuant to a contract with a provider licensed by the Department of Behavioral Health and Developmental Services, who has been trained in the administration of insulin and glucagon and who administers or assists with the administration of insulin or administers glucagon to a person diagnosed as having diabetes who requires insulin injections or for whom glucagon has been prescribed for the emergency treatment of hypoglycemia in accordance with § 54.1-3408 shall not be liable for any civil damages for ordinary negligence in acts or omissions resulting from the rendering of such treatment if the insulin is administered in accordance with the prescriber's instructions or such person has reason to believe that the individual receiving the glucagon is suffering or is about to suffer life-threatening hypoglycemia. Whenever any employee of a provider licensed by the Department of Behavioral Health and Developmental Services or a person who provides services pursuant to a contract with a provider licensed by the Department of Behavioral Health and Developmental Services is covered by the immunity granted herein, the provider shall not be liable for any civil damages for ordinary negligence in acts or omissions resulting from the rendering of such insulin or glucagon treatment.

15. Is an employee of a provider licensed by the Department of Behavioral Health and Developmental Services, or provides services pursuant to a contract with a provider licensed by the Department of Behavioral Health and Developmental Services, who has been trained in the administration of epinephrine and who administers or assists in the administration of epinephrine to a person believed in good faith to be having an anaphylactic reaction in accordance with the prescriber's instructions shall not be liable for any civil damages for ordinary negligence in acts or omissions resulting from the rendering of such treatment.

16. In good faith prescribes, dispenses, or administers naloxone or other opioid antagonist used for overdose reversal in an emergency to an individual who is believed to be experiencing or about to experience a life-threatening opiate overdose shall not be liable for any civil damages for ordinary negligence in acts or omissions resulting from the rendering of such treatment if acting in accordance with the provisions of subsection X of § 54.1-3408 or in his role as a member of an emergency medical services agency.

B. Any licensed physician serving without compensation as the operational medical director for an emergency medical services agency that holds a valid license as an emergency medical services agency issued by the Commissioner of Health shall not be liable for any civil damages for any act or omission resulting from the rendering of emergency medical services in good faith by the personnel of such licensed agency unless such act or omission was the result of such physician's gross negligence or willful misconduct.

Any person serving without compensation as a dispatcher for any licensed public or nonprofit emergency medical services agency in the Commonwealth shall not be liable for any civil damages for any act or omission resulting from the rendering of emergency services in good faith by the personnel of such licensed agency unless such act or omission was the result of such dispatcher's gross negligence or willful misconduct.

Any individual, certified by the State Office of Emergency Medical Services as an emergency medical services instructor and pursuant to a written agreement with such office, who, in good faith and in the performance of his duties, provides instruction to persons for certification or recertification as a certified basic life support or advanced life support emergency medical services provider shall not be liable for any civil damages for acts or omissions on his part directly relating to his activities on behalf of such office unless such act or omission was the result of such emergency medical services instructor's gross negligence or willful misconduct.

Any licensed physician serving without compensation as a medical advisor to an E-911 system in the Commonwealth shall not be liable for any civil damages for any act or omission resulting from rendering medical advice in good faith to establish protocols to be used by the personnel of the E-911 service, as defined in § 58.1-1730, when answering emergency calls unless such act or omission was the result of such physician's gross negligence or willful misconduct.

Any licensed physician who directs the provision of emergency medical services, as authorized by the State Board of Health, through a communications device shall not be liable for any civil damages for any act or omission resulting from the rendering of such emergency medical services unless such act or omission was the result of such physician's gross negligence or willful misconduct.

Any licensed physician serving without compensation as a supervisor of an AED in the Commonwealth shall not be liable for any civil damages for any act or omission resulting from rendering medical advice in good faith to the owner of the AED relating to personnel training, local emergency medical services coordination, protocol approval, AED deployment strategies, and equipment maintenance plans and records unless such act or omission was the result of such physician's gross negligence or willful misconduct.

C. Any communications services provider, as defined in § 58.1-647, including mobile service, and any provider of Voice-over-Internet Protocol service, in the Commonwealth shall not be liable for any civil damages for any act or omission resulting from rendering such service with or without charge related to emergency calls unless such act or omission was the result of such service provider's gross negligence or willful misconduct.

Any volunteer engaging in rescue or recovery work at a mine, or any mine operator voluntarily providing personnel to engage in rescue or recovery work at a mine not owned or operated by such operator, shall not be liable for civil damages for acts or omissions resulting from the rendering of such rescue or recovery work in good faith unless such act or omission was the result of gross negligence or willful misconduct. For purposes of this subsection, "Voice-over-Internet Protocol service" or "VoIP service" means any Internet protocol-enabled services utilizing a broadband connection, actually originating or terminating in Internet Protocol from either or both ends of a channel of communication offering real time, multidirectional voice functionality, including, but not limited to, services similar to traditional telephone service.

D. Nothing contained in this section shall be construed to provide immunity from liability arising out of the operation of a motor vehicle.

E. For the purposes of this section, "compensation" shall not be construed to include (i) the salaries of police, fire, or other public officials or personnel who render such emergency assistance; (ii) the salaries or wages of employees of a coal producer engaging in emergency medical services or first aid services pursuant to the provisions of § 45.1-161.38, 45.1-161.101, 45.1-161.199, or 45.1-161.263; (iii) complimentary lift tickets, food, lodging, or other gifts provided as a gratuity to volunteer members of the National Ski Patrol System, Inc., by any resort, group, or agency; (iv) the salary of any person who (a) owns an AED for the use at the scene of an emergency, (b) trains individuals, in courses approved by the Board of Health, to operate AEDs at the scene of emergencies, (c) orders AEDs for use at the scene of emergencies, or (d) operates an AED at the scene of an emergency; or (v) expenses reimbursed to any person providing care or assistance pursuant to this section.

For the purposes of this section, "emergency medical services provider" shall include a person licensed or certified as such or its equivalent by any other state when he is performing services that he is licensed or certified to perform by such other state in caring for a patient in transit in the Commonwealth, which care originated in such other state.

Further, the public shall be urged to receive training on how to use CPR and an AED in order to acquire the skills and confidence to respond to emergencies using both CPR and an AED.

History.

Code 1950, § 54-276.9; 1962, c. 449; 1964, c. 568; 1968, c. 796; 1972, c. 578; 1975, c. 508; 1977, c. 441; 1978, cc. 94, 707; 1979, cc. 713, 729; 1980, c. 419; 1983, c. 72; 1984, cc. 493, 577; 1987, cc. 260, 382; 1990, c. 898; 1996, c. 899; 1997, cc. 334, 809; 1998, cc. 493, 500; 1999, cc. 570, 1000; 2000, cc. 928, 1064; 2003, cc. 18, 978, 1020; 2005, c. 426; 2006, c. 780; 2008, c. 229; 2012, cc. 787, 833; 2013, cc. 183, 267, 300, 336, 617; 2014, c. 468; 2015, cc. 340, 387, 502, 503, 725, 732, 752; 2016, c. 144.

§ 8.01-225.01. Certain immunity for health care providers during disasters under specific circumstances.

A. In the absence of gross negligence or willful misconduct, any health care provider who responds to a disaster by delivering health care to persons injured in such disaster shall be immune from civil liability for any injury or wrongful death arising from abandonment by such health care provider of any person to whom such health care provider owes a duty to provide health care when (i) a state or local emergency has been or is subsequently declared; and (ii) the provider was unable to provide the requisite health care to the person to whom he owed such duty of care as a result of the provider's voluntary or mandatory response to the relevant disaster.

B. In the absence of gross negligence or willful misconduct, any hospital or other entity credentialing health care providers to deliver health care in response to a disaster shall be immune from civil liability for any cause of action arising out of such credentialing or granting of practice privileges if (i) a state or local emergency has been or is subsequently declared and (ii) the hospital has followed procedures for such credentialing and granting of practice privileges that are consistent with the applicable standards of an approved national accrediting organization for granting emergency practice privileges.

C. For the purposes of this section:

"Approved national accrediting organization" means an organization granted authority by the Centers for Medicare and Medicaid Services to ensure compliance with Medicare conditions of participation pursuant to § 1865 of Title XVIII of the Social Security Act (42 U.S.C. § 1395bb);

"Disaster" means any "disaster," "emergency," or "major disaster" as those terms are used and defined in § 44-146.16; and

"Health care provider" means those professions defined as such in § 8.01-581.1.

D. The immunity provided by this section shall be in addition to, and shall not be in lieu of, any immunities provided in other state or federal law, including, but not limited to, §§ 8.01-225 and 44-146.23.

History.
2003, c. 507; 2008, cc. 121, 157; 2014, c. 320.

§ 8.01-225.02. Certain liability protection for health care providers during disasters.

A. In the absence of gross negligence or willful misconduct, any health care provider who responds to a disaster shall not be liable for any injury or wrongful death of any person arising from the delivery or withholding of health care when (i) a state or local emergency has been or is subsequently declared in response to such disaster, and (ii) the emergency and subsequent conditions caused a lack of resources, attributable to the disaster, rendering the health care provider unable to provide the level or manner of care that otherwise would have been required in the absence of the emergency and which resulted in the injury or wrongful death at issue.

B. For purposes of this section:

"Disaster" means any "disaster," "emergency," or "major disaster" as those terms are used and defined in § 44-146.16; and

"Health care provider" has the same definition as provided in § 8.01-581.1.

History.
2008, cc. 121, 157.

§ 8.01-225.1. Immunity for team physicians.

Any physician, surgeon or chiropractor licensed to practice by the Board of Medicine in the Commonwealth who, in the absence of gross negligence or willful misconduct, renders emergency medical care or emergency treatment to a participant in an athletic event sponsored by a public, private or religious elementary, middle or high school while acting without compensation as a team physician, shall not be liable for civil damages resulting from any act or omission related to such care or treatment.

History.
1989, c. 436; 1993, c. 702; 2005, c. 928.

§ 8.01-225.2. Immunity for those rendering emergency care to animals.

Any person, including a person licensed to practice veterinary medicine, who in good faith and without compensation renders emergency care or treatment to an injured animal at the scene of an emergency or accident shall not be liable for any injuries to such animals resulting from the rendering of such care or treatment.

History.
1998, c. 669.

§ 8.01-225.3. Immunity for volunteer first responders en route to an emergency.

Notwithstanding any other provision of law, no volunteer firefighter or volunteer emergency medical services personnel shall be liable for any injury to persons or property arising out of the operation of an emergency vehicle as defined in § 46.2-920 when such volunteer is en route to respond to a fire or to render emergency care or assistance to any ill or injured person at the scene of an accident, fire, or life-threatening emergency and the emergency vehicle displays warning lights as provided in § 46.2-1022 or 46.2-1023 and sounds a siren, exhaust whistle, or air horn, unless such injury results from gross negligence or willful or wanton misconduct. The immunity provided by this section shall be in addition to, not in lieu of, any other applicable immunity provided by state or federal law, including § 2.2-3605 or 27-6.02.

History.
2015, c. 417.

§ 8.01-226. Duty of care to law-enforcement officers and firefighters, etc.

An owner or occupant of real property containing premises normally open to the public shall, with respect to such premises, owe to firefighters, Department of Emergency Management hazardous materials officers, nonfirefighter regional hazardous materials emergency response team members, and law-enforcement officers who in the performance of their duties come upon that portion of the premises normally open to the public the duty to maintain the same in a reasonably safe condition or to warn of dangers thereon of which he knows or has reason to know, whether or not such premises are at the time open to the public.

An owner or occupant of real property containing premises not normally open to the public shall, with respect to such premises, owe the same duty to firefighters, Department of Emergency Management hazardous materials officers, nonfirefighter regional hazardous materials emergency response team members, and law-enforcement officers who he knows or has reason to know are upon, about to come upon or imminently likely to come upon that portion of the premises not normally open to the public.

While otherwise engaged in the performance of his duties, a law-enforcement officer, Department of Emergency Management hazardous materials officer, nonfirefighter regional hazardous materials emergency response team member, or firefighter shall be owed a duty of ordinary care.

For purposes of this section, the term *"law-enforcement officers"* shall mean only police officers, sheriffs and deputy sheriffs and the term "firefighter" includes (i) emergency medical personnel and (ii) special forest wardens designated pursuant to § 10.1-1135.

History.
1987, c. 442; 1992, c. 731; 1996, cc. 646, 660; 2000, c. 962.

ARTICLE 23.

DRUG DEALER LIABILITY ACT.

§ 8.01-227.6. Law-enforcement officer or agency; health care provider not liable under certain conditions.

A law-enforcement officer or agency shall not be liable under this article if acting in furtherance of an official investigation. A health care provider who in good faith and in compliance with state or federal law, sells, administers, furnishes or distributes a controlled substance shall not be liable under this article.

History.
2002, c. 863.

CHAPTER 5.

VENUE.

§ 8.01-261. Category A or preferred venue.

In the actions listed in this section, the forums enumerated shall be deemed preferred places of venue and may be referred to as "Category A" in this title. Venue laid in any other forum shall be subject to objection; however, if more than one preferred place of venue applies, any such place shall be a proper forum. The following forums are designated as places of preferred venue for the action specified:

1. In actions for review of, appeal from, or enforcement of state administrative regulations, decisions, or other orders:

a. If the moving or aggrieved party is other than the Commonwealth or an agency thereof, then the county or city wherein such party:

(1) Resides;

(2) Regularly or systematically conducts affairs or business activity; or

(3) Wherein such party's property affected by the administrative action is located.

b. If the moving or aggrieved party is the Commonwealth or an agency thereof, then the county or city wherein the respondent or a party defendant:

(1) Resides;

(2) Regularly or systematically conducts affairs or business activity; or

(3) Has any property affected by the administrative action.

c. If subdivisions 1 a and 1 b do not apply, then the county or city wherein the alleged violation of the administrative regulation, decision, or other order occurred.

2. Except as provided in subdivision 1 of this section, where the action is against one or more officers of the Commonwealth in an official capacity, the county or city where any such person has his official office.

3. The county or city wherein the subject land, or a part thereof, is situated in the following actions:

a. To recover or partition land;

b. To subject land to a debt;

c. To sell, lease, or encumber the land of persons under disabilities;

d. [Repealed.]

e. To sell wastelands;

f. To establish boundaries;

g. For unlawful entry or detainer;

h. For ejectment; or

i. To remove clouds on title.

4. [Reserved.]

5. In actions for writs of mandamus, prohibition, or certiorari, except such as may be issued by the Supreme Court, the county or city wherein is the record or proceeding to which the writ relates.

6. In actions on bonds required for public contract, the county or city in which the public project, or any part thereof, is situated.

7. In actions to impeach or establish a will, the county or city wherein the will was probated, or, if not probated at the time of the action, where the will may be properly offered for probate.

8., 9. [Repealed.]

10. In actions on any contract between a transportation district and a component government, any county or city any part of which is within such transportation district.

11. In attachments,

a. With reference to the principal defendant and those liable with or to him, venue shall be determined as if the principal defendant were the sole defendant; or

b. In the county or city in which the principal defendant has estate or has debts owing to him.

12. [Repealed.]

13. a. In any action for the collection of state, county, or municipal taxes, any one of the following counties or cities shall be deemed preferred places of venue:

(1) Wherein the taxpayer resides;

(2) Wherein the taxpayer owns real or personal property;

(3) Wherein the taxpayer has a registered office, or regularly or systematically conducts business; or

(4) In case of withdrawal from the Commonwealth by a delinquent taxpayer, wherein venue was

proper at the time the taxes in question were assessed or at the time of such withdrawal.

b. In any action for the correction of an erroneous assessment of state taxes and tax refunds, any one of the following counties or cities shall be deemed preferred places of venue:

(1) Wherein the taxpayer resides;

(2) Wherein the taxpayer has a registered office or regularly or systematically conducts business;

(3) Wherein the taxpayer's real or personal property involved in such a proceeding is located; or

(4) The Circuit Court of the City of Richmond.

14. In proceedings by writ of quo warranto:

a. The city or county wherein any of the defendants reside;

b. If the defendant is a corporation, the city or county where its registered office is or where its mayor, rector, president, or other chief officer resides; or

c. If there is no officer or none of the defendants reside in the Commonwealth, venue shall be in the City of Richmond.

15. In proceedings to award an injunction:

a. To any judgment or judicial proceeding of a circuit court, venue shall be in the court in the county or city in which the judgment was rendered or such proceeding is pending;

b. To any judgment or judicial proceeding of a district court, venue shall be in the circuit court of the county or city in which the judgment was rendered or such proceeding is pending; or

c. To any other act or proceeding, venue shall be in the circuit court of the county or city in which the act is to be done, or being done, or is apprehended to be done or the proceeding is pending.

16. [Repealed.]

17. In disbarment or suspension proceedings against any attorney-at-law, in the county or city where the defendant:

a. Resides;

b. Has his principal office or place of practice when the proceeding is commenced;

c. Resided or had such principal office or place of practice when any misconduct complained of occurred; or

d. Has any pending case as to which any misconduct took place.

18. In actions under the Virginia Tort Claims Act, Article 18.1 (§ 8.01-195.1 et seq.) of Chapter 3 of this title:

a. The county or city where the claimant resides;

b. The county or city where the act or omission complained of occurred; or

c. If the claimant resides outside the Commonwealth and the act or omission complained of occurred outside the Commonwealth, the City of Richmond.

19. In suits for annulment, affirmance, or divorce, the county or city in which the parties last cohabited, or at the option of the plaintiff, in the county or city in which the defendant resides, if a resident of this Commonwealth, and in cases in which an order of publication may be issued against the defendant under § 8.01-316, venue may also be in the county or city in which the plaintiff resides.

20. In distress actions, in the county or city when the premises yielding the rent, or some part thereof, may be or where goods liable to distress may be found.

History.

1977, c. 617; 1978, c. 334; 1979, c. 331; 1985, c. 433; 1987, c. 567; 1988, c. 766; 1989, c. 556; 1990, c. 831; 1993, c. 841.

§ 8.01-262. Category B or permissible venue.

In any actions to which this chapter applies except those actions enumerated in Category A where preferred venue is specified, one or more of the following counties or cities shall be permissible forums, such forums being sometimes referred to as "Category B" in this title:

1. Wherein the defendant resides or has his principal place of employment or, if the defendant is not an individual, wherein its principal office or principal place of business is located;

2. Wherein the defendant has a registered office, has appointed an agent to receive process, or such agent has been appointed by operation of the law; or, in case of withdrawal from the Commonwealth by such defendant, wherein venue herein was proper at the time of such withdrawal;

3. Provided there exists any practical nexus to the forum including, but not limited to, the location of fact witnesses, plaintiffs, or other evidence to the action, wherein the defendant regularly conducts substantial business activity, or in the case of withdrawal from the Commonwealth by such defendant, wherein venue herein was proper at the time of such withdrawal;

4. Wherein the cause of action, or any part thereof, arose;

5. In actions to recover or partition personal property, whether tangible or intangible, the county or city:

a. Wherein such property is physically located; or

b. Wherein the evidence of such property is located;

c. And if subdivisions a and b do not apply, wherein the plaintiff resides.

6. In actions against a fiduciary as defined in § 8.01-2 appointed under court authority, the county or city wherein such fiduciary qualified;

7. In actions for improper message transmission or misdelivery wherein the message was transmitted or delivered or wherein the message was accepted for delivery or was misdelivered;

8. In actions arising based on delivery of goods, wherein the goods were received;

9. If there is no other forum available in subdivisions 1 through 8 of this category, then the county or city where the defendant has property or debts

owing to him subject to seizure by any civil process; or

10. Wherein any of the plaintiffs reside if (i) all of the defendants are unknown or are nonresidents of the Commonwealth or if (ii) there is no other forum available under any other provisions of § 8.01-261 or this section.

History.
1977, c. 617; 1978, c. 414; 1979, c. 331; 1985, c. 213; 1999, c. 73; 2004, c. 979; 2013, cc. 71, 103.

CHAPTER 8.
PROCESS.

Article 4.

Who to Be Served.

ARTICLE 4.
WHO TO BE SERVED.

§ 8.01-307. Definition of terms "motor vehicle" and "nonresident" in motor vehicle and aircraft accident cases.

For the purpose of §§ 8.01-308 through 8.01-313:

1. The term *"motor vehicle"* shall mean every vehicle which is self-propelled or designed for self-propulsion and every vehicle drawn by or designed to be drawn by a motor vehicle and includes every device in, upon, or by which any person or property is or can be transported or drawn upon a highway, except devices moved by human or animal power and devices used exclusively upon stationary rails or tracks.

2. The term *"nonresident"* includes any person who, though a resident of the Commonwealth when the accident or collision specified in § 8.01-308 or § 8.01-309 occurred, has been continuously outside the Commonwealth for at least sixty days next preceding the date when process is left with the Commissioner of the Department of Motor Vehicles or the Secretary of the Commonwealth and includes any person against whom an order of publication may be issued under the provisions of § 8.01-316.

History.
Code 1950, § 8-67.1; 1950, p. 620; 1952, c. 681; 1956, c. 64; 1966, c. 518; 1977, c. 617.

§ 8.01-308. Service on Commissioner of the Department of Motor Vehicles as agent for nonresident motor vehicle operator.

Any operation in the Commonwealth of a motor vehicle by a nonresident, including those nonresidents defined in subdivision 2 of § 8.01-307, either in person or by an agent or employee, shall be deemed equivalent to an appointment by such nonresident of the Commissioner of the Department of Motor Vehicles, and his successors in office, to be the attorney or statutory agent of such nonresident for the purpose of service of process in any action against him growing out of any accident or collision in which such nonresident, his agent, or his employee may be involved while operating motor vehicles in this Commonwealth. Acceptance by a nonresident of the rights and privileges conferred by Article 5 (§ 46.2-655 et seq.) of Chapter 6 of Title 46.2 shall have the same effect under this section as the operation of such motor vehicle, by such nonresident, his agent, or his employee.

History.
Code 1950, § 8-67.1; 1950, p. 620; 1952, c. 681; 1956, c. 64; 1966, c. 518; 1977, c. 617.

§ 8.01-309. Service on Secretary of Commonwealth as agent of nonresident operator or owner of aircraft.

Any nonresident owner or operator of any aircraft that is operated over and above the land and waters of the Commonwealth or uses aviation facilities within the Commonwealth, shall by such operation and use appoint the Secretary of the Commonwealth as his statutory agent for the service of process in any action against him growing out of any accident or collision occurring within or above the Commonwealth in which such aircraft is involved.

History.
Code 1950, § 8-67.4; 1952, c. 384; 1954, c. 333; 1977, c. 617.

§ 8.01-310. How service made on Commissioner and Secretary; appointment binding.

A. Service of process on either the Commissioner of the Department of Motor Vehicles as authorized under § 8.01-308 or on the Secretary of the Commonwealth as authorized under § 8.01-309 shall be made by the plaintiff or his agent or the sheriff leaving a copy of such process together with the fee for service of process on parties, in the amount prescribed in § 2.2-409, for each party to be thus served, in the hands, or in the office, of the Commissioner or the Secretary, and such service shall be sufficient upon the nonresident and shall be effective on the date when service is made on the Commissioner or the Secretary. All fees collected by the Commissioner pursuant to the provisions of this section shall be paid into the state treasury and shall be set aside as a special fund to be used to meet the expenses of the Department of Motor Vehicles.

B. Appointment of the Commissioner or Secretary as attorney or agent for the service of process on a nonresident under § 8.01-308 or 8.01-309 shall be irrevocable and binding upon the executor or other personal representative of such nonresident:

1. Where a nonresident has died before the commencement of an action against him regarding an accident or collision under § 8.01-308 or 8.01-309 shall be irrevocable and binding upon the executor or other personal representative of such nonresident; or

2. Where a nonresident dies after the commencement of an action against him regarding an accident or collision under § 8.01-308 or 8.01-309, the action shall continue and shall be irrevocable and binding upon his executor, administrator, or other personal representative with such additional notice of the pendency of the action as the court deems proper.

History.

Code 1950, §§ 8-67.2, 8-67.4; 1952, c. 384; 1954, c. 333; 1970, c. 680; 1972, c. 408; 1976, c. 26; 1977, c. 617; 1987, c. 696; 1992, c. 459; 2000, c. 579; 2013, c. 113.

§ 8.01-311. Continuance of action where service made on Commissioner or Secretary.

The court, in which an action is pending against a nonresident growing out of an accident or collision as specified in §§ 8.01-308 and 8.01-309, may order such continuances as necessary to afford such nonresident reasonable opportunity to defend the action.

History.

Code 1950, § 8-67.3; 1954, c. 547; 1977, c. 617.

§ 8.01-312. Effect of service on statutory agent; duties of such agent.

A. Service of process on the statutory agent shall have the same legal force and validity as if served within the Commonwealth personally upon the person for whom it is intended. It shall be the duty of the statutory agent to:

1. Provide a receipt to a party seeking service who serves process on the statutory agent by hand delivery or any other method that does not provide a return of service or other means showing the date on which service on the statutory agent was accomplished. The party seeking service shall be responsible for filing such receipt in the office of the clerk of court in which the action is pending;

2. Forthwith send by registered or certified mail, with return receipt requested, a copy of the process to the person named therein and for whom the statutory agent is receiving the process; and

3. File an affidavit of compliance with this section with the papers in the action; this filing shall be made in the office of the clerk of the court in which the action is pending.

B. Unless otherwise provided by § 8.01-313 and subject to the provisions of § 8.01-316, the address for the mailing of the process required by this section shall be that as provided by the party seeking service.

C. The time for a nonresident to respond to process sent by the statutory agent shall run from the date when the affidavit of compliance is filed in the office of the clerk of the court in which the action is pending.

History.

Code 1950, § 8-67.2; 1954, c. 333; 1970, c. 680; 1972, c. 408; 1976, c. 26; 1977, c. 617; 2013, c. 113.

§ 8.01-313. Specific addresses for mailing by statutory agent.

A. For the statutory agent appointed pursuant to §§ 8.01-308 and 8.01-309, the address for the mailing of the process as required by § 8.01-312 shall be the last known address of the nonresident or, where appropriate under subdivision 1 or 2 of § 8.01-310 B, of the executor, administrator, or other personal representative of the nonresident. However, upon the filing of an affidavit by the plaintiff that he does not know and is unable with due diligence to ascertain any post-office address of such nonresident, service of process on the statutory agent shall be sufficient without the mailing otherwise required by this section. Provided further that:

1. In the case of a nonresident defendant licensed by the Commonwealth to operate a motor vehicle, the last address reported by such defendant to the Department of Motor Vehicles as his address on an application for or renewal of a driver's license shall be deemed to be the address of the defendant for the purpose of the mailing required by this section if no other address is known, and, in any case in which the affidavit provided for in § 8.01-316 of this chapter is filed, such a defendant, by so notifying the Department of such an address, and by failing to notify the Department of any change therein, shall be deemed to have appointed the Commissioner of the Department of Motor Vehicles his statutory agent for service of process in an action arising out of operation of a motor vehicle by him in the Commonwealth, and to have accepted as valid service such mailing to such address; or

2. In the case of a nonresident defendant not licensed by the Commonwealth to operate a motor vehicle, the address shown on the copy of the report of accident required by § 46.2-372 filed by or for him with the Department, and on file at the office of the Department, or the address reported by such a defendant to any state or local police officer, or

sheriff investigating the accident sued on, if no other address is known, shall be conclusively presumed to be a valid address of such defendant for the purpose of the mailing provided for in this section, and his so reporting of an incorrect address, or his moving from the address so reported without making provision for forwarding to him of mail directed thereto, shall be deemed to be a waiver of notice and a consent to and acceptance of service of process served upon the Commissioner of the Department of Motor Vehicles as provided in this section.

B. For the statutory agent appointed pursuant to § 64.2-1426, the address for the mailing of process as required by § 8.01-312 shall be the address of the fiduciary's statutory agent as contained in the written consent most recently filed with the clerk of the circuit court wherein the qualification of such fiduciary was had or, in the event of the death, removal, resignation or absence from the Commonwealth of such statutory agent, or in the event that such statutory agent cannot with due diligence be found at such address, the address of the clerk of such circuit court.

History.

Code 1950, § 8-67.2; 1954, c. 333; 1970, c. 680; 1972, c. 408; 1976, c. 26; 1977, c. 617; 1983, c. 467; 1984, c. 780; 1991, c. 672.

CHAPTER 9.

PERSONAL JURISDICTION IN CERTAIN ACTIONS.

Section

§ 8.01-328. Person defined.

As used in this chapter, "person" includes an individual, his executor, administrator, or other personal representative, or a corporation, partnership, association or any other legal or commercial entity, whether or not a citizen or domiciliary of this Commonwealth and whether or not organized under the laws of this Commonwealth.

History.

Code 1950, § 8-81.1; 1964, c. 331; 1977, c. 617.

§ 8.01-328.1. When personal jurisdiction over person may be exercised.

A. A court may exercise personal jurisdiction over a person, who acts directly or by an agent, as to a cause of action arising from the person's:

1. Transacting any business in this Commonwealth;
2. Contracting to supply services or things in this Commonwealth;
3. Causing tortious injury by an act or omission in this Commonwealth;
4. Causing tortious injury in this Commonwealth by an act or omission outside this Commonwealth if he regularly does or solicits business, or engages in any other persistent course of conduct, or derives substantial revenue from goods used or consumed or services rendered, in this Commonwealth;
5. Causing injury in this Commonwealth to any person by breach of warranty expressly or impliedly made in the sale of goods outside this Commonwealth when he might reasonably have expected such person to use, consume, or be affected by the goods in this Commonwealth, provided that he also regularly does or solicits business, or engages in any other persistent course of conduct, or derives substantial revenue from goods used or consumed or services rendered in this Commonwealth;
6. Having an interest in, using, or possessing real property in this Commonwealth;
7. Contracting to insure any person, property, or risk located within this Commonwealth at the time of contracting;
8. Having (i) executed an agreement in this Commonwealth which obligates the person to pay spousal support or child support to a domiciliary of this Commonwealth, or to a person who has satisfied the residency requirements in suits for annulments or divorce for members of the armed forces or foreign service officers of the United States pursuant to § 20-97 provided proof of service of process on a nonresident party is made by a law-enforcement officer or other person authorized to serve process in the jurisdiction where the nonresident party is located, (ii) been ordered to pay spousal support or child support pursuant to an order entered by any court of competent jurisdiction in this Commonwealth having in personam jurisdiction over such person, or (iii) shown by personal conduct in this Commonwealth, as alleged by affidavit, that the person conceived or fathered a child in this Commonwealth;
9. Having maintained within this Commonwealth a matrimonial domicile at the time of separation of the parties upon which grounds for divorce or separate maintenance is based, or at the time a cause of action arose for divorce or separate maintenance or at the time of commencement of such suit, if the other party to the matrimonial relationship resides herein; or
10. Having incurred a liability for taxes, fines, penalties, interest, or other charges to any political subdivision of the Commonwealth.

Jurisdiction in subdivision 9 is valid only upon proof of service of process pursuant to § 8.01-296 on the nonresident party by a person authorized under the provisions of § 8.01-320. Jurisdiction under subdivision 8 (iii) of this subsection is valid only upon proof of personal service on a nonresident pursuant to § 8.01-320.

B. Using a computer or computer network located in the Commonwealth shall constitute an act in the Commonwealth. For purposes of this subsection, "use" and "computer network" shall have the same meanings as those contained in § 18.2-152.2.

C. When jurisdiction over a person is based solely upon this section, only a cause of action arising from acts enumerated in this section may be asserted against him; however, nothing contained in this chapter shall limit, restrict or otherwise affect the jurisdiction of any court of this Commonwealth over foreign corporations which are subject to service of process pursuant to the provisions of any other statute.

History.

Code 1950, § 8-81.2; 1964, c. 331; 1977, c. 617; 1978, c. 132; 1981, c. 6; 1982, c. 313; 1983, c. 428; 1984, c. 609; 1986, c. 275; 1987, c. 594; 1988, cc. 866, 878; 1992, c. 571; 1999, cc. 886, 904, 905; 2001, c. 221; 2007, c. 533; 2009, c. 582.

§ 8.01-329. Service of process or notice; service on Secretary of Commonwealth.

A. When the exercise of personal jurisdiction is authorized by this chapter, service of process or notice may be made in the same manner as is provided for in Chapter 8 (§ 8.01-285 et seq.) in any other case in which personal jurisdiction is exercised over such a party, or process or notice may be served on any agent of such person in the county or city in the Commonwealth in which that agent resides or on the Secretary of the Commonwealth of Virginia, hereinafter referred to in this section as the "Secretary," who, for this purpose, shall be deemed to be the statutory agent of such person.

B. When service is to be made on the Secretary, the party or his agent or attorney seeking service shall file an affidavit with the court, stating either (i) that the person to be served is a nonresident or (ii) that, after exercising due diligence, the party seeking service has been unable to locate the person to be served. In either case, such affidavit shall set forth the last known address of the person to be served. For the mailing, by the clerk to the party or his agent or attorney, in accordance with subsection C, of verification of the effective date of service of process, the person filing an affidavit may leave a self-addressed, stamped envelope with the clerk.

When the person to be served is a resident, the signature of an attorney, party or agent of the person seeking service on such affidavit shall constitute a certificate by him that process has been delivered to the sheriff or to a disinterested person as permitted by § 8.01-293 for execution and, if the sheriff or disinterested person was unable to execute such service, that the person seeking service has made a bona fide attempt to determine the actual place of abode or location of the person to be served.

C. Service of such process or notice on the Secretary shall be made by the plaintiff's, his agent's or the sheriff's leaving a copy of the process or notice, together with a copy of the affidavit called for in subsection B and the fee prescribed in § 2.2-409 in the office of the Secretary in the City of Richmond, Virginia. Service of process or notice on the Secretary may be made by mail if such service otherwise meets the requirements of this section. Such service shall be sufficient upon the person to be served and shall be effective on the date when service is made on the Secretary. It shall be the duty of the Secretary to:

1. Provide a receipt to a party seeking service who serves process on the Secretary by hand delivery or any other method that does not provide a return of service or other means showing the date on which service on the Secretary was accomplished. The party seeking service shall be responsible for filing such receipt in the office of the clerk of the court in which the action is pending;

2. Forthwith send by certified mail, return receipt requested, to the person or persons to be served at the last known post-office address of such person notice of such service, a copy of the process or notice, and a copy of the affidavit; and

3. Forthwith file with the papers in the action a certificate of compliance herewith by the Secretary or someone designated by him for that purpose and having knowledge of such compliance.

Upon receipt of the certificate of compliance, the clerk of the court shall mail verification of the date the certificate of compliance was filed with the court to the person who filed the affidavit required by subsection B, in the self-addressed, stamped envelope, if any, provided to the clerk at the time of filing of the affidavit. The clerk shall not be required to mail verification unless the self-addressed, stamped envelope has been provided. The time for the person to be served to respond to process sent by the Secretary shall run from the date when the certificate of compliance is filed in the office of the clerk of the court in which the action is pending.

D. Service of process in actions brought on a warrant or motion for judgment pursuant to § 16.1-79 or 16.1-81 shall be void and of no effect when such service of process is received by the Secretary within ten days of any return day set by the warrant. In such cases, the Secretary shall return the process or notice, the copy of the affidavit, and the prescribed fee to the plaintiff or his agent. A copy of the notice of the rejection shall be sent to the clerk of the court in which the action was filed.

E. The Secretary shall maintain a record of each notice of service sent to a person for a period of two years. The record maintained by the Secretary shall include the name of the plaintiff or the person seeking service, the name of the person to be served, the date service was received by the Secretary, the date notice of service was forwarded to the person to be served, and the date the certificate of compliance was sent by the Secretary to the appropriate court. The Secretary shall not be required to maintain any other records pursuant to this section.

History.
Code 1950, § 8-813; 1977, c. 617; 1979, c. 31; 1986, c. 388; 1987, cc. 449, 450, 459; 1990, c. 741; 1998, c. 259; 2001, c. 29; 2013, c. 113.

§ 8.01-330. Jurisdiction on any other basis authorized.

A court of this State may exercise jurisdiction on any other basis authorized by law.

History.
Code 1950, § 8-81.5; 1964, c. 331; 1977, c. 617.

CHAPTER 11.
JURIES.

Article 1.

When Jury Trial May Be Had.

Article 2.

Jurors.

Article 4.

Jury Service.

ARTICLE 1.
WHEN JURY TRIAL MAY BE HAD.

§ 8.01-336. Jury trial of right; waiver of jury trial; court-ordered jury trial; trial by jury of plea in equity; equitable claim.

A. The right of trial by jury as declared in Article I, Section 11 of the Constitution of Virginia and by statutes thereof shall be preserved inviolate to the parties. Unless waived, any demand for a trial by jury in a civil case made in compliance with the Rules of Supreme Court of Virginia shall be sufficient, with no further notice, hearing, or order, to proceed thereon.

B. *Waiver of jury trial.* — In any action at law in which the recovery sought is greater than $20, exclusive of interest, unless one of the parties demands that the case or any issue thereof be tried by a jury, or in a criminal action in which trial by jury is dispensed with as provided by law, the whole matter of law and fact may be heard and judgment given by the court.

C. *Court-ordered jury trial.* — Notwithstanding any provision in this Code to the contrary, in any action asserting a claim at law in which there has been no demand for trial by jury by any party, a circuit court may on its own motion direct one or more issues, including an issue of damages, to be tried by a jury.

D. *Trial by jury of plea in equity.* — In any action in which a plea has been filed to an equitable claim, and the allegations of such plea are denied by the plaintiff, either party may have the issue tried by jury.

E. *Suit on equitable claim.* — In any suit on an equitable claim, the court may, of its own motion or upon motion of any party, supported by such party's affidavit that the case will be rendered doubtful by conflicting evidence of another party, direct an issue to be tried before an advisory jury.

History.
Code 1950, §§ 8-208.21, 8-211, 8-212, 8-213, 8-214; 1954, c. 333; 1973, c. 439; 1974, c. 611; 1975, c. 578; 1977, c. 617; 2005, c. 681; 2014, c. 172.

ARTICLE 2.
JURORS.

§ 8.01-341. Who are exempt from jury service.

The following shall be exempt from serving on juries in civil and criminal cases:

1. The President and Vice President of the United States,
2. The Governor, Lieutenant Governor and Attorney General of the Commonwealth,
3. The members of both houses of Congress,
4. The members of the General Assembly, while in session or during a period when the member would be entitled to a legislative continuance as a matter of right under § 30-5,
5. Licensed practicing attorneys,
6. The judge of any court, members of the State Corporation Commission, members of the Virginia Workers' Compensation Commission, and magistrates,
7. Sheriffs, deputy sheriffs, state police, and police in counties, cities and towns,
8. The superintendent of the penitentiary and his assistants and the persons composing the guard,
9. Superintendents and jail officers, as defined in § 53.1-1, of regional jails.

History.
Code 1950, § 8-208.6; 1973, c. 439; 1977, cc. 458, 617; 1978, cc. 176, 340; 1980, c. 535; 1982, c. 315; 1987, c. 256; 1990, c. 758; 1993, c. 572; 1998, c. 83.

§ 8.01-341.1. Exemptions from jury service upon request.

Any of the following persons may serve on juries in civil and criminal cases but shall be exempt from jury service upon his request:

1. through 3. [Repealed.]

4. A mariner actually employed in maritime service;

5. through 7. [Repealed.]

8. A person who has legal custody of and is necessarily and personally responsible for a child or children 16 years of age or younger requiring continuous care by him during normal court hours, or any mother who is breast-feeding a child;

9. A person who is necessarily and personally responsible for a person having a physical or mental impairment requiring continuous care by him during normal court hours;

10. Any person over 70 years of age;

11. Any person whose spouse is summoned to serve on the same jury panel;

12. Any person who is the only person performing services for a business, commercial or agricultural enterprise and whose services are so essential to the operations of the business, commercial or agricultural enterprise that such enterprise must close or cease to function if such person is required to perform jury duty;

13. Any person who is the only person performing services for a political subdivision as a firefighter, as defined in § 65.2-102, and whose services are so essential to the operations of the political subdivision that such political subdivision will suffer an undue hardship in carrying out such services if such person is required to perform jury duty;

14. Any person employed by the Office of the Clerk of the House of Delegates, the Office of the Clerk of the Senate, the Division of Legislative Services, and the Division of Legislative Automated Systems; however, this exemption shall apply only to jury service starting (i) during the period beginning 60 days prior to the day any regular session commences and ending 30 days after the day of adjournment of such session and (ii) during the period beginning seven days prior to the day any reconvened or special session commences and ending seven days after the day of adjournment of such session;

15. Any general registrar, member of a local electoral board, or person appointed or employed by either the general registrar or the local electoral board, except officers of election appointed pursuant to Article 5 (§ 24.2-115 et seq.) of Chapter 1 of Title 24.2; however, this exemption shall apply only to jury service starting (i) during the period beginning 90 days prior to any election and continuing through election day, (ii) during the period to ascertain the results of the election and continuing for 10 days after the local electoral board certifies the results of the election under § 24.2-671 or the State Board of Elections certifies the results of the election under § 24.2-679, or (iii) during the period of an election recount or contested election pursuant to Chapter 8 (§ 24.2-800 et seq.) of Title 24.2. Any officer of election shall be exempt from jury service only on election day and during the periods set forth in clauses (ii) and (iii); and

16. Any member of the armed services of the United States or the diplomatic service of the United States appointed under the Foreign Service Act (22 U.S.C. § 3901 et seq.) who will be serving outside of the United States at the time of such jury service.

History.

Code 1970, § 8-208.6:1; 1977, c. 458; 1987, c. 256; 1997, c. 693; 1999, c. 153; 2004, c. 106; 2005, c. 195; 2011, cc. 389, 708; 2012, c. 98.

§ 8.01-341.2. Deferral or limitation of jury service for particular occupational inconvenience.

The court, on its own motion, may exempt any person from jury service for a particular term of court, or limit that person's service to particular dates of that term, if serving on a jury during that term or certain dates of that term of court would cause such person a particular occupational inconvenience. Any such person who is selected for jury service, and who is exempted under the provisions of this section, shall not be discharged from his obligation to serve on a jury, but such obligation shall only be deferred until the term of court next after such particular occupational inconvenience shall end.

History.

1981, c. 108; 1987, c. 155.

§ 8.01-342. Restrictions on amount of jury service permitted.

A. The jury commissioners shall not include on the jury list provided for in § 8.01-345 the name of any person who has been called and reported to any state court for jury duty at any time during the period of three years next preceding the date of completion of such jury list.

B. If such person has been called and reported for jury duty in the trial of any case, either civil or criminal, at any one term of a court, he shall not be permitted to serve as a juror in any civil or criminal case, at any other term of that court during the three-year period set forth in subsection A of this section, unless all the persons whose names are in the jury box have been drawn to serve during such three-year period; however, such person shall be permitted to serve on any special jury ordered pursuant to § 8.01-362 and on any grand jury.

History.

Code 1950, §§ 8-208.7, 8-208.10; 1973, c. 439; 1974, c. 369; 1977, cc. 451, 617; 1984, c. 165; 1992, c. 312; 1994, c. 27.

ARTICLE 4.
JURY SERVICE.

§ 8.01-356. Failure of juror to appear.

If any juror who has been given due notice to appear in court shall fail to do so without sufficient excuse, he shall be fined not less than $50 nor more than $200.

History.
Code 1950, § 8-208.18; 1973, c. 439; 1977, c. 617; 2004, c. 116.

CHAPTER 17.
JUDGMENTS AND DECREES GENERALLY.

Article 5.

Keeping of Docket Books; Execution Thereon; Disposal of Exhibits.

ARTICLE 5.
KEEPING OF DOCKET BOOKS; EXECUTION THEREON; DISPOSAL OF EXHIBITS.

§ 8.01-446.1. Keeping of docket books by clerk of court using micrographic process; form.

Whenever judgments are docketed in the judgment lien book in the office of the clerk of the circuit court and are recorded by a procedural micrographic process as provided in § 17.1-240, or by any other method or process which renders impractical or impossible the subsequent entry of notations upon the docketed judgment, an appropriate certificate of assignment, release, partial release, certified copy of any order, or other separate instrument setting forth the necessary information as provided in this section shall be recorded and indexed according to law. Such instrument shall conform substantially with the following form:

TYPE OF FILING (Check One) ORIGINAL BOOK # ..... PAGE ....
( ) Assignment (or instrument no)
( ) Release ORIGINAL DATE DOCKETED: ......
( ) Partial Release
( ) Credit(s)
( ) Additional Debtor(s)
( ) New Name of Debtor

Date of Judgment:
Amount of Judgment:
Plaintiff(s):

Defendant(s):

Assignee (If assignment): ....

Payments (If credits): AMOUNT .... DATE PAID ......

(Complete below if additional debtor or change of name of debtor)

Debtor:
Social Security Number of Debtor (Last Four Digits) (If known):

Given under my hand this ...... day of ...., ...

....
(Plaintiff) (Attorney for Plaintiff)
(Authorized Agent for Plaintiff)

Any judgment creditor who knowingly gives false information upon such certificate made under this section shall be guilty of a Class 1 misdemeanor.

History.
1985, c. 48; 2008, cc. 823, 833.

CHAPTER 27.

VIRGINIA PRISONER LITIGATION REFORM ACT.

Section

§ 8.01-689. Short title.

This chapter shall be known and may be cited as the "Virginia Prisoner Litigation Reform Act."

History.
2002, c. 871.

§ 8.01-690. Applicability provisions.

The provisions of this chapter shall apply to all pro se civil actions for money damages brought under the laws of this Commonwealth, or for injunctive, declaratory or mandamus relief, brought by prisoners incarcerated in any state or local correctional facility, or operated pursuant to the Corrections Private Management Act (§ 53.1-261 et seq.).

History.
2002, c. 871.

§ 8.01-691. Payment of filing fees and costs by prisoners; when in forma pauperis status granted.

A prisoner seeking in forma pauperis status shall provide the court with a certified copy of his inmate trust account for the preceding twelve months. Any prisoner granted leave to proceed in forma pauperis shall nonetheless make payments, in equal installments as the court directs, towards satisfaction of the filing fee and costs. If the court determines the prisoner has had no deposits in his inmate trust account for the preceding six months, the court shall permit the prisoner to proceed without paying the filing fee and costs. However, the filing fee and costs shall be taxed as costs at the end of the case. Any prisoner failing to make any payment when due shall have his case dismissed without prejudice.

History.
2002, c. 871.

§ 8.01-692. When in forma pauperis status denied.

The court shall deny in forma pauperis status to any prisoner who has had three or more cases or appeals dismissed by any federal or state court for being frivolous, malicious, or for failure to state a claim, unless the prisoner shows that he is in imminent danger of serious physical injury at the time of filing his motion for judgment or the court determines that it would be manifest injustice to deny in forma pauperis status.

History.
2002, c. 871.

§ 8.01-693. Venue of prisoner actions.

Notwithstanding any other provision of law, no prisoner action shall be filed except in the city or county in which the prison is located where the prisoner was housed when his cause of action arose. When an action is filed in an improper venue, upon motion of the defendant or the court sua sponte, the court shall transfer the case to the proper venue.

History.
2002, c. 871.

§ 8.01-694. Service of process; time for response.

In any action in which any defendant is the Commonwealth or one of its officers, employees, or agents, upon the grant of in forma pauperis status or receipt of the filing fee and costs, the court shall serve the Office of the Attorney General with a copy of the motion for judgment and all necessary supporting papers. The Office of the Attorney General shall have no fewer than thirty days from receipt in which to file responsive pleadings. The prisoner's failure to state his claims in a written motion for judgment plainly stating facts sufficient to support his cause of action, accompanied by all necessary supporting documentation, may be grounds for dismissal of the action.

History.
2002, c. 871; 2009, c. 372.

§ 8.01-695. When argument held; when discovery permitted.

Oral argument on any motion in any prisoner civil action shall be heard orally only at the request of the court; whenever possible, the court shall rule upon the record before it. No prisoner shall be permitted to request subpoenas for witnesses or documents, or file discovery requests, until the court has ruled upon any demurrer, plea or motion to dismiss. Where a case proceeds past the initial dispositive motions, the court shall require the prisoner seeking discovery to demonstrate that his requests are relevant and material to the issues in the case. No subpoena for witnesses or documents shall issue unless a judge of the court has reviewed the subpoena request and specifically authorized a subpoena to issue. The court shall exercise its discretion in determining the scope of the subpoena and may condition its issuance on such terms as the court finds appropriate. The court shall take into account the burden placed upon the object of the subpoena in relation to the needs of the case, the amount in controversy, and the importance of the issues at stake in the litigation.

History.
2002, c. 871; 2006, c. 435.

§ 8.01-696. Summary judgment; pro se prisoner civil action.

Notwithstanding the provisions of § 8.01-420, any time after commencement of a pro se prisoner civil action, a party may move for summary judgment on all issues based upon the pleadings, any admissions, and supporting affidavits. The adverse party may serve supporting affidavits within 10 days after service of the motion. The judgment sought shall be rendered forthwith if the pleadings, admissions, and affidavits show that there is no genuine issue of material fact and that the moving party is entitled to a judgment as a matter of law.

History.
2006, c. 435.

§ 8.01-697. Access to Department of Corrections records.

All records maintained by the Department of Corrections in the name of individual prisoners, including prisoner medical records, shall be the property of the Department. Notwithstanding the provisions of § 32.1-127.1:03, in any civil suit subject to this chapter, where the Commonwealth, an agency of the Commonwealth, an employee of the Commonwealth, or a private contractor providing services to the Department of Corrections is named as a defendant, the Director of the Department may share any records maintained by the Department in the name of the prisoner filing suit with counsel representing the above-named defendants.

History.
2006, c. 435.

TITLE 9.

COMMISSIONS, BOARDS AND INSTITUTIONS GENERALLY.

[Repealed.]

TITLE 9.1.

COMMONWEALTH PUBLIC SAFETY.

CHAPTER 1.

DEPARTMENT OF CRIMINAL JUSTICE SERVICES.

Article 4.

Private Security Services Businesses.

Article 4.1.

Special Conservators of the Peace.

Article 6.

Crime Prevention Programs.

ARTICLE 4.

PRIVATE SECURITY SERVICES BUSINESSES.

§ 9.1-138. Definitions.

In addition to the definitions set forth in § 9.1-101, as used in this article, unless the context requires a different meaning:

"Alarm respondent" means an individual who responds to the signal of an alarm for the purpose of detecting an intrusion of the home, business or property of the end user.

"Armed" means a private security registrant who carries or has immediate access to a firearm in the performance of his duties.

"Armed security officer" means a natural person employed to (i) safeguard and protect persons and property or (ii) deter theft, loss, or concealment of any tangible or intangible personal property on the premises he is contracted to protect, and who carries or has access to a firearm in the performance of his duties.

"Armored car personnel" means persons who transport or offer to transport under armed security from one place to another, money, negotiable instruments or other valuables in a specially equipped motor vehicle with a high degree of security and certainty of delivery.

"Business advertising material" means display advertisements in telephone directories, letterhead, business cards, local newspaper advertising and contracts.

"Central station dispatcher" means an individual who monitors burglar alarm signal devices, burglar alarms or any other electrical, mechanical or electronic device used (i) to prevent or detect burglary, theft, shoplifting, pilferage or similar losses; (ii) to prevent or detect intrusion; or (iii) primarily to summon aid for other emergencies.

"Certification" means the method of regulation indicating that qualified persons have met the minimum requirements as private security services training schools, private security services instructors, compliance agents, or certified detector canine handler examiners.

"Compliance agent" means an individual who owns or is employed by a licensed private security services business to ensure the compliance of the private security services business with this title.

"Computer or digital forensic services" means the use of highly specialized expertise for the recovery, authentication, and analysis of electronic data or computer usage.

"Courier" means any armed person who transports or offers to transport from one place to another documents or other papers, negotiable or nonnegotiable instruments, or other small items of value that require expeditious services.

"Detector canine" means any dog that detects drugs or explosives.

"Detector canine handler" means any individual who uses a detector canine in the performance of private security duties.

"Detector canine handler examiner" means any individual who examines the proficiency and reliability of detector canines and detector canine handlers in the detection of drugs or explosives.

"Detector canine team" means the detector canine handler and his detector canine performing private security duties.

"Electronic security business" means any person who engages in the business of or undertakes to (i) install, service, maintain, design or consult in the design of any electronic security equipment to an end user; (ii) respond to or cause a response to electronic security equipment for an end user; or (iii) have access to confidential information concerning the design, extent, status, password, contact list, or location of an end user's electronic security equipment.

"Electronic security employee" means an individual who is employed by an electronic security business in any capacity which may give him access to information concerning the design, extent, status, password, contact list, or location of an end user's electronic security equipment.

"Electronic security equipment" means (i) electronic or mechanical alarm signaling devices including burglar alarms or holdup alarms used to safeguard and protect persons and property; or (ii) cameras used to detect intrusions, concealment or theft, to safeguard and protect persons and property. This shall not include tags, labels, and other devices that are attached or affixed to items offered for sale, library books, and other protected articles as part of an electronic article surveillance and theft detection and deterrence system.

"Electronic security sales representative" means an individual who sells electronic security equipment on behalf of an electronic security business to the end user.

"Electronic security technician" means an individual who installs, services, maintains or repairs electronic security equipment.

"Electronic security technician's assistant" means an individual who works as a laborer under the supervision of the electronic security technician in the course of his normal duties, but who may not make connections to any electronic security equipment.

"Employed" means to be in an employer/employee relationship where the employee is providing work in exchange for compensation and the employer directly controls the employee's conduct and pays some taxes on behalf of the employee. The term "employed" shall not be construed to include independent contractors.

"End user" means any person who purchases or leases electronic security equipment for use in that person's home or business.

"Firearms training verification" means the verification of successful completion of either initial or retraining requirements for handgun or shotgun training, or both.

"General public" means individuals who have access to areas open to all and not restricted to any particular class of the community.

"Key cutting" means making duplicate keys from an existing key and includes no other locksmith services.

"License number" means the official number issued to a private security services business licensed by the Department.

"Locksmith" means any individual that performs locksmith services, or advertises or represents to the general public that the individual is a locksmith even if the specific term locksmith is substituted with any other term by which a reasonable person could construe that the individual possesses special skills relating to locks or locking devices, including use of the words lock technician, lockman, safe technician, safeman, boxman, unlocking technician, lock installer, lock opener, physical security technician or similar descriptions.

"Locksmith services" mean selling, servicing, rebuilding, repairing, rekeying, repinning, changing the combination to an electronic or mechanical locking device; programming either keys to a device or the device to accept electronic controlled keys; originating keys for locks or copying keys; adjusting or installing locks or deadbolts, mechanical or electronic locking devices, egress control devices, safes, and vaults; opening, defeating or bypassing locks or latching mechanisms in a manner other than intended by the manufacturer; with or without compensation for the general public or on property not his own nor under his own control or authority.

"Natural person" means an individual person.

"Personal protection specialist" means any individual who engages in the duties of providing close protection from bodily harm to any person.

"Private investigator" means any individual who engages in the business of, or accepts employment to make, investigations to obtain information on (i) crimes or civil wrongs; (ii) the location, disposition, or recovery of stolen property; (iii) the cause of accidents, fires, damages, or injuries to persons or to property; or (iv) evidence to be used before any court, board, officer, or investigative committee.

"Private security services business" means any person engaged in the business of providing, or who undertakes to provide, armored car personnel, security officers, personal protection specialists, private investigators, couriers, security canine handlers, security canine teams, detector canine handlers, detector canine teams, alarm respondents, locksmiths, central station dispatchers, electronic security employees, electronic security sales representatives or electronic security technicians and their assistants to another person under contract, express or implied.

"Private security services instructor" means any individual certified by the Department to provide mandated instruction in private security subjects for a certified private security services training school.

"Private security services registrant" means any qualified individual who has met the requirements under this article to perform the duties of alarm respondent, locksmith, armored car personnel, central station dispatcher, courier, electronic security sales representative, electronic security technician, electronic security technician's assistant, personal protection specialist, private investigator, security canine handler, detector canine handler, unarmed security officer or armed security officer.

"Private security services training school" means any person certified by the Department to provide instruction in private security subjects for the training of private security services business personnel in accordance with this article.

"Registration" means a method of regulation whereby certain personnel employed by a private security services business are required to register with the Department pursuant to this article.

"Registration category" means any one of the following categories: (i) unarmed security officer and armed security officer/courier, (ii) security canine handler, (iii) armored car personnel, (iv) private investigator, (v) personal protection specialist, (vi) alarm respondent, (vii) central station dispatcher, (viii) electronic security sales representative, (ix) electronic security technician, (x) electronic technician's assistant, (xi) detector canine handler, or (xii) locksmith.

"Security canine" means a dog that has attended, completed, and been certified as a security canine by a certified security canine handler instructor in accordance with approved Department procedures and certification guidelines. "Security canines" shall not include detector dogs.

"Security canine handler" means any individual who utilizes his security canine in the performance of private security duties.

"Security canine team" means the security canine handler and his security canine performing private security duties.

"Supervisor" means any individual who directly or indirectly supervises registered or certified private security services business personnel.

"Unarmed security officer" means a natural person who performs the functions of observation, detection, reporting, or notification of appropriate authorities or designated agents regarding persons or property on the premises he is contracted to protect, and who does not carry or have access to a firearm in the performance of his duties.

History.

1976, c. 737, § 54-729.27; 1977, c. 376, § 54.1-1900; 1980, c. 425, cc. 57, 779; 1988, c. 765; 1992, c. 578, § 9-183.1; 1994, cc. 45, 335, 810; 1995, c. 79; 1996, c. 541; 1997, c. 80; 1998, cc. 122, 807; 1999, c. 33; 2001, cc. 821, 844; 2003, c. 124; 2004, c. 470; 2005, c. 365; 2008, c. 638; 2009, c. 375; 2011, c. 263.

§ 9.1-139. Licensing, certification, and registration required; qualifications; temporary licenses.

A. No person shall engage in the private security services business or solicit private security business in the Commonwealth without having obtained a license from the Department. No person shall be issued a private security services business license until a compliance agent is designated in writing on forms provided by the Department. The compliance agent shall ensure the compliance of the private security services business with this article and shall meet the qualifications and perform the duties required by the regulations adopted by the Board. A compliance agent shall have either a minimum of (i) three years of managerial or supervisory experience in a private security services business; with a federal, state or local law-enforcement agency; or in a related field or (ii) five years of experience in a private security services business; with a federal, state or local law-enforcement agency; or in a related field.

B. No person shall act as private security services training school or solicit students for private security training in the Commonwealth without being certified by the Department. No person shall be issued a private security services training school certification until a school director is designated in writing on forms provided by the Department. The school director shall ensure the compliance of the school with the provisions of this article and shall meet the qualifications and perform the duties required by the regulations adopted by the Board.

C. No person shall be employed by a licensed private security services business in the Commonwealth as armored car personnel, courier, armed security officer, detector canine handler, unarmed security officer, security canine handler, private investigator, personal protection specialist, alarm respondent, locksmith, central station dispatcher, electronic security sales representative, electronic security technician's assistant, or electronic security technician without possessing a valid registration issued by the Department, except as provided in this article. Notwithstanding any other provision of this article, a licensed private security services business may hire as an independent contractor a personal protection specialist or private investigator who has been issued a registration by the Department.

D. A temporary license may be issued in accordance with Board regulations for the purpose of awaiting the results of the state and national fingerprint search. However, no person shall be issued a temporary license until (i) he has designated a compliance agent who has complied with the compulsory minimum training standards established by the Board pursuant to subsection A of § 9.1-141 for compliance agents, (ii) each principal of the business has submitted his fingerprints for a National Criminal Records search and a Virginia Criminal History Records search, and (iii) he has met all other requirements of this article and Board regulations.

E. No person shall be employed by a licensed private security services business in the Commonwealth unless such person is certified or registered in accordance with this chapter.

F. A temporary registration may be issued in accordance with Board regulations for the purpose of awaiting the results of the state and national fingerprint search. However, no person shall be issued a temporary registration until he has (i) complied with, or been exempted from the compulsory minimum training standards established by the Board, pursuant to subsection A of § 9.1-141, for armored car personnel, couriers, armed security officers, detector canine handlers, unarmed security officers, security canine handlers, private investigators, personal protection specialists, alarm respondents, locksmith, central station dispatchers, electronic security sales representatives, electronic security technician's assistants, or electronic security technicians, (ii) submitted his fingerprints to be used for the conduct of a National Criminal Records search and a Virginia Criminal History Records search, and (iii) met all other requirements of this article and Board regulations.

G. A temporary certification as a private security instructor or private security training school may be issued in accordance with Board regulations for the purpose of awaiting the results of the state and national fingerprint search. However, no person shall be issued a temporary certification as a private security services instructor until he has (i) met the education, training and experience requirements established by the Board and (ii) submitted his fingerprints to be used for the conduct of a National Criminal Records search and a Virginia Criminal History Records search. No person shall be issued a temporary certification as a private security services training school until (a) he has designated a training director, (b) each principal of the training school has submitted his fingerprints to be used for the conduct of a National Criminal Records search and a Virginia Criminal History Records search, and (c) he has met all other requirements of this article and Board regulations.

H. A licensed private security services business in the Commonwealth shall not employ as an unarmed security officer, electronic security technician's assistant, unarmed alarm respondent, central station dispatcher, electronic security sales representative, locksmith, or electronic security technician, any person who has not complied with, or been exempted from, the compulsory minimum training standards established by the Board, pursuant to subsection A of § 9.1-141, except that such person may be so employed for not more than 90 days while completing compulsory minimum training standards.

I. No person shall be employed as an electronic security employee, electronic security technician's assistant, unarmed alarm respondent, locksmith, central station dispatcher, electronic security sales representative, electronic security technician or supervisor until he has submitted his fingerprints to the Department to be used for the conduct of a National Criminal Records search and a Virginia Criminal History Records search. The provisions of this subsection shall not apply to an out-of-state central station dispatcher meeting the requirements of subdivision 19 of § 9.1-140.

J. The compliance agent of each licensed private security services business in the Commonwealth shall maintain documentary evidence that each private security registrant and certified employee employed by his private security services business has complied with, or been exempted from, the compulsory minimum training standards required by the Board. Before January 1, 2003, the compliance agent shall ensure that an investigation to determine suitability of each unarmed security officer employee has been conducted, except that any such unarmed security officer, upon initiating a request for such investigation under the provisions of subdivision A 11 of § 19.2-389, may be employed for up to 30 days pending completion of such investigation. After January 1, 2003, no person shall be employed as an unarmed security officer until he has submitted his fingerprints to the Department for the conduct of a National Criminal Records search and a Virginia Criminal History Records search. Any person who was employed as an unarmed security officer prior to January 1, 2003, shall submit his fingerprints to the Department in accordance with subsection B of § 9.1-145.

K. No person with a criminal conviction for a misdemeanor involving (i) moral turpitude, (ii) assault and battery, (iii) damage to real or personal property, (iv) controlled substances or imitation controlled substances as defined in Article 1 (§ 18.2-247 et seq.) of Chapter 7 of Title 18.2, (v) prohibited sexual behavior as described in Article 7 (§ 18.2-61 et seq.) of Chapter 4 of Title 18.2, or (vi) firearms, or any felony shall be (a) employed as a registered or certified employee by a private security services business or training school, or (b) issued a private security services registration, certification as an unarmed security officer, electronic security employee or technician's assistant, a private security services training school or instructor certification, compliance agent certification, or a private security services business license, except that, upon written request, the Director of the Department may waive such prohibition. Any grant or denial of such waiver shall be made in writing within 30 days of receipt of the written request and shall state the reasons for such decision.

L. The Department may grant a temporary exemption from the requirement for licensure, certification, or registration for a period of not more than 30 days in a situation deemed an emergency by the Department.

M. All private security services businesses and private security services training schools in the Commonwealth shall include their license or certification number on all business advertising materials.

N. A licensed private security services business in the Commonwealth shall not employ as armored car personnel any person who has not complied with, or been exempted from, the compulsory minimum training standards established by the Board pursuant to subsection A of § 9.1-141, except such person may serve as a driver of an armored car for not more than 90 days while completing compulsory minimum training standards, provided such person does not possess or have access to a firearm while serving as a driver.

History.

1976, c. 737, § 54-729.29; 1977, c. 376, § 54.1-1902; 1978, cc. 28, 428; 1984, cc. 57, 779; 1988, cc. 48, 765; 1991, c. 589; 1992, c. 578, § 9-183.3; 1994, cc. 45, 47, 810; 1995, c. 79; 1996, c. 541; 1998, cc. 53, 122, 807; 2000, c. 26; 2001, cc. 821, 844; 2002, cc. 578, 597; 2003, c. 124; 2004, c. 470; 2008, c. 638; 2015, c. 202; 2016, c. 561.

§ 9.1-140. Exceptions from article; training requirements for out-of-state central station dispatchers.

The provisions of this article shall not apply to:

1. An officer or employee of the United States, the Commonwealth, or a political subdivision of either, while the officer or employee is performing his official duties;

2. A person, except a private investigator as defined in § 9.1-138, engaged exclusively in the business of obtaining and furnishing information regarding an individual's financial rating or a person engaged in the business of a consumer reporting agency as defined by the Federal Fair Credit Reporting Act;

3. An attorney licensed to practice in Virginia or his employees;

4. The legal owner of personal property which has been sold under any security agreement while performing acts relating to the repossession of such property;

5. A person receiving compensation for private employment as a security officer, or receiving compensation under the terms of a contract, express or implied, as a security officer, who is also a law-enforcement officer as defined by § 9.1-101 and employed by the Commonwealth or any of its political subdivisions;

6. Any person appointed under § 46.2-2003 or 56-353 while engaged in the employment contemplated thereunder, unless they have successfully completed training mandated by the Department;

7. Persons who conduct investigations as a part of the services being provided as a claims adjuster, by a claims adjuster who maintains an ongoing claims adjusting business, and any natural person employed by the claims adjuster to conduct investigations for the claims adjuster as a part of the services being provided as a claims adjuster;

8. Any natural person otherwise required to be registered pursuant to § 9.1-139 who is employed by a business that is not a private security services business for the performance of his duties for his employer. Any such employee, however, who carries a firearm and is in direct contact with the general public in the performance of his duties shall possess a valid registration with the Department as required by this article;

9. Persons, sometimes known as "shoppers," employed to purchase goods or services solely for the purpose of determining or assessing the efficiency, loyalty, courtesy, or honesty of the employees of a business establishment;

10. Licensed or registered private investigators from other states entering Virginia during an inves-

tigation originating in their state of licensure or registration when the other state offers similar reciprocity to private investigators licensed and registered by the Commonwealth;

11. Unarmed regular employees of telephone public service companies where the regular duties of such employees consist of protecting the property of their employers and investigating the usage of telephone services and equipment furnished by their employers, their employers' affiliates, and other communications common carriers;

12. An end user;

13. A material supplier who renders advice concerning the use of products sold by an electronics security business and who does not provide installation, monitoring, repair or maintenance services for electronic security equipment;

14. Members of the security forces who are directly employed by electric public service companies;

15. Any professional engineer or architect licensed in accordance with Chapter 4 (§ 54.1-400 et seq.) of Title 54.1 to practice in the Commonwealth, or his employees;

16. Any person who only performs telemarketing or schedules appointments without access to information concerning the electronic security equipment purchased by an end user;

17. Any certified forensic scientist employed as an expert witness for the purpose of possibly testifying as an expert witness;

18. Members of the security forces who are directly employed by shipyards engaged in the construction, design, overhaul or repair of nuclear vessels for the United States Navy;

19. An out-of-state central station dispatcher employed by a private security services business licensed by the Department provided he (i) possesses and maintains a valid license, registration, or certification as a central station dispatcher issued by the regulatory authority of the state in which he performs the monitoring duties and (ii) has submitted his fingerprints to the regulatory authority for the conduct of a national criminal history records search;

20. Any person, or independent contractor or employee of any person, who (i) exclusively contracts directly with an agency of the federal government to conduct background investigations and (ii) possesses credentials issued by such agency authorizing such person, subcontractor or employee to conduct background investigations;

21. Any person whose occupation is limited to the technical reconstruction of the cause of accidents involving motor vehicles as defined in § 46.2-100, regardless of whether the information resulting from the investigation is to be used before a court, board, officer, or investigative committee, and who is not otherwise a private investigator as defined in § 9.1-138;

22. Retail merchants performing locksmith services, selling locks or engaged in key cutting activities conducted at the business location who do not represent themselves to the general public as locksmiths;

23. Law-enforcement, fire, rescue, emergency service personnel, or other persons performing locksmith services in an emergency situation without compensation and who do not represent themselves to the general public as locksmiths;

24. Motor vehicle dealers as defined in § 46.2-1500 performing locksmith services who do not represent themselves to the general public as locksmiths;

25. Taxicab and towing businesses performing locksmith services that do not represent themselves to the general public as locksmiths;

26. Contractors licensed under Chapter 11 (§ 54.1-1100 et seq.) of Title 54.1 performing locksmith services when acting within the scope of such license who do not represent themselves to the general public as locksmiths;

27. Any contractor as defined in § 54.1-1100 (i) who is exempt from the licensure requirements of Chapter 11 (§ 54.1-1100 et seq.) of Title 54.1, (ii) where the total value referred to in a single contract or project is less than $1,000, (iii) when the performance of locksmith services is ancillary to the work performed by such contractor, and (iv) who does not represent himself to the general public as a locksmith;

28. Any individual, employed by a retail merchant that also holds a private security services business license as a locksmith, where such individual's duties relating to such license are limited to key cutting and the key cutting is performed under the direct supervision of the licensee;

29. Any individual engaged in (i) computer or digital forensic services as defined in § 9.1-138 or in the acquisition, review, or analysis of digital or computer-based information, in order to obtain or furnish information for evidentiary purposes or to provide expert testimony before a court, or (ii) network or system vulnerability testing, including network scans and risk assessment and analysis of computers connected to a network;

30. Employees and sales representatives of a retailer of electronic security equipment, provided such employees and sales representatives (i) sell electronic security equipment at a store location, online, or by telephone, but not at the end user's premises; (ii) are not electronic security technicians; and (iii) do not have access to end user confidential information regarding the end user's electronic security equipment; or

31. A certified public accountant authorized to practice in the Commonwealth under Chapter 44 (§ 54.1-4400 et seq.) of Title 54.1 or his employees.

History.

1976, c. 737, § 54-729.28; 1977, c. 376, § 54.1-1901; 1981, c. 538; 1983, c. 569; 1984, c. 375; 1988, c. 765; 1992, c. 578, § 9-183.2; 1994, cc. 45, 810; 1995, c. 79; 1996, cc. 541, 543, 576; 1997, cc. 80, 204; 2000, c. 26; 2001, cc. 388, 650, 821, 844; 2002, cc. 578, 597; 2003, c.

136; 2008, c. 638; 2009, c. 225; 2011, c. 263; 2013, c. 411; 2014, c. 214.

§ 9.1-140.01. Exemption from training requirements; central station dispatchers employed by central stations certified by a Nationally Recognized Testing Laboratory.

Central station dispatchers employed by a central station that is certified by a Nationally Recognized Testing Laboratory (NRTL) shall be exempt from the training requirements of this article. For the purposes of this section, "Nationally Recognized Testing Laboratory" means the designation given by the federal Occupational Safety and Health Administration (OSHA) to a private sector testing facility that provides product safety testing and certification services.

History.
2014, c. 610.

§ 9.1-140.1. Registration; waiver of examination; locksmiths.

Notwithstanding any other provision of this article, unless an applicant is found by the Board to have engaged in any act that would constitute grounds for disciplinary action, the Board shall issue a registration, without examination, to any applicant who provides satisfactory proof to the Board of having been actively and continuously providing locksmith services immediately prior to July 1, 2008, for at least two years.

History.
2008, c. 638.

§ 9.1-141. Powers of Board relating to private security services business.

A. The Board may adopt regulations in accordance with the Administrative Process Act (§ 2.2-4000 et seq.), establishing compulsory minimum, entry-level, in-service, and advanced training standards for persons employed by private security services businesses in classifications defined in § 9.1-138. The regulations may include provisions delegating to the Board's staff the right to inspect the facilities and programs of persons conducting training to ensure compliance with the law and Board regulations. In establishing compulsory training standards for each of the classifications defined in § 9.1-138, the Board shall be guided by the policy of this section to secure the public safety and welfare against incompetent or unqualified persons engaging in the activities regulated by this section and Article 4 (§ 9.1-138 et seq.) of this chapter. The regulations may provide for partial exemption from such compulsory, entry-level training for persons having previous employment as law-enforcement officers for a local, state or the federal government, to include units of the United States armed forces, or for persons employed in classifications defined in § 9.1-138. However, no such exemption shall be granted to persons having less than five continuous years of such employment, nor shall an exemption be provided for any person whose employment as a law-enforcement officer or whose employment as a private security services business employee was terminated because of his misconduct or incompetence. The regulations may include separate provisions for full exemption from compulsory training for persons having previous training that meets or exceeds the minimum training standards and has been approved by the Department. However, no such exemption shall be granted to persons whose employment as a private security services business employee was terminated because of his misconduct or incompetence. No regulation adopted by the Board shall prevent any person employed by an electronic security business, other than an alarm respondent, or as a locksmith from carrying a firearm in the course of his duties when such person carries with him a valid concealed handgun permit issued in accordance with § 18.2-308.

B. The Board may enter into an agreement with other states for reciprocity or recognition of private security services businesses and their employees, duly licensed by such states. The agreements shall allow those businesses and their employees to provide and perform private security services within the Commonwealth to secure the public safety and welfare against incompetent, unqualified, unscrupulous, or unfit persons engaging in the activities of private security services businesses.

C. The Board may adopt regulations in accordance with the Administrative Process Act (§ 2.2-4000 et seq.) to secure the public safety and welfare against incompetent, unqualified, unscrupulous, or unfit persons engaging in the activities of private security services businesses that:

1. Establish the qualifications of applicants for registration, certification, or licensure under Article 4 (§ 9.1-138) of this chapter;

2. Examine, or cause to be examined, the qualifications of each applicant for registration, certification, or licensure, including when necessary the preparation, administration, and grading of examinations;

3. Certify qualified applicants for private security training schools and instructors or license qualified applicants as practitioners of private security services businesses;

4. Levy and collect fees for registration, certification, or licensure and renewal that are sufficient to cover all expenses for administration and operation of a program of registration, certification, and licensure for private security services businesses and training schools;

5. Are necessary to ensure continued competency, and to prevent deceptive or misleading practices by practitioners and effectively administer the regulatory system adopted by the Board;

6. Receive complaints concerning the conduct of any person whose activities are regulated by the Board, to conduct investigations, and to take appropriate disciplinary action if warranted; and

7. Revoke, suspend or fail to renew a registration, certification, or license for just cause as enumerated in Board regulations.

D. In adopting its regulations under subsections A and C, the Board shall seek the advice of the Private Security Services Advisory Board established pursuant to § 9.1-143.

History.

1981, c. 632, § 9-182; 1990, c. 354; 1992, c. 578; 1994, cc. 45, 335, 810; 1995, c. 79; 1998, cc. 122, 807; 2001, c. 844; 2009, c. 375; 2013, c. 69; 2014, c. 32.

§ 9.1-142. Powers of Department relating to private security services businesses.

A. In addition to the powers otherwise conferred upon it by law, the Department may:

1. Charge each applicant for licensure, certification or registration a nonrefundable fee as established by the Board to cover the costs of the Department for processing an application for a registration, certification or license, and enforcement of these regulations, and other costs associated with the maintenance of this program of regulation.

2. Charge nonrefundable fees for private security services training as established by the Board for processing school certifications and enforcement of training standards.

3. Conduct investigations to determine the suitability of applicants for registration, licensure, or certification of compliance agents, training schools, and instructors. For purposes of this investigation, the Department shall have access to criminal history record information maintained by the Central Criminal Records Exchange of the Department of State Police and shall conduct a background investigation, to include a National Criminal Records search and a Virginia Criminal History Records search.

4. Issue subpoenas. The Director or a designated subordinate may make an ex parte application to the circuit court for the city or county wherein evidence sought is kept or wherein a licensee does business, for the issuance of a subpoena duces tecum in furtherance of the investigation of a sworn complaint within the jurisdiction of the Department or the Board to request production of any relevant records, documents and physical or other evidence of any person, partnership, association or corporation licensed or regulated by the Department pursuant to this article. The court may issue and compel compliance with such a subpoena upon a showing of reasonable cause. Upon determining that reasonable cause exists to believe that evidence may be destroyed or altered, the court may issue a subpoena duces tecum requiring the immediate production of evidence.

5. Recover costs of the investigation and adjudication of violations of this article or Board regulations. Such costs may be recovered from the respondent when a sanction is imposed to fine or place on probation, suspend, revoke, or deny the issuance of any license, certification, or registration. Such costs shall be in addition to any monetary penalty which may be imposed. All costs recovered shall be deposited into the state treasury to the credit of the Private Security Services Regulatory Fund.

6. Institute proceedings to enjoin any person from engaging in any lawful act enumerated in § 9.1-147. Such proceedings shall be brought in the name of the Commonwealth by the Department in circuit court of the city or county in which the unlawful act occurred or in which the defendant resides.

B. The Director, or agents appointed by him, shall be vested with the authority to administer oaths or affirmations for the purpose of receiving complaints and conducting investigations of violations of this article, or any Board regulation promulgated pursuant to authority given by this article. Information concerning alleged criminal violations shall be turned over to law-enforcement officers in appropriate jurisdictions. Agents shall be vested with authority to serve such paper or process issued by the Department or the Board under regulations approved by the Board.

History.

1976, c. 737, § 54-729.30; 1977, c. 376, § 54.1-1903; 1984, cc. 57, 779; 1985, c. 448; 1988, c. 765; 1991, c. 589; 1992, c. 578, § 9-183.4; 1994, c. 46; 1998, cc. 122, 807; 2001, c. 844.

§ 9.1-143. Private Security Services Advisory Board; membership.

The Private Security Services Advisory Board is established as an advisory board within the meaning of § 2.2-2100, in the executive branch of state government. The Private Security Services Advisory Board shall consist of 15 members as follows: two members shall be private investigators; two shall be representatives of electronic security businesses; two members shall be representatives of locksmith businesses; three shall be representatives of private security services businesses providing security officers, armed couriers, detector canine handlers, or security canine handlers; one shall be a representative of a private security services business providing armored car personnel; one shall be a representative of a private security services business involving personal protection specialists; one shall be a certified private security services instructor; one shall be a special conservator of the peace appointed pursuant to § 19.2-13; one shall be a licensed bail bondsman and one shall be a representative of law enforcement. The Private Security Services Advisory Board shall be appointed by the Criminal Justice Services Board and shall advise the Criminal Justice Services Board on all issues relating to regulation of private security services businesses.

History.

1976, c. 737, § 54-729.30; 1977, c. 376, § 54.1-1904; 1984, cc. 57, 779; 1985, c. 448; 1988, c. 765; 1992, c. 578, § 9-183.5; 1994, c. 810; 1997, c. 79; 2001, c. 844; 2003, c. 922; 2004, c. 460; 2008, c. 638; 2009, c. 375.

§ 9.1-144. Bond or insurance required; actions against bond.

A. Every person licensed as a private security services business under subsection A of § 9.1-139 or certified as a private security services training school under subsection B of § 9.1-139 shall, at the time of receiving the license or certification and before the license or certification shall be operative, file with the Department (i) a cash bond or evidence that the licensee or certificate holder is covered by a surety bond, executed by a surety company authorized to do business in the Commonwealth, in a reasonable amount to be fixed by the Department, conditioned upon the faithful and honest conduct of his business or employment; or (ii) evidence of a policy of liability insurance in an amount and with coverage as fixed by the Department. The bond or liability insurance shall be maintained for so long as the licensee or certificate holder is licensed or certified by the Department.

Every personal protection specialist and private investigator who has been issued a registration by the Department and is hired as an independent contractor by a licensed private security services business shall maintain comprehensive general liability insurance in a reasonable amount to be fixed by the Department, evidence of which shall be provided to the private security services business prior to the hiring of such independent contractor pursuant to subsection C of § 9.1-139.

B. If any person aggrieved by the misconduct of any person licensed or certified under subsection A or B of § 9.1-139 recovers judgment against the licensee or certificate holder, which judgment is unsatisfied in whole or in part, such person may bring an action in his own name on the bond of the licensee or certificate holder.

History.

1976, c. 737, § 54-729.31; 1988, c. 765, § 54.1-1905; 1992, c. 578, § 9-183.6; 1998, cc. 122, 807; 2001, c. 844; 2015, c. 202.

§ 9.1-145. Fingerprints required; penalty.

A. Each applicant for initial registration, licensure or certification as a compliance agent, private security services training school or instructor or unarmed security officer under the provisions of this article and every person employed as an electronic security employee or electronic security technician's assistant shall submit his fingerprints to the Department on a form provided by the Department. The Department shall use the applicant's fingerprints and personal descriptive information for the conduct of a National Criminal Records search and a Virginia Criminal History Records search.

B. Each currently certified unarmed security officer applying for renewal between January 1, 2003, and December 31, 2004, shall submit his fingerprints to the Department on a form provided by the Department. The Department shall use the applicant's fingerprints and personal descriptive information for the conduct of a National Criminal Records search and a Virginia Criminal History Records search.

C. The Department may suspend the registration, license or certification of any applicant who is subsequently convicted of a misdemeanor involving (i) moral turpitude, (ii) assault and battery, (iii) damage to real or personal property, (iv) controlled substances or imitation controlled substances as defined in Article 1 (§ 18.2-247 et seq.) of Chapter 7 of Title 18.2, (v) prohibited sexual behavior as described in Article 7 (§ 18.2-61 et seq.) of Chapter 4 of Title 18.2, or (vi) firearms or any felony.

D. Any person willfully and intentionally making a false statement in the personal descriptive information required on the fingerprint card is guilty of a Class 5 felony.

History.

1976, c. 737, § 54-729.32; 1988, c. 765, § 54.1-1906; 1992, c. 578, § 9-183.7; 1994, c. 810; 1995, c. 79; 1998, cc. 122, 807; 2001, c. 844; 2002, cc. 578, 597.

§ 9.1-146. Limitation on powers of registered armed security officers.

Compliance with the provisions of this article shall not itself authorize any person to carry a concealed weapon or exercise any powers of a conservator of the peace. A registered armed security officer of a private security services business while at a location which the business is contracted to protect shall have the power to effect an arrest for an offense occurring (i) in his presence on such premises or (ii) in the presence of a merchant, agent, or employee of the merchant the private security business has contracted to protect, if the merchant, agent, or employee had probable cause to believe that the person arrested had shoplifted or committed willful concealment of goods as contemplated by § 18.2-106. For the purposes of § 19.2-74, a registered armed security officer of a private security services business shall be considered an arresting officer.

History.

1976, c. 737, § 54-729.33; 1978, c. 560, § 54.1-1907; 1980, c. 425; 1988, cc. 48, 765; 1992, c. 578, § 9-183.8; 1994, c. 45; 2001, c. 844.

§ 9.1-147. Unlawful conduct generally; penalty.

A. It shall be unlawful for any person to:

1. Practice any trade or profession licensed, certified or registered under this article without obtaining the necessary license, certification or registration required by statute or regulation;

2. Materially misrepresent facts in an application for licensure, certification or registration;

3. Willfully refuse to furnish the Department information or records required or requested pursuant to statute or regulation; and

4. Violate any statute or regulation governing the practice of the private security services businesses or training schools regulated by this article.

B. Any person who is convicted of willful violation of subsection A shall be guilty of a Class 1 misdemeanor. Any person convicted of a third or subsequent offense under this section during a thirty-six-month period shall be guilty of a Class 6 felony.

History.
1992, c. 578, § 9-183.11; 1998, cc. 122, 807; 2001, c. 844.

§ 9.1-148. Unlawful procurement of a license; penalty.

A. It shall be unlawful for any person to:

1. Procure, or assist another to procure, through theft, fraud or other illegal means, a registration or license, by giving to, or receiving from, any person any information, oral, written or printed, during the administration of the examination, which is intended to, or will, assist any person taking the examination in passing the examination and obtaining the required registration or license;

2. Attempt to procure, through theft, fraud or other illegal means, any questions intended to be used by the Department conducting the examination, or the answers to the questions;

3. Promise or offer any valuable or other consideration to a person having access to the questions or answers as an inducement to procure for delivery to the promisor, or any other person, a copy of any questions or answers.

B. No person, other than a designee of the Department, shall procure or have in his possession prior to the beginning of an examination, without written authority of the Department, any question intended to be used by the Department, or receive or furnish to any person taking the examination, prior to or during the examination, any written or printed material purporting to be answers to, or aid in answering such questions;

C. If an examination is divided into separate parts, each of the parts shall be deemed an examination for the purposes of this section.

D. Any person convicted of a violation of subsections A or B shall be guilty of a Class 2 misdemeanor.

History.
1992, c. 578, § 9-183.10; 2001, c. 844.

§ 9.1-149. Unlicensed activity prohibited; penalty.

A. No person:

1. Required to possess a registration under subsection C of § 9.1-139 shall be employed by a private security services business, except as provided in this article, as armored car personnel, courier, armed security officer, security canine handler, personal protection specialist, private investigator, alarm respondent, central station dispatcher, electronic security sales representative or electronic security technician without possessing a valid registration.

2. Licensed or required to be licensed under subsection A of § 9.1-139 shall employ or otherwise utilize, except as provided in this article, as armored car personnel, courier, armed security officer, security canine handler, personal protection specialist, private investigator, alarm respondent, central station dispatcher, electronic security sales representative or electronic security technician, any person not possessing a valid registration.

3. Required to possess an instructor certification under subsection D of § 9.1-139 shall provide mandated instruction, except as provided in § 9.1-141 and Board regulations, without possessing a valid private security instructor certification.

4. Certified or required to be certified as a private security services training school under subsection B of § 9.1-139 shall employ or otherwise utilize, except as provided in § 9.1-141 and Board regulations, as a private security instructor, any person not possessing a valid instructor certification.

B. No compliance agent employed or otherwise utilized by a person licensed or required to be licensed under subsection A of § 9.1-139 shall:

1. Employ or otherwise utilize as an unarmed security officer, except as provided in this article, any individual for whom the compliance agent does not possess documentary evidence of compliance with, or exemption from, the compulsory minimum training standards established by the Board for unarmed security officers and before January 1, 2003, maintain documentary evidence that an investigation to determine suitability has been conducted.

2. Employ or otherwise utilize as an electronic security technician's assistant, except as provided in this article, any individual for whom the compliance agent does not possess documentary evidence of compliance with, or exemption from, the compulsory minimum training standards established by the Board for electronic security technician's assistants.

C. Any person convicted of a violation of subsections A or B shall be guilty of a Class 1 misdemeanor.

History.
1976, c. 737, § 54-729.34; 1980, c. 425, § 54.1-1908; 1988, cc. 48, 765; 1992, c. 578, § 9-183.9; 1994, cc. 45, 810; 1995, c. 79; 1998, cc. 122, 807; 2001, c. 844; 2002, cc. 578, 597.

§ 9.1-149.1. Unlawful advertisement for regulated services; notice; penalty.

A. It shall be unlawful for any person to place before the public through any medium an advertisement for services in the Commonwealth requiring a license, certification, or registration under this article unless the individual who will perform such services possesses the necessary license, certification, or registration at the time of the posting.

B. Whenever the Board receives information that an advertisement has been placed in violation of this section, the Board shall provide notice to the entity publishing the advertisement to the public.

C. Any person who is convicted of a violation of subsection A is guilty of a Class 1 misdemeanor.

History.
2014, c. 396.

§ 9.1-150. Monetary penalty.

Any person required to be licensed, certified or registered by the Board pursuant to this article who violates any statute or Board regulation who is not criminally prosecuted is subject to the monetary penalty provided in this section. If the Board determines that such person has violated any statute or Board regulation, the Board shall determine the amount of the monetary penalty for the violation, which shall not exceed $2,500 for each violation. The penalty may be sued for and recovered in the name of the Commonwealth. The monetary penalty shall be paid into the state treasury to the credit of the Literary Fund in accordance with § 19.2-353.

History.
1992, c. 578, § 9-183.12; 1994, c. 810; 1998, cc. 122, 807; 2001, c. 844; 2011, cc. 821, 854.

ARTICLE 4.1.

SPECIAL CONSERVATORS OF THE PEACE.

§ 9.1-150.1. Definitions.

In addition to the definitions set forth in § 9.1-101, as used in this article, unless the context requires a different meaning:

"Special conservator of the peace" means any individual appointed pursuant to § 19.2-13 on or after September 15, 2004.

History.
2003, c. 922.

§ 9.1-150.2. Powers of Criminal Justice Services Board relating to special conservators of the peace appointed pursuant to § 19.2-13.

The Board shall adopt regulations establishing compulsory minimum, entry-level, in-service, and advanced training standards for special conservators of the peace. The regulations may include provisions delegating to the Board's staff the right to inspect the facilities and programs of persons conducting training to ensure compliance with the law and its regulations. In establishing compulsory training standards for special conservators of the peace, the Board shall require training to be obtained at a criminal justice training academy established pursuant to § 15.2-1747, or at a private security training school certified by the Department, and shall ensure the public safety and welfare against incompetent or unqualified persons engaging in the activities regulated by this section. The regulations may provide for exemption from training of persons having previous employment as law-enforcement officers for a state or the federal government. However, no such exemption shall be granted to persons having less than five continuous years of such employment, nor shall an exemption be provided for any person whose employment as a law-enforcement officer was terminated because of his misconduct or incompetence or who has been decertified as a law-enforcement officer. The regulations may include provisions for exemption from such training for persons having previous training that meets or exceeds the minimum training standards and has been approved by the Department. The Board may also adopt regulations that (i) establish the qualifications of applicants for registration; (ii) cause to be examined the qualifications of each applicant for registration; (iii) provide for collection of fees for registration and renewal that are sufficient to cover all expenses for administration and operation of a program of registration; (iv) ensure continued competency and prevent deceptive or misleading practices by practitioners; (v) effectively administer the regulatory system promulgated by the Board; (vi) provide for receipt of complaints concerning the conduct of any person whose activities are regulated by the Board; (vii) provide for investigations, and appropriate disciplinary action if warranted; and (viii) allow the Board to revoke, suspend or refuse to renew a registration, certification, or license for just cause as enumerated in regulations of the Board. The Board shall adopt compulsory, entry-level training standards that shall not exceed, but shall be a minimum of 98 hours for unarmed special conservators of the peace and that shall not exceed, but shall be a minimum of 130 hours for armed special conservators of the peace. In adopting its regulations, the Board shall seek the advice of the Private Security Services Advisory Board established pursuant to § 9.1-143.

History.
2003, c. 922; 2015, cc. 766, 772.

§ 9.1-150.3. Powers of Department of Criminal Justice Services relating to special conservators of the peace appointed pursuant to § 19.2-13.

A. In addition to the powers otherwise conferred upon it by law, the Department may (i) charge each applicant for registration a nonrefundable fee as established by the Board to cover the costs of the Department for processing an application for registration, and enforcement of the regulations, and other costs associated with the maintenance of the program of regulation; (ii) charge nonrefundable fees for private security services training as established by the Board for processing school certifications and enforcement of training standards; and (iii) conduct investigations to determine the suitability of applicants for registration, including a drug and alcohol screening. For purposes of this investigation, the Department shall require the applicant to provide personal descriptive information to be forwarded, along with the applicant's fingerprints, to the Central Criminal Records Exchange for the purpose of conducting a Virginia criminal history records search. The Central Criminal Records Exchange shall forward the fingerprints and personal description to the Federal Bureau of Investigation for the purpose of obtaining a national criminal record check.

B. The Director or his designee may make an ex parte application to the circuit court for the city or county wherein evidence sought is kept or wherein a licensee does business for the issuance of a subpoena duces tecum in furtherance of the investigation of a sworn complaint within the jurisdiction of the Department or the Board to request production of any relevant records, documents and physical or other evidence of any person, partnership, association or corporation licensed or regulated by the Department pursuant to this article. The court may issue and compel compliance with such a subpoena upon a showing of reasonable cause. Upon determining that reasonable cause exists to believe that evidence may be destroyed or altered, the court may issue a subpoena duces tecum requiring the immediate production of evidence. Costs of the investigation and adjudication of violations of this article or Board regulations may be recovered. All costs recovered shall be deposited into the state treasury to the credit of the Conservators of the Peace Regulatory Fund. Such proceedings shall be brought in the name of the Commonwealth by the Department in the circuit court of the city or county in which the unlawful act occurred or in which the defendant resides. The Director, or agents appointed by him, shall have the authority to administer oaths or affirmations for the purpose of receiving complaints and conducting investigations of violations of this article, or any regulation promulgated hereunder and to serve process issued by the Department or the Board.

History.
2003, c. 922.

§ 9.1-150.4. Unlawful conduct; penalties.

A. It shall be unlawful for any person to (i) misrepresent facts in an application for registration; (ii) willfully refuse to furnish the Department information or records required or requested pursuant to statute or regulation; or (iii) violate any statute or regulation governing the practice of special conservators of the peace regulated by this article or § 19.2-13.

B. Any person registered by the Department pursuant to § 19.2-13 who the Department or the Board determines has violated any statute or Board regulation and who is not criminally prosecuted shall be subject to a monetary penalty not to exceed $2,500 for each violation. The penalty may be sued for and recovered in the name of the Commonwealth and shall be paid into the state treasury to the credit of the Literary Fund in accordance with § 19.2-353.

C. Any person who is convicted of a willful violation of the provisions of this article or § 19.2-13 is guilty of a Class 1 misdemeanor. Any person convicted of a third or subsequent offense under this article or § 19.2-13 during a 36-month period is guilty of a Class 6 felony.

History.
2003, c. 922.

ARTICLE 6.
CRIME PREVENTION PROGRAMS.

§§ 9.1-158 through 9.1-160: Repealed by Acts 2011, cc. 821 and 854, cl. 2.

§ 9.1-161. (Effective until October 1, 2016) Crime prevention specialists; duties.

The Board shall adopt regulations establishing minimum standards for certification of crime prevention specialists. Such regulations shall require that the chief law-enforcement officer of the locality or the campus police departments of institutions of higher education established by Chapter 17 (§ 23-232 et seq.) of Title 23 wherein the person serves shall approve the certification before a candidate for certification may serve as a crime prevention specialist. A crime prevention specialist shall have the duty to:

1. Provide citizens living within his jurisdiction information concerning personal safety and the security of property, and other matters relating to the reduction of criminal opportunity;
2. Provide business establishments within his jurisdiction information concerning business and employee security, and other matters relating to reduction of criminal activity;
3. Provide citizens and businesses within his jurisdiction assistance in forming and maintaining neighborhood and business watch groups and other community-based crime prevention programs;
4. Provide assistance to other units of government within his jurisdiction in developing plans and

procedures related to the reduction of criminal activity within government and the community; and

5. Promote the reduction and prevention of crime within his jurisdiction and the Commonwealth.

History.

1994, cc. 60, 868, § 9-173.19; 2001, c. 844; 2004, c. 466.

§ 9.1-161. (Effective October 1, 2016) Crime prevention specialists; duties.

The Board shall adopt regulations establishing minimum standards for certification of crime prevention specialists. Such regulations shall require that the chief law-enforcement officer of the locality or the campus police departments of institutions of higher education established by Article 3 (§ 23.1-809 et seq.) of Chapter 8 of Title 23.1 wherein the person serves shall approve the certification before a candidate for certification may serve as a crime prevention specialist. A crime prevention specialist shall have the duty to:

1. Provide citizens living within his jurisdiction information concerning personal safety and the security of property, and other matters relating to the reduction of criminal opportunity;

2. Provide business establishments within his jurisdiction information concerning business and employee security, and other matters relating to reduction of criminal activity;

3. Provide citizens and businesses within his jurisdiction assistance in forming and maintaining neighborhood and business watch groups and other community-based crime prevention programs;

4. Provide assistance to other units of government within his jurisdiction in developing plans and procedures related to the reduction of criminal activity within government and the community; and

5. Promote the reduction and prevention of crime within his jurisdiction and the Commonwealth.

History.

1994, cc. 60, 868, § 9-173.19; 2001, c. 844; 2004, c. 466.

§ 9.1-162. Eligibility for crime prevention specialists.

Any employee of a local, state or federal government agency who serves in a law-enforcement, crime prevention or criminal justice capacity is eligible to be trained and certified as a crime prevention specialist.

The chief executive of any local, state or federal government agency may designate one or more employees in his department or office, who serves in a law-enforcement, crime prevention or criminal justice capacity, to be trained and certified as a crime prevention specialist.

No person who is a candidate for certification shall serve as a crime prevention specialist unless his certification is approved by the chief law-enforcement officer of the locality wherein the person serves.

History.

1994, cc. 60, 868, § 9-173.20; 2001, c. 844; 2002, c. 209; 2004, c. 466.

CHAPTER 4.

LINE OF DUTY ACT.

Section

§ 9.1-400. (Effective until July 1, 2017) Title of chapter; definitions.

A. This chapter shall be known and designated as the Line of Duty Act.

B. As used in this chapter, unless the context requires a different meaning:

"Beneficiary" means the spouse of a deceased person and such persons as are entitled to take under the will of a deceased person if testate, or as his heirs at law if intestate.

"Deceased person" means any individual whose death occurs on or after April 8, 1972, as the direct or proximate result of the performance of his duty, including the presumptions under §§ 27-40.1, 27-40.2, 51.1-813, and 65.2-402, as a law-enforcement officer of the Commonwealth or any of its political subdivisions; a correctional officer as defined in § 53.1-1; a jail officer; a regional jail or jail farm superintendent; a sheriff, deputy sheriff, or city sergeant or deputy city sergeant of the City of

Richmond; a police chaplain; a member of any fire company or department or emergency medical services agency that has been recognized by an ordinance or a resolution of the governing body of any county, city, or town of the Commonwealth as an integral part of the official safety program of such county, city, or town; a member of any fire company providing fire protection services for facilities of the Virginia National Guard; a member of the Virginia National Guard or the Virginia Defense Force while such member is serving in the Virginia National Guard or the Virginia Defense Force on official state duty or federal duty under Title 32 of the United States Code; any special agent of the Virginia Alcoholic Beverage Control Board; any regular or special conservation police officer who receives compensation from a county, city, or town or from the Commonwealth appointed pursuant to the provisions of § 29.1-200; any commissioned forest warden appointed under the provisions of § 10.1-1135; any member or employee of the Virginia Marine Resources Commission granted the power of arrest pursuant to § 28.2-900; any Department of Emergency Management hazardous materials officer; any other employee of the Department of Emergency Management who is performing official duties of the agency, when those duties are related to a major disaster or emergency, as defined in § 44-146.16, that has been or is later declared to exist under the authority of the Governor in accordance with § 44-146.28; any employee of any county, city, or town performing official emergency management or emergency services duties in cooperation with the Department of Emergency Management, when those duties are related to a major disaster or emergency, as defined in § 44-146.16, that has been or is later declared to exist under the authority of the Governor in accordance with § 44-146.28 or a local emergency, as defined in § 44-146.16, declared by a local governing body; any nonfirefighter regional hazardous materials emergency response team member; any conservation officer of the Department of Conservation and Recreation commissioned pursuant to § 10.1-115; or any full-time sworn member of the enforcement division of the Department of Motor Vehicles appointed pursuant to § 46.2-217.

"Disabled person" means any individual who, as the direct or proximate result of the performance of his duty in any position listed in the definition of deceased person in this section, has become mentally or physically incapacitated so as to prevent the further performance of duty where such incapacity is likely to be permanent. The term shall also include any state employee included in the definition of a deceased person who was disabled on or after January 1, 1966.

"Line of duty" means any action the deceased or disabled person was obligated or authorized to perform by rule, regulation, condition of employment or service, or law.

History.

1995, cc. 112, 156, 597, §§ 2.1-133.5, 2.1-133.6; 1996, cc. 66, 174; 1998, c. 712; 2001, cc. 678, 844; 2003, cc. 37, 41, 1005; 2004, c. 30; 2005, cc. 907, 910; 2006, c. 824; 2007, c. 87; 2011, cc. 572, 586; 2012, cc. 374, 458, 573; 2015, cc. 38, 502, 503, 730.

§ 9.1-400. (Effective July 1, 2017) Title of chapter; definitions.

A. This chapter shall be known and designated as the Line of Duty Act.

B. As used in this chapter, unless the context requires a different meaning:

"Beneficiary" means the spouse of a deceased person and such persons as are entitled to take under the will of a deceased person if testate, or as his heirs at law if intestate.

(Effective until July 1, 2018) *"Deceased person"* means any individual whose death occurs on or after April 8, 1972, in the line of duty as the direct or proximate result of the performance of his duty, including the presumptions under §§ 27-40.1, 27-40.2, 51.1-813, 65.2-402, and 65.2-402.1 if his position is covered by the applicable statute, as a law-enforcement officer of the Commonwealth or any of its political subdivisions; a correctional officer as defined in § 53.1-1; a jail officer; a regional jail or jail farm superintendent; a sheriff, deputy sheriff, or city sergeant or deputy city sergeant of the City of Richmond; a police chaplain; a member of any fire company or department or emergency medical services agency that has been recognized by an ordinance or a resolution of the governing body of any county, city, or town of the Commonwealth as an integral part of the official safety program of such county, city, or town; a member of any fire company providing fire protection services for facilities of the Virginia National Guard; a member of the Virginia National Guard or the Virginia Defense Force while such member is serving in the Virginia National Guard or the Virginia Defense Force on official state duty or federal duty under Title 32 of the United States Code; any special agent of the Virginia Alcoholic Beverage Control Board; any regular or special conservation police officer who receives compensation from a county, city, or town or from the Commonwealth appointed pursuant to the provisions of § 29.1-200; any commissioned forest warden appointed under the provisions of § 10.1-1135; any member or employee of the Virginia Marine Resources Commission granted the power of arrest pursuant to § 28.2-900; any Department of Emergency Management hazardous materials officer; any other employee of the Department of Emergency Management who is performing official duties of the agency, when those duties are related to a major disaster or emergency, as defined in § 44-146.16, that has been or is later declared to exist under the authority of the Governor in accordance with § 44-146.28; any employee of any county, city, or town performing official emergency management or emergency services duties in cooperation with the Department of Emergency Management, when those duties are related to a major disaster or emergency, as defined in § 44-146.16, that has been or is later declared to exist under the authority of the Governor in accordance with § 44-146.28 or a local emergency, as defined in § 44-146.16, declared by a local governing body; any nonfirefighter regional hazardous materials emergency response team member; any conservation officer of the Department of Conservation and Recreation commissioned pursuant to § 10.1-115; or any full-time sworn member of the enforcement division of the Department of Motor Vehicles appointed pursuant to § 46.2-217.

(Effective July 1, 2018) *"Deceased person"* means any individual whose death occurs on or after April 8, 1972, in the line of duty as the direct or proximate result of the performance of his duty, including the presumptions under §§ 27-40.1, 27-40.2, 51.1-813, 65.2-402, and 65.2-402.1 if his position is covered by the applicable statute, as a law-enforcement officer of the Commonwealth or any of its political subdivisions; a correctional officer as defined in § 53.1-1; a jail officer; a regional jail or jail farm superintendent; a sheriff, deputy sheriff, or city sergeant or deputy city sergeant of the City of Richmond; a police chaplain; a member of any fire company or department or emergency medical services agency that has been recognized by an ordinance or a resolution of the governing body of any county, city, or town of the Commonwealth as an integral part of the official safety program of such county, city, or town; a member of any fire company providing fire protection services for facilities of the Virginia National Guard; a member of the Virginia National Guard or the Virginia Defense Force while such member is serving in the Virginia National Guard or the Virginia Defense Force on official state duty or federal duty under Title 32 of the United States Code; any special agent of the Virginia Alcoholic Beverage Control Authority; any regular or special conservation police officer who receives compensation from a county, city, or town or from the Commonwealth appointed pursuant to the provisions of § 29.1-200; any commissioned forest warden appointed under the provisions of § 10.1-1135; any member or employee of the Virginia Marine Resources Commission granted the power of arrest pursuant to § 28.2-900; any Department of Emergency Management hazardous materials officer; any other employee of the Department of Emergency Management who is performing official duties of the agency, when those duties are related to a major disaster or emergency, as defined in § 44-146.16, that has been or is later declared to exist under the authority of the Governor in accordance with § 44-146.28; any employee of any county, city, or town performing official emergency management or emergency services duties in cooperation with the Department of Emergency Management, when those duties are related to a major disaster or emergency, as defined in § 44-146.16, that has been or is later declared to exist under the authority of the Governor in accordance with § 44-146.28 or a local emergency, as defined in § 44-146.16, declared by a local governing body; any nonfirefighter regional hazardous materials emergency response team member; any conservation officer of the Department of Conservation and Recreation commissioned pursuant to § 10.1-115; or any full-time sworn member of the enforcement division of the Department of Motor Vehicles appointed pursuant to § 46.2-217.

"Disabled person" means any individual who has been determined to be mentally or physically incapacitated so as to prevent the further performance of his duties at the time of his disability where such incapacity is likely to be permanent, and whose incapacity occurs in the line of duty as the direct or proximate result of the performance of his duty, including the presumptions under §§ 27-40.1, 27-40.2, 51.1-813, 65.2-402, and 65.2-402.1 if his position is covered by the applicable statute, in any position listed in the definition of deceased person in this section. "Disabled person" does not include any individual who has been determined to be no longer disabled pursuant to subdivision A 2 of § 9.1-404. Disabled person also does not include any individual during any period in which his health insurance coverage in the LODA Health Benefits Plan is suspended pursuant to subdivision C 4 of § 9.1-401. "Disabled person" includes any state employee included in the definition of a deceased person who was disabled on or after January 1, 1966.

"Eligible dependent" for purposes of continued health insurance pursuant to § 9.1-401 means the natural or adopted child or children of a deceased person or disabled person or of a deceased or disabled person's eligible spouse, including any children born as the result of a pregnancy or adopted pursuant to a preadoptive agreement, either of which occurred prior to the time of the employee's death or disability. Eligibility will continue until the end of the year in which the eligible dependent reaches age 26 or when the eligible dependent ceases to be eligible based on the Virginia Administrative Code or administrative guidance as determined by the Department of Human Resource Management.

"Eligible spouse" for purposes of continued health insurance pursuant to § 9.1-401 means the spouse of a deceased person or a disabled person at the time of the death or disability. Eligibility will continue until the eligible spouse dies, ceases to be married to a disabled person, or in the case of the spouse of a deceased person, dies, remarries, or otherwise ceases to be eligible based on the Virginia Administrative Code or administrative guidance as determined by the Department of Human Resource Management.

"Employee" means any person who would be covered or whose spouse, dependents, or beneficiaries would be covered under the benefits of this chapter if the person became a disabled person or a deceased person.

"Employer" means (i) the employer of a person who is a covered employee or (ii) in the case of a

volunteer who is a member of any fire company or department or rescue squad described in the definition of "deceased person," the county, city, or town that by ordinance or resolution recognized such fire company or department or rescue squad as an integral part of the official safety program of such locality.

"Fund" means the Line of Duty Death and Health Benefits Trust Fund established pursuant to § 9.1-400.1.

"Line of duty" means any action the deceased or disabled person was obligated or authorized to perform by rule, regulation, condition of employment or service, or law.

"LODA Health Benefits Plans" means the separate health benefits plans established pursuant to § 9.1-401.

"Nonparticipating employer" means any employer that is a political subdivision of the Commonwealth that elected on or before July 1, 2012, to directly fund the cost of benefits provided under this chapter and not participate in the Fund.

"Participating employer" means any employer that is a state agency or is a political subdivision of the Commonwealth that did not make an election to become a nonparticipating employer.

"VRS" means the Virginia Retirement System.

History.
1995, cc. 112, 156, 597, §§ 2.1-133.5, 2.1-133.6; 1996, cc. 66, 174; 1998, c. 712; 2001, cc. 678, 844; 2003, cc. 37, 41, 1005; 2004, c. 30; 2005, cc. 907, 910; 2006, c. 824; 2007, c. 87; 2011, cc. 572, 586; 2012, cc. 374, 458, 573; 2015, cc. 38, 502, 503, 730; 2016, c. 677.

§ 9.1-400.1. (Effective July 1, 2017) Line of Duty Death and Health Benefits Trust Fund.

A. There is hereby established a permanent and perpetual fund to be known as the Line of Duty Death and Health Benefits Trust Fund, consisting of such moneys as may be appropriated by the General Assembly, contributions or reimbursements from participating and nonparticipating employers, gifts, bequests, endowments, or grants from the United States government or its agencies or instrumentalities, net income from the investment of moneys held in the Fund, and any other available sources of funds, public and private. Any moneys remaining in the Fund at the end of a biennium shall not revert to the general fund but shall remain in the Fund. Interest and income earned from the investment of such moneys shall remain in the Fund and be credited to it. The moneys in the Fund shall be (i) deemed separate and independent trust funds, (ii) segregated and accounted for separately from all other funds of the Commonwealth, and (iii) administered solely in the interests of the persons who are covered under the benefits provided pursuant to this chapter. Deposits to and assets of the Fund shall not be subject to the claims of creditors.

B. The Virginia Retirement System shall invest, reinvest, and manage the assets of the Fund as provided in § 51.1-124.39 and shall be reimbursed from the Fund for such activities as provided in that section.

C. The Fund shall be used to provide the benefits under this chapter related to disabled persons, deceased persons, eligible dependents, and eligible spouses on behalf of participating employers and to pay related administrative costs.

D. Each participating employer shall make annual contributions to the Fund and provide information as determined by VRS. The amount of the contribution for each participating employer shall be determined on a current disbursement basis in accordance with the provisions of this section. If any participating employer fails to remit contributions or other fees or costs associated with the Fund, VRS shall inform the State Comptroller and the affected participating employer of the delinquent amount. In calculating the delinquent amount, VRS may impose an interest rate of one percent per month of delinquency. The State Comptroller shall forthwith transfer such delinquent amount, plus interest, from any moneys otherwise distributable to such participating employer.

History.
2016, c. 677.

§ 9.1-401. (Effective until July 1, 2017) Continued health insurance coverage for disabled persons, their spouses and dependents, and for the surviving spouse and dependents of certain deceased law-enforcement officers, firefighters, etc.

A. The surviving spouse and any dependents of a deceased person shall be afforded continued health insurance coverage, the cost of which shall be paid in full out of the general fund of the state treasury.

B. If the disabled person's disability (i) occurred while in the line of duty as the direct or proximate result of the performance of his duty or (ii) was subject to the provisions of §§ 27-40.1, 27-40.2, 51.1-813 or § 65.2-402, and arose out of and in the course of his employment, the disabled person, his surviving spouse and any dependents shall be afforded continued health insurance coverage. The cost of such health insurance coverage shall be paid in full out of the general fund of the state treasury.

C. The continued health insurance coverage provided by this section shall be the same plan of benefits which the deceased or disabled person was entitled to on the last day of his active duty or comparable benefits established as a result of a replacement plan.

D. For any spouse, continued health insurance provided by this section shall terminate upon such spouse's death or coverage by alternate health insurance.

E. For dependents, continued health insurance provided by this section shall terminate upon such dependent's death, marriage, coverage by alternate health insurance or twenty-first birthday. Continued health care insurance shall be provided beyond the dependent's twenty-first birthday if the dependent is a full-time college student and shall continue until such time as the dependent ceases to be a full-time student or reaches his twenty-fifth birthday, whichever occurs first. Continued health care insurance shall also be provided beyond the dependent's twenty-first birthday if the dependent is mentally or physically disabled, and such coverage shall continue until three months following the cessation of the disability.

F. For any disabled person, continued health insurance provided by this section shall automatically terminate upon the disabled person's death, recovery or return to full duty in any position listed in the definition of deceased person in § 9.1-400.

History.

1998, c. 712, § 2.1-133.7:1; 2000, c. 616; 2001, c. 844.

§ 9.1-401. (Effective July 1, 2017) Continued health insurance coverage for employees, eligible spouses, and eligible dependents.

A. Employees, eligible spouses, and eligible dependents shall be afforded continued health insurance coverage as provided in this section, the cost of which shall be paid by the nonparticipating employer to the Department of Human Resource Management or from the Fund on behalf of a participating employer, as applicable. If any disabled person is receiving the benefits described in this section and would otherwise qualify for the health insurance credit described in Chapter 14 (§ 51.1-1400 et seq.) of Title 51.1, the amount of such credit shall be deposited into the Line of Duty Death and Health Benefits Trust Fund or paid to the nonparticipating employer, as applicable, from the health insurance credit trust fund, in a manner prescribed by VRS.

B. 1. The continued health insurance coverage provided by this section for all disabled persons, eligible spouses, and eligible dependents shall be through separate plans, referred to as the LODA Health Benefits Plans (the Plans), administered by the Department of Human Resource Management. The Plans shall comply with all applicable federal and state laws and shall be modeled upon state employee health benefits program plans. Funding of the Plans' reserves and contingency shall be provided through a line of credit, the amount of which shall be based on an actuarially determined estimate of liabilities. The Department of Human Resource Management shall be reimbursed for health insurance premiums and all reasonable costs incurred and associated, directly and indirectly, in performing the duties pursuant to this section (i) from the Line of Duty Death and Health Benefits Trust Fund for costs related to disabled persons, deceased persons, eligible dependents, and eligible spouses on behalf of participating employers and (ii) from a nonparticipating employer for premiums and costs related to disabled persons, deceased persons, eligible dependents, and eligible spouses for which the nonparticipating employer is responsible. If any nonparticipating employer fails to remit such premiums and costs, the Department of Human Resource Management shall inform the State Comptroller and the affected nonparticipating employer of the delinquent amount. In calculating the delinquent amount, the Department of Human Resource Management may impose an interest rate of one percent per month of delinquency. The State Comptroller shall forthwith transfer such delinquent amount, plus interest, from any moneys otherwise distributable to such nonparticipating employer.

2. In the event that temporary health care insurance coverage is needed for employees, eligible spouses, and eligible dependents during the period of transition into the LODA Health Benefits Plans, the Department of Human Resource Management is authorized to acquire and provide temporary transitional health insurance coverage. The type and source of the transitional health plans shall be within the sole discretion of the Department of Human Resource Management. Transitional coverage for eligible dependents shall comply with the eligibility criteria of the transitional plans until enrollment in the LODA Health Benefits Plan can be completed.

C. 1. a. Except as provided in subdivision 2 and any other law, continued health insurance coverage in any LODA Health Benefits Plans shall not be provided to any person (i) whose coverage under the Plan is based on a deceased person's death or a disabled person's disability occurring on or after July 1, 2017 and (ii) who is eligible for Medicare due to age.

b. Coverage in the LODA Health Benefits Plans shall also cease for any person upon his death.

2. The provisions of subdivision 1 a shall not apply to any disabled person who is eligible for Medicare due to disability under Social Security Disability Insurance or a Railroad Retirement Board Disability Annuity. The Department of Human Resource Management may provide such disabled person coverage under a LODA Health Benefits Plan that is separate from the plan for other persons.

3. Continued health insurance under this section shall also terminate upon the disabled person's return to full duty in any position listed in the definition of deceased person in § 9.1-400. Such disabled person shall promptly notify the participating or nonparticipating employer, VRS, and the Department of Human Resource Management upon his return to work.

4. Such continued health insurance shall be suspended for the year following a calendar year in which the disabled person has earned income in an amount equal to or greater than the salary of the

position held by the disabled person at the time of disability, indexed annually based upon the annual increases in the United States Average Consumer Price Index for all items, all urban consumers (CPI-U), as published by the Bureau of Labor Statistics of the U.S. Department of Labor. Such suspension shall cease the year following a calendar year in which the disabled person has not earned such amount of income. The disabled person shall notify the participating or nonparticipating employer, VRS, and the Department of Human Resource Management no later than January 15 of the year following any year in which he earns income of such amount, and notify the participating or nonparticipating employer, VRS, and the Department of Human Resource Management when he no longer is earning such amount. Upon request, a disabled person shall provide VRS and the Department of Human Resource Management with documentation of earned income.

History.
1998, c. 712, § 2.1-133.7:1; 2000, c. 616; 2001, c. 844; 2016, c. 677.

§ 9.1-401.1. Supplemental short-term disability benefit for state police officers.

A state police officer who is a participating employee, as defined in § 51.1-1100, and who incurs a work-related injury in the line of duty, shall receive supplemental short-term disability coverage, pursuant to § 51.1-1121, that provides income replacement for 100 percent of the officer's creditable compensation for the first six months and, pursuant to a certification by the Superintendent of State Police, based on a medical evaluation, that the officer is likely to return to service within another six months, up to one calendar year, that the officer is disabled, without regard to the officer's number of months of state service. Except as provided in this section with regard to the rate of income replacement and the duration of supplemental short-term disability coverage, such state police officers shall be eligible for work-related, supplemental short-term disability benefits upon the same terms and conditions that apply to other participating employees pursuant to Article 4 (§ 51.1-1119 et seq.) of Chapter 11 of Title 51.1. Upon the expiration of the one-calendar-year period, such state police officers shall be eligible for supplemental long-term disability benefits as provided in § 51.1-1123.

History.
2010, c. 654.

§ 9.1-402. (Effective until July 1, 2017) Payments to beneficiaries of certain deceased law-enforcement officers, firefighters, etc., and retirees.

A. The beneficiary of a deceased person whose death occurred on or before December 31, 2005, while in the line of duty as the direct or proximate result of the performance of his duty shall be entitled to receive the sum of $75,000, which shall be payable out of the general fund of the state treasury, in gratitude for and in recognition of his sacrifice on behalf of the people of the Commonwealth.

B. The beneficiary of a deceased person whose death occurred on or after January 1, 2006, while in the line of duty as the direct or proximate result of the performance of his duty shall be entitled to receive the sum of $100,000, which shall be payable out of the general fund of the state treasury, in gratitude for and in recognition of his sacrifice on behalf of the people of the Commonwealth.

C. Subject to the provisions of §§ 27-40.1, 27-40.2, 51.1-813, or § 65.2-402, if the deceased person's death (i) arose out of and in the course of his employment or (ii) was within five years from his date of retirement, his beneficiary shall be entitled to receive the sum of $25,000, which shall be payable out of the general fund of the state treasury.

History.
1995, cc. 156, 597, § 2.1-133.7; 2000, c. 314; 2001, c. 844; 2006, c. 878.

§ 9.1-402. (Effective July 1, 2017) Payments to beneficiaries of certain deceased law-enforcement officers, firefighters, etc., and retirees.

A. The beneficiary of a deceased person whose death occurred on or before December 31, 2005, while in the line of duty as the direct or proximate result of the performance of his duty shall be entitled to receive the sum of $75,000, which shall be paid by the nonparticipating employer or from the Fund on behalf of a participating employer, as applicable, in gratitude for and in recognition of his sacrifice on behalf of the people of the Commonwealth.

B. The beneficiary of a deceased person whose death occurred on or after January 1, 2006, while in the line of duty as the direct or proximate result of the performance of his duty shall be entitled to receive the sum of $100,000, which shall be paid by the nonparticipating employer or from the Fund on behalf of a participating employer, as applicable, in gratitude for and in recognition of his sacrifice on behalf of the people of the Commonwealth.

C. Subject to the provisions of § 27-40.1, 27-40.2, 51.1-813, or 65.2-402, if the deceased person's death (i) arose out of and in the course of his employment or (ii) was within five years from his date of retirement, his beneficiary shall be entitled to receive the sum of $25,000, which shall be paid by the nonparticipating employer or from the Fund on behalf of a participating employer, as applicable.

History.
1995, cc. 156, 597, § 2.1-133.7; 2000, c. 314; 2001, c. 844; 2006, c. 878; 2016, c. 677.

§ 9.1-402.1. (Effective until July 1, 2017) Payments for burial expenses.

It is the intent of the General Assembly that expeditious payments for burial expenses be made for persons whose death is determined to be a direct and proximate result of their performance in the line of duty as defined by the Line of Duty Act. The State Comptroller is hereby authorized to release, at the request of the family of a person who may be subject to the line of duty death benefits, payments to a funeral service provider for burial and transportation costs. These payments would be advanced from the death benefit that would be due to the beneficiary of the deceased person if it is determined that the person qualifies for line of duty coverage. Expenses advanced under this provision shall not exceed the coverage amounts outlined in § 65.2-512. In the event a determination is made that the death is not subject to the line of duty benefits, the Virginia Retirement System or other retirement fund to which the deceased is a member will deduct from benefit payments otherwise due to be paid to the beneficiaries of the deceased payments previously paid by the State Comptroller for burial and related transportation expenses and return such funds to the State Comptroller. The State Comptroller shall have the right to file a claim with the Virginia Workers' Compensation Commission against any employer to recover burial and related transportation expenses advanced under this provision.

History.

2012, cc. 90, 576.

§ 9.1-402.1. (Effective July 1, 2017) Payments for burial expenses.

It is the intent of the General Assembly that expeditious payments for burial expenses be made for deceased persons whose death is determined to be a direct and proximate result of their performance in the line of duty as defined by the Line of Duty Act. Upon the approval of VRS, at the request of the family of a person who may be subject to the line of duty death benefits, payments shall be made to a funeral service provider for burial and transportation costs by the nonparticipating employer or from the Fund on behalf of a participating employer, as applicable. These payments would be advanced from the death benefit that would be due to the beneficiary of the deceased person if it is determined that the person qualifies for line of duty coverage. Expenses advanced under this provision shall not exceed the coverage amounts outlined in § 65.2-512. In the event a determination is made that the death is not subject to the line of duty benefits, VRS or other Virginia governmental retirement fund of which the deceased is a member will deduct from benefit payments otherwise due to be paid to the beneficiaries of the deceased payments previously paid for burial and related transportation expenses and return such funds to the nonparticipating employer or to the Fund on behalf of a participating employer, as applicable. The Virginia Retirement System shall have the right to file a claim with the Virginia Workers' Compensation Commission against any employer to recover burial and related transportation expenses advanced under this provision.

History.

2012, cc. 90, 576; 2016, c. 677.

§ 9.1-403. (Effective until July 1, 2017) Claim for payment; costs.

A. Every beneficiary, disabled person or his spouse, or dependent of a deceased or disabled person shall present his claim to the chief officer, or his designee, of the appropriate division or department that last employed the deceased or disabled person on forms to be provided by the State Comptroller's office.

B. In the case of a police department or a sheriff's office that is part of or administered by the Commonwealth or any political subdivision thereof, the chief officer, or his designee, of such department or office shall investigate and report upon the circumstances surrounding the deceased or disabled person and report his findings to the Comptroller within 10 business days after completion of the investigation. The Comptroller, the Attorney General, or any such chief officer, in his discretion, may submit a request to the Superintendent of the Department of State Police to perform the investigation pursuant to subsection C.

C. In all other cases, upon receipt of the claim the chief officer, or his designee, of the appropriate division or department shall submit a request to the Superintendent of the Department of the State Police, who shall investigate and report upon the circumstances surrounding the deceased or disabled person, calling upon the additional information and services of any other appropriate agents or agencies of the Commonwealth. The Superintendent, or his designee, shall report his findings to the Comptroller within 10 business days after completion of the investigation. The Department of State Police shall take action to conduct the investigation as expeditiously as possible. The Department shall be reimbursed for the cost of investigations conducted pursuant to this section from the appropriate employer that last employed the deceased or disabled employee.

D. Within 10 business days of being notified by an employee, or an employee's representative, that such employee is permanently and totally disabled due to a work-related injury suffered in the line of duty, the agency or department employing the disabled person shall provide him with information about the continued health insurance coverage provided under this act and the process for initiating a claim. The employer shall assist in filing a claim, unless such assistance is waived by the employee or the employee's representative.

History.

1995, c. 156, § 2.1-133.8; 1998, c. 712; 2001, cc. 427, 844; 2007, c. 90; 2009, cc. 393, 580.

§ 9.1-403. (Effective July 1, 2017) Claim for payment; costs.

A. Every beneficiary, disabled person or his spouse, or dependent of a deceased or disabled person shall present his claim to the chief officer, or his designee, of the employer for which the disabled or deceased person last worked on forms to be provided by VRS. Upon receipt of a claim, the chief officer or his designee shall forward the claim to VRS within seven days. The Virginia Retirement System shall determine eligibility for benefits under this chapter. The Virginia Retirement System may request assistance in obtaining information necessary to make an eligibility determination from the Department of State Police. The Department of State Police shall take action to conduct the investigation as expeditiously as possible. The Department of State Police shall be reimbursed from the Fund or the nonparticipating employer, as applicable, for the cost of searching for and obtaining information requested by VRS. The Virginia Retirement System shall be reimbursed for the reasonable costs incurred for making eligibility determinations by nonparticipating employers or from the Fund on behalf of participating employers, as applicable. If any nonparticipating employer fails to reimburse VRS for reasonable costs incurred in making an eligibility determination, VRS shall inform the State Comptroller and the affected nonparticipating employer of the delinquent amount. In calculating the delinquent amount, VRS may impose an interest rate of one percent per month of delinquency. The State Comptroller shall forthwith transfer such delinquent amount, plus interest, from any moneys otherwise distributable to such nonparticipating employer.

B. 1. Within 10 business days of being notified by an employee, or an employee's representative, that such employee is permanently and totally disabled due to a work-related injury suffered in the line of duty, the agency or department employing the employee shall provide him with information about the continued health insurance coverage provided under this chapter and the process for initiating a claim. The employer shall assist in filing a claim, unless such assistance is waived by the employee or the employee's representative.

2. Within 10 business days of having knowledge that a deceased person's surviving spouse, dependents, or beneficiaries may be entitled to benefits under this chapter, the employer for which the deceased person last worked shall provide the surviving spouse, dependents, or beneficiaries, as applicable, with information about the benefits provided under this chapter and the process for initiating a claim. The employer shall assist in filing a claim, unless such assistance is waived by the surviving spouse, dependents, or beneficiaries.

C. Within 30 days of receiving a claim pursuant to subsection A, an employer may submit to VRS any evidence that could assist in determining the eligibility of a claim. However, when the claim involves a presumption under § 65.2-402 or 65.2-402.1, VRS shall provide an employer additional time to submit evidence as is necessary not to exceed nine months from the date the employer received a claim pursuant to subsection A. Any such evidence submitted by the employer shall be included in the agency record for the claim.

History.

1995, c. 156, § 2.1-133.8; 1998, c. 712; 2001, cc. 427, 844; 2007, c. 90; 2009, cc. 393, 580; 2016, c. 677.

§ 9.1-404. (Effective until July 1, 2017) Order of Comptroller.

A. If it appears to the Comptroller that the requirements of either subsection A or B of § 9.1-402 have been satisfied, he shall issue his warrant in the appropriate amount for payment out of the general fund of the state treasury to the surviving spouse or to such persons and subject to such conditions as may be proper in his administrative discretion, and in the event there is no beneficiary, the Comptroller shall issue the payment to the estate of the deceased person. The Comptroller shall issue a decision, and payment, if appropriate, shall be made no later than forty-five days following receipt of the report required under § 9.1-403.

B. If it appears to the Comptroller that the requirements of either subsection A or B of § 9.1-401 have been satisfied, he shall issue his warrants in the appropriate amounts for payment from the general fund of the state treasury to ensure continued health care coverage for the persons designated under § 9.1-401. The Comptroller shall issue a decision, and payments, if appropriate, shall commence no later than forty-five days following receipt of the report required under § 9.1-403. The payments shall be retroactive to the first date that the disability existed.

History.

1995, cc. 156, 597, § 2.1-133.9; 1998, c. 712; 2001, c. 844.

§ 9.1-404. (Effective July 1, 2017) Order of the Virginia Retirement System.

A. 1. The Virginia Retirement System shall make an eligibility determination within 45 days of receiving all necessary information for determining eligibility for a claim filed under § 9.1-403. If benefits under this chapter are due, VRS shall notify the nonparticipating employer, which shall provide the benefits within 15 days of such notice, or VRS shall pay the benefits from the Fund on behalf of the participating employer within 15 days of the determination, as applicable. The payments shall be retroactive to the first date that the disabled person was no longer eligible for health insurance coverage subsidized by his employer.

2. Two years after an individual has been determined to be a disabled person, VRS may require the disabled person to renew the determination through a process established by VRS. If a disabled person refuses to submit to the determination renewal process described in this subdivision, then benefits under this chapter shall cease for the individual, any eligible dependents, and an eligible spouse until the individual complies. If such individual does not comply within six months from the date of the initial request for a renewed determination, then benefits under this chapter shall permanently cease for the individual, any eligible dependents, and an eligible spouse. If VRS issues a renewed determination that an individual is no longer a disabled person, then benefits under this chapter shall permanently cease for the individual, any eligible dependents, and an eligible spouse. If VRS issues a renewed determination that an individual remains a disabled person, then VRS may require the disabled person to renew the determination five years after such renewed determination through a process established by VRS. The Virginia Retirement System may require the disabled person to renew the determination at any time if VRS has information indicating that the person may no longer be disabled.

B. The Virginia Retirement System shall be reimbursed for all reasonable costs incurred and associated, directly and indirectly, in performing the duties pursuant to this chapter (i) from the Line of Duty Death and Health Benefits Trust Fund for costs related to disabled persons, deceased persons, eligible dependents, and eligible spouses on behalf of participating employers and (ii) from a nonparticipating employer for premiums and costs related to disabled persons, deceased persons, eligible dependents, and eligible spouses for which the nonparticipating employer is responsible.

C. The Virginia Retirement System may develop policies and procedures necessary to carry out the provisions of this chapter.

History.

1995, cc. 156, 597, § 2.1-133.9; 1998, c. 712; 2001, c. 844; 2016, c. 677.

§ 9.1-405. (Effective until July1, 2017) Appeal from decision of Comptroller.

Any beneficiary, disabled person or his spouse or dependent of a deceased or disabled person aggrieved by the decision of the Comptroller shall present a petition to the court in which the will of the deceased person is probated or in which the personal representative of the deceased person is qualified or might qualify or in the jurisdiction in which the disabled person resides.

The Commonwealth shall be represented in such proceeding by the Attorney General or his designee. The court shall proceed as chancellor without a jury. If it appears to the court that the requirements of this chapter have been satisfied, the judge shall enter an order to that effect. The order shall also direct the Comptroller to issue his warrant in the appropriate amount for the payment out of the general fund of the state treasury to such persons and subject to such conditions as may be proper. If, in the case of a deceased person, there is no beneficiary, the judge shall direct such payment as is due under § 9.1-402 to the estate of the deceased person.

History.

1995, cc. 156, 597, § 2.1-133.10; 1998, c. 712; 2001, c. 844.

§ 9.1-405. (Effective July 1, 2017) Appeal from decision of Virginia Retirement System.

Any beneficiary, disabled person or eligible spouse or eligible dependent of a deceased or disabled person aggrieved by the decision of VRS may appeal the decision through a process established by VRS. Any such process may utilize a medical board as described in § 51.1-124.23. An employer may submit information related to the claim and may participate in any informal fact-finding proceeding that is included in such process established by VRS. Upon completion of the appeal process, the final determination issued by VRS shall constitute a case decision as defined in § 2.2-4001. Any beneficiary, disabled person, or eligible spouse or eligible dependent of a deceased or disabled person aggrieved by, and claiming the unlawfulness of, such case decision shall have a right to seek judicial review thereof in accordance with Article 5 (§ 2.2-4025 et seq.) of the Administrative Process Act. The employer shall not have a right to seek such judicial review.

History.

1995, cc. 156, 597, § 2.1-133.10; 1998, c. 712; 2001, c. 844; 2016, c. 677.

§ 9.1-406. (Repealed effective July 1, 2017) Appeals.

Appeals from judgments entered pursuant to this chapter shall be allowed as in civil actions generally.

History.

1995, c. 156, § 2.1-133.11; 2001, c. 844; 2005, c. 681.

§ 9.1-407. (Effective until July 1, 2017) Training.

Any law-enforcement or public safety officer entitled to benefits under this Chapter shall receive training concerning the benefits available to himself or his beneficiary in case of disability or death in the line of duty. The Secretary of Public Safety and Homeland Security shall develop training information to be distributed to agencies and localities with employees subject to this chapter. The agency or locality shall be responsible for providing the training. Such training shall not count towards in-service training requirements for law-enforcement officers pursuant to § 9.1-102.

History.
2006, c. 535; 2014, cc. 115, 490.

§ 9.1-407. (Effective July 1, 2017) Training.

Any law-enforcement or public safety officer entitled to benefits under this chapter shall receive training within 30 days of his employment, and again every two years thereafter, concerning the benefits available to himself or his beneficiary in case of disability or death in the line of duty. The Secretary of Public Safety and Homeland Security shall develop training information to be distributed to agencies and localities with employees subject to this chapter. The agency or locality shall be responsible for providing the training. Such training shall not count toward in-service training requirements for law-enforcement officers pursuant to § 9.1-102 and shall include, but not be limited to, the general rules for intestate succession described in § 64.2-200 that may be applicable to the distribution of benefits provided under § 9.1-402.

History.
2006, c. 535; 2014, cc. 115, 490; 2016, c. 677.

§ 9.1-408. Records of investigation confidential.

Evidence and documents obtained by or created by, and the report of investigation prepared by, the Department of State Police in carrying out the provisions of this chapter shall (i) be deemed confidential, (ii) be exempt from disclosure under the Freedom of Information Act (§ 2.2-3700 et seq.), and (iii) not be released in whole or in part by any person to any person except as provided in this chapter.

History.
2010, c. 568.

CHAPTER 5.

LAW-ENFORCEMENT OFFICERS PROCEDURAL GUARANTEE ACT.

Section

Section

§ 9.1-500. (Effective until July 1, 2018) Definitions.

As used in this chapter, unless the context requires a different meaning:

"Agency" means the Department of State Police, the Division of Capitol Police, the Virginia Marine Resources Commission, the Virginia Port Authority, the Department of Game and Inland Fisheries, the Department of Alcoholic Beverage Control, the Department of Conservation and Recreation, or the Department of Motor Vehicles; or the political subdivision or the campus police department of any public institution of higher education of the Commonwealth employing the law-enforcement officer.

"Law-enforcement officer" means any person, other than a Chief of Police or the Superintendent of the Department of State Police, who, in his official capacity, is (i) authorized by law to make arrests and (ii) a nonprobationary officer of one of the following agencies:

a. The Department of State Police, the Division of Capitol Police, the Virginia Marine Resources Commission, the Virginia Port Authority, the Department of Game and Inland Fisheries, the Department of Alcoholic Beverage Control, the Department of Motor Vehicles, or the Department of Conservation and Recreation;

b. The police department, bureau or force of any political subdivision or the campus police department of any public institution of higher education of the Commonwealth where such department, bureau or force has 10 or more law-enforcement officers; or

c. Any conservation police officer as defined in § 9.1-101.

For the purposes of this chapter, "law-enforcement officer" shall not include the sheriff's department of any city or county.

History.
1978, c. 19, § 2.1-116.1; 1979, c. 592; 1983, c. 357; 1995, c. 730; 2001, c. 844; 2007, cc. 87, 364.

§ 9.1-500. (Effective July 1, 2018) Definitions.

As used in this chapter, unless the context requires a different meaning:

"Agency" means the Department of State Police, the Division of Capitol Police, the Virginia Marine Resources Commission, the Virginia Port Authority, the Department of Game and Inland Fisheries, the Virginia Alcoholic Beverage Control Authority, the Department of Conservation and Recreation, or the Department of Motor Vehicles; or the political subdivision or the campus police department of any public institution of higher education of the Commonwealth employing the law-enforcement officer.

"Law-enforcement officer" means any person, other than a Chief of Police or the Superintendent of the Department of State Police, who, in his official capacity, is (i) authorized by law to make arrests and (ii) a nonprobationary officer of one of the following agencies:

a. The Department of State Police, the Division of Capitol Police, the Virginia Marine Resources Commission, the Virginia Port Authority, the Department of Game and Inland Fisheries, the Virginia Alcoholic Beverage Control Authority, the Department of Motor Vehicles, or the Department of Conservation and Recreation;

b. The police department, bureau or force of any political subdivision or the campus police department of any public institution of higher education of the Commonwealth where such department, bureau or force has 10 or more law-enforcement officers; or

c. Any conservation police officer as defined in § 9.1-101.

For the purposes of this chapter, "law-enforcement officer" shall not include the sheriff's department of any city or county.

History.

1978, c. 19, § 2.1-116.1; 1979, c. 592; 1983, c. 357; 1995, c. 730; 2001, c. 844; 2007, cc. 87, 364; 2015, cc. 38, 730.

§ 9.1-501. Conduct of investigation.

The provisions of this section shall apply whenever an investigation by an agency focuses on matters which could lead to the dismissal, demotion, suspension or transfer for punitive reasons of a law-enforcement officer:

1. Any questioning of the officer shall take place at a reasonable time and place as designated by the investigating officer, preferably when the officer under investigation is on duty and at the office of the command of the investigating officer or at the office of the local precinct or police unit of the officer being investigated, unless matters being investigated are of such a nature that immediate action is required.

2. Prior to the officer being questioned, he shall be informed of (i) the name and rank of the investigating officer and of any individual to be present during the questioning and (ii) the nature of the investigation.

3. When a blood or urine specimen is taken from a law-enforcement officer for the purpose of determining whether the officer has used drugs or alcohol, the specimen shall be divided and placed into two separate containers. One specimen shall be tested while the other is held in a proper manner to preserve the specimen by the facility collecting or testing the specimen. Should the first specimen test positive, the law-enforcement officer shall have the right to require the second specimen be sent to a laboratory of his choice for independent testing in accordance generally with the procedures set forth in §§ 18.2-268.1 through 18.2-268.12. The officer shall notify the chief of his agency in writing of his request within 10 days of being notified of positive specimen results. The laboratory chosen by the officer shall be accredited or certified by one or more of the following bodies: the American Society of Crime Laboratory Directors/Laboratory Accreditation Board (ASCLD/LAB), the College of American Pathologists (CAP), the United States Department of Health and Human Services Substance Abuse and Mental Health Services Administration (SAMHSA), or the American Board of Forensic Toxicology (ABFT).

History.

1978, c. 19, § 2.1-116.2; 1992, c. 221; 1993, c. 229; 2001, c. 844; 2005, cc. 868, 881.

§ 9.1-502. Notice of charges; response; election to proceed under grievance procedure of local governing body.

A. Before any dismissal, demotion, suspension without pay or transfer for punitive reasons may be imposed, the following rights shall be afforded:

1. The law-enforcement officer shall be notified in writing of all charges, the basis therefor, and the action which may be taken;

2. The law-enforcement officer shall be given an opportunity, within a reasonable time limit after the date of the written notice provided for above, to respond orally and in writing to the charges. The time limit shall be determined by the agency, but in no event shall it be less than five calendar days unless agreed to by the law-enforcement officer;

3. In making his response, the law-enforcement officer may be assisted by counsel at his own expense; and

4. The law-enforcement officer shall be given written notification of his right to initiate a grievance under the grievance procedure established by the local governing body pursuant to §§ 15.2-1506 and 15.2-1507. A copy of the local governing body's grievance procedure shall be provided to the law-enforcement officer upon his request.

B. A law-enforcement officer may proceed under either the local governing body's grievance procedure or the law-enforcement officer's procedural guarantees, but not both.

History.

1978, c. 19, § 2.1-116.4; 1987, c. 461; 2001, c. 844.

§ 9.1-503. Personal assets of officers.

No law-enforcement officer shall be required or requested to disclose any item of his property, income, assets, source of income, debts, or personal or domestic expenditures, including those of any member of his family or household, unless (i) such information is necessary in investigating a possible conflict of interest with respect to the performance of his official duties(ii) such disclosure is required by law, or (iii) such information is related to an investigation. Nothing in this section shall preclude an agency from requiring the law-enforcement officer to disclose any place of off-duty employment and where he may be contacted.

History.
1978, c. 19, § 2.1-116.3; 2001, c. 844.

§ 9.1-504. Hearing; hearing panel recommendations.

A. Whenever a law-enforcement officer is dismissed, demoted, suspended or transferred for punitive reasons, he may, within a reasonable amount of time following such action, as set by the agency, request a hearing. If such request is timely made, a hearing shall be held within a reasonable amount of time set by the agency. However, the hearing shall not be set later than fourteen calendar days following the date of request unless a later date is agreed to by the law-enforcement officer. At the hearing, the law-enforcement officer and his agency shall be afforded the opportunity to present evidence, examine and cross-examine witnesses. The law-enforcement officer shall also be given the opportunity to be represented by counsel at the hearing unless the officer and agency are afforded, by regulation, the right to counsel in a subsequent de novo hearing.

B. The hearing shall be conducted by a panel consisting of one member from within the agency selected by the grievant, one member from within the agency of equal rank of the grievant but no more than two ranks above appointed by the agency head, and a third member from within the agency to be selected by the other two members. In the event that such two members cannot agree upon their selection, the chief judge of the judicial circuit wherein the duty station of the grievant lies shall choose such third member. The hearing panel may, and on the request of either the law-enforcement officer or his agency shall, issue subpoenas requiring the testimony of witnesses who have refused or failed to appear at the hearing. The hearing panel shall rule on the admissibility of the evidence. A record shall be made of the hearing.

C. At the option of the agency, it may, in lieu of complying with the provisions of § 9.1-502, give the law-enforcement officer a statement, in writing, of the charges, the basis therefor, the action which may be taken, and provide a hearing as provided for in this section prior to dismissing, demoting, suspending or transferring for punitive reasons the law-enforcement officer.

D. The recommendations of the hearing panel, and the reasons therefor, shall be in writing and transmitted promptly to the law-enforcement officer or his attorney and to the chief executive officer of the law-enforcement agency. Such recommendations shall be advisory only, but shall be accorded significant weight.

History.
1978, c. 19, §§ 2.1-116.5, 2.1-116.7; 1980, c. 191; 2001, c. 844.

§ 9.1-505. Immediate suspension.

Nothing in this chapter shall prevent the immediate suspension without pay of any law-enforcement officer whose continued presence on the job is deemed to be a substantial and immediate threat to the welfare of his agency or the public, nor shall anything in this chapter prevent the suspension of a law-enforcement officer for refusing to obey a direct order issued in conformance with the agency's written and disseminated regulations. In such a case, the law-enforcement officer shall, upon request, be afforded the rights provided for under this chapter within a reasonable amount of time set by the agency.

History.
1978, c. 19, § 2.1-116.6; 2001, c. 844.

§ 9.1-506. Informal counseling not prohibited.

Nothing in this chapter shall be construed to prohibit the informal counseling of a law-enforcement officer by a supervisor in reference to a minor infraction of policy or procedure which does not result in disciplinary action being taken against the law-enforcement officer.

History.
1978, c. 19, § 2.1-116.8; 2001, c. 844.

§ 9.1-507. Chapter accords minimum rights.

The rights accorded law-enforcement officers in this chapter are minimum rights and all agencies shall adopt grievance procedures that are consistent with this chapter. However, an agency may provide for additional rights of law-enforcement officers in its grievance procedure.

History.
1978, c. 19, § 2.1-116.9; 2001, c. 844.

CHAPTER 6.

CIVILIAN PROTECTION IN CASES OF POLICE MISCONDUCT.

Section

§ 9.1-600. Civilian protection in cases of police misconduct; minimum standards.

A. State, local, and other public law-enforcement agencies, which have ten or more law-enforcement officers, shall have procedures as established in subsection B, allowing citizen submission of complaints regarding the conduct of the law-enforcement agency, law-enforcement officers in the agency, or employees of the agency.

B. Law-enforcement agencies shall ensure, at a minimum, that in the case of all written complaints:

1. The general public has access to the required forms and information concerning the submission of complaints;

2. The law-enforcement agency assists individuals in filing complaints; and

3. Adequate records are maintained of the nature and disposition of such cases.

History.

1993, c. 722, § 2.1-116.9:6; 2001, cc. 153, 844.

CHAPTER 9.

SEX OFFENDER AND CRIMES AGAINST MINORS REGISTRY ACT.

Section

§ 9.1-900. Purpose of the Sex Offender and Crimes Against Minors Registry.

The purpose of the Sex Offender and Crimes Against Minors Registry (Registry) shall be to assist the efforts of law-enforcement agencies and others to protect their communities and families from repeat sex offenders and to protect children from becoming victims of criminal offenders by helping to prevent such individuals from being allowed to work directly with children.

History.

2003, c. 584.

§ 9.1-901. Persons for whom registration required.

A. Every person convicted on or after July 1, 1994, including a juvenile tried and convicted in the circuit court pursuant to § 16.1-269.1, whether sentenced as an adult or juvenile, of an offense set forth in § 9.1-902 and every juvenile found delinquent of an offense for which registration is required under subsection G of § 9.1-902 shall register and reregister as required by this chapter. Every person serving a sentence of confinement on or after July 1, 1994, for a conviction of an offense set forth in § 9.1-902 shall register and reregister as required by this chapter. Every person under community supervision as defined by § 53.1-1 or any similar form of supervision under the laws of the United States or any political subdivision thereof, on or after July 1, 1994, resulting from a conviction of an offense set forth in § 9.1-902 shall register and reregister as required by this chapter.

B. Every person found not guilty by reason of insanity on or after July 1, 2007, of an offense set forth in § 9.1-902 shall register and reregister as required by this chapter. Every person in the custody of the Commissioner of Behavioral Health and Developmental Services, or on conditional release on or after July 1, 2007, because of a finding of not guilty by reason of insanity of an offense set forth in § 9.1-902 shall register and reregister as required by this chapter.

C. Unless a specific effective date is otherwise provided, all provisions of the Sex Offender and Crimes Against Minors Registry Act shall apply retroactively. This subsection is declaratory of existing law.

History.

2003, c. 584; 2005, c. 586; 2007, cc. 718, 744; 2009, cc. 813, 840.

§ 9.1-902. Offenses requiring registration.

A. For purposes of this chapter:

"Offense for which registration is required" includes:

1. Any offense listed in subsection B;
2. Criminal homicide;
3. Murder;
4. A sexually violent offense;
5. Any offense similar to those listed in subdivisions 1 through 4 under the laws of any foreign country or any political subdivision thereof, the United States or any political subdivision thereof; and
6. Any offense for which registration in a sex offender and crimes against minors registry is required under the laws of the jurisdiction where the offender was convicted.

B. The offenses included under this subsection include any violation of, attempted violation of, or conspiracy to violate:

1. § 18.2-63 unless registration is required pursuant to subdivision E 1; § 18.2-64.1; former § 18.2-67.2:1; § 18.2-90 with the intent to commit rape; former § 18.1-88 with the intent to commit rape; any felony violation of § 18.2-346; any violation of subdivision (4) of § 18.2-355; any violation of subsection C of § 18.2-357.1; subsection B or C of § 18.2-374.1:1; former subsection D of § 18.2-374.1:1 as it was in effect from July 1, 1994, through June 30, 2007; former clause (iv) of subsection B of § 18.2-374.3 as it was in effect on June 30, 2007; subsection B, C, or D of § 18.2-374.3; or a third or subsequent conviction of (i) § 18.2-67.4, (ii) § 18.2-67.4:2, (iii) subsection C of § 18.2-67.5, or (iv) § 18.2-386.1.

If the offense was committed on or after July 1, 2006, § 18.2-91 with the intent to commit any felony offense listed in this section; subsection A of § 18.2-374.1:1; or a felony under § 18.2-67.5:1.

2. Where the victim is a minor or is physically helpless or mentally incapacitated as defined in § 18.2-67.10, subsection A of § 18.2-47, clause (i) of § 18.2-48, § 18.2-67.4, subsection C of § 18.2-67.5, § 18.2-361, § 18.2-366, or a felony violation of former § 18.1-191.

3. § 18.2-370.6.

4. If the offense was committed on or after July 1, 2016, and where the perpetrator is 18 years of age or older and the victim is under the age of 13, any violation of § 18.2-51.2.

5. If the offense was committed on or after July 1, 2016, any violation of § 18.2-356 punishable as a Class 3 felony or any violation of § 18.2-357 punishable as a Class 3 felony.

C. "Criminal homicide" means a homicide in conjunction with a violation of, attempted violation of, or conspiracy to violate clause (i) of § 18.2-371 or § 18.2-371.1, when the offenses arise out of the same incident.

D. "Murder" means a violation of, attempted violation of, or conspiracy to violate § 18.2-31 or § 18.2-32 where the victim is (i) under 15 years of age or (ii) where the victim is at least 15 years of age but under 18 years of age and the murder is related to an offense listed in this section or a violation of former § 18.1-21 where the victim is (a) under 15 years of age or (b) at least 15 years of age but under 18 years of age and the murder is related to an offense listed in this section.

E. "Sexually violent offense" means a violation of, attempted violation of, or conspiracy to violate:

1. Clause (ii) and (iii) of § 18.2-48, former § 18.1-38 with the intent to defile or, for the purpose of concubinage or prostitution, a felony violation of subdivision (2) or (3) of former § 18.1-39 that involves assisting or aiding in such an abduction, § 18.2-61, former § 18.1-44 when such act is accomplished against the complaining witness's will, by force, or through the use of the complaining witness's mental incapacity or physical helplessness, or if the victim is under 13 years of age, subsection A of § 18.2-63 where the perpetrator is more than five years older than the victim, § 18.2-67.1, § 18.2-67.2, § 18.2-67.3, former § 18.1-215 when the complaining witness is under 13 years of age, § 18.2-67.4 where the perpetrator is 18 years of age or older and the victim is under the age of six, subsections A and B of § 18.2-67.5, § 18.2-370, subdivision (1), (2), or (4) of former § 18.1-213, former § 18.1-214, § 18.2-370.1, or § 18.2-374.1; or

2. § 18.2-63, § 18.2-64.1, former § 18.2-67.2:1, § 18.2-90 with the intent to commit rape or, where the victim is a minor or is physically helpless or mentally incapacitated as defined in § 18.2-67.10, subsection A of § 18.2-47, § 18.2-67.4, subsection C of § 18.2-67.5, clause (i) of § 18.2-48, § 18.2-361, § 18.2-366, or subsection C of § 18.2-374.1:1. An offense listed under this subdivision shall be deemed a sexually violent offense only if the person has been convicted or adjudicated delinquent of any two or more such offenses, provided that person had been at liberty between such convictions or adjudications;

3. If the offense was committed on or after July 1, 2006, § 18.2-91 with the intent to commit any felony offense listed in this section. An offense listed under this subdivision shall be deemed a sexually violent offense only if the person has been convicted or adjudicated delinquent of any two or more such offenses, provided that the person had been at liberty between such convictions or adjudications; or

4. Chapter 117 (18 U.S.C. § 2421 et seq.) of Title 18 of the United States Code or sex trafficking (as described in § 1591 of Title 18, U.S.C.).

F. "Any offense listed in subsection B," "criminal homicide" as defined in this section, "murder" as defined in this section, and "sexually violent offense" as defined in this section includes (i) any similar offense under the laws of any foreign country or any political subdivision thereof, the United States or any political subdivision thereof or (ii) any offense for which registration in a sex offender and crimes against minors registry is required under the laws of the jurisdiction where the offender was convicted.

G. Juveniles adjudicated delinquent shall not be required to register; however, where the offender is a juvenile over the age of 13 at the time of the offense who is tried as a juvenile and is adjudicated delinquent on or after July 1, 2005, of any offense for which registration is required, the court may, in its discretion and upon motion of the attorney for the Commonwealth, find that the circumstances of the offense require offender registration. In making its determination, the court shall consider all of the following factors that are relevant to the case: (i) the degree to which the delinquent act was committed with the use of force, threat or intimidation, (ii) the age and maturity of the complaining witness, (iii) the age and maturity of the offender, (iv) the difference in the ages of the complaining witness and the offender, (v) the nature of the relationship between the complaining witness and the offender, (vi) the offender's prior criminal history, and (vii) any other aggravating or mitigating factors relevant to the case. The attorney for the Commonwealth may file such a motion at any time during which the offender is within the jurisdiction of the court for the offense that is the basis for such motion. Prior to any hearing on such motion, the court shall appoint a qualified and competent attorney-at-law to represent the offender unless an attorney has been retained and appears on behalf of the offender or counsel has already been appointed.

H. Prior to entering judgment of conviction of an offense for which registration is required if the victim of the offense was a minor, physically helpless, or mentally incapacitated, when the indictment, warrant, or information does not allege that the victim of the offense was a minor, physically helpless, or mentally incapacitated, the court shall determine by a preponderance of the evidence whether the victim of the offense was a minor, physically helpless, or mentally incapacitated, as defined in § 18.2-67.10, and shall also determine the age of the victim at the time of the offense if it determines the victim to be a minor. When such a determination is required, the court shall advise the defendant of its determination and of the defendant's right to make a motion to withdraw a plea of guilty or nolo contendere pursuant to § 19.2-296. If the court grants the defendant's motion to withdraw his plea of guilty or of nolo contendere, his case shall be heard by another judge, unless the parties agree otherwise. Failure to make such determination or so advise the defendant does not otherwise invalidate the underlying conviction.

History.

2003, cc. 584, 732; 2004, cc. 414, 444; 2005, cc. 586, 603, 631; 2006, cc. 857, 875, 914, 931; 2007, cc. 463, 718, 759, 823; 2008, cc. 592, 747, 772, 877; 2010, c. 858; 2012, c. 243; 2013, cc. 750, 781; 2014, cc. 546, 649, 706; 2015, cc. 690, 691; 2016, c. 586.

§ 9.1-903. Registration procedures.

A. Every person convicted, including juveniles tried and convicted in the circuit courts pursuant to § 16.1-269.1, whether sentenced as an adult or juvenile, of an offense for which registration is required and every juvenile found delinquent of an offense for which registration is required under subsection G of § 9.1-902 shall be required upon conviction to register and reregister with the Department of State Police. The court shall order the person to provide to the local law-enforcement agency of the county or city where he physically resides all information required by the State Police for inclusion in the Registry. The court shall immediately remand the person to the custody of the local law-enforcement agency for the purpose of obtaining the person's fingerprints and photographs of a type and kind specified by the State Police for inclusion in the Registry. Upon conviction, the local law-enforcement agency shall forthwith forward to the State Police all the necessary registration information.

B. Every person required to register shall register in person within three days of his release from confinement in a state, local or juvenile correctional facility, in a state civil commitment program for sexually violent predators or, if a sentence of confinement is not imposed, within three days of suspension of the sentence or in the case of a juvenile of disposition. A person required to register shall register, and as part of the registration shall submit to be photographed, submit to have a sample of his blood, saliva, or tissue taken for DNA (deoxyribonucleic acid) analysis and submission to the DNA databank to determine identification characteristics specific to the person, provide electronic mail address information, any instant message, chat or other Internet communication name or identity information that the person uses or intends to use, submit to have his fingerprints and palm prints taken, provide information regarding his place of employment, and provide motor vehicle, watercraft and aircraft registration information for all motor vehicles, watercraft and aircraft owned by him. The local law-enforcement agency shall obtain from the person who presents himself for registration or reregistration one set of fingerprints, electronic mail address information, any instant message, chat or other Internet communication name or identity information that the person uses or intends to use, one set of palm prints, place of employment information, motor vehicle, watercraft and aircraft registration information for all motor vehicles, watercraft and aircraft owned by the registrant, proof of residency and a photograph of a type and kind specified by the State Police for inclusion in the Registry and advise the person of his duties regarding reregistration. The local law-enforcement agency shall obtain from the person who presents himself for registration a sample of his blood, saliva or tissue taken for DNA (deoxyribonucleic acid) analysis to determine identification characteristics specific to the person. If a sample has been previously taken from the person, as indicated by the Local Inmate Data System (LIDS), no additional sample shall be taken. The local law-enforcement agency shall forthwith forward to the State Police all necessary registration information.

C. To establish proof of residence in Virginia, a person who has a permanent physical address shall present one photo-identification form issued by a governmental agency of the Commonwealth which contains the person's complete name, gender, date of birth and complete physical address. The local law-enforcement agency shall forthwith forward to the State Police a copy of the identification presented by the person required to register.

D. Any person required to register shall also reregister in person with the local law-enforcement agency following any change of name or any change of residence, whether within or without the Commonwealth. The person shall register in person with the local law-enforcement agency within three days following his change of name. If his new residence is within the Commonwealth, the person shall register in person with the local law-enforcement agency where his new residence is located within three days following his change in residence. If the new residence is located outside of the Commonwealth, the person shall register in person with the local law-enforcement agency where he previously registered within 10 days prior to his change of residence. If a probation or parole officer becomes aware of a change of name or residence for any of his probationers or parolees required to register, the probation or parole officer shall notify the State Police forthwith of learning of the change. Whenever a person subject to registration changes residence to another state, the State Police shall notify the designated law-enforcement agency of that state.

E. Any person required to register shall reregister in person with the local law-enforcement agency where his residence is located within three days following any change of the place of employment, whether within or without the Commonwealth. If a probation or parole officer becomes aware of a change of the place of employment for any of his probationers or parolees required to register, the probation or parole officer shall notify the State Police forthwith upon learning of the change of the person's place of employment. Whenever a person subject to registration changes his place of employment to another state, the State Police shall notify the designated law-enforcement agency of that state.

F. Any person required to register shall reregister in person with the local law-enforcement agency where his residence is located within three days following any change of owned motor vehicle, watercraft and aircraft registration information, whether within or without the Commonwealth. If a probation or parole officer becomes aware of a change of owned motor vehicle, watercraft and aircraft registration information for any of his probationers or parolees required to register, the probation or parole officer shall notify the State Police forthwith upon learning of the change of the person's owned motor vehicle, watercraft and aircraft registration information. Whenever a person required to register changes his owned motor vehicle, watercraft and aircraft registration information to another state, the State Police shall notify the designated law-enforcement agency of that state.

G. Any person required to register shall reregister either in person or electronically with the local law-enforcement agency where his residence is located within 30 minutes following any change of the electronic mail address information, any instant message, chat or other Internet communication name or identity information that the person uses or intends to use, whether within or without the Commonwealth. If a probation or parole officer becomes aware of a change of the electronic mail address information, any instant message, chat or other Internet communication name or identity information for any of his probationers or parolees required to register, the probation or parole officer shall notify the State Police forthwith upon learning of the change.

H. The registration shall be maintained in the Registry and shall include the person's name, any former name if he has lawfully changed his name during the period for which he is required to register, all aliases that he has used or under which he may have been known, the date and locality of the conviction for which registration is required, his fingerprints and a photograph of a type and kind specified by the State Police, his date of birth, social security number, current physical and mailing address and a description of the offense or offenses for which he was convicted. The registration shall also include the locality of the conviction and a description of the offense or offenses for previous convictions for the offenses set forth in § 9.1-902.

I. The local law-enforcement agency shall forthwith forward to the State Police all necessary registration or reregistration information received by it. Upon receipt of registration or reregistration information the State Police shall forthwith notify the chief law-enforcement officer of the locality listed as the person's address on the registration and reregistration.

J. If a person required to register does not have a legal residence, such person shall designate a location that can be located with reasonable specificity where he resides or habitually locates himself. For the purposes of this section, "residence" shall include such a designated location. If the person wishes to change such designated location, he shall do it pursuant to the terms of this section.

History.

2003, c. 584; 2004, c. 834; 2005, c. 586; 2006, cc. 857, 914; 2007, cc. 718, 759, 823; 2008, c. 220; 2010, c. 843; 2014, c. 677.

§ 9.1-904. Reregistration.

A. Every person required to register, other than a person convicted of a sexually violent offense or murder, shall reregister with the State Police on an annual basis from the date of the initial registration. Every person convicted of a sexually violent offense or murder shall reregister with the State Police every 90 days from the date of initial registration. Reregistration means that the person has notified the State Police, confirmed his current physical and mailing address and electronic mail address information, any instant message, chat or other Internet communication name or identity information that he uses or intends to use, and provided such other information, including identifying information, which the State Police may require. Upon registration and as may be necessary thereafter, the State Police shall provide the person with an address verification form to be used for reregistration. The form shall contain in bold print a statement indicating that failure to comply with the registration required is punishable as provided in § 18.2-472.1. Upon registration and as may be necessary thereafter, the person shall likewise be required to execute a consent form consistent with applicable law that authorizes a business or organization that offers electronic communications or remote computer services to provide to the Department of State Police any information pertaining to that person necessary to determine the veracity of his electronic identity information in the registry.

B. Any person convicted of a violation of § 18.2-472.1, other than a person convicted of a sexually violent offense or murder, shall reregister with the State Police every 180 days from the date of such conviction. Any person convicted of a violation of § 18.2-472.1, in which such person was included on the Registry for a conviction of a sexually violent offense or murder, shall reregister with the State Police every 30 days from the date of conviction. Reregistration means the person has notified the State Police, confirmed his current physical and mailing address and electronic mail address information, any instant message, chat or other Internet communication name or identity information that he uses or intends to use, and provided such other information, including identifying information, which the State Police may require. Upon registration and as may be necessary thereafter, the State Police shall provide the person with an address verification form to be used for reregistration. The form shall state the registration requirements and contain in bold print a statement indicating that failure to comply with the registration requirements is punishable as provided in § 18.2-472.1.

C. Every person required to register pursuant to this chapter shall submit to be photographed by a local law-enforcement agency every two years commencing with the date of initial registration. Photographs shall be in color, be taken with the registrant facing the camera, and clearly show the registrant's face and shoulders only. No person other than the registrant may appear in the photograph submitted. The photograph shall indicate the registrant's full name, date of birth and the date the photograph was taken. The local law-enforcement agency shall forthwith forward the photograph and the registration form to the State Police. Where practical, the local law-enforcement agency may electronically transfer a digital photograph containing the required information to the Sex Offender and Crimes Against Minors Registry within the State Police.

History.
2003, c. 584; 2006, cc. 857, 914; 2007, cc. 759, 823.

§ 9.1-905. New residents and nonresident offenders; registration required.

A. All persons required to register shall register within three days of establishing a residence in the Commonwealth.

B. Nonresident offenders entering the Commonwealth for an extended visit, for employment, to carry on a vocation, or as a student attending school who are required to register in their state of residence or who would be required to register if a resident of the Commonwealth shall, within three days of entering the Commonwealth for an extended visit, accepting employment or enrolling in school in the Commonwealth, be required to register and reregister in person with the local law-enforcement agency.

C. To document employment or school attendance in Virginia a person shall present proof of enrollment as a student or suitable proof of temporary employment in the Commonwealth and one photo-identification form issued by a governmental agency of the person's state of residence which contains the person's complete name, gender, date of birth and complete address.

D. For purposes of this section:

"Employment" and *"carry on a vocation"* include employment that is full-time or part-time for a period of time exceeding 14 days or for an aggregate period of time exceeding 30 days during any calendar year, whether financially compensated, volunteered, or for the purpose of government or educational benefit.

"Extended visit" means a period of visitation for any purpose in the Commonwealth of 30 days or more.

"Student" means a person who is enrolled on a full-time or part-time basis, in any public or private educational institution, including any secondary school, trade or professional institution, or institution of higher education.

History.
2003, c. 584; 2005, c. 603; 2006, cc. 857, 914.

§ 9.1-906. Enrollment or employment at institution of higher learning; information required.

A. Persons required to register or reregister who are enrolled in or employed at institutions of higher learning shall, in addition to other registration requirements, indicate on their registration and reregistration form the name and location of the institution attended by or employing the registrant whether such institution is within or without the Commonwealth. In addition, persons required to register or reregister shall notify the local law-enforcement agency in person within three days of any change in their enrollment or employment status with an institution of higher learning. The local law-enforcement agency shall forthwith forward to the State Police all necessary registration or reregistration information received by it.

B. Upon receipt of a registration or reregistration indicating enrollment or employment with an institute of higher learning or notification of a change in status, the State Police shall notify the chief law-enforcement officer of the institution's law-enforcement agency or, if there is no institutional law-enforcement agency, the local law-enforcement agency serving that institution, of the registration, reregistration, or change in status. The law-enforcement agency receiving notification under this section shall make such information available upon request.

C. For purposes of this section:

"Employment" includes full- or part-time, temporary or permanent or contractual employment at an institution of higher learning either with or without compensation.

"Enrollment" includes both full- and part-time.

"Institution of higher learning" means any post-secondary school, trade or professional institution, or institution of higher education.

History.

2003, c. 584; 2006, cc. 857, 914.

§ 9.1-907. Procedures upon a failure to register or reregister.

A. Whenever it appears from the records of the State Police that a person has failed to comply with the duty to register or reregister, the State Police shall promptly investigate and, if there is probable cause to believe a violation has occurred, obtain a warrant or assist in obtaining an indictment charging a violation of § 18.2-472.1 in the jurisdiction in which the person last registered or reregistered or, if the person failed to comply with the duty to register, in the jurisdiction in which the person was last convicted of an offense for which registration or reregistration is required or if the person was convicted of an offense requiring registration outside the Commonwealth, in the jurisdiction in which the person resides. The State Police shall forward to the jurisdiction an affidavit signed by a custodian of the records that such person failed to comply with the duty to register or reregister. If such affidavit is admitted into evidence, it shall constitute prima facie evidence of the failure to comply with the duty to register or reregister in any trial or hearing for the violation of § 18.2-472.1, provided that in a trial or hearing other than a preliminary hearing, the requirements of subsection G of § 18.2-472.1 have been satisfied and the accused has not objected to the admission of the affidavit pursuant to subsection H of § 18.2-472.1. The State Police shall also promptly notify the local law-enforcement agency of the jurisdiction of the person's last known residence as shown in the records of the State Police.

B. Nothing in this section shall prohibit a law-enforcement officer employed by a sheriff's office or police department of a locality from enforcing the provisions of this chapter, including obtaining a warrant, or assisting in obtaining an indictment for a violation of § 18.2-472.1. The local law-enforcement agency shall notify the State Police forthwith of such actions taken pursuant to this chapter or under the authority granted pursuant to this section.

C. The State Police shall physically verify or cause to be physically verified the registration information within 30 days of the initial registration and semiannually each year thereafter and within 30 days of a change of address of those persons who are not under the control of the Department of Corrections or community supervision as defined by § 53.1-1, who are required to register pursuant to this chapter. Whenever it appears that a person has provided false registration information, the State Police shall promptly investigate and, if there is probable cause to believe that a violation has occurred, obtain a warrant or assist in obtaining an indictment charging a violation of § 18.2-472.1 in the jurisdiction in which the person last registered or reregistered. The State Police shall forward to the jurisdiction an affidavit signed by a custodian of the records that such person failed to comply with the provisions of this chapter. If such affidavit is admitted into evidence, it shall constitute prima facie evidence of the failure to comply with the provisions of this chapter in any trial or hearing for the violation of § 18.2-472.1, provided that in a trial or hearing other than a preliminary hearing, the requirements of subsection G of § 18.2-472.1 have been satisfied and the accused has not objected to the admission of the affidavit pursuant to subsection H of § 18.2-472.1. The State Police shall also promptly notify the local law-enforcement agency of the jurisdiction of the person's last known residence as shown in the records of the State Police.

D. The Department of Corrections or community supervision as defined by § 53.1-1 shall physically verify or cause to be physically verified by the State Police the registration information within 30 days of the original registration and semiannually each year thereafter and within 30 days of a change of address of all persons who are under the control of the Department of Corrections or community supervision, and those who are under supervision pursuant to § 37.2-919, who are required to register pursuant to this chapter. The Department of Corrections or community supervision, upon request, shall provide the State Police the verification information, in an electronic format approved by the State Police, regarding persons under their control who are required to register pursuant to the chapter. Whenever it appears that a person has provided false registration information, the Department of Corrections or community supervision shall promptly notify the State Police, who shall investigate and, if there is probable cause to believe that a violation has occurred, obtain a warrant or assist in obtaining an indictment charging a violation of § 18.2-472.1 in the jurisdiction in which the person last registered or reregistered. The State Police shall forward to the jurisdiction an affidavit signed by a custodian of the records that such person failed to comply with the provisions of this chapter. If such affidavit is admitted into evidence, it shall constitute prima facie evidence of the failure to comply with the provisions of this chapter in any trial or hearing for the violation of § 18.2-472.1, provided that in a trial or hearing other than a preliminary hearing, the requirements of subsection G of § 18.2-472.1 have been satisfied and the accused has not objected to the admission of the affidavit pursuant to subsection H of § 18.2-472.1. The State Police shall also promptly notify the local law-enforcement agency of the jurisdiction of the person's last known residence as shown in the records of the State Police.

History.

2003, c. 584; 2005, c. 603; 2006, cc. 857, 914; 2007, c. 718; 2009, Sp. Sess. I, cc. 1, 4; 2010, c. 858; 2015, cc. 81, 598.

§ 9.1-908. Duration of registration requirement.

Any person required to register or reregister shall be required to register until the duty to register and reregister is terminated by a court order as set forth in § 9.1-910, except that any person who has been convicted of (i) any sexually violent offense, (ii) murder or (iii) former § 18.2-67.2:1 shall have a continuing duty to reregister for life.

Any period of confinement in a federal, state or local correctional facility, hospital or any other institution or facility during the otherwise applicable period shall toll the registration period and the duty to reregister shall be extended. Persons confined in a federal, state, or local correctional facility shall not be required to reregister until released from custody. Persons civilly committed pursuant to Chapter 9 (§ 37.2-900 et seq.) of Title 37.2 shall not be required to reregister until released from custody. Persons confined in a federal, state, or local correctional facility or civilly committed pursuant to Chapter 9 (§ 37.2-900 et seq.) of Title 37.2 shall notify the Registry within three days following any change of name.

History.

2003, c. 584; 2005, c. 631; 2006, cc. 857, 914; 2007, c. 718; 2008, c. 877; 2010, c. 858; 2014, c. 677.

§ 9.1-909. Relief from registration or reregistration.

A. Upon expiration of three years from the date upon which the duty to register as a sexually violent offender or murderer is imposed, the person required to register may petition the court in which he was convicted or, if the conviction occurred outside of the Commonwealth, the circuit court in the jurisdiction where he currently resides, for relief from the requirement to reregister every 90 days. After five years from the date of his last conviction for a violation of § 18.2-472.1, a sexually violent offender or murderer may petition for relief from the requirement to reregister monthly. A person who is required to register may similarly petition the circuit court for relief from the requirement to reregister every 180 days after five years from the date of his last conviction for a violation of § 18.2-472.1. The court shall hold a hearing on the petition, on notice to the attorney for the Commonwealth, to determine whether the person suffers from a mental abnormality or a personality disorder that makes the person a menace to the health and safety of others or significantly impairs his ability to control his sexual behavior. Prior to the hearing the court shall order a comprehensive assessment of the applicant by a panel of three certified sex offender treatment providers as defined in § 54.1-3600. A report of the assessment shall be filed with the court prior to the hearing. The costs of the assessment shall be taxed as costs of the proceeding.

If, after consideration of the report and such other evidence as may be presented at the hearing, the court finds by clear and convincing evidence that the person does not suffer from a mental abnormality or a personality disorder that makes the person a menace to the health and safety of others or significantly impairs his ability to control his sexual behavior, the petition shall be granted and the duty to reregister more frequently than once a year shall be terminated. The court shall promptly notify the State Police upon entry of an order granting the petition. The person shall, however, be under a continuing duty to register annually for life. If the petition is denied, the duty to reregister with the same frequency as before shall continue. An appeal from the denial of a petition shall lie to the Supreme Court.

A petition for relief pursuant to this subsection may not be filed within three years from the date on which any previous petition for such relief was denied.

B. The duly appointed guardian of a person convicted of an offense requiring registration or reregistration as either a sex offender, sexually violent offender or murderer, who due to a physical condition is incapable of (i) reoffending and (ii) reregistering, may petition the court in which the person was convicted for relief from the requirement to reregister. The court shall hold a hearing on the petition, on notice to the attorney for the Commonwealth, to determine whether the person suffers from a physical condition that makes the person (i) no longer a menace to the health and safety of others and (ii) incapable of reregistering. Prior to the hearing the court shall order a comprehensive assessment of the applicant by at least two licensed physicians other than the person's primary care physician. A report of the assessment shall be filed with the court prior to the hearing. The costs of the assessment shall be taxed as costs of the proceeding.

If, after consideration of the report and such other evidence as may be presented at the hearing, the court finds by clear and convincing evidence that due to his physical condition the person (i) no longer poses a menace to the health and safety of others and (ii) is incapable of reregistering, the petition shall be granted and the duty to reregister shall be terminated. However, for a person whose duty to reregister was terminated under this subsection, the Department of State Police shall, annually for sex offenders and quarterly for persons convicted of sexually violent offenses and murder, verify and report to the attorney for the Commonwealth in the jurisdiction in which the person resides that the person continues to suffer from the physical condition that resulted in such termination.

The court shall promptly notify the State Police upon entry of an order granting the petition to terminate the duty to reregister.

If the petition is denied, the duty to reregister shall continue. An appeal from the denial of a petition shall be to the Virginia Supreme Court.

A petition for relief pursuant to this subsection may not be filed within three years from the date on which any previous petition for such relief was denied.

If, at any time, the person's physical condition changes so that he is capable of reoffending or reregistering, the attorney for the Commonwealth shall file a petition with the circuit court in the jurisdiction where the person resides and the court shall hold a hearing on the petition, with notice to the person and his guardian, to determine whether the person still suffers from a physical condition that makes the person (i) no longer a menace to the health and safety of others and (ii) incapable of reregistering. If the petition is granted, the duty to reregister shall commence from the date of the court's order. An appeal from the denial or granting of a petition shall be to the Virginia Supreme Court. Prior to the hearing the court shall order a comprehensive assessment of the applicant by at least two licensed physicians other than the person's primary care physician. A report of the assessment shall be filed with the court prior to the hearing. The costs of the assessment shall be taxed as costs of the proceeding.

History.
2003, c. 584; 2006, cc. 857, 914.

§ 9.1-910. Removal of name and information from Registry.

A. Any person required to register, other than a person who has been convicted of any (i) sexually violent offense, (ii) two or more offenses for which registration is required, (iii) a violation of former § 18.2-67.2:1, or (iv) murder, may petition the circuit court in which he was convicted or the circuit court in the jurisdiction where he then resides for removal of his name and all identifying information from the Registry. A petition may not be filed earlier than 15 years, or 25 years for violations of § 18.2-64.1, subsection C of § 18.2-374.1:1, or subsection C, D, or E of § 18.2-374.3, after the date of initial registration nor earlier than 15 years, or 25 years for violations of § 18.2-64.1, subsection C of § 18.2-374.1:1, or subsection C, D, or E of § 18.2-374.3, from the date of his last conviction for (a) a violation of § 18.2-472.1 or (b) any felony. A petition may not be filed until all court ordered treatment, counseling, and restitution has been completed. The court shall obtain a copy of the petitioner's complete criminal history and registration and reregistration history from the Registry and then hold a hearing on the petition at which the applicant and any interested persons may present witnesses and other evidence. The Commonwealth shall be made a party to any action under this section. If, after such hearing, the court is satisfied that such person no longer poses a risk to public safety, the court shall grant the petition. In the event the petition is not granted, the person shall wait at least 24 months from the date of the denial to file a new petition for removal from the Registry.

B. The State Police shall remove from the Registry the name of any person and all identifying information upon receipt of an order granting a petition pursuant to subsection A.

History.
2003, c. 584; 2005, c. 631; 2006, cc. 857, 914; 2007, c. 718; 2008, c. 877.

§ 9.1-911. Registry maintenance.

The Registry shall include conviction data received from the courts, including the disposition records for juveniles tried and convicted in the circuit courts pursuant to § 16.1-269.1, on convictions for offenses for which registration is required and registrations and reregistrations received from persons required to do so. The Registry shall also include a separate indication that a person has been convicted of a sexually violent offense. The State Police shall forthwith transmit the appropriate information as required by the Federal Bureau of Investigation for inclusion in the National Sex Offender Registry.

History.
2003, c. 584.

§ 9.1-912. Registry access and dissemination; fees.

A. Except as provided in § 9.1-913 and subsection B or C of this section, Registry information shall be disseminated upon request made directly to the State Police or to the State Police through a local law-enforcement agency. Such information may be disclosed to any person requesting information on a specific individual in accordance with subsection B. The State Police shall make Registry information available, upon request, to criminal justice agencies including local law-enforcement agencies through the Virginia Criminal Information Network (VCIN).

Registry information provided under this section shall be used for the purposes of the administration of criminal justice, for the screening of current or prospective employees or volunteers or otherwise for the protection of the public in general and children in particular. The Superintendent of State Police may by regulation establish a fee not to exceed $15 for responding to requests for information from the Registry. Any fees collected shall be deposited in a special account to be used to offset the costs of administering the Registry.

B. Information regarding a specific person shall be disseminated upon receipt of an official request form that may be submitted directly to the State Police or to the State Police through a local law-enforcement agency. The official request form shall include a statement of the reason for the request; the name and address of the person requesting the information; the name, address and, if known, the social security number of the person about whom information is sought; and such other information as the State Police may require to ensure reliable identification.

C. Registry information regarding all registered offender's electronic mail address information, any instant message, chat or other Internet communication name or identity information may be electronically transmitted by the Department of State Police to a business or organization that offers electronic communication or remote computing services for the purpose of prescreening users or for comparison with information held by the requesting business or organization. In order to obtain the information from the Department of State Police, the requesting business or organization that offers electronic communication or remote computing services shall agree to notify the Department of State Police forthwith when a comparison indicates that any such registered sex offender's electronic mail address information, any instant message, chat or other Internet communication name or identity information is being used on their system. The requesting business or organization shall also agree that the information will not be further disseminated.

History.

2003, c. 584; 2007, cc. 759, 823.

§ 9.1-913. Public dissemination by means of the Internet.

The State Police shall develop and maintain a system for making certain Registry information on persons convicted of an offense for which registration is required publicly available by means of the Internet. The information to be made available shall include the offender's name; all aliases that he has used or under which he may have been known; the date and locality of the conviction and a brief description of the offense; his age, current address, and photograph; his current work address; the name of any institution of higher education at which he is currently enrolled; and such other information as the State Police may from time to time determine is necessary to preserve public safety, including but not limited to the fact that an individual is wanted for failing to register or reregister. The system shall be secure and not capable of being altered except by the State Police. The system shall be updated each business day with newly received registrations and reregistrations. The State Police shall remove all information that it knows to be inaccurate from the Internet system.

History.

2003, c. 584; 2005, c. 603; 2006, cc. 857, 914; 2016, c. 335.

§ 9.1-914. Automatic notification of registration to certain entities; electronic notification to requesting persons.

Any school, day-care service and child-minding service, state-regulated or state-licensed child day center, child day program, children's residential facility, family day home, assisted living facility or foster home as defined in § 63.2-100, nursing home or certified nursing facility as defined in § 32.1-123, association of a common interest community as defined in § 55-528, and institution of higher education may request from the State Police and, upon compliance with the requirements therefor established by the State Police, shall be eligible to receive from the State Police electronic notice of the registration or reregistration of any sex offender and if such entities do not have the capability of receiving such electronic notice, the entity may register with the State Police to receive written notification of sex offender registration or reregistration. Within three business days of receipt by the State Police of registration or reregistration, the State Police shall electronically or in writing notify an entity listed above that has requested such notification, has complied with the requirements established by the State Police and is located in the same or a contiguous zip code area as the address of the offender as shown on the registration.

The Virginia Council for Private Education shall annually provide the State Police, in an electronic format approved by the State Police, with the location of every private school in the Commonwealth that is accredited through one of the approved accrediting agencies of the Council, and an electronic mail address for each school if available, for purposes of receiving notice under this section.

Any person may request from the State Police and, upon compliance with the requirements therefor established by the State Police, shall be eligible to receive from the State Police electronic notice of the registration or reregistration of any sex offender. Within three business days of receipt by the State Police of registration or reregistration, the State Police shall electronically notify a person who has requested such notification, has complied with the requirements established by the State Police and is located in the same or a contiguous zip code area as the address of the offender as shown on the registration.

The State Police shall establish reasonable guidelines governing the automatic dissemination of Registry information, which may include the payment of a fee, whether a one-time fee or a regular assessment, to maintain the electronic access. The fee, if any, shall defray the costs of establishing and maintaining the electronic notification system and notice by mail.

For the purposes of this section:

"Child-minding service" means provision of temporary custodial care or supervisory services for the minor child of another;

"Day-care service" means provision of supplementary care and protection during a part of the day for the minor child of another; and

"School" means any public, religious or private educational institution, including any preschool, elementary school, secondary school, post-secondary school, trade or professional institution, or institution of higher education.

History.
2003, c. 584; 2005, c. 928; 2006, cc. 857, 914; 2007, cc. 119, 164; 2016, c. 424.

§ 9.1-915. Regulations.

The Superintendent of State Police shall promulgate regulations and develop forms to implement and enforce this chapter; including the operation and maintenance of the Registry and the removal of records on persons who are deceased, whose convictions have been reversed or who have been pardoned, and those for whom an order of removal or relief from frequent registration has been entered. Such regulations and forms shall not be subject to the provisions of Article 2 (§ 2.2-4006 et seq.) of the Administrative Process Act.

History.
2003, c. 584.

§ 9.1-916. Requests for Registry data by Virginia Criminal Sentencing Commission; confidentiality.

Upon request of the Virginia Criminal Sentencing Commission, the Department of State Police shall provide the Commission with Registry data in an electronic format. The Commission may use the data for research, evaluative or statistical purposes only and shall ensure the confidentiality and security of the data.

History.
2003, c. 391.

§ 9.1-917. Limitation on liability.

No liability shall be imposed upon any law-enforcement official who disseminates information or fails to disseminate information in good faith compliance with the requirements of this chapter, but this provision shall not be construed to grant immunity for gross negligence or willful misconduct.

History.
2003, c. 584.

§ 9.1-918. Misuse of registry or supplement information; penalty.

Use of registry information or information from the Supplement to the Registry established pursuant to § 9.1-923 for purposes not authorized by this chapter is prohibited, the unlawful use of the information contained in or derived from the Registry or Supplement for purposes of intimidating or harassing another is prohibited, and a willful violation of this chapter is a Class 1 misdemeanor. For purposes of this section, absent other aggravating circumstances, the mere republication or reasonable distribution of material contained on or derived from the publicly available Internet sex offender database shall not be deemed intimidation or harassment.

History.
2003, c. 584; 2006, cc. 857, 914; 2015, cc. 594, 603.

§ 9.1-919. Notice of penalty on forms and documents.

The Virginia Criminal Information Network and any form or document used by the Department of State Police to disseminate information from the Registry shall provide notice that any unauthorized use of the information with the intent to harass or intimidate another is a crime punishable as a Class 1 misdemeanor.

History.
2003, c. 391.

§ 9.1-920. Liberal construction.

This chapter, being necessary for the welfare of the Commonwealth and its inhabitants, shall be liberally construed to effect the purposes hereof.

History.
2003, c. 584; 2015, c. 709.

§ 9.1-921. Exemption of information systems from provisions related to the Virginia Information Technologies Agency.

The provisions of Chapter 20.1 (§ 2.2-2005 et seq.) of Title 2.2 shall not apply to the Sex Offender and Crimes Against Minors Registry pursuant to Chapter 9 (§ 9.1-900 et seq.) of Title 9.1, operated by the Department of State Police or to information technology as defined in § 2.2-2006 operated by the Department of Juvenile Justice, Department of Corrections or the Virginia Compensation Board that interact, furnish, update, contain or exchange information with the Sex Offender and Crimes Against Minors Registry.

History.
2006, cc. 857, 914.

§ 9.1-922. Use of Registry data by Statewide Automated Victim Notification (SAVIN) system; confidentiality.

Upon request of the Compensation Board, the Department of State Police shall provide the Statewide Automated Victim Notification (SAVIN) system with Registry data in an electronic format. The Board or its contractor may use the data for verification of registrant status and notification of victims and law enforcement regarding changes in status of persons on the Registry and shall ensure the confidentiality and security of the data.

History.
2008, cc. 76, 338.

§ 9.1-923. Supplement to the Sex Offender and Crimes Against Minors Registry established.

A. The Superintendent of State Police shall establish a Supplement to the Registry of information composed of persons who were convicted of an offense listed in subsection B on or after July 1, 1980, and before July 1, 1994, but whose names are not on the Registry. Access to the Supplement to the Registry shall be made available to the public on the website of the Department of State Police and shall contain the following information for each person: name, year of birth, the date of the conviction, the jurisdiction in which the conviction occurred, the person's age on the date of the conviction, the offense of which he was convicted, and the Code of Virginia section of the conviction.

B. Information on the following offenses where the conviction occurred on or after July 1, 1980, and before July 1, 1994, shall be listed in the Supplement: clause (i) of § 18.2-48 if the victim was a minor; clauses (ii) and (iii) of § 18.2-48; § 18.2-61; § 18.2-63 if the victim was under 13 years of age; subsection A of § 18.2-63 if the offender was more than five years older than the victim; §§ 18.2-67.1, 18.2-67.2, and 18.2-67.3; § 18.2-67.4 if the victim was a minor; subsections A and B of § 18.2-67.5; subsection C of § 18.2-67.5 if the victim was a minor; § 18.2-361 if the victim was a minor; and §§ 18.2-370, 18.2-370.1, and 18.2-374.1.

C. Persons whose names and conviction information appear on the Supplement are not subject to the registration requirements of this chapter and are not considered persons for whom registration is required unless they are required to register pursuant to other provisions of this chapter.

D. A person whose name and conviction information appear on the Supplement may, regardless of the date of conviction, petition the circuit court in which he was convicted or the circuit court where he then resides for removal of his name and conviction information from the Supplement if the offense he was convicted of would qualify for removal from the Registry under § 9.1-910. A petition may not be filed until all court ordered treatment, counseling, and restitution has been completed. The court shall obtain a copy of the petitioner's complete criminal history and then hold a hearing on the petition at which the applicant and any interested persons may present witnesses and other evidence. The Commonwealth shall be made a party to any action under this subsection. If after such a hearing, the court is satisfied that such person does not pose a risk to public safety, the court shall grant the petition. In the event the petition is not granted, the person shall wait at least 24 months from the date of denial to file a new petition for removal from the Supplement. The State Police shall remove from the Supplement the name and conviction information upon receipt of an order granting a petition pursuant to this subsection.

E. The Superintendent of State Police shall complete the Supplement to the Registry prior to January 1, 2016.

History.
2015, cc. 594, 603.

CHAPTER 10.
RETIRED LAW ENFORCEMENT IDENTIFICATION.

Section

§ 9.1-1000. Retired law-enforcement officers; photo identification cards.

Upon the retirement of a law-enforcement officer, as defined in § 9.1-101, the employing department or agency shall, upon request of the retiree, issue the individual a photo identification card indicating that such individual is a retired law-enforcement officer of that department or agency. Upon request, such a card shall also be issued to any law-enforcement officer who retired before July 1, 2004.

History.
2004, c. 419.

CHAPTER 13.

DOMESTIC AND SEXUAL ASSAULT POLICIES.

§ 9.1-1300. Domestic violence policies and procedures for law-enforcement agencies in the Commonwealth.

The Virginia Department of State Police and the police and sheriff's departments of every political subdivision in the Commonwealth shall establish an arrest policy and procedures for domestic violence and family abuse cases. Any local police or sheriff's department is authorized to adopt an arrest policy that prescribes additional requirements under this section. Any policies and procedures established under this section shall at a minimum provide guidance to law-enforcement officers on the following:

1. The department's arrest policy;
2. The standards for determining who is the predominant physical aggressor pursuant to § 19.2-81.3;
3. The standards for completion of a required incident report to be filed with the department including the existence of any special circumstances which would dictate a course of action other than arrest;
4. The department's policy on providing transportation to an allegedly abused person;
5. The legal and community resources available to allegedly abused persons in the department's jurisdiction;
6. The department's policy on domestic violence incidents involving law-enforcement officers; and
7. The department's policy on the handling of cases involving repeat offenders of family abuse or domestic violence.

History.
2008, cc. 600, 771.

§ 9.1-1301. Sexual assault policies for law-enforcement agencies in the Commonwealth; memoranda of understanding with institutions of higher education.

A. The Virginia Department of State Police and the police and sheriff's departments of every political subdivision in the Commonwealth and every campus police department shall establish written policies and procedures regarding a law-enforcement officer's response to an alleged criminal sexual assault in violation of Article 7 (§ 18.2-61 et seq.) of Chapter 4 of Title 18.2. Such policies shall, at a minimum, provide guidance as to the department's policy on (i) training; (ii) compliance with §§ 19.2-9.1 and 19.2-165.1; (iii) transportation of alleged sexual assault victims; and (iv) the provision of information on legal and community resources available to alleged victims of sexual assault.

B. The primary law-enforcement agency of each locality that contains a public institution of higher education or nonprofit private institution of higher education shall cooperate in establishing a written memorandum of understanding with any such institution of higher education, if requested, to address the prevention of and response to criminal sexual assault as set forth in Article 7 (§ 18.2-61 et seq.) of Chapter 4 of Title 18.2.

History.
2008, cc. 600, 771; 2016, c. 481.

TITLE 10.1.

CONSERVATION.

SUBTITLE II.

ACTIVITIES ADMINISTERED BY OTHER ENTITIES.

CHAPTER 11.

FOREST RESOURCES AND THE DEPARTMENT OF FORESTRY.

Article 6.

Forest Wardens and Fires.

ARTICLE 6.

FOREST WARDENS AND FIRES.

§ 10.1-1139. Who may be summoned to aid forest warden.

Any forest warden to whom written instructions have been issued by the State Forester authorizing him to employ persons to assist in suppressing forest fires, shall have the authority to summon as many able-bodied persons between eighteen and fifty years of age as may, in his discretion, be reasonably necessary to assist in extinguishing any forest fire in any county or city of the Commonwealth which is organized for forest fire control under the direction of the State Forester. Any person summoned by a forest warden to fight a forest fire shall be paid at the rate of pay provided in the Department of Forestry wage scale for fire fighting in effect in the county or city, or part thereof, in which the fire is fought. Wardens shall not summon for such service any person while engaged in maintaining the rights-of-way of railroads for the safe passage of trains, nor any station agent, operator or other person while engaged in duties necessary for the safe operation of trains.

Any person summoned who fails or refuses to assist in fighting the fire, unless the failure is due to physical inability or other valid reason, shall be guilty of a Class 4 misdemeanor.

History.

Code 1950, § 10-59; 1964, c. 79; 1973, c. 401; 1986, c. 188; 1988, c. 891.

§ 10.1-1142. Regulating the burning of woods, brush, etc.; penalties.

A. It shall be unlawful for any owner or lessee of land to set fire to, or to procure another to set fire to, any woods, brush, logs, leaves, grass, debris, or other inflammable material upon such land unless he previously has taken all reasonable care and precaution, by having cut and piled the same or carefully cleared around the same, to prevent the spread of such fire to lands other than those owned or leased by him. It shall also be unlawful for any employee of any such owner or lessee of land to set fire to or to procure another to set fire to any woods, brush, logs, leaves, grass, debris, or other inflammable material, upon such land unless he has taken similar precautions to prevent the spread of such fire to any other land.

B. Except as provided in subsection C, during the period February 15 through April 30 of each year, even though the precautions required by the foregoing subsection have been taken, it shall be unlawful, in any county or city or portion thereof organized for forest fire control under the direction of the State Forester, for any person to set fire to, or to procure another to set fire to, any brush, leaves, grass, debris or field containing dry grass or other inflammable material capable of spreading fire, located in or within 300 feet of any woodland, brushland, or field containing dry grass or other inflammable material, except between the hours of 4:00 p.m. and 12:00 midnight.

The provisions of this subsection shall not apply to any fires which may be set on federal lands.

C. Subsection B shall not apply to any fire set during the period beginning February 15 through April 30 of each year, if:

1. The fire is set for "prescribed burning" that is conducted in accordance with a "prescription" and managed by a "certified prescribed burn manager" as those terms are defined in § 10.1-1150.1;

2. The burn is conducted in accordance with § 10.1-1150.4;

3. The State Forester has, prior to February 1, approved the prescription for the burn; and

4. The burn is being conducted for one of the following purposes: (i) control of exotic and invasive plant species that cannot be accomplished at other times of the year; (ii) wildlife habitat establishment and maintenance that cannot be accomplished at other times of the year; or (iii) management necessary for natural heritage resources.

The State Forester may on the day of any burn planned to be conducted pursuant to this subsection revoke his approval of the prescription for the burn if hazardous fire conditions exist. The State Forester may revoke the certification of any certified prescribed burn manager who violates any provision of this subsection.

D. Any person who builds a fire in the open air, or uses a fire built by another in the open air, within 150 feet of any woodland, brushland or field containing dry grass or other inflammable material, shall totally extinguish the fire before leaving the area and shall not leave the fire unattended.

E. Any person violating any provisions of this section shall be guilty of a Class 3 misdemeanor for each separate offense. If any forest fire originates as a result of the violation by any person of any provision of this section, such person shall, in addition to the above penalty, be liable to the Commonwealth for the full amount of all expenses incurred by the Commonwealth in suppressing such fire. Such amounts shall be recoverable by action brought by the State Forester in the name of the Commonwealth on behalf of the Commonwealth and credited to the Forestry Operations Fund.

History.

Code 1950, §§ 10-62, 10-63; 1964, c. 79; 1986, c. 188; 1988, c. 891; 1996, cc. 74, 1008; 2001, c. 319; 2006, c. 228.

§ 10.1-1143. Throwing inflammable objects from vehicle on highway while in or near certain lands.

It shall be unlawful for any person to throw, toss or drop from a vehicle moving or standing on a highway any lighted smoking material, lighted match, lighted material of any nature, or any bomb or device liable to set fire to inflammable material on the ground while in or near any forestland, brushland or field containing inflammable vegetation or trash.

Any person violating the provisions of this section shall be guilty of a Class 2 misdemeanor for each separate offense.

History.

1954, c. 35, § 10-64.1; 1986, c. 188; 1988, c. 891.

CHAPTER 14.
VIRGINIA WASTE MANAGEMENT ACT.

Article 7.

Transportation of Hazardous Materials.

Article 7.1.

Transportation of Solid and Medical Wastes on State Waters.

Article 7.2.

Transportation of Municipal Solid and Medical Waste by Truck.

Article 8.

Penalties, Enforcement and Judicial Review.

ARTICLE 7.
TRANSPORTATION OF HAZARDOUS MATERIALS.

§ 10.1-1450. Waste Management Board to promulgate regulations regarding hazardous materials.

The Board shall promulgate regulations designating the manner and method by which hazardous materials shall be loaded, unloaded, packed, identified, marked, placarded, stored and transported. Such regulations shall be no more restrictive than any applicable federal laws or regulations.

History.
1986, c. 492, § 10-305; 1988, c. 891; 1992, c. 208; 1997, c. 260.

§ 10.1-1451. Enforcement of article and regulations.

The Department of State Police and all other law-enforcement officers of the Commonwealth who have satisfactorily completed the course in Hazardous Materials Compliance and Enforcement as prescribed by the U.S. Department of Transportation, Research and Special Programs Administration, Office of Hazardous Materials Transportation, in federal safety regulations and safety inspection procedures pertaining to the transportation of hazardous materials, shall enforce the provisions of this article, and any rule or regulation promulgated hereunder. Those law-enforcement officers certified to enforce the provisions of this article and any regulation promulgated hereunder, shall annually receive in-service training in current federal safety regulations and safety inspection procedures pertaining to the transportation of hazardous materials.

History.
1986, c. 492, § 10-306; 1988, cc. 14, 891.

§ 10.1-1452. Article not to preclude exercise of certain regulatory powers.

The provisions of this article shall not preclude the exercise of the statutory and regulatory powers of any agency, department or political subdivision of the Commonwealth having statutory authority to regulate hazardous materials on specified highways or portions thereof.

History.
1986, c. 492, § 10-307; 1988, c. 891.

§ 10.1-1453. Exceptions.

This article shall not apply to regular military or naval forces of the United States, the duly authorized militia of any state or territory thereof, police or fire departments, or sheriff's offices and regional jails of this Commonwealth, provided the same are acting within their official capacity and in the performance of their duties, or to the transportation of hazardous radioactive materials in accordance with § 44-146.30.

History.
1986, c. 492, § 10-308; 1988, c. 891; 1995, c. 112.

§ 10.1-1454. Transportation under United States regulations.

Any person transporting hazardous materials in accordance with regulations promulgated under the laws of the United States, shall be deemed to have complied with the provisions of this article, except when such transportation is excluded from regulation under the laws or regulations of the United States.

History.
1986, c. 492, § 10-309; 1988, c. 891.

ARTICLE 7.1.

TRANSPORTATION OF SOLID AND MEDICAL WASTES ON STATE WATERS.

§ 10.1-1454.1. Regulation of wastes transported by water.

A. The Board shall develop regulations governing the commercial transport, loading and off-loading of nonhazardous solid waste (except scrap metal, dredged material, recyclable construction demolition debris being transported directly to a processing facility for recycling or reuse, and source-separated recyclables), municipal and industrial sludge, and regulated medical waste by ship, barge or other vessel upon the navigable waters of the Commonwealth as are necessary to protect the health, safety, and welfare of the citizens of the Commonwealth and to protect the Commonwealth's environment and natural resources from pollution, impairment or destruction. Included in the regulations shall be provisions governing (i) the issuance of permits by rule to facilities receiving nonhazardous solid waste (except scrap metal, dredged material, recyclable construction demolition debris being transported directly to a processing facility for recycling or reuse, and source-separated recyclables), municipal and industrial sludge, and regulated medical waste from a ship, barge or other vessel transporting such wastes upon the navigable waters of the Commonwealth and (ii) to the extent allowable under federal law and regulation, the commercial transport of nonhazardous solid wastes (except scrap metal, dredged material, recyclable construction demolition debris being transported directly to a processing facility for recycling or reuse, and source-separated recyclables), municipal and industrial sludge, and regulated medical waste upon the navigable waters of the Commonwealth and the loading and off-loading of ships, barges and other vessels transporting such waste.

B. 1. Included in the regulations shall be requirements, to the extent allowable under federal law, that: (a) containers holding wastes be watertight and be designed, constructed, secured and maintained so as to prevent the escape of wastes, liquids and odors and to prevent the loss or spillage of wastes in the event of an accident; (b) containers be tested at least two times a year and be accompanied by a certification from the container owner that such testing has shown that the containers are watertight; (c) each container be listed on a manifest designed to assure that the waste being transported in each container is suitable for the destination facility; and (d) containers be secured to the barges to prevent accidents during transportation, loading and unloading.

2. For the purposes of this section and the regulations promulgated hereunder, a container shall satisfy clauses (a) and (b) of subdivision B 1, if it meets the following requirements:

a. Each container shall be certified for special service by a Delegated Approval Authority approved by the U.S. Coast Guard in accordance with 49 CFR Parts 450 through 453 as having met the requirements for the approval of prototype containers described in §§ 1.5 and 1.17.2 of the Rules for Certification of Cargo Containers, 1998, American Bureau of Shipping, including a special container prototype test as follows: a minimum internal head of three inches of water shall be applied to all sides, seams, bottom and top of the container for at least 15 minutes of each side, seam, bottom and top, during which the container shall remain free from the escape of water.

b. Each container shall be certified by the Delegated Approval Authority as having passed the following test when the container is placed in service and at least once every six months thereafter while it remains in service:

(1) Each container shall have a minimum internal head of 24 inches of water applied to the container in an upright position for at least 15 minutes during which the container shall remain free from the escape of water. All wastewater and contaminated water resulting from this test procedure shall be disposed of in compliance with the applicable regulations of the State Water Control Board.

(2) Each container shall be visually inspected for damage on all sides, plus the top and bottom, and shall have no visible holes, gaps, or structural damage affecting its integrity or performance.

c. Following each unloading of solid waste from a container, each container shall be visually inspected, as practical, at the solid waste management facility immediately upon unloading for damage on all sides, plus top and bottom, and shall have no visible holes, gaps, or structural damage affecting its integrity or performance.

3. It shall be a violation of this chapter if during transportation, holding, or storage operations, or in the event of an accident, there is an: (i) entry of liquids into a container; (ii) escape, loss, or spillage of wastes or liquids from a container; or (iii) escape of odors from a container.

C. A facility utilized to receive nonhazardous solid waste (except scrap metal, dredged material, recyclable construction demolition debris being transported directly to a processing facility for recycling or reuse, and source-separated recyclables), municipal and industrial sludge, or regulated medical waste from a ship, barge or other vessel regulated pursuant to subsection A, arriving at the facility upon the navigable waters of the Commonwealth, is a solid waste management facility and is subject to the requirements of this chapter. On and after the effective date of the regulations promulgated under subsection A, no new or existing facilities shall receive any wastes regulated under subsection A from a ship, barge or other vessel without a permit issued in accordance with the Board's regulations.

D. 1. The Board shall, by regulation, establish a fee schedule, payable by the owner or operator of any ship, barge or other vessel carrying, loading or off-loading waste regulated under this article on the navigable waters of the Commonwealth, for the purpose of funding the administrative and enforcement costs of this article associated with such operations including, but not limited to, the inspection and monitoring of such ships, barges or other vessels to ensure compliance with this article, and for funding activities authorized by this section to abate pollution caused by barging of waste, to improve water quality, or for other waste-related purposes.

2. The owner or operator of a facility permitted to receive wastes regulated under this article from a ship, barge or other vessel shall be assessed a permit fee in accordance with the criteria set forth in § 10.1-1402.1. However, such fees shall also include an additional amount to cover the Department's costs for facility inspections that it shall conduct on at least a quarterly basis.

3. The fees collected pursuant to this article shall be deposited into a separate account within the Virginia Waste Management Board Permit Program Fund (§ 10.1-1402.2) and shall be treated as are other moneys in that fund except that they shall only be used for the purposes of this article, and for funding purposes authorized by this article to abate pollution caused by barging of waste, to improve water quality, or for other waste-related purposes.

E. The Board shall promulgate regulations requiring owners and operators of ships, barges and other vessels transporting wastes regulated under this article to demonstrate financial responsibility sufficient to comply with the requirements of this article as a condition of operation. Regulations governing the amount of any financial responsibility required shall take into consideration: (i) the risk of potential damage or injury to state waters and the impairment of beneficial uses that may result from spillage or leakage from the ship, barge or vessel; (ii) the potential costs of containment and cleanup; and (iii) the nature and degree of injury or interference with general health, welfare and property that may result.

F. The owner or operator of a ship, barge or other vessel from which there is spillage or loss to state waters of wastes subject to regulations under this article shall immediately report such spillage or loss in accordance with the regulations of the Board and shall immediately take all such actions as may be necessary to contain and remove such wastes from state waters.

G. No person shall transport wastes regulated under this article on the navigable waters of the Commonwealth by ship, barge or other vessel unless such ship, barge or vessel and the containers carried thereon are designed, constructed, loaded, operated and maintained so as to prevent the escape of liquids, waste and odors and to prevent the loss or spillage of waste in the event of an accident. A violation of this subsection shall be a Class 1 misdemeanor. For the purposes of this subsection, the term "odors" means any emissions that cause an odor objectionable to individuals of ordinary sensibility.

H. The Director may grant variances for the commercial transport, loading, and off-loading of solid waste on waters of the Commonwealth from the requirements of this section provided: (i) travel on state waters is minimized; (ii) the solid waste is easily identifiable, is not hazardous, and is containerized so as to prevent the escape of liquids, waste, and odors; (iii) the containers are secured to the vessel to prevent spillage; (iv) the amount of solid waste transported does not exceed 300 tons annually; and (v) the activity will not occur when weather conditions pose a risk of the vessel losing its load.

History.

1998, cc. 705, 717; 1999, c. 608; 2003, c. 830; 2005, cc. 130, 232; 2006, c. 477.

§ **10.1-1454.2:** Repealed by Acts 2003, c. 830.

ARTICLE 7.2.

TRANSPORTATION OF MUNICIPAL SOLID AND MEDICAL WASTE BY TRUCK.

§ **10.1-1454.3:** Repealed by Acts 2007, c. 23, cl. 2.

ARTICLE 8.

PENALTIES, ENFORCEMENT AND JUDICIAL REVIEW.

§ 10.1-1455. Penalties and enforcement.

A. Any person who violates any provision of this chapter, any condition of a permit or certification, or any regulation or order of the Board shall, upon such finding by an appropriate circuit court, be assessed a civil penalty of not more than $32,500 for each day of such violation. All civil penalties under this section shall be recovered in a civil action brought by the Attorney General in the name of the Commonwealth. Such civil penalties shall be paid into the state treasury and deposited by the State Treasurer into the Virginia Environmental Emergency Response Fund pursuant to Chapter 25 (§ 10.1-2500 et seq.) of this title.

B. In addition to the penalties provided above, any person who knowingly transports any hazardous waste to an unpermitted facility; who knowingly transports, treats, stores, or disposes of hazardous waste without a permit or in violation of a permit; or who knowingly makes any false statement or representation in any application, disclosure statement, label, manifest, record, report, permit, or other document filed, maintained, or used for purposes of hazardous waste program compliance shall be guilty of a felony punishable by a term of imprisonment of not less than one year nor more than five years and a fine of not more than $32,500 for each violation, either or both. The provisions of this subsection shall be deemed to constitute a lesser included offense of the violation set forth under subsection I.

Each day of violation of each requirement shall constitute a separate offense.

C. The Board is authorized to issue orders to require any person to comply with the provisions of any law administered by the Board, the Director or the Department, any condition of a permit or certification, or any regulations promulgated by the Board or to comply with any case decision, as defined in § 2.2-4001, of the Board or Director. Any such order shall be issued only after a hearing in accordance with § 2.2-4020 with at least 30 days' notice to the affected person of the time, place and purpose thereof. Such order shall become effective not less than 15 days after mailing a copy thereof by certified mail to the last known address of such person. The provisions of this section shall not affect the authority of the Board to issue separate orders and regulations to meet any emergency as provided in § 10.1-1402.

D. Any person willfully violating or refusing, failing or neglecting to comply with any regulation or order of the Board or the Director, any condition of a permit or certification or any provision of this chapter shall be guilty of a Class 1 misdemeanor unless a different penalty is specified.

Any person violating or failing, neglecting, or refusing to obey any lawful regulation or order of the Board or the Director, any condition of a permit or certification or any provision of this chapter may be compelled in a proceeding instituted in an appropriate court by the Board or the Director to obey such regulation, permit, certification, order or provision of this chapter and to comply therewith by injunction, mandamus, or other appropriate remedy.

E. Without limiting the remedies which may be obtained in this section, any person violating or failing, neglecting or refusing to obey any injunction, mandamus or other remedy obtained pursuant to this section shall be subject, in the discretion of the court, to a civil penalty not to exceed $32,500 for each violation. Such civil penalties shall be paid into the state treasury and deposited by the State Treasurer into the Virginia Environmental Emergency Response Fund pursuant to Chapter 25 of this title. Each day of violation of each requirement shall constitute a separate offense. Such civil penalties may, in the discretion of the court assessing them, be directed to be paid into the treasury of the county, city or town in which the violation occurred, to be used to abate environmental pollution in such manner as the court may, by order, direct, except that where the owner in violation is the county, city or town itself, or its agent, the court shall direct the penalty to be paid into the state treasury and deposited by the State Treasurer into the Virginia Environmental Emergency Response Fund pursuant to Chapter 25 of this title.

F. With the consent of any person who has violated or failed, neglected or refused to obey any regulation or order of the Board or the Director, any condition of a permit or any provision of this chapter, the Board may provide, in an order issued by the Board against such person, for the payment of civil charges for past violations in specific sums, not to exceed the limits specified in this section. Such civil charges shall be instead of any appropriate civil penalty which could be imposed under this section. Such civil charges shall be paid into the state treasury and deposited by the State Treasurer into the Virginia Environmental Emergency Response Fund pursuant to Chapter 25 of this title.

G. In addition to all other available remedies, the Board may issue administrative orders for the violation of (i) any law or regulation administered by the Board; (ii) any condition of a permit or certificate issued pursuant to this chapter; or (iii) any case decision or order of the Board. Issuance of an administrative order shall be a case decision as defined in § 2.2-4001 and shall be issued only after a hearing before a hearing officer appointed by the Supreme Court in accordance with § 2.2-4020. Orders issued pursuant to this subsection may include civil penalties of up to $32,500 per violation not to exceed $100,000 per order, and may compel the taking of corrective actions or the cessation of any activity upon which the order is based. The Board may assess penalties under this subsection if (a) the person has been issued at least two written notices of alleged violation by the Department for the same or substantially related violations at the same site, (b) such violations have not been resolved by demonstration that there was no violation, by an order issued by the Board or the Director, or by other means, (c) at least 130 days have passed since the issuance of the first notice of alleged violation, and (d) there is a finding that such violations have occurred after a hearing conducted in accordance with this subsection. The actual amount of any penalty assessed shall be based upon the severity of the violations, the extent of any potential or actual environmental harm, the compliance history of the facility or person, any economic benefit realized from the noncompliance, and the ability of the person to pay the penalty. The Board shall provide the person with the calculation for the proposed penalty prior to any hearing conducted for the issuance of an order that assesses penalties pursuant to this subsection. Penalties shall be paid to the state treasury and deposited by the State Treasurer into the Virginia Environmental Emergency Response Fund (§ 10.1-2500 et seq.). The issuance of a notice of alleged violation by the Department shall not be considered a case decision as defined in § 2.2-4001. Any notice of alleged violation shall include a description of each violation, the specific provision of law violated, and information on the process for obtaining a final decision or fact finding from the Department on whether or not a violation has occurred, and nothing in this section shall preclude an owner from seeking such a determination. Orders issued pursuant to this subsection shall become effective five days after having been delivered to the affected persons or mailed by certified mail to the last known address of such persons. Should the Board find that any person is adversely affecting the public health, safety or welfare, or the environment, the Board shall, after a reasonable attempt to give notice, issue, without a hearing, an emergency administrative order directing the person to cease the activity immediately and undertake any needed corrective action, and shall within 10 days hold a hearing, after reasonable notice as to the time and place thereof to the person, to affirm, modify, amend or cancel the emergency administrative order. If the Board finds that a person who has been issued an administrative order or an emergency administrative order is not complying with the order's terms, the Board may utilize the enforcement and penalty provisions of this article to secure compliance.

H. In addition to all other available remedies, the Department and generators of recycling residues shall have standing to seek enforcement by injunction of conditions which are specified by applicants in order to receive the priority treatment of their permit applications pursuant to § 10.1-1408.1.

I. Any person who knowingly transports, treats, stores, disposes of, or exports any hazardous waste in violation of this chapter or in violation of the regulations promulgated by the Board and who knows at the time that he thereby places another person in imminent danger of death or serious bodily injury, shall, upon conviction, be guilty of a felony punishable by a term of imprisonment of not less than two years nor more than 15 years and a fine of not more than $250,000, either or both. A defendant that is not an individual shall, upon conviction of violating this section, be subject to a fine not exceeding the greater of $1 million or an amount that is three times the economic benefit realized by the defendant as a result of the offense. The maximum penalty shall be doubled with respect to both fine and imprisonment for any subsequent conviction of the same person.

J. Criminal prosecutions under this chapter shall be commenced within three years after discovery of the offense, notwithstanding the provisions of any other statute.

K. The Board shall be entitled to an award of reasonable attorneys' fees and costs in any action brought by the Board under this section in which it substantially prevails on the merits of the case, unless special circumstances would make an award unjust.

L. The Board shall develop and provide an opportunity for public comment on guidelines and procedures that contain specific criteria for calculating the appropriate penalty for each violation based upon the severity of the violations, the extent of any potential or actual environmental harm, the compliance history of the facility or person, any economic benefit realized from the noncompliance, and the ability of the person to pay the penalty.

History.

1986, c. 492, § 10-310; 1988, c. 891; 1990, cc. 12, 781, 912, 919; 1991, c. 718; 1993, c. 23; 1998, c. 837; 1999, c. 876; 2005, cc. 133, 706.

§ 10.1-1456. Right of entry to inspect, etc.; warrants.

Upon presentation of appropriate credentials and upon consent of the owner or custodian, the Director or his designee shall have the right to enter at any reasonable time onto any property to inspect, investigate, evaluate, conduct tests or take samples for testing as he reasonably deems necessary in order to determine whether the provisions of any law administered by the Board, Director or Department, any regulations of the Board, any order of the Board or Director or any conditions in a permit, license or certificate issued by the Board or Director are being complied with. If the Director or his designee is denied entry, he may apply to an appropriate circuit court for an inspection warrant authorizing such investigation, evaluation, inspection, testing or taking of samples for testing as provided in Chapter 24 (§ 19.2-393 et seq.) of Title 19.2.

History.

1986, c. 492, § 10-311; 1988, c. 891.

§ 10.1-1457. Judicial review.

A. Except as provided in subsection B, any person aggrieved by a final decision of the Board or Director under this chapter shall be entitled to judicial review thereof in accordance with the Administrative Process Act (§ 2.2-4000 et seq.).

B. Any person who has participated, in person or by the submittal of written comments, in the public comment process related to a final decision of the Board or Director under § 10.1-1408.1 or § 10.1-1426 and who has exhausted all available administrative remedies for review of the Board's or

Director's decision, shall be entitled to judicial review thereof in accordance with the Administrative Process Act (§ 2.2-4000 et seq.) if such person meets the standard for obtaining judicial review of a case or controversy pursuant to Article III of the United States Constitution. A person shall be deemed to meet such standard if (i) such person has suffered an actual or imminent injury which is an invasion of a legally protected interest and which is concrete and particularized; (ii) such injury is fairly traceable to the decision of the Board and not the result of the independent action of some third party not before the court; and (iii) such injury will likely be redressed by a favorable decision by the court.

History.
1986, c. 492, § 10-312; 1988, c. 891; 1996, c. 1032.

§ 10.1-1458. Persons to provide plans, specifications, and information.

Every person the Department has reason to believe is generating, storing, transporting, disposing of, or treating waste shall, on request of the Department, furnish such plans, specifications, and information as the Department may require in the discharge of its duties under this chapter. Trade secret information included within any plans, specifications, or information submitted pursuant to this section shall be excluded from the provisions of the Virginia Freedom of Information Act as provided in subdivision 26 of § 2.2-3705.6. At all times, the Department may disclose such trade secret information to the appropriate officials of the Environmental Protection Agency pursuant to the requirements of the federal Solid Waste Disposal Act, 42 U.S.C. § 3251, et seq., or as otherwise required by law.

History.
2013, c. 54.

TITLE 14.1.
COSTS, FEES, SALARIES AND ALLOWANCES.

[Repealed.]

TITLE 15.1.
COUNTIES, CITIES AND TOWNS.

[Repealed.]

TITLE 15.2.
COUNTIES, CITIES AND TOWNS.

SUBTITLE I.
GENERAL PROVISIONS; CHARTERS; OTHER FORMS AND ORGANIZATION OF COUNTIES.

CHAPTER 8.
URBAN COUNTY EXECUTIVE FORM OF GOVERNMENT.

Article 2.

Departments and Commissions.

ARTICLE 2.
DEPARTMENTS AND COMMISSIONS.

§ 15.2-836.1. Animal protection police officer.

The department of police, if established in accordance with Chapter 17 (§ 15.2-1700 et seq.), may include an animal protection police officer who shall have all of the powers of an animal control officer, as defined in § 3.2-6500, conferred by general law and one or more deputy animal protection police officers to assist the animal protection police officer in the performance of his duties. An animal protection officer and his deputies also shall have all of the powers vested in law-enforcement officers, as defined in § 9.1-101, if they meet the minimum qualifications and have been certified under §§ 15.2-1705 and 15.2-1706.

History.
2016, c. 498.

SUBTITLE II.

POWERS OF LOCAL GOVERNMENT.

CHAPTER 9.

GENERAL POWERS OF LOCAL GOVERNMENTS.

Article 5.

Additional Powers.

ARTICLE 5.

ADDITIONAL POWERS.

§ 15.2-968.01. Parking in certain residential areas.

Notwithstanding any other provision of general law, localities may by ordinance permit the parking of vehicles within residential areas in a public right-of-way that constitutes a part of the state highway system so long as the vehicle does not obstruct the right-of-way.

History.
2015, c. 233.

§ 15.2-968.1. Use of photo-monitoring systems to enforce traffic light signals.

A. The governing body of any county, city, or town may provide by ordinance for the establishment of a traffic signal enforcement program imposing monetary liability on the operator of a motor vehicle for failure to comply with traffic light signals in such locality in accordance with the provisions of this section. Each such locality may install and operate traffic light signal photo-monitoring systems at no more than one intersection for every 10,000 residents within each county, city, or town at any one time, provided, however, that within planning District 8, each such locality may install and operate traffic light signal photo-monitoring systems at no more than 10 intersections, or at no more than one intersection for every 10,000 residents within each county, city, or town, whichever is greater, at any one time.

B. The operator of a vehicle shall be liable for a monetary penalty imposed pursuant to this section if such vehicle is found, as evidenced by information obtained from a traffic light signal violation monitoring system, to have failed to comply with a traffic light signal within such locality.

C. Proof of a violation of this section shall be evidenced by information obtained from a traffic light signal violation monitoring system authorized pursuant to this section. A certificate, sworn to or affirmed by a law-enforcement officer employed by a locality authorized to impose penalties pursuant to this section, or a facsimile thereof, based upon inspection of photographs, microphotographs, videotape, or other recorded images produced by a traffic light signal violation monitoring system, shall be prima facie evidence of the facts contained therein. Any photographs, microphotographs, videotape, or other recorded images evidencing such a violation shall be available for inspection in any proceeding to adjudicate the liability for such violation pursuant to an ordinance adopted pursuant to this section.

D. In the prosecution for a violation of any local ordinance adopted as provided in this section, prima facie evidence that the vehicle described in the summons issued pursuant to this section was operated in violation of such ordinance, together with proof that the defendant was at the time of such violation the owner, lessee, or renter of the vehicle, shall constitute in evidence a rebuttable presumption that such owner, lessee, or renter of the vehicle was the person who committed the violation. Such presumption shall be rebutted if the owner, lessee, or renter of the vehicle (i) files an affidavit by regular mail with the clerk of the general district court that he was not the operator of the vehicle at the time of the alleged violation or (ii) testifies in open court under oath that he was not the operator of the vehicle at the time of the alleged violation. Such presumption shall also be rebutted if a certified copy of a police report, showing that the vehicle had been reported to the police as stolen prior to the time of the alleged violation of this section, is presented, prior to the return date established on the summons issued pursuant to this section, to the court adjudicating the alleged violation.

E. For purposes of this section, "owner" means the registered owner of such vehicle on record with the Department of Motor Vehicles. For purposes of this section, "traffic light signal violation monitoring system" means a vehicle sensor installed to work in conjunction with a traffic light that automatically produces two or more photographs, two or more microphotographs, video, or other recorded images of each vehicle at the time it is used or operated in violation of § 46.2-833, 46.2-835, or 46.2-836. For each such vehicle, at least one recorded image shall be of the vehicle before it has illegally entered the intersection, and at least one recorded image shall be of the same vehicle after it has illegally entered that intersection.

F. Imposition of a penalty pursuant to this section shall not be deemed a conviction as an operator and shall not be made part of the operating record of the person upon whom such liability is imposed, nor shall it be used for insurance purposes in the provision of motor vehicle insurance coverage. No monetary penalty imposed under this section shall exceed $50, nor shall it include court costs. Any finding in a district court that an operator has violated an ordinance adopted as provided in this section shall be appealable to the circuit court in a civil proceeding.

G. A summons for a violation of this section may be executed pursuant to § 19.2-76.2. Notwithstanding the provisions of § 19.2-76, a summons for a violation of this section may be executed by mailing by first class mail a copy thereof to the owner, lessee, or renter of the vehicle. In the case of a vehicle owner, the copy shall be mailed to the address contained in the records of the Department of Motor Vehicles; in the case of a vehicle lessee or renter, the copy shall be mailed to the address contained in the records of the lessor or renter. Every such mailing shall include, in addition to the summons, a notice of (i) the summoned person's ability to rebut the presumption that he was the operator of the vehicle at the time of the alleged violation through the filing of an affidavit as provided in subsection D and (ii) instructions for filing such affidavit, including the address to which the affidavit is to be sent. If the summoned person fails to appear on the date of return set out in the summons mailed pursuant to this section, the summons shall be executed in the manner set out in § 19.2-76.3. No proceedings for contempt or arrest of a person summoned by mailing shall be instituted for failure to appear on the return date of the summons. Any summons executed for a violation of this section shall provide to the person summoned at least 30 business days from the mailing of the summons to inspect information collected by a traffic light signal violation monitoring system in connection with the violation.

H. Information collected by a traffic light signal violation monitoring system installed and operated pursuant to subsection A shall be limited exclusively to that information that is necessary for the enforcement of traffic light violations. On behalf of a locality, a private entity that operates a traffic light signal violation monitoring system may enter into an agreement with the Department of Motor Vehicles, in accordance with the provisions of subdivision B 21 of § 46.2-208, to obtain vehicle owner information regarding the registered owners of vehicles that fail to comply with a traffic light signal. Information provided to the operator of a traffic light signal violation monitoring system shall be protected in a database with security comparable to that of the Department of Motor Vehicles' system, and used only for enforcement against individuals who violate the provisions of this section. Notwithstanding any other provision of law, all photographs, microphotographs, electronic images, or other personal information collected by a traffic light signal violation monitoring system shall be used exclusively for enforcing traffic light violations and shall not (i) be open to the public; (ii) be sold or used for sales, solicitation, or marketing purposes; (iii) be disclosed to any other entity except as may be necessary for the enforcement of a traffic light violation or to a vehicle owner or operator as part of a challenge to the violation; or (iv) be used in a court in a pending action or proceeding unless the action or proceeding relates to a violation of § 46.2-833, 46.2-835, or 46.2-836 or requested upon order from a court of competent jurisdiction. Information collected under this section pertaining to a specific violation shall be purged and not retained later than 60 days after the collection of any civil penalties. If a locality does not execute a summons for a violation of this section within 10 business days, all information collected pertaining to that suspected violation shall be purged within two business days. Any locality operating a traffic light signal violation monitoring system shall annually certify compliance with this section and make all records pertaining to such system available for inspection and audit by the Commissioner of Highways or the Commissioner of the Department of Motor Vehicles or his designee. Any person who discloses personal information in violation of the provisions of this subsection shall be subject to a civil penalty of $1,000 per disclosure. Any unauthorized use or disclosure of such personal information shall be grounds for termination of the agreement between the Department of Motor Vehicles and the private entity.

I. A private entity may enter into an agreement with a locality to be compensated for providing the traffic light signal violation monitoring system or equipment, and all related support services, to include consulting, operations and administration. However, only a law-enforcement officer employed by a locality may swear to or affirm the certificate required by subsection C. No locality shall enter into an agreement for compensation based on the number of violations or monetary penalties imposed.

J. When selecting potential intersections for a traffic light signal violation monitoring system, a locality shall consider factors such as (i) the accident rate for the intersection, (ii) the rate of red light violations occurring at the intersection (number of violations per number of vehicles), (iii) the difficulty experienced by law-enforcement officers in patrol cars or on foot in apprehending violators, and (iv) the ability of law-enforcement officers to apprehend violators safely within a reasonable distance from the violation. Localities may consider the risk to pedestrians as a factor, if applicable.

K. Before the implementation of a traffic light signal violation monitoring system at an intersection, the locality shall complete an engineering safety analysis that addresses signal timing and other location-specific safety features. The length of the yellow phase shall be established based on the recommended methodology of the Institute of Transportation Engineers. No traffic light signal violation monitoring system shall be implemented or utilized for a traffic signal having a yellow signal phase length of less than three seconds. All traffic light signal violation monitoring systems shall provide a minimum 0.5-second grace period between the time the signal turns red and the time the first violation is recorded. If recommended by the engineering safety analysis, the locality shall make reasonable location-specific safety improvements, including signs and pavement markings.

L. Any locality that uses a traffic light signal violation monitoring system shall evaluate the system on a monthly basis to ensure all cameras and traffic signals are functioning properly. Evaluation results shall be made available to the public.

M. Any locality that uses a traffic light signal violation monitoring system to enforce traffic light signals shall place conspicuous signs within 500 feet of the intersection approach at which a traffic light signal violation monitoring system is used. There shall be a rebuttable presumption that such signs were in place at the time of the commission of the traffic light signal violation.

N. Prior to or coincident with the implementation or expansion of a traffic light signal violation monitoring system, a locality shall conduct a public awareness program, advising the public that the locality is implementing or expanding a traffic light signal violation monitoring system.

O. Notwithstanding any other provision of this section, if a vehicle depicted in images recorded by a traffic light signal photo-monitoring system is owned, leased, or rented by a county, city, or town, then the county, city, or town may access and use the recorded images and associated information for employee disciplinary purposes.

History.

2007, cc. 836, 903; 2010, c. 175; 2012, cc. 805, 836; 2014, c. 163; 2015, c. 714.

§ 15.2-973. Ordinances imposing license taxes on owners of certain motor vehicles.

Any locality may adopt an ordinance imposing a license tax, in an amount not exceeding $100 annually, upon the owners of motor vehicles that do not display current license plates and that are not exempted from the requirements of displaying such license plates under the provisions of Article 6 (§ 46.2-662 et seq.) of Chapter 6 of Title 46.2, §§ 46.2-1554 and 46.2-1555, are not in a public dump, in an "automobile graveyard" as defined in § 33.2-804, or in the possession of a licensed junk dealer or licensed motor vehicle dealer. Nothing in this section shall be applicable to any vehicle being held or stored by or at the direction of any governmental authority, to any vehicle owned by a member of the armed forces on active duty or to any vehicle regularly stored within a structure. Nothing in this section shall be applicable to motor vehicles that are stored on private property for the purpose of restoration or repair or for removing parts for the repair of another vehicle.

History.

1970, c. 380, § 15.1-27.1; 1977, c. 557; 1982, c. 216; 1988, c. 484; 1997, c. 587; 2013, c. 347.

Editor's note.

References in this section were updated at the direction of the Virginia Code Commission to conform to the recodification of Title 33.2 by Acts 2014, c. 805, effective October 1, 2014.

The 2013 amendments.

The 2013 amendment by c. 347 substituted "that" for "which" twice in the first sentence, deleted the former second sentence which read; "Such ordinance shall exempt from such tax any vehicles which are stored on private property for a period not in excess of sixty days, for the purpose of removing parts for the repair of another vehicle," and added the last sentence.

CHAPTER 11.
POWERS OF CITIES AND TOWNS.

Article 1.

Uniform Charter Powers.

ARTICLE 1.
UNIFORM CHARTER POWERS.

§ 15.2-1123.1. Lynchburg Regional Airport police department.

The City of Lynchburg may by ordinance establish an airport police department at the Lynchburg Regional Airport. The authority of the airport police department shall be limited to real property owned, leased, or controlled by the Airport. Such authority shall not supersede the authority, duties, or jurisdiction vested by law with the local police department or sheriff's office, including as provided in §§ 15.2-1609 and 15.2-1704. The airport police department and airport police officers shall be subject to and comply with the Constitution of the United States; the Constitution of Virginia; the laws governing municipal police departments, including the provisions of §§ 9.1-600, 15.2-1705 through 15.2-1708, 15.2-1719, 15.2-1721, and 15.2-1722; and any regulations adopted by the Criminal Justice Services Board that the Department of Criminal Justice Services designates as applicable to private police departments. Any person employed as an airport police officer pursuant to this section shall meet all requirements, including the minimum compulsory training requirements, for law-enforcement officers pursuant to Chapter 1 (§ 9.1-100 et seq.) of Title 9.1. An airport police officer is not entitled to benefits under the Line of Duty Act (§ 9.1-400 et seq.) or under the Virginia Retirement System, is not a "qualified law-enforcement officer" or "qualified retired law-enforcement officer" within the meaning of the federal Law Enforcement Officers Safety Act, 18 U.S.C. § 926B et seq., and shall not be deemed an employee of the Commonwealth. The airport police department may use the word "police" to describe its sworn officers and may join a regional criminal justice academy created pursuant to Article 5 (§ 15.2-1747 et seq.) of Chapter 17 of Title 15.2.

History.
2015, c. 213.

§ 15.2-1124. Police jurisdiction over lands, buildings and structures; jurisdiction of offenses; appeals; jurisdiction in certain public buildings with magistrate's offices.

A. Lands, buildings or structures provided and operated by a municipality for any purpose defined in this article shall be under the police jurisdiction of the municipal corporation for the enforcement of its regulations respecting the use or occupancy thereof. All police officers of the municipal corporation shall have jurisdiction to make arrests on such land and in such buildings or structures for violations of such regulations. Such criminal case shall be prosecuted in the locality in which the offense was committed.

B. In any public building that is located in Henry County adjoining a municipal corporation and that contains a magistrate's office which serves the municipal corporation, the sheriff, any deputy sheriff, and any police officer of the municipal corporation shall have the same powers which such sheriff, deputy sheriff or police officer would have in the municipal corporation itself. The courts of the municipal corporation and the locality in which such public building is located shall have concurrent jurisdiction of any offense committed against or any escape from any such sheriff, deputy sheriff, or police officer in such public building, provided that the sheriff, deputy sheriff, or police officer was present in the public building while in the performance of his official duties. Such police powers and concurrent jurisdiction shall also apply during travel between the municipal corporation and the public building by such sheriff, deputy sheriffs, and police officers while in the performance of their official duties. For purposes of this subsection, a "public building" shall include the surrounding grounds of such building.

History.
Code 1950, § 15-77.51; 1958, c. 328; 1962, c. 623, § 15.1-887; 1997, cc. 587, 739; 2007, c. 813; 2014, c. 543.

CHAPTER 15.

LOCAL GOVERNMENT PERSONNEL, QUALIFICATION FOR OFFICE, BONDS, DUAL OFFICE HOLDING AND CERTAIN LOCAL GOVERNMENT OFFICERS.

Article 1.

General Provisions for Certain Officers and Employees.

Section

ARTICLE 1.

GENERAL PROVISIONS FOR CERTAIN OFFICERS AND EMPLOYEES.

§ 15.2-1511. Allowances to injured officials and employees and their dependents.

The governing body of any locality is authorized in its discretion to make allowances by appropriation of funds, payable in monthly or semimonthly installments, for the relief of any of its officials, employees, police officers, firefighters, sheriffs or deputy sheriffs, town sergeants and town deputy sergeants, or their dependents, who suffer injury or death as defined in Title 65.2, whether such injury was suffered or death occurs before or after June 29, 1948 (which date is the effective date of the section). The allowance shall not exceed the salary or wage being paid such official, employee, police officer, firefighter, sheriff or deputy sheriff, town sergeants and town deputy sergeants, at the time of such injury or death, and the payment of the allowance shall not extend beyond the period of disability resulting from such injury. In case death results from the injury, the allowance may be made for the dependents as defined in Title 65.2. In localities which have established retirement or pension systems for injured, retired or superannuated officials, employees, members of police or fire departments, sheriffs, deputy sheriffs, town sergeants and deputy sergeants, or for the dependents of those killed in line of duty, the agencies provided for the administration of such systems shall determine the existence of such injury or cause of death before any appropriation to pay such allowance is made and shall determine the extent of and period of disability resulting from such injury and the cause in case of death. All sums paid to any such official, employee, police officer, firefighter, sheriff or deputy sheriff, town sergeants and deputy sergeants, as compensation under Title 65.2 and all sums paid to the dependents of such official, employee, police officer, firefighter, sheriff or deputy sheriff, town sergeant and deputy sergeant, if he is killed, and all sums paid under any retirement or pension system shall be deducted from the allowance made under this section in such installments as the agency determines. If the agency determines that any official, employee, police officer, firefighter, sheriff or deputy sheriff, town sergeant and deputy sergeant, who suffered injury in the line of duty is engaged or is able to engage in a gainful occupation, then the allowance shall be reduced by the agency to an amount which, together with the amount earnable by him, equals the allowance. Should the earning capacity of the official, employee, police officer, firefighter, sheriff or deputy sheriff, town sergeant and deputy sergeant, be later changed, such allowance may be further modified, up or down, provided the new allowance shall not exceed the amount of the allowance originally made nor an amount which, when added to the amount earnable by him, exceeds such allowance.

The death of, or any condition or impairment of health of, any member of a local police department, or of a sheriff or deputy sheriff, caused by hypertension or heart disease resulting in total or partial disability shall be presumed to have been suffered in the line of duty unless the contrary be shown by competent evidence; provided that prior to making any claim based upon such presumption for retirement, sickness or other benefits on account of such death or total or partial disability, such member, sheriff, or deputy sheriff, shall have been found free from hypertension or heart disease, as the case may be, by a physical examination which shall include such appropriate laboratory and other diagnostic studies as such governing body shall prescribe and which shall have been conducted by physicians whose qualifications shall have been prescribed by such governing body. In the case of a claim for disability, that any such member, sheriff, or deputy sheriff, shall, if requested by such governing body or its authorized representative, submit himself to physical examination by any physician designated by such governing body, such examination to include such tests or studies as may reasonably be prescribed by the physician so designated. Such member, sheriff or deputy sheriff, or claimant shall have the right to have present at such examination, at his own expense, any qualified physician he may designate. In the case of a claim for death benefits, any person entitled to make a claim for such benefits, claiming that such person's death was suffered in the line of duty, shall submit the body of the deceased to a postmortem examination to be performed by the medical examiner for the county, city or town appointed under § 32.1-282.

History.
Code 1950, § 15-555; 1950, p. 315; 1954, c. 246; 1960, c. 487; 1962, c. 623, § 15.1-134; 1971, Ex. Sess., c. 155; 1973, c. 499; 1976, c. 769; 1977, c. 326; 1997, c. 587.

§ 15.2-1511.01. Allowances to injured deputy sheriffs.

A. In addition to the allowances provided in § 15.2-1511, any deputy sheriff who suffers injury as defined in Title 65.2 and whose allowance as provided in § 15.2-1511 is less than 100 percent of his regular compensation shall be entitled to use any accrued vacation, compensatory, or sick leave to supplement the allowance so as to receive 100 percent of his regular compensation. In no case shall a deputy sheriff use such accrued leave so as to receive more than 100 percent of his regular compensation.

B. The governing body of a locality shall continue to pay the employer's share of the cost of health insurance to the same extent paid for other employees of the locality covered by the health insurance plan for a deputy sheriff who participates in the employer-provided health plan who suffers a compensable injury as defined under Title 65.2 so long as the deputy sheriff remains employed by the locality.

History.
2008, cc. 335, 766.

CHAPTER 16.
LOCAL CONSTITUTIONAL OFFICERS, COURTHOUSES AND SUPPLIES.

Article 3.

Sheriff.

ARTICLE 3.
SHERIFF.

§ 15.2-1613. Operation of sheriff's office.

Any county or city may appropriate funds for the operation of the sheriff's office.

In addition to those items listed in § 15.2-1615.1, counties and cities shall provide at their expense in accordance with standards set forth in § 15.2-1610 a reasonable number of uniforms and items of personal equipment required by the sheriff to carry out his official duties.

History.
1986, c. 139, § 15.1-137.3; 1990, c. 68; 1997, c. 587.

§ 15.2-1613.1. Processing fee may be imposed on certain individuals.

Any county or city may by ordinance authorize a processing fee not to exceed $25 on any individual admitted to a county, city, or regional jail following conviction. The fee shall be ordered as a part of court costs collected by the clerk, deposited into the account of the treasurer of the county or city and shall be used by the local sheriff's office to defray the costs of processing arrested persons into local or regional jails. If processing costs are incurred by a regional jail rather than a local sheriff's office, the fees collected pursuant to such ordinance may be used by the regional jail to defray the costs of processing arrested persons. Where costs are incurred by a sheriff's office and a regional jail the fees collected pursuant to such ordinance may be divided proportionately as determined by the local governing body or bodies, between the sheriff's office and the regional jail. Where costs are incurred by a police department for booking or fingerprinting services, the fees collected pursuant to such ordinance may be divided proportionately as determined by the local governing body or bodies, between the sheriff's office and the police department.

History.
2002, c. 840; 2003, c. 623; 2011, cc. 300, 664.

CHAPTER 17.
POLICE AND PUBLIC ORDER.

Article 1.
General Provisions.

Article 2.
Interjurisdictional Law-Enforcement Authority and Agreements.

Article 3.
Auxiliary Police Forces in Localities.

Article 4.
Special Police Officers in Localities.

Article 5.
Criminal Justice Training Academies.

ARTICLE 1. GENERAL PROVISIONS.

§ 15.2-1700. Preservation of peace and good order.

Any locality may provide for the protection of its inhabitants and property and for the preservation of peace and good order therein.

History.

Code 1950, § 15-556; 1962, c. 623, § 15.1-137; 1997, c. 587.

§ 15.2-1701. Organization of police forces.

Any locality may, by ordinance, provide for the organization of its authorized police forces. Such forces shall include a chief of police, and such officers and other personnel as appropriate.

When a locality provides for a police department, the chief of police shall be the chief law-enforcement officer of that locality. However, in towns, the chief law-enforcement officer may be called the town sergeant.

History.

1979, c. 333, § 15.1-131.7; 1997, c. 587.

§ 15.2-1702. Referendum required prior to establishment of county police force.

A. A county shall not establish a police force unless (i) such action is first approved by the voters of the county in accordance with the provisions of this section and (ii) the General Assembly enacts appropriate authorizing legislation.

B. The governing body of any county shall petition the court, by resolution, asking that a referendum be held on the question, "Shall a police force be established in the county and the sheriff's office be relieved of primary law-enforcement responsibilities?" The court, by order entered of record in accordance with Article 5 (§ 24.2-681 et seq.) of Chapter 6 of Title 24.2, shall require the regular election officials of the county to open the polls and take the sense of the voters on the question as herein provided.

The clerk of the circuit court for the county shall publish notice of the election in a newspaper of general circulation in the county once a week for three consecutive weeks prior to the election. The notice shall contain the ballot question and a statement of not more than 500 words on the proposed question. The explanation shall be presented in plain English, shall be limited to a neutral explanation, and shall not present arguments by either proponents or opponents of the proposal. The attorney for the county or city or, if there is no county or city attorney, the attorney for the Commonwealth shall prepare the explanation. "Plain English" means written in nontechnical, readily understandable language using words of common everyday usage and avoiding legal terms and phrases or other terms and words of art whose usage or special meaning primarily is limited to a particular field or profession.

C. The county may expend public funds to produce and distribute neutral information concerning the referendum; provided, however, public funds may not be used to promote a particular position on the question, either in the notice called for in subsection B, or in any other distribution of information to the public.

D. The regular election officers of the county shall open the polls on the date specified in such order and conduct the election in the manner provided by law. The election shall be by ballot which shall be prepared by the electoral board of the county and on which shall be printed the following:

"Shall a police force be established in the county and the sheriff's office be relieved of primary law-enforcement responsibilities?

☐ Yes

☐ No"

The ballots shall be counted, returns made and canvassed as in other elections, and the results certified by the electoral board to the court ordering the election. If a majority of the voters voting in the election vote "Yes," the court shall enter an order proclaiming the results of the election and a duly certified copy of such order shall be transmitted to the governing body of the county. The governing body shall proceed to establish a police force following the enactment of authorizing legislation by the General Assembly.

E. After a referendum has been conducted pursuant to this section, no subsequent referendum shall be conducted pursuant to this section in the same county for a period of four years from the date of the prior referendum.

History.

1983, c. 341, § 15.1-131.6:1; 1993, c. 630; 1997, c. 587; 2000, c. 298.

§ 15.2-1703. Referendum to abolish county police force.

The police force in any county which established the force subsequent to July 1, 1983, may be abolished and its responsibilities assumed by the sheriff's office after a referendum held pursuant to this section.

Either (i) the voters of the county by petition signed by not less than ten percent of the registered voters therein on the January 1 preceding the filing of the petition or (ii) the governing body of the county, by resolution, may petition the circuit court for the county that a referendum be held on the question, "Shall the county police force be abolished and its responsibilities assumed by the county sheriff's office?" The court, by order entered of record in accordance with Article 5 (§ 24.2-681 et seq.) of

Chapter 6 of Title 24.2, shall require the regular election officials of the county at the next general election held in the county to open the polls and take the sense of the voters on the question as herein provided. The clerk of the circuit court for the county shall publish notice of the election in a newspaper of general circulation in the county once a week for three consecutive weeks prior to the election.

The ballot shall be printed as follows:

"Shall the county police force be abolished and its responsibilities assumed by the county sheriff's office?

☐ Yes

☐ No"

The election shall be held and the results certified as provided in § 24.2-684. If a majority of the voters voting in the election vote in favor of the question, the court shall enter an order proclaiming the results of the election, and a duly certified copy of such order shall be transmitted to the governing body of the county. The governing body shall proceed with the necessary action to abolish the police force and transfer its responsibilities to the sheriff's office, to become effective on July 1 following the referendum.

Once a referendum has been held pursuant to this section, no further referendum shall be held pursuant to this section within four years thereafter.

History.

1988, c. 660, § 15.1-131.6:2; 1997, c. 587.

§ 15.2-1704. Powers and duties of police force.

A. The police force of a locality is hereby invested with all the power and authority which formerly belonged to the office of constable at common law and is responsible for the prevention and detection of crime, the apprehension of criminals, the safeguard of life and property, the preservation of peace and the enforcement of state and local laws, regulations, and ordinances.

B. A police officer has no authority in civil matters, except (i) to execute and serve temporary detention and emergency custody orders and any other powers granted to law-enforcement officers in § 16.1-340, 16.1-340.1, 37.2-808, or 37.2-809, (ii) to serve an order of protection pursuant to §§ 16.1-253.1, 16.1-253.4, and 16.1-279.1, (iii) to execute all warrants or summons as may be placed in his hands by any magistrate serving the locality and to make due return thereof, and (iv) to deliver, serve, execute, and enforce orders of isolation and quarantine issued pursuant to §§ 32.1-48.09, 32.1-48.012, and 32.1-48.014 and to deliver, serve, execute, and enforce an emergency custody order issued pursuant to § 32.1-48.02. A town police officer, after receiving training under subdivision 8 of § 9.1-102, may, with the concurrence of the local sheriff, also serve civil papers, and make return thereof, only when the town is the plaintiff and the defendant can be found within the corporate limits of the town.

History.

Code 1950, § 15-557; 1960, c. 167; 1962, c. 623, § 15.1-138; 1982, c. 38; 1984, c. 661; 1992, cc. 729, 742; 1995, c. 844; 1997, c. 587; 1998, c. 425; 1999, c. 495; 2007, c. 724; 2008, cc. 551, 691; 2010, cc. 778, 825.

§ 15.2-1705. Minimum qualifications; waiver.

A. The chief of police and all police officers of any locality, all deputy sheriffs and jail officers in this Commonwealth, and all law-enforcement officers as defined in § 9.1-101 who enter upon the duties of such office after July 1, 1994, are required to meet the following minimum qualifications for office. Such person shall (i) be a citizen of the United States, (ii) be required to undergo a background investigation including fingerprint-based criminal history records inquiries to both the Central Criminal Records Exchange and the Federal Bureau of Investigation, (iii) have a high school education or have passed a high school equivalency examination approved by the Board of Education, (iv) possess a valid driver's license if required by the duties of office to operate a motor vehicle, (v) undergo a physical examination, subsequent to a conditional offer of employment, conducted under the supervision of a licensed physician, (vi) be at least eighteen years of age, (vii) not have been convicted of or pled guilty or no contest to a felony or any offense that would be a felony if committed in the Commonwealth, and (viii) not have produced a positive result on a pre-employment drug screening, if such screening is required by the hiring law-enforcement agency or jail, where the positive result cannot be explained to the law-enforcement agency or jail administrator's satisfaction. In addition, all such officers who enter upon the duties of such office on or after July 1, 2013, shall not have been convicted of or pled guilty or no contest to (a) any misdemeanor involving moral turpitude, including but not limited to petit larceny under § 18.2-96, or any offense involving moral turpitude that would be a misdemeanor if committed in the Commonwealth, (b) any misdemeanor sex offense in the Commonwealth, another state, or the United States, including but not limited to sexual battery under § 18.2-67.4 or consensual sexual intercourse with a minor 15 or older under clause (ii) of § 18.2-371, or (c) domestic assault under § 18.2-57.2 or any offense that would be domestic assault under the laws of another state or the United States.

B. Upon request of a sheriff or chief of police, or the director or chief executive of any agency or department employing law-enforcement officers as defined in § 9.1-101, or jail officers as defined in § 53.1-1, the Department of Criminal Justice Services is hereby authorized to waive the requirements for qualification as set out in subsection A of this section for good cause shown.

History.

1982, c. 442, § 15.1-131.8; 1988, c. 396; 1994, cc. 850, 905; 1995, c. 112; 1997, c. 587; 2013, cc. 307, 468; 2014, c. 84.

§ 15.2-1706. Certification through training required for all law-enforcement officers; waiver of requirements.

A. All law-enforcement officers as defined in § 9.1-101 and all jail officers as defined in § 53.1-1 must be certified through the successful completion of training at an approved criminal justice training academy in order to remain eligible for appointment or employment. In order to obtain such certification, all entry level law-enforcement officers seeking certification on or after July 1, 2003, shall successfully complete statewide certification examinations developed and administered by the Department of Criminal Justice Services. The Department may delegate administration of the examinations to an approved criminal justice training academy and may revoke such delegation at its discretion. The appointee's or employee's hiring agency must provide the Department of Criminal Justice Services with verification that law-enforcement or jail officers first hired after July 1, 1994, have met the minimum standards set forth in § 15.2-1705.

B. The requirement for the successful completion of the law-enforcement certification examination may be waived by the Department of Criminal Justice Services based upon previous law-enforcement experience and training. To be eligible for such waiver, the individual must have applied for and been granted an exemption or partial exemption in accordance with § 9.1-116.

History.

1994, cc. 850, 905, § 15.1-131.8:1; 1995, c. 112; 1997, c. 587; 1999, c. 635; 2002, c. 345; 2004, c. 477.

§ 15.2-1707. Decertification of law-enforcement officers.

A. The sheriff, chief of police, or agency administrator shall notify the Criminal Justice Services Board in writing when any certified law-enforcement or jail officer currently employed by his agency has (i) been convicted of or pled guilty or no contest to a felony or any offense that would be a felony if committed in the Commonwealth, (ii) been convicted of or pled guilty or no contest to a Class 1 misdemeanor involving moral turpitude or any offense that would be any misdemeanor involving moral turpitude, including but not limited to petit larceny under § 18.2-96, or any offense involving moral turpitude that would be a misdemeanor if committed in the Commonwealth, (iii) been convicted of or pled guilty or no contest to any misdemeanor sex offense in the Commonwealth, another state, or the United States, including but not limited to sexual battery under § 18.2-67.4 or consensual sexual intercourse with a minor 15 or older under clause (ii) of § 18.2-371, (iv) been convicted of or pled guilty or no contest to domestic assault under § 18.2-57.2 or any offense that would be domestic assault under the laws of another state or the United States, (v) failed to comply with or maintain compliance with mandated training requirements, or (vi) refused to submit to a drug screening or has produced a positive result on a drug screening reported to the employing agency, where the positive result cannot be explained to the agency administrator's satisfaction. Notification shall also be provided in writing for any employee who resigned or was terminated in advance of being convicted or found guilty of an offense that requires decertification or who resigned or was terminated in advance of a pending drug screening. The notification, where appropriate, shall be accompanied by a copy of the judgment of conviction. Upon receiving such notice from the sheriff, chief of police, or agency administrator, or from an attorney for the Commonwealth, the Criminal Justice Services Board shall decertify such law-enforcement or jail officer. Such officer shall not have the right to serve as a law-enforcement officer within the Commonwealth until his certification has been reinstated by the Board.

B. When a conviction has not become final, the Board may decline to decertify the officer until the conviction becomes final, after considering the likelihood of irreparable damage to the officer if such officer is decertified during the pendency of an ultimately successful appeal, the likelihood of injury or damage to the public if the officer is not decertified, and the seriousness of the offense.

C. The Department of Criminal Justice Services is hereby authorized to waive the requirements for decertification as set out in subsection A for good cause shown.

D. The Criminal Justice Services Board may initiate decertification proceedings against any former law-enforcement or jail officer whom the Board has found to have been convicted of an offense that requires decertification or who has failed to comply with or maintain compliance with mandated training requirements.

History.

1994, cc. 850, 905, § 15.1-131.8:2; 1995, c. 112; 1997, c. 587; 2013, cc. 307, 468.

§ 15.2-1708. Notice of decertification.

A. Service of notice. The Board shall, within ten days of decertification, serve notice upon an affected officer, in person or by certified mail, and upon the law-enforcement or jail agency employing said officer, by certified mail, specifying the action taken and remedies available. The Board shall stay final action until the period for requesting a hearing expires.

B. Decertification hearing. Any law-enforcement or jail officer who has been decertified may, within thirty days of receipt of notice served by the Board, request, by certified mail, a hearing which shall be granted by the Board. Upon receipt of such request, the Board shall set a date, time, and place for the hearing within sixty days and serve notice by certified mail upon the affected officer. The Board, or a committee thereof, shall conduct such hearing. The affected officer may be represented by counsel. In the absence of a request for hearing, decertification shall, without further proceedings, become final thirty days after the initial notice.

C. Standard of review. The decertification of a law-enforcement or jail officer under § 15.2-1707 shall be sustained by the Board unless such law-enforcement or jail officer shows, by a preponderance of the evidence, good cause for his certification to be reinstated.

D. Final decision after request for hearing. The Board shall render a final decision within thirty days.

E. Notice of final action. The Board shall notify the officer and the law-enforcement or jail agency involved, by certified mail, of the final action regarding decertification.

F. Reinstatement after decertification. Any officer who is decertified may, after a period of not less than five years, petition the Board to be considered for reinstatement of certification.

History.

1994, cc. 850, 905, § 15.1-131.8:3; 1995, c. 112; 1997, c. 587.

§ 15.2-1709. Employer immunity from liability; disclosure of information regarding former deputy sheriffs and law-enforcement officers.

Any sheriff or chief of police, the director or chief executive of any agency or department employing deputy sheriffs or law-enforcement officers as defined § 9.1-101, or jail officers as defined in § 53.1-1, and the Director of the Department of Criminal Justice Services or his designee who discloses information about a former deputy sheriff's or law-enforcement officer's or jail officer's job performance to a prospective law-enforcement or jail employer of the former appointee or employee is presumed to be acting in good faith and, unless lack of good faith is shown by clear and convincing evidence, is immune from civil liability for such disclosure or its consequences. For purposes of this section, the presumption of good faith is rebutted upon a showing that the information disclosed by the former employer was knowingly false or deliberately misleading, was rendered with malicious purpose, or violated any civil right of the former employee or appointee.

History.

1994, cc. 850, 905, § 15.1-131.8:4; 1995, c. 112; 1997, c. 587.

§ 15.2-1710. Fees and other compensation.

A police officer shall not receive any fee or other compensation out of the state treasury or the treasury of a locality for any service rendered under the provisions of this chapter other than the salary paid him by the locality and a fee as a witness in cases arising under the criminal laws of the Commonwealth. A police officer shall not receive any fee as a witness in any case arising under the ordinances of his locality, nor for attendance as a witness before any magistrate serving his locality. However, if it is necessary or expedient for him to travel beyond the limits of the locality in his capacity as a police officer, he shall be entitled to his actual expenses, as provided by law for other expenses in criminal cases.

Nothing in this section shall be construed as prohibiting a police officer of a locality from claiming and receiving any reward which may be offered for the arrest and detention of any offender against the criminal laws of this or any other state or nation.

History.

Code 1950, § 15-557; 1960, c. 167; 1962, c. 623, § 15.1-138; 1982, c. 38; 1984, c. 661; 1992, cc. 729, 742; 1995, c. 844; 1997, c. 587; 2008, cc. 551, 691.

§ 15.2-1711. Providing legal fees and expenses for law-enforcement officers; repayment to locality of two-thirds of amount by Compensation Board.

If any law-enforcement officer is investigated, arrested or indicted or otherwise prosecuted on any criminal charge arising out of any act committed in the discharge of his official duties, and no charges are brought, the charge is subsequently dismissed or upon trial he is found not guilty, the governing body of the locality wherein he is appointed may reimburse such officer for reasonable legal fees and expenses incurred by him in defense of such investigation or charge; such reimbursement shall be paid from the treasury of the locality.

When a governing body reimburses its sheriff or a law-enforcement officer in the sheriff's employment for reasonable legal fees and expenses as provided for in this section, then, upon certification of the reimbursement to the Chairman of the Compensation Board by the presiding officer of the governing body, the Compensation Board shall pay to the applicable locality two-thirds of the amount so certified.

History.

1975, c. 31, § 15.1-131.6; 1979, c. 600; 1980, c. 106; 1985, c. 321; 1997, c. 587.

§ 15.2-1712. Employment of off-duty officers.

Notwithstanding the provisions of §§ 2.2-3100 through 2.2-3127, any locality may adopt an ordinance which permits law-enforcement officers and deputy sheriffs in such locality to engage in off-duty employment which may occasionally require the use of their police powers in the performance of such employment. Such ordinance may include reasonable rules to apply to such off-duty employment, or it may delegate the promulgation of such reasonable rules to the chief of the respective police departments or the sheriff of the county or city.

History.
1978, c. 537, § 15.1-133.1; 1997, c. 587.

§ 15.2-1713. Localities authorized to offer and pay rewards in felony and misdemeanor cases.

When any felony or misdemeanor has been committed, or there has been any attempt to commit a felony in any locality, the governing body of the locality or its duly authorized agent may offer and pay a reward for the arrest and final conviction of the person or persons who committed the felony or misdemeanor or attempted to commit the felony. The reward may be paid out of the general fund of such locality.

History.
1983, c. 525, § 15.1-137.2; 1984, c. 661; 1997, c. 587.

§ 15.2-1713.1. Local "Crime Stoppers" programs; confidentiality.

A. As used in this section, a "Crime Stoppers," "crime solvers," "crime line," or other similarly named organization is defined as a private, nonprofit Virginia corporation governed by a civilian volunteer board of directors that is operated on a local or statewide level that (i) offers anonymity to persons providing information to the organization, (ii) accepts and expends donations for cash rewards to persons who report to the organization information about alleged criminal activity and that the organization forwards to the appropriate law-enforcement agency, and (iii) is established as a cooperative alliance between the news media, the community, and law-enforcement officials.

B. Evidence of a communication or any information contained therein between a person submitting a report of an alleged criminal act to a "Crime Stoppers" organization and the person who accepted the report on behalf of the organization is not admissible in a court proceeding. Law-enforcement agencies receiving information concerning alleged criminal activity from a "Crime Stoppers" organization shall maintain confidentiality pursuant to subdivision A 3 of § 2.2-3706.

History.
2003, cc. 754, 760; 2013, c. 695.

§ 15.2-1714. Establishing police lines, perimeters, or barricades.

Whenever fires, accidents, wrecks, explosions, crimes, riots, or other emergency situations where life, limb, or property may be endangered may cause persons to collect on the public streets, alleys, highways, parking lots, or other public area, the chief law-enforcement officer of any locality or that officer's authorized representative who is responsible for the security of the scene may establish such areas, zones, or perimeters by the placement of police lines or barricades as are reasonably necessary to (i) preserve the integrity of evidence at such scenes, (ii) notwithstanding the provisions of §§ 46.2-888 through 46.2-891, facilitate the movement of vehicular and pedestrian traffic into, out of, and around the scene, (iii) permit firefighters, police officers, and emergency medical services personnel to perform necessary operations unimpeded, and (iv) protect persons and property.

Any police line or barricade erected for these purposes shall be clearly identified by wording such as "Police Line — DO NOT CROSS" or other similar wording. If material or equipment is not available for identifying the prohibited area, then a verbal warning by identifiable law-enforcement officials positioned to indicate a location of a police line or barricade shall be given to any person or persons attempting to cross police lines or barricades without proper authorization.

Such scene may be secured no longer than is reasonably necessary to effect the above-described purposes. Nothing in this section shall limit or otherwise affect the authority of, or be construed to deny access to such scene by, any person charged by law with the responsibility of rendering assistance at or investigating any such fires, accidents, wrecks, explosions, crimes or riots.

Personnel from information services such as press, radio, and television, when gathering news, shall be exempt from the provisions of this section except that it shall be unlawful for such persons to obstruct the police, firefighters, or emergency medical services personnel in the performance of their duties at such scene. Such personnel shall proceed at their own risk.

History.
1984, c. 533, § 15.1-140.1; 1990, c. 327; 1997, c. 587; 2015, cc. 502, 503.

§ 15.2-1715. Authority to declare Intensified Drug Enforcement Jurisdictions; expenditure of funds.

Whenever, in the judgment of the Governor or his designee, a locality or multi-jurisdictional area is confronted with a drug trafficking problem of such a magnitude as to warrant additional resources to supplement the efforts of local officials responsible for the apprehension and prosecution of persons engaged in drug trafficking activities, he may declare such areas Intensified Drug Enforcement Jurisdictions. Upon such declaration, the Governor, or his designee, may make available funds from the Intensified Drug Enforcement Jurisdictions Fund provided for in § 9.1-105.

History.
1990, c. 971, § 15.1-131.12; 1997, c. 587.

§ 15.2-1716. Reimbursement of expenses incurred in responding to DUI and related incidents.

A. Any locality may provide by ordinance that a person convicted of violating any of the following provisions shall, at the time of sentencing or in a separate civil action, be liable to the locality or to any responding volunteer fire company or department or volunteer emergency medical services agency, or both, for restitution of reasonable expenses incurred by the locality for responding law enforcement, firefighting, and emergency medical services, including those incurred by the sheriff's office of such locality, or by any volunteer fire or volunteer emergency medical services agency, or by any combination of the foregoing, when providing an appropriate emergency response to any accident or incident related to such violation. The ordinance may further provide that a person convicted of violating any of the following provisions shall, at the time of sentencing or in a separate civil action, be liable to the locality or to any responding volunteer fire or volunteer emergency medical services agency, or both, for restitution of reasonable expenses incurred by the locality when issuing any related arrest warrant or summons, including the expenses incurred by the sheriff's office of such locality, or by any volunteer fire or volunteer emergency medical services agency, or by any combination of the foregoing:

1. The provisions of § 18.2-36.1, 18.2-51.4, 18.2-266, 18.2-266.1, 29.1-738, 29.1-738.02, or 46.2-341.24, or a similar ordinance, when such operation of a motor vehicle, engine, train or watercraft while so impaired is the proximate cause of the accident or incident;
2. The provisions of Article 7 (§ 46.2-852 et seq.) of Chapter 8 of Title 46.2 relating to reckless driving, when such reckless driving is the proximate cause of the accident or incident;
3. The provisions of Article 1 (§ 46.2-300 et seq.) of Chapter 3 of Title 46.2 relating to driving without a license or driving with a suspended or revoked license; and
4. The provisions of § 46.2-894 relating to improperly leaving the scene of an accident.

B. Personal liability under this section for reasonable expenses of an appropriate emergency response pursuant to subsection A shall not exceed $1,000 in the aggregate for a particular accident, arrest, or incident occurring in such locality. In determining the "reasonable expenses," a locality may bill a flat fee of $350 or a minute-by-minute accounting of the actual costs incurred. As used in this section, "appropriate emergency response" includes all costs of providing law-enforcement, firefighting, and emergency medical services. The court may order as restitution the reasonable expenses incurred by the locality for responding law enforcement, firefighting, and emergency medical services. The provisions of this section shall not preempt or limit any remedy available to the Commonwealth, to the locality, or to any volunteer emergency medical services agency to recover the reasonable expenses of an emergency response to an accident or incident not involving impaired driving, operation of a vehicle, or other conduct as set forth herein.

History.
1994, c. 617, § 15.1-132.1; 1995, cc. 683, 685, 830; 1997, cc. 587, 691; 2001, c. 505; 2003, c. 796; 2004, c. 273; 2005, cc. 148, 366; 2006, c. 679; 2009, c. 245; 2010, c. 343; 2015, cc. 502, 503.

§ 15.2-1716.1. Reimbursement of expenses incurred in responding to terrorism hoax incident or bomb threat.

Any locality may provide by ordinance that any person who is convicted of a violation of subsection B or C of § 18.2-46.6 or of a felony violation of § 18.2-83 or 18.2-84, when his violation of such section is the proximate cause of any incident resulting in an appropriate emergency response, shall be liable at the time of sentencing or in a separate civil action to the locality or to any volunteer emergency medical services agency, or both, which may provide such emergency response for the reasonable expense thereof, in an amount not to exceed $1,000 in the aggregate for a particular incident occurring in such locality. In determining the "reasonable expense," a locality may bill a flat fee of $250 or a minute-by-minute accounting of the actual costs incurred. As used in this section, "appropriate emergency response" includes all costs of providing law-enforcement, firefighting, and emergency medical services. The provisions of this section shall not preempt or limit any remedy available to the Commonwealth, to the locality, or to any volunteer emergency medical services agency to recover the reasonable expenses of an emergency response to an incident not involving a terroristic hoax or an act undertaken in violation of § 18.2-83 or 18.2-84 as set forth herein.

History.
2002, cc. 588, 623; 2005, c. 479; 2015, cc. 502, 503; 2016, c. 213.

§ 15.2-1716.2. Methamphetamine lab cleanup costs; localities may charge for reimbursement.

Any locality may provide by ordinance that any person who is convicted of an offense for manufacture of methamphetamine pursuant to § 18.2-248 or 18.2-248.03 shall be liable at the time of sentencing or in a separate civil action to the locality or to any other law-enforcement entity for the expense in cleaning up any methamphetamine lab related to the conviction. The amount charged shall not exceed the actual expenses associated with cleanup, removal, or repair of the affected property or the replacement cost of personal protective equipment used.

History.
2012, cc. 517, 616.

§ 15.2-1717. Preventing interference with pupils at schools.

Localities may adopt any reasonable ordinance necessary to prevent any improper interference with or annoyance of the pupils attending or boarding at any schools situated in such locality.

History.

Code 1950, § 15-558; 1962, c. 623, § 15.1-139; 1973, c. 401; 1984, c. 661; 1997, c. 587.

§ 15.2-1717.1. Designation of police to enforce trespass violations.

Any locality may by ordinance establish a procedure whereby the owner, lessee, custodian, or person lawfully in charge as those terms are used in § 18.2-119, of real property may designate the local law-enforcement agency as a "person lawfully in charge of the property" for the purpose of forbidding another to go or remain upon the lands, buildings or premises as specified in the designation. The ordinance shall require that any such designation be in writing and on file with the local law-enforcement agency.

History.

1999, c. 275; 2002, c. 328.

§ 15.2-1718. Receipt of missing child reports.

No police or sheriff's department shall establish or maintain any policy which requires the observance of any waiting period before accepting a missing child report as defined in § 52-32. Upon receipt of a missing child report by any police or sheriff's department, the department shall immediately, but in all cases within two hours of receiving the report, enter identifying and descriptive data about the child into the Virginia Criminal Information Network and the National Crime Information Center Systems, forward the report to the Missing Children Information Clearinghouse within the Department of State Police, notify all other law-enforcement agencies in the area, and initiate an investigation of the case.

History.

1985, c. 259, § 15.1-131.9; 1990, c. 239; 1997, c. 587; 2004, cc. 248, 443.

§ 15.2-1718.1. Receipt of missing senior adult reports.

A. No police or sheriff's department shall establish or maintain any policy which requires the observance of any waiting period before accepting a missing senior adult report. Upon receipt of a missing senior adult report by any police or sheriff's department, the department shall immediately, but in all cases within two hours of receiving the report, enter identifying and descriptive data about the senior adult into the Virginia Criminal Information Network and the National Crime Information Center Systems, forward the report to the Department of State Police, notify all other law-enforcement agencies in the area, and initiate an investigation of the case.

B. For purposes of this section:

"Missing senior adult report" means a report prepared in a format prescribed by the Superintendent of State Police for use by law-enforcement agencies to report missing senior adult information and photograph to the Department of State Police.

History.

2007, cc. 486, 723.

§ 15.2-1718.2. Receipt of critically missing adult reports.

A. No police or sheriff's department shall establish or maintain any policy that requires the observance of any waiting period before accepting a critically missing adult report. Upon receipt of a critically missing adult report by any police or sheriff's department, the department shall immediately, but in all cases within two hours of receiving the report, enter identifying and descriptive data about the critically missing adult into the Virginia Criminal Information Network and the National Crime Information Center Systems, forward the report to the Department of State Police, notify all other law-enforcement agencies in the area, and initiate an investigation of the case.

B. For purposes of this section:

"Critically missing adult" means any missing adult 21 years of age or older whose disappearance indicates a credible threat to the health and safety of the adult as determined by a law-enforcement agency and under such other circumstances as deemed appropriate after consideration of all known circumstances.

"Critically missing adult report" means a report prepared in a format prescribed by the Superintendent of State Police for use by law-enforcement agencies to report critically missing adult information, including a photograph, to the Department of State Police.

History.

2015, cc. 205, 223.

§ 15.2-1719. Disposal of unclaimed property in possession of sheriff or police.

Any locality may provide by ordinance for (i) the public sale in accordance with the provisions of this section or (ii) the retention for use by the law-enforcement agency, of any unclaimed personal property which has been in the possession of its law-enforcement agencies and unclaimed for a period of more than 60 days, after payment of a reasonable storage fee to the sheriff or other agency storing such property. No storage fee shall be charged or accounted for if such property has been stored by and is to be retained by the sheriff's office or other law-enforcement agency. As used herein, "unclaimed personal property" shall be any personal property belonging to another which has been acquired by a law-enforcement officer pursuant to his duties, which is not needed in any criminal prosecution, which has not been claimed by its rightful owner and which the State Treasurer has indicated will be declined if remitted under the Uniform Disposition of Unclaimed Property Act (§ 55-210.1 et seq.). Unclaimed bicycles and mopeds may also be disposed of in accordance with § 15.2-1720. Unclaimed firearms may also be disposed of in accordance with § 15.2-1721.

Prior to the sale or retention for use by the law-enforcement agency of any unclaimed item, the chief of police, sheriff or their duly authorized agents shall make reasonable attempts to notify the rightful owner of the property, obtain from the attorney for the Commonwealth in writing a statement advising that the item is not needed in any criminal prosecution, and cause to be published in a newspaper of general circulation in the locality once a week for two successive weeks, notice that there will be a public display and sale of unclaimed personal property. Such property, including property selected for retention by the law-enforcement agency, shall be described generally in the notice, together with the date, time and place of the sale and shall be made available for public viewing at the sale. The chief of police, sheriff or their duly authorized agents shall pay from the proceeds of sale the costs of advertisement, removal, storage, investigation as to ownership and liens, and notice of sale. The balance of the funds shall be held by such officer for the owner and paid to the owner upon satisfactory proof of ownership. Any unclaimed item retained for use by the law-enforcement agency shall become the property of the locality served by the agency and shall be retained only if, in the opinion of the chief law-enforcement officer, there is a legitimate use for the property by the agency and that retention of the item is a more economical alternative than purchase of a similar or equivalent item.

If no claim has been made by the owner for the property or proceeds of such sale within 60 days of the sale, the remaining funds shall be deposited in the general fund of the locality and the retained property may be placed into use by the law-enforcement agency. Any such owner shall be entitled to apply to the locality within three years from the date of the sale and, if timely application is made therefor and satisfactory proof of ownership of the funds or property is made, the locality shall pay the remaining proceeds of the sale or return the property to the owner without interest or other charges or compensation. No claim shall be made nor any suit, action or proceeding be instituted for the recovery of such funds or property after three years from the date of the sale.

History.

1982, c. 163, § 15.1-133.01; 1994, c. 144; 1997, c. 587; 2010, c. 333.

§ 15.2-1720. Localities authorized to license bicycles, electric power-assisted bicycles, mopeds, and electric personal assistive mobility devices; disposition of unclaimed bicycles, electric power-assisted bicycles, mopeds, and electric personal assistive mobility devices.

Any locality may, by ordinance, (i) provide for the public sale or donation to a charitable organization of any bicycle, electric personal assistive mobility device, electric power-assisted bicycle, or moped that has been in the possession of the police or sheriff's department, unclaimed, for more than thirty days; (ii) require every resident owner of a bicycle, electric power-assisted bicycle, electric personal assistive mobility device, or moped to obtain a license therefor and a license plate, tag, or adhesive license decal of such design and material as the ordinance may prescribe, to be substantially attached to the bicycle, electric personal assistive mobility device, electric power-assisted bicycle, or moped; (iii) prescribe the license fee, the license application forms and the license form; and (iv) prescribe penalties for operating a bicycle, electric personal assistive mobility device, electric power-assisted bicycle, or moped on public roads or streets within the locality without an attached license plate, tag, or adhesive decal. The ordinance shall require the license plates, tags, or adhesive decals to be provided by and at the cost of the locality. Any locality may provide that the license plates, tags, or adhesive decals shall be valid for the life of the bicycles, electric personal assistive mobility devices, electric power-assisted bicycles, and mopeds to which they are attached or for such other period as it may prescribe and may prescribe such fee therefor as it may deem reasonable. When any town license is required as provided for herein, the license shall be in lieu of any license required by any county ordinance. Any bicycle, electric personal assistive mobility device, electric power-assisted bicycle, or moped found and delivered to the police or sheriff's department by a private person that thereafter remains unclaimed for thirty days after the final date of publication as required herein may be given to the finder; however, the location and description of the bicycle, electric personal assistive mobility device, electric power-assisted bicycle, or moped shall be published at least once a week for two successive weeks in a newspaper of general circulation within the locality. In addition, if there is a license, tag, or adhesive license decal affixed to the bicycle, electric personal assistive mobility device, or electric power-assisted bicycle, or moped, the record owner shall be notified directly.

History.

Code 1950, § 15-554; 1962, c. 623, § 15.1-133; 1968, c. 24; 1970,

c. 285; 1975, c. 76; 1986, c. 52; 1994, c. 449; 1997, c. 587; 2001, c. 834; 2002, c. 254; 2013, c. 783.

§ 15.2-1721. Disposal of unclaimed firearms or other weapons in possession of sheriff or police.

Any locality may destroy unclaimed firearms and other weapons which have been in the possession of law-enforcement agencies for a period of more than 120 days. For the purposes of this section, "unclaimed firearms and other weapons" means any firearm or other weapon belonging to another which has been acquired by a law-enforcement officer pursuant to his duties, which is not needed in any criminal prosecution, which has not been claimed by its rightful owner and which the State Treasurer has indicated will be declined if remitted under the Uniform Disposition of Unclaimed Property Act (§ 55-210.1 et seq.).

At the discretion of the chief of police, sheriff, or their duly authorized agents, unclaimed firearms and other weapons may be destroyed by any means which renders the firearms and other weapons permanently inoperable. Prior to the destruction of such firearms and other weapons, the chief of police, sheriff, or their duly authorized agents shall comply with the notice provision contained in § 15.2-1719.

In lieu of destroying any such unclaimed firearm, the locality may donate the firearm to the Department of Forensic Science, upon agreement of the Department.

History.
1990, c. 324, § 15.1-133.01:1; 1997, c. 587; 2015, c. 220.

§ 15.2-1722. Disclosure of criminal records; limitations.

A. It shall be the duty of the sheriff or chief of police of every locality to insure, in addition to other records required by law, the maintenance of adequate personnel, arrest, investigative, reportable incidents, and noncriminal incidents records necessary for the efficient operation of a law-enforcement agency. Failure of a sheriff or a chief of police to maintain such records or failure to relinquish such records to his successor in office shall constitute a misdemeanor. Former sheriffs or chiefs of police shall be allowed access to such files for preparation of a defense in any suit or action arising from the performance of their official duties as sheriff or chief of police. The enforcement of this section shall be the duty of the attorney for the Commonwealth of the county or city wherein the violation occurs.

B. For purposes of this section, the following definitions shall apply:

"Arrest records" means a compilation of information, centrally maintained in law-enforcement custody, of any arrest or temporary detention of an individual, including the identity of the person arrested or detained, the nature of the arrest or detention, and the charge, if any.

"Investigative records" means the reports of any systematic inquiries or examinations into criminal or suspected criminal acts which have been committed, are being committed, or are about to be committed.

"Noncriminal incidents records" means compilations of noncriminal occurrences of general interest to law-enforcement agencies, such as missing persons, lost and found property, suicides and accidental deaths.

"Personnel records" means those records maintained on each and every individual employed by a law-enforcement agency which reflect personal data concerning the employee's age, length of service, amount of training, education, compensation level, and other pertinent personal information.

"Reportable incidents records" means a compilation of complaints received by a law-enforcement agency and action taken by the agency in response thereto.

History.
1975, c. 290, § 15.1-135.1; 1979, c. 686; 1981, c. 284; 1997, c. 587; 1999, cc. 703, 726.

§ 15.2-1723. Validation of certain police forces.

Any police force in existence on July 1, 1980, whose existence is authorized or was authorized by any provision of law, general or special, that was repealed by Chapter 333 of the Acts of Assembly of 1979 is hereby validated and shall continue. Any police force in existence on December 1, 1996, whose existence is authorized or was authorized by any provision of law, general or special, that is repealed by this act is hereby validated and shall continue.

History.
1979, c. 333, § 15.1-142.2; 1983, c. 576; 1997, c. 587.

ARTICLE 2.

INTERJURISDICTIONAL LAW-ENFORCEMENT AUTHORITY AND AGREEMENTS.

§ 15.2-1724. (Effective until October 1, 2016) Police and other officers may be sent beyond territorial limits.

Whenever the necessity arises (i) for the enforcement of laws designed to control or prohibit the use or sale of controlled drugs as defined in § 54.1-3401 or laws contained in Article 3 (§ 18.2-47 et seq.) of Chapter 4 or Article 3 (§ 18.2-344 et seq.) of Chapter 8 of Title 18.2, (ii) in response to any law-enforcement emergency involving any immediate threat to life or public safety, (iii) during the execution of the provisions of Article 4 (§ 37.2-808 et seq.) of Chapter 8 of Title 37.2 or § 16.1-340 or 16.1-340.1 relating to orders for temporary detention or emergency custody for mental health evaluation or (iv) during any emergency resulting from the existence of a state of war, internal disorder, or fire, flood, epidemic or other public disaster, the police officers and other officers, agents and employees of any locality, the police officers of the Division of Capitol Police, and the police of any state-supported institution of higher learning appointed pursuant to § 23-233 may, together with all necessary equipment, lawfully go or be sent beyond the territorial limits of such locality, such agency, or such state-supported institution of higher learning to any point within or without the Commonwealth to assist in meeting such emergency or need, or while enroute to a part of the jurisdiction which is only accessible by roads outside the jurisdiction. However, the police of any state-supported institution of higher learning may be sent only to a locality within the Commonwealth, or locality outside the Commonwealth, whose boundaries are contiguous with the locality in which such institution is located. No member of a police force of any state-supported institution of higher learning shall be sent beyond the territorial limits of the locality in which such institution is located unless such member has met the requirements established by the Department of Criminal Justice Services as provided in clause (i) of subdivision 2 of § 9.1-102.

In such event the acts performed for such purpose by such police officers or other officers, agents or employees and the expenditures made for such purpose by such locality, such agency, or a state-supported institution of higher learning shall be deemed conclusively to be for a public and governmental purpose, and all of the immunities from liability enjoyed by a locality, agency, or a state-supported institution of higher learning when acting through its police officers or other officers, agents or employees for a public or governmental purpose within its territorial limits shall be enjoyed by it to the same extent when such locality, agency, or a state-supported institution of higher learning within the Commonwealth is so acting, under this section or under other lawful authority, beyond its territorial limits.

The police officers and other officers, agents and employees of any locality, agency, or a state-supported institution of higher learning when acting hereunder or under other lawful authority beyond the territorial limits of such locality, agency, or such state-supported institution of higher learning shall have all of the immunities from liability and exemptions from laws, ordinances and regulations and shall have all of the pension, relief, disability, workers' compensation and other benefits enjoyed by them while performing their respective duties within the territorial limits of such locality, agency, or such state-supported institution of higher learning.

History.

Code 1950, § 15-552; 1962, c. 623, § 15.1-131; 1968, c. 800; 1971, Ex. Sess., c. 238; 1976, c. 457; 1977, c. 79; 1979, c. 503; 1984, c. 779; 1992, c. 566; 1993, c. 860; 1995, c. 844; 1997, c. 587; 2008, c. 437; 2010, cc. 778, 825; 2013, c. 428.

§ 15.2-1724. (Effective October 1, 2016) Police and other officers may be sent beyond territorial limits.

Whenever the necessity arises (i) for the enforcement of laws designed to control or prohibit the use or sale of controlled drugs as defined in § 54.1-3401 or laws contained in Article 3 (§ 18.2-47 et seq.) of Chapter 4 or Article 3 (§ 18.2-344 et seq.) of Chapter 8 of Title 18.2, (ii) in response to any law-enforcement emergency involving any immediate threat to life or public safety, (iii) during the execution of the provisions of Article 4 (§ 37.2-808 et seq.) of Chapter 8 of Title 37.2 or § 16.1-340 or 16.1-340.1 relating to orders for temporary detention or emergency custody for mental health evaluation or (iv) during any emergency resulting from the existence of a state of war, internal disorder, or fire, flood, epidemic or other public disaster, the police officers and other officers, agents and employees of any locality, the police officers of the Division of Capitol Police, and the police of any state-supported institution of higher learning appointed pursuant to subsection B of § 23.1-812 may, together with all necessary equipment, lawfully go or be sent beyond the territorial limits of such locality, such agency, or such state-supported institution of higher learning to any point within or without the Commonwealth to assist in meeting such emergency or need, or while enroute to a part of the jurisdiction which is only accessible by roads outside the jurisdiction. However, the police of any state-supported institution of higher learning may be sent only to a locality within the Commonwealth, or locality outside the Commonwealth, whose boundaries are contiguous with the locality in which such institution is located. No member of a police force of any state-supported institution of higher learning shall be sent beyond the territorial limits of the locality in which such institution is located unless such member has met the requirements established by the Department of Criminal Justice Services as provided in clause (i) of subdivision 2 of § 9.1-102.

In such event the acts performed for such purpose by such police officers or other officers, agents or employees and the expenditures made for such purpose by such locality, such agency, or a state-supported institution of higher learning shall be deemed conclusively to be for a public and governmental purpose, and all of the immunities from liability enjoyed by a locality, agency, or a state-supported institution of higher learning when acting through its police officers or other officers, agents or employees for a public or governmental purpose within its territorial limits shall be enjoyed by it to the same extent when such locality, agency, or a state-supported institution of higher learning within the Commonwealth is so acting, under this section or under other lawful authority, beyond its territorial limits.

The police officers and other officers, agents and employees of any locality, agency, or a state-supported institution of higher learning when acting hereunder or under other lawful authority beyond the territorial limits of such locality, agency, or such state-supported institution of higher learning shall have all of the immunities from liability and exemptions from laws, ordinances and regulations and shall have all of the pension, relief, disability, workers' compensation and other benefits enjoyed by them while performing their respective duties within the territorial limits of such locality, agency, or such state-supported institution of higher learning.

History.
Code 1950, § 15-552; 1962, c. 623, § 15.1-131; 1968, c. 800; 1971, Ex. Sess., c. 238; 1976, c. 457; 1977, c. 79; 1979, c. 503; 1984, c. 779; 1992, c. 566; 1993, c. 860; 1995, c. 844; 1997, c. 587; 2008, c. 437; 2010, cc. 778, 825; 2013, c. 428.

§ 15.2-1725. Extending police power of localities over lands lying beyond boundaries thereof; jurisdiction of courts.

Any locality owning and operating an airport, public hospital, sanitarium, nursing home, public water supply or watershed, public park, recreational area, sewage disposal plant or system, public landing, dock, wharf or canal, public school, public utility, public buildings and other public property located beyond the limits of the locality shall have and may exercise full police power over the property, and over persons using the property, and may, by ordinance, prescribe rules for the operation and use of the property and for the conduct of all persons using the property and may, further, provide penalties for the violation of such rules contained in an ordinance; such penalties, however, shall not exceed those provided by general law for misdemeanors. However, no ordinances in conflict with an ordinance of the jurisdiction wherein the property is located shall be enacted.

Any locality which maintains or operates in whole or in part any property enumerated in this section may lawfully send its law-enforcement officers to the property owned beyond the limits of the locality for the purpose of protecting the property, keeping order therein, or otherwise enforcing the laws of the Commonwealth and ordinances of the locality owning the property as such laws and ordinances may relate to the operation and use thereof. The law-enforcement officer shall have power to make an arrest for a violation of any law or ordinance relating to the operation and use of the property. The district court in the city or town where the offense occurs shall have jurisdiction of all cases arising therein, and the district court of the county where the offense occurs shall have jurisdiction of all cases arising therein.

It shall be the duty of the attorney for the Commonwealth for the locality wherein the offense occurs to prosecute all violators of the ordinances of the locality that pertain to the operation and use of the property enumerated in this section.

History.
Code 1950, § 15-560.1; 1952, c. 382; 1962, c. 623, § 15.1-142; 1979, c. 333; 1997, c. 587.

§ 15.2-1725.1. Concurrent jurisdiction; limitations.

For the purposes of local public safety regulatory authority and enforcement, the territorial limits of the City of Virginia Beach shall extend from its coastal shorelines, the coastal shorelines of Camp Pendleton, the coastal shorelines of First Landing State Park, and the coastal shorelines of False Cape State Park in a perpendicular direction for three miles into the Atlantic Ocean and Chesapeake Bay waters. This territorial jurisdiction shall be concurrent with the jurisdiction of the Commonwealth. No ordinance enacted under this authority shall conflict with the laws or regulations promulgated by the Commonwealth or any of its agencies. This authority shall not extend to the regulatory authority held by the Virginia Marine Resources Commission as provided in § 28.2-101.

History.
2012, c. 809.

§ 15.2-1726. (Effective until October 1, 2016) Agreements for consolidation of police departments or for cooperation in furnishing police services.

Any locality may, in its discretion, enter into a reciprocal agreement with any other locality, any agency of the federal government exercising police powers, the police of any state-supported institution of higher learning appointed pursuant to § 23-233, the Division of Capitol Police, any private police department certified by the Department of Criminal Justice Services, or any combination of the foregoing, for such periods and under such conditions as the contracting parties deem advisable, for cooperation in the furnishing of police services. Such agreements may include designation of mutually agreed-upon boundary lines between contiguous localities for purposes of organizing 911 dispatch and response and clarifying issues related to coverage under workers' compensation and risk management laws. Such agreements may also include provisions allowing for the loan of unmarked police vehicles. Such localities also may enter into an agreement for the cooperation in the furnishing of police services with the Department of State Police. The governing body of any locality also may, in its discretion, enter into a reciprocal agreement with any other locality, or combination thereof, for the consolidation of police departments or divisions or departments thereof. Subject to the conditions of the agreement, all police officers, officers, agents and other employees of such consolidated or cooperating police departments shall have the same powers, rights, benefits, privileges and immunities in every jurisdiction subscribing to such agreement, including the authority to make arrests in every such jurisdiction subscribing to the agreement; however, no police officer of any locality shall have authority to enforce federal laws unless specifically empowered to do so by statute, and no federal law-enforcement officer shall have authority to enforce the laws of the Commonwealth unless specifically empowered to do so by statute.

The governing body of a county also may enter into a tripartite contract with the governing body of any town, one or more, in such county and the sheriff for such county for the purpose of having the sheriff furnish law-enforcement services in the town. The contract shall be structured as a service contract and may have such other terms and conditions as the contracting parties deem advisable. The sheriff and any deputy sheriff serving as a town law-enforcement officer shall have authority to enforce such town's ordinances. Likewise, subject to the conditions of the contract, the sheriff and deputy sheriffs while serving as a town's law-enforcement officers shall have the same powers, rights, benefits, privileges and immunities as those of regular town police officers. The sheriff under any such contract shall be the town's chief of police.

History.

1970, c. 271, § 15.1-131.3; 1978, c. 9; 1984, c. 622; 1989, c. 294; 1994, c. 268; 1997, c. 587; 2008, c. 437; 2013, cc. 250, 472, 594, 775; 2014, c. 581.

§ 15.2-1726. (Effective October 1, 2016) Agreements for consolidation of police departments or for cooperation in furnishing police services.

Any locality may, in its discretion, enter into a reciprocal agreement with any other locality, any agency of the federal government exercising police powers, the police of any state-supported institution of higher learning appointed pursuant to subsection B of § 23.1-812, the Division of Capitol Police, any private police department certified by the Department of Criminal Justice Services, or any combination of the foregoing, for such periods and under such conditions as the contracting parties deem advisable, for cooperation in the furnishing of police services. Such agreements may include designation of mutually agreed-upon boundary lines between contiguous localities for purposes of organizing 911 dispatch and response and clarifying issues related to coverage under workers' compensation and risk management laws. Such agreements may also include provisions allowing for the loan of unmarked police vehicles. Such localities also may enter into an agreement for the cooperation in the furnishing of police services with the Department of State Police. The governing body of any locality also may, in its discretion, enter into a reciprocal agreement with any other locality, or combination thereof, for the consolidation of police departments or divisions or departments thereof. Subject to the conditions of the agreement, all police officers, officers, agents and other employees of such consolidated or cooperating police departments shall have the same powers, rights, benefits, privileges and immunities in every jurisdiction subscribing to such agreement, including the authority to make arrests in every such jurisdiction subscribing to the agreement; however, no police officer of any locality shall have authority to enforce federal laws unless specifically empowered to do so by statute, and no federal law-enforcement officer shall have authority to enforce the laws of the Commonwealth unless specifically empowered to do so by statute.

The governing body of a county also may enter into a tripartite contract with the governing body of any town, one or more, in such county and the sheriff for such county for the purpose of having the sheriff furnish law-enforcement services in the town. The contract shall be structured as a service contract and may have such other terms and conditions as the contracting parties deem advisable. The sheriff and any deputy sheriff serving as a town law-enforcement officer shall have authority to enforce such town's ordinances. Likewise, subject to the conditions of the contract, the sheriff and deputy sheriffs while serving as a town's law-enforcement officers shall have the same powers, rights, benefits, privileges and immunities as those of regular town police officers. The sheriff under any such contract shall be the town's chief of police.

History.

1970, c. 271, § 15.1-131.3; 1978, c. 9; 1984, c. 622; 1989, c. 294; 1994, c. 268; 1997, c. 587; 2008, c. 437; 2013, cc. 250, 472, 594, 775; 2014, c. 581.

§ 15.2-1727. Reciprocal agreements with localities outside the Commonwealth.

A locality or a state-supported or private institution of higher learning may, in its discretion, enter into reciprocal agreements for such periods as it deems advisable with any locality outside the Commonwealth, including the District of Columbia, in order to establish and carry into effect a plan to provide mutual aid through the furnishing of its police and other employees and agents, together with all necessary equipment, in the event of such need or emergency as provided herein. No state-supported or private institution of higher learning shall enter into such agreement unless the agreement provides that each of the parties to such agreement shall: (i) waive any and all claims against all the other parties thereto which may arise out of their activities outside their respective jurisdictions under such agreement and (ii) indemnify and save harmless the other parties to such agreement from all claims by third parties for property damage or personal injury which may arise out of the activities of the other parties to such agreement outside their respective jurisdictions under such agreement. Parties responding to a reciprocal agreement for mutual aid between localities shall be liable to third parties only to the extent permitted under and in accordance with the laws of the state of the party rendering aid.

The principal law-enforcement officer in any locality or of a state-supported or private institution of higher learning having a reciprocal agreement with a jurisdiction outside the Commonwealth for police mutual aid under the provisions hereof shall be responsible for directing the activities of all police officers and other officers and agents coming into his jurisdiction under the reciprocal agreement. While operating under the terms of the reciprocal agreement, the principal law-enforcement officer is empowered to authorize all police officers and other officers and agents from outside the Commonwealth to enforce the laws of the Commonwealth of Virginia to the same extent as if they were duly authorized law-enforcement officers of the locality or a state-supported or private institution of higher learning in Virginia.

The governing body of any locality or a state-supported or private institution of higher learning in the Commonwealth is authorized to procure or extend the necessary public liability insurance to cover claims arising out of mutual aid agreements executed with other localities outside the Commonwealth.

The police officers, and other officers, agents and employees of a locality or a state-supported or private institution of higher learning serving in a jurisdiction outside the Commonwealth under a reciprocal agreement entered into pursuant hereto are authorized to carry out the duties and functions provided for in the agreement under the command and supervision of the chief law-enforcement officer of the jurisdiction outside the Commonwealth.

In counties where no police department has been established and the sheriff is the chief law-enforcement officer, the sheriff may enter into mutual aid agreements and furnish and receive such assistance as provided by this section. Sheriffs and their deputies providing assistance pursuant to such a mutual aid agreement shall enjoy all of the authority, immunities and benefits as provided herein for police officers, including full police powers.

History.

Code 1950, § 15-552; 1962, c. 623, § 15.1-131; 1968, c. 800; 1971, Ex. Sess., c. 238; 1976, c. 457; 1977, c. 79; 1979, c. 503; 1984, c. 779; 1992, c. 566; 1993, c. 860; 1995, c. 844; 1997, cc. 587, 638, 668; 2004, c. 769; 2007, c. 724.

§ 15.2-1728. Mutual aid agreements between police departments and federal authorities.

In any case where exclusive jurisdiction over any property or territory has been granted by the Commonwealth to the United States government, or to a department or agency thereof, the governing body of any contiguous locality or the Division of Capitol Police may enter into a mutual aid agreement with the appropriate federal authorities to authorize police cooperation and assistance within such property or territory. Subject to the conditions of any such agreement, all police officers and agents of the contracting governing body or agency shall have the same powers, rights, benefits, privileges and immunities while acting in the performance of their duties on the property or territory under federal authority as are lawfully conferred upon them within their own jurisdictions.

History.

1987, c. 33, § 15.1-131.10; 1997, c. 587; 2008, c. 437.

§ 15.2-1729. Agreements for enforcement of state and county laws by federal officers on federal property.

A. The governing body of any county may enter into an agreement with the United States government or a department or agency thereof, under the terms of which agreement law-enforcement officers employed by such government, including but not limited to members of the United States Park Police, may enforce the laws of such county and the Commonwealth on federally owned properties within such county, and on the highways located therein and other public places abutting such properties. In the event such an agreement is entered into, all of the provisions of §§ 15.2-1724 and 15.2-1727 shall be applicable, mutatis mutandis.

B. The governing body of any county governed under the provisions of Chapter 8 (§ 15.2-800 et seq.) of Title 15.2 may enter into an agreement with the United States government or a department or agency thereof, under the terms of which agreement law-enforcement officers employed by such government, including but not limited to members of the United States Park Police, may enforce the laws of such county and the Commonwealth on federally owned properties within such county, and on the highways and other public places abutting such properties. In the event such an agreement is entered into, all of the provisions of §§ 15.2-1724 and 15.2-1727 shall be applicable, mutatis mutandis.

History.
1972, c. 743, § 15.1-131.4; 1997, cc. 537, 587.

§ 15.2-1730. Calling upon law-enforcement officers of counties, cities or towns for assistance.

In case of an emergency declared by the chief law-enforcement officer of a locality, such officer may call upon the chief law-enforcement officer of towns within his county and the chief law-enforcement officer of an adjoining county or city, or towns in adjoining counties for assistance from him or his deputies or other police officers, without the necessity for deputizing such deputies or officers. Such deputies or officers shall have full police powers in such locality as are conferred upon them by law during the period of such emergency.

History.
1974, c. 633, § 15.1-131.5; 1976, c. 206; 1997, c. 587.

§ 15.2-1730.1. Authority and immunity of sheriffs and deputies.

In counties where no police department has been established and the sheriff is the chief law-enforcement officer, the sheriff may enter into agreements with any other governmental entity providing law-enforcement services in the Commonwealth, and may furnish and receive interjurisdictional law-enforcement assistance for all law-enforcement purposes, including those described in this chapter, and for purposes of Chapter 3.2 (§ 44-146.13 et seq.) of Title 44. Sheriffs and their deputies, providing or receiving such assistance, shall have all the authority, benefits, immunity from liability and exemptions from laws, ordinances and regulations as officers acting within their own jurisdictions.

History.
1999, c. 352.

ARTICLE 3.

AUXILIARY POLICE FORCES IN LOCALITIES.

§ 15.2-1731. Establishment, etc., authorized; powers, authority and immunities generally.

A. Localities, for the further preservation of the public peace, safety, and good order of the community, may establish, equip, and maintain auxiliary police forces that have all the powers and authority and all the immunities of full-time law-enforcement officers, if all such forces have met the training requirements established by the Department of Criminal Justice Services under § 9.1-102.

B. Notwithstanding any other provision of this section, an auxiliary officer shall be exempted from any initial training requirement established under § 9.1-102 until a date one year subsequent to the approval by the Criminal Justice Services Board of compulsory minimum training standards for auxiliary police officers, except that (i) any such officer shall not be permitted to carry or use a firearm while serving as an auxiliary police officer unless such officer has met the firearms training requirements established in accordance with in-service training standards for law-enforcement officers as prescribed by the Criminal Justice Services Board, and (ii) any such officer shall have one year following the approval by the Board to comply with the compulsory minimum training standards.

History.
1968, c. 157, § 15.1-159.2; 1987, c. 421; 1988, c. 864; 1997, c. 587; 2012, c. 827.

§ 15.2-1732. Appropriations for equipment and maintenance.

Localities may make such appropriations as may be necessary to arm, equip, uniform and maintain such auxiliary police force.

History.
1968, c. 157, § 15.1-159.3; 1997, c. 587.

§ 15.2-1733. Appointment of auxiliary police officers; revocation of appointment; uniform; organization; rules and regulations.

The governing body of the locality may appoint or provide for the appointment as auxiliary police officers as many persons of good character as it deems necessary, not to exceed the number fixed by ordinance adopted by the governing body, and their appointment shall be revocable at any time by the governing body. The governing body may prescribe the uniform, organization, and such rules as it deems necessary for the operation of the auxiliary police force.

History.
1968, c. 157, § 15.1-159.4; 1997, c. 587.

§ 15.2-1734. Calling auxiliary police officers into service; police officers performing service to wear uniform; exception.

A. A locality may call into service or provide for calling into service such auxiliary police officers as may be deemed necessary (i) in time of public emergency, (ii) at such times as there are insufficient numbers of regular police officers to preserve the peace, safety and good order of the community, or (iii) at any time for the purpose of training such auxiliary police officers. At all times when performing such service, the members of the auxiliary police force shall wear the uniform prescribed by the governing body.

B. Members of any auxiliary police force who have been trained in accordance with the provisions of § 15.2-1731 may be called into service by the chief of police of any locality to aid and assist regular police officers in the performance of their duties.

C. When the duties of an auxiliary police officer are such that the wearing of the prescribed uniform would adversely limit the effectiveness of the auxiliary police officer's ability to perform his prescribed duties, then clothing appropriate for the duties to be performed may be required by the chief of police.

History.

1968, c. 157, § 15.1-159.5; 1987, c. 421; 1988, c. 190; 1997, c. 587.

§ 15.2-1735. Acting beyond limits of jurisdiction of locality.

The members of any such auxiliary police force shall not be required to act beyond the limits of the jurisdiction of any such locality except when called upon to protect any public property belonging to the locality which may be located beyond its boundaries, or as provided in § 15.2-1736.

History.

1968, c. 157, § 15.1-159.6; 1997, c. 587.

§ 15.2-1736. (Effective until October 1, 2016) Mutual aid agreements among governing bodies of localities.

The governing bodies of localities, institutions of higher learning having a police force appointed pursuant to § 23-233, and institutions of higher education having a private police force, as well as sheriffs, and the Director of the Department of Conservation and Recreation with commissioned conservation officers, or any combination thereof may, by proper resolutions, enter in and become a party to contracts or mutual aid agreements for the use of their joint forces, both regular and auxiliary, their equipment and materials to maintain peace and good order. However, no such institution of higher learning shall enter into such agreement with another institution of higher education in a noncontiguous locality without the consent of all localities within which such institutions are located. Any police or other law-enforcement officer, regular or auxiliary, while performing his duty under any such contract or agreement, shall have the same authority in such locality as he has within the locality where he was appointed.

In counties where no police department has been established, the sheriff may, in his discretion, enter into mutual aid agreements as provided by this section.

History.

1968, c. 157, § 15.1-159.7; 1987, c. 421; 1994, c. 268; 1997, cc. 587, 604; 2002, cc. 684, 709, 876; 2005, c. 87; 2006, c. 286; 2009, cc. 461, 609; 2010, c. 523.

§ 15.2-1736. (Effective October 1, 2016) Mutual aid agreements among governing bodies of localities.

The governing bodies of localities, institutions of higher learning having a police force appointed pursuant to subsection B of § 23.1-812, and institutions of higher education having a private police force, as well as sheriffs, and the Director of the Department of Conservation and Recreation with commissioned conservation officers, or any combination thereof may, by proper resolutions, enter in and become a party to contracts or mutual aid agreements for the use of their joint forces, both regular and auxiliary, their equipment and materials to maintain peace and good order. However, no such institution of higher learning shall enter into such agreement with another institution of higher education in a noncontiguous locality without the consent of all localities within which such institutions are located. Any police or other law-enforcement officer, regular or auxiliary, while performing his duty under any such contract or agreement, shall have the same authority in such locality as he has within the locality where he was appointed.

In counties where no police department has been established, the sheriff may, in his discretion, enter into mutual aid agreements as provided by this section.

History.

1968, c. 157, § 15.1-159.7; 1987, c. 421; 1994, c. 268; 1997, cc. 587, 604; 2002, cc. 684, 709, 876; 2005, c. 87; 2006, c. 286; 2009, cc. 461, 609; 2010, c. 523.

ARTICLE 4.

SPECIAL POLICE OFFICERS IN LOCALITIES.

§§ 15.2-1737 through 15.2-1746: Repealed by Acts 2014, c. 543, cl. 2.

ARTICLE 5.

CRIMINAL JUSTICE TRAINING ACADEMIES.

§ 15.2-1747. Creation of academies.

A. The governing bodies of two or more localities or other political subdivisions or other public bodies hereinafter collectively referred to as "governmental units," may by ordinance or resolution enter into an agreement which creates a regional criminal justice academy under an appropriate name and title containing the words "criminal justice academy" or "criminal justice training academy" which shall be a public body politic and corporate. Any regional criminal justice training academy created under this article shall also be subject to the requirements of § 9.1-102.

B. The agreement shall set forth (i) the name of the academy, (ii) the governmental subdivision in which its principal office shall be situated, (iii) the effective date of the organization of the academy and the duration of the agreement, (iv) the composition of the board of directors of the academy which may include representation of each locality, political subdivision or governmental entity party to the agreement, the members of which shall be the governing body of the academy, (v) the method for selection and the terms of office of the board of directors, (vi) the voting rights of the directors which need not be equal, (vii) the procedure for amendment of the agreement, and (viii) such other matters as the governmental units creating the academy deem appropriate. Sheriffs and members of the governing bodies of the governmental units as well as other public officials or employees may be members of the board of directors.

C. Any governmental unit not a party to an original agreement creating an academy under this section or § 15.2-1300 may join the academy only by two-thirds vote of the board of directors of the academy. The governing body of the governmental unit seeking to join the academy shall request membership by resolution or ordinance. The board of directors shall provide for the addition of the joining governmental unit to the academy and the number, terms of office, and voting rights of members of the board of directors, if any, to be appointed by the joining governmental unit.

D. A governmental unit may withdraw from an academy created under this section or § 15.2-1300 only by two-thirds vote of the board of directors of the academy. The governing body of the governmental unit seeking to withdraw from the academy shall signify its desire by resolution or ordinance. The board of directors shall consider requests to withdraw in October 2001, and in October of every fifth year thereafter. No requests to withdraw shall be considered at any other time, unless agreed to unanimously. Any withdrawal approved by the board of directors shall be effective on June 30 of the following year. The board of directors shall provide for the conditions of withdrawal.

D1. The Division of Capitol Police may become a party to an agreement creating an academy or may join an existing academy. The Chief of the Capitol Police is authorized to enter into such agreement as necessary to join an academy. The chief or his designee may serve as a member of the board of directors of such academy, and in accordance with the bylaws of the academy, may serve as a member of the executive committee or other committee of the academy.

E. The chairman of the academy board shall serve as a member and as the chairman of an executive committee. The composition of the remaining membership of the executive committee, the term of office of its members and any alternate members, procedures for the conduct of its meetings, and any limitations upon the general authority of the executive committee shall be established in the bylaws of the academy. The bylaws shall also establish any other special standing committees, advisory, technical or otherwise, as the board of directors shall deem desirable for the transaction of its affairs.

History.

1993, c. 935, § 15.1-159.7:1; 1997, c. 587; 2000, c. 772; 2002, c. 350; 2010, c. 516.

§ 15.2-1748. Powers of the academies.

A. Upon organization of an academy, it shall be a public body corporate and politic, the purposes of which shall be to establish and conduct training for public law-enforcement and correctional officers, those being trained to be public law-enforcement and correctional officers, other personnel who assist or support such officers, and those persons seeking appointments as special conservators of the peace pursuant to § 19.2-13. The persons trained by an academy need not be employed by a locality that has joined in the agreement creating the academy.

B. Criminal justice training academies may:

1. Adopt and have a common seal and alter that seal at the pleasure of the board of directors;
2. Sue and be sued;
3. Adopt bylaws and make rules and regulations for the conduct of its business;
4. Make and enter into all contracts or agreements, as it may determine are necessary, incidental or convenient to the performance of its duties and to the execution of the powers granted under this article;
5. Apply for and accept, disburse and administer for itself or for a member governmental unit any loans or grants of money, materials or property from any private or charitable source, the United States of America, the Commonwealth, any agency or instrumentality thereof, or from any other source;
6. Employ engineers, attorneys, planners and such other professional experts or consultants, and general and clerical employees as may be deemed necessary and prescribe such experts, consultants, and employees' powers, duties, and compensation;
7. Perform any acts authorized under this article through or by means of its own officers, agents and employees, or by contracts with any person, firm or corporation;
8. Acquire, whether by purchase, exchange, gift, lease or otherwise, any interest in real or personal property, and improve, maintain, equip and furnish academy facilities;
9. Lease, sell, exchange, donate and convey any interest in any or all of its projects, property or facilities in furtherance of the purposes of the academy as set forth in this article;
10. Accept contributions, grants and other financial assistance from the United States of America and its agencies or instrumentalities thereof, the

Commonwealth, any political subdivision, agency or public instrumentality thereof or from any other source, for or in aid of the construction, acquisition, ownership, maintenance or repair of the academy facilities, for the payment of principal of, or interest on, any bond of the academy, or other costs incident thereto, or make loans in furtherance of the purposes of this article of such money, contributions, grants, and other financial assistance, and comply with such conditions and to execute such agreements, trust indentures, and other legal instruments as may be necessary, convenient or desirable and agree to such terms and conditions as may be imposed;

11. Borrow money from any source for capital purposes or to cover current expenditures in any given year in anticipation of the collection of revenues;

12. Mortgage and pledge any or all of its projects, property or facilities or parts thereof and pledge the revenues therefrom or from any part thereof as security for the payment of principal and premium, if any, and interest on any bonds, notes or other evidences of indebtedness;

13. Create an executive committee which may exercise the powers and authority of the academy under this article pursuant to authority delegated to it by the board of directors;

14. Establish fees or other charges for the training services provided;

15. Exercise the powers granted in the agreement creating the academy; and

16. Execute any and all instruments and do and perform any and all acts necessary, convenient or desirable for its purposes or to carry out the powers expressly given in this article.

History.

1993, c. 935, § 15.1-159.7:2; 1997, c. 587; 2015, cc. 766, 772.

§ 15.2-1749. Revenue bonds.

A. Each academy is hereby authorized, after a resolution adopted by a majority of its board of directors, to issue, at one time or from time to time, revenue bonds of the academy on a taxable or tax-exempt basis for the purpose of acquiring, purchasing, constructing, reconstructing, or improving training facilities and acquiring necessary land or equipment therefor, and to refund any bonds issued for such purposes. The bonds of each issue shall be dated, shall mature at such time or times not exceeding forty years from their issue date or dates and shall bear interest at such fixed or variable rate or rates as may be determined by the board of directors, and may be made redeemable before maturity at the option of the board of directors at such price or prices and under such terms and conditions as may be fixed by the authority prior to the issuance of the bonds. The board of directors shall determine the form of the bonds, including any interest coupons to be attached thereto, and the manner of execution of the bonds, and shall affix the denomination or denominations of the bonds and the place or places of payment of principal and interest, which may be at any bank or trust company within or outside the Commonwealth. In case any officer whose signature or a facsimile of whose signature appears on any bonds or coupons ceases to be such officer before the delivery of such bonds, such signature or facsimile shall nevertheless be valid and sufficient for all purposes the same as if he had remained in office until such delivery. Notwithstanding any of the other provisions of this article or any recitals in any bonds issued under the provisions of this article, all such bonds shall be deemed to be negotiable instruments under the laws of this Commonwealth. The bonds may be issued in coupon or registered form or both, as the board of directors may determine, and provision may be made for the registration of any coupon bonds as to principal alone and also as to both principal and interest, and for the reconversion into coupon bonds of any bonds registered as to both principal and interest. The board of directors may sell such bonds in such manner, either at public or private sale, and for such price as it may determine to be for the best interests of the academy.

B. The resolution providing for the issuance of revenue bonds, and any trust agreement securing such bonds, may also contain such limitations upon the issuance of additional revenue bonds as the board of directors may deem proper and such additional bonds as shall be issued under such restriction and limitations as may be prescribed by such resolution or trust agreement.

C. Bonds may be issued under the provisions of this article without obtaining the consent of any commission, board, bureau, or agency of the Commonwealth or of any political subdivision and without any other proceedings or conditions as are specifically required by this article.

D. Bonds issued under the provisions of this article shall not be deemed to constitute a debt of the Commonwealth or of any political subdivision thereof or a pledge of the faith and credit of the Commonwealth or of any political subdivision thereof. The bonds shall be payable solely from revenues or other property of the academy specifically pledged for such purpose.

E. "Bonds" or "revenue bonds" as used in this article shall embrace notes, bonds and other obligations authorized to be issued pursuant to this article.

History.

1993, c. 935, § 15.1-159.7:3; 1997, c. 587.

§ 15.2-1750. Governmental units authorized to appropriate or lend funds.

The governmental units which are parties of the agreement creating the academy or which arrange to have personnel trained at the academy are authorized to appropriate or lend funds; pay fees or charges for services; convey by sale, lease or gift real or personal property, or any interest therein; provide services to the academy; or enter into such other contracts with the academy as may be appropriate to carry out any other power granted to those localities or the academy.

History.
1993, c. 935, § 15.1-159.7:4; 1997, c. 587.

§ 15.2-1751. Exemption from taxation.

Any academy created under the provisions of this article shall not be required to pay taxes or assessments upon any project or upon any property acquired or used by it or upon the income therefrom and income derived from bonds shall be exempt at all times from every kind and nature of taxation by this Commonwealth or by any of its political subdivisions, municipal corporations, or public agencies of any kind.

History.
1993, c. 935, § 15.1-159.7:5; 1997, c. 587.

§ 15.2-1752. Governmental immunity.

Any academy created pursuant to this article shall be deemed to be a governmental entity exercising essential governmental powers. Any such academy; its directors, officers, and employees; and any person serving as a trainer at the academy who is certified by the Department of Criminal Justice Services or any person who is a criminal justice academy approved instructor shall be entitled to immunity in any civil action or proceeding for damages or injury to any person or property of any person to the same extent that counties and their officers and employees are immune. Members of the board of directors of the academy shall have the same immunity as members of county boards of supervisors.

History.
1993, c. 935, § 15.1-159.7:6; 1997, c. 587; 2013, cc. 66, 99.

§ 15.2-1753. Liability of board members.

No member of the board of directors of an academy shall be personally liable for any indebtedness, obligation or other liability of an academy, barring willful misconduct.

History.
1993, c. 935, § 15.1-159.7:7; 1997, c. 587.

CHAPTER 20.
STREETS AND ALLEYS.

Article 5.

Miscellaneous.

ARTICLE 5.
MISCELLANEOUS.

§ 15.2-2018. Use of certain public property without consent or franchise.

Notwithstanding the provisions of subsection A of § 15.2-2000, any person or corporation, except a public service corporation, that occupies or uses any streets, avenues, parks, bridges or any other public places or public property or any public easement of a county, in a manner not permitted to the general public, without having first obtained the consent of the governing body of such county or a franchise therefor, shall be guilty of a Class 4 misdemeanor. Each day's continuance thereof shall be a separate offense. Such occupancy or use shall be deemed a nuisance. The court trying the case may cause the nuisance to be abated and commit the offenders and all their agents and employees engaged in such offenses to jail until the order of the court is obeyed.

History.
1983, c. 613, § 15.1-512.1; 1997, c. 587.

§ 15.2-2028. Regulation of traffic.

Every locality may regulate and control the operation of motor and other vehicles and the movement of vehicular and pedestrian travel and traffic on streets, highways, roads, alleys, bridges, viaducts, subways, underpasses and other public rights-of-way and places, provided such regulations shall not be inconsistent with the provisions of Chapter 13 (§ 46.2-1300 et seq.) of Title 46.2.

History.
Code 1950, § 15-77.55; 1958, c. 328; 1962, c. 623, § 15.1-891; 1997, c. 587.

§ 15.2-2029. Regulation of transportation of certain materials.

Any locality may regulate the transportation of hay, coal, gasoline, explosives or other articles through the streets of the locality.

History.
Code 1950, § 15-6; 1960, c. 528; 1962, c. 623, § 15.1-14; 1970, c. 453; 1973, c. 402; 1990, c. 58; 1997, c. 587.

CHAPTER 21.
FRANCHISES; SALE AND LEASE OF CERTAIN MUNICIPAL PUBLIC PROPERTY; PUBLIC UTILITIES.

Article 1.

Franchises; Sale and Lease of Certain Public Property.

ARTICLE 1.
FRANCHISES; SALE AND LEASE OF CERTAIN PUBLIC PROPERTY.

§ 15.2-2107. Persons occupying or using streets, etc., contrary to law.

Any person occupying or using any of the streets, avenues, parks, bridges or any other public places or public property or any public easement of any description of a city or town, in a manner not permitted to the general public, without having first legally obtained the consent of the city or town shall be guilty of a Class 4 misdemeanor. Each day's continuance thereof shall be a separate offense. Such occupancy or use shall be deemed a nuisance. The court trying the case may cause the nuisance to be abated and commit the offenders and all their agents and employees engaged in such offenses to jail until the order of the court is obeyed.

History.
Code 1950, § 15-736; 1962, c. 623, § 15.1-316; 1983, c. 613; 1997, c. 587.

CHAPTER 28.
VIRGINIA INDOOR CLEAN AIR ACT.

§§ **15.2-2800 through 15.2-2810:** Repealed by Acts 2009, cc. 153 and 154, cl. 2, effective December 1, 2009.

TITLE 16.1.
COURTS NOT OF RECORD.

CHAPTER 4.1.
DISTRICT COURTS.

Article 5.

Financing of the District System.

ARTICLE 5.
FINANCING OF THE DISTRICT SYSTEM.

§ 16.1-69.48:1. Fixed fee for misdemeanors, traffic infractions and other violations in district court; additional fees to be added.

A. Assessment of the fees provided for in this section shall be based on (i) an appearance for court hearing in which there has been a finding of guilty; (ii) a written appearance with waiver of court hearing and entry of guilty plea; (iii) for a defendant failing to appear, a trial in his or her absence resulting in a finding of guilty; (iv) an appearance for court hearing in which the court requires that the defendant successfully complete traffic school, a mature driver motor vehicle crash prevention course, or a driver improvement clinic, in lieu of a finding of guilty; (v) a deferral of proceedings pursuant to §§ 4.1-305, 16.1-278.8, 16.1-278.9, 18.2-57.3, 18.2-251 or 19.2-303.2; or (vi) proof of compliance with law under §§ 46.2-104 and 46.2-1158.02.

In addition to any other fee prescribed by this section, a fee of $35 shall be taxed as costs whenever a defendant fails to appear, unless, after a hearing requested by such person, good cause is shown for such failure to appear. No defendant with multiple charges arising from a single incident shall be taxed the applicable fixed fee provided in subsection B, C, or D more than once for a single appearance or trial in absence related to that incident. However, when a defendant who has multiple charges arising from the same incident and who has been assessed a fixed fee for one of those charges is later convicted of another charge that arises from that same incident and that has a higher fixed fee, he shall be assessed the difference between the fixed fee earlier assessed and the higher fixed fee.

A defendant with charges which arise from separate incidents shall be taxed a fee for each incident even if the charges from the multiple incidents are disposed of in a single appearance or trial in absence.

In addition to the fixed fees assessed pursuant to this section, in the appropriate cases, the clerk shall also assess any costs otherwise specifically provided by statute.

B. In misdemeanors tried in district court, except for those proceedings provided for in subsection C, there shall be assessed as court costs a fixed fee of $61. The amount collected, in whole or in part, for the fixed fee shall be apportioned, as provided by law, to the following funds in the fractional amounts designated:

1. Processing fee (General Fund) (.573770);
2. Virginia Crime Victim-Witness Fund (.049180);
3. Regional Criminal Justice Training Academies Fund (.016393);
4. Courthouse Construction/Maintenance Fund (.032787);
5. Criminal Injuries Compensation Fund (.098361);
6. Intensified Drug Enforcement Jurisdiction Fund (.065574);
7. Sentencing/supervision fee (General Fund) (.131148); and
8. Virginia Sexual and Domestic Violence Victim Fund (.032787).

C. In criminal actions and proceedings in district court for a violation of any provision of Article 1 (§ 18.2-247 et seq.) of Chapter 7 of Title 18.2, there shall be assessed as court costs a fixed fee of $136. The amount collected, in whole or in part, for the fixed fee shall be apportioned, as provided by law, to the following funds in the fractional amounts designated:

1. Processing fee (General Fund) (.257353);
2. Virginia Crime Victim-Witness Fund (.022059);
3. Regional Criminal Justice Training Academies Fund (.007353);
4. Courthouse Construction/Maintenance Fund (.014706);
5. Criminal Injuries Compensation Fund (.044118);
6. Intensified Drug Enforcement Jurisdiction Fund (.029412);
7. Drug Offender Assessment and Treatment Fund (.551471);
8. Forensic laboratory fee and sentencing/supervision fee (General Fund) (.058824); and
9. Virginia Sexual and Domestic Violence Victim Fund (.014706).

D. In traffic infractions tried in district court, there shall be assessed as court costs a fixed fee of $51. The amount collected, in whole or in part, for the fixed fee shall be apportioned, as provided by law, to the following funds in the fractional amounts designated:

1. Processing fee (General Fund) (.764706);
2. Virginia Crime Victim-Witness Fund (.058824);
3. Regional Criminal Justice Training Academies Fund (.019608);
4. Courthouse Construction/Maintenance Fund (.039216);
5. Intensified Drug Enforcement Jurisdiction Fund (.078431); and
6. Virginia Sexual and Domestic Violence Victim Fund (.039216).

History.

Code 1950, § 14-132; 1956, c. 556; 1956, Ex. Sess., c. 10; 1958, c. 286; 1960, cc. 278, 368; 1962, c. 546; 1964, c. 386, § 14.1-123; 1968, c. 639; 1970, c. 553; 1975, c. 591; 1977, c. 585; 1978, c. 605; 1979, cc. 525, 594; 1982, cc. 494, 569; 1983, c. 499; 1989, c. 595; 1990, c. 971; 1992, cc. 555, 558; 1995, c. 371; 1996, cc. 62, 976; 1997, c. 215; 1998, c. 872; 2003, cc. 883, 1039; 2004, cc. 371, 375, 1004; 2005, c. 631; 2006, c. 288; 2009, c. 756; 2010, c. 874; 2011, cc. 283, 890; 2014, c. 282.

§ 16.1-69.48:1.02. Additional fee assessed for conviction requiring computer analysis.

In addition to the fees provided for by § 16.1-69.48:1, upon a finding of guilty of any charge or charges in which any computer forensic analysis revealed evidence used at trial of a defendant, the defendant may be assessed costs in an amount equal to the actual cost of the computer forensic analysis not to exceed $100 for each computer analyzed by any state or local law-enforcement agency. Upon motion and submission to the court of an affidavit by the law-enforcement agency setting forth the number of computers analyzed and the total amount of costs requested, the court shall determine the appropriate amount to be assessed and order such amount paid to the law-enforcement agency.

History.

2011, c. 511.

CHAPTER 11.

JUVENILE AND DOMESTIC RELATIONS DISTRICT COURTS.

Article 1.

General Provisions.

Article 2.

Organization and Personnel.

Article 3.

Jurisdiction and Venue.

Article 4.

Immediate Custody, Arrest, Detention and Shelter Care.

Article 5.

Intake, Petition and Notice.

Article 6.

Appointment of Counsel.

Article 7.

Transfer and Waiver.

Article 8.

Adjudication.

Article 9.

Disposition.

ARTICLE 1.
GENERAL PROVISIONS.

§ 16.1-226. Short title.

The short title of the statutes embraced in this chapter is "Juvenile and Domestic Relations District Court Law."

History.
Code 1950, § 16.1-139; 1956, c. 555; 1972, c. 708; 1973, c. 546; 1977, c. 559.

§ 16.1-227. Purpose and intent.

This law shall be construed liberally and as remedial in character, and the powers hereby conferred are intended to be general to effect the beneficial purposes herein set forth. It is the intention of this law that in all proceedings the welfare of the child and the family, the safety of the community and the protection of the rights of victims are the paramount concerns of the Commonwealth and to the end that these purposes may be attained, the judge shall possess all necessary and incidental powers and authority, whether legal or equitable in their nature.

This law shall be interpreted and construed so as to effectuate the following purposes:

1. To divert from or within the juvenile justice system, to the extent possible, consistent with the protection of the public safety, those children who can be cared for or treated through alternative programs;

2. To provide judicial procedures through which the provisions of this law are executed and enforced and in which the parties are assured a fair hearing and their constitutional and other rights are recognized and enforced;

3. To separate a child from such child's parents, guardian, legal custodian or other person standing in loco parentis only when the child's welfare is endangered or it is in the interest of public safety and then only after consideration of alternatives to out-of-home placement which afford effective protection to the child, his family, and the community; and

4. To protect the community against those acts of its citizens, both juveniles and adults, which are harmful to others and to reduce the incidence of delinquent behavior and to hold offenders accountable for their behavior.

History.
Code 1950, § 16.1-140; 1956, c. 555; 1977, c. 559; 1990, c. 554; 1991, c. 392; 1996, cc. 755, 914.

§ 16.1-228. Definitions.

When used in this chapter, unless the context otherwise requires:

"Abused or neglected child" means any child:

1. Whose parents or other person responsible for his care creates or inflicts, threatens to create or inflict, or allows to be created or inflicted upon such child a physical or mental injury by other than accidental means, or creates a substantial risk of death, disfigurement or impairment of bodily or mental functions, including, but not limited to, a child who is with his parent or other person responsible for his care either (i) during the manufacture or attempted manufacture of a Schedule I or II controlled substance, or (ii) during the unlawful sale of such substance by that child's parents or other

person responsible for his care, where such manufacture, or attempted manufacture or unlawful sale would constitute a felony violation of § 18.2-248;

2. Whose parents or other person responsible for his care neglects or refuses to provide care necessary for his health; however, no child who in good faith is under treatment solely by spiritual means through prayer in accordance with the tenets and practices of a recognized church or religious denomination shall for that reason alone be considered to be an abused or neglected child;

3. Whose parents or other person responsible for his care abandons such child;

4. Whose parents or other person responsible for his care commits or allows to be committed any sexual act upon a child in violation of the law;

5. Who is without parental care or guardianship caused by the unreasonable absence or the mental or physical incapacity of the child's parent, guardian, legal custodian, or other person standing in loco parentis;

6. Whose parents or other person responsible for his care creates a substantial risk of physical or mental injury by knowingly leaving the child alone in the same dwelling, including an apartment as defined in § 55-79.2, with a person to whom the child is not related by blood or marriage and who the parent or other person responsible for his care knows has been convicted of an offense against a minor for which registration is required as a violent sexual offender pursuant to § 9.1-902; or

7. Who has been identified as a victim of sex trafficking or severe forms of trafficking as defined in the Trafficking Victims Protection Act of 2000, 22 U.S.C § 7102 et seq., and in the Justice for Victims of Trafficking Act of 2015, 42 U.S.C. § 5101 et seq.

If a civil proceeding under this chapter is based solely on the parent having left the child at a hospital or emergency medical services agency, it shall be an affirmative defense that such parent safely delivered the child to a hospital that provides 24-hour emergency services or to an attended emergency medical services agency that employs emergency medical services personnel, within 14 days of the child's birth. For purposes of terminating parental rights pursuant to § 16.1-283 and placement for adoption, the court may find such a child is a neglected child upon the ground of abandonment.

"Adoptive home" means the place of residence of any natural person in which a child resides as a member of the household and in which he has been placed for the purposes of adoption or in which he has been legally adopted by another member of the household.

"Adult" means a person 18 years of age or older.

"Ancillary crime" or *"ancillary charge"* means any delinquent act committed by a juvenile as a part of the same act or transaction as, or which constitutes a part of a common scheme or plan with, a delinquent act which would be a felony if committed by an adult.

"Boot camp" means a short term secure or nonsecure juvenile residential facility with highly structured components including, but not limited to, military style drill and ceremony, physical labor, education and rigid discipline, and no less than six months of intensive aftercare.

"Child," "juvenile," or *"minor"* means a person less than 18 years of age.

"Child in need of services" means (i) a child whose behavior, conduct or condition presents or results in a serious threat to the well-being and physical safety of the child or (ii) a child under the age of 14 whose behavior, conduct or condition presents or results in a serious threat to the well-being and physical safety of another person; however, no child who in good faith is under treatment solely by spiritual means through prayer in accordance with the tenets and practices of a recognized church or religious denomination shall for that reason alone be considered to be a child in need of services, nor shall any child who habitually remains away from or habitually deserts or abandons his family as a result of what the court or the local child protective services unit determines to be incidents of physical, emotional or sexual abuse in the home be considered a child in need of services for that reason alone.

However, to find that a child falls within these provisions, (i) the conduct complained of must present a clear and substantial danger to the child's life or health or to the life or health of another person, (ii) the child or his family is in need of treatment, rehabilitation or services not presently being received, and (iii) the intervention of the court is essential to provide the treatment, rehabilitation or services needed by the child or his family.

"Child in need of supervision" means:

1. A child who, while subject to compulsory school attendance, is habitually and without justification absent from school, and (i) the child has been offered an adequate opportunity to receive the benefit of any and all educational services and programs that are required to be provided by law and which meet the child's particular educational needs, (ii) the school system from which the child is absent or other appropriate agency has made a reasonable effort to effect the child's regular attendance without success, and (iii) the school system has provided documentation that it has complied with the provisions of § 22.1-258; or

2. A child who, without reasonable cause and without the consent of his parent, lawful custodian or placement authority, remains away from or deserts or abandons his family or lawful custodian on more than one occasion or escapes or remains away without proper authority from a residential care facility in which he has been placed by the court, and (i) such conduct presents a clear and substantial danger to the child's life or health, (ii) the child or his family is in need of treatment, rehabilitation or services not presently being received, and (iii) the intervention of the court is essential to provide the

treatment, rehabilitation or services needed by the child or his family.

"Child welfare agency" means a child-placing agency, child-caring institution or independent foster home as defined in § 63.2-100.

"The court" or the *"juvenile court"* or the *"juvenile and domestic relations court"* means the juvenile and domestic relations district court of each county or city.

"Delinquent act" means (i) an act designated a crime under the law of the Commonwealth, or an ordinance of any city, county, town, or service district, or under federal law, (ii) a violation of § 18.2-308.7, or (iii) a violation of a court order as provided for in § 16.1-292, but shall not include an act other than a violation of § 18.2-308.7, which is otherwise lawful, but is designated a crime only if committed by a child. For purposes of §§ 16.1-241 and 16.1-278.9, the term shall include a refusal to take a blood or breath test in violation of § 18.2-268.2 or a similar ordinance of any county, city, or town.

"Delinquent child" means a child who has committed a delinquent act or an adult who has committed a delinquent act prior to his 18th birthday, except where the jurisdiction of the juvenile court has been terminated under the provisions of § 16.1-269.6.

"Department" means the Department of Juvenile Justice and *"Director"* means the administrative head in charge thereof or such of his assistants and subordinates as are designated by him to discharge the duties imposed upon him under this law.

"Family abuse" means any act involving violence, force, or threat that results in bodily injury or places one in reasonable apprehension of death, sexual assault, or bodily injury and that is committed by a person against such person's family or household member. Such act includes, but is not limited to, any forceful detention, stalking, criminal sexual assault in violation of Article 7 (§ 18.2-61 et seq.) of Chapter 4 of Title 18.2, or any criminal offense that results in bodily injury or places one in reasonable apprehension of death, sexual assault, or bodily injury.

"Family or household member" means (i) the person's spouse, whether or not he or she resides in the same home with the person, (ii) the person's former spouse, whether or not he or she resides in the same home with the person, (iii) the person's parents, stepparents, children, stepchildren, brothers, sisters, half-brothers, half-sisters, grandparents and grandchildren, regardless of whether such persons reside in the same home with the person, (iv) the person's mother-in-law, father-in-law, sons-in-law, daughters-in-law, brothers-in-law and sisters-in-law who reside in the same home with the person, (v) any individual who has a child in common with the person, whether or not the person and that individual have been married or have resided together at any time, or (vi) any individual who cohabits or who, within the previous 12 months, cohabited with the person, and any children of either of them then residing in the same home with the person.

"Foster care services" means the provision of a full range of casework, treatment and community services for a planned period of time to a child who is abused or neglected as defined in § 63.2-100 or in need of services as defined in this section and his family when the child (i) has been identified as needing services to prevent or eliminate the need for foster care placement, (ii) has been placed through an agreement between the local board of social services or a public agency designated by the community policy and management team and the parents or guardians where legal custody remains with the parents or guardians, (iii) has been committed or entrusted to a local board of social services or child welfare agency, or (iv) has been placed under the supervisory responsibility of the local board pursuant to § 16.1-293.

"Independent living arrangement" means placement of a child at least 16 years of age who is in the custody of a local board or licensed child-placing agency and has been placed by the local board or licensed child-placing agency in a living arrangement in which he does not have daily substitute parental supervision.

"Independent living services" means services and activities provided to a child in foster care 14 years of age or older and who has been committed or entrusted to a local board of social services, child welfare agency, or private child-placing agency. "Independent living services" may also mean services and activities provided to a person who was in foster care on his 18th birthday and has not yet reached the age of 21 years. Such services shall include counseling, education, housing, employment, and money management skills development and access to essential documents and other appropriate services to help children or persons prepare for self-sufficiency.

"Intake officer" means a juvenile probation officer appointed as such pursuant to the authority of this chapter.

"Jail" or *"other facility designed for the detention of adults"* means a local or regional correctional facility as defined in § 53.1-1, except those facilities utilized on a temporary basis as a court holding cell for a child incident to a court hearing or as a temporary lock-up room or ward incident to the transfer of a child to a juvenile facility.

"The judge" means the judge or the substitute judge of the juvenile and domestic relations district court of each county or city.

"This law" or *"the law"* means the Juvenile and Domestic Relations District Court Law embraced in this chapter.

"Legal custody" means (i) a legal status created by court order which vests in a custodian the right to have physical custody of the child, to determine and redetermine where and with whom he shall live, the right and duty to protect, train and discipline him and to provide him with food, shelter, education and ordinary medical care, all subject to any residual

parental rights and responsibilities or (ii) the legal status created by court order of joint custody as defined in § 20-107.2.

"Permanent foster care placement" means the place of residence in which a child resides and in which he has been placed pursuant to the provisions of §§ 63.2-900 and 63.2-908 with the expectation and agreement between the placing agency and the place of permanent foster care that the child shall remain in the placement until he reaches the age of majority unless modified by court order or unless removed pursuant to § 16.1-251 or 63.2-1517. A permanent foster care placement may be a place of residence of any natural person or persons deemed appropriate to meet a child's needs on a long-term basis.

"Residual parental rights and responsibilities" means all rights and responsibilities remaining with the parent after the transfer of legal custody or guardianship of the person, including but not limited to the right of visitation, consent to adoption, the right to determine religious affiliation and the responsibility for support.

"Secure facility" or *"detention home"* means a local, regional or state public or private locked residential facility that has construction fixtures designed to prevent escape and to restrict the movement and activities of children held in lawful custody.

"Shelter care" means the temporary care of children in physically unrestricting facilities.

"State Board" means the State Board of Juvenile Justice.

"Status offender" means a child who commits an act prohibited by law which would not be criminal if committed by an adult.

"Status offense" means an act prohibited by law which would not be an offense if committed by an adult.

"Violent juvenile felony" means any of the delinquent acts enumerated in subsection B or C of § 16.1-269.1 when committed by a juvenile 14 years of age or older.

History.

Code 1950, § 16.1-141; 1956, c. 555; 1972, c. 708; 1973, c. 546; 1974, cc. 44, 45; 1977, c. 559; 1978, c. 605; 1979, c. 15; 1981, c. 491; 1984, c. 631; 1985, c. 260; 1986, cc. 281, 308; 1987, c. 632; 1988, c. 794; 1990, cc. 704, 769, 842; 1991, c. 534; 1992, cc. 742, 830, 886; 1993, cc. 435, 467, 494; 1994, cc. 859, 865, 949; 1996, cc. 755, 914; 1999, cc. 453, 665, 697, 721; 2002, cc. 810, 818; 2003, cc. 538, 547, 835; 2004, cc. 245, 753; 2006, c. 868; 2008, cc. 475, 483; 2011, cc. 445, 480; 2015, cc. 502, 503; 2016, c. 631.

§ 16.1-229. This chapter controlling in event of conflict.

Whenever any specific provision of this chapter differs from or is in conflict with any provision or requirement of any other chapters of this title relating to the same or a similar subject, then such specific provision shall be controlling with respect to such subject or requirement.

History.

Code 1950, § 16.1-142; 1956, c. 555; 1977, c. 559.

ARTICLE 2.

ORGANIZATION AND PERSONNEL.

§ 16.1-235.1. Provision of court services; replacement intake officers.

The chief judge may make arrangements for a replacement intake officer from another court service unit to ensure the capability of a prompt response in matters under § 16.1-255 or 16.1-260 during hours the court is closed. The replacement intake officer shall have all the authority and power of an intake officer of that district when authorized in writing by the appointing authority and by the chief judge of that district.

History.

2002, c. 700; 2012, cc. 164, 456.

§ 16.1-236. Supervisory officers.

In any court where more than one probation or parole officer or other court services staff has been appointed under the provisions of this law, one or more probation or parole officers may be designated to serve in a supervisory position, other than court services unit director, by the Director, if it is a state-operated court services unit, or by the local governing body, if it is a locally operated court services unit.

The transfer, demotion, or separation of supervisory officers, other than court services unit directors, of state court service units shall be under the authority of the Director and shall be only for good cause shown, after consulting with the judge or judges of that juvenile and domestic relations district court, and in accordance with the Virginia Personnel Act (§ 2.2-2900 et seq.). The transfer, demotion or separation of supervisory officers of local court service units shall be under the authority of the local governing body and shall be only for good cause shown, after consulting with the judge or judges of that juvenile and domestic relations district court and after due notice and opportunity to be heard.

History.

Code 1950, § 16.1-207; 1956, c. 555; 1972, c. 708; 1973, c. 546; 1974, c. 673; 1977, c. 559; 2001, c. 853; 2003, c. 648.

§ 16.1-236.1. Court services unit directors.

A. State-operated court services units. A court services unit director shall be designated for each state-operated court services unit. The judge or judges of the juvenile and domestic relations district court shall, from a list of eligible persons submitted by the Director appoint one court services unit director for the state-operated court services unit serving that district court. The list of eligible persons shall be developed in accordance with state personnel laws and regulations, and Department policies and procedures.

If any list of eligible persons submitted by the Director is unsatisfactory to the judge or judges, the judge or judges may request the Director to submit a new list containing the names of additional eligible persons. Upon such request by the judge or judges, the Director shall develop and submit a new list of eligible persons in accordance with state personnel laws and regulations, and Department policies and procedures.

The transfer, demotion, or separation of a court services unit director, appointed pursuant to this subsection shall be under the authority of the Director and shall be only for good cause shown, after consulting with the judge or judges of that juvenile and domestic relations district court, and in accordance with the Virginia Personnel Act (§ 2.2-2900 et seq.).

B. Locally operated court services units. A court services unit director shall be designated for each locally operated court services unit. The judge or judges of the juvenile and domestic relations district court shall, from a list of eligible persons submitted by the governing body or bodies of the district, appoint one court services unit director for the locally operated court services unit serving that district court. The list of eligible persons shall be in accordance with locally established qualifications that are consistent with state personnel laws and regulations, and Department policies and procedures.

If any list of eligible persons submitted by the governing body or bodies of the district is unsatisfactory to the judge or judges, the judge or judges may request the governing body or bodies to submit a new list containing the names of additional eligible persons. Upon such request by the judge or judges, the governing body or bodies shall develop and submit a new list of eligible persons in accordance with locally established qualifications that are consistent with state personnel laws and regulations, and Department policies and procedures.

The transfer, demotion, or separation of a court services unit director appointed pursuant to this subsection shall be under the authority of the local governing body or bodies and shall be only for good cause shown after consulting with the judge or judges of that juvenile and domestic relations district court and in accordance with the Virginia Personnel Act (§ 2.2-2900 et seq.).

History.

2003, c. 648.

§ 16.1-237. Powers, duties and functions of probation and parole officers.

In addition to any other powers and duties imposed by this law, a probation or parole officer appointed hereunder shall:

A. Investigate all cases referred to him by the judge or any person designated so to do, and shall render reports of such investigation as required;

B. Supervise persons placed under his supervision and shall keep informed concerning the conduct and condition of every person under his supervision by visiting, requiring reports and in other ways, and shall report thereon as required;

C. Under the general supervision of the director of the court service unit, investigate complaints and accept for informal supervision cases wherein such handling would best serve the interests of all concerned;

D. Use all suitable methods not inconsistent with conditions imposed by the court to aid and encourage persons on probation or parole and to bring about improvement in their conduct and condition;

E. Furnish to each person placed on probation or parole a written statement of the conditions of his probation or parole and instruct him regarding the same;

F. Keep records of his work including photographs and perform such other duties as the judge or other person designated by the judge or the Director shall require;

G. Have the authority to administer oaths and take acknowledgements for the purposes of §§ 16.1-259 and 16.1-260 to facilitate the processes of intake and petition;

H. Have the powers of arrest of a police officer and the power to carry a concealed weapon when specifically so authorized by the judge; and

I. Determine by reviewing the Local Inmate Data System or the Juvenile Tracking System (JTS) upon intake and again prior to discharge whether a blood, saliva, or tissue sample has been taken for DNA analysis for each offender required to submit a sample pursuant to § 16.1-299.1 and, if no sample has been taken, require an offender to submit a sample for DNA analysis.

History.

Code 1950, § 16.1-208; 1956, c. 555; 1964, c. 516; 1972, c. 708; 1973, c. 546; 1974, c. 464; 1977, c. 559; 2001, c. 853; 2007, c. 528; 2009, c. 726.

ARTICLE 3.

JURISDICTION AND VENUE.

§ 16.1-241. Jurisdiction; consent for abortion.

The judges of the juvenile and domestic relations district court elected or appointed under this law shall be conservators of the peace within the corporate limits of the cities and the boundaries of the counties for which they are respectively chosen and within one mile beyond the limits of such cities and counties. Except as hereinafter provided, each juvenile and domestic relations district court shall have, within the limits of the territory for which it is created, exclusive original jurisdiction, and within one mile beyond the limits of said city or county, concurrent jurisdiction with the juvenile court or courts of the adjoining city or county, over all cases, matters and proceedings involving:

A. The custody, visitation, support, control or disposition of a child:

1. Who is alleged to be abused, neglected, in need of services, in need of supervision, a status offender, or delinquent except where the jurisdiction of the juvenile court has been terminated or divested;

2. Who is abandoned by his parent or other custodian or who by reason of the absence or physical or mental incapacity of his parents is without parental care and guardianship;

2a. Who is at risk of being abused or neglected by a parent or custodian who has been adjudicated as having abused or neglected another child in the care of the parent or custodian;

3. Whose custody, visitation or support is a subject of controversy or requires determination. In such cases jurisdiction shall be concurrent with and not exclusive of courts having equity jurisdiction, except as provided in § 16.1-244;

4. Who is the subject of an entrustment agreement entered into pursuant to § 63.2-903 or 63.2-1817 or whose parent or parents for good cause desire to be relieved of his care and custody;

5. Where the termination of residual parental rights and responsibilities is sought. In such cases jurisdiction shall be concurrent with and not exclusive of courts having equity jurisdiction, as provided in § 16.1-244; and

6. Who is charged with a traffic infraction as defined in § 46.2-100.

In any case in which the juvenile is alleged to have committed a violent juvenile felony enumerated in subsection B of § 16.1-269.1, and for any charges ancillary thereto, the jurisdiction of the juvenile court shall be limited to conducting a preliminary hearing to determine if there is probable cause to believe that the juvenile committed the act alleged and that the juvenile was 14 years of age or older at the time of the commission of the alleged offense, and any matters related thereto. In any case in which the juvenile is alleged to have committed a violent juvenile felony enumerated in subsection C of § 16.1-269.1, and for all charges ancillary thereto, if the attorney for the Commonwealth has given notice as provided in subsection C of § 16.1-269.1, the jurisdiction of the juvenile court shall be limited to conducting a preliminary hearing to determine if there is probable cause to believe that the juvenile committed the act alleged and that the juvenile was 14 years of age or older at the time of the commission of the alleged offense, and any matters related thereto. A determination by the juvenile court following a preliminary hearing pursuant to subsection B or C of § 16.1-269.1 to certify a charge to the grand jury shall divest the juvenile court of jurisdiction over the charge and any ancillary charge. In any case in which a transfer hearing is held pursuant to subsection A of § 16.1-269.1, if the juvenile court determines to transfer the case, jurisdiction of the juvenile court over the case shall be divested as provided in § 16.1-269.6.

In all other cases involving delinquent acts, and in cases in which an ancillary charge remains after a violent juvenile felony charge has been dismissed or a violent juvenile felony has been reduced to a lesser offense not constituting a violent juvenile felony, the jurisdiction of the juvenile court shall not be divested unless there is a transfer pursuant to subsection A of § 16.1-269.1.

The authority of the juvenile court to adjudicate matters involving the custody, visitation, support, control or disposition of a child shall not be limited to the consideration of petitions filed by a mother, father or legal guardian but shall include petitions filed at any time by any party with a legitimate interest therein. A party with a legitimate interest shall be broadly construed and shall include, but not be limited to, grandparents, step-grandparents, stepparents, former stepparents, blood relatives and family members. A party with a legitimate interest shall not include any person (i) whose parental rights have been terminated by court order, either voluntarily or involuntarily, (ii) whose interest in the child derives from or through a person whose parental rights have been terminated by court order, either voluntarily or involuntarily, including, but not limited to, grandparents, stepparents, former stepparents, blood relatives and family members, if the child subsequently has been legally adopted, except where a final order of adoption is entered pursuant to § 63.2-1241, or (iii) who has been convicted of a violation of subsection A of § 18.2-61, § 18.2-63, subsection B of § 18.2-366, or an equivalent offense of another state, the United States, or any foreign jurisdiction, when the child who is the subject of the petition was conceived as a result of such violation. The authority of the juvenile court to consider a petition involving the custody of a child shall not be proscribed or limited where the child has previously been awarded to the custody of a local board of social services.

B. The admission of minors for inpatient treatment in a mental health facility in accordance with the provisions of Article 16 (§ 16.1-335 et seq.) and the involuntary admission of a person with mental illness or judicial certification of eligibility for admission to a training center for persons with intellectual disability in accordance with the provisions of Chapter 8 (§ 37.2-800 et seq.) of Title 37.2. Jurisdiction of the involuntary admission and certification of adults shall be concurrent with the general district court.

C. Except as provided in subsections D and H, judicial consent to such activities as may require parental consent may be given for a child who has been separated from his parents, guardian, legal custodian or other person standing in loco parentis and is in the custody of the court when such consent is required by law.

D. Judicial consent for emergency surgical or medical treatment for a child who is neither married nor has ever been married, when the consent of his parent, guardian, legal custodian or other person standing in loco parentis is unobtainable because such parent, guardian, legal custodian or other person standing in loco parentis (i) is not a resident of the Commonwealth, (ii) has his whereabouts unknown, (iii) cannot be consulted with promptness, reasonable under the circumstances, or (iv) fails to give such consent or provide such treatment when requested by the judge to do so.

E. Any person charged with deserting, abandoning or failing to provide support for any person in violation of law.

F. Any parent, guardian, legal custodian or other person standing in loco parentis of a child:

1. Who has been abused or neglected;

2. Who is the subject of an entrustment agreement entered into pursuant to § 63.2-903 or 63.2-1817 or is otherwise before the court pursuant to subdivision A 4; or

3. Who has been adjudicated in need of services, in need of supervision, or delinquent, if the court finds that such person has by overt act or omission induced, caused, encouraged or contributed to the conduct of the child complained of in the petition.

G. Petitions filed by or on behalf of a child or such child's parent, guardian, legal custodian or other person standing in loco parentis for the purpose of obtaining treatment, rehabilitation or other services that are required by law to be provided for that child or such child's parent, guardian, legal custodian or other person standing in loco parentis. Jurisdiction in such cases shall be concurrent with and not exclusive of that of courts having equity jurisdiction as provided in § 16.1-244.

H. Judicial consent to apply for a work permit for a child when such child is separated from his parents, legal guardian or other person standing in loco parentis.

I. The prosecution and punishment of persons charged with ill-treatment, abuse, abandonment or neglect of children or with any violation of law that causes or tends to cause a child to come within the purview of this law, or with any other offense against the person of a child. In prosecution for felonies over which the court has jurisdiction, jurisdiction shall be limited to determining whether or not there is probable cause.

J. All offenses in which one family or household member is charged with an offense in which another family or household member is the victim and all offenses under § 18.2-49.1.

In prosecution for felonies over which the court has jurisdiction, jurisdiction shall be limited to determining whether or not there is probable cause. Any objection based on jurisdiction under this subsection shall be made before a jury is impaneled and sworn in a jury trial or, in a nonjury trial, before the earlier of when the court begins to hear or receive evidence or the first witness is sworn, or it shall be conclusively waived for all purposes. Any such objection shall not affect or be grounds for challenging directly or collaterally the jurisdiction of the court in which the case is tried.

K. Petitions filed by a natural parent, whose parental rights to a child have been voluntarily relinquished pursuant to a court proceeding, to seek a reversal of the court order terminating such parental rights. No such petition shall be accepted, however, after the child has been placed in the home of adoptive parents.

L. Any person who seeks spousal support after having separated from his spouse. A decision under this subdivision shall not be res judicata in any subsequent action for spousal support in a circuit court. A circuit court shall have concurrent original jurisdiction in all causes of action under this subdivision.

M. Petitions filed for the purpose of obtaining an order of protection pursuant to § 16.1-253.1, 16.1-253.4, or 16.1-279.1, and all petitions filed for the purpose of obtaining an order of protection pursuant to § 19.2-152.8, 19.2-152.9, or 19.2-152.10 if either the alleged victim or the respondent is a juvenile.

N. Any person who escapes or remains away without proper authority from a residential care facility in which he had been placed by the court or as a result of his commitment to the Virginia Department of Juvenile Justice.

O. Petitions for emancipation of a minor pursuant to Article 15 (§ 16.1-331 et seq.).

P. Petitions for enforcement of administrative support orders entered pursuant to Chapter 19 (§ 63.2-1900 et seq.) of Title 63.2, or by another state in the same manner as if the orders were entered by a juvenile and domestic relations district court upon the filing of a certified copy of such order in the juvenile and domestic relations district court.

Q. Petitions for a determination of parentage pursuant to Chapter 3.1 (§ 20-49.1 et seq.) of Title 20. A circuit court shall have concurrent original jurisdiction to the extent provided for in § 20-49.2.

R. [Repealed.]

S. Petitions filed by school boards against parents pursuant to §§ 16.1-241.2 and 22.1-279.3.

T. Petitions to enforce any request for information or subpoena that is not complied with or to review any refusal to issue a subpoena in an administrative appeal regarding child abuse and neglect pursuant to § 63.2-1526.

U. Petitions filed in connection with parental placement adoption consent hearings pursuant to § 63.2-1233. Such proceedings shall be advanced on the docket so as to be heard by the court within 10 days of filing of the petition, or as soon thereafter as practicable so as to provide the earliest possible disposition.

V. Petitions filed for the purpose of obtaining the court's assistance with the execution of consent to an adoption when the consent to an adoption is executed pursuant to the laws of another state and the laws of that state provide for the execution of consent to an adoption in the court of the Commonwealth.

W. Petitions filed by a juvenile seeking judicial authorization for a physician to perform an abortion if a minor elects not to seek consent of an authorized person.

After a hearing, a judge shall issue an order authorizing a physician to perform an abortion, without the consent of any authorized person, if he finds that (i) the minor is mature enough and well enough informed to make her abortion decision, in consultation with her physician, independent of the wishes of any authorized person, or (ii) the minor is not mature enough or well enough informed to make such decision, but the desired abortion would be in her best interest.

If the judge authorizes an abortion based on the best interests of the minor, such order shall expressly state that such authorization is subject to the physician or his agent giving notice of intent to perform the abortion; however, no such notice shall be required if the judge finds that such notice would not be in the best interest of the minor. In determining whether notice is in the best interest of the minor, the judge shall consider the totality of the circumstances; however, he shall find that notice is not in the best interest of the minor if he finds that (i) one or more authorized persons with whom the minor regularly and customarily resides is abusive or neglectful, and (ii) every other authorized person, if any, is either abusive or neglectful or has refused to accept responsibility as parent, legal guardian, custodian or person standing in loco parentis.

The minor may participate in the court proceedings on her own behalf, and the court may appoint a guardian ad litem for the minor. The court shall advise the minor that she has a right to counsel and shall, upon her request, appoint counsel for her.

Notwithstanding any other provision of law, the provisions of this subsection shall govern proceedings relating to consent for a minor's abortion. Court proceedings under this subsection and records of such proceedings shall be confidential. Such proceedings shall be given precedence over other pending matters so that the court may reach a decision promptly and without delay in order to serve the best interests of the minor. Court proceedings under this subsection shall be heard and decided as soon as practicable but in no event later than four days after the petition is filed.

An expedited confidential appeal to the circuit court shall be available to any minor for whom the court denies an order authorizing an abortion without consent or without notice. Any such appeal shall be heard and decided no later than five days after the appeal is filed. The time periods required by this subsection shall be subject to subsection B of § 1-210. An order authorizing an abortion without consent or without notice shall not be subject to appeal.

No filing fees shall be required of the minor at trial or upon appeal.

If either the original court or the circuit court fails to act within the time periods required by this subsection, the court before which the proceeding is pending shall immediately authorize a physician to perform the abortion without consent of or notice to an authorized person.

Nothing contained in this subsection shall be construed to authorize a physician to perform an abortion on a minor in circumstances or in a manner that would be unlawful if performed on an adult woman.

A physician shall not knowingly perform an abortion upon an unemancipated minor unless consent has been obtained or the minor delivers to the physician a court order entered pursuant to this section and the physician or his agent provides such notice as such order may require. However, neither consent nor judicial authorization nor notice shall be required if the minor declares that she is abused or neglected and the attending physician has reason to suspect that the minor may be an abused or neglected child as defined in § 63.2-100 and reports the suspected abuse or neglect in accordance with § 63.2-1509; or if there is a medical emergency, in which case the attending physician shall certify the facts justifying the exception in the minor's medical record.

For purposes of this subsection:

"Authorization" means the minor has delivered to the physician a notarized, written statement signed by an authorized person that the authorized person knows of the minor's intent to have an abortion and consents to such abortion being performed on the minor.

"Authorized person" means (i) a parent or duly appointed legal guardian or custodian of the minor or (ii) a person standing in loco parentis, including, but not limited to, a grandparent or adult sibling with whom the minor regularly and customarily resides and who has care and control of the minor. Any person who knows he is not an authorized person and who knowingly and willfully signs an authorization statement consenting to an abortion for a minor is guilty of a Class 3 misdemeanor.

"Consent" means that (i) the physician has given notice of intent to perform the abortion and has received authorization from an authorized person, or (ii) at least one authorized person is present with the minor seeking the abortion and provides written authorization to the physician, which shall be witnessed by the physician or an agent thereof. In either case, the written authorization shall be incorporated into the minor's medical record and maintained as a part thereof.

"Medical emergency" means any condition which, on the basis of the physician's good faith clinical judgment, so complicates the medical condition of the pregnant minor as to necessitate the immediate abortion of her pregnancy to avert her death or for

which a delay will create a serious risk of substantial and irreversible impairment of a major bodily function.

"Notice of intent to perform the abortion" means that (i) the physician or his agent has given actual notice of his intention to perform such abortion to an authorized person, either in person or by telephone, at least 24 hours previous to the performance of the abortion; or (ii) the physician or his agent, after a reasonable effort to notify an authorized person, has mailed notice to an authorized person by certified mail, addressed to such person at his usual place of abode, with return receipt requested, at least 72 hours prior to the performance of the abortion.

"Perform an abortion" means to interrupt or terminate a pregnancy by any surgical or nonsurgical procedure or to induce a miscarriage as provided in § 18.2-72, 18.2-73, or 18.2-74.

"Unemancipated minor" means a minor who has not been emancipated by (i) entry into a valid marriage, even though the marriage may have been terminated by dissolution; (ii) active duty with any of the Armed Forces of the United States; (iii) willingly living separate and apart from his or her parents or guardian, with the consent or acquiescence of the parents or guardian; or (iv) entry of an order of emancipation pursuant to Article 15 (§ 16.1-331 et seq.).

X. Petitions filed pursuant to Article 17 (§ 16.1-349 et seq.) relating to standby guardians for minor children.

The ages specified in this law refer to the age of the child at the time of the acts complained of in the petition.

Notwithstanding any other provision of law, no fees shall be charged by a sheriff for the service of any process in a proceeding pursuant to subdivision A 3, except as provided in subdivision A 6 of § 17.1-272, or subsection B, D, M, or R.

Notwithstanding the provisions of § 18.2-71, any physician who performs an abortion in violation of subsection W shall be guilty of a Class 3 misdemeanor.

History.

Code 1950, § 16.1-158; 1956, c. 555; 1960, c. 388; 1968, c. 225; 1970, cc. 232, 600; 1973, c. 440; 1976, cc. 42, 324; 1977, cc. 525, 559; 1978, c. 648; 1979, cc. 597, 605, 628; 1980, cc. 527, 529; 1981, cc. 454, 475, 488, 491, 501, 502, 510; 1982, c. 46; 1983, c. 280; 1984, cc. 631, 645, 651, 665, 669; 1985, c. 270; 1986, cc. 59, 506; 1987, c. 632; 1988, cc. 797, 906; 1989, cc. 368, 733; 1990, cc. 704, 975; 1991, cc. 511, 715; 1992, cc. 585, 742; 1994, cc. 575, 719, 813, 859, 949; 1995, cc. 7, 665, 772, 826, 852; 1996, cc. 755, 914; 1997, cc. 690, 708; 1998, c. 829; 1999, cc. 697, 721, 1028; 2000, c. 830; 2003, cc. 229, 960, 962; 2004, c. 588; 2005, cc. 716, 839, 890; 2007, cc. 284, 370; 2008, cc. 164, 201; 2010, c. 402; 2012, cc. 424, 476, 507, 637; 2014, c. 653.

§ 16.1-241.1: Repealed by Acts 2002, c. 305.

§ 16.1-241.2. Proceedings against certain parents.

A. Upon the failure of a parent to comply with the provisions of § 22.1-279.3, the school board may, by petition to the juvenile and domestic relations court, proceed against such parent for willful and unreasonable refusal to participate in efforts to improve the student's behavior as follows:

1. If the court finds that the parent has willfully and unreasonably failed to meet, pursuant to a request of the principal as set forth in subsection D of § 22.1-279.3, to review the school board's standards of student conduct and the parent's responsibility to assist the school in disciplining the student, maintaining order, or ensuring the child's school attendance, and to discuss improvement of the child's behavior, school attendance, or educational progress, it may order the parent to so meet; or

2. If the court finds that the parent has willfully and unreasonably failed to accompany a suspended student to meet with school officials pursuant to subsection F of § 22.1-279.3, or upon the student receiving a second suspension or being expelled, it may order (i) the student or his parent to participate in such programs or such treatment as the court deems appropriate to improve the student's behavior, including, but not limited to, extended day programs and summer school or other education programs and counseling, or (ii) the student or his parent to be subject to such conditions and limitations as the court deems appropriate for the supervision, care, and rehabilitation of the student or his parent; in addition, the court may order the parent to pay a civil penalty not to exceed $500.

The court may use its contempt power to enforce any order entered under this section.

B. The civil penalties established pursuant to this section shall be enforceable in the juvenile and domestic relations court or its successor in interest in which the student's school is located and shall be paid into a fund maintained by the appropriate local governing body to support programs or treatments designed to improve the behavior and school attendance of students as described in subdivision 2 of subsection G of § 22.1-279.3. Upon the failure to pay any civil penalties imposed by this section and § 22.1-279.3, the attorney for the appropriate county, city, or town shall enforce the collection of such civil penalties.

C. For the purposes of this section and § 22.1-279.3, *"parent"* or *"parents"* means any parent, guardian, legal custodian, or other person having control or charge of a child.

History.

1994, c. 813; 1995, c. 852; 1996, c. 771; 2004, c. 573.

§ 16.1-241.3. Newborn children; substance abuse.

Upon the filing of a petition alleging that an investigation has been commenced in response to a report of suspected abuse or neglect of the child based upon a factor specified in subsection B of § 63.2-1509, the court may enter any order authorized pursuant to this chapter which the court deems necessary to protect the health and welfare of the child pending final disposition of the investigation pursuant to Chapter 15 (§ 63.2-1500 et seq.) of Title 63.2 or other proceedings brought pursuant to this chapter. Such orders may include, but shall not be limited to, an emergency removal order pursuant to § 16.1-251, a preliminary protective order pursuant to § 16.1-253 or an order authorized pursuant to subdivisions A 1 through 4 of § 16.1-278.2. The fact that an order was entered pursuant to this section shall not be admissible as evidence in any criminal, civil or administrative proceeding other than a proceeding to enforce the order.

The order shall be effective for a limited duration not to exceed the period of time necessary to conclude the investigation and any proceedings initiated pursuant to Chapter 15 (§ 63.2-1500 et seq.) of Title 63.2, but shall be a final order subject to appeal.

History.

1998, cc. 704, 716; 2002, c. 860; 2012, cc. 504, 640.

§ 16.1-242. Retention of jurisdiction.

When jurisdiction has been obtained by the court in the case of any child, such jurisdiction may be retained by the court until such person becomes twenty-one years of age, except when the person is in the custody of the Department or when jurisdiction is divested under the provisions of § 16.1-244. In any event, when such person reaches the age of twenty-one and a prosecution has not been commenced against him, he shall be proceeded against as an adult, even if he was a juvenile when the offense was committed.

History.

Code 1950, § 16.1-159; 1956, c. 555; 1977, c. 559; 1978, c. 740; 1992, c. 509.

§ 16.1-242.1. Retention of jurisdiction; appeals involving children in foster care.

Upon appeal to the circuit court of any case involving a child placed in foster care and in any appeal to the Court of Appeals or Supreme Court of Virginia, the juvenile court shall retain jurisdiction to continue to hear petitions filed pursuant to §§ 16.1-282 and 16.1-282.1. Orders of the juvenile court in such cases shall continue to be reviewed and enforced by the juvenile court until the circuit court, Court of Appeals or Supreme Court rules otherwise.

History.

1998, c. 550.

§ 16.1-243. Venue.

A. Original venue:

1. Cases involving children, other than support or where protective order issued: Proceedings with respect to children under this law, except support proceedings as provided in subdivision 2 or family abuse proceedings as provided in subdivision 3, shall:

a. Delinquency: If delinquency is alleged, be commenced in the city or county where the acts constituting the alleged delinquency occurred or they may, with the written consent of the child and the attorney for the Commonwealth for both jurisdictions, be commenced in the city or county where the child resides;

b. Custody or visitation: In cases involving custody or visitation, be commenced in the court of the city or county which, in order of priority, (i) is the home of the child at the time of the filing of the petition, or had been the home of the child within six months before the filing of the petition and the child is absent from the city or county because of his removal or retention by a person claiming his custody or for other reasons, and a parent or person acting as a parent continues to live in the city or county, (ii) has significant connection with the child and in which there is substantial evidence concerning the child's present or future care, protection, training and personal relationships, (iii) is where the child is physically present and the child has been abandoned or it is necessary in an emergency to protect the child because he has been subjected to or threatened with mistreatment or abuse or is otherwise neglected or dependent or (iv) it is in the best interest of the child for the court to assume jurisdiction as no other city or county is an appropriate venue under the preceding provisions of this subdivision;

c. Adoption: In parental placement adoption consent hearings pursuant to §§ 16.1-241, 63.2-1233, and 63.2-1237, be commenced in any city or county, provided, however, that diligent efforts shall first be made to commence such hearings (i) in the city or county where the child to be adopted was born, (ii) in the city or county where the birth parent(s) reside, or (iii) in the city or county where the prospective adoptive parent(s) reside. In cases in which a hearing is commenced in a city or county other than one described in clauses (i) through (iii), the petitioner shall certify in writing to the court that diligent efforts to commence a hearing in such city or county have been made but have proven ineffective; and

d. All other cases: In all other proceedings, be commenced in the city or county where the child resides or in the city or county where the child is present when the proceedings are commenced.

2. Support: Proceedings that involve child or spousal support or child and spousal support, exclusive of proceedings arising under Chapter 5 (§ 20-61 et seq.) of Title 20, shall be commenced in the city or county where either party resides or in the city or county where the respondent is present when the proceeding commences.

3. Family abuse: Proceedings in which an order of protection is sought as a result of family abuse shall be commenced where (i) either party has his or her

principal residence (ii) the abuse occurred or (iii) a protective order was issued if at the time the proceeding is commenced the order is in effect to protect the petitioner or a family or household member of the petitioner.

B. Transfer of venue:

1. Generally: Except in custody, visitation and support cases, if the child resides in a city or county of the Commonwealth and the proceeding is commenced in a court of another city or county, that court may at any time, on its own motion or a motion of a party for good cause shown, transfer the proceeding to the city or county of the child's residence for such further action or proceedings as the court receiving the transfer may deem proper. However, such transfer may occur only after adjudication in delinquency proceedings.

2. Custody and visitation: In custody and visitation cases, if venue lies in one of several cities or counties, the court in which the motion for transfer is made shall determine which such city or county is the most appropriate venue unless the parties mutually agree to the selection of venue. In the consideration of the motion, the best interests of the child shall determine the most appropriate forum.

3. Support: In support proceedings, exclusive of proceedings arising under Chapter 5 of Title 20, if the respondent resides in a city or county in the Commonwealth and the proceeding is commenced in a court of another city or county, that court may, at any time on its own motion or a motion of a party for good cause shown or by agreement of the parties, transfer the proceeding to the city or county of the respondent's residence for such further action or proceedings as the court receiving the transfer may deem proper. For the purposes of determining venue of cases involving support, the respondent's residence shall include any city or county in which the respondent has resided within the last six months prior to the commencement of the proceeding or in which the respondent is residing at the time that the motion for transfer of venue is made. If venue is transferable to one of several cities or counties, the court in which the motion for transfer is made shall determine which such city or county is the most appropriate venue unless the parties mutually agree to the selection of such venue.

When the support proceeding is a companion case to a child custody or visitation proceeding, the provisions governing venue in the proceeding involving the child's custody or visitation shall govern.

4. Subsequent transfers: Any court receiving a transferred proceeding as provided in this section may in its discretion transfer such proceeding to a court in an appropriate venue for good cause shown based either upon changes in circumstances or mistakes of fact or upon agreement of the parties. In any transfer of venue in cases involving children, the best interests of the child shall be considered in deciding if and to which court a transfer of venue would be appropriate.

5. Enforcement of orders for support, maintenance and custody: Any juvenile and domestic relations district court to which a suit is transferred for enforcement of orders pertaining to support, maintenance, care or custody pursuant to § 20-79 (c) may transfer the case as provided in this section.

C. Records: Originals of all legal and social records pertaining to the case shall accompany the transfer of venue. Records imaged from the original documents shall be considered original documents for purposes of the transfer of venue. The transferor court may, in its discretion, retain copies as it deems appropriate.

History.

Code 1950, § 16.1-160; 1956, c. 555; 1977, c. 559; 1985, c. 367; 1987, cc. 598, 608, 620; 1989, c. 545; 1995, cc. 772, 826; 1996, c. 866; 2000, c. 830; 2010, cc. 717, 760; 2012, c. 424.

§ 16.1-244. Concurrent jurisdiction; exceptions.

A. Nothing contained in this law shall deprive any other court of the concurrent jurisdiction to determine the custody of children upon a writ of habeas corpus under the law, or to determine the custody, guardianship, visitation or support of children when such custody, guardianship, visitation or support is incidental to the determination of causes pending in such courts, nor deprive a circuit court of jurisdiction to determine spousal support in a suit for separate maintenance. However, when a suit for divorce has been filed in a circuit court, in which the custody, guardianship, visitation or support of children of the parties or spousal support is raised by the pleadings and a hearing, including a pendente lite hearing, is set by the circuit court on any such issue for a date certain or on a motions docket to be heard within 21 days of the filing, the juvenile and domestic relations district courts shall be divested of the right to enter any further decrees or orders to determine custody, guardianship, visitation or support when raised for such hearing and such matters shall be determined by the circuit court unless both parties agreed to a referral to the juvenile court. Nothing in this section shall deprive a circuit court of the authority to refer any such case to a commissioner for a hearing or shall deprive the juvenile and domestic relations district courts of the jurisdiction to enforce its valid orders prior to the entry of a conflicting order of any circuit court for any period during which the order was in effect or to temporarily place a child in the custody of any person when that child has been adjudicated abused, neglected, in need of services or delinquent subsequent to the order of any circuit court.

B. Jurisdiction of cases involving violations of federal law by a child shall be concurrent and shall be assumed only if waived by the federal court or the United States attorney.

History.

Code 1950, § 16.1-161; 1956, c. 555; 1977, c. 559; 1978, c. 740;

1984, cc. 657, 669; 1985, c. 183; 1987, c. 36; 1989, c. 509; 1990, c. 600; 2000, c. 781; 2003, c. 129.

§ 16.1-245. Transfer from other courts.

If, during the pendency of a proceeding in any other court, it is ascertained for the first time that exclusive jurisdiction lies within the juvenile and domestic relations district court, such court shall forthwith transfer the case, together with all papers, documents and evidence connected therewith, to the juvenile and domestic relations district court of the city or county having jurisdiction. The court making the transfer shall determine who is to have custody of the child pending action by the juvenile and domestic relations district court pursuant to § 16.1-247. If, during the pendency of a proceeding in the juvenile and domestic relations district court, it is ascertained for the first time that exclusive jurisdiction lies in the general district or circuit court, the juvenile and domestic relations district court shall likewise transfer the case to the appropriate court.

History.
Code 1950, § 16.1-175; 1956, c. 555; 1977, c. 559; 1992, c. 496.

§ 16.1-245.1. Medical evidence admissible in juvenile and domestic relations district court.

In any civil case heard in a juvenile and domestic relations district court involving allegations of child abuse or neglect or family abuse, any party may present evidence, by a report from the treating or examining health care provider as defined in § 8.01-581.1 or the records of a hospital, medical facility or laboratory at which the treatment, examination or laboratory analysis was performed, or both, as to the extent, nature, and treatment of any physical condition or injury suffered by a person and the examination of the person or the result of the laboratory analysis.

A medical report shall be admitted if the party intending to present such evidence at trial or hearing gives the opposing party or parties a copy of the evidence and written notice of intention to present it at least ten days, or in the case of a preliminary removal hearing under § 16.1-252 or § 16.1-253.1 at least twenty-four hours, prior to the trial or hearing and if attached to such evidence is a sworn statement of the treating or examining health care provider or laboratory analyst who made the report that (i) the information contained therein is true, accurate, and fully describes the nature and extent of the physical condition or injury and (ii) the patient named therein was the person treated or examined by such health care provider; or, in the case of a laboratory analysis, that the information contained therein is true and accurate.

A hospital or other medical facility record shall be admitted if attached to it is a sworn statement of the custodian thereof that the same is a true and accurate copy of the record of such hospital or other medical facility. If thereafter a party summons the health care provider or custodian making such statement to testify in proper person or by deposition taken de bene esse, the court shall determine which party shall pay the fees and costs for such appearance or depositions, or may apportion the same among the parties in such proportion as the ends of justice may require. If such health care provider or custodian is not subject to subpoena for cross-examination in court or by a deposition de bene esse, then the court shall allow a reasonable opportunity for the party seeking the subpoena for such health care provider or custodian to obtain his testimony as the ends of justice may require.

History.
1990, c. 560; 1996, c. 866; 2000, c. 163.

ARTICLE 4.

IMMEDIATE CUSTODY, ARREST, DETENTION AND SHELTER CARE.

§ 16.1-246. When and how child may be taken into immediate custody.

No child may be taken into immediate custody except:

A. With a detention order issued by the judge, the intake officer or the clerk, when authorized by the judge, of the juvenile and domestic relations district court in accordance with the provisions of this law or with a warrant issued by a magistrate; or

B. When a child is alleged to be in need of services or supervision and (i) there is a clear and substantial danger to the child's life or health or (ii) the assumption of custody is necessary to ensure the child's appearance before the court; or

C. When, in the presence of the officer who makes the arrest, a child has committed an act designated a crime under the law of this Commonwealth, or an ordinance of any city, county, town or service district, or under federal law and the officer believes that such is necessary for the protection of the public interest; or

C1. When a child has committed a misdemeanor offense involving (i) shoplifting in violation of § 18.2-103, (ii) assault and battery or (iii) carrying a weapon on school property in violation of § 18.2-308.1 and, although the offense was not committed in the presence of the officer who makes the arrest, the arrest is based on probable cause on reasonable complaint of a person who observed the alleged offense; or

D. When there is probable cause to believe that a child has committed an offense which if committed by an adult would be a felony; or

E. When a law-enforcement officer has probable cause to believe that a person committed to the Department of Juvenile Justice as a child has run away or that a child has escaped from a jail or detention home; or

F. When a law-enforcement officer has probable cause to believe a child has run away from a residential, child-caring facility or home in which he had been placed by the court, the local department of social services or a licensed child welfare agency; or

G. When a law-enforcement officer has probable cause to believe that a child (i) has run away from home or (ii) is without adult supervision at such hours of the night and under such circumstances that the law-enforcement officer reasonably concludes that there is a clear and substantial danger to the child's welfare; or

H. When a child is believed to be in need of inpatient treatment for mental illness as provided in § 16.1-340.

History.

Code 1950, § 16.1-194; 1956, c. 555; 1958, c. 344; 1974, cc. 585, 671; 1977, c. 559; 1978, cc. 643, 740; 1979, c. 701; 1981, c. 487; 1982, c. 683; 1985, c. 540; 1990, cc. 635, 642, 743, 744, 975; 2002, c. 747.

§ 16.1-247. Duties of person taking child into custody.

A. A person taking a child into custody pursuant to the provisions of subsection A of § 16.1-246, during such hours as the court is open, shall, with all practicable speed, and in accordance with the provisions of this law and the orders of court pursuant thereto, bring the child to the judge or intake officer of the court and the judge, intake officer or arresting officer shall, in the most expeditious manner practicable, give notice of the action taken, together with a statement of the reasons for taking the child into custody, orally or in writing to the child's parent, guardian, legal custodian or other person standing in loco parentis.

B. A person taking a child into custody pursuant to the provisions of subsection B, C, or D of § 16.1-246, during such hours as the court is open, shall, with all practicable speed, and in accordance with the provisions of this law and the orders of court pursuant thereto:

1. Release the child to such child's parents, guardian, custodian or other suitable person able and willing to provide supervision and care for such child and issue oral counsel and warning as may be appropriate; or

2. Release the child to such child's parents, guardian, legal custodian or other person standing in loco parentis upon their promise to bring the child before the court when requested; or

3. If not released, bring the child to the judge or intake officer of the court and, in the most expeditious manner practicable, give notice of the action taken, together with a statement of the reasons for taking the child into custody, in writing to the judge or intake officer, and the judge, intake officer or arresting officer shall give notice of the action taken orally or in writing to the child's parent, guardian, legal custodian or other person standing in loco parentis. Nothing herein shall prevent the child from being held for the purpose of administering a blood or breath test to determine the alcoholic content of his blood where the child has been taken into custody pursuant to § 18.2-266.

C. A person taking a child into custody pursuant to the provisions of subsections E and F of § 16.1-246, during such hours as the court is open, shall, with all practicable speed and in accordance with the provisions of this law and the orders of court pursuant thereto:

1. Release the child to the institution, facility or home from which he ran away or escaped; or

2. If not released, bring the child to the judge or intake officer of the court and, in the most expeditious manner practicable, give notice of the action taken, together with a statement of the reasons for taking the child into custody, in writing to the judge or intake officer, and the judge, intake officer or arresting officer shall give notice of the action taken orally or in writing to the institution, facility or home in which the child had been placed and orally or in writing to the child's parent, guardian, legal custodian or other person standing in loco parentis.

D. A person taking a child into custody pursuant to the provisions of subsection A of § 16.1-246, during such hours as the court is not open, shall with all practicable speed and in accordance with the provisions of this law and the orders of court pursuant thereto:

1. Release the child taken into custody pursuant to a warrant on bail or recognizance pursuant to Chapter 9 (§ 19.2-119 et seq.) of Title 19.2; or

2. Place the child in a detention home or in shelter care; or

3. Place the child in a jail subject to the provisions of § 16.1-249.

E. A person taking a child into custody pursuant to the provisions of subsection B, C, or D of § 16.1-246 during such hours as the court is not open, shall:

1. Release the child pursuant to the provisions of subdivision B 1 or B 2 of this section; or

2. Release the child on bail or recognizance pursuant to Chapter 9 (§ 19.2-119 et seq.) of Title 19.2; or

3. Place the child taken into custody pursuant to subsection B of § 16.1-246 in shelter care after the issuance of a detention order pursuant to § 16.1-255; or

4. Place the child taken into custody pursuant to subsection C or D of § 16.1-246 in shelter care or in a detention home after the issuance of a warrant by a magistrate; or

5. Place the child in a jail subject to the provisions of § 16.1-249 after the issuance of a warrant by a magistrate or after the issuance of a detention order pursuant to § 16.1-255; or

6. In addition to any other provisions of this subsection, detain the child for a reasonably necessary period of time in order to administer a breath or

blood test to determine the alcohol content of his blood, if such child was taken into custody pursuant to § 18.2-266.

F. A person taking a child into custody pursuant to the provisions of subsection E of § 16.1-246, during such hours as the court is not open, shall:

1. Release the child to the institution or facility from which he ran away or escaped; or

2. Detain the child in a detention home or in a jail subject to the provisions of § 16.1-249 after the issuance of a warrant by a magistrate or after the issuance of a detention order pursuant to § 16.1-255.

G. A person taking a child into custody pursuant to the provisions of subsection F of § 16.1-246, during such hours as the court is not open, shall:

1. Release the child to the facility or home from which he ran away; or

2. Detain the child in shelter care after the issuance of a detention order pursuant to § 16.1-255 or after the issuance of a warrant by a magistrate.

H. If a parent, guardian or other custodian fails, when requested, to bring the child before the court as provided in subdivisions B 2 and E 1, the court may issue a detention order directing that the child be taken into custody and be brought before the court.

I. A law-enforcement officer taking a child into custody pursuant to the provisions of subsection G of § 16.1-246 shall notify the intake officer of the juvenile court of the action taken. The intake officer shall determine if the child's conduct or situation is within the jurisdiction of the court and if a petition should be filed on behalf of the child. If the intake officer determines that a petition should not be filed, the law-enforcement officer shall as soon as practicable:

1. Return the child to his home;

2. Release the child to such child's parents, guardian, legal custodian or other person standing in loco parentis;

3. Place the child in shelter care for a period not longer than 24 hours after the issuance of a detention order pursuant to § 16.1-255; or

4. Release the child.

During the period of detention authorized by this subsection no child shall be confined in any detention home, jail or other facility for the detention of adults.

J. If a child is taken into custody pursuant to the provisions of subsection B, F, or G of § 16.1-246 by a law-enforcement officer during such hours as the court is not in session and the child is not released or transferred to a facility or institution in accordance with subsection E, G, or I of this section, the child shall be held in custody only so long as is reasonably necessary to complete identification, investigation and processing. The child shall be held under visual supervision in a nonlocked, multipurpose area which is not designated for residential use. The child shall not be handcuffed or otherwise secured to a stationary object.

K. When an adult is taken into custody pursuant to a warrant, detention order, or capias alleging a delinquent act committed when he was a juvenile, he may be released on bail or recognizance pursuant to Chapter 9 (§ 19.2-119 et seq.) of Title 19.2. An intake officer shall have the authority to issue a capias for an adult under the age of 21 who is alleged to have committed, before attaining the age of 18, an offense that would be a crime if committed by an adult.

History.

Code 1950, § 16.1-197; 1956, c. 550; 1958, c. 344; 1973, c. 440; 1974, c. 584; 1975, c. 248; 1977, c. 559; 1978, c. 643; 1979, c. 701; 1984, c. 567; 1992, cc. 728, 830; 2004, cc. 415, 439; 2012, c. 253; 2016, c. 626.

§ 16.1-248: Repealed by Acts 1985, c. 260.

Cross references.

For present provisions as to criteria for detention or shelter care, see § 16.1-248.1.

§ 16.1-248.1. Criteria for detention or shelter care.

A. A juvenile taken into custody whose case is considered by a judge, intake officer or magistrate pursuant to § 16.1-247 shall immediately be released, upon the ascertainment of the necessary facts, to the care, custody and control of such juvenile's parent, guardian, custodian or other suitable person able and willing to provide supervision and care for such juvenile, either on bail or recognizance pursuant to Chapter 9 (§ 19.2-119 et seq.) of Title 19.2 or under such conditions as may be imposed or otherwise. However, at any time prior to an order of final disposition, a juvenile may be detained in a secure facility, pursuant to a detention order or warrant, only upon a finding by the judge, intake officer, or magistrate, that there is probable cause to believe that the juvenile committed the act alleged, and that at least one of the following conditions is met:

1. The juvenile is alleged to have (a) violated the terms of his probation or parole when the charge for which he was placed on probation or parole would have been a felony or Class 1 misdemeanor if committed by an adult; (b) committed an act that would be a felony or Class 1 misdemeanor if committed by an adult; or (c) violated any of the provisions of § 18.2-308.7, and there is clear and convincing evidence that:

a. Considering the seriousness of the current offense or offenses and other pending charges, the seriousness of prior adjudicated offenses, the legal status of the juvenile and any aggravating and mitigating circumstances, the liberty of the juvenile, constitutes a clear and substantial threat to the person or property of others;

b. The liberty of the juvenile would present a clear and substantial threat of serious harm to such juvenile's life or health; or

c. The juvenile has threatened to abscond from the court's jurisdiction during the pendency of the instant proceedings or has a record of willful failure to appear at a court hearing within the immediately preceding 12 months.

2. The juvenile has absconded from a detention home or facility where he has been directed to remain by the lawful order of a judge or intake officer.

3. The juvenile is a fugitive from a jurisdiction outside the Commonwealth and subject to a verified petition or warrant, in which case such juvenile may be detained for a period not to exceed that provided for in § 16.1-323 while arrangements are made to return the juvenile to the lawful custody of a parent, guardian or other authority in another state.

4. The juvenile has failed to appear in court after having been duly served with a summons in any case in which it is alleged that the juvenile has committed a delinquent act or that the child is in need of services or is in need of supervision; however, a child alleged to be in need of services or in need of supervision may be detained for good cause pursuant to this subsection only until the next day upon which the court sits within the county or city in which the charge against the child is pending, and under no circumstances longer than 72 hours from the time he was taken into custody. If the 72-hour period expires on a Saturday, Sunday, legal holiday or day on which the court is lawfully closed, the 72 hours shall be extended to the next day that is not a Saturday, Sunday, legal holiday or day on which the court is lawfully closed.

5. The juvenile failed to adhere to the conditions imposed upon him by the court, intake officer or magistrate following his release upon a Class 1 misdemeanor charge or a felony charge.

When a juvenile is placed in secure detention, the detention order shall state the offense for which the juvenile is being detained, and, to the extent practicable, other pending and previous charges.

B. Any juvenile not meeting the criteria for placement in a secure facility shall be released to a parent, guardian or other person willing and able to provide supervision and care under such conditions as the judge, intake officer or magistrate may impose. However, a juvenile may be placed in shelter care if:

1. The juvenile is eligible for placement in a secure facility;

2. The juvenile has failed to adhere to the directions of the court, intake officer or magistrate while on conditional release;

3. The juvenile's parent, guardian or other person able to provide supervision cannot be reached within a reasonable time;

4. The juvenile does not consent to return home;

5. Neither the juvenile's parent or guardian nor any other person able to provide proper supervision can arrive to assume custody within a reasonable time; or

6. The juvenile's parent or guardian refuses to permit the juvenile to return home and no relative or other person willing and able to provide proper supervision and care can be located within a reasonable time.

C. When a juvenile is detained in a secure facility, the juvenile's probation officer may review such placement for the purpose of seeking a less restrictive alternative to confinement in that secure facility.

D. The criteria for continuing the juvenile in detention or shelter care as set forth in this section shall govern the decisions of all persons involved in determining whether the continued detention or shelter care is warranted pending court disposition. Such criteria shall be supported by clear and convincing evidence in support of the decision not to release the juvenile.

E. Nothing in this section shall be construed to deprive the court of its power to punish a juvenile summarily for contempt for acts set forth in § 18.2-456, other than acts of disobedience of the court's dispositional order which are committed outside the presence of the court.

F. A detention order may be issued pursuant to subdivision 2 of subsection A by the committing court or by the court in the jurisdiction from which the juvenile fled or where he was taken into custody.

G. The court is authorized to detain a juvenile based upon the criteria set forth in subsection A at any time after a delinquency petition has been filed, both prior to adjudication and after adjudication pending final disposition subject to the time limitations set forth in § 16.1-277.1.

H. If the intake officer or magistrate releases the juvenile, either on bail or recognizance or under such conditions as may be imposed, no motion to revoke bail, or change such conditions may be made unless (i) the juvenile has violated a term or condition of his release, or is convicted of or taken into custody for an additional offense, or (ii) the attorney for the Commonwealth presents evidence that incorrect or incomplete information regarding the factors in subsection A was relied upon by the intake officer or magistrate establishing the initial terms of release. If the juvenile court releases the juvenile, either on bail or recognizance or under such conditions as may be imposed, over the objection of the attorney for the Commonwealth, the attorney for the Commonwealth may appeal such decision to the circuit court. The order of the juvenile court releasing the juvenile shall remain in effect until the circuit court, Court of Appeals or Supreme Court rules otherwise.

History.

1977, c. 559; 1979, c. 701; 1985, c. 260; 1986, c. 517; 1987, c. 632; 1989, c. 725; 1990, c. 257; 1996, cc. 755, 914; 2000, c. 836; 2001, c.

837; 2002, cc. 55, 359; 2003, cc. 104, 851; 2004, c. 374; 2005, c. 647; 2010, c. 683; 2011, c. 644.

§ 16.1-248.2. Mental health screening and assessment for certain juveniles.

Whenever a juvenile is placed in a secure facility pursuant to § 16.1-248.1, the staff of the facility shall gather such information from the juvenile and the probation officer as is reasonably available and deemed necessary by the facility staff. As part of the intake procedures at each such facility, the staff shall ascertain the juvenile's need for a mental health assessment. If it is determined that the juvenile needs such an assessment, the assessment shall take place within twenty-four hours of such determination. The community services board serving the jurisdiction where the facility is located shall be responsible for conducting the assessments and shall be compensated from funds appropriated to the Department of Juvenile Justice for this purpose. The Department of Juvenile Justice shall develop criteria and a compensation plan for such assessments.

History.
1996, cc. 755, 914; 1998, c. 434.

§ 16.1-248.3. Medical records of juveniles in secure facility.

Whenever a juvenile is placed in a secure facility or a shelter care facility pursuant to § 16.1-248.1, the director of the facility or his designee shall be entitled to obtain medical records concerning the juvenile from a provider. Prior to using the authority granted by this section to obtain such records, the director of the facility or his designee shall make a reasonable attempt to obtain consent for the release of the records from the juvenile's parent or legal guardian or, in instances where the juvenile may consent pursuant to § 54.1-2969, from the juvenile. The director of the facility or his designee may proceed to obtain the records from the provider if such consent is refused or is not readily obtainable and the records are necessary (i) for the provision of health care to the juvenile, (ii) to protect the health and safety of the juvenile or other residents or staff of the facility or (iii) to maintain the security and safety of the facility.

The director or his designee shall document in writing the reason that the records were requested and that a reasonable attempt was made to obtain consent for the release of records and that consent was refused or not readily obtainable.

No person to whom disclosure of records was made pursuant to this section shall redisclose or otherwise reveal the records, beyond the purpose for which such disclosure was made, without first obtaining specific consent to redisclose from the juvenile's parent or legal guardian or, in instances where the juvenile may consent pursuant to § 54.1-2969, from the juvenile.

Substance abuse records subject to federal regulations, Confidentiality of Alcohol and Drug Abuse Patient Records, 42 C.F.R. Part 2, shall not be subject to the provisions of this section. The disclosure of results of a test for human immunodeficiency virus shall not be permitted except as provided in § 32.1-36.1.

The definitions of "provider" and "records" in § 32.1-127.1:03 shall apply to this section.

History.
2003, c. 983.

§ 16.1-249. Places of confinement for juveniles.

A. If it is ordered that a juvenile remain in detention or shelter care pursuant to § 16.1-248.1, such juvenile may be detained, pending a court hearing, in the following places:

1. An approved foster home or a home otherwise authorized by law to provide such care;
2. A facility operated by a licensed child welfare agency;
3. If a juvenile is alleged to be delinquent, in a detention home or group home approved by the Department;
4. Any other suitable place designated by the court and approved by the Department;
5. To the extent permitted by federal law, a separate juvenile detention facility located upon the site of an adult regional jail facility established by any county, city or any combination thereof constructed after 1994, approved by the Department of Juvenile Justice and certified by the Board of Juvenile Justice for the holding and detention of juveniles.

B. No juvenile shall be detained or confined in any jail or other facility for the detention of adult offenders or persons charged with crime except as provided in subsection D, E, F or G of this section.

C. The official in charge of a jail or other facility for the detention of adult offenders or persons charged with crime shall inform the court immediately when a juvenile who is or appears to be under the age of 18 years is received at the facility, and shall deliver him to the court upon request, or transfer him to a detention facility designated by the court.

D. When a case is transferred to the circuit court in accordance with the provisions of subsection A of § 16.1-269.1 and an order is entered by the circuit court in accordance with § 16.1-269.6, or in accordance with the provisions of § 16.1-270 where the juvenile has waived the jurisdiction of the district court, or when the district court has certified a charge to the grand jury pursuant to subsection B or C of § 16.1-269.1, the juvenile, if in confinement, shall be placed in a juvenile secure facility, unless the court determines that the juvenile is a threat to the security or safety of the other juveniles detained or the staff of the facility, in which case the court may transfer the juvenile to a jail or other facility for the detention of adults and need no longer be entirely separate and removed from adults.

E. If, in the judgment of the custodian, a juvenile has demonstrated that he is a threat to the security or safety of the other juveniles detained or the staff of the home or facility, the judge shall determine whether such juvenile should be transferred to another juvenile facility or, if the child is 14 years of age or older, a jail or other facility for the detention of adults; provided, that (i) the detention is in a room or ward entirely separate and removed from adults, (ii) adequate supervision is provided, and (iii) the facility is approved by the State Board of Corrections for detention of juveniles.

F. If, in the judgment of the custodian, it has been demonstrated that the presence of a juvenile in a facility creates a threat to the security or safety of the other juveniles detained or the staff of the home or facility, the custodian may transfer the juvenile to another juvenile facility, or, if the child is 14 years of age or older, a jail or other facility for the detention of adults pursuant to the limitations of clauses (i), (ii) and (iii) of subsection E for a period not to exceed six hours prior to a court hearing and an additional six hours after the court hearing unless a longer period is ordered pursuant to subsection E.

G. If a juvenile 14 years of age or older is charged with an offense which, if committed by an adult, would be a felony or Class 1 misdemeanor, and the judge or intake officer determines that secure detention is needed for the safety of the juvenile or the community, such juvenile may be detained for a period not to exceed six hours prior to a court hearing and six hours after the court hearing in a temporary lock-up room or ward for juveniles while arrangements are completed to transfer the juvenile to a juvenile facility. Such room or ward may be located in a building which also contains a jail or other facility for the detention of adults, provided (i) such room or ward is totally separate and removed from adults or juveniles transferred to the circuit court pursuant to Article 7 (§ 16.1-269.1 et seq.) of this chapter, (ii) constant supervision is provided, and (iii) the facility is approved by the State Board of Corrections for the detention of juveniles. The State Board of Corrections is authorized and directed to prescribe minimum standards for temporary lock-up rooms and wards based on the requirements set out in this subsection.

G1. Any juvenile who has been ordered detained in a secure detention facility pursuant to § 16.1-248.1 may be held incident to a court hearing (i) in a court holding cell for a period not to exceed six hours provided the juvenile is entirely separate and removed from detained adults or (ii) in a nonsecure area provided constant supervision is provided.

H. If a judge, intake officer or magistrate orders the predispositional detention of persons 18 years of age or older, such detention shall be in an adult facility; however, if the predispositional detention is ordered for a violation of the terms and conditions of release from a juvenile correctional center, the judge, intake officer or magistrate may order such detention be in a juvenile facility.

I. The Departments of Corrections, Juvenile Justice and Criminal Justice Services shall assist the localities or combinations thereof in implementing this section and ensuring compliance herewith.

History.

1977, c. 559; 1979, c. 655; 1983, c. 336; 1985, c. 260; 1988, c. 886; 1989, c. 557; 1993, c. 435; 1994, cc. 859, 904, 949; 1995, cc. 746, 748, 798, 802; 1996, cc. 755, 914; 1998, cc. 576, 830; 2002, c. 558; 2004, cc. 415, 439; 2010, c. 739.

§ 16.1-249.1. Places of confinement to give notice of intake of certain persons.

A. At the time of receipt of any person, for whom registration with the Sex Offender and Crimes Against Minors Registry is required pursuant to Chapter 9 (§ 9.1-900 et seq.) of Title 9.1 into a secure facility, the secure facility shall obtain from that person all necessary registration information, including fingerprints and photographs of a type and kind approved by the Department of State Police. A person required to register shall register and submit to be photographed as part of the registration. The facility shall forthwith forward the registration information to the Department of State Police on the date of the receipt of the prisoner.

B. Whenever a person required to register has failed to comply with the provisions of subsection A, the facility shall promptly investigate or request the State Police promptly investigate and, if there is probable cause to believe a violation has occurred, obtain a warrant, or assist in obtaining an indictment charging a violation of § 18.2-472.1 in the jurisdiction in which the person was received. The facility shall notify the State Police forthwith of such actions taken pursuant to this section.

History.

2006, cc. 857, 914.

§ 16.1-250. Procedure for detention hearing.

A. When a child has been taken into immediate custody and not released as provided in § 16.1-247 or § 16.1-248.1, such child shall appear before a judge on the next day on which the court sits within the county or city wherein the charge against the child is pending. In the event the court does not sit within the county or city on the following day, such child shall appear before a judge within a reasonable time, not to exceed 72 hours, after he has been taken into custody. If the 72-hour period expires on a Saturday, Sunday or other legal holiday, the 72 hours shall be extended to the next day which is not a Saturday, Sunday or legal holiday. In the event the court does not sit on the following day within the county or city wherein the charge against the child is pending, the court may conduct the hearing in another county or city, but only if two-way electronic video and audio communication is available in the courthouse of the county or city wherein the charge is pending.

B. The appearance of the child, the attorney for the Commonwealth, the attorney for the child and the parent, guardian, legal custodian or other person standing in loco parentis may be by (i) personal appearance before the judge or (ii) use of two-way electronic video and audio communication. If two-way electronic video and audio communication is used, a judge may exercise all powers conferred by law and all communications and proceedings shall be conducted in the same manner as if the appearance were in person, and any documents filed may be transmitted by electronically transmitted facsimile process. The facsimile may be served or executed by the officer or person to whom sent, and returned in the same manner, and with the same force, effect, authority, and liability as an original document. All signatures thereon shall be treated as original signatures. Any two-way electronic video and audio communication system used for an appearance shall meet the standards as set forth in subsection B of § 19.2-3.1.

C. Notice of the detention hearing or any rehearing, either oral or written, stating the time, place and purpose of the hearing shall be given to the parent, guardian, legal custodian or other person standing in loco parentis if he can be found, to the child's attorney, to the child if 12 years of age or older and to the attorney for the Commonwealth.

D. During the detention hearing, the parties shall be informed of the child's right to remain silent with respect to any allegation of delinquency and of the contents of the petition. The attorney for the child and the attorney for the Commonwealth shall be given the opportunity to be heard.

E. If the judge finds that there is not probable cause to believe that the child committed the delinquent act alleged, the court shall order his release. If the judge finds that there is probable cause to believe that the child committed the delinquent act alleged but that the full-time detention of a child who is alleged to be delinquent is not required, the court shall order his release, and in so doing, the court may impose one or more of the following conditions singly or in combination:

1. Place the child in the custody of a parent, guardian, legal custodian or other person standing in loco parentis under their supervision, or under the supervision of an organization or individual agreeing to supervise him;

2. Place restrictions on the child's travel, association or place of abode during the period of his release;

3. Impose any other condition deemed reasonably necessary and consistent with the criteria for detaining children specified in § 16.1-248.1; or

4. Release the child on bail or recognizance in accordance with the provisions of Chapter 9 (§ 19.2-119 et seq.) of Title 19.2.

F. An order releasing a child on any of the conditions specified in this section may, at any time, be amended to impose additional or different conditions of release or to return the child who is alleged to be delinquent to custody for failure to conform to the conditions previously imposed.

G. All relevant and material evidence helpful in determining probable cause under this section or the need for detention may be admitted by the court even though not competent in a hearing on the petition.

H. If the child is not released and a parent, guardian, legal custodian or other person standing in loco parentis is not notified and does not appear or does not waive appearance at the hearing, upon the written request of such person stating that such person is willing and available to supervise the child upon release from detention and to return the child to court for all scheduled proceedings on the pending charges, the court shall rehear the matter on the next day on which the court sits within the county or city wherein the charge against the child is pending. If the court does not sit within the county or city on the following day, such hearing shall be held before a judge within a reasonable time, not to exceed 72 hours, after the request.

I. In considering probable cause under this section, if the court deems it necessary to summon witnesses to assist in such determination then the hearing may be continued and the child remain in detention, but in no event longer than three consecutive days, exclusive of Saturdays, Sundays, and legal holidays.

History.

1977, c. 559; 1979, c. 338; 1985, c. 260; 1986, c. 542; 1988, c. 220; 1989, c. 549; 1992, c. 508; 1995, c. 451; 2004, c. 437; 2006, c. 89.

§ **16.1-250.1:** Repealed by Acts 2004, c. 437, cl. 2, effective July 1, 2005.

§ 16.1-251. Emergency removal order.

A. A child may be taken into immediate custody and placed in shelter care pursuant to an emergency removal order in cases in which the child is alleged to have been abused or neglected. Such order may be issued ex parte by the court upon a petition supported by an affidavit or by sworn testimony in person before the judge or intake officer which establishes that:

1. The child would be subjected to an imminent threat to life or health to the extent that severe or irremediable injury would be likely to result if the child were returned to or left in the custody of his parents, guardian, legal custodian or other person standing in loco parentis pending a final hearing on the petition.

2. Reasonable efforts have been made to prevent removal of the child from his home and there are no alternatives less drastic than removal of the child from his home which could reasonably protect the

child's life or health pending a final hearing on the petition. The alternatives less drastic than removal may include but not be limited to the provision of medical, educational, psychiatric, psychological, homemaking or other similar services to the child or family or the issuance of a preliminary protective order pursuant to § 16.1-253.

If the petitioner fails to obtain an emergency removal order within four hours of taking custody of the child, the affidavit or sworn testimony before the judge or intake officer shall state the reasons therefor.

When a child is removed from his home and there is no reasonable opportunity to provide preventive services, reasonable efforts to prevent removal shall be deemed to have been made.

B. Whenever a child is taken into immediate custody pursuant to an emergency removal order, a hearing shall be held in accordance with § 16.1-252 as soon as practicable, but in no event later than five business days after the removal of the child.

C. In the emergency removal order the court shall give consideration to temporary placement of the child with a relative or other interested individual, including grandparents, under the supervision of the local department of social services, until such time as the hearing in accordance with § 16.1-252 is held.

D. The local department of social services having "legal custody" of a child as defined in § 16.1-228 (i) shall not be required to comply with the requirements of this section in order to redetermine where and with whom the child shall live, notwithstanding that the child had been placed with a natural parent.

History.

1977, c. 559; 1984, c. 499; 1985, c. 584; 1986, c. 308; 1990, c. 769; 2000, c. 385; 2003, c. 508.

§ 16.1-252. Preliminary removal order; hearing.

A. A preliminary removal order in cases in which a child is alleged to have been abused or neglected may be issued by the court after a hearing wherein the court finds that reasonable efforts have been made to prevent removal of the child from his home. The hearing shall be in the nature of a preliminary hearing rather than a final determination of custody.

B. Prior to the removal hearing, notice of the hearing shall be given at least 24 hours in advance of the hearing to the guardian ad litem for the child, to the parents, guardian, legal custodian or other person standing in loco parentis of the child and to the child if he or she is 12 years of age or older. If notice to the parents, guardian, legal custodian or other person standing in loco parentis cannot be given despite diligent efforts to do so, the hearing shall be held nonetheless, and the parents, guardian, legal custodian or other person standing in loco parentis shall be afforded a later hearing on their motion regarding a continuation of the summary removal order. The notice provided herein shall include (i) the time, date and place for the hearing; (ii) a specific statement of the factual circumstances which allegedly necessitate removal of the child; and (iii) notice that child support will be considered if a determination is made that the child must be removed from the home.

C. All parties to the hearing shall be informed of their right to counsel pursuant to § 16.1-266.

D. At the removal hearing the child and his parent, guardian, legal custodian or other person standing in loco parentis shall have the right to confront and cross-examine all adverse witnesses and evidence and to present evidence on their own behalf. If the child was 14 years of age or under on the date of the alleged offense and is 16 or under at the time of the hearing, the child's attorney or guardian ad litem, or if the child has been committed to the custody of the Department of Social Services, the local department of social services, may apply for an order from the court that the child's testimony be taken in a room outside the courtroom and be televised by two-way closed-circuit television. The provisions of § 63.2-1521 shall apply, mutatis mutandis, to the use of two-way closed-circuit television except that the person seeking the order shall apply for the order at least 48 hours before the hearing, unless the court for good cause shown allows the application to be made at a later time.

E. In order for a preliminary order to issue or for an existing order to be continued, the petitioning party or agency must prove:

1. The child would be subjected to an imminent threat to life or health to the extent that severe or irremediable injury would be likely to result if the child were returned to or left in the custody of his parents, guardian, legal custodian or other person standing in loco parentis pending a final hearing on the petition; and

2. Reasonable efforts have been made to prevent removal of the child from his home and there are no alternatives less drastic than removal of the child from his home which could reasonably and adequately protect the child's life or health pending a final hearing on the petition. The alternatives less drastic than removal may include but not be limited to the provision of medical, educational, psychiatric, psychological, homemaking or other similar services to the child or family or the issuance of a preliminary protective order pursuant to § 16.1-253.

When a child is removed from his home and there is no reasonable opportunity to provide preventive services, reasonable efforts to prevent removal shall be deemed to have been made.

F. If the court determines that pursuant to subsection E hereof the removal of the child is proper, the court shall:

1. Order that the child be placed in the temporary care and custody of a suitable person, subject to the

provisions of subsection F1 of this section and under the supervision of the local department of social services, with consideration being given to placement in the temporary care and custody of a relative or other interested individual, including grandparents, until such time as the court enters an order of disposition pursuant to § 16.1-278.2, or, if such placement is not available, in the care and custody of a suitable agency;

2. Order that reasonable visitation be allowed between the child and his parents, guardian, legal custodian or other person standing in loco parentis, and between the child and his siblings, if such visitation would not endanger the child's life or health; and

3. Order that the parent or other legally obligated person pay child support pursuant to § 16.1-290.

In addition, the court may enter a preliminary protective order pursuant to § 16.1-253 imposing requirements and conditions as specified in that section which the court deems appropriate for protection of the welfare of the child.

F1. Prior to the entry of an order pursuant to subsection F of this section transferring temporary custody of the child to a relative or other interested individual, including grandparents, the court shall consider whether the relative or other interested individual is one who (i) is willing and qualified to receive and care for the child; (ii) is willing to have a positive, continuous relationship with the child; and (iii) is willing and has the ability to protect the child from abuse and neglect. The court's order transferring temporary custody to a relative or other interested individual should provide for compliance with any preliminary protective order entered on behalf of the child in accordance with the provisions of § 16.1-253; initiation and completion of the investigation as directed by the court and court review of the child's placement required in accordance with the provisions of § 16.1-278.2; and, as appropriate, ongoing provision of social services to the child and the temporary custodian.

G. At the conclusion of the preliminary removal order hearing, the court shall determine whether the allegations of abuse or neglect have been proven by a preponderance of the evidence. Any finding of abuse or neglect shall be stated in the court order. However, if, before such a finding is made, a person responsible for the care and custody of the child, the child's guardian ad litem or the local department of social services objects to a finding being made at the hearing, the court shall schedule an adjudicatory hearing to be held within 30 days of the date of the initial preliminary removal hearing. The adjudicatory hearing shall be held to determine whether the allegations of abuse and neglect have been proven by a preponderance of the evidence. Parties who are present at the preliminary removal order hearing shall be given notice of the date set for the adjudicatory hearing and parties who are not present shall be summoned as provided in § 16.1-263. The hearing shall be held and an order may be entered, although a party to the preliminary removal order hearing fails to appear and is not represented by counsel, provided personal or substituted service was made on the person, or the court determines that such person cannot be found, after reasonable effort, or in the case of a person who is without the Commonwealth, the person cannot be found or his post office address cannot be ascertained after reasonable effort.

The preliminary removal order and any preliminary protective order issued shall remain in full force and effect pending the adjudicatory hearing.

H. If the preliminary removal order includes a finding of abuse or neglect and the child is removed from his home or a preliminary protective order is issued, a dispositional hearing shall be held pursuant to § 16.1-278.2. The dispositional hearing shall be scheduled at the time of the preliminary removal order hearing and shall be held within 60 days of the preliminary removal order hearing. If an adjudicatory hearing is requested pursuant to subsection G, the dispositional hearing shall nonetheless be scheduled at the initial preliminary removal order hearing. All parties present at the preliminary removal order hearing shall be given notice of the date scheduled for the dispositional hearing; parties who are not present shall be summoned to appear as provided in § 16.1-263.

I. The local department of social services having "legal custody" of a child as defined in § 16.1-228 (i) shall not be required to comply with the requirements of this section in order to redetermine where and with whom the child shall live, notwithstanding that the child had been placed with a natural parent.

J. Violation of any order issued pursuant to this section shall constitute contempt of court.

History.

1977, c. 559; 1984, c. 499; 1985, c. 584; 1986, c. 308; 1990, c. 769; 1994, c. 42; 1995, c. 817; 1997, c. 790; 1999, c. 668; 2000, c. 385; 2008, c. 397; 2013, c. 130.

§ 16.1-253. Preliminary protective order.

A. Upon the motion of any person or upon the court's own motion, the court may issue a preliminary protective order, after a hearing, if necessary to protect a child's life, health, safety or normal development pending the final determination of any matter before the court. The order may require a child's parents, guardian, legal custodian, other person standing in loco parentis or other family or household member of the child to observe reasonable conditions of behavior for a specified length of time. These conditions shall include any one or more of the following:

1. To abstain from offensive conduct against the child, a family or household member of the child or any person to whom custody of the child is awarded;

2. To cooperate in the provision of reasonable services or programs designed to protect the child's life, health or normal development;

3. To allow persons named by the court to come into the child's home at reasonable times designated by the court to visit the child or inspect the fitness of the home and to determine the physical or emotional health of the child;

4. To allow visitation with the child by persons entitled thereto, as determined by the court;

5. To refrain from acts of commission or omission which tend to endanger the child's life, health or normal development;

6. To refrain from such contact with the child or family or household members of the child, as the court may deem appropriate, including removal of such person from the residence of the child. However, prior to the issuance by the court of an order removing such person from the residence of the child, the petitioner must prove by a preponderance of the evidence that such person's probable future conduct would constitute a danger to the life or health of such child, and that there are no less drastic alternatives which could reasonably and adequately protect the child's life or health pending a final determination on the petition; or

7. To grant the person on whose behalf the order is issued the possession of any companion animal as defined in § 3.2-6500 if such person meets the definition of owner in § 3.2-6500.

B. A preliminary protective order may be issued ex parte upon motion of any person or the court's own motion in any matter before the court, or upon petition. The motion or petition shall be supported by an affidavit or by sworn testimony in person before the judge or intake officer which establishes that the child would be subjected to an imminent threat to life or health to the extent that delay for the provision of an adversary hearing would be likely to result in serious or irremediable injury to the child's life or health. If an ex parte order is issued without an affidavit being presented, the court, in its order, shall state the basis upon which the order was entered, including a summary of the allegations made and the court's findings. Following the issuance of an ex parte order the court shall provide an adversary hearing to the affected parties within the shortest practicable time not to exceed five business days after the issuance of the order.

C. Prior to the hearing required by this section, notice of the hearing shall be given at least 24 hours in advance of the hearing to the guardian ad litem for the child, to the parents, guardian, legal custodian, or other person standing in loco parentis of the child, to any other family or household member of the child to whom the protective order may be directed and to the child if he or she is 12 years of age or older. The notice provided herein shall include (i) the time, date and place for the hearing and (ii) a specific statement of the factual circumstances which allegedly necessitate the issuance of a preliminary protective order.

D. All parties to the hearing shall be informed of their right to counsel pursuant to § 16.1-266.

E. At the hearing the child, his or her parents, guardian, legal custodian or other person standing in loco parentis and any other family or household member of the child to whom notice was given shall have the right to confront and cross-examine all adverse witnesses and evidence and to present evidence on their own behalf.

F. If a petition alleging abuse or neglect of a child has been filed, at the hearing pursuant to this section the court shall determine whether the allegations of abuse or neglect have been proven by a preponderance of the evidence. Any finding of abuse or neglect shall be stated in the court order. However, if, before such a finding is made, a person responsible for the care and custody of the child, the child's guardian ad litem or the local department of social services objects to a finding being made at the hearing, the court shall schedule an adjudicatory hearing to be held within 30 days of the date of the initial preliminary protective order hearing. The adjudicatory hearing shall be held to determine whether the allegations of abuse and neglect have been proven by a preponderance of the evidence. Parties who are present at the hearing shall be given notice of the date set for the adjudicatory hearing and parties who are not present shall be summoned as provided in § 16.1-263. The adjudicatory hearing shall be held and an order may be entered, although a party to the hearing fails to appear and is not represented by counsel, provided personal or substituted service was made on the person, or the court determines that such person cannot be found, after reasonable effort, or in the case of a person who is without the Commonwealth, the person cannot be found or his post office address cannot be ascertained after reasonable effort.

Any preliminary protective order issued shall remain in full force and effect pending the adjudicatory hearing.

G. If at the preliminary protective order hearing held pursuant to this section the court makes a finding of abuse or neglect and a preliminary protective order is issued, a dispositional hearing shall be held pursuant to § 16.1-278.2. The court shall forthwith, but in all cases no later than the end of the business day on which the order was issued, enter and transfer electronically to the Virginia Criminal Information Network the respondent's identifying information and the name, date of birth, sex, and race of each protected person provided to the court. A copy of the preliminary protective order containing any such identifying information shall be forwarded forthwith to the primary law-enforcement agency responsible for service and entry of protective orders. Upon receipt of the order by the primary law-enforcement agency, the agency shall forthwith verify and enter any modification as necessary to the identifying information and other appropriate information required by the Department of State Police into the Virginia Criminal Information Network established and maintained by the Department of State Police pursuant to Chapter 2 (§ 52-12 et seq.) of Title 52 and the order shall be served forthwith on the allegedly abusing person in person as provided in § 16.1-264 and due return made to the court. However, if the order is issued by the circuit court, the clerk of the circuit court shall forthwith forward an attested copy of the order containing the respondent's identifying information and the name, date of birth, sex, and race of each protected person provided to the court to the primary law-enforcement agency providing service and entry of protective orders and upon receipt of the order, the primary law-enforcement agency shall enter the name of the person subject to the order and other appropriate information required by the Department of State Police into the Virginia Criminal Information Network established and maintained by the Department pursuant to Chapter 2 (§ 52-12 et seq.) of Title 52 and the order shall be served forthwith upon the allegedly abusing person in person as provided in § 16.1-264. Upon service, the agency making service shall enter the date and time of service and other appropriate information required by the Department of State Police into the Virginia Criminal Information Network and make due return to the court. The preliminary order shall specify a date for the dispositional hearing. The dispositional hearing shall be scheduled at the time of the hearing pursuant to this section, and shall be held within 60 days of this hearing. If an adjudicatory hearing is requested pursuant to subsection F, the dispositional hearing shall nonetheless be scheduled at the hearing pursuant to this section. All parties present at the hearing shall be given notice of the date and time scheduled for the dispositional hearing; parties who are not present shall be summoned to appear as provided in § 16.1-263.

H. Nothing in this section enables the court to remove a child from the custody of his or her parents, guardian, legal custodian or other person standing in loco parentis, except as provided in § 16.1-278.2, and no order hereunder shall be entered against a person over whom the court does not have jurisdiction.

I. Neither a law-enforcement agency, the attorney for the Commonwealth, a court nor the clerk's office, nor any employee of them, may disclose, except among themselves, the residential address, telephone number, or place of employment of the person protected by the order or that of the family of such person, except to the extent that disclosure is (i) required by law or the Rules of the Supreme Court, (ii) necessary for law-enforcement purposes, or (iii) permitted by the court for good cause.

J. Violation of any order issued pursuant to this section shall constitute contempt of court.

K. The court shall forthwith, but in all cases no later than the end of the business day on which the order was issued, enter and transfer electronically to the Virginia Criminal Information Network the respondent's identifying information and the name, date of birth, sex, and race of each protected person provided to the court. A copy of the preliminary protective order containing any such identifying information shall be forwarded forthwith to the primary law-enforcement agency responsible for service and entry of protective orders. Upon receipt of the order by the primary law-enforcement agency, the agency shall forthwith verify and enter any modification as necessary to the identifying information and other appropriate information required by the Department of State Police into the Virginia Criminal Information Network established and maintained by the Department pursuant to Chapter 2 (§ 52-12 et seq.) of Title 52 and the order shall be served forthwith on the allegedly abusing person in person as provided in § 16.1-264 and due return made to the court. However, if the order is issued by the circuit court, the clerk of the circuit court shall forthwith forward an attested copy of the order containing the respondent's identifying information and the name, date of birth, sex, and race of each protected person provided to the court to the primary law-enforcement agency providing service and entry of protective orders and upon receipt of the order, the primary law-enforcement agency shall enter the name of the person subject to the order and other appropriate information required by the Department of State Police into the Virginia Criminal Information Network established and maintained by the Department pursuant to Chapter 2 (§ 52-12 et seq.) of Title 52 and the order shall be served forthwith on the allegedly abusing person in person as provided in § 16.1-264. Upon service, the agency making service shall enter the date and time of service and other appropriate information required by the Department of State Police into the Virginia Criminal Information Network and make due return to the court. The preliminary order shall specify a date for the full hearing.

Upon receipt of the return of service or other proof of service pursuant to subsection C of § 16.1-264, the clerk shall forthwith forward an attested copy of the preliminary protective order to the primary law-enforcement agency and the agency shall forthwith verify and enter any modification as necessary into the Virginia Criminal Information Network as described above. If the order is later dissolved or modified, a copy of the dissolution or modification order shall also be attested, forwarded forthwith to the primary law-enforcement agency responsible for service and entry of protective orders, and upon receipt of the order by the primary law-enforcement agency, the agency shall forthwith verify and enter any modification as necessary to the identifying information and other appropriate information required by the Department of State Police into the Virginia Criminal Information Network as described above and the order shall be served forthwith and due return made to the court.

L. No fee shall be charged for filing or serving any petition or order pursuant to this section.

History.

1977, c. 559; 1985, c. 595; 1986, c. 308; 1987, c. 497; 1996, c. 866; 1997, c. 790; 1998, c. 550; 2002, cc. 508, 810, 818; 2008, cc. 73, 246; 2009, c. 732; 2013, c. 130; 2014, c. 346.

§ 16.1-253.1. Preliminary protective orders in cases of family abuse; confidentiality.

A. Upon the filing of a petition alleging that the petitioner is or has been, within a reasonable period of time, subjected to family abuse, the court may issue a preliminary protective order against an allegedly abusing person in order to protect the health and safety of the petitioner or any family or household member of the petitioner. The order may be issued in an ex parte proceeding upon good cause shown when the petition is supported by an affidavit or sworn testimony before the judge or intake officer. Immediate and present danger of family abuse or evidence sufficient to establish probable cause that family abuse has recently occurred shall constitute good cause. Evidence that the petitioner has been subjected to family abuse within a reasonable time and evidence of immediate and present danger of family abuse may be established by a showing that (i) the allegedly abusing person is incarcerated and is to be released from incarceration within 30 days following the petition or has been released from incarceration within 30 days prior to the petition, (ii) the crime for which the allegedly abusing person was convicted and incarcerated involved family abuse against the petitioner, and (iii) the allegedly abusing person has made threatening contact with the petitioner while he was incarcerated, exhibiting a renewed threat to the petitioner of family abuse.

A preliminary protective order may include any one or more of the following conditions to be imposed on the allegedly abusing person:

1. Prohibiting acts of family abuse or criminal offenses that result in injury to person or property.
2. Prohibiting such contacts by the respondent with the petitioner or family or household members of the petitioner as the court deems necessary for the health or safety of such persons.
3. Granting the petitioner possession of the premises occupied by the parties to the exclusion of the allegedly abusing person; however, no such grant of possession shall affect title to any real or personal property.
4. Enjoining the respondent from terminating any necessary utility service to a premises that the petitioner has been granted possession of pursuant to subdivision 3 or, where appropriate, ordering the respondent to restore utility services to such premises.
5. Granting the petitioner temporary possession or use of a motor vehicle owned by the petitioner alone or jointly owned by the parties to the exclusion of the allegedly abusing person; however, no such grant of possession or use shall affect title to the vehicle.
6. Requiring that the allegedly abusing person provide suitable alternative housing for the petitioner and any other family or household member and, where appropriate, requiring the respondent to pay deposits to connect or restore necessary utility services in the alternative housing provided.
7. Granting the petitioner the possession of any companion animal as defined in § 3.2-6500 if such petitioner meets the definition of owner in § 3.2-6500.
8. Any other relief necessary for the protection of the petitioner and family or household members of the petitioner.

B. The court shall forthwith, but in all cases no later than the end of the business day on which the order was issued, enter and transfer electronically to the Virginia Criminal Information Network the respondent's identifying information and the name, date of birth, sex, and race of each protected person provided to the court. A copy of a preliminary protective order containing any such identifying information shall be forwarded forthwith to the primary law-enforcement agency responsible for service and entry of protective orders. Upon receipt of the order by the primary law-enforcement agency, the agency shall forthwith verify and enter any modification as necessary to the identifying information and other appropriate information required by the Department of State Police into the Virginia Criminal Information Network established and maintained by the Department pursuant to Chapter 2 (§ 52-12 et seq.) of Title 52 and the order shall be served forthwith on the allegedly abusing person in person as provided in § 16.1-264 and due return made to the court. However, if the order is issued by the circuit court, the clerk of the circuit court shall forthwith forward an attested copy of the order containing the respondent's identifying information and the name, date of birth, sex, and race of each protected person provided to the court to the primary law-enforcement agency providing service and entry of protective orders and upon receipt of the order, the primary law-enforcement agency shall enter the name of the person subject to the order and other appropriate information required by the Department of State Police into the Virginia Criminal Information Network established and maintained by the Department pursuant to Chapter 2 (§ 52-12 et seq.) of Title 52 and the order shall be served forthwith on the allegedly abusing person in person as provided in § 16.1-264. Upon service, the agency making service shall enter the date and time of service and other appropriate information required by the Department of State Police into the Virginia Criminal Information Network and make due return to the court. The preliminary order shall specify a date for the full hearing. The hearing shall be held within 15 days of the issuance of the preliminary order. If the respondent fails to appear at this hearing because the respondent was not personally served, or if personally served was incarcerated and not transported to the hearing, the court may extend the protective order for a period not to exceed six months. The extended protective order shall be served forthwith on the respondent. However, upon motion of the respondent and for good cause shown, the court may continue the hearing. The preliminary order shall remain in effect until the hearing. Upon request after the order is issued, the clerk shall provide the petitioner with a copy of the order and information regarding the date and time of service. The order shall further specify that either party may at any time file a motion with the court requesting a hearing to dissolve or modify the order. The hearing on the motion shall be given precedence on the docket of the court.

Upon receipt of the return of service or other proof of service pursuant to subsection C of § 16.1-264, the clerk shall forthwith forward an attested copy of the preliminary protective order to the primary law-enforcement agency, and the agency shall forthwith verify and enter any modification as necessary into the Virginia Criminal Information Network as described above. If the order is later dissolved or modified, a copy of the dissolution or modification order shall also be attested, forwarded forthwith to the primary law-enforcement agency responsible for service and entry of protective orders, and upon receipt of the order by the primary law-enforcement agency, the agency shall forthwith verify and enter any modification as necessary to the identifying information and other appropriate information required by the Department of State Police into the Virginia Criminal Information Network as described above and the order shall be served forthwith and due return made to the court.

C. The preliminary order is effective upon personal service on the allegedly abusing person. Except as otherwise provided in § 16.1-253.2, a violation of the order shall constitute contempt of court.

D. At a full hearing on the petition, the court may issue a protective order pursuant to § 16.1-279.1 if the court finds that the petitioner has proven the allegation of family abuse by a preponderance of the evidence.

E. Neither a law-enforcement agency, the attorney for the Commonwealth, a court nor the clerk's office, nor any employee of them, may disclose, except among themselves, the residential address, telephone number, or place of employment of the person protected by the order or that of the family of such person, except to the extent that disclosure is (i) required by law or the Rules of the Supreme Court, (ii) necessary for law-enforcement purposes, or (iii) permitted by the court for good cause.

F. As used in this section, "copy" includes a facsimile copy.

G. No fee shall be charged for filing or serving any petition or order pursuant to this section.

History.

1984, c. 631; 1987, c. 497; 1988, c. 165; 1992, c. 886; 1994, c. 907; 1996, c. 866; 1997, c. 603; 1998, c. 684; 2000, cc. 34, 654; 2001, c. 101; 2002, cc. 508, 810, 818; 2006, c. 308; 2007, c. 205; 2008, cc. 73, 246; 2009, cc. 343, 732; 2011, cc. 445, 480; 2014, c. 346.

§ 16.1-253.2. Violation of provisions of protective orders; penalty.

A. In addition to any other penalty provided by law, any person who violates any provision of a protective order issued pursuant to § 16.1-253, 16.1-253.1, 16.1-253.4, 16.1-278.14, or 16.1-279.1 or subsection B of § 20-103, when such violation involves a provision of the protective order that prohibits such person from (i) going or remaining upon land, buildings, or premises; (ii) further acts of family abuse; or (iii) committing a criminal offense, or which prohibits contacts by the respondent with the allegedly abused person or family or household members of the allegedly abused person as the court deems appropriate, is guilty of a Class 1 misdemeanor. The punishment for any person convicted of a second offense of violating a protective order, when the offense is committed within five years of the prior conviction and when either the instant or prior offense was based on an act or threat of violence, shall include a mandatory minimum term of confinement of 60 days. Any person convicted of a third or subsequent offense of violating a protective order, when the offense is committed within 20 years of the first conviction and when either the instant or one of the prior offenses was based on an act or threat of violence is guilty of a Class 6 felony and the punishment shall include a mandatory minimum term of confinement of six months. The mandatory minimum terms of confinement prescribed for violations of this section shall be served consecutively with any other sentence.

B. In addition to any other penalty provided by law, any person who, while knowingly armed with a firearm or other deadly weapon, violates any provision of a protective order with which he has been served issued pursuant to § 16.1-253, 16.1-253.1, 16.1-253.4, 16.1-278.14, or 16.1-279.1 or subsection B of § 20-103 is guilty of a Class 6 felony.

C. If the respondent commits an assault and battery upon any party protected by the protective order resulting in bodily injury to the party or stalks any party protected by the protective order in violation of § 18.2-60.3, he is guilty of a Class 6 felony. Any person who violates such a protective order by furtively entering the home of any protected party while the party is present, or by entering and remaining in the home of the protected party until the party arrives, is guilty of a Class 6 felony, in addition to any other penalty provided by law.

D. Upon conviction of any offense hereunder for which a mandatory minimum term of confinement is not specified, the person shall be sentenced to a term of confinement and in no case shall the entire term imposed be suspended. Upon conviction, the court shall, in addition to the sentence imposed, enter a protective order pursuant to § 16.1-279.1 for a specified period not exceeding two years from the date of conviction.

History.

1987, c. 700; 1988, c. 501; 1991, cc. 534, 715; 1992, c. 886; 1996, c. 866; 2003, c. 219; 2004, cc. 972, 980; 2007, cc. 745, 923; 2012, c. 637; 2013, cc. 761, 774; 2016, cc. 583, 585, 638.

§ 16.1-253.3: Repealed by Acts 1992, c. 886.

§ 16.1-253.4. Emergency protective orders authorized in certain cases; penalty.

A. Any judge of a circuit court, general district court, juvenile and domestic relations district court or magistrate may issue a written or oral ex parte emergency protective order pursuant to this section in order to protect the health or safety of any person.

B. When a law-enforcement officer or an allegedly abused person asserts under oath to a judge or magistrate, and on that assertion or other evidence the judge or magistrate (i) finds that a warrant for a violation of § 18.2-57.2 has been issued or issues a warrant for violation of § 18.2-57.2 and finds that there is probable danger of further acts of family abuse against a family or household member by the respondent or (ii) finds that reasonable grounds exist to believe that the respondent has committed family abuse and there is probable danger of a further such offense against a family or household member by the respondent, the judge or magistrate shall issue an ex parte emergency protective order, except if the respondent is a minor, an emergency protective order shall not be required, imposing one or more of the following conditions on the respondent:

1. Prohibiting acts of family abuse or criminal offenses that result in injury to person or property;

2. Prohibiting such contacts by the respondent with the allegedly abused person or family or household members of the allegedly abused person, including prohibiting the respondent from being in the physical presence of the allegedly abused person or family or household members of the allegedly abused person, as the judge or magistrate deems necessary to protect the safety of such persons;

3. Granting the family or household member possession of the premises occupied by the parties to the exclusion of the respondent; however, no such grant of possession shall affect title to any real or personal property; and

4. Granting the petitioner the possession of any companion animal as defined in § 3.2-6500 if such petitioner meets the definition of owner in § 3.2-6500.

When the judge or magistrate considers the issuance of an emergency protective order pursuant to clause (i), he shall presume that there is probable danger of further acts of family abuse against a family or household member by the respondent unless the presumption is rebutted by the allegedly abused person.

C. An emergency protective order issued pursuant to this section shall expire at 11:59 p.m. on the third day following issuance. If the expiration occurs on a day that the court is not in session, the emergency protective order shall be extended until 11:59 p.m. on the next day that the juvenile and domestic relations district court is in session. When issuing an emergency protective order under this section, the judge or magistrate shall provide the protected person or the law-enforcement officer seeking the emergency protective order with the form for use in filing petitions pursuant to § 16.1-253.1 and written information regarding protective orders that shall include the telephone numbers of domestic violence agencies and legal referral sources on a form prepared by the Supreme Court. If these forms are provided to a law-enforcement officer, the officer may provide these forms to the protected person when giving the emergency protective order to the protected person. The respondent may at any time file a motion with the court requesting a hearing to dissolve or modify the order issued hereunder. The hearing on the motion shall be given precedence on the docket of the court.

D. A law-enforcement officer may request an emergency protective order pursuant to this section and, if the person in need of protection is physically or mentally incapable of filing a petition pursuant to § 16.1-253.1 or 16.1-279.1, may request the extension of an emergency protective order for an additional period of time not to exceed three days after expiration of the original order. The request for an emergency protective order or extension of an order may be made orally, in person or by electronic means, and the judge of a circuit court, general district court, or juvenile and domestic relations district court or a magistrate may issue an oral emergency protective order. An oral emergency protective order issued pursuant to this section shall be reduced to writing, by the law-enforcement officer requesting the order or the magistrate on a preprinted form approved and provided by the Supreme Court of Virginia. The completed form shall include a statement of the grounds for the order asserted by the officer or the allegedly abused person.

E. The court or magistrate shall forthwith, but in all cases no later than the end of the business day on which the order was issued, enter and transfer electronically to the Virginia Criminal Information Network the respondent's identifying information and the name, date of birth, sex, and race of each protected person provided to the court or magistrate. A copy of an emergency protective order issued pursuant to this section containing any such identifying information shall be forwarded forthwith to the primary law-enforcement agency responsible for service and entry of protective orders. Upon receipt of the order by the primary law-enforcement agency, the agency shall forthwith verify and enter any modification as necessary to the identifying information and other appropriate information required by the Department of State Police into the Virginia Criminal Information Network established and maintained by the Department pursuant to Chapter 2 (§ 52-12 et seq.) of Title 52 and the order shall be served forthwith upon the respondent and due return made to the court. However, if the order is issued by the circuit court, the clerk of the circuit court shall forthwith forward an attested copy of the order containing the respondent's identifying information and the name, date of birth, sex, and race of each protected person provided to the court to the primary law-enforcement agency providing service and entry of protective orders and upon receipt of the order, the primary law-enforcement agency shall enter the name of the person subject to the order and other appropriate information required by the Department of State Police into the Virginia Criminal Network established and maintained by the Department pursuant to Chapter 2 (§ 52-12 et seq.) of Title 52 and the order shall be served forthwith on the respondent. Upon service, the agency making service shall enter the date and time of service and other appropriate information required by the Department of State Police into the Virginia Criminal Information Network and make due return to the court. One copy of the order shall be given to the allegedly abused person when it is issued, and one copy shall be filed with the written report required by subsection D of § 19.2-81.3. The judge or magistrate who issues an oral order pursuant to an electronic request by a law-enforcement officer shall verify the written order to determine whether the officer who reduced it to writing accurately transcribed the contents of the oral order. The original copy shall be filed with the clerk of the juvenile and domestic relations district court within five business days of the issuance of the order. If the order is later dissolved or modified, a copy of the dissolution or modification order shall also be attested, forwarded forthwith to the primary law-enforcement agency responsible for service and entry of protective orders, and upon receipt of the order by the primary law-enforcement agency, the agency shall forthwith verify and enter any modification as necessary to the identifying information and other appropriate information required by the Department of State Police into the Virginia Criminal Information Network as described above and the order shall be served forthwith and due return made to the court. Upon request, the clerk shall provide the allegedly abused person with information regarding the date and time of service.

F. The availability of an emergency protective order shall not be affected by the fact that the family or household member left the premises to avoid the danger of family abuse by the respondent.

G. The issuance of an emergency protective order shall not be considered evidence of any wrongdoing by the respondent.

H. As used in this section, "law-enforcement officer" means (i) any full-time or part-time employee of a police department or sheriff's office which is part of or administered by the Commonwealth or any political subdivision thereof and who is responsible for the prevention and detection of crime and the enforcement of the penal, traffic, or highway laws of the Commonwealth; (ii) any member of an auxiliary police force established pursuant to § 15.2-1731; and (iii) any special conservator of the peace who meets the certification requirements for a law-enforcement officer as set forth in § 15.2-1706. Part-time employees are compensated officers who are not full-time employees as defined by the employing police department or sheriff's office.

I. Neither a law-enforcement agency, the attorney for the Commonwealth, a court nor the clerk's office, nor any employee of them, may disclose, except among themselves, the residential address, telephone number, or place of employment of the person protected by the order or that of the family of such person, except to the extent that disclosure is (i) required by law or the Rules of the Supreme Court, (ii) necessary for law-enforcement purposes, or (iii) permitted by the court for good cause.

J. As used in this section:

"Copy" includes a facsimile copy.

"Physical presence" includes (i) intentionally maintaining direct visual contact with the petitioner or (ii) unreasonably being within 100 feet from the petitioner's residence or place of employment.

K. No fee shall be charged for filing or serving any petition or order pursuant to this section.

L. Except as provided in § 16.1-253.2, a violation of a protective order issued under this section shall constitute contempt of court.

History.

1991, c. 715; 1992, c. 742; 1994, c. 907; 1996, c. 866; 1997, c. 603; 1998, cc. 677, 684; 1999, c. 807; 2001, c. 474; 2002, cc. 508, 706, 810, 818; 2007, cc. 396, 661; 2008, cc. 73, 246; 2009, c. 732; 2011, cc. 445, 480; 2012, cc. 637, 827; 2014, cc. 346, 779, 797; 2016, c. 455.

§ 16.1-254. Responsibility for and limitation on transportation of children.

A. The detention home having custody or responsibility for supervision of a child pursuant to §§ 16.1-246, 16.1-247, 16.1-248.1, 16.1-249, and 16.1-250 shall be responsible for transportation of the child to all local medical appointments, dental appointments, psychological and psychiatric evaluations. Transportation of youth to special placements pursuant to § 16.1-286 shall be the responsibility of the court service unit.

B. However, the chief judge of the juvenile and domestic relations district court, on the basis of guidelines approved by the Board, shall designate the appropriate agencies in each county, city and town, other than the Department of State Police, to be responsible for (i) the transportation of violent and disruptive children and (ii) the transportation of children to destinations other than those set forth in subsection A of this section, pursuant to §§ 16.1-246, 16.1-247, 16.1-248.1, 16.1-249, and 16.1-250, and as otherwise ordered by the judge.

No child shall be transported with adults suspected of or charged with criminal acts.

History.

Code 1950, § 16.1-196; 1956, c. 555; 1958, c. 344; 1971, Ex. Sess., c. 109; 1973, c. 440; 1974, c. 358; 1977, c. 559; 1979, c. 202; 1990, cc. 629, 673.

§ 16.1-255. Limitation on issuance of detention orders for juveniles; appearance by juvenile.

No detention order shall be issued for any juvenile except when authorized by the judge or intake officer of a juvenile court or by a magistrate as provided in § 16.1-256.

In matters involving the issuance of detention orders each state or local court service unit shall ensure the capability of a prompt response by an intake officer who is either on duty or on call.

A child may appear before an intake officer either (i) by personal appearance before the intake officer or (ii) by the use of two-way electronic video and audio communication. All communications and proceedings shall be conducted in the same manner and the intake officer shall have the same powers as if the appearance were in person. Any documents filed may be transmitted by facsimile and the facsimile and any signatures thereon shall serve, for all purposes, as an original document. Any two-way electronic video and audio communication system used shall comply with the provisions of subsection B of § 19.2-3.1.

History.

1977, c. 559; 1985, c. 260; 1996, cc. 755, 914; 1997, c. 862; 2002, c. 700.

§ 16.1-256. Limitations as to issuance of warrants for juveniles; detention orders.

No warrant of arrest shall be issued for any juvenile by a magistrate, except as follows:

1. As provided in § 16.1-260 on appeal from a decision of an intake officer; or
2. Upon a finding of probable cause to believe that the child is in need of services or is a delinquent, when (i) the court is not open and (ii) the judge and the intake officer of the juvenile and domestic relations district court are not reasonably available. For purposes of this section, the phrase "not reasonably available" means that neither the judge nor the intake officer of the juvenile and domestic relations district court could be reached after the appearance by the juvenile before a magistrate or that neither could arrive within one hour after he was contacted.

When a magistrate is authorized to issue a warrant pursuant to subdivision 2, he may also issue a detention order, if the criteria for detention set forth in § 16.1-248.1 have been satisfied.

Warrants issued pursuant to this section shall be delivered forthwith to the juvenile court.

History.

Code 1950, § 16.1-195; 1956, c. 555; 1958, c. 344; 1973, c. 440; 1977, c. 559; 1979, c. 701; 1980, c. 234; 1981, c. 184; 1983, c. 349; 1986, c. 295; 1996, cc. 755, 914.

§ 16.1-257. Interference with or obstruction of officer; concealment or removal of child.

No person shall interfere with or obstruct any officer, juvenile probation officer or other officer or employee of the court in the discharge of his duties under this law, nor remove or conceal or cause to be removed or concealed any child in order that he or she may not be brought before the court, nor interfere with or remove or attempt to remove any child who is in the custody of the court or of an officer or who has been lawfully committed under this law. Any person willfully violating any provision of this section is guilty of a Class 1 misdemeanor.

History.

Code 1950, § 16.1-191; 1956, c. 555; 1977, c. 559.

ARTICLE 5.

INTAKE, PETITION AND NOTICE.

§ 16.1-260. Intake; petition; investigation.

A. All matters alleged to be within the jurisdiction of the court shall be commenced by the filing of a petition, except as provided in subsection H and in § 16.1-259. The form and content of the petition shall be as provided in § 16.1-262. No individual shall be required to obtain support services from the Department of Social Services prior to filing a petition seeking support for a child. Complaints, requests, and the processing of petitions to initiate a case shall be the responsibility of the intake officer. However, (i) the attorney for the Commonwealth of the city or county may file a petition on his own motion with the clerk; (ii) designated nonattorney employees of the Department of Social Services may complete, sign, and file petitions and motions relating to the establishment, modification, or enforcement of support on forms approved by the Supreme Court of Virginia with the clerk; (iii) designated nonattorney employees of a local department of social services may complete, sign, and file with the clerk, on forms approved by the Supreme Court of Virginia, petitions for foster care review, petitions for permanency planning hearings, petitions to establish paternity, motions to establish or modify support, motions to amend or review an order, and motions for a rule to show cause; and (iv) any attorney may file petitions on behalf of his client with the clerk except petitions alleging that the subject of the petition is a child alleged to be in need of services, in need of supervision, or delinquent. Complaints alleging abuse or neglect of a child shall be referred initially to the local department of social services in accordance with the provisions of Chapter 15 (§ 63.2-1500 et seq.) of Title 63.2. Motions and other subsequent pleadings in a case shall be filed directly with the clerk. The intake officer or clerk with whom the petition or motion is filed shall inquire whether the petitioner is receiving child support services or public assistance. No individual who is receiving support services or public assistance shall be denied the right to file a petition or motion to establish, modify, or enforce an order for support of a child. If the petitioner is seeking or receiving child support services or public assistance, the clerk, upon issuance of process, shall forward a copy of the petition or motion, together with notice of the court date, to the Division of Child Support Enforcement.

B. The appearance of a child before an intake officer may be by (i) personal appearance before the intake officer or (ii) use of two-way electronic video and audio communication. If two-way electronic video and audio communication is used, an intake officer may exercise all powers conferred by law. All communications and proceedings shall be conducted in the same manner as if the appearance were in person, and any documents filed may be transmitted by facsimile process. The facsimile may be served or executed by the officer or person to whom sent, and returned in the same manner, and with the same force, effect, authority, and liability as an original document. All signatures thereon shall be treated as original signatures. Any two-way electronic video and audio communication system used for an appearance shall meet the standards as set forth in subsection B of § 19.2-3.1.

When the court service unit of any court receives a complaint alleging facts which may be sufficient to invoke the jurisdiction of the court pursuant to § 16.1-241, the unit, through an intake officer, may proceed informally to make such adjustment as is practicable without the filing of a petition or may authorize a petition to be filed by any complainant having sufficient knowledge of the matter to establish probable cause for the issuance of the petition.

An intake officer may proceed informally on a complaint alleging a child is in need of services, in need of supervision, or delinquent only if the juvenile (i) is not alleged to have committed a violent juvenile felony or (ii) has not previously been proceeded against informally or adjudicated delinquent for an offense that would be a felony if committed by an adult. A petition alleging that a juvenile committed a violent juvenile felony shall be filed with the court. A petition alleging that a juvenile is delinquent for an offense that would be a felony if committed by an adult shall be filed with the court if the juvenile had previously been proceeded against informally by intake or had been adjudicated delinquent for an offense that would be a felony if committed by an adult.

If a juvenile is alleged to be a truant pursuant to a complaint filed in accordance with § 22.1-258 and the attendance officer has provided documentation to the intake officer that the relevant school division has complied with the provisions of § 22.1-258, then the intake officer shall file a petition with the court. The intake officer may defer filing the complaint for 90 days and proceed informally by developing a truancy plan. The intake officer may proceed informally only if the juvenile has not previously been proceeded against informally or adjudicated in need of supervision for failure to comply with compulsory school attendance as provided in § 22.1-254. The juvenile and his parent or parents, guardian, or other person standing in loco parentis must agree, in writing, for the development of a truancy plan. The truancy plan may include requirements that the juvenile and his parent or parents, guardian, or other person standing in loco parentis participate in such programs, cooperate in such treatment, or be subject to such conditions and limitations as necessary to ensure the juvenile's compliance with compulsory school attendance as provided in § 22.1-254. The intake officer may refer the juvenile to the appropriate public agency for the purpose of developing a truancy plan using an interagency interdisciplinary team approach. The team may include qualified personnel who are reasonably available from the appropriate department of social services, community services board, local school division, court service unit, and other appropriate and available public and private agencies and may be the family assessment and planning team established pursuant to § 2.2-5207. If at the end of the 90-day period the juvenile has not successfully completed the truancy plan or the truancy program, then the intake officer shall file the petition.

Whenever informal action is taken as provided in this subsection on a complaint alleging that a child is in need of services, in need of supervision, or delinquent, the intake officer shall (i) develop a plan for the juvenile, which may include restitution and the performance of community service, based upon community resources and the circumstances which resulted in the complaint, (ii) create an official record of the action taken by the intake officer and file such record in the juvenile's case file, and (iii) advise the juvenile and the juvenile's parent, guardian, or other person standing in loco parentis and the complainant that any subsequent complaint alleging that the child is in need of supervision or delinquent based upon facts which may be sufficient to invoke the jurisdiction of the court pursuant to § 16.1-241 will result in the filing of a petition with the court.

C. The intake officer shall accept and file a petition in which it is alleged that (i) the custody, visitation, or support of a child is the subject of controversy or requires determination, (ii) a person has deserted, abandoned, or failed to provide support for any person in violation of law, (iii) a child or such child's parent, guardian, legal custodian, or other person standing in loco parentis is entitled to treatment, rehabilitation, or other services which are required by law, (iv) family abuse has occurred and a protective order is being sought pursuant to § 16.1-253.1, 16.1-253.4, or 16.1-279.1, or (v) an act of violence, force, or threat has occurred, a protective order is being sought pursuant to § 19.2-152.8, 19.2-152.9, or 19.2-152.10, and either the alleged victim or the respondent is a juvenile. If any such complainant does not file a petition, the intake officer may file it. In cases in which a child is alleged to be abused, neglected, in need of services, in need of supervision, or delinquent, if the intake officer believes that probable cause does not exist, or that the authorization of a petition will not be in the best interest of the family or juvenile or that the matter may be effectively dealt with by some agency other than the court, he may refuse to authorize the filing of a petition. The intake officer shall provide to a person seeking a protective order pursuant to § 16.1-253.1, 16.1-253.4, or 16.1-279.1 a written explanation of the conditions, procedures and time limits applicable to the issuance of protective orders pursuant to § 16.1-253.1, 16.1-253.4, or 16.1-279.1. If the person is seeking a protective order pursuant to § 19.2-152.8, 19.2-152.9, or 19.2-152.10, the intake officer shall provide a written explanation of the conditions, procedures, and time limits applicable to the issuance of protective orders pursuant to § 19.2-152.8, 19.2-152.9, or 19.2-152.10.

D. Prior to the filing of any petition alleging that a child is in need of supervision, the matter shall be reviewed by an intake officer who shall determine whether the petitioner and the child alleged to be in need of supervision have utilized or attempted to utilize treatment and services available in the community and have exhausted all appropriate nonjudicial remedies which are available to them. When the intake officer determines that the parties have not attempted to utilize available treatment or services or have not exhausted all appropriate nonjudicial remedies which are available, he shall refer the petitioner and the child alleged to be in need of supervision to the appropriate agency, treatment facility, or individual to receive treatment or services, and a petition shall not be filed. Only after the intake officer determines that the parties have made a reasonable effort to utilize available community treatment or services may he permit the petition to be filed.

E. If the intake officer refuses to authorize a petition relating to an offense that if committed by an adult would be punishable as a Class 1 misdemeanor or as a felony, the complainant shall be notified in writing at that time of the complainant's right to apply to a magistrate for a warrant. If a magistrate determines that probable cause exists, he shall issue a warrant returnable to the juvenile and domestic relations district court. The warrant shall be delivered forthwith to the juvenile court, and the intake officer shall accept and file a petition founded upon the warrant. If the court is closed and the magistrate finds that the criteria for detention or shelter care set forth in § 16.1-248.1 have been satisfied, the juvenile may be detained pursuant to the warrant issued in accordance with this subsection. If the intake officer refuses to authorize a petition relating to a child in need of services or in need of supervision, a status offense, or a misdemeanor other than Class 1, his decision is final.

Upon delivery to the juvenile court of a warrant issued pursuant to subdivision 2 of § 16.1-256, the intake officer shall accept and file a petition founded upon the warrant.

F. The intake officer shall notify the attorney for the Commonwealth of the filing of any petition which alleges facts of an offense which would be a felony if committed by an adult.

G. Notwithstanding the provisions of Article 12 (§ 16.1-299 et seq.), the intake officer shall file a report with the division superintendent of the school division in which any student who is the subject of a petition alleging that such student who is a juvenile has committed an act, wherever committed, which would be a crime if committed by an adult, or that such student who is an adult has committed a crime and is alleged to be within the jurisdiction of the court. The report shall notify the division superintendent of the filing of the petition and the nature of the offense, if the violation involves:

1. A firearm offense pursuant to Article 4 (§ 18.2-279 et seq.), 5 (§ 18.2-288 et seq.), 6 (§ 18.2-299 et seq.), 6.1 (§ 18.2-307.1 et seq.), or 7 (§ 18.2-308.1 et seq.) of Chapter 7 of Title 18.2;
2. Homicide, pursuant to Article 1 (§ 18.2-30 et seq.) of Chapter 4 of Title 18.2;
3. Felonious assault and bodily wounding, pursuant to Article 4 (§ 18.2-51 et seq.) of Chapter 4 of Title 18.2;
4. Criminal sexual assault, pursuant to Article 7 (§ 18.2-61 et seq.) of Chapter 4 of Title 18.2;
5. Manufacture, sale, gift, distribution or possession of Schedule I or II controlled substances, pursuant to Article 1 (§ 18.2-247 et seq.) of Chapter 7 of Title 18.2;
6. Manufacture, sale or distribution of marijuana pursuant to Article 1 (§ 18.2-247 et seq.) of Chapter 7 of Title 18.2;
7. Arson and related crimes, pursuant to Article 1 (§ 18.2-77 et seq.) of Chapter 5 of Title 18.2;
8. Burglary and related offenses, pursuant to §§ 18.2-89 through 18.2-93;
9. Robbery pursuant to § 18.2-58;
10. Prohibited criminal street gang activity pursuant to § 18.2-46.2;
11. Recruitment of other juveniles for a criminal street gang activity pursuant to § 18.2-46.3; or
12. An act of violence by a mob pursuant to § 18.2-42.1.

The failure to provide information regarding the school in which the student who is the subject of the petition may be enrolled shall not be grounds for refusing to file a petition.

The information provided to a division superintendent pursuant to this section may be disclosed only as provided in § 16.1-305.2.

H. The filing of a petition shall not be necessary:

1. In the case of violations of the traffic laws, including offenses involving bicycles, hitchhiking and other pedestrian offenses, game and fish laws, or a violation of the ordinance of any city regulating surfing or any ordinance establishing curfew violations, animal control violations, or littering violations. In such cases the court may proceed on a summons issued by the officer investigating the violation in the same manner as provided by law for adults. Additionally, an officer investigating a motor vehicle accident may, at the scene of the accident or at any other location where a juvenile who is involved in such an accident may be located, proceed on a summons in lieu of filing a petition.

2. In the case of seeking consent to apply for the issuance of a work permit pursuant to subsection H of § 16.1-241.

3. In the case of a misdemeanor violation of § 18.2-250.1, 18.2-266, 18.2-266.1, or 29.1-738, or the commission of any other alcohol-related offense, provided the juvenile is released to the custody of a parent or legal guardian pending the initial court date. The officer releasing a juvenile to the custody of a parent or legal guardian shall issue a summons to the juvenile and shall also issue a summons requiring the parent or legal guardian to appear before the court with the juvenile. Disposition of the charge shall be in the manner provided in § 16.1-278.8, 16.1-278.8:01, or 16.1-278.9. If the juvenile so charged with a violation of § 18.2-51.4, 18.2-266, 18.2-266.1, 18.2-272, or 29.1-738 refuses to provide a sample of blood or breath or samples of both blood and breath for chemical analysis pursuant to §§ 18.2-268.1 through 18.2-268.12 or 29.1-738.2, the provisions of these sections shall be followed except that the magistrate shall authorize execution of the warrant as a summons. The summons shall be served on a parent or legal guardian and the juvenile, and a copy of the summons shall be forwarded to the court in which the violation is to be tried. When a violation of § 18.2-250.1 is charged by summons, the juvenile shall be entitled to have the charge referred to intake for consideration of informal proceedings pursuant to subsection B, provided such right is exercised by written notification to the clerk not later than 10 days prior to trial. At the time such summons alleging a violation of § 18.2-250.1 is served, the officer shall also serve upon the juvenile written notice of the right to have the charge referred to intake on a form approved by the Supreme Court and make return of such service to the court. If the officer fails to make such service or return, the court shall dismiss the summons without prejudice.

4. In the case of offenses which, if committed by an adult, would be punishable as a Class 3 or Class 4 misdemeanor. In such cases the court may direct that an intake officer proceed as provided in § 16.1-237 on a summons issued by the officer investigating the violation in the same manner as provided by law for adults provided that notice of the summons to appear is mailed by the investigating officer within five days of the issuance of the summons to a parent or legal guardian of the juvenile.

I. Failure to comply with the procedures set forth in this section shall not divest the juvenile court of the jurisdiction granted it in § 16.1-241.

History.

Code 1950, § 16.1-164; 1956, c. 555; 1972, cc. 672, 835; 1973, c. 440; 1977, c. 559; 1979, c. 701; 1982, c. 91; 1983, c. 349; 1985, c. 488; 1986, c. 381; 1987, cc. 203, 632; 1988, cc. 792, 803; 1990, c. 742; 1991, cc. 496, 511, 534; 1992, cc. 502, 527, 542; 1993, c. 981; 1995, cc. 347, 429; 1996, cc. 755, 914; 1997, c. 862; 1999, cc. 54, 526, 952; 2002, c. 747; 2003, c. 587; 2004, cc. 105, 255, 309, 416, 517, 558; 2006, c. 677; 2008, cc. 136, 845; 2009, cc. 385, 726; 2010, c. 742; 2011, cc. 384, 410, 825; 2012, c. 637; 2013, c. 746; 2014, cc. 674, 719; 2016, c. 704.

§ 16.1-261. Statements made at intake or mental health screening and assessment.

Statements made by a child to the intake officer or probation officer during the intake process or during a mental health screening or assessment conducted pursuant to § 16.1-248.2 and prior to a hearing on the merits of the petition filed against the child, shall not be admissible at any stage of the proceedings.

History.

1977, c. 559; 1996, cc. 755, 914.

§ 16.1-262. Form and content of petition.

A. The petition shall contain the facts below indicated:

"Commonwealth of Virginia, In re ...." a
(name of child)
child under eighteen years of age.

"In the Juvenile and Domestic Relations District Court of the county (or city) of ...."

1. Statement of name, age, date of birth, if known, and residence of the child.

2. Statement of names and residence of his parents, guardian, legal custodian or other person standing in loco parentis and spouse, if any.

3. Statement of names and residence of the nearest known relatives if no parent or guardian can be found.

4. Statement of the specific facts which allegedly bring the child within the purview of this law. If the petition alleges a delinquent act, it shall make reference to the applicable sections of the Code which designate the act a crime.

5. Statement as to whether the child is in custody, and if so, the place of detention or shelter care, and

the time the child was taken into custody, and the time the child was placed in detention or shelter care.

B. If the subject of the petition is an adult, the petition shall not state or include the name of or any information concerning the parents, guardians, legal custodian, or person standing in loco parentis of the adult subject of the petition except as may be necessary to state the conduct alleged in the petition.

C. If any of the facts herein required to be stated are not known by the petitioner, the petition shall so state. The petition shall be verified, except that petitions filed under § 63.2-1237 may be signed by the petitioner's counsel, and may be upon information.

In accordance with § 16.1-69.32, the Supreme Court may formulate rules for the form and content of petitions in the juvenile court concerning matters related to the custody, visitation or support of a child and the protection, support or maintenance of an adult where the provisions of this section are not appropriate.

History.

Code 1950, § 16.1-165; 1956, c. 555; 1977, c. 559; 1979, c. 615; 1984, c. 631; 1995, cc. 772, 826; 2000, c. 830; 2016, c. 626.

§ 16.1-263. Summonses.

A. After a petition has been filed, the court shall direct the issuance of summonses, one directed to the juvenile, if the juvenile is twelve or more years of age, and another to at least one parent, guardian, legal custodian or other person standing in loco parentis, and such other persons as appear to the court to be proper or necessary parties to the proceedings.

After a petition has been filed against an adult pursuant to subsection C or D of § 16.1-259, the court shall direct the issuance of a summons against the adult.

The summons shall require them to appear personally before the court at the time fixed to answer or testify as to the allegations of the petition. Where the custodian is summoned and such person is not a parent of the juvenile in question, a parent shall also be served with a summons. The court may direct that other proper or necessary parties to the proceedings be notified of the pendency of the case, the charge and the time and place for the hearing.

Any such summons shall be deemed a mandate of the court, and willful failure to obey its requirements shall subject any person guilty thereof to liability for punishment for contempt. Upon the failure of any person to appear as ordered in the summons, the court shall immediately issue an order for such person to show cause why he should not be held in contempt.

The parent, guardian, legal custodian, or other person standing in loco parentis shall not be summoned to appear or be punished for failure to appear in cases of adults who are brought before the court pursuant to subsection C or D of § 16.1-259 unless such person is summoned as a witness.

B. The summons shall advise the parties of their right to counsel as provided in § 16.1-266. A copy of the petition shall accompany each summons for the initial proceedings. The summons shall include notice that in the event that the juvenile is committed to the Department or to a secure local facility, at least one parent or other person legally obligated to care for and support the juvenile may be required to pay a reasonable sum for support and treatment of the juvenile pursuant to § 16.1-290. Notice of subsequent proceedings shall be provided to all parties in interest. In all cases where a party is represented by counsel and counsel has been provided with a copy of the petition and due notice as to time, date and place of the hearing, such action shall be deemed due notice to such party, unless such counsel has notified the court that he no longer represents such party.

C. The judge may endorse upon the summons an order directing a parent or parents, guardian or other custodian having the custody or control of the juvenile to bring the juvenile to the hearing.

D. A party, other than the juvenile, may waive service of summons by written stipulation or by voluntary appearance at the hearing.

E. No such summons or notification shall be required if the judge shall certify on the record that (i) the identity of a parent or guardian is not reasonably ascertainable or (ii) in cases in which it is alleged that a juvenile has committed a delinquent act, crime, status offense or traffic infraction or is in need of services or supervision, the location, or in the case of a parent or guardian located outside of the Commonwealth the location or mailing address, of a parent or guardian is not reasonably ascertainable. An affidavit of the mother that the identity of the father is not reasonably ascertainable shall be sufficient evidence of this fact, provided there is no other evidence before the court which would refute such an affidavit. In cases referred to in clause (ii), an affidavit of a law-enforcement officer or juvenile probation officer that the location of a parent or guardian is not reasonably ascertainable shall be sufficient evidence of this fact, provided that there is no other evidence before the court which would refute the affidavit.

History.

Code 1950, §§ 16.1-166, 16.1-172; 1956, c. 555; 1974, c. 620; 1975, c. 128; 1977, c. 559; 1978, cc. 613, 740; 1996, cc. 755, 914; 1997, c. 441; 1999, c. 952; 2004, c. 573; 2016, c. 626.

§ 16.1-264. Service of summons; proof of service; penalty.

A. If a party designated in subsection A of § 16.1-263 to be served with a summons can be found within the Commonwealth, the summons shall be served upon him in person or by substituted service as prescribed in subdivision 2 of § 8.01-296.

If a party designated to be served in § 16.1-263 is without the Commonwealth but can be found or his address is known, or can with reasonable diligence be ascertained, service of summons may be made either by delivering a copy thereof to him personally or by mailing a copy thereof to him by certified mail return receipt requested.

If after reasonable effort a party other than the person who is the subject of the petition cannot be found or his post-office address cannot be ascertained, whether he is within or without the Commonwealth, the court may order service of the summons upon him by publication in accordance with the provisions of §§ 8.01-316 and 8.01-317.

A1. Any person who is subject to an emergency protective order issued pursuant to § 16.1-253.4 or 19.2-152.8 shall have been personally served with the protective order if a law-enforcement officer, as defined in § 9.1-101, personally provides to such person a notification of the issuance of the order, which shall be on a form approved by the Executive Secretary of the Supreme Court of Virginia, provided that all of the information and individual requirements of the order are included on the form. The officer making service shall enter or cause to be entered the date and time of service and other appropriate information required by the Department of State Police into the Virginia Criminal Information Network and make due return to the court.

B. Service of summons may be made under the direction of the court by sheriffs, their deputies and police officers in counties and cities or by any other suitable person designated by the court. However, in any case in which custody or visitation of a minor child or children is at issue and a summons is issued for the attendance and testimony of a teacher or other school personnel who is not a party to the proceeding, if such summons is served on school property, it shall be served only by a sheriff or his deputy.

C. Proof of service may be made by the affidavit of the person other than an officer designated in subsection B hereof who delivers a copy of the summons to the person summoned, but if served by a state, county or municipal officer his return shall be sufficient without oath.

D. The summons shall be considered a mandate of the court and willful failure to obey its requirements shall subject any person guilty thereof to liability for punishment as for contempt.

History.

Code 1950, §§ 16.1-167 to 16.1-170; 1956, c. 555; 1977, c. 559; 1984, c. 594; 1987, c. 632; 1991, c. 62; 2004, c. 588; 2011, c. 482.

§ 16.1-265. Subpoena; attorney-issued subpoena.

Upon application of a party and pursuant to the rules of the Supreme Court of Virginia for the issuance of subpoenas, the clerk of the court shall issue, and the court on its own motion may issue, subpoenas requiring attendance and testimony of witnesses and production of records, documents or other tangible objects at any hearing.

Subpoenas duces tecum for medical records shall be subject to the provisions of §§ 8.01-413 and 32.1-127.1:03 except that no separate fee shall be imposed. A subpoena may also be issued in a civil proceeding by an attorney-at-law who is an active member of the Virginia State Bar at the time of issuance, as an officer of the court. Any such subpoena shall be on a form approved by the Committee on District Courts, signed by the attorney as if a pleading and shall include the attorney's address. A copy, together with the attorney's certificate of service pursuant to Rule 1:12, shall be mailed or delivered to the clerk's office of the court in which the case is pending on the day of issuance by the attorney. The law governing subpoenas issued by a clerk shall apply mutatis mutandis, except that attorneys may not issue subpoenas in those cases in which they may not issue a summons as provided in § 8.01-407. When an attorney-at-law transmits one or more subpoenas or subpoenas duces tecum to a sheriff to be served in his jurisdiction, the provisions in § 8.01-407 regarding such transmittals shall apply. A sheriff shall not be required to serve an attorney-issued subpoena that is not issued at least five business days prior to the date production of evidence is required.

If the time for compliance with a subpoena issued by an attorney is less than 14 days after service of the subpoena, the person to whom it is directed may serve upon the party issuing the subpoena a written objection setting forth any grounds therefor. If objection is made, the party on whose behalf the subpoena was issued and served shall not be entitled to compliance, except pursuant to an order of the court, but may, upon notice to the person to whom the subpoena was directed, move for an order to compel compliance. Upon such timely motion, the court may quash, modify or sustain the subpoena.

History.

1977, c. 559; 2000, c. 813; 2004, c. 335.

ARTICLE 6.

APPOINTMENT OF COUNSEL.

§ 16.1-266. Appointment of counsel and guardian ad litem.

A. Prior to the hearing by the court of any case involving a child who is alleged to be abused or neglected or who is the subject of an entrustment agreement or a petition seeking termination of residual parental rights or who is otherwise before the court pursuant to subdivision A 4 of § 16.1-241 or § 63.2-1230, the court shall appoint a discreet and competent attorney-at-law as guardian ad litem to represent the child pursuant to § 16.1-266.1.

B. Prior to the detention hearing held pursuant to § 16.1-250, the court shall appoint a qualified and competent attorney-at-law to represent the child unless an attorney has been retained and appears on behalf of the child. For the purposes of appointment of counsel for the detention hearing held pursuant to § 16.1-250 only, a child's indigence shall be presumed. Nothing in this subsection shall prohibit a judge from releasing a child from detention prior to appointment of counsel.

C. Subsequent to the detention hearing, if any, and prior to the adjudicatory or transfer hearing by the court of any case involving a child who is alleged to be in need of services, in need of supervision or delinquent, such child and his parent, guardian, legal custodian or other person standing in loco parentis shall be informed by a judge, clerk or probation officer of the child's right to counsel and of the liability of the parent, guardian, legal custodian or other person standing in loco parentis for the costs of such legal services pursuant to § 16.1-267 and be given an opportunity to:

1. Obtain and employ counsel of the child's own choice; or

2. Request that the court appoint counsel, provided that before counsel is appointed or the court continues any appointment previously made pursuant to subsection B, the court shall determine that the child is indigent within the contemplation of the law pursuant to guidelines set forth in § 19.2-159 by requiring the child's parent, guardian, legal custodian or other person standing in loco parentis to complete a statement of indigence substantially in the form provided by § 19.2-159 and a financial statement, and upon determination of indigence the court shall appoint an attorney from the list maintained by the Indigent Defense Commission pursuant to § 19.2-163.01 to represent the child; or

3. Waive the right to representation by an attorney, if the court finds the child and the parent, guardian, legal custodian or other person standing in loco parentis of the child consent, in writing, and such waiver is consistent with the interests of the child. Such written waiver shall be in accordance with law and shall be filed with the court records of the case. A child who is alleged to have committed an offense that would be a felony if committed by an adult, may waive such right only after he consults with an attorney and the court determines that his waiver is free and voluntary. The waiver shall be in writing, signed by both the child and the child's attorney and shall be filed with the court records of the case.

D. A judge, clerk or probation officer shall inform the parent or guardian of his right to counsel prior to the adjudicatory hearing of a petition in which a child is alleged to be abused or neglected or at risk of abuse or neglect as provided in subdivision A 2a of § 16.1-241 and prior to a hearing at which a parent could be subjected to the loss of residual parental rights. In addition, prior to the hearing by the court of any case involving any other adult charged with abuse or neglect of a child, this adult shall be informed of his right to counsel. This adult and the parent or guardian shall be given an opportunity to:

1. Obtain and employ counsel of the parent's, guardian's or other adult's own choice; or

2. If the court determines that the parent, guardian or other adult is indigent within the contemplation of the law pursuant to the guidelines set forth in § 19.2-159, a statement substantially in the form provided by § 19.2-159 and a financial statement shall be executed by such parent, guardian or other adult and the court shall appoint an attorney-at-law to represent him; or

3. Waive the right to representation by an attorney in accordance with the provisions of § 19.2-160.

If the identity or location of a parent or guardian is not reasonably ascertainable or a parent or guardian fails to appear, the court shall consider appointing an attorney-at-law to represent the interests of the absent parent or guardian, and the hearing may be held.

Prior to a hearing at which a child is the subject of an initial foster care plan filed pursuant to § 16.1-281, a foster care review hearing pursuant to § 16.1-282 and a permanency planning hearing pursuant to § 16.1-282.1, the court shall consider appointing counsel to represent the child's parent or guardian.

E. In those cases described in subsections A, B, C and D, which in the discretion of the court require counsel or a guardian ad litem to represent the child or children or the parent or guardian or other adult party in addition to the representation provided in those subsections, a discreet and competent attorney-at-law may be appointed by the court as counsel or a guardian ad litem.

F. In all other cases which in the discretion of the court require counsel or a guardian ad litem, or both, to represent the child or children or the parent or guardian, discreet and competent attorneys-at-law may be appointed by the court. However, in cases where the custody of a child or children is the subject of controversy or requires determination and each of the parents or other persons claiming a right to custody is represented by counsel, the court shall not appoint counsel or a guardian ad litem to represent the interests of the child or children unless the court finds, at any stage in the proceedings in a specific case, that the interests of the child or children are not otherwise adequately represented.

G. Any state or local agency, department, authority or institution and any school, hospital, physician or other health or mental health care provider shall permit a guardian ad litem or counsel for the child appointed pursuant to this section to inspect and copy, without the consent of the child or his parents, any records relating to the child whom the guardian or counsel represents upon presentation by him of a copy of the court order appointing him or a court order specifically allowing him such access. Upon request therefor by the guardian ad litem or counsel for the child made at least 72 hours in advance, a mental health care provider shall make himself available to conduct a review and interpretation of the child's treatment records which are specifically related to the investigation. Such a request may be made in lieu of or in addition to inspection and copying of the records.

History.

Code 1950, §§ 16.1-173, 63.1-248.12; 1956, c. 555; 1966, c. 709; 1968, c. 581; 1970, c. 87; 1973, c. 440; 1974, c. 513; 1975, cc. 341, 465, 559; 1977, c. 559; 1980, c. 572; 1982, c. 451; 1984, c. 709; 1985, c. 260; 1987, c. 632; 1994, c. 36; 1997, c. 790; 2002, c. 687; 2003, c. 98; 2004, cc. 66, 437, 884, 921, 1014; 2005, c. 427.

§ 16.1-266.1. Standards for attorneys appointed as guardians ad litem; list of qualified attorneys; attorneys appointed for parents or guardians.

A. On or before January 1, 1995, the Judicial Council of Virginia, in conjunction with the Virginia State Bar and the Virginia Bar Association, shall adopt standards for attorneys appointed as guardians ad litem pursuant to § 16.1-266. The standards shall, insofar as practicable, take into consideration the following criteria: (i) license or permission to practice law in Virginia, (ii) current training in the roles, responsibilities and duties of guardian ad litem representation, (iii) familiarity with the court system and general background in juvenile law, and (iv) demonstrated proficiency in this area of the law.

B. The Judicial Council shall maintain a list of attorneys admitted to practice law in Virginia who are qualified to serve as guardians ad litem based upon the standards and shall make the names available to the courts. If no attorney who is on the list is reasonably available, a judge in his discretion may appoint any discreet and competent attorney who is admitted to practice law in Virginia.

C. Counsel appointed for a parent or guardian pursuant to subsection D of § 16.1-266 shall be selected from the list of attorneys who are qualified to serve as guardians ad litem. If no attorney who is on the list is reasonably available or appropriate considering the circumstances of the parent or case, a judge in his discretion may appoint any discreet and competent attorney who is admitted to practice law in Virginia.

History.

1994, c. 36; 1995, c. 273; 2016, cc. 182, 509.

§ 16.1-266.2. Appointment of pro bono counsel by judges of the First and Second Judicial District in certain cases.

The judges of the juvenile and domestic relations district court of the First and Second Judicial District are authorized to appoint pro bono counsel for alleged victims in family abuse cases in which the court is authorized to issue a preliminary protective order under § 16.1-253.1, or an emergency protective order under § 16.1-253.4. Such counsel shall have no prosecutorial authority except as granted in writing by the attorney for the Commonwealth for the jurisdiction in which the representation is to occur.

Any attorney appointed under the provisions of this section shall be a volunteer and serve without compensation and shall be subject to any rules adopted by the court and approved by the Virginia Supreme Court providing for the establishment and conduct of a project providing pro bono services to victims of family abuse.

History.

1995, c. 806.

§ 16.1-267. Compensation of appointed counsel.

A. When the court appoints counsel to represent a child pursuant to subsection A of § 16.1-266 and, after an investigation by the court services unit, finds that the parents are financially able to pay for the attorney and refuse to do so, the court shall assess costs against the parents for such legal services in the maximum amount of that awarded the attorney by the court under the circumstances of the case, considering such factors as the ability of the parents to pay and the nature and extent of the counsel's duties in the case. Such amount shall not exceed the maximum amount specified in subdivision 1 of § 19.2-163 if the action is in district court.

When the court appoints counsel to represent a child pursuant to subsection B or C of § 16.1-266 and, after an investigation by the court services unit, finds that the parents are financially able to pay for the attorney in whole or in part and refuse to do so, the court shall assess costs in whole or in part against the parents for such legal services in the amount awarded the attorney by the court. Such amount shall not exceed $100 if the action is in circuit court or the maximum amount specified in subdivision 1 of § 19.2-163 if the action is in district court. In determining the financial ability of the parents to pay for an attorney to represent the child, the court shall utilize the financial statement required by § 19.2-159.

In all other cases, except as provided in § 16.1-343, counsel appointed to represent a child shall be compensated for his services pursuant to § 19.2-163.

B. When the court appoints counsel to represent a parent, guardian or other adult pursuant to § 16.1-266, such counsel shall be compensated for his services pursuant to § 19.2-163.

History.

Code 1950, § 16.1-173; 1956, c. 555; 1966, c. 709; 1968, c. 581; 1970, c. 87; 1973, c. 440; 1974, c. 513; 1975, cc. 465, 559; 1977, c.

559; 1981, c. 213; 1984, c. 709; 1986, c. 425; 1993, c. 344; 2004, cc. 342, 437.

§ 16.1-268. Order of appointment.

The order of appointment of counsel pursuant to § 16.1-266 shall be filed with and become a part of the record of such proceeding. The attorney so appointed shall represent the child or parent, guardian or other adult at any such hearing and at all other stages of the proceeding unless relieved or replaced in the manner provided by law.

History.
1977, c. 559.

ARTICLE 7.
TRANSFER AND WAIVER.

§ 16.1-269: Repealed by Acts 1994, cc. 859 and 949.

Cross references.
For disposition of court-ordered studies and reports, see Rule 8:5, Juvenile and Domestic Relations District Court Rules. For rule providing for discovery in transfer hearing, see Rule 8:15, Juvenile and Domestic Relations District Court Rules.

§ 16.1-269.1. Trial in circuit court; preliminary hearing; direct indictment; remand.

A. Except as provided in subsections B and C, if a juvenile 14 years of age or older at the time of an alleged offense is charged with an offense which would be a felony if committed by an adult, the court shall, on motion of the attorney for the Commonwealth and prior to a hearing on the merits, hold a transfer hearing and may retain jurisdiction or transfer such juvenile for proper criminal proceedings to the appropriate circuit court having criminal jurisdiction of such offenses if committed by an adult. Any transfer to the appropriate circuit court shall be subject to the following conditions:

1. Notice as prescribed in §§ 16.1-263 and 16.1-264 shall be given to the juvenile and his parent, guardian, legal custodian or other person standing in loco parentis; or attorney;

2. The juvenile court finds that probable cause exists to believe that the juvenile committed the delinquent act as alleged or a lesser included delinquent act which would be a felony if committed by an adult;

3. The juvenile is competent to stand trial. The juvenile is presumed to be competent and the burden is on the party alleging the juvenile is not competent to rebut the presumption by a preponderance of the evidence; and

4. The court finds by a preponderance of the evidence that the juvenile is not a proper person to remain within the jurisdiction of the juvenile court. In determining whether a juvenile is a proper person to remain within the jurisdiction of the juvenile court, the court shall consider, but not be limited to, the following factors:

a. The juvenile's age;

b. The seriousness and number of alleged offenses, including (i) whether the alleged offense was committed in an aggressive, violent, premeditated, or willful manner; (ii) whether the alleged offense was against persons or property, with greater weight being given to offenses against persons, especially if death or bodily injury resulted; (iii) whether the maximum punishment for such an offense is greater than 20 years confinement if committed by an adult; (iv) whether the alleged offense involved the use of a firearm or other dangerous weapon by brandishing, threatening, displaying or otherwise employing such weapon; and (v) the nature of the juvenile's participation in the alleged offense;

c. Whether the juvenile can be retained in the juvenile justice system long enough for effective treatment and rehabilitation;

d. The appropriateness and availability of the services and dispositional alternatives in both the criminal justice and juvenile justice systems for dealing with the juvenile's problems;

e. The record and previous history of the juvenile in this or other jurisdictions, including (i) the number and nature of previous contacts with juvenile or circuit courts, (ii) the number and nature of prior periods of probation, (iii) the number and nature of prior commitments to juvenile correctional centers, (iv) the number and nature of previous residential and community-based treatments, (v) whether previous adjudications and commitments were for delinquent acts that involved the infliction of serious bodily injury, and (vi) whether the alleged offense is part of a repetitive pattern of similar adjudicated offenses;

f. Whether the juvenile has previously absconded from the legal custody of a juvenile correctional entity in this or any other jurisdiction;

g. The extent, if any, of the juvenile's degree of intellectual disability or mental illness;

h. The juvenile's school record and education;

i. The juvenile's mental and emotional maturity; and

j. The juvenile's physical condition and physical maturity.

No transfer decision shall be precluded or reversed on the grounds that the court failed to consider any of the factors specified in subdivision 4.

B. The juvenile court shall conduct a preliminary hearing whenever a juvenile 14 years of age or older is charged with murder in violation of § 18.2-31, 18.2-32 or 18.2-40, or aggravated malicious wounding in violation of § 18.2-51.2.

C. The juvenile court shall conduct a preliminary hearing whenever a juvenile 14 years of age or older is charged with murder in violation of § 18.2-33; felonious injury by mob in violation of § 18.2-41; abduction in violation of § 18.2-48; malicious wounding in violation of § 18.2-51; malicious wounding of a law-enforcement officer in violation of § 18.2-51.1; felonious poisoning in violation of § 18.2-54.1; adulteration of products in violation of § 18.2-54.2; robbery in violation of § 18.2-58 or carjacking in violation of § 18.2-58.1; rape in violation of § 18.2-61; forcible sodomy in violation of § 18.2-67.1; object sexual penetration in violation of § 18.2-67.2; manufacturing, selling, giving, distributing, or possessing with intent to manufacture, sell, give, or distribute a controlled substance or an imitation controlled substance in violation of § 18.2-248 if the juvenile has been previously adjudicated delinquent on two or more occasions of violating § 18.2-248 provided the adjudications occurred after the juvenile was at least 14 years of age; manufacturing, selling, giving, distributing, or possessing with intent to manufacture, sell, give, or distribute methamphetamine in violation of § 18.2-248.03 if the juvenile has been previously adjudicated delinquent on two or more occasions of violating § 18.2-248.03 provided the adjudications occurred after the juvenile was at least 14 years of age; or felonious manufacturing, selling, giving, distributing, or possessing with intent to manufacture, sell, give, or distribute anabolic steroids in violation of § 18.2-248.5 if the juvenile has been previously adjudicated delinquent on two or more occasions of violating § 18.2-248.5 provided the adjudications occurred after the juvenile was at least 14 years of age, provided the attorney for the Commonwealth gives written notice of his intent to proceed pursuant to this subsection. The notice shall be filed with the court and mailed or delivered to counsel for the juvenile or, if the juvenile is not then represented by counsel, to the juvenile and a parent, guardian or other person standing in loco parentis with respect to the juvenile at least seven days prior to the preliminary hearing. If the attorney for the Commonwealth elects not to give such notice, or if he elects to withdraw the notice prior to certification of the charge to the grand jury, he may proceed as provided in subsection A.

D. Upon a finding of probable cause pursuant to a preliminary hearing under subsection B or C, the juvenile court shall certify the charge, and all ancillary charges, to the grand jury. Such certification shall divest the juvenile court of jurisdiction as to the charge and any ancillary charges. Nothing in this subsection shall divest the juvenile court of jurisdiction over any matters unrelated to such charge and ancillary charges which may otherwise be properly within the jurisdiction of the juvenile court.

If the court does not find probable cause to believe that the juvenile has committed the violent juvenile felony as charged in the petition or warrant or if the petition or warrant is terminated by dismissal in the juvenile court, the attorney for the Commonwealth may seek a direct indictment in the circuit court. If the petition or warrant is terminated by nolle prosequi in the juvenile court, the attorney for the Commonwealth may seek an indictment only after a preliminary hearing in juvenile court.

If the court finds that the juvenile was not 14 years of age or older at the time of the alleged commission of the offense or that the conditions specified in subdivision A 1, 2, or 3 have not been met, the case shall proceed as otherwise provided for by law.

E. An indictment in the circuit court cures any error or defect in any proceeding held in the juvenile court except with respect to the juvenile's age. If an indictment is terminated by nolle prosequi, the Commonwealth may reinstate the proceeding by seeking a subsequent indictment.

History.

1994, cc. 859, 949; 1996, cc. 755, 914; 1997, c. 862; 2012, cc. 476, 507, 772.

§ 16.1-269.2. Admissibility of statement; investigation and report; bail.

A. Statements made by the juvenile at the transfer hearing provided for under § 16.1-269.1 shall not be admissible against him over objection in any criminal proceedings following the transfer, except for purposes of impeachment.

B. Prior to a transfer hearing pursuant to subsection A of § 16.1-269.1, a study and report to the court, in writing, relevant to the factors set out in subdivision A 4 of § 16.1-269.1, as well as an assessment of any affiliation with a criminal street gang as defined in § 18.2-46.1, shall be made by the probation services or other qualified agency designated by the court. Upon motion of the attorney for the Commonwealth for a transfer hearing pursuant to subsection A of § 16.1-269.1, the attorney for the Commonwealth shall provide notice to the designated probation services or other qualified agency of the need for a transfer report. Counsel for the juvenile and the attorney for the Commonwealth shall have full access to the study and report and any other report or data concerning the juvenile which are available to the court. The court shall not consider the report until a finding has been made concerning probable cause. If the court so orders, the study and report may be expanded to include matters provided for in § 16.1-273, whereupon it may also serve as the report required by this subsection, but on the condition that it will not be submitted to the judge who will preside at any subsequent hearings except as provided for by law.

C. After the completion of the hearing, whether or not the juvenile court decides to retain jurisdiction over the juvenile or transfer such juvenile for criminal proceedings in the circuit court, the juvenile court shall set bail for the juvenile in accordance with Chapter 9 (§ 19.2-119 et seq.) of Title 19.2, if bail has not already been set.

History.

1994, cc. 859, 949; 1999, c. 350; 2005, cc. 590, 843.

§ 16.1-269.3. Retention by juvenile court; appeal.

If a case is not transferred following a transfer hearing or is not certified following a probable cause hearing, the judge who conducted the hearing shall not, over the objection of any interested party, preside at the adjudicatory hearing on the petition, but rather it shall be presided over by another judge of that court. If the attorney for the Commonwealth deems it to be in the public interest, and the juvenile is fourteen years of age or older he may, within ten days after the juvenile court's final decision to retain the case in accordance with subsection A of § 16.1-269.1, file a notice of appeal of the decision to the appropriate circuit court. A copy of such notice shall be furnished at the same time to the counsel for the juvenile.

History.
1994, cc. 859, 949; 1996, cc. 755, 914.

§ 16.1-269.4. Transfer to circuit court; appeal by juvenile.

If the juvenile court transfers the case pursuant to subsection A of § 16.1-269.1, the juvenile may, within ten days after the juvenile court's final decision, file a notice of appeal of the decision to the appropriate circuit court. A copy of the notice shall be furnished at the same time to the attorney for the Commonwealth.

History.
1994, cc. 859, 949; 1996, cc. 755, 914.

§ 16.1-269.5. Placement of juvenile.

The juvenile court may order placement of the transferred juvenile in either a local correctional facility as approved by the State Board of Corrections pursuant to the limitations of subsections D and E of § 16.1-249 or a juvenile detention facility.

History.
1994, cc. 859, 949; 1995, cc. 746, 798, 802; 2010, c. 739.

§ 16.1-269.6. Circuit court hearing; jury; termination of juvenile court jurisdiction; objections and appeals.

A. Within seven days after receipt of notice of an appeal from the transfer decision pursuant to subsection A of § 16.1-269.1, by either the attorney for the Commonwealth or the juvenile, or if an appeal to such a decision to transfer is not noted, upon expiration of the time in which to note such an appeal, the clerk of the court shall forward to the circuit court all papers connected with the case, including any report required by subsection B of § 16.1-269.2, as well as a written court order setting forth the reasons for the juvenile court's decision. Within seven days after receipt of notice of an appeal, the clerk shall forward copies of the order to the attorney for the Commonwealth and other counsel of record.

B. The circuit court, when practicable, shall, within 45 days after receipt of the case from the juvenile court pursuant to subsection A of § 16.1-269.1, (i) if either the juvenile or the attorney for the Commonwealth has appealed the transfer decision, examine all such papers, reports and orders and conduct a hearing to take further evidence on the issue of transfer, to determine if there has been substantial compliance with subsection A of § 16.1-269.1, but without redetermining whether the juvenile court had sufficient evidence to find probable cause; and (ii) enter an order either remanding the case to the juvenile court or advising the attorney for the Commonwealth that he may seek an indictment. A juvenile held continuously in secure detention shall be released from confinement if there is no hearing on the merits of his case within 45 days of the filing of the appeal. The circuit court may extend the time limitations for a reasonable period of time based upon good cause shown, provided the basis for such extension is recorded in writing and filed among the papers of the proceedings. However, in cases where a charge has been certified by the juvenile court to the grand jury pursuant to subsection B or C of § 16.1-269.1, the attorney for the Commonwealth may seek an indictment upon such charge and any ancillary charge without obtaining an order of the circuit court advising him that he may do so.

C. The circuit court order advising the attorney for the Commonwealth that he may seek an indictment shall divest the juvenile court of its jurisdiction over the case as well as the juvenile court's jurisdiction over any other allegations of delinquency arising from the same act, transaction or scheme giving rise to the charge for which the juvenile has been transferred. In addition, upon conviction of the juvenile following transfer or certification and trial as an adult, the circuit court shall issue an order terminating the juvenile court's jurisdiction over that juvenile with respect to any future criminal acts alleged to have been committed by such juvenile and with respect to any pending allegations of delinquency which have not been disposed of by the juvenile court at the time of the criminal conviction. However, such an order terminating the juvenile court's jurisdiction shall not apply to any allegations of criminal conduct that would properly be within the jurisdiction of the juvenile and domestic relations district court if the defendant were an adult. Upon receipt of the order terminating the juvenile court's jurisdiction over the juvenile, the clerk of the juvenile court shall forward any pending petitions of delinquency for proceedings in the appropriate general district court.

D. The judge of the circuit court who reviewed the case after receipt from the juvenile court shall not, over the objection of any interested party, preside over the trial of such charge or charges.

E. Any objection to the jurisdiction of the circuit court pursuant to this article shall be waived if not made before arraignment.

F. The time period beginning with the filing of a notice of appeal pursuant to § 16.1-269.3 or § 16.1-269.4 and ending with the order of the circuit court disposing of the appeal shall not be included as applying to the provisions of § 19.2-243.

History.

1994, cc. 859, 949; 1996, cc. 755, 914; 1997, c. 862; 2003, c. 144; 2004, c. 468; 2010, c. 739.

§ 16.1-270. Waiver of jurisdiction of juvenile court in certain cases.

At any time prior to commencement of the adjudicatory hearing, a juvenile fourteen years of age or older charged with an offense which if committed by an adult could be punishable by confinement in a state correctional facility, with the written consent of his counsel, may elect in writing to waive the jurisdiction of the juvenile court and have his case transferred to the appropriate circuit court, in which event his case shall thereafter be dealt with in the same manner as if he had been transferred pursuant to this article.

History.

Code 1950, § 16.1-176.2; 1973, c. 440; 1977, c. 559; 1994, cc. 859, 949.

§ 16.1-271. Subsequent offenses by juvenile.

Conviction of a juvenile as an adult pursuant to the provisions of this chapter shall preclude the juvenile court from taking jurisdiction of such juvenile for subsequent offenses committed by that juvenile.

Any juvenile who is tried and convicted in a circuit court as an adult under the provisions of this article shall be considered and treated as an adult in any criminal proceeding resulting from any alleged future criminal acts and any pending allegations of delinquency which have not been disposed of by the juvenile court at the time of the criminal conviction.

All procedures and dispositions applicable to adults charged with such a criminal offense shall apply in such cases, including, but not limited to, arrest; probable cause determination by a magistrate or grand jury; the use of a warrant, summons, or capias instead of a petition to initiate the case; adult bail; preliminary hearing and right to counsel provisions; trial in a court having jurisdiction over adults; and trial and sentencing as an adult. The provisions of this article regarding a transfer hearing shall not be applicable to such juveniles.

History.

1977, c. 559; 1989, c. 675; 1990, c. 668; 1994, cc. 859, 949; 2007, c. 221.

§ 16.1-272. Power of circuit court over juvenile offender.

A. In any case in which a juvenile is indicted, the offense for which he is indicted and all ancillary charges shall be tried in the same manner as provided for in the trial of adults, except as otherwise provided with regard to sentencing. Upon a finding of guilty of any charge, the court shall fix the sentence without the intervention of a jury. Nothing in this subsection shall be construed to require a court to review the results of an investigation completed pursuant to § 16.1-273.

1. If a juvenile is convicted of a violent juvenile felony, for that offense and for all ancillary crimes the court may order that (i) the juvenile serve a portion of the sentence as a serious juvenile offender under § 16.1-285.1 and the remainder of such sentence in the same manner as provided for adults; (ii) the juvenile serve the entire sentence in the same manner as provided for adults; or (iii) the portion of the sentence to be served in the same manner as provided for adults be suspended conditioned upon successful completion of such terms and conditions as may be imposed in a juvenile court upon disposition of a delinquency case including, but not limited to, commitment under subdivision A 14 of § 16.1-278.8 or § 16.1-285.1.

2. If the juvenile is convicted of any other felony, the court may sentence or commit the juvenile offender in accordance with the criminal laws of this Commonwealth or may in its discretion deal with the juvenile in the manner prescribed in this chapter for the hearing and disposition of cases in the juvenile court, including, but not limited to, commitment under § 16.1-285.1 or may in its discretion impose an adult sentence and suspend the sentence conditioned upon successful completion of such terms and conditions as may be imposed in a juvenile court upon disposition of a delinquency case.

3. If the juvenile is not convicted of a felony but is convicted of a misdemeanor, the court shall deal with the juvenile in the manner prescribed by law for the disposition of a delinquency case in the juvenile court.

B. If the circuit court decides to deal with the juvenile in the same manner as a case in the juvenile court and places the juvenile on probation, the juvenile may be supervised by a juvenile probation officer.

C. Whether the court sentences and commits the juvenile as a juvenile under this chapter or under the criminal law, in cases where the juvenile is convicted of a felony in violation of § 18.2-61, 18.2-63, 18.2-64.1, 18.2-67.1, 18.2-67.2, 18.2-67.3, 18.2-67.5, 18.2-370 or 18.2-370.1 or, where the victim is a minor or is physically helpless or mentally incapacitated as defined in § 18.2-67.10, subsection B of § 18.2-361 or subsection B of § 18.2-366, the clerk shall make the report required by § 19.2-390 to the Sex Offender and Crimes Against Minors Registry established pursuant to Chapter 9 (§ 9.1-900 et seq.) of Title 9.1.

D. A juvenile sentenced pursuant to clause (i) of subdivision A 1 shall be eligible to earn sentence credits in the manner prescribed by § 53.1-202.2 for the portion of the sentence served as a serious juvenile offender under § 16.1-285.1.

E. If the court sentences the juvenile as a juvenile under this chapter, the clerk shall provide a copy of the court's final order or judgment to the court service unit in the same locality as the juvenile court to which the case had been transferred.

History.

Code 1950, § 16.1-177; 1956, c. 555; 1977, c. 559; 1994, c. 362; 1996, cc. 755, 914; 2000, c. 793; 2002, c. 511; 2003, c. 584; 2005, c. 590; 2007, c. 460; 2008, c. 517; 2014, cc. 20, 249.

§ 16.1-272.1. Claim of error to be raised within one year.

In addition to any other curative provisions, waivers, procedural defaults, or requirements for timely objection, including but not limited to those in subsection J of § 16.1-241, subsection E of § 16.1-269.1 and subsection E of § 16.1-269.6, any claim of error or defect under this chapter, jurisdictional or otherwise, that is not raised within one year from the date of final judgment of the circuit court or one year from the effective date of this act, whichever is later, shall not constitute a ground for relief in any judicial proceeding.

History.

2000, c. 418.

ARTICLE 8.

ADJUDICATION.

§ 16.1-273. Court may require investigation of social history and preparation of victim impact statement.

A. When a juvenile and domestic relations district court or circuit court has adjudicated any case involving a child subject to the jurisdiction of the court hereunder, except for a traffic violation, a violation of the game and fish law, or a violation of any city ordinance regulating surfing or establishing curfew violations, the court before final disposition thereof may require an investigation, which (i) shall include a drug screening and (ii) may, and for the purposes of subdivision A 14 or A 17 of § 16.1-278.8 shall, include a social history of the physical, mental, and social conditions, including an assessment of any affiliation with a criminal street gang as defined in § 18.2-46.1, and personality of the child and the facts and circumstances surrounding the violation of law. However, in the case of a juvenile adjudicated delinquent on the basis of an act committed on or after January 1, 2000, which would be a felony if committed by an adult, or a violation under Article 1 (§ 18.2-247 et seq.) or Article 1.1 (§ 18.2-265.1 et seq.) of Chapter 7 of Title 18.2 and such offense would be punishable as a Class 1 or Class 2 misdemeanor if committed by an adult, the court shall order the juvenile to undergo a drug screening. If the drug screening indicates that the juvenile has a substance abuse or dependence problem, an assessment shall be completed by a certified substance abuse counselor as defined in § 54.1-3500 employed by the Department of Juvenile Justice or by a locally operated court services unit or by an individual employed by or currently under contract to such agencies and who is specifically trained to conduct such assessments under the supervision of such counselor.

B. The court also shall, on motion of the attorney for the Commonwealth with the consent of the victim, or may in its discretion, require the preparation of a victim impact statement in accordance with the provisions of § 19.2-299.1 if the court determines that the victim may have suffered significant physical, psychological, or economic injury as a result of the violation of law.

History.

Code 1950, § 16.1-164; 1956, c. 555; 1972, cc. 672, 835; 1973, c. 440; 1977, cc. 559, 627; 1993, c. 603; 1998, cc. 783, 840; 1999, cc. 350, 891, 913; 2000, cc. 1020, 1041; 2005, c. 843; 2007, c. 510; 2014, cc. 20, 249.

§ 16.1-274. Time for filing of reports; copies furnished to attorneys; amended reports; fees.

A. Whenever any court directs an investigation pursuant to subdivision A of § 16.1-237 or § 16.1-273 or 9.1-153, or an evaluation pursuant to § 16.1-278.5, the probation officer, court-appointed special advocate, or other agency conducting such investigation shall file such report with the clerk of the court directing the investigation. The clerk shall furnish a copy of such report to all attorneys representing parties in the matter before the court no later than 72 hours, and in cases of child custody, 15 days, prior to the time set by the court for hearing the matter. If such probation officer or other agency discovers additional information or a change in circumstance after the filing of the report, an amended report shall be filed forthwith and a copy sent to each person who received a copy of the original report. Whenever such a report is not filed or an amended report is filed, the court shall grant such continuance of the proceedings as justice requires. All attorneys receiving such report or amended report shall return such to the clerk upon the conclusion of the hearing and shall not make copies of such report or amended report or any portion thereof. However, the chief judge of each juvenile and domestic relations district court may provide for an alternative means of copying and distributing reports or amended reports filed pursuant to § 9.1-153.

B. Notwithstanding the provisions of §§ 16.1-69.48:2 and 17.1-275, when the court directs the appropriate local department of social services to conduct supervised visitation or directs the appropriate local department of social services or court services unit to conduct an investigation pursuant to § 16.1-273 or to provide mediation services in matters involving a child's custody, visitation, or support, the court shall assess a fee against the petitioner, the respondent, or both, in accordance with fee schedules established by the appropriate local board of social services when the service is provided by a local department of social services or by a court services unit. The fee schedules shall include (i) standards for determining the paying party's or parties' ability to pay and (ii) a scale of fees based on the paying party's or parties' income and family size and the actual cost of the services provided. The fee charged shall not exceed the actual cost of the service. The fee shall be assessed as a cost of the case and shall be paid as prescribed by the court to the local department of social services, locally operated court services unit or Department of Juvenile Justice, whichever performed the service, unless payment is waived. The method and medium for payment for such services shall be determined by the local department of social services, Department of Juvenile Justice, or the locally operated court services unit that provided the services.

C. When a local department of social services or any court services unit is requested by another local department or court services unit in the Commonwealth or by a similar department or entity in another state to conduct an investigation involving a child's custody, visitation or support pursuant to § 16.1-273 or, in the case of a request from another state pursuant to a provision corresponding to § 16.1-273, or to provide mediation services, or for a local department of social services to provide supervised visitation, the local department or the court services unit performing the service may require payment of fees prior to conducting the investigation or providing mediation services or supervised visitation.

History.

Code 1950, § 16.1-208.1; 1972, c. 111; 1975, c. 286; 1977, c. 559; 1983, c. 174; 1987, c. 5; 1989, c. 725; 1990, c. 752; 1991, cc. 534, 618; 1992, c. 554; 1993, c. 975; 2001, c. 364; 2006, c. 675; 2012, cc. 164, 456.

§ 16.1-274.1. Admission of evidence of juvenile's age.

In any proceeding in a district court or circuit court where a juvenile is alleged to have committed a delinquent act, the Commonwealth shall be permitted to introduce evidence establishing the age of the juvenile at any time prior to adjudication of the case.

History.

1994, c. 913; 1996, cc. 755, 914.

§ 16.1-274.2. Certain education records as evidence.

A. In any proceeding where (i) a juvenile is alleged to have committed a delinquent act that would be a misdemeanor if committed by an adult and whether such act was committed intentionally or willfully by the juvenile is an element of the delinquent act and (ii) such act was committed (a) during school hours, and during school-related or school-sponsored activities upon the property of a public or private elementary or secondary school or child day center; (b) on any school bus as defined in § 46.2-100; or (c) upon any property, public or private, during hours when such property is solely being used by a public or private elementary or secondary school for a school-related or school-sponsored activity, the juvenile shall be permitted to introduce into evidence as relevant to whether he acted intentionally or willfully any document created prior to the commission of the alleged delinquent act that relates to (a) an Individualized Education Program developed pursuant to the federal Individuals with Disabilities Education Act, 20 U.S.C. § 1400 et seq.; (b) a Section 504 Plan prepared pursuant to § 504 of the federal Rehabilitation Act of 1973, 29 U.S.C. § 794; (c) a behavioral intervention plan as defined in 8VAC20-81-10; or (d) a functional behavioral assessment as defined in 8VAC20-81-10.

Any such document shall be admitted as evidence of the facts stated therein.

B. At least 10 days prior to the commencement of the proceeding in which a document listed in subsection A will be offered as evidence, the juvenile intending to offer the document shall notify the attorney for the Commonwealth, in writing, of the intent to offer the document and shall provide or make available copies of the document to be introduced.

C. Copies of documents listed in subsection A shall be received as evidence, provided that such copies are authenticated to be true and accurate copies by the custodian thereof, or by the person to whom the custodian reports if they are different. An affidavit signed by the custodian of such documents, or by the person to whom the custodian reports if they are different, stating that such documents are true and accurate copies of such documents shall be valid authentication for the purposes of this section.

D. Upon motion of the juvenile, any document admitted pursuant to this section shall be placed under seal by the court.

History.

2016, c. 726.

§ 16.1-275. Physical and mental examinations and treatment; nursing and medical care.

The juvenile court or the circuit court may cause any juvenile within its jurisdiction under the provisions of this law to be physically examined and treated by a physician or to be examined and treated at a local mental health center. If no such appropriate facility is available locally, the court may order the juvenile to be examined and treated by any physician or psychiatrist or examined by a clinical psychologist. The Commissioner of Behavioral Health and Developmental Services shall provide for distribution a list of appropriate mental health centers available throughout the Commonwealth. Upon the written recommendation of the person examining the juvenile that an adequate evaluation of the juvenile's treatment needs can only be performed in an inpatient hospital setting, the court shall have the power to send any such juvenile to a state mental hospital for not more than 10 days for the purpose of obtaining a recommendation for the treatment of the juvenile. No juvenile sent to a state mental hospital pursuant to this provision shall be held or cared for in any maximum security unit where adults determined to be criminally insane reside; the juvenile shall be kept separate and apart from such adults. However, the Commissioner of Behavioral Health and Developmental Services may place a juvenile who has been certified to the circuit court for trial as an adult pursuant to § 16.1-269.6 or 16.1-270 or who has been convicted as an adult of a felony in the circuit court in a unit appropriate for the care and treatment of persons under a criminal charge when, in his discretion, such placement is necessary to protect the security or safety of other patients, staff or the public.

Whenever the parent or other person responsible for the care and support of a juvenile is determined by the court to be financially unable to pay the costs of such examination as ordered by the juvenile court or the circuit court, such costs may be paid according to procedures and rates adopted by the Department from funds appropriated in the general appropriation act for the Department.

The juvenile court or the circuit court may cause any juvenile within its jurisdiction who is found to be delinquent for an offense that is eligible for commitment pursuant to subdivision A 14 of § 16.1-278.8 or § 16.1-285.1 to be placed in the temporary custody of the Department of Juvenile Justice for a period of time not to exceed 30 days for diagnostic assessment services after the adjudicatory hearing and prior to final disposition of his or her case. Prior to such a placement, the Department shall determine that the personnel, services and space are available in the appropriate correctional facility for the care, supervision and study of such juvenile and that the juvenile's case is appropriate for referral for diagnostic services.

Whenever a juvenile concerning whom a petition has been filed appears to be in need of nursing, medical or surgical care, the juvenile court or the circuit court may order the parent or other person responsible for the care and support of the juvenile to provide such care in a hospital or otherwise and to pay the expenses thereof. If the parent or other person is unable or fails to provide such care, the juvenile court or the circuit court may refer the matter to the authority designated in accordance with law for the determination of eligibility for such services in the county or city in which such juvenile or his parents have residence or legal domicile.

In any such case, if a parent who is able to do so fails or refuses to comply with the order, the juvenile court or the circuit court may proceed against him as for contempt or may proceed against him for nonsupport.

History.

Code 1950, § 16.1-190; 1956, c. 555; 1972, c. 354; 1975, c. 430; 1976, c. 321; 1977, c. 559; 1978, c. 739; 1982, c. 636; 1983, c. 358; 1984, c. 44; 1988, cc. 47, 826; 1990, c. 975; 1994, cc. 859, 949; 2004, c. 321; 2009, cc. 813, 840; 2012, cc. 164, 456.

§ 16.1-276. Fees and travel expenses of witnesses.

The judge may authorize the payment of the fees and mileage provided by law in § 19.2-278 of any witness or person summoned or otherwise required to appear at the hearing of any case coming within the jurisdiction of the court, which sum shall be paid by the State Treasurer out of funds appropriated in the general appropriations act to the Supreme Court of Virginia.

History.

Code 1950, § 16.1-171; 1956, c. 555; 1977, c. 559; 1982, c. 636.

§ **16.1-276.1:** Repealed by Acts 2002, c. 305.

§ 16.1-276.2. Transportation orders in certain proceedings.

In any proceeding (i) pursuant to subdivisions 2, 4 or 5 of subsection A of § 16.1-241, (ii) pursuant to subsections K or U of § 16.1-241, (iii) involving a child who is alleged to be abused or neglected, or (iv) involving a child who is before the court pursuant to §§ 16.1-281, 16.1-282 or § 16.1-282.1, if the judge finds that the presence at a hearing of a prisoner in a state, local or regional correctional institution is essential to the just adjudication and disposition of the proceeding, the judge may issue an order to the Director of the Department of Corrections or the administrator of the state, local or regional correctional institution to deliver such witness to the sheriff of the jurisdiction of the court issuing the order. Such orders shall be executed in accordance with § 8.01-410. Any such orders shall issue only upon consideration of the importance of the personal appearance of the person.

The party seeking the testimony of such prisoner shall advance a sum sufficient to defray the expenses and compensation of the officers, which the court shall tax as costs. When the party seeking the attendance of the prisoner is an agency of the

Commonwealth or when the attendance is sought on motion of the court, no sum shall be advanced to defray the expenses or compensation of the correctional officers and sheriff nor shall any such sum be taxed as costs.

History.
2001, c. 513.

§ 16.1-276.3. Use of telephonic communication systems or electronic video and audio communication systems to conduct hearing.

Notwithstanding any other provision of law, in any civil proceeding under this chapter in which a party or witness is incarcerated or when otherwise authorized by the court, the court may, in its discretion, conduct any hearing using a telephonic communication system or an electronic audio and video communication system to provide for the appearance of any parties and witnesses. Any electronic audio and video communication system used to conduct such a hearing shall meet the standards set forth in subsection B of § 19.2-3.1.

History.
2001, c. 513.

§ 16.1-277: Repealed by Acts 1999, c. 889.

§ 16.1-277.01. Approval of entrustment agreement.

A. In any case in which a child has been entrusted pursuant to § 63.2-903 or 63.2-1817 to the local board of social services or to a child welfare agency, a petition for approval of the entrustment agreement by the board or agency:

1. Shall be filed within a reasonable period of time, no later than 89 days after the execution of an entrustment agreement for less than 90 days, if the child is not returned to the caretaker from whom he was entrusted within that period;
2. Shall be filed within a reasonable period of time, not to exceed 30 days after the execution of an entrustment agreement for 90 days or longer or for an unspecified period of time, if such entrustment agreement does not provide for the termination of all parental rights and responsibilities with respect to the child; and
3. May be filed in the case of a permanent entrustment agreement which provides for the termination of all parental rights and responsibilities with respect to the child.

The board or agency shall file a foster care plan pursuant to § 16.1-281 to be heard with any petition for approval of an entrustment agreement.

B. Upon the filing of a petition for approval of an entrustment agreement pursuant to subsection A of § 16.1-241, the court shall appoint a guardian ad litem to represent the child in accordance with the provisions of § 16.1-266, and shall schedule the matter for a hearing to be held as follows: within 45 days of the filing of a petition pursuant to subdivision A 1, A 2 or A 3, except where an order of publication has been ordered by the court, in which case the hearing shall be held within 75 days of the filing of the petition. The court shall provide notice of the hearing and a copy of the petition to the following, each of whom shall be a party entitled to participate in the proceeding:

1. The local board of social services or child welfare agency;
2. The child, if he is 12 years of age or older;
3. The guardian ad litem for the child; and
4. The child's parents, guardian, legal custodian or other person standing in loco parentis to the child.

No such notification shall be required, however, if the judge certifies on the record that the identity of the parent or guardian is not reasonably ascertainable. A birth father shall be given notice of the proceedings if he is an acknowledged father pursuant to § 20-49.1, adjudicated pursuant to § 20-49.8, or presumed pursuant to § 63.2-1202, or has registered with the Putative Father Registry pursuant to Article 7 (§ 63.2-1249 et seq.). An affidavit of the mother that the identity of the father is not reasonably ascertainable shall be sufficient evidence of this fact, provided there is no other evidence before the court which would refute such an affidavit. Failure to register with the Putative Father Registry pursuant to Article 7 (§ 63.2-1249 et seq.) of Chapter 12 of Title 63.2 shall be evidence that the identity of the father is not reasonably ascertainable. The hearing shall be held and an order may be entered, although a parent, guardian, legal custodian or person standing in loco parentis fails to appear and is not represented by counsel, provided personal or substituted service was made on the person, or the court determines that such person cannot be found, after reasonable effort, or in the case of a person who is without the Commonwealth, the person cannot be found or his post office address cannot be ascertained after reasonable effort. However, when a petition seeks approval of a permanent entrustment agreement which provides for the termination of all parental rights and responsibilities with respect to the child, a summons shall be served upon the parent or parents and the other parties specified in § 16.1-263. The summons or notice of hearing shall clearly state the consequences of a termination of residual parental rights. Service shall be made pursuant to § 16.1-264. The remaining parent's parental rights may be terminated even though that parent has not entered into an entrustment agreement if the court finds, based upon clear and convincing evidence, that it is in the best interest of the child and that (i) the identity of the parent is not reasonably ascertainable; (ii) the identity and whereabouts of the parent are known or reasonably ascertainable, and the parent is personally served with notice of the termination proceeding pursuant to § 8.01-296 or 8.01-320; (iii) the whereabouts of the parent are not reasonably ascertainable and the parent is given notice of the termination proceedings by certified or registered mail to the last known address and such parent fails to object to the proceedings within 15 days of the mailing of such notice; or (iv) the whereabouts of the parent are not reasonably ascertainable and the parent is given notice of the termination proceedings through an order of publication pursuant to §§ 8.01-316 and 8.01-317, and such parent fails to object to the proceedings.

C. At the hearing held pursuant to this section, the court shall hear evidence on the petition filed and shall review the foster care plan for the child filed by the local board or child welfare agency in accordance with § 16.1-281.

D. At the conclusion of the hearing, the court shall make a finding, based upon a preponderance of the evidence, whether approval of the entrustment agreement is in the best interest of the child. However, if the petition seeks approval of a permanent entrustment agreement which provides for the termination of all parental rights and responsibilities with respect to the child, the court shall make a finding, based upon clear and convincing evidence, whether termination of parental rights is in the best interest of the child. If the court makes either of these findings, the court may make any of the orders of disposition permitted in a case involving an abused or neglected child pursuant to § 16.1-278.2. Any such order transferring legal custody of the child shall be made in accordance with the provisions of subdivision A 5 of § 16.1-278.2 and shall be subject to the provisions of subsection D1. This order shall include, but need not be limited to, the following findings: (i) that there is no less drastic alternative to granting the requested relief; and (ii) that reasonable efforts have been made to prevent removal and that continued placement in the home would be contrary to the welfare of the child, if the order transfers legal custody of the child to a local board of social services. At any time subsequent to the transfer of legal custody of the child pursuant to this section, a birth parent or parents of the child and the pre-adoptive parent or parents may enter into a written post-adoption contact and communication agreement in accordance with the provisions of § 16.1-283.1 and Article 1.1 (§ 63.2-1220.2 et seq.) of Chapter 12 of Title 63.2. The court shall not require a written post-adoption contact and communication agreement as a precondition to entry of an order in any case involving the child.

The effect of the court's order approving a permanent entrustment agreement is to terminate an entrusting parent's residual parental rights. Any order terminating parental rights shall be accompanied by an order (i) continuing or granting custody to a local board of social services or to a licensed child-placing agency or (ii) granting custody or guardianship to a relative or other interested individual. Such an order continuing or granting custody to a local board of social services or to a licensed child-placing agency shall indicate whether that board or agency shall have the authority to place the child for adoption and consent thereto. A final order terminating parental rights pursuant to this section renders the approved entrustment agreement irrevocable. Such order may be appealed in accordance with the provisions of § 16.1-296.

D1. Any order transferring custody of the child to a relative or other interested individual pursuant to subsection D shall be entered only upon a finding, based upon a preponderance of the evidence, that the relative or other interested individual is one who (i) after an investigation as directed by the court, is found by the court to be willing and qualified to receive and care for the child; (ii) is willing to have a positive, continuous relationship with the child; (iii) is committed to providing a permanent, suitable home for the child; and (iv) is willing and has the ability to protect the child from abuse and neglect; and the order shall so state. The court's order transferring custody to a relative or other interested individual should further provide for, as appropriate, any terms and conditions which would promote the child's interest and welfare; ongoing provision of social services to the child and the child's custodian; and court review of the child's placement.

E. The local board or licensed child-placing agency to which authority is given to place the child for adoption and consent thereto after an order terminating parental rights is entered pursuant to this section shall file a written Adoption Progress Report with the juvenile court on the progress being made to place the child in an adoptive home. The report shall be filed with the court every six months from the date of the final order terminating parental rights until a final order of adoption is entered on behalf of the child in the circuit court. At the conclusion of the hearing at which termination of parental rights is ordered and authority is given to the local board or licensed child-placing agency to place the child for adoption, the juvenile court shall schedule a date by which the board or agency shall file the first Adoption Progress Report required by this section. A copy of the Adoption Progress Report shall be sent by the court to the guardian ad litem for the child. The court may schedule a hearing on the report with or without the request of a party.

History.

1999, c. 889; 2000, c. 385; 2006, c. 825; 2009, cc. 98, 260; 2010, c. 331.

§ 16.1-277.02. Petition for relief of care and custody.

A. Requests for petitions for relief of the care and custody of a child shall be referred initially to the local department of social services for investigation and the provision of services, if appropriate, in accordance with the provisions of § 63.2-319 or

Chapter 15 (§ 63.2-1500 et seq.) of Title 63.2. Upon the filing of a petition for relief of a child's care and custody pursuant to subdivision A 4 of § 16.1-241, the court shall appoint a guardian ad litem to represent the child in accordance with the provisions of § 16.1-266, and shall schedule the matter for a hearing on the petition. Such hearing on the petition may include partial or final disposition of the matter. The court shall provide notice of the hearing and a copy of the petition to the following, each of whom shall be a party entitled to participate in the proceeding:

1. The child, if he is 12 years of age or older;
2. The guardian ad litem for the child;
3. The child's parents, custodian or other person standing in loco parentis to the child. No such notification shall be required, however, if the judge certifies on the record that the identity of the parent is not reasonably ascertainable. An affidavit of the mother that the identity of the father is not reasonably ascertainable shall be sufficient evidence of this fact, provided there is no other evidence before the court which would refute such an affidavit. The hearing on the petition shall be held pursuant to this section although a parent fails to appear and is not represented by counsel, provided personal or substituted service was made on the parent, or the court determines that such person cannot be found, after reasonable effort, or in the case of a person who is without the Commonwealth, the person cannot be found or his post office address cannot be ascertained after reasonable effort. However, in the case of a hearing to grant a petition for permanent relief of custody and terminate a parent's residual parental rights, notice to the parent whose rights may be affected shall be provided in accordance with the provisions of §§ 16.1-263 and 16.1-264; and
4. The local board of social services. Upon receiving notice of the hearing pursuant to this section, the local board of social services shall investigate the matter and provide services, as appropriate, in accordance with the provisions of § 63.2-319 or Chapter 15 (§ 63.2-1500 et seq.) of Title 63.2.

B. At the hearing, the local board of social services, the child, the child's parents, guardian, legal custodian or other person standing in loco parentis and any other family or household member of the child to whom notice was given shall have the right to confront and cross-examine all adverse witnesses and evidence and to present evidence on their own behalf.

C. At the conclusion of the hearing on the petition, the court shall make a finding, based upon a preponderance of the evidence, whether there is good cause shown for the petitioner's desire to be relieved of the child's care and custody, unless the petition seeks permanent relief of custody and termination of parental rights. If the petition seeks permanent relief of custody and termination of parental rights, the court shall make a finding, based upon clear and convincing evidence, whether termination of parental rights is in the best interest of the child. If the court makes either of these findings, the court may enter:

1. A preliminary protective order pursuant to § 16.1-253;
2. An order that requires the local board of social services to provide services to the family as required by law;
3. An order that is consistent with any of the dispositional alternatives pursuant to § 16.1-278.3; or
4. Any combination of these orders.

Any such order transferring legal custody of the child shall be made in accordance with the provisions of subdivision A 5 of § 16.1-278.2 and shall be subject to the provisions of subsection C1. This order shall include, but need not be limited to, the following findings: (i) that there is no less drastic alternative to granting the requested relief; and (ii) that reasonable efforts have been made to prevent removal and that continued placement in the home would be contrary to the welfare of the child, if the order transfers legal custody of the child to a local board of social services. Any order terminating residual parental rights shall be accompanied by an order continuing or granting custody to a local board of social services, to a licensed child-placing agency or the granting of custody or guardianship to a relative or other interested individual. Such an order continuing or granting custody to a local board of social services or to a licensed child-placing agency shall indicate whether that board or agency shall have the authority to place the child for adoption and consent thereto. At any time subsequent to the transfer of legal custody of the child pursuant to this section, a birth parent or parents of the child and the pre-adoptive parent or parents may enter into a written post-adoption contact and communication agreement in accordance with the provisions of § 16.1-283.1 and Article 1.1 (§ 63.2-1220.2 et seq.) of Chapter 12 of Title 63.2. The court shall not require a written post-adoption contact and communication agreement as a precondition to entry of an order in any case involving the child.

The court shall schedule a subsequent hearing within 60 days of the hearing held pursuant to this section: (a) to enter a final order of disposition pursuant to § 16.1-278.3 or (b) if the child is placed in foster care, for review of the foster care plan filed pursuant to § 16.1-281. If a party is required to be present at the subsequent hearing, and (1) is present at the hearing on the petition, the party shall be given notice of the date set for the subsequent hearing; (2) if not present, shall be summoned as provided in § 16.1-263.

C1. Any order transferring temporary custody of the child to a relative or other interested individual pursuant to subsection C shall be entered only upon a finding, based upon a preponderance of the evidence, that the relative or other interested individual is one who (i) is found by the court to be willing and qualified to receive and care for the child; (ii) is willing to have a positive, continuous relationship with the child; and (iii) is willing and has the ability to protect the child from abuse and neglect. The court's order transferring temporary custody to a relative or other interested individual should further provide for compliance with any preliminary protective order entered on behalf of the child in accordance with the provisions of § 16.1-253; and, as appropriate, ongoing provision of social services to the child and the child's custodian; and court review of the child's placement with the relative or other individual. Any final order transferring custody of the child to a relative or other interested individual pursuant to this section shall, in addition, be entered only after an investigation as directed by the court and upon a finding, stated in the court's order, that the relative or other interested individual is one who satisfies clauses (i), (ii), and (iii) and is committed to providing a permanent, suitable home for the child.

D. The local board or licensed child-placing agency to which authority is given to place the child for adoption and consent thereto after an order terminating parental rights is entered pursuant to this section shall file a written Adoption Progress Report with the juvenile court on the progress being made to place the child in an adoptive home. The report shall be filed with the court every six months from the date of the final order terminating parental rights until a final order of adoption is entered on behalf of the child in the circuit court. At the conclusion of the hearing at which termination of parental rights is ordered and authority is given to the local board or licensed child-placing agency to place the child for adoption, the juvenile court shall schedule a date by which the board or agency shall file the first Adoption Progress Report required by this section. A copy of the Adoption Progress Report shall be sent by the court to the guardian ad litem for the child. The court may schedule a hearing on the report with or without the request of a party.

History.
1999, c. 889; 2000, c. 385; 2009, cc. 98, 260; 2010, c. 331; 2013, c. 130.

§ 16.1-277.1. Time limitation.

A. When a child is held continuously in secure detention, he shall be released from confinement if there is no adjudicatory or transfer hearing conducted by the court for the matters upon which he was detained within twenty-one days from the date he was first detained.

B. If a child is not held in secure detention or is released from same after having been confined, an adjudicatory or transfer hearing on the matters charged in the petition or petitions issued against him shall be conducted within 120 days from the date the petition or petitions are filed.

C. When a child is held in secure detention after the completion of his adjudicatory hearing or is detained when the juvenile court has retained jurisdiction as a result of a transfer hearing, he shall be released from such detention if the disposition hearing is not completed within thirty days from the date of the adjudicatory or transfer hearing.

D. The time limitations provided for in this section shall be tolled during any period in which (i) the whereabouts of the child are unknown, (ii) the child has escaped from custody, or (iii) the child has failed to appear pursuant to a court order. The limitations also may be extended by the court for a reasonable period of time based upon good cause shown, provided that the basis for such extension is recorded in writing and filed among the papers of the proceedings. For the purposes of this section, good cause includes, but is not limited to, extension of limitations necessary to obtain the presence of a witness to testify regarding the results of scientific analyses or examinations.

History.
1985, c. 260; 1988, c. 220; 1999, c. 58; 2009, Sp. Sess. I, cc. 1, 4.

§ 16.1-277.2. Rejection of plea agreement; recusal.

Upon rejecting a plea agreement in any delinquency matter, a judge shall immediately recuse himself from any further proceedings on the same matter unless the parties agree otherwise.

History.
2014, c. 165.

ARTICLE 9.

DISPOSITION.

§ 16.1-278. Cooperation of certain agencies, officials, institutions and associations.

A. The judge may order, after notice and opportunity to be heard, any state, county or municipal officer or employee or any governmental agency or other governmental institution to render only such information, assistance, services and cooperation as may be provided for by state or federal law or an ordinance of any city, county or town.

The officer, employee, agency or institution may appeal such order to the circuit court in accordance with § 16.1-296. The circuit court shall advance such appeals on its docket and may stay the order of the juvenile court during the pendency of the appeal. The circuit court may affirm or reverse the order of the juvenile court. Upon reversal, the circuit court may remand the case to the juvenile court for an alternative disposition.

B. The court is authorized to cooperate with and make use of the services of all public or private societies or organizations which seek to protect or aid children or families, in order that the court may be assisted in giving the children and families within its jurisdiction such care, protection and assistance as will best enhance their welfare.

History.
Code 1950, § 16.1-156; 1956, c. 555; 1977, c. 559; 1980, c. 245.

§ 16.1-278.1. Definitions.

As used in this article, unless the context clearly indicates otherwise:

"Parent" includes parent, guardian, legal custodian, or other person standing in loco parentis.

"Public service project" means any governmental or quasi-governmental agency project or any project of a nonprofit corporation or association operated exclusively for charitable or community purposes.

History.
1991, c. 534.

§ 16.1-278.2. Abused, neglected, or abandoned children or children without parental care.

A. Within 60 days of a preliminary removal order hearing held pursuant to § 16.1-252 or a hearing on a preliminary protective order held pursuant to § 16.1-253, a dispositional hearing shall be held if the court found abuse or neglect and (i) removed the child from his home or (ii) entered a preliminary protective order. Notice of the dispositional hearing shall be provided to the child's parent, guardian, legal custodian, or other person standing in loco parentis in accordance with § 16.1-263. The hearing shall be held and a dispositional order may be entered, although a parent, guardian, legal custodian, or person standing in loco parentis fails to appear and is not represented by counsel, provided personal or substituted service was made on the person, or the court determines that such person cannot be found, after reasonable effort, or in the case of a person who is without the Commonwealth, the person cannot be found or his post office address cannot be ascertained after reasonable effort. Notice shall also be provided to the local department of social services, the guardian ad litem and, if appointed, the court-appointed special advocate.

If a child is found to be (a) abused or neglected; (b) at risk of being abused or neglected by a parent or custodian who has been adjudicated as having abused or neglected another child in his care; or (c) abandoned by his parent or other custodian, or without parental care and guardianship because of his parent's absence or physical or mental incapacity, the juvenile court or the circuit court may make any of the following orders of disposition to protect the welfare of the child:

1. Enter an order pursuant to the provisions of § 16.1-278;

2. Permit the child to remain with his parent, subject to such conditions and limitations as the court may order with respect to such child and his parent or other adult occupant of the same dwelling;

3. Prohibit or limit contact as the court deems appropriate between the child and his parent or other adult occupant of the same dwelling whose presence tends to endanger the child's life, health or normal development. The prohibition may exclude any such individual from the home under such conditions as the court may prescribe for a period to be determined by the court but in no event for longer than 180 days from the date of such determination. A hearing shall be held within 150 days to determine further disposition of the matter that may include limiting or prohibiting contact for another 180 days;

4. Permit the local board of social services or a public agency designated by the community policy and management team to place the child, subject to the provisions of § 16.1-281, in suitable family homes, child-caring institutions, residential facilities, or independent living arrangements with legal custody remaining with the parents or guardians. The local board or public agency and the parents or guardians shall enter into an agreement which shall specify the responsibilities of each for the care and control of the child. The board or public agency that places the child shall have the final authority to determine the appropriate placement for the child.

Any order allowing a local board or public agency to place a child where legal custody remains with the parents or guardians as provided in this section shall be entered only upon a finding by the court that reasonable efforts have been made to prevent placement out of the home and that continued placement in the home would be contrary to the welfare of the child; and the order shall so state.

5. After a finding that there is no less drastic alternative, transfer legal custody, subject to the provisions of § 16.1-281, to any of the following:

a. A relative or other interested individual subject to the provisions of subsection A1 of this section;

b. A child welfare agency, private organization or facility that is licensed or otherwise authorized by law to receive and provide care for such child; however, a court shall not transfer legal custody of an abused or neglected child to an agency, organization or facility out of the Commonwealth without the approval of the Commissioner of Social Services; or

c. The local board of social services of the county or city in which the court has jurisdiction or, at the discretion of the court, to the local board of the county or city in which the child has residence if other than the county or city in which the court has jurisdiction. The local board shall accept the child for care and custody, provided that it has been given reasonable notice of the pendency of the case and an opportunity to be heard. However, in an emergency in the county or city in which the court has jurisdiction, the local board may be required to accept a child for a period not to exceed 14 days without prior notice or an opportunity to be heard if the judge entering the placement order describes the emergency and the need for such temporary placement in the order. Nothing in this section shall prohibit the commitment of a child to any local board of social services in the Commonwealth when the local board consents to the commitment. The board to which the child is committed shall have the final authority to determine the appropriate placement for the child.

Any order authorizing removal from the home and transferring legal custody of a child to a local board of social services as provided in this section shall be entered only upon a finding by the court that reasonable efforts have been made to prevent removal and that continued placement in the home would be contrary to the welfare of the child; and the order shall so state.

6. Transfer legal custody pursuant to subdivision 5 of this section and order the parent to participate in such services and programs or to refrain from such conduct as the court may prescribe; or

7. Terminate the rights of the parent pursuant to § 16.1-283.

A1. Any order transferring custody of the child to a relative or other interested individual pursuant to subdivision A 5 a shall be entered only upon a finding, based upon a preponderance of the evidence, that the relative or other interested individual is one who, after an investigation as directed by the court, (i) is found by the court to be willing and qualified to receive and care for the child; (ii) is willing to have a positive, continuous relationship with the child; (iii) is committed to providing a permanent, suitable home for the child; and (iv) is willing and has the ability to protect the child from abuse and neglect; and the order shall so state. The court's order transferring custody to a relative or other interested individual should further provide for, as appropriate, any terms or conditions which would promote the child's interest and welfare; ongoing provision of social services to the child and the child's custodian; and court review of the child's placement.

B. If the child has been placed in foster care, at the dispositional hearing the court shall review the foster care plan for the child filed in accordance with § 16.1-281 by the local department of social services, a public agency designated by the community policy and management team which places a child through an agreement with the parents or guardians where legal custody remains with the parents or guardians, or child welfare agency.

C. Any preliminary protective orders entered on behalf of the child shall be reviewed at the dispositional hearing and may be incorporated, as appropriate, in the dispositional order.

D. A dispositional order entered pursuant to this section is a final order from which an appeal may be taken in accordance with § 16.1-296.

History.

1991, c. 534; 1994, c. 865; 1997, c. 790; 2000, c. 385; 2002, c. 747; 2013, c. 130.

§ 16.1-278.3. Relief of care and custody.

A. Within 60 days of a hearing on a petition for relief of the care and custody of any child pursuant to § 16.1-277.02 at which the court found (i) good cause for the petitioner's desire to be relieved of a child's care and custody or (ii) that permanent relief of custody and termination of residual parental rights is in the best interest of the child, a dispositional hearing shall be held, if a final order disposing of the matter was not entered at the conclusion of the hearing on the petition held pursuant to § 16.1-277.02.

B. Notice of the dispositional hearing shall be provided to the local department of social services, the guardian ad litem for the child, the child if he is at least 12 years of age, and the child's parents, custodian or other person standing in loco parentis. However, if a parent's residual parental rights were terminated at the hearing on the petition held pursuant to § 16.1-277.02, no such notice of the hearing pursuant to this section shall be provided to the parent. The hearing shall be held and a dispositional order may be entered, although a parent, guardian, legal custodian or person standing in loco parentis fails to appear and is not represented by counsel, provided personal or substituted service was made on the person, or the court determines that the person cannot be found, after reasonable effort, or in the case of a person who is without the Commonwealth, the person cannot be found or his post office address cannot be ascertained after reasonable effort. However, in the case of a hearing to grant a petition for permanent relief of custody and terminate a parent's residual parental rights, notice to the parent whose rights may be affected shall be provided in accordance with the provisions of §§ 16.1-263 and 16.1-264.

C. The court may make any of the orders of disposition permitted in a case involving an abused or neglected child pursuant to § 16.1-278.2. Any such order transferring legal custody of the child shall be made in accordance with the provisions of subdivision A 5 of § 16.1-278.2 and shall be subject to the provisions of subsection D1. This order shall include, but need not be limited to, the following findings: (i) that there is no less drastic alternative to granting the requested relief; and (ii) that reasonable efforts have been made to prevent removal and that continued placement in the home would be contrary to the welfare of the child, if the order transfers legal custody of the child to a local board of social services. Any preliminary protective orders entered on behalf of the child shall be reviewed at the dispositional hearing and may be incorporated, as appropriate, in the dispositional order. If the child has been placed in foster care, at the dispositional hearing the court shall review the foster care plan for the child filed by the local board of social services or child welfare agency in accordance with § 16.1-281.

D. If the parent or other custodian seeks to be relieved permanently of the care and custody of any child and the court finds by clear and convincing evidence that termination of the parent's parental rights is in the best interest of the child, the court may terminate the parental rights of that parent. If the remaining parent has not petitioned for permanent relief of the care and custody of the child, the remaining parent's parental rights may be terminated in accordance with the provisions of § 16.1-283. Any order terminating parental rights shall be accompanied by an order (i) continuing or granting custody to a local board of social services or to a licensed child-placing agency, or (ii) granting custody or guardianship to a relative or other interested individual. Such an order continuing or granting custody to a local board of social services or to a licensed child-placing agency shall indicate whether that board or agency shall have the authority to place the child for adoption and consent thereto. Proceedings under this section shall be advanced on the docket so as to provide for their earliest practicable disposition. At any time subsequent to the transfer of legal custody of the child pursuant to this section, a birth parent or parents of the child and the pre-adoptive parent or parents may enter into a written post-adoption contact and communication agreement in accordance with the provisions of § 16.1-283.1 and Article 1.1 (§ 63.2-1220.2 et seq.) of Chapter 12 of Title 63.2. The court shall not require a written post-adoption contact and communication agreement as a precondition to entry of an order in any case involving the child.

D1. Any order transferring custody of the child to a relative or other interested individual pursuant to subsection C or D shall be entered only upon a finding, based upon a preponderance of the evidence, that the relative or other interested individual is one who, after an investigation as directed by the court, (i) is found by the court to be willing and qualified to receive and care for the child; (ii) is willing to have a positive, continuous relationship with the child; (iii) is committed to providing a permanent, suitable home for the child; and (iv) is willing and has the ability to protect the child from abuse and neglect; and the order shall so state. The court's order transferring custody to a relative or other interested individual should further provide for, as appropriate, any terms or conditions which would promote the child's interest and welfare; ongoing provision of social services to the child and the child's custodian; and court review of the child's placement.

E. The local board or licensed child-placing agency to which authority is given to place the child for adoption and consent thereto after an order terminating parental rights is entered pursuant to this section shall file a written Adoption Progress Report with the juvenile court on the progress being made to place the child in an adoptive home. The report shall be filed with the court every six months from the date of the final order terminating parental rights until a final order of adoption is entered on behalf of the child in the circuit court. At the conclusion of the hearing at which termination of parental rights is ordered and authority is given to the local board or licensed child-placing agency to place the child for adoption, the juvenile court shall schedule a date by which the board or agency shall file the first Adoption Progress Report required by this section. A copy of the Adoption Progress Report shall be sent by the court to the guardian ad litem for the child. The court may schedule a hearing on the report with or without the request of a party.

F. A dispositional order entered pursuant to this section is a final order from which an appeal may be taken in accordance with § 16.1-296.

History.

1991, c. 534; 1999, c. 889; 2000, c. 385; 2009, cc. 98, 260; 2010, c. 331; 2013, c. 130.

§ 16.1-278.4. Children in need of services.

If a child is found to be in need of services or a status offender, the juvenile court or the circuit court may make any of the following orders of disposition for the supervision, care and rehabilitation of the child:

1. Enter an order pursuant to the provisions of § 16.1-278.
2. Permit the child to remain with his parent subject to such conditions and limitations as the court may order with respect to such child and his parent.
3. Order the parent with whom the child is living to participate in such programs, cooperate in such treatment or be subject to such conditions and limitations as the court may order and as are designed for the rehabilitation of the child and his parent.
4. Beginning July 1, 1992, in the case of any child fourteen years of age or older, where the court finds that the child is not able to benefit appreciably from further schooling, the court may excuse the child from further compliance with any legal requirement of compulsory school attendance as provided under § 22.1-254 or authorize the child, notwithstanding the provisions of any other law, to be employed in any occupation which is not legally declared hazardous for children under the age of eighteen.
5. Permit the local board of social services or a public agency designated by the community policy and management team to place the child, subject to the provisions of § 16.1-281, in suitable family homes, child caring-institutions, residential facilities, or independent living arrangements with legal custody remaining with the parents or guardians. The local board or public agency and the parents or guardians shall enter into an agreement which shall specify the responsibilities of each for the care and control of the child. The board or public agency that places the child shall have the final authority to determine the appropriate placement for the child.

Any order allowing a local board or public agency to place a child where legal custody remains with the parents or guardians as provided in this section shall be entered only upon a finding by the court that reasonable efforts have been made to prevent placement out of the home and that continued placement in the home would be contrary to the welfare of the child, and the order shall so state.

6. Transfer legal custody to any of the following:

a. A relative or other individual who, after study, is found by the court to be qualified to receive and care for the child;

b. A child welfare agency, private organization or facility that is licensed or otherwise authorized by law to receive and provide care for such child. The court shall not transfer legal custody of a child in need of services to an agency, organization or facility out of the Commonwealth without the approval of the Commissioner of Social Services; or

c. The local board of social services of the county or city in which the court has jurisdiction or, at the discretion of the court, to the local board of the county or city in which the child has residence if other than the county or city in which the court has jurisdiction. The local board shall accept the child for care and custody, provided that it has been given reasonable notice of the pendency of the case and an opportunity to be heard. However, in an emergency in the county or city in which the court has jurisdiction, the local board may be required to accept a child for a period not to exceed fourteen days without prior notice or an opportunity to be heard if the judge entering the placement order describes the emergency and the need for such temporary placement in the order. Nothing in this subdivision shall prohibit the commitment of a child to any local board of social services in the Commonwealth when the local board consents to the commitment. The board to which the child is committed shall have the final authority to determine the appropriate placement for the child.

Any order authorizing removal from the home and transferring legal custody of a child to a local board of social services as provided in this subdivision shall be entered only upon a finding by the court that reasonable efforts have been made to prevent removal and that continued placement in the home would be contrary to the welfare of the child, and the order shall so state.

7. Require the child to participate in a public service project under such conditions as the court prescribes.

History.

1991, c. 534; 1994, c. 865; 1997, c. 463; 1999, cc. 488, 552; 2002, c. 747.

§ 16.1-278.5. Children in need of supervision.

A. If a child is found to be in need of supervision, the court shall, before final disposition of the case, direct the appropriate public agency to evaluate the child's service needs using an interdisciplinary team approach. The team shall consist of qualified personnel who are reasonably available from the appropriate department of social services, community services board, local school division, court service unit and other appropriate and available public and private agencies and may be the family assessment and planning team established pursuant to § 2.2-5207. A report of the evaluation shall be filed as provided in § 16.1-274 A. In lieu of directing an evaluation be made, the court may consider the report concerning the child of an interdisciplinary team which met not more than ninety days prior to the court's making a finding that the child is in need of supervision.

B. The court may make any of the following orders of disposition for the supervision, care and rehabilitation of the child:

1. Enter any order of disposition authorized by § 16.1-278.4 for a child found to be in need of services;

2. Place the child on probation under such conditions and limitations as the court may prescribe including suspension of the child's driver's license upon terms and conditions which may include the issuance of a restricted license for those purposes set forth in subsection E of § 18.2-271.1;

3. Order the child and/or his parent to participate in such programs, cooperate in such treatment or be subject to such conditions and limitations as the court may order and as are designed for the rehabilitation of the child;

4. Require the child to participate in a public service project under such conditions as the court may prescribe; or

5. a. Beginning July 1, 1992, in the case of any child subject to compulsory school attendance as provided in § 22.1-254, where the court finds that the child's parent is in violation of §§ 22.1-254, 22.1-255, 22.1-265, or § 22.1-267, in addition to any penalties provided in § 22.1-263 or § 22.1-265, the court may order the parent with whom the child is living to participate in such programs, cooperate in such treatment, or be subject to such conditions and limitations as the court may order and as are designed for the rehabilitation of the child and/or the parent. Upon the failure of the parent to so participate or cooperate, or to comply with the conditions and limitations that the court orders, the court may impose a fine of not more than $100 for each day in which the person fails to comply with the court order.

b. If the court finds that the parent has willfully disobeyed a lawful process, judgment, decree, or court order requiring such person to comply with the compulsory school attendance law, in addition to any conditions or limitations that the court may order or any penalties provided by §§ 16.1-278.2 through 16.1-278.19, 22.1-263 or § 22.1-265, the court may impose the penalty authorized by § 18.2-371.

C. Any order entered pursuant to this section shall be provided in writing to the child, his parent or legal custodian, and to the child's attorney and shall contain adequate notice of the provisions of § 16.1-292 regarding willful violation of such order.

History.

1991, c. 534; 1992, cc. 837, 880; 1996, c. 45; 1997, c. 210.

§ 16.1-278.6. Status offenders.

If a child is alleged to be a status offender, including but not limited to those cases in which the juvenile is alleged to have committed a curfew violation or a violation of the law regarding tobacco, the juvenile court or the circuit court may enter any order of disposition authorized by § 16.1-278.4.

History.

1991, c. 534; 1997, c. 463.

§ 16.1-278.7. Commitment to Department of Juvenile Justice.

Only a juvenile who is adjudicated as a delinquent and is 11 years of age or older may be committed to the Department of Juvenile Justice. In cases where a waiver of an investigation has been granted pursuant to subdivision A 14 or A 17 of § 16.1-278.8, at the time a court commits a child to the Department of Juvenile Justice the court shall order an investigation pursuant to § 16.1-273 to be completed within 15 days. No juvenile court or circuit court shall order the commitment of any child jointly to the Department of Juvenile Justice and to a local board of social services or transfer the custody of a child jointly to a court service unit of a juvenile court and to a local board of social services. Any person sentenced and committed to an active term of incarceration in the Department of Corrections who is, at the time of such sentencing, in the custody of the Department of Juvenile Justice, upon pronouncement of sentence, shall be immediately transferred to the Department of Corrections.

History.

1991, c. 534; 2000, cc. 954, 981, 988; 2007, c. 510; 2014, cc. 20, 249.

§ 16.1-278.7:01. Department to give notice of the receipt of certain persons.

A. At the time or receipt of any person, for whom registration with the Sex Offender and Crimes Against Minors Registry is required pursuant to Chapter 9 (§ 9.1-900 et seq.) of Title 9.1, the Department shall obtain from that person all necessary registration information, including fingerprints and photographs of a type and kind approved by the Department of State Police. A person required to register shall register and submit to be photographed as part of the registration. The Department shall forthwith forward the registration information and photograph to the Department of State Police on the date of the receipt of the person.

B. Whenever a person required to register has failed to comply with the provisions of subsection A, the Department shall promptly investigate or request the State Police promptly investigate and, if there is probable cause to believe a violation has occurred, obtain a warrant or petition or assist in obtaining an indictment charging a violation of § 18.2-472.1 in the jurisdiction in which the person was received. The Department shall notify the State Police forthwith of such actions taken pursuant to this section.

History.

2006, cc. 857, 914.

§ 16.1-278.7:02. Department to give notice of Sex Offender and Crimes Against Minors Registry requirements to certain persons.

A. Prior to the release or discharge of any persons for whom registration with the Sex Offender and Crimes Against Minors Registry is required pursuant to Chapter 9 (§ 9.1-900 et seq.) of Title 9.1, the Department shall give notice to the persons of his duty to register with the State Police. A person required to register shall register, submit to be photographed as part of the registration, and provide information regarding place of employment, if available, to the Department. The Department shall also obtain from that person all necessary registration information, including fingerprints and photographs of a type and kind approved by the Department of State Police; inform the person of his duties regarding reregistration and change of address; and inform the person of his duty to register. The Department of Juvenile Justice shall forward the registration information to the Department of State Police on the date of the person's release or discharge.

B. Whenever a person required to register has failed to comply with the provisions of subsection A, the Department shall promptly investigate or request the State Police promptly investigate and, if there is probable cause to believe a violation has occurred, obtain a warrant or assist in obtaining an indictment charging a violation of § 18.2-472.1 in the jurisdiction in which the person was discharged. The Department shall notify the State Police forthwith of such actions taken pursuant to this section.

History.

2006, cc. 857, 914.

§ 16.1-278.8. Delinquent juveniles.

A. If a juvenile is found to be delinquent, except where such finding involves a refusal to take a blood or breath test in violation of § 18.2-268.2 or a similar ordinance, the juvenile court or the circuit court may make any of the following orders of disposition for his supervision, care and rehabilitation:

1. Enter an order pursuant to the provisions of § 16.1-278;

2. Permit the juvenile to remain with his parent, subject to such conditions and limitations as the court may order with respect to the juvenile and his parent;

3. Order the parent of a juvenile living with him to participate in such programs, cooperate in such treatment or be subject to such conditions and limitations as the court may order and as are designed for the rehabilitation of the juvenile and his parent;

4. Defer disposition for a specific period of time established by the court with due regard for the gravity of the offense and the juvenile's history, after which time the charge may be dismissed by the judge if the juvenile exhibits good behavior during the period for which disposition is deferred;

4a. Defer disposition and place the juvenile in the temporary custody of the Department to attend a boot camp established pursuant to § 66-13 provided bed space is available for confinement and the juvenile (i) has been found delinquent for an offense that would be a Class 1 misdemeanor or felony if committed by an adult, (ii) has not previously been and is not currently being adjudicated delinquent or found guilty of a violent juvenile felony, (iii) has not previously attended a boot camp, (iv) has not previously been committed to and received by the Department, and (v) has had an assessment completed by the Department or its contractor concerning the appropriateness of the candidate for a boot camp. Upon the juvenile's withdrawal, removal or refusal to comply with the terms and conditions of participation in the program, he shall be brought before the court for a hearing at which the court may impose any other disposition as authorized by this section which could have been imposed at the time the juvenile was placed in the custody of the Department;

5. Without entering a judgment of guilty and with the consent of the juvenile and his attorney, defer disposition of the delinquency charge for a specific period of time established by the court with due regard for the gravity of the offense and the juvenile's history, and place the juvenile on probation under such conditions and limitations as the court may prescribe. Upon fulfillment of the terms and conditions, the court shall discharge the juvenile and dismiss the proceedings against him. Discharge and dismissal under these provisions shall be without adjudication of guilt;

6. Order the parent of a juvenile with whom the juvenile does not reside to participate in such programs, cooperate in such treatment or be subject to such conditions and limitations as the court may order and as are designed for the rehabilitation of the juvenile where the court determines this participation to be in the best interest of the juvenile and other parties concerned and where the court determines it reasonable to expect the parent to be able to comply with such order;

7. Place the juvenile on probation under such conditions and limitations as the court may prescribe;

7a. Place the juvenile on probation and order treatment for the abuse or dependence on alcohol or drugs in a program licensed by the Department of Behavioral Health and Developmental Services for the treatment of juveniles for substance abuse provided that (i) the juvenile has received a substance abuse screening and assessment pursuant to § 16.1-273 and that such assessment reasonably indicates that the commission of the offense was motivated by, or closely related to, the habitual use of alcohol or drugs and indicates that the juvenile is in need of treatment for this condition; (ii) the juvenile has not previously been and is not currently being adjudicated for a violent juvenile felony; and (iii) such facility is available. Upon the juvenile's withdrawal, removal, or refusal to comply with the conditions of participation in the program, he shall be brought before the court for a hearing at which the court may impose any other disposition authorized by this section. The court shall review such placements at 30-day intervals;

8. Impose a fine not to exceed $500 upon such juvenile;

9. Suspend the motor vehicle and driver's license of such juvenile or impose a curfew on the juvenile as to the hours during which he may operate a motor vehicle. Any juvenile whose driver's license is suspended may be referred for an assessment and subsequent referral to appropriate services, upon such terms and conditions as the court may order. The court, in its discretion and upon a demonstration of hardship, may authorize the use of a restricted permit to operate a motor vehicle by any juvenile who enters such program for any of the purposes set forth in subsection E of § 18.2-271.1 or for travel to and from school. The restricted permit shall be issued in accordance with the provisions of such subsection. However, only an abstract of the court order that identifies the juvenile and the conditions under which the restricted license is to be issued shall be sent to the Department of Motor Vehicles.

If a curfew is imposed, the juvenile shall surrender his driver's license, which shall be held in the physical custody of the court during any period of curfew restriction. The court shall send an abstract of any order issued under the provisions of this section to the Department of Motor Vehicles, which shall preserve a record thereof. Notwithstanding the provisions of Article 12 (§ 16.1-299 et seq.) of this chapter or the provisions of Title 46.2, this record shall be available only to all law-enforcement officers, attorneys for the Commonwealth and courts. A copy of the court order, upon which shall be noted all curfew restrictions, shall be provided to the juvenile and shall contain such information regarding the juvenile as is reasonably necessary to identify him. The juvenile may operate a motor vehicle under the court order in accordance with its terms.

Any juvenile who operates a motor vehicle in violation of any restrictions imposed pursuant to this section shall be guilty of a violation of § 46.2-301.

The Department of Motor Vehicles shall refuse to issue a driver's license to any juvenile denied a driver's license until such time as is stipulated in the court order or until notification by the court of withdrawal of the order imposing the curfew;

10. Require the juvenile to make restitution or reparation to the aggrieved party or parties for actual damages or loss caused by the offense for which the juvenile was found to be delinquent;

11. Require the juvenile to participate in a public service project under such conditions as the court prescribes;

12. In case of traffic violations, impose only those penalties that are authorized to be imposed on adults for such violations. However, for those violations punishable by confinement if committed by an adult, confinement shall be imposed only as authorized by this title;

13. Transfer legal custody to any of the following:

a. A relative or other individual who, after study, is found by the court to be qualified to receive and care for the juvenile;

b. A child welfare agency, private organization or facility that is licensed or otherwise authorized by law to receive and provide care for such juvenile. The court shall not transfer legal custody of a delinquent juvenile to an agency, organization or facility outside of the Commonwealth without the approval of the Director; or

c. The local board of social services of the county or city in which the court has jurisdiction or, at the discretion of the court, to the local board of the county or city in which the juvenile has residence if other than the county or city in which the court has jurisdiction. The board shall accept the juvenile for care and custody, provided that it has been given reasonable notice of the pendency of the case and an opportunity to be heard. However, in an emergency in the county or city in which the court has jurisdiction, such local board may be required to temporarily accept a juvenile for a period not to exceed 14 days without prior notice or an opportunity to be heard if the judge entering the placement order describes the emergency and the need for such temporary placement in the order. Nothing in this subdivision shall prohibit the commitment of a juvenile to any local board of social services in the Commonwealth when such local board consents to the commitment. The board to which the juvenile is committed shall have the final authority to determine the appropriate placement for the juvenile. Any order authorizing removal from the home and transferring legal custody of a juvenile to a local board of social services as provided in this subdivision shall be entered only upon a finding by the court that reasonable efforts have been made to prevent removal and that continued placement in the home would be contrary to the welfare of the juvenile, and the order shall so state;

14. Unless waived by an agreement between the attorney for the Commonwealth and the juvenile and his attorney or other legal representative, upon consideration of the results of an investigation completed pursuant to § 16.1-273, commit the juvenile to the Department of Juvenile Justice, but only if he is 11 years of age or older and the current offense is (i) an offense that would be a felony if committed by an adult, (ii) an offense that would be a Class 1 misdemeanor if committed by an adult and the juvenile has previously been found to be delinquent based on an offense that would be a felony if committed by an adult, or (iii) an offense that would be a Class 1 misdemeanor if committed by an adult and the juvenile has previously been adjudicated delinquent of three or more offenses that would be a Class 1 misdemeanor if committed by an adult, and each such offense was not a part of a common act, transaction or scheme;

15. Impose the penalty authorized by § 16.1-284;

16. Impose the penalty authorized by § 16.1-284.1;

17. Unless waived by an agreement between the attorney for the Commonwealth and the juvenile and his attorney or other legal representative, upon consideration of the results of an investigation completed pursuant to § 16.1-273, impose the penalty authorized by § 16.1-285.1;

18. Impose the penalty authorized by § 16.1-278.9; or

19. Require the juvenile to participate in a gang-activity prevention program including, but not limited to, programs funded under the Virginia Juvenile Community Crime Control Act pursuant to § 16.1-309.7, if available, when a juvenile has been found delinquent of any of the following violations: § 18.2-51, 18.2-51.1, 18.2-52, 18.2-53, 18.2-55, 18.2-56, 18.2-57, 18.2-57.2, 18.2-121, 18.2-127, 18.2-128, 18.2-137, 18.2-138, 18.2-146, or 18.2-147, or any violation of a local ordinance adopted pursuant to § 15.2-1812.2.

B. If the court finds a juvenile delinquent of any of the following offenses, the court shall require the juvenile to make at least partial restitution or reparation for any property damage, for loss caused by the offense, or for actual medical expenses incurred by the victim as a result of the offense: § 18.2-51, 18.2-51.1, 18.2-52, 18.2-53, 18.2-55, 18.2-56, 18.2-57, 18.2-57.2, 18.2-121, 18.2-127, 18.2-128, 18.2-137, 18.2-138, 18.2-146, or 18.2-147; or for any violation of a local ordinance adopted pursuant to § 15.2-1812.2. The court shall further require the juvenile to participate in a community service project under such conditions as the court prescribes.

History.

1991, c. 534; 1992, c. 830; 1994, cc. 859, 949; 1996, cc. 755, 914; 1997, c. 318; 1999, cc. 350, 622; 2000, cc. 954, 978, 981, 988, 1020, 1041; 2004, cc. 325, 462; 2005, c. 810; 2009, cc. 813, 840; 2014, cc. 20, 249.

§ 16.1-278.8:01. Juveniles found delinquent of first drug offense; screening; assessment; drug tests; costs and fees; education or treatment programs.

Whenever any juvenile who has not previously been found delinquent of any offense under Article 1 (§ 18.2-247 et seq.) of Chapter 7 of Title 18.2 or under any statute of the United States or of any state relating to narcotic drugs, marijuana, or stimulant, depressant or hallucinogenic drugs, or has not previously had a proceeding against him for a violation of such an offense dismissed as provided in § 18.2-251, is found delinquent of any offense concerning the use, in any manner, of drugs, controlled substances, narcotics, marijuana, noxious chemical substances and like substances, the juvenile court or the circuit court shall require such juvenile to undergo a substance abuse screening pursuant to § 16.1-273 and to submit to such periodic substance abuse testing, to include alcohol testing, as may be directed by the court. Such testing shall be conducted by a court services unit of the Department of Juvenile Justice, or by a locally operated court services unit or by personnel of any program or agency approved by the Department. The cost of such testing ordered by the court shall be paid by the Commonwealth from funds appropriated to the Department for this purpose. The court shall also order the juvenile to undergo such treatment or education program for substance abuse, if available, as the court deems appropriate based upon consideration of the substance abuse assessment. The treatment or education shall be provided by a program licensed by the Department of Behavioral Health and Developmental Services or by a similar program available through a facility or program operated by or under contract to the Department of Juvenile Justice or a locally operated court services unit or a program funded through the Virginia Juvenile Community Crime Control Act (§ 16.1-309.2 et seq.).

History.

2000, cc. 1020, 1041; 2009, cc. 813, 840; 2011, cc. 384, 410; 2014, cc. 674, 719.

§ 16.1-278.9. Delinquent children; loss of driving privileges for alcohol, firearm, and drug offenses; truancy.

A. If a court has found facts which would justify a finding that a child at least 13 years of age at the time of the offense is delinquent and such finding involves (i) a violation of § 18.2-266 or of a similar ordinance of any county, city or town, (ii) a refusal to take a blood or breath test in violation of § 18.2-268.2, (iii) a felony violation of § 18.2-248, 18.2-248.1 or 18.2-250, (iv) a misdemeanor violation of § 18.2-248, 18.2-248.1, or 18.2-250 or a violation of § 18.2-250.1, (v) the unlawful purchase, possession or consumption of alcohol in violation of § 4.1-305 or the unlawful drinking or possession of alcoholic beverages in or on public school grounds in violation of § 4.1-309, (vi) public intoxication in violation of § 18.2-388 or a similar ordinance of a county, city or town, (vii) the unlawful use or possession of a handgun or possession of a "streetsweeper" as defined below, or (viii) a violation of § 18.2-83, the court shall order, in addition to any other penalty that it may impose as provided by law for the offense, that the child be denied a driver's license. In addition to any other penalty authorized by this section, if the offense involves a violation designated under clause (i) and the child was transporting a person 17 years of age or younger, the court shall impose the additional fine and order community service as provided in § 18.2-270. If the offense involves a violation designated under clause (i), (ii), (iii) or (viii), the denial of a driver's license shall be for a period of one year or until the juvenile reaches the age of 17, whichever is longer, for a first such offense or for a period of one year or until the juvenile reaches the age of 18, whichever is longer, for a second or subsequent such offense. If the offense involves a violation designated under clause (iv), (v) or (vi) the denial of driving privileges shall be for a period of six months unless the offense is committed by a child under the age of 16 years and three months, in which case the child's ability to apply for a driver's license shall be delayed for a period of six months following the date he reaches the age of 16 and three months. If the offense involves a first violation designated under clause (v) or (vi), the court shall impose the license sanction and may enter a judgment of guilt or, without entering a judgment of guilt, may defer disposition of the delinquency charge until such time as the court disposes of the case pursuant to subsection F of this section. If the offense involves a violation designated under clause (iii) or (iv), the court shall impose the license sanction and shall dispose of the delinquency charge pursuant to the provisions of this chapter or § 18.2-251. If the offense involves a violation designated under clause (vii), the denial of driving privileges shall be for a period of not less than 30 days, except when the offense involves possession of a concealed handgun or a striker 12, commonly called a "streetsweeper," or any semi-automatic folding stock shotgun of like kind with a spring tension drum magazine capable of holding 12 shotgun shells, in which case the denial of driving privileges shall be for a period of two years unless the offense is committed by a child under the age of 16 years and three months, in which event the child's ability to apply for a driver's license shall be delayed for a period of two years following the date he reaches the age of 16 and three months.

A1. If a court finds that a child at least 13 years of age has failed to comply with school attendance and meeting requirements as provided in § 22.1-258, the court shall order the denial of the child's driving privileges for a period of not less than 30 days. If such failure to comply involves a child under the age of 16 years and three months, the child's ability to apply for a driver's license shall be delayed for a period of not less than 30 days following the date he reaches the age of 16 and three months.

If the court finds a second or subsequent such offense, it may order the denial of a driver's license for a period of one year or until the juvenile reaches the age of 18, whichever is longer, or delay the child's ability to apply for a driver's license for a period of one year following the date he reaches the age of 16 and three months, as may be appropriate.

B. Any child who has a driver's license at the time of the offense or at the time of the court's finding as provided in subsection A1 shall be ordered to surrender his driver's license, which shall be held in the physical custody of the court during any period of license denial.

C. The court shall report any order issued under this section to the Department of Motor Vehicles, which shall preserve a record thereof. The report and the record shall include a statement as to whether the child was represented by or waived counsel or whether the order was issued pursuant to subsection A1 of this section. Notwithstanding the provisions of Article 12 (§ 16.1-299 et seq.) of this chapter or the provisions of Title 46.2, this record shall be available only to all law-enforcement officers, attorneys for the Commonwealth and courts. No other record of the proceeding shall be forwarded to the Department of Motor Vehicles unless the proceeding results in an adjudication of guilt pursuant to subsection F.

The Department of Motor Vehicles shall refuse to issue a driver's license to any child denied a driver's license until such time as is stipulated in the court order or until notification by the court of withdrawal of the order of denial under subsection E.

D. If the finding as to the child involves a violation designated under clause (i), (ii), (iii) or (vi) of subsection A, the child may be referred to a certified alcohol safety action program in accordance with § 18.2-271.1 upon such terms and conditions as the court may set forth. If the finding as to such child involves a violation designated under clause (iii), (iv), (v), (vii) or (viii) of subsection A, such child may be referred to appropriate rehabilitative or educational services upon such terms and conditions as the court may set forth.

The court, in its discretion and upon a demonstration of hardship, may authorize the use of a restricted permit to operate a motor vehicle by any child who has a driver's license at the time of the offense or at the time of the court's finding as provided in subsection A1 for any of the purposes set forth in subsection E of § 18.2-271.1 or for travel to and from school, except that no restricted license shall be issued for travel to and from home and school when school-provided transportation is available and no restricted license shall be issued if the finding as to such child involves a violation designated under clause (iii) or (iv) of subsection A, or if it involves a second or subsequent violation of any offense designated in subsection A or a second finding by the court of failure to comply with school attendance and meeting requirements as provided in subsection A1. The issuance of the restricted permit shall be set forth within the court order, a copy of which shall be provided to the child, and shall specifically enumerate the restrictions imposed and contain such information regarding the child as is reasonably necessary to identify him. The child may operate a motor vehicle under the court order in accordance with its terms. Any child who operates a motor vehicle in violation of any restrictions imposed pursuant to this section shall be guilty of a violation of § 46.2-301.

E. Upon petition made at least 90 days after issuance of the order, the court may review and withdraw any order of denial of a driver's license if for a first such offense or finding as provided in subsection A1. For a second or subsequent such offense or finding, the order may not be reviewed and withdrawn until one year after its issuance.

F. If the finding as to such child involves a first violation designated under clause (vii) of subsection A, upon fulfillment of the terms and conditions prescribed by the court and after the child's driver's license has been restored, the court shall or, in the event the violation resulted in the injury or death of any person or if the finding involves a violation designated under clause (i), (ii), (v), or (vi) of subsection A, may discharge the child and dismiss the proceedings against him. Discharge and dismissal under these provisions shall be without an adjudication of guilt but a record of the proceeding shall be retained for the purpose of applying this section in subsequent proceedings. Failure of the child to fulfill such terms and conditions shall result in an adjudication of guilt. If the finding as to such child involves a violation designated under clause (iii) or (iv) of subsection A, the charge shall not be dismissed pursuant to this subsection but shall be disposed of pursuant to the provisions of this chapter or § 18.2-251. If the finding as to such child involves a second violation under clause (v), (vi) or (vii) of subsection A, the charge shall not be dismissed pursuant to this subsection but shall be disposed of under § 16.1-278.8.

History.

1991, cc. 534, 696; 1992, cc. 701, 736, 830; 1993, cc. 482, 866, 972; 1994, c. 338; 2000, c. 835; 2001, cc. 248, 266; 2002, cc. 519, 755; 2003, c. 118; 2005, c. 895; 2007, c. 731; 2010, cc. 522, 569, 570.

§ 16.1-278.10. Traffic infractions.

In cases involving a child who is charged with a traffic infraction, the court may impose only those penalties which are authorized to be imposed on adults for such infractions.

History.
1991, c. 534.

§ 16.1-278.11. Mental illness and intellectual disability.

In cases involving a person who is involuntarily admitted because of a mental illness or is judicially certified as eligible for admission to a training center for persons with intellectual disability, disposition shall be in accordance with the provisions of Chapter 8 (§ 37.2-800 et seq.) of Title 37.2. A child shall not be committed pursuant to §§ 16.1-278.2 through 16.1-278.8 or the provisions of Title 37.2 to a maximum security unit within any state hospital where adults determined to be criminally insane reside.

History.
1991, c. 534; 2005, c. 716; 2012, cc. 476, 507.

§ 16.1-278.12. When judicial consent in lieu of parental consent authorized.

In cases involving judicial consent to the matters set out in subsections C and D of § 16.1-241, the juvenile court or the circuit court providing consent may also make any appropriate order to protect the health and welfare of the child.

History.
1991, c. 534.

§ 16.1-278.13. Work permits; petitions for treatment, etc.

In cases involving judicial consent to apply for a work permit for a child, the juvenile court shall enter an order either granting, in whole or in part, consent to such application or withholding such consent as is appropriate to protect the health and welfare of the child.

In cases involving petitions filed by or on behalf of a child or such child's parent to obtain treatment, rehabilitation or other services required by law to be provided for such persons, the juvenile court or the circuit court may enter an order in accordance with § 16.1-278.

History.
1991, cc. 511, 534.

§ 16.1-278.14. Criminal jurisdiction; protective orders; family offenses.

In cases involving the violation of any law, regulation or ordinance for the education, protection or care of children or involving offenses committed by one family or household member against another, the juvenile court or the circuit court may impose a penalty prescribed by applicable sections of the Code and may impose conditions and limitations upon the defendant to protect the health or safety of family or household members, including, but not limited to, a protective order as provided in § 16.1-279.1, treatment and counseling for the defendant and payment by the defendant for crisis shelter care for the complaining family or household member.

History.
1991, c. 534; 1992, c. 742; 1996, c. 866.

§ 16.1-279.1. Protective order in cases of family abuse.

A. In cases of family abuse, including any case involving an incarcerated or recently incarcerated respondent against whom a preliminary protective order has been issued pursuant to § 16.1-253.1, the court may issue a protective order to protect the health and safety of the petitioner and family or household members of the petitioner. A protective order issued under this section may include any one or more of the following conditions to be imposed on the respondent:

1. Prohibiting acts of family abuse or criminal offenses that result in injury to person or property;
2. Prohibiting such contacts by the respondent with the petitioner or family or household members of the petitioner as the court deems necessary for the health or safety of such persons;
3. Granting the petitioner possession of the residence occupied by the parties to the exclusion of the respondent; however, no such grant of possession shall affect title to any real or personal property;
4. Enjoining the respondent from terminating any necessary utility service to the residence to which the petitioner was granted possession pursuant to subdivision 3 or, where appropriate, ordering the respondent to restore utility services to that residence;
5. Granting the petitioner temporary possession or use of a motor vehicle owned by the petitioner alone or jointly owned by the parties to the exclusion of the respondent and enjoining the respondent from terminating any insurance, registration, or taxes on the motor vehicle and directing the respondent to maintain the insurance, registration, and taxes, as appropriate; however, no such grant of possession or use shall affect title to the vehicle;
6. Requiring that the respondent provide suitable alternative housing for the petitioner and, if appropriate, any other family or household member and where appropriate, requiring the respondent to pay deposits to connect or restore necessary utility services in the alternative housing provided;
7. Ordering the respondent to participate in treatment, counseling or other programs as the court deems appropriate;
8. Granting the petitioner the possession of any companion animal as defined in § 3.2-6500 if such petitioner meets the definition of owner in § 3.2-6500; and
9. Any other relief necessary for the protection of the petitioner and family or household members of

the petitioner, including a provision for temporary custody or visitation of a minor child.

A1. If a protective order is issued pursuant to subsection A, the court may also issue a temporary child support order for the support of any children of the petitioner whom the respondent has a legal obligation to support. Such order shall terminate upon the determination of support pursuant to § 20-108.1.

B. The protective order may be issued for a specified period of time up to a maximum of two years. The protective order shall expire at 11:59 p.m. on the last day specified or at 11:59 p.m. on the last day of the two-year period if no date is specified. Prior to the expiration of the protective order, a petitioner may file a written motion requesting a hearing to extend the order. Proceedings to extend a protective order shall be given precedence on the docket of the court. If the petitioner was a family or household member of the respondent at the time the initial protective order was issued, the court may extend the protective order for a period not longer than two years to protect the health and safety of the petitioner or persons who are family or household members of the petitioner at the time the request for an extension is made. The extension of the protective order shall expire at 11:59 p.m. on the last day specified or at 11:59 p.m. on the last day of the two-year period if no date is specified. Nothing herein shall limit the number of extensions that may be requested or issued.

C. A copy of the protective order shall be served on the respondent and provided to the petitioner as soon as possible. The court, including a circuit court if the circuit court issued the order, shall forthwith, but in all cases no later than the end of the business day on which the order was issued, enter and transfer electronically to the Virginia Criminal Information Network the respondent's identifying information and the name, date of birth, sex, and race of each protected person provided to the court and shall forthwith forward the attested copy of the protective order containing any such identifying information to the primary law-enforcement agency responsible for service and entry of protective orders. Upon receipt of the order by the primary law-enforcement agency, the agency shall forthwith verify and enter any modification as necessary to the identifying information and other appropriate information required by the Department of State Police into the Virginia Criminal Information Network established and maintained by the Department pursuant to Chapter 2 (§ 52-12 et seq.) of Title 52 and the order shall be served forthwith upon the respondent and due return made to the court. Upon service, the agency making service shall enter the date and time of service and other appropriate information required by the Department of State Police into the Virginia Criminal Information Network and make due return to the court. If the order is later dissolved or modified, a copy of the dissolution or modification order shall also be attested, forwarded forthwith to the primary law-enforcement agency responsible for service and entry of protective orders, and upon receipt of the order by the primary law-enforcement agency, the agency shall forthwith verify and enter any modification as necessary to the identifying information and other appropriate information required by the Department of State Police into the Virginia Criminal Information Network as described above and the order shall be served forthwith and due return made to the court.

D. Except as otherwise provided in § 16.1-253.2, a violation of a protective order issued under this section shall constitute contempt of court.

E. The court may assess costs and attorneys' fees against either party regardless of whether an order of protection has been issued as a result of a full hearing.

F. Any judgment, order or decree, whether permanent or temporary, issued by a court of appropriate jurisdiction in another state, the United States or any of its territories, possessions or Commonwealths, the District of Columbia or by any tribal court of appropriate jurisdiction for the purpose of preventing violent or threatening acts or harassment against or contact or communication with or physical proximity to another person, including any of the conditions specified in subsection A, shall be accorded full faith and credit and enforced in the Commonwealth as if it were an order of the Commonwealth, provided reasonable notice and opportunity to be heard were given by the issuing jurisdiction to the person against whom the order is sought to be enforced sufficient to protect such person's due process rights and consistent with federal law. A person entitled to protection under such a foreign order may file the order in any juvenile and domestic relations district court by filing with the court an attested or exemplified copy of the order. Upon such a filing, the clerk shall forthwith forward an attested copy of the order to the primary law-enforcement agency responsible for service and entry of protective orders which shall, upon receipt, enter the name of the person subject to the order and other appropriate information required by the Department of State Police into the Virginia Criminal Information Network established and maintained by the Department pursuant to Chapter 2 (§ 52-12 et seq.) of Title 52. Where practical, the court may transfer information electronically to the Virginia Criminal Information Network.

Upon inquiry by any law-enforcement agency of the Commonwealth, the clerk shall make a copy available of any foreign order filed with that court. A law-enforcement officer may, in the performance of his duties, rely upon a copy of a foreign protective order or other suitable evidence which has been provided to him by any source and may also rely upon the statement of any person protected by the order that the order remains in effect.

G. Either party may at any time file a written motion with the court requesting a hearing to dissolve or modify the order. Proceedings to dissolve or modify a protective order shall be given precedence on the docket of the court.

H. As used in this section:

"Copy" includes a facsimile copy; and

"Protective order" includes an initial, modified or extended protective order.

I. Neither a law-enforcement agency, the attorney for the Commonwealth, a court nor the clerk's office, nor any employee of them, may disclose, except among themselves, the residential address, telephone number, or place of employment of the person protected by the order or that of the family of such person, except to the extent that disclosure is (i) required by law or the Rules of the Supreme Court, (ii) necessary for law-enforcement purposes, or (iii) permitted by the court for good cause.

J. No fee shall be charged for filing or serving any petition or order pursuant to this section.

History.

1984, c. 631; 1987, c. 497; 1992, c. 886; 1994, cc. 360, 521, 739, 907; 1996, cc. 866, 900, 945; 1997, c. 603; 1998, c. 684; 2000, cc. 34, 654; 2002, cc. 508, 810, 818; 2004, cc. 972, 980; 2006, c. 308; 2008, cc. 73, 246; 2009, cc. 343, 732; 2010, cc. 425, 468; 2011, cc. 445, 480; 2012, cc. 152, 261; 2014, cc. 318, 346, 613; 2016, c. 102.

§ 16.1-283.2. Restoration of parental rights.

A. If a child is in the custody of the local department of social services and a pre-adoptive parent or parents have not been identified and approved for the child, the child's guardian ad litem or the local board of social services may file a petition to restore the previously terminated parental rights of the child's parent under the following circumstances:

1. The child is at least 14 years of age;

2. The child was previously adjudicated to be an abused or neglected child, child in need of services, child in need of supervision, or delinquent child;

3. The parent's rights were terminated under a final order pursuant to subsection B, C, or D of § 16.1-283 at least two years prior to the filing of the petition to restore parental rights;

4. The child has not achieved his permanency goal or the permanency goal was achieved but not sustained; and

5. The child, if he is 14 years of age or older, and the parent whose rights are to be reinstated consent to the restoration of the parental rights.

B. Notwithstanding the provisions of subsection A, the court may accept (i) a petition involving a child younger than 14 years of age if (a) the child is the sibling of a child for whom a petition for restoration of parental rights has been filed and the child who is younger than 14 years of age meets all other criteria for restoration of parental rights set forth in subsection A, or (b) the child's guardian ad litem and the local department of social services jointly file the petition for restoration; or (ii) a petition filed before the expiration of the two-year period following termination of parental rights if the child will turn 18 before the expiration of the two-year period, and the court finds that accepting such a petition is in the best interest of the child.

C. The court shall set a hearing on the petition and serve notice of the hearing along with a copy of the petition on the former parent of the child whose rights are the subject of the petition, any other parent who retains legal rights to the child, the child's court-appointed special advocate, if one has been appointed, and either the child's guardian ad litem or the local board of social services, whichever is not the petitioner.

D. If the court finds, based upon clear and convincing evidence, that the parent is willing and able to (i) receive and care for the child; (ii) have a positive, continuous relationship with the child; (iii) provide a permanent, suitable home for the child; and (iv) protect the child from abuse and neglect, the court may enter an order permitting the local board of social services to place the child with the former parent whose rights are the subject of the petition, subject to the requirements of the placement plan developed pursuant to subsection E and for visitation required pursuant to subsection F.

E. Within 60 days of the filing of the petition for restoration of parental rights and prior to the entry of an order pursuant to subsection D, the local board of social services shall develop a written placement plan for the child, which shall (i) describe the programs, services, and other supports that shall be offered to the child and the former parent with whom the child has been placed and (ii) set forth requirements for the participation of the former parent with whom the child has been placed in programs and services described in the placement plan and the conduct of the child's former parent with whom the child has been placed. Such plan shall be incorporated into the order entered pursuant to subsection D.

F. Following the placement of a child with his former parent following entry of an order pursuant to subsection D, the director of the local department of social services shall cause the child to be visited by an agent of such local board or local department at least three times within the six-month period immediately following placement of the child in order to evaluate the suitability of the placement and the progress of the former parent toward remedying the factors and conditions that led to or required continuation of the child's foster care placement; however, no less than 90 days shall elapse between the first visit and the last visit. At least one of the visits shall be conducted in the home of the former parent whose rights are the subject of the petition in the presence of the former parent.

G. Upon completion of the visitation required pursuant to subsection F, the director of the local department of social services shall make a written report to the court, in such form as the Commissioner of Social Services may prescribe, describing (i) findings made as a result of the visits required pursuant to subsection F and (ii) findings and information related to the former parent's compliance with requirements of the placement plan developed pursuant to subsection E.

H. Upon receipt of the report required pursuant to subsection G, the court shall set a hearing on the petition for restoration of parental rights and serve notice of the hearing, along with a copy of the report required pursuant to subsection G, on the former parent of the child whose rights are the subject of the petition, any other parent who retains legal rights to the child, the child's court-appointed special advocate, if one has been appointed, and the child's guardian ad litem.

I. If, upon consideration of the report required pursuant to subsection G, the court finds by clear and convincing evidence that the restoration of parental rights is in the child's best interest, the court shall enter an order restoring the parental rights of the child's parent. In determining whether restoration is in the best interest of the child, the court shall consider the following:

1. Whether the parent whose rights are to be reinstated agrees to the reinstatement and has substantially remedied the conditions that led to or required continuation of the child's foster care placement;

2. The age and maturity of the child and whether the child consents to the reinstatement of the former parent's rights, if the child is 14 years of age or older, or the child's preference with regard to the reinstatement of the former parent's rights, if the child is younger than 14 years of age;

3. Whether the restoration of parental rights will present a risk to the child's life, health, or development;

4. Whether the restoration of parental rights will affect benefits available to the child; and

5. Other material changes in circumstances, if any, that warrant the granting of the petition.

J. The court may revoke its order permitting the placement of a child with his former parent pursuant to subsection D at any time prior to entry of an order restoring parental rights to the former parent of the child, for good cause shown, on its own motion or on the motion of the child's guardian ad litem or the local department.

K. A petition for restoration of parental rights filed while the child is younger than 18 years of age shall not become invalid because the child reaches 18 years of age prior to the entry of an order of restoration of parental rights. Any order restoring parental rights to a parent of a child pursuant to this section entered after a child reaches 18 years of age, where the petition was filed prior to the child turning 18 years of age, shall have the same effect as if the child was under 18 years of age at the time the order was entered by the court.

L. The granting of a petition under this section does not vacate the findings of fact or conclusions of law contained in the original order that terminated the parental rights of the child's parent.

History.

2013, cc. 338, 685.

§ 16.1-284. When adult sentenced for juvenile offense.

A. When the juvenile court sentences an adult who has committed, before attaining the age of 18, an offense that would be a crime if committed by an adult, the court may impose, for each offense, the penalties that are authorized to be imposed on adults for such violations, not to exceed the punishment for a Class 1 misdemeanor, provided that the total jail sentence imposed shall not exceed 36 continuous months and the total fine shall not exceed $2,500 or the court may order a disposition as provided in subdivision A 4, 5, 7, 11, 12, 14, or 17 and subsection B of § 16.1-278.8.

B. A person sentenced pursuant to this section shall be entitled to good time credit as authorized by § 53.1-116.

History.

Code 1950, § 16.1-177.1; 1956, c. 555; 1973, c. 440; 1977, c. 559; 1978, c. 142; 1980, c. 235; 1983, c. 336; 1985, c. 260; 1996, cc. 755, 914; 2016, c. 626.

§ 16.1-284.1. Placement in secure local facility.

A. If a juvenile 14 years of age or older is found to have committed an offense which if committed by an adult would be punishable by confinement in a state or local correctional facility as defined in § 53.1-1, and the court determines (i) that the juvenile has not previously been and is not currently adjudicated delinquent of a violent juvenile felony or found guilty of a violent juvenile felony, (ii) that the juvenile has not been released from the custody of the Department within the previous 18 months, (iii) that the interests of the juvenile and the community require that the juvenile be placed under legal restraint or discipline, and (iv) that other placements authorized by this title will not serve the best interests of the juvenile, then the court may order the juvenile confined in a detention home or other secure facility for juveniles for a period not to exceed six months from the date the order is entered, for a single offense or multiple offenses. However, if the single offense or multiple offenses, which if committed by an adult would be punishable as a felony or a Class 1 misdemeanor, caused the death of any person, then the court may order the juvenile confined in a detention home or other secure facility for juveniles for a period not to exceed 12 months from the date the order is entered.

The period of confinement ordered may exceed 30 calendar days if the juvenile has had an assessment completed by the secure facility to which he is ordered concerning the appropriateness of the placement.

B. If the period of confinement in a detention home or other secure facility for juveniles is to exceed 30 calendar days, and the juvenile is eligible for commitment pursuant to subdivision A 14 of § 16.1-278.8, then the court shall order the juvenile committed to the Department, but suspend such commitment. In suspending the commitment to the Department as provided for in this subsection, the court shall specify conditions for the juvenile's satisfactory completion of one or more community or facility based treatment programs as may be appropriate for the juvenile's rehabilitation.

C. During any period of confinement which exceeds 30 calendar days ordered pursuant to this section, the court shall conduct a mandatory review hearing at least once during each 30 days and at such other times upon the request of the juvenile's probation officer, for good cause shown. If it appears at such hearing that the purpose of the order of confinement has been achieved, the juvenile shall be released on probation for such period and under such conditions as the court may specify and remain subject to the order suspending commitment to the State Department of Juvenile Justice. If the juvenile's commitment to the Department has been suspended as provided in subsection B of this section, and if the court determines at the first or any subsequent review hearing that the juvenile is consistently failing to comply with the conditions specified by the court or the policies and program requirements of the facility, then the court shall order that the juvenile be committed to the State Department of Juvenile Justice. If the court determines at the first or any subsequent review hearing that the juvenile is not actively involved in any community facility based treatment program through no fault of his own, then the court shall order that the juvenile be released under such conditions as the court may specify subject to the suspended commitment.

C1. The appearance of the juvenile before the court for a hearing pursuant to subsection C may be by (i) personal appearance before the judge or (ii) use of two-way electronic video and audio communication. If two-way electronic video and audio communication is used, a judge may exercise all powers conferred by law and all communications and proceedings shall be conducted in the same manner as if the appearance were in person, and any documents filed may be transmitted by facsimile process. A facsimile may be served or executed by the officer or person to whom sent, and returned in the same manner, and with the same force, effect, authority, and liability as an original document. All signatures thereon shall be treated as original signatures. Any two-way electronic video and audio communication system used for an appearance shall meet the standards as set forth in subsection B of § 19.2-3.1.

D. A juvenile may only be ordered confined pursuant to this section to a facility in compliance with standards established by the State Board for such placements. Standards for these facilities shall require juveniles placed pursuant to this section for a period which exceeds 30 calendar days be provided separate services for their rehabilitation, consistent with the intent of this section.

E. The Department of Juvenile Justice shall assist the localities or combinations thereof in implementing this section consistent with the statewide plan required by § 16.1-309.4 and pursuant to standards promulgated by the State Board, in order to ensure the availability and reasonable access of each court to the facilities the use of which is authorized by this section.

History.

1985, c. 260; 1989, c. 733; 1995, cc. 696, 699; 1996, cc. 755, 914; 2000, c. 978; 2001, c. 140; 2012, c. 94; 2013, c. 651; 2015, c. 391.

§ 16.1-285. Duration of commitments.

Except as provided in § 16.1-285.1, all commitments under this chapter shall be for an indeterminate period having regard to the welfare of the juvenile and interests of the public, but no juvenile committed hereunder shall be held or detained longer than thirty-six continuous months or after such juvenile has attained the age of twenty-one years. However, the thirty-six month limitation shall not apply in cases of commitment for an act of murder or manslaughter. The Department shall have the authority to discharge any juvenile or person from its custody, including releasing a juvenile or person to parole supervision, in accordance with policies and procedures established by the State Board and with other provisions of law. Parole supervision programs shall be operated through the court services units established pursuant to § 16.1-233. A juvenile or person who violates the conditions of his parole granted pursuant to this section may be proceeded against for a revocation or modification of parole status pursuant to § 16.1-291.

History.

Code 1950, § 16.1-180; 1956, c. 555; 1977, c. 559; 1985, cc. 260, 388; 1996, cc. 755, 914; 2000, cc. 954, 981, 988; 2001, c. 853.

§ 16.1-285.1. Commitment of serious offenders.

A. In the case of a juvenile fourteen years of age or older who has been found guilty of an offense which would be a felony if committed by an adult, and either (i) the juvenile is on parole for an offense which would be a felony if committed by an adult, (ii) the juvenile was committed to the state for an offense which would be a felony if committed by an adult within the immediately preceding twelve months, (iii) the felony offense is punishable by a term of confinement of greater than twenty years if the felony was committed by an adult, or (iv) the juvenile has been previously adjudicated delinquent for an offense which if committed by an adult would be a felony punishable by a term of confinement of twenty years or more, and the circuit court, or the juvenile or family court, as the case may be, finds that commitment under this section is necessary to meet the rehabilitative needs of the juvenile and would serve the best interests of the community, then the court may order the juvenile committed to the Department of Juvenile Justice for placement in a juvenile correctional center for the period of time prescribed pursuant to this section.

Alternatively, in order to determine if a juvenile, transferred from a juvenile and domestic relations district court to a circuit court pursuant to § 16.1-269.1, appropriately qualifies for commitment pursuant to this section, notwithstanding the inapplicability of the qualification criteria set forth in clauses (i) through (iv), the circuit court may consider the commitment criteria set forth in subdivisions 1, 2, and 3 of subsection B as well as other components of the juvenile's life history and, if upon such consideration in the opinion of the court the needs of the juvenile and the interests of the community would clearly best be served by commitment hereunder, may so commit the juvenile.

B. Prior to committing any juvenile pursuant to this section, the court shall consider:

1. The juvenile's age;

2. The seriousness and number of the present offenses, including (i) whether the offense was committed in an aggressive, violent, premeditated, or willful manner; (ii) whether the offense was against persons or property, with greater weight being given to offenses against persons, especially if death or injury resulted; (iii) whether the offense involved the use of a firearm or other dangerous weapon by brandishing, displaying, threatening with or otherwise employing such weapon; and (iv) the nature of the juvenile's participation in the alleged offense;

3. The record and previous history of the juvenile in this or any other jurisdiction, including (i) the number and nature of previous contacts with courts, (ii) the number and nature of prior periods of probation, (iii) the number and nature of prior commitments to juvenile correctional centers, (iv) the number and nature of previous residential and community-based treatments, (v) whether previous adjudications and commitments were for delinquent acts that involved the infliction of serious bodily injury, and (vi) whether the offense is part of a repetitive pattern of similar adjudicated offenses; and

4. The Department's estimated length of stay.

Such commitment order must be supported by a determination that the interests of the juvenile and community require that the juvenile be placed under legal restraint or discipline and that the juvenile is not a proper person to receive treatment or rehabilitation through other juvenile programs or facilities.

C. In ordering commitment pursuant to this section, the court shall specify a period of commitment not to exceed seven years or the juvenile's twenty-first birthday, whichever shall occur first. The court may also order a period of determinate or indeterminate parole supervision to follow the commitment but the total period of commitment and parole supervision shall not exceed seven years or the juvenile's twenty-first birthday, whichever occurs first.

D. Upon receipt of a juvenile committed under the provisions of this section, the Department shall evaluate the juvenile for the purpose of considering placement of the juvenile in an appropriate juvenile correctional center for the time prescribed by the committing court. Such a placement decision shall be made based on the availability of treatment programs at the facility; the level of security at the facility; the offense for which the juvenile has been committed; and the welfare, age and gender of the juvenile.

E. The court which commits the juvenile to the Department under this section shall have continuing jurisdiction over the juvenile throughout his commitment. The continuing jurisdiction of the court shall not prevent the Department from removing the juvenile from a juvenile correctional center without prior court approval for the sole purposes of routine or emergency medical treatment, routine educational services, or family emergencies.

F. Any juvenile committed under the provisions of this section shall not be released at a time earlier than that specified by the court in its dispositional order except as provided for in § 16.1-285.2. The Department may petition the committing court for a hearing as provided for in § 16.1-285.2 for an earlier release of the juvenile when good cause exists for an earlier release. In addition, the Department shall petition the committing court for a determination as to the continued commitment of each juvenile sentenced under this section at least sixty days prior to the second anniversary of the juvenile's date of commitment and sixty days prior to each annual anniversary thereafter.

History.

1985, c. 260; 1989, c. 717; 1992, c. 484; 1994, cc. 859, 949; 1996, cc. 755, 914; 2001, c. 563.

§ 16.1-285.2. Release and review hearing for serious offender.

A. Upon receipt of a petition of the Department of Juvenile Justice for a hearing concerning a juvenile committed under § 16.1-285.1, the court shall schedule a hearing within thirty days and shall appoint counsel for the juvenile pursuant to § 16.1-266. The court shall provide a copy of the petition, the progress report required by this section, and notice of the time and place of the hearing to (i) the juvenile, (ii) the juvenile's parent, legal guardian, or person standing in loco parentis, (iii) the juvenile's guardian ad litem, if any, (iv) the juvenile's legal counsel, and (v) the attorney for the Commonwealth who prosecuted the juvenile during the delinquency proceeding. The attorney for the Commonwealth shall provide notice of the time and place of the hearing by first-class mail to the last known address of any victim of the offense for which the juvenile was committed if such victim has submitted a written request for notification to the attorney for the Commonwealth.

B. The petition shall be filed in the committing court and shall be accompanied by a progress report from the Department. This report shall describe (i) the facility and living arrangement provided for the juvenile by the Department, (ii) the services and treatment programs afforded the juvenile, (iii) the juvenile's progress toward treatment goals and objectives, which shall include a summary of his educational progress, (iv) the juvenile's potential for danger to either himself or the community, and (v) a comprehensive aftercare plan for the juvenile.

B1. The appearance of the juvenile before the court may be by (i) personal appearance before the judge, or (ii) use of two-way electronic video and audio communication. If two-way electronic video and audio communication is used, a judge may exercise all powers conferred by law and all communications and proceedings shall be conducted in the same manner as if the appearance were in person, and any documents filed may be transmitted by facsimile process. A facsimile may be served or executed by the officer or person to whom sent, and returned in the same manner, and with the same force, effect, authority, and liability as an original document. All signatures thereon shall be treated as original signatures. Any two-way electronic video and audio communication system used for an appearance shall meet the standards as set forth in subsection B of § 19.2-3.1.

C. At the hearing the court shall consider the progress report. The court may also consider additional evidence from (i) probation officers, the juvenile correctional center, treatment professionals, and the court service unit; (ii) the juvenile, his legal counsel, parent, guardian or family member; or (iii) other sources the court deems relevant. The hearing and all records relating thereto shall be governed by the confidentiality provisions of Article 12 (§ 16.1-299 et seq.) of this chapter.

D. At the conclusion of the hearing, the court shall order (i) continued commitment of the juvenile to the Department for completion of the original determinate period of commitment or such lesser time as the court may order or (ii) release of the juvenile under such terms and conditions as the court may prescribe. In making a determination under this section, the court shall consider (i) the experiences and character of the juvenile before and after commitment, (ii) the nature of the offenses that the juvenile was found to have committed, (iii) the manner in which the offenses were committed, (iv) the protection of the community, (v) the recommendations of the Department, and (vi) any other factors the court deems relevant. The order of the court shall be final and not subject to appeal.

E. In the case of a juvenile convicted as an adult and committed as a serious offender under subdivision A 1 of § 16.1-272, at the conclusion of the review hearing, the circuit court shall order (i) the juvenile to begin serving any adult sentence in whole or in part that may include any remaining part of the original determinate period of commitment, or (ii) the suspension of the unserved portion of the adult sentence in whole or in part based upon the juvenile's successful completion of the commitment as a serious offender, or (iii) the continued commitment of the juvenile to the Department for completion of the original determinate period of commitment or such lesser time as the court may order, or (iv) the release of the juvenile under such terms and conditions as the court may prescribe.

History.

1994, cc. 859, 949; 1995, c. 536; 1996, cc. 755, 914; 2002, c. 511.

ARTICLE 12.

CONFIDENTIALITY AND EXPUNGEMENT.

§ 16.1-299. Fingerprints and photographs of juveniles.

A. All duly constituted police authorities having the power of arrest shall take fingerprints and photographs of any juvenile who is taken into custody and charged with a delinquent act an arrest for which, if committed by an adult, is required to be reported to the Central Criminal Records Exchange pursuant to subsection A of § 19.2-390. Whenever fingerprints are taken, they shall be maintained separately from adult records and a copy shall be filed with the juvenile court on forms provided by the Central Criminal Records Exchange.

B. If a juvenile of any age (i) is convicted of a felony, (ii) is adjudicated delinquent of an offense that would be a felony if committed by an adult, (iii) has a case involving an offense, which would be a felony if committed by an adult, that is dismissed pursuant to the deferred disposition provisions of § 16.1-278.8, or (iv) is convicted or adjudicated delinquent of any other offense for which a report to the Central Criminal Records Exchange is required by subsection C of § 19.2-390 if the offense were committed by an adult, copies of his fingerprints and a report of the disposition shall be forwarded to the Central Criminal Records Exchange and to the jurisdiction making the arrest by the clerk of the court which heard the case.

C. If a petition or warrant is not filed against a juvenile whose fingerprints or photographs have been taken in connection with an alleged violation of law, the fingerprint card, all copies of the fingerprints and all photographs shall be destroyed 60 days after fingerprints were taken. If a juvenile charged with a delinquent act other than a violent juvenile felony or a crime ancillary thereto is found not guilty, or in any other case resulting in a disposition for which fingerprints are not required to be forwarded to the Central Criminal Records Exchange, the court shall order that the fingerprint card, all copies of the fingerprints and all photographs be destroyed within six months of the date of disposition of the case.

History.

1977, c. 559; 1978, c. 383; 1979, c. 267; 1982, c. 514; 1985, c. 211; 1986, c. 264; 1993, cc. 468, 926; 1994, cc. 859, 949; 1996, cc. 755, 914; 1997, c. 657; 2000, c. 431; 2004, c. 464; 2008, c. 636.

§ 16.1-299.1. Sample required for DNA analysis upon conviction or adjudication of felony.

A juvenile convicted of a felony or adjudicated delinquent on the basis of an act which would be a felony if committed by an adult shall have a sample of his blood, saliva or tissue taken for DNA analysis provided the juvenile was 14 years of age or older at the time of the commission of the offense.

The provisions of Article 1.1 (§ 19.2-310.2 et seq.) of Chapter 18 of Title 19.2 shall apply to all persons and all DNA samples taken as required by this section, mutatis mutandis.

The Department of Juvenile Justice shall verify that a DNA sample required to be taken has been received by the Department of Forensic Science. In any case where a DNA sample has not been received, the Department of Juvenile Justice shall notify the court and the court shall require the person to submit a sample for DNA analysis.

History.

1996, cc. 755, 914; 1998, c. 280; 2003, cc. 150, 607; 2007, c. 528.

§ **16.1-299.2:** Repealed by Acts 2005, c. 843, cl. 2.

§ 16.1-301. Confidentiality of juvenile law-enforcement records; disclosures to school principal and others.

A. The court shall require all law-enforcement agencies to take special precautions to ensure that law-enforcement records concerning a juvenile are protected against disclosure to any unauthorized person. The police departments of the cities of the Commonwealth, and the police departments or sheriffs of the counties, as the case may be, shall keep separate records as to violations of law other than violations of motor vehicle laws committed by juveniles. Such records with respect to such juvenile shall not be open to public inspection nor their contents disclosed to the public unless a juvenile 14 years of age or older is charged with a violent juvenile felony as specified in subsections B and C of § 16.1-269.1.

B. Notwithstanding any other provision of law, the chief of police or sheriff of a jurisdiction or his designee may disclose, for the protection of the juvenile, his fellow students and school personnel, to the school principal that a juvenile is a suspect in or has been charged with (i) a violent juvenile felony, as specified in subsections B and C of § 16.1-269.1; (ii) a violation of any of the provisions of Article 1 (§ 18.2-77 et seq.) of Chapter 5 of Title 18.2; or (iii) a violation of law involving any weapon as described in subsection A of § 18.2-308. If a chief of police, sheriff or a designee has disclosed to a school principal pursuant to this section that a juvenile is a suspect in or has been charged with a crime listed above, upon a court disposition of a proceeding regarding such crime in which a juvenile is adjudicated delinquent, convicted, found not guilty or the charges are reduced, the chief of police, sheriff or a designee shall, within 15 days of the expiration of the appeal period, if there is no notice of appeal, provide notice of the disposition ordered by the court to the school principal to whom disclosure was made. If the court defers disposition or if charges are withdrawn, dismissed or nolle prosequi, the chief of police, sheriff or a designee shall, within 15 days of such action provide notice of such action to the school principal to whom disclosure was made. If charges are withdrawn in intake or handled informally without a court disposition or if charges are not filed within 90 days of the initial disclosure, the chief of police, sheriff or a designee shall so notify the school principal to whom disclosure was made. In addition to any other disclosure that is permitted by this subsection, the principal in his discretion may provide such information to a threat assessment team established by the local school division. No member of a threat assessment team shall (a) disclose any juvenile record information obtained pursuant to this section or (b) use such information for any purpose other than evaluating threats to students and school personnel. For the purposes of this subsection, "principal" also refers to the chief administrator of any private primary or secondary school.

C. Inspection of law-enforcement records concerning juveniles shall be permitted only by the following:

1. A court having the juvenile currently before it in any proceeding;

2. The officers of public and nongovernmental institutions or agencies to which the juvenile is currently committed, and those responsible for his supervision after release;

3. Any other person, agency, or institution, by order of the court, having a legitimate interest in the case or in the work of the law-enforcement agency;

4. Law-enforcement officers of other jurisdictions, by order of the court, when necessary for the discharge of their current official duties;

5. The probation and other professional staff of a court in which the juvenile is subsequently convicted of a criminal offense for the purpose of a presentence report or other dispositional proceedings, or by offi-

cials of penal institutions and other penal facilities to which he is committed, or by a parole board in considering his parole or discharge or in exercising supervision over him;

6. The juvenile, parent, guardian or other custodian and counsel for the juvenile by order of the court; and

7. As provided in §§ 19.2-389.1 and 19.2-390.

D. The police departments of the cities and towns and the police departments or sheriffs of the counties may release, upon request to one another and to state and federal law-enforcement agencies, and to law-enforcement agencies in other states, current information on juvenile arrests. The information exchanged shall be used by the receiving agency for current investigation purposes only and shall not result in the creation of new files or records on individual juveniles on the part of the receiving agency.

E. Upon request, the police departments of the cities and towns and the police departments or sheriffs of the counties may release current information on juvenile arrests or juvenile victims to the Virginia Workers' Compensation Commission solely for purposes of determining whether to make an award to the victim of a crime, and such information shall not be disseminated or used by the Commission for any other purpose than provided in § 19.2-368.3.

F. Nothing in this section shall prohibit the exchange of other criminal investigative or intelligence information among law-enforcement agencies.

G. Nothing in this section shall prohibit the disclosure of law-enforcement records concerning a juvenile to a court services unit-authorized diversion program in accordance with this chapter, which includes programs authorized by subdivision 1 of § 16.1-227 and § 16.1-260. Such records shall not be further disclosed by the authorized diversion program or any participants therein. Law-enforcement officers may prohibit a disclosure to such a program to protect a criminal investigation or intelligence information.

History.

Code 1950, § 16.1-163; 1956, c. 555; 1977, cc. 559, 618; 1978, c. 740; 1981, c. 175; 1993, cc. 468, 926; 1994, cc. 859, 949; 1995, c. 752; 1996, cc. 755, 914; 1997, c. 430; 2000, c. 211; 2001, c. 770; 2003, c. 119; 2005, c. 683; 2009, c. 286; 2013, c. 769; 2016, c. 234.

§ 16.1-302. Dockets, indices and order books; when hearings and records private; right to public hearing; presence of juvenile in court.

A. Every juvenile court shall keep a separate docket of cases arising under this law.

B. Every circuit court shall keep a separate docket, index, and, for entry of its orders, a separate order book or file for cases on appeal from the juvenile court except: (i) cases involving support pursuant to § 20-61 or subdivisions A 3, F or L of § 16.1-241; (ii) cases involving criminal offenses committed by adults which are commenced on a warrant or a summons as described in Title 19.2; and (iii) cases involving civil commitments of adults pursuant to Title 37.2. Such cases shall be docketed on the appropriate docket and the orders in such cases shall be entered in the appropriate order book as used with similar cases commenced in circuit court.

C. The general public shall be excluded from all juvenile court hearings and only such persons admitted as the judge shall deem proper. However, proceedings in cases involving an adult charged with a crime and hearings held on a petition or warrant alleging that a juvenile fourteen years of age or older committed an offense which would be a felony if committed by an adult shall be open. Subject to the provisions of subsection D for good cause shown, the court may, sua sponte or on motion of the accused or the attorney for the Commonwealth close the proceedings. If the proceedings are closed, the court shall state in writing its reasons and the statement shall be made a part of the public record.

D. In any hearing held for the purpose of adjudicating an alleged violation of any criminal law, or law defining a traffic infraction, the juvenile or adult so charged shall have a right to be present and shall have the right to a public hearing unless expressly waived by such person. The chief judge may provide by rule that any juvenile licensed to operate a motor vehicle who has been charged with a traffic infraction may waive court appearance and admit to the infraction or infractions charged if he or she and a parent, legal guardian, or person standing in loco parentis to the juvenile appear in person at the court or before a magistrate or sign and either mail or deliver to the court or magistrate a written form of appearance, plea and waiver, provided that the written form contains the notarized signature of the parent, legal guardian, or person standing in loco parentis to the juvenile.. An emancipated juvenile charged with a traffic infraction shall have the opportunity to waive court appearance and admit to the infraction or infractions if he or she appears in person at the court or before a magistrate or signs and either mails or delivers to the court or magistrate a written form of appearance, plea, and waiver, provided that the written plea form containing the signature of the emancipated juvenile is accompanied by a notarized sworn statement which details the facts supporting the claim of emancipated status. Whenever the sole purpose of a proceeding is to determine the custody of a child of tender years, the presence of such juvenile in court may be waived by the judge at any stage thereof.

History.

Code 1950, § 16.1-162; 1956, c. 555; 1958, c. 353; 1971, Ex. Sess., c. 228; 1975, c. 334; 1977, cc. 559, 585; 1978, c. 605; 1979, c. 393; 1983, c. 293; 1996, cc. 755, 914.

§ 16.1-302.1. Right of victim or representative to attend certain proceedings; notice of hearings.

During proceedings involving petitions or warrants alleging that a juvenile is delinquent, including proceedings on appeal, a victim may remain in the courtroom and shall not be excluded unless the court determines in its discretion, that the presence of the victim would impair the conduct of a fair trial. In any such case involving a minor victim, the court may permit an adult chosen by the minor victim to be present in the courtroom during the proceedings in addition to or in lieu of the minor's parent or guardian.

The attorney for the Commonwealth shall give prior notice of any such proceedings and changes in the scheduling thereof to any known victim and to any known adult chosen in accordance with this section by a minor victim at the address or telephone number, or both, provided in writing by such persons.

History.

1996, cc. 755, 914; 2000, c. 339.

§ 16.1-308. Effect of adjudication on status of child.

Except as otherwise provided by law for a juvenile found guilty of a felony in circuit court whose case is disposed of in the same manner as an adult criminal case, a finding of guilty on a petition charging delinquency under the provisions of this law shall not operate to impose any of the civil disabilities ordinarily imposed by conviction for a crime, nor shall any such finding operate to disqualify the child for employment by any state or local governmental agency.

Nothing in this section shall prohibit the State Police or a police department or sheriff's office that is a part of or administered by the Commonwealth or any political subdivision thereof from denying employment to a person who had been adjudicated delinquent where such denial is based on the nature and gravity of the offense, the time since adjudication, the time since completion of any sentence, and the nature of the job sought.

History.

Code 1950, § 16.1-179; 1956, c. 555; 1977, c. 559; 1996, cc. 755, 914; 2011, c. 622.

§ 16.1-309. Penalty.

A. Except as provided in §§ 16.1-299, 16.1-300, 16.1-301, 16.1-305 and 16.1-307, any person who (i) files a petition, (ii) receives a petition or has access to court records in an official capacity, (iii) participates in the investigation of allegations which form the basis of a petition, (iv) is interviewed concerning such allegations and whose information is derived solely from such interview or (v) is present during any court proceeding, who discloses or makes use of or knowingly permits the use of identifying information not otherwise available to the public concerning a juvenile who is suspected of being or is the subject of a proceeding within the jurisdiction of the juvenile court pursuant to subdivisions 1 through 5 of subsection A of § 16.1-241 or who is in the custody of the State Department of Juvenile Justice, which information is directly or indirectly derived from the records or files of a law-enforcement agency, court or the Department of Juvenile Justice or acquired in the course of official duties, shall be guilty of a Class 3 misdemeanor.

B. The provisions of this section shall not apply to any law-enforcement officer or school employee who discloses to school personnel identifying information concerning a juvenile who is suspected of committing or has committed a delinquent act that has met applicable criteria of § 16.1-260 and is committed or alleged to have been committed on school property during a school-sponsored activity or on the way to or from such activity, if the disclosure is made solely for the purpose of enabling school personnel to take appropriate disciplinary action within the school setting against the juvenile. Further, the provisions of this section shall not apply to school personnel who disclose information obtained pursuant to §§ 16.1-305.1 and 22.1-288.2, if the disclosure is made in compliance with those sections.

History.

1977, c. 559; 1978, c. 626; 1979, c. 481; 1989, cc. 520, 733; 1993, cc. 645, 889; 1994, cc. 835, 913; 1996, cc. 755, 914; 2003, c. 119.

§ 16.1-309.1. Exception as to confidentiality.

A. Notwithstanding any other provision of this article, where consideration of public interest requires, the judge shall make available to the public the name and address of a juvenile and the nature of the offense for which a juvenile has been adjudicated delinquent (i) for an act which would be a Class 1, 2, or 3 felony, forcible rape, robbery or burglary or a related offense as set out in Article 2 (§ 18.2-89 et seq.) of Chapter 5 of Title 18.2 if committed by an adult or (ii) in any case where a juvenile is sentenced as an adult in circuit court.

B. 1. a. At any time prior to disposition, if a juvenile charged with a delinquent act which would constitute a felony if committed by an adult, or held in custody by a law-enforcement officer, or held in a secure facility pursuant to such charge becomes a fugitive from justice, the attorney for the Commonwealth or, upon notice to the Commonwealth's attorney, the Department of Juvenile Justice or a locally operated court services unit, may, with notice to the juvenile's attorney of record, petition the court having jurisdiction of the offense to authorize public release of the juvenile's name, age, physical description and photograph, the charge for which he is sought or for which he was adjudicated and any other information which may expedite his apprehension. Upon a showing that the juvenile is a fugitive and for good cause, the court shall order release of this information to the public. If a juvenile charged with a delinquent act that would constitute a felony if committed by an adult, or held in custody by a law-enforcement officer, or held in a secure facility pursuant to such charge becomes a fugitive from justice at a time when the court is not in session, the Commonwealth's attorney, the Department of Juvenile Justice, or a locally operated court services unit may, with notice to the juvenile's attorney of record, authorize the public release of the juvenile's name, age, physical description and photograph, the charge for which he is sought, and any other information which may expedite his apprehension.

b. At any time prior to disposition, if a juvenile charged with a delinquent act which would constitute a misdemeanor if committed by an adult, or held in custody by a law-enforcement officer, or held in a secure facility pursuant to such charge becomes a fugitive from justice, the attorney for the Commonwealth may, with notice to the juvenile's attorney of record, petition the court having jurisdiction of the offense to authorize public release of the juvenile's name, age, physical description and photograph, the charge for which he is sought or for which he was adjudicated and any other information which may expedite his apprehension. Upon a showing that the juvenile is a fugitive and for good cause, the court shall order release of this information to the public. If a juvenile charged with a delinquent act that would constitute a misdemeanor if committed by an adult, or held in custody by a law-enforcement officer, or held in a secure facility pursuant to such charge becomes a fugitive from justice at a time when the court is not in session, the attorney for the Commonwealth may, with notice to the juvenile's attorney of record, authorize the public release of the juvenile's name, age, physical description and photograph, the charge for which he is sought, and any other information which may expedite his apprehension.

2. After final disposition, if a juvenile (i) found to have committed a delinquent act becomes a fugitive from justice or (ii) who has been committed to the Department of Juvenile Justice pursuant to subdivision 14 of § 16.1-278.8 or 16.1-285.1 becomes a fugitive from justice by escaping from a facility operated by or under contract with the Department or from the custody of any employee of such facility, the Department may release to the public the juvenile's name, age, physical description and photograph, the charge for which he is sought or for which he was committed, and any other information which may expedite his apprehension. The Department shall promptly notify the attorney for the Commonwealth of the jurisdiction in which the juvenile was tried whenever information is released pursuant to this subdivision. If a juvenile specified in clause (i) being held after disposition in a secure facility not operated by or under contract with the Department becomes a fugitive by such escape, the attorney for the Commonwealth of the locality in which the facility is located may release the information as provided in this subdivision.

C. Whenever a juvenile 14 years of age or older is charged with a delinquent act that would be a criminal violation of Article 2 (§ 18.2-38 et seq.) of Chapter 4 of Title 18.2, a felony involving a weapon, a felony violation of Article 1 (§ 18.2-247 et seq.) of Chapter 7 of Title 18.2, or an "act of violence" as defined in subsection A of § 19.2-297.1 if committed by an adult, the judge may, where consideration of the public interest requires, make the juvenile's name and address available to the public.

D. Upon the request of a victim of a delinquent act that would be a felony or that would be a misdemeanor violation of § 16.1-253.2, 18.2-57, 18.2-57.2, 18.2-60.3, 18.2-60.4, 18.2-67.4, or 18.2-67.5 if committed by an adult, the court may order that such victim be informed of the charge or charges brought, the findings of the court, and the disposition of the case. For purposes of this section, "victim" shall be defined as in § 19.2-11.01.

E. Upon request, the judge or clerk may disclose if an order of emancipation of a juvenile pursuant to § 16.1-333 has been entered, provided (i) the order is not being appealed, (ii) the order has not been terminated, or (iii) there has not been a judicial determination that the order is void ab initio.

F. Notwithstanding any other provision of law, a copy of any court order that imposes a curfew or other restriction on a juvenile may be provided to the chief law-enforcement officer of the county or city wherein the juvenile resides. The chief law-enforcement officer shall only disclose information contained in the court order to other law-enforcement officers in the conduct of official duties.

G. Notwithstanding any other provision of law, where consideration of public safety requires, the Department and locally operated court service unit shall release information relating to a juvenile's criminal street gang involvement, if any, and the criminal street gang-related activity and membership of others, as criminal street gang is defined in § 18.2-46.1, obtained from an investigation or supervision of a juvenile and shall include the identity or identifying information of the juvenile; however, the Department and local court service unit shall not release the identifying information of a juvenile not affiliated with or involved in a criminal street gang unless that information relates to a specific criminal act. Such information shall be released to any State Police, local police department, sheriff's office, or law-enforcement task force that is a part of or administered by the Commonwealth or any political subdivision thereof, and that is responsible for the prevention and detection of crime and the enforcement of the penal, traffic, or highway laws of the Commonwealth. The exchange of information shall be for the purpose of an investigation into criminal street gang activity.

H. Notwithstanding any other provision of Article 12 (§ 16.1-299 et seq.), an intake officer shall report to the Bureau of Immigration and Customs Enforcement of the United States Department of Homeland Security a juvenile who has been detained in a secure facility based on an allegation that the juvenile committed a violent juvenile felony and who the intake officer has probable cause to believe is in the United States illegally.

History.
1979, c. 94; 1981, c. 307; 1986, c. 506; 1988, c. 749; 1993, c. 297; 1994, cc. 499, 542; 1995, cc. 558, 687, 804; 1997, cc. 434, 452; 1999, c. 710; 2000, cc. 563, 603; 2005, c. 364; 2006, cc. 259, 309, 682; 2008, c. 798; 2010, cc. 367, 472, 526; 2014, c. 230.

ARTICLE 12.1.

VIRGINIA JUVENILE COMMUNITY CRIME CONTROL ACT.

§ 16.1-309.2. Purpose and intent.

The General Assembly, to ensure the imposition of appropriate and just sanctions and to make the most efficient use of correctional resources for those juveniles before intake on complaints or the court on petitions alleging that the juvenile is a child in need of services, child in need of supervision, or delinquent, has determined that it is in the best interest of the Commonwealth to establish a community-based system of progressive intensive sanctions and services that correspond to the severity of offense and treatment needs. The purpose of this system shall be to deter crime by providing immediate, effective punishment that emphasizes accountability of the juvenile offender for his actions as well as reduces the pattern of repeat offending. In furtherance of this purpose, counties, cities or combinations thereof are encouraged to develop, implement, operate and evaluate programs and services responsive to their specific juvenile offender needs and juvenile crime trends.

This article shall be interpreted and construed to accomplish the following purposes:

1. Promote an adequate level of services to be available to every juvenile and domestic relations district court.

2. Ensure local autonomy and flexibility in addressing juvenile crime.

3. Encourage a public and private partnership in the design and delivery of services for juveniles who come before intake on a complaint or the court on a petition alleging a child is in need of services, in need of supervision or delinquent.

4. Emphasize parental responsibility and provide community-based services for juveniles and their families which hold them accountable for their behavior.

5. Establish a locally driven statewide planning process for the allocation of state resources.

6. Promote the development of an adequate service capacity for juveniles before intake on a complaint or the court on petitions alleging status or delinquent offenses.

History.
1995, cc. 698, 840; 1996, cc. 671, 682.

§ 16.1-309.3. Establishment of a community-based system of services; biennial local plan; quarterly report.

A. Any county, city or combination thereof may establish a community-based system pursuant to this article, which shall provide, or arrange to have accessible, a variety of predispositional and postdispositional services. These services may include, but are not limited to, diversion, community service, restitution, house arrest, intensive juvenile supervision, substance abuse assessment and testing, first-time offender programs, intensive individual and family treatment, structured day treatment and structured residential programs, aftercare/parole community supervision and residential and nonresidential services for juvenile offenders who are before intake on complaints or the court on petitions alleging that the juvenile is delinquent, in need of services or in need of supervision but shall not include secure detention for the purposes of this article. Such community-based systems shall be based on an annual review of court-related data and an objective assessment of the need for services and programs for juveniles before intake on complaints or the court on petitions alleging that the juvenile is a child in need of services, in need of supervision, or delinquent. The community- based system shall be developed after consultation with the judge or judges of the juvenile and domestic relations district court, the director of the court services unit, the community policy and management team established under § 2.2-5205, and, if applicable, the director of any program established pursuant to § 66-26.

B. Community-based services instituted pursuant to this article shall be administered by a county, city or combination thereof, and may be administered through a community policy and management team established under § 2.2-5204 or a commission established under § 16.1-315. Such programs and services may be provided by qualified public or private agencies, pursuant to appropriate contracts. Any commission established under § 16.1-315 providing predispositional and postdispositional services prior to the enactment of this article which serves the City of Chesapeake or the City of Hampton shall directly receive the proportion of funds calculated under § 16.1-309.7 on behalf of the owner localities. The funds received shall be allocated directly to the member localities. Any member locality which elects to withdraw from the commission shall be entitled to its full allocation as provided in §§ 16.1-309.6 and 16.1-309.7. The Department of

Juvenile Justice shall provide technical assistance to localities, upon request, for establishing or expanding programs or services pursuant to this article.

C. Funds provided to implement the provisions of this article shall not be used to supplant funds established as the state pool of funds under § 2.2-5211.

D. Any county, city or combination thereof which establishes a community-based system pursuant to this article shall biennially submit to the State Board for approval a local plan for the development, implementation and operation of such services, programs and facilities pursuant to this article. The plan shall provide (i) the projected number of juveniles served by alternatives to secure detention and (ii) any reduction in secure detention rates and commitments to state care as a result of programs funded pursuant to this article. The State Board shall solicit written comments on the plan from the judge or judges of the juvenile and domestic relations court, the director of the court services unit, and if applicable, the director of programs established pursuant to § 66-26. Prior to the initiation of any new services, the plan shall also include a cost comparison for the private operation of such services.

E. Each locality shall report quarterly to the Director the data required by the Department to measure progress on stated objectives and to evaluate programs and services within such locality's plan.

History.
1995, cc. 698, 840; 1996, cc. 671, 682; 1997, c. 347; 2000, cc. 195, 806; 2007, c. 813.

§ 16.1-309.4. Statewide plan for juvenile services.

It shall be the duty of the Department of Juvenile Justice to devise, develop and promulgate a statewide plan for the establishment and maintenance of a range of institutional and community-based, diversion, predispositional and postdispositional services to be reasonably accessible to each court. The Department shall be responsible for the collection and dissemination of the required court data necessary for the development of the plan. The plan shall utilize the information provided by local plans submitted under § 16.1-309.3. The plan shall be submitted to the Board on or before July 1 in odd-numbered years. The plan shall include a biennial forecast with appropriate annual updates as may be required of future juvenile correctional center and detention home needs.

History.
1995, cc. 698, 840; 1996, cc. 671, 682, 755, 914.

§ 16.1-309.5. Construction, etc., of detention homes and other facilities; reimbursement in part by Commonwealth.

A. The Commonwealth shall reimburse any county, city or any combination thereof for one-half the cost of construction, enlargement, renovation, purchase or rental of a detention home or other facilities the plans and specifications of which were approved by the Board and the Governor in accordance with the provisions of subsection C of this section.

B. The construction, renovation, purchase, rental, maintenance and operation of a detention home or other facilities established by a county, city or any combination thereof and the necessary expenses incurred in operating such facilities shall be the responsibility of the county, city or any combination thereof.

C. The Board shall promulgate regulations to include criteria to serve as guidelines in evaluating requests for such reimbursements and to ensure the geographically equitable distribution of state funds provided for such purpose. Priority funding shall be given to multijurisdictional initiatives. No such reimbursement for costs of construction shall be made, however, unless the plans and specifications, including the need for additional personnel therefor, have been submitted to the Governor and the construction has been approved by him. Such reimbursement shall be paid by the State Treasurer out of funds appropriated to the Department. In the event that a county or city requests and receives financial assistance from other public fund sources outside the provisions of this law, the total financial assistance and reimbursement shall not exceed the total construction cost of the project exclusive of land and site improvement costs, and such funds shall not be considered state funds.

History.
1995, cc. 698, 840; 2000, cc. 562, 601.

§ 16.1-309.6. How state appropriations for operating costs of Juvenile Community Crime Control Act programs determined; notice of financial aid.

The Governor's proposed biennial budget shall include, for each fiscal year, an appropriation for operating costs for Juvenile Community Crime Control Act programs. The proposed appropriation shall include amounts for compensating counties, cities and combinations thereof which elect to establish a system of community-based services pursuant to this article. Upon approval pursuant to the provisions of this article, any county, city or combination thereof which utilized predispositional or postdispositional block grant services or programs in fiscal year 1995 shall contribute an amount not less than the sum of its fiscal year 1995 expenditures for child care day placements in predispositional and postdispositional block grant alternatives to secure detention for implementation of its local plan. Such amount shall not include any expenditures in fiscal year 1995 for secure detention and placements made pursuant to § 2.2-5211.

The Department shall review annually the costs of operating services, programs and facilities pursuant to this article and recommend adjustments to maintain the Commonwealth's proportionate share. The Department shall no later than the fifteenth day following adjournment sine die of the General Assembly provide each county and city an estimate of funds appropriated pursuant to this article.

History.
1995, cc. 698, 840; 1996, cc. 671, 682; 1998, c. 54.

§ 16.1-309.7. Determination of payment.

A. The Commonwealth shall provide financial assistance to localities whose plans have been approved pursuant to subsection D of § 16.1-309.3 in quarterly payments based on the annual calculated costs which shall be determined as follows:

1. For community diversion services, one-half of the calculated costs as determined by the following factors: (i) the statewide daily average costs for predispositional nonresidential services and (ii) the total number of children in need of services and children in need of supervision complaints diverted at intake by the locality in the previous year.

2. For predispositional community-based services, three-quarters of the calculated costs as determined by the following factors: (i) the statewide daily average cost evenly divided for predispositional community-based residential and nonresidential services and (ii) the number of arrests of juveniles based on the locality's most recent year available Uniform Crime Reports for (a) one-third of all Part 1 crimes against property, (b) one-third of all drug offenses and (c) all remaining Part 2 arrests.

3. For postdispositional community-based services for adjudicated juveniles, one-half of the calculated costs as determined by the following factors: (i) the statewide average daily costs for postdispositional community-based nonresidential services and (ii) the locality's total number of juveniles, who, in the previous year, were adjudicated delinquent for the first time.

4. For postdispositional community-based services for juveniles adjudicated delinquent for a second or subsequent offense, one-half of the calculated costs as determined by the following factors: (i) the statewide average daily costs evenly divided for postdispositional community-based residential and nonresidential services and (ii) the locality's total number of court dispositions which, in the previous year, adjudicated juveniles as (a) delinquent for a second or subsequent offense, (b) children in need of services, or (c) children in need of supervision, less those juveniles receiving services under the provisions of §§ 16.1-285.1 and 16.1-286.

B. Any moneys distributed by the Commonwealth under this article which are unexpended at the end of each fiscal year within a biennium shall be retained by the county, city or combination thereof and subsequently expended for operating expenses of Juvenile Community Crime Control Act programs. Any surplus funds remaining at the end of a biennium shall be returned to the state treasury.

History.
1995, cc. 698, 840; 1996, cc. 820, 970.

§ 16.1-309.8. Costs of maintenance of juveniles in Community Crime Control Act programs.

Any county, city or combination thereof operating a Juvenile Community Crime Control Act program may collect from any locality of this Commonwealth from which a juvenile is placed in its program a daily rate calculated to allow the operating locality or localities to meet but not exceed the costs of providing services. Additionally, this rate may not be higher than the rate charged other counties, cities or combinations thereof using the same program.

History.
1995, cc. 698, 840; 1996, cc. 671, 682; 1998, c. 538.

§ 16.1-309.9. Establishment of standards; determination of compliance.

A. The State Board of Juvenile Justice shall develop, promulgate and approve standards for the development, implementation, operation and evaluation of the range of community-based programs, services and facilities authorized by this article. The State Board shall also approve minimum standards for the construction and equipment of detention homes or other facilities and for food, clothing, medical attention, and supervision of juveniles to be housed in these facilities and programs.

B. The State Board may prohibit, by its order, the placement of juveniles in any place of residence which does not comply with the minimum standards. It may limit the number of juveniles to be detained or housed in a detention home or other facility and may designate some other place of detention or housing for juveniles who would otherwise be held therein.

C. The Department shall periodically review all services established and annually review expenditures made under this article to determine compliance with the approved local plans and operating standards. If the Department determines that a program is not in substantial compliance with the approved plan or standards, the Department may suspend all or any portion of financial aid made available to the locality until there is compliance.

D. Orders of the State Board of Juvenile Justice shall be enforced by circuit courts as is provided for the enforcement of orders of the State Board of Corrections under § 53.1-70.

History.
1995, cc. 698, 840.

§ 16.1-309.10. Visitation and management of detention homes; other facilities; reports of superintendent.

In the event that a detention home, group home or other residential care facility for children in need of services or delinquent or alleged delinquent youth is established by a county, city, or any combination thereof, it shall be subject to visitation, inspection and regulation by the State Board or its agents, and shall be furnished and operated so far as possible as a family home under the management of a superintendent. It shall be the duty of the superintendent to furnish the Department such reports and other statistical data relating to the operation of such detention homes, group homes or other residential care facilities for children in need of services or delinquent or alleged delinquent youth as may be required by the Director.

History.
1995, cc. 698, 840.

ARTICLE 18.

JUVENILE COMPETENCY.

§ 16.1-356. Raising question of competency to stand trial; evaluation and determination of competency.

A. If, at any time after the attorney for the juvenile has been retained or appointed pursuant to a delinquency proceeding and before the end of trial, the court finds, sua sponte or upon hearing evidence or representations of counsel for the juvenile or the attorney for the Commonwealth, that there is probable cause to believe that the juvenile lacks substantial capacity to understand the proceedings against him or to assist his attorney in his own defense, the court shall order that a competency evaluation be performed by at least one psychiatrist, clinical psychologist, licensed professional counselor, licensed clinical social worker, or licensed marriage and family therapist, who is qualified by training and experience in the forensic evaluation of juveniles.

The Commissioner of Behavioral Health and Developmental Services shall approve the training and qualifications for individuals authorized to conduct juvenile competency evaluations and provide restoration services to juveniles pursuant to this article. The Commissioner shall also provide all juvenile courts with a list of guidelines for the court to use in the determination of qualifying individuals as experts in matters relating to juvenile competency and restoration.

B. The evaluation shall be performed on an outpatient basis at a community services board or behavioral health authority, juvenile detention home or juvenile justice facility unless the court specifically finds that (i) the results of the outpatient competency evaluation indicate that hospitalization of the juvenile for evaluation of competency is necessary or (ii) the juvenile is currently hospitalized in a psychiatric hospital. If one of these findings is made, the court, under authority of this subsection, may order the juvenile sent to a hospital designated by the Commissioner of Behavioral Health and Developmental Services as appropriate for the evaluation of juveniles against whom a delinquency petition has been filed.

C. The court shall require the attorney for the Commonwealth to provide to the evaluators appointed under subsection A any information relevant to the evaluation, including, but not limited to (i) a copy of the warrant or petition, (ii) the names and addresses of the attorney for the Commonwealth, the attorney for the juvenile, and the judge ordering the evaluation; and (iii) information about the alleged offense. The court shall require the attorney for the juvenile to provide to the evaluator only the psychiatric records and other information that is deemed relevant to the evaluation of competency. The moving party shall provide the evaluator a summary of the reasons for the evaluation request. All information required by this subsection shall be provided to the evaluator within 96 hours of the issuance of the court order requiring the evaluation and when applicable, shall be submitted prior to admission to the facility providing the inpatient evaluation. If the 96-hour period expires on a Saturday, Sunday or other legal holiday, the 96 hours shall be extended to the next day which is not a Saturday, Sunday or legal holiday.

D. If the juvenile is hospitalized under the provisions of subsection B, the juvenile shall be hospitalized for such time as the director of the hospital deems necessary to perform an adequate evaluation of the juvenile's competency, but not to exceed 10 days from the date of admission to the hospital. All evaluations shall be completed and the report filed with the court within 14 days of receipt by the evaluator of all information required under subsection C.

E. Upon completion of the evaluation, the evaluator shall promptly and in no event exceeding 14 days after receipt of all required information submit the report in writing to the court and the attorneys of record concerning (i) the juvenile's capacity to understand the proceedings against him; (ii) his ability to assist his attorney; and (iii) his need for services in the event he is found incompetent, including a description of the suggested necessary services and least restrictive setting to assist the juvenile in restoration to competency. No statements of the juvenile relating to the alleged offense shall be included in the report.

F. After receiving the report described in subsection E, the court shall promptly determine whether the juvenile is competent to stand trial for adjudication or disposition. A hearing on the juvenile's competency is not required unless one is requested by the attorney for the Commonwealth or the attorney for the juvenile or when required under § 16.1-357 B. If a hearing is held, the party alleging that the juvenile is incompetent shall bear the burden of proving by a preponderance of the evidence the juvenile's incompetency. The juvenile shall have the right to notice of the hearing and the right to personally participate in and introduce evidence at the hearing.

If the juvenile is otherwise able to understand the charges against him and assist in his defense, a finding of incompetency shall not be made based solely on any or all of the following: (i) the juvenile's age or developmental factors, (ii) the juvenile's claim to be unable to remember the time period surrounding the alleged offense, or (iii) the fact that the juvenile is under the influence of medication.

History.

1999, cc. 958, 997; 2000, c. 337; 2005, c. 110; 2009, cc. 813, 840.

§ 16.1-357. Disposition when juvenile found incompetent.

A. Upon finding pursuant to subsection F of § 16.1-356 that the juvenile is incompetent, the court shall order that the juvenile receive services to restore his competency in either a nonsecure community setting or a secure facility as defined in § 16.1-228. A copy of the order shall be forwarded to the Commissioner of Behavioral Health and Developmental Services, who shall arrange for the provision of restoration services in a manner consistent with the order. Any report submitted pursuant to subsection E of § 16.1-356 shall be made available to the agent providing restoration.

B. If the court finds the juvenile incompetent but restorable to competency in the foreseeable future, it shall order restoration services for up to three months. At the end of three months from the date restoration is ordered under subsection A of this section, if the juvenile remains incompetent in the opinion of the agent providing restoration, the agent shall so notify the court and make recommendations concerning disposition of the juvenile. The court shall hold a hearing according to the procedures specified in subsection F of § 16.1-356 and, if it finds the juvenile unrestorably incompetent, shall order one of the dispositions pursuant to § 16.1-358. If the court finds the juvenile incompetent but restorable to competency, it may order continued restoration services for additional three-month periods, provided a hearing pursuant to subsection F of § 16.1-356 is held at the completion of each such period and the juvenile continues to be incompetent but restorable to competency in the foreseeable future.

C. If, at any time after the juvenile is ordered to undergo services under subsection A of this section, the agent providing restoration believes the juvenile's competency is restored, the agent shall immediately send a report to the court as prescribed in subsection E of § 16.1-356. The court shall make a ruling on the juvenile's competency according to the procedures specified in subsection F of § 16.1-356.

History.

1999, cc. 958, 997; 2009, cc. 813, 840.

§ 16.1-358. Disposition of the unrestorably incompetent juvenile.

If, at any time after the juvenile is ordered to undergo services pursuant to subsection A of § 16.1-357, the agent providing restoration concludes that the juvenile is likely to remain incompetent for the foreseeable future, he shall send a report to the court so stating. The report shall also indicate whether, in the agent's opinion, the juvenile should be (i) committed pursuant to Article 16 (§ 16.1-335 et seq.) of this chapter or, if the juvenile has reached the age of eighteen years at the time of the competency determination, pursuant to Article 5 (§ 37.2-814 et seq.) of Chapter 8 of Title 37.2, (ii) certified pursuant to § 37.2-806, (iii) provided other services by the court, or (iv) released. Upon receipt of the report, the court shall make a competency determination according to the procedures specified in subsection F of § 16.1-356. If the court finds that the juvenile is incompetent and is likely to remain so for the foreseeable future, it shall order that the juvenile (i) be committed pursuant to Article 16 (§ 16.1-335 et seq.) of this chapter or, if the juvenile has reached the age of eighteen years at the time of the competency determination, pursuant to Article 5 (§ 37.2-814 et seq.) of Chapter 8 of Title 37.2, (ii) be certified pursuant to § 37.2-806, (iii) have a child in need of services petition filed on his behalf pursuant to § 16.1-260 D, or (iv) be released. If the court finds the juvenile incompetent but restorable to competency in the foreseeable future, it may order restoration services continued until three months have elapsed from the date of the provision of restoration ordered under subsection A of § 16.1-357.

If not dismissed without prejudice at an earlier time, charges against an unrestorably incompetent juvenile shall be dismissed in compliance with the time frames as follows: in the case of a charge which would be a misdemeanor, one year from the date of the juvenile's arrest for such charge; and in the case of a charge which would be a felony, three years from the date of the juvenile's arrest for such charges.

History.

1999, cc. 958, 997; 2000, c. 216.

§ 16.1-359. Litigating certain issues when the juvenile is incompetent.

A finding of incompetency does not preclude the adjudication, at any time before trial, of a motion objecting to the sufficiency of the petition, nor does it preclude the adjudication of similar legal objections which, in the court's opinion, may be undertaken without the personal participation of the juvenile.

History.
1999, cc. 958, 997.

§ 16.1-360. Disclosure by juvenile during evaluation or restoration; use at guilt phase of trial adjudication or disposition hearing.

No statement or disclosure by the juvenile concerning the alleged offense made during a competency evaluation ordered pursuant to § 16.1-356, or services ordered pursuant to § 16.1-357 may be used against the juvenile at the adjudication or disposition hearings as evidence or as a basis for such evidence.

History.
1999, cc. 958, 997.

§ 16.1-361. Compensation of experts.

Each psychiatrist, clinical psychologist, licensed clinical social worker, licensed professional counselor, licensed marriage and family therapist, or other expert appointed by the court to render professional service pursuant to § 16.1-356, shall receive a reasonable fee for such service. With the exception of services provided by state hospitals or training centers, the fee shall be determined in each instance by the court that appointed the expert, in accordance with guidelines established by the Supreme Court after consultation with the Department of Behavioral Health and Developmental Services. If any such expert is required to appear as a witness in any hearing held pursuant to § 16.1-356, he shall receive mileage and a fee of $100 for each day during which he is required to serve. An itemized account of expenses, duly sworn to, must be presented to the court, and when allowed shall be certified to the Supreme Court for payment out of the state treasury, and be charged against the appropriations made to pay criminal charges. Allowance for the fee and for the per diem authorized shall also be made by order of the court, duly certified to the Supreme Court for payment out of the appropriation to pay criminal charges.

History.
1999, cc. 958, 997; 2000, c. 337; 2005, c. 110; 2009, cc. 813, 840; 2012, cc. 476, 507.

TITLE 17.
COURTS OF RECORD.

[Repealed.]

TITLE 17.1.
COURTS OF RECORD.

CHAPTER 1.
GENERAL PROVISIONS.

§ 17.1-112. Sheriff to attend court as its officer.

Neither the Supreme Court nor the Court of Appeals shall be attended by any sheriff in the City of Richmond. In all other cases, the sheriff of the county or city in which any court is held shall attend it and act as its officer.

History.
Code 1919, § 5963, § 17-13; 1984, c. 703; 1998, c. 872.

§ 17.1-128.1. Recording evidence and incidents of trial in certain misdemeanor cases.

In any misdemeanor case in circuit court for which no recording verbatim of the evidence and incidents of trial either by a court reporter or by mechanical or electronic devices approved by the court will be used, the court shall allow the defendant, the Commonwealth, or both to record the evidence and incidents of trial by mechanical or electronic device to aid counsel in producing a thorough, complete, and accurate written statement of facts in lieu of transcript for purposes of any appeal. The recording shall not be made a part of the record unless otherwise permitted.

History.
2014, c. 78.

CHAPTER 2.
CLERKS, CLERKS' OFFICES AND RECORDS.

Article 7.

Fees.

ARTICLE 7.

FEES.

§ 17.1-275.1. Fixed felony fee.

Upon conviction of any and each felony charge or upon a deferred disposition of proceedings in circuit court in the case of any and each felony disposition deferred pursuant to the terms and conditions of § 16.1-278.8, 16.1-278.9, 18.2-61, 18.2-67.1, or 18.2-251, there shall be assessed as court costs a fee of $375, to be known as the fixed felony fee.

The amount collected, in whole or in part, for the fixed felony fee shall be apportioned, as provided by law, to the following funds in the fractional amounts designated:

1. Sentencing/supervision fee (General Fund) (.4705067);
2. Forensic science fund (.1033333);
3. Court reporter fund (.0887200);
4. Witness expenses/expert witness fund (.0053333);
5. Virginia Crime Victim-Witness Fund (.0080000);
6. Intensified Drug Enforcement Jurisdiction Fund (.0106667);
7. Criminal Injuries Compensation Fund (.0800000);
8. Commonwealth's attorney fund (state share) (.0533333);
9. Commonwealth's attorney fund (local share) (.0533333);
10. Regional Criminal Justice Academy Training Fund (.0026667);
11. Warrant fee (.0320000);
12. Courthouse construction/maintenance fund (.0053333); and
13. Clerk of the circuit court (.0867733).

History.

1999, c. 9; 2002, c. 831; 2003, c. 1039; 2005, c. 631; 2011, c. 565.

§ 17.1-275.2. Fixed fee for felony reduced to misdemeanor.

In circuit court, upon the conviction of a person of any and each misdemeanor reduced from a felony charge, or upon a deferred disposition of proceedings in the case of any and each misdemeanor reduced from a felony charge and deferred pursuant to the terms and conditions of § 4.1-305, 16.1-278.8, 16.1-278.9, 18.2-57.3, or 19.2-303.2, there shall be assessed as court costs a fee of $227, to be known as the fixed fee for felony reduced to misdemeanor. However, this section shall not apply to those proceedings provided for in § 17.1-275.8.

The amount collected, in whole or in part, for the fixed fee for felony reduced to misdemeanor shall be apportioned to the following funds in the fractional amounts designated:

1. Sentencing/supervision fee (General Fund) (.1695154);
2. Forensic science fund (.1707048);
3. Court reporter fund (.1465639);
4. Witness expenses/expert witness fund (.0088106);
5. Virginia Crime Victim-Witness Fund (.0132159);
6. Intensified Drug Enforcement Jurisdiction Fund (.0176211);
7. Criminal Injuries Compensation Fund (.0881057);
8. Commonwealth's attorney fund (state share) (.0881057);
9. Commonwealth's attorney fund (local share) (.0881057);
10. Regional Criminal Justice Academy Training Fund (.0044053);
11. Warrant fee (.0528634);
12. Courthouse construction/maintenance fund (.0088106); and
13. Clerk of the circuit court (.1431718).

History.

1999, c. 9; 2002, c. 831; 2003, c. 1039; 2005, c. 631; 2011, c. 565.

§ 17.1-275.3. Fixed felony revocation fee.

Upon the partial or full revocation of suspension of sentence or probation of a convicted felon pursuant to § 19.2-306, other than a revocation for failure to pay previously assessed court costs, there shall be assessed as court costs a fee of $158 to be known as the fixed felony revocation fee. A single fixed felony revocation fee shall be assessed per defendant per hearing without regard to the number of revocations being considered.

The amount collected, in whole or in part, for the fixed felony revocation fee shall be apportioned to the following funds in the fractional amounts designated:

1. Virginia Crime Victim-Witness Fund (.0189873);

2. Intensified Drug Enforcement Jurisdiction Fund (.0253165);
3. Court reporter fund (.2105696);
4. Witness expenses/expert witness fund (.0126582);
5. Commonwealth's attorney fund (state share) (.1265823);
6. Commonwealth's attorney fund (local share) (.1265823);
7. Criminal Injuries Compensation Fund (.1898734);
8. Regional Criminal Justice Academy Training Fund (.0063291);
9. Warrant fee (.0759494); and
10. Clerk of the circuit court (.2071519).

History.
1999, c. 9; 2003, c. 1039; 2011, c. 565.

§ 17.1-275.4. Fixed misdemeanor reduced from felony revocation fee.

In circuit court, when a person whose charge was reduced from a felony charge is convicted of a misdemeanor and subsequently suffers partial or full revocation of his suspension of sentence or probation pursuant to § 19.2-306, other than a revocation for failure to pay previously assessed court costs, he shall be assessed as court costs a fee of $114.50 to be known as the fixed misdemeanor reduced from felony revocation fee. A single fixed misdemeanor reduced from felony revocation fee shall be assessed per defendant per hearing without regard to the number of misdemeanor revocations being considered except that if a revocation of probation or suspended sentence upon a felony conviction is also being considered at the same revocation proceeding, a single fixed felony revocation fee shall apply instead. The amount collected, in whole or in part, for the fixed misdemeanor reduced from felony revocation fee shall be apportioned, as provided by law, to the following funds in the fractional amounts designated:
1. Virginia Crime Victim-Witness Fund (.0262009);
2. Intensified Drug Enforcement Jurisdiction Fund (.0349345);
3. Witness expenses/expert witness fund (.0174672);
4. Commonwealth's attorney fund (state share) (.1746725);
5. Commonwealth's attorney fund (local share) (.1746725);
6. Criminal Injuries Compensation Fund (.1746725);
7. Regional Criminal Justice Training Academy Fund (.0087336);
8. Warrant fee, as prescribed by § 17.1-272 (.1048035); and
9. Clerk of the circuit court (.2838428).

History.
1999, c. 9; 2002, c. 831; 2003, c. 1039; 2011, c. 565.

§ 17.1-275.5. Amounts to be added; judgment in favor of the Commonwealth.

A. The clerk shall assess, in addition to the fees provided for by § 17.1-275.1, 17.1-275.2, 17.1-275.3, 17.1-275.4, 17.1-275.7, 17.1-275.8, 17.1-275.9, 17.1-275.10, 17.1-275.11, 17.1-275.11:1, or 17.1-275.12, the following costs:
1. Any amount paid by the Commonwealth for legal representation of the defendant;
2. Any amount paid for trial transcripts;
3. Extradition costs;
4. Costs of psychiatric evaluation;
5. Costs taxed against the defendant as appellant under Rule 5A:30 of the Rules of the Supreme Court;
6. Any fee for a returned check or disallowed credit card charge assessed pursuant to subdivision A 28 of § 17.1-275;
7. Any jury costs;
8. Any assessment made pursuant to subdivision A 10 of § 17.1-275;
9. Any fees prescribed in §§ 18.2-268.8 and 46.2-341.26:8;
10. Any court costs related to an ignition interlock device;
11. Any fee for testing for HIV;
12. Any fee for processing an individual admitted to jail as prescribed in § 15.2-1613.1;
13. Any fee for courthouse security personnel as prescribed in § 53.1-120;
14. Any fee for a DNA sample as prescribed in § 19.2-310.2;
15. Reimbursement to the Commonwealth of medical fees as prescribed in § 19.2-165.1;
16. Any fee for a local criminal justice training academy as prescribed in § 9.1-106;
17. Any fee prescribed by §§ 16.1-69.48:1.01 and 17.1-275.11;
18. Any expenses charged pursuant to subsection B or F of § 19.2-187.1; and
19. Any fee for an electronic summons system as prescribed in § 17.1-279.1.

B. The total amount of assessments described in subsection A, including (i) the fees provided for by § 17.1-275.1, 17.1-275.2, 17.1-275.3, 17.1-275.4, 17.1-275.7, 17.1-275.8, 17.1-275.9, 17.1-275.10, 17.1-275.11, 17.1-275.11:1, or 17.1-275.12 and (ii) all other fines and costs, shall be docketed by the clerk as a judgment against the defendant in favor of the Commonwealth in accordance with § 8.01-446.

History.
1999, c. 9; 2002, c. 831; 2003, cc. 1001, 1022, 1039; 2010, c. 555; 2012, c. 714; 2013, c. 263; 2014, c. 325; 2015, c. 641.

§ 17.1-275.6. Fees collected from court reporter fund.

Notwithstanding any other provision of law, in any court in which electronic devices are used for recording testimony, a sum not to exceed twenty dollars for each day or part of a day of the trial shall be paid by the clerk, from the court reporter fund as set forth in §§ 17.1-275.1, 17.1-275.2 and 17.1-275.3, or a sum not to exceed five dollars for each day or part of a day of the trial of a case wherein costs are assessed pursuant to § 17.1-275.8 shall be paid by the clerk, from the court reporter fund as set forth in § 17.1-275.8, into a special fund to be used for the purpose of repairing, replacing or supplementing such electronic devices or, if a sufficient amount is available, to pay the purchase price of such devices in whole or in part. For the purpose of this section, repairing shall include maintenance and service contracts. Fees collected under this article shall be retained locally and shall not be subject to the provisions of § 17.1-286.

History.
2000, c. 875; 2002, c. 831.

§ 17.1-275.7. Fixed misdemeanor fee.

In circuit court, upon (i) conviction of any and each misdemeanor, not originally charged as a felony; (ii) a deferred disposition of proceedings in the case of any and each misdemeanor not originally charged as a felony and deferred pursuant to the terms and conditions of § 4.1-305, 16.1-278.8, 16.1-278.9, 18.2-57.3, or 19.2-303.2; (iii) any and each conviction of a traffic infraction or referral to a driver improvement clinic or traffic school in lieu of a finding of guilt for a traffic infraction; or (iv) proof of compliance with law under §§ 46.2-104 and 46.2-1158.02, there shall be assessed as court costs a fee of $80, to be known as the fixed misdemeanor fee. However, this section shall not apply to those proceedings provided for in § 17.1-275.8. This fee shall be in addition to any fee assessed in the district court.

The amount collected, in whole or in part, for the fixed misdemeanor fee shall be apportioned, as provided by law, to the following funds in the fractional amounts designated:

1. Sentencing/supervision fee (General Fund) (.0125000);
2. Witness expenses/expert witness fee (General Fund) (.0250000);
3. Virginia Crime Victim-Witness Fund (.0375000);
4. Intensified Drug Enforcement Jurisdiction Fund (.0500000);
5. Criminal Injuries Compensation Fund (.2500000);
6. Commonwealth's Attorney Fund (state share) (.0937500);
7. Commonwealth's Attorney Fund (local share) (.0937500);
8. Regional Criminal Justice Academy Training Fund (.0125000);
9. Warrant fee, as prescribed by § 17.1-272 (.1500000);
10. Courthouse Construction/Maintenance Fund (.0250000); and
11. Clerk of the circuit court (.2500000).

History.
2002, c. 831; 2003, c. 1039; 2005, c. 631; 2009, c. 756; 2011, cc. 283, 565.

§ 17.1-275.8. Fixed drug misdemeanor fee.

In circuit court, upon conviction of any and each misdemeanor charge, whether or not originally charged as a felony, for a violation of any provision of Article 1 (§ 18.2-247 et seq.) of Chapter 7 of Title 18.2, or upon a deferred disposition of proceedings in the case of any and each misdemeanor charge, whether or not originally charged as a felony, deferred pursuant to the terms and conditions of § 18.2-251, there shall be assessed as court costs a fee of $296.50, to be known as the fixed drug misdemeanor fee. This fee shall be in addition to any fee assessed in the district court.

The amount collected, in whole or in part, for the fixed drug misdemeanor fee shall be apportioned, as provided by law, to the following funds in the fractional amounts designated:

1. Sentencing/supervision fee (General Fund) (.1264755);
2. Court Reporter Fund (.0168634);
3. Witness expenses/expert witness fee (General Fund) (.0067454);
4. Virginia Crime Victim-Witness Fund (.0101180);
5. Intensified Drug Enforcement Jurisdiction Fund (.0134907);
6. Criminal Injuries Compensation Fund (.0674536);
7. Commonwealth's Attorney Fund (state share) (.0252951);
8. Commonwealth's Attorney Fund (local share) (.0252951);
9. Regional Criminal Justice Academy Training Fund (.0033727);
10. Warrant fee, as prescribed by § 17.1-272 (.0404722);
11. Courthouse Construction/Maintenance Fund (.0067454);
12. Clerk of the circuit court (.0674536);
13. Forensic laboratory fee (General Fund) (.3372681); and
14. Drug Offender Assessment and Treatment Fund (.2529511).

History.
2002, c. 831; 2003, c. 1039; 2004, c. 1004; 2011, c. 565.

§ 17.1-275.9. Fixed misdemeanor revocation fee.

In circuit court, when a person is convicted of a misdemeanor not originally charged as a felony and subsequently suffers partial or full revocation of his suspension of sentence or probation pursuant to § 19.2-306, he shall be assessed as court costs a fee of $77 to be known as the fixed misdemeanor revocation fee. A single fixed misdemeanor revocation fee shall be assessed per defendant per hearing without regard to the number of misdemeanor revocations being considered, except that if a revocation of probation or suspended sentence upon a felony conviction is also being considered at the same revocation proceeding, a single fixed felony revocation fee shall apply instead. The amount collected, in whole or in part, for the fixed misdemeanor revocation fee shall be apportioned, as provided by law, to the following funds in the fractional amounts designated:

1. Virginia Crime Victim-Witness Fund (.0389610);
2. Intensified Drug Enforcement Jurisdiction Fund (.0519481);
3. Witness expenses/expert witness fee (General Fund) (.0259740);
4. Commonwealth's Attorney Fund (state share) (.0974026);
5. Commonwealth's Attorney Fund (local share) (.0974026);
6. Criminal Injuries Compensation Fund (.2597403);
7. Regional Criminal Justice Training Academy Fund (.0129870);
8. Warrant fee, as prescribed by § 17.1-272 (.1558442); and
9. Clerk of the circuit court (.2597403).

History.
2002, c. 831; 2003, c. 1039; 2011, c. 565.

§ 17.1-275.10. Additional fee.

Beginning May 1, 2003, in addition to the fees set forth in §§ 17.1-275.1, 17.1-275.2, 17.1-275.3, 17.1-275.4, 17.1-275.7, 17.1-275.8, and 17.1-275.9, there shall be assessed as court costs, a fee of $2, at the same time fees in such sections are assessed. All fees collected pursuant to this section shall be deposited into the Intensified Drug Enforcement Jurisdiction Fund.

History.
2003, c. 1042, cl. 9.

§ 17.1-275.11. Additional fee assessed for conviction of certain offenses.

Beginning May 1, 2003, the clerk shall assess a person, in addition to the fees provided for by §§ 17.1-275.1, 17.1-275.2, 17.1-275.3, 17.1-275.4, 17.1-275.5, 17.1-275.7, 17.1-275.8, and 17.1-275.9, a fee of $100 upon conviction of any and each charge of a violation of §§ 18.2-36.1, 18.2-51.4, 18.2-266, 18.2-266.1, 18.2-268.3, 46.2-341.24 or § 46.2-341.26:3, or any similar local ordinance.

History.
2003, c. 1042, cl. 9.

§ 17.1-275.11:1. Additional fee assessed for conviction requiring computer analysis.

In addition to the fees provided for by §§ 17.1-275.1 through 17.1-275.5, 17.1-275.7, 17.1-275.8, and 17.1-275.9, upon a finding of guilty of any charge or charges in which any computer forensic analysis revealed evidence used at trial of a defendant, the defendant may be assessed costs in an amount equal to the actual cost of the computer forensic analysis not to exceed $100 for each computer analyzed by any state or local law-enforcement agency. Upon motion and submission to the court of an affidavit by the law-enforcement agency setting forth the number of computers analyzed and the total amount of costs requested, the court shall determine the appropriate amount to be assessed and order such amount paid to the law-enforcement agency.

History.
2011, c. 511.

§ 17.1-275.12. Additional fee for Internet Crimes Against Children Fund.

In addition to the fees provided for by §§ 16.1-69.48:1, 16.1-69.48:1.01, 17.1-275.1, 17.1-275.2, 17.1-275.3, 17.1-275.4, 17.1-275.5, 17.1-275.7, 17.1-275.8, 17.1-275.9, 17.1-275.10, and 17.1-275.11, a fee of $15 upon each felony or misdemeanor conviction shall be assessed as court costs. All fees collected pursuant to this section shall be deposited into the state treasury and credited to the Internet Crimes Against Children Fund.

There is hereby established in the state treasury the Internet Crimes Against Children Fund. Such fund shall consist of all fees collected under this section, moneys appropriated directly to the Fund, and any other grants or gifts made to the Fund. Moneys in the Fund shall be disbursed in the following manner: to the Virginia State Police, 33.3333 percent of the total annual deposits to support the Northern Virginia Internet Crimes Against Children program; to the Department of Criminal Justice Services, 33.3333 percent of the total annual deposits to support the Southern Virginia Internet Crimes Against Children program; to the Department of Criminal Justice Services, 27.7777 percent of the total annual deposits to support grants and training and equipment for local law-enforcement agencies' use in investigating and prosecuting Internet crimes against children; and to the Department of Social Services, 5.5555 percent of the total annual deposits to support the Virginia Child Protection Accountability System established under § 63.2-1530.

History.
2010, c. 685; 2014, c. 794.

ARTICLE 8.
SECURE REMOTE ACCESS.

§ 17.1-293. Posting and availability of certain information on the Internet; prohibitions.

A. Notwithstanding Chapter 37 (§ 2.2-3700 et seq.) of Title 2.2 or subsection B, it shall be unlawful for any court clerk to disclose the social security number or other identification numbers appearing on driver's licenses or information on credit cards, debit cards, bank accounts, or other electronic billing and payment systems that was supplied to a court clerk for the purpose of paying fees, fines, taxes, or other charges collected by such court clerk. The prohibition shall not apply where disclosure of such information is required (i) to conduct or complete the transaction for which such information was submitted or (ii) by other law or court order.

B. Beginning January 1, 2004, no court clerk shall post on the Internet any document that contains the following information: (i) an actual signature, (ii) a social security number, (iii) a date of birth identified with a particular person, (iv) the maiden name of a person's parent so as to be identified with a particular person, (v) any financial account number or numbers, or (vi) the name and age of any minor child.

C. Each such clerk shall post notice that includes a list of the documents routinely posted on its website. However, the clerk shall not post information on his website that includes private activity for private financial gain.

D. Nothing in this section shall be construed to prohibit access to any original document as provided by law.

E. This section shall not apply to the following:

1. Providing access to any document among the land records via secure remote access pursuant to § 17.1-294;
2. Postings related to legitimate law-enforcement purposes;
3. Postings of historical, genealogical, interpretive, or educational documents and information about historic persons and events;
4. Postings of instruments and records filed or recorded that are more than 100 years old;
5. Providing secure remote access to any person, his counsel, or staff which counsel directly supervises to documents filed in matters to which such person is a party;
6. Providing official certificates and certified records in digital form of any document maintained by the clerk pursuant to § 17.1-258.3:2; and
7. Providing secure remote access to nonconfidential court records, subject to any fees charged by the clerk, to members in good standing with the Virginia State Bar and their authorized agents, pro hac vice attorneys authorized by the court for purposes of the practice of law, and such governmental agencies as authorized by the clerk.

F. Nothing in this section shall prohibit the Supreme Court or any other court clerk from providing online access to a case management system that may include abstracts of case filings and proceedings in the courts of the Commonwealth.

G. The court clerk shall be immune from suit arising from any acts or omissions relating to providing remote access on the Internet pursuant to this section unless the clerk was grossly negligent or engaged in willful misconduct.

This subsection shall not be construed to limit, withdraw, or overturn any defense or immunity already existing in statutory or common law, or to affect any cause of action accruing prior to July 1, 2005.

H. Nothing in this section shall be construed to permit any data accessed by secure remote access to be sold or posted on any other website or in any way redistributed to any third party, and the clerk, in his discretion, may deny secure remote access to ensure compliance with these provisions. However, the data accessed by secure remote access may be included in products or services provided to a third party of the subscriber provided that (i) such data is not made available to the general public and (ii) the subscriber maintains administrative, technical, and security safeguards to protect the confidentiality, integrity, and limited availability of the data.

History.

2007, cc. 548, 626; 2010, c. 430; 2011, cc. 557, 625, 689, 715; 2012, c. 234; 2013, c. 77; 2014, c. 460.

CHAPTER 3.
SUPREME COURT.

Article 1.

Composition, Jurisdiction, etc.

ARTICLE 1.
COMPOSITION, JURISDICTION, ETC.

§ 17.1-312. Where criminal jurisdiction exercised.

The appellate jurisdiction of the Supreme Court in any criminal case may be exercised at any place of session, no matter where the court may have been held which rendered the judgment in such case.

History.

Code 1919, § 5870, § 17-110; 1998, c. 872.

§ 17.1-313. Review of death sentence.

A. A sentence of death, upon the judgment thereon becoming final in the circuit court, shall be reviewed on the record by the Supreme Court.

B. The proceeding in the circuit court shall be transcribed as expeditiously as practicable, and the transcript filed forthwith upon transcription with the clerk of the circuit court, who shall, within ten days after receipt of the transcript, compile the record as provided in Rule 5:14 and transmit it to the Supreme Court.

C. In addition to consideration of any errors in the trial enumerated by appeal, the court shall consider and determine:

1. Whether the sentence of death was imposed under the influence of passion, prejudice or any other arbitrary factor; and

2. Whether the sentence of death is excessive or disproportionate to the penalty imposed in similar cases, considering both the crime and the defendant.

D. In addition to the review and correction of errors in the trial of the case, with respect to review of the sentence of death, the court may:

1. Affirm the sentence of death;

2. Commute the sentence of death to imprisonment for life; or

3. Remand to the trial court for a new sentencing proceeding.

E. The Supreme Court may accumulate the records of all capital felony cases tried within such period of time as the court may determine. The court shall consider such records as are available as a guide in determining whether the sentence imposed in the case under review is excessive. Such records as are accumulated shall be made available to the circuit courts.

F. Sentence review shall be in addition to appeals, if taken, and review and appeal may be consolidated. The defendant and the Commonwealth shall have the right to submit briefs within time limits imposed by the court, either by rule or order, and to present oral argument.

G. The Supreme Court shall, in setting its docket, give priority to the review of cases in which the sentence of death has been imposed over other cases pending in the Court. In setting its docket, the Court shall also give priority to the consideration and disposition of petitions for writs of habeas corpus filed by prisoners held under sentence of death.

History.
1977, c. 492, §§ 17-110.1, 17-110.2; 1983, c. 519; 1995, c. 503; 1998, c. 872.

CHAPTER 6.
COSTS GENERALLY.

Section

§ 17.1-617. Number of witnesses paid fees in criminal cases.

Not more than the maximum number of witnesses provided for herein shall be paid out of the state treasury in criminal cases.

The maximum number that may be (i) caused to be summoned by an attorney for the Commonwealth in any one case to go before a grand jury — five; (ii) used before a court not of record in the trial of any criminal case — five; and (iii) caused to be summoned by an attorney for the Commonwealth for the trial of any criminal case — ten.

Nothing herein shall be construed to limit (i) the number of witnesses that may be authorized by any court or the judge thereof to be used when the necessity for additional witnesses appears to the court or judge and the consent of the court or judge is first obtained or (ii) the number of witnesses that a grand jury may of its own motion summon.

History.
Code 1950, § 14-192; 1964, c. 386, § 14.1-195; 1998, c. 872.

§ 17.1-618. Allowances for jurors; expenses of keeping jury together; fees of jury commissioners and commissioner in chancery for drawing of juries.

Every person summoned as a juror in a civil or criminal case shall be entitled to thirty dollars for each day of attendance upon the court for expenses of travel incident to jury service and other necessary and reasonable costs as the court may direct. Jurors summoned from another political subdivision pursuant to § 8.01-363 may be allowed by the court, in addition to the above allowance, their actual expenses. When kept together overnight under the supervision of the court, the jurors and the sheriff or his deputies keeping the jury shall be furnished suitable board and lodging. Reimbursement for board and lodging shall be set by the judge in an amount not to exceed the amount authorized by travel regulations promulgated pursuant to § 2.2-2823. Allowances and other costs will be allowed a juror in only one case the same day.

Every person serving as a jury commissioner and every person serving as a commissioner in chancery for the drawing of juries for a circuit court of this Commonwealth may be allowed, by the court appointing him, a fee not exceeding thirty dollars per day for the time actually engaged in such work and such other necessary and reasonable costs as the court may direct.

History.

Code 1950, § 8-208.33; 1954, c. 709; 1958, cc. 216, 303; 1960, c. 366; 1964, c. 268, § 14.1-195.1; 1968, c. 632; 1969, Ex. Sess., c. 20; 1972, c. 719; 1973, c. 439; 1974, c. 220; 1975, c. 193; 1976, c. 308; 1977, c. 624; 1978, c. 230; 1980, cc. 593, 594; 1982, c. 610; 1983, c. 495; 1984, c. 512; 1993, cc. 345, 635; 1996, c. 332; 1998, c. 872.

§ 17.1-619. How jurors paid.

A. The compensation and allowances of persons attending the court as jurors in all felony cases shall be paid by the Commonwealth. Jurors in misdemeanor cases shall be paid by the Commonwealth unless the charge is written on a local warrant or summons, in which case the jurors shall be paid by the political subdivision in which the summons is issued. Jurors in all civil cases shall be paid by the political subdivision in which the summons is issued. Payment in all cases shall be by negotiable check, warrant, cash, or electronic transfer upon the Commonwealth, or the political subdivision, as the case may be.

When, during the same day any juror is entitled to compensation from both the Commonwealth and from the political subdivision in which he has served, the court shall divide the pay for such day between the Commonwealth and the political subdivision. It shall be the duty of the sheriff at the term of the court during which an allowance is made or has been made under this section, to furnish the clerk of the court with a statement showing the number and names of the jurors in attendance upon the court.

B. A county or city may provide by local ordinance that a juror may direct in writing that compensation due him be paid to the court service unit or to any other agency, authority or organization which is ancillary to and provides services to the courts of the county or city.

History.

Code 1950, § 8-208.34; 1954, c. 709; 1958, c. 303; 1960, c. 366; 1968, c. 632, § 14.1-195.2; 1969, Ex. Sess., c. 20; 1972, c. 719; 1973, c. 739; 1974, c. 208; 1975, c. 193; 1977, c. 624; 1982, c. 610; 1991, c. 78; 1998, c. 872; 2005, c. 173.

§ 17.1-620. When juror not entitled to compensation.

No person shall be entitled to receive any compensation for service as a juror if he departs without the leave of the court, or, being summoned as a witness for the Commonwealth, charges for his attendance as such.

History.

Code 1950, § 8-208.35; 1973, c. 439, § 14.1-195.3; 1977, c. 624; 1998, c. 872.

§ 17.1-621. Clerk to make entry on minutes stating amount due and by whom payable.

The clerk of any court in which juries are impaneled shall, before its final adjournment at each term, and under the direction of the court, make an entry upon its minutes stating the amount to which each juror is entitled for his services or attendance during the term, and specifying how much is payable by the Commonwealth, and how much by the political subdivision.

History.

Code 1950, § 8-208.36; 1973, c. 439, § 14.1-195.4; 1977, c. 624; 1998, c. 872.

§ 17.1-622. Clerk to transmit orders making allowances to Supreme Court, treasurer and jurors.

Such clerk shall immediately, after the adjournment of the court, transmit to the Supreme Court a list of all orders under § 17.1-621 making allowances against the Commonwealth, and to the treasurer of the political subdivision a list of all such orders making allowances against the political subdivision, with a certificate to the correctness of the list and the aggregate amount thereof annexed thereto and signed by the judge of the court and himself, and such clerk shall also deliver to each juror copies of any orders making an allowance to him, whether the same be payable by the Commonwealth or by the political subdivision.

History.

Code 1950, § 8-208.37; 1973, c. 439, § 14.1-195.5; 1977, c. 624; 1978, c. 195; 1998, c. 872.

§ 17.1-623. Payment of allowances.

The treasurer of such political subdivision shall upon demand pay to such juror the amount allowed him by negotiable check, cash, or electronic transfer which shall be repaid to such treasurer out of the public treasury or out of the political subdivision levy, as the case may be, upon the production of satisfactory proof that the same has been actually paid by him. But such treasurer shall not be repaid any allowance made against the Commonwealth unless it appear on the list directed to be sent to the Supreme Court. No such allowance shall be paid unless presented within two years from the time of rendering the service.

History.

Code 1950, § 8-208.38; 1973, c. 439, § 14.1-195.6; 1975, c. 193; 1977, c. 624; 1978, c. 195; 1998, c. 872; 2005, c. 173.

§ 17.1-626.1. Recovery of costs in civil actions for bad checks.

A. In any civil action by a holder to recover the sum payable of a check drawn by the defendant on which payment has been refused by the payor bank because the drawer had no account or insufficient funds, or in any civil action following an arrest under § 18.2-181 or 18.2-182, the court, upon a determination that the plaintiff has prevailed, shall add the following amounts, as costs, to the amount due to the plaintiff for the check: (i) the sum of $30 to defray the cost of processing the returned check; and (ii) the base wage of one employee for time actually spent acting as a witness for the Commonwealth; provided, however, that the total amount of allowable costs granted under the provisions of this section shall not exceed the sum of $250 excluding restitution for the amount of the check.

B. Such award of costs shall be contingent upon a finding (i) that the plaintiff complied with the provisions in § 18.2-183 relating to notice and (ii) that the defendant failed to deliver payment or evidence of bank error to the plaintiff within five days after receipt of such notice.

History.
1977, c. 329, § 6.1-118.1; 2010, cc. 343, 794.

§ 17.1-629. No judgment for costs against Commonwealth; exception.

In no case, civil or criminal, whether in a court of record or a court not of record, except when otherwise specially provided, shall there be a judgment for costs against the Commonwealth.

History.
Code 1950, § 14-197; 1964, c. 386, § 14.1-201; 1998, c. 872.

TITLE 18.2.

CRIMES AND OFFENSES GENERALLY.

CHAPTER 1.

IN GENERAL.

Article 1.

Transition Provisions.

Article 2.

Construction and Definitions.

Article 3.

Classification of Criminal Offenses and Punishment Therefor.

ARTICLE 1.

TRANSITION PROVISIONS.

§ 18.2-1. Repealing clause.

All acts and parts of acts, all sections of this Code, and all provisions of municipal charters, inconsistent with the provisions of this title, are, except as herein otherwise provided, repealed to the extent of such inconsistency.

History.
1975, cc. 14, 15.

§ 18.2-2. Effect of repeal of Title 18.1 and enactment of this title.

The repeal of Title 18.1, effective as of October 1, 1975, shall not affect any act or offense done or committed, or any penalty or forfeiture incurred, or any right established, accrued or accruing on or before such date, or any prosecution, suit or action pending on that day. Except as herein otherwise provided, neither the repeal of Title 18.1 nor the enactment of this title shall apply to offenses committed prior to October 1, 1975, and prosecutions for such offenses shall be governed by the prior law, which is continued in effect for that purpose. For the purposes of this section, an offense was committed prior to October 1, 1975, if any of the essential elements of the offense occurred prior thereto.

History.
1975, cc. 14, 15.

§ 18.2-3. Certain notices, recognizances and processes validated.

Any notice given, recognizance taken, or process or writ issued before October 1, 1975, shall be valid although given, taken or to be returned to a day after such date, in like manner as if this title had been effective before the same was given, taken or issued.

History.
1975, cc. 14, 15.

§ 18.2-4. References to former sections, articles and chapters of Title 18.1 and others.

Whenever in this title any of the conditions, requirements, provisions or contents of any section, article or chapter of Title 18.1 or any other title of this Code as such titles existed prior to October 1, 1975, are transferred in the same or in modified form to a new section, article or chapter of this title or any other title of this Code and whenever any such former section, article or chapter is given a new number in this or any other title, all references to any such former section, article or chapter of Title 18.1 or such other title appearing elsewhere in this Code than in this title shall be construed to apply to the new or renumbered section, article or chapter containing such conditions, requirements, provisions or contents or portions thereof.

History.
1975, cc. 14, 15.

ARTICLE 2.
CONSTRUCTION AND DEFINITIONS.

§ 18.2-5: Repealed by Acts 2005, c. 839, cl. 10, effective October 1, 2005.

§ 18.2-6. Meaning of certain terms.

As used in this title:

The word *"court,"* unless otherwise clearly indicated by the context in which it appears, shall mean and include any court vested with appropriate jurisdiction under the Constitution and laws of this Commonwealth.

The word *"judge,"* unless otherwise clearly indicated by the context in which it appears, shall mean and include any judge, associate judge or substitute judge, or police justice, of any court.

The words *"motor vehicle," "semitrailer," "trailer"* and *"vehicle"* shall have the respective meanings assigned to them by § 46.2-100.

History.
Code 1950, § 18.1-5; 1960, c. 358; 1975, cc. 14, 15.

§ 18.2-7. Criminal act not to merge civil remedy.

The commission of a crime shall not stay or merge any civil remedy.

History.
Code 1950, § 18.1-7; 1960, c. 358; 1975, cc. 14, 15.

ARTICLE 3.
CLASSIFICATION OF CRIMINAL OFFENSES AND PUNISHMENT THEREFOR.

§ 18.2-8. Felonies, misdemeanors and traffic infractions defined.

Offenses are either felonies or misdemeanors. Such offenses as are punishable with death or confinement in a state correctional facility are felonies; all other offenses are misdemeanors. Traffic infractions are violations of public order as defined in § 46.2-100 and not deemed to be criminal in nature.

History.
Code 1950, § 18.1-6; 1960, c. 358; 1975, cc. 14, 15; 1977, c. 585.

§ 18.2-9. Classification of criminal offenses.

(1) Felonies are classified, for the purposes of punishment and sentencing, into six classes:
(a) Class 1 felony
(b) Class 2 felony
(c) Class 3 felony
(d) Class 4 felony
(e) Class 5 felony
(f) Class 6 felony.

(2) Misdemeanors are classified, for the purposes of punishment and sentencing, into four classes:
(a) Class 1 misdemeanor
(b) Class 2 misdemeanor
(c) Class 3 misdemeanor
(d) Class 4 misdemeanor.

History.
1975, cc. 14, 15.

§ 18.2-10. Punishment for conviction of felony; penalty.

The authorized punishments for conviction of a felony are:

(a) For Class 1 felonies, death, if the person so convicted was 18 years of age or older at the time of the offense and is not determined to be mentally retarded pursuant to § 19.2-264.3:1.1, or imprisonment for life and, subject to subdivision (g), a fine of not more than $100,000. If the person was under 18 years of age at the time of the offense or is determined to be mentally retarded pursuant to § 19.2-264.3:1.1, the punishment shall be imprisonment for life and, subject to subdivision (g), a fine of not more than $100,000.

(b) For Class 2 felonies, imprisonment for life or for any term not less than 20 years and, subject to subdivision (g), a fine of not more than $100,000.

(c) For Class 3 felonies, a term of imprisonment of not less than five years nor more than 20 years and, subject to subdivision (g), a fine of not more than $100,000.

(d) For Class 4 felonies, a term of imprisonment of not less than two years nor more than 10 years and, subject to subdivision (g), a fine of not more than $100,000.

(e) For Class 5 felonies, a term of imprisonment of not less than one year nor more than 10 years, or in the discretion of the jury or the court trying the case without a jury, confinement in jail for not more than 12 months and a fine of not more than $2,500, either or both.

(f) For Class 6 felonies, a term of imprisonment of not less than one year nor more than five years, or in the discretion of the jury or the court trying the case without a jury, confinement in jail for not more than 12 months and a fine of not more than $2,500, either or both.

(g) Except as specifically authorized in subdivision (e) or (f), or in Class 1 felonies for which a sentence of death is imposed, the court shall impose either a sentence of imprisonment together with a fine, or imprisonment only. However, if the defendant is not a natural person, the court shall impose only a fine.

For any felony offense committed (i) on or after January 1, 1995, the court may, and (ii) on or after July 1, 2000, shall, except in cases in which the court orders a suspended term of confinement of at least six months, impose an additional term of not less than six months nor more than three years, which shall be suspended conditioned upon successful completion of a period of post-release supervision pursuant to § 19.2-295.2 and compliance with such other terms as the sentencing court may require. However, such additional term may only be imposed when the sentence includes an active term of incarceration in a correctional facility.

For a felony offense prohibiting proximity to children as described in subsection A of § 18.2-370.2, the sentencing court is authorized to impose the punishment set forth in that section in addition to any other penalty provided by law.

History.

1975, cc. 14, 15; 1977, c. 492; 1990, c. 788; 1991, c. 7; 1994, 2nd Sp. Sess., cc. 1, 2; 1995, c. 427; 2000, cc. 361, 767, 770; 2003, cc. 1031, 1040; 2006, cc. 36, 733; 2008, c. 579.

§ 18.2-11. Punishment for conviction of misdemeanor.

The authorized punishments for conviction of a misdemeanor are:

(a) For Class 1 misdemeanors, confinement in jail for not more than twelve months and a fine of not more than $2,500, either or both.

(b) For Class 2 misdemeanors, confinement in jail for not more than six months and a fine of not more than $1,000, either or both.

(c) For Class 3 misdemeanors, a fine of not more than $500.

(d) For Class 4 misdemeanors, a fine of not more than $250.

For a misdemeanor offense prohibiting proximity to children as described in subsection A of § 18.2-370.2, the sentencing court is authorized to impose the punishment set forth in subsection B of that section in addition to any other penalty provided by law.

History.

1975, cc. 14, 15; 1990, c. 788; 2000, c. 770.

§ 18.2-12. Same; where no punishment or maximum punishment prescribed.

A misdemeanor for which no punishment or no maximum punishment is prescribed by statute shall be punishable as a Class 1 misdemeanor.

History.

Code 1950, § 18.1-9; 1960, c. 358; 1975, cc. 14, 15.

§ 18.2-12.1. Mandatory minimum punishment; definition.

"Mandatory minimum" wherever it appears in this Code means, for purposes of imposing punishment upon a person convicted of a crime, that the court shall impose the entire term of confinement, the full amount of the fine and the complete requirement of community service prescribed by law. The court shall not suspend in full or in part any punishment described as mandatory minimum punishment.

History.

2004, c. 461.

§ 18.2-13. Same; by reference.

Where a statute in this Code prescribes punishment by stating that the offense is a misdemeanor, or that it is punishable as provided for in § 18.2-12, the offense shall be deemed to be a Class 1 misdemeanor.

History.
1975, cc. 14, 15.

§ 18.2-14. How unclassified offenses punished.

Offenses defined in Title 18.2 and in other titles in the Code, for which punishment is prescribed without specification as to the class of the offense, shall be punished according to the punishment prescribed in the section or sections thus defining the offense.

History.
1975, cc. 14, 15.

§ 18.2-15. Place of punishment.

Imprisonment for conviction of a felony shall be by confinement in a state correctional facility, unless in Class 5 and Class 6 felonies the jury or court trying the case without a jury fixes the punishment at confinement in jail. Imprisonment for conviction of a misdemeanor shall be by confinement in jail.

History.
1975, cc. 14, 15.

§ 18.2-16. How common-law offenses punished.

A common-law offense, for which punishment is prescribed by statute, shall be punished only in the mode so prescribed.

History.
Code 1950, § 18.1-8; 1960, c. 358; 1975, cc. 14, 15.

§ 18.2-17. When capital punishment inflicted.

No crime shall be punished with death unless it be authorized by statute.

History.
Code 1950, § 18.1-10; 1960, c. 358; 1975, cc. 14, 15.

CHAPTER 2.
PRINCIPALS AND ACCESSORIES.

§ 18.2-18. How principals in second degree and accessories before the fact punished.

In the case of every felony, every principal in the second degree and every accessory before the fact may be indicted, tried, convicted and punished in all respects as if a principal in the first degree; provided, however, that except in the case of a killing for hire under the provisions of subdivision 2 of § 18.2-31 or a killing pursuant to the direction or order of one who is engaged in a continuing criminal enterprise under the provisions of subdivision 10 of § 18.2-31 or a killing pursuant to the direction or order of one who is engaged in the commission of or attempted commission of an act of terrorism under the provisions of subdivision 13 of § 18.2-31, an accessory before the fact or principal in the second degree to a capital murder shall be indicted, tried, convicted and punished as though the offense were murder in the first degree.

History.
Code 1950, § 18.1-11; 1960, c. 358; 1975, cc. 14, 15; 1977, c. 478; 1997, c. 313; 2002, cc. 588, 623.

§ 18.2-19. How accessories after the fact punished; certain exceptions.

Every accessory after the fact is guilty of (i) a Class 6 felony in the case of a homicide offense that is punishable by death or as a Class 2 felony or (ii) a Class 1 misdemeanor in the case of any other felony. However, no person in the relation of husband or wife, parent or grandparent, child or grandchild, brother or sister, by consanguinity or affinity, or servant to the offender, who, after the commission of a felony, shall aid or assist a principal felon or accessory before the fact to avoid or escape from prosecution or punishment, shall be deemed an accessory after the fact.

History.
Code 1950, §§ 18.1-11, 18.1-12; 1960, c. 358; 1975, cc. 14, 15; 2014, c. 668.

§ 18.2-20: Reserved.

§ 18.2-21. When and where accessories tried; how indicted.

An accessory, either before or after the fact, may, whether the principal felon be convicted or not, or be amenable to justice or not, be indicted, tried, convicted and punished in the county or corporation in which he became accessory, or in which the principal felon might be indicted. Any such accessory before the fact may be indicted either with such principal or separately.

History.
Code 1950, § 18.1-13; 1960, c. 358; 1975, cc. 14, 15.

CHAPTER 3.
INCHOATE OFFENSES.

Article 1.

Conspiracies.

Section

Article 2.

Attempts.

ARTICLE 1.
CONSPIRACIES.

§ 18.2-22. Conspiracy to commit felony.

(a) If any person shall conspire, confederate or combine with another, either within or without this Commonwealth, to commit a felony within this Commonwealth, or if he shall so conspire, confederate or combine with another within this Commonwealth to commit a felony either within or without this Commonwealth, he shall be guilty of a felony which shall be punishable as follows:

(1) Every person who so conspires to commit an offense which is punishable by death shall be guilty of a Class 3 felony;

(2) Every person who so conspires to commit an offense which is a noncapital felony shall be guilty of a Class 5 felony; and

(3) Every person who so conspires to commit an offense the maximum punishment for which is confinement in a state correctional facility for a period of less than five years shall be confined in a state correctional facility for a period of one year, or, in the discretion of the jury or the court trying the case without a jury, may be confined in jail not exceeding twelve months and fined not exceeding $500, either or both.

(b) However, in no event shall the punishment for a conspiracy to commit an offense exceed the maximum punishment for the commission of the offense itself.

(c) Jurisdiction for the trial of any person accused of a conspiracy under this section shall be in the county or city wherein any part of such conspiracy is planned or in the county or city wherein any act is done toward the consummation of such plan or conspiracy.

(d) The penalty provisions of this section shall not apply to any person who conspires to commit any offense defined in Chapter 34 of Title 54.1 or of Article 1 (§ 18.2-247 et seq.), Chapter 7 of this title. The penalty for any such violation shall be as provided in § 18.2-256.

History.
Code 1950, § 18.1-15.3; 1972, c. 484; 1973, c. 399; 1975, cc. 14, 15; 1983, c. 19.

Crimes and Offenses

§ 18.2-23. Conspiring to trespass or commit larceny.

A. If any person shall conspire, confederate or combine with another or others in the Commonwealth to go upon or remain upon the lands, buildings or premises of another, or any part, portion or area thereof, having knowledge that any of them have been forbidden, either orally or in writing, to do so by the owner, lessee, custodian or other person lawfully in charge thereof, or having knowledge that any of them have been forbidden to do so by a sign or signs posted on such lands, buildings, premises or part, portion or area thereof at a place or places where it or they may reasonably be seen, he shall be deemed guilty of a Class 3 misdemeanor.

B. If any person shall conspire, confederate or combine with another or others in the Commonwealth to commit larceny or counsel, assist, aid or abet another in the performance of a larceny, where the aggregate value of the goods or merchandise involved is more than $200, he is guilty of a felony punishable by confinement in a state correctional facility for not less than one year nor more than 20 years. The willful concealment of goods or merchandise of any store or other mercantile establishment, while still on the premises thereof, shall be prima facie evidence of an intent to convert and defraud the owner thereof out of the value of the goods or merchandise. A violation of this subsection constitutes a separate and distinct felony.

C. Jurisdiction for the trial of any person charged under this section shall be in the county or city wherein any part of such conspiracy is planned, or in the county or city wherein any act is done toward the consummation of such plan or conspiracy.

History.
Code 1950, § 18.1-15.1; 1960, cc. 99, 358; 1975, cc. 14, 15; 2003, c. 831.

§ 18.2-23.1. Completed substantive offense bars conviction for conspiracy.

Notwithstanding any other provision of this article or of § 18.2-256, in any case where a defendant has been tried and convicted of an act he has also conspired to commit, such defendant shall be subject to conviction only for the completed substantive offense and not thereafter be convicted for the underlying conspiracy.

History.
1985, c. 376.

§ 18.2-24: Reserved.

ARTICLE 2.

ATTEMPTS.

§ 18.2-25. Attempts to commit capital offenses; how punished.

If any person attempts to commit an offense which is punishable with death, he shall be guilty of a Class 2 felony.

History.
Code 1950, § 18.1-16; 1960, c. 358; 1975, cc. 14, 15; 1985, c. 280.

§ 18.2-26. Attempts to commit noncapital felonies; how punished.

Every person who attempts to commit an offense which is a noncapital felony shall be punished as follows:

(1) If the felony attempted is punishable by a maximum punishment of life imprisonment or a term of years in excess of twenty years, an attempt thereat shall be punishable as a Class 4 felony.

(2) If the felony attempted is punishable by a maximum punishment of twenty years' imprisonment, an attempt thereat shall be punishable as a Class 5 felony.

(3) If the felony attempted is punishable by a maximum punishment of less than twenty years' imprisonment, an attempt thereat shall be punishable as a Class 6 felony.

History.
Code 1950, §§ 18.1-17, 18.1-18; 1960, c. 358; 1975, cc. 14, 15; 1994, c. 639.

§ 18.2-27. Attempts to commit misdemeanors; how punished.

Every person who attempts to commit an offense which is a misdemeanor shall be punishable by the same punishment prescribed for the offense the commission of which was the object of the attempt.

History.
Code 1950, § 18.1-19; 1960, c. 358; 1972, c. 52; 1975, cc. 14, 15.

§ 18.2-28. Maximum punishment for attempts.

Any provision in this article notwithstanding, in no event shall the punishment for an attempt to commit an offense exceed the maximum punishment had the offense been committed.

History.
Code 1950, § 18.1-20; 1960, c. 358; 1975, cc. 14, 15.

§ 18.2-29. Criminal solicitation; penalty.

Any person who commands, entreats, or otherwise attempts to persuade another person to commit a felony other than murder, shall be guilty of a Class 6 felony. Any person age eighteen or older who commands, entreats, or otherwise attempts to persuade another person under age eighteen to commit a felony other than murder, shall be guilty of a Class 5 felony. Any person who commands, entreats, or otherwise attempts to persuade another person to commit a murder is guilty of a felony punishable by confinement in a state correctional facility for a term not less than five years or more than forty years.

History.
1975, cc. 14, 15; 1994, cc. 364, 440; 2002, cc. 615, 635.

CHAPTER 4.

CRIMES AGAINST THE PERSON.

Article 1.

Homicide.

Article 2.

Crimes by Mobs.

Article 2.1.

Crimes by Gangs.

Article 2.2.

Terrorism Offenses.

Article 3.

Kidnapping and Related Offenses.

Article 4.

Assaults and Bodily Woundings.

Article 5.

Robbery.

Article 6.

Extortion and Other Threats.

Article 7.

Criminal Sexual Assault.

Crimes and Offenses

Article 8.

Seduction.

Article 9.

Abortion.

ARTICLE 1.
HOMICIDE.

§ 18.2-30. Murder and manslaughter declared felonies.

Any person who commits capital murder, murder of the first degree, murder of the second degree, voluntary manslaughter, or involuntary manslaughter, shall be guilty of a felony.

History.
1975, cc. 14, 15.

§ 18.2-31. Capital murder defined; punishment.

The following offenses shall constitute capital murder, punishable as a Class 1 felony:

1. The willful, deliberate, and premeditated killing of any person in the commission of abduction, as defined in § 18.2-48, when such abduction was committed with the intent to extort money or a pecuniary benefit or with the intent to defile the victim of such abduction;

2. The willful, deliberate, and premeditated killing of any person by another for hire;

3. The willful, deliberate, and premeditated killing of any person by a prisoner confined in a state or local correctional facility as defined in § 53.1-1, or while in the custody of an employee thereof;

4. The willful, deliberate, and premeditated killing of any person in the commission of robbery or attempted robbery;

5. The willful, deliberate, and premeditated killing of any person in the commission of, or subsequent to, rape or attempted rape, forcible sodomy or attempted forcible sodomy or object sexual penetration;

6. The willful, deliberate, and premeditated killing of a law-enforcement officer as defined in § 9.1-101, a fire marshal appointed pursuant to § 27-30 or a deputy or an assistant fire marshal appointed pursuant to § 27-36, when such fire marshal or deputy or assistant fire marshal has police powers as set forth in §§ 27-34.2 and 27-34.2:1, an auxiliary police officer appointed or provided for pursuant to §§ 15.2-1731 and 15.2-1733, an auxiliary deputy sheriff appointed pursuant to § 15.2-1603, or any law-enforcement officer of another state or the United States having the power to arrest for a felony under the laws of such state or the United States, when such killing is for the purpose of interfering with the performance of his official duties;

7. The willful, deliberate, and premeditated killing of more than one person as a part of the same act or transaction;

8. The willful, deliberate, and premeditated killing of more than one person within a three-year period;

9. The willful, deliberate, and premeditated killing of any person in the commission of or attempted commission of a violation of § 18.2-248, involving a Schedule I or II controlled substance, when such killing is for the purpose of furthering the commission or attempted commission of such violation;

10. The willful, deliberate, and premeditated killing of any person by another pursuant to the direction or order of one who is engaged in a continuing criminal enterprise as defined in subsection I of § 18.2-248;

11. The willful, deliberate, and premeditated killing of a pregnant woman by one who knows that the woman is pregnant and has the intent to cause the involuntary termination of the woman's pregnancy without a live birth;

12. The willful, deliberate, and premeditated killing of a person under the age of fourteen by a person age twenty-one or older;

13. The willful, deliberate, and premeditated killing of any person by another in the commission of or attempted commission of an act of terrorism as defined in § 18.2-46.4;

14. The willful, deliberate, and premeditated killing of a justice of the Supreme Court, a judge of the Court of Appeals, a judge of a circuit court or district court, a retired judge sitting by designation or under temporary recall, or a substitute judge appointed under § 16.1-69.9:1 when the killing is for the purpose of interfering with his official duties as a judge; and

15. The willful, deliberate, and premeditated killing of any witness in a criminal case after a subpoena has been issued for such witness by the court, the clerk, or an attorney, when the killing is for the purpose of interfering with the person's duties in such case.

If any one or more subsections, sentences, or parts of this section shall be judged unconstitutional or invalid, such adjudication shall not affect, impair, or invalidate the remaining provisions thereof but shall be confined in its operation to the specific provisions so held unconstitutional or invalid.

History.

Code 1950, §§ 18.1-21, 53-291; 1960, c. 358; 1962, c. 42; 1966, c. 300; 1970, c. 648; 1973, c. 403; 1975, cc. 14, 15; 1976, c. 503; 1977, c. 478; 1979, c. 582; 1980, c. 221; 1981, c. 607; 1982, c. 636; 1983, c. 175; 1985, c. 428; 1988, c. 550; 1989, c. 527; 1990, c. 746; 1991, c. 232; 1995, c. 340; 1996, cc. 876, 959; 1997, cc. 235, 313, 514, 709; 1998, c. 887; 2002, cc. 588, 623; 2007, cc. 844, 845, 846; 2010, cc. 399, 428, 475.

§ 18.2-32. First and second degree murder defined; punishment.

Murder, other than capital murder, by poison, lying in wait, imprisonment, starving, or by any willful, deliberate, and premeditated killing, or in the commission of, or attempt to commit, arson, rape, forcible sodomy, inanimate or animate object sexual penetration, robbery, burglary or abduction, except as provided in § 18.2-31, is murder of the first degree, punishable as a Class 2 felony.

All murder other than capital murder and murder in the first degree is murder of the second degree and is punishable by confinement in a state correctional facility for not less than five nor more than forty years.

History.

Code 1950, § 18.1-21; 1960, c. 358; 1962, c. 42; 1975, cc. 14, 15; 1976, c. 503; 1977, cc. 478, 492; 1981, c. 397; 1993, cc. 463, 490; 1998, c. 281.

§ 18.2-32.1. Murder of a pregnant woman; penalty.

The willful and deliberate killing of a pregnant woman without premeditation by one who knows that the woman is pregnant and has the intent to cause the involuntary termination of the woman's pregnancy without a live birth shall be punished by a term of imprisonment of not less than ten years nor more than forty years.

History.

1997, c. 709.

§ 18.2-32.2. Killing a fetus; penalty.

A. Any person who unlawfully, willfully, deliberately, maliciously and with premeditation kills the fetus of another is guilty of a Class 2 felony.

B. Any person who unlawfully, willfully, deliberately and maliciously kills the fetus of another is guilty of a felony punishable by confinement in a state correctional facility for not less than five nor more than 40 years.

History.

2004, cc. 1023, 1026.

§ 18.2-32.3. Human infant; independent and separate existence.

For the purposes of this article, the fact that the umbilical cord has not been cut or that the placenta remains attached shall not be considered in determining whether a human infant has achieved an independent and separate existence.

History.

2010, cc. 810, 851.

§ 18.2-33. Felony homicide defined; punishment.

The killing of one accidentally, contrary to the intention of the parties, while in the prosecution of some felonious act other than those specified in §§ 18.2-31 and 18.2-32, is murder of the second degree and is punishable by confinement in a state correctional facility for not less than five years nor more than forty years.

History.

1975, cc. 14, 15; 1999, c. 282.

§ 18.2-34: Reserved.

§ 18.2-35. How voluntary manslaughter punished.

Voluntary manslaughter is punishable as a Class 5 felony.

History.

Code 1950, § 18.1-24; 1960, c. 358; 1972, cc. 14, 15.

§ 18.2-36. How involuntary manslaughter punished.

Involuntary manslaughter is punishable as a Class 5 felony.

History.

Code 1950, § 18.1-25; 1960, c. 358; 1975, cc. 14, 15; 1982, c. 301.

§ 18.2-36.1. Certain conduct punishable as involuntary manslaughter.

A. Any person who, as a result of driving under the influence in violation of clause (ii), (iii), or (iv) of § 18.2-266 or any local ordinance substantially similar thereto unintentionally causes the death of another person, shall be guilty of involuntary manslaughter.

B. If, in addition, the conduct of the defendant was so gross, wanton and culpable as to show a reckless disregard for human life, he shall be guilty of aggravated involuntary manslaughter, a felony punishable by a term of imprisonment of not less than one nor more than 20 years, one year of which shall be a mandatory minimum term of imprisonment.

Crimes and Offenses

C. The provisions of this section shall not preclude prosecution under any other homicide statute. This section shall not preclude any other revocation or suspension required by law. The driver's license of any person convicted under this section shall be revoked pursuant to subsection B of § 46.2-391.

History.
1989, cc. 554, 574; 1992, c. 862; 1994, cc. 635, 682; 1999, cc. 945, 987; 2000, cc. 956, 982; 2004, c. 461.

§ 18.2-36.2. Involuntary manslaughter; operating a watercraft while under the influence; penalties.

A. Any person who, as a result of operating a watercraft or motorboat in violation of clause (ii), (iii), or (iv) of subsection B of § 29.1-738 or a similar local ordinance, unintentionally causes the death of another person, is guilty of involuntary manslaughter.

B. If, in addition, the conduct of the defendant was so gross, wanton, and culpable as to show a reckless disregard for human life, he shall be guilty of aggravated involuntary manslaughter, a felony punishable by a term of imprisonment of not less than one nor more than 20 years, one year of which shall be a mandatory minimum term of imprisonment.

C. The provisions of this section shall not preclude prosecution under any other homicide statute. The court shall order any person convicted under this section not to operate a watercraft or motorboat that is underway upon the waters of the Commonwealth. After five years have passed from the date of the conviction, the convicted person may petition the court that entered the conviction for the right to operate a watercraft or motorboat upon the waters of the Commonwealth. Upon consideration of such petition, the court may restore the right to operate a watercraft or motorboat subject to such terms and conditions as the court deems appropriate, including the successful completion of a water safety alcohol rehabilitation program described in § 29.1-738.5.

History.
2005, c. 376.

§ 18.2-37. How and where homicide prosecuted and punished if death occur without the Commonwealth.

If any person be stricken or poisoned in this Commonwealth, and die by reason thereof out of this Commonwealth, the offender shall be as guilty, and shall be prosecuted and punished, as if the death had occurred in the county or corporation in which the stroke or poison was given or administered.

History.
Code 1950, § 18.1-26; 1960, c. 358; 1975, cc. 14, 15.

ARTICLE 2.
CRIMES BY MOBS.

§ 18.2-38. "Mob" defined.

Any collection of people, assembled for the purpose and with the intention of committing an assault or a battery upon any person or an act of violence as defined in § 19.2-297.1, without authority of law, shall be deemed a *"mob."*

History.
Code 1950, § 18.1-27; 1960, c. 358; 1975, cc. 14, 15; 1999, c. 623.

§ 18.2-39. "Lynching" defined.

Any act of violence by a mob upon the body of any person, which shall result in the death of such person, shall constitute a *"lynching."*

History.
Code 1950, § 18.1-28; 1960, c. 358; 1975, cc. 14, 15.

§ 18.2-40. Lynching deemed murder.

Every lynching shall be deemed murder. Any and every person composing a mob and any and every accessory thereto, by which any person is lynched, shall be guilty of murder, and upon conviction, shall be punished as provided in Article 1 (§ 18.2-30 et seq.) of this chapter.

History.
Code 1950, § 18.1-29; 1960, c. 358; 1975, cc. 14, 15.

§ 18.2-41. Shooting, stabbing, etc., with intent to maim, kill, etc., by mob.

Any and every person composing a mob which shall maliciously or unlawfully shoot, stab, cut or wound any person, or by any means cause him bodily injury with intent to maim, disable, disfigure or kill him, shall be guilty of a Class 3 felony.

History.
Code 1950, § 18.1-30; 1960, c. 358; 1975, cc. 14, 15.

§ 18.2-42. Assault or battery by mob.

Any and every person composing a mob which shall commit a simple assault or battery shall be guilty of a Class 1 misdemeanor.

History.
Code 1950, § 18.1-31; 1960, c. 358; 1975, cc. 14, 15.

§ 18.2-42.1. Acts of violence by mob.

Any and every person composing a mob which commits an act of violence as defined in § 19.2-297.1 shall be guilty of that act of violence and, upon conviction, shall be punished as provided in the section of this title which makes that act of violence unlawful.

History.
1999, c. 623.

§ 18.2-43. Apprehension and prosecution of participants in lynching.

The attorney for the Commonwealth of any county or city in which a lynching may occur shall promptly and diligently endeavor to ascertain the identity of the persons who in any way participated therein, or who composed the mob which perpetrated the same, and have them apprehended, and shall promptly proceed with the prosecution of any and all persons so found; and to the end that such offenders may not escape proper punishment, such attorney for the Commonwealth may be assisted in all such endeavors and prosecutions by the Attorney General, or other prosecutors designated by the Governor for the purpose; and the Governor may have full authority to spend such sums as he may deem necessary for the purpose of seeking out the identity, and apprehending the members of such mob.

History.
Code 1950, § 18.1-32; 1960, c. 358; 1975, cc. 14, 15.

§ 18.2-44. Civil liability for lynching.

No provisions of this article shall be construed to relieve any member of a mob from civil liability to the personal representative of the victim of a lynching.

History.
Code 1950, § 18.1-33; 1960, c. 358; 1975, cc. 14, 15.

§ 18.2-45. Persons suffering death from mob attempting to lynch another person.

Every person suffering death from a mob attempting to lynch another person shall come within the provisions of this article, and his personal representative shall be entitled to relief in the same manner and to the same extent as if he were the originally intended victim of such mob.

History.
Code 1950, § 18.1-34; 1960, c. 358; 1975, cc. 14, 15.

§ 18.2-46. Venue.

Venue for all actions and prosecutions under any of the provisions of this article shall be in the county or city wherein a lynching or other violation of any of the provisions of this article may have occurred, or of the county or city from which the person lynched or assaulted may have been taken as aforesaid.

History.
Code 1950, § 18.1-35; 1960, c. 358; 1975, cc. 14, 15; 2004, c. 144.

ARTICLE 2.1.
CRIMES BY GANGS.

§ 18.2-46.1. Definitions.

As used in this article unless the context requires otherwise or it is otherwise provided:

"Act of violence" means those felony offenses described in subsection A of § 19.2-297.1.

"Criminal street gang" means any ongoing organization, association, or group of three or more persons, whether formal or informal, (i) which has as one of its primary objectives or activities the commission of one or more criminal activities; (ii) which has an identifiable name or identifying sign or symbol; and (iii) whose members individually or collectively have engaged in the commission of, attempt to commit, conspiracy to commit, or solicitation of two or more predicate criminal acts, at least one of which is an act of violence, provided such acts were not part of a common act or transaction.

"Predicate criminal act" means (i) an act of violence; (ii) any violation of § 18.2-31, 18.2-42, 18.2-46.3, 18.2-51, 18.2-51.1, 18.2-51.2, 18.2-51.3, 18.2-51.6, 18.2-52, 18.2-52.1, 18.2-53, 18.2-53.1, 18.2-55, 18.2-56.1, 18.2-57, 18.2-57.2, 18.2-59, 18.2-83, 18.2-89, 18.2-90, 18.2-95, 18.2-108.1, 18.2-121, 18.2-127, 18.2-128, 18.2-137, 18.2-138, 18.2-146, 18.2-147, 18.2-248.01, 18.2-248.03, 18.2-255, 18.2-255.2, 18.2-279, 18.2-282.1, 18.2-286.1, 18.2-287.4, 18.2-289, 18.2-300, 18.2-308.1, 18.2-308.2, 18.2-308.2:01, 18.2-308.4, 18.2-355, 18.2-356, 18.2-357, or 18.2-357.1; (iii) a felony violation of § 18.2-60.3; (iv) a felony violation of § 18.2-248 or of 18.2-248.1 or a conspiracy to commit a felony violation of § 18.2-248 or 18.2-248.1; (v) any violation of a local ordinance adopted pursuant to § 15.2-1812.2; or (vi) any substantially similar offense under the laws of another state or territory of the United States, the District of Columbia, or the United States.

History.
2000, c. 332; 2004, cc. 396, 435, 462, 867; 2005, cc. 764, 813; 2006, cc. 262, 319, 844, 895; 2007, c. 499; 2012, c. 364; 2013, cc. 573, 645; 2014, cc. 674, 719; 2015, cc. 690, 691.

§ 18.2-46.2. Prohibited criminal street gang participation; penalty.

A. Any person who actively participates in or is a member of a criminal street gang and who knowingly and willfully participates in any predicate criminal act committed for the benefit of, at the direction of, or in association with any criminal street gang shall be guilty of a Class 5 felony. However, if such participant in or member of a criminal street gang is age eighteen years or older and knows or has reason to know that such criminal street gang also includes a juvenile member or participant, he shall be guilty of a Class 4 felony.

B. Violation of this section shall constitute a separate and distinct offense. If the acts or activities

Crimes and Offenses

violating this section also violate another provision of law, a prosecution under this section shall not prohibit or bar any prosecution or proceeding under such other provision or the imposition of any penalties provided for thereby.

History.
2000, c. 332.

§ 18.2-46.3. Recruitment of persons for criminal street gang; penalty.

A. Any person who solicits, invites, recruits, encourages or otherwise causes or attempts to cause another to actively participate in or become a member of what he knows to be a criminal street gang is guilty of a Class 1 misdemeanor. Any person age 18 years or older who solicits, invites, recruits, encourages or otherwise causes or attempts to cause a juvenile to actively participate in or become a member of what he knows to be a criminal street gang is guilty of a Class 6 felony.

B. Any person who, in order to encourage an individual (a) to join a criminal street gang, (b) to remain as a participant in or a member of a criminal street gang, or (c) to submit to a demand made by a criminal street gang to commit a felony violation of this title, (i) uses force against the individual or a member of his family or household or (ii) threatens force against the individual or a member of his family or household, which threat would place any person in reasonable apprehension of death or bodily injury, is guilty of a Class 6 felony. The definition of "family or household member" set forth in § 16.1-228 applies to this section.

History.
2000, c. 332; 2004, cc. 396, 435.

§ 18.2-46.3:1. Third or subsequent conviction of criminal street gang crimes.

Upon a felony conviction of § 18.2-46.2 or § 18.2-46.3, where it is alleged in the warrant, information or indictment on which a person is convicted that (i) such person has been previously convicted twice under any combination of § 18.2-46.2 or § 18.2-46.3, within 10 years of the third or subsequent offense, and (ii) each such offense occurred on different dates, such person is guilty of a Class 3 felony.

History.
2004, cc. 396, 435, 847.

§ 18.2-46.3:2. Forfeiture.

All property, both personal and real, of any kind or character used in substantial connection with, intended for use in the course of, derived from, traceable to, or realized through, including any profit or interest derived from, any conduct in violation of any provision of this article is subject to civil forfeiture to the Commonwealth. Further, all property, both personal and real, of any kind or character used or intended to be used in substantial connection with, during the course of, derived from, traceable to, or realized through, including any profit or interest derived from, criminal street gang member recruitment as prohibited under § 18.2-46.3 is subject to civil forfeiture to the Commonwealth. The forfeiture proceeding shall utilize the provisions of Chapter 22.1 (§ 19.2-386.1 et seq.) of Title 19.2 and the procedures specified therein shall apply, mutatis mutandis, to all forfeitures under this article. The application of one civil remedy under the article does not preclude the application of any other remedy, civil or criminal, under this article or any other provision of the Code.

History.
2004, cc. 396, 435.

§ 18.2-46.3:3. Enhanced punishment for gang activity taking place in a gang-free zone; penalties.

Any person who violates § 18.2-46.2 (i) upon the property, including buildings and grounds, of any public or private elementary, secondary, or postsecondary school, or any public or private two-year or four-year institution of higher education; (ii) upon public property or any property open to public use within 1,000 feet of such school property; (iii) on any school bus as defined in § 46.2-100; or (iv) upon the property, including buildings and grounds, of any publicly owned or operated community center or any publicly owned or operated recreation center is guilty of a felony punishable as specified in § 18.2-46.2, and shall be sentenced to a mandatory minimum term of imprisonment of two years to be served consecutively with any other sentence. A person who violates subsection A of § 18.2-46.3 upon any property listed in this section is guilty of a Class 6 felony, except that any person 18 years of age or older who violates subsection A of § 18.2-46.3 upon any property listed in this section, when such offense is committed against a juvenile, is guilty of a Class 5 felony. Any person who violates subsection B of § 18.2-46.3 upon any property listed in this section is guilty of a Class 5 felony. It is a violation of this section if the person violated § 18.2-46.2 or 18.2-46.3 on the property described in clauses (i) through (iii) regardless of where the person intended to commit such violation.

History.
2005, cc. 764, 813; 2010, c. 364; 2013, cc. 761, 774.

ARTICLE 2.2. TERRORISM OFFENSES.

§ 18.2-46.4. Definitions.

As used in this article unless the context requires otherwise or it is otherwise provided:

"Act of terrorism" means an act of violence as defined in clause (i) of subdivision A of § 19.2-297.1 committed with the intent to (i) intimidate the civilian population at large; or (ii) influence the conduct or activities of the government of the United States, a state or locality through intimidation.

"Base offense" means an act of violence as defined in clause (i) of subdivision A of § 19.2-297.1 committed with the intent required to commit an act of terrorism.

"Weapon of terrorism" means any device or material that is designed, intended or used to cause death, bodily injury or serious bodily harm, through the release, dissemination, or impact of (i) poisonous chemicals; (ii) an infectious biological substance; or (iii) release of radiation or radioactivity.

History.
2002, cc. 588, 623.

§ 18.2-46.5. Committing, conspiring and aiding and abetting acts of terrorism prohibited; penalty.

A. Any person who commits or conspires to commit, or aids and abets the commission of an act of terrorism, as defined in § 18.2-46.4, is guilty of a Class 2 felony if the base offense of such act of terrorism may be punished by life imprisonment, or a term of imprisonment of not less than twenty years.

B. Any person who commits, conspires to commit, or aids and abets the commission of an act of terrorism, as defined in § 18.2-46.4, is guilty of a Class 3 felony if the maximum penalty for the base offense of such act of terrorism is a term of imprisonment or incarceration in jail of less than twenty years.

C. Any person who solicits, invites, recruits, encourages, or otherwise causes or attempts to cause another to participate in an act or acts of terrorism, as defined in § 18.2-46.4, is guilty of a Class 4 felony.

History.
2002, cc. 588, 623; 2007, c. 409.

§ 18.2-46.6. Possession, manufacture, distribution, etc. of weapon of terrorism or hoax device prohibited; penalty.

A. Any person who, with the intent to commit an act of terrorism, possesses, uses, sells, gives, distributes or manufactures (i) a weapon of terrorism or (ii) a "fire bomb," "explosive material," or "device," as those terms are defined in § 18.2-85, is guilty of a Class 2 felony.

B. Any person who, with the intent to commit an act of terrorism, possesses, uses, sells, gives, distributes or manufactures any device or material that by its design, construction, content or characteristics appears to be or appears to contain a (i) weapon of terrorism or (ii) a "fire bomb," "explosive material," or "device," as those terms are defined in § 18.2-85, but that is an imitation of any such weapon of terrorism, "fire bomb," "explosive material," or "device" is guilty of a Class 3 felony.

C. Any person who, with the intent to (i) intimidate the civilian population, (ii) influence the conduct or activities of the government of the United States, a state or locality through intimidation, (iii) compel the emergency evacuation of any place of assembly, building or other structure or any means of mass transportation, or (iv) place any person in reasonable apprehension of bodily harm, uses, sells, gives, distributes or manufactures any device or material that by its design, construction, content or characteristics appears to be or appears to contain a weapon of terrorism, but that is an imitation of any such weapon of terrorism is guilty of a Class 6 felony.

History.
2002, cc. 588, 623.

§ 18.2-46.7. Act of bioterrorism against agricultural crops or animals; penalty.

Any person who maliciously destroys or devastates agricultural crops or agricultural animals having a value of $2,500 or more through the use of an infectious biological substance with the intent to (i) intimidate the civilian population or (ii) influence the conduct or activities of the government of the United States, a state or locality through intimidation, is guilty of a Class 3 felony.

For the purposes of this section *"agricultural animal"* means all livestock and poultry as defined in § 3.2-5900 and *"agricultural crop"* means cultivated plants or produce, including grain, silage, forages, oilseeds, vegetables, fruits, nursery stock or turf grass.

History.
2002, cc. 588, 623.

§ 18.2-46.8. Venue.

Venue for any violation of this article may be had in the county or city where such crime is alleged to have occurred or where any act in furtherance of an act prohibited by this article was committed.

History.
2002, cc. 588, 623.

§ 18.2-46.9: Repealed by Acts 2004, c. 995.

Cross references.
For current provisions concerning seizure of property used in connection with or derived from terrorism, see § 19.2-386.15.

§ 18.2-46.10. Violation of sections within article separate and distinct offenses.

A violation of any section in this article shall constitute a separate and distinct offense. If the acts or activities violating any section within this article also violate another provision of law, a prosecution under any section in this article shall not prohibit or bar any prosecution or proceeding under such other provision or the imposition of any penalties provided for thereby.

History.
2002, cc. 588, 623.

ARTICLE 3. KIDNAPPING AND RELATED OFFENSES.

§ 18.2-47. Abduction and kidnapping defined; punishment.

A. Any person who, by force, intimidation or deception, and without legal justification or excuse, seizes, takes, transports, detains or secretes another person with the intent to deprive such other person of his personal liberty or to withhold or conceal him from any person, authority or institution lawfully entitled to his charge, shall be deemed guilty of "abduction."

B. Any person who, by force, intimidation or deception, and without legal justification or excuse, seizes, takes, transports, detains or secretes another person with the intent to subject him to forced labor or services shall be deemed guilty of "abduction." For purposes of this subsection, the term "intimidation" shall include destroying, concealing, confiscating, withholding, or threatening to withhold a passport, immigration document, or other governmental identification or threatening to report another as being illegally present in the United States.

C. The provisions of this section shall not apply to any law-enforcement officer in the performance of his duty. The terms "abduction" and "kidnapping" shall be synonymous in this Code. Abduction for which no punishment is otherwise prescribed shall be punished as a Class 5 felony.

D. If an offense under subsection A is committed by the parent of the person abducted and punishable as contempt of court in any proceeding then pending, the offense shall be a Class 1 misdemeanor in addition to being punishable as contempt of court. However, such offense, if committed by the parent of the person abducted and punishable as contempt of court in any proceeding then pending and the person abducted is removed from the Commonwealth by the abducting parent, shall be a Class 6 felony in addition to being punishable as contempt of court.

History.
Code 1950, §§ 18.1-36, 18.1-37; 1960, c. 358; 1975, cc. 14, 15; 1979, c. 663; 1980, c. 506; 1997, c. 747; 2009, c. 662.

§ 18.2-48. Abduction with intent to extort money or for immoral purpose.

Abduction (i) of any person with the intent to extort money or pecuniary benefit, (ii) of any person with intent to defile such person, (iii) of any child under sixteen years of age for the purpose of concubinage or prostitution, (iv) of any person for the purpose of prostitution, or (v) of any minor for the purpose of manufacturing child pornography shall be punishable as a Class 2 felony. If the sentence imposed for a violation of (ii), (iii), (iv), or (v) includes a term of confinement less than life imprisonment, the judge shall impose, in addition to any active sentence, a suspended sentence of no less than 40 years. This suspended sentence shall be suspended for the remainder of the defendant's life subject to revocation by the court.

History.
Code 1950, § 18.1-38; 1960, c. 358; 1966, c. 214; 1975, cc. 14, 15; 1993, c. 317; 1997, c. 747; 2006, cc. 853, 914; 2011, c. 785.

§ 18.2-48.1. Abduction by prisoners or committed persons; penalty.

Any person confined in a state, local, or community correctional facility or committed to the Department of Juvenile Justice in any juvenile correctional center, or in the custody of an employee thereof, or who has escaped from any such facility or from any person in charge of such prisoner or committed person, who abducts or takes any person hostage is guilty of a Class 3 felony.

History.
1985, c. 526; 1986, c. 414; 2013, cc. 707, 782.

§ 18.2-49. Threatening, attempting or assisting in such abduction.

Any person who (1) threatens, or attempts, to abduct any other person with intent to extort money, or pecuniary benefit, or (2) assists or aids in the abduction of, or threatens to abduct, any person with the intent to defile such person, or (3) assists or aids in the abduction of, or threatens to abduct, any female under sixteen years of age for the purpose of concubinage or prostitution, shall be guilty of a Class 5 felony.

History.
Code 1950, § 18.1-39; 1960, c. 358; 1966, c. 214; 1975, cc. 14, 15.

§ 18.2-49.1. Violation of court order regarding custody and visitation; penalty.

A. Any person who knowingly, wrongfully and intentionally withholds a child from either of a child's parents or other legal guardian in a clear and significant violation of a court order respecting the custody or visitation of such child, provided such child is withheld outside of the Commonwealth, is guilty of a Class 6 felony.

B. Any person who knowingly, wrongfully and intentionally engages in conduct that constitutes a clear and significant violation of a court order respecting the custody or visitation of a child is guilty of a Class 3 misdemeanor upon conviction of a first offense. Any person who commits a second violation of this section within 12 months of a first conviction is guilty of a Class 2 misdemeanor, and any person who commits a third violation occurring within 24 months of the first conviction is guilty of a Class 1 misdemeanor.

History.

1987, c. 704; 1989, c. 486; 1994, c. 575; 2002, cc. 576, 596; 2003, c. 261.

§ 18.2-50. Disclosure of information and assistance to law-enforcement officers required.

Whenever it is brought to the attention of the members of the immediate family of any person that such person has been abducted, or that threats or attempts have been made to abduct any such person, such members shall make immediate report thereof to the police or other law-enforcement officers of the county, city or town where such person resides, and shall render all such possible assistance to such officers in the capture and conviction of the person or persons guilty of the alleged offense. Any person violating any of the provisions of this section shall be guilty of a Class 2 misdemeanor.

History.

Code 1950, § 18.1-40; 1960, c. 358; 1975, cc. 14, 15.

§ 18.2-50.1: Repealed by Acts 1992, c. 479.

Cross references.

For present provisions as to emergency control of telephone service in hostage or barricaded person situation, see § 18.2-50.2.

§ 18.2-50.2. Emergency control of telephone service in hostage or barricaded person situation.

A. The Superintendent of the State Police or the chief law-enforcement officer or sheriff of any county, city or town may designate one or more law-enforcement officers with appropriate technical training or expertise as a hostage and barricade communications specialist.

B. Each telephone company providing service to Virginia residents shall designate a department or one or more individuals to provide liaison with law-enforcement agencies for the purposes of this section and shall designate telephone numbers, not exceeding two, at which such law-enforcement liaison department or individual can be contacted.

C. The supervising law-enforcement officer, who has jurisdiction in any situation in which there is probable cause to believe that the criminal enterprise of hostage holding is occurring or that a person has barricaded himself within a structure and poses an immediate threat to the life, safety or property of himself or others, may order a telephone company, or a hostage and barricade communications specialist to interrupt, reroute, divert, or otherwise control any telephone communications service involved in the hostage or barricade situation for the purpose of preventing telephone communication by a hostage holder or barricaded person with any person other than a law-enforcement officer or a person authorized by the officer.

D. A hostage and barricade communication specialist shall be ordered to act under subsection C only if the telephone company providing service in the area has been contacted and requested to act under subsection C or an attempt to contact has been made, using the telephone company's designated liaison telephone numbers and:

1. The officer's attempt to contact after ten rings for each call is unsuccessful;

2. The telephone company declines to respond to the officer's request because of a threat of personal injury to its employees; or

3. The telephone company indicates when contacted that it will be unable to respond appropriately to the officer's request within a reasonable time from the receipt of the request.

E. The supervising law-enforcement officer may give an order under subsection C only after that supervising law-enforcement officer has given or attempted to give written notification or oral notification of the hostage or barricade situation to the telephone company providing service to the area in which it is occurring. If an order is given on the basis of an oral notice, the oral notice shall be followed by a written confirmation of that notice within forty-eight hours of the order.

F. Good faith reliance on an order by a supervising law-enforcement officer who has the real or apparent authority to issue an order under this section shall constitute a complete defense to any action against a telephone company or a telephone company employee that rises out of attempts by the telephone company or the employees of the telephone company to comply with such an order.

History.

1992, c. 479.

§ 18.2-50.3. Enticing, etc., another into a dwelling house with intent to commit certain felonies; penalty.

Any person who commits a violation of § 18.2-31, 18.2-32, 18.2-32.1, 18.2-48, 18.2-51.2, 18.2-58, 18.2-61, 18.2-67.1, or 18.2-67.2 within a dwelling house and who, with the intent to commit a felony listed in this section, enticed, solicited, requested, or otherwise caused the victim to enter such dwelling house is guilty of a Class 6 felony. A violation of this section is a separate and distinct felony.

History.

2015, c. 392.

ARTICLE 4.
ASSAULTS AND BODILY WOUNDINGS.

§ 18.2-51. Shooting, stabbing, etc., with intent to maim, kill, etc.

If any person maliciously shoot, stab, cut, or wound any person or by any means cause him bodily injury, with the intent to maim, disfigure, disable, or kill, he shall, except where it is otherwise provided, be guilty of a Class 3 felony. If such act be done unlawfully but not maliciously, with the intent aforesaid, the offender shall be guilty of a Class 6 felony.

History.
Code 1950, § 18.1-65; 1960, c. 358; 1975, cc. 14, 15.

§ 18.2-51.1. Malicious bodily injury to law-enforcement officers, firefighters, search and rescue personnel, or emergency medical services personnel; penalty; lesser-included offense.

If any person maliciously causes bodily injury to another by any means including the means set out in § 18.2-52, with intent to maim, disfigure, disable or kill, and knowing or having reason to know that such other person is a law-enforcement officer, as defined hereinafter, firefighter, as defined in § 65.2-102, search and rescue personnel as defined hereinafter, or emergency medical services personnel, as defined in § 32.1-111.1 engaged in the performance of his public duties as a law-enforcement officer, firefighter, search and rescue personnel, or emergency medical services personnel, such person is guilty of a felony punishable by imprisonment for a period of not less than five years nor more than 30 years and, subject to subdivision (g) of § 18.2-10, a fine of not more than $100,000. Upon conviction, the sentence of such person shall include a mandatory minimum term of imprisonment of two years.

If any person unlawfully, but not maliciously, with the intent aforesaid, causes bodily injury to another by any means, knowing or having reason to know such other person is a law-enforcement officer, firefighter, as defined in § 65.2-102, search and rescue personnel, or emergency medical services personnel, engaged in the performance of his public duties as a law-enforcement officer, firefighter, search and rescue personnel, or emergency medical services personnel as defined in § 32.1-111.1, he is guilty of a Class 6 felony, and upon conviction, the sentence of such person shall include a mandatory minimum term of imprisonment of one year.

Nothing in this section shall be construed to affect the right of any person charged with a violation of this section from asserting and presenting evidence in support of any defenses to the charge that may be available under common law.

As used in this section, "law-enforcement officer" means any full-time or part-time employee of a police department or sheriff's office that is part of or administered by the Commonwealth or any political subdivision thereof, who is responsible for the prevention or detection of crime and the enforcement of the penal, traffic, or highway laws of the Commonwealth; any conservation officer of the Department of Conservation and Recreation commissioned pursuant to § 10.1-115; any conservation police officer appointed pursuant to § 29.1-200; and auxiliary police officers appointed or provided for pursuant to §§ 15.2-1731 and 15.2-1733 and auxiliary deputy sheriffs appointed pursuant to § 15.2-1603.

As used in this section, "search and rescue personnel" means any employee or member of a search and rescue organization that is authorized by a resolution or ordinance duly adopted by the governing body of any county, city, or town of the Commonwealth or any member of a search and rescue organization operating under a memorandum of understanding with the Virginia Department of Emergency Management.

The provisions of § 18.2-51 shall be deemed to provide a lesser-included offense hereof.

History.
1983, c. 578; 1985, c. 444; 1994, cc. 205, 427; 1997, cc. 8, 120; 2002, cc. 588, 623; 2004, cc. 461, 841; 2007, c. 87; 2010, c. 344; 2015, cc. 502, 503.

§ 18.2-51.2. Aggravated malicious wounding; penalty.

A. If any person maliciously shoots, stabs, cuts or wounds any other person, or by any means causes bodily injury, with the intent to maim, disfigure, disable or kill, he shall be guilty of a Class 2 felony if the victim is thereby severely injured and is caused to suffer permanent and significant physical impairment.

B. If any person maliciously shoots, stabs, cuts or wounds any other woman who is pregnant, or by any other means causes bodily injury, with the intent to maim, disfigure, disable or kill the pregnant woman or to cause the involuntary termination of her pregnancy, he shall be guilty of a Class 2 felony if the victim is thereby severely injured and is caused to suffer permanent and significant physical impairment.

C. For purposes of this section, the involuntary termination of a woman's pregnancy shall be deemed a severe injury and a permanent and significant physical impairment.

History.
1986, c. 460; 1991, c. 670; 1997, c. 709.

§ 18.2-51.3. Prohibition against reckless endangerment of others by throwing objects from places higher than one story; penalty.

A. It shall be unlawful for any person, with the intent to cause injury to another, to intentionally throw from a balcony, roof top, or other place more than one story above ground level any object capable of causing any such injury.

B. A violation of this section shall be punishable as a Class 6 felony.

History.
1990, c. 761.

§ 18.2-51.4. Maiming, etc., of another resulting from driving while intoxicated.

A. Any person who, as a result of driving while intoxicated in violation of § 18.2-266 or any local ordinance substantially similar thereto in a manner so gross, wanton and culpable as to show a reckless disregard for human life, unintentionally causes the serious bodily injury of another person resulting in permanent and significant physical impairment shall be guilty of a Class 6 felony. The driver's license of any person convicted under this section shall be revoked pursuant to subsection B of § 46.2-391.

B. The provisions of Article 2 (§ 18.2-266 et seq.) of Chapter 7 of Title 18.2 shall apply, mutatis mutandis, upon arrest for a violation of this section.

History.
1997, c. 691; 1999, cc. 945, 987; 2000, cc. 956, 982.

§ 18.2-51.5. Maiming, etc., of another resulting from operating a watercraft while intoxicated; penalty.

A. Any person who, as a result of operating a watercraft or motorboat in violation of subsection B of § 29.1-738 or a similar local ordinance in a manner so gross, wanton, and culpable as to show reckless disregard for human life, unintentionally causes the serious bodily injury of another person resulting in permanent and significant physical impairment is guilty of a Class 6 felony. The court shall order any person convicted under this section not to operate a watercraft or motorboat that is underway upon the waters of the Commonwealth. After two years have passed from the date of the conviction, the convicted person may petition the court that entered the conviction for the right to operate a watercraft or motorboat upon the waters of the Commonwealth. Upon consideration of such petition, the court may restore the right to operate a watercraft or motorboat subject to such terms and conditions as the court deems appropriate, including the successful completion of a water safety alcohol rehabilitation program described in § 29.1-738.5.

B. The provisions of Article 3 (§ 29.1-734 et seq.) of Chapter 7 of Title 29.1 shall apply, mutatis mutandis, upon arrest for a violation of this section.

History.
2007, cc. 379, 679.

§ 18.2-51.6. Strangulation of another; penalty.

Any person who, without consent, impedes the blood circulation or respiration of another person by knowingly, intentionally, and unlawfully applying pressure to the neck of such person resulting in the wounding or bodily injury of such person is guilty of strangulation, a Class 6 felony.

History.
2012, cc. 577, 602.

§ 18.2-52. Malicious bodily injury by means of any caustic substance or agent or use of any explosive or fire.

If any person maliciously causes any other person bodily injury by means of any acid, lye or other caustic substance or agent or use of any explosive or fire, he shall be guilty of a felony and shall be punished by confinement in a state correctional facility for a period of not less than five years nor more than thirty years. If such act is done unlawfully but not maliciously, the offender shall be guilty of a Class 6 felony.

History.
Code 1950, § 18.1-67; 1960, c. 358; 1975, cc. 14, 15, 604; 1995, c. 439.

§ 18.2-52.1. Possession of infectious biological substances or radiological agents; penalties.

A. Any person who possesses, with the intent thereby to injure another, an infectious biological substance or radiological agent is guilty of a Class 5 felony.

B. Any person who (i) destroys or damages, or attempts to destroy or damage, any facility, equipment or material involved in the sale, manufacturing, storage or distribution of an infectious biological substance or radiological agent, with the intent to injure another by releasing the substance, or (ii) manufactures, sells, gives, distributes or uses an infectious biological substance or radiological agent with the intent to injure another is guilty of a Class 4 felony.

C. Any person who maliciously and intentionally causes any other person bodily injury by means of an infectious biological substance or radiological agent is guilty of a felony and shall be punished by confinement in a state correctional facility for a period of not less than five years nor more than 30 years.

An *"infectious biological substance"* includes any bacteria, viruses, fungi, protozoa, or rickettsiae capable of causing death or serious bodily injury. This definition shall not include HIV as defined in § 18.2-67.4:1, syphilis or hepatitis B.

A *"radiological agent"* includes any substance able to release radiation at levels that are capable of causing death or serious bodily injury.

History.
1996, c. 769; 2002, cc. 588, 623, 816; 2004, c. 833.

§ 18.2-53. Shooting, etc., in committing or attempting a felony.

If any person, in the commission of, or attempt to commit, felony, unlawfully shoot, stab, cut or wound another person he shall be guilty of a Class 6 felony.

History.
Code 1950, § 18.1-68; 1960, c. 358; 1975, cc. 14, 15.

§ 18.2-53.1. Use or display of firearm in committing felony.

It shall be unlawful for any person to use or attempt to use any pistol, shotgun, rifle, or other firearm or display such weapon in a threatening manner while committing or attempting to commit murder, rape, forcible sodomy, inanimate or animate object sexual penetration as defined in § 18.2-67.2, robbery, carjacking, burglary, malicious wounding as defined in § 18.2-51, malicious bodily injury to a law-enforcement officer as defined in § 18.2-51.1, aggravated malicious wounding as defined in § 18.2-51.2, malicious wounding by mob as defined in § 18.2-41 or abduction. Violation of this section shall constitute a separate and distinct felony and any person found guilty thereof shall be sentenced to a mandatory minimum term of imprisonment of three years for a first conviction, and to a mandatory minimum term of five years for a second or subsequent conviction under the provisions of this section. Such punishment shall be separate and apart from, and shall be made to run consecutively with, any punishment received for the commission of the primary felony.

History.
1975, cc. 624, 628; 1976, c. 371; 1980, c. 333; 1982, c. 654; 1991, c. 506; 1992, cc. 191, 726; 1993, cc. 549, 835; 1994, c. 950; 2004, c. 461.

§ 18.2-54. Conviction of lesser offenses under certain indictments.

On any indictment for maliciously shooting, stabbing, cutting or wounding a person or by any means causing him bodily injury, with intent to maim, disfigure, disable or kill him, or of causing bodily injury by means of any acid, lye or other caustic substance or agent, the jury or the court trying the case without a jury may find the accused not guilty of the offense charged but guilty of unlawfully doing such act with the intent aforesaid, or of assault and battery if the evidence warrants.

History.
Code 1950, § 19.1-251; 1960, c. 366; 1975, cc. 14, 15.

§ 18.2-54.1. Attempts to poison.

If any person administers or attempts to administer any poison or destructive substance in food, drink, prescription or over-the-counter medicine, or otherwise, or poisons any spring, well, waterworks as defined in § 32.1-167, or reservoir of water with intent to kill or injure another person, he shall be guilty of a Class 3 felony.

History.
Code 1950, § 18.1-64; 1960, c. 358; 1975, cc. 14, 15; 1983, c. 129; 2006, c. 300.

§ 18.2-54.2. Adulteration of food, drink, drugs, cosmetics, etc.; penalty.

Any person who adulterates or causes to be adulterated any food, drink, prescription or over-the-counter medicine, cosmetic or other substance with the intent to kill or injure any individual who ingests, inhales or uses such substance shall be guilty of a Class 3 felony.

History.
1983, c. 129.

§ 18.2-55. Bodily injuries caused by prisoners, state juvenile probationers and state and local adult probationers or adult parolees.

A. It shall be unlawful for a person confined in a state, local or regional correctional facility as defined in § 53.1-1; in a secure facility or detention home as defined in § 16.1-228 or in any facility designed for the secure detention of juveniles; or while in the custody of an employee thereof to knowingly and willfully inflict bodily injury on:

1. An employee thereof, or
2. Any other person lawfully admitted to such facility, except another prisoner or person held in legal custody, or
3. Any person who is supervising or working with prisoners or persons held in legal custody, or
4. Any such employee or other person while such prisoner or person held in legal custody is committing any act in violation of § 53.1-203.

B. It shall be unlawful for an accused, probationer or parolee under the supervision of, or being investigated by, (i) a probation or parole officer whose powers and duties are defined in § 16.1-237 or § 53.1-145, (ii) a local pretrial services officer associated with an agency established pursuant to Article 5 (§ 19.2-152.2) of Chapter 9 of Title 19.2, or (iii) a local community-based probation officer associated with an agency established pursuant to Article 9 (§ 9.1-173 et seq.) of Chapter 1 of Title 9.1, to knowingly and willfully inflict bodily injury on such officer while he is in the performance of his duty, knowing or having reason to know that the officer is engaged in the performance of his duty.

Any person violating any provision of this section is guilty of a Class 5 felony.

History.
1975, cc. 14, 15; 1977, c. 553; 1982, c. 636; 1985, c. 508; 1996, c. 527; 1999, cc. 618, 658; 2001, cc. 818, 848; 2007, c. 133.

§ 18.2-55.1. Hazing of youth gang members unlawful; criminal liability.

It shall be unlawful to cause bodily injury by hazing (i) any member of a criminal street gang as defined in § 18.2-46.1, or (ii) a person seeking to become a member of a youth gang or criminal street gang. Any person found guilty of hazing is guilty of a Class 1 misdemeanor.

For the purposes of this section, *"hazing"* means to recklessly or intentionally endanger the health or safety of a person or to inflict bodily injury on a person in connection with or for the purpose of initiation, admission into or affiliation with or as a condition for continued membership in a youth gang or criminal street gang regardless of whether the person so endangered or injured participated voluntarily in the relevant activity.

History.
2004, c. 850; 2005, c. 843.

§ 18.2-56. Hazing unlawful; civil and criminal liability; duty of school, etc., officials; penalty.

It shall be unlawful to haze so as to cause bodily injury, any student at any school, college, or university.

Any person found guilty thereof shall be guilty of a Class 1 misdemeanor.

Any person receiving bodily injury by hazing shall have a right to sue, civilly, the person or persons guilty thereof, whether adults or infants.

The president or other presiding official of any school, college or university receiving appropriations from the state treasury shall, upon satisfactory proof of the guilt of any student hazing another student, sanction and discipline such student in accordance with the institution's policies and procedures. The institution's policies and procedures shall provide for expulsions or other appropriate discipline based on the facts and circumstances of each case and shall be consistent with the model policies established by the Department of Education or the State Council of Higher Education for Virginia, as applicable. The president or other presiding official of any school, college or university receiving appropriations from the state treasury shall report hazing which causes bodily injury to the attorney for the Commonwealth of the county or city in which such school, college or university is, who shall take such action as he deems appropriate.

For the purposes of this section, "hazing" means to recklessly or intentionally endanger the health or safety of a student or students or to inflict bodily injury on a student or students in connection with or for the purpose of initiation, admission into or affiliation with or as a condition for continued membership in a club, organization, association, fraternity, sorority, or student body regardless of whether the student or students so endangered or injured participated voluntarily in the relevant activity.

History.
Code 1950, § 18.1-71; 1960, c. 358; 1975, cc. 14, 15; 2003, cc. 62, 67; 2014, c. 627.

§ 18.2-56.1. Reckless handling of firearms; reckless handling while hunting.

A. It shall be unlawful for any person to handle recklessly any firearm so as to endanger the life, limb or property of any person. Any person violating this section shall be guilty of a Class 1 misdemeanor.

A1. Any person who handles any firearm in a manner so gross, wanton, and culpable as to show a reckless disregard for human life and causes the serious bodily injury of another person resulting in permanent and significant physical impairment is guilty of a Class 6 felony.

B. If this section is violated while the person is engaged in hunting, trapping or pursuing game, the trial judge may, in addition to the penalty imposed by the jury or the court trying the case without a jury, revoke such person's hunting or trapping license and privileges to hunt or trap while possessing a firearm for a period of one to five years.

C. Upon a revocation pursuant to subsection B hereof, the clerk of the court in which the case is tried pursuant to this section shall forthwith send to the Department of Game and Inland Fisheries (i) such person's revoked hunting or trapping license or notice that such person's privilege to hunt or trap while in possession of a firearm has been revoked and (ii) a notice of the length of revocation imposed. The Department shall keep a list which shall be furnished upon request to any law-enforcement officer, the attorney for the Commonwealth or court in this Commonwealth, and such list shall contain the names and addresses of all persons whose license or privilege to hunt or trap while in possession of a firearm has been revoked and the court which took such action.

D. If any person whose license to hunt and trap, or whose privilege to hunt and trap while in possession of a firearm, has been revoked pursuant to this section, thereafter hunts or traps while in possession of a firearm, he shall be guilty of a Class 1 misdemeanor, and, in addition to any penalty imposed by the jury or the court trying the case without a jury, the trial judge may revoke such person's hunting or trapping license and privileges to hunt or trap while in possession of a firearm for a period of one year to life. The clerk of the court shall notify the Department of Game and Inland Fisheries as is provided in subsection C herein.

History.

1977, c. 194; 1985, c. 182; 1991, c. 384; 2010, c. 183; 2011, c. 684; 2014, cc. 444, 579.

§ 18.2-56.2. Allowing access to firearms by children; penalty.

A. It shall be unlawful for any person to recklessly leave a loaded, unsecured firearm in such a manner as to endanger the life or limb of any child under the age of fourteen. Any person violating the provisions of this subsection shall be guilty of a Class 3 misdemeanor.

B. It shall be unlawful for any person knowingly to authorize a child under the age of twelve to use a firearm except when the child is under the supervision of an adult. Any person violating this subsection shall be guilty of a Class 1 misdemeanor. For purposes of this subsection, *"adult"* shall mean a parent, guardian, person standing in loco parentis to the child or a person twenty-one years or over who has the permission of the parent, guardian, or person standing in loco parentis to supervise the child in the use of a firearm.

History.

1991, c. 537; 1994, c. 832.

§ 18.2-57. Assault and battery; penalty.

A. Any person who commits a simple assault or assault and battery is guilty of a Class 1 misdemeanor, and if the person intentionally selects the person against whom a simple assault is committed because of his race, religious conviction, color or national origin, the penalty upon conviction shall include a term of confinement of at least six months, 30 days of which shall be a mandatory minimum term of confinement.

B. However, if a person intentionally selects the person against whom an assault and battery resulting in bodily injury is committed because of his race, religious conviction, color or national origin, the person is guilty of a Class 6 felony, and the penalty upon conviction shall include a term of confinement of at least six months, 30 days of which shall be a mandatory minimum term of confinement.

C. In addition, if any person commits an assault or an assault and battery against another knowing or having reason to know that such other person is a judge, a magistrate, a law-enforcement officer as defined in subsection F, a correctional officer as defined in § 53.1-1, a person directly involved in the care, treatment, or supervision of inmates in the custody of the Department of Corrections or an employee of a local or regional correctional facility directly involved in the care, treatment, or supervision of inmates in the custody of the facility, a person directly involved in the care, treatment, or supervision of persons in the custody of or under the supervision of the Department of Juvenile Justice, an employee or other individual who provides control, care, or treatment of sexually violent predators committed to the custody of the Department of Behavioral Health and Developmental Services, a firefighter as defined in § 65.2-102, or a volunteer firefighter or any emergency medical services personnel member who is employed by or is a volunteer of an emergency medical services agency or as a member of a bona fide volunteer fire department or volunteer emergency medical services agency, regardless of whether a resolution has been adopted by the governing body of a political subdivision recognizing such firefighters or emergency medical services personnel as employees, engaged in the performance of his public duties anywhere in the Commonwealth, such person is guilty of a Class 6 felony, and, upon conviction, the sentence of such person shall include a mandatory minimum term of confinement of six months.

Nothing in this subsection shall be construed to affect the right of any person charged with a violation of this section from asserting and presenting evidence in support of any defenses to the charge that may be available under common law.

D. In addition, if any person commits a battery against another knowing or having reason to know that such other person is a full-time or part-time employee of any public or private elementary or secondary school and is engaged in the performance of his duties as such, he is guilty of a Class 1 misdemeanor and the sentence of such person upon conviction shall include a sentence of 15 days in jail, two days of which shall be a mandatory minimum term of confinement. However, if the offense is committed by use of a firearm or other weapon prohibited on school property pursuant to § 18.2-308.1, the person shall serve a mandatory minimum sentence of confinement of six months.

E. In addition, any person who commits a battery against another knowing or having reason to know that such individual is a health care provider as defined in § 8.01-581.1 who is engaged in the performance of his duties as an emergency health care provider in an emergency room of a hospital or clinic or on the premises of any other facility rendering emergency medical care is guilty of a Class 1 misdemeanor. The sentence of such person, upon conviction, shall include a term of confinement of 15 days in jail, two days of which shall be a mandatory minimum term of confinement.

F. As used in this section:

"Judge" means any justice or judge of a court of record of the Commonwealth including a judge designated under § 17.1-105, a judge under temporary recall under § 17.1-106, or a judge pro tempore

under § 17.1-109, any member of the State Corporation Commission, or of the Virginia Workers' Compensation Commission, and any judge of a district court of the Commonwealth or any substitute judge of such district court.

(Effective until July 1, 2018) *"Law-enforcement officer"* means any full-time or part-time employee of a police department or sheriff's office that is part of or administered by the Commonwealth or any political subdivision thereof who is responsible for the prevention or detection of crime and the enforcement of the penal, traffic or highway laws of the Commonwealth, any conservation officer of the Department of Conservation and Recreation commissioned pursuant to § 10.1-115, any special agent of the Department of Alcoholic Beverage Control, conservation police officers appointed pursuant to § 29.1-200, full-time sworn members of the enforcement division of the Department of Motor Vehicles appointed pursuant to § 46.2-217, and any employee with internal investigations authority designated by the Department of Corrections pursuant to subdivision 11 of § 53.1-10, and such officer also includes jail officers in local and regional correctional facilities, all deputy sheriffs, whether assigned to law-enforcement duties, court services or local jail responsibilities, auxiliary police officers appointed or provided for pursuant to §§ 15.2-1731 and 15.2-1733, auxiliary deputy sheriffs appointed pursuant to § 15.2-1603, police officers of the Metropolitan Washington Airports Authority pursuant to § 5.1-158, and fire marshals appointed pursuant to § 27-30 when such fire marshals have police powers as set out in §§ 27-34.2 and 27-34.2:1.

(Effective July 1, 2018) *"Law-enforcement officer"* means any full-time or part-time employee of a police department or sheriff's office that is part of or administered by the Commonwealth or any political subdivision thereof who is responsible for the prevention or detection of crime and the enforcement of the penal, traffic or highway laws of the Commonwealth, any conservation officer of the Department of Conservation and Recreation commissioned pursuant to § 10.1-115, any special agent of the Virginia Alcoholic Beverage Control Authority, conservation police officers appointed pursuant to § 29.1-200, full-time sworn members of the enforcement division of the Department of Motor Vehicles appointed pursuant to § 46.2-217, and any employee with internal investigations authority designated by the Department of Corrections pursuant to subdivision 11 of § 53.1-10, and such officer also includes jail officers in local and regional correctional facilities, all deputy sheriffs, whether assigned to law-enforcement duties, court services or local jail responsibilities, auxiliary police officers appointed or provided for pursuant to §§ 15.2-1731 and 15.2-1733, auxiliary deputy sheriffs appointed pursuant to § 15.2-1603, police officers of the Metropolitan Washington Airports Authority pursuant to § 5.1-158, and fire marshals appointed pursuant to § 27-30 when such fire marshals have police powers as set out in §§ 27-34.2 and 27-34.2:1.

"School security officer" means an individual who is employed by the local school board for the purpose of maintaining order and discipline, preventing crime, investigating violations of school board policies and detaining persons violating the law or school board policies on school property, a school bus or at a school-sponsored activity and who is responsible solely for ensuring the safety, security and welfare of all students, faculty and staff in the assigned school.

G. "Simple assault" or "assault and battery" shall not be construed to include the use of, by any school security officer or full-time or part-time employee of any public or private elementary or secondary school while acting in the course and scope of his official capacity, any of the following: (i) incidental, minor or reasonable physical contact or other actions designed to maintain order and control; (ii) reasonable and necessary force to quell a disturbance or remove a student from the scene of a disturbance that threatens physical injury to persons or damage to property; (iii) reasonable and necessary force to prevent a student from inflicting physical harm on himself; (iv) reasonable and necessary force for self-defense or the defense of others; or (v) reasonable and necessary force to obtain possession of weapons or other dangerous objects or controlled substances or associated paraphernalia that are upon the person of the student or within his control.

In determining whether a person was acting within the exceptions provided in this subsection, due deference shall be given to reasonable judgments that were made by a school security officer or full-time or part-time employee of any public or private elementary or secondary school at the time of the event.

History.

1975, cc. 14, 15; 1994, c. 658; 1997, c. 833; 1999, cc. 771, 1036; 2000, cc. 288, 682; 2001, c. 129; 2002, c. 817; 2004, cc. 420, 461; 2006, cc. 270, 709, 829; 2008, c. 460; 2009, c. 257; 2011, cc. 230, 233, 374; 2013, cc. 698, 707, 711, 748, 782; 2014, cc. 663, 714; 2015, cc. 38, 196, 730; 2016, c. 420.

§ 18.2-57.01. Pointing laser at law-enforcement officer unlawful; penalty.

If any person, knowing or having reason to know another person is a law-enforcement officer as defined in § 18.2-57, a probation or parole officer appointed pursuant to § 53.1-143, a correctional officer as defined in § 53.1-1, or a person employed by the Department of Corrections directly involved in the care, treatment or supervision of inmates in the custody of the Department engaged in the performance of his public duties as such, intentionally projects at such other person a beam or a point of light from a laser, a laser gun sight, or any device that simulates a laser, shall be guilty of a Class 2 misdemeanor.

History.
2000, c. 350.

§ 18.2-57.02. Disarming a law-enforcement or correctional officer; penalty.

Any person who knows or has reason to know a person is a law-enforcement officer as defined in § 18.2-57, a correctional officer as defined in § 53.1-1, or a person employed by the Department of Corrections directly involved in the care, treatment or supervision of inmates in the custody of the Department, who is engaged in the performance of his duties as such and, with the intent to impede or prevent any such person from performing his official duties, knowingly and without the person's permission removes a chemical irritant weapon or impact weapon from the possession of the officer or deprives the officer of the use of the weapon is guilty of a Class 1 misdemeanor. However, if the weapon removed or deprived in violation of this section is the officer's firearm or stun weapon as defined in § 18.2-308.1, he shall be guilty of a Class 6 felony. A violation of this section shall constitute a separate and distinct offense.

History.
2001, c. 2; 2007, c. 519.

§ 18.2-57.1: Repealed by Acts 1997, c. 833.

Editor's note.
This section was amended by Acts 1997, cc. 8 and 120. At the direction of the Code Commission, the repeal by Acts 1997, c. 833, was implemented. For comparable current provisions, see § 18.2-57, which was amended by Acts 1997, c. 833.

§ 18.2-57.2. Assault and battery against a family or household member; penalty.

A. Any person who commits an assault and battery against a family or household member is guilty of a Class 1 misdemeanor.

B. Upon a conviction for assault and battery against a family or household member, where it is alleged in the warrant, petition, information, or indictment on which a person is convicted, that such person has been previously convicted of two offenses against a family or household member of (i) assault and battery against a family or household member in violation of this section, (ii) malicious wounding or unlawful wounding in violation of § 18.2-51, (iii) aggravated malicious wounding in violation of § 18.2-51.2, (iv) malicious bodily injury by means of a substance in violation of § 18.2-52, (v) strangulation in violation of § 18.2-51.6, or (vi) an offense under the law of any other jurisdiction which has the same elements of any of the above offenses, in any combination, all of which occurred within a period of 20 years, and each of which occurred on a different date, such person is guilty of a Class 6 felony.

C. Whenever a warrant for a violation of this section is issued, the magistrate shall issue an emergency protective order as authorized by § 16.1-253.4, except if the defendant is a minor, an emergency protective order shall not be required.

D. The definition of "family or household member" in § 16.1-228 applies to this section.

History.
1991, c. 238; 1992, cc. 526, 886; 1996, c. 866; 1997, c. 603; 1999, cc. 697, 721, 807; 2004, cc. 448, 738; 2009, c. 726; 2014, c. 660.

§ 18.2-57.3. Persons charged with first offense of assault and battery against a family or household member may be placed on local community-based probation; conditions; education and treatment programs; costs and fees; violations; discharge.

A. When a person is charged with a simple assault in violation of subsection A of § 18.2-57 where the victim was a family or household member of the person or a violation of § 18.2-57.2, the court may defer the proceedings against such person, without a finding of guilt, and place him on probation under the terms of this section.

B. For a person to be eligible for such deferral, the court shall find that (i) the person was an adult at the time of the commission of the offense, (ii) the person has not previously been convicted of any offense under this article or under any statute of the United States or of any state or any ordinance of any local government relating to an assault or assault and battery against a family or household member, (iii) the person has not previously had a proceeding against him for violation of such an offense dismissed as provided in this section, (iv) the person pleads guilty to, or enters a plea of not guilty or nolo contendere and the court finds the evidence is sufficient to find the person guilty of, simple assault in violation of subsection A of § 18.2-57 where the victim was a family or household member of the person or a violation of § 18.2-57.2, and (v) the person consents to such deferral.

C. The court shall (i) where a local community-based probation services agency established pursuant to Article 9 (§ 9.1-173 et seq.) of Chapter 1 of Title 9.1 is available, order that the eligible person be placed with such agency and require, as a condition of local community-based probation, the person to successfully complete all treatment, education programs or services, or any combination thereof indicated by an assessment or evaluation obtained by the local community-based probation services agency if such assessment, treatment or education services are available; or (ii) require successful completion of treatment, education programs or services, or any combination thereof, such as, in the opinion of the court, may be best suited to the needs of the person.

D. The court shall require the person entering such education or treatment program or services under the provisions of this section to pay all or part of the costs of the program or services, including the costs of any assessment, evaluation, testing, education and treatment, based upon the person's ability to pay. Such programs or services shall offer a sliding-scale fee structure or other mechanism to assist participants who are unable to pay the full costs of the required programs or services.

The court shall order the person to be of good behavior for a total period of not less than two years following the deferral of proceedings, including the period of supervised probation, if available.

The court shall, unless done at arrest, order the person to report to the original arresting law-enforcement agency to submit to fingerprinting.

E. Upon fulfillment of the terms and conditions specified in the court order, the court shall discharge the person and dismiss the proceedings against him. Discharge and dismissal under this section shall be without adjudication of guilt and is a conviction only for the purposes of applying this section in subsequent proceedings. No charges dismissed pursuant to this section shall be eligible for expungement under § 19.2-392.2.

F. Upon violation of a term or condition of supervised probation or of the period of good behavior, the court may enter an adjudication of guilt and proceed as otherwise provided by law.

G. Notwithstanding any other provision of this section, whenever a court places a person on probation upon terms and conditions pursuant to this section, such action shall be treated as a conviction for purposes of Article 6.1 (§ 18.2-307.1 et seq.) of Chapter 7.

History.
1999, c. 963; 2000, c. 1040; 2003, cc. 33, 38; 2004, c. 377; 2007, c. 133; 2009, cc. 313, 347; 2013, c. 746; 2016, cc. 422, 742.

§ 18.2-57.4. Reporting findings of assault and battery to military family advocacy representatives.

If any active duty member of the United States Armed Forces is found guilty of a violation of § 18.2-57.2 or § 18.2-57.3, the court shall report the conviction to family advocacy representatives of the United States Armed Forces.

History.
2004, c. 681.

ARTICLE 5.

ROBBERY.

§ 18.2-58. How punished.

If any person commit robbery by partial strangulation, or suffocation, or by striking or beating, or by other violence to the person, or by assault or otherwise putting a person in fear of serious bodily harm, or by the threat or presenting of firearms, or other deadly weapon or instrumentality whatsoever, he shall be guilty of a felony and shall be punished by confinement in a state correctional facility for life or any term not less than five years.

History.
Code 1950, § 18.1-91; 1960, c. 358; 1966, c. 361; 1975, cc. 14, 15, 605; 1978, c. 608.

§ 18.2-58.1. Carjacking; penalty.

A. Any person who commits carjacking, as herein defined, shall be guilty of a felony punishable by imprisonment for life or a term not less than fifteen years.

B. As used in this section, *"carjacking"* means the intentional seizure or seizure of control of a motor vehicle of another with intent to permanently or temporarily deprive another in possession or control of the vehicle of that possession or control by means of partial strangulation, or suffocation, or by striking or beating, or by other violence to the person, or by assault or otherwise putting a person in fear of serious bodily harm, or by the threat or presenting of firearms, or other deadly weapon or instrumentality whatsoever. *"Motor vehicle"* shall have the same meaning as set forth in § 46.2-100.

C. The provisions of this section shall not preclude the applicability of any other provision of the criminal law of the Commonwealth which may apply to any course of conduct which violates this section.

History.
1993, c. 500.

ARTICLE 6.

EXTORTION AND OTHER THREATS.

§ 18.2-59. Extortion of money, property or pecuniary benefit.

Any person who (i) threatens injury to the character, person, or property of another person, (ii) accuses him of any offense, (iii) threatens to report him as being illegally present in the United States, or (iv) knowingly destroys, conceals, removes, confiscates, withholds or threatens to withhold, or possesses any actual or purported passport or other immigration document, or any other actual or purported government identification document, of another person, and thereby extorts money, property, or pecuniary benefit or any note, bond, or other evidence of debt from him or any other person, is guilty of a Class 5 felony.

For the purposes of this section, injury to property includes the sale, distribution, or release of identifying information defined in clauses (iii) through (xii) of subsection C of § 18.2-186.3, but does not include the distribution or release of such information by a person who does so with the intent to obtain money, property or a pecuniary benefit to which he reasonably believes he is lawfully entitled.

History.
Code 1950, § 18.1-184; 1960, c. 358; 1975, cc. 14, 15; 2006, c. 313; 2007, cc. 453, 547; 2010, c. 298.

§ 18.2-60. Threats of death or bodily injury to a person or member of his family; threats to commit serious bodily harm to persons on school property; penalty.

A. 1. Any person who knowingly communicates, in a writing, including an electronically transmitted communication producing a visual or electronic message, a threat to kill or do bodily injury to a person, regarding that person or any member of his family, and the threat places such person in reasonable apprehension of death or bodily injury to himself or his family member, is guilty of a Class 6 felony. However, any person who violates this subsection with the intent to commit an act of terrorism as defined in § 18.2-46.4 is guilty of a Class 5 felony.

2. Any person who communicates a threat, in a writing, including an electronically transmitted communication producing a visual or electronic message, to kill or do bodily harm, (i) on the grounds or premises of any elementary, middle or secondary school property, (ii) at any elementary, middle or secondary school-sponsored event or (iii) on a school bus to any person or persons, regardless of whether the person who is the object of the threat actually receives the threat, and the threat would place the person who is the object of the threat in reasonable apprehension of death or bodily harm, is guilty of a Class 6 felony.

B. Any person who orally makes a threat to any employee of any elementary, middle or secondary school, while on a school bus, on school property or at a school-sponsored activity, to kill or to do bodily injury to such person, is guilty of a Class 1 misdemeanor.

A prosecution pursuant to this section may be either in the county, city or town in which the communication was made or received.

History.
Code 1950, § 18.1-257; 1960, c. 358; 1973, c. 118; 1975, cc. 14, 15; 1994, c. 265; 1998, cc. 687, 788; 2001, cc. 644, 653; 2002, cc. 588, 623.

§ 18.2-60.1. Threatening the Governor or his immediate family.

Any person who shall knowingly and willfully send, deliver or convey, or cause to be sent, delivered or conveyed, to the Governor or his immediate family any threat to take the life of or inflict bodily harm upon the Governor or his immediate family, whether such threat be oral or written, shall be guilty of a Class 6 felony.

History.
1982, c. 568.

§ 18.2-60.2. Members of the Governor's immediate family.

As used in § 18.2-60.1, the immediate family of the Governor shall include any parent, sibling, child, grandchild, spouse, parent of a spouse, and spouse of a sibling, child or grandchild who resides in the same household as the Governor.

History.
1982, c. 568.

§ 18.2-60.3. Stalking; penalty.

A. Any person, except a law-enforcement officer, as defined in § 9.1-101, and acting in the performance of his official duties, and a registered private investigator, as defined in § 9.1-138, who is regulated in accordance with § 9.1-139 and acting in the course of his legitimate business, who on more than one occasion engages in conduct directed at another person with the intent to place, or when he knows or reasonably should know that the conduct places that other person in reasonable fear of death, criminal sexual assault, or bodily injury to that other person or to that other person's family or household member is guilty of a Class 1 misdemeanor. If the person contacts or follows or attempts to contact or follow the person at whom the conduct is directed after being given actual notice that the person does not want to be contacted or followed, such actions shall be prima facie evidence that the person intended to place that other person, or reasonably should have known that the other person was placed, in reasonable fear of death, criminal sexual assault, or bodily injury to himself or a family or household member.

B. Any person who is convicted of a second offense of subsection A occurring within five years of a prior conviction of such an offense under this section or for a substantially similar offense under the law of any other jurisdiction is guilty of a Class 6 felony.

C. A person may be convicted under this section irrespective of the jurisdiction or jurisdictions within the Commonwealth wherein the conduct described in subsection A occurred, if the person engaged in that conduct on at least one occasion in the jurisdiction where the person is tried. Evidence of any such conduct that occurred outside the Commonwealth may be admissible, if relevant, in any prosecution under this section provided that the prosecution is based upon conduct occurring within the Commonwealth.

D. Upon finding a person guilty under this section, the court shall, in addition to the sentence imposed, issue an order prohibiting contact between the defendant and the victim or the victim's family or household member.

E. The Department of Corrections, sheriff or regional jail director shall give notice prior to the release from a state correctional facility or a local or regional jail of any person incarcerated upon conviction of a violation of this section, to any victim of the offense who, in writing, requests notice, or to any person designated in writing by the victim. The notice shall be given at least 15 days prior to release of a person sentenced to a term of incarceration of more than 30 days or, if the person was sentenced to a term of incarceration of at least 48 hours but no more than 30 days, 24 hours prior to release. If the person escapes, notice shall be given as soon as practicable following the escape. The victim shall keep the Department of Corrections, sheriff or regional jail director informed of the current mailing address and telephone number of the person named in the writing submitted to receive notice.

All information relating to any person who receives or may receive notice under this subsection shall remain confidential and shall not be made available to the person convicted of violating this section.

For purposes of this subsection, "release" includes a release of the offender from a state correctional facility or a local or regional jail (i) upon completion of his term of incarceration or (ii) on probation or parole.

No civil liability shall attach to the Department of Corrections nor to any sheriff or regional jail director or their deputies or employees for a failure to comply with the requirements of this subsection.

F. For purposes of this section:

"Family or household member" has the same meaning as provided in § 16.1-228.

History.

1992, c. 888; 1994, cc. 360, 521, 739; 1995, c. 824; 1996, cc. 540, 866; 1998, c. 570; 2001, c. 197; 2002, c. 377; 2013, c. 759; 2016, cc. 545, 696, 745.

§ 18.2-60.4. Violation of protective orders; penalty.

A. Any person who violates any provision of a protective order issued pursuant to § 19.2-152.8, 19.2-152.9, or 19.2-152.10 is guilty of a Class 1 misdemeanor. Conviction hereunder shall bar a finding of contempt for the same act. The punishment for any person convicted of a second offense of violating a protective order, when the offense is committed within five years of the prior conviction and when either the instant or prior offense was based on an act or threat of violence, shall include a mandatory minimum term of confinement of 60 days. Any person convicted of a third or subsequent offense of violating a protective order, when the offense is committed within 20 years of the first conviction and when either the instant or one of the prior offenses was based on an act or threat of violence, is guilty of a Class 6 felony and the punishment shall include a mandatory minimum term of confinement of six months. The mandatory minimum terms of confinement prescribed for violations of this section shall be served consecutively with any other sentence.

B. In addition to any other penalty provided by law, any person who, while knowingly armed with a firearm or other deadly weapon, violates any provision of a protective order with which he has been served issued pursuant to § 19.2-152.8, 19.2-152.9, or 19.2-152.10 is guilty of a Class 6 felony.

C. If the respondent commits an assault and battery upon any party protected by the protective order resulting in bodily injury to the party or stalks any party protected by the protective order in violation of § 18.2-60.3, he is guilty of a Class 6 felony. Any person who violates such a protective order by furtively entering the home of any protected party while the party is present, or by entering and remaining in the home of the protected party until the party arrives, is guilty of a Class 6 felony, in addition to any other penalty provided by law.

D. Upon conviction of any offense hereunder for which a mandatory minimum term of confinement is not specified, the person shall be sentenced to a term of confinement and in no case shall the entire term imposed be suspended.

E. Upon conviction, the court shall, in addition to the sentence imposed, enter a protective order pursuant to § 19.2-152.10 for a specified period not exceeding two years from the date of conviction.

History.

1998, c. 569; 2003, c. 219; 2011, cc. 445, 480; 2013, cc. 761, 774; 2016, cc. 583, 585, 638.

§ 18.2-60.5. Unauthorized use of electronic tracking device; penalty.

A. Any person who installs or places an electronic tracking device through intentionally deceptive means and without consent, or causes an electronic tracking device to be installed or placed through intentionally deceptive means and without consent, and uses such device to track the location of any person is guilty of a Class 3 misdemeanor.

B. The provisions of this section shall not apply to the installation, placement, or use of an electronic tracking device by:

1. A law-enforcement officer, judicial officer, probation or parole officer, or employee of the Department of Corrections when any such person is engaged in the lawful performance of official duties and in accordance with other state or federal law;

2. The parent or legal guardian of a minor when tracking (i) the minor or (ii) any person authorized by the parent or legal guardian as a caretaker of the minor at any time when the minor is under the person's sole care;

3. A legally authorized representative of an incapacitated adult, as defined in § 18.2-369;

4. The owner of fleet vehicles, when tracking such vehicles;

Crimes and Offenses

5. An electronic communications provider to the extent that such installation, placement, or use is disclosed in the provider's terms of use, privacy policy, or similar document made available to the customer; or

6. A registered private investigator, as defined in § 9.1-138, who is regulated in accordance with § 9.1-139 and is acting in the normal course of his business and with the consent of the owner of the property upon which the electronic tracking device is installed and placed. However, such exception shall not apply if the private investigator is working on behalf of a client who is subject to a protective order under § 16.1-253, 16.1-253.1, 16.1-253.4, 16.1-279.1, 19.2-152.8, 19.2-152.9, 19.2-152.10, or subsection B of § 20-103, or if the private investigator knows or should reasonably know that the client seeks the private investigator's services to aid in the commission of a crime.

C. For the purposes of this section:

"Electronic tracking device" means an electronic or mechanical device that permits a person to remotely determine or track the position and movement of another person.

"Fleet vehicle" means (i) one or more motor vehicles owned by a single entity and operated by employees or agents of the entity for business or government purposes, (ii) motor vehicles held for lease or rental to the general public, or (iii) motor vehicles held for sale by motor vehicle dealers.

History.
2013, c. 434.

ARTICLE 7.
CRIMINAL SEXUAL ASSAULT.

§ 18.2-61. Rape.

A. If any person has sexual intercourse with a complaining witness, whether or not his or her spouse, or causes a complaining witness, whether or not his or her spouse, to engage in sexual intercourse with any other person and such act is accomplished (i) against the complaining witness's will, by force, threat or intimidation of or against the complaining witness or another person; or (ii) through the use of the complaining witness's mental incapacity or physical helplessness; or (iii) with a child under age 13 as the victim, he or she shall be guilty of rape.

B. A violation of this section shall be punishable, in the discretion of the court or jury, by confinement in a state correctional facility for life or for any term not less than five years; and in addition:

1. For a violation of clause (iii) of subsection A where the offender is more than three years older than the victim, if done in the commission of, or as part of the same course of conduct as, or as part of a common scheme or plan as a violation of (i) subsection A of § 18.2-47 or § 18.2-48, (ii) § 18.2-89, 18.2-90, or 18.2-91, or (iii) § 18.2-51.2, the punishment shall include a mandatory minimum term of confinement of 25 years; or

2. For a violation of clause (iii) of subsection A where it is alleged in the indictment that the offender was 18 years of age or older at the time of the offense, the punishment shall include a mandatory minimum term of confinement for life.

The mandatory minimum terms of confinement prescribed for violations of this section shall be served consecutively with any other sentence. If the term of confinement imposed for any violation of clause (iii) of subsection A, where the offender is more than three years older than the victim, is for a term less than life imprisonment, the judge shall impose, in addition to any active sentence, a suspended sentence of no less than 40 years. This suspended sentence shall be suspended for the remainder of the defendant's life, subject to revocation by the court.

There shall be a rebuttable presumption that a juvenile over the age of 10 but less than 12, does not possess the physical capacity to commit a violation of this section. In any case deemed appropriate by the court, all or part of any sentence imposed for a violation under this section against a spouse may be suspended upon the defendant's completion of counseling or therapy, if not already provided, in the manner prescribed under § 19.2-218.1 if, after consideration of the views of the complaining witness and such other evidence as may be relevant, the court finds such action will promote maintenance of the family unit and will be in the best interest of the complaining witness.

C. Upon a finding of guilt under this section, when a spouse is the complaining witness in any case tried by the court without a jury, the court, without entering a judgment of guilt, upon motion of the defendant who has not previously had a proceeding against him for violation of this section dismissed pursuant to this subsection and with the consent of the complaining witness and the attorney for the Commonwealth, may defer further proceedings and place the defendant on probation pending completion of counseling or therapy, if not already provided, in the manner prescribed under § 19.2-218.1. If the defendant fails to so complete such counseling or therapy, the court may make final disposition of the case and proceed as otherwise provided. If such counseling is completed as prescribed under § 19.2-218.1, the court may discharge the defendant and dismiss the proceedings against him if, after consideration of the views of the complaining witness and such other evidence as may be relevant, the court finds such action will promote maintenance of the family unit and be in the best interest of the complaining witness.

History.
Code 1950, § 18.1-44; 1960, c. 358; 1972, c. 394; 1975, cc. 14, 15, 606; 1981, c. 397; 1982, c. 506; 1986, c. 516; 1994, cc. 339, 772, 794;

Crimes and Offenses

1997, c. 330; 1999, c. 367; 2002, cc. 810, 818; 2005, c. 631; 2006, cc. 853, 914; 2012, cc. 575, 605; 2013, cc. 761, 774.

§ 18.2-62. Testing of certain persons for human immunodeficiency virus or hepatitis B or C viruses.

A. As soon as practicable following arrest, the attorney for the Commonwealth may request, after consultation with any complaining witness, that any person charged with (i) any crime involving sexual assault pursuant to this article, (ii) any offenses against children as prohibited by §§ 18.2-361, 18.2-366, 18.2-370, and 18.2-370.1, or (iii) any assault and battery in which the complaining witness was exposed to body fluids of the person arrested, be requested to submit to testing for infection with human immunodeficiency virus or hepatitis B or C viruses. The person so charged shall be counseled about the meaning of the test, about acquired immunodeficiency syndrome or hepatitis B or C viruses, and about the transmission and prevention of infection with human immunodeficiency virus or hepatitis B or C viruses.

If the person so charged refuses to submit to the test or the competency of the person to consent to the test is at issue, the court with jurisdiction of the case shall hold a hearing to determine whether there is probable cause that the individual has committed the crime with which he is charged. If the court finds probable cause, the court shall order the accused to undergo testing for infection with human immunodeficiency virus or hepatitis B or C viruses. The court may enter such an order in the absence of the defendant if the defendant is represented at the hearing by counsel or a guardian ad litem. The court's finding shall be without prejudice to either the Commonwealth or the person charged and shall not be evidence in any proceeding, civil or criminal.

B. At any point following indictment, arrest by warrant, or service of a petition in the case of a juvenile, of any crime involving sexual assault pursuant to this article or any offenses against children as prohibited by §§ 18.2-361, 18.2-366, 18.2-370, and 18.2-370.1, the attorney for the Commonwealth may request, or after consultation with a complaining witness and, upon the request of the complaining witness shall request, and the court shall order the defendant to submit to testing for infection with human immunodeficiency virus or hepatitis B or C viruses within 48 hours, and follow-up testing as may be medically appropriate. Any test conducted following indictment, arrest by warrant, or service of a petition shall be in addition to such tests as may have been conducted following arrest pursuant to subsection A.

C. Confirmatory tests shall be conducted before any test result shall be determined to be positive. The results of the tests for infection with human immunodeficiency virus or hepatitis B or C viruses shall be confidential as provided in § 32.1-36.1; however, the Department of Health shall also disclose the results to any victim and offer appropriate counseling as provided by subsection B of § 32.1-37.2. The Department shall conduct surveillance and investigation in accordance with § 32.1-39.

The results of such tests shall not be admissible as evidence in any criminal proceeding.

The cost of such tests shall be paid by the Commonwealth and taxed as part of the cost of such criminal proceedings.

History.

1990, c. 957; 1992, cc. 500, 587; 1993, c. 512; 2001, c. 862; 2005, c. 661; 2008, c. 756.

§ 18.2-63. Carnal knowledge of child between thirteen and fifteen years of age.

A. If any person carnally knows, without the use of force, a child thirteen years of age or older but under fifteen years of age, such person shall be guilty of a Class 4 felony.

B. If any person carnally knows, without the use of force, a child thirteen years of age or older but under fifteen years of age who consents to sexual intercourse and the accused is a minor and such consenting child is three years or more the accused's junior, the accused shall be guilty of a Class 6 felony. If such consenting child is less than three years the accused's junior, the accused shall be guilty of a Class 4 misdemeanor.

In calculating whether such child is three years or more a junior of the accused minor, the actual dates of birth of the child and the accused, respectively, shall be used.

C. For the purposes of this section, (i) a child under the age of thirteen years shall not be considered a consenting child and (ii) "carnal knowledge" includes the acts of sexual intercourse, cunnilingus, fellatio, anilingus, anal intercourse, and animate and inanimate object sexual penetration.

History.

Code 1950, § 18.1-44; 1960, c. 358; 1972, c. 394; 1975, cc. 14, 15, 606; 1981, c. 397; 1993, c. 852; 2007, c. 718.

§ 18.2-63.1. Death of victim.

When the death of the victim occurs in connection with an offense under this article, it shall be immaterial in the prosecution thereof whether the alleged offense occurred before or after the death of the victim.

History.

1978, c. 803; 1981, c. 397.

§ 18.2-64: Repealed by Acts 1981, c. 397.

§ 18.2-64.1. Carnal knowledge of certain minors.

If any person providing services, paid or unpaid, to juveniles under the purview of the Juvenile and

Domestic Relations District Court Law, or to juveniles who have been committed to the custody of the State Department of Juvenile Justice, carnally knows, without the use of force, any minor fifteen years of age or older, when such minor is confined or detained in jail, is detained in any facility mentioned in § 16.1-249, or has been committed to the custody of the Department of Juvenile Justice pursuant to § 16.1-278.8, knowing or having good reason to believe that (i) such minor is in such confinement or detention status, (ii) such minor is a ward of the Department of Juvenile Justice, or (iii) such minor is on probation, furlough, or leave from or has escaped or absconded from such confinement, detention, or custody, he shall be guilty of a Class 6 felony.

For the purposes of this section, "carnal knowledge" includes the acts of sexual intercourse, cunnilingus, fellatio, anallingus, anal intercourse, and animate and inanimate object sexual penetration.

History.

1977, c. 304; 1981, c. 397; 1989, c. 733; 1991, c. 534; 1993, c. 852.

§ 18.2-64.2. Carnal knowledge of an inmate, parolee, probationer, detainee, or pretrial or posttrial offender; penalty.

An accused is guilty of carnal knowledge of an inmate, parolee, probationer, detainee, or pretrial defendant or posttrial offender if he is an employee or contractual employee of, or a volunteer with, a state or local correctional facility or regional jail, the Department of Corrections, the Department of Juvenile Justice, a secure facility or detention home, as defined in § 16.1-228, a state or local court services unit, as defined in § 16.1-235, a local community-based probation services agency or a pretrial services agency; is in a position of authority over the inmate, probationer, parolee, detainee, or a pretrial defendant or posttrial offender; knows that the inmate, probationer, parolee, detainee, or pretrial defendant or posttrial offender is under the jurisdiction of the state or local correctional facility, a regional jail, the Department of Corrections, the Department of Juvenile Justice, a secure facility or detention home, as defined in § 16.1-228, a state or local court services unit, as defined in § 16.1-235, a local community-based probation services agency, or a pretrial services agency; and carnally knows, without the use of force, threat or intimidation (i) an inmate who has been committed to jail or convicted and sentenced to confinement in a state or local correctional facility or regional jail or (ii) a probationer, parolee, detainee, or a pretrial defendant or posttrial offender under the jurisdiction of the Department of Corrections, the Department of Juvenile Justice, a secure facility or detention home, as defined in § 16.1-228, a state or local court services unit, as defined in § 16.1-235, a local community-based probation services agency, a pretrial services agency, a local or regional jail for the purposes of imprisonment, a work program or any other parole/probationary or pretrial services program or agency. Such offense is a Class 6 felony.

An accused is guilty of carnal knowledge of a pretrial defendant or posttrial offender if he (a) is an owner or employee of the bail bond company that posted the pretrial defendant's or posttrial offender's bond, (b) has the authority to revoke the pretrial defendant's or posttrial offender's bond, and (c) carnally knows, without use of force, threat, or intimidation, a pretrial defendant or posttrial offender. Such offense is a Class 1 misdemeanor.

For the purposes of this section, "carnal knowledge" includes the acts of sexual intercourse, cunnilingus, fellatio, anallingus, anal intercourse and animate or inanimate object sexual penetration.

History.

1999, c. 294; 2000, c. 1040; 2001, c. 385; 2007, c. 133; 2013, c. 602.

§ 18.2-65: Repealed by Acts 1981, c. 397.

§ 18.2-66: Repealed by Acts 2008, cc. 174 and 206, cl. 2.

§ 18.2-67. Depositions of complaining witnesses in cases of criminal sexual assault and attempted criminal sexual assault.

Before or during the trial for an offense or attempted offense under this article, the judge of the court in which the case is pending, with the consent of the accused first obtained in open court, by an order of record, may direct that the deposition of the complaining witness be taken at a time and place designated in the order, and the judge may adjourn the taking thereof to such other time and places as he may deem necessary. Such deposition shall be taken before a judge of a circuit court in the county or city in which the offense was committed or the trial is had, and the judge shall rule upon all questions of evidence, and otherwise control the taking of the same as though it were taken in open court. At the taking of such deposition the attorney for the Commonwealth, as well as the accused and his attorneys, shall be present and they shall have the same rights in regard to the examination of such witness as if he or she were testifying in open court. No other person shall be present unless expressly permitted by the judge. Such deposition shall be read to the jury at the time such witness might have testified if such deposition had not been taken, and shall be considered by them, and shall have the same force and effect as though such testimony had been given orally in court. The judge may, in like manner, direct other depositions of the complaining witness, in rebuttal or otherwise, which shall be taken and read in the manner and under the conditions herein prescribed as to the first deposition. The cost of taking such depositions shall be paid by the Commonwealth.

History.

Code 1950, § 18.1-47; 1960, c. 358; 1975, cc. 14, 15, 606; 1981, c. 397.

§ 18.2-67.01: Not in effect.

Editor's note.

This section, which was enacted by Acts 1987, c. 448, was to become effective only if reenacted by the 1988 Session of the General Assembly. This section was not reenacted at the 1988 Session and therefore did not become effective.

§ 18.2-67.1. Forcible sodomy.

A. An accused shall be guilty of forcible sodomy if he or she engages in cunnilingus, fellatio, anilingus, or anal intercourse with a complaining witness whether or not his or her spouse, or causes a complaining witness, whether or not his or her spouse, to engage in such acts with any other person, and

1. The complaining witness is less than 13 years of age; or

2. The act is accomplished against the will of the complaining witness, by force, threat or intimidation of or against the complaining witness or another person, or through the use of the complaining witness's mental incapacity or physical helplessness.

B. Forcible sodomy is a felony punishable by confinement in a state correctional facility for life or for any term not less than five years; and in addition:

1. For a violation of subdivision A 1, where the offender is more than three years older than the victim, if done in the commission of, or as part of the same course of conduct as, or as part of a common scheme or plan as a violation of (i) subsection A of § 18.2-47 or § 18.2-48, (ii) § 18.2-89, 18.2-90, or 18.2-91, or (iii) § 18.2-51.2, the punishment shall include a mandatory minimum term of confinement of 25 years; or

2. For a violation of subdivision A 1 where it is alleged in the indictment that the offender was 18 years of age or older at the time of the offense, the punishment shall include a mandatory minimum term of confinement for life.

The mandatory minimum terms of confinement prescribed for violations of this section shall be served consecutively with any other sentence. If the term of confinement imposed for any violation of subdivision A 1, where the offender is more than three years older than the victim, is for a term less than life imprisonment, the judge shall impose, in addition to any active sentence, a suspended sentence of no less than 40 years. This suspended sentence shall be suspended for the remainder of the defendant's life, subject to revocation by the court.

In any case deemed appropriate by the court, all or part of any sentence imposed for a violation under this section against a spouse may be suspended upon the defendant's completion of counseling or therapy, if not already provided, in the manner prescribed under § 19.2-218.1 if, after consideration of the views of the complaining witness and such other evidence as may be relevant, the court finds such action will promote maintenance of the family unit and will be in the best interest of the complaining witness.

C. Upon a finding of guilt under this section, when a spouse is the complaining witness in any case tried by the court without a jury, the court, without entering a judgment of guilt, upon motion of the defendant who has not previously had a proceeding against him for violation of this section dismissed pursuant to this subsection and with the consent of the complaining witness and the attorney for the Commonwealth, may defer further proceedings and place the defendant on probation pending completion of counseling or therapy, if not already provided, in the manner prescribed under § 19.2-218.1. If the defendant fails to so complete such counseling or therapy, the court may make final disposition of the case and proceed as otherwise provided. If such counseling is completed as prescribed under § 19.2-218.1, the court may discharge the defendant and dismiss the proceedings against him if, after consideration of the views of the complaining witness and such other evidence as may be relevant, the court finds such action will promote maintenance of the family unit and be in the best interest of the complaining witness.

History.

1981, c. 397; 1986, c. 516; 1994, cc. 772, 794; 1999, c. 367; 2005, c. 631; 2006, cc. 853, 914; 2012, cc. 575, 605; 2013, cc. 761, 774.

§ 18.2-67.2. Object sexual penetration; penalty.

A. An accused shall be guilty of inanimate or animate object sexual penetration if he or she penetrates the labia majora or anus of a complaining witness, whether or not his or her spouse, other than for a bona fide medical purpose, or causes such complaining witness to so penetrate his or her own body with an object or causes a complaining witness, whether or not his or her spouse, to engage in such acts with any other person or to penetrate, or to be penetrated by, an animal, and

1. The complaining witness is less than 13 years of age; or

2. The act is accomplished against the will of the complaining witness, by force, threat or intimidation of or against the complaining witness or another person, or through the use of the complaining witness's mental incapacity or physical helplessness.

B. Inanimate or animate object sexual penetration is a felony punishable by confinement in the state correctional facility for life or for any term not less than five years; and in addition:

1. For a violation of subdivision A 1, where the offender is more than three years older than the victim, if done in the commission of, or as part of the same course of conduct as, or as part of a common scheme or plan as a violation of (i) subsection A of

§ 18.2-47 or § 18.2-48, (ii) § 18.2-89, 18.2-90, or 18.2-91, or (iii) § 18.2-51.2, the punishment shall include a mandatory minimum term of confinement of 25 years; or

2. For a violation of subdivision A 1 where it is alleged in the indictment that the offender was 18 years of age or older at the time of the offense, the punishment shall include a mandatory minimum term of confinement for life.

The mandatory minimum terms of confinement prescribed for violations of this section shall be served consecutively with any other sentence. If the term of confinement imposed for any violation of subdivision A 1, where the offender is more than three years older than the victim, is for a term less than life imprisonment, the judge shall impose, in addition to any active sentence, a suspended sentence of no less than 40 years. This suspended sentence shall be suspended for the remainder of the defendant's life, subject to revocation by the court.

In any case deemed appropriate by the court, all or part of any sentence imposed for a violation under this section against a spouse may be suspended upon the defendant's completion of counseling or therapy, if not already provided, in the manner prescribed under § 19.2-218.1 if, after consideration of the views of the complaining witness and such other evidence as may be relevant, the court finds such action will promote maintenance of the family unit and will be in the best interest of the complaining witness.

C. Upon a finding of guilt under this section, when a spouse is the complaining witness in any case tried by the court without a jury, the court, without entering a judgment of guilt, upon motion of the defendant who has not previously had a proceeding against him for violation of this section dismissed pursuant to this subsection and with the consent of the complaining witness and the attorney for the Commonwealth, may defer further proceedings and place the defendant on probation pending completion of counseling or therapy, if not already provided, in the manner prescribed under § 19.2-218.1. If the defendant fails to so complete such counseling or therapy, the court may make final disposition of the case and proceed as otherwise provided. If such counseling is completed as prescribed under § 19.2-218.1, the court may discharge the defendant and dismiss the proceedings against him if, after consideration of the views of the complaining witness and such other evidence as may be relevant, the court finds such action will promote maintenance of the family unit and be in the best interest of the complaining witness.

History.

1981, c. 397; 1982, c. 508; 1986, c. 516; 1988, c. 437; 1993, c. 549; 1994, cc. 772, 794; 1999, c. 367; 2005, c. 631; 2006, cc. 853, 914; 2012, cc. 575, 605; 2013, cc. 761, 774.

§ **18.2-67.2:1:** Repealed by Acts 2005, c. 631, cl. 2.

§ 18.2-67.3. Aggravated sexual battery; penalty.

A. An accused shall be guilty of aggravated sexual battery if he or she sexually abuses the complaining witness, and

1. The complaining witness is less than 13 years of age, or

2. The act is accomplished through the use of the complaining witness's mental incapacity or physical helplessness, or

3. The offense is committed by a parent, step-parent, grandparent, or step-grandparent and the complaining witness is at least 13 but less than 18 years of age, or

4. The act is accomplished against the will of the complaining witness by force, threat or intimidation, and

a. The complaining witness is at least 13 but less than 15 years of age, or

b. The accused causes serious bodily or mental injury to the complaining witness, or

c. The accused uses or threatens to use a dangerous weapon.

B. Aggravated sexual battery is a felony punishable by confinement in a state correctional facility for a term of not less than one nor more than 20 years and by a fine of not more than $100,000.

History.

1981, c. 397; 1993, c. 590; 2004, c. 843; 2005, cc. 185, 406.

§ 18.2-67.4. Sexual battery.

A. An accused is guilty of sexual battery if he sexually abuses, as defined in § 18.2-67.10, (i) the complaining witness against the will of the complaining witness, by force, threat, intimidation, or ruse, (ii) within a two-year period, more than one complaining witness or one complaining witness on more than one occasion intentionally and without the consent of the complaining witness, (iii) an inmate who has been committed to jail or convicted and sentenced to confinement in a state or local correctional facility or regional jail, and the accused is an employee or contractual employee of, or a volunteer with, the state or local correctional facility or regional jail; is in a position of authority over the inmate; and knows that the inmate is under the jurisdiction of the state or local correctional facility or regional jail, or (iv) a probationer, parolee, or a pretrial defendant or posttrial offender under the jurisdiction of the Department of Corrections, a local community-based probation services agency, a pretrial services agency, a local or regional jail for the purposes of imprisonment, a work program or any other parole/probationary or pretrial services or agency and the accused is an employee or contractual employee of, or a volunteer with, the Department of Corrections, a local community-based probation services agency, a pretrial services agency or a local or regional jail; is in a position of authority over an offender; and knows that the offender is under the jurisdiction of the Department of Corrections, a local community-based probation services agency, a pretrial services agency or a local or regional jail.

B. Sexual battery is a Class 1 misdemeanor.

History.

1981, c. 397; 1997, c. 643; 1999, c. 294; 2000, cc. 832, 1040; 2006, c. 284; 2007, c. 133; 2014, c. 656.

§ 18.2-67.4:1. Infected sexual battery; penalty.

A. Any person who, knowing he is infected with HIV, syphilis, or hepatitis B, has sexual intercourse, cunnilingus, fellatio, anallingus or anal intercourse with the intent to transmit the infection to another person is guilty of a Class 6 felony.

B. Any person who, knowing he is infected with HIV, syphilis, or hepatitis B, has sexual intercourse, cunnilingus, fellatio, anallingus or anal intercourse with another person without having previously disclosed the existence of his infection to the other person is guilty of a Class 1 misdemeanor.

C. "HIV" means the human immunodeficiency virus or any other related virus that causes acquired immunodeficiency syndrome (AIDS).

Nothing in this section shall prevent the prosecution of any other crime against persons under Chapter 4 (§ 18.2-30 et seq.) of this title. Any person charged with a violation of this section alleging he is infected with HIV shall be subject to the testing provisions of § 18.2-62.

History.

2000, c. 831; 2004, c. 449.

§ 18.2-67.4:2. Sexual abuse of a child under 15 years of age; penalty.

Any adult who, with lascivious intent, commits an act of sexual abuse, as defined in § 18.2-67.10, with any child 13 years of age or older but under 15 years of age is guilty of a Class 1 misdemeanor.

History.

2007, c. 463.

§ 18.2-67.5. Attempted rape, forcible sodomy, object sexual penetration, aggravated sexual battery, and sexual battery.

A. An attempt to commit rape, forcible sodomy, or inanimate or animate object sexual penetration shall be punishable as a Class 4 felony.

B. An attempt to commit aggravated sexual battery shall be a felony punishable as a Class 6 felony.

C. An attempt to commit sexual battery is a Class 1 misdemeanor.

History.

1981, c. 397; 1993, c. 549.

§ 18.2-67.5:1. Punishment upon conviction of third misdemeanor offense.

When a person is convicted of sexual battery in violation of § 18.2-67.4, attempted sexual battery in violation of subsection C of § 18.2-67.5, a violation of § 18.2-371 involving consensual intercourse, anal intercourse, cunnilingus, fellatio, or anilingus with a child, indecent exposure of himself or procuring another to expose himself in violation of § 18.2-387, or a violation of § 18.2-130, and it is alleged in the warrant, information, or indictment on which the person is convicted and found by the court or jury trying the case that the person has previously been convicted within the 10-year period immediately preceding the offense charged of two or more of the offenses specified in this section, each such offense occurring on a different date, he is guilty of a Class 6 felony.

History.

1994, c. 468; 2006, c. 875; 2014, c. 794.

§ 18.2-67.5:2. Punishment upon conviction of certain subsequent felony sexual assault.

A. Any person convicted of (i) more than one offense specified in subsection B or (ii) one of the offenses specified in subsection B of this section and one of the offenses specified in subsection B of § 18.2-67.5:3 when such offenses were not part of a common act, transaction or scheme, and who has been at liberty as defined in § 53.1-151 between each conviction shall, upon conviction of the second or subsequent such offense, be sentenced to the maximum term authorized by statute for such offense, and shall not have all or any part of such sentence suspended, provided it is admitted, or found by the jury or judge before whom the person is tried, that he has been previously convicted of at least one of the specified offenses.

B. The provisions of subsection A shall apply to felony convictions for:

1. Carnal knowledge of a child between thirteen and fifteen years of age in violation of § 18.2-63 when the offense is committed by a person over the age of eighteen;
2. Carnal knowledge of certain minors in violation of § 18.2-64.1;
3. Aggravated sexual battery in violation of § 18.2-67.3;
4. Crimes against nature in violation of subsection B of § 18.2-361;
5. Adultery or fornication with one's own child or grandchild in violation of § 18.2-366;
6. Taking indecent liberties with a child in violation of § 18.2-370 or § 18.2-370.1; or
7. Conspiracy to commit any offense listed in subdivisions 1 through 6 pursuant to § 18.2-22.

C. For purposes of this section, prior convictions shall include (i) adult convictions for felonies under the laws of any state or the United States that are substantially similar to those listed in subsection B and (ii) findings of not innocent, adjudications or convictions in the case of a juvenile if the juvenile offense is substantially similar to those listed in subsection B, the offense would be a felony if committed by an adult in the Commonwealth and the offense was committed less than twenty years before the second offense.

The Commonwealth shall notify the defendant in writing, at least thirty days prior to trial, of its intention to seek punishment pursuant to this section.

History.

1995, c. 834; 2000, c. 333.

§ 18.2-67.5:3. Punishment upon conviction of certain subsequent violent felony sexual assault.

A. Any person convicted of more than one offense specified in subsection B, when such offenses were not part of a common act, transaction or scheme, and who has been at liberty as defined in § 53.1-151 between each conviction shall, upon conviction of the second or subsequent such offense, be sentenced to life imprisonment and shall not have all or any portion of the sentence suspended, provided it is admitted, or found by the jury or judge before whom he is tried, that he has been previously convicted of at least one of the specified offenses.

B. The provisions of subsection A shall apply to convictions for:

1. Rape in violation of § 18.2-61;
2. Forcible sodomy in violation of § 18.2-67.1;
3. Object sexual penetration in violation of § 18.2-67.2;
4. Abduction with intent to defile in violation of § 18.2-48; or
5. Conspiracy to commit any offense listed in subdivisions 1 through 4 pursuant to § 18.2-22.

C. For purposes of this section, prior convictions shall include (i) adult convictions for felonies under the laws of any state or the United States that are substantially similar to those listed in subsection B and (ii) findings of not innocent, adjudications or convictions in the case of a juvenile if the juvenile offense is substantially similar to those listed in subsection B, the offense would be a felony if committed by an adult in the Commonwealth and the offense was committed less than twenty years before the second offense.

The Commonwealth shall notify the defendant in the indictment, information, or warrant, at least thirty days prior to trial, of its intention to seek punishment pursuant to this section.

History.

1995, c. 834; 2007, c. 506.

§ 18.2-67.6. Proof of physical resistance not required.

The Commonwealth need not demonstrate that the complaining witness cried out or physically resisted the accused in order to convict the accused of an offense under this article, but the absence of such resistance may be considered when relevant to show that the act alleged was not against the will of the complaining witness.

History.

1981, c. 397.

§ 18.2-67.7. Admission of evidence (Supreme Court Rule 2:412 derived from this section).

A. In prosecutions under this article, or under clause (iii) or (iv) of § 18.2-48, 18.2-370, 18.2-370.01, or 18.2-370.1, general reputation or opinion evidence of the complaining witness's unchaste character or prior sexual conduct shall not be admitted. Unless the complaining witness voluntarily agrees otherwise, evidence of specific instances of his or her prior sexual conduct shall be admitted only if it is relevant and is:

1. Evidence offered to provide an alternative explanation for physical evidence of the offense charged which is introduced by the prosecution, limited to evidence designed to explain the presence of semen, pregnancy, disease, or physical injury to the complaining witness's intimate parts; or
2. Evidence of sexual conduct between the complaining witness and the accused offered to support a contention that the alleged offense was not accomplished by force, threat or intimidation or through the use of the complaining witness's mental incapacity or physical helplessness, provided that the sexual conduct occurred within a period of time reasonably proximate to the offense charged under the circumstances of this case; or
3. Evidence offered to rebut evidence of the complaining witness's prior sexual conduct introduced by the prosecution.

B. Nothing contained in this section shall prohibit the accused from presenting evidence relevant to show that the complaining witness had a motive to fabricate the charge against the accused. If such evidence relates to the past sexual conduct of the complaining witness with a person other than the accused, it shall not be admitted and may not be referred to at any preliminary hearing or trial unless the party offering same files a written notice generally describing the evidence prior to the introduction of any evidence, or the opening statement of either counsel, whichever first occurs, at the preliminary hearing or trial at which the admission of the evidence may be sought.

C. Evidence described in subsections A and B of this section shall not be admitted and may not be referred to at any preliminary hearing or trial until the court first determines the admissibility of that evidence at an evidentiary hearing to be held before the evidence is introduced at such preliminary hearing or trial. The court shall exclude from the evidentiary hearing all persons except the accused, the complaining witness, other necessary witnesses, and required court personnel. If the court determines that the evidence meets the requirements of subsections A and B of this section, it shall be admissible before the judge or jury trying the case in the ordinary course of the preliminary hearing or trial. If the court initially determines that the evidence is inadmissible, but new information is discovered during the course of the preliminary hearing or trial which may make such evidence admissible, the court shall determine in an evidentiary hearing whether such evidence is admissible.

History.

1981, c. 397; 2007, c. 890; 2011, c. 785.

§ 18.2-67.7:1. Evidence of similar crimes in child sexual offense cases (Supreme Court Rule 2:413 derived from this section).

A. In a criminal case in which the defendant is accused of a felony sexual offense involving a child victim, evidence of the defendant's conviction of another sexual offense or offenses is admissible and may be considered for its bearing on any matter to which it is relevant.

B. The Commonwealth shall provide to the defendant 14 days prior to trial notice of its intention to introduce copies of final orders evidencing the defendant's qualifying prior criminal convictions. Such notice shall include (i) the date of each prior conviction, (ii) the name and jurisdiction of the court where each prior conviction was obtained, and (iii) each offense of which the defendant was convicted. Prior to commencement of the trial, the Commonwealth shall provide to the defendant photocopies of certified copies of the final orders that it intends to introduce.

C. This section shall not be construed to limit the admission or consideration of evidence under any other section or rule of court.

D. For purposes of this section, "sexual offense" means any offense or any attempt or conspiracy to engage in any offense described in Article 7 (§ 18.2-61 et seq.) of Chapter 4 or § 18.2-370, 18.2-370.01, or 18.2-370.1 or any substantially similar offense under the laws of another state or territory of the United States, the District of Columbia, or the United States.

E. Evidence offered in a criminal case pursuant to the provisions of this section shall be subject to exclusion in accordance with the Virginia Rules of Evidence, including but not limited to Rule 2:403.

History.

2014, c. 782.

§ 18.2-67.8. Closed preliminary hearings.

In preliminary hearings for offenses charged under this article or under §§ 18.2-361, 18.2-366, 18.2-370 or § 18.2-370.1, the court may, on its own motion or at the request of the Commonwealth, the complaining witness, the accused, or their counsel, exclude from the courtroom all persons except officers of the court and persons whose presence, in the judgment of the court, would be supportive of the complaining witness or the accused and would not impair the conduct of a fair hearing.

History.

1981, c. 397; 1993, c. 440.

§ 18.2-67.9. Testimony by child victims and witnesses using two-way closed-circuit television.

A. The provisions of this section shall apply to an alleged victim who was fourteen years of age or under at the time of the alleged offense and is sixteen or under at the time of the trial and to a witness who is fourteen years of age or under at the time of the trial.

In any criminal proceeding, including preliminary hearings, involving an alleged offense against a child, relating to a violation of the laws pertaining to kidnapping (§ 18.2-47 et seq.), criminal sexual assault (§ 18.2-61 et seq.) or family offenses pursuant to Article 4 (§ 18.2-362 et seq.) of Chapter 8 of Title 18.2, or involving an alleged murder of a person of any age, the attorney for the Commonwealth or the defendant may apply for an order from the court that the testimony of the alleged victim or a child witness be taken in a room outside the courtroom and be televised by two-way closed-circuit television. The party seeking such order shall apply for the order at least seven days before the trial date or at least seven days before such other preliminary proceeding to which the order is to apply.

B. The court may order that the testimony of the child be taken by closed-circuit television as provided in subsection A if it finds that the child is unavailable to testify in open court in the presence of the defendant, the jury, the judge, and the public, for any of the following reasons:

1. The child's persistent refusal to testify despite judicial requests to do so;

2. The child's substantial inability to communicate about the offense; or

3. The substantial likelihood, based upon expert opinion testimony, that the child will suffer severe emotional trauma from so testifying.

Any ruling on the child's unavailability under this subsection shall be supported by the court with findings on the record or with written findings in a court not of record.

C. In any proceeding in which closed-circuit television is used to receive testimony, the attorney for the Commonwealth and the defendant's attorney shall be present in the room with the child, and the child shall be subject to direct and cross-examination. The only other persons allowed to be present in the room with the child during his testimony shall be those persons necessary to operate the closed-circuit equipment, and any other person whose presence is determined by the court to be necessary to the welfare and well-being of the child.

D. The child's testimony shall be transmitted by closed-circuit television into the courtroom for the defendant, jury, judge and public to view. The defendant shall be provided with a means of private, contemporaneous communication with his attorney during the testimony.

E. Notwithstanding any other provision of law, none of the cost of the two-way closed-circuit television shall be assessed against the defendant.

History.
1988, c. 846; 1999, c. 668; 2001, c. 410.

§ 18.2-67.10. General definitions.

As used in this article:

1. *"Complaining witness"* means the person alleged to have been subjected to rape, forcible sodomy, inanimate or animate object sexual penetration, marital sexual assault, aggravated sexual battery, or sexual battery.

2. *"Intimate parts"* means the genitalia, anus, groin, breast, or buttocks of any person.

3. *"Mental incapacity"* means that condition of the complaining witness existing at the time of an offense under this article which prevents the complaining witness from understanding the nature or consequences of the sexual act involved in such offense and about which the accused knew or should have known.

4. *"Physical helplessness"* means unconsciousness or any other condition existing at the time of an offense under this article which otherwise rendered the complaining witness physically unable to communicate an unwillingness to act and about which the accused knew or should have known.

5. The complaining witness's *"prior sexual conduct"* means any sexual conduct on the part of the complaining witness which took place before the conclusion of the trial, excluding the conduct involved in the offense alleged under this article.

6. *"Sexual abuse"* means an act committed with the intent to sexually molest, arouse, or gratify any person, where:

a. The accused intentionally touches the complaining witness's intimate parts or material directly covering such intimate parts;

b. The accused forces the complaining witness to touch the accused's, the witness's own, or another person's intimate parts or material directly covering such intimate parts;

c. If the complaining witness is under the age of 13, the accused causes or assists the complaining witness to touch the accused's, the witness's own, or another person's intimate parts or material directly covering such intimate parts; or

d. The accused forces another person to touch the complaining witness's intimate parts or material directly covering such intimate parts.

History.
1981, c. 397; 1987, c. 277; 1993, c. 549; 1994, c. 568; 2004, c. 741.

ARTICLE 8.

SEDUCTION.

§§ 18.2-68 through 18.2-70: Repealed by Acts 1994, c. 59.

ARTICLE 9.

ABORTION.

§ 18.2-71. Producing abortion or miscarriage, etc.; penalty.

Except as provided in other sections of this article, if any person administer to, or cause to be taken by a woman, any drug or other thing, or use means, with intent to destroy her unborn child, or to produce abortion or miscarriage, and thereby destroy such child, or produce such abortion or miscarriage, he shall be guilty of a Class 4 felony.

History.
Code 1950, § 18.1-62; 1960, c. 358; 1970, c. 508; 1975, cc. 14, 15.

§ 18.2-71.1. Partial birth infanticide; penalty.

A. Any person who knowingly performs partial birth infanticide and thereby kills a human infant is guilty of a Class 4 felony.

B. For the purposes of this section, *"partial birth infanticide"* means any deliberate act that (i) is intended to kill a human infant who has been born alive, but who has not been completely extracted or expelled from its mother, and that (ii) does kill such infant, regardless of whether death occurs before or after extraction or expulsion from its mother has been completed.

The term "partial birth infanticide" shall not under any circumstances be construed to include any of the following procedures: (i) the suction curettage abortion procedure, (ii) the suction aspiration abortion procedure, (iii) the dilation and evacuation abortion procedure involving dismemberment of the fetus prior to removal from the body of the mother, or (iv) completing delivery of a living human infant and severing the umbilical cord of any infant who has been completely delivered.

C. For the purposes of this section, *"human infant who has been born alive"* means a product of human conception that has been completely or substantially expelled or extracted from its mother, regardless of the duration of pregnancy, which after such expulsion or extraction breathes or shows any other evidence of life such as beating of the heart, pulsation of the umbilical cord, or definite movement of voluntary muscles, whether or not the umbilical cord has been cut or the placenta is attached.

D. For purposes of this section, *"substantially expelled or extracted from its mother"* means, in the case of a headfirst presentation, the infant's entire head is outside the body of the mother, or, in the case of breech presentation, any part of the infant's trunk past the navel is outside the body of the mother.

E. This section shall not prohibit the use by a physician of any procedure that, in reasonable medical judgment, is necessary to prevent the death of the mother, so long as the physician takes every medically reasonable step, consistent with such procedure, to preserve the life and health of the infant. A procedure shall not be deemed necessary to prevent the death of the mother if completing the delivery of the living infant would prevent the death of the mother.

F. The mother may not be prosecuted for any criminal offense based on the performance of any act or procedure by a physician in violation of this section.

History.

2003, cc. 961, 963.

§ 18.2-72. When abortion lawful during first trimester of pregnancy.

Notwithstanding any of the provisions of § 18.2-71, it shall be lawful for any physician licensed by the Board of Medicine to practice medicine and surgery, to terminate or attempt to terminate a human pregnancy or aid or assist in the termination of a human pregnancy by performing an abortion or causing a miscarriage on any woman during the first trimester of pregnancy.

History.

1975, cc. 14, 15.

§ 18.2-73. When abortion lawful during second trimester of pregnancy.

Notwithstanding any of the provisions of § 18.2-71 and in addition to the provisions of § 18.2-72, it shall be lawful for any physician licensed by the Board of Medicine to practice medicine and surgery, to terminate or attempt to terminate a human pregnancy or aid or assist in the termination of a human pregnancy by performing an abortion or causing a miscarriage on any woman during the second trimester of pregnancy and prior to the third trimester of pregnancy provided such procedure is performed in a hospital licensed by the State Department of Health or operated by the Department of Behavioral Health and Developmental Services.

History.

1975, cc. 14, 15; 2009, cc. 813, 840.

§ 18.2-74. When abortion or termination of pregnancy lawful after second trimester of pregnancy.

Notwithstanding any of the provisions of § 18.2-71 and in addition to the provisions of §§ 18.2-72 and 18.2-73, it shall be lawful for any physician licensed by the Board of Medicine to practice medicine and surgery to terminate or attempt to terminate a human pregnancy or aid or assist in the termination of a human pregnancy by performing an abortion or causing a miscarriage on any woman in a stage of pregnancy subsequent to the second trimester provided the following conditions are met:

(a) Said operation is performed in a hospital licensed by the Virginia State Department of Health or operated by the Department of Behavioral Health and Developmental Services.

(b) The physician and two consulting physicians certify and so enter in the hospital record of the woman, that in their medical opinion, based upon their best clinical judgment, the continuation of the pregnancy is likely to result in the death of the woman or substantially and irremediably impair the mental or physical health of the woman.

(c) Measures for life support for the product of such abortion or miscarriage must be available and utilized if there is any clearly visible evidence of viability.

History.

1975, cc. 14, 15; 2009, cc. 813, 840.

§ 18.2-74.1. Abortion, etc., when necessary to save life of woman.

In the event it is necessary for a licensed physician to terminate a human pregnancy or assist in the termination of a human pregnancy by performing an abortion or causing a miscarriage on any woman in order to save her life, in the opinion of the physician so performing the abortion or causing the miscarriage, §§ 18.2-71, 18.2-73 and 18.2-74 shall not be applicable.

History.

Code 1950, § 18.1-62.3; 1970, c. 508; 1975, cc. 14, 15.

§ 18.2-74.2: Repealed by Acts 2003, cc. 961 and 963.

Cross references.

As to prohibition against partial birth infanticide, and penalty therefor, see § 18.2-71.1.

§ 18.2-75. Conscience clause.

Nothing in §§ 18.2-72, 18.2-73 or § 18.2-74 shall require a hospital or other medical facility or physician to admit any patient under the provisions hereof for the purpose of performing an abortion. In addition, any person who shall state in writing an objection to any abortion or all abortions on personal, ethical, moral or religious grounds shall not be required to participate in procedures which will result in such abortion, and the refusal of such person, hospital or other medical facility to participate therein shall not form the basis of any claim for damages on account of such refusal or for any disciplinary or recriminatory action against such person, nor shall any such person be denied employment because of such objection or refusal. The written objection shall remain in effect until such person shall revoke it in writing or terminate his association with the facility with which it is filed.

History.

Code 1950, § 18.1-63.1; 1974, c. 679; 1975, cc. 14, 15.

§ 18.2-76. Informed written consent required; civil penalty.

A. Before performing any abortion or inducing any miscarriage or terminating a pregnancy as provided in § 18.2-72, 18.2-73, or 18.2-74, the physician shall obtain the informed written consent of the pregnant woman. However, if the woman has been adjudicated incapacitated by any court of competent jurisdiction or if the physician knows or has good reason to believe that such woman is incapacitated as adjudicated by a court of competent jurisdiction, then only after permission is given in writing by a parent, guardian, committee, or other person standing in loco parentis to the woman, may the physician perform the abortion or otherwise terminate the pregnancy.

B. At least 24 hours before the performance of an abortion, a qualified medical professional trained in sonography and working under the supervision of a physician licensed in the Commonwealth shall perform fetal transabdominal ultrasound imaging on the patient undergoing the abortion for the purpose of determining gestational age. If the pregnant woman lives at least 100 miles from the facility where the abortion is to be performed, the fetal ultrasound imaging shall be performed at least two hours before the abortion. The ultrasound image shall contain the dimensions of the fetus and accurately portray the presence of external members and internal organs of the fetus, if present or viewable. Determination of gestational age shall be based upon measurement of the fetus in a manner consistent with standard medical practice in the community for determining gestational age. When only the gestational sac is visible during ultrasound imaging, gestational age may be based upon measurement of the gestational sac. If gestational age cannot be determined by a transabdominal ultrasound, then the patient undergoing the abortion shall be verbally offered other ultrasound imaging to determine gestational age, which she may refuse. A print of the ultrasound image shall be made to document the measurements that have been taken to determine the gestational age of the fetus.

The provisions of this subsection shall not apply if the woman seeking an abortion is the victim of rape or incest, if the incident was reported to law-enforcement authorities. Nothing herein shall preclude the physician from using any ultrasound imaging that he considers to be medically appropriate pursuant to the standard medical practice in the community.

C. The qualified medical professional performing fetal ultrasound imaging pursuant to subsection B shall verbally offer the woman an opportunity to view the ultrasound image, receive a printed copy of the ultrasound image and hear the fetal heart tones pursuant to standard medical practice in the community, and shall obtain from the woman written certification that this opportunity was offered and whether or not it was accepted and, if applicable, verification that the pregnant woman lives at least 100 miles from the facility where the abortion is to be performed. A printed copy of the ultrasound image shall be maintained in the woman's medical record at the facility where the abortion is to be performed for the longer of (i) seven years or (ii) the extent required by applicable federal or state law.

D. For purposes of this section:

"Informed written consent" means the knowing and voluntary written consent to abortion by a pregnant woman of any age, without undue inducement or any element of force, fraud, deceit, duress, or other form of constraint or coercion by the physician who is to perform the abortion or his agent. The basic information to effect such consent, as required by this subsection, shall be provided by telephone or in person to the woman at least 24 hours before the abortion by the physician who is to perform the abortion, by a referring physician, or by a licensed professional or practical nurse working under the direct supervision of either the physician who is to perform the abortion or the referring physician; however, the information in subdivision 5 may be provided instead by a licensed health-care professional working under the direct supervision of either the physician who is to perform the abortion or the referring physician. This basic information shall include:

1. A full, reasonable and comprehensible medical explanation of the nature, benefits, and risks of and alternatives to the proposed procedures or protocols to be followed in her particular case;

2. An instruction that the woman may withdraw her consent at any time prior to the performance of the procedure;

3. An offer for the woman to speak with the physician who is to perform the abortion so that he may answer any questions that the woman may have and provide further information concerning the procedures and protocols;

4. A statement of the probable gestational age of the fetus at the time the abortion is to be performed and that fetal ultrasound imaging shall be performed prior to the abortion to confirm the gestational age; and

5. An offer to review the printed materials described in subsection F. If the woman chooses to review such materials, they shall be provided to her in a respectful and understandable manner, without prejudice and intended to give the woman the opportunity to make an informed choice and shall be provided to her at least 24 hours before the abortion or mailed to her at least 72 hours before the abortion by first-class mail or, if the woman requests, by certified mail, restricted delivery. This offer for the woman to review the material shall advise her of the following: (i) the Department of Health publishes printed materials that describe the unborn child and list agencies that offer alternatives to abortion; (ii) medical assistance benefits may be available for prenatal care, childbirth and neonatal care, and that more detailed information on the availability of such assistance is contained in the printed materials published by the Department; (iii) the father of the unborn child is liable to assist in the support of her child, even in instances where he has offered to pay for the abortion, that assistance in the collection of such support is available, and that more detailed information on the availability of such assistance is contained in the printed materials published by the Department; (iv) she has the right to review the materials printed by the Department and that copies will be provided to her free of charge if she chooses to review them; and (v) a statewide list of public and private agencies and services that provide ultrasound imaging and auscultation of fetal heart tone services free of charge. Where the woman has advised that the pregnancy is the result of a rape, the information in clause (iii) may be omitted.

The information required by this subsection may be provided by telephone or in person.

E. The physician need not obtain the informed written consent of the woman when the abortion is to be performed pursuant to a medical emergency or spontaneous miscarriage. "Medical emergency" means any condition which, on the basis of the physician's good faith clinical judgment, so complicates the medical condition of a pregnant woman as to necessitate the immediate abortion of her pregnancy to avert her death or for which a delay will create a serious risk of substantial and irreversible impairment of a major bodily function.

F. On or before October 1, 2001, the Department of Health shall publish, in English and in each language which is the primary language of two percent or more of the population of the Commonwealth, the following printed materials in such a way as to ensure that the information is easily comprehensible:

1. Geographically indexed materials designed to inform the woman of public and private agencies and services available to assist a woman through pregnancy, upon childbirth and while the child is dependent, including, but not limited to, information on services relating to (i) adoption as a positive alternative, (ii) information relative to counseling services, benefits, financial assistance, medical care and contact persons or groups, (iii) paternity establishment and child support enforcement, (iv) child development, (v) child rearing and stress management, (vi) pediatric and maternal health care, and (vii) public and private agencies and services that provide ultrasound imaging and auscultation of fetal heart tone services free of charge. The materials shall include a comprehensive list of the names and telephone numbers of the agencies, or, at the option of the Department of Health, printed materials including a toll-free, 24-hour-a-day telephone number which may be called to obtain, orally, such a list and description of agencies in the locality of the caller and of the services they offer;

2. Materials designed to inform the woman of the probable anatomical and physiological characteristics of the human fetus at two-week gestational increments from the time when a woman can be known to be pregnant to full term, including any relevant information on the possibility of the fetus's survival and pictures or drawings representing the development of the human fetus at two-week gestational increments. Such pictures or drawings shall contain the dimensions of the fetus and shall be realistic and appropriate for the stage of pregnancy depicted. The materials shall be objective, nonjudgmental and designed to convey only accurate scientific information about the human fetus at the various gestational ages; and

3. Materials containing objective information describing the methods of abortion procedures commonly employed, the medical risks commonly associated with each such procedure, the possible detrimental psychological effects of abortion, and the medical risks commonly associated with carrying a child to term.

The Department of Health shall make these materials available at each local health department and, upon request, to any person or entity, in reasonable numbers and without cost to the requesting party.

G. Any physician who fails to comply with the provisions of this section shall be subject to a $2,500 civil penalty.

History.

Code 1950, § 18.1-62.1; 1970, c. 508; 1972, c. 823; 1975, cc. 14, 15; 1979, c. 250; 1997, c. 801; 2001, cc. 473, 477; 2003, c. 784; 2012, c. 131.

§ 18.2-76.1. Encouraging or promoting abortion.

If any person, by publication, lecture, advertisement, or by the sale or circulation of any publication, or through the use of a referral agency for profit, or in any other manner, encourage or promote the performing of an abortion or the inducing of a miscarriage in this Commonwealth which is prohibited under this article, he shall be guilty of a Class 3 misdemeanor.

History.
Code 1950, § 18.1-63; 1960, c. 358; 1972, c. 725; 1975, cc. 14, 15.

§ 18.2-76.2: Repealed by Acts 2015, c. 709, cl. 2.

CHAPTER 5.

CRIMES AGAINST PROPERTY.

Crimes and Offenses

Article 1.

Arson and Related Crimes.

Article 2.

Burglary and Related Offenses.

Article 3.

Larceny and Receiving Stolen Goods.

Article 4.

Embezzlement and Fraudulent Conversions.

Article 5.

Trespass to Realty.

Article 6.

Damage to Realty and Personalty Thereon.

Article 7.

Damage to and Tampering With Property.

Article 7.1.

Computer Crimes.

Article 7.2.

Fraudulent Procurement, Sale, or Receipt of Telephone Records.

Article 8.

Offenses Relating to Railroads and Other Utilities.

ARTICLE 1.
ARSON AND RELATED CRIMES.

§ 18.2-77. Burning or destroying dwelling house, etc.

A. If any person maliciously (i) burns, or by use of any explosive device or substance destroys, in whole or in part, or causes to be burned or destroyed, or (ii) aids, counsels or procures the burning or destruction of any dwelling house or manufactured home whether belonging to himself or another, or any occupied hotel, hospital, mental health facility, or other house in which persons usually dwell or lodge, any occupied railroad car, boat, vessel, or river craft in which persons usually dwell or lodge, or any occupied jail or prison, or any occupied church or occupied building owned or leased by a church that is immediately adjacent to a church, he shall be guilty of a felony, punishable by imprisonment for life or for any period not less than five years and, subject to subdivision g of § 18.2-10, a fine of not more than $100,000. Any person who maliciously sets fire to anything, or aids, counsels or procures the setting fire to anything, by the burning whereof such occupied dwelling house, manufactured home, hotel, hospital, mental health facility or other house, or railroad car, boat, vessel, or river craft, jail or prison, church or building owned or leased by a church that is immediately adjacent to a church, is burned shall be guilty of a violation of this subsection.

B. Any such burning or destruction when the building or other place mentioned in subsection A is unoccupied, shall be punishable as a Class 4 felony.

C. For purposes of this section, "church" shall be defined as in § 18.2-127.

History.

Code 1950, § 18.1-75; 1960, c. 358; 1975, cc. 14, 15; 1977, c. 63; 1978, c. 443; 1993, c. 406; 1997, c. 832.

§ 18.2-78. What not deemed dwelling house.

No outhouse, not adjoining a dwelling house, nor under the same roof, although within the curtilage thereof, shall be deemed a part of such dwelling house, within the meaning of this chapter, unless some person usually lodge therein at night.

History.

Code 1950, § 18.1-77; 1960, c. 358; 1975, cc. 14, 15.

§ 18.2-79. Burning or destroying meeting house, etc.

If any person maliciously burns, or by the use of any explosive device or substance, maliciously destroys, in whole or in part, or causes to be burned or destroyed, or aids, counsels, or procures the burning or destroying, of any meeting house, courthouse, townhouse, college, academy, schoolhouse, or other building erected for public use except an asylum, hotel, jail, prison or church or building owned or leased by a church that is immediately adjacent to a church, or any banking house, warehouse, storehouse, manufactory, mill, or other house, whether the property of himself or of another person, not usually occupied by persons lodging therein at night, at a time when any person is therein, or if he maliciously sets fire to anything, or causes to be set on fire, or aids, counsels, or procures the setting on fire of anything, by the burning whereof any building mentioned in this section is burned, at a time when any person is therein, he shall be guilty of a Class 3 felony. If such offense is committed when no person is in such building mentioned in this section, the offender shall be guilty of a Class 4 felony.

History.

Code 1950, § 18.1-78; 1960, c. 358; 1975, cc. 14, 15; 1997, c. 832.

§ 18.2-80. Burning or destroying any other building or structure.

If any person maliciously, or with intent to defraud an insurance company or other person, burn, or by the use of any explosive device or substance, maliciously destroy, in whole or in part, or cause to be burned or destroyed, or aid, counsel or procure the burning or destruction of any building, bridge, lock, dam or other structure, whether the property of himself or of another, at a time when any person is therein or thereon, the burning or destruction whereof is not punishable under any other section of this chapter, he shall be guilty of a Class 3 felony. If he commits such offense at a time when no person is in such building, or other structure, and such building, or other structure, with the property therein, be of the value of $200, or more, he shall be guilty of a Class 4 felony, and if it and the property therein be of less value, he shall be guilty of a Class 1 misdemeanor.

History.

Code 1950, §§ 18.1-80, 18.1-81, 18.1-85; 1960, c. 358; 1975, cc. 14, 15; 1981, c. 197.

§ 18.2-81. Burning or destroying personal property, standing grain, etc.

If any person maliciously, or with intent to defraud an insurance company or other person, set fire to or burn or destroy by any explosive device or substance, or cause to be burned, or destroyed by any explosive device or substance, or aid, counsel, or procure the burning or destroying by any explosive device or substance, of any personal property, standing grain or other crop, he shall, if the thing burnt or destroyed, be of the value of $200 or more, be guilty of a Class 4 felony; and if the thing burnt or destroyed be of less value, he shall be guilty of a Class 1 misdemeanor.

History.

Code 1950, §§ 18.1-79, 18.1-85; 1960, c. 358; 1972, c. 53; 1975, cc. 14, 15; 1981, c. 197.

§ 18.2-82. Burning building or structure while in such building or structure with intent to commit felony.

If any person while in any building or other structure unlawfully, with intent to commit a felony therein, shall burn or cause to be burned, in whole or in part, such building or other structure, the burning of which is not punishable under any other section of this chapter, he shall be guilty of a Class 4 felony.

History.

Code 1950, § 18.1-80.1; 1970, c. 356; 1975, cc. 14, 15.

§ 18.2-83. Threats to bomb or damage buildings or means of transportation; false information as to danger to such buildings, etc.; punishment; venue.

A. Any person (a) who makes and communicates to another by any means any threat to bomb, burn, destroy or in any manner damage any place of assembly, building or other structure, or any means of transportation, or (b) who communicates to another, by any means, information, knowing the same to be false, as to the existence of any peril of bombing, burning, destruction or damage to any such place of assembly, building or other structure, or any means of transportation, shall be guilty of a Class 5 felony; provided, however, that if such person be under fifteen years of age, he shall be guilty of a Class 1 misdemeanor.

B. A violation of this section may be prosecuted either in the jurisdiction from which the communication was made or in the jurisdiction where the communication was received.

History.

Code 1950, §§ 18.1-78.1 through 18.2-78.4; 1960, c. 358; 1975, cc. 14, 15; 1982, c. 502.

§ 18.2-84. Causing, inciting, etc., commission of act proscribed by § 18.2-83.

Any person fifteen years of age or over, including the parent of any child, who shall cause, encourage, incite, entice or solicit any person, including a child, to commit any act proscribed by the provisions of § 18.2-83, shall be guilty of a Class 5 felony.

History.

Code 1950, § 18.1-78.5; 1960, c. 358; 1975, cc. 14, 15.

§ 18.2-85. Manufacture, possession, use, etc., of fire bombs or explosive materials or devices; penalties.

For the purpose of this section:

"Device" means any instrument, apparatus or contrivance, including its component parts, that is capable of producing or intended to produce an explosion but shall not include fireworks as defined in § 27-95.

"Explosive material" means any chemical compound, mechanical mixture or device that is commonly used or can be used for the purpose of producing an explosion and which contains any oxidizing and combustive agents or other ingredients in such proportions, quantities or packaging that an ignition by fire, friction, concussion, percussion, detonation or by any part of the compound or mixture may cause a sudden generation of highly heated gases. These materials include, but are not limited to, gunpowder, powders for blasting, high explosives, blasting materials, fuses (other than electric circuit breakers), detonators, and other detonating agents and smokeless powder.

"Fire bomb" means any container of a flammable material such as gasoline, kerosene, fuel oil, or other chemical compound, having a wick composed of any material or a device or other substance which, if set or ignited, is capable of igniting such flammable material or chemical compound but does not include a similar device commercially manufactured and used solely for the purpose of illumination or cooking.

"Hoax explosive device" means any device which by its design, construction, content or characteristics appears to be or to contain a bomb or other destructive device or explosive but which is an imitation of any such device or explosive.

Any person who (i) possesses materials with which fire bombs or explosive materials or devices can be made with the intent to manufacture fire bombs or explosive materials or devices or, (ii) manufactures, transports, distributes, possesses or uses a fire bomb or explosive materials or devices shall be guilty of a Class 5 felony. Any person who constructs, uses, places, sends, or causes to be sent any hoax explosive device so as to intentionally cause another person to believe that such device is a bomb or explosive shall be guilty of a Class 6 felony.

Nothing in this section shall prohibit the authorized manufacture, transportation, distribution, use or possession of any material, substance, or device by a member of the armed forces of the United States, fire fighters or law-enforcement officers, nor shall it prohibit the manufacture, transportation, distribution, use or possession of any material, substance or device to be used solely for scientific research, educational purposes or for any lawful purpose, subject to the provisions of §§ 27-97 and 27-97.2.

History.

Code 1950, § 18.1-78.6; 1968, c. 249; 1972, c. 126; 1975, cc. 14, 15, 497; 1976, c. 526; 1977, c. 326; 1990, cc. 644, 647; 1992, c. 540; 2000, cc. 951, 1065; 2002, cc. 588, 623; 2005, c. 204.

§ 18.2-86. Setting fire to woods, fences, grass, etc.

If any person maliciously set fire to any wood, fence, grass, straw or other thing capable of spreading fire on land, he shall be guilty of a Class 6 felony.

History.

Code 1950, § 18.1-82; 1960, c. 358; 1968, c. 362; 1975, cc. 14, 15.

§ 18.2-87. Setting woods, etc., on fire intentionally whereby another is damaged or jeopardized.

Any person who intentionally sets or procures another to set fire to any woods, brush, leaves, grass, straw, or any other inflammable substance capable of spreading fire, and who intentionally allows the fire to escape to lands not his own, whereby the property of another is damaged or jeopardized, shall be guilty of a Class 1 misdemeanor, and shall be liable for the full amount of all expenses incurred in fighting the fire.

History.

Code 1950, § 18.1-83; 1960, c. 358; 1975, cc. 14, 15; 1988, c. 403.

§ 18.2-87.1. Setting off chemical bombs capable of producing smoke in certain public buildings.

It shall be unlawful for any person to willfully and intentionally set off or cause to be set off any chemical bomb capable of producing smoke in any building used for public assembly or regularly used by the public including, but not limited to, schools, theaters, stores, office buildings, shopping malls, coliseums and arenas. Any person convicted of a violation of this section shall be guilty of a Class 2 misdemeanor.

History.
1976, c. 153.

§ 18.2-88. Carelessly damaging property by fire.

If any person carelessly, negligently or intentionally set any woods or marshes on fire, or set fire to any stubble, brush, straw, or any other substance capable of spreading fire on lands, whereby the property of another is damaged or jeopardized, he shall be guilty of a Class 4 misdemeanor, and shall be liable for the full amount of all expenses incurred in fighting the fire.

History.
Code 1950, § 18.1-84; 1960, c. 358; 1975, cc. 14, 15.

ARTICLE 2.
BURGLARY AND RELATED OFFENSES.

§ 18.2-89. Burglary; how punished.

If any person break and enter the dwelling house of another in the nighttime with intent to commit a felony or any larceny therein, he shall be guilty of burglary, punishable as a Class 3 felony; provided, however, that if such person was armed with a deadly weapon at the time of such entry, he shall be guilty of a Class 2 felony.

History.
Code 1950, § 18.1-86; 1960, c. 358; 1975, cc. 14, 15.

§ 18.2-90. Entering dwelling house, etc., with intent to commit murder, rape, robbery or arson; penalty.

If any person in the nighttime enters without breaking or in the daytime breaks and enters or enters and conceals himself in a dwelling house or an adjoining, occupied outhouse or in the nighttime enters without breaking or at any time breaks and enters or enters and conceals himself in any building permanently affixed to realty, or any ship, vessel or river craft or any railroad car, or any automobile, truck or trailer, if such automobile, truck or trailer is used as a dwelling or place of human habitation, with intent to commit murder, rape, robbery or arson in violation of §§ 18.2-77, 18.2-79 or § 18.2-80, he shall be deemed guilty of statutory burglary, which offense shall be a Class 3 felony. However, if such person was armed with a deadly weapon at the time of such entry, he shall be guilty of a Class 2 felony.

History.
Code 1950, § 18.1-88; 1960, c. 358; 1970, c. 381; 1975, cc. 14, 15; 1985, c. 110; 1992, c. 546; 1997, c. 832; 2004, c. 842.

§ 18.2-91. Entering dwelling house, etc., with intent to commit larceny, assault and battery or other felony.

If any person commits any of the acts mentioned in § 18.2-90 with intent to commit larceny, or any felony other than murder, rape, robbery or arson in violation of §§ 18.2-77, 18.2-79 or § 18.2-80, or if any person commits any of the acts mentioned in § 18.2-89 or § 18.2-90 with intent to commit assault and battery, he shall be guilty of statutory burglary, punishable by confinement in a state correctional facility for not less than one or more than twenty years or, in the discretion of the jury or the court trying the case without a jury, be confined in jail for a period not exceeding twelve months or fined not more than $2,500, either or both. However, if the person was armed with a deadly weapon at the time of such entry, he shall be guilty of a Class 2 felony.

History.
Code 1950, § 18.1-89; 1960, c. 358; 1962, c. 505; 1970, c. 381; 1975, cc. 14, 15, 602; 1991, c. 710; 1992, c. 486; 1996, c. 1040; 1997, c. 832.

§ 18.2-92. Breaking and entering dwelling house with intent to commit other misdemeanor.

If any person break and enter a dwelling house while said dwelling is occupied, either in the day or nighttime, with the intent to commit any misdemeanor except assault and battery or trespass, he shall be guilty of a Class 6 felony. However, if the person was armed with a deadly weapon at the time of such entry, he shall be guilty of a Class 2 felony.

History.
Code 1950, § 18.1-88.1; 1968, c. 530; 1970, c. 381; 1975, cc. 14, 15; 1992, c. 486.

§ 18.2-93. Entering bank, armed, with intent to commit larceny.

If any person, armed with a deadly weapon, shall enter any banking house, in the daytime or in the nighttime, with intent to commit larceny of money, bonds, notes, or other evidence of debt therein, he shall be guilty of a Class 2 felony.

History.
Code 1950, § 18.1-90; 1960, c. 358; 1975, cc. 14, 15.

§ 18.2-94. Possession of burglarious tools, etc.

If any person have in his possession any tools, implements or outfit, with intent to commit burglary, robbery or larceny, upon conviction thereof he shall be guilty of a Class 5 felony. The possession of such burglarious tools, implements or outfit by any person other than a licensed dealer, shall be prima facie evidence of an intent to commit burglary, robbery or larceny.

History.
Code 1950, § 18.1-87; 1960, c. 358; 1970, c. 587; 1975, cc. 14, 15.

ARTICLE 3.

LARCENY AND RECEIVING STOLEN GOODS.

§ 18.2-95. Grand larceny defined; how punished.

Any person who (i) commits larceny from the person of another of money or other thing of value of $5 or more, (ii) commits simple larceny not from the person of another of goods and chattels of the value of $200 or more, or (iii) commits simple larceny not from the person of another of any firearm, regardless of the firearm's value, shall be guilty of grand larceny, punishable by imprisonment in a state correctional facility for not less than one nor more than twenty years or, in the discretion of the jury or court trying the case without a jury, be confined in jail for a period not exceeding twelve months or fined not more than $2,500, either or both.

History.
Code 1950, § 18.1-100; 1960, c. 358; 1966, c. 247; 1975, cc. 14, 15, 603; 1980, c. 175; 1991, c. 710; 1992, c. 822; 1998, c. 821.

§ 18.2-96. Petit larceny defined; how punished.

Any person who:

1. Commits larceny from the person of another of money or other thing of value of less than $5, or
2. Commits simple larceny not from the person of another of goods and chattels of the value of less than $200, except as provided in subdivision (iii) of § 18.2-95, shall be deemed guilty of petit larceny, which shall be punishable as a Class 1 misdemeanor.

History.
Code 1950, § 18.1-101; 1960, c. 358; 1966, c. 247; 1975, cc. 14, 15; 1980, c. 175; 1992, c. 822.

§ 18.2-96.1. Identification of certain personalty.

A. The owner of personal property may permanently mark such property, including any part thereof, for the purpose of identification with the social security number of the owner, preceded by the letters "VA."

B. [Repealed.]

C. It shall be unlawful for any person to remove, alter, deface, destroy, conceal, or otherwise obscure the manufacturer's serial number or marks, including personalty marked with a social security number preceded by the letters "VA," from such personal property or any part thereof, without the consent of the owner, with intent to render it or other property unidentifiable.

D. It shall be unlawful for any person to possess such personal property or any part thereof, without the consent of the owner, knowing that the manufacturer's serial number or any other distinguishing identification number or mark, including personalty marked with a social security number preceded by the letters "VA," has been removed, altered, defaced, destroyed, concealed, or otherwise obscured with the intent to violate the provisions of this section.

E. A person in possession of such property which is otherwise in violation of this section may apply in writing to the Bureau of Criminal Investigation, Virginia State Police, for assignment of a number for the personal property providing he can show that he is the lawful owner of the property. If a number is issued in conformity with the provisions of this section, then the person to whom it was issued and any person to whom the property is lawfully disposed of shall not be in violation of this section. This subsection shall apply only when the application has been filed by a person prior to arrest or authorization of a warrant of arrest for that person by a court.

F. Any person convicted of an offense under this section, when the value of the personalty is less than $200, shall be guilty of a Class 1 misdemeanor and, when the value of the personalty is $200 or more, shall be guilty of a Class 5 felony.

History.
1981, c. 165; 1982, c. 382.

§ 18.2-97. Larceny of certain animals and poultry.

Any person who shall be guilty of the larceny of a dog, horse, pony, mule, cow, steer, bull or calf shall be guilty of a Class 5 felony; and any person who shall be guilty of the larceny of any poultry of the value of $5 dollars or more, but of the value of less than $200, or of a sheep, lamb, swine, or goat, of the value of less than $200, shall be guilty of a Class 6 felony.

History.
Code 1950, § 18.1-102; 1960, c. 358; 1962, c. 15; 1966, c. 247; 1975, cc. 14, 15; 1981, c. 197.

§ 18.2-97.1. Removal of a transmitting device; penalty.

Any person who removes an electronic or radio transmitting device from a dog, falcon, hawk, or owl without the permission of the owner and with the intent to prevent or hinder the owner from locating the dog, falcon, hawk, or owl is guilty of a Class 1

Crimes and Offenses

misdemeanor. Upon a finding of guilt, the court shall order that the defendant pay as restitution the actual value of any dog, falcon, hawk, or owl lost or killed as a result of such removal. The court may also order restitution to the owner for any lost breeding revenues.

History.

2007, cc. 484, 721; 2011, c. 191.

§ 18.2-98. Larceny of bank notes, checks, etc., or any book of accounts.

If any person steal any bank note, check, or other writing or paper of value, whether the same represents money and passes as currency, or otherwise, or any book of accounts, for or concerning money or goods due or to be delivered, he shall be deemed guilty of larceny thereof, and may be charged for such larceny under § 18.2-95 or 18.2-96, and if convicted shall receive the same punishment, according to the value of the thing stolen, prescribed for the punishment of the larceny of goods and chattels. The provisions of this section shall be construed to embrace all bank notes and papers of value representing money and passing as currency, whether the same be the issue of this Commonwealth or any other state, or of the United States, or of any corporation, and shall include all other papers of value, of whatever description. In a prosecution under this section, the money due on or secured by the writing, paper or book, and remaining unsatisfied, or which in any event might be collected thereon, or the value of the property or money affected thereby, shall be deemed to be the value of the article stolen.

History.

Code 1950, §§ 18.1-104, 18.1-105; 1960, c. 358; 1975, cc. 14, 15; 2009, c. 591.

§ 18.2-98.1: Repealed by Acts 1984, c. 751.

Cross references.

For present provisions as to computer crimes, see § 18.2-152.1 et seq.

§ 18.2-99. Larceny of things fixed to the freehold.

Things which savor of the realty, and are at the time they are taken part of the freehold, whether they be of the substance or produce thereof, or affixed thereto, shall be deemed goods and chattels of which larceny may be committed, although there be no interval between the severing and taking away.

History.

Code 1950, § 18.1-106; 1960, c. 358; 1975, cc. 14, 15.

§ 18.2-100. Removal of crop by tenant before rents and advances are satisfied.

It shall be unlawful for any person renting the lands of another, either for a share of the crop or for money consideration, to remove therefrom, without the consent of the landlord, any part of such crop until the rents and advances are satisfied. Every such offense shall be punishable as a Class 3 misdemeanor.

History.

Code 1950, § 18.1-115; 1960, c. 358; 1975, cc. 14, 15.

§ 18.2-101. Selling, etc., of goods distrained or levied on.

If any person fraudulently sell, pledge, encumber, remove, destroy, receive or secrete any goods, chattels or other personal property of any kind whatsoever that has been distrained or levied upon, with intent to defeat such distress or levy, he shall be deemed guilty of the larceny thereof.

History.

Code 1950, § 18.1-108; 1960, c. 358; 1975, cc. 14, 15.

§ 18.2-102. Unauthorized use of animal, aircraft, vehicle or boat; consent; accessories or accomplices.

Any person who shall take, drive or use any animal, aircraft, vehicle, boat or vessel, not his own, without the consent of the owner thereof and in the absence of the owner, and with intent temporarily to deprive the owner thereof of his possession thereof, without intent to steal the same, shall be guilty of a Class 6 felony; provided, however, that if the value of such animal, aircraft, vehicle, boat or vessel shall be less than $200, such person shall be guilty of a Class 1 misdemeanor. The consent of the owner of an animal, aircraft, vehicle, boat or vessel to its taking, driving or using shall not in any case be presumed or implied because of such owner's consent on a previous occasion to the taking, driving or using of such animal, aircraft, vehicle, boat or vessel by the same or a different person. Any person who assists in, or is a party or accessory to, or an accomplice in, any such unauthorized taking, driving or using shall be subject to the same punishment as if he were the principal offender.

History.

Code 1950, § 18.1-164; 1960, c. 358; 1970, c. 8; 1975, cc. 14, 15; 1981, c. 197.

§ 18.2-102.1. Removal of shopping cart from store premises.

(1) The term *"shopping cart"* when used in this section means those push carts of the type or types

which are commonly provided by grocery stores, drugstores, or other merchant stores or markets for the use of the public in transporting commodities in stores and markets from the store to a place outside the store.

(2) It shall be unlawful for any person to remove a shopping cart from the premises, of the owner of such shopping cart without the consent, of the owner or of his agent, servant, or employee given at the time of such removal. For the purpose of this section, the premises shall include all the parking area set aside by the owner, or on behalf of the owner, for the parking of cars for the convenience of the patrons of the owner.

(3) Any person convicted of a violation under subsection (2) shall be guilty of a Class 3 misdemeanor.

History.
Code 1950, § 18.1-117.2; 1975, c. 269.

§ 18.2-102.2. Unauthorized use of dairy milk cases or milk crates; penalty.

It shall be unlawful for any person to:

1. Buy, sell, or dispose of any milk case or milk crate bearing the name or label of the owner without the written consent of the owner or his designated agent;
2. Refuse, upon written demand of the owner or his designated agent, to return to the owner or his designated agent any milk case or milk crate bearing the name or label of the owner; or
3. Deface, obliterate, erase, cover up, or otherwise remove or conceal any name, label, registered trademark, insignia, or other business identification of an owner of a milk case or milk crate without the consent of the owner, for the purpose of destroying or removing from the milk case or milk crate evidence of its ownership.

A violation of this section shall be punishable as a Class 4 misdemeanor.

For purposes of this section, milk cases or milk crates shall be deemed to bear a name or label of an owner when there is imprinted or attached on the case or crate a name, insignia, mark, business identification, or label showing ownership or sufficient information to ascertain ownership. The term *"milk case"* or *"milk crate"* means a wire or plastic container which holds sixteen quarts or more of beverage and is used by distributors or retailers or their agents as a means to transport, store, or carry dairy products.

History.
1990, c. 452.

§ 18.2-103. Concealing or taking possession of merchandise; altering price tags; transferring goods from one container to another; counseling, etc., another in performance of such acts.

Whoever, without authority, with the intention of converting goods or merchandise to his own or another's use without having paid the full purchase price thereof, or of defrauding the owner of the value of the goods or merchandise, (i) willfully conceals or takes possession of the goods or merchandise of any store or other mercantile establishment, or (ii) alters the price tag or other price marking on such goods or merchandise, or transfers the goods from one container to another, or (iii) counsels, assists, aids or abets another in the performance of any of the above acts, when the value of the goods or merchandise involved in the offense is less than $200, shall be guilty of petit larceny and, when the value of the goods or merchandise involved in the offense is $200 or more, shall be guilty of grand larceny. The willful concealment of goods or merchandise of any store or other mercantile establishment, while still on the premises thereof, shall be prima facie evidence of an intent to convert and defraud the owner thereof out of the value of the goods or merchandise.

History.
Code 1950, § 18.1-126; 1960, c. 358; 1970, c. 652; 1975, cc. 14, 15; 1994, c. 706.

§ 18.2-104. Punishment for conviction of misdemeanor larceny.

When a person is convicted of an offense of larceny or any offense deemed to be or punished as larceny under any provision of the Code, and it is alleged in the warrant, indictment or information on which he is convicted, and admitted, or found by the jury or judge before whom he is tried, that he has been before convicted in the Commonwealth of Virginia or in another jurisdiction for any offense of larceny or any offense deemed or punishable as larceny, or of any substantially similar offense in any other jurisdiction, regardless of whether the prior convictions were misdemeanors, felonies or a combination thereof, he shall be confined in jail not less than thirty days nor more than twelve months; and for a third, or any subsequent offense, he shall be guilty of a Class 6 felony.

History.
Code 1950, § 18.1-126.1; 1970, c. 652; 1975, cc. 14, 15; 1980, c. 174; 1987, c. 178; 1994, c. 706.

§ 18.2-104.1. Liability upon conviction under § 18.2-103.

Any person who has been convicted of violating the provisions of § 18.2-103 shall be civilly liable to the owner for the retail value of any goods and merchandise illegally converted and not recovered by the owner, and for all costs incurred in prosecuting such person under the provisions of § 18.2-103. Such costs shall be limited to actual expenses, including the base wage of one employee acting as a witness for the Commonwealth and suit costs. Provided, however, the total amount of allowable costs granted hereunder shall not exceed $250, excluding the retail value of the goods and merchandise.

History.
1976, c. 577.

§ 18.2-105: Repealed by Acts 2004, c. 462.

Cross references.
For current provisions relating to exemption from civil liability in connection with arrest or detention of a person suspected of shoplifting, see § 8.01-226.9.

§ 18.2-105.1. Detention of suspected shoplifter.

A merchant, agent or employee of the merchant, who has probable cause to believe that a person has shoplifted in violation of § 18.2-95 or § 18.2-96 or § 18.2-103, on the premises of the merchant, may detain such person for a period not to exceed one hour pending arrival of a law-enforcement officer.

History.
1976, c. 515.

§ 18.2-105.2. Manufacture, sale, etc., of devices to shield against electronic detection of shoplifting prohibited; penalty.

It shall be unlawful to manufacture, sell, offer for sale, distribute or possess any specially coated or laminated bag or other device primarily designed and intended to shield shoplifted merchandise from detection by an anti-theft electronic alarm sensor, with the intention that the same be used to aid in the shoplifting of merchandise. A violation of this section shall be punishable as a Class 1 misdemeanor.

History.
1984, c. 386; 2003, c. 831.

§ 18.2-106. "Agents of the merchant" defined.

As used in this article *"agents of the merchant"* shall include attendants at any parking lot owned or leased by the merchant, or generally used by customers of the merchant through any contract or agreement between the owner of the parking lot and the merchant.

History.
Code 1950, § 18.1-128; 1960, c. 358; 1975, cc. 14, 15.

§ 18.2-107. Theft or destruction of public records by others than officers.

If any person steal or fraudulently secrete or destroy a public record or part thereof, including a microphotographic copy thereof, he shall, if the offense be not embraced by § 18.2-472 be guilty of a Class 6 felony.

History.
Code 1950, § 18.1-308; 1960, c. 358; 1974, c. 649; 1975, cc. 14, 15; 1977, c. 107.

§ 18.2-108. Receiving, etc., stolen goods.

A. If any person buys or receives from another person, or aids in concealing, any stolen goods or other thing, knowing the same to have been stolen, he shall be deemed guilty of larceny thereof, and may be proceeded against, although the principal offender is not convicted.

B. If any person buys or receives any goods or other thing, used in the course of a criminal investigation by law enforcement that such person believes to have been stolen, he shall be deemed guilty of larceny thereof.

History.
Code 1950, § 18.1-107; 1960, c. 358; 1975, cc. 14, 15; 2008, c. 578.

§ 18.2-108.01. Larceny with intent to sell or distribute; sale of stolen property; penalty.

A. Any person who commits larceny of property with a value of $200 or more with the intent to sell or distribute such property is guilty of a felony punishable by confinement in a state correctional facility for not less than two years nor more than 20 years. The larceny of more than one item of the same product is prima facie evidence of intent to sell or intent to distribute for sale.

B. Any person who sells, attempts to sell or possesses with intent to sell or distribute any stolen property with an aggregate value of $200 or more where he knew or should have known that the property was stolen is guilty of a Class 5 felony.

C. A violation of this section constitutes a separate and distinct offense.

History.
2003, c. 831.

§ 18.2-108.1. Receipt of stolen firearm.

Notwithstanding the provisions of § 18.2-108, any person who buys or receives a firearm from another person or aids in concealing a firearm, knowing that the firearm was stolen, shall be guilty of a Class 6 felony and may be proceeded against although the principal offender is not convicted.

History.
1988, c. 358; 1998, c. 821.

§ 18.2-109. Receipt or transfer of possession of stolen vehicle, aircraft or boat.

Any person who, with intent to procure or pass title to a vehicle, aircraft, boat or vessel, which he knows or has reason to believe has been stolen, shall receive or transfer possession of the same from one to another or who shall with like intent have in his possession any vehicle, aircraft, boat or vessel which he knows or has reason to believe has been stolen, and who is not an officer of the law engaged at the time in the performance of his duty as an officer, shall be guilty of a Class 6 felony.

History.
Code 1950, § 18.1-165; 1960, c. 358; 1975, cc. 14, 15.

§ 18.2-110: Repealed by Acts 2004, c. 995.

Cross references.
For current provisions as to forfeiture of motor vehicles used in commission of certain crimes, see § 19.2-386.16.

ARTICLE 4.

EMBEZZLEMENT AND FRAUDULENT CONVERSIONS.

§ 18.2-111. Embezzlement deemed larceny; indictment.

If any person wrongfully and fraudulently use, dispose of, conceal or embezzle any money, bill, note, check, order, draft, bond, receipt, bill of lading or any other personal property, tangible or intangible, which he shall have received for another or for his employer, principal or bailor, or by virtue of his office, trust, or employment, or which shall have been entrusted or delivered to him by another or by any court, corporation or company, he shall be guilty of embezzlement. Proof of embezzlement shall be sufficient to sustain the charge of larceny. Any person convicted hereunder shall be deemed guilty of larceny and may be indicted as for larceny and upon conviction shall be punished as provided in § 18.2-95 or § 18.2-96.

History.
Code 1950, § 18.1-109; 1960, c. 358; 1975, cc. 14, 15; 1979, c. 349; 1994, c. 555; 2003, c. 733.

§ 18.2-111.1: Repealed by Acts 2004, c. 459.

§ 18.2-111.2. Failure to pay withheld child support; embezzlement.

If any employer withholds money from the pay of his employee for the purpose of paying administrative or court-ordered child support on behalf of the employee and then wrongfully and fraudulently fails to make payment of the money withheld, the employer shall be guilty of embezzlement.

History.
1999, c. 56.

§ 18.2-112. Embezzlement by officers, etc., of public or other funds; default in paying over funds evidence of guilt.

If any officer, agent or employee of the Commonwealth or of any city, town, county, or any other political subdivision, or the deputy of any such officer having custody of public funds, or other funds coming into his custody under his official capacity, knowingly misuse or misappropriate the same or knowingly dispose thereof otherwise than in accordance with law, he shall be guilty of a Class 4 felony; and any default of such officer, agent, employee or deputy in paying over any such funds to the proper authorities when required by law to do so shall be deemed prima facie evidence of his guilt.

History.
Code 1950, § 18.1-110; 1960, c. 358; 1973, c. 15; 1975, cc. 14, 15; 1979, c. 585.

§ 18.2-112.1. Misuse of public assets; penalty.

A. For purposes of this section, "public assets" means personal property belonging to or paid for by the Commonwealth, or any city, town, county, or any other political subdivision, or the labor of any person other than the accused that is paid for by the Commonwealth, or any city, town, county, or any other political subdivision.

B. Any full-time officer, agent, or employee of the Commonwealth, or of any city, town, county, or any other political subdivision who, without lawful authorization, uses or permits the use of public assets for private or personal purposes unrelated to the duties and office of the accused or any other legitimate government interest when the value of such use exceeds $1,000 in any 12-month period, is guilty of a Class 4 felony.

C. Any county, city, or town shall be permitted to adopt a local ordinance that provides that any non-full-time officer, agent, employee, or elected official of the county, city, or town who, without lawful authorization, uses or permits the use of public assets for private or personal purposes unrelated to the duties and office of the accused or any other legitimate government interest when the value of such use exceeds $1,000 in any 12-month period is guilty of a Class 1 misdemeanor.

History.
2008, cc. 738, 755; 2014, c. 321.

§ 18.2-113. Fraudulent entries, etc., in accounts by officers or clerks of financial institutions, joint stock companies or corporations; penalty.

If any officer or clerk of any financial institution, joint stock company or corporation makes, alters or omits to make any entry in any account kept in or by such financial institution, company or corporation, with intent, in so doing, to conceal the true state of such account, or to defraud such financial institution, company or corporation, or to enable or assist any person to obtain money to which he was not entitled, such officer or clerk shall be guilty of a Class 4 felony.

History.

Code 1950, § 18.1-111; 1960, c. 358; 1975, cc. 14, 15; 1996, c. 77; 2003, c. 740.

§ 18.2-114: Repealed by Acts 2004, c. 459.

§ 18.2-114.1. When collection of money by commissioner, etc., larceny.

If any special commissioner or receiver, appointed by any court to collect money, and required by law, or decree of the court, to give bond before collecting the same, shall collect such money, or any part thereof, without giving such bond, and fail properly to account for the same, he shall be deemed guilty of larceny of the money so collected and not so accounted for.

History.

1978, c. 718.

§ 18.2-115. Fraudulent conversion or removal of property subject to lien or title to which is in another.

Whenever any person is in possession of any personal property, including motor vehicles or farm products, in any capacity, the title or ownership of which he has agreed in writing shall be or remain in another, or on which he has given a lien, and such person so in possession shall fraudulently sell, pledge, pawn or remove such property from the premises where it has been agreed that it shall remain, and refuse to disclose the location thereof, or otherwise dispose of the property or fraudulently remove the same from the Commonwealth, without the written consent of the owner or lienor or the person in whom the title is, or, if such writing be a deed of trust, without the written consent of the trustee or beneficiary in such deed of trust, he shall be deemed guilty of the larceny thereof.

In any prosecution hereunder, the fact that such person after demand therefor by the lienholder or person in whom the title or ownership of the property is, or his agent, shall fail or refuse to disclose to such claimant or his agent the location of the property, or to surrender the same, shall be prima facie evidence of the violation of the provisions of this section. In the case of farm products, failure to pay the proceeds of the sale of the farm products to the secured party, lienholder or person in whom the title or ownership of the property is, or his agent, within ten days after the sale or other disposition of the farm products unless otherwise agreed by the lender and borrower in the obligation of indebtedness, note or other evidence of the debt shall be prima facie evidence of a violation of the provisions of this section. The venue of prosecutions against persons fraudulently removing any such property, including motor vehicles, from the Commonwealth shall be the county or city in which such property or motor vehicle was purchased or in which the accused last had a legal residence.

This section shall not be construed to interfere with the rights of any innocent third party purchasing such property, unless such writing shall be docketed or recorded as provided by law.

History.

Code 1950, § 18.1-116; 1960, c. 358; 1975, cc. 14, 15; 1986, c. 484.

§ 18.2-115.1. Unlawful sublease of a motor vehicle; penalty.

A. It shall be unlawful for any person, for profit in the course of business, who is not a party to a lease contract, conditional sales contract, or security agreement which transfers any right or interest in a motor vehicle, knowing that the motor vehicle is subject to a lease, security interest or lien, to:

1. Obtain or exercise control over a motor vehicle and sell, transfer, assign, or lease the motor vehicle to another person without the prior written authorization of the secured creditor, lessor, or lienholder if he receives compensation or other consideration for the sale, transfer, assignment, or lease of the motor vehicle; or

2. Assist, cause, or arrange the actual or purported sale, transfer, assignment, or lease of a motor vehicle to another person without the prior written authorization of the secured creditor, lessor, or lienholder if he receives compensation or other consideration for assisting, causing, or arranging the sale, transfer, assignment, or lease of the motor vehicle.

B. A violation of this section is punishable as a Class 3 misdemeanor.

C. This section shall not apply to any employee acting upon request of his employer.

D. This section shall not apply if the entire indebtedness owed under or secured by the lease, conditional sales contract, or security agreement through the date of payment is paid in full and received by the lessor or secured party within thirty days after the sale, transfer, assignment, or lease of the motor vehicle.

History.

1990, c. 844; 1993, c. 608.

§ 18.2-116. Failure to pay for or return goods delivered for selection or approval.

If any person shall solicit and obtain from any merchant any goods, wares or merchandise for examination or approval, and shall thereafter, upon written demand, refuse or fail to return the same to such merchant in unused condition, or to pay for the same, such person so offending shall be deemed guilty of the larceny thereof. But the provisions of this section shall not apply unless such written demand be made within five days after delivery, and unless the goods, wares or merchandise shall have attached to them or to the package in which they are contained a label, card or tag containing the words, "Delivered for selection or approval."

History.
Code 1950, § 18.1-117; 1960, c. 358; 1975, cc. 14, 15.

§ 18.2-117. Failure of bailee to return animal, aircraft, vehicle or boat.

If any person comes into the possession as bailee of any animal, aircraft, vehicle, boat or vessel, and fail to return the same to the bailor, in accordance with the bailment agreement, he shall be deemed guilty of larceny thereof and receive the same punishment, according to the value of the thing stolen, prescribed for the punishment of the larceny of goods and chattels. The failure to return to the bailor such animal, aircraft, vehicle, boat or vessel, within five days from the time the bailee has agreed in writing to return the same shall be prima facie evidence of larceny by such bailee of such animal, aircraft, vehicle, boat or vessel.

History.
Code 1950, § 18.1-163; 1960, c. 358; 1975, cc. 14, 15.

§ 18.2-118. Fraudulent conversion or removal of leased personal property.

A. Whenever any person is in possession or control of any personal property, by virtue of or subject to a written lease of such property, except property described in § 18.2-117 or in the Virginia Lease-Purchase Agreement Act (§ 59.1-207.17 et seq.), and such person so in possession or control shall, with intent to defraud, sell, secrete, or destroy the property, or dispose of the property for his own use, or fraudulently remove the same from the Commonwealth without the written consent of the lessor thereof, or fail to return such property to the lessor thereof within 30 days after expiration of the lease or rental period for such property stated in such written lease, he shall be deemed guilty of the larceny thereof.

B. The fact that such person signs the lease or rental agreement with a name other than his own, or fails to return such property to the lessor thereof within 30 days after the giving of written notice to such person that the lease or rental period for such property has expired, shall be prima facie evidence of intent to defraud. For purposes of this section, notice mailed by certified mail and addressed to such person at the address of the lessee stated in the lease, shall be sufficient giving of written notice under this section.

C. The venue of prosecution under this section shall be the county or city in which such property was leased or in which such accused person last had a legal residence.

D. The court shall order a person found guilty of an offense under this section to make restitution as the court deems appropriate to the lessor. Such restitution may include (i) the cost of repairing such property; (ii) if the property is not returned or cannot reasonably be repaired, the actual value of such property; and (iii) any reasonable loss of revenue by the lessor resulting from the fraudulent conversion or removal of such property.

History.
Code 1950, § 18.1-117.1; 1966, c. 474; 1975, cc. 14, 15; 1978, c. 675; 2013, c. 536; 2014, c. 56.

ARTICLE 5.

TRESPASS TO REALTY.

§ 18.2-119. Trespass after having been forbidden to do so; penalties.

If any person without authority of law goes upon or remains upon the lands, buildings or premises of another, or any portion or area thereof, after having been forbidden to do so, either orally or in writing, by the owner, lessee, custodian, or the agent of any such person, or other person lawfully in charge thereof, or after having been forbidden to do so by a sign or signs posted by or at the direction of such persons or the agent of any such person or by the holder of any easement or other right-of-way authorized by the instrument creating such interest to post such signs on such lands, structures, premises or portion or area thereof at a place or places where it or they may be reasonably seen, or if any person, whether he is the owner, tenant or otherwise entitled to the use of such land, building or premises, goes upon, or remains upon such land, building or premises after having been prohibited from doing so by a court of competent jurisdiction by an order issued pursuant to §§ 16.1-253, 16.1-253.1, 16.1-253.4, 16.1-278.2 through 16.1-278.6, 16.1-278.8, 16.1-278.14, 16.1-278.15, 16.1-279.1, 19.2-152.8, 19.2-152.9 or § 19.2-152.10 or an ex parte order issued pursuant to § 20-103, and after having been served with such order, he shall be guilty of a Class 1 misdemeanor. This section shall not be construed to affect in any way the provisions of §§ 18.2-132 through 18.2-136.

History.
Code 1950, § 18.1-173; 1960, c. 358; 1975, cc. 14, 15; 1982, c. 169; 1987, cc. 625, 705; 1991, c. 534; 1998, cc. 569, 684; 2011, c. 195.

§ 18.2-119.1. Validity of signs forbidding trespass; penalty.

If any person knowingly and intentionally posts No Trespassing signs on the land of another without the permission of a person authorized to post such signs on that land, he shall be guilty of a Class 3 misdemeanor.

History.
1999, c. 274.

§ 18.2-120. Instigating, etc., such trespass by others; preventing service to persons not forbidden to trespass.

If any person shall solicit, urge, encourage, exhort, instigate or procure another or others to go upon or remain upon the lands, buildings, or premises of another, or any part, portion or area thereof, knowing such other person or persons to have been forbidden, either orally or in writing, to do so by the owner, lessee, custodian or other person lawfully in charge thereof, or knowing such other person or persons to have been forbidden to do so by a sign or signs posted on such lands, buildings, premises or part, portion or area thereof at a place or places where it or they may reasonably be seen; or if any person shall, on such lands, buildings, premises or part, portion or area thereof prevent or seek to prevent the owner, lessee, custodian, person in charge or any of his employees from rendering service to any person or persons not so forbidden, he shall be guilty of a Class 1 misdemeanor.

History.
Code 1950, § 18.1-173.1; 1960, c. 358; 1975, cc. 14, 15.

§ 18.2-121. Entering property of another for purpose of damaging it, etc.

It shall be unlawful for any person to enter the land, dwelling, outhouse or any other building of another for the purpose of damaging such property or any of the contents thereof or in any manner to interfere with the rights of the owner, user or the occupant thereof to use such property free from interference.

Any person violating the provisions of this section shall be guilty of a Class 1 misdemeanor. However, if a person intentionally selects the property entered because of the race, religious conviction, color or national origin of the owner, user or occupant of the property, the person shall be guilty of a Class 6 felony, and the penalty upon conviction shall include a term of confinement of at least six months, 30 days of which shall be a mandatory minimum term of confinement.

History.
Code 1950, § 18.1-183; 1960, c. 358; 1975, cc. 14, 15; 1994, c. 658; 1997, c. 833; 2004, c. 461.

§ 18.2-121.1. Permitting certain animals to run at large.

The owner or manager of any animal mentioned in § 55-316, who shall knowingly permit such animal to run at large in any county or portion thereof, under quarantine, shall be deemed to be guilty of a Class 4 misdemeanor.

History.
Code 1950, § 8-885; 1977, c. 624.

§ 18.2-121.2. Trespass by spotlight on agricultural land.

If any person shall willfully use a spotlight or similar lighting apparatus to cast a light upon private property used for livestock or crops without the written permission of the person in legal possession of such property, he shall be guilty of a Class 3 misdemeanor.

The prohibition of this section shall not apply to light cast by (i) permanently installed outdoor lighting fixtures, (ii) headlamps on vehicles moving in normal travel on public or private roads, (iii) railroad locomotives or rolling stock being operated on the tracks or right-of-way of a railroad company, (iv) aircraft or watercraft, (v) apparatus used by employees of any public utility in maintaining the utility's lines and equipment, (vi) emergency medical services vehicles used by emergency medical services personnel or fire apparatus used by members of fire departments in the performance of their official duties, (vii) apparatus used by any law-enforcement officer in the performance of his official duties, or (viii) farm machinery or motor vehicles being used in normal farming operations.

History.
1981, c. 460; 2015, cc. 502, 503.

§ 18.2-122: Repealed by Acts 1998, c. 6.

§ 18.2-123: Repealed by Acts 2004, c. 459.

§ 18.2-124. Jurisdiction over offenses committed in Capitol Square.

The Circuit Court of the City of Richmond shall have jurisdiction to try cases of offenses committed in Capitol Square except as hereinafter provided. The district court of the City of Richmond shall have jurisdiction to try misdemeanor cases arising under § 18.2-122, and all other offenses committed in the Capitol Square of which it would have jurisdiction if committed within the corporate limits and jurisdiction of the city; and the Capitol Police, or any member thereof, shall have the same authority to arrest and to swear out warrants for offenses committed on the Capitol Square as policemen of the City of Richmond have to arrest or to swear out warrants for offenses committed within the jurisdiction of the city.

History.

Code 1950, § 2.1-97; 1966, c. 677; 1975, cc. 14, 15; 2004, c. 459.

§ 18.2-125. Trespass at night upon any cemetery.

If any person, without the consent of the owner, proprietor or custodian, go or enter in the nighttime, upon the premises, property, driveways or walks of any cemetery, either public or private, for any purpose other than to visit the burial lot or grave of some member of his family, he shall be guilty of a Class 4 misdemeanor.

History.

Code 1950, § 18.1-181; 1960, c. 358; 1975, cc. 14, 15.

§ 18.2-126. Violation of sepulture; defilement of a dead human body; penalties.

A. If a person unlawfully disinters or displaces a dead human body, or any part of a dead human body which has been deposited in any vault, grave or other burial place, he is guilty of a Class 4 felony.

B. If a person willfully and intentionally physically defiles a dead human body he is guilty of a Class 6 felony. For the purposes of this section, the term "defile" shall not include any autopsy or the recovery of organs or tissues for transplantation, or any other lawful purpose.

History.

Code 1950, § 18.1-243; 1960, c. 358; 1975, cc. 14, 15; 1995, c. 306.

§ 18.2-127. Injuries to churches, church property, cemeteries, burial grounds, etc.; penalty.

A. Any person who willfully or maliciously commits any of the following acts is guilty of a Class 1 misdemeanor:

1. Destroys, removes, cuts, breaks, or injures any tree, shrub, or plant on any church property or within any cemetery or lot of any memorial or monumental association;

2. Destroys, mutilates, injures, or removes and carries away any flowers, wreaths, vases, or other ornaments placed within any church or on church property, or placed upon or around any grave, tomb, monument, or lot in any cemetery, graveyard, or other place of burial; or

3. Obstructs proper ingress to and egress from any church or any cemetery or lot belonging to any memorial or monumental association.

B. Any person who willfully or maliciously destroys, mutilates, defaces, injures, or removes any object or structure permanently attached or affixed within any church or on church property, any tomb, monument, gravestone, or other structure placed within any cemetery, graveyard, or place of burial, or within any lot belonging to any memorial or monumental association, or any fence, railing, or other work for the protection or ornament of any tomb, monument, gravestone, or other structure aforesaid, or of any cemetery lot within any cemetery is guilty of a Class 6 felony. A person convicted under this section who is required to pay restitution by the court shall be required to pay restitution to the church, if the property damaged is property of the church, or to the owner of a cemetery, if the property damaged is located within such cemetery regardless of whether the property damaged is owned by the cemetery or by another person.

C. This section shall not apply to any work which is done by the authorities of a church or congregation in the maintenance or improvement of any church property or any burial ground or cemetery belonging to it and under its management or control and which does not injure or result in the removal of a tomb, monument, gravestone, grave marker or vault. For purposes of this section, "church" shall mean any place of worship, and "church property" shall mean any educational building or community center owned or rented by a church.

History.

Code 1950, § 18.1-244; 1960, c. 358; 1975, cc. 14, 15; 1982, c. 561; 1983, c. 579; 1990, c. 510; 2004, c. 203.

§ 18.2-128. Trespass upon church or school property.

A. Any person who, without the consent of some person authorized to give such consent, goes or enters upon, in the nighttime, the premises or property of any church or upon any school property for any purpose other than to attend a meeting or service held or conducted in such church or school property, shall be guilty of a Class 3 misdemeanor.

B. It shall be unlawful for any person, whether or not a church member or student, to enter upon or remain upon any church or school property in violation of (i) any direction to vacate the property by a person authorized to give such direction or (ii) any posted notice which contains such information, posted at a place where it reasonably may be seen. Each time such person enters upon or remains on the posted premises or after such direction that person refuses to vacate such property, it shall constitute a separate offense.

A violation of this subsection shall be punishable as a Class 1 misdemeanor, except that any person, other than a parent, who violates this subsection on school property with the intent to abduct a student shall be guilty of a Class 6 felony.

C. For purposes of this section: (i) *"school property"* includes a school bus as defined in § 46.2-100 and (ii) *"church"* means any place of worship and includes any educational building or community center owned or leased by a church.

History.
Code 1950, § 18.1-182; 1960, c. 358; 1975, cc. 14, 15; 1988, c. 497; 1989, c. 680; 1993, c. 961; 1994, c. 326; 1995, cc. 493, 642; 1997, c. 779.

§ 18.2-129: Repealed by Acts 1989, c. 680.

Cross references.
As to trespass upon church or school property, see § 18.2-128.

§ 18.2-130. Peeping or spying into dwelling or enclosure.

A. It shall be unlawful for any person to enter upon the property of another and secretly or furtively peep, spy or attempt to peep or spy into or through a window, door or other aperture of any building, structure, or other enclosure of any nature occupied or intended for occupancy as a dwelling, whether or not such building, structure or enclosure is permanently situated or transportable and whether or not such occupancy is permanent or temporary, or to do the same, without just cause, upon property owned by him and leased or rented to another under circumstances that would violate the occupant's reasonable expectation of privacy.

B. It shall be unlawful for any person to use a peephole or other aperture to secretly or furtively peep, spy or attempt to peep or spy into a restroom, dressing room, locker room, hotel room, motel room, tanning bed, tanning booth, bedroom or other location or enclosure for the purpose of viewing any nonconsenting person who is totally nude, clad in undergarments, or in a state of undress exposing the genitals, pubic area, buttocks or female breast and the circumstances are such that the person would otherwise have a reasonable expectation of privacy.

C. The provisions of this section shall not apply to a lawful criminal investigation or a correctional official or local or regional jail official conducting surveillance for security purposes or during an investigation of alleged misconduct involving a person committed to the Department of Corrections or to a local or regional jail.

D. As used in this section, *"peephole"* means any hole, crack or other similar opening through which a person can see.

E. A violation of this section is a Class 1 misdemeanor.

History.
Code 1950, § 18.1-174; 1960, c. 358; 1975, cc. 14, 15; 1992, c. 520; 1999, c. 351; 2003, cc. 81, 87.

§ 18.2-131. Trespass upon licensed shooting preserve.

It shall be unlawful for any person to trespass on a licensed shooting preserve. Any person convicted of such trespass shall be guilty of a Class 4 misdemeanor and shall be responsible for all damage. Owners or keepers of dogs trespassing on preserves shall be responsible for all damage done by such dogs.

History.
Code 1950, § 29-49; 1975, cc. 14, 15.

§ 18.2-132. Trespass by hunters and fishers.

Any person who goes on the lands, waters, ponds, boats or blinds of another to hunt, fish or trap without the consent of the landowner or his agent shall be deemed guilty of a Class 3 misdemeanor.

History.
Code 1950, § 29-165; 1954, c. 155; 1962, c. 469; 1975, cc. 14, 15.

§ 18.2-132.1. Trespass by hunters using dogs; penalty.

Any person who intentionally releases hunting dogs on the lands of another which have been posted in accordance with the provisions of § 18.2-134.1 to hunt without the consent of the landowner or his agent is guilty of a Class 3 misdemeanor. A second or subsequent violation of this section within three years is a Class 1 misdemeanor and, upon conviction, the court shall revoke such person's hunting or trapping license for a period of one year. The fact that hunting dogs are present on the lands of another alone is not sufficient evidence to prove that the person acted intentionally.

History.
2016, c. 373.

§ 18.2-133. Refusal of person on land, etc., of another to identify himself.

Any person who goes on the lands, waters, ponds, boats or blinds of another to hunt, fish, or trap and willfully refuses to identify himself when requested by the landowner or his agent so to do shall be deemed guilty of a Class 4 misdemeanor.

History.
Code 1950, § 29-165.1; 1954, c. 156; 1962, c. 469; 1975, cc. 14, 15.

§ 18.2-134. Trespass on posted property.

Any person who goes on the lands, waters, ponds, boats or blinds of another, which have been posted in accordance with the provisions of § 18.2-134.1, to hunt, fish or trap except with the written consent of or in the presence of the owner or his agent shall be guilty of a Class 1 misdemeanor.

History.
Code 1950, § 29-166; 1954, c. 155; 1962, c. 469; 1975, cc. 14, 15; 1987, c. 603.

§ 18.2-134.1. Method of posting lands.

A. The owner or lessee of property described in § 18.2-134 may post property by (i) placing signs prohibiting hunting, fishing or trapping where they may reasonably be seen; or (ii) placing identifying paint marks on trees or posts at each road entrance and adjacent to public roadways and public waterways adjoining the property. Each paint mark shall be a vertical line of at least two inches in width and at least eight inches in length and the center of the mark shall be no less than three feet nor more than six feet from the ground or normal water surface. Such paint marks shall be readily visible to any person approaching the property.

B. The type and color of the paint to be used for posting shall be prescribed by the Department of Game and Inland Fisheries.

History.
1987, c. 603.

§ 18.2-135. Destruction of posted signs; posting land of another.

Any person who shall mutilate, destroy or take down any "posted," "no hunting" or similar sign or poster on the lands or waters of another, or who shall post such sign or poster on the lands or waters of another, without the consent of the landowner or his agent, shall be deemed guilty of a Class 3 misdemeanor and his hunting, fishing, and trapping license and privileges shall be revoked for a period of one to five years from the date of conviction.

History.
Code 1950, § 29-167; 1962, c. 469; 1975, cc. 14, 15; 2010, c. 183.

§ 18.2-136. Right of certain hunters to go on lands of another; carrying firearms or bows and arrows prohibited.

Fox hunters and coon hunters, when the chase begins on other lands, may follow their dogs on prohibited lands, and hunters of all other game, when the chase begins on other lands, may go upon prohibited lands to retrieve their dogs, falcons, hawks, or owls but may not carry firearms or bows and arrows on their persons or hunt any game while thereon. The use of vehicles to retrieve dogs, falcons, hawks, or owls on prohibited lands shall be allowed only with the permission of the landowner or his agent. Any person who goes on prohibited lands to retrieve his dogs, falcons, hawks, or owls pursuant to this section and who willfully refuses to identify himself when requested by the landowner or his agent to do so is guilty of a Class 4 misdemeanor.

History.
Code 1950, § 29-168; 1964, c. 600; 1975, cc. 14, 15; 1988, c. 593; 1991, cc. 317, 327; 2007, cc. 145, 658; 2011, c. 191.

§ 18.2-136.1. Enforcement of §§ 18.2-131 through 18.2-135.

Conservation police officers, sheriffs and all other law-enforcement officers shall enforce the provisions of §§ 18.2-131, 18.2-132, 18.2-133, 18.2-134 and 18.2-135.

History.
1975, cc. 14, 15.

ARTICLE 6.

DAMAGE TO REALTY AND PERSONALTY THEREON.

§ 18.2-137. Injuring, etc., any property, monument, etc.

A. If any person unlawfully destroys, defaces, damages or removes without the intent to steal any property, real or personal, not his own, or breaks down, destroys, defaces, damages or removes without the intent to steal, any monument or memorial for war veterans described in § 15.2-1812, any monument erected for the purpose of marking the site of any engagement fought during the War between the States, or for the purpose of designating the boundaries of any city, town, tract of land, or any tree marked for that purpose, he shall be guilty of a Class 3 misdemeanor; provided that the court may, in its discretion, dismiss the charge if the locality or organization responsible for maintaining the injured property, monument, or memorial files a written affidavit with the court stating it has received full payment for the injury.

B. If any person intentionally causes such injury, he shall be guilty of (i) a Class 1 misdemeanor if the value of or damage to the property, memorial or monument is less than $1,000 or (ii) a Class 6 felony if the value of or damage to the property, memorial or monument is $1,000 or more. The amount of loss caused by the destruction, defacing, damage or removal of such property, memorial or monument may be established by proof of the fair market cost of repair or fair market replacement value. Upon conviction, the court may order that the defendant pay restitution.

History.
Code 1950, § 18.1-172; 1960, c. 358; 1975, cc. 14, 15, 598; 1990, c. 933; 1999, c. 625.

§ 18.2-138. Damaging public buildings, etc.; penalty.

Any person who willfully and maliciously (i) breaks any window or door of the Capitol, any courthouse, house of public worship, college, school house, city or town hall, or other public building or library, (ii) damages or defaces the Capitol or any other public building or any statuary in the Capitol, on the Capitol Square, or in or on any other public buildings or public grounds, or (iii) destroys any property in any of such buildings shall be guilty of a Class 6 felony if damage to the property is $1,000 or more or a Class 1 misdemeanor if the damage is less than $1,000.

Any person who willfully and unlawfully damages or defaces any book, newspaper, magazine, pamphlet, map, picture, manuscript, or other property located in any library, reading room, museum, or other educational institution shall be guilty of a Class 6 felony if damage to the property is $1,000 or more or a Class 1 misdemeanor if the damage is less than $1,000.

History.

Code 1950, § 18.1-177; 1960, c. 358; 1975, cc. 14, 15; 1990, c. 454.

§ 18.2-138.1: Repealed by Acts 2004, c. 462.

Cross references.

For current provisions relating to willful and malicious damage to or defacement of public or private facilities, see § 15.2-1812.2.

§ 18.2-139. Injuries to trees, fences or herbage on grounds of Capitol, or in any public square.

If any person:

(1) Cut down, pull up, girdle or otherwise injure or destroy any tree growing in the grounds of the Capitol, or in any public square or grounds, without the consent of the Governor, or of the circuit court of the county or city in which such grounds or square is situated; or

(2) Willfully and maliciously injure the fences or herbage of the Capitol grounds, or of any such square or grounds,

he shall be guilty of a Class 3 misdemeanor.

History.

Code 1950, § 18.1-180; 1960, c. 358; 1975, cc. 14, 15.

§ 18.2-140. Destruction of trees, shrubs, etc.

It shall be unlawful for any person to pick, pull, pull up, tear, tear up, dig, dig up, cut, break, injure, burn or destroy, in whole or in part, any tree, shrub, vine, plant, flower or turf found, growing or being upon the land of another, or upon any land reserved, set aside or maintained by the Commonwealth as a public park, or as a refuge or sanctuary for wild animals, birds or fish, or upon any land reserved, set aside or maintained as a public park by a park authority created under the provisions of § 15.2-5702, without having previously obtained the permission in writing of such other or his agent or of the superintendent or custodian of such park, refuge or sanctuary so to do, unless the same be done under the personal direction of such owner, his agent, tenant or lessee or superintendent or custodian of such park, refuge or sanctuary.

Any person violating this section shall be guilty of a Class 3 misdemeanor; provided, however, that the approval of the owner, his agent, tenant or lessee, or the superintendent or custodian of such park or sanctuary afterwards given in writing or in open court shall be a bar to further prosecution or suit.

History.

Code 1950, § 18.1-178; 1960, c. 358; 1975, cc. 14, 15; 1976, c. 757; 1998, c. 81.

§ 18.2-141. Cutting or destroying trees; carrying axe, saw, etc., while hunting.

It shall be unlawful for any person while hunting for game or wildlife on the property of another to carry any axe other than a belt axe with a handle less than twenty inches, saw or other tool or instrument customarily used for the purpose of cutting, felling, mutilating or destroying trees without obtaining prior permission of the landowner. Any person violating the provisions of this section shall be guilty of a Class 3 misdemeanor.

Conservation police officers, sheriffs and all law-enforcement officers shall enforce the provisions of this section.

History.

Code 1950, § 18.1-179; 1960, c. 358; 1975, cc. 14, 15.

§ 18.2-142: Repealed by Acts 1979, c. 252.

Cross references.

For present provisions making it unlawful to damage caves, see § 10.1-1000 et seq.

§ 18.2-143. Pulling down fences or leaving open gates.

If any person, without permission of the owner, pull down the fence of another and leave the same down, or, without permission, open and leave open the gate of another, or any gate across a public road established by order of court, or if any person other than the owner or owners of the lands through which a line of railroad runs open and leave open a gate at any public or private crossing of the right-of-way of a railroad, he shall be guilty of a Class 4 misdemeanor.

History.

Code 1950, § 18.1-176; 1960, c. 358; 1975, cc. 14, 15.

ARTICLE 7.

DAMAGE TO AND TAMPERING WITH PROPERTY.

§ 18.2-144. Maiming, killing or poisoning animals, fowl, etc.

Except as otherwise provided for by law, if any person maliciously shoot, stab, wound or otherwise cause bodily injury to, or administer poison to or expose poison with intent that it be taken by, any horse, mule, pony, cattle, swine or other livestock of another, with intent to maim, disfigure, disable or kill the same, or if he do any of the foregoing acts to any animal of his own with intent to defraud any insurer thereof, he shall be guilty of a Class 5 felony. If any person do any of the foregoing acts to any fowl or to any companion animal with any of the aforesaid intents, he shall be guilty of a Class 1 misdemeanor, except that any second or subsequent offense shall be a Class 6 felony if the current offense or any previous offense resulted in the death of an animal or the euthanasia of an animal based on the recommendation of a licensed veterinarian upon determination that such euthanasia was necessary due to the condition of the animal, and such condition was a direct result of a violation of this section.

History.

Code 1950, § 18.1-159; 1960, c. 358; 1964, c. 400; 1975, cc. 14, 15; 1977, c. 598; 1978, c. 559; 1999, c. 620.

§ 18.2-144.1. Prohibition against killing or injuring police animals; penalty.

It shall be unlawful for any person to maliciously shoot, stab, wound or otherwise cause bodily injury to, or administer poison to or expose poison with intent that it be taken by a dog, horse or other animal owned, used or trained by a law-enforcement agency, regional jail or the Department of Corrections while such animal is performing his lawful duties or is being kept in a kennel, pen or stable while off duty. A violation of this section shall be punishable as a Class 5 felony. The court shall order that the defendant pay restitution for the cost of any animal killed or rendered unable to perform its duties. Such cost shall include training expenses.

History.

1989, c. 558; 1998, c. 8.

§ 18.2-144.2. Prohibition against making a false representation of ownership of an animal to a public or private animal shelter; penalty.

A. It shall be unlawful for any person to deliver or release any animal not owned by that person to a public or private animal shelter or humane society, as these terms are defined in § 3.2-6500, or to any other similar facility for animals, or any agent thereof, and to falsely represent to such facility or agent that such person is the owner of the animal.

B. A violation of subsection A is a Class 1 misdemeanor.

C. No public or private animal shelter, humane society or other similar facility for animals, or the directors or employees of any such business or facility, shall, in the absence of gross negligence, be civilly liable for accepting and disposing of any animal in good faith from a person who falsely claims to be the owner of the animal.

History.

1994, c. 885; 2014, c. 148.

§ 18.2-145. Protection of homing pigeons.

It shall be unlawful for any person at any time or in any manner to hunt, pursue, take, capture, wound, maim, disfigure, or kill any homing pigeon of another person, or to make use of any pit or pitfall, scaffold, cage, snare, trap, net, baited hook or similar device or drug, poison chemical or explosive, for the purpose of injuring, capturing or killing any such homing pigeon, provided that any officer, employee or agent of a city or county acting pursuant to authority of an ordinance thereof may take, capture and kill pigeons in, on and about any building or structure devoted to business, commercial or industrial purposes when any pigeons are using such premises for roosting, resting or congregating thereon; all pigeons taken upon such premises shall be conclusively deemed not to be homing pigeons or the property of any person.

Any person violating any of the foregoing provisions shall be guilty of a Class 3 misdemeanor.

History.

Code 1950, § 18.1-160; 1960, c. 358; 1975, cc. 14, 15.

§ 18.2-145.1. Damaging or destroying research farm product; penalty; restitution.

A. Any person or entity that (i) maliciously damages or destroys any farm product, as defined in § 3.2-4709 and (ii) knows the product is grown for testing or research purposes in the context of product development in conjunction or coordination with a private research facility or a university or any federal, state or local government agency is guilty of a Class 1 misdemeanor if the value of the farm product was less than $200, or a Class 6 felony if the value of the farm product was $200 or more.

B. The court shall order the defendant to make restitution in accordance with § 19.2-305.1 for the damage or destruction caused. For the purpose of awarding restitution under this section, the court shall determine the market value of the farm product prior to its damage or destruction and, in so doing, shall include the cost of: (i) production, (ii) research, (iii) testing, (iv) replacement and (v) product development directly related to the product damaged or destroyed.

History.

2001, cc. 547, 572.

§ 18.2-146. Breaking, injuring, defacing, destroying or preventing the operation of vehicle, aircraft or boat.

Any person who shall individually or in association with one or more others willfully break, injure, tamper with or remove any part or parts of any vehicle, aircraft, boat or vessel for the purpose of injuring, defacing or destroying said vehicle, aircraft, boat or vessel, or temporarily or permanently preventing its useful operation, or for any purpose against the will or without the consent of the owner of such vehicle, aircraft, boat or vessel, or who shall in any other manner willfully or maliciously interfere with or prevent the running or operation of such vehicle, aircraft, boat or vessel, shall be guilty of a Class 1 misdemeanor.

History.
Code 1950, § 18.1-166; 1960, c. 358; 1975, cc. 14, 15.

§ 18.2-147. Entering or setting in motion, vehicle, aircraft, boat, locomotive or rolling stock of railroad; exceptions.

Any person who shall, without the consent of the owner or person in charge of a vehicle, aircraft, boat, vessel, locomotive or other rolling stock of a railroad, climb into or upon such vehicle, aircraft, boat, vessel, locomotive or other rolling stock of a railroad, with intent to commit any crime, malicious mischief, or injury thereto, or who, while a vehicle, aircraft, boat, vessel, locomotive or other rolling stock of a railroad is at rest and unattended, shall attempt to manipulate any of the levers and starting crank or other device, brakes or mechanism thereof or to set into motion such vehicle, aircraft, boat, vessel, locomotive or other rolling stock of a railroad, with the intent to commit any crime, malicious mischief, or injury thereto, shall be guilty of a Class 1 misdemeanor, except that the foregoing provision shall not apply when any such act is done in an emergency or in furtherance of public safety or by or under the direction of an officer in the regulation of traffic or performance of any other official duty.

History.
Code 1950, § 18.1-167; 1960, c. 358; 1975, cc. 14, 15.

§ 18.2-147.1. Breaking and entering into railroad cars, motortrucks, aircraft, etc., or pipeline systems.

Any person who breaks the seal or lock of any railroad car, vessel, aircraft, motortruck, wagon or other vehicle or of any pipeline system, containing shipments of freight or express or other property, or breaks and enters any such vehicle or pipeline system with the intent to commit larceny or any felony therein shall be guilty of a Class 4 felony; provided, however, that if such person is armed with a firearm at the time of such breaking and entering, he shall be guilty of a Class 3 felony.

History.
1979, c. 336.

§ 18.2-147.2. Devices for puncturing motor vehicle tires.

It shall be unlawful for any person to manufacture, distribute, have in his possession or place upon any highway or private property jackrocks which are primarily designed for the purpose of disabling motor vehicles by the puncturing of tires by anyone other than a law-enforcement officer. Any person convicted of unlawful manufacture, distribution, possession or use of such device shall be guilty of a Class 1 misdemeanor. A law-enforcement officer who is lawfully engaged in the discharge of his duties shall not be subject to the provisions of this section.

History.
1982, c. 253; 2007, c. 437.

§ 18.2-148. Bona fide repossession under lien.

The provisions of §§ 18.2-102, 18.2-146 and 18.2-147 shall not apply to a bona fide repossession of a vehicle, aircraft, boat or vessel by the holder of a lien on such vehicle, aircraft, boat or vessel, or by the agents or employees of such lienholder.

History.
Code 1950, § 18.1-168; 1960, c. 358; 1975, cc. 14, 15.

§ 18.2-149. Injury to hired animal, aircraft, vehicle or boat.

If any person after having rented or leased from any other person an animal, aircraft, vehicle, boat or vessel shall willfully injure or damage the same, by hard or reckless driving or using, or by using the same in violation of any statute of this Commonwealth, or allow or permit any other person so to do, or hire the same to any other person without the consent of the bailor, such person shall be guilty of a Class 3 misdemeanor.

History.
Code 1950, § 18.1-161; 1960, c. 358; 1975, cc. 14, 15.

§ 18.2-150. Willfully destroying vessel, etc.

If any person willfully scuttle, cast away or otherwise dispose of, or in any manner destroy, except as otherwise provided, a ship, vessel or other watercraft, with intent to injure or defraud any owner thereof or of any property on board the same, or any insurer of such ship, vessel or other watercraft, or any part thereof, or of any such property on board the same, if the same be of the value of $200, he shall be guilty of a Class 4 felony, but if it be of less value than $200, he shall be guilty of a Class 1 misdemeanor.

History.
Code 1950, § 18.1-170; 1960, c. 358; 1975, cc. 14, 15; 1981, c. 197.

§ 18.2-151. Opening or carrying away pumps, etc., used for dispensing gasoline, etc.

If any person, with intent to commit larceny therefrom, break and open, or open, or carry away, any pump, tank, or other similar equipment or container used for dispensing or storing kerosene, gasoline or motor oils, he shall be guilty of a Class 6 felony.

History.
Code 1950, § 18.1-169; 1960, c. 358; 1975, cc. 14, 15.

§ 18.2-151.1. Injuring, destroying, removing, or tampering with firefighting equipment; penalty.

Any person who injures, destroys, removes, tampers with, or otherwise interferes with the operation of (i) any equipment or apparatus used for fighting fires or for protecting property or human life by a fire company or fire department, as those terms are defined in § 27-6.01, or (ii) any emergency medical services vehicle, as defined in § 32.1-111.1, intending to temporarily or permanently prevent the useful operation of such equipment or apparatus is guilty of a Class 1 misdemeanor.

History.
2016, c. 687.

§ 18.2-152. Stealing from or tampering with parking meter, vending machine, pay telephone, etc.

Any person who enters, forces or attempts to force an entrance into, tampers with, or inserts any part of an instrument into any parking meter, vending machine, pay telephone, money changing machine, or any other device designed to receive money, with intent to steal therefrom, shall for the first conviction thereof be guilty of a Class 1 misdemeanor, and for any subsequent conviction of a violation thereof shall be guilty of a Class 6 felony.

History.
Code 1950, § 18.1-125.1; 1968, c. 518; 1975, cc. 14, 15.

ARTICLE 7.1.
COMPUTER CRIMES.

§ 18.2-152.1. Short title.

This article shall be known and may be cited as the "Virginia Computer Crimes Act."

History.
1984, c. 751.

§ 18.2-152.2. Definitions; computer crimes.

For purposes of this article:

"Commercial electronic mail" means electronic mail, the primary purpose of which is the advertisement or promotion of a commercial product or service.

"Computer" means a device that accepts information in digital or similar form and manipulates it for a result based on a sequence of instructions. Such term does not include simple calculators, automated typewriters, facsimile machines, or any other specialized computing devices that are preprogrammed to perform a narrow range of functions with minimal end-user or operator intervention and are dedicated to a specific task.

"Computer data" means any representation of information, knowledge, facts, concepts, or instructions which is being prepared or has been prepared and is intended to be processed, is being processed, or has been processed in a computer or computer network. "Computer data" may be in any form, whether readable only by a computer or only by a human or by either, including, but not limited to, computer printouts, magnetic storage media, punched cards, or stored internally in the memory of the computer.

"Computer network" means two or more computers connected by a network.

"Computer operation" means arithmetic, logical, monitoring, storage or retrieval functions and any combination thereof, and includes, but is not limited to, communication with, storage of data to, or retrieval of data from any device or human hand manipulation of electronic or magnetic impulses. A "computer operation" for a particular computer may also be any function for which that computer was generally designed.

"Computer program" means an ordered set of data representing coded instructions or statements that, when executed by a computer, causes the computer to perform one or more computer operations.

"Computer services" means computer time or services, including data processing services, Internet services, electronic mail services, electronic message services, or information or data stored in connection therewith.

"Computer software" means a set of computer programs, procedures and associated documentation concerned with computer data or with the operation of a computer, computer program, or computer network.

"Electronic mail service provider" (EMSP) means any person who (i) is an intermediary in sending or receiving electronic mail and (ii) provides to end-users of electronic mail services the ability to send or receive electronic mail.

"Financial instrument" includes, but is not limited to, any check, draft, warrant, money order, note, certificate of deposit, letter of credit, bill of exchange, credit or debit card, transaction authorization mechanism, marketable security, or any computerized representation thereof.

"Network" means any combination of digital transmission facilities and packet switches, routers, and similar equipment interconnected to enable the exchange of computer data.

"Owner" means an owner or lessee of a computer or a computer network or an owner, lessee, or

Crimes and Offenses

licensee of computer data, computer programs or computer software.

"Person" shall include any individual, partnership, association, corporation or joint venture.

"Property" shall include:

1. Real property;
2. Computers and computer networks;
3. Financial instruments, computer data, computer programs, computer software and all other personal property regardless of whether they are:

a. Tangible or intangible;

b. In a format readable by humans or by a computer;

c. In transit between computers or within a computer network or between any devices which comprise a computer; or

d. Located on any paper or in any device on which it is stored by a computer or by a human; and

4. Computer services.

"Spam" means unsolicited commercial electronic mail. Spam shall not include commercial electronic mail transmitted to a recipient with whom the sender has an existing business or personal relationship.

A person *"uses"* a computer or computer network when he attempts to cause or causes a computer or computer network to perform or to stop performing computer operations.

A person is *"without authority"* when he knows or reasonably should know that he has no right, agreement, or permission or acts in a manner knowingly exceeding such right, agreement, or permission.

History.
1984, c. 751; 1999, cc. 886, 904, 905; 2000, c. 627; 2003, cc. 987, 1016; 2005, cc. 761, 812, 827; 2009, cc. 321, 376; 2010, c. 489.

§ 18.2-152.3. Computer fraud; penalty.

Any person who uses a computer or computer network, without authority and:

1. Obtains property or services by false pretenses;
2. Embezzles or commits larceny; or
3. Converts the property of another;

is guilty of the crime of computer fraud.

If the value of the property or services obtained is $200 or more, the crime of computer fraud shall be punishable as a Class 5 felony. Where the value of the property or services obtained is less than $200, the crime of computer fraud shall be punishable as a Class 1 misdemeanor.

History.
1984, c. 751; 1985, c. 322; 2003, cc. 987, 1016; 2005, cc. 747, 761, 827, 837.

§ 18.2-152.3:1. Transmission of unsolicited commercial electronic mail (spam); penalty.

A. Any person who:

1. Uses a computer or computer network with the intent to falsify or forge electronic mail transmission information or other routing information in any manner in connection with the transmission of spam through or into the computer network of an electronic mail service provider or its subscribers; or

2. Knowingly sells, gives, or otherwise distributes or possesses with the intent to sell, give, or distribute software that (i) is primarily designed or produced for the purpose of facilitating or enabling the falsification of the transmission information or other routing information of spam; (ii) has only limited commercially significant purpose or use other than to facilitate or enable the falsification of the transmission information or other routing information of spam; or (iii) is marketed by that person acting alone or with another for use in facilitating or enabling the falsification of the transmission information or other routing information of spam is guilty of a Class 1 misdemeanor.

B. Any person who commits a violation of subdivision A 1 when (i) the volume of spam transmitted exceeded 10,000 attempted recipients in any 24-hour time period, 100,000 attempted recipients in any 30-day time period, or one million attempted recipients in any one-year time period or (ii) revenue generated from a specific transmission of spam exceeded $1,000 or the total revenue generated from all spam transmitted to any EMSP exceeded $50,000, is guilty of a Class 6 felony.

C. Any person who knowingly hires, employs, uses, or permits any minor to assist in the transmission of spam in violation of subsection B is guilty of a Class 6 felony.

History.
2003, cc. 987, 1016; 2010, c. 489.

§ 18.2-152.4. Computer trespass; penalty.

A. It shall be unlawful for any person, with malicious intent, to:

1. Temporarily or permanently remove, halt, or otherwise disable any computer data, computer programs or computer software from a computer or computer network;

2. Cause a computer to malfunction, regardless of how long the malfunction persists;

3. Alter, disable, or erase any computer data, computer programs or computer software;

4. Effect the creation or alteration of a financial instrument or of an electronic transfer of funds;

5. Use a computer or computer network to cause physical injury to the property of another;

6. Use a computer or computer network to make or cause to be made an unauthorized copy, in any form, including, but not limited to, any printed or electronic form of computer data, computer programs or computer software residing in, communicated by, or produced by a computer or computer network;

7. [Repealed.]

8. Install or cause to be installed, or collect information through, computer software that records all

or a majority of the keystrokes made on the computer of another without the computer owner's authorization; or

9. Install or cause to be installed on the computer of another, computer software for the purpose of (i) taking control of that computer so that it can cause damage to another computer or (ii) disabling or disrupting the ability of the computer to share or transmit instructions or data to other computers or to any related computer equipment or devices, including but not limited to printers, scanners, or fax machines.

B. Any person who violates this section is guilty of computer trespass, which shall be a Class 1 misdemeanor. If there is damage to the property of another valued at $1,000 or more caused by such person's act in violation of this section, the offense shall be a Class 6 felony. If a person installs or causes to be installed computer software in violation of this section on more than five computers of another, the offense shall be a Class 6 felony. If a person violates subdivision A 8, the offense shall be a Class 6 felony.

C. Nothing in this section shall be construed to interfere with or prohibit terms or conditions in a contract or license related to computers, computer data, computer networks, computer operations, computer programs, computer services, or computer software or to create any liability by reason of terms or conditions adopted by, or technical measures implemented by, a Virginia-based electronic mail service provider to prevent the transmission of unsolicited electronic mail in violation of this article. Nothing in this section shall be construed to prohibit the monitoring of computer usage of, the otherwise lawful copying of data of, or the denial of computer or Internet access to a minor by a parent or legal guardian of the minor.

History.
1984, c. 751; 1985, c. 322; 1990, c. 663; 1998, c. 892; 1999, cc. 886, 904, 905; 2002, c. 195; 2003, cc. 987, 1016; 2005, cc. 761, 812, 827; 2007, c. 483.

§ 18.2-152.5. Computer invasion of privacy; penalties.

A. A person is guilty of the crime of computer invasion of privacy when he uses a computer or computer network and intentionally examines without authority any employment, salary, credit or any other financial or identifying information, as defined in clauses (iii) through (xiii) of subsection C of § 18.2-186.3, relating to any other person. "Examination" under this section requires the offender to review the information relating to any other person after the time at which the offender knows or should know that he is without authority to view the information displayed.

B. The crime of computer invasion of privacy shall be punishable as a Class 1 misdemeanor.

C. Any person who violates this section after having been previously convicted of a violation of this section or any substantially similar laws of any other state or of the United States is guilty of a Class 6 felony.

D. Any person who violates this section and sells or distributes such information to another is guilty of a Class 6 felony.

E. Any person who violates this section and uses such information in the commission of another crime is guilty of a Class 6 felony.

F. This section shall not apply to any person collecting information that is reasonably needed to (i) protect the security of a computer, computer service, or computer business, or to facilitate diagnostics or repair in connection with such computer, computer service, or computer business or (ii) determine whether the computer user is licensed or authorized to use specific computer software or a specific computer service.

History.
1984, c. 751; 1985, c. 398; 2001, c. 358; 2005, cc. 747, 761, 827, 837.

§ 18.2-152.5:1. Using a computer to gather identifying information; penalties.

A. It is unlawful for any person, other than a law-enforcement officer, as defined in § 9.1-101, and acting in the performance of his official duties, to use a computer to obtain, access, or record, through the use of material artifice, trickery or deception, any identifying information, as defined in clauses (iii) through (xiii) of subsection C of § 18.2-186.3. Any person who violates this section is guilty of a Class 6 felony.

B. Any person who violates this section and sells or distributes such information to another is guilty of a Class 5 felony.

C. Any person who violates this section and uses such information in the commission of another crime is guilty of a Class 5 felony.

History.
2005, cc. 747, 760, 761, 827, 837.

§ 18.2-152.6. Theft of computer services; penalties.

Any person who willfully obtains computer services without authority is guilty of the crime of theft of computer services, which shall be punishable as a Class 1 misdemeanor. If the theft of computer services is valued at $2,500 or more, he is guilty of a Class 6 felony.

History.
1984, c. 751; 1985, c. 322; 2003, cc. 987, 1016; 2005, cc. 746, 761, 827.

§ 18.2-152.7. Personal trespass by computer; penalty.

A. A person is guilty of the crime of personal trespass by computer when he uses a computer or computer network to cause physical injury to an individual.

B. If committed maliciously, the crime of personal trespass by computer shall be punishable as a Class 3 felony. If such act is done unlawfully but not maliciously, the crime of personal trespass by computer shall be punishable as a Class 6 felony.

History.
1984, c. 751; 1985, c. 322; 2003, cc. 987, 1016; 2005, cc. 746, 761, 827.

§ 18.2-152.7:1. Harassment by computer; penalty.

If any person, with the intent to coerce, intimidate, or harass any person, shall use a computer or computer network to communicate obscene, vulgar, profane, lewd, lascivious, or indecent language, or make any suggestion or proposal of an obscene nature, or threaten any illegal or immoral act, he shall be guilty of a Class 1 misdemeanor.

History.
2000, c. 849.

§ 18.2-152.8. Property capable of embezzlement.

For purposes of §§ 18.2-95, 18.2-96, 18.2-108, and 18.2-111, personal property subject to embezzlement, larceny, or receiving stolen goods shall include:

1. Computers and computer networks;
2. Financial instruments, computer data, computer programs, computer software and all other personal property regardless of whether they are:
   a. Tangible or intangible;
   b. In a format readable by humans or by a computer;
   c. In transit between computers or within a computer network or between any devices which comprise a computer; or
   d. Located on any paper or in any device on which it is stored by a computer or by a human; and
3. Computer services.

History.
1984, c. 751; 2005, cc. 746, 761, 827.

§§ 18.2-152.9, 18.2-152.10: Repealed by Acts 2005, cc. 746, 761, and 827, cl. 2.

§ 18.2-152.11. Article not exclusive.

The provisions of this article shall not be construed to preclude the applicability of any other provision of the criminal law of this Commonwealth which presently applies or may in the future apply to any transaction or course of conduct which violates this article, unless such provision is clearly inconsistent with the terms of this article.

History.
1984, c. 751.

§ 18.2-152.12. Civil relief; damages.

A. Any person whose property or person is injured by reason of a violation of any provision of this article or by any act of computer trespass set forth in subdivisions A 1 through A 8 of § 18.2-152.4 regardless of whether such act is committed with malicious intent may sue therefor and recover for any damages sustained and the costs of suit. Without limiting the generality of the term, "damages" shall include loss of profits.

B. If the injury under this article arises from the transmission of spam in contravention of the authority granted by or in violation of the policies set by the electronic mail service provider where the defendant has knowledge of the authority or policies of the EMSP or where the authority or policies of the EMSP are available on the electronic mail service provider's website, the injured person, other than an electronic mail service provider, may also recover attorneys' fees and costs, and may elect, in lieu of actual damages, to recover the lesser of $10 for each and every spam message transmitted in violation of this article, or $25,000 per day. The injured person shall not have a cause of action against the electronic mail service provider that merely transmits the spam over its computer network. Transmission of electronic mail from an organization to its members shall not be deemed to be spam.

C. If the injury under this article arises from the transmission of spam in contravention of the authority granted by or in violation of the policies set by the electronic mail service provider where the defendant has knowledge of the authority or policies of the EMSP or where the authority or policies of the EMSP are available on the electronic mail service provider's website, an injured electronic mail service provider may also recover attorneys' fees and costs, and may elect, in lieu of actual damages, to recover $1 for each and every intended recipient of a spam message where the intended recipient is an end user of the EMSP or $25,000 for each day an attempt is made to transmit a spam message to an end user of the EMSP. In calculating the statutory damages under this provision, the court may adjust the amount awarded as necessary, but in doing so shall take into account the number of complaints to the EMSP generated by the defendant's messages, the defendant's degree of culpability, the defendant's prior history of such conduct, and the extent of economic gain resulting from the conduct. Transmission of electronic mail from an organization to its members shall not be deemed to be spam.

D. At the request of any party to an action brought pursuant to this section, the court may, in its discretion, conduct all legal proceedings in such a way as to protect the secrecy and security of the computer, computer network, computer data, computer program and computer software involved in order to prevent possible recurrence of the same or a similar act by another person and to protect any trade secrets of any party and in such a way as to protect the privacy of nonparties who complain about violations of this section.

E. The provisions of this article shall not be construed to limit any person's right to pursue any additional civil remedy otherwise allowed by law.

F. A civil action under this section must be commenced before expiration of the time period prescribed in § 8.01-40.1. In actions alleging injury arising from the transmission of spam, personal jurisdiction may be exercised pursuant to § 8.01-328.1.

History.

1984, c. 751; 1985, c. 92; 1999, cc. 886, 904, 905; 2003, cc. 987, 1016; 2005, cc. 746, 761, 827; 2010, cc. 489, 529.

§ 18.2-152.13: Repealed by Acts 2015, c. 709, cl. 2.

§ 18.2-152.14. Computer as instrument of forgery.

The creation, alteration, or deletion of any computer data contained in any computer or computer network, which if done on a tangible document or instrument would constitute forgery under Article 1 (§ 18.2-168 et seq.) of Chapter 6 of this Title, will also be deemed to be forgery. The absence of a tangible writing directly created or altered by the offender shall not be a defense to any crime set forth in Article 1 (§ 18.2-168 et seq.) of Chapter 6 of this Title if a creation, alteration, or deletion of computer data was involved in lieu of a tangible document or instrument.

History.

1984, c. 751; 1985, c. 322.

§ 18.2-152.15. Encryption used in criminal activity.

Any person who willfully uses encryption to further any criminal activity shall be guilty of an offense which is separate and distinct from the predicate criminal activity and punishable as a Class 1 misdemeanor.

"Encryption" means the enciphering of intelligible data into unintelligible form or the deciphering of unintelligible data into intelligible form.

History.

1999, c. 455.

§ 18.2-152.16: Repealed by Acts 2004, c. 995.

Cross references.

For current provisions as to forfeitures for computer crimes, see § 19.2-386.17.

ARTICLE 7.2.

FRAUDULENT PROCUREMENT, SALE, OR RECEIPT OF TELEPHONE RECORDS.

§ 18.2-152.17. Fraudulent procurement, sale, or receipt of telephone records.

A. Whoever (i) knowingly procures, attempts to procure, solicits, or conspires with another to procure a telephone record by fraudulent means; (ii) knowingly sells, or attempts to sell, a telephone record without the authorization of the customer to whom the record pertains; or (iii) receives a telephone record knowing that such record has been obtained by fraudulent means is guilty of a Class 1 misdemeanor.

B. As used in this section:

"Procure" in regard to such a telephone record means to obtain by any means, whether electronically, in writing, or in oral form, with or without consideration.

"Telecommunications carrier" means any person that provides commercial telephone services to a customer, irrespective of the communications technology used to provide such service, including, but not limited to, traditional wireline or cable telephone service; cellular, broadband PCS, or other wireless telephone service; microwave, satellite, or other terrestrial telephone service; and voice over Internet telephone service.

"Telephone record" means information retained by a telecommunications carrier that relates to the telephone number dialed by the customer or the incoming number of a call directed to a customer, or other data related to such calls typically contained on a customer telephone bill such as the time the call started and ended, the duration of the call, the time of day the call was made, and any charges applied. For purposes of this section, any information collected and retained by customers utilizing Caller I.D., or other similar technology, does not constitute a telephone record.

C. Nothing in this section shall be construed to prevent any action by a law-enforcement agency, or any officer or employee of such agency, from obtaining telephone records in connection with the performance of the official duties of the agency.

D. Nothing in this section shall be construed to prohibit a telecommunications carrier from obtaining, using, disclosing, or permitting access to any telephone record, either directly or indirectly through its agents (i) in compliance with a subpoena or subpoena duces tecum or as otherwise authorized by law; (ii) with the lawful consent of the customer or subscriber; (iii) as may be necessarily incident to the rendition of the service or to the protection of the rights or property of the provider of that service, or to protect users of those services and other carriers from fraudulent, abusive, or unlawful use of, subscription to, such services; (iv) to a governmental entity, if the telecommunications carrier reasonably believes that an emergency involving immediate danger of death or serious physical injury to any person justifies disclosure of the information; or (v) to the National Center for Missing and Exploited Children, in connection with a report submitted thereto under the Victims of Child Abuse Act of 1990.

Crimes and Offenses

E. Venue for the trial of any person charged with an offense under this section may be in the locality in which:

1. Any act was performed in furtherance of any course of conduct in violation of this section;

2. The accused has his principal place of business in the Commonwealth;

3. Any accused had control or possession of any proceeds of the violation or of any books, records, documents, property, financial instrument, telephone record, or other material or objects that were used in furtherance of the violation;

4. From which, to which, or through which any access to a telecommunication carrier was made whether by wires, electromagnetic waves, microwaves, optics or any other means of communication; or

5. The accused resides, or resided at the time of the offense.

History.

2006, c. 469.

ARTICLE 8.

OFFENSES RELATING TO RAILROADS AND OTHER UTILITIES.

§ 18.2-153. Obstructing or injuring canal, railroad, power line, etc.

If any person maliciously obstruct, remove or injure any part of a canal, railroad or urban, suburban or interurban electric railway, or any lines of any electric power company, or any bridge or fixture thereof, or maliciously obstruct, tamper with, injure or remove any machinery, engine, car, trolley, supply or return wires or any other work thereof, or maliciously open, close, displace, tamper with or injure any switch, switch point, switch lever, signal lever or signal of any such company, whereby the life of any person on such canal, railroad, urban, suburban or interurban electric railway, is put in peril, he shall be guilty of a Class 4 felony; and, in the event of the death of any such person resulting from such malicious act, the person so offending shall be deemed guilty of murder, the degree to be determined by the jury or the court trying the case without a jury.

If any such act be committed unlawfully, but not maliciously, the person so offending shall be guilty of a Class 6 felony; and in the event of the death of any such person resulting from such unlawful act, the person so offending shall be deemed guilty of involuntary manslaughter.

History.

Code 1950, § 18.1-147; 1960, c. 358; 1975, cc. 14, 15.

§ 18.2-154. Shooting at or throwing missiles, etc., at train, car, vessel, etc.; penalty.

Any person who maliciously shoots at, or maliciously throws any missile at or against, any train or cars on any railroad or other transportation company or any vessel or other watercraft, or any motor vehicle or other vehicles when occupied by one or more persons, whereby the life of any person on such train, car, vessel, or other watercraft, or in such motor vehicle or other vehicle, may be put in peril, is guilty of a Class 4 felony. In the event of the death of any such person, resulting from such malicious shooting or throwing, the person so offending is guilty of murder in the second degree. However, if the homicide is willful, deliberate, and premeditated, he is guilty of murder in the first degree.

If any such act is committed unlawfully, but not maliciously, the person so offending is guilty of a Class 6 felony and, in the event of the death of any such person, resulting from such unlawful act, the person so offending is guilty of involuntary manslaughter.

If any person commits a violation of this section by maliciously or unlawfully shooting, with a firearm, at a conspicuously marked law-enforcement, fire, or emergency medical services vehicle, the sentence imposed shall include a mandatory minimum term of imprisonment of one year to be served consecutively with any other sentence.

History.

Code 1950, § 18.1-152; 1960, c. 358; 1975, cc. 14, 15; 1990, c. 426; 2004, c. 461; 2005, c. 143; 2013, cc. 761, 774; 2015, cc. 502, 503.

§ 18.2-155. Injuring, etc., signal used by railroad.

If any person maliciously injure, destroy, molest, or remove any switchlamp, flag or other signal used by any railroad, or any line, wire, post, lamp or any other structure or mechanism used in connection with any signal on a railroad, or destroys or in any manner interferes with the proper working of any signal on a railroad, whereby the life of any person is or may be put in peril he shall be guilty of a Class 4 felony; and in the event of the death of such person resulting from such malicious injuring, destroying or removing, the person so offending shall be deemed guilty of murder, the degree to be determined by the jury or the court trying the case without a jury. If such act be done unlawfully but not maliciously the offender shall be guilty of a Class 1 misdemeanor, provided that in the event of the death of any such person resulting from such unlawful injuring, destroying or removing, the person so offending shall be deemed guilty of involuntary manslaughter.

History.
Code 1950, § 18.1-153; 1960, c. 358; 1975, cc. 14, 15.

§ 18.2-156. Taking or removing waste or packing from journal boxes.

If any person shall willfully and maliciously take or remove the waste or packing from any journal box of any locomotive, engine, tender, carriage, coach, car, caboose or truck used or operated upon any railroad, whether the same be operated by steam or electricity, he shall be guilty of a Class 6 felony.

History.
Code 1950, § 18.1-151; 1960, c. 358; 1975, cc. 14, 15.

§ 18.2-157. Injury to fences or cattle stops along line of railroad.

Any person who shall willfully or maliciously cut, break down, injure or destroy any fence erected along the line of any railroad for the purpose of fencing the track or depot grounds of such road, or shall break down, injure or destroy any cattle stop along the line of any railroad, shall be guilty of a Class 3 misdemeanor.

History.
Code 1950, § 18.1-155; 1960, c. 358; 1975, cc. 14, 15.

§ 18.2-158. Driving, etc., animal on track to recover damages.

If any person, with a view to the recovery of damages against a railroad company, willfully ride, drive, or lead any animal, or otherwise contrive for any animal to go, on the railroad track of such company, and such animal is by reason thereof killed or injured, he shall be guilty of a Class 3 misdemeanor.

History.
Code 1950, § 18.1-154; 1960, c. 358; 1975, cc. 14, 15.

§ 18.2-159. Trespassing on railroad track.

Any person who goes upon the track of a railroad other than to pass over such road at a public or private crossing, or who willfully rides, drives or leads any animal or contrives for any animal to go on such track except to cross as aforesaid, without the consent of the railroad company or person operating such road, shall be guilty of a Class 4 misdemeanor. A second violation of the provisions of this section occurring within two years of the first violation shall be punishable as a Class 3 misdemeanor. A third or subsequent violation of the provisions of this section occurring within two years of a second or a subsequent violation shall be punishable as a Class 1 misdemeanor. This section shall not apply to any section of track which has been legally abandoned pursuant to an order of a federal or state agency having jurisdiction over the track and is not being used for railroad service.

For purposes of this section, track shall mean the rail, ties, and ballast of the railroad.

History.
Code 1950, § 18.1-148; 1960, c. 358; 1975, cc. 14, 15; 1993, c. 845.

§ 18.2-160. Trespassing on railroad trains.

If any person, not being a passenger or employee, shall be found trespassing upon any railroad car or train of any railroad in this Commonwealth, by riding on any car, or any part thereof, on its arrival, stay or departure at or from any station or depot of such railroad, or on the passage of any such car or train over any part of any such railroad, such person shall be guilty of a Class 4 misdemeanor.

History.
Code 1950, § 18.1-150; 1960, c. 358; 1975, cc. 14, 15.

§ 18.2-160.1. Boarding or riding transportation district train without lawful payment of fare; penalty.

A. It is unlawful for any person to board or ride a train operated by, or under contract with, a transportation district created pursuant to the Transportation District Act of 1964 (§ 33.2-1900 et seq.) of Title 33.2 when he fails or refuses to pay the posted fare published by the transportation district, or fails to properly validate a train ticket of the transportation district. A violation of this subsection continues from the point of boarding through termination of the train's scheduled trip. Any person who violates the provisions of this subsection is subject to a civil penalty of $100.

B. It is unlawful for any person to board or ride a train operated by, or under contract with, a transportation district created pursuant to the Transportation District Act of 1964 (§ 33.2-1900 et seq.) of Title 33.2 with a validated ticket and to willfully use the ticket outside the designated zone of the paid ride. A violation of this subsection continues throughout the time that such ticket is used outside the designated zone of the paid ride. Any person who violates the provisions of this subsection is subject to a civil penalty of $100.

C. It is unlawful for any person to board or ride a train operated by, or under contract with, a transportation district created pursuant to the Transportation District Act of 1964 (§ 33.2-1900 et seq.) of Title 33.2 when he uses a fraudulent or counterfeit ticket as a means to evade payment of the posted fare published by the transportation district. A violation of this subsection continues from the point of boarding through termination of the train's scheduled trip. A violation of this subsection is punishable as a Class 2 misdemeanor with a fine of not less than $500 for a first violation and with a fine of not less than $750 for a second or subsequent conviction when the second or subsequent conviction occurs more than 24 hours after but within 365 days of a prior violation.

D. Any person who has been convicted of violating subsection C shall be civilly liable to the Commonwealth and the transportation district for all costs incurred in prosecuting such person. The costs shall be limited to actual expenses, including the base wage of one employee acting as a witness for the Commonwealth and suit costs, but the total costs recovered shall not exceed the maximum amount of the fine that may be imposed for the offense.

History.

1988, c. 762; 1991, c. 241; 2009, c. 760; 2010, cc. 445, 837; 2012, c. 676.

Editor's note.

References in this section were updated at the direction of the Virginia Code Commission to conform to the recodification of Title 33.2 by Acts 2014, c. 805, effective October 1, 2014.

§ 18.2-160.2. Trespassing on public transportation; penalty.

Any person who enters or remains upon or within a vehicle operated by a public transportation service without the permission of, or after having been forbidden to do so by, the owner, lessee, or authorized operator thereof is guilty of a Class 4 misdemeanor.

"Public transportation service" means passenger transportation service provided by bus, rail or other surface conveyance that provides transportation to the general public on a regular and continuing basis.

History.

2007, c. 461.

§ 18.2-160.3. Fare enforcement inspectors; failure to produce proof of payment of fare; penalty.

A. For the purposes of this section, "eligible entity" means any transit operation in Planning District 8 that is owned or operated directly or indirectly by a political subdivision of the Commonwealth or any governmental entity established by an interstate compact of which Virginia is a signatory.

B. Any eligible entity that either directly or by contract operates any form of mass transit may appoint fare enforcement inspectors and establish the qualifications required for their appointment. Fare enforcement inspectors shall have the power to (i) request patrons at transit boarding locations or on transit vehicles to show proof of payment of the applicable fare; (ii) inspect the proof of payment for validity; (iii) issue a civil summons for violations authorized by this section; (iv) assist with crowd control while on a transit vehicle or at a transit boarding location; and (v) perform such other customer service and safety duties as may be assigned by the eligible entity. The powers of fare enforcement inspectors are limited to those powers enumerated in this section, and fare enforcement inspectors are not required to be law-enforcement officers. The powers of fare enforcement inspectors appointed pursuant to this section shall be exercisable anywhere in the Commonwealth where the appointing eligible entity operates transit service. Fare enforcement inspectors shall report to the department or agency designated by the appointing eligible entity.

C. It shall be unlawful for any person to board or ride a transit operation operated by an eligible entity when he fails or refuses to pay the applicable fare or refuses to produce valid proof of payment of the fare upon request of a fare enforcement inspector. Any person who violates this section shall be liable for a civil penalty of not more than $100. Any person summoned for a violation may make an appearance in person or in writing by mail to the department of finance or the treasurer of the locality, or the designee of the department of finance or the treasurer, where the violation occurred as specified on the summons prior to the date fixed for trial in court. Any person so appearing may enter a waiver of trial, admit liability, and pay the civil penalty established for the violation charged. Such persons shall be informed of their right to stand trial and that a signature to an admission of liability will have the same force and effect as a judgment of court. If a person charged with a violation does not elect to enter a waiver of trial and admit liability, the violation shall be brought by the eligible entity or the locality in which the violation occurred and tried as a civil case in the general district court in the same manner and with the same right of appeal as provided for by law. In any trial for a violation authorized by this section, it shall be the burden of the eligible entity or locality in which the violation occurred to show the liability of the violator by a preponderance of the evidence. The penalty for failure to pay the established fare on transit properties covered by another provision of law shall be governed by that provision and not by this section.

D. The governing bodies of counties, cities, and towns may adopt ordinances not in conflict with the provisions of this section to appoint fare enforcement inspectors and prescribe their duties in such counties, cities, and towns.

E. The penalty imposed by this section shall not apply to a law-enforcement officer while he is engaged in the performance of his official duties.

History.

2014, cc. 281, 447.

§ 18.2-161: Repealed by Acts 2004, c. 459.

§ 18.2-162. Damage or trespass to public services or utilities.

Any person who shall intentionally destroy or damage any facility which is used to furnish oil, telegraph, telephone, electric, gas, sewer, wastewater or water service to the public, shall be guilty of a Class 4 felony, provided that in the event the destruction or damage may be remedied or repaired for $200 or less such act shall constitute a Class 3 misdemeanor. On electric generating property marked with no trespassing signs, the security personnel of a utility may detain a trespasser for a period not to exceed one hour pending arrival of a law-enforcement officer.

Notwithstanding any other provisions of this title, any person who shall intentionally destroy or damage, or attempt to destroy or damage, any such facility, equipment or material connected therewith, the destruction or damage of which might, in any manner, threaten the release of radioactive materials or ionizing radiation beyond the areas in which they are normally used or contained, shall be guilty of a Class 4 felony, provided that in the event the destruction or damage results in the death of another due to exposure to radioactive materials or ionizing radiation, such person shall be guilty of a Class 2 felony; provided further, that in the event the destruction or damage results in injury to another, such person shall be guilty of a Class 3 felony.

History.
Code 1950, § 18.1-158; 1960, c. 358; 1964, c. 224; 1966, c. 446; 1975, cc. 14, 15; 1980, c. 548; 1981, c. 197; 1985, c. 299; 1992, c. 352.

§ 18.2-162.1. Diverting wastewater line; diverting or wasting public water supply.

Any person who willfully and maliciously (i) diverts any public wastewater or sewer line or (ii) diverts or wastes any public water supply by tampering with any fire hydrant shall be guilty of a Class 2 misdemeanor.

History.
1980, c. 140; 1992, c. 352.

§ 18.2-163. Tampering with metering device; diverting service; civil liability.

A. Any person who (i) tampers with any metering device incident to the facilities set forth in § 18.2-162, or otherwise intentionally prevents such a metering device from properly registering the degree, amount or quantity of service supplied, or (ii) diverts such service, except telephonic or electronic extension service not owned or controlled by any such company without authorization from the owner of the facility furnishing the service to the public, shall be guilty of a Class 1 misdemeanor.

B. The presence of any metering device found to have been altered, tampered with, or bypassed in a manner that would cause the metering device to inaccurately measure and register the degree, amount or quantity of service supplied or which would cause the service to be diverted from the recording apparatus of the meter shall be prima facie evidence of intent to violate and of the violation of this section by the person to whose benefit it is that such service be unmetered, unregistered or diverted.

C. The court may order restitution for the value of the services unlawfully used and for all costs. Such costs shall be limited to actual expenses, including the base wages of employees acting as witnesses for the Commonwealth, and suit costs. However, the total amount of allowable costs granted hereunder shall not exceed $250, excluding the value of the service.

History.
Code 1950, § 18.1-158.1; 1966, c. 446; 1975, cc. 14, 15; 1976, c. 273; 1978, c. 813; 1992, c. 525.

§ 18.2-164. Unlawful use of, or injury to, telephone and telegraph lines; copying or obstructing messages; penalty.

A. If any person commits any of the following acts, he is guilty of a Class 2 misdemeanor:

1. Maliciously injure, molest, cut down, or destroy any telephone or telegraph line, wire, cable, pole, tower, or the material or property belonging thereto;
2. Maliciously cut, break, tap, or make any connection with any telephone or telegraph line, wire, cable, or instrument of any telegraph or telephone company which has legally acquired the right-of-way by purchase, condemnation, or otherwise;
3. Maliciously copy in any unauthorized manner any message, either social, business, or otherwise, passing over any telephone or telegraph line, wire, cable, or wireless telephone transmission in the Commonwealth;
4. Willfully or maliciously prevent, obstruct, or delay by any means or contrivance whatsoever the sending, conveyance, or delivery in the Commonwealth of any authorized communication by or through any telephone or telegraph line, wire, cable, or wireless transmission device under the control of any telephone or telegraph company doing business in the Commonwealth;
5. Maliciously aid, agree with, employ, or conspire with any unauthorized person or persons unlawfully to do or cause to be done any of the acts hereinbefore mentioned.

B. If any person, with the intent to prevent another person from summoning law-enforcement, fire, or rescue services:

1. Commits any act set forth in subsection A; or
2. Maliciously prevents or interferes with telephone or telegraph communication by disabling or destroying any device that enables such communi-

cation, whether wired or wireless, he is guilty of a Class 1 misdemeanor.

History.

Code 1950, § 18.1-156; 1960, c. 358; 1975, cc. 14, 15; 2002, cc. 810, 818; 2006, c. 457.

§ 18.2-165. Unlawful use of, or injury to, television or radio signals and equipment.

Any person who shall willfully or maliciously break, injure or otherwise destroy or damage any of the posts, wires, towers or other materials or fixtures employed in the construction or use of any line of a television coaxial cable, or a microwave radio system, or willfully or maliciously interfere with such structure so erected, or in any way attempt to lead from its uses or make use of the electrical signal or any portion thereof properly belonging to or in use or in readiness to be made use of for the purpose of using said electrical signal from any television coaxial cable company or microwave system or owner of such property, shall be guilty of a Class 3 misdemeanor.

History.

Code 1950, § 18.1-157; 1960, c. 358; 1975, cc. 14, 15.

§ 18.2-165.1. Tampering with or unlawful use of cable television service.

Any person who (i) shall knowingly obtain or attempt to obtain cable television service from another by means, artifice, trick, deception or device without the payment to the operator of such service of all lawful compensation for each type of service obtained; (ii) shall knowingly, and with intent to profit thereby from any consideration received or expected, assist or instruct any other person in obtaining or attempting to obtain any cable television service without the payment to the operator of said service of all lawful compensation; (iii) shall knowingly tamper or otherwise interfere with or connect to by any means whether mechanical, electrical, acoustical or other, any cables, wires, or other devices used for the distribution of cable television service without authority from the operator of such service; or (iv) shall knowingly sell, rent, lend, promote, offer or advertise for sale, rental or use any device of any description or any plan for making or assembling the same to any person, with knowledge that the person intends to use such device or plan to do any of the acts hereinbefore mentioned or if the device or plan was represented either directly or indirectly by the person distributing it as having the ability to facilitate the doing of any of the acts hereinbefore mentioned, shall be guilty of a Class 6 felony if convicted under clause (ii) or (iv) above and shall be guilty of a Class 1 misdemeanor if convicted under clause (i) or (iii) above.

As used herein, cable television service shall include any and all services provided by or through the facilities of any cable television system or closed circuit coaxial cable communications system or any microwave, satellite or similar transmission service used in connection with any cable television system or other similar closed circuit coaxial cable communications system.

In any prosecution under this section, the existence on property in the actual possession of the accused, of any connection, wire, conductor, or any device whatsoever, which permits the use of cable television service without the same being reported for payment to and specifically authorized by the operator of the cable television service shall be prima facie evidence of intent to violate and of the violation of this section by the accused.

Nothing contained in this section shall be construed so as to abrogate or interfere with any contract right or remedy of any person having a contract with the owner of a television coaxial cable, or a cablevision system, or a microwave radio system.

History.

1978, c. 712; 1979, c. 500; 1981, c. 197; 1991, c. 502.

§ 18.2-165.2. Unlawful interference with emergency two-way radio communications; penalty.

A. It shall be unlawful for any person to knowingly and willfully (i) interfere with the transmission of a radio communication, the purpose of which is to inform or to inquire about an emergency or (ii) transmit false information about an emergency.

B. For the purposes of this section, *"emergency"* means a condition or circumstance in which an individual is or is reasonably believed by the person transmitting the communication to be in imminent danger of death or serious bodily harm or in which property is in imminent danger of damage or destruction.

C. Any person who violates the provisions of this section shall be guilty of a Class 1 misdemeanor.

History.

1985, c. 100.

§ 18.2-166. Disclosing or inducing disclosure of certain information concerning customers of telephone companies.

Any person:

(1) Who is an employee of a telephone company, or an employee of a company which prints or otherwise handles lists of telephone customers for a telephone company and who discloses to another the names, addresses, or telephone numbers of any two or more customers of telephone service, knowing that such disclosure is without the consent of the telephone company furnishing said service; or

(2) Who knowingly induces such an employee to make such disclosure by giving, offering, or promising to such employee any gift, gratuity, or thing of

value, or by doing or promising to do any act beneficial to such employee; or

(3) Who takes, copies, or compiles any list containing the aforesaid information knowing that such conduct is without the consent of the telephone company furnishing said service; or

(4) Who attempts, aids or abets another, or conspires with another, to commit any of the aforesaid acts,

shall be guilty of a Class 3 misdemeanor.

History.
Code 1950, § 18.1-417.1; 1968, c. 332; 1975, cc. 14, 15.

§ 18.2-167. Selling or transferring certain telephonic instruments.

(a) It shall be unlawful for any person knowingly to make, sell, offer or advertise for sale, possess, or give or otherwise transfer to another any instrument, apparatus, equipment, or device or plans or instructions for making or assembling any instrument, apparatus, equipment or device which has been designed, adapted, used, or employed with the intent or for the purpose of (1) obtaining long distance toll telephone or telegraph service or the transmission of a long distance toll message, signal, or other communication by telephone or telegraph, or over telephone or telegraph facilities, without the payment of charges for any such long distance message, signal or other communication; or (2) concealing or assisting another to conceal from any supplier of telephone or telegraph service or from any person charged with the responsibility of enforcing this section, the existence or place of origin or of destination of any long distance toll message, signal, or other communication by telephone or telegraph, or over telephone or telegraph facilities. Persons violating any provision of this section shall be guilty of a Class 3 misdemeanor.

(b) Any such instrument, apparatus, equipment or device, or plans or instructions therefor, may be seized by court order or under a warrant; and, upon a final conviction of any person owning the seized materials, or having any ownership interest therein, for a violation of any provision of this section, the instrument, apparatus, equipment, device, or plans or instructions shall be ordered destroyed as contraband by the court in which the person is convicted.

History.
Code 1950, § 18.1-238.3; 1966, c. 445; 1975, cc. 14, 15.

§ 18.2-167.1. Interception or monitoring of customer telephone calls; penalty.

It shall be unlawful for any person, firm or corporation to intercept or monitor, or attempt to intercept or monitor, the transmission of a message, signal or other communication by telephone between an employee or other agent of such person, firm or corporation and a customer of such person, firm or corporation.

The provisions of this section shall not apply if the person, firm or corporation gives notice to such employee or agent that such monitoring may occur at any time during the course of such employment.

Any person, firm or corporation violating the provisions of this section shall be guilty of a Class 4 misdemeanor. The provisions of this section shall not apply to any wiretap or other interception of any communication authorized pursuant to Chapter 6 of Title 19.2 (§ 19.2-61 et seq.).

History.
1982, c. 380.

CHAPTER 6.

CRIMES INVOLVING FRAUD.

Article 1.

Forgery.

Article 2.

Impersonation.

Article 3.

False Pretenses.

Article 4.

Bad Check Law.

Crimes and Offenses

Article 5.

False Representations to Obtain Property or Credit.

Article 5.1.

Offenses Involving Electronic Communication Devices.

Article 6.

Offenses Relating to Credit Cards.

Article 7.

Miscellaneous False and Fraudulent Acts.

Article 8.

Misrepresentations and Other Offenses Connected With Sales.

Crimes and Offenses

ARTICLE 1.
FORGERY.

§ 18.2-168. Forging public records, etc.

If any person forge a public record, or certificate, return, or attestation, of any public officer or public employee, in relation to any matter wherein such certificate, return, or attestation may be received as legal proof, or utter, or attempt to employ as true, such forged record, certificate, return, or attestation, knowing the same to be forged, he shall be guilty of a Class 4 felony.

History.
Code 1950, § 18.1-92; 1960, c. 358; 1975, cc. 14, 15; 1976, c. 146.

§ 18.2-169. Forging, or keeping an instrument for forging, a seal.

If any person forge, or keep or conceal any instrument for the purpose of forging, the seal of the Commonwealth, the seal of a court, or of any public office, or body politic or corporate in this Commonwealth, he shall be guilty of a Class 4 felony.

History.
Code 1950, § 18.1-93; 1960, c. 358; 1975, cc. 14, 15.

§ 18.2-170. Forging coin or bank notes.

If any person (1) forge any coin, note or bill current by law or usage in this Commonwealth or any note or bill of a banking company, (2) fraudulently make any base coin, or a note or bill purporting to be the note or bill of a banking company, when such company does not exist, or (3) utter, or attempt to employ as true, or sell, exchange, or deliver, or offer to sell, exchange, or deliver, or receive on sale, exchange, or delivery, with intent to utter or employ, or to have the same uttered or employed as true, any such false, forged, or base coin, note or bill, knowing it to be so, he shall be guilty of a Class 4 felony.

History.
Code 1950, § 18.1-94; 1960, c. 358; 1975, cc. 14, 15.

§ 18.2-171. Making or having anything designed for forging any writing, etc.

If any person engrave, stamp, or cast, or otherwise make or mend, any plate, block, press, or other thing, adapted and designed for the forging and false making of any writing or other thing, the forging or false making whereof is punishable by this chapter, or if such person have in possession any such plate, block, press, or other thing, with intent to use, or cause or permit it to be used, in forging or false making any such writing or other thing, he shall be guilty of a Class 4 felony.

History.
Code 1950, § 18.1-95; 1960, c. 358; 1975, cc. 14, 15.

§ 18.2-172. Forging, uttering, etc., other writings.

If any person forge any writing, other than such as is mentioned in §§ 18.2-168 and 18.2-170, to the prejudice of another's right, or utter, or attempt to employ as true, such forged writing, knowing it to be forged, he shall be guilty of a Class 5 felony. Any person who shall obtain, by any false pretense or token, the signature of another person, to any such

Crimes and Offenses

writing, with intent to defraud any other person, shall be deemed guilty of the forgery thereof, and shall be subject to like punishment.

History.
Code 1950, § 18.1-96; 1960, c. 358; 1975, cc. 14, 15.

§ 18.2-172.1. Falsifying or altering and fraudulently using transcripts or diplomas; penalty.

Any person who materially falsifies or alters a transcript or diploma from an institution of postsecondary education and fraudulently uses the same for pecuniary gain or in furtherance of such person's education shall be guilty of a Class 3 misdemeanor.

History.
1983, c. 91.

§ 18.2-172.2. Maliciously affixing another's signature to writing; penalty.

Any person who maliciously affixes a facsimile or likeness of the signature of another person to any writing without the permission of that person and with the intent to create the false impression that the writing was signed by that person is guilty of a Class 1 misdemeanor.

History.
2008, c. 595.

§ 18.2-173. Having in possession forged coin or bank notes.

If any person have in his possession forged bank notes or forged or base coin, such as are mentioned in § 18.2-170, knowing the same to be forged or base, with the intent to utter or employ the same as true, or to sell, exchange, or deliver them, so as to enable any other person to utter or employ them as true, he shall, if the number of such notes or coins in his possession at the same time, be ten or more, be guilty of a Class 6 felony; and if the number be less than ten, he shall be guilty of a Class 3 misdemeanor.

History.
Code 1950, § 18.1-97; 1960, c. 358; 1975, cc. 14, 15.

ARTICLE 2.

IMPERSONATION.

§ 18.2-174. Impersonating law-enforcement officer; penalty.

Any person who falsely assumes or exercises the functions, powers, duties, and privileges incident to the office of sheriff, police officer, marshal, or other peace officer, or any local, city, county, state, or federal law-enforcement officer, or who falsely assumes or pretends to be any such officer, is guilty of a Class 1 misdemeanor. A second or subsequent offense is punishable as a Class 6 felony.

History.
Code 1950, § 18.1-311; 1960, c. 358; 1975, cc. 14, 15; 2013, cc. 410, 431, 638.

§ 18.2-174.1. Impersonating certain public safety personnel; penalty.

Any person who willfully impersonates, with the intent to make another believe he is, an emergency medical services provider, firefighter, special forest warden designated pursuant to § 10.1-1135, fire marshal, or fire chief is guilty of a Class 1 misdemeanor. A second or subsequent offense is punishable as a Class 6 felony.

History.
1993, c. 403; 2000, c. 962; 2002, c. 536; 2013, c. 431; 2015, cc. 502, 503.

§ 18.2-175. Unlawful wearing of officer's uniform or insignia; unlawful use of vehicle with word "police" shown thereon.

No person, not such an officer as is referred to in § 19.2-78, shall wear any such uniform as is designated pursuant to the provisions of such section or wear an insignia or markings containing the Seal of the Commonwealth or the insignia of any such officer's uniform, nor shall any person not such an officer, or not authorized by such officer, or not authorized by the military police of the armed forces or of the National Guard, or not authorized by the military police of other governmental agencies, use or cause to be used on the public roads or highways of this Commonwealth, any motor vehicle bearing markings with the word "police" shown thereon. However, the prohibition against wearing an insignia or markings containing the Seal of the Commonwealth shall not apply to any certified firefighter or to any certified or licensed emergency medical personnel. Any violation of this section shall be a Class 1 misdemeanor.

History.
Code 1950, § 18.1-312; 1960, c. 358; 1966, c. 420; 1968, c. 675; 1975, cc. 14, 15; 1979, c. 704; 1991, c. 424.

§ 18.2-176. Unauthorized wearing or displaying on motor vehicles of any button, insignia or emblem of certain associations or societies or of Southern Cross of Honor.

(a) No person shall wear the button or insignia of any order of police, trade union or veterans' organization or display upon a motor vehicle the insignia or emblem of any automobile club, medical society, order of police, trade union or veterans' organization or use such button, insignia or emblem to obtain aid or assistance unless entitled to wear, display or use the same under the constitution, bylaws, rules or regulations of the organization concerned.

(b) No person shall wear any Southern Cross of Honor when not entitled to do so by the regulations under which such Crosses of Honor are given.

(c) A violation of this section shall be a Class 3 misdemeanor.

History.

Code 1950, § 18.1-410; 1960, c. 358; 1964, c. 124; 1975, cc. 14, 15.

§ 18.2-177. Illegal use of insignia.

Any person who shall willfully wear, exhibit, display, print, or use, for any purpose, the badge, motto, button, decoration, charm, emblem, rosette, or other insignia of any such association or organization mentioned in § 2.2-411, duly registered under Article 2 (§ 2.2-411 et seq.) of Chapter 4, Title 2.2, unless he shall be entitled to use and wear the same under the constitution and bylaws, rules and regulations of such association or organization, shall be guilty of a Class 4 misdemeanor.

History.

Code 1950, § 2.1-80; 1966, c. 677; 1975, cc. 14, 15.

§ 18.2-177.1. False representation of military status; penalty.

A. It is unlawful for any person, with the intent to obtain any services, to falsely represent himself to be a member or veteran of the United States Armed Forces, Armed Forces Reserves, or National Guard by wearing the uniform or any medal or insignia authorized for use by the members or veterans of the United States Armed Forces, Armed Forces Reserves, or National Guard by federal or state law or regulation and obtain any services through such false representation.

B. It is unlawful for any person, with the intent to obtain any services, to falsely represent himself as a recipient of any decoration or medal created by federal or state law or regulation to honor the members or veterans of the United States Armed Forces, Armed Forces Reserves, or National Guard and obtain any services through such false representation.

C. A violation of this section is a Class 1 misdemeanor.

D. The provisions of this section shall not preclude prosecution under any other statute.

History.

2016, c. 236.

ARTICLE 3. FALSE PRETENSES.

§ 18.2-178. Obtaining money or signature, etc., by false pretense.

A. If any person obtain, by any false pretense or token, from any person, with intent to defraud, money, a gift certificate or other property that may be the subject of larceny, he shall be deemed guilty of larceny thereof; or if he obtain, by any false pretense or token, with such intent, the signature of any person to a writing, the false making whereof would be forgery, he shall be guilty of a Class 4 felony.

B. Venue for the trial of any person charged with an offense under this section may be in the county or city in which (i) any act was performed in furtherance of the offense, or (ii) the person charged with the offense resided at the time of the offense.

History.

Code 1950, § 18.1-118; 1960, c. 358; 1975, cc. 14, 15; 2001, c. 131; 2006, c. 321.

§ 18.2-178.1. Financial exploitation of mentally incapacitated persons; penalty.

A. It is unlawful for any person who knows or should know that another person suffers from mental incapacity to, through the use of that other person's mental incapacity, take, obtain, or convert money or other thing of value belonging to that other person with the intent to permanently deprive him thereof. Any person who violates this section shall be deemed guilty of larceny.

B. Venue for the trial of an accused charged with a violation of this section shall be in any county or city in which (i) any act was performed in furtherance of the offense or (ii) the accused resided at the time of the offense.

C. This section shall not apply to a transaction or disposition of money or other thing of value in which the accused acted for the benefit of the person with mental incapacity or made a good faith effort to assist such person with the management of his money or other thing of value.

D. As used in this section, "mental incapacity" means that condition of a person existing at the time of the offense described in subsection A that prevents him from understanding the nature or consequences of the transaction or disposition of money or other thing of value involved in such offense.

History.

2013, cc. 419, 452.

§ 18.2-179. Unlawful operation of coin box telephone, parking meter, vending machine, etc.

Any person who shall operate, cause to be operated, or attempt to operate or cause to be operated any coin box telephone, parking meter, vending machine or other machine that operates on the coin-in-the-slot principle, whether of like kind or not, designed only to receive lawful coin of the United States of America, in connection with the use or enjoyment of telephone or telegraph service, parking privileges or any other service, or the sale of merchandise or other property, by means of a slug, or any false, counterfeit, mutilated, sweated or foreign coin, or by any means, method, trick or device whatsoever, not authorized by the owner, lessee or licensee of such coin box telephone, parking meter, vending machine or other machine; or who shall obtain or receive telephone or telegraph service, parking privileges, merchandise, or any other service or property from any such coin box telephone, parking meter, vending machine or other machines, designed only to receive lawful coin of the United States of America, without depositing in or surrendering to such coin box telephone, parking meter, vending machine, or other machine lawful coin of the United States of America to the amount required therefor by the owner, lessee or licensee of such coin box telephone, parking meter, vending machine or other machine, shall be guilty of a Class 3 misdemeanor.

History.
Code 1950, § 28.1-124; 1960, c. 358; 1975, cc. 14, 15.

§ 18.2-180. Manufacture, etc., of slugs, etc., for such unlawful use.

Any person who, with intent to cheat or defraud the owner, lessee, licensee or other person entitled to the contents of any such coin box telephone, parking meter, vending machine or other machine operated on the coin-in-the-slot principle, designed only to receive lawful coin of the United States of America, in connection with the use of any such coin box telephone, parking meter, vending machine or other machine, or who, knowing or having reason to believe that the same is intended for such unlawful use, shall manufacture, sell, offer to sell, advertise for sale or give away any slug, device or substance whatsoever, intended or calculated to be placed or deposited in any such coin box telephone, parking meter, vending machine or other machine, shall be guilty of a Class 3 misdemeanor.

The manufacture, sale, offer for sale, advertisement for sale, giving away or possession of any such slug, device or substance whatsoever, intended or calculated to be placed or deposited in any such coin box telephone, parking meter, vending machine or other machine that operates on the coin-in-the-slot principle, shall be prima facie evidence of intent to cheat or defraud within the meaning of this section and § 18.2-179.

History.
Code 1950, § 18.1-125; 1960, c. 358; 1975, cc. 14, 15.

ARTICLE 4.
BAD CHECK LAW.

§ 18.2-181. Issuing bad checks, etc., larceny.

Any person who, with intent to defraud, shall make or draw or utter or deliver any check, draft, or order for the payment of money, upon any bank, banking institution, trust company, or other depository, knowing, at the time of such making, drawing, uttering or delivering, that the maker or drawer has not sufficient funds in, or credit with, such bank, banking institution, trust company, or other depository, for the payment of such check, draft or order, although no express representation is made in reference thereto, shall be guilty of larceny; and, if this check, draft, or order has a represented value of $200 or more, such person shall be guilty of a Class 6 felony. In cases in which such value is less than $200, the person shall be guilty of a Class 1 misdemeanor.

The word *"credit"* as used herein, shall be construed to mean any arrangement or understanding with the bank, trust company, or other depository for the payment of such check, draft or order.

Any person making, drawing, uttering or delivering any such check, draft or order in payment as a present consideration for goods or services for the purposes set out in this section shall be guilty as provided herein.

History.
Code 1950, § 6.1-115; 1966, c. 584; 1975, cc. 14, 15; 1978, c. 791; 1981, c. 230.

§ 18.2-181.1. Issuance of bad checks.

It shall be a Class 6 felony for any person, within a period of ninety days, to issue two or more checks, drafts or orders for the payment of money in violation of § 18.2-181, which have an aggregate represented value of $200 or more and which (i) are drawn upon the same account of any bank, banking institution, trust company or other depository and (ii) are made payable to the same person, firm or corporation.

History.
1988, c. 496.

§ 18.2-182. Issuing bad checks on behalf of business firm or corporation in payment of wages; penalty.

Any person who shall make, draw, or utter, or deliver any check, draft, or order for the payment of money, upon any bank, banking institution, trust company or other depository on behalf of any business firm or corporation, for the purpose of paying wages to any employee of such firm or corporation, or for the purpose of paying for any labor performed by any person for such firm or corporation, knowing, at the time of such making, drawing, uttering or delivering, that the account upon which such check, draft or order is drawn has not sufficient funds, or credit with, such bank, banking institution, trust company or other depository, for the payment of such check, draft or order, although no express representation is made in reference thereto, shall be guilty of a Class 1 misdemeanor; except that if this check, draft, or order has a represented value of $200 or more, such person shall be guilty of a Class 6 felony.

The word "credit," as used herein, shall be construed to mean any arrangement or understanding with the bank, banking institution, trust company, or other depository for the payment of such check, draft or order.

In addition to the criminal penalty set forth herein, such person shall be personally liable in any civil action brought upon such check, draft or order.

History.
Code 1950, § 6.1-116; 1966, c. 584; 1975, cc. 14, 15; 2005, c. 598.

§ 18.2-182.1. Issuing bad checks in payment of taxes.

Any person who shall make, draw, utter, or deliver two or more checks, drafts, or orders within a period of ninety days which have an aggregate represented value of $1,000 or more, for the payment of money upon any bank, banking institution, trust company, or other depository on behalf of any taxpayer for the payment of any state tax under § 58.1-486 or § 58.1-637, knowing, at the time of such making, drawing, uttering, or delivering, that the account upon which such check, draft, or order is drawn has not sufficient funds or credit with such bank, banking institution, trust company, or other depository for the payment of such check, draft, or order, although no express representation is made in reference thereto, shall be guilty of a Class 1 misdemeanor.

The word "credit," as used herein, means any arrangement or understanding with the bank, banking institution, trust company, or other depository for the payment of such check, draft, or order.

History.
1992, c. 763.

§ 18.2-183. Issuance of bad check prima facie evidence of intent and knowledge; notice by certified or registered mail.

In any prosecution or action under the preceding sections, the making or drawing or uttering or delivery of a check, draft, or order, payment of which is refused by the drawee because of lack of funds or credit shall be prima facie evidence of intent to defraud or of knowledge of insufficient funds in, or credit with, such bank, banking institution, trust company or other depository unless such maker or drawer, or someone for him, shall have paid the holder thereof the amount due thereon, together with interest, and protest fees (if any), within five days after receiving written notice that such check, draft, or order has not been paid to the holder thereof. Notice mailed by certified or registered mail, evidenced by return receipt, to the last known address of the maker or drawer shall be deemed sufficient and equivalent to notice having been received by the maker or drawer.

If such check, draft or order shows on its face a printed or written address, home, office, or otherwise, of the maker or drawer, then the foregoing notice, when sent by certified or registered mail to such address, with or without return receipt requested, shall be deemed sufficient and equivalent to notice having been received by the maker or drawer, whether such notice shall be returned undelivered or not.

When a check is drawn on a bank in which the maker or drawer has no account, it shall be presumed that such check was issued with intent to defraud, and the five-day notice set forth above shall not be required in such case.

History.
Code 1950, § 6.1-117; 1966, c. 584; 1975, cc. 14, 15.

§ 18.2-184. Presumption as to notation attached to check, draft or order.

In any prosecution or action under the preceding sections, any notation attached to or stamped upon a check, draft or order which is refused by the drawee because of lack of funds or credit, bearing the terms "not sufficient funds," "uncollected funds," "account closed," or "no account in this name," or words of similar import, shall be prima facie evidence that such notation is true and correct.

History.
Code 1950, § 6.1-117.1; 1970, c. 695; 1974, c. 322; 1975, cc. 14, 15.

§ 18.2-185. Evidence and presumptions in malicious prosecution actions after issuance of bad check.

In any civil action growing out of an arrest under § 18.2-181 or § 18.2-182, no evidence of statements or representations as to the status of the check, draft, order or deposit involved, or of any collateral agreement with reference to the check, draft, or order, shall be admissible unless such statements, or representations, or collateral agreement, be written upon the instrument at the time it is given by the drawer.

If payment of any check, draft, or order for the payment of money be refused by the bank, banking institution, trust company or other depository upon which such instrument is drawn, and the person who drew or uttered such instrument be arrested or prosecuted under the provisions of § 18.2-181 or § 18.2-182, for failure or refusal to pay such instrument, the one who arrested or caused such person to be arrested and prosecuted, or either, shall be conclusively deemed to have acted with reasonable or probable cause in any suit for damages that may be brought by the person who drew or uttered such instrument, if the one who arrested or caused such person to be arrested and prosecuted, or either, shall have, before doing so, presented or caused such instrument to be presented to the depository on which it was drawn where it was refused, and then waited five days after notice, as provided in § 18.2-183, without the amount due under the provisions of such instrument being paid.

History.
Code 1950, § 6.1-118; 1966, c. 584; 1975, cc. 14, 15.

ARTICLE 5. FALSE REPRESENTATIONS TO OBTAIN PROPERTY OR CREDIT.

§ 18.2-186. False statements to obtain property or credit.

A. A person shall be guilty of a Class 1 misdemeanor if he makes, causes to be made or conspires to make directly, indirectly or through an agency, any materially false statement in writing, knowing it to be false and intending that it be relied upon, concerning the financial condition or means or ability to pay of himself, or of any other person for whom he is acting, or any firm or corporation in which he is interested or for which he is acting, for the purpose of procuring, for his own benefit or for the benefit of such person, firm or corporation, the delivery of personal property, the payment of cash, the making of a loan or credit, the extension of a credit, the discount of an account receivable, or the making, acceptance, discount, sale or endorsement of a bill of exchange or promissory note.

B. Any person who knows that a false statement has been made in writing concerning the financial condition or ability to pay of himself or of any person for whom he is acting, or any firm or corporation in which he is interested or for which he is acting and who, with intent to defraud, procures, upon the faith thereof, for his own benefit, or for the benefit of the person, firm or corporation in which he is interested or for which he is acting, any such delivery, payment, loan, credit, extension, discount making, acceptance, sale or endorsement, shall, if the value of the thing or the amount of the loan, credit or benefit obtained is $200 or more, be guilty of grand larceny or, if the value is less than $200, be guilty of petit larceny.

C. Venue for the trial of any person charged with an offense under this section may be in the county or city in which (i) any act was performed in furtherance of the offense, or (ii) the person charged with the offense resided at the time of the offense.

D. As used in this section, "in writing" shall include information transmitted by computer, facsimile, e-mail, Internet, or any other electronic medium, and shall not include information transmitted by any such medium by voice transmission.

History.
Code 1950, § 18.1-119; 1960, c. 358; 1966, c. 247; 1975, cc. 14, 15; 1981, c. 197; 1991, c. 546; 2006, c. 321; 2007, c. 518.

§ 18.2-186.1: Repealed by Acts 1981, c. 255.

Cross references.
For present provisions covering similar subject matter to the repealed section, see § 32.1-310 et seq.

§ 18.2-186.2. False statements or failure to disclose material facts in order to obtain aid or benefits under any local, state or federal housing assistance program.

Any person who (i) knowingly makes or causes to be made either directly or indirectly or through any agent or agency, any false statement in writing with the intent that it shall be relied upon, or fails to disclose any material fact concerning the financial means or ability to pay of himself or of any other person for whom he is acting, for the purpose of procuring aid and benefits available under any local, state or federally funded housing assistance program, or (ii) knowingly fails to disclose a change in circumstances in order to obtain or continue to receive under any such program aid or benefits to which he is not entitled or who knowingly aids and abets another person in the commission of any such act is guilty of a Class 1 misdemeanor.

History.
1980, c. 303.

§ 18.2-186.3. Identity theft; penalty; restitution; victim assistance.

A. It shall be unlawful for any person, without the authorization or permission of the person or persons who are the subjects of the identifying information, with the intent to defraud, for his own use or the use of a third person, to:

1. Obtain, record, or access identifying information which is not available to the general public that would assist in accessing financial resources, obtaining identification documents, or obtaining benefits of such other person;

2. Obtain money, credit, loans, goods, or services through the use of identifying information of such other person;

3. Obtain identification documents in such other person's name; or

4. Obtain, record, or access identifying information while impersonating a law-enforcement officer or an official of the government of the Commonwealth.

B. It shall be unlawful for any person without the authorization or permission of the person who is the subject of the identifying information, with the intent to sell or distribute the information to another to:

1. Fraudulently obtain, record, or access identifying information that is not available to the general public that would assist in accessing financial resources, obtaining identification documents, or obtaining benefits of such other person;

2. Obtain money, credit, loans, goods, or services through the use of identifying information of such other person;

3. Obtain identification documents in such other person's name; or

4. Obtain, record, or access identifying information while impersonating a law-enforcement officer or an official of the Commonwealth.

B1. It shall be unlawful for any person to use identification documents or identifying information of another person, whether that person is dead or alive, or of a false or fictitious person, to avoid summons, arrest, prosecution, or to impede a criminal investigation.

C. As used in this section, "identifying information" shall include but not be limited to: (i) name; (ii) date of birth; (iii) social security number; (iv) driver's license number; (v) bank account numbers; (vi) credit or debit card numbers; (vii) personal identification numbers (PIN); (viii) electronic identification codes; (ix) automated or electronic signatures; (x) biometric data; (xi) fingerprints; (xii) passwords; or (xiii) any other numbers or information that can be used to access a person's financial resources, obtain identification, act as identification, or obtain money, credit, loans, goods, or services.

D. Violations of this section shall be punishable as a Class 1 misdemeanor. Any violation resulting in financial loss of greater than $200 shall be punishable as a Class 6 felony. Any second or subsequent conviction shall be punishable as a Class 6 felony. Any violation of subsection B where five or more persons' identifying information has been obtained, recorded, or accessed in the same transaction or occurrence shall be punishable as a Class 5 felony. Any violation of subsection B where 50 or more persons' identifying information has been obtained, recorded, or accessed in the same transaction or occurrence shall be punishable as a Class 4 felony. Any violation resulting in the arrest and detention of the person whose identification documents or identifying information were used to avoid summons, arrest, prosecution, or to impede a criminal investigation shall be punishable as a Class 5 felony. In any proceeding brought pursuant to this section, the crime shall be considered to have been committed in any locality where the person whose identifying information was appropriated resides, or in which any part of the offense took place, regardless of whether the defendant was ever actually in such locality.

E. Upon conviction, in addition to any other punishment, a person found guilty of this offense shall be ordered by the court to make restitution as the court deems appropriate to any person whose identifying information was appropriated or to the estate of such person. Such restitution may include the person's or his estate's actual expenses associated with correcting inaccuracies or errors in his credit report or other identifying information.

F. Upon the request of a person whose identifying information was appropriated, the Attorney General may provide assistance to the victim in obtaining information necessary to correct inaccuracies or errors in his credit report or other identifying information; however, no legal representation shall be afforded such person.

History.

2000, c. 349; 2001, c. 423; 2003, cc. 847, 914, 918; 2004, c. 450; 2006, cc. 455, 496; 2007, c. 441; 2009, cc. 314, 380; 2013, cc. 420, 466.

§ 18.2-186.3:1. Identity fraud; consumer reporting agencies; police reports.

A. A consumer may report a case of identity theft to the law-enforcement agency in the jurisdiction where he resides. If a consumer, as defined by the Fair Credit Reporting Act, 15 U.S.C. § 1681 et seq., submits to a consumer reporting agency, as defined by the Fair Credit Reporting Act, 15 U.S.C. § 1681 et seq., a copy of a valid police report, the consumer reporting agency shall, within 30 days of receipt thereof, block the reporting of any information that the consumer alleges appears on his credit report, as defined by the Fair Credit Reporting Act, 15 U.S.C. § 1681 et seq., as a result of a violation of § 18.2-186.3. The consumer reporting agency shall promptly notify the furnisher of the information that a police report has been filed, that a block has been requested, and the effective date of the block.

B. Consumer reporting agencies may decline to block or may rescind any block of consumer information if, in the exercise of good faith and reasonable judgment, the consumer reporting agency believes that: (i) the information was blocked due to a misrepresentation of a material fact by the consumer; (ii) the information was blocked due to fraud, in which the consumer participated, or of which the consumer had knowledge, and which may for purposes of this section be demonstrated by circumstantial evidence; (iii) the consumer agrees that portions of the blocked information or all of it were blocked in error; (iv) the consumer knowingly obtained or should have known that he obtained possession of goods, services, or moneys as a result of the blocked transaction or transactions; or (v) the consumer reporting agency, in the exercise of good faith and reasonable judgment, has substantial reason based on specific, verifiable facts to doubt the authenticity of the consumer's report of a violation of § 18.2-186.3.

C. If blocked information is unblocked pursuant to this section, the consumer shall be notified in the same manner as consumers are notified of the reinsertion of information pursuant to the Fair Credit Reporting Act at 15 U.S.C. § 1681i, as amended. The prior presence of the blocked information in the consumer reporting agency's file on the consumer is not evidence of whether the consumer knew or should have known that he obtained possession of any goods, services, or moneys.

D. A consumer reporting agency shall accept the consumer's version of the disputed information and correct the disputed item when the consumer submits to the consumer reporting agency documentation obtained from the source of the item in dispute or from public records confirming that the report was inaccurate or incomplete, unless the consumer reporting agency, in the exercise of good faith and reasonable judgment, has substantial reason based on specific, verifiable facts to doubt the authenticity of the documentation submitted and notifies the consumer in writing of that decision, explaining its reasons for unblocking the information and setting forth the specific, verifiable facts on which the decision is based.

E. A consumer reporting agency shall delete from a consumer credit report inquiries for credit reports based upon credit requests that the consumer reporting agency verifies were initiated as a result of a violation of § 18.2-186.3.

F. The provisions of this section do not apply to (i) a consumer reporting agency that acts as a reseller of credit information by assembling and merging information contained in the databases of other consumer reporting agencies, and that does not maintain a permanent database of credit information from which new consumer credit reports are produced, (ii) a check services or fraud prevention services company that issues reports on incidents of fraud or authorizations for the purpose of approving or processing negotiable instruments, electronic funds transfers, or similar payment methods, or (iii) a demand deposit account information service company that issues reports regarding account closures due to fraud, substantial overdrafts, automatic teller machine abuse or similar negative information regarding a consumer to inquiring banks or other financial institutions for use only in reviewing a consumer request for a demand deposit account at the inquiring bank or financial institution.

History.

2003, cc. 914, 918; 2006, c. 298.

§ 18.2-186.4. Use of a person's identity with the intent to coerce, intimidate, or harass; penalty.

It shall be unlawful for any person, with the intent to coerce, intimidate, or harass another person, to publish the person's name or photograph along with identifying information as defined in clauses (iii) through (ix), or clause (xii) of subsection C of § 18.2-186.3, or identification of the person's primary residence address. Any person who violates this section is guilty of a Class 1 misdemeanor.

Any person who violates this section knowing or having reason to know that person is a law-enforcement officer, as defined in § 9.1-101, is guilty of a Class 6 felony. The sentence shall include a mandatory minimum term of confinement of six months.

History.

2001, cc. 775, 782; 2007, c. 736; 2010, c. 767.

§ 18.2-186.4:1. Internet publication of personal information of certain public officials.

A. The Commonwealth shall not publish on the Internet the personal information of any public official if a court has, pursuant to subsection B, ordered that the official's personal information is prohibited from publication and the official has made a demand in writing to the Commonwealth, accompanied by the order of the court, that the Commonwealth not publish such information.

B. Any public official may petition a circuit court for an order prohibiting the publication on the Internet, by the Commonwealth, of the official's personal information. The petition shall set forth the specific reasons that the official seeks the order. The court shall issue such an order only if it finds that (i) there exists a threat to the official or a person who resides with him that would result from publication of the information or (ii) the official has demonstrated a reasonable fear of a risk to his safety or the safety of someone who resides with him that would result from publication of the information on the Internet.

C. If the Commonwealth publishes the public official's personal information on the Internet prior to receipt of a written demand by the official under subsection A, it shall remove the information from publication on the Internet within 48 hours of receipt of the written demand.

D. A written demand made by any public official pursuant to this section shall be effective for four years as follows:

1. For a law-enforcement officer, if the officer remains continuously employed as a law-enforcement officer throughout the four-year period;

2. For a federal or state judge or justice, if such public official continuously serves throughout the four-year period; and

3. For an attorney for the Commonwealth, if such public official continuously serves throughout the four-year period.

E. For purposes of this section:

"Commonwealth" means any agency or political subdivision of the Commonwealth of Virginia.

"Law-enforcement officer" means the same as that term is defined in § 9.1-101, 5 U.S.C. § 8331(20), excluding officers whose duties relate to detention as defined in 5 U.S.C. § 8331(20), and any other federal officer or agent who is credentialed with the authority to enforce federal law.

"Personal information" means home address, home telephone numbers, personal cell phone numbers, or personal email address.

"Publication" and *"publishes"* means intentionally communicating personal information to, or otherwise making personal information available to, and accessible by, the general public through the Internet or other online service.

"Public official" means any state or federal judge or justice, law-enforcement officer, or attorney for the Commonwealth.

F. No provision of this section shall apply to lists of registered voters and persons who voted, voter registration records, or lists of absentee voters prepared or provided under Title 24.2.

History.

2010, c. 767; 2012, c. 143; 2014, c. 170.

§ 18.2-186.5. Expungement of false identity information from police and court records; Identity Theft Passport.

Any person whose name or other identification has been used without his consent or authorization by another person who has been charged or arrested using such name or identification may file a petition with the court for relief pursuant to § 19.2-392.2. A person who has petitioned the court pursuant to § 19.2-392.2 as a result of a violation of § 18.2-186.3, may submit to the Attorney General a certified copy of a court order obtained pursuant to § 19.2-392.2. Upon receipt by the Attorney General of a certified copy of the court order and upon request by such person, the Office of the Attorney General, in cooperation with the State Police, may issue an "Identity Theft Passport" stating that such an order has been submitted. The Office of the Attorney General shall provide access to identity theft information to (i) criminal justice agencies and (ii) individuals who have submitted a court order pursuant to this section. When the Office of the Attorney General issues an Identity Theft Passport, it shall transmit a record of the issuance of the passport to the Department of Motor Vehicles. The Department shall note on the individual's driver abstract that a court order was obtained pursuant to § 19.2-392.2 and that an Identity Theft Passport has been issued. The provisions of § 2.2-3808 shall not apply to this section.

History.

2003, cc. 914, 918; 2004, c. 450; 2006, c. 298; 2011, c. 619.

§ 18.2-186.6. Breach of personal information notification.

A. As used in this section:

"Breach of the security of the system" means the unauthorized access and acquisition of unencrypted and unredacted computerized data that compromises the security or confidentiality of personal information maintained by an individual or entity as part of a database of personal information regarding multiple individuals and that causes, or the individual or entity reasonably believes has caused, or will cause, identity theft or other fraud to any resident of the Commonwealth. Good faith acquisition of personal information by an employee or agent of an individual or entity for the purposes of the individual or entity is not a breach of the security of the system, provided that the personal information is not used for a purpose other than a lawful purpose of the individual or entity or subject to further unauthorized disclosure.

"Encrypted" means the transformation of data through the use of an algorithmic process into a form in which there is a low probability of assigning meaning without the use of a confidential process or key, or the securing of the information by another method that renders the data elements unreadable or unusable.

"Entity" includes corporations, business trusts, estates, partnerships, limited partnerships, limited liability partnerships, limited liability companies, associations, organizations, joint ventures, governments, governmental subdivisions, agencies, or instrumentalities or any other legal entity, whether for profit or not for profit.

"Financial institution" has the meaning given that term in 15 U.S.C. § 6809(3).

"Individual" means a natural person.

"Notice" means:

1. Written notice to the last known postal address in the records of the individual or entity;

2. Telephone notice;

3. Electronic notice; or

4. Substitute notice, if the individual or the entity required to provide notice demonstrates that the cost of providing notice will exceed $50,000, the affected class of Virginia residents to be notified exceeds 100,000 residents, or the individual or the entity does not have sufficient contact information or consent to provide notice as described in subdivisions 1, 2, or 3 of this definition. Substitute notice consists of all of the following:

a. E-mail notice if the individual or the entity has e-mail addresses for the members of the affected class of residents;

b. Conspicuous posting of the notice on the website of the individual or the entity if the individual or the entity maintains a website; and

c. Notice to major statewide media.

Crimes and Offenses

Notice required by this section shall not be considered a debt communication as defined by the Fair Debt Collection Practices Act in 15 U.S.C. § 1692a.

Notice required by this section shall include a description of the following:

(1) The incident in general terms;

(2) The type of personal information that was subject to the unauthorized access and acquisition;

(3) The general acts of the individual or entity to protect the personal information from further unauthorized access;

(4) A telephone number that the person may call for further information and assistance, if one exists; and

(5) Advice that directs the person to remain vigilant by reviewing account statements and monitoring free credit reports.

"Personal information" means the first name or first initial and last name in combination with and linked to any one or more of the following data elements that relate to a resident of the Commonwealth, when the data elements are neither encrypted nor redacted:

1. Social security number;

2. Driver's license number or state identification card number issued in lieu of a driver's license number; or

3. Financial account number, or credit card or debit card number, in combination with any required security code, access code, or password that would permit access to a resident's financial accounts.

The term does not include information that is lawfully obtained from publicly available information, or from federal, state, or local government records lawfully made available to the general public.

"Redact" means alteration or truncation of data such that no more than the following are accessible as part of the personal information:

1. Five digits of a social security number; or

2. The last four digits of a driver's license number, state identification card number, or account number.

B. If unencrypted or unredacted personal information was or is reasonably believed to have been accessed and acquired by an unauthorized person and causes, or the individual or entity reasonably believes has caused or will cause, identity theft or another fraud to any resident of the Commonwealth, an individual or entity that owns or licenses computerized data that includes personal information shall disclose any breach of the security of the system following discovery or notification of the breach of the security of the system to the Office of the Attorney General and any affected resident of the Commonwealth without unreasonable delay. Notice required by this section may be reasonably delayed to allow the individual or entity to determine the scope of the breach of the security of the system and restore the reasonable integrity of the system. Notice required by this section may be delayed if, after the individual or entity notifies a law-enforcement agency, the law-enforcement agency determines and advises the individual or entity that the notice will impede a criminal or civil investigation, or homeland or national security. Notice shall be made without unreasonable delay after the law-enforcement agency determines that the notification will no longer impede the investigation or jeopardize national or homeland security.

C. An individual or entity shall disclose the breach of the security of the system if encrypted information is accessed and acquired in an unencrypted form, or if the security breach involves a person with access to the encryption key and the individual or entity reasonably believes that such a breach has caused or will cause identity theft or other fraud to any resident of the Commonwealth.

D. An individual or entity that maintains computerized data that includes personal information that the individual or entity does not own or license shall notify the owner or licensee of the information of any breach of the security of the system without unreasonable delay following discovery of the breach of the security of the system, if the personal information was accessed and acquired by an unauthorized person or the individual or entity reasonably believes the personal information was accessed and acquired by an unauthorized person.

E. In the event an individual or entity provides notice to more than 1,000 persons at one time pursuant to this section, the individual or entity shall notify, without unreasonable delay, the Office of the Attorney General and all consumer reporting agencies that compile and maintain files on consumers on a nationwide basis, as defined in 15 U.S.C. § 1681a(p), of the timing, distribution, and content of the notice.

F. An entity that maintains its own notification procedures as part of an information privacy or security policy for the treatment of personal information that are consistent with the timing requirements of this section shall be deemed to be in compliance with the notification requirements of this section if it notifies residents of the Commonwealth in accordance with its procedures in the event of a breach of the security of the system.

G. An entity that is subject to Title V of the Gramm-Leach-Bliley Act (15 U.S.C. § 6801 et seq.) and maintains procedures for notification of a breach of the security of the system in accordance with the provision of that Act and any rules, regulations, or guidelines promulgated thereto shall be deemed to be in compliance with this section.

H. An entity that complies with the notification requirements or procedures pursuant to the rules, regulations, procedures, or guidelines established by the entity's primary or functional state or federal regulator shall be in compliance with this section.

I. Except as provided by subsections J and K, pursuant to the enforcement duties and powers of the Office of the Attorney General, the Attorney

General may bring an action to address violations of this section. The Office of the Attorney General may impose a civil penalty not to exceed $150,000 per breach of the security of the system or a series of breaches of a similar nature that are discovered in a single investigation. Nothing in this section shall limit an individual from recovering direct economic damages from a violation of this section.

J. A violation of this section by a state-chartered or licensed financial institution shall be enforceable exclusively by the financial institution's primary state regulator.

K. A violation of this section by an individual or entity regulated by the State Corporation Commission's Bureau of Insurance shall be enforced exclusively by the State Corporation Commission.

L. The provisions of this section shall not apply to criminal intelligence systems subject to the restrictions of 28 C.F.R. Part 23 that are maintained by law-enforcement agencies of the Commonwealth and the organized Criminal Gang File of the Virginia Criminal Information Network (VCIN), established pursuant to Chapter 2 (§ 52-12 et seq.) of Title 52.

History.
2008, cc. 566, 801.

§ 18.2-187: Repealed by Acts 1978, c. 807.

Cross references.
For present section covering the subject matter of the repealed section, see § 18.2-187.1.

§ 18.2-187.1. Obtaining or attempting to obtain oil, electric, gas, water, telephone, telegraph, cable television or electronic communication service without payment; penalty; civil liability.

A. It shall be unlawful for any person knowingly, with the intent to defraud, to obtain or attempt to obtain, for himself or for another, oil, electric, gas, water, telephone, telegraph, cable television or electronic communication service by the use of any false information, or in any case where such service has been disconnected by the supplier and notice of disconnection has been given.

B. It shall be unlawful for any person to obtain or attempt to obtain oil, electric, gas, water, telephone, telegraph, cable television or electronic communication service by the use of any scheme, device, means or method, or by a false application for service with intent to avoid payment of lawful charges therefor.

B1. It shall be unlawful for any person to obtain, or attempt to obtain, electronic communication service as defined in § 18.2-190.1 by the use of an unlawful electronic communication device as defined in § 18.2-190.1.

C. The word "notice" as used in subsection A shall be notice given in writing to the person to whom the service was assigned. The sending of a notice in writing by registered or certified mail in the United States mail, duly stamped and addressed to such person at his last known address, requiring delivery to the addressee only with return receipt requested, and the actual signing of the receipt for such mail by the addressee, shall be prima facie evidence that such notice was duly received.

D. Any person who violates any provisions of this section, if the value of service, credit or benefit procured is $200 or more, shall be guilty of a Class 6 felony; or if the value is less than $200, shall be guilty of a Class 1 misdemeanor. In addition, the court may order restitution for the value of the services unlawfully used and for all costs. Such costs shall be limited to actual expenses, including the base wages of employees acting as witnesses for the Commonwealth, and suit costs. However, the total amount of allowable costs granted hereunder shall not exceed $250, excluding the value of the service.

E. Any party providing oil, electric, gas, water, telephone, telegraph, cable television or electronic communication service who is aggrieved by a violation of this section may, in a civil proceeding in any court of competent jurisdiction, seek both injunctive and equitable relief, and an award of damages, including attorney's fees and costs. In addition to any other remedy provided by law, the party aggrieved may recover an award of actual damages or $500 whichever is greater for each action.

History.
1978, c. 807; 1981, c. 197; 1992, c. 525; 1993, c. 439; 2002, c. 671; 2003, c. 354.

§ 18.2-187.2. Audiovisual recording of motion pictures unlawful; penalty.

A. It shall be unlawful for any person to operate an audiovisual recording function of a device in a commercial theater, excluding the lobby and other common areas, to record a motion picture or any portion thereof without the consent of the owner or lessee of the theater. Any person who violates the provisions of this section is guilty of a Class 1 misdemeanor.

B. The owner or lessee of a commercial theater where a motion picture is being exhibited, or his authorized agent or employee, who has probable cause to believe that a person has made a recording in violation of subsection A on the premises of the owner or lessee, may detain such person for a period not to exceed one hour pending arrival of a law-enforcement officer. Such owner, lessee, agent or employee shall not be held civilly liable for unlawful detention if such detention does not exceed one hour, slander, malicious prosecution, false imprisonment, false arrest, or assault and battery of the person so arrested or detained, whether such arrest or detention takes place on the premises of the owner or lessee or after close pursuit from such premises, provided that, in causing the arrest or detention of such person, the owner, lessee, agent or employee had at the time of such arrest or detention probable cause to believe the person was making or had made an illegal recording in violation of subsection A.

C. This section shall not apply to any lawfully authorized investigative, law-enforcement, protective, or intelligence gathering activity by an agent or employee of the Commonwealth or the federal government.

D. The term "audiovisual recording function" means that component of an analog or digital photographic or video camera or other device developed with the capability to record or transmit a motion picture or any part thereof.

History.
2004, c. 759.

§ 18.2-188. Defrauding hotels, motels, campgrounds, boardinghouses, etc.

It shall be unlawful for any person, without paying therefor, and with the intent to cheat or defraud the owner or keeper to:

1. Put up at a hotel, motel, campground or boardinghouse;
2. Obtain food from a restaurant or other eating house;
3. Gain entrance to an amusement park; or
4. Without having an express agreement for credit, procure food, entertainment or accommodation from any hotel, motel, campground, boardinghouse, restaurant, eating house or amusement park.

It shall be unlawful for any person, with intent to cheat or defraud the owner or keeper out of the pay therefor to obtain credit at a hotel, motel, campground, boardinghouse, restaurant or eating house for food, entertainment or accommodation by means of any false show of baggage or effects brought thereto.

It shall be unlawful for any person, with intent to cheat or defraud, to obtain credit at a hotel, motel, campground, boardinghouse, restaurant, eating house or amusement park for food, entertainment or accommodation through any misrepresentation or false statement.

It shall be unlawful for any person, with intent to cheat or defraud, to remove or cause to be removed any baggage or effects from a hotel, motel, campground, boardinghouse, restaurant or eating house while there is a lien existing thereon for the proper charges due from him for fare and board furnished.

Any person who violates any provision of this section shall, if the value of service, credit or benefit procured or obtained is $200 or more, be guilty of a Class 5 felony; or if the value is less than $200, a Class 1 misdemeanor.

History.
Code 1950, § 18.1-120; 1960, c. 358; 1974, c. 615; 1975, cc. 14, 15; 1977, c. 178; 1981, c. 197; 1993, c. 575.

§ 18.2-188.1. Defrauding person having a lien on an animal; penalty.

It shall be unlawful to remove or cause any horse or other animal to be removed from the possession of the owner or keeper of a livery stable or other person having a lien on the horse or animal for keep, support and care pursuant to § 43-32, with intent to defraud or cheat the lienholder. A violation of this section shall be punishable as a Class 2 misdemeanor.

History.
1990, c. 639.

§ 18.2-189. Defrauding keeper of motor vehicles or watercraft.

A person shall be guilty of a Class 2 misdemeanor if he:

1. Stores a motor vehicle, boat or other watercraft with any person, firm or corporation engaged in the business of conducting a garage, marina, watercraft dealership or other facility for the (i) storage of motor vehicles, boats or other watercraft, (ii) furnishing of supplies to motor vehicles, boats or other watercraft, or (iii) alteration or repair of motor vehicles, boats or other watercraft, and obtains storage, supplies, alterations or repairs for such motor vehicle, boat or other watercraft, without having an express agreement for credit, or procures storage, supplies, alterations or repairs on account of such motor vehicle, boat or other watercraft so stored, without paying therefor, and with the intent to cheat or defraud the owner or keeper of the garage, marina or boat repair facility; or
2. With such intent, obtains credit at the garage, marina, watercraft dealership or boat repair facility for such storage, supplies, alterations or repairs through any misrepresentation or false statement; or
3. With such intent, removes or causes to be removed any such motor vehicle, boat or other watercraft from any such garage, marina, watercraft dealership or boat repair facility while there is a lien existing thereon for the proper charges due from him for storage, supplies, alterations or repairs furnished thereon, in accordance with the provisions of § 43-32, 43-33, 46.2-644.01, or § 46.2-644.02.

History.
Code 1950, § 18.1-121; 1960, c. 358; 1975, cc. 14, 15; 1978, c. 245; 1988, c. 414; 2009, c. 664.

§ 18.2-190. Fraudulent misrepresentation as to breed of bull or cattle.

Any person who, in the sale, gift or transfer, of any bull or cattle, knowingly shall make any false representation that such bull is registered, or entitled to registration, in some recognized standard and accredited herd of cattle, or three-quarters blood of such breed, or that such cattle are from such a herd or breed of cattle, shall be guilty of a Class 1 misdemeanor.

History.
Code 1950, §§ 18.1-185, 18.1-186; 1960, c. 358; 1975, cc. 14, 15.

ARTICLE 5.1.

OFFENSES INVOLVING ELECTRONIC COMMUNICATION DEVICES.

§ 18.2-190.1. Definitions.

As used in this article, unless the context requires a different meaning:

"Electronic communication device" means (i) any type of instrument, device, machine, equipment or software that is capable of transmitting, acquiring, encrypting, decrypting or receiving any signs, signals, writings, images and sounds or intelligence of any nature by wire, radio, optical or other electromagnetic systems or (ii) any part, accessory or component of such an instrument, device, machine, equipment or software, including, but not limited to, any computer circuit, computer chip, security module, smart card, electronic mechanism, or other component, accessory or part, that is capable of facilitating the transmission, acquisition, encryption, decryption or reception of signs, signals, writings, images, and sounds or intelligence of any nature by wire, radio, optical or other electromagnetic systems.

"Electronic communication service" means any service provided for a charge or compensation to facilitate the lawful origination, transmission, emission or reception of signs, signals, writings, images and sounds or intelligence of any nature through the use of an electronic communication device as that term is defined in this section.

"Electronic communication service provider" means any person or entity providing any electronic communication service including (i) any person or entity owning or operating any cable television, satellite, Internet-based, telephone, wireless, microwave, fiber optic, data transmission or radio distribution network, system or facility; (ii) any person or entity that for a fee supplies equipment or services to an electronic communication service provider; and (iii) any person or entity providing an electronic communication service directly or indirectly using any of the systems, networks, or facilities described in clause (i).

"Equipment or materials used to manufacture an unlawful electronic communication device" means (i) a scanner capable of intercepting the electronic serial number or mobile identification number of a cellular or other wireless telephone; (ii) electronic software or hardware capable of altering or changing the factory-installed electronic serial number of a cellular or other wireless telephone or a computer containing such software; (iii) a list of cellular or other wireless telephone electronic serial numbers with their associated mobile identification numbers; or (iv) a part, accessory or component of an unlawful electronic communications device possessed or used in the manufacture of such device including any electronic serial number, computer software, mobile identification number, service access card, account number, or personal identification number used to acquire, receive, use, decrypt or transmit an electronic communication service without the actual consent or knowledge of the electronic communication service provider.

"Manufacture of an unlawful electronic communication device" means to make, produce or assemble an unlawful electronic communication device, or to modify, alter, program or reprogram an electronic communication device to be capable of performing any of the illegal functions of an unlawful electronic communication device as that term is defined in this section.

"Sell" means to sell, exchange, lease, give or dispose of to another or to offer or agree to do the same.

"Unlawful electronic communication device" means any electronic communication device that has been manufactured, designed, developed, altered, modified, programmed or reprogrammed, alone or in conjunction with another electronic communication device, so as to be capable of facilitating the disruption, acquisition, receipt, transmission, retransmission or decryption of an electronic communication service without the actual consent or knowledge of the electronic communication service provider. Such unlawful devices include, but are not limited to (i) any device, technology, product, service, equipment, computer software, or any component or part thereof, primarily distributed, sold, designed, assembled, developed, manufactured, modified, programmed, reprogrammed or used for the purpose of facilitating the unauthorized receipt of, transmission of, disruption of, decryption of, access to, or acquisition of any electronic communication service provided by any electronic communication service provider; and (ii) any type of instrument, device, machine, equipment, technology, or software that is primarily designed, assembled, manufactured, developed, sold, distributed, possessed, used or offered, promoted or advertised for the purpose of defeating or circumventing any technology, device or software, or any component or part thereof, used by the provider, owner or licensee of any electronic communication service or of any data, audio or video programs or transmissions, to protect any such electronic communication, data, audio or video services, programs or transmissions from unauthorized receipt, acquisition, access, decryption, disclosure, communication, transmission or retransmission.

History.
1993, c. 439; 1998, c. 518; 2002, c. 671; 2003, c. 354.

Crimes and Offenses

§ 18.2-190.2. Possession of an unlawful electronic communication device or equipment etc., used to manufacture such device; penalty.

A person who knowingly possesses (i) an unlawful electronic communication device or (ii) equipment or materials used to manufacture an unlawful electronic communication device as defined in § 18.2-190.1 with the intent to manufacture an unlawful electronic communication device shall be guilty of a Class 6 felony unless such possession is by an electronic communication equipment manufacturer while lawfully acting in that capacity, or a facilities-based electronic communication service provider licensed by the Federal Communications Commission or by a law-enforcement agency.

History.
1993, c. 439; 1998, c. 518; 2002, c. 671; 2003, c. 354.

§ 18.2-190.3. Sale of an unlawful electronic communication device; penalty.

A person who (i) knowingly sells an unlawful electronic communication device or (ii) sells material, including hardware, data, computer software or other information or equipment, knowing, or having reason to know, that the purchaser or a third person intends to use such material in the manufacture of an unlawful electronic communication device, shall be guilty of a Class 6 felony.

History.
1993, c. 439; 1998, c. 518; 2002, c. 671; 2003, c. 354.

§ 18.2-190.4. Manufacture of an unlawful electronic communication device; penalty.

A person who knowingly manufactures an unlawful electronic communication device shall be guilty of a Class 6 felony.

History.
1993, c. 439; 1998, c. 518; 2002, c. 671; 2003, c. 354.

§ 18.2-190.5. Separate offenses; penalty.

For purposes of imposing criminal penalties for violations of §§ 18.2-190.3 and 18.2-190.4, the commission of the prohibited activity regarding each unlawful electronic communication device shall be deemed a separate offense.

History.
2002, c. 671; 2003, c. 354.

§ 18.2-190.6. Restitution.

The court may, in addition to any other sentence authorized by law, require a person convicted of violating § 18.2-190.3 or § 18.2-190.4 to make restitution in the manner provided in § 19.2-305.1.

History.
2002, c. 671.

§ 18.2-190.7: Repealed by Acts 2004, c. 995.

Cross references.
For current provisions as to forfeiture of unlawful electronic communication devices, see § 19.2-386.18.

§ 18.2-190.8. Civil relief; damages.

Any electronic communication service provider aggrieved by a violation of this article may seek both injunctive and equitable relief and an award of damages including attorney's fees and costs. In addition to any other remedy provided by law, the party aggrieved may recover an award of actual damages or $500, whichever is greater, for each unlawful electronic communications device involved in the action. In any case in which the court finds that the violation was committed for purposes of commercial advantage or financial gain, the award shall be increased by an amount not to exceed three times the actual damages sustained or $1,500 for each unlawful electronic communications device involved, whichever is greater.

History.
2002, c. 671; 2003, c. 354.

ARTICLE 6. OFFENSES RELATING TO CREDIT CARDS.

§ 18.2-191. Definitions.

The following words and phrases as used in this article, unless a different meaning is plainly required by the context, shall have the following meanings:

"Acquirer" means a business organization, financial institution or an agent of a business organization or financial institution that authorizes a merchant to accept payment by credit card or credit card number for money, goods, services or anything else of value.

"Cardholder" means the person or organization named on the face of a credit card to whom or for whose benefit the credit card is issued by an issuer.

"Credit card" means any instrument or device, whether known as a credit card, credit plate, payment device number, or by any other name, issued with or without fee by an issuer for the use of the cardholder in obtaining money, goods, services or anything else of value on credit. For the purpose of this article, "credit card" shall also include a similar device, whether known as a debit card, or any other name, issued with or without fee by an issuer for the use of the cardholder in obtaining money, goods, services or anything else of value by charging the account of the cardholder with a bank or any other person even though no credit is thereby extended.

"Expired credit card" means a credit card which is no longer valid because the term shown on it has elapsed.

"Issuer" means the business organization or financial institution or its duly authorized agent which issues a credit card.

"Payment device number" means any code, account number or other means of account access, other than a check, draft or similar paper instrument, that can be used to obtain money, goods, services or anything else of value, or to initiate a transfer of funds. "Payment device number" does not include an encoded or truncated credit card number or payment device number.

"Receives" or *"receiving"* means acquiring possession or control of the credit card number or payment device number or accepting the same as security for a loan.

"Revoked credit card" means a credit card which is no longer valid because permission to use it has been suspended or terminated by the issuer.

"Sales draft" means a paper form evidencing a purchase of goods, services or anything else of value from a merchant through the use of a credit card.

"Cash advance/withdrawal draft" means a paper form evidencing a cash advance or withdrawal from a bank or other financial institution through the use of a credit card.

History.

Code 1950, § 18.1-125.2; 1968, c. 480; 1975, cc. 14, 15; 1977, c. 103; 1980, c. 99; 1985, c. 266; 1991, c. 546.

§ 18.2-192. Credit card theft.

(1) A person is guilty of credit card or credit card number theft when:

(a) He takes, obtains or withholds a credit card or credit card number from the person, possession, custody or control of another without the cardholder's consent or who, with knowledge that it has been so taken, obtained or withheld, receives the credit card or credit card number with intent to use it or sell it, or to transfer it to a person other than the issuer or the cardholder; or

(b) He receives a credit card or credit card number that he knows to have been lost, mislaid, or delivered under a mistake as to the identity or address of the cardholder, and who retains possession with intent to use, to sell or to transfer the credit card or credit card number to a person other than the issuer or the cardholder; or

(c) He, not being the issuer, sells a credit card or credit card number or buys a credit card or credit card number from a person other than the issuer; or

(d) He, not being the issuer, during any twelve-month period, receives credit cards or credit card numbers issued in the names of two or more persons which he has reason to know were taken or retained under circumstances which constitute a violation of § 18.2-194 and subdivision (1) (c) of this section.

(2) Credit card or credit card number theft is grand larceny and is punishable as provided in § 18.2-95.

History.

Code 1950, § 18.1-125.3; 1968, c. 480; 1975, cc. 14, 15; 1976, c. 318; 1985, c. 266.

§ 18.2-193. Credit card forgery.

(1) A person is guilty of credit card forgery when:

(a) With intent to defraud a purported issuer, a person or organization providing money, goods, services or anything else of value, or any other person, he falsely makes or falsely embosses a purported credit card or utters such a credit card; or

(b) He, not being the cardholder or a person authorized by him, with intent to defraud the issuer, or a person or organization providing money, goods, services or anything else of value, or any other person, signs a credit card; or

(c) He, not being the cardholder or a person authorized by him, with intent to defraud the issuer, or a person or organization providing money, goods, services or anything else of value, or any other person, forges a sales draft or cash advance/withdrawal draft, or uses a credit card number of a card of which he is not the cardholder, or utters, or attempts to employ as true, such forged draft knowing it to be forged.

(2) A person falsely makes a credit card when he makes or draws, in whole or in part, a device or instrument which purports to be the credit card of a named issuer but which is not such a credit card because the issuer did not authorize the making or drawing, or alters a credit card which was validly issued.

(3) A person falsely embosses a credit card when, without the authorization of the named issuer, he completes a credit card by adding any of the matter, other than the signature of the cardholder, which an issuer requires to appear on the credit card before it can be used by a cardholder. Conviction of credit card forgery shall be punishable as a Class 5 felony.

History.

Code 1950, § 18.1-125.4; 1968, c. 480; 1975, cc. 14, 15; 1980, c. 99; 1985, c. 266.

§ 18.2-194. Unauthorized possession of two or more signed credit cards or credit card numbers.

When a person, other than the cardholder or a person authorized by him, possesses two or more credit cards which are signed or two or more credit card numbers, such possession shall be prima facie evidence that said cards or credit card numbers were obtained in violation of § 18.2-192.

History.

Code 1950, § 18.1-125.5; 1968, c. 480; 1975, cc. 14, 15; 1985, c. 266; 2005, c. 157.

§ 18.2-195. Credit card fraud; conspiracy; penalties.

(1) A person is guilty of credit card fraud when, with intent to defraud any person, he:

(a) Uses for the purpose of obtaining money, goods, services or anything else of value a credit card or credit card number obtained or retained in violation of § 18.2-192 or a credit card or credit card number which he knows is expired or revoked;

(b) Obtains money, goods, services or anything else of value by representing (i) without the consent of the cardholder that he is the holder of a specified card or credit card number or (ii) that he is the holder of a card or credit card number and such card or credit card number has not in fact been issued;

(c) Obtains control over a credit card or credit card number as security for debt; or

(d) Obtains money from an issuer by use of an unmanned device of the issuer or through a person other than the issuer when he knows that such advance will exceed his available credit with the issuer and any available balances held by the issuer.

(2) A person who is authorized by an issuer to furnish money, goods, services or anything else of value upon presentation of a credit card or credit card number by the cardholder, or any agent or employee of such person, is guilty of a credit card fraud when, with intent to defraud the issuer or the cardholder, he:

(a) Furnishes money, goods, services or anything else of value upon presentation of a credit card or credit card number obtained or retained in violation of § 18.2-192, or a credit card or credit card number which he knows is expired or revoked;

(b) Fails to furnish money, goods, services or anything else of value which he represents or causes to be represented in writing or by any other means to the issuer that he has furnished; or

(c) Remits to an issuer or acquirer a record of a credit card or credit card number transaction which is in excess of the monetary amount authorized by the cardholder.

(3) Conviction of credit card fraud is punishable as a Class 1 misdemeanor if the value of all money, goods, services and other things of value furnished in violation of this section, or if the difference between the value of all money, goods, services and anything else of value actually furnished and the value represented to the issuer to have been furnished in violation of this section, does not exceed $200 in any six-month period; conviction of credit card fraud is punishable as a Class 6 felony if such value exceeds $200 in any six-month period.

(4) Any person who conspires, confederates or combines with another, (i) either within or without the Commonwealth to commit credit card fraud within the Commonwealth or (ii) within the Commonwealth to commit credit card fraud within or without the Commonwealth, is guilty of a Class 6 felony.

History.

Code 1950, § 18.1-125.6; 1968, c. 480; 1975, cc. 14, 15; 1978, c. 364; 1980, c. 99; 1981, c. 197; 1985, c. 266; 1991, c. 546.

§ 18.2-195.1. Credit card factoring.

A. Any authorized person who presents to the issuer or acquirer for payment a credit card or credit card number transaction record of a sale which was not made by such person or his agent or employee, without the express authorization of the acquirer and with intent to defraud the issuer, acquirer or cardholder, is guilty of a Class 5 felony. If such act is done without authorization of the acquirer but without intent to defraud, he shall be guilty of a Class 1 misdemeanor.

B. Any person who, without the express authorization of the acquirer and with intent to defraud the issuer, acquirer or cardholder, employs or otherwise causes an authorized person to remit to an acquirer or issuer a credit card transaction record of sale that was not made by the authorized person is guilty of a Class 5 felony. If such act is done without the authorization of the acquirer but without intent to defraud, he shall be guilty of a Class 1 misdemeanor.

C. As used in this section, *"authorized person"* means a person authorized by the acquirer to furnish money, goods, services or anything else of value upon presentation of a credit card or credit card number by a cardholder and includes an agent or employee of a person having such authority.

History.

1991, c. 546.

§ 18.2-195.2. Fraudulent application for credit card; penalties.

A. A person shall be guilty of a Class 1 misdemeanor if he makes, causes to be made or conspires to make, directly, indirectly or through an agency, any materially false statement in writing concerning the financial condition or means or ability to pay of himself or of any other person for whom he is acting or any firm or corporation in which he is interested or for which he is acting, knowing the statement to be false and intending that it be relied upon for the purpose of procuring a credit card. However, if the statement is made in response to an unrequested written solicitation from the issuer or an agent of the issuer to apply for a credit card, he shall be guilty of a Class 4 misdemeanor.

B. A person who knows that a false statement has been made in writing concerning the financial condition or ability to pay of himself or of any person for whom he is acting or any firm or corporation in which he is interested or for which he is acting and who with intent to defraud, procures a credit card, upon the faith of such false statement, for his own benefit, or for the benefit of the person, firm or corporation in which he is interested or for which he is acting, and obtains by use of the credit card, money, property, services or any thing of value, is guilty of grand larceny if the value of whatever is obtained is $200 or more or petit larceny if the value is less than $200.

C. As used in this section, "in writing" shall include information transmitted by computer, facsimile, e-mail, Internet, or any other electronic medium, and shall not include information transmitted by any such medium by voice transmission.

History.

1991, c. 546; 2007, c. 518.

§ 18.2-196. Criminal possession of credit card forgery devices.

(1) A person is guilty of criminal possession of credit card forgery devices when:

(a) He is a person other than the cardholder and possesses two or more incomplete credit cards, with intent to complete them without the consent of the issuer; or

(b) He possesses, with knowledge of its character, machinery, plates or any other contrivance designed to reproduce instruments purporting to be credit cards of an issuer who has not consented to the preparation of such credit cards.

(2) A credit card is incomplete if part of the matter, other than the signature of the cardholder, which an issuer requires to appear on the credit card before it can be used by a cardholder, has not yet been stamped, embossed, imprinted or written upon.

Conviction of criminal possession of credit card forgery devices is punishable as a Class 6 felony.

History.

Code 1950, § 18.1-125.7; 1968, c. 480; 1975, cc. 14, 15.

§ 18.2-196.1. Unlawful use of payment card scanning devices and re-encoders; penalty.

A. Any person who with malicious intent uses a scanning device or a re-encoder on the payment card of another without the permission of the authorized payment card user is guilty of a Class 1 misdemeanor.

B. Any person who violates this section and sells or distributes such information to another is guilty of a Class 6 felony.

C. Any person who violates this section and uses such information in the commission of another crime is guilty of a Class 6 felony.

D. For the purposes of this section:

1. *"Authorized payment card user"* means any person with the authorization or permission to use any payment card to obtain, purchase, or receive goods, services, money, or anything else of value from a merchant.

2. *"Merchant"* means an owner or operator of any mercantile establishment or any agent, employee, lessee, consignee, officer, director, franchisee, or independent contractor of such owner or operator who receives from an authorized payment card user or someone he believes to be an authorized payment card user, a payment card or information from a payment card, or what he believes to be a payment card or information from a payment card, as the instrument for obtaining, purchasing or receiving goods, services, money, or anything else of value from him.

3. *"Payment card"* means a credit card, charge card, debit card, hotel key card, stored-value card, white plastic, or any other card containing encoded information that allows an authorized payment card user to obtain, purchase, or receive goods, services, money, or anything else of value from a merchant.

4. *"Re-encoder"* means an electronic device that transfers encoded information from the magnetic strip or stripe of a payment card onto the magnetic strip or stripe of a different payment card.

5. *"Scanning device"* means a scanner, reader, or any other electronic device that is used to access, read, scan, obtain, memorize, temporarily store, or permanently store encoded information on the magnetic strip or stripe of a payment card.

History.

2005, c. 166.

§ 18.2-197. Criminally receiving goods and services fraudulently obtained.

A person is guilty of criminally receiving goods and services fraudulently obtained when he receives money, goods, services or anything else of value obtained in violation of subsection (1) of § 18.2-195 with the knowledge or belief that the same were obtained in violation of subsection (1) of § 18.2-195. Conviction of criminal receipt of goods and services fraudulently obtained is punishable as a Class 1 misdemeanor if the value of all money, goods, services and anything else of value, obtained in violation of this section, does not exceed $200 in any six-month period; conviction of criminal receipt of goods and services fraudulently obtained is punishable as a Class 6 felony if such value exceeds $200 in any six-month period.

History.

Code 1950, § 18.1-125.8; 1968, c. 480; 1975, cc. 14, 15; 1981, c. 197.

§ 18.2-198. Obtaining airline, railroad, steamship, etc., ticket at discount price.

A person who obtains at a discount price a ticket issued by an airline, railroad, steamship or other transportation company from other than an apparent agent of such company which was acquired in violation of subsection (1) of § 18.2-195 without reasonable inquiry to ascertain that the person from whom it was obtained had a legal right to possess it shall be presumed to know that such ticket was acquired under circumstances constituting a violation of subsection (1) of § 18.2-195.

History.
Code 1950, § 18.1-125.9; 1968, c. 480; 1975, cc. 14, 15.

§ 18.2-198.1. Venue.

Notwithstanding the provisions of § 19.2-244, a prosecution for a violation of this article may be had in any county or city in which (i) any act in furtherance of the crime was committed or (ii) an issuer or acquirer, or an agent of either, sustained a financial loss as a result of the offense. A prosecution for a violation of § 18.2-192 may be had in any county or city where a credit card number is used, is attempted to be used, or is possessed with intent to violate § 18.2-193, 18.2-195, or 18.2-197.

History.
1991, c. 546; 2008, c. 797.

§ 18.2-199. Penalties for violation of article.

Persons violating any provision of this article for which no other specific punishment is provided for shall be guilty of a Class 6 felony.

History.
Code 1950, § 18.1-125.10; 1968, c. 480; 1975, cc. 14, 15.

ARTICLE 7.
MISCELLANEOUS FALSE AND FRAUDULENT ACTS.

§ 18.2-200. Failure to perform promise to deliver crop, etc., in return for advances.

If any person obtain from another an advance of money, merchandise or other thing, upon a promise in writing that he will send or deliver to such other person his crop or other property, and fraudulently fail or refuse to perform such promise, and also fail to make good such advance, he shall be deemed guilty of the larceny of such money, merchandise or other thing.

History.
Code 1950, § 18.1-113; 1960, c. 358; 1975, cc. 14, 15.

§ 18.2-200.1. Failure to perform promise for construction, etc., in return for advances.

If any person obtain from another an advance of money, merchandise or other thing, of value, with fraudulent intent, upon a promise to perform construction, removal, repair or improvement of any building or structure permanently annexed to real property, or any other improvements to such real property, including horticulture, nursery or forest products, and fail or refuse to perform such promise, and also fail to substantially make good such advance, he shall be deemed guilty of the larceny of such money, merchandise or other thing if he fails to return such advance within fifteen days of a request to do so sent by certified mail, return receipt requested, to his last known address or to the address listed in the contract.

History.
1980, c. 459; 1987, c. 358.

§ 18.2-201. Advances secured by fraudulent promise to perform agricultural labor.

If any person enter into a contract of employment, oral or written, for the performance of personal service to be rendered within one year, in and about the cultivation of the soil, and, at any time during the pendency of such contract, thereby obtain from the landowner, or the person so engaged in the cultivation of the soil, advances of money or other thing of value under such contract, with intent to injure or defraud his employer, and fraudulently refuses or fails to perform such service or to refund such money or other thing of value so obtained, he shall be guilty of a Class 3 misdemeanor. But no prosecution hereunder shall be commenced more than sixty days after the breach of such contract.

History.
Code 1950, § 18.1-114; 1960, c. 358; 1975, cc. 14, 15.

§§ 18.2-202, 18.2-203: Repealed by Acts 2004, c. 459.

§ 18.2-204. False statement for the purpose of defrauding industrial sick benefit company.

Any agent, physician or other person who shall knowingly or willfully make any false or fraudulent statement or representation of any material fact:

(1) In or with reference to any application for insurance in any industrial sick benefit company licensed, or which may be licensed, to do business in this Commonwealth,

(2) As to the death or disability of a policy or certificate holder in any such company,

(3) For the purpose of procuring or attempting to procure the payment of any false or fraudulent claim against any such company, or

(4) For the purpose of obtaining or attempting to obtain any money from or benefit in any such company,

shall be guilty of a Class 3 misdemeanor.

Any such person who shall willfully make a false statement of any material fact or thing in a sworn statement as to the death or disability of a policy or certificate holder in any such company for the purpose of procuring payment of a benefit named in the policy or certificate of such holder, shall be guilty of perjury, and shall be proceeded against and punished as provided by the statutes of this Commonwealth in relation to the crime of perjury.

History.
Code 1950, § 18.1-122; 1960, c. 358; 1975, cc. 14, 15.

§ 18.2-204.1. Fraudulent use of birth certificates, etc.; penalty.

A. Any person who obtains or possesses a fictitious birth certificate or the birth certificate of another for the purpose of establishing a false identity for himself is guilty of a Class 1 misdemeanor. Any person who manufactures, sells, or transfers a fictitious birth certificate or the birth certificate of another for the purpose of establishing a false identity for himself or for another person is guilty of a Class 6 felony.

B. Except as provided in subsection A, any person who obtains, possesses, sells, or transfers any document for the purpose of establishing a false status, occupation, membership, license or identity for himself or any other person is guilty of a Class 1 misdemeanor.

C. Any person who obtains, possesses, sells, or transfers such birth certificate or document with the intent that such certificate or document be used to purchase a firearm is guilty of a Class 6 felony.

D. The provisions of this section shall not apply to members of state, federal, county, city or town law-enforcement agencies in the performance of their duties.

E. The provisions of this section shall not preclude prosecution under any other statute.

History.
1978, c. 615; 1979, c. 479; 1981, c. 593; 2003, cc. 889, 914, 918; 2006, c. 271; 2011, c. 401.

§ 18.2-204.2. Manufacture, sale, etc., or possession of fictitious, facsimile or simulated official license or identification; penalty.

A. Except as provided in subsection D of § 18.2-204.1, it shall be unlawful for any person to manufacture, advertise for sale, sell or possess any fictitious, facsimile or simulated driver's license issued by any state, territory or possession of the United States, the District of Columbia, the Commonwealth of Puerto Rico or any foreign country or government; United States Armed Forces identification card; United States passport or foreign government visa; Virginia Department of Motor Vehicles special identification card; official identification issued by any other federal, state or foreign government agency; or official university or college student identification card, or in any way reproduce any identification card or facsimile thereof in such a manner that it could be mistaken for a valid license or identification of any type specified in this subsection.

B. Any person manufacturing, advertising for sale, selling or reproducing such card or facsimile thereof shall be guilty of a Class 1 misdemeanor.

C. Any person possessing any such card or facsimile thereof shall be guilty of a Class 2 misdemeanor.

D. The provisions of this section shall not preclude an election to prosecute under § 18.2-172, except to prosecute for forgery or uttering of such license or identification card or facsimile thereof as proof of age.

History.
1980, c. 281; 1989, c. 705; 1992, c. 531; 2006, cc. 445, 484; 2011, c. 401.

§ 18.2-204.3. Transfers for the sole or primary purpose of obtaining a lower unemployment tax rate; penalty.

A. Any person who transfers or attempts to transfer any trade or business to another person, where the sole or primary purpose of the transfer is to obtain a lower unemployment tax rate, is guilty of a Class 1 misdemeanor.

B. Any person who knowingly advises another person to transfer any trade or business to another person where the sole or primary purpose of the transfer is to obtain a lower unemployment tax rate, is guilty of a Class 1 misdemeanor.

C. Any person who is found guilty of more than two such actions under subsections A or B is guilty of a Class 6 felony.

D. It shall be the duty of the attorney for the Commonwealth to whom the Commission shall report, pursuant to subsection B of § 60.2-500, any violation of this section, to determine whether to proceed with prosecution.

History.
2005, cc. 47, 91.

§ 18.2-205. False pretense in obtaining registration of cattle and other animals and giving false pedigree.

Every person who by any false pretense shall obtain from any club, association, society or company for improving the breed of cattle, horses, sheep, swine or other domestic animals the registration of any animal in the herd register or other register of any such club, association, society or company, or a transfer of any such registration, and every person who shall knowingly give a false pedigree of any animal shall be guilty of a Class 3 misdemeanor.

History.
Code 1950, § 18.1-123; 1960, c. 358; 1975, cc. 14, 15.

§ 18.2-206. Procuring an animal, aircraft, vehicle or boat with intent to defraud.

If any person procure any such animal, aircraft, vehicle, boat or vessel mentioned in § 18.2-149 by fraud or by misrepresenting himself as some other person or with the intent to cheat or defraud such other person, he shall be guilty of a Class 1 misdemeanor. The failure to pay the rental for or damage to such animal, aircraft, vehicle, boat or vessel, or absconding without paying such rental or damage, shall be prima facie evidence of the intent to defraud at the time of renting or leasing such animal, aircraft, vehicle, boat or vessel.

History.
Code 1950, § 18.1-162; 1960, c. 358; 1975, cc. 14, 15.

§ 18.2-207. Making false entry, etc., in marriage register, etc.

If any clerk of a court, commissioner of the revenue, physician, surgeon, medical examiner or minister celebrating a marriage, or clerk or keeper of the records of any religious society, shall, in any book, register, record, certificate or copy which such person is by Title 20 (§ 20-13 et seq.) required to keep, make, or give, knowingly make any false, erroneous, or fraudulent entry, record, registration, or written statement, he shall, for every such offense, be guilty of a Class 3 misdemeanor.

History.
Code 1950, § 18.1-98; 1960, c. 358; 1975, cc. 14, 15.

§ 18.2-208. Making false statement, etc., for marriage record, etc.

If any person, upon whose information or statement any record or registration may lawfully be made under Title 20 (§ 20-13 et seq.), knowingly give any false information, or make any false statement to be used for the purpose of making any such record or registration, he shall, for every such offense, be guilty of a Class 4 misdemeanor.

History.
Code 1950, § 18.1-99; 1960, c. 358; 1975, cc. 14, 15.

§ 18.2-209. False publications.

Any person who knowingly and willfully states, delivers or transmits by any means whatever to any publisher, or employee of a publisher, of any newspaper, magazine, or other publication or to any owner, or employee of an owner, of any radio station, television station, news service or cable service, any false and untrue statement, knowing the same to be false or untrue, concerning any person or corporation, with intent that the same shall be published, broadcast or otherwise disseminated, shall be guilty of a Class 3 misdemeanor.

History.
Code 1950, § 18.1-407; 1960, c. 358; 1975, cc. 14, 15; 1978, c. 359.

§ 18.2-209.1. Penalties for false certificate or failure to give bond.

A. If any clerk make a certificate as to any bond of a special commissioner appointed under Article 11 (§ 8.01-96 et seq.) of Chapter 3 of Title 8.01, knowing it to be false, he shall be guilty of a Class 3 misdemeanor, and shall, upon conviction, be removed from his office.

B. If any special commissioner appointed under Article 11 of Chapter 3 of Title 8.01 shall advertise property for sale or rent, and shall sell or rent the same before he shall have given bond as is required by § 8.01-99, he shall be guilty of a Class 3 misdemeanor.

History.
1978, c. 718.

§ 18.2-209.2. Failure of clerk to give notice of appointment of special commissioner to collect purchase money or rent.

If any clerk fail to give notice as required by § 8.01-103 of a special commissioner, he shall be guilty of a Class 4 misdemeanor.

History.
1978, c. 718.

§ 18.2-210. Stamping, etc., on newspapers, any word, etc., to cause belief it was done by publisher; circulating such newspapers.

No person, without first obtaining the consent of the publisher so to do, shall affix to, or place or insert in, or print, stamp or impress upon any newspaper or any part thereof, after the same shall have been issued for circulation by the publisher thereof, any word, figure, design, picture, emblem or advertisement with intent to cause, or which when so affixed, placed, inserted, printed, stamped or impressed may cause, the public to believe that such word, figure, design, picture, emblem or advertisement was affixed, placed, printed, inserted, stamped or impressed in and upon such newspaper by the publisher of the same as a part thereof.

No person shall knowingly circulate, distribute or sell, or cause to be circulated, distributed or sold, any newspaper upon which has been so affixed, placed, inserted, printed, stamped or impressed any word, figure, design, picture, emblem or advertisement in violation of the terms hereof.

Any person violating the provisions hereof shall be guilty of a Class 4 misdemeanor. Each violation shall constitute a separate offense.

History.
Code 1950, § 18.1-409; 1960, c. 358; 1964, c. 560; 1975, cc. 14, 15.

§ 18.2-211: Repealed by Acts 2004, c. 459.

§ 18.2-212. Calling or summoning emergency medical services vehicle or firefighting apparatus without just cause; maliciously activating fire alarms in public buildings; venue.

A. Any person who without just cause therefor calls or summons, by telephone or otherwise, any emergency medical services vehicle or firefighting apparatus, or any person who maliciously activates a manual or automatic fire alarm in any building used for public assembly or for other public use, including, but not limited to, schools, theaters, stores, office buildings, shopping centers and malls, coliseums, and arenas, regardless of whether an emergency medical services vehicle or fire apparatus responds or not, is guilty of a Class 1 misdemeanor.

B. A violation of this section may be prosecuted either in the jurisdiction from which the call or summons was made or in the jurisdiction where the call or summons was received.

History.
Code 1950, § 18.1-412; 1960, c. 358; 1975, cc. 14, 15; 1976, c. 75; 1982, c. 502; 2015, cc. 502, 503.

§ 18.2-212.1. Unlawful for person not blind or incapacitated to carry white, white tipped with red or metallic cane.

It is unlawful for any person, unless totally or partially blind or otherwise incapacitated, while on any public street or highway to carry in a raised or extended position a cane or walking stick which is metallic or white in color or white tipped with red. Any person violating any provisions of this section shall be guilty of a Class 4 misdemeanor.

History.
Code 1950, §§ 46.1-238, 46.1-239; 1958, c. 541; 1964, c. 20; 1975, cc. 14, 15.

§ 18.2-213. Simulation of warrants, processes, writs and notices.

Any person who, for the purpose of collecting money, shall knowingly deliver, mail, send or otherwise use or cause to be used any paper or writing simulating or intended to simulate any warrant, process, writ, notice of execution lien or notice of motion for judgment shall be guilty of a Class 4 misdemeanor.

History.
Code 1950, § 18.1-313; 1960, c. 358; 1975, cc. 14, 15.

§ 18.2-213.1. Obtaining certification as small, women-owned, or minority-owned business by deception; penalty.

A. Except as otherwise provided by § 18.2-498.3, a person shall be guilty of a Class 1 misdemeanor if, in the course of business, he:

1. Fraudulently obtains or retains certification as a small, women-owned, or minority-owned business;
2. Willfully makes a false statement knowing it to be untrue, whether by affidavit, report or other representation, to an official or employee of a public body for the purpose of influencing the certification or denial of certification of any business entity as a small, women-owned, or minority-owned business;
3. Willfully obstructs or impedes any agency official or employee who is investigating the qualifications of a business entity which has requested certification as a small, women-owned, or minority-owned business; or
4. Fraudulently obtains public moneys reserved for or allocated or available to small, women-owned, or minority-owned businesses.

B. For the purposes of this section, "minority-owned business," and "small business" and "women-owned business" shall have the same meaning as those terms are defined in § 2.2-1604.

History.
1987, c. 689; 1989, c. 570; 2006, cc. 831, 921; 2009, c. 869; 2013, c. 482; 2015, cc. 696, 697.

§ 18.2-213.2. Filing false lien or encumbrance against another.

Any person who maliciously files a lien or encumbrance in a public record against the real or personal property of another knowing that such lien or encumbrance is false is guilty of a Class 5 felony. The court in its conviction order or in a separate order, shall direct the clerk of any jurisdiction in which a false lien or encumbrance has been filed to release from record such lien or encumbrance specifically described in the conviction order or separate order, including any notice or memorandum of lien. Such lien or encumbrance shall be deemed invalid and shall be treated as if it was never filed.

History.
2013, c. 454.

ARTICLE 8.
MISREPRESENTATIONS AND OTHER OFFENSES CONNECTED WITH SALES.

§ 18.2-214. Changing or removing, etc., trademarks, identification marks, etc.

Any person, firm, association or corporation who or which intentionally removes, defaces, alters,

Crimes and Offenses

changes, destroys or obliterates in any manner or way or who causes to be removed, defaced, altered, changed, destroyed or obliterated in any manner or way any trademark, distinguishment or identification number, serial number or mark on or from any article or device, in order to secrete its identification with intent to defraud, shall be guilty of a Class 1 misdemeanor.

History.
Code 1950, § 59.1-42; 1968, c. 439; 1975, cc. 14, 15.

§ 18.2-214.1. Penalties for failure to report removal or alteration of identification or serial number on business machines.

It shall be unlawful for any person, firm, association, or corporation regularly engaged in the business of repairing, selling, renting or leasing of business machines to fail to report any business machine which such person, firm, association, or corporation knows has an altered or removed identification or serial number. The report shall be made to the appropriate law-enforcement agency for the county, city, or town where such business machine is located.

For purposes of this section, the term "business machines" includes, but is not limited to, typewriters, adding machines, check-writing machines, cash registers, calculators, addressing machines, copying, and accounting equipment, and recording equipment.

Any person, firm, association, or corporation violating the provisions of this section shall be guilty of a Class 4 misdemeanor.

History.
1981, c. 186; 1982, c. 154.

§ 18.2-215. Removal or alteration of identification numbers on household electrical appliances; possession of such appliances.

No person, firm, association or corporation, either individually or in association with one or more other persons, firms, associations or corporations shall remove, change or alter the serial number or other identification number stamped upon, cut into or attached as a permanent part of any household or electrical or electronic appliance where such number was stamped upon, cut into or attached to such appliance by the manufacturer thereof.

No person, firm, association or corporation shall knowingly have in his or its possession for the purpose of resale or keep in his possession for a period in excess of forty-eight hours without reporting such possession to the appropriate law-enforcement agency in his county, town or city a household or electrical or electronic appliance, with knowledge that the serial number or other identification number has been removed, changed or altered.

Any person, firm, association or corporation violating the provisions of this section shall be guilty of a Class 1 misdemeanor.

History.
Code 1950, § 59.1-43; 1968, c. 439; 1975, cc. 14, 15; 1976, c. 305.

§ 18.2-216. Untrue, deceptive or misleading advertising, inducements, writings or documents.

A. Any person, firm, corporation or association who, with intent to sell or in anywise dispose of merchandise, securities, service or anything offered by such person, firm, corporation or association, directly or indirectly, to the public for sale or distribution or with intent to increase the consumption thereof, or to induce the public in any manner to enter into any obligation relating thereto, or to acquire title thereto, or any interest therein, makes, publishes, disseminates, circulates or places before the public, or causes, directly or indirectly to be made, published, disseminated, circulated or placed before the public, in a newspaper or other publications, or in the form of a book, notice, handbill, poster, blueprint, map, bill, tag, label, circular, pamphlet or letter or in any other way, an advertisement of any sort regarding merchandise, securities, service, land, lot or anything so offered to the public, which advertisement contains any promise, assertion, representation or statement of fact which is untrue, deceptive or misleading, or uses any other method, device or practice which is fraudulent, deceptive or misleading to induce the public to enter into any obligation, shall be guilty of a Class 1 misdemeanor.

The actions prohibited in this section, shall be construed as including (i) the advertising in any manner by any person of any goods, wares or merchandise as a bankrupt stock, receiver's stock or trustee's stock, if such stock contains any goods, wares or merchandise put therein subsequent to the date of the purchase by such advertiser of such stock, and if such advertisement of any such stock fail to set forth the fact that such stock contains other goods, wares or merchandise put therein, subsequent to the date of the purchase by such advertiser of such stock in type as large as the type used in any other part of such advertisement, including the caption of the same, it shall be a violation of this section; and (ii) the use of any writing or document which appears to be, but is not in fact a negotiable check, negotiable draft or other negotiable instrument unless the writing clearly and conspicuously, in at least 14-point bold type, bears the phrase "THIS IS NOT A CHECK" printed on its face.

B. An allegation made by a plaintiff in a civil pleading that a defendant real estate licensee has violated this section shall be stated with particularity.

History.
Code 1950, § 59.1-44; 1968, c. 439; 1975, cc. 14, 15, 507; 2005, c. 150; 2014, cc. 650, 696.

§ 18.2-216.1. Unauthorized use of name or picture of any person; punishment.

A person, firm, or corporation that knowingly uses for advertising purposes, or for the purpose of trade, the name, portrait, or picture of any person resident in the Commonwealth, without having first obtained the written consent of such person, or if dead, of his surviving consort, or if none, his next of kin, or, if a minor, of his or her parent or guardian, as well as that of such minor, shall be deemed guilty of a misdemeanor and be fined not less than $50 nor more than $1,000.

History.
Code 1950, § 8-650; 1977, c. 624.

§ 18.2-217. Advertising merchandise, etc., for sale with intent not to sell at price or terms advertised; prima facie evidence of violation.

(a) Any person, firm, corporation or association who in any manner advertises or offers for sale to the public any merchandise, goods, commodity, service or thing with intent not to sell, or with intent not to sell at the price or upon the terms advertised or offered, shall be guilty of a Class 1 misdemeanor.

(b) In any prosecution or civil action under this section, the refusal by any person, firm, corporation or association or any employee, agent or servant thereof to sell, or the refusal to sell at the price or upon the terms advertised or offered, any merchandise, goods, commodity, service or thing advertised or offered for sale to the public, shall be prima facie evidence of a violation of this section; provided, that this subsection shall not apply when it is clearly stated in the advertisement or offer by which such merchandise, goods, commodity, service or thing is advertised or offered for sale to the public, that the advertiser or offeror has a limited quantity or amount of such merchandise, goods, commodity, service or thing for sale, and the advertiser or offeror at the time of such advertisement or offer did in fact have at least such quantity or amount for sale.

History.
Code 1950, § 59.1-45; 1968, c. 439; 1972, c. 217; 1975, cc. 14, 15.

§ 18.2-218. Failure to indicate goods, etc., are "seconds," "irregulars," "secondhand," etc.

Any person, firm, corporation or association who in any manner knowingly advertises or offers for sale to the public any merchandise, goods, commodity or thing which is defective, blemished, secondhand or used, or which has been designated by the manufacturer thereof as "seconds," "irregulars," "imperfects," "not first class," or words of similar import without clearly and unequivocally indicating in the advertisement or offer of the merchandise, goods, commodity or thing or the articles, units or parts, thereof so advertised or offered for sale to the public is defective, blemished, secondhand or used or consists of "seconds," "irregulars," "imperfects" or "not first class," shall be guilty of a Class 1 misdemeanor.

History.
Code 1950, § 59.1-46; 1968, c. 439; 1975, cc. 14, 15.

§ 18.2-219: Repealed by Acts 1992, c. 768.

Cross references.
For present provisions relating to advertising former or comparative price of merchandise, etc., see § 59.1-207.40 et seq.

§ 18.2-220. Use of word "wholesale" or "wholesaler."

Any person, firm, corporation or association who in any manner in any advertisement or offer for sale to the public of any merchandise, goods, commodity or thing uses the words "wholesale" or "wholesaler" to represent or describe the nature of its business shall be guilty of a Class 1 misdemeanor, unless such person, firm, corporation or association is actually engaged in selling at wholesale the merchandise, goods, commodity or thing advertised or offered for sale.

History.
Code 1950, § 59.1-48; 1968, c. 439; 1975, cc. 14, 15.

§ 18.2-221. Advertising new or used automobiles or trucks.

Any person, firm, corporation or association engaged in selling new or used automobiles or trucks to the public shall be guilty of a Class 2 misdemeanor unless, in any printed advertisement or printed offer in which a price is stated, the following is included: (a) the make, year, and model of such automobile or truck; (b) if reference is made to items of optional equipment which are not included in the advertised price, the additional cost of each such items of optional equipment; and (c) if the manufacturer's suggested retail price is stated, whether such price is an F.O.B. factory or delivered price.

History.
Code 1950, § 59.1-49; 1968, c. 439; 1975, cc. 14, 15; 1985, c. 420.

§ 18.2-222. Misrepresentation as to source of merchandise; penalty.

No person, firm, corporation or association selling or offering for sale any article or merchandise, shall in any manner represent, contrary to fact, that the article was made for, or acquired directly or indirectly from, the United States government or its military or naval forces or any agency of the United

States government, or that it has been disposed of by the United States government.

Any person, firm, corporation or association violating any provision of this section shall be guilty of a Class 3 misdemeanor.

History.

Code 1950, § 59.1-53; 1968, c. 439; 1975, cc. 14, 15; 1983, c. 290.

§ 18.2-223. "Going out of business" sales; permit required.

It shall be unlawful for any person to advertise, or conduct, a sale for the purpose of discontinuing a retail business, or to modify the word "sale" in any advertisement with the words "going out of business" or any other words which tend to insinuate that the retail business is to be discontinued and the merchandise liquidated, unless such person obtains a permit to conduct such sale from the city, town or county, or from each city, town or county, wherein such sale is to be conducted.

A violation of the provisions of this section shall be punishable as a Class 1 misdemeanor.

History.

Code 1950, § 59.1-53.1; 1972, c. 399; 1975, cc. 14, 15.

§ 18.2-224. "Going out of business" sales; counties, cities and towns to issue permits; inspections; application for permit; inventory required; commingling of other goods prohibited; duration; additional permits; inclusion of permit number and dates in advertisements; fee.

Every county, town and city shall issue permits to retail merchants for special sales as required by § 18.2-223 upon the application of such merchant and shall inspect the advertisement and conducting of such sale to insure that it is being advertised and conducted in conformity with the required permit.

All applications for special sale permits shall be accompanied by an inventory, including the kind and quantity of all goods which are to be offered for sale during the sale and only the goods specified in the inventory list may be advertised or sold during the sale period. Goods not included on the inventory of special sale goods shall not be commingled with or added to the special sale goods. Each county, city or town shall have the right to revoke a special sale permit upon proof that goods not appearing on the original inventory of special sale goods have been commingled with or added to the special sale goods.

Each special sale permit shall be valid for a period of no longer than sixty days, and any extension of that time shall constitute a new special sale and shall require an additional permit and inventory. A maximum of one permit beyond the initial sixty-day permit may be granted solely for the purpose of liquidating only those goods contained in the initial inventory list which remain unsold.

Any person who advertises such sale shall conspicuously include in the advertisement the permit number assigned for the sale by the city, town or county wherein the sale is to be conducted and the effective dates of the sale as authorized in the permit.

Each county, town and city is authorized to charge a fee for the issuance of special sale permits. Such fee shall not exceed sixty-five dollars for each permit.

History.

Code 1950, § 59.1-53.2; 1972, c. 399; 1975, cc. 14, 15; 1983, c. 445; 1988, c. 779; 1992, c. 562.

§ 18.2-225. Misrepresentations as to agricultural products.

Misrepresentation by advertising in the press or by radio or by television, or misrepresentation by letter, statement, mark representing grade, quality or condition, label or otherwise in handling, selling, offering or exposing for sale any agricultural commodities is hereby prohibited.

Any person, firm, association or corporation who shall violate any of the provisions of this section shall be guilty of a Class 3 misdemeanor.

The Director of the Division of Marketing, with the approval of the Commissioner of Agriculture and Consumer Services, may, in his discretion, cause prosecutions for violations of this section to be instituted through the attorneys for the Commonwealth, or otherwise, in counties or cities of the Commonwealth where in his opinion violations of this section are found.

History.

Code 1950, § 59.1-54; 1968, c. 439; 1975, cc. 14, 15.

§ 18.2-226. Fraud and misrepresentation in sale of liquid fuels, lubricating oils and similar products.

It shall be unlawful for any person, firm, association or corporation, to store, sell, expose for sale or offer for sale any liquid fuels, lubricating oils or other similar products, in any manner whatsoever, so as to deceive or tend to deceive the purchaser as to the nature, quality and identity of the product so sold or offered for sale.

History.

Code 1950, § 59.1-55; 1968, c. 439; 1975, cc. 14, 15.

§ 18.2-227. Same; sale from pump indicating other brand.

It shall be unlawful for any person, firm, association or corporation to store, keep, expose for sale, offer for sale or sell, from any tank or container, or from any pump or other distributing device or equipment, any other liquid fuels, lubricating oils or other similar products than those indicated by the name, trade name, symbol, sign or other distinguishing mark or device of the manufacturer or distributor, appearing upon the tank, container, pump or other distributing equipment from which the same are sold, offered for sale or distributed.

History.
Code 1950, § 59.1-56; 1968, c. 439; 1975, cc. 14, 15.

§ 18.2-228. Same; imitating indicia of other brands.

It shall be unlawful, for any person, firm, association or corporation to disguise or camouflage his or their own equipment by imitating the design, symbol or trade name of the equipment under which recognized brands of liquid fuels, lubricating oils and similar products are generally marketed.

History.
Code 1950, § 59.1-57; 1968, c. 439; 1975, cc. 14, 15.

§ 18.2-229. Same; false trade name or mixing brands.

It shall be unlawful for any person, firm, association or corporation to expose for sale, offer for sale or sell, under any trademark or trade name in general use, any liquid fuels, lubricating oils or other like products, except those manufactured or distributed by the manufacturer or distributor marketing liquid fuels, lubricating oils or other like products under such trademark or trade name, or to substitute, mix or adulterate the liquid fuels, lubricating oils or other similar products sold, offered for sale or distributed under such trademark or trade name.

History.
Code 1950, § 59.1-58; 1968, c. 439; 1975, cc. 14, 15.

§ 18.2-230. Same; assisting in violation of §§ 18.2-226 through 18.2-229.

It shall be unlawful for any person, firm, association or corporation to aid or assist any other person, firm, association or corporation in the violation of the provisions of §§ 18.2-226 through 18.2-229 by depositing or delivering into any tank, receptacle or other container any other liquid fuels, lubricating oils or like products than those intended to be stored therein and distributed therefrom, as indicated by the name of the manufacturer or distributor or the trademark or trade name of the product displayed on the container itself, or on the pump or other distributing device used in connection therewith.

History.
Code 1950, § 59.1-59; 1968, c. 439; 1975, cc. 14, 15.

§ 18.2-231. Same; label required.

There shall be firmly attached to or painted at or near the point of outlet from which lubricating oil is drawn or poured out for sale or delivery a sign or label consisting of the word or words in letters not less than one inch in height comprising the brand or trade name of such lubricating oil. But if any lubricating oil shall have no brand or trade name, the above sign or label shall consist of the words "lubricating oil, no brand."

History.
Code 1950, § 59.1-60; 1968, c. 439; 1975, cc. 14, 15.

§ 18.2-232. Same; punishment for violation of §§ 18.2-226 through 18.2-231.

Any person, firm, association or corporation or any officer, agent or employee thereof who shall violate any provision of §§ 18.2-226 through 18.2-231, shall be guilty of a Class 3 misdemeanor; and a second or any subsequent offense shall be punishable as a Class 1 misdemeanor.

History.
Code 1950, § 59.1-61; 1968, c. 439; 1975, cc. 14, 15.

§ 18.2-233. Sale of goods marked "sterling" and "sterling silver."

A person who makes or sells or offers to sell or dispose of or has in his possession with intent to sell or dispose of any article of merchandise marked, stamped or branded with the words "sterling" or "sterling silver," or encased or enclosed in any box, package, cover or wrapper, or other thing in or by which such article is packed, enclosed or otherwise prepared for sale or disposition, having thereon any engraving or printed label, stamp, imprint, mark or trademark indicating or denoting by such marking, stamping, branding, engraving or printing that such article is silver, sterling silver or solid silver, unless nine hundred and twenty-five one-thousandths part of the component parts of the metal of which such article is manufactured is pure silver, shall be guilty of a Class 2 misdemeanor.

History.
Code 1950, § 59.1-62; 1968, c. 439; 1975, cc. 14, 15.

§ 18.2-234. Sale of goods marked "coin" and "coin silver."

A person who makes or sells or offers to sell or dispose of, or has in his possession with intent to sell or dispose of, any article of merchandise marked, stamped or branded with words "coin" or "coin silver," or encased or enclosed in any box, package, cover, wrapper or other thing in or by which such article is packed, enclosed, or otherwise prepared for sale or disposition, having thereon any engraving or printed label, stamp, imprint, mark or trademark indicating or denoting by such marking, stamping, branding, engraving or printing that such article is coin or coin silver, unless nine hundred one-thousandths part of the component parts of the metal of which such article is manufactured is pure silver, shall be guilty of a Class 2 misdemeanor.

History.
Code 1950, § 59.1-63; 1968, c. 439; 1975, cc. 14, 15.

§ 18.2-235. Regulating sale of merchandise made of gold.

Any person who marks or sells or offers to sell or dispose of or has in his possession with intent to sell or dispose of any article of merchandise made of gold of a less carat of fineness than is stamped or marked on it or of a less carat of fineness than is engraved, stamped or imprinted on the tag, card, box, label, package, wrapper, cover or other thing in or by which such article is packed, enclosed or otherwise prepared for sale or disposition shall be guilty of a Class 2 misdemeanor.

History.
Code 1950, § 59.1-64; 1968, c. 439; 1975, cc. 14, 15.

§ 18.2-236: Repealed by Acts 2006, cc. 392 and 485, cl. 2, effective July 1, 2006.

Cross references.
For current provisions as to penalties for improperly labeling food as kosher and halal, see § 3.2-5124.

§ 18.2-237. Buying, etc., certain secondhand materials; intent; possession.

If any person buy or receive secondhand grate baskets, keys, bells and bell fixtures, gas fixtures, water fixtures, water pipes, gas pipes, or any part of such fixtures or pipes with intent to defraud, he shall be guilty of a Class 2 misdemeanor. Possession of any such secondhand baskets, keys, bells and bell fixtures, water fixtures, gas fixtures, water pipes, gas pipes, or any part of such fixtures or pipes if bought or received from any other person than the manufacturer thereof or his authorized agent or the owner thereof shall be prima facie evidence of such intent.

History.
Code 1950, § 59.1-66; 1968, c. 439; 1975, cc. 14, 15.

§ 18.2-238. Buying, etc., pig iron, etc., with intent to defraud; possession; evidence of intent.

If any person buy or receive pig iron or railroad, telephone, telegraph, coal mining, industrial, manufacturing or public utility iron, brass, copper, metal or any composition thereof with intent to defraud, he shall be guilty of a Class 6 felony. Possession of any pig iron or railroad, telephone, telegraph, coal mining, industrial, manufacturing or public utility iron, brass, copper, metal or any composition thereof, if bought or received from any other person than the manufacturer thereof or his authorized agent or of a regularly licensed dealer therein, shall be prima facie evidence of such intent.

History.
Code 1950, § 59.1-67; 1968, c. 439; 1975, cc. 14, 15.

§ 18.2-239. Pyramid promotional schemes; misdemeanor; definitions; contracts void.

Every person who contrives, prepares, sets up, operates, advertises or promotes any pyramid promotional scheme shall be guilty of a Class 1 misdemeanor. For the purposes of this section:

(1) *"Compensation"* means the transfer of money or anything of value.

"Compensation" does not mean payment based on sales of goods or services to persons who are not participants in the scheme and who are not purchasing in order to participate in the scheme;

(2) *"Consideration"* means the payment of cash or the purchase of goods, services, or intangible property;

(3) *"Promotes"* means inducing one or more other persons to become a participant; and

(4) *"Pyramid promotional scheme"* means any plan or operation by which a person gives consideration for the opportunity to receive compensation a majority of which is derived from the introduction of other persons into the plan or operation rather than from the sale or consumption of goods, services, or intangible property by a participant or other persons introduced into the plan or operation.

All contracts and agreements, now existing or hereafter formed, whereof the whole or any part of the consideration is given for the right to participate in pyramid promotional scheme programs, are against public policy, void and unenforceable.

Any violation of the provisions of this section shall constitute a prohibited practice under the provisions of § 59.1-200 and shall be subject to any and all of the enforcement provisions of the Virginia Consumer Protection Act (§ 59.1-196 et seq.).

History.
Code 1950, §§ 59.1-67.1, 59.1-67.2; 1970, c. 450; 1975, cc. 14, 15; 2008, cc. 791, 842.

§ 18.2-240. Same; injunction.

Any attorney for the Commonwealth may petition a court of competent jurisdiction to enjoin the further prosecution of any pyramid promotional scheme as defined in § 18.2-239, and to appoint receivers to secure and distribute in an equitable manner any assets received by any participant as a result of such scheme, any such distribution to effect reimbursement, to the extent possible, for uncompensated payments made to become a participant in the scheme. The procedure in any such suit shall be similar to the procedure in other suits for equitable relief, except that no bond shall be required upon the granting of either a temporary or permanent injunction therein. Any person who organizes an endless chain scheme and, either directly or through an agent, promotes such scheme within the Commonwealth shall be deemed subject to the personal jurisdiction of such court of competent jurisdiction under §§ 8.01-328 through 8.01-330, and shall be liable for reasonable costs and attorneys' fees in such suit.

History.
Code 1950, § 59.1-67.3; 1970, c. 450; 1975, cc. 14, 15.

§ 18.2-241. Acceptance of promissory notes in payment for food sold at retail.

As used in this section, *"food"* includes food, groceries and beverages, for human consumption. *"Retailer"* means a person who sells food for consumption and not for resale.

It shall be unlawful for any retailer to accept, in payment for any food sold by him to a customer, a promissory note or notes for an amount in excess of twice the sales price of food delivered by him to the customer. As used in this section the word *"delivered"* means that actual physical delivery into the exclusive custody and control of the customer is made within seven days of the receipt of the note by the seller.

Any person who violates the provisions of this section shall be guilty of a Class 3 misdemeanor.

History.
Code 1950, § 59.1-68; 1968, c. 439; 1975, cc. 14, 15.

§ 18.2-242. Use of games, lotteries, etc., for promoting sale of certain products.

(a) No retail establishment in this Commonwealth shall use any game, contest, lottery or other scheme or device, whereby a person or persons may receive gifts, prizes or gratuities as determined by chance for the purpose of promoting, furthering or advertising the sale of any product or products having both a federal and state excise tax placed upon it, and the fact that no purchase is required in order to participate in such game, contest, lottery or scheme shall not exclude such game, contest, lottery or scheme from the provisions of this section.

(b) Any person violating the provision of this section shall be guilty of a Class 3 misdemeanor.

History.
Code 1950, § 59.1-68.01; 1970, c. 764; 1975, cc. 14, 15.

§ 18.2-242.1. Certain referral transactions in connection with consumer sales or leases prohibited; effect of such transactions.

(a) For the purpose of this section, the term *"consumer sale or lease of goods or services"* means the sale or lease of goods or services which are purchased or leased by a natural person primarily for a personal, family or household purpose, and not for resale.

(b) With respect to a consumer sale or lease of goods or services, no seller or lessor shall give or offer to give a rebate or discount or otherwise pay or offer to pay value to the buyer or lessee as an inducement for the sale or lease in return for the buyer's giving to the seller or lessor the names of prospective buyers or lessees, or otherwise aiding the seller or lessor in entering into a transaction with another buyer or lessee, if the earning of the rebate, discount, or other value is contingent upon the occurrence of any sale, lease, appointment, demonstration, interview, conference, seminar, bailment, testimonial or endorsement subsequent to the time the buyer or lessee enters into the agreement of sale or lease.

(c) Agreements made in whole or in part pursuant to a referral transaction as above described shall be void and unenforceable by the seller or lessor. The buyer or lessee shall be entitled to retain the goods, services or money received pursuant to a referral transaction without obligation to make any further or future payments of any sort on the transaction total, or he shall be entitled to avoid the transaction and to recover from the seller or lessor any sums paid to the seller or lessor pursuant to the transaction.

History.
Code 1950, § 59.1-68.02; 1975, c. 3; 1976, c. 641.

§ 18.2-243. When issuer or distributor of advertisements not guilty of violation; inadvertent error.

A person, firm, corporation or association who or which, for compensation, issues or distributes any advertisement or offer, written, printed, oral or otherwise, in reliance upon the copy or information supplied him by the advertiser or offeror, shall not be deemed to have violated the provisions of this article, nor shall an inadvertent error on the part of any such person, firm, corporation or association be deemed a violation of such provisions.

History.
Code 1950, § 59.1-51; 1968, c. 439; 1975, cc. 14, 15.

§ 18.2-244. Right to select clientele or customers not affected.

Nothing in this article shall be deemed to impair the right of any person, firm, corporation or association to select its clientele or customers.

History.
Code 1950, § 59.1-52; 1968, c. 439; 1975, cc. 14, 15.

§ 18.2-245. Enjoining violation of this article.

(a) Any person, firm, corporation or association who violates any one or more of the sections in this article, may be enjoined by any court of competent jurisdiction notwithstanding the existence of an adequate remedy at law. In any action under this section, it shall not be necessary that damages be alleged or proved.

(b) Actions for injunctive relief under this section may be brought by an attorney for the Commonwealth in the name of the Commonwealth of Virginia upon their own complaint or upon the complaint of any person, firm, corporation or association. The bringing of an action under this section shall not prevent the institution or continuation of criminal proceedings against the same defendant or defendants.

History.
Code 1950, § 59.1-50; 1968, c. 439; 1975, cc. 14, 15.

§ 18.2-246. Penalty in general for violations.

Unless otherwise provided, any person who shall violate any provision of any section in this article shall be guilty of a Class 1 misdemeanor.

History.
Code 1950, § 59.1-68.1; 1968, c. 439; 1975, cc. 14, 15.

ARTICLE 9.

VIRGINIA COMPREHENSIVE MONEY LAUNDERING ACT.

§ 18.2-246.1. Title.

This article shall be known and may be cited as the "Virginia Comprehensive Money Laundering Act."

History.
1999, c. 348.

§ 18.2-246.2. Definitions.

"Conduct" or *"conducts"* includes initiating, concluding, participating in, or assisting in a financial transaction.

"Financial transaction" means any purchase, sale, trade, loan, pledge, investment, gift, transfer, transmission, transportation, delivery, deposit, withdrawal, payment, transfer between accounts, exchange of currency, extension of credit, purchase or sale of monetary instruments, use of a safe-deposit box, or any other acquisition or disposition of monetary instruments by any means including the movement of funds by wire or other electronic means, which is knowingly designed in whole or in part to conceal or disguise the nature, location, source, ownership or control of the property involved in the transaction.

"Monetary instruments" means (i) coin or currency of the United States or of any other country, travelers' checks, personal checks, bank checks, cashier's checks, credit cards, debit cards, and money orders or (ii) securities or other negotiable instruments, in bearer form or otherwise.

"Person" includes any individual, partnership, association, corporation or joint venture.

"Proceeds" means property acquired or derived, directly or indirectly, from, produced through, realized through, or caused by an act or omission and includes property, real or personal, of any kind.

"Property" means anything of value, and includes any interest therein, including any benefit, privilege, claim or right with respect to anything of value, whether real or personal, tangible or intangible.

History.
1999, c. 348; 2003, cc. 541, 549.

§ 18.2-246.3. Money laundering; penalties.

A. It shall be unlawful for any person knowingly to conduct a financial transaction where the person knows the property involved in the transaction represents the proceeds of an activity which is punishable as a felony under the laws of the Commonwealth, another state or territory of the United States, the District of Columbia, or the United States. A violation of this section is punishable by imprisonment of not more than forty years or a fine of not more than $500,000 or by both imprisonment and a fine.

B. Any person who, for compensation, converts cash into negotiable instruments or electronic funds for another, knowing the cash is the proceeds of some form of activity which is punishable as a felony under the laws of the Commonwealth, another state or territory of the United States, the District of Columbia, or the United States, shall be guilty of a Class 1 misdemeanor. Any second or subsequent violation of this subsection shall be punishable as a Class 6 felony.

History.
1999, c. 348.

§ 18.2-246.4: Repealed by Acts 2004, c. 995.

Cross references.
For current provisions as to seizure of property used in connection with money laundering, see § 19.2-386.19.

§ 18.2-246.5. Forfeiture of business license or registration upon conviction of sale or distribution of imitation controlled substance; money laundering.

Any person, firm or corporation holding a license or registration to operate any business as required by either state or local law shall forfeit such license or registration upon conviction of a violation of (i) § 18.2-248 relating to an imitation controlled substance or (ii) § 18.2-246.3 relating to money laundering. Upon a conviction under this section the attorney for the Commonwealth shall notify any appropriate agency.

History.
1999, c. 348.

ARTICLE 10.

CIGARETTE DELIVERY SALE REQUIREMENTS.

§ 18.2-246.6. Definitions.

For purposes of this article:

"Adult" means a person who is at least the legal minimum purchasing age.

(Effective until July 1, 2018) *"Board"* means the Virginia Alcoholic Beverage Control Board.

(Effective July 1, 2018) *"Board"* means the Board of Directors of the Virginia Alcoholic Beverage Control Authority.

"Consumer" means an individual who is not permitted as a wholesaler pursuant to § 58.1-1011 or who is not a retailer.

"Delivery sale" means any sale of cigarettes to a consumer in the Commonwealth regardless of whether the seller is located in the Commonwealth where either (i) the purchaser submits the order for such sale by means of a telephonic or other method of voice transmission, the mails or any other delivery service, or the Internet or other online service; or (ii) the cigarettes are delivered by use of the mails or a delivery service. A sale of cigarettes not for personal consumption to a person who is a wholesale dealer or retail dealer, as such terms are defined in § 58.1-1000, shall not be a delivery sale. A delivery of cigarettes, not through the mail or by a common carrier, to a consumer performed by the owner, employee or other individual acting on behalf of a retailer authorized to sell such cigarettes shall not be a delivery sale.

"Delivery service" means any person who is engaged in the commercial delivery of letters, packages, or other containers.

"Legal minimum purchasing age" is the minimum age at which an individual may legally purchase cigarettes in the Commonwealth.

"Mails" or *"mailing"* means the shipment of cigarettes through the United States Postal Service.

"Shipping container" means a container in which cigarettes are shipped in connection with a delivery sale.

"Shipping documents" means bills of lading, airbills, or any other documents used to evidence the undertaking by a delivery service to deliver letters, packages, or other containers.

History.
2003, c. 1010; 2005, c. 839; 2015, cc. 38, 730.

§ 18.2-246.7. Requirements for delivery sales.

A. No person shall make a delivery sale of cigarettes to any individual who is under the legal minimum purchase age in the Commonwealth.

B. Each person accepting a purchase order for a delivery sale shall comply with:

1. The age verification requirements set forth in § 18.2-246.8;
2. The disclosure requirements set forth in § 18.2-246.9;
3. The shipping requirements set forth in § 18.2-246.10;
4. The registration and reporting requirements set forth in § 18.2-246.11;
5. The tax collection requirements set forth in § 18.2-246.12; and
6. All other laws of the Commonwealth generally applicable to sales of cigarettes that occur entirely within the Commonwealth, including, but not limited to, those laws imposing: (i) excise taxes, (ii) sales taxes, and (iii) license and revenue-stamping requirements.

History.
2003, c. 1010.

§ 18.2-246.8. Age verification requirements.

A. No person shall mail, ship, or otherwise deliver cigarettes in connection with a delivery sale unless prior to the first delivery sale to a consumer such person:

1. Obtains from the prospective consumer a certification that includes (i) a reliable confirmation that the consumer is at least the legal minimum purchase age, and (ii) a statement signed by the prospective consumer in writing that certifies the prospective consumer's address and that the consumer is at least 18 years of age. Such statement shall also confirm (a) that the prospective consumer understands that signing another person's name to such certification is illegal, (b) that the sale of cigarettes to individuals under the legal minimum purchase age is illegal, and (c) that the purchase of cigarettes by individuals under the legal minimum purchase age is illegal under the laws of the Commonwealth;
2. Makes a good faith effort to verify the information contained in the certification provided by the prospective consumer pursuant to subsection A against a commercially available database of valid, government-issued identification that contains the date of birth or age of the individual placing the order, or obtains a photocopy or other image of the valid, government-issued identification stating the date of birth or age of the individual placing the order;
3. Provides to the prospective consumer, via e-mail or other means, a notice that meets the requirements of § 18.2-246.9; and

Crimes and Offenses

4. Receives payment for the delivery sale from the prospective consumer by a credit or debit card that has been issued in such consumer's name or by a check drawn on the consumer's account.

B. Persons accepting purchase orders made via the Internet for delivery sales may request that prospective consumers provide their e-mail addresses.

History.
2003, c. 1010.

§ 18.2-246.9. Disclosure requirements.

The notice required under subdivision A 3 of § 18.2-246.8 shall include:

1. A prominent and clearly legible statement that cigarette sales to consumers below the legal minimum purchase age are illegal;

2. A prominent and clearly legible statement that consists of one of the warnings set forth in section 4(a)(1) of the Federal Cigarette Labeling and Advertising Act (15 U.S.C. § 1333(a)(1)) rotated on a quarterly basis;

3. A prominent and clearly legible statement that sales of cigarettes are restricted to those consumers who provide verifiable proof of age in accordance with § 18.2-246.8; and

4. A prominent and clearly legible statement that cigarette sales are subject to tax under § 58.1-1001, and an explanation of how such tax has been, or is to be, paid with respect to such delivery sale.

History.
2003, c. 1010.

§ 18.2-246.10. Shipping requirements.

Each person who mails, ships, or otherwise delivers cigarettes in connection with a delivery sale:

1. Shall include as part of the shipping documents a clear and conspicuous statement providing as follows: "Cigarettes: Virginia Law Prohibits Shipping to Individuals Under 18, and Requires the Payment of all Applicable Taxes";

2. Shall use a method of mailing, shipping, or delivery that obligates the delivery service or any party making delivery to require (i) the consumer placing the purchase order for the delivery sale, or an adult of legal minimum purchase age, to sign to accept delivery of the shipping container, and (ii) proof, in the form of a valid, government-issued identification bearing a photograph of the individual who signs to accept delivery of the shipping container, demonstrating that he is either the addressee who is of legal minimum purchase age or another adult of legal minimum purchase age. However, proof of the legal minimum purchase age shall be required only if such individual appears to be under 27 years of age; and

3. Shall provide to the delivery service retained for such delivery sale evidence of full compliance with § 18.2-246.12.

History.
2003, c. 1010.

§ 18.2-246.11. Registration and reporting requirements.

A. Prior to making delivery sales or mailing, shipping, or otherwise delivering cigarettes in connection with any such delivery sales, every person shall file with the Board and with the Attorney General a statement setting forth such person's name, trade name, and the address of such person's principal place of business and any other place of business.

B. Not later than the tenth day of each calendar month, each person that has made a delivery sale or mailed, shipped, or otherwise delivered cigarettes in connection with any such delivery sale during the previous calendar month shall file with the Board and with the Attorney General a report in the format prescribed by the Board, which may include an electronic format, that provides for each and every such delivery sale:

1. The name and address of the consumer to whom such delivery sale was made;

2. The brand or brands of the cigarettes that were sold in such delivery sale; and

3. The quantity of cigarettes that were sold in such delivery sale.

C. Any person who satisfies the requirements of § 376 of Title 15 of the United States Code shall be deemed to satisfy the requirements of this section.

D. For purposes of any penalty that may be imposed for a violation of this section, a failure to file a particular statement or report with both the Board and the Attorney General shall constitute a single violation.

History.
2003, c. 1010; 2009, c. 847.

§ 18.2-246.12. Collection of taxes.

Each person accepting a purchase order for a delivery sale shall collect and remit to the Board all cigarette taxes imposed by the Commonwealth with respect to such delivery sale, except that such collection and remission shall not be required to the extent such person has obtained proof (in the form of the presence of applicable revenue stamps or otherwise) that such taxes already have been paid to the Commonwealth. In the event the Board finds that any tax imposed by the Commonwealth and administered by the Department of Taxation has not been collected and remitted, the Board shall provide the Department of Taxation with a notification of such sale which shall include:

1. The name and address of the consumer to whom such sale was made;

2. The name and address of the seller of the cigarettes;

3. The brand or brands of the cigarettes that were sold in such sale; and

4. The quantity of cigarettes that were sold in such sale.

History.
2003, c. 1010.

§ 18.2-246.13. Civil penalties; penalties.

A. In addition to any criminal penalties for violations of this article and except for civil penalties otherwise provided in this article, a first violation of any provision of this article shall be punishable by a civil penalty of no more than $1,000. A second or subsequent violation of any provision of this article shall be punishable by a civil penalty of no more than $10,000.

B. Any prospective consumer who knowingly submits a false certification under subdivision A 1 of § 18.2-246.8 shall be subject to a civil penalty of no more than $5,000 for each such offense.

C. Any person failing to collect or remit to the Board or the Department of Taxation any tax required in connection with a delivery sale shall be assessed, in addition to any other applicable penalty, a civil penalty of no more than five times the retail value of the cigarettes involved.

D. Any civil penalty collected under this article shall be paid to the general fund.

E. Any person who fails to file the statement required by subsection A of § 18.2-246.11 and thereafter makes a delivery sale is guilty of a Class 1 misdemeanor and for any second or subsequent offense is guilty of a violation of § 18.2-498.3.

F. Any person who knowingly and with the intent to defraud, mislead, or deceive makes a statement filed as required by subsection A of § 18.2-246.11 which is false is guilty of a violation of § 18.2-498.3. Each such filed statement containing one or more false statements shall constitute a separate offense.

G. Any person who fails to make the report required by subsection B of § 18.2-246.11 is guilty of a Class 1 misdemeanor and for any second or subsequent offense is guilty of a violation of § 18.2-498.3.

H. Any person who knowingly and with the intent to defraud, mislead, or deceive makes a materially false statement in any report required by subsection B of § 18.2-246.11 is guilty of a violation of § 18.2-498.3. Each such report containing one or more false statements constitutes a separate offense.

History.
2003, c. 1010; 2004, c. 995; 2009, c. 847; 2013, c. 625.

§ 18.2-246.14. Counterfeit cigarettes; penalty; civil penalty.

A. It is unlawful to distribute or possess counterfeit cigarettes.

B. Any person who knowingly distributes or possesses with the intent to distribute a total quantity of less than 10 cartons of counterfeit cigarettes is guilty of a Class 1 misdemeanor. Any person who is convicted of a second or subsequent offense involving a total quantity of less than 10 cartons of counterfeit cigarettes is guilty of a Class 6 felony, provided that the accused was at liberty as defined in § 53.1-151 between each conviction, and it is admitted, or found by the jury or judge before whom the person is tried, that the accused was previously convicted of a violation of this subsection. Any person who knowingly distributes or possesses with the intent to distribute a total quantity of 10 or more cartons of counterfeit cigarettes is guilty of a Class 6 felony.

C. Any person who knowingly violates subsection A with a total quantity of less than two cartons of cigarettes shall be punished by a civil penalty of no more than $1,000. Any person who knowingly violates subsection A shall, for a second or subsequent offense involving a total quantity of less than two cartons of cigarettes, be punished by a civil penalty of no more than $5,000 and, if applicable, the revocation by the Department of Taxation of his wholesale dealer license.

D. Any person who knowingly violates subsection A with a total quantity of two or more cartons of cigarettes shall be punished by a civil penalty of no more than $2,000. Any person who knowingly violates subsection A shall, for a second or subsequent offense involving a total quantity of two or more cartons of cigarettes, be punished by a civil penalty of no more than $50,000 and, if applicable, the revocation by the Department of Taxation of his wholesale dealer license.

For purposes of this section, counterfeit cigarettes shall include but not be limited to cigarettes that (i) have false manufacturing labels, (ii) are not manufactured by the manufacturer indicated on the container, or (iii) have affixed to the container a false tax stamp.

History.
2003, c. 1010; 2004, c. 995; 2013, c. 625.

§ 18.2-246.15. Enforcement.

The Attorney General is authorized to enforce the provisions of this article. The Attorney General may assess the civil penalties authorized by this article, with the concurrence of the attorney for the Commonwealth pursuant to § 2.2-511, may prosecute criminal violations under this article, and may bring an action in the appropriate court to collect assessed penalties or prevent or restrain violations of this article by any person, or any person controlling such person. The Board and the State Department of Taxation shall cooperate with the Attorney General in his enforcement efforts and provide to the Attorney General all information and documentation in their possession necessary for the Attorney General to accomplish such enforcement.

History.
2003, c. 1010; 2009, c. 847; 2013, c. 625.

CHAPTER 7.

CRIMES INVOLVING HEALTH AND SAFETY.

Article 1.

Drugs.

Article 1.1.

Drug Paraphernalia.

Article 1.2.

Sale of Ephedrine or Related Compounds.

Article 1.3.

Dextromethorphan Distribution Act.

Article 2.

Driving Motor Vehicle, etc., While Intoxicated.

Article 3.

Transporting Dangerous Articles.

Article 3.1.

Transportation of Hazardous Materials.

Article 4.

Dangerous Use of Firearms or Other Weapons.

Article 5.

Uniform Machine Gun Act.

Article 6.

"Sawed-off" Shotgun and "Sawed-off" Rifle Act.

Article 6.1.

Concealed Weapons and Concealed Handgun Permits.

Article 7.

Other Illegal Weapons.

ARTICLE 1.

DRUGS.

§ 18.2-247. Use of terms "controlled substances," "marijuana," "Schedules I, II, III, IV, V and VI," "imitation controlled substance" and "counterfeit controlled substance" in Title 18.2.

A. Wherever the terms *"controlled substances"* and *"Schedules I, II, III, IV, V and VI"* are used in Title 18.2, such terms refer to those terms as they are used or defined in the Drug Control Act (§ 54.1-3400 et seq.).

B. The term *"imitation controlled substance"* when used in this article means (i) a counterfeit controlled substance or (ii) a pill, capsule, tablet, or substance in any form whatsoever which is not a controlled substance subject to abuse, and:

1. Which by overall dosage unit appearance, including color, shape, size, marking and packaging or by representations made, would cause the likelihood that such a pill, capsule, tablet, or substance in any other form whatsoever will be mistaken for a controlled substance unless such substance was introduced into commerce prior to the initial introduction into commerce of the controlled substance which it is alleged to imitate; or

2. Which by express or implied representations purports to act like a controlled substance as a stimulant or depressant of the central nervous system and which is not commonly used or recognized for use in that particular formulation for any purpose other than for such stimulant or depressant effect, unless marketed, promoted, or sold as permitted by the United States Food and Drug Administration.

C. In determining whether a pill, capsule, tablet, or substance in any other form whatsoever, is an "imitation controlled substance," there shall be considered, in addition to all other relevant factors, comparisons with accepted methods of marketing for legitimate nonprescription drugs for medicinal purposes rather than for drug abuse or any similar nonmedicinal use, including consideration of the packaging of the drug and its appearance in overall finished dosage form, promotional materials or representations, oral or written, concerning the drug, and the methods of distribution of the drug and where and how it is sold to the public.

D. The term *"marijuana"* when used in this article means any part of a plant of the genus Cannabis, whether growing or not, its seeds or resin; and every compound, manufacture, salt, derivative, mixture, or preparation of such plant, its seeds, or its resin. Marijuana shall not include any oily extract containing one or more cannabinoids unless such extract contains less than 12 percent of tetrahydrocannabinol by weight, or the mature stalks of such plant, fiber produced from such stalk, oil or cake made from the seed of such plant, unless such stalks, fiber, oil or cake is combined with other parts of plants of the genus Cannabis.

E. The term *"counterfeit controlled substance"* means a controlled substance that, without authorization, bears, is packaged in a container or wrapper that bears, or is otherwise labeled to bear, the trademark, trade name, or other identifying mark, imprint or device or any likeness thereof, of a drug manufacturer, processor, packer, or distributor other than the manufacturer, processor, packer, or distributor who did in fact so manufacture, process, pack or distribute such drug.

History.
1975, cc. 14, 15; 1979, c. 435; 1982, c. 462; 1984, c. 684; 1992, c. 756; 1999, cc. 661, 722; 2004, c. 688.

§ 18.2-248. Manufacturing, selling, giving, distributing, or possessing with intent to manufacture, sell, give, or distribute a controlled substance or an imitation controlled substance prohibited; penalties.

A. Except as authorized in the Drug Control Act (§ 54.1-3400 et seq.), it shall be unlawful for any person to manufacture, sell, give, distribute, or possess with intent to manufacture, sell, give or distribute a controlled substance or an imitation controlled substance.

B. In determining whether any person intends to manufacture, sell, give or distribute an imitation controlled substance, the court may consider, in addition to all other relevant evidence, whether any distribution or attempted distribution of such pill, capsule, tablet or substance in any other form whatsoever included an exchange of or a demand for money or other property as consideration, and, if so, whether the amount of such consideration was substantially greater than the reasonable value of such pill, capsule, tablet or substance in any other form whatsoever, considering the actual chemical composition of such pill, capsule, tablet or substance in any other form whatsoever and, where applicable, the price at which over-the-counter substances of like chemical composition sell.

C. Except as provided in subsection C1, any person who violates this section with respect to a controlled substance classified in Schedule I or II shall upon conviction be imprisoned for not less than five nor more than 40 years and fined not more than $500,000. Upon a second conviction of such a violation, and it is alleged in the warrant, indictment, or information that the person has been before convicted of such an offense or of a substantially similar offense in any other jurisdiction, which offense would be a felony if committed in the Commonwealth, and such prior conviction occurred before the date of the offense alleged in the warrant, indictment, or information, any such person may, in the discretion of the court or jury imposing the sentence, be sentenced to imprisonment for life or for any period not less than five years, three years of which shall be a mandatory minimum term of imprisonment to be served consecutively with any other sentence, and he shall be fined not more than $500,000.

When a person is convicted of a third or subsequent offense under this subsection and it is alleged in the warrant, indictment or information that he has been before convicted of two or more such offenses or of substantially similar offenses in any other jurisdiction which offenses would be felonies if committed in the Commonwealth and such prior convictions occurred before the date of the offense alleged in the warrant, indictment, or information, he shall be sentenced to imprisonment for life or for a period of not less than 10 years, 10 years of which shall be a mandatory minimum term of imprisonment to be served consecutively with any other sentence, and he shall be fined not more than $500,000.

Any person who manufactures, sells, gives, distributes or possesses with the intent to manufacture, sell, give, or distribute the following is guilty of a felony punishable by a fine of not more than $1 million and imprisonment for five years to life, five years of which shall be a mandatory minimum term of imprisonment to be served consecutively with any other sentence:

1. 100 grams or more of a mixture or substance containing a detectable amount of heroin;

2. 500 grams or more of a mixture or substance containing a detectable amount of:

a. Coca leaves, except coca leaves and extracts of coca leaves from which cocaine, ecgonine, and derivatives of ecgonine or their salts have been removed;

b. Cocaine, its salts, optical and geometric isomers, and salts of isomers;

c. Ecgonine, its derivatives, their salts, isomers, and salts of isomers; or

d. Any compound, mixture, or preparation that contains any quantity of any of the substances referred to in subdivisions 2a through 2c;

3. 250 grams or more of a mixture or substance described in subdivisions 2a through 2d that contain cocaine base; or

4. 10 grams or more of methamphetamine, its salts, isomers, or salts of its isomers or 20 grams or more of a mixture or substance containing a detectable amount of methamphetamine, its salts, isomers, or salts of its isomers.

The mandatory minimum term of imprisonment to be imposed for a violation of this subsection shall not be applicable if the court finds that:

a. The person does not have a prior conviction for an offense listed in subsection C of § 17.1-805;

b. The person did not use violence or credible threats of violence or possess a firearm or other dangerous weapon in connection with the offense or induce another participant in the offense to do so;

c. The offense did not result in death or serious bodily injury to any person;

d. The person was not an organizer, leader, manager, or supervisor of others in the offense, and was not engaged in a continuing criminal enterprise as defined in subsection I; and

e. Not later than the time of the sentencing hearing, the person has truthfully provided to the Commonwealth all information and evidence the person has concerning the offense or offenses that were part of the same course of conduct or of a common scheme or plan, but the fact that the person has no relevant or useful other information to provide or that the Commonwealth already is aware of the information shall not preclude a determination by the court that the defendant has complied with this requirement.

C1. Any person who violates this section with respect to the manufacturing of methamphetamine, its salts, isomers, or salts of its isomers or less than 200 grams of a mixture or substance containing a detectable amount of methamphetamine, its salts, isomers, or salts of its isomers shall, upon conviction, be imprisoned for not less than 10 nor more than 40 years and fined not more than $500,000. Upon a second conviction of such a violation, any such person may, in the discretion of the court or jury imposing the sentence, be sentenced to imprisonment for life or for any period not less than 10 years, and be fined not more than $500,000. When a person is convicted of a third or subsequent offense under this subsection and it is alleged in the warrant, indictment, or information that he has been previously convicted of two or more such offenses or of substantially similar offenses in any other jurisdiction, which offenses would be felonies if committed in the Commonwealth and such prior convictions occurred before the date of the offense alleged in the warrant, indictment, or information, he shall be sentenced to imprisonment for life or for a period not less than 10 years, three years of which shall be a mandatory minimum term of imprisonment to be served consecutively with any other sentence and he shall be fined not more than $500,000.

Upon conviction, in addition to any other punishment, a person found guilty of this offense shall be ordered by the court to make restitution, as the court deems appropriate, to any innocent property owner whose property is damaged, destroyed, or otherwise rendered unusable as a result of such methamphetamine production. This restitution shall include the person's or his estate's estimated or actual expenses associated with cleanup, removal, or repair of the affected property. If the property that is damaged, destroyed, or otherwise rendered unusable as a result of such methamphetamine production is property owned in whole or in part by the person convicted, the court shall order the person to pay to the Methamphetamine Cleanup Fund authorized in § 18.2-248.04 the reasonable estimated or actual expenses associated with cleanup, removal, or repair of the affected property or, if actual or estimated expenses cannot be determined, the sum of $10,000. The convicted person shall also pay the cost of certifying that any building that is cleaned up or repaired pursuant to this section is safe for human occupancy according to the guidelines established pursuant to § 32.1-11.7.

D. If such person proves that he gave, distributed or possessed with intent to give or distribute a controlled substance classified in Schedule I or II only as an accommodation to another individual who is not an inmate in a community correctional facility, local correctional facility or state correctional facility as defined in § 53.1-1 or in the custody of an employee thereof, and not with intent to profit thereby from any consideration received or expected nor to induce the recipient or intended recipient of the controlled substance to use or become addicted to or dependent upon such controlled substance, he shall be guilty of a Class 5 felony.

E. If the violation of the provisions of this article consists of the filling by a pharmacist of the prescription of a person authorized under this article to issue the same, which prescription has not been received in writing by the pharmacist prior to the filling thereof, and such written prescription is in fact received by the pharmacist within one week of the time of filling the same, or if such violation consists of a request by such authorized person for the filling by a pharmacist of a prescription which has not been received in writing by the pharmacist and such prescription is, in fact, written at the time of such request and delivered to the pharmacist within one week thereof, either such offense shall constitute a Class 4 misdemeanor.

E1. Any person who violates this section with respect to a controlled substance classified in Schedule III except for an anabolic steroid classified in Schedule III, constituting a violation of § 18.2-248.5, shall be guilty of a Class 5 felony.

E2. Any person who violates this section with respect to a controlled substance classified in Schedule IV shall be guilty of a Class 6 felony.

E3. Any person who proves that he gave, distributed or possessed with the intent to give or distribute a controlled substance classified in Schedule III or IV, except for an anabolic steroid classified in Schedule III, constituting a violation of § 18.2-248.5, only as an accommodation to another individual who is not an inmate in a community correctional facility, local correctional facility or state correctional facility as defined in § 53.1-1 or in the custody of an employee thereof, and not with the intent to profit thereby from any consideration received or expected nor to induce the recipient or intended recipient of the controlled substance to use or become addicted to or dependent upon such controlled substance, is guilty of a Class 1 misdemeanor.

F. Any person who violates this section with respect to a controlled substance classified in Schedule V or Schedule VI or an imitation controlled substance which imitates a controlled substance classified in Schedule V or Schedule VI, shall be guilty of a Class 1 misdemeanor.

G. Any person who violates this section with respect to an imitation controlled substance which imitates a controlled substance classified in Schedule I, II, III, or IV shall be guilty of a Class 6 felony. In any prosecution brought under this subsection, it is not a defense to a violation of this subsection that the defendant believed the imitation controlled substance to actually be a controlled substance.

H. Any person who manufactures, sells, gives, distributes or possesses with the intent to manufacture, sell, give or distribute the following:

1. 1.0 kilograms or more of a mixture or substance containing a detectable amount of heroin;

2. 5.0 kilograms or more of a mixture or substance containing a detectable amount of:

a. Coca leaves, except coca leaves and extracts of coca leaves from which cocaine, ecgonine, and derivatives of ecgonine or their salts have been removed;

b. Cocaine, its salts, optical and geometric isomers, and salts of isomers;

c. Ecgonine, its derivatives, their salts, isomers, and salts of isomers; or

d. Any compound, mixture, or preparation which contains any quantity of any of the substances referred to in subdivisions a through c;

3. 2.5 kilograms or more of a mixture or substance described in subdivision 2 which contains cocaine base;

4. 100 kilograms or more of a mixture or substance containing a detectable amount of marijuana; or

5. 100 grams or more of methamphetamine, its salts, isomers, or salts of its isomers or 200 grams or more of a mixture or substance containing a detectable amount of methamphetamine, its salts, isomers, or salts of its isomers shall be guilty of a felony punishable by a fine of not more than $1 million and imprisonment for 20 years to life, 20 years of which shall be a mandatory minimum sentence. Such mandatory minimum sentence shall not be applicable if the court finds that (i) the person does not have a prior conviction for an offense listed in subsection C of § 17.1-805; (ii) the person did not use violence or credible threats of violence or possess a firearm or other dangerous weapon in connection with the offense or induce another participant in the offense to do so; (iii) the offense did not result in death or serious bodily injury to any person; (iv) the person was not an organizer, leader, manager, or supervisor of others in the offense, and was not engaged in a continuing criminal enterprise as defined in subsection I of this section; and (v) not later than the time of the sentencing hearing, the person has truthfully provided to the Commonwealth all information and evidence the person has concerning the offense or offenses that were part of the same course of conduct or of a common scheme or plan, but the fact that the person has no relevant or useful other information to provide or that the Commonwealth already is aware of the information shall not preclude a determination by the court that the defendant has complied with this requirement.

H1. Any person who was the principal or one of several principal administrators, organizers or leaders of a continuing criminal enterprise shall be guilty of a felony if (i) the enterprise received at least $100,000 but less than $250,000 in gross receipts during any 12-month period of its existence from the manufacture, importation, or distribution of heroin or cocaine or ecgonine or methamphetamine or the derivatives, salts, isomers, or salts of isomers thereof or marijuana or (ii) the person engaged in the enterprise to manufacture, sell, give, distribute or possess with the intent to manufacture, sell, give or distribute the following during any 12-month period of its existence:

1. At least 1.0 kilograms but less than 5.0 kilograms of a mixture or substance containing a detectable amount of heroin;

2. At least 5.0 kilograms but less than 10 kilograms of a mixture or substance containing a detectable amount of:

a. Coca leaves, except coca leaves and extracts of coca leaves from which cocaine, ecgonine, and derivatives of ecgonine or their salts have been removed;

b. Cocaine, its salts, optical and geometric isomers, and salts of isomers;

c. Ecgonine, its derivatives, their salts, isomers, and salts of isomers; or

d. Any compound, mixture, or preparation which contains any quantity of any of the substances referred to in subdivisions a through c;

3. At least 2.5 kilograms but less than 5.0 kilograms of a mixture or substance described in subdivision 2 which contains cocaine base;

4. At least 100 kilograms but less than 250 kilograms of a mixture or substance containing a detectable amount of marijuana; or

5. At least 100 grams but less than 250 grams of methamphetamine, its salts, isomers, or salts of its isomers or at least 200 grams but less than 1.0 kilograms of a mixture or substance containing a detectable amount of methamphetamine, its salts, isomers, or salts of its isomers.

A conviction under this section shall be punishable by a fine of not more than $1 million and imprisonment for 20 years to life, 20 years of which shall be a mandatory minimum sentence.

H2. Any person who was the principal or one of several principal administrators, organizers or leaders of a continuing criminal enterprise if (i) the enterprise received $250,000 or more in gross receipts during any 12-month period of its existence from the manufacture, importation, or distribution of heroin or cocaine or ecgonine or methamphetamine or the derivatives, salts, isomers, or salts of isomers thereof or marijuana or (ii) the person engaged in the enterprise to manufacture, sell, give, distribute or possess with the intent to manufacture, sell, give or distribute the following during any 12-month period of its existence:

1. At least 5.0 kilograms of a mixture or substance containing a detectable amount of heroin;

2. At least 10 kilograms of a mixture or substance containing a detectable amount of:

a. Coca leaves, except coca leaves and extracts of coca leaves from which cocaine, ecgonine, and derivatives of ecgonine or their salts have been removed;

b. Cocaine, its salts, optical and geometric isomers, and salts of isomers;

c. Ecgonine, its derivatives, their salts, isomers, and salts of isomers; or

d. Any compound, mixture, or preparation which contains any quantity of any of the substances referred to in subdivisions a through c;

3. At least 5.0 kilograms of a mixture or substance described in subdivision 2 which contains cocaine base;

4. At least 250 kilograms of a mixture or substance containing a detectable amount of marijuana; or

5. At least 250 grams of methamphetamine, its salts, isomers, or salts of its isomers or at least 1.0 kilograms of a mixture or substance containing a detectable amount of methamphetamine, its salts, isomers, or salts of its isomers shall be guilty of a felony punishable by a fine of not more than $1 million and imprisonment for life, which shall be served with no suspension in whole or in part. Such punishment shall be made to run consecutively with any other sentence. However, the court may impose a mandatory minimum sentence of 40 years if the court finds that the defendant substantially cooperated with law-enforcement authorities.

I. For purposes of this section, a person is engaged in a continuing criminal enterprise if (i) he violates any provision of this section, the punishment for which is a felony and either (ii) such violation is a part of a continuing series of violations of this section which are undertaken by such person in concert with five or more other persons with respect to whom such person occupies a position of organizer, a supervisory position, or any other position of management, and from which such person obtains substantial income or resources or (iii) such violation is committed, with respect to methamphetamine or other controlled substance classified in Schedule I or II, for the benefit of, at the direction of, or in association with any criminal street gang as defined in § 18.2-46.1.

J. Except as authorized in the Drug Control Act (§ 54.1-3400 et seq.), any person who possesses any two or more different substances listed below with the intent to manufacture methamphetamine, methcathinone, or amphetamine is guilty of a Class 6 felony: liquified ammonia gas, ammonium nitrate, ether, hypophosphorus acid solutions, hypophosphite salts, hydrochloric acid, iodine crystals or tincture of iodine, phenylacetone, phenylacetic acid, red phosphorus, methylamine, methyl formamide, lithium, sodium metal, sulfuric acid, sodium hydroxide, potassium dichromate, sodium dichromate, potassium permanganate, chromium trioxide, methylbenzene, methamphetamine precursor drugs, trichloroethane, or 2-propanone.

K. The term "methamphetamine precursor drug," when used in this article, means a drug or product containing ephedrine, pseudoephedrine, or phenylpropanolamine or any of their salts, optical isomers, or salts of optical isomers.

History.

Code 1950, § 54-524.101:1; 1972, c. 798; 1973, c. 479; 1974, c. 586; 1975, cc. 14, 15; 1976, c. 614; 1977, c. 409; 1978, cc. 177, 779; 1979, c. 435; 1982, cc. 276, 462; 1985, c. 569; 1986, c. 453; 1988, c. 355; 1990, c. 82; 1991, c. 13; 1992, cc. 685, 737, 756; 1995, c. 538; 1999, c. 722; 2000, cc. 1020, 1041; 2004, c. 461; 2005, cc. 174, 759, 796, 923, 941; 2006, cc. 697, 759; 2008, cc. 79, 618; 2009, c. 750; 2012, cc. 219, 710, 844; 2013, c. 426; 2014, c. 513.

§ 18.2-248.01. Transporting controlled substances into the Commonwealth; penalty.

Except as authorized in the Drug Control Act (§ 54.1-3400 et seq.) it is unlawful for any person to transport into the Commonwealth by any means with intent to sell or distribute one ounce or more of cocaine, coca leaves or any salt, compound, derivative or preparation thereof as described in Schedule II of the Drug Control Act or one ounce or more of any other Schedule I or II controlled substance or five or more pounds of marijuana. A violation of this section shall constitute a separate and distinct felony. Upon conviction, the person shall be sentenced to not less than five years nor more than 40 years imprisonment, three years of which shall be a mandatory minimum term of imprisonment, and a fine not to exceed $1,000,000. A second or subsequent conviction hereunder shall be punishable by a mandatory minimum term of imprisonment of 10 years, which shall be served consecutively with any other sentence.

History.

1992, c. 723; 2000, cc. 1020, 1041; 2004, c. 461.

§ 18.2-248.02. Allowing a minor or incapacitated person to be present during manufacture or attempted manufacture of methamphetamine prohibited; penalties.

Any person 18 years of age or older who knowingly allows (i) a minor under the age of 15, (ii) a minor 15 years of age or older with whom he maintains a custodial relationship, including but not limited to as a parent, step-parent, grandparent, step-grandparent, or who stands in loco parentis with respect to such minor, or (iii) a mentally incapacitated or physically helpless person of any age, to be present in the same dwelling, apartment as defined by § 55-79.2, unit of a hotel as defined in § 35.1-1, garage, shed, or vehicle during the manufacture or attempted manufacture of methamphetamine as prohibited by subsection C1 of § 18.2-248 is guilty of a felony punishable by imprisonment for not less than 10 nor more than 40 years. This penalty shall be in addition to and served consecutively with any other sentence.

History.
2005, cc. 923, 941; 2013, c. 743.

§ 18.2-248.03. Manufacturing, selling, giving, distributing, or possessing with intent to manufacture, sell, give, or distribute methamphetamine; penalty.

A. Notwithstanding any other provision of law, any person who manufactures, sells, gives, distributes, or possesses with intent to manufacture, sell, give, or distribute 28 grams or more of a mixture or substance containing a detectable amount of methamphetamine, its salts, isomers, or salts of its isomers is guilty of a felony punishable by a fine of not more than $500,000 and imprisonment for not less than five nor more than 40 years, three years of which shall be a mandatory minimum term of imprisonment to be served consecutively with any other sentence.

B. Notwithstanding any other provision of law, any person who manufactures, sells, gives, distributes, or possesses with intent to manufacture, sell, give, or distribute 227 grams or more of a mixture or substance containing a detectable amount of methamphetamine, its salts, isomers, or salts of its isomers is guilty of a felony punishable by a fine of not more than $1 million and imprisonment for not less than five years nor more than life, five years of which shall be a mandatory minimum term of imprisonment to be served consecutively with any other sentence.

History.
2008, cc. 858, 874.

§ 18.2-248.04. Methamphetamine Cleanup Fund established.

There is hereby created in the state treasury a special nonreverting fund to be known as the Methamphetamine Cleanup Fund, hereafter referred to as "the Fund." The Fund shall be established on the books of the Comptroller. All moneys assessed against a person convicted of manufacture of methamphetamine as methamphetamine cleanup funds pursuant to subsection C1 of § 18.2-248 shall be paid into the state treasury and credited to the Fund. Interest earned on moneys in the Fund shall remain in the Fund and be credited to it. Any moneys remaining in the Fund, including interest thereon, at the end of each fiscal year shall not revert to the general fund but shall remain in the Fund. Moneys in the Fund shall be used solely for the purposes of restoration to an environmentally sound state sites used for the criminal manufacture of methamphetamine. Expenditures and disbursements from the Fund shall be made by the State Treasurer on warrants issued by the Comptroller upon written request signed by any agency of the Commonwealth, law-enforcement agency, or locality with the responsibility for and engaged in a specific methamphetamine site cleanup.

History.
2012, c. 219.

§ 18.2-248.1. Penalties for sale, gift, distribution or possession with intent to sell, give or distribute marijuana.

Except as authorized in the Drug Control Act, Chapter 34 of Title 54.1, it shall be unlawful for any person to sell, give, distribute or possess with intent to sell, give or distribute marijuana.

(a) Any person who violates this section with respect to:

(1) Not more than one-half ounce of marijuana is guilty of a Class 1 misdemeanor;

(2) More than one-half ounce but not more than five pounds of marijuana is guilty of a Class 5 felony;

(3) More than five pounds of marijuana is guilty of a felony punishable by imprisonment of not less than five nor more than 30 years.

If such person proves that he gave, distributed or possessed with intent to give or distribute marijuana only as an accommodation to another individual and not with intent to profit thereby from any consideration received or expected nor to induce the recipient or intended recipient of the marijuana to use or become addicted to or dependent upon such marijuana, he shall be guilty of a Class 1 misdemeanor.

(b) Any person who gives, distributes or possesses marijuana as an accommodation and not with intent to profit thereby, to an inmate of a state or local correctional facility as defined in § 53.1-1, or in the custody of an employee thereof shall be guilty of a Class 4 felony.

(c) Any person who manufactures marijuana, or possesses marijuana with the intent to manufacture such substance, not for his own use is guilty of a felony punishable by imprisonment of not less than five nor more than 30 years and a fine not to exceed $10,000.

(d) When a person is convicted of a third or subsequent felony offense under this section and it is alleged in the warrant, indictment or information that he has been before convicted of two or more felony offenses under this section or of substantially similar offenses in any other jurisdiction which offenses would be felonies if committed in the Commonwealth and such prior convictions occurred before the date of the offense alleged in the warrant, indictment or information, he shall be sentenced to imprisonment for life or for any period not less than five years, five years of which shall be a mandatory minimum term of imprisonment to be served consecutively with any other sentence and he shall be fined not more than $500,000.

History.

1979, c. 435; 1986, c. 467; 2000, cc. 819, 1020, 1041; 2004, c. 461; 2006, cc. 697, 759.

§ 18.2-248.1:1: Repealed by Acts 2014, cc. 674 and 719, cl. 2.

§ 18.2-248.2: Repealed by Acts 1981, c. 598.

Cross references.

For present provisions concerning drug paraphernalia, see §§ 18.2-265.1 through 18.2-265.5.

§ 18.2-248.3. Professional use of imitation controlled substances.

No civil or criminal liability shall be imposed by virtue of this article on any person licensed under the Drug Control Act, Chapter 34 of Title 54.1, who manufactures, sells, gives or distributes an imitation controlled substance for use as a placebo by a licensed practitioner in the course of professional practice or research.

History.

1982, c. 462.

§ 18.2-248.4. Advertisement of imitation controlled substances prohibited; penalty.

It shall be a Class 1 misdemeanor for any person knowingly to sell or display for sale, or to distribute, whether or not any charge is made therefor, any book, pamphlet, handbill or other printed matter which he knows is intended to promote the distribution of an imitation controlled substance.

History.

1982, c. 462.

§ 18.2-248.5. Illegal stimulants and steroids; penalty.

A. Except as authorized in the Drug Control Act (§ 54.1-3400 et seq.), Chapter 34 of Title 54.1, it shall be unlawful for any person to knowingly manufacture, sell, give, distribute or possess with intent to manufacture, sell, give or distribute any anabolic steroid.

A violation of subsection A shall be punishable by a term of imprisonment of not less than one year nor more than 10 years or, in the discretion of the jury or the court trying the case without a jury, confinement in jail for not more than 12 months or a fine of not more than $20,000, either or both. Any person violating the provisions of this subsection shall, upon conviction, be incarcerated for a mandatory minimum term of six months to be served consecutively with any other sentence.

B. It shall be unlawful for any person to knowingly sell or otherwise distribute, without prescription, to a minor any pill, capsule or tablet containing any combination of caffeine and ephedrine sulfate.

A violation of this subsection B shall be punishable as a Class 1 misdemeanor.

History.

1984, c. 620; 1988, c. 428; 1989, c. 567; 2000, cc. 1020, 1041; 2004, c. 461.

§§ 18.2-248.6, 18.2-248.7: Repealed by Acts 1999, c. 348, cl. 2.

§ 18.2-248.8: Repealed by Acts 2012, cc. 160 and 252, cl. 2, effective January 1, 2013.

Cross references.

For current provisions related to penalty for sale of methamphetamine precursors ephedrine and pseudoephedrine, see § 18.2-265.7.

§ 18.2-249: Repealed by Acts 2004, c. 995.

Cross references.

For current provisions as to seizure of property used in connection with or derived from illegal drug transactions, see § 19.2-386.22.

§ 18.2-250. Possession of controlled substances unlawful.

A. It is unlawful for any person knowingly or intentionally to possess a controlled substance unless the substance was obtained directly from, or pursuant to, a valid prescription or order of a practitioner while acting in the course of his professional practice, or except as otherwise authorized by the Drug Control Act (§ 54.1-3400 et seq.).

Upon the prosecution of a person for a violation of this section, ownership or occupancy of premises or vehicle upon or in which a controlled substance was found shall not create a presumption that such person either knowingly or intentionally possessed such controlled substance.

(a) Any person who violates this section with respect to any controlled substance classified in Schedule I or II of the Drug Control Act shall be guilty of a Class 5 felony, except that any person other than an inmate of a penal institution as defined in § 53.1-1 or in the custody of an employee thereof who violates this section with respect to a cannabimimetic agent is guilty of a Class 1 misdemeanor.

(b) Any person other than an inmate of a penal institution as defined in § 53.1-1 or in the custody of an employee thereof, who violates this section with respect to a controlled substance classified in Schedule III shall be guilty of a Class 1 misdemeanor.

(b1) Violation of this section with respect to a controlled substance classified in Schedule IV shall be punishable as a Class 2 misdemeanor.

(b2) Violation of this section with respect to a controlled substance classified in Schedule V shall be punishable as a Class 3 misdemeanor.

(c) Violation of this section with respect to a controlled substance classified in Schedule VI shall be punishable as a Class 4 misdemeanor.

B. The provisions of this section shall not apply to members of state, federal, county, city or town law-enforcement agencies, jail officers, or correctional officers, as defined in § 53.1-1, certified as handlers of dogs trained in the detection of controlled substances when possession of a controlled substance or substances is necessary in the performance of their duties.

History.

Code 1950, § 54-524.101:2; 1972, c. 798; 1973, c. 64; 1975, cc. 14, 15; 1976, c. 614; 1978, cc. 151, 177, 179; 1979, c. 435; 1980, c. 285; 1991, c. 649; 1998, c. 116; 2014, cc. 674, 719.

§ 18.2-250.1. Possession of marijuana unlawful.

A. It is unlawful for any person knowingly or intentionally to possess marijuana unless the substance was obtained directly from, or pursuant to, a valid prescription or order of a practitioner while acting in the course of his professional practice, or except as otherwise authorized by the Drug Control Act (§ 54.1-3400 et seq.).

Upon the prosecution of a person for violation of this section, ownership or occupancy of the premises or vehicle upon or in which marijuana was found shall not create a presumption that such person either knowingly or intentionally possessed such marijuana.

Any person who violates this section is guilty of a misdemeanor and shall be confined in jail not more than 30 days and fined not more than $500, either or both; any person, upon a second or subsequent conviction of a violation of this section, is guilty of a Class 1 misdemeanor.

B. The provisions of this section shall not apply to members of state, federal, county, city, or town law-enforcement agencies, jail officers, or correctional officers, as defined in § 53.1-1, certified as handlers of dogs trained in the detection of controlled substances when possession of marijuana is necessary for the performance of their duties.

C. In any prosecution under this section involving marijuana in the form of cannabidiol oil or THC-A oil as those terms are defined in § 54.1-3408.3, it shall be an affirmative defense that the individual possessed such oil pursuant to a valid written certification issued by a practitioner in the course of his professional practice pursuant to § 54.1-3408.3 for treatment or to alleviate the symptoms of (i) the individual's intractable epilepsy or (ii) if such individual is the parent or legal guardian of a minor, such minor's intractable epilepsy. If the individual files the valid written certification with the court at least 10 days prior to trial and causes a copy of such written certification to be delivered to the attorney for the Commonwealth, such written certification shall be prima facie evidence that such oil was possessed pursuant to a valid written certification.

History.

1979, c. 435; 1991, c. 649; 1998, c. 116; 2015, cc. 7, 8.

§ 18.2-251. Persons charged with first offense may be placed on probation; conditions; substance abuse screening, assessment treatment and education programs or services; drug tests; costs and fees; violations; discharge.

Whenever any person who has not previously been convicted of any offense under this article or under any statute of the United States or of any state relating to narcotic drugs, marijuana, or stimulant, depressant, or hallucinogenic drugs, or has not previously had a proceeding against him for violation of such an offense dismissed as provided in this section, pleads guilty to or enters a plea of not guilty to possession of a controlled substance under § 18.2-250 or to possession of marijuana under § 18.2-250.1, the court, upon such plea if the facts found by the court would justify a finding of guilt, without entering a judgment of guilt and with the consent of the accused, may defer further proceedings and place him on probation upon terms and conditions.

As a term or condition, the court shall require the accused to undergo a substance abuse assessment pursuant to § 18.2-251.01 or 19.2-299.2, as appropriate, and enter treatment and/or education program or services, if available, such as, in the opinion of the court, may be best suited to the needs of the accused based upon consideration of the substance abuse assessment. The program or services may be located in the judicial district in which the charge is brought or in any other judicial district as the court may provide. The services shall be provided by (i) a program licensed by the Department of Behavioral Health and Developmental Services, by a similar program which is made available through the Department of Corrections, (ii) a local community-based probation services agency established pursuant to § 9.1-174, or (iii) an ASAP program certified by the Commission on VASAP.

The court shall require the person entering such program under the provisions of this section to pay all or part of the costs of the program, including the costs of the screening, assessment, testing, and treatment, based upon the accused's ability to pay unless the person is determined by the court to be indigent.

As a condition of probation, the court shall require the accused (i) to successfully complete treatment or education program or services, (ii) to remain drug and alcohol free during the period of probation and submit to such tests during that period as may be necessary and appropriate to determine if the accused is drug and alcohol free, (iii) to make reasonable efforts to secure and maintain employment, and (iv) to comply with a plan of at least 100 hours of community service for a felony and up to 24 hours of community service for a misdemeanor. Such testing shall be conducted by personnel of the supervising probation agency or personnel of any program or agency approved by the supervising probation agency.

The court shall, unless done at arrest, order the accused to report to the original arresting law-enforcement agency to submit to fingerprinting.

Upon violation of a term or condition, the court may enter an adjudication of guilt and proceed as otherwise provided. Upon fulfillment of the terms and conditions, the court shall discharge the person and dismiss the proceedings against him. Discharge and dismissal under this section shall be without adjudication of guilt and is a conviction only for the purposes of applying this section in subsequent proceedings.

Notwithstanding any other provision of this section, whenever a court places an individual on probation upon terms and conditions pursuant to this section, such action shall be treated as a conviction for purposes of §§ 18.2-259.1, 22.1-315, and 46.2-390.1, and the driver's license forfeiture provisions of those sections shall be imposed. The provisions of this paragraph shall not be applicable to any offense for which a juvenile has had his license suspended or denied pursuant to § 16.1-278.9 for the same offense.

History.

Code 1950, § 54-524.101:3; 1972, c. 798; 1975, cc. 14, 15; 1976, c. 181; 1979, c. 435; 1983, c. 513; 1991, c. 482; 1992, cc. 58, 833; 1993, c. 410; 1997, c. 380; 1998, cc. 688, 783, 840; 2000, cc. 1020, 1041; 2001, cc. 430, 450, 827; 2007, c. 133; 2009, cc. 813, 840; 2011, cc. 384, 410; 2014, cc. 674, 719.

§ 18.2-251.01. Substance abuse screening and assessment for felony convictions.

A. When a person is convicted of a felony, not a capital offense, committed on or after January 1, 2000, he shall be required to undergo a substance abuse screening and, if the screening indicates a substance abuse or dependence problem, an assessment by a certified substance abuse counselor as defined in § 54.1-3500 employed by the Department of Corrections or by an agency employee under the supervision of such counselor. If the person is determined to have a substance abuse problem, the court shall require him to enter treatment and/or education program or services, if available, which, in the opinion of the court, is best suited to the needs of the person. The program or services may be located in the judicial district in which the conviction was had or in any other judicial district as the court may provide. The treatment and/or education program or services shall be licensed by the Department of Behavioral Health and Developmental Services or shall be a similar program or services which are made available through the Department of Corrections if the court imposes a sentence of one year or more or, if the court imposes a sentence of 12 months or less, by a similar program or services available through a local or regional jail, a local community-based probation services agency established pursuant to § 9.1-174, or an ASAP program certified by the Commission on VASAP. The services agency or program may require the person entering such program or services under the provisions of this section to pay a fee for the education and treatment component, or both, based upon the defendant's ability to pay.

B. As a condition of any suspended sentence and probation, the court shall order the person to undergo periodic testing and treatment for substance abuse, if available, as the court deems appropriate based upon consideration of the substance abuse assessment.

History.

1998, cc. 783, 840; 1999, cc. 891, 913; 2000, cc. 1020, 1041; 2007, c. 133; 2009, cc. 813, 840.

§ 18.2-251.02. Drug Offender Assessment and Treatment Fund.

There is hereby established in the state treasury the Drug Offender Assessment and Treatment Fund which shall consist of moneys received from fees imposed on certain drug offense convictions pursuant to subdivisions A 10 and A 11 of § 17.1-275 and § 16.1-69.48:3. All interest derived from the deposit and investment of moneys in the Fund shall be credited to the Fund. Any moneys not appropriated by the General Assembly shall remain in the Drug Offender Assessment and Treatment Fund and shall not be transferred or revert to the general fund at the end of any fiscal year. All moneys in the Fund shall be subject to annual appropriation by the General Assembly to the Department of Corrections, the Department of Juvenile Justice, and the Commission on VASAP to implement and operate the offender substance abuse screening and assessment program; the Department of Criminal Justice Services for the support of community-based probation and local pretrial services agencies; and the Office of the Executive Secretary of the Supreme Court of

Virginia for the support of drug treatment court programs.

History.
1998, cc. 783, 840; 2003, c. 606; 2004, c. 1004.

§ 18.2-251.03. Safe reporting of overdoses.

A. For purposes of this section, "overdose" means a life-threatening condition resulting from the consumption or use of a controlled substance, alcohol, or any combination of such substances.

B. It shall be an affirmative defense to prosecution of an individual for the unlawful purchase, possession, or consumption of alcohol pursuant to § 4.1-305, possession of a controlled substance pursuant to § 18.2-250, possession of marijuana pursuant to § 18.2-250.1, intoxication in public pursuant to § 18.2-388, or possession of controlled paraphernalia pursuant to § 54.1-3466 if:

1. Such individual, in good faith, seeks or obtains emergency medical attention for himself, if he is experiencing an overdose, or for another individual, if such other individual is experiencing an overdose, by contemporaneously reporting such overdose to a firefighter, as defined in § 65.2-102, emergency medical services personnel, as defined in § 32.1-111.1, a law-enforcement officer, as defined in § 9.1-101, or an emergency 911 system;

2. Such individual remains at the scene of the overdose or at any alternative location to which he or the person requiring emergency medical attention has been transported until a law-enforcement officer responds to the report of an overdose. If no law-enforcement officer is present at the scene of the overdose or at the alternative location, then such individual shall cooperate with law enforcement as otherwise set forth herein;

3. Such individual identifies himself to the law-enforcement officer who responds to the report of the overdose;

4. If requested by a law-enforcement officer, such individual substantially cooperates in any investigation of any criminal offense reasonably related to the controlled substance, alcohol, or combination of such substances that resulted in the overdose; and

5. The evidence for the prosecution of an offense enumerated in this subsection was obtained as a result of the individual seeking or obtaining emergency medical attention.

C. No individual may assert the affirmative defense provided for in this section if the person sought or obtained emergency medical attention for himself or another individual during the execution of a search warrant or during the conduct of a lawful search or a lawful arrest.

D. This section does not establish an affirmative defense for any individual or offense other than those listed in subsection B.

History.
2015, cc. 418, 436.

§ 18.2-251.1. Possession or distribution of marijuana for medical purposes permitted.

A. No person shall be prosecuted under § 18.2-250 or § 18.2-250.1 for the possession of marijuana or tetrahydrocannabinol when that possession occurs pursuant to a valid prescription issued by a medical doctor in the course of his professional practice for treatment of cancer or glaucoma.

B. No medical doctor shall be prosecuted under § 18.2-248 or § 18.2-248.1 for dispensing or distributing marijuana or tetrahydrocannabinol for medical purposes when such action occurs in the course of his professional practice for treatment of cancer or glaucoma.

C. No pharmacist shall be prosecuted under §§ 18.2-248 to 18.2-248.1 for dispensing or distributing marijuana or tetrahydrocannabinol to any person who holds a valid prescription of a medical doctor for such substance issued in the course of such doctor's professional practice for treatment of cancer or glaucoma.

History.
1979, c. 435.

§ 18.2-251.2. Possession and distribution of flunitrazepam; enhanced penalty.

Notwithstanding the provisions of §§ 54.1-3446 and 54.1-3452, the drug flunitrazepam shall be deemed to be listed on Schedule I for the purposes of penalties for violations of the Drug Control Act (§ 54.1-3400 et seq.). Any person knowingly manufacturing, selling, giving, distributing or possessing the drug flunitrazepam shall be punished under the penalties prescribed for such violations in accordance with §§ 18.2-248 and 18.2-250.

History.
1997, c. 595.

§ 18.2-251.3. Possession and distribution of gamma-butyrolactone; 1, 4-butanediol; enhanced penalty.

Any person who knowingly manufactures, sells, gives, distributes or possesses with the intent to distribute the substances gamma-butyrolactone; or 1, 4-butanediol, when intended for human consumption shall be guilty of a Class 3 felony.

History.
2000, c. 348.

§ 18.2-251.4. Defeating drug and alcohol screening tests; penalty.

A. It is unlawful for a person to:

1. Sell, give away, distribute, transport or market human urine in the Commonwealth with the intent

of using the urine to defeat a drug or alcohol screening test;

2. Attempt to defeat a drug or alcohol screening test by the substitution of a sample;

3. Adulterate a urine or other bodily fluid sample with the intent to defraud a drug or alcohol screening test.

B. A violation of this section is a Class 1 misdemeanor.

History.

2001, c. 379.

§ 18.2-252. Suspended sentence conditioned upon substance abuse screening, assessment, testing, and treatment or education.

The trial judge or court trying the case of any person found guilty of violating any law concerning the use, in any manner, of drugs, controlled substances, narcotics, marijuana, noxious chemical substances and like substances, shall condition any suspended sentence by first requiring such person to agree to undergo a substance abuse screening pursuant to § 18.2-251.01 and to submit to such periodic substance abuse testing, to include alcohol testing, as may be directed by the court. Such testing shall be conducted by the supervising probation agency or by personnel of any program or agency approved by the supervising probation agency. The cost of such testing ordered by the court shall be paid by the Commonwealth and taxed as a part of the costs of such criminal proceedings. The judge or court shall order the person, as a condition of any suspended sentence, to undergo such treatment or education for substance abuse, if available, as the judge or court deems appropriate based upon consideration of the substance abuse assessment. The treatment or education shall be provided by a program or agency licensed by the Department of Behavioral Health and Developmental Services, by a similar program or services available through the Department of Corrections if the court imposes a sentence of one year or more or, if the court imposes a sentence of 12 months or less, by a similar program or services available through a local or regional jail, a local community-based probation services agency established pursuant to § 9.1-174, or an ASAP program certified by the Commission on VASAP.

History.

Code 1950, § 54-524.101:4; 1973, c. 473; 1975, cc. 14, 15; 1979, c. 435; 1998, cc. 783, 840; 2000, cc. 1020, 1041; 2007, c. 133; 2009, cc. 813, 840.

§§ 18.2-253 through 18.2-253.2: Repealed by Acts 2004, c. 995.

Cross references.

For current provisions as to seizure and custody of controlled substances, see §§ 19.2-386.23 through 19.2-386.25.

§ 18.2-254. Commitment of convicted person for treatment for substance abuse.

A. Whenever any person who has not previously been convicted of any offense under this article or under any statute of the United States or of any state relating to narcotic drugs, marijuana, stimulant, depressant, or hallucinogenic drugs or has not previously had a proceeding against him for violation of such an offense dismissed as provided in § 18.2-251 is found guilty of violating any law concerning the use, in any manner, of drugs, controlled substances, narcotics, marijuana, noxious chemical substances, and like substances, the judge or court shall require such person to undergo a substance abuse screening pursuant to § 18.2-251.01 and to submit to such periodic substance abuse testing, to include alcohol testing, as may be directed by the court. The cost of such testing ordered by the court shall be paid by the Commonwealth and taxed as a part of the costs of the criminal proceedings. The judge or court shall also order the person to undergo such treatment or education for substance abuse, if available, as the judge or court deems appropriate based upon consideration of the substance abuse assessment. The treatment or education shall be provided by a program or agency licensed by the Department of Behavioral Health and Developmental Services or by a similar program or services available through the Department of Corrections if the court imposes a sentence of one year or more or, if the court imposes a sentence of 12 months or less, by a similar program or services available through a local or regional jail, a local community-based probation services agency established pursuant to § 9.1-174, or an ASAP program certified by the Commission on VASAP.

B. The court trying the case of any person alleged to have committed any offense designated by this article or by the Drug Control Act (§ 54.1-3400 et seq.) or in any other criminal case in which the commission of the offense was motivated by or closely related to the use of drugs and determined by the court, pursuant to a substance abuse screening and assessment, to be in need of treatment for the use of drugs may commit, based upon a consideration of the substance abuse assessment, such person, upon his conviction, to any facility for the treatment of persons with substance abuse, licensed by the Department of Behavioral Health and Developmental Services, if space is available in such facility, for a period of time not in excess of the maximum term of imprisonment specified as the penalty for conviction of such offense or, if sentence was determined by a jury, not in excess of the term of imprisonment as set by such jury. Confinement under such commitment shall be, in all regards, treated as confinement in a penal institution and the person so committed may be convicted of escape if he leaves the place of commitment without authority. A charge of escape may be prosecuted in either the jurisdiction where the treatment facility is located or the jurisdiction where the person was sentenced to commitment. The court may revoke such commitment at any time and transfer the person to an appropriate state or local correctional facility. Upon presentation of a certified statement from the director of the treatment facility to the effect that the confined person has successfully responded to treatment, the court may release such confined person prior to the termination of the period of time for which such person was confined and may suspend the remainder of the term upon such conditions as the court may prescribe.

C. The court trying a case in which commission of the offense was related to the defendant's habitual abuse of alcohol and in which the court determines, pursuant to a substance abuse screening and assessment, that such defendant is in need of treatment, may commit, based upon a consideration of the substance abuse assessment, such person, upon his conviction, to any facility for the treatment of persons with substance abuse licensed by the Department of Behavioral Health and Developmental Services, if space is available in such facility, for a period of time not in excess of the maximum term of imprisonment specified as the penalty for conviction. Confinement under such commitment shall be, in all regards, treated as confinement in a penal institution and the person so committed may be convicted of escape if he leaves the place of commitment without authority. The court may revoke such commitment at any time and transfer the person to an appropriate state or local correctional facility. Upon presentation of a certified statement from the director of the treatment facility to the effect that the confined person has successfully responded to treatment, the court may release such confined person prior to the termination of the period of time for which such person was confined and may suspend the remainder of the term upon such conditions as the court may prescribe.

History.

Code 1950, § 54-524.102; 1972, c. 758; 1974, c. 447; 1975, cc. 14, 15; 1978, c. 640; 1979, cc. 413, 435; 1992, c. 852; 1998, c. 724; 2000, cc. 1020, 1041; 2004, c. 130; 2005, c. 716; 2007, c. 133; 2009, cc. 813, 840.

§ 18.2-254.1. Drug Treatment Court Act.

A. This section shall be known and may be cited as the "Drug Treatment Court Act."

B. The General Assembly recognizes that there is a critical need in the Commonwealth for effective treatment programs that reduce the incidence of drug use, drug addiction, family separation due to parental substance abuse, and drug-related crimes. It is the intent of the General Assembly by this section to enhance public safety by facilitating the creation of drug treatment courts as means by which to accomplish this purpose.

C. The goals of drug treatment courts include: (i) reducing drug addiction and drug dependency among offenders; (ii) reducing recidivism; (iii) reducing drug-related court workloads; (iv) increasing personal, familial and societal accountability among offenders; and, (v) promoting effective planning and use of resources among the criminal justice system and community agencies.

D. Drug treatment courts are specialized court dockets within the existing structure of Virginia's court system offering judicial monitoring of intensive treatment and strict supervision of addicts in drug and drug-related cases. Local officials must complete a recognized planning process before establishing a drug treatment court program.

E. Administrative oversight for implementation of the Drug Treatment Court Act shall be conducted by the Supreme Court of Virginia. The Supreme Court of Virginia shall be responsible for (i) providing oversight for the distribution of funds for drug treatment courts; (ii) providing technical assistance to drug treatment courts; (iii) providing training for judges who preside over drug treatment courts; (iv) providing training to the providers of administrative, case management, and treatment services to drug treatment courts; and (v) monitoring the completion of evaluations of the effectiveness and efficiency of drug treatment courts in the Commonwealth.

F. A state drug treatment court advisory committee shall be established to (i) evaluate and recommend standards for the planning and implementation of drug treatment courts; (ii) assist in the evaluation of their effectiveness and efficiency; and (iii) encourage and enhance cooperation among agencies that participate in their planning and implementation. The committee shall be chaired by the Chief Justice of the Supreme Court of Virginia or his designee and shall include a member of the Judicial Conference of Virginia who presides over a drug treatment court; a district court judge; the Executive Secretary or his designee; the directors of the following executive branch agencies: Department of Corrections, Department of Criminal Justice Services, Department of Juvenile Justice, Department of Behavioral Health and Developmental Services, Department of Social Services; a representative of the following entities: a local community-based probation and pretrial services agency, the Commonwealth's Attorney's Association, the Virginia Indigent Defense Commission, the Circuit Court Clerk's Association, the Virginia Sheriff's Association, the Virginia Association of Chiefs of Police, the Commission on VASAP, and two representatives designated by the Virginia Drug Court Association.

G. Each jurisdiction or combination of jurisdictions that intend to establish a drug treatment court or continue the operation of an existing one shall establish a local drug treatment court advisory committee. Jurisdictions that establish separate adult and juvenile drug treatment courts may establish an advisory committee for each such court. Each advisory committee shall ensure quality, efficiency, and fairness in the planning, implementation, and operation of the drug treatment court or courts that serve the jurisdiction or combination of jurisdictions. Advisory committee membership shall include, but shall not be limited to the following people or their designees: (i) the drug treatment court judge; (ii) the attorney for the Commonwealth, or, where applicable, the city or county attorney who has responsibility for the prosecution of misdemeanor offenses; (iii) the public defender or a member of the local criminal defense bar in jurisdictions in which there is no public defender; (iv) the clerk of the court in which the drug treatment court is located; (v) a representative of the Virginia Department of Corrections, or the Department of Juvenile Justice, or both, from the local office which serves the jurisdiction or combination of jurisdictions; (vi) a representative of a local community-based probation and pretrial services agency; (vii) a local law-enforcement officer; (viii) a representative of the Department of Behavioral Health and Developmental Services or a representative of local drug treatment providers; (ix) the drug court administrator; (x) a representative of the Department of Social Services; (xi) county administrator or city manager; and (xii) any other people selected by the drug treatment court advisory committee.

H. Each local drug treatment court advisory committee shall establish criteria for the eligibility and participation of offenders who have been determined to be addicted to or dependent upon drugs. Subject to the provisions of this section, neither the establishment of a drug treatment court nor anything herein shall be construed as limiting the discretion of the attorney for the Commonwealth to prosecute any criminal case arising therein which he deems advisable to prosecute, except to the extent the participating attorney for the Commonwealth agrees to do so. As defined in § 17.1-805 or 19.2-297.1, adult offenders who have been convicted of a violent criminal offense within the preceding 10 years, or juvenile offenders who previously have been adjudicated not innocent of any such offense within the preceding 10 years, shall not be eligible for participation in any drug treatment court established or continued in operation pursuant to this section.

I. Each drug treatment court advisory committee shall establish policies and procedures for the operation of the court to attain the following goals: (i) effective integration of drug and alcohol treatment services with criminal justice system case processing; (ii) enhanced public safety through intensive offender supervision and drug treatment; (iii) prompt identification and placement of eligible participants; (iv) efficient access to a continuum of alcohol, drug, and related treatment and rehabilitation services; (v) verified participant abstinence through frequent alcohol and other drug testing; (vi) prompt response to participants' noncompliance with program requirements through a coordinated strategy; (vii) ongoing judicial interaction with each drug court participant; (viii) ongoing monitoring and evaluation of program effectiveness and efficiency; (ix) ongoing interdisciplinary education and training in support of program effectiveness and efficiency; and (x) ongoing collaboration among drug treatment courts, public agencies, and community-based organizations to enhance program effectiveness and efficiency.

J. Participation by an offender in a drug treatment court shall be voluntary and made pursuant only to a written agreement entered into by and between the offender and the Commonwealth with the concurrence of the court.

K. Nothing in this section shall preclude the establishment of substance abuse treatment programs and services pursuant to the deferred judgment provisions of § 18.2-251.

L. Each offender shall contribute to the cost of the substance abuse treatment he receives while participating in a drug treatment court pursuant to guidelines developed by the drug treatment court advisory committee.

M. Nothing contained in this section shall confer a right or an expectation of a right to treatment for an offender or be construed as requiring a local drug treatment court advisory committee to accept for participation every offender.

N. The Office of the Executive Secretary shall, with the assistance of the state drug treatment court advisory committee, develop a statewide evaluation model and conduct ongoing evaluations of the effectiveness and efficiency of all local drug treatment courts. A report of these evaluations shall be submitted to the General Assembly by December 1 of each year. Each local drug treatment court advisory committee shall submit evaluative reports to the Office of the Executive Secretary as requested.

O. Notwithstanding any other provision of this section, no drug treatment court shall be established subsequent to March 1, 2004, unless the jurisdiction or jurisdictions intending or proposing to establish such court have been specifically granted permission under the Code of Virginia to establish such court. The provisions of this subsection shall not apply to any drug treatment court established on or before March 1, 2004, and operational as of July 1, 2004.

P. Subject to the requirements and conditions established by the state Drug Treatment Court Advisory Committee, there shall be established a drug treatment court in the following jurisdictions: the City of Chesapeake and the City of Newport News.

Q. Subject to the requirements and conditions established by the state Drug Treatment Court Advisory Committee, there shall be established a drug treatment court in the Juvenile and Domestic Relations District Court for the County of Franklin, provided that such court is funded solely through local sources.

R. Subject to the requirements and conditions established by the state Drug Treatment Court Advisory Committee, there shall be established a drug treatment court in the City of Bristol and the County of Tazewell, provided that the court is funded within existing state and local appropriations.

History.

2004, c. 1004; 2005, cc. 519, 602; 2006, cc. 175, 341; 2007, c. 133; 2009, cc. 205, 281, 294, 813, 840; 2010, c. 258.

§ 18.2-255. Distribution of certain drugs to persons under 18 prohibited; penalty.

A. Except as authorized in the Drug Control Act, Chapter 34 (§ 54.1-3400 et seq.) of Title 54.1, it shall be unlawful for any person who is at least 18 years of age to knowingly or intentionally (i) distribute any drug classified in Schedule I, II, III or IV or marijuana to any person under 18 years of age who is at least three years his junior or (ii) cause any person under 18 years of age to assist in such distribution of any drug classified in Schedule I, II, III or IV or marijuana. Any person violating this provision shall upon conviction be imprisoned in a state correctional facility for a period not less than 10 nor more than 50 years, and fined not more than $100,000. Five years of the sentence imposed for a conviction under this section involving a Schedule I or II controlled substance or one ounce or more of marijuana shall be a mandatory minimum sentence. Two years of the sentence imposed for a conviction under this section involving less than one ounce of marijuana shall be a mandatory minimum sentence.

B. It shall be unlawful for any person who is at least 18 years of age to knowingly or intentionally (i) distribute any imitation controlled substance to a person under 18 years of age who is at least three years his junior or (ii) cause any person under 18 years of age to assist in such distribution of any imitation controlled substance. Any person violating this provision shall be guilty of a Class 6 felony.

History.

Code 1950, § 54-524.103; 1970, c. 650; 1972, c. 798; 1975, cc. 14, 15; 1976, c. 614; 1979, c. 435; 1982, c. 462; 1990, cc. 720, 864, 866; 1992, cc. 708, 724; 2000, cc. 1020, 1041; 2004, c. 461; 2011, cc. 384, 410; 2014, cc. 674, 719.

§ 18.2-255.1. Distribution, sale or display of printed material advertising instruments for use in administering marijuana or controlled substances to minors; penalty.

It shall be a Class 1 misdemeanor for any person knowingly to sell, distribute, or display for sale to a minor any book, pamphlet, periodical or other printed matter which he knows advertises for sale any instrument, device, article, or contrivance for advertised use in unlawfully ingesting, smoking, administering, preparing or growing marijuana or a controlled substance.

History.

1980, c. 737; 2011, cc. 384, 410; 2014, cc. 674, 719.

§ 18.2-255.2. Prohibiting the sale or manufacture of drugs on or near certain properties; penalty.

A. It shall be unlawful for any person to manufacture, sell or distribute or possess with intent to sell, give or distribute any controlled substance, imitation controlled substance, or marijuana while:

1. Upon the property, including buildings and grounds, of any public or private elementary, secondary, or post secondary school, or any public or private two-year or four-year institution of higher education, or any clearly marked licensed child day center as defined in § 63.2-100;
2. Upon public property or any property open to public use within 1,000 feet of the property described in subdivision 1;
3. On any school bus as defined in § 46.2-100;
4. Upon a designated school bus stop, or upon either public property or any property open to public use which is within 1,000 feet of such school bus stop, during the time when school children are waiting to be picked up and transported to or are being dropped off from school or a school-sponsored activity;
5. Upon the property, including buildings and grounds, of any publicly owned or publicly operated recreation or community center facility or any public library; or
6. Upon the property of any state facility as defined in § 37.2-100 or upon public property or property open to public use within 1,000 feet of such an institution. It is a violation of the provisions of this section if the person possessed the controlled substance, imitation controlled substance, or marijuana on the property described in subdivisions 1 through 6, regardless of where the person intended to sell, give or distribute the controlled substance, imitation controlled substance, or marijuana. Nothing in this section shall prohibit the authorized distribution of controlled substances.

B. Violation of this section shall constitute a separate and distinct felony. Any person violating the provisions of this section shall, upon conviction, be imprisoned for a term of not less than one year nor more than five years and fined not more than $100,000. A second or subsequent conviction hereunder for an offense involving a controlled substance classified in Schedule I, II, or III of the Drug Control Act (§ 54.1-3400 et seq.) or more than one-half ounce of marijuana shall be punished by a mandatory minimum term of imprisonment of one year to be served consecutively with any other sentence. However, if such person proves that he sold such controlled substance or marijuana only as an accommodation to another individual and not with intent

Crimes and Offenses

to profit thereby from any consideration received or expected nor to induce the recipient or intended recipient of the controlled substance or marijuana to use or become addicted to or dependent upon such controlled substance or marijuana, he is guilty of a Class 1 misdemeanor.

C. If a person commits an act violating the provisions of this section, and the same act also violates another provision of law that provides for penalties greater than those provided for by this section, then nothing in this section shall prohibit or bar any prosecution or proceeding under that other provision of law or the imposition of any penalties provided for thereby.

History.

1982, c. 594; 1989, cc. 619, 682, 709; 1990, cc. 617, 622; 1991, c. 268; 1991, 1st Sp. Sess., c. 14; 1993, cc. 30, 708, 729; 1999, c. 873; 2000, cc. 1020, 1041; 2003, cc. 80, 91; 2004, c. 461; 2005, c. 716; 2006, c. 325; 2011, cc. 384, 410; 2014, cc. 674, 719.

§ 18.2-256. Conspiracy.

Any person who conspires to commit any offense defined in this article or in the Drug Control Act (§ 54.1-3400 et seq.) is punishable by imprisonment or fine or both which may not be less than the minimum punishment nor exceed the maximum punishment prescribed for the offense, the commission of which was the object of the conspiracy.

History.

Code 1950, § 54-524.104; 1970, c. 650; 1972, c. 798; 1975, cc. 14, 15; 1978, c. 130.

§ 18.2-257. Attempts.

(a) Any person who attempts to commit any offense defined in this article or in the Drug Control Act (§ 54.1-3400 et seq.) which is a felony shall be imprisoned for not less than one nor more than ten years; provided, however, that any person convicted of attempting to commit a felony for which a lesser punishment may be imposed may be punished according to such lesser penalty.

(b) Any person who attempts to commit any offense defined in this article or in the Drug Control Act which is a misdemeanor shall be guilty of a Class 2 misdemeanor; provided, however, that any person convicted of attempting to commit a misdemeanor for which a lesser punishment may be imposed may be punished according to such lesser penalty.

History.

Code 1950, § 54-524.104:1; 1972, c. 798; 1973, c. 447; 1975, cc. 14, 15; 1979, c. 435.

§ 18.2-258. Certain premises deemed common nuisance; penalty.

Any office, store, shop, restaurant, dance hall, theater, poolroom, clubhouse, storehouse, warehouse, dwelling house, apartment, building of any kind, vehicle, vessel, boat, or aircraft, which with the knowledge of the owner, lessor, agent of any such lessor, manager, chief executive officer, operator, or tenant thereof, is frequented by persons under the influence of illegally obtained controlled substances or marijuana, as defined in § 54.1-3401, or for the purpose of illegally obtaining possession of, manufacturing or distributing controlled substances or marijuana, or is used for the illegal possession, manufacture or distribution of controlled substances or marijuana shall be deemed a common nuisance. Any such owner, lessor, agent of any such lessor, manager, chief executive officer, operator, or tenant who knowingly permits, establishes, keeps or maintains such a common nuisance is guilty of a Class 1 misdemeanor and, for a second or subsequent offense, a Class 6 felony.

History.

Code 1950, § 54-524.104:2; 1972, c. 736; 1973, c. 400; 1975, cc. 14, 15; 1979, c. 435; 1990, c. 948; 1992, cc. 248, 538; 2004, c. 462; 2011, cc. 384, 410; 2014, cc. 674, 719.

§ 18.2-258.01. Enjoining nuisances involving illegal drug transactions.

The attorney for the Commonwealth, or any citizen of the county, city, or town, where such a nuisance as is described in § 18.2-258 exists, may, in addition to the remedies given in and punishment imposed by this chapter, maintain a suit in equity in the name of the Commonwealth to enjoin the same; provided, however, the attorney for the Commonwealth shall not be required to prosecute any suit brought by a citizen under this section. In every case where the bill charges, on the knowledge or belief of complainant, and is sworn to by two witnesses, that a nuisance exists as described in § 18.2-258, a temporary injunction may be granted as soon as the bill is presented to the court provided reasonable notice has been given. The injunction shall enjoin and restrain any owners, tenants, their agents, employees, and any other person from contributing to or maintaining the nuisance and may impose such other requirements as the court deems appropriate. If, after hearing, the court finds that the material allegations of the bill are true, although the premises complained of may not then be unlawfully used, it shall continue the injunction against such persons or premises for such period of time as it deems appropriate, with the right to dissolve the injunction upon a proper showing by the owner of the premises.

History.

1990, c. 948.

§ 18.2-258.02. Maintaining a fortified drug house; penalty.

Any office, store, shop, restaurant, dance hall, theater, poolroom, clubhouse, storehouse, warehouse, dwelling house, apartment or building or structure of any kind which is (i) substantially altered from its original status by means of reinforcement with the intent to impede, deter or delay lawful entry by a law-enforcement officer into such structure, (ii) being used for the purpose of manufacturing or distributing controlled substances or marijuana, and (iii) the object of a valid search warrant, shall be considered a fortified drug house. Any person who maintains or operates a fortified drug house is guilty of a Class 5 felony.

History.
1996, c. 913; 2011, cc. 384, 410; 2014, cc. 674, 719.

§ 18.2-258.1. Obtaining drugs, procuring administration of controlled substances, etc., by fraud, deceit or forgery.

A. It shall be unlawful for any person to obtain or attempt to obtain any drug or procure or attempt to procure the administration of any controlled substance or marijuana: (i) by fraud, deceit, misrepresentation, embezzlement, or subterfuge; (ii) by the forgery or alteration of a prescription or of any written order; (iii) by the concealment of a material fact; or (iv) by the use of a false name or the giving of a false address.

B. It shall be unlawful for any person to furnish false or fraudulent information in or omit any information from, or willfully make a false statement in, any prescription, order, report, record, or other document required by Chapter 34 (§ 54.1-3400 et seq.) of Title 54.1.

C. It shall be unlawful for any person to use in the course of the manufacture or distribution of a controlled substance or marijuana a license number which is fictitious, revoked, suspended, or issued to another person.

D. It shall be unlawful for any person, for the purpose of obtaining any controlled substance or marijuana to falsely assume the title of, or represent himself to be, a manufacturer, wholesaler, pharmacist, physician, dentist, veterinarian or other authorized person.

E. It shall be unlawful for any person to make or utter any false or forged prescription or false or forged written order.

F. It shall be unlawful for any person to affix any false or forged label to a package or receptacle containing any controlled substance.

G. This section shall not apply to officers and employees of the United States, of this Commonwealth or of a political subdivision of this Commonwealth acting in the course of their employment, who obtain such drugs for investigative, research or analytical purposes, or to the agents or duly authorized representatives of any pharmaceutical manufacturer who obtain such drugs for investigative, research or analytical purposes and who are acting in the course of their employment; provided that such manufacturer is licensed under the provisions of the Federal Food, Drug and Cosmetic Act; and provided further, that such pharmaceutical manufacturer, its agents and duly authorized representatives file with the Board such information as the Board may deem appropriate.

H. Except as otherwise provided in this subsection, any person who shall violate any provision herein shall be guilty of a Class 6 felony.

Whenever any person who has not previously been convicted of any offense under this article or under any statute of the United States or of any state relating to narcotic drugs, marijuana, or stimulant, depressant, or hallucinogenic drugs, or has not previously had a proceeding against him for violation of such an offense dismissed, or reduced as provided in this section, pleads guilty to or enters a plea of not guilty to the court for violating this section, upon such plea if the facts found by the court would justify a finding of guilt, the court may place him on probation upon terms and conditions.

As a term or condition, the court shall require the accused to be evaluated and enter a treatment and/or education program, if available, such as, in the opinion of the court, may be best suited to the needs of the accused. This program may be located in the judicial circuit in which the charge is brought or in any other judicial circuit as the court may provide. The services shall be provided by a program certified or licensed by the Department of Behavioral Health and Developmental Services. The court shall require the person entering such program under the provisions of this section to pay all or part of the costs of the program, including the costs of the screening, evaluation, testing and education, based upon the person's ability to pay unless the person is determined by the court to be indigent.

As a condition of supervised probation, the court shall require the accused to remain drug free during the period of probation and submit to such tests during that period as may be necessary and appropriate to determine if the accused is drug free. Such testing may be conducted by the personnel of any screening, evaluation, and education program to which the person is referred or by the supervising agency.

Unless the accused was fingerprinted at the time of arrest, the court shall order the accused to report to the original arresting law-enforcement agency to submit to fingerprinting.

Upon violation of a term or condition, the court may enter an adjudication of guilt upon the felony and proceed as otherwise provided. Upon fulfillment of the terms and conditions of probation, the court shall find the defendant guilty of a Class 1 misdemeanor.

History.
1977, c. 558; 1979, c. 435; 1992, c. 76; 1997, c. 542; 2009, cc. 813, 840; 2011, cc. 384, 410; 2014, cc. 674, 719.

§ 18.2-258.2. Assisting individuals in unlawfully procuring prescription drugs; penalty.

Unless otherwise specifically authorized by law, any person who, for compensation, knowingly assists another in unlawfully procuring prescription drugs from a pharmacy or other source he knows is not licensed, registered or permitted by the licensing authority of the Commonwealth, any other state or territory of the United States, or the United States, is guilty of a Class 1 misdemeanor and, upon a second or subsequent conviction, a Class 6 felony.

History.
2004, c. 620.

§ 18.2-259. Penalties to be in addition to civil or administrative sanctions.

Any penalty imposed for violation of this article or of the Drug Control Act (§ 54.1-3400 et seq.) shall be in addition to, and not in lieu of, any civil or administrative penalty or sanction authorized by law.

History.
Code 1950, § 54-524.105; 1970, c. 650; 1975, cc. 14, 15.

§ 18.2-259.1. Forfeiture of driver's license for violations of article.

A. In addition to any other sanction or penalty imposed for a violation of this article, the (i) judgment of conviction under this article or (ii) placement on probation following deferral of further proceedings under § 18.2-251 or subsection H of § 18.2-258.1 for any such offense shall of itself operate to deprive the person so convicted or placed on probation after deferral of proceedings under § 18.2-251 or subsection H of § 18.2-258.1 of the privilege to drive or operate a motor vehicle, engine, or train in the Commonwealth for a period of six months from the date of such judgment or placement on probation. Such license forfeiture shall be in addition to and shall run consecutively with any other license suspension, revocation or forfeiture in effect or imposed upon the person so convicted or placed on probation. However, a juvenile who has had his license suspended or denied pursuant to § 16.1-278.9 shall not have his license forfeited pursuant to this section for the same offense.

B. The court trying the case shall order any person so convicted or placed on probation to surrender his driver's license to be disposed of in accordance with the provisions of § 46.2-398 and shall notify the Department of Motor Vehicles of any such conviction entered and of the license forfeiture to be imposed.

C. In those cases where the court determines there are compelling circumstances warranting an exception, the court may provide that any individual be issued a restricted license to operate a motor vehicle for any of the purposes set forth in subsection E of § 18.2-271.1. No restricted license issued pursuant to this subsection shall permit any person to operate a commercial motor vehicle as defined in the Virginia Commercial Driver's License Act (§ 46.2-341.1 et seq.). The court shall order the surrender of such person's license in accordance with the provisions of subsection B and shall forward to the Commissioner of the Department of Motor Vehicles a copy of its order entered pursuant to this subsection. This order shall specifically enumerate the restrictions imposed and contain such information regarding the person to whom such a permit is issued as is reasonably necessary to identify such person. The court shall also provide a copy of its order to such person who may operate a motor vehicle on the order until receipt from the Commissioner of the Department of Motor Vehicles of a restricted license, but only if the order provides for a restricted license for that period. A copy of the order and, after receipt thereof, the restricted license shall be carried at all times by such person while operating a motor vehicle. The court may require a person issued a restricted permit under the provisions of this subsection to be monitored by an alcohol safety action program during the period of license suspension. Any violation of the terms of the restricted license or of any condition set forth by the court related thereto, or any failure to remain drug-free during such period shall be reported forthwith to the court by such program. Any person who operates a motor vehicle in violation of any restriction imposed pursuant to this section shall be guilty of a violation of § 46.2-301.

History.
1992, cc. 58, 833; 1993, c. 920; 1994, cc. 403, 545; 1999, c. 45; 2000, c. 325; 2001, cc. 645, 779.

§ 18.2-260. Prescribing, dispensing, etc., drug except as authorized in article and Drug Control Act; violations for which no penalty provided.

It shall be unlawful for any person to prescribe, administer or dispense any drug except as authorized in the Drug Control Act (§ 54.1-3400 et seq.) or in this article. Any person who violates any provision of the Drug Control Act or of this article, for which no penalty is elsewhere specified in this article or in Article 7 (§ 54.1-3466 et seq.) of the Drug Control Act, shall be guilty of a Class 1 misdemeanor.

History.
Code 1950, § 54-524.106; 1970, c. 650; 1973, c. 548; 1975, cc. 14, 15.

§ 18.2-260.1. Falsifying patient records.

Any person who, with the intent to defraud, falsifies any patient record shall be guilty of a Class 1 misdemeanor.

History.
1997, c. 619; 2011, c. 204.

§ 18.2-261. Monetary penalty.

Any person licensed by the State Board of Pharmacy who violates any of the provisions of the Drug Control Act (§ 54.1-3400 et seq.) or of this article, and who is not criminally prosecuted, shall be subject to the monetary penalty provided in this section. If, by a majority vote, the Board shall determine that the respondent is guilty of the violation complained of, the Board shall proceed to determine the amount of the monetary penalty for such violation, which shall not exceed the sum of $1,000 for each violation. Such penalty may be sued for and recovered in the name of the Commonwealth.

History.
Code 1950, § 54-524.107; 1970, c. 650; 1975, cc. 14, 15; 1980, c. 678.

§ 18.2-262. Witnesses not excused from testifying or producing evidence because of self-incrimination.

No person shall be excused from testifying or from producing books, papers, correspondence, memoranda or other records for the Commonwealth as to any offense alleged to have been committed by another under this article or under the Drug Control Act (§ 54.1-3400 et seq.) by reason of his testimony or other evidence tending to incriminate himself, but the testimony given and evidence so produced by such person on behalf of the Commonwealth when called for by the trial judge or court trying the case, or by the attorney for the Commonwealth, or when summoned by the Commonwealth and sworn as a witness by the court or the clerk and sent before the grand jury, shall be in no case used against him nor shall he be prosecuted as to the offense as to which he testifies. Any person who refuses to testify or produce books, papers, correspondence, memoranda or other records, shall be guilty of a Class 2 misdemeanor.

History.
Code 1950, § 54-524.107:1; 1971, Ex. Sess., c. 170; 1975, cc. 14, 15; 1984, c. 667.

§ 18.2-263. Unnecessary to negative exception, etc.; burden of proof of exception, etc.

In any complaint, information, or indictment, and in any action or proceeding brought for the enforcement of any provision of this article or of the Drug Control Act (§ 54.1-3400 et seq.), it shall not be necessary to negative any exception, excuse, proviso, or exemption contained in this article or in the Drug Control Act, and the burden of proof of any such exception, excuse, proviso, or exemption shall be upon the defendant.

History.
Code 1950, § 54-524.108; 1970, c. 650; 1975, cc. 14, 15.

§ 18.2-264. Inhaling drugs or other noxious chemical substances or causing, etc., others to do so.

A. It shall be unlawful, except under the direction of a practitioner as defined in § 54.1-3401, for any person deliberately to smell or inhale any drugs or any other noxious chemical substances including but not limited to fingernail polish or model airplane glue, containing any ketones, aldehydes, organic acetates, ether, chlorinated hydrocarbons or vapors, with the intent to become intoxicated, inebriated, excited, stupefied or to dull the brain or nervous system.

Any person violating the provisions of this subsection shall be guilty of a Class 1 misdemeanor.

B. It shall be unlawful for any person, other than one duly licensed, deliberately to cause, invite or induce any person to smell or inhale any drugs or any other noxious substances or chemicals containing any ketone, aldehydes, organic acetates, ether, chlorinated hydrocarbons or vapors with the intent to intoxicate, inebriate, excite, stupefy or to dull the brain or nervous system of such person.

Any person violating the provisions of this subsection shall be guilty of a Class 2 misdemeanor.

History.
Code 1950, § 18.1-70.1; 1968, c. 391; 1969, Ex. Sess., c. 19; 1973, c. 27; 1975, cc. 14, 15; 1993, c. 416.

§ 18.2-264.01: Repealed by Acts 2002, c. 831, cl. 2, effective July 1, 2003.

§ 18.2-264.1: Repealed by Acts 1994, c. 432.

§ 18.2-265: Repealed by Acts 1979, c. 638.

ARTICLE 1.1. DRUG PARAPHERNALIA.

§ 18.2-265.1. Definition.

As used in this article, the term *"drug paraphernalia"* means all equipment, products, and materials of any kind which are either designed for use or which are intended by the person charged with violating § 18.2-265.3 for use in planting, propagating, cultivating, growing, harvesting, manufacturing, compounding, converting, producing, processing, preparing, strength testing, analyzing, packaging, repackaging, storing, containing, concealing, injecting, ingesting, inhaling, or otherwise introducing into the human body marijuana or a controlled substance. It includes, but is not limited to:

1. Kits intended for use or designed for use in planting, propagating, cultivating, growing or har-

vesting of marijuana or any species of plant which is a controlled substance or from which a controlled substance can be derived;

2. Kits intended for use or designed for use in manufacturing, compounding, converting, producing, processing, or preparing marijuana or controlled substances;

3. Isomerization devices intended for use or designed for use in increasing the potency of marijuana or any species of plant which is a controlled substance;

4. Testing equipment intended for use or designed for use in identifying or in analyzing the strength or effectiveness of marijuana or controlled substances;

5. Scales and balances intended for use or designed for use in weighing or measuring marijuana or controlled substances;

6. Diluents and adulterants, such as quinine hydrochloride, mannitol, or mannite, intended for use or designed for use in cutting controlled substances;

7. Separation gins and sifters intended for use or designed for use in removing twigs and seeds from, or in otherwise cleaning or refining, marijuana;

8. Blenders, bowls, containers, spoons, and mixing devices intended for use or designed for use in compounding controlled substances;

9. Capsules, balloons, envelopes, and other containers intended for use or designed for use in packaging small quantities of marijuana or controlled substances;

10. Containers and other objects intended for use or designed for use in storing or concealing marijuana or controlled substances;

11. Hypodermic syringes, needles, and other objects intended for use or designed for use in parenterally injecting controlled substances into the human body;

12. Objects intended for use or designed for use in ingesting, inhaling, or otherwise introducing marijuana, cocaine, hashish, or hashish oil into the human body, such as:

a. Metal, wooden, acrylic, glass, stone, plastic, or ceramic pipes with or without screens, permanent screens, hashish heads, or punctured metal bowls;

b. Water pipes;

c. Carburetion tubes and devices;

d. Smoking and carburetion masks;

e. Roach clips, meaning objects used to hold burning material, such as a marijuana cigarette, that has become too small or too short to be held in the hand;

f. Miniature cocaine spoons, and cocaine vials;

g. Chamber pipes;

h. Carburetor pipes;

i. Electric pipes;

j. Air-driven pipes;

k. Chillums;

l. Bongs;

m. Ice pipes or chillers.

History.

1981, c. 598; 1983, c. 535.

§ 18.2-265.2. Evidence to be considered in cases under this article.

In determining whether an object is drug paraphernalia, the court may consider, in addition to all other relevant evidence, the following:

1. Constitutionally admissible statements by the accused concerning the use of the object;

2. The proximity of the object to marijuana or controlled substances, which proximity is actually known to the accused;

3. Instructions, oral or written, provided with the object concerning its use;

4. Descriptive materials accompanying the object which explain or depict its use;

5. National and local advertising within the actual knowledge of the accused concerning its use;

6. The manner in which the object is displayed for sale;

7. Whether the accused is a legitimate supplier of like or related items to the community, such as a licensed distributor or dealer of tobacco products;

8. Evidence of the ratio of sales of the objects defined in § 18.2-265.1 to the total sales of the business enterprise;

9. The existence and scope of legitimate uses for the object in the community;

10. Expert testimony concerning its use or the purpose for which it was designed;

11. Relevant evidence of the intent of the accused to deliver it to persons who he knows, or should reasonably know, intend to use the object with an illegal drug. The innocence of an owner, or of anyone in control of the object, as to a direct violation of this article shall not prevent a finding that the object is intended for use or designed for use as drug paraphernalia.

History.

1981, c. 598; 1983, c. 535.

§ 18.2-265.3. Penalties for sale, etc., of drug paraphernalia.

A. Any person who sells or possesses with intent to sell drug paraphernalia, knowing, or under circumstances where one reasonably should know, that it is either designed for use or intended by such person for use to illegally plant, propagate, cultivate, grow, harvest, manufacture, compound, convert, produce, process, prepare, test, analyze, pack, repack, store, contain, conceal, inject, ingest, inhale, or otherwise introduce into the human body marijuana or a controlled substance, shall be guilty of a Class 1 misdemeanor.

B. Any person eighteen years of age or older who violates subsection A hereof by selling drug paraphernalia to a minor who is at least three years junior to the accused in age shall be guilty of a Class 6 felony.

C. Any person eighteen years of age or older who distributes drug paraphernalia to a minor shall be guilty of a Class 1 misdemeanor.

History.
1981, c. 598; 1983, c. 535; 1984, c. 31.

§ 18.2-265.4: Repealed by Acts 2004, c. 995.

Cross references.
For current provisions as to seizure and forfeiture of drug paraphernalia, see § 19.2-386.26.

§ 18.2-265.5. Advertisement of drug paraphernalia prohibited; penalty.

It shall be unlawful for any person to place in any newspaper, magazine, handbill or other publication any advertisement, knowing or under circumstances where one reasonably should know, that the purpose of the advertisement, in whole or in part, is to promote the sale of objects designed or intended by such person for use as drug paraphernalia. A violation of this section shall be punishable as a Class 1 misdemeanor.

History.
1983, c. 535.

ARTICLE 1.2.

SALE OF EPHEDRINE OR RELATED COMPOUNDS.

§ 18.2-265.6. Definitions.

As used in this article, unless the context requires a different meaning:

"Department" means the Department of State Police.

"Ephedrine or related compounds" means ephedrine and pseudoephedrine base or their salts, isomers, or salts of isomers.

"Pharmacy" means any establishment or institution from which drugs, medicines, or medicinal chemicals are dispensed or offered for sale or on which a sign is displayed bearing the words "apothecary," "druggist," "drugs," "drug store," "drug sundries," "medicine store," "pharmacist," "pharmacy," or "prescriptions filled" or any similar words intended to indicate that the practice of pharmacy is being conducted pursuant to a license issued under Chapter 33 (§ 54.1-3300 et seq.) of Title 54.1.

"Retail distributor" means an entity licensed to conduct business in the Commonwealth that offers for sale to the public at a retail outlet any nonprescription compound, mixture, or preparation containing ephedrine or related compounds.

"System" or *"electronic system"* means a real-time electronic recordkeeping and monitoring system for the sale of ephedrine or related compounds.

History.
2012, cc. 160, 252.

§ 18.2-265.7. Sale of the methamphetamine precursors ephedrine or related compounds; penalty.

A. The sale of any product containing ephedrine or related compounds sold by a pharmacy or retail distributor shall be limited to no more than 3.6 grams per day and 9 grams per 30-day period per individual customer. The limits shall apply to the total amount of base ephedrine or related compounds contained in the products and not to the overall weight of the products.

B. Ephedrine or related compounds shall only be displayed for sale behind a store counter that is not accessible to consumers or in a locked case that requires assistance by a store employee for customer access.

C. Any person purchasing, receiving, or otherwise acquiring ephedrine or related compounds shall, prior to taking possession, present photo identification issued by a government or an educational institution.

D. The pharmacy or retail distributor shall maintain a written log or electronic system with the purchaser's name and address, birth date, and signature; the product name and quantity sold; and the date and time of the transaction. Unless exempt under subsection B of § 18.2-265.8 or § 18.2-265.11, the pharmacy or retail distributor shall use the electronic recordkeeping and monitoring system to report all nonprescription sales of any product containing ephedrine or related compounds.

E. The purchaser shall sign the record acknowledging an understanding of the applicable sales limit and that providing false statements or misrepresentations may subject the purchaser to criminal penalties under § 1001 of Title 18 of the United States Code.

F. The pharmacy or retail distributor shall maintain records of all sales required to be entered into the electronic system or written log for a period of two years from the date of the last entry.

G. The provisions of this article do not apply to sales of ephedrine or related compounds pursuant to a valid prescription.

H. Any person who willfully violates this section is guilty of a Class 1 misdemeanor.

History.
2012, cc. 160, 252.

§ 18.2-265.8. Real-time electronic recording of sales of ephedrine or related compounds; memorandum of understanding.

A. The Department shall enter into a memorandum of understanding with an appropriate entity to establish the Commonwealth's participation in a real-time electronic recordkeeping and monitoring system for the sale of ephedrine or related com-

Crimes and Offenses

pounds. The memorandum of understanding shall include the following:

1. A real-time electronic recordkeeping and monitoring system shall be provided at no charge to the Commonwealth or to participating pharmacies and retail distributors and shall be approved by the Department.

2. The system shall provide, at no charge to participating pharmacies and retail distributors, appropriate training, 24-hour online support, and a toll-free telephone help line that is staffed 24 hours a day.

3. The system shall be able to communicate in real time with similar systems operated in other states and the District of Columbia and similar systems containing information submitted by more than one state.

4. The system shall comply with information exchange standards adopted by the National Information Exchange Model.

5. The system shall include a stop sales alert, which shall be a notification that completion of the sale would result in the seller or purchaser violating the quantity limits set forth in § 18.2-265.7, with an override function that may be used by a pharmacy or retail distributor under the circumstances set forth in § 18.2-265.9 and shall record each instance in which the override function is utilized.

6. The system shall provide for the recording of the following:

a. The date and time of the transaction;

b. The name, address, date of birth, and photo identification number of the purchaser; the type of identification; and the government or educational institution of issuance;

c. The number of packages purchased; the total number of grams of ephedrine or related compounds per package; and the name of the compound, mixture, or preparation containing ephedrine or related compounds; and

d. The signature of the purchaser or unique number connecting the transaction to a paper signature maintained at the retail premises.

7. The system shall ensure that submitted data is retained within the system for at least two years from the date of submission.

B. The Department shall provide a process for a pharmacy or retail distributor to apply for, obtain, and periodically renew an exemption from the requirement to report transactions to the electronic system if the pharmacy or retail distributor lacks broadband access or maintains a sales volume of less than 72 grams of ephedrine or related compounds in a 30-day period.

C. The Superintendent of State Police shall promulgate regulations pursuant to the Administrative Process Act (§ 2.2-4000 et seq.) for the implementation of this section. Regulations adopted under this section shall be deemed a customary police function for purposes of subdivision B 6 of § 2.2-4002.

History.
2012, cc. 160, 252.

§ 18.2-265.9. Stop sales alerts; interruption of electronic system.

A. A pharmacy or retail distributor shall not complete the sale if the system generates a stop sales alert unless the individual distributing the ephedrine or related compound has a reasonable fear of imminent bodily harm if the sale is not completed.

B. In the event of a mechanical or electronic interruption of the system, the pharmacy or retail establishment shall maintain a written log of sales of ephedrine or related compounds until the system is restored. The information written in the log shall be transmitted to the system as soon as practicable after the system is restored.

History.
2012, cc. 160, 252.

§ 18.2-265.10. Exemption from participation in electronic system; requirement to maintain log.

Any pharmacy or retail distributor that has been granted an exemption from participation in the system pursuant to subsection B of § 18.2-265.8 shall forward to the Department every seven days by fax or electronic means a legible copy of the log required by § 18.2-265.7.

History.
2012, cc. 160, 252.

§ 18.2-265.11. Exemption from participation in electronic system and maintenance of a written log.

A. The following entities shall not be required to participate in the electronic system and shall not be required to maintain a written log:

1. Licensed manufacturers that manufacture and lawfully distribute products in the channels of commerce.

2. Wholesalers that lawfully distribute products in the channels of commerce.

3. Inpatient pharmacies of health care facilities licensed in the Commonwealth.

4. Licensed long-term health care facilities.

5. Government-operated health care clinics or departments or centers.

6. Physicians who dispense drugs pursuant to § 54.1-3304.

7. Pharmacies located in correctional facilities.

8. Government-operated or industry-operated medical facilities serving the employees of the Commonwealth or local or federal government.

B. Purchases of ephedrine or related compounds pursuant to a valid prescription are not required to be reported to the system or entered into a written log.

C. The sale of a single package containing no more than 60 milligrams of ephedrine or related compounds to an individual is not required to be reported to the system or entered into a log provided it is an isolated sale.

History.
2012, cc. 160, 252.

§ 18.2-265.12. Authority to access data, records, and reports.

The Department or other law-enforcement agency of the Commonwealth or any federal agency conducting a criminal investigation involving the manufacture of methamphetamine consistent with state or federal law may access data, records, and reports regarding the sale of ephedrine or related compounds. In addition, such information may be accessed if relevant to proceedings in any court, investigatory grand jury, or special grand jury that has been impaneled in accordance with the provisions of Chapter 13 (§ 19.2-191 et seq.) of Title 19.2.

The Superintendent of State Police shall promulgate regulations, pursuant to the Administrative Process Act (§ 2.2-4000 et seq.), for the implementation of this section. Regulations adopted under this section shall be deemed a customary police function for purposes of subdivision B 6 of § 2.2-4002.

History.
2012, cc. 160, 252.

§ 18.2-265.13. Confidentiality of data in possession of Department.

All data, records, and reports related to the sale of ephedrine or related compounds to retail customers and any abstracts of such data, records, and reports that are in the possession of the Department pursuant to this article shall be confidential and exempt from the Virginia Freedom of Information Act (§ 2.2-3700 et seq.) and the Government Data Collection and Dissemination Practices Act (§ 2.2-3800 et seq.).

History.
2012, cc. 160, 252.

§ 18.2-265.14. Prohibition on disclosure of information by entity operating the system.

The entity operating the system pursuant to the memorandum of understanding with the Department shall not use or disclose the information collected on behalf of the Department from a pharmacy or retail distributor for any purpose other than (i) to ensure compliance with this article or the federal Combat Methamphetamine Epidemic Act of 2005, (ii) to comply with the United States government or a political subdivision thereof for law-enforcement purposes pursuant to state or federal law, or (iii) to facilitate a product recall necessary to protect public health and safety.

History.
2012, cc. 160, 252.

§ 18.2-265.15. Prohibition on disclosure of information by pharmacy or retail distributor; civil immunity.

A pharmacy or retail distributor that sells any product containing ephedrine or related compounds shall not use or disclose the information in the system or a written log for any purpose other than (i) to ensure compliance with this article or the federal Combat Methamphetamine Epidemic Act of 2005, (ii) to comply with the United States government or a political subdivision thereof for law-enforcement purposes pursuant to state or federal law, or (iii) to facilitate a product recall necessary to protect public health and safety. A pharmacy or retail distributor shall report information in the written log or electronic system to law-enforcement personnel upon request, and any pharmacy or retail distributor that in good faith releases such information to federal, state, or local law-enforcement officers, or to any person acting on behalf of such officers, shall be immune from civil liability for the release unless the release constitutes gross negligence or intentional, wanton, or willful misconduct.

History.
2012, cc. 160, 252.

§ 18.2-265.16. Compliance with statutory provisions; civil immunity.

Absent gross negligence, recklessness, or willful misconduct, any pharmacy or retail distributor utilizing the system or written log in compliance with this article shall be immune from civil liability as a result of actions or omissions in carrying out such statutory duties.

History.
2012, cc. 160, 252.

§ 18.2-265.17. Exemption of information systems from provisions related to the Virginia Information Technologies Agency.

The provisions of Chapter 20.1 (§ 2.2-2005 et seq.) of Title 2.2 shall not apply to this article.

History.
2012, cc. 160, 252.

§ 18.2-265.18. Failure to report certain sales; penalty.

Any person subject to the recordkeeping and reporting requirements set forth in this article that

Crimes and Offenses

willfully fails to report nonprescription sales of ephedrine or related compounds is guilty of a Class 1 misdemeanor.

History.
2012, cc. 160, 252.

ARTICLE 1.3.

DEXTROMETHORPHAN DISTRIBUTION ACT.

§ 18.2-265.19. Definitions.

As used in this article, unless the context requires a different meaning:

"Dextromethorphan" means the dextrorotatory isomer of 3-methoxy-N-methylmorphinan and its salts.

"Pharmacy" means any establishment or institution from which drugs, medicines, or medicinal chemicals are dispensed or offered for sale or on which a sign is displayed bearing the words "apothecary," "druggist," "drugs," "drug store," "drug sundries," "medicine store," "pharmacist," "pharmacy," "prescriptions filled," or any similar words intended to indicate that the practice of pharmacy is being conducted pursuant to a license issued under Chapter 33 (§ 54.1-3300 et seq.) of Title 54.1.

"Retail distributor" means an entity licensed to conduct business in the Commonwealth that offers for sale to the public at a retail outlet any nonprescription compound, mixture, or preparation containing dextromethorphan.

"Unfinished dextromethorphan" means dextromethorphan in the form of a "bulk drug substance" as defined in § 54.1-3401.

History.
2014, cc. 101, 362.

§ 18.2-265.20. Sale or distribution of dextromethorphan to minors; purchase by minors; civil penalty.

A. It is unlawful for any pharmacy or retail distributor knowingly or intentionally to sell or distribute any product containing dextromethorphan to a minor.

B. A pharmacy or retail distributor, or its employee or agent, shall not sell or distribute a product containing dextromethorphan unless the purchaser presents a federal, state, or local government-issued document that contains a photograph and the birth date of the purchaser that shows that the purchaser is at least 18 years of age or unless from the purchaser's outward appearance the pharmacy or retail distributor would reasonably presume the purchaser to be 25 years of age or older.

C. It is unlawful for any minor knowingly or intentionally to purchase any product containing dextromethorphan.

D. Any pharmacy or retail distributor, or its employee or agent, that violates subsection A or any minor who violates subsection C is subject to a civil penalty of $25. Any pharmacy or retail distributor, or its employee or agent, that violates subsection B shall receive a notice of noncompliance and, upon any subsequent violation of subsection B, shall be subject to a civil penalty of $25. Such penalty shall be collected by the attorney for the Commonwealth for the locality where the violation occurred, and the proceeds shall be deposited into the Literary Fund.

E. The provisions of this section shall not apply if the product was obtained directly from, or pursuant to, a valid prescription or order of a practitioner while acting in the course of his professional practice, or except as otherwise authorized by the Drug Control Act (§ 54.1-3400 et seq.).

History.
2014, cc. 101, 362.

§ 18.2-265.21. Possession or distribution of unfinished dextromethorphan; penalty.

Any person who distributes or possesses with the intent to distribute unfinished dextromethorphan who is not registered under § 510 of the Federal Food, Drug, and Cosmetic Act (21 U.S.C. § 321 et seq.) or otherwise authorized by the Drug Control Act (§ 54.1-3400 et seq.) to distribute or possess unfinished dextromethorphan is guilty of a Class 1 misdemeanor. This section does not apply to a common carrier that receives or possesses unfinished dextromethorphan for the purpose of distributing such unfinished dextromethorphan between persons registered under § 510 of the Federal Food, Drug, and Cosmetic Act (21 U.S.C. § 321 et seq.) or otherwise authorized by the Drug Control Act (§ 54.1-3400 et seq.) to distribute or possess unfinished dextromethorphan.

History.
2014, cc. 101, 362.

ARTICLE 2.

DRIVING MOTOR VEHICLE, ETC., WHILE INTOXICATED.

§ 18.2-266. Driving motor vehicle, engine, etc., while intoxicated, etc.

It shall be unlawful for any person to drive or operate any motor vehicle, engine or train (i) while such person has a blood alcohol concentration of 0.08 percent or more by weight by volume or 0.08 grams or more per 210 liters of breath as indicated by a chemical test administered as provided in this article, (ii) while such person is under the influence of alcohol, (iii) while such person is under the influence of any narcotic drug or any other self-administered intoxicant or drug of whatsoever nature, or any combination of such drugs, to a degree which impairs his ability to drive or operate any motor vehicle, engine or train safely, (iv) while such person is under the combined influence of alcohol and any drug or drugs to a degree which impairs his ability to drive or operate any motor vehicle, engine or train safely, or (v) while such person has a blood concentration of any of the following substances at a level that is equal to or greater than: (a) 0.02 milligrams of cocaine per liter of blood, (b) 0.1 milligrams of methamphetamine per liter of blood, (c) 0.01 milligrams of phencyclidine per liter of blood, or (d) 0.1 milligrams of 3,4-methylenedioxymethamphetamine per liter of blood. A charge alleging a violation of this section shall support a conviction under clauses (i), (ii), (iii), (iv), or (v).

For the purposes of this article, the term "motor vehicle" includes mopeds, while operated on the public highways of this Commonwealth.

History.

Code 1950, § 18.1-54; 1960, c. 358; 1975, cc. 14, 15; 1977, c. 637; 1984, c. 666; 1986, c. 635; 1987, c. 661; 1992, c. 830; 1994, cc. 359, 363; 1996, c. 439; 2005, cc. 616, 845.

§ 18.2-266.1. Persons under age 21 driving after illegally consuming alcohol; penalty.

A. It shall be unlawful for any person under the age of 21 to operate any motor vehicle after illegally consuming alcohol. Any such person with a blood alcohol concentration of 0.02 percent or more by weight by volume or 0.02 grams or more per 210 liters of breath but less than 0.08 by weight by volume or less than 0.08 grams per 210 liters of breath as indicated by a chemical test administered as provided in this article shall be in violation of this section.

B. A violation of this section is a Class 1 misdemeanor. Punishment shall include (i) forfeiture of such person's license to operate a motor vehicle for a period of one year from the date of conviction and (ii) a mandatory minimum fine of $500 or performance of a mandatory minimum of 50 hours of community service. This suspension period shall be in addition to the suspension period provided under § 46.2-391.2. The penalties and license forfeiture provisions set forth in §§ 16.1-278.9, 18.2-270 and 18.2-271 shall not apply to a violation of this section. Any person convicted of a violation of this section shall be eligible to attend an Alcohol Safety Action Program under the provisions of § 18.2-271.1 and may, in the discretion of the court, be issued a restricted license during the term of license suspension.

C. Notwithstanding §§ 16.1-278.8 and 16.1-278.9, upon adjudicating a juvenile delinquent based upon a violation of this section, the juvenile and domestic relations district court shall order disposition as provided in subsection B.

History.

1994, cc. 359, 363; 1995, c. 31; 2003, c. 605; 2008, c. 729; 2009, c. 660; 2011, cc. 134, 683.

§ 18.2-267. Preliminary analysis of breath to determine alcoholic content of blood.

A. Any person who is suspected of a violation of § 18.2-266, 18.2-266.1, subsection B of § 18.2-272, or a similar ordinance shall be entitled, if such equipment is available, to have his breath analyzed to determine the probable alcoholic content of his blood. The person shall also be entitled, upon request, to observe the process of analysis and to see the blood-alcohol reading on the equipment used to perform the breath test. His breath may be analyzed by any police officer of the Commonwealth, or of any county, city or town, or by any member of a sheriff's department in the normal discharge of his duties.

B. The Department of Forensic Science shall determine the proper method and equipment to be used in analyzing breath samples taken pursuant to this section and shall advise the respective police and sheriff's departments of the same.

C. Any person who has been stopped by a police officer of the Commonwealth, or of any county, city or town, or by any member of a sheriff's department and is suspected by such officer to be guilty of an offense listed in subsection A, shall have the right to refuse to permit his breath to be so analyzed, and his failure to permit such analysis shall not be evidence in any prosecution for an offense listed in subsection A.

D. Whenever the breath sample analysis indicates that alcohol is present in the person's blood, the officer may charge the person with a violation of an offense listed in subsection A. The person so charged shall then be subject to the provisions of §§ 18.2-268.1 through 18.2-268.12, or of a similar ordinance.

E. The results of the breath analysis shall not be admitted into evidence in any prosecution for an offense listed in subsection A, the purpose of this section being to permit a preliminary analysis of the alcoholic content of the blood of a person suspected of having committed an offense listed in subsection A.

F. Police officers or members of any sheriff's department shall, upon stopping any person suspected of having committed an offense listed in subsection A, advise the person of his rights under the provisions of this section.

G. Nothing in this section shall be construed as limiting the provisions of §§ 18.2-268.1 through 18.2-268.12.

History.

Code 1950, § 18.1-54.1; 1970, c. 511; 1975, cc. 14, 15; 1979, c. 717; 1985, cc. 355, 609; 1990, c. 825; 1992, c. 830; 1994, cc. 359, 363; 1996, cc. 154, 952; 2004, c. 1013; 2005, cc. 757, 840, 868, 881.

§ 18.2-268: Repealed by Acts 1992, c. 830.

Cross references.

For present provisions relating to chemical testing to determine alcohol or drug content of blood, see § 18.2-268.1 et seq.

§ 18.2-268.1. Chemical testing to determine alcohol or drug content of blood; definitions.

As used in §§ 18.2-268.2 through 18.2-268.12, unless the context clearly indicates otherwise:

The phrase *"alcohol or drug"* means alcohol, a drug or drugs, or any combination of alcohol and a drug or drugs.

The phrase *"blood or breath"* means either or both.

"Chief police officer" means the sheriff in any county not having a chief of police, the chief of police of any county having a chief of police, the chief of police of the city, or the sergeant or chief of police of the town in which the charge will be heard, or their authorized representatives.

"Department" means the Department of Forensic Science.

"Director" means the Director of the Department of Forensic Science.

"License" means any driver's license, temporary driver's license, or instruction permit authorizing the operation of a motor vehicle upon the highways.

"Ordinance" means a county, city or town ordinance.

History.

1992, c. 830; 2005, cc. 868, 881.

§ 18.2-268.2. Implied consent to post-arrest testing to determine drug or alcohol content of blood.

A. Any person, whether licensed by Virginia or not, who operates a motor vehicle upon a highway, as defined in § 46.2-100, in the Commonwealth shall be deemed thereby, as a condition of such operation, to have consented to have samples of his blood, breath, or both blood and breath taken for a chemical test to determine the alcohol, drug, or both alcohol and drug content of his blood, if he is arrested for violation of § 18.2-266, 18.2-266.1, or subsection B of § 18.2-272 or of a similar ordinance within three hours of the alleged offense.

B. Any person so arrested for a violation of clause (i) or (ii) of § 18.2-266 or both, § 18.2-266.1 or subsection B of § 18.2-272 or of a similar ordinance shall submit to a breath test. If the breath test is unavailable or the person is physically unable to submit to the breath test, a blood test shall be given. The accused shall, prior to administration of the test, be advised by the person administering the test that he has the right to observe the process of analysis and to see the blood-alcohol reading on the equipment used to perform the breath test. If the equipment automatically produces a written printout of the breath test result, the printout, or a copy, shall be given to the accused.

C. A person, after having been arrested for a violation of clause (iii), (iv), or (v) of § 18.2-266 or § 18.2-266.1 or subsection B of § 18.2-272 or of a similar ordinance, may be required to submit to a blood test to determine the drug or both drug and alcohol content of his blood. When a person, after having been arrested for a violation of § 18.2-266 (i) or (ii) or both, submits to a breath test in accordance with subsection B or refuses to take or is incapable of taking such a breath test, he may be required to submit to tests to determine the drug or both drug and alcohol content of his blood if the law-enforcement officer has reasonable cause to believe the person was driving under the influence of any drug or combination of drugs, or the combined influence of alcohol and drugs.

History.

1992, c. 830; 1993, c. 746; 1994, cc. 359, 363; 1995, c. 23; 2002, c. 748; 2004, c. 1013; 2005, cc. 616, 757, 840.

§ 18.2-268.3. Refusal of tests; penalties; procedures.

A. It shall be unlawful for a person who is arrested for a violation of § 18.2-266, 18.2-266.1, or subsection B of § 18.2-272 or of a similar ordinance to unreasonably refuse to have samples of his blood or breath or both blood and breath taken for chemical tests to determine the alcohol or drug content of his blood as required by § 18.2-268.2 and any person who so unreasonably refuses is guilty of a violation of this section.

B. When a person is arrested for a violation of § 18.2-51.4, 18.2-266, 18.2-266.1 or, subsection B of § 18.2-272 or of a similar ordinance and such person refuses to permit blood or breath or both blood and breath samples to be taken for testing as required by § 18.2-268.2, the arresting officer shall advise the person, from a form provided by the Office of the Executive Secretary of the Supreme Court, that (i) a person who operates a motor vehicle upon a highway in the Commonwealth is deemed thereby, as a condition of such operation, to have consented to have samples of his blood and breath taken for chemical tests to determine the alcohol or drug content of his blood, (ii) a finding of unreasonable refusal to consent may be admitted as evidence at a criminal trial, (iii) the unreasonable refusal to do so constitutes grounds for the revocation of the privilege of operating a motor vehicle upon the highways of the Commonwealth, (iv) the criminal penalty for unreasonable refusal within 10 years of a prior conviction for driving while intoxicated or unreasonable refusal is a Class 2 misdemeanor, and (v) the criminal penalty for unreasonable refusal within 10 years of any two prior convictions for driving while intoxicated or unreasonable refusal is a Class 1 misdemeanor. The form from which the arresting officer shall advise the person arrested shall contain a brief statement of the law requiring the taking of blood or breath samples, a statement that a finding of unreasonable refusal to consent may be admitted as evidence at a criminal trial, and the penalties for refusal. The Office of the Executive Secretary of the Supreme Court shall make the form available on the Internet and the form shall be considered an official publication of the Commonwealth for the purposes of § 8.01-388.

C. The arresting officer shall, under oath before the magistrate, execute the form and certify, (i) that the defendant has refused to permit blood or breath or both blood and breath samples to be taken for testing; (ii) that the officer has read the portion of the form described in subsection B to the arrested person; (iii) that the arrested person, after having had the portion of the form described in subsection B read to him, has refused to permit such sample or samples to be taken; and (iv) how many, if any, violations of this section, § 18.2-266, or any offense described in subsection E of § 18.2-270 the arrested person has been convicted of within the last 10 years. Such sworn certification shall constitute probable cause for the magistrate to issue a warrant or summons charging the person with unreasonable refusal. The magistrate shall attach the executed and sworn advisement form to the warrant or summons. The warrant or summons for a first offense under this section shall be executed in the same manner as a criminal warrant or summons. If the person arrested has been taken to a medical facility for treatment or evaluation of his medical condition, the arresting officer may read the advisement form to the person at the medical facility, and issue, on the premises of the medical facility, a summons for a violation of this section in lieu of securing a warrant or summons from the magistrate. The magistrate or arresting officer, as the case may be, shall forward the executed advisement form and warrant or summons to the appropriate court.

D. A first violation of this section is a civil offense and subsequent violations are criminal offenses. For a first offense the court shall suspend the defendant's privilege to drive for a period of one year. This suspension period is in addition to the suspension period provided under § 46.2-391.2.

If a person is found to have violated this section and within 10 years prior to the date of the refusal he was found guilty of any of the following: a violation of this section, a violation of § 18.2-266, or a violation of any offense listed in subsection E of § 18.2-270, arising out of separate occurrences or incidents, he is guilty of a Class 2 misdemeanor and the court shall suspend the defendant's privilege to drive for a period of three years. This suspension period is in addition to the suspension period provided under § 46.2-391.2.

If a person is found guilty of a violation of this section and within 10 years prior to the date of the refusal he was found guilty of any two of the following: a violation of this section, a violation of § 18.2-266, or a violation of any offense listed in subsection E of § 18.2-270 arising out of separate occurrences or incidents, he is guilty of a Class 1 misdemeanor and the court shall suspend the defendant's privilege to drive for a period of three years. This suspension period is in addition to the suspension period provided under § 46.2-391.2.

History.

1992, c. 830; 1994, cc. 359, 363; 1997, c. 691; 2001, cc. 654, 779; 2004, cc. 985, 1013, 1022; 2004, Sp. Sess. I, c. 2; 2005, cc. 757, 840; 2009, c. 239.

§ 18.2-268.4. Trial and appeal for refusal.

A. Venue for the trial of the warrant or summons shall lie in the court of the county or city in which the offense of driving under the influence of intoxicants or other offense listed in subsection A of § 18.2-268.3 is to be tried.

B. The procedure for appeal and trial of a first offense of § 18.2-268.3 shall be the same as provided by law for misdemeanors; if requested by either party on appeal to the circuit court, trial by jury shall be as provided in Article 4 (§ 19.2-260 et seq.) of Chapter 15 of Title 19.2, and the Commonwealth shall be required to prove its case beyond a reasonable doubt.

C. If the defendant pleads guilty to a violation of § 18.2-266, 18.2-266.1, or subsection B of § 18.2-272 or of a similar ordinance, the court may dismiss the warrant or summons.

The court shall dispose of the defendant's license in accordance with the provisions of § 46.2-398; however, the defendant's license shall not be returned during any period of suspension imposed under § 46.2-391.2.

History.

1992, c. 830; 1994, cc. 151, 359, 363; 2004, cc. 985, 1013; 2005, cc. 757, 840, 943.

§ 18.2-268.5. Qualifications and liability of persons authorized to take blood sample; procedure for taking samples.

For purposes of this article, only a physician, registered nurse, licensed practical nurse, phlebotomist, graduate laboratory technician or a technician or nurse designated by order of a circuit court acting upon the recommendation of a licensed physician, using soap and water, polyvinylpyrrolidone iodine, pvp iodine, povidone iodine or benzalkonium chloride to cleanse the part of the body from which the blood is taken and using instruments sterilized by the accepted steam sterilizer or some other sterilizer which will not affect the accuracy of the test, or using chemically clean sterile disposable syringes, shall withdraw blood for the purpose of determining its alcohol or drug or both alcohol and drug content. It is a Class 3 misdemeanor to reuse single-use-only needles or syringes. No civil liability shall attach to any person authorized to withdraw blood as a result of the act of withdrawing blood as provided in this section from any person submitting thereto, provided the blood was withdrawn according to recognized medical procedures. However, the person shall not be relieved from liability for negligence in the withdrawing of any blood sample.

No person arrested for a violation of § 18.2-266, 18.2-266.1, or subsection B of § 18.2-272, or a similar ordinance shall be required to execute in favor of any person or corporation a waiver or release of liability in connection with the withdrawal of blood and as a condition precedent to the withdrawal of blood as provided for in this section.

History.

1992, c. 830; 1994, cc. 359, 363; 2004, cc. 150, 440, 1013; 2005, cc. 757, 840.

§ 18.2-268.6. Transmission of blood samples.

The blood sample withdrawn pursuant to § 18.2-268.5 shall be placed in vials provided or approved by the Department of Forensic Science. The vials shall be sealed by the person taking the sample or at his direction. The person who seals the vials shall complete the prenumbered certificate of blood withdrawal forms and attach one form to each vial. The completed withdrawal certificate for each vial shall show the name of the accused, the name of the person taking the blood sample, the date and time the blood sample was taken and information identifying the arresting or accompanying officer. The vials shall be placed in a container provided by the Department, and the container shall be sealed to prevent tampering with the vials. The arresting or accompanying officer shall take possession of the container as soon as the vials are placed in the container and sealed, and shall promptly transport or mail the container to the Department.

History.

1992, c. 830; 2001, c. 561; 2003, cc. 933, 936; 2005, cc. 868, 881.

§ 18.2-268.7. Transmission of blood test samples; use as evidence.

A. Upon receipt of a blood sample forwarded to the Department for analysis pursuant to § 18.2-268.6, the Department shall have it examined for its alcohol or drug or both alcohol and drug content and the Director shall execute a certificate of analysis indicating the name of the accused; the date, time and by whom the blood sample was received and examined; a statement that the seal on the vial had not been broken or otherwise tampered with; a statement that the container and vial were provided or approved by the Department and that the vial was one to which the completed withdrawal certificate was attached; and a statement of the sample's alcohol or drug or both alcohol and drug content. The Director shall remove the withdrawal certificate from the vial and either (i) attach it to the certificate of analysis and state in the certificate of analysis that it was so removed and attached or (ii) electronically scan it into the Department's Laboratory Information Management System and place the original withdrawal certificate in its case-specific file. The certificate of analysis and the withdrawal certificate shall be returned or electronically transmitted to the clerk of the court in which the charge will be heard.

B. After completion of the analysis, the Department shall preserve the remainder of the blood until at least 90 days have lapsed from the date the blood was drawn. During this 90-day period, the accused may, by motion filed before the court in which the charge will be heard, with notice to the Department, request an order directing the Department to transmit the remainder of the blood sample to an independent laboratory retained by the accused for analysis. The Department shall destroy the remainder of the blood sample if no notice of a motion to transmit the remaining blood sample is received during the 90-day period.

C. When a blood sample taken in accordance with the provisions of §§ 18.2-268.2 through 18.2-268.6 is forwarded for analysis to the Department, a report of the test results shall be filed in that office. Upon proper identification of the certificate of withdrawal, the certificate of analysis, with the withdrawal certificate attached, shall, when attested by the Director, be admissible in any court as evidence of the facts therein stated and of the results of such analysis (i) in any criminal proceeding, provided the requirements of subsection A of § 19.2-187.1 have been satisfied and the accused has not objected to the admission of the certificate pursuant to subsection B of § 19.2-187.1, or (ii) in any civil proceeding. On motion of the accused, the report of analysis prepared for the remaining blood sample shall be admissible in evidence provided the report is duly attested by a person performing such analysis and the independent laboratory that performed the analysis is accredited or certified to conduct forensic blood alcohol/drug testing by one or more of the following bodies: American Society of Crime Laboratory Directors/Laboratory Accreditation Board (ASCLD/LAB); College of American Pathologists (CAP); United States Department of Health and Human Services Substance Abuse and Mental Health Services Administration (SAMHSA); or American Board of Forensic Toxicology (ABFT).

Upon request of the person whose blood was analyzed, the test results shall be made available to him.

The Director may delegate or assign these duties to an employee of the Department.

History.

1992, c. 830; 1993, c. 688; 1994, cc. 337, 359, 363; 2003, cc. 933, 936; 2005, cc. 868, 881; 2009, Sp. Sess. I, cc. 1, 4; 2014, c. 328.

§ 18.2-268.8. Fees.

Payment for withdrawing blood shall not exceed $25, which shall be paid out of the appropriation for criminal charges. If the person whose blood sample was withdrawn is subsequently convicted for a violation of § 18.2-266, 18.2-266.1, or subsection B of § 18.2-272 or of a similar ordinance, or is placed under the purview of a probational, educational, or rehabilitational program as set forth in § 18.2-271.1, the amount charged by the person withdrawing the sample shall be taxed as part of the costs of the criminal case and shall be paid into the general fund of the state treasury.

If the person whose blood sample was withdrawn is subsequently convicted for violation of § 18.2-266, 18.2-266.1, or subsection B of § 18.2-272 or a similar ordinance, a fee of $25 for testing the first blood sample by the Department shall be taxed as part of the costs of the criminal case and shall be paid into the general fund of the state treasury.

History.

1992, c. 830; 1994, cc. 359, 363; 2001, c. 561; 2003, cc. 933, 936; 2004, c. 1013; 2005, cc. 757, 840, 868, 881.

§ 18.2-268.9. Assurance of breath-test validity; use of breath-test results as evidence.

A. To be capable of being considered valid as evidence in a prosecution under § 18.2-266, 18.2-266.1, or subsection B of § 18.2-272, or a similar ordinance, chemical analysis of a person's breath shall be performed by an individual possessing a valid license to conduct such tests, with a type of equipment and in accordance with methods approved by the Department.

B. The Department shall establish a training program for all individuals who are to administer the breath tests. Upon a person's successful completion of the training program, the Department may license him to conduct breath-test analyses. Such license shall identify the specific types of breath test equipment upon which the individual has successfully completed training. Any individual conducting a breath test under the provisions of § 18.2-268.2 shall issue a certificate which will indicate that the test was conducted in accordance with the Department's specifications, the name of the accused, that prior to administration of the test the accused was advised of his right to observe the process and see the blood alcohol reading on the equipment used to perform the breath test, the date and time the sample was taken from the accused, the sample's alcohol content, and the name of the person who examined the sample. This certificate, when attested by the individual conducting the breath test on equipment maintained by the Department, shall be admissible in any court as evidence of the facts therein stated and of the results of such analysis (i) in any criminal proceeding, provided that the requirements of subsection A of § 19.2-187.1 have been satisfied and the accused has not objected to the admission of the certificate pursuant to subsection B of § 19.2-187.1, or (ii) in any civil proceeding. Any such certificate of analysis purporting to be signed by a person authorized by the Department shall be admissible in evidence without proof of seal or signature of the person whose name is signed to it. A copy of the certificate shall be promptly delivered to the accused. Copies of Department records relating to any breath test conducted pursuant to this section shall be admissible provided such copies are authenticated as true copies either by the custodian thereof or by the person to whom the custodian reports.

The officer making the arrest, or anyone with him at the time of the arrest, or anyone participating in the arrest of the accused, if otherwise qualified to conduct such test as provided by this section, may administer the breath test and analyze the results.

History.

1992, c. 830; 1994, cc. 359, 363; 1996, cc. 154, 952; 1997, c. 256; 1999, c. 273; 2004, c. 1013; 2005, cc. 757, 840, 868, 881; 2006, c. 101; 2009, Sp. Sess. I, cc. 1, 4.

§ 18.2-268.10. Evidence of violation of driving under the influence offenses.

A. In any trial for a violation of § 18.2-266, 18.2-266.1, or subsection B of § 18.2-272 or a similar ordinance, the admission of the blood or breath test results shall not limit the introduction of any other relevant evidence bearing upon any question at issue before the court, and the court shall, regardless of the result of any blood or breath tests, consider other relevant admissible evidence of the condition of the accused. If the test results indicate the presence of any drug other than alcohol, the test results shall be admissible, except in a prosecution under clause (v) of § 18.2-266, only if other competent evidence has been presented to relate the presence of the drug or drugs to the impairment of the accused's ability to drive or operate any motor vehicle, engine or train safely.

B. The failure of an accused to permit a blood or breath sample to be taken to determine the alcohol or drug content of his blood is not evidence and shall not be subject to comment by the Commonwealth at the trial of the case, except in rebuttal or pursuant to subsection C; nor shall the fact that a blood or breath test had been offered the accused be evidence or the subject of comment by the Commonwealth, except in rebuttal or pursuant to subsection C.

C. Evidence of a finding against the defendant under § 18.2-268.3 for his unreasonable refusal to permit a blood or breath sample to be taken to determine the alcohol or drug content of his blood shall be admissible into evidence, upon the motion of the Commonwealth or the defendant, for the sole purpose of explaining the absence at trial of a chemical test of such sample. When admitted pursuant to this subsection such evidence shall not be considered evidence of the accused's guilt.

D. The court or jury trying the case involving a violation of clause (ii), (iii) or (iv) of § 18.2-266 or

§ 18.2-266.1, or a similar ordinance shall determine the innocence or guilt of the defendant from all the evidence concerning his condition at the time of the alleged offense.

History.

1992, c. 830; 1994, cc. 359, 363; 2001, c. 654; 2004, c. 1013; 2005, cc. 616, 757, 840.

§ 18.2-268.11. Substantial compliance.

The steps set forth in §§ 18.2-268.2 through 18.2-268.9 relating to taking, handling, identifying, and disposing of blood or breath samples are procedural and not substantive. Substantial compliance shall be sufficient. Failure to comply with any steps or portions thereof shall not of itself be grounds for finding the defendant not guilty, but shall go to the weight of the evidence and shall be considered with all the evidence in the case; however, the defendant shall have the right to introduce evidence on his own behalf to show noncompliance with the aforesaid procedures or any part thereof, and that as a result his rights were prejudiced.

History.

1992, c. 830; 2003, cc. 933, 936.

§ 18.2-268.12. Ordinances.

The governing bodies of counties, cities and towns are authorized to adopt ordinances paralleling the provisions of §§ 18.2-268.1 through 18.2-268.11.

History.

1992, c. 830.

§ 18.2-269. Presumptions from alcohol or drug content of blood.

A. In any prosecution for a violation of § 18.2-36.1 or clause (ii), (iii) or (iv) of § 18.2-266, or any similar ordinance, the amount of alcohol or drugs in the blood of the accused at the time of the alleged offense as indicated by a chemical analysis of a sample of the accused's blood or breath to determine the alcohol or drug content of his blood in accordance with the provisions of §§ 18.2-268.1 through 18.2-268.12 shall give rise to the following rebuttable presumptions:

(1) If there was at that time 0.05 percent or less by weight by volume of alcohol in the accused's blood or 0.05 grams or less per 210 liters of the accused's breath, it shall be presumed that the accused was not under the influence of alcohol intoxicants at the time of the alleged offense;

(2) If there was at that time in excess of 0.05 percent but less than 0.08 percent by weight by volume of alcohol in the accused's blood or 0.05 grams but less than 0.08 grams per 210 liters of the accused's breath, such facts shall not give rise to any presumption that the accused was or was not under the influence of alcohol intoxicants at the time of the alleged offense, but such facts may be considered with other competent evidence in determining the guilt or innocence of the accused;

(3) If there was at that time 0.08 percent or more by weight by volume of alcohol in the accused's blood or 0.08 grams or more per 210 liters of the accused's breath, it shall be presumed that the accused was under the influence of alcohol intoxicants at the time of the alleged offense; or

(4) If there was at that time an amount of the following substances at a level that is equal to or greater than: (a) 0.02 milligrams of cocaine per liter of blood, (b) 0.1 milligrams of methamphetamine per liter of blood, (c) 0.01 milligrams of phencyclidine per liter of blood, or (d) 0.1 milligrams of 3,4-methylenedioxymethamphetamine per liter of blood, it shall be presumed that the accused was under the influence of drugs at the time of the alleged offense to a degree which impairs his ability to drive or operate any motor vehicle, engine or train safely.

B. The provisions of this section shall not apply to and shall not affect any prosecution for a violation of § 46.2-341.24.

History.

Code 1950, § 18.1-57; 1960, c. 358; 1964, c. 240; 1966, c. 636; 1972, c. 757; 1973, c. 459; 1975, cc. 14, 15; 1977, c. 638; 1983, c. 504; 1986, c. 635; 1989, cc. 554, 574, 705; 1992, c. 830; 1994, cc. 359, 363; 2005, c. 616.

§ 18.2-270. Penalty for driving while intoxicated; subsequent offense; prior conviction.

A. Except as otherwise provided herein, any person violating any provision of § 18.2-266 shall be guilty of a Class 1 misdemeanor with a mandatory minimum fine of $250. If the person's blood alcohol level as indicated by the chemical test administered as provided in this article or by any other scientifically reliable chemical test performed on whole blood under circumstances reliably establishing the identity of the person who is the source of the blood and the accuracy of the results (i) was at least 0.15, but not more than 0.20, he shall be confined in jail for an additional mandatory minimum period of five days or, (ii) if the level was more than 0.20, for an additional mandatory minimum period of 10 days.

B. 1. Any person convicted of a second offense committed within less than five years after a prior offense under § 18.2-266 shall upon conviction of the second offense be punished by a mandatory minimum fine of $500 and by confinement in jail for not less than one month nor more than one year. Twenty days of such confinement shall be a mandatory minimum sentence.

2. Any person convicted of a second offense committed within a period of five to 10 years of a prior offense under § 18.2-266 shall upon conviction of the second offense be punished by a mandatory minimum fine of $500 and by confinement in jail for

not less than one month. Ten days of such confinement shall be a mandatory minimum sentence.

3. Upon conviction of a second offense within 10 years of a prior offense, if the person's blood alcohol level as indicated by the chemical test administered as provided in this article or by any other scientifically reliable chemical test performed on whole blood under circumstances reliably establishing the identity of the person who is the source of the blood and the accuracy of the results (i) was at least 0.15, but not more than 0.20, he shall be confined in jail for an additional mandatory minimum period of 10 days or, (ii) if the level was more than 0.20, for an additional mandatory minimum period of 20 days. In addition, such person shall be fined a mandatory minimum fine of $500.

C. 1. Any person convicted of three offenses of § 18.2-266 committed within a 10-year period shall upon conviction of the third offense be guilty of a Class 6 felony. The sentence of any person convicted of three offenses of § 18.2-266 committed within a 10-year period shall include a mandatory minimum sentence of 90 days, unless the three offenses were committed within a five-year period, in which case the sentence shall include a mandatory minimum sentence of confinement for six months. In addition, such person shall be fined a mandatory minimum fine of $1,000.

2. A person who has been convicted of § 18.2-36.1, 18.2-36.2, 18.2-51.4, 18.2-51.5, or a felony violation of § 18.2-266 shall upon conviction of a subsequent violation of § 18.2-266 be guilty of a Class 6 felony. The punishment of any person convicted of such a subsequent violation of § 18.2-266 shall include a mandatory minimum term of imprisonment of one year and a mandatory minimum fine of $1,000.

3. The punishment of any person convicted of a fourth or subsequent offense of § 18.2-266 committed within a 10-year period shall, upon conviction, include a mandatory minimum term of imprisonment of one year. In addition, such person shall be fined a mandatory minimum fine of $1,000.

4. The vehicle solely owned and operated by the accused during the commission of a felony violation of § 18.2-266 shall be subject to seizure and forfeiture. After an arrest for a felony violation of § 18.2-266, the Commonwealth may file an information in accordance with § 19.2-386.34.

D. In addition to the penalty otherwise authorized by this section or § 16.1-278.9, any person convicted of a violation of § 18.2-266 committed while transporting a person 17 years of age or younger shall be (i) fined an additional minimum of $500 and not more than $1,000 and (ii) sentenced to a mandatory minimum period of confinement of five days.

E. For the purpose of determining the number of offenses committed by, and the punishment appropriate for, a person under this section, an adult conviction of any person, or finding of guilty in the case of a juvenile, under the following shall be considered a conviction of § 18.2-266: (i) the provisions of § 18.2-36.1 or the substantially similar laws of any other state or of the United States, (ii) the provisions of §§ 18.2-51.4, 18.2-266, former § 18.1-54 (formerly § 18-75), the ordinance of any county, city or town in this Commonwealth or the laws of any other state or of the United States substantially similar to the provisions of § 18.2-51.4, or § 18.2-266, or (iii) the provisions of subsection A of § 46.2-341.24 or the substantially similar laws of any other state or of the United States.

F. Mandatory minimum punishments imposed pursuant to this section shall be cumulative, and mandatory minimum terms of confinement shall be served consecutively. However, in no case shall punishment imposed hereunder exceed the applicable statutory maximum Class 1 misdemeanor term of confinement or fine upon conviction of a first or second offense, or Class 6 felony term of confinement or fine upon conviction of a third or subsequent offense.

History.

Code 1950, § 18.1-58; 1960, c. 358; 1962, c. 302; 1975, cc. 14, 15; 1982, c. 301; 1983, c. 504; 1989, c. 705; 1991, cc. 370, 710; 1992, c. 891; 1993, c. 972; 1997, c. 691; 1999, cc. 743, 945, 949, 987; 2000, cc. 784, 956, 958, 980, 982; 2002, c. 759; 2003, cc. 573, 591; 2004, cc. 461, 937, 946, 950, 957, 958, 962; 2006, cc. 82, 314; 2009, c. 229; 2012, cc. 283, 756; 2013, cc. 415, 655; 2014, c. 707.

§ 18.2-270.01. Multiple offenders; payment to Trauma Center Fund.

A. The court shall order any person convicted of a violation of §§ 18.2-36.1, 18.2-51.4, 18.2-266, 18.2-266.1 or § 46.2-341.24 who has been convicted previously of one or more violations of any of those sections or any ordinance, any law of another state, or any law of the United States substantially similar to the provisions of those sections within 10 years of the date of the current offense to pay $50 to the Trauma Center Fund for the purpose of defraying the costs of providing emergency medical care to victims of automobile accidents attributable to alcohol or drug use.

B. There is hereby established in the state treasury a special nonreverting fund to be known as the Trauma Center Fund. The Fund shall consist of any moneys paid into it by virtue of operation of subsection A hereof and any moneys appropriated thereto by the General Assembly and designated for the Fund. Any moneys deposited to or remaining in the Fund during or at the end of each fiscal year or biennium, including interest thereon, shall not revert to the general fund but shall remain in the Fund and be available for allocation in ensuing fiscal years. The Department of Health shall award and administer grants from the Trauma Center Fund to appropriate trauma centers based on the cost to provide emergency medical care to victims of automobile accidents. The Department of Health shall develop, on or before October 1, 2004, written criteria for the awarding of such grants that shall be evaluated and, if necessary, revised on an annual basis.

History.
2004, c. 999.

§ 18.2-270.1. Ignition interlock systems; penalty.

A. For purposes of this section and § 18.2-270.2:

"Commission" means the Commission on VASAP.

"Department" means the Department of Motor Vehicles.

"Ignition interlock system" means a device that (i) connects a motor vehicle ignition system to an analyzer that measures a driver's blood alcohol content; (ii) prevents a motor vehicle ignition from starting if a driver's blood alcohol content exceeds 0.02 percent; and (iii) is equipped with the ability to perform a rolling retest and to electronically log the blood alcohol content during ignition, attempted ignition and rolling retest.

"Rolling retest" means a test of the vehicle operator's blood alcohol content required at random intervals during operation of the vehicle, which triggers the sounding of the horn and flashing of lights if (i) the test indicates that the operator has a blood alcohol content which exceeds 0.02 percent or (ii) the operator fails to take the test.

B. In addition to any penalty provided by law for a conviction under § 18.2-51.4 or 18.2-266 or a substantially similar ordinance of any county, city or town, any court of proper jurisdiction shall, as a condition of a restricted license, prohibit an offender from operating a motor vehicle that is not equipped with a functioning, certified ignition interlock system for any period of time not to exceed the period of license suspension and restriction, not less than six consecutive months without alcohol-related violations of the interlock requirements. The court shall, for a conviction under § 18.2-51.4, a second or subsequent offense of § 18.2-266 or a substantially similar ordinance of any county, city or town, or as a condition of license restoration pursuant to subsection C of § 18.2-271.1 or § 46.2-391, require that such a system be installed on each motor vehicle, as defined in § 46.2-100, owned by or registered to the offender, in whole or in part, for such period of time. Such condition shall be in addition to any purposes for which a restricted license may be issued pursuant to § 18.2-271.1. The court may order the installation of an ignition interlock system to commence immediately upon conviction. A fee of $20 to cover court and administrative costs related to the ignition interlock system shall be paid by any such offender to the clerk of the court. The court shall require the offender to install an electronic log device with the ignition interlock system on a vehicle designated by the court to measure the blood alcohol content at each attempted ignition and random rolling retest during operation of the vehicle. The offender shall be enrolled in and supervised by an alcohol safety action program pursuant to § 18.2-271.1 and to conditions established by regulation under § 18.2-270.2 by the Commission during the period for which the court has ordered installation of the ignition interlock system. The offender shall be further required to provide to such program, at least quarterly during the period of court ordered ignition interlock installation, a printout from such electronic log indicating the offender's blood alcohol content during such ignitions, attempted ignitions, and rolling retests, and showing attempts to circumvent or tamper with the equipment.

C. In any case in which the court requires the installation of an ignition interlock system, the court shall order the offender not to operate any motor vehicle that is not equipped with such a system for the period of time that the interlock restriction is in effect. The clerk of the court shall file with the Department of Motor Vehicles a copy of the order, which shall become a part of the offender's operator's license record maintained by the Department. The Department shall issue to the offender for the period during which the interlock restriction is imposed a restricted license which shall appropriately set forth the restrictions required by the court under this subsection and any other restrictions imposed upon the offender's driving privilege, and shall also set forth any exception granted by the court under subsection F.

D. The offender shall be ordered to provide the appropriate ASAP program, within 30 days of the effective date of the order of court, proof of the installation of the ignition interlock system. The Program shall require the offender to have the system monitored and calibrated for proper operation at least every 30 days by an entity approved by the Commission under the provisions of § 18.2-270.2 and to demonstrate proof thereof. The offender shall pay the cost of leasing or buying and monitoring and maintaining the ignition interlock system. Absent good cause shown, the court may revoke the offender's driving privilege for failing to (i) timely install such system or (ii) have the system properly monitored and calibrated.

E. No person shall start or attempt to start a motor vehicle equipped with an ignition interlock system for the purpose of providing an operable motor vehicle to a person who is prohibited under this section from operating a motor vehicle that is not equipped with an ignition interlock system. No person shall tamper with, or in any way attempt to circumvent the operation of, an ignition interlock system that has been installed in the motor vehicle of a person under this section. Except as authorized in subsection F, no person shall knowingly furnish a motor vehicle not equipped with a functioning ignition interlock system to any person prohibited under subsection B from operating any motor vehicle which is not equipped with such system. A violation of this subsection is punishable as a Class 1 misdemeanor.

F. Any person prohibited from operating a motor vehicle under subsection B may, solely in the course of his employment, operate a motor vehicle which is owned or provided by his employer without installation of an ignition interlock system, if the court expressly permits such operation as a condition of a restricted license at the request of the employer, but such person may not operate a school bus, school vehicle, or a commercial motor vehicle as defined in § 46.2-341.4. This subsection shall not apply if such employer is an entity wholly or partially owned or controlled by the person otherwise prohibited from operating a vehicle without an ignition interlock system.

G. The Commission shall promulgate such regulations and forms as are necessary to implement the procedures outlined in this section.

History.

1995, c. 486; 1996, c. 841; 1997, c. 691; 1998, cc. 783, 840; 1999, c. 734; 2000, cc. 958, 980; 2004, c. 961; 2007, c. 686; 2008, c. 862; 2012, cc. 141, 570; 2014, c. 707.

§ 18.2-270.2. Ignition interlock system; certification by Commission on VASAP; regulations; sale or lease; monitoring use; reports.

A. The Executive Director of the Commission on VASAP or his designee shall, pursuant to approval by the Commission, certify ignition interlock systems for use in this Commonwealth and adopt regulations and forms for the installation, maintenance and certification of such ignition interlock systems.

The regulations adopted shall include requirements that ignition interlock systems:

1. Do not impede the safe operation of the vehicle;
2. Minimize opportunities to be bypassed, circumvented or tampered with, and provide evidence thereof;
3. Correlate accurately with established measures of blood alcohol content and be calibrated according to the manufacturer's specifications;
4. Work accurately and reliably in an unsupervised environment;
5. Have the capability to provide an accurate written measure of blood alcohol content for each ignition, attempted ignition, and rolling retest, and record each attempt to circumvent or tamper with the equipment;
6. Minimize inconvenience to other users;
7. Be manufactured or distributed by an entity responsible for installation, user training, service, and maintenance, and meet the safety and operational requirements promulgated by the National Highway Transportation Safety Administration;
8. Operate reliably over the range of motor vehicle environments or motor vehicle manufacturing standards;
9. Be manufactured by an entity which is adequately insured against liability, in an amount established by the Commission, including product liability and installation and maintenance errors;
10. Provide for an electronic log of the driver's experience with the system with an information management system capable of electronically delivering information to the agency supervising the interlock user within twenty-four hours of the collection of such information from the datalogger; and
11. Provide for a rolling retest of the operator's blood alcohol content.

Such regulations shall also provide for the establishment of a fund, using a percentage of fees received by the manufacturer or distributor providing ignition interlock services, to afford persons found by the court to be indigent all or part of the costs of an ignition interlock system.

The Commission shall design and adopt a warning label to be affixed to an ignition interlock system upon installation. The warning label shall state that a person tampering with, or attempting to circumvent the ignition interlock system shall be guilty of a Class 1 misdemeanor and, upon conviction, shall be subject to a fine or incarceration or both.

The Commission shall publish a list of certified ignition interlock systems and shall ensure that such systems are available throughout the Commonwealth. The local alcohol safety action program shall make the list available to eligible offenders, who shall have the responsibility and authority to choose which certified ignition interlock company will supply the offender's equipment. A manufacturer or distributor of an ignition interlock system that seeks to sell or lease the ignition interlock system to persons subject to the provisions of § 18.2-270.1 shall pay the reasonable costs of obtaining the required certification, as set forth by the Commission.

B. A person may not sell or lease or offer to sell or lease an ignition interlock system to any person subject to the provisions of § 18.2-270.1 unless:

1. The system has been certified by the Commission; and
2. The warning label adopted by the Commission is affixed to the system.

C. A manufacturer or distributor of an ignition interlock system shall provide such services as may be required at no cost to the Commonwealth. Such services shall include a toll free, twenty-four-hour telephone number for the users of ignition interlock systems.

History.

1995, c. 486; 2000, cc. 341, 362.

§ 18.2-271. Forfeiture of driver's license for driving while intoxicated.

A. Except as provided in § 18.2-271.1, the judgment of conviction if for a first offense under § 18.2-266 or for a similar offense under any county, city, or town ordinance, or for a first offense under subsection A of § 46.2-341.24, shall of itself operate to deprive the person so convicted of the privilege to drive or operate any motor vehicle, engine or train in the Commonwealth for a period of one year from the date of such judgment. This suspension period shall be in addition to the suspension period provided under § 46.2-391.2.

B. If a person (i) is tried on a process alleging a second offense of violating § 18.2-266 or subsection A of § 46.2-341.24, or any substantially similar local ordinance, or law of any other jurisdiction, within ten years of a first offense for which the person was convicted, or found guilty in the case of a juvenile, under § 18.2-266 or subsection A of § 46.2-341.24 or any valid local ordinance or any law of any other jurisdiction substantially similar to § 18.2-266 or subsection A of § 46.2-341.24 and (ii) is convicted thereof, such conviction shall of itself operate to deprive the person so convicted of the privilege to drive or operate any motor vehicle, engine or train in the Commonwealth for a period of three years from the date of the judgment of conviction and such person shall have his license revoked as provided in subsection A of § 46.2-391. The court trying such case shall order the surrender of the person's driver's license, to be disposed of in accordance with § 46.2-398, and shall notify such person that his license has been revoked for a period of three years and that the penalty for violating that revocation is as set out in § 46.2-391. This suspension period shall be in addition to the suspension period provided under § 46.2-391.2. Any period of license suspension or revocation imposed pursuant to this section, in any case, shall run consecutively with any period of suspension for failure to permit a blood or breath sample to be taken as required by §§ 18.2-268.1 through 18.2-268.12 or §§ 46.2-341.26:1 through 46.2-341.26:11 or any period of suspension for a previous violation of § 18.2-266, 18.2-266.1, or 46.2-341.24.

C. If a person (i) is tried on a process alleging (a) a felony conviction of § 18.2-266 or (b) a third or subsequent offense of violating § 18.2-266 or subsection A of § 46.2-341.24, or any substantially similar local ordinance, or law of any other jurisdiction, within 10 years of two other offenses for which the person was convicted, or found not innocent in the case of a juvenile, under § 18.2-266 or subsection A of § 46.2-341.24 or any valid local ordinance or any law of any other jurisdiction substantially similar to § 18.2-266 or subsection A of § 46.2-341.24 and (ii) is convicted thereof, such conviction shall of itself operate to deprive the person so convicted of the privilege to drive or operate any motor vehicle, engine or train in the Commonwealth and such person shall not be eligible for participation in a program pursuant to § 18.2-271.1 and shall, upon such conviction, have his license revoked as provided in subsection B of § 46.2-391. The court trying such case shall order the surrender of the person's driver's license, to be disposed of in accordance with § 46.2-398, and shall notify such person that his license has been revoked indefinitely and that the penalty for violating that revocation is as set out in § 46.2-391.

D. Notwithstanding any other provision of this section, the period of license revocation or suspension shall not begin to expire until the person convicted has surrendered his license to the court or to the Department of Motor Vehicles.

E. The provisions of this section shall not apply to, and shall have no effect upon, any disqualification from operating a commercial motor vehicle imposed under the provisions of the Commercial Driver's License Act (§ 46.2-341.1 et seq.).

History.

Code 1950, § 18.1-59; 1960, c. 358; 1962, c. 625; 1964, c. 240; 1972, c. 757; 1975, cc. 14, 15; 1982, c. 301; 1983, c. 504; 1984, cc. 623, 673; 1989, c. 705; 1990, c. 949; 1992, cc. 722, 830, 891; 1994, cc. 359, 363; 2000, cc. 956, 982; 2001, c. 739; 2002, c. 873; 2010, c. 521; 2013, cc. 415, 655.

§ 18.2-271.1. Probation, education, and rehabilitation of person charged or convicted; person convicted under law of another state or federal law.

A. Any person convicted of a first or second offense of § 18.2-266, or any ordinance of a county, city, or town similar to the provisions thereof, or provisions of subsection A of § 46.2-341.24, shall be required by court order, as a condition of probation or otherwise, to enter into and successfully complete an alcohol safety action program in the judicial district in which such charge is brought or in any other judicial district upon such terms and conditions as the court may set forth. However, upon motion of a person convicted of any such offense following an assessment of the person conducted by an alcohol safety action program, the court, for good cause, may decline to order participation in such a program if the assessment by the alcohol safety action program indicates that intervention is not appropriate for such person. In no event shall such persons be permitted to enter any such program which is not certified as meeting minimum standards and criteria established by the Commission on the Virginia Alcohol Safety Action Program (VASAP) pursuant to this section and to § 18.2-271.2. However, any person charged with a violation of a first or second offense of § 18.2-266, or any ordinance of a county, city, or town similar to the provisions thereof, or provisions of subsection A of § 46.2-341.24, may, at any time prior to trial, enter into an alcohol safety action program in the judicial district in which such charge is brought or in any other judicial district. Any person who enters into such program prior to trial may pre-qualify with the program to have an ignition interlock system installed on any motor vehicle owned or operated by him. However, no ignition interlock company shall install an ignition interlock system on any such vehicle until a court issues to the person a restricted license with the ignition interlock restriction.

B. The court shall require the person entering such program under the provisions of this section to pay a fee of no less than $250 but no more than $300. A reasonable portion of such fee, as may be determined by the Commission on VASAP, but not to exceed 10 percent, shall be forwarded monthly to be deposited with the State Treasurer for expenditure by the Commission on VASAP, and the balance shall be held in a separate fund for local administration of driver alcohol rehabilitation programs. Upon a positive finding that the defendant is indigent, the court may reduce or waive the fee. In addition to the costs of the proceeding, fees as may reasonably be required of defendants referred for intervention under any such program may be charged.

C. Upon conviction of a violation of § 18.2-266 or any ordinance of a county, city or town similar to the provisions thereof, or subsection A of § 46.2-341.24, the court shall impose the sentence authorized by § 18.2-270 or 46.2-341.28 and the license revocation as authorized by § 18.2-271. In addition, if the conviction was for a second offense committed within less than 10 years after a first such offense, the court shall order that restoration of the person's license to drive be conditioned upon the installation of an ignition interlock system on each motor vehicle, as defined in § 46.2-100, owned by or registered to the person, in whole or in part, for a period of six months beginning at the end of the three year license revocation, unless such a system has already been installed for six months prior to that time pursuant to a restricted license order under subsection E of this section. Upon a finding that a person so convicted is required to participate in the program described herein, the court shall enter the conviction on the warrant, and shall note that the person so convicted has been referred to such program. The court may then proceed to issue an order in accordance with subsection E of this section, if the court finds that the person so convicted is eligible for a restricted license. If the court finds good cause for a person not to participate in such program or subsequently that such person has violated, without good cause, any of the conditions set forth by the court in entering the program, the court shall dispose of the case as if no program had been entered, in which event the revocation provisions of § 46.2-389 and subsection A of § 46.2-391 shall be applicable to the conviction. The court shall, upon final disposition of the case, send a copy of its order to the Commissioner of the Department of Motor Vehicles. If such order provides for the issuance of a restricted license, the Commissioner of the Department of Motor Vehicles, upon receipt thereof, shall issue a restricted license. Appeals from any such disposition shall be allowed as provided by law. The time within which an appeal may be taken shall be calculated from the date of the final disposition of the case or any motion for rehearing, whichever is later.

D. Any person who has been convicted under the law of another state or the United States of an offense substantially similar to the provisions of § 18.2-266 or subsection A of § 46.2-341.24, and whose privilege to operate a motor vehicle in this Commonwealth is subject to revocation under the provisions of § 46.2-389 and subsection A of § 46.2-391, may petition the general district court of the county or city in which he resides that he be given probation and assigned to a program as provided in subsection A of this section and that, upon entry into such program, he be issued an order in accordance with subsection E of this section. If the court finds that such person would have qualified therefor if he had been convicted in this Commonwealth of a violation of § 18.2-266 or subsection A of § 46.2-341.24, the court may grant the petition and may issue an order in accordance with subsection E of this section as to the period of license suspension or revocation imposed pursuant to § 46.2-389 or subsection A of § 46.2-391. The court shall, as a condition of a restricted license, prohibit such person from operating a motor vehicle that is not equipped with a functioning certified ignition interlock system for a period of time not to exceed the period of license suspension and restriction, not less than six consecutive months without alcohol-related violations of interlock requirements. Such order shall be conditioned upon the successful completion of a program by the petitioner. If the court subsequently finds that such person has violated any of the conditions set forth by the court, the court shall dispose of the case as if no program had been entered and shall notify the Commissioner, who shall revoke the person's license in accordance with the provisions of § 46.2-389 or subsection A of § 46.2-391. A copy of the order granting the petition or subsequently revoking or suspending such person's license to operate a motor vehicle shall be forthwith sent to the Commissioner of the Department of Motor Vehicles.

No period of license suspension or revocation shall be imposed pursuant to this subsection which, when considered together with any period of license suspension or revocation previously imposed for the same offense under the law of another state or the United States, results in such person's license being suspended for a period in excess of the maximum periods specified in this subsection.

E. Except as otherwise provided herein, whenever a person enters a certified program pursuant to this section, and such person's license to operate a motor vehicle, engine or train in the Commonwealth has been suspended or revoked, the court may, in its discretion and for good cause shown, provide that such person be issued a restricted permit to operate a motor vehicle for any of the following purposes: (i) travel to and from his place of employment; (ii) travel to and from an alcohol rehabilitation or safety action program; (iii) travel during the hours of such person's employment if the operation of a motor vehicle is a necessary incident of such employment; (iv) travel to and from school if such person is a student, upon proper written verification to the court that such person is enrolled in a continuing program of education; (v) travel for health care services, including medically necessary transportation of an elderly parent or, as designated by the court, any person residing in the person's household with a serious medical problem upon written verification of need by a licensed health professional; (vi) travel necessary to transport a minor child under the care of such person to and from school, day care, and facilities housing medical service providers; (vii) travel to and from court-ordered visitation with a child of such person; (viii) travel to a screening, evaluation and education program entered pursuant to § 18.2-251 or subsection H of § 18.2-258.1; (ix) travel to and from court appearances in which he is a subpoenaed witness or a party and appointments with his probation officer and to and from any programs required by the court or as a condition of probation; (x) travel to and from a place of religious worship one day per week at a specified time and place; (xi) travel to and from appointments approved by the Division of Child Support Enforcement of the Department of Social Services as a requirement of participation in an administrative or court-ordered intensive case monitoring program for child support for which the participant maintains written proof of the appointment, including written proof of the date and time of the appointment, on his person; (xii) travel to and from jail to serve a sentence when such person has been convicted and sentenced to confinement in jail and pursuant to § 53.1-131.1 the time to be served is on weekends or nonconsecutive days; or (xiii) travel to and from the facility that installed or monitors the ignition interlock in the person's vehicle. No restricted license issued pursuant to this subsection shall permit any person to operate a commercial motor vehicle as defined in the Virginia Commercial Driver's License Act (§ 46.2-341.1 et seq.). The court shall order the surrender of such person's license to operate a motor vehicle to be disposed of in accordance with the provisions of § 46.2-398 and shall forward to the Commissioner of the Department of Motor Vehicles a copy of its order entered pursuant to this subsection, which shall specifically enumerate the restrictions imposed and contain such information regarding the person to whom such a permit is issued as is reasonably necessary to identify such person. The court shall also provide a copy of its order to the person so convicted who may operate a motor vehicle on the order until receipt from the Commissioner of the Department of Motor Vehicles of a restricted license, if the order provides for a restricted license for that time period. A copy of such order and, after receipt thereof, the restricted license shall be carried at all times while operating a motor vehicle. Any person who operates a motor vehicle in violation of any restrictions imposed pursuant to this section shall be guilty of a violation of § 18.2-272. Such restricted license shall be conditioned upon enrollment within 15 days in, and successful completion of, a program as described in subsection A of this section. No restricted license shall be issued during the first four months of a revocation imposed pursuant to subsection B of § 18.2-271 or subsection A of § 46.2-391 for a second offense of the type described therein committed within 10 years of a first such offense. No restricted license shall be issued during the first year of a revocation imposed pursuant to subsection B of § 18.2-271 or subsection A of § 46.2-391 for a second offense of the type described therein committed within five years of a first such offense. No restricted license shall be issued during any revocation period imposed pursuant to subsection C of § 18.2-271 or subsection B of § 46.2-391. Notwithstanding the provisions of § 46.2-411, the fee charged pursuant to § 46.2-411 for reinstatement of the driver's license of any person whose privilege or license has been suspended or revoked as a result of a violation of § 18.2-266, subsection A of § 46.2-341.24 or of any ordinance of a county, city or town, or of any federal law or the laws of any other state similar to the provisions of § 18.2-266 or subsection A of § 46.2-341.24 shall be $105. Forty dollars of such reinstatement fee shall be retained by the Department of Motor Vehicles as provided in § 46.2-411, $40 shall be transferred to the Commission on VASAP, and $25 shall be transferred to the Commonwealth Neurotrauma Initiative Trust Fund.

F. The court shall have jurisdiction over any person entering such program under any provision of this section until such time as the case has been disposed of by either successful completion of the program, or revocation due to ineligibility or violation of a condition or conditions imposed by the court, whichever shall first occur. Revocation proceedings shall be commenced by notice to show cause why the court should not revoke the privilege afforded by this section. Such notice shall be made by first-class mail to the last known address of such person, and shall direct such person to appear before the court in response thereto on a date contained in such notice, which shall not be less than 10 days from the date of mailing of the notice. Failure to appear in response to such notice shall of itself be grounds for revocation of such privilege. Notice of revocation under this subsection shall be sent forthwith to the Commissioner of the Department of Motor Vehicles.

G. For the purposes of this section, any court which has convicted a person of a violation of § 18.2-266, subsection A of § 46.2-341.24 or any ordinance of a county, city or town similar to the provisions of § 18.2-266 shall have continuing jurisdiction over such person during any period of license revocation related to that conviction, for the limited purposes of (i) referring such person to a certified alcohol safety action program, (ii) providing for a restricted permit for such person in accordance with the provisions of subsection E, and (iii) imposing terms, conditions and limitations for actions taken pursuant to clauses (i) and (ii), whether or not it took either such action at the time of the conviction. This continuing jurisdiction is subject to the limitations of subsection E that provide that no restricted license shall be issued during a revocation imposed pursuant to subsection C of § 18.2-271 or subsection B of § 46.2-391 or during the first four months or first year, whichever is applicable, of the revocation imposed pursuant to subsection B of § 18.2-271 or subsection A of § 46.2-391. The provisions of this subsection shall apply to a person convicted of a violation of § 18.2-266, subsection A of § 46.2-341.24 or any ordinance of a county, city or town similar to the provisions of § 18.2-266 on, after and at any time prior to July 1, 2003.

H. The State Treasurer, the Commission on VASAP or any city or county is authorized to accept any gifts or bequests of money or property, and any grant, loan, service, payment or property from any source, including the federal government, for the purpose of driver alcohol education. Any such gifts, bequests, grants, loans or payments shall be deposited in the separate fund provided in subsection B.

I. The Commission on VASAP, or any county, city, town, or any combination thereof may establish and, if established, shall operate, in accordance with the standards and criteria required by this subsection, alcohol safety action programs in connection with highway safety. Each such program shall operate under the direction of a local independent policy board chosen in accordance with procedures approved and promulgated by the Commission on VASAP. Local sitting or retired district court judges who regularly hear or heard cases involving driving under the influence and are familiar with their local alcohol safety action programs may serve on such boards. The Commission on VASAP shall establish minimum standards and criteria for the implementation and operation of such programs and shall establish procedures to certify all such programs to ensure that they meet the minimum standards and criteria stipulated by the Commission. The Commission shall also establish criteria for the administration of such programs for public information activities, for accounting procedures, for the auditing requirements of such programs and for the allocation of funds. Funds paid to the Commonwealth hereunder shall be utilized in the discretion of the Commission on VASAP to offset the costs of state programs and local programs run in conjunction with any county, city or town and costs incurred by the Commission. The Commission shall submit an annual report as to actions taken at the close of each calendar year to the Governor and the General Assembly.

J. Notwithstanding any other provisions of this section or of § 18.2-271, nothing in this section shall permit the court to suspend, reduce, limit, or otherwise modify any disqualification from operating a commercial motor vehicle imposed under the provisions of the Virginia Commercial Driver's License Act (§ 46.2-341.1 et seq.).

History.

1975, c. 601; 1976, cc. 612, 691; 1977, c. 240; 1978, c. 352; 1979, c. 353; 1980, c. 589; 1981, c. 195; 1982, c. 301; 1983, c. 504; 1984, c. 778; 1986, cc. 552, 590; 1987, cc. 465, 663; 1988, cc. 781, 858, 859, 888; 1989, c. 705; 1990, c. 949; 1991, cc. 131, 491; 1992, c. 559; 1993, cc. 527, 919; 1994, cc. 359, 363, 870; 1996, c. 984; 1997, cc. 472, 508; 1998, c. 703; 1999, c. 743; 2000, cc. 958, 970, 980; 2001, cc. 182, 645, 779; 2002, c. 806; 2003, c. 290; 2004, c. 720; 2007, cc. 194, 553; 2009, c. 295; 2010, cc. 446, 682; 2011, c. 592; 2012, cc. 141, 570; 2014, c. 707; 2015, cc. 506, 729.

§ 18.2-271.2. Commission on VASAP; purpose; membership; terms; meetings; staffing; compensation and expenses; chairman's executive summary.

A. There is hereby established in the legislative branch of state government the Commission on the Virginia Alcohol Safety Action Program (VASAP). The Commission shall administer and supervise the state system of local alcohol and safety action programs, develop and maintain operation and performance standards for local alcohol and safety action programs, and allocate funding to such programs. The Commission shall have a total membership of 15 members that shall consist of six legislative members and nine nonlegislative citizen members. Members shall be appointed as follows: four current or former members of the House Committee for Courts of Justice, to be appointed by the Speaker of the House of Delegates; two members of the Senate Committee for Courts of Justice, to be appointed by the Senate Committee on Rules; three sitting or retired judges, one each from the circuit, general district and juvenile and domestic relations district courts, who regularly hear or heard cases involving driving under the influence and are familiar with their local alcohol safety action programs, to be appointed by the Chairman of the Committee on District Courts; two directors of local alcohol safety action programs, to be appointed by the legislative members of the Commission; one representative from the law-enforcement profession, to be appointed by the Speaker of the House and one nonlegislative citizen at large, to be appointed by the Senate Committee on Rules; one representative from the Virginia Department of Motor Vehicles whose duties are substantially related to matters to be addressed by the Commission to be appointed by the Commissioner of the Department of Motor Vehicles, and one representative from the Department of Behavioral Health and Developmental Services whose duties also substantially involve such matters, to be appointed by the Commissioner of Behavioral Health and Developmental Services. Legislative members shall serve terms coincident with their terms of office. In accordance with the staggered terms previously established, nonlegislative citizen members shall serve two-year terms. All members may be reappointed. Appointments to fill vacancies, other than by expiration of a term, shall be made for the unexpired terms. Any appointment to fill a vacancy shall be made in the same manner as the original appointment.

B. The Commission shall meet at least four times each year at such places as it may from time to time designate. A majority of the members shall constitute a quorum. The Commission shall elect a chairman and vice-chairman from among its membership.

The Commission shall be empowered to establish and ensure the maintenance of minimum standards and criteria for program operations and performance, accounting, auditing, public information and administrative procedures for the various local alcohol safety action programs and shall be responsible for overseeing the administration of the statewide VASAP system. Such programs shall be certified by the Commission in accordance with procedures set forth in the Commission on VASAP Certification Manual. The Commission shall also oversee program plans, operations and performance and a system for allocating funds to cover deficits that may occur in the budgets of local programs.

C. The Commission shall appoint and employ and, at its pleasure, remove an executive director and such other persons as it may deem necessary, and determine their duties and fix their salaries or compensation.

D. The Commission shall appoint a Virginia Alcohol Safety Action Program Advisory Board to make recommendations to the Commission regarding its duties and administrative functions. The membership of such Board shall be appointed in the discretion of the Commission and include personnel from (i) local safety action programs, (ii) the State Board of Behavioral Health and Developmental Services, community services boards, or behavioral health authorities and (iii) other community mental health services organizations. An assistant attorney general who provides counsel in matters relating to driving under the influence shall also be appointed to the Board.

E. Legislative members of the Commission shall receive compensation as provided in § 30-19.12. Funding for the costs of compensation of legislative members shall be provided by the Commission. All members shall be reimbursed for all reasonable and necessary expenses as provided in §§ 2.2-2813 and 2.2-2825 to be paid out of that portion of moneys paid in VASAP defendant entry fees which is forwarded to the Virginia Alcohol Safety Action Program.

F. The chairman of the Commission shall submit to the Governor and the General Assembly an annual executive summary of the interim activity and work of the Commission no later than the first day of each regular session of the General Assembly. The executive summary shall be submitted as provided in the procedures of the Division of Legislative Automated Systems for the processing of legislative documents and reports and shall be posted on the General Assembly's website.

History.

1986, c. 580; 1988, cc. 781, 859, 888; 1990, cc. 1, 317; 1992, c. 560; 1993, c. 757; 2003, c. 885; 2005, c. 758; 2009, cc. 813, 840.

§ 18.2-271.3: Repealed by Acts 1999, c. 734.

§ 18.2-271.4. Oath of office.

Every case manager, and any other employee who is designated by the director of any VASAP-certified local alcohol safety action program operated pursuant to this article to provide probation and related services, shall take an oath of office as prescribed in § 49-1, by a person authorized to administer oaths pursuant to § 49-3, before entering the duties of his office.

History.

2001, cc. 380, 396.

§ 18.2-272. Driving after forfeiture of license.

A. Any person who drives or operates any motor vehicle, engine or train in the Commonwealth during the time for which he was deprived of the right to do so (i) upon conviction of a violation of § 18.2-268.3 or of an offense set forth in subsection E of § 18.2-270, (ii) by § 18.2-271 or 46.2-391.2, (iii) after his license has been revoked pursuant to § 46.2-389 or 46.2-391, or (iv) in violation of the terms of a restricted license issued pursuant to subsection E of § 18.2-271.1, is guilty of a Class 1 misdemeanor except as otherwise provided in § 46.2-391, and is subject to administrative revocation of his driver's license pursuant to §§ 46.2-389 and 46.2-391. Any person convicted of three violations of this section committed within a 10-year period is guilty of a Class 6 felony.

Nothing in this section or § 18.2-266, 18.2-270 or 18.2-271, shall be construed as conflicting with or repealing any ordinance or resolution of any city, town or county which restricts still further the right of such persons to drive or operate any such vehicle or conveyance.

B. Regardless of compliance with any other restrictions on his privilege to drive or operate a motor vehicle, it shall be a violation of this section for any person whose privilege to drive or operate a motor vehicle has been restricted, suspended or revoked because of a violation of § 18.2-36.1, 18.2-51.4, 18.2-266, 18.2-268.3, 46.2-341.24, or a similar ordinance or law of another state or the United States to drive or operate a motor vehicle while he has a blood alcohol content of 0.02 percent or more.

Any person suspected of a violation of this subsection shall be entitled to a preliminary breath test in accordance with the provisions of § 18.2-267, shall be deemed to have given his implied consent to have samples of his blood, breath or both taken for analysis pursuant to the provisions of § 18.2-268.2, and, when charged with a violation of this subsection, shall be subject to the provisions of §§ 18.2-268.1 through 18.2-268.12.

C. Any person who drives or operates a motor vehicle without a certified ignition interlock system as required by § 46.2-391.01 is guilty of a Class 1 misdemeanor and is subject to administrative revocation of his driver's license pursuant to §§ 46.2-389 and 46.2-391.

History.
Code 1950, § 18.1-60; 1960, c. 358; 1975, cc. 14, 15; 1988, c. 859; 1991, c. 64; 2004, cc. 948, 1013; 2005, cc. 757, 840; 2006, c. 390; 2007, c. 258; 2009, cc. 71, 255.

§ 18.2-273. Report of conviction to Department of Motor Vehicles.

The clerk of every court of record and the judge of every court not of record shall, within thirty days after final conviction of any person in his court under the provisions of this article, report the fact thereof and the name, post-office address and street address of such person, together with the license plate number on the vehicle operated by such person to the Commissioner of the Department of Motor Vehicles who shall preserve a record thereof in his office.

History.
Code 1950, § 18.1-61; 1960, c. 358; 1975, cc. 14, 15.

ARTICLE 3.

TRANSPORTING DANGEROUS ARTICLES.

§§ 18.2-274 through 18.2-278: Repealed by Acts 1980, c. 759.

Cross references.
For present provisions as to transportation of hazardous materials, see § 10.1-1450 et seq.

ARTICLE 3.1.

TRANSPORTATION OF HAZARDOUS MATERIALS.

§§ 18.2-278.1 through 18.2-278.7: Repealed by Acts 1986, c. 492.

Cross references.
As to the transportation of hazardous materials, see now § 10.1-1450 et seq.

ARTICLE 4.

DANGEROUS USE OF FIREARMS OR OTHER WEAPONS.

§ 18.2-279. Discharging firearms or missiles within or at building or dwelling house; penalty.

If any person maliciously discharges a firearm within any building when occupied by one or more persons in such a manner as to endanger the life or lives of such person or persons, or maliciously shoots at, or maliciously throws any missile at or against any dwelling house or other building when occupied by one or more persons, whereby the life or lives of any such person or persons may be put in peril, the person so offending is guilty of a Class 4 felony. In the event of the death of any person, resulting from such malicious shooting or throwing, the person so offending is guilty of murder in the second degree. However, if the homicide is willful, deliberate and premeditated, he is guilty of murder in the first degree.

If any such act be done unlawfully, but not maliciously, the person so offending is guilty of a Class 6 felony; and, in the event of the death of any person resulting from such unlawful shooting or throwing, the person so offending is guilty of involuntary manslaughter. If any person willfully discharges a firearm within or shoots at any school building whether occupied or not, he is guilty of a Class 4 felony.

History.
Code 1950, §§ 18.1-66, 18.1-152; 1960, c. 358; 1975, cc. 14, 15; 1992, c. 738; 2005, c. 143.

§ 18.2-280. Willfully discharging firearms in public places.

A. If any person willfully discharges or causes to be discharged any firearm in any street in a city or town, or in any place of public business or place of public gathering, and such conduct results in bodily injury to another person, he shall be guilty of a Class 6 felony. If such conduct does not result in bodily injury to another person, he shall be guilty of a Class 1 misdemeanor.

B. If any person willfully discharges or causes to be discharged any firearm upon the buildings and grounds of any public, private or religious elementary, middle or high school, he shall be guilty of a Class 4 felony, unless he is engaged in a program or curriculum sponsored by or conducted with permission of a public, private or religious school.

C. If any person willfully discharges or causes to be discharged any firearm upon any public property within 1,000 feet of the property line of any public, private or religious elementary, middle or high school property he shall be guilty of a Class 4 felony, unless he is engaged in lawful hunting.

D. This section shall not apply to any law-enforcement officer in the performance of his official duties nor to any other person whose said willful act is otherwise justifiable or excusable at law in the protection of his life or property, or is otherwise specifically authorized by law.

E. Nothing in this statute shall preclude the Commonwealth from electing to prosecute under any other applicable provision of law instead of this section.

History.

Code 1950, § 18.1-69; 1960, c. 358; 1975, cc. 14, 15; 1992, c. 735; 1999, c. 996; 2001, c. 712; 2005, c. 928.

§ 18.2-281. Setting spring gun or other deadly weapon.

It shall be unlawful for any person to set or fix in any manner any firearm or other deadly weapon so that it may be discharged or activated by a person coming in contact therewith or with any string, wire, spring, or any other contrivance attached thereto or designed to activate such weapon remotely. Any person violating this section shall be guilty of a Class 6 felony.

History.

Code 1950, § 18.1-69.1; 1966, c. 422; 1975, cc. 14, 15.

§ 18.2-282. Pointing, holding, or brandishing firearm, air or gas operated weapon or object similar in appearance; penalty.

A. It shall be unlawful for any person to point, hold or brandish any firearm or any air or gas operated weapon or any object similar in appearance, whether capable of being fired or not, in such manner as to reasonably induce fear in the mind of another or hold a firearm or any air or gas operated weapon in a public place in such a manner as to reasonably induce fear in the mind of another of being shot or injured. However, this section shall not apply to any person engaged in excusable or justifiable self-defense. Persons violating the provisions of this section shall be guilty of a Class 1 misdemeanor or, if the violation occurs upon any public, private or religious elementary, middle or high school, including buildings and grounds or upon public property within 1,000 feet of such school property, he shall be guilty of a Class 6 felony.

B. Any police officer in the performance of his duty, in making an arrest under the provisions of this section, shall not be civilly liable in damages for injuries or death resulting to the person being arrested if he had reason to believe that the person being arrested was pointing, holding, or brandishing such firearm or air or gas operated weapon, or object that was similar in appearance, with intent to induce fear in the mind of another.

C. For purposes of this section, the word *"firearm"* means any weapon that will or is designed to or may readily be converted to expel single or multiple projectiles by the action of an explosion of a combustible material. The word *"ammunition,"* as used herein, shall mean a cartridge, pellet, ball, missile or projectile adapted for use in a firearm.

History.

Code 1950, § 18.1-69.2; 1968, c. 513; 1975, cc. 14, 15; 1990, cc. 588, 599; 1992, c. 735; 2003, c. 976; 2005, c. 928.

§ 18.2-282.1. Brandishing a machete or other bladed weapon with intent to intimidate; penalty.

It shall be unlawful for any person to point, hold, or brandish a machete or any weapon, with an exposed blade 12 inches or longer, with the intent of intimidating any person or group of persons and in a manner that reasonably demonstrates that intent. This section shall not apply to any person engaged in excusable or justifiable self-defense. A person who violates this section is guilty of a Class 1 misdemeanor or, if the violation occurs upon any public, private, or religious elementary, middle, or high school, including buildings and grounds or upon public property within 1,000 feet of such school property, he is guilty of a Class 6 felony.

History.

2006, cc. 844, 895.

§ 18.2-283. Carrying dangerous weapon to place of religious worship.

If any person carry any gun, pistol, bowie knife, dagger or other dangerous weapon, without good and sufficient reason, to a place of worship while a meeting for religious purposes is being held at such place he shall be guilty of a Class 4 misdemeanor.

History.

Code 1950, § 18.1-241; 1960, c. 358; 1962, c. 411; 1975, cc. 14, 15.

§ 18.2-283.1. Carrying weapon into courthouse.

It shall be unlawful for any person to possess in or transport into any courthouse in this Commonwealth any (i) gun or other weapon designed or intended to propel a missile or projectile of any kind, (ii) frame, receiver, muffler, silencer, missile, projectile or ammunition designed for use with a dangerous weapon and (iii) any other dangerous weapon, including explosives, stun weapons as defined in § 18.2-308.1, and those weapons specified in subsection A of § 18.2-308. Any such weapon shall be subject to seizure by a law-enforcement officer. A violation of this section is punishable as a Class 1 misdemeanor.

The provisions of this section shall not apply to any police officer, sheriff, law-enforcement agent or official, conservation police officer, conservator of the peace, magistrate, court officer, judge, or city or county treasurer while in the conduct of such person's official duties.

History.

1988, c. 615; 2004, c. 995; 2007, cc. 87, 519; 2012, c. 295.

§ 18.2-284. Selling or giving toy firearms.

No person shall sell, barter, exchange, furnish, or dispose of by purchase, gift or in any other manner any toy gun, pistol, rifle or other toy firearm, if the same shall, by action of an explosion of a combustible material, discharge blank or ball charges. Any person violating the provisions of this section shall be guilty of a Class 4 misdemeanor. Each sale of any of the articles hereinbefore specified to any person shall constitute a separate offense.

Nothing in this section shall be construed as preventing the sale of what are commonly known as cap pistols.

History.

Code 1950, § 18.1-347; 1960, c. 348; 1975, cc. 14, 15; 2003, c. 976.

§ 18.2-285. Hunting with firearms while under influence of intoxicant or narcotic drug; penalty.

It shall be unlawful for any person to hunt wildlife with a firearm, bow and arrow, or crossbow in the Commonwealth of Virginia while he is (i) under the influence of alcohol; (ii) under the influence of any narcotic drug or any other self-administered intoxicant or drug of whatsoever nature, or any combination of such drugs, to a degree that impairs his ability to hunt with a firearm, bow and arrow, or crossbow safely; or (iii) under the combined influence of alcohol and any drug or drugs to a degree that impairs his ability to hunt with a firearm, bow and arrow, or crossbow safely. Any person who violates the provisions of this section is guilty of a Class 1 misdemeanor. Conservation police officers, sheriffs and all other law-enforcement officers shall enforce the provisions of this section.

History.

Code 1950, § 29-140.1; 1952, c. 96; 1962, c. 469; 1975, cc. 14, 15; 1999, c. 543; 2005, c. 507.

§ 18.2-286. Shooting in or across road or in street.

If any person discharges a firearm, crossbow or bow and arrow in or across any road, or within the right-of-way thereof, or in a street of any city or town, he shall, for each offense, be guilty of a Class 4 misdemeanor.

The provisions of this section shall not apply to firing ranges or shooting matches maintained, and supervised or approved, by law-enforcement officers and military personnel in performance of their lawful duties.

History.

Code 1950, § 33.1-349; 1970, c. 322; 1975, cc. 14, 15; 1993, c. 322; 1994, c. 18.

§ 18.2-286.1. Shooting from vehicles so as to endanger persons; penalty.

Any person who, while in or on a motor vehicle, intentionally discharges a firearm so as to create the risk of injury or death to another person or thereby cause another person to have a reasonable apprehension of injury or death shall be guilty of a Class 5 felony. Nothing in this section shall apply to a law-enforcement officer in the performance of his duties.

History.

1990, c. 951.

§ 18.2-287: Repealed by Acts 2004, c. 462.

Cross references.

For current provisions authorizing counties to regulate carrying of loaded firearms on public highways, see § 15.2-1209.1.

§ 18.2-287.01. Carrying weapon in air carrier airport terminal.

It shall be unlawful for any person to possess or transport into any air carrier airport terminal in the Commonwealth any (i) gun or other weapon designed or intended to propel a missile or projectile of any kind, (ii) frame, receiver, muffler, silencer, missile, projectile or ammunition designed for use with a dangerous weapon, and (iii) any other dangerous weapon, including explosives, stun weapons as defined in § 18.2-308.1, and those weapons specified in subsection A of § 18.2-308. Any such weapon shall be subject to seizure by a law-enforcement officer. A violation of this section is punishable as a Class 1 misdemeanor. Any weapon possessed or transported in violation of this section shall be forfeited to the Commonwealth and disposed of as provided in § 19.2-386.28.

The provisions of this section shall not apply to any police officer, sheriff, law-enforcement agent or official, conservation police officer, conservator of the peace employed by the air carrier airport, or retired law-enforcement officer qualified pursuant to subsection C of § 18.2-308.016, nor shall the provisions of this section apply to any passenger of an airline who, to the extent otherwise permitted by law, transports a lawful firearm, weapon, or ammunition into or out of an air carrier airport terminal for the sole purposes, respectively, of (i) presenting such firearm, weapon, or ammunition to U.S. Customs agents in advance of an international flight, in order to comply with federal law, (ii) checking such firearm, weapon, or ammunition with his luggage, or (iii) retrieving such firearm, weapon, or ammunition from the baggage claim area.

Any other statute, rule, regulation, or ordinance specifically addressing the possession or transportation of weapons in any airport in the Commonwealth shall be invalid, and this section shall control.

History.

2004, c. 894; 2007, cc. 87, 519; 2013, c. 746; 2016, c. 257.

§ 18.2-287.1: Repealed by Acts 2004, c. 462.

Cross references.

For current provisions concerning regulation of transportation of loaded rifle or shotgun, see § 15.2-915.2.

§ 18.2-287.2. Wearing of body armor while committing a crime; penalty.

Any person who, while committing a crime of violence as defined in § 18.2-288 (2) or a felony violation of § 18.2-248 or subdivision (a) 2 or 3 of § 18.2-248.1, has in his possession a firearm or knife and is wearing body armor designed to diminish the effect of the impact of a bullet or projectile shall be guilty of a Class 4 felony.

History.
1990, c. 936; 1997, c. 311.

§ 18.2-287.3: Repealed by Acts 1993, cc. 467, 494.

Cross references.
As to present provisions relating to possession or transportation of certain firearms by persons under the age of eighteen, see § 18.2-308.7.

§ 18.2-287.4. Carrying loaded firearms in public areas prohibited; penalty.

It shall be unlawful for any person to carry a loaded (a) semi-automatic center-fire rifle or pistol that expels single or multiple projectiles by action of an explosion of a combustible material and is equipped at the time of the offense with a magazine that will hold more than 20 rounds of ammunition or designed by the manufacturer to accommodate a silencer or equipped with a folding stock or (b) shotgun with a magazine that will hold more than seven rounds of the longest ammunition for which it is chambered on or about his person on any public street, road, alley, sidewalk, public right-of-way, or in any public park or any other place of whatever nature that is open to the public in the Cities of Alexandria, Chesapeake, Fairfax, Falls Church, Newport News, Norfolk, Richmond, or Virginia Beach or in the Counties of Arlington, Fairfax, Henrico, Loudoun, or Prince William.

The provisions of this section shall not apply to law-enforcement officers, licensed security guards, military personnel in the performance of their lawful duties, or any person having a valid concealed handgun permit or to any person actually engaged in lawful hunting or lawful recreational shooting activities at an established shooting range or shooting contest. Any person violating the provisions of this section shall be guilty of a Class 1 misdemeanor.

The exemptions set forth in §§ 18.2-308 and 18.2-308.016 shall apply, mutatis mutandis, to the provisions of this section.

History.
1991, c. 570; 1992, c. 790; 2003, c. 976; 2004, c. 995; 2005, c. 160; 2007, c. 813; 2016, c. 257.

ARTICLE 5.

UNIFORM MACHINE GUN ACT.

§ 18.2-288. Definitions.

When used in this article:

(1) *"Machine gun"* applies to any weapon which shoots or is designed to shoot automatically more than one shot, without manual reloading, by a single function of the trigger.

(2) *"Crime of violence"* applies to and includes any of the following crimes or an attempt to commit any of the same, namely, murder, manslaughter, kidnapping, rape, mayhem, assault with intent to maim, disable, disfigure or kill, robbery, burglary, housebreaking, breaking and entering and larceny.

(3) *"Person"* applies to and includes firm, partnership, association or corporation.

History.
Code 1950, § 18.1-258; 1960, c. 358; 1975, cc. 14, 15.

§ 18.2-289. Use of machine gun for crime of violence.

Possession or use of a machine gun in the perpetration or attempted perpetration of a crime of violence is hereby declared to be a Class 2 felony.

History.
Code 1950, § 18.1-259; 1960, c. 358; 1975, cc. 14, 15.

§ 18.2-290. Use of machine gun for aggressive purpose.

Unlawful possession or use of a machine gun for an offensive or aggressive purpose is hereby declared to be a Class 4 felony.

History.
Code 1950, § 18.1-260; 1960, c. 358; 1968, c. 229; 1975, cc. 14, 15.

§ 18.2-291. What constitutes aggressive purpose.

Possession or use of a machine gun shall be presumed to be for an offensive or aggressive purpose:

(1) When the machine gun is on premises not owned or rented for bona fide permanent residence or business occupancy by the person in whose possession the machine gun may be found;

(2) When the machine gun is in the possession of, or used by, a person who has been convicted of a crime of violence in any court of record, state or federal, of the United States of America, its territories or insular possessions;

(3) When the machine gun has not been registered as required in § 18.2-295; or

(4) When empty or loaded shells which have been or are susceptible of use in the machine gun are found in the immediate vicinity thereof.

History.
Code 1950, § 18.1-261; 1960, c. 358; 1975, cc. 14, 15.

§ 18.2-292. Presence prima facie evidence of use.

The presence of a machine gun in any room, boat or vehicle shall be prima facie evidence of the possession or use of the machine gun by each person occupying the room, boat, or vehicle where the weapon is found.

History.
Code 1950, § 18.1-262; 1960, c. 358; 1975, cc. 14, 15.

§ 18.2-293. What article does not apply to.

The provisions of this article shall not be applicable to:

(1) The manufacture for, and sale of, machine guns to the armed forces or law-enforcement officers of the United States or of any state or of any political subdivision thereof, or the transportation required for that purpose; and

(2) Machine guns and automatic arms issued to the national guard of Virginia by the United States or such arms used by the United States army or navy or in the hands of troops of the national guards of other states or territories of the United States passing through Virginia, or such arms as may be provided for the officers of the State Police or officers of penal institutions.

History.
Code 1950, § 18.1-263; 1960, c. 358; 1975, cc. 14, 15.

§ 18.2-293.1. What article does not prohibit.

Nothing contained in this article shall prohibit or interfere with:

(1) The possession of a machine gun for scientific purposes, or the possession of a machine gun not usable as a weapon and possessed as a curiosity, ornament, or keepsake; and

(2) The possession of a machine gun for a purpose manifestly not aggressive or offensive.

Provided, however, that possession of such machine guns shall be subject to the provisions of § 18.2-295.

History.
Code 1950, § 18.1-263; 1960, c. 358; 1975, cc. 14, 15.

§ 18.2-294. Manufacturer's and dealer's register; inspection of stock.

Every manufacturer or dealer shall keep a register of all machine guns manufactured or handled by him. This register shall show the model and serial number, date of manufacture, sale, loan, gift, delivery or receipt of every machine gun, the name, address, and occupation of the person to whom the machine gun was sold, loaned, given or delivered, or from whom it was received. Upon demand every manufacturer or dealer shall permit any marshal, sheriff or police officer to inspect his entire stock of machine guns, parts, and supplies therefor, and shall produce the register, herein required, for inspection. A violation of any provisions of this section shall be punishable as a Class 3 misdemeanor.

History.
Code 1950, § 18.1-264; 1960, c. 358; 1975, cc. 14, 15.

§ 18.2-295. Registration of machine guns.

Every machine gun in this Commonwealth shall be registered with the Department of State Police within twenty-four hours after its acquisition or, in the case of semi-automatic weapons which are converted, modified or otherwise altered to become machine guns, within twenty-four hours of the conversion, modification or alteration. Blanks for registration shall be prepared by the Superintendent of State Police, and furnished upon application. To comply with this section the application as filed shall be notarized and shall show the model and serial number of the gun, the name, address and occupation of the person in possession, and from whom and the purpose for which, the gun was acquired or altered. The Superintendent of State Police shall upon registration required in this section forthwith furnish the registrant with a certificate of registration, which shall be valid as long as the registrant remains the same. Certificates of registration shall be retained by the registrant and produced by him upon demand by any peace officer. Failure to keep or produce such certificate for inspection shall be a Class 3 misdemeanor, and any peace officer, may without warrant, seize the machine gun and apply for its confiscation as provided in § 18.2-296. Upon transferring a registered machine gun, the transferor shall forthwith notify the Superintendent in writing, setting forth the date of transfer and name and address of the transferee. Failure to give the required notification shall constitute a Class 3 misdemeanor. Registration data shall not be subject to inspection by the public.

History.
Code 1950, § 18.1-265; 1960, c. 358; 1972, c. 199; 1975, cc. 14, 15; 1978, c. 618; 1988, c. 460.

§ 18.2-296. Search warrants for machine guns.

Warrant to search any house or place and seize any machine gun possessed in violation of this article may issue in the same manner and under the same restrictions as provided by law for stolen property, and any court of record, upon application of the attorney for the Commonwealth, a police officer or conservator of the peace, may order any machine gun, thus or otherwise legally seized, to be confiscated and either destroyed or delivered to a peace officer of the Commonwealth or a political subdivision thereof.

History.
Code 1950, § 18.1-266; 1960, c. 358; 1975, cc. 14, 15.

§ 18.2-297. How article construed.

This article shall be so interpreted and construed as to effectuate its general purpose to make uniform the law of those states which enact it.

History.
Code 1950, § 18.1-267; 1960, c. 358; 1975, cc. 14, 15.

§ 18.2-298. Short title of article.

This article may be cited as the "Uniform Machine Gun Act."

History.
Code 1950, § 18.1-268; 1960, c. 358; 1975, cc. 14, 15.

ARTICLE 6.

"SAWED-OFF" SHOTGUN AND "SAWED-OFF" RIFLE ACT.

§ 18.2-299. Definitions.

When used in this article:

"Sawed-off shotgun" means any weapon, loaded or unloaded, originally designed as a shoulder weapon, utilizing a self-contained cartridge from which a number of ball shot pellets or projectiles may be fired simultaneously from a smooth or rifled bore by a single function of the firing device and which has a barrel length of less than 18 inches for smooth bore weapons and 16 inches for rifled weapons. Weapons of less than .225 caliber shall not be included.

"Sawed-off rifle" means a rifle of any caliber, loaded or unloaded, which expels a projectile by action of an explosion of a combustible material and is designed as a shoulder weapon with a barrel or barrels length of less than 16 inches or which has been modified to an overall length of less than 26 inches.

"Crime of violence" applies to and includes any of the following crimes or an attempt to commit any of the same, namely, murder, manslaughter, kidnapping, rape, mayhem, assault with intent to maim, disable, disfigure or kill, robbery, burglary, housebreaking, breaking and entering and larceny.

"Person" applies to and includes firm, partnership, association or corporation.

History.
Code 1950, § 18.1-268.1; 1968, c. 661; 1975, cc. 14, 15; 1992, c. 580; 2004, c. 930.

§ 18.2-300. Possession or use of "sawed-off" shotgun or rifle.

A. Possession or use of a "sawed-off" shotgun or "sawed-off" rifle in the perpetration or attempted perpetration of a crime of violence is a Class 2 felony.

B. Possession or use of a "sawed-off" shotgun or "sawed-off" rifle for any other purpose, except as permitted by this article and official use by those persons permitted possession by § 18.2-303, is a Class 4 felony.

History.
Code 1950, § 18.1-268.2; 1968, c. 661; 1975, cc. 14, 15; 1978, c. 710; 1992, c. 580.

§§ 18.2-301, 18.2-302: Repealed by Acts 1978, c. 710.

§ 18.2-303. What article does not apply to.

The provisions of this article shall not be applicable to:

(1) The manufacture for, and sale of, "sawed-off" shotguns or "sawed-off" rifles to the armed forces or law-enforcement officers of the United States or of any state or of any political subdivision thereof, or the transportation required for that purpose; and

(2) "Sawed-off" shotguns, "sawed-off" rifles and automatic arms issued to the National Guard of Virginia by the United States or such arms used by the United States Army or Navy or in the hands of troops of the national guards of other states or territories of the United States passing through Virginia, or such arms as may be provided for the officers of the State Police or officers of penal institutions.

History.
Code 1950, § 18.1-268.5; 1968, c. 661; 1975, cc. 14, 15; 1992, c. 580.

§ 18.2-303.1. What article does not prohibit.

Nothing contained in this article shall prohibit or interfere with the possession of a "sawed-off" shotgun or "sawed-off" rifle for scientific purposes, the possession of a "sawed-off" shotgun or "sawed-off" rifle possessed in compliance with federal law or the possession of a "sawed-off" shotgun or "sawed-off" rifle not usable as a firing weapon and possessed as a curiosity, ornament, or keepsake.

History.
Code 1950, § 18.1-268.5; 1968, c. 661; 1975, cc. 14, 15; 1976, c. 351; 1992, c. 580; 1993, c. 449.

§ 18.2-304. Manufacturer's and dealer's register; inspection of stock.

Every manufacturer or dealer shall keep a register of all "sawed-off" shotguns and "sawed-off" rifles manufactured or handled by him. This register shall show the model and serial number, date of manufacture, sale, loan, gift, delivery or receipt of every "sawed-off" shotgun and "sawed-off" rifle, the name, address, and occupation of the person to whom the "sawed-off" shotgun or "sawed-off" rifle was sold, loaned, given or delivered, or from whom it was received. Upon demand every manufacturer or dealer shall permit any marshal, sheriff or police officer to inspect his entire stock of "sawed-off" shotguns and "sawed-off" rifles, and "sawed-off" shotgun or "sawed-off" rifle barrels, and shall produce the register, herein required, for inspection. A violation of any provision of this section shall be punishable as a Class 3 misdemeanor.

History.
Code 1950, § 18.1-268.6; 1968, c. 661; 1975, cc. 14, 15; 1992, c. 580.

§ 18.2-305: Repealed by Acts 1976, c. 351.

§ 18.2-306. Search warrants for "sawed-off" shotguns and rifles; confiscation and destruction.

Warrant to search any house or place and seize any "sawed-off" shotgun or "sawed-off" rifle possessed in violation of this article may issue in the same manner and under the same restrictions as provided by law for stolen property, and any court of record, upon application of the attorney for the Commonwealth, a police officer or conservator of the peace, may order any "sawed-off" shotgun or "sawed-off" rifle thus or otherwise legally seized, to be confiscated and either destroyed or delivered to a peace officer of the Commonwealth or a political subdivision thereof.

History.
Code 1950, § 18.1-268.8; 1968, c. 661; 1975, cc. 14, 15; 1992, c. 580.

§ 18.2-307. Short title of article.

This article may be cited as the "Sawed-Off Shotgun and Sawed-Off Rifle Act."

History.
Code 1950, § 18.1-268.9; 1968, c. 661; 1975, cc. 14, 15; 1992, c. 580.

ARTICLE 6.1.

CONCEALED WEAPONS AND CONCEALED HANDGUN PERMITS.

§ 18.2-307.1. Definitions.

As used in this article, unless the context requires a different meaning:

"Ballistic knife" means any knife with a detachable blade that is propelled by a spring-operated mechanism.

"Handgun" means any pistol or revolver or other firearm, except a machine gun, originally designed, made, and intended to fire a projectile by means of an explosion of a combustible material from one or more barrels when held in one hand.

"Law-enforcement officer" means those individuals defined as a law-enforcement officer in § 9.1-101, law-enforcement agents of the armed forces of the United States and the Naval Criminal Investigative Service, and federal agents who are otherwise authorized to carry weapons by federal law. "Law-enforcement officer" also means any sworn full-time law-enforcement officer employed by a law-enforcement agency of the United States or any state or political subdivision thereof, whose duties are substantially similar to those set forth in § 9.1-101.

"Lawfully admitted for permanent residence" means the status of having been lawfully accorded the privilege of residing permanently in the United States as an immigrant in accordance with the immigration laws, such status not having changed.

"Personal knowledge" means knowledge of a fact that a person has himself gained through his own senses, or knowledge that was gained by a law-enforcement officer or prosecutor through the performance of his official duties.

"Spring stick" means a spring-loaded metal stick activated by pushing a button that rapidly and forcefully telescopes the weapon to several times its original length.

History.
2013, c. 746.

§ 18.2-308. Carrying concealed weapons; exceptions; penalty.

A. If any person carries about his person, hidden from common observation, (i) any pistol, revolver, or other weapon designed or intended to propel a missile of any kind by action of an explosion of any combustible material; (ii) any dirk, bowie knife, switchblade knife, ballistic knife, machete, razor, slingshot, spring stick, metal knucks, or blackjack; (iii) any flailing instrument consisting of two or more rigid parts connected in such a manner as to allow them to swing freely, which may be known as a nun chahka, nun chuck, nunchaku, shuriken, or fighting chain; (iv) any disc, of whatever configuration, having at least two points or pointed blades which is designed to be thrown or propelled and which may be known as a throwing star or oriental dart; or (v) any weapon of like kind as those enumerated in this subsection, he is guilty of a Class 1 misdemeanor. A second violation of this section or a conviction under this section subsequent to any conviction under any substantially similar ordinance of any county, city, or town shall be punishable as a Class 6 felony, and a third or subsequent such violation shall be punishable as a Class 5 felony. For the purpose of this section, a weapon shall be deemed to be hidden from common observation when it is observable but is of such deceptive appearance as to disguise the weapon's true nature. It shall be an affirmative defense to a violation of clause (i) regarding a handgun, that a person had been issued, at the time of the offense, a valid concealed handgun permit.

B. This section shall not apply to any person while in his own place of abode or the curtilage thereof.

C. Except as provided in subsection A of § 18.2-308.012, this section shall not apply to:

1. Any person while in his own place of business;
2. Any law-enforcement officer, or retired law-enforcement officer pursuant to § 18.2-308.016, wherever such law-enforcement officer may travel in the Commonwealth;
3. Any person who is at, or going to or from, an established shooting range, provided that the weapons are unloaded and securely wrapped while being transported;
4. Any regularly enrolled member of a weapons collecting organization who is at, or going to or from,

Crimes and Offenses

a bona fide weapons exhibition, provided that the weapons are unloaded and securely wrapped while being transported;

5. Any person carrying such weapons between his place of abode and a place of purchase or repair, provided the weapons are unloaded and securely wrapped while being transported;

6. Any person actually engaged in lawful hunting, as authorized by the Board of Game and Inland Fisheries, under inclement weather conditions necessitating temporary protection of his firearm from those conditions, provided that possession of a handgun while engaged in lawful hunting shall not be construed as hunting with a handgun if the person hunting is carrying a valid concealed handgun permit;

7. Any attorney for the Commonwealth or assistant attorney for the Commonwealth, wherever such attorney may travel in the Commonwealth;

8. Any person who may lawfully possess a firearm and is carrying a handgun while in a personal, private motor vehicle or vessel and such handgun is secured in a container or compartment in the vehicle or vessel;

9. Any enrolled participant of a firearms training course who is at, or going to or from, a training location, provided that the weapons are unloaded and securely wrapped while being transported; and

10. Any judge or justice of the Commonwealth, wherever such judge or justice may travel in the Commonwealth.

D. This section shall also not apply to any of the following individuals while in the discharge of their official duties, or while in transit to or from such duties:

1. Carriers of the United States mail;

2. Officers or guards of any state correctional institution;

3. Conservators of the peace, except that a judge or justice of the Commonwealth, an attorney for the Commonwealth, or an assistant attorney for the Commonwealth may carry a concealed handgun pursuant to subdivisions C 7 and 10. However, the following conservators of the peace shall not be permitted to carry a concealed handgun without obtaining a permit as provided in this article: (i) notaries public; (ii) registrars; (iii) drivers, operators, or other persons in charge of any motor vehicle carrier of passengers for hire; or (iv) commissioners in chancery;

4. Noncustodial employees of the Department of Corrections designated to carry weapons by the Director of the Department of Corrections pursuant to § 53.1-29; and

5. Harbormaster of the City of Hopewell.

History.

Code 1950, § 18.1-269; 1960, c. 358; 1964, c. 130; 1975, cc. 14, 15, 594; 1976, c. 302; 1978, c. 715; 1979, c. 642; 1980, c. 238; 1981, c. 376; 1982, cc. 71, 553; 1983, c. 529; 1984, cc. 360, 720; 1985, c. 427; 1986, cc. 57, 451, 625, 641; 1987, cc. 592, 707; 1988, cc. 359, 793; 1989, cc. 538, 542; 1990, cc. 640, 648, 825; 1991, c. 637; 1992, cc. 510, 705; 1993, cc. 748, 861; 1994, cc. 375, 697; 1995, c. 829; 1997, cc. 916, 921, 922; 1998, cc. 662, 670, 846, 847; 1999, cc. 628, 666, 679; 2001, cc. 25, 384, 657; 2002, cc. 699, 728, 826; 2004, cc. 355, 423, 462, 876, 885, 900, 901, 903, 905, 926, 995, 1012; 2005, cc. 344, 420, 424, 441, 839; 2006, c. 886; 2007, cc. 87, 272, 408, 455; 2008, cc. 69, 75, 80, 309, 464, 742; 2009, cc. 235, 779, 780; 2010, cc. 387, 433, 576, 586, 602, 677, 700, 709, 740, 741, 754, 841, 863; 2011, cc. 231, 234, 384, 410; 2012, cc. 132, 175, 291, 557, 776; 2013, cc. 559, 746; 2014, cc. 45, 225, 450; 2015, cc. 38, 221, 730; 2016, cc. 257, 589, 672.

§ 18.2-308.01. Carrying a concealed handgun with a permit.

A. The prohibition against carrying a concealed handgun in clause (i) of subsection A of § 18.2-308 shall not apply to a person who has a valid concealed handgun permit issued pursuant to this article. The person issued the permit shall have such permit on his person at all times during which he is carrying a concealed handgun and shall display the permit and a photo identification issued by a government agency of the Commonwealth or by the U.S. Department of Defense or U.S. State Department (passport) upon demand by a law-enforcement officer. A person to whom a nonresident permit is issued shall have such permit on his person at all times when he is carrying a concealed handgun in the Commonwealth and shall display the permit on demand by a law-enforcement officer. A person whose permit is extended due to deployment shall carry with him and display, upon request of a law-enforcement officer, a copy of the documents required by subsection B of § 18.2-308.010.

B. Failure to display the permit and a photo identification upon demand by a law-enforcement officer shall be punishable by a $25 civil penalty, which shall be paid into the state treasury. Any attorney for the Commonwealth of the county or city in which the alleged violation occurred may bring an action to recover the civil penalty. A court may waive such penalty upon presentation to the court of a valid permit and a government-issued photo identification. Any law-enforcement officer may issue a summons for the civil violation of failure to display the concealed handgun permit and photo identification upon demand.

C. The granting of a concealed handgun permit pursuant to this article shall not thereby authorize the possession of any handgun or other weapon on property or in places where such possession is otherwise prohibited by law or is prohibited by the owner of private property.

History.

2013, c. 746.

§ 18.2-308.02. Application for a concealed handgun permit; Virginia resident or domiciliary.

A. Any person 21 years of age or older may apply in writing to the clerk of the circuit court of the county or city in which he resides, or if he is a member of the United States armed forces, the county or city in which he is domiciled, for a five-year permit to carry a concealed handgun. There shall be no requirement regarding the length of time an applicant has been a resident or domiciliary of the county or city. The application shall be made under oath before a notary or other person qualified to take oaths and shall be made only on a form prescribed by the Department of State Police, in consultation with the Supreme Court, requiring only that information necessary to determine eligibility for the permit. No information or documentation other than that which is allowed on the application in accordance with this section may be requested or required by the clerk or the court.

B. The court shall require proof that the applicant has demonstrated competence with a handgun and the applicant may demonstrate such competence by one of the following, but no applicant shall be required to submit to any additional demonstration of competence, nor shall any proof of demonstrated competence expire:

1. Completing any hunter education or hunter safety course approved by the Department of Game and Inland Fisheries or a similar agency of another state;

2. Completing any National Rifle Association firearms safety or training course;

3. Completing any firearms safety or training course or class available to the general public offered by a law-enforcement agency, junior college, college, or private or public institution or organization or firearms training school utilizing instructors certified by the National Rifle Association or the Department of Criminal Justice Services;

4. Completing any law-enforcement firearms safety or training course or class offered for security guards, investigators, special deputies, or any division or subdivision of law enforcement or security enforcement;

5. Presenting evidence of equivalent experience with a firearm through participation in organized shooting competition or current military service or proof of an honorable discharge from any branch of the armed services;

6. Obtaining or previously having held a license to carry a firearm in the Commonwealth or a locality thereof, unless such license has been revoked for cause;

7. Completing any firearms training or safety course or class, including an electronic, video, or online course, conducted by a state-certified or National Rifle Association-certified firearms instructor;

8. Completing any governmental police agency firearms training course and qualifying to carry a firearm in the course of normal police duties; or

9. Completing any other firearms training which the court deems adequate.

A photocopy of a certificate of completion of any of the courses or classes; an affidavit from the instructor, school, club, organization, or group that conducted or taught such course or class attesting to the completion of the course or class by the applicant; or a copy of any document that shows completion of the course or class or evidences participation in firearms competition shall constitute evidence of qualification under this subsection.

C. The making of a materially false statement in an application under this article shall constitute perjury, punishable as provided in § 18.2-434.

D. The clerk of court shall withhold from public disclosure the applicant's name and any other information contained in a permit application or any order issuing a concealed handgun permit, except that such information shall not be withheld from any law-enforcement officer acting in the performance of his official duties or from the applicant with respect to his own information. The prohibition on public disclosure of information under this subsection shall not apply to any reference to the issuance of a concealed handgun permit in any order book before July 1, 2008; however, any other concealed handgun records maintained by the clerk shall be withheld from public disclosure.

E. An application is deemed complete when all information required to be furnished by the applicant, including the fee for a concealed handgun permit as set forth in § 18.2-308.03, is delivered to and received by the clerk of court before or concomitant with the conduct of a state or national criminal history records check.

History.

2013, cc. 659, 746; 2014, cc. 16, 401, 549.

§ 18.2-308.03. Fees for concealed handgun permits.

A. The clerk shall charge a fee of $10 for the processing of an application or issuing of a permit, including his costs associated with the consultation with law-enforcement agencies. The local law-enforcement agency conducting the background investigation may charge a fee not to exceed $35 to cover the cost of conducting an investigation pursuant to this article. The $35 fee shall include any amount assessed by the U.S. Federal Bureau of Investigation for providing criminal history record information, and the local law-enforcement agency shall forward the amount assessed by the U.S. Federal Bureau of Investigation to the State Police with the fingerprints taken from any nonresident applicant. The State Police may charge a fee not to exceed $5 to cover its costs associated with processing the application. The total amount assessed for processing an application for a permit shall not exceed $50, with such fees to be paid in one sum to the person who receives the application. Payment may be made by any method accepted by that court for payment of other fees or penalties. No payment shall be required until the application is received by the court as a complete application.

B. **(Effective until July 1, 2018)** No fee shall be charged for the issuance of such permit to a person who has retired from service (i) as a magistrate in the Commonwealth; (ii) as a special agent with the Alcoholic Beverage Control Board or as a law-enforcement officer with the Department of State Police, the Department of Game and Inland Fisheries, or a sheriff or police department, bureau, or force of any political subdivision of the Commonwealth, after completing 15 years of service or after reaching age 55; (iii) as a law-enforcement officer with the U.S. Federal Bureau of Investigation, Bureau of Alcohol, Tobacco and Firearms, Secret Service Agency, Drug Enforcement Administration, United States Citizenship and Immigration Services, U.S. Customs and Border Protection, Department of State Diplomatic Security Service, U.S. Marshals Service, or Naval Criminal Investigative Service, after completing 15 years of service or after reaching age 55; (iv) as a law-enforcement officer with any police or sheriff's department within the United States, the District of Columbia, or any of the territories of the United States, after completing 15 years of service; (v) as a law-enforcement officer with any combination of the agencies listed in clauses (ii) through (iv), after completing 15 years of service; (vi) as a designated boarding team member or boarding officer of the United States Coast Guard, after completing 15 years of service or after reaching age 55; or (vii) as a correctional officer as defined in § 53.1-1 after completing 15 years of service.

B. **(Effective July 1, 2018)** No fee shall be charged for the issuance of such permit to a person who has retired from service (i) as a magistrate in the Commonwealth; (ii) as a special agent with the Virginia Alcoholic Beverage Control Authority or as a law-enforcement officer with the Department of State Police, the Department of Game and Inland Fisheries, or a sheriff or police department, bureau, or force of any political subdivision of the Commonwealth, after completing 15 years of service or after reaching age 55; (iii) as a law-enforcement officer with the U.S. Federal Bureau of Investigation, Bureau of Alcohol, Tobacco and Firearms, Secret Service Agency, Drug Enforcement Administration, United States Citizenship and Immigration Services, U.S. Customs and Border Protection, Department of State Diplomatic Security Service, U.S. Marshals Service, or Naval Criminal Investigative Service, after completing 15 years of service or after reaching age 55; (iv) as a law-enforcement officer with any police or sheriff's department within the United States, the District of Columbia, or any of the territories of the United States, after completing 15 years of service; (v) as a law-enforcement officer with any combination of the agencies listed in clauses (ii) through (iv), after completing 15 years of service; (vi) as a designated boarding team member or boarding officer of the United States Coast Guard, after completing 15 years of service or after reaching age 55; or (vii) as a correctional officer as defined in § 53.1-1 after completing 15 years of service.

History.

2013, cc. 135, 559, 746; 2015, cc. 38, 730.

§ 18.2-308.04. Processing of the application and issuance of a concealed handgun permit.

A. The clerk of court shall enter on the application the date on which the application and all other information required to be submitted by the applicant is received.

B. Upon receipt of the completed application, the court shall consult with either the sheriff or police department of the county or city and receive a report from the Central Criminal Records Exchange.

C. The court shall issue the permit via United States mail and notify the State Police of the issuance of the permit within 45 days of receipt of the completed application unless it is determined that the applicant is disqualified. Any order denying issuance of the permit shall be in accordance with § 18.2-308.08. If the applicant is later found by the court to be disqualified after a five-year permit has been issued, the permit shall be revoked.

D. A court may authorize the clerk to issue concealed handgun permits, without judicial review, to applicants who have submitted complete applications, for whom the criminal history records check does not indicate a disqualification and, after consulting with either the sheriff or police department of the county or city, about which application there are no outstanding questions or issues. The court clerk shall be immune from suit arising from any acts or omissions relating to the issuance of concealed handgun permits without judicial review pursuant to this section unless the clerk was grossly negligent or engaged in willful misconduct. This section shall not be construed to limit, withdraw, or overturn any defense or immunity already existing in statutory or common law, or to affect any cause of action accruing prior to July 1, 2010.

E. The permit to carry a concealed handgun shall specify only the following information: name, address, date of birth, gender, height, weight, color of hair, color of eyes, and signature of the permittee; the signature of the judge issuing the permit, of the clerk of court who has been authorized to sign such permits by the issuing judge, or of the clerk of court who has been authorized to issue such permits pursuant to subsection D; the date of issuance; and the expiration date. The permit to carry a concealed handgun shall be no larger than two inches wide by three and one-fourth inches long and shall be of a uniform style prescribed by the Department of State Police.

History.

2013, c. 746.

§ 18.2-308.05. Issuance of a de facto permit.

If the court has not issued the permit or determined that the applicant is disqualified within 45 days of the date of receipt noted on the application, the clerk shall certify on the application that the

45-day period has expired, and mail or send via electronic mail a copy of the certified application to the applicant within five business days of the expiration of the 45-day period. The certified application shall serve as a de facto permit, which shall expire 90 days after issuance, and shall be recognized as a valid concealed handgun permit when presented with a valid government-issued photo identification pursuant to subsection A of § 18.2-308.01, until the court issues a five-year permit or finds the applicant to be disqualified. If the applicant is found to be disqualified after the de facto permit is issued, the applicant shall surrender the de facto permit to the court and the disqualification shall be deemed a denial of the permit and a revocation of the de facto permit.

History.
2013, c. 746.

§ 18.2-308.06. Nonresident concealed handgun permits.

A. Nonresidents of the Commonwealth 21 years of age or older may apply in writing to the Virginia Department of State Police for a five-year permit to carry a concealed handgun. Every applicant for a nonresident concealed handgun permit shall submit two photographs of a type and kind specified by the Department of State Police for inclusion on the permit and shall submit fingerprints on a card provided by the Department of State Police for the purpose of obtaining the applicant's state or national criminal history record. As a condition for issuance of a concealed handgun permit, the applicant shall submit to fingerprinting by his local or state law-enforcement agency and provide personal descriptive information to be forwarded with the fingerprints through the Central Criminal Records Exchange to the U.S. Federal Bureau of Investigation for the purpose of obtaining criminal history record information regarding the applicant and obtaining fingerprint identification information from federal records pursuant to criminal investigations by state and local law-enforcement agencies. The application shall be made under oath before a notary or other person qualified to take oaths on a form provided by the Department of State Police, requiring only that information necessary to determine eligibility for the permit. If the permittee is later found by the Department of State Police to be disqualified, the permit shall be revoked and the person shall return the permit after being so notified by the Department of State Police. The permit requirement and restriction provisions of subsection C of § 18.2-308.02 and § 18.2-308.09 shall apply, mutatis mutandis, to the provisions of this subsection.

B. The applicant shall demonstrate competence with a handgun by one of the following:

1. Completing a hunter education or hunter safety course approved by the Virginia Department of Game and Inland Fisheries or a similar agency of another state;

2. Completing any National Rifle Association firearms safety or training course;

3. Completing any firearms safety or training course or class available to the general public offered by a law-enforcement agency, junior college, college, or private or public institution or organization or firearms training school utilizing instructors certified by the National Rifle Association or the Department of Criminal Justice Services or a similar agency of another state;

4. Completing any law-enforcement firearms safety or training course or class offered for security guards, investigators, special deputies, or any division or subdivision of law enforcement or security enforcement;

5. Presenting evidence of equivalent experience with a firearm through participation in organized shooting competition approved by the Department of State Police or current military service or proof of an honorable discharge from any branch of the armed services;

6. Obtaining or previously having held a license to carry a firearm in the Commonwealth or a locality thereof, unless such license has been revoked for cause;

7. Completing any firearms training or safety course or class, including an electronic, video, or on-line course, conducted by a state-certified or National Rifle Association-certified firearms instructor;

8. Completing any governmental police agency firearms training course and qualifying to carry a firearm in the course of normal police duties; or

9. Completing any other firearms training that the Virginia Department of State Police deems adequate.

A photocopy of a certificate of completion of any such course or class; an affidavit from the instructor, school, club, organization, or group that conducted or taught such course or class attesting to the completion of the course or class by the applicant; or a copy of any document that shows completion of the course or class or evidences participation in firearms competition shall satisfy the requirement for demonstration of competence with a handgun.

C. The Department of State Police may charge a fee not to exceed $100 to cover the cost of the background check and issuance of the permit. Any fees collected shall be deposited in a special account to be used to offset the costs of administering the nonresident concealed handgun permit program.

D. The permit to carry a concealed handgun shall contain only the following information: name, address, date of birth, gender, height, weight, color of hair, color of eyes, and photograph of the permittee; the signature of the Superintendent of the Virginia Department of State Police or his designee; the date of issuance; and the expiration date.

E. The Superintendent of the State Police shall promulgate regulations, pursuant to the Administrative Process Act (§ 2.2-4000 et seq.), for the implementation of an application process for obtaining a nonresident concealed handgun permit.

History.
2013, c. 746.

§ 18.2-308.07. Entry of information into the Virginia Criminal Information Network.

A. An order issuing a concealed handgun permit pursuant to § 18.2-308.04, or the copy of the permit application certified by the clerk as a de facto permit pursuant to § 18.2-308.05, shall be provided to the State Police and the law-enforcement agencies of the county or city by the clerk of the court. The State Police shall enter the permittee's name and description in the Virginia Criminal Information Network so that the permit's existence and current status will be made known to law-enforcement personnel accessing the Network for investigative purposes.

B. The Department of State Police shall enter the name and description of a person issued a nonresident permit pursuant to § 18.2-308.06 in the Virginia Criminal Information Network so that the permit's existence and current status are known to law-enforcement personnel accessing the Network for investigative purposes.

C. The State Police shall withhold from public disclosure permittee information submitted to the State Police for purposes of entry into the Virginia Criminal Information Network, except that such information shall not be withheld from any law-enforcement agency, officer, or authorized agent thereof acting in the performance of official law-enforcement duties, nor shall such information be withheld from an entity that has a valid contract with any local, state, or federal law-enforcement agency for the purpose of performing official duties of the law-enforcement agency. However, nothing in this subsection shall be construed to prohibit the release of (i) records by the State Police concerning permits issued to nonresidents of the Commonwealth pursuant to § 18.2-308.06 or (ii) statistical summaries, abstracts, or other records containing information in an aggregate form that does not identify any individual permittees.

History.
2013, c. 746.

§ 18.2-308.08. Denial of a concealed handgun permit; appeal.

A. Only a circuit court judge may deny issuance of a concealed handgun permit to a Virginia resident or domiciliary who has applied for a permit pursuant to § 18.2-308.04. Any order denying issuance of a concealed handgun permit shall state the basis for the denial of the permit, including, if applicable, any reason under § 18.2-308.09 that is the basis of the denial, and the clerk shall provide notice, in writing, upon denial of the application, of the applicant's right to an ore tenus hearing and the requirements for perfecting an appeal of such order.

B. Upon request of the applicant made within 21 days, the court shall place the matter on the docket for an ore tenus hearing. The applicant may be represented by counsel, but counsel shall not be appointed, and the rules of evidence shall apply. The final order of the court shall include the court's findings of fact and conclusions of law.

C. Any person denied a permit to carry a concealed handgun by the circuit court may present a petition for review to the Court of Appeals. The petition for review shall be filed within 60 days of the expiration of the time for requesting an ore tenus hearing, or if an ore tenus hearing is requested, within 60 days of the entry of the final order of the circuit court following the hearing. The petition shall be accompanied by a copy of the original papers filed in the circuit court, including a copy of the order of the circuit court denying the permit. Subject to the provisions of subsection B of § 17.1-410, the decision of the Court of Appeals or judge shall be final. Notwithstanding any other provision of law, if the decision to deny the permit is reversed upon appeal, taxable costs incurred by the person shall be paid by the Commonwealth.

History.
2013, c. 746.

§ 18.2-308.09. Disqualifications for a concealed handgun permit.

The following persons shall be deemed disqualified from obtaining a permit:

1. An individual who is ineligible to possess a firearm pursuant to § 18.2-308.1:1, 18.2-308.1:2, or 18.2-308.1:3 or the substantially similar law of any other state or of the United States.

2. An individual who was ineligible to possess a firearm pursuant to § 18.2-308.1:1 and who was discharged from the custody of the Commissioner pursuant to § 19.2-182.7 less than five years before the date of his application for a concealed handgun permit.

3. An individual who was ineligible to possess a firearm pursuant to § 18.2-308.1:2 and whose competency or capacity was restored pursuant to § 64.2-2012 less than five years before the date of his application for a concealed handgun permit.

4. An individual who was ineligible to possess a firearm under § 18.2-308.1:3 and who was released from commitment less than five years before the date of this application for a concealed handgun permit.

5. An individual who is subject to a restraining order, or to a protective order and prohibited by § 18.2-308.1:4 from purchasing, possessing, or transporting a firearm.

6. An individual who is prohibited by § 18.2-308.2 from possessing or transporting a firearm, except that a permit may be obtained in accordance with subsection C of that section.

7. An individual who has been convicted of two or more misdemeanors within the five-year period immediately preceding the application, if one of the misdemeanors was a Class 1 misdemeanor, but the judge shall have the discretion to deny a permit for two or more misdemeanors that are not Class 1. Traffic infractions and misdemeanors set forth in Title 46.2 shall not be considered for purposes of this disqualification.

8. An individual who is addicted to, or is an unlawful user or distributor of, marijuana, synthetic cannabinoids, or any controlled substance.

9. An individual who has been convicted of a violation of § 18.2-266 or a substantially similar local ordinance, or of public drunkenness, or of a substantially similar offense under the laws of any other state, the District of Columbia, the United States, or its territories within the three-year period immediately preceding the application, or who is a habitual drunkard as determined pursuant to § 4.1-333.

10. An alien other than an alien lawfully admitted for permanent residence in the United States.

11. An individual who has been discharged from the armed forces of the United States under dishonorable conditions.

12. An individual who is a fugitive from justice.

13. An individual who the court finds, by a preponderance of the evidence, based on specific acts by the applicant, is likely to use a weapon unlawfully or negligently to endanger others. The sheriff, chief of police, or attorney for the Commonwealth may submit to the court a sworn, written statement indicating that, in the opinion of such sheriff, chief of police, or attorney for the Commonwealth, based upon a disqualifying conviction or upon the specific acts set forth in the statement, the applicant is likely to use a weapon unlawfully or negligently to endanger others. The statement of the sheriff, chief of police, or the attorney for the Commonwealth shall be based upon personal knowledge of such individual or of a deputy sheriff, police officer, or assistant attorney for the Commonwealth of the specific acts, or upon a written statement made under oath before a notary public of a competent person having personal knowledge of the specific acts.

14. An individual who has been convicted of any assault, assault and battery, sexual battery, discharging of a firearm in violation of § 18.2-280 or 18.2-286.1 or brandishing of a firearm in violation of § 18.2-282 within the three-year period immediately preceding the application.

15. An individual who has been convicted of stalking.

16. An individual whose previous convictions or adjudications of delinquency were based on an offense that would have been at the time of conviction a felony if committed by an adult under the laws of any state, the District of Columbia, the United States or its territories. For purposes of this disqualifier, only convictions occurring within 16 years following the later of the date of (i) the conviction or adjudication or (ii) release from any incarceration imposed upon such conviction or adjudication shall be deemed to be "previous convictions." Disqualification under this subdivision shall not apply to an individual with previous adjudications of delinquency who has completed a term of service of no less than two years in the Armed Forces of the United States and, if such person has been discharged from the Armed Forces of the United States, received an honorable discharge.

17. An individual who has a felony charge pending or a charge pending for an offense listed in subdivision 14 or 15.

18. An individual who has received mental health treatment or substance abuse treatment in a residential setting within five years prior to the date of his application for a concealed handgun permit.

19. An individual not otherwise ineligible pursuant to this article, who, within the three-year period immediately preceding the application for the permit, was found guilty of any criminal offense set forth in Article 1 (§ 18.2-247 et seq.) or former § 18.2-248.1:1 or of a criminal offense of illegal possession or distribution of marijuana, synthetic cannabinoids, or any controlled substance, under the laws of any state, the District of Columbia, or the United States or its territories.

20. An individual, not otherwise ineligible pursuant to this article, with respect to whom, within the three-year period immediately preceding the application, upon a charge of any criminal offense set forth in Article 1 (§ 18.2-247 et seq.) or former § 18.2-248.1:1 or upon a charge of illegal possession or distribution of marijuana, synthetic cannabinoids, or any controlled substance under the laws of any state, the District of Columbia, or the United States or its territories, the trial court found that the facts of the case were sufficient for a finding of guilt and disposed of the case pursuant to § 18.2-251 or the substantially similar law of any other state, the District of Columbia, or the United States or its territories.

History.
2013, c. 746; 2014, cc. 674, 719; 2016, cc. 48, 49, 337.

§ 18.2-308.010. Renewal of concealed handgun permit.

A. 1. Persons who previously have held a concealed handgun permit shall be issued, upon application as provided in § 18.2-308.02, a new five-year permit unless it is found that the applicant is subject to any of the disqualifications set forth in § 18.2-308.09. Persons who previously have been issued a concealed handgun permit pursuant to this article shall not be required to appear in person to apply for a new five-year permit pursuant to this section, and the application for the new permit may be submitted via the United States mail. The circuit court that receives the application shall promptly notify an applicant if the application is incomplete or if the fee submitted for the permit pursuant to § 18.2-308.03 is incorrect.

2. If a new five-year permit is issued while an existing permit remains valid, the new five-year permit shall become effective upon the expiration date of the existing permit, provided that the application is received by the court at least 90 days but no more than 180 days prior to the expiration of the existing permit.

3. Any order denying issuance of the new permit shall be in accordance with subsection A of § 18.2-308.08.

B. If a permit holder is a member of the Virginia National Guard, armed forces of the United States, or the Armed Forces Reserves of the United States, and his five-year permit expires during an active-duty military deployment outside of the permittee's county or city of residence, such permit shall remain valid for 90 days after the end date of the deployment. In order to establish proof of continued validity of the permit, such a permittee shall carry with him and display, upon request of a law-enforcement officer, a copy of the permittee's deployment orders or other documentation from the permittee's commanding officer that order the permittee to travel outside of his county or city of residence and that indicate the start and end date of such deployment.

History.
2013, c. 746.

§ 18.2-308.011. Replacement permits.

A. The clerk of a circuit court that issued a valid concealed handgun permit shall, upon presentation of the valid permit and proof of a new address of residence by the permit holder, issue a replacement permit specifying the permit holder's new address. The clerk of court shall forward the permit holder's new address of residence to the State Police. The State Police may charge a fee not to exceed $5, and the clerk of court issuing the replacement permit may charge a fee not to exceed $5. The total amount assessed for processing a replacement permit pursuant to this subsection shall not exceed $10, with such fees to be paid in one sum to the person who receives the information for the replacement permit.

B. The clerk of a circuit court that issued a valid concealed handgun permit shall, upon submission of a notarized statement by the permit holder that the permit was lost or destroyed or that the permit holder has undergone a legal name change, issue a replacement permit. The replacement permit shall have the same expiration date as the permit that was lost, destroyed, or issued to the permit holder under a previous name. The clerk shall issue the replacement permit within 10 business days of receiving the notarized statement and may charge a fee not to exceed $5.

History.
2013, c. 746; 2014, cc. 16, 549.

§ 18.2-308.012. Prohibited conduct.

A. Any person permitted to carry a concealed handgun who is under the influence of alcohol or illegal drugs while carrying such handgun in a public place is guilty of a Class 1 misdemeanor. Conviction of any of the following offenses shall be prima facie evidence, subject to rebuttal, that the person is "under the influence" for purposes of this section: manslaughter in violation of § 18.2-36.1, maiming in violation of § 18.2-51.4, driving while intoxicated in violation of § 18.2-266, public intoxication in violation of § 18.2-388, or driving while intoxicated in violation of § 46.2-341.24. Upon such conviction that court shall revoke the person's permit for a concealed handgun and promptly notify the issuing circuit court. A person convicted of a violation of this subsection shall be ineligible to apply for a concealed handgun permit for a period of five years.

B. **(Effective until July 1, 2018)** No person who carries a concealed handgun onto the premises of any restaurant or club as defined in § 4.1-100 for which a license to sell and serve alcoholic beverages for on-premises consumption has been granted by the Virginia Alcoholic Beverage Control Board under Title 4.1 may consume an alcoholic beverage while on the premises. A person who carries a concealed handgun onto the premises of such a restaurant or club and consumes alcoholic beverages is guilty of a Class 2 misdemeanor. However, nothing in this subsection shall apply to a federal, state, or local law-enforcement officer.

B. **(Effective July 1, 2018)** No person who carries a concealed handgun onto the premises of any restaurant or club as defined in § 4.1-100 for which a license to sell and serve alcoholic beverages for on-premises consumption has been granted by the Virginia Alcoholic Beverage Control Authority under Title 4.1 may consume an alcoholic beverage while on the premises. A person who carries a concealed handgun onto the premises of such a restaurant or club and consumes alcoholic beverages is guilty of a Class 2 misdemeanor. However, nothing in this subsection shall apply to a federal, state, or local law-enforcement officer.

History.
2013, c. 746; 2015, cc. 38, 730.

§ 18.2-308.013. Suspension or revocation of permit.

A. Any person convicted of an offense that would disqualify that person from obtaining a permit under § 18.2-308.09 or who violates subsection C of

§ 18.2-308.02 shall forfeit his permit for a concealed handgun and surrender it to the court. Upon receipt by the Central Criminal Records Exchange of a record of the arrest, conviction, or occurrence of any other event that would disqualify a person from obtaining a concealed handgun permit under § 18.2-308.09, the Central Criminal Records Exchange shall notify the court having issued the permit of such disqualifying arrest, conviction, or other event. Upon receipt of such notice of a conviction, the court shall revoke the permit of a person disqualified pursuant to this subsection, and shall promptly notify the State Police and the person whose permit was revoked of the revocation.

B. An individual who has a felony charge pending or a charge pending for an offense listed in subdivision 14 or 15 of § 18.2-308.09, holding a permit for a concealed handgun, may have the permit suspended by the court before which such charge is pending or by the court that issued the permit.

C. The court shall revoke the permit of any individual for whom it would be unlawful to purchase, possess, or transport a firearm under § 18.2-308.1:2 or 18.2-308.1:3, and shall promptly notify the State Police and the person whose permit was revoked of the revocation.

History.
2013, c. 746.

§ 18.2-308.014. Reciprocity.

A. A valid concealed handgun or concealed weapon permit or license issued by another state shall authorize the holder of such permit or license who is at least 21 years of age to carry a concealed handgun in the Commonwealth, provided (i) the issuing authority provides the means for instantaneous verification of the validity of all such permits or licenses issued within that state, accessible 24 hours a day if available; (ii) the permit or license holder carries a photo identification issued by a government agency of any state or by the U.S. Department of Defense or U.S. Department of State and displays the permit or license and such identification upon demand by a law-enforcement officer; and (iii) the permit or license holder has not previously had a Virginia concealed handgun permit revoked. The Superintendent of State Police shall enter into agreements for reciprocal recognition with such other states that require an agreement to be in place before such state will recognize a Virginia concealed handgun permit as valid in such state. The Attorney General shall provide the Superintendent with any legal assistance or advice necessary for the Superintendent to perform his duties set forth in this subsection. If the Superintendent determines that another state requires that an agreement for reciprocal recognition be executed by the Attorney General or otherwise formally approved by the Attorney General as a condition of such other state's entering into an agreement for reciprocal recognition, the Attorney General shall (a) execute such agreement or otherwise formally approve such agreement and (b) return to the Superintendent the executed agreement or, in a form deemed acceptable by such other state, documentation of his formal approval of such agreement within 30 days after the Superintendent notifies the Attorney General, in writing, that he is required to execute or otherwise formally approve such agreement.

B. For the purposes of participation in concealed handgun reciprocity agreements with other jurisdictions, the official government-issued law-enforcement identification card issued to an active-duty law-enforcement officer in the Commonwealth who is exempt from obtaining a concealed handgun permit under this article shall be deemed a concealed handgun permit.

History.
2013, c. 746; 2016, cc. 46, 47.

§ 18.2-308.015. Inclusion of Supreme Court website on application.

For the purposes of understanding the law relating to the use of deadly and lethal force, the Department of State Police, in consultation with the Supreme Court on the development of the application for a concealed handgun permit under this article, shall include a reference to the Virginia Supreme Court website address or the Virginia Reports on the application.

History.
2013, c. 746.

§ 18.2-308.016. (Effective until October 1, 2016) Retired law-enforcement officers; carrying a concealed handgun.

A. Except as provided in subsection A of § 18.2-308.012, § 18.2-308 shall not apply to:

1. Any State Police officer retired from the Department of State Police, any officer retired from the Division of Capitol Police, any local law-enforcement officer, auxiliary police officer or animal control officer retired from a police department or sheriff's office within the Commonwealth, any special agent retired from the State Corporation Commission or the Virginia Alcoholic Beverage Control Board, any employee with internal investigations authority designated by the Department of Corrections pursuant to subdivision 11 of § 53.1-10 retired from the Department of Corrections, any conservation police officer retired from the Department of Game and Inland Fisheries, any Virginia Marine Police officer retired from the Law Enforcement Division of the Virginia Marine Resources Commission, any campus police officer appointed under Chapter 17 (§ 23-232 et seq.) of Title 23 retired from a campus police department, any retired member of the enforcement division of the Department of Motor Vehicles ap-

pointed pursuant to § 46.2-217, and any retired investigator of the security division of the Virginia Lottery, other than an officer or agent terminated for cause, (i) with a service-related disability; (ii) following at least 10 years of service with any such law-enforcement agency, commission, board, or any combination thereof; (iii) who has reached 55 years of age; or (iv) who is on long-term leave from such law-enforcement agency or board due to a service-related injury, provided such officer carries with him written proof of consultation with and favorable review of the need to carry a concealed handgun issued by the chief law-enforcement officer of the last such agency from which the officer retired or the agency that employs the officer or, in the case of special agents, issued by the State Corporation Commission or the Virginia Alcoholic Beverage Control Board. A copy of the proof of consultation and favorable review shall be forwarded by the chief, Commission, or Board to the Department of State Police for entry into the Virginia Criminal Information Network. The chief law-enforcement officer shall not without cause withhold such written proof if the retired law-enforcement officer otherwise meets the requirements of this section. An officer set forth in clause (iv) who receives written proof of consultation to carry a concealed handgun shall surrender such proof of consultation upon return to work or upon termination of employment with the law-enforcement agency. Notice of the surrender shall be forwarded to the Department of State Police for entry into the Virginia Criminal Information Network. However, if such officer retires on disability because of the service-related injury, and would be eligible under clause (i) for written proof of consultation to carry a concealed handgun, he may retain the previously issued written proof of consultation.

2. Any person who is eligible for retirement with at least 20 years of service with a law-enforcement agency, commission, or board mentioned in subdivision 1 who has resigned in good standing from such law-enforcement agency, commission, or board to accept a position covered by a retirement system that is authorized under Title 51.1, provided such person carries with him written proof of consultation with and favorable review of the need to carry a concealed handgun issued by the chief law-enforcement officer of the agency from which he resigned or, in the case of special agents, issued by the State Corporation Commission or the Virginia Alcoholic Beverage Control Board. A copy of the proof of consultation and favorable review shall be forwarded by the chief, Commission, or Board to the Department of State Police for entry into the Virginia Criminal Information Network. The chief law-enforcement officer shall not without cause withhold such written proof if the law-enforcement officer otherwise meets the requirements of this section.

3. Any State Police officer who is a member of the organized reserve forces of any of the Armed Services of the United States or National Guard, while such officer is called to active military duty, provided such officer carries with him written proof of consultation with and favorable review of the need to carry a concealed handgun issued by the Superintendent of State Police. The proof of consultation and favorable review shall be valid as long as the officer is on active military duty and shall expire when the officer returns to active law-enforcement duty. The issuance of the proof of consultation and favorable review shall be entered into the Virginia Criminal Information Network. The Superintendent of State Police shall not without cause withhold such written proof if the officer is in good standing and is qualified to carry a weapon while on active law-enforcement duty.

B. For purposes of complying with the federal Law Enforcement Officers Safety Act of 2004, a retired or resigned law-enforcement officer who receives proof of consultation and review pursuant to this section shall have the opportunity to annually participate, at the retired or resigned law-enforcement officer's expense, in the same training and testing to carry firearms as is required of active law-enforcement officers in the Commonwealth. If such retired or resigned law-enforcement officer meets the training and qualification standards, the chief law-enforcement officer shall issue the retired or resigned officer certification, valid one year from the date of issuance, indicating that the retired or resigned officer has met the standards of the agency to carry a firearm.

C. A retired or resigned law-enforcement officer who receives proof of consultation and review pursuant to this section may annually participate and meet the training and qualification standards to carry firearms as is required of active law-enforcement officers in the Commonwealth. If such retired or resigned law-enforcement officer meets the training and qualification standards, the chief law-enforcement officer shall issue the retired or resigned officer certification, valid one year from the date of issuance, indicating that the retired or resigned officer has met the standards of the Commonwealth to carry a firearm. A copy of the certification indicating that the retired or resigned officer has met the standards of the Commonwealth to carry a firearm shall be forwarded by the chief, Commission, or Board to the Department of State Police for entry into the Virginia Criminal Information Network.

D. For all purposes, including for the purpose of applying the reciprocity provisions of § 18.2-308.014, any person granted the privilege to carry a concealed handgun pursuant to this section, while carrying the proof of consultation and favorable review required, shall be deemed to have been issued a concealed handgun permit.

History.

2016, cc. 209, 257, 421.

§ 18.2-308.016. (Effective October 1, 2016, until July 1, 2018) Retired law-enforcement officers; carrying a concealed handgun.

A. Except as provided in subsection A of § 18.2-308.012, § 18.2-308 shall not apply to:

1. Any State Police officer retired from the Department of State Police, any officer retired from the Division of Capitol Police, any local law-enforcement officer, auxiliary police officer or animal control officer retired from a police department or sheriff's office within the Commonwealth, any special agent retired from the State Corporation Commission or the Virginia Alcoholic Beverage Control Board, any employee with internal investigations authority designated by the Department of Corrections pursuant to subdivision 11 of § 53.1-10 retired from the Department of Corrections, any conservation police officer retired from the Department of Game and Inland Fisheries, any Virginia Marine Police officer retired from the Law Enforcement Division of the Virginia Marine Resources Commission, any campus police officer appointed under Article 3 (§ 23.1-809 et seq.) of Chapter 8 of Title 23.1 retired from a campus police department, any retired member of the enforcement division of the Department of Motor Vehicles appointed pursuant to § 46.2-217, and any retired investigator of the security division of the Virginia Lottery, other than an officer or agent terminated for cause, (i) with a service-related disability; (ii) following at least 10 years of service with any such law-enforcement agency, commission, board, or any combination thereof; (iii) who has reached 55 years of age; or (iv) who is on long-term leave from such law-enforcement agency or board due to a service-related injury, provided such officer carries with him written proof of consultation with and favorable review of the need to carry a concealed handgun issued by the chief law-enforcement officer of the last such agency from which the officer retired or the agency that employs the officer or, in the case of special agents, issued by the State Corporation Commission or the Virginia Alcoholic Beverage Control Board. A copy of the proof of consultation and favorable review shall be forwarded by the chief, Commission, or Board to the Department of State Police for entry into the Virginia Criminal Information Network. The chief law-enforcement officer shall not without cause withhold such written proof if the retired law-enforcement officer otherwise meets the requirements of this section. An officer set forth in clause (iv) who receives written proof of consultation to carry a concealed handgun shall surrender such proof of consultation upon return to work or upon termination of employment with the law-enforcement agency. Notice of the surrender shall be forwarded to the Department of State Police for entry into the Virginia Criminal Information Network. However, if such officer retires on disability because of the service-related injury, and would be eligible under clause (i) for written proof of consultation to carry a concealed handgun, he may retain the previously issued written proof of consultation.

2. Any person who is eligible for retirement with at least 20 years of service with a law-enforcement agency, commission, or board mentioned in subdivision 1 who has resigned in good standing from such law-enforcement agency, commission, or board to accept a position covered by a retirement system that is authorized under Title 51.1, provided such person carries with him written proof of consultation with and favorable review of the need to carry a concealed handgun issued by the chief law-enforcement officer of the agency from which he resigned or, in the case of special agents, issued by the State Corporation Commission or the Virginia Alcoholic Beverage Control Board. A copy of the proof of consultation and favorable review shall be forwarded by the chief, Commission, or Board to the Department of State Police for entry into the Virginia Criminal Information Network. The chief law-enforcement officer shall not without cause withhold such written proof if the law-enforcement officer otherwise meets the requirements of this section.

3. Any State Police officer who is a member of the organized reserve forces of any of the Armed Services of the United States or National Guard, while such officer is called to active military duty, provided such officer carries with him written proof of consultation with and favorable review of the need to carry a concealed handgun issued by the Superintendent of State Police. The proof of consultation and favorable review shall be valid as long as the officer is on active military duty and shall expire when the officer returns to active law-enforcement duty. The issuance of the proof of consultation and favorable review shall be entered into the Virginia Criminal Information Network. The Superintendent of State Police shall not without cause withhold such written proof if the officer is in good standing and is qualified to carry a weapon while on active law-enforcement duty.

B. For purposes of complying with the federal Law Enforcement Officers Safety Act of 2004, a retired or resigned law-enforcement officer who receives proof of consultation and review pursuant to this section shall have the opportunity to annually participate, at the retired or resigned law-enforcement officer's expense, in the same training and testing to carry firearms as is required of active law-enforcement officers in the Commonwealth. If such retired or resigned law-enforcement officer meets the training and qualification standards, the chief law-enforcement officer shall issue the retired or resigned officer certification, valid one year from the date of issuance, indicating that the retired or resigned officer has met the standards of the agency to carry a firearm.

C. A retired or resigned law-enforcement officer who receives proof of consultation and review pursuant to this section may annually participate and meet the training and qualification standards to carry firearms as is required of active law-enforcement officers in the Commonwealth. If such retired or resigned law-enforcement officer meets the training and qualification standards, the chief law-enforcement officer shall issue the retired or resigned officer certification, valid one year from the date of issuance, indicating that the retired or resigned officer has met the standards of the Commonwealth to carry a firearm. A copy of the certification indicating that the retired or resigned officer has met the standards of the Commonwealth to carry a firearm shall be forwarded by the chief, Commission, or Board to the Department of State Police for entry into the Virginia Criminal Information Network.

D. For all purposes, including for the purpose of applying the reciprocity provisions of § 18.2-308.014, any person granted the privilege to carry a concealed handgun pursuant to this section, while carrying the proof of consultation and favorable review required, shall be deemed to have been issued a concealed handgun permit.

History.

2016, cc. 209, 257, 421.

§ 18.2-308.016. (Effective July 1, 2018) Retired law-enforcement officers; carrying a concealed handgun.

A. Except as provided in subsection A of § 18.2-308.012, § 18.2-308 shall not apply to:

1. Any State Police officer retired from the Department of State Police, any officer retired from the Division of Capitol Police, any local law-enforcement officer, auxiliary police officer or animal control officer retired from a police department or sheriff's office within the Commonwealth, any special agent retired from the State Corporation Commission or the Virginia Alcoholic Beverage Control Authority, any employee with internal investigations authority designated by the Department of Corrections pursuant to subdivision 11 of § 53.1-10 retired from the Department of Corrections, any conservation police officer retired from the Department of Game and Inland Fisheries, any Virginia Marine Police officer retired from the Law Enforcement Division of the Virginia Marine Resources Commission, any campus police officer appointed under Article 3 (§ 23.1-809 et seq.) of Chapter 8 of Title 23.1 retired from a campus police department, any retired member of the enforcement division of the Department of Motor Vehicles appointed pursuant to § 46.2-217, and any retired investigator of the security division of the Virginia Lottery, other than an officer or agent terminated for cause, (i) with a service-related disability; (ii) following at least 10 years of service with any such law-enforcement agency, commission, board, or any combination thereof; (iii) who has reached 55 years of age; or (iv) who is on long-term leave from such law-enforcement agency or board due to a service-related injury, provided such officer carries with him written proof of consultation with and favorable review of the need to carry a concealed handgun issued by the chief law-enforcement officer of the last such agency from which the officer retired or the agency that employs the officer or, in the case of special agents, issued by the State Corporation Commission or the Virginia Alcoholic Beverage Control Authority. A copy of the proof of consultation and favorable review shall be forwarded by the chief, Commission, or Board to the Department of State Police for entry into the Virginia Criminal Information Network. The chief law-enforcement officer shall not without cause withhold such written proof if the retired law-enforcement officer otherwise meets the requirements of this section. An officer set forth in clause (iv) who receives written proof of consultation to carry a concealed handgun shall surrender such proof of consultation upon return to work or upon termination of employment with the law-enforcement agency. Notice of the surrender shall be forwarded to the Department of State Police for entry into the Virginia Criminal Information Network. However, if such officer retires on disability because of the service-related injury, and would be eligible under clause (i) for written proof of consultation to carry a concealed handgun, he may retain the previously issued written proof of consultation.

2. Any person who is eligible for retirement with at least 20 years of service with a law-enforcement agency, commission, or board mentioned in subdivision 1 who has resigned in good standing from such law-enforcement agency, commission, or board to accept a position covered by a retirement system that is authorized under Title 51.1, provided such person carries with him written proof of consultation with and favorable review of the need to carry a concealed handgun issued by the chief law-enforcement officer of the agency from which he resigned or, in the case of special agents, issued by the State Corporation Commission or the Virginia Alcoholic Beverage Control Authority. A copy of the proof of consultation and favorable review shall be forwarded by the chief, Commission, or Board to the Department of State Police for entry into the Virginia Criminal Information Network. The chief law-enforcement officer shall not without cause withhold such written proof if the law-enforcement officer otherwise meets the requirements of this section.

3. Any State Police officer who is a member of the organized reserve forces of any of the Armed Services of the United States or National Guard, while such officer is called to active military duty, provided such officer carries with him written proof of consultation with and favorable review of the need to carry a concealed handgun issued by the Superintendent of State Police. The proof of consultation and favorable review shall be valid as long as the officer is on active military duty and shall expire when the officer returns to active law-enforcement duty. The issuance of the proof of consultation and favorable

review shall be entered into the Virginia Criminal Information Network. The Superintendent of State Police shall not without cause withhold such written proof if the officer is in good standing and is qualified to carry a weapon while on active law-enforcement duty.

B. For purposes of complying with the federal Law Enforcement Officers Safety Act of 2004, a retired or resigned law-enforcement officer who receives proof of consultation and review pursuant to this section shall have the opportunity to annually participate, at the retired or resigned law-enforcement officer's expense, in the same training and testing to carry firearms as is required of active law-enforcement officers in the Commonwealth. If such retired or resigned law-enforcement officer meets the training and qualification standards, the chief law-enforcement officer shall issue the retired or resigned officer certification, valid one year from the date of issuance, indicating that the retired or resigned officer has met the standards of the agency to carry a firearm.

C. A retired or resigned law-enforcement officer who receives proof of consultation and review pursuant to this section may annually participate and meet the training and qualification standards to carry firearms as is required of active law-enforcement officers in the Commonwealth. If such retired or resigned law-enforcement officer meets the training and qualification standards, the chief law-enforcement officer shall issue the retired or resigned officer certification, valid one year from the date of issuance, indicating that the retired or resigned officer has met the standards of the Commonwealth to carry a firearm. A copy of the certification indicating that the retired or resigned officer has met the standards of the Commonwealth to carry a firearm shall be forwarded by the chief, Commission, or Board to the Department of State Police for entry into the Virginia Criminal Information Network.

D. For all purposes, including for the purpose of applying the reciprocity provisions of § 18.2-308.014, any person granted the privilege to carry a concealed handgun pursuant to this section, while carrying the proof of consultation and favorable review required, shall be deemed to have been issued a concealed handgun permit.

History.

2016, cc. 209, 257, 421.

ARTICLE 7. OTHER ILLEGAL WEAPONS.

§ 18.2-308.1. Possession of firearm, stun weapon, or other weapon on school property prohibited; penalty.

A. If any person knowingly possesses any (i) stun weapon as defined in this section; (ii) knife, except a pocket knife having a folding metal blade of less than three inches; or (iii) weapon, including a weapon of like kind, designated in subsection A of § 18.2-308, other than a firearm; upon (a) the property of any public, private or religious elementary, middle or high school, including buildings and grounds; (b) that portion of any property open to the public and then exclusively used for school-sponsored functions or extracurricular activities while such functions or activities are taking place; or (c) any school bus owned or operated by any such school, he shall be guilty of a Class 1 misdemeanor.

B. If any person knowingly possesses any firearm designed or intended to expel a projectile by action of an explosion of a combustible material while such person is upon (i) any public, private or religious elementary, middle or high school, including buildings and grounds; (ii) that portion of any property open to the public and then exclusively used for school-sponsored functions or extracurricular activities while such functions or activities are taking place; or (iii) any school bus owned or operated by any such school, he shall be guilty of a Class 6 felony.

C. If any person knowingly possesses any firearm designed or intended to expel a projectile by action of an explosion of a combustible material within a public, private or religious elementary, middle or high school building and intends to use, or attempts to use, such firearm, or displays such weapon in a threatening manner, such person shall be guilty of a Class 6 felony and sentenced to a mandatory minimum term of imprisonment of five years to be served consecutively with any other sentence.

The exemptions set out in §§ 18.2-308 and 18.2-308.016 shall apply, mutatis mutandis, to the provisions of this section. The provisions of this section shall not apply to (i) persons who possess such weapon or weapons as a part of the school's curriculum or activities; (ii) a person possessing a knife customarily used for food preparation or service and using it for such purpose; (iii) persons who possess such weapon or weapons as a part of any program sponsored or facilitated by either the school or any organization authorized by the school to conduct its programs either on or off the school premises; (iv) any law-enforcement officer, or retired law-enforcement officer qualified pursuant to subsection C of § 18.2-308.016; (v) any person who possesses a knife or blade which he uses customarily in his trade; (vi) a person who possesses an unloaded firearm that is in a closed container, or a knife having a metal blade, in or upon a motor vehicle, or an unloaded shotgun or rifle in a firearms rack in or upon a motor vehicle; (vii) a person who has a valid concealed handgun permit and possesses a concealed handgun while in a motor vehicle in a parking lot, traffic circle, or other means of vehicular ingress or egress to the school; or (viii) an armed security officer, licensed pursuant to Article 4 (§ 9.1-138 et seq.) of Chapter 1 of Title 9.1, hired by a private or religious school for the protection of students and employees as authorized by such school. For the purposes of this paragraph, "weapon" includes a knife having a metal blade of three inches or longer and "closed container" includes a locked vehicle trunk.

As used in this section:

"Stun weapon" means any device that emits a momentary or pulsed output, which is electrical, audible, optical or electromagnetic in nature and which is designed to temporarily incapacitate a person.

History.

1979, c. 467; 1988, c. 493; 1990, cc. 635, 744; 1991, c. 579; 1992, cc. 727, 735; 1995, c. 511; 1999, cc. 587, 829, 846; 2001, c. 403; 2003, cc. 619, 976; 2004, cc. 128, 461; 2005, cc. 830, 928; 2007, c. 519; 2011, c. 282; 2013, c. 416; 2015, c. 289; 2016, c. 257.

§ 18.2-308.1:1. Purchase, possession or transportation of firearms by persons acquitted by reason of insanity; penalty.

A. It shall be unlawful for any person acquitted by reason of insanity and committed to the custody of the Commissioner of Behavioral Health and Developmental Services, pursuant to Chapter 11.1 (§ 19.2-182.2 et seq.) of Title 19.2, on a charge of treason, any felony or any offense punishable as a misdemeanor under Title 54.1 or a Class 1 or Class 2 misdemeanor under this title, except those misdemeanor violations of (i) Article 2 (§ 18.2-266 et seq.) of Chapter 7 of this title, (ii) Article 2 (§ 18.2-415 et seq.) of Chapter 9 of this title, or (iii) § 18.2-119, or (iv) an ordinance of any county, city, or town similar to the offenses specified in (i), (ii), or (iii), to knowingly and intentionally purchase, possess, or transport any firearm. A violation of this subsection shall be punishable as a Class 1 misdemeanor.

B. Any person so acquitted may, upon discharge from the custody of the Commissioner, petition the general district court in the city or county in which he resides to restore his right to purchase, possess or transport a firearm. A copy of the petition shall be mailed or delivered to the attorney for the Commonwealth for the jurisdiction where the petition was filed who shall be entitled to respond and represent the interests of the Commonwealth. The court shall conduct a hearing if requested by either party. If the court determines, after receiving and considering evidence concerning the circumstances regarding the disability referred to in subsection A and the person's criminal history, treatment record, and reputation as developed through character witness statements, testimony, or other character evidence, that the person will not be likely to act in a manner dangerous to public safety and that the granting of the relief would not be contrary to the public interest, the court shall grant the petition. Any person denied relief by the general district court may petition the circuit court for a de novo review of the denial. Upon a grant of relief in any court, the court shall enter a written order granting the petition, in which event the provisions of subsection A do not apply. The clerk of court shall certify and forward forthwith to the Central Criminal Records Exchange, on a form provided by the Exchange, a copy of any such order.

C. As used in this section, "treatment record" shall include copies of health records detailing the petitioner's psychiatric history, which shall include the records pertaining to the commitment or adjudication that is the subject of the request for relief pursuant to this section.

History.

1990, c. 692; 2008, cc. 788, 854, 869; 2009, cc. 813, 840; 2010, c. 781; 2011, c. 775.

§ 18.2-308.1:2. Purchase, possession or transportation of firearm by persons adjudicated legally incompetent or mentally incapacitated; penalty.

A. It shall be unlawful for any person who has been adjudicated (i) legally incompetent pursuant to former § 37.1-128.02 or former § 37.1-134, (ii) mentally incapacitated pursuant to former § 37.1-128.1 or former § 37.1-132 or (iii) incapacitated pursuant to Chapter 20 (§ 64.2-2000 et seq.) of Title 64.2 to purchase, possess, or transport any firearm. A violation of this subsection shall be punishable as a Class 1 misdemeanor.

B. Any person whose competency or capacity has been restored pursuant to former § 37.1-134.1, former § 37.2-1012, or § 64.2-2012 may petition the general district court in the city or county in which he resides to restore his right to purchase, possess or transport a firearm. A copy of the petition shall be mailed or delivered to the attorney for the Commonwealth for the jurisdiction where the petition was filed who shall be entitled to respond and represent the interests of the Commonwealth. The court shall conduct a hearing if requested by either party. If the court determines, after receiving and considering evidence concerning the circumstances regarding the disability referred to in subsection A and the person's criminal history, treatment record, and reputation as developed through character witness statements, testimony, or other character evidence, that the person will not be likely to act in a manner dangerous to public safety and that the granting of the relief would not be contrary to the public interest, the court shall grant the petition. Any person denied relief by the general district court may petition the circuit court for a de novo review of the denial. Upon a grant of relief in any court, the court shall enter a written order granting the petition, in which event the provisions of subsection A do not apply. The clerk of court shall certify and forward forthwith to the Central Criminal Records Exchange, on a form provided by the Exchange, a copy of any such order.

C. As used in this section, "treatment record" shall include copies of health records detailing the petitioner's psychiatric history, which shall include the records pertaining to the commitment or adjudication that is the subject of the request for relief pursuant to this section.

History.

1994, c. 907; 1997, c. 921; 2004, c. 995; 2011, c. 775.

§ 18.2-308.1:3. Purchase, possession or transportation of firearm by persons involuntarily admitted or ordered to outpatient treatment; penalty.

A. It shall be unlawful for any person involuntarily admitted to a facility or ordered to mandatory outpatient treatment pursuant to § 19.2-169.2, involuntarily admitted to a facility or ordered to mandatory outpatient treatment as the result of a commitment hearing pursuant to Article 5 (§ 37.2-814 et seq.) of Chapter 8 of Title 37.2, or who was the subject of a temporary detention order pursuant to § 37.2-809 and subsequently agreed to voluntary admission pursuant to § 37.2-805 to purchase, possess or transport a firearm. A violation of this subsection shall be punishable as a Class 1 misdemeanor.

B. Any person prohibited from purchasing, possessing or transporting firearms under this section may, at any time following his release from involuntary admission to a facility, his release from an order of mandatory outpatient treatment, or his release from voluntary admission pursuant to § 37.2-805 following the issuance of a temporary detention order, petition the general district court in the city or county in which he resides to restore his right to purchase, possess or transport a firearm. A copy of the petition shall be mailed or delivered to the attorney for the Commonwealth for the jurisdiction where the petition was filed who shall be entitled to respond and represent the interests of the Commonwealth. The court shall conduct a hearing if requested by either party. If the court determines, after receiving and considering evidence concerning the circumstances regarding the disabilities referred to in subsection A and the person's criminal history, treatment record, and reputation as developed through character witness statements, testimony, or other character evidence, that the person will not likely act in a manner dangerous to public safety and that granting the relief would not be contrary to the public interest, the court shall grant the petition. Any person denied relief by the general district court may petition the circuit court for a de novo review of the denial. Upon a grant of relief in any court, the court shall enter a written order granting the petition, in which event the provisions of subsection A do not apply. The clerk of court shall certify and forward forthwith to the Central Criminal Records Exchange, on a form provided by the Exchange, a copy of any such order.

C. As used in this section, "treatment record" shall include copies of health records detailing the petitioner's psychiatric history, which shall include the records pertaining to the commitment or adjudication that is the subject of the request for relief pursuant to this section.

History.

1994, c. 907; 2004, c. 995; 2008, cc. 751, 788; 2010, c. 781; 2011, c. 775.

§ 18.2-308.1:4. Purchase or transportation of firearm by persons subject to protective orders; penalties.

A. It is unlawful for any person who is subject to (i) a protective order entered pursuant to § 16.1-253.1, 16.1-253.4, 16.1-278.2, 16.1-279.1, 19.2-152.8, 19.2-152.9, or 19.2-152.10; (ii) an order issued pursuant to subsection B of § 20-103; (iii) an order entered pursuant to subsection E of § 18.2-60.3; (iv) a preliminary protective order entered pursuant to subsection F of § 16.1-253 where a petition alleging abuse or neglect has been filed; or (v) an order issued by a tribunal of another state, the United States or any of its territories, possessions, or commonwealths, or the District of Columbia pursuant to a statute that is substantially similar to those cited in clauses (i), (ii), (iii), or (iv) to purchase or transport any firearm while the order is in effect. Any person with a concealed handgun permit shall be prohibited from carrying any concealed firearm, and shall surrender his permit to the court entering the order, for the duration of any protective order referred to herein. A violation of this subsection is a Class 1 misdemeanor.

B. In addition to the prohibition set forth in subsection A, it is unlawful for any person who is subject to a protective order entered pursuant to § 16.1-279.1 or an order issued by a tribunal of another state, the United States or any of its territories, possessions, or commonwealths, or the District of Columbia pursuant to a statute that is substantially similar to § 16.1-279.1 to knowingly possess any firearm while the order is in effect, provided that for a period of 24 hours after being served with a protective order in accordance with subsection C of § 16.1-279.1 such person may continue to possess and, notwithstanding the provisions of subsection A, transport any firearm possessed by such person at the time of service for the purposes of selling or transferring any such firearm to any person who is not otherwise prohibited by law from possessing such firearm. A violation of this subsection is a Class 6 felony.

History.

1994, c. 907; 1996, c. 866; 1998, c. 569; 2001, c. 357; 2002, cc. 783, 865; 2004, c. 995; 2011, cc. 373, 402; 2013, c. 759; 2016, cc. 48, 49.

§ 18.2-308.1:5. Purchase or transportation of firearm by persons convicted of certain drug offenses prohibited.

Any person who, within a 36-consecutive-month period, has been convicted of two misdemeanor offenses under subsection B of former § 18.2-248.1:1, § 18.2-250 or 18.2-250.1 shall be ineligible to purchase or transport a handgun. However, upon expiration of a period of five years from the date of the second conviction and provided the person has not been convicted of any such offense within that period, the ineligibility shall be removed.

History.

1995, c. 577; 2011, cc. 384, 410; 2014, cc. 674, 719.

§ 18.2-308.2. Possession or transportation of firearms, firearms ammunition, stun weapons, explosives or concealed weapons by convicted felons; penalties; petition for permit; when issued.

A. It shall be unlawful for (i) any person who has been convicted of a felony; (ii) any person adjudicated delinquent as a juvenile 14 years of age or older at the time of the offense of murder in violation of § 18.2-31 or 18.2-32, kidnapping in violation of § 18.2-47, robbery by the threat or presentation of firearms in violation of § 18.2-58, or rape in violation of § 18.2-61; or (iii) any person under the age of 29 who was adjudicated delinquent as a juvenile 14 years of age or older at the time of the offense of a delinquent act which would be a felony if committed by an adult, other than those felonies set forth in clause (ii), whether such conviction or adjudication occurred under the laws of the Commonwealth, or any other state, the District of Columbia, the United States or any territory thereof, to knowingly and intentionally possess or transport any firearm or ammunition for a firearm, any stun weapon as defined by § 18.2-308.1, or any explosive material, or to knowingly and intentionally carry about his person, hidden from common observation, any weapon described in subsection A of § 18.2-308. However, such person may possess in his residence or the curtilage thereof a stun weapon as defined by § 18.2-308.1. Any person who violates this section shall be guilty of a Class 6 felony. However, any person who violates this section by knowingly and intentionally possessing or transporting any firearm and who was previously convicted of a violent felony as defined in § 17.1-805 shall be sentenced to a mandatory minimum term of imprisonment of five years. Any person who violates this section by knowingly and intentionally possessing or transporting any firearm and who was previously convicted of any other felony within the prior 10 years shall be sentenced to a mandatory minimum term of imprisonment of two years. The mandatory minimum terms of imprisonment prescribed for violations of this section shall be served consecutively with any other sentence.

B. The prohibitions of subsection A shall not apply to (i) any person who possesses a firearm, ammunition for a firearm, explosive material or other weapon while carrying out his duties as a member of the Armed Forces of the United States or of the National Guard of Virginia or of any other state, (ii) any law-enforcement officer in the performance of his duties, (iii) any person who has been pardoned or whose political disabilities have been removed pursuant to Article V, Section 12 of the Constitution of Virginia provided the Governor, in the document granting the pardon or removing the person's political disabilities, may expressly place conditions upon the reinstatement of the person's right to ship, transport, possess or receive firearms, (iv) any person whose right to possess firearms or ammunition has been restored under the law of another state subject to conditions placed upon the reinstatement of the person's right to ship, transport, possess, or receive firearms by such state, or (v) any person adjudicated delinquent as a juvenile who has completed a term of service of no less than two years in the Armed Forces of the United States and, if such person has been discharged from the Armed Forces of the United States, received an honorable discharge and who is not otherwise prohibited under clause (i) or (ii) of subsection A.

C. Any person prohibited from possessing, transporting, or carrying a firearm, ammunition for a firearm, or a stun weapon under subsection A may petition the circuit court of the jurisdiction in which he resides or, if the person is not a resident of the Commonwealth, the circuit court of any county or city where such person was last convicted of a felony or adjudicated delinquent of a disqualifying offense pursuant to subsection A, for a permit to possess or carry a firearm, ammunition for a firearm, or a stun weapon; however, no person who has been convicted of a felony shall be qualified to petition for such a permit unless his civil rights have been restored by the Governor or other appropriate authority. A copy of the petition shall be mailed or delivered to the attorney for the Commonwealth for the jurisdiction where the petition was filed who shall be entitled to respond and represent the interests of the Commonwealth. The court shall conduct a hearing if requested by either party. The court may, in its discretion and for good cause shown, grant such petition and issue a permit. The provisions of this section relating to firearms, ammunition for a firearm, and stun weapons shall not apply to any person who has been granted a permit pursuant to this subsection.

C1. Any person who was prohibited from possessing, transporting or carrying explosive material under subsection A may possess, transport or carry such explosive material if his right to possess, transport or carry explosive material has been restored pursuant to federal law.

D. For the purpose of this section:

"Ammunition for a firearm" means the combination of a cartridge, projectile, primer, or propellant designed for use in a firearm other than an antique firearm as defined in § 18.2-308.2:2.

"Explosive material" means any chemical compound mixture, or device, the primary or common

purpose of which is to function by explosion; the term includes, but is not limited to, dynamite and other high explosives, black powder, pellet powder, smokeless gun powder, detonators, blasting caps and detonating cord but shall not include fireworks or permissible fireworks as defined in § 27-95.

History.
1979, c. 474; 1982, c. 515; 1983, c. 233; 1986, cc. 409, 641; 1987, c. 108; 1988, c. 237; 1989, cc. 514, 531; 1993, cc. 468, 926; 1994, cc. 859, 949; 1999, cc. 829, 846; 2001, cc. 811, 854; 2002, c. 362; 2003, c. 110; 2004, cc. 429, 461, 995; 2005, cc. 600, 833; 2007, c. 519; 2008, c. 752; 2009, c. 236; 2010, c. 781; 2015, cc. 200, 767; 2016, c. 337.

§ 18.2-308.2:01. Possession or transportation of certain firearms by certain persons.

A. It shall be unlawful for any person who is not a citizen of the United States or who is not a person lawfully admitted for permanent residence to knowingly and intentionally possess or transport any assault firearm or to knowingly and intentionally carry about his person, hidden from common observation, an assault firearm.

B. It shall be unlawful for any person who is not a citizen of the United States and who is not lawfully present in the United States to knowingly and intentionally possess or transport any firearm or to knowingly and intentionally carry about his person, hidden from common observation, any firearm. A violation of this section shall be punishable as a Class 6 felony.

C. For purposes of this section, *"assault firearm"* means any semi-automatic center-fire rifle or pistol that expels single or multiple projectiles by action of an explosion of a combustible material and is equipped at the time of the offense with a magazine which will hold more than 20 rounds of ammunition or designed by the manufacturer to accommodate a silencer or equipped with a folding stock.

History.
1993, c. 674; 2003, c. 976; 2004, cc. 347, 995; 2008, c. 408.

§ 18.2-308.2:1. Prohibiting the selling, etc., of firearms to certain persons.

Any person who sells, barters, gives or furnishes, or has in his possession or under his control with the intent of selling, bartering, giving or furnishing, any firearm to any person he knows is prohibited from possessing or transporting a firearm pursuant to § 18.2-308.1:1, 18.2-308.1:2, 18.2-308.1:3, 18.2-308.2, subsection B of § 18.2-308.2:01, or § 18.2-308.7 shall be guilty of a Class 4 felony. However, this prohibition shall not be applicable when the person convicted of the felony, adjudicated delinquent or acquitted by reason of insanity has (i) been issued a permit pursuant to subsection C of § 18.2-308.2 or been granted relief pursuant to subsection B of § 18.2-308.1:1, or § 18.2-308.1:2 or 18.2-308.1:3 (ii) been pardoned or had his political disabilities removed in accordance with subsection B of § 18.2-308.2 or (iii) obtained a permit to ship, transport, possess or receive firearms pursuant to the laws of the United States.

History.
1988, c. 327; 1990, c. 692; 1993, cc. 467, 494, 882, 926; 2004, c. 995; 2008, c. 408; 2011, c. 775; 2013, c. 797.

§ 18.2-308.2:2. Criminal history record information check required for the transfer of certain firearms.

A. Any person purchasing from a dealer a firearm as herein defined shall consent in writing, on a form to be provided by the Department of State Police, to have the dealer obtain criminal history record information. Such form shall include only the written consent; the name, birth date, gender, race, citizenship, and social security number and/or any other identification number; the number of firearms by category intended to be sold, rented, traded, or transferred; and answers by the applicant to the following questions: (i) has the applicant been convicted of a felony offense or found guilty or adjudicated delinquent as a juvenile 14 years of age or older at the time of the offense of a delinquent act that would be a felony if committed by an adult; (ii) is the applicant subject to a court order restraining the applicant from harassing, stalking, or threatening the applicant's child or intimate partner, or a child of such partner, or is the applicant subject to a protective order; and (iii) has the applicant ever been acquitted by reason of insanity and prohibited from purchasing, possessing or transporting a firearm pursuant to § 18.2-308.1:1 or any substantially similar law of any other jurisdiction, been adjudicated legally incompetent, mentally incapacitated or adjudicated an incapacitated person and prohibited from purchasing a firearm pursuant to § 18.2-308.1:2 or any substantially similar law of any other jurisdiction, or been involuntarily admitted to an inpatient facility or involuntarily ordered to outpatient mental health treatment and prohibited from purchasing a firearm pursuant to § 18.2-308.1:3 or any substantially similar law of any other jurisdiction.

B. 1. No dealer shall sell, rent, trade or transfer from his inventory any such firearm to any other person who is a resident of Virginia until he has (i) obtained written consent and the other information on the consent form specified in subsection A, and provided the Department of State Police with the name, birth date, gender, race, citizenship, and social security and/or any other identification number and the number of firearms by category intended to be sold, rented, traded or transferred and (ii) requested criminal history record information by a telephone call to or other communication authorized by the State Police and is authorized by subdivision 2 to complete the sale or other such transfer. To establish personal identification and residence in

Virginia for purposes of this section, a dealer must require any prospective purchaser to present one photo-identification form issued by a governmental agency of the Commonwealth or by the United States Department of Defense that demonstrates that the prospective purchaser resides in Virginia. For the purposes of this section and establishment of residency for firearm purchase, residency of a member of the armed forces shall include both the state in which the member's permanent duty post is located and any nearby state in which the member resides and from which he commutes to the permanent duty post. A member of the armed forces whose photo identification issued by the Department of Defense does not have a Virginia address may establish his Virginia residency with such photo identification and either permanent orders assigning the purchaser to a duty post, including the Pentagon, in Virginia or the purchaser's Leave and Earnings Statement. When the photo identification presented to a dealer by the prospective purchaser is a driver's license or other photo identification issued by the Department of Motor Vehicles, and such identification form contains a date of issue, the dealer shall not, except for a renewed driver's license or other photo identification issued by the Department of Motor Vehicles, sell or otherwise transfer a firearm to the prospective purchaser until 30 days after the date of issue of an original or duplicate driver's license unless the prospective purchaser also presents a copy of his Virginia Department of Motor Vehicles driver's record showing that the original date of issue of the driver's license was more than 30 days prior to the attempted purchase.

In addition, no dealer shall sell, rent, trade, or transfer from his inventory any assault firearm to any person who is not a citizen of the United States or who is not a person lawfully admitted for permanent residence.

Upon receipt of the request for a criminal history record information check, the State Police shall (a) review its criminal history record information to determine if the buyer or transferee is prohibited from possessing or transporting a firearm by state or federal law, (b) inform the dealer if its record indicates that the buyer or transferee is so prohibited, and (c) provide the dealer with a unique reference number for that inquiry.

2. The State Police shall provide its response to the requesting dealer during the dealer's request, or by return call without delay. If the criminal history record information check indicates the prospective purchaser or transferee has a disqualifying criminal record or has been acquitted by reason of insanity and committed to the custody of the Commissioner of Behavioral Health and Developmental Services, the State Police shall have until the end of the dealer's next business day to advise the dealer if its records indicate the buyer or transferee is prohibited from possessing or transporting a firearm by state or federal law. If not so advised by the end of the dealer's next business day, a dealer who has fulfilled the requirements of subdivision 1 may immediately complete the sale or transfer and shall not be deemed in violation of this section with respect to such sale or transfer. In case of electronic failure or other circumstances beyond the control of the State Police, the dealer shall be advised immediately of the reason for such delay and be given an estimate of the length of such delay. After such notification, the State Police shall, as soon as possible but in no event later than the end of the dealer's next business day, inform the requesting dealer if its records indicate the buyer or transferee is prohibited from possessing or transporting a firearm by state or federal law. A dealer who fulfills the requirements of subdivision 1 and is told by the State Police that a response will not be available by the end of the dealer's next business day may immediately complete the sale or transfer and shall not be deemed in violation of this section with respect to such sale or transfer.

3. Except as required by subsection D of § 9.1-132, the State Police shall not maintain records longer than 30 days, except for multiple handgun transactions for which records shall be maintained for 12 months, from any dealer's request for a criminal history record information check pertaining to a buyer or transferee who is not found to be prohibited from possessing and transporting a firearm under state or federal law. However, the log on requests made may be maintained for a period of 12 months, and such log shall consist of the name of the purchaser, the dealer identification number, the unique approval number and the transaction date.

4. On the last day of the week following the sale or transfer of any firearm, the dealer shall mail or deliver the written consent form required by subsection A to the Department of State Police. The State Police shall immediately initiate a search of all available criminal history record information to determine if the purchaser is prohibited from possessing or transporting a firearm under state or federal law. If the search discloses information indicating that the buyer or transferee is so prohibited from possessing or transporting a firearm, the State Police shall inform the chief law-enforcement officer in the jurisdiction where the sale or transfer occurred and the dealer without delay.

5. Notwithstanding any other provisions of this section, rifles and shotguns may be purchased by persons who are citizens of the United States or persons lawfully admitted for permanent residence but residents of other states under the terms of subsections A and B upon furnishing the dealer with one photo-identification form issued by a governmental agency of the person's state of residence and one other form of identification determined to be acceptable by the Department of Criminal Justice Services.

6. For the purposes of this subsection, the phrase "dealer's next business day" shall not include December 25.

C. No dealer shall sell, rent, trade or transfer from his inventory any firearm, except when the transaction involves a rifle or a shotgun and can be accomplished pursuant to the provisions of subdivision B 5 to any person who is not a resident of Virginia unless he has first obtained from the Department of State Police a report indicating that a search of all available criminal history record information has not disclosed that the person is prohibited from possessing or transporting a firearm under state or federal law. The dealer shall obtain the required report by mailing or delivering the written consent form required under subsection A to the State Police within 24 hours of its execution. If the dealer has complied with the provisions of this subsection and has not received the required report from the State Police within 10 days from the date the written consent form was mailed to the Department of State Police, he shall not be deemed in violation of this section for thereafter completing the sale or transfer.

D. Nothing herein shall prevent a resident of the Commonwealth, at his option, from buying, renting or receiving a firearm from a dealer in Virginia by obtaining a criminal history record information check through the dealer as provided in subsection C.

E. If any buyer or transferee is denied the right to purchase a firearm under this section, he may exercise his right of access to and review and correction of criminal history record information under § 9.1-132 or institute a civil action as provided in § 9.1-135, provided any such action is initiated within 30 days of such denial.

F. Any dealer who willfully and intentionally requests, obtains, or seeks to obtain criminal history record information under false pretenses, or who willfully and intentionally disseminates or seeks to disseminate criminal history record information except as authorized in this section shall be guilty of a Class 2 misdemeanor.

G. For purposes of this section:

"Actual buyer" means a person who executes the consent form required in subsection B or C, or other such firearm transaction records as may be required by federal law.

"Antique firearm" means:

1. Any firearm (including any firearm with a matchlock, flintlock, percussion cap, or similar type of ignition system) manufactured in or before 1898;

2. Any replica of any firearm described in subdivision 1 of this definition if such replica (i) is not designed or redesigned for using rimfire or conventional centerfire fixed ammunition or (ii) uses rimfire or conventional centerfire fixed ammunition that is no longer manufactured in the United States and that is not readily available in the ordinary channels of commercial trade;

3. Any muzzle-loading rifle, muzzle-loading shotgun, or muzzle-loading pistol that is designed to use black powder, or a black powder substitute, and that cannot use fixed ammunition. For purposes of this subdivision, the term "antique firearm" shall not include any weapon that incorporates a firearm frame or receiver, any firearm that is converted into a muzzle-loading weapon, or any muzzle-loading weapon that can be readily converted to fire fixed ammunition by replacing the barrel, bolt, breechblock, or any combination thereof; or

4. Any curio or relic as defined in this subsection.

"Assault firearm" means any semi-automatic center-fire rifle or pistol which expels single or multiple projectiles by action of an explosion of a combustible material and is equipped at the time of the offense with a magazine which will hold more than 20 rounds of ammunition or designed by the manufacturer to accommodate a silencer or equipped with a folding stock.

"Curios or relics" means firearms that are of special interest to collectors by reason of some quality other than is associated with firearms intended for sporting use or as offensive or defensive weapons. To be recognized as curios or relics, firearms must fall within one of the following categories:

1. Firearms that were manufactured at least 50 years prior to the current date, which use rimfire or conventional centerfire fixed ammunition that is no longer manufactured in the United States and that is not readily available in the ordinary channels of commercial trade, but not including replicas thereof;

2. Firearms that are certified by the curator of a municipal, state, or federal museum that exhibits firearms to be curios or relics of museum interest; and

3. Any other firearms that derive a substantial part of their monetary value from the fact that they are novel, rare, bizarre, or because of their association with some historical figure, period, or event. Proof of qualification of a particular firearm under this category may be established by evidence of present value and evidence that like firearms are not available except as collectors' items, or that the value of like firearms available in ordinary commercial channels is substantially less.

"Dealer" means any person licensed as a dealer pursuant to 18 U.S.C. § 921 et seq.

"Firearm" means any handgun, shotgun, or rifle that will or is designed to or may readily be converted to expel single or multiple projectiles by action of an explosion of a combustible material.

"Handgun" means any pistol or revolver or other firearm originally designed, made and intended to fire single or multiple projectiles by means of an explosion of a combustible material from one or more barrels when held in one hand.

"Lawfully admitted for permanent residence" means the status of having been lawfully accorded the privilege of residing permanently in the United States as an immigrant in accordance with the immigration laws, such status not having changed.

H. The Department of Criminal Justice Services shall promulgate regulations to ensure the identity, confidentiality and security of all records and data provided by the Department of State Police pursuant to this section.

I. **(Effective until October 1, 2016)** The provisions of this section shall not apply to (i) transactions between persons who are licensed as firearms importers or collectors, manufacturers or dealers pursuant to 18 U.S.C. § 921 et seq.; (ii) purchases by or sales to any law-enforcement officer or agent of the United States, the Commonwealth or any local government, or any campus police officer appointed under Chapter 17 (§ 23-232 et seq.) of Title 23; or (iii) antique firearms, curios or relics.

I. **(Effective October 1, 2016)** The provisions of this section shall not apply to (i) transactions between persons who are licensed as firearms importers or collectors, manufacturers or dealers pursuant to 18 U.S.C. § 921 et seq.; (ii) purchases by or sales to any law-enforcement officer or agent of the United States, the Commonwealth or any local government, or any campus police officer appointed under Article 3 (§ 23.1-809 et seq.) of Chapter 8 of Title 23.1; or (iii) antique firearms, curios or relics.

J. The provisions of this section shall not apply to restrict purchase, trade or transfer of firearms by a resident of Virginia when the resident of Virginia makes such purchase, trade or transfer in another state, in which case the laws and regulations of that state and the United States governing the purchase, trade or transfer of firearms shall apply. A National Instant Criminal Background Check System (NICS) check shall be performed prior to such purchase, trade or transfer of firearms.

J1. All licensed firearms dealers shall collect a fee of $2 for every transaction for which a criminal history record information check is required pursuant to this section, except that a fee of $5 shall be collected for every transaction involving an out-of-state resident. Such fee shall be transmitted to the Department of State Police by the last day of the month following the sale for deposit in a special fund for use by the State Police to offset the cost of conducting criminal history record information checks under the provisions of this section.

K. Any person willfully and intentionally making a materially false statement on the consent form required in subsection B or C or on such firearm transaction records as may be required by federal law, shall be guilty of a Class 5 felony.

L. Except as provided in § 18.2-308.2:1, any dealer who willfully and intentionally sells, rents, trades or transfers a firearm in violation of this section shall be guilty of a Class 6 felony.

L1. Any person who attempts to solicit, persuade, encourage, or entice any dealer to transfer or otherwise convey a firearm other than to the actual buyer, as well as any other person who willfully and intentionally aids or abets such person, shall be guilty of a Class 6 felony. This subsection shall not apply to a federal law-enforcement officer or a law-enforcement officer as defined in § 9.1-101, in the performance of his official duties, or other person under his direct supervision.

M. Any person who purchases a firearm with the intent to (i) resell or otherwise provide such firearm to any person who he knows or has reason to believe is ineligible to purchase or otherwise receive from a dealer a firearm for whatever reason or (ii) transport such firearm out of the Commonwealth to be resold or otherwise provided to another person who the transferor knows is ineligible to purchase or otherwise receive a firearm, shall be guilty of a Class 4 felony and sentenced to a mandatory minimum term of imprisonment of one year. However, if the violation of this subsection involves such a transfer of more than one firearm, the person shall be sentenced to a mandatory minimum term of imprisonment of five years. The prohibitions of this subsection shall not apply to the purchase of a firearm by a person for the lawful use, possession, or transport thereof, pursuant to § 18.2-308.7, by his child, grandchild, or individual for whom he is the legal guardian if such child, grandchild, or individual is ineligible, solely because of his age, to purchase a firearm.

N. Any person who is ineligible to purchase or otherwise receive or possess a firearm in the Commonwealth who solicits, employs or assists any person in violating subsection M shall be guilty of a Class 4 felony and shall be sentenced to a mandatory minimum term of imprisonment of five years.

O. Any mandatory minimum sentence imposed under this section shall be served consecutively with any other sentence.

P. All driver's licenses issued on or after July 1, 1994, shall carry a letter designation indicating whether the driver's license is an original, duplicate or renewed driver's license.

Q. Prior to selling, renting, trading, or transferring any firearm owned by the dealer but not in his inventory to any other person, a dealer may require such other person to consent to have the dealer obtain criminal history record information to determine if such other person is prohibited from possessing or transporting a firearm by state or federal law. The Department of State Police shall establish policies and procedures in accordance with 28 C.F.R. § 25.6 to permit such determinations to be made by the Department of State Police, and the processes established for making such determinations shall conform to the provisions of this section.

History.

1989, c. 745; 1990, cc. 594, 692; 1991, cc. 515, 525, 716; 1992, cc. 637, 872; 1993, cc. 451, 461, 486, 493, 674; 1994, c. 624; 1997, c. 341; 1998, c. 844; 2002, c. 695; 2003, cc. 833, 976; 2004, cc. 354, 461, 837, 904, 922; 2005, cc. 578, 859; 2007, c. 509; 2008, cc. 854, 869; 2009, cc. 813, 840; 2011, c. 235; 2012, cc. 37, 257, 776; 2013, cc. 450, 662, 761, 774, 797; 2015, c. 759; 2016, cc. 697, 727.

§ 18.2-308.2:3. Criminal background check required for employees of a gun dealer to transfer firearms; exemptions; penalties.

A. No person, corporation, or proprietorship licensed as a firearms dealer pursuant to 18 U.S.C. § 921 et seq. shall employ any person to act as a seller, whether full-time or part-time, permanent, temporary, paid or unpaid, for the transfer of firearms under § 18.2-308.2:2, if such employee would be prohibited from possessing a firearm under § 18.2-308.1:1, 18.2-308.1:2, or 18.2-308.1:3, subsection B of § 18.2-308.1:4, or § 18.2-308.2 or 18.2-308.2:01 or is an illegal alien, or is prohibited from purchasing or transporting a firearm pursuant to subsection A of § 18.2-308.1:4 or § 18.2-308.1:5.

B. Prior to permitting an applicant to begin employment, the dealer shall obtain a written statement or affirmation from the applicant that he is not disqualified from possessing a firearm and shall submit the applicant's fingerprints and personal descriptive information to the Central Criminal Records Exchange to be forwarded to the Federal Bureau of Investigation (FBI) for the purpose of obtaining national criminal history record information regarding the applicant.

C. Prior to August 1, 2000, the dealer shall obtain written statements or affirmations from persons employed before July 1, 2000, to act as a seller under § 18.2-308.2:2 that they are not disqualified from possessing a firearm. Within five working days of the employee's next birthday, after August 1, 2000, the dealer shall submit the employee's fingerprints and personal descriptive information to the Central Criminal Records Exchange to be forwarded to the Federal Bureau of Investigation (FBI) for the purpose of obtaining national criminal history record information regarding the request.

C1. In lieu of submitting fingerprints pursuant to this section, any dealer holding a valid federal firearms license (FFL) issued by the Bureau of Alcohol, Tobacco and Firearms (ATF) may submit a sworn and notarized affidavit to the Department of State Police on a form provided by the Department, stating that the dealer has been subjected to a record check prior to the issuance and that the FFL was issued by the ATF. The affidavit may also contain the names of any employees that have been subjected to a record check and approved by the ATF. This exemption shall apply regardless of whether the FFL was issued in the name of the dealer or in the name of the business. The affidavit shall contain the valid FFL number, state the name of each person requesting the exemption, together with each person's identifying information, including their social security number and the following statement: "I hereby swear, under the penalty of perjury, that as a condition of obtaining a federal firearms license, each person requesting an exemption in this affidavit has been subjected to a fingerprint identification check by the Bureau of Alcohol, Tobacco and Firearms and the Bureau of Alcohol, Tobacco and Firearms subsequently determined that each person satisfied the requirements of 18 U.S.C. § 921 et seq. I understand that any person convicted of making a false statement in this affidavit is guilty of a Class 5 felony and that in addition to any other penalties imposed by law, a conviction under this section shall result in the forfeiture of my federal firearms license."

D. The Department of State Police, upon receipt of an individual's record or notification that no record exists, shall submit an eligibility report to the requesting dealer within 30 days of the applicant beginning his duties for new employees or within 30 days of the applicant's birthday for a person employed prior to July 1, 2000.

E. If any applicant is denied employment because of information appearing on the criminal history record and the applicant disputes the information upon which the denial was based, the Central Criminal Records Exchange shall, upon written request, furnish to the applicant the procedures for obtaining a copy of the criminal history record from the Federal Bureau of Investigation. The information provided to the dealer shall not be disseminated except as provided in this section.

F. The applicant shall bear the cost of obtaining the criminal history record unless the dealer, at his option, decides to pay such cost.

G. Upon receipt of the request for a criminal history record information check, the State Police shall establish a unique number for that firearm seller. Beginning September 1, 2001, the firearm seller's signature, firearm seller's number and the dealer's identification number shall be on all firearm transaction forms. The State Police shall void the firearm seller's number when a disqualifying record is discovered. The State Police may suspend a firearm seller's identification number upon the arrest of the firearm seller for a potentially disqualifying crime.

H. This section shall not restrict the transfer of a firearm at any place other than at a dealership or at any event required to be registered as a gun show.

I. Any person who willfully and intentionally requests, obtains, or seeks to obtain criminal history record information under false pretenses, or who willfully and intentionally disseminates or seeks to disseminate criminal history record information except as authorized by this section and § 18.2-308.2:2, shall be guilty of a Class 2 misdemeanor.

J. Any person willfully and intentionally making a materially false statement on the personal descriptive information required in this section shall be guilty of a Class 5 felony. Any person who offers for transfer any firearm in violation of this section shall be guilty of a Class 1 misdemeanor. Any dealer who willfully and knowingly employs or permits a person to act as a firearm seller in violation of this section shall be guilty of a Class 1 misdemeanor.

K. There is no civil liability for any seller for the actions of any purchaser or subsequent transferee of a firearm lawfully transferred pursuant to this section.

L. The provisions of this section requiring a seller's background check shall not apply to a licensed dealer.

M. Any person who willfully and intentionally makes a false statement in the affidavit as set out in subdivision C 1 shall be guilty of a Class 5 felony.

N. For purposes of this section:

"Dealer" means any person, corporation or proprietorship licensed as a dealer pursuant to 18 U.S.C. § 921 et seq.

"Firearm" means any handgun, shotgun, or rifle that will or is designed to or may readily be converted to expel single or multiple projectiles by action of an explosion of a combustible material.

"Place of business" means any place or premises where a dealer may lawfully transfer firearms.

"Seller" means for the purpose of any single sale of a firearm any person who is a dealer or an agent of a dealer, who may lawfully transfer firearms and who actually performs the criminal background check in accordance with the provisions of § 18.2-308.2:2.

"Transfer" means any act performed with intent to sell, rent, barter, trade or otherwise transfer ownership or permanent possession of a firearm at the place of business of a dealer.

History.

2000, c. 794; 2002, c. 880; 2003, c. 976; 2016, cc. 48, 49.

§ 18.2-308.2:4. Firearm verification check; penalty.

A. For the purposes of this section:

"Dealer" means any person licensed as a dealer pursuant to 18 U.S.C. § 921 et seq.

"Department" means the Department of State Police.

"Firearm" means any handgun, shotgun, or rifle that will or is designed to or may readily be converted to expel single or multiple projectiles by action of an explosion of a combustible material.

B. A dealer who is receiving by sale, transfer, or trade a firearm from a person who is not a dealer may choose to obtain a verification check from the Department to determine if the firearm has been reported to a law-enforcement agency as lost or stolen. If a dealer chooses to obtain a verification check, the procedures in this section shall be followed.

C. The person selling, transferring, or trading the firearm to the dealer shall present a valid photo identification issued by a state or federal governmental agency and shall consent in writing, on a form to be provided by the Department, to have the dealer obtain a verification check to determine if the firearm has been reported to a law-enforcement agency as lost or stolen. Such form shall include only the written consent; the name, address, birth date, gender, race, and verifiable government identification number on the photo identification presented by the person selling, transferring, or trading the firearm; and the serial number, caliber, make, and, if available, model of the firearm.

D. A dealer shall (i) obtain written consent and identifying information on the consent form specified in subsection C; (ii) provide the Department with the serial number, caliber, make, and, if available, model of the firearm intended to be sold, traded, or transferred to the dealer; (iii) request a verification check by telephone or other manner authorized by the Department; and (iv) receive information from the Department as to whether the firearm has been reported to a law-enforcement agency as lost or stolen.

To establish personal identification and residence for purposes of this section, a dealer shall require a prospective transferee to present one photo-identification form containing a verifiable identification number issued by a governmental agency of the Commonwealth, a similar photo-identification form from another state government or by the U.S. Department of Defense, or other documentation of residence determined acceptable by the Department.

E. Upon receipt of the request for a verification check, the Department shall (i) query firearms databases to determine if the firearm has been reported to a law-enforcement agency as lost or stolen, (ii) inform the dealer if the firearm has been reported to a law-enforcement agency as lost or stolen, and (iii) provide the dealer with a unique response for that inquiry.

The Department shall provide its response to the requesting dealer electronically or by return call without delay. If the verification check discloses that the firearm cannot be lawfully sold, transferred, or traded, the Department shall have until the end of the dealer's next business day to advise the dealer that its records indicate the firearm cannot be lawfully sold, transferred, or traded pursuant to state or federal law.

In the case of electronic failure or other circumstances beyond the control of the Department, the dealer shall be advised immediately of the reason for such delay and be given an estimate of the length of such delay. After such notification, the Department shall, as soon as possible but in no event later than the end of the dealer's next business day, inform the requesting dealer if the firearm cannot be lawfully sold, transferred, or traded pursuant to state or federal law.

F. The Department shall maintain a log of requests made for a period of 12 months from the date the request was made, consisting of the serial number, caliber, make, and, if available, model of the firearm; the dealer identification number; and the transaction date.

G. The dealer shall maintain the consent form for a period of 12 months from the date of the transaction if the firearm is determined to be lost or stolen.

If the firearm is determined not to be lost or stolen, the consent form shall be destroyed by the dealer within two weeks from the date of such determination.

H. The Superintendent of State Police shall promulgate regulations to ensure the identity, confidentiality, and security of all records and data provided pursuant to this section.

I. The provisions of this section shall not apply to transactions between persons who are licensed as firearms importers, manufacturers, or dealers pursuant to 18 U.S.C. § 921 et seq.

J. Any person who willfully and intentionally makes a material false statement on the consent form is guilty of a Class 1 misdemeanor.

History.
2014, c. 821.

§ 18.2-308.3. Use or attempted use of restricted ammunition in commission or attempted commission of crimes prohibited; penalty.

A. When used in this section:

"Restricted firearm ammunition" applies to bullets, projectiles or other types of ammunition that are: (i) coated with or contain, in whole or in part, polytetrafluorethylene or a similar product, (ii) commonly known as "KTW" bullets or "French Arcanes," or (iii) any cartridges containing bullets coated with a plastic substance with other than lead or lead alloy cores, jacketed bullets with other than lead or lead alloy cores, or cartridges of which the bullet itself is wholly comprised of a metal or metal alloy other than lead. This definition shall not be construed to include shotgun shells or solid plastic bullets.

B. It shall be unlawful for any person to knowingly use or attempt to use restricted firearm ammunition while committing or attempting to commit a crime. Violation of this section shall constitute a separate and distinct felony and any person found guilty thereof shall be guilty of a Class 5 felony.

History.
1983, c. 602; 1988, c. 530.

§ 18.2-308.4. Possession of firearms while in possession of certain substances.

A. It shall be unlawful for any person unlawfully in possession of a controlled substance classified in Schedule I or II of the Drug Control Act (§ 54.1-3400 et seq.) of Title 54.1 to simultaneously with knowledge and intent possess any firearm. A violation of this subsection is a Class 6 felony and constitutes a separate and distinct felony.

B. It shall be unlawful for any person unlawfully in possession of a controlled substance classified in Schedule I or II of the Drug Control Act (§ 54.1-3400 et seq.) to simultaneously with knowledge and intent possess any firearm on or about his person. A violation of this subsection is a Class 6 felony and constitutes a separate and distinct felony and any person convicted hereunder shall be sentenced to a mandatory minimum term of imprisonment of two years. Such punishment shall be separate and apart from, and shall be made to run consecutively with, any punishment received for the commission of the primary felony.

C. It shall be unlawful for any person to possess, use, or attempt to use any pistol, shotgun, rifle, or other firearm or display such weapon in a threatening manner while committing or attempting to commit the illegal manufacture, sale, distribution, or the possession with the intent to manufacture, sell, or distribute a controlled substance classified in Schedule I or Schedule II of the Drug Control Act (§ 54.1-3400 et seq.) or more than one pound of marijuana. A violation of this subsection is a Class 6 felony, and constitutes a separate and distinct felony and any person convicted hereunder shall be sentenced to a mandatory minimum term of imprisonment of five years. Such punishment shall be separate and apart from, and shall be made to run consecutively with, any punishment received for the commission of the primary felony.

History.
1987, c. 285; 1990, c. 625; 1992, c. 707; 1993, c. 831; 1999, cc. 829, 846; 2003, c. 949; 2004, cc. 461, 995; 2011, cc. 384, 410; 2014, cc. 674, 719.

§ 18.2-308.5. Manufacture, import, sale, transfer or possession of plastic firearm prohibited.

It shall be unlawful for any person to manufacture, import, sell, transfer or possess any plastic firearm. As used in this section, *"plastic firearm"* means any firearm, including machine guns and sawed-off shotguns as defined in this chapter, containing less than 3.7 ounces of electromagnetically detectable metal in the barrel, slide, cylinder, frame or receiver of which, when subjected to inspection by X-ray machines commonly used at airports, does not generate an image that accurately depicts its shape. A violation of this section shall be punishable as a Class 5 felony.

History.
1989, c. 663; 2004, c. 995.

§ 18.2-308.6: Repealed by Acts 2009, c. 288, cl. 1.

§ 18.2-308.7. Possession or transportation of certain firearms by persons under the age of 18; penalty.

It shall be unlawful for any person under 18 years of age to knowingly and intentionally possess or transport a handgun or assault firearm anywhere in the Commonwealth. For the purposes of this section, "handgun" means any pistol or revolver or other

Crimes and Offenses

firearm originally designed, made and intended to fire single or multiple projectiles by means of an explosion of a combustible material from one or more barrels when held in one hand and "assault firearm" means any (i) semi-automatic centerfire rifle or pistol which expels single or multiple projectiles by action of an explosion of a combustible material and is equipped at the time of the offense with a magazine which will hold more than 20 rounds of ammunition or designed by the manufacturer to accommodate a silencer or equipped with a folding stock or (ii) shotgun with a magazine which will hold more than seven rounds of the longest ammunition for which it is chambered. A violation of this section shall be a Class 1 misdemeanor.

This section shall not apply to:

1. Any person (i) while in his home or on his property; (ii) while in the home or on the property of his parent, grandparent, or legal guardian; or (iii) while on the property of another who has provided prior permission, and with the prior permission of his parent or legal guardian if the person has the landowner's written permission on his person while on such property;

2. Any person who, while accompanied by an adult, is at, or going to and from, a lawful shooting range or firearms educational class, provided that the weapons are unloaded while being transported;

3. Any person actually engaged in lawful hunting or going to and from a hunting area or preserve, provided that the weapons are unloaded while being transported; and

4. Any person while carrying out his duties in the Armed Forces of the United States or the National Guard of this Commonwealth or any other state.

History.

1993, cc. 467, 494; 2003, c. 976; 2004, c. 995.

§ 18.2-308.8. Importation, sale, possession or transfer of Striker 12's prohibited; penalty.

It shall be unlawful for any person to import, sell, possess or transfer the following firearms: the Striker 12, commonly called a *"streetsweeper,"* or any semi-automatic folding stock shotgun of like kind with a spring tension drum magazine capable of holding twelve shotgun shells. A violation of this section shall be punishable as a Class 6 felony.

History.

1993, c. 888.

§ 18.2-309. Furnishing certain weapons to minors; penalty.

A. If any person sells, barters, gives or furnishes, or causes to be sold, bartered, given or furnished, to any minor a dirk, switchblade knife or bowie knife, having good cause to believe him to be a minor, such person shall be guilty of a Class 1 misdemeanor.

B. If any person sells, barters, gives or furnishes, or causes to be sold, bartered, given or furnished, to any minor a handgun, having good cause to believe him to be a minor, such person shall be guilty of a Class 6 felony. This subsection shall not apply to any transfer made between family members or for the purpose of engaging in a sporting event or activity.

History.

Code 1950, § 18.1-344; 1960, c. 358; 1975, cc. 14, 15; 1992, c. 487; 1993, c. 855.

§ 18.2-310: Repealed by Acts 2004, c. 995.

Cross references.

For current provisions as to forfeiture of certain weapons used in commission of criminal offense, see § 19.2-386.29.

§ 18.2-311. Prohibiting the selling or having in possession blackjacks, etc.

If any person sells or barters, or exhibits for sale or for barter, or gives or furnishes, or causes to be sold, bartered, given or furnished, or has in his possession, or under his control, with the intent of selling, bartering, giving or furnishing, any blackjack, brass or metal knucks, any disc of whatever configuration having at least two points or pointed blades which is designed to be thrown or propelled and which may be known as a throwing star or oriental dart, switchblade knife, ballistic knife as defined in § 18.2-307.1, or like weapons, such person is guilty of a Class 4 misdemeanor. The having in one's possession of any such weapon shall be prima facie evidence, except in the case of a conservator of the peace, of his intent to sell, barter, give or furnish the same.

History.

Code 1950, § 18.1-271; 1960, c. 358; 1975, cc. 14, 15; 1985, c. 394; 1988, c. 359; 2013, c. 746.

§ 18.2-311.1. Removing, altering, etc., serial number or other identification on firearm.

Any person, firm, association or corporation who or which intentionally removes, defaces, alters, changes, destroys or obliterates in any manner or way or who or which causes to be removed, defaced, altered, changed, destroyed or obliterated in any manner or way the name of the maker, model, manufacturer's or serial number, or any other mark or identification on any pistol, shotgun, rifle, machine gun or any other firearm shall be guilty of a Class 1 misdemeanor.

History.

1975, c. 590.

§ 18.2-311.2. Third conviction of firearm offenses; penalty.

On a third or subsequent conviction of any offense contained in Article 4, 5, 6, or 7 of Chapter 7

(§ 18.2-247 et seq.) of Title 18.2, which would ordinarily be punished as a Class 1 misdemeanor, where it is alleged in the information or indictment on which the person is convicted, that (i) such person has been twice previously convicted of a violation of any Class 1 misdemeanor or felony offense contained in either Article 4, 5, 6, or 7 of Chapter 7 of Title 18.2 or § 18.2-53.1, or of a substantially similar offense under the law of any other jurisdiction of the United States, and (ii) each such violation occurred on a different date, such person shall be guilty of a Class 6 felony.

History.
1994, c. 731.

ARTICLE 8.
MISCELLANEOUS DANGEROUS CONDUCT.

§ 18.2-312. Illegal use of tear gas, phosgene and other gases.

If any person maliciously release or cause or procure to be released in any private home, place of business or place of public gathering any tear gas, mustard gas, phosgene gas or other noxious or nauseating gases or mixtures of chemicals designed to, and capable of, producing vile or injurious or nauseating odors or gases, and bodily injury results to any person from such gas or odor, the offending person shall be guilty of a Class 3 felony.

If such act be done unlawfully, but not maliciously, the offending person shall be guilty of a Class 6 felony.

Nothing herein contained shall prevent the use of tear gas or other gases by police officers or other peace officers in the proper performance of their duties, or by any person or persons in the protection of person, life or property.

History.
Code 1950, § 18.1-70; 1960, c. 358; 1975, cc. 14, 15.

§ 18.2-313. Handling or using snakes so as to endanger human life or health.

It shall be unlawful for any person, or persons, to display, exhibit, handle or use any poisonous or dangerous snake or reptile in such a manner as to endanger the life or health of any person.

Any person violating the provisions of this section shall be guilty of a Class 4 misdemeanor.

History.
Code 1950, § 18.1-72; 1960, c. 358; 1975, cc. 14, 15.

§ 18.2-313.1. Withholding information about possibly rabid animal; penalty.

It shall be unlawful for any person to (i) knowingly withhold information from, or knowingly give false information to, any lawfully authorized governmental agent which would reasonably lead to the discovery or location and capture of any animal reasonably identifiable as one that has potentially exposed a human being to rabies; (ii) upon the request of an animal control officer, a law-enforcement officer, or an official of the Department of Health, willfully fail to grant access to any animal owned, harbored, or kept by that person that is suspected of having caused a rabies exposure to a human being; or (iii) upon notice by an animal control officer, a law-enforcement officer, or an official of the Department of Health, willfully fail to comply with a confinement, isolation, or quarantine order.

Any person violating the provisions of this section shall be guilty of a Class 2 misdemeanor.

History.
1989, c. 491; 2010, c. 834.

§ 18.2-313.2. Introduction of snakehead fish or zebra mussel; penalty.

Any person who knowingly introduces into the Commonwealth any snakehead fish of the family Channidae, or knowingly places or causes to be placed into state waters any zebra mussel (Dreissena polymorpha) or the larvae thereof, without a permit from the Director of Game and Inland Fisheries issued pursuant to § 29.1-575 is guilty of a Class 1 misdemeanor.

History.
2005, c. 916.

§ 18.2-314. Failing to secure medical attention for injured child.

Any parent or other person having custody of a minor child which child shows evidence of need for medical attention as the result of physical injury inflicted by an act of any member of the household, whether the injury was intentional or unintentional, who knowingly fails or refuses to secure prompt and adequate medical attention, or who conspires to prevent the securing of such attention, for such minor child, shall be guilty of a Class 1 misdemeanor; provided, however, that any parent or other person having custody of a minor child that is being furnished Christian Science treatment by a duly accredited Christian Science practitioner shall not, for that reason alone, be considered in violation of this section.

History.
Code 1950, § 18.1-74.2; 1966, c. 578; 1975, cc. 14, 15.

§ 18.2-315: Repealed by Acts 1980, c. 173.

§ 18.2-316. Duty of persons causing well or pit to be dug to fill it before abandonment.

Any person who has caused to be dug on his own land or the land of another any well or pit, shall fill such well or pit with earth so that the same shall not be dangerous to human beings, animals or fowls before such well or such pit is abandoned; and any person owning land whereon any such well or pit is located shall in the same manner fill with earth any such well or pit which has been abandoned, provided such person has knowledge of the existence of such well or pit.

But in the case of mining operations in lieu of filling the shaft or pit the owner or operator thereof on ceasing operations in such shaft or pit shall securely fence the same and keep the same at all times thereafter securely fenced.

Any person violating any provision of this section shall be deemed guilty of a Class 3 misdemeanor.

History.
Code 1950, § 18.1-73; 1960, c. 358; 1975, cc. 14, 15.

§ 18.2-317. Covers to be kept on certain wells.

Every person owning or occupying any land on which there is a well having a diameter greater than six inches and which is more than ten feet deep shall at all times keep the same covered in such a manner as not to be dangerous to human beings, animals or fowls.

Any person violating the provisions of this section shall be guilty of a Class 3 misdemeanor.

History.
Code 1950, § 18.1-74; 1960, c. 358; 1975, cc. 14, 15.

§ 18.2-318. Authority of counties, cities and towns to require and regulate well covers.

Notwithstanding the provisions of § 18.2-317, the governing body of any county, city or town may adopt ordinances requiring persons owning or occupying any land within such county, city or town on which there is a well having a diameter greater than six inches and which is more than ten feet deep to keep the same covered in such a manner as not to be dangerous to human beings, animals or fowls.

Any such ordinance may specify and require reasonable minimum standards for the construction, installation and maintenance of such covers, including the manner in which any concrete used in connection therewith shall be reinforced, and may prescribe punishment for violations not inconsistent with general law.

History.
Code 1950, § 18.1-74.1; 1962, c. 525; 1975, cc. 14, 15.

§ 18.2-319. Discarding or abandoning iceboxes, etc.; precautions required.

It shall be unlawful for any person, firm or corporation to discard, abandon, leave or allow to remain in any place any icebox, refrigerator or other container, device or equipment of any kind with an interior storage area of more than two cubic feet of clear space which is airtight, without first removing the door or doors or hinges from such icebox, refrigerator, container, device or equipment.

This section shall not apply to any icebox, refrigerator, container, device or equipment which is being used for the purpose for which it was originally designed, or is being used for display purposes by any retail or wholesale merchant, or is crated, strapped or locked to such an extent that it is impossible for a child to obtain access to any airtight compartment thereof.

Any violation of the provisions of this section shall be punishable as a Class 3 misdemeanor.

History.
Code 1950, § 18.1-415; 1960, c. 358; 1975, cc. 14, 15.

§ 18.2-320. Sale, etc., of plastic bags; warning required.

(a) No person shall sell, offer for sale, or deliver, or offer for delivery, or give away any plastic bag or partial plastic bag intended to enclose freshly cleaned clothing, the length of which totals twenty-five inches or more and the material of which is less than one mil (1/1000 inch) in thickness; unless such plastic bag bears the following warning statement, or a warning statement which the Commissioner of Health has approved as the equivalent thereof:

"WARNING: To avoid danger of suffocation, keep this plastic bag away from babies and children. Do not use this bag in cribs, beds, carriages or playpens."

(b) Such warning statement shall be imprinted in a prominent place on the plastic bag or shall appear on a label securely attached to the bag in a prominent place, and shall be printed in legible type of at least thirty-six point type.

(c) Violators of this section shall be guilty of a Class 3 misdemeanor.

History.
Code 1950, § 18.1-415.1; 1968, c. 340; 1975, cc. 14, 15.

§ 18.2-321. Using X ray, fluoroscope, etc., in the fitting of footwear.

It shall be unlawful for any person to use any X ray, fluoroscope, or other equipment or apparatus employing roentgen rays, in the fitting of shoes or other footwear. This section shall not apply to any licensed physician or surgeon in the practice of his profession. Any person violating the provisions of this section shall be guilty of a Class 3 misdemeanor.

History.
Code 1950, § 18.1-416; 1960, c. 358; 1975, cc. 14, 15.

§ 18.2-322. Expectorating in public places.

No person shall spit, expectorate, or deposit any sputum, saliva, mucus, or any form of saliva or sputum upon the floor, stairways, or upon any part of any public building or place where the public assemble, or upon the floor of any part of any public conveyance, or upon any sidewalk abutting on any public street, alley or lane of any town or city.

Any person violating any provision of this section shall be guilty of a Class 4 misdemeanor.

History.
Code 1950, § 32-69; 1975, cc. 14, 15.

§ 18.2-322.1: Repealed by Acts 1997, c. 391.

§ 18.2-323. Leaving disabled or dead animal in road, or allowing dead animal to remain unburied.

If any person cast any dead animal into a road or knowingly permit any dead animal to remain unburied upon his property when offensive to the public or, having in custody any maimed, diseased, disabled or infirm animal, leave it to lie or be in a street, road or public place, he shall be guilty of a Class 3 misdemeanor.

History.
Code 1950, § 32-70.1; 1958, c. 548; 1970, c. 72; 1975, cc. 14, 15.

§ 18.2-323.01. Prohibition against disposal of dead body; penalty.

It shall be unlawful for any person to dispose of a dead body as defined in § 32.1-249 (i) on private property without the written permission of the landowner or (ii) on public property.

A violation of this section shall be punishable as a Class 1 misdemeanor.

History.
1992, c. 883.

§ 18.2-323.02. Prohibition against concealment of dead body; penalty.

Any person who transports, secretes, conceals or alters a dead body, as defined in § 32.1-249, with malicious intent and to prevent detection of an unlawful act or to prevent the detection of the death or the manner or cause of death is guilty of a Class 6 felony.

History.
2007, c. 436.

§ 18.2-323.1. Drinking while operating a motor vehicle; possession of open container while operating a motor vehicle and presumption; penalty.

A. It shall be unlawful for any person to consume an alcoholic beverage while driving a motor vehicle upon a public highway of this Commonwealth.

B. A rebuttable presumption that the driver has consumed an alcoholic beverage in violation of this section shall be created if (i) an open container is located within the passenger area of the motor vehicle, (ii) the alcoholic beverage in the open container has been at least partially removed and (iii) the appearance, conduct, odor of alcohol, speech or other physical characteristic of the driver of the motor vehicle may be reasonably associated with the consumption of an alcoholic beverage.

For the purposes of this section:

"Open container" means any vessel containing an alcoholic beverage, except the originally sealed manufacturer's container.

"Passenger area" means the area designed to seat the driver of any motor vehicle, any area within the reach of the driver, including an unlocked glove compartment, and the area designed to seat passengers. This term shall not include the trunk of any passenger vehicle, the area behind the last upright seat of a passenger van, station wagon, hatchback, sport utility vehicle or any similar vehicle, the living quarters of a motor home, or the passenger area of a motor vehicle designed, maintained or used primarily for the transportation of persons for compensation, including a bus, taxi, or limousine, while engaged in the transportation of such persons.

C. A violation of this section is punishable as a Class 4 misdemeanor.

History.
1989, c. 343; 2002, c. 890.

§ 18.2-324. Throwing or depositing certain substances upon highway; removal of such substances.

No person shall throw or deposit or cause to be deposited upon any highway any glass bottle, glass, nail, tack, wire, can, or any other substance likely to injure any person or animal, or damage any vehicle upon such highway, nor shall any person throw or deposit or cause to be deposited upon any highway any soil, sand, mud, gravel or other substances so as to create a hazard to the traveling public. Any person who drops, or permits to be dropped or thrown, upon any highway any destructive, hazardous or injurious material shall immediately remove the same or cause it to be removed. Any person removing a wrecked or damaged vehicle from a highway shall remove any glass or other injurious substance dropped upon the highway from such vehicle. Any persons violating the provisions of this section shall be guilty of a Class 1 misdemeanor.

This section shall not apply to the use, by a law-enforcement officer while in the discharge of official duties, of any device designed to deflate tires. The Division of Purchase and Supply shall, pursuant to § 2.2-1112, set minimum standards for such devices and shall give notice of such standards to law-enforcement offices in the Commonwealth. No such device shall be used which does not meet or exceed the standards.

History.
Code 1950, § 33.1-350; 1970, c. 322; 1975, cc. 14, 15; 1997, c. 136.

§ 18.2-324.1. Punishment for violation of §§ 55-298.1 through 55-298.5, relating to electric fences.

The violation of any provision of §§ 55-298.1 through 55-298.5 shall constitute a Class 1 misdemeanor.

History.
Code 1950, § 8-868.2; 1960, c. 384; 1977, c. 624.

CHAPTER 8.

CRIMES INVOLVING MORALS AND DECENCY.

Article 1.

Gambling.

Article 1.1.

Bingo and Raffles.

Article 1.1:1.

Charitable Gaming.

Article 2.

Sunday Offenses.

Article 3.

Commercial Sex Trafficking, Prostitution, etc.

Article 4.

Family Offenses; Crimes Against Children, etc.

Article 5.

Obscenity and Related Offenses.

Article 6.

Prohibited Sales and Loans to Juveniles.

Article 7.

Cruelty to Animals.

Article 8.

Offenses Involving Animals.

ARTICLE 1.
GAMBLING.

§ 18.2-325. Definitions.

1. "Illegal gambling" means the making, placing or receipt of any bet or wager in the Commonwealth of money or other thing of value, made in exchange for a chance to win a prize, stake or other consideration or thing of value, dependent upon the result of any game, contest or any other event the outcome of which is uncertain or a matter of chance, whether such game, contest or event occurs or is to occur inside or outside the limits of the Commonwealth.

For the purposes of this subdivision and notwithstanding any provision in this section to the contrary, the making, placing, or receipt of any bet or wager of money or other thing of value shall include the purchase of a product, Internet access, or other thing, which purchase credits the purchaser with free points or other measurable units that may be (i) risked by the purchaser for an opportunity to win additional points or other measurable units that are redeemable by the purchaser for money or (ii) redeemed by the purchaser for money, and but for the free points or other measurable units, with regard to clauses (i) and (ii), the purchase of the product, Internet access, or other thing (a) would be of insufficient value in and of itself to justify the purchase or (b) is merely incidental to the chance to win money.

2. "Interstate gambling" means the conduct of an enterprise for profit which engages in the purchase or sale within the Commonwealth of any interest in

Crimes and Offenses

a lottery of another state or country whether or not such interest is an actual lottery ticket, receipt, contingent promise to pay, order to purchase, or other record of such interest.

3. "Gambling device" includes:

a. Any device, machine, paraphernalia, equipment, or other thing, including books, records and other papers, which are actually used in an illegal gambling operation or activity, and

b. Any machine, apparatus, implement, instrument, contrivance, board or other thing, or electronic or video versions thereof, including but not limited to those dependent upon the insertion of a coin or other object for their operation, which operates, either completely automatically or with the aid of some physical act by the player or operator, in such a manner that, depending upon elements of chance, it may eject something of value or determine the prize or other thing of value to which the player is entitled; provided, however, that the return to the user of nothing more than additional chances or the right to use such machine is not deemed something of value within the meaning of this subsection; and provided further, that machines that only sell, or entitle the user to, items of merchandise of equivalent value that may differ from each other in composition, size, shape or color, shall not be deemed gambling devices within the meaning of this subsection.

Such devices are no less gambling devices if they indicate beforehand the definite result of one or more operations but not all the operations. Nor are they any less a gambling device because, apart from their use or adaptability as such, they may also sell or deliver something of value on a basis other than chance.

4. "Operator" includes any person, firm or association of persons, who conducts, finances, manages, supervises, directs or owns all or part of an illegal gambling enterprise, activity or operation.

History.
1975, cc. 14, 15; 1992, c. 423; 2010, c. 877; 2011, cc. 879, 887.

§ 18.2-325.1: Repealed by Acts 2011, cc. 879 and 887, cl. 2.

§ 18.2-326. Penalty for illegal gambling.

Except as otherwise provided in this article, any person who illegally gambles or engages in interstate gambling as defined in § 18.2-325 shall be guilty of a Class 3 misdemeanor. If an association or pool of persons illegally gamble, each person therein shall be guilty of illegal gambling.

However, if any person makes, places, or receives any bet or wager of money or other thing of value on a horse race in the Commonwealth, whether the race is inside or outside the limits of the Commonwealth at any place or through any means other than (i) at a racetrack licensed by the Virginia Racing Commission pursuant to Chapter 29 (§ 59.1-364 et seq.) of Title 59.1 or (ii) at a satellite facility or through advance deposit account wagering, as those terms are defined in § 59.1-365, licensed by the Virginia Racing Commission pursuant to Chapter 29 (§ 59.1-364 et seq.) of Title 59.1, such person shall be guilty of a Class 1 misdemeanor. For the purposes of this paragraph, venue shall be in any county or city in which any act was performed in furtherance of any course of conduct constituting illegal gambling.

History.
Code 1950, § 18.1-316; 1960, c. 358; 1973, c. 463; 1975, cc. 14, 15; 1992, c. 423; 2011, c. 732.

§ 18.2-327. Winning by fraud; penalty.

If any person while gambling cheats or by fraudulent means wins or acquires for himself or another money or any other valuable thing, he shall be fined not less than five nor more than ten times the value of such winnings. This penalty shall be in addition to any other penalty imposed under this article.

History.
Code 1950, § 18.1-318; 1960, c. 358; 1975, cc. 14, 15.

§ 18.2-328. Conducting illegal gambling operation; penalties.

The operator of an illegal gambling enterprise, activity or operation shall be guilty of a Class 6 felony. However, any such operator who engages in an illegal gambling operation which (i) has been or remains in substantially continuous operation for a period in excess of thirty days or (ii) has gross revenue of $2,000 or more in any single day shall be fined not more than $20,000 and imprisoned not less than one year nor more than ten years.

As used in this section, the term *"gross revenue"* means the total amount of illegal gambling transactions handled, dealt with, received by or placed with such operation, as distinguished from any net figure or amount from which deductions are taken, without regard to whether money or any other thing of value actually changes hands.

History.
Code 1950, § 18.1-318.1; 1972, c. 364; 1975, cc. 14, 15; 1983, c. 331.

§ 18.2-329. Owners, etc., of gambling place permitting its continuance; penalty.

If the owner, lessee, tenant, occupant or other person in control of any place or conveyance, knows, or reasonably should know, that it is being used for illegal gambling, and permits such gambling to continue without having notified a law-enforcement officer of the presence of such illegal gambling activity, he shall be guilty of a Class 1 misdemeanor.

History.
Code 1950, §§ 18.1-319, 18.1-324, 18.1-337, 18.1-339; 1960, c. 358; 1968, c. 401; 1975, cc. 14, 15.

§ 18.2-330. Accessories to gambling activity; penalty.

Any person, firm or association of persons, other than those persons specified in other sections of this article, who knowingly aids, abets or assists in the operation of an illegal gambling enterprise, activity or operation, shall be guilty of a Class 1 misdemeanor.

History.
Code 1950, §§ 18.1-319, 18.1-325; 1960, c. 358; 1968, c. 401; 1975, cc. 14, 15; 1984, c. 625.

§ 18.2-331. Illegal possession, etc., of gambling device; penalty.

A person is guilty of illegal possession of a gambling device when he manufactures, sells, transports, rents, gives away, places or possesses, or conducts or negotiates any transaction affecting or designed to affect ownership, custody or use of any gambling device, believing or having reason to believe that the same is to be used in the advancement of unlawful gambling activity. Violation of any provision of this section shall constitute a Class 1 misdemeanor.

History.
Code 1950, §§ 18.1-323, 18.1-329, 18.1-330; 1960, c. 358; 1962, c. 633; 1964, c. 371; 1975, cc. 14, 15.

§ 18.2-332. Certain acts not deemed "consideration" in prosecution under this article.

In any prosecution under this article, no consideration shall be deemed to have passed or been given because of any person's attendance upon the premises of another; his execution, mailing or delivery of an entry blank; his answering of questions, verbally or in writing; his witnessing of a demonstration or other proceeding; or any one or more thereof, where no charge is made to, paid by, or any purchase required of him in connection therewith.

History.
Code 1950, § 18.1-340.1; 1960, c. 226; 1975, cc. 14, 15.

§ 18.2-333. Exceptions to article; certain sporting events.

Nothing in this article shall be construed to prevent any contest of speed or skill between men, animals, fowl or vehicles, where participants may receive prizes or different percentages of a purse, stake or premium dependent upon whether they win or lose or dependent upon their position or score at the end of such contest.

Any participant who, for the purpose of competing for any such purse, stake or premium offered in any such contest, knowingly and fraudulently enters any contestant other than the contestant purported to be entered or knowingly and fraudulently enters a contestant in a class in which it does not belong, shall be guilty of a Class 3 misdemeanor.

History.
Code 1950, §§ 18.1-319, 18.1-322; 1960, c. 358; 1968, c. 401; 1975, cc. 14, 15.

§ 18.2-334. Exception to article; private residences.

Nothing in this article shall be construed to make it illegal to participate in a game of chance conducted in a private residence, provided such private residence is not commonly used for such games of chance and there is no operator as defined in subsection 4 of § 18.2-325.

History.
Code 1950, § 18.1-327; 1960, c. 358; 1975, cc. 14, 15; 1992, c. 423.

§ 18.2-334.1: Defeated at referendum.

Editor's note.
This section, relating to horse racing and pari-mutuel betting, was enacted by Acts 1978, c. 600. The 1978 act, which also enacted §§ 59.1-216 through 59.1-254, was made subject to referendum held Nov. 7, 1978, and provided that, if approved, the act would become effective Jan. 1, 1979. The act was defeated at the referendum, and therefore never went into effect.

§ 18.2-334.2. Same; bingo games, raffles and duck races conducted by certain organizations.

Nothing in this article shall apply to any bingo game, instant bingo, network bingo, raffle, or duck race conducted solely by organizations as defined in § 18.2-340.16 which have received a permit as set forth in § 18.2-340.25, or which are exempt from the permit requirement under § 18.2-340.23.

History.
1979, c. 420; 1993, c. 513; 1995, c. 837; 2013, cc. 36, 350.

§ 18.2-334.3. Exemptions to article; state lottery.

Nothing in this article shall apply to any lottery conducted by the Commonwealth of Virginia pursuant to Chapter 40 of Title 58.1.

History.
1987, c. 531.

§ 18.2-334.4. Exemptions to article; pari-mutuel wagering.

Nothing in this article shall be construed to make it illegal to participate in any race meeting or pari-mutuel wagering conducted in accordance with Chapter 29 (§ 59.1-364 et seq.) of Title 59.1.

History.
1988, c. 855.

§ 18.2-335: Repealed by Acts 1979, c. 420.

Cross references.
For present provisions as to bingo games and raffles, see § 18.2-334.2 and Article 1.1:1 (§ 18.2-340.15 et seq.) of this chapter.

§ 18.2-336: Repealed by Acts 2004, c. 995.

Cross references.
For current provisions as to forfeiture of money, gambling devices, etc., seized from illegal gambling enterprise, see § 19.2-386.30.

§ 18.2-337. Immunity of witnesses from prosecution.

No witness called by the Commonwealth or by the court, giving evidence either before the grand jury or in any prosecution under this article, shall ever be prosecuted for the offense being prosecuted concerning which he testifies. Such witness shall be compelled to testify and for refusing to do so may be punished for contempt.

History.
Code 1950, § 19.1-266; 1960, c. 366; 1975, cc. 14, 15.

§ 18.2-338. Enforcement of § 18.2-331 by Governor and Attorney General.

If it shall come to the knowledge of the Governor that § 18.2-331 is not being enforced in any county, city or town, the Governor may call upon the Attorney General to direct its enforcement in such county, city or town, and thereupon the Attorney General may instruct the attorney for the Commonwealth, sheriff and chief of police, if any, of such county, or the attorney for the Commonwealth and chief of police of such city, or the attorney for the Commonwealth of the county in which such town is located and the chief of police or sergeant of such town, to take such steps as may be necessary to insure the enforcement of such section in such county, city or town, and if any such officers, after receiving such instructions, shall thereafter fail or refuse to exercise diligence in the enforcement of § 18.2-331, the Attorney General shall make report thereof in writing to the Governor and to the judge of the circuit court having jurisdiction over the acts thereby prohibited, and thereupon the Attorney General upon being directed so to do by the Governor, shall take such steps as he may deem proper in directing the institution and prosecution of criminal proceedings, to secure the enforcement of § 18.2-331.

History.
Code 1950, § 18.1-334; 1960, c. 358; 1975, cc. 14, 15.

§ 18.2-339. Enjoining offenses relating to gambling.

Whenever any person shall be engaged in committing, or in permitting to be committed, or shall be about to commit, or permit, any act prohibited by any one or more of the sections in this article, the attorney for the Commonwealth of the county or city in which such act is being, or is about to be, committed or permitted, or the Attorney General of the Commonwealth, may institute and maintain a suit in equity in the appropriate court, in the name of the Commonwealth, upon the relation of such attorney for the Commonwealth, or the Attorney General, to enjoin and restrain such person from committing, or permitting, such prohibited act or acts. The procedure in any such suit shall be similar to the procedure in other suits for injunctions, except that no bond shall be required upon the granting of either a temporary or permanent injunction therein.

History.
Code 1950, § 18.1-343; 1960, c. 358; 1975, cc. 14, 15.

§ 18.2-340. County ordinances prohibiting illegal gambling.

The governing body of any county may adopt ordinances prohibiting illegal gambling, including a provision for forfeiture proceedings in accordance with Chapter 22.1 (§ 19.2-386.1 et seq.) of Title 19.2. Such ordinances shall not conflict with the provisions of this article or with other state laws and any penalties provided for violation of such ordinances shall not exceed a fine of $2,500 or confinement in jail for 12 months, either or both.

History.
Code 1950, § 18.1-344; 1960, c. 358; 1975, cc. 14, 15; 1991, c. 710; 2012, cc. 283, 756.

ARTICLE 1.1.

BINGO AND RAFFLES.

§§ 18.2-340.1 through 18.2-340.14: Repealed by Acts 1995, c. 837, effective July 1, 1996.

ARTICLE 1.1:1.

CHARITABLE GAMING.

§ 18.2-340.15. State control of charitable gaming.

A. Charitable gaming as authorized herein shall be permitted in the Commonwealth as a means of funding qualified organizations but shall be conducted only in strict compliance with the provisions of this article. The Department of Agriculture and Consumer Services is vested with control of all charitable gaming in the Commonwealth. The

Charitable Gaming Board shall have the power to prescribe regulations and conditions under which such gaming shall be conducted to ensure that it is conducted in a manner consistent with the purpose for which it is permitted.

B. The conduct of any charitable gaming is a privilege that may be granted or denied by the Department of Agriculture and Consumer Services or its duly authorized representatives in its discretion in order to effectuate the purposes set forth in this article.

History.

1995, c. 837; 2003, c. 884; 2006, c. 644; 2008, cc. 387, 689.

§ 18.2-340.16. Definitions.

As used in this article, unless the context requires a different meaning:

"Bingo" means a specific game of chance played with (i) individual cards having randomly numbered squares ranging from one to 75, (ii) Department-approved electronic devices that display facsimiles of bingo cards and are used for the purpose of marking and monitoring players' cards as numbers are called, or (iii) Department-approved cards, in which prizes are awarded on the basis of designated numbers on such cards conforming to a predetermined pattern of numbers selected at random.

"Board" means the Charitable Gaming Board created pursuant to § 2.2-2455.

"Bona fide member" means an individual who participates in activities of a qualified organization other than such organization's charitable gaming activities.

"Charitable gaming" or *"charitable games"* means those raffles and games of chance explicitly authorized by this article.

"Charitable gaming supplies" includes bingo cards or sheets, devices for selecting bingo numbers, instant bingo cards, pull-tab cards and seal cards, and any other equipment or product manufactured for or intended to be used in the conduct of charitable games. However, for the purposes of this article, charitable gaming supplies shall not include items incidental to the conduct of charitable gaming such as markers, wands, or tape.

"Commissioner" means the Commissioner of the Department of Agriculture and Consumer Services.

"Conduct" means the actions associated with the provision of a gaming operation during and immediately before or after the permitted activity, which may include, but not be limited to, (i) selling bingo cards or packs, electronic devices, instant bingo or pull-tab cards, or raffle tickets, (ii) calling bingo games, (iii) distributing prizes, and (iv) any other services provided by volunteer workers.

"Department" means the Department of Agriculture and Consumer Services.

"Fair market rental value" means the rent that a rental property will bring when offered for lease by a lessor who desires to lease the property but is not obligated to do so and leased by a lessee under no necessity of leasing.

"Gaming expenses" means prizes, supplies, costs of publicizing gaming activities, audit and administration or permit fees, and a portion of the rent, utilities, accounting and legal fees and such other reasonable and proper expenses as are directly incurred for the conduct of charitable gaming.

"Gross receipts" means the total amount of money generated by an organization from charitable gaming before the deduction of expenses, including prizes.

"Instant bingo," "pull tabs," or *"seal cards"* means specific games of chance played by the random selection of one or more individually prepacked cards, including Department-approved electronic versions thereof, with winners being determined by the preprinted or predetermined appearance of concealed letters, numbers or symbols that must be exposed by the player to determine wins and losses and may include the use of a seal card which conceals one or more numbers or symbols that have been designated in advance as prize winners. Such cards may be dispensed by electronic or mechanical equipment.

"Jackpot" means a bingo game that the organization has designated on its game program as a jackpot game in which the prize amount is greater than $100.

"Landlord" means any person or his agent, firm, association, organization, partnership, or corporation, employee, or immediate family member thereof, which owns and leases, or leases any premises devoted in whole or in part to the conduct of bingo games, and any person residing in the same household as a landlord.

"Management" means the provision of oversight of a gaming operation, which may include, but is not limited to, the responsibilities of applying for and maintaining a permit or authorization, compiling, submitting and maintaining required records and financial reports, and ensuring that all aspects of the operation are in compliance with all applicable statutes and regulations.

"Network bingo" means a specific bingo game in which pari-mutuel play is permitted.

"Network bingo provider" means a person licensed by the Department to operate network bingo.

"Operation" means the activities associated with production of a charitable gaming activity, which may include, but not be limited to (i) the direct on-site supervision of the conduct of charitable gaming; (ii) coordination of volunteers; and (iii) all responsibilities of charitable gaming designated by the organization's management.

"Organization" means any one of the following:

1. A volunteer fire department or volunteer emergency medical services agency or auxiliary unit thereof that has been recognized in accordance with § 15.2-955 by an ordinance or resolution of the political subdivision where the volunteer fire depart-

ment or volunteer emergency medical services agency is located as being a part of the safety program of such political subdivision;

2. An organization operated exclusively for religious, charitable, community or educational purposes;

3. An athletic association or booster club or a band booster club established solely to raise funds for school-sponsored athletic or band activities for a public school or private school accredited pursuant to § 22.1-19 or to provide scholarships to students attending such school;

4. An association of war veterans or auxiliary units thereof organized in the United States;

5. A fraternal association or corporation operating under the lodge system;

6. A local chamber of commerce; or

7. Any other nonprofit organization that raises funds by conducting raffles that generate annual gross receipts of $40,000 or less, provided such gross receipts from the raffle, less expenses and prizes, are used exclusively for charitable, educational, religious or community purposes.

"Pari-mutuel play" means an integrated network operated by a licensee of the Department comprised of participating charitable organizations for the conduct of network bingo games in which the purchase of a network bingo card by a player automatically includes the player in a pool with all other players in the network, and where the prize to the winning player is awarded based on a percentage of the total amount of network bingo cards sold in a particular network.

"Qualified organization" means any organization to which a valid permit has been issued by the Department to conduct charitable gaming or any organization that is exempt pursuant to § 18.2-340.23.

"Raffle" means a lottery in which the prize is won by (i) a random drawing of the name or prearranged number of one or more persons purchasing chances or (ii) a random contest in which the winning name or preassigned number of one or more persons purchasing chances is determined by a race involving inanimate objects floating on a body of water, commonly referred to as a "duck race."

"Reasonable and proper business expenses" means business expenses actually incurred by a qualified organization in the conduct of charitable gaming and not otherwise allowed under this article or under Board regulations on real estate and personal property tax payments, travel expenses, payments of utilities and trash collection services, legal and accounting fees, costs of business furniture, fixtures and office equipment and costs of acquisition, maintenance, repair or construction of an organization's real property. For the purpose of this definition, salaries and wages of employees whose primary responsibility is to provide services for the principal benefit of an organization's members shall not qualify as a business expense. However, payments made pursuant to § 51.1-1204 to the Volunteer Firefighters' and Rescue Squad Workers' Service Award Fund shall be deemed a reasonable and proper business expense.

"Supplier" means any person who offers to sell, sells or otherwise provides charitable gaming supplies to any qualified organization.

History.

1995, c. 837; 1996, c. 919; 1997, cc. 777, 838; 1998, cc. 57, 398; 1999, c. 534; 2002, cc. 282, 340; 2003, c. 884; 2006, c. 644; 2007, cc. 160, 264; 2008, cc. 387, 689; 2009, c. 121; 2010, c. 429; 2013, cc. 36, 350; 2015, cc. 502, 503.

§ 18.2-340.17: Repealed by Acts 2003, c. 884, cl. 2.

§ 18.2-340.18. Powers and duties of the Department.

The Department shall have all powers and duties necessary to carry out the provisions of this article and to exercise the control of charitable gaming as set forth in § 18.2-340.15. Such powers and duties shall include but not be limited to the following:

1. The Department is vested with jurisdiction and supervision over all charitable gaming authorized under the provisions of this article and including all persons that conduct or provide goods, services or premises used in the conduct of charitable gaming. It may employ such persons as are necessary to ensure that charitable gaming is conducted in conformity with the provisions of this article and the regulations of the Board. The Department shall designate such agents and employees as it deems necessary and appropriate who shall be sworn to enforce the provisions of this article and the criminal laws of the Commonwealth and who shall be law-enforcement officers as defined in § 9.1-101.

2. The Department, its agents and employees and any law-enforcement officers charged with the enforcement of charitable gaming laws shall have free access to the offices, facilities or any other place of business of any organization, including any premises devoted in whole or in part to the conduct of charitable gaming. These individuals may enter such places or premises for the purpose of carrying out any duty imposed by this article, securing records required to be maintained by an organization, investigating complaints, or conducting audits.

3. The Department may compel the production of any books, documents, records, or memoranda of any organizations or supplier involved in the conduct of charitable gaming for the purpose of satisfying itself that this article and its regulations are strictly complied with. In addition, the Department may require the production of an annual balance sheet and operating statement of any person granted a permit pursuant to the provisions of this article and may require the production of any contract to which such person is or may be a party.

4. The Department may issue subpoenas for the attendance of witnesses before it, administer oaths,

and compel production of records or other documents and testimony of such witnesses whenever, in the judgment of the Department, it is necessary to do so for the effectual discharge of its duties.

5. The Department may compel any person conducting charitable gaming to file with the Department such documents, information or data as shall appear to the Department to be necessary for the performance of its duties.

6. The Department may enter into arrangements with any governmental agency of this or any other state or any locality in the Commonwealth or any agency of the federal government for the purposes of exchanging information or performing any other act to better ensure the proper conduct of charitable gaming.

7. The Department may issue a charitable gaming permit while the permittee's tax-exempt status is pending approval by the Internal Revenue Service.

8. The Department shall report annually to the Governor and the General Assembly, which report shall include a financial statement of the operation of the Department and any recommendations for legislation applicable to charitable gaming in the Commonwealth.

9. The Department, its agents and employees may conduct such audits, in addition to those required by § 18.2-340.31, as they deem necessary and desirable.

10. The Department may limit the number of organizations for which a person may manage, operate or conduct charitable games.

11. The Department may report any alleged criminal violation of this article to the appropriate attorney for the Commonwealth for appropriate action.

History.

1995, c. 837; 1997, cc. 777, 838; 2003, c. 884; 2006, c. 644; 2014, c. 208.

§ 18.2-340.19. Regulations of the Board.

A. The Board shall adopt regulations that:

1. Require, as a condition of receiving a permit, that the applicant use a predetermined percentage of its gross receipts for (i) those lawful religious, charitable, community or educational purposes for which the organization is specifically chartered or organized or (ii) those expenses relating to the acquisition, construction, maintenance or repair of any interest in real property involved in the operation of the organization and used for lawful religious, charitable, community or educational purposes. The regulation may provide for a graduated scale of percentages of gross receipts to be used in the foregoing manner based upon factors the Board finds appropriate to and consistent with the purpose of charitable gaming.

2. Specify the conditions under which a complete list of the organization's members who participate in the management, operation or conduct of charitable gaming may be required in order for the Board to ascertain the percentage of Virginia residents in accordance with subdivision A 3 of § 18.2-340.24.

Membership lists furnished to the Board or Department in accordance with this subdivision shall not be a matter of public record and shall be exempt from disclosure under the provisions of the Freedom of Information Act (§ 2.2-3700 et seq.).

3. Prescribe fees for processing applications for charitable gaming permits. Such fees may reflect the nature and extent of the charitable gaming activity proposed to be conducted.

4. Establish requirements for the audit of all reports required in accordance with § 18.2-340.30.

5. Define electronic and mechanical equipment used in the conduct of charitable gaming. Board regulations shall include capacity for such equipment to provide full automatic daubing as numbers are called. For the purposes of this subdivision, electronic or mechanical equipment for instant bingo, pull tabs, or seal cards shall include such equipment that displays facsimiles of instant bingo, pull tabs, or seal cards and are used solely for the purpose of dispensing or opening such paper or electronic cards, or both; but shall not include (i) devices operated by dropping one or more coins or tokens into a slot and pulling a handle or pushing a button or touchpoint on a touchscreen to activate one to three or more reels marked into horizontal segments by varying symbols, where the predetermined prize amount depends on how and how many of the symbols line up when the rotating reels come to rest, or (ii) other similar devices that display flashing lights or illuminations, or bells, whistles, or other sounds, solely intended to entice players to play.

6. Prescribe the conditions under which a qualified organization may (i) provide food and nonalcoholic beverages to its members who participate in the management, operation or conduct of bingo; (ii) permit members who participate in the management, operation or conduct of bingo to play bingo; and (iii) subject to the provisions of subdivision 13 of § 18.2-340.33, permit nonmembers to participate in the conduct of bingo so long as the nonmembers are under the direct supervision of a bona fide member of the organization during the bingo game.

7. Prescribe the conditions under which a qualified organization may sell raffle tickets for a raffle drawing that will be held outside the Commonwealth pursuant to subsection B of § 18.2-340.26.

8. Prescribe the conditions under which persons who are bona fide members of a qualified organization or a child, above the age of 13 years, of a bona fide member of such organization may participate in the conduct or operation of bingo games.

9. Prescribe the conditions under which a person below the age of 18 years may play bingo, provided such person is accompanied by his parent or legal guardian.

Crimes and Offenses

10. Require all qualified organizations that are subject to Board regulations to post in a conspicuous place in every place where charitable gaming is conducted a sign which bears a toll-free telephone number for "Gamblers Anonymous" or other organization which provides assistance to compulsive gamblers.

11. Prescribe the conditions under which a qualified organization may sell network bingo cards in accordance with § 18.2-340.28:1 and establish a percentage of proceeds derived from network bingo sales to be allocated to (i) prize pools, (ii) the organization conducting the network bingo, and (iii) the network bingo provider. The regulations shall also establish procedures for the retainage and ultimate distribution of any unclaimed prize.

B. In addition to the powers and duties granted pursuant to § 2.2-2456 and this article, the Board may, by regulation, approve variations to the card formats for bingo games provided such variations result in bingo games that are conducted in a manner consistent with the provisions of this article. Board-approved variations may include, but are not limited to, bingo games commonly referred to as player selection games and 90-number bingo.

History.

1995, c. 837; 1996, c. 919; 1997, cc. 777, 838; 1998, c. 845; 2001, c. 833; 2003, c. 884; 2006, c. 644; 2010, cc. 429, 572; 2013, cc. 36, 350.

§ 18.2-340.20. Denial, suspension or revocation of permit; hearings and appeals.

A. The Department may deny, suspend or revoke the permit of any organization found not to be in strict compliance with the provisions of this article and the regulations of the Board only after the proposed action by the Department has been reviewed and approved by the Board. The action of the Department in denying, suspending or revoking any permit shall be subject to the Administrative Process Act (§ 2.2-4000 et seq.).

B. Except as provided in §§ 18.2-340.25, 18.2-340.30 and 18.2-340.36, no permit to conduct charitable gaming shall be denied, suspended or revoked except upon notice stating the proposed basis for such action and the time and place for the hearing. At the discretion of the Department, hearings may be conducted by hearing officers who shall be selected from the list prepared by the Executive Secretary of the Supreme Court. After a hearing on the issues, the Department may refuse to issue or may suspend or revoke any such permit if it determines that the organization has not complied with the provisions of this article or the regulations of the Board.

C. Any person aggrieved by a refusal of the Department to issue any permit, the suspension or revocation of a permit, or any other action of the Department may seek review of such action in accordance with Article 4 (§ 2.2-4025 et seq.) of the Administrative Process Act.

History.

1995, c. 837; 1996, c. 573; 1997, cc. 777, 838; 2000, c. 1000; 2001, c. 813; 2002, c. 282; 2003, c. 884; 2004, c. 213; 2006, c. 644; 2010, c. 711.

§ 18.2-340.21: Repealed by Acts 2003, c. 884, cl. 2.

Cross references.

As to the Charitable Gaming Board, see § 2.2-2452 et seq.

§ 18.2-340.22. Only raffles, bingo, network bingo, and instant bingo games permitted; prizes not gaming contracts.

A. This article permits qualified organizations to conduct raffles, bingo, network bingo, and instant bingo games. All games not explicitly authorized by this article or Board regulations adopted in accordance with § 18.2-340.18 are prohibited.

B. The award of any prize money for any charitable game shall not be deemed to be part of any gaming contract within the purview of § 11-14.

C. Nothing in this article shall prohibit an organization from using the Virginia Lottery's Pick-3 number or any number or other designation selected by the Virginia Lottery in connection with any lottery, as the basis for determining the winner of a raffle.

History.

1995, c. 837; 1997, cc. 777, 838; 2003, c. 884; 2013, cc. 36, 350; 2014, c. 225.

§ 18.2-340.23. Organizations exempt from certain permits and fees.

A. No organization that reasonably expects, based on prior charitable gaming annual results or any other quantifiable method, to realize gross receipts of $40,000 or less in any 12-month period shall be required to (i) notify the Department of its intention to conduct charitable gaming or (ii) comply with Board regulations. If any organization's actual gross receipts for the 12-month period exceed $40,000, the Department may require the organization to file by a specified date the report required by § 18.2-340.30.

B. Any volunteer fire department or volunteer emergency medical services agency or auxiliary unit thereof that has been recognized in accordance with § 15.2-955 by an ordinance or resolution of the political subdivision where the volunteer fire department or volunteer emergency medical services agency is located as being part of the safety program of such political subdivision shall be exempt from the payment of application fees required by § 18.2-340.25 and the payment of audit fees required by § 18.2-340.31. Nothing in this subsection shall be construed as exempting volunteer fire departments and volunteer emergency medical services agencies from any other provisions of this article or other Board regulations.

C. Nothing in this section shall prevent the Department from conducting any investigation or audit it deems appropriate to ensure an organization's compliance with the provisions of this article and, to the extent applicable, Board regulations.

History.

1995, c. 837; 1997, cc. 777, 838; 2003, c. 884; 2006, c. 644; 2009, c. 121; 2015, cc. 502, 503.

§ 18.2-340.24. Eligibility for permit; exceptions; where valid.

A. To be eligible for a permit to conduct charitable gaming, an organization shall:

1. Have been in existence and met on a regular basis in the Commonwealth for a period of at least three years immediately prior to applying for a permit.

The three-year residency requirement shall not apply (i) to any lodge or chapter of a national or international fraternal order or of a national or international civic organization which is exempt under § 501(c) of the United States Internal Revenue Code and which has a lodge or chapter holding a charitable gaming permit issued under the provisions of this article anywhere within the Commonwealth; (ii) to booster clubs which have been operating for less than three years and which have been established solely to raise funds for school-sponsored activities in public schools or private schools accredited pursuant to § 22.1-19; (iii) to recently established volunteer fire and rescue companies or departments, after county, city or town approval; or (iv) to an organization which relocates its meeting place on a permanent basis from one jurisdiction to another, complies with the requirements of subdivision 2 of this section, and was the holder of a valid permit at the time of its relocation.

2. Be operating currently and have always been operated as a nonprofit organization.

3. Have at least 50 percent of its membership consist of residents of the Commonwealth; however, if an organization (i) does not consist of bona fide members and (ii) is exempt under § 501(c)(3) of the United States Internal Revenue Code, the Board shall exempt such organizations from the requirements of this subdivision.

B. Any organization whose gross receipts from all charitable gaming exceeds or can be expected to exceed $40,000 in any calendar year shall have been granted tax-exempt status pursuant to § 501(c) of the United States Internal Revenue Code. At the same time tax-exempt status is sought from the Internal Revenue Service, the same documentation may be filed with the Department in conjunction with an application for a charitable gaming permit. If such documentation is filed, the Department may, after reviewing such documentation it deems necessary, issue a charitable gaming permit.

C. A permit shall be valid only for the locations, dates, and times designated in the permit.

History.

1995, c. 837; 1996, c. 919; 2003, c. 884; 2006, c. 644; 2009, c. 121; 2014, c. 208.

§ 18.2-340.25. Permit required; application fee; form of application.

A. Except as provided for in § 18.2-340.23, prior to the commencement of any charitable game, an organization shall obtain a permit from the Department.

B. All complete applications for a permit shall be acted upon by the Department within 45 days from the filing thereof. Upon compliance by the applicant with the provisions of this article, and at the discretion of the Department, a permit may be issued. All permits when issued shall be valid for the period specified in the permit unless it is sooner suspended or revoked. No permit shall be valid for longer than two years. The application shall be a matter of public record.

All permits shall be subject to regulation by the Department to ensure the public safety and welfare in the operation of charitable games. The permit shall only be granted after a reasonable investigation has been conducted by the Department. The Department may require any prospective employee, permit holder or applicant to submit to fingerprinting and to provide personal descriptive information to be forwarded along with employee's, licensee's or applicant's fingerprints through the Central Criminal Records Exchange to the Federal Bureau of Investigation for the purposes of obtaining criminal history record information regarding such prospective employee, permit holder or applicant. The Central Criminal Records Exchange upon receipt of a prospective employee, licensee or applicant record or notification that no record exists, shall forward the report to the Commissioner of the Department or his designee, who shall belong to a governmental entity. However, nothing in this subsection shall be construed to require the routine fingerprinting of volunteer bingo workers.

C. In no case shall an organization receive more than one permit allowing it to conduct charitable gaming; however, nothing in this section shall be construed to prohibit granting special permits pursuant to § 18.2-340.27.

D. Application for a charitable gaming permit shall be made on forms prescribed by the Department and shall be accompanied by payment of the fee for processing the application.

E. Applications for renewal of permits shall be made in accordance with Board Regulations. If a complete renewal application is received 45 days or more prior to the expiration of the permit, the permit shall continue to be effective until such time as the Department has taken final action. Otherwise, the permit shall expire at the end of its term.

F. The failure to meet any of the requirements of § 18.2-340.24 shall cause the automatic denial of the permit, and no organization shall conduct any charitable gaming until the requirements are met and a permit is obtained.

History.

1995, c. 837; 1997, cc. 777, 838; 1999, c. 361; 2003, c. 884; 2006, cc. 211, 644; 2008, cc. 387, 689.

§ 18.2-340.26. Sale of raffle tickets; drawings.

A. Except as provided in subsection B, a qualified organization may sell raffle tickets both in and out of the jurisdiction designated in its permit and shall conduct the drawing within the Commonwealth.

B. A qualified organization may sell raffle tickets for a raffle drawing which will be held outside the Commonwealth, provided the raffle is conducted in accordance with (i) the regulations of the Board and (ii) the laws and regulations of the jurisdiction in which the raffle drawing will be held.

C. Before a prize drawing, each stub or other detachable section of each ticket sold or won through some other authorized charitable game conducted by the same organization holding the raffle, shall be placed into a receptacle from which the winning tickets are drawn. The receptacle shall be designed so that each ticket placed in it has an equal chance of being drawn.

History.

1995, c. 837; 1997, cc. 777, 838; 2001, c. 833; 2003, c. 884; 2006, c. 644; 2008, c. 573.

§ 18.2-340.26:1. Sale of instant bingo, pull tabs or seal cards; proceeds not counted as gross receipts.

A. Instant bingo, pull tabs or seal cards may be sold only upon the premises owned or exclusively leased by the organization and at such times as the portion of the premises in which the instant bingo, pull tabs or seal cards are sold is open only to members and their guests. Nothing in this article shall be construed to prohibit the conduct of games of chance involving the sale of pull tabs or seal cards, commonly known as last sale games, conducted in accordance with this section.

B. The proceeds from instant bingo, pull tabs or seal cards shall not be included in determining the gross receipts for a qualified organization provided the gaming (i) is limited exclusively to members of the organization and their guests, (ii) is not open to the general public, and (iii) there is no public solicitation or advertisement made regarding such gaming.

History.

2001, c. 833; 2006, c. 644; 2007, c. 196.

§ 18.2-340.26:2. Sale of instant bingo, pull tabs, or seal cards by certain booster clubs.

As a part of its annual fund-raising event, any qualified organization that is an athletic association or booster club or a band booster club may sell instant bingo, pull tabs, or seal cards provided that (i) the sale is limited to a single event in a calendar year and (ii) the event is open to the public. The Department may require organizations authorized under this section to make such financial reporting as it deems necessary.

Nothing in this section shall be construed as exempting organizations authorized to sell instant bingo, pull tabs, or seal cards under this section from any other provisions of this article or other Board regulations.

History.

2007, c. 160.

§ 18.2-340.27. Conduct of bingo games; special permits.

A. A qualified organization shall accept only cash or, at its option, checks or debit cards in payment of any charges or assessments for players to participate in bingo games. However, no such organization shall accept postdated checks in payment of any charges or assessments for players to participate in bingo games.

B. No qualified organization or any person on the premises shall extend lines of credit or accept any credit or other electronic fund transfer other than debit cards in payment of any charges or assessments for players to participate in bingo games.

C. Bingo games may be held by qualified organizations no more frequently than two calendar days in any calendar week, except in accordance with subsection E.

D. No more than two sessions of bingo games may be held by qualified organizations in any calendar day, nor shall there be more than 55 bingo games per session.

E. A special permit may be granted a qualified organization which entitles it to conduct more frequent operations of bingo games during carnivals, fairs and state, federal or religious holidays, which shall be designated in the permit.

F. Any organization may conduct bingo games only in the county, city or town or in any adjoining county, city or town in which they regularly have been in existence or met. The Department may approve exceptions to this requirement where there is a special circumstance or documented need.

History.

1995, c. 837; 2006, c. 644; 2010, c. 429.

§ 18.2-340.28. Conduct of instant bingo, network bingo, pull tabs and seal cards.

A. Any organization qualified to conduct bingo games pursuant to the provisions of this article may play instant bingo, network bingo, pull tabs, or seal cards as a part of such bingo game and, if a permit is required pursuant to § 18.2-340.25, such games shall be played only at such location and at such times as designated in the permit for regular bingo games.

B. Any organization conducting instant bingo, network bingo, pull tabs, or seal cards shall maintain a record of the date, quantity and card value of instant bingo supplies purchased as well as the name and address of the supplier of such supplies. The organization shall also maintain a written invoice or receipt from a nonmember of the organization verifying any information required by this subsection. Such supplies shall be paid for only by check drawn on the gaming account of the organization. A complete inventory of all such gaming supplies shall be maintained by the organization on the premises where the gaming is being conducted.

C. No qualified organization shall sell any instant bingo, network bingo, pull tabs, or seal cards to any individual younger than 18 years of age. No individual younger than 18 years of age shall play or redeem any instant bingo, network bingo, pull tabs, or seal cards.

History.

1995, c. 837; 1997, cc. 777, 838; 2006, c. 644; 2013, cc. 36, 350.

§ 18.2-340.28:1. Conduct of network bingo.

A. Any organization qualified to conduct bingo games pursuant to the provisions of this article may sell network bingo cards as a part of a regular bingo game and, if a permit is required pursuant to § 18.2-340.25, network bingo shall be sold only at such location and at such times as designated in the permit for regular bingo games.

B. Any organization selling network bingo cards shall maintain a record of the date and quantity of network bingo cards purchased from a licensed network bingo provider. The organization shall also maintain a written invoice or receipt from a licensed supplier verifying any information required by this subsection. Such supplies shall be paid for only by check drawn on the gaming account of the organization or by electronic fund transfer. A complete inventory of all such gaming supplies shall be maintained by the organization on the premises where network bingo cards are sold.

C. No qualified organization shall sell any network bingo cards to any individual younger than 18 years of age. No individual younger than 18 years of age shall play or redeem any network bingo cards.

D. A qualified organization shall accept only cash or, at its option, checks or debit cards in payment of any charges or assessments for players to participate in any network bingo game. However, no such organization shall accept postdated checks in payment of any charges or assessments for players to participate in network bingo games.

E. No qualified organization or any person on the premises shall extend lines of credit or accept any credit or other electronic fund transfer other than debit cards in payment of any charges or assessments for players to participate in network bingo games.

F. No qualified organization shall conduct network bingo more frequently than one day in any calendar week, which shall not be the same day of each week.

G. No network bingo games shall be permitted in the social quarters of an organization that are open only to the organization's members and their guests.

H. No qualified organization shall sell network bingo cards on the Internet or other online service or allow the play of network bingo on the Internet or other online service. However, the location where network bingo games are conducted shall be equipped with a video monitor, television, or video screen, or any other similar means of visually displaying a broadcast or signal, that relays live, real-time video of the numbers as they are called by a live caller. The Internet or other online service may be used to relay information about winning players.

I. Qualified organizations may award network bingo prizes on a graduated scale; however, no single network bingo prize shall exceed $25,000.

J. Nothing in this section shall be construed to prohibit an organization from participating in more than one network bingo network.

History.

2013, cc. 36, 350.

§ 18.2-340.29. Joint operation of bingo games; written reports; joint permit required.

A. Any two or more qualified organizations may jointly organize and conduct bingo games provided both have fully complied with all other provisions of this article.

B. Any two or more qualified organizations jointly conducting such games shall be (i) subject to the same restrictions and prohibitions contained in this article that would apply to a single organization conducting bingo games and (ii) required to furnish to the Department a written report setting forth the location where such games will be held, the division of manpower, costs, and proceeds for each game to be jointly conducted.

Upon a finding that the division of manpower and costs for each game bears a reasonable relationship to the division of proceeds, the Department shall issue a joint permit.

C. No bingo game shall be jointly conducted until the joint permit issued pursuant to subsection B is obtained by the organizations.

Crimes and Offenses

History.
1995, c. 837; 2003, c. 884; 2006, c. 644.

§ 18.2-340.30. Reports of gross receipts and disbursements required; form of reports; failure to file.

A. Each qualified organization shall keep a complete record of all inventory of charitable gaming supplies purchased, all receipts from its charitable gaming operation, and all disbursements related to such operation. Except as provided in § 18.2-340.23, each qualified organization shall file at least annually, on a form prescribed by the Department, a report of all such receipts and disbursements, the amount of money on hand attributable to charitable gaming as of the end of the period covered by the report and any other information related to its charitable gaming operation that the Department may require. In addition, the Board, by regulation, may require any qualified organization whose net receipts exceed a specified amount during any three-month period to file a report of its receipts and disbursements for such period. All reports filed pursuant to this section shall be a matter of public record.

B. All reports required by this section shall be filed on or before the date prescribed by the Department. The Board, by regulation, shall establish a schedule of late fees to be assessed for any organization that fails to submit required reports by the due date.

C. Except as provided in § 18.2-340.23, each qualified organization shall designate or compensate an outside individual or group who shall be responsible for filing an annual, and, if required, quarterly, financial report if the organization goes out of business or otherwise ceases to conduct charitable gaming activities. The Department shall require such reports as it deems necessary until all proceeds of any charitable gaming have been used for the purposes specified in § 18.2-340.19 or have been disbursed in a manner approved by the Department.

D. Each qualified organization shall maintain for three years a complete written record of (i) all charitable gaming sessions using Department prescribed forms or reasonable facsimiles thereof approved by the Department; (ii) the name and address of each individual to whom is awarded any charitable gaming prize or jackpot that meets or exceeds the requirements of Internal Revenue Service Publication 3079, as well as the amount of the award; and (iii) an itemized record of all receipts and disbursements, including operating costs and use of proceeds incurred in operating bingo games.

E. The failure to file reports within 30 days of the time such reports are due shall cause the automatic revocation of the permit, and no organization shall conduct any bingo game or raffle thereafter until the report is properly filed and a new permit is obtained. However, the Department may grant an extension of time for filing such reports for a period not to exceed 45 days if requested by an organization, provided the organization requests an extension within 15 days of the time such reports are due and all projected fees are paid. For the term of any such extension, the organization's permit shall not be automatically revoked, such organization may continue to conduct charitable gaming, and no new permit shall be required.

History.
1995, c. 837; 1997, cc. 777, 838; 1999, c. 360; 2003, c. 884; 2006, c. 644; 2007, c. 541; 2014, c. 208.

§ 18.2-340.30:1: Repealed by Acts 2010, c. 429, cl. 2.

§ 18.2-340.31. Audit of reports; exemption; audit and administration fee.

A. All reports filed pursuant to § 18.2-340.30 shall be subject to audit by the Department in accordance with Board regulations. The Department may engage the services of independent certified public accountants to perform any audits deemed necessary to fulfill the Department's responsibilities under this article.

B. The Department shall prescribe a reasonable audit and administration fee to be paid by any organization conducting charitable gaming under a permit issued by the Department unless the organization is exempt from such fee pursuant to § 18.2-340.23. Such fee shall not exceed one and one-quarter percent of the gross receipts which an organization reports pursuant to § 18.2-340.30. The audit and administration fee shall accompany each report for each calendar quarter.

C. The audit and administration fee shall be payable to the Treasurer of Virginia. All such fees received by the Treasurer of Virginia shall be separately accounted for and shall be used only by the Department for the purposes of auditing and regulating charitable gaming.

History.
1995, c. 837; 1997, cc. 777, 838; 2003, c. 884; 2006, c. 644.

§ 18.2-340.32: Repealed by Acts 2004, c. 462.

Cross references.
For current provisions as to regulation of bingo and instant bingo, see § 15.2-912.2.

§ 18.2-340.33. Prohibited practices.

In addition to those other practices prohibited by this article, the following acts or practices are prohibited:

1. No part of the gross receipts derived by a qualified organization may be used for any purpose other than (i) reasonable and proper gaming expenses, (ii) reasonable and proper business expenses, (iii) those lawful religious, charitable, com-

munity or educational purposes for which the organization is specifically chartered or organized, and (iv) expenses relating to the acquisition, construction, maintenance, or repair of any interest in the real property involved in the operation of the organization and used for lawful religious, charitable, community or educational purposes. For the purposes of clause (iv), such expenses may include the expenses of a corporation formed for the purpose of serving as the real estate holding entity of a qualified organization, provided (a) such holding entity is qualified as a tax exempt organization under § 501(c) of the Internal Revenue Code and (b) the membership of the qualified organization is identical to such holding entity.

2. Except as provided in § 18.2-340.34:1, no qualified organization shall enter into a contract with or otherwise employ for compensation any person for the purpose of organizing, managing, or conducting any charitable games. However, organizations composed of or for deaf or blind persons may use a part of their gross receipts for costs associated with providing clerical assistance in the management and operation but not the conduct of charitable gaming.

The provisions of this subdivision shall not prohibit the joint operation of bingo games held in accordance with § 18.2-340.29.

3. No person shall pay or receive for use of any premises devoted, in whole or in part, to the conduct of any charitable games, any consideration in excess of the current fair market rental value of such property. Fair market rental value consideration shall not be based upon or determined by reference to a percentage of the proceeds derived from the operation of any charitable games or to the number of people in attendance at such charitable games.

4. No building or other premises shall be utilized in whole or in part for the purpose of conducting charitable gaming more frequently than two calendar days in any one calendar week. However, no building or other premises owned by (i) a qualified organization which is exempt from taxation pursuant to § 501(c) of the Internal Revenue Code or (ii) any county, city or town shall be utilized in whole or in part for the purpose of conducting bingo games more frequently than four calendar days in any one calendar week.

The provisions of this subdivision shall not apply to the playing of bingo games pursuant to a special permit issued in accordance with § 18.2-340.27.

5. No person shall participate in the management or operation of any charitable game unless such person is and, for a period of at least 30 days immediately preceding such participation, has been a bona fide member of the organization. For any organization that is not composed of members, a person who is not a bona fide member may volunteer in the conduct of a charitable game as long as that person is directly supervised by a bona fide official member of the organization.

The provisions of this subdivision shall not apply to (i) persons employed as clerical assistants by qualified organizations composed of or for deaf or blind persons; (ii) employees of a corporate sponsor of a qualified organization, provided such employees' participation is limited to the management, operation or conduct of no more than one raffle per year; (iii) the spouse or family member of any such bona fide member of a qualified organization provided at least one bona fide member is present; or (iv) persons employed by a qualified organization authorized to sell pull tabs or seal cards in accordance with § 18.2-340.16, provided (a) such sales are conducted by no more than two on-duty employees, (b) such employees receive no compensation for or based on the sale of the pull tabs or seal cards, and (c) such sales are conducted in the private social quarters of the organization.

6. No person shall receive any remuneration for participating in the management, operation or conduct of any charitable game, except that:

a. Persons employed by organizations composed of or for deaf or blind persons may receive remuneration not to exceed $30 per event for providing clerical assistance in the management and operation but not the conduct of charitable games only for such organizations;

b. Persons under the age of 19 who sell raffle tickets for a qualified organization to raise funds for youth activities in which they participate may receive nonmonetary incentive awards or prizes from the organization;

c. Remuneration may be paid to off-duty law-enforcement officers from the jurisdiction in which such bingo games are played for providing uniformed security for such bingo games even if such officer is a member of the sponsoring organization, provided the remuneration paid to such member is in accordance with off-duty law-enforcement personnel work policies approved by the local law-enforcement official and further provided that such member is not otherwise engaged in the management, operation or conduct of the bingo games of that organization, or to private security services businesses licensed pursuant to § 9.1-139 providing uniformed security for such bingo games, provided that employees of such businesses shall not otherwise be involved in the management, operation, or conduct of the bingo games of that organization;

d. A member of a qualified organization lawfully participating in the management, operation or conduct of a bingo game may be provided food and nonalcoholic beverages by such organization for on-premises consumption during the bingo game provided the food and beverages are provided in accordance with Board regulations; and

e. Remuneration may be paid to bingo managers or callers who have a current registration certificate issued by the Department in accordance with § 18.2-340.34:1, or who are exempt from such registration requirement. Such remuneration shall not exceed $100 per session.

7. No landlord shall, at bingo games conducted on the landlord's premises, (i) participate in the conduct, management, or operation of any bingo games; (ii) sell, lease or otherwise provide for consideration any bingo supplies, including, but not limited to, bingo cards, instant bingo cards, or other game pieces; or (iii) require as a condition of the lease or by contract that a particular manufacturer, distributor or supplier of bingo supplies or equipment be used by the organization.

The provisions of this subdivision shall not apply to any qualified organization conducting bingo games on its own behalf at premises owned by it.

8. No qualified organization shall enter into any contract with or otherwise employ or compensate any member of the organization on account of the sale of bingo supplies or equipment.

9. No organization shall award any bingo prize money or any merchandise valued in excess of the following amounts:

a. No bingo door prize shall exceed $50 for a single door prize or $250 in cumulative door prizes in any one session;

b. No regular bingo or special bingo game prize shall exceed $100;

c. No instant bingo, pull tab, or seal card prize for a single card shall exceed $1,000;

d. Except as provided in subdivision 9, no bingo jackpot of any nature whatsoever shall exceed $1,000, nor shall the total amount of bingo jackpot prizes awarded in any one session exceed $1,000. Proceeds from the sale of bingo cards and the sheets used for bingo jackpot games shall be accounted for separately from the bingo cards or sheets used for any other bingo games; and

e. No single network bingo prize shall exceed $25,000. Proceeds from the sale of network bingo cards shall be accounted for separately from bingo cards and sheets used for any other bingo game.

10. The provisions of subdivision 9 shall not apply to:

Any progressive bingo game, in which (a) a regular or special prize, not to exceed $100, is awarded on the basis of predetermined numbers or patterns selected at random and (b) a progressive prize, not to exceed $500 for the initial progressive prize and $5,000 for the maximum progressive prize, is awarded if the predetermined numbers or patterns are covered when a certain number of numbers is called, provided (i) there are no more than six such games per session per organization, (ii) the amount of increase of the progressive prize per session is no more than $100, (iii) the bingo cards or sheets used in such games are sold separately from the bingo cards or sheets used for any other bingo games, (iv) the organization separately accounts for the proceeds from such sale, and (v) such games are otherwise operated in accordance with the Department's rules of play.

11. No organization shall award any raffle prize valued at more than $100,000.

The provisions of this subdivision shall not apply to a raffle conducted no more than once per calendar year by a qualified organization qualified as a tax-exempt organization pursuant to § 501(c) of the Internal Revenue Code for a prize consisting of a lot improved by a residential dwelling where 100 percent of the moneys received from such a raffle, less deductions for the fair market value for the cost of acquisition of the land and materials, are donated to lawful religious, charitable, community, or educational organizations specifically chartered or organized under the laws of the Commonwealth and qualified as a § 501(c) tax-exempt organization.

12. No qualified organization composed of or for deaf or blind persons which employs a person not a member to provide clerical assistance in the management and operation but not the conduct of any charitable games shall conduct such games unless it has in force fidelity insurance, as defined in § 38.2-120, written by an insurer licensed to do business in the Commonwealth.

13. No person shall participate in the management or operation of any charitable game if he has ever been convicted of any felony or if he has been convicted of any misdemeanor involving fraud, theft, or financial crimes within the preceding five years. No person shall participate in the conduct of any charitable game if, within the preceding 10 years, he has been convicted of any felony or if, within the preceding five years he has been convicted of any misdemeanor involving fraud, theft, or financial crimes. In addition, no person shall participate in the management, operation or conduct of any charitable game if that person, within the preceding five years, has participated in the management, operation, or conduct of any charitable game which was found by the Department or a court of competent jurisdiction to have been operated in violation of state law, local ordinance or Board regulation.

14. Qualified organizations jointly conducting bingo games pursuant to § 18.2-340.29 shall not circumvent any restrictions and prohibitions which would otherwise apply if a single organization were conducting such games. These restrictions and prohibitions shall include, but not be limited to, the frequency with which bingo games may be held, the value of merchandise or money awarded as prizes, or any other practice prohibited under this section.

15. A qualified organization shall not purchase any charitable gaming supplies for use in the Commonwealth from any person who is not currently registered with the Department as a supplier pursuant to § 18.2-340.34.

16. Unless otherwise permitted in this article, no part of an organization's charitable gaming gross receipts shall be used for an organization's social or recreational activities.

History.

1995, c. 837; 1996, c. 919; 1997, cc. 777, 838; 1998, cc. 57, 398; 1999, c. 534; 2000, c. 1000; 2001, c. 754; 2002, c. 282; 2003, c. 884;

2004, c. 275; 2005, cc. 776, 826; 2006, c. 644; 2007, cc. 226, 790; 2008, c. 352; 2010, c. 429; 2013, cc. 36, 350.

§ 18.2-340.34. Suppliers of charitable gaming supplies; manufacturers of electronic games of chance systems; permit; qualification; suspension, revocation or refusal to renew certificate; maintenance, production, and release of records.

A. No person shall offer to sell, sell or otherwise provide charitable gaming supplies to any qualified organization and no manufacturer shall distribute electronic games of chance systems for charitable gaming in the Commonwealth unless and until such person has made application for and has been issued a permit by the Department. An application for permit shall be made on forms prescribed by the Department and shall be accompanied by a fee in the amount of $1,000. Each permit shall remain valid for a period of one year from the date of issuance. Application for renewal of a permit shall be accompanied by a fee in the amount of $1,000 and shall be made on forms prescribed by the Department.

B. The Board shall have authority to prescribe by regulation reasonable criteria consistent with the provisions of this article for the registration of suppliers and manufacturers of electronic games of chance systems for charitable gaming. The Department may refuse to issue a permit to any supplier or manufacturer who has, or which has any officer, director, partner, or owner who has (i) been convicted of or pleaded nolo contendere to a felony in any state or federal court or has been convicted of any offense which, if committed in the Commonwealth, would be a felony; (ii) been convicted of or pleaded nolo contendere to a crime involving gambling; (iii) had any license, permit, certificate or other authority related to activities defined as charitable gaming in the Commonwealth suspended or revoked in the Commonwealth or in any other jurisdiction; (iv) failed to file or has been delinquent in excess of one year in the filing of any tax returns or the payment of any taxes due the Commonwealth; or (v) failed to establish a registered office or registered agent in the Commonwealth if so required by § 13.1-634 or 13.1-763.

C. The Department may suspend, revoke or refuse to renew the permit of any supplier or manufacturer for any conduct described in subsection B or for any violation of this article or regulation of the Board. Before taking any such action, the Department shall give the supplier or manufacturer a written statement of the grounds upon which it proposes to take such action and an opportunity to be heard. Every hearing in a contested case shall be conducted in accordance with the Administrative Process Act (§ 2.2-4000 et seq.).

D. Each supplier shall document each sale of charitable gaming supplies, including electronic games of chance systems, and other items incidental to the conduct of charitable gaming, such as markers, wands or tape, to a qualified organization on an invoice which clearly shows (i) the name and address of the qualified organization to which such supplies or items were sold; (ii) the date of the sale; (iii) the name or form and serial number of each deal of instant bingo cards and pull-tab raffle cards, the quantity of deals sold and the price per deal paid by the qualified organization; (iv) the serial number of the top sheet in each packet of bingo paper, the serial number for each series of uncollated bingo paper, and the cut, color and quantity of bingo paper sold; and (v) any other information with respect to charitable gaming supplies, including electronic games of chance systems, or other items incidental to the conduct of charitable gaming as the Board may prescribe by regulation. A legible copy of the invoice shall accompany the charitable gaming supplies when delivered to the qualified organization.

Each manufacturer of electronic games of chance systems shall document each distribution of such systems to a qualified organization or supplier on an invoice which clearly shows (i) the name and address of the qualified organization or supplier to which such systems were distributed; (ii) the date of distribution; (iii) the serial number of each such system; and (iv) any other information with respect to electronic games of chance systems as the Board may prescribe by regulation. A legible copy of the invoice shall accompany the electronic games of chance systems when delivered to the qualified organization or supplier.

E. Each supplier and manufacturer shall maintain a legible copy of each invoice required by subsection D for a period of three years from the date of sale. Each supplier and manufacturer shall make such documents immediately available for inspection and copying to any agent or employee of the Department upon request made during normal business hours. This subsection shall not limit the right of the Department to require the production of any other documents in the possession of the supplier or manufacturer which relate to its transactions with qualified organizations. All documents and other information of a proprietary nature furnished to the Department in accordance with this subsection shall not be a matter of public record and shall be exempt from disclosure under the provisions of the Freedom of Information Act (§ 2.2-3700 et seq.).

History.

1995, c. 837; 1996, c. 919; 1997, cc. 777, 838; 1999, c. 534; 2003, c. 884; 2006, c. 644; 2007, c. 264.

§ 18.2-340.34:1. Bingo managers and callers; remuneration; registration; qualification; suspension, revocation or refusal to renew certificate; exceptions.

A. No person shall receive remuneration as a bingo manager or caller from any qualified organi-

Crimes and Offenses

zation unless and until such person has made application for and has been issued a registration certificate by the Department. Application for registration shall be made on forms prescribed by the Department and shall be accompanied by a fee in the amount of $75. Each registration certificate shall remain valid for a period of one year from the date of issuance. Application for renewal of a registration certificate shall be accompanied by a fee in the amount of $75 and shall be made on forms prescribed by the Department.

B. As a condition of registration as a bingo manager, the applicant shall (i) have been a bona fide member of the qualified organization for at least 12 consecutive months prior to making application for registration and (ii) be required to complete a reasonable training course developed and conducted by the Department.

As a condition of registration as a bingo caller, the applicant shall be required to complete a reasonable training course developed and conducted by the Department.

The Department may refuse to register any bingo manager or caller who has (a) been convicted of or pleaded nolo contendere to a felony in any state or federal court or has been convicted of any offense which, if committed in the Commonwealth, would be a felony; (b) been convicted of or pleaded nolo contendere to a crime involving gambling; (c) had any license, permit, certificate, or other authority related to activities defined as charitable gaming in the Commonwealth suspended or revoked in the Commonwealth or in any other jurisdiction; or (d) failed to file or has been delinquent in excess of one year in the filing of any tax returns or the payment of any taxes due the Commonwealth.

C. The Department may suspend, revoke, or refuse to renew the registration certificate of any bingo manager or caller for any conduct described in subsection B or for any violation of this article or regulations of the Board. Before taking any such action, the Department shall give the bingo manager or caller a written statement of the grounds upon which it proposes to take such action and an opportunity to be heard. Every hearing in a contested case shall be conducted in accordance with the Administrative Process Act (§ 2.2-4000 et seq.).

D. The provisions of subsection A requiring registration for bingo callers with the Department shall not apply to a bingo caller for a volunteer fire department or volunteer emergency medical services agency or auxiliary unit thereof that has been recognized in accordance with § 15.2-955 by an ordinance or resolution of the political subdivision where the volunteer fire department or volunteer emergency medical services agency is located as being a part of the safety program of such political subdivision.

History.

2005, cc. 776, 826; 2007, cc. 226, 347; 2015, cc. 502, 503.

§ 18.2-340.34:2. Licensing of network bingo providers; qualification; suspension, revocation, or refusal to renew license; maintenance, production, and release of records.

A. No person shall sell or offer to sell or otherwise provide access to a network bingo network to any qualified organization unless and until such person has made application for and has been issued a license by the Department. An application for license shall be made on forms prescribed by the Department and shall be accompanied by a fee in the amount of $500. Each license shall remain valid for a period of two years from the date of issuance. Application for renewal of a license shall be accompanied by a fee in the amount of $500 and shall be made on forms prescribed by the Department.

B. The Board shall have authority to prescribe by regulation reasonable criteria consistent with the provisions of this article for the licensure of network bingo providers. The Department may refuse to issue a license to any network bingo provider that has any officer, director, partner, or owner who has (i) been convicted of or pleaded nolo contendere to a felony in any state or federal court or has been convicted of any offense that, if committed in the Commonwealth, would be a felony; (ii) been convicted of or pleaded nolo contendere to a crime involving gambling; (iii) had any license, permit, certificate, or other authority related to activities defined as charitable gaming in the Commonwealth suspended or revoked in the Commonwealth or in any other jurisdiction; (iv) failed to file or been delinquent in excess of one year in the filing of any tax returns or the payment of any taxes due the Commonwealth; or (v) failed to establish a registered office or registered agent in the Commonwealth if so required by § 13.1-634 or 13.1-763.

C. The Department may suspend, revoke, or refuse to renew the license of any network bingo provider for any conduct described in subsection B or for any violation of this article or regulation of the Board. Before taking any such action, the Department shall give the network bingo provider a written statement of the grounds upon which it proposes to take such action and an opportunity to be heard. Every hearing in a contested case shall be conducted in accordance with the Administrative Process Act (§ 2.2-4000 et seq.).

D. The Department by regulation shall require network bingo providers to have onsite independent supervision of network bingo games as the numbers are called.

E. Each network bingo provider shall document each sale of network bingo supplies and other items incidental to the conduct of network bingo to a qualified organization on an invoice that clearly shows (i) the name and address of the qualified organization to which such supplies or items were sold; (ii) the date of the sale; (iii) the name or form and serial number of each network bingo card, the quantity of cards sold, and the price per card paid by the qualified organization; and (iv) any other information required by the Department. A legible copy of the invoice shall accompany the network bingo supplies when delivered to the qualified organization.

F. Each network bingo provider shall maintain a legible copy of each invoice required by subsection E for a period of three years from the date of sale. Each network bingo provider shall make such documents immediately available for inspection and copying to any agent or employee of the Department upon request made during normal business hours. This subsection shall not limit the right of the Department to require the production of any other documents in the possession of the network bingo provider that relate to its transactions with qualified organizations. All documents and other information of a proprietary nature furnished to the Department in accordance with this subsection shall be exempt from disclosure under the provisions of the Freedom of Information Act (§ 2.2-3700 et seq.).

History.
2013, cc. 36, 350.

§ 18.2-340.35. Assistance from Department of State Police.

The Department of the State Police, upon request of the Department, shall assist in the conduct of investigations by the Department.

History.
1995, c. 837; 2003, c. 884.

§ 18.2-340.36. Suspension of permit.

A. When any officer charged with the enforcement of the charitable gaming laws of the Commonwealth has reasonable cause to believe that the conduct of charitable gaming is being conducted by an organization in violation of this article or the regulations of the Board, he may apply to any judge, magistrate, or other person having authority to issue criminal warrants for the immediate suspension of the permit of the organization conducting the bingo game or raffle. If the judge, magistrate, or person to whom such application is presented is satisfied that probable cause exists to suspend the permit, he shall suspend the permit. Immediately upon such suspension, the officer shall notify the organization in writing of such suspension.

B. Written notice specifying the particular basis for the immediate suspension shall be provided by the officer to the organization within one business day of the suspension and a hearing held thereon by the Department or its designated hearing officer within 10 days of the suspension unless the organization consents to a later date. No charitable gaming shall be conducted by the organization until the suspension has been lifted by the Department or a court of competent jurisdiction.

History.
1995, c. 837; 2003, c. 884.

§ 18.2-340.37. Criminal penalties.

A. Any person who violates the provisions of this article or who willfully and knowingly files, or causes to be filed, a false application, report or other document or who willfully and knowingly makes a false statement, or causes a false statement to be made, on any application, report or other document required to be filed with or made to the Department shall be guilty of a Class 1 misdemeanor.

B. Each day in violation shall constitute a separate offense.

C. Any person who converts funds derived from any charitable gaming to his own or another's use, when the amount of funds is less than $200, shall be guilty of petit larceny and, when the amount of funds is $200 or more, shall be guilty of grand larceny. The provisions of this section shall not preclude the applicability of any other provision of the criminal law of the Commonwealth that may apply to any course of conduct that violates this section.

History.
1995, c. 837; 1996, c. 919; 2003, c. 884; 2006, c. 644.

§ 18.2-340.38: Repealed by Acts 2001, c. 754, cl. 2.

ARTICLE 2.
SUNDAY OFFENSES.

§§ 18.2-341 through 18.2-343: Repealed by Acts 2004, c. 608.

ARTICLE 3.
COMMERCIAL SEX TRAFFICKING, PROSTITUTION, ETC.

§ 18.2-344. Fornication.

Any person, not being married, who voluntarily shall have sexual intercourse with any other person, shall be guilty of fornication, punishable as a Class 4 misdemeanor.

History.
Code 1950, §§ 18.1-188, 18.1-190; 1960, c. 358; 1975, cc. 14, 15.

§ 18.2-345: Repealed by Acts 2013, c. 621.

§ 18.2-346. Prostitution; commercial sexual conduct; commercial exploitation of a minor; penalties.

A. Any person who, for money or its equivalent, (i) commits adultery, fornication, or any act in violation of § 18.2-361, performs cunnilingus, fellatio,

Crimes and Offenses

or anilingus upon or by another person, or engages in anal intercourse or (ii) offers to commit adultery, fornication, or any act in violation of § 18.2-361, perform cunnilingus, fellatio, or anilingus upon or by another person, or engage in anal intercourse and thereafter does any substantial act in furtherance thereof is guilty of prostitution, which is punishable as a Class 1 misdemeanor.

B. Any person who offers money or its equivalent to another for the purpose of engaging in sexual acts as enumerated in subsection A and thereafter does any substantial act in furtherance thereof is guilty of solicitation of prostitution, which is punishable as a Class 1 misdemeanor. However, any person who solicits prostitution from a minor (i) 16 years of age or older is guilty of a Class 6 felony or (ii) younger than 16 years of age is guilty of a Class 5 felony.

History.
Code 1950, § 18.1-194; 1960, c. 358; 1975, cc. 14, 15; 1980, c. 534; 1993, c. 609; 2013, cc. 417, 467; 2014, c. 794.

§ 18.2-346.1. Testing of convicted prostitutes and injection drug users for infection with human immunodeficiency viruses and hepatitis C; limited disclosure.

A. As soon as practicable following conviction of any person for violation of § 18.2-346 or 18.2-361, or any violation of Article 1 (§ 18.2-247 et seq.) or 1.1 (§ 18.2-265.1 et seq.) of Chapter 7 involving the possession, sale, or use of a controlled substance in a form amenable to intravenous use; or the possession, sale, or use of hypodermic syringes, needles, or other objects designed or intended for use in parenterally injecting controlled substances into the human body, such person shall be required to submit to testing for infection with human immunodeficiency viruses and hepatitis C. The convicted person shall receive counseling from personnel of the Department of Health concerning (i) the meaning of the test, (ii) acquired immunodeficiency syndrome and hepatitis C, and (iii) the transmission and prevention of infection with human immunodeficiency viruses and hepatitis C.

B. Tests for human immunodeficiency viruses shall be conducted to confirm any initial positive test results before any test result shall be determined to be positive for infection. The results of such test shall be confidential as provided in § 32.1-36.1 and shall be disclosed to the person who is the subject of the test and to the Department of Health as required by § 32.1-36. The Department shall conduct surveillance and investigation in accordance with the requirements of § 32.1-39.

C. Upon receiving a report of a positive test for hepatitis C, the State Health Commissioner may share protected health information relating to such positive test with relevant sheriffs' offices, the state police, local police departments, adult or youth correctional facilities, salaried or volunteer firefighters, paramedics or emergency medical technicians, officers of the court, and regional or local jails (i) to the extent necessary to advise exposed individuals of the risk of infection and to enable exposed individuals to seek appropriate testing and treatment, and (ii) as may be needed to prevent and control disease and is deemed necessary to prevent serious harm and serious threats to the health and safety of individuals and the public.

The disclosed protected health information shall be held confidential; no person to whom such information is disclosed shall redisclose or otherwise reveal the protected health information without first obtaining the specific authorization from the individual who was the subject of the test for such redisclosure.

Such protected health information shall only be used to protect the health and safety of individuals and the public in conformance with the regulations concerning patient privacy promulgated by the federal Department of Health and Human Services, as such regulations may be amended.

D. The results of the tests shall not be admissible in any criminal proceeding related to prostitution or drug use.

The cost of the tests shall be paid by the Commonwealth and taxed as part of the cost of such criminal proceedings.

History.
1990, c. 913; 2005, c. 438.

§ 18.2-347. Keeping, residing in or frequenting a bawdy place; "bawdy place" defined.

It shall be unlawful for any person to keep any bawdy place, or to reside in or at or visit, for immoral purposes, any such bawdy place. Each and every day such bawdy place shall be kept, resided in or visited, shall constitute a separate offense. In a prosecution under this section the general reputation of the place may be proved.

As used in this Code, *"bawdy place"* shall mean any place within or without any building or structure which is used or is to be used for lewdness, assignation or prostitution.

History.
Code 1950, §§ 18.1-195, 18.1-196; 1960, c. 358; 1975, cc. 14, 15.

§ 18.2-348. Aiding prostitution or illicit sexual intercourse, etc.

It is unlawful for any person or any officer, employee, or agent of any firm, association, or corporation, with knowledge of, or good reason to believe, the immoral purpose of such visit, to take or transport or assist in taking or transporting, or offer to take or transport on foot or in any way, any person to a place, whether within or without any building or structure, used or to be used for the purpose of lewdness, assignation, or prostitution within the Commonwealth, or to procure or assist in procuring for the purpose of illicit sexual intercourse, anal intercourse, cunnilingus, fellatio, or anilingus or any act violative of § 18.2-361, or to give any information or direction to any person with intent to enable such person to commit an act of prostitution.

History.

Code 1950, § 18.1-197; 1960, c. 358; 1975, cc. 14, 15; 1980, c. 534; 2014, c. 794.

§ 18.2-349. Using vehicles to promote prostitution or unlawful sexual intercourse.

It shall be unlawful for any owner or chauffeur of any vehicle, with knowledge or reason to believe the same is to be used for such purpose, to use the same or to allow the same to be used for the purpose of prostitution or unlawful sexual intercourse, or to aid or promote such prostitution or unlawful sexual intercourse by the use of any such vehicle.

History.

Code 1950, § 18.1-198; 1960, c. 358; 1975, cc. 14, 15.

§ 18.2-350. Confinement of convicted prostitutes and persons violating §§ 18.2-347 through 18.2-349.

Every person convicted of being a prostitute and every person convicted of violating any of the provisions of §§ 18.2-347 through 18.2-349 shall be guilty of a Class 1 misdemeanor; provided, however, that in any case in which a city or county farm or hospital is available for the confinement of persons so convicted, confinement may be in such farm or hospital, in the discretion of the court or judge.

History.

Code 1950, § 18.1-199; 1960, c. 358; 1975, cc. 14, 15.

§§ 18.2-351 through 18.2-353: Repealed by Acts 2004, c. 459.

§ 18.2-354: Reserved.

§ 18.2-355. Taking, detaining, etc., person for prostitution, etc., or consenting thereto; human trafficking.

Any person who:

(1) For purposes of prostitution or unlawful sexual intercourse, takes any person into, or persuades, encourages or causes any person to enter, a bawdy place, or takes or causes such person to be taken to any place against his or her will for such purposes; or

(2) Takes or detains a person against his or her will with the intent to compel such person, by force, threats, persuasions, menace or duress, to marry him or her or to marry any other person, or to be defiled; or

(3) Being parent, guardian, legal custodian or one standing in loco parentis of a person, consents to such person being taken or detained by any person for the purpose of prostitution or unlawful sexual intercourse; or

(4) For purposes of prostitution, takes any minor into, or persuades, encourages, or causes any minor to enter, a bawdy place, or takes or causes such person to be taken to any place for such purposes; is guilty of pandering.

A violation of subdivision (1), (2), or (3) is punishable as a Class 4 felony. A violation of subdivision (4) is punishable as a Class 3 felony.

History.

Code 1950, § 18.1-204; 1960, c. 358; 1975, cc. 14, 15; 1980, c. 534; 1997, c. 555; 2014, cc. 649, 706; 2015, c. 395.

§ 18.2-356. Receiving money for procuring person; penalties.

Any person who receives any money or other valuable thing for or on account of (i) procuring for or placing in a house of prostitution or elsewhere any person for the purpose of causing such person to engage in unlawful sexual intercourse, anal intercourse, cunnilingus, fellatio, or anilingus or any act in violation of § 18.2-361 or (ii) causing any person to engage in forced labor or services, concubinage, prostitution, or the manufacture of any obscene material or child pornography is guilty of a Class 4 felony. Any person who violates clause (i) or (ii) with a person under the age of 18 is guilty of a Class 3 felony.

History.

Code 1950, § 18.1-206; 1960, c. 358; 1975, cc. 14, 15; 1980, c. 534; 2011, c. 785; 2014, c. 794; 2015, cc. 690, 691.

§ 18.2-357. Receiving money from earnings of male or female prostitute; penalties.

Any person who shall knowingly receive any money or other valuable thing from the earnings of any male or female engaged in prostitution, except for a consideration deemed good and valuable in law, shall be guilty of pandering, punishable as a Class 4 felony. Any person who violates this section by receiving money or other valuable thing from a person under the age of 18 is guilty of a Class 3 felony.

History.

Code 1950, § 18.1-208; 1960, c. 358; 1975, cc. 14, 15; 1980, c. 534; 2015, cc. 690, 691.

§ 18.2-357.1. Commercial sex trafficking; penalties.

A. Any person who, with the intent to receive money or other valuable thing or to assist another in

Crimes and Offenses

receiving money or other valuable thing from the earnings of a person from prostitution or unlawful sexual intercourse in violation of subsection A of § 18.2-346, solicits, invites, recruits, encourages, or otherwise causes or attempts to cause a person to violate subsection A of § 18.2-346 is guilty of a Class 5 felony.

B. Any person who violates subsection A through the use of force, intimidation, or deception is guilty of a Class 4 felony.

C. Any adult who violates subsection A with a person under the age of 18 is guilty of a Class 3 felony.

History.
2015, cc. 690, 691.

§ **18.2-358:** Repealed by Acts 2004, c. 459.

§ 18.2-359. Venue for criminal sexual assault or where any person transported for criminal sexual assault, attempted criminal sexual assault, or purposes of unlawful sexual intercourse, crimes against nature, and indecent liberties with children; venue for such crimes when coupled with a violent felony.

A. Any person transporting or attempting to transport through or across the Commonwealth any person for the purposes of unlawful sexual intercourse, anal intercourse, cunnilingus, fellatio, or anilingus or prostitution, or for the purpose of committing any crime specified in § 18.2-361, 18.2-370, or 18.2-370.1, or for the purposes of committing or attempting to commit criminal sexual assault under Article 7 (§ 18.2-61 et seq.) of Chapter 4, may be presented, indicted, tried, and convicted in any county or city in which any part of such transportation occurred.

B. Venue for the trial of any person charged with committing or attempting to commit any crime specified in § 18.2-361, 18.2-370, or 18.2-370.1, or sexual assault under Article 7 (§ 18.2-61 et seq.) of Chapter 4 may be had in the county or city in which such crime is alleged to have occurred or, with the concurrence of the attorney for the Commonwealth in the county or city in which the crime is alleged to have occurred, in any county or city through which the victim was transported by the defendant prior to the commission of such offense.

C. Venue for the trial of any person charged with committing or attempting to commit criminal sexual assault under Article 7 (§ 18.2-61 et seq.) of Chapter 4 against a person under 18 years of age may be had in the county or city in which such crime is alleged to have occurred or, when the county or city where the offense is alleged to have occurred cannot be determined, then in the county or city where the person under 18 years of age resided at the time of the offense.

D. Venue for the trial of any person charged with committing or attempting to commit (i) any crime specified in § 18.2-361, 18.2-370, or 18.2-370.1, or criminal sexual assault under Article 7 (§ 18.2-61 et seq.) of Chapter 4 and (ii) any violent felony as defined in § 17.1-805 or any act of violence as defined in § 19.2-297.1 arising out of the same incident, occurrence, or transaction may be had in the county or city in which any such crime is alleged to have occurred or, with the concurrence of the attorney for the Commonwealth in the county or city in which the crime is alleged to have occurred, in any county or city through which the victim was transported by the defendant in the commission of such offense.

History.
Code 1950, § 18.1-210; 1960, c. 358; 1975, cc. 14, 15; 1976, c. 54; 1978, c. 610; 1981, c. 397; 2004, c. 869; 2011, c. 763; 2014, c. 794; 2015, c. 555.

§ 18.2-360. Competency of persons to testify in prosecutions under §§ 18.2-355 through 18.2-361.

Any male or female referred to in §§ 18.2-355 through 18.2-361 shall be a competent witness in any prosecution under such sections to testify to any and all matters, including conversations by or with the accused with third persons in his or her presence, notwithstanding he or she may have married the accused either before or after the violation of any of the provisions of this section; but such witness shall not be compelled to testify after such marriage.

History.
Code 1950, § 18.1-211; 1960, c. 358; 1975, cc. 14, 15; 1980, c. 534.

§ 18.2-361. Crimes against nature; penalty.

A. If any person carnally knows in any manner any brute animal or voluntarily submits to such carnal knowledge, he is guilty of a Class 6 felony.

B. Any person who performs or causes to be performed cunnilingus, fellatio, anilingus, or anal intercourse upon or by his daughter or granddaughter, son or grandson, brother or sister, or father or mother is guilty of a Class 5 felony. However, if a parent or grandparent commits any such act with his child or grandchild and such child or grandchild is at least 13 but less than 18 years of age at the time of the offense, such parent or grandparent is guilty of a Class 3 felony.

C. For the purposes of this section, parent includes step-parent, grandparent includes step-grandparent, child includes step-child, and grandchild includes step-grandchild.

History.
Code 1950, § 18.1-212; 1960, c. 358; 1968, c. 427; 1975, cc. 14, 15; 1977, c. 285; 1981, c. 397; 1993, c. 450; 2005, c. 185; 2014, c. 794.

ARTICLE 4.

FAMILY OFFENSES; CRIMES AGAINST CHILDREN, ETC.

§ 18.2-362. Person marrying when husband or wife is living; penalty; venue.

If any person, being married, shall, during the life of the husband or wife, marry another person in this Commonwealth, or if the marriage with such other person take place out of the Commonwealth, shall thereafter cohabit with such other person in this Commonwealth, he or she shall be guilty of a Class 4 felony. Venue for a violation of this section may be in the county or city where the subsequent marriage occurred or where the parties to the subsequent marriage cohabited.

History.
Code 1950, § 20-41; 1975, cc. 14, 15; 2003, c. 99.

§ 18.2-363. Leaving Commonwealth to evade law against bigamy.

If any persons, resident in this Commonwealth, one of whom has a husband or wife living, shall, with the intention of returning to reside in this Commonwealth, go into another state or country and there intermarry and return to and reside in this Commonwealth cohabiting as man and wife, such marriage shall be governed by the same law, in all respects, as if it had been solemnized in this Commonwealth.

History.
Code 1950, § 20-44; 1975, cc. 14, 15.

§ 18.2-364. Exceptions to preceding sections.

Sections 18.2-362 and 18.2-363 shall not extend to a person whose husband or wife shall have been continuously absent from such person for seven years next before marriage of such person to another, and shall not have been known by such person to be living within that time; nor to a person who can show that the second marriage was contracted in good faith under a reasonable belief that the former consort was dead; nor to a person who shall, at the time of the subsequent marriage, have been divorced from the bond of the former marriage; nor to a person whose former marriage was void.

History.
Code 1950, § 20-42; 1975, cc. 14, 15.

§ 18.2-365. Adultery defined; penalty.

Any person, being married, who voluntarily shall have sexual intercourse with any person not his or her spouse shall be guilty of adultery, punishable as a Class 4 misdemeanor.

History.
Code 1950, §§18.1-187, 18.1-190; 1960, c. 358; 1975, cc. 14, 15.

§ 18.2-366. Adultery and fornication by persons forbidden to marry; incest.

A. Any person who commits adultery or fornication with any person whom he or she is forbidden by law to marry shall be guilty of a Class 1 misdemeanor except as provided by subsection B.

B. Any person who commits adultery or fornication with his daughter or granddaughter, or with her son or grandson, or her father or his mother, shall be guilty of a Class 5 felony. However, if a parent or grandparent commits adultery or fornication with his or her child or grandchild, and such child or grandchild is at least thirteen years of age but less than eighteen years of age at the time of the offense, such parent or grandparent shall be guilty of a Class 3 felony.

C. For the purposes of this section, parent includes step-parent, grandparent includes step-grandparent, child includes a step-child, and grandchild includes a step-grandchild.

History.
Code 1950, § 18.1-191; 1960, c. 358; 1975, cc. 14, 15; 1981, c. 397; 1993, c. 703; 2014, c. 542.

§ 18.2-367: Repealed by Acts 2004, c. 459.

§ 18.2-368. Placing or leaving wife for prostitution; penalty.

Any person who, by force, fraud, intimidation, or threats, places or leaves or procures any other person to place or leave his wife in a bawdy place for the purpose of prostitution or unlawful sexual intercourse, anal intercourse, cunnilingus, fellatio, or anilingus is guilty of pandering, punishable as a Class 4 felony.

History.
Code 1950, § 18.1-207; 1960, c. 358; 1975, cc. 14, 15; 2014, c. 794.

§ 18.2-369. Abuse and neglect of incapacitated adults; penalty.

A. It shall be unlawful for any responsible person to abuse or neglect any incapacitated adult as defined in this section. Any responsible person who abuses or neglects an incapacitated adult in violation of this section and the abuse or neglect does not result in serious bodily injury or disease to the incapacitated adult is guilty of a Class 1 misdemeanor. Any responsible person who is convicted of a second or subsequent offense under this subsection is guilty of a Class 6 felony.

B. Any responsible person who abuses or neglects an incapacitated adult in violation of this section and the abuse or neglect results in serious bodily injury or disease to the incapacitated adult is guilty of a Class 4 felony. Any responsible person who abuses or neglects an incapacitated adult in violation of this section and the abuse or neglect results in the death of the incapacitated adult is guilty of a Class 3 felony.

C. For purposes of this section:

"Abuse" means (i) knowing and willful conduct that causes physical injury or pain or (ii) knowing and willful use of physical restraint, including confinement, as punishment, for convenience or as a substitute for treatment, except where such conduct or physical restraint, including confinement, is a part of care or treatment and is in furtherance of the health and safety of the incapacitated person.

"Incapacitated adult" means any person 18 years of age or older who is impaired by reason of mental illness, intellectual disability, physical illness or disability, advanced age or other causes to the extent the adult lacks sufficient understanding or capacity to make, communicate or carry out reasonable decisions concerning his well-being.

"Neglect" means the knowing and willful failure by a responsible person to provide treatment, care, goods or services which results in injury to the health or endangers the safety of an incapacitated adult.

"Responsible person" means a person who has responsibility for the care, custody or control of an incapacitated person by operation of law or who has assumed such responsibility voluntarily, by contract or in fact.

"Serious bodily injury or disease" shall include but not be limited to (i) disfigurement, (ii) a fracture, (iii) a severe burn or laceration, (iv) mutilation, (v) maiming, or (vi) life-threatening internal injuries or conditions, whether or not caused by trauma.

D. No responsible person shall be in violation of this section whose conduct was (i) in accordance with the informed consent of the incapacitated person or a person authorized to consent on his behalf; (ii) in accordance with a declaration by the incapacitated person under the Natural Death Act of Virginia (§ 54.1-2981 et seq.) or with the provisions of a valid medical power of attorney; (iii) in accordance with the wishes of the incapacitated person or a person authorized to consent on behalf of the incapacitated person and in accord with the tenets and practices of a church or religious denomination; (iv) incident to necessary movement of, placement of or protection from harm to the incapacitated person; or (v) a bona fide, recognized or approved practice to provide medical care.

History.

1992, c. 551; 1994, c. 620; 2000, c. 796; 2001, c. 181; 2004, c. 863; 2007, cc. 562, 653; 2012, cc. 476, 507.

§ 18.2-370. Taking indecent liberties with children; penalties.

A. Any person 18 years of age or over, who, with lascivious intent, knowingly and intentionally commits any of the following acts with any child under the age of 15 years is guilty of a Class 5 felony:

(1) Expose his or her sexual or genital parts to any child to whom such person is not legally married or propose that any such child expose his or her sexual or genital parts to such person; or

(2) [Repealed.]

(3) Propose that any such child feel or fondle his own sexual or genital parts or the sexual or genital parts of such person or propose that such person feel or fondle the sexual or genital parts of any such child; or

(4) Propose to such child the performance of an act of sexual intercourse, anal intercourse, cunnilingus, fellatio, or anilingus or any act constituting an offense under § 18.2-361; or

(5) Entice, allure, persuade, or invite any such child to enter any vehicle, room, house, or other place, for any of the purposes set forth in the preceding subdivisions of this subsection.

B. Any person 18 years of age or over who, with lascivious intent, knowingly and intentionally receives money, property, or any other remuneration for allowing, encouraging, or enticing any person under the age of 18 years to perform in or be a subject of sexually explicit visual material as defined in § 18.2-374.1 or who knowingly encourages such person to perform in or be a subject of sexually explicit material is guilty of a Class 5 felony.

C. Any person who is convicted of a second or subsequent violation of this section is guilty of a Class 4 felony, provided that (i) the offenses were not part of a common act, transaction or scheme; (ii) the accused was at liberty as defined in § 53.1-151 between each conviction; and (iii) it is admitted, or found by the jury or judge before whom the person is tried, that the accused was previously convicted of a violation of this section.

D. Any parent, step-parent, grandparent, or step-grandparent who commits a violation of either this section or clause (v) or (vi) of subsection A of § 18.2-370.1 (i) upon his child, step-child, grandchild, or step-grandchild who is at least 15 but less than 18 years of age is guilty of a Class 5 felony or (ii) upon his child, step-child, grandchild, or step-grandchild less than 15 years of age is guilty of a Class 4 felony.

History.

Code 1950, §§ 18.1-213 through 18.1-215; 1960, c. 358; 1973, c. 131; 1975, cc. 14, 15; 1979, c. 348; 1981, c. 397; 1986, c. 503; 2000, c. 333; 2001, cc. 776, 840; 2005, cc. 185, 762; 2013, cc. 423, 470; 2014, c. 794.

§ 18.2-370.01. Indecent liberties by children; penalty.

Any child over the age of thirteen years but under the age of eighteen who, with lascivious intent, knowingly and intentionally exposes his or her sexual or genital parts to any other child under the age of fourteen years who, measured by actual dates of birth, is five or more years the accused's junior, or proposes that any such child expose his or her sexual or genital parts to such person, shall be guilty of a Class 1 misdemeanor.

History.
1998, c. 825.

§ 18.2-370.1. Taking indecent liberties with child by person in custodial or supervisory relationship; penalties.

A. Any person 18 years of age or older who, except as provided in § 18.2-370, maintains a custodial or supervisory relationship over a child under the age of 18 and is not legally married to such child and such child is not emancipated who, with lascivious intent, knowingly and intentionally (i) proposes that any such child feel or fondle the sexual or genital parts of such person or that such person feel or handle the sexual or genital parts of the child; or (ii) proposes to such child the performance of an act of sexual intercourse, anal intercourse, cunnilingus, fellatio, or anilingus or any act constituting an offense under § 18.2-361; or (iii) exposes his or her sexual or genital parts to such child; or (iv) proposes that any such child expose his or her sexual or genital parts to such person; or (v) proposes to the child that the child engage in sexual intercourse, sodomy or fondling of sexual or genital parts with another person; or (vi) sexually abuses the child as defined in subdivision 6 of § 18.2-67.10 is guilty of a Class 6 felony.

B. Any person who is convicted of a second or subsequent violation of this section is guilty of a Class 5 felony, provided that (i) the offenses were not part of a common act, transaction or scheme; (ii) the accused was at liberty as defined in § 53.1-151 between each conviction; and (iii) it is admitted, or found by the jury or judge before whom the person is tried, that the accused was previously convicted of a violation of this section.

History.
1982, c. 521; 1986, c. 503; 1991, c. 517; 2001, c. 840; 2005, c. 185; 2014, c. 794.

§ 18.2-370.2. Sex offenses prohibiting proximity to children; penalty.

A. *"Offense prohibiting proximity to children"* means a violation or an attempt to commit a violation of (i) subsection A of § 18.2-47, clause (ii) or (iii) of § 18.2-48, subsection B of § 18.2-361, or subsection B of § 18.2-366, where the victim of one of the foregoing offenses was a minor, or (ii) subsection A (iii) of § 18.2-61, §§ 18.2-63, 18.2-64.1, subdivision A 1 of § 18.2-67.1, subdivision A 1 of § 18.2-67.2, or subdivision A 1 or A 4 (a) of § 18.2-67.3, or §§ 18.2-370, 18.2-370.1, clause (ii) of § 18.2-371, §§ 18.2-374.1, 18.2-374.1:1 or § 18.2-379. As of July 1, 2006, "offense prohibiting proximity to children" shall include a violation of § 18.2-472.1, when the offense requiring registration was one of the foregoing offenses.

B. Every adult who is convicted of an offense prohibiting proximity to children when the offense occurred on or after July 1, 2000, shall as part of his sentence be forever prohibited from loitering within 100 feet of the premises of any place he knows or has reason to know is a primary, secondary or high school. In addition, every adult who is convicted of an offense prohibiting proximity to children when the offense occurred on or after July 1, 2006, shall as part of his sentence be forever prohibited from loitering within 100 feet of the premises of any place he knows or has reason to know is a child day program as defined in § 63.2-100.

C. Every adult who is convicted of an offense prohibiting proximity to children, when the offense occurred on or after July 1, 2008, shall as part of his sentence be forever prohibited from going, for the purpose of having any contact whatsoever with children that are not in his custody, within 100 feet of the premises of any place owned or operated by a locality that he knows or should know is a playground, athletic field or facility, or gymnasium.

A violation of this section is punishable as a Class 6 felony.

History.
2000, c. 770; 2006, cc. 857, 914; 2008, c. 579.

§ 18.2-370.3. Sex offenses prohibiting residing in proximity to children; penalty.

A. Every adult who is convicted of an offense occurring on or after July 1, 2006, where the offender is more than three years older than the victim, of one of the following qualifying offenses: (i) clause (iii) of subsection A of § 18.2-61, (ii) subdivision A 1 of § 18.2-67.1, or (iii) subdivision A 1 of § 18.2-67.2, shall be forever prohibited from residing within 500 feet of the premises of any place he knows or has reason to know is a child day center as defined in § 63.2-100, or a primary, secondary, or high school. A violation of this section is a Class 6 felony. The provisions of this section shall only apply if the qualifying offense was done in the commission of, or as a part of the same course of conduct as, or as part of a common scheme or plan as a violation of (i) subsection A of § 18.2-47 or § 18.2-48, (ii) § 18.2-89, 18.2-90, or 18.2-91, or (iii) § 18.2-51.2.

B. An adult who is convicted of an offense as specified in subsection A of this section and has established a lawful residence shall not be in violation of this section if a child day center or a primary, secondary, or high school is established within 500 feet of his residence subsequent to his conviction.

C. Every adult who is convicted of an offense occurring on or after July 1, 2008, where the offender is more than three years older than the victim, of one of the following qualifying offenses: (i) clause (iii) of subsection A of § 18.2-61, (ii) subdivision A 1 of § 18.2-67.1, or (iii) subdivision A 1 of

§ 18.2-67.2, shall be forever prohibited from residing within 500 feet of the boundary line of any place he knows is a public park when such park (i) is owned and operated by a county, city or town, (ii) shares a boundary line with a primary, secondary, or high school and (iii) is regularly used for school activities. A violation of this section is a Class 6 felony. The provisions of this section shall only apply if the qualifying offense was done in the commission of, or as a part of the same course of conduct as, or as part of a common scheme or plan as a violation of (i) subsection A of § 18.2-47 or § 18.2-48, (ii) § 18.2-89, 18.2-90, or 18.2-91, or (iii) § 18.2-51.2.

D. An adult who is convicted of an offense as specified in subsection C and has established a lawful residence shall not be in violation of this section if a public park that (i) is owned and operated by a county, city or town, (ii) shares a boundary line with a primary, secondary, or high school, and (iii) is regularly used for school activities, is established within 500 feet of his residence subsequent to his conviction.

History.
2006, cc. 857, 914; 2008, c. 726.

§ 18.2-370.4. Sex offenses prohibiting working on school property; penalty.

A. Every adult who has been convicted of an offense occurring on or after July 1, 2006, where the offender is more than three years older than the victim, of one of the following qualifying offenses: (i) clause (iii) of subsection A of § 18.2-61, (ii) subdivision A 1 of § 18.2-67.1, or (iii) subdivision A 1 of § 18.2-67.2, shall be forever prohibited from working or engaging in any volunteer activity on property he knows or has reason to know is public or private elementary or secondary school or child day center property. A violation of this section is punishable as a Class 6 felony. The provisions of this section shall only apply if the qualifying offense was done in the commission of, or as a part of the same course of conduct of, or as part of a common scheme or plan as a violation of (i) subsection A of § 18.2-47 or 18.2-48, (ii) § 18.2-89, 18.2-90, or 18.2-91, or (iii) § 18.2-51.2.

B. An employer of a person who violates this section, or any person who procures volunteer activity by a person who violates this section, and the school or child day center where the violation of this section occurred, are immune from civil liability unless they had actual knowledge that such person had been convicted of an offense listed in subsection A.

History.
2006, cc. 853, 857, 914.

§ 18.2-370.5. Sex offenses prohibiting entry onto school or other property; penalty.

A. Every adult who is convicted of a sexually violent offense, as defined in § 9.1-902, shall be prohibited from entering or being present (i) during school hours, and during school-related or school-sponsored activities upon any property he knows or has reason to know is a public or private elementary or secondary school or child day center property; (ii) on any school bus as defined in § 46.2-100; or (iii) upon any property, public or private, during hours when such property is solely being used by a public or private elementary or secondary school for a school-related or school-sponsored activity.

B. The provisions of clauses (i) and (iii) of subsection A shall not apply to such adult if (i) he is a lawfully registered and qualified voter, and is coming upon such property solely for purposes of casting his vote; (ii) he is a student enrolled at the school; or (iii) he has obtained a court order pursuant to subsection C allowing him to enter and be present upon such property, has obtained the permission of the school board or of the owner of the private school or child day center or their designee for entry within all or part of the scope of the lifted ban, and is in compliance with such school board's, school's or center's terms and conditions and those of the court order.

C. Every adult who is prohibited from entering upon school or child day center property pursuant to subsection A may after notice to the attorney for the Commonwealth and either (i) the proprietor of the child day center, (ii) the Superintendent of Public Instruction and the chairman of the school board of the school division in which the school is located, or (iii) the chief administrator of the school if such school is not a public school, petition the circuit court in the county or city where the school or child day center is located for permission to enter such property. The court shall direct that the petitioner shall cause notice of the time and place of the hearing on his petition to be published once a week for two successive weeks in a newspaper meeting the requirements of § 8.01-324. The newspaper notice shall contain a provision stating that written comments regarding the petition may be submitted to the clerk of court at least five days prior to the hearing. For good cause shown, the court may issue an order permitting the petitioner to enter and be present on such property, subject to whatever restrictions of area, reasons for being present, or time limits the court deems appropriate.

D. A violation of this section is punishable as a Class 6 felony.

History.
2007, cc. 284, 370; 2008, c. 781; 2010, c. 402; 2011, cc. 648, 796, 855; 2015, c. 688.

§ 18.2-370.6. Penetration of mouth of child with lascivious intent; penalty.

Any person 18 years of age or older who, with lascivious intent, kisses a child under the age of 13 on the mouth while knowingly and intentionally penetrating the mouth of such child with his tongue is guilty of a Class 1 misdemeanor.

History.
2008, c. 772.

§ 18.2-371. Causing or encouraging acts rendering children delinquent, abused, etc.; penalty; abandoned infant.

Any person 18 years of age or older, including the parent of any child, who (i) willfully contributes to, encourages, or causes any act, omission, or condition that renders a child delinquent, in need of services, in need of supervision, or abused or neglected as defined in § 16.1-228 or (ii) engages in consensual sexual intercourse or anal intercourse with or performs cunnilingus, fellatio, or anilingus upon or by a child 15 or older not his spouse, child, or grandchild is guilty of a Class 1 misdemeanor. This section shall not be construed as repealing, modifying, or in any way affecting §§ 18.2-18, 18.2-19, 18.2-61, 18.2-63, and 18.2-347.

If the prosecution under this section is based solely on the accused parent having left the child at a hospital or emergency medical services agency, it shall be an affirmative defense to prosecution of a parent under this section that such parent safely delivered the child to a hospital that provides 24-hour emergency services or to an attended emergency medical services agency that employs emergency medical services personnel, within the first 14 days of the child's life. In order for the affirmative defense to apply, the child shall be delivered in a manner reasonably calculated to ensure the child's safety.

History.
Code 1950, § 18.1-14; 1960, c. 358; 1975, cc. 14, 15; 1981, cc. 397, 568; 1990, c. 797; 1991, c. 295; 1993, c. 411; 2003, cc. 816, 822; 2006, c. 935; 2008, cc. 174, 206; 2014, c. 794; 2015, cc. 502, 503.

§ 18.2-371.1. Abuse and neglect of children; penalty; abandoned infant.

A. Any parent, guardian, or other person responsible for the care of a child under the age of 18 who by willful act or willful omission or refusal to provide any necessary care for the child's health causes or permits serious injury to the life or health of such child is guilty of a Class 4 felony. For purposes of this subsection, "serious injury" includes but is not limited to (i) disfigurement, (ii) a fracture, (iii) a severe burn or laceration, (iv) mutilation, (v) maiming, (vi) forced ingestion of dangerous substances, and (vii) life-threatening internal injuries. For purposes of this subsection, "willful act or willful omission" includes operating or engaging in the conduct of a child welfare agency as defined in § 63.2-100 without first obtaining a license such person knows is required by Subtitle IV (§ 63.2-1700 et seq.) of Title 63.2 or after such license has been revoked or has expired and not been renewed.

B. 1. Any parent, guardian, or other person responsible for the care of a child under the age of 18 whose willful act or omission in the care of such child was so gross, wanton, and culpable as to show a reckless disregard for human life is guilty of a Class 6 felony.

2. If a prosecution under this subsection is based solely on the accused parent having left the child at a hospital or emergency medical services agency, it shall be an affirmative defense to prosecution of a parent under this subsection that such parent safely delivered the child to a hospital that provides 24-hour emergency services or to an attended emergency medical services agency that employs emergency medical services personnel, within the first 14 days of the child's life. In order for the affirmative defense to apply, the child shall be delivered in a manner reasonably calculated to ensure the child's safety.

C. Any parent, guardian, or other person having care, custody, or control of a minor child who in good faith is under treatment solely by spiritual means through prayer in accordance with the tenets and practices of a recognized church or religious denomination shall not, for that reason alone, be considered in violation of this section.

History.
1981, c. 568; 1988, c. 228; 1990, c. 638; 1993, c. 628; 2003, cc. 816, 822; 2006, c. 935; 2015, cc. 502, 503; 2016, c. 705.

§ 18.2-371.2. Prohibiting purchase or possession of tobacco products, nicotine vapor products, and alternative nicotine products by minors or sale of tobacco products, nicotine vapor products, and alternative nicotine products to minors.

A. No person shall sell to, distribute to, purchase for, or knowingly permit the purchase by any person less than 18 years of age, knowing or having reason to believe that such person is less than 18 years of age, any tobacco product, nicotine vapor product, or alternative nicotine product.

Tobacco products may be sold from a vending machine only if the machine is (i) posted with a notice, in a conspicuous manner and place, indicating that the purchase or possession of tobacco products by minors is unlawful and (ii) located in a place which is not open to the general public and is not generally accessible to minors. An establishment which prohibits the presence of minors unless accompanied by an adult is not open to the general public.

B. No person less than 18 years of age shall attempt to purchase, purchase, or possess any tobacco product, nicotine vapor product, or alternative nicotine product. The provisions of this subsection shall not be applicable to the possession of tobacco products, nicotine vapor products, or alternative nicotine products by a person less than 18 years of age making a delivery of tobacco products, nicotine vapor products, or alternative nicotine products in pursuance of his employment. This subsection shall not apply to purchase, attempt to purchase, or possession by a law-enforcement officer or his agent when the same is necessary in the performance of his duties.

C. No person shall sell a tobacco product, nicotine vapor product, or alternative nicotine product to any individual who does not demonstrate, by producing a driver's license or similar photo identification issued by a government agency, that the individual is at least 18 years of age. Such identification is not required from an individual whom the person has reason to believe is at least 18 years of age or who the person knows is at least 18 years of age. Proof that the person demanded, was shown, and reasonably relied upon a photo identification stating that the individual was at least 18 years of age shall be a defense to any action brought under this subsection. In determining whether a person had reason to believe an individual is at least 18 years of age, the trier of fact may consider, but is not limited to, proof of the general appearance, facial characteristics, behavior, and manner of the individual.

This subsection shall not apply to mail order or Internet sales, provided that the person offering the tobacco product, nicotine vapor product, or alternative nicotine product for sale through mail order or the Internet (i) prior to the sale of the tobacco product, nicotine vapor product, or alternative nicotine product verifies that the purchaser is at least 18 years of age through a commercially available database that is regularly used by businesses or governmental entities for the purpose of age and identity verification and (ii) uses a method of mailing, shipping, or delivery that requires the signature of a person at least 18 years of age before the tobacco product, nicotine vapor product, or alternative nicotine product will be released to the purchaser.

D. A violation of subsection A or C by an individual or by a separate retail establishment that involves a nicotine vapor product, alternative nicotine product, or tobacco product other than a bidi is punishable by a civil penalty not to exceed $100 for a first violation, a civil penalty not to exceed $200 for a second violation, and a civil penalty not to exceed $500 for a third or subsequent violation.

A violation of subsection A or C by an individual or by a separate retail establishment that involves the sale, distribution, or purchase of a bidi is punishable by a civil penalty in the amount of $500 for a first violation, a civil penalty in the amount of $1,000 for a second violation, and a civil penalty in the amount of $2,500 for a third or subsequent violation. Where a defendant retail establishment offers proof that it has trained its employees concerning the requirements of this section, the court shall suspend all of the penalties imposed hereunder. However, where the court finds that a retail establishment has failed to so train its employees, the court may impose a civil penalty not to exceed $1,000 in lieu of any penalties imposed hereunder for a violation of subsection A or C involving a nicotine vapor product, alternative nicotine product, or tobacco product other than a bidi.

A violation of subsection B is punishable by a civil penalty not to exceed $100 for a first violation and a civil penalty not to exceed $250 for a second or subsequent violation. A court may, as an alternative to the civil penalty, and upon motion of the defendant, prescribe the performance of up to 20 hours of community service for a first violation of subsection B and up to 40 hours of community service for a second or subsequent violation. If the defendant fails or refuses to complete the community service as prescribed, the court may impose the civil penalty. Upon a violation of subsection B, the judge may enter an order pursuant to subdivision A 9 of § 16.1-278.8.

Any attorney for the Commonwealth of the county or city in which an alleged violation occurred may bring an action to recover the civil penalty, which shall be paid into the state treasury. Any law-enforcement officer may issue a summons for a violation of subsection A, B, or C.

E. 1. Cigarettes shall be sold only in sealed packages provided by the manufacturer, with the required health warning. The proprietor of every retail establishment that offers for sale any tobacco product, nicotine vapor product, or alternative nicotine product shall post in a conspicuous manner and place a sign or signs indicating that the sale of tobacco products, nicotine vapor products, or alternative nicotine products to any person under 18 years of age is prohibited by law. Any attorney for the county, city, or town in which an alleged violation of this subsection occurred may enforce this subsection by civil action to recover a civil penalty not to exceed $50. The civil penalty shall be paid into the local treasury. No filing fee or other fee or cost shall be charged to the county, city, or town which instituted the action.

2. For the purpose of compliance with regulations of the Substance Abuse and Mental Health Services Administration published at 61 Federal Register 1492, the Department of Agriculture and Consumer Services may promulgate regulations which allow the Department to undertake the activities necessary to comply with such regulations.

3. Any attorney for the county, city, or town in which an alleged violation of this subsection occurred may enforce this subsection by civil action to recover a civil penalty not to exceed $100. The civil penalty shall be paid into the local treasury. No filing fee or other fee or cost shall be charged to the county, city, or town which instituted the action.

F. Nothing in this section shall be construed to create a private cause of action.

G. **(Effective until July 1, 2018)** Agents of the Virginia Alcoholic Beverage Control Board designated pursuant to § 4.1-105 may issue a summons for any violation of this section.

G. **(Effective July 1, 2018)** Agents of the Virginia Alcoholic Beverage Control Authority designated pursuant to § 4.1-105 may issue a summons for any violation of this section.

H. As used in this section:

"Alternative nicotine product" means any noncombustible product containing nicotine that is intended for human consumption, whether chewed, absorbed, dissolved, or ingested by any other means. "Alternative nicotine product" does not include any nicotine vapor product, tobacco product, or product regulated as a drug or device by the U.S. Food and Drug Administration (FDA) under Chapter V (21 U.S.C. § 351 et seq.) of the Federal Food, Drug, and Cosmetic Act.

"Bidi" means a product containing tobacco that is wrapped in temburni leaf (diospyros melanoxylon) or tendu leaf (diospyros exculpra), or any other product that is offered to, or purchased by, consumers as a bidi or beedie.

"Nicotine vapor product" means any noncombustible product containing nicotine that employs a heating element, power source, electronic circuit, or other electronic, chemical, or mechanical means, regardless of shape or size, that can be used to produce vapor from nicotine in a solution or other form. "Nicotine vapor product" includes any electronic cigarette, electronic cigar, electronic cigarillo, electronic pipe, or similar product or device and any cartridge or other container of nicotine in a solution or other form that is intended to be used with or in an electronic cigarette, electronic cigar, electronic cigarillo, electronic pipe, or similar product or device. "Nicotine vapor product" does not include any product regulated by the FDA under Chapter V (21 U.S.C. § 351 et seq.) of the Federal Food, Drug, and Cosmetic Act.

"Tobacco product" means any product made of tobacco and includes cigarettes, cigars, smokeless tobacco, pipe tobacco, bidis, and wrappings. "Tobacco product" does not include any nicotine vapor product, alternative nicotine product, or product that is regulated by the FDA under Chapter V (21 U.S.C. § 351 et seq.) of the Federal Food, Drug, and Cosmetic Act.

"Wrappings" includes papers made or sold for covering or rolling tobacco or other materials for smoking in a manner similar to a cigarette or cigar.

History.

1986, c. 406; 1991, c. 558; 1993, c. 631; 1994, c. 305; 1995, c. 675; 1996, cc. 509, 517; 1997, cc. 812, 882; 1998, c. 363; 1999, c. 1020; 2000, c. 883; 2003, cc. 114, 615; 2014, cc. 357, 394; 2015, cc. 38, 730, 739, 756.

§ 18.2-371.3. Tattooing or body piercing of minors.

No person shall tattoo or perform body piercing for hire or consideration on a person less than eighteen years of age, knowing or having reason to believe such person is less than eighteen years of age except (i) in the presence of the person's parent or guardian, or (ii) when done by or under the supervision of a medical doctor, registered nurse or other medical services personnel licensed pursuant to Title 54.1 in the performance of their duties.

In addition, no person shall tattoo or perform body piercing on any client unless he complies with the Centers for Disease Control and Prevention's guidelines for "Universal Blood and Body Fluid Precautions" and provides the client with the following disclosure:

1. Tattooing and body piercing are invasive procedures in which the skin is penetrated by a foreign object.

2. If proper sterilization and antiseptic procedures are not followed by tattoo artists and body piercers, there is a risk of transmission of bloodborne pathogens and other infections, including, but not limited to, human immunodeficiency viruses and hepatitis B or C viruses.

3. Tattooing and body piercing may cause allergic reactions in persons sensitive to dyes or the metals used in ornamentation.

4. Tattooing and body piercing may involve discomfort or pain for which appropriate anesthesia cannot be legally made available by the person performing the tattoo or body piercing unless such person holds the appropriate license from a Virginia health regulatory board.

A person who violates this section is guilty of a Class 1 misdemeanor.

For the purposes of this section:

"Body-piercing" means the act of penetrating the skin to make a hole, mark, or scar, generally permanent in nature. "Body piercing" does not include the use of a mechanized, presterilized ear-piercing system that penetrates the outer perimeter or lobe of the ear or both.

"Tattoo" means to place any design, letter, scroll, figure, symbol or any other mark upon or under the skin of any person with ink or any other substance resulting in the permanent coloration of the skin, including permanent make-up or permanent jewelry, by the aid of needles or any other instrument designed to touch or puncture the skin.

History.

1997, c. 586; 2000, c. 842; 2001, c. 270; 2006, c. 692.

§ 18.2-371.4. Prohibiting the sale of novelty lighters to juveniles.

A. "Novelty lighter" means a mechanical or electrical device containing a combustible fuel typically used for lighting cigarettes, cigars, or pipes that is (i) designed to resemble a cartoon character, toy, gun, watch, musical instrument, vehicle, animal, food, or beverage, or (ii) a fanciful article that plays musical notes, has flashing lights, or has other entertaining features that are appealing to or intended for use by juveniles. A novelty lighter may operate on any fuel, including butane, isobutene, or liquid fuel.

B. "Novelty lighter" does not include (i) a lighter without fuel and that is incapable of being fueled, (ii) a lighter lacking a device necessary to produce combustion or a flame, (iii) a mechanical or electrical device primarily used to ignite fuel for fireplaces or for charcoal or gas grills, (iv) a lighter manufactured prior to 1980, or (v) a standard disposable lighter that is printed or decorated with logos, labels, decals, or artwork, or heat shrinkable sleeves.

C. Novelty lighters that are available for purchase at a retail establishment shall be located in a place that is not open to the general public.

D. Any individual who sells a novelty lighter to a person he knows or has reason to know is a juvenile is subject to a civil penalty of no more than $100.

E. This section may be enforced by the State Fire Marshal's Office, local fire marshals appointed pursuant to § 27-34.2 or 27-34.2:1, or law-enforcement officers.

History.
2009, c. 668.

ARTICLE 5.

OBSCENITY AND RELATED OFFENSES.

§ 18.2-372. "Obscene" defined.

The word *"obscene"* where it appears in this article shall mean that which, considered as a whole, has as its dominant theme or purpose an appeal to the prurient interest in sex, that is, a shameful or morbid interest in nudity, sexual conduct, sexual excitement, excretory functions or products thereof or sadomasochistic abuse, and which goes substantially beyond customary limits of candor in description or representation of such matters and which, taken as a whole, does not have serious literary, artistic, political or scientific value.

History.
Code 1950, § 18.1-227; 1960, c. 233; 1975, cc. 14, 15.

§ 18.2-373. Obscene items enumerated.

Obscene items shall include:

(1) Any obscene book;

(2) Any obscene leaflet, pamphlet, magazine, booklet, picture, painting, bumper sticker, drawing, photograph, film, negative, slide, motion picture, videotape recording;

(3) Any obscene figure, object, article, instrument, novelty device, or recording or transcription used or intended to be used in disseminating any obscene song, ballad, words, or sounds; or

(4) Any obscene writing, picture or similar visual representation, or sound recording, stored in an electronic or other medium retrievable in a perceivable form.

History.
Code 1950, § 18.1-229; 1960, c. 233; 1975, cc. 14, 15; 1981, c. 293; 1989, c. 546; 2000, c. 1009.

§ 18.2-374. Production, publication, sale, possession, etc., of obscene items.

It shall be unlawful for any person knowingly to:

(1) Prepare any obscene item for the purposes of sale or distribution; or

(2) Print, copy, manufacture, produce, or reproduce any obscene item for purposes of sale or distribution; or

(3) Publish, sell, rent, lend, transport in intrastate commerce, or distribute or exhibit any obscene item, or offer to do any of these things; or

(4) Have in his possession with intent to sell, rent, lend, transport, or distribute any obscene item. Possession in public or in a public place of any obscene item as defined in this article shall be deemed prima facie evidence of a violation of this section.

For the purposes of this section, *"distribute"* shall mean delivery in person, by mail, messenger or by any other means by which obscene items as defined in this article may pass from one person, firm or corporation to another.

History.
Code 1950, § 18.1-228; 1960, c. 233; 1962, c. 289; 1970, c. 204; 1975, cc. 14, 15.

§ 18.2-374.1. Production, publication, sale, financing, etc., of child pornography; presumption as to age.

A. For purposes of this article and Article 4 (§ 18.2-362 et seq.) of this chapter, "child pornography" means sexually explicit visual material which utilizes or has as a subject an identifiable minor. An identifiable minor is a person who was a minor at the time the visual depiction was created, adapted, or modified; or whose image as a minor was used in creating, adapting or modifying the visual depiction; and who is recognizable as an actual person by the person's face, likeness, or other distinguishing characteristic, such as a unique birthmark or other recognizable feature; and shall not be construed to require proof of the actual identity of the identifiable minor.

For the purposes of this article and Article 4 (§ 18.2-362 et seq.) of this chapter, the term "sexually explicit visual material" means a picture, photograph, drawing, sculpture, motion picture film, digital image, including such material stored in a computer's temporary Internet cache when three or more images or streaming videos are present, or similar visual representation which depicts sexual bestiality, a lewd exhibition of nudity, as nudity is defined in § 18.2-390, or sexual excitement, sexual conduct or sadomasochistic abuse, as also defined in § 18.2-390, or a book, magazine or pamphlet which contains such a visual representation. An undeveloped photograph or similar visual material may be sexually explicit material notwithstanding that processing or other acts may be required to make its sexually explicit content apparent.

B. A person shall be guilty of production of child pornography who:

1. Accosts, entices or solicits a person less than 18 years of age with intent to induce or force such person to perform in or be a subject of child pornography; or

2. Produces or makes or attempts or prepares to produce or make child pornography; or

3. Who knowingly takes part in or participates in the filming, photographing, or other production of child pornography by any means; or

4. Knowingly finances or attempts or prepares to finance child pornography.

5. [Repealed.]

B1. [Repealed.]

C1. Any person who violates this section, when the subject of the child pornography is a child less than 15 years of age, shall be punished by not less than five years nor more than 30 years in a state correctional facility. However, if the person is at least seven years older than the subject of the child pornography the person shall be punished by a term of imprisonment of not less than five years nor more than 30 years in a state correctional facility, five years of which shall be a mandatory minimum term of imprisonment. Any person who commits a second or subsequent violation of this section where the person is at least seven years older than the subject shall be punished by a term of imprisonment of not less than 15 years nor more than 40 years, 15 years of which shall be a mandatory minimum term of imprisonment.

C2. Any person who violates this section, when the subject of the child pornography is a person at least 15 but less than 18 years of age, shall be punished by not less than one year nor more than 20 years in a state correctional facility. However, if the person is at least seven years older than the subject of the child pornography the person shall be punished by term of imprisonment of not less than three years nor more than 30 years in a state correctional facility, three years of which shall be a mandatory minimum term of imprisonment. Any person who commits a second or subsequent violation of this section when he is at least seven years older than the subject shall be punished by a term of imprisonment of not less than 10 years nor more than 30 years, 10 years of which shall be a mandatory minimum term of imprisonment.

C3. The mandatory minimum terms of imprisonment prescribed for violations of this section shall be served consecutively with any other sentence.

D. For the purposes of this section it may be inferred by text, title or appearance that a person who is depicted as or presents the appearance of being less than 18 years of age in sexually explicit visual material is less than 18 years of age.

E. Venue for a prosecution under this section may lie in the jurisdiction where the unlawful act occurs or where any sexually explicit visual material associated with a violation of this section is produced, reproduced, found, stored, or possessed.

History.
1979, c. 348; 1983, c. 524; 1986, c. 585; 1992, c. 234; 1995, c. 839; 2007, cc. 418, 759, 823; 2013, cc. 761, 774; 2015, c. 709.

§ 18.2-374.1:1. Possession, reproduction, distribution, solicitation, and facilitation of child pornography; penalty.

A. Any person who knowingly possesses child pornography is guilty of a Class 6 felony.

B. Any person who commits a second or subsequent violation of subsection A is guilty of a Class 5 felony.

C. Any person who knowingly (i) reproduces by any means, including by computer, sells, gives away, distributes, electronically transmits, displays, purchases, or possesses with intent to sell, give away, distribute, transmit, or display child pornography or (ii) commands, entreats, or otherwise attempts to persuade another person to send, submit, transfer or provide to him any child pornography in order to gain entry into a group, association, or assembly of persons engaged in trading or sharing child pornography shall be punished by not less than five years nor more than 20 years in a state correctional facility. Any person who commits a second or subsequent violation under this subsection shall be punished by a term of imprisonment of not less than five years nor more than 20 years in a state correctional facility, five years of which shall be a mandatory minimum term of imprisonment. The mandatory minimum terms of imprisonment prescribed for violations of this section shall be served consecutively with any other sentence.

D. Any person who intentionally operates an Internet website for the purpose of facilitating the payment for access to child pornography is guilty of a Class 4 felony.

E. All child pornography shall be subject to lawful seizure and forfeiture pursuant to § 19.2-386.31.

F. For purposes of this section it may be inferred by text, title or appearance that a person who is depicted as or presents the appearance of being less than 18 years of age in sexually explicit visual material is less than 18 years of age.

G. Venue for a prosecution under this section may lie in the jurisdiction where the unlawful act occurs or where any child pornography is produced, reproduced, found, stored, received, or possessed in violation of this section.

H. The provisions of this section shall not apply to any such material that is possessed for a bona fide medical, scientific, governmental, law-enforcement, or judicial purpose by a physician, psychologist, scientist, attorney, employee of a law-enforcement agency, judge, or clerk who possesses such material in the course of conducting his professional duties as such.

History.

1992, c. 745; 1993, c. 853; 1994, c. 511; 1999, c. 659; 2003, cc. 935, 938; 2004, c. 995; 2007, cc. 759, 823; 2009, c. 379; 2011, cc. 399, 416; 2012, c. 369; 2013, cc. 761, 774; 2014, c. 291; 2015, c. 428.

§ 18.2-374.1:2: Repealed by Acts 2007, cc. 759 and 823, cl. 2.

§ 18.2-374.2: Repealed by Acts 2004, c. 995.

Cross references.

For current provisions as to seizure and forfeiture of property used in connection with production of sexually explicit items involving children, see § 19.2-386.31.

§ 18.2-374.3. Use of communications systems to facilitate certain offenses involving children.

A. As used in subsections C, D, and E, "use a communications system" means making personal contact or direct contact through any agent or agency, any print medium, the United States mail, any common carrier or communication common carrier, any electronic communications system, the Internet, or any telecommunications, wire, computer network, or radio communications system.

B. It is unlawful for any person to use a communications system, including but not limited to computers or computer networks or bulletin boards, or any other electronic means for the purposes of procuring or promoting the use of a minor for any activity in violation of § 18.2-370 or 18.2-374.1. A violation of this subsection is a Class 6 felony.

C. It is unlawful for any person 18 years of age or older to use a communications system, including but not limited to computers or computer networks or bulletin boards, or any other electronic means, for the purposes of soliciting, with lascivious intent, any person he knows or has reason to believe is a child younger than 15 years of age to knowingly and intentionally:

1. Expose his sexual or genital parts to any child to whom he is not legally married or propose that any such child expose his sexual or genital parts to such person;

2. Propose that any such child feel or fondle his own sexual or genital parts or the sexual or genital parts of such person or propose that such person feel or fondle the sexual or genital parts of any such child;

3. Propose to such child the performance of an act of sexual intercourse, anal intercourse, cunnilingus, fellatio, or anilingus or any act constituting an offense under § 18.2-361; or

4. Entice, allure, persuade, or invite any such child to enter any vehicle, room, house, or other place, for any purposes set forth in the preceding subdivisions.

Any person who violates this subsection is guilty of a Class 5 felony. However, if the person is at least seven years older than the child he knows or has reason to believe is less than 15 years of age, the person shall be punished by a term of imprisonment of not less than five years nor more than 30 years in a state correctional facility, five years of which shall be mandatory minimum term of imprisonment. Any person who commits a second or subsequent violation of this subsection when the person is at least seven years older than the child he knows or has reason to believe is less than 15 years of age shall be punished by a term of imprisonment of not less than 10 years nor more than 40 years, 10 years of which shall be a mandatory minimum term of imprisonment.

D. Any person who uses a communications system, including but not limited to computers or computer networks or bulletin boards, or any other electronic means, for the purposes of soliciting, with lascivious intent, any child he knows or has reason to believe is at least 15 years of age but younger than 18 years of age to knowingly and intentionally commit any of the activities listed in subsection C if the person is at least seven years older than the child is guilty of a Class 5 felony. Any person who commits a second or subsequent violation of this subsection shall be punished by a term of imprisonment of not less than one nor more than 20 years, one year of which shall be a mandatory minimum term of imprisonment.

E. Any person 18 years of age or older who uses a communications system, including but not limited to computers or computer networks or bulletin boards, or any other electronic means, for the purposes of soliciting any person he knows or has reason to believe is a child younger than 18 years of age for (i) any activity in violation of § 18.2-355 or 18.2-361, (ii) any activity in violation of § 18.2-374.1, or (iii) a violation of § 18.2-374.1:1 is guilty of a Class 5 felony.

History.

1992, c. 699; 1999, c. 659; 2003, cc. 935, 938; 2004, cc. 414, 444, 459, 864; 2007, cc. 759, 823; 2013, cc. 423, 470; 2014, c. 794.

§ 18.2-374.4. Display of child pornography or grooming video or materials to a child unlawful; penalty.

A. Any person 18 years of age or older who displays child pornography or a grooming video or materials to a child under 13 years of age with the intent to entice, solicit, or encourage the child to engage in the fondling of the sexual or genital parts of another or the fondling of his sexual or genital parts by another, sexual intercourse, cunnilingus, fellatio, anilingus, anal intercourse, or object sexual penetration is guilty of a Class 6 felony.

B. "Grooming video or materials" means a cartoon, animation, image, or series of images depicting a child engaged in the fondling of the sexual or genital parts of another or the fondling of his sexual or genital parts by another, masturbation, sexual intercourse, cunnilingus, fellatio, anilingus, anal intercourse, or object sexual penetration.

History.
2012, c. 624.

§ 18.2-375. Obscene exhibitions and performances.

It shall be unlawful for any person knowingly to:

(1) Produce, promote, prepare, present, manage, direct, carry on or participate in, any obscene exhibitions or performances, including the exhibition or performance of any obscene motion picture, play, drama, show, entertainment, exposition, tableau or scene; provided, that no employee of any person or legal entity operating a theatre, garden, building, structure, room or place which presents such obscene exhibition or performance shall be subject to prosecution under this section if the employee is not the manager of the theatre or an officer of such entity, and has no financial interest in such theatre other than receiving salary and wages; or

(2) Own, lease or manage any theatre, garden, building, structure, room or place and lease, let, lend or permit such theatre, garden, building, structure, room or place to be used for the purpose of presenting such obscene exhibition or performance or to fail to post prominently therein the name and address of a person resident in the locality who is the manager of such theatre, garden, building, structure, room or place.

History.
Code 1950, § 18.1-230; 1960, c. 233; 1971, Ex. Sess., c. 191; 1975, cc. 14, 15.

§ 18.2-376. Advertising, etc., obscene items, exhibitions or performances.

It shall be unlawful for any person knowingly to prepare, print, publish, or circulate, or cause to be prepared, printed, published or circulated, any notice or advertisement of any obscene item proscribed in § 18.2-373, or of any obscene performance or exhibition proscribed in § 18.2-375, stating or indicating where such obscene item, exhibition, or performance may be purchased, obtained, seen or heard.

History.
Code 1950, § 18.1-231; 1960, c. 233; 1975, cc. 14, 15.

§ 18.2-376.1. Enhanced penalties for using a computer in certain violations.

Any person who uses a computer in connection with a violation of §§ 18.2-374, 18.2-375, or § 18.2-376 is guilty of a separate and distinct Class 1 misdemeanor, and for a second or subsequent such offense within 10 years of a prior such offense is guilty of a Class 6 felony, the penalties to be imposed in addition to any other punishment otherwise prescribed for a violation of any of those sections.

History.
2003, cc. 987, 1016.

§ 18.2-377. Placards, posters, bills, etc.

It shall be unlawful for any person knowingly to expose, place, display, post up, exhibit, paint, print, or mark, or cause to be exposed, placed, displayed, posted, exhibited, painted, printed or marked, in or on any building, structure, billboard, wall or fence, or on any street, or in or upon any public place, any placard, poster, banner, bill, writing, or picture which is obscene, or which advertises or promotes any obscene item proscribed in § 18.2-373 or any obscene exhibition or performance proscribed in § 18.2-375, or knowingly to permit the same to be displayed on property belonging to or controlled by him.

History.
Code 1950, § 18.1-232; 1960, c. 233; 1975, cc. 14, 15.

§ 18.2-378. Coercing acceptance of obscene articles or publications.

It shall be unlawful for any person, firm, association or corporation, as a condition to any sale, allocation, consignment or delivery for resale of any paper, magazine, book, periodical or publication to require that the purchaser or consignee receive for resale any other article, book, or other publication which is obscene; nor shall any person, firm, association or corporation deny or threaten to deny any franchise or impose or threaten to impose any penalty, financial or otherwise, by reason of the failure or refusal of any person to accept such articles, books, or publications, or by reason of the return thereof.

History.
Code 1950, § 18.1-233; 1960, c. 233; 1975, cc. 14, 15.

§ 18.2-379. Employing or permitting minor to assist in offense under article.

It shall be unlawful for any person knowingly to hire, employ, use or permit any minor to do or assist in doing any act or thing constituting an offense under this article.

History.
Code 1950, § 18.1-234; 1960, c. 233; 1975, cc. 14, 15.

§ 18.2-380. Punishment for first offense.

Any person, firm, association or corporation convicted for the first time of an offense under §§ 18.2-

374, 18.2-375, 18.2-376, 18.2-377, 18.2-378 or § 18.2-379, shall be guilty of a Class 1 misdemeanor.

History.
Code 1950, § 18.1-235.1; 1968, c. 662; 1975, cc. 14, 15; 1983, c. 412; 1985, c. 279.

§ 18.2-381. Punishment for subsequent offenses; additional penalty for owner.

Any person, firm, association or corporation convicted of a second or other subsequent offense under § 18.2-374, 18.2-375, 18.2-376, 18.2-377, 18.2-378, or 18.2-379 is guilty of a Class 6 felony. However, if the person, firm, association or corporation convicted of such subsequent offense is the owner of the business establishment where each of the offenses occurred, a fine of not more than $10,000 shall be imposed in addition to the penalties otherwise prescribed by this section.

History.
Code 1950, § 18.1-236.1; 1960, c. 233; 1968, c. 662; 1975, cc. 14, 15; 1983, c. 412; 2015, c. 428.

§ 18.2-382. Photographs, slides and motion pictures.

Every person who knowingly:

(1) Photographs himself or any other person, for purposes of preparing an obscene film, photograph, negative, slide or motion picture for purposes of sale or distribution; or

(2) Models, poses, acts, or otherwise assists in the preparation of any obscene film, photograph, negative, slide or motion picture for purposes of sale or distribution;

shall be guilty of a Class 3 misdemeanor.

History.
Code 1950, § 18.1-235; 1960, c. 233; 1970, c. 204; 1975, cc. 14, 15.

§ 18.2-383. Exceptions to application of article.

Nothing contained in this article shall be construed to apply to:

(1) The purchase, distribution, exhibition, or loan of any book, magazine, or other printed or manuscript material by any library, school, or institution of higher learning, supported by public appropriation;

(2) The purchase, distribution, exhibition, or loan of any work of art by any museum of fine arts, school, or institution of higher learning, supported by public appropriation;

(3) The exhibition or performance of any play, drama, tableau, or motion picture by any theatre, museum of fine arts, school or institution of higher learning, supported by public appropriation.

History.
Code 1950, § 18.1-236.2; 1960, c. 233; 1966, c. 516; 1975, cc. 14, 15.

§ 18.2-384. Proceeding against book alleged to be obscene.

(1) Whenever he has reasonable cause to believe that any person is engaged in the sale or commercial distribution of any obscene book, any citizen or the attorney for the Commonwealth of any county or city, or city attorney, in which the sale or commercial distribution of such book occurs may institute a proceeding in the circuit court in said city or county for adjudication of the obscenity of the book.

(2) The proceeding shall be instituted by filing with the court a petition:

(a) Directed against the book by name or description;

(b) Alleging the obscene nature of the book; and

(c) Listing the names and addresses, if known, of the author, publisher, and all other persons interested in its sale or commercial distribution.

(3) Upon the filing of a petition pursuant to this article, the court in term or in vacation shall forthwith examine the book alleged to be obscene. If the court find no probable cause to believe the book obscene, the judge thereof shall dismiss the petition; but if the court find probable cause to believe the book obscene, the judge thereof shall issue an order to show cause why the book should not be adjudicated obscene.

(4) The order to show cause shall be:

(a) Directed against the book by name or description;

(b) Published once a week for two successive weeks in a newspaper of general circulation within the county or city in which the proceeding is filed;

(c) If their names and addresses are known, served by registered mail upon the author, publisher, and all other persons interested in the sale or commercial distribution of the book; and

(d) Returnable twenty-one days after its service by registered mail or the commencement of its publication, whichever is later.

(5) When an order to show cause is issued pursuant to this article, and upon four days' notice to be given to the persons and in the manner prescribed by the court, the court may issue a temporary restraining order against the sale or distribution of the book alleged to be obscene.

(6) On or before the return date specified in the order to show cause, the author, publisher, and any person interested in the sale or commercial distribution of the book may appear and file an answer. The court may by order permit any other person to appear and file an answer amicus curiae.

(7) If no one appears and files an answer on or before the return date specified in the order to show cause, the court, upon being satisfied that the book is obscene, shall order the clerk of court to enter judgment that the book is obscene, but the court in its discretion may except from its judgment a restricted category of persons to whom the book is not obscene.

(8) If an appearance is entered and an answer filed, the court shall order the proceeding set on the calendar for a prompt hearing. The court shall conduct the hearing in accordance with the rules of civil procedure applicable to the trial of cases by the court without a jury. At the hearing, the court shall receive evidence, including the testimony of experts, if such evidence be offered, pertaining to:

(a) The artistic, literary, medical, scientific, cultural and educational values, if any, of the book considered as a whole;

(b) The degree of public acceptance of the book, or books of similar character, within the county or city in which the proceeding is brought;

(c) The intent of the author and publisher of the book;

(d) The reputation of the author and publisher;

(e) The advertising, promotion, and other circumstances relating to the sale of the book;

(f) The nature of classes of persons, including scholars, scientists, and physicians, for whom the book may not have prurient appeal, and who may be subject to exception pursuant to subsection (7).

(9) In making a decision on the obscenity of the book, the court shall consider, among other things, the evidence offered pursuant to subsection (8), if any, and shall make a written determination upon every such consideration relied upon in the proceeding in his findings of fact and conclusions of law or in a memorandum accompanying them.

(10) If he finds the book not obscene, the court shall order the clerk of court to enter judgment accordingly. If he finds the book obscene, the court shall order the clerk of court to enter judgment that the book is obscene, but the court, in its discretion, may except from its judgment a restricted category of persons to whom the book is not obscene.

(11) While a temporary restraining order made pursuant to subsection (5) is in effect, or after the entry of a judgment pursuant to subsection (7), or after the entry of judgment pursuant to subsection (10), any person who publishes, sells, rents, lends, transports in intrastate commerce, or commercially distributes or exhibits the book, or has the book in his possession with intent to publish, sell, rent, lend, transport in intrastate commerce, or commercially distribute or exhibit the book, is presumed to have knowledge that the book is obscene under §§ 18.2-372 through 18.2-378 of this article.

(12) Any party to the proceeding, including the petitioner, may appeal from the judgment of the court to the Supreme Court of Virginia, as otherwise provided by law.

(13) It is expressly provided that the petition and proceeding authorized under this article, relating to books alleged to be obscene, shall be intended only to establish scienter in cases where the establishment of such scienter is thought to be useful or desirable by the petitioner; and the provisions of § 18.2-384 shall in nowise be construed to be a necessary prerequisite to the filing of criminal charges under this article.

History.

Code 1950, § 18.1-236.3; 1960, c. 233; 1975, cc. 14, 15.

§ 18.2-385. Section 18.2-384 applicable to motion picture films.

The provisions of § 18.2-384 shall apply mutatis mutandis in the case of motion picture film.

History.

Code 1950, § 18.1-236.4; 1966, c. 516; 1975, cc. 14, 15.

§ 18.2-386. Showing previews of certain motion pictures.

It shall be unlawful for any person to exhibit any trailer or preview of any motion picture which has a motion picture industry rating which would not permit persons in the audience viewing the feature motion picture to see the complete motion picture from which the trailer or preview is taken. Persons violating the provisions of this section shall be guilty of a Class 1 misdemeanor.

History.

Code 1950, § 18.1-246.1; 1970, c. 504; 1975, cc. 14, 15.

§ 18.2-386.1. Unlawful creation of image of another; penalty.

A. It shall be unlawful for any person to knowingly and intentionally create any videographic or still image by any means whatsoever of any nonconsenting person if (i) that person is totally nude, clad in undergarments, or in a state of undress so as to expose the genitals, pubic area, buttocks or female breast in a restroom, dressing room, locker room, hotel room, motel room, tanning bed, tanning booth, bedroom or other location; or (ii) the videographic or still image is created by placing the lens or image-gathering component of the recording device in a position directly beneath or between a person's legs for the purpose of capturing an image of the person's intimate parts or undergarments covering those intimate parts when the intimate parts or undergarments would not otherwise be visible to the general public; and when the circumstances set forth in clause (i) or (ii) are otherwise such that the person being recorded would have a reasonable expectation of privacy.

B. The provisions of this section shall not apply to any videographic or still image created by any means whatsoever by (i) law-enforcement officers pursuant to a criminal investigation which is otherwise lawful or (ii) correctional officials and local or regional jail officials for security purposes or for investigations of alleged misconduct involving a person committed to the Department of Corrections or to a local or regional jail, or to any sound recording of an oral conversation made as a result of any videotaping or filming pursuant to Chapter 6 (§ 19.2-61 et seq.) of Title 19.2.

Crimes and Offenses

C. A violation of subsection A shall be punishable as a Class 1 misdemeanor.

D. A violation of subsection A involving a nonconsenting person under the age of 18 shall be punishable as a Class 6 felony.

E. Where it is alleged in the warrant, information, or indictment on which the person is convicted and found by the court or jury trying the case that the person has previously been convicted within the 10-year period immediately preceding the offense charged of two or more of the offenses specified in this section, each such offense occurring on a different date, and when such offenses were not part of a common act, transaction, or scheme, and such person has been at liberty as defined in § 53.1-151 between each conviction, he shall be guilty of a Class 6 felony.

History.
1994, c. 640; 2004, c. 844; 2005, c. 375; 2008, c. 732; 2014, c. 399.

§ 18.2-386.2. Unlawful dissemination or sale of images of another; penalty.

A. Any person who, with the intent to coerce, harass, or intimidate, maliciously disseminates or sells any videographic or still image created by any means whatsoever that depicts another person who is totally nude, or in a state of undress so as to expose the genitals, pubic area, buttocks, or female breast, where such person knows or has reason to know that he is not licensed or authorized to disseminate or sell such videographic or still image is guilty of a Class 1 misdemeanor. However, if a person uses services of an Internet service provider, an electronic mail service provider, or any other information service, system, or access software provider that provides or enables computer access by multiple users to a computer server in committing acts prohibited under this section, such provider shall not be held responsible for violating this section for content provided by another person.

B. Venue for a prosecution under this section may lie in the jurisdiction where the unlawful act occurs or where any videographic or still image created by any means whatsoever is produced, reproduced, found, stored, received, or possessed in violation of this section.

C. The provisions of this section shall not preclude prosecution under any other statute.

History.
2014, c. 399.

§ 18.2-387. Indecent exposure.

Every person who intentionally makes an obscene display or exposure of his person, or the private parts thereof, in any public place, or in any place where others are present, or procures another to so expose himself, shall be guilty of a Class 1 misdemeanor. No person shall be deemed to be in violation of this section for breastfeeding a child in any public place or any place where others are present.

History.
Code 1950, § 18.1-236; 1960, c. 233; 1975, cc. 14, 15; 1994, c. 398.

§ 18.2-387.1. Obscene sexual display; penalty.

Any person who, while in any public place where others are present, intending that he be seen by others, intentionally and obscenely as defined in § 18.2-372, engages in actual or explicitly simulated acts of masturbation, is guilty of a Class 1 misdemeanor.

History.
2005, c. 422.

§ 18.2-388. Profane swearing and intoxication in public; penalty; transportation of public inebriates to detoxification center.

If any person profanely curses or swears or is intoxicated in public, whether such intoxication results from alcohol, narcotic drug or other intoxicant or drug of whatever nature, he shall be deemed guilty of a Class 4 misdemeanor. In any area in which there is located a court-approved detoxification center a law-enforcement officer may authorize the transportation, by police or otherwise, of public inebriates to such detoxification center in lieu of arrest; however, no person shall be involuntarily detained in such center.

History.
Code 1950, § 18.1-237; 1960, c. 358; 1964, c. 434; 1975, cc. 14, 15; 1979, c. 654; 1982, c. 666; 1983, c. 187; 1990, c. 965.

§ 18.2-389: Repealed by Acts 2004, c. 462.

Cross references.
For current provisions as to adoption of ordinances prohibiting obscenity, see § 15.2-926.2.

ARTICLE 6.
PROHIBITED SALES AND LOANS TO JUVENILES.

§ 18.2-390. Definitions.

As used in this article:

(1) *"Juvenile"* means a person less than 18 years of age.

(2) *"Nudity"* means a state of undress so as to expose the human male or female genitals, pubic area or buttocks with less than a full opaque covering, or the showing of the female breast with less than a fully opaque covering of any portion thereof below the top of the nipple, or the depiction of covered or uncovered male genitals in a discernibly turgid state.

(3) *"Sexual conduct"* means actual or explicitly simulated acts of masturbation, homosexuality, sexual intercourse, or physical contact in an act of apparent sexual stimulation or gratification with a person's clothed or unclothed genitals, pubic area, buttocks or, if such be female, breast.

(4) *"Sexual excitement"* means the condition of human male or female genitals when in a state of sexual stimulation or arousal.

(5) *"Sadomasochistic abuse"* means actual or explicitly simulated flagellation or torture by or upon a person who is nude or clad in undergarments, a mask or bizarre costume, or the condition of being fettered, bound or otherwise physically restrained on the part of one so clothed.

(6) *"Harmful to juveniles"* means that quality of any description or representation, in whatever form, of nudity, sexual conduct, sexual excitement, or sadomasochistic abuse, when it (a) predominantly appeals to the prurient, shameful or morbid interest of juveniles, (b) is patently offensive to prevailing standards in the adult community as a whole with respect to what is suitable material for juveniles, and (c) is, when taken as a whole, lacking in serious literary, artistic, political or scientific value for juveniles.

(7) *"Knowingly"* means having general knowledge of, or reason to know, or a belief or ground for belief which warrants further inspection or inquiry of both (a) the character and content of any material described herein which is reasonably susceptible of examination by the defendant, and (b) the age of the juvenile, provided however, that an honest mistake shall constitute an excuse from liability hereunder if the defendant made a reasonable bona fide attempt to ascertain the true age of such juvenile.

(8) *"Video or computer game"* means an object or device that stores recorded data or instructions, receives data or instructions generated by a person who uses it, and, by processing the data or instructions, creates an interactive game capable of being played, viewed, or experienced on or through a computer, television gaming system, console, or other technology.

History.

Code 1950, § 18.1-236.6; 1970, c. 560; 1975, cc. 14, 15, 492; 1976, c. 504; 2006, c. 463.

§ 18.2-391. Unlawful acts; penalties.

A. It shall be unlawful for any person to sell, rent or loan to a juvenile, knowing or having reason to know that such person is a juvenile, or to knowingly display for commercial purpose in a manner whereby juveniles may examine and peruse:

1. Any picture, photography, drawing, sculpture, motion picture in any format or medium, video or computer game, electronic file or message containing an image, or similar visual representation or image of a person or portion of the human body which depicts sexually explicit nudity, sexual conduct or sadomasochistic abuse and which is harmful to juveniles, or

2. Any book, pamphlet, magazine, printed matter however reproduced, electronic file or message containing words, or sound recording which contains any matter enumerated in subdivision 1 of this subsection, or explicit and detailed verbal descriptions or narrative accounts of sexual excitement, sexual conduct or sadomasochistic abuse and which, taken as a whole, is harmful to juveniles.

However, if a person uses services of an Internet service provider or an electronic mail service provider in committing acts prohibited under this subsection, such Internet service provider or electronic mail service provider shall not be held responsible for violating this subsection.

B. It shall be unlawful for any person knowingly to sell to a juvenile an admission ticket or pass, or knowingly to admit a juvenile to premises whereon there is exhibited a motion picture, show or other presentation which, in whole or in part, depicts sexually explicit nudity, sexual conduct or sadomasochistic abuse and which is harmful to juveniles or to exhibit any such motion picture at any such premises which are not designed to prevent viewing from any public way of such motion picture by juveniles not admitted to any such premises.

C. It shall be unlawful for any juvenile falsely to represent to any person mentioned in subsection A or subsection B hereof, or to his agent, that such juvenile is 18 years of age or older, with the intent to procure any material set forth in subsection A, or with the intent to procure such juvenile's admission to any motion picture, show or other presentation, as set forth in subsection B.

D. It shall be unlawful for any person knowingly to make a false representation to any person mentioned in subsection A or subsection B hereof or to his agent, that he is the parent or guardian of any juvenile, or that any juvenile is 18 years of age, with the intent to procure any material set forth in subsection A, or with the intent to procure such juvenile's admission to any motion picture, show or other presentation, as set forth in subsection B.

E. No person shall sell, rent, or loan any item described in subdivision A 1 or A 2 to any individual who does not demonstrate his age in accordance with the provisions of subsection C of § 18.2-371.2.

F. A violation of subsection A, B, C, or D is a Class 1 misdemeanor. A person or separate retail establishment who violates subsection E shall be liable for a civil penalty not to exceed $100 for a first violation, a civil penalty not to exceed $200 for a second violation, and a civil penalty not to exceed $500 for a third or subsequent violation.

History.

Code 1950, § 18.1-236.7; 1970, c. 560; 1972, c. 421; 1975, cc. 14, 15; 1976, c. 504; 1985, c. 506; 1987, c. 356; 1999, c. 936; 2000, c. 1009; 2001, c. 451; 2006, c. 463.

§ 18.2-391.1. Exceptions to application of article.

Nothing contained in this article shall be construed to apply to:

1. The purchase, distribution, exhibition, or loan of any work of art, book, magazine, or other printed or manuscript material by any accredited museum, library, school, or institution of higher learning.

2. The exhibition or performance of any play, drama, tableau, or motion picture by any theatre, museum, school or institution of higher learning, either supported by public appropriation or which is an accredited institution supported by private funds.

History.
1977, c. 480.

ARTICLE 7.
CRUELTY TO ANIMALS.

§§ 18.2-392 through 18.2-403: Repealed by Acts 1984, c. 492.

Cross references.
For the comprehensive animal laws, see now § 3.2-5900 et seq. As to offenses involving animals, see now § 18.2-403.1 et seq.

ARTICLE 8.
OFFENSES INVOLVING ANIMALS.

§ 18.2-403.1. Offenses involving animals — Class 1 misdemeanors.

The following unlawful acts and offenses against animals shall constitute and be punished as a Class 1 misdemeanor:

1. Violation of subsection A of § 3.2-6570 pertaining to cruelty to animals, except as provided for second or subsequent violations in that section.

2. Violation of § 3.2-6508 pertaining to transporting animals under certain conditions.

3. Making a false claim or receiving money on a false claim under § 3.2-6553 pertaining to compensation for livestock and poultry killed by dogs.

4. Violation of § 3.2-6518 pertaining to boarding establishments and groomers as defined in § 3.2-6500.

History.
1984, c. 492; 1992, c. 177; 1993, c. 174; 1996, c. 249; 1999, c. 620.

§ 18.2-403.2. Offenses involving animals — Class 3 misdemeanors.

The following unlawful acts and offenses against animals shall constitute and be punished as a Class 3 misdemeanor:

1. Violation of § 3.2-6511 pertaining to the failure of a shopkeeper or pet dealer to provide adequate care to animals.

2. Violation of § 3.2-6509 pertaining to the misrepresentation of an animal's condition by the shopkeeper or pet dealer.

3. Violation of § 3.2-6504 pertaining to the abandonment of animals.

4. Violation of § 3.2-6510 pertaining to the sale of baby fowl.

5. Violation of clause (iii) of subsection A of § 3.2-6570 pertaining to soring horses.

6. Violation of § 3.2-6519 pertaining to notice of consumer remedies required to be supplied by boarding establishments.

History.
1984, c. 492; 1992, c. 177; 1993, c. 174; 1999, c. 620; 2003, c. 787; 2008, cc. 543, 707.

§ 18.2-403.3. Offenses involving animals — Class 4 misdemeanors.

The following unlawful acts and offenses against animals shall constitute and be punished as a Class 4 misdemeanor:

1. Violation of § 3.2-6566 pertaining to interference of agents charged with preventing cruelty to animals.

2. Violation of § 3.2-6573 pertaining to shooting pigeons.

3. Violation of § 3.2-6554 pertaining to disposing of the body of a dead companion animal.

4. Violation of ordinances passed pursuant to §§ 3.2-6522 and 3.2-6525 pertaining to rabid dogs and preventing the spread of rabies and the running at large of vicious dogs.

5. Violation of an ordinance passed pursuant to § 3.2-6539 requiring dogs to be on a leash.

6. Failure by any person to secure and exhibit the permits required by § 29.1-422 pertaining to field trails, night trails and foxhounds.

7. Diseased dogs. — For the owner of any dog with a contagious or infectious disease to permit such dog to stray from his premises if such disease is known to the owner.

8. License application. — For any person to make a false statement in order to secure a dog or cat license to which he is not entitled.

9. License tax. — For any dog or cat owner to fail to pay any license tax required by § 3.2-6530 before February 1 for the year in which it is due. In addition, the court may order confiscation and the proper disposition of the dog or cat.

10. Concealing a dog or cat. — For any person to conceal or harbor any dog or cat on which any required license tax has not been paid.

11. Removing collar and tag. — For any person, except the owner or custodian, to remove a legally acquired license tag from a dog or cat without the permission of the owner or custodian.

12. Violation of § 3.2-6503 pertaining to care of animals by owner.

History.
1984, c. 492; 1993, cc. 174, 817.

§ 18.2-403.4. Unauthorized release of animals; penalty.

Any person who intentionally releases an animal, as defined in § 3.2-6500, lawfully confined for scientific, research, commercial, agricultural or educational purposes without the consent of the owner or custodian of the animal and with the intent to impede or obstruct any such lawful purpose shall be guilty of a Class 1 misdemeanor.

History.
1992, c. 307.

CHAPTER 9.

CRIMES AGAINST PEACE AND ORDER.

Article 1.

Riot and Unlawful Assembly.

Article 2.

Disorderly Conduct.

Article 3.

Abusive and Insulting Language.

Article 4.

Picketing of Dwelling Places.

Article 5.

Activities Tending to Cause Violence.

Article 6.

Unlawful Use of Telephones.

Article 7.

Places of Amusement and Dance Halls.

Article 8.

Unlawful Paramilitary Activity.

ARTICLE 1.

RIOT AND UNLAWFUL ASSEMBLY.

§ 18.2-404. Obstructing free passage of others.

Any person or persons who in any public place or on any private property open to the public unreasonably or unnecessarily obstructs the free passage of other persons to and from or within such place or property and who shall fail or refuse to cease such obstruction or move on when requested to do so by the owner or lessee or agent or employee of such owner or lessee or by a duly authorized law-enforcement officer shall be guilty of a Class 1 misdemeanor. Nothing in this section shall be construed to prohibit lawful picketing.

History.
Code 1950, § 18.1-254.01; 1968, c. 608; 1975, cc. 14, 15.

§ 18.2-405. What constitutes a riot; punishment.

Any unlawful use, by three or more persons acting together, of force or violence which seriously jeopardizes the public safety, peace or order is riot.

Crimes and Offenses

Every person convicted of participating in any riot shall be guilty of a Class 1 misdemeanor.

If such person carried, at the time of such riot, any firearm or other deadly or dangerous weapon, he shall be guilty of a Class 5 felony.

History.
Code 1950, §§ 18.1-254.1, 18.1-254.2; 1968, c. 460; 1971, Ex. Sess., c. 251; 1975, cc. 14, 15.

§ 18.2-406. What constitutes an unlawful assembly; punishment.

Whenever three or more persons assembled share the common intent to advance some lawful or unlawful purpose by the commission of an act or acts of unlawful force or violence likely to jeopardize seriously public safety, peace or order, and the assembly actually tends to inspire persons of ordinary courage with well-grounded fear of serious and immediate breaches of public safety, peace or order, then such assembly is an unlawful assembly. Every person who participates in any unlawful assembly shall be guilty of a Class 1 misdemeanor. If any such person carried, at the time of his participation in an unlawful assembly, any firearm or other deadly or dangerous weapon, he shall be guilty of a Class 5 felony.

History.
Code 1950, §§ 18.1-254.1, 18.1-254.3; 1968, c. 460; 1971, Ex. Sess., c. 251; 1975, cc. 14, 15.

§ 18.2-407. Remaining at place of riot or unlawful assembly after warning to disperse.

Every person, except the owner or lessee of the premises, his family and nonrioting guests, and public officers and persons assisting them, who remains at the place of any riot or unlawful assembly after having been lawfully warned to disperse, shall be guilty of a Class 3 misdemeanor.

History.
Code 1950, § 18.1-254.4; 1968, c. 460; 1971, Ex. Sess., c. 251; 1975, cc. 14, 15.

§ 18.2-408. Conspiracy; incitement, etc., to riot.

Any person who conspires with others to cause or produce a riot, or directs, incites, or solicits other persons who participate in a riot to acts of force or violence, shall be guilty of a Class 5 felony.

History.
Code 1950, § 18.1-254.5:1; 1971, Ex. Sess., c. 251; 1975, cc. 14, 15.

§ 18.2-409. Resisting or obstructing execution of legal process.

Every person acting jointly or in combination with any other person to resist or obstruct the execution of any legal process shall be guilty of a Class 1 misdemeanor.

History.
Code 1950, § 18.1-254.6; 1968, c. 460; 1975, cc. 14, 15.

§ 18.2-410. Power of Governor to summon law-enforcement agencies, national guard, etc., to execute process or preserve the peace.

If it appears to the Governor that the power of the locality is not sufficient to enable the sheriff or other officer to execute process delivered to him or to suppress riots and to preserve the peace, he may order law-enforcement agencies, national guard, militia or other agencies of the Commonwealth or localities as may be necessary to execute such process and to preserve the peace. All persons so ordered or summoned by the Governor are required to attend and act. Any person who, without lawful cause, refuses or neglects to obey the command, shall be guilty of a Class 1 misdemeanor.

History.
Code 1950, § 18.1-254.7; 1968, c. 460; 1975, cc. 14, 15.

§ 18.2-411. Dispersal of unlawful or riotous assemblies; duties of officers.

When any number of persons, whether armed or not, are unlawfully or riotously assembled, the sheriff of the county and his deputies, the police officials of the county, city or town, and any assigned militia, or any of them, shall go among the persons assembled or as near to them as safety will permit and command them in the name of the Commonwealth immediately to disperse. If upon such command the persons unlawfully assembled do not disperse immediately, such sheriff, officer or militia may use such force as is reasonably necessary to disperse them and to arrest those who fail or refuse to disperse. To accomplish this end, the sheriff or other law-enforcement officer may request and use the assistance and services of private citizens. Every endeavor shall be used, both by such sheriff or other officers and by the officer commanding any other force, which can be made consistently with the preservation of life, to induce or force those unlawfully assembled to disperse before an attack is made upon those unlawfully assembled by which their lives may be endangered.

History.
Code 1950, §§ 18.1-254.8, 18.1-254.9; 1968, c. 460; 1975, cc. 14, 15.

§ 18.2-412. Immunity of officers and others in quelling a riot or unlawful assembly.

No liability, criminal or civil, shall be imposed upon any person authorized to disperse or assist in dispersing a riot or unlawful assembly for any action of such person which was taken after those rioting or unlawfully assembled had been commanded to disperse, and which action was reasonably necessary under all the circumstances to disperse such riot or unlawful assembly or to arrest those who failed or refused to disperse.

History.
Code 1950, §§ 18.1-254.8, 18.1-254.9; 1968, c. 460; 1975, cc. 14, 15.

§ 18.2-413. Commission of certain offenses in county, city or town declared by Governor to be in state of riot or insurrection.

Any person, who after the publication of a proclamation by the Governor, or who after lawful notice to disperse and retire, resists or aids in resisting the execution of process in any county, city or town declared to be in a state of riot or insurrection, or who aids or attempts the rescue or escape of another from lawful custody or confinement, or who resists or aids in resisting a force ordered out by the Governor or any sheriff or other officer to quell or suppress an insurrection or riot, shall be guilty of a Class 5 felony.

History.
Code 1950, § 18.1-254.10; 1968, c. 460; 1975, cc. 14, 15.

§ 18.2-414. Injury to property or persons by persons unlawfully or riotously assembled.

If any person or persons, unlawfully or riotously assembled, pull down, injure, or destroy, or begin to pull down, injure or destroy any dwelling house or other building, or assist therein, or perpetrate any premeditated injury on the person of another, he shall be guilty of a Class 6 felony.

History.
Code 1950, § 18.1-254.11; 1968, c. 460; 1975, cc. 14, 15.

§ 18.2-414.1. Obstructing emergency medical services agency personnel in performance of mission; penalty.

Any person who unreasonably or unnecessarily obstructs the delivery of emergency medical services by emergency medical services agency personnel, whether governmental, private, or volunteer, or who fails or refuses to cease such obstruction or move on when requested to do so by emergency medical services personnel going to or at the site at which emergency medical services are required is guilty of a Class 2 misdemeanor.

History.
1976, c. 233; 2002, c. 560; 2015, cc. 502, 503.

§ 18.2-414.2. Crossing established police lines, perimeters or barricades.

It shall be unlawful for any person to cross or remain within police lines or barricades which have been established pursuant to § 15.2-1714 without proper authorization.

Any person violating the provisions of this section shall be guilty of a Class 3 misdemeanor.

History.
1984, c. 533; 1990, c. 327.

ARTICLE 2.
DISORDERLY CONDUCT.

§ 18.2-415. Disorderly conduct in public places.

A person is guilty of disorderly conduct if, with the intent to cause public inconvenience, annoyance or alarm, or recklessly creating a risk thereof, he:

A. In any street, highway, public building, or while in or on a public conveyance, or public place engages in conduct having a direct tendency to cause acts of violence by the person or persons at whom, individually, such conduct is directed; or

B. Willfully or being intoxicated, whether willfully or not, and whether such intoxication results from self-administered alcohol or other drug of whatever nature, disrupts any funeral, memorial service, or meeting of the governing body of any political subdivision of this Commonwealth or a division or agency thereof, or of any school, literary society or place of religious worship, if the disruption (i) prevents or interferes with the orderly conduct of the funeral, memorial service, or meeting or (ii) has a direct tendency to cause acts of violence by the person or persons at whom, individually, the disruption is directed; or

C. Willfully or while intoxicated, whether willfully or not, and whether such intoxication results from self-administered alcohol or other drug of whatever nature, disrupts the operation of any school or any activity conducted or sponsored by any school, if the disruption (i) prevents or interferes with the orderly conduct of the operation or activity or (ii) has a direct tendency to cause acts of violence by the person or persons at whom, individually, the disruption is directed.

However, the conduct prohibited under subdivision A, B or C of this section shall not be deemed to include the utterance or display of any words or to include conduct otherwise made punishable under this title.

The person in charge of any such building, place, conveyance, meeting, operation or activity may eject therefrom any person who violates any provision of this section, with the aid, if necessary, of any persons who may be called upon for such purpose.

The governing bodies of counties, cities and towns are authorized to adopt ordinances prohibiting and punishing the acts and conduct prohibited by this section, provided that the punishment fixed therefor shall not exceed that prescribed for a Class 1 misdemeanor. A person violating any provision of this section shall be guilty of a Class 1 misdemeanor.

History.

Code 1950, §§ 18.1-239, 18.1-240, 18.1-253.1 through 18.1-253.3; 1960, c. 358; 1968, c. 639; 1969, Ex. Sess., c. 2; 1970, c. 374; 1975, cc. 14, 15; 1976, c. 244; 1990, c. 627; 2006, c. 250.

ARTICLE 3.
ABUSIVE AND INSULTING LANGUAGE.

§ 18.2-416. Punishment for using abusive language to another.

If any person shall, in the presence or hearing of another, curse or abuse such other person, or use any violent abusive language to such person concerning himself or any of his relations, or otherwise use such language, under circumstances reasonably calculated to provoke a breach of the peace, he shall be guilty of a Class 3 misdemeanor.

History.

Code 1950, § 18.1-255; 1960, c. 358; 1975, cc. 14, 15.

§ 18.2-417. Slander and libel.

Any person who shall falsely utter and speak, or falsely write and publish, of and concerning any female of chaste character, any words derogatory of such female's character for virtue and chastity, or imputing to such female acts not virtuous and chaste, or who shall falsely utter and speak, or falsely write and publish, of and concerning another person, any words which from their usual construction and common acceptation are construed as insults and tend to violence and breach of the peace or shall use grossly insulting language to any female of good character or reputation, shall be guilty of a Class 3 misdemeanor.

The defendant shall be entitled to prove upon trial in mitigation of the punishment, the provocation which induced the libelous or slanderous words, or any other fact or circumstance tending to disprove malice, or lessen the criminality of the offense.

History.

Code 1950, § 18.1-256; 1960, c. 358; 1973, c. 526; 1975, cc. 14, 15.

ARTICLE 4.
PICKETING OF DWELLING PLACES.

§ 18.2-418. Declaration of policy.

It is hereby declared that the protection and preservation of the home is the keystone of democratic government; that the public health and welfare and the good order of the community require that members of the community enjoy in their homes a feeling of well-being, tranquility, and privacy, and when absent from their homes carry with them the sense of security inherent in the assurance that they may return to the enjoyment of their homes; that the practice of picketing before or about residences and dwelling places causes emotional disturbance and distress to the occupants; that such practice has as its object the harassing of such occupants; and without resort to such practice, full opportunity exists, and under the terms and provisions of this article will continue to exist, for the exercise of freedom of speech and other constitutional rights; and that the provisions hereinafter enacted are necessary in the public interest, to avoid the detrimental results herein set forth.

History.

Code 1950, § 18.1-367.1; 1970, c. 711; 1975, cc. 14, 15.

§ 18.2-419. Picketing or disrupting tranquility of home.

Any person who shall engage in picketing before or about the residence or dwelling place of any individual, or who shall assemble with another person or persons in a manner which disrupts or threatens to disrupt any individual's right to tranquility in his home, shall be guilty of a Class 3 misdemeanor. Each day on which a violation of this section occurs shall constitute a separate offense.

Nothing herein shall be deemed to prohibit (1) the picketing in any lawful manner, during a labor dispute, of the place of employment involved in such labor dispute; (2) the picketing in any lawful manner of a construction site; or (3) the holding of a meeting or assembly on any premises commonly used for the discussion of subjects of general public interest.

Notwithstanding the penalties herein provided, any court of general equity jurisdiction may enjoin conduct, or threatened conduct, proscribed by this article, and may in any such proceeding award damages, including punitive damages, against the persons found guilty of actions made unlawful by this section.

History.

Code 1950, §§ 18.1-367.2 through 18.1-367.6; 1970, c. 711; 1975, cc. 14, 15.

ARTICLE 5.
ACTIVITIES TENDING TO CAUSE VIOLENCE.

§ 18.2-420. "Clandestine organization" defined.

"Clandestine organization" means: any organization (1) which conceals, or attempts to conceal, its

name, activities or membership, or the names, activities or membership of any chapter, branch, unit or affiliate thereof, by the use of cover-names, codes, or any deceptive practice or other means, or (2) whose members shall be required, urged, or instructed, or shall adopt any practice, to conceal their membership or affiliation and that of others in or with such organization, or (3) whose members shall take any oath or pledge, or shall administer any such oath or pledge to those associated with them, to maintain in secrecy any matter or knowledge committed to them by the organization or by any member thereof, or (4) which shall transact business or advance any purpose at any secret meeting or meetings which are guarded or secured against intrusion by persons not associated with it, and (5) whose purpose, policy or activity includes the unlawful use of violence, threats, or intimidation in accomplishing any of its objectives.

History.
Code 1950, § 18.1-380.1; 1968, c. 792; 1975, cc. 14, 15.

§ 18.2-421. Information to be filed by clandestine organization with State Corporation Commission.

Every existing membership corporation and every existing unincorporated association which is a clandestine organization as defined in § 18.2-420, shall file with the clerk of the State Corporation Commission a sworn copy of its constitution, bylaws, rules, regulations, and oath of membership, together with a roster of its membership and a list of its officers for the current year. Every such corporation and association shall, in case its constitution, bylaws, rules, regulations or oath of membership or any part thereof be revised, changed or amended, within ten days after such revision or amendment, file with the clerk of the State Corporation Commission a sworn copy of such revised, changed or amended constitution, bylaw, rule, regulation or oath of membership. Every such corporation or association shall, within thirty days after a change has been made in its officers, file with the clerk of the State Corporation Commission a sworn statement showing such change. Every such corporation or association shall, at intervals of six months, file with the clerk of the State Corporation Commission, a sworn statement showing the names and addresses of such additional members as have been received in such corporation or association during such interval.

The violation of any provision of this section shall constitute a Class 3 misdemeanor.

The provisions of §§ 18.2-420 and 18.2-421 shall not apply to fraternal organizations which are organized for charitable, benevolent, and educational objectives and whose transactions and list of members are open for public inspection.

History.
Code 1950, § 18.1-380.2; 1968, c. 792; 1975, cc. 14, 15.

§ 18.2-422. Prohibition of wearing of masks in certain places; exceptions.

It shall be unlawful for any person over 16 years of age to, with the intent to conceal his identity, wear any mask, hood or other device whereby a substantial portion of the face is hidden or covered so as to conceal the identity of the wearer, to be or appear in any public place, or upon any private property in this Commonwealth without first having obtained from the owner or tenant thereof consent to do so in writing. However, the provisions of this section shall not apply to persons (i) wearing traditional holiday costumes; (ii) engaged in professions, trades, employment or other activities and wearing protective masks which are deemed necessary for the physical safety of the wearer or other persons; (iii) engaged in any bona fide theatrical production or masquerade ball; or (iv) wearing a mask, hood or other device for bona fide medical reasons upon (a) the advice of a licensed physician or osteopath and carrying on his person an affidavit from the physician or osteopath specifying the medical necessity for wearing the device and the date on which the wearing of the device will no longer be necessary and providing a brief description of the device, or (b) the declaration of a disaster or state of emergency by the Governor in response to a public health emergency where the emergency declaration expressly waives this section, defines the mask appropriate for the emergency, and provides for the duration of the waiver. The violation of any provisions of this section is a Class 6 felony.

History.
Code 1950, §§ 18.1-364, 18.1-367; 1960, c. 358; 1975, cc. 14, 15; 1986, c. 19; 2010, cc. 262, 420; 2014, c. 167.

§ 18.2-423. Burning cross on property of another or public place with intent to intimidate; penalty; prima facie evidence of intent.

It shall be unlawful for any person or persons, with the intent of intimidating any person or group of persons, to burn, or cause to be burned, a cross on the property of another, a highway or other public place. Any person who shall violate any provision of this section shall be guilty of a Class 6 felony.

Any such burning of a cross shall be prima facie evidence of an intent to intimidate a person or group of persons.

History.
Code 1950, §§ 18.1-365 through 18.1-367; 1960, c. 358; 1968, c. 350; 1975, cc. 14, 15; 1983, c. 337.

§ 18.2-423.01. Burning object on property of another or a highway or other public place with intent to intimidate; penalty.

A. Any person who, with the intent of intimidating any person or group of persons, burns an object

Crimes and Offenses

on the private property of another without permission, is guilty of a Class 6 felony.

B. Any person who, with the intent of intimidating any person or group of persons, burns an object on a highway or other public place in a manner having a direct tendency to place another person in reasonable fear or apprehension of death or bodily injury is guilty of a Class 6 felony.

History.
2002, cc. 589, 600.

§ 18.2-423.1. Placing swastika on certain property with intent to intimidate; penalty; prima facie evidence of intent.

It shall be unlawful for any person or persons, with the intent of intimidating another person or group of persons, to place or cause to be placed a swastika on any church, synagogue or other building or place used for religious worship, or on any school, educational facility or community center owned or operated by a church or religious body.

A violation of this section shall be punishable as a Class 6 felony.

For the purposes of this section, any such placing of a swastika shall be prima facie evidence of an intent to intimidate another person or group of persons.

History.
1983, c. 337.

§ 18.2-423.2. Displaying noose on property of another or a highway or other public place with intent to intimidate; penalty.

A. Any person who, with the intent of intimidating any person or group of persons, displays a noose on the private property of another without permission is guilty of a Class 6 felony.

B. Any person who, with the intent of intimidating any person or group of persons, displays a noose on a highway or other public place in a manner having a direct tendency to place another person in reasonable fear or apprehension of death or bodily injury is guilty of a Class 6 felony.

History.
2009, c. 277.

ARTICLE 6.

UNLAWFUL USE OF TELEPHONES.

§§ 18.2-424, 18.2-425: Repealed by Acts 2007, c. 467, cl. 2.

§ 18.2-425.1: Repealed by Acts 2009, c. 699, cl. 2.

Cross references.
For current provisions restricting certain solicitation calls, see Automatic Dialing-Announcing Devices, Chapter 44.1 (§ 59.1-518.1 et seq.) of Title 59.1.

§ 18.2-426. "Emergency call" and "emergency personnel" defined.

As used in this article:

"Emergency call" means a call to report a fire or summon police, or for emergency medical services, in a situation where human life or property is in jeopardy and the prompt summoning of aid is essential.

"Emergency personnel" means any persons, paid or volunteer, who receive calls for dispatch of police, fire, or emergency medical services personnel, and includes law-enforcement officers, firefighters, including special forest wardens designated pursuant to § 10.1-1135, and emergency medical services personnel.

History.
Code 1950, § 18.1-370; 1960, c. 358; 1975, cc. 14, 15; 1995, c. 791; 2000, c. 962; 2007, c. 467; 2015, cc. 502, 503.

§ 18.2-427. Use of profane, threatening, or indecent language over public airways or by other methods.

Any person who uses obscene, vulgar, profane, lewd, lascivious, or indecent language, or makes any suggestion or proposal of an obscene nature, or threatens any illegal or immoral act with the intent to coerce, intimidate, or harass any person, over any telephone or citizens band radio, in this Commonwealth, is guilty of a Class 1 misdemeanor.

"Over any telephone" includes, for purposes of this section, any electronically transmitted communication producing a visual or electronic message that is received or transmitted by cellular telephone or other wireless telecommunications device.

History.
Code 1950, § 18.1-238; 1960, c. 358; 1964, c. 577; 1975, cc. 14, 15; 1976, c. 312; 1984, c. 592; 2010, c. 565; 2011, c. 246.

§ 18.2-428. Giving certain false information to another by telephone.

If any person maliciously advises or informs another over any telephone in this Commonwealth of the death of, accident to, injury to, illness of, or disappearance of some third party, knowing the same to be false, he shall be guilty of a Class 1 misdemeanor.

History.
Code 1950, § 18.1-238.1; 1962, c. 225; 1975, cc. 14, 15.

§ 18.2-429. Causing telephone or pager to ring with intent to annoy.

A. Any person who, with or without intent to communicate but with intent to annoy any other person, causes any telephone or digital pager, not his own, to ring or to otherwise signal, and any person who permits or condones the use of any telephone under his control for such purpose, is guilty of a Class 3 misdemeanor. A second or subsequent conviction under this subsection is punishable as a Class 2 misdemeanor if such prior conviction occurred before the date of the offense charged.

B. Any person who, with or without intent to converse, but with intent to annoy, harass, hinder or delay emergency personnel in the performance of their duties as such, causes a telephone to ring, which is owned or leased for the purpose of receiving emergency calls by a public or private entity providing fire, police or emergency medical services, and any person who knowingly permits the use of a telephone under his control for such purpose, is guilty of a Class 1 misdemeanor.

History.
Code 1950, § 18.1-238.2; 1962, c. 495; 1975, cc. 14, 15; 1989, c. 59; 1995, cc. 410, 478, 791; 2012, c. 133; 2015, cc. 502, 503.

§ 18.2-430. Venue for offenses under this article.

Any person violating any of the provisions of this article may be prosecuted either in the county or city from which he called or in the county or city in which the call was received.

History.
Code 1950, § 18.1-238; 1960, c. 358; 1964, c. 577; 1975, cc. 14, 15.

§ 18.2-431. Duty of telephone companies; notices in directories.

(1) It shall be the duty, on pain of contempt of court, of each telephone company in this Commonwealth to furnish immediately in response to a subpoena issued by a circuit court such information as it, its officers and employees may possess which, in the opinion of the court, may aid in the apprehension of persons suspected of violating the provisions of this article or the provisions of § 18.2-83 or § 18.2-212.

(2) Every telephone directory distributed to the public which lists the calling numbers of telephones or of any telephone exchange located in this Commonwealth shall contain a notice which explains the offenses made punishable under this article, such notice to be printed in type which conforms with and is comparable to other type on the same page, and to be placed in a prominent place in such directory. Any violation of this subsection shall be punishable as a Class 4 misdemeanor.

History.
Code 1950, §§ 18.1-238, 18.1-371; 1960, c. 358; 1964, c. 577; 1975, cc. 14, 15; 1982, c. 502.

§ 18.2-431.1. Illegal conveyance or possession of cellular telephone or other wireless telecommunications device by prisoner or committed person; penalty.

A. It is unlawful for any person without authorization to provide or cause to be provided a cellular telephone or other wireless telecommunications device to an incarcerated prisoner or person committed to the Department of Juvenile Justice in any juvenile correctional center.

B. It is unlawful for an incarcerated prisoner or person committed to the Department of Juvenile Justice in any juvenile correctional center without authorization to possess a cellular telephone or other wireless telecommunications device during the period of his incarceration.

C. Any violation of this section is a Class 6 felony.

History.
2005, c. 171; 2013, cc. 707, 782; 2015, c. 601.

ARTICLE 7. PLACES OF AMUSEMENT AND DANCE HALLS.

§§ 18.2-432, 18.2-433: Repealed by Acts 2004, c. 462.

Cross references.
For current provisions as to regulation of dance halls by counties, cities and towns, see § 15.2-912.3.

ARTICLE 8. UNLAWFUL PARAMILITARY ACTIVITY.

§ 18.2-433.1. Definitions.

As used in this article:

"Civil disorder" means any public disturbance within the United States or any territorial possessions thereof involving acts of violence by assemblages of three or more persons, which causes an immediate danger of or results in damage or injury to the property or person of any other individual.

"Explosive or incendiary device" means (i) dynamite and all other forms of high explosives, (ii) any explosive bomb, grenade, missile, or similar device, or (iii) any incendiary bomb or grenade, fire bomb, or similar device, including any device which consists of or includes a breakable container including a flammable liquid or compound, and a wick composed of any material which, when ignited, is capable of igniting such flammable liquid or compound, and can be carried or thrown by one individual acting alone.

"Firearm" means any weapon that will or is designed to or may readily be converted to expel single or multiple projectiles by the action of an explosion of a combustible material; or the frame or receiver of any such weapon.

"Law-enforcement officer" means any officer as defined in § 9.1-101 or any such officer or member of the armed forces of the United States, any state, any political subdivision of a state, or the District of Columbia, and such term shall specifically include, but shall not be limited to, members of the National Guard, as defined in § 101(c) of Title 10, United States Code, members of the organized militia of any state or territory of the United States, the Commonwealth of Puerto Rico, or the District of Columbia, not included within the definition of National Guard as defined by such § 101(c), and members of the Armed Forces of the United States.

History.
1987, c. 720; 2003, c. 976; 2004, c. 263.

§ 18.2-433.2. Paramilitary activity prohibited.

A person shall be guilty of unlawful paramilitary activity, punishable as a Class 5 felony if he:

1. Teaches or demonstrates to any other person the use, application, or making of any firearm, explosive or incendiary device, or technique capable of causing injury or death to persons, knowing or having reason to know or intending that such training will be employed for use in, or in furtherance of, a civil disorder; or

2. Assembles with one or more persons for the purpose of training with, practicing with, or being instructed in the use of any firearm, explosive or incendiary device, or technique capable of causing injury or death to persons, intending to employ such training for use in, or in furtherance of, a civil disorder.

History.
1987, c. 720.

§ 18.2-433.3. Exceptions.

Nothing contained in this article shall be construed to apply to:

1. Any act of a law-enforcement officer performed in the otherwise lawful performance of the officer's official duties;

2. Any activity, undertaken without knowledge of or intent to cause or further a civil disorder, which is intended to teach or practice self-defense or self-defense techniques such as karate clubs or self-defense clinics, and similar lawful activity;

3. Any facility, program or lawful activity related to firearms instruction and training intended to teach the safe handling and use of firearms; or

4. Any other lawful sports or activities related to the individual recreational use or possession of firearms, including but not limited to hunting activities, target shooting, self-defense and firearms collection.

Notwithstanding any language contained herein, no activity of any individual, group, organization or other entity engaged in the lawful display or use of firearms or other weapons or facsimiles thereof shall be deemed to be in violation of this statute.

History.
1987, c. 720.

CHAPTER 10.

CRIMES AGAINST THE ADMINISTRATION OF JUSTICE.

Article 1.

Perjury.

Article 2.

Bribery and Related Offenses.

Article 3.

Bribery of Public Servants and Party Officials.

Article 4.

Barratry.

Article 5.

Contempt of Court.

ARTICLE 1.

PERJURY.

§ 18.2-434. What deemed perjury; punishment and penalty.

If any person to whom an oath is lawfully administered on any occasion willfully swears falsely on such occasion touching any material matter or thing, or if a person falsely make oath that any other person is 18 years of age or older in order to obtain a marriage license for such other person, or if any person in any written declaration, certificate, verification, or statement under penalty of perjury pursuant to § 8.01-4.3 willfully subscribes as true any material matter which he does not believe is true, he is guilty of perjury, punishable as a Class 5 felony. Upon the conviction of any person for perjury, such person thereby shall be adjudged forever incapable of holding any office of honor, profit or trust under the Constitution of Virginia, or of serving as a juror.

History.
Code 1950, §§ 18.1-273 through 18.1-275; 1960, c. 358; 1972, c. 823; 1975, cc. 14, 15; 2005, c. 423.

§ 18.2-435. Giving conflicting testimony on separate occasions as to same matter; indictment; sufficiency of evidence.

It shall likewise constitute perjury for any person, with the intent to testify falsely, to knowingly give testimony under oath as to any material matter or thing and subsequently to give conflicting testimony under oath as to the same matter or thing. In any indictment for such perjury, it shall be sufficient to allege the offense by stating that the person charged therewith did, knowingly and with the intent to testify falsely, on one occasion give testimony upon a certain matter and, on a subsequent occasion, give different testimony upon the same matter. Upon the trial on such indictment, it shall be sufficient to prove that the defendant, knowingly and with the intent to testify falsely, gave such differing testimony and that the differing testimony was given on two separate occasions.

History.
Code 1950, § 18.1-276; 1960, c. 358; 1975, cc. 14, 15.

§ 18.2-436. Inducing another to give false testimony; sufficiency of evidence.

If any person procure or induce another to commit perjury or to give false testimony under oath in violation of any provision of this article, he shall be punished as prescribed in § 18.2-434.

In any prosecution under this section, it shall be sufficient to prove that the person alleged to have given false testimony shall have been procured, induced, counselled or advised to give such testimony by the party charged.

History.
Code 1950, § 18.1-277; 1960, c. 358; 1975, cc. 14, 15.

§ 18.2-437. Immunity of witnesses.

No witness called by the attorney for the Commonwealth, or by the court, and required to give evidence for the prosecution in a proceeding under this article shall ever be proceeded against for the offense concerning which he testified. Such witness shall be compelled to testify and may be punished for contempt for refusing to do so.

History.
Code 1950, § 18.1-277; 1960, c. 358; 1975, cc. 14, 15.

ARTICLE 2.

BRIBERY AND RELATED OFFENSES.

§ 18.2-438. Bribes to officers or candidates for office.

If any person corruptly give, offer or promise to any executive, legislative or judicial officer, sheriff or police officer, or to any candidate for such office, either before or after he shall have taken his seat, any gift or gratuity, with intent to influence his act, vote, opinion, decision or judgment on any matter, question, cause or proceeding, which is or may be then pending, or may by law come or be brought before him in his official capacity, he shall be guilty of a Class 4 felony and shall forfeit to the Commonwealth any such gift or gratuity given. This section shall also apply to a resident of this Commonwealth who, while temporarily absent therefrom for that purpose, shall make such gift, offer or promise.

History.
Code 1950, § 18.1-278; 1960, c. 358; 1975, cc. 14, 15; 1978, c. 123.

§ 18.2-439. Acceptance of bribe by officer or candidate.

If any executive, legislative or judicial officer, sheriff or police officer, or any candidate for such office, accept in this Commonwealth, or if, being resident in this Commonwealth, such officer or candidate shall go out of this Commonwealth and accept and afterwards return to and reside in this Commonwealth, any gift or gratuity or any promise to make a gift or do any act beneficial to such officer or candidate under an agreement, or with an understanding, that his vote, opinion or judgment shall be given on any particular side of any question, cause or proceeding which is or may be by law brought before him in his official capacity or that in such capacity he shall make any particular nomination or appointment or take or fail to take any particular action or perform any duty required by law, he shall be guilty of a Class 4 felony and shall forfeit his office and be forever incapable of holding any office of honor, profit or trust under the Constitution of Virginia. The word candidate as used in this section and § 18.2-438, shall mean anyone who has filed his candidacy with the appropriate electoral official or who is a candidate as defined in § 24.2-101.

History.
Code 1950, § 18.1-279; 1960, c. 358; 1975, cc. 14, 15.

§ 18.2-440. Bribes to officers to prevent service of process.

If any officer authorized to serve legal process receive any money or other thing of value for omitting or delaying to perform any duty pertaining to his office, he shall be guilty of a Class 2 misdemeanor.

History.
Code 1950, § 18.1-281; 1960, c. 358; 1975, cc. 14, 15.

§ 18.2-441. Giving bribes to, or receiving bribes by, commissioners, jurors, etc.

If any person give, offer or promise to give any money or other thing of value to a commissioner appointed by a court, auditor, arbitrator, umpire or juror (although not impaneled), with intent to bias his opinion or influence his decision in relation to any matter in which he is acting or is to act, or if any such commissioner, auditor, arbitrator, umpire or juror corruptly take or receive such money or other thing, he shall be guilty of a Class 4 felony.

History.
Code 1950, § 18.1-282; 1960, c. 358; 1975, cc. 14, 15.

§ 18.2-441.1. Bribery of witnesses.

If any person give, offer, or promise to give any money or other thing of value to anyone with intent to prevent such person from testifying as a witness in any civil or criminal proceeding or with intent to cause that person to testify falsely, he shall be guilty of a Class 6 felony.

History.
1978, c. 612.

§ 18.2-442. Bribery of participants in games, contests or sports.

Whoever gives, promises or offers any valuable thing to any professional or amateur participant or prospective participant in any game, contest or sport, with intent to influence him to lose or try to lose or cause to be lost or to limit his or his team's margin of victory in any professional or amateur game, contest or sport in which such participant is taking part or expects to take part, or has any duty or connection therewith, shall be guilty of a Class 5 felony.

History.
Code 1950, § 18.1-402; 1960, c. 358; 1975, cc. 14, 15.

§ 18.2-443. Solicitation or acceptance of bribes by participants or by managers, coaches or trainers.

A professional or amateur participant or prospective participant in any game, contest or sport or a manager, coach or trainer of any team or individual participant or prospective participant in any such game, contest or sport, who solicits or accepts any valuable thing to influence him to lose or try to lose or cause to be lost or to limit his or his team's margin of victory in any game, contest or sport in which he is taking part, or expects to take part, or has any duty or connection therewith, shall be guilty of a Class 5 felony.

History.
Code 1950, § 18.1-403; 1960, c. 358; 1975, cc. 14, 15.

§ 18.2-444. Corruptly influencing, or being influenced as, agents, etc.

(1) Any person who gives, offers or promises to an agent, employee or servant any gift or gratuity whatever, without the knowledge and consent of the principal, employer or master of such agent, employee or servant, with intent to influence his action to the prejudice of his principal's, employer's or master's business; or

(2) An agent, employee or servant who, without the knowledge and consent of his principal, employer or master requests or accepts a gift or gratuity or a promise to make a gift or to do an act beneficial to himself, under an agreement or with an understanding that he shall act in any particular manner as to his principal's, employer's or master's business; or

(3) An agent, employee or servant who, being authorized to procure materials, supplies or other articles either by purchase or contract for his principal, employer or master or to employ service or labor for his principal, employer or master receives directly or indirectly, for himself or for another, a commission, discount or bonus from the person who makes such sale or contract, or furnishes such materials, supplies or other articles, or from a person who renders such service or labor; or

(4) Any person who gives or offers such an agent, employee or servant such commission, discount or bonus;

shall be guilty of a Class 3 misdemeanor.

History.
Code 1950, § 18.1-404; 1960, c. 358; 1975, cc. 14, 15.

§ 18.2-444.1: Reserved.

§ 18.2-444.2. Giving or accepting a fee or gift for purposes of influencing decisions of financial institution.

A. No officer, director, or employee of a financial institution or subsidiary, affiliate or holding company thereof, or stockholder owning ten percent or more of the issued capital stock of any such financial institution or holding company, shall accept, receive or acquire any fee, gift, property interest, or other thing of value with the intent to influence the decision of the financial institution, subsidiary, affiliate or holding company with regard to any extension of credit, investment, or purchase or sale of assets by such financial institution, subsidiary, affiliate or holding company. No person shall give, provide or cause to be transferred to any such officer, director, employee or stockholder, any fee, gift, property interest or other thing of value with the intent to influence the decision of the financial institution, subsidiary, affiliate or holding company with regard to any extension of credit, investment or purchase or sale of assets by the financial institution, subsidiary, affiliate or holding company. The foregoing provisions shall not apply to salary, wages, fees or other compensation or consideration paid by, or expenses paid or reimbursed by, such financial institution, subsidiary, affiliate or holding company. The violation of this section shall be punishable as a Class 6 felony.

B. The provisions of this section shall not apply to any such officer, director, employee or stockholder who is a member of a firm of licensed brokers, in buying for or from or selling to, or for the account of, the financial institution, in the ordinary course of business, real estate or bonds, stocks, or other evidences of debt at the usual rate of commission for such service, if the officer, director, employee or stockholder notifies the board of directors of the financial institution, its cashier or secretary, in writing, that such services will be rendered for compensation prior to the rendition of the services or within five business days following the commencement of the services. If a continuing business relationship exists, an annual disclosure may be made.

C. The provisions of this section shall not apply to fees paid to any such officer, director, employee, or stockholder who renders services to a borrower outside of his relationship with the financial institution in connection with the preparation of a loan application, or in connection with the closing of a loan, in evaluating the security or affecting a lien on the collateral, where the fact of rendition of such services for compensation is disclosed in writing to the board of directors of the financial institution, or its cashier or secretary, prior to the time such services are rendered or within five business days following the commencement of the services. If a continuing business relationship exists, an annual disclosure may be made.

History.
Code 1950, § 6.1-121; 1966, c. 584; 1981, c. 339; 1991, c. 501; 1992, c. 318.

§ 18.2-445. Immunity of witnesses.

No witness called by the court or attorney for the Commonwealth and giving evidence for the prosecution, either before the grand jury or the court in any prosecution, under this article shall ever be proceeded against for any offense of giving, or offering to give, or accepting a bribe committed by him at the

Crimes and Offenses

time and place indicated in such prosecution; but such witness shall be compelled to testify, and for refusing to answer questions may, by the court, be punished for contempt.

History.
Code 1950, §§ 18.1-280, 18.1-405; 1960, c. 358; 1975, cc. 14, 15.

ARTICLE 3.

BRIBERY OF PUBLIC SERVANTS AND PARTY OFFICIALS.

§ 18.2-446. Definitions.

The following words and phrases when used in this article shall have the meanings respectively ascribed to them in this section except where the context clearly requires a different meaning:

(1) *"Benefits"* means a gain or advantage, or anything regarded by the beneficiary as a gain or advantage, including a benefit to any other person or entity in whose welfare he is interested, but shall not mean an advantage promised generally to a group or class of voters as a consequence of public measures which a candidate engages to support or oppose;

(2) *"Party official"* means a person who holds an elective or appointive post in a political party in the United States by virtue of which he directs or conducts, or participates in directing or conducting party affairs at any level of responsibility;

(3) *"Pecuniary benefit"* means a benefit in the form of money, property, commercial interest or anything else the primary significance of which is economic gain;

(4) *"Public servant"* means any officer or employee of this Commonwealth or any political subdivision thereof, including members of the General Assembly and judges, and any person participating as a juror, advisor, consultant or otherwise, in performing any governmental function; but the term does not include witnesses;

(5) *"Administrative proceeding"* means any proceeding other than a judicial proceeding, the outcome of which is required to be based on a record or documentation prescribed by law including specifically, but not limited to, proceedings before a planning commission and board of zoning appeals.

History.
Code 1950, § 18.1-282.1; 1968, c. 552; 1975, cc. 14, 15.

§ 18.2-447. When person guilty of bribery.

A person shall be guilty of bribery under the provisions of this article:

(1) If he offers, confers or agrees to confer upon another (a) any pecuniary benefit as consideration for or to obtain or influence the recipient's decision, opinion, recommendation, vote or other exercise of discretion as a public servant or party official, or (b) any benefit as consideration for or to obtain or influence either the recipient's decision, opinion, recommendation, vote or other exercise of official discretion in a judicial or administrative proceeding or the recipient's violation of a known legal duty as a public servant or party official; or

(2) If he accepts or agrees to accept from another (a) any pecuniary benefit offered, conferred or agreed to be conferred as consideration for or to obtain or influence the recipient's decision, opinion, recommendation, vote or other exercise of discretion as a public servant or party official, or (b) any benefit offered, conferred or agreed to be conferred as consideration for or to obtain or influence either the recipient's decision, opinion, recommendation, vote or other exercise of official discretion in a judicial or administrative proceeding or the recipient's violation of a known legal duty as a public servant or party official; or

(3) If he solicits from another (a) any pecuniary benefit or promise of pecuniary benefit as consideration for or in exchange for his decision, opinion, recommendation, vote or other exercise of discretion as a public servant or party official, or (b) any benefit or promise of benefit as consideration for or in exchange for his decision, opinion, recommendation, vote or other exercise of official discretion in a judicial or administrative proceeding or his violation of a known legal duty as a public servant or party official.

History.
Code 1950, § 18.1-282.2; 1968, c. 552; 1975, cc. 14, 15.

§ 18.2-448. Certain matters not to constitute defenses.

It shall be no defense to any prosecution under § 18.2-447 that a person whom the actor sought to influence was not qualified to act in the desired way, whether because he had not yet assumed office, or lacked jurisdiction, or for any other reason. Also it shall be no defense to a prosecution under § 18.2-447 that a resident of this Commonwealth charged with committing an act of bribery was temporarily absent from this Commonwealth at the time such act was committed.

History.
Code 1950, § 18.1-282.3; 1968, c. 552; 1975, cc. 14, 15.

§ 18.2-449. Punishment.

Any person found guilty of bribery under the provisions of this article shall be guilty of a Class 4 felony, and if such person be a public servant he shall in addition forfeit his public office and shall be forever incapable of holding any public office in this Commonwealth.

History.
Code 1950, § 18.1-282.4; 1968, c. 552; 1975, cc. 14, 15.

§ 18.2-450. Immunity of witnesses.

No witness called by the court or attorney for the Commonwealth and giving evidence for the prosecution, either before the grand jury or the court in any prosecution under this article shall ever be proceeded against for any offense of giving, or offering to give, or accepting a bribe committed by him at the time and place indicated in such prosecution; but such witness shall be compelled to testify, and for refusing to answer questions, may by the court, be punished for contempt.

History.
Code 1950, § 18.1-282.3; 1968, c. 552; 1975, cc. 14, 15.

ARTICLE 4.
BARRATRY.

§ 18.2-451. Definitions; application and construction of article.

(a) *"Barratry"* is the offense of stirring up litigation.

(b) A *"barrator"* is an individual, partnership, association or corporation who or which stirs up litigation.

(c) *"Stirring up litigation"* means instigating or attempting to instigate a person or persons to institute a suit at law or equity.

(d) *"Instigating"* means bringing it about that all or part of the expenses of the litigation are paid by the barrator or by a person or persons (other than the plaintiffs) acting in concert with the barrator, unless the instigation is justified.

(e) *"Justified"* means that the instigator is related by blood or marriage to the plaintiff whom he instigates, or that the instigator is entitled by law to share with the plaintiff in money or property that is the subject of the litigation or that the instigator has a direct interest in the subject matter of the litigation or occupies a position of trust in relation to the plaintiff; or that the instigator is acting on behalf of a duly constituted legal aid society approved by the Virginia State Bar which offers advice or assistance in all kinds of legal matters to all members of the public who come to it for advice or assistance and are unable because of poverty to pay legal fees.

(f) *"Direct interest"* means a personal right or a pecuniary right or liability.

This article shall not be applicable to attorneys who are parties to contingent fee contracts with their clients where the attorney does not protect the client from payment of the costs and expense of litigation, nor shall this article apply to any matter involving annexation, zoning, bond issues, or the holding or results of any election or referendum, nor shall this article apply to suits pertaining to or affecting possession of or title to real or personal property, regardless of ownership, nor shall this article apply to suits involving the legality of assessment or collection of taxes or the rates thereof, nor shall this article apply to suits involving rates or charges or services by common carriers or public utilities, nor shall this article apply to criminal prosecutions, nor to the payment of attorneys by legal aid societies approved by the Virginia State Bar, nor to proceedings to abate nuisances. Nothing herein shall be construed to be in derogation of the constitutional rights of real parties in interest to employ counsel or to prosecute any available legal remedy under the laws of this Commonwealth.

History.
Code 1950, § 18.1-388; 1960, c. 358; 1975, cc. 14, 15.

§ 18.2-452. Barratry unlawful.

Any person, if an individual, who shall engage in barratry shall be guilty of a Class 1 misdemeanor; and if a corporation, may be fined not more than $10,000. If the corporation be a foreign corporation, its certificate of authority to transact business in Virginia shall be revoked by the State Corporation Commission.

History.
Code 1950, §§ 18.1-389, 18.1-390; 1960, c. 358; 1975, cc. 14, 15.

§ 18.2-453. Aiders and abettors.

A person who aids and abets a barrator by giving money or rendering services to or for the use or benefit of the barrator for committing barratry shall be guilty of barratry and punished as provided in § 18.2-452.

History.
Code 1950, § 18.1-391; 1960, c. 358; 1975, cc. 14, 15.

§ 18.2-454. Enjoining barratry.

Suits to enjoin barratry may be brought by the Attorney General or the attorney for the Commonwealth in the appropriate circuit court.

History.
Code 1950, § 18.1-392; 1960, c. 358; 1975, cc. 14, 15.

§ 18.2-455. Unprofessional conduct; revocation of license.

Conduct that is made illegal by this article on the part of an attorney at law or any person holding license from the Commonwealth to engage in a profession is unprofessional conduct. Upon hearing pursuant to the provisions of § 54.1-3935, or other statute applicable to the profession concerned, if the defendant be found guilty of barratry, his license to practice law or any other profession shall be revoked for such period as provided by law.

History.
Code 1950, § 18.1-393; 1960, c. 358; 1975, cc. 14, 15.

Crimes and Offenses

ARTICLE 5.
CONTEMPT OF COURT.

§ 18.2-456. Cases in which courts and judges may punish summarily for contempt.

The courts and judges may issue attachments for contempt, and punish them summarily, only in the cases following:

(1) Misbehavior in the presence of the court, or so near thereto as to obstruct or interrupt the administration of justice;

(2) Violence, or threats of violence, to a judge or officer of the court, or to a juror, witness or party going to, attending or returning from the court, for or in respect of any act or proceeding had or to be had in such court;

(3) Vile, contemptuous or insulting language addressed to or published of a judge for or in respect of any act or proceeding had, or to be had, in such court, or like language used in his presence and intended for his hearing for or in respect of such act or proceeding;

(4) Misbehavior of an officer of the court in his official character;

(5) Disobedience or resistance of an officer of the court, juror, witness or other person to any lawful process, judgment, decree or order of the court.

History.
Code 1950, § 18.1-292; 1960, c. 358; 1975, cc. 14, 15.

§ 18.2-457. Fine and imprisonment by court limited unless jury impaneled.

No court shall, without a jury, for any such contempt as is mentioned in the first class embraced in § 18.2-456, impose a fine exceeding $250 or imprison more than ten days; but in any such case the court may, without an indictment, information or any formal pleading, impanel a jury to ascertain the fine or imprisonment proper to be inflicted and may give judgment according to the verdict.

History.
Code 1950, § 18.1-295; 1960, c. 358; 1975, cc. 14, 15; 1999, c. 626.

§ 18.2-458. Power of judge of district court to punish for contempt.

A judge of a district court shall have the same power and jurisdiction as a judge of a circuit court to punish summarily for contempt, but in no case shall the fine exceed $250, or the imprisonment exceed ten days, for the same contempt.

History.
Code 1950, § 18.1-293; 1960, c. 358; 1975, cc. 14, 15; 1999, c. 626.

§ 18.2-459. Appeal from sentence of such judge.

Any person sentenced to pay a fine, or to confinement, under § 18.2-458, may appeal therefrom to the circuit court of the county or city in which the sentence was pronounced, upon entering into recognizance before the sentencing judge, with surety and in penalty deemed sufficient, to appear before such circuit court to answer for the offense. If such appeal be taken, a certificate of the conviction and the particular circumstances of the offense, together with the recognizance, shall forthwith be transmitted by the sentencing judge to the clerk of such circuit court, who shall immediately deliver the same to the judge thereof. Such judge, sitting without a jury, shall hear the case upon the certificate and any legal testimony adduced on either side, and make such order therein as may seem to him proper.

History.
Code 1950, § 18.1-294; 1960, c. 358; 1975, cc. 14, 15; 2013, c. 615.

ARTICLE 6.
INTERFERENCE WITH ADMINISTRATION OF JUSTICE.

§ 18.2-460. Obstructing justice; penalty.

A. If any person without just cause knowingly obstructs a judge, magistrate, justice, juror, attorney for the Commonwealth, witness, any law-enforcement officer, or animal control officer employed pursuant to § 3.2-6555 in the performance of his duties as such or fails or refuses without just cause to cease such obstruction when requested to do so by such judge, magistrate, justice, juror, attorney for the Commonwealth, witness, law-enforcement officer, or animal control officer employed pursuant to § 3.2-6555, he shall be guilty of a Class 1 misdemeanor.

B. Except as provided in subsection C, any person who, by threats or force, knowingly attempts to intimidate or impede a judge, magistrate, justice, juror, attorney for the Commonwealth, witness, any law-enforcement officer, or an animal control officer employed pursuant to § 3.2-6555 lawfully engaged in his duties as such, or to obstruct or impede the administration of justice in any court, is guilty of a Class 1 misdemeanor.

C. If any person by threats of bodily harm or force knowingly attempts to intimidate or impede a judge, magistrate, justice, juror, attorney for the Commonwealth, witness, any law-enforcement officer, lawfully engaged in the discharge of his duty, or to obstruct or impede the administration of justice in any court relating to a violation of or conspiracy to violate § 18.2-248 or subdivision (a) (3), (b) or (c) of § 18.2-248.1, or § 18.2-46.2 or § 18.2-46.3, or relating to the violation of or conspiracy to violate any violent felony offense listed in subsection C of § 17.1-805, he shall be guilty of a Class 5 felony.

D. Any person who knowingly and willfully makes any materially false statement or representation to a law-enforcement officer or an animal control officer employed pursuant to § 3.2-6555 who is in the course of conducting an investigation of a crime by another is guilty of a Class 1 misdemeanor.

History.
Code 1950, § 18.1-310; 1960, c. 358; 1975, cc. 14, 15; 1976, c. 269; 1984, c. 571; 1989, c. 506; 1993, c. 747; 1996, c. 718; 1999, cc. 770, 800; 2002, cc. 527, 810, 818; 2003, cc. 111, 149; 2004, cc. 396, 435; 2007, cc. 220, 282; 2009, c. 242.

§ 18.2-460.1. Unlawful disclosure of existence of order authorizing wire or oral interception of communication.

Except as provided in Chapter 6 (§ 19.2-61 et seq.) of Title 19.2, it shall be unlawful for any person who, by virtue of his position of authority or in the course of his employment by a court, a public utility, a law-enforcement agency, or by any other agency of state or local government, obtains knowledge of the fact that an order authorizing interception of wire or oral communication has been entered or is sought to be entered, intentionally to disclose such information to any person, except in the performance of his duties. Persons violating this section shall be guilty of a Class 1 misdemeanor.

Nothing herein precludes a court authorizing an interception under this chapter from prohibiting any other person from disclosing the existence of an order, interception, or device and imposing contempt sanctions for any willful disclosure.

History.
1980, c. 339.

§ 18.2-461. Falsely summoning or giving false reports to law-enforcement officials.

It shall be unlawful for any person (i) to knowingly give a false report as to the commission of any crime to any law-enforcement official with intent to mislead, or (ii) without just cause and with intent to interfere with the operations of any law-enforcement official, to call or summon any law-enforcement official by telephone or other means, including engagement or activation of an automatic emergency alarm. Violation of the provisions of this section shall be punishable as a Class 1 misdemeanor.

History.
Code 1950, § 18.1-401; 1960, c. 358; 1975, cc. 14, 15; 1996, cc. 753, 815.

§ 18.2-462. Concealing or compounding offenses; penalties.

A. Except as provided in subsection B, if any person knowing of the commission of an offense takes any money or reward, or an engagement therefor, upon an agreement or understanding, expressed or implied, to compound or conceal such offense, or not to prosecute therefor, or not to give evidence thereof, he shall, if such offense is a felony, be guilty of a Class 2 misdemeanor; and if such offense is not a felony, unless it is punishable merely by forfeiture to him, he shall be guilty of a Class 4 misdemeanor.

B. Any person, other than the victim of the crime or the husband, wife, parent, grandparent, child, grandchild, brother, or sister, by consanguinity or affinity of the offender, who with actual knowledge of the commission by another of any felony offense under Chapter 4 (§ 18.2-30 et seq.) of this title, willfully conceals, alters, dismembers, or destroys any item of physical evidence with the intent to delay, impede, obstruct, prevent, or hinder the investigation, apprehension, prosecution, conviction, or punishment of any person regarding such offense is guilty of a Class 6 felony.

History.
Code 1950, § 18.1-303; 1960, c. 358; 1975, cc. 14, 15; 2005, c. 408.

§ 18.2-462.1. Use of police radio during commission of crime.

Any person who has in his possession or who uses a device capable of receiving a police radio signal, message, or transmission, while in the commission of a felony, is guilty of a Class 1 misdemeanor. A prosecution for or conviction of the crime of use or possession of a police radio is not a bar to conviction for any other crime committed while possessing or using the police radio.

History.
1992, c. 499.

§ 18.2-463. Refusal to aid officer in execution of his office.

If any person on being required by any sheriff or other officer refuse or neglect to assist him: (1) in the execution of his office in a criminal case, (2) in the preservation of the peace, (3) in the apprehending or securing of any person for a breach of the peace, or (4) in any case of escape or rescue, he shall be guilty of a Class 2 misdemeanor.

History.
Code 1950, § 18.301; 1960, c. 358; 1975, cc. 14, 15.

§ 18.2-464. Failure to obey order of conservator of the peace.

If any person, being required by a conservator of the peace on view of a breach of the peace or other offense to bring before him the offender, refuse or neglect to obey the conservator of the peace, he shall be guilty of a Class 2 misdemeanor; and if the conservator of the peace declare himself or be known to be such to the person so refusing or neglecting, ignorance of his office shall not be pleaded as an excuse.

History.

Code 1950, § 18.1-302; 1960, c. 358; 1975, cc. 14, 15.

§ 18.2-465. Officer summoning juror to act impartially.

If any sheriff or other officer corruptly, or through favor or ill-will, summon a juror, with intent that such juror shall find a verdict for or against either party, he shall be guilty of a Class 3 misdemeanor, and forfeit his office; and he shall be forever incapable of holding any office of honor, profit or trust under the Constitution of Virginia.

History.

Code 1950, § 18.1-296; 1960, c. 358; 1975, cc. 14, 15.

§ 18.2-465.1. Penalizing employee for court appearance or service on jury panel.

Any person who is summoned to serve on jury duty or any person, except a defendant in a criminal case, who is summoned or subpoenaed to appear in any court of law or equity when a case is to be heard or who, having appeared, is required in writing by the court to appear at any future hearing, shall neither be discharged from employment, nor have any adverse personnel action taken against him, nor shall he be required to use sick leave or vacation time, as a result of his absence from employment due to such jury duty or court appearance, upon giving reasonable notice to his employer of such court appearance or summons. No person who is summoned and appears for jury duty for four or more hours, including travel time, in one day shall be required to start any work shift that begins on or after 5:00 p.m. on the day of his appearance for jury duty or begins before 3:00 a.m. on the day following the day of his appearance for jury duty. Any employer violating the provisions of this section is guilty of a Class 3 misdemeanor.

History.

1981, c. 609; 1985, c. 436; 1988, c. 415; 2000, c. 295; 2002, c. 423; 2004, c. 800; 2005, c. 931.

§ 18.2-466. Corruptly procuring juror to be summoned.

If any person procure or attempt to procure a juror to be summoned, with intent that such juror shall find a verdict for or against either party, he shall be guilty of a Class 3 misdemeanor.

History.

Code 1950, § 18.1-297; 1960, c. 358; 1975, cc. 14, 15.

§ 18.2-467. Fraud in drawing jurors, etc.

If any person be guilty of any fraud, either by tampering with the jury box prior to a draft, or in drawing a juror, or in returning into the jury box the name of any person which has lawfully been drawn out and drawing and substituting another in his stead, or in any other way in drawing of jurors, he shall be guilty of a Class 1 misdemeanor.

History.

Code 1950, § 18.1-298; 1960, c. 358; 1975, cc. 14, 15.

§ 18.2-468. Making sound recordings of jury deliberations.

If any person shall install or cause to be installed or use or cause to be used any microphone or device designed for recording or transmitting for recording sound in any jury room in this Commonwealth for the purpose of recording the deliberations of any jury or for the purpose of preparing a summary of such deliberations, he shall be guilty of a Class 6 felony.

History.

Code 1950, § 18.1-299; 1960, c. 358; 1975, cc. 14, 15.

§ 18.2-469. Officer refusing, delaying, etc., to execute process for criminal.

If any officer willfully and corruptly refuse to execute any lawful process requiring him to apprehend or confine a person convicted of, or charged with, an offense, or willfully and corruptly omit or delay to execute such process, whereby such person shall escape and go at large, such officer shall be guilty of a Class 3 misdemeanor.

History.

Code 1950, § 18.1-300; 1960, c. 358; 1975, cc. 14, 15.

§ 18.2-470. Extortion by officer.

If any officer, for performing an official duty for which a fee or compensation is allowed or provided by law, knowingly demand and receive a greater fee or compensation than is so allowed or provided, he shall be guilty of a Class 4 misdemeanor.

History.

Code 1950, § 18.1-304; 1960, c. 358; 1975, cc. 14, 15.

§ 18.2-471. Fraudulent issue of fee bills.

If any person authorized by law to charge fees for services performed by him and issue bills therefor fraudulently issue a fee bill for a service not performed by him, or for more than he is entitled to, he shall be guilty of a Class 3 misdemeanor and shall forfeit his office and be forever incapable of holding office of honor, profit or trust under the Constitution of Virginia.

History.
Code 1950, §§ 18.1-305, 18.1-307; 1960, c. 358; 1975, cc. 14, 15.

§ 18.2-471.1. Destruction of human biological evidence; penalty.

Any clerk of court or other public official who willfully violates an order entered pursuant to § 19.2-270.4:1 is guilty of a Class 6 felony.

History.
2006, c. 913.

§ 18.2-472. False entries or destruction of records by officers.

If a clerk of any court or other public officer fraudulently make a false entry, or erase, alter, secrete or destroy any record, including a microphotographic copy, in his keeping and belonging to his office, he shall be guilty of a Class 1 misdemeanor and shall forfeit his office and be forever incapable of holding any office of honor, profit or trust under the Constitution of Virginia.

History.
Code 1950, §§ 18.1-306, 18.1-307; 1960, c. 358; 1975, cc. 14, 15; 1977, c. 107.

§ 18.2-472.1. Providing false information or failing to provide registration information; penalty; prima facie evidence.

A. Any person subject to Chapter 9 (§ 9.1-900 et seq.) of Title 9.1, other than a person convicted of a sexually violent offense or murder as defined in § 9.1-902, who knowingly fails to register or reregister, or who knowingly provides materially false information to the Sex Offender and Crimes Against Minors Registry is guilty of a Class 1 misdemeanor. A second or subsequent conviction for an offense under this subsection is a Class 6 felony.

B. Any person convicted of a sexually violent offense or murder, as defined in § 9.1-902, who knowingly fails to register or reregister, or who knowingly provides materially false information to the Sex Offender and Crimes Against Minors Registry is guilty of a Class 6 felony. A second or subsequent conviction for an offense under this subsection is a Class 5 felony.

C. A prosecution pursuant to this section shall be brought in the city or county where the offender can be found or where the offender last registered or reregistered or, if the offender failed to comply with the duty to register, where the offender was last convicted of an offense for which registration or reregistration is required.

D. At any preliminary hearing pursuant to this section, an affidavit from the State Police issued as required in § 9.1-907 shall be admitted into evidence as prima facie evidence of the failure to comply with the duty to register or reregister. A copy of such affidavit shall be provided to the registrant or his counsel seven days prior to hearing or trial by the attorney for the Commonwealth.

E. The accused in any preliminary hearing in which an affidavit from the State Police issued as required in § 9.1-907 is offered into evidence pursuant to this section shall have the right to summon and call a custodian of records issuing the affidavit and examine him in the same manner as if he had been called as an adverse witness. Such witness shall appear at the cost of the Commonwealth.

F. At any trial or hearing other than a preliminary hearing conducted pursuant to this section, an affidavit from the State Police issued as required in § 9.1-907 shall constitute prima facie evidence of the failure to comply with the duty to register or reregister, provided the requirements of subsection G have been satisfied and the accused has not objected to the admission of the affidavit pursuant to subsection H.

G. If the attorney for the Commonwealth intends to offer the affidavit into evidence in lieu of testimony at a trial or hearing, other than a preliminary hearing, he shall:

1. Provide by mail, delivery, or otherwise, a copy of the affidavit to counsel of record for the accused, or to the accused if he is proceeding pro se, at no charge, no later than 28 days prior to the hearing or trial;

2. Provide simultaneously with the copy of the affidavit so provided under subdivision 1 a notice to the accused of his right to object to having the affidavit admitted without the presence and testimony of a custodian of the records; and

3. File a copy of the affidavit and notice with the clerk of the court hearing the matter on the day that the affidavit and notice are provided to the accused.

H. In any trial or hearing, other than a preliminary hearing, the accused may object in writing to admission of the affidavit, in lieu of testimony, as evidence of the facts stated therein. Such objection shall be filed with the court hearing the matter, with a copy to the attorney for the Commonwealth, no more than 14 days after the affidavit and notice were filed with the clerk by the attorney for the Commonwealth, or the objection shall be deemed waived. If timely objection is made, the affidavit shall not be admissible into evidence unless (i) the objection is waived by the accused or his counsel in writing or before the court, or (ii) the parties stipulate before the court to the admissibility of the affidavit.

I. Where a custodian of the records is not available for hearing or trial and the attorney for the Commonwealth has used due diligence to secure the presence of the person, the court shall order a continuance. Any continuances ordered pursuant to this subsection shall total not more than 90 days if the accused has been held continuously in custody and not more than 180 days if the accused has not been held continuously in custody.

J. Any objection by counsel for the accused, or the accused if he is proceeding pro se, to timeliness of the receipt of notice required by subsection G shall be made before hearing or trial upon his receipt of actual notice unless the accused did not receive actual notice prior to hearing or trial. A showing by the Commonwealth that the notice was mailed, delivered, or otherwise provided in compliance with the time requirements of this section shall constitute prima facie evidence that the notice was timely received by the accused. If the court finds upon the accused's objection made pursuant to this subsection, that he did not receive timely notice pursuant to subsection G, the accused's objection shall not be deemed waived and if the objection is made prior to hearing or trial, a continuance shall be ordered if requested by either party. Any continuance ordered pursuant to this subsection shall be subject to the time limitations set forth in subsection I.

K. For the purposes of this section any conviction for a substantially similar offense under the laws of (i) any foreign country or any political subdivision thereof, or (ii) any state or territory of the United States or any political subdivision thereof, the District of Columbia, or the United States shall be considered a prior conviction.

History.

1997, c. 747; 1999, c. 845; 2001, c. 365; 2003, c. 584; 2006, cc. 857, 914, 931; 2008, c. 218; 2009, Sp. Sess. I, cc. 1, 4; 2010, c. 656; 2011, c. 285.

ARTICLE 7.

ESCAPE OF, COMMUNICATIONS WITH AND DELIVERIES TO PRISONERS.

§ 18.2-473. Persons aiding escape of prisoner or child.

When a person is lawfully detained as a prisoner in any jail or prison or held in custody, or when a child is placed in a local juvenile detention home, or committed to the Department of Juvenile Justice in any juvenile correctional center, or Reception and Diagnostic Center for Children or held in custody, if any person: (1) conveys anything into the jail, prison, juvenile detention home, juvenile correctional center or Reception and Diagnostic Center for Children with intent to facilitate a person's escape therefrom, (2) in any way aids such prisoner or child to escape, or in an attempt to escape, from such jail, prison, juvenile detention home, juvenile correctional center, Reception and Diagnostic Center for Children or custody, or (3) forcibly takes, or attempts to take him therefrom, such person, if the taking or escape is effected, shall, if the prisoner or child was detained on conviction, commitment or charge of felony, be confined in a state correctional facility not less than one year nor more than five years. If the same is not effected, or if the prisoner or child was not detained on such conviction, commitment or charge, he shall be guilty of a Class 1 misdemeanor.

History.

Code 1950, § 18.1-284; 1960, c. 358; 1975, cc. 14, 15; 1984, c. 587; 1989, c. 733; 1996, cc. 755, 914.

§ 18.2-473.1. Communication with prisoners or committed person; penalty.

It shall be unlawful for any person outside of any state or local correctional facility or any juvenile correctional center, other than the jailers or custodial officers in charge of the prisoners or in charge of the persons committed to the Department of Juvenile Justice, to communicate without authority by word or sign with the intent to disrupt institutional operations with any prisoner confined within a state or local correctional facility or with any person committed to the Department of Juvenile Justice in any juvenile correctional center. Any person violating this section is guilty of a Class 4 misdemeanor.

History.

1982, c. 636; 2000, c. 286; 2013, cc. 707, 782.

§ 18.2-474. Delivery of articles to prisoners or committed person.

No person shall willfully in any manner deliver, or attempt to deliver, to any prisoner confined under authority of the Commonwealth of Virginia, or of any political subdivision thereof, or to any person committed to the Department of Juvenile Justice in any juvenile correctional center, any article of any nature whatsoever, without first securing the permission of the person in whose charge such prisoner or committed person is, and who may in his discretion grant or refuse permission. Any person violating this section is guilty of a Class 1 misdemeanor.

Nothing herein contained shall be construed to repeal or amend § 18.2-473.

History.

Code 1950, § 18.1-285; 1960, c. 358; 1975, cc. 14, 15; 2013, cc. 707, 782.

§ 18.2-474.1. Delivery of drugs, firearms, explosives, etc., to prisoners or committed persons.

Notwithstanding the provisions of § 18.2-474, any person who shall willfully in any manner deliver, attempt to deliver, or conspire with another to deliver to any prisoner confined under authority of the Commonwealth of Virginia, or of any political subdivision thereof, or to any person committed to the Department of Juvenile Justice in any juvenile correctional center, any drug which is a controlled substance regulated by the Drug Control Act in Chapter 34 (§ 54.1-3400 et seq.) of Title 54.1 or marijuana is guilty of a Class 5 felony. Any person who shall willfully in any manner so deliver or attempt to deliver or conspire to deliver to any such prisoner or confined or committed person, firearms, ammunitions, or explosives of any nature is guilty of a Class 3 felony.

Nothing herein contained shall be construed to repeal or amend § 18.2-473.

History.
1975, c. 608; 1982, c. 490; 2011, cc. 384, 410; 2013, cc. 707, 782; 2014, cc. 674, 719.

§ 18.2-475. Officers, etc., voluntarily allowing person convicted, charged, or adjudicated delinquent of felony to escape; penalty.

If any sheriff, jailer, or other officer, or any guard or other person summoned or employed by any such sheriff, jailer, or other officer, voluntarily allows a prisoner or person committed to the Department of Juvenile Justice convicted of, charged with, or adjudicated delinquent of a felony to escape from his custody, he is guilty of a Class 4 felony.

History.
Code 1950, § 18.1-286; 1960, c. 358; 1975, cc. 14, 15; 1983, c. 360; 2013, cc. 707, 782.

§ 18.2-476. Officers, etc., willfully and deliberately permitting person convicted of, charged with, or adjudicated delinquent of a nonfelonious offense to escape or willfully refusing to receive person; penalty.

If any sheriff, jailer, or other officer, or any guard or other person summoned or employed by such sheriff, jailer, or other officer, willfully and deliberately permits a prisoner or person committed to the Department of Juvenile Justice convicted of, charged with, or adjudicated delinquent of an offense not a felony, to escape from his custody, or willfully refuses to receive into his custody a person lawfully committed thereto, he is guilty of a Class 2 misdemeanor.

History.
Code 1950, § 18.1-287; 1960, c. 358; 1975, cc. 14, 15; 1983, c. 360; 2013, cc. 707, 782.

§ 18.2-477. Prisoner escaping from jail; how punished.

If any person confined in jail or in custody after conviction of a criminal offense shall escape by force or violence, other than by setting fire thereto, he shall be guilty of a Class 6 felony. The term of confinement under this section shall commence from the expiration of the former sentence.

History.
Code 1950, § 18.1-288; 1960, c. 358; 1962, c. 506; 1975, cc. 14, 15; 1985, c. 555.

§ 18.2-477.1. Escapes from juvenile facility; penalty.

A. It shall be unlawful for any person to escape or remain away without proper authority from a group home or other residential care facility for children in need of services, delinquent or alleged delinquent youths in which he had been placed by the juvenile and domestic relations court or as a result of his commitment as a juvenile to the Department of Juvenile Justice. Any person violating this subsection shall be taken into custody and brought before the juvenile and domestic relations court. The court may find the person in violation of § 16.1-292 or, if the court finds the person amenable to further treatment in a juvenile facility, the court may return him to the custody of the Department.

B. It shall be unlawful for any person to escape or remain away without proper authority from a secure facility operated by or under contract with the Department of Juvenile Justice or from a secure juvenile detention facility in which he had been placed by the juvenile and domestic relations court or as a result of his commitment as a juvenile to the Department of Juvenile Justice. Any person who escapes from a facility specified in this subsection by force or by violence shall be guilty of a Class 6 felony or, if violation of this subsection occurs other than by force or violence, a Class 1 misdemeanor.

History.
1985, c. 435; 1989, c. 733; 1993, c. 840; 1994, c. 490; 1997, c. 749.

§ 18.2-477.2. Punishment for certain offenses committed within a secure juvenile facility or detention home.

It shall be unlawful for a person committed to the Department of Juvenile Justice in any juvenile correctional center or detained in a secure juvenile facility or detention home to commit any of the offenses enumerated in § 53.1-203. A violation of this section shall be punishable as a Class 6 felony, except that a violation of subdivision 6 of § 53.1-203 is a Class 5 felony.

History.
1999, c. 21; 2007, c. 521; 2013, cc. 707, 782.

§ 18.2-478. Escape from jail or custody by force or violence without setting fire to jail.

If any person lawfully imprisoned in jail and not tried or sentenced on a criminal offense escapes from jail by force or violence, other than by setting fire thereto or if any person lawfully in the custody of any police officer on a charge of criminal offense escapes from such custody by force or violence, he shall be guilty of a Class 6 felony.

History.
Code 1950, § 18.1-289; 1960, c. 358; 1975, cc. 14, 15; 1985, c. 555.

§ 18.2-479. Escape without force or violence or setting fire to jail.

A. Except as provided in subsection B, any person lawfully confined in jail or lawfully in the custody of

Crimes and Offenses

any court, officer of the court, or of any law-enforcement officer for violation of his probation or parole or on a charge or conviction of a misdemeanor, who escapes, other than by force or violence or by setting fire to the jail, is guilty of a Class 1 misdemeanor.

B. Any person, lawfully confined in jail or lawfully in the custody of any court, officer of the court, or of any law-enforcement officer on a charge or conviction of a felony, who escapes, other than by force or violence or by setting fire to the jail, is guilty of a Class 6 felony.

History.
Code 1950, § 18.1-290; 1960, c. 358; 1975, cc. 14, 15; 1985, c. 555; 2005, c. 573.

§ 18.2-479.1. Resisting arrest; fleeing from a law-enforcement officer; penalty.

A. Any person who intentionally prevents or attempts to prevent a law-enforcement officer from lawfully arresting him, with or without a warrant, is guilty of a Class 1 misdemeanor.

B. For purposes of this section, intentionally preventing or attempting to prevent a lawful arrest means fleeing from a law-enforcement officer when (i) the officer applies physical force to the person, or (ii) the officer communicates to the person that he is under arrest and (a) the officer has the legal authority and the immediate physical ability to place the person under arrest, and (b) a reasonable person who receives such communication knows or should know that he is not free to leave.

History.
2003, cc. 112, 805.

§ 18.2-480. Escape, etc., by setting fire to jail.

If any person lawfully imprisoned in jail escape, or attempt to escape therefrom, by setting fire thereto, he shall be guilty of a Class 4 felony.

History.
Code 1950, § 18.1-291; 1960, c. 358; 1975, cc. 14, 15.

§ 18.2-480.1. Admissibility of records of Department of Corrections in escape cases.

In any prosecution for, or preliminary hearing for, the offense of escape under this article or Title 53.1, the records maintained by the Department of Corrections or the Department of Juvenile Justice, when such records are duly attested by the custodian of such records, shall be admissible in evidence as evidence of the fact, location and dates of confinement, provided that the records shall be filed with the clerk of the court hearing the case at least seven days prior to the trial or preliminary hearing. On motion of the accused, the court may require the custodian to appear as a witness and be subject to cross-examination; provided such motion is made within a reasonable time prior to the day on which the case is set for trial; and provided further, that the custodian so appearing shall be considered the Commonwealth's witness.

History.
1976, c. 394; 1989, c. 733.

CHAPTER 11.

OFFENSES AGAINST THE SOVEREIGNTY OF THE COMMONWEALTH.

Article 1.

Treason and Related Offenses.

Article 2.

Uniform Flag Act.

ARTICLE 1.

TREASON AND RELATED OFFENSES.

§ 18.2-481. Treason defined; how proved and punished.

Treason shall consist only in:

(1) Levying war against the Commonwealth;

(2) Adhering to its enemies, giving them aid and comfort;

(3) Establishing, without authority of the legislature, any government within its limits separate from the existing government;

(4) Holding or executing, in such usurped government, any office, or professing allegiance or fidelity to it; or

(5) Resisting the execution of the laws under color of its authority.

Such treason, if proved by the testimony of two witnesses to the same overt act, or by confession in court, shall be punishable as a Class 2 felony.

History.
Code 1950, § 18.1-418; 1960, c. 358; 1975, cc. 14, 15.

§ 18.2-482. Misprision of treason.

If any person knowing of such treason shall not, as soon as may be, give information thereof to the Governor, or some conservator of the peace, he shall be guilty of a Class 6 felony.

History.
Code 1950, § 18.1-419; 1960, c. 358; 1975, cc. 14, 15.

§ 18.2-483. Attempting, or instigating others, to establish usurped government.

If any person attempt to establish any such usurped government and commit any overt act therefor or by writing or speaking endeavor to instigate others to establish such government, he shall be guilty of a Class 1 misdemeanor.

History.
Code 1950, § 18.1-420; 1960, c. 358; 1975, cc. 14, 15.

§ 18.2-484. Advocacy of change in government by force, violence or other unlawful means.

It shall be unlawful for any person, group, or organization to advocate any change, by force, violence, or other unlawful means in the government of the Commonwealth of Virginia or any of its subdivisions or in the government of the United States of America.

It shall be unlawful for any person to join, assist or otherwise contribute to any group or organization which, to the knowledge of such person, advocates or has as its purpose, aim or objective, any change, by force, violence, or other unlawful means in the government of the Commonwealth of Virginia or any of its subdivisions or in the government of the United States of America.

Violation of this section shall be punishable as a Class 6 felony.

Nothing herein shall be construed to limit or prohibit the advocacy, orally or otherwise, of any change, by peaceful means, in the government of the Commonwealth or any of its subdivisions or in the government of the United States.

History.
Code 1950, § 18.1-421; 1960, c. 358; 1962, c. 343; 1975, cc. 14, 15.

§ 18.2-485. Conspiring to incite one race to insurrection against another race.

If any person conspire with another to incite the population of one race to acts of violence and war against the population of another race, he shall, whether such acts of violence and war be made or not, be guilty of a Class 4 felony.

History.
Code 1950, § 18.1-422; 1960, c. 358; 1975, cc. 14, 15.

ARTICLE 2.

UNIFORM FLAG ACT.

§ 18.2-486. Definition of flag, standard, etc.

The words flag, standard, color, ensign or shield, as used in this article, shall include any flag, standard, color, ensign or shield, or copy, picture or representation thereof, made of any substance or represented or produced thereon, and of any size, evidently purporting to be such flag, standard, color, ensign or shield of the United States, or of this Commonwealth, or a copy, picture or representation thereof.

History.
Code 1950, § 18.1-423; 1960, c. 358; 1975, cc. 14, 15.

§ 18.2-487. Exhibition or display.

No person shall, in any manner, for exhibition or display:

(1) Place or cause to be placed any word, figure, mark, picture, design, drawing or advertisement of any nature upon any flag, standard, color, ensign or shield of the United States or of this Commonwealth, or authorized by any law of the United States or of this Commonwealth;

(2) Expose to public view any such flag, standard, color, ensign or shield upon which shall have been printed, painted or otherwise produced, or to which shall have been attached, appended, affixed or annexed, any such word, figure, mark, picture, design, drawing or advertisement; or

(3) Expose to public view for sale, manufacture or otherwise, or sell, give or have in possession for sale, for gift or for use for any purpose, any substance, being an article of merchandise, or receptacle, or thing for holding or carrying merchandise, upon or to which shall have been produced or attached any such flag, standard, color, ensign or shield, in order to advertise, call attention to, decorate, mark or distinguish such article or substance.

History.
Code 1950, § 18.1-424; 1960, c. 358; 1975, cc. 14, 15.

§ 18.2-488. Mutilating, defacing, etc.

No person shall publicly burn with contempt, mutilate, deface, defile, trample upon, or wear with intent to defile any such flag, standard, color, ensign or shield.

History.
Code 1950, § 18.1-425; 1960, c. 358; 1968, c. 349; 1975, cc. 14, 15, 493.

§ 18.2-488.1. Flag at half mast for certain public safety personnel killed in the line of duty.

A. As used in this section, unless the context requires a different meaning:

"Emergency medical services provider" means the same as that term is defined in § 32.1-111.1 and any member of a volunteer emergency medical services agency.

"Firefighter" means the same as that term is defined in § 9.1-300, and any member of a volunteer fire department.

"Police officer" means any full-time or part-time employee of a police department or sheriff's office which is a part of or administered by the Commonwealth or any political subdivision thereof and who is responsible for the prevention and detection of crime and the enforcement of the penal, traffic, or highway laws of the Commonwealth.

"Service member" means a member of the United States armed forces, Virginia National Guard, or Virginia Defense Force.

B. Whenever a service member, police officer, firefighter, or emergency medical services provider who is a resident of Virginia is killed in the line of duty, all flags, state and local, flown at any building owned and operated by the Commonwealth shall be flown at half staff or mast for one day to honor and acknowledge respect for those who made the supreme sacrifice.

C. The Department of General Services shall develop procedures to effectuate the purposes of this section.

History.
2012, c. 767; 2015, cc. 502, 503.

§ 18.2-489. To what article applies.

This article shall not apply to any act permitted by the statutes of the United States or by the laws of this Commonwealth, or by the United States armed forces regulations, nor shall it apply to any printed or written document or production, stationery, ornament, picture or jewelry whereon shall be depicted such flag, standard, color, ensign or shield, with no design or words thereon and disconnected with any advertisement.

History.
Code 1950, § 18.1-426; 1960, c. 358; 1975, cc. 14, 15.

§ 18.2-490. Penalty.

Any violation of this article shall be punishable as a Class 1 misdemeanor.

The provisions of this section shall not apply to § 18.2-488.1.

History.
Code 1950, § 18.1-427; 1960, c. 358; 1968, c. 349; 1975, cc. 14, 15; 2012, c. 767.

§ 18.2-491. Construction.

This article shall be so construed as to effectuate its general purpose, and to make uniform the laws of the states which enact it.

History.
Code 1950, § 18.1-428; 1960, c. 358; 1975, cc. 14, 15.

§ 18.2-492. Short title.

This article may be cited as the Uniform Flag Act.

History.
Code 1950, § 18.1-429; 1960, c. 358; 1975, cc. 14, 15.

CHAPTER 12. MISCELLANEOUS.

Article 1.

Liquefied Petroleum Gas Containers.

Article 1.1.

Virginia Governmental Frauds Act.

Article 2.

Conspiracy to Injure Another in Trade, Business or Profession.

Article 3.

Miscellaneous Offenses in General.

ARTICLE 1.

LIQUEFIED PETROLEUM GAS CONTAINERS.

§ 18.2-493. Definitions.

As used in this article, unless the text indicates otherwise:

(a) *"Person"* shall mean any person, firm or corporation.

(b) *"Owner"* shall mean any person who holds a written bill of sale under which title or ownership to a container was transferred to such person, or any manufacturer of a container who has not sold or transferred ownership thereof by written bill of sale.

(c) *"Liquefied petroleum gas"* shall mean any material which is composed predominately of any of the following hydrocarbons or mixtures of the same: propane, propylene, butanes (normal butane and isobutane) and butylenes.

History.
Code 1950, § 18.1-400.1; 1970, c. 442; 1975, cc. 14, 15.

§ 18.2-494. Unlawful use of, filling or refilling or trafficking in containers.

No person except the owner thereof or person authorized in writing by the owner shall fill or refill with liquefied petroleum gas, or any other gas or compound, a liquefied petroleum gas container; or buy, sell, offer for sale, give, take, loan, deliver or permit to be delivered, or otherwise use, dispose of, or traffic in a liquefied petroleum gas container or containers if the container bears upon the surface thereof in plainly legible characters the name, initials, mark or other device of the owner; nor shall any person other than the owner of a liquefied petroleum gas container or a person authorized in writing by the owner deface, erase, obliterate, cover up, or otherwise remove or conceal any name, mark, initial or device thereon.

History.
Code 1950, § 18.1-400.2; 1970, c. 442; 1975, cc. 14, 15.

§ 18.2-495. Presumptive evidence.

The use of a liquefied petroleum gas container or containers by any person other than the person whose name, mark, initial or device is on the liquefied petroleum gas container or containers, without written consent, or purchase of the marked and distinguished liquefied petroleum gas container for the sale of liquefied petroleum gas or filling or refilling with liquefied petroleum gas, or possession of the liquefied petroleum gas containers by any person other than the person having his name, mark, initial or other device thereon, without the written consent of such owner, is presumptive evidence of the unlawful use, filling or refilling, or trafficking in of such liquefied petroleum gas containers.

History.
Code 1950, § 18.1-400.3; 1970, c. 442; 1975, cc. 14, 15.

§ 18.2-496. Punishment for violation.

Any person who fails to comply with any of the foregoing provisions of this article is guilty of a Class 3 misdemeanor for each separate offense.

History.
Code 1950, § 18.1-400.4; 1970, c. 442; 1975, cc. 14, 15.

§ 18.2-497. Fines and costs.

The costs incurred in the enforcement of this article shall be assessed and collected in the same manner as in criminal cases, and all fines collected by virtue of this article shall be turned over in the same manner and for the same purposes as criminal and misdemeanor fines are disposed of by law.

History.
Code 1950, § 18.1-400.5; 1970, c. 442; 1975, cc. 14, 15.

§ 18.2-498. Exempt containers.

Nothing in this article applies to or shall be construed to affect a liquefied petroleum gas container having a total capacity of five gallons or less.

History.
Code 1950, § 18.1-400.6; 1970, c. 442; 1975, cc. 14, 15.

ARTICLE 1.1.

VIRGINIA GOVERNMENTAL FRAUDS ACT.

§ 18.2-498.1. Short title.

This article shall be known and cited as the Virginia Governmental Frauds Act.

History.
1980, c. 472.

§ 18.2-498.2. Definitions.

When used in this article, the term:

1. *"Person"* includes any natural person, any trust or association of persons, formal or otherwise, or any corporation, partnership, company or other legal or commercial entity.

2. *"Commercial dealing"* shall mean any offer, acceptance, agreement, or solicitation to sell or offer to sell or distribute goods, services or construction, to the Commonwealth of Virginia, or any local gov-

ernment within the Commonwealth or any department or agency thereof.

History.
1980, c. 472.

§ 18.2-498.3. Misrepresentations prohibited.

Any person, in any commercial dealing in any matter within the jurisdiction of any department or agency of the Commonwealth of Virginia, or any local government within the Commonwealth or any department or agency thereof, who knowingly falsifies, conceals, misleads, or covers up by any trick, scheme, or device a material fact, or makes any false, fictitious or fraudulent statements or representations, or makes or uses any false writing or document knowing the same to contain any false, fictitious or fraudulent statement or entry, shall be guilty of a Class 6 felony.

History.
1980, c. 472.

§ 18.2-498.4. Duty to provide certified statement.

A. The Commonwealth, or any department or agency thereof, and any local government or any department or agency thereof, may require that any person seeking, offering or agreeing to transact business or commerce with it, or seeking, offering or agreeing to receive any portion of the public funds or moneys, submit a certification that the offer or agreement or any claim resulting therefrom is not the result of, or affected by, any act of collusion with another person engaged in the same line of business or commerce; or any act of fraud punishable under this article.

B. Any person required to submit a certified statement as provided in subsection A above who knowingly makes a false statement shall be guilty of a Class 6 felony.

History.
1980, c. 472.

§ 18.2-498.5. Actions on behalf of Commonwealth or localities.

The Attorney General on behalf of the Commonwealth, or the attorney for the Commonwealth, on behalf of the county or city as the case may be may institute actions and proceedings for any and all violations occurring within their jurisdictions.

History.
1980, c. 472.

ARTICLE 2.

CONSPIRACY TO INJURE ANOTHER IN TRADE, BUSINESS OR PROFESSION.

§ 18.2-499. Combinations to injure others in their reputation, trade, business or profession; rights of employees.

A. Any two or more persons who combine, associate, agree, mutually undertake or concert together for the purpose of (i) willfully and maliciously injuring another in his reputation, trade, business or profession by any means whatever or (ii) willfully and maliciously compelling another to do or perform any act against his will, or preventing or hindering another from doing or performing any lawful act, shall be jointly and severally guilty of a Class 1 misdemeanor. Such punishment shall be in addition to any civil relief recoverable under § 18.2-500.

B. Any person who attempts to procure the participation, cooperation, agreement or other assistance of any one or more persons to enter into any combination, association, agreement, mutual understanding or concert prohibited in subsection A of this section shall be guilty of a violation of this section and subject to the same penalties set out in subsection A.

C. This section shall not affect the right of employees lawfully to organize and bargain concerning wages and conditions of employment, and take other steps to protect their rights as provided under state and federal laws.

History.
Code 1950, § 18.1-74.1:1; 1964, c. 623; 1972, c. 469; 1975, cc. 14, 15; 1994, c. 534.

§ 18.2-500. Same; civil relief; damages and counsel fees; injunctions.

A. Any person who shall be injured in his reputation, trade, business or profession by reason of a violation of § 18.2-499, may sue therefor and recover three-fold the damages by him sustained, and the costs of suit, including a reasonable fee to plaintiff's counsel, and without limiting the generality of the term, "damages" shall include loss of profits.

B. Whenever a person shall duly file a civil action in the circuit court of any county or city against any person alleging violations of the provisions of § 18.2-499 and praying that such party defendant be restrained and enjoined from continuing the acts complained of, such court shall have jurisdiction to hear and determine the issues involved, to issue injunctions pendente lite and permanent injunctions and to decree damages and costs of suit, including reasonable counsel fees to complainants' and defendants' counsel.

History.
Code 1950, § 18.1-74.1:2; 1964, c. 623; 1975, cc. 14, 15; 2003, c. 578; 2005, c. 681.

§ 18.2-501. Same; protection of persons testifying or producing evidence.

(a) No natural person shall be prosecuted or be subjected to any penalty or forfeiture for or on account of any transaction, matter or thing concerning which he may testify or produce evidence, documentary or otherwise, in any action, suit, or prosecution authorized by this article; provided, that no person so testifying shall be exempt from prosecution or punishment for perjury committed in so testifying.

(b) As used in this article a *"person"* is any person, firm, corporation, partnership or association.

History.
Code 1950, § 18.1-74.1:3; 1964, c. 623; 1975, cc. 14, 15.

ARTICLE 2.1.

SPORTS AGENTS REGULATION ACT.

Editor's note.
Acts 1989, c. 530, cl. 2 provided that this article (§§ 18.2-501.1 through 18.2-501.5) would not become effective until reenacted by the 1990 Session of the General Assembly. The article was not reenacted, and therefore, never became effective.

ARTICLE 3.

MISCELLANEOUS OFFENSES IN GENERAL.

§ 18.2-502. Medical referral for profit.

(a) No person, firm, partnership, association or corporation, or agent or employee thereof, shall for profit engage in any business which in whole or in part includes the referral or recommendation of persons to a physician, hospital, health related facility, or dispensary for any form of medical care or treatment of any ailment or physical condition unless the person is advised of the criteria of selection of the physicians, hospitals, health-related facilities or dispensaries considered for the referral or recommendation. The acceptance of a fee or charge for any such referral or recommendation shall create a presumption that the business is engaged in such service for profit. A violation of the provisions of this section shall be punishable as a Class 1 misdemeanor.

(b) Whenever there is a violation of this section, in addition to the criminal sanctions, an application may be made by the Attorney General to the circuit court of the city or county in which the offense occurred, to issue an injunction, and upon notice to the defendant of not less than five days, to enjoin and restrain the continuance of such violation. If it appears to the satisfaction of the court or judge that the defendant has, in fact, violated this section, an injunction may be issued by such court or judge enjoining and restraining any further violation, without requiring proof that any person has, in fact, been injured or damaged thereby. Nothing in this section shall be construed to limit, prohibit, forbid or prevent any licensed physician or practitioner of the healing arts in the ordinary course of his professional practice from making referrals or recommendations to other members of such groups, so long as no fee is received for such referral or recommendation.

The criminal and civil provisions of this section shall not apply to any individual association or corporation not organized or incorporated for pecuniary profit or financial gain, or to any organization or association which is exempt from taxation pursuant to § 501 (c) of Title 26 of the United States Code (Int. Rev. Code of 1954).

(c) Nothing in this section shall be construed to authorize any division of fees prohibited by § 54.1-2962 or any remuneration for referral prohibited by federal law or regulation.

History.
Code 1950, § 18.1-417.2; 1972, c. 642; 1975, cc. 14, 15; 1986, c. 632.

§ 18.2-502.1. Weight loss centers or clinics; disclosure.

No weight loss center or clinic shall, in its name or advertisements, use the words "physicians" or "doctors" or refer to its clients as "patients" or indicate that "medical teams" are available in its facility unless (i) the facility employs at least one registered nurse full-time and employs or contracts with at least one physician licensed by the Board of Medicine for services or consultation in connection with the facility's activities; or (ii) the facility is under the full-time supervision of a physician; or (iii) the clinic or program is operated by or in conjunction with a licensed hospital. Any physician affiliated with a weight loss center or clinic for purposes of consultation or supervision shall have primary responsibility for decisions made within the scope of that affiliation relating to the provision of medical services or care to persons using the services of that facility and shall have primary responsibility for medical decisions relating to the evaluation of the appropriateness of the admission of persons to the weight loss program. Any person who violates the provisions of this section shall be guilty of a Class 1 misdemeanor.

History.
1988, c. 765.

§ 18.2-502.2. Warning required for certain medical tests; penalty.

No commercial medical testing kit designed for consumer home use shall be sold in this Commonwealth unless a warning is provided to the consumer to the effect that such tests may produce erroneous results and that medical testing is more accurate when performed by professionals within the controlled conditions of a laboratory. The consumer shall be advised to seek professional medical consultation and, if recommended, another test for validation of such test results.

Any person who violates the provisions of this section shall be guilty of a Class 4 misdemeanor.

History.
1989, c. 142.

§ 18.2-503. Possession or duplication of certain keys.

(a) No person shall knowingly possess any key to the lock of any building or other property owned by the Commonwealth of Virginia, or a department, division, agency or political subdivision thereof, without receiving permission from a person duly authorized to give such permission to possess such key.

(b) No person, without receiving permission from a person duly authorized to give such permission, shall knowingly duplicate, copy or make a facsimile of any key to a lock of a building or other property owned by the Commonwealth of Virginia, or a department, division, agency or political subdivision thereof.

Violation of this section shall constitute a Class 3 misdemeanor.

History.
Code 1950, § 18.1-408.1; 1972, c. 139; 1975, cc. 14, 15; 1984, c. 61.

§ 18.2-504. Destroying or concealing wills.

If any person fraudulently destroy or conceal any will or codicil, with intent to prevent the probate thereof, he shall be guilty of a Class 6 felony.

History.
Code 1950, § 18.1-309; 1960, c. 358; 1975, cc. 14, 15.

§ 18.2-504.1. Unlawful change of name; punishment.

If any person residing in this Commonwealth changes his name or assumes another name, unlawfully, he shall be guilty of a Class 3 misdemeanor.

History.
Code 1950, § 8-577.1; 1956, c. 402; 1973, c. 401; 1976, c. 115; 1977, c. 624.

§ 18.2-505. Preparation, etc., of papers to be submitted for academic credit.

(a) No person shall prepare, cause to be prepared or sell any term paper, thesis, dissertation or other written material for another person, for profit, with the knowledge, or under circumstances in which he should reasonably have known, that such term paper, thesis, dissertation or other written material is to be submitted by any other person for academic credit at any public or private college, university or other institution of higher learning in this Commonwealth.

(b) No person shall make or disseminate, with the intent to induce any other person to enter into any obligation relating thereto, any statement, written or oral, that he will prepare or cause to be prepared, any term paper, thesis, dissertation or other written material, to be sold for profit, for or on behalf of any person who has been assigned the written preparation of such term paper, thesis, dissertation or other written material for academic credit at any public or private college, university or other institution of higher learning in this Commonwealth.

History.
Code 1950, § 18.1-371.1; 1974, c. 342; 1975, cc. 14, 15.

§ 18.2-506. "Person" and "prepare" defined.

(a) As used in this article, *"person"* means any individual, partnership, corporation or association.

(b) As used in this article, *"prepare"* means to put into condition for intended use. "Prepare" does not include the mere typing or assembling of papers, nor the mere furnishing of information or research.

History.
Code 1950, § 18.1-371.2; 1974, c. 342; 1975, cc. 14, 15.

§ 18.2-507. Injunctions against violation of § 18.2-505.

Whenever a college, university or other institution of higher learning in this Commonwealth shall duly file a civil action in the circuit court of any county or city against any person alleging violations of the provisions of § 18.2-505, and praying that such party defendant be restrained and enjoined from continuing the acts complained of, such court shall have jurisdiction to hear and determine the issues involved, to issue injunctions pendente lite and permanent injunctions and to decree damages and costs of suit, including reasonable counsel fees to complainants' counsel.

History.
Code 1950, § 18.1-371.3; 1974, c. 342; 1975, cc. 14, 15; 2005, c. 681.

§ 18.2-508. Penalties.

Any person found guilty of violating any provision of § 18.2-505 shall be guilty of a misdemeanor and shall be punished by a fine not to exceed $1,000.

History.
Code 1950, § 18.1-371.4; 1974, c. 342; 1975, cc. 14, 15.

§ 18.2-509. Employment of lights under certain circumstances.

Any person in any motor vehicle or otherwise who, between a half hour after sunset on any day and a half hour before sunrise the following day, employs a light attached to such vehicle, or employs a spotlight to cast a light beyond the surface of the roadway upon any poultry house or other building inhabited by animals that causes such animals to panic or become injured, except upon his own land or upon private land on which he has permission, shall be guilty of a Class 4 misdemeanor.

History.
1976, c. 332.

§ 18.2-510. Burial or cremation of animals or fowls which have died.

When the owner of any animal or grown fowl which has died knows of such death, such owner shall forthwith have its body cremated or buried or request such service from an officer or other person designated for the purpose. If the owner fails to do so, any judge of a general district court, after notice to the owner if he can be ascertained, shall cause any such dead animal or fowl to be cremated or buried by an officer or other person designated for the purpose. Such officer or other person shall be entitled to recover of the owner of every such animal or fowl that is cremated or buried the actual cost of the cremation or burial and a reasonable fee to be recovered in the same manner as officers' fees are recovered, free from all exemptions in favor of such owner. Any person violating the provisions of this section shall be guilty of a Class 4 misdemeanor.

Nothing in this section shall be deemed to require the burial or cremation of the whole or portions of any animal or fowl which is to be used for food or in any commercial manner.

This section shall not apply to any county until the governing body thereof shall adopt the same.

History.
Code 1950, § 32-70; 1979, c. 716; 1981, c. 578; 2008, c. 345.

§ 18.2-511. Sale of certain military grave markers prohibited.

Any person who sells or offers for sale any military grave marker of one or more deceased persons who served in the military service of the Commonwealth, the United States, or any of the states thereof, shall be assessed a $100 civil penalty payable to the Literary Fund.

The provisions of this section shall not apply to the sale or offer for sale of such grave marker if it was (i) conveyed with real property to which it remains affixed, (ii) sold or offered for sale following manufacture or fabrication and prior to initial installation or dedication, or (iii) lawfully acquired.

History.
2004, c. 299.

§ 18.2-511.1. Smoking in proximity to a medical oxygen source in a health care facility; penalty.

Any person who smokes or uses an open flame within 25 feet of a medical oxygen source in a health care facility, as defined in § 15.2-2820, when the area is posted as an area where smoking and open flame are prohibited is guilty of a Class 2 misdemeanor.

History.
2007, c. 430; 2009, cc. 153, 154.

CHAPTER 13.

VIRGINIA RACKETEER INFLUENCED AND CORRUPT ORGANIZATION ACT.

Section

§ 18.2-512. Short title.

This chapter may be cited as the "Virginia Racketeer Influenced and Corrupt Organization (RICO) Act."

History.
2004, cc. 883, 996.

§ 18.2-513. Definitions.

As used in this chapter, the term:

"Criminal street gang" shall be as defined in § 18.2-46.1.

"Enterprise" includes any of the following: sole proprietorship, partnership, corporation, business trust, criminal street gang; or other group of three or more individuals associated for the purpose of criminal activity.

"Proceeds" shall be as defined in § 18.2-246.2.

"Racketeering activity" means to commit, attempt to commit, conspire to commit, or to solicit, coerce, or intimidate another person to commit two or more of the following offenses: Article 2.1 (§ 18.2-46.1 et seq.) of Chapter 4 of this title, § 18.2-460; a felony offense of §§ 3.2-4212, 3.2-4219, 10.1-1455, 18.2-31, 18.2-32, 18.2-32.1, 18.2-33, 18.2-35, Article 2.2 (§ 18.2-46.4 et seq.) of Chapter 4 of this title,

Crimes and Offenses

§§ 18.2-47, 18.2-48, 18.2-48.1, 18.2-49, 18.2-51, 18.2-51.2, 18.2-52, 18.2-53, 18.2-55, 18.2-58, 18.2-59, 18.2-77, 18.2-79, 18.2-80, 18.2-89, 18.2-90, 18.2-91, 18.2-92, 18.2-93, 18.2-95, Article 4 (§ 18.2-111 et seq.) of Chapter 5 of this title, Article 1 (§ 18.2-168 et seq.) of Chapter 6 of this title, §§ 18.2-178, 18.2-186, Article 6 (§ 18.2-191 et seq.) of Chapter 6 of this title, Article 9 (§ 18.2-246.1 et seq.) of Chapter 6 of this title, § 18.2-246.13, Article 1 (§ 18.2-247 et seq.) of Chapter 7 of this title, §§ 18.2-279, 18.2-286.1, 18.2-289, 18.2-300, 18.2-308.2, 18.2-308.2:1, 18.2-328, 18.2-348, 18.2-355, 18.2-356, 18.2-357, 18.2-357.1, 18.2-368, 18.2-369, 18.2-374.1, Article 8 (§ 18.2-433.1 et seq.) of Chapter 9 of this title, Article 1 (§ 18.2-434 et seq.) of Chapter 10 of this title, Article 2 (§ 18.2-438 et seq.) of Chapter 10 of this title, Article 3 (§ 18.2-446 et seq.) of Chapter 10 of this title, Article 1.1 (§ 18.2-498.1 et seq.) of Chapter 12 of this title, § 3.2-6571, 18.2-516, 32.1-314, 58.1-1008.2, 58.1-1017, or 58.1-1017.1; or any substantially similar offenses under the laws of any other state, the District of Columbia, the United States or its territories.

History.
2004, cc. 883, 996; 2008, c. 681; 2009, cc. 662, 847; 2013, c. 626; 2015, cc. 690, 691.

§ 18.2-514. Racketeering offenses.

A. It shall be unlawful for an enterprise, or for any person who occupies a position of organizer, supervisor, or manager of an enterprise, to receive any proceeds known to have been derived directly from racketeering activity and to use or invest an aggregate of $10,000 or more of such proceeds in the acquisition of any title to, or any right, interest, or equity in, real property, or in the establishment or operation of any enterprise.

B. It shall be unlawful for any enterprise, or for any person who occupies a position of organizer, supervisor, or manager of an enterprise, to directly acquire or maintain any interest in or control of any enterprise or real property through racketeering activity.

C. It shall be unlawful for any person employed by, or associated with, any enterprise to conduct or participate, directly or indirectly, in such enterprise through racketeering activity.

D. It shall be unlawful for any person to conspire to violate any of the provisions of subsection A, B, or C.

E. Each violation of this section is a separate and distinct felony punishable in accordance with § 18.2-515.

History.
2004, cc. 883, 996; 2009, c. 847.

§ 18.2-515. Criminal penalties; forfeiture.

A. Any person or enterprise convicted of engaging in activity in violation of the provisions of § 18.2-514 is guilty of a felony punishable by imprisonment for not less than five years nor more than 40 years and a fine of not more than $1 million. A second or subsequent offense shall be punishable as a Class 2 felony and a fine of not more than $2 million.

The court may order any such person or enterprise to be divested of any interest in any enterprise or real property identified in § 18.2-514; order the dissolution or reorganization of such enterprise; and order the suspension or revocation of any license, permit, or prior approval granted to such enterprise or person by any agency of the Commonwealth or political subdivision thereof.

B. All property, real or personal, including money, together with any interest or profits derived from the investment of such money, used in substantial connection with, intended for use in the course of, or traceable to, conduct in violation of any provision of § 18.2-514 is subject to civil forfeiture to the Commonwealth. The forfeiture proceeding shall be conducted pursuant to the provisions of Chapter 22.1 (§ 19.2-386.1 et seq.) of Title 19.2.

History.
2004, cc. 883, 996; 2012, c. 511.

§ 18.2-516. Prohibition of illegal money transmitting.

A. Any person who controls, manages, or owns all or part of an enterprise, engaged in money transmission as defined in § 6.2-1900, and transmits money, which he knows or should have known was derived from or traceable to racketeering activity, is guilty of a Class 6 felony.

B. All property, real or personal, including money, used in substantial connection with, intended for use in the course of, or traceable to, conduct in violation of any provision of subsection A is subject to civil forfeiture to the Commonwealth. The forfeiture proceeding shall be conducted pursuant to the provisions of Chapter 22.1 (§ 19.2-386.1 et seq.) of Title 19.2.

History.
2004, cc. 883, 996.

§ 18.2-517. Venue for prosecution.

For the purposes of venue, any violation of this chapter shall be considered to have been committed in any county or city:

1. In which any act was performed in furtherance of any course of conduct that violates this chapter;
2. That is the principal place of the enterprise in the Commonwealth;
3. In which any offender had control or possession of any proceeds of a violation of this chapter, or of any records, or any other material or objects, which were used in furtherance of a violation;
4. In which any offender resides; or
5. Any place of venue under Article 2 (§ 19.2-244 et seq.) of Chapter 15 of Title 19.2.

History.
2004, cc. 883, 996.

TITLE 19.2.
CRIMINAL PROCEDURE.

CHAPTER 1.
GENERAL PROVISIONS.

§ 19.2-1. Repealing clause.

All acts and parts of acts, all sections of this Code, and all provisions of municipal charters, inconsistent with the provisions of this title, are, except as herein otherwise provided, repealed to the extent of such inconsistency.

History.
1975, c. 495.

§ 19.2-2. Effect of repeal of Title 19.1 and enactment of this title.

The repeal of Title 19.1 effective as of October 1, 1975, shall not affect any act or offense done or committed, or any penalty or forfeiture incurred, or any right established, accrued, or accruing on or before such date, or any prosecution, suit or action pending on that day. Except as herein otherwise provided, neither the repeal of Title 19.1 nor the enactment of this title shall apply to offenses committed prior to October 1, 1975, and prosecutions for such offenses shall be governed by the prior law, which is continued in effect for that purpose. For the purposes of this section, an offense was committed prior to October 1, 1975, if any of the essential elements of the offense occurred prior thereto.

History.
1975, c. 495.

§ 19.2-3. Certain notices, recognizances and processes validated.

Any notice given, recognizance taken, or process or writ issued before October 1, 1975, shall be valid although given, taken or to be returned to a day after such date, in like manner as if this title had been effective before the same was given, taken or issued.

History.
1975, c. 495.

§ 19.2-3.1. Personal appearance by two-way electronic video and audio communication; standards.

A. Where an appearance is required or permitted before a magistrate, intake officer or, prior to trial, before a judge, the appearance may be by (i) personal appearance before the magistrate, intake officer or judge or (ii) use of two-way electronic video and audio communication. If two-way electronic video and audio communication is used, a magistrate, intake officer or judge may exercise all powers conferred by law and all communications and proceedings shall be conducted in the same manner as if the appearance were in person. If two-way electronic video and audio communication is available for use by a district court for the conduct of a hearing to determine bail or to determine representation by counsel, the court shall use such communication in any such proceeding that would otherwise require the transportation of a person from outside the jurisdiction of the court in order to appear in person before the court. Any documents transmitted between the magistrate, intake officer, or judge and the person appearing before the magistrate, intake officer, or judge may be transmitted by electronically transmitted facsimile process or other electronic method. The facsimile or other electronically generated document may be served or executed by the officer or person to whom sent, and returned in the same manner, and with the same force, effect, authority, and liability as an original document. All signatures thereon shall be treated as original signatures.

B. Any two-way electronic video and audio communication system used for an appearance shall meet the following standards:

1. The persons communicating must simultaneously see and speak to one another;
2. The signal transmission must be live, real time;
3. The signal transmission must be secure from interception through lawful means by anyone other than the persons communicating; and
4. Any other specifications as may be promulgated by the Chief Justice of the Supreme Court.

History.
1991, c. 41; 1996, cc. 755, 914; 2006, c. 285; 2009, cc. 94, 623; 2010, c. 800.

§ 19.2-4. References to former sections, articles or chapters of Titles 18.1 and 19.1.

Whenever in this title any of the conditions, requirements, provisions or contents of any section, article or chapter of Titles 18.1 and 19.1, as such titles existed prior to October 1, 1975, are transferred in the same or in modified form to a new section, article or chapter of this title or of Title 18.2, and whenever any such former section, article or chapter is given a new number in this title or in Title 18.2, all references to any such former section, article or chapter of Title 19.1 or of Title 18.1 appearing elsewhere in this Code than in this title or in Title 18.2, shall be construed to apply to the new or renumbered section, article or chapter containing such conditions, requirements, provisions or contents or portions thereof.

History.
1975, c. 495.

§ 19.2-5. Meaning of certain terms.

As used in this title, unless otherwise clearly indicated by the context in which it appears:

"Court" means any court vested with appropriate jurisdiction under the Constitution and laws of the Commonwealth.

"Court not of record" and *"district court"* shall have the respective meanings assigned to them in Chapter 4.1 (§ 16.1-69.1 et seq.) of Title 16.1.

"Judge" means any judge, associate judge or substitute judge of any court or any magistrate.

History.

Code 1950, § 19.1-5; 1960, c. 366; 1975, c. 495; 2005, c. 839; 2008, cc. 551, 691.

§ 19.2-6. Appointive power of circuit courts.

Unless otherwise specifically provided, whenever an appointive power is given to the judge of a circuit court, that power shall be exercised by a majority of the judges of the circuit. In case of a tie, such fact shall be communicated to the Chief Justice of the Supreme Court, who shall appoint a circuit judge from another circuit who shall act as a tie breaker. Where the power of appointment is to be exercised by a majority of the judges of the Second Judicial Circuit and such appointment is to a local post, board or commission in Accomack or Northampton County, the resident judge or judges of the County of Accomack or Northampton shall exercise such appointment power as if he or they comprise the majority of the judges of the Circuit.

History.

1975, c. 495; 1977, c. 288; 1994, c. 407.

§ 19.2-7. Rewards for arrest of persons convicted of or charged with offenses; rewards for conviction of unknown offenders.

The Governor may offer a reward for apprehending and securing any person convicted of an offense or charged therewith, who shall have escaped from lawful custody or confinement, or for apprehending and securing any person charged with an offense, who, there is reason to fear, cannot be arrested in the common course of proceeding. The Governor may also offer a reward for the detection and conviction of the person guilty of an offense when such offense has been committed but the person guilty thereof is unknown.

Any sheriff, deputy sheriff, sergeant, deputy sergeant or any other officer may claim and receive any reward which may be offered for the arrest and detention of any offender against the criminal laws of this or any other state or nation.

History.

Code 1950, §§ 19.1-6, 19.1-6.1; 1960, c. 366; 1962, c. 513; 1964, c. 171; 1975, c. 495.

§ 19.2-8. Limitation of prosecutions.

A prosecution for a misdemeanor, or any pecuniary fine, forfeiture, penalty or amercement, shall be commenced within one year next after there was cause therefor, except that a prosecution for petit larceny may be commenced within five years, and for an attempt to produce abortion, within two years after commission of the offense.

A prosecution for any misdemeanor violation of § 54.1-3904 shall be commenced within two years of the discovery of the offense.

A prosecution for violation of laws governing the placement of children for adoption without a license pursuant to § 63.2-1701 shall be commenced within one year from the date of the filing of the petition for adoption.

A prosecution for making a false statement or representation of a material fact knowing it to be false or knowingly failing to disclose a material fact, to obtain or increase any benefit or other payment under the Virginia Unemployment Compensation Act (§ 60.2-100 et seq.) shall be commenced within three years next after the commission of the offense.

A prosecution for any violation of § 10.1-1320, 62.1-44.32 (b), 62.1-194.1, or Article 11 (§ 62.1-44.34:14 et seq.) of Chapter 3.1 of Title 62.1 that involves the discharge, dumping or emission of any toxic substance as defined in § 32.1-239 shall be commenced within three years next after the commission of the offense.

Prosecution of Building Code violations under § 36-106 shall commence within one year of discovery of the offense by the building official, provided that such discovery occurs within two years of the date of initial occupancy or use after construction of the building or structure, or the issuance of a certificate of use and occupancy for the building or structure, whichever is later. However, prosecutions under § 36-106 relating to the maintenance of existing buildings or structures as contained in the Uniform Statewide Building Code shall commence within one year of the issuance of a notice of violation for the offense by the building official.

Prosecution of any misdemeanor violation of § 54.1-111 shall commence within one year of the discovery of the offense by the complainant, but in no case later than five years from occurrence of the offense.

Prosecution of any misdemeanor violation of any professional licensure requirement imposed by a locality shall commence within one year of the discovery of the offense by the complainant, but in no case later than five years from occurrence of the offense.

Prosecution of nonfelonious offenses which constitute malfeasance in office shall commence within two years next after the commission of the offense.

Prosecution of any violation of § 55-79.87, 55-79.88, 55-79.89, 55-79.90, 55-79.93, 55-79.94, 55-79.95, 55-79.103, or any rule adopted under or order issued pursuant to § 55-79.98, shall commence within three years next after the commission of the offense.

Prosecution of illegal sales or purchases of wild birds, wild animals and freshwater fish under § 29.1-553 shall commence within three years after commission of the offense.

Prosecution of violations under Title 58.1 for offenses involving false or fraudulent statements, documents or returns, or for the offense of willfully attempting in any manner to evade or defeat any tax or the payment thereof, or for the offense of willfully failing to pay any tax, or willfully failing to make any return at the time or times required by law or regulations shall commence within three years next after the commission of the offense, unless a longer period is otherwise prescribed.

Prosecution of violations of subsection A or B of § 3.2-6570 shall commence within five years of the commission of the offense, except violations regarding agricultural animals shall commence within one year of the commission of the offense.

A prosecution for a violation of § 18.2-386.1 shall be commenced within five years of the commission of the offense.

A prosecution for any violation of the Campaign Finance Disclosure Act, Chapter 9.3 (§ 24.2-945 et seq.) of Title 24.2, shall commence within one year of the discovery of the offense but in no case more than three years after the date of the commission of the offense.

A prosecution of a crime that is punishable as a misdemeanor pursuant to the Virginia Computer Crimes Act (§ 18.2-152.1 et seq.) or pursuant to § 18.2-186.3 for identity theft shall be commenced before the earlier of (i) five years after the commission of the last act in the course of conduct constituting a violation of the article or (ii) one year after the existence of the illegal act and the identity of the offender are discovered by the Commonwealth, by the owner, or by anyone else who is damaged by such violation.

A prosecution of a misdemeanor under § 18.2-64.2, 18.2-67.4, 18.2-67.4:1, 18.2-67.4:2, 18.2-67.5, or 18.2-370.6 where the victim is a minor at the time of the offense shall be commenced no later than one year after the victim reaches majority.

A prosecution for a violation of § 18.2-260.1 shall be commenced within three years of the commission of the offense.

Nothing in this section shall be construed to apply to any person fleeing from justice or concealing himself within or without the Commonwealth to avoid arrest or be construed to limit the time within which any prosecution may be commenced for desertion of a spouse or child or for neglect or refusal or failure to provide for the support and maintenance of a spouse or child.

History.
Code 1950, § 19.1-8; 1960, c. 366; 1974, c. 466; 1975, c. 495; 1976, cc. 114, 620; 1977, c. 108; 1978, c. 730; 1979, c. 243; 1980, c. 496; 1981, c. 31, 1984, c. 601; 1987, c. 488; 1990, cc. 575, 976; 1992, cc. 177, 435, 650; 1996, c. 484; 1998, c. 566; 1999, c. 620; 2005, cc. 746, 761, 827; 2006, cc. 193, 787, 892; 2008, c. 769; 2011, cc. 118, 143, 494, 553; 2014, c. 169; 2015, c. 176; 2016, cc. 233, 253.

§ 19.2-8.1. Prosecution for murder or manslaughter; passage of time not a limitation.

A prosecution for murder or manslaughter, whether at common law or under the Code of Virginia, may be instituted regardless of the time elapsed between the act or omission causing the death of the victim and the death of the victim.

History.
2009, c. 278.

§ 19.2-9. Prosecution of certain criminal cases removed from state to federal courts; costs.

When any person indicted in the courts of this Commonwealth for a violation of its laws, has his case removed to the district court of the United States under 28 U.S.C. § 1442, it shall be the duty of the attorney for the Commonwealth for the county or city in which any such indictment is found to prosecute any such case in the United States district court to which the same shall be so removed, and for his services in this behalf he shall be paid a fee of $100 for each case tried by him in such United States district court, and mileage at the rate now allowed by law to the members of the General Assembly for all necessary travel in going to and returning from such court, to be paid on his account when approved by the Attorney General.

A per diem of one dollar and fifty cents for each day of actual attendance upon such United States district court and mileage at a rate as provided by law for every mile of necessary travel in going to and returning from such court shall be paid out of the state treasury to each witness for the Commonwealth in every such case upon accounts therefor against the Commonwealth, certified by the attorney for the Commonwealth prosecuting such case and approved by the Attorney General.

It shall not be the duty of the Attorney General to appear for the Commonwealth in such cases unless he can do so without interfering with the efficient discharge of the duties imposed upon him by law; but he may appear with the attorney for the Commonwealth prosecuting such case in any case when the interests of the Commonwealth may in his judgment require his presence.

The Comptroller shall from time to time draw his warrants upon the state treasury in favor of the parties entitled to be paid the above compensation and expenses, or their assigns, upon bills certified and approved as above prescribed.

History.
Code 1950, § 19.1-14; 1960, c. 366; 1975, c. 495.

§ 19.2-9.1. Written notice required for complaining witness who is requested to take polygraph test.

A. For offenses not specified in subsection B, if a complaining witness is requested to submit to a polygraph examination during the course of a criminal investigation, such witness shall be informed in writing prior to the examination that (i) the exami-

Criminal Procedure

nation is voluntary, (ii) the results thereof are inadmissible as evidence and (iii) the agreement of the complaining witness to submit thereto shall not be the sole condition for initiating or continuing the criminal investigation.

B. No law-enforcement officer, attorney for the Commonwealth, or other government official shall ask or require a victim of an alleged sex offense to submit to a polygraph examination or other truth-telling device as a condition for proceeding with the investigation of such an offense. If a victim is requested to submit to a polygraph examination during the course of a criminal investigation, such victim shall be informed in writing of the provisions of subsection A and that the refusal of a victim to submit to such an examination shall not prevent the investigation, charging, or prosecution of the offense.

C. A "sex offense," for the purposes of this section, shall mean any offense set forth in Article 7 (§ 18.2-61 et seq.) of Chapter 4 of Title 18.2.

History.
1994, c. 336; 2008, cc. 512, 748.

§ 19.2-10. Outlawry abolished.

No proceeding of outlawry shall hereafter be instituted or prosecuted.

History.
Code 1950, § 19.1-15; 1960, c. 366; 1975, c. 495.

§ 19.2-10.1. Subpoena duces tecum for obtaining records concerning banking and credit cards.

A. A financial institution as defined in § 6.2-604, money transmitter as defined in § 6.2-1900, or commercial businesses providing credit history or credit reports; or an issuer as defined in § 6.2-424 shall disclose a record or other information pertaining to a customer, to a law-enforcement officer pursuant to a subpoena duces tecum issued pursuant to this section.

1. In order to obtain such records, the law-enforcement official shall provide a statement of the facts documenting the reasons that the records or other information sought are relevant to a legitimate law-enforcement inquiry, relating to a named person or persons, to the attorney for the Commonwealth. A court shall issue a subpoena duces tecum upon motion of the Commonwealth only if the court finds that there is probable cause to believe that a crime has been committed and to believe the records sought or other information sought, including electronic data and electronic communications, are relevant to a legitimate law-enforcement inquiry into that offense. The court may issue a subpoena duces tecum under this section regardless of whether any criminal charges have been filed.

2. A court issuing an order pursuant to this section, on a motion made promptly by the financial institution or credit card issuer, or enterprise may quash or modify the subpoena duces tecum, if the information or records requested are unusually voluminous in nature or compliance with such subpoena duces tecum would otherwise cause an undue burden on such provider.

B. No cause of action shall lie in any court against a financial institution or credit card issuer, or enterprise, its officers, employees, agents, or other specified persons for providing information, facilities, or assistance in accordance with the terms of a subpoena duces tecum under this section.

C. Upon issuance of a subpoena duces tecum under this section, the statement shall be temporarily sealed by the court upon application of the attorney for the Commonwealth for good cause shown in an ex parte proceeding. Any individual arrested and claiming to be aggrieved by the order may move the court for the unsealing of the statement, and the burden of proof with respect to continued sealing shall be upon the Commonwealth.

D. Any and all records received by law enforcement pursuant to this section shall be utilized only for a reasonable amount of time and only for a legitimate law-enforcement purpose. Upon the completion of the investigation the records shall be submitted to the court by the attorney for the Commonwealth along with a proposed order requiring the records to be sealed. Upon entry of such order, the court shall seal the records in accordance with the requirements contained in subsection C.

History.
2003, cc. 223, 541, 549; 2004, cc. 883, 996; 2010, cc. 702, 794.

§ 19.2-10.2. Administrative subpoena issued for record from provider of electronic communication service or remote computing service.

A. A provider of electronic communication service or remote computing service that is transacting or has transacted any business in the Commonwealth shall disclose a record or other information pertaining to a subscriber to or customer of such service, excluding the contents of electronic communications as required by § 19.2-70.3, to an attorney for the Commonwealth or the Attorney General pursuant to an administrative subpoena issued under this section.

1. In order to obtain such records or other information, the attorney for the Commonwealth or the Attorney General shall certify on the face of the subpoena that there is reason to believe that the records or other information being sought are relevant to a legitimate law-enforcement investigation concerning violations of §§ 18.2-47, 18.2-48, 18.2-49, 18.2-346, 18.2-347, 18.2-348, 18.2-349, 18.2-355, 18.2-356, 18.2-357, 18.2-374.1, and 18.2-374.1:1, former § 18.2-374.1:2, and § 18.2-374.3.

2. Upon written certification by the attorney for the Commonwealth or the Attorney General that

there is a reason to believe that the victim is under the age of 18 and that notification or disclosure of the existence of the subpoena will endanger the life or physical safety of an individual, or lead to flight from prosecution, the destruction of or tampering with evidence, the intimidation of potential witnesses, or otherwise seriously jeopardize an investigation, the subpoena shall include a provision ordering the service provider not to notify or disclose the existence of the subpoena to another person, other than an attorney to obtain legal advice, for a period of 30 days after the date on which the service provider responds to the subpoena.

3. On a motion made promptly by the electronic communication service or remote computing service provider, a court of competent jurisdiction may quash or modify the administrative subpoena if the records or other information requested are unusually voluminous in nature or if compliance with the subpoena would otherwise cause an undue burden on the service provider.

B. All records or other information received by an attorney for the Commonwealth or the Attorney General pursuant to an administrative subpoena issued under this section shall be used only for a reasonable length of time not to exceed 30 days and only for a legitimate law-enforcement purpose. Upon completion of the investigation, the records or other information held by the attorney for the Commonwealth or the Attorney General shall be destroyed if no prosecution is initiated. The existence of such a subpoena shall be disclosed upon motion of an accused.

C. No cause of action shall lie in any court against an electronic communication service or remote computing service provider, its officers, employees, agents, or other specified persons for providing information, facilities, or assistance in accordance with the terms of an administrative subpoena issued under this section.

D. Records or other information pertaining to a subscriber to or customer of such service means name, address, local and long distance telephone connection records, or records of session times and durations, length of service, including start date, and types of service utilized, telephone or instrument number or other subscriber number or identity, including any temporarily assigned network address, and means and source of payment for such service.

E. Nothing in this section shall require the disclosure of information in violation of any federal law.

History.
2007, cc. 802, 814; 2014, c. 166; 2015, cc. 544, 625.

§ 19.2-10.3. Reasonable suspicion required to stop, board, or inspect a noncommercial vessel on navigable waters of the Commonwealth.

A. Notwithstanding any other provision of law, no law-enforcement officer charged with enforcing laws or regulations on the navigable waters of the Commonwealth shall stop, board, or inspect any noncommercial vessel on the navigable waters of the Commonwealth unless such officer has reasonable suspicion that a violation of law or regulation exists.

B. The provisions of subsection A shall not apply to lawful stops, boardings, or inspections conducted by conservation police officers, as defined in § 29.1-100, or the Virginia Marine Police for the purposes of inspecting hunting, fishing, and trapping licenses pursuant to §§ 28.2-231 and 29.1-337 or creel and bag limit inspections pursuant to § 29.1-209, nor shall it prohibit lawful boating safety checkpoints conducted by conservation police officers and Virginia Marine Police in accordance with established agency policy.

History.
2015, c. 484.

§ 19.2-11. Procedure in contempt cases.

No court or judge shall impose a fine upon a juror, witness or other person for disobedience of its process or any contempt, unless he either be present in court at the time, or shall have been served with a rule, returnable to a certain time, requiring him to show cause why the fine should not be imposed and shall have failed to appear and show cause.

History.
Code 1950, § 19.1-16; 1960, c. 366; 1968, c. 639; 1975, c. 495.

CHAPTER 1.1.
CRIME VICTIM AND WITNESS RIGHTS ACT.

Section

§ 19.2-11.01. Crime victim and witness rights.

A. In recognition of the Commonwealth's concern for the victims and witnesses of crime, it is the purpose of this chapter to ensure that the full impact of crime is brought to the attention of the courts of the Commonwealth; that crime victims and witnesses are treated with dignity, respect and sensitivity; and that their privacy is protected to the extent permissible under law. It is the further purpose of this chapter to ensure that victims and witnesses are informed of the rights provided to them under the laws of the Commonwealth; that they receive authorized services as appropriate; and that they have the opportunity to be heard by law-enforcement agencies, attorneys for the Commonwealth, corrections agencies and the judiciary at all critical stages of the criminal justice process to the extent permissible under law. Unless otherwise stated and subject to the provisions of § 19.2-11.1, it shall be the responsibility of a locality's crime victim and witness assistance program to provide the information and assistance required by this chapter, including verification that the standardized form listing the specific rights afforded to crime victims has been received by the victim.

As soon as practicable after identifying a victim of a crime, the investigating law-enforcement agency shall provide the victim with a standardized form listing the specific rights afforded to crime victims. The form shall include a telephone number by which the victim can receive further information and assistance in securing the rights afforded crime victims, the name, address and telephone number of the office of the attorney for the Commonwealth, the name, address and telephone number of the investigating law-enforcement agency, and a summary of the victim's rights under § 40.1-28.7:2.

1. Victim and witness protection and law-enforcement contacts.

a. In order that victims and witnesses receive protection from harm and threats of harm arising out of their cooperation with law-enforcement, or prosecution efforts, they shall be provided with information as to the level of protection which may be available pursuant to § 52-35 or to any other federal, state or local program providing protection, and shall be assisted in obtaining this protection from the appropriate authorities.

b. Victims and witnesses shall be provided, where available, a separate waiting area during court proceedings that affords them privacy and protection from intimidation, and that does not place the victim in close proximity to the defendant or the defendant's family.

2. Financial assistance.

a. Victims shall be informed of financial assistance and social services available to them as victims of a crime, including information on their possible right to file a claim for compensation from the Crime Victims' Compensation Fund pursuant to Chapter 21.1 (§ 19.2-368.1 et seq.) of this title and on other available assistance and services.

b. Victims shall be assisted in having any property held by law-enforcement agencies for evidentiary purposes returned promptly in accordance with §§ 19.2-270.1 and 19.2-270.2.

c. Victims shall be advised that restitution is available for damages or loss resulting from an offense and shall be assisted in seeking restitution in accordance with §§ 19.2-305, 19.2-305.1, Chapter 21.1 (§ 19.2-368.1 et seq.) of this title, Article 21 (§ 58.1-520 et seq.) of Chapter 3 of Title 58.1, and other applicable laws of the Commonwealth.

3. Notices.

a. Victims and witnesses shall be (i) provided with appropriate employer intercession services to ensure that employers of victims and witnesses will cooperate with the criminal justice process in order to minimize an employee's loss of pay and other benefits resulting from court appearances and (ii) advised that pursuant to § 18.2-465.1 it is unlawful for an employer to penalize an employee for appearing in court pursuant to a summons or subpoena.

b. Victims shall receive advance notification when practicable from the attorney for the Commonwealth of judicial proceedings relating to their case and shall be notified when practicable of any change in court dates in accordance with § 19.2-265.01 if they have provided their names, current addresses and telephone numbers.

c. Victims shall receive notification, if requested, subject to such reasonable procedures as the Attorney General may require pursuant to § 2.2-511, from the Attorney General of the filing and disposition of any appeal or habeas corpus proceeding involving their case.

d. Victims shall be notified by the Department of Corrections or a sheriff or jail superintendent (i) in whose custody an escape, change of name, transfer, release or discharge of a prisoner occurs pursuant to the provisions of §§ 53.1-133.02 and 53.1-160 or (ii) when an accused is released on bail, if they have provided their names, current addresses and telephone numbers in writing. Such notification may be provided through the Virginia Statewide VINE (Victim Information and Notification Everyday) System or other similar electronic or automated system.

e. Victims shall be advised that, in order to protect their right to receive notices and offer input, all agencies and persons having such duties must have current victim addresses and telephone numbers given by the victims. Victims shall also be advised that any such information given shall be confidential as provided by § 19.2-11.2.

4. Victim input.

a. Victims shall be given the opportunity, pursuant to § 19.2-299.1, to prepare a written victim impact statement prior to sentencing of a defendant and may provide information to any individual or agency charged with investigating the social history of a person or preparing a victim impact statement under the provisions of §§ 16.1-273 and 53.1-155 or any other applicable law.

b. Victims shall have the right to remain in the courtroom during a criminal trial or proceeding pursuant to the provisions of § 19.2-265.01.

c. On motion of the attorney for the Commonwealth, victims shall be given the opportunity, pursuant to §§ 19.2-264.4 and 19.2-295.3, to testify prior to sentencing of a defendant regarding the impact of the offense.

d. In a felony case, the attorney for the Commonwealth, upon the victim's written request, shall consult with the victim either verbally or in writing (i) to inform the victim of the contents of a proposed plea agreement and (ii) to obtain the victim's views about the disposition of the case, including the victim's views concerning dismissal, pleas, plea negotiations and sentencing. However, nothing in this section shall limit the ability of the attorney for the Commonwealth to exercise his discretion on behalf of the citizens of the Commonwealth in the disposition of any criminal case. The court shall not accept the plea agreement unless it finds that, except for good cause shown, the Commonwealth has complied with clauses (i) and (ii). Good cause shown shall include, but not be limited to, the unavailability of the victim due to incarceration, hospitalization, failure to appear at trial when subpoenaed, or change of address without notice.

Upon the victim's written request, the victim shall be notified in accordance with subdivision A 3 b of any proceeding in which the plea agreement will be tendered to the court.

The responsibility to consult with the victim under this subdivision shall not confer upon the defendant any substantive or procedural rights and shall not affect the validity of any plea entered by the defendant.

5. Courtroom assistance.

a. Victims and witnesses shall be informed that their addresses and telephone numbers may not be disclosed, pursuant to the provisions of §§ 19.2-11.2 and 19.2-269.2, except when necessary for the conduct of the criminal proceeding.

b. Victims and witnesses shall be advised that they have the right to the services of an interpreter in accordance with §§ 19.2-164 and 19.2-164.1.

c. Victims and witnesses of certain sexual offenses shall be advised that there may be a closed preliminary hearing in accordance with § 18.2-67.8 and, if a victim was 14 years of age or younger on the date of the offense and is 16 or under at the time of the trial, or a witness to the offense is 14 years of age or younger at the time of the trial, that two-way closed-circuit television may be used in the taking of testimony in accordance with § 18.2-67.9.

6. Post trial assistance.

a. Within 30 days of receipt of a victim's written request after the final trial court proceeding in the case, the attorney for the Commonwealth shall notify the victim in writing, of (i) the disposition of the case, (ii) the crimes of which the defendant was convicted, (iii) the defendant's right to appeal, if known, and (iv) the telephone number of offices to contact in the event of nonpayment of restitution by the defendant.

b. If the defendant has been released on bail pending the outcome of an appeal, the agency that had custody of the defendant immediately prior to his release shall notify the victim as soon as practicable that the defendant has been released.

c. If the defendant's conviction is overturned, and the attorney for the Commonwealth decides to retry the case or the case is remanded for a new trial, the victim shall be entitled to the same rights as if the first trial did not take place.

B. For purposes of this chapter, "victim" means (i) a person who has suffered physical, psychological, or economic harm as a direct result of the commission of (a) a felony, (b) assault and battery in violation of § 18.2-57 or 18.2-57.2, stalking in violation of § 18.2-60.3, a violation of a protective order in violation of § 16.1-253.2 or 18.2-60.4, sexual battery in violation of § 18.2-67.4, attempted sexual battery in violation of § 18.2-67.5, or maiming or driving while intoxicated in violation of § 18.2-51.4 or 18.2-266, or (c) a delinquent act that would be a felony or a misdemeanor violation of any offense enumerated in clause (b) if committed by an adult; (ii) a spouse or child of such a person; (iii) a parent or legal guardian of such a person who is a minor; (iv) for the purposes of subdivision A 4 only, a current or former foster parent or other person who has or has had physical custody of such a person who is a minor, for six months or more or for the majority of the minor's life; or (v) a spouse, parent, sibling, or legal guardian of such a person who is physically or mentally incapacitated or was the victim of a homicide; however, "victim" does not mean a parent, child, spouse, sibling, or legal guardian who commits a felony or other enumerated criminal offense against a victim as defined in clause (i).

C. Officials and employees of the judiciary, including court services units, law-enforcement agencies, the Department of Corrections, attorneys for the Commonwealth and public defenders, shall be provided with copies of this chapter by the Department of Criminal Justice Services or a crime victim and witness assistance program. Each agency, officer or employee who has a responsibility or responsibilities to victims under this chapter or other applicable law shall make reasonable efforts to become informed about these responsibilities and to ensure that victims and witnesses receive such information and services to which they may be entitled under applicable law, provided that no liability or cause of action shall arise from the failure to make such efforts or from the failure of such victims or witnesses to receive any such information or services.

History.

1995, c. 687; 1996, c. 546; 1997, c. 691; 1998, c. 485; 1999, cc. 668, 702, 844; 2000, cc. 272, 827; 2001, cc. 410, 530, 549; 2002, cc. 310, 810, 818; 2003, cc. 103, 751, 764; 2006, c. 241; 2007, cc. 94, 109, 423; 2014, c. 230.

§ 19.2-11.1. Establishment of crime victim-witness assistance programs; funding; minimum standards.

Any local governmental body which establishes, operates and maintains a crime victim and witness assistance program, whose funding is provided in whole or part by grants administered by the Department of Criminal Justice Services pursuant to § 9.1-104, shall operate the program in accordance with guidelines which shall be established by the Department to implement the provisions of this chapter and other applicable laws establishing victims' rights.

History.
1988, c. 542; 1994, cc. 361, 598; 1995, c. 687; 1996, c. 545.

§ 19.2-11.2. Crime victim's right to nondisclosure of certain information; exceptions; testimonial privilege.

Upon request of any witness in a criminal prosecution under § 18.2-46.2, 18.2-46.3, or 18.2-248 or of any violent felony as defined by subsection C of § 17.1-805, or any crime victim, neither a law-enforcement agency, the attorney for the Commonwealth, the counsel for a defendant, a court nor the Department of Corrections, nor any employee of any of them, may disclose, except among themselves, the residential address, telephone number, or place of employment of the witness or victim or a member of the witness' or victim's family, except to the extent that disclosure is (i) of the site of the crime, (ii) required by law or Rules of the Supreme Court, (iii) necessary for law-enforcement purposes or preparation for court proceedings, or (iv) permitted by the court for good cause.

Except with the written consent of the victim, a law-enforcement agency may not disclose to the public information which directly or indirectly identifies the victim of a crime involving any sexual assault, sexual abuse or family abuse, except to the extent that disclosure is (i) of the site of the crime, (ii) required by law, (iii) necessary for law-enforcement purposes, or (iv) permitted by the court for good cause. In addition, at the request of the victim to the Court of Appeals of Virginia or the Supreme Court of Virginia hearing, on or after July 1, 2007, the case of a crime involving any sexual assault or sexual abuse, no appellate decision shall contain the first or last name of the victim.

Nothing herein shall limit the right to examine witnesses in a court of law or otherwise affect the conduct of any criminal proceeding.

History.
1994, cc. 845, 931; 2002, cc. 810, 818; 2005, cc. 764, 813; 2007, c. 503; 2014, c. 744.

§ 19.2-11.3. Virginia Crime Victim-Witness Fund.

There is hereby established the Virginia Crime Victim-Witness Fund as a special nonreverting fund to be administered by the Department of Criminal Justice Services to support victim and witness services that meet the minimum standards prescribed for such programs under § 19.2-11.1. A portion of the sum collected pursuant to §§ 16.1-69.48:1, 17.1-275.1, 17.1-275.2, 17.1-275.3, 17.1-275.4, 17.1-275.7, 17.1-275.8, and 17.1-275.9, as specified in these sections, shall be deposited into the state treasury to the credit of this Fund. The Fund shall be distributed according to grant procedures adopted pursuant to § 9.1-104 and shall be established on the books of the Comptroller. Any funds remaining in such Fund at the end of the biennium shall not revert to the general fund, but shall remain in the Fund. Interest earned on the Fund shall be credited to the Fund.

History.
1995, c. 371; 2002, c. 831.

§ 19.2-11.4. Establishment of victim-offender reconciliation program.

A. Any Crime Victim and Witness Assistance Program may establish a victim-offender reconciliation program to provide an opportunity after conviction for a victim, at his request and upon the subsequent agreement of the offender, to:

1. Meet with the offender in a safe, controlled environment in accordance with the policies established pursuant to subsection B of § 53.1-30;
2. Give to the offender, either orally or in writing, a summary of the financial, emotional, and physical effects of the offense on the victim or the victim's family; and
3. Discuss a proposed restitution agreement which may be submitted for consideration by the sentencing court for damages incurred by the victim as a result of the offense.

B. If the victim chooses to participate in a victim-offender reconciliation program under this section, the victim shall execute a waiver releasing the Crime Victim and Witness Assistance Program, attorney for the offender and the attorney for the Commonwealth from civil and criminal liability for actions taken by the victim or offender as a result of participation by the victim or the offender in a victim-offender reconciliation program.

C. A victim shall not be required to participate in a victim-offender reconciliation program under this section.

D. The failure of any person to participate in a reconciliation program pursuant to this section shall not be used directly or indirectly at sentencing.

History.
1995, c. 628; 2010, c. 844.

CHAPTER 1.2.

PHYSICAL EVIDENCE RECOVERY KITS.

Section

§ 19.2-11.5. Definitions.

As used in this chapter, unless the context requires a different meaning:

"Anonymous physical evidence recovery kit" means a physical evidence recovery kit that is collected from a victim of sexual assault through a forensic medical examination where the victim elects, at the time of the examination, not to report the sexual assault offense to a law-enforcement agency.

"Department" means the Virginia Department of Forensic Science.

"Division" means the Division of Consolidated Laboratory Services of the Virginia Department of General Services.

"Health care provider" means any hospital, clinic, or other medical facility that provides forensic medical examinations to victims of sexual assault.

"Law-enforcement agency" means the state or local law-enforcement agency with the primary responsibility for investigating an alleged sexual assault offense case and includes the employees of that agency.

"Physical evidence recovery kit" means any evidence collection kit supplied by the Department to health care providers for use in collecting evidence from victims of sexual assault during forensic medical examinations or to the Office of the Chief Medical Examiner for use during death investigations to collect evidence from decedents who may be victims of sexual assault.

"Sexual assault offense" means a violation or attempted violation of any offense enumerated in Article 7 (§ 18.2-61 et seq.) of Chapter 4 of Title 18.2 or of any offense specified in § 18.2-361, 18.2-370, or 18.2-370.1.

"Victim of sexual assault" means any person who undergoes a forensic medical examination for the collection of a physical evidence recovery kit connected to a sexual assault offense.

History.
2016, cc. 332, 698.

§ 19.2-11.6. Anonymous physical evidence recovery kits.

A. When a victim of sexual assault who undergoes a forensic medical examination elects not to report the offense to law enforcement, the health care provider shall inform the victim that the physical evidence recovery kit shall be forwarded to the Division for storage as an anonymous physical evidence recovery kit. The health care provider shall further inform the victim of the length of time the anonymous physical evidence recovery kit will be stored by the Division and how the victim can have the anonymous physical evidence recovery kit released to a law-enforcement agency at a later date. The health care provider shall forward the anonymous physical evidence recovery kit to the Division in accordance with the policies and procedures established by the Division.

B. The Division shall store any anonymous physical evidence recovery kit received for a minimum of two years. After two years, the Division may destroy the anonymous physical evidence recovery kit or, in its discretion or upon request of the victim or the law-enforcement agency, may elect to retain the anonymous physical evidence recovery kit for a longer period of time. Upon notification from either the law-enforcement agency or the attorney for the Commonwealth that the victim has elected to report the offense to the law-enforcement agency, the Division shall release the anonymous physical evidence recovery kit to the law-enforcement agency.

History.
2016, cc. 332, 698.

§ 19.2-11.7. Law enforcement taking possession of physical evidence recovery kits.

A. A health care provider that has collected a physical evidence recovery kit from a victim of sexual assault who has elected to report the offense shall forthwith notify the law-enforcement agency that such kit has been collected.

B. A law-enforcement agency that receives notice from a health care provider that a physical evidence recovery kit has been collected shall forthwith take possession of the physical evidence recovery kit.

History.
2016, cc. 332, 698.

§ 19.2-11.8. Submission of physical evidence recovery kits to the Department.

A. A law-enforcement agency that receives a physical evidence recovery kit shall submit the physical evidence recovery kit to the Department for analysis within 60 days of receipt, except under the following circumstances: (i) it is an anonymous physical evidence recovery kit that shall be forwarded to the Division for storage; (ii) the physical evidence recovery kit was collected by the Office of the Chief Medical Examiner as part of a routine death investigation, and the medical examiner and the law-enforcement agency agree that analysis is not warranted; (iii) the physical evidence recovery kit is connected to an offense that occurred outside of the Commonwealth; or (iv) the physical evidence recovery kit was determined by the law-enforcement agency not to be connected to a criminal offense.

B. Upon completion of analysis, the Department shall return the physical evidence recovery kit to the submitting law-enforcement agency. Upon receipt of the physical evidence recovery kit from the Department, the law-enforcement agency shall store the physical evidence recovery kit for a period of 10 years or until two years after the victim reaches the age of majority if the victim was a minor at the time of collection, whichever is longer. After the mandatory retention period has lapsed, the law-enforcement agency may destroy the physical evidence recovery kit or, in its discretion, may elect to retain the physical evidence recovery kit for a longer period of time.

C. The DNA profiles developed from physical evidence recovery kits submitted to the Department for analysis pursuant to this section shall be uploaded into any local, state, or national DNA data bank only if eligible as determined by Department procedures and in accordance with state and federal law.

History.
2016, cc. 332, 698.

§ 19.2-11.9. Lack of compliance with procedures.

The failure of a law-enforcement agency to take possession of a physical evidence recovery kit as provided in this chapter or to submit a physical evidence recovery kit to the Department within the time period prescribed under this chapter does not alter the authority of the law-enforcement agency to take possession of the physical evidence recovery kit or to submit the physical evidence recovery kit to the Department under this chapter or the authority of the Department to accept and analyze the physical evidence recovery kit or to maintain or upload any developed DNA profiles from the physical evidence recovery kit into any local, state, or national DNA data bank if eligible as determined by Department procedures and in accordance with state and federal law.

A person accused or convicted of committing a crime against a sexual assault victim has no standing to object to any failure to comply with the requirements of this chapter, and the failure to comply with the requirements of this chapter is not grounds for challenging the admissibility of the evidence or setting aside the conviction or sentence.

History.
2016, cc. 332, 698.

§ 19.2-11.10. Expungement of DNA profile.

If the Department receives written confirmation from a law-enforcement agency or attorney for the Commonwealth that a DNA profile that has been uploaded pursuant to this chapter into any local, state, or national DNA data bank was determined not to be connected to a criminal offense or that the DNA profile is of an individual who is not the putative perpetrator, the Department shall expunge the DNA profile from the DNA data bank.

The detention, arrest, or conviction of a person based upon a data bank match or data bank information is not invalidated if it is determined that the sample was obtained, placed, or retained in the data bank in good faith pursuant to this chapter, and evidence based upon or derived from the DNA record shall not be excluded by a court.

History.
2016, cc. 332, 698.

§ 19.2-11.11. Victim's right to notification of scientific analysis information.

A. In addition to the rights provided under Chapter 1.1 (§ 19.2-11.01 et seq.), a victim of sexual assault, a parent or guardian of a victim of a sexual assault who was a minor at the time of the offense, or a close relative of a deceased victim of sexual assault shall have the right to request and receive information from the law-enforcement agency regarding (i) the submission of any physical evidence recovery kit for forensic analysis that was collected from the victim during the investigation of the offense; (ii) the status of any analysis being performed on any evidence that was collected during the investigation of the offense; and (iii) the results of any analysis, unless disclosing this information would interfere with the investigation or prosecution of the offense, in which case the victim, parent, guardian, or relative shall be informed of the estimated date on which the information may be disclosed, if known.

B. The victim, parent, guardian, or relative who requests to be notified under subsection A must provide a current address and telephone number to the attorney for the Commonwealth and to the law-enforcement agency that is investigating the offense and keep such information updated.

History.
2016, cc. 332, 698.

CHAPTER 2.

CONSERVATORS OF THE PEACE AND SPECIAL POLICEMEN.

Article 1.

Appointment.

Article 2.

Powers and Duties.

Article 3.

Appeals.

ARTICLE 1.

APPOINTMENT.

§ 19.2-12. Who are conservators of the peace.

Every judge and attorney for the Commonwealth throughout the Commonwealth and every magistrate within the geographical area for which he is appointed or elected, shall be a conservator of the peace. In addition, every commissioner in chancery, while sitting as such commissioner; any special agent or law-enforcement officer of the United States Department of Justice, National Marine Fisheries Service of the United States Department of Commerce, Department of Treasury, Department of Agriculture, Department of Defense, Department of State, Office of the Inspector General of the Department of Transportation, Department of Homeland Security, and Department of Interior; any inspector, law-enforcement official or police personnel of the United States Postal Service; any United States marshal or deputy United States marshal whose duties involve the enforcement of the criminal laws of the United States; any officer of the Virginia Marine Police; any criminal investigator of the Department of Professional and Occupational Regulation, who meets the minimum law-enforcement training requirements established by the Department of Criminal Justice Services for in-service training; any criminal investigator of the United States Department of Labor; any special agent of the United States Naval Criminal Investigative Service, any special agent of the National Aeronautics and Space Administration, and any sworn municipal park ranger, who has completed all requirements under § 15.2-1706, shall be a conservator of the peace, while engaged in the performance of their official duties.

History.

Code 1950, § 19.1-20; 1960, c. 366; 1968, c. 639; 1972, c. 549; 1975, c. 495; 1978, c. 697; 1981, cc. 572, 587; 1990, c. 558; 1991, cc. 74, 338; 1994, cc. 375, 569, 626; 1997, c. 34; 2001, cc. 3, 31; 2002, cc. 86, 605, 789; 2004, c. 1009; 2005, c. 372; 2006, c. 88; 2007, c. 224; 2015, cc. 75, 126.

§ 19.2-13. Special conservators of the peace; authority; jurisdiction; registration; liability of employers; penalty; report.

A. Upon the submission of an application, which shall include the results of the background investigation conducted pursuant to subsection C, from (i) any sheriff or chief of police of any county, city, or town; (ii) any corporation authorized to do business in the Commonwealth; (iii) the owner, proprietor, or authorized custodian of any place within the Commonwealth; or (iv) any museum owned and managed by the Commonwealth, a circuit court judge of any county or city shall appoint special conservators of the peace who shall serve as such for such length of time as the court may designate, but not exceeding four years under any one appointment, during which time the court shall retain jurisdiction over the appointment order, upon a showing by the applicant of a necessity for the security of property or the peace and presentation of evidence that the person or persons to be appointed as a special conservator of the peace possess a valid registration issued by the Department of Criminal Justice Services in accordance with the provisions of subsection C. Upon an application made pursuant to clause (ii), (iii), or (iv), the court shall, prior to entering the order of appointment, transmit a copy of the application to the local attorney for the Commonwealth and the local sheriff or chief of police who may submit to the court a sworn, written statement indicating whether the order of appointment should be granted. However, a judge may deny the appointment for good cause, and shall state the specific reasons for the denial in writing in the order denying the appointment. A judge also may revoke the appointment order for good cause shown, upon the filing of a sworn petition by the attorney for the Commonwealth, sheriff, or chief of police for any locality in which the special conservator of the peace is authorized to serve or by the Department of Criminal Justice Services. Prior to revocation, a hearing shall be set and the special conservator of the peace shall be given notice and the opportunity to be heard. The judge may temporarily suspend the appointment pending the hearing for good cause shown. A hearing on the petition shall be heard by the court as soon as practicable. If the appointment order is suspended or revoked, the clerk of court shall notify the Department of Criminal Justice Services, the Department of State Police, the applicable local law-enforcement agencies in all cities and counties where the special conservator of the peace is authorized to serve, and the employer of the special conservator of the peace.

The order of appointment may provide that a special conservator of the peace shall have all the powers, functions, duties, responsibilities and authority of any other conservator of the peace within such geographical limitations as the court may deem appropriate within the confines of the county, city or town that makes application or on the real property where the corporate applicant is located, or any real property contiguous to such real property, limited, except as provided in subsection F, to the city or county wherein application has been made, whenever such special conservator of the peace is engaged in the performance of his duties as such. The order may provide that the special conservator of the peace shall have the authority to make an arrest outside of such geographical limitations if the arrest results from a close pursuit that was initiated when the special conservator of the peace was within the confines of the area wherein he has been authorized to have the powers and authority of a special conservator of the peace; the order may further delineate a geographical limitation or distance beyond which the special conservator of the peace may not effectuate such an arrest that follows from a close pursuit. The order shall require the special conservator of the peace to comply with the provisions of the United States Constitution and the Constitution of Virginia. The order shall not identify the special conservator of the peace as a law-enforcement officer pursuant to § 9.1-101. The order may provide, however, that the special conservator of the peace is a "law-enforcement officer" for the purposes of Article 4 (§ 37.2-808 et seq.) of Chapter 8 of Title 37.2 or Article 16 (§ 16.1-335 et seq.) of Chapter 11 of Title 16.1, but such designation shall not qualify the special conservator of the peace as a "qualified law-enforcement officer" or "qualified retired law-enforcement officer" within the meaning of the federal Law Enforcement Officer Safety Act, 18 U.S.C. § 926(B) et seq., and the order of appointment shall specifically state this. Upon request and for good cause shown, the order may also provide that the special conservator of the peace is authorized to use the seal of the Commonwealth in a badge or other credential of office as the court may deem appropriate. Upon request and for good cause shown, the order may also provide that the special conservator of the peace may use the title "police" on any badge or uniform worn in the performance of his duties as such. The order may also provide that a special conservator of the peace who has completed the minimum training standards established by the Criminal Justice Services Board, has the authority to affect arrests, using up to the same amount of force as would be allowed to a law-enforcement officer employed by the Commonwealth or any of its political subdivisions when making a lawful arrest. The order shall prohibit blue flashing lights, but upon request and for good cause shown may provide that the special conservator of the peace may use flashing lights and sirens on any vehicle used by the special conservator of the peace when he is in the performance of his duties. Prior to granting an application for appointment, the circuit court shall ensure that the applicant has met the registration requirements established by the Criminal Justice Services Board.

B. All applications and orders for appointments of special conservators of the peace shall be submitted on forms developed by the Office of the Executive Secretary of the Supreme Court of Virginia in consultation with the Department of Criminal Justice Services and shall specify the duties for which the applicant is qualified. The applications and orders shall specify the geographic limitations consistent with subsection A.

C. No person shall seek appointment as a special conservator of the peace from a circuit court judge without possessing a valid registration issued by the Department of Criminal Justice Services, except as provided in this section. Applicants for registration may submit an application on or after January 1, 2004. A temporary registration may be issued in accordance with regulations established by the Criminal Justice Services Board while awaiting the results of a state and national fingerprint search. However, no person shall be issued a valid registration or temporary registration until he has (i) complied with, or been exempted from the compulsory minimum training standards as set forth in this section; (ii) submitted his fingerprints on a form provided by the Department to be used for the conduct of a national criminal records search and a Virginia criminal history records search; (iii) submitted the results of a background investigation, performed by any state or local law-enforcement agency, which may, at its discretion, charge a reasonable fee to the applicant and which shall include a review of the applicant's criminal history records and may include a review of the applicant's school records, employment records, or interviews with persons possessing general knowledge of the applicant's character and fitness for such appointment; and (iv) met all other requirements of this article and Board regulations. No person with a criminal conviction for a misdemeanor involving (a) moral turpitude, (b) assault and battery, (c) damage to real or personal property, (d) controlled substances or imitation controlled substances as defined in Article 1 (§ 18.2-247 et seq.) of Chapter 7 of Title 18.2, (e) prohibited sexual behavior as described in Article 7 (§ 18.2-61 et seq.) of Chapter 4 of Title 18.2, or (f) firearms, or any felony, or who is required to register with the Sex Offender and Crimes Against Minors Registry pursuant to Chapter 9 (§ 9.1-900 et seq.) of Title 9.1, or who is prohibited from possessing, transporting, or purchasing a firearm shall be eligible for registration or appointment as a special conservator of the peace. A special conservator of the peace shall report if he is arrested for, charged with, or convicted of any misdemeanor or felony offense or becomes ineligible for registration or appointment as a special conservator of the peace pursuant to this subsection to the Department of Criminal Justice Services and the chief law-enforcement officer of all localities in which he is authorized to serve within three days of such arrest or of becoming ineligible for registration or appointment as a special conservator of the peace. Any appointment for a special conservator of the peace shall be eligible for suspension and revocation after a hearing pursuant to subsection A if the special conservator of the peace is convicted of any offense listed in this subsection or becomes ineligible for registration or appointment as a special conservator of the peace pursuant to this subsection. All appointments for special conservators of the peace shall become void on September 15, 2004, unless they have obtained a valid registration issued by the Department of Criminal Justice Services.

D. Each person registered as or seeking registration as a special conservator of the peace shall be covered by evidence of a policy of liability insurance or self-insurance in an amount and with coverage as fixed by the Board. Any person who is aggrieved by the misconduct of any person registered as a special conservator of the peace and recovers a judgment against the registrant, which is unsatisfied in whole or in part, may bring an action in his own name against the insurance policy of the registrant.

E. Effective July 1, 2015, all persons currently appointed or seeking appointment or reappointment as a special conservator of the peace are required to register with the Department of Criminal Justice Services, regardless of any other standing the person may have as a law-enforcement officer or other position requiring registration or licensure by the Department. The employer of any special conservator of the peace shall notify the circuit court, the Department of Criminal Justice Services, the Department of State Police, and the chief law-enforcement officer of all localities in which the special conservator of the peace is authorized to serve within 30 days after the date such individual has left employment and all powers of the special conservator of the peace shall be void. Failure to provide such notification shall be punishable by a fine of $250 plus an additional $50 per day for each day such notice is not provided.

F. When the application is made by any sheriff or chief of police, the circuit court shall specify in the order of appointment the name of the applicant authorized under subsection A and the geographic jurisdiction of the special conservator of the peace. Such appointments shall be limited to the city or county wherein application has been made. When the application is made by any corporation authorized to do business in the Commonwealth, any owner, proprietor, or authorized custodian of any place within the Commonwealth, or any museum owned and managed by the Commonwealth, the circuit court shall specify in the order of appointment the name of the applicant authorized under subsection A and the specific real property where the special conservator of the peace is authorized to serve. Such appointments shall be limited to the specific real property within the county, city, or town wherein application has been made. In the case of a corporation or other business, the court appointment may also include, for good cause shown, any real property owned or leased by the corporation or business, including any subsidiaries, in other specifically named cities and counties, but shall provide that the powers of the special conservator of the peace do not extend beyond the boundaries of such real property. The clerk of the appointing circuit court shall transmit to the Department of State Police, the clerk of the circuit court of each locality where the special conservator of the peace is authorized to serve, and the sheriff or chief of police of each such locality a copy of the order of appointment that shall specify the following information: the person's complete name, address, date of birth, social security number, gender, race, height, weight, color of hair, color of eyes, firearm authority or limitation as set forth in subsection G, date of the order, and other information as may be required by the Department of State Police. The Department of State Police shall enter the person's name and other information into the Virginia Criminal Information Network established and maintained by the Department pursuant to Chapter 2 (§ 52-12 et seq.) of Title 52. The Department of State Police may charge a fee not to exceed $10 to cover its costs associated with processing these orders. Each special conservator of the peace so appointed on application shall present his credentials to the chief of police or sheriff or his designee of all jurisdictions where he has conservator powers. If his powers are limited to certain areas of real property owned or leased by a corporation or business, he shall also provide notice of the exact physical addresses of those areas. Each special conservator shall provide to the circuit court a temporary registration letter issued by the Department of Criminal Justice Services to include the results of the background check prior to seeking an appointment by the circuit court. Once the applicant receives the appointment from the circuit court the applicant shall file the appointment order and a copy of the application with the Department of Criminal Justice Services in order to receive his special conservator of the peace registration document. If the court appointment includes any real property owned or leased by the corporation or business in other specifically named cities and counties not within the city or county wherein application has been made, the clerk of the appointing court shall transmit a copy of the order of appointment to (i) the clerk of the circuit court for each jurisdiction where the special conservator of the peace is authorized to serve and (ii) the sheriff or chief of police of each jurisdiction where the special conservator of the peace is authorized to serve.

If any such special conservator of the peace is the employee, agent or servant of another, his appointment as special conservator of the peace shall not relieve his employer, principal or master from civil liability to another arising out of any wrongful action or conduct committed by such special conservator of the peace while within the scope of his employment.

Effective July 1, 2002, no person employed by a local school board as a school security officer, as defined in § 9.1-101, shall be eligible for appointment as a conservator for purposes of maintaining safety in a public school in the Commonwealth. All appointments of special conservators of the peace granted to school security officers as defined in § 9.1-101 prior to July 1, 2002 are void.

G. The court may limit or prohibit the carrying of weapons by any special conservator of the peace initially appointed on or after July 1, 1996, while the appointee is within the scope of his employment as such.

H. The governing body of any locality or the sheriff of a county where no police department has been established may enter into mutual aid agreements with any entity employing special conservators of the peace that is located in such locality for the use of their joint forces and their equipment and materials to maintain peace and good order. Any law-enforcement officer or special conservator of the peace, while performing his duty under any such agreement, shall have the same authority as lawfully conferred on him within his own jurisdiction.

History.

Code 1950, § 19.1-28; 1960, c. 366; 1974, cc. 44, 45; 1975, c. 495; 1976, c. 220; 1982, c. 523; 1989, c. 455; 1996, cc. 850, 956; 2001, c. 249; 2002, cc. 605, 836, 868; 2003, c. 922; 2004, c. 401; 2005, c. 498; 2006, c. 290; 2007, cc. 380, 481; 2008, c. 795; 2010, cc. 530, 778, 825; 2013, cc. 105, 122; 2015, cc. 602, 766, 772; 2016, c. 551.

§ 19.2-13.1. Application for special conservator of the peace by locality.

No official or employee of a school board or county, city, or town, its departments, or its agents shall submit an application for the appointment of a special conservator of the peace without attaching a written assessment from the chief law-enforcement officer of the locality stating the need for the appointment and recommending any limitations that should be included in the order of appointment to the application submitted to the court pursuant to subsection A of § 19.2-13.

History.

2016, c. 416.

§ 19.2-14. Conservators of the peace for fairgrounds and cemeteries; bond required.

The superintendent or other person in charge of any fairgrounds or any public or private cemetery shall, for the purpose of maintaining order and enforcing the criminal and police laws of the Commonwealth, or the county or city in which such fairgrounds or cemetery is situated, have all the powers, functions, duties, responsibilities and authority of a conservator of the peace within the fairgrounds or cemetery over which he may have charge and within one-half of a mile around the same.

The provisions of § 19.2-13 relative to the giving of bond and the liability of an employer, principal or master, shall be applicable to every person exercising any powers of a conservator of the peace under this section.

History.

Code 1950, § 19.1-32; 1960, c. 366; 1975, c. 495.

§ 19.2-15. When conservator appointed under § 19.2-13 need not be a citizen.

Any such conservator appointed under the provisions of § 19.2-13 whose jurisdiction is limited to the grounds attached to an airport, need not be a citizen of the Commonwealth if the proprietors of such airport shall, before any such conservator shall enter upon the duties of the office, enter into bond with approved surety before the clerk of the circuit court having jurisdiction over such airport in the penalty of $1,000 for each conservator so appointed, with condition for the faithful discharge of his official duties.

History.

Code 1950, § 19.1-29; 1960, c. 366; 1975, c. 495.

§ 19.2-16: Repealed by Acts 1994, c. 205.

§ 19.2-17: Repealed by Acts 1996, c. 850.

ARTICLE 2.

POWERS AND DUTIES.

§ 19.2-18. Powers and duties generally.

Every conservator of the peace shall have authority to arrest without a warrant in such instances as are set out in §§ 19.2-19 and 19.2-81. Upon making an arrest without a warrant, the conservator of the peace shall proceed in accordance with the provisions of § 19.2-22 or § 19.2-82 as the case may be.

History.

Code 1950, § 19.1-20; 1960, c. 366; 1968, c. 639; 1972, c. 549; 1975, c. 495.

§ 19.2-19. Recognizance to keep the peace; when required.

If any person threatens to kill or injure another or to commit violence or injury against his person or property, or to unlawfully trespass upon his property, he shall be required to give a recognizance to keep the peace for such period not to exceed one year as the court hearing the complaint may determine.

History.

Code 1950, §§ 19.1-26, 19.1-27; 1960, c. 366; 1975, c. 495; 1978, c. 500.

§ 19.2-20. Same; complaint and issuance of warrant therefor.

If complaint be made to any magistrate or judge that a person should be required to give a recognizance to keep the peace due to any of the reasons set forth in § 19.2-19, such magistrate or judge shall examine on oath the complainant, and any witness who may be produced, reduce the complaint to writing, and cause it to be signed by the complainant; and if probable cause is established, such magistrate or judge shall issue a warrant, reciting the complaint, and requiring the person complained of forthwith to be apprehended and brought before the district court having appropriate jurisdiction.

History.
Code 1950, § 19.1-21; 1960, c. 366; 1975, c. 495; 1978, c. 500; 1979, c. 708.

§ 19.2-21. Same; procedure when accused appears.

When such person appears, if the judge, on hearing the parties, considers that there is not good cause for the complaint, he shall discharge such person, and may give judgment in his favor against the complainant for his costs. If he considers that there is good cause therefor, he may require a recognizance of the person against whom it is, and give judgment against him for the costs of the prosecution, or any part thereof; and, unless such recognizance be given, he shall commit him to jail by a warrant, stating the sum and time in and for which the recognizance is directed. The person given judgment under this section for costs may issue a writ of fieri facias thereon, if an appeal be not allowed; and proceedings thereupon may be according to §§ 16.1-99 through 16.1-101.

History.
Code 1950, § 19.1-22; 1960, c. 366; 1975, c. 495; 1978, c. 500.

§ 19.2-22. Same; arrest without a warrant.

A person arrested without a warrant by any conservator of the peace or other law-enforcement officer for any of the acts set forth in § 19.2-19 committed in the presence of such conservator of the peace or law-enforcement officer, shall be brought forthwith before a magistrate or judge, and proceedings shall be had in accordance with §§ 19.2-20 and 19.2-21.

History.
1975, c. 495.

§ 19.2-23. Payment of fees or mileage allowances into county or city treasury.

Any conservator or policeman appointed under the provisions of this chapter shall not be entitled to fees or mileage for performance of his duties as such conservator or policeman.

History.
Code 1950, § 19.1-31; 1960, c. 366; 1975, c. 495.

ARTICLE 3.

APPEALS.

§ 19.2-24. When appeal may be taken; witnesses recognized; bail.

Any person from whom a recognizance is required under the provisions of this chapter or who has been committed to jail for failure to give security therefor, may appeal to the circuit court of the county or city, and, in such case, the judge from whose judgment the appeal is taken shall recognize such of the witnesses as he thinks proper; provided, however, that the person taking the appeal may be required to give bail, with good security, for his appearance at the circuit court of the county or city.

History.
Code 1950, § 19.1-23; 1960, c. 366; 1975, c. 495; 1978, c. 500.

§ 19.2-25. Power of court on appeal.

The court may dismiss the complaint or affirm the judgment, and make what order it sees fit as to the costs. If it award costs against the appellant, the recognizance which he may have given shall stand as security therefor. When there is a failure to prosecute the appeal, such recognizance shall remain in force, although there be no order of affirmance. On any appeal the court may require of the appellant a new recognizance if it see fit.

Any person committed to jail under this chapter may be discharged by the circuit court of the county or city on such terms as it may deem reasonable.

History.
Code 1950, §§ 19.1-24, 19.1-25; 1960, c. 366; 1975, c. 495.

CHAPTER 3.

MAGISTRATES.

Article 1.

Transition Provisions.

Article 2.

Abolition of Justice of the Peace System.

Criminal Procedure

Article 3.

The Magistrate System.

Article 4.

Supervision.

Article 5.

Jurisdiction and Powers.

Article 6.

Compensation and Fees.

ARTICLE 1.

TRANSITION PROVISIONS.

§ 19.2-26. Repeal of inconsistent statutes, municipal charters, etc.

All acts and parts of acts, all sections of this Code, and all provisions of municipal charters, inconsistent with the provisions of this title, are, except as herein otherwise provided, repealed to the extent of such inconsistency.

History.
Code 1950, § 19.1-374; 1973, c. 545; 1975, c. 495.

§ 19.2-27. Effect of repeal of Title 39.1 on prior acts, offenses, etc.

The repeal of Title 39.1 effective as of January 1, 1974, shall not affect any act or offense done or committed or any penalty or forfeiture incurred, or any right established, accrued, or accruing on or before such date, or any prosecution, suit or action pending on that day.

History.
Code 1950, § 19.1-375; 1973, c. 545; 1975, c. 495.

§ 19.2-28. Certain notices, recognizances and processes validated.

Any notice given, recognizance taken, or process or writ issued, before January 1, 1974, shall be valid although given, taken or to be returned to a day after such date, in like manner as if this title had been effective before the same was given, taken or issued.

History.
Code 1950, § 19.1-376; 1973, c. 545; 1975, c. 495.

§ 19.2-29. References to former sections, articles and chapters in Title 39.1.

Whenever in Chapter 3 (§ 19.2-26 et seq.) of this title any of the conditions, requirements, provisions or contents of any section, article or chapter of Title 39.1, as such title existed prior to January 1, 1974, are transferred in the same or modified form to a new section, article or chapter, and whenever any such former section, article or chapter is given a new number in Chapter 3 of this title all references to any such former section, article or chapter of Title 39.1 appearing elsewhere in this Code than in Chapter 3 of this title shall be construed to apply to the new or renumbered section, article or chapter containing such conditions, requirements, provisions or contents or portions thereof.

History.
Code 1950, § 19.1-377; 1973, c. 545; 1975, c. 495; 2002, c. 310.

ARTICLE 2.

ABOLITION OF JUSTICE OF THE PEACE SYSTEM.

§ 19.2-30: Repealed by Acts 2008, cc. 551 and 691, cl. 2.

§ 19.2-31. Abolition of office of issuing justice.

Effective January 1, 1974, the office of issuing justice as provided for in Chapter 2 (§ 39.1-20 et seq.) of Title 39.1 having been abolished, nevertheless, any such special justice of the peace in office December 31, 1973, and elected by the town council for a specific term to expire after that date, may continue in office for the remainder of that term. If he continues in office as provided herein, such justice shall exercise the same powers, perform the same duties, and receive such compensation as he was receiving as of December 31, 1973.

History.
Code 1950, § 19.1-379; 1973, c. 545; 1975, c. 495.

§ 19.2-32. References to justices of the peace.

References in law to justices of the peace shall be deemed to apply to magistrates unless the provisions of Chapter 3 (§ 19.2-26 et seq.) of this title shall render such reference inapplicable.

History.
Code 1950, § 19.1-380; 1973, c. 545; 1975, c. 495; 2002, c. 310.

ARTICLE 3.
THE MAGISTRATE SYSTEM.

§ 19.2-33. Office of magistrate.

The office of magistrate shall be vested with all the authority, duties and obligations previously vested in the office of justice of the peace prior to January 1, 1974.

History.
Code 1950, § 19.1-381; 1973, c. 545; 1975, c. 495.

§ 19.2-34. Number of magistrates.

There shall be appointed as many magistrates as are necessary for the effective administration of justice. The positions of all employees of the magistrate system shall be authorized by the Committee on District Courts established pursuant to § 16.1-69.33.

History.
Code 1950, § 19.1-382; 1973, c. 545; 1974, c. 484; 1975, c. 495; 1976, c. 138; 1977, c. 198; 1981, c. 4; 1992, c. 55; 2008, cc. 551, 691.

§ 19.2-35. Appointment; supervision generally.

Magistrates and any other personnel in the office of the magistrate shall be appointed by the Executive Secretary of the Supreme Court of Virginia in consultation with the chief judges of the circuit courts having jurisdiction within the region. Each magistrate shall be appointed to serve one or more of the magisterial regions created by the Executive Secretary. Each magisterial region shall be comprised of one or more judicial districts. The Executive Secretary shall have full supervisory authority over the magistrates so appointed. Notwithstanding any other provision of law, the only methods for the selection of magistrates shall be as set out in this section.

No person shall be appointed under this section until he has submitted his fingerprints to be used for the conduct of a national criminal records search and a Virginia criminal history records search. No person with a criminal conviction for a felony shall be appointed as a magistrate.

History.
Code 1950, § 19.1-383; 1973, c. 545; 1974, c. 484; 1975, c. 495; 1976, c. 138; 1981, c. 4; 1988, c. 511; 2002, c. 310; 2004, cc. 370, 452; 2008, cc. 551, 691.

§ 19.2-36. Chief magistrates.

A. The Executive Secretary of the Supreme Court of Virginia may appoint chief magistrates, for the purpose of assisting in the training of the magistrates and being responsible to the Executive Secretary for the conduct of the magistrates and to further assist the Office of the Executive Secretary in the operation of one or more of the magisterial regions. The chief magistrate shall exercise direct daily supervision over the magistrates he supervises and shall have the power to suspend without pay a magistrate after consultation and with the concurrence of the Executive Secretary.

B. To be eligible for appointment as chief magistrate, a person shall meet all of the qualifications of a magistrate under § 19.2-37 and must be a member in good standing of the Virginia State Bar. His appointment as chief magistrate shall terminate effective on the date on which his membership in good standing ceases. The requirements of this subsection relating to membership in the Virginia State Bar shall not apply to any person appointed as a chief magistrate before July 1, 2008, who continues in that capacity without a break in service.

History.
Code 1950, § 19.1-384; 1973, c. 545; 1974, c. 484; 1975, c. 495; 1984, c. 37; 2004, c. 370; 2008, cc. 551, 691.

§ 19.2-37. Magistrates; eligibility for appointment; restrictions on activities.

A. Any person who is a United States citizen and resident of the Commonwealth may be appointed to the office of magistrate under this title subject to the limitations of Chapter 28 (§ 2.2-2800 et seq.) of Title 2.2 and of this section.

B. Every person appointed as a magistrate on and after July 1, 2008, shall be required to have a bachelor's degree from an accredited institution of higher education. A person initially appointed as a magistrate prior to July 1, 2008, who continues in office without a break in service is not required to have a bachelor's degree from an accredited institution of higher education.

C. A person shall not be eligible for appointment as a magistrate under the provisions of this title: (a) if such person is a law-enforcement officer; (b) if such person or his spouse is a clerk, deputy or assistant clerk, or employee of any such clerk of a district or circuit court, provided that the Committee on District Courts may authorize a magistrate to assist in the district court clerk's office on a part-time basis; (c) if the parent, child, spouse, or sibling of such person is a district or circuit court judge in the magisterial region where he will serve; or (d) if such person is the chief executive officer, or a member of the board of supervisors, town or city council, or other governing body for any political subdivision of the Commonwealth.

D. No magistrate shall issue any warrant or process in complaint of his spouse, child, grandchild,

Criminal Procedure

parent, grandparent, parent-in-law, child-in-law, brother, sister, brother-in-law or sister-in-law, nephew, niece, uncle, aunt, first cousin, guardian or ward.

E. A magistrate may not engage in any other activity for financial gain during the hours that he is serving on duty as a magistrate. A magistrate may not be employed outside his duty hours without the prior written approval of the Executive Secretary.

F. No person appointed as a magistrate on or after July 1, 2008, may engage in the practice of law.

G. A magistrate who is designated as a marriage celebrant under § 20-25 may not accept a fee, a gratuity, or any other thing of value for exercise of authority as a marriage celebrant.

History.

Code 1950, § 19.1-385; 1973, c. 545; 1975, c. 495; 1976, c. 138; 1978, cc. 463, 760; 1984, c. 41; 1985, c. 45; 1986, c. 202; 1996, c. 112; 1999, c. 267; 2004, c. 830; 2008, cc. 551, 691.

§ 19.2-38. Probationary period; compensation and benefits; vacancies; revocation of appointment.

Persons appointed as magistrates under the provisions of this chapter shall serve at the pleasure of the Executive Secretary. Upon appointment by the Executive Secretary, every magistrate shall serve initially for a nine-month probationary period during which the magistrate must complete the minimum training program as established by the Committee on District Courts and satisfactorily complete a certification examination. Any magistrate who fails to successfully pass the certification examination shall not serve beyond the nine-month probationary period. The probationary period described in this section shall not apply to any magistrate serving on July 1, 2008, who has successfully completed the minimum training program and passed the certification examination, provided there is no break in service after July 1, 2008. Magistrates shall be entitled to compensation and other benefits only from the time they take office.

History.

Code 1950, § 19.1-386; 1973, c. 545; 1974, c. 484; 1975, c. 495; 1980, c. 505; 2004, c. 370; 2008, cc. 551, 691.

§ 19.2-38.1. Training standards; training prerequisite to reappointment; waiver.

The Committee on District Courts shall establish minimum training and certification standards for magistrates in accordance with such rules and regulations as may be established by the Committee. Every magistrate shall comply with these standards and shall complete the minimum training standards as a prerequisite for continuing to serve as magistrate beyond the nine-month probationary period as established by § 19.2-38. The Committee on District Courts upon request may waive any portion of the minimum training standards for an individual magistrate.

History.

1980, c. 505; 1985, c. 132; 1995, c. 611; 2008, cc. 551, 691.

§ 19.2-39. Bond.

Every magistrate appointed under the provisions of this chapter shall enter into bond in the sum of $5,000, made payable to the Commonwealth, before a clerk of a circuit court, for the faithful performance of his duties. The premium for such bond shall be paid by the Commonwealth. Provided, however, that in lieu of specific bonds, the Committee on District Courts may in its discretion procure faithful performance of duty blanket bonds for all magistrates and for the penalty contained in this section, unless in the discretion of the Committee, bonds with a larger penalty should be obtained. Such blanket bonds shall be made payable to the Commonwealth and shall cover all funds handled by a magistrate whether such funds belong to the Commonwealth or any political subdivision thereof. Provided further, that in those instances where specific bonds for magistrates are in effect, the Committee on District Courts may, whenever it deems it advisable, terminate such specific bonds upon obtaining a blanket bond covering such magistrates with appropriate refunds or credit being made for the unearned premiums on the specific bonds terminated. A copy of any such blanket bond so procured shall be filed with the State Comptroller and with the clerk of the respective circuit courts. The premiums for such blanket bonds shall be paid by the Commonwealth.

History.

Code 1950, § 19.1-387; 1973, c. 545; 1974, c. 484; 1975, c. 495; 2008, cc. 551, 691.

§ 19.2-40: Repealed by Acts 1980, c. 758.

ARTICLE 4.

SUPERVISION.

§ 19.2-41: Repealed by Acts 2008, cc. 551 and 691, cl. 2.

§ 19.2-42: Repealed by Acts 2004, c. 327.

§ 19.2-43. Duty of Executive Secretary of Supreme Court.

It shall be the duty of the Executive Secretary of the Supreme Court to exercise general supervisory power over the administration of magistrates and adopt such policies as are deemed necessary to supplement or clarify the provisions of this chapter with respect to such magistrates, to include fixing the time and place such magistrates shall serve. The Executive Secretary shall conduct training sessions and meetings for magistrates and provide information and materials for their use. He may appoint one or more magistrates to assist him and, in addition, require annual reports to be filed by the magistrates on their work as such, fees associated therewith and other information pertinent to their office, on forms to be furnished by him. The Executive Secretary may appoint and employ such personnel as are needed to manage the magistrate system and carry out the duties and responsibilities conferred upon the Executive Secretary by this chapter.

History.

Code 1950, § 19.1-392; 1973, c. 545; 1974, c. 484; 1975, c. 495; 2008, cc. 551, 691.

ARTICLE 5. JURISDICTION AND POWERS.

§ 19.2-44. Territorial jurisdiction.

A magistrate shall be authorized to exercise the powers conferred on magistrates by this title only in the magisterial region or regions for which he is appointed, except that a magistrate may issue search warrants in accordance with the provisions of Chapter 5 (§ 19.2-52 et seq.) throughout the Commonwealth. A magistrate may exercise all powers conferred on magistrates by this title throughout the Commonwealth when so authorized by the Executive Secretary upon a determination that such assistance is necessary.

History.

Code 1950, § 19.1-393; 1973, c. 545; 1974, c. 484; 1975, c. 495; 1976, c. 138; 1995, c. 551; 2008, cc. 551, 691; 2014, cc. 305, 310.

Criminal Procedure

§ 19.2-44.1: Repealed by Acts 1976, c. 138.

Cross references.

For present provisions as to substitute magistrates, see § 19.2-35.

§ 19.2-45. Powers enumerated.

A magistrate shall have the following powers only:

(1) To issue process of arrest in accord with the provisions of §§ 19.2-71 to 19.2-82 of the Code;

(2) To issue search warrants in accord with the provisions of §§ 19.2-52 to 19.2-60 of the Code;

(3) To admit to bail or commit to jail all persons charged with offenses subject to the limitations of and in accord with general laws on bail;

(4) The same power to issue warrants and subpoenas as is conferred upon district courts and as limited by the provisions of §§ 19.2-71 through 19.2-82. A copy of all felony warrants issued at the request of a citizen shall be promptly delivered to the attorney for the Commonwealth for the county or city in which the warrant is returnable. Upon the request of the attorney for the Commonwealth, a copy of any misdemeanor warrant issued at the request of a citizen shall be delivered to the attorney for the Commonwealth for such county or city. All attachments, warrants and subpoenas shall be returnable before a district court or any court of limited jurisdiction continued in operation pursuant to § 16.1-70.1;

(5) To issue civil warrants directed to the sheriff or constable of the county or city wherein the defendant resides, together with a copy thereof, requiring him to summon the person against whom the claim is, to appear before a district court on a certain day, not exceeding 30 days from the date thereof to answer such claim. If there be two or more defendants and any defendant resides outside the jurisdiction in which the warrant is issued, the summons for such defendant residing outside the jurisdiction may be directed to the sheriff of the county or city of his residence, and such warrant may be served and returned as provided in § 16.1-80;

(6) To administer oaths and take acknowledgments;

(7) To act as conservators of the peace;

(8), (9) [Repealed.]

(10) To perform such other acts or functions specifically authorized by law.

History.

Code 1950, § 19.1-394; 1973, c. 545; 1974, c. 484; 1975, c. 495; 1976, c. 471; 1977, c. 332; 1978, cc. 500, 605; 1985, c. 77; 2007, cc. 122, 373; 2008, cc. 551, 691; 2009, cc. 291, 344.

ARTICLE 6. COMPENSATION AND FEES.

§ 19.2-46. Compensation.

The salaries of all magistrates shall be fixed and paid as provided in § 19.2-46.1. The salaries referred to herein shall be in lieu of all fees which may accrue to the recipient by virtue of his office.

History.

Code 1950, § 19.1-395; 1973, c. 545; 1974, c. 484; 1975, c. 495; 1980, c. 139; 2008, cc. 551, 691.

§ 19.2-46.1. Salaries to be fixed by the Executive Secretary; limitations; mileage allowance.

Salaries of magistrates and any other personnel in the office of the magistrate shall be fixed by the Executive Secretary of the Supreme Court. Such salaries shall be fixed by the Executive Secretary at least annually at such time as he deems proper and as soon as practicable thereafter certified to the Comptroller.

In determining the salary of any magistrate, the Executive Secretary shall consider the work load of and territory and population served by the magistrate and such other factors he deems relevant.

The governing body of any county or city may add to the fixed compensation of magistrates such amount as the governing body may appropriate with the total amount not to exceed 50 percent of the amount paid by the Commonwealth to magistrates provided such additional compensation was in effect on June 30, 2008, for such magistrates and any magistrate receiving such additional compensation continues in office without a break in service. However, the total amount of additional compensation may not be increased after June 30, 2008. No additional amount paid by a local governing body shall be chargeable to the Executive Secretary of the Supreme Court, nor shall it remove or supersede any authority, control or supervision of the Executive Secretary or Committee on District Courts.

History.
1973, c. 545, § 14.1-44.2; 1974, c. 484; 1975, c. 334; 1981, c. 4; 1995, cc. 331, 378; 1998, c. 872; 2008, cc. 551, 691.

§ 19.2-46.2. Full-time magistrates; certification for retirement coverage.

The Committee on District Courts shall certify to the director of the Virginia Retirement System the names of those magistrates serving on a regular full-time basis. Certification by the Committee shall qualify a magistrate as a state employee, for purposes of §§ 51.1-124.3 and 51.1-152 of the Virginia Retirement System (§ 51.1-124.1 et seq.), effective on the date given in the certificate as the date on which such magistrate first served on a regular full-time basis on or after January 1, 1974.

History.
1974, c. 353, § 14.1-44.2:1; 1998, c. 872.

§ 19.2-47. Magistrate not to receive claims or evidence of debt for collection.

No magistrate shall receive claims or evidence of debt for collection; and it shall be unlawful for any magistrate to receive claims of any kind for collection, or to accept or receive money or any other things of value by way of commission or compensation for or on account of any collection made by or through him on any such claim, either before or after judgment. Any magistrate violating this section shall be guilty of a Class 1 misdemeanor.

History.
Code 1950, § 19.1-396; 1973, c. 545; 1975, c. 495.

§ 19.2-47.1. Disposition of funds.

All funds paid to and collected by or on behalf of a magistrate shall be paid promptly to the appropriate district court clerk, circuit court clerk, commissioner in chancery, department of the Commonwealth, federal agency or as otherwise authorized by statute.

History.
1973, c. 545, § 14.1-44.4; 1980, c. 356; 1987, c. 22; 1998, c. 872.

§ 19.2-48. Audits.

The Auditor of Public Accounts shall audit the records of all magistrates who serve any county or city when auditing the records of the district courts of such county or city or upon request of the chief district judge of the district in which such county or city is located.

History.
Code 1950, § 19.1-397; 1973, c. 545; 1975, c. 495; 1980, c. 195; 2008, cc. 551, 691.

§ 19.2-48.1. Quarters for magistrates.

A. The counties and cities served by a magistrate or magistrates shall provide suitable quarters for such magistrates, including a site for any videoconferencing equipment necessary to provide remote access to such magistrates. Insofar as possible, such quarters should be located in a public facility and should be appropriate to conduct the affairs of a judicial officer as well as provide convenient access to the public and law-enforcement officers. The county or city shall also provide all furniture and other equipment necessary for the efficient operation of the office.

B. Wherever practical, the office of magistrate shall be located at the county seat. However, offices may be located at other locations in the county, or city adjacent thereto, whenever such additional offices are necessary to effect the efficient administration of justice.

History.
1975, c. 495; 1981, c. 5; 1988, c. 510; 2008, cc. 551, 691.

CHAPTER 4.
SPECIAL MAGISTRATES.

§§ 19.2-49 through 19.2-51: Repealed by Acts 1980, c. 758.

CHAPTER 5.
SEARCH WARRANTS.

Section

§ 19.2-52. When search warrant may issue.

Except as provided in § 19.2-56.1, search warrants, based upon complaint on oath supported by an affidavit as required in § 19.2-54, may be issued by any judge, magistrate or other person having authority to issue criminal warrants, if he be satisfied from such complaint and affidavit that there is reasonable and probable cause for the issuance of such search warrant.

History.
Code 1950, § 19.1-83; 1960, c. 366; 1975, c. 495; 1986, c. 636.

§ 19.2-53. What may be searched and seized.

A. Search warrants may be issued for the search of or for specified places, things or persons, and seizure therefrom of the following things as specified in the warrant:

1. Weapons or other objects used in the commission of crime;
2. Articles or things the sale or possession of which is unlawful;
3. Stolen property or the fruits of any crime;
4. Any object, thing, or person, including without limitation, documents, books, papers, records or body fluids, constituting evidence of the commission of crime.

Notwithstanding any other provision in this chapter to the contrary, no search warrant may be issued as a substitute for a witness subpoena.

B. Any search warrant issued for the search and seizure of a computer, computer network, or other device containing electronic or digital information shall be deemed to include the search and seizure of the physical components and the electronic or digital information contained in any such computer, computer network, or other device.

C. Any search, including the search of the contents of any computer, computer network, or other device conducted pursuant to subsection B, may be conducted in any location and is not limited to the location where the evidence was seized.

History.
Code 1950, § 19.1-84; 1960, c. 366; 1962, c. 519; 1966, c. 363; 1970, c. 650; 1974, c. 113; 1975, c. 495; 1981, c. 559; 2015, c. 501.

§ 19.2-53.1. Taking blood samples pursuant to search warrant; immunity.

No cause of action shall lie in any court against any person authorized by law to withdraw blood pursuant to a search warrant issued in accordance with § 19.2-53 when that person is acting in accordance with such warrant, except in cases of negligence in the withdrawing of blood or willful misconduct.

History.
2015, c. 425.

§ 19.2-54. Affidavit preliminary to issuance of search warrant; general search warrant prohibited; effect of failure to file affidavit.

No search warrant shall be issued until there is filed with the officer authorized to issue the same an affidavit of some person reasonably describing the place, thing, or person to be searched, the things or persons to be searched for thereunder, alleging briefly material facts, constituting the probable cause for the issuance of such warrant and alleging substantially the offense in relation to which such search is to be made and that the object, thing, or person searched for constitutes evidence of the commission of such offense. The affidavit may be filed by electronically transmitted (i) facsimile process or (ii) electronic record as defined in § 59.1-480. Such affidavit shall be certified by the officer who issues such warrant and delivered in person; mailed by certified mail, return receipt requested; or delivered by electronically transmitted facsimile process or by use of filing and security procedures as defined in the Uniform Electronic Transactions Act (§ 59.1-479 et seq.) for transmitting signed documents, by such officer or his designee or agent, to the clerk of the circuit court of the county or city wherein the search is made, with a copy of the affidavit also being delivered to the clerk of the circuit court of the county or city where the warrant is issued, if in a different county or city, within seven days after the issuance of such warrant and shall by such clerks be preserved as a record and shall at all times be subject to inspection by the public after the warrant that is the subject of the affidavit has been executed or 15 days after issuance of the warrant, whichever is earlier; however, such affidavit, any warrant issued pursuant thereto, any return made thereon, and any order sealing the affidavit, warrant, or return may be temporarily sealed for a specific period of time by the appropriate court upon application of the attorney for the Commonwealth for good cause shown in an ex parte hearing. Any individual arrested and claiming to be aggrieved by such search and seizure or any person who claims to be entitled to lawful possession of such property seized may move the appropriate court for the unsealing of such affidavit, warrant, and return. The

Criminal Procedure

burden of proof with respect to continued sealing shall be upon the Commonwealth. Each such clerk shall maintain an index of all such affidavits filed in his office in order to facilitate inspection. No such warrant shall be issued on an affidavit omitting such essentials, and no general warrant for the search of a house, place, compartment, vehicle or baggage shall be issued. The term "affidavit" as used in this section, means statements made under oath or affirmation and preserved verbatim.

Failure of the officer issuing such warrant to file the required affidavit shall not invalidate any search made under the warrant unless such failure shall continue for a period of 30 days. If the affidavit is filed prior to the expiration of the 30-day period, nevertheless, evidence obtained in any such search shall not be admissible until a reasonable time after the filing of the required affidavit.

History.

Code 1950, § 19.1-85; 1960, c. 366; 1973, c. 502; 1975, c. 495; 1976, c. 552; 1977, c. 109; 1979, c. 583; 1980, c. 362; 1981, c. 559; 1989, c. 719; 2006, c. 285; 2007, c. 212; 2008, cc. 147, 183; 2011, cc. 196, 219; 2012, c. 5.

§ 19.2-55. Issuing general search warrant or search warrant without affidavit deemed malfeasance.

Any person having authority to issue criminal warrants who wilfully and knowingly issues a general search warrant or a search warrant without the affidavit required by § 19.2-54 shall be deemed guilty of a malfeasance.

History.

Code 1950, § 19.1-89; 1960, c. 366; 1975, c. 495.

§ 19.2-56. To whom search warrant directed; what it shall command; warrant to show date and time of issuance; copy of affidavit to be part of warrant and served therewith; warrants not executed within 15 days.

The judge, magistrate or other official authorized to issue criminal warrants, shall issue a search warrant if he finds from the facts or circumstances recited in the affidavit that there is probable cause for the issuance thereof.

Every search warrant shall be directed to (i) the sheriff, sergeant, or any policeman of the county, city or town in which the place to be searched is located, (ii) any law-enforcement officer or agent employed by the Commonwealth and vested with the powers of sheriffs and police, or (iii) jointly to any such sheriff, sergeant, policeman or law-enforcement officer or agent and an agent, special agent or officer of the Federal Bureau of Investigation, the Bureau of Alcohol, Tobacco and Firearms of the United States Treasury, the United States Naval Criminal Investigative Service, the United States Department of Homeland Security, any inspector, law-enforcement official or police personnel of the United States Postal Service, or the Drug Enforcement Administration. The warrant shall (i) name the affiant, (ii) recite the offense in relation to which the search is to be made, (iii) name or describe the place to be searched, (iv) describe the property or person to be searched for, and (v) recite that the magistrate has found probable cause to believe that the property or person constitutes evidence of a crime (identified in the warrant) or tends to show that a person (named or described therein) has committed or is committing a crime.

The warrant shall command that the place be forthwith searched, either in day or night, and that the objects or persons described in the warrant, if found there, be seized. An inventory shall be produced before a court having jurisdiction of the offense in relation to which the warrant was issued as provided in § 19.2-57.

Any such warrant as provided in this section shall be executed by the policeman or other law-enforcement officer or agent into whose hands it shall come or be delivered. If the warrant is directed jointly to a sheriff, sergeant, policeman or law-enforcement officer or agent of the Commonwealth and a federal agent or officer as otherwise provided in this section, the warrant may be executed jointly or by the policeman, law-enforcement officer or agent into whose hands it is delivered. No other person may be permitted to be present during or participate in the execution of a warrant to search a place except (i) the owners and occupants of the place to be searched when permitted to be present by the officer in charge of the conduct of the search and (ii) persons designated by the officer in charge of the conduct of the search to assist or provide expertise in the conduct of the search.

Any search warrant for records or other information pertaining to a subscriber to, or customer of, an electronic communication service or remote computing service, whether a domestic corporation or foreign corporation, that is transacting or has transacted any business in the Commonwealth, to be executed upon such service provider may be executed within or without the Commonwealth by hand, United States mail, commercial delivery service, facsimile, or other electronic means upon the service provider. Notwithstanding the provisions of § 19.2-57, the officer executing a warrant pursuant to this paragraph shall endorse the date of execution thereon and shall file the warrant, with the inventory attached (or a notation that no property was seized) and the accompanying affidavit, unless such affidavit was made by voice or videotape recording, within three days after the materials ordered to be produced are received by the officer from the service provider. The return shall be made in the circuit court clerk's office for the jurisdiction wherein the warrant was issued. Saturdays, Sundays, or any federal or state legal holiday shall not be used in computing the three-day filing period.

Electronic communication service or remote computing service providers, whether a foreign or domestic corporation, shall also provide the contents of electronic communications pursuant to a search warrant issued under this section and § 19.2-70.3 using the same process described in the preceding paragraph.

Every search warrant shall contain the date and time it was issued. However, the failure of any such search warrant to contain the date and time it was issued shall not render the warrant void, provided that the date and time of issuing of said warrant is established by competent evidence.

The judge, magistrate, or other official authorized to issue criminal warrants shall attach a copy of the affidavit required by § 19.2-54, which shall become a part of the search warrant and served therewith. However, this provision shall not be applicable in any case in which the affidavit is made by means of a voice or videotape recording or where the affidavit has been sealed pursuant to § 19.2-54.

Any search warrant not executed within 15 days after issuance thereof shall be returned to, and voided by, the officer who issued such search warrant.

For the purposes of this section:

"Foreign corporation" means any corporation or other entity, whose primary place of business is located outside of the boundaries of the Commonwealth, that makes a contract or engages in a terms of service agreement with a resident of the Commonwealth to be performed in whole or in part by either party in the Commonwealth, or a corporation that has been issued a certificate of authority pursuant to § 13.1-759 to transact business in the Commonwealth. The making of the contract or terms of service agreement or the issuance of a certificate of authority shall be considered to be the agreement of the foreign corporation or entity that a search warrant or subpoena, which has been properly served on it, has the same legal force and effect as if served personally within the Commonwealth.

"Properly served" means delivery of a search warrant or subpoena by hand, by United States mail, by commercial delivery service, by facsimile or by any other manner to any officer of a corporation or its general manager in the Commonwealth, to any natural person designated by it as agent for the service of process, or if such corporation has designated a corporate agent, to any person named in the latest annual report filed pursuant to § 13.1-775.

History.

Code 1950, § 19.1-86; 1960, c. 366; 1968, c. 572; 1975, c. 495; 1977, c. 289; 1979, c. 584; 1980, c. 573; 1981, c. 559; 1984, cc. 491, 598; 1988, c. 50; 1989, c. 719; 2000, c. 783; 2001, cc. 183, 205; 2007, c. 416; 2009, c. 725; 2015, cc. 75, 126.

§ 19.2-56.1. Warrant issued for search of attorney's office.

A. Any warrant sought for the search of a premises or the contents thereof belonging to or under the control of any licensed attorney-at-law to search for evidence of any crime solely involving a client of such attorney shall be issued only by a circuit court judge. Any evidence seized pursuant to this section shall be inventoried forthwith by the clerk of the issuing court and sealed by the issuing judge. As soon thereafter as is practicable, the issuing judge shall conduct an in camera inspection of the seized evidence in the presence of the attorney from whom the evidence was seized. Following such inspection the issuing judge shall return any evidence so seized which is determined to be within the scope of the attorney-client privilege and not otherwise subject to seizure.

B. Nothing herein shall bar the standing of the client to challenge the admissibility of any evidence seized pursuant to this section in any trial or proceeding.

History.

1986, c. 636.

§ 19.2-56.2. Application for and issuance of search warrant for a tracking device; installation and use.

A. As used in this section, unless the context requires a different meaning:

"Judicial officer" means a judge, magistrate, or other person authorized to issue criminal warrants.

"Law-enforcement officer" shall have the same meaning as in § 9.1-101.

"Tracking device" means an electronic or mechanical device that permits a person to remotely determine or track the position or movement of a person or object. "Tracking device" includes devices that store geographic data for subsequent access or analysis and devices that allow for the real-time monitoring of movement.

"Use of a tracking device" includes the installation, maintenance, and monitoring of a tracking device but does not include the interception of wire, electronic, or oral communications or the capture, collection, monitoring, or viewing of images.

B. A law-enforcement officer may apply for a search warrant from a judicial officer to permit the use of a tracking device. Each application for a search warrant authorizing the use of a tracking device shall be made in writing, upon oath or affirmation, to a judicial officer for the circuit in which the tracking device is to be installed, or where there is probable cause to believe the offense for which the tracking device is sought has been committed, is being committed, or will be committed.

The law-enforcement officer shall submit an affidavit, which may be filed by electronically transmitted (i) facsimile process or (ii) electronic record as defined in § 59.1-480, and shall include:

1. The identity of the applicant and the identity of the law-enforcement agency conducting the investigation;

2. The identity of the vehicle, container, item, or object to which, in which, or on which the tracking device is to be attached, placed, or otherwise installed; the name of the owner or possessor of the vehicle, container, item, or object described, if known; and the jurisdictional area in which the vehicle, container, item, or object described is expected to be found, if known;

3. Material facts constituting the probable cause for the issuance of the search warrant and alleging substantially the offense in relation to which such tracking device is to be used and a showing that probable cause exists that the information likely to be obtained will be evidence of the commission of such offense; and

4. The name of the county or city where there is probable cause to believe the offense for which the tracking device is sought has been committed, is being committed, or will be committed.

C. 1. If the judicial officer finds, based on the affidavit submitted, that there is probable cause to believe that a crime has been committed, is being committed, or will be committed and that there is probable cause to believe the information likely to be obtained from the use of the tracking device will be evidence of the commission of such offense, the judicial officer shall issue a search warrant authorizing the use of the tracking device. The search warrant shall authorize the use of the tracking device from within the Commonwealth to track a person or property for a reasonable period of time, not to exceed 30 days from the issuance of the search warrant. The search warrant shall authorize the collection of the tracking data contained in or obtained from the tracking device but shall not authorize the interception of wire, electronic, or oral communications or the capture, collection, monitoring, or viewing of images.

2. The affidavit shall be certified by the judicial officer who issues the search warrant and shall be delivered to and preserved as a record by the clerk of the circuit court of the county or city where there is probable cause to believe the offense for which the tracking device has been sought has been committed, is being committed, or will be committed. The affidavit shall be delivered by the judicial officer in person; mailed by certified mail, return receipt requested; or delivered by electronically transmitted facsimile process or by use of filing and security procedures as defined in the Uniform Electronic Transactions Act (§ 59.1-479 et seq.) for transmitting signed documents.

3. By operation of law, the affidavit, search warrant, return, and any other related materials or pleadings shall be sealed. Upon motion of the Commonwealth or the owner or possessor of the vehicle, container, item, or object that was tracked, the circuit court may unseal such documents if it appears that the unsealing is consistent with the ends of justice or is necessary to reasonably inform such person of the nature of the evidence to be presented against him or to adequately prepare for his defense.

4. The circuit court may, for good cause shown, grant one or more extensions, not to exceed 30 days each.

D. 1. The search warrant shall command the law-enforcement officer to complete the installation authorized by the search warrant within 15 days after issuance of the search warrant.

2. The law-enforcement officer executing the search warrant shall enter on it the exact date and time the device was installed and the period during which it was used.

3. Law-enforcement officers shall be permitted to monitor the tracking device during the period authorized in the search warrant, unless the period is extended as provided for in this section.

4. Law-enforcement officers shall remove the tracking device as soon as practical, but not later than 10 days after the use of the tracking device has ended. Upon request, and for good cause shown, the circuit court may grant one or more extensions for such removal for a period not to exceed 10 days each.

5. In the event that law-enforcement officers are unable to remove the tracking device as required by subdivision 4, the law-enforcement officers shall disable the device, if possible, and all use of the tracking device shall cease.

6. Within 10 days after the use of the tracking device has ended, the executed search warrant shall be returned to the circuit court of the county or city where there is probable cause to believe the offense for which the tracking device has been sought has been committed, is being committed, or will be committed, as designated in the search warrant, where it shall be preserved as a record by the clerk of the circuit court.

E. Within 10 days after the use of the tracking device has ended, a copy of the executed search warrant shall be served on the person who was tracked and the person whose property was tracked. Service may be accomplished by delivering a copy to the person who, or whose property, was tracked or by leaving a copy with any individual found at the person's usual place of abode who is a member of the person's family, other than a temporary sojourner or guest, and who is 16 years of age or older and by mailing a copy to the person's last known address. Upon request, and for good cause shown, the circuit court may grant one or more extensions for such service for a period not to exceed 30 days each. Good cause shall include, but not be limited to, a continuing criminal investigation, the potential for intimidation, the endangerment of an individual, or the preservation of evidence.

F. The disclosure or publication, without authorization of a circuit court, by a court officer, law-enforcement officer, or other person responsible for the administration of this section of the existence of a search warrant issued pursuant to this section, application for such search warrant, any affidavit filed in support of such warrant, or any return or data obtained as a result of such search warrant that is sealed by operation of law is punishable as a Class 1 misdemeanor.

History.
2012, cc. 636, 679.

§ 19.2-57. Execution and return of warrant; list of property seized.

The warrant shall be executed by the search of the place described in the warrant and, if property described in the warrant is found there, by the seizure of the property. The officer who seizes any property shall prepare an inventory thereof, under oath. An inventory of any seized property shall be produced before the circuit court of the county or city where the search was conducted. The officer executing the warrant shall endorse the date of execution thereon and the officer or his designee shall file the warrant, with the inventory attached (or a notation that no property was seized) and the accompanying affidavit, unless such affidavit was made by voice or videotape recording, within three days after the execution of such search warrant in the circuit court clerk's office, wherein the search was made, as provided in § 19.2-54. Saturdays, Sundays, or any federal or state legal holiday shall not be used in computing the three-day filing period. The officer, or his designee or agent, may file the warrant, inventory, and accompanying affidavit by delivering them in person, or by mailing them certified mail, return receipt requested, or delivering them by electronically transmitted facsimile process.

History.
Code 1950, § 19.1-87.1; 1970, c. 416; 1973, c. 11; 1975, c. 495; 1976, cc. 142, 552; 1977, c. 109; 1980, c. 573; 1984, c. 491; 2008, cc. 147, 183.

§ 19.2-58. Disposition of property seized.

If any such warrant be executed by the seizure of property, or of any other of the things aforesaid, the same shall be safely kept by the direction of such judge or court, to be used as evidence, and thereafter be disposed of as provided by law; provided, however, that any such property seized under such warrant which is not used in evidence and any property which is stolen or embezzled property shall be restored to its owner, and the things mentioned in § 19.2-53 may be burnt or otherwise destroyed, under such direction, as soon as there is no further need for its use as evidence unless it is otherwise expressly provided by law.

History.
Code 1950, § 19.1-87; 1960, c. 366; 1975, c. 495.

§ 19.2-59. Search without warrant prohibited; when search without warrant lawful.

No officer of the law or any other person shall search any place, thing or person, except by virtue of and under a warrant issued by a proper officer. Any officer or other person searching any place, thing or person otherwise than by virtue of and under a search warrant, shall be guilty of malfeasance in office. Any officer or person violating the provisions of this section shall be liable to any person aggrieved thereby in both compensatory and punitive damages. Any officer found guilty of a second offense under this section shall, upon conviction thereof, immediately forfeit his office, and such finding shall be deemed to create a vacancy in such office to be filled according to law.

Provided, however, that any officer empowered to enforce the game laws or marine fisheries laws as set forth in Title 28.2 may without a search warrant enter for the purpose of enforcing such laws, any freight yard or room, passenger depot, baggage room or warehouse, storage room or warehouse, train, baggage car, passenger car, express car, Pullman car or freight car of any common carrier, or any boat, automobile or other vehicle; but nothing in this proviso contained shall be construed to permit a search of any occupied berth or compartment on any passenger car or boat or any baggage, bag, trunk, box or other closed container without a search warrant.

History.
Code 1950, § 19.1-88; 1960, c. 366; 1975, c. 495; 1976, c. 293; 1978, c. 721; 1997, c. 147.

§ 19.2-59.1. Strip searches prohibited; exceptions; how strip searches conducted.

A. No person in custodial arrest for a traffic infraction, Class 3 or Class 4 misdemeanor, or a violation of a city, county, or town ordinance, which is punishable by no more than thirty days in jail shall be strip searched unless there is reasonable cause to believe on the part of a law-enforcement officer authorizing the search that the individual is concealing a weapon. All strip searches conducted under this section shall be performed by persons of the same sex as the person arrested and on premises where the search cannot be observed by persons not physically conducting the search.

B. A regional jail superintendent or the chief of police or the sheriff of the county or city shall develop a written policy regarding strip searches.

C. A search of any body cavity must be performed under sanitary conditions and a search of any body cavity, other than the mouth, shall be conducted either by or under the supervision of medically trained personnel.

D. Strip searches authorized pursuant to the exceptions stated in subsection A of this section shall be conducted by a law-enforcement officer as defined in § 9.1-101.

E. The provisions of this section shall not apply when the person is taken into custody by or remanded to a law-enforcement officer pursuant to a circuit or district court order.

F. For purposes of this section, *"strip search"* shall mean having an arrested person remove or arrange some or all of his clothing so as to permit a visual inspection of the genitals, buttocks, anus, female breasts, or undergarments of such person.

G. Nothing in this section shall prohibit a sheriff or a regional jail superintendent from requiring that inmates take hot water and soap showers and be subjected to visual inspection upon assignment to the general population area of the jail or upon determination by the sheriff or regional jail superintendent that the inmate must be held at the jail by reason of his inability to post bond after reasonable opportunity to do so.

History.
1981, c. 608; 1995, c. 112.

§ 19.2-60. Motion for return of seized property and to suppress.

A person aggrieved by an allegedly unlawful search or seizure may move the court to return any seized property and to suppress it for use as evidence. The court shall receive evidence on any issue of fact necessary to the decision of the motion. If the motion is granted by a court of record, any seized property shall be restored as soon as practicable unless otherwise subject to lawful detention, and such property shall not be admissible in evidence at any hearing or trial. If the motion is granted by a court not of record, such property shall not be admissible in evidence at any hearing or trial before that court, but the ruling shall have no effect on any hearing or trial in a court of record.

History.
1975, c. 495.

§ 19.2-60.1. Use of unmanned aircraft systems by public bodies; search warrant required.

A. As used in this section, unless the context requires a different meaning:

"Unmanned aircraft" means an aircraft that is operated without the possibility of human intervention from within or on the aircraft.

"Unmanned aircraft system" means an unmanned aircraft and associated elements, including communication links, sensing devices, and the components that control the unmanned aircraft.

B. No state or local government department, agency, or instrumentality having jurisdiction over criminal law enforcement or regulatory violations, including but not limited to the Department of State Police, and no department of law enforcement as defined in § 15.2-836 of any county, city, or town shall utilize an unmanned aircraft system except during the execution of a search warrant issued pursuant to this chapter or an administrative or inspection warrant issued pursuant to law.

C. Notwithstanding the prohibition in this section, an unmanned aircraft system may be deployed without a warrant (i) when an Amber Alert is activated pursuant to § 52-34.3, (ii) when a Senior Alert is activated pursuant to § 52-34.6, (iii) when a Blue Alert is activated pursuant to § 52-34.9, (iv) where use of an unmanned aircraft system is determined to be necessary to alleviate an immediate danger to any person, (v) for training exercises related to such uses, or (vi) if a person with legal authority consents to the warrantless search.

D. The warrant requirements of this section shall not apply when such systems are utilized to support the Commonwealth for purposes other than law enforcement, including damage assessment, traffic assessment, flood stage assessment, and wildfire assessment. Nothing herein shall prohibit use of unmanned aircraft systems for private, commercial, or recreational use or solely for research and development purposes by institutions of higher education and other research organizations or institutions.

E. Evidence obtained through the utilization of an unmanned aircraft system in violation of this section is not admissible in any criminal or civil proceeding.

F. In no case may a weaponized unmanned aircraft system be deployed in the Commonwealth or its use facilitated in the Commonwealth by a state or local government department, agency, or instrumentality or department of law enforcement in the Commonwealth except in operations at the Space Port and Naval/Aegis facilities at Wallops Island.

G. Nothing herein shall apply to the Armed Forces of the United States or the Virginia National Guard while utilizing unmanned aircraft systems during training required to maintain readiness for its federal mission or when facilitating training for other U.S. Department of Defense units.

History.
2015, cc. 764, 774.

CHAPTER 6. INTERCEPTION OF WIRE, ELECTRONIC OR ORAL COMMUNICATIONS.

Section

§ 19.2-61. Definitions.

As used in this chapter:

"Aggrieved person" means a person who was a party to any intercepted wire, electronic or oral communication or a person against whom the interception was directed;

"Aural transfer" means a transfer containing the human voice at any point between and including the point of origin and the point of reception;

"Communications common carrier" means any person engaged as a common carrier for hire in communication by wire or radio or in radio transmission of energy;

"Contents" when used with respect to any wire, electronic or oral communication, includes any information concerning the substance, purport or meaning of that communication;

"Electronic, mechanical or other device" means any device or apparatus that can be used to intercept a wire, electronic or oral communication other than:

(a) Any telephone or telegraph instrument, equipment or facility, or any component thereof, (i) furnished to the subscriber or user by a provider of wire or electronic communication service in the ordinary course of its business and being used by the subscriber or user in the ordinary course of its business or furnished by the subscriber or user for connection to the facilities of such service and used in the ordinary course of the subscriber's or user's business; or (ii) being used by a communications common carrier in the ordinary course of its business, or by an investigative or law-enforcement officer in the ordinary course of his duties;

(b) A hearing aid or similar device being used to correct subnormal hearing to not better than normal;

"Electronic communication" means any transfer of signs, signals, writing, images, sounds, data, or intelligence of any nature transmitted in whole or in part by a wire, radio, electromagnetic, photoelectronic or photooptical system. The term does not include:

1. Any wire communication or oral communication as defined herein;

2. Any communication made through a tone-only paging device;

3. Any communication from an electronic or mechanical device which permits the tracking of the movement of a person or object; or

4. Any electronic funds transfer information stored by a financial institution in a communications system used for the electronic storage and transfer of funds;

"Electronic communication service" means any service which provides to users thereof the ability to send or receive wire or electronic communications;

"Electronic communication system" means any wire, radio, electromagnetic, photooptical or photoelectronic facilities for the transmission of wire or electronic communications, and any computer facilities or related electronic equipment for the electronic storage of such communications;

"Electronic storage" means any temporary, intermediate storage of a wire or electronic communication incidental to the electronic transmission thereof and any storage of such communication by an electronic communication service for purposes of backup protection of such communication;

"Intercept" means any aural or other means of acquisition of the contents of any wire, electronic or oral communication through the use of any electronic, mechanical or other device;

"Investigative or law-enforcement officer" means any officer of the United States or of a state or political subdivision thereof, who is empowered by law to conduct investigations of or to make arrests for offenses enumerated in this chapter, and any attorney authorized by law to prosecute or participate in the prosecution of such offenses;

"Judge of competent jurisdiction" means a judge of any circuit court of the Commonwealth with general criminal jurisdiction;

"Monitor" or *"monitoring"* means the actual auditory or visual acquisition of an intercepted communication by any means;

"Oral communication" means any oral communication uttered by a person exhibiting an expectation that such communication is not subject to interception under circumstances justifying such expectations but does not include any electronic communication;

"Pen register" means a device or process that records or decodes dialing, routing, addressing or signaling information transmitted by an instrument or facility from which a wire or electronic communication is transmitted; however, such information shall not include the contents of any communication. The term does not include any device or process used by a provider or customer of a wire or electronic communication service for billing, or recording as an incident to billing, for communications services provided by such provider or any device or process used by a provider or customer of a wire communication service for cost accounting or other like purposes in the ordinary course of the provider's or customer's business;

"Person" means any employee or agent of the Commonwealth or a political subdivision thereof, and any individual, partnership, association, joint stock company, trust or corporation;

"Readily accessible to the general public" means, with respect to a radio communication, that such communication is not (i) scrambled or encrypted; (ii) transmitted using modulation techniques whose essential parameters have been withheld from the public with the intention of preserving the privacy of such communication; (iii) carried on a subcarrier or other signal subsidiary to a radio transmission; (iv) transmitted over a communication system provided by a communications common carrier, unless the communication is a tone-only paging system communication; or (v) transmitted on frequencies allocated under Part 25, subpart D, E, or F of Part 74, or Part 94 of the Rules of the Federal Communications Commission, unless, in the case of a communication transmitted on a frequency allocated under Part 74 that is not exclusively allocated to broadcast auxiliary services, the communication is a two-way voice communication by radio;

"Remote computing service" means the provision to the public of computer storage or processing services by means of an electronic communications system;

"Trap and trace device" means a device or process that captures the incoming electronic or other impulses that identify the originating number or other dialing, routing, addressing and signaling information reasonably likely to identify the source of a wire or electronic communication; however, such information shall not include the contents of any communication;

"User" means any person or entity who uses an electronic communication service and is duly authorized by the provider of such service to engage in such use;

"Wire communication" means any aural transfer made in whole or in part through the use of facilities for the transmission of communications by the aid of wire, cable, or other like connection, including the use of such connection in a switching station, furnished or operated by any person engaged in providing or operating such facilities for the transmission of communications.

History.

Code 1950, § 19.1-89.1; 1973, c. 442; 1975, c. 495; 1988, c. 889; 2002, cc. 588, 623; 2005, c. 934.

§ 19.2-62. Interception, disclosure, etc., of wire, electronic or oral communications unlawful; penalties; exceptions.

A. Except as otherwise specifically provided in this chapter any person who:

1. Intentionally intercepts, endeavors to intercept or procures any other person to intercept or endeavor to intercept, any wire, electronic or oral communication;

2. Intentionally uses, endeavors to use, or procures any other person to use or endeavor to use any electronic, mechanical or other device to intercept any oral communication;

3. Intentionally discloses, or endeavors to disclose, to any other person the contents of any wire, electronic or oral communication knowing or having reason to know that the information was obtained through the interception of a wire, electronic or oral communication; or

4. Intentionally uses, or endeavors to use, the contents of any wire, electronic or oral communication, knowing or having reason to know that the information was obtained through the interception of a wire, electronic or oral communication; shall be guilty of a Class 6 felony.

B. 1. It shall not be unlawful under this chapter for an operator of a switchboard, or an officer, employee or agent of a provider of wire or electronic communications service, whose facilities are used in the transmission of a wire communication, to intercept, disclose or use that communication in the normal course of his employment while engaged in any activity which is a necessary incident to the rendition of his service or to the protection of the rights or property of the provider of that service. However, a provider of wire communication service to the public shall not utilize service observing or random monitoring except for mechanical or service quality control checks. It shall not be a criminal offense under this chapter for providers of wire or electronic communications service, their officers, employees and agents, landlords, custodians, or other persons pursuant to a court order under this chapter, to provide information facilities or technical assistance to an investigative or law-enforcement officer, who, pursuant to this chapter, is authorized to intercept a wire, electronic or oral communication.

2. It shall not be a criminal offense under this chapter for a person to intercept a wire, electronic or oral communication, where such person is a party to the communication or one of the parties to the communication has given prior consent to such interception.

3. It shall not be a criminal offense under this chapter for any person:

(a) To intercept or access an electronic communication made through an electronic communication system that is configured so that such electronic communication is readily accessible to the general public;

(b) To intercept any radio communication which is transmitted (i) by any station for the use of the general public, or that relates to ships, aircraft, vehicles, or persons in distress, (ii) by any governmental, law-enforcement, civil defense, private land mobile, or public safety communications system, including police and fire, readily accessible to the general public, (iii) by a station operating on an authorized frequency within the bands allocated to

Criminal Procedure

the amateur, citizens band, or general mobile radio services; or (iv) by any marine or aeronautical communications system;

(c) To intercept any wire or electronic communication the transmission of which is causing harmful interference to any lawfully operating station or consumer electronic equipment, to the extent necessary to identify the source of such interference;

(d) Using the same frequency to intercept any radio communication made through a system that utilizes frequencies monitored by individuals engaged in the provision or the use of such system, if such communication is not scrambled or encrypted;

(e) To use a pen register or a trap and trace device pursuant to §§ 19.2-70.1 and 19.2-70.2; or

(f) Who is a provider of electronic communication service to record the fact that a wire or electronic communication was initiated or completed in order to protect such provider, another provider furnishing service toward the completion of the wire or electronic communication, or a user of that service, from fraudulent, unlawful or abusive use of such service.

C. A person or entity providing an electronic communication service to the public shall not intentionally divulge the contents of any communication, other than one to such person or entity or an agent thereof, while in transmission on that service to any person or entity other than an addressee or intended recipient of such communication or an agent of the addressee or intended recipient. However, a person or entity providing electronic communication service to the public may divulge the contents of any such communication:

1. As authorized in subdivision B 1 of this section or § 19.2-67;

2. With the lawful consent of the originator or any addressee or intended recipient of such communication;

3. To a person employed or authorized, or whose facilities are used, to forward such communication to its destination; or

4. Which were inadvertently obtained by the service provider and which appear to pertain to the commission of a crime, to a law-enforcement agency.

Conduct otherwise an offense under this subsection that consists of or relates to the interception of a satellite transmission that is not encrypted or scrambled and that is transmitted (i) to a broadcasting station for purposes of retransmission to the general public, or (ii) as an audio subcarrier intended for redistribution to facilities open to the public, but not including data transmissions or telephone calls, is not an offense under this section unless the conduct is for the purposes of direct or indirect commercial advantage or private financial gain. Further, private viewing of a satellite video communication that is not scrambled or encrypted and interception of a radio communication that is transmitted on frequencies allocated under subpart D of Part 74 of the Rules of the Federal Communications Commission that is not scrambled or encrypted when the viewing or interception is not done for a tortious or illegal purpose or for purposes of direct or indirect commercial advantage or private commercial gain, shall not be offenses under this chapter.

Violation of this subsection shall be punishable as a Class 1 misdemeanor.

History.

Code 1950, § 19.1-89.2; 1973, c. 442; 1975, c. 495; 1988, c. 889; 2004, c. 149.

§ 19.2-63. Manufacture, possession, sale or advertising of certain devices unlawful; penalties; exceptions.

A. Except as otherwise specifically provided in this chapter, any person who intentionally:

1. Manufactures, assembles, possesses, or sells any electronic, mechanical, or other device, knowing or having reason to know that the design of such device renders it primarily useful for the purpose of the surreptitious interception of wire, electronic or oral communications; or

2. Places in any newspaper, magazine, handbill, or other publication any advertisement of:

(a) Any electronic, mechanical, or other device knowing or having reason to know that the design of such device renders it primarily useful for the purpose of the surreptitious interception of wire, electronic or oral communications, or

(b) Any other electronic, mechanical, or other device where such advertisement promotes the use of such device for the purpose of the surreptitious interception of wire, electronic or oral communications; shall be guilty of a Class 6 felony.

B. It shall not be unlawful under this section for:

1. A provider of wire or electronic communication service or an officer, agent, or employee of, or a person under contract with, such provider in the normal course of the provider's business, or

2. An officer, agent, or employee of, or a person under contract with the United States, the Commonwealth or a political subdivision thereof, in the normal course of the activities of the United States, the Commonwealth, or a political subdivision thereof, to manufacture, assemble, possess, or sell any electronic, mechanical, or other device knowing or having reason to know that the design of such device renders it primarily useful for the purpose of the surreptitious interception of wire, electronic or oral communications.

History.

Code 1950, § 19.1-89.3; 1973, c. 442; 1975, c. 495; 1988, c. 889.

§ 19.2-63.1. Supervision and control of devices; unauthorized possession.

Any electronic, mechanical or other device as defined in this chapter which is in the possession of

Criminal Procedure

any sheriff's office or police department of a county, city or town, or in the possession of any employee of such office, shall be under the direct control and supervision of the sheriff or chief of police of the office or department or his designee who is an employee of the office or department. Unauthorized possession of any such device under the provisions of this section by any such employee is unlawful, notwithstanding the provisions of subdivision B 2 of § 19.2-63, and a Class 1 misdemeanor.

History.
1978, c. 63; 1988, c. 889; 2011, c. 193.

§ 19.2-64. Forfeiture of unlawful devices.

Any electronic, mechanical or other device used, manufactured, assembled, possessed, sold, or advertised in violation of § 19.2-62 or § 19.2-63 may be seized and forfeited to the Commonwealth, and turned over to the court of record in the city or county in which it was seized and such property shall be disposed of in such manner as the court may direct.

History.
Code 1950, § 19.1-89.4; 1973, c. 442; 1975, c. 495.

§ 19.2-65. When intercepted communications and evidence derived therefrom not to be received in evidence.

Whenever any wire or oral communication has been intercepted, no part of the contents of such communication and no evidence derived therefrom may be received in evidence in any trial, hearing or other proceeding in or before any court, grand jury, department, officer, commission, regulatory body, legislative committee or other agency of this Commonwealth or a political subdivision thereof if the disclosure of that information would be in violation of this chapter.

History.
Code 1950, § 19.1-89.5; 1973, c. 442; 1975, c. 495.

§ 19.2-66. When Attorney General or Chief Deputy Attorney General may apply for order authorizing interception of communications.

A. The Attorney General or Chief Deputy Attorney General, if the Attorney General so designates in writing, in any case where the Attorney General is authorized by law to prosecute or pursuant to a request in his official capacity of an attorney for the Commonwealth in any city or county, may apply to a judge of competent jurisdiction for an order authorizing the interception of wire, electronic or oral communications by the Department of State Police, when such interception may reasonably be expected to provide evidence of the commission of a felonious offense of extortion, bribery, kidnapping, murder, any felony violation of § 18.2-248 or 18.2-248.1, any felony violation of Chapter 29 (§ 59.1-364 et seq.) of Title 59.1, any felony violation of Article 2 (§ 18.2-38 et seq.), Article 2.1 (§ 18.2-46.1 et seq.), Article 2.2 (§ 18.2-46.4 et seq.), Article 5 (§ 18.2-58 et seq.), Article 6 (§ 18.2-59 et seq.) or any felonies that are not Class 6 felonies in Article 7 (§ 18.2-61 et seq.) of Chapter 4 of Title 18.2, or any conspiracy to commit any of the foregoing offenses. The Attorney General or Chief Deputy Attorney General may apply for authorization for the observation or monitoring of the interception by a police department of a county or city, by a sheriff's office, or by law-enforcement officers of the United States. Such application shall be made, and such order may be granted, in conformity with the provisions of § 19.2-68.

B. The application for an order under subsection B of § 19.2-68 shall be made as follows:

1. In the case of an application for a wire or electronic interception, a judge of competent jurisdiction shall have the authority to issue an order under subsection B of § 19.2-68 if there is probable cause to believe that an offense was committed, is being committed, or will be committed or the person or persons whose communications are to be intercepted live, work, subscribe to a wire or electronic communication system, maintain an address or a post office box, or are making the communication within the territorial jurisdiction of the court.

2. In the case of an application for an oral intercept, a judge of competent jurisdiction shall have the authority to issue an order under subsection B of § 19.2-68 if there is probable cause to believe that an offense was committed, is being committed, or will be committed or the physical location of the oral communication to be intercepted is within the territorial jurisdiction of the court.

C. For the purposes of an order entered pursuant to subsection B of § 19.2-68 for the interception of a wire or electronic communication, such communication shall be deemed to be intercepted in the jurisdiction where the order is entered, regardless of the physical location or the method by which the communication is captured or routed to the monitoring location.

History.
Code 1950, § 19.1-89.6; 1973, c. 442; 1975, c. 495; 1976, c. 271; 1979, c. 602; 1982, cc. 40, 274; 1988, cc. 855, 889; 2002, cc. 588, 623; 2004, c. 122; 2005, c. 934; 2011, cc. 403, 414; 2013, cc. 448, 664.

§ 19.2-67. Disclosure of information obtained by authorized means.

A. Any investigative or law-enforcement officer, or police officer of a county or city, who, by any means authorized by this chapter, has obtained knowledge of the contents of any wire, electronic or oral communication, or evidence derived therefrom, may disclose such contents to another investigative or law-enforcement officer, or police officer of a county or city, to the extent that such disclosure is appropriate to the proper performance of the official duties of the officer making or receiving the disclosure.

B. Any investigative or law-enforcement officer or police officer of a county or city, who, by any means authorized by this chapter, has obtained knowledge of the contents of any wire, electronic or oral communication or evidence derived therefrom may use such contents to the extent such use is appropriate to the proper performance of his official duties.

C. Any person who has received, by any means authorized by this chapter, any information concerning a wire, electronic or oral communication, or evidence derived therefrom intercepted in accordance with the provisions of this chapter may disclose the contents of that communication or such derivative evidence while giving testimony under oath or affirmation in any criminal proceeding for an offense specified in § 19.2-66, or any conspiracy or attempt to commit the same, in any court of the United States or of any state or in any federal or state grand jury proceeding.

D. No wire, electronic or oral communication which is a privileged communication between the parties to the conversation which is intercepted in accordance with, or in violation of, the provisions of this chapter shall lose its privileged character, nor shall it be disclosed or used in any way.

E. When an investigative or law-enforcement officer, or police officer of a county or city, while engaged in intercepting wire, electronic or oral communications in the manner authorized herein, or observing or monitoring such interception intercepts, observes or monitors wire, electronic or oral communications relating to offenses other than those specified in the order of authorization, the contents thereof, and evidence derived therefrom, shall not be disclosed or used as provided in subsections A, B and C of this section, unless such communications or derivative evidence relates to a felony, in which case use or disclosure may be made as provided in subsections A, B and C of this section. Such use and disclosure pursuant to subsection C of this section shall be permitted only when approved by a judge of competent jurisdiction where such judge finds, on subsequent application, that such communications were otherwise intercepted in accordance with the provisions of this chapter. Violations of this subsection E shall be punishable as provided in § 19.2-62.

History.

Code 1950, § 19.1-89.7; 1973, c. 442; 1975, c. 495; 1976, c. 231; 1979, c. 602; 1983, c. 536; 1988, c. 889.

§ 19.2-68. Application for and issuance of order authorizing interception; contents of order; recording and retention of intercepted communications, applications and orders; notice to parties; introduction in evidence of information obtained.

A. Each application for an order authorizing the interception of a wire, electronic or oral communication shall be made in writing upon oath or affirmation to the appropriate judge of competent jurisdiction and shall state the applicant's authority to make such application. Each application shall be verified by the Attorney General to the best of his knowledge and belief and shall include the following information:

1. The identity of the attorney for the Commonwealth and law-enforcement officer who requested the Attorney General to apply for such order;

2. A full and complete statement of the facts and circumstances relied upon by the applicant to justify his belief that an order should be issued, including (i) details as to the particular offense that has been, is being or is about to be committed, (ii) except as provided in subsection I, a particular description of the nature and location of the facilities from which or the place where the communication is to be intercepted, (iii) a particular description of the type of communications sought to be intercepted, (iv) the identity of the person, if known, committing the offense and whose communications are to be intercepted;

3. A full and complete statement as to whether or not other investigative procedures have been tried and failed or why they reasonably appear to be unlikely to succeed if tried or to be too dangerous;

4. A statement of the period of time for which the interception is required to be maintained. If the nature of the investigation is such that the authorization for interception should not automatically terminate when the described type of communication has been first obtained, a particular description of facts establishing probable cause to believe that additional communications of the same type will occur thereafter;

5. A full and complete statement of the facts concerning all previous applications known to the individual authorizing and making the application, made to any judge for authorization to intercept wire, electronic or oral communications involving any of the same persons, facilities or places specified in the application, and the action taken by the judge on each such application;

6. Where the application is for the extension of an order, a statement setting forth the results thus far obtained from the interception, or a reasonable explanation of the failure to obtain such results; and

7. If authorization is requested for observation or monitoring by a police department of a county or city, by a sheriff's office, or by law-enforcement officers of the United States, a statement containing the name of the police department, sheriff's office, or United States agency and an explanation of the reasons such observation or monitoring is necessary.

The judge may require the applicant to furnish additional testimony or documentary evidence in support of the application.

B. Upon such application the judge may enter an ex parte order, as requested or as modified, authorizing interception of wire, electronic or oral communications if the judge determines on the basis of the facts submitted by the applicant that:

1. There is probable cause for belief that an individual is committing, has committed or is about to commit an offense enumerated in § 19.2-66 of this chapter;

2. There is probable cause for belief that particular communications concerning that offense will be obtained through such interception;

3. Normal investigative procedures have been tried and have failed, or reasonably appear to be unlikely to succeed if tried, or to be too dangerous; and interception under this chapter is the only alternative investigative procedure available;

4. Except as provided in subsection I, there is probable cause for belief that the facilities from which, or the place where, the wire, electronic or oral communications are to be intercepted are being used, or are about to be used, in connection with the commission of such offense, or are leased to, listed in the name of, or commonly used by such person;

5. A wire, electronic or oral communication authorized to be intercepted pursuant to this section may be monitored at any location within the Commonwealth of Virginia.

C. Each order authorizing the interception of any wire, electronic or oral communication shall specify:

1. The identity of the person, if known, whose communications are to be intercepted;

2. The nature and location of the communications facilities as to which, or the place where, authority to intercept is granted;

3. A particular description of the type of communication sought to be intercepted, and a statement of the particular offense enumerated in § 19.2-66 to which it relates;

4. That such interception is to be conducted only by the Department of State Police;

5. If observation or monitoring by the police department of a county or city, by a sheriff's office, or by law-enforcement officers of the United States is authorized, only that police department, sheriff's office, or agency or the officers from any police department of a town which originated the investigation leading to the application shall observe or monitor the interception; and

6. The period of time during which such interception is authorized, including a statement as to whether or not the interception shall automatically terminate when the described communication has been first obtained.

An order authorizing the interception of a wire, electronic or oral communication shall, upon request of the applicant, direct that a provider of wire or electronic communications service, landlord, custodian or other person shall furnish the Department of State Police forthwith all information, facilities and technical assistance necessary to accomplish the interception unobtrusively and with a minimum of interference with the services that such service provider, landlord, custodian or person is providing the person whose communications are to be intercepted. Any provider of wire or electronic communications service, landlord, custodian or other person furnishing such facilities or technical assistance shall be compensated therefor by the Commonwealth for reasonable and actual expenses incurred in providing such facilities or assistance, to be paid out of the criminal fund.

D. No order entered under this section may authorize the interception of any wire, electronic or oral communication for any period longer than is necessary to achieve the objective of the authorization, nor in any event longer than 30 days which period begins to run on the earlier of the day on which the investigative or law-enforcement officer begins to conduct an interception under the order or 10 days after the date of entry of the order. Extensions of an order may be granted, but only upon application for an extension made in accordance with subsection A of this section and the court's making the findings required by subsection B of this section. The period of extension shall be no longer than the authorizing judge deems necessary to achieve the purposes for which it was granted and in no event for longer than 30 days. Every order and extension thereof shall contain a provision that the authorization to intercept shall be executed as soon as practicable, shall be conducted in such a way as to minimize the interception of communications not otherwise subject to interception under this chapter, and must terminate upon attainment of the authorized objective, or in any event in 30 days. In the event the intercepted communication is in a code or foreign language, and an expert in that foreign language or code is not reasonably available during the interception period, minimization may be accomplished as soon as practicable after such interception.

E. Whenever an order authorizing interception is entered pursuant to this chapter, the order shall require reports to be made to the judge who issued the order showing what progress has been made toward achievement of the authorized objective and the need for continued interception. Such reports shall be made at such intervals as the judge shall require.

F. 1. The contents of any wire, electronic or oral communication intercepted by any means authorized by this chapter shall, if possible, be recorded on tape or wire or other comparable device. Should it not be possible to record the intercepted communication, a detailed resume of such communication shall forthwith be reduced to writing and filed with the court. The recording of the contents of any wire, electronic or oral communication under this subsection shall be done in such way as will protect the recording from editing or other alterations and shall not be duplicated except upon order of the court as hereafter provided. Immediately upon the expiration of the period of the order, or extensions thereof, such recording or detailed resume shall be made available to the judge issuing such order and sealed under his directions. Custody of any recordings or detailed resumes shall be vested with the court and shall not be destroyed for a period of 10 years from the date of the order and then only by direction of the court; provided, however, should any interception fail to reveal any information related to the offense or offenses for which it was authorized, such recording or resume shall be destroyed after the expiration of 60 days after the notice required by subdivision 4 of this subsection is served. Duplicate recordings may be made for use or disclosure pursuant to the provisions of subsections A and B of § 19.2-67 for investigations. The presence of the seal provided for by this subsection, or a satisfactory explanation for the absence thereof, shall be a prerequisite for the use or disclosure of the contents of any wire, electronic or oral communication or evidence derived therefrom under subsection C of § 19.2-67.

2. Applications made and orders granted or denied under this chapter shall be sealed by the judge. Custody of the applications and orders shall be wherever the judge directs. Such applications and orders shall be disclosed only upon a showing of good cause before a judge of competent jurisdiction and shall not be destroyed except on order of the issuing or denying judge, and in any event shall be kept for 10 years.

3. Any violation of the provisions of this subsection may be punished as contempt of the issuing or denying court.

4. Within a reasonable time but not later than 90 days after the filing of an application for an order of authorization which is denied or the termination of the period of an order or extensions thereof, the issuing or denying judge shall cause to be served, on the persons named in the order or the application, and such other parties to intercepted communications as the judge may determine in his discretion that is in the interest of justice, an inventory which shall include notice of:

(a) The fact of the entry of the order or the application;

(b) The date of the entry and the period of authorized interception, or the denial of the application;

(c) The fact that during the period wire, electronic or oral communications were or were not intercepted; and

(d) The fact that unless he files a motion with the court within 60 days after the service of notice upon him, the recordation or resume may be destroyed in accordance with subdivision 1 of this subsection.

The judge, upon the filing of a motion, shall make available to such person or his counsel for inspection the intercepted communications, applications and orders. The serving of the inventory required by this subsection may be postponed for additional periods, not to exceed 30 days each, upon the ex parte showing of good cause to a judge of competent jurisdiction.

G. The contents of any intercepted wire, electronic or oral communication or evidence derived therefrom shall not be received in evidence or otherwise disclosed in any trial, hearing or other proceeding in a state court unless each party to the communication and to such proceeding, not less than 10 days before the trial, hearing or proceeding, has been furnished with a copy of the court order, accompanying application under which the interception was authorized and the contents of any intercepted wire, electronic or oral communication that is to be used in any trial, hearing or other proceeding in a state court. This 10-day period may be waived by the judge if he finds that it was not possible to furnish the party with the above information 10 days before the trial, hearing or proceeding and that the party will not be prejudiced by the delay in receiving such information; provided that such information in any event shall be given prior to the day of the trial, and the inability to comply with such 10-day period shall be grounds for the granting of a continuance to either party.

The judge who considers an application for an interception under this chapter, whether issuing or denying the order, shall be disqualified from presiding at any trial resulting from or in any manner connected with such interception, regardless of whether the evidence acquired thereby is used in such trial.

H. Any aggrieved person in any trial, hearing or proceeding in or before any court, department, officer, agency, regulatory body or other authority of the Commonwealth, or a political subdivision thereof, may move to suppress the contents of any intercepted wire, electronic or oral communication, or evidence derived therefrom, on the grounds that:

1. The communication was unlawfully intercepted, or was not intercepted in compliance with this chapter; or

2. The order of the authorization or approval under which it was intercepted is insufficient on its face; or

3. The interception was not made in conformity with the order of authorization or approval; or

4. The interception is not admissible into evidence in any trial, proceeding or hearing in a state court under the applicable rules of evidence.

Such motion shall be made before the trial, hearing or proceeding unless there was no opportunity to make such motion or the person was not aware of the grounds of the motion. If the motion is granted pursuant to subdivision 1, 2 or 3 of this subsection, the contents of the intercepted wire, electronic or oral communication or evidence derived therefrom shall be treated as having been obtained in violation of this chapter. The judge, upon the filing of such motion by the aggrieved person, shall make available to the aggrieved person, or his counsel, for inspection the intercepted communication.

I. The requirements of subdivision 2 of subsection A and subdivision 4 of subsection B of this section relating to the specification of the facilities from which, or the place where, the communication is to be intercepted do not apply if:

1. In the case of an application with respect to the interception of an oral communication:

(a) The application contains a full and complete statement as to why such specification is not practical and identifies the person committing the offense and whose communications are to be intercepted; and

(b) The judge finds that such specification is not practical; or

2. In the case of an application with respect to a wire or electronic communication:

(a) the application identifies the person believed to be committing the offense and whose communications are to be intercepted and the applicant makes a showing of a purpose, on the part of that person, to thwart interception by changing facilities; and

(b) the judge finds that such purpose has been adequately shown.

The interception of a communication under an order issued pursuant to this subsection shall not begin until the facilities from which, or the place where, the communication is to be intercepted is ascertained by the person implementing the interception order. A provider of wire or electronic communications service that has received an order issued pursuant to this subdivision 2 may move the court to modify or quash the order on the ground that its assistance with respect to the interception cannot be performed in a timely or reasonable fashion. The court, upon notice to the Attorney General, shall decide the motion expeditiously.

History.

Code 1950, § 19.1-89.8; 1973, c. 442; 1975, c. 495; 1976, c. 163; 1977, c. 335; 1979, c. 602; 1980, c. 244; 1988, c. 889; 2002, c. 91; 2005, c. 934; 2013, cc. 448, 664.

§ 19.2-69. Civil action for unlawful interception, disclosure or use.

Any person whose wire, electronic or oral communication is intercepted, disclosed or used in violation of this chapter shall (i) have a civil cause of action against any person who intercepts, discloses or uses, or procures any other person to intercept, disclose or use such communications, and (ii) be entitled to recover from any such person:

1. Actual damages but not less than liquidated damages computed at the rate of $400 a day for each day of violation or $4,000, whichever is higher, provided that liquidated damages shall be computed at the rate of $800 a day for each day of violation or $8,000, whichever is higher, if the wire, electronic, or oral communication intercepted, disclosed, or used is between (i) a husband and wife; (ii) an attorney and client; (iii) a licensed practitioner of the healing arts and patient; (iv) a licensed professional counselor, licensed clinical social worker, licensed psychologist, or licensed marriage and family therapist and client; or (v) a clergy member and person seeking spiritual counsel or advice;

2. Punitive damages; and

3. A reasonable attorney's fee and other litigation costs reasonably incurred.

A good faith reliance on a court order or legislative authorization shall constitute a complete defense to any civil or criminal action brought under this chapter or under any other law.

History.

Code 1950, § 19.1-89.9; 1973, c. 442; 1975, c. 495; 1988, c. 889; 2010, c. 343; 2015, c. 672.

§ 19.2-70. Reports to be filed by courts and Attorney General.

All courts of the Commonwealth and the Attorney General shall file all reports required by 18 U.S.C.A. § 2519. The Attorney General shall file a written report with the Clerks of the Senate and House of Delegates on or before December 31 of each year setting forth the number of applications made pursuant to this chapter, the number of interceptions authorized, the number of arrests resulting from each application, the number of convictions including a breakdown by offense, the cost of each application granted and the number of requests denied. Such information shall be made available by such Clerks to any member of the General Assembly upon request. However, notwithstanding the above requirements, no report shall be made concerning a granted application until after all inventories associated with such application are served pursuant to subdivision F 4 of § 19.2-68.

History.

Code 1950, § 19.1-89.10; 1973, c. 442; 1975, c. 495; 2011, cc. 403, 414.

§ 19.2-70.1. General prohibition on pen register and trap and trace device use; exceptions.

Except as provided in this section, no person may install or use a pen register or a trap and trace device without first obtaining a court order under § 19.2-70.2.

However, a court order shall not be required for use of a pen register or trap and trace device by a provider of electronic or wire communication service (i) relating to the operation, maintenance, and testing of a wire or electronic communication service or to the protection of the rights or property of the provider, or to the protection of users of that service from abuse of service or unlawful use of service; (ii) to record the fact that a wire or electronic communication was initiated or completed in order to protect such provider, another provider furnishing service toward the completion of the wire communication, or a user of that service, from fraudulent, unlawful or abusive use of service; or (iii) where the consent of the user of that service has been obtained.

Any person who knowingly violates this section shall be guilty of a Class 1 misdemeanor.

History.

1988, c. 889.

§ 19.2-70.2. Application for and issuance of order for a pen register or trap and trace device; assistance in installation and use.

A. An investigative or law-enforcement officer may make application for an order or an extension of an order authorizing or approving the installation and use of a pen register or a trap and trace device, in writing under oath or equivalent affirmation, to a court of competent jurisdiction. The application shall include:

1. The identity of the officer making the application and the identity of the law-enforcement agency conducting the investigation; and

2. A certification by the applicant that the information likely to be obtained is relevant to an ongoing criminal investigation being conducted by that agency.

The application may include a request that the order require information, facilities and technical assistance necessary to accomplish the installation be furnished.

B. An application for an ex parte order authorizing the installation and use of a pen register or trap and trace device may be filed in the jurisdiction where the ongoing criminal investigation is being conducted; where there is probable cause to believe that an offense was committed, is being committed, or will be committed; or where the person or persons who subscribe to the wire or electronic communication system live, work, or maintain an address or a post office box. For the purposes of an order entered pursuant to this section for the installation and use of a pen register or trap and trace device, such installation shall be deemed to occur in the jurisdiction where the order is entered, regardless of the physical location or the method by which the information is captured or routed to the law-enforcement officer that made the application. Upon application, the court shall enter an ex parte order authorizing the installation and use of a pen register or a trap and trace device if the court finds that the investigative or law-enforcement officer has certified to the court that the information likely to be obtained by such installation and use is relevant to an ongoing criminal investigation.

The order shall specify:

1. The identity, if known, of the person in whose name the telephone line or other facility to which the pen register or trap and trace device is to be attached or applied is listed or to whom the line or other facility is leased;

2. The identity, if known, of the person who is the subject of the criminal investigation;

3. The attributes of the communications to which the order applies, including the number or other identifier and, if known, the location of the telephone line or other facility to which the pen register or trap and trace device is to be attached or applied; and

4. A statement of the offense to which the information likely to be obtained by the pen register or trap and trace device relates.

C. Installation and use of a pen register or a trap and trace device shall be authorized for a period not to exceed 60 days. Extensions of the order may be granted, but only upon application made and order issued in accordance with this section. The period of an extension shall not exceed 60 days.

D. An order authorizing or approving the installation and use of a pen register or a trap and trace device shall direct that:

1. The order and application be sealed until otherwise ordered by the court;

2. Information, facilities and technical assistance necessary to accomplish the installation be furnished if requested in the application; and

3. The person owning or leasing the line or other facility to which the pen register or trap and trace device is attached or applied, or who is obligated by the order to provide assistance to the applicant, not disclose the existence of the pen register or trap and trace device or the existence of the investigation to the listed subscriber, or to any other person, unless or until otherwise ordered by the court.

E. Upon request of an investigative or a law-enforcement officer authorized by the court to install and use a pen register, a provider of wire or electronic communication service, a landlord, custodian or any other person so ordered by the court shall, as soon as practicable, furnish the officer with all information, facilities, and technical assistance necessary to accomplish the installation of the pen register unobtrusively and with a minimum of interference with the services that the person so ordered by the court accords the party with respect to whom the installation and use is to take place.

F. Upon request of an investigative or law-enforcement officer authorized by the court to receive the results of a trap and trace device under this section, a provider of wire or electronic communication service, a landlord, custodian or any other person so ordered by the court shall, as soon as practicable, install the device on the appropriate line and furnish the officer with all additional information, facilities and technical assistance, including installation and operation of the device, unobtrusively and with a minimum of interference with the services that the person so ordered by the court accords the party with respect to whom the installation and use is to take place. Unless otherwise ordered by the court, the results of the trap and trace device shall be furnished to the investigative or law-enforcement officer designated by the court at reasonable intervals during regular business hours for the duration of the order. Where the law-enforcement agency implementing an ex parte order under this subsection seeks to do so by installing and using its own pen register or trap and trace device on a packet-switched data network of a provider of electronic communication service to the public, the agency shall ensure that a record will be maintained that will identify (i) any officer or officers who installed the device and any officer or officers who accessed the device to obtain information from the network; (ii) the date and time the device was installed, the date and time the device was uninstalled, and the date, time, and duration of each time the device is accessed to obtain information; (iii) the configuration of the device at the time of its installation and any subsequent modification thereof; and (iv) any information that has been collected by the device. To the extent that the pen register or trap and trace device can be set automatically to record this information electronically, the record shall be maintained electronically throughout the installation and use of such device. The record maintained hereunder shall be provided ex parte and under seal of the court that entered the ex parte order authorizing the installation and use of the device within 30 days after termination of the order, including any extensions thereof.

G. A provider of a wire or electronic communication service, a landlord, custodian or other person who furnishes facilities or technical assistance pursuant to this section shall be reasonably compensated for reasonable and actual expenses incurred in providing such facilities and assistance. The expenses shall be paid out of the criminal fund.

H. No cause of action shall lie in any court against a provider of a wire or electronic communication service, its officers, employees, agents or other specified persons for providing information, facilities, or assistance in accordance with the terms of a court order issued pursuant to this section. Good faith reliance on a court order, a legislative authorization or a statutory authorization is a complete defense against any civil or criminal action based upon a violation of this chapter.

History.

1988, c. 889; 2002, cc. 588, 623; 2005, c. 934; 2016, c. 231.

§ 19.2-70.3. Obtaining records concerning electronic communication service or remote computing service.

A. A provider of electronic communication service or remote computing service, which, for purposes of subdivisions 2, 3, and 4, includes a foreign corporation that provides such services, shall disclose a record or other information pertaining to a subscriber to or customer of such service, excluding the contents of electronic communications and real-time location data, to an investigative or law-enforcement officer only pursuant to:

1. A subpoena issued by a grand jury of a court of the Commonwealth;
2. A search warrant issued by a magistrate, general district court, or circuit court;
3. A court order issued by a circuit court for such disclosure issued as provided in subsection B; or
4. The consent of the subscriber or customer to such disclosure.

B. A court shall issue an order for disclosure under this section only if the investigative or law-enforcement officer shows that there is reason to believe the records or other information sought are relevant and material to an ongoing criminal investigation, or the investigation of any missing child as defined in § 52-32, missing senior adult as defined in § 52-34.4, or an incapacitated person as defined in § 64.2-2000 who meets the definition of a missing senior adult except for the age requirement. Upon issuance of an order for disclosure under this section, the order and any written application or statement of facts may be sealed by the court for 90 days for good cause shown upon application of the attorney for the Commonwealth in an ex parte proceeding. The order and any written application or statement of facts may be sealed for additional 90-day periods for good cause shown upon subsequent application of the attorney for the Commonwealth in an ex parte proceeding. A court issuing an order pursuant to this section, on a motion made promptly by the service provider, may quash or modify the order, if the information or records requested are unusually voluminous in nature or compliance with such order would otherwise cause an undue burden on such provider.

C. Except as provided in subsection D or E, a provider of electronic communication service or remote computing service, including a foreign corporation that provides such services, shall disclose the contents of electronic communications or real-time location data to an investigative or law-enforcement officer only pursuant to a search warrant issued by a magistrate, a juvenile and domestic relations district court, a general district court, or a circuit court, based upon complaint on oath supported by an affidavit as required in § 19.2-54, or judicial officer or court of any of the several states of the United States or its territories, or the District of Columbia when the warrant issued by such officer or such court complies with the provisions of subsection G.

In the case of a search warrant directed to a foreign corporation, the affidavit shall state that the complainant believes that the records requested are actually or constructively possessed by a foreign corporation that provides electronic communication service or remote computing service within the Commonwealth of Virginia. If satisfied that probable cause has been established for such belief and as required by Chapter 5 (§ 19.2-52 et seq.), the magistrate, the juvenile and domestic relations district court, the general district court, or the circuit court shall issue a warrant identifying those records to be searched for and commanding the person seeking such warrant to properly serve the warrant upon the foreign corporation. A search warrant for real-time location data shall be issued if the magistrate, the juvenile and domestic relations district court, the general district court, or the circuit court is satisfied that probable cause has been established that the real-time location data sought is relevant to a crime that is being committed or has been committed or that an arrest warrant exists for the person whose real-time location data is sought.

D. A provider of electronic communication service or remote computing service, including a foreign corporation that provides such services, shall disclose a record or other information pertaining to a subscriber to or customer of such service, including real-time location data but excluding the contents of electronic communications, to an investigative or law-enforcement officer pursuant to an administrative subpoena issued pursuant to § 19.2-10.2 concerning a violation of § 18.2-374.1 or 18.2-374.1:1, former § 18.2-374.1:2, or § 18.2-374.3 when the information sought is relevant and material to an ongoing criminal investigation.

E. When disclosure of real-time location data is not prohibited by federal law, an investigative or law-enforcement officer may obtain real-time location data without a warrant in the following circumstances:

1. To respond to the user's call for emergency services;

2. With the informed, affirmative consent of the owner or user of the electronic device concerned if (i) the device is in his possession; (ii) the owner or user knows or believes that the device is in the possession of an employee or agent of the owner or user with the owner's or user's consent; or (iii) the owner or user knows or believes that the device has been taken by a third party without the consent of the owner or user;

3. With the informed, affirmative consent of the legal guardian or next of kin of the owner or user, if reasonably available, if the owner or user is reasonably believed to be deceased, is reported missing, or is unable to be contacted; or

4. If the investigative or law-enforcement officer reasonably believes that an emergency involving the immediate danger to a person requires the disclosure, without delay, of real-time location data concerning a specific person and that a warrant cannot be obtained in time to prevent the identified danger.

No later than three business days after seeking disclosure of real-time location data pursuant to this subsection, the investigative or law-enforcement officer seeking the information shall file with the appropriate court a written statement setting forth the facts giving rise to the emergency and the facts as to why the person whose real-time location data was sought is believed to be important in addressing the emergency.

F. In order to comply with the requirements of § 19.2-54, any search of the records of a foreign corporation shall be deemed to have been made in the same place wherein the search warrant was issued.

G. A Virginia corporation or other entity that provides electronic communication services or remote computing services to the general public, when properly served with a search warrant and affidavit in support of the warrant, issued by a judicial officer or court of any of the several states of the United States or its territories, or the District of Columbia with jurisdiction over the matter, to produce a record or other information pertaining to a subscriber to or customer of such service, including real-time location data, or the contents of electronic communications, or both, shall produce the record or other information, including real-time location data, or the contents of electronic communications as if that warrant had been issued by a Virginia court. The provisions of this subsection shall only apply to a record or other information, including real-time location data, or contents of electronic communications relating to the commission of a criminal offense that is substantially similar to (i) a violent felony as defined in § 17.1-805, (ii) an act of violence as defined in § 19.2-297.1, (iii) any offense for which registration is required pursuant to § 9.1-902, (iv) computer fraud pursuant to § 18.2-152.3, or (v) identity theft pursuant to § 18.2-186.3. The search warrant shall be enforced and executed in the Commonwealth as if it were a search warrant described in subsection C.

H. The provider of electronic communication service or remote computing service may verify the authenticity of the written reports or records that it discloses pursuant to this section by providing an affidavit from the custodian of those written reports or records or from a person to whom said custodian reports certifying that they are true and complete copies of reports or records and that they are prepared in the regular course of business. When so authenticated, no other evidence of authenticity shall be necessary. The written reports and records, excluding the contents of electronic communications, shall be considered business records for purposes of the business records exception to the hearsay rule.

I. No cause of action shall lie in any court against a provider of a wire or electronic communication service or remote computing service or such provider's officers, employees, agents, or other specified persons for providing information, facilities, or assistance in accordance with the terms of a court order, warrant, administrative subpoena, or subpoena under this section or the provisions of subsection E.

J. A search warrant or administrative subpoena for the disclosure of real-time location data pursuant to this section shall require the provider to provide ongoing disclosure of such data for a reasonable period of time, not to exceed 30 days. A court may, for good cause shown, grant one or more extensions, not to exceed 30 days each.

K. An investigative or law-enforcement officer shall not use any device to obtain electronic communications or collect real-time location data from an electronic device without first obtaining a search warrant authorizing the use of the device if, in order to obtain the contents of such electronic communications or such real-time location data from the provider of electronic communication service or remote computing service, such officer would be required to obtain a search warrant pursuant to this section. However, an investigative or law-enforcement officer may use such a device without first obtaining a search warrant under the circumstances set forth in subsection E. For purposes of subdivision E 4, the investigative or law-enforcement officer using such a device shall be considered to be the possessor of the real-time location data.

L. Upon issuance of any subpoena, search warrant, or order for disclosure issued under this section, upon written certification by the attorney for the Commonwealth that there is a reason to believe that the victim is under the age of 18 and that notification or disclosure of the existence of the subpoena, search warrant, or order will endanger the life or physical safety of an individual, or lead to flight from prosecution, the destruction of or tampering with evidence, the intimidation of potential witnesses, or otherwise seriously jeopardize an investigation, the court may in an ex parte proceeding order a provider of electronic communication service or remote computing service not to disclose for a period of 90 days the existence of the subpoena, search warrant, or order and written application or statement of facts to another person, other than an attorney to obtain legal advice. The nondisclosure order may be renewed for additional 90-day periods for good cause shown upon subsequent application of the attorney for the Commonwealth in an ex parte proceeding. A court issuing an order for disclosure pursuant to this section, on a motion made promptly by the service provider, may quash or modify the order if the information or records requested are unusually voluminous in nature or compliance with such order would otherwise cause an undue burden on such provider.

M. For the purposes of this section:

"Electronic device" means a device that enables access to, or use of, an electronic communication service, remote computing service, or location information service, including a global positioning service or other mapping, locational, or directional information service.

"Foreign corporation" means any corporation or other entity, whose primary place of business is located outside of the boundaries of the Commonwealth, that makes a contract or engages in a terms of service agreement with a resident of the Commonwealth to be performed in whole or in part by either party in the Commonwealth, or a corporation that has been issued a certificate of authority pursuant to § 13.1-759 to transact business in the Commonwealth. The making of the contract or terms of service agreement or the issuance of a certificate of authority shall be considered to be the agreement of the foreign corporation or entity that a search warrant or subpoena, which has been properly served on it, has the same legal force and effect as if served personally within the Commonwealth.

"Properly served" means delivery of a search warrant or subpoena by hand, by United States mail, by commercial delivery service, by facsimile or by any other manner to any officer of a corporation or its general manager in the Commonwealth, to any natural person designated by it as agent for the service of process, or if such corporation has designated a corporate agent, to any person named in the latest annual report filed pursuant to § 13.1-775.

"Real-time location data" means any data or information concerning the current location of an electronic device that, in whole or in part, is generated, derived from, or obtained by the operation of the device.

History.

1988, c. 889; 2009, c. 378; 2010, cc. 319, 473, 582, 720, 721; 2011, c. 392; 2014, c. 388; 2015, cc. 43, 634; 2016, cc. 549, 576, 616.

CHAPTER 7.

ARREST.

Section

§ 19.2-71. Who may issue process of arrest.

A. Process for the arrest of a person charged with a criminal offense may be issued by the judge, or clerk of any circuit court, any general district court, any juvenile and domestic relations district court, or any magistrate as provided for in Chapter 3 (§ 19.2-26 et seq.) of this title. However, no magistrate may issue an arrest warrant for a felony offense upon the basis of a complaint by a person other than a law-enforcement officer or an animal control officer without prior authorization by the attorney for the Commonwealth or by a law-enforcement agency having jurisdiction over the alleged offense.

B. No law-enforcement officer shall seek issuance of process by any judicial officer, for the arrest of a person for the offense of capital murder as defined in § 18.2-31, without prior authorization by the attorney for the Commonwealth. Failure to comply with the provisions of this subsection shall not be (i) a basis upon which a warrant may be quashed or deemed invalid, (ii) deemed error upon which a conviction or sentence may be reversed or vacated, or (iii) a basis upon which a court may prevent or delay execution of sentence.

History.

Code 1950, § 19.1-90; 1960, c. 366; 1975, c. 495; 1999, c. 266; 2002, c. 310; 2009, cc. 291, 344; 2010, c. 240; 2011, cc. 205, 223.

§ 19.2-72. When it may issue; what to recite and require.

On complaint of a criminal offense to any officer authorized to issue criminal warrants he shall examine on oath the complainant and any other witnesses, or when such officer shall suspect that an offense punishable otherwise than by a fine has been committed he may, without formal complaint, issue a summons for witnesses and shall examine such witnesses. A written complaint shall be required if the complainant is not a law-enforcement officer; however, if no arrest warrant is issued in response to a written complaint made by such complainant, the written complaint shall be returned to the complainant. If upon such examination such officer finds that there is probable cause to believe the accused has committed an offense, such officer shall issue a warrant for his arrest, except that no magistrate may issue an arrest warrant for a felony offense upon the basis of a complaint by a person other than a law-enforcement officer or an animal control officer without prior authorization by the attorney for the Commonwealth or by a law-enforcement agency having jurisdiction over the alleged offense. The warrant shall (i) be directed to an appropriate officer or officers, (ii) name the accused or, if his name is unknown, set forth a description by which he can be identified with reasonable certainty, (iii) describe the offense charged with reasonable certainty, (iv) command that the accused be arrested and brought before a court of appropriate jurisdiction in the county, city or town in which the offense was allegedly committed, and (v) be signed by the issuing officer. The warrant shall require the officer to whom it is directed to summon such witnesses as shall be therein named to appear and give evidence on the examination. But in a city or town having a police force, the warrant shall be directed "To any policeman, sheriff or his deputy sheriff of such city (or town)," and shall be executed by the policeman, sheriff or his deputy sheriff into whose hands it shall come or be delivered. A sheriff or his deputy may execute an arrest warrant throughout the county in which he serves and in any city or town surrounded thereby and effect an arrest in any city or town surrounded thereby as a result of a criminal act committed during the execution of such warrant. A jail officer as defined in § 53.1-1 employed at a regional jail or jail farm is authorized to execute a warrant of arrest upon an accused in his jail. The venue for the prosecution of such criminal act shall be the jurisdiction in which the offense occurred.

History.

Code 1950, § 19.1-91; 1960, c. 366; 1975, c. 495; 1991, c. 420; 2000, c. 170; 2007, c. 412; 2009, cc. 291, 344; 2010, c. 240; 2011, cc. 205, 223; 2013, c. 207; 2016, c. 204.

§ 19.2-73. Issuance of summons instead of warrant in certain cases.

A. In any misdemeanor case or in any class of misdemeanor cases, or in any case involving complaints made by any state or local governmental official or employee having responsibility for the enforcement of any statute, ordinance or administrative regulation, the magistrate or other issuing authority having jurisdiction may issue a summons instead of a warrant when there is reason to believe that the person charged will appear in the courts having jurisdiction over the trial of the offense charged.

B. If any person under suspicion for driving while intoxicated has been taken to a medical facility for treatment or evaluation of his medical condition, the officer at the medical facility may issue, on the premises of the medical facility, a summons for a violation of § 18.2-266, 18.2-266.1, 18.2-272 or 46.2-341.24 and for refusal of tests in violation of subsection A of § 18.2-268.3 or subsection A of § 46.2-341.26:3, in lieu of securing a warrant and without having to detain that person, provided that the officer has probable cause to place him under arrest. The issuance of such summons shall be deemed an arrest for purposes of Article 2 (§ 18.2-266 et seq.) of Chapter 7 of Title 18.2.

C. Any person on whom such summons is served shall appear on the date set forth in same, and if such person fails to appear in such court at such time and on such date then he shall be treated in accordance with the provisions of § 19.2-128, regardless of the disposition of, and in addition to, the charge upon which he was originally arrested.

History.
Code 1950, § 19.1-146; 1972, c. 461; 1975, c. 495; 1978, c. 500; 1981, c. 382; 2005, c. 425; 2010, c. 840.

§ 19.2-73.1. Notice of issuance of warrant or summons; appearance; failure to appear.

In any misdemeanor case or in any class of misdemeanor cases and in a Class 5 or Class 6 felony case, the chief of police of the city or county or his designee, or the sheriff or deputy sheriff of the county, if the county has no police department, in which the case is pending may notify the accused of the issuance of the warrant or summons and direct the accused to appear at the time and place directed for the purpose of the execution of the summons or warrant. However, the issuing judicial officer may direct the execution of such process prior to any such notification. If the accused does not appear, then the warrant or summons shall be executed and returned as provided by § 19.2-76.

History.
1979, c. 335; 1991, c. 162; 1993, c. 350.

§ 19.2-73.2. Law-enforcement officers to issue subpoenas; penalty.

Law-enforcement officers as defined in § 9.1-101 and state police officers, in the course of their duties, in the investigation of any Class 3 or Class 4 misdemeanor or any traffic infraction, may, within seventy-two hours of the time of the offense, issue a subpoena to any witness to appear in court and testify with respect to any such criminal charge or traffic infraction brought against any person as a result of such investigation. The return of service thereof shall be made within seventy-two hours after service to the appropriate court clerk. A subpoena so issued shall have the same force and effect as if issued by the court.

Any person failing to appear in response to a subpoena issued as provided in this section shall be punished as provided by law.

History.
1995, c. 335.

§ 19.2-74. Issuance and service of summons in place of warrant in misdemeanor case; issuance of summons by special conservators of the peace.

A. 1. Whenever any person is detained by or is in the custody of an arresting officer for any violation committed in such officer's presence which offense is a violation of any county, city or town ordinance or of any provision of this Code punishable as a Class 1 or Class 2 misdemeanor or any other misdemeanor for which he may receive a jail sentence, except as otherwise provided in Title 46.2, or for offenses listed in subsection D of § 19.2-81, or an arrest on a warrant charging an offense for which a summons may be issued, and when specifically authorized by the judicial officer issuing the warrant, the arresting officer shall take the name and address of such person and issue a summons or otherwise notify him in writing to appear at a time and place to be specified in such summons or notice. Upon the giving by such person of his written promise to appear at such time and place, the officer shall forthwith release him from custody. However, if any such person shall fail or refuse to discontinue the unlawful act, the officer may proceed according to the provisions of § 19.2-82.

Anything in this section to the contrary notwithstanding, if any person is believed by the arresting officer to be likely to disregard a summons issued under the provisions of this subsection, or if any person is reasonably believed by the arresting officer to be likely to cause harm to himself or to any other person, a magistrate or other issuing authority having jurisdiction shall proceed according to the provisions of § 19.2-82.

2. Whenever any person is detained by or is in the custody of an arresting officer for a violation of any county, city, or town ordinance or of any provision of this Code, punishable as a Class 3 or Class 4 misdemeanor or any other misdemeanor for which he cannot receive a jail sentence, except as otherwise provided in Title 46.2, or to the offense of public drunkenness as defined in § 18.2-388, the arresting officer shall take the name and address of such person and issue a summons or otherwise notify him in writing to appear at a time and place to be

specified in such summons or notice. Upon the giving of such person of his written promise to appear at such time and place, the officer shall forthwith release him from custody. However, if any such person shall fail or refuse to discontinue the unlawful act, the officer may proceed according to the provisions of § 19.2-82.

3. Any person so summoned shall not be held in custody after the issuance of such summons for the purpose of complying with the requirements of Chapter 23 (§ 19.2-387 et seq.) of this title. Reports to the Central Criminal Records Exchange concerning such persons shall be made after a disposition of guilt is entered as provided for in § 19.2-390.

Any person refusing to give such written promise to appear under the provisions of this section shall be taken immediately by the arresting or other police officer before a magistrate or other issuing authority having jurisdiction, who shall proceed according to provisions of § 19.2-82.

Any person who willfully violates his written promise to appear, given in accordance with this section, shall be treated in accordance with the provisions of § 19.2-128, regardless of the disposition of, and in addition to, the charge upon which he was originally arrested.

Any person charged with committing any violation of § 18.2-407 may be arrested and immediately brought before a magistrate who shall proceed as provided in § 19.2-82.

B. Conservators of the peace appointed under Chapter 2 (§ 19.2-12 et seq.) may issue summonses pursuant to this section, if such officers are in uniform or displaying a badge of office. On application, the chief law-enforcement officer of the county or city shall supply each officer with a supply of summons forms, for which such officer shall account pursuant to regulation of such chief law-enforcement officer.

C. The summons used by a law-enforcement officer pursuant to this section shall be in form the same as the uniform summons for motor vehicle law violations as prescribed pursuant to § 46.2-388.

History.

Code 1950, § 19.1-92.1; 1973, c. 98; 1974, c. 481; 1975, c. 495; 1976, c. 753; 1978, c. 500; 1979, cc. 679, 680; 1980, c. 492; 1981, c. 382; 1982, cc. 485, 500; 1984, c. 24; 1988, c. 455; 1995, c. 471; 2010, c. 840; 2014, c. 543.

§ **19.2-74.1:** Repealed by Acts 1981, c. 382.

§ 19.2-75. Copy of process to be left with accused; exception.

Except as provided in § 46.2-936, any process issued against a person charged with a criminal offense shall be in duplicate and the officer serving such process shall leave a copy with the person charged.

History.

Code 1950, § 19.1-92; 1960, c. 366; 1975, c. 495.

§ 19.2-76. Execution and return of warrant, capias or summons; arrest outside county or city where charge is to be tried.

A law-enforcement officer may execute within his jurisdiction a warrant, capias or summons issued anywhere in the Commonwealth. A jail officer as defined in § 53.1-1 employed at a regional jail or jail farm may execute upon a person being held in his jail a warrant, capias or summons issued anywhere in the Commonwealth. A warrant or capias shall be executed by the arrest of the accused, and a summons shall be executed by delivering a copy to the accused personally.

If the accused is a corporation, partnership, unincorporated association or legal entity other than an individual, a summons may be executed by service on the entity in the same manner as provided in Title 8.01 for service of process on that entity in a civil proceeding. However, if the summons is served on the entity by delivery to a registered agent or to any other agent who is not an officer, director, managing agent or employee of the entity, such agent shall not be personally subject to penalty for failure to appear as provided in § 19.2-128, nor shall the agent be subject to punishment for contempt for failure to appear under his summons as provided in § 19.2-129.

The law-enforcement officer or jail officer executing a warrant or capias shall endorse the date of execution thereon and make return thereof to a judicial officer. The law-enforcement officer executing a summons shall endorse the date of execution thereon and make return thereof to the court to which the summons is returnable.

Whenever a person is arrested upon a warrant or capias in a county or city other than that in which the charge is to be tried, the law-enforcement officer or jail officer making the arrest shall either (i) bring the accused forthwith before a judicial officer in the locality where the arrest was made or where the charge is to be tried or (ii) commit the accused to the custody of an officer from the county or city where the charge is to be tried who shall bring the accused forthwith before a judicial officer in the county or city in which the charge is to be tried. The judicial officer before whom the accused is brought shall immediately conduct a bail hearing and either admit the accused to bail or commit him to jail for transfer forthwith to the county or city where the charge is to be tried.

History.
Code 1950, §§ 19.1-98, 19.1-99; 1960, c. 366; 1975, c. 495; 1979, c. 661; 1993, c. 431; 1994, c. 933; 1997, c. 10; 1998, c. 615; 2013, c. 207.

§ 19.2-76.1. Submission of quarterly reports concerning unexecuted felony and misdemeanor warrants and other criminal process; destruction; dismissal.

It shall be the duty of the chief law-enforcement officer of the police department or sheriff's office, whichever is responsible for such service, in each county, town or city of the Commonwealth to submit quarterly reports to the attorney for the Commonwealth for the county, town or city concerning unexecuted felony and misdemeanor arrest warrants, summonses, capiases or other unexecuted criminal processes as hereinafter provided. The reports shall list those existing felony arrest warrants in his possession that have not been executed within seven years of the date of issuance, those misdemeanor arrest warrants, summonses and capiases and other criminal processes in his possession that have not been executed within three years from the date of issuance, and those unexecuted misdemeanor arrest warrants, summonses and capiases in his possession that were issued for a now deceased person, based on mistaken identity or as a result of any other technical or legal error. The reports shall be submitted in writing no later than the tenth day of April, July, October, and January of each year, together with the unexecuted felony and misdemeanor warrants, or other unexecuted criminal processes listed therein. Upon receipt of the report and the warrants listed therein, the attorney for the Commonwealth shall petition the circuit court of the county or city for the destruction of such unexecuted felony and misdemeanor warrants, summonses, capiases or other unexecuted criminal processes. The attorney for the Commonwealth may petition that certain of the unexecuted warrants, summonses, capiases and other unexecuted criminal processes not be destroyed based upon justifiable continuing, active investigation of the cases. The circuit court shall order the destruction of each such unexecuted felony warrant and each unexecuted misdemeanor warrant, summons, capias and other criminal process except (i) any warrant which charges capital murder and (ii) any unexecuted criminal process whose preservation is deemed justifiable by the court. No arrest shall be made under the authority of any warrant or other process which has been ordered destroyed pursuant to this section. Nothing in this section shall be construed to relate to or affect the time within which a prosecution for a felony or a misdemeanor shall be commenced.

Notwithstanding the foregoing, an attorney for the Commonwealth may at any time move for the dismissal and destruction of any unexecuted warrant or summons issued by a magistrate upon presentation of such warrant or summons to the court in which the warrant or summons would otherwise be returnable. The court shall not order the dismissal and destruction of any warrant which charges capital murder and shall not order the dismissal and destruction of an unexecuted criminal process whose preservation is deemed justifiable by the court. Dismissal of such a warrant or summons shall be without prejudice.

As used herein, the term "chief law-enforcement officer" refers to the chiefs of police of cities, counties and towns and sheriffs of cities and counties, unless a political subdivision has otherwise designated its chief law-enforcement officer by appropriate resolution or ordinance, in which case the local designation shall be controlling.

History.
1976, c. 252; 1979, c. 34; 1982, c. 608; 1985, c. 199; 1990, c. 626; 1991, c. 542; 1993, c. 550; 2003, c. 147; 2010, c. 652; 2011, cc. 336, 347.

§ 19.2-76.2. Mailing of summons in certain cases.

Notwithstanding the provisions of § 19.2-76, whenever a summons for a violation of a county, city or town parking ordinance is served in any county, city or town it may be executed by mailing by first-class mail a copy thereof to the address of the owner of the vehicle as shown on the records of the Department of Motor Vehicles. In addition, whenever a summons for a violation of a county, city or town trash ordinance punishable as a misdemeanor under § 15.2-901 is served in any county, city or town, it may be executed by mailing a copy by first-class mail to the person who occupies the subject premises. If the person fail to appear on the date of return set out in the summons mailed pursuant to this section, the summons shall be executed in the manner set out in § 19.2-76.3 of this Code.

No proceedings for contempt or arrest of a person summoned by mailing shall be instituted for his failure to appear on the return date of the summons.

History.
1977, c. 233; 1978, c. 781; 1983, c. 254; 1984, c. 119.

§ 19.2-76.3. Failure to appear on return date for summons issued under § 19.2-76.2.

A. If any person fails to appear on the date of the return contained in the summons issued in accordance with § 19.2-76.2, then a summons shall be delivered to the sheriff of the county, city, or town or to another authorized process server for service on that person as set out in § 8.01-296.

B. If such person then fails to appear on the date of return as contained in the summons so issued, a summons shall be executed in the manner set out in § 19.2-76.

C. No proceedings for contempt or arrest of any person summoned under the provisions of this section shall be instituted unless such person has been personally served with a summons and has failed to appear on the return date contained therein.

History.
1983, c. 254; 1994, c. 642; 2016, cc. 242, 354.

§ 19.2-77. Escape, flight and pursuit; arrest anywhere in Commonwealth.

Whenever a person in the custody of an officer shall escape or whenever a person shall flee from an officer attempting to arrest him, such officer, with or without a warrant, may pursue such person anywhere in the Commonwealth and, when actually in close pursuit, may arrest him wherever he is found. If the arrest is made in a county or city adjoining that from which the accused fled, or in any area of the Commonwealth within one mile of the boundary of the county or city from which he fled, the officer may forthwith return the accused before the proper official of the county or city from which he fled. If the arrest is made beyond the foregoing limits, the officer shall proceed according to the provisions of § 19.2-76, and if such arrest is made without a warrant, the officer shall procure a warrant from the magistrate serving the county or city wherein the arrest was made, charging the accused with the offense committed in the county or city from which he fled.

History.
Code 1950, § 19.1-94; 1960, c. 366; 1975, c. 495; 1992, c. 881; 2008, cc. 551, 691.

§ 19.2-78. Uniform of officer making arrest.

All officers whose duties are to make arrests acting under the authority of any law of this Commonwealth or any subdivision thereof, who shall make any arrest, search or seizure on any public road or highway of this Commonwealth shall be dressed at the time of making any such arrest, search or seizure in such uniform as he may customarily wear in the performance of his duties which will clearly show him to casual observation to be an officer.

Nothing in this section shall render unlawful any arrest, search or seizure by an officer who is not in such customary uniform.

History.
Code 1950, §§ 19.1-95, 19.1-96; 1960, c. 366; 1975, c. 495.

§ 19.2-79. Arrest by officers of other states of United States.

Any member of a duly organized state, county or municipal peace unit of another state of the United States who enters this Commonwealth in close pursuit, and continues within this Commonwealth in such close pursuit, of a person in order to arrest him on the ground that he has committed a felony in such other state shall have the same authority to arrest and hold in custody such person as members of a duly organized state, county or municipal peace unit of this Commonwealth have to arrest and hold in custody a person on the ground that he has committed a felony in this Commonwealth, if the state from which such person has fled extends similar privileges to any member of a duly organized state, county or municipal peace unit of this Commonwealth.

If an arrest is made in this Commonwealth by an officer of another state in accordance with the provisions of the first paragraph of this section, he shall without unnecessary delay take the person arrested before a judge of a general district court, or of the circuit court, of the county or city in which the arrest was made, who shall conduct a hearing for the purpose of determining the lawfulness of the arrest. If the judge determines that the arrest was lawful he shall commit the person arrested to await for a reasonable time the issuance of an extradition warrant by the Governor. If the judge determines that the arrest was unlawful he shall discharge the person arrested.

The first paragraph of this section shall not be construed so as to make unlawful any arrest in this Commonwealth which would otherwise be lawful.

For the purpose of this section the word "State" shall include the District of Columbia.

History.
Code 1950, § 19.1-97; 1960, c. 366; 1975, c. 495.

§ 19.2-80. Duty of arresting officer; bail.

In any case in which an officer does not issue a summons pursuant to § 19.2-74 or § 46.2-936, a law-enforcement officer making an arrest under a warrant or capias shall bring the arrested person without unnecessary delay before a judicial officer. The judicial officer shall immediately conduct a bail hearing and either admit the accused to bail or commit him to jail. However, if (i) the accused is charged with a misdemeanor and is brought before a judge of the court having jurisdiction to try the case and (ii) both the accused and the Commonwealth consent, the judge may proceed to trial instead of conducting a bail hearing.

History.
Code 1950, § 19.1-98; 1960, c. 366; 1975, c. 495; 1979, c. 679; 1986, c. 327; 1997, c. 10.

§ 19.2-80.1. When arrested person operating motor vehicle; how vehicle removed from scene of arrest.

In any case in which a police officer arrests the operator of a motor vehicle and there is no legal cause for the retention of the motor vehicle by the officer, the officer shall allow the person arrested to designate another person who is present at the scene of the arrest and a licensed driver to drive the motor vehicle from the scene to a place designated by the person arrested. If such a designation is not made, the officer may cause the vehicle to be taken to the nearest appropriate place for safekeeping.

History.
1981, c. 306.

§ 19.2-80.2. Duty of arresting officer; providing magistrate or court with criminal history information.

In any case in which an officer proceeds under §§ 19.2-76, 19.2-80 and 19.2-82, such officer shall, to the extent possible, obtain and provide the magistrate or court with the arrested person's criminal history information prior to any proceeding under Article 1 (§ 19.2-119 et seq.) of Chapter 9 of this title. A pretrial services agency established pursuant to § 19.2-152.2 may, in lieu of the arresting officer, provide the criminal history to the magistrate or court.

History.
1999, cc. 829, 846; 2007, c. 133.

§ 19.2-81. (Effective until July 1, 2018) Arrest without warrant authorized in certain cases.

A. The following officers shall have the powers of arrest as provided in this section:

1. Members of the State Police force of the Commonwealth;

2. Sheriffs of the various counties and cities, and their deputies;

3. Members of any county police force or any duly constituted police force of any city or town of the Commonwealth;

4. The Commissioner, members and employees of the Marine Resources Commission granted the power of arrest pursuant to § 28.2-900;

5. Regular conservation police officers appointed pursuant to § 29.1-200;

6. United States Coast Guard and United States Coast Guard Reserve commissioned, warrant, and petty officers authorized under § 29.1-205 to make arrests;

7. Conservation officers appointed pursuant to § 10.1-115;

8. Full-time sworn members of the enforcement division of the Department of Motor Vehicles appointed pursuant to § 46.2-217;

9. Special agents of the Virginia Alcoholic Beverage Control Authority; and

10. **(Effective until October 1, 2016)** Campus police officers appointed under Chapter 17 (§ 23-232 et seq.) of Title 23.

10. **(Effective October 1, 2016)** Campus police officers appointed under Article 3 (§ 23.1-809 et seq.) of Chapter 8 of Title 23.1.

B. Such officers may arrest without a warrant any person who commits any crime in the presence of the officer and any person whom he has reasonable grounds or probable cause to suspect of having committed a felony not in his presence.

Such officers may arrest without a warrant any person whom the officer has probable cause to suspect of operating any watercraft or motorboat while (i) intoxicated in violation of subsection B of § 29.1-738 or a substantially similar ordinance of any county, city, or town in the Commonwealth or (ii) in violation of an order issued pursuant to § 29.1-738.4 and may thereafter transfer custody of the person arrested to another officer, who may obtain a warrant based upon statements made to him by the arresting officer.

C. Any such officer may, at the scene of any accident involving a motor vehicle, watercraft as defined in § 29.1-733.2 or motorboat, or at any hospital or medical facility to which any person involved in such accident has been transported, or in the apprehension of any person charged with the theft of any motor vehicle, on any of the highways or waters of the Commonwealth, upon reasonable grounds to believe, based upon personal investigation, including information obtained from eyewitnesses, that a crime has been committed by any person then and there present, apprehend such person without a warrant of arrest. For purposes of this section, "the scene of any accident " shall include a reasonable location where a vehicle or person involved in an accident has been moved at the direction of a law-enforcement officer to facilitate the clearing of the highway or to ensure the safety of the motoring public.

D. Such officers may, within three hours of the alleged offense, arrest without a warrant at any location any person whom the officer has probable cause to suspect of driving or operating a motor vehicle, watercraft or motorboat while intoxicated in violation of § 18.2-266, 18.2-266.1, 46.2-341.24, or subsection B of § 29.1-738; or a substantially similar ordinance of any county, city, or town in the Commonwealth, whether or not the offense was committed in such officer's presence. Such officers may, within three hours of the alleged offense, arrest without a warrant at any location any person whom the officer has probable cause to suspect of operating a watercraft or motorboat in violation of an order issued pursuant to § 29.1-738.4, whether or not the offense was committed in such officer's presence.

E. Such officers may arrest, without a warrant or a capias, persons duly charged with a crime in another jurisdiction upon receipt of a photocopy of a warrant or a capias, telegram, computer printout, facsimile printout, a radio, telephone or teletype message, in which photocopy of a warrant, telegram, computer printout, facsimile printout, radio, telephone or teletype message shall be given the name or a reasonably accurate description of such person wanted and the crime alleged.

F. Such officers may arrest, without a warrant or a capias, for an alleged misdemeanor not committed in his presence when the officer receives a radio message from his department or other law-enforcement agency within the Commonwealth that a warrant or capias for such offense is on file.

G. Such officers may also arrest without a warrant for an alleged misdemeanor not committed in their presence involving (i) shoplifting in violation of § 18.2-96 or 18.2-103 or a similar local ordinance, (ii) carrying a weapon on school property in violation of § 18.2-308.1, (iii) assault and battery, (iv) brandishing a firearm in violation of § 18.2-282, or (v) destruction of property in violation of § 18.2-137, when such property is located on premises used for business or commercial purposes, or a similar local ordinance, when any such arrest is based on probable cause upon reasonable complaint of the person who observed the alleged offense. The arresting officer may issue a summons to any person arrested under this section for a misdemeanor violation involving shoplifting.

History.

Code 1950, § 19.1-100; 1960, c. 366; 1974, c. 241; 1975, c. 495; 1976, cc. 515, 570; 1977, c. 97; 1979, c. 268; 1982, c. 272; 1983, c. 206; 1984, c. 534; 1985, c. 507; 1988, cc. 353, 744, 752, 853; 1989, c. 726; 1990, cc. 635, 744, 784; 1995, c. 465; 1996, cc. 866, 929, 1015; 1998, c. 684; 2004, c. 949; 2005, cc. 88, 435; 2008, cc. 460, 737; 2010, c. 840; 2011, cc. 510, 643; 2012, c. 776; 2013, c. 787; 2014, c. 543; 2015, cc. 38, 730.

§ 19.2-81. (Effective July 1, 2018) Arrest without warrant authorized in certain cases.

A. The following officers shall have the powers of arrest as provided in this section:

1. Members of the State Police force of the Commonwealth;
2. Sheriffs of the various counties and cities, and their deputies;
3. Members of any county police force or any duly constituted police force of any city or town of the Commonwealth;
4. The Commissioner, members and employees of the Marine Resources Commission granted the power of arrest pursuant to § 28.2-900;
5. Regular conservation police officers appointed pursuant to § 29.1-200;
6. United States Coast Guard and United States Coast Guard Reserve commissioned, warrant, and petty officers authorized under § 29.1-205 to make arrests;
7. Conservation officers appointed pursuant to § 10.1-115;
8. Full-time sworn members of the enforcement division of the Department of Motor Vehicles appointed pursuant to § 46.2-217;
9. Special agents of the Virginia Alcoholic Beverage Control Authority; and
10. Campus police officers appointed under Article 3 (§ 23.1-809 et seq.) of Chapter 8 of Title 23.1.

B. Such officers may arrest without a warrant any person who commits any crime in the presence of the officer and any person whom he has reasonable grounds or probable cause to suspect of having committed a felony not in his presence.

Such officers may arrest without a warrant any person whom the officer has probable cause to suspect of operating any watercraft or motorboat while (i) intoxicated in violation of subsection B of § 29.1-738 or a substantially similar ordinance of any county, city, or town in the Commonwealth or (ii) in violation of an order issued pursuant to § 29.1-738.4 and may thereafter transfer custody of the person arrested to another officer, who may obtain a warrant based upon statements made to him by the arresting officer.

C. Any such officer may, at the scene of any accident involving a motor vehicle, watercraft as defined in § 29.1-733.2 or motorboat, or at any hospital or medical facility to which any person involved in such accident has been transported, or in the apprehension of any person charged with the theft of any motor vehicle, on any of the highways or waters of the Commonwealth, upon reasonable grounds to believe, based upon personal investigation, including information obtained from eyewitnesses, that a crime has been committed by any person then and there present, apprehend such person without a warrant of arrest. For purposes of this section, "the scene of any accident" shall include a reasonable location where a vehicle or person involved in an accident has been moved at the direction of a law-enforcement officer to facilitate the clearing of the highway or to ensure the safety of the motoring public.

D. Such officers may, within three hours of the alleged offense, arrest without a warrant at any location any person whom the officer has probable cause to suspect of driving or operating a motor vehicle, watercraft or motorboat while intoxicated in violation of § 18.2-266, 18.2-266.1, 46.2-341.24, or subsection B of § 29.1-738; or a substantially similar ordinance of any county, city, or town in the Commonwealth, whether or not the offense was committed in such officer's presence. Such officers may, within three hours of the alleged offense, arrest without a warrant at any location any person whom the officer has probable cause to suspect of operating a watercraft or motorboat in violation of an order issued pursuant to § 29.1-738.4, whether or not the offense was committed in such officer's presence.

E. Such officers may arrest, without a warrant or a capias, persons duly charged with a crime in another jurisdiction upon receipt of a photocopy of a warrant or a capias, telegram, computer printout, facsimile printout, a radio, telephone or teletype message, in which photocopy of a warrant, telegram, computer printout, facsimile printout, radio, telephone or teletype message shall be given the name or a reasonably accurate description of such person wanted and the crime alleged.

F. Such officers may arrest, without a warrant or a capias, for an alleged misdemeanor not committed in his presence when the officer receives a radio message from his department or other law-enforcement agency within the Commonwealth that a warrant or capias for such offense is on file.

G. Such officers may also arrest without a warrant for an alleged misdemeanor not committed in their presence involving (i) shoplifting in violation of § 18.2-96 or 18.2-103 or a similar local ordinance, (ii) carrying a weapon on school property in violation of § 18.2-308.1, (iii) assault and battery, (iv) brandishing a firearm in violation of § 18.2-282, or (v) destruction of property in violation of § 18.2-137, when such property is located on premises used for business or commercial purposes, or a similar local ordinance, when any such arrest is based on probable cause upon reasonable complaint of the person who observed the alleged offense. The arresting officer may issue a summons to any person arrested under this section for a misdemeanor violation involving shoplifting.

History.

Code 1950, § 19.1-100; 1960, c. 366; 1974, c. 241; 1975, c. 495; 1976, cc. 515, 570; 1977, c. 97; 1979, c. 268; 1982, c. 272; 1983, c. 206; 1984, c. 534; 1985, c. 507; 1988, cc. 353, 744, 752, 853; 1989, c. 726; 1990, cc. 635, 744, 784; 1995, c. 465; 1996, cc. 866, 929, 1015; 1998, c. 684; 2004, c. 949; 2005, cc. 88, 435; 2008, cc. 460, 737; 2010, c. 840; 2011, cc. 510, 643; 2012, c. 776; 2013, c. 787; 2014, c. 543; 2015, cc. 38, 730.

§ 19.2-81.1. Arrest without warrant by correctional officers in certain cases.

Any correctional officer, as defined in § 53.1-1, may arrest, in the same manner as provided in § 19.2-81, persons for crimes involving:

(a) The escape of an inmate from a correctional institution, as defined in § 53.1-1;

(b) Assisting an inmate to escape from a correctional institution, as defined in § 53.1-1;

(c) The delivery of contraband to an inmate in violation of § 18.2-474 or § 18.2-474.1; and

(d) Any other criminal offense which may contribute to the disruption of the safety, welfare, or security of the population of a correctional institution.

History.

1976, c. 752.

§ 19.2-81.2. Power of correctional officers and designated noncustodial employees to detain.

A. A correctional officer, as defined in § 53.1-1, who has completed the minimum training standards established by the Department of Criminal Justice Services, or other noncustodial employee of the Department of Corrections who has been designated to carry a weapon by the Director of the Department of Corrections pursuant to § 53.1-29 of the Code and who has completed the basic course in detention training as approved by the Department of Criminal Justice Services, may, while on duty in or on the grounds of a correctional institution, or with custody of prisoners without the confines of a correctional institution, detain any person whom he has reasonable suspicion to believe has committed a violation of §§ 18.2-473 through 18.2-475, or of aiding or abetting a prisoner in violating the provisions of § 53.1-203. Such detention shall be for the purpose of summoning a law-enforcement officer in order that the law-enforcement officer can arrest the person who is alleged to have violated any of the above sections.

B. Any employee of the Department of Corrections having the authority to detain any person pursuant to subsection A hereof shall not be held civilly liable for unlawful detention, slander, malicious prosecution, false imprisonment, false arrest, or assault and battery of the person so detained, whether such detention takes place within or without the grounds of a correctional institution, provided that, in causing the detention of such person, the employee had at the time of the detention reasonable suspicion to believe that the person committed a violation for which the detention was undertaken.

C. It is the purpose and intent of this section to ensure that the safety, stability, welfare and security of correctional institutions be preserved insofar as possible.

History.

1976, c. 740; 1979, c. 642; 1984, cc. 720, 779.

§ 19.2-81.3. Arrest without a warrant authorized in cases of assault and battery against a family or household member and stalking and for violations of protective orders; procedure, etc.

A. Any law-enforcement officer with the powers of arrest may arrest without a warrant for an alleged violation of § 18.2-57.2, 18.2-60.4, or 16.1-253.2 regardless of whether such violation was committed in his presence, if such arrest is based on probable cause or upon personal observations or the reasonable complaint of a person who observed the alleged offense or upon personal investigation.

B. A law-enforcement officer having probable cause to believe that a violation of § 18.2-57.2 or 16.1-253.2 has occurred shall arrest and take into custody the person he has probable cause to believe, based on the totality of the circumstances, was the predominant physical aggressor unless there are special circumstances which would dictate a course of action other than an arrest. The standards for determining who is the predominant physical aggressor shall be based on the following considerations: (i) who was the first aggressor, (ii) the protection of the health and safety of family and household members, (iii) prior complaints of family abuse by the allegedly abusing person involving the family or household members, (iv) the relative severity of the injuries inflicted on persons involved in the incident, (v) whether any injuries were inflicted in self-defense, (vi) witness statements, and (vii) other observations.

C. A law-enforcement officer having probable cause to believe that a violation of § 18.2-60.4 has occurred that involves physical aggression shall arrest and take into custody the person he has probable cause to believe, based on the totality of the circumstances, was the predominant physical aggressor unless there are special circumstances which would dictate a course of action other than an arrest. The standards for determining who is the predominant physical aggressor shall be based on the following considerations: (i) who was the first aggressor, (ii) the protection of the health and safety of the person to whom the protective order was issued and the person's family and household members, (iii) prior acts of violence, force, or threat, as defined in § 19.2-152.7:1, by the person against whom the protective order was issued against the person protected by the order or the protected person's family or household members, (iv) the relative severity of the injuries inflicted on persons involved in the incident, (v) whether any injuries were inflicted in self-defense, (vi) witness statements, and (vii) other observations.

D. Regardless of whether an arrest is made, the officer shall file a written report with his department, which shall state whether any arrests were made, and if so, the number of arrests, specifically including any incident in which he has probable cause to believe family abuse has occurred, and, where required, including a complete statement in writing that there are special circumstances that would dictate a course of action other than an arrest. The officer shall provide the allegedly abused person or the person protected by an order issued pursuant to § 19.2-152.8, 19.2-152.9, or 19.2-152.10, both orally and in writing, information regarding the legal and community resources available to the allegedly abused person or person protected by the order. Upon request of the allegedly abused person or person protected by the order, the department shall make a summary of the report available to the allegedly abused person or person protected by the order.

E. In every case in which a law-enforcement officer makes an arrest under this section for a violation of § 18.2-57.2, he shall petition for an emergency protective order as authorized in § 16.1-253.4 when the person arrested and taken into custody is brought before the magistrate, except if the person arrested is a minor, a petition for an emergency protective order shall not be required. Regardless of whether an arrest is made, if the officer has probable cause to believe that a danger of acts of family abuse exists, the law-enforcement officer shall seek an emergency protective order under § 16.1-253.4, except if the suspected abuser is a minor, a petition for an emergency protective order shall not be required.

F. A law-enforcement officer investigating any complaint of family abuse, including but not limited to assault and battery against a family or household member shall, upon request, transport, or arrange for the transportation of an abused person to a hospital or safe shelter, or to appear before a magistrate. Any local law-enforcement agency may adopt a policy requiring an officer to transport or arrange for transportation of an abused person as provided in this subsection.

G. The definition of "family or household member" in § 16.1-228 applies to this section.

H. **(Effective until October 1, 2016)** As used in this section, "law-enforcement officer" means (i) any full-time or part-time employee of a police department or sheriff's office which is part of or administered by the Commonwealth or any political subdivision thereof, and any campus police officer appointed under Chapter 17 (§ 23-232 et seq.) of Title 23, and who is responsible for the prevention and detection of crime and the enforcement of the penal, traffic or highway laws of this Commonwealth; (ii) any member of an auxiliary police force established pursuant to § 15.2-1731; and (iii) any special conservator of the peace who meets the certification requirements for a law-enforcement officer as set forth in § 15.2-1706. Part-time employees are compensated officers who are not full-time employees as defined by the employing police department or sheriff's office.

H. **(Effective October 1, 2016)** As used in this section, "law-enforcement officer" means (i) any full-time or part-time employee of a police department or sheriff's office which is part of or administered by the Commonwealth or any political subdivision thereof, and any campus police officer appointed under Article 3 (§ 23.1-809 et seq.) of Chapter 8 of Title 23.1, and who is responsible for the prevention and detection of crime and the enforcement of the penal, traffic or highway laws of this Commonwealth; (ii) any member of an auxiliary police force established pursuant to § 15.2-1731; and (iii) any special conservator of the peace who meets the certification requirements for a law-enforcement officer as set forth in § 15.2-1706. Part-time employees are compensated officers who are not full-time employees as defined by the employing police department or sheriff's office.

History.

1991, c. 715; 1992, c. 886; 1995, cc. 413, 433; 1996, c. 866; 1997, c. 603; 1998, c. 569; 1999, cc. 697, 721, 807; 2002, cc. 810, 818; 2004, c. 1016; 2008, cc. 551, 691; 2011, cc. 445, 480; 2012, cc. 776, 827; 2014, cc. 779, 797.

§ **19.2-81.4:** Repealed by Acts 2008, cc. 600 and 771, cl. 2.

Cross references.

For current provisions as to arrest policies and procedures in domestic violence and family abuse cases, see § 9.1-1300.

§ 19.2-81.5. Cooperation with a law-enforcement officer.

Upon receipt of a request and documentation of an indictment or issuance of a warrant from a law-enforcement agency, any public agency within the Commonwealth may disclose to the requesting law-enforcement agency from agency records, to the extent permitted by federal law, the address of an individual who has been indicted or for whom a warrant for arrest for a crime punishable by incarceration has been issued.

History.
1998, c. 436.

§ 19.2-81.6. Authority of law-enforcement officers to arrest illegal aliens.

All law-enforcement officers enumerated in § 19.2-81 shall have the authority to enforce immigration laws of the United States, pursuant to the provisions of this section. Any law-enforcement officer enumerated in § 19.2-81 may, in the course of acting upon reasonable suspicion that an individual has committed or is committing a crime, arrest the individual without a warrant upon receiving confirmation from the Bureau of Immigration and Customs Enforcement of the United States Department of Homeland Security that the individual (i) is an alien illegally present in the United States, and (ii) has previously been convicted of a felony in the United States and deported or left the United States after such conviction. Upon receiving such confirmation, the officer shall take the individual forthwith before a magistrate or other issuing authority and proceed pursuant to § 19.2-82.

History.
2004, cc. 360, 412.

§ 19.2-82. Procedure upon arrest without warrant.

A. A person arrested without a warrant shall be brought forthwith before a magistrate or other issuing authority having jurisdiction who shall proceed to examine the officer making the arrest under oath. If the magistrate or other issuing authority having jurisdiction has lawful probable cause upon which to believe that a criminal offense has been committed, and that the person arrested has committed such offense, he shall issue either a warrant under the provisions of § 19.2-72 or a summons under the provisions of § 19.2-73.

As used in this section the term "brought before a magistrate or other issuing authority having jurisdiction" shall include a personal appearance before such authority or any two-way electronic video and audio communication meeting the requirements of § 19.2-3.1, in order that the accused and the arresting officer may simultaneously see and speak to such magistrate or authority. If electronic means are used, any documents filed may be transmitted in accordance with § 19.2-3.1.

If a warrant is issued the case shall thereafter be disposed of under the provisions of §§ 19.2-183 through 19.2-190, if the issuing officer is a judge; under the provisions of §§ 19.2-119 through 19.2-134, if the issuing officer is a magistrate or other issuing officer having jurisdiction.

If such warrant or summons is not issued, the person so arrested shall be released.

B. A warrant may be issued pursuant to this section, where the person has been arrested in accordance with § 19.2-81.6, and the magistrate or other issuing authority examines the officer making the arrest under oath, and finds lawful probable cause to believe the arrested individual meets the conditions of clauses (i) and (ii) of § 19.2-81.6. If such warrant is issued, it shall recite § 19.2-81.6 and the applicable violation of federal criminal law previously confirmed with Immigration and Customs Enforcement. Upon the person being taken into federal custody, such state warrant shall be dismissed. Any warrant issued under this subsection shall expire within 72 hours, or when the person is taken into federal custody, whichever occurs first. Recurrent applications for a warrant under this subsection shall not be permitted within a six-month period except where confirmation has been received from Immigration and Customs Enforcement that the arrested person will be taken into federal custody.

History.
Code 1950, § 19.1-100.1; 1968, c. 639; 1975, c. 495; 1981, c. 382; 1983, c. 564; 1984, c. 766; 1991, c. 41; 2002, c. 310; 2004, cc. 360, 412; 2009, c. 669.

§ 19.2-82.1. Giving false identity to law-enforcement officer; penalty.

Any person who falsely identifies himself to a law-enforcement officer with the intent to deceive the law-enforcement officer as to his real identity after having been lawfully detained and after being requested to identify himself by a law-enforcement officer, is guilty of a Class 1 misdemeanor.

History.
2006, c. 387.

§ 19.2-83: Repealed by Acts 1994, c. 273.

§ 19.2-83.1. Report of arrest of school employees and adult students for certain offenses.

A. Every state official or agency and every sheriff, police officer, or other local law-enforcement officer or conservator of the peace having the power to arrest for a felony, upon arresting a person who is known or discovered by the arresting official to be a full-time, part-time, permanent, or temporary teacher or other employee in any public school division in this Commonwealth for a felony or a Class 1 misdemeanor or an equivalent offense in another state shall file a report of such arrest with the division superintendent of the employing division as soon as practicable. The contents of the report required pursuant to this section shall be utilized by the local school division solely to implement the provisions of subsection B of § 22.1-296.2 and § 22.1-315.

B. Every state official or agency and every sheriff, police officer, or other local law-enforcement officer or conservator of the peace having the power to arrest for a felony, shall file a report, as soon as practicable, with the division superintendent of the school division in which the student is enrolled upon arresting a person who is known or discovered by the arresting official to be a student age 18 or older in any public school division in this Commonwealth for:

1. A firearm offense pursuant to Article 4 (§ 18.2-279 et seq.), 5 (§ 18.2-288 et seq.), 6 (§ 18.2-299 et seq.), 6.1 (§ 18.2-307.1 et seq.), or 7 (§ 18.2-308.1 et seq.) of Chapter 7 of Title 18.2;

2. Homicide, pursuant to Article 1 (§ 18.2-30 et seq.) of Chapter 4 of Title 18.2;

3. Felonious assault and bodily wounding, pursuant to Article 4 (§ 18.2-51 et seq.) of Chapter 4 of Title 18.2;

4. Criminal sexual assault, pursuant to Article 7 (§ 18.2-61 et seq.) of Chapter 4 of Title 18.2;

5. Manufacture, sale, gift, distribution or possession of Schedule I or II controlled substances, pursuant to Article 1 (§ 18.2-247 et seq.) of Chapter 7 of Title 18.2;

6. Manufacture, sale or distribution of marijuana pursuant to Article 1 (§ 18.2-247 et seq.) of Chapter 7 of Title 18.2;

7. Arson and related crimes, pursuant to Article 1 (§ 18.2-77 et seq.) of Chapter 5 of Title 18.2;

8. Burglary and related offenses, pursuant to §§ 18.2-89 through 18.2-93;

9. Robbery pursuant to § 18.2-58;

10. Prohibited criminal street gang activity pursuant to § 18.2-46.2; or

11. Recruitment of juveniles for criminal street gang pursuant to § 18.2-46.3.

History.

1991, c. 2; 1996, cc. 958, 960; 1997, c. 721; 2001, c. 591; 2004, c. 517; 2011, cc. 384, 410; 2013, c. 746; 2014, cc. 674, 719.

§ 19.2-83.2. Jail officer to ascertain citizenship of inmate.

Whenever any person is taken into custody at any jail, the sheriff or other officer in charge of such facility shall inquire as to whether the person (i) was born in a country other than the United States, and (ii) is a citizen of a country other than the United States. The sheriff or other officer in charge of such facility shall make an immigration alien query to the Law Enforcement Support Center of the United States Immigration and Customs Enforcement for any person who (i) was born in a country other than the United States, and (ii) is a citizen of a country other than the United States, or for whom the answer to (i) or (ii) is unknown. The sheriff or other officer in charge shall communicate the results of any immigration alien query to the Local Inmate Data System of the State Compensation Board. The State Compensation Board shall communicate, on a monthly basis, the results of any immigration alien query that results in a confirmation that the person is illegally present in the United States to the Central Criminal Records Exchange of the Department of State Police in a format approved by the Exchange. The information received by the Central Criminal Records Exchange concerning the person's immigration status shall be recorded in the person's criminal history record.

History.

2008, cc. 180, 415.

CHAPTER 8. EXTRADITION OF CRIMINALS.

Article 1.

Fugitives From Foreign Nations.

Section

Article 2.

Uniform Criminal Extradition Act.

ARTICLE 1.

FUGITIVES FROM FOREIGN NATIONS.

§ 19.2-84. Governor to surrender on requisition of President.

The Governor shall whenever required by the executive authority of the United States, pursuant to the Constitution and laws thereof, deliver over to justice any person found within the Commonwealth, who is charged with having committed any crime without the jurisdiction of the United States.

History.
Code 1950, § 19.1-47; 1960, c. 366; 1975, c. 495.

ARTICLE 2.

UNIFORM CRIMINAL EXTRADITION ACT.

§ 19.2-85. Definitions.

When appearing in this chapter:

(1) The term *"Governor"* includes any person performing the functions of Governor by authority of the law of this Commonwealth;

(2) The term *"executive authority"* includes the Governor, and any person performing the functions of Governor in a state other than this Commonwealth;

(3) The term *"State,"* referring to a state other than this Commonwealth, includes any other state or territory, organized or unorganized, of the United States of America, and the District of Columbia; and

(4) The term *"judge"* means a judge of a court of record having criminal jurisdiction.

History.
Code 1950, § 19.1-49; 1960, c. 366; 1975, c. 495.

§ 19.2-86. Fugitives from justice; duty of Governor.

Subject to the provisions of this chapter, the provisions of the Constitution of the United States controlling, and any and all acts of Congress enacted in pursuance thereof, the Governor shall have arrested and delivered up to the executive authority of any other of the United States any person charged in that state with treason, felony, or other crime, who has fled from justice and is found in this Commonwealth.

History.
Code 1950, § 19.1-50; 1960, c. 366; 1975, c. 495.

§ 19.2-87. Form of demand.

No demand for the extradition of a person charged with, or convicted of, crime in another state shall be recognized by the Governor unless in writing alleging, except in cases arising under § 19.2-91, that the accused was present in the demanding state at the time of the commission of the alleged crime and that thereafter he fled from such state, and accompanied: (1) by a copy of an indictment found, (2) by a copy or an information supported by an affidavit filed in the state having jurisdiction of the crime, (3) by a copy of an affidavit made before a magistrate in such state together with a copy of any warrant which was issued thereupon, or (4) by a copy of a judgment of conviction or of a sentence imposed in execution thereof together with a statement by the executive authority of the demanding state that the person claimed has escaped from confinement or has broken the terms of his bail, probation or parole. The indictment, information or affidavit made before the magistrate must substantially charge the person demanded with having committed a crime under the law of that state; and the copy of the indictment, information, affidavit, judgment of conviction or sentence must be authenticated by the executive authority making the demand.

History.
Code 1950, § 19.1-51; 1960, c. 366; 1975, c. 495.

§ 19.2-88. Governor may investigate case.

When a demand shall be made upon the Governor by the executive authority of another state for the surrender of a person so charged with, or convicted of, crime, the Governor may call upon the Attorney General or any other officer of this Commonwealth to investigate or assist in investigating the demand and to report to him the situation and circumstances of the person so demanded and whether he ought to be surrendered.

History.
Code 1950, § 19.1-52; 1960, c. 366; 1975, c. 495.

§ 19.2-89. Extradition of persons imprisoned or awaiting trial in another state.

When it is desired to have returned to this Commonwealth a person charged in this Commonwealth with a crime and such person is imprisoned or is held under criminal proceedings then pending

Criminal Procedure

against him in another state, the Governor may agree with the executive authority of such other state for the extradition of such person before the conclusion of such proceedings or his term of sentence in such other state, upon condition that such person be returned to such other state at the expense of this Commonwealth as soon as the prosecution in this Commonwealth is terminated.

History.
Code 1950, § 19.1-53; 1960, c. 366; 1975, c. 495.

§ 19.2-90. Extradition of persons who have left demanding state involuntarily.

The Governor may also surrender on demand of the executive authority of any other state any person in this Commonwealth who is charged in the manner provided in §§ 19.2-109 to 19.2-111, with having violated the laws of the state whose executive authority is making the demand, even though such person left the demanding state involuntarily.

History.
Code 1950, § 19.1-54; 1960, c. 366; 1975, c. 495.

§ 19.2-91. Extradition of persons not in demanding state at time of commission of crime.

The Governor may also surrender, on demand of the executive authority of any other state, any person in this Commonwealth charged in such other state in the manner provided in § 19.2-87 with committing an act in this Commonwealth, or in a third state, intentionally resulting in a crime in the state whose executive authority is making the demand. The provisions of this chapter not otherwise inconsistent shall apply to such cases, even though the accused was not in that state at the time of the commission of the crime, and has not fled therefrom.

History.
Code 1950, § 19.1-55; 1960, c. 366; 1975, c. 495.

§ 19.2-92. Issuance of Governor's warrant of arrest; its recitals.

If the Governor decides that a demand for the extradition of a person, charged with, or convicted of, crime in another state should be complied with, he shall sign a warrant of arrest, which shall be sealed with the state seal, and be directed to the sheriff or sergeant of any county or city or to any peace officer or other person whom he may think fit to entrust with the execution thereof. The warrant must substantially recite the facts necessary to the validity of its issuance. Any electronically transmitted facsimile of a Governor's warrant shall be treated as an original document, provided the original is received within four working days of receipt of the facsimile.

History.
Code 1950, § 19.1-56; 1960, c. 366; 1975, c. 495; 2001, cc. 214, 226; 2011, c. 59.

§ 19.2-93. Manner and place of execution of warrant.

Such warrant shall authorize the officer or other person to whom it is directed to arrest the accused at any time and at any place where he may be found within the Commonwealth and to command the aid of all peace officers or other persons in the execution of the warrant and to deliver the accused, subject to the provisions of this chapter, to the duly authorized agent of the demanding state.

History.
Code 1950, § 19.1-57; 1960, c. 366; 1975, c. 495.

§ 19.2-94. Assistance to arresting officer.

Every officer or other person empowered to make the arrest, as provided in the preceding section, shall have the same authority, in arresting the accused, to command assistance therein as the sheriffs and sergeants of the several counties and cities of this Commonwealth have by law in the execution of any criminal process directed to them, with like penalties against those who refuse to render their assistance.

History.
Code 1950, § 19.1-58; 1960, c. 366; 1975, c. 495.

§ 19.2-95. Rights of accused persons; application for writ of habeas corpus.

No person arrested upon such warrant shall be delivered over to the agent whom the executive authority demanding him shall have appointed to receive him unless he shall first be taken forthwith before a judge of a circuit or general district court in the Commonwealth, who shall inform him of the demand made for his surrender and of the crime with which he is charged, and that he has the right to demand and procure legal counsel; and if the prisoner or his counsel shall state that he or they desire to test the legality of his arrest, the judge shall fix a reasonable time to be allowed him within which to apply for a writ of habeas corpus. When such writ is applied for, notice thereof and of the time and place of hearing thereon shall be given to the attorney for the Commonwealth of the county or city in which the arrest is made and in which the accused is in custody, and to the agent of the demanding state.

History.
Code 1950, § 19.1-59; 1960, c. 366; 1975, c. 495; 2005, c. 839.

§ 19.2-96. Penalty for noncompliance with preceding section.

Any officer who shall deliver to the agent for extradition of the demanding state a person in his custody under the Governor's warrant in willful disobedience to the last preceding section shall be guilty of a Class 1 misdemeanor.

History.
Code 1950, § 19.1-60; 1960, c. 366; 1975, c. 495.

§ 19.2-97. Confinement in jail when necessary.

The officer or persons executing the Governor's warrant of arrest, or the agent of the demanding state to whom the prisoner may have been delivered, may, when necessary, confine the prisoner in the jail of any county or city through which he may pass; and the keeper of such jail shall receive and safely keep the prisoner until the officer or person having charge of him is ready to proceed on his route, such officer or person being chargeable with the expense of keeping.

History.
Code 1950, § 19.1-61; 1960, c. 366; 1975, c. 495.

§ 19.2-98. Same; for prisoners being taken through Commonwealth.

The officer or agent of a demanding state to whom a prisoner may have been delivered following extradition proceedings in another state or to whom a prisoner may have been delivered after waiving extradition in such other state, and who is passing through this Commonwealth with such prisoner for the purpose of returning immediately such prisoner to the demanding state may, when necessary, confine the prisoner in the jail of any county or city through which he may pass; and the keeper of such jail shall receive and safely keep the prisoner until the officer or agent having charge of him is ready to proceed on his route, such officer or agent, however, being chargeable with the expense of keeping, provided, however, that such officer or agent shall deliver to the jailer the warrant or legal order authorizing custody of the prisoner. Such prisoner shall not be entitled to demand a new requisition while in this Commonwealth.

History.
Code 1950, § 19.1-62; 1960, c. 366; 1975, c. 495.

§ 19.2-99. Arrest prior to requisition.

Whenever: (1) any person within this Commonwealth shall be charged on the oath of any credible person before any judge, magistrate or other officer authorized to issue criminal warrants in this Commonwealth with the commission of any crime in any other state and, except in cases arising under § 19.2-91, (a) with having fled from justice, (b) with having been convicted of a crime in that state and of having escaped from confinement, or (c) of having broken the terms of his bail, probation, or parole, or (2) complaint shall have been made before any such judge, magistrate or other officer in this Commonwealth setting forth on the affidavit of any credible person in another state that a crime has been committed in such other state and that the accused has been charged in such state with the commission of the crime, and, except in cases arising under § 19.2-91, (a) has fled from justice, (b) having been convicted of a crime in that state has escaped from confinement, or (c) broken the terms of his bail, probation or parole, and that the accused is believed to be in this Commonwealth, such judge, magistrate or other officer shall issue a warrant directed to any sheriff or to any peace officer commanding him to apprehend the person named therein, wherever he may be found in this Commonwealth, and to bring him before any judge who may be available in or convenient of access to the place where the arrest may be made, to answer the charge of complaint and affidavit. A certified copy of the sworn charge or complaint and affidavit upon which the warrant is issued shall be attached to the warrant.

History.
Code 1950, § 19.1-63; 1960, c. 366; 1975, c. 495.

§ 19.2-100. Arrest without warrant.

The arrest of a person may be lawfully made also by any peace officer or private person without a warrant upon reasonable information that the accused stands charged in the courts of a state with a crime punishable by death or imprisonment for a term exceeding one year. But when so arrested the accused shall be taken before a judge, magistrate or other officer authorized to issue criminal warrants in this Commonwealth with all practicable speed and complaint made against him under oath setting forth the ground for the arrest as in the preceding section; and thereafter his answer shall be heard as if he had been arrested on a warrant.

History.
Code 1950, § 19.1-64; 1960, c. 366; 1975, c. 495.

§ 19.2-101. Confinement to await requisition; bail.

If from the examination before the judge it appears that the person held pursuant to either of the two preceding sections is the person charged with having committed the crime alleged and, except in cases arising under § 19.2-91, that he has fled from justice, the judge shall, by a warrant reciting the accusation, commit him to jail for such a time, not exceeding thirty days, specified in the warrant as will enable the arrest of the accused to be made under a warrant of the Governor on a requisition of the executive authority of the state having jurisdiction of the offense, unless the accused give bail as provided in the next section, or until he shall be legally discharged.

History.
Code 1950, § 19.1-65; 1960, c. 366; 1975, c. 495.

§ 19.2-102. In what cases bail allowed; conditions of bond.

Unless the offense with which the prisoner is charged is shown to be an offense punishable by death or life imprisonment under the laws of the state in which it was committed, any judge, magistrate or other person authorized by law to admit persons to bail in this Commonwealth may admit the person arrested to bail by bond, with sufficient sureties, and in such sum as he deems proper, conditioned upon his appearance before a judge at a time specified in such bond and upon his surrender for arrest upon the warrant of the Governor of this Commonwealth.

History.
Code 1950, § 19.1-66; 1960, c. 366; 1975, c. 495.

§ 19.2-103. Discharge, recommitment or renewal of bail.

If the accused is not arrested under warrant of the Governor by the expiration of the time specified in the warrant or bond, any judge in this Commonwealth may discharge him or may recommit him for a further period not to exceed sixty days, or such judge may again take bail for his appearance and surrender, as provided in the preceding section, but within a period not to exceed sixty days after the date of such new bond.

History.
Code 1950, § 19.1-67; 1960, c. 366; 1975, c. 495.

§ 19.2-104. Forfeiture of bail.

If the prisoner is admitted to bail and fails to appear and surrender himself according to the conditions of his bond, any judge of a circuit or general district court by proper order, shall declare the bond forfeited and order his immediate arrest without warrant if he be within this Commonwealth. Recovery may be had on such bond in the name of the Commonwealth as in the case of other bonds given by the accused in criminal proceedings within this Commonwealth.

History.
Code 1950, § 19.1-68; 1960, c. 366; 1975, c. 495.

§ 19.2-105. Persons under criminal prosecution in this Commonwealth at time of requisition.

If a criminal prosecution has been instituted against such person under the laws of this Commonwealth and is still pending, the Governor, in his discretion, either may surrender him on demand of the executive authority of another state or hold him until he has been tried and discharged or convicted and punished in this Commonwealth.

History.
Code 1950, § 19.1-69; 1960, c. 366; 1975, c. 495.

§ 19.2-106. When guilt or innocence of accused inquired into.

The guilt or innocence of the accused as to the crime of which he is charged may not be inquired into by the Governor or in any proceeding after the demand for extradition accompanied by a charge of crime in legal form as above provided shall have been presented to the Governor, except as it may be involved in identifying the person held as the person charged with the crime.

History.
Code 1950, § 19.1-70; 1960, c. 366; 1975, c. 495.

§ 19.2-107. Governor may recall warrant or issue alias.

The Governor may recall his warrant of arrest or may issue another warrant whenever he deems it proper.

History.
Code 1950, § 19.1-71; 1960, c. 366; 1975, c. 495.

§ 19.2-108. Fugitives from this Commonwealth; duty of Governor.

Whenever the Governor shall demand a person charged with crime or with escaping from confinement or breaking the terms of his bail, probation or parole in this Commonwealth, from the executive authority of any other state, or from the chief justice or an associate justice of the Supreme Court of the District of Columbia authorized to receive such demand under the laws of the United States, he shall issue a warrant under the seal of this Commonwealth to some agent commanding him to receive the person so charged if delivered to him and convey him to the proper officer of the county or city in this Commonwealth in which the offense was committed. Nothing herein shall prevent the sheriff or police chief of a county or city who has been directed to execute such warrant from authorizing a private prisoner transportation company meeting the minimum qualifications set by the Department of Criminal Justice Services to receive and return the person to the Commonwealth.

History.
Code 1950, § 19.1-72; 1960, c. 366; 1975, c. 495; 2009, c. 848.

§ 19.2-109. Application for requisition for return of person charged with crime.

When the return to this Commonwealth of a person charged with crime in this Commonwealth is required, the attorney for the Commonwealth shall present to the Governor his written application for a requisition for the return of the person charged, in which application shall be stated the name of the person so charged, the crime charged against him, the approximate time, place and circumstances of its commission, the state in which he is believed to be, including the location of the accused therein at the time the application is made, and certifying that, in the opinion of the attorney for the Commonwealth, the ends of justice require the arrest and return of the accused to this Commonwealth for trial and that the proceeding is not instituted to enforce a private claim.

History.
Code 1950, § 19.1-73; 1960, c. 366; 1975, c. 495.

§ 19.2-110. Application for requisition for return of escaped convict, etc.

When the return to this Commonwealth is required of a person who has been convicted of a crime in this Commonwealth and has escaped from confinement or broken the terms of his bail, probation or parole, the attorney for the Commonwealth, of the county or city in which the offense was committed, or the warden of the institution or sheriff of the county or city from which the escape was made, shall present to the Governor a written application for a requisition for the return of such person, in which application shall be stated the name of the person, the crime of which he was convicted, the circumstances of his escape from confinement or of the breach of the terms of his bail, probation or parole and the state in which he is believed to be, including the location of the person therein at the time application is made.

History.
Code 1950, § 19.1-74; 1960, c. 366; 1975, c. 495.

§ 19.2-111. Form of such applications; copies, etc.

The application shall be verified by affidavit, shall be executed in duplicate and shall be accompanied by two certified copies of the indictment returned, or information and affidavit filed, or of the complaint made to the judge of a circuit or general district court or other officer issuing the warrant stating the offense with which the accused is charged, or of the judgment of conviction or of the sentence. The attorney for the Commonwealth, warden or sheriff may also attach such further affidavits and other documents in duplicate as he shall deem proper to be submitted with such application. One copy of the application, with the action of the Governor indicated by endorsement thereon, and one of the certified copies of the indictment, complaint, information, and affidavits, or of the judgment of conviction or of the sentence shall be filed in the office of the Secretary of the Commonwealth, to remain of record in that office. The other copies of all papers shall be forwarded with the Governor's requisition.

History.
Code 1950, § 19.1-75; 1960, c. 366; 1975, c. 495.

§ 19.2-112. Costs and expenses of extradition.

A. The expenses incident to the extradition of any person under the four preceding sections may be paid out of the state treasury, on warrants of the Comptroller issued upon vouchers signed by the Governor, or such other person as may be designated by him for such purpose.

B. If the person extradited is found guilty, or if the person was extradited after illegally leaving the Commonwealth while on parole or on probation, the person extradited, and not the Commonwealth, shall be responsible for the costs and expenses of extradition. The state treasury shall continue to reimburse local jurisdictions for the costs and expenses of extradition. The fugitive shall pay the costs and expenses of his extradition into the state treasury.

History.
Code 1950, § 19.1-76; 1960, c. 366; 1975, c. 495; 1999, c. 322; 2002, c. 622.

§ 19.2-113. Immunity from service of process in certain civil actions.

A person brought into this Commonwealth by, or after waiver of, extradition based on a criminal charge shall not be subject to service of personal process in civil actions arising out of the same facts as the criminal proceeding to answer which he is being or has been returned, until he has been convicted in the criminal proceeding, or, if acquitted, until he has had reasonable opportunity to return to the state from which he was extradited.

History.
Code 1950, § 19.1-77; 1960, c. 366; 1975, c. 495.

§ 19.2-114. Written waiver of extradition proceedings.

Any person arrested in this Commonwealth charged with having committed any crime in another state or alleged to have escaped from confinement, or broken the terms of his bail, probation or parole may waive the issuance and service of the warrant provided for in §§ 19.2-92 and 19.2-93 and all other procedures incidental to extradition proceedings by executing or subscribing in the presence of a judge of a circuit or district court within this Commonwealth a writing which states that he consents to return to the demanding state. However, before the waiver is executed or subscribed by the person, it shall be the duty of the judge to inform the person of his rights to the issuance and service of a warrant of extradition and to obtain a writ of habeas corpus as provided for in § 19.2-95.

If and when such consent has been duly executed, it shall forthwith be forwarded to the office of the Governor and filed therein. The judge shall direct the officer having the person in custody to promptly deliver him to the duly accredited agent of the demanding state, and shall deliver or cause to be delivered to such agent a copy of the consent.

This section shall not be deemed to limit the rights of the accused person to return voluntarily and without formality to the demanding state, nor shall this waiver procedure be deemed to be an executive procedure or to limit the powers, rights or duties of the officers of the demanding state or of this Commonwealth.

History.
Code 1950, § 19.1-78; 1960, c. 366; 1975, c. 495; 1992, c. 306.

§ 19.2-115. Nonwaiver by this Commonwealth.

Nothing in this chapter contained shall be deemed to constitute a waiver by this Commonwealth of its right, power or privilege to try such demanded person for crime committed within this Commonwealth, or of its right, power or privilege to regain custody of such person by extradition proceedings or otherwise for the purpose of trial, sentence or punishment for any crime committed within this Commonwealth, nor shall any proceedings had under this chapter which result in, or fail to result in, extradition be deemed a waiver by this Commonwealth of any of its rights, privileges or jurisdiction in any way whatsoever.

History.
Code 1950, § 19.1-79; 1960, c. 366; 1975, c. 495.

§ 19.2-116. No right of asylum; no immunity from other criminal prosecutions while in this Commonwealth.

After a person has been brought back to this Commonwealth by, or after waiver of, extradition proceedings he may be tried in this Commonwealth for other crimes which he may be charged with having committed here as well as that specified in the requisition for his extradition.

History.
Code 1950, § 19.1-80; 1960, c. 366; 1975, c. 495.

§ 19.2-117. Interpretation of article.

The provisions of this article shall be so interpreted and construed as to effectuate its general purposes to make uniform the law of those states which enact statutes similar thereto.

History.
Code 1950, § 19.1-81; 1960, c. 366; 1975, c. 495.

§ 19.2-118. Short title.

This article may be cited as the Uniform Criminal Extradition Act.

History.
Code 1950, § 19.1-82; 1960, c. 366; 1975, c. 495.

CHAPTER 9.

BAIL AND RECOGNIZANCES.

Article 1.

Bail.

Section

Article 2.

Recognizances.

Criminal Procedure

Article 3.

Satisfaction and Discharge.

Article 4.

Bail Bondsmen.

Article 5.

Pretrial Services Act.

ARTICLE 1.
BAIL.

§ 19.2-119. Definitions.

As used in this chapter:

"Bail" means the pretrial release of a person from custody upon those terms and conditions specified by order of an appropriate judicial officer.

"Bond" means the posting by a person or his surety of a written promise to pay a specific sum, secured or unsecured, ordered by an appropriate judicial officer as a condition of bail to assure performance of the terms and conditions contained in the recognizance.

"Criminal history" means records and data collected by criminal justice agencies or persons consisting of identifiable descriptions and notations of arrests, detentions, indictments, informations or other formal charges, and any deposition arising therefrom.

"Judicial officer" means, unless otherwise indicated, any magistrate serving the jurisdiction, any judge of a district court and the clerk or deputy clerk of any district court or circuit court within their respective cities and counties, any judge of a circuit court, any judge of the Court of Appeals and any justice of the Supreme Court of Virginia.

"Person" means any accused, or any juvenile taken into custody pursuant to § 16.1-246.

"Recognizance" means a signed commitment by a person to appear in court as directed and to adhere to any other terms ordered by an appropriate judicial officer as a condition of bail.

History.

Code 1950, § 19.1-109.1; 1973, c. 485; 1974, c. 114; 1975, c. 495; 1984, c. 703; 1991, c. 581; 1993, c. 636; 1999, cc. 829, 846; 2008, cc. 551, 691.

§ 19.2-120. Admission to bail.

Prior to conducting any hearing on the issue of bail, release or detention, the judicial officer shall, to the extent feasible, obtain the person's criminal history.

A. A person who is held in custody pending trial or hearing for an offense, civil or criminal contempt, or otherwise shall be admitted to bail by a judicial officer, unless there is probable cause to believe that:

1. He will not appear for trial or hearing or at such other time and place as may be directed, or

2. His liberty will constitute an unreasonable danger to himself or the public.

B. The judicial officer shall presume, subject to rebuttal, that no condition or combination of conditions will reasonably assure the appearance of the person or the safety of the public if the person is currently charged with:

1. An act of violence as defined in § 19.2-297.1;

2. An offense for which the maximum sentence is life imprisonment or death;

3. A violation of § 18.2-248, 18.2-248.01, 18.2-255, or 18.2-255.2 involving a Schedule I or II controlled substance if (i) the maximum term of imprisonment is 10 years or more and the person was previously convicted of a like offense or (ii) the person was previously convicted as a "drug kingpin" as defined in § 18.2-248;

4. A violation of § 18.2-308.1, 18.2-308.2, or 18.2-308.4 and which relates to a firearm and provides for a mandatory minimum sentence;

5. Any felony, if the person has been convicted of two or more offenses described in subdivision 1 or 2, whether under the laws of the Commonwealth or substantially similar laws of the United States;

6. Any felony committed while the person is on release pending trial for a prior felony under federal or state law or on release pending imposition or execution of sentence or appeal of sentence or conviction;

7. An offense listed in subsection B of § 18.2-67.5:2 and the person had previously been convicted of an offense listed in § 18.2-67.5:2 or a substantially similar offense under the laws of any state or the United States and the judicial officer finds probable cause to believe that the person who is currently charged with one of these offenses committed the offense charged;

8. A violation of § 18.2-374.1 or 18.2-374.3 where the offender has reason to believe that the solicited person is under 15 years of age and the offender is at least five years older than the solicited person;

9. A violation of § 18.2-46.2, 18.2-46.3, 18.2-46.5, or 18.2-46.7;

10. A violation of § 18.2-36.1, 18.2-51.4, 18.2-266, or 46.2-341.24 and the person has, within the past five years of the instant offense, been convicted three times on different dates of a violation of any combination of these Code sections, or any ordinance of any county, city, or town or the laws of any other state or of the United States substantially similar thereto, and has been at liberty between each conviction;

11. A second or subsequent violation of § 16.1-253.2 or 18.2-60.4 or a substantially similar offense under the laws of any state or the United States;

12. A violation of subsection B of § 18.2-57.2;

13. A violation of subsection C of § 18.2-460 charging the use of threats of bodily harm or force to knowingly attempt to intimidate or impede a witness; or

14. A violation of § 18.2-51.6 if the alleged victim is a family or household member as defined in § 16.1-228.

C. The judicial officer shall presume, subject to rebuttal, that no condition or combination of conditions will reasonably assure the appearance of the person or the safety of the public if the person is being arrested pursuant to § 19.2-81.6.

D. A judicial officer who is a magistrate, clerk, or deputy clerk of a district court or circuit court may not admit to bail, that is not set by a judge, any person who is charged with an offense giving rise to a rebuttable presumption against bail as set out in subsection B or C without the concurrence of an attorney for the Commonwealth. For a person who is charged with an offense giving rise to a rebuttable presumption against bail, any judge may set or admit such person to bail in accordance with this section after notice and an opportunity to be heard has been provided to the attorney for the Commonwealth.

E. The court shall consider the following factors and such others as it deems appropriate in determining, for the purpose of rebuttal of the presumption against bail described in subsection B, whether there are conditions of release that will reasonably assure the appearance of the person as required and the safety of the public:

1. The nature and circumstances of the offense charged;

2. The history and characteristics of the person, including his character, physical and mental condition, family ties, employment, financial resources, length of residence in the community, community ties, past conduct, history relating to drug or alcohol abuse, criminal history, membership in a criminal street gang as defined in § 18.2-46.1, and record concerning appearance at court proceedings; and

3. The nature and seriousness of the danger to any person or the community that would be posed by the person's release.

F. The judicial officer shall inform the person of his right to appeal from the order denying bail or fixing terms of bond or recognizance consistent with § 19.2-124.

G. If the judicial officer sets a secured bond and the person engages the services of a licensed bail bondsman, the magistrate executing recognizance for the accused shall provide the bondsman, upon request, with a copy of the person's Virginia criminal history record, if readily available, to be used by the bondsman only to determine appropriate reporting requirements to impose upon the accused upon his release. The bondsman shall pay a $15 fee payable to the state treasury to be credited to the Literary Fund, upon requesting the defendant's Virginia criminal history record issued pursuant to § 19.2-389. The bondsman shall review the record on the premises and promptly return the record to the magistrate after reviewing it.

History.

1975, c. 495; 1978, c. 755; 1979, c. 649; 1987, c. 390; 1991, c. 581; 1993, c. 636; 1996, c. 973; 1997, cc. 6, 476; 1999, cc. 829, 846; 2000, c. 797; 2002, cc. 588, 623; 2004, cc. 308, 360, 406, 412, 461, 819, 954, 959; 2005, c. 132; 2006, c. 504; 2007, cc. 134, 386, 745, 923; 2008, c. 596; 2010, c. 862; 2011, cc. 445, 450, 480; 2012, c. 467; 2015, c. 413.

§ 19.2-120.1. Presumption of no bail for illegal aliens charged with certain crimes.

A. In addition to the presumption against the admission to bail under subsection B of § 19.2-120, the judicial officer shall presume, subject to rebuttal, that no condition or combination of conditions will reasonably assure the appearance of the person or the safety of the public if (i) the person is currently charged with an offense listed in subsection A of § 19.2-297.1, subsection C of § 17.1-805, any offense under Chapter 4 (§ 18.2-30 et seq.) of Title 18.2 except any offense under subsection A of § 18.2-57.2, any felony offense under Article 1 (§ 18.2-247 et seq.) of Chapter 7 of Title 18.2, or any offense under Article 2 (§ 18.2-266 et seq.), or any local ordinance substantially similar thereto, 4 (§ 18.2-279 et seq.), 5 (§ 18.2-288 et seq.), 6 (§ 18.2-299 et seq.), 6.1 (§ 18.2-307.1 et seq.), or 7 (§ 18.2-308.1 et seq.) of Chapter 7 of Title 18.2, and (ii) the person has been identified as being illegally present in the United States by United States Immigration and Customs Enforcement.

B. Notwithstanding subsection A, no presumption shall exist under this section as to any misdemeanor offense, or any felony offense under Article 1 (§ 18.2-247 et seq.) of Chapter 7 of Title 18.2, unless United States Immigration and Customs Enforcement has guaranteed that, in all such cases in the Commonwealth, it will issue a detainer for the initiation of removal proceedings and agree to reimburse for the cost of incarceration from the time of the issuance of the detainer.

History.

2008, cc. 469, 834; 2013, c. 746.

§ 19.2-121. Fixing terms of bail.

If the person is admitted to bail, the terms thereof shall be such as, in the judgment of any official granting or reconsidering the same, will be reasonably fixed to assure the appearance of the accused and to assure his good behavior pending trial. The judicial officer shall take into account (i) the nature and circumstances of the offense; (ii) whether a firearm is alleged to have been used in the offense; (iii) the weight of the evidence; (iv) the financial resources of the accused or juvenile and his ability to pay bond; (v) the character of the accused or juvenile including his family ties, employment or involvement in education; (vi) his length of residence in the community; (vii) his record of convictions; (viii) his appearance at court proceedings or flight to avoid prosecution or failure to appear at court proceedings; (ix) whether the person is likely to obstruct or attempt to obstruct justice, or threaten, injure, or intimidate, or attempt to threaten, injure, or intimidate a prospective witness, juror, or victim; and (x) any other information available which the court considers relevant to the determination of whether the accused or juvenile is unlikely to appear for court proceedings.

In any case where the accused has appeared and otherwise met the conditions of bail, no bond therefor shall be used to satisfy fines and costs unless agreed to by the person who posted such bond.

History.

1975, c. 495; 1978, c. 755; 1980, c. 190; 1991, c. 581; 1992, c. 576; 1993, c. 636; 1999, cc. 829, 846.

§ 19.2-122: Repealed by Acts 1986, c. 327.

§ 19.2-123. Release of accused on secured or unsecured bond or promise to appear; conditions of release.

A. Any person arrested for a felony who has previously been convicted of a felony, or who is presently on bond for an unrelated arrest in any jurisdiction, or who is on probation or parole, may be released only upon a secure bond. This provision may be waived with the approval of the judicial officer and with the concurrence of the attorney for the Commonwealth or the attorney for the county, city or town. Subject to the foregoing, when a person is arrested for either a felony or a misdemeanor, any judicial officer may impose any one or any combination of the following conditions of release:

1. Place the person in the custody and supervision of a designated person, organization or pretrial services agency which, for the purposes of this section, shall not include a court services unit established pursuant to § 16.1-233;

2. Place restrictions on the travel, association or place of abode of the person during the period of release and restrict contacts with household members for a specified period of time;

2a. Require the execution of an unsecured bond;

3. Require the execution of a secure bond which at the option of the accused shall be satisfied with sufficient solvent sureties, or the deposit of cash in lieu thereof. Only the actual value of any interest in real estate or personal property owned by the proposed surety shall be considered in determining solvency and solvency shall be found if the value of the proposed surety's equity in the real estate or personal property equals or exceeds the amount of the bond;

3a. Require that the person do any or all of the following: (i) maintain employment or, if unemployed, actively seek employment; (ii) maintain or commence an educational program; (iii) avoid all contact with an alleged victim of the crime and with any potential witness who may testify concerning the offense; (iv) comply with a specified curfew; (v) refrain from possessing a firearm, destructive device, or other dangerous weapon; (vi) refrain from excessive use of alcohol, or use of any illegal drug or any controlled substance not prescribed by a health care provider; and (vii) submit to testing for drugs and alcohol until the final disposition of his case;

3b. Place a prohibition on a person who holds an elected constitutional office and who is accused of a felony arising from the performance of his duties from physically returning to his constitutional office;

3c. Require the accused to accompany the arresting officer to the jurisdiction's fingerprinting facility and submit to having his photograph and fingerprints taken prior to release; or

4. Impose any other condition deemed reasonably necessary to assure appearance as required, and to assure his good behavior pending trial, including a condition requiring that the person return to custody after specified hours or be placed on home electronic incarceration pursuant to § 53.1-131.2 or, when the person is required to execute a secured bond, be subject to monitoring by a GPS (Global Positioning System) tracking device, or other similar device. The defendant may be ordered by the court to pay the cost of the device.

Upon satisfaction of the terms of recognizance, the accused shall be released forthwith.

In addition, where the accused is an individual receiving services in a state training center for individuals with intellectual disability, the judicial officer may place the individual in the custody of the director of the training center, if the director agrees to accept custody. The director is hereby authorized to take custody of the individual and to maintain him at the training center prior to a trial or hearing under such circumstances as will reasonably assure the appearance of the accused for the trial or hearing.

B. In any jurisdiction served by a pretrial services agency which offers a drug or alcohol screening or testing program approved for the purposes of this subsection by the chief general district court judge, any such person charged with a crime may be requested by such agency to give voluntarily a urine sample, submit to a drug or alcohol screening, or take a breath test for presence of alcohol. A sample may be analyzed for the presence of phencyclidine (PCP), barbiturates, cocaine, opiates or such other drugs as the agency may deem appropriate prior to any hearing to establish bail. The judicial officer and agency shall inform the accused or juvenile being screened or tested that test results shall be used by a judicial officer only at a bail hearing and only to determine appropriate conditions of release or to reconsider the conditions of bail at a subsequent hearing. All screening or test results, and any pretrial investigation report containing the screening or test results, shall be confidential with access thereto limited to judicial officers, the attorney for the Commonwealth, defense counsel, other pretrial service agencies, any criminal justice agency as defined in § 9.1-101 and, in cases where a juvenile is screened or tested, the parents or legal guardian or custodian of such juvenile. However, in no event shall the judicial officer have access to any screening or test result prior to making a bail release determination or to determining the amount of bond, if any. Following this determination, the judicial officer shall consider the screening or test results and the screening or testing agency's report and accompanying recommendations, if any, in setting appropriate conditions of release. In no event shall a decision regarding a release determination be subject to reversal on the sole basis of such screening or test results. Any accused or juvenile whose urine sample has tested positive for such drugs and who is admitted to bail may, as a condition of release, be ordered to refrain from use of alcohol or illegal drugs and may be required to be tested on a periodic basis until final disposition of his case to ensure his compliance with the order. Sanctions for a violation of any condition of release, which violations shall include subsequent positive drug or alcohol test results or failure to report as ordered for testing, may be imposed in the discretion of the judicial officer and may include imposition of more stringent conditions of release, contempt of court proceedings or revocation of release. Any test given under the provisions of this subsection which yields a positive drug or alcohol test result shall be reconfirmed by a second test if the person tested denies or contests the initial drug or alcohol test positive result. The results of any drug or alcohol test conducted pursuant to this subsection shall not be admissible in any judicial proceeding other than for the imposition of sanctions for a violation of a condition of release.

C. [Repealed.]

D. Nothing in this section shall be construed to prevent an officer taking a juvenile into custody from releasing that juvenile pursuant to § 16.1-247. If any condition of release imposed under the provisions of this section is violated, a judicial officer may issue a capias or order to show cause why the recognizance should not be revoked.

E. Nothing in this section shall be construed to prevent a court from imposing a recognizance or bond designed to secure a spousal or child support obligation pursuant to § 16.1-278.16, Chapter 5 (§ 20-61 et seq.) of Title 20, or § 20-114 in addition to any recognizance or bond imposed pursuant to this chapter.

History.

Code 1950, § 19.1-109.2; 1973, c. 485; 1975, c. 495; 1978, cc. 500, 755; 1979, c. 518; 1981, c. 528; 1984, c. 707; 1989, c. 369; 1991, cc. 483, 512, 581, 585; 1992, c. 576; 1993, c. 636; 1999, cc. 829, 846; 2000, cc. 885, 1020, 1041; 2001, c. 201; 2006, c. 296; 2008, cc. 129, 884; 2011, cc. 799, 837; 2012, cc. 476, 507; 2013, c. 614; 2014, c. 466.

§ 19.2-124. Appeal from bail, bond, or recognizance order.

A. If a judicial officer denies bail to a person, requires excessive bond, or fixes unreasonable terms of a recognizance under this article, the person may appeal the decision of the judicial officer.

If the initial bail decision on a charge brought by a warrant or district court capias is made by a magistrate, clerk, or deputy clerk, the person shall first appeal to the district court in which the case is pending.

If the initial bail decision on a charge brought by direct indictment or presentment or circuit court capias is made by a magistrate, clerk, or deputy clerk, the person shall first appeal to the circuit court in which the case is pending.

If the appeal of an initial bail decision is taken on any charge originally pending in a district court after that charge has been appealed, certified, or transferred to a circuit court, the person shall first appeal to the circuit court in which the case is pending.

Any bail decision made by a judge of a court may be appealed successively by the person to the next higher court, up to and including the Supreme Court of Virginia, where permitted by law.

B. The attorney for the Commonwealth may appeal a bail, bond, or recognizance decision to the same court to which the accused person is required to appeal under subsection A.

C. In a matter not governed by subsection B or C of § 19.2-120 or § 19.2-120.1, the court granting or denying such bail may, upon appeal thereof, and for good cause shown, stay execution of such order for so long as reasonably practicable for the party to obtain an expedited hearing before the next higher court. When a district court grants bail over the presumption against bail in a matter that is governed by subsection B or C of § 19.2-120 or § 19.2-120.1, and upon notice by the Commonwealth of its appeal of the court's decision, the court shall stay execution of such order for so long as reasonably practical for the Commonwealth to obtain an expedited hearing before the circuit court, but in no event more than five days, unless the defendant requests a hearing date outside the five-day limit.

No such stay under this subsection may be granted after any person who has been granted bail has been released from custody on such bail.

D. No filing or service fees shall be assessed or collected for any appeal taken pursuant to this section.

History.

Code 1950, §§ 19.1-109.3, 19.1-112; 1960, c. 366; 1973, cc. 130, 485; 1975, c. 495; 1978, c. 755; 1984, c. 703; 1991, c. 581; 1999, cc. 829, 846; 2007, cc. 462, 549; 2010, cc. 404, 592; 2013, cc. 408, 474; 2016, c. 621.

§ 19.2-125. Release pending appeal from conviction in court not of record.

A person who has been convicted of an offense in a district court and who has noted an appeal shall be given credit for any bond that he may have posted in the court from which he appeals and shall be treated in accordance with the provisions of this article.

History.

Code 1950, § 19.1-109.4; 1973, c. 485; 1975, c. 495; 1978, c. 755; 1999, cc. 829, 846.

§ 19.2-126: Repealed by Acts 1999, cc. 829 and 846.

§ 19.2-127. Conditions of release of material witness.

If it appears by affidavit that the testimony of a person is material in any criminal proceeding, and it reasonably appears that it will be impossible to secure his presence by a subpoena, a judge shall inquire into the conditions of his release pursuant to this article.

History.

Code 1950, § 19.1-109.6; 1973, c. 485; 1975, c. 495; 1999, cc. 829, 846.

§ 19.2-128. Penalties for failure to appear.

A. Whoever, having been released pursuant to this chapter or § 19.2-319 or on a summons pursuant to § 19.2-73 or § 19.2-74, willfully fails to appear before any court or judicial officer as required, shall, after notice to all interested parties, incur a forfeiture of any security which may have been given or pledged for his release, unless one of the parties can show good cause for excusing the absence, or unless the court, in its sound discretion, shall determine that neither the interests of justice nor the power of the court to conduct orderly proceedings will be served by such forfeiture.

B. Any person (i) charged with a felony offense or (ii) convicted of a felony offense and execution of sentence is suspended pursuant to § 19.2-319 who willfully fails to appear before any court as required shall be guilty of a Class 6 felony.

C. Any person (i) charged with a misdemeanor offense or (ii) convicted of a misdemeanor offense and execution of sentence is suspended pursuant to § 19.2-319 who willfully fails to appear before any court as required shall be guilty of a Class 1 misdemeanor.

History.

Code 1950, § 19.1-109.7; 1973, c. 485; 1975, c. 495; 1981, c. 382; 1982, c. 271; 1999, c. 821.

§ 19.2-129. Power of court to punish for contempt.

Nothing in this chapter shall interfere with or prevent the exercise by any court of the Commonwealth of its power to punish for contempt, except that a person shall not be sentenced for contempt and under the provisions of § 19.2-128 for the same absence.

History.

Code 1950, § 19.1-109.8; 1973, c. 485; 1975, c. 495.

§ 19.2-130. Bail in subsequent proceeding arising out of initial arrest.

Any person admitted to bail by a judge or clerk of a district court or by a magistrate shall not be required to be admitted to bail in any subsequent proceeding arising out of the initial arrest unless the court having jurisdiction of such subsequent proceeding deems the initial amount of bond or security taken inadequate. When the court having jurisdiction of the proceeding believes the amount of bond or security inadequate or excessive, it may change the amount of such bond or security, require new and additional sureties, or set other terms of bail as are appropriate to the case, including, but not limited to, drug and alcohol monitoring. The court may, after notice to the parties, initiate a proceeding to alter the terms and conditions of bail on its own motion.

History.

Code 1950, § 19.1-111.1; 1972, c. 366; 1975, c. 495; 1978, c. 755; 1991, c. 581; 2008, cc. 363, 812.

§ 19.2-130.1. Bail terms set by court on a capias to be honored by magistrate.

A magistrate who is to set the terms of bail of a person arrested and brought before him pursuant to § 19.2-234 shall, unless circumstances exist that require him to set more restrictive terms, set the terms of bail in accordance with the order of the court that issued the capias, if such an order is affixed to or made a part of the capias by the court.

History.

2010, cc. 312, 375; 2011, c. 112.

§ 19.2-131. Bail for person held in jurisdiction other than that of trial.

In any case in which a person charged with a misdemeanor or felony, or a juvenile taken into custody pursuant to § 16.1-246 is held in some county, city or town other than that in which he is to be tried upon such charge, he may be admitted to bail by any judicial officer of the county, city or town in which he is so held in accordance with the provisions of law concerning the granting of bail in cases in which persons are so admitted to bail, when held in the county, city or town in which they are to be tried.

In such case, such judicial officer before whom he is brought may, without trial or examination, let him to bail, upon taking a recognizance for his appearance before the court having cognizance of the case. The fact of taking such recognizance shall be certified by the court or officer taking it upon the warrant under which such person was arrested or taken into custody and the warrant and recognizance shall be returned forthwith to the clerk of the court before whom the accused or juvenile taken into custody pursuant to § 16.1-246 is to appear. And to such court, the judicial officer who issued such warrant shall recognize or cause to be summoned such witnesses as he may think proper.

History.

Code 1950, §§ 19.1-118, 19.1-119; 1960, c. 366; 1975, c. 495; 1978, c. 755; 1992, c. 576.

§ 19.2-132. Motion to increase amount of bond fixed by judicial officer; when bond may be increased.

If the amount of any bond fixed by a judicial officer is subsequently deemed insufficient, or the security taken inadequate, or if it appears that bail should have been denied or that the person has violated a term or condition of his release, or has been convicted of or arrested for a felony or misdemeanor, the attorney for the Commonwealth of the county or city in which the person is held for trial may, on reasonable notice to the person and, if such person has been admitted to bail, to any surety on the bond of such person, move the appropriate judicial officer to increase the amount of such bond or to revoke bail. The court may grant such motion and may require new or additional sureties therefor, or both or revoke bail. Any surety in a bond for the appearance of such person may take from his principal collateral or other security to indemnify such surety against liability. The failure to notify the surety will not prohibit the court from proceeding with the bond hearing.

The court ordering any increase in the amount of such bond, ordering new or additional sureties, or revoking such bail may, upon appeal, and for good cause shown, stay execution of such order for so long as reasonably practicable for such person to obtain an expedited hearing before the court to which such order has been appealed.

History.

Code 1950, § 19.1-120; 1960, c. 366; 1975, c. 495; 1978, c. 755; 1989, c. 519; 1991, c. 581; 1999, cc. 829, 846; 2010, cc. 404, 592; 2013, cc. 408, 474.

§§ 19.2-132.1, 19.2-133: Repealed by Acts 1991, c. 581.

Cross references.

For current provision relating to when accused admitted to bail may be subject to a motion to increase his bond, see § 19.2-132.

§ 19.2-134. When bail piece to be delivered to accused; form of bail piece.

In all cases in which recognizances, at the suit of the Commonwealth, may have been, or shall hereafter be entered into, it shall be the duty of the clerk of the court in which, or in the clerk's office of which, any recognizance is filed, to deliver to the accused and his sureties upon request, a bail piece, in substance, as follows: "A. B. of the county or city of ......, is delivered to bail, unto C. D. of the county or city of ......, at the suit of the Commonwealth. Given under my hand, this day of ...., in the year ...."

History.

Code 1950, § 19.1-123; 1960, c. 366; 1975, c. 495; 1991, c. 581; 1992, c. 576.

ARTICLE 2.

RECOGNIZANCES.

§ 19.2-135. Commitment for trial; recognizance; notice to attorney for Commonwealth; remand on violation of condition.

When a judicial officer considers that there is sufficient cause for charging the accused or juvenile taken into custody pursuant to § 16.1-246 with a felony, unless it be a case wherein it is otherwise specially provided, the commitment shall be for trial or hearing. Any recognizance taken of the accused or juvenile shall be upon the following conditions: (1) that he appear to answer for the offense with which he is charged before the court or judge before whom the case will be tried at such time as may be stated in the recognizance and at any time or times to which the proceedings may be continued and before any court or judge thereafter in which proceedings on the charge are held; (2) that he shall not depart from the Commonwealth unless the judicial officer taking recognizance or a court in a subsequent proceeding specifically waives such requirement; and (3) that he shall keep the peace and be of good behavior until the case is finally disposed of. Every such recognizance shall also include a waiver such as is required by § 49-12 in relation to the bonds therein mentioned and though such waiver be not expressed in the recognizance it shall be deemed to be included therein in like manner and with the same effect as if it was so expressed. The judge shall return to the clerk of the court wherein the accused or juvenile is to be tried, or the case be heard as soon as may be, a certificate of the nature of the offense, showing whether the accused or juvenile was committed to jail or recognized for his appearance; and the clerk, as soon as may be, shall inform the attorney for the Commonwealth of such certificate.

The court may, in its discretion, in the event of a violation of any condition of a recognizance taken pursuant to this section, remand the principal to jail until the case is finally disposed of, and if the principal is remanded to jail, the surety is discharged from liability.

When a recognizance is taken of a witness in a case against an accused or juvenile, the condition thereof shall be that he appear to give evidence in such case and that he shall not depart from the Commonwealth without the leave of such court or judge.

History.
Code 1950, §§ 19.1-125, 19.1-128, 19.1-133; 1960, c. 366; 1968, c. 639; 1975, c. 495; 1977, c. 287; 1978, c. 755; 1979, c. 735; 1988, c. 688; 1992, c. 576.

§ 19.2-136. How bonds in recognizances payable; penalty.

Bonds in recognizances in criminal or juvenile cases shall be payable to the county or city in which the case is prosecuted. The treasurer or director of finance of such locality may engage in collection activity regarding the judgment of default rendered pursuant to § 19.2-143. Any responses to the judgment of default rendered pursuant to § 19.2-143 shall be filed with the court, with notice given to such locality. Every bond under this title shall be in such sum as the court or officer requiring it may direct.

History.
Code 1950, § 19.1-127; 1960, c. 366; 1973, c. 485; 1975, c. 495; 1978, c. 755; 1991, c. 581; 2011, c. 802; 2012, c. 408.

§ 19.2-137. Order of court on recognizance.

When such recognizance is taken by a court of a person to answer a charge or of a witness to give evidence it shall be sufficient for the order of the court taking the recognizance to state that the party or parties recognized were duly recognized upon a bond in such sum as the court may have directed with such surety as the court may have accepted for his or their appearance before such court at such time as may have been prescribed by the court to answer for the offense with which such person is charged or to give evidence, as the case may be.

History.
Code 1950, § 19.1-129; 1960, c. 366; 1975, c. 495; 1991, c. 581.

§§ 19.2-138 through 19.2-140: Repealed by Acts 1987, c. 670.

Cross references.
As to cash bonds, see § 19.2-143.

§ 19.2-141. How recognizance taken for incapacitated or insane person or one under disability.

A recognizance which would be taken of a person but for his being a minor, insane or otherwise mentally incapacitated, may be taken of another person and without further surety, if such other person is deemed sufficient, for the performance by such minor, insane or otherwise incapacitated person, of the conditions of the recognizance.

History.
Code 1950, § 19.1-134; 1960, c. 366; 1975, c. 495; 1997, c. 801.

§ 19.2-142. Where recognizance taken out of court to be sent.

A person taking a recognizance out of court shall forthwith transmit it to the clerk of the court for appearance before which it is taken; or, if it be not for appearance before a court, to the clerk of the circuit court of the county or city in which it is taken; and it shall remain filed in the clerk's office.

History.
Code 1950, § 19.1-136; 1960, c. 366; 1975, c. 495.

§ 19.2-143. Where default recorded; process on recognizance; forfeiture on recognizance; when copy may be used; cash bond.

When a person, under recognizance in a case, either as party or witness, fails to perform the condition of appearance thereof, if it is to appear before a court of record, or a district court, a hearing shall be held upon reasonable notice to all parties affording them opportunity to show cause why the recognizance or any part thereof should not be forfeited. The show cause notice shall be issued within 45 days of the breach of the condition of appearance.

If the court finds the recognizance or any part thereof should be forfeited, the default shall be recorded therein, unless the defendant or juvenile is brought before the court within 150 days of the findings of default. After 150 days of the finding of default, his default shall be recorded therein, and if it is to appear before a district court, his default shall be entered by the judge of such court, on the case papers unless the defendant or juvenile has been delivered or appeared before the court. The process on any such forfeited recognizance shall be issued from the court before which the appearance was to be, and wherein such forfeiture was recorded or entered. Any such process issued by a judge shall be made returnable before, and tried by, such judge, who shall promptly transmit to the clerk of the circuit court of his county or city wherein deeds are recorded an abstract of such judgment as he may render thereon, which shall be forthwith docketed by the clerk of such court.

If the defendant or juvenile appears before or is delivered to the court within 24 months of the findings of default, the court shall remit any bond previously ordered forfeited by the courts, less such costs as the court may direct.

If it is brought to the attention of the court that the defendant or juvenile is incarcerated in another state or country within 48 months of the finding of default, thereby preventing his delivery or appearance within that period, the court shall remit any bond previously ordered forfeited. If the defendant or juvenile left the Commonwealth with the permission of the court, the bond shall be remitted without deduction of costs; otherwise, the cost of returning him to the Commonwealth shall be deducted from the bond.

Evidence that the defendant or juvenile is incarcerated or subject to court process in another jurisdiction on the day his appearance is required or a medical certificate from a duly licensed physician that the defendant was physically unable to so appear shall be considered evidence of good cause why the recognizance should not be forfeited.

If such recognizance so forfeited is not for such appearance, process thereon shall be issued from the court in which it was taken, or the court to which it was made returnable, and in a proceeding in one court on a recognizance entered in another a copy thereof shall be evidence in like manner as the original would be if it had been entered in the court wherein the proceeding is being had thereon.

However, when any defendant or juvenile who posted a cash bond and failed to appear is tried in his absence and is convicted, the court or judge trying the case shall first apply the cash bond, or so much thereof as may be necessary, to the payment of any fines or costs, or both, adjudged against the defendant or juvenile or imposed by law. Any remaining funds shall be forfeited without further notice. However, if a rehearing is granted, the court may remit part or all of such cash bond not applied ultimately to fines or costs, and order a refund of the same by the State Treasurer, or by the treasurer or director of finance of the locality, if the bond was collected by a locality pursuant to § 19.2-136, but only if good cause is shown.

If the defendant or juvenile posted a cash bond and failed to appear, but is not tried in his absence, the bond shall be forfeited promptly without further notice. However, if the defendant or juvenile appears in court within 60 days after the bond is forfeited, the judge may remit part or all of any bond previously forfeited and order a refund of the same by the State Treasurer, or by the treasurer or director of finance of the locality, if the bond was collected by a locality pursuant to § 19.2-136.

History.

Code 1950, § 19.1-137; 1960, c. 366; 1962, c. 499; 1970, c. 371; 1973, c. 409; 1975, c. 495; 1978, c. 755; 1979, c. 735; 1987, c. 670; 1988, c. 443; 1990, c. 624; 2000, c. 885; 2003, c. 840; 2005, c. 585; 2006, cc. 296, 316; 2011, c. 802; 2012, c. 408.

§ 19.2-144. Forfeiture of recognizance while in military or naval service.

If in any motion, action, suit or other proceeding made or taken in any court of this Commonwealth on a forfeited bail bond or forfeited recognizance, or to enforce the payment of the bond in any manner or any judgment thereon, or to forfeit any bail bond or recognizance, it appears that the person for whose alleged default such bail bond or recognizance was forfeited or judgment rendered, or such motion is made or proceeding taken, was prevented from complying with the condition of such bail bond or recognizance by reason of his having enlisted or been drafted in the army or navy of the United States, then judgment or decree on such motion, action, suit or other proceeding shall be given for the defendant.

History.

Code 1950, § 19.1-139; 1960, c. 366; 1975, c. 495; 1991, c. 581.

§ 19.2-145. How penalty remitted.

When in an action or on a motion to extend the period for enforcement of a judgment on a recognizance the penalty is adjudged to be forfeited the court may on an application of a defendant or juvenile remit the penalty or any part of it and render judgment on such terms and conditions as it deems reasonable.

History.

Code 1950, § 19.1-140; 1960, c. 366; 1975, c. 495; 1978, c. 755; 1982, c. 153.

§ 19.2-146. Defects in form of recognizance not to defeat action or judgment.

No action or judgment on a recognizance shall be defeated or arrested by reason of any defect in the form of the recognizance, if it appear to have been taken by a court or officer authorized to take it and be substantially sufficient.

History.

Code 1950, § 19.1-141; 1960, c. 366; 1975, c. 495.

§ 19.2-147. Docketing judgment on forfeited recognizance or bond.

Whenever a judgment is entered in any court of record in favor of the Commonwealth of Virginia upon a forfeited recognizance or bond, the clerk of the court in which the judgment is rendered shall certify an abstract of the same to the clerk of the circuit court of the county or city wherein the judgment debtor resides or of any city or county in which he may own real property, who shall thereupon enter the abstract of judgment upon his judgment docket.

History.

Code 1950, § 19.1-142; 1960, c. 366; 1975, c. 495; 1994, c. 432.

§ 19.2-148. Surety discharged on payment of amount, etc., into court.

A surety on a bond in a recognizance may, after default, pay into the court from which the process has issued, or may issue thereon, the amount for which he is bound, with such costs as the court may direct, and be thereupon discharged.

History.
Code 1950, § 19.1-143; 1960, c. 366; 1975, c. 495; 1991, c. 581.

§ 19.2-149. How surety on a bond in recognizance may surrender principal and be discharged from liability.

A bail bondsman or his licensed bail enforcement agent on a bond in a recognizance may at any time arrest his principal and surrender him to the court before which the recognizance was taken or before which such principal's appearance is required, or to the sheriff, sergeant or jailer of the county or city wherein the court before which such principal's appearance is required is located; in addition to the above authority, upon the application of the surety, the court, or the clerk thereof, before which the recognizance was taken, or before which such principal's appearance is required, or any magistrate shall issue a capias for the arrest of such principal, and such capias may be executed by such bail bondsman or his licensed bail enforcement agent, or by any sheriff, sergeant or police officer, and the person executing such capias shall deliver such principal and such capias to the sheriff or jailer of the county or the sheriff, sergeant or jailer of the city in which the appearance of such principal is required, and thereupon the surety or the property bail bondsman shall be discharged from liability for any act of the principal subsequent thereto. Such sheriff, sergeant or jailer shall thereafter deliver such capias to the clerk of such court, with his endorsement thereon acknowledging delivery of such principal to his custody. If a magistrate issues a capias pursuant to this section, the magistrate shall transmit a copy of the capias to the court before which such principal's appearance is required by the close of business on the next day that is not a Saturday, Sunday, legal holiday, or day on which the court is lawfully closed.

History.
Code 1950, § 19.1-144; 1960, c. 366; 1975, c. 495; 1991, c. 581; 2004, c. 460; 2015, c. 622.

§ 19.2-150. Proceeding when surety surrenders principal.

If the surrender is to the court, the court shall make such order as it deems proper; if the surrender is to a sheriff or jailer, the officer to whom the accused has been surrendered shall give the surety a certificate of the fact. After such surrender the person shall be treated in accordance with the provisions of Article 1 (§ 19.2-119 et seq.) of Chapter 9 of this title unless the court or judge thereof has reason to believe that no one or more conditions of release will reasonably assure that the person will not flee or pose a danger to any other person or to the community.

History.
Code 1950, § 19.1-145; 1960, c. 366; 1973, c. 485; 1975, c. 495; 1978, c. 755; 1999, cc. 829, 846.

ARTICLE 3.
SATISFACTION AND DISCHARGE.

§ 19.2-151. Satisfaction and discharge of assault and similar charges.

When a person is in jail or under a recognizance to answer a charge of assault and battery or other misdemeanor, or has been indicted for an assault and battery or other misdemeanor for which there is a remedy by civil action, unless the offense was committed (i) by or upon any law-enforcement officer, (ii) riotously in violation of §§ 18.2-404 to 18.2-407, (iii) against a family or household member in violation of § 18.2-57.2, or (iv) with intent to commit a felony, if the person injured appears before the court which made the commitment or took the recognizance, or before the court in which the indictment is pending, and acknowledges in writing that he has received satisfaction for the injury, the court may, in its discretion, by an order, supersede the commitment, discharge the recognizance, or dismiss the prosecution, upon payment by the defendant of costs accrued to the Commonwealth or any of its officers.

History.
Code 1950, § 19.1-18; 1960, c. 366; 1968, c. 639; 1975, c. 495; 1997, c. 532; 1999, c. 963.

§ 19.2-152. Order discharging recognizance or superseding commitment; judgment for costs.

Every order discharging a recognizance shall be filed with the clerk before the session of the court at which the party was to appear. Where a person is held under a commitment, any order superseding a commitment shall be delivered to the jailer, who shall forthwith discharge the witnesses, if any, and the accused or juvenile, and judgment against the accused or juvenile shall be entered in the court for the costs of the prosecution.

History.
Code 1950, § 19.1-19; 1960, c. 366; 1975, c. 495; 1978, c. 755.

ARTICLE 4.
BAIL BONDSMEN.

§§ 19.2-152.1 through 19.2-152.1:7: Repealed by Acts 2004, c. 460, effective July 1, 2005.

ARTICLE 5.
PRETRIAL SERVICES ACT.

§ 19.2-152.2. Purpose; establishment of pretrial services and services agencies.

It is the purpose of this article to provide more effective protection of society by establishing pretrial services agencies that will assist judicial officers in discharging their duties pursuant to Article 1 (§ 19.2-119 et seq.) of Chapter 9 of this title. Such agencies are intended to provide better information and services for use by judicial officers in determining the risk to public safety and the assurance of appearance of persons age 18 or over or persons under the age of 18 who have been transferred for trial as adults held in custody and charged with an offense, other than an offense punishable by death, who are pending trial or hearing. Any city, county or combination thereof may establish a pretrial services agency and any city, county or combination thereof required to submit a community-based corrections plan pursuant to § 53.1-82.1 shall establish a pretrial services agency.

History.
1994, 2nd Sp. Sess., cc. 1, 2; 1999, cc. 829, 846; 2004, c. 378; 2007, c. 133.

§ 19.2-152.3. Department of Criminal Justice Services to prescribe standards; biennial plan.

The Department of Criminal Justice Services shall prescribe standards for the development, implementation, operation and evaluation of services authorized by this article. The Department of Criminal Justice Services shall develop risk assessment and other instruments to be used by pretrial services agencies in assisting judicial officers in discharging their duties pursuant to Article 1 (§ 19.2-119 et seq.) of Chapter 9 of this title. Any city, county or combination thereof which establishes pretrial services pursuant to this article shall submit a biennial plan to the Department of Criminal Justice Services for review and approval.

History.
1994, 2nd Sp. Sess., cc. 1, 2; 1999, cc. 829, 846; 2007, c. 133.

§ 19.2-152.4. Mandated services.

Any city, county or combination thereof which elects or is required to establish a pretrial services agency shall provide all information and services for use by judicial officers as set forth in Article 1 (§ 19.2-119 et seq.) of Chapter 9 of this title.

History.
1994, 2nd Sp. Sess., cc. 1, 2; 1999, cc. 829, 846; 2007, c. 133.

§ 19.2-152.4:1. Form of oath of office for local pretrial services officer; authorization to seek capias.

Every pretrial services officer who is an employee of a local pretrial services agency established by any city, county or combination thereof or operated pursuant to this article shall take an oath of office as prescribed in § 49-1 and to provide services pursuant to the requirements of this article before entering the duties of his office. The oath of office shall be taken before any general district or circuit court judge in any county or city which has established services for use by judicial officers pursuant to this article.

In addition, any officer of a pretrial services agency established or operated pursuant to this article may seek a capias from any judicial officer for the arrest of any person under the agency's custody and supervision for failure to comply with any conditions of release imposed by a judicial officer, for failure to comply with the conditions of pretrial supervision as established by a pretrial services agency, or when there is reason to believe that the person will fail to appear, will leave, or has left the jurisdiction to avoid prosecution.

History.
2000, c. 1040; 2007, c. 133.

§ 19.2-152.4:2. Confidentiality of records of and reports on adult persons under investigation by or in the custody or supervision of a local pretrial services agency.

A. Any pretrial investigation report prepared by a local pretrial services officer is confidential and is exempt from the Virginia Freedom of Information Act (§ 2.2-3700 et seq.). Such reports shall be filed as a part of the case record. Such reports shall be sealed upon receipt by the court and made available only by court order; except that such reports shall be available upon request to (i) any criminal justice agency, as defined in § 9.1-101, of this or any other state or of the United States; (ii) any agency where the accused is referred for assessment or treatment; or (iii) counsel for the person who is the subject of the report.

B. Any report on the progress of an accused under the supervision or custody of a pretrial services agency and any information relative to the identity of or inferring personal characteristics of an accused, including demographic information, diagnostic summaries, records of office visits, medical, substance abuse, psychiatric or psychological records or information, substance abuse screening, assessment and testing information, and other sensitive information not explicitly classified as criminal history record information, is exempt from the Virginia Freedom of Information Act (§ 2.2-3700 et seq.). However, such information may be disseminated to criminal justice agencies as defined in § 9.1-101 in the discretion of the custodian of these records.

History.
2002, c. 769; 2007, c. 133.

§ 19.2-152.4:3. Duties and responsibilities of local pretrial services officers.

A. Each local pretrial services officer, for the jurisdictions served, shall:

1. Investigate and interview defendants arrested on state and local warrants and who are detained in jails located in jurisdictions served by the agency while awaiting a hearing before any court that is considering or reconsidering bail, at initial appearance, advisement or arraignment, or at other subsequent hearings;

2. Present a pretrial investigation report with recommendations to assist courts in discharging their duties related to granting or reconsidering bail;

3. Supervise and assist all defendants residing within the jurisdictions served and placed on pretrial supervision by any judicial officer within the jurisdictions to ensure compliance with the terms and conditions of bail;

4. Conduct random drug and alcohol tests on any defendant under supervision for whom a judicial officer has ordered testing or who has been required to refrain from excessive use of alcohol or use of any illegal drug or controlled substance or other defendant-specific condition of bail related to alcohol or substance abuse;

5. Seek a capias from any judicial officer pursuant to § 19.2-152.4:1 for any defendant placed under supervision or the custody of the agency who fails to comply with the conditions of bail or supervision, when continued liberty or noncompliance presents a risk of flight, a risk to public safety or risk to the defendant;

6. Seek an order to show cause why the defendant should not be required to appear before the court in those cases requiring a subsequent hearing before the court;

7. Provide defendant-based information to assist any law-enforcement officer with the return to custody of defendants placed on supervision for which a capias has been sought; and

8. Keep such records and make such reports as required by the Commonwealth of Virginia Department of Criminal Justice Services.

B. Each local pretrial services officer, for the jurisdictions served, may provide the following optional services, as appropriate and when available resources permit:

1. Conduct, subject to court approval, drug and alcohol screenings, or tests at investigation pursuant to subsection B of § 19.2-123 or following release to supervision, and conduct or facilitate the preparation of screenings or assessments or both pursuant to state approved protocols;

2. Facilitate placement of defendants in a substance abuse education or treatment program or services or other education or treatment service when ordered as a condition of bail;

3. Sign for the custody of any defendant investigated by a pretrial services officer, and released by a court to pretrial supervision as the sole term and condition of bail or when combined with an unsecured bond;

4. Provide defendant information and investigation services for those who are detained in jails located in jurisdictions served by the agency and are awaiting an initial bail hearing before a magistrate;

5. Supervise defendants placed by any judicial officer on home electronic monitoring as a condition of bail and supervision;

6. Prepare, for defendants investigated, the financial statement-eligibility determination form for indigent defense services; and

7. Subject to approved procedures and if so requested by the court, coordinate for defendants investigated, services for court-appointed counsel and for interpreters for foreign-language speaking and hearing-impaired defendants.

History.
2003, c. 603; 2007, c. 133; 2008, cc. 551, 691.

§ 19.2-152.5. Community criminal justice boards.

Each city, county or combination thereof establishing a pretrial services agency shall also establish a community criminal justice board pursuant to § 9.1-178.

History.
1994, 2nd Sp. Sess., cc. 1, 2; 2007, c. 133.

§ 19.2-152.6. Withdrawal from pretrial services.

Any participating city or county may, at the beginning of any calendar quarter, by ordinance or resolution of its governing authority, notify the Department of Criminal Justice Services of its intention to withdraw from participation in pretrial services. Such withdrawal shall be effective as of the last day of the quarter in which such notice is given.

History.
1994, 2nd Sp. Sess., cc. 1, 2; 2007, c. 133.

§ 19.2-152.7. Funding; failure to comply.

Counties and cities shall be required to establish a pretrial services agency only to the extent funded by the Commonwealth through the general appropriation act. The Department of Criminal Justice Services shall periodically review each agency established under this article to determine compliance with the submitted plan and operating standards. If the Department determines that any agency is not in substantial compliance with the submitted plan or standards, the Department may suspend all or any portion of financial aid made available to the locality for purposes of this article until there is compliance.

History.
1994, 2nd Sp. Sess., cc. 1, 2; 2007, c. 133.

CHAPTER 9.1.
PROTECTIVE ORDERS.

Section

§ 19.2-152.7:1. Definitions.

As used in this chapter:

"Act of violence, force, or threat" means any act involving violence, force, or threat that results in bodily injury or places one in reasonable apprehension of death, sexual assault, or bodily injury. Such act includes, but is not limited to, any forceful detention, stalking, criminal sexual assault in violation of Article 7 (§ 18.2-61 et seq.) of Chapter 4 of Title 18.2, or any criminal offense that results in bodily injury or places one in reasonable apprehension of death, sexual assault, or bodily injury.

History.
2011, cc. 445, 480.

§ 19.2-152.8. Emergency protective orders authorized.

A. Any judge of a circuit court, general district court, juvenile and domestic relations district court or magistrate may issue a written or oral ex parte emergency protective order pursuant to this section in order to protect the health or safety of any person.

B. When a law-enforcement officer or an alleged victim asserts under oath to a judge or magistrate that such person is being or has been subjected to an act of violence, force, or threat and on that assertion or other evidence the judge or magistrate finds that (i) there is probable danger of a further such act being committed by the respondent against the alleged victim or (ii) a petition or warrant for the arrest of the respondent has been issued for any criminal offense resulting from the commission of an act of violence, force, or threat, the judge or magistrate shall issue an ex parte emergency protective order imposing one or more of the following conditions on the respondent:

1. Prohibiting acts of violence, force, or threat or criminal offenses resulting in injury to person or property;

2. Prohibiting such contacts by the respondent with the alleged victim or the alleged victim's family or household members, including prohibiting the respondent from being in the physical presence of the alleged victim or the alleged victim's family or household members, as the judge or magistrate deems necessary to protect the safety of such persons;

3. Such other conditions as the judge or magistrate deems necessary to prevent (i) acts of violence, force, or threat, (ii) criminal offenses resulting in injury to person or property, or (iii) communication or other contact of any kind by the respondent; and

4. Granting the petitioner the possession of any companion animal as defined in § 3.2-6500 if such petitioner meets the definition of owner in § 3.2-6500.

C. An emergency protective order issued pursuant to this section shall expire at 11:59 p.m. on the third day following issuance. If the expiration occurs on a day that the court is not in session, the emergency protective order shall be extended until 11:59 p.m. on the next day that the court which issued the order is in session. The respondent may at any time file a motion with the court requesting a hearing to dissolve or modify the order. The hearing on the motion shall be given precedence on the docket of the court.

D. A law-enforcement officer may request an emergency protective order pursuant to this section and, if the person in need of protection is physically or mentally incapable of filing a petition pursuant to § 19.2-152.9 or 19.2-152.10, may request the extension of an emergency protective order for an additional period of time not to exceed three days after expiration of the original order. The request for an emergency protective order or extension of an order may be made orally, in person or by electronic means, and the judge of a circuit court, general district court, or juvenile and domestic relations district court or a magistrate may issue an oral emergency protective order. An oral emergency protective order issued pursuant to this section shall be reduced to writing, by the law-enforcement officer requesting the order or the magistrate, on a preprinted form approved and provided by the Supreme Court of Virginia. The completed form shall include a statement of the grounds for the order asserted by the officer or the alleged victim of such crime.

E. The court or magistrate shall forthwith, but in all cases no later than the end of the business day on which the order was issued, enter and transfer electronically to the Virginia Criminal Information Network the respondent's identifying information and the name, date of birth, sex, and race of each protected person provided to the court or magistrate. A copy of an emergency protective order issued pursuant to this section containing any such identifying information shall be forwarded forthwith to the primary law-enforcement agency responsible for service and entry of protective orders. Upon receipt of the order by the primary law-enforcement agency, the agency shall forthwith verify and enter any modification as necessary to the identifying information and other appropriate information required by the Department of State Police into the Virginia Criminal Information Network established and maintained by the Department pursuant to Chapter 2 (§ 52-12 et seq.) of Title 52 and the order shall be served forthwith upon the respondent and due return made to the court. However, if the order is issued by the circuit court, the clerk of the circuit court shall forthwith forward an attested copy of the order containing the respondent's identifying information and the name, date of birth, sex, and race of each protected person provided to the court to the primary law-enforcement agency providing service and entry of protective orders and upon receipt of the order, the primary law-enforcement agency shall enter the name of the person subject to the order and other appropriate information required by the Department of State Police into the Virginia Criminal Information Network established and maintained by the Department pursuant to Chapter 2 (§ 52-12 et seq.) of Title 52 and the order shall be served forthwith upon the respondent. Upon service, the agency making service shall enter the date and time of service and other appropriate information required into the Virginia Criminal Information Network and make due return to the court. One copy of the order shall be given to the alleged victim of such crime. The judge or magistrate who issues an oral order pursuant to an electronic request by a law-enforcement officer shall verify the written order to determine whether the officer who reduced it to writing accurately transcribed the contents of the oral order. The original copy shall be filed with the clerk of the appropriate district court within five business days of the issuance of the order. If the order is later dissolved or modified, a copy of the dissolution or modification order shall also be attested, forwarded forthwith to the primary law-enforcement agency responsible for service and entry of protective orders, and upon receipt of the order by the primary law-enforcement agency, the agency shall forthwith verify and enter any modification as necessary to the identifying information and other appropriate information required by the Department of State Police into the Virginia Criminal Information Network as described above and the order shall be served forthwith and due return made to the court. Upon request, the clerk shall provide the alleged victim of such crime with information regarding the date and time of service.

F. The issuance of an emergency protective order shall not be considered evidence of any wrongdoing by the respondent.

G. As used in this section, a "law-enforcement officer" means any (i) person who is a full-time or part-time employee of a police department or sheriff's office which is part of or administered by the Commonwealth or any political subdivision thereof and who is responsible for the prevention and detection of crime and the enforcement of the penal, traffic or highway laws of the Commonwealth and (ii) member of an auxiliary police force established pursuant to § 15.2-1731. Part-time employees are compensated officers who are not full-time employees as defined by the employing police department or sheriff's office.

H. Neither a law-enforcement agency, the attorney for the Commonwealth, a court nor the clerk's office, nor any employee of them, may disclose, except among themselves, the residential address, telephone number, or place of employment of the person protected by the order or that of the family of such person, except to the extent that disclosure is (i) required by law or the Rules of the Supreme Court, (ii) necessary for law-enforcement purposes, or (iii) permitted by the court for good cause.

I. As used in this section:

"Copy" includes a facsimile copy.

"Physical presence" includes (i) intentionally maintaining direct visual contact with the petitioner or (ii) unreasonably being within 100 feet from the petitioner's residence or place of employment.

J. No fee shall be charged for filing or serving any petition pursuant to this section.

K. No emergency protective order shall be issued pursuant to this section against a law-enforcement officer for any action arising out of the lawful performance of his duties.

History.

1997, c. 831; 1998, cc. 569, 684; 1999, c. 371; 2001, c. 474; 2002, cc. 507, 706, 810, 818; 2003, c. 730; 2008, cc. 73, 246; 2009, cc. 341, 732; 2011, cc. 445, 480; 2012, cc. 146, 637, 827; 2014, c. 346; 2016, c. 455.

§ 19.2-152.9. Preliminary protective orders.

A. Upon the filing of a petition alleging that (i) the petitioner is or has been, within a reasonable period of time, subjected to an act of violence, force, or threat, or (ii) a petition or warrant has been issued for the arrest of the alleged perpetrator for any criminal offense resulting from the commission of an act of violence, force, or threat, the court may issue a preliminary protective order against the alleged perpetrator in order to protect the health and safety of the petitioner or any family or household member of the petitioner. The order may be issued in an ex parte proceeding upon good cause shown when the petition is supported by an affidavit or sworn testimony before the judge or intake officer. Immediate and present danger of any act of violence, force, or threat or evidence sufficient to establish probable cause that an act of violence, force, or threat has recently occurred shall constitute good cause.

A preliminary protective order may include any one or more of the following conditions to be imposed on the respondent:

1. Prohibiting acts of violence, force, or threat or criminal offenses that may result in injury to person or property;

2. Prohibiting such other contacts by the respondent with the petitioner or the petitioner's family or household members as the court deems necessary for the health and safety of such persons;

3. Such other conditions as the court deems necessary to prevent (i) acts of violence, force, or threat, (ii) criminal offenses that may result in injury to person or property, or (iii) communication or other contact of any kind by the respondent; and

4. Granting the petitioner the possession of any companion animal as defined in § 3.2-6500 if such petitioner meets the definition of owner in § 3.2-6500.

B. The court shall forthwith, but in all cases no later than the end of the business day on which the order was issued, enter and transfer electronically to the Virginia Criminal Information Network the respondent's identifying information and the name, date of birth, sex, and race of each protected person provided to the court. A copy of a preliminary protective order containing any such identifying information shall be forwarded forthwith to the primary law-enforcement agency responsible for service and entry of protective orders. Upon receipt of the order by the primary law-enforcement agency, the agency shall forthwith verify and enter any modification as necessary to the identifying information and other appropriate information required by the Department of State Police into the Virginia Criminal Information Network established and maintained by the Department pursuant to Chapter 2 (§ 52-12 et seq.) of Title 52 and the order shall be served forthwith on the alleged perpetrator in person as provided in § 16.1-264, and due return made to the court. However, if the order is issued by the circuit court, the clerk of the circuit court shall forthwith forward an attested copy of the order containing the respondent's identifying information and the name, date of birth, sex, and race of each protected person provided to the court to the primary law-enforcement agency providing service and entry of protective orders and upon receipt of the order, the primary law-enforcement agency shall enter the name of the person subject to the order and other appropriate information required by the Department of State Police into the Virginia Criminal Information Network established and maintained by the Department pursuant to Chapter 2 (§ 52-12 et seq.) of Title 52 and the order shall be served forthwith on the alleged perpetrator in person as provided in § 16.1-264. Upon service, the agency making service shall enter the date and time of service and other appropriate information required by the Department of State Police into the Virginia Criminal Information Network and make due return to the court. The preliminary order shall specify a date for the full hearing. The hearing shall be held within 15 days of the issuance of the preliminary order. If the respondent fails to appear at this hearing because the respondent was not personally served, the court may extend the protective order for a period not to exceed six months. The extended protective order shall be served as soon as possible on the respondent. However, upon motion of the respondent and for good cause shown, the court may continue the hearing. The preliminary order shall remain in effect until the hearing. Upon request after the order is issued, the clerk shall provide the petitioner with a copy of the order and information regarding the date and time of service. The order shall further specify that either party may at any time file a motion with the court requesting a hearing to dissolve or modify the order. The hearing on the motion shall be given precedence on the docket of the court.

Upon receipt of the return of service or other proof of service pursuant to subsection C of § 16.1-264, the clerk shall forthwith forward an attested copy of the preliminary protective order to primary law-enforcement agency and the agency shall forthwith verify and enter any modification as necessary into the Virginia Criminal Information Network as described above. If the order is later dissolved or modified, a copy of the dissolution or modification order shall also be attested, forwarded forthwith to the primary law-enforcement agency responsible for service and entry of protective orders, and upon receipt of the order by the primary law-enforcement agency, the agency shall forthwith verify and enter any modification as necessary to the identifying information and other appropriate information required by the Department of State Police into the Virginia Criminal Information Network as described above and the order shall be served forthwith and due return made to the court.

C. The preliminary order is effective upon personal service on the alleged perpetrator. Except as otherwise provided, a violation of the order shall constitute contempt of court.

D. At a full hearing on the petition, the court may issue a protective order pursuant to § 19.2-152.10 if the court finds that the petitioner has proven the allegation that the petitioner is or has been, within a reasonable period of time, subjected to an act of violence, force, or threat by a preponderance of the evidence.

E. No fees shall be charged for filing or serving petitions pursuant to this section.

F. Neither a law-enforcement agency, the attorney for the Commonwealth, a court nor the clerk's office, nor any employee of them, may disclose, except among themselves, the residential address, telephone number, or place of employment of the person protected by the order or that of the family of such person, except to the extent that disclosure is (i) required by law or the Rules of the Supreme Court, (ii) necessary for law-enforcement purposes, or (iii) permitted by the court for good cause.

G. As used in this section, "copy" includes a facsimile copy.

History.

1997, c. 831; 1998, cc. 569, 684; 1999, c. 371; 2001, c. 101; 2002, cc. 507, 810, 818; 2003, c. 730; 2008, cc. 73, 128, 246; 2009, cc. 341, 732; 2011, cc. 445, 480; 2014, c. 346.

§ 19.2-152.10. Protective order.

A. The court may issue a protective order pursuant to this chapter to protect the health and safety of the petitioner and family or household members of a petitioner upon (i) the issuance of a petition or warrant for, or a conviction of, any criminal offense resulting from the commission of an act of violence, force, or threat or (ii) a hearing held pursuant to subsection D of § 19.2-152.9. A protective order issued under this section may include any one or more of the following conditions to be imposed on the respondent:

1. Prohibiting acts of violence, force, or threat or criminal offenses that may result in injury to person or property;
2. Prohibiting such contacts by the respondent with the petitioner or family or household members of the petitioner as the court deems necessary for the health or safety of such persons;
3. Any other relief necessary to prevent (i) acts of violence, force, or threat, (ii) criminal offenses that may result in injury to person or property, or (iii) communication or other contact of any kind by the respondent; and
4. Granting the petitioner the possession of any companion animal as defined in § 3.2-6500 if such petitioner meets the definition of owner in § 3.2-6500.

B. The protective order may be issued for a specified period of time up to a maximum of two years. The protective order shall expire at 11:59 p.m. on the last day specified or at 11:59 p.m. on the last day of the two-year period if no date is specified. Prior to the expiration of the protective order, a petitioner may file a written motion requesting a hearing to extend the order. Proceedings to extend a protective order shall be given precedence on the docket of the court. The court may extend the protective order for a period not longer than two years to protect the health and safety of the petitioner or persons who are family or household members of the petitioner at the time the request for an extension is made. The extension of the protective order shall expire at 11:59 p.m. on the last day specified or at 11:59 p.m. on the last day of the two-year period if no date is specified. Nothing herein shall limit the number of extensions that may be requested or issued.

C. A copy of the protective order shall be served on the respondent and provided to the petitioner as soon as possible. The court, including a circuit court if the circuit court issued the order, shall forthwith, but in all cases no later than the end of the business day on which the order was issued, enter and transfer electronically to the Virginia Criminal Information Network the respondent's identifying information and the name, date of birth, sex, and race of each protected person provided to the court and shall forthwith forward the attested copy of the protective order and containing any such identifying information to the primary law-enforcement agency responsible for service and entry of protective orders. Upon receipt of the order by the primary law-enforcement agency, the agency shall forthwith verify and enter any modification as necessary to the identifying information and other appropriate information required by the Department of State Police into the Virginia Criminal Information Network established and maintained by the Department pursuant to Chapter 2 (§ 52-12 et seq.) of Title 52 and the order shall be served forthwith upon the respondent and due return made to the court. Upon service, the agency making service shall enter the date and time of service and other appropriate information required into the Virginia Criminal Information Network and make due return to the court. If the order is later dissolved or modified, a copy of the dissolution or modification order shall also be attested, forwarded forthwith to the primary law-enforcement agency responsible for service and entry of protective orders, and upon receipt of the order by the primary law-enforcement agency, the agency shall forthwith verify and enter any modification as necessary to the identifying information and other appropriate information required by the Department of State Police into the Virginia Criminal Information Network as described above and the order shall be served forthwith and due return made to the court.

D. Except as otherwise provided, a violation of a protective order issued under this section shall constitute contempt of court.

E. The court may assess costs and attorneys' fees against either party regardless of whether an order of protection has been issued as a result of a full hearing.

F. Any judgment, order or decree, whether permanent or temporary, issued by a court of appropriate jurisdiction in another state, the United States or any of its territories, possessions or Commonwealths, the District of Columbia or by any tribal court of appropriate jurisdiction for the purpose of preventing violent or threatening acts or harassment against or contact or communication with or physical proximity to another person, including any of the conditions specified in subsection A, shall be accorded full faith and credit and enforced in the Commonwealth as if it were an order of the Commonwealth, provided reasonable notice and opportunity to be heard were given by the issuing jurisdiction to the person against whom the order is sought to be enforced sufficient to protect such person's due process rights and consistent with federal law. A person entitled to protection under such a foreign order may file the order in any appropriate district court by filing with the court, an attested or exemplified copy of the order. Upon such a filing, the clerk shall forthwith forward an attested copy of the order to the primary law-enforcement agency responsible for service and entry of protective orders which shall, upon receipt, enter the name of the person subject to the order and other appropriate information required by the Department of State Police into the Virginia Criminal Information Network established and maintained by the Department pursuant to Chapter 2 (§ 52-12 et seq.) of Title 52. Where practical, the court may transfer information electronically to the Virginia Criminal Information Network.

Upon inquiry by any law-enforcement agency of the Commonwealth, the clerk shall make a copy available of any foreign order filed with that court. A law-enforcement officer may, in the performance of his duties, rely upon a copy of a foreign protective order or other suitable evidence which has been provided to him by any source and may also rely upon the statement of any person protected by the order that the order remains in effect.

G. Either party may at any time file a written motion with the court requesting a hearing to dissolve or modify the order. Proceedings to modify or dissolve a protective order shall be given precedence on the docket of the court.

H. Neither a law-enforcement agency, the attorney for the Commonwealth, a court nor the clerk's office, nor any employee of them, may disclose, except among themselves, the residential address, telephone number, or place of employment of the person protected by the order or that of the family of such person, except to the extent that disclosure is (i) required by law or the Rules of the Supreme Court, (ii) necessary for law-enforcement purposes, or (iii) permitted by the court for good cause.

I. No fees shall be charged for filing or serving petitions pursuant to this section.

J. As used in this section:

"Copy" includes a facsimile copy; and

"Protective order" includes an initial, modified or extended protective order.

History.

1997, c. 831; 1998, cc. 569, 684; 1999, c. 371; 2002, cc. 507, 810, 818; 2003, c. 730; 2008, cc. 73, 246; 2009, cc. 341, 732; 2010, cc. 425, 468; 2011, cc. 445, 480; 2012, cc. 152, 261; 2014, c. 346.

§ 19.2-152.11. Venue for protective orders.

Proceedings in which a protective order is sought pursuant to this chapter shall be commenced where (i) either party has his principal residence; (ii) the act of violence, force, or threat by the respondent against the petitioner occurred; or (iii) a protective order was issued if, at the time the proceeding is commenced, the order is in effect to protect the petitioner or a family or household member of the petitioner.

History.

2012, c. 637.

§ 19.2-152.12. Compensation for required representation of respondents.

Notwithstanding any other provision of law, when, in a proceeding pursuant to this chapter, representation of a respondent by counsel is required under the Servicemembers Civil Relief Act (50 U.S.C. § 3901 et seq.) or a guardian ad litem is required by law and there is no other provision for the compensation of counsel or a guardian ad litem, the court may order such counsel or guardian ad litem to be compensated for services pursuant to § 19.2-163.

History.

2015, cc. 545, 556.

CHAPTER 10.

DISABILITY OF JUDGE OR ATTORNEY FOR COMMONWEALTH; COURT-APPOINTED COUNSEL; INTERPRETERS; TRANSCRIPTS.

Article 1.

Disability of Judge.

Article 2.

Disability of Attorney for Commonwealth.

Article 3.

Appointment of Attorney for Accused.

Article 3.1.

Indigent Defense.

ARTICLE 1.

DISABILITY OF JUDGE.

§ 19.2-153. When judge cannot sit on trial; how another judge procured to try the case.

When the judge of a circuit court in which a prosecution is pending is connected with the accused or party injured, or is so situated in respect to the case as in his opinion to render it improper that he should preside at the trial, or if he has rejected a plea bargain agreement submitted by both parties and the parties do not agree that he may hear the case, he shall enter the fact of record and the clerk of the court shall at once certify this fact to the Chief Justice of the Supreme Court and thereupon another judge shall be appointed, in the manner prescribed by § 17.1-105, to preside at the trial.

History.

Code 1950, § 19.1-7; 1960, c. 366; 1975, c. 495; 1984, c. 585; 1985, c. 253.

§ 19.2-154. Death or disability of judge during trial; how another judge procured to continue with trial.

If by reason of death, sickness or other disability the judge who presided at a criminal jury trial is unable to proceed with and finish the trial, another judge of that court or a judge designated by the Chief Justice of the Supreme Court or by a justice designated by him for that purpose, may proceed with and finish the trial or, in his discretion, may grant and preside at a new trial. If by reason of such disability, the judge who presided at any trial is unable to perform the duties to be performed by the court after a finding of guilty by the jury or the court, another judge of that court, or a judge designated as provided in the preceding sentence, may perform those duties or, in his discretion, may grant and preside at a new trial. Before proceeding with the trial or performing such duties, such judge shall certify that he has familiarized himself with the record of the trial.

History.

1975, c. 495.

ARTICLE 2.

DISABILITY OF ATTORNEY FOR COMMONWEALTH.

§ 19.2-155. Disqualification or temporary disability of attorney for Commonwealth; appointment of substitute; powers, duties and compensation of such appointee.

If the attorney for the Commonwealth of any county or city is connected by blood or marriage with the accused, or is so situated with respect to such accused as to render it improper, in his opinion, concurred in by the judge, for him to act, or if such attorney for the Commonwealth of any county or city is unable to act, or to attend to his official duties as attorney for the Commonwealth, due to sickness, disability or other reason of a temporary nature, then upon notification by such attorney for the Commonwealth, or upon the certificate of his attending physician, or the clerk of the court, which fact shall be entered of record, the judge of the circuit court shall appoint from another jurisdiction an attorney for the Commonwealth or an assistant attorney for the Commonwealth, with the consent of such attorney for the Commonwealth or assistant, who is not authorized by law to engage in private practice for such case or cases, term or terms of court, or period or periods of time, as may be necessary or desirable, and the same to be forthwith entered of record. However, if the circuit court determines that the appointment of such attorney for the Commonwealth or such assistant attorney for the Commonwealth is not appropriate or that such an attorney or assistant is unavailable, or for other good cause, then the circuit court may appoint an attorney-at-law who shall be compensated pursuant to § 19.2-332. Such appointee shall act in place of, and otherwise perform the duties and exercise the powers of, such disqualified or disabled attorney for the Commonwealth, in regard to such case or cases, for the term or terms of the court, or the period or periods of time, for which the appointment and designation is made, or until the disqualified or disabled attorney for the Commonwealth shall again be able to attend to his duties as such. Nothing herein shall prevent a court from appointing as a special assistant attorney for the Commonwealth, without additional compensation, an attorney employed by a state agency when such appointment is requested by the attorney for the Commonwealth and the court determines such appointment will aid in the prosecution of a particular case or cases.

An attorney for the Commonwealth or assistant attorney for the Commonwealth who is required by law to devote full time to his duties as such shall not receive additional compensation for services rendered on appointment pursuant to this section. However, such attorney for the Commonwealth or assistant may receive reimbursement for actual expenses incurred, as approved by the Compensation Board to be paid by the Compensation Board, provided such expenses are not otherwise reimbursed by the county or city which he is elected or appointed to serve or by the Compensation Board.

History.

Code 1950, §§ 19.1-9, 19.1-10; 1960, c. 366; 1975, c. 495; 1983, c. 362; 1985, c. 321; 1996, c. 968.

§ 19.2-156. Prolonged absence of attorney for Commonwealth.

If it shall be necessary for the attorney for the Commonwealth of any county or city to absent himself for a prolonged period of time from the performance of the duties of his office, then, upon notification by such attorney for the Commonwealth, or by the court on its own motion, and the facts being entered of record, the judge of the circuit court shall appoint an attorney-at-law as acting attorney for the Commonwealth to serve for such length of time as may be necessary. Such acting attorney for the Commonwealth shall act in place of and otherwise perform the duties and exercise the powers of such regular attorney for the Commonwealth, and while so acting shall receive the salary and allowance for expenses fixed by the State Compensation Board for such regular attorney for the Commonwealth, who during such length of time shall not receive any such salary or allowance.

History.

Code 1950, § 19.1-11; 1960, c. 366; 1975, c. 495.

ARTICLE 3.

APPOINTMENT OF ATTORNEY FOR ACCUSED.

§ 19.2-157. Duty of court when accused appears without counsel.

Except as may otherwise be provided in §§ 16.1-266 through 16.1-268, whenever a person charged with a criminal offense the penalty for which may be death or confinement in the state correctional facility or jail, including charges for revocation of suspension of imposition or execution of sentence or probation, appears before any court without being represented by counsel, the court shall inform him of his right to counsel. The accused shall be allowed a reasonable opportunity to employ counsel or, if appropriate, the statement of indigence provided for in § 19.2-159 may be executed.

History.

Code 1950, §§ 19.1-241.1, 19.1-241.7; 1964, c. 657; 1966, c. 460; 1973, c. 316; 1975, c. 495; 1978, c. 362.

§ 19.2-158. When person not free on bail shall be informed of right to counsel and amount of bail.

Every person charged with an offense described in § 19.2-157, who is not free on bail or otherwise, shall be brought before the judge of a court not of record, unless the circuit court issues process commanding the presence of the person, in which case the person shall be brought before the circuit court, on the first day on which such court sits after the person is charged, at which time the judge shall inform the accused of the amount of his bail and his right to counsel. If the court not of record sits on a day prior to the scheduled sitting of the court which issued process, the person shall be brought before the court not of record. The court shall also hear and consider motions by the person or Commonwealth relating to bail or conditions of release pursuant to Article 1 (§ 19.2-119 et seq.) of Chapter 9 of this title. Absent good cause shown, a hearing on bail or conditions of release shall be held as soon as practicable but in no event later than three calendar days, excluding Saturdays, Sundays, and legal holidays, following the making of such motion.

No hearing on the charges against the accused shall be had until the foregoing conditions have been complied with, and the accused shall be allowed a reasonable opportunity to employ counsel of his own choice, or, if appropriate, the statement of indigence provided for in § 19.2-159 may be executed.

History.

Code 1950, §§ 19.1-241.2, 19.1-241.8; 1964, c. 657; 1966, c. 460; 1973, c. 316; 1975, c. 495; 1998, c. 773; 1999, cc. 829, 846; 2014, c. 515.

§ 19.2-159. Determination of indigency; guidelines; statement of indigence; appointment of counsel.

A. If the accused shall claim that he is indigent, and the charge against him is a criminal offense which may be punishable by death or confinement in the state correctional facility or jail, subject to the provisions of § 19.2-160, the court shall determine from oral examination of the accused or other competent evidence whether or not the accused is indigent within the contemplation of law pursuant to the guidelines set forth in this section.

B. In making its finding, the court shall determine whether or not the accused is a current recipient of a state or federally funded public assistance program for the indigent. If the accused is a current recipient of such a program and does not waive his right to counsel or retain counsel on his own behalf, he shall be presumed eligible for the appointment of counsel. This presumption shall be rebuttable where the court finds that a more thorough examination of the financial resources of the defendant is necessary. If the accused shall claim to be indigent and is not presumptively eligible under the provisions of this section, then a thorough examination of the financial resources of the accused shall be made with consideration given to the following:

1. The net income of the accused, which shall include his total salary and wages minus deductions required by law. The court also shall take into account income and amenities from other sources including but not limited to social security funds, union funds, veteran's benefits, other regular support from an absent family member, public or private employee pensions, dividends, interests, rents, estates, trusts, or gifts.

2. All assets of the accused which are convertible into cash within a reasonable period of time without causing substantial hardship or jeopardizing the ability of the accused to maintain home and employment. Assets shall include all cash on hand as well as in checking and savings accounts, stocks, bonds, certificates of deposit, and tax refunds. All personal property owned by the accused which is readily convertible into cash shall be considered, except property exempt from attachment. Any real estate owned by the accused shall be considered in terms of the amounts which could be raised by a loan on the property. For purposes of eligibility determination, the income, assets, and expenses of the spouse, if any, who is a member of the accused's household, shall be considered, unless the spouse was the victim of the offense or offenses allegedly committed by the accused.

3. Any exceptional expenses of the accused and his family which would, in all probability, prohibit him from being able to secure private counsel. Such items shall include but not be limited to costs for medical care, family support obligations, and child care payments.

The available funds of the accused shall be calculated as the sum of his total income and assets less the exceptional expenses as provided in paragraph 3 above. If the accused does not waive his right to counsel or retain counsel on his own behalf, counsel shall be appointed for the accused if his available funds are equal to or below 125 percent of the federal poverty income guidelines prescribed for the size of the household of the accused by the federal Department of Health and Human Services. The Supreme Court of Virginia shall be responsible for distributing to all courts the annual updates of the federal poverty income guidelines made by the Department.

If the available funds of the accused exceed 125 percent of the federal poverty income guidelines and the accused fails to employ counsel and does not waive his right to counsel, the court may, in exceptional circumstances, and where the ends of justice so require, appoint an attorney to represent the accused. However, in making such appointments, the court shall state in writing its reasons for so doing. The written statement by the court shall be included in the permanent record of the case.

C. If the court determines that the accused is indigent as contemplated by law pursuant to the guidelines set forth in this section, the court shall provide the accused with a statement which shall contain the following:

"I have been advised this .... day of ...., 20 .., by the (name of court) court of my right to representation by counsel in the trial of the charge pending against me; I certify that I am without means to employ counsel and I hereby request the court to appoint counsel for me."

.... (signature of accused)

The court shall also require the accused to complete a written financial statement to support the claim of indigency and to permit the court to determine whether or not the accused is indigent within the contemplation of law. The accused shall execute the said statements under oath, and the said court shall appoint competent counsel to represent the accused in the proceeding against him, including an appeal, if any, until relieved or replaced by other counsel.

The executed statements by the accused and the order of appointment of counsel shall be filed with and become a part of the record of such proceeding.

All other instances in which the appointment of counsel is required for an indigent shall be made in accordance with the guidelines prescribed in this section.

D. Except in jurisdictions having a public defender, or unless (i) the public defender is unable to represent the defendant by reason of conflict of interest or (ii) the court finds that appointment of other counsel is necessary to attain the ends of justice, counsel appointed by the court for representation of the accused shall be selected by a fair system of rotation among members of the bar practicing before the court whose names are on the list maintained by the Indigent Defense Commission pursuant to § 19.2-163.01. If no attorney who is on the list maintained by the Indigent Defense Commission is reasonably available, the court may appoint as counsel an attorney not on the list who has otherwise demonstrated to the court's satisfaction an appropriate level of training and experience. The court shall provide notice to the Commission of the appointment of the attorney.

History.

Code 1950, § 19.1-241.3; 1964, c. 657; 1966, c. 460; 1975, c. 495; 1976, c. 553; 1978, c. 720; 1984, c. 709; 2004, cc. 884, 921; 2006, cc. 680, 708; 2008, cc. 122, 154.

§ 19.2-159.1. Interrogation by court; filing; change in circumstances; investigation by attorney for Commonwealth.

A. The court shall thoroughly interrogate any person making the statement of indigency required in § 19.2-159 and shall further advise such person of the penalty which might result from false swearing, as provided in § 19.2-161.

B. The statement and oath of the defendant shall be filed with the papers in the case, and shall follow and be in effect at all stages of the proceedings against him without further oath. In the event the defendant undergoes a change of circumstances so that he is no longer indigent, the defendant shall thereupon obtain private counsel and shall forthwith advise the court of the change of circumstances. The court shall grant reasonable continuance to allow counsel to be obtained and to prepare for trial. When private counsel has been retained, appointed counsel shall forthwith be relieved of further responsibility and compensated for his services, pro rata, pursuant to § 19.2-163.

C. Upon the request of the court, it shall be the duty of the attorney for the Commonwealth of the county or city in which such statement and oath was made to make an investigation as to the indigency of the defendant, or of any other person making such statement. The attorney for the Commonwealth is authorized to delegate the responsibility for such investigation to any subordinate in his office, or to any agency, state or local, which possesses the facilities to quickly make such investigation. Such investigation shall be reduced to writing and forwarded to the court in which the statement and oath was made within fourteen days after such request by the court is made. Such report shall be placed with the papers in the case.

History.

Code 1950, § 19.1-241.3:1; 1975, c. 580; 1977, c. 6; 1981, c. 289; 1984, c. 709.

§ 19.2-160. Appointment of counsel or waiver of right.

If the charge against the accused is a crime the penalty for which may be incarceration, and the accused is not represented by counsel, the court shall ascertain by oral examination of the accused whether or not the accused desires to waive his right to counsel.

In the event the accused desires to waive his right to counsel, and the court ascertains that such waiver is voluntary and intelligently made, then the court shall provide the accused with a statement to be executed by the accused to document his waiver. The statement shall be in a form designed and provided by the Supreme Court. Any executed statement herein provided for shall be filed with and become a part of the record of such proceeding.

In the absence of a waiver of counsel by the accused, and if he shall claim that he is indigent, the court shall proceed in the same manner as is provided in § 19.2-159.

Should the defendant refuse or otherwise fail to sign either of the statements described in this section and § 19.2-159, the court shall note such refusal on the record. Such refusal shall be deemed to be a waiver of the right to counsel, and the court, after so advising the accused and offering him the opportunity to rescind his refusal shall, if such refusal is not rescinded and the accused's signature given, proceed to hear and decide the case. However, if, prior to the commencement of the trial, the court states in writing, either upon the request of the attorney for the Commonwealth or, in the absence of the attorney for the Commonwealth, upon the court's own motion, that a sentence of incarceration will not be imposed if the defendant is convicted, the court may try the case without appointing counsel, and in such event no sentence of incarceration shall be imposed.

History.

Code 1950, § 19.1-241.9; 1973, c. 316; 1975, c. 495; 1978, c. 365; 1979, c. 468; 1983, c. 97; 1989, c. 385.

§ 19.2-161. Penalty for false swearing with regard to statement of indigence.

Any person charged with a felony who shall falsely swear or who shall execute the statement provided for in § 19.2-159 knowing such statement to be false, shall be guilty of perjury, punishable as a Class 5 felony.

Any person charged with a misdemeanor punishable by confinement in jail who shall falsely swear or who shall execute the statement provided for in § 19.2-159 knowing such statement to be false shall be guilty of a Class 1 misdemeanor.

History.

Code 1950, §§ 19.1-241.6, 19.1-241.12; 1964, c. 657; 1973, c. 316; 1975, c. 495.

§ 19.2-162. Continuances to be granted if necessary.

Courts before which criminal proceedings are pending shall afford such continuances and take such other action as is necessary to comply with the provisions of this chapter.

History.

Code 1950, §§ 19.1-241.4, 19.1-241.10; 1964, c. 657; 1973, c. 316; 1975, c. 495.

§ 19.2-163. Compensation of court-appointed counsel.

Upon submission to the court, for which appointed representation is provided, of a detailed accounting of the time expended for that representation, made within 30 days of the completion of all proceedings in that court, counsel appointed to represent an indigent accused in a criminal case shall be compensated for his services on an hourly basis at a rate set by the Supreme Court of Virginia in a total amount not to exceed the amounts specified in the following schedule:

1. In a district court, a sum not to exceed $120, provided that, notwithstanding the foregoing limitation, the court in its discretion, and subject to guidelines issued by the Executive Secretary of the Supreme Court of Virginia, may waive the limitation of fees up to (i) an additional $120 when the effort expended, the time reasonably necessary for the particular representation, the novelty and difficulty of the issues, or other circumstances warrant such a waiver; or (ii) an amount up to $650 to defend, in the case of a juvenile, an offense that would be a felony if committed by an adult that may be punishable by confinement in the state correctional facility for a period of more than 20 years, or a charge of violation of probation for such offense, when the effort expended, the time reasonably necessary for the particular representation, the novelty and difficulty of the issues, or other circumstances warrant such a waiver; or (iii) such other amount as may be provided by law. Such amount shall be allowed in any case wherein counsel conducts the defense of a single charge against the indigent through to its conclusion or a charge of violation of probation at any hearing conducted under § 19.2-306; thereafter, compensation for additional charges against the same accused also conducted by the same counsel shall be allowed on the basis of additional time expended as to such additional charges;

2. In a circuit court (i) to defend a felony charge that may be punishable by death an amount deemed reasonable by the court; (ii) to defend a felony charge that may be punishable by confinement in the state correctional facility for a period of more than 20 years, or a charge of violation of probation for such offense, a sum not to exceed $1,235, provided that, notwithstanding the foregoing limitation, the court in its discretion, and subject to guidelines issued by the Executive Secretary of the Supreme Court of Virginia, may waive the limitation of fees up to an additional $850 when the effort expended, the time reasonably necessary for the particular representation, the novelty and difficulty of the issues, or other circumstances warrant such a waiver; (iii) to defend any other felony charge, or a charge of violation of probation for such offense, a sum not to exceed $445, provided that, notwithstanding the foregoing limitation, the court in its discretion, and subject to guidelines issued by the Executive Secretary of the Supreme Court of Virginia, may waive the limitation of fees up to an additional $155 when the effort expended, the time reasonably necessary for the particular representation, the novelty and difficulty of the issues, or other circumstances warrant such a waiver; and (iv) in the circuit court only, to defend any misdemeanor charge punishable by confinement in jail or a charge of violation of probation for such offense, a sum not to exceed $158. In the event any case is required to be retried due to a mistrial for any cause or reversed on appeal, the court may allow an additional fee for each case in an amount not to exceed the amounts allowable in the initial trial. In the event counsel is appointed to defend an indigent charged with a felony that may be punishable by death, such counsel shall continue to receive compensation as provided in this paragraph for defending such a felony, regardless of whether the charge is reduced or amended to a felony that may not be punishable by death, prior to final disposition of the case. In the event counsel is appointed to defend an indigent charged with any other felony, such counsel shall receive compensation as provided in this paragraph for defending such a felony, regardless of whether the charge is reduced or amended to a misdemeanor or lesser felony prior to final disposition of the case in either the district court or circuit court.

Counsel appointed to represent an indigent accused in a criminal case, who are not public defenders, may request an additional waiver exceeding the amounts provided for in this section. The request for any additional amount shall be submitted to the presiding judge, in writing, with a detailed accounting of the time spent and the justification for the additional amount. The presiding judge shall determine, subject to guidelines issued by the Executive Secretary of the Supreme Court of Virginia, whether the request for an additional amount is justified in whole or in part, by considering the effort expended and the time reasonably necessary for the particular representation, and, if so, shall forward the request as approved to the chief judge of the circuit court or district court for approval.

If at any time the funds appropriated to pay for waivers under this section become insufficient, the Executive Secretary of the Supreme Court of Virginia shall so certify to the courts and no further waivers shall be approved.

The circuit or district court shall direct the payment of such reasonable expenses incurred by such court-appointed counsel as it deems appropriate under the circumstances of the case. Counsel appointed by the court to represent an indigent charged with repeated violations of the same section of the Code of Virginia, with each of such violations arising out of the same incident, occurrence, or transaction, shall be compensated in an amount not to exceed the fee prescribed for the defense of a single charge, if such offenses are tried as part of the same judicial proceeding. The trial judge shall consider any guidelines established by the Supreme Court but shall have the sole discretion to fix the amount of compensation to be paid counsel appointed by the court to defend a felony charge that may be punishable by death.

The circuit or district court shall direct that the foregoing payments shall be paid out by the Commonwealth, if the defendant is charged with a violation of a statute, or by the county, city or town, if the defendant is charged with a violation of a county, city or town ordinance, to the attorney so appointed to defend such person as compensation for such defense.

Counsel representing a defendant charged with a Class 1 felony, or counsel representing an indigent prisoner under sentence of death in a state habeas corpus proceeding, may submit to the court, on a monthly basis, a statement of all costs incurred and fees charged by him in the case during that month. Whenever the total charges as are deemed reasonable by the court for which payment has not previously been made or requested exceed $1,000, the court may direct that payment be made as otherwise provided in this section.

When such directive is entered upon the order book of the court, the Commonwealth, county, city or town, as the case may be, shall provide for the payment out of its treasury of the sum of money so specified. If the defendant is convicted, the amount allowed by the court to the attorney appointed to defend him shall be taxed against the defendant as a part of the costs of prosecution and, if collected, the same shall be paid to the Commonwealth, or the county, city or town, as the case may be. In the event that counsel for the defendant requests a waiver of the limitations on compensation, the court shall assess against the defendant an amount equal to the pre-waiver compensation limit specified in this section for each charge for which the defendant was convicted. An abstract of such costs shall be docketed in the judgment docket and execution lien book maintained by such court.

Any statement submitted by an attorney for payments due him for indigent representation or for representation of a child pursuant to § 16.1-266 shall, after the submission of the statement, be forwarded forthwith by the clerk to the Commonwealth, county, city or town, as the case may be, responsible for payment.

For the purposes of this section, the defense of a case may be considered conducted through to its conclusion and an appointed counsel entitled to compensation for his services in the event an indigent accused fails to appear in court subject to a capias for his arrest or a show cause summons for his failure to appear and remains a fugitive from justice for one year following the issuance of the capias or the summons to show cause, and appointed counsel has appeared at a hearing on behalf of the accused.

Effective July 1, 2007, the Executive Secretary of the Supreme Court of Virginia shall track and report the number and category of offenses charged involving adult and juvenile offenders in cases in which court-appointed counsel is assigned. The Executive Secretary shall also track and report the amounts paid by waiver above the initial cap to court-appointed counsel. The Executive Secretary shall provide these reports to the Governor, members of the House Appropriations Committee, and members of the Senate Finance Committee on a quarterly basis.

History.

Code 1950, §§ 14.1-184, 14.1-184.1, 19.1-241.5, 19.1-241.11; 1964, cc. 386, 651, 657; 1968, c. 481; 1973, c. 316; 1975, c. 495; 1976, c. 553; 1980, c. 626; 1981, cc. 472, 486; 1985, c. 525; 1986, c. 425; 1987, c. 638; 1988, cc. 465, 472; 1989, c. 565; 1994, c. 451; 1995, cc. 571, 713; 1997, c. 492; 1998, cc. 440, 451; 2000, cc. 436, 448; 2001, c. 509; 2006, c. 332; 2007, cc. 938, 946; 2008, c. 760; 2009, c. 284.

ARTICLE 3.1.
INDIGENT DEFENSE.

§ 19.2-163.01. Virginia Indigent Defense Commission established; powers and duties.

A. The Virginia Indigent Defense Commission (hereinafter Indigent Defense Commission or Commission) is established. The Commission shall be supervisory and shall have sole responsibility for the powers, duties, operations, and responsibilities set forth in this section.

The Commission shall have the following powers and duties:

1. To publicize and enforce the qualification standards for attorneys seeking eligibility to serve as court-appointed counsel for indigent defendants pursuant to § 19.2-159.

2. To develop initial training courses for attorneys who wish to begin serving as court-appointed counsel, and to review and certify legal education courses that satisfy the continuing requirements for attorneys to maintain their eligibility for receiving court appointments.

3. To maintain a list of attorneys admitted to practice law in Virginia who are qualified to serve as court-appointed counsel for indigent defendants based upon the official standards and to disseminate the list by July 1 of each year and updates throughout the year to the Office of the Executive Secretary of the Supreme Court for distribution to the courts. In establishing and updating the list, the Commission shall consider all relevant factors, including but not limited to, the attorney's background, experience, and training and the Commission's assessment

of whether the attorney is competent to provide quality legal representation.

4. To establish official standards of practice for court-appointed counsel and public defenders to follow in representing their clients, and guidelines for the removal of an attorney from the official list of those qualified to receive court appointments and to notify the Office of the Executive Secretary of the Supreme Court of any attorney whose name has been removed from the list.

5. To develop initial training courses for public defenders and to review and certify legal education courses that satisfy the continuing requirements for public defenders to maintain their eligibility.

6. To periodically review and report to the Virginia State Crime Commission, the House and the Senate Committees for Courts of Justice, the House Committee on Appropriations, and the Senate Committee on Finance on the caseload handled by each public defender office.

7. To maintain all public defender and regional capital defender offices established by the General Assembly.

8. To hire and employ and, at its pleasure, remove an executive director, counsel, and such other persons as it deems necessary, and to authorize the executive director to appoint, after prior notice to the Commission, a deputy director, and for each of the above offices a public defender or capital defender, as the case may be, who shall devote his full time to his duties and not engage in the private practice of law.

9. To authorize the public defender or capital defender to employ such assistants as authorized by the Commission.

10. To authorize the public defender or capital defender to employ such staff, including secretarial and investigative personnel, as may be necessary to carry out the duties imposed upon the public defender office.

11. To authorize the executive director of the Commission, in consultation with the public defender or capital defender to secure such office space as needed, to purchase or rent office equipment, to purchase supplies and to incur such expenses as are necessary to carry out the duties imposed upon him.

12. To approve requests for appropriations and receive and expend moneys appropriated by the General Assembly of Virginia, to receive other moneys as they become available to it and expend the same in order to carry out the duties imposed upon it.

13. To require and ensure that each public defender office collects and maintains caseload data and fields in a case management database on an annual basis.

14. To report annually on or before October 1 to the Virginia State Crime Commission, the House and Senate Committees for Courts of Justice, the House Committee on Appropriations, and the Senate Committee on Finance on the state of indigent criminal defense in the Commonwealth, including Virginia's ranking amongst the 50 states in terms of pay allowed for court-appointed counsel appointed pursuant to § 19.2-159 or subdivision C 2 of § 16.1-266.

B. The Commission shall adopt rules and procedures for the conduct of its business. The Commission may delegate to the executive director or, in the absence of the executive director, the deputy executive director, such powers and duties conferred upon the Commission as it deems appropriate, including powers and duties involving the exercise of discretion. The Commission shall ensure that the executive director complies with all Commission and statutory directives. Such rules and procedures may include the establishment of committees and the delegation of authority to the committees. The Commission shall review and confirm by a vote of the Commission its rules and procedures and any delegation of authority to the executive director at least every three years.

C. The executive director shall, with the approval of the Commission, fix the compensation of each public defender and all other personnel in each public defender office. The executive director shall also exercise and perform such other powers and duties as may be lawfully delegated to him and such powers and duties as may be conferred or imposed upon him by law.

History.

2004, cc. 884, 921; 2005, c. 230; 2006, cc. 429, 501; 2007, c. 371; 2008, cc. 536, 815; 2010, c. 314.

§ 19.2-163.01:1. Supplementing compensation of public defender.

A. The governing body of any county or city may supplement the compensation of the public defender or any of his deputies or employees above the compensation fixed by the executive director, in such amounts as it may deem expedient. Such additional compensation shall be wholly payable from the funds of any such county or city.

B. Due to the privileged and protected nature of the attorney-client relationship and the statutory scope of representation provided in §§ 19.2-157 and 19.2-163.3, no county or city providing a supplement to compensation under this section shall place any condition or requirement upon the receipt of such funds.

C. Funds provided by any county or city under this section shall be paid directly to the employees with notice to the Indigent Defense Commission of any amount so provided.

History.

2008, cc. 536, 815; 2010, c. 314.

§ 19.2-163.02. Membership of Indigent Defense Commission; expenses.

The Virginia Indigent Defense Commission shall consist of 14 members as follows: the chairmen of the House and Senate Committees for Courts of Justice or their designees who shall be members of the Courts of Justice committees; the chairman of the Virginia State Crime Commission or his designee; the Executive Secretary of the Supreme Court or his designee; two attorneys officially designated by the Virginia State Bar; two persons appointed by the Governor; three persons appointed by the Speaker of the House of Delegates; and three persons appointed by the Senate Committee on Rules. At least one of the appointments made by the Governor, one of the appointments made by the Speaker, and one of the appointments made by the Senate Committee on Rules, shall be an attorney in private practice with a demonstrated interest in indigent defense issues. Persons who are appointed by virtue of their office shall hold terms coincident with their terms of office. If the chairman of the Virginia State Crime Commission is (i) the chairman of the House Committee for Courts of Justice, then the vice-chairman of the Committee shall serve in the position designated for the Committee chairman or (ii) the chairman of the Senate Committee for Courts of Justice, then the Senate Committee on Rules, upon the recommendation of the chairman of the Committee, shall appoint a member of the Committee to serve in the position designated for the Committee chairman. All other members shall be appointed for terms of three years and may be reappointed.

The Commission shall elect a chairman and a vice-chairman from among its membership annually. The chairman or his designee shall preside at all regular and called meetings of the Commission and shall have no additional duties or authority unless set by statute or by resolution of the Commission and annually confirmed by the Commission. A majority of the members shall constitute a quorum. The Commission shall meet at least four times each year. The meetings of the Commission shall be held at the call of the chairman or whenever three of the members so request.

Members shall be paid reasonable and necessary expenses incurred in the performance of their duties. Legislative members shall receive compensation as provided in § 30-19.12 and nonlegislative citizen members shall receive compensation for their services as provided in §§ 2.2-2813 and 2.2-2825.

History.

2004, cc. 884, 921; 2005, cc. 176, 758; 2006, cc. 429, 501; 2008, c. 115.

§ 19.2-163.03. Qualifications for court-appointed counsel.

A. Initial qualification requirements. An attorney seeking to represent an indigent accused in a criminal case, in addition to being a member in good standing of the Virginia State Bar, shall meet the specific criteria required for each type or level of case. The following criteria shall be met for qualification and subsequent court appointment:

1. Misdemeanor case. To initially qualify to serve as counsel appointed pursuant to § 19.2-159 for an indigent defendant charged with a misdemeanor, the attorney shall:

(i) if an active member of the Virginia State Bar for less than one year, have completed six hours of MCLE-approved continuing legal education developed by the Indigent Defense Commission, or

(ii) if an active member of the Virginia State Bar for one year or more, either complete the six hours of approved continuing legal education developed by the Commission, or certify to the Commission that he has represented, in a district court within the past year, four or more defendants charged with misdemeanors, or

(iii) be qualified pursuant to this section to serve as counsel for an indigent defendant charged with a felony.

2. Felony case.

a. To initially qualify to serve as counsel appointed pursuant to § 19.2-159 for an indigent defendant charged with a felony, the attorney shall (i) have completed the six hours of MCLE-approved continuing legal education developed by the Commission, and (ii) certify that he has participated as either lead counsel or co-counsel in four felony cases from their beginning through to their final resolution, including appeals, if any.

b. If the attorney has been an active member of the Virginia State Bar for more than one year and certifies that he has participated, within the past year, as lead counsel in four felony cases through to their final resolution, including appeals, if any, the requirement to complete six hours of continuing legal education and the requirement to participate as co-counsel shall be waived.

c. If the attorney has been an active member of the Virginia State Bar for more than one year and certifies that he has participated, within the past five years, as lead counsel in five felony cases through to their final resolution, including appeals, if any, the requirement to participate as either lead counsel or co-counsel in four felony cases within the past year shall be waived.

3. Juvenile and domestic relations case.

a. To initially qualify to serve as appointed counsel in a juvenile and domestic relations district court pursuant to subdivision C 2 of § 16.1-266, the attorney shall (i) have completed the six hours of MCLE-approved continuing legal education developed by the Commission, (ii) have completed four additional hours of MCLE-approved continuing legal education on representing juveniles developed by the Commission, and (iii) certify that he has participated as either lead counsel or co-counsel in four cases involving juveniles in a juvenile and domestic relations district court.

b. If the attorney has been an active member of the Virginia State Bar for more than one year and certifies that he has, within the past year, been lead counsel in four cases involving juveniles in juvenile and domestic relations district court, the requirement to complete the 10 hours of continuing legal education shall be waived.

c. If the attorney has been an active member of the Virginia State Bar for more than one year and certifies that he has participated, within the past five years in five cases involving juveniles in a juvenile and domestic relations district court, the requirement to participate as either lead counsel or co-counsel in four juvenile cases shall be waived.

B. Requalification requirements. After initially qualifying as provided in subsection A, an attorney shall maintain his eligibility for certification biennially by notifying the Commission of completion of at least six hours of Commission and MCLE-approved continuing legal education. The Commission shall provide information on continuing legal education programs that have been approved.

In addition, to maintain eligibility to accept court appointments under subdivision C 2 of § 16.1-266, an attorney shall complete biennially thereafter four additional hours of MCLE-approved continuing legal education on representing juveniles, certified by the Commission.

C. Waiver and exceptions. The Commission or the court before which a matter is pending, may, in its discretion, waive the requirements set out in this section for individuals who otherwise demonstrate their level of training and experience. A waiver of such requirements pursuant to this subsection shall not form the basis for a claim of error at trial, on appeal, or in any habeas corpus proceeding.

History.
2004, cc. 884, 921; 2006, c. 708; 2007, c. 571.

§ 19.2-163.04. Public Defender offices.

Public defender offices are established in:
a. The City of Virginia Beach;
b. The City of Petersburg;
c. The Cities of Buena Vista, Lexington, Staunton and Waynesboro and the Counties of Augusta and Rockbridge;
d. The City of Roanoke;
e. The City of Portsmouth;
f. The City of Richmond;
g. The Counties of Clarke, Frederick, Page, Shenandoah and Warren, and the City of Winchester;
h. The City and County of Fairfax;
i. The City of Alexandria;
j. The City of Radford and the Counties of Bland, Pulaski and Wythe;
k. The Counties of Fauquier, Loudoun and Rappahannock;
l. The City of Suffolk;
m. The City of Franklin and the Counties of Isle of Wight and Southampton;
n. The County of Bedford;
o. The City of Danville;
p. The Counties of Halifax, Lunenburg and Mecklenburg;
q. The City of Fredericksburg and the Counties of King George, Stafford and Spotsylvania;
r. The City of Lynchburg;
s. The City of Martinsville and the Counties of Henry and Patrick;
t. The City of Charlottesville and the County of Albemarle;
u. The City of Norfolk;
v. The County of Arlington and the City of Falls Church;
w. The City of Newport News;
x. The City of Chesapeake; and
y. The City of Hampton.

History.
2004, cc. 884, 921; 2004, Sp. Sess. I, c. 4, cl. 2; 2005, c. 951; 2006, Sp. Sess. I, c. 2; 2016, cc. 164, 312.

ARTICLE 4.
PUBLIC DEFENDERS.

§§ 19.2-163.1, 19.2-163.2: Repealed by Acts 2004, cc. 884 and 921.

Cross references.
For current provisions relating to public defenders offices, see § 19.2-163.04.

§ 19.2-163.3. Duties of public defenders.

Public defenders shall carry out the following duties in accordance with the guidance, policies, and authorizations of the Indigent Defense Commission:

(a) To assist the executive director of the Commission in securing office space, to employ a staff, to fix salaries and to do such other things necessary to carry out the duties imposed upon them with the approval of the Commission.

(b) To represent or supervise assistants in representing within their respective jurisdictions as set out in § 19.2-163.04 indigent persons charged with a crime or offense when such persons are entitled to be represented by law by court-appointed counsel in a court of record or a court not of record.

(c) To represent or supervise assistants in representing indigent persons who are entitled to be represented by court-appointed counsel in an appeal of their conviction to the Court of Appeals or the Supreme Court of Virginia.

(d) To submit such reports as required by the Commission.

History.
Code 1950, § 19.1-32.4; 1972, c. 800; 1975, c. 495; 1978, c. 698; 1979, c. 194; 1990, c. 734; 1992, c. 80; 2007, c. 680.

§ 19.2-163.4. Inapplicability of §§ 17.1-606 and 19.2-163 where public defender offices established; exception.

In counties and cities in which public defender offices are established pursuant to § 19.2-163.04, defense services for indigents charged with jailable offenses shall be provided by the public defenders unless (i) the public defender is unable to represent the defendant or petitioner by reason of conflict of interest or (ii) the court finds that appointment of other counsel is necessary to attain the ends of justice. Except for the provisions of § 19.2-163 relating to reasonable expenses, §§ 17.1-606 and 19.2-163 shall not apply when defense services are provided by the public defenders.

History.
Code 1950, § 19.1-32.5; 1972, c. 800; 1975, cc. 476, 495; 1992, c. 80; 1994, c. 415.

§ 19.2-163.4:1. Repayment of representation costs by convicted persons.

In any case in which an attorney from a public defender or capital defender office represents an indigent person charged with an offense and such person is convicted, the sum that would have been allowed a court-appointed attorney as compensation and as reasonable expenses shall be taxed against the person defended as a part of the costs of the prosecution, and, if collected, shall be paid to the Commonwealth or, if payment was made to the Commonwealth by a locality for defense of a local ordinance violation, to the appropriate county, city or town. An abstract of such costs shall be docketed in the judgment lien docket and execution book of the court.

History.
2004, cc. 884, 921.

§ 19.2-163.5. Legal services to public defenders and/or assistant public defenders.

At the request of a public defender, the Attorney General shall provide legal services to such attorney, his assistants, or members of his staff in any proceeding brought against him, his assistants, or staff for money damages, when the cause of action allegedly arises out of the duties of his office.

Any costs chargeable against the defendant or defendants in any such case shall be paid by the Commonwealth from the appropriation for the payment of criminal charges.

History.
1978, c. 698.

§ 19.2-163.6: Repealed by Acts 2004, c. 884 and 921.

ARTICLE 4.1.
COUNSEL IN CAPITAL CASES.

§ 19.2-163.7. Counsel in capital cases.

In any case in which an indigent defendant is charged with a capital offense, the judge of the circuit court, upon request for the appointment of counsel, shall appoint at least two attorneys from the list or lists established by the Supreme Court and the Indigent Defense Commission or as provided in subsection C of § 19.2-163.8 to represent the defendant at trial and, if the defendant is sentenced to death, on appeal. In all cases where counsel is appointed under this section after July 1, 2004, one of the attorneys appointed shall be from a capital defense unit maintained by the Indigent Defense Commission. This section shall be construed in conformity with the provisions of § 19.2-163.4. If prior to indictment the attorney for the Commonwealth declares in writing that the Commonwealth will not seek the death penalty, the capital defense unit attorney may upon motion before the circuit court seek to withdraw as counsel. The circuit court judge having heard the motion to withdraw shall permit the capital defense unit attorney to withdraw and shall appoint another attorney pursuant to the provisions of § 19.2-159. If the sentence of death is affirmed on appeal, the court shall, within 30 days after the decision of the Supreme Court of Virginia, appoint counsel from the same list, or such other list as the Supreme Court and the Commission may establish, to represent an indigent prisoner under sentence of death in a state habeas corpus proceeding. The Attorney General shall have no standing to object to the appointment of counsel for the petitioner.

History.
1991, c. 664; 1995, c. 503; 2001, c. 766; 2002, c. 614; 2004, cc. 329, 884, 921.

§ 19.2-163.8. List of qualified attorneys.

A. The Supreme Court and the Indigent Defense Commission, in conjunction with the Virginia State Bar, shall adopt standards for attorneys admitted to practice law in Virginia who are qualified to represent defendants charged with capital murder or sentenced to death, which take into consideration, to the extent practicable, the following criteria: (i) license or permission to practice law in Virginia; (ii) general background in criminal litigation; (iii) demonstrated experience in felony practice at trial and appeal; (iv) experience in death penalty litigation; (v) familiarity with the requisite court system; (vi) current training in death penalty litigation; (vii) current training in the analysis and introduction of forensic evidence, including deoxyribonucleic acid (DNA) testing and the evidence of a DNA profile comparison to prove or disprove the identity of any person; and (viii) demonstrated proficiency and commitment to quality representation.

B. The Supreme Court and the Indigent Defense Commission shall maintain a list of attorneys admitted to practice law in Virginia who are qualified to represent defendants charged with capital murder or sentenced to death. In establishing such a list, the Court and the Commission shall consider all relevant factors, including but not limited to, the attorney's background, experience, and training and the Court's and the Commission's assessment of whether the attorney is competent to provide quality legal representation.

C. Notwithstanding the requirements of § 19.2-163.7, the judge of the circuit court may appoint counsel who is not included on the list, but who otherwise qualifies under the standards established and maintained by the Court and the Commission.

D. Noncompliance with the requirements of this article shall not form the basis for a claim of error at trial, on appeal, or in any habeas corpus proceeding. The performance of habeas corpus counsel appointed pursuant to this article shall not form a basis for relief in any subsequent habeas corpus proceeding.

E. The Supreme Court and the Indigent Defense Commission shall, in conjunction with the Virginia State Bar, promulgate and thereafter maintain standards for the qualifications of counsel who shall be considered eligible to be placed on the list of qualified attorneys.

History.
1991, c. 664; 2001, c. 766; 2004, cc. 884, 921.

ARTICLE 5.
INTERPRETERS.

§ 19.2-164. Interpreters for non-English-speaking persons (Supreme Court Rule 2:507 derived in part from this section).

In any criminal case in which a non-English-speaking person is the accused, an interpreter for the non-English-speaking person shall be appointed. In any criminal case in which a non-English-speaking person is a victim or witness, an interpreter shall be appointed by the judge of the court in which the case is to be heard unless the court finds that the person does not require the services of a court-appointed interpreter. An English-speaking person fluent in the language of the country of the accused, a victim or a witness shall be appointed by the judge of the court in which the case is to be heard, unless such person obtains an interpreter of his own choosing who is approved by the court as being competent. The compensation of an interpreter appointed by the court pursuant to this section shall be fixed by the court in accordance with guidelines set by the Judicial Council of Virginia and shall be paid from the general fund of the state treasury as part of the expense of trial. Such fee shall not be assessed as part of the costs unless (i) an interpreter has been appointed for the defendant, (ii) the defendant fails to appear, (iii) the interpreter appears in the case and no other case on that date, and (iv) the defendant is convicted of a failure to appear on that date the interpreter appeared in the case, then the court, in its discretion, may assess as costs the fee paid to the interpreter. Whenever a person communicates through an interpreter to any person under such circumstances that the communication would be privileged, and such person could not be compelled to testify as to the communications, this privilege shall also apply to the interpreter. The provisions of this section shall apply in both circuit courts and district courts.

History.
Code 1950, § 19.1-246.1; 1966, c. 240; 1974, c. 110; 1975, c. 495; 1978, c. 601; 1982, c. 444; 1985, c. 396; 1995, c. 546; 1996, c. 402; 2003, c. 1011; 2007, c. 383.

§ 19.2-164.1. Interpreters for the deaf (Supreme Court Rule 2:507 derived in part from this section).

In any criminal case in which a deaf person is the accused, an interpreter for the deaf person shall be appointed. In any criminal case in which a deaf person is the victim or a witness, an interpreter for the deaf person shall be appointed by the court in which the case is to be heard unless the court finds that the deaf person does not require the services of a court-appointed interpreter and the deaf person waives his rights. Such interpreter shall be procured by the judge of the court in which the case is to be heard through the Department for the Deaf and Hard-of-Hearing.

The compensation of an interpreter appointed by the court pursuant to this section shall be fixed by the court and paid from the general fund of the state treasury as part of the expense of trial. Such fee shall not be assessed as part of the costs.

Any person entitled to the services of an interpreter under this section may waive these services for all or a portion of the proceedings. Such a waiver shall be made by the person upon the record after an opportunity to consult with legal counsel. A judicial officer, utilizing an interpreter obtained in accordance with this section, shall explain to the deaf person the nature and effect of any waiver. Any waiver shall be approved in writing by the deaf person's legal counsel. If the person does not have legal counsel, approval shall be made in writing by a judicial officer. A person who waives his right to an interpreter may provide his own interpreter at his own expense without regard to whether the interpreter is qualified under this section.

The provisions of this section shall apply in both circuit courts and district courts.

Whenever a person communicates through an interpreter to any person under such circumstances that the communication would be privileged, and such person could not be compelled to testify as to the communications, this privilege shall also apply to the interpreter.

In any judicial proceeding, the judge on his own motion or on the motion of a party to the proceeding may order all of the testimony of a deaf person and the interpretation thereof to be visually electronically recorded for use in verification of the official transcript of the proceedings.

History.
1982, c. 444; 1985, c. 396; 1995, c. 546; 1996, c. 402.

ARTICLE 6.

RECORDING EVIDENCE AND INCIDENTS OF TRIAL.

§ 19.2-165. Recording evidence and incidents of trial in felony cases; cost of recording; cost of transcripts; certified transcript deemed prima facie correct; request for copy of transcript.

In all felony cases, the court or judge trying the case shall by order entered of record provide for the recording verbatim of the evidence and incidents of trial either by a court reporter or by mechanical or electronic devices approved by the court. The expense of reporting or recording the trial of criminal cases shall be paid by the Commonwealth out of the appropriation for criminal charges, upon approval of the trial judge. However, if the defendant is convicted, the Commonwealth shall be entitled to receive the amount allocated to the court reporter fund under the fixed felony fee. Localities that maintain mechanical or electronic devices for this purpose shall be entitled to retain their reasonable expenses attributable to the cost of operating and maintaining such equipment. The clerk shall receive the evidence at the time of admission of such evidence by the court and shall maintain control over such evidence until the time such evidence is transferred on appeal, or destroyed or returned in accordance with law.

In all felony cases where it appears to the court from the affidavit of the defendant and other evidence that the defendant intends to seek an appeal and is financially unable to pay such costs or to bear the expense of a copy of the transcript of the evidence for an appeal, the trial court shall, upon the motion of counsel for the defendant, order the evidence transcribed for such appeal and all costs therefor paid by the Commonwealth out of the appropriation for criminal charges. If the conviction is not reversed, all costs paid by the Commonwealth, under the provisions hereof, shall be assessed against the defendant.

The reporter or other individual designated to report and record the trial shall file the original shorthand notes or other original records with the clerk of the circuit court who shall preserve them in the public records of the court for not less than five years if an appeal was taken and a transcript was prepared, or ten years if no appeal was taken. The transcript in any case certified by the reporter or other individual designated to report and record the trial shall be deemed prima facie a correct statement of the evidence and incidents of trial.

Upon the request of any counsel of record, or of any party not represented by counsel, and upon payment of the reasonable cost thereof, the court reporter covering any proceeding shall provide the requesting party with a copy of the transcript of such proceeding or any requested portion thereof.

The court shall not direct the court reporter to cease recording any portion of the proceeding without the consent of all parties or of their counsel of record.

The administration of this section shall be under the direction of the Supreme Court of Virginia.

History.
Code 1950, § 17-30.1; 1952, c. 642; 1956, c. 699; 1962, c. 419; 1964, c. 533; 1968, c. 358; 1975, cc. 495, 640; 1983, c. 505; 1984, c. 752; 1994, c. 497; 1999, c. 9; 2014, c. 291.

§ 19.2-165.1. Payment of medical fees in certain criminal cases; reimbursement.

A. Except as provided in subsection B, all medical fees expended in the gathering of evidence for all criminal cases where medical evidence is necessary to establish a crime has occurred and for cases involving abuse of children under the age of 18 shall be paid by the Commonwealth out of the appropriation for criminal charges, provided that any medical evaluation, examination, or service rendered be performed by a physician or facility specifically designated by the attorney for the Commonwealth in the city or county having jurisdiction of such case for such a purpose. If no such physician or facility is reasonably available in such city or county, then the attorney for the Commonwealth may designate a physician or facility located outside and adjacent to such city or county.

Where there has been no prior designation of such a physician or facility, such medical fees shall be paid out of the appropriation for criminal charges upon authorization by the attorney for the Commonwealth of the city or county having jurisdiction over the case. Such authorization may be granted prior to or within 48 hours after the medical evaluation, examination, or service rendered.

B. All medical fees expended in the gathering of evidence through physical evidence recovery kit examinations conducted on victims complaining of sexual assault under Article 7 (§ 18.2-61 et seq.) of Chapter 4 of Title 18.2 shall be paid by the Commonwealth pursuant to subsection F of § 19.2-368.11:1. Victims complaining of sexual assault shall not be required to participate in the criminal justice system or cooperate with law-enforcement authorities in order to be provided with such forensic medical exams.

C. Upon conviction of the defendant in any case requiring the payment of medical fees authorized by this section, the court shall order that the defendant reimburse the Commonwealth for payment of such fees.

History.
1976, c. 292; 1982, c. 507; 1987, c. 330; 1997, c. 322; 1999, c. 853; 2000, c. 292; 2003, cc. 28, 772; 2008, cc. 203, 251.

§ 19.2-166. Court reporters.

Each judge of a court of record having jurisdiction over criminal proceedings shall be authorized, in all felony cases and habeas corpus proceedings to appoint a court reporter to report proceedings or to operate mechanical or electrical devices for recording proceedings, to transcribe the report or record of such proceedings, to perform any stenographic work related to such report, record or transcript including work pertinent to the court's findings of fact and conclusions of law pertinent thereto. Such reporter shall be paid by the Commonwealth on a per diem or work basis as appropriate out of the appropriation for criminal charges.

History.
Code 1950, § 17-30.1:1; 1968, c. 486; 1975, c. 495; 2003, c. 140.

CHAPTER 11.

PROCEEDINGS ON QUESTION OF INSANITY.

Section

Section

§ 19.2-167. Accused not to be tried while insane or feebleminded.

No person shall, while he is insane or feebleminded, be tried for a criminal offense.

History.
Code 1950, § 19.1-227; 1960, c. 366; 1964, c. 231; 1968, c. 789; 1975, c. 495.

§ 19.2-168. Notice to Commonwealth of intention to present evidence of insanity; continuance if notice not given.

In any case in which a person charged with a crime intends (i) to put in issue his sanity at the time of the crime charged and (ii) to present testimony of an expert to support his claim on this issue at his trial, he, or his counsel, shall give notice in writing to the attorney for the Commonwealth, at least 60 days prior to his trial, of his intention to present such evidence. However, if the period between indictment and trial is less than 120 days, the person or his counsel shall give such notice no later than 60 days following indictment. In the event that such notice is not given, and the person proffers such evidence at his trial as a defense, then the court may in its discretion, either allow the Commonwealth a continuance or, under appropriate circumstances, bar the defendant from presenting such evidence. The period of any such continuance shall not be counted for speedy trial purposes under § 19.2-243.

History.
Code 1950, § 19.1-227.1; 1970, c. 336; 1975, c. 495; 1986, c. 535; 2008, c. 372.

§ 19.2-168.1. Evaluation on motion of the Commonwealth after notice.

A. If the attorney for the defendant gives notice pursuant to § 19.2-168, and the Commonwealth thereafter seeks an evaluation of the defendant's sanity at the time of the offense, the court shall appoint one or more qualified mental health experts to perform such an evaluation. The court shall order the defendant to submit to such an evaluation and advise the defendant on the record in court that a refusal to cooperate with the Commonwealth's expert could result in exclusion of the defendant's expert evidence. The qualification of the experts shall be governed by subsection A of § 19.2-169.5. The location of the evaluation shall be governed by subsection B of § 19.2-169.5. The attorney for the Commonwealth shall be responsible for providing the experts the information specified in subsection C of § 19.2-169.5. After performing their evaluation, the experts shall report their findings and opinions, and provide copies of psychiatric, psychological, medical or other records obtained during the course of the evaluation to the attorneys for the Commonwealth and the defense. The evaluator shall also send a redacted copy of the report removing references to the defendant's name, date of birth, case number, and court of jurisdiction to the Commissioner of Behavioral Health and Developmental Services for the purpose of peer review to establish and maintain the list of approved evaluators described in subsection A of § 19.2-169.5.

B. If the court finds, after hearing evidence presented by the parties, that the defendant has refused to cooperate with an evaluation requested by the Commonwealth, it may admit evidence of such refusal or, in the discretion of the court, bar the defendant from presenting expert psychiatric or psychological evidence at trial on the issue of his sanity at the time of the offense.

History.
1982, c. 653; 1986, c. 535; 2016, c. 445.

§ 19.2-169: Repealed by Acts 1982, c. 653.

Cross references.
For present provisions covering the subject matter of the repealed section, see §§ 19.2-168.1 and 19.2-169.1.

§ 19.2-169.1. Raising question of competency to stand trial or plead; evaluation and determination of competency.

A. Raising competency issue; appointment of evaluators. — If, at any time after the attorney for the defendant has been retained or appointed and before the end of trial, the court finds, upon hearing evidence or representations of counsel for the defendant or the attorney for the Commonwealth, that there is probable cause to believe that the defendant, whether a juvenile transferred pursuant to § 16.1-269.1 or adult, lacks substantial capacity to understand the proceedings against him or to assist his attorney in his own defense, the court shall order that a competency evaluation be performed by at least one psychiatrist or clinical psychologist who (i) has performed forensic evaluations; (ii) has successfully completed forensic evaluation training recognized by the Commissioner of Behavioral Health and Developmental Services; (iii) has demonstrated to the Commissioner competence to perform forensic evaluations; and (iv) is included on a list of approved evaluators maintained by the Commissioner.

B. Location of evaluation. — The evaluation shall be performed on an outpatient basis at a mental health facility or in jail unless the court specifically finds that outpatient evaluation services are unavailable or unless the results of outpatient evaluation indicate that hospitalization of the defendant for evaluation on competency is necessary. If the court finds that hospitalization is necessary, the court, under authority of this subsection, may order the defendant sent to a hospital designated by the Commissioner of Behavioral Health and Developmental Services as appropriate for evaluations of persons under criminal charge. The defendant shall be hospitalized for such time as the director of the hospital deems necessary to perform an adequate evaluation of the defendant's competency, but not to exceed 30 days from the date of admission to the hospital.

C. Provision of information to evaluators. — The court shall require the attorney for the Commonwealth to provide to the evaluators appointed under subsection A any information relevant to the evaluation, including, but not limited to (i) a copy of the warrant or indictment; (ii) the names and addresses of the attorney for the Commonwealth, the attorney for the defendant, and the judge ordering the evaluation; (iii) information about the alleged crime; and (iv) a summary of the reasons for the evaluation request. The court shall require the attorney for the defendant to provide any available psychiatric records and other information that is deemed relevant. The court shall require that information be provided to the evaluator within 96 hours of the issuance of the court order pursuant to this section.

D. The competency report. — Upon completion of the evaluation, the evaluators shall promptly submit a report in writing to the court and the attorneys of record concerning (i) the defendant's capacity to understand the proceedings against him; (ii) his ability to assist his attorney; and (iii) his need for treatment in the event he is found incompetent but restorable, or incompetent for the foreseeable future. If a need for restoration treatment is identified pursuant to clause (iii), the report shall state whether inpatient or outpatient treatment is recommended. No statements of the defendant relating to the time period of the alleged offense shall be included in the report. The evaluator shall also send a redacted copy of the report removing references to the defendant's name, date of birth, case number, and court of jurisdiction to the Commissioner of Behavioral Health and Developmental Services for the purpose of peer review to establish and maintain the list of approved evaluators described in subsection A.

E. The competency determination. — After receiving the report described in subsection D, the court shall promptly determine whether the defendant is competent to stand trial. A hearing on the defendant's competency is not required unless one is requested by the attorney for the Commonwealth or the attorney for the defendant, or unless the court has reasonable cause to believe the defendant will be hospitalized under § 19.2-169.2. If a hearing is held, the party alleging that the defendant is incompetent shall bear the burden of proving by a preponderance of the evidence the defendant's incompetency. The defendant shall have the right to notice of the hearing, the right to counsel at the hearing and the right to personally participate in and introduce evidence at the hearing.

The fact that the defendant claims to be unable to remember the time period surrounding the alleged offense shall not, by itself, bar a finding of competency if the defendant otherwise understands the charges against him and can assist in his defense. Nor shall the fact that the defendant is under the influence of medication bar a finding of competency if the defendant is able to understand the charges against him and assist in his defense while medicated.

History.
1982, c. 653; 1983, c. 373; 1985, c. 307; 2003, c. 735; 2007, c. 781; 2009, cc. 813, 840; 2014, cc. 329, 739; 2016, c. 445.

§ 19.2-169.2. Disposition when defendant found incompetent.

A. Upon finding pursuant to subsection E of § 19.2-169.1 that the defendant, including a juvenile transferred pursuant to § 16.1-269.1, is incompetent, the court shall order that the defendant receive treatment to restore his competency on an outpatient basis or, if the court specifically finds that the defendant requires inpatient hospital treatment, at a hospital designated by the Commissioner of Behavioral Health and Developmental Services as appropriate for treatment of persons under criminal charge. Any psychiatric records and other information that have been deemed relevant and submitted by the attorney for the defendant pursuant to subsection C of § 19.2-169.1 and any reports submitted pursuant to subsection D of § 19.2-169.1 shall be made available to the director of the community services board or behavioral health authority or his designee or to the director of the treating inpatient facility or his designee within 96 hours of the issuance of the court order requiring treatment to restore the defendant's competency. If the 96-hour period expires on a Saturday, Sunday, or other legal holiday, the 96 hours shall be extended to the next day that is not a Saturday, Sunday, or legal holiday.

B. If, at any time after the defendant is ordered to undergo treatment under subsection A of this section, the director of the community services board or behavioral health authority or his designee or the director of the treating inpatient facility or his designee believes the defendant's competency is restored, the director or his designee shall immediately send a report to the court as prescribed in subsection D of § 19.2-169.1. The court shall make a ruling on the defendant's competency according to the procedures specified in subsection E of § 19.2-169.1.

C. The clerk of court shall certify and forward forthwith to the Central Criminal Records Exchange, on a form provided by the Exchange, a copy of an order for treatment issued pursuant to subsection A.

History.
1982, c. 653; 2003, c. 735; 2007, c. 781; 2008, cc. 751, 788; 2009, cc. 813, 840; 2014, cc. 373, 408.

§ 19.2-169.3. Disposition of the unrestorably incompetent defendant; capital murder charge; sexually violent offense charge.

A. If, at any time after the defendant is ordered to undergo treatment pursuant to subsection A of § 19.2-169.2, the director of the community services board or behavioral health authority or his designee or the director of the treating inpatient facility or his designee concludes that the defendant is likely to remain incompetent for the foreseeable future, he shall send a report to the court so stating. The report shall also indicate whether, in the board, authority, or inpatient facility director's or his designee's opinion, the defendant should be released, committed pursuant to Article 5 (§ 37.2-814 et seq.) of Chapter 8 of Title 37.2, committed pursuant to Chapter 9 (§ 37.2-900 et seq.) of Title 37.2, or certified pursuant to § 37.2-806 in the event he is found to be unrestorably incompetent. Upon receipt of the report, the court shall make a competency determination according to the procedures specified in subsection E of § 19.2-169.1. If the court finds that the defendant is incompetent and is likely to remain so for the foreseeable future, it shall order that he be (i) released, (ii) committed pursuant to Article 5 (§ 37.2-814 et seq.) of Chapter 8 of Title 37.2, or (iii) certified pursuant to § 37.2-806. However, if the court finds that the defendant is incompetent and is likely to remain so for the foreseeable future and the defendant has been charged with a sexually violent offense, as defined in § 37.2-900, he shall be screened pursuant to the procedures set forth in §§ 37.2-903 and 37.2-904. If the court finds the defendant incompetent but restorable to competency in the foreseeable future, it may order treatment continued until six months have elapsed from the date of the defendant's initial admission under subsection A of § 19.2-169.2.

B. At the end of six months from the date of the defendant's initial admission under subsection A of § 19.2-169.2 if the defendant remains incompetent in the opinion of the board, authority, or inpatient facility director or his designee, the director or his designee shall so notify the court and make recommendations concerning disposition of the defendant as described in subsection A. The court shall hold a hearing according to the procedures specified in subsection E of § 19.2-169.1 and, if it finds the defendant unrestorably incompetent, shall order one of the dispositions described in subsection A. If the court finds the defendant incompetent but restorable to competency, it may order continued treatment under subsection A of § 19.2-169.2 for additional six-month periods, provided a hearing pursuant to subsection E of § 19.2-169.1 is held at the completion of each such period and the defendant continues to be incompetent but restorable to competency in the foreseeable future.

C. If any defendant has been charged with a misdemeanor in violation of Article 3 (§ 18.2-95 et seq.) of Chapter 5 of Title 18.2 or Article 5 (§ 18.2-119 et seq.) of Chapter 5 of Title 18.2, other than a misdemeanor charge pursuant to § 18.2-130 or Article 2 (§ 18.2-415 et seq.) of Chapter 9 of Title 18.2, and is being treated pursuant to subsection A of § 19.2-169.2, and after 45 days has not been restored to competency, the director of the community service board, behavioral health authority, or the director of the treating inpatient facility, or any of their designees, shall send a report indicating the defendant's status to the court. The report shall also indicate whether the defendant should be released or committed pursuant to § 37.2-817 or certified pursuant to § 37.2-806. Upon receipt of the report, if the court determines that the defendant is still incompetent, the court shall order that the defendant be released, committed, or certified, and may dismiss the charges against the defendant.

D. Unless an incompetent defendant is charged with capital murder or the charges against an incompetent criminal defendant have been previously dismissed, charges against an unrestorably incompetent defendant shall be dismissed on the date upon which his sentence would have expired had he been convicted and received the maximum sentence for the crime charged, or on the date five years from the date of his arrest for such charges, whichever is sooner.

E. If the court orders an unrestorably incompetent defendant to be screened pursuant to the procedures set forth in §§ 37.2-903 and 37.2-904, it shall order the attorney for the Commonwealth in the jurisdiction wherein the defendant was charged and the Commissioner of Behavioral Health and Developmental Services to provide the Director of the Department of Corrections with any information relevant to the review, including, but not limited to: (i) a copy of the warrant or indictment, (ii) a copy of the defendant's criminal record, (iii) information about the alleged crime, (iv) a copy of the competency report completed pursuant to § 19.2-169.1, and (v) a copy of the report prepared by the director of the defendant's community services board, behavioral health authority, or treating inpatient facility or his designee pursuant to this section. The court shall further order that the defendant be held in the custody of the Department of Behavioral Health and Developmental Services for secure confinement and treatment until the Commitment Review Committee's and Attorney General's review and any subsequent hearing or trial are completed. If the court receives notice that the Attorney General has declined to file a petition for the commitment of an unrestorably incompetent defendant as a sexually violent predator after conducting a review pursuant to § 37.2-905, the court shall order that the defendant be released, committed pursuant to Article 5 (§ 37.2-814 et seq.) of Chapter 8 of Title 37.2, or certified pursuant to § 37.2-806.

F. In any case when an incompetent defendant is charged with capital murder, notwithstanding any other provision of this section, the charge shall not be dismissed and the court having jurisdiction over the capital murder case may order that the defendant receive continued treatment under subsection A of § 19.2-169.2 for additional six-month periods without limitation, provided that (i) a hearing pursuant to subsection E of § 19.2-169.1 is held at the completion of each such period, (ii) the defendant remains incompetent, (iii) the court finds continued treatment to be medically appropriate, and (iv) the defendant presents a danger to himself or others.

G. The attorney for the Commonwealth may bring charges that have been dismissed against the defendant when he is restored to competency.

History.

1982, c. 653; 1999, cc. 946, 985; 2003, cc. 915, 919, 989, cls. 4, 5, 1018, cls. 4, 5, 1042, cls. 10, 11; 2006, cc. 863, 914; 2007, cc. 781, 876; 2008, cc. 406, 796; 2009, cc. 813, 840; 2012, cc. 668, 800.

§ 19.2-169.4. Litigating certain issues when the defendant is incompetent.

A finding of incompetency does not preclude the adjudication, at any time before trial, of a motion objecting to the sufficiency of the indictment, nor does it preclude the adjudication of similar legal objections which, in the court's opinion, may be undertaken without the personal participation of the defendant.

History.

1982, c. 653.

§ 19.2-169.5. Evaluation of sanity at the time of the offense; disclosure of evaluation results.

A. Raising issue of sanity at the time of offense; appointment of evaluators. — If, at any time before trial, the court finds, upon hearing evidence or representations of counsel for the defendant, that there is probable cause to believe that the defendant's sanity will be a significant factor in his defense and that the defendant is financially unable to pay for expert assistance, the court shall appoint one or more qualified mental health experts to evaluate the defendant's sanity at the time of the offense and, where appropriate, to assist in the development of an insanity defense. Such mental health expert shall be a psychiatrist or a clinical psychologist who (i) has performed forensic examinations, (ii) has successfully completed forensic evaluation training recognized by the Commissioner of Behavioral Health and Developmental Services, (iii) has demonstrated to the Commissioner competence to perform forensic evaluations, and (iv) is included on a list of approved evaluators maintained by the Commissioner. The defendant shall not be entitled to a mental health expert of his own choosing or to funds to employ such expert.

B. Location of evaluation. — The evaluation shall be performed on an outpatient basis, at a mental health facility or in jail, unless the court specifically finds that outpatient services are unavailable, or unless the results of the outpatient evaluation indicate that hospitalization of the defendant for further evaluation of his sanity at the time of the offense is necessary. If either finding is made, the court, under authority of this subsection, may order that the defendant be sent to a hospital designated by the Commissioner of Behavioral Health and Developmental Services as appropriate for evaluation of the defendant under criminal charge. The defendant shall be hospitalized for such time as the director of the hospital deems necessary to perform an adequate evaluation of the defendant's sanity at the time of the offense, but not to exceed 30 days from the date of admission to the hospital.

C. Provision of information to evaluator. — The court shall require the party making the motion for the evaluation, and such other parties as the court deems appropriate, to provide to the evaluators appointed under subsection A any information relevant to the evaluation, including, but not limited to (i) copy of the warrant or indictment; (ii) the names and addresses of the attorney for the Commonwealth, the attorney for the defendant and the judge who appointed the expert; (iii) information pertaining to the alleged crime, including statements by the defendant made to the police and transcripts of preliminary hearings, if any; (iv) a summary of the reasons for the evaluation request; (v) any available psychiatric, psychological, medical or social records that are deemed relevant; and (vi) a copy of the defendant's criminal record, to the extent reasonably available.

D. The evaluators shall prepare a full report concerning the defendant's sanity at the time of the offense, including whether he may have had a significant mental disease or defect which rendered him insane at the time of the offense. The report shall be prepared within the time period designated by the court, said period to include the time necessary to obtain and evaluate the information specified in subsection C.

E. Disclosure of evaluation results. — The report described in subsection D shall be sent solely to the attorney for the defendant and shall be deemed to be protected by the lawyer-client privilege. However, the Commonwealth shall be given the report in all felony cases, the results of any other evaluation of the defendant's sanity at the time of the offense, and copies of psychiatric, psychological, medical, or other records obtained during the course of any such evaluation, after the attorney for the defendant gives notice of an intent to present psychiatric or psychological evidence pursuant to § 19.2-168. In addition, in all cases, the evaluator shall send a redacted copy of the report removing references to the defendant's name, date of birth, case number, and court of jurisdiction to the Commissioner of Behavioral Health and Developmental Services for the purpose of peer review to establish and maintain the list of approved evaluators described in subsection A.

F. In any case where the defendant obtains his own expert to evaluate the defendant's sanity at the time of the offense, the provisions of subsections D and E, relating to the disclosure of the evaluation results, shall apply.

History.
1982, c. 653; 1986, c. 535; 1987, c. 439; 1996, cc. 937, 980; 2005, c. 428; 2009, cc. 813, 840; 2016, c. 445.

§ 19.2-169.6. Inpatient psychiatric hospital admission from local correctional facility.

A. Any inmate of a local correctional facility who is not subject to the provisions of § 19.2-169.2 may be hospitalized for psychiatric treatment at a hospital designated by the Commissioner of Behavioral Health and Developmental Services as appropriate for treatment of persons under criminal charge if:

1. The court with jurisdiction over the inmate's case, if it is still pending, on the petition of the person having custody over an inmate or on its own motion, holds a hearing at which the inmate is represented by counsel and finds by clear and convincing evidence that (i) the inmate has a mental illness; (ii) there exists a substantial likelihood that, as a result of a mental illness, the inmate will, in the near future, (a) cause serious physical harm to himself or others as evidenced by recent behavior causing, attempting, or threatening harm and any other relevant information or (b) suffer serious harm due to his lack of capacity to protect himself from harm as evidenced by recent behavior and any other relevant information; and (iii) the inmate requires treatment in a hospital rather than the local correctional facility. Prior to making this determination, the court shall consider the examination conducted in accordance with § 37.2-815 and the preadmission screening report prepared in accordance with § 37.2-816 and conducted in-person or by means of a two-way electronic video and audio communication system as authorized in § 37.2-804.1 by an employee or designee of the local community services board or behavioral health authority who is skilled in the assessment and treatment of mental illness, who is not providing treatment to the inmate, and

who has completed a certification program approved by the Department of Behavioral Health and Developmental Services as provided in § 37.2-809. The examiner appointed pursuant to § 37.2-815, if not physically present at the hearing, shall be available whenever possible for questioning during the hearing through a two-way electronic video and audio or telephonic communication system as authorized in § 37.2-804.1. Any employee or designee of the local community services board or behavioral health authority, as defined in § 37.2-809, representing the board or authority that prepared the preadmission screening report shall attend the hearing in person or, if physical attendance is not practicable, shall participate in the hearing through a two-way electronic video and audio communication system as authorized in § 37.2-804.1. When the hearing is held outside the service area of the community services board or behavioral health authority that prepared the preadmission screening report, and it is not practicable for a representative of the board or authority to attend or participate in the hearing, arrangements shall be made by the board or authority for an employee or designee of the board or authority serving the area in which the hearing is held to attend or participate on behalf of the board or authority that prepared the preadmission screening report; or

2. Upon petition by the person having custody over an inmate, a magistrate finds probable cause to believe that (i) the inmate has a mental illness; (ii) there exists a substantial likelihood that, as a result of a mental illness, the inmate will, in the near future, (a) cause serious physical harm to himself or others as evidenced by recent behavior causing, attempting, or threatening harm and any other relevant information or (b) suffer serious harm due to his lack of capacity to protect himself from harm as evidenced by recent behavior and any other relevant information; and (iii) the inmate requires treatment in a hospital rather than a local correctional facility, and the magistrate issues a temporary detention order for the inmate. Prior to the filing of the petition, the person having custody shall arrange for an evaluation of the inmate conducted in-person or by means of a two-way electronic video and audio communication system as authorized in § 37.2-804.1 by an employee or designee of the local community services board or behavioral health authority who is skilled in the assessment and treatment of mental illness and who has completed a certification program approved by the Department as provided in § 37.2-809. After considering the evaluation of the employee or designee of the local community services board or behavioral health authority, and any other information presented, and finding that probable cause exists to meet the criteria, the magistrate may issue a temporary detention order in accordance with the applicable procedures specified in §§ 37.2-809 through 37.2-813. The person having custody over the inmate shall notify the court having jurisdiction over the inmate's case, if it is still pending, and the inmate's attorney prior to the detention pursuant to a temporary detention order or as soon thereafter as is reasonable.

Upon detention pursuant to this subdivision, a hearing shall be held either before the court having jurisdiction over the inmate's case or before a district court judge or a special justice, as defined in § 37.2-100, in accordance with the provisions of §§ 37.2-815 through 37.2-821, in which case the inmate shall be represented by counsel as specified in § 37.2-814. The hearing shall be held within 72 hours of execution of the temporary detention order issued pursuant to this subdivision. If the 72-hour period terminates on a Saturday, Sunday, legal holiday, or day on which the court is lawfully closed, the inmate may be detained until the close of business on the next day that is not a Saturday, Sunday, legal holiday, or day on which the court is lawfully closed. Any employee or designee of the local community services board or behavioral health authority, as defined in § 37.2-809, representing the board or authority that prepared the preadmission screening report shall attend the hearing in person or, if physical attendance is not practicable, shall participate in the hearing through a two-way electronic video and audio communication system as authorized in § 37.2-804.1. When the hearing is held outside the service area of the community services board or behavioral health authority that prepared the preadmission screening report, and it is not practicable for a representative of the board or authority to attend or participate in the hearing, arrangements shall be made by the board or authority for an employee or designee of the board or authority serving the area in which the hearing is held to attend or participate on behalf of the board or authority that prepared the preadmission screening report. The judge or special justice conducting the hearing may order the inmate hospitalized if, after considering the examination conducted in accordance with § 37.2-815, the preadmission screening report prepared in accordance with § 37.2-816, and any other available information as specified in subsection C of § 37.2-817, he finds by clear and convincing evidence that (1) the inmate has a mental illness; (2) there exists a substantial likelihood that, as a result of a mental illness, the inmate will, in the near future, (a) cause serious physical harm to himself or others as evidenced by recent behavior causing, attempting, or threatening harm and any other relevant information or (b) suffer serious harm due to his lack of capacity to protect himself from harm as evidenced by recent behavior and any other relevant information; and (3) the inmate requires treatment in a hospital rather than a local correctional facility. The examiner appointed pursuant to § 37.2-815, if not physically present at the hearing, shall be available whenever possible for questioning during the hearing through a two-way electronic video and audio or telephonic communication system as authorized in § 37.2-804.1. The examination and the preadmission screening report shall be admitted into evidence at the hearing.

B. In no event shall an inmate have the right to make application for voluntary admission as may be otherwise provided in § 37.2-805 or 37.2-814 or be subject to an order for mandatory outpatient treatment as provided in § 37.2-817.

C. If an inmate is hospitalized pursuant to this section and his criminal case is still pending, the court having jurisdiction over the inmate's case may order that the admitting hospital evaluate the inmate's competency to stand trial and his mental state at the time of the offense pursuant to §§ 19.2-169.1 and 19.2-169.5.

D. An inmate may not be hospitalized longer than 30 days under subsection A unless the court which has criminal jurisdiction over him or a district court judge or a special justice, as defined in § 37.2-100, holds a hearing and orders the inmate's continued hospitalization in accordance with the provisions of subdivision A 2. If the inmate's hospitalization is continued under this subsection by a court other than the court which has jurisdiction over his criminal case, the facility at which the inmate is hospitalized shall notify the court with jurisdiction over his criminal case and the inmate's attorney in the criminal case, if the case is still pending.

E. Hospitalization may be extended in accordance with subsection D for periods of 60 days for inmates awaiting trial, but in no event may such hospitalization be continued beyond trial, nor shall such hospitalization act to delay trial, as long as the inmate remains competent to stand trial. Hospitalization may be extended in accordance with subsection D for periods of 180 days for an inmate who has been convicted and not yet sentenced, or for an inmate who has been convicted of a crime and is in the custody of a local correctional facility after sentencing, but in no event may such hospitalization be continued beyond the date upon which his sentence would have expired had he received the maximum sentence for the crime charged. Any inmate who has not completed service of his sentence upon discharge from the hospital shall serve the remainder of his sentence.

F. For any inmate who has been convicted and not yet sentenced, or who has been convicted of a crime and is in the custody of a local correctional facility after sentencing, the time the inmate is confined in a hospital for psychiatric treatment shall be deducted from any term for which he may be sentenced to any penal institution, reformatory or elsewhere.

G. Any health care provider, as defined in § 32.1-127.1:03, or other provider rendering services to an inmate who is the subject of a proceeding under this section, upon request, shall disclose to a magistrate, the court, the inmate's attorney, the inmate's guardian ad litem, the examiner appointed pursuant to § 37.2-815, the community service board or behavioral health authority preparing the preadmission screening pursuant to § 37.2-816, or the sheriff or administrator of the local correctional facility any and all information that is necessary and appropriate to enable each of them to perform his duties under this section. These health care providers and other service providers shall disclose to one another health records and information where necessary to provide care and treatment to the inmate and to monitor that care and treatment. Health records disclosed to a sheriff or administrator of the local correctional facility shall be limited to information necessary to protect the sheriff or administrator of the local correctional facility and his employees, the inmate, or the public from physical injury or to address the health care needs of the inmate. Information disclosed to a law-enforcement officer shall not be used for any other purpose, disclosed to others, or retained.

Any health care provider disclosing records pursuant to this section shall be immune from civil liability for any harm resulting from the disclosure, including any liability under the federal Health Insurance Portability and Accountability Act (42 U.S.C. § 1320d et seq.), as amended, unless the person or provider disclosing such records intended the harm or acted in bad faith.

H. Any order entered where an inmate is the subject of proceedings under this section shall provide for the disclosure of medical records pursuant to subsection G. This subsection shall not preclude any other disclosures as required or permitted by law.

I. As used in this section, "person having custody over an inmate" means the sheriff or other person in charge of the local correctional facility where the inmate is incarcerated at the time of the filing of a petition for the psychiatric treatment of the inmate.

History.

1982, c. 653; 1986, c. 629; 1987, c. 96; 1990, c. 76; 1995, c. 844; 2005, c. 716; 2008, cc. 779, 782, 850, 870; 2010, cc. 340, 406; 2012, c. 801; 2014, cc. 499, 538, 691; 2016, cc. 357, 599.

§ 19.2-169.7. Disclosure by defendant during evaluation or treatment; use at guilt phase of trial.

No statement or disclosure by the defendant concerning the alleged offense made during a competency evaluation ordered pursuant to § 19.2-169.1, a mental state at the time of the offense evaluation ordered pursuant to § 19.2-169.5, or treatment ordered pursuant to § 19.2-169.2 or § 19.2-169.6 may be used against the defendant at trial as evidence or as a basis for such evidence, except on the issue of his mental condition at the time of the offense after he raises the issue pursuant to § 19.2-168.

History.

1982, c. 653.

§ 19.2-169.8. Orders for evaluation or treatment; duties of clerk; copies.

A. Whenever a court orders an evaluation pursuant to § 19.2-168.1, 19.2-169.1, or 19.2-169.5 or orders treatment pursuant to § 19.2-169.2 or 19.2-169.6, the clerk of the court shall provide a copy of the order to the appointed evaluator or to the director of the community services board, behavioral health authority, or hospital named in the order as soon as practicable but no later than the close of business on the next business day following entry of the order. The party requesting the evaluation pursuant to § 19.2-168.1, 19.2-169.1, or 19.2-169.5, the attorney for the Commonwealth if treatment is ordered pursuant to § 19.2-169.2, or the petitioner if treatment is ordered pursuant to § 19.2-169.6 shall be responsible for providing to the court the name, address, and other contact information for the appointed evaluator or the director of the community services board, behavioral health authority, or hospital unless the court or clerk already has this information. The appointed evaluator or the director of the community services board, behavioral health authority, or hospital shall acknowledge receipt of the order to the clerk of the court on a form developed by the Office of the Executive Secretary of the Supreme Court of Virginia as soon as practicable but no later than the close of business on the next business day following receipt of the order.

B. No person shall be liable for any act or omission relating to the performance of any requirement set forth in subsection A unless the person was grossly negligent or engaged in willful misconduct.

History.
2016, cc. 446, 449.

§§ 19.2-170 through 19.2-174: Repealed by Acts 1982, c. 653.

Cross references.
For present provisions covering the subject matter of the repealed sections, see §§ 19.2-168.1 and 19.2-169.1 through 19.2-169.7.

§ 19.2-174.1. Information required prior to admission to a mental health facility.

Prior to any person being placed into the custody of the Commissioner for evaluation or treatment pursuant to §§ 19.2-169.2, 19.2-169.3, 19.2-169.6, 19.2-182.2, and 19.2-182.3, and Chapter 9 (§ 37.2-900 et seq.) of Title 37.2, the court or special justice shall provide the Commissioner with the following, if available: (i) the commitment order, (ii) the names and addresses for the attorney for the Commonwealth, the attorney for the person and the judge holding jurisdiction over the person, (iii) a copy of the warrant or indictment, and (iv) a copy of the criminal incident information as defined in § 2.2-3706 or a copy of the arrest report or a summary of the facts relating to the crime. The party requesting the placement into the Commissioner's custody or, in the case of admissions pursuant to §§ 19.2-169.3 and 19.2-169.6, and Chapter 9 (§ 37.2-900 et seq.) of Title 37.2, the person having custody over the defendant or inmate shall gather the above information for submission to the court at the hearing. If the information is not available at the hearing, it shall be provided by the party requesting placement or the person having custody directly to the Commissioner within 96 hours of the person being placed into the Commissioner's custody. If the 96-hour period expires on a Saturday, Sunday or legal holiday, the 96 hours shall be extended to the next day that is not a Saturday, Sunday or legal holiday.

History.
1995, c. 645; 1999, cc. 946, 985; 2001, c. 837; 2003, c. 989, cls. 4, 5, 1018, cls. 4, 5, 1042, cls. 10, 11; 2010, cc. 340, 406.

§ 19.2-175. Compensation of experts.

Each psychiatrist, clinical psychologist or other expert appointed by the court to render professional service pursuant to § 19.2-168.1, 19.2-169.1, 19.2-169.5, 19.2-182.8, 19.2-182.9, 19.2-264.3:1, 19.2-264.3:3 or 19.2-301, who is not regularly employed by the Commonwealth of Virginia except by the University of Virginia School of Medicine and the Medical College of Virginia Commonwealth University, shall receive a reasonable fee for such service. For any psychiatrist, clinical psychologist, or other expert appointed by the court to render such professional services who is regularly employed by the Commonwealth of Virginia, except by the University of Virginia School of Medicine or the Medical College of Virginia Commonwealth University, the fee shall be paid only for professional services provided during nonstate hours that have been approved by his employing agency as being beyond the scope of his state employment duties. The fee shall be determined in each instance by the court that appointed the expert, in accordance with guidelines established by the Supreme Court after consultation with the Department of Behavioral Health and Developmental Services. Except in capital murder cases the fee shall not exceed $750, but in addition if any such expert is required to appear as a witness in any hearing held pursuant to such sections, he shall receive mileage and a fee of $100 for each day during which he is required so to serve. An itemized account of expense, duly sworn to, must be presented to the court, and when allowed shall be certified to the Supreme Court for payment out of the state treasury, and be charged against the appropriations made to pay criminal charges. Allowance for the fee and for the per diem authorized shall also be made by order of the court, duly certified to the Supreme Court for payment out of the appropriation to pay criminal charges.

History.
Code 1950, § 19.1-233; 1960, c. 366; 1968, c. 657; 1970, c. 640; 1975, c. 495; 1976, c. 140; 1978, cc. 195, 794; 1979, c. 516; 1982, c.

653; 1986, c. 535; 1990, c. 697; 1995, c. 645; 2003, cc. 1031, 1040; 2006, cc. 114, 170; 2007, c. 829; 2009, cc. 813, 840; 2010, cc. 340, 406.

§ **19.2-176:** Repealed by Acts 2010, cc. 340 and 406, cl. 2.

§ **19.2-177:** Repealed by Acts 1988, cc. 787, 873.

Cross references.

As to determination of mental illness after sentencing, see now § 19.2-177.1.

§ **19.2-177.1:** Repealed by Acts 2010, cc. 340 and 406, cl. 2.

§ 19.2-178. Where prisoner kept when no vacancy in facility or hospital.

When a court shall have entered any of the orders provided for in § 19.2-168.1, 19.2-169.1, 19.2-169.5, or 19.2-169.6, the sheriff of the county or city or the proper officer of the penal institution shall immediately proceed to ascertain whether a vacancy exists at the proper facility or hospital and until it is ascertained that there is a vacancy such person shall be kept in the jail of such county or city or in such custody as the court may order, or in the penal institution in which he is confined, until there is room in such facility or hospital. Any person whose care and custody is herein provided for shall be taken to and from the facility or hospital to which he was committed by an officer of the penal institution having custody of him, or by the sheriff of the county or city whose court issued the order of commitment, and the expenses incurred in such removals shall be paid by such penal institution, county or city.

History.

Code 1950, § 19.1-236; 1960, c. 366; 1975, c. 495; 1995, c. 645; 2010, cc. 340, 406.

§ **19.2-179:** Repealed by Acts 1981, c. 310.

§ 19.2-180. Sentence or trial of prisoner when restored to sanity.

When a prisoner whose trial or sentence was suspended by reason of his being found to be insane or feebleminded, has been found to be mentally competent and is brought from a hospital and committed to jail, if already convicted, he shall be sentenced, and if not, the court shall proceed to try him as if no delay had occurred on account of his insanity or feeblemindedness.

History.

Code 1950, § 19.1-238; 1960, c. 366; 1975, c. 495.

§ **19.2-181:** Repealed by Acts 1991, c. 427.

Cross references.

For provisions pertaining to disposition of persons acquitted by reason of insanity, see § 19.2-182.2 et seq.

§ 19.2-182. Representation by counsel in proceeding for commitment.

A. In any proceeding for commitment under this title, the judge before whom or upon whose order the proceeding is being held shall ascertain if the person whose commitment is sought is represented by counsel. If the person is not represented by counsel, the judge shall appoint an attorney at law to represent him in the proceeding. The attorney shall receive a fee of $150 for his services, to be paid by the Commonwealth.

B. Any attorney representing any person in any proceeding for commitment under this title shall, prior to such proceeding, personally consult with such person.

History.

Code 1950, § 19.1-239.1; 1966, c. 715; 1975, c. 495; 1991, c. 427; 2016, c. 474.

§ **19.2-182.1:** Repealed by Acts 1982, c. 653.

CHAPTER 11.1.

DISPOSITION OF PERSONS ACQUITTED BY REASON OF INSANITY.

§ 19.2-182.2. Verdict of acquittal by reason of insanity to state the fact; temporary custody and evaluation.

When the defense is insanity of the defendant at the time the offense was committed, the jurors shall be instructed, if they acquit him on that ground, to state the fact with their verdict. The court shall place the person so acquitted (the acquittee) in temporary custody of the Commissioner of Behav-

Criminal Procedure

ioral Health and Developmental Services (hereinafter referred to in this chapter as the Commissioner) for evaluation as to whether the acquittee may be released with or without conditions or requires commitment. The evaluation shall be conducted by (i) one psychiatrist and (ii) one clinical psychologist. The psychiatrist or clinical psychologist shall be skilled in the diagnosis of mental illness and intellectual disability and qualified by training and experience to perform such evaluations. The Commissioner shall appoint both evaluators, at least one of whom shall not be employed by the hospital in which the acquittee is primarily confined. The evaluators shall determine whether the acquittee currently has mental illness or intellectual disability and shall assess the acquittee and report on his condition and need for hospitalization with respect to the factors set forth in § 19.2-182.3. The evaluators shall conduct their examinations and report their findings separately within 45 days of the Commissioner's assumption of custody. Copies of the report shall be sent to the acquittee's attorney, the attorney for the Commonwealth for the jurisdiction where the person was acquitted and the community services board or behavioral health authority as designated by the Commissioner. If either evaluator recommends conditional release or release without conditions of the acquittee, the court shall extend the evaluation period to permit the hospital in which the acquittee is confined and the appropriate community services board or behavioral health authority to jointly prepare a conditional release or discharge plan, as applicable, prior to the hearing.

History.

1991, c. 427; 1993, c. 295; 1996, cc. 937, 980; 2007, cc. 485, 565; 2009, cc. 813, 840; 2012, cc. 476, 507.

§ 19.2-182.3. Commitment; civil proceedings.

Upon receipt of the evaluation report and, if applicable, a conditional release or discharge plan, the court shall schedule the matter for hearing on an expedited basis, giving the matter priority over other civil matters before the court, to determine the appropriate disposition of the acquittee. Except as otherwise ordered by the court, the attorney who represented the defendant at the criminal proceedings shall represent the acquittee through the proceedings pursuant to this section. The matter may be continued on motion of either party for good cause shown. The acquittee shall be provided with adequate notice of the hearing, of the right to be present at the hearing, the right to the assistance of counsel in preparation for and during the hearing, and the right to introduce evidence and cross-examine witnesses at the hearing. The hearing is a civil proceeding.

At the conclusion of the hearing, the court shall commit the acquittee if it finds that he has mental illness or intellectual disability and is in need of inpatient hospitalization. For the purposes of this chapter, mental illness includes any mental illness, as defined in § 37.2-100, in a state of remission when the illness may, with reasonable probability, become active. The decision of the court shall be based upon consideration of the following factors:

1. To what extent the acquittee has mental illness or intellectual disability, as those terms are defined in § 37.2-100;

2. The likelihood that the acquittee will engage in conduct presenting a substantial risk of bodily harm to other persons or to himself in the foreseeable future;

3. The likelihood that the acquittee can be adequately controlled with supervision and treatment on an outpatient basis; and

4. Such other factors as the court deems relevant.

If the court determines that an acquittee does not need inpatient hospitalization solely because of treatment or habilitation he is currently receiving, but the court is not persuaded that the acquittee will continue to receive such treatment or habilitation, it may commit him for inpatient hospitalization. The court shall order the acquittee released with conditions pursuant to §§ 19.2-182.7, 19.2-182.8, and 19.2-182.9 if it finds that he is not in need of inpatient hospitalization but that he meets the criteria for conditional release set forth in § 19.2-182.7. If the court finds that the acquittee does not need inpatient hospitalization nor does he meet the criteria for conditional release, it shall release him without conditions, provided the court has approved a discharge plan prepared by the appropriate community services board or behavioral health authority in consultation with the appropriate hospital staff.

History.

1991, c. 427; 1993, c. 295; 2005, c. 716; 2012, cc. 476, 507.

§ 19.2-182.4. Confinement and treatment; interfacility transfers; out-of-hospital visits; notice of change in treatment.

A. Upon commitment of an acquittee for inpatient hospitalization, the Commissioner shall determine the appropriate placement for him, based on his clinical needs and security requirements. The Commissioner may make interfacility transfers and treatment and management decisions regarding acquittees in his custody without obtaining prior approval of or review by the committing court. If the Commissioner is of the opinion that a temporary visit from the hospital would be therapeutic for the acquittee and that such visit would pose no substantial danger to others, the Commissioner may grant such visit not to exceed forty-eight hours.

B. The Commissioner shall give notice of the granting of an unescorted community visit to any victim of a felony offense against the person punishable by more than five years in prison that resulted in the charges on which the acquittee was acquitted or the next-of-kin of the victim at the last known address, provided the person seeking notice submits a written request for such notice to the Commissioner.

C. The Commissioner shall notify the attorney for the Commonwealth for the committing jurisdiction in writing of changes in an acquittee's course of treatment which will involve authorization for the acquittee to leave the grounds of the hospital in which he is confined.

History.

1991, c. 427; 1993, c. 295; 2006, c. 358.

§ 19.2-182.5. Review of continuation of confinement hearing; procedure and reports; disposition.

A. The committing court shall conduct a hearing twelve months after the date of commitment to assess the need for inpatient hospitalization of each acquittee who is acquitted of a felony by reason of insanity. A hearing for assessment shall be conducted at yearly intervals for five years and at biennial intervals thereafter. The court shall schedule the matter for hearing as soon as possible after it becomes due, giving the matter priority over all pending matters before the court.

B. Prior to the hearing, the Commissioner shall provide to the court a report evaluating the acquittee's condition and recommending treatment, to be prepared by a psychiatrist or a psychologist. The psychologist who prepares the report shall be a clinical psychologist and any evaluating psychiatrist or clinical psychologist shall be skilled in the diagnosis of mental illness and qualified by training and experience to perform forensic evaluations. If the examiner recommends release or the acquittee requests release, the acquittee's condition and need for inpatient hospitalization shall be evaluated by a second person with such credentials who is not currently treating the acquittee. A copy of any report submitted pursuant to this subsection shall be sent to the attorney for the Commonwealth for the jurisdiction from which the acquittee was committed.

C. The acquittee shall be provided with adequate notice of the hearing, of the right to be present at the hearing, the right to the assistance of counsel in preparation for and during the hearing, and the right to introduce evidence and cross-examine witnesses at the hearing. Written notice of the hearing shall be provided to the attorney for the Commonwealth for the committing jurisdiction. The hearing is a civil proceeding.

According to the determination of the court following the hearing, and based upon the report and other evidence provided at the hearing, the court shall (i) release the acquittee from confinement if he does not need inpatient hospitalization and does not meet the criteria for conditional release set forth in § 19.2-182.7, provided the court has approved a discharge plan prepared jointly by the hospital staff and the appropriate community services board or behavioral health authority; (ii) place the acquittee on conditional release if he meets the criteria for conditional release, and the court has approved a conditional release plan prepared jointly by the hospital staff and the appropriate community services board or behavioral health authority; or (iii) order that he remain in the custody of the Commissioner if he continues to require inpatient hospitalization based on consideration of the factors set forth in § 19.2-182.3.

D. An acquittee who is found not guilty of a misdemeanor by reason of insanity on or after July 1, 2002, shall remain in the custody of the Commissioner pursuant to this chapter for a period not to exceed one year from the date of acquittal. If, prior to or at the conclusion of one year, the Commissioner determines that the acquittee meets the criteria for conditional release or release without conditions pursuant to § 19.2-182.7, emergency custody pursuant to § 37.2-808, temporary detention pursuant to §§ 37.2-809 to 37.2-813, or involuntary commitment pursuant to Article 5 (§ 37.2-814 et seq.) of Chapter 8 of Title 37.2, he shall petition the committing court. Written notice of an acquittee's scheduled release shall be provided by the Commissioner to the attorney for the Commonwealth for the committing jurisdiction not less than thirty days prior to the scheduled release. The Commissioner's duty to file a petition upon such determination shall not preclude the ability of any other person meeting the requirements of § 37.2-808 to file the petition.

History.

1991, c. 427; 1993, c. 295; 1996, cc. 937, 980; 2002, c. 750; 2007, cc. 485, 565.

§ 19.2-182.6. Petition for release; conditional release hearing; notice; disposition.

A. The Commissioner may petition the committing court for conditional or unconditional release of the acquittee at any time he believes the acquittee no longer needs hospitalization. The petition shall be accompanied by a report of clinical findings supporting the petition with respect to the factors set forth in § 19.2-182.3 and by a conditional release or discharge plan, as applicable, prepared jointly by the hospital and the appropriate community services board or behavioral health authority. The acquittee may petition the committing court for release only once in each year in which no annual judicial review is required pursuant to § 19.2-182.5. The party petitioning for release shall transmit a copy of the petition to the attorney for the Commonwealth for the committing jurisdiction.

B. 1. When a petition for release is made by the acquittee, the court shall order the Commissioner to appoint two persons in the same manner as set forth in § 19.2-182.2 to assess and report on the acquittee's need for inpatient hospitalization by reviewing his condition with respect to the factors set forth in § 19.2-182.3. The evaluators shall conduct their evaluations and report their finding in accordance with the provisions of § 19.2-182.2, except that the evaluations shall be completed and findings reported within 45 days of issuance of the court's order for evaluation.

2. When a petition for release is made by the Commissioner no further evaluations of the acquittee shall be required unless otherwise deemed necessary by the court. If the court determines that further evaluation is necessary, the court shall order the Commissioner to appoint two persons in the same manner as set forth in § 19.2-182.2 to assess and report on the acquittee's need for inpatient hospitalization by reviewing his condition with respect to the factors set forth in § 19.2-182.3. The evaluators shall conduct their evaluations and report their finding in accordance with the provisions of § 19.2-182.2, except that the evaluations shall be completed and findings reported within 45 days of issuance of the court's order for evaluation.

The Commissioner shall give notice of the hearing to any victim of the act resulting in the charges on which the acquittee was acquitted or the next of kin of the victim at the last known address, provided the person submits a written request for such notification to the Commissioner.

C. Upon receipt of the reports of evaluation, the court shall conduct a hearing on the petition. The hearing shall be scheduled on an expedited basis and given priority over other civil matters before the court. The acquittee shall be provided with adequate notice of the hearing, of the right to be present at the hearing, the right to the assistance of counsel in preparation for and during the hearing, and the right to introduce evidence and cross-examine witnesses. Written notice of the hearing shall be provided to the attorney for the Commonwealth for the committing jurisdiction. The hearing is a civil proceeding.

At the conclusion of the hearing, based upon the report and other evidence provided at the hearing, the court shall order the acquittee (i) released from confinement if he does not need inpatient hospitalization and does not meet the criteria for conditional release set forth in § 19.2-182.3, provided the court has approved a discharge plan prepared jointly by the hospital and the appropriate community services board or behavioral health authority; (ii) placed on conditional release if he meets the criteria for such release as set forth in § 19.2-182.7, and the court has approved a conditional release plan prepared jointly by the hospital and the appropriate community services board or behavioral health authority; or (iii) retained in the custody of the Commissioner if he continues to require inpatient hospitalization based on consideration of the factors set forth in § 19.2-182.3.

D. Persons committed pursuant to this chapter shall be released only in accordance with the procedures set forth governing release and conditional release.

History.

1991, c. 427; 1993, c. 295; 2007, cc. 485, 565, 785.

§ 19.2-182.7. Conditional release; criteria; conditions; reports.

At any time the court considers the acquittee's need for inpatient hospitalization pursuant to this chapter, it shall place the acquittee on conditional release if it finds that (i) based on consideration of the factors which the court must consider in its commitment decision, he does not need inpatient hospitalization but needs outpatient treatment or monitoring to prevent his condition from deteriorating to a degree that he would need inpatient hospitalization; (ii) appropriate outpatient supervision and treatment are reasonably available; (iii) there is significant reason to believe that the acquittee, if conditionally released, would comply with the conditions specified; and (iv) conditional release will not present an undue risk to public safety. The court shall subject a conditionally released acquittee to such orders and conditions it deems will best meet the acquittee's need for treatment and supervision and best serve the interests of justice and society.

The community services board or behavioral health authority as designated by the Commissioner shall implement the court's conditional release orders and shall submit written reports to the court on the acquittee's progress and adjustment in the community no less frequently than every six months. An aquittee's conditional release shall not be revoked solely because of his voluntary admission to a state hospital.

After a finding by the court that the acquittee has violated the conditions of his release but does not require inpatient hospitalization pursuant to § 19.2-182.8, the court may hold the acquittee in contempt of court for violation of the conditional release order.

History.

1991, c. 427; 1999, cc. 700, 746; 2007, cc. 485, 565; 2008, c. 810.

§ 19.2-182.8. Revocation of conditional release.

If at any time the court that released an acquittee pursuant to § 19.2-182.7 finds reasonable ground to believe that an acquittee on conditional release (i) has violated the conditions of his release or is no longer a proper subject for conditional release based on application of the criteria for conditional release and (ii) requires inpatient hospitalization, it may order an evaluation of the acquittee by a psychiatrist or clinical psychologist, provided the psychiatrist or clinical psychologist is qualified by training and experience to perform forensic evaluations. If the court, based on the evaluation and after hearing evidence on the issue, finds by a preponderance of the evidence that an acquittee on conditional release (a) has violated the conditions of his release or is no longer a proper subject for conditional release based on application of the criteria for conditional release and (b) has mental illness or intellectual disability and requires inpatient hospitalization, the court may revoke the acquittee's conditional release and order him returned to the custody of the Commissioner.

At any hearing pursuant to this section, the acquittee shall be provided with adequate notice of the hearing, of the right to be present at the hearing, the right to the assistance of counsel in preparation for and during the hearing, and the right to introduce evidence and cross-examine witnesses at the hearing. The hearing shall be scheduled on an expedited basis and shall be given priority over other civil matters before the court. Written notice of the hearing shall be provided to the attorney for the Commonwealth for the committing jurisdiction. The hearing is a civil proceeding.

History.

1991, c. 427; 1993, c. 295; 1996, cc. 937, 980; 2006, cc. 343, 369, 370; 2008, c. 810; 2012, cc. 476, 507.

§ 19.2-182.9. Emergency custody of conditionally released acquittee.

When exigent circumstances do not permit compliance with revocation procedures set forth in § 19.2-182.8, any district court judge or a special justice, as defined in § 37.2-100, or a magistrate may issue an emergency custody order, upon the sworn petition of any responsible person or upon his own motion based upon probable cause to believe that an acquittee on conditional release (i) has violated the conditions of his release or is no longer a proper subject for conditional release and (ii) requires inpatient hospitalization. The emergency custody order shall require the acquittee within his judicial district to be taken into custody and transported to a convenient location where a person designated by the community services board or behavioral health authority who is skilled in the diagnosis and treatment of mental illness shall evaluate such acquittee and assess his need for inpatient hospitalization. A law-enforcement officer who, based on his observation or the reliable reports of others, has probable cause to believe that any acquittee on conditional release has violated the conditions of his release and is no longer a proper subject for conditional release and requires emergency evaluation to assess the need for inpatient hospitalization, may take the acquittee into custody and transport him to an appropriate location to assess the need for hospitalization without prior judicial authorization. The evaluation shall be conducted immediately. The acquittee shall remain in custody until a temporary detention order is issued or until he is released, but in no event shall the period of custody exceed eight hours. If it appears from all evidence readily available (a) that the acquittee has violated the conditions of his release or is no longer a proper subject for conditional release and (b) that he requires emergency evaluation to assess the need for inpatient hospitalization, the district court judge or a special justice, as defined in § 37.2-100, or magistrate, upon the advice of such person skilled in the diagnosis and treatment of mental illness, may issue a temporary detention order authorizing the executing officer to place the acquittee in an appropriate institution for a period not to exceed 72 hours prior to a hearing. If the 72-hour period terminates on a Saturday, Sunday, legal holiday, or day on which the court is lawfully closed, the acquittee may be detained until the next day which is not a Saturday, Sunday, legal holiday, or day on which the court is lawfully closed.

The committing court or any district court judge or a special justice, as defined in § 37.2-100, shall have jurisdiction to hear the matter. Prior to the hearing, the acquittee shall be examined by a psychiatrist or licensed clinical psychologist, provided the psychiatrist or clinical psychologist is skilled in the diagnosis of mental illness, who shall certify whether the person is in need of hospitalization. At the hearing the acquittee shall be provided with adequate notice of the hearing, of the right to be present at the hearing, the right to the assistance of counsel in preparation for and during the hearing, and the right to introduce evidence and cross-examine witnesses at the hearing. Following the hearing, if the court determines, based on a preponderance of the evidence presented at the hearing, that the acquittee (1) has violated the conditions of his release or is no longer a proper subject for conditional release and (2) has mental illness or intellectual disability and is in need of inpatient hospitalization, the court shall revoke the acquittee's conditional release and place him in the custody of the Commissioner.

When an acquittee on conditional release pursuant to this chapter is taken into emergency custody, detained, or hospitalized, such action shall be considered to have been taken pursuant to this section, notwithstanding the fact that his status as an insanity acquittee was not known at the time of custody, detention, or hospitalization. Detention or hospitalization of an acquittee pursuant to provisions of law other than those applicable to insanity acquittees pursuant to this chapter shall not render the detention or hospitalization invalid. If a person's status as an insanity acquittee on conditional release is not recognized at the time of emergency custody or detention, at the time his status as such is verified, the provisions applicable to such persons shall be applied and the court hearing the matter shall notify the committing court of the proceedings.

History.

1991, c. 427; 1993, c. 295; 1996, cc. 937, 980; 2001, c. 837; 2005, c. 716; 2006, cc. 343, 370; 2008, c. 810; 2009, cc. 21, 838; 2012, cc. 476, 507; 2014, cc. 499, 538, 691, 761.

§ 19.2-182.10. Release of person whose conditional release was revoked.

If an acquittee is returned to the custody of the Commissioner for inpatient treatment pursuant to revocation proceedings, and his condition improves to the degree that, within 60 days of resumption of custody following the hearing, the acquittee, in the opinion of hospital staff treating the acquittee and the supervising community services board or behavioral health authority, is an appropriate candidate for conditional release, he may be, with the approval of the court, conditionally released as if revocation had not taken place. If treatment is required for longer than 60 days, the acquittee shall be returned to the custody of the Commissioner for a period of hospitalization and treatment which is governed by the provisions of this chapter applicable to committed acquittees.

History.
1991, c. 427; 1993, c. 295; 2006, cc. 199, 225; 2007, cc. 485, 565.

§ 19.2-182.11. Modification or removal of conditions; notice; objections; review.

A. The committing court may modify conditions of release or remove conditions placed on release pursuant to § 19.2-182.7, upon petition of the supervising community services board or behavioral health authority, the attorney for the Commonwealth, or the acquittee or upon its own motion based on reports of the supervising community services board or behavioral health authority. However, the acquittee may petition only annually commencing six months after the conditional release order is issued. Upon petition, the court shall require the supervising community services board or behavioral health authority to provide a report on the acquittee's progress while on conditional release.

B. As it deems appropriate based on the community services board's or behavioral health authority's report and any other evidence provided to it, the court may issue a proposed order for modification or removal of conditions. The court shall provide notice of the order, and their right to object to it within ten days of its issuance, to the acquittee, the supervising community services board or behavioral health authority and the attorney for the Commonwealth for the committing jurisdiction and for the jurisdiction where the acquittee is residing on conditional release. The proposed order shall become final if no objection is filed within ten days of its issuance. If an objection is so filed, the court shall conduct a hearing at which the acquittee, the attorney for the Commonwealth, and the supervising community services board or behavioral health authority have an opportunity to present evidence challenging the proposed order. At the conclusion of the hearing, the court shall issue an order specifying conditions of release or removing existing conditions of release.

History.
1991, c. 427; 2007, cc. 485, 565.

§ 19.2-182.12. Representation of Commonwealth and acquittee.

The attorney for the Commonwealth shall represent the Commonwealth in all proceedings held pursuant to this chapter. The court shall appoint counsel for the acquittee unless the acquittee waives his right to counsel. The court shall consider appointment of the person who represented the acquittee at the last proceeding.

History.
1991, c. 427; 1993, c. 295.

§ 19.2-182.13. Authority of Commissioner; delegation to board; liability.

The Commissioner may delegate any of the duties and powers imposed on or granted to him by this chapter to an administrative board composed of persons with demonstrated expertise in such matters. The Department of Behavioral Health and Developmental Services shall assist the board in its administrative and technical duties. Members of the board shall exercise their powers and duties without compensation and shall be immune from personal liability while acting within the scope of their duties except for intentional misconduct.

History.
1991, c. 427; 2009, cc. 813, 840.

§ 19.2-182.14. Escape of persons placed or committed; penalty.

Any person placed in the temporary custody of the Commissioner pursuant to § 19.2-182.2 or committed to the custody of the Commissioner pursuant to § 19.2-182.3 who escapes from such custody shall be guilty of a Class 6 felony.

History.
1993, c. 295.

§ 19.2-182.15. Escape of persons placed on conditional release; penalty.

Any person placed on conditional release pursuant to § 19.2-182.7 who leaves the Commonwealth without permission from the court which conditionally released the person shall be guilty of a Class 6 felony.

History.
1993, c. 295.

§ 19.2-182.16. Copies of orders to Commissioner.

Copies of all orders and notices issued pursuant to this chapter shall be sent to the Commissioner of the

Criminal Procedure

Department of Behavioral Health and Developmental Services.

History.
1993, c. 295; 2009, cc. 813, 840.

CHAPTER 12.
PRELIMINARY HEARING.

§ 19.2-183. Examination of witnesses; assistance of counsel; evidentiary matters and remedies; power to adjourn case.

A. The judge before whom any person is brought for an offense shall, as soon as may be practical, in the presence of such person, examine on oath the witnesses for and against him. Before conducting the hearing or accepting a waiver of the hearing, the judge shall advise the accused of his right to counsel and, if the accused is indigent and the offense charged be punishable by confinement in jail or the state correctional facility, the judge shall appoint counsel as provided by law.

B. At the hearing the judge shall, in the presence of the accused, hear testimony presented for and against the accused in accordance with the rules of evidence applicable to criminal trials in this Commonwealth. In felony cases, the accused shall not be called upon to plead, but he may cross-examine any witness who testifies on behalf of the Commonwealth or on behalf of any other defendant, introduce witnesses in his own behalf, and testify in his own behalf.

C. A judge may adjourn a trial, pending before him, not exceeding 10 days at one time, without the consent of the accused.

D. At any preliminary hearing under this section, certificates of analysis and reports prepared pursuant to §§ 19.2-187 and 19.2-188 shall be admissible without the testimony of the person preparing such certificate or report.

History.
Code 1950, §§ 19.1-101, 19.1-102; 1960, c. 366; 1968, c. 639; 1973, c. 485; 1975, c. 495; 1982, c. 513; 2010, c. 555.

§ 19.2-183.1. Joint preliminary hearings.

Upon motion of the attorney for the Commonwealth, preliminary hearings for persons alleged to have participated in contemporaneous and related acts or occurrences or in a series of such acts or occurrences constituting an offense or offenses may be heard jointly if jurisdiction over each person and offense lies in the same court, unless the court finds that such joint preliminary hearing would constitute prejudice to a defendant. Upon such a finding, the court shall order that the preliminary hearing for that defendant be held separately.

History.
1993, cc. 462, 489.

§ 19.2-184. Witnesses may be separated (Subsection (a) of Supreme Court Rule 2:615 derived in part from this section).

While a witness is under such examination all other witnesses may by order of the judge be excluded from the place of examination and kept separate from each other.

History.
Code 1950, § 19.1-104; 1960, c. 366; 1968, c. 639; 1975, c. 495.

§ 19.2-185. Testimony may be reduced to writing and subscribed.

When the judge deems it proper the testimony of the witnesses may be reduced to writing, and, if required by him, shall be signed by them respectively.

The judge of the court of record to which the case may be or has been certified may order the testimony of the witnesses at the preliminary hearing to be reduced to writing.

History.
Code 1950, § 19.1-105; 1960, c. 366; 1968, c. 639; 1975, c. 495.

§ 19.2-186. When accused to be discharged, tried, committed or bailed by judge.

The judge shall discharge the accused if he considers that there is not sufficient cause for charging him with the offense.

If a judge considers that there is sufficient cause only to charge the accused with an offense which the judge has jurisdiction to try, then he shall try the accused for such offense and convict him if he deems him guilty and pass judgment upon him in accordance with law just as if the accused had first been brought before him on a warrant charging him with such offense.

If a judge considers that there is sufficient cause to charge the accused with an offense that he does not have jurisdiction to try then he shall certify the case to the appropriate court having jurisdiction and shall commit the accused to jail or let him to bail pursuant to the provisions of Article 1 (§ 19.2-119 et seq.) of Chapter 9 of this title.

History.

Code 1950, § 19.1-106; 1960, c. 366; 1968, c. 639; 1973, c. 485; 1975, c. 495; 1999, cc. 829, 846.

§ 19.2-187. Admission into evidence of certain certificates of analysis.

In any hearing or trial of any criminal offense or in any proceeding brought pursuant to Chapter 22.1 (§ 19.2-386.1 et seq.), a certificate of analysis of a person performing an analysis or examination, duly attested by such person, shall be admissible in evidence as evidence of the facts therein stated and the results of the analysis or examination referred to therein, provided (i) the certificate of analysis is filed with the clerk of the court hearing the case at least seven days prior to the proceeding if the attorney for the Commonwealth intends to offer it into evidence in a preliminary hearing or the accused intends to offer it into evidence in any hearing or trial, or (ii) the requirements of subsection A of § 19.2-187.1 have been satisfied and the accused has not objected to the admission of the certificate pursuant to subsection B of § 19.2-187.1, when any such analysis or examination is performed in any laboratory operated by the Division of Consolidated Laboratory Services or the Department of Forensic Science or authorized by such Department to conduct such analysis or examination, or performed by a person licensed by the Department of Forensic Science pursuant to § 18.2-268.9 or 46.2-341.26:9 to conduct such analysis or examination, or performed by the Federal Bureau of Investigation, the United States Postal Service, the federal Bureau of Alcohol, Tobacco and Firearms, the Naval Criminal Investigative Service, the National Fish and Wildlife Forensics Laboratory, the federal Drug Enforcement Administration, the Forensic Document Laboratory of the U.S. Department of Homeland Security, or the U.S. Secret Service Laboratory.

In a hearing or trial in which the provisions of subsection A of § 19.2-187.1 do not apply, a copy of such certificate shall be mailed or delivered by the clerk or attorney for the Commonwealth to counsel of record for the accused at no charge at least seven days prior to the hearing or trial upon request made by such counsel to the clerk with notice of the request to the attorney for the Commonwealth. The request to the clerk shall be on a form prescribed by the Supreme Court and filed with the clerk at least 10 days prior to the hearing or trial. In the event that a request for a copy of a certificate is filed with the clerk with respect to a case that is not yet before the court, the clerk shall advise the requester that he must resubmit the request at such time as the case is properly before the court in order for such request to be effective. If, upon proper request made by counsel of record for the accused, a copy of such certificate is not mailed or delivered by the clerk or attorney for the Commonwealth to counsel of record for the accused in a timely manner in accordance with this section, the accused shall be entitled to continue the hearing or trial.

The certificate of analysis of any examination conducted by the Department of Forensic Science relating to a controlled substance or marijuana shall be mailed or forwarded by personnel of the Department of Forensic Science to the attorney for the Commonwealth of the jurisdiction where such offense may be heard. The attorney for the Commonwealth shall acknowledge receipt of the certificate on forms provided by the laboratory.

Any such certificate of analysis purporting to be signed, either by hand or by electronic means, by any such person shall be admissible as evidence in such hearing or trial without any proof of the seal or signature or of the official character of the person whose name is signed to it. The attestation signature of a person performing the analysis or examination may be either hand or electronically signed.

For the purposes of this section and §§ 19.2-187.01, 19.2-187.1, and 19.2-187.2, the term "certificate of analysis" includes reports of analysis and results of laboratory examination.

History.

Code 1950, § 19.1-106.1; 1974, c. 200; 1975, c. 495; 1976, c. 245; 1983, c. 178; 1984, c. 607; 1988, c. 494; 1990, cc. 737, 825; 1992, c. 56; 1994, cc. 41, 375; 1995, c. 437; 1999, c. 296; 2000, c. 336; 2002, c. 832; 2005, cc. 868, 881; 2006, c. 294; 2009, Sp. Sess. I, cc. 1, 4; 2010, c. 656; 2011, cc. 384, 410, 645; 2014, cc. 328, 674, 719; 2015, cc. 75, 126.

§ 19.2-187.01. Certificate of analysis as evidence of chain of custody of material described therein.

A report of analysis duly attested by the person performing such analysis or examination in any laboratory operated by (i) the Division of Consolidated Laboratory Services, the Department of Forensic Science or any of its regional laboratories, or by any laboratory authorized by such Division or

Department to conduct such analysis or examination; (ii) the Federal Bureau of Investigation; (iii) the federal Bureau of Alcohol, Tobacco and Firearms; (iv) the Naval Criminal Investigative Service; (v) the federal Drug Enforcement Administration; (vi) the United States Postal Service; (vii) the U.S. Secret Service; or (viii) the Forensic Document Laboratory of the U.S. Department of Homeland Security shall be prima facie evidence in a criminal or civil proceeding as to the custody of the material described therein from the time such material is received by an authorized agent of such laboratory until such material is released subsequent to such analysis or examination. Any such certificate of analysis purporting to be signed by any such person shall be admissible as evidence in such hearing or trial without any proof of the seal or signature or of the official character of the person whose name is signed to it. The signature of the person who received the material for the laboratory on the request for laboratory examination form shall be deemed prima facie evidence that the person receiving the material was an authorized agent and that such receipt constitutes proper receipt by the laboratory for purposes of this section.

History.
1979, c. 364; 1989, c. 458; 1990, cc. 548, 825; 1991, c. 687; 1993, c. 32; 1994, c. 375; 1995, c. 437; 2005, cc. 868, 881; 2011, c. 645; 2015, cc. 75, 126.

§ 19.2-187.02. Admissibility of written reports or records of blood alcohol tests conducted in the regular course of providing emergency medical treatment.

A. Notwithstanding any other provision of law, the written reports or records of blood alcohol tests conducted upon persons receiving medical treatment in a hospital or emergency room are admissible in evidence as a business records exception to the hearsay rule in prosecutions for any violation of § 18.2-266 (driving while intoxicated) or a substantially similar local ordinance, § 18.2-36.1 (involuntary manslaughter resulting from driving while intoxicated), § 18.2-36.2 (involuntary manslaughter resulting from boating while intoxicated), § 18.2-51.4 (maiming resulting from driving while intoxicated), § 18.2-51.5 (maiming resulting from boating while intoxicated), § 29.1-738 (boating while intoxicated), or § 46.2-341.24 (driving a commercial vehicle while intoxicated).

B. The provisions of law pertaining to confidentiality of medical records and medical treatment shall not be applicable to reports or records of blood alcohol tests sought or admitted as evidence under the provisions of this section in prosecutions as specified in subsection A. Owners or custodians of such reports or records may disclose them, in accordance with regulations concerning patient privacy promulgated by the U.S. Department of Health and Human Services, without obtaining consent or authorization for such disclosure. No person who is involved in taking blood or conducting blood alcohol tests shall be liable for civil damages for breach of confidentiality or unauthorized release of medical records because of the evidentiary use of blood alcohol test results under this section, or as a result of that person's testimony given pursuant to this section.

History.
2002, c. 749; 2005, c. 801; 2007, cc. 379, 679.

§ 19.2-187.1. Procedures for notifying accused of certificate of analysis; waiver; continuances.

A. In any trial and in any hearing other than a preliminary hearing, in which the attorney for the Commonwealth intends to offer a certificate of analysis into evidence in lieu of testimony pursuant to § 19.2-187, the attorney for the Commonwealth shall:

1. Provide by mail, delivery, or otherwise, a copy of the certificate to counsel of record for the accused, or to the accused if he is proceeding pro se, at no charge, no later than 28 days prior to the hearing or trial;

2. Provide simultaneously with the copy of the certificate so provided under subdivision 1 a notice to the accused of his right to object to having the certificate admitted without the person who performed the analysis or examination being present and testifying;

2a. When the attorney for the Commonwealth intends to present such testimony through two-way video conferencing, attach to the copy of the certificate provided under subdivision 1 a notice on a page separate from the notice in subdivision 2 specifying that the person who performed the analysis or examination may testify by two-way video conferencing and that the accused has a right to object to such two-way video testimony; and

3. File a copy of the certificate and notice with the clerk of the court hearing the matter (i) on the day that the certificate and notice are provided to the accused or (ii) in the case of a breath test certificate for a violation of any offense listed in subsection E of § 18.2-270, no later than three business days following the day that the certificate and notice are provided to the accused.

B. The accused may object in writing to admission of the certificate of analysis, in lieu of testimony, as evidence of the facts stated therein and of the results of the analysis or examination. Such objection shall be filed with the court hearing the matter, with a copy to the attorney for the Commonwealth, no more than 14 days after the certificate and notice were filed with the clerk by the attorney for the Commonwealth or the objection shall be deemed waived. If timely objection is made, the certificate shall not be admissible into evidence unless (i) the testimony of the person who performed the analysis or examination is admitted into evidence describing the facts and results of the analysis or examination during the Commonwealth's case-in-chief at the hearing or trial and that person is present and subject to cross-examination by the accused, (ii) the objection is waived by the accused or his counsel in writing or before the court, or (iii) the parties stipulate before the court to the admissibility of the certificate. If the accused demands, at hearing or trial, the presence of the person who performed the analysis or examination and he is thereafter found guilty of the charge or charges for which he demanded the presence of such witness, $50 for expenses related to the witness's appearance at hearing or trial shall be charged to the accused as court costs.

B1. When the attorney for the Commonwealth gives notice to the accused of intent to present testimony by two-way video conferencing, the accused may object in writing to the admission of such testimony and may file an objection as provided in subsection B. The provisions of subsection B shall apply to such objection mutatis mutandis.

B2. The two-way video testimony permitted by this section shall comply with the provisions of subsection B of § 19.2-3.1. In addition, unless otherwise agreed by the parties and the court, (i) all orders pertaining to witnesses apply to witnesses testifying by video conferencing; (ii) upon request, all materials read or used by the witness during his testimony shall be identified on the video; and (iii) any witness testifying by video conferencing shall certify at the conclusion of his testimony, under penalty of perjury, that he did not engage in any off-camera communications with any person during his testimony.

C. Where the person who performed the analysis and examination is not available for hearing or trial and the attorney for the Commonwealth has used due diligence to secure the presence of the person, the court shall order a continuance. Any continuances ordered pursuant to this subsection shall total not more than 90 days if the accused has been held continuously in custody and not more than 180 days if the accused has not been held continuously in custody.

D. Any objection by counsel for the accused, or the accused if he is proceeding pro se, to timeliness of the receipt of notice required by subsection A shall be made before hearing or trial upon his receipt of actual notice unless the accused did not receive actual notice prior to hearing or trial. A showing by the Commonwealth that the notice was mailed, delivered, or otherwise provided in compliance with the time requirements of this section shall constitute prima facie evidence that the notice was timely received by the accused. If the court finds upon the accused's objection made pursuant to this subsection, that he did not receive timely notice pursuant to subsection A, the accused's objection shall not be deemed waived and if the objection is made prior to hearing or trial, a continuance shall be ordered if requested by either party. Any continuance ordered pursuant to this subsection shall be subject to the time limitations set forth in subsection C.

E. Nothing in this section shall prohibit the admissibility of a certificate of analysis when the person who performed the analysis and examination testifies at trial or the hearing concerning the facts stated therein and of the results of the analysis or examination.

F. The accused in any hearing or trial in which a certificate of analysis is offered into evidence shall have the right to call the person performing such analysis or examination or involved in the chain of custody as a witness therein, and examine him in the same manner as if he had been called as an adverse witness. Such witness shall be summoned and appear at the cost of the Commonwealth; however, if the accused calls the person performing such analysis or examination as a witness and is found guilty of the charge or charges for which such witness is summoned, $50 for expenses related to that witness's appearance at hearing or trial shall be charged to the accused as court costs.

History.

1976, c. 245; 1979, c. 364; 2009, Sp. Sess. I, cc. 1, 4; 2010, cc. 555, 656, 800; 2011, c. 32.

§ 19.2-187.2. Procedure for subpoena duces tecum of analysis evidence.

No subpoena duces tecum shall issue for the production of writings or documents used to reach the conclusion contained in a certificate of analysis prepared pursuant to § 19.2-187 except upon affidavit that the requested writings or documents are material. Upon a showing by the Commonwealth that the production of such writings and documents would place an undue burden on the Department of Forensic Science, the court may order that the subpoena duces tecum be satisfied by making the writings and documents available for inspection by the requesting party at the laboratory site where the analysis was performed or at the laboratory operated by the Department of Forensic Science which is closest to the court in which the case is pending.

History.

1993, c. 629; 2005, cc. 868, 881.

§ 19.2-188. Reports by Chief Medical Examiner received as evidence.

A. Reports of investigations made by the Chief Medical Examiner, his assistants or medical examiners, and the records and certified reports of autopsies made under the authority of Title 32.1, shall be received as evidence in any court or other proceeding, and copies of photographs, laboratory findings and reports in the office of the Chief Medical Examiner or any medical examiner, when duly attested by the Chief Medical Examiner or one of his Assistant Chief Medical Examiners, shall be received as evidence in any court or other proceeding for any purpose for which the original could be received without proof of the official character or the person whose name is signed thereto.

B. Any statement of fact or of opinion in such reports and records concerning the physical or medical cause of death and not alleging any conduct by the accused shall be admissible as competent evidence of the cause of death in any preliminary hearing.

History.
Code 1950, § 19.1-45; 1960, c. 366; 1975, c. 495; 2003, c. 459; 2009, c. 640.

§ 19.2-188.1. Testimony regarding identification of controlled substances.

A. In any preliminary hearing on a violation of Article 1 (§ 18.2-247 et seq.) of Chapter 7 of Title 18.2 or a violation of subdivision 6 of § 53.1-203, any law-enforcement officer shall be permitted to testify as to the results of field tests that have been approved by the Department of Forensic Science pursuant to regulations adopted in accordance with the Administrative Process Act (§ 2.2-4000 et seq.), regarding whether or not any substance the identity of which is at issue in such hearing is a controlled substance, imitation controlled substance, or marijuana, as defined in § 18.2-247.

B. In any trial for a violation of § 18.2-250.1, any law-enforcement officer shall be permitted to testify as to the results of any marijuana field test approved as accurate and reliable by the Department of Forensic Science pursuant to regulations adopted in accordance with the Administrative Process Act (§ 2.2-4000 et seq.), regarding whether or not any plant material, the identity of which is at issue, is marijuana provided the defendant has been given written notice of his right to request a full chemical analysis. Such notice shall be on a form approved by the Supreme Court and shall be provided to the defendant prior to trial.

In any case in which the person accused of a violation of § 18.2-250.1, or the attorney of record for the accused, desires a full chemical analysis of the alleged plant material, he may, by motion prior to trial before the court in which the charge is pending, request such a chemical analysis. Upon such motion, the court shall order that the analysis be performed by the Department of Forensic Science and shall prescribe in its order the method of custody, transfer, and return of evidence submitted for chemical analysis.

History.
1991, c. 477; 1993, c. 33; 2005, cc. 868, 881; 2006, c. 447; 2013, c. 60.

§ 19.2-188.2. Certificate of surgeon as evidence.

A. In any criminal proceeding, the certificate of a duly qualified surgeon stating that he has removed organs or other body parts from a decedent for transplant in accordance with Chapter 8 (§ 32.1-277 et seq.) of Title 32.1, shall be admissible in evidence as evidence of the facts stated therein. The certificate shall be competent evidence to show that such organs or body parts were functional at the time of recovery and not affected by any injury or illness that caused the decedent's death.

B. A copy of the certificate shall be filed with the attorney for the Commonwealth in the jurisdiction in which the decedent's fatal injury occurred. The certificate shall not be admitted into evidence unless the attorney for the Commonwealth has provided a copy of the certificate to counsel for the defendant at least fourteen days prior to the proceeding in which it is to be offered into evidence.

C. Any such certificate, when properly notarized, purporting to be signed by the surgeon who removed the organs or other body parts shall be admissible in evidence without proof of seal or signature of the person whose name is signed to it. In any hearing or trial the accused shall have the right to call the person signing the certificate and the provisions of § 19.2-187.1 shall apply, mutatis mutandis.

History.
1997, c. 557.

§ 19.2-188.3. Admissibility of affidavits by government officials regarding a search of government records (Subdivision (10)(b) of Supreme Court Rule 2:803 derived from this section).

In any hearing or trial, an affidavit signed by a government official who is competent to testify, deemed to have custody of an official record, or signed by his designee, stating that after a diligent search, no record or entry of such record is found to exist among the records in his custody, is admissible as evidence that his office has no such record or entry, provided that, if the hearing or trial is a proceeding other than a preliminary hearing, the procedures set forth in subsection G of § 18.2-472.1 for admission of an affidavit have been satisfied, mutatis mutandis, and the accused has not objected to the admission of the affidavit pursuant to the procedures set forth in subsection H of § 18.2-472.1, mutatis mutandis. Nothing in this section shall be construed to affect the admissibility of affidavits in civil cases under § 8.01-390.

History.
2010, c. 464; 2011, c. 285.

§ 19.2-189. Commitment of accused for further examination.

If the accused be committed, it shall be by an order of the judge stating that he is committed for further examination on a day specified in the order. And on that day he may be brought before such judge by his verbal order to the officer by whom he was committed, or by a written order to a different person.

History.
Code 1950, § 19.1-107; 1960, c. 366; 1968, c. 639; 1975, c. 495.

§ 19.2-190. To whom, and when, examination and recognizance to be certified.

Every examination and recognizance for a felony taken under this chapter, shall, by the person taking it, be certified to the clerk of the circuit court of the county or city in which the party charged is to be tried, or the witness is to appear, on or before the first day of its next term. If he fails he may be compelled to do so by attachment as for a contempt.

History.
Code 1950, § 19.1-108; 1960, c. 366; 1975, c. 495.

§ 19.2-190.1. Certification of ancillary misdemeanor offenses.

Upon certification of any felony offense pursuant to this chapter, the court shall also certify any ancillary misdemeanor offense to the clerk of the circuit court provided that the attorney for the Commonwealth and the accused consent to such certification. Any misdemeanor offense certified pursuant to this section shall proceed in the same manner as a misdemeanor appealed to circuit court pursuant to § 16.1-136.

History.
2015, c. 548.

CHAPTER 13.
GRAND JURIES.

Article 1.

In General.

Article 2.

Regular Grand Juries.

Article 3.

Special Grand Juries.

Article 4.

Multi-Jurisdiction Grand Juries.

ARTICLE 1.
IN GENERAL.

§ 19.2-191. Functions of a grand jury.

The functions of a grand jury are twofold:

(1) To consider bills of indictment prepared by the attorney for the Commonwealth and to determine whether as to each such bill there is sufficient probable cause to return such indictment "a true bill."

(2) To investigate and report on any condition that involves or tends to promote criminal activity, either in the community or by any governmental authority, agency or official thereof. These functions may be exercised by either a special grand jury or a regular grand jury as hereinafter provided.

History.
1975, c. 495; 1980, c. 517; 2001, c. 4.

§ 19.2-192. Secrecy in grand jury proceedings.

Except as otherwise provided in this chapter, every attorney for the Commonwealth, special counsel, sworn investigator, and member of a regular, special, or multi-jurisdiction grand jury shall keep secret all proceedings which occurred during sessions of the grand jury; provided, however, in a prosecution for perjury of a witness examined before a regular grand jury, a regular grand juror may be required by the court to testify as to the testimony given by such witness before the regular grand jury.

History.
1975, c. 495; 2014, c. 389.

§ 19.2-192.1. Sealing of indictment.

Upon ex parte motion by the Commonwealth and for good cause shown, the circuit court may seal an indictment until such time as the defendant is arrested.

History.
2002, c. 130.

ARTICLE 2.
REGULAR GRAND JURIES.

§ 19.2-193. Number of regular grand juries.

There shall be a regular grand jury at each term of the circuit court of each county and city, unless the court, on the motion of the attorney for the Commonwealth or with his concurrence, finds that it is unnecessary or impractical to impanel a grand jury for the particular term and enters an order to that effect.

Whenever the number of cases to be considered by the grand jury at a given term is so great as to hamper the intelligent consideration thereof by a single grand jury, the court may order two or more regular grand juries to be impanelled to sit separately at the same or a different time during the term.

Whenever a regular grand jury has been discharged, the court, during the term, may impanel another regular grand jury.

History.
Code 1950, § 19.1-147; 1960, c. 366; 1975, c. 495.

§ 19.2-194. When and how grand jurors to be selected and summoned; lists to be delivered to clerk.

The judge or judges regularly presiding in the circuit court of each county and city shall annually, in the month of June, July, or August, select from citizens of the county or city at least 60 persons and not more than 120 persons 18 years of age or over, of honesty, intelligence, impartiality, and good demeanor and suitable in all respects to serve as grand jurors, who, except as hereinafter provided, shall be the grand jurors for the county or city from which they are selected for the next 12 months. The judge or judges making the selection shall at once furnish to the clerk of the circuit court a list of those selected for that county or city.

The clerk, not more than 20 days before the commencement of each term of his court at which a regular grand jury is required, shall issue a venire facias to the sheriff of his county or city, commanding him to summon not less than five nor more than nine of the persons selected as aforesaid (the number to be designated by the judge of the court by an order entered of record) to be named in the writ to appear on the first day of the court to serve as grand jurors. Those persons who are to be summoned shall be randomly selected but no such person shall be required to appear more than once until all the others have been summoned once, nor more than twice until the others have been twice summoned, and so on. The Circuit Court of James City County, or the judge thereof in vacation, shall select the grand jurors for each court from such county and the City of Williamsburg in such proportion from each as he may think proper.

Any person who has legal custody of and is responsible for a child 16 years of age or younger or a person having a mental or physical impairment requiring continuous care during normal court hours shall be excused from jury service upon his request.

History.
Code 1950, § 19.1-148; 1960, c. 366; 1971, Ex. Sess., c. 262; 1973, cc. 401, 439; 1974, c. 618; 1975, c. 495; 1991, c. 226; 2003, c. 825; 2004, c. 306; 2008, c. 644.

§ 19.2-195. Number and qualifications of grand jurors.

A regular grand jury shall consist of not less than five nor more than seven persons. Each grand juror shall be a citizen of this Commonwealth, eighteen years of age or over, and shall have been a resident of this Commonwealth one year and of the county or corporation in which the court is to be held six months, and in other respects a qualified juror, and, when the grand juror is for a circuit court of a county, not an inhabitant of a city, except in those cases in which the circuit court of the county has jurisdiction in the city.

History.
Code 1950, § 19.1-150; 1960, c. 366; 1973, c. 439; 1974, c. 617; 1975, c. 495; 1991, c. 226.

§ 19.2-196. How deficiency of jurors supplied.

If a sufficient number of grand jurors do not appear, the court may order the deficiency to be supplied from the bystanders or from a list furnished by the judge to the sheriff or sergeant.

History.
Code 1950, § 19.1-151; 1960, c. 366; 1975, c. 495.

§ 19.2-197. Foreman of grand jury; oaths of jurors and witnesses.

From among the persons summoned who attend the court shall select a foreman who shall be sworn as follows: "You shall diligently inquire, and true presentment make, of all such matters as may be given you in charge, or come to your knowledge, touching the present service. You shall present no person through prejudice or ill-will, nor leave any unpresented through fear or favor, but in all your presentments you shall present the truth, the whole truth, and nothing but the truth. So help you God." The other grand jurors shall afterwards be sworn as follows: "The same oath that your foreman has taken on his part, you and each of you shall observe and keep on your part. So help you God." Any witness testifying before the grand jury may be sworn by the foreman.

History.
Code 1950, § 19.1-152; 1960, c. 366; 1975, c. 495.

§ 19.2-198. When new foreman or juror may be sworn in.

If the foreman or any grand juror, at any time after being sworn, fail or be unable to attend another may be sworn in his stead.

History.
Code 1950, § 19.1-153; 1960, c. 366; 1975, c. 495.

§ 19.2-199. Judge to charge grand jury.

The grand jury, after being sworn, shall be charged by the judge of the court and shall then be sent to their room. In the charge given by the court to a regular grand jury, the court shall instruct it to advise the court after their considerations of the bills of indictment whether it desires to be impanelled as a special grand jury to consider any matters provided for in subdivision (2) of § 19.2-191.

History.
Code 1950, § 19.1-154; 1960, cc. 366, 467; 1975, c. 495.

§ 19.2-200. Duties of grand jury.

The grand jury shall inquire of and present all felonies, misdemeanors and violations of penal laws committed within the jurisdiction of the respective courts wherein it is sworn; except that no presentment shall be made of a matter for which there is no corporal punishment, but only a fine, where the fine is limited to an amount not exceeding five dollars. After a regular grand jury has concluded its deliberation on bills of indictment and made its return thereon, the court shall inquire of it whether it recommends that a special grand jury be impanelled to perform any of the functions provided for in subdivision (2) of § 19.2-191. If a majority of the grand jurors responds in the affirmative, the court shall impanel so many of that jury as answer in the affirmative and are also willing to serve thereon, plus any additional members as may be necessary to complete the panel, as a special grand jury and if a minority of the grand jurors responds in the affirmative, the court may impanel a special grand jury in the same manner.

History.
Code 1950, § 19.1-155; 1960, c. 366; 1975, c. 495; 1978, c. 741; 1980, c. 134.

§ 19.2-201. Officers to give information of violation of penal laws to attorney for Commonwealth.

Every commissioner of the revenue, sheriff, constable or other officer shall promptly give information of the violation of any penal law to the attorney for the Commonwealth, who shall forthwith institute and prosecute all necessary and proper proceedings in such case, whether in the name of the Commonwealth or of a county or corporation, and may in such case issue or cause to be issued a summons for any witnesses he may deem material to give evidence before the court or grand jury. Except as otherwise provided in this chapter, no attorney for the Commonwealth shall go before any grand jury except when duly sworn to testify as a witness, but he may advise the foreman of a regular grand jury or any member or members thereof in relation to the discharge of their duties.

History.
Code 1950, § 19.1-156; 1960, c. 366; 1975, c. 495.

§ 19.2-202. How indictments found and presentment made.

At least four of a regular grand jury must concur in finding or making an indictment or presentment. It may make a presentment or find an indictment upon the information of two or more of its own body, or on the testimony of witnesses called on by the grand jury, or sent to it by the court. If only one of their number can testify as to an offense, he shall be sworn as any other witness. When a presentment or indictment is so made or found, the names of the grand jurors giving the information, or of the witnesses, shall be written at the foot of the presentment or indictment.

History.
Code 1950, § 19.1-157; 1960, c. 366; 1975, c. 495.

§ 19.2-203. Indictments ignored may be sent to another grand jury; what irregularities not to vitiate indictment, etc.

Although a bill of indictment be returned not a true bill the same or another bill of indictment against the same person for the same offense may be sent to, and acted on, by the same or another grand jury. No irregularity in the time or manner of selecting the jurors, or in the writ of venire facias, or in the manner of executing the same, shall vitiate any presentment, indictment or finding of a grand jury.

History.
Code 1950, § 19.1-158; 1960, c. 366; 1975, c. 495.

§ 19.2-204. Penalties on officers and jurors for failure of duty.

A court whose officer fails without good cause, when it is his duty, to summon a grand jury and return a list of its names shall fine him twenty dollars. A person summoned and failing to attend a court as a grand juror shall be fined by the court not less than five dollars nor more than twenty dollars, unless, after being summoned to show cause against the fine, he gives a reasonable excuse for his failure.

History.
Code 1950, § 19.1-159; 1960, c. 366; 1975, c. 495.

§ 19.2-205. Pay and mileage of grand jurors.

Every person who serves upon a grand jury, regular or special, shall receive the same compensation and mileage allowed jurors in civil cases by § 17.1-618 and the same shall be paid out of the county or corporation levy.

History.
Code 1950, § 19.1-160; 1960, c. 366; 1974, c. 207; 1975, c. 495.

ARTICLE 3.

SPECIAL GRAND JURIES.

§ 19.2-206. When impanelled.

A. Special grand juries may be impanelled by a circuit court (i) at any time upon its own motion, (ii) upon recommendation of a minority of the members of a regular grand jury that a special grand jury be impanelled, to perform the functions provided for in subdivision (2) of § 19.2-191, or (iii) upon request of the attorney for the Commonwealth to investigate and report on any condition that involves or tends to promote criminal activity and consider bills of indictment to determine whether there is sufficient probable cause to return each such indictment as a "true bill."

B. A special grand jury shall be impanelled by a circuit court upon the recommendation of a majority of the members of a regular grand jury if the court finds probable cause to believe that a crime has been committed which should be investigated by a special grand jury impanelled to perform the functions provided for in subdivision (2) of § 19.2-191.

History.
Code 1950, § 19.1-149; 1960, c. 366; 1975, c. 495; 1978, c. 741; 1980, c. 134; 1987, c. 136; 2001, c. 4.

§ 19.2-207. Composition of a special grand jury.

Special grand juries shall consist of not less than seven and not more than 11 members, and shall be summoned from a list prepared by the court. Members of a special grand jury shall possess the same qualifications as those prescribed for members of a regular grand jury, including indifferent in the cause to be conducted by the special grand jury. In order to determine a potential juror's qualifications, the presiding judge shall examine each juror individually and under oath. He shall then certify in writing and not under seal that he has examined the members of the special grand jury and has found that they are qualified and are impartial and disinterested in the subject matter and outcome of the investigation. The examination shall be recorded by a court reporter and conducted pursuant to the requirements of secrecy provided for in this chapter. The court shall appoint one of the members as foreman.

History.
1975, c. 495; 2008, c. 644.

§ 19.2-208. Subpoena power of special grand jury.

The special grand jury may subpoena persons to appear before it to testify and to produce specified records, papers, and documents or other tangible things, but before any witness testifies, he shall be warned by the foreman that he need not answer any questions or produce any evidence that would tend to incriminate him, and that the witness may have counsel of his own procurement present when he appears to testify, and at the same time the foreman also shall warn each witness that he may later be called upon to testify in any case that might grow out of the investigation and report of the special grand jury.

A witness who has been called to testify or produce specified records, papers and documents or other tangible things before a grand jury requested by the attorney for the Commonwealth, and who refuses to testify or produce specified records, papers and documents or other tangible things by expressly invoking his right not to incriminate himself, may be compelled to testify or produce specified records, papers and documents or other tangible things by the presiding judge. Such witness who refuses to testify or produce specified records, papers and documents or other tangible things after being ordered to do so by the presiding judge may be held in contempt and may be incarcerated until the contempt is purged by compliance with the order or the grand jury is discharged. When a witness is compelled to testify or produce specified records, papers and documents or other tangible things after expressly invoking his right not to incriminate himself, and the presiding judge has determined that the assertion of the right is bona fide, the compelled testimony, or any information directly or indirectly derived from such testimony or other information, shall not be used against the witness in any criminal proceeding except a prosecution for perjury.

Notwithstanding the provisions of this section, all provisions of this Code relative to immunity granted to witnesses who testify before a grand jury shall remain applicable.

The foreman shall administer the oath prescribed by law for witnesses, and any member of the special grand jury may examine a witness.

History.
1975, c. 495; 2001, c. 4; 2003, c. 565.

§ 19.2-209. Presence of counsel for a witness.

Any witness appearing before a special grand jury shall have the right to have counsel of his own procurement present when he testifies. Such counsel shall have the right to consult with and advise the witness during his examination, but shall not have the right to conduct an examination of his own of the witness.

History.
1975, c. 495.

§ 19.2-210. Presence of attorney for the Commonwealth.

The attorney for the Commonwealth shall not be present at any time while the special grand jury is in session except that during the investigatory stage of its proceedings he may be present. When the special grand jury is impanelled upon motion of the court or recommendation of a regular grand jury, he may be present during the investigatory stage only when his presence is requested by the special grand jury and may interrogate witnesses provided the special grand jury requests or consents to such interrogation. When the special grand jury was impanelled upon his request, he may examine any witness called to testify or produce evidence, but his examination of a witness shall in no way affect the right of any grand juror to examine the witness.

The attorney for the Commonwealth shall not be present during or after the investigative stage of the proceedings at any time while the special grand jury is discussing, evaluating or considering the testimony of a witness or is deliberating in order to reach decisions or prepare its report, except that he may be present when his legal advice is requested by the special grand jury.

History.
1975, c. 495; 2001, c. 4.

§ 19.2-211. Provision for special counsel and other personnel.

At the request of the special grand jury, the court may designate special counsel to assist it in its work, and may also provide it with appropriate specialized personnel for investigative purposes.

History.
1975, c. 495.

§ 19.2-212. Provision for court reporter; use and disposition of notes, tapes and transcriptions.

A. A court reporter shall be provided for a special grand jury to record, manually or electronically, and transcribe all oral testimony taken before a special grand jury, but such reporter shall not be present during any stage of its deliberations. The notes, tapes and transcriptions of the reporter are for the sole use of the special grand jury, and the contents thereof shall not be divulged by anyone except as hereinafter provided. After the special grand jury has completed its use of the notes, tapes and transcriptions, the foreman shall cause them to be sealed, the container dated, and delivered to the court.

The court shall cause the sealed container to be kept safely. If any witness testifying before the special grand jury is prosecuted subsequently for perjury, the court, on motion of either the attorney for the Commonwealth or the defendant, shall permit them both to have access to the testimony given by the defendant when a witness before the special grand jury, and the testimony shall be admissible in the perjury case.

If no prosecution for perjury is instituted within three years from the date of the report of the special grand jury, the court shall cause the sealed container to be destroyed; however, on motion of the attorney for the Commonwealth, the court may extend the time period for destruction if the grand jury was impanelled at the request of the attorney for the Commonwealth.

B. Upon motion to the presiding judge, the attorney for the Commonwealth shall be permitted to review any evidence that was presented to the special grand jury, and shall be permitted to make notes and to duplicate portions of the evidence as he deems necessary for use in a criminal investigation or proceeding. The attorney for the Commonwealth shall maintain the secrecy of all information obtained from a review or duplication of the evidence presented to the special grand jury. Upon motion to the presiding judge by a person indicted after a special grand jury investigation, similar permission to review, note or duplicate evidence shall be extended if it appears that the permission is consistent with the ends of justice and is necessary to reasonably inform such person of the nature of the evidence to be presented against him, or to adequately prepare his defense.

History.
1975, c. 495; 2001, c. 4; 2003, c. 96; 2008, c. 644.

§ 19.2-213. Report by special grand jury; return of true bill.

At the conclusion of its investigation and deliberation, a special grand jury impanelled by the court on its own motion or on recommendation of a regular grand jury shall file a report of its findings with the court, including therein any recommendations that it may deem appropriate, after which it shall be discharged. Such report shall be sealed and not open to public inspection, other than by order of the court.

A majority, but not less than five, of the members of a special grand jury convened upon request of the attorney for the Commonwealth must concur in order to return a "true bill" of indictment. A "true bill" may be returned upon the testimony of, or evidence produced by, any witness who was called by the grand jury, upon evidence presented or sent to it.

History.
1975, c. 495; 1978, c. 638; 2001, c. 4.

§ 19.2-213.1. Discharge of special grand jury.

If a special grand jury has not filed a report pursuant to § 19.2-213 within six months of its impanelling, the circuit court appointing it shall discharge it; provided, however, if such court, in its discretion, determines that the special grand jury is making progress in its investigation, the court may direct that special grand jury to continue its investigation pursuant to this article.

History.
1978, c. 638.

§ 19.2-214. Prosecutions resulting from report.

Any bill of indictment for alleged criminal offenses, which may follow as a result of the report of the special grand jury, shall be prepared by the attorney for the Commonwealth for presentation to a regular grand jury.

History.
1975, c. 495.

§ 19.2-215. Costs of special grand jury.

All costs incurred for services provided by the court for a special grand jury shall be paid by the Commonwealth.

History.
1975, c. 495.

ARTICLE 4. MULTI-JURISDICTION GRAND JURIES.

§ 19.2-215.1. Functions of a multijurisdiction grand jury.

The functions of a multijurisdiction grand jury are:

1. To investigate any condition that involves or tends to promote criminal violations of:

a. Title 10.1 for which punishment as a felony is authorized;

b. § 13.1-520;

c. §§ 18.2-47 and 18.2-48;

d. §§ 18.2-111 and 18.2-112;

e. Article 6 (§ 18.2-59 et seq.) of Chapter 4 of Title 18.2;

f. Article 7.1 (§ 18.2-152.1 et seq.) of Chapter 5 of Title 18.2;

g. Article 1 (§ 18.2-247 et seq.) and Article 1.1 (§ 18.2-265.1 et seq.) of Chapter 7 of Title 18.2;

h. Article 1 (§ 18.2-325 et seq.) and Article 1.1:1 (§ 18.2-340.15 et seq.) of Chapter 8 of Title 18.2, Chapter 29 (§ 59.1-364 et seq.) of Title 59.1 or any other provision prohibiting, limiting, regulating, or otherwise affecting gaming or gambling activity;

i. § 18.2-434, when violations occur before a multijurisdiction grand jury;

j. Article 2 (§ 18.2-438 et seq.) and Article 3 (§ 18.2-446 et seq.) of Chapter 10 of Title 18.2;

k. § 18.2-460 for which punishment as a felony is authorized;

l. Article 1.1 (§ 18.2-498.1 et seq.) of Chapter 12 of Title 18.2;

m. Article 1 (§ 32.1-310 et seq.) of Chapter 9 of Title 32.1;

n. Chapter 4.2 (§ 59.1-68.6 et seq.) of Title 59.1;

o. Article 9 (§ 3.2-6570 et seq.) of Chapter 65 of Title 3.2;

p. Article 1 (§ 18.2-30 et seq.) of Chapter 4 of Title 18.2;

q. Article 2.1 (§ 18.2-46.1 et seq.) and Article 2.2 (§ 18.2-46.4 et seq.) of Chapter 4 of Title 18.2;

r. Article 5 (§ 18.2-186 et seq.) and Article 6 (§ 18.2-191 et seq.) of Chapter 6 of Title 18.2;

s. Chapter 6.1 (§ 59.1-92.1 et seq.) of Title 59.1;

t. § 18.2-178 where the violation involves insurance fraud;

u. § 18.2-346 for which punishment as a felony is authorized or § 18.2-355, 18.2-356, 18.2-357, or 18.2-357.1;

v. Article 9 (§ 18.2-246.1 et seq.) of Chapter 6 of Title 18.2;

w. Article 2 (§ 18.2-38 et seq.) of Chapter 4 of Title 18.2;

x. Malicious felonious assault and malicious bodily wounding under Article 4 (§ 18.2-51 et seq.) of Chapter 4 of Title 18.2;

y. Article 5 (§ 18.2-58 et seq.) of Chapter 4 of Title 18.2;

z. Felonious sexual assault under Article 7 (§ 18.2-61 et seq.) of Chapter 4 of Title 18.2;

aa. Arson in violation of § 18.2-77 when the structure burned was occupied or a Class 3 felony violation of § 18.2-79;

bb. Chapter 13 (§ 18.2-512 et seq.) of Title 18.2;

cc. § 18.2-246.14 and Chapter 10 (§ 58.1-1000 et seq.) of Title 58.1; and

dd. Any other provision of law when such condition is discovered in the course of an investigation that a multijurisdiction grand jury is otherwise authorized to undertake and to investigate any condition that involves or tends to promote any attempt, solicitation or conspiracy to violate the laws enumerated in this section.

2. To report evidence of any criminal offense enumerated in subdivision 1 and for which a court reporter has recorded all oral testimony as provided by § 19.2-215.9 to the attorney for the Commonwealth or United States attorney of any jurisdiction where such offense could be prosecuted or investigated, or to the chief law-enforcement officer of any jurisdiction where such offense could be prosecuted or investigated, or to a sworn investigator designated pursuant to § 19.2-215.6, or, when appropriate, to the Attorney General.

3. To consider bills of indictment prepared by a special counsel to determine whether there is sufficient probable cause to return each such indictment as a "true bill." Only bills of indictment which allege an offense enumerated in subdivision 1 may be submitted to a multijurisdiction grand jury.

4. The provisions of this section shall not abrogate the authority of an attorney for the Commonwealth in a particular jurisdiction to determine the course of a prosecution in that jurisdiction.

History.

1983, c. 543; 1991, c. 616; 1995, c. 552; 2000, c. 359; 2002, cc. 588, 623; 2004, cc. 396, 435; 2008, c. 704; 2009, c. 491; 2011, c. 504; 2013, cc. 83, 314, 459; 2014, cc. 389, 422, 534; 2015, cc. 690, 691.

§ 19.2-215.2. Application for such grand jury.

Provided the Attorney General has approved the application in writing prior to submission, application for a multi-jurisdiction grand jury may be made to the Supreme Court of Virginia by two or more attorneys for the Commonwealth from jurisdictions which would be within the original scope of the investigation. The application shall be in writing and shall state (i) which jurisdictions will be involved in the original scope of the investigation, (ii) in which jurisdiction it is requested that the multi-jurisdiction grand jury be convened, (iii) the name or names of the attorneys for the Commonwealth or their assistants who will serve as special counsel to the grand jury, (iv) the name of the attorney who shall direct the grand jury proceedings. The presiding judge may extend or limit the jurisdictional territory of the investigation, for good cause shown, upon the motion of a grand jury already convened. Notice of every such application shall be given to the attorneys for the Commonwealth in the jurisdictions named in the application and, if the original scope of the investigation is extended into other jurisdictions, notice of such extension shall be given to the attorneys for the Commonwealth in the jurisdictions into which the investigation is extended.

History.

1983, c. 543.

§ 19.2-215.3. When impaneled; impaneling order.

Upon application by two or more attorneys for the Commonwealth, the Chief Justice of the Supreme Court, or any justice designated by the Chief Justice, may within twenty days thereafter order the impaneling of a multi-jurisdiction grand jury for a term of twelve months. The term of such a grand jury may be extended for successive periods of not more than six months by the Chief Justice, or by any justice designated by the Chief Justice, upon the petition of a majority of the members of the grand jury.

The impaneling order shall designate the jurisdiction requested on the application as the jurisdiction where the multi-jurisdiction grand jury shall be convened and shall, unless all judges of that circuit have recused themselves, appoint a judge of the circuit court of that jurisdiction as the presiding judge. The impaneling order shall also designate special counsel and each special counsel who will assist the multi-jurisdiction grand jury as listed in the application. The presiding judge shall substitute or appoint additional special counsel upon motion of special counsel.

History.

1983, c. 543; 2010, c. 438.

§ 19.2-215.4. Number and qualifications of jurors; grand jury list; when convened; compensation of jurors.

A. A multi-jurisdiction grand jury shall consist of not less than seven nor more than 11 members. Each member of a multi-jurisdiction grand jury shall be a citizen of this Commonwealth, 18 years of age or older, and a resident of this Commonwealth for one year and of one of the jurisdictions named in the application for six months.

B. The presiding judge shall determine the number of grand jurors to be drawn and shall draw them so that, to the extent practicable, each of the jurisdictions named in the application is represented by at least one juror residing in that jurisdiction, but in no event shall said panel have more than 11 members. The grand jurors shall be summoned from a list prepared by the presiding judge. In the preparation of this list, the presiding judge shall select only persons who have been selected as regular grand jurors pursuant to the provisions of § 19.2-194 in the jurisdiction named in the application. Members of a multi-jurisdiction grand jury shall possess the same qualifications as those prescribed for members of a regular grand jury, including indifference in the cause.

C. The provisions of § 19.2-192 dealing with secrecy in grand jury proceedings are incorporated herein by reference.

D. The presiding judge shall determine the time, date and place within the designated jurisdiction where the multi-jurisdiction grand jury is to be convened. The presiding judge shall also appoint one of the grand jurors to serve as foreman. Members of the multi-jurisdiction grand jury shall be compensated according to the provisions of § 19.2-205. The expense of a multi-jurisdiction grand jury shall be borne by the Commonwealth.

History.
1983, c. 543; 2008, c. 644.

§ 19.2-215.5. Subpoena power; counsel for witness; oath.

A multi-jurisdiction grand jury has statewide subpoena power and, through special counsel, may subpoena persons to appear before it to testify and may subpoena the production of evidence, with or without the custodian of records at the election of special counsel, in the form of specified records, papers, documents, or other tangible things. Such subpoenas shall be returnable for a specific meeting of the multi-jurisdiction grand jury. Mileage and such other reasonable expenses as are approved by the presiding judge shall be paid such persons from funds appropriated for such purpose.

A witness before a multi-jurisdiction grand jury shall be entitled to the presence of counsel in the grand jury room, but he may not participate in the proceedings.

The foreman shall administer the oath required by law for witnesses.

History.
1983, c. 543; 2014, c. 389.

§ 19.2-215.6. Role and presence of special counsel; examination of witnesses; sworn investigators.

Special counsel may be present during the investigatory stage of a multi-jurisdiction grand jury proceeding and may examine any witness who is called to testify or produce evidence. The examination of a witness by special counsel shall in no way affect the right of any grand juror to examine the witness.

At the request of special counsel, the presiding judge shall designate specialized personnel for investigative purposes. Such personnel shall be designated as a sworn investigator and shall be administered an oath to maintain the secrecy of all proceedings of the multi-jurisdiction grand jury. A sworn investigator is permitted to discuss multi-jurisdiction grand jury proceedings with any other sworn investigator or special counsel and may participate in multi-jurisdiction grand jury proceedings at the request of special counsel or the grand jury. Any specialized personnel who have been administered an oath to maintain the secrecy of all proceedings of the multi-jurisdiction grand jury before July 1, 2014, and who continue to serve in that position are deemed to be sworn investigators under this section.

Special counsel and sworn investigators, however, may not be present at any time during the deliberations of a multi-jurisdiction grand jury except when the grand jury requests the legal advice of special counsel as to specific questions of law.

History.
1983, c. 543; 2014, c. 389.

§ 19.2-215.7. Warnings given to witnesses; when witness in contempt; use of testimony compelled after witness invokes right against self-incrimination.

A. Every witness testifying before a multi-jurisdiction grand jury shall be warned by special counsel or by the foreman of the grand jury that he need not answer any question that would tend to incriminate him, and that he may later be called upon to testify in any case that may result from the grand jury proceedings.

B. A witness who has been called to testify or produce evidence before a multi-jurisdiction grand jury, and who refuses to testify or produce evidence by expressly invoking his right not to incriminate himself, may be compelled to testify or produce evidence by the presiding judge. A witness who refuses to testify or produce evidence after being ordered to do so by the presiding judge may be held in contempt and may be incarcerated until the contempt is purged by compliance with the order.

C. When a witness is compelled to testify or produce evidence after expressly invoking his right not to incriminate himself, and the presiding judge has determined that the assertion of the right is bona fide, the compelled testimony, or any information directly or indirectly derived from such testimony or other information, shall not be used against the witness in any criminal proceeding except a prosecution for perjury.

History.
1983, c. 543.

§ 19.2-215.8. Returning a "true bill" of indictment; jurisdiction to be set out.

In order to return a "true bill" of indictment, a majority, but in no instance less than five, of the multi-jurisdiction grand jurors must concur in that finding. A multi-jurisdiction grand jury may return a "true bill" of indictment upon the testimony of, or evidence produced by, any witness who was called by the grand jury, upon evidence presented to it by special counsel, or upon evidence sent to it by the presiding judge.

Every "true bill" of indictment returned by a multi-jurisdiction grand jury shall state in which jurisdiction or jurisdictions the offense is alleged to have occurred. Thereafter, when venue is proper in more than one jurisdiction, the presiding judge who directed the grand jury proceeding shall elect in which one of the jurisdictions named in the indictment the indictment is to be prosecuted.

History.
1983, c. 543.

§ 19.2-215.9. Court reporter provided; safekeeping of transcripts, notes, etc.; when disclosure permitted; access to record of testimony and evidence.

A. A court reporter shall be provided for a multi-jurisdiction grand jury to record, manually or electronically, and transcribe all oral testimony taken before a multi-jurisdiction grand jury, but such a reporter shall not be present during any stage of its deliberations. Such transcription shall include the original or copies of all documents, reports, or other evidence presented to the multi-jurisdiction grand jury. The notes, tapes, and transcriptions of the reporter are for the use of the multi-jurisdiction grand jury, and the contents thereof shall not be used or divulged by anyone except as provided in this article. After the multi-jurisdiction grand jury has completed its use of the notes, tapes, and transcriptions, the foreman shall cause them to be delivered to the clerk of the circuit court in whose jurisdiction the multi-jurisdiction grand jury sits, with copies provided to special counsel. Upon motion of special counsel, the presiding judge may order that such notes, tapes, and transcriptions be destroyed at the direction of special counsel by any means the presiding judge deems sufficient, provided that at least seven years have passed from the date of the multi-jurisdiction grand jury proceeding where such notes, tapes, and transcriptions were made.

B. The clerk shall cause the notes, tapes, and transcriptions or other evidence to be kept safely. Upon motion to the presiding judge, special counsel or the attorney for the Commonwealth or United States attorney of any jurisdiction where the offense could be prosecuted or investigated shall be permitted to review any of the evidence which was presented to the multi-jurisdiction grand jury and shall be permitted to make notes and to duplicate portions of the evidence as he deems necessary for use in a criminal investigation or proceeding. Special counsel, the attorney for the Commonwealth, or the United States attorney shall maintain the secrecy of all information obtained from a review or duplication of the evidence presented to the multi-jurisdiction grand jury, except that this information may be disclosed pursuant to the provisions of subdivision 2 of § 19.2-215.1. A United States attorney satisfies his duty to maintain secrecy of information obtained from a review or duplication of evidence presented to the multi-jurisdiction grand jury if such information is maintained in accordance with the Federal Rules of Criminal Procedure. Upon motion to the presiding judge by a person indicted by a multi-jurisdiction grand jury or by a person being prosecuted with evidence presented to a multi-jurisdiction grand jury, similar permission to review, note, or duplicate evidence shall be extended.

C. If any witness who testified or produced evidence before the multi-jurisdiction grand jury is prosecuted on the basis of his testimony or the evidence he produced, or if any witness is prosecuted for perjury on the basis of his testimony or the evidence he produced before the multi-jurisdiction grand jury, the presiding judge, on motion of either special counsel or the defendant, shall permit the defendant access to the testimony of or evidence produced by the defendant before the multi-jurisdiction grand jury. The testimony and the evidence produced by the defendant before the multi-jurisdiction grand jury shall then be admissible in the trial of the criminal offense with which the defendant is charged (i) to establish a charge of perjury in the Commonwealth's case-in-chief on the basis of his testimony before the multi-jurisdiction grand jury and (ii) for the purpose of impeaching the defendant in the trial of any other criminal matter, provided the testimony or evidence being used for impeachment was produced by the defendant voluntarily before the multi-jurisdiction grand jury.

History.
1983, c. 543; 2014, c. 389; 2016, c. 262.

§ 19.2-215.10. Participation by Office of Attorney General; assistance of special counsel permitted in certain prosecutions.

Upon request by the applicants or upon motion to the presiding judge by special counsel, the Office of Attorney General may participate as special counsel in the multi-jurisdiction grand jury proceedings and any prosecutions arising therefrom. In any prosecution arising out of the multi-jurisdiction grand jury, the attorney for the Commonwealth may also obtain the assistance of the special counsel to the grand jury as a special assistant attorney for the Commonwealth.

History.
1983, c. 543.

§ 19.2-215.11. Discharge of grand jury.

At any time during the original or extended term of a multi-jurisdiction grand jury, the presiding judge may discharge the grand jury if, in the opinion of the presiding judge, the existence of the multi-jurisdiction grand jury is no longer necessary.

History.
1983, c. 543.

CHAPTER 14.

PRESENTMENTS, INDICTMENTS AND INFORMATIONS.

ARTICLE 1.

NECESSITY FOR INDICTMENT, ETC.

§ 19.2-216. Definition of indictment, presentment and information.

An indictment is a written accusation of crime, prepared by the attorney for the Commonwealth and returned "a true bill" upon the oath or affirmation of a legally impanelled grand jury.

A presentment is a written accusation of crime prepared and returned by a grand jury from their own knowledge or observation, without any bill of indictment laid before them.

An information is a written accusation of crime or a complaint for forfeiture of property or money or for imposition of a penalty, prepared and presented by a competent public official upon his oath of office.

History.
1975, c. 495.

§ 19.2-217. When information filed; prosecution for felony to be by indictment or presentment; waiver; process to compel appearance of accused.

An information may be filed by the attorney for the Commonwealth based upon a complaint in writing verified by the oath of a competent witness; but no person shall be put upon trial for any felony, unless an indictment or presentment shall have first been found or made by a grand jury in a court of competent jurisdiction or unless such person, by writing signed by such person before the court having jurisdiction to try such felony or before the judge of such court shall have waived such indictment or presentment, in which event he may be tried on a warrant or information. If the accused be in custody, or has been recognized or summoned to answer such information, presentment or indictment, no other process shall be necessary; but the court may, in its discretion, issue process to compel the appearance of the accused.

History.
Code 1950, § 19.1-162; 1960, c. 366; 1975, c. 495.

§ 19.2-217.1. Central file of capital murder indictments.

Upon the return by a grand jury of an indictment for capital murder and the arrest of the defendant, the clerk of the circuit court in which such indictment is returned shall forthwith file a certified copy of the indictment with the clerk of the Supreme Court of Virginia. All such indictments shall be maintained in a single place by the clerk of the Supreme Court, and shall be available to members of the public upon request. Failure to comply with the provisions of this section shall not be (i) a basis upon which an indictment may be quashed or deemed invalid; (ii) deemed error upon which a conviction may be reversed or a sentence vacated; or (iii) a basis upon which a court may prevent or delay execution of a sentence.

History.
1993, c. 319.

§ 19.2-218. Preliminary hearing required for person arrested on charge of felony; waiver.

No person who is arrested on a charge of felony shall be denied a preliminary hearing upon the question of whether there is reasonable ground to believe that he committed the offense and no indictment shall be returned in a court of record against any such person prior to such hearing unless such hearing is waived in writing by the accused.

History.
Code 1950, § 19.1-163.1; 1960, c. 389; 1975, c. 495.

§ 19.2-218.1. Preliminary hearings involving certain sexual crimes against spouses.

A. In any preliminary hearing of a charge for a violation under § 18.2-61, 18.2-67.1, or 18.2-67.2 where the complaining witness is the spouse of the accused, upon a finding of probable cause the court may request that its court services unit, in consultation with any appropriate social services organization, local community services board, or other community mental health services organization, prepare a report analyzing the feasibility of providing counseling or other forms of therapy for the accused and the probability such treatment will be successful. Based upon this report and any other relevant evidence, the court may, with the consent of the accused, the complaining witness and the attorney for the Commonwealth in any case involving a violation of § 18.2-61, 18.2-67.1, or 18.2-67.2, authorize the accused to submit to and complete a designated course of counseling or therapy. In such case, the hearing shall be adjourned until such time as counseling or therapy is completed or terminated. Upon the completion of counseling or therapy by the accused and after consideration of a final evaluation to be furnished to the court by the person responsible for conducting such counseling or therapy and such further report of the court services unit as the court may require, and after consideration of the views of the complaining witness, the court, in its discretion, may discharge the accused if the court finds such action will promote maintenance of the family unit and be in the best interest of the complaining witness.

B. No statement or disclosure by the accused concerning the alleged offense made during counseling or any other form of therapy ordered pursuant to this section or § 18.2-61, 18.2-67.1, 18.2-67.2, or 19.2-218.2 may be used against the accused in any trial as evidence, nor shall any evidence against the accused be admitted which was discovered through such statement or disclosure.

History.
1986, c. 516; 2005, c. 631; 2012, cc. 476, 507.

§ 19.2-218.2. Hearing before juvenile and domestic relations district court required for persons accused of certain violations against their spouses.

A. In any case involving a violation of § 18.2-61, 18.2-67.1, or 18.2-67.2 where the complaining witness is the spouse of the accused, where a preliminary hearing pursuant to § 19.2-218.1 has not been held prior to indictment or trial, the court shall refer the case to the appropriate juvenile and domestic relations district court for a hearing to determine whether counseling or therapy is appropriate prior to further disposition unless the hearing is waived in writing by the accused. The court conducting this hearing may order counseling or therapy for the accused in compliance with the guidelines set forth in § 19.2-218.1.

B. After such hearing pursuant to which the accused has completed counseling or therapy and upon the recommendation of the juvenile and domestic relations district court judge conducting the hearing, the judge of the circuit court may dismiss the charge with the consent of the attorney for the Commonwealth and if the court finds such action will promote maintenance of the family unit and be in the best interest of the complaining witness.

History.
1986, c. 516; 2005, c. 631.

§ 19.2-219. When capias need not be issued; summons; judgment.

No capias need be issued on a presentment or indictment of an offense for which there is no punishment but a fine or forfeiture, limited to an amount not exceeding twenty dollars; but a summons to answer such presentment or indictment may be issued against the accused; and if it be served ten days before the return day thereof, and he does not appear, judgment may be rendered against him for the penalty. If he appear, the court may, unless he demand a jury, hear and determine the matter and give judgment thereon.

History.
Code 1950, § 19.1-164; 1960, c. 366; 1975, c. 495.

ARTICLE 2.
FORM AND REQUISITES.

§ 19.2-220. Contents of indictment in general.

The indictment or information shall be a plain, concise and definite written statement, (1) naming the accused, (2) describing the offense charged, (3) identifying the county, city or town in which the accused committed the offense, and (4) reciting that the accused committed the offense on or about a certain date. In describing the offense, the indictment or information may use the name given to the offense by the common law, or the indictment or information may state so much of the common law or statutory definition of the offense as is sufficient to advise what offense is charged.

History.
1975, c. 495.

§ 19.2-221. Form of prosecutions generally; murder and manslaughter.

The prosecutions for offenses against the Commonwealth, unless otherwise provided, shall be by presentment, indictment or information. While any form of presentment, indictment or information which informs the accused of the nature and cause of the accusation against him shall be good the following shall be deemed sufficient for murder and manslaughter:

Commonwealth of Virginia .... county (or city) to-wit: The grand jurors of the Commonwealth of Virginia, in and for the body of the county (or city) of ...., upon their oaths present that A .... B ...., on the .... day of ...., 20 ...., in the county (or city) of .... feloniously did kill and murder one C .... D .... against the peace and dignity of the Commonwealth.

A grand jury may, in case of homicide, which in their opinion amounts to manslaughter only, and not to murder, find an indictment against the accused for manslaughter and in such case the indictment shall be sufficient if it be in form or effect as follows:

Commonwealth of Virginia .... county (or city) to-wit: The grand jurors of the Commonwealth of Virginia, in and for the body of the county (or city) of ...., upon their oaths present that A .... B ...., on the .... day of ...., 20 ...., in the county (or city) of .... feloniously and unlawfully did kill and slay one C .... D ...., against the peace and dignity of the Commonwealth.

History.
Code 1950, § 19.1-166; 1960, c. 366; 1975, c. 495.

§ 19.2-222: Repealed by Acts 1996, c. 676.

§ 19.2-223. Charging several acts of embezzlement; description of money.

In a prosecution against a person accused of embezzling or fraudulently converting to his own use bullion, money, bank notes or other security for money or items of personal property subject to larceny it shall be lawful in the same indictment or accusation to charge and thereon to proceed against the accused for any number of distinct acts of such embezzlements or fraudulent conversions which may have been committed by him within six months from the first to the last of the acts charged in the indictment; and it shall be sufficient to allege the embezzlement or fraudulent conversion to be of money without specifying any particular money, gold, silver, note or security. Such allegation, so far as it regards the description of the property, shall be sustained if the accused be proved to have embezzled any bullion, money, bank note or other security for money or items of personal property subject to larceny although the particular species be not proved.

And in a prosecution for the larceny of United States currency or for obtaining United States currency by a false pretense or token, or for receiving United States currency knowing the same to have been stolen, it shall be sufficient if the accused be proved guilty of the larceny of national bank notes or United States treasury notes, certificates for either gold or silver coin, fractional coin, currency, or any other form of money issued by the United States government, or of obtaining the same by false pretense or token, or of receiving the same knowing it to have been stolen although the particular species be not proved.

History.
Code 1950, § 19.1-168; 1960, c. 366; 1975, c. 495; 1989, c. 370.

§ 19.2-224. In prosecution for forgery, unnecessary to set forth copy of forged instrument.

In a prosecution for forging or altering any instrument or other thing, or attempting to employ as true any forged instrument or other thing, or for any of the offenses mentioned in Article 1 (§ 18.2-168 et seq.) of Chapter 6 of Title 18.2, it shall not be necessary to set forth any copy or facsimile of such instrument or other thing; but it shall be sufficient to describe the same in such manner as would sustain an indictment for stealing such instrument or other thing, supposing it to be the subject of larceny.

History.
Code 1950, § 19.1-169; 1960, c. 366; 1975, c. 495.

§ 19.2-225. Allegation of intent.

Where an intent to injure, defraud or cheat is required to constitute an offense, it shall be sufficient, in an indictment or accusation therefor, to allege generally an intent to injure, defraud or cheat without naming the person intended to be injured, defrauded or cheated; and it shall be sufficient, and not be deemed a variance, if there appear to be an intent to injure, defraud or cheat the United States, or any state, or any county, corporation, officer or person.

History.
Code 1950, § 19.1-170; 1960, c. 366; 1975, c. 495.

§ 19.2-226. What defects in indictments not to vitiate them.

No indictment or other accusation shall be quashed or deemed invalid:

(1) For omitting to set forth that it is upon the oaths of the jurors or upon their oaths and affirmations;

(2) For the insertion of the words "upon their oath," instead of "upon their oaths";

(3) For not in terms alleging that the offense was committed "within the jurisdiction of the court" when the averments show that the case is one of which the court has jurisdiction;

(4) For the omission or misstatement of the title, occupation, estate, or degree of the accused or of the name or place of his residence;

(5) For omitting the words "with force and arms" or the statement of any particular kind of force and arms;

(6) For omitting to state, or stating imperfectly, the time at which the offense was committed when time is not the essence of the offense;

(7) For failing to allege the kind or value of an instrument which caused death or to allege that it was of no value;

(8) For omitting to charge the offense to be "against the form of the statute or statutes";

(9) For the omission or insertion of any other words of mere form or surplusage; or

(10) For omitting or stating incorrectly the Virginia crime code references for the particular offense or offenses covered.

Nor shall it be abated for any misnomer of the accused; but the court may, in case of a misnomer appearing before or in the course of a trial, forthwith cause the indictment or accusation to be amended according to the fact.

History.
Code 1950, § 19.1-172; 1960, c. 366; 1975, c. 495; 2003, c. 148.

§ 19.2-227. When judgment not to be arrested or reversed.

Judgment in any criminal case shall not be arrested or reversed upon any exception or objection made after a verdict to the indictment or other accusation, unless it be so defective as to be in violation of the Constitution.

History.
Code 1950, § 19.1-165; 1960, c. 366; 1975, c. 495.

§ 19.2-228. Name and address of complaining witness to be written on indictment, etc., for misdemeanor.

In a prosecution for a misdemeanor the name and address of the complaining witness, if there be one, shall be written at the foot of the presentment, indictment or information when it is made, found or filed. In case the grand jury that brings in such presentment or indictment or the attorney for the Commonwealth who files such information fail to write the name of a complaining witness at the foot of the presentment, indictment or information, then the name of a complaining witness may be entered of record as such by the court on the motion of the defendant or the attorney for the Commonwealth at any time before the judgment.

History.
Code 1950, § 19.1-173; 1960, c. 366; 1975, c. 495.

§ 19.2-229. When complaining witness required to give security for costs.

For good cause the court may require a complaining witness to give security for the costs and if he fails to do so dismiss the prosecution at his costs.

History.
Code 1950, § 19.1-174; 1960, c. 366; 1975, c. 495.

§ 19.2-230. Bill of particulars.

A court of record may direct the filing of a bill of particulars at any time before trial. A motion for a bill of particulars shall be made before a plea is entered and at least seven days before the day fixed for trial and the bill of particulars shall be filed within such time as is fixed by the court.

History.
1975, c. 495.

ARTICLE 3. AMENDMENTS.

§ 19.2-231. Amendment of indictment, presentment or information.

If there be any defect in form in any indictment, presentment or information, or if there shall appear to be any variance between the allegations therein and the evidence offered in proof thereof, the court may permit amendment of such indictment, presentment or information, at any time before the jury returns a verdict or the court finds the accused guilty or not guilty, provided the amendment does not change the nature or character of the offense charged. After any such amendment the accused shall be arraigned on the indictment, presentment or information as amended, and shall be allowed to plead anew thereto, if he so desires, and the trial shall proceed as if no amendment had been made; but if the court finds that such amendment operates as a surprise to the accused, he shall be entitled, upon request, to a continuance of the case for a reasonable time.

History.
Code 1950, §§ 19.1-175 through 19.1-177; 1960, c. 366; 1975, c. 495.

ARTICLE 4. PROCESS.

§ 19.2-232. What process to be awarded against accused on indictment, etc.

When an indictment or presentment is found or made, or information filed, the court, or the judge thereof, shall award process against the accused to answer the same, if he be not in custody. Such process, if the prosecution be for a felony, shall be a capias; if it be for a misdemeanor, for which imprisonment may be imposed, it may be a capias or summons, in the discretion of the court or judge; in all other cases, it shall be, in the first instance a summons, but if a summons be returned executed and the defendant does not appear, or be returned not found, the court or judge may award a capias. The officer serving the summons or capias shall also serve a copy of the indictment, presentment or information therewith.

History.
Code 1950, § 19.1-178; 1960, c. 366; 1975, c. 495; 1980, c. 349.

§ 19.2-233. How awarded, directed, returnable and executed.

Sections 8.01-292 and 8.01-295 shall apply to process in criminal, as well as in civil cases; and the court may, in the same case against the same person, award at the same time, or different times, several writs of summons or capias directed to officers of different counties or cities. An officer having a capias under which the accused is let to bail shall give a certificate of the fact, which shall protect him against any other capias which may have been issued for the same offense. A summons shall be served by delivering a copy thereof to the party in person and the clerk issuing such summons shall deliver or transmit therewith as many copies thereof as there are persons named therein on whom it is to be served.

History.
Code 1950, § 19.1-179; 1960, c. 366; 1975, c. 495.

§ 19.2-234. Procedure when person arrested under capias.

An officer who, under a capias from any court, arrests a person accused of an offense shall proceed in accordance with § 19.2-80 and Article 1 (§ 19.2-119 et seq.) of Chapter 9 of Title 19.2 regarding bail.

History.
Code 1950, § 19.1-183; 1960, c. 366; 1975, c. 495; 1986, c. 327.

§ 19.2-235. Clerks to mail process to officers in other counties, etc.

The clerk of every court shall forward, by mail, all process issued for the Commonwealth, directed to the officer of any county or city other than his own.

History.
Code 1950, § 19.1-181; 1960, c. 366; 1975, c. 495.

§ 19.2-236. Where process of arrest may be executed.

When process of arrest in a criminal prosecution is issued from a court, either against a party accused or a witness, the officer to whom it is directed or delivered may execute it in any part of the Commonwealth.

History.
Code 1950, § 19.1-182; 1960, c. 366; 1975, c. 495.

§ 19.2-237. Process on indictment or presentment for misdemeanor.

On any indictment or presentment for a misdemeanor process shall be issued immediately. If the accused appear and plead to the charge, the trial shall proceed without delay, unless good cause for continuance be shown. If, in any misdemeanor case the accused fails to appear and plead, when required the court may either award a capias or proceed to trial in the same manner as if the accused had appeared, plead not guilty and waived trial by jury, provided, that the court shall not in any such case enforce a jail sentence.

History.
Code 1950, §§ 19.1-180, 19.1-184; 1960, c. 366; 1975, c. 495; 1979, c. 468.

§ 19.2-238. Summons against corporation; proceedings; expense of publication.

A summons against a corporation to answer an indictment, presentment or information may be served as provided in §§ 8.01-299 through 8.01-301; and if the defendant after being so served fail to appear, the court may proceed to trial and judgment, without further process, as if the defendant had appeared, plead not guilty and waived trial by jury. And when, in any such case, publication of a copy of the process is required according to such sections, the expense of such publication may be certified by the court to the Comptroller, and shall be paid out of the state treasury; but the same shall be taxed with other costs and collected from the defendant, if judgment be for the Commonwealth, and be paid into the state treasury by the officer collecting the same.

History.
Code 1950, § 19.1-186; 1960, c. 366; 1975, c. 495.

Criminal Procedure

CHAPTER 15.
TRIAL AND ITS INCIDENTS.

Article 1.

Jurisdiction.

Article 2.

Venue.

Article 3.

Arraignment; Pleas; Trial Without Jury.

Article 4.

Trial by Jury.

Article 4.1.

Trial of Capital Cases.

Article 5.

Miscellaneous Provisions.

ARTICLE 1. JURISDICTION.

§ 19.2-239. Jurisdiction in criminal cases.

The circuit courts, except where otherwise provided, shall have exclusive original jurisdiction for the trial of all presentments, indictments and informations for offenses committed within their respective circuits.

History.
Code 1950, § 19.1-187; 1960, c. 366; 1975, c. 495.

§ 19.2-240. Clerks shall make out criminal docket.

Before every term of any court in which criminal cases are to be tried the clerk of the court shall make out a separate docket of criminal cases then pending, in the following order, numbering the same:

1. Felony cases;
2. Misdemeanor cases.

He shall docket all felony cases in the order in which the indictments are found and all misdemeanor cases in the order in which the presentments or indictments are found or informations are filed or appeals are allowed by magistrates and as soon as any presentments or indictments are made at a term of court he shall forthwith docket the same in the order required above.

Traffic infractions shall be docketed with misdemeanor cases.

Cases appealed from the juvenile and domestic relations district court shall not be placed on the criminal docket except for cases involving criminal offenses committed by adults as provided in § 16.1-302. Cases transferred to a circuit court from a juvenile and domestic relations district court pursuant to Article 7 (§ 16.1-269.1 et seq.) of Chapter 11 of Title 16.1 shall be docketed as provided in this section upon return of a true bill of indictment by the grand jury.

History.
Code 1950, § 19.1-189; 1960, c. 366; 1975, c. 495; 1977, c. 585; 1990, c. 258; 1994, cc. 859, 949.

§ 19.2-241. Time within which court to set criminal cases for trial.

The judge of each circuit court shall fix a day of his court when the trial of criminal cases will commence, and may make such general or special order in reference thereto, and to the summoning of witnesses, as may seem proper, but all criminal cases shall be disposed of before civil cases, unless the court shall direct otherwise.

When an indictment is found against a person for felony or when an appeal has been perfected from the conviction of a misdemeanor or traffic infraction, the accused, if in custody, or if he appear according to his recognizance, may be tried at the same term and shall be tried within the time limits fixed in § 19.2-243; provided that no trial shall be held on the first day of the term unless it be with consent of the attorney for the Commonwealth and the accused and his attorney.

History.
Code 1950, §§ 19.1-188 through 19.1-190; 1960, c. 366; 1972, c. 705; 1975, c. 495; 1977, c. 585; 1978, c. 410.

§ 19.2-242. Accused discharged from jail if not indicted in time.

A person in jail on a criminal charge shall be discharged from imprisonment if a presentment, indictment or information be not found or filed against him before the end of the second term of the court at which he is held to answer, unless it appear to the court that material witnesses for the Commonwealth have been enticed or kept away or are prevented from attendance by sickness or inevitable accident, and except, also, in the cases provided in §§ 19.2-168.1 and 19.2-169.1. A discharge under the provisions of this section shall not, however, prevent a reincarceration after a presentment or indictment has been found.

History.
Code 1950, § 19.1-163; 1960, c. 366; 1975, c. 495.

§ 19.2-243. Limitation on prosecution of felony due to lapse of time after finding of probable cause; misdemeanors; exceptions.

Where a district court has found that there is probable cause to believe that an adult has committed a felony, the accused, if he is held continuously in custody thereafter, shall be forever discharged from prosecution for such offense if no trial is commenced in the circuit court within five months from the date such probable cause was found by the district court; and if the accused is not held in custody but has been recognized for his appearance in the circuit court to answer for such offense, he shall be forever discharged from prosecution therefor if no trial is commenced in the circuit court within nine months from the date such probable cause was found.

If there was no preliminary hearing in the district court, or if such preliminary hearing was waived by the accused, the commencement of the running of the five and nine months periods, respectively, set forth in this section, shall be from the date an indictment or presentment is found against the accused.

If an indictment or presentment is found against the accused but he has not been arrested for the offense charged therein, the five and nine months periods, respectively, shall commence to run from the date of his arrest thereon.

Where a case is before a circuit court on appeal from a conviction of a misdemeanor or traffic infraction in a district court, the accused shall be forever discharged from prosecution for such offense if the trial de novo in the circuit court is not commenced (i) within five months from the date of the conviction if the accused has been held continuously in custody or (ii) within nine months of the date of the conviction if the accused has been recognized for his appearance in the circuit court to answer for such offense.

The provisions of this section shall not apply to such period of time as the failure to try the accused was caused:

1. By his insanity or by reason of his confinement in a hospital for care and observation;

2. By the witnesses for the Commonwealth being enticed or kept away, or prevented from attending by sickness or accident;

3. By the granting of a separate trial at the request of a person indicted jointly with others for a felony;

4. By continuance granted on the motion of the accused or his counsel, or by concurrence of the accused or his counsel in such a motion by the attorney for the Commonwealth, or by the failure of the accused or his counsel to make a timely objection to such a motion by the attorney for the Commonwealth, or by reason of his escaping from jail or failing to appear according to his recognizance;

5. By continuance ordered pursuant to subsection I or J of § 18.2-472.1 or subsection C or D of § 19.2-187.1;

6. By the inability of the jury to agree in their verdict; or

7. By a natural disaster, civil disorder, or act of God.

But the time during the pendency of any appeal in any appellate court shall not be included as applying to the provisions of this section.

For the purposes of this section, an arrest on an indictment or warrant or information or presentment is deemed to have occurred only when such indictment, warrant, information, or presentment or the summons or capias to answer such process is served or executed upon the accused and a trial is deemed commenced at the point when jeopardy would attach or when a plea of guilty or nolo contendere is tendered by the defendant. The lodging of a detainer or its equivalent shall not constitute an arrest under this section.

History.

Code 1950, § 19.1-191; 1960, c. 366; 1974, c. 391; 1975, c. 495; 1984, c. 618; 1988, c. 33; 1993, c. 425; 1995, cc. 37, 352; 2002, c. 743; 2005, c. 650; 2007, c. 944; 2009, Sp. Sess. I, cc. 1, 4.

ARTICLE 2.

VENUE.

§ 19.2-244. Venue in general.

A. Except as otherwise provided by law, the prosecution of a criminal case shall be had in the county or city in which the offense was committed. Except as to motions for a change of venue, all other questions of venue must be raised before verdict in cases tried by a jury and before the finding of guilty in cases tried by the court without a jury.

B. If an offense has been committed within the Commonwealth and it cannot readily be determined within which county or city the offense was committed, venue for the prosecution of the offense may be had in the county or city (i) in which the defendant resides; (ii) if the defendant is not a resident of the Commonwealth, in which the defendant is apprehended; or (iii) if the defendant is not a resident of the Commonwealth and is not apprehended in the Commonwealth, in which any related offense was committed.

History.

1975, c. 495; 2015, cc. 632, 637.

§ 19.2-245. Offenses committed without and made punishable within Commonwealth; embezzlement or larceny committed within Commonwealth; where prosecuted.

Prosecution for offenses committed wholly or in part without and made punishable within this Commonwealth may be in any county or city in which the offender is found or to which he is sent by any judge or court; and if any person shall commit larceny or embezzlement beyond the jurisdiction of this Commonwealth and bring the stolen property into the same he shall be liable to prosecution and punishment for larceny or embezzlement in any county or city into which he shall have taken the property as if the same had been wholly committed therein; and if any person shall commit larceny or embezzlement within this Commonwealth and take the stolen property into any county or city other than the county or city within which the same was committed he shall be liable to prosecution and punishment for such larceny or embezzlement in any such county or city into which he shall have taken the property as if the same had been wholly committed therein; provided, that if any person shall commit embezzlement within this Commonwealth he shall be liable as aforesaid or to prosecution and punishment for his offense in the county or city in which he was legally obligated to deliver the embezzled funds or property.

History.
Code 1950, § 19.1-220; 1960, c. 366; 1975, c. 495; 1977, c. 216.

§ 19.2-245.01. Offenses involving reports or statements concerning cigarette sales or stamping.

Any criminal violation of Chapter 42 (§ 3.2-4200 et seq.) of Title 3.2, Article 10 (§ 18.2-246.6 et seq.) of Chapter 6 of Title 18.2, or § 18.2-514 involving reports or statements concerning cigarette sales or stamping may be prosecuted in the City of Richmond.

History.
2009, c. 847; 2013, c. 625.

§ 19.2-245.1. Forgery; where prosecuted.

If any person commits forgery, that forgery may be prosecuted in any county or city (i) where the writing was forged, or where the same was used or passed, or attempted to be used or passed, or deposited or placed with another person, firm, association, or corporation either for collection or credit for the account of any person, firm, association, or corporation or (ii) where the writing is found in the possession of the defendant.

History.
1979, c. 30; 2000, c. 327.

§ 19.2-245.2. Tax offenses; where prosecuted.

If an offense involving tax, as defined in Title 58.1, is committed, that offense may be prosecuted in either any county or city where a false or fraudulent tax return, document, or statement was filed, or the county or city where the offender resides. However, venue shall not be in the City of Richmond solely because a false or fraudulent tax return, document or statement was filed directly with the Department of Taxation.

History.
1990, c. 631.

§ 19.2-246. Injury inflicted by person within Commonwealth upon one outside Commonwealth.

If a mortal wound or other violence or injury be inflicted by a person within this Commonwealth upon one outside of the same, or upon one in this Commonwealth who afterwards dies from the effect thereof out of the Commonwealth, the offender shall be amenable to prosecution and punishment for the offense in the courts of the county or city in which he was at the time of the commission thereof as if the same had been committed in such county or city.

History.
Code 1950, § 19.1-221; 1960, c. 366; 1975, c. 495.

§ 19.2-247. Venue in certain homicide cases.

Where evidence exists that a homicide has been committed either within or without the Commonwealth, under circumstances that make it unknown where such crime was committed, the homicide and any related offenses shall be amenable to prosecution in the courts of the county or city where the body or any part thereof of the victim may be found or, if the victim was removed from the Commonwealth for medical treatment prior to death and died outside the Commonwealth, in the courts of the county or city from which the victim was removed for medical treatment prior to death, as if the offense has been committed in such county or city. In a prosecution for capital murder pursuant to subdivision 8 of § 18.2-31, the offense may be prosecuted in any jurisdiction in the Commonwealth in which any one of the killings may be prosecuted.

History.
Code 1950, § 19.1-221.1; 1973, c. 308; 1975, c. 495; 1996, c. 959; 2002, c. 503; 2015, cc. 632, 637.

§ 19.2-248. Venue when mortal wound, etc., inflicted in one county and death ensues in another.

If a mortal wound, or other violence or injury, be inflicted, or poison administered in one county or city, and death ensues therefrom in another county or city, the offense may be prosecuted in either.

History.
Code 1950, § 19.1-223; 1960, c. 366; 1975, c. 495.

§ 19.2-249. Offenses committed on boundary of two counties, two cities, or county and city, etc.; where prosecuted.

An offense committed on the boundary of two counties, or on the boundary of two cities, or on the boundary of a county and city, or within 300 yards thereof, may be alleged to have been committed, and may be prosecuted and punished, in either county, in either city, or the county or city, and any sheriff, deputy sheriff, or other police officer shall have jurisdiction to make arrests and preserve the peace for a like distance on either side of the boundary line between such counties, such cities, or such county and city.

History.
Code 1950, § 19.1-222; 1960, c. 366; 1975, c. 495; 1978, c. 354; 2003, c. 116.

§ 19.2-249.1. Offenses committed within towns situated in two or more counties; where prosecuted.

An offense or traffic infraction committed within a town situated in two or more counties within the

Commonwealth may be alleged to have been committed, and may be prosecuted and punished, in any one of such counties.

History.
1984, c. 278.

§ 19.2-249.2. Venue for prosecution of computer and other crimes.

For the purpose of venue, any violation of the Virginia Computer Crimes Act (§ 18.2-152.1 et seq.) or § 18.2-386.1 shall be considered to have been committed in any county or city:

1. In which any act was performed in furtherance of any course of conduct that violated any provision listed above;
2. In which the owner has his principal place of business in the Commonwealth;
3. In which any offender had control or possession of any proceeds of the violation or of any books, records, documents, property, financial instrument, computer software, computer program, computer data, or other material or objects that were used in furtherance of the violation;
4. From which, to which, or through which any access to a computer or computer network was made whether by wires, electromagnetic waves, microwaves, optics or any other means of communication;
5. In which the offender resides; or
6. In which any computer that is an object or an instrument of the violation is located at the time of the alleged offense.

History.
2005, cc. 746, 761, 827; 2015, c. 423.

§ 19.2-250. How far jurisdiction of corporate authorities extends.

A. Notwithstanding any other provision of this article and except as provided in subsection B hereof, the jurisdiction of the corporate authorities of each town or city, in criminal cases involving offenses against the Commonwealth, shall extend within the Commonwealth one mile beyond the corporate limits of such town or city; except that such jurisdiction of the corporate authorities of towns situated in counties having a density of population in excess of 300 inhabitants per square mile, or in counties adjacent to cities having a population of 170,000 or more, shall extend for 300 yards beyond the corporate limits of such town or, in the case of the criminal jurisdiction of an adjacent county, for 300 yards within such town.

B. Notwithstanding any other provision of this article, the jurisdiction of the authorities of Chesterfield County and Henrico County, in criminal cases involving offenses against the Commonwealth, shall extend one mile beyond the limits of such county into the City of Richmond.

History.
Code 1950, § 15.1-141; 1962, c. 623; 1975, c. 495; 1978, c. 379; 1998, c. 428; 2007, c. 813.

§ 19.2-251. When and how venue may be changed.

A circuit court may, on motion of the accused or of the Commonwealth, for good cause, order the venue for the trial of a criminal case in such court to be changed to some other circuit court. Such motion when made by the accused may be made in his absence upon a petition signed and sworn to by him.

Whenever the mayor of any city, or the sheriff of any county, shall call on the Governor for military force to protect the accused from violence, the judge of the circuit court of the city or county having jurisdiction of the offense shall, upon a petition signed and sworn to by the accused, whether he be present or not, at once order the venue to be changed to the circuit court of a city or county sufficiently remote from the place where the offense was committed to insure the safe and impartial trial of the accused.

History.
Code 1950, § 19.1-224; 1960, c. 366; 1975, c. 495.

§ 19.2-252. Court ordering change of venue may admit accused to bail and recognize witnesses; remand of accused not admitted to bail.

When the venue is so changed, the court making the order may admit the accused to bail and shall recognize the witnesses and the accused if admitted to bail and the bail be given, to appear on some certain day before the court to which the case is removed; if the accused be not admitted to bail or the bail required be not given, the court shall remand him to its own jail and order its officer to remove him thence to the jail of the court to which the case is removed, so that he shall be there before the day for the appearance of the witnesses.

History.
Code 1950, § 19.1-225; 1960, c. 366; 1975, c. 495.

§ 19.2-253. Procedure upon and after change of venue.

The clerk of the court which orders a change of venue shall certify copies of the recognizances aforesaid and of the record of the case to the clerk of the court to which the case is removed, who shall thereupon issue a venire facias, directed to the officer of such court; and such court shall proceed with the case as if the prosecution had been originally therein; and for that purpose the certified copies aforesaid shall be sufficient.

History.
Code 1950, § 19.1-226; 1960, c. 366; 1975, c. 495.

ARTICLE 3.

ARRAIGNMENT; PLEAS; TRIAL WITHOUT JURY.

§ 19.2-254. Arraignment; pleas; when court may refuse to accept plea; rejection of plea agreement; recusal.

Arraignment shall be conducted in open court. It shall consist of reading to the accused the charge on which he will be tried and calling on him to plead thereto. In a felony case, arraignment is not necessary when waived by the accused. In a misdemeanor case, arraignment is not necessary when waived by the accused or his counsel, or when the accused fails to appear.

An accused may plead not guilty, guilty or nolo contendere. The court may refuse to accept a plea of guilty to any lesser offense included in the charge upon which the accused is arraigned; but, in misdemeanor and felony cases the court shall not refuse to accept a plea of nolo contendere.

With the approval of the court and the consent of the Commonwealth, a defendant may enter a conditional plea of guilty in a misdemeanor or felony case in circuit court, reserving the right, on appeal from the judgment, to a review of the adverse determination of any specified pretrial motion. If the defendant prevails on appeal, he shall be allowed to withdraw his plea.

Upon rejecting a plea agreement in any criminal matter, a judge shall immediately recuse himself from any further proceedings on the same matter unless the parties agree otherwise.

History.
1975, c. 495; 1987, c. 357; 2014, cc. 52, 165.

§ 19.2-254.1. Procedure in traffic infraction cases.

In a traffic infraction case, as defined in § 46.2-100, involving an offense included in the uniform fine schedule established pursuant to § 16.1-69.40:1, a defendant may elect to enter a written appearance and waive court hearing, except in instances in which property damage or personal injury resulted. Arraignment is not necessary when waived by the accused or his counsel, when the accused fails to appear, or when such written appearance has been elected.

An accused may plead not guilty, guilty, or nolo contendere; and the court shall not refuse to accept a plea of nolo contendere. A plea of guilty may be entered in writing without court appearance.

When an accused tenders payment without executing a written waiver of court hearing and entry of guilty plea, such tender of payment shall itself be deemed a waiver of court hearing and entry of guilty plea.

In districts with traffic violations bureaus on July 1, 1977, the chief judge of the district may designate the traffic violations bureau for the receipt of a written appearance, waiver of court hearing and guilty plea.

History.
1977, c. 585; 1978, c. 605; 1992, c. 54.

§ 19.2-254.2. Procedure in nontraffic offenses for which prepayment is authorized.

In any prepayable nontraffic offense case as defined in § 16.1-69.40:2 a defendant may elect to enter a written appearance and waive court hearing. Arraignment is not necessary when waived by the accused or his counsel, when the accused fails to appear, or when such written appearance has been elected.

An accused may plead not guilty, guilty, or nolo contendere; and the court shall not refuse to accept a plea of nolo contendere. A plea of guilty may be entered in writing without court appearance.

When an accused tenders payment without executing a written waiver of court hearing and entry of guilty plea, such tender of payment shall itself be deemed a waiver of court hearing and entry of guilty plea. Likewise when a person charged with a prepayable nontraffic offense fails to enter a written or court appearance, he shall be deemed to have waived court hearing and the case may be heard in his absence. In all other respects prepayable traffic offenses shall be treated as all other misdemeanors.

History.
1978, c. 605; 1992, c. 54.

§ 19.2-255. Defendant allowed to plead several matters of law or fact.

The defendant in any criminal prosecution may plead as many several matters, whether of law or fact, as he shall think necessary, and he may file pleas in bar at the same time with pleas in abatement, or within a reasonable time thereafter; but the issues on the pleas in abatement shall be first tried.

History.
Code 1950, § 19.1-242; 1960, c. 366; 1975, c. 495.

§ 19.2-256. Approvers.

Approvers shall not be admitted in any case.

History.
Code 1950, § 19.1-244; 1960, c. 366; 1975, c. 495.

§ 19.2-257. Trial without jury in felony cases.

Upon a plea of guilty in a felony case, tendered in person by the accused after being advised by coun-

Criminal Procedure

sel, the court shall hear and determine the case without the intervention of a jury; or if the accused plead not guilty, with his consent after being advised by counsel and the concurrence of the attorney for the Commonwealth and of the court entered of record, the court shall hear and determine the case without the intervention of a jury. In such cases the court shall have and exercise all the powers, privileges and duties given to juries by any statute relating to crimes and punishments.

History.
Code 1950, § 19.1-192; 1960, c. 366; 1975, c. 495.

§ 19.2-258. Trial of misdemeanors by court without jury; failure to appear deemed waiver of jury.

In all cases of a misdemeanor upon a plea of guilty, tendered in person by the accused or his counsel, the court shall hear and determine the case without the intervention of a jury. If the accused plead not guilty, in person or by his counsel, the court, in its discretion, with the concurrence of the accused and the attorney for the Commonwealth, may hear and determine the case without the intervention of a jury. In each instance the court shall have and exercise all the powers and duties vested in juries by any statute relating to crimes and punishments.

When a person charged with a misdemeanor has been admitted to bail or released upon his own recognizance for his appearance before a court of record having jurisdiction of the case, for a hearing thereon and fails to appear in accordance with the condition of his bail or recognizance, he shall be deemed to have waived trial by a jury and the case may be heard in his absence as upon a plea of not guilty.

History.
Code 1950, § 19.1-193; 1960, c. 366; 1975, c. 495.

§ 19.2-258.1. Trial of traffic infractions; measure of proof; failure to appear.

For any traffic infraction cases tried in a district court, the court shall hear and determine the case without the intervention of a jury. For any traffic infraction case appealed to a circuit court, the defendant shall have the right to trial by jury. The defendant shall be presumed innocent until proven guilty beyond a reasonable doubt.

When a person charged with a traffic infraction fails to enter a written or court appearance, he shall be deemed to have waived court hearing and the case may be heard in his absence, after which he shall be notified of the court's finding. He shall be advised that if he fails to comply with any order of the court therein, the court may order suspension of his driver's license as provided in § 46.2-395 but the court shall not issue a warrant for his failure to appear pursuant to § 46.2-938.

History.
1977, c. 585; 1978, c. 605; 1989, c. 705; 2001, c. 414.

§ 19.2-259. On trial for felony, accused to be present; when court may enter plea for him, and trial go on.

A person tried for felony shall be personally present during the trial. If when arraigned he will not plead or answer and does not confess his guilt the court shall have the plea of not guilty entered and the trial shall proceed as if the accused had put in that plea. But for the purposes of this section a motion for a continuance, whether made before or after arraignment, shall not be deemed to be part of the trial.

History.
Code 1950, § 19.1-240; 1960, c. 366; 1975, c. 495.

ARTICLE 4.

TRIAL BY JURY.

§ 19.2-260. Provisions of Title 8.01 apply except as provided in this article.

Except as otherwise provided in this article, trial by jury in criminal cases shall be regulated as provided for in Chapter 11 (§ 8.01-336 et seq.) of Title 8.01.

History.
1975, c. 495; 1977, c. 624.

§ 19.2-261. Charging grand jury in presence of person selected as juror.

The court shall not charge the grand jury in the presence of any person selected as a juror to try any person indicted by the said grand jury. A violation of this provision shall constitute reversible error in any criminal case tried by a jury composed of one or more such veniremen.

History.
Code 1950, § 8-208.20; 1973, c. 439; 1975, c. 495.

§ 19.2-262. Waiver of jury trial; numbers of jurors in criminal cases; how jurors selected from panel.

A. In any criminal case in which trial by jury is dispensed with as provided by law, the whole matter of law and fact shall be heard and judgment given by the court. In appeals from juvenile and domestic relations district courts, the infant, through his guardian ad litem or counsel, may waive a jury.

B. Twelve persons from a panel of not less than 20 shall constitute a jury in a felony case. Seven persons from a panel of not less than 13 shall constitute a jury in a misdemeanor case.

C. The parties or their counsel, beginning with the attorney for the Commonwealth, shall alternately strike off one name from the panel until the number remaining shall be reduced to the number required for a jury.

D. In any case in which persons indicted for felony are tried jointly, if counsel or the accused are unable to agree on the full number to be stricken, or, if for any other reason counsel or the accused fail or refuse to strike off the full number of jurors allowed such party, the clerk shall place in a box ballots bearing the names of the jurors whose names have not been stricken and shall cause to be drawn from the box such number of ballots as may be necessary to complete the number of strikes allowed the party or parties failing or refusing to strike. Thereafter, if the opposing side is entitled to further strikes, they shall be made in the usual manner.

History.
Code 1950, § 8-208.21; 1973, c. 439; 1974, c. 611; 1975, cc. 495, 578; 1979, c. 230; 1997, cc. 516, 518; 2005, c. 356.

§ 19.2-262.1. Joinder of defendants.

On motion of the Commonwealth, for good cause shown, the court shall order persons charged with participating in contemporaneous and related acts or occurrences or in a series of acts or occurrences constituting an offense or offenses, to be tried jointly unless such joint trial would constitute prejudice to a defendant. If the court finds that a joint trial would constitute prejudice to a defendant, the court shall order severance as to that defendant or provide such other relief justice requires.

History.
1993, cc. 462, 489; 1997, c. 518.

§ 19.2-263: Repealed by Acts 1993, cc. 462 and 489.

Cross references.
As to present provisions relating to severance of a joint trial, see § 19.2-262.1.

§ 19.2-263.1. Contact between judge and juror prohibited.

No judge shall communicate in any way with a juror in a criminal proceeding concerning the juror's conduct or any aspect of the case during the course of the trial outside the presence of the parties or their counsel.

History.
1985, c. 176.

§ 19.2-263.2. Jury instructions.

A proposed jury instruction submitted by a party, which constitutes an accurate statement of the law applicable to the case, shall not be withheld from the jury solely for its nonconformance with model jury instructions.

History.
1992, c. 522.

§ 19.2-263.3. Juror information confidential.

A. The court may, upon motion of either party or its own motion, and for good cause shown, issue an order regulating the disclosure of the personal information of a juror who has been impaneled in a criminal trial to any person, other than to counsel for either party. Good cause shown includes, but is not limited to, a determination by the court that there is a likelihood of bribery, tampering, or physical injury to or harassment of a juror if his personal information is disclosed. An order regulating the disclosure of information may be modified, and the personal information of the jurors in a criminal case may be disseminated to a person having a legitimate interest or need for the information, with restrictions upon its use and further dissemination as may be deemed appropriate by the court.

B. In addition to the provisions of subsection A, the Supreme Court shall prescribe and publish rules that provide for the protection of the personal information of a juror in a criminal trial.

C. For purposes of this section, *"personal information"* means any information collected by the court, clerk, or jury commissioner at any time about a person who is selected to sit on a criminal jury and includes, but is not limited to, a juror's name, age, occupation, home and business addresses, telephone numbers, email addresses, and any other identifying information that would assist another in locating or contacting the juror.

History.
2008, c. 538.

§ 19.2-264. When jury need not be kept together in felony case; sufficient compliance with requirement that jury be kept together.

In any case of a felony the jury shall not be kept together unless the court otherwise directs. Whenever a jury is required to be kept together, it shall be deemed sufficient compliance although the court for good cause permits one or more of such jurors to be separated from the others; provided all such jurors, whether separated or not, be kept in charge of officers provided therefor.

History.
Code 1950, §§ 8-208.31, 8-208.32; 1973, c. 439; 1975, c. 495.

§ 19.2-264.1. Views by juries.

The jury in any criminal case may, at the request of either the attorney for the Commonwealth or any defendant, be taken to view the premises or place in question, or any property, matter or thing relating to the case, when it shall appear to the court that such view is necessary to a just decision.

History.

Code 1950, § 8-216; 1977, c. 624.

ARTICLE 4.1.

TRIAL OF CAPITAL CASES.

§ 19.2-264.2. Conditions for imposition of death sentence.

In assessing the penalty of any person convicted of an offense for which the death penalty may be imposed, a sentence of death shall not be imposed unless the court or jury shall (1) after consideration of the past criminal record of convictions of the defendant, find that there is a probability that the defendant would commit criminal acts of violence that would constitute a continuing serious threat to society or that his conduct in committing the offense for which he stands charged was outrageously or wantonly vile, horrible or inhuman in that it involved torture, depravity of mind or an aggravated battery to the victim; and (2) recommend that the penalty of death be imposed.

History.

1977, c. 492.

§ 19.2-264.3. Procedure for trial by jury.

A. In any case in which the offense may be punishable by death which is tried before a jury the court shall first submit to the jury the issue of guilt or innocence of the defendant of the offense charged in the indictment, or any other offense supported by the evidence for which a lesser punishment is provided by law and the penalties therefor.

B. If the jury finds the defendant guilty of an offense for which the death penalty may not be imposed, it shall fix the punishment as provided in § 19.2-295.1.

C. If the jury finds the defendant guilty of an offense which may be punishable by death, then a separate proceeding before the same jury shall be held as soon as is practicable on the issue of the penalty, which shall be fixed as is provided in § 19.2-264.4.

If the sentence of death is subsequently set aside or found invalid, and the defendant or the Commonwealth requests a jury for purposes of resentencing, the court shall impanel a different jury on the issue of penalty.

History.

1977, c. 492; 1983, c. 519; 1994, cc. 828, 860, 862, 881.

§ 19.2-264.3:1. Expert assistance when defendant's mental condition relevant to capital sentencing.

A. Upon (i) motion of the attorney for a defendant charged with or convicted of capital murder and (ii) a finding by the court that the defendant is financially unable to pay for expert assistance, the court shall appoint one or more qualified mental health experts to evaluate the defendant and to assist the defense in the preparation and presentation of information concerning the defendant's history, character, or mental condition, including (i) whether the defendant acted under extreme mental or emotional disturbance at the time of the offense; (ii) whether the capacity of the defendant to appreciate the criminality of his conduct or to conform his conduct to the requirements of the law was significantly impaired at the time of the offense; and (iii) whether there are any other factors in mitigation relating to the history or character of the defendant or the defendant's mental condition at the time of the offense. The mental health expert appointed pursuant to this section shall be (i) a psychiatrist, a clinical psychologist, or an individual with a doctorate degree in clinical psychology who has successfully completed forensic evaluation training as approved by the Commissioner of Behavioral Health and Developmental Services and (ii) qualified by specialized training and experience to perform forensic evaluations. The defendant shall not be entitled to a mental health expert of the defendant's own choosing or to funds to employ such expert.

B. Evaluations performed pursuant to subsection A may be combined with evaluations performed pursuant to § 19.2-169.5 and shall be governed by subsections B and C of § 19.2-169.5.

C. The expert appointed pursuant to subsection A shall submit to the attorney for the defendant a report concerning the history and character of the defendant and the defendant's mental condition at the time of the offense. The report shall include the expert's opinion as to (i) whether the defendant acted under extreme mental or emotional disturbance at the time of the offense, (ii) whether the capacity of the defendant to appreciate the criminality of his conduct or to conform his conduct to the requirements of the law was significantly impaired, and (iii) whether there are any other factors in mitigation relating to the history or character of the defendant or the defendant's mental condition at the time of the offense.

D. The report described in subsection C shall be sent solely to the attorney for the defendant and shall be protected by the attorney-client privilege. However, the Commonwealth shall be given the report and the results of any other evaluation of the defendant's mental condition conducted relative to the sentencing proceeding and copies of psychiatric, psychological, medical or other records obtained during the course of such evaluation, after the attorney for the defendant gives notice of an intent to present psychiatric or psychological evidence in mitigation pursuant to subsection E.

E. In any case in which a defendant charged with capital murder intends, in the event of conviction, to present testimony of an expert witness to support a claim in mitigation relating to the defendant's history, character or mental condition, he or his attorney shall give notice in writing to the attorney for the Commonwealth, at least 60 days before trial, of his intention to present such testimony. In the event that such notice is not given and the defendant tenders testimony by an expert witness at the sentencing phase of the trial, then the court may, in its discretion, upon objection of the Commonwealth, either allow the Commonwealth a continuance or, under appropriate circumstances, bar the defendant from presenting such evidence.

F. 1. If the attorney for the defendant gives notice pursuant to subsection E and the Commonwealth thereafter seeks an evaluation concerning the existence or absence of mitigating circumstances relating to the defendant's mental condition at the time of the offense, the court shall appoint one or more qualified experts to perform such an evaluation. The court shall order the defendant to submit to such an evaluation, and advise the defendant on the record in court that a refusal to cooperate with the Commonwealth's expert could result in exclusion of the defendant's expert evidence. The qualification of the experts shall be governed by subsection A. The location of the evaluation shall be governed by subsection B of § 19.2-169.5. The attorney for the Commonwealth shall be responsible for providing the experts the information specified in subsection C of § 19.2-169.5. After performing their evaluation, the experts shall report their findings and opinions and provide copies of psychiatric, psychological, medical or other records obtained during the course of the evaluation to the attorneys for the Commonwealth and the defense.

2. If the court finds, after hearing evidence presented by the parties, out of the presence of the jury, that the defendant has refused to cooperate with an evaluation requested by the Commonwealth, the court may admit evidence of such refusal or, in the discretion of the court, bar the defendant from presenting his expert evidence.

G. [Repealed.]

History.

1986, c. 535; 1987, c. 439; 1996, cc. 937, 980; 2003, cc. 1031, 1040; 2009, cc. 813, 840; 2010, c. 559.

§ 19.2-264.3:1.1. Capital cases; determination of mental retardation.

A. As used in this section and § 19.2-264.3:1.2, the following definition applies:

"Mentally retarded" means a disability, originating before the age of 18 years, characterized concurrently by (i) significantly subaverage intellectual functioning as demonstrated by performance on a standardized measure of intellectual functioning administered in conformity with accepted professional practice, that is at least two standard deviations below the mean and (ii) significant limitations in adaptive behavior as expressed in conceptual, social and practical adaptive skills.

B. Assessments of mental retardation under this section and § 19.2-264.3:1.2 shall conform to the following requirements:

1. Assessment of intellectual functioning shall include administration of at least one standardized measure generally accepted by the field of psychological testing and appropriate for administration to the particular defendant being assessed, taking into account cultural, linguistic, sensory, motor, behavioral and other individual factors. All such measures shall be reported as a range of scores calculated by adding and subtracting the standard error of measurement identified by the test publisher to the defendant's earned score. Testing of intellectual functioning shall be carried out in conformity with accepted professional practice, and whenever indicated, the assessment shall include information from multiple sources. The Commissioner of Behavioral Health and Developmental Services shall maintain an exclusive list of standardized measures of intellectual functioning generally accepted by the field of psychological testing.

2. Assessment of adaptive behavior shall be based on multiple sources of information, including clinical interview, psychological testing and educational, correctional and vocational records. The assessment shall include at least one standardized measure generally accepted by the field of psychological testing for assessing adaptive behavior and appropriate for administration to the particular defendant being assessed, unless not feasible. In reaching a clinical judgment regarding whether the defendant exhibits significant limitations in adaptive behavior, the examiner shall give performance on standardized measures whatever weight is clinically appropriate in light of the defendant's history and characteristics and the context of the assessment.

3. Assessment of developmental origin shall be based on multiple sources of information generally accepted by the field of psychological testing and appropriate for the particular defendant being assessed, including, whenever available, educational, social service, medical records, prior disability assessments, parental or caregiver reports, and other collateral data, recognizing that valid clinical assessment conducted during the defendant's childhood may not have conformed to current practice standards.

C. In any case in which the offense may be punishable by death and is tried before a jury, the issue of mental retardation, if raised by the defendant in accordance with the notice provisions of subsection E of § 19.2-264.3:1.2, shall be determined by the jury as part of the sentencing proceeding required by § 19.2-264.4.

In any case in which the offense may be punishable by death and is tried before a judge, the issue of mental retardation, if raised by the defendant in accordance with the notice provisions of subsection E of § 19.2-264.3:1.2, shall be determined by the judge as part of the sentencing proceeding required by § 19.2-264.4.

The defendant shall bear the burden of proving that he is mentally retarded by a preponderance of the evidence.

D. The verdict of the jury, if the issue of mental retardation is raised, shall be in writing, and, in addition to the forms specified in § 19.2-264.4, shall include one of the following forms:

(1) "We the jury, on the issue joined, having found the defendant guilty of (here set out the statutory language of the offense charged), and that the defendant has proven by a preponderance of the evidence that he is mentally retarded, fix his punishment at (i) imprisonment for life or (ii) imprisonment for life and a fine of $________.

Signed ________________ foreman"

or

(2) "We the jury, on the issue joined, having found the defendant guilty of (here set out the statutory language of the offense charged) find that the defendant has not proven by a preponderance of the evidence that he is mentally retarded.

Signed ________________ foreman"

History.

2003, cc. 1031, 1040; 2009, cc. 813, 840; 2015, c. 360.

§ 19.2-264.3:1.2. Expert assistance when issue of defendant's mental retardation relevant to capital sentencing.

A. Upon (i) motion of the attorney for a defendant charged with or convicted of capital murder and (ii) a finding by the court that the defendant is financially unable to pay for expert assistance, the court shall appoint one or more qualified mental health experts to assess whether or not the defendant is mentally retarded and to assist the defense in the preparation and presentation of information concerning the defendant's mental retardation. The mental health expert appointed pursuant to this section shall be (a) a psychiatrist, a clinical psychologist or an individual with a doctorate degree in clinical psychology, (b) skilled in the administration, scoring and interpretation of intelligence tests and measures of adaptive behavior and (c) qualified by experience and by specialized training, approved by the Commissioner of Behavioral Health and Developmental Services, to perform forensic evaluations. The defendant shall not be entitled to a mental health expert of the defendant's own choosing or to funds to employ such expert.

B. Evaluations performed pursuant to subsection A may be combined with evaluations performed pursuant to § 19.2-169.1, 19.2-169.5, or 19.2-264.3:1.

C. The expert appointed pursuant to subsection A shall submit to the attorney for the defendant a report assessing whether the defendant is mentally retarded. The report shall include the expert's opinion as to whether the defendant is mentally retarded.

D. The report described in subsection C shall be sent solely to the attorney for the defendant and shall be protected by the attorney-client privilege. However, the Commonwealth shall be given a copy of the report, the results of any other evaluation of the defendant's mental retardation and copies of psychiatric, psychological, medical or other records obtained during the course of the evaluation, after the attorney for the defendant gives notice of an intent to present evidence of mental retardation pursuant to subsection E.

E. In any case in which a defendant charged with capital murder intends, in the event of conviction, to present testimony of an expert witness to support a claim that he is mentally retarded, he or his attorney shall give notice in writing to the attorney for the Commonwealth, at least 21 days before trial, of his intention to present such testimony. In the event that such notice is not given and the defendant tenders testimony by an expert witness at the sentencing phase of the trial, then the court may, in its discretion, upon objection of the Commonwealth, either allow the Commonwealth a continuance or, under appropriate circumstances, bar the defendant from presenting such evidence.

F. 1. If the attorney for the defendant gives notice pursuant to subsection E and the Commonwealth thereafter seeks an evaluation concerning the existence or absence of the defendant's mental retardation, the court shall appoint one or more qualified experts to perform such an evaluation. The court shall order the defendant to submit to such an evaluation, and advise the defendant on the record in court that a refusal to cooperate with the Commonwealth's experts could result in exclusion of the defendant's expert evidence. The qualification of the experts shall be governed by subsection A. The attorney for the Commonwealth shall be responsible for providing the experts the information specified in subsection C of § 19.2-169.5. After performing their evaluation, the experts shall report their findings and opinions and provide copies of psychiatric, psychological, medical or other records obtained during the course of the evaluation to the attorneys for the Commonwealth and the defense.

2. If the court finds, after hearing evidence presented by the parties, out of the presence of the jury, that the defendant has refused to cooperate with an evaluation requested by the Commonwealth, the court may admit evidence of such refusal or, in the discretion of the court, bar the defendant from presenting his expert evidence.

History.

2003, cc. 1031, 1040; 2009, cc. 813, 840.

§ 19.2-264.3:1.3. Expert assistance for indigent defendants in capital cases.

A. In any case in which an indigent defendant (i) is charged with a capital offense and (ii) is found by the court to be financially unable to pay for expert assistance, the defendant or his attorney may, upon notice to the Commonwealth, move in circuit court for the court to designate another judge in the same circuit to hear an ex parte request for the appointment of a qualified expert to assist in the preparation of the defendant's defense. No ex parte proceeding, communication, or request may be considered pursuant to this section unless a proper showing is made in an adversarial proceeding before the trial judge demonstrating a particularized need for confidentiality. Any such proceeding, communication, or request shall be transcribed and made part of the record available for appellate review or any other post conviction review.

B. The motion for the appointment of a qualified expert shall be in writing, filed under seal, and shall be heard ex parte as soon as practicable by the designated judge. Upon hearing the ex parte request, the designated judge shall find, by clear and convincing evidence, a particularized need for confidentiality has been demonstrated before considering the request for expert services. After a hearing upon the motion, the court may order the appointment of a qualified expert upon a showing that the provision of the requested expert services would materially assist the defendant in preparing his defense and the lack of such confidential assistance would result in a fundamentally unfair trial. Any expert appointed pursuant to this subsection shall be compensated in accordance with § 19.2-332. The designated judge shall direct requests for scientific investigations to the Department of Forensic Science or Division of Consolidated Laboratory Services whenever practicable.

C. All ex parte hearings conducted under this section shall be on the record, and the record of the hearings, together with all papers filed and orders entered in connection with ex parte requests for expert assistance, shall be kept under seal as part of the record of the case. Following decision on the motion, whether it is granted or denied, the motion shall remain under seal. On motion of any party, and for good cause shown, the court may unseal the record after the trial is concluded. Following final judgment and after all appeals have been exhausted, the court shall unseal all records and other material sealed pursuant to this section. No ex parte ruling by a designated judge pursuant to this section in a proceeding where the Commonwealth is excluded shall be the subject of a claim of error on appeal, or form the basis for relief in any post-conviction litigation on behalf of the defendant.

D. This section does not apply to the appointment of a mental health expert pursuant to § 19.2-264.3:1 or 19.2-264.3:1.2.

History.
2010, c. 789.

§ 19.2-264.3:2. Notice to the defendant of intention to present evidence of unadjudicated criminal conduct.

Upon motion of the defendant, in any case in which the offense for which the defendant is to be tried may be punishable by death, if the attorney for the Commonwealth intends to introduce during a sentencing proceeding held pursuant to § 19.2-264.4 evidence of defendant's unadjudicated criminal conduct, the attorney for the Commonwealth shall give notice in writing to the attorney for the defendant of such intention. The notice shall include a description of the alleged unadjudicated criminal conduct and, to the extent such information is available, the time and place such conduct will be alleged to have occurred.

The court shall specify the time by which such notice shall be given.

History.
1993, c. 377.

§ 19.2-264.3:3. Limitations on use of statements or disclosure by defendant during evaluations.

No statement or disclosure by the defendant made during a competency evaluation performed pursuant to § 19.2-169.1, an evaluation performed pursuant to § 19.2-169.5 to determine sanity at the time of the offense, treatment provided pursuant to § 19.2-169.2 or § 19.2-169.6, a mental condition evaluation performed pursuant to § 19.2-264.3:1 or a mental retardation evaluation performed pursuant to § 19.2-264.3:1.2, and no evidence derived from any such statements or disclosures may be introduced against the defendant at the sentencing phase of a capital murder trial for the purpose of proving the aggravating circumstances specified in § 19.2-264.4. Such statements or disclosures shall be admissible in rebuttal only when relevant to issues in mitigation raised by the defense.

History.
2003, cc. 1031, 1040.

§ 19.2-264.3:4. Notice of expert testimony in capital case.

Whenever the defendant, the defendant's attorney, or the attorney for the Commonwealth in a capital case intends to introduce expert opinion testimony at trial, the defendant, defendant's attorney, or attorney for the Commonwealth shall notify the opposing party in writing of such party's intention to present such testimony at least 60 days before the trial. The written notice shall include copies of any written reports of the witness, a summary of the proposed expert testimony that describes the witness's opinions and the basis and reasons for those opinions, and the witness's qualifications and contact information.

History.
2010, c. 789.

§ 19.2-264.4. Sentence proceeding.

A. Upon a finding that the defendant is guilty of an offense which may be punishable by death, a proceeding shall be held which shall be limited to a determination as to whether the defendant shall be sentenced to death or life imprisonment. Upon request of the defendant, a jury shall be instructed that for all Class 1 felony offenses committed after January 1, 1995, a defendant shall not be eligible for parole if sentenced to imprisonment for life. In case of trial by jury, where a sentence of death is not recommended, the defendant shall be sentenced to imprisonment for life.

A1. In any proceeding conducted pursuant to this section, the court shall permit the victim, as defined in § 19.2-11.01, upon the motion of the attorney for the Commonwealth, and with the consent of the victim, to testify in the presence of the accused regarding the impact of the offense upon the victim. The court shall limit the victim's testimony to the factors set forth in clauses (i) through (vi) of subsection A of § 19.2-299.1.

B. In cases of trial by jury, evidence may be presented as to any matter which the court deems relevant to sentence, except that reports under the provisions of § 19.2-299, or under any rule of court, shall not be admitted into evidence.

Evidence which may be admissible, subject to the rules of evidence governing admissibility, may include the circumstances surrounding the offense, the history and background of the defendant, and any other facts in mitigation of the offense. Facts in mitigation may include, but shall not be limited to, the following: (i) the defendant has no significant history of prior criminal activity, (ii) the capital felony was committed while the defendant was under the influence of extreme mental or emotional disturbance, (iii) the victim was a participant in the defendant's conduct or consented to the act, (iv) at the time of the commission of the capital felony, the capacity of the defendant to appreciate the criminality of his conduct or to conform his conduct to the requirements of law was significantly impaired, (v) the age of the defendant at the time of the commission of the capital offense, or (vi) even if § 19.2-264.3:1.1 is inapplicable as a bar to the death penalty, the subaverage intellectual functioning of the defendant.

C. The penalty of death shall not be imposed unless the Commonwealth shall prove beyond a reasonable doubt that there is a probability based upon evidence of the prior history of the defendant or of the circumstances surrounding the commission of the offense of which he is accused that he would commit criminal acts of violence that would constitute a continuing serious threat to society, or that his conduct in committing the offense was outrageously or wantonly vile, horrible or inhuman, in that it involved torture, depravity of mind or aggravated battery to the victim.

D. In the event the jury cannot agree as to the penalty, the court shall dismiss the jury, and impose a sentence of imprisonment for life.

History.
1977, c. 492; 1980, c. 160; 1990, cc. 316, 754; 1998, c. 485; 2000, c. 838; 2003, cc. 1031, 1040; 2010, c. 658.

§ 19.2-264.5. Post-sentence reports.

When the punishment of any person has been fixed at death, the court shall, before imposing sentence, direct a probation officer of the court to thoroughly investigate the history of the defendant and any and all other relevant facts, to the end that the court may be fully advised as to whether the sentence of death is appropriate and just. Reports shall be made, presented and filed as provided in § 19.2-299 except that, notwithstanding any other provision of law, such reports shall in all cases contain a Victim Impact Statement. Such statement shall contain the same information and be prepared in the same manner as Victim Impact Statements prepared pursuant to § 19.2-299.1. After consideration of the report, and upon good cause shown, the court may set aside the sentence of death and impose a sentence of imprisonment for life. Notwithstanding any other provision of law, if the court sets aside the sentence of death and imposes a sentence of imprisonment for life, it shall include in the sentencing order an explanation for the reduction in sentence.

History.
1977, c. 492; 1993, c. 978; 2004, c. 298.

ARTICLE 5.
MISCELLANEOUS PROVISIONS.

§ 19.2-265. Opening statement of counsel.

On the trial of any case of felony or misdemeanor and before any evidence is submitted on either side, the attorney for the Commonwealth and counsel for the accused, respectively, shall have the right to make an opening statement of their case.

History.
Code 1950, § 19.1-245; 1960, c. 366; 1975, c. 495.

§ 19.2-265.01. Victims, certain members of the family and support persons not to be excluded.

During the trial of every criminal case and in all court proceedings attendant to trial, whether before, during or after trial, including any proceedings occurring after an appeal by the defendant or the Commonwealth, at which attendance by the defendant is permitted, whether in a circuit or district court, any victim as defined in § 19.2-11.01 may remain in the courtroom and shall not be excluded unless the court determines, in its discretion, the presence of the victim would impair the conduct of a fair trial. In any case involving a minor victim, the court may permit an adult chosen by the minor to be present in the courtroom during any proceedings in addition to or in lieu of the minor's parent or guardian.

The attorney for the Commonwealth shall give prior notice when practicable of such trial and attendant proceedings and changes in the scheduling thereof to any known victim and to any known adult chosen in accordance with this section by a minor victim, at the address or telephone number, or both, provided in writing by such person.

History.
1993, cc. 447, 452; 1994, cc. 361, 598; 1995, c. 687; 1996, c. 546; 1999, c. 844; 2000, c. 339.

§ 19.2-265.1. Exclusion of witnesses (Subsection (a) of Supreme Court Rule 2:615 derived in part from this section and subsection (c) of Supreme Court Rule 2:615 derived from this section).

In the trial of every criminal case, the court, whether a court of record or a court not of record, may upon its own motion and shall upon the motion of either the attorney for the Commonwealth or any defendant, require the exclusion of every witness to be called, including, but not limited to, police officers or other investigators; however, each defendant who is an individual and one officer or agent of each defendant which is a corporation or association shall be exempt from the rule of this section as a matter of right. Additionally, any victim as defined in § 19.2-11.01 who is to be called as a witness shall be exempt from the rule of this section as a matter of law unless, in accordance with the provisions of § 19.2-265.01, his exclusion is otherwise required.

History.
Code 1950, § 8-211.1; 1966, c. 268; 1975, c. 652; 1977, c. 624; 1990, c. 572; 2004, c. 311.

§ 19.2-265.2. Judicial notice of laws (Supreme Court Rule 2:202 derived in part from this section).

A. Whenever, in any criminal case it becomes necessary to ascertain what the law, statutory or otherwise, of this Commonwealth, of another state, of the United States, of another country, or of any political subdivision or agency of the same is, or was, at any time, the court shall take judicial notice thereof whether specially pleaded or not.

B. The court, in taking such notice, shall consult any book, record, register, journal, or other official document or publication purporting to contain, state, or explain such law, and may consider any evidence or other information or argument that is offered on the subject.

History.
1978, c. 328.

§ 19.2-265.3. Nolle prosequi; discretion of court upon good cause shown.

Nolle prosequi shall be entered only in the discretion of the court, upon motion of the Commonwealth with good cause therefor shown.

History.
1979, c. 641.

§ 19.2-265.4. Failure to provide discovery.

A. In any criminal prosecution for a felony in a circuit court or for a misdemeanor brought on direct indictment, the attorney for the Commonwealth shall have a duty to adequately and fully provide discovery as provided under Rule 3A:11 of the Rules of the Supreme Court. Rule 3A:11 shall be construed to apply to such felony and misdemeanor prosecutions. This duty to disclose shall be continuing and shall apply to any additional evidence or material discovered by the Commonwealth prior to or during trial which is subject to discovery or inspection and has been previously requested by the accused. In any criminal prosecution for a misdemeanor by trial de novo in circuit court, the attorney for the Commonwealth shall have a duty to adequately and fully provide discovery as provided under Rule 7C:5 of the Rules of the Supreme Court.

B. If at any time during the course of the proceedings it is brought to the attention of the court that the attorney for the Commonwealth has failed to comply with this section, the court may order the Commonwealth to permit the discovery or inspection, grant a continuance, or prohibit the Commonwealth from introducing evidence not disclosed, or the court may enter such other order as it deems just under the circumstances.

History.
1985, c. 538; 1995, c. 504; 2004, c. 348.

§ 19.2-265.5. Prosecuting misdemeanor cases without attorney.

Notwithstanding any of the provisions of § 19.2-265.1, whenever in a misdemeanor case neither an attorney for the Commonwealth nor any other attorney for the prosecution is present, the complaining witness may be allowed to remain in court throughout the entire trial if necessary for the orderly presentation of witnesses for the prosecution.

History.
1987, c. 659.

§ 19.2-265.6. Effect of dismissal of criminal charges.

No dismissal of any criminal charge by a court shall bar subsequent prosecution of the charge unless jeopardy attached at the earlier proceeding or unless the dismissal order explicitly states that the dismissal is with prejudice.

History.
2007, c. 419.

§ 19.2-266. Exclusion of persons from trial; photographs and broadcasting permitted under designated guidelines; exceptions.

In the trial of all criminal cases, whether the same be felony or misdemeanor cases, the court may, in its discretion, exclude from the trial any persons whose presence would impair the conduct of a fair trial, provided that the right of the accused to a public trial shall not be violated.

A court may solely in its discretion permit the taking of photographs in the courtroom during the progress of judicial proceedings and the broadcasting of judicial proceedings by radio or television and the use of electronic or photographic means for the perpetuation of the record or parts thereof in criminal and in civil cases, but only in accordance with the rules set forth hereunder. In addition to such rules, the Supreme Court and the Court of Appeals shall have the authority to promulgate any other rules they deem necessary to govern electronic media and still photography coverage in their respective courts. The following rules shall serve as guidelines, and a violation of these rules may be punishable as contempt:

Coverage Allowed.

1. The presiding judge shall at all times have authority to prohibit, interrupt or terminate electronic media and still photography coverage of public judicial proceedings. The presiding judge shall advise the parties of such coverage in advance of the proceedings and shall allow the parties to object thereto. For good cause shown, the presiding judge may prohibit coverage in any case and may restrict coverage as he deems appropriate to meet the ends of justice.

2. Coverage of the following types of judicial proceedings shall be prohibited: adoption proceedings, juvenile proceedings, child custody proceedings, divorce proceedings, temporary and permanent spousal support proceedings, proceedings concerning sexual offenses, proceedings for the hearing of motions to suppress evidence, proceedings involving trade secrets, and in camera proceedings.

3. Coverage of the following categories of witnesses shall be prohibited: police informants, minors, undercover agents and victims and families of victims of sexual offenses.

4. Coverage of jurors shall be prohibited expressly at any stage of a judicial proceeding, including that portion of a proceeding during which a jury is selected. The judge shall inform all potential jurors at the beginning of the jury selection process of this prohibition.

5. To protect the attorney-client privilege and the right to counsel, there shall be no recording or broadcast of sound from such conferences which occur in a court facility between attorneys and their clients, between co-counsel of a client, between adverse counsel, or between counsel and the presiding judge held at the bench or in chambers.

Location of Equipment and Personnel.

1. The location of recording and camera equipment shall be strictly regulated so as not to be intrusive.

2. Media personnel shall not enter or leave the courtroom once the proceedings are in session except during a court recess or adjournment.

3. Electronic media equipment and still photography equipment shall not be taken into the courtroom or removed from the designated media area except at the following times:

a. Prior to the convening of proceedings;

b. During any luncheon recess;

c. During any court recess with the permission of the trial judge; and

d. After adjournment for the day of the proceedings.

Official Representatives of the Media.

The Virginia Association of Broadcasters and the Virginia Press Association may designate one person to represent the television media, one person to represent the radio broadcasters, and one person to represent still photographers in each jurisdiction in which electronic media and still photographic coverage is desired. The names of the persons so designated shall be forwarded to the chief judge of the court in the county or city in which coverage is desired so that arrangements can be made for the "pooling" of equipment and personnel. Such persons shall also be the only persons authorized to speak for the media to the presiding judge concerning the coverage of any judicial proceedings.

Equipment and Personnel.

1. No distracting lights or sounds shall be permitted.

2. Not more than two television cameras shall be permitted in any proceeding.

3. Not more than one still photographer, utilizing not more than two still cameras with not more than

two lenses for each camera and related equipment for print purposes, shall be permitted in any proceeding.

4. Not more than one audio system for broadcast purposes shall be permitted in any proceeding.

Audio pickup for all media purposes shall be accomplished with existing audio systems present in the court facility. If no technically suitable audio system exists in the court facility, microphones and related wiring essential for media purposes may be installed and maintained at media expense. The microphones and wiring must be unobtrusive and shall be located in places designated in advance of any proceeding by the chief judge of the court in which coverage is desired.

5. Any "pooling" arrangements among the media required by these limitations on equipment and personnel shall be the sole responsibility of the media without calling upon the presiding judge to mediate any dispute as to the appropriate media representative or equipment authorized to cover a particular proceeding. In the absence of advance media agreement on disputed equipment or personnel issues, the presiding judge may exclude all contesting media personnel from a proceeding.

6. In no event shall the number of personnel in the designated area exceed the number necessary to operate the designated equipment.

7. Only television photographic and audio equipment which does not produce distracting sound or light shall be employed to cover judicial proceedings. No artificial lighting device of any kind shall be employed in connection with the television camera.

8. Only still camera equipment which does not produce distracting sound or light shall be employed to cover judicial proceedings. No artificial lighting device of any kind shall be employed in connection with a still camera.

9. With the concurrence of the chief judge of the court in which coverage is desired, modifications and additions may be made in light sources existing in the facility, provided such modifications or additions are installed and maintained without public expense.

Impermissible Use of Media Material.

None of the film, video tape, still photographs or audio reproductions developed during or by virtue of coverage of a judicial proceeding shall be admissible as evidence (i) in the proceeding out of which it arose, (ii) in any proceeding subsequent and collateral thereto, or (iii) upon any retrial or appeal of such proceedings.

All electronic media and still photography coverage of public judicial proceedings authorized by this section, with the exception of electronic or photographic means authorized for the perpetuation of the record or parts thereof shall be conducted at no cost to the Commonwealth.

History.

Code 1950, § 19.1-246; 1960, c. 366; 1971, Ex. Sess., c. 28; 1975, c. 495; 1978, c. 477; 1987, c. 580; 1989, c. 582; 1990, c. 243; 1992, c. 557.

§ 19.2-266.1. Conviction of lesser offense on indictment for homicide.

In any trial upon an indictment charging homicide, the jury or the court may find the accused not guilty of the specific offense charged in the indictment, but guilty of any degree of homicide supported by the evidence for which a lesser punishment is provided by law.

History.

1975, c. 495.

§ 19.2-266.2. Defense objections to be raised before trial; hearing; bill of particulars.

A. Defense motions or objections seeking (i) suppression of evidence on the grounds such evidence was obtained in violation of the provisions of the Fourth, Fifth or Sixth Amendments to the Constitution of the United States or Article I, Section 8, 10 or 11 of the Constitution of Virginia proscribing illegal searches and seizures and protecting rights against self-incrimination; (ii) dismissal of a warrant, information, or indictment or any count or charge thereof on the ground that: (a) the defendant would be deprived of a speedy trial in violation of the provisions of the Sixth Amendment to the Constitution of the United States, Article I, Section 8 of the Constitution of Virginia, or § 19.2-243; or (b) the defendant would be twice placed in jeopardy in violation of the provisions of the Fifth Amendment to the Constitution of the United States or Article I, Section 8 of the Constitution of Virginia; or (iii) dismissal of a warrant, information, or indictment or any count or charge thereof on the ground that a statute upon which it was based is unconstitutional shall be raised by motion or objection.

B. Such a motion or objection in a proceeding in circuit court shall be raised in writing, before trial. The motions or objections shall be filed and notice given to opposing counsel not later than seven days before trial in circuit court or, if made under clause (ii) of subsection A, at such time prior to trial in circuit court as the grounds for the motion or objection shall arise, whichever occurs last. A hearing on all such motions or objections shall be held not later than three days prior to trial in circuit court, unless such period is waived by the accused, as set by the trial judge. The circuit court may, however, for good cause shown and in the interest of justice, permit the motions or objections to be raised at a later time.

C. To assist the defense in filing such motions or objections in a timely manner, the circuit court shall, upon motion of the defendant, direct the Commonwealth to file a bill of particulars pursuant to § 19.2-230. The circuit court shall fix the time within which such bill of particulars is to be filed. Upon further

Criminal Procedure

motion of the defendant, the circuit court may, upon a showing of good cause, direct the Commonwealth to supplement its bill of particulars. The attorney for the Commonwealth shall certify that the matters stated in the bill of particulars are true and accurate to the best of his knowledge and belief.

D. In a criminal proceeding in district court, any motion or objection as described in subsection A may be raised prior to or at such proceeding. In the event such a motion or objection is raised, the district court shall, upon motion of the Commonwealth grant a continuance for good cause shown.

History.

1987, c. 710; 2005, cc. 622, 694; 2006, cc. 578, 862.

§ 19.2-266.3. Continuances; appearances of parties.

When the court grants a continuance in advance of the date of a scheduled trial or hearing, if the defendant acknowledges in writing, on a form provided by the Office of the Executive Secretary of the Supreme Court, that he promises to appear in court on the date and time of the newly scheduled trial or hearing, the court shall not require counsel or the defendant to appear on the date when the trial or hearing was originally scheduled. However, if the defendant is in violation of the terms of his pretrial release or has failed to appear at any court proceeding, the court may require the defendant to appear on the date when the trial or hearing was originally scheduled as a condition of any continuance granted.

History.

2013, c. 154.

CHAPTER 16.

EVIDENCE AND WITNESSES.

Article 1.

In General.

Article 2.

Witnesses From or for Another State.

ARTICLE 1.

IN GENERAL.

§ 19.2-267. Provisions applicable to witnesses in criminal as well as civil cases; obligation to attend; summons.

Sections 8.01-396.1, 8.01-402, 8.01-405, 8.01-407, and 8.01-408 to 8.01-410, inclusive, shall apply to a criminal as well as a civil case in all respects, except that a witness in a criminal case shall be obliged to attend, and may be proceeded against for failing to do so, although there may not previously have been any payment, or tender to him of anything for attendance, mileage, or tolls. In a criminal case a summons for a witness may be issued by the attorney for the Commonwealth or other attorney charged with the responsibility for the prosecution of a violation of any ordinance or by the attorney for the defendant; however, any attorney who issues such a summons shall, at the time of the issuance, file with the clerk of the court the names and addresses of such witnesses except to the extent protected under § 19.2-11.2.

History.
Code 1950, § 19.1-262; 1960, c. 366; 1962, c. 374; 1975, c. 495; 1977, c. 624; 1991, c. 38; 1994, c. 543; 2007, c. 552; 2008, c. 124; 2014, c. 744.

§ 19.2-267.1. Authority of law-enforcement officer to issue summons to witness; failure to appear.

A summons may be issued by a law-enforcement officer during the course of his immediate investigation of an alleged misdemeanor for which an arrest warrant is not required pursuant to § 19.2-81 to any person he reasonably believes was a witness to the offense. The summons shall command the person to appear and testify at the trial of any criminal charge brought against any person as the result of the offense.

A summons issued pursuant to this section shall have the same force as if issued by the court. The failure of any person so summoned to appear after receiving written notice of the date, time and place of the trial at least five days prior to the trial shall be punishable as contempt of the court in accordance with § 18.2-456 (5).

History.
1983, c. 224.

§ 19.2-267.2. Response to subpoena for information stored in electronic format.

When a subpoena has been served pursuant to Rule 3A:12 of the Rules of the Supreme Court on a person who is not a party to the action requiring the production of information that is stored in an electronic format, the person shall produce a tangible copy of the information. If a tangible copy cannot be produced, the person shall permit the parties to review the information on a computer or by electronic means during normal business hours, provided that the information can be accessed and isolated. If a tangible copy cannot reasonably be produced and the information is commingled with information other than that requested in the subpoena and cannot reasonably be isolated, the person may file a motion for a protective order or motion to quash.

History.
2002, c. 764.

§ 19.2-268. Right of accused to testify.

In any case of felony or misdemeanor, the accused may be sworn and examined in his own behalf, and if so sworn and examined, he shall be deemed to have waived his privilege of not giving evidence against himself, and shall be subject to cross-examination as any other witness; but his failure to testify shall create no presumption against him, nor be the subject of any comment before the court or jury by the prosecuting attorney.

History.
Code 1950, § 19.1-264; 1960, c. 366; 1975, c. 495.

§ 19.2-268.1. Contradiction by prior inconsistent writing (Subdivision (b)(i) of Supreme Court Rule 2:613 derived in part from this section).

A witness in a criminal case may be cross-examined as to previous statements made by him in writing or reduced into writing, relative to the subject matter of the proceeding, without such writing being shown to him; but if it is intended to contradict such witness by the writing, his attention must, before such contradictory proof can be given, be called to the particular occasion on which the writing is supposed to have been made, and he may be asked if he did not make a writing of the purport of the one to be offered to contradict him, and if he denies making it, or does not admit its execution, it shall then be shown to him, and if he admits its genuineness, he shall be allowed to make his own explanation of it; but it shall be competent for the court at any time during the trial to require the production of the writing for its inspection, and the court may thereupon make such use of it for the purpose of the trial as it may think best.

History.
Code 1950, § 8-293; 1958, c. 380; 1960, c. 114; 1964, c. 356; 1977, c. 624.

§ 19.2-268.2. Recent complaint hearsay exception (Subdivision (23) of Supreme Court Rule 2:803 derived from this section).

Notwithstanding any other provision of law, in any prosecution for criminal sexual assault under Article 7 (§ 18.2-61 et seq.) of Chapter 4 of Title 18.2, a violation of §§ 18.2-361, 18.2-366, 18.2-370 or § 18.2-370.1, the fact that the person injured made complaint of the offense recently after commission of the offense is admissible, not as independent evidence of the offense, but for the purpose of corroborating the testimony of the complaining witness.

History.
1993, c. 592.

§ 19.2-268.3. Admissibility of statements by children in certain cases.

A. As used in this section, "offense against children" means a violation or an attempt to violate

§ 18.2-31, 18.2-32, or 18.2-35, subsection A of § 18.2-47, § 18.2-48, 18.2-51, 18.2-51.2, 18.2-51.6, 18.2-52, 18.2-54.1, 18.2-54.2, 18.2-61, 18.2-67.1, 18.2-67.2, or 18.2-67.3, subsection B of § 18.2-346 if punishable as a felony, § 18.2-355, 18.2-356, 18.2-357, or 18.2-357.1, subsection B of § 18.2-361, subsection B of § 18.2-366, § 18.2-370, 18.2-370.1, 18.2-371.1, 18.2-374.1, 18.2-374.1:1, 18.2-374.3, or 18.2-374.4, § 18.2-386.1 if punishable as a felony, or § 40.1-103.

B. An out-of-court statement made by a child who is under 13 years of age at the time of trial or hearing who is the alleged victim of an offense against children describing any act directed against the child relating to such alleged offense shall not be excluded as hearsay under Rule 2:802 of the Rules of Supreme Court of Virginia if both of the following apply:

1. The court finds, in a hearing conducted prior to a trial, that the time, content, and totality of circumstances surrounding the statement provide sufficient indicia of reliability so as to render it inherently trustworthy. In determining such trustworthiness, the court may consider, among other things, the following factors:

a. The child's personal knowledge of the event;

b. The age, maturity, and mental state of the child;

c. The credibility of the person testifying about the statement;

d. Any apparent motive the child may have to falsify or distort the event, including bias or coercion;

e. Whether the child was suffering pain or distress when making the statement; and

f. Whether extrinsic evidence exists to show the defendant's opportunity to commit the act; and

2. The child:

a. Testifies; or

b. Is declared by the court to be unavailable as a witness; when the child has been declared unavailable, such statement may be admitted pursuant to this section only if there is corroborative evidence of the act relating to an alleged offense against children.

C. At least 14 days prior to the commencement of the proceeding in which a statement will be offered as evidence, the party intending to offer the statement shall notify the opposing party, in writing, of the intent to offer the statement and shall provide or make available copies of the statement to be introduced.

D. This section shall not be construed to limit the admission of any statement offered under any other hearsay exception or applicable rule of evidence.

History.

2016, cc. 542, 553.

§ 19.2-269. Convicts as witnesses (Supreme Court Rule 2:609 derived from this section).

A person convicted of a felony or perjury shall not be incompetent to testify, but the fact of conviction may be shown in evidence to affect his credit.

History.

Code 1950, § 19.1-265; 1960, c. 366; 1975, c. 495.

§ 19.2-269.1. Inmates as witnesses in criminal cases.

Whenever the Commonwealth or a defendant in a criminal prosecution in any circuit court in this Commonwealth requires as a witness in his behalf, an inmate in a state or local correctional facility as defined in § 53.1-1, the court, on the application of such defendant or his attorney, or the attorney for the Commonwealth, shall issue an order to the Director of the Department of Corrections to deliver such witness to the sheriff of the jurisdiction of the court issuing the order. If authorized by the court, the clerk of the circuit court or a deputy clerk may issue these orders on behalf of the court. The sheriff shall go where such witness may then be and carry him to the court to testify as such witness, and after he has testified and been released as such witness, carry him back to the place whence he came, for all of which service the sheriff shall be paid out of the criminal expense funds in the state treasury such compensation as the court in which the case is pending may certify to be reasonable.

History.

Code 1950, § 8-300; 1966, c. 227; 1974, cc. 44, 45; 1977, c. 624; 2002, cc. 515, 544.

§ 19.2-269.2. Nondisclosure of addresses or telephone numbers of crime victims and witnesses.

During any criminal proceeding, upon motion of the defendant or the attorney for the Commonwealth, a judge may prohibit testimony as to the current residential or business address or telephone number of a victim or witness if the judge determines that this information is not material under the circumstances of the case.

History.

1989, c. 170; 1994, cc. 845, 931.

§ 19.2-270. When statement by accused as witness not received as evidence.

In a criminal prosecution, other than for perjury, or in an action on a penal statute, evidence shall not be given against the accused of any statement made by him as a witness upon a legal examination, in a criminal or civil action, unless such statement was made when examined as a witness in his own behalf.

History.

Code 1950, § 19.1-267; 1960, c. 366; 1975, c. 495; 1988, c. 366.

§ 19.2-270.1. Use of photographs as evidence in certain larceny and burglary prosecutions.

In any prosecution for larceny under the provisions of §§ 18.2-95, 18.2-96 or § 18.2-98, or for shoplifting under the provisions of § 18.2-103, or for burglary under the provisions of §§ 18.2-89, 18.2-90, 18.2-91 or § 18.2-92, photographs of the goods, merchandise, money or securities alleged to have been taken or converted shall be deemed competent evidence of such goods, merchandise, money or securities and shall be admissible in any proceeding, hearing or trial of the case to the same extent as if such goods, merchandise, money or securities had been introduced as evidence. Such photographs shall bear a written description of the goods, merchandise, money or securities alleged to have been taken or converted, the name of the owner of such goods, merchandise, money or securities and the manner of the identification of same by such owner, or the name of the place wherein the alleged offense occurred, the name of the accused, the name of the arresting or investigating police officer or conservator of the peace, the date of the photograph and the name of the photographer. Such writing shall be made under oath by the arresting or investigating police officer or conservator of the peace, and the photographs identified by the signature of the photographer. Upon the filing of such photograph and writing with the police authority or court holding such goods and merchandise as evidence, such goods or merchandise shall be returned to their owner, or the proprietor or manager of the store or establishment wherein the alleged offense occurred.

History.

1976, c. 577; 1985, c. 184; 1987, c. 493; 1995, c. 447.

§ 19.2-270.1:1. Computer and electronic data in obscenity, etc. cases; access to defendant.

When computer data or electronic data, stored in any form, the possession of which is otherwise unlawful, are seized as evidence in a criminal prosecution of any offense involving obscenity or child pornography, neither the original data nor a copy thereof shall be released to the defendant or his counsel, nor shall a court order the release of such evidence to the defendant or his counsel except as provided herein. The defendant and his counsel shall be allowed the reasonable opportunity to review such evidence in accordance with the rules of discovery. Upon a finding that the production of the original data or a copy thereof to counsel or his designee is necessary and material to the defense of the accused, the court may order such production only under terms that restrict access to specifically identified recipients, prohibit any duplication of the data beyond what is reasonably necessary for the purpose of the production, and require the return of the data to the law-enforcement agency maintaining custody or control of the seized data for appropriate disposition.

History.

2006, c. 601.

§ 19.2-270.2. Disposition of money, securities or documents seized upon arrest, etc., and pertinent as evidence.

A. When in the course of investigation or arrest, the investigating or arresting officer shall seize or come into the possession of moneys, cash, or negotiable or nonnegotiable instruments or securities, hereinafter called "moneys or securities," taken or retained unlawfully from a financial institution or other person, and such moneys or securities, or a portion thereof, shall be pertinent evidence in a pending prosecution or appeal therefrom, the officer or agency having possession thereof, may retain, pending such prosecution or appeal thereof, sufficient of such moneys or securities as shall be necessary to prove the crime of grand larceny or other crimes requiring a specific amount in value. The court upon motion of the attorney for the Commonwealth and for good cause shown may order the release of all moneys or securities, subject to the provisions of this section. The remaining excess moneys or securities, if any, may be released to the owner thereof, upon proper receipt therefor, which release shall be with the consent of the attorney for the Commonwealth. The officer or agency authorizing such release shall make an appropriate record of such moneys or securities released, including designation or copying of serial numbers, and such record or receipt shall be admissible into evidence in any proceeding, hearing or trial of the case to the same extent as if such moneys or securities had been introduced. Such record or receipt shall contain the name of the financial institution or person from whom such moneys or securities were taken, the place from which taken, the name of the accused, and the name of the arresting officer or officers coming into initial possession of such moneys or securities. Pictures shall be taken of any instruments or securities and such pictures shall be attached to the receipt or record above and shall contain further, in the case of such copying, the date of the photograph and the name of the photographer.

B. When in the course of investigation or arrest, the investigating or arresting officer seizes or comes into the possession of moneys or securities under the provisions of this section, and such moneys or securities, or a portion thereof, are introduced as an exhibit in a prosecution or appeal therefrom, the court may, with the consent of the attorney for the Commonwealth, authorize the clerk of the circuit court, upon all appeal rights being exhausted, to deposit such moneys or cash in an interest-bearing account.

History.

1980, c. 423; 1991, c. 680; 1995, c. 447.

§ 19.2-270.3. Admissible evidence as to identity of party presenting bad check, draft or order.

In any prosecution under § 18.2-181 or § 18.2-182 for the presentation of a bad check, draft or order, the following shall be admissible in any proceeding, hearing or trial of the case:

1. The unpaid or dishonored check, draft or order, bearing a notation thereon of the full name, residence address, home telephone number, and either the driver's license, social security or other governmentally issued identification number of the person who delivered such check, draft or order to the payee, the cashing party or its representative, and bearing the initials of the representative of the payee or cashing party to whom the check, draft or order was delivered, as evidence that such information was transcribed on such check, draft or order at the time of such delivery; or

2. A composite photograph of the check, draft or order, and of the person delivering such check, draft or order, and of other documentation identifying such person, such as a driver's license, social security card, or other governmentally issued identification card, taken together at the time the check, draft or order was delivered by such person to the payee, the cashing party or its representative.

If such evidence is introduced, it may invoke an inference sufficient for the trier of fact to find that the person whose identifying information appears on the check, draft or order was the person who delivered the check, draft or order in question to the payee, cashing party or its representative.

History.

1981, c. 292; 1991, c. 633.

§ 19.2-270.4. When donation, destruction, or return of exhibits received in evidence authorized.

A. Except as provided in § 19.2-270.4:1 and unless objection with sufficient cause is made, the trial court in any criminal case may order the donation or destruction of any or all exhibits received in evidence during the course of the trial (i) in any misdemeanor case, at any time after the expiration of the time for filing an appeal from the final judgment of the court if no appeal is taken or if an appeal is taken, at any time after exhaustion of all appellate remedies and (ii) in any felony case, upon notice in the sentencing order or otherwise to the attorney for the Commonwealth, the defendant at his last known address, and attorney of record for the defendant in the case, after more than one year has expired from exhaustion of all appellate remedies, or, if no appeal is taken, after more than one year from the time for seeking appellate remedies has expired; and in the event the defendant is found not guilty by a court of law, the court may, upon entry of the final order, order the destruction, donation, or return of the exhibits; provided, however, if a petition for writ of habeas corpus is filed within such one-year period, then such order shall not be entered until exhaustion of such habeas corpus proceedings. Notwithstanding the foregoing, in all cases concluded prior to July 1, 2005, the notice requirement in this section shall not apply. The order of donation or destruction may require that photographs be made of all exhibits ordered to be donated or destroyed and that such photographs be appropriately labeled for future identification. In addition, the order shall state the nature of the exhibit subject to donation or destruction, identify the case in which such exhibit was received and from whom such exhibit was received, if known, and the manner by which the exhibit is to be destroyed or to whom donated. However, any money introduced into evidence, unless it is stolen from a third party, shall be subject to forfeiture by law-enforcement officials as otherwise provided by law, and if no forfeiture action is taken or if funds remain after any such forfeiture, the clerk shall escheat such funds as otherwise provided by law. No notice to the defendant shall be required in the case of exhibits the disposal or destruction of which is controlled by § 19.2-386.23 or 19.2-386.24, in any case in which such exhibits may be seized and forfeited to the Commonwealth under Chapter 22.1 (§ 19.2-386.1 et seq.) or Chapter 22.2 (§ 19.2-386.15 et seq.), or any other forfeiture provisions, or in any case where such exhibits are deemed contraband.

B. Except as provided in § 19.2-270.4:1, a circuit court for good cause shown, on notice to the attorney for the Commonwealth and any attorney for a defendant in the case, may order the return of any or all exhibits to the owners thereof, notwithstanding the pendency of any appeal or petition for a writ of habeas corpus. The order may be upon such conditions as the court deems appropriate for future identification and inclusion in the record of a case subject to retrial. In addition, the owner shall acknowledge in a sworn affidavit to be filed with the record of the case, that he has retaken possession of such exhibit or exhibits.

C. Any photographs taken pursuant to an order of donation or destruction or an order returning exhibits to the owners shall be retained with the record in the case and, if necessary, shall be admissible in any subsequent trial of the same cause, subject to all other rules of evidence.

D. Upon petition of any organization which is exempt from taxation under § 501 (c) (3) of the

Internal Revenue Code, the court in its sound discretion may order the donation of an exhibit to such charitable organization.

History.

1984, c. 621; 1989, c. 481; 1994, c. 536; 2001, cc. 873, 874, 875; 2008, c. 805; 2010, cc. 352, 366, 454.

§ 19.2-270.4:1. Storage, preservation and retention of human biological evidence in felony cases.

A. Notwithstanding any provision of law or rule of court, upon motion of a person convicted of a felony but not sentenced to death or his attorney of record to the circuit court that entered the judgment for the offense, the court shall order the storage, preservation, and retention of specifically identified human biological evidence or representative samples collected or obtained in the case for a period of up to 15 years from the time of conviction, unless the court determines, in its discretion, that the evidence should be retained for a longer period of time. Upon the filing of such a motion, the defendant may request a hearing for the limited purpose of identifying the human biological evidence or representative samples that are to be stored in accordance with the provisions of this section. Upon the granting of the motion, the court shall order the clerk of the circuit court to transfer all such evidence to the Department of Forensic Science. The Department of Forensic Science shall store, preserve, and retain such evidence. If the evidence is not within the custody of the clerk at the time the order is entered, the court shall order the governmental entity having custody of the evidence to transfer such evidence to the Department of Forensic Science. Upon the entry of an order under this subsection, the court may upon motion or upon good cause shown, with notice to the convicted person, his attorney of record and the attorney for the Commonwealth, modify the original storage order, as it relates to time of storage of the evidence or samples, for a period of time greater than or less than that specified in the original order.

B. In the case of a person sentenced to death, the court that entered the judgment shall, in all cases, order any human biological evidence or representative samples to be transferred by the governmental entity having custody to the Department of Forensic Science. The Department of Forensic Science shall store, preserve, and retain such evidence until the judgment is executed. If the person sentenced to death has his sentence reduced, then such evidence shall be transferred from the Department to the original investigating law-enforcement agency for storage as provided in this section.

C. Pursuant to standards and guidelines established by the Department of Forensic Science, the order shall state the method of custody, transfer and return of any evidence to insure and protect the Commonwealth's interest in the integrity of the evidence. Pursuant to standards and guidelines established by the Department of Forensic Science, the Department of Forensic Science, local law-enforcement agency or other custodian of the evidence shall take all necessary steps to preserve, store, and retain the evidence and its chain of custody for the period of time specified.

D. In any proceeding under this section, the court, upon a finding that the physical evidence is of such a nature, size or quantity that storage, preservation or retention of all of the evidence is impractical, may order the storage of only representative samples of the evidence. The Department of Forensic Science shall take representative samples, cuttings or swabbings and retain them. The remaining evidence shall be handled according to § 19.2-270.4 or as otherwise provided for in the Code.

E. An action under this section or the performance of any attorney representing the petitioner under this section shall not form the basis for relief in any habeas corpus or appellate proceeding. Nothing in this section shall create any cause of action for damages against the Commonwealth, or any of its political subdivisions or officers, employees or agents of the Commonwealth or its political subdivisions.

History.

2001, cc. 873, 874, 875; 2002, c. 832; 2005, cc. 868, 881.

§ 19.2-270.5. DNA profile admissible in criminal proceeding.

In any criminal proceeding, DNA (deoxyribonucleic acid) testing shall be deemed to be a reliable scientific technique and the evidence of a DNA profile comparison may be admitted to prove or disprove the identity of any person. This section shall not otherwise limit the introduction of any relevant evidence bearing upon any question at issue before the court, including the accuracy and reliability of the procedures employed in the collection and analysis of a particular DNA sample. The court shall, regardless of the results of the DNA analysis, if any, consider such other relevant evidence of the identity of the accused as shall be admissible in evidence.

At least twenty-one days prior to commencement of the proceeding in which the results of a DNA analysis will be offered as evidence, the party intending to offer the evidence shall notify the opposing party, in writing, of the intent to offer the analysis and shall provide or make available copies of the profiles and the report or statement to be introduced. In the event that such notice is not given, and the person proffers such evidence, then the court may in its discretion either allow the opposing party a continuance or, under appropriate circumstances, bar the person from presenting such evidence. The period of any such continuance shall not be counted for speedy trial purposes under § 19.2-243. If the opposing party intends to object to the admissibility of such evidence he shall give written notice of that fact and the basis for his objections at least ten days prior to commencement of the proceedings.

History.
1990, c. 669; 1997, c. 315; 2002, cc. 627, 885.

§ 19.2-270.6. Evidence of abuse admissible in certain criminal trials (Supreme Court Rule 2:409 derived from this section).

In any criminal prosecution alleging personal injury or death, or the attempt to cause personal injury or death, relevant evidence of repeated physical and psychological abuse of the accused by the victim shall be admissible, subject to the general rules of evidence.

History.
1993, c. 5.

§ 19.2-270.7. Determining decibel level of sound with proper equipment; certificate as to accuracy of equipment.

A law-enforcement officer may use equipment deemed proper pursuant to subsection C of § 2.2-1112 to determine the decibel level of any sound, including noise. The results of such determinations shall be accepted as prima facie evidence of the decibel level of the sound in any court or legal proceeding where the decibel level of the sound is at issue.

In any court or legal proceeding in which any question arises about the calibration or accuracy of such equipment used to determine the decibel level of sound, a certificate, or a true copy thereof, showing the calibration or testing for accuracy of the equipment, and when and by whom the calibration or test was made, shall be admissible as evidence of the facts therein stated. No calibration or testing of such equipment shall be valid for longer than 12 months.

History.
2010, c. 558.

§ 19.2-271. Certain judicial officers incompetent to testify under certain circumstances; exceptions (Supreme Court Rule 2:605 derived from this section).

No judge shall be competent to testify in any criminal or civil proceeding as to any matter which came before him in the course of his official duties.

Except as otherwise provided in this section, no clerk of any court, magistrate, or other person having the power to issue warrants, shall be competent to testify in any criminal or civil proceeding as to any matter which came before him in the course of his official duties. Such person shall be competent to testify in any criminal proceeding wherein the defendant is charged with perjury or pursuant to the provisions of § 18.2-460 or in any proceeding authorized pursuant to § 19.2-353.3. Notwithstanding any other provision of this section, any judge, clerk of any court, magistrate, or other person having the power to issue warrants, who is the victim of a crime, shall not be incompetent solely because of his office to testify in any criminal or civil proceeding arising out of the crime.

History.
Code 1950, §§ 19.1-267, 19.1-268; 1960, c. 366; 1975, c. 495; 1976, c. 269; 1989, c. 738; 1990, c. 602; 2015, c. 635.

§ 19.2-271.1. Competency of husband and wife to testify.

Husband and wife shall be competent witnesses to testify for or against each other in criminal cases, except as otherwise provided.

History.
Code 1950, § 8-287; 1977, c. 624.

§ 19.2-271.2. Testimony of husband and wife in criminal cases (Subsection (b) of Supreme Court Rule 2:504 derived from this section).

In criminal cases husband and wife shall be allowed, and, subject to the rules of evidence governing other witnesses, may be compelled to testify in behalf of each other, but neither shall be compelled to be called as a witness against the other, except (i) in the case of a prosecution for an offense committed by one against the other, against a minor child of either, or against the property of either; (ii) in any case where either is charged with forgery of the name of the other or uttering or attempting to utter a writing bearing the allegedly forged signature of the other; or (iii) in any proceeding relating to a violation of the laws pertaining to criminal sexual assault (§§ 18.2-61 through 18.2-67.10), crimes against nature (§ 18.2-361) involving a minor as a victim and provided the defendant and the victim are not married to each other, incest (§ 18.2-366), or abuse of children (§§ 18.2-370 through 18.2-371). The failure of either husband or wife to testify, however, shall create no presumption against the accused, nor be the subject of any comment before the court or jury by any attorney.

Except in the prosecution for a criminal offense as set forth in (i), (ii) or (iii) above, in any criminal proceeding, a person has a privilege to refuse to disclose, and to prevent anyone else from disclosing, any confidential communication between his spouse and him during their marriage, regardless of whether he is married to that spouse at the time he objects to disclosure. For the purposes of this section, *"confidential communication"* means a communication made privately by a person to his spouse that is not intended for disclosure to any other person.

History.

Code 1950, § 8-288; 1950, p. 664; 1958, c. 231; 1960, c. 469; 1977, c. 624; 1988, c. 482; 1993, c. 637; 1996, c. 423; 2005, c. 809.

§ 19.2-271.3. Communications between ministers of religion and persons they counsel or advise (Supreme Court Rule 2:503 derived in part from this section).

No regular minister, priest, rabbi or accredited practitioner over the age of eighteen years, of any religious organization or denomination usually referred to as a church, shall be required in giving testimony as a witness in any criminal action to disclose any information communicated to him by the accused in a confidential manner, properly entrusted to him in his professional capacity and necessary to enable him to discharge the functions of his office according to the usual course of his practice or discipline, where such person so communicating such information about himself or another is seeking spiritual counsel and advice relative to and growing out of the information so imparted.

History.

1985, c. 570.

§ 19.2-271.4. Privileged communications by certain public safety personnel.

A. A person who is a member of a critical incident stress management team, established pursuant to subdivision A 13 of § 32.1-111.3, shall not disclose nor be compelled to testify regarding any information communicated to him by emergency medical services or public safety personnel who are the subjects of peer support services regarding a critical incident. Such information shall also be exempt from the Virginia Freedom of Information Act (§ 2.2-3700 et seq.).

B. A person whose communications are privileged under subsection A may waive the privilege.

C. The provisions of this section shall not apply when:

1. Criminal activity is revealed;

2. A member of a critical incident stress management team is a witness or a party to a critical incident that prompted the peer support services;

3. A member of a critical incident stress management team reveals the content of privileged information to prevent a crime against any other person or a threat to public safety;

4. The privileged information reveals intent to defraud or deceive the investigation into the critical incident; or

5. A member of a critical incident stress management team reveals the content of privileged information to the employer of the emergency medical services or public safety personnel regarding criminal acts committed or information that would indicate that the emergency medical services or public safety personnel pose a threat to themselves or others.

History.

2012, cc. 148, 320.

ARTICLE 2.

WITNESSES FROM OR FOR ANOTHER STATE.

§ 19.2-272. Definitions.

"Witness" as used in this article shall include a person whose testimony is desired in any proceeding or investigation by a grand jury or in a criminal action, prosecution or proceeding.

The word *"state"* shall include any territory of the United States and the District of Columbia.

The word *"summons"* shall include a subpoena (both subpoena ad testificandum and subpoena duces tecum), order or other notice requiring the appearance of a witness or production of documents.

History.

Code 1950, § 19.1-269; 1960, c. 366; 1975, c. 495; 1988, c. 34.

§ 19.2-273. Certificate that witness is needed in another state; hearing.

If a judge of a court of record in any state which by its laws has made provisions for commanding persons within that state to attend and testify in this Commonwealth certifies under the seal of such court (1) that there is a criminal prosecution pending in such court or that a grand jury investigation has commenced or is about to commence, (2) that a person being within this Commonwealth is a material witness in such prosecution or grand jury investigation and (3) that his presence will be required for a specified number of days, upon presentation of such certificate to any judge of a court of record in the county or city in which such person is, such judge shall fix a time and place for hearing and shall make an order directing the witness to appear at a time and place certain for the hearing.

History.

Code 1950, § 19.1-270; 1960, c. 366; 1975, c. 495.

§ 19.2-274. When court to order witness to attend.

If at such hearing the judge determines that the witness is material and necessary, that it will not cause undue hardship to the witness to be compelled to attend and testify in the prosecution or grand jury investigation in the other state and that the laws of the state in which the prosecution is pending, or grand jury investigation has commenced or is about to commence (and of any other state through which the witness may be required to pass by ordinary course of travel) will give to him protection from arrest and the service of civil and criminal process, the judge shall issue a summons, with a copy of the certificate attached, directing the witness to attend and testify in the court where the prosecution is pending, or where a grand jury investigation has commenced or is about to commence at a time and place specified in the summons. In any such hearing the certificate shall be prima facie evidence of all the facts stated therein.

History.

Code 1950, § 19.1-271; 1960, c. 366; 1975, c. 495.

§ 19.2-275. Arrest of witness.

If the certificate recommends that the witness be taken into immediate custody and delivered to an officer of the requesting state to assure his attendance in the requesting state, such judge may, in lieu of notification of the hearing, direct that such witness be forthwith brought before him for the hearing; and the judge at the hearing being satisfied of the desirability of such custody and delivery, for which determination the certificate shall be prima facie proof of such desirability, may, in lieu of issuing subpoena or summons, order that the witness be forthwith taken into custody and delivered to an officer of the requesting state.

History.

Code 1950, § 19.1-272; 1960, c. 366; 1975, c. 495.

§ 19.2-276. Penalty for failure to attend and testify.

If the witness who is summoned as above provided, after being paid or tendered by some properly authorized person reimbursement for reasonable travel and lodging expenses as provided in § 2.2-2823 for each day he is required to travel and attend as a witness, fails without good cause to attend and testify as directed in the summons, he shall be punished in the manner provided for the punishment of any witness who disobeys a Virginia circuit court summons.

History.

Code 1950, § 19.1-273; 1960, c. 366; 1975, c. 495; 1987, c. 125.

§ 19.2-277. Summoning witnesses in another state to testify in this Commonwealth.

If a person in any state which by its laws has made provision for commanding persons within its borders to attend and testify in criminal prosecutions or grand jury investigations commenced or about to commence in this Commonwealth is a material witness in a prosecution pending in a court of record in this Commonwealth, or in a grand jury investigation which has commenced or is about to commence, a judge of such court may issue a certificate under the seal of the court stating these facts and specifying the number of days the witness will be required. The certificate may include a recommendation that the witness be taken into immediate custody and delivered to an officer of this Commonwealth to assure his attendance in this Commonwealth. This certificate shall be presented to a judge of a court of record in the county in which the witness is found.

History.

Code 1950, § 19.1-274; 1960, c. 366; 1975, c. 495.

§ 19.2-278. Reimbursement for daily mileage to such witnesses; issuance of warrant necessary to make tender.

If the witness is summoned to attend and testify in this Commonwealth he shall receive such reimbursement for his daily mileage as prescribed in § 2.2-2823 for each day that he is required to travel and attend as a witness. A witness who has appeared in accordance with the provisions of the summons shall not be required to remain within this Commonwealth a longer period of time than the period mentioned in the certificate, unless otherwise ordered by the court.

The judge issuing the certificate prescribed in § 19.2-277 may, by order, direct the clerk of the court involved to issue such warrant or warrants payable out of the state treasury, as may be necessary to make the tender hereinabove prescribed; and after the entry of such order, such clerk, upon application of the attorney for the Commonwealth of the county or city involved, or of the accused, if certificate for the attendance of witness has been issued by such judge on his behalf as authorized by § 19.2-330, shall issue such warrant or warrants and deliver them to the said attorney for the Commonwealth, who shall, forthwith, cause such tender to be made. Upon issuance of any such warrant or warrants said clerk shall deliver a certified copy of the court's order to the Supreme Court, and the said warrant or warrants shall be paid out of the state treasury upon presentation.

Unless and until appropriate forms shall be obtained, such warrants may be issued on the regular forms provided for the payment of witness fees and allowances, but in such event the clerk issuing the same shall make a notation thereon that they were issued pursuant to the provisions of this section.

History.

Code 1950, § 19.1-275; 1960, c. 366; 1972, c. 719; 1975, c. 495; 1976, c. 308; 1977, c. 483; 1978, c. 195.

§ 19.2-279. Penalty for failure of such witnesses to testify.

If such witness, after coming into this Commonwealth, fails without good cause to attend and testify as directed in the summons, he shall be punished in the manner provided for the punishment of any witness who disobeys a summons issued from a court of record in this Commonwealth.

History.
Code 1950, § 19.1-276; 1960, c. 366; 1975, c. 495.

§ 19.2-280. Exemption of such witnesses from arrest or service of process.

If a person comes into this Commonwealth in obedience to a summons directing him to attend and testify in this Commonwealth he shall not while in this Commonwealth pursuant to such summons be subject to arrest or the service of process, civil or criminal, in connection with matters which arose before his entrance into this Commonwealth under the summons.

If a person passes through this Commonwealth while going to another state in obedience to a summons to attend and testify in that state or while returning therefrom, he shall not while so passing through this Commonwealth be subject to arrest or the service of process, civil or criminal, in connection with matters which arose before his entrance into this Commonwealth under the summons.

History.
Code 1950, § 19.1-277; 1960, c. 366; 1975, c. 495.

§ 19.2-281. Construction of article.

This article shall be so interpreted and construed as to effectuate its general purpose to make uniform the law of the states which enact it.

History.
Code 1950, § 19.1-278; 1960, c. 366; 1975, c. 495.

§ 19.2-282. How article cited.

This article may be cited as the "Uniform Act to Secure the Attendance of Witnesses from without a State in Criminal Proceedings."

History.
Code 1950, § 19.1-279; 1960, c. 366; 1975, c. 495.

CHAPTER 17.

CONVICTIONS; EFFECT THEREOF.

Article 1.

Proof and Verdicts.

Article 2.

Former Jeopardy.

Article 3.

Conviction of Aliens.

ARTICLE 1.

PROOF AND VERDICTS.

§ 19.2-283. How accused may be convicted of felony.

No person shall be convicted of felony, unless by his confession of guilt in court, or by his plea, or by the verdict of a jury, accepted and recorded by the court, or by judgment of the court trying the case without a jury according to law.

History.
Code 1950, § 19.1-248; 1960, c. 366; 1975, c. 495.

§ 19.2-284. Proof of ownership in offense relating to property.

In a prosecution for an offense committed upon, relating to or affecting real estate, or for stealing, embezzling, destroying, injuring or fraudulently receiving or concealing any personal estate it shall be sufficient to prove that when the offense was committed the actual or constructive possession, or a general or special property, in the whole or any part of such estate was in the person or entity alleged in the indictment or other accusation to be the owner thereof.

History.
Code 1950, § 19.1-247; 1960, c. 366; 1975, c. 495.

§ 19.2-285. Accused guilty of part of offense charged; sentence; on new trial what tried.

If a person indicted of a felony be by the jury acquitted of part of the offense charged, he shall be sentenced for such part as he is so convicted of, if the same be substantially charged in the indictment, whether it be felony or misdemeanor. If the verdict be set aside and a new trial granted the accused, he shall not be tried for any higher offense than that of which he was convicted on the last trial.

History.
Code 1950, § 19.1-249; 1960, c. 366; 1975, c. 495.

§ 19.2-286. Conviction of attempt or as accessory on indictment for felony; effect of general verdict of not guilty.

On an indictment for felony the jury may find the accused not guilty of the felony but guilty of an attempt to commit such felony, or of being an accessory thereto; and a general verdict of not guilty, upon such indictment, shall be a bar to a subsequent prosecution for an attempt to commit such felony, or of being an accessory thereto.

History.
Code 1950, § 19.1-254; 1960, c. 366; 1975, c. 495.

§ 19.2-287. Verdict and judgment, when jury agree as to some and disagree as to others.

When two or more persons are charged and tried jointly, the jury may render a verdict as to any of them as to whom they agree. Thereupon judgment shall be entered according to the verdict; and as to the others the case shall be tried by another jury.

History.
Code 1950, § 19.1-256; 1960, c. 366; 1975, c. 495.

§ 19.2-288. Verdict when accused found guilty of punishable homicide.

If a person indicted for murder be found by the jury guilty of any punishable homicide, they shall in their verdict fix the degree thereof and ascertain the extent of the punishment to be inflicted within the bounds prescribed by §§ 18.2-30 to 18.2-36.

History.
Code 1950, § 19.1-250; 1960, c. 366; 1975, c. 495.

§ 19.2-289. Conviction of petit larceny.

In a prosecution for grand larceny, if it be found that the thing stolen is of less value than $200, the jury may find the accused guilty of petit larceny.

History.
Code 1950, § 19.1-252; 1960, c. 366; 1966, c. 247; 1975, c. 495; 1981, c. 197.

§ 19.2-290. Conviction of petit larceny though thing stolen worth more than $200.

In a prosecution for petit larceny, though the thing stolen be of the value of $200 or more, the jury may find the accused guilty; and upon a conviction under this section or § 19.2-289 the accused shall be sentenced for petit larceny.

History.
Code 1950, § 19.1-253; 1960, c. 366; 1966, c. 247; 1975, c. 495; 1981, c. 197.

§ 19.2-291. Faulty counts; motion to strike; general verdict of guilty.

When there are several counts in the indictment one or more of which are faulty, the accused may move to strike the faulty count or counts or move the court to instruct the jury to disregard them. If he does neither and a general verdict of guilty is found, judgment shall be entered against the accused, if any count be good, though others be faulty, unless the court can plainly see that the verdict could not have been found on the good count. If the accused demurs to the faulty count or moves the court to instruct the jury to disregard it and his demurrer or motion is overruled and there is a general verdict of guilty and it cannot be seen on which count the verdict was founded, if the jury has been discharged, it shall be set aside; but if it is manifest that it could not have been found on the bad count, the verdict shall be allowed to stand.

History.
Code 1950, § 19.1-255; 1960, c. 366; 1975, c. 495.

§ 19.2-291.1. Report of conviction of school employees for certain offenses.

The clerk of any circuit court or any district court in the Commonwealth shall report to the Superintendent of Public Instruction and the division superintendent of any employing school division the conviction of any person, known by such clerk to hold a license issued by the Board of Education, for any felony involving the sexual molestation, physical or sexual abuse, or rape of a child or involving drugs pursuant to Article 1 (§ 18.2-247 et seq.) of Chapter 7 of Title 18.2.

History.
2008, cc. 474, 827.

ARTICLE 2.

FORMER JEOPARDY.

§ 19.2-292. Acquittal by jury on merits bar to further prosecution for same offense.

A person acquitted upon the facts and merits on a former trial, may plead such acquittal in bar of a second prosecution for the same offense, notwithstanding any defect in the form or substance of the indictment or accusation on which he was acquitted, unless the case be for a violation of the law relating to the state revenue and the acquittal be reversed on a writ of error on behalf of the Commonwealth.

History.
Code 1950, § 19.1-257; 1960, c. 366; 1975, c. 495.

§ 19.2-293. When acquittal not a bar to further prosecution for same offense.

A person acquitted of an offense on the ground of a variance between the allegations and the proof of the indictment or other accusation, or upon an exception to the form or substance thereof, may be arraigned again on a new indictment or other proper accusation, and tried and convicted for the same offense, notwithstanding such former acquittal.

History.
Code 1950, § 19.1-258; 1960, c. 366; 1975, c. 495.

§ 19.2-294. Offense against two or more statutes or ordinances.

If the same act be a violation of two or more statutes, or of two or more ordinances, or of one or more statutes and also one or more ordinances, conviction under one of such statutes or ordinances shall be a bar to a prosecution or proceeding under the other or others. Furthermore, if the same act be a violation of both a state and a federal statute, a prosecution under the federal statute shall be a bar to a prosecution under the state statute. The provisions of this section shall not apply to any offense involving an act of terrorism as defined in § 18.2-46.4.

For purposes of this section, a prosecution under a federal statute shall be deemed to be commenced once jeopardy has attached.

History.
Code 1950, § 19.1-259; 1960, c. 366; 1975, c. 495; 1987, c. 241; 2002, cc. 588, 623; 2003, c. 736.

§ 19.2-294.1. Dismissal of one of dual charges for driving while intoxicated and reckless driving upon conviction of other charge.

Whenever any person is charged with a violation of § 18.2-266 or any similar ordinances of any county, city, or town and with reckless driving in violation of § 46.2-852 or any ordinance of any county, city or town incorporating § 46.2-852, growing out of the same act or acts and is convicted of one of these charges, the court shall dismiss the remaining charge.

History.
Code 1950, § 19.1-259.1; 1960, c. 493; 1975, c. 495; 1997, c. 691; 2004, c. 937.

ARTICLE 3.

CONVICTION OF ALIENS.

§ 19.2-294.2. Procedure when aliens convicted of certain felonies; duties of probation and parole officer.

A. Whenever a person is (i) convicted in a circuit court of any felony and (ii) referred to a probation or parole officer for a report pursuant to § 19.2-299, or for probation supervision, the probation or parole officer shall inquire as to the citizenship of such person. If upon inquiry it is determined that the person may be an alien based upon his failure to produce evidence of United States citizenship, the probation or parole officer shall report this determination to the Central Criminal Records Exchange of the Department of State Police on forms provided by the Exchange.

B. The inquiry required by this section need not be made if it is apparent that a report on alien status has previously been made to the Central Criminal Records Exchange pursuant to this section.

C. It shall be the responsibility of the Central Criminal Records Exchange of the Department of State Police to review arrest reports submitted by law-enforcement agencies and reports of suspected alien-status inquiries made by probation or parole officers, and to report within sixty days of final disposition to the Law Enforcement Support Center of the United States Immigration and Customs Enforcement the identity of all convicted offenders suspected of being an alien.

History.
1985, c. 247; 1994, c. 579; 2008, cc. 180, 415.

CHAPTER 18.

SENTENCE; JUDGMENT; EXECUTION OF SENTENCE.

Article 1.

General Provisions.

Article 1.1.

DNA Analysis and Data Bank.

Article 2.

Indeterminate Commitment.

Article 3.

Boot Camp Incarceration Program.

Article 4.

Detention Center Incarceration Program.

Article 5.

Diversion Center Incarceration Program.

ARTICLE 1.
GENERAL PROVISIONS.

§ 19.2-295. Ascertainment of punishment.

A. Within the limits prescribed by law, the term of confinement in the state correctional facility or in jail and the amount of fine, if any, of a person convicted of a criminal offense, shall be ascertained by the jury, or by the court in cases tried without a jury.

B. In any case in which a jury has fixed a sentence as provided in this chapter and the sentence is modified by the court pursuant to the authority contained within this chapter, the court shall file with the record of the case a written explanation of such modification including the cause therefor.

History.

Code 1950, §§ 19.1-291, 19.1-292; 1960, c. 366; 1975, c. 495; 2007, c. 259.

§ 19.2-295.1. Sentencing proceeding by the jury after conviction.

In cases of trial by jury, upon a finding that the defendant is guilty of a felony or a Class 1 misdemeanor, or upon a finding in the trial de novo of an appealed misdemeanor conviction that the defendant is guilty of a Class 1 misdemeanor, a separate proceeding limited to the ascertainment of punishment shall be held as soon as practicable before the same jury. At such proceeding, the Commonwealth may present any victim impact testimony pursuant to § 19.2-295.3 and shall present the defendant's prior criminal history, including prior convictions and the punishments imposed, by certified, attested or exemplified copies of the final order, including

Criminal Procedure

adult convictions and juvenile convictions and adjudications of delinquency. Prior convictions shall include convictions and adjudications of delinquency under the laws of any state, the District of Columbia, the United States or its territories. The Commonwealth shall provide to the defendant 14 days prior to trial notice of its intention to introduce copies of final orders evidencing the defendant's prior criminal history, including prior convictions and punishments imposed. Such notice shall include (i) the date of each prior conviction, (ii) the name and jurisdiction of the court where each prior conviction was had, (iii) each offense of which he was convicted, and (iv) the punishment imposed. Prior to commencement of the trial, the Commonwealth shall provide to the defendant photocopies of certified copies of the final orders which it intends to introduce at sentencing. After the Commonwealth has introduced in its case-in-chief of the sentencing phase such evidence of prior convictions or victim impact testimony, or both, or if no such evidence is introduced, the defendant may introduce relevant, admissible evidence related to punishment. Nothing in this section shall prevent the Commonwealth or the defendant from introducing relevant, admissible evidence in rebuttal.

If the jury cannot agree on a punishment, the court shall impanel a different jury to ascertain punishment, unless the defendant, the attorney for the Commonwealth, and the court agree, in the manner provided in § 19.2-257, that the court shall fix punishment.

If the sentence imposed pursuant to this section is subsequently set aside or found invalid solely due to an error in the sentencing proceeding, the court shall impanel a different jury to ascertain punishment, unless the defendant, the attorney for the Commonwealth and the court agree, in the manner provided in § 19.2-257, that the court shall fix punishment.

History.

1994, cc. 828, 860, 862, 881; 1995, c. 567; 1996, c. 664; 2001, c. 389; 2007, cc. 388, 478; 2012, c. 134.

§ 19.2-295.2. Postrelease supervision of felons sentenced for offenses committed on and after January 1, 1995, and on and after July 1, 2000.

A. At the time the court imposes sentence upon a conviction for any felony offense committed (i) on or after January 1, 1995, the court may, and (ii) on or after July 1, 2000, shall, in addition to any other punishment imposed if such other punishment includes an active term of incarceration in a state or local correctional facility, except in cases in which the court orders a suspended term of confinement of at least six months, impose a term of postrelease supervision of not less than six months nor more than three years, as the court may determine. Such additional term shall be suspended and the defendant placed under postrelease supervision upon release from the active term of incarceration. The period of supervision shall be established by the court; however, such period shall not be less than six months nor more than three years. Periods of postrelease supervision imposed pursuant to this section upon more than one felony conviction may be ordered to run concurrently. Periods of postrelease supervision imposed pursuant to this section may be ordered to run concurrently with any period of probation the defendant may also be subject to serve.

B. The period of postrelease supervision shall be under the supervision and review of the Virginia Parole Board. The Board shall review each felon prior to release and establish conditions of postrelease supervision. Failure to successfully abide by such terms and conditions shall be grounds to terminate the period of postrelease supervision and recommit the defendant to the Department of Corrections or to the local correctional facility from which he was previously released. Procedures for any such termination and recommitment shall be conducted in the same manner as procedures for the revocation of parole.

C. Postrelease supervision programs shall be operated through the probation and parole districts established pursuant to § 53.1-141.

D. Nothing in this section shall be construed to prohibit the court from exercising any authority otherwise granted by law.

History.

1994, 2nd Sp. Sess., cc. 1, 2; 1995, cc. 502, 574; 2000, c. 767.

§ 19.2-295.2:1. Postrelease supervision of felons sentenced for certain offenses committed on or after July 1, 2006.

A. For offenses committed on or after July 1, 2006:

1. At the time the court imposes a sentence upon a conviction for a first violation of subsection A of § 18.2-472.1 the court shall impose an added term of postrelease supervision of six months.

2. For a second or subsequent violation of subsection A of § 18.2-472.1 when both violations occurred after July 1, 2006, or a first violation of subsection B of § 18.2-472.1, the court shall impose an added term of postrelease supervision by the Department of Corrections of two years.

3. For a second or subsequent violation of subsection B of § 18.2-472.1 when both violations occurred after July 1, 2006, the court shall impose an added term of postrelease supervision by the Department of Corrections of five years.

Any terms of postrelease supervision imposed pursuant to this section shall be in addition to any other punishment imposed, including any periods of active incarceration or suspended periods of incarceration, if any.

B. The court shall order that any term of postrelease supervision imposed pursuant to this section be suspended, and the defendant be placed on active supervision under a postrelease supervision program operated by the Department of Corrections. The court shall order that the defendant be subject to electronic monitoring by means of a GPS (Global Positioning System) tracking device, or other similar device during this period of postrelease supervision. Failure to successfully abide by the terms and conditions of the postrelease supervision program shall be grounds to terminate the period of postrelease supervision and recommit the defendant to the Department of Corrections or to a local correctional facility. Procedures for any such termination shall be conducted after a hearing in the court which originally sentenced the defendant, conducted in a manner consistent with a revocation hearing under § 19.2-306, mutatis mutandis.

C. Nothing in this section shall be construed to prohibit the court from exercising any authority otherwise granted by law.

History.

2006, cc. 857, 914.

§ 19.2-295.3. Admission of victim impact testimony.

Whether by trial or upon a plea of guilty, upon a finding that the defendant is guilty of a felony, the court shall permit the victim, as defined in § 19.2-11.01, upon motion of the attorney for the Commonwealth, to testify in the presence of the accused regarding the impact of the offense upon the victim. The court shall limit the victim's testimony to the factors set forth in clauses (i) through (vi) of subsection A of § 19.2-299.1. In the case of trial by jury, the court shall permit the victim to testify at the sentencing hearing conducted pursuant to § 19.2-295.1 or in the case of trial by the court or a guilty plea, the court shall permit the victim to testify before the court prior to the imposition of a sentence. Victim impact testimony in all capital murder cases shall be admitted in accordance with § 19.2-264.4.

History.

1998, c. 485; 2004, c. 310.

§ 19.2-296. Withdrawal of plea of guilty.

A motion to withdraw a plea of guilty or nolo contendere may be made only before sentence is imposed or imposition of a sentence is suspended; but to correct manifest injustice, the court within twenty-one days after entry of a final order may set aside the judgment of conviction and permit the defendant to withdraw his plea.

History.

1975, c. 495.

§ 19.2-297: Repealed by Acts 1994, c. 706.

§ 19.2-297.1. Sentence of person twice previously convicted of certain violent felonies.

A. Any person convicted of two or more separate acts of violence when such offenses were not part of a common act, transaction or scheme, and who has been at liberty as defined in § 53.1-151 between each conviction, shall, upon conviction of a third or subsequent act of violence, be sentenced to life imprisonment and shall not have all or any portion of the sentence suspended, provided it is admitted, or found by the jury or judge before whom he is tried, that he has been previously convicted of two or more such acts of violence. For the purposes of this section, *"act of violence"* means (i) any one of the following violations of Chapter 4 (§ 18.2-30 et seq.) of Title 18.2:

a. First and second degree murder and voluntary manslaughter under Article 1 (§ 18.2-30 et seq.);

b. Mob-related felonies under Article 2 (§ 18.2-38 et seq.);

c. Any kidnapping or abduction felony under Article 3 (§ 18.2-47 et seq.);

d. Any malicious felonious assault or malicious bodily wounding under Article 4 (§ 18.2-51 et seq.);

e. Robbery under § 18.2-58 and carjacking under § 18.2-58.1;

f. Except as otherwise provided in § 18.2-67.5:2 or § 18.2-67.5:3, criminal sexual assault punishable as a felony under Article 7 (§ 18.2-61 et seq.); or

g. Arson in violation of § 18.2-77 when the structure burned was occupied or a Class 3 felony violation of § 18.2-79.

(ii) conspiracy to commit any of the violations enumerated in clause (i) of this section; and (iii) violations as a principal in the second degree or accessory before the fact of the provisions enumerated in clause (i) of this section.

B. Prior convictions shall include convictions under the laws of any state or of the United States for any offense substantially similar to those listed under "act of violence" if such offense would be a felony if committed in the Commonwealth.

The Commonwealth shall notify the defendant in writing, at least thirty days prior to trial, of its intention to seek punishment pursuant to this section.

C. Any person sentenced to life imprisonment pursuant to this section shall not be eligible for parole and shall not be eligible for any good conduct allowance or any earned sentence credits under Chapter 6 (§ 53.1-186 et seq.) of Title 53.1. However, any person subject to the provisions of this section, other than a person who was sentenced under subsection A of § 18.2-67.5:3 for criminal sexual assault convictions specified in subdivision f, (i) who has reached the age of sixty-five or older and who has served at least five years of the sentence imposed or (ii) who has reached the age of sixty or older and who has served at least ten years of the sentence imposed may petition the Parole Board for conditional release. The Parole Board shall promulgate regulations to implement the provisions of this subsection.

History.
1994, cc. 828, 860, 862, 881; 1994, 2nd Sp. Sess., cc. 1, 2; 1995, c. 834; 1996, c. 539.

§ 19.2-298. Pronouncement of sentence.

After a finding of guilty, sentence shall be pronounced, or decision to suspend the imposition of sentence shall be announced, without unreasonable delay. Pending pronouncement, the court may commit the accused to jail or may continue or alter the bail except that in those cases where the accused is convicted of a murder in the first degree, the court shall commit him to jail and he shall not be allowed bail pending the pronouncement of sentence. Before pronouncing the sentence, the court shall inquire of the accused if he desires to make a statement and if he desires to advance any reason why judgment should not be pronounced against him.

Whenever any person willfully and knowingly fails to surrender or submit to the custody of a sheriff as ordered by a court, any law-enforcement officer, with or without a warrant, may arrest such person anywhere in the Commonwealth. If the arrest is made in the county or city in which the person was ordered to surrender, or in an adjoining county or city, the officer may forthwith return the accused before the proper court. If the arrest is made beyond the foregoing limits, the officer shall proceed according to the provisions of § 19.2-76, and if such arrest is made without a warrant, the officer shall procure a warrant from the magistrate serving the county or city wherein the arrest was made, charging the accused with contempt of court.

History.
1975, c. 495; 1976, c. 285; 2009, c. 192.

§ 19.2-298.01. Use of discretionary sentencing guidelines.

A. In all felony cases, other than Class 1 felonies, the court shall (i) have presented to it the appropriate discretionary sentencing guidelines worksheets and (ii) review and consider the suitability of the applicable discretionary sentencing guidelines established pursuant to Chapter 8 (§ 17.1-800 et seq.) of Title 17.1. Before imposing sentence, the court shall state for the record that such review and consideration have been accomplished and shall make the completed worksheets a part of the record of the case and open for inspection. In cases tried by a jury, the jury shall not be presented any information regarding sentencing guidelines.

B. In any felony case, other than Class 1 felonies, in which the court imposes a sentence which is either greater or less than that indicated by the discretionary sentencing guidelines, the court shall file with the record of the case a written explanation of such departure.

C. In felony cases, other than Class 1 felonies, tried by a jury and in felony cases tried by the court without a jury upon a plea of not guilty, the court shall direct a probation officer of such court to prepare the discretionary sentencing guidelines worksheets. In felony cases tried upon a plea of guilty, including cases which are the subject of a plea agreement, the court shall direct a probation officer of such court to prepare the discretionary sentencing guidelines worksheets, or, with the concurrence of the accused, the court and the attorney for the Commonwealth, the worksheets shall be prepared by the attorney for the Commonwealth.

D. Except as provided in subsection E, discretionary sentencing guidelines worksheets prepared pursuant to this section shall be subject to the same distribution as presentence investigation reports prepared pursuant to subsection A of § 19.2-299.

E. Following the entry of a final order of conviction and sentence in a felony case, the clerk of the circuit court in which the case was tried shall cause a copy of such order or orders, the original of the discretionary sentencing guidelines worksheets prepared in the case, and a copy of any departure explanation prepared pursuant to subsection B to be forwarded to the Virginia Criminal Sentencing Commission within five days. Similarly, the statement required by §§ 19.2-295 and 19.2-303 and regarding departure from or modification of a sentence fixed by a jury shall be forwarded to the Virginia Criminal Sentencing Commission.

F. The failure to follow any or all of the provisions of this section or the failure to follow any or all of the provisions of this section in the prescribed manner shall not be reviewable on appeal or the basis of any other post-conviction relief.

G. The provisions of this section shall apply only to felony cases in which the offense is committed on or after January 1, 1995, and for which there are discretionary sentencing guidelines. For purposes of the discretionary sentencing guidelines only, a person sentenced to a boot camp incarceration program pursuant to § 19.2-316.1, a detention center incarceration program pursuant to § 19.2-316.2 or a diversion center incarceration program pursuant to § 19.2-316.3 shall be deemed to be sentenced to a term of incarceration.

History.
1994, 2nd Sp. Sess., cc. 1, 2; 1996, c. 552; 1997, c. 345; 1998, cc. 200, 353; 1999, c. 286; 2007, c. 259.

§§ 19.2-298.1 through 19.2-298.4: Repealed by Acts 2003, c. 584.

Cross references.
For current registration provisions, see the Sex Offender and Crimes Against Minors Registry Act, §§ 9.1-900 et seq.

§ 19.2-299. Investigations and reports by probation officers in certain cases.

A. When a person is tried in a circuit court (i) upon a charge of assault and battery in violation of

§ 18.2-57 or 18.2-57.2, stalking in violation of § 18.2-60.3, sexual battery in violation of § 18.2-67.4, attempted sexual battery in violation of § 18.2-67.5, or driving while intoxicated in violation of § 18.2-266, and is adjudged guilty of such charge, unless waived by the court and the defendant and the attorney for the Commonwealth, the court may, or on motion of the defendant shall; or (ii) upon a felony charge not set forth in subdivision (iii) below, the court may when there is a plea agreement between the defendant and the Commonwealth and shall when the defendant pleads guilty without a plea agreement or is found guilty by the court after a plea of not guilty; or (iii) the court shall when a person is charged and adjudged guilty of a felony violation, or conspiracy to commit or attempt to commit a felony violation, of § 18.2-46.2, 18.2-46.3, 18.2-48, clause (2) or (3) of § 18.2-49, § 18.2-61, 18.2-63, 18.2-64.1, 18.2-64.2, 18.2-67.1, 18.2-67.2, 18.2-67.3, 18.2-67.4:1, 18.2-67.5, 18.2-67.5:1, 18.2-355, 18.2-356, 18.2-357, 18.2-361, 18.2-362, 18.2-366, 18.2-368, 18.2-370, 18.2-370.1, or 18.2-370.2, or any attempt to commit or conspiracy to commit any felony violation of § 18.2-67.5, 18.2-67.5:2, or 18.2-67.5:3, direct a probation officer of such court to thoroughly investigate and report upon the history of the accused, including a report of the accused's criminal record as an adult and available juvenile court records, any information regarding the accused's participation or membership in a criminal street gang as defined in § 18.2-46.1, and all other relevant facts, to fully advise the court so the court may determine the appropriate sentence to be imposed. Unless the defendant or the attorney for the Commonwealth objects, the court may order that the report contain no more than the defendant's criminal history, any history of substance abuse, any physical or health-related problems as may be pertinent, and any applicable sentencing guideline worksheets. This expedited report shall be subject to all the same procedures as all other sentencing reports and sentencing guidelines worksheets. The probation officer, after having furnished a copy of this report at least five days prior to sentencing to counsel for the accused and the attorney for the Commonwealth for their permanent use, shall submit his report in advance of the sentencing hearing to the judge in chambers, who shall keep such report confidential. Counsel for the accused may provide the accused with a copy of the presentence report. The probation officer shall be available to testify from this report in open court in the presence of the accused, who shall have been provided with a copy of the presentence report by his counsel or advised of its contents and be given the right to cross-examine the investigating officer as to any matter contained therein and to present any additional facts bearing upon the matter. The report of the investigating officer shall at all times be kept confidential by each recipient, and shall be filed as a part of the record in the case. Any report so filed shall be made available only by court order and shall be sealed upon final order by the court, except that such reports or copies thereof shall be available at any time to any criminal justice agency, as defined in § 9.1-101, of this or any other state or of the United States; to any agency where the accused is referred for treatment by the court or by probation and parole services; and to counsel for any person who has been indicted jointly for the same felony as the person subject to the report. Subject to the limitations set forth in § 37.2-901, any report prepared pursuant to the provisions hereof shall without court order be made available to counsel for the person who is the subject of the report if that person (i) is charged with a felony subsequent to the time of the preparation of the report or (ii) has been convicted of the crime or crimes for which the report was prepared and is pursuing a post-conviction remedy. The presentence report shall be in a form prescribed by the Department of Corrections. In all cases where such report is not ordered, a simplified report shall be prepared on a form prescribed by the Department of Corrections. For the purposes of this subsection, information regarding the accused's participation or membership in a criminal street gang may include the characteristics, specific rivalries, common practices, social customs and behavior, terminology, and types of crimes that are likely to be committed by that criminal street gang.

B. As a part of any presentence investigation conducted pursuant to subsection A when the offense for which the defendant was convicted was a felony, the court probation officer shall advise any victim of such offense in writing that he may submit to the Virginia Parole Board a written request (i) to be given the opportunity to submit to the Board a written statement in advance of any parole hearing describing the impact of the offense upon him and his opinion regarding the defendant's release and (ii) to receive copies of such other notifications pertaining to the defendant as the Board may provide pursuant to subsection B of § 53.1-155.

C. As part of any presentence investigation conducted pursuant to subsection A when the offense for which the defendant was convicted was a felony drug offense set forth in Article 1 (§ 18.2-247 et seq.) of Chapter 7 of Title 18.2, the presentence report shall include any known association of the defendant with illicit drug operations or markets.

D. As a part of any presentence investigation conducted pursuant to subsection A, when the offense for which the defendant was convicted was a felony, not a capital offense, committed on or after January 1, 2000, the defendant shall be required to undergo a substance abuse screening pursuant to § 18.2-251.01.

History.

Code 1950, § 53-278.1; 1952, c. 233; 1972, c. 516; 1974, c. 121; 1975, cc. 371, 495; 1979, c. 286; 1980, c. 733; 1981, c. 263; 1983, c. 541; 1987, c. 676; 1989, c. 169; 1991, cc. 43, 229; 1992, c. 77; 1993, cc. 466, 492; 1994, 2nd Sp. Sess., cc. 1, 2; 1995, cc. 687, 778; 1997,

Criminal Procedure

c. 691; 1998, cc. 783, 840; 1999, cc. 891, 903, 913; 2001, c. 647; 2003, cc. 146, 613; 2004, cc. 308, 459, 819; 2005, cc. 188, 219, 631; 2006, cc. 99, 863, 914, 916; 2010, c. 223.

§ 19.2-299.1. When Victim Impact Statement required; contents; uses.

The presentence report prepared pursuant to § 19.2-299 shall, with the consent of the victim, as defined in § 19.2-11.01, in all cases involving offenses other than capital murder, include a Victim Impact Statement. Victim Impact Statements in all cases involving capital murder shall be prepared and submitted in accordance with the provisions of § 19.2-264.5.

A Victim Impact Statement shall be kept confidential and shall be sealed upon entry of the sentencing order. If prepared by someone other than the victim, it shall (i) identify the victim, (ii) itemize any economic loss suffered by the victim as a result of the offense, (iii) identify the nature and extent of any physical or psychological injury suffered by the victim as a result of the offense, (iv) detail any change in the victim's personal welfare, lifestyle or familial relationships as a result of the offense, (v) identify any request for psychological or medical services initiated by the victim or the victim's family as a result of the offense, and (vi) provide such other information as the court may require related to the impact of the offense upon the victim.

If the court does not order a presentence investigation and report, the attorney for the Commonwealth shall, at the request of the victim, submit a Victim Impact Statement. In any event, a victim shall be advised by the local crime victim and witness assistance program that he may submit in his own words a written Victim Impact Statement prepared by the victim or someone the victim designates in writing.

The Victim Impact Statement may be considered by the court in determining the appropriate sentence. A copy of the statement prepared pursuant to this section shall be made available to the defendant or counsel for the defendant without court order at least five days prior to the sentencing hearing. The statement shall not be admissible in any civil proceeding for damages arising out of the acts upon which the conviction was based. The statement, however, may be utilized by the Virginia Workers' Compensation Commission in its determinations on claims by victims of crimes pursuant to Chapter 21.1 (§ 19.2-368.1 et seq.) of this title.

History.
1983, c. 541; 1984, c. 282; 1987, c. 676; 1989, c. 374; 1993, cc. 436, 569; 1995, cc. 687, 720; 1996, c. 398.

§ 19.2-299.2. Alcohol and substance abuse screening and assessment for designated Class 1 misdemeanor convictions.

A. When a person is convicted of any offense committed on or after January 1, 2000, under Article 1 (§ 18.2-247 et seq.) or Article 1.1 (§ 18.2-265.1 et seq.) of Chapter 7 of Title 18.2, and such offense is punishable as a Class 1 misdemeanor, or when a person is convicted for a second offense of petit larceny, the court shall order the person to undergo a substance abuse screening as part of the sentence if the defendant's sentence includes probation supervision by a local community-based probation services agency established pursuant to Article 9 (§ 9.1-173 et seq.) of Chapter 1 of Title 9.1 or participation in a local alcohol safety action program. Whenever a court requires a person to enter into and successfully complete an alcohol safety action program pursuant to § 18.2-271.1 for a second offense of the type described therein, or orders an evaluation of a person to be conducted by an alcohol safety action program pursuant to any provision of § 46.2-391, the alcohol safety action program shall assess such person's degree of alcohol abuse before determining the appropriate level of treatment to be provided or to be recommended for such person being evaluated pursuant to § 46.2-391.

The court may order such screening upon conviction as part of the sentence of any other Class 1 misdemeanor if the defendant's sentence includes probation supervision by a local community-based probation services agency established pursuant to Article 9 (§ 9.1-173 et seq.) of Chapter 1 of Title 9.1, participation in a local alcohol safety action program or any other sanction and the court has reason to believe the defendant has a substance abuse or dependence problem.

B. A substance abuse screening ordered pursuant to this section shall be conducted by the local alcohol safety action program. When an offender is ordered to enter local community-based probation services established pursuant to Article 9 (§ 9.1-173 et seq.) of Chapter 1 of Title 9.1, rather than the local alcohol safety action program, the local community-based probation services agency shall be responsible for the screening. However, if a local community-based probation services agency has not been established for the locality, the local alcohol safety action program shall conduct the screening as part of the sentence.

C. If the screening indicates that the person has a substance abuse or dependence problem, an assessment shall be completed and if the assessment confirms that the person has a substance abuse or dependence problem, as a condition of a suspended sentence and probation, the court shall order the person to complete the substance abuse education and intervention component, or both as appropriate, of the local alcohol safety action program or such other agency providing treatment programs or services, if available, such as in the opinion of the court would be best suited to the needs of the person. If the referral is to the local alcohol safety action program, the program may charge a fee for the education and intervention component, or both, not to exceed $300, based upon the defendant's ability to pay.

History.

1998, cc. 783, 840; 1999, cc. 891, 913; 2000, cc. 958, 980, 1040; 2007, c. 133; 2008, c. 762.

§ 19.2-300. Deferring for mental examination sentence of person convicted of offense indicating sexual abnormality.

In the case of the conviction in any circuit court of any person for any criminal offense which indicates sexual abnormality, the trial judge may on his own initiative, or shall upon application of the attorney for the Commonwealth, the defendant, or counsel for defendant or other person acting for the defendant, defer sentence until the report of a mental examination conducted as provided in § 19.2-301 of the defendant can be secured to guide the judge in determining what disposition shall be made of the defendant.

History.

Code 1950, § 53-278.2; 1950, p. 897; 1970, c. 62; 1975, c. 495; 1990, c. 697.

§ 19.2-301. Judge shall require examination under § 19.2-300; by whom made; report; expenses of psychiatrist.

The judge shall order the defendant examined by at least one psychiatrist or clinical psychologist who is qualified by specialized training and experience to perform such evaluations. Upon a finding by the court that a psychiatrist or clinical psychologist is not reasonably available for the instant case, the court may appoint a state licensed clinical social worker who has been certified by the Commonwealth as a sex offender treatment provider as defined in § 54.1-3600 and qualified by experience and by specialized training approved by the Commissioner of Behavioral Health and Developmental Services to perform such evaluations. The examination shall be performed on an outpatient basis at a mental health facility or in jail. However, if the court specifically finds that outpatient examination services are unavailable or if the results of outpatient examination indicate that hospitalization of the defendant for further examination is necessary, the court may order the defendant sent to a hospital designated by the Commissioner of Behavioral Health and Developmental Services as appropriate for examination of persons convicted of crimes. The defendant shall then be hospitalized for such time as the director of the hospital deems necessary to perform an adequate examination, but not to exceed 30 days from the date of admission to the hospital. Upon completion of the examination, the examiners shall prepare a written report of their findings and conclusions and shall furnish copies of such report to the defendant, counsel for the defendant, and the attorney for the Commonwealth at least five days prior to sentencing and shall furnish a copy of the report to the judge in advance of the sentencing hearing. The report of the examiners shall at all times be kept confidential by each recipient, except to the extent necessary for the prosecution or defense of any offense, and shall be filed as part of the record in the case and the defendant's copy shall be returned to the court at the conclusion of sentencing. Any report so filed shall be sealed upon the entry of the sentencing order by the court and made available only by court order, except that such report or copies thereof shall be available at any time to the office of the Attorney General for assessment for civil commitment as provided in Chapter 9 (§ 37.2-900 et seq.) of Title 37.2; any criminal justice agency, as defined in § 9.1-101, of this or any other state or of the United States; to any agency where the accused is referred for treatment by the court or by probation and parole services; and to counsel for any person who has been indicted jointly for the same felony as the person who is the subject of the report. Any such report shall without court order be made available to counsel for the person who is the subject of the report if that person is charged with a felony subsequent to the time of the preparation of the report.

History.

Code 1950, § 53-278.3; 1950, p. 898; 1970, c. 62; 1975, cc. 286, 495; 1990, c. 697; 2002, c. 662; 2003, c. 886; 2007, c. 440; 2009, cc. 813, 840.

§ 19.2-302. Construction and administration of §§ 19.2-300 and 19.2-301.

Nothing contained in § 19.2-300 or 19.2-301 shall be construed to conflict with or repeal any statute in regard to the Department of Behavioral Health and Developmental Services, and such sections shall be administered with due regard to the authority of, and in cooperation with, the Commissioner of Behavioral Health and Developmental Services.

History.

Code 1950, § 53-278.4; 1950, p. 898; 1975, c. 495; 2009, cc. 813, 840.

§ 19.2-303. Suspension or modification of sentence; probation; taking of fingerprints and blood, saliva, or tissue sample as condition of probation.

After conviction, whether with or without jury, the court may suspend imposition of sentence or suspend the sentence in whole or part and in addition may place the defendant on probation under such conditions as the court shall determine, including monitoring by a GPS (Global Positioning System) tracking device, or other similar device, or may, as a condition of a suspended sentence, require the defendant to make at least partial restitution to the aggrieved party or parties for damages or loss caused by the offense for which convicted, or to perform community service, or both, under terms and conditions which shall be entered in writing by the court. The defendant may be ordered by the

Criminal Procedure

court to pay the cost of the GPS tracking device or other similar device. If, however, the court suspends or modifies any sentence fixed by a jury pursuant to § 19.2-295, the court shall file a statement of the reasons for the suspension or modification in the same manner as the statement required pursuant to subsection B of § 19.2-298.01. The judge, after convicting the defendant of a felony, shall determine whether a copy of the defendant's fingerprints are on file at the Central Criminal Records Exchange. In any case where fingerprints are not on file, the judge shall require that fingerprints be taken as a condition of probation. Such fingerprints shall be submitted to the Central Criminal Records Exchange under the provisions of subsection D of § 19.2-390.

In those courts having electronic access to the Local Inmate Data System (LIDS) within the courtroom, prior to or upon sentencing, the clerk of court shall also determine by reviewing LIDS whether a blood, saliva, or tissue sample has been taken for DNA analysis and submitted to the DNA data bank maintained by the Department of Forensic Science pursuant to Article 1.1 (§ 19.2-310.2 et seq.) of Chapter 18 of this title. In any case in which the clerk has determined that a DNA sample or analysis is not stored in the DNA data bank, or in any case in which electronic access to LIDS is not available in the courtroom, the court shall order that the defendant appear within 30 days before the sheriff or probation officer and allow the sheriff or probation officer to take the required sample. The order shall also require that, if the defendant has not appeared and allowed the sheriff or probation officer to take the required sample by the date stated in the order, then the sheriff or probation officer shall report to the court the defendant's failure to appear and provide the required sample.

After conviction and upon sentencing of an active participant or member of a criminal street gang, the court may, as a condition for suspending the imposition of the sentence in whole or in part or for placing the accused on probation, place reasonable restrictions on those persons with whom the accused may have contact. Such restrictions may include prohibiting the accused from having contact with anyone whom he knows to be a member of a criminal street gang, except that contact with a family or household member, as defined in § 16.1-228, shall be permitted unless expressly prohibited by the court.

In any case where a defendant is convicted of a violation of § 18.2-48, 18.2-61, 18.2-63, 18.2-67.1, 18.2-67.2, 18.2-67.3, 18.2-370, or 18.2-370.1, committed on or after July 1, 2006, and some portion of the sentence is suspended, the judge shall order that the period of suspension shall be for a length of time at least equal to the statutory maximum period for which the defendant might originally have been sentenced to be imprisoned, and the defendant shall be placed on probation for that period of suspension subject to revocation by the court. The conditions of probation may include such conditions as the court shall determine, including active supervision. Where the conviction is for a violation of clause (iii) of subsection A of § 18.2-61, subdivision A 1 of § 18.2-67.1, or subdivision A 1 of § 18.2-67.2, the court shall order that at least three years of the probation include active supervision of the defendant under a postrelease supervision program operated by the Department of Corrections, and for at least three years of such active supervision, the defendant shall be subject to electronic monitoring by means of a GPS (Global Positioning System) tracking device, or other similar device.

If a person is sentenced to jail upon conviction of a misdemeanor or a felony, the court may, at any time before the sentence has been completely served, suspend the unserved portion of any such sentence, place the person on probation for such time as the court shall determine, or otherwise modify the sentence imposed.

If a person has been sentenced for a felony to the Department of Corrections but has not actually been transferred to a receiving unit of the Department, the court which heard the case, if it appears compatible with the public interest and there are circumstances in mitigation of the offense, may, at any time before the person is transferred to the Department, suspend or otherwise modify the unserved portion of such a sentence. The court may place the person on probation for such time as the court shall determine.

History.

1975, c. 495; 1982, cc. 458, 636; 1983, c. 431; 1984, c. 32; 1992, c. 391; 1993, c. 448; 2006, cc. 436, 483, 853, 914; 2007, cc. 259, 528; 2011, cc. 799, 837.

§ 19.2-303.1. Fixing period of suspension of sentence.

In any case where a court suspends the imposition or execution of a sentence, it may fix the period of suspension for a reasonable time, having due regard to the gravity of the offense, without regard to the maximum period for which the defendant might have been sentenced.

History.

1982, c. 636.

§ 19.2-303.2. Persons charged with first offense may be placed on probation.

Whenever any person who has not previously been convicted of any felony pleads guilty to or enters a plea of not guilty to any crime against property constituting a misdemeanor, under Articles 5, 6, 7 and 8 of Chapter 5 (§ 18.2-119 et seq.) of Title 18.2, the court, upon such plea if the facts found by the court would justify a finding of guilt, without entering a judgment of guilt and with the consent of the accused, may defer further proceedings and place him on probation subject to terms and conditions, which may include restitution for losses caused, set by the court. Upon violation of a term or condition, the court may enter an adjudication of guilt and proceed as otherwise provided. Upon fulfillment of the terms and conditions, the court shall discharge the person and dismiss the proceedings against him. Discharge and dismissal under this section shall be without adjudication of guilt and is a conviction only for the purpose of applying this section in subsequent proceedings.

History.
1985, c. 617.

§ 19.2-303.3. Sentence to local community-based probation services; services agency; requirements for participation; sentencing; and removal from probation; payment of costs towards supervision and services.

A. Any offender who is (i) convicted on or after July 1, 1995, of a misdemeanor or a felony that is not a felony act of violence as defined in § 19.2-297.1, and for which the court imposes a total sentence of 12 months or less, and (ii) no younger than 18 years of age or is considered an adult at the time of conviction may be sentenced to a local community-based probation services agency established pursuant to § 9.1-174 by the local governing bodies within that judicial district or circuit.

B. In those courts having electronic access to the Local Inmate Data System (LIDS) within the courtroom, at the time of sentencing, the clerk of court shall determine by reviewing LIDS, in any case where there is a felony conviction, whether a sample of the offender's blood, saliva, or tissue or an analysis of the sample is stored in the DNA data bank maintained by the Department of Forensic Science pursuant to Article 1.1 (§ 19.2-310.2 et seq.) of Chapter 18 of this title. If the clerk has determined that a DNA sample or analysis is not stored in the DNA data bank, or in any case in which electronic access to LIDS is not available in the courtroom, the court shall order that the offender appear within 30 days before the sheriff or community-based probation officer and allow the sheriff or community-based probation officer to take the required sample. The order shall also require that, if the offender has not appeared and allowed the sheriff or community-based probation officer to take the required sample by the date stated in the order, then the sheriff or community-based probation officer shall report to the court the offender's failure to appear and provide the required sample. The court may order the offender placed under local community-based probation services pursuant to § 9.1-174 upon a determination by the court that the offender may benefit from these services and is capable of returning to society as a productive citizen with a reasonable amount of supervision and intervention including services set forth in § 9.1-176. All or part of any sentence imposed that has been suspended, shall be conditioned upon the offender's successful completion of local community-based probation services established pursuant to § 9.1-174.

The court may impose terms and conditions of supervision as it deems appropriate, including that the offender abide by any additional requirements of supervision imposed or established by the local community-based probation services agency during the period of probation supervision.

C. Any sworn officer of a local community-based probation services agency established or operated pursuant to the Comprehensive Community Corrections Act for Local-Responsible Offenders (§ 9.1-173 et seq.) may seek a capias from any judicial officer for the arrest of any person on local community-based probation and under its supervision for (i) intractable behavior; (ii) refusal to comply with the terms and conditions imposed by the court; (iii) refusal to comply with the requirements of local community-based probation supervision established by the agency; or (iv) the commission of a new offense while on local community-based probation and under agency supervision. Upon arrest, the offender shall be brought for a hearing before the court of appropriate jurisdiction. After finding that the offender (a) exhibited intractable behavior as defined herein; (b) refused to comply with terms and conditions imposed by the court; (c) refused to comply with the requirements of local community-based probation supervision established by the agency; or (d) committed a new offense while on local community-based probation and under agency supervision, the court may revoke all or part of the suspended sentence and supervision, and commit the offender to serve whatever sentence was originally imposed or impose such other terms and conditions of probation as it deems appropriate or, in a case where the proceeding has been deferred, enter an adjudication of guilt and proceed as otherwise provided by law.

"Intractable behavior" is that behavior that, in the determination of the court, indicates an offender's unwillingness or inability to conform his behavior to that which is necessary for successful completion of local community-based probation or that the offender's behavior is so disruptive as to threaten the successful completion of the program by other participants.

D. An offender sentenced to or provided a deferred proceeding and placed on community-based probation pursuant to this section may be required to pay an amount towards the costs of his supervision and services received in accordance with subsection D of § 9.1-182.

History.
1994, 2nd Sp. Sess., cc. 1, 2; 1995, cc. 502, 574; 1999, c. 372; 2000, c. 1040; 2006, c. 883; 2007, cc. 133, 528.

§ 19.2-303.4. Payment of costs when proceedings deferred and defendant placed on probation.

A circuit or district court, which has deferred further proceedings, without entering a judgment of guilt, and placed a defendant on probation subject to terms and conditions pursuant to § 4.1-305, 16.1-278.8, 16.1-278.9, 18.2-57.3, 18.2-61, 18.2-67.1, 18.2-67.2, 18.2-251 or 19.2-303.2, shall impose upon the defendant costs.

History.
1995, c. 485; 2000, c. 186; 2002, c. 831; 2005, c. 631.

§ 19.2-303.5. (Expires July 1, 2017) Immediate sanction probation programs.

There may be established in the Commonwealth up to four immediate sanction probation programs in accordance with the following provisions:

1. As a condition of a sentence suspended pursuant to § 19.2-303, a court may order a defendant convicted of a crime, other than a violent crime as defined in subsection C of § 17.1-805, to participate in an immediate sanction probation program.

2. If a participating offender fails to comply with any term or condition of his probation and the alleged probation violation is not that the offender committed a new crime or infraction, (i) his probation officer shall immediately issue a noncompliance letter pursuant to § 53.1-149 authorizing his arrest at any location in the Commonwealth and (ii) his probation violation hearing shall take priority on the court's docket. The probation officer may, in any event, exercise any other lawful authority he may have with respect to the offender.

3. When a participating offender is arrested pursuant to subdivision 2, the court shall conduct an immediate sanction hearing unless (i) the alleged probation violation is that the offender committed a new crime or infraction; (ii) the alleged probation violation is that the offender absconded for more than seven days; or (iii) the offender, attorney for the Commonwealth, or the court objects to such immediate sanction hearing. If the court conducts an immediate sanction hearing, it shall proceed pursuant to subdivision 4. Otherwise, the court shall proceed pursuant to § 19.2-306.

4. At the immediate sanction hearing, the court shall receive the noncompliance letter, which shall be admissible as evidence, and may receive other evidence. If the court finds good cause to believe that the offender has violated the terms or conditions of his probation, it may (i) revoke no more than 30 days of the previously suspended sentence and (ii) continue or modify any existing terms and conditions of probation. If the court does not modify the terms and conditions of probation or remove the defendant from the program, the previously ordered terms and conditions of probation shall continue to apply. The court may remove the offender from the immediate sanction probation program at any time.

5. The provisions of this section shall expire on July 1, 2017.

History.
2010, c. 845; 2014, c. 314; 2016, c. 201.

§ 19.2-304. Increasing or decreasing probation period and modification of conditions.

The court may subsequently increase or decrease the probation period and may revoke or modify any condition of probation, but only upon a hearing after reasonable notice to both the defendant and the attorney for the Commonwealth.

History.
Code 1950, § 53-273; 1974, c. 205; 1975, c. 495.

§ 19.2-305. Requiring fines, costs, restitution for damages, support or community services from probationer.

A. While on probation the defendant may be required to pay in one or several sums a fine or costs, or both such fine and costs, imposed at the time of being placed on probation as a condition of such probation, and the failure of the defendant to pay such fine or costs, or both such fine and costs, at the prescribed time or times may be deemed a breach of such probation. The provisions of this subsection shall also apply to any person ordered to pay costs pursuant to § 19.2-303.3.

B. A defendant placed on probation following conviction may be required to make at least partial restitution or reparation to the aggrieved party or parties for damages or loss caused by the offense for which conviction was had, or may be required to provide for the support of his wife or others for whose support he may be legally responsible, or may be required to perform community services. The defendant may submit a proposal to the court for making restitution, for providing for support or for performing community services.

C. No defendant shall be kept under supervised probation solely because of his failure to make full payment of fines, fees, or costs, provided that, following notice by the probation and parole officer to each court and attorney for the Commonwealth in whose jurisdiction any fines, fees, or costs are owed by the defendant, no such court or attorney for the Commonwealth objects to his removal from supervised probation.

History.
Code 1950, § 53-274; 1962, c. 143; 1975, c. 495; 1977, c. 682; 1978, c. 716; 1984, c. 32; 1995, c. 485; 2009, c. 240.

§ 19.2-305.1. Restitution for property damage or loss; community service.

A. Notwithstanding any other provision of law, no person convicted of a crime in violation of any provision in Title 18.2, which resulted in property damage or loss, shall be placed on probation or have his sentence suspended unless such person shall make at least partial restitution for such property damage or loss, or shall be compelled to perform community services, or both, or shall submit a plan for doing that which appears to the court to be feasible under the circumstances.

B. Notwithstanding any other provision of law, any person who, on or after July 1, 1995, commits, and is convicted of, a crime in violation of any provision in Title 18.2 shall make at least partial restitution for any property damage or loss caused by the crime or for any medical expenses or expenses directly related to funeral or burial incurred by the victim or his estate as a result of the crime, may be compelled to perform community services and, if the court so orders, shall submit a plan for doing that which appears to be feasible to the court under the circumstances.

B1. Notwithstanding any other provision of law, any person, who on or after July 1, 2005 commits and is convicted of a crime in violation of § 18.2-248 involving the manufacture of any controlled substance, may be ordered, upon presentation of suitable evidence of such costs, by the court to reimburse the Commonwealth or the locality for the costs incurred by the jurisdiction, as the case may be, for the removal and remediation associated with the illegal manufacture of any controlled substance by the defendant.

B2. Notwithstanding any other provision of law, any person who, on or after July 1, 2015, commits and is convicted of a violation of § 18.2-138 for damage to the Capitol or any building, monument, statuary, artwork, or other state property in Capitol Square, or at any other property assigned to the Capitol Police, shall be ordered to pay restitution to the Commonwealth for the full amount of damages. Any person who, on or after July 1, 2015, commits and is convicted of a violation of § 18.2-405, 18.2-407, or 18.2-408 in Capitol Square, or at any other property assigned to the Capitol Police, shall be ordered to pay restitution to the Commonwealth for the full amount of damages to the Capitol or any building, monument, statuary, artwork, or other state property in Capitol Square, or at any other property assigned to the Capitol Police, to which damage is caused during such riot or unlawful assembly. In any prosecution under § 18.2-138, 18.2-405, 18.2-407, or 18.2-408, testimony of the Division of Engineering and Buildings of the Department of General Services or the Division of Risk Management shall be admissible as evidence of value or extent of damages or cost of repairs to the Capitol or any building, monument, statuary, artwork, or other state property in Capitol Square, or at any other property assigned to the Capitol Police. For the purposes of this subsection, "Capitol Square" means the grounds and the interior and exterior of all buildings in that area in the City of Richmond bounded by Bank, Governor, Broad, and Ninth Streets. "Capitol Square" includes the exterior of all state buildings that are at least 50 years old and bordering the boundary streets.

C. At or before the time of sentencing, the court shall receive and consider any plan for making restitution submitted by the defendant. The plan shall include the defendant's home address, place of employment and address, social security number and bank information. If the court finds such plan to be reasonable and practical under the circumstances, it may consider probation or suspension of whatever portion of the sentence that it deems appropriate. By order of the court incorporating the defendant's plan or a reasonable and practical plan devised by the court, the defendant shall make restitution while he is free on probation or work release or following his release from confinement. Additionally, the court may order that the defendant make restitution during his confinement, if feasible, based upon both his earning capacity and net worth as determined by the court at sentencing.

D. At the time of sentencing, the court shall determine the amount to be repaid by the defendant and the terms and conditions thereof. If community service work is ordered, the court shall determine the terms and conditions upon which such work shall be performed. The court shall include such findings in the judgment order. The order shall specify that sums paid under such order shall be paid to the clerk, who shall disburse such sums as the court may, by order, direct. Any court desiring to participate in the Setoff Debt Collection Act (§§ 58.1-520 through 58.1-535) for the purpose of collecting fines or costs or providing restitution shall, at the time of sentencing, obtain the social security number of each defendant.

E. Unreasonable failure to execute the plan by the defendant shall result in revocation of the probation or imposition of the suspended sentence. A hearing shall be held in accordance with the provisions of this Code relating to revocation of probation or imposition of a suspended sentence before either such action is taken.

E1. A defendant convicted of an offense under § 18.2-374.1, 18.2-374.1:1, or 18.2-374.3 shall be ordered to pay mandatory restitution to the victim of the offense in an amount as determined by the court. For purposes of this subsection, "victim" means a person who is depicted in a still or videographic image involved in an offense under § 18.2-374.1, 18.2-374.1:1, or 18.2-374.3.

The Commonwealth shall make reasonable efforts to notify victims of offenses under § 18.2-374.1, 18.2-374.1:1, or 18.2-374.3.

F. If restitution is ordered to be paid by the defendant to the victim of a crime and the victim can no longer be located or identified, the clerk shall deposit any such restitution collected to the Criminal Injuries Compensation Fund for the benefit of crime victims. The administrator shall reserve a sum sufficient in the Fund from which he shall make prompt payment to the victim for any proper claims. Before making the deposit he shall record the name, last known address and amount of restitution due each victim appearing from the clerk's report to be entitled to restitution.

G. If restitution pursuant to § 19.2-305 or this section is ordered to be paid by the defendant to the victim of a crime or other entity, and the Criminal Injuries Compensation Fund has made any payments to or on behalf of the victim for any loss, damage, or expenses included in the restitution order, then upon presentation by the Fund of a written request that sets forth the amount of payments made by the Fund to the victim or on the victim's behalf, the entity collecting restitution shall pay to the Fund as much of the restitution collected as will reimburse the Fund for its payments made to the victim or on the victim's behalf.

History.

1977, c. 682; 1978, c. 131; 1981, c. 224; 1984, cc. 32, 269; 1994, c. 197; 1995, cc. 434, 687; 2000, c. 775; 2002, cc. 810, 818; 2003, c. 982; 2005, c. 591; 2011, cc. 575, 588; 2013, c. 273; 2015, cc. 312, 550.

§ 19.2-305.2. Amount of restitution; enforcement.

A. The court, when ordering restitution pursuant to § 19.2-305.1, may require that such defendant, in the case of an offense resulting in damage to or loss or destruction of property of a victim of the offense (i) return the property to the owner or (ii) if return of the property is impractical or impossible, pay an amount equal to the greater of the value of the property at the time of the offense or the value of the property at the time of sentencing.

B. An order of restitution may be docketed as provided in § 8.01-446 when so ordered by the court or upon written request of the victim and may be enforced by a victim named in the order to receive the restitution in the same manner as a judgment in a civil action.

History.

1988, c. 679; 1989, c. 386.

§ 19.2-305.3: Repealed by Acts 1997, c. 140.

§ 19.2-305.4. When interest to be paid on award of restitution.

The court, when ordering restitution pursuant to § 19.2-305 or 19.2-305.1, may provide in the order for interest on the restitution. If the court orders the payment of interest, it shall accrue from the date of the loss or damage unless the court specifies a different date in the order, at the rate specified in § 6.2-302.

History.

1996, c. 544; 2001, c. 122; 2005, cc. 14, 79.

§ 19.2-306. Revocation of suspension of sentence and probation.

A. In any case in which the court has suspended the execution or imposition of sentence, the court may revoke the suspension of sentence for any cause the court deems sufficient that occurred at any time within the probation period, or within the period of suspension fixed by the court. If neither a probation period nor a period of suspension was fixed by the court, then the court may revoke the suspension for any cause the court deems sufficient that occurred within the maximum period for which the defendant might originally have been sentenced to be imprisoned.

B. The court may not conduct a hearing to revoke the suspension of sentence unless the court issues process to notify the accused or to compel his appearance before the court within one year after the expiration of the period of probation or the period of suspension or, in the case of a failure to pay restitution, within three years after such expiration. If neither a probation period nor a period of suspension was fixed by the court, then the court shall issue process within one year after the expiration of the maximum period for which the defendant might originally have been sentenced to be incarcerated. Such notice and service of process may be waived by the defendant, in which case the court may proceed to determine whether the defendant has violated the conditions of suspension.

C. If the court, after hearing, finds good cause to believe that the defendant has violated the terms of suspension, then: (i) if the court originally suspended the imposition of sentence, the court shall revoke the suspension, and the court may pronounce whatever sentence might have been originally imposed or (ii) if the court originally suspended the execution of the sentence, the court shall revoke the suspension and the original sentence shall be in full force and effect. The court may again suspend all or any part of this sentence and may place the defendant upon terms and conditions or probation.

D. If any court has, after hearing, found no cause to impose a sentence that might have been originally imposed, or to revoke a suspended sentence or probation, then any further hearing to impose a sentence or revoke a suspended sentence or probation, based solely on the alleged violation for which the hearing was held, shall be barred.

E. Nothing contained herein shall be construed to deprive any person of his right to appeal in the manner provided by law to the circuit court having criminal jurisdiction from a judgment or order revoking any suspended sentence.

History.

Code 1950, § 53-275; 1958, c. 468; 1970, c. 275; 1975, c. 495; 1978, c. 687; 2002, c. 628; 2016, c. 718.

§ 19.2-307. Contents of judgment order.

The judgment order shall set forth the plea, the verdict or findings and the adjudication and sentence, whether or not the case was tried by jury, and if not, whether the consent of the accused was concurred in by the court and the attorney for the Commonwealth. If the accused is found not guilty, or for any other reason is entitled to be discharged, judgment shall be entered accordingly. If an accused is tried at one time for two or more offenses, the court may enter one judgment order respecting all such offenses. The final judgment order shall be entered on a form promulgated by the Supreme Court.

History.
1975, c. 495; 1996, c. 60.

§ 19.2-308. When two or more sentences run concurrently.

When any person is convicted of two or more offenses, and sentenced to confinement, such sentences shall not run concurrently, unless expressly ordered by the court.

History.
Code 1950, § 19.1-294; 1960, c. 366; 1975, c. 495.

§ 19.2-308.1. When sentence may run concurrently with sentence in another jurisdiction.

Notwithstanding any other provision of law, in the event that a person is convicted of a criminal offense in any court of this Commonwealth and such person has also been sentenced to imprisonment for a term of one year or more by a court of the United States, or any other state or territory, and, at the time of sentencing in this Commonwealth, is incarcerated in a federal or state penal institution, the court may order the sentence to run concurrently with the sentence imposed by such other court.

History.
1977, c. 344.

§ 19.2-309. Sentence of confinement for conviction of a combination of felony and misdemeanor offenses.

When any person is convicted of a combination of felony and misdemeanor offenses and sentenced to confinement therefor, in determining the sequence of confinement, the felony sentence and commitment shall take precedence and such person shall first be committed to serve the felony sentence.

History.
Code 1950, § 19.1-295; 1960, c. 366; 1975, c. 495.

§ 19.2-309.1: Sentence of confinement to jail farms maintained by the Cities of Danville, Martinsville and Newport News [Not set out.] (1988, cc. 764, 785.)

Editor's note.
This section, relating to confinement to jail farms maintained by the Cities of Danville, Martinsville, and Newport News, was enacted by Acts 1988, cc. 764 and 785. In furtherance of the general policy of the Virginia Code Commission to include in the Code only provisions having general and permanent application, this section, which is limited in its purpose and scope, is not set out here, but attention is called to it by this reference.

§ 19.2-310. Transfer of prisoners to custody of Director of Department of Corrections.

Every person sentenced by a court to the Department of Corrections upon conviction of a felony shall be conveyed to an appropriate receiving unit operated by the Department in the manner hereinafter provided. The clerk of the court in which the person is sentenced shall forthwith transmit to the Central Criminal Records Exchange the report of dispositions required by § 19.2-390. The clerk of the court within 30 days from the date of the judgment shall forthwith transmit to the Director of the Department a certified copy or copies of the order of trial and a certified copy of the complete final order, and if he fails to do so shall forfeit $50. The clerk of the court may transmit or make available a copy or copies of such orders electronically. Such copy or copies shall contain, as nearly as ascertainable, the birth date of the person sentenced. The sheriff shall certify to the Director of the Department any jail credits to which the person to be confined is entitled at such time as that person is transferred to the custody of the Director of the Department.

Following receipt of the order of trial and a certified copy of the complete final order, the Director or his designee shall dispatch a correctional officer to the county or city with a warrant directed to the sheriff authorizing him to deliver the prisoner to the correctional officer whose duty it shall be to take charge of the person and convey him to an appropriate receiving unit designated by the Director or his designee. The Director or his designee shall allocate space available in the receiving unit or units by giving first priority to the transportation, as the transportation facilities of the Department may permit, of those persons held in jails who in the opinion of the Director or his designee except as required by § 53.1-20 require immediate transportation to a receiving unit. In making such a determination of priority, the Director shall give due regard to the capacity of local as well as state correctional facilities and, to the extent feasible, shall seek to balance between local and state correctional facilities the excess of prisoners requiring detention.

History.
Code 1950, § 19.1-296; 1960, c. 366; 1966, c. 522; 1970, c. 67; 1972, c. 358; 1974, cc. 44, 45; 1975, c. 495; 1981, c. 529; 1982, cc. 476, 636; 1986, c. 606; 1990, cc. 676, 768; 2010, c. 352; 2011, c. 470.

§ 19.2-310.01. Transmission of sentencing documents.

Within thirty days of the receipt of a request from the Department of Corrections for certified copies of sentencing documents for any misdemeanor conviction, the clerk of the court receiving such request shall transmit the requested documents to the Director of the Department. In accordance with the provisions of § 17.1-267, the requested documents shall be provided to the Director without the payment of any fee.

History.
1992, c. 498.

§ 19.2-310.1: Repealed by Acts 1982, c. 636.

Cross references.
For present provisions covering the subject matter of the repealed section, see § 53.1-21, subdivision B 4.

ARTICLE 1.1.

DNA ANALYSIS AND DATA BANK.

§ 19.2-310.2. Blood, saliva, or tissue sample required for DNA analysis upon conviction of certain crimes; fee.

A. Every person convicted of a felony on or after July 1, 1990, every person convicted of a felony offense under Article 7 (§ 18.2-61 et seq.) of Chapter 4 of Title 18.2 who was incarcerated on July 1, 1989, and every person convicted of a misdemeanor violation of § 16.1-253.2, 18.2-60.3, 18.2-60.4, 18.2-67.4, 18.2-67.4:1, 18.2-67.4:2, 18.2-67.5, 18.2-102, 18.2-121, 18.2-130, 18.2-370.6, 18.2-387, 18.2-387.1, or 18.2-479.1 shall have a sample of his blood, saliva or tissue taken for DNA (deoxyribonucleic acid) analysis to determine identification characteristics specific to the person. If a sample has been previously taken from the person as indicated by the Local Inmate Data System (LIDS), no additional sample shall be taken. The Department of Forensic Science shall provide to LIDS the most current information submitted to the DNA data bank on a weekly basis and shall remove from LIDS and the data bank persons no longer eligible to be in the data bank. A fee of $53 shall be charged for the withdrawal of this sample. The fee shall be taxed as part of the costs of the criminal case resulting in the conviction and $15 of the fee shall be paid into the general fund of the locality where the sample was taken and $38 of the fee shall be paid into the general fund of the state treasury. This fee shall only be taxed one time regardless of the number of samples taken. The assessment provided for herein shall be in addition to any other fees prescribed by law. The analysis shall be performed by the Department of Forensic Science or other entity designated by the Department. The identification characteristics of the profile resulting from the DNA analysis shall be stored and maintained by the Department in a DNA data bank and shall be made available only as provided in § 19.2-310.5.

B. After July 1, 1990, the blood, saliva, or tissue sample shall be taken prior to release from custody. Notwithstanding the provisions of § 53.1-159, any person convicted of an offense listed in subsection A who is in custody after July 1, 1990, shall provide a blood, saliva, or tissue sample prior to his release. Every person so convicted after July 1, 1990, who is not sentenced to a term of confinement shall provide a blood, saliva, or tissue sample as a condition of such sentence. A person required under this section to submit a sample for DNA analysis is not relieved from this requirement regardless of whether no blood, saliva, or tissue sample has been taken from the person or, if a sample has been taken, whether the sample or the results from the analysis of a sample cannot be found in the DNA data bank maintained by the Department of Forensic Science.

C. Nothing in this section shall prevent the Department of Forensic Science from including the identification characteristics of an individual's DNA profile in the DNA data bank as ordered by a circuit court pursuant to a lawful plea agreement.

D. A collection or placement of a sample for DNA analysis that was taken or retained in good faith does not invalidate the sample's use in the data bank pursuant to the provisions of this article. The detention, arrest, or conviction of a person based upon a data bank match or data bank information is not invalidated if it is determined that the sample was obtained, placed, or retained in the data bank in good faith, or if the conviction or juvenile adjudication that resulted in the collection of the DNA sample was subsequently vacated or otherwise altered in any future proceeding, including but not limited to post-trial or post-fact-finding motions, appeals, or collateral attacks.

E. The Virginia Department of Corrections and the Department of Forensic Science shall, on a quarterly basis, compare databases of offenders under the custody or supervision of the Department of Corrections with the DNA data bank of the Department of Forensic Science. The Virginia Department of Corrections shall require a DNA sample of those offenders under its custody or supervision if they are not identified in the DNA data bank.

F. The Department of State Police shall verify that a DNA sample required to be taken for the Sex Offender and Crimes Against Minors Registry pursuant to § 9.1-903 has been received by the Department of Forensic Science. In any instance where a DNA sample has not been received, the Department of State Police or its designee shall obtain from the person required to register a sample for DNA analysis.

G. Each community-based probation services agency established pursuant to § 9.1-174 shall determine by reviewing the Local Inmate Data System upon intake and again prior to discharge whether a blood, saliva, or tissue sample has been taken for DNA analysis for each offender required to submit a sample pursuant to this section and, if no sample has been taken, require an offender to submit a sample for DNA analysis.

H. The sheriff or regional jailer shall determine by reviewing the Local Inmate Data System upon intake and again prior to release whether a blood, saliva, or tissue sample has been taken for DNA analysis for each offender required to submit a sample pursuant to this section and, if no sample has been taken, require an offender to submit a sample for DNA analysis.

History.

1990, c. 669; 1993, c. 33; 1996, cc. 154, 952; 1998, c. 280; 2002, cc. 54, 753, 773; 2005, cc. 868, 881; 2007, c. 528; 2011, c. 247; 2015, cc. 193, 209, 437.

§ 19.2-310.2:1. Saliva or tissue sample required for DNA analysis after arrest for a violent felony.

Every person arrested for the commission or attempted commission of a violent felony as defined in § 19.2-297.1 or a violation or attempt to commit a violation of § 18.2-31, 18.2-89, 18.2-90, 18.2-91, or 18.2-92, shall have a sample of his saliva or tissue taken for DNA (deoxyribonucleic acid) analysis to determine identification characteristics specific to the person. After a determination by a magistrate or a grand jury that probable cause exists for the arrest, a sample shall be taken prior to the person's release from custody. The analysis shall be performed by the Department of Forensic Science or other entity designated by the Department. The identification characteristics of the profile resulting from the DNA analysis shall be stored and maintained by the Department in a DNA data bank and shall be made available as provided in § 19.2-310.5.

The clerk of the court shall notify the Department of final disposition of the criminal proceedings. If the charge for which the sample was taken is dismissed or the defendant is acquitted at trial, the Department shall destroy the sample and all records thereof, provided there is no other pending qualifying warrant or capias for an arrest or felony conviction that would otherwise require that the sample remain in the data bank.

History.

2002, cc. 753, 773; 2003, c. 150; 2004, c. 445; 2005, cc. 868, 881; 2006, c. 182.

§ 19.2-310.3. Procedures for withdrawal of blood, saliva or tissue sample for DNA analysis.

Each sample required pursuant to § 19.2-310.2 from persons who are to be incarcerated shall be withdrawn at the receiving unit or at such other place as is designated by the Department of Corrections or, in the case of a juvenile, the Department of Juvenile Justice. The required samples from persons who are not sentenced to a term of confinement shall be withdrawn at a time and place specified by the sentencing court. Only a correctional health nurse technician or a physician, registered nurse, licensed practical nurse, graduate laboratory technician, or phlebotomist shall withdraw any blood sample to be submitted for analysis. No civil liability shall attach to any person authorized to withdraw blood, saliva or tissue as provided herein as a result of the act of withdrawing blood, saliva or tissue from any person submitting thereto, provided the blood, saliva or tissue was withdrawn according to recognized medical procedures. However, no person shall be relieved from liability for negligence in the withdrawing of any blood, saliva or tissue sample.

Chemically clean sterile disposable needles and vacuum draw tubes or swabs shall be used for all samples. The tube or envelope containing the sample shall be sealed and labeled with the subject's name, social security number, date of birth, race and gender; the name of the person collecting the sample; and the date and place of collection. The tubes or envelopes containing the samples shall be secured to prevent tampering with the contents. The steps herein set forth relating to the taking, handling, identification, and disposition of blood, saliva or tissue samples are procedural and not substantive. Substantial compliance therewith shall be deemed to be sufficient. The samples shall be transported to the Department of Forensic Science not more than 15 days following withdrawal and shall be analyzed and stored in the DNA data bank in accordance with §§ 19.2-310.4 and 19.2-310.5.

History.

1990, c. 669; 1997, c. 862; 1998, c. 280; 2003, c. 150; 2004, c. 440; 2005, cc. 868, 881.

§ 19.2-310.3:1. Procedures for taking saliva or tissue sample for DNA analysis.

A. Each sample required pursuant to § 19.2-310.2:1 from persons arrested shall be taken before release from custody at such place as is designated by the law-enforcement agency responsible for arrest booking in the jurisdiction. Samples shall be taken in accordance with procedures adopted by the Department of Forensic Science. The sample shall be sealed and labeled with the subject's name, social security number, date of birth, race and gender; the name of the person collecting the sample; the date and place of collection; information identifying the arresting or accompanying officer; and the offense for which the person was arrested. The sample shall be secured to prevent tampering with the contents and be accompanied by a copy of the arrest warrant or capias. The steps herein set forth relating to the taking, handling, identification, and disposition of saliva or tissue samples are procedural and not substantive. The sample shall be transported to the Department of Forensic Science not more than 15 days following withdrawal and shall be analyzed and stored in the DNA data bank in accordance with §§ 19.2-310.4 and 19.2-310.5.

B. Substantial compliance therewith shall be deemed to be sufficient. If a sample has been previously taken from the individual as indicated by the Local Inmate Data System (LIDS), no additional sample shall be taken. No civil liability shall attach to any person authorized to take saliva or tissue as provided herein as a result of the act of taking saliva or tissue from any person submitting thereto, provided the saliva or tissue was taken according to recognized medical procedures. However, no person shall be relieved from liability for negligence in the taking of any saliva or tissue sample.

History.
2002, cc. 753, 773; 2003, c. 150; 2005, cc. 868, 881.

§ 19.2-310.4. Procedures for conducting DNA analysis of blood, saliva or tissue sample.

Whether or not the results of an analysis are to be included in the data bank, the Department shall conduct the DNA analysis in accordance with procedures adopted by the Department to determine identification characteristics specific to the individual whose sample is being analyzed. The Director or his designated representative shall complete and maintain on file a form indicating the name of the person whose sample is to be analyzed, the date and by whom the blood, saliva or tissue sample was received and examined, and a statement that the seal on the tube or envelope containing the sample had not been broken or otherwise tampered with. The remainder of a blood, saliva or tissue sample submitted for analysis and inclusion in the data bank pursuant to § 19.2-310.2 or 19.2-310.2:1 may be divided, labeled as provided for the original sample, and securely stored by the Department in accordance with specific procedures adopted by regulation of the Department to ensure the integrity and confidentiality of the samples. All or part of the remainder of that sample may be used only (i) to create a statistical data base provided no identifying information on the individual whose sample is being analyzed is included or (ii) for retesting by the Department to validate or update the original analysis.

A report of the results of a DNA analysis conducted by the Department as authorized, including the profile and identifying information, shall be made and maintained at the Department. A certificate and the results of the analysis shall be admissible in any court as evidence of the facts therein stated. Except as specifically provided in this section and § 19.2-310.5, the results of the analysis shall be securely stored and shall remain confidential.

History.
1990, c. 669; 1998, c. 280; 2002, cc. 753, 773; 2003, c. 150; 2005, cc. 868, 881.

§ 19.2-310.5. DNA data bank.

A. It shall be the duty of the Department to receive samples of human biological evidence and to analyze, classify, and file the results of DNA identification characteristics profiles of samples of human biological evidence submitted pursuant to § 19.2-310.2 or 19.2-310.2:1 and to make such information available as provided in this section. The results of an analysis and comparison of evidence submitted to the Department pursuant to § 9.1-1101 to the identification characteristics of human biological evidence so analyzed, classified, and filed shall be made available directly to duly authorized members of federal, state, and local law-enforcement agencies or private police departments that have been designated as criminal justice agencies by the Department of Criminal Justice Services as defined by § 9.1-101, attorneys for the Commonwealth or attorneys for the United States Department of Justice, or the Office of the Chief Medical Examiner upon request made in furtherance of an official investigation or prosecution of any criminal offense, or to an accused or his attorney pursuant to § 9.1-1104. The Department shall confirm whether or not there is a DNA profile on file for a specific individual if a federal, state or local law-enforcement officer requests that information in furtherance of an official investigation of any criminal offense. The name of the requestor and the purpose for which the information is requested shall be maintained on file with the Department.

B. The Department shall adopt regulations governing (i) the methods of obtaining information from the data bank in accordance with this section and (ii) procedures for verification of the identity and authority of the requestor. The Department shall specify the positions in that agency which require regular access to the data bank and samples submitted as a necessary function of the job.

C. The Department shall create a separate statistical data base comprised of DNA profiles of samples of human biological evidence of persons whose identity is unknown. Nothing in this section or § 19.2-310.6 shall prohibit the Department from sharing or otherwise disseminating the information in the statistical data base with law-enforcement or criminal justice agencies within or without the Commonwealth.

D. The Department may charge a reasonable fee to search and provide a comparative analysis of DNA profiles in the data bank to any authorized law-enforcement agency outside of the Commonwealth.

History.
1990, c. 669; 1998, c. 280; 2000, c. 284; 2002, cc. 753, 773; 2005, cc. 868, 881; 2010, c. 502; 2011, cc. 66, 171, 638.

§ 19.2-310.6. Unauthorized uses of DNA data bank; forensic samples; penalties.

Any person who, without authority, disseminates information contained in the data bank shall be guilty of a Class 3 misdemeanor. Any person who disseminates, receives, or otherwise uses or attempts to so use information in the data bank, knowing that such dissemination, receipt, or use is for a purpose other than as authorized by law, shall be guilty of a Class 1 misdemeanor.

Except as authorized by law, any person who, for purposes of having DNA analysis performed, obtains or attempts to obtain any sample submitted to the Department of Forensic Science for analysis shall be guilty of a Class 5 felony.

History.

1990, c. 669; 2005, cc. 868, 881.

§ 19.2-310.7. Expungement when DNA taken for a conviction.

A person whose DNA profile has been included in the data bank pursuant to § 19.2-310.2 may request expungement on the grounds that the conviction on which the authority for including his DNA profile was based has been reversed and the case dismissed. Provided that the person's DNA profile is not otherwise required to be included in the data bank pursuant to § 9.1-903, 16.1-299.1, 19.2-310.2, or 19.2-310.2:1, the Department of Forensic Science shall purge all records and identifiable information in the data bank pertaining to the person and destroy all samples from the person upon receipt of (i) a written request for expungement pursuant to this section and (ii) a certified copy of the court order reversing and dismissing the conviction.

History.

1990, c. 669; 2002, cc. 753, 773; 2005, cc. 868, 881; 2015, cc. 209, 437.

Criminal Procedure

ARTICLE 2.
INDETERMINATE COMMITMENT.

§ 19.2-311. Indeterminate commitment to Department of Corrections in certain cases; duration and character of commitment; concurrence by Department.

A. The judge, after a finding of guilt, when fixing punishment in those cases specifically enumerated in subsection B of this section, may, in his discretion, in lieu of imposing any other penalty provided by law and, with consent of the person convicted, commit such person for a period of four years, which commitment shall be indeterminate in character. In addition, the court shall impose a period of confinement which shall be suspended. Subject to the provisions of subsection C hereof, such persons shall be committed to the Department of Corrections for confinement in a state facility for youthful offenders established pursuant to § 53.1-63. Such confinement shall be followed by at least one and one-half years of supervisory parole, conditioned on good behavior. The sentence of indeterminate commitment and eligibility for continuous evaluation and parole under § 19.2-313 shall remain in effect but eligibility for use of programs and facilities established pursuant to § 53.1-63 shall lapse if such person (i) exhibits intractable behavior as defined in § 53.1-66 or (ii) is convicted of a second criminal offense which is a felony. A sentence imposed for any second criminal offense shall run consecutively with the indeterminate sentence.

B. The provisions of subsection A of this section shall be applicable to first convictions in which the person convicted:

1. Committed the offense of which convicted before becoming twenty-one years of age;

2. Was convicted of a felony offense other than any of the following: capital murder, murder in the first degree or murder in the second degree or a violation of §§ 18.2-61, 18.2-67.1, 18.2-67.2 or subdivision A 1 of § 18.2-67.3; and

3. Is considered by the judge to be capable of returning to society as a productive citizen following a reasonable amount of rehabilitation.

C. Subsequent to a finding of guilt and prior to fixing punishment, the Department of Corrections shall, concurrently with the evaluation required by § 19.2-316, review all aspects of the case to determine whether (i) such defendant is physically and emotionally suitable for the program, (ii) such indeterminate sentence of commitment is in the best interest of the Commonwealth and of the person convicted, and (iii) facilities are available for the confinement of such person. After the review such person shall be again brought before the court, which shall review the findings of the Department. The court may impose a sentence as authorized in subsection A, or any other penalty provided by law.

D. Upon the defendant's failure to complete the program established pursuant to § 53.1-63 or to comply with the terms and conditions through no fault of his own, the defendant shall be brought before the court for hearing. Notwithstanding the provisions for pronouncement of sentence as set forth in § 19.2-306, the court, after hearing, may pronounce whatever sentence was originally imposed, pronounce a reduced sentence, or impose such other terms and conditions of probation as it deems appropriate.

History.

Code 1950, § 19.1-295.1; 1966, c. 579; 1974, cc. 44, 45; 1975, c. 495; 1976, c. 498; 1980, c. 531; 1988, c. 38; 1990, c. 701; 1994, cc. 859, 949; 1996, cc. 755, 914; 1997, c. 387; 2000, cc. 668, 690.

§ **19.2-312:** Repealed by Acts 1990, c. 701.

§ 19.2-313. Eligibility for release.

Any person committed under the provisions of § 19.2-311 shall be eligible for release at the discretion of the Parole Board upon certification by the Director of the Department of Corrections that the person has successfully completed the program established pursuant to § 53.1-63 and a determination that he has demonstrated that such release is compatible with the interests of society and of such person and his successful rehabilitation to that extent. The Department and Parole Board shall make continuous evaluation of his progress to determine his readiness for release. All such persons, in any event, shall be released after four years' confinement. Any person committed under § 19.2-311 who was convicted of a misdemeanor and is determined to be unsuitable for the program established pursuant to § 53.1-63 shall be released after one year of confinement or the maximum confinement for the misdemeanor whichever is less.

History.

Code 1950, § 19.1-295.3; 1966, c. 579; 1975, cc. 495, 571; 2000, cc. 668, 690.

§ 19.2-314. Supervision of persons released.

Every person released under § 19.2-313 shall receive intensive parole supervision for a period of at least one and one-half years and may have parole supervision continued for a longer period, if the Parole Board deems it advisable.

History.

Code 1950, § 19.1-295.4; 1966, c. 579; 1975, c. 495; 2000, cc. 668, 690.

§ 19.2-315. Compliance with terms and conditions of parole; time on parole not counted as part of commitment period.

Every person on parole under § 19.2-314 shall comply with such terms and conditions as may be prescribed by the Board according to § 53.1-157 and shall be subject to the penalties imposed by law for a violation of such terms and conditions. Notwithstanding any other provision of the Code, if parole is revoked as a result of any such violation, such person may be returned to the institution established pursuant to § 53.1-63 upon the direction of the Parole Board with the concurrence of the Department of Corrections, provided such person has not been convicted since his release on parole of an offense constituting a felony under the laws of the Commonwealth. Time on parole shall not be counted as part of the four-year period of commitment under this section. In addition, such person may be brought before the sentencing court for imposition of all or part of the suspended sentence.

History.

Code 1950, § 19.1-295.5; 1966, c. 579; 1975, c. 495; 1984, c. 33; 2000, cc. 668, 690.

§ 19.2-316. Evaluation and report prior to determining punishment.

Following conviction and prior to sentencing, the court shall order such defendant committed to the Department of Corrections for a period not to exceed 60 days from the date of referral for evaluation and diagnosis by the Department to determine the person's potential for rehabilitation through confinement and treatment in the facilities and programs established pursuant to § 53.1-63. The evaluation and diagnosis shall include a complete physical and mental examination of the defendant and may be conducted by the Department of Corrections at any state or local facility, probation and parole office, or other location deemed appropriate by the Department. The Department of Corrections shall conduct the evaluation and diagnosis and shall review all aspects of the case within 60 days from the date of conviction or revocation of ordinary probation and shall recommend that the defendant be committed to the facility established pursuant to § 53.1-63 upon finding that (i) such defendant is physically and emotionally suitable for the program, (ii) such commitment is in the best interest of the Commonwealth and the defendant, and (iii) facilities are available for confinement of the defendant.

If the Director of the Department of Corrections determines such person should be confined in a facility other than one established pursuant to § 53.1-63, a written report giving the reasons for such decision shall be submitted to the sentencing court. The court shall not be bound by such written report in the matter of determining punishment. Additionally, the person may be committed or transferred to a state hospital operated by the Department of Behavioral Health and Developmental Services or other mental health hospital, as provided by law, during such 60-day period.

History.

Code 1950, § 19.1-295.6; 1966, c. 579; 1974, cc. 44, 1975, c. 495; 1990, c. 701; 2000, cc. 668, 690; 2012, cc. 476, 507.

ARTICLE 3.

BOOT CAMP INCARCERATION PROGRAM.

§ 19.2-316.1. Eligibility for participation; evaluation; sentencing; withdrawal or removal from program.

An individual may be eligible to be sentenced as provided herein if he (i) is convicted on or after January 1, 1991, of a nonviolent felony, or is deemed by the court to be nonviolent in character, (ii) is no older than twenty-four at the time of conviction for the offense, (iii) has never before been incarcerated upon a felony conviction in a correctional facility of any state, the District of Columbia, the United States or its territories, and (iv) has not been confined for more than twelve months nor for more than one term of confinement in a local correctional facility of any such jurisdiction; however, confinement for misdemeanor traffic convictions shall not be considered in determining eligibility.

Following conviction and prior to sentencing, upon motion of the defendant, the court may order such defendant committed to the Department of Corrections for a period not to exceed sixty days from the date of referral or the date of revocation of ordinary probation, as the case may be, for evaluation and diagnosis by the Department to determine suitability for participation in the Boot Camp Incarceration Program established pursuant to § 53.1-67.1. The evaluation and diagnosis shall include a complete physical and mental examination of the defendant and may be conducted by the Department of Corrections at any state or local facility, probation and parole office, or other location deemed appropriate by the Department.

The Department of Corrections shall conduct the evaluation and diagnosis and shall review all aspects of the case within sixty days from the date of conviction or revocation of ordinary probation and shall recommend that the defendant be committed to the Boot Camp Incarceration Program upon finding that (i) such defendant is physically and emotionally suitable for the program, (ii) such commitment is in the best interest of the Commonwealth and the defendant, and (iii) facilities are available for confinement of the defendant.

Upon receipt of such a recommendation and written consent of the defendant to participate in the program, and a determination by the court that the defendant will benefit from the program and is capable of returning to society as a productive citizen following a reasonable amount of intensive supervision and rehabilitation including program components set forth in § 53.1-67.1, and the defendant would otherwise be committed to the Department of Corrections for a period of confinement, the court shall impose such sentence of confinement as authorized by law and suspend the sentence and place the defendant on probation. Such probation shall be conditioned upon the defendant's entry into and successful completion of a Boot Camp Incarceration Program established by the Department of Corrections pursuant to § 53.1-67.1. The court may impose such other terms and conditions of probation as it deems appropriate.

Upon the defendant's (i) voluntary withdrawal from the program, (ii) removal from the program by the Department of Corrections for intractable behavior, or (iii) refusal to comply with the terms and conditions of probation imposed by the court, the defendant shall be brought before the court for hearing. Upon a finding that the defendant voluntarily chooses to withdraw from the program, exhibited intractable behavior as defined herein, or refused to comply with terms and conditions of probation, the court may revoke all or part of the suspended sentence and probation. Upon revocation of the suspension and probation, the provisions of §§ 53.1-191, 53.1-196 and 53.1-198 through 53.1-201 shall apply retroactively to the date of sentencing.

Upon the defendant's failure to complete the program or to comply with the terms and conditions of probation imposed by the court through no fault of his own, the defendant shall be brought before the court for hearing. Notwithstanding the provisions for pronouncement of sentence as set forth in § 19.2-306, the court, after hearing, may pronounce whatever sentence was originally imposed, pronounce a reduced sentence, or impose such other terms and conditions of probation as it deems appropriate.

"Intractable behavior" means that behavior which, in the determination of the Department of Corrections, (i) indicates an inmate's unwillingness or inability to conform his behavior to that necessary to his successful completion of the program or (ii) is so disruptive as to threaten the successful completion of the program by other participants.

"Nonviolent felony" means any felony except those considered an "act of violence" pursuant to § 19.2-297.1 or any attempt to commit any of those crimes.

History.

1990, c. 474; 1992, c. 861; 1994, c. 926; 1995, c. 117; 1996, cc. 809, 938; 2000, c. 769.

ARTICLE 4.

DETENTION CENTER INCARCERATION PROGRAM.

§ 19.2-316.2. Eligibility for participation in detention center incarceration program; evaluation; sentencing; withdrawal or removal from program.

A. A defendant who otherwise would have been sentenced to incarceration for a nonviolent felony as defined in § 19.2-316.1 or who has been previously incarcerated for a nonviolent felony as defined in § 19.2-316.1 but otherwise meets the following criteria and (i) who is determined by the court to need more security or supervision than provided by the diversion center incarceration program under § 53.1-67.7, (ii) whose age or physical condition disqualifies him from the Boot Camp Incarceration Program under § 53.1-67.1, and (iii) who can benefit from a regimented environment and structured program, may be considered for commitment to a detention center established under § 53.1-67.8 as follows:

1. Following conviction and prior to imposition of sentence or following a finding that the defendant's probation should be revoked, upon motion of the defendant or the attorney for the Commonwealth or upon the court's own motion, the court may order such defendant committed to the Department of

Corrections for a period not to exceed 60 days from the date of commitment for evaluation and diagnosis by the Department to determine suitability for participation in the Detention Center Incarceration Program. The evaluation and diagnosis shall include a complete physical and mental examination of the defendant and may be conducted by the Department at any state or local correctional facility, probation and parole office, or other location deemed appropriate by the Department. When a defendant who has not been charged with a new criminal offense and who may be subject to a revocation of probation, scores incarceration on the probation violation guidelines and agrees to participate, the probation and parole officer, with the approval of the court, may commit the defendant to the Department for such evaluation, for a period not to exceed 60 days.

2. Upon determination that (i) such defendant is physically and emotionally suited for the program, (ii) such commitment is in the best interest of the Commonwealth and the defendant, and (iii) facilities are available for the confinement of the defendant, the Department shall recommend to the court in writing that the defendant be committed to the Detention Center Incarceration Program.

3. Upon receipt of such a recommendation and a determination by the court that the defendant will benefit from the program and is capable of returning to society as a productive citizen following successful completion of the program, and if the defendant would otherwise be committed to the Department, the court (i) shall impose sentence, suspend the sentence, and place the defendant on probation or (ii) following a finding that the defendant has violated the terms and conditions of his probation previously ordered, shall place the defendant on probation pursuant to this section. Such probation shall be conditioned upon the defendant's entry into and successful completion of the Detention Center Incarceration Program. The court shall order that, upon successful completion of the program, the defendant shall be released from confinement and be under intensive probation supervision for a period to be specified by the court followed by an additional period of regular probation of not less than one year. The court shall further order that the defendant, following release from confinement, shall (a) make reasonable efforts to secure and maintain employment, (b) comply with a plan of restitution or community service, (c) comply with a plan for payment of fines, if any, and costs of court, and (d) undergo appropriate substance abuse treatment, if necessary. The court may impose such other terms and conditions of probation as it deems appropriate. A sentence to the Detention Center Incarceration Program shall not be imposed as an addition to an active sentence to a state correctional facility.

4. Upon the defendant's (i) voluntary withdrawal from the program, (ii) removal from the program by the Department for intractable behavior as defined in § 19.2-316.1, or (iii) failure to comply with the terms and conditions of probation, the court shall cause the defendant to show cause why his probation and suspension of sentence should not be revoked. Upon a finding that the defendant voluntarily withdrew from the program, was removed from the program by the Department for intractable behavior, or failed to comply with the terms and conditions of probation, the court may revoke all or part of the probation and suspended sentence and commit the defendant as otherwise provided in this chapter.

B. Any offender as described in § 19.2-316.1 paroled under § 53.1-155 or mandatorily released under § 53.1-159 and for whom probable cause that a violation of parole or of the terms and conditions of mandatory release, other than for the occurrence of a new felony or Class 1 or Class 2 misdemeanor, has been determined under § 53.1-165, may be considered by the Parole Board for commitment to a detention center as established under § 53.1-67.8 as follows:

1. The Parole Board or its authorized hearing officer, with the violator's consent, may order the violator to be evaluated and diagnosed by the Department of Corrections to determine suitability for participation in the Detention Center Incarceration Program. The evaluation and diagnosis may be conducted by the Department at any state or local correctional facility, probation or parole office, or other location deemed appropriate by the Department.

2. Upon determination that (i) such commitment is in the best interest of the Commonwealth and the violator and (ii) facilities are available for the confinement of the violator, or upon receipt of a defendant's voluntary participation form from the probation and parole officer and a determination that (i) and (ii) have been met, the Department shall recommend to the Parole Board in writing that the violator be committed to the Detention Center Incarceration Program. The Department shall have the final authority to determine an individual's suitability for the program.

3. Upon receipt of such a recommendation and a determination by the Parole Board that the violator will benefit from the program and is capable of returning to society as a productive citizen following successful completion of the program, the violator shall be placed under parole supervision for a period of not less than one year. The Parole Board may impose such other terms and conditions of parole or mandatory release as it deems appropriate.

4. Upon the violator's (i) voluntary withdrawal from the program, (ii) removal from the program for intractable behavior as defined in § 19.2-316.1, or (iii) failure to comply with the terms and conditions of parole or mandatory release, the Department shall conduct a preliminary parole violation hearing to determine if probable cause exists to revoke his parole or mandatory release. Upon a finding that the violator voluntarily withdrew from the program,

was removed from the program by the Department for intractable behavior, or failed to comply with the terms and conditions of parole or mandatory release, the Parole Board shall revoke parole or mandatory release and recommit the violator as provided in § 53.1-165.

History.
1994, 2nd Sp. Sess., cc. 1, 2; 1995, cc. 502, 574; 2000, c. 338; 2002, c. 604; 2005, cc. 512, 580; 2008, cc. 362, 761.

ARTICLE 5.

DIVERSION CENTER INCARCERATION PROGRAM.

§ 19.2-316.3. Eligibility for participation in diversion center incarceration program; evaluation; sentencing; withdrawal or removal from program; payment for costs.

A. A defendant (i) who otherwise would have been sentenced to incarceration for a nonviolent felony as defined in § 19.2-316.1 and who the court determines requires more security or supervision than provided by intensive probation supervision or (ii) whose suspension of sentence would otherwise be revoked after a finding that the defendant has violated the terms and conditions of probation for a nonviolent felony as defined in § 19.2-316.1, may be considered for commitment to a diversion center established under § 53.1-67.7 as follows:

1. Following conviction and prior to imposition of sentence or following a finding that the defendant's probation should be revoked, upon motion of the defendant or the attorney for the Commonwealth or upon the court's own motion, the court may order such defendant committed to the Department of Corrections for a period not to exceed 45 days from the date of commitment for evaluation and diagnosis by the Department to determine suitability for participation in the Diversion Center Incarceration Program. The evaluation and diagnosis may be conducted by the Department at any state or local correctional facility, probation and parole office, or other location deemed appropriate by the Department. When a defendant who has not been charged with a new criminal offense and who may be subject to a revocation of probation, scores incarceration on the probation violation guidelines and agrees to participate, the probation and parole officer, with the approval of the court, may commit the defendant to the Department for such evaluation, for a period not to exceed 45 days.

2. Upon determination that (i) such commitment is in the best interest of the Commonwealth and the defendant and (ii) facilities are available for the confinement of the defendant, the Department shall recommend to the court in writing that the defendant be committed to the Diversion Center Incarceration Program.

3. Upon receipt of such a recommendation and a determination by the court that the defendant will benefit from the program and is capable of returning to society as a productive citizen following successful completion of the program, and if the defendant would otherwise be committed to the Department, the court (i) shall impose sentence, suspend the sentence, and place the defendant on probation pursuant to this section or (ii) following a finding that the defendant has violated the terms and conditions of his probation previously ordered, shall place the defendant on probation pursuant to this section. Such probation shall be conditioned upon the defendant's entry into and successful completion of the Diversion Center Incarceration Program. The court shall order that, upon successful completion of the program, the defendant shall be released from confinement and be under intensive probation supervision for a period to be specified by the court followed by an additional period of regular probation of not less than one year. The court shall further order that the defendant, prior to release from confinement, shall (a) make reasonable efforts to secure and maintain employment, (b) comply with a plan of restitution or community service, (c) comply with a plan for payment of fines, if any, and costs of court, and (d) undergo substance abuse treatment, if necessary. The court may impose such other terms and conditions of probation as it deems appropriate. A sentence to the Diversion Center Incarceration Program shall not be imposed in addition to an active sentence to a state correctional facility.

4. Upon the defendant's (i) voluntary withdrawal from the program, (ii) removal from the program by the Department for intractable behavior as defined in § 19.2-316.1, or (iii) failure to comply with the terms and conditions of probation, the court shall cause the defendant to show cause why his probation and suspension of sentence should not be revoked. Upon a finding that the defendant voluntarily withdrew from the program, was removed from the program by the Department for intractable behavior, or failed to comply with the terms and conditions of probation, the court may revoke all or part of the probation and suspended sentence, and commit the defendant as otherwise provided in this chapter.

B. Any offender as described in § 19.2-316.1 paroled under § 53.1-155 or mandatorily released under § 53.1-159 and for whom probable cause that a violation of parole or of the terms and conditions of mandatory release, other than the occurrence of a new felony or Class 1 or Class 2 misdemeanor, has been determined under § 53.1-165, may be considered by the Parole Board for commitment to a diversion center as established under § 53.1-67.7 as follows:

1. The Parole Board or its authorized hearing officer, with the violator's consent or upon receipt of a defendant's written voluntary agreement to participate form from the probation and parole officer,

may order the violator to be evaluated and diagnosed by the Department of Corrections to determine suitability for participation in the Diversion Center Incarceration Program. The evaluation and diagnosis may be conducted by the Department at any state or local correctional facility, probation or parole office, or other location deemed appropriate by the Department.

2. Upon determination that (i) such commitment is in the best interest of the Commonwealth and the violator and (ii) facilities are available for the confinement of the violator, the Department shall recommend to the Parole Board in writing that the violator be committed to the Diversion Center Incarceration Program. The Department shall have the final authority to determine an individual's suitability for the program.

3. Upon receipt of such a recommendation and a determination by the Parole Board that the violator will benefit from the program and is capable of returning to society as a productive citizen following successful completion of the program and if the violator would otherwise be committed to the Department, the Parole Board shall restore the violator to parole supervision conditioned upon entry into and successful completion of the Diversion Center Incarceration Program. The Parole Board shall order that, upon successful completion of the program, the violator shall be placed under parole supervision for a period of not less than one year. The Parole Board may impose such other terms and conditions of parole or mandatory release as it deems appropriate. The time spent in the program shall not be counted as service of any part of a term of imprisonment for which he was sentenced upon his conviction.

4. Upon the violator's (i) voluntary withdrawal from the program, (ii) removal from the program by the Department for intractable behavior as defined in § 19.2-316.1, or (iii) failure to comply with the terms and conditions of parole or mandatory release, the Parole Board may revoke parole or mandatory release and recommit the violator as provided in § 53.1-165.

C. A person sentenced pursuant to this article shall be required to pay an amount to be determined by the Board of Corrections pursuant to regulation to defray the cost of his keep.

History.

1994, 2nd Sp. Sess., cc. 1, 2; 1995, cc. 502, 574; 2000, c. 338; 2002, c. 604; 2005, c. 604; 2008, cc. 384, 757.

CHAPTER 19.

EXCEPTIONS AND WRITS OF ERROR.

Section

§ 19.2-317. When writ of error lies in criminal case for accused; when for Commonwealth; when for county, city or town.

A. A writ of error shall lie in a criminal case to the judgment of a circuit court or the judge thereof, from the Court of Appeals as provided in § 17.1-406. It shall lie in any such case for the accused and if the case is for the violation of any law relating to the state revenue, it shall lie also for the Commonwealth.

B. A writ of error shall also lie for any county, city or town from the Supreme Court to the judgment of any circuit court declaring an ordinance of such county, city or town to be unconstitutional or otherwise invalid, except when the violation of any such ordinance is made a misdemeanor by state statute.

C. A writ of error shall also lie for the Commonwealth from the Supreme Court to a judgment of the Court of Appeals in a criminal case, except where the decision of the Court of Appeals is made final under § 17.1-410 or § 19.2-408.

History.

Code 1950, § 19.1-282; 1960, c. 366; 1975, c. 495; 1984, c. 703; 1997, c. 358.

§ 19.2-317.1: Repealed by Acts 1990, c. 74.

§ 19.2-318. Appeal on writ of error to judgment for contempt.

From a judgment for any civil contempt of court an appeal may be taken to the Court of Appeals. A writ of error shall lie from the Court of Appeals to a judgment for criminal contempt of court. This section shall also be construed to authorize an appeal from or writ of error to a judgment of a circuit court rendered on appeal from a judgment of a district court for civil or criminal contempt.

History.

Code 1950, § 19.1-283; 1960, c. 366; 1968, c. 639; 1975, c. 495; 1979, c. 649; 1984, c. 703.

Criminal Procedure

§ 19.2-319. When execution of sentence to be suspended; bail; appeal from denial.

If a person sentenced by a circuit court to death or confinement in the state correctional facility indicates an intention to apply for a writ of error, the circuit court shall postpone the execution of such sentence for such time as it may deem proper.

In any other criminal case wherein judgment is given by any court to which a writ of error lies, and in any case of judgment for any civil or criminal contempt, from which an appeal may be taken or to which a writ of error lies, the court giving such judgment may postpone the execution thereof for such time and on such terms as it deems proper.

In any case after conviction if the sentence, or the execution thereof, is suspended in accordance with this section, or for any other cause, the court, or the judge thereof, may, and in any case of a misdemeanor shall, set bail in such penalty and for appearance at such time as the nature of the case may require; provided that, if the conviction was for a violent felony as defined in § 19.2-297.1 and the defendant was sentenced to serve a period of incarceration not subject to suspension, then the court shall presume, subject to rebuttal, that no condition or combination of conditions of bail will reasonably assure the appearance of the convicted person or the safety of the public.

In any case in which the court denies bail, the reason for such denial shall be stated on the record of the case. A writ of error from the Court of Appeals shall lie to any such judgment refusing bail or requiring excessive bail, except that in any case where a person has been sentenced to death, a writ of error shall lie from the Supreme Court. Upon review by the Court of Appeals or the Supreme Court, if the decision by the trial court to deny bail is overruled, the appellate court shall either set bail or remand the matter to circuit court for such further action regarding bail as the appellate court directs.

History.

Code 1950, § 19.1-281; 1960, c. 366; 1975, c. 495; 1979, c. 649; 1984, c. 703; 1987, c. 175; 1988, c. 524; 1999, c. 821; 2008, cc. 126, 146.

§ 19.2-320. Petitioner for writ of error to comply with Rules of Court.

Any party for whom a writ of error lies may apply therefor by complying with the provisions of the Rules of the Supreme Court of Virginia relative to the appeal of criminal cases to the Court of Appeals, or where an appeal is taken to the Supreme Court, with the Rules of the Supreme Court relative to appeal of criminal cases to the Supreme Court.

History.

Code 1950, § 19.1-284; 1960, c. 366; 1975, c. 495; 1984, c. 703.

§ 19.2-321. With whom petition for writ of error filed.

A. The petition to the Court of Appeals shall be filed with the Clerk of the Court in the manner and within the time provided by law.

B. The petition in a case wherein a writ of error lies from the Supreme Court shall be filed with the Clerk of that Court in the manner and within the time provided by law.

History.

Code 1950, § 19.1-285; 1960, c. 366; 1975, c. 495; 1976, c. 615; 1984, c. 703.

§ 19.2-321.1. Motion in the Court of Appeals for delayed appeal in criminal cases.

A. *Filing and content of motion.* — When, due to the error, neglect, or fault of counsel representing the appellant, or of the court reporter, or of the circuit court or an officer or employee thereof, an appeal in a criminal case has (i) never been initiated; (ii) been dismissed for failure to adhere to proper form, procedures, or time limits in the perfection of the appeal; or (iii) been denied or the conviction has been affirmed, for failure to file or timely file the indispensable transcript or written statement of facts as required by law or by the Rules of the Supreme Court; then a motion for leave to pursue a delayed appeal may be filed in the Court of Appeals within six months after the appeal has been dismissed or denied, the conviction has been affirmed, or the circuit court judgment sought to be appealed has become final, whichever is later. Such motion shall identify the circuit court and the style, date, and circuit court record number of the judgment sought to be appealed, and, if one was assigned in a prior attempt to appeal the judgment, shall give the Court of Appeals record number in that proceeding, and shall set forth the specific facts establishing the said error, neglect, or fault. If the error, neglect, or fault is alleged to be that of an attorney representing the appellant, the motion shall be accompanied by the affidavit of the attorney whose error, neglect, or fault is alleged, verifying the specific facts alleged in the motion, and certifying that the appellant is not personally responsible, in whole or in part, for the error, neglect, or fault causing loss of the original opportunity for appeal.

B. *Service, response, and disposition.* — Such motion shall be served on the attorney for the Commonwealth or, if a petition for appeal was granted in the original attempt to appeal, upon the Attorney General, in accordance with the Rules of the Supreme Court. If the Commonwealth disputes the facts alleged in the motion, or contends that those facts do not entitle the appellant to a delayed appeal under this section, the motion shall be denied without prejudice to the appellant's right to seek a delayed appeal by means of petition for a writ of

Criminal Procedure

habeas corpus. Otherwise, the Court of Appeals shall, if the motion meets the requirements of this section, grant appellant leave to initiate or re-initiate pursuit of the appeal.

C. *Time limits when motion granted.* — If the motion is granted, all computations of time under the Rules of the Supreme Court shall run from the date of the order of the Court of Appeals granting the motion, or if the appellant has been determined to be indigent, from the date of the order by the circuit court appointing counsel to represent the appellant in the delayed appeal, whichever is later.

D. *Applicability.* — The provisions of this section shall not apply to cases in which the appellant is responsible, in whole or in part, for the error, neglect, or fault causing loss of the original opportunity for appeal, nor shall it apply in cases where the claim of error, neglect, or fault has already been alleged and rejected in a prior judicial proceeding.

History.
2005, c. 836; 2011, c. 278.

§ 19.2-321.2. Motion in the Supreme Court for delayed appeal in criminal cases.

A. *Filing and content of motion.* — When, due to the error, neglect, or fault of counsel representing the appellant, or of the court reporter, or of the Court of Appeals or the circuit court or an officer or employee of either, an appeal from the Court of Appeals to the Supreme Court in a criminal case has (i) never been initiated; (ii) been dismissed for failure to adhere to proper form, procedures, or time limits in the perfection of the appeal; or (iii) been denied or the conviction has been affirmed, for failure to file or timely file the indispensable transcript or written statement of facts as required by law or by the Rules of the Supreme Court; then a motion for leave to pursue a delayed appeal may be filed in the Supreme Court within six months after the appeal has been dismissed or denied, the conviction has been affirmed, or the Court of Appeals judgment sought to be appealed has become final, whichever is later. Such motion shall identify by the style, date, and Court of Appeals record number of the judgment sought to be appealed, and, if one was assigned in a prior attempt to appeal the judgment to the Supreme Court, shall give the record number assigned in the Supreme Court in that proceeding, and shall set forth the specific facts establishing the said error, neglect, or fault. If the error, neglect, or fault is alleged to be that of an attorney representing the appellant, the motion shall be accompanied by the affidavit of the attorney whose error, neglect, or fault is alleged, verifying the specific facts alleged in the motion, and certifying that the appellant is not personally responsible, in whole or in part, for the error, neglect, or fault causing loss of the original opportunity for appeal.

B. *Service, response, and disposition.* — Such motion shall be served on the attorney for the Commonwealth or, if a petition for appeal was granted in the Court of Appeals or in the Supreme Court in the original attempt to appeal, upon the Attorney General, in accordance with Rule 5:4 of the Supreme Court. If the Commonwealth disputes the facts alleged in the motion, or contends that those facts do not entitle the appellant to a delayed appeal under this section, the motion shall be denied without prejudice to the appellant's right to seek a delayed appeal by means of petition for a writ of habeas corpus. Otherwise, the Supreme Court shall, if the motion meets the requirements of this section, grant appellant leave to initiate or re-initiate pursuit of the appeal from the Court of Appeals to the Supreme Court.

C. *Time limits when motion granted.* — If the motion is granted, all computations of time under the Rules of the Supreme Court shall run from the date of the order of the Supreme Court granting the motion, or if the appellant has been determined to be indigent, from the date of the order by the circuit court appointing counsel to represent the appellant in the delayed appeal, whichever is later.

D. *Applicability.* — The provisions of this section shall not apply to cases in which the appellant is responsible, in whole or in part, for the error, neglect, or fault causing loss of the original opportunity for appeal, nor shall it apply in cases where the claim of error, neglect, or fault has already been alleged and rejected in a prior judicial proceeding, nor shall it apply in cases in which a sentence of death has been imposed.

History.
2005, c. 836; 2011, c. 278.

§ 19.2-322: Repealed by Acts 1984, c. 703.

Cross references.
As to suspension of execution of judgment on appeal, see now § 19.2-322.1.

§ 19.2-322.1. Suspension of execution of judgment on appeal.

Execution of a judgment from which an appeal to the Court of Appeals or the Supreme Court is sought may be suspended during an appeal provided the appeal is timely prosecuted and an appeal bond is filed as provided in § 8.01-676.1.

History.
1984, c. 703.

§ 19.2-323. Denial by judge or justice no bar to allowance by Court.

The denial of a writ of error by a judge or justice of an appellate court, in the vacation of that court, shall not prevent the allowance of the writ by the Court, if by it deemed proper, on presentation of the petition to that Court at its next term.

History.
Code 1950, § 19.1-287; 1960, c. 366; 1975, c. 495; 1976, c. 615; 1984, c. 703.

§ 19.2-324. Decision of appellate court.

The court from which a writ of error lies shall affirm the judgment, if there be no error therein, and reverse the same in whole or in part, if erroneous, and enter such judgment as the court whose error is sought to be corrected ought to have entered; or remand the cause and direct a new trial; affirming in those cases where the voices on both sides are equal.

History.
Code 1950, § 19.1-288; 1960, c. 366; 1975, c. 495.

§ 19.2-324.1. Erroneously admitted evidence; appeal.

In appeals to the Court of Appeals or the Supreme Court, when a challenge to a conviction rests on a claim that the evidence was insufficient because the trial court improperly admitted evidence, the reviewing court shall consider all evidence admitted at trial to determine whether there is sufficient evidence to sustain the conviction. If the reviewing court determines that evidence was erroneously admitted and that such error was not harmless, the case shall be remanded for a new trial if the Commonwealth elects to have a new trial.

History.
2013, c. 675.

§ 19.2-325. Provisions which apply to criminal as well as civil cases; when plaintiff in error unable to pay printing costs.

Sections 8.01-675.1, 8.01-675.2, 8.01-675.3, 8.01-684 and 17.1-328 shall apply as well to criminal cases as to civil cases. In a felony case in the Court of Appeals or the Supreme Court, if the plaintiff in error files with the Clerk of the Court an affidavit that he is unable to pay or secure to be paid the costs of printing the record in the case, together with a certificate of the judge of the trial court to the effect that he has investigated the matter and is of opinion that the plaintiff in error is unable to pay, or secure to be paid, such costs, the printing shall be done as if the costs had been paid and the clerk shall not be required to account for and pay the same into the state treasury. However, if the costs are not paid or secured to be paid and upon the hearing of the case the judgment of the court below is wholly affirmed by the Court of Appeals and no appeal granted by the Supreme Court, or wholly affirmed by the Supreme Court where appeal is granted, the Court in affirming the judgment shall also give judgment in behalf of the Commonwealth against the plaintiff in error for the amount of the costs to be taxed by its clerk.

History.
Code 1950, § 19.1-289; 1960, c. 366; 1975, c. 495; 1984, c. 703.

§ 19.2-326. Payment of expenses of appeals of indigent defendants.

In any felony or misdemeanor case wherein the judge of the circuit court, from the affidavit of the defendant or any other evidence certifies that the defendant is financially unable to pay his attorneys' fees, costs and expenses incident to an appeal, the court to which an appeal is taken shall order the payment of such attorneys' fees in an amount not less than $300, costs or necessary expenses of such attorneys in an amount deemed reasonable by the court, by the Commonwealth out of the appropriation for criminal charges. If the conviction is upheld on appeal, the attorney's fees, costs and necessary expenses of such attorney paid by the Commonwealth under the provisions hereof shall be assessed against the defendant.

History.
Code 1950, § 17-30.2; 1962, c. 419; 1964, c. 651; 1975, c. 495; 1980, c. 626; 1984, c. 703.

§ 19.2-327. How judgment of appellate court certified and entered.

The judgment of the Court of Appeals or of the Supreme Court shall be certified to the court to whose judgment the writ of error was allowed. The court or the clerk thereof shall cause the same to be entered on its order book as its own judgment.

History.
Code 1950, § 19.1-290; 1960, c. 366; 1975, c. 495; 1984, c. 703.

CHAPTER 19.1.

SCIENTIFIC ANALYSIS OF NEWLY DISCOVERED OR UNTESTED SCIENTIFIC EVIDENCE.

Section

§ 19.2-327.01: Repealed by Acts 2004, c. 337.

§ 19.2-327.1. Motion by a convicted felon or person adjudicated delinquent for scientific analysis of newly discovered or previously untested scientific evidence; procedure.

A. Notwithstanding any other provision of law or rule of court, any person convicted of a felony or any person who was adjudicated delinquent by a circuit court of an offense that would be a felony if committed by an adult may, by motion to the circuit court that entered the original conviction or the adjudication of delinquency, apply for a new scientific investigation of any human biological evidence related to the case that resulted in the felony conviction or adjudication of delinquency if: (i) the evidence was not known or available at the time the conviction or adjudication of delinquency became final in the circuit court or the evidence was not previously subjected to testing because the testing procedure was not available at the Department of Forensic Science at the time the conviction or adjudication of delinquency became final in the circuit court; (ii) the evidence is subject to a chain of custody sufficient to establish that the evidence has not been altered, tampered with, or substituted in any way; (iii) the testing is materially relevant, noncumulative, and necessary and may prove the actual innocence of the convicted person or the person adjudicated delinquent; (iv) the testing requested involves a scientific method employed by the Department of Forensic Science; and (v) the person convicted or adjudicated delinquent has not unreasonably delayed the filing of the petition after the evidence or the test for the evidence became available at the Department of Forensic Science.

B. The petitioner shall assert categorically and with specificity, under oath, the facts to support the items enumerated in subsection A and (i) the crime for which the person was convicted or adjudicated delinquent, (ii) the reason or reasons the evidence was not known or tested by the time the conviction or adjudication of delinquency became final in the circuit court, and (iii) the reason or reasons that the newly discovered or untested evidence may prove the actual innocence of the person convicted or adjudicated delinquent. Such motion shall contain all relevant allegations and facts that are known to the petitioner at the time of filing and shall enumerate and include all previous records, applications, petitions, and appeals and their dispositions.

C. The petitioner shall serve a copy of such motion upon the attorney for the Commonwealth. The Commonwealth shall file its response to the motion within 30 days of the receipt of service. The court shall, no sooner than 30 and no later than 90 days after such motion is filed, hear the motion. Motions made by a petitioner under a sentence of death shall be given priority on the docket.

D. The court shall, after a hearing on the motion, set forth its findings specifically as to each of the items enumerated in subsections A and B and either (i) dismiss the motion for failure to comply with the requirements of this section or (ii) dismiss the motion for failure to state a claim upon which relief can be granted or (iii) order that the testing be done by the Department of Forensic Science based on a finding of clear and convincing evidence that the requirements of subsection A have been met.

E. The court shall order the tests to be performed by the Department of Forensic Science and prescribe in its order, pursuant to standards and guidelines established by the Department, the method of custody, transfer, and return of evidence submitted for scientific investigation sufficient to insure and protect the Commonwealth's interest in the integrity of the evidence. The results of any such testing shall be furnished simultaneously to the court, the petitioner and his attorney of record and the attorney for the Commonwealth. The Department of Forensic Science shall give testing priority to cases in which a sentence of death has been imposed. The results of any tests performed and any hearings held pursuant to this section shall become a part of the record.

F. Nothing in this section shall constitute grounds to delay setting an execution date pursuant to § 53.1-232.1 or to grant a stay of execution that has been set pursuant to clause (iii) or (iv) of § 53.1-232.1.

G. An action under this section or the performance of any attorney representing the petitioner under this section shall not form the basis for relief in any habeas corpus proceeding or any other appeal. Nothing in this section shall create any cause of action for damages against the Commonwealth or any of its political subdivisions or any officers, employees or agents of the Commonwealth or its political subdivisions.

H. In any petition filed pursuant to this chapter, the petitioner is entitled to representation by counsel subject to the provisions of Article 3 (§ 19.2-157 et seq.) of Chapter 10.

History.
2001, cc. 873, 874; 2005, cc. 868, 881; 2013, c. 170.

CHAPTER 19.2.

ISSUANCE OF WRIT OF ACTUAL INNOCENCE.

Section

§ 19.2-327.2. Issuance of writ of actual innocence based on biological evidence.

Notwithstanding any other provision of law or rule of court, upon a petition of a person who was convicted of a felony upon a plea of not guilty or who was adjudicated delinquent upon a plea of not guilty by a circuit court of an offense that would be a felony if committed by an adult, or for any person, regardless of the plea, sentenced to death, or convicted or adjudicated delinquent of (i) a Class 1 felony, (ii) a Class 2 felony, or (iii) any felony for which the maximum penalty is imprisonment for life, the Supreme Court shall have the authority to issue writs of actual innocence under this chapter. The writ shall lie to the circuit court that entered the felony conviction or adjudication of delinquency and that court shall have the authority to conduct hearings, as provided for in § 19.2-327.5, on such a petition as directed by order from the Supreme Court.

History.
2001, cc. 873, 874; 2009, cc. 139, 320; 2013, c. 170.

§ 19.2-327.2:1. Petition for writ of actual innocence joined by Attorney General; release of prisoner; bond hearing.

The Attorney General may join in a petition for a writ of actual innocence made pursuant to § 19.2-327.2. When such petition is so joined, the petitioner may file a copy of the petition and attachments thereto and the Attorney General's answer with the circuit court that entered the felony conviction and move the court for a hearing to consider release of the person on bail pursuant to Chapter 9 (§ 19.2-119 et seq.). Upon hearing and for good cause shown, the court may order the person released from custody subject to the terms and conditions of bail so established, pending a ruling by the Supreme Court on the writ under § 19.2-327.5.

History.
2015, c. 66.

§ 19.2-327.3. Contents and form of the petition based on previously unknown or untested human biological evidence of actual innocence.

A. The petitioner shall allege categorically and with specificity, under oath, the following: (i) the crime for which the petitioner was convicted or the offense for which the petitioner was adjudicated delinquent, and that such conviction or adjudication of delinquency was upon a plea of not guilty or that the person is under a sentence of death or convicted of (a) a Class 1 felony, (b) a Class 2 felony, or (c) any felony for which the maximum penalty is imprisonment for life; (ii) that the petitioner is actually innocent of the crime for which he was convicted or adjudicated delinquent; (iii) an exact description of the human biological evidence and the scientific testing supporting the allegation of innocence; (iv) that the evidence was not previously known or available to the petitioner or his trial attorney of record at the time the conviction or adjudication of delinquency became final in the circuit court, or if known, the reason that the evidence was not subject to the scientific testing set forth in the petition; (v) the date the test results under § 19.2-327.1 became known to the petitioner or any attorney of record; (vi) that the petitioner or his attorney of record has filed the petition within 60 days of obtaining the test results under § 19.2-327.1; (vii) the reason or reasons the evidence will prove that no rational trier of fact would have found proof of guilt or delinquency beyond a reasonable doubt; and (viii) for any conviction or adjudication of delinquency that became final in the circuit court after June 30, 1996, that the evidence was not available for testing under § 9.1-1104. The Supreme Court may issue a stay of execution pending proceedings under the petition. Nothing in this chapter shall constitute grounds to delay setting an execution date pursuant to § 53.1-232.1 or to grant a stay of execution that has been set pursuant to clause (iii) or (iv) of § 53.1-232.1.

B. Such petition shall contain all relevant allegations of facts that are known to the petitioner at the time of filing and shall enumerate and include all previous records, applications, petitions, and appeals and their dispositions. A copy of any test results shall be filed with the petition. The petition shall be filed on a form provided by the Supreme Court. If the petitioner fails to submit a completed form, the Court may dismiss the petition or return the petition to the prisoner pending the completion of such form. The petitioner shall be responsible for all statements contained in the petition. Any false statement in the petition, if such statement is knowingly or willfully made, shall be a ground for prosecution and conviction of perjury as provided for in § 18.2-434.

C. The Supreme Court shall not accept the petition unless it is accompanied by a duly executed return of service in the form of a verification that a copy of the petition and all attachments has been served on the attorney for the Commonwealth of the jurisdiction where the conviction or adjudication of delinquency occurred and the Attorney General or an acceptance of service signed by these officials, or any combination thereof. The Attorney General shall have 30 days after receipt of the record by the clerk of the Supreme Court in which to file a response to the petition. The response may contain a proffer of any evidence pertaining to the guilt or delinquency or innocence of the petitioner that is not included in the record of the case, including evidence that was suppressed at trial.

D. The Supreme Court may, when the case has been before a trial or appellate court, inspect the record of any trial or appellate court action, and the Court may, in any case, award a writ of certiorari to the clerk of the respective court below, and have brought before the Court the whole record or any part of any record.

E. In any petition filed pursuant to this chapter, the petitioner is entitled to representation by counsel subject to the provisions of Article 3 (§ 19.2-157 et seq.) of Chapter 10.

History.
2001, cc. 873, 874; 2003, c. 131; 2005, cc. 868, 881; 2009, cc. 139, 320; 2013, cc. 170, 180.

§ 19.2-327.4. Determination by the Supreme Court for findings of fact by the circuit court.

If the Supreme Court determines from the petition, from any hearing on the petition, from a review of the records of the case, including the record of any hearing on a motion to test evidence pursuant to § 9.1-1104, or from any response from the Attorney General that a resolution of the case requires further development of the facts under this chapter, the court may order the circuit court to conduct a hearing within 90 days after the order has been issued to certify findings of fact with respect to such issues as the Supreme Court shall direct. The record and certified findings of fact of the circuit court shall be filed in the Supreme Court within 30 days after the hearing is concluded. The petitioner or his attorney of record, the attorney for the Commonwealth and the Attorney General shall be served a copy of the order stating the specific purpose and evidence for which the hearing has been ordered.

History.
2001, cc. 873, 874; 2005, cc. 868, 881.

§ 19.2-327.5. Relief under writ.

Upon consideration of the petition, the response by the Commonwealth, previous records of the case, the record of any hearing held under this chapter and the record of any hearings held pursuant to § 19.2-327.1, and if applicable, any findings certified from the circuit court pursuant to § 19.2-327.4, the Supreme Court shall either dismiss the petition for failure to state a claim or assert grounds upon which relief shall be granted; or upon a hearing the Court shall (i) dismiss the petition for failure to establish allegations sufficient to justify the issuance of the writ or (ii) only upon a finding of clear and convincing evidence that the petitioner has proven all of the allegations contained in clauses (iv) through (viii) of subsection A of § 19.2-327.3, and upon a finding that no rational trier of fact would have found proof of guilt or delinquency beyond a reasonable doubt, grant the writ, and vacate the conviction or adjudication of delinquency, or in the event that the Court finds that no rational trier of fact would have found sufficient evidence beyond a reasonable doubt as to one or more elements of the offense for which the petitioner was convicted or adjudicated delinquent, but the Court finds that there remains in the original trial record evidence sufficient to find the petitioner guilty or delinquent beyond a reasonable doubt of a lesser included offense, the Court shall modify the conviction or adjudication of delinquency accordingly and remand the case to the circuit court for resentencing. The burden of proof in a proceeding brought pursuant to this chapter shall be upon the convicted or delinquent person seeking relief. If a writ vacating a conviction or adjudication of delinquency is granted, the Court shall forward a copy of the writ to the circuit court, where an order of expungement shall be immediately granted.

History.
2001, cc. 873, 874; 2007, cc. 465, 824, 883, 905; 2009, cc. 139, 320; 2013, cc. 170, 180.

§ 19.2-327.6. Claims of relief.

An action under this chapter or the performance of any attorney representing the petitioner under this chapter shall not form the basis for relief in any habeas corpus or appellate proceeding. Nothing in this chapter shall create any cause of action for damages against the Commonwealth or any of its political subdivisions or any officers, employees or agents of the Commonwealth or its political subdivisions.

History.
2001, cc. 873, 874.

CHAPTER 19.3.

ISSUANCE OF WRIT OF ACTUAL INNOCENCE BASED ON NONBIOLOGICAL EVIDENCE.

Section

§ 19.2-327.10. Issuance of writ of actual innocence based on nonbiological evidence.

Notwithstanding any other provision of law or rule of court, upon a petition of a person who was convicted of a felony upon a plea of not guilty, or the petition of a person who was adjudicated delinquent, upon a plea of not guilty, by a circuit court of an offense that would be a felony if committed by an adult, the Court of Appeals shall have the authority to issue writs of actual innocence under this chapter. Only one such writ based upon such conviction or adjudication of delinquency may be filed by a petitioner. The writ shall lie to the circuit court that entered the conviction or the adjudication of delinquency and that court shall have the authority to conduct hearings, as provided for in this chapter, on such a petition as directed by order from the Court of Appeals. In accordance with §§ 17.1-411 and 19.2-317, either party may appeal a final decision of the Court of Appeals to the Supreme Court of Virginia. Upon an appeal from the Court of Appeals, the Supreme Court of Virginia shall have the authority to issue writs in accordance with the provisions of this chapter.

History.
2004, c. 1024; 2013, c. 170.

§ 19.2-327.10:1. Petition for writ of actual innocence joined by Attorney General; release of prisoner; bond hearing.

The Attorney General may join in a petition for a writ of actual innocence made pursuant to § 19.2-327.10. When such petition is so joined, the petitioner may file a copy of the petition and attachments thereto and the Attorney General's answer with the circuit court that entered the felony conviction and move the court for a hearing to consider release of the person on bail pursuant to Chapter 9 (§ 19.2-119 et seq.). Upon hearing and for good cause shown, the court may order the person released from custody subject to the terms and conditions of bail so established, pending a ruling by the Court of Appeals on the writ under § 19.2-327.13.

History.
2015, c. 66.

§ 19.2-327.11. Contents and form of the petition based on previously unknown or unavailable evidence of actual innocence.

A. The petitioner shall allege categorically and with specificity, under oath, all of the following: (i) the crime for which the petitioner was convicted or the offense for which the petitioner was adjudicated delinquent, and that such conviction or adjudication of delinquency was upon a plea of not guilty; (ii) that the petitioner is actually innocent of the crime for which he was convicted or the offense for which he was adjudicated delinquent; (iii) an exact description of the previously unknown or unavailable evidence supporting the allegation of innocence; (iv) that such evidence was previously unknown or unavailable to the petitioner or his trial attorney of record at the time the conviction or adjudication of delinquency became final in the circuit court; (v) the date the previously unknown or unavailable evidence became known or available to the petitioner, and the circumstances under which it was discovered; (vi) that the previously unknown or unavailable evidence is such as could not, by the exercise of diligence, have been discovered or obtained before the expiration of 21 days following entry of the final order of conviction or adjudication of delinquency by the circuit court; (vii) the previously unknown or unavailable evidence is material and, when considered with all of the other evidence in the current record, will prove that no rational trier of fact would have found proof of guilt or delinquency beyond a reasonable doubt; and (viii) the previously unknown or unavailable evidence is not merely cumulative, corroborative or collateral. Nothing in this chapter shall constitute grounds to delay setting an execution date pursuant to § 53.1-232.1 or to grant a stay of execution that has been set pursuant to clause (iii) or (iv) of § 53.1-232.1 or to delay or stay any other appeals following conviction or adjudication of delinquency, or petitions to any court. Human biological evidence may not be used as the sole basis for seeking relief under this writ but may be used in conjunction with other evidence.

B. Such petition shall contain all relevant allegations of facts that are known to the petitioner at the time of filing, shall be accompanied by all relevant documents, affidavits and test results, and shall enumerate and include all relevant previous records, applications, petitions, and appeals and their dispositions. The petition shall be filed on a form provided by the Supreme Court. If the petitioner fails to submit a completed form, the Court of Appeals may dismiss the petition or return the petition to the petitioner pending the completion of such form. Any false statement in the petition, if such statement is knowingly or willfully made, shall be a ground for prosecution of perjury as provided for in § 18.2-434.

C. In cases brought by counsel for the petitioner, the Court of Appeals shall not accept the petition unless it is accompanied by a duly executed return of service in the form of a verification that a copy of the petition and all attachments have been served on the attorney for the Commonwealth of the jurisdiction where the conviction or adjudication of delinquency occurred and the Attorney General, or an acceptance of service signed by these officials, or any combination thereof. In cases brought by petitioners pro se, the Court of Appeals shall not accept the petition unless it is accompanied by a certificate that a copy of the petition and all attachments have been sent, by certified mail, to the attorney for the Commonwealth of the jurisdiction where the conviction or adjudication of delinquency occurred and the Attorney General. If the Court of Appeals does not summarily dismiss the petition, it shall so notify in writing the Attorney General, the attorney for the Commonwealth, and the petitioner. The Attorney General shall have 60 days after receipt of such notice in which to file a response to the petition that may be extended for good cause shown; however, nothing shall prevent the Attorney General from filing an earlier response. The response may contain a proffer of any evidence pertaining to the guilt or delinquency or innocence of the petitioner that is not included in the record of the case, including evidence that was suppressed at trial.

D. The Court of Appeals may inspect the record of any trial or appellate court action, and the Court may, in any case, award a writ of certiorari to the clerk of the respective court below, and have brought before the Court the whole record or any part of any record. If, in the judgment of the Court, the petition fails to state a claim, or if the assertions of previously unknown or unavailable evidence, even if true, would fail to qualify for the granting of relief under this chapter, the Court may dismiss the petition summarily, without any hearing or a response from the Attorney General.

E. In any petition filed pursuant to this chapter that is not summarily dismissed, the petitioner is entitled to representation by counsel subject to the provisions of Article 3 (§ 19.2-157 et seq.) and Article 4 (§ 19.2-163.3 et seq.) of Chapter 10. The Court of Appeals may, in its discretion, appoint counsel prior to deciding whether a petition should be summarily dismissed.

History.
2004, c. 1024; 2013, cc. 170, 180.

§ 19.2-327.12. Determination by Court of Appeals for findings of fact by the circuit court.

If the Court of Appeals determines from the petition, from any hearing on the petition, from a review of the records of the case, or from any response from the Attorney General that a resolution of the case requires further development of the facts, the court may order the circuit court in which the order of conviction or the adjudication of delinquency was originally entered to conduct a hearing within 90 days after the order has been issued to certify findings of fact with respect to such issues as the Court of Appeals shall direct. The record and certified findings of fact of the circuit court shall be filed in the Court of Appeals within 30 days after the hearing is concluded. The petitioner or his attorney of record, the attorney for the Commonwealth and the Attorney General shall be served a copy of the order stating the specific purpose and evidence for which the hearing has been ordered.

History.
2004, c. 1024; 2013, c. 170.

§ 19.2-327.13. Relief under writ.

Upon consideration of the petition, the response by the Commonwealth, previous records of the case, the record of any hearing held under this chapter and, if applicable, any findings certified from the circuit court pursuant to an order issued under this chapter, the Court of Appeals, if it has not already summarily dismissed the petition, shall either dismiss the petition for failure to state a claim or assert grounds upon which relief shall be granted; or the Court shall (i) dismiss the petition for failure to establish previously unknown or unavailable evidence sufficient to justify the issuance of the writ, or (ii) only upon a finding that the petitioner has proven by clear and convincing evidence all of the allegations contained in clauses (iv) through (viii) of subsection A of § 19.2-327.11, and upon a finding that no rational trier of fact would have found proof of guilt or delinquency beyond a reasonable doubt, grant the writ, and vacate the conviction or finding of delinquency, or in the event that the Court finds that no rational trier of fact would have found sufficient evidence beyond a reasonable doubt as to one or more elements of the offense for which the petitioner was convicted or adjudicated delinquent, but the Court finds that there remains in the original trial record evidence sufficient to find the petitioner guilty or delinquent beyond a reasonable doubt of a lesser included offense, the Court shall modify the order of conviction or delinquency accordingly and remand the case to the circuit court that entered the conviction or adjudication of delinquency for resentencing. The burden of proof in a proceeding brought pursuant to this chapter shall be upon the convicted or delinquent person seeking relief. If a writ vacating a conviction or adjudication of delinquency is granted, and no appeal is made to the Supreme Court, or the Supreme Court denies the Commonwealth's petition for appeal or upholds the decision of the Court of Appeals to grant the writ, the Court of Appeals shall forward a copy of the writ to the circuit court, where an order of expungement shall be immediately granted.

History.
2004, c. 1024; 2007, cc. 465, 824, 883, 905; 2013, cc. 170, 180.

§ 19.2-327.14. Claims of relief.

An action under this chapter or the actions of any attorney representing the petitioner under this chapter shall not form the basis for relief in any habeas corpus proceeding. Nothing in this chapter shall create any cause of action for damages against the Commonwealth or any of its political subdivisions.

History.
2004, c. 1024.

CHAPTER 20.

TAXATION AND ALLOWANCE OF COSTS.

Section

§ 19.2-328. When jailers and sheriffs to summon or employ guards and other persons; allowances therefor.

Whenever in the discretion of the court it is necessary for the safekeeping of a prisoner under charge of, or sentence for, crime, whether the prisoner be in jail, hospital, court or elsewhere, the court may order the jailer to summon a sufficient guard, and whenever ordered by the court to do so, the sheriff of any county or city shall summon or employ temporarily such person or persons as may be needed to preserve proper order or otherwise to aid the court in its proper operation and functioning, and for such guard or other service the court may allow therefor so much as it deems proper, not exceeding the hourly equivalent of the minimum annual salary paid a full-time deputy sheriff who performs like services in the same county or city; in addition, mileage and other expenses for rendering the services shall be paid for each person, the same to be paid out of the budget allotted to the sheriff as approved by the Compensation Board, except when payment for such guard is otherwise provided under the provisions of § 53.1-94 of the Code of Virginia.

History.
Code 1950, § 19.1-308; 1960, c. 366; 1972, c. 225; 1973, c. 401; 1975, c. 495; 1981, c. 386; 1985, c. 321.

§ 19.2-329. Allowance to witnesses.

Sections 17.1-612 to 17.1-616, inclusive, shall apply to a person attending as a witness, under a recognizance or summons in a criminal case, as well as to a person attending under a summons in a civil case, except that a person residing out of this Commonwealth, who attends a court therein as a witness, shall be allowed by the court a proper compensation for attendance and travel to and from the place of his abode, the amount of the same to be fixed by the court.

History.
Code 1950, § 19.1-312; 1960, c. 366; 1975, c. 495; 1977, c. 483.

§ 19.2-330. Compensation to witnesses from out of Commonwealth.

Any witness from without the Commonwealth whose attendance is compelled under the provisions of Chapter 16, Article 2 (§ 19.2-272 et seq.) of this title shall be deemed to render a service within the meaning of § 19.2-332 and the compensation and expenses of such witness, whether on behalf of the Commonwealth or the accused, may be paid out of the state treasury in accordance with the provisions of such section. But the compensation and expenses of any witness summoned on behalf of an accused shall not be certified to the state treasury as a compensation under such section except in cases when the court or judge thereof is satisfied that the defendant is without means to pay same and is unable to provide the costs incident thereto.

History.
Code 1950, § 19.1-313; 1960, c. 366; 1975, c. 495.

§ 19.2-331. When Commonwealth pays witnesses in case of misdemeanor.

Payment shall not be made out of the state treasury to a witness attending for the Commonwealth in any prosecution for a misdemeanor unless it appears that the sum to which the witness is entitled cannot be obtained:

(1) If it be a case wherein there is a prosecutor and the defendant is convicted, by reason of the insolvency of the defendant, or

(2) If it be a case in which there is no prosecutor, by reason of the acquittal or insolvency of the defendant or other cause.

History.
Code 1950, § 19.1-314; 1960, c. 366; 1975, c. 495.

§ 19.2-332. Compensation to officer or other person for services not otherwise compensable.

Whenever in a criminal case an officer or other person renders any service required by law for which no specific compensation is provided, or whenever any other service has been rendered pursuant to the request or prior approval of the court, the court shall allow therefor such sum as it deems reasonable, including mileage at a rate provided by law, and such allowance shall be paid out of the state treasury from the appropriation for criminal charges on the certificate of the court stating the nature of the service. This section shall not prevent any payment under § 2.2-816, which could have been made if this section had not been enacted.

This section shall not be construed to authorize the payment of any additional compensation to an officer or other employee of the Commonwealth who is compensated for his services exclusively by salary unless it be otherwise expressly provided by law.

History.
Code 1950, § 19.1-315; 1960, c. 366; 1972, c. 719; 1975, c. 495.

§ 19.2-333. No state fees to attorney for the Commonwealth.

No fee to an attorney for the Commonwealth shall be payable out of the state treasury, unless it be expressly so provided.

History.
Code 1950, § 19.1-316; 1960, c. 366; 1975, c. 495.

§ 19.2-334. By whom certificate of allowance to be made; vouchers to accompany it; proof of correctness; what entry to state.

Any other expense incident to a proceeding in a criminal case which is payable out of the state treasury otherwise than under §§ 2.2-816, 19.2-330 or § 19.2-332 shall be certified by the court. If it be a judge of a district court exercising jurisdiction, it shall be certified by such judge to the Supreme Court. With the certificate of allowance there shall be transmitted to the Supreme Court the vouchers on which it is made. The court, in passing upon any account for fees or expenses required to be certified by it under this section, before certifying the account, may, in its discretion, require proof of the correctness of any item thereof.

The entry of such certificate of allowance shall state how much thereof is on account of each person prosecuted.

History.
Code 1950, §§ 19.1-317, 19.1-318; 1960, c. 366; 1975, c. 495; 1978, c. 195; 1979, c. 465.

§ 19.2-335. Judge of district court to certify to clerk of circuit court costs of proceedings in criminal cases before him.

A judge of a district court before whom there is any proceeding in a criminal case, including any proceeding which has been deferred upon probation of the defendant pursuant to § 16.1-278.8, 16.1-278.9, 18.2-61, 18.2-67.1, 18.2-67.2, 18.2-251 or 19.2-303.2, shall certify to the clerk of the circuit court of his county or city, and a judge or court before whom there is, in a criminal case, any proceeding preliminary to conviction in another court, upon receiving information of the conviction from the clerk of the court wherein it is, shall certify to such clerk, all the expenses incident to such proceedings which are payable out of the state treasury.

History.
Code 1950, § 19.1-319; 1960, c. 366; 1968, c. 639; 1975, c. 495; 1995, c. 485; 2005, c. 631.

§ 19.2-336. Clerk to make up statement of whole cost, and issue execution therefor.

In every criminal case the clerk of the circuit court in which the accused is found guilty or is placed on probation during deferral of the proceedings pursuant to § 16.1-278.8, 16.1-278.9, 18.2-61, 18.2-67.1, 18.2-67.2, 18.2-251 or 19.2-303.2, or, if the conviction is in a district court, the clerk to which the judge thereof certifies as aforesaid, shall, as soon as may be, make up a statement of all the expenses incident to the prosecution, including such as are certified under § 19.2-335, and execution for the amount of such expenses shall be issued and proceeded with. Chapter 21 (§ 19.2-339 et seq.) shall apply thereto in like manner as if, on the day of completing the statement, there was a judgment in such court in favor of the Commonwealth against the accused for such amount as a fine. However, in any case in which an accused waives trial by jury, at least 10 days before trial, but the Commonwealth or the court trying the case refuses to so waive, then the cost of the jury shall not be included in such statement or judgment recorded pursuant to § 17.1-275.5.

History.
Code 1950, § 19.1-320; 1960, c. 366; 1970, c. 429; 1975, c. 495; 1978, c. 716; 1995, c. 485; 2005, c. 631; 2012, c. 714.

§ 19.2-337. Claims not presented in time to be disallowed.

If by reason of the failure of a person to present his claim in due time a sum be not included in such execution which would have been included if so presented, such claim, unless there be good cause for the failure, shall be disallowed.

History.
Code 1950, § 19.1-321; 1960, c. 366; 1975, c. 495.

§ 19.2-338. Collection by town of cost of transporting prisoners.

(1) Notwithstanding any provision of any charter or any law to the contrary, any town may provide that any person convicted of violating any ordinance of the town may be charged, in addition to all other costs, fines, fees and charges, the costs of transporting such person so convicted to and from a jail or other penal institution outside the corporate limits of such town designated by the town as a place of confinement for persons arrested for violating the ordinances of the town and required to be held in jail pending trial upon such charge. The cost of such transportation shall be taxed as a part of the costs payable by persons convicted of violating such ordinances.

(2) No officer transporting any person convicted of violating any ordinance of the town, as provided in subsection (1) hereof, shall charge or be paid, nor shall such town receive directly or indirectly, more than the cost of transporting such person when more than one person is transported.

History.
Code 1950, § 19.1-322; 1960, c. 366; 1975, c. 495; 1995, c. 51.

CHAPTER 21.

RECOVERY OF FINES AND PENALTIES.

Article 1.

Proceedings to Recover.

Article 2.

Reports, etc., of Fines and Costs.

Article 3.

Collection and Disposition of Fines.

Article 4.

Payment of Fines and Costs on Installment Basis, etc.

Article 5.

Receipts for Fines.

Article 6.

Relief from Fines and Penalties.

ARTICLE 1.

PROCEEDINGS TO RECOVER.

§ 19.2-339. Word "fine" construed.

Whenever the word *"fine"* is used in this chapter, it shall be construed to refer solely to the pecuniary penalty imposed by a court or jury upon a defendant who has been found guilty of a crime. The word "fine" shall not include other forfeitures, penalties, costs, amercements or the like, even though they follow as a consequence of conviction of crime.

History.
Code 1950, § 19.1-323; 1960, c. 366; 1975, c. 495.

§ 19.2-340. Fines; how recovered; in what name.

When any statute or ordinance prescribes a fine, unless it is otherwise expressly provided or would be inconsistent with the manifest intention of the General Assembly, it shall be paid to the Commonwealth if prescribed by a statute and recoverable by presentment, indictment, information or warrant and paid to the locality if prescribed by an ordinance and recoverable by warrant. Fines imposed and costs taxed in a criminal or traffic prosecution, including a prosecution for a violation of an ordinance adopted pursuant to § 46.2-1220, for committing an offense shall constitute a judgment and, if not paid at the time they are imposed, execution may issue thereon in the same manner as upon any other monetary judgment, subject to the period of limitations provided by § 19.2-341.

History.
Code 1950, § 19.1-324; 1960, c. 366; 1975, c. 495; 1995, c. 438.

§ 19.2-340.1. Disposition of fines in criminal cases.

When a law-enforcement officer of (i) the Department of State Police or (ii) any other division of the state government makes an arrest or issues a summons for a violation of a provision of the Code of Virginia, the person arrested or summoned shall be charged with a violation of that Code provision and shall not be charged with a substantially similar local ordinance. All fines collected upon conviction of any person so arrested or summoned shall be credited to the Literary Fund.

History.
2012, c. 749.

§ 19.2-341. Penalties other than fines; how recovered; in what name; limitation of actions.

When any statute or ordinance prescribes a monetary penalty other than a fine, unless it is otherwise expressly provided or would be inconsistent with the manifest intention of the General Assembly, it shall be paid to the Commonwealth if prescribed by a statute and paid to the locality if prescribed by an ordinance and recoverable by warrant, presentment, indictment, or information. Penalties imposed and costs taxed in any such proceeding shall constitute a judgment and, if not paid at the time they are imposed, execution may issue thereon in the same manner as upon any other monetary judgment. No such proceeding of any nature, however, shall be brought or had for the recovery of such a penalty or costs due the Commonwealth or any political subdivision thereof, unless within twenty years from the date of the offense or delinquency giving rise to imposition of such penalty if imposed by a circuit court, or within ten years if imposed by a general district court.

History.
Code 1950, § 19.1-324; 1960, c. 366; 1975, c. 495; 1983, c. 499; 1995, c. 438.

§ 19.2-342. Where and in what court proceeding to be.

In a proceeding under § 19.2-341, such warrant, presentment, indictment or information shall be in the county or city wherein the offense was committed or the delinquency occurred.

History.
Code 1950, § 19.1-325; 1960, c. 366; 1975, c. 495.

§§ 19.2-343, 19.2-344: Reserved.

ARTICLE 2.
REPORTS, ETC., OF FINES AND COSTS.

§§ 19.2-345, 19.2-346: Repealed by Acts 1988, c. 509.

§ 19.2-347: Repealed by Acts 1983, c. 499.

ARTICLE 3.
COLLECTION AND DISPOSITION OF FINES.

§ 19.2-348. Attorneys for Commonwealth or clerks to superintend issue of executions, etc.

The attorney for the Commonwealth or the clerk of the circuit court shall superintend the issuing of all executions or judgments for fines and penalties going wholly or in part to the Commonwealth or a county, city or town, in the circuit court or appropriate district court of his county or city.

History.
Code 1950, § 19.1-341.1; 1960, c. 366; 1975, c. 495; 1983, c. 499; 1992, c. 623; 1994, c. 811.

§ 19.2-349. Responsibility for collections; clerks to report unsatisfied fines, etc.; duty of attorneys for Commonwealth; duties of Department of Taxation.

A. The clerk of the circuit court and district court of every county and city shall submit to the judge of his court, the Department of Taxation, the State Compensation Board and the attorney for the Commonwealth of his county or city a monthly report of all fines, costs, forfeitures and penalties which are delinquent more than 30 days, including court-ordered restitution of a sum certain, imposed in his court for a violation of state law or a local ordinance which remain unsatisfied, including those which are delinquent in installment payments. The monthly report shall include the social security number or driver's license number of the defendant, if known, and such other information as the Department of Taxation and the Compensation Board deem appropriate. The Executive Secretary shall make the report required by this subsection on behalf of those clerks who participate in the Supreme Court's automated information system.

B. It shall be the duty of the attorney for the Commonwealth to cause proper proceedings to be instituted for the collection and satisfaction of all fines, costs, forfeitures, penalties and restitution. The attorney for the Commonwealth shall determine whether it would be impractical or uneconomical for such service to be rendered by the office of the attorney for the Commonwealth. If the defendant does not enter into an installment payment agreement under § 19.2-354, the attorney for the Com-

Criminal Procedure

monwealth and the clerk may agree to a process by which collection activity may be commenced 30 days after judgment.

If the attorney for the Commonwealth does not undertake collection, he shall contract with (i) private attorneys or private collection agencies, (ii) enter into an agreement with a local governing body, (iii) enter into an agreement with the county or city treasurer, or (iv) use the services of the Department of Taxation, upon such terms and conditions as may be established by guidelines promulgated by the Office of the Attorney General, the Executive Secretary of the Supreme Court with the Department of Taxation and the Compensation Board. If the attorney for the Commonwealth undertakes collection, he shall follow the procedures established by the Department of Taxation and the Compensation Board. Such guidelines shall not supersede contracts between attorneys for the Commonwealth and private attorneys and collection agencies when active collection efforts are being undertaken. As part of such contract, private attorneys or collection agencies shall be given access to the social security number of the defendant in order to assist in the collection effort. Any such private attorney shall be subject to the penalties and provisions of § 18.2-186.3.

The fees of any private attorneys or collection agencies shall be paid on a contingency fee basis out of the proceeds of the amounts collected. However, in no event shall such attorney or collection agency receive a fee for amounts collected by the Department of Taxation under the Setoff Debt Collection Act (§ 58.1-520 et seq.). A local treasurer undertaking collection pursuant to an agreement with the attorney for the Commonwealth may collect the administrative fee authorized by § 58.1-3958.

C. The Department of Taxation and the State Compensation Board shall be responsible for the collection of any judgment which remains unsatisfied or does not meet the conditions of § 19.2-354. Persons owing such unsatisfied judgments or failing to comply with installment payment agreements under § 19.2-354 shall be subject to the delinquent tax collection provisions of Title 58.1. The Department of Taxation and the State Compensation Board shall establish procedures to be followed by clerks of courts, attorneys for the Commonwealth, other state agencies and any private attorneys or collection agents and may employ private attorneys or collection agencies, or engage other state agencies to collect the judgment. The Department of Taxation and the Commonwealth shall be entitled to deduct a fee for services from amounts collected for violations of local ordinances.

The Department of Taxation and the State Compensation Board shall annually report to the Governor and the General Assembly the total of fines, costs, forfeitures and penalties assessed, collected, and unpaid and those which remain unsatisfied or do not meet the conditions of § 19.2-354 by each circuit and district court. The report shall include the procedures established by the Department of Taxation and the State Compensation Board pursuant to this section and a plan for increasing the collection of unpaid fines, costs, forfeitures and penalties. The Auditor of Public Accounts shall annually report to the Governor, the Executive Secretary of the Supreme Court and the General Assembly as to the adherence of clerks of courts, attorneys for the Commonwealth and other state agencies to the procedures established by the Department of Taxation and the State Compensation Board.

History.

Code 1950, § 19.1-341.2; 1960, c. 366; 1975, c. 495; 1979, c. 469; 1983, cc. 415, 499; 1988, cc. 742, 750, 770, 852; 1991, c. 202; 1992, c. 623; 1993, c. 269; 1994, cc. 841, 945; 2001, c. 414; 2003, c. 262; 2006, c. 359; 2007, c. 551; 2012, c. 615.

§ 19.2-349.1. Receipt of unpaid fines, costs, forfeitures, penalties, or restitution by Department of Motor Vehicles.

At the direction of the Committee on District Courts or at the request of a circuit court clerk, the Executive Secretary of the Supreme Court may enter into an agreement with the Commissioner of the Department of Motor Vehicles authorizing the Department of Motor Vehicles to receive, on behalf of a district or circuit court, payment of any delinquent fines, costs, forfeitures, and penalties, including any court-ordered restitution of a sum certain, imposed by a court for the violation of a state law or a local ordinance. However, in no case shall the Department of Motor Vehicles be authorized to establish an installment plan for any such payments or to receive partial payment of the full amount imposed by the court for the violation of a state law or a local ordinance.

For each such payment it receives, the Department of Motor Vehicles may impose and collect a processing fee, to be used to defray the costs of the transaction to the Department. Such transaction fee shall be $2, unless payment is made by credit card or debit card and the merchant's fees and other transaction costs imposed by the card issuer are charged to the Department of Motor Vehicles, in which case the processing fee shall be the greater of (i) $2 or (ii) an amount not to exceed four percent of the amount of the payment. The Department may also collect any processing fee charged by a private vendor operating under contract to distribute to the court payments received by the Department. All processing fees imposed and collected by the Department of Motor Vehicles under this section shall be in addition to the other fees specified in this chapter. All such processing fees collected by the Department of Motor Vehicles shall be paid into the state treasury as provided in § 46.2-206 and used to meet the expenses of the Department of Motor Vehicles. The service charge provided under § 46.2-212.1 shall not be added to the processing fee authorized under this section. Other fees specified in this chapter, including those payable pursuant to collections contracts made by attorneys for the Commonwealth, shall not be diminished or offset due to receipt of payments by the Department of Motor Vehicles.

History.
2015, c. 228.

§ 19.2-350. When sheriff not to receive fines.

No sheriff or other law-enforcement officer shall receive any fine, penalty or costs imposed by a court not of record, except under process duly issued.

History.
Code 1950, § 19.1-342; 1960, c. 366; 1975, c. 495.

§ 19.2-351. How fines disposed of; informer.

Although a law may allow an informer or person prosecuting to have part of a fine or penalty, the whole thereof shall go to the Commonwealth, unless the name of such informer or prosecutor be endorsed on, or written at the foot of, the presentment at the time it is made, or of the indictment before it is presented to the grand jury, or of the information before it is filed, or of the writ issued in the action, or the process on the warrant, or the notice of the motion before service of such writ, process, or notice.

History.
Code 1950, § 19.1-344; 1960, c. 366; 1975, c. 495.

§ 19.2-352. Officers to pay fines to clerks; default; forfeiture, etc.

Every sheriff or other officer receiving money under a writ of fieri facias or capias pro fine shall pay the same to the clerk of the court from which such process issued, on or before the return day of such process; and if such sheriff or other officer fail to pay the money, or fail to return such writ of fieri facias or capias pro fine, he shall, for every such failure, unless good cause be shown therefor, forfeit twenty dollars; and the clerk shall, within ten days from the return day of such process, report the failure to pay such money, or to return such process, to the attorney for the Commonwealth, who shall proceed at once against such officer in default to recover such money and the forfeiture aforesaid.

History.
Code 1950, § 19.1-345; 1960, c. 366; 1975, c. 495.

§ 19.2-353. Certain fines paid into Literary Fund.

The proceeds of all fines and penalties collected for offenses committed against the Commonwealth, and directed by Article VIII, Section 8 of the Constitution of Virginia to be set apart as a part of a perpetual and permanent literary fund, shall be paid and collected only in lawful money of the United States, and shall be paid into the state treasury to the credit of the Literary Fund, and shall be used for no other purpose whatsoever.

History.
Code 1950, § 19.1-346; 1960, c. 366; 1971, Ex. Sess., c. 1; 1975, c. 495.

§ 19.2-353.1. Fieri facias and proceedings thereon.

Any writ of fieri facias issued under this chapter and the proceedings on the same shall conform to the writ of fieri facias and proceedings thereon under Article 19 (§ 8.01-196 et seq.) of Chapter 3 of Title 8.01.

History.
Code 1950, § 19.1-347; 1960, c. 366; 1975, c. 495.

§ 19.2-353.2: Repealed by Acts 1988, cc. 770, 852.

§ 19.2-353.3. Acceptance of checks and credit or debit cards in lieu of money; additional fee.

Notwithstanding the provisions of § 19.2-353, personal checks and credit or debit cards shall be accepted in lieu of money to collect and secure all fees, fines, restitution, forfeiture, penalties and costs collected for offenses tried in a district court, including motor vehicle violations, committed against the Commonwealth or against any county, city or town. Notwithstanding the provisions of § 19.2-353, personal checks shall be accepted in lieu of money to collect and secure all fees, fines, restitution, forfeiture, penalties and costs collected for offenses tried in a circuit court, including motor vehicle violations, committed against the Commonwealth or against any county, city or town. The clerk of any circuit court shall not be required to but may, in his discretion, accept credit or debit card payment in lieu of money to collect and secure all fees, including filing fees, fines, restitution, forfeitures, penalties, and costs collected. The Committee on District Courts shall devise a procedure for approving and accepting checks and credit or debit cards that shall be accepted by the district courts. Court personnel shall not be held to be guarantors of the payment made in such manner and shall not be personally liable for any sums uncollected. The clerk of the court, in addition to any fees, fines, restitution, forfeiture, penalties or costs, may add to such payment a sum not to exceed four percent of the amount paid for the transaction, or a flat fee not to exceed $2 per transaction, as a reasonable convenience fee for the acceptance of a credit or debit card.

If a check is returned unpaid by the financial institution on which it is drawn or notice is received from the credit or debit card issuer that payment will not be made, for any reason, the fees, fine, restitution, forfeiture, penalty or costs shall be treated as unpaid, and the court may pursue all available remedies to obtain payment. The clerk of the court to whom the dishonored check or credit or debit card was tendered may impose a fee of $50 or 10 percent of the value of the payment, whichever is greater, in addition to the fine and costs already imposed.

The clerk of court may refuse acceptance of checks or credit or debit cards of an individual if (i) he has been convicted of a violation of Chapter 6 (§ 18.2-168 et seq.) of Title 18.2 in which a check, credit or debit card, or credit or debit card information was used to commit the offense, (ii) he has previously tendered to the court a check which was not ultimately honored or a credit or debit card or credit or debit card information which did not ultimately result in payment by the credit or debit card issuer, (iii) authorization of payment is not given by the bank or credit or debit card issuer, (iv) the validity of the check or credit or debit card cannot be verified, or (v) the payee of the check is other than the court.

History.

1979, c. 525; 1988, cc. 770, 852; 1990, c. 899; 1994, cc. 432, 841, 945; 1997, c. 819; 1998, cc. 720, 731; 2001, cc. 481, 501; 2009, c. 594; 2012, cc. 420, 714.

§ **19.2-353.4:** Repealed by Acts 1988, cc. 770, 852.

§ 19.2-353.5. Interest on fines and costs.

No interest shall accrue on any fine or costs imposed in a criminal case or in a case involving a traffic infraction for a period of 40 days from the date of the final judgment imposing such fine or costs or during any period the defendant is incarcerated. A person who owes fines and costs on which interest has accrued during a period of incarceration may move any court in which he owes fines and costs to waive the interest that accrued on such fines and costs during such period of incarceration. Upon certification of the period of incarceration by the superintendent, warden, or other official in charge of a correctional facility on a form developed by the Office of the Executive Secretary of the Supreme Court, such interest shall be waived. In no event shall interest accrue in such cases during any period in which a fine, costs, or both a fine and costs are being paid in deferred or installment payments pursuant to an order of the court. Whenever interest on any unpaid fine or costs accrues, it shall accrue at the judgment rate of interest set forth in § 6.2-302.

History.

1987, c. 648; 1988, cc. 106, 508; 1995, cc. 375, 566; 1996, c. 226; 2016, c. 282.

ARTICLE 4.

PAYMENT OF FINES AND COSTS ON INSTALLMENT BASIS, ETC.

§ 19.2-354. Authority of court to order payment of fine, costs, forfeitures, penalties or restitution in installments or upon other terms and conditions; community work in lieu of payment.

A. Whenever (i) a defendant, convicted of a traffic infraction or a violation of any criminal law of the Commonwealth or of any political subdivision thereof, or found not innocent in the case of a juvenile, is sentenced to pay a fine, restitution, forfeiture or penalty and (ii) the defendant is unable to make payment of the fine, restitution, forfeiture, or penalty and costs within 30 days of sentencing, the court shall order the defendant to pay such fine, restitution, forfeiture or penalty and any costs which the defendant may be required to pay in deferred payments or installments. The court assessing the fine, restitution, forfeiture, or penalty and costs may authorize the clerk to establish and approve individual deferred or installment payment agreements. Any payment agreement authorized under this section shall be consistent with the Rules of Supreme Court of Virginia, including any required minimum payments or other required conditions. The requirements established by the Rules of Supreme Court of Virginia shall be posted in the clerk's office and on the court's website, if a website is available. As a condition of every such agreement, a defendant who enters into an installment or deferred payment agreement shall promptly inform the court of any change of mailing address during the term of the agreement. If the defendant is unable to make payment within 30 days of sentencing, the court may assess a one-time fee not to exceed $10 to cover the costs of management of the defendant's account until such account is paid in full. This one-time fee shall not apply to cases in which costs are assessed pursuant to § 17.1-275.1, 17.1-275.2, 17.1-275.3, 17.1-275.4, 17.1-275.7, 17.1-275.8, or 17.1-275.9. Installment or deferred payment agreements shall include terms for payment if the defendant participates in a program as provided in subsection B or C. The court, if such sum or sums are not paid in full by the date ordered, shall proceed in accordance with § 19.2-358.

B. When a person sentenced to the Department of Corrections or a local correctional facility owes any fines, costs, forfeitures, restitution or penalties, he shall be required as a condition of participating in any work release, home/electronic incarceration or nonconsecutive days program as set forth in § 53.1-60, 53.1-131, 53.1-131.1, or 53.1-131.2 to either make full payment or make payments in accordance with his installment or deferred payment agreement while participating in such program. If, after the person has an installment or deferred payment agreement, the person fails to pay as ordered, his participation in the program may be terminated until all fines, costs, forfeitures, restitution and penalties are satisfied. The Director of the Department of Corrections and any sheriff or other administrative head of any local correctional facility shall withhold such ordered payments from any amounts due to such person. Distribution of the money collected shall be made in the following order of priority to:

1. Meet the obligation of any judicial or administrative order to provide support and such funds shall be disbursed according to the terms of such order;
2. Pay any fines, restitution or costs as ordered by the court;
3. Pay travel and other such expenses made necessary by his work release employment or participation in an education or rehabilitative program, including the sums specified in § 53.1-150; and
4. Defray the offender's keep.

The balance shall be credited to the offender's account or sent to his family in an amount the offender so chooses.

The Board of Corrections shall promulgate regulations governing the receipt of wages paid to persons participating in such programs, the withholding of payments and the disbursement of appropriate funds.

C. The court shall establish a program and may provide an option to any person upon whom a fine and costs have been imposed to discharge all or part of the fine or costs by earning credits for the performance of community service work before or after imprisonment. The program shall specify the rate at which credits are earned and provide for the manner of applying earned credits against the fine or costs. The court shall have such other authority as is reasonably necessary for or incidental to carrying out this program.

D. When the court has authorized deferred payment or installment payments, the clerk shall give notice to the defendant that upon his failure to pay as ordered he may be fined or imprisoned pursuant to § 19.2-358 and his privilege to operate a motor vehicle will be suspended pursuant to § 46.2-395.

E. The failure of the defendant to enter into a deferred payment or installment payment agreement with the court or the failure of the defendant to make payments as ordered by the agreement shall allow the Tax Commissioner to act in accordance with § 19.2-349 to collect all fines, costs, forfeitures and penalties.

History.

Code 1950, § 19.1-347.1; 1971 Ex. Sess., c. 250; 1975, c. 495; 1977, c. 585; 1982, c. 244; 1984, c. 32; 1986, c. 230; 1988, cc. 770, 852; 1994, cc. 841, 945; 1995, cc. 380, 441; 1996, c. 273; 1998, c. 831; 1999, c. 9; 2001, c. 414; 2002, c. 831; 2009, c. 741; 2012, c. 615; 2015, c. 265; 2016, c. 282.

§ 19.2-355. Petition of defendant.

(a) In determining whether the defendant is unable to pay such fine forthwith, the court may require such defendant to file a petition, under oath, with the court, upon a form provided by the court, setting forth the financial condition of the defendant.

(b) Such form shall be a questionnaire, and shall include, but shall not be limited to: the name and residence of the defendant; his occupation, if any; his family status and the number of persons dependent upon him; his monthly income; whether or not his dependents are employed and, if so, their approximate monthly income; his banking accounts, if any; real estate owned by the defendant, or any interest he may have in real estate; income produced therefrom; any independent income accruing to the defendant; tangible and intangible personal property owned by the defendant, or in which he may have an interest; and a statement listing the approximate indebtedness of the defendant to other persons. Such form shall also include a payment plan of the defendant, if the court should exercise its discretion in permitting the payment of such fine and costs in installments or other conditions to be fixed by the court. At the end of such form there shall be printed in bold face type, in a distinctive color the following: THIS STATEMENT IS MADE UNDER OATH, ANY FALSE STATEMENT OF A MATERIAL FACT TO ANY QUESTION CONTAINED HEREIN SHALL CONSTITUTE PERJURY UNDER THE PROVISIONS OF § 18.2-434 OF THE CODE OF VIRGINIA. THE MAXIMUM PENALTY FOR PERJURY IS CONFINEMENT IN THE PENITENTIARY FOR A PERIOD OF TEN YEARS. A copy of the petition shall be retained by the defendant.

(c) If the defendant is unable to read or write, the court, or the clerk, may assist the defendant in completing the petition and require him to affix his mark thereto. The consequences of the making of a false statement shall be explained to such defendant.

History.

Code 1950, § 19.1-347.2; 1971, Ex. Sess., c. 250; 1975, c. 495.

§ 19.2-356. Payment of fine or costs as condition of probation or suspension of sentence.

If a defendant is placed on probation, or imposition or execution of sentence is suspended, or both, the court may make payment of any fine, or costs, or fine and costs, either on a certain date or on an installment basis, a condition of probation or suspension of sentence.

History.
Code 1950, § 19.1-347.3; 1971, Ex. Sess., c. 250; 1975, c. 495; 1987, c. 238.

§ 19.2-357. Requiring that defendant be of peace and good behavior until fine and costs are paid.

If a defendant is permitted to pay a fine or fine and costs on an installment basis, or under such other conditions as the court shall fix under the provisions of § 19.2-354, the court may require as a condition that the defendant be of peace and good behavior until the fine and costs are paid.

History.
Code 1950, § 19.1-347.4; 1971, Ex. Sess., c. 250; 1975, c. 495.

§ 19.2-358. Procedure on default in deferred payment or installment payment of fine, costs, forfeiture, restitution or penalty.

A. When an individual obligated to pay a fine, costs, forfeiture, restitution or penalty defaults in the payment or any installment payment, the court upon the motion of the Commonwealth in the case of a conviction of a violation of a state law, or attorney for a locality or for the Commonwealth in the event of a conviction of a violation of a local law or ordinance, or upon its own motion, may require him to show cause why he should not be confined in jail or fined for nonpayment. A show cause proceeding shall not be required prior to issuance of a capias if an order to appear on a date certain in the event of nonpayment was issued pursuant to subsection A of § 19.2-354 and the defendant failed to appear.

B. Following the order to show cause or following a capias issued for a defendant's failure to comply with a court order to appear issued pursuant to subsection A of § 19.2-354, unless the defendant shows that his default was not attributable to an intentional refusal to obey the sentence of the court, or not attributable to a failure on his part to make a good faith effort to obtain the necessary funds for payment, or unless the defendant shows that any failure to appear was not attributable to an intentional refusal to obey the order of the court, the court may order the defendant confined as for a contempt for a term not to exceed sixty days or impose a fine not to exceed $500. The court may provide in its order that payment or satisfaction of the amounts in default at any time will entitle the defendant to his release from such confinement or, after entering the order, may at any time reduce the sentence for good cause shown, including payment or satisfaction of such amounts.

C. If it appears that the default is excusable under the standards set forth in subsection B hereof, the court may enter an order allowing the defendant additional time for payment, reducing the amount due or of each installment, or remitting the unpaid portion in whole or in part.

D. Nothing in this section shall be deemed to alter or interfere with the collection of fines by any means authorized for the enforcement of money judgments rendered in favor of the Commonwealth or any locality within the Commonwealth.

History.
Code 1950, § 19.1-347.6; 1973, c. 342; 1975, c. 495; 1977, c. 223; 1987, c. 238; 1988, cc. 770, 852; 1992, c. 485; 1994, c. 546.

ARTICLE 5.

RECEIPTS FOR FINES.

§ 19.2-359. Official receipts to be given for fines.

Every officer collecting a fine, fine and costs or costs when no fine is imposed shall give an official receipt therefor to the person making the payment, and the clerk of the court shall use the official receipt in receipting to a court not of record for payments made to the clerk; and when the fine, fine and costs or costs are collected by execution, the clerk shall receipt to the officer making payment to him upon the official receipts.

History.
Code 1950, § 19.1-348; 1960, c. 366; 1975, c. 495.

§ 19.2-360. Forms of receipts; distribution; record of disposition.

The Executive Secretary of the Supreme Court shall prescribe and prepare forms of official receipts for fines and distribute them to the clerks of the circuit courts and to the clerks of the district courts for their use. A record of the disposition of each receipt form shall be maintained as prescribed by the Executive Secretary.

History.
Code 1950, § 19.1-349; 1960, c. 366; 1972, c. 97; 1975, c. 495; 1977, c. 465.

§ 19.2-361. Misuse, misappropriation or willful failure to account for fines is embezzlement.

If any officer misuse, misappropriate, or willfully fail to return or account for, a fine collected by him he shall be deemed guilty of embezzlement and shall be punished as for the embezzlement of public funds and the failure, without good cause, to produce or account for any receipt form received by him shall be prima facie evidence of his embezzlement of the amount represented thereby.

History.
Code 1950, § 19.1-350; 1960, c. 366; 1975, c. 495.

ARTICLE 6.

RELIEF FROM FINES AND PENALTIES.

§ 19.2-362. Court not to remit fine or penalty, other than fine for contempt, except as provided in § 19.2-358.

No court shall remit any fine or penalty, except for a contempt, which the court during the same term may remit either wholly or in part, and except as provided in § 19.2-358. This section shall not impair the judicial power of the court to set aside a verdict or judgment, or to grant a new trial.

History.
Code 1950, § 19.1-351; 1960, c. 366; 1971, Ex. Sess., c. 250; 1975, c. 495.

§ 19.2-363. Authority of Governor to grant relief from fines and penalties.

The Governor shall have power, in his discretion, to remit, in whole or in part, fines and penalties, in all cases of felony or misdemeanor, after conviction, whether paid into the state treasury or not, except when judgment shall have been rendered against any person for contempt of court, for nonperformance of or disobedience to some order, decree or judgment of such court, or when the fine or penalty has been imposed by the State Corporation Commission, or when the prosecution has been carried on by the House of Delegates. The Governor may, in his discretion, remit, refund or release, in whole or in part, any forfeited recognizance or any judgment rendered thereon, provided, in the opinion of the Governor, the evidence accompanying such application warrants the granting of the relief asked for. But the provisions of the three following sections and § 19.2-368 shall be complied with as a condition precedent to such action by the Governor; provided, that when the party against whom the fine or penalty has been imposed and judgment rendered therefor has departed this life leaving a spouse or children surviving, the Governor may remit such fine or penalty upon the certificate of the judge of the circuit court of the county or city wherein such fine or penalty was imposed and judgment rendered, that to enforce the same against the estate, real or personal, of the decedent, would impose hardship upon the spouse or children. In any case when the Governor remits, in whole or in part, a fine or penalty, if the same has been paid into the state treasury, on the order of the Governor such fine or penalty or so much thereof as is remitted shall be paid by the State Treasurer, on the warrant of the Comptroller, out of the fund into which the fine or penalty was paid.

History.
Code 1950, § 19.1-352; 1960, c. 366; 1975, c. 495.

§ 19.2-364. Petition for relief; in what court filed; notice to attorney for Commonwealth.

Such person or his personal representative, as the case may be, shall file a petition in the clerk's office of the circuit court of the county or city wherein such fine or penalty was imposed, or such liability established, at least fifteen days before the term of the court at which the same is to be heard, and shall set forth the grounds upon which relief is asked. Ten days' notice thereof in writing shall be given to the attorney for the Commonwealth of the county or city.

History.
Code 1950, § 19.1-353; 1960, c. 366; 1975, c. 495.

§ 19.2-365. Duties of attorney for Commonwealth upon filing of such petition.

The attorney for the Commonwealth, at or before the hearing of such petition, shall file an answer to the same. He shall cause to be summoned such witnesses and shall introduce all such testimony as may be necessary and proper to protect the interest of the Commonwealth; and the petitioner may cause to be summoned such witnesses and shall introduce all such testimony as may be necessary and proper to protect his interest.

History.
Code 1950, § 19.1-354; 1960, c. 366; 1975, c. 495.

§ 19.2-366. Duty of court in which petition filed; certificate and opinion.

The court wherein such petition is filed shall hear all such testimony as may be offered, either by the petitioner or attorney for the Commonwealth, and after the evidence has been heard shall cause to be made out by the clerk of the court a certificate of the facts proved, and file with the same an opinion, in writing, as to the propriety of granting the relief prayed for.

History.
Code 1950, § 19.1-355; 1960, c. 366; 1975, c. 495.

§ 19.2-367. Proceedings to be according to common law.

All proceedings had before the court under the provisions of the three preceding sections shall be according to the course of the common-law practice, except that no formal pleadings shall be necessary.

History.
Code 1950, § 19.1-356; 1960, c. 366; 1975, c. 495.

§ 19.2-368. Course of proceeding when relief asked of the Governor.

Whenever application shall be made to the Governor by or on behalf of any person desiring to be relieved, in whole or in part, of any such fine or penalty, the petition, answer, certificate of facts, and opinion of the court provided for in §§ 19.2-364, 19.2-365 and 19.2-366, duly authenticated by the clerk of the court, shall accompany the application, which shall be in writing. In all cases in which the Governor shall remit a fine or penalty he shall issue his order to the clerk of the court by which such fine or penalty was imposed; or if such fine or penalty was imposed by a court not of record, to the clerk of the circuit court of the county or city in which the judge of such court not of record holds office, and such court shall, at its next term, or immediately, if then in session, cause such order to be spread upon the law order book of its court; and the clerk of such court shall immediately, upon the receipt of such order, mark the judgment for such fine or penalty, and costs, or so much thereof as the person may have been relieved of, "remitted by the Governor," upon the Judgment Lien Docket of the court of the county or city in which it may have been recorded. The Governor shall communicate to the General Assembly at each session the particulars of every case of fine or penalty remitted, with his reason for remitting the same.

History.
Code 1950, § 19.1-357; 1960, c. 366; 1975, c. 495.

CHAPTER 21.1.
COMPENSATING VICTIMS OF CRIME.

Section

Section

§ 19.2-368.1. Findings; legislative intent.

The General Assembly finds that many innocent persons suffer personal physical injury or death as a result of criminal acts or in their efforts to prevent crime or apprehend persons committing or attempting to commit crimes. Such persons or their dependents may thereby suffer disability, incur financial hardships or become dependent upon public assistance. The General Assembly finds and determines that there is a need for governmental financial assistance for such victims of crime. Therefore, it is the intent of the General Assembly that aid, care and support be provided by the Commonwealth as a matter of moral responsibility for such victims of crime.

History.
1976, c. 605.

§ 19.2-368.2. Definitions.

For the purpose of this chapter:

"Claimant" means the person filing a claim pursuant to this chapter.

"Commission" means the Virginia Workers' Compensation Commission.

"Crime" means an act committed by any person in the Commonwealth of Virginia which would constitute a crime as defined by the Code of Virginia or at common law. However, no act involving the operation of a motor vehicle which results in injury shall constitute a crime for the purpose of this chapter unless the injuries (i) were intentionally inflicted through the use of such vehicle or (ii) resulted from a violation of § 18.2-51.4 or 18.2-266 or from a felony violation of § 46.2-894.

"Family," when used with reference to a person, means (i) any person related to such person within the third degree of consanguinity or affinity, (ii) any person residing in the same household with such person, or (iii) a spouse.

"Sexual abuse" means sexual abuse as defined in subdivision 6 of § 18.2-67.10 and acts constituting rape, sodomy, object sexual penetration or sexual battery as defined in Article 7 (§ 18.2-61 et seq.) of Chapter 4 of Title 18.2.

"Victim" means a person who suffers personal physical injury or death as a direct result of a crime including a person who is injured or killed as a result of foreign terrorism or who suffers personal emotional injury as a direct result of being the subject of a violent felony offense as defined in subsection C of § 17.1-805, or stalking as described in § 18.2-60.3, or attempted robbery or abduction.

History.

1976, c. 605; 1984, c. 619; 1988, c. 748; 1990, c. 620; 1997, cc. 528, 691; 1998, c. 484; 1999, c. 286; 2001, c. 855; 2008, c. 590; 2012, c. 38.

§ 19.2-368.3. Powers and duties of Commission.

The Commission shall have the following powers and duties in the administration of the provisions of this chapter:

1. To adopt, promulgate, amend and rescind suitable rules and regulations to carry out the provisions and purposes of this chapter, to include a distinct policy (i) for the payment of physical evidence recovery kit examinations and (ii) to require each health care provider as defined in § 8.01-581.1 that provides services under this chapter to negotiate with the Commission or its designee to establish prospective agreements relating to rates for payment of claims for such services allowed under § 19.2-368.11:1, such rates to discharge the obligation to the provider in full except where the provider is an agency of the Commonwealth and the claimant receives a third party recovery in addition to the payment from the Fund.

2. Notwithstanding the provisions of § 2.2-3706, to acquire from the attorneys for the Commonwealth, State Police, local police departments, sheriffs' departments, and the Chief Medical Examiner such investigative results, information and data as will enable the Commission to determine if, in fact, a crime was committed or attempted, and the extent, if any, to which the victim or claimant was responsible for his own injury. These data shall include prior adult arrest records and juvenile court disposition records of the offender. For such purposes and in accordance with § 16.1-305, the Commission may also acquire from the juvenile and domestic relations district courts a copy of the order of disposition relating to the crime. The use of any information received by the Commission pursuant to this subdivision shall be limited to carrying out the purposes set forth in this section, and this information shall be confidential and shall not be disseminated further. The agency from which the information is requested may submit original reports, portions thereof, summaries, or such other configurations of information as will comply with the requirements of this section.

3. To hear and determine all claims for awards filed with the Commission pursuant to this chapter, and to reinvestigate or reopen cases as the Commission deems necessary.

4. To require and direct medical examination of victims.

5. To hold hearings, administer oaths or affirmations, examine any person under oath or affirmation and to issue summonses requiring the attendance and giving of testimony of witnesses and require the production of any books, papers, documentary or other evidence. The powers provided in this subsection may be delegated by the Commission to any member or employee thereof.

6. To take or cause to be taken affidavits or depositions within or without the Commonwealth.

7. To render each year to the Governor and to the General Assembly a written report of its activities.

8. To accept from the government of the United States grants of federal moneys for disbursement under the provisions of this chapter.

History.

1976, c. 605; 1984, c. 619; 1986, c. 422; 1990, c. 551; 1992, c. 547; 1998, c. 484; 1999, cc. 703, 726; 2008, cc. 203, 251; 2010, c. 780.

§ 19.2-368.3:1. Crime victims' ombudsman.

A. The Commission shall employ a crime victims' ombudsman and adequate staff to facilitate the prompt review and resolution of crime victim compensation claims and to assure that crime victims' rights are safeguarded and protected during the claims process. The ombudsman shall report directly to the Commission.

B. The ombudsman shall ensure that all parties, including service providers and Criminal Injuries Compensation Fund personnel, are acting in the best interests of the crime victim. The ombudsman shall also provide assistance to crime victims in filling out the necessary forms for compensation and obtaining necessary documentation.

History.

1998, c. 484.

§ 19.2-368.4. Persons eligible for awards.

A. The following persons shall be eligible for awards pursuant to this chapter unless the award would directly and unjustly benefit the person who is criminally responsible:

1. A victim of a crime or the parent or guardian of a minor who is the victim of a crime.

2. A surviving spouse, parent, grandparent, sibling or child, including posthumous children, of a victim of a crime who died as a direct result of such crime.

3. Any person, except a law-enforcement officer engaged in the performance of his duties, who is injured or killed while trying to prevent a crime or an attempted crime from occurring in his presence, or trying to apprehend a person who had committed a crime in his presence or had, in fact, committed a felony.

4. A surviving spouse, parent, grandparent, sibling or child, including posthumous children, of any person who dies as a direct result of trying to prevent a crime or attempted crime from occurring in his presence, or trying to apprehend a person who had committed a crime in his presence or had, in fact, committed a felony.

5. Any other person legally dependent for his principal support upon a victim of crime who dies as

a result of such crime, or legally dependent for his principal support upon any person who dies as a direct result of trying to prevent a crime or an attempted crime from occurring in his presence or trying to apprehend a person who had committed a crime in his presence or had, in fact, committed a felony.

B. A person who is criminally responsible for the crime upon which a claim is based, or an accomplice or accessory of such person, shall not be eligible to receive an award with respect to such claim.

C. A resident of Virginia who is the victim of a crime occurring outside Virginia and any other person as defined in subsection A who is injured as a result of a crime occurring outside Virginia shall be eligible for an award pursuant to this chapter if (i) the person would be eligible for benefits had the crime occurred in Virginia and (ii) the state, country or territory in which the crime occurred does not have a crime victims' compensation program deemed eligible pursuant to the provisions of the federal Victims of Crime Act and does not compensate nonresidents.

History.

1976, c. 605; 1977, c. 215; 1978, c. 210; 1981, c. 592; 1984, c. 747; 1985, c. 446; 1986, c. 422; 1988, c. 406; 1990, c. 550; 1996, c. 86; 2002, c. 665.

§ 19.2-368.5. Filing of claims; deferral of proceedings; restitution.

A. A claim may be filed by a person eligible to receive an award, as provided in § 19.2-368.4, or if such person is a minor, by his parent or guardian. In any case in which the person entitled to make a claim is incapacitated, the claim may be filed on his behalf by his guardian, conservator or such other individual authorized to administer his estate.

B. A claim shall be filed by the claimant not later than one year after the occurrence of the crime upon which such claim is based, or not later than one year after the death of the victim. However, (i) in cases involving claims made on behalf of a minor or a person who is incapacitated, the provisions of subsection A of § 8.01-229 shall apply to toll the one-year period; (ii) in cases involving claims made by a victim against profits of crime held in escrow pursuant to Chapter 21.2 (§ 19.2-368.19 et seq.) of this title, the claim shall be filed within five years of the date of the special order of escrow; and (iii) in cases involving claims of sexual abuse of a minor, the claim shall be filed within 10 years after the minor's eighteenth birthday. For good cause shown, the Commission may extend the time for filing for a crime committed on or after July 1, 2001.

In the case of a crime committed on or after July 1, 1977, and before July 1, 2001, for which a claim was not filed in a timely manner, the Commission may, for good cause shown, extend the time for filing if the attorney for the Commonwealth sends written notification to the Commission that the crime is being investigated as a result of newly discovered evidence. For any claim filed pursuant to this paragraph, the Commission shall only consider expenses and loss of earnings that the claimant accrues after the date of newly discovered evidence as stipulated in the written notification by the attorney for the Commonwealth.

C. Claims shall be filed in the office of the Commission in person, by mail, or by electronic means in accordance with standards approved by the Commission. The Commission shall accept for filing all claims submitted by persons eligible under subsection A of this section and alleging the jurisdictional requirements set forth in this chapter and meeting the requirements as to form in the rules and regulations of the Commission.

D. Upon filing of a claim pursuant to this chapter, the Commission shall promptly notify the attorney for the Commonwealth of the jurisdiction wherein the crime is alleged to have occurred. If, within 10 days after such notification, the attorney for the Commonwealth so notified advises the Commission that a criminal prosecution is pending upon the same alleged crime, the Commission shall defer all proceedings under this chapter until such time as such criminal prosecution has been concluded in the circuit court unless notification is received from the attorney for the Commonwealth that no objection is made to a continuation of the investigation and determination of the claim. When such criminal prosecution has been concluded in the circuit court the attorney for the Commonwealth shall promptly so notify the Commission. Nothing in this section shall be construed to mean that the Commission is to defer proceedings upon the filing of an appeal, nor shall this section be construed to limit the authority of the Commission to grant emergency awards as hereinafter provided. Upon awarding a claim pursuant to this chapter, the Commission shall promptly notify the attorney for the Commonwealth of the jurisdiction wherein the crime is alleged to have occurred. If a criminal prosecution occurs regarding the same alleged crime, the attorney for the Commonwealth shall request the court to order restitution. However, neither the lack of a restitution order, nor the failure of the attorney for the Commonwealth to request such an order, shall preclude the Fund from exercising its subrogation rights pursuant to § 19.2-368.15. Any such restitution shall be paid over to the Comptroller for deposit into the Criminal Injuries Compensation Fund to the extent of the amount of the award paid from the Fund.

History.

1976, c. 605; 1977, c. 215; 1978, c. 122; 1986, c. 457; 1992, c. 681; 1997, c. 801; 1998, c. 484; 2001, cc. 363, 855; 2002, c. 665; 2005, c. 683; 2006, c. 414; 2009, c. 381; 2014, cc. 251, 665; 2016, c. 456.

§ 19.2-368.5:1. Failure to perfect claim; denial.

Notwithstanding the provisions of § 19.2-368.5, if, following the initial filing of a claim, a claimant fails to take such further steps to support or perfect the claim as may be required by the Commission within 180 days after written notice of such requirement is sent by the Commission to the claimant, the claimant shall be deemed in default. If the claimant is in default, the Commission shall notify the claimant that the claim is denied and the claimant shall be forever barred from reasserting it; however, the Commission may reopen the proceeding upon a showing by claimant that the failure to do the acts required by the Commission was beyond the control of the claimant.

History.
1981, c. 302; 1998, c. 484.

§ 19.2-368.5:2. Effect of filing a claim; stay of debt collection activities by health care providers.

A. Whenever a person files a claim under this chapter, all health care providers, as defined in § 8.01-581.1 that have been given notice of a pending claim, shall refrain from all debt collection activities relating to medical treatment received by the person in connection with such claim until an award is made on the claim or until a claim is determined to be noncompensable pursuant to § 19.2-368.11:1. The statute of limitations for collection of such debt shall be tolled during the period in which the applicable health care provider is required to refrain from debt collection activities hereunder.

B. For the purpose of this section, *"debt collection activities"* means repeatedly calling or writing to the claimant and threatening either to turn the matter over to a debt collection agency or to an attorney for collection, enforcement or filing of other process. The term shall not include routine billing or inquiries about the status of the claim.

History.
2005, c. 683.

§ 19.2-368.6. Assignment of claims; investigation; hearing; confidentiality of records; decisions.

A. A claim, when accepted for filing, shall be properly investigated, and, if necessary, assigned by the chairman to a commissioner, deputy commissioner or other proper party for disposition. All claims arising from the death of an individual shall be considered together by the same person.

B. The person to whom such claim is assigned shall examine the papers filed in support of the claim and shall thereupon cause an investigation to be conducted into the validity of the claim. The investigation shall include, but not be limited to, an examination of police, court and official records and reports concerning the crime, and an examination of medical and hospital reports relating to the injury upon which the claim is based. Health care providers, as defined in § 8.01-581.1, shall provide medical and hospital reports relating to the diagnosis and treatment of the injury upon which the claim is based to the Commission, upon request.

C. Claims shall be investigated and determined, regardless of whether the alleged criminal has been apprehended or prosecuted for, or convicted of, any crime based upon the same incident, or has been acquitted, or found not guilty of the crime in question owing to a lack of criminal responsibility or other legal exemption.

D. There shall be a rebuttable presumption that the claimant did not contribute to and was not responsible for the infliction of his injury.

E. The person to whom a claim is assigned may decide the claim in favor of a claimant on the basis of the papers filed in support thereof and the report of the investigation of the claim. If he is unable to decide the claim, upon the basis of the said papers and report, he shall order a hearing. At the hearing any relevant evidence, not legally privileged, shall be admissible. The hearing of any claim involving a claimant or victim who is a juvenile shall be closed. All records, papers, and reports involving such claim shall be confidential except as to the amount of the award and nonidentifying information concerning the claimant or victim.

F. For purposes of this chapter, confidentiality provided for by law applicable to a claimant's or victim's juvenile court records shall not be applicable to the extent that the Commission shall have access to those records only for the purposes set forth in this chapter.

G. After examining the papers filed in support of the claim, and the report of investigation, and after a hearing, if any, a decision shall be made either granting an award pursuant to § 19.2-368.11:1 of this chapter or denying the claim.

H. The person making a decision shall issue a written report setting forth such decision and his reasons therefor, and shall notify the claimant and furnish him a copy of such report.

History.
1976, c. 605; 1977, c. 215; 1994, c. 834; 1997, c. 528; 1998, c. 484.

§ 19.2-368.7. Review by Commission.

A. The claimant may, within forty-five days from the date of the report, apply in writing to the Commission for review of the decision by the full Commission. The Commission may extend the time for filing under this section for good cause shown.

B. Upon receipt of an application pursuant to subsection A of this section, or upon its own motion, the Commission shall review the record and affirm or modify the decision of the person to whom the claim was assigned. The action of the Commission in affirming or modifying such decision shall be final. If the Commission receives no application pursuant to subsection A of this section, or takes no action upon its own motion, the decision of the person to whom the claim was assigned shall become the final decision of the Commission.

C. The Commission shall promptly notify the claimant and the Comptroller of the final decision of the Commission and furnish each with a copy of the report setting forth the decision.

History.

1976, c. 605; 1977, c. 215; 1986, c. 457; 1989, c. 335; 2000, c. 455; 2001, c. 363.

§ 19.2-368.8. Reinvestigation of decision; reconsideration of award; judicial review.

A. The Commission, on its own motion, or upon request of the claimant, may reinvestigate or reopen a decision making or denying an award. Except for claims of sexual abuse that occurred while the victim was a minor, the Commission shall not reopen or reinvestigate a case after the expiration of two years from the date of submission of the original claim. Any claim involving the sexual abuse of a minor that has been denied before July 1, 2001, because it was not timely filed may, upon application filed with the Commission, be reconsidered provided the application for reconsideration is filed within ten years after the minor's eighteenth birthday.

B. The Commission shall reconsider, at least annually, every award upon which periodic payments are being made. An order or reconsideration of an award shall not require refund of amounts previously paid unless the award was obtained by fraud. The right of reconsideration does not affect the finality of a Commission decision for the purposes of judicial review.

C. Within thirty days of the date of the report containing the final decision of the Commission, the claimant may, if in his judgment the award is improper, appeal such decision to the Court of Appeals, as provided in § 65.2-706. The Attorney General may appear in such proceedings as counsel for the Commission.

History.

1976, c. 605; 1977, c. 215; 1984, c. 703; 2001, c. 855; 2002, c. 665.

§ 19.2-368.9. Emergency awards.

Notwithstanding any other provisions of this chapter, if it appears to the Commission, that (1) such claim is one with respect to which an award probably will be made, and (2) undue hardship will result to the claimant if immediate payment is not made, the Commission may make an emergency award to the claimant, pending a final decision in the case, provided that (i) the amount of such emergency award shall not exceed $3,000, (ii) the amount of such emergency award shall be deducted from any final award made to the claimant, and (iii) the excess of the amount of such emergency award over the final award, or the full amount of the emergency award if no final award is made, shall be repaid by the claimant to the Commission.

History.

1976, c. 605; 1977, c. 215; 1985, c. 446; 2014, c. 665.

§ 19.2-368.10. When awards to be made; reporting crime and cooperation with law enforcement.

No award shall be made unless the Commission finds that:

1. A crime was committed;
2. Such crime directly resulted in an individual becoming a victim as defined in § 19.2-368.2, on whose behalf a claim is filed; and
3. Police records show that such crime was promptly reported to the proper authorities. In no case may an award be made where the police records show that such report was made more than 120 hours after the occurrence of such crime, unless the Commission, for good cause shown, finds the delay to have been justified. The provisions of this subdivision shall not apply to claims of sexual abuse that occurred while the victim was a minor.

The Commission, upon finding that any claimant or award recipient has not fully cooperated with all law-enforcement agencies, may deny, reduce or withdraw any award, as the case may be.

History.

1976, c. 605; 1977, c. 215; 1985, c. 446; 2001, c. 855; 2005, c. 683.

§ 19.2-368.11: Repealed by Acts 1986, c. 457.

§ 19.2-368.11:1. Amount of award.

A. Compensation for Total Loss of Earnings: An award made pursuant to this chapter for total loss of earnings which results directly from incapacity incurred by a crime victim shall be payable during total incapacity to the victim or to such other eligible person, at a weekly compensation rate equal to 66 ⅔ percent of the victim's average weekly wages. The total amount of weekly compensation shall not exceed $600. The victim's average weekly wages shall be determined as provided in § 65.2-101.

B. Compensation for Partial Loss of Earnings: An award made pursuant to this chapter for partial loss of earnings which results directly from incapacity incurred by a crime victim shall be payable during incapacity at a weekly rate equal to 66 ⅔ percent of the difference between the victim's average weekly wages before the injury and the weekly wages which the victim is able to earn thereafter. The combined total of actual weekly earnings and compensation for partial loss of earnings shall not exceed $600 per week.

C. Compensation for Loss of Earnings of Parent of Minor Victim: The parent or guardian of a minor crime victim may receive compensation for loss of earnings, calculated as specified in subsections A and B, for time spent obtaining medical treatment for the child and for accompanying the child to, attending or participating in investigative, prosecutorial, judicial, adjudicatory and post-conviction proceedings.

D. Compensation for Dependents of a Victim Who Is Killed: If death results to a victim of crime entitled to benefits, dependents of the victim shall be entitled to compensation in accordance with the provisions of §§ 65.2-512 and 65.2-515 in an amount not to exceed the maximum aggregate payment or the maximum weekly compensation which would have been payable to the deceased victim under this section.

E. Compensation for Unreimbursed Medical Costs, Funeral Expenses, Services, etc.: Awards may also be made on claims or portions of claims based upon the claimant's actual expenses incurred as are determined by the Commission to be appropriate, for (i) unreimbursed medical expenses or indebtedness reasonably incurred for medical expenses; (ii) expenses reasonably incurred in obtaining ordinary and necessary services in lieu of those the victim would have performed, for the benefit of himself and his family, if he had not been a victim of crime; (iii) expenses directly related to funeral or burial, not to exceed $5,000; (iv) expenses attributable to pregnancy resulting from forcible rape; (v) mental health counseling for survivors as defined under subdivisions A 2 and A 4 of § 19.2-368.4, not to exceed $3,500 per claim; (vi) reasonable and necessary moving expenses, not to exceed $2,000, incurred by a victim or survivors as defined under subdivisions A 2 and A 4 of § 19.2-368.4; and (vii) any other reasonable and necessary expenses and indebtedness incurred as a direct result of the injury or death upon which such claim is based, not otherwise specifically provided for. Notwithstanding any other provision of law, a person who is not eligible for an award under subsection A of § 19.2-368.4 who pays expenses directly related to funeral or burial is eligible for reimbursement subject to the limitations of this section.

F. Notwithstanding the provisions of subdivision 3 of § 19.2-368.10, §§ 19.2-368.5, 19.2-368.5:1, 19.2-368.6, 19.2-368.7, 19.2-368.8, subsection G of this section, and § 19.2-368.16, the Criminal Injuries Compensation Fund shall pay for physical evidence recovery kit examinations conducted on victims of sexual assault. Any individual that submits to and completes a physical evidence recovery kit examination shall be considered to have met the reporting and cooperation requirements of this chapter. Funds paid for physical evidence recovery kit collection shall not be offset against the Fund's maximum allowable award as provided in subsection H. Payments may be subject to negotiated agreements with the provider. Healthcare providers that complete physical evidence recovery kit examinations may bill the Fund directly subject to the provisions of § 19.2-368.5:2. The Commission shall develop policies for a distinct payment process for physical evidence recovery kit examination expenses as required under subdivision 1 of § 19.2-368.3.

In order for the Fund to consider additional crime-related expenses, victims shall file with the Fund following the provisions of this chapter and Criminal Injuries Compensation Fund policy.

G. Any claim made pursuant to this chapter shall be reduced by the amount of any payments received or to be received as a result of the injury from or on behalf of the person who committed the crime or from any other public or private source, including an emergency award by the Commission pursuant to § 19.2-368.9.

H. To qualify for an award under this chapter, a claim must have a minimum value of $100, and payments for injury or death to a victim of crime, to the victim's dependents or to others entitled to payment for covered expenses, after being reduced as provided in subsection G, shall not exceed $25,000 in the aggregate.

History.

1986, c. 457; 1988, c. 748; 1989, c. 335; 1990, c. 552; 1992, c. 687; 1996, c. 86; 1998, c. 484; 2000, c. 847; 2002, c. 665; 2005, c. 683; 2007, c. 381; 2008, cc. 203, 251; 2014, c. 665.

Criminal Procedure

§ 19.2-368.12. Awards not subject to execution or attachment; apportionment; reductions.

A. No award made pursuant to this chapter shall be subject to execution or attachment other than for expenses resulting from the injury which is the basis for the claim.

B. If there are two or more persons entitled to an award as a result of the death of a person which is the direct result of a crime, the award shall be apportioned among the claimants.

C. In determining the amount of an award, the Commission shall determine whether, because of his conduct, the victim of such crime contributed to the infliction of his injury, and the Commission shall reduce the amount of the award or reject the claim altogether, in accordance with such determination; provided, however, that the Commission may disregard for this purpose the responsibility of the victim for his own injury where the record shows that such responsibility was attributable to efforts by the victim to prevent a crime or an attempted crime from occurring in his presence, or to apprehend a person who had committed a crime in his presence or had, in fact, committed a felony.

History.

1976, c. 605; 1977, c. 215; 1989, c. 335.

§ 19.2-368.13: Repealed by Acts 1984, c. 619.

§ 19.2-368.14. Public record; exception.

Except as provided in § 19.2-368.6 concerning juvenile claimants or victims, the record of any proceedings under this chapter shall be a public record; provided, however, that any record or report obtained by the Commission, the confidentiality of which is protected by any other law or regulation, shall remain confidential, subject to such law or regulation.

History.
1976, c. 605; 1994, c. 834.

§ 19.2-368.15. Subrogation of Commonwealth to claimant's right of action; lien in favor of the Commonwealth; disposition of funds collected.

Acceptance of an award made pursuant to this chapter shall subrogate the Commonwealth, to the extent of such award, to any right or right of action accruing to the claimant or the victim to recover payments on account of losses resulting from the crime with respect to which the award is made. However, except as otherwise provided in subsection G of § 19.2-305.1, the Commonwealth shall not institute any proceedings in connection with its right of subrogation under this section within one year from the date of commission of the crime, unless any claimant or victim's right or action shall have been previously terminated. All funds collected by the Commonwealth in a proceeding instituted pursuant to this section shall be paid over to the Comptroller for deposit into the Criminal Injuries Compensation Fund.

Whenever any person receives an award from the Criminal Injuries Compensation Fund, the Commonwealth shall have a lien for the total amount paid by the Fund, or any portion thereof compromised pursuant to the authority granted under § 2.2-514, on the claim of such injured person or his personal representative against the person, firm, or corporation who is alleged to have caused such injuries. The Fund's lien shall be inferior to any lien for payment of reasonable attorney fees and costs, but shall be superior to all other liens created by § 8.01-66.2. The injured person may file a petition or motion to reduce the lien and apportion the recovery pursuant to § 8.01-66.9. The Fund's lien shall become effective when notice is provided pursuant to § 8.01-66.5 and liability shall attach pursuant to § 8.01-66.6.

History.
1976, c. 605; 1983, c. 227; 2013, c. 273.

§ 19.2-368.16. Claims to be made under oath.

All claims shall be made under oath. Any person who asserts a false claim under the provisions of this chapter shall be guilty of perjury and, in addition, shall be subject to prosecution under the provisions of Article 3 (§ 18.2-95 et seq.) of Chapter 5 of Title 18.2, and shall further forfeit any benefit received and shall reimburse and repay the Commonwealth for payments received or paid on his behalf pursuant to any of the provisions hereunder.

History.
1976, c. 605.

§ 19.2-368.17. Public information program.

The Commission shall establish and conduct a public information program to assure extensive and continuing publicity and public awareness of the provisions of this chapter. The public information program shall include brochures, posters and public service advertisements for television, radio and print media for dissemination to the public of information regarding the right to compensation for innocent victims of crime, including information on the right to file a claim, the scope of coverage, and the procedures to be utilized incident thereto.

Whenever a crime which directly resulted in personal physical injury to, or death of, an individual is reported within the time required by § 19.2-368.10, the law-enforcement agency to which the report is made shall make reasonable efforts, where practicable, to notify the victim or other potential claimant in writing on forms prepared by the Commission of his or her possible right to file a claim under this chapter. In any event, no liability or cause of action shall arise from the failure to so notify a victim of crime or other potential claimant.

History.
1976, c. 605; 1986, cc. 457, 472.

§ 19.2-368.18. Criminal Injuries Compensation Fund.

A. There is hereby created a special fund to be administered by the Comptroller, known as the Criminal Injuries Compensation Fund.

B. Whenever the costs provided for in §§ 17.1-275.1, 17.1-275.2, 17.1-275.3, 17.1-275.4, 17.1-275.7, 17.1-275.8, or § 17.1-275.9 or subsections B or C of § 16.1-69.48:1 are assessed, a portion of the costs, as specified in those sections, shall be paid over to the Comptroller to be deposited into the Criminal Injuries Compensation Fund. Under no condition shall a political subdivision be held liable for the payment of this sum.

C. No claim shall be accepted under the provisions of this chapter when the crime that gave rise to such claim occurred prior to July 1, 1977.

D. Sums available in the Criminal Injuries Compensation Fund shall be used for the purpose of payment of the costs and expenses necessary for the administration of this chapter and for the payment of claims pursuant to this chapter.

E. All revenues deposited into the Criminal Injuries Compensation Fund, and appropriated for the purposes of this chapter, shall be immediately available for the payment of claims.

Criminal Procedure

History.
1976, c. 605; 1978, c. 413; 1980, c. 521; 1985, c. 230; 1988, c. 748; 1993, c. 434; 1996, cc. 760, 976; 2002, c. 831.

CHAPTER 21.2.
PROFITS FROM CRIME.

Section

§ 19.2-368.19. Definitions.

For purposes of this chapter, the following terms shall have the following meanings unless the context requires otherwise:

"Defendant" means any person who pleads guilty to, is convicted of, or is found not guilty by reason of insanity with respect to a felony resulting in physical injury to or death of another person.

"Division" means the Division of Crime Victims' Compensation.

"Interested party" means the victim, the defendant, and any transferee of proceeds due the defendant under a contract, the person with whom the defendant has contracted, the prosecuting attorney for the Commonwealth, and the Division of Crime Victims' Compensation.

"Victim" means a person who suffers personal, physical, mental, emotional, or pecuniary loss as a direct result of a crime and includes the spouse, parent, child, or sibling of the victim.

History.
1990, c. 549; 1992, c. 681.

§ 19.2-368.20. Special order of escrow.

A. Any proceeds or profits received or to be received directly or indirectly, except property that may be forfeited to the Commonwealth pursuant to §§ 19.2-386.15 through 19.2-386.31, by a defendant or a transferee of that defendant from any source, as a direct or indirect result of his crime or sentence, or the notoriety which such crime or sentence has conferred upon him, shall be subject to a special order of escrow.

B. Income from the defendant's employment in a position unrelated to his crime or the notoriety which such crime has conferred upon him but obtained through the assistance of or rehabilitative training by correctional or mental health programs or personnel shall not be subject to a special order of escrow under this section, and nothing in this section shall be construed to prohibit or hinder the return of property belonging to victims of crime to its rightful owners. Any proceeds from a contract relating to a depiction or discussion of the defendant's crime in a movie, book, newspaper, magazine, radio or television production, or live entertainment or publication of any kind shall not be subject to a special order of escrow unless an integral part of the work is a depiction or discussion of the defendant's crime or an impression of the defendant's thoughts, opinions, or emotions regarding such crime.

C. Upon petition of the attorney for the Commonwealth filed at any time after conviction of such defendant or his acquittal by reason of insanity and after notice to the interested parties, a hearing upon the motion and a finding for the Commonwealth, for good cause shown, any circuit court in which the petition is filed shall order that such proceeds be subject to a special order of escrow.

1. The petition shall be filed in the circuit court of the jurisdiction where the defendant was convicted or acquitted by reason of insanity.

2. The petition shall set forth in general terms the causes for entry of the special order of escrow, and be signed by the attorney for the Commonwealth.

3. Upon the filing of the petition, the clerk shall forthwith issue a warrant directed to the sheriff or other law-enforcement officer of the county or city, commanding him to take the property into his possession and hold the same subject to further proceedings in the cause. If for any cause the warrant was not executed, other like warrants may be successively issued until one is executed. The officer serving the warrant shall take the property into his possession and forthwith return the warrant and report to the clerk in writing.

4. Any person concerned in interest may appear and make defense to the petition, which may be done by answer on oath.

5. When the case is ready for trial, such issues of fact as are made by the pleadings, or as the court may direct, the court shall determine the whole matter of law and fact.

6. Expenses and costs incurred in the proceedings shall be paid as the court, in its discretion, shall determine; except that no costs shall be adjudged against the Commonwealth.

An order issued under this section shall require that the defendant and the person with whom the defendant contracts pay to the Division any proceeds due the defendant under the contract and the proceeds shall be placed in a special escrow account for the victims of the defendant's crime.

History.
1990, c. 549; 1992, c. 681; 2006, c. 414.

§ 19.2-368.21. Distribution.

A. Proceeds paid to the Division under § 19.2-368.20 shall be retained in escrow in the Criminal Injuries Compensation Fund for five years after the date of the order, but during that five-year period may be levied upon to satisfy a money judgment rendered by a court or award of the Workers' Compensation Commission in favor of a victim of an offense for which the defendant has been convicted or acquitted by reason of insanity, or a legal representative of the victim.

B. If ordered by a circuit court in the interest of justice, after motion, notice to all interested parties, and opportunity for hearing, such escrow fund shall be used to:

1. First, satisfy court ordered restitution against a defendant and in favor of a victim;

2. Satisfy a money judgment rendered in the court hearing the matter, in favor of a victim of any offense for which the defendant has been convicted;

3. Pay for legal representation of the defendant in criminal proceedings, including the appeals process, to the extent the defendant's representation was paid for by the Commonwealth or an agency thereof. No more than 25% of the total proceeds in escrow may be used for legal representation; and

4. Pay any fines or costs assessed against the defendant by a court of the Commonwealth.

C. At the end of the five-year period, the remaining proceeds shall be paid into the Literary Fund. However, (i) if a civil action under this section is pending against the defendant, the proceeds shall be held in escrow until completion of the action or (ii) if the defendant has appealed his conviction and the appeals process is not final, the proceeds shall be held in escrow until the appeals process is final, and upon disposition of the charges favorable to the defendant, the Division shall immediately pay any money in the escrow account to the defendant.

History.
1990, c. 549; 1992, c. 681; 2006, c. 414.

§ 19.2-368.22. Actions to defeat chapter void.

Any action taken by any person convicted of a felony, whether by way of execution of a power of attorney, creation of corporate entities, or otherwise, to defeat the purpose of this chapter shall be void.

History.
1990, c. 549; 1992, c. 59.

CHAPTER 22.

ENFORCEMENT OF FORFEITURES.

Section

§§ 19.2-369 through 19.2-386: Repealed by Acts 2012, cc. 283 and 756, cl. 2.

Cross references.
For current provisions as to enforcement of forfeitures, see Chapter 22 (§ 19.2-386.1 et seq.).

CHAPTER 22.1.

ENFORCEMENT OF FORFEITURES.

Section

§ 19.2-386.1. Commencing an action of forfeiture.

Except as otherwise specifically provided by law, whenever any property is forfeited to the Commonwealth by reason of the violation of any law, or if any statute provides for the forfeiture of any property or money, or if any property or money be seized as forfeited for a violation of any of the provisions of this Code, the Commonwealth shall follow the procedures set forth in this chapter.

An action against any property subject to seizure under the provisions of Chapter 22.2 (§ 19.2-386.15 et seq.) shall be commenced by the filing of an information in the clerk's office of the circuit court. Any information shall be filed in the name of the Commonwealth by the attorney for the Commonwealth or may be filed by the Attorney General if so requested by the attorney for the Commonwealth. Venue for an action of forfeiture shall lie in the county or city where (i) the property is located, (ii) the property is seized, or (iii) an owner of the property could be prosecuted for the illegal conduct alleged to give rise to the forfeiture. Such information shall (a) name as parties defendant all owners and lienholders then known or of record and the trustees named in any deed of trust securing such lienholder, (b) specifically describe the property, (c) set forth in general terms the grounds for forfeiture of the named property, (d) pray that the same be condemned and sold or otherwise be disposed of according to law, and (e) ask that all persons concerned or interested be notified to appear and show cause why such property should not be forfeited. In all cases, an information shall be filed within three years of the date of actual discovery by the Commonwealth of the last act giving rise to the forfeiture or the action for forfeiture will be barred.

History.
1989, c. 690; 1991, c. 560; 2002, cc. 588, 623; 2004, c. 995; 2012, cc. 283, 756.

§ 19.2-386.2. Seizure of named property.

A. When any property subject to seizure under Chapter 22.2 (§ 19.2-386.15 et seq.) or other provision under the Code has not been seized at the time an information naming that property is filed, the clerk of the circuit court or a judge of the circuit court, upon motion of the attorney for the Commonwealth wherein the information is filed, shall issue a warrant to the sheriff or other state or local law-enforcement officer authorized to serve criminal process in the jurisdiction where the property is located, describing the property named in the complaint and authorizing its immediate seizure.

B. In all cases of seizure of real property, a notice of lis pendens shall be filed with the clerk of the circuit court of the county or city wherein the property is located and shall be indexed in the land records in the name or names of those persons whose interests appear to be affected thereby.

C. When any property is seized for the purposes of forfeiture under Chapter 22.2 (§ 19.2-386.15 et seq.) or other forfeiture provision under the Code, the agency seizing the property shall, as soon as practicable after the seizure, conduct an inventory of the seized property and shall, as soon as practicable, provide a copy of the inventory to the owner. An agency's failure to provide a copy of an inventory pursuant to this subsection shall not invalidate any forfeiture.

D. When any property is seized for the purposes of forfeiture under Chapter 22.2 (§ 19.2-386.15 et seq.) or other forfeiture provision under the Code, and an information naming that property has not been filed, neither the agency seizing the property nor any other law-enforcement agency may request, require, or in any manner induce any person who asserts ownership, lawful possession, or any lawful right to the property to waive his interest in or rights to the property until an information has been filed.

History.

1989, c. 690; 2002, cc. 588, 623; 2004, c. 995; 2006, c. 766; 2012, cc. 283, 756; 2015, c. 769; 2016, cc. 203, 423.

§ 19.2-386.2:1. Notice to Commissioner of Department of Motor Vehicles; duties of Commissioner.

If the property seized is a motor vehicle required by the motor vehicle laws of Virginia to be registered, the attorney for the Commonwealth shall forthwith notify the Commissioner of the Department of Motor Vehicles, by certified mail, or electronically in a format prescribed by the Commissioner, of such seizure and the motor number of the vehicle so seized, and the Commissioner shall promptly certify to such attorney for the Commonwealth the name and address of the person in whose name such vehicle is registered, together with the name and address of any person holding a lien thereon. The Commissioner shall also forthwith notify such registered owner and lienor, in writing, of the reported seizure and the county or city wherein such seizure was made.

The certificate of the Commissioner, concerning such registration and lien, shall be received in evidence in any proceeding, either civil or criminal, under any provision of this chapter, in which such facts may be material to the issue involved.

History.

2012, cc. 283, 756; 2016, cc. 203, 423.

§ 19.2-386.3. Notice of seizure for forfeiture and notice of motion for judgment.

A. If an information has not been filed, then upon seizure of any property under Chapter 22.2 (§ 19.2-386.15 et seq.) or other provision under the Code, the agency seizing the property shall forthwith notify in writing the attorney for the Commonwealth in the county or city in which the seizure occurred, who shall, within 21 days of receipt of such notice, file a notice of seizure for forfeiture with the clerk of the circuit court. Such notice of seizure for forfeiture shall specifically describe the property seized, set forth in general terms the grounds for seizure, identify the date on which the seizure occurred, and identify all owners and lien holders then known or of record, including the treasurer of the locality in which the seized property is located. The clerk shall forthwith mail by first-class mail notice of seizure for forfeiture to the last known address of all identified owners and lien holders. When property has been seized under Chapter 22.2 (§ 19.2-386.15 et seq.) or other provision under the Code prior to filing an information, then an information against that property shall be filed within 90 days of the date of seizure or the property shall be released to the owner or lien holder.

B. Except as to corporations, all parties defendant shall be served, in accordance with § 8.01-296, with a copy of the information and a notice to appear prior to any motion for default judgment on the information. The notice shall contain a statement warning the party defendant that his interest in the property shall be subject to forfeiture to the Commonwealth unless within 30 days after service on him of the notice, or before the date set forth in the order of publication with respect to the notice, an answer under oath is filed in the proceeding setting forth (i) the nature of the defendant's claim, (ii) the exact right, title or character of the ownership or interest in the property and the evidence thereof, and (iii) the reason, cause, exemption or defense he may have against the forfeiture of his interest in the property, including but not limited to the exemptions set forth in § 19.2-386.8. Service upon corporations shall be made in accordance with § 8.01-299 or subdivision 1 or 2 of § 8.01-301; however, if such service cannot be thus made, it shall be made by publication in accordance with § 8.01-317.

History.
1989, c. 690; 1991, c. 560; 1996, c. 673; 2002, cc. 588, 623; 2004, c. 995; 2011, c. 83; 2012, cc. 283, 756.

§ 19.2-386.4. Records and handling of seized property.

Any agency seizing property under § 19.2-386.2, Chapter 22.2 (§ 19.2-386.15 et seq.), or other provision under the Code, pending forfeiture and final disposition, may do any of the following:

1. Place the property under constructive seizure by posting notice of seizure for forfeiture on the property or by filing notice of seizure for forfeiture in any appropriate public record relating to property;
2. Remove the property to a storage area for safekeeping or, if the property is a negotiable instrument or money, deposit it in an interest-bearing account;
3. Remove the property to a place designated by the circuit court in the county or city wherein the property was seized; or
4. Provide for another custodian or agency to take custody of the property and remove it to an appropriate location within or without the jurisdiction of the circuit court in the county or city wherein the property was seized or in which the complaint was filed.

A report regarding the type of property subject to forfeiture and its handling pursuant to this section and § 19.2-386.5, and the final disposition of the property shall be filed by the seizing agency with the Department of Criminal Justice Services in accordance with regulations promulgated by the Board.

History.
1989, c. 690; 1991, c. 560; 2002, cc. 588, 623; 2004, c. 995; 2012, cc. 283, 756.

§ 19.2-386.5. Release of seized property.

At any time prior to the filing of an information, the attorney for the Commonwealth in the county or city in which the property has been seized pursuant to Chapter 22.2 (§ 19.2-386.15 et seq.) or other provision under the Code may, in his discretion, upon the payment of costs incident to the custody of the seized property, return the seized property to an owner or lien holder, without requiring that the owner or lien holder post bond as provided in § 19.2-386.6, if he believes the property is properly exempt from forfeiture pursuant to § 19.2-386.8.

History.
1989, c. 690; 2002, cc. 588, 623; 2004, c. 995; 2012, cc. 283, 756.

§ 19.2-386.6. Bond to secure possession.

If the owner or lien holder of the named property desires to obtain possession thereof before the hearing on the information filed against the same, such property shall be appraised by the clerk of the court where such information is filed. The clerk shall promptly cause the property to be appraised at its fair cash value, and forthwith make return thereof in writing to the court. Any appraisal fee shall be taxed as costs as provided in § 19.2-386.12. Upon the return of the appraisal, the owner or lien holder may give a bond payable to the Commonwealth, in a penalty of the amount equal to the appraised value of the property plus the court costs which may accrue, with security to be approved by the clerk and conditioned for the performance of the final judgment of the court, on the trial of the information. A further condition shall be that, if upon the hearing on the information, the judgment of the court is that such property, or any part thereof, or such interest and equity as the owner or lien holder may have therein, is forfeited, judgment may thereupon be entered against the obligors on such bond for the penalty thereof, without further or other proceedings against them thereon, to be discharged by the payment of the appraised value of the property so seized and forfeited, and costs. Upon such judgment, execution may issue, on which the clerk shall endorse, "No security to be taken." Upon giving of the bond, the property shall be delivered to the owner or lien holder.

History.
1989, c. 690.

§ 19.2-386.7. Sale of property liable to deterioration.

If the property seized is perishable or liable to deterioration, decay, or injury by being detained in custody pending the proceedings, the circuit court for the county or city in which the information is filed or in which the property is located, may order the same to be sold upon such notice as the court, in its discretion, may deem proper and hold the proceeds of sale pending the final disposition of such proceedings.

History.
1989, c. 690.

§ 19.2-386.8. Exemptions.

The following exemptions shall apply to property otherwise subject to forfeiture:

1. No conveyance used by any person as a lawfully certified common carrier in the transaction of business as a common carrier may be forfeited under the provisions of this section unless the owner of the conveyance was a consenting party or privy to the conduct giving rise to forfeiture or knew or had reason to know of it.
2. No conveyance may be forfeited under the provisions of this section for any conduct committed by a person other than the owner while the conveyance was unlawfully in the possession of a person other than the owner in violation of the criminal laws of this Commonwealth, or any other state, the

District of Columbia, the United States or any territory thereof.

3. No owner's interest may be forfeited under this chapter if the court finds that:

a. He did not know and had no reason to know of the conduct giving rise to forfeiture;

b. He was a bona fide purchaser for value without notice;

c. The conduct giving rise to forfeiture occurred without his connivance or consent, express or implied; or

d. The conduct giving rise to forfeiture was committed by a tenant of a residential or commercial property owned by a landlord, and the landlord did not know or have reason to know of the tenant's conduct.

4. No lien holder's interest may be forfeited under this chapter if the court finds that:

a. The lien holder did not know of the conduct giving rise to forfeiture at the time the lien was granted;

b. The lien holder held a bona fide lien on the property subject to forfeiture and had perfected the same in the manner prescribed by law prior to seizure of the property; and

c. The conduct giving rise to forfeiture occurred without his connivance or consent, express or implied.

In the event the interest has been sold to a bona fide purchaser for value in order to avoid the provisions of this chapter, the Commonwealth shall have a right of action against the seller of the property for the proceeds of the sale.

History.
1989, c. 690; 2005, c. 883.

§ 19.2-386.9. Appearance by owner or lien holder.

Any person claiming to be an owner or lien holder of the named property may appear at any time within thirty days after service on him of notice to appear or on or before the date certain set forth in any order of publication under § 8.01-317 or such longer time as the court in its discretion may allow to prevent a miscarriage of justice. Any person without actual or constructive notice of the forfeiture proceedings claiming to be an owner or lienholder may appear at any time before final judgment of the trial court and be made a party to the action. Such appearance shall be by answer, under oath, which shall clearly set forth (i) the nature of the defendant's claim; (ii) the exact right, title or character of the ownership or interest in the property and the evidence thereof; and (iii) the reason, cause, exemption or defense he may have against the forfeiture of the property.

History.
1989, c. 690; 1991, c. 560.

§ 19.2-386.10. Forfeiture; default judgment; remission; trial.

A. A party defendant who fails to appear as provided in § 19.2-386.9 shall be in default. The forfeiture shall be deemed established as to the interest of any party in default upon entry of judgment as provided in § 19.2-386.11. Within 21 days after entry of judgment, any party defendant against whom judgment has been so entered may petition the Department of Criminal Justice Services for remission of his interest in the forfeited property. For good cause shown and upon proof by a preponderance of the evidence that the party defendant's interest in the property is exempt under subdivision 2, 3, or 4 of § 19.2-386.8, the Department of Criminal Justice Services shall grant the petition and direct the state treasury to either (i) remit to the party defendant an amount not exceeding the party defendant's interest in the proceeds of sale of the forfeited property after deducting expenses incurred and payable pursuant to subsection B of § 19.2-386.12 or (ii) convey clear and absolute title to the forfeited property in extinguishment of such interest.

If any party defendant appears in accordance with § 19.2-386.9, the court shall proceed to trial of the case, unless trial by jury is demanded by the Commonwealth or any party defendant. At trial, the Commonwealth has the burden of proving by clear and convincing evidence that the property is subject to forfeiture under this chapter. Upon such a showing by the Commonwealth, the claimant has the burden of proving by a preponderance of the evidence that the claimant's interest in the property is exempt under subdivision 2, 3, or 4 of § 19.2-386.8.

B. The information and trial thereon shall be independent of any criminal proceeding against any party or other person for violation of law. However, upon motion and for good cause shown, the court may stay a forfeiture proceeding that is related to any warrant, indictment, or information.

History.
1989, c. 690; 1991, c. 560; 2016, cc. 203, 423, 664.

§ 19.2-386.11. Judgment of condemnation; destruction.

A. If the forfeiture is established, the judgment shall be that the property be condemned as forfeited to the Commonwealth subject to any remission granted under subsection A of § 19.2-386.10 and further that the same be sold, unless (i) a sale thereof has been already made under § 19.2-386.7, (ii) the court determines that the property forfeited is of such minimal value that the sale would not be in the best interest of the Commonwealth or (iii) the court finds that the property may be subject to return to a participating agency. If the court finds that the property may be subject to return to an agency participating in the seizure in accordance with subsection C of § 19.2-386.14, the order shall provide for storage of the property until the determination to return it is made or, if return is not made, for sale of the property as provided in this section and § 19.2-386.12. If sale has been made, the judgment shall be against the proceeds of sale, subject to the rights of any lien holder whose interest is not forfeited. If the property condemned has been delivered to the claimant under § 19.2-386.6, further judgment shall be against the obligors in the bond for the penalty thereof, to be discharged by the payment of the appraised value of the property, upon which judgment, process of execution shall be awarded and the clerk shall endorse thereon, "No security is to be taken."

B. Forfeited cash and negotiable instruments shall be disposed of pursuant to the provisions of § 19.2-386.12.

C. Contraband, the sale or possession of which is unlawful, weapons and property not sold because of the minimal value thereof, may be ordered destroyed by the court.

History.

1989, c. 690; 1991, c. 560; 1993, c. 484.

§ 19.2-386.12. Sale of forfeited property.

A. Any sale of forfeited property shall be made for cash, after due advertisement. The sale shall be by public sale or other commercially feasible means authorized by the court in the order of forfeiture and shall vest in the purchaser a clear and absolute title to the property sold subject to the rights of any lien holder whose interest is not forfeited. The proceeds of sale, and whatever may be realized on any bond given under § 19.2-386.6, and any money forfeited shall be paid over to the state treasury into a special fund of the Department of Criminal Justice Services in accordance with § 19.2-386.14.

B. In all cases of forfeiture under this section, the actual expenses incident to the custody, preservation, and management of the seized property prior to forfeiture, the actual expenses incident to normal legal proceedings to perfect the Commonwealth's interest in the seized property through forfeiture, and the actual expenses incident to the sale thereof, including commissions, shall be taxed as costs and shall be paid to the person or persons who incurred these costs out of the net proceeds from the sale of such property. If there are no proceeds, the actual expenses shall be paid by the Commonwealth from the Criminal Fund. Actual expenses in excess of the available net proceeds shall be paid by the Commonwealth from the Criminal Fund. The party or parties in interest to any forfeiture proceeding commenced under this section shall be entitled to reasonable attorney's fees and costs if the forfeiture proceeding is terminated in favor of such party or parties. Such fees and costs shall be paid by the Commonwealth from the Criminal Fund.

The residue, if any, shall be paid and disbursed as provided in subsection A of § 19.2-386.10 and § 19.2-386.14 and regulations promulgated by the Criminal Justice Services Board.

History.

1989, c. 690; 1991, c. 560.

§ 19.2-386.13. Writ of error and supersedeas.

For the purpose of review on a writ of error or supersedeas, a final judgment or order in the cause shall be deemed a final judgment or order within the meaning of subsection A of § 8.01-670.

History.

1989, c. 690; 2005, c. 681.

§ 19.2-386.14. Sharing of forfeited assets.

A. All cash, negotiable instruments, and proceeds from a sale conducted pursuant to § 19.2-386.7 or 19.2-386.12, after deduction of expenses, fees, and costs as provided in § 19.2-386.12, shall, as soon after entry of the forfeiture as is practicable, be distributed in a manner consistent with this chapter and Article VIII, Section 8 of the Constitution of Virginia.

A1. All cash, negotiable instruments and proceeds from a sale conducted pursuant to § 19.2-386.7 or 19.2-386.12, after deduction of expenses, fees and costs as provided in § 19.2-386.12, shall, as soon after entry of the forfeiture as is practicable, be paid over to the state treasury into a special fund of the Department of Criminal Justice Services for distribution in accordance with this section. The forfeited property and proceeds, less 10 percent, shall be made available to federal, state and local agencies to promote law enforcement in accordance with this section and regulations adopted by the Criminal Justice Services Board to implement the asset-sharing program.

The 10 percent retained by the Department shall be held in a nonreverting fund, known as the Asset Sharing Administrative Fund. Administrative costs incurred by the Department to manage and operate the asset-sharing program shall be paid from the Fund. Any amounts remaining in the Fund after payment of these costs shall be used to promote state or local law-enforcement activities. Distributions from the Fund for these activities shall be based upon need and shall be made from time to time in accordance with regulations promulgated by the Board.

B. Any federal, state or local agency or office that directly participated in the investigation or other law-enforcement activity which led, directly or indirectly, to the seizure and forfeiture shall be eligible for, and may petition the Department for, return of the forfeited asset or an equitable share of the net proceeds, based upon the degree of participation in the law-enforcement effort resulting in the forfeiture, taking into account the total value of all property forfeited and the total law-enforcement effort with respect to the violation of law on which the forfeiture is based. Upon finding that the petitioning agency is eligible for distribution and that all participating agencies agree on the equitable share of each, the Department shall distribute each share directly to the appropriate treasury of the participating agency.

If all eligible participating agencies cannot agree on the equitable shares of the net proceeds, the shares shall be determined by the Criminal Justice Services Board in accordance with regulations which shall specify the criteria to be used by the Board in assessing the degree of participation in the law-enforcement effort resulting in the forfeiture.

C. After the order of forfeiture is entered concerning any motor vehicle, boat, aircraft, or other tangible personal property, any seizing agency may (i) petition the Department for return of the property that is not subject to a grant or pending petition for remission or (ii) request the circuit court to order the property destroyed. Where all the participating agencies agree upon the equitable distribution of the tangible personal property, the Department shall return the property to those agencies upon finding that (a) the agency meets the criteria for distribution as set forth in subsection B and (b) the agency has a clear and reasonable law-enforcement need for the forfeited property.

If all eligible participating agencies cannot agree on the distribution of the property, distribution shall be determined by the Criminal Justice Services Board as in subsection B, taking into consideration the clear and reasonable law-enforcement needs for the property which the agencies may have. In order to equitably distribute tangible personal property, the Criminal Justice Services Board may require the agency receiving the property to reimburse the Department in cash for the difference between the fair market value of the forfeited property and the agency's equitable share as determined by the Criminal Justice Services Board.

If a seizing agency has received property for its use pursuant to this section, when the agency disposes of the property (1) by sale, the proceeds shall be distributed as set forth in this section; or (2) by destruction pursuant to a court order, the agency shall do so in a manner consistent with this section.

D. All forfeited property, including its proceeds or cash equivalent, received by a participating state or local agency pursuant to this section shall be used to promote law enforcement but shall not be used to supplant existing programs or funds. The Board shall promulgate regulations establishing an audit procedure to ensure compliance with this section.

E. On or after July 1, 2012, but before July 1, 2014, local seizing agencies may contribute cash funds and proceeds from forfeited property to the Virginia Public Safety Foundation to support the construction of the Commonwealth Public Safety Memorial. Any funds contributed by seizing agencies shall be contributed only after an internal analysis to determine that such contributions will not negatively impact law-enforcement training or operations.

F. The Department shall report annually on or before December 31 to the Governor and the General Assembly the amount of all cash, negotiable instruments, and proceeds from sales conducted pursuant to § 19.2-386.7 or 19.2-386.12 that were forfeited to the Commonwealth, including the amount of all forfeitures distributed to the Literary Fund. Such report shall also detail the amount distributed by the Department to each federal, state, or local agency or office pursuant to this section, and the amount each state or local agency or office received from federal asset forfeiture proceedings. The Department shall ensure that such report is available to the public.

History.

1991, c. 560; 2012, cc. 126, 283, 373, 756; 2016, cc. 203, 423.

CHAPTER 22.2.

MISCELLANEOUS FORFEITURE PROVISIONS.

Section

§ 19.2-386.15. Seizure of property used in connection with or derived from terrorism.

A. The following property shall be subject to lawful seizure by any law-enforcement officer charged with enforcing the provisions of Article 2.2 (§ 18.2-46.4 et seq.) of Chapter 4 of Title 18.2: all moneys or other property, real or personal, together with any interest or profits derived from the investment of such money and used in substantial connection with an act of terrorism as defined in § 18.2-46.4.

B. All seizures and forfeitures under this section shall be governed by the procedures contained in Chapter 22.1 (§ 19.2-386.1 et seq.) of this title.

History.
2002, cc. 588, 623, § 18.2-46.9; 2004, c. 995.

§ 19.2-386.16. Forfeiture of motor vehicles used in commission of certain crimes.

A. Any vehicle knowingly used by the owner thereof or used by another with his knowledge of and during the commission of, or in an attempt to commit, a second or subsequent offense of § 18.2-346, 18.2-347, 18.2-348, 18.2-349, 18.2-355, 18.2-356 or 18.2-357 or of a similar ordinance of any county, city or town or knowingly used for the transportation of any stolen goods, chattels or other property, when the value of such stolen goods, chattels or other property is $200 or more, or any stolen property obtained as a result of a robbery, without regard to the value of the property, shall be forfeited to the Commonwealth. The vehicle shall be seized by any law-enforcement officer arresting the operator of such vehicle for the criminal offense, and delivered to the sheriff of the county or city in which the offense occurred. The officer shall take a receipt therefor.

B. Any vehicle knowingly used by the owner thereof or used by another with his knowledge of and during the commission of, or in an attempt to commit, a misdemeanor violation of subsection D of § 18.2-47 or a felony violation of (i) Article 3 (§ 18.2-47 et seq.) of Chapter 4 of Title 18.2 or (ii) § 18.2-357 where the prostitute is a minor, shall be forfeited to the Commonwealth. The vehicle shall be seized by any law-enforcement officer arresting the operator of such vehicle for the criminal offense, and delivered to the sheriff of the county or city in which the offense occurred. The officer shall take a receipt therefor.

C. Forfeiture of such vehicle shall be enforced as is provided in Chapter 22.1 (§ 19.2-386.1 et seq.).

History.
Code 1950, §§ 18.1-103, 18.1-107.1; 1960, c. 358; 1966, c. 247; 1970, c. 353; 1975, cc. 14, 15, § 18.2-110; 1981, c. 188; 1982, c. 509; 1992, cc. 310, 725; 1993, cc. 609, 866; 2004, c. 995; 2010, c. 710; 2011, cc. 818, 852; 2012, cc. 283, 756.

§ 19.2-386.17. Forfeitures for computer crimes.

All moneys and other income, including all proceeds earned but not yet received by a defendant from a third party as a result of the defendant's violations of Article 7.1 (§ 18.2-152.1 et seq.) of Chapter 5 of Title 18.2, and all computer equipment, all computer software, and all personal property used in connection with any violation of such article known by the owner thereof to have been used in violation of such article, shall be subject to lawful seizure by a law-enforcement officer and forfeiture by the Commonwealth in accordance with the procedures set forth in Chapter 22.1 (§ 19.2-386.1 et seq.) of this title, applied mutatis mutandis.

History.
2003, cc. 987, 1016, § 18.2-152.16; 2004, c. 995.

§ 19.2-386.18. Forfeiture of unlawful electronic communication devices.

Any unlawful electronic communication device possessed, manufactured or sold in violation of §§ 18.2-190.2, 18.2-190.3 or § 18.2-190.4 may be seized and forfeited to the Commonwealth, and turned over to the circuit court in the city or county in which it was seized and such property shall be disposed of as provided by law.

History.
2002, c. 671, § 18.2-190.7; 2003, c. 354; 2004, c. 995.

§ 19.2-386.19. Seizure of property used in connection with money laundering.

The following property shall be subject to lawful seizure by any officer charged with enforcing the provisions of Article 9 (§ 18.2-246.1 et seq.) of Chapter 6 of Title 18.2: (i) all money, equipment, motor vehicles, and all other personal and real property of any kind or character used in substantial connection with the laundering of proceeds of some form of activity punishable as a felony under the laws of the Commonwealth, another state or territory of the United States, the District of Columbia, or the United States; (ii) all money or other property, real or personal, traceable to the proceeds of some form of activity punishable as a felony under the laws of the Commonwealth, another state or territory of the United States, the District of Columbia, or the United States, together with any interest or profits derived from the investment of such proceeds or other property; and (iii) all money, equipment, motor vehicles, and all other personal and real property of any kind or character used to or intended to be used to promote money laundering. Real property shall not be subject to seizure unless the minimum prescribed punishment for the violation is a term of imprisonment of not less than five years. All seizures and forfeitures under this section shall be governed by Chapter 22.1 (§ 19.2-386.1 et seq.), and the procedures specified therein shall apply, mutatis mutandis, to all forfeitures under Article 9 (§ 18.2-246.1 et seq.) of Chapter 6 of Title 18.2.

History.
1999, c. 348, § 18.2-246.4; 2003, cc. 541, 549; 2004, c. 995; 2012, cc. 283, 756.

§ 19.2-386.20. Forfeiture of cigarettes sold or attempted to be sold in an unlawful delivery sale.

Any cigarettes sold or attempted to be sold in a delivery sale in violation of Article 10 (§ 18.2-246.6 et seq.) of Chapter 6 of Title 18.2 shall be forfeited to the Commonwealth and destroyed. All fixtures, equipment, materials and personal property used in substantial connection with a delivery sale or attempted delivery sale in a knowing and intentional violation of such article shall be subject to seizure and forfeiture according to the procedures contained in Chapter 22.1 (§ 19.2-386.1 et seq.) of this title, applied mutatis mutandis.

History.
2004, c. 995.

§ 19.2-386.21. (Effective until July 1, 2018) Forfeiture of counterfeit and contraband cigarettes.

Counterfeit cigarettes possessed in violation of § 18.2-246.14 and cigarettes possessed in violation of § 58.1-1017 or 58.1-1017.1 shall be subject to seizure, forfeiture, and destruction or court-ordered assignment for use by a law-enforcement undercover operation by the Virginia Alcoholic Beverage Control Board or any law-enforcement officer of the Commonwealth. However, any undercover operation that makes use of counterfeit cigarettes shall ensure that the counterfeit cigarettes remain under the control and command of law enforcement and shall not be distributed to a member of the general public who is not the subject of a criminal investigation. All fixtures, equipment, materials, and personal property used in substantial connection with (i) the sale or possession of counterfeit cigarettes in a knowing and intentional violation of Article 10 (§ 18.2-246.6 et seq.) of Chapter 6 of Title 18.2 or (ii) the sale or possession of cigarettes in a knowing and intentional violation of § 58.1-1017 or 58.1-1017.1 shall be subject to seizure and forfeiture according to the procedures contained in Chapter 22.1 (§ 19.2-386.1 et seq.), applied mutatis mutandis.

History.
2004, c. 995; 2013, c. 627; 2014, cc. 422, 458.

§ 19.2-386.21. (Effective July 1, 2018) Forfeiture of counterfeit and contraband cigarettes.

Counterfeit cigarettes possessed in violation of § 18.2-246.14 and cigarettes possessed in violation of § 58.1-1017 or 58.1-1017.1 shall be subject to seizure, forfeiture, and destruction or court-ordered assignment for use by a law-enforcement undercover operation by the Virginia Alcoholic Beverage Control Authority or any law-enforcement officer of the Commonwealth. However, any undercover operation that makes use of counterfeit cigarettes shall ensure that the counterfeit cigarettes remain under the control and command of law enforcement and shall not be distributed to a member of the general public who is not the subject of a criminal investigation. All fixtures, equipment, materials, and personal property used in substantial connection with (i) the sale or possession of counterfeit cigarettes in a knowing and intentional violation of Article 10 (§ 18.2-246.6 et seq.) of Chapter 6 of Title 18.2 or (ii) the sale or possession of cigarettes in a knowing and intentional violation of § 58.1-1017 or 58.1-1017.1 shall be subject to seizure and forfeiture according to the procedures contained in Chapter 22.1 (§ 19.2-386.1 et seq.), applied mutatis mutandis.

History.
2004, c. 995; 2013, c. 627; 2014, cc. 422, 458; 2015, cc. 38, 730.

§ 19.2-386.22. Seizure of property used in connection with or derived from illegal drug transactions.

A. The following property shall be subject to lawful seizure by any officer charged with enforcing the provisions of Article 1 (§ 18.2-247 et seq.) of Chapter 7 of Title 18.2: (i) all money, medical equipment, office equipment, laboratory equipment, motor vehicles, and all other personal and real property of any kind or character, used in substantial connection with (a) the illegal manufacture, sale or distribution of controlled substances or possession with intent to sell or distribute controlled substances in violation of § 18.2-248, (b) the sale or distribution of marijuana or possession with intent to distribute marijuana in violation of subdivisions (a)(2), (a)(3) and (c) of § 18.2-248.1, or (c) a drug-related offense in violation of § 18.2-474.1; (ii) everything of value furnished, or intended to be furnished, in exchange for a controlled substance in violation of § 18.2-248 or for marijuana in violation of § 18.2-248.1 or for a controlled substance or marijuana in violation of § 18.2-474.1; and (iii) all moneys or other property, real or personal, traceable to such an exchange, together with any interest or profits derived from the investment of such money or other property. Under the provisions of clause (i), real property shall not be subject to lawful seizure unless the minimum prescribed punishment for the violation is a term of not less than five years.

B. All seizures and forfeitures under this section shall be governed by the procedures contained in Chapter 22.1 (§ 19.2-386.1 et seq.).

History.

Code 1950, § 18.1-346; 1960, c. 358; 1970, c. 650; 1972, c. 799; 1973, c. 171; 1975, cc. 14, 15, § 18.2-249; 1976, c. 132; 1979, c. 435; 1982, c. 462; 1985, c. 569; 1986, cc. 449, 485; 1988, cc. 575, 753; 1989, cc. 638, 690; 1993, c. 825; 1999, c. 269; 2004, c. 995; 2011, cc. 384, 410; 2014, cc. 674, 719.

§ 19.2-386.23. Disposal of seized controlled substances, marijuana, and paraphernalia.

A. All controlled substances, imitation controlled substances, marijuana, or paraphernalia, the lawful possession of which is not established or the title to which cannot be ascertained, which have come into the custody of a peace officer or have been seized in connection with violations of Chapter 7 (§ 18.2-247 et seq.) of Title 18.2, shall be forfeited and disposed of as follows:

1. Upon written application by (i) the Department of Forensic Science, (ii) the Department of State Police, or (iii) any police department or sheriff's office in a locality, the court may order the forfeiture of any such substance or paraphernalia to the Department of Forensic Science, the Department of State Police, or to such police department or sheriff's office for research and training purposes and for destruction pursuant to regulations of the United States Department of Justice Drug Enforcement Administration and of the Board of Pharmacy once these purposes have been fulfilled.

2. In the event no application is made under subdivision 1, the court shall order the destruction of all such substances or paraphernalia, which order shall state the existence and nature of the substance or paraphernalia, the quantity thereof, the location where seized, the person or persons from whom the substance or paraphernalia was seized, if known, and the manner whereby such item shall be destroyed. However, the court may order that paraphernalia identified in subdivision 5 of § 18.2-265.1 not be destroyed and that it be given to a person or entity that makes a showing to the court of sufficient need for the property and an ability to put the property to a lawful and publicly beneficial use. A return under oath, reporting the time, place and manner of destruction shall be made to the court by the officer to whom the order is directed. A copy of the order and affidavit shall be made a part of the record of any criminal prosecution in which the substance or paraphernalia was used as evidence and shall, thereafter, be prima facie evidence of its contents. In the event a law-enforcement agency recovers, seizes, finds, is given or otherwise comes into possession of any such substances or paraphernalia that are not evidence in a trial in the Commonwealth, the chief law-enforcement officer of the agency or his designee may, with the written consent of the appropriate attorney for the Commonwealth, order destruction of same; provided that a statement under oath, reporting a description of the substances and paraphernalia destroyed and the time, place and manner of destruction, is made to the chief law-enforcement officer by the officer to whom the order is directed.

B. No such substance or paraphernalia used or to be used in a criminal prosecution under Chapter 7 (§ 18.2-247 et seq.) of Title 18.2 shall be disposed of as provided by this section until all rights of appeal have been exhausted, except as provided in § 19.2-386.24.

C. The amount of any specific controlled substance, or imitation controlled substance, retained by any law-enforcement agency pursuant to a court order issued under this section shall not exceed five pounds, or 25 pounds in the case of marijuana. Any written application to the court for controlled substances, imitation controlled substances, or marijuana, shall certify that the amount requested shall not result in the requesting agency's exceeding the limits allowed by this subsection.

D. A law-enforcement agency that retains any controlled substance, imitation controlled substance, or marijuana, pursuant to a court order issued under this section shall (i) be required to conduct an inventory of such substance on a monthly basis, which shall include a description and weight of the substance, and (ii) destroy such substance pursuant to subdivision A 1 when no longer needed for research and training purposes. A written report outlining the details of the inventory shall be made to the chief law-enforcement officer of the agency within 10 days of the completion of the inventory, and the agency shall detail the substances that were used for research and training pursuant to a court order in the immediately preceding fiscal year. Destruction of such substance shall be certified to the court along with a statement prepared under oath, reporting a description of the substance destroyed, and the time, place, and manner of destruction.

History.

Code 1950, § 54-524.101:5; 1973, c. 470; 1974, c. 113; 1975, cc. 14, 15, 607, § 18.2-253; 1979, cc. 435, 646; 1982, c. 462; 1990, c. 825; 1995, c. 578; 2001, c. 195; 2004, c. 995; 2005, cc. 868, 881; 2006, c. 107; 2011, cc. 384, 410; 2014, cc. 99, 254, 674, 686, 719; 2015, c. 429.

§ 19.2-386.24. Destruction of seized controlled substances or marijuana prior to trial.

Where seizures of controlled substances or marijuana are made in excess of 10 pounds in connection with any prosecution or investigation under Chapter 7 (§ 18.2-247 et seq.) of Title 18.2, the appropriate law-enforcement agency may retain 10 pounds of the substance randomly selected from the seized substance for representative purposes as evidence and destroy the remainder of the seized substance.

Before any destruction is carried out under this section, the law-enforcement agency shall cause the material seized to be photographed with identification case numbers or other means of identification and shall prepare a report identifying the seized material. It shall also notify the accused, or other interested party, if known, or his attorney, at least five days in advance that the photography will take place and that they may be present. Prior to any destruction under this section, the law-enforcement agency shall also notify the accused or other interested party, if known, and his attorney at least seven days prior to the destruction of the time and place the destruction will occur. Any notice required under the provisions of this section shall be by first-class mail to the last known address of the person required to be notified. In addition to the substance retained for representative purposes as evidence, all photographs and records made under this section and properly identified shall be admissible in any court proceeding for any purposes for which the seized substance itself would have been admissible.

History.

1979, c. 646, § 18.2-253.1; 1980, c. 179; 2004, c. 995; 2011, cc. 384, 410; 2014, cc. 674, 719.

§ 19.2-386.25. Judge may order law-enforcement agency to maintain custody of controlled substances, etc.

Upon request of the clerk of any court, a judge of the court may order a law-enforcement agency to take into its custody or to maintain custody of substantial quantities of any controlled substances, imitation controlled substances, chemicals, marijuana, or paraphernalia used or to be used in a criminal prosecution under Chapter 7 (§ 18.2-247 et seq.) of Title 18.2. The court in its order may make provision for ensuring integrity of these items until further order of the court.

History.

1985, c. 377, § 18.2-253.2; 2004, c. 995; 2011, cc. 384, 410; 2014, cc. 674, 719.

§ 19.2-386.26. Seizure and forfeiture of drug paraphernalia.

All drug paraphernalia as defined in Article 1.1 (§ 18.2-247 et seq.) of Chapter 7 of Title 18.2 shall be forfeited to the Commonwealth and may be seized and disposed of in the same manner as provided in § 19.2-386.23, subject to the rights of an innocent lienor, to be recognized as under § 19.2-386.8.

History.

1981, c. 598, § 18.2-265.4; 1993, c. 866; 2004, c. 995; 2012, cc. 283, 756.

§ 19.2-386.27. Forfeiture of firearms carried in violation of Article 6.1 (§ 18.2-307.1 et seq.).

Any weapon used in the commission of a violation of Article 6.1 (§ 18.2-307.1 et seq.) of Chapter 7 of Title 18.2 shall be forfeited to the Commonwealth and may be seized by an officer as forfeited, and such as may be needed for police officers, conservators of the peace, and the Department of Forensic Science shall be devoted to that purpose, subject to any registration requirements of federal law, and the remainder shall be disposed of as provided in § 19.2-386.29.

History.

2004, c. 995; 2005, cc. 868, 881; 2013, c. 746.

§ 19.2-386.28. Forfeiture of weapons that are concealed, possessed, transported or carried in violation of law.

Any firearm, stun weapon as defined by § 18.2-308.1, or any weapon concealed, possessed, transported or carried in violation of § 18.2-283.1, 18.2-287.01, 18.2-287.4, 18.2-308.1:2, 18.2-308.1:3, 18.2-308.1:4, 18.2-308.2, 18.2-308.2:01, 18.2-308.2:1, 18.2-308.4, 18.2-308.5, 18.2-308.7, or 18.2-308.8 shall be forfeited to the Commonwealth and disposed of as provided in § 19.2-386.29.

History.

2004, c. 995; 2007, c. 519; 2013, c. 746.

§ 19.2-386.29. Forfeiture of certain weapons used in commission of criminal offense.

All pistols, shotguns, rifles, dirks, bowie knives, switchblade knives, ballistic knives, razors, slingshots, brass or metal knucks, blackjacks, stun weapons, and other weapons used by any person in the commission of a criminal offense, shall, upon conviction of such person, be forfeited to the Commonwealth by order of the court trying the case. The court shall dispose of such weapons as it deems proper by entry of an order of record. Such disposition may include the destruction of the weapons or, subject to any registration requirements of federal law, sale of the firearms to a licensed dealer in such firearms in accordance with the provisions of Chapter 22.1 (§ 19.2-386.1 et seq.) regarding sale of property forfeited to the Commonwealth.

The court may authorize the seizing law-enforcement agency to use the weapon for a period of time as specified in the order. When the seizing agency ceases to so use the weapon, it shall be disposed of as otherwise provided in this section.

However, upon petition to the court and notice to the attorney for the Commonwealth, the court, upon good cause shown, shall return any such weapon to its lawful owner after conclusion of all relevant proceedings if such owner (i) did not know and had no reason to know of the conduct giving rise to the forfeiture and (ii) is not otherwise prohibited by law from possessing the weapon. The owner shall acknowledge in a sworn affidavit to be filed with the record in the case or cases that he has retaken possession of the weapon involved.

History.

Code 1950, § 18.1-270; 1960, c. 358; 1975, cc. 14, 15, § 18.2-310; 1986, cc. 445, 641; 1988, c. 359; 1990, cc. 556, 944; 2004, c. 995; 2007, c. 519; 2012, cc. 283, 756.

§ 19.2-386.30. Forfeiture of money, gambling devices, etc., seized from illegal gambling enterprise; innocent owners or lienors.

All money, gambling devices, office equipment and other personal property used in connection with an illegal gambling enterprise or activity, and all money, stakes and things of value received or proposed to be received by a winner in any illegal gambling transaction, which are lawfully seized by any law-enforcement officer or which shall lawfully come into his custody, shall be forfeited to the Commonwealth in accordance with the procedures contained in Chapter 22.1 (§ 19.2-386.1 et seq.).

History.

Code 1950, §§ 18.1-321, 18.1-323, 18.1-333, 18.1-341; 1960, c. 358; 1975, cc. 14, 15, 576, § 18.2-336; 2004, c. 995; 2012, cc. 283, 756.

§ 19.2-386.31. Seizure and forfeiture of property used in connection with the exploitation and solicitation of children.

All audio and visual equipment, electronic equipment, devices and other personal property used in connection with the possession, production, distribution, publication, sale, possession with intent to distribute or making of child pornography that constitutes a violation of § 18.2-374.1 or 18.2-374.1:1, or in connection with the solicitation of a person less than 18 years of age that constitutes a violation of § 18.2-374.3 shall be subject to lawful seizure by a law-enforcement officer and shall be subject to forfeiture to the Commonwealth pursuant to Chapter 22.1 (§ 19.2-386.1 et seq.). The Commonwealth shall file an information and notice of seizure in accordance with the procedures in Chapter 22.1 (§ 19.2-386.1 et seq.); however, any forfeiture action shall be stayed until conviction of the person whose property is subject to forfeiture. Upon his conviction, the court may dispose of the issue of forfeiture or may continue the civil case allowing the defendant time to answer, at the court's discretion.

History.

1986, c. 596, § 18.2-374.2; 1999, c. 659; 2004, c. 995; 2007, cc. 134, 386; 2012, cc. 283, 756.

§ 19.2-386.32. Seizure and forfeiture of property used in connection with the abduction of children.

All moneys and other property, real and personal, owned by a person and used to further the abduction of a child in violation of § 18.2-47, 18.2-48, or 18.2-48.1 are subject to lawful seizure by a law-enforcement officer and are subject to forfeiture to the Commonwealth pursuant to Chapter 22.1 (§ 19.2-386.1 et seq.) by order of the court in which a conviction under § 18.2-47, 18.2-48, or 18.2-48.1 is obtained.

History.

2011, cc. 818, 852; 2012, cc. 283, 756.

§ 19.2-386.33. Forfeiture of money, etc., derived from violation of §§ 2.2-3103 through 2.2-3112.

In addition to any other fine or penalty provided by law, any money or other thing of value derived by an officer or employee from a violation of §§ 2.2-3103 through 2.2-3112 shall be forfeited, in accordance with the procedures contained in Chapter 22.1 (§ 19.2-386.1 et seq.). If the thing of value received by the officer or employee in violation of §§ 2.2-3103 through 2.2-3112 increases in value between the time of the violation and the time of discovery of the violation, the greater value shall determine the amount of forfeiture.

History.

2012, cc. 283, 756.

§ 19.2-386.34. Forfeiture of vehicle used in a felony violation of § 18.2-266.

The vehicle solely owned and operated by the accused during the commission of a felony violation of § 18.2-266 shall be subject to seizure and forfeiture. After an arrest upon a felony violation of § 18.2-266, the vehicle may be forfeited to the Commonwealth pursuant to the procedures set forth in Chapter 22.1 (§ 19.2-386.1 et seq.). Any seizure shall be stayed until conviction and the exhaustion of all appeals at which time, if the information has been filed, the Commonwealth shall give notice of seizure to all appropriate parties pursuant to § 19.2-386.3.

An immediate family member of the owner of any motor vehicle for which an information has been filed under this section who was not the driver at the time of the violation may petition the court in which such information was filed for the release of the motor vehicle. If the immediate family member proves by a preponderance of the evidence that his immediate family has only one motor vehicle and will suffer a substantial hardship if that motor vehicle is seized and forfeited, the court, in its discretion, may release the vehicle.

In the event the vehicle was sold to a bona fide purchaser subsequent to the arrest but prior to seizure in order to avoid seizure and forfeiture, the Commonwealth shall have a right of action against the seller for the proceeds of the sale.

History.
2012, cc. 283, 756.

§ 19.2-386.35. Seizure of property used in connection with certain offenses.

All money, equipment, motor vehicles, and other personal and real property of any kind or character together with any interest or profits derived from the investment of such proceeds or other property that (i) was used in connection with the commission of, or in an attempt to commit, a violation of subsection B of § 18.2-47, § 18.2-48 or 18.2-59, subsection B of § 18.2-346, or § 18.2-347, 18.2-348, 18.2-349, 18.2-355, 18.2-356, 18.2-357, 18.2-357.1, 40.1-29, 40.1-100.2, or 40.1-103; (ii) is traceable to the proceeds of some form of activity that violates subsection B of § 18.2-47, § 18.2-48 or 18.2-59, subsection B of § 18.2-346, or § 18.2-347, 18.2-348, 18.2-349, 18.2-355, 18.2-356, 18.2-357, 40.1-29, 40.1-100.2, or 40.1-103; or (iii) was used to or intended to be used to promote some form of activity that violates subsection B of § 18.2-47, § 18.2-48 or 18.2-59, subsection B of § 18.2-346, or § 18.2-347, 18.2-348, 18.2-349, 18.2-355, 18.2-356, 18.2-357, 40.1-29, 40.1-100.2, or 40.1-103 is subject to lawful seizure by a law-enforcement officer and subject to forfeiture to the Commonwealth pursuant to Chapter 22.1 (§ 19.2-386.1 et seq.). Any forfeiture action under this section shall be stayed until conviction, and property eligible for forfeiture pursuant to this section shall be forfeited only upon the entry of a final judgment of conviction for an offense listed in this section; if no such judgment is entered, all property seized pursuant to this section shall be released from seizure.

Real property shall not be subject to seizure unless the minimum prescribed punishment for the violation is a term of imprisonment of not less than five years.

All seizures and forfeitures under this section shall be governed by Chapter 22.1 (§ 19.2-386.1 et seq.), and the procedures specified therein shall apply, mutatis mutandis, to all forfeitures under this section.

History.
2014, c. 658; 2015, cc. 690, 691.

CHAPTER 23.
CENTRAL CRIMINAL RECORDS EXCHANGE.

Section

§ 19.2-387. Exchange to operate as a division of Department of State Police; authority of Superintendent of State Police.

A. The Central Criminal Records Exchange shall operate as a separate division within the Department of State Police and shall be the sole criminal record-keeping agency of the Commonwealth, except for (i) the Department of Juvenile Justice pursuant to Chapter 10 (§ 16.1-222 et seq.) of Title 16.1, (ii) the Department of Motor Vehicles, (iii) for purposes of the DNA data bank, the Department of Forensic Science and (iv) for the purpose of making parole determinations pursuant to subdivisions 1, 2, 3 and 5 of § 53.1-136, the Virginia Parole Board.

B. The Superintendent of State Police is hereby authorized to employ such personnel, establish such offices, and acquire such equipment as shall be necessary to carry out the purposes of this chapter and is also authorized to enter into agreements with other state agencies for services to be performed for it by employees of such other agencies.

History.
Code 1950, § 19.1-19.1:1; 1970, c. 101; 1975, c. 495; 1988, c. 541; 1990, c. 669; 1993, c. 313; 2001, cc. 203, 215; 2003, c. 431; 2005, cc. 868, 881.

§ 19.2-387.1. Protective Order Registry; maintenance; access.

A. The Department of State Police shall keep and maintain a computerized Protective Order Registry. The purpose of the Registry shall be to assist the efforts of law-enforcement agencies to protect their communities and their citizens. The Department of

State Police shall make Registry information available, upon request, to criminal justice agencies, including local law-enforcement agencies, through the Virginia Criminal Information Network (VCIN). Registry information provided under this section shall be used only for the purposes of the administration of criminal justice.

B. No liability shall be imposed upon any law-enforcement official who disseminates information or fails to disseminate information in good faith compliance with the requirements of this section, but this provision shall not be construed to grant immunity for gross negligence or willful misconduct.

History.
2002, cc. 810, 818.

§ 19.2-388. Duties and authority of Exchange.

A. It shall be the duty of the Central Criminal Records Exchange to receive, classify and file criminal history record information as defined in § 9.1-101 and other records required to be reported to it by §§ 16.1-299 and 19.2-390. The Exchange is authorized to prepare and furnish to all state and local law-enforcement officials and agencies; to clerks of circuit courts, general district courts, and juvenile and domestic relations district courts; and to corrections and penal officials, forms which shall be used for the making of such reports.

B. Juvenile records received pursuant to § 16.1-299 shall be maintained separately from adult records.

Criminal Procedure

History.
Code 1950, § 19.1-19.2; 1966, c. 669; 1968, c. 537; 1970, c. 118; 1975, c. 495; 1976, c. 771; 1982, c. 33; 1993, cc. 468, 926; 1996, cc. 755, 914.

§ 19.2-389. Dissemination of criminal history record information.

A. Criminal history record information shall be disseminated, whether directly or through an intermediary, only to:

1. Authorized officers or employees of criminal justice agencies, as defined by § 9.1-101, for purposes of the administration of criminal justice and the screening of an employment application or review of employment by a criminal justice agency with respect to its own employees or applicants, and dissemination to the Virginia Parole Board, pursuant to this subdivision, of such information on all state-responsible inmates for the purpose of making parole determinations pursuant to subdivisions 1, 2, 3, and 5 of § 53.1-136 shall include collective dissemination by electronic means every 30 days. For purposes of this subdivision, criminal history record information includes information sent to the Central Criminal Records Exchange pursuant to §§ 37.2-819 and 64.2-2014 when disseminated to any full-time or part-time employee of the State Police, a police department or sheriff's office that is a part of or administered by the Commonwealth or any political subdivision thereof, and who is responsible for the prevention and detection of crime and the enforcement of the penal, traffic or highway laws of the Commonwealth for the purposes of the administration of criminal justice;

2. Such other individuals and agencies that require criminal history record information to implement a state or federal statute or executive order of the President of the United States or Governor that expressly refers to criminal conduct and contains requirements or exclusions expressly based upon such conduct, except that information concerning the arrest of an individual may not be disseminated to a noncriminal justice agency or individual if an interval of one year has elapsed from the date of the arrest and no disposition of the charge has been recorded and no active prosecution of the charge is pending;

3. Individuals and agencies pursuant to a specific agreement with a criminal justice agency to provide services required for the administration of criminal justice pursuant to that agreement which shall specifically authorize access to data, limit the use of data to purposes for which given, and ensure the security and confidentiality of the data;

4. Individuals and agencies for the express purpose of research, evaluative, or statistical activities pursuant to an agreement with a criminal justice agency that shall specifically authorize access to data, limit the use of data to research, evaluative, or statistical purposes, and ensure the confidentiality and security of the data;

5. Agencies of state or federal government that are authorized by state or federal statute or executive order of the President of the United States or Governor to conduct investigations determining employment suitability or eligibility for security clearances allowing access to classified information;

6. Individuals and agencies where authorized by court order or court rule;

7. Agencies of any political subdivision of the Commonwealth, public transportation companies owned, operated or controlled by any political subdivision, and any public service corporation that operates a public transit system owned by a local government for the conduct of investigations of applicants for employment, permit, or license whenever, in the interest of public welfare or safety, it is necessary to determine under a duly enacted ordinance if the past criminal conduct of a person with a conviction record would be compatible with the nature of the employment, permit, or license under consideration;

7a. Commissions created pursuant to the Transportation District Act of 1964 (§ 33.2-1900 et seq.) of Title 33.2 and their contractors, for the conduct of investigations of individuals who have been offered a position of employment whenever, in the interest of public welfare or safety and as authorized in the

Transportation District Act of 1964, it is necessary to determine if the past criminal conduct of a person with a conviction record would be compatible with the nature of the employment under consideration;

8. Public or private agencies when authorized or required by federal or state law or interstate compact to investigate (i) applicants for foster or adoptive parenthood or (ii) any individual, and the adult members of that individual's household, with whom the agency is considering placing a child or from whom the agency is considering removing a child due to abuse or neglect, on an emergency, temporary, or permanent basis pursuant to §§ 63.2-901.1 and 63.2-1505, subject to the restriction that the data shall not be further disseminated to any party other than a federal or state authority or court as may be required to comply with an express requirement of law;

9. To the extent permitted by federal law or regulation, public service companies as defined in § 56-1, for the conduct of investigations of applicants for employment when such employment involves personal contact with the public or when past criminal conduct of an applicant would be incompatible with the nature of the employment under consideration;

10. The appropriate authority for purposes of granting citizenship and for purposes of international travel, including, but not limited to, issuing visas and passports;

11. A person requesting a copy of his own criminal history record information as defined in § 9.1-101 at his cost, except that criminal history record information shall be supplied at no charge to a person who has applied to be a volunteer with (i) a Virginia affiliate of Big Brothers/Big Sisters of America; (ii) a volunteer fire company; (iii) the Volunteer Emergency Families for Children; (iv) any affiliate of Prevent Child Abuse, Virginia; (v) any Virginia affiliate of Compeer; or (vi) any board member or any individual who has been offered membership on the board of a Crime Stoppers, Crime Solvers or Crime Line program as defined in § 15.2-1713.1;

12. Administrators and board presidents of and applicants for licensure or registration as a child welfare agency as defined in § 63.2-100 for dissemination to the Commissioner of Social Services' representative pursuant to § 63.2-1702 for the conduct of investigations with respect to employees of and volunteers at such facilities, caretakers, and other adults living in family day homes or homes approved by family day systems, and foster and adoptive parent applicants of private child-placing agencies, pursuant to §§ 63.2-1719, 63.2-1720, 63.2-1720.1, 63.2-1721, and 63.2-1721.1, subject to the restriction that the data shall not be further disseminated by the facility or agency to any party other than the data subject, the Commissioner of Social Services' representative or a federal or state authority or court as may be required to comply with an express requirement of law for such further dissemination;

13. The school boards of the Commonwealth for the purpose of screening individuals who are offered or who accept public school employment and those current school board employees for whom a report of arrest has been made pursuant to § 19.2-83.1;

14. The Virginia Lottery for the conduct of investigations as set forth in the Virginia Lottery Law (§ 58.1-4000 et seq.), and the Department of Agriculture and Consumer Services for the conduct of investigations as set forth in Article 1.1:1 (§ 18.2-340.15 et seq.) of Chapter 8 of Title 18.2;

15. Licensed nursing homes, hospitals and home care organizations for the conduct of investigations of applicants for compensated employment in licensed nursing homes pursuant to § 32.1-126.01, hospital pharmacies pursuant to § 32.1-126.02, and home care organizations pursuant to § 32.1-162.9:1, subject to the limitations set out in subsection E;

16. Licensed assisted living facilities and licensed adult day care centers for the conduct of investigations of applicants for compensated employment in licensed assisted living facilities and licensed adult day care centers pursuant to § 63.2-1720, subject to the limitations set out in subsection F;

17. **(Effective until July 1, 2018)** The Alcoholic Beverage Control Board for the conduct of investigations as set forth in § 4.1-103.1;

17. **(Effective July 1, 2018)** The Virginia Alcoholic Beverage Control Authority for the conduct of investigations as set forth in § 4.1-103.1;

18. The State Board of Elections and authorized officers and employees thereof and general registrars appointed pursuant to § 24.2-110 in the course of conducting necessary investigations with respect to voter registration, limited to any record of felony convictions;

19. The Commissioner of Behavioral Health and Developmental Services for those individuals who are committed to the custody of the Commissioner pursuant to §§ 19.2-169.2, 19.2-169.6, 19.2-182.2, 19.2-182.3, 19.2-182.8, and 19.2-182.9 for the purpose of placement, evaluation, and treatment planning;

20. Any alcohol safety action program certified by the Commission on the Virginia Alcohol Safety Action Program for (i) assessments of habitual offenders under § 46.2-360, (ii) interventions with first offenders under § 18.2-251, or (iii) services to offenders under § 18.2-51.4, 18.2-266, or 18.2-266.1;

21. Residential facilities for juveniles regulated or operated by the Department of Social Services, the Department of Education, or the Department of Behavioral Health and Developmental Services for the purpose of determining applicants' fitness for employment or for providing volunteer or contractual services;

22. The Department of Behavioral Health and Developmental Services and facilities operated by the Department for the purpose of determining an individual's fitness for employment pursuant to departmental instructions;

23. Pursuant to § 22.1-296.3, the governing boards or administrators of private elementary or secondary schools which are accredited pursuant to § 22.1-19 or a private organization coordinating such records information on behalf of such governing boards or administrators pursuant to a written agreement with the Department of State Police;

24. Public and nonprofit private colleges and universities for the purpose of screening individuals who are offered or accept employment;

25. **(Effective until October 1, 2016)** Members of a threat assessment team established by a local school board pursuant to § 22.1-79.4, by a public institution of higher education pursuant to § 23-9.2:10, or by a private nonprofit institution of higher education, for the purpose of assessing or intervening with an individual whose behavior may present a threat to safety; however, no member of a threat assessment team shall redisclose any criminal history record information obtained pursuant to this section or otherwise use any record of an individual beyond the purpose that such disclosure was made to the threat assessment team;

25. **(Effective October 1, 2016)** Members of a threat assessment team established by a local school board pursuant to § 22.1-79.4, by a public institution of higher education pursuant to § 23.1-805, or by a private nonprofit institution of higher education, for the purpose of assessing or intervening with an individual whose behavior may present a threat to safety; however, no member of a threat assessment team shall redisclose any criminal history record information obtained pursuant to this section or otherwise use any record of an individual beyond the purpose that such disclosure was made to the threat assessment team;

26. Executive directors of community services boards or the personnel director serving the community services board for the purpose of determining an individual's fitness for employment, approval as a sponsored residential service provider, or permission to enter into a shared living arrangement with a person receiving medical assistance services pursuant to a waiver pursuant to §§ 37.2-506 and 37.2-607;

27. Executive directors of behavioral health authorities as defined in § 37.2-600 for the purpose of determining an individual's fitness for employment, approval as a sponsored residential service provider, or permission to enter into a shared living arrangement with a person receiving medical assistance services pursuant to a waiver pursuant to §§ 37.2-506 and 37.2-607;

28. The Commissioner of Social Services for the purpose of locating persons who owe child support or who are alleged in a pending paternity proceeding to be a putative father, provided that only the name, address, demographics and social security number of the data subject shall be released;

29. Authorized officers or directors of agencies licensed pursuant to Article 2 (§ 37.2-403 et seq.) of Chapter 4 of Title 37.2 by the Department of Behavioral Health and Developmental Services for the purpose of determining if any applicant who accepts employment in any direct care position or requests approval as a sponsored residential service provider or permission to enter into a shared living arrangement with a person receiving medical assistance services pursuant to a waiver has been convicted of a crime that affects his fitness to have responsibility for the safety and well-being of individuals with mental illness, intellectual disability, or substance abuse pursuant to §§ 37.2-416, 37.2-506, and 37.2-607;

30. The Commissioner of the Department of Motor Vehicles, for the purpose of evaluating applicants for and holders of a motor carrier certificate or license subject to the provisions of Chapters 20 (§ 46.2-2000 et seq.) and 21 (§ 46.2-2100 et seq.) of Title 46.2;

31. The chairmen of the Committees for Courts of Justice of the Senate or the House of Delegates for the purpose of determining if any person being considered for election to any judgeship has been convicted of a crime;

32. Heads of state agencies in which positions have been identified as sensitive for the purpose of determining an individual's fitness for employment in positions designated as sensitive under Department of Human Resource Management policies developed pursuant to § 2.2-1201.1. Dissemination of criminal history record information to the agencies shall be limited to those positions generally described as directly responsible for the health, safety and welfare of the general populace or protection of critical infrastructures;

33. The Office of the Attorney General, for all criminal justice activities otherwise permitted under subdivision A 1 and for purposes of performing duties required by the Civil Commitment of Sexually Violent Predators Act (§ 37.2-900 et seq.);

34. Shipyards, to the extent permitted by federal law or regulation, engaged in the design, construction, overhaul, or repair of nuclear vessels for the United States Navy, including their subsidiary companies, for the conduct of investigations of applications for employment or for access to facilities, by contractors, leased laborers, and other visitors;

35. Any employer of individuals whose employment requires that they enter the homes of others, for the purpose of screening individuals who apply for, are offered, or have accepted such employment;

36. Public agencies when and as required by federal or state law to investigate (i) applicants as providers of adult foster care and home-based services or (ii) any individual with whom the agency is considering placing an adult on an emergency, temporary, or permanent basis pursuant to § 63.2-1601.1, subject to the restriction that the data shall not be further disseminated by the agency to any party other than a federal or state authority or court as may be required to comply with an express

requirement of law for such further dissemination, subject to limitations set out in subsection G;

37. The Department of Medical Assistance Services, or its designee, for the purpose of screening individuals who, through contracts, subcontracts, or direct employment, volunteer, apply for, are offered, or have accepted a position related to the provision of transportation services to enrollees in the Medicaid Program or the Family Access to Medical Insurance Security (FAMIS) Program, or any other program administered by the Department of Medical Assistance Services;

38. The State Corporation Commission for the purpose of investigating individuals who are current or proposed members, senior officers, directors, and principals of an applicant or person licensed under Chapter 16 (§ 6.2-1600 et seq.) or Chapter 19 (§ 6.2-1900 et seq.) of Title 6.2. Notwithstanding any other provision of law, if an application is denied based in whole or in part on information obtained from the Central Criminal Records Exchange pursuant to Chapter 16 or 19 of Title 6.2, the Commissioner of Financial Institutions or his designee may disclose such information to the applicant or its designee;

39. The Department of Professional and Occupational Regulation for the purpose of investigating individuals for initial licensure pursuant to § 54.1-2106.1;

40. The Department for Aging and Rehabilitative Services and the Department for the Blind and Vision Impaired for the purpose of evaluating an individual's fitness for various types of employment and for the purpose of delivering comprehensive vocational rehabilitation services pursuant to Article 11 (§ 51.5-170 et seq.) of Chapter 14 of Title 51.5 that will assist the individual in obtaining employment;

41. Bail bondsmen, in accordance with the provisions of § 19.2-120;

42. The State Treasurer for the purpose of determining whether a person receiving compensation for wrongful incarceration meets the conditions for continued compensation under § 8.01-195.12;

43. The Department of Social Services and directors of local departments of social services for the purpose of screening individuals seeking to enter into a contract with the Department of Social Services or a local department of social services for the provision of child care services for which child care subsidy payments may be provided;

44. The Department of Juvenile Justice to investigate any parent, guardian, or other adult members of a juvenile's household when completing a predispositional or postdispositional report required by § 16.1-273 or a Board of Juvenile Justice regulation promulgated pursuant to § 16.1-233; and

45. Other entities as otherwise provided by law.

Upon an ex parte motion of a defendant in a felony case and upon the showing that the records requested may be relevant to such case, the court shall enter an order requiring the Central Criminal Records Exchange to furnish the defendant, as soon as practicable, copies of any records of persons designated in the order on whom a report has been made under the provisions of this chapter.

Notwithstanding any other provision of this chapter to the contrary, upon a written request sworn to before an officer authorized to take acknowledgments, the Central Criminal Records Exchange, or the criminal justice agency in cases of offenses not required to be reported to the Exchange, shall furnish a copy of conviction data covering the person named in the request to the person making the request; however, such person on whom the data is being obtained shall consent in writing, under oath, to the making of such request. A person receiving a copy of his own conviction data may utilize or further disseminate that data as he deems appropriate. In the event no conviction data is maintained on the data subject, the person making the request shall be furnished at his cost a certification to that effect.

B. Use of criminal history record information disseminated to noncriminal justice agencies under this section shall be limited to the purposes for which it was given and may not be disseminated further.

C. No criminal justice agency or person shall confirm the existence or nonexistence of criminal history record information for employment or licensing inquiries except as provided by law.

D. Criminal justice agencies shall establish procedures to query the Central Criminal Records Exchange prior to dissemination of any criminal history record information on offenses required to be reported to the Central Criminal Records Exchange to ensure that the most up-to-date disposition data is being used. Inquiries of the Exchange shall be made prior to any dissemination except in those cases where time is of the essence and the normal response time of the Exchange would exceed the necessary time period. A criminal justice agency to whom a request has been made for the dissemination of criminal history record information that is required to be reported to the Central Criminal Records Exchange may direct the inquirer to the Central Criminal Records Exchange for such dissemination. Dissemination of information regarding offenses not required to be reported to the Exchange shall be made by the criminal justice agency maintaining the record as required by § 15.2-1722.

E. Criminal history information provided to licensed nursing homes, hospitals and to home care organizations pursuant to subdivision A 15 shall be limited to the convictions on file with the Exchange for any offense specified in §§ 32.1-126.01, 32.1-126.02, and 32.1-162.9:1.

F. Criminal history information provided to licensed assisted living facilities and licensed adult day care centers pursuant to subdivision A 16 shall be limited to the convictions on file with the Exchange for any offense specified in § 63.2-1720.

G. Criminal history information provided to public agencies pursuant to subdivision A 36 shall be limited to the convictions on file with the Exchange for any offense specified in § 63.2-1719.

H. Upon receipt of a written request from an employer or prospective employer, the Central Criminal Records Exchange, or the criminal justice agency in cases of offenses not required to be reported to the Exchange, shall furnish at the employer's cost a copy of conviction data covering the person named in the request to the employer or prospective employer making the request, provided that the person on whom the data is being obtained has consented in writing to the making of such request and has presented a photo-identification to the employer or prospective employer. In the event no conviction data is maintained on the person named in the request, the requesting employer or prospective employer shall be furnished at his cost a certification to that effect. The criminal history record search shall be conducted on forms provided by the Exchange.

History.

Code 1950, § 19.1-19.2; 1966, c. 669; 1968, c. 537; 1970, c. 118; 1975, c. 495; 1976, c. 771; 1977, c. 626; 1978, c. 350; 1979, c. 480; 1981, c. 207; 1985, c. 360; 1987, cc. 130, 131; 1988, c. 851; 1989, c. 544; 1990, c. 766; 1991, c. 342; 1992, cc. 422, 641, 718, 746, 791, 844; 1993, cc. 48, 313, 348; 1994, cc. 34, 670, 700, 830; 1995, cc. 409, 645, 731, 781, 809; 1996, cc. 428, 432, 747, 881, 927, 944; 1997, cc. 169, 177, 606, 691, 721, 743, 796, 895; 1998, cc. 113, 405, 445, 882; 1999, cc. 383, 685; 2001, cc. 552, 582; 2002, cc. 370, 587, 606; 2003, c. 731; 2005, cc. 149, 914, 928; 2006, cc. 257, 277, 644; 2007, cc. 12, 361, 495, 572; 2008, cc. 387, 689, 863; 2009, cc. 667, 813, 840; 2010, cc. 189, 340, 406, 456, 524, 563, 862; 2011, cc. 432, 449; 2012, cc. 40, 189, 386, 476, 507, 803, 835; 2013, cc. 165, 176, 261, 407, 491, 582; 2014, cc. 225, 454; 2015, cc. 38, 343, 540, 730, 758, 770; 2016, cc. 454, 554, 574.

Editor's note.

References in this section were updated at the direction of the Virginia Code Commission to conform to the recodification of Title 33.2 by Acts 2014, c. 805, effective October 1, 2014.

§ 19.2-389.1. (Effective until October 1, 2016) Dissemination of juvenile record information.

Record information maintained in the Central Criminal Records Exchange pursuant to the provisions of § 16.1-299 shall be disseminated only (i) to make the determination as provided in §§ 18.2-308.2 and 18.2-308.2:2 of eligibility to possess or purchase a firearm; (ii) to aid in the preparation of a pretrial investigation report prepared by a local pretrial services agency established pursuant to Article 5 (§ 19.2-152.2 et seq.) of Chapter 9, a presentence or post-sentence investigation report pursuant to § 19.2-264.5 or 19.2-299 or in the preparation of the discretionary sentencing guidelines worksheets pursuant to subsection C of § 19.2-298.01; (iii) to aid local community-based probation services agencies established pursuant to the Comprehensive Community Corrections Act for Local-Responsible Offenders (§ 9.1-173 et seq.) with investigating or serving adult local-responsible offenders and all court service units serving juvenile delinquent offenders; (iv) for fingerprint comparison utilizing the fingerprints maintained in the Automated Fingerprint Information System (AFIS) computer; (v) to attorneys for the Commonwealth to secure information incidental to sentencing and to attorneys for the Commonwealth and probation officers to prepare the discretionary sentencing guidelines worksheets pursuant to subsection C of § 19.2-298.01; (vi) to any full-time or part-time employee of the State Police, a police department or sheriff's office that is a part of or administered by the Commonwealth or any political subdivision thereof, and who is responsible for the prevention and detection of crime and the enforcement of the penal, traffic or highway laws of the Commonwealth, for purposes of the administration of criminal justice as defined in § 9.1-101; (vii) to the Department of Forensic Science to verify its authority to maintain the juvenile's sample in the DNA data bank pursuant to § 16.1-299.1; (viii) to the Office of the Attorney General, for all criminal justice activities otherwise permitted and for purposes of performing duties required by the Civil Commitment of Sexually Violent Predators Act (§ 37.2-900 et seq.); (ix) to the Virginia Criminal Sentencing Commission for research purposes; (x) to members of a threat assessment team established by a school board pursuant to § 22.1-79.4, by a public institution of higher education pursuant to § 23-9.2:10, or by a private nonprofit institution of higher education, to aid in the assessment or intervention with individuals whose behavior may present a threat to safety; however, no member of a threat assessment team shall redisclose any juvenile record information obtained pursuant to this section or otherwise use any record of an individual beyond the purpose that such disclosure was made to the threat assessment team; and (xi) to any full-time or part-time employee of the State Police or a police department or sheriff's office that is a part of or administered by the Commonwealth or any political subdivision thereof for the purpose of screening any person for full-time or part-time employment with the State Police or a police department or sheriff's office that is a part of or administered by the Commonwealth or any political subdivision thereof.

History.

1993, cc. 468, 926; 1996, cc. 755, 870, 914; 2002, c. 701; 2003, cc. 107, 432; 2005, cc. 868, 881, 914; 2006, c. 502; 2007, c. 133; 2010, cc. 456, 524; 2011, c. 622; 2012, c. 386; 2016, c. 554.

§ 19.2-389.1. (Effective October 1, 2016) Dissemination of juvenile record information.

Record information maintained in the Central Criminal Records Exchange pursuant to the provisions of § 16.1-299 shall be disseminated only (i) to make the determination as provided in §§ 18.2-

Criminal Procedure

308.2 and 18.2-308.2:2 of eligibility to possess or purchase a firearm; (ii) to aid in the preparation of a pretrial investigation report prepared by a local pretrial services agency established pursuant to Article 5 (§ 19.2-152.2 et seq.) of Chapter 9, a presentence or post-sentence investigation report pursuant to § 19.2-264.5 or 19.2-299 or in the preparation of the discretionary sentencing guidelines worksheets pursuant to subsection C of § 19.2-298.01; (iii) to aid local community-based probation services agencies established pursuant to the Comprehensive Community Corrections Act for Local-Responsible Offenders (§ 9.1-173 et seq.) with investigating or serving adult local-responsible offenders and all court service units serving juvenile delinquent offenders; (iv) for fingerprint comparison utilizing the fingerprints maintained in the Automated Fingerprint Information System (AFIS) computer; (v) to attorneys for the Commonwealth to secure information incidental to sentencing and to attorneys for the Commonwealth and probation officers to prepare the discretionary sentencing guidelines worksheets pursuant to subsection C of § 19.2-298.01; (vi) to any full-time or part-time employee of the State Police, a police department or sheriff's office that is a part of or administered by the Commonwealth or any political subdivision thereof, and who is responsible for the prevention and detection of crime and the enforcement of the penal, traffic or highway laws of the Commonwealth, for purposes of the administration of criminal justice as defined in § 9.1-101; (vii) to the Department of Forensic Science to verify its authority to maintain the juvenile's sample in the DNA data bank pursuant to § 16.1-299.1; (viii) to the Office of the Attorney General, for all criminal justice activities otherwise permitted and for purposes of performing duties required by the Civil Commitment of Sexually Violent Predators Act (§ 37.2-900 et seq.); (ix) to the Virginia Criminal Sentencing Commission for research purposes; (x) to members of a threat assessment team established by a school board pursuant to § 22.1-79.4, by a public institution of higher education pursuant to § 23.1-805, or by a private nonprofit institution of higher education, to aid in the assessment or intervention with individuals whose behavior may present a threat to safety; however, no member of a threat assessment team shall redisclose any juvenile record information obtained pursuant to this section or otherwise use any record of an individual beyond the purpose that such disclosure was made to the threat assessment team; and (xi) to any full-time or part-time employee of the State Police or a police department or sheriff's office that is a part of or administered by the Commonwealth or any political subdivision thereof for the purpose of screening any person for full-time or part-time employment with the State Police or a police department or sheriff's office that is a part of or administered by the Commonwealth or any political subdivision thereof.

History.

1993, cc. 468, 926; 1996, cc. 755, 870, 914; 2002, c. 701; 2003, cc. 107, 432; 2005, cc. 868, 881, 914; 2006, c. 502; 2007, c. 133; 2010, cc. 456, 524; 2011, c. 622; 2012, c. 386; 2016, c. 554.

§ 19.2-389.2. Background checks of applicants of the Metropolitan Washington Airports Authority.

The police department of the Metropolitan Washington Airports Authority as established in Chapter 10 (§ 5.1-152 et seq.) of Title 5.1 may require an applicant, upon conditional offer of employment with the Authority, to submit to fingerprinting and to provide personal descriptive information to be forwarded along with the applicant's fingerprints through the Central Criminal Records Exchange and the Federal Bureau of Investigation for the purpose of obtaining criminal history record information regarding such applicant.

The Central Criminal Records Exchange, upon receipt of an applicant's record or notification that no record exists, shall make a report to the chief of the police department of the Authority or his designee, provided the designee is an employee of the police department of the Authority. In determining whether a criminal conviction directly relates to a position, the Authority shall consider the following criteria: (i) the nature and seriousness of the crime; (ii) the relationship of the crime to the work to be performed in the position applied for; (iii) the extent to which the position applied for might offer an opportunity to engage in further criminal activity of the same type as that in which the applicant had been involved; (iv) the relationship of the crime to the ability, capacity, or fitness required to perform the duties and discharge the responsibilities of the position being sought; (v) the extent and nature of the applicant's past criminal activity; (vi) the age of the applicant at the time of the commission of the crime; (vii) the amount of time that has elapsed since the applicant's last involvement in the commission of a crime; (viii) the conduct and work activity of the applicant prior to and following the criminal activity; and (ix) evidence of the applicant's rehabilitation or rehabilitative effort while incarcerated or following release.

If an applicant is denied employment because of information appearing in his criminal history record, the Authority shall notify the applicant that information obtained from the Central Criminal Records Exchange contributed to such denial. The criminal history record information obtained pursuant to this section shall be used solely to determine an applicant's eligibility for employment by the Authority and access to restricted areas of Ronald Reagan Washington National Airport and Washington Dulles International Airport in compliance with 49 U.S.C. § 44936 and shall otherwise be confidential.

History.

2014, c. 57.

§ 19.2-390. Reports to be made by local law-enforcement officers, conservators of the peace, clerks of court, Secretary of the Commonwealth and Corrections officials to State Police; material submitted by other agencies.

A. 1. Every state official or agency having the power to arrest, the sheriffs of counties, the police officials of cities and towns, and any other local law-enforcement officer or conservator of the peace having the power to arrest for a felony shall make a report to the Central Criminal Records Exchange, on forms provided by it, of any arrest, including those arrests involving the taking into custody of, or service of process upon, any person on charges resulting from an indictment, presentment or information, the arrest on capias or warrant for failure to appear, and the service of a warrant for another jurisdiction, on any of the following charges:

a. Treason;

b. Any felony;

c. Any offense punishable as a misdemeanor under Title 54.1; or

d. Any misdemeanor punishable by confinement in jail (i) under Title 18.2 or 19.2, except an arrest for a violation of § 18.2-119, Article 2 (§ 18.2-415 et seq.) of Chapter 9 of Title 18.2, or any similar ordinance of any county, city or town, (ii) under § 20-61, or (iii) under § 16.1-253.2.

The reports shall contain such information as is required by the Exchange and shall be accompanied by fingerprints of the individual arrested. Effective January 1, 2006, the corresponding photograph of the individual arrested shall accompany the report. Fingerprint cards prepared by a law-enforcement agency for inclusion in a national criminal justice file shall be forwarded to the Exchange for transmittal to the appropriate bureau. Nothing in this section shall preclude each local law-enforcement agency from maintaining its own separate photographic database. Fingerprints and photographs required to be taken pursuant to this subsection or subdivision A 3c of § 19.2-123 may be taken at the facility where the magistrate is located, including a regional jail, even if the accused is not committed to jail.

2. For persons arrested and released on summonses in accordance with § 19.2-74, such report shall not be required until (i) a conviction is entered and no appeal is noted or if an appeal is noted, the conviction is upheld upon appeal or the person convicted withdraws his appeal; (ii) the court dismisses the proceeding pursuant to § 18.2-251; or (iii) an acquittal by reason of insanity pursuant to § 19.2-182.2 is entered. Upon such conviction or acquittal, the court shall remand the individual to the custody of the office of the chief law-enforcement officer of the county or city. It shall be the duty of the chief law-enforcement officer, or his designee who may be the arresting officer, to ensure that such report is completed after a determination of guilt or acquittal by reason of insanity. The court shall require the officer to complete the report immediately following the person's conviction or acquittal, and the individual shall be discharged from custody forthwith, unless the court has imposed a jail sentence to be served by him or ordered him committed to the custody of the Commissioner of Behavioral Health and Developmental Services.

B. Within 72 hours following the receipt of (i) a warrant or capias for the arrest of any person on a charge of a felony or (ii) a Governor's warrant of arrest of a person issued pursuant to § 19.2-92, the law-enforcement agency which received the warrant shall enter the person's name and other appropriate information required by the Department of State Police into the "information systems" known as the Virginia Criminal Information Network (VCIN), established and maintained by the Department pursuant to Chapter 2 (§ 52-12 et seq.) of Title 52 and the National Crime Information Center (NCIC), maintained by the Federal Bureau of Investigation. The report shall include the person's name, date of birth, social security number and such other known information which the State Police or Federal Bureau of Investigation may require. Where feasible and practical, the magistrate or court issuing the warrant or capias may transfer information electronically into VCIN. When the information is electronically transferred to VCIN, the court or magistrate shall forthwith forward the warrant or capias to the local police department or sheriff's office. When criminal process has been ordered destroyed pursuant to § 19.2-76.1, the law-enforcement agency destroying such process shall ensure the removal of any information relating to the destroyed criminal process from the VCIN and NCIC.

B1. Within 72 hours following the receipt of a written statement issued by a parole officer pursuant to § 53.1-149 or 53.1-162 authorizing the arrest of a person who has violated the provisions of his post-release supervision or probation, the law-enforcement agency that received the written statement shall enter, or cause to be entered, the person's name and other appropriate information required by the Department of State Police into the "information systems" known as the Virginia Criminal Information Network (VCIN), established and maintained by the Department pursuant to Chapter 2 (§ 52-12 et seq.) of Title 52.

C. The clerk of each circuit court and district court shall make an electronic report to the Central Criminal Records Exchange of (i) any dismissal, indefinite postponement or continuance, charge still pending due to mental incompetency or incapacity, nolle prosequi, acquittal, or conviction of, including any sentence imposed, or failure of a grand jury to return a true bill as to, any person charged with an offense listed in subsection A, including any action which may have resulted from an indictment, presentment or information, and (ii) any adjudication of delinquency based upon an act which, if committed by an adult, would require fingerprints to be filed pursuant to subsection A. In the case of offenses not required to be reported to the Exchange by subsection A, the reports of any of the foregoing dispositions shall be filed by the law-enforcement agency making the arrest with the arrest record required to be maintained by § 15.2-1722. Upon conviction of any person, including juveniles tried and convicted in the circuit courts pursuant to § 16.1-269.1, whether sentenced as adults or juveniles, for an offense for which registration is required as defined in § 9.1-902, the clerk shall within seven days of sentencing submit a report to the Sex Offender and Crimes Against Minors Registry. The report to the Registry shall include the name of the person convicted and all aliases which he is known to have used, the date and locality of the conviction for which registration is required, his date of birth, social security number, last known address, and specific reference to the offense for which he was convicted. No report of conviction or adjudication in a district court shall be filed unless the period allowed for an appeal has elapsed and no appeal has been perfected. In the event that the records in the office of any clerk show that any conviction or adjudication has been nullified in any manner, he shall also make a report of that fact to the Exchange and, if appropriate, to the Registry. In addition, each clerk of a circuit court, upon receipt of certification thereof from the Supreme Court, shall report to the Exchange or the Registry, or to the law-enforcement agency making the arrest in the case of offenses not required to be reported to the Exchange, on forms provided by the Exchange or Registry, as the case may be, any reversal or other amendment to a prior sentence or disposition previously reported. When criminal process is ordered destroyed pursuant to § 19.2-76.1, the clerk shall report such action to the law-enforcement agency that entered the warrant or capias into the VCIN.

D. In addition to those offenses enumerated in subsection A of this section, the Central Criminal Records Exchange may receive, classify and file any other fingerprints, photographs, and records of arrest or confinement submitted to it by any law-enforcement agency or any correctional institution.

E. Corrections officials, sheriffs, and jail superintendents of regional jails, responsible for maintaining correctional status information, as required by the regulations of the Department of Criminal Justice Services, with respect to individuals about whom reports have been made under the provisions of this chapter shall make reports of changes in correctional status information to the Central Criminal Records Exchange. The reports to the Exchange shall include any commitment to or release or escape from a state or local correctional facility, including commitment to or release from a parole or probation agency.

F. Any pardon, reprieve or executive commutation of sentence by the Governor shall be reported to the Exchange by the office of the Secretary of the Commonwealth.

G. Officials responsible for reporting disposition of charges, and correctional changes of status of individuals under this section, including those reports made to the Registry, shall adopt procedures reasonably designed at a minimum (i) to ensure that such reports are accurately made as soon as feasible by the most expeditious means and in no instance later than 30 days after occurrence of the disposition or correctional change of status and (ii) to report promptly any correction, deletion, or revision of the information.

H. Upon receiving a correction, deletion, or revision of information, the Central Criminal Records Exchange shall notify all criminal justice agencies known to have previously received the information.

As used in this section:

"Chief law-enforcement officer" means the chief of police of cities and towns and sheriffs of counties, unless a political subdivision has otherwise designated its chief law-enforcement officer by appropriate resolution or ordinance, in which case the local designation shall be controlling.

"Electronic report" means a report transmitted to, or otherwise forwarded to, the Central Criminal Records Exchange in an electronic format approved by the Exchange. The report shall contain the name of the person convicted and all aliases which he is known to have used, the date and locality of the conviction, his date of birth, social security number, last known address, and specific reference to the offense including the Virginia Code section and any subsection, the Virginia crime code for the offense, and the offense tracking number for the offense for which he was convicted.

History.

Code 1950, § 19.1-19.3; 1966, c. 669; 1968, c. 724; 1970, c. 191; 1971, Ex. Sess., c. 107; 1974, c. 575; 1975, cc. 495, 584; 1976, cc. 336, 572, 771; 1978, cc. 467, 825; 1979, c. 378; 1981, c. 529; 1982, cc. 33, 535; 1990, cc. 100, 692; 1992, c. 391; 1993, cc. 448, 468, 926; 1994, cc. 362, 428, 432; 1996, cc. 429, 755, 806, 914; 1997, cc. 27, 509, 747, 801; 2001, cc. 516, 536, 565; 2003, cc. 27, 584, 727; 2004, cc. 284, 406; 2005, cc. 187, 229; 2008, cc. 73, 246; 2009, cc. 249, 813, 840; 2010, c. 273; 2013, c. 614.

§ 19.2-390.01. Use of Virginia crime code references required.

If any criminal warrant, indictment, information, presentment, petition, summons, charging document issued by a magistrate, or dispositional document from a criminal trial, involves a jailable offense, it shall include the Virginia crime code references for the particular offense or offenses covered. When Virginia crime codes are provided on charging and dispositional documents, the Virginia crime codes shall be recorded and stored for adult offenders in: criminal history computer systems maintained by the State Police; court case management computer systems maintained by the Supreme Court of Virginia; probation and parole case management computer systems maintained by the Department of Corrections and the Virginia Parole Board; pretrial and community-based probation case management computer systems maintained by the Department of Criminal Justice Services; and jail management computer systems maintained by the State Compensation Board. The Department of Juvenile Justice shall record and store Virginia crime codes for particular offenses related to juveniles in case management computer systems.

Virginia crime codes shall only be used to facilitate administration and research, and shall not have any legal standing as they relate to a particular offense or offenses.

History.

2003, c. 148; 2007, c. 133.

§ 19.2-390.02. Policies and procedures for law enforcement to conduct in-person and photo lineups.

The Department of State Police and each local police department and sheriff's office shall establish a written policy and procedure for conducting in-person and photographic lineups.

History.

2005, cc. 187, 229.

§ 19.2-390.1. Sex Offender and Crimes Against Minors Registry; maintenance; access.

The Department of State Police shall keep and maintain a Sex Offender and Crimes Against Minors Registry, separate and apart from all other records maintained by it.

The Superintendent of State Police shall organize, equip, and staff, within the Department of State Police, the Sex Offender and Crimes Against Minors Registry. The Superintendent shall appoint and designate personnel as he deems necessary to carry out all duties and assignments related to the Sex Offender and Crimes Against Minors Registry as required by Chapter 9 (§ 9.1-900 et seq.) of Title 9.1.

History.

1994, c. 362; 1996, cc. 418, 542, 880; 1997, cc. 670, 672, 747; 1998, cc. 785, 834; 2000, c. 250; 2003, c. 584; 2006, cc. 857, 914.

§ 19.2-390.2: Repealed by Acts 2003, c. 584, cl. 2.

Cross references.

For current provisions relating to automatic notification of registration to certain entities, see § 9.1-914.

§ 19.2-390.3. Child Pornography Images Registry; maintenance; access.

A. The Office of the Attorney General, in cooperation with the Department of State Police, shall keep and maintain a Child Pornography Registry to be located within the State Police, separate and apart from all other records maintained by either department. The purpose of the Registry shall be to assist the efforts of law-enforcement agencies statewide to protect their communities from repeat child pornographers and to protect children from becoming victims of criminal offenders by aiding in identifying victims and perpetrators. Criminal justice agencies, including law-enforcement agencies, may request of the State Police a search and comparison of child pornography images contained within the Registry with those images obtained by criminal justice agencies during the course of official investigations.

B. The Registry shall include images of sexually explicit visual material in any form including any picture, photograph, drawing, sculpture, motion picture film, digital image or similar visual representation, presented as evidence and used in any conviction for any offense enumerated in §§ 18.2-374.1 and 18.2-374.1:1.

C. Registry information provided under this section shall be used for the purposes of the administration of criminal justice or for the protection of the public in general and children in particular. Use of the information or the images contained therein for purposes not authorized by this section is prohibited and a willful violation of this section with the intent to harass or intimidate another shall be punished as a Class 6 felony.

D. The Virginia Criminal Information Network and any form or document used by the Department of State Police to disseminate information from the Registry shall provide notice that any unauthorized possession, use or dissemination of the information or images is a crime punishable as a Class 6 felony.

History.

2003, cc. 935, 938.

§ 19.2-391. Records to be made available to Exchange by state officials and agencies; duplication of records.

Each state official and agency shall make available to the Central Criminal Records Exchange such of their records as are pertinent to its functions and shall cooperate with the Exchange in the development and use of equipment and facilities on a joint basis, where feasible. No state official or agency shall maintain records which are a duplication of the records on deposit in the Central Criminal Records Exchange, except to the extent necessary for efficient internal administration of such agency. Furthermore, the Virginia Parole Board may receive and use electronically disseminated criminal history record information from the Central Criminal Records Exchange as required to make parole determinations pursuant to subdivisions 1, 2, 3, and 5 of § 53.1-136, provided the data is (i) temporarily stored with the Board solely for operational purposes, (ii) purged within thirty days of receipt of updated data by the Board, and (iii) accessed and viewed solely by Parole Board members and authorized staff pursuant to § 9.1-101 and § 9.1-130.

History.

Code 1950, § 19.1-19.4; 1966, c. 669; 1975, c. 495; 1993, c. 313.

§ 19.2-392. Fingerprints and photographs by police authorities.

A. All duly constituted police authorities having the power of arrest may take the fingerprints and photographs of: (i) any person arrested by them and charged with a felony or a misdemeanor an arrest for which is to be reported by them to the Central Criminal Records Exchange, or (ii) any person who pleads guilty or is found guilty after being summoned in accordance with § 19.2-74. Such authorities shall make such records available to the Central Criminal Records Exchange. Such authorities are authorized to provide, on the request of duly appointed law-enforcement officers, copies of any fingerprint records they may have, and to furnish services and technical advice in connection with the taking, classifying and preserving of fingerprints and fingerprint records.

B. Such police authorities may establish and collect a reasonable fee not to exceed $10 for the first card and $5 for each successive card for the taking of fingerprints when voluntarily requested by any person for purposes other than criminal violations.

History.

Code 1950, § 19.1-19.6; 1968, c. 722; 1975, c. 495; 1978, c. 825; 1985, c. 306; 2005, c. 347.

§ 19.2-392.01. Judges may require taking of fingerprints and photographs in certain misdemeanor cases.

The judge of a district court may, in his discretion, on motion of the attorney for the Commonwealth, require the duly constituted police officers of the county, city or town within the territorial jurisdiction of the court to take the fingerprints and photograph of any person who has been arrested and charged with a misdemeanor other than a misdemeanor which is a violation of any provision of Title 46.2.

History.

1995, c. 407; 1996, cc. 755, 914.

§ 19.2-392.02. National criminal background checks by businesses and organizations regarding employees or volunteers providing care to children, or the elderly or disabled.

A. For purposes of this section:

"Barrier crime" means any offense set forth in § 63.2-1719 or 63.2-1726.

"Barrier crime information" means the following facts concerning a person who has been arrested for, or has been convicted of, a barrier crime, regardless of whether the person was a juvenile or adult at the time of the arrest or conviction: full name, race, sex, date of birth, height, weight, fingerprints, a brief description of the barrier crime or offenses for which the person has been arrested or has been convicted, the disposition of the charge, and any other information that may be useful in identifying persons arrested for or convicted of a barrier crime.

"Care" means the provision of care, treatment, education, training, instruction, supervision, or recreation to children or the elderly or disabled.

"Department" means the Department of State Police.

"Employed by" means any person who is employed by, volunteers for, seeks to be employed by, or seeks to volunteer for a qualified entity.

"Identification document" means a document made or issued by or under the authority of the United States government, a state, a political subdivision of a state, a foreign government, political subdivision of a foreign government, an international governmental or an international quasi-governmental organization that, when completed with information concerning a particular individual, is of a type intended or commonly accepted for the purpose of identification of individuals.

"Provider" means a person who (i) is employed by a qualified entity and has, seeks to have, or may have unsupervised access to a child or to an elderly or disabled person to whom the qualified entity provides care; (ii) is a volunteer of a qualified entity and has, seeks to have, or may have unsupervised access to a child to whom the qualified entity provides care; or (iii) owns, operates, or seeks to own or operate a qualified entity.

"Qualified entity" means a business or organization that provides care to children or the elderly or disabled, whether governmental, private, for profit, nonprofit or voluntary, except organizations exempt pursuant to subdivision A 10 of § 63.2-1715.

B. A qualified entity may request the Department of State Police to conduct a national criminal background check on any provider who is employed by such entity. No qualified entity may request a national criminal background check on a provider until such provider has:

1. Been fingerprinted; and

2. Completed and signed a statement, furnished by the entity, that includes (i) his name, address, and date of birth as it appears on a valid identification document; (ii) a disclosure of whether or not the provider has ever been convicted of or is the subject of pending charges for a criminal offense within or outside the Commonwealth, and if the provider has been convicted of a crime, a description of the crime and the particulars of the conviction; (iii) a notice to the provider that the entity may request a background check; (iv) a notice to the provider that he is entitled to obtain a copy of any background check report, to challenge the accuracy and completeness

of any information contained in any such report, and to obtain a prompt determination as to the validity of such challenge before a final determination is made by the Department; and (v) a notice to the provider that prior to the completion of the background check the qualified entity may choose to deny the provider unsupervised access to children or the elderly or disabled for whom the qualified entity provides care.

C. Upon receipt of (i) a qualified entity's written request to conduct a background check on a provider, (ii) the provider's fingerprints, and (iii) a completed, signed statement as described in subsection B, the Department shall make a determination whether the provider has been convicted of or is the subject of charges of a barrier crime. To conduct its determination regarding the provider's barrier crime information, the Department shall access the national criminal history background check system, which is maintained by the Federal Bureau of Investigation and is based on fingerprints and other methods of identification, and shall access the Central Criminal Records Exchange maintained by the Department. If the Department receives a background report lacking disposition data, the Department shall conduct research in whatever state and local recordkeeping systems are available in order to obtain complete data. The Department shall make reasonable efforts to respond to a qualified entity's inquiry within 15 business days.

D. Any background check conducted pursuant to this section for a provider employed by a private entity shall be screened by the Department of State Police. If the provider has been convicted of or is under indictment for a barrier crime, the qualified entity shall be notified that the provider is not qualified to work or volunteer in a position that involves unsupervised access to children or the elderly or disabled.

E. Any background check conducted pursuant to this section for a provider employed by a governmental entity shall be provided to that entity.

F. In the case of a provider who desires to volunteer at a qualified entity and who is subject to a national criminal background check, the Department and the Federal Bureau of Investigation may each charge the provider the lesser of $18 or the actual cost to the entity of the background check conducted with the fingerprints.

G. The failure to request a criminal background check pursuant to subsection B shall not be considered negligence per se in any civil action.

History.
2000, c. 860; 2005, c. 217; 2015, cc. 758, 770.

CHAPTER 23.1.
EXPUNGEMENT OF CRIMINAL RECORDS.

Section

§ 19.2-392.1. Statement of policy.

The General Assembly finds that arrest records can be a hindrance to an innocent citizen's ability to obtain employment, an education and to obtain credit. It further finds that the police and court records of those of its citizens who have been absolutely pardoned for crimes for which they have been unjustly convicted can also be a hindrance. This chapter is intended to protect such persons from the unwarranted damage which may occur as a result of being arrested and convicted.

History.
1977, c. 675; 1984, c. 642.

§ 19.2-392.2. Expungement of police and court records.

A. If a person is charged with the commission of a crime or any offense defined in Title 18.2, and

1. Is acquitted, or

2. A nolle prosequi is taken or the charge is otherwise dismissed, including dismissal by accord and satisfaction pursuant to § 19.2-151, he may file a petition setting forth the relevant facts and requesting expungement of the police records and the court records relating to the charge.

B. If any person whose name or other identification has been used without his consent or authorization by another person who has been charged or arrested using such name or identification, he may file a petition with the court disposing of the charge for relief pursuant to this section. Such person shall not be required to pay any fees for the filing of a petition under this subsection. A petition filed under this subsection shall include one complete set of the petitioner's fingerprints obtained from a law-enforcement agency.

C. The petition with a copy of the warrant or indictment if reasonably available shall be filed in the circuit court of the county or city in which the case was disposed of by acquittal or being otherwise dismissed and shall contain, except where not reasonably available, the date of arrest and the name of

Criminal Procedure

the arresting agency. Where this information is not reasonably available, the petition shall state the reason for such unavailability. The petition shall further state the specific criminal charge to be expunged, the date of final disposition of the charge as set forth in the petition, the petitioner's date of birth, and the full name used by the petitioner at the time of arrest.

D. A copy of the petition shall be served on the attorney for the Commonwealth of the city or county in which the petition is filed. The attorney for the Commonwealth may file an objection or answer to the petition or may give written notice to the court that he does not object to the petition within 21 days after it is served on him.

E. The petitioner shall obtain from a law-enforcement agency one complete set of the petitioner's fingerprints and shall provide that agency with a copy of the petition for expungement. The law-enforcement agency shall submit the set of fingerprints to the Central Criminal Records Exchange (CCRE) with a copy of the petition for expungement attached. The CCRE shall forward under seal to the court a copy of the petitioner's criminal history, a copy of the source documents that resulted in the CCRE entry that the petitioner wishes to expunge, and the set of fingerprints. Upon completion of the hearing, the court shall return the fingerprint card to the petitioner. If no hearing was conducted, upon the entry of an order of expungement or an order denying the petition for expungement, the court shall cause the fingerprint card to be destroyed unless, within 30 days of the date of the entry of the order, the petitioner requests the return of the fingerprint card in person from the clerk of the court or provides the clerk of the court a self-addressed, stamped envelope for the return of the fingerprint card.

F. After receiving the criminal history record information from the CCRE, the court shall conduct a hearing on the petition. If the court finds that the continued existence and possible dissemination of information relating to the arrest of the petitioner causes or may cause circumstances which constitute a manifest injustice to the petitioner, it shall enter an order requiring the expungement of the police and court records, including electronic records, relating to the charge. Otherwise, it shall deny the petition. However, if the petitioner has no prior criminal record and the arrest was for a misdemeanor violation, the petitioner shall be entitled, in the absence of good cause shown to the contrary by the Commonwealth, to expungement of the police and court records relating to the charge, and the court shall enter an order of expungement. If the attorney for the Commonwealth of the county or city in which the petition is filed (i) gives written notice to the court pursuant to subsection D that he does not object to the petition and (ii) when the charge to be expunged is a felony, stipulates in such written notice that the continued existence and possible dissemination of information relating to the arrest of the petitioner causes or may cause circumstances which constitute a manifest injustice to the petitioner, the court may enter an order of expungement without conducting a hearing.

G. The Commonwealth shall be made party defendant to the proceeding. Any party aggrieved by the decision of the court may appeal, as provided by law in civil cases.

H. Notwithstanding any other provision of this section, when the charge is dismissed because the court finds that the person arrested or charged is not the person named in the summons, warrant, indictment or presentment, the court dismissing the charge shall, upon motion of the person improperly arrested or charged, enter an order requiring expungement of the police and court records relating to the charge. Such order shall contain a statement that the dismissal and expungement are ordered pursuant to this subsection and shall be accompanied by the complete set of the petitioner's fingerprints filed with his petition. Upon the entry of such order, it shall be treated as provided in subsection K.

I. Notwithstanding any other provision of this section, when a person has been granted an absolute pardon for the commission of a crime that he did not commit, he may file in the circuit court of the county or city in which the conviction occurred a petition setting forth the relevant facts and requesting expungement of the police records and the court records relating to the charge and conviction, and the court shall enter an order requiring expungement of the police and court records relating to the charge and conviction. Such order shall contain a statement that the expungement is ordered pursuant to this subsection. Upon the entry of such order, it shall be treated as provided in subsection K.

J. Upon receiving a copy of a writ vacating a conviction pursuant to § 19.2-327.5 or 19.2-327.13, the court shall enter an order requiring expungement of the police and court records relating to the charge and conviction. Such order shall contain a statement that the expungement is ordered pursuant to this subsection. Upon the entry of the order, it shall be treated as provided in subsection K.

K. Upon the entry of an order of expungement, the clerk of the court shall cause a copy of such order to be forwarded to the Department of State Police, which shall, pursuant to rules and regulations adopted pursuant to § 9.1-134, direct the manner by which the appropriate expungement or removal of such records shall be effected.

L. Costs shall be as provided by § 17.1-275, but shall not be recoverable against the Commonwealth. If the court enters an order of expungement, the clerk of the court shall refund to the petitioner such costs paid by the petitioner.

M. Any order entered where (i) the court or parties failed to strictly comply with the procedures set forth in this section or (ii) the court enters an order of expungement contrary to law, shall be voidable upon motion and notice made within three years of the entry of such order.

History.
1977, c. 675; 1983, c. 394; 1984, c. 642; 1990, c. 603; 1992, c. 697; 2001, cc. 40, 345; 2007, cc. 465, 824, 883, 905; 2009, c. 618; 2011, c. 362; 2015, c. 426; 2016, c. 617.

§ 19.2-392.3. Disclosure of expunged records.

A. It shall be unlawful for any person having or acquiring access to an expunged court or police record to open or review it or to disclose to another person any information from it without an order from the court which ordered the record expunged.

B. Upon a verified petition filed by the attorney for the Commonwealth alleging that the record is needed by a law-enforcement agency for purposes of employment application as an employee of a law-enforcement agency or for a pending criminal investigation and that the investigation will be jeopardized or that life or property will be endangered without immediate access to the record, the court may enter an ex parte order, without notice to the person, permitting such access. An ex parte order may permit a review of the record, but may not permit a copy to be made of it.

C. Any person who willfully violates this section is guilty of a Class 1 misdemeanor.

History.
1977, c. 675; 1978, c. 713.

§ 19.2-392.4. Prohibited practices by employers, educational institutions, agencies, etc., of state and local governments.

A. An employer or educational institution shall not, in any application, interview, or otherwise, require an applicant for employment or admission to disclose information concerning any arrest or criminal charge against him that has been expunged. An applicant need not, in answer to any question concerning any arrest or criminal charge that has not resulted in a conviction, include a reference to or information concerning arrests or charges that have been expunged.

B. Agencies, officials, and employees of the state and local governments shall not, in any application, interview, or otherwise, require an applicant for a license, permit, registration, or governmental service to disclose information concerning any arrest or criminal charge against him that has been expunged. An applicant need not, in answer to any question concerning any arrest or criminal charge that has not resulted in a conviction, include a reference to or information concerning charges that have been expunged. Such an application may not be denied solely because of the applicant's refusal to disclose information concerning any arrest or criminal charge against him that has been expunged.

C. A person who willfully violates this section is guilty of a Class 1 misdemeanor for each violation.

History.
1977, c. 675.

CHAPTER 24. INSPECTION WARRANTS.

§ 19.2-393. Definitions.

An *"inspection warrant"* is an order in writing, made in the name of the Commonwealth, signed by any judge of the circuit court whose territorial jurisdiction encompasses the property or premises to be inspected or entered, and directed to a state or local official, commanding him to enter and to conduct any inspection, testing or collection of samples for testing required or authorized by state or local law or regulation in connection with the manufacturing, emitting or presence of a toxic substance, and which describes, either directly or by reference to any accompanying or attached supporting affidavit, the property or premises where the inspection, testing or collection of samples for testing is to occur. Such warrant shall be sufficiently accurate in description so that the official executing the warrant and the owner or custodian of the property or premises can reasonably determine from the warrant the activity, condition, circumstance, object or property of which inspection, testing or collection of samples for testing is authorized.

For the purposes of this chapter, *"manufacturing"* means producing, formulating, packaging, or diluting any substance for commercial sale or resale; *"emitting"* means the release of any substance, whether or not intentional or avoidable, into the work environment, into the air, into the water, or otherwise into the human environment; and *"toxic substance"* means any substance, including (i) any raw material, intermediate product, catalyst, final product and by-product of any operation conducted in a commercial establishment and (ii) any biological organism, that has the capacity, through its physical, chemical, or biological properties, to pose a substantial risk to humans, aquatic organisms or any other animal of illness, death or impairment of normal functions, either immediately or over a period of time.

History.
1976, c. 625; 1979, c. 122.

§ 19.2-394. Issuance of warrant.

An inspection warrant may be issued for any inspection, testing or collection of samples for testing or for any administrative search authorized by state or local law or regulation in connection with the presence, manufacturing or emitting of toxic substances, whether or not such warrant be constitutionally required. Nothing in this chapter shall be construed to require issuance of an inspection warrant where a warrant is not constitutionally required or to exclude any other lawful means of search, inspection, testing or collection of samples for testing, whether without warrant or pursuant to a search warrant issued under any other provision of the Code of Virginia. No inspection warrant shall be issued pursuant to this chapter except upon probable cause, supported by affidavit, particularly describing the place, things or persons to be inspected or tested and the purpose for which the inspection, testing or collection of samples for testing is to be made. Probable cause shall be deemed to exist if either reasonable legislative or administrative standards for conducting such inspection, testing or collection of samples for testing are satisfied with respect to the particular place, things or persons or there exists probable cause to believe that there is a condition, object, activity or circumstance which legally justifies such inspection, testing or collection of samples for testing. The supporting affidavit shall contain either a statement that consent to inspect, test or collect samples for testing has been sought and refused or facts or circumstances reasonably justifying the failure to seek such consent in order to enforce effectively the state or local law or regulation which authorizes such inspection, testing or collection of samples for testing. The issuing judge may examine the affiant under oath or affirmation to verify the accuracy of any matter indicated by the statement in the affidavit. After issuing a warrant under this section, the judge shall file the affidavit in the manner prescribed by § 19.2-54.

History.
1976, c. 625; 1979, c. 122; 2014, c. 354.

§ 19.2-395. Duration of warrant.

An inspection warrant shall be effective for the time specified therein, for a period of not more than ten days, unless extended or renewed by the judicial officer who signed and issued the original warrant, upon satisfying himself that such extension or renewal is in the public interest. Such warrant shall be executed and returned to the clerk of the circuit court of the city or county wherein the inspection was made within the time specified in the warrant or within the extended or renewed time. After the expiration of such time, the warrant, unless executed shall be void.

History.
1976, c. 625; 2014, c. 354.

§ 19.2-396. Conduct of inspection, testing or collection of samples for testing; special procedure for dwelling.

An inspection, testing or collection of samples for testing pursuant to such warrant may not be made in the absence of the owner, custodian or possessor of the particular place, things or persons unless specifically authorized by the issuing judge upon a showing that such authority is reasonably necessary to effectuate the purpose of the law or regulation being enforced. An entry pursuant to this warrant shall not be made forcibly, except that the issuing judge may expressly authorize a forcible entry where facts are shown sufficient to create a reasonable suspicion of an immediate threat to public health or safety, or where facts are shown establishing that reasonable attempts to serve a previous warrant have been unsuccessful. In the case of entry into a dwelling, prior consent must be sought and refused and notice that a warrant has been issued must be given at least twenty-four hours before the warrant is executed, unless the issuing judge finds that failure to seek consent is justified and that there is a reasonable suspicion of an immediate threat to public health or safety.

History.
1976, c. 625; 1979, c. 122.

§ 19.2-397. Refusal to permit authorized inspection; penalty.

Any person who willfully refuses to permit an inspection, testing or collection of samples for testing lawfully authorized by warrant issued pursuant to this chapter shall be guilty of a Class 3 misdemeanor.

History.
1976, c. 625; 1979, c. 122.

CHAPTER 25.

APPEALS BY THE COMMONWEALTH.

Section

§ 19.2-398. When appeal by the Commonwealth allowed.

A. In a felony case a pretrial appeal from a circuit court may be taken by the Commonwealth from:

1. An order of a circuit court dismissing a warrant, information or indictment, or any count or charge thereof on the ground that (i) the defendant was deprived of a speedy trial in violation of the provisions of the Sixth Amendment to the Constitution of the United States, Article I, Section 8 of the Constitution of Virginia, or § 19.2-243; or (ii) the defendant would be twice placed in jeopardy in violation of the provisions of the Fifth Amendment to the Constitution of the United States or Article I, Section 8 of the Constitution of Virginia; or

2. An order of a circuit court prohibiting the use of certain evidence at trial on the grounds such evidence was obtained in violation of the provisions of the Fourth, Fifth or Sixth Amendments to the Constitution of the United States or Article I, Section 8, 10 or 11 of the Constitution of Virginia prohibiting illegal searches and seizures and protecting rights against self-incrimination, provided the Commonwealth certifies that the appeal is not taken for purpose of delay and that the evidence is substantial proof of a fact material in the proceeding.

B. A petition for appeal may be taken by the Commonwealth in a felony case from any order of release on conditions pursuant to Article 1 (§ 19.2-119 et seq.) of Chapter 9 of this title.

C. A petition for appeal may be taken by the Commonwealth in a felony case after conviction where the sentence imposed by the circuit court is contrary to mandatory sentencing or restitution terms required by statute.

D. Nothing in this chapter shall affect the Commonwealth's right to appeal in civil matters or cases involving a violation of law relating to the state revenue or appeals pursuant to § 17.1-411 or subsection C of § 19.2-317.

E. A pretrial appeal may be taken in any criminal case from an order of a circuit court dismissing a warrant, information, summons, delinquency petition, or indictment, or any count or charge thereof, on the ground that a statute or local ordinance on which the order is based is unconstitutional.

History.
1985, c. 510; 1987, c. 710; 1998, c. 251; 1999, cc. 829, 846; 2002, cc. 611, 692; 2003, c. 109; 2005, cc. 622, 694; 2006, cc. 571, 876.

§ 19.2-399. Defense objections to be raised before trial; hearing; bill of particulars.

Editor's note.
This section is now codified at § 19.2-266.2.

§ 19.2-400. Appeal lies to the Court of Appeals; time for filing notice.

An appeal taken pursuant to § 19.2-398, including such an appeal in a capital murder case, shall lie to the Court of Appeals of Virginia.

No appeal shall be allowed the Commonwealth pursuant to subsection A of § 19.2-398 unless within seven days after entry of the order of the circuit court from which the appeal is taken, and before a jury is impaneled and sworn if there is to be trial by jury or, in cases to be tried without a jury, before the court begins to hear or receive evidence or the first witness is sworn, whichever occurs first, the Commonwealth files a notice of appeal with the clerk of the trial court. If the appeal relates to suppressed evidence, the attorney for the Commonwealth shall certify in the notice of appeal that the appeal is not taken for the purpose of delay and that the evidence is substantial proof of a fact material to the proceeding. All other requirements related to the notice of appeal shall be governed by Part Five A of the Rules of the Supreme Court. Upon the filing of a timely notice of appeal, the order from which the pretrial appeal is taken and further trial proceedings in the circuit court, except for a bail hearing, shall thereby be suspended pending disposition of the appeal.

An appeal by the Commonwealth pursuant to subsection C of § 19.2-398 shall be governed by Part Five A of the Rules of the Supreme Court.

History.
1987, c. 710; 2003, c. 109.

§ 19.2-401. Cross appeal; when allowed; time for filing.

The defendant shall have no independent right of appeal pursuant to § 19.2-398. If the Commonwealth appeals, the defendant may cross appeal from any orders from which the Commonwealth may appeal, pursuant to § 19.2-398. The defendant shall be under no obligation to defend an appeal filed by the Commonwealth. However, when an appeal is taken by the Commonwealth, and the defendant wishes to defend or cross appeal, the circuit court shall, where the defendant is indigent, appoint counsel to represent the defendant on appeal. The remuneration to be awarded appointed counsel shall be governed by § 19.2-326.

In pretrial appeals, the defendant shall file a notice of cross appeal with the clerk of the circuit court within seven days following the notice of appeal filed by the Commonwealth.

Any brief on cross appeal shall be consolidated with the defendant's brief as appellee, if any.

History.
1987, c. 710; 2003, c. 109.

§ 19.2-402. Petition for appeal; brief in opposition; time for filing.

A. When a notice of appeal has been filed pursuant to § 19.2-400, the Commonwealth may petition the Court of Appeals for an appeal pursuant to § 19.2-398. The Commonwealth shall be represented by the attorney for the Commonwealth prosecuting the case.

B. The provisions of this subsection apply only to pretrial appeals. The petition for a pretrial appeal shall be filed with the clerk of the Court of Appeals not more than 14 days after the notice of transcript or written statement of facts required by § 19.2-405 is filed or, if there are objections thereto, within 14 days after the judge signs the transcript or written statement of facts. The accused may file a brief in opposition with the clerk of the Court of Appeals within 14 days after the filing of the petition for pretrial appeal. If the accused has filed a notice of cross appeal, he shall file a petition for cross appeal to be consolidated with, and filed within the same time period as, his brief in opposition. The Commonwealth may file a brief in opposition to any petition for cross appeal within 10 days after the petition for cross appeal is filed. Except as specifically provided in this section, all other requirements for the petition for pretrial appeal and brief in opposition shall conform as nearly as practicable to Part Five A of the Rules of the Supreme Court of Virginia.

History.
1987, c. 710; 2003, c. 109; 2014, cc. 33, 294.

§ 19.2-403. Procedures on petition for pretrial appeal.

The procedures on a pretrial appeal to the Court of Appeals by the Commonwealth pursuant to § 19.2-398, and on a cross appeal of a pretrial appeal by the accused pursuant to § 19.2-401, shall be governed by the provisions of subsections C and D of § 17.1-407. The Court of Appeals, however, shall grant or deny the petition for a pretrial appeal, and the petition for cross appeal, if any, not later than 30 days after the brief in opposition is timely filed or the time for such filing has expired.

No petition for rehearing may be filed in any pretrial appeal pursuant to this chapter. If the petition for a pretrial appeal pursuant to this chapter is denied, the Court's mandate shall immediately issue and the clerk of the Court of Appeals shall return the record forthwith to the clerk of the trial court.

History.
1987, c. 710; 2003, c. 109.

§ 19.2-404. Procedures on awarded pretrial appeal.

This section applies only to pretrial appeals. If the Court of Appeals grants the Commonwealth's petition for a pretrial appeal, the Attorney General shall thereafter represent the Commonwealth during that appeal.

The Commonwealth shall file its opening brief in the office of the clerk of the Court of Appeals within 25 days after the date of the certificate awarding the appeal. The brief of the appellee shall be filed in the office of the clerk of the Court of Appeals within 25 days after the filing of the Commonwealth's opening brief. The Commonwealth may then file a reply brief, including its response to any cross appeal, in the office of the clerk of the Court of Appeals within 15 days after the filing of the brief of the accused. With the permission of a judge of the Court of Appeals, the time for filing any brief may be extended for good cause shown. Four copies of each brief shall be filed and three copies shall be mailed or delivered to opposing counsel on or before the date of filing. Except as specifically provided in this section, all other requirements of the brief shall conform as nearly as practicable to Part Five A of the Rules of the Supreme Court of Virginia. The Court of Appeals shall accelerate the appeal on its docket and render its decision not later than 60 days after the filing of the appellee's brief or after the time for filing such brief has expired.

When the opinion is rendered by the Court of Appeals, the mandate shall immediately issue and the clerk of the Court of Appeals shall return the record forthwith to the clerk of the trial court. No petition for rehearing may be filed.

History.
1987, c. 710; 2003, c. 109.

§ 19.2-405. Pretrial appeals; record on appeal; transcript; written statement of facts; time for filing.

This section applies only to pretrial appeals. The record on appeal shall conform, as nearly as practicable, to the requirements of Part Five A of the Rules of the Supreme Court for the record on appeal, except as hereinafter provided. The transcript or written statement of facts shall be filed with the clerk of the circuit court from which the appeal is being taken, no later than 25 days following entry of the order of the circuit court. Upon motion of the Commonwealth, the Court of Appeals may grant an extension of up to 45 days for filing the transcript or written statement of facts for good cause shown. If a transcript or written statement of facts is filed, the Commonwealth shall file with the clerk of the circuit court a notice, signed by the attorney for the Commonwealth, who is counsel for the appellant, identifying the transcript or written statement of facts and reciting its filing with the clerk. There shall be appended to the notice a certificate by the attorney for the Commonwealth that a copy of the notice has been mailed or delivered to opposing counsel. The notice of filing of the transcript or written statement of facts shall be filed within three days of the filing of the transcript or written statement of facts or within 14 days of the order of the circuit court, whichever is later.

Any party may object to the transcript or written statement of facts on the ground that it is erroneous or incomplete. Notice of the objection specifying the errors alleged or deficiencies asserted shall be tendered to the trial judge within 10 days after the notice of filing of the transcript or written statement of facts is filed in the office of the clerk. The trial judge shall, within three days after the filing of such objection, either overrule the objection, or take steps deemed necessary to make the record complete or certify the respect in which the record is incomplete, and sign the transcript or written statement of facts to verify its accuracy. The clerk of the trial court shall forthwith transmit the record to the clerk of the Court of Appeals.

History.
1987, c. 710; 2003, c. 109; 2014, cc. 33, 294.

§ 19.2-406. Bail pending pretrial appeal.

This section applies only to pretrial appeals. Upon a pretrial appeal being taken by the Commonwealth pursuant to § 19.2-398, if the defendant moves the trial court for release on bail, that court shall promptly, but in no event later than three days after the Commonwealth's notice of appeal is filed, hold a hearing to determine the issue of bail. The burden shall be upon the Commonwealth to show good cause why the bail should not be reduced or the accused released on his own recognizance. If it is determined that the accused shall be released on bail, bail shall be set and determined in accordance with Article 1 (§ 19.2-119 et seq.) of Chapter 9 of this title.

History.
1987, c. 710; 1999, cc. 829, 846; 2003, c. 109.

§ 19.2-407. Review by the Supreme Court.

Pursuant to § 17.1-409, the Supreme Court in its discretion may certify an appeal taken pursuant to § 19.2-398, or a cross appeal taken pursuant to § 19.2-401, for expedited review by the Supreme Court before it has been determined by the Court of Appeals. Such certification may be made only when the Supreme Court determines that at least one of the conditions set forth in subsection B of § 17.1-409 exists.

History.
1987, c. 710.

§ 19.2-408. Finality of decision of the Court of Appeals in pretrial appeals.

The decision of the Court of Appeals shall be final for purposes of a pretrial appeal pursuant to § 19.2-398, or a cross appeal of a pretrial appeal taken pursuant to § 19.2-401, and no further pretrial appeal shall lie to the Supreme Court.

History.
1987, c. 710; 2003, c. 109.

§ 19.2-409. Exclusion of pretrial appeal period from time within which accused must be tried; reconsideration of issues after conviction.

This section applies only to pretrial appeals. The provisions of § 19.2-243 shall not apply to the period of time commencing when the Commonwealth's notice of pretrial appeal is filed pursuant to this chapter and ending 60 days after the Court of Appeals or Supreme Court issues its mandate disposing of the pretrial appeal. Such finality of the Court of Appeals' decision shall not preclude a defendant, if he is convicted, from requesting the Court of Appeals or Supreme Court on direct appeal to reconsider an issue which was the subject of the pretrial appeal.

History.
1987, c. 710; 2003, c. 109; 2007, c. 414.

TITLE 20.
DOMESTIC RELATIONS.

CHAPTER 2.
MARRIAGE GENERALLY.

Section

§ 20-28. Penalty for celebrating marriage without license.

If any person knowingly perform the ceremony of marriage without lawful license, or officiate in celebrating the rites of marriage without being authorized by law to do so, he shall be confined in jail not exceeding one year, and fined not exceeding $500.

History.
Code 1919, § 4542.

§ 20-32: Repealed by Acts 2010, c. 352, cl. 2.

§ 20-33. Penalty for clerk issuing license contrary to law.

If any clerk of a court knowingly issue a marriage license contrary to law, he shall be confined in jail not exceeding one year, and fined not exceeding $500.

History.
Code 1919, § 4541.

CHAPTER 3.
UNLAWFUL MARRIAGES GENERALLY.

§ 20-45.2. Marriage between persons of same sex.

A marriage between persons of the same sex is prohibited. Any marriage entered into by persons of the same sex in another state or jurisdiction shall be void in all respects in Virginia and any contractual rights created by such marriage shall be void and unenforceable.

History.
1975, c. 644; 1997, cc. 354, 365.

§ 20-45.3. Civil unions between persons of same sex.

A civil union, partnership contract or other arrangement between persons of the same sex purporting to bestow the privileges or obligations of marriage is prohibited. Any such civil union, partnership contract or other arrangement entered into by persons of the same sex in another state or jurisdiction shall be void in all respects in Virginia and any contractual rights created thereby shall be void and unenforceable.

History.
2004, c. 983.

CHAPTER 5.
DESERTION AND NONSUPPORT.

§ 20-61. Desertion or nonsupport of wife, husband or children in necessitous circumstances.

Any spouse who without cause deserts or willfully neglects or refuses or fails to provide for the support and maintenance of his or her spouse, and any parent who deserts or willfully neglects or refuses or fails to provide for the support and maintenance of his or her child under the age of eighteen years of age, or child of whatever age who is crippled or otherwise incapacitated from earning a living, the spouse, child or children being then and there in necessitous circumstances, shall be guilty of a misdemeanor and upon conviction shall be punished by a fine of not exceeding $500, or confinement in jail not exceeding twelve months, or both, or on work release employment as provided in § 53.1-131 for a period of not less than ninety days nor more than twelve months; or in lieu of the fine or confinement being imposed upon conviction by the court or by verdict of a jury he or she may be required by the court to suffer a forfeiture of an amount not exceeding the sum of $1,000 and the fine or forfeiture may be directed by the court to be paid in whole or in part to the spouse, or to the guardian, curator, custodian or trustee of the minor child or children, or to some discreet person or responsible organization designated by the court to receive it. This section shall not apply to the parent of a child of whatever age, if the child qualifies for and is receiving aid under a federal or state program for aid to the permanently and totally disabled; or is an adult and meets the visual requirements for aid to the blind; and for this purpose any state agency shall use only the financial resources of the child of whatever age in determining eligibility; however, such parent is subject to prosecution under this section for the desertion or nonsupport of a spouse or of another child who is not receiving such aid.

History.
1944, p. 210; Michie Suppl. 1946, § 1936; 1950, p. 613; 1954, c. 481; 1960, c. 275; 1966, c. 360; 1970, c. 284; 1972, cc. 460, 845; 1973, cc. 315, 346; 1974, c. 464; 1975, c. 644; 1976, c. 462; 2010, c. 619.

TITLE 22.1.
EDUCATION.

CHAPTER 12.
PUPIL TRANSPORTATION.

Article 1.
General Provisions.

ARTICLE 1.

GENERAL PROVISIONS.

§ 22.1-176. Transportation of pupils authorized; when fee may be charged; contributions; regulations of Board of Education.

A. School boards may provide for the transportation of pupils, but nothing herein contained shall be construed as requiring such transportation except as provided in § 22.1-221.

B. When a school board provides transportation to pupils for extracurricular activities, other than those covered by an activity fund, which are sponsored by the pupils' school apart from the regular instructional program and which the pupils are not required to attend or participate in, the school board may accept contributions for such transportation or charge each pupil utilizing such transportation a reasonable fee not to exceed his pro rata share of the cost of providing such transportation. A school board may waive such fees for any pupil whose parent or guardian is financially unable to pay them.

C. When a school board provides transportation to pupils for field trips which are a part of the program of the pupils' school or are sponsored by such school, the school board may accept contributions for such transportation.

D. The Board of Education shall promulgate such regulations as shall be in the public interest to effect the intent of this section.

History.

Code 1950, §§ 22-72.1, 22-97.1; 1954, c. 291; 1956, Ex. Sess., c. 60; 1959, Ex. Sess., c. 79, § 1; 1968, c. 501; 1970, c. 156; 1971, Ex. Sess., c. 161; 1972, c. 86; 1975, cc. 308, 328; 1976, c. 99; 1978, cc. 430, 527; 1980, c. 559.

§ 22.1-176.1. Agreements to provide transportation for nonpublic school pupils.

Local school boards may enter into agreements with nonpublic schools within the school division to provide student transportation to and from such schools and school field trips under such terms and conditions as the local school boards deem appropriate and responsible. Such terms may include arrangements relating to cost-sharing, fees, insurance, and liability.

History.

2007, c. 476; 2016, cc. 57, 145.

§ 22.1-177. Regulations.

A. The Board may make regulations relating to the construction, design, operation, equipment, and color of public school buses and shall have the authority to issue an order prohibiting the operation on public streets and highways of any public school bus that does not comply with such regulations. Any such order shall be enforced by the Department of State Police.

B. Local school boards may, notwithstanding any regulation to the contrary, display decals depicting the flag of the United States on the sides and rear of school buses as long as any such decal does not obstruct the name of the school division or the number of the school bus and is no larger than 100 square inches. In addition, local school boards may, notwithstanding any regulation to the contrary, display decals relating to school bus safety. Local school divisions shall be responsible for the cost of the decals. Such decal shall not obstruct the name of the school division or the number of the school bus.

C. No regulation of the Board shall unreasonably limit the authority of any local school division to purchase and use school buses using compressed natural gas or other alternative fuels or convert its school buses to use compressed natural gas or other alternative fuels.

D. Any local school board may, notwithstanding any regulation to the contrary, sell or transfer any of its school buses to another school division or purchase a used school bus from another school division or a school bus dealer as long as the school bus (i) conforms to the specifications relating to construction and design effective in the Commonwealth on the date of manufacture; (ii) has a valid Virginia State Police inspection; and (iii) has not reached the end of its useful life according to the school bus replacement schedule utilized by the Department of Education as required by the general appropriation act.

History.

Code 1950, § 22-276; 1958, c. 274; 1980, c. 559; 1991, c. 191; 2003, c. 162; 2007, c. 104; 2013, c. 778; 2015, c. 559.

§ 22.1-178. Requirements for persons employed to drive school buses.

A. No school board shall hire, employ, or enter into any agreement with any person for the purposes of operating a school bus transporting pupils unless the person proposed to so operate such school bus shall:

1. Have a physical examination of a scope prescribed by the Board of Education with the advice of the Medical Society of Virginia and furnish a form prescribed by the Board of Education showing the results of such examination.

2. Furnish a statement or copy of records from the Department of Motor Vehicles showing that the records of such Department do not disclose that the

person, within the preceding five years, has been convicted upon a charge of driving under the influence of alcohol or drugs, convicted of a felony or assigned to any alcohol safety action program or driver alcohol rehabilitation program pursuant to § 18.2-271.1 or, within the preceding 12 months, has been convicted of two or more moving traffic violations or required to attend a driver improvement clinic by the Commissioner of the Department of Motor Vehicles pursuant to § 46.2-498.

3. Furnish a statement signed by two reputable persons who reside in the school division or in the applicant's community that the person is of good moral character.

4. Exhibit a license showing the person has successfully undertaken the examination prescribed by § 46.2-339.

5. Have reached the age of 18 on the first day of the school year.

B. Any school board may require proof of current certification or training in emergency first aid, cardiopulmonary resuscitation, and the use of an automated external defibrillator as a condition to employment to operate a school bus transporting pupils.

C. School boards may require persons accepting employment after July 1, 1994, as a driver of a school bus transporting pupils to agree, as a condition of employment, to submit to alcohol and controlled substance testing. Any such tests shall be conducted in compliance with Board of Education regulations.

D. The documents required pursuant to subdivisions A 1 and A 2 shall be furnished annually prior to the anniversary date of the employment agreement as a condition to continuing employment to operate a school bus.

E. The documents required pursuant to this section shall be filed with, and made a part of, the records of the school board employing such person as a school bus operator.

F. The State Department of Education shall furnish to the several division superintendents the necessary forms to be used by applicants in furnishing the information required by this section. Insofar as practicable, such forms shall be designed to limit paperwork, avoid the possibility of mistake, and furnish all parties involved with a complete and accurate record of the information required.

G. The physical examination required by subsection A may be performed and the report of the results signed by a licensed nurse practitioner or physician assistant.

History.

Code 1950, § 22-276.1; 1962, c. 544; 1966, c. 604; 1970, c. 696; 1972, c. 359; 1973, c. 170; 1976, cc. 116, 123; 1977, c. 393; 1978, c. 322; 1979, c. 126; 1980, c. 559; 1992, c. 130; 1993, c. 285; 1994, c. 104; 1998, c. 287; 2001, c. 445; 2006, c. 396; 2013, cc. 498, 530.

§ 22.1-179: Repealed by Acts 1992, c. 130, effective March 3, 1992.

§ 22.1-180. Requirements for persons employed to transport pupils attending religious or private schools.

No person, partnership, association or corporation operating any religious or private school shall hire, employ or enter into any agreement with any person for the purpose of transporting pupils by motor vehicle unless such person shall present the documents and meet the qualifications required of operators of public school buses by subsection A of § 22.1-178. The State Department of Education shall furnish the forms prescribed for the purposes of § 22.1-178 to any person, partnership, association or corporation who shall request such forms for the purpose of compliance with this section.

History.

Code 1950, § 22-276.2; 1968, c. 432; 1980, c. 559; 2005, c. 928.

§ 22.1-181. Training program for school bus operators.

The Board of Education shall develop a training program for persons applying for employment, and employed, to operate school buses and shall promote its implementation.

History.

Code 1950, § 22-276.3; 1977, c. 393; 1980, c. 559.

§ 22.1-182. Use of school buses for public purposes.

The school board of any school division may enter into agreements with the governing body of any county, city or town in the school division, any state agency or any agency established or identified pursuant to United States Public Law 89-73 or any law amendatory or supplemental thereto providing for the use of the school buses of such school division by such agency or by departments, boards, commissions or officers of such county, city or town for public purposes, including transportation for the elderly. Each such agreement shall provide for reimbursing the school board in full for the proportionate share of any and all costs, both fixed and variable, of such buses incurred by such school board attributable to the use of such buses pursuant to such agreement. The governing body, state agency or agency established or identified pursuant to United States Public Law 89-73 or any law amendatory or supplemental thereto shall indemnify and hold harmless the school board from any and all liability of the school board by virtue of use of such buses pursuant to an agreement authorized herein.

History.

Code 1950, § 22-151.2; 1973, c. 368; 1975, c. 633; 1980, c. 559.

§ 22.1-183. When warning lights and identification to be covered.

It shall be unlawful for a school bus licensed in this Commonwealth to be operated on the public highways of this Commonwealth for the purpose of transporting persons or commodities other than school personnel, school children or elderly or mentally or physically handicapped persons unless the lettered identification and school bus traffic warning lights on the front and rear of such bus are covered with some opaque detachable material. This section shall not apply to any such bus when operated by a salesman or demonstrator in connection with a prospective sale or delivery of a bus.

History.
Code 1950, §§ 22-151.2, 22-280.1; 1973, c. 368; 1975, c. 633; 1980, c. 559.

§ 22.1-184. School bus emergency drills.

At every public school having public school buses there shall be held, at least once during the first ninety calendar days of each school session and oftener if necessary, a drill in leaving school buses under emergency circumstances.

History.
Code 1950, § 22-280.2; 1964, c. 174; 1980, c. 559.

§ 22.1-185. Shelters on bus routes.

The governing body of any county, city or town may expend funds for the construction and maintenance at points on school bus routes of such shelters, platforms or other structures as it may deem necessary or convenient for the protection and comfort of children of school age who go to such points to meet school buses.

History.
Code 1950, § 22-282; 1980, c. 559.

§ 22.1-186. Payments for transportation of pupils.

The regulations of the Board of Education governing state payments for pupil transportation shall provide for payments to school divisions for pupil transportation provided by the school divisions both through systems operated by the school divisions and through contracts with public transportation facilities.

History.
Code 1950, § 22-283.1; 1972, c. 699; 1980, c. 559.

§ 22.1-187. Exemption from payment of tolls by certain students, etc.

It shall be unlawful to collect any toll for the use of any road, highway, bridge or ferry in this Commonwealth, except those financed under the Transportation Development and Revenue Bond Act (§ 33.2-1700 et seq.) or other act authorizing the construction by the State or a political subdivision thereof of projects financed by the issuance of bonds payable solely from tolls and other revenues of the project, (i) by any student or other person using the road, highway, bridge or ferry daily for going to or from immediate attendance upon any school, college, or other educational institution in this Commonwealth, or classes in water safety training conducted under the auspices of the American Red Cross or (ii) by the vehicle carrying the student or other person.

Any such student or other person or the parent or guardian of any such student may apply for and receive from the principal of any school, college, or other educational institution in this Commonwealth a card certifying that the student or other person uses such road, highway, bridge or ferry daily for regularly attending such school, college, educational institution or classes. Such card exhibited to the person in charge of any tollgate on any road, highway, bridge or ferry in this Commonwealth shall be accepted in lieu of all charges for the passage through such tollgate of any such student, person or the vehicle carrying him when using the road, highway, bridge or ferry daily for going to or from immediate attendance upon any such school, college, other educational institution, or classes.

Any person using any such card, except for the purpose herein specified, shall be guilty of a Class 4 misdemeanor.

History.
Code 1950, § 22-277; 1956, c. 237; 1958, c. 465; 1980, c. 559.

Editor's note.
References in this section were updated at the direction of the Virginia Code Commission to conform to the recodification of Title 33.2 by Acts 2014, c. 805, effective October 1, 2014.

CHAPTER 13.

PROGRAMS, COURSES OF INSTRUCTION AND TEXTBOOKS.

Article 1.

Programs and Courses of Instruction Generally.

ARTICLE 1.

PROGRAMS AND COURSES OF INSTRUCTION GENERALLY.

§ 22.1-205. Driver education programs.

A. The Board of Education shall establish for the public school system a standardized program of driver education in the safe operation of motor vehicles. Such program shall consist of classroom training and behind-the-wheel driver training. However, any student who participates in such a pro-

Education

gram of driver education shall meet the academic requirements established by the Board, and no student in a course shall be permitted to operate a motor vehicle without a license or permit to do so issued by the Department of Motor Vehicles. The program shall include instruction concerning (i) alcohol and drug abuse, (ii) aggressive driving, (iii) distracted driving, (iv) motorcycle awareness, (v) organ and tissue donor awareness, (vi) fuel-efficient driving practices, and (vii) in Planning District 8, for any student completing a driver education program beginning in academic year 2010 — 2011, an additional minimum 90-minute parent/student driver education component included as part of the in-classroom portion of the driver education curriculum, requiring the participation of the student's parent or guardian and emphasizing parental responsibilities regarding juvenile driver behavior, juvenile driving restrictions pursuant to the Code of Virginia, and the dangers of driving while intoxicated and underage consumption of alcohol. Such instruction shall be developed by the Department in cooperation with the Virginia Alcohol Safety Action Program, the Department of Health, and the Department of Behavioral Health and Developmental Services, as appropriate. Such program shall require a minimum number of miles driven during the behind-the-wheel driver training.

B. The Board shall assist school divisions by preparation, publication and distribution of competent driver education instructional materials to ensure a more complete understanding of the responsibilities and duties of motor vehicle operators.

C. Each school board shall determine whether to offer the program of driver education in the safe operation of motor vehicles and, if offered, whether such program shall be an elective or a required course. In addition to the fee approved by the Board of Education pursuant to the appropriation act that allows local school boards to charge a per pupil fee for behind-the-wheel driver education, the Board of Education may authorize a local school board's request to assess a surcharge in order to further recover program costs that exceed state funds distributed through basic aid to school divisions offering driver education programs. Each school board may waive the fee or the surcharge in total or in part for those students it determines cannot pay the fee or surcharge. Only school divisions complying with the standardized program and regulations established by the Board of Education and the provisions of § 46.2-335 shall be entitled to participate in the distribution of state funds appropriated for driver education.

School boards in Planning District 8 shall make the 90-minute parent/student driver education component available to all students and their parents or guardians who are in compliance with § 22.1-254.

D. The actual initial driving instruction shall be conducted, with motor vehicles equipped as may be required by regulation of the Board of Education, on private or public property removed from public highways if practicable; if impracticable, then, at the request of the school board, the Commissioner of Highways shall designate a suitable section of road near the school to be used for such instruction. Such section of road shall be marked with signs, which the Commissioner of Highways shall supply, giving notice of its use for driving instruction. Such signs shall be removed at the close of the instruction period. No vehicle other than those used for driver training shall be operated between such signs at a speed in excess of 25 miles per hour. Violation of this limit shall be a Class 4 misdemeanor.

E. The Board of Education may, in its discretion, promulgate regulations for the use and certification of paraprofessionals as teaching assistants in the driver education programs of school divisions.

F. The Board of Education shall approve correspondence courses for the classroom training component of driver education. These correspondence courses shall be consistent in quality with instructional programs developed by the Board for classroom training in the public schools. Students completing the correspondence courses for classroom training, who are eligible to take behind-the-wheel driver training, may receive behind-the-wheel driver training (i) from a public school, upon payment of the required fee, if the school division offers behind-the-wheel driver training and space is available, (ii) from a driver training school licensed by the Department of Motor Vehicles, or (iii) in the case of a home schooling parent or guardian instructing his own child who meets the requirements for home school instruction under § 22.1-254.1 or subdivision B 1 of § 22.1-254, from a behind-the-wheel training course approved by the Board. Nothing herein shall be construed to require any school division to provide behind-the-wheel driver training to nonpublic school students.

History.

Code 1950, § 22-235.1; 1962, c. 482; 1966, c. 208; 1968, c. 433; 1974, c. 154; 1980, c. 559; 1988, c. 105; 1989, c. 392; 1998, c. 96; 1999, c. 928; 2000, cc. 82, 651; 2001, cc. 659, 665; 2002, cc. 177, 386; 2003, c. 951; 2007, c. 278; 2009, cc. 785, 813, 840; 2010, c. 663; 2011, c. 346; 2013, cc. 585, 646.

CHAPTER 14.
PUPILS.

Article 1.
Compulsory School Attendance.

Section

ARTICLE 1.

COMPULSORY SCHOOL ATTENDANCE.

§ 22.1-254. Compulsory attendance required; excuses and waivers; alternative education program attendance; exemptions from article.

A. Except as otherwise provided in this article, every parent, guardian, or other person in the Commonwealth having control or charge of any child who will have reached the fifth birthday on or before September 30 of any school year and who has not passed the eighteenth birthday shall, during the period of each year the public schools are in session and for the same number of days and hours per day as the public schools, send such child to a public school or to a private, denominational, or parochial school or have such child taught by a tutor or teacher of qualifications prescribed by the Board of Education and approved by the division superintendent, or provide for home instruction of such child as described in § 22.1-254.1.

As prescribed in the regulations of the Board of Education, the requirements of this section may also be satisfied by sending a child to an alternative program of study or work/study offered by a public, private, denominational, or parochial school or by a public or private degree-granting institution of higher education. Further, in the case of any five-year-old child who is subject to the provisions of this subsection, the requirements of this section may be alternatively satisfied by sending the child to any public educational pre-kindergarten program, including a Head Start program, or in a private, denominational, or parochial educational pre-kindergarten program.

Instruction in the home of a child or children by the parent, guardian, or other person having control or charge of such child or children shall not be classified or defined as a private, denominational or parochial school.

The requirements of this section shall apply to (i) any child in the custody of the Department of Juvenile Justice or the Department of Corrections who has not passed his eighteenth birthday and (ii) any child whom the division superintendent has required to take a special program of prevention, intervention, or remediation as provided in subsection C of § 22.1-253.13:1 and in § 22.1-254.01. The requirements of this section shall not apply to (a) any person 16 through 18 years of age who is housed in an adult correctional facility when such person is actively pursuing the achievement of a passing score on a high school equivalency examination approved by the Board of Education but is not enrolled in an individual student alternative education plan pursuant to subsection E, and (b) any child who has obtained a high school diploma or its equivalent, a certificate of completion, or has achieved a passing score on a high school equivalency examination approved by the Board of Education, or who has otherwise complied with compulsory school attendance requirements as set forth in this article.

B. A school board shall excuse from attendance at school:

1. Any pupil who, together with his parents, by reason of bona fide religious training or belief is conscientiously opposed to attendance at school. For purposes of this subdivision, "bona fide religious training or belief" does not include essentially political, sociological or philosophical views or a merely personal moral code; and

2. On the recommendation of the juvenile and domestic relations district court of the county or city in which the pupil resides and for such period of time as the court deems appropriate, any pupil who, together with his parents, is opposed to attendance at a school by reason of concern for such pupil's health, as verified by competent medical evidence, or by reason of such pupil's reasonable apprehension for personal safety when such concern or apprehen-

sion in that pupil's specific case is determined by the court, upon consideration of the recommendation of the principal and division superintendent, to be justified.

C. Each local school board shall develop policies for excusing students who are absent by reason of observance of a religious holiday. Such policies shall ensure that a student shall not be deprived of any award or of eligibility or opportunity to compete for any award, or of the right to take an alternate test or examination, for any which he missed by reason of such absence, if the absence is verified in a manner acceptable to the school board.

D. A school board may excuse from attendance at school:

1. On recommendation of the principal and the division superintendent and with the written consent of the parent or guardian, any pupil who the school board determines, in accordance with regulations of the Board of Education, cannot benefit from education at such school; or

2. On recommendation of the juvenile and domestic relations district court of the county or city in which the pupil resides, any pupil who, in the judgment of such court, cannot benefit from education at such school.

E. Local school boards may allow the requirements of subsection A to be met under the following conditions:

For a student who is at least 16 years of age, there shall be a meeting of the student, the student's parents, and the principal or his designee of the school in which the student is enrolled in which an individual student alternative education plan shall be developed in conformity with guidelines prescribed by the Board, which plan must include:

a. Career guidance counseling;

b. Mandatory enrollment and attendance in a preparatory program for passing a high school equivalency examination approved by the Board of Education or other alternative education program approved by the local school board with attendance requirements that provide for reporting of student attendance by the chief administrator of such preparatory program or approved alternative education program to such principal or his designee;

c. Mandatory enrollment in a program to earn a Board of Education-approved career and technical education credential, such as the successful completion of an industry certification, a state licensure examination, a national occupational competency assessment, or the Virginia workplace readiness skills assessment;

d. Successful completion of the course in economics and personal finance required to earn a Board of Education-approved high school diploma;

e. Counseling on the economic impact of failing to complete high school; and

f. Procedures for reenrollment to comply with the requirements of subsection A.

A student for whom an individual student alternative education plan has been granted pursuant to this subsection and who fails to comply with the conditions of such plan shall be in violation of the compulsory school attendance law, and the division superintendent or attendance officer of the school division in which such student was last enrolled shall seek immediate compliance with the compulsory school attendance law as set forth in this article.

Students enrolled with an individual student alternative education plan shall be counted in the average daily membership of the school division.

F. A school board may, in accordance with the procedures set forth in Article 3 (§ 22.1-276.01 et seq.) of Chapter 14 and upon a finding that a school-age child has been (i) charged with an offense relating to the Commonwealth's laws, or with a violation of school board policies, on weapons, alcohol or drugs, or intentional injury to another person; (ii) found guilty or not innocent of a crime that resulted in or could have resulted in injury to others, or of an offense that is required to be disclosed to the superintendent of the school division pursuant to subsection G of § 16.1-260; (iii) suspended pursuant to § 22.1-277.05; or (iv) expelled from school attendance pursuant to § 22.1-277.06 or 22.1-277.07 or subsection B of § 22.1-277, require the child to attend an alternative education program as provided in § 22.1-209.1:2 or 22.1-277.2:1.

G. Whenever a court orders any pupil into an alternative education program, including a program preparing students for a high school equivalency examination approved by the Board of Education, offered in the public schools, the local school board of the school division in which the program is offered shall determine the appropriate alternative education placement of the pupil, regardless of whether the pupil attends the public schools it supervises or resides within its school division.

The juvenile and domestic relations district court of the county or city in which a pupil resides or in which charges are pending against a pupil, or any court in which charges are pending against a pupil, may require the pupil who has been charged with (i) a crime that resulted in or could have resulted in injury to others, (ii) a violation of Article 1 (§ 18.2-77 et seq.) of Chapter 5 of Title 18.2, or (iii) any offense related to possession or distribution of any Schedule I, II, or III controlled substances to attend an alternative education program, including, but not limited to, night school, adult education, or any other education program designed to offer instruction to students for whom the regular program of instruction may be inappropriate.

This subsection shall not be construed to limit the authority of school boards to expel, suspend, or exclude students, as provided in §§ 22.1-277.04, 22.1-277.05, 22.1-277.06, 22.1-277.07, and 22.1-277.2. As used in this subsection, the term "charged" means that a petition or warrant has been filed or is pending against a pupil.

H. Within one calendar month of the opening of school, each school board shall send to the parents or guardian of each student enrolled in the division a copy of the compulsory school attendance law and the enforcement procedures and policies established by the school board.

I. The provisions of this article shall not apply to:

1. Children suffering from contagious or infectious diseases while suffering from such diseases;

2. Children whose immunizations against communicable diseases have not been completed as provided in § 22.1-271.2;

3. Children under 10 years of age who live more than two miles from a public school unless public transportation is provided within one mile of the place where such children live;

4. Children between the ages of 10 and 17, inclusive, who live more than 2.5 miles from a public school unless public transportation is provided within 1.5 miles of the place where such children live; and

5. Children excused pursuant to subsections B and D.

Further, any child who will not have reached his sixth birthday on or before September 30 of each school year whose parent or guardian notifies the appropriate school board that he does not wish the child to attend school until the following year because the child, in the opinion of the parent or guardian, is not mentally, physically, or emotionally prepared to attend school, may delay the child's attendance for one year.

The distances specified in subdivisions 3 and 4 of this subsection shall be measured or determined from the child's residence to the entrance to the school grounds or to the school bus stop nearest the entrance to the residence of such children by the nearest practical routes which are usable for walking or riding. Disease shall be established by the certificate of a reputable practicing physician in accordance with regulations adopted by the Board of Education.

History.

Code 1950, § 22-275.1; 1952, c. 279; 1959, Ex. Sess., c. 72; 1968, c. 178; 1974, c. 199; 1976, cc. 681, 713; 1978, c. 518; 1980, c. 559; 1984, c. 436; 1989, c. 515; 1990, c. 797; 1991, c. 295; 1993, c. 903; 1996, cc. 163, 916, 964; 1997, c. 828; 1999, cc. 488, 552; 2000, c. 184; 2001, cc. 688, 820; 2003, c. 119; 2004, c. 251; 2006, c. 335; 2010, c. 605; 2012, cc. 454, 642; 2014, c. 84.

§ 22.1-254.01. Certain students required to attend summer school or after-school sessions.

The division superintendent may seek immediate compliance with the compulsory school attendance law as set forth in § 22.1-254 after a reasonable effort to seek the student's attendance in the summer school program or after-school session has failed, including direct notification of the parents of such student of the attendance requirement and failure of the parents to secure the student's attendance, when:

1. A student is required to take a special program of prevention, intervention, or remediation in a public summer school program or to participate in another form of remediation as provided in subsection C of § 22.1-253.13:1 and in accordance with clause (ii) of subsection A of § 22.1-254; and

2. The division superintendent determines that remediation of the student's poor academic performance, passage of the Standards of Learning Assessment in grades three through eight, or promotion is related directly to the student's attendance in the summer school program or participation in another form of remediation.

History.

1996, c. 163; 1997, cc. 466, 828; 1998, cc. 602, 627, 902; 1999, cc. 488, 552; 2006, cc. 41, 834.

§ 22.1-254.02. Students transferring from a public school.

When a student transfers from a school division, such school division to the extent practicable, shall obtain written or electronic documentation of such transfer, in order to make an informed status classification of such student in an information management system prescribed by the Board of Education.

History.

2008, c. 422.

§ 22.1-254.2. Testing for high school equivalency; eligibility; guidelines.

A. The Board of Education shall establish a program of testing for high school equivalency through which a person may pass a high school equivalency examination approved by the Board of Education through which persons may earn a high school equivalency certificate or may earn a diploma as provided in subsection F of § 22.1-253.13:4. The following persons may participate in the testing program:

1. Persons who are at least 18 years of age and not enrolled in public school or not otherwise meeting the school attendance requirements set forth in § 22.1-254;

2. Persons 16 years of age or older who have been instructed by their parents in their home pursuant to § 22.1-254.1 and who have completed such home school instruction;

3. Persons who have been excused from school attendance pursuant to subsections B and D of § 22.1-254;

4. Persons for whom an individual student alternative education plan has been granted pursuant to subsection E of § 22.1-254;

5. Persons 16 through 18 years of age who are housed in adult correctional facilities and who are actively pursuing a passing score on a high school equivalency examination approved by the Board of Education but who are not enrolled in an individual

student alternative education plan pursuant to subsection E of § 22.1-254;

6. Persons 16 years of age or older who have been expelled from school pursuant to §§ 22.1-277.06 through 22.1-277.08; and

7. Persons required by court order to participate in the testing program.

Under no circumstances shall persons under the age of 16 be eligible for the testing program.

B. From such funds as may be appropriated for this purpose, local school boards shall implement programs of preparation and testing for high school equivalency consistent with guidelines to be developed by the Board of Education. Such guidelines shall include a provision that allows preparatory and testing programs to be offered jointly by two or more school boards.

History.

1989, c. 225; 1997, c. 458; 1999, cc. 488, 552; 2003, c. 688; 2004, cc. 251, 939, 955; 2006, c. 335; 2010, c. 605; 2014, c. 84.

§ 22.1-255. Nonresident children.

Any person who has residing with him for a period of sixty days or more any child within the ages prescribed in § 22.1-254 whose parents or guardians reside in another state or the District of Columbia shall be subject to the provisions of § 22.1-254 and shall pay or cause to be paid any tuition charges for such child that may be required pursuant to § 22.1-5 or shall return such child to the home of his parents or legal guardians.

History.

Code 1950, § 22-220; 1958, c. 628; 1968, c. 178; 1976, cc. 681, 713; 1978, c. 140; 1980, c. 559.

§ 22.1-262. Complaint to court when parent fails to comply with law.

A list of persons notified pursuant to § 22.1-261 shall be sent by the attendance officer to the appropriate school principal. If the parent (i) fails to comply with the provisions of § 22.1-261 within the time specified in the notice; or (ii) fails to comply with the provisions of § 22.1-254; or (iii) refuses to participate in the development of the plan to resolve the student's nonattendance or in the conference provided for in § 22.1-258, it shall be the duty of the attendance officer, with the knowledge and approval of the division superintendent, to make complaint against the pupil's parent in the name of the Commonwealth before the juvenile and domestic relations district court. If proceedings are instituted against the parent for failure to comply with the provisions of § 22.1-258, the attendance officer is to provide documentation to the court regarding the school division's compliance with § 22.1-258. In addition thereto, such child may be proceeded against as a child in need of services or a child in need of supervision as provided in Chapter 11 (§ 16.1-226 et seq.) of Title 16.1.

History.

Code 1950, § 22-275.11; 1959, Ex. Sess., c. 72; 1976, c. 98; 1980, c. 559; 1990, c. 797; 1991, c. 295; 1996, cc. 891, 964; 1999, c. 526.

§ 22.1-263. Violation constitutes misdemeanor.

Any person violating the provisions of either § 22.1-254, except for clause (ii) of subsection A, §§ 22.1-255, 22.1-258, 22.1-267, or the parental responsibility provisions relating to compulsory school attendance included in § 22.1-279.3, shall be guilty of a Class 3 misdemeanor. Upon a finding that a person knowingly and willfully violated any provision of § 22.1-254, except for clause (ii) of subsection A, or any provision of §§ 22.1-255, 22.1-258, or § 22.1-267 and that such person has been convicted previously of a violation of any provision of § 22.1-254, except for clause (ii) of subsection A, or any provision of §§ 22.1-255, 22.1-258 or § 22.1-267, such person shall be guilty of a Class 2 misdemeanor.

History.

Code 1950, § 22-275.5; 1959, Ex. Sess., c. 72; 1976, c. 283; 1980, c. 559; 1990, c. 797; 1991, c. 295; 1996, cc. 891, 964; 1999, cc. 488, 526, 552; 2004, c. 573.

§ 22.1-264. Misdemeanor to make false statements as to age.

Any person who makes a false statement concerning the age of a child between the ages set forth in § 22.1-254 for the purpose of evading the provisions of this article shall be guilty of a Class 4 misdemeanor.

History.

Code 1950, § 22-275.18; 1959, Ex. Sess., c. 72; 1968, c. 178; 1976, cc. 283, 681, 713; 1980, c. 559.

§ 22.1-264.1. Misdemeanor to make false statements as to school division or attendance zone residency; penalty.

Any person who knowingly makes a false statement concerning the residency of a child, as determined by § 22.1-3, in a particular school division or school attendance zone, for the purposes of (i) avoiding the tuition charges authorized by § 22.1-5 or (ii) enrollment in a school outside the attendance zone in which the student resides, shall be guilty of a Class 4 misdemeanor and shall be liable to the school division in which the child was enrolled as a result of such false statements for tuition charges, pursuant to § 22.1-5, for the time the student was enrolled in such school division.

History.

2005, c. 178; 2006, c. 143.

§ 22.1-265. Inducing children to absent themselves.

Any person who induces or attempts to induce any child to be absent unlawfully from school or who knowingly employs or harbors, while school is in session, any child absent unlawfully shall be guilty of a Class 3 misdemeanor and may be subject to the penalties provided by subdivision 5 a of subsection B of § 16.1-278.5 or § 18.2-371. Upon a finding that a person knowingly and willfully violated the provisions of this section and that such person has been convicted previously of a violation of this section, such person shall be guilty of a Class 2 misdemeanor.

History.

Code 1950, § 22-275.19; 1959, Ex. Sess., c. 72; 1976, c. 283; 1980, c. 559; 1990, c. 797; 1991, cc. 295, 534; 1996, cc. 891, 916, 964.

§ 22.1-266. Law-enforcement officers and truant children.

A. Notwithstanding the provisions of § 16.1-246, any law-enforcement officer as defined in § 9.1-101 or any attendance officer may pick up any child who (i) is reported to be truant from a public school by a school principal or division superintendent or (ii) the law-enforcement officer or attendance officer reasonably determines to be a public school student and by reason of the child's age and circumstances is either truant from public school or has been expelled from school and has been required to attend an alternative education program pursuant to § 22.1-254 or § 22.1-277.2:1, and may deliver such child to the appropriate public school, alternative education program, or truancy center and personnel thereof without charging the parent or guardian of such child with a violation of any provision of law.

B. Any such law-enforcement officer or attendance officer shall not be liable for any civil damages for any acts or omissions resulting from picking up or delivering a public school child as provided in subsection A when such acts or omissions are within the scope of the employment of such law-enforcement officer or attendance officer and are taken in good faith, unless such acts or omissions were the result of gross negligence or willful misconduct. This subsection shall not be construed to limit, withdraw or overturn any defense or immunity already existing in statutory or common law or to affect any claim occurring prior to the effective date of this law.

C. For the purposes of this section, "truancy center" means a facility or site operated by a school division, sometimes jointly with the local law-enforcement agency, and designated for receiving children who have been retrieved by a law-enforcement officer or attendance officer for truancy from school.

History.

Code 1950, § 22-275.11:1; 1976, c. 692; 1978, c. 215; 1980, c. 559; 1999, cc. 395, 1023; 2001, cc. 688, 820.

§ 22.1-267. Proceedings against habitually absent child.

Any child permitted by any parent, guardian, or other person having control thereof to be habitually absent from school contrary to the provisions of this article may be proceeded against as a child in need of supervision as provided in Chapter 11 (§ 16.1-226 et seq.) of Title 16.1.

History.

Code 1950, § 22-275.20; 1959, Ex. Sess., c. 72; 1976, c. 98; 1980, c. 559; 1990, c. 797; 1991, c. 295.

ARTICLE 3.
DISCIPLINE.

§§ 22.1-277.01 through 22.1-277.03: Repealed by Acts 2001, cc. 688 and 820, cl. 2.

Cross references.

As to optional education programs for kindergarten through grade five, see § 22.1-200.1.

§ 22.1-277.04. Short-term suspension; procedures; readmission.

A pupil may be suspended for not more than ten school days by either the school principal, any assistant principal, or, in their absence, any teacher. The principal, assistant principal, or teacher may suspend the pupil after giving the pupil oral or written notice of the charges against him and, if he denies them, an explanation of the facts as known to school personnel and an opportunity to present his version of what occurred. In the case of any pupil whose presence poses a continuing danger to persons or property, or whose presence is an ongoing threat of disruption, the pupil may be removed from school immediately and the notice, explanation of facts, and opportunity to present his version shall be given as soon as practicable thereafter.

Upon suspension of any pupil, the principal, assistant principal, or teacher responsible for such suspension shall report the facts of the case in writing to the division superintendent or his designee and the parent of the pupil suspended. The division superintendent or his designee shall review forthwith the action taken by the principal, assistant principal, or teacher upon a petition for such review by any party in interest and confirm or disapprove such action based on an examination of the record of the pupil's behavior.

The decision of the division superintendent or his designee may be appealed to the school board or a committee thereof in accordance with regulations of the school board; however, the decision of the division superintendent or his designee shall be final if so prescribed by school board regulations.

The school board shall require that any oral or written notice to the parent of a student who is suspended from school attendance for not more than ten days include notification of the length of the suspension, information regarding the availability of community-based educational programs, alternative education programs or other educational options, and of the student's right to return to regular school attendance upon the expiration of the suspension. The costs of any community-based educational program, or alternative education program or educational option, which is not a part of the educational program offered by the school division, shall be borne by the parent of the student.

History.

1998, c. 806, § 22.1-277.03; 2001, cc. 688, 820.

§ 22.1-277.05. Long-term suspensions; procedures; readmission.

A. A pupil may be suspended from attendance at school for more than ten days after providing written notice to the pupil and his parent of the proposed action and the reasons therefor and of the right to a hearing before the school board, or a committee thereof, or the superintendent or his designee, in accordance with regulations of the school board. If the regulations provide for a hearing by the superintendent or his designee, the regulations shall also provide for an appeal of the decision to the full school board. Such appeal shall be decided by the school board within thirty days.

If the regulations provide for a hearing by a committee of the school board, the regulations shall also provide that such committee may confirm or disapprove the suspension of a student. Any such committee of the school board shall be composed of at least three members. If the committee's decision is not unanimous, the pupil or his parent may appeal the committee's decision to the full school board. Such appeal shall be decided by the school board within thirty days.

B. A school board shall include in the written notice of a suspension for more than ten days required by this section, notification of the length of the suspension. In the case of a suspension for more than ten days, such written notice shall provide information concerning the availability of community-based educational, alternative education, or intervention programs. Such notice shall also state that the student is eligible to return to regular school attendance upon the expiration of the suspension or to attend an appropriate alternative education program approved by the school board during or upon the expiration of the suspension. The costs of any community-based educational, alternative education, or intervention program that is not a part of the educational program offered by the school division that the student may attend during his suspension shall be borne by the parent of the student.

Nothing in this section shall be construed to prohibit the school board from permitting or requiring students suspended pursuant to this section to attend an alternative education program provided by the school board for the term of such suspension.

History.

1998, c. 806, § 22.1-277.03; 2001, cc. 688, 820.

§ 22.1-277.06. Expulsions; procedures; readmission.

A. Pupils may be expelled from attendance at school after written notice to the pupil and his parent of the proposed action and the reasons therefor and of the right to a hearing before the school board or a committee thereof in accordance with regulations of the school board.

If the regulations provide for a hearing by a committee of the school board, the regulations shall also provide that such committee may confirm or disapprove the expulsion of a student. Any such committee of the school board shall be composed of at least three members. If the committee's decision is not unanimous, the pupil or his parent may appeal the committee's decision to the full school board. Such appeal shall be decided by the school board within 30 days.

The regulations shall also provide for subsequent confirmation or disapproval of the proposed expulsion by the school board, or a committee thereof, as may be provided in regulation, regardless of whether the pupil exercised the right to a hearing.

B. The written notice required by this section shall include notification of the length of the expulsion and shall provide information to the parent of the student concerning the availability of community-based educational, training, and intervention programs. Such notice shall state further whether or not the student is eligible to return to regular school attendance, or to attend an appropriate alternative education program approved by the school board, or an adult education program offered by the school division, during or upon the expiration of the expulsion, and the terms or conditions of such readmission. The costs of any community-based educational, training, or intervention program that is not a part of the educational program offered by the school division that the student may attend during his expulsion shall be borne by the parent of the student.

Nothing in this section shall be construed to prohibit the school board from permitting or requiring students expelled pursuant to this section to attend an alternative education program provided by the school board for the term of such expulsion.

If the school board determines that the student is ineligible to return to regular school attendance or to attend during the expulsion an alternative education program or an adult education program in the school division, the written notice shall also advise the parent of such student that the student may petition the school board for readmission to be effective one calendar year from the date of his expulsion, and of the conditions, if any, under which readmission may be granted.

School boards shall establish, by regulation, a schedule pursuant to which such students may apply and reapply for readmission to school. Such schedule shall be designed to ensure that any initial petition for readmission will be reviewed by the school board or a committee thereof, or the division superintendent, and, if granted, would enable the student to resume school attendance one calendar year from the date of the expulsion. If the division superintendent or a committee of the school board denies such petition, the student may petition the school board for review of such denial.

C. Recommendations for expulsion for actions other than those specified in §§ 22.1-277.07 and 22.1-277.08 shall be based on consideration of the following factors:

1. The nature and seriousness of the violation;
2. The degree of danger to the school community;
3. The student's disciplinary history, including the seriousness and number of previous infractions;
4. The appropriateness and availability of an alternative education placement or program;
5. The student's age and grade level;
6. The results of any mental health, substance abuse, or special education assessments;
7. The student's attendance and academic records; and
8. Such other matters as he deems appropriate.

No decision to expel a student shall be reversed on the grounds that such factors were not considered.

Nothing in this subsection shall be deemed to preclude a school board from considering any of these factors as "special circumstances" for purposes of §§ 22.1-277.07 and 22.1-277.08.

History.

1998, c. 806, § 22.1-277.03; 2001, cc. 688, 820; 2005, c. 96.

§ 22.1-277.07. Expulsion of students under certain circumstances; exceptions.

A. In compliance with the federal Improving America's Schools Act of 1994 (Part F-Gun-Free Schools Act of 1994), a school board shall expel from school attendance for a period of not less than one year any student whom such school board has determined, in accordance with the procedures set forth in this article, to have possessed a firearm on school property or at a school-sponsored activity as prohibited by § 18.2-308.1 or to have possessed a firearm or destructive device as defined in subsection E, a firearm muffler or firearm silencer, or a pneumatic gun as defined in subsection E of § 15.2-915.4 on school property or at a school-sponsored activity. A school administrator, pursuant to school board policy, or a school board may, however, determine, based on the facts of a particular situation, that special circumstances exist and no disciplinary action or another disciplinary action or another term of expulsion is appropriate. A school board may promulgate guidelines for determining what constitutes special circumstances. In addition, a school board may, by regulation, authorize the division superintendent or his designee to conduct a preliminary review of such cases to determine whether a disciplinary action other than expulsion is appropriate. Such regulations shall ensure that, if a determination is made that another disciplinary action is appropriate, any such subsequent disciplinary action is to be taken in accordance with the procedures set forth in this article. Nothing in this section shall be construed to require a student's expulsion regardless of the facts of the particular situation.

B. The Board of Education is designated as the state education agency to carry out the provisions of the federal Improving America's Schools Act of 1994 and shall administer the funds to be appropriated to the Commonwealth under this act.

C. Each school board shall revise its standards of student conduct no later than three months after the date on which this act becomes effective. Local school boards requesting moneys apportioned to the Commonwealth through the federal Improving America's Schools Act of 1994 shall submit to the Department of Education an application requesting such assistance. Applications for assistance shall include:

1. Documentation that the local school board has adopted and implemented student conduct policies in compliance with this section; and
2. A description of the circumstances pertaining to expulsions imposed under this section, including (i) the schools from which students were expelled under this section, (ii) the number of students expelled from each such school in the school division during the school year, and (iii) the types of firearms involved in the expulsions.

D. No school operating a Junior Reserve Officers Training Corps (JROTC) program shall prohibit the JROTC program from conducting marksmanship training when such training is a normal element of such programs. Such programs may include training in the use of pneumatic guns. The administration of a school operating a JROTC program shall cooperate with the JROTC staff in implementing such marksmanship training.

E. As used in this section:

"Destructive device" means (i) any explosive, incendiary, or poison gas, bomb, grenade, rocket having a propellant charge of more than four ounces, missile having an explosive or incendiary charge of more than one-quarter ounce, mine, or other similar device; (ii) any weapon, except a shotgun or a shotgun shell generally recognized as particularly suitable for sporting purposes, by whatever name known that will, or may be readily converted to, expel a projectile by the action of an explosive or other propellant, and that has any barrel with a bore of more than one-half inch in diameter that is homemade or was not made by a duly licensed weapon manufacturer, any fully automatic firearm, any sawed-off shotgun or sawed-off rifle as defined in § 18.2-299 or any firearm prohibited from civilian ownership by federal law; and (iii) any combination of parts either designed or intended for use in converting any device into any destructive device described in this subsection and from which a destructive device may be readily assembled. "Destruc-

Education

tive device" does not include any device that is not designed or redesigned for use as a weapon, or any device originally designed for use as a weapon and that is redesigned for use as a signaling, pyrotechnic, line-throwing, safety, or other similar device, nor shall it include any antique firearm as defined in subsection G of § 18.2-308.2:2.

"Firearm" means any weapon, including a starter gun, that will, or is designed or may readily be converted to, expel single or multiple projectiles by the action of an explosion of a combustible material or the frame or receiver of any such weapon. "Firearm" does not include any pneumatic gun, as defined in subsection E of § 15.2-915.4.

"One year" means 365 calendar days as required in federal regulations.

"School property" means any real property owned or leased by the school board or any vehicle owned or leased by the school board or operated by or on behalf of the school board.

F. The exemptions set out in §§ 18.2-308 and 18.2-308.016 regarding concealed weapons shall apply, mutatis mutandis, to the provisions of this section. The provisions of this section shall not apply to persons who possess such firearm or firearms or pneumatic guns as a part of the curriculum or other programs sponsored by the schools in the school division or any organization permitted by the school to use its premises or to any law-enforcement officer while engaged in his duties as such.

G. This section shall not be construed to diminish the authority of the Board of Education or the Governor concerning decisions on whether, or the extent to which, Virginia shall participate in the federal Improving America's Schools Act of 1994, or to diminish the Governor's authority to coordinate and provide policy direction on official communications between the Commonwealth and the United States government.

History.
1995, cc. 724, 801; 1999, cc. 707, 1027; 2000, c. 523, § 22.1-277.01; 2001, cc. 688, 820; 2003, cc. 843, 976; 2004, c. 930; 2006, c. 703; 2013, c. 288; 2014, cc. 109, 312, 765; 2016, c. 257.

§ 22.1-277.07:1. Policies prohibiting possession of firearms.

Notwithstanding any other provision of law to the contrary, each school division may develop and implement procedures addressing disciplinary actions against students, and may establish disciplinary policies prohibiting the possession of firearms on school property, school buses, and at school-sponsored activities.

History.
2004, c. 560.

§ 22.1-277.08. Expulsion of students for certain drug offenses.

A. School boards shall expel from school attendance any student whom such school board has determined, in accordance with the procedures set forth in this article, to have brought a controlled substance, imitation controlled substance, or marijuana as defined in § 18.2-247 onto school property or to a school-sponsored activity. A school administrator, pursuant to school board policy, or a school board may, however, determine, based on the facts of a particular situation, that special circumstances exist and no disciplinary action or another disciplinary action or another term of expulsion is appropriate. A school board may, by regulation, authorize the division superintendent or his designee to conduct a preliminary review of such cases to determine whether a disciplinary action other than expulsion is appropriate. Such regulations shall ensure that, if a determination is made that another disciplinary action is appropriate, any such subsequent disciplinary action is to be taken in accordance with the procedures set forth in this article. Nothing in this section shall be construed to require a student's expulsion regardless of the facts of the particular situation.

B. Each school board shall revise its standards of student conduct to incorporate the requirements of this section no later than three months after the date on which this act becomes effective.

History.
1998, c. 655; 1999, cc. 706, 732, § 22.1-277.01:1; 2001, cc. 688, 820; 2011, cc. 384, 410; 2014, cc. 109, 312, 577, 674, 719, 765.

§ 22.1-277.1: Repealed by Acts 2001, cc. 688 and 820, cl. 2.

Cross references.
Former § 22.1-277.1, relating to the disciplinary authority of school boards under certain circumstances, was derived from Acts 1990, c. 835; 1995, cc. 724, 755, 801; 1998, c. 355; 1999, c. 457; 2000, c. 577.

§ 22.1-277.2:1. Disciplinary authority of school boards under certain circumstances; alternative education program.

A. A school board may, in accordance with the procedures set forth in this article, require any student who has been (i) charged with an offense relating to the Commonwealth's laws, or with a violation of school board policies, on weapons, alcohol or drugs, or intentional injury to another person, or with an offense that is required to be disclosed to the superintendent of the school division pursuant to subsection G of § 16.1-260; (ii) found guilty or not innocent of an offense relating to the Commonwealth's laws on weapons, alcohol, or drugs, or of a crime that resulted in or could have resulted in injury to others, or of an offense that is required to be disclosed to the superintendent of the school division pursuant to subsection G of § 16.1-260; (iii) found to have committed a serious offense or repeated offenses in violation of school board policies;

(iv) suspended pursuant to § 22.1-277.05; or (v) expelled pursuant to § 22.1-277.06, 22.1-277.07, or 22.1-277.08, or subsection B of § 22.1-277, to attend an alternative education program. A school board may require such student to attend such programs regardless of where the crime occurred. School boards may require any student who has been found, in accordance with the procedures set forth in this article, to have been in possession of, or under the influence of, drugs or alcohol on a school bus, on school property, or at a school-sponsored activity in violation of school board policies, to undergo evaluation for drug or alcohol abuse, or both, and, if recommended by the evaluator and with the consent of the student's parent, to participate in a treatment program.

As used in this section, the term "charged" means that a petition or warrant has been filed or is pending against a pupil.

B. A school board may adopt regulations authorizing the division superintendent or his designee to require students to attend an alternative education program consistent with the provisions of subsection A after (i) written notice to the student and his parent that the student will be required to attend an alternative education program and (ii) notice of the opportunity for the student or his parent to participate in a hearing to be conducted by the division superintendent or his designee regarding such placement. The decision of the superintendent or his designee regarding such alternative education placement shall be final unless altered by the school board, upon timely written petition, as established in regulation, by the student or his parent, for a review of the record by the school board.

C. A school board may adopt regulations authorizing the principal or his designee to impose a short-term suspension, pursuant to § 22.1-277.04, upon a student who has been charged with an offense involving intentional injury enumerated in subsection G of § 16.1-260, to another student in the same school pending a decision as to whether to require that such student attend an alternative education program.

History.
1990, c. 835; 1995, cc. 724, 755, 801; 1998, c. 355; 1999, c. 457; 2000, c. 577, § 22.1-277.1; 2001, cc. 688, 820; 2003, c. 119; 2009, c. 208.

§ 22.1-279.1. Corporal punishment prohibited.

A. No teacher, principal or other person employed by a school board or employed in a school operated by the Commonwealth shall subject a student to corporal punishment. This prohibition of corporal punishment shall not be deemed to prevent (i) the use of incidental, minor or reasonable physical contact or other actions designed to maintain order and control; (ii) the use of reasonable and necessary force to quell a disturbance or remove a student from the scene of a disturbance which threatens physical injury to persons or damage to property; (iii) the use of reasonable and necessary force to prevent a student from inflicting physical harm on himself; (iv) the use of reasonable and necessary force for self-defense or the defense of others; or (v) the use of reasonable and necessary force to obtain possession of weapons or other dangerous objects or controlled substances or paraphernalia which are upon the person of the student or within his control.

B. In determining whether a person was acting within the exceptions provided in this section, due deference shall be given to reasonable judgments at the time of the event which were made by a teacher, principal or other person employed by a school board or employed in a school operated by the Commonwealth.

C. For the purposes of this section, "corporal punishment" means the infliction of, or causing the infliction of, physical pain on a student as a means of discipline.

This definition shall not include physical pain, injury or discomfort caused by the use of incidental, minor or reasonable physical contact or other actions designed to maintain order and control as permitted in subdivision (i) of subsection A of this section or the use of reasonable and necessary force as permitted by subdivisions (ii), (iii), (iv), and (v) of subsection A of this section, or by participation in practice or competition in an interscholastic sport, or participation in physical education or an extracurricular activity.

History.
1989, c. 287; 1995, c. 681.

§ 22.1-279.3:1. Reports of certain acts to school authorities.

A. Reports shall be made to the division superintendent and to the principal or his designee on all incidents involving (i) the assault or assault and battery, without bodily injury, of any person on a school bus, on school property, or at a school-sponsored activity; (ii) the assault and battery that results in bodily injury, sexual assault, death, shooting, stabbing, cutting, or wounding of any person, or stalking of any person as described in § 18.2-60.3, on a school bus, on school property, or at a school-sponsored activity; (iii) any conduct involving alcohol, marijuana, a controlled substance, imitation controlled substance, or an anabolic steroid on a school bus, on school property, or at a school-sponsored activity, including the theft or attempted theft of student prescription medications; (iv) any threats against school personnel while on a school bus, on school property or at a school-sponsored activity; (v) the illegal carrying of a firearm, as defined in § 22.1-277.07, onto school property; (vi) any illegal conduct involving firebombs, explosive materials or devices, or hoax explosive devices, as defined in § 18.2-85, or explosive or incendiary devices, as defined in § 18.2-433.1, or chemical bombs, as described in § 18.2-

87.1, on a school bus, on school property, or at a school-sponsored activity; (vii) any threats or false threats to bomb, as described in § 18.2-83, made against school personnel or involving school property or school buses; or (viii) the arrest of any student for an incident occurring on a school bus, on school property, or at a school-sponsored activity, including the charge therefor.

B. Notwithstanding the provisions of Article 12 (§ 16.1-299 et seq.) of Chapter 11 of Title 16.1, local law-enforcement authorities shall report, and the principal or his designee and the division superintendent shall receive such reports, on offenses, wherever committed, by students enrolled at the school if the offense would be a felony if committed by an adult or would be a violation of the Drug Control Act (§ 54.1-3400 et seq.) and occurred on a school bus, on school property, or at a school-sponsored activity, or would be an adult misdemeanor involving any incidents described in clauses (i) through (viii) of subsection A, and whether the student is released to the custody of his parent or, if 18 years of age or more, is released on bond. As part of any report concerning an offense that would be an adult misdemeanor involving an incident described in clauses (i) through (viii) of subsection A, local law-enforcement authorities and attorneys for the Commonwealth shall be authorized to disclose information regarding terms of release from detention, court dates, and terms of any disposition orders entered by the court, to the superintendent of such student's school division, upon request by the superintendent, if, in the determination of the law-enforcement authority or attorney for the Commonwealth, such disclosure would not jeopardize the investigation or prosecution of the case. No disclosures shall be made pursuant to this section in violation of the confidentiality provisions of subsection A of § 16.1-300 or the record retention and redisclosure provisions of § 22.1-288.2. Further, any school superintendent who receives notification that a juvenile has committed an act that would be a crime if committed by an adult pursuant to subsection G of § 16.1-260 shall report such information to the principal of the school in which the juvenile is enrolled.

C. The principal or his designee shall submit a report of all incidents required to be reported pursuant to this section to the superintendent of the school division. The division superintendent shall annually report all such incidents to the Department of Education for the purpose of recording the frequency of such incidents on forms that shall be provided by the Department and shall make such information available to the public.

In submitting reports of such incidents, principals and division superintendents shall accurately indicate any offenses, arrests, or charges as recorded by law-enforcement authorities and required to be reported by such authorities pursuant to subsection B.

A division superintendent who knowingly fails to comply or secure compliance with the reporting requirements of this subsection shall be subject to the sanctions authorized in § 22.1-65. A principal who knowingly fails to comply or secure compliance with the reporting requirements of this section shall be subject to sanctions prescribed by the local school board, which may include, but need not be limited to, demotion or dismissal.

The principal or his designee shall also notify the parent of any student involved in an incident required pursuant to this section to be reported, regardless of whether disciplinary action is taken against such student or the nature of the disciplinary action. Such notice shall relate to only the relevant student's involvement and shall not include information concerning other students.

Whenever any student commits any reportable incident as set forth in this section, such student shall be required to participate in such prevention and intervention activities as deemed appropriate by the superintendent or his designee. Prevention and intervention activities shall be identified in the local school division's drug and violence prevention plans developed pursuant to the federal Improving America's Schools Act of 1994 (Title IV — Safe and Drug-Free Schools and Communities Act).

D. Except as may otherwise be required by federal law, regulation, or jurisprudence, the principal shall immediately report to the local law-enforcement agency any act enumerated in clauses (ii) through (vii) of subsection A that may constitute a criminal offense and may report to the local law-enforcement agency any incident described in clause (i) of subsection A. Nothing in this section shall require delinquency charges to be filed or prevent schools from dealing with school-based offenses through graduated sanctions or educational programming before a delinquency charge is filed with the juvenile court.

Further, except as may be prohibited by federal law, regulation, or jurisprudence, the principal shall also immediately report any act enumerated in clauses (ii) through (v) of subsection A that may constitute a criminal offense to the parents of any minor student who is the specific object of such act. Further, the principal shall report that the incident has been reported to local law enforcement as required by law and that the parents may contact local law enforcement for further information, if they so desire.

E. A statement providing a procedure and the purpose for the requirements of this section shall be included in school board policies required by § 22.1-253.13:7.

The Board of Education shall promulgate regulations to implement this section, including, but not limited to, establishing reporting dates and report formats.

F. For the purposes of this section, "parent" or "parents" means any parent, guardian or other person having control or charge of a child.

G. This section shall not be construed to diminish the authority of the Board of Education or to diminish the Governor's authority to coordinate and provide policy direction on official communications between the Commonwealth and the United States government.

History.

1981, c. 189; 1990, cc. 517, 797; 1991, c. 295; 1994, cc. 265, 285; 1995, cc. 759, 773; 1996, cc. 916, 964; 1999, c. 970; 2000, cc. 79, 611, § 22.1-280.1; 2001, cc. 688, 820; 2002, c. 388; 2003, cc. 899, 954; 2004, cc. 517, 542, 939, 955; 2005, cc. 461, 484, 528; 2006, c. 146; 2010, c. 525; 2011, cc. 384, 410; 2013, c. 800; 2014, cc. 674, 719.

§ 22.1-279.7. Guidelines for student searches.

The Board of Education shall develop, in consultation with the Office of the Attorney General, guidelines for school boards for the conduct of student searches, including random locker searches, voluntary and mandatory drug testing, and strip searches, consistent with relevant state and federal laws and constitutional principles.

School boards shall adopt and revise, in accordance with the requirements of this section, regulations governing student searches that are consistent with the guidelines of the Board.

History.

1998, c. 655; 1999, c. 650; 2000, c. 648, § 22.1-277.01:2; 2001, cc. 688, 820; 2003, c. 899.

§ 22.1-279.9. Development of programs to prevent crime and violence.

All school boards shall develop, in cooperation with the local law-enforcement agencies, juvenile and domestic relations court judges and personnel, parents, and the community at large, programs to prevent violence and crime on school property and at school-sponsored events, which shall include prevention of hazing. Activities designed to prevent the recurrence of violence and crime, including hazing, may include such interventions as education relating to Virginia's criminal law, school crime lines, peer mediation, conflict resolution, community service requirements, and any program focused on demonstrating the consequences of violence and crime. School boards are encouraged to develop and use a network of volunteer services in implementing these prevention activities.

History.

2001, cc. 688, 820; 2004, c. 574.

§ 22.1-280.1: Repealed by Acts 2001, cc. 688 and 820, cl. 2.

Cross references.

Former § 22.1-280.1, requiring reports of certain acts to school authorities was derived from Acts 1981, c. 189; 1990, cc. 517, 797; 1991, c. 295; 1994, cc. 265, 285; 1995, cc. 759, 773; 1996, cc. 916, 964; 1999, c. 970; 2000, cc. 79, 611.

§ 22.1-280.2. School crime line defined; development of school crime lines authorized; local school boards' authority; Board of Education to promulgate regulations.

A. As used in this section:

"School crime line" means a confidential, anonymous system providing inducements for students to report any unlawful act occurring in school buildings or on school grounds or during school-sponsored activities to local law-enforcement authorities which is established as a cooperative alliance between the local school board, news media, the community, and law-enforcement officials or through a separate, nonprofit corporation governed by a board of directors or as part of a local "Crime Stoppers" program.

B. In order to reduce crime and violence within the school divisions in the Commonwealth, any local school board may develop a school crime line program as a joint, self-sustaining, cooperative alliance with news media, the community, and law-enforcement authorities to receive, screen, and reward student reports of unlawful acts committed in school buildings or on school grounds or at school functions, when such reports lead to arrests or recovery of contraband or stolen property. Police or other law-enforcement personnel shall staff every school crime line program, receive reported information from anonymous student callers, screen such information, and direct information for further investigation, as may be appropriate.

C. Such programs may be established (i) by a local school board as a joint, self-sustaining, cooperative alliance with news media, the community, and law-enforcement authorities; (ii) through a separate nonprofit corporation initiated jointly by the local school board, news media, the community, and law-enforcement authorities and governed by a board of directors; or (iii) as part of a local "Crime Stoppers" program.

The governing board of any separate nonprofit school crime line corporation shall include broad-based community representation and shall, through its bylaws, set the policy, coordinate fund raising, and formulate a system of rewards. Prior to implementation of any school crime line program and annually thereafter, the local school board shall review and approve, as complying with the Board of Education's regulations for implementation of school crime lines, its regulations or the bylaws of any nonprofit school crime line corporation or the bylaws of any nonprofit "Crime Stoppers" corporation operating a school crime line. No school crime line program shall be implemented or revised without first obtaining the local school board's approval. Every local school board developing a school crime line program shall also notify all students and their parents or other custodian of the procedures and policies governing the program prior to implementation and annually thereafter.

D. By July 1, 1994, the Board of Education shall promulgate regulations for the implementation of school crime lines, including, but not limited to, appropriate fund raising, and the appropriateness of and limitations on rewards. In developing the regulations, the Board shall, in consultation with the Office of the Attorney General, address issues relating to civil rights, privacy, and any other question of law, including the civic duty to report crime without compensation.

E. Local school boards may establish, as a separate account, a school crime line fund, consisting of private contributions, local appropriations specifically designated for such purposes, and such funds as may be appropriated for this purpose by the Commonwealth pursuant to the appropriation act. No state or local funds appropriated for educational purposes shall be used to implement a school crime line.

History.

1993, c. 361; 1994, c. 721.

§ 22.1-280.2:1. Employment of school safety personnel.

Local school boards may employ school security officers, as defined in § 9.1-101 for the purposes set forth therein.

History.

2002, cc. 836, 868.

§ 22.1-280.2:2. Public School Security Equipment Grant Act of 2013.

A. This section shall be known and may be cited as the "Public School Security Equipment Grant Act of 2013."

B. For purposes of this section:

"Authority" means the Virginia Public School Authority.

"Department" means the Department of Education.

"Eligible school division" means a (i) local school division or (ii) regional vocational center, special education center, alternative education center, or academic year Governor's School serving public school students in grades K through 12. The term shall also include the Virginia School for the Deaf and the Blind.

"Local school division" means a school division with schools subject to state accreditation and whose students are required to be reported in fall membership for grades K through 12.

C. The Authority shall issue bonds for the purpose of grant payments to eligible school divisions of the Commonwealth to be used exclusively for purchasing security equipment for schools, including any related installation, which is designed to improve and help ensure the safety of students attending public schools in Virginia. Such grants shall not be used to pay for security equipment that is not included or described in a grant application approved by the Department pursuant to subsection D. The amount of grants provided to each eligible school division pursuant to this section shall not exceed $100,000 for each fiscal year of the Commonwealth. Funds for the payment of such grants shall be provided from the issuance of bonds by the Authority, provided that the Authority shall not issue more than an aggregate of $6 million in bonds, after all costs, for such grants during each fiscal year of the Commonwealth. In addition, the Authority shall ensure that no more than an aggregate principal amount of $30 million in bonds issued under this section shall be outstanding at any time. Eligible school divisions seeking a grant shall apply to the Department, which shall be responsible for administering the grant program.

The Authority shall work with the Department to determine the schedule for the issuance of the bonds, which shall be based in part upon eligible school divisions having sufficient funds to purchase such security equipment. The payment of debt service on such bonds shall be as provided in the general appropriation act.

Such grants shall be in addition to all other grants made to local governments, school boards, or school divisions according to law. In addition, such grants shall not replace or be in lieu of loans to local school boards or interest rate subsidy payments to local school boards pursuant to Chapter 11.1 (§ 22.1-175.1 et seq.) of Title 22.1, and the issuance of such bonds and the payment of such grants shall not, except as herein provided, affect or otherwise amend the provisions of such chapter as they relate to the powers and duties of the Authority, local school boards, local governments, or any other entity.

D. Based on the criteria developed by the Department in collaboration with the Department of Criminal Justice Services, eligible school divisions shall apply for a grant by August 1 of each year. As a condition of receiving a grant, a local match of 25 percent of the grant amount shall be required. The Superintendent of Public Instruction is authorized to reduce the local match for local school divisions with a composite index of local ability-to-pay less than 0.2000, including any such school division participating in a regional vocational center, special education center, alternative education center, or academic year Governor's School. The Virginia School for the Deaf and the Blind shall be exempt from the match requirement.

Grants shall be awarded by the Department on a competitive basis. As part of the application for a grant, each eligible school division shall (i) identify with specificity the security equipment for which grants are being sought, as well as the estimated costs to purchase and install the security equipment, and (ii) certify that it is the intent of the eligible school division to purchase the security equipment within six months of approval of any grant by the Department.

If the Department determines that a grant shall be paid to an eligible school division under this section, it shall provide a written certification to the chairman of the Authority directing him to make a grant payment in a specific amount to the eligible school division. The Department, however, shall not make such written certification until it has established that the Authority has sufficient funds to make such grant payment. The Authority shall only make grant payments to an eligible school division for the grants provided under this section upon receipt of such written certification. The Authority shall make such grant payments, and in the amounts as directed by the Department, within 30 days of receipt of the certification.

E. The Department shall develop guidelines concerning the requirements for applying for a grant and the administration of such grants. Such guidelines shall not be subject to the Administrative Process Act (§ 2.2-4000 et seq.).

F. In the event that two or more local school divisions became one local school division, whether by consolidation of only the local school divisions or by consolidation of the local governments, such resulting local school division shall be eligible for grants on the basis of the same number of local school divisions as existed prior to September 30, 2012.

G. The Authority shall take all necessary and proper steps as it is authorized to take under law to carry out the provisions of this section.

H. Beginning in 2014, the Department shall make an annual report to the General Assembly by September 1 of each year reporting (i) the total grants paid during the immediately prior fiscal year to each eligible school division and (ii) a general description of the security equipment purchased by eligible school divisions.

History.

2013, c. 608.

ARTICLE 5.
PUPIL RECORDS.

§ 22.1-288.1. Notation in school records of missing children; local law-enforcement cooperation.

A. Each school board shall receive reports of disappearances of any children living within the school division from local law enforcement pursuant to § 52-31.1.

B. Upon notification by a local law-enforcement agency of a child's disappearance, the principal of any school in which the child was enrolled at the time of the disappearance shall indicate, by mark, in the child's cumulative record that the child has been reported as missing. Upon notification by law enforcement that the child is located, the principal shall remove the mark from the record.

C. Upon receiving a request from any school or person for copies of the cumulative records and birth certificate of any child who has been reported by a local law-enforcement agency to be missing, the school being requested to transfer the records shall immediately notify the law-enforcement agency that provided the report to the school of the child's disappearance of the location of the school or person requesting the cumulative records and birth certificate of the child, without alerting the requestor of such report.

D. For the purposes of this section, a "mark" shall mean an electronic or other indicator that (i) is readily apparent on the student's record and (ii) will immediately alert any school personnel that the record is that of a missing child.

History.

1990, c. 295; 2006, c. 295.

CHAPTER 16.
SCHOOLS FOR STUDENTS WITH DISABILITIES.

Section

§ 22.1-323. Licenses generally.

A. No person shall open, operate or conduct any school for students with disabilities in this Commonwealth without a license to operate such school issued by the Board of Education. A license shall be issued for a school if it is in compliance with the regulations of the Board issued pursuant to this chapter, any fee for such license has been paid, and its facilities are approved by the Board after an inspection by the Department. No such license shall be transferable. The license shall be prominently displayed on the premises of the school in a place open for inspection by any interested person during the hours of operation.

B. Any license issued to a residential school for students with disabilities, except a provisional or conditional license issued pursuant to § 22.1-323.1, may, upon written notification to the school, expire on a date subsequent to its stated expiration date and determined at the discretion of the Board, but in no case later than three years from the effective date. Licenses issued to residential schools for students with disabilities which are effective on or after July 1, 1992, may be issued for periods of up to three successive years. Licenses may be issued to private day special education schools for periods of up to three successive years.

C. The Superintendent or his authorized agents may make unannounced inspections of each school for students with disabilities each year.

History.
Code 1950, § 22-330.21; 1970, c. 665; 1972, c. 523; 1980, c. 559; 1992, c. 666; 1994, c. 258; 2004, c. 991.

§ 22.1-331. Violations.

Any person who opens, operates or conducts any school without a license required by this chapter shall be guilty of a Class 2 misdemeanor. Each day such person permits the school to be open and operate without such a license shall constitute a separate offense.

History.
Code 1950, § 22-330.31; 1970, c. 665; 1980, c. 559; 2004, c. 991.

TITLE 23.
EDUCATIONAL INSTITUTIONS.
[REPEALED EFFECTIVE OCTOBER 1, 2016]

CHAPTER 1.
GENERAL PROVISIONS.

§ 23-9.2:4. (Repealed effective October 1, 2016) Payments to institutions of higher education for certain courses taken by law-enforcement officers.

The State Department of Criminal Justice Services is hereby authorized and directed to enter into contracts to make payments to accredited institutions of higher education within this Commonwealth for tuition, books and mandatory fees for law-enforcement officers of the Commonwealth, or its political subdivisions, departments or authorities, or of any county, city or town thereof enrolled on a full-time or part-time basis in courses included in an undergraduate or graduate program which leads to a degree or certificate in an area related to law enforcement or an area suitable for law-enforcement officers. No payments shall be made pursuant to this section to any institution of higher education operating within this Commonwealth whose primary campus is outside this Commonwealth. Assistance under this section may be granted only on behalf of an applicant who enters into an agreement to continue to serve as a law-enforcement officer in Virginia upon completion of his course of study for a period at least as long as the length of the course of study undertaken and paid for under the provisions of this section, and in the event such service is not completed, to repay the full amount of such payments on the terms and in the manner the State Department of Criminal Justice Services may prescribe.

Any person receiving the benefit of funds expended pursuant to this section shall be required to make reimbursement of such funds if he fails to satisfactorily complete the course or courses for which the funds were expended.

Any reimbursement of money advanced under the provisions of this section shall be returned to the State Department of Criminal Justice Services and used in accordance with the purposes of this section.

History.
1972, c. 697; 1974, c. 162; 1977, c. 162; 1982, c. 18; 1986, c. 236.

§ 23-9.2:15. (Repealed effective October 1, 2016) Reporting of acts of sexual violence.

A. For purposes of this section:

"Campus" means (i) any building or property owned or controlled by an institution of higher education within the same reasonably contiguous geographic area of the institution and used by the institution in direct support of, or in a manner related to, the institution's educational purposes, including residence halls, and (ii) any building or property that is within or reasonably contiguous to the area described in clause (i) that is owned by the institution but controlled by another person, is frequently used by students, and supports institutional purposes, such as a food or other retail vendor.

"Noncampus building or property" means (i) any building or property owned or controlled by a student organization officially recognized by an institution of higher education or (ii) any building or property owned or controlled by an institution of higher education that is used in direct support of, or in relation to, the institution's educational purposes, is frequently used by students, and is not within the same reasonably contiguous geographic area of the institution.

"Public property" means all public property, including thoroughfares, streets, sidewalks, and parking facilities, that is within the campus, or immediately adjacent to and accessible from the campus.

"Responsible employee" means a person employed by a public institution of higher education or private nonprofit institution of higher education who has the authority to take action to redress sexual vio-

lence, who has been given the duty of reporting acts of sexual violence or any other misconduct by students to the Title IX coordinator or other appropriate institution designee, or whom a student could reasonably believe has this authority or duty.

"Sexual violence" means physical sexual acts perpetrated against a person's will or where a person is incapable of giving consent.

"Title IX coordinator" means an employee designated by a public institution of higher education or private nonprofit institution of higher education to coordinate the institution's efforts to comply with and carry out the institution's responsibilities under Title IX (20 U.S.C. § 1681 et seq.). If no such employee has been designated by the institution, the institution shall designate an employee who will be responsible for receiving information of alleged acts of sexual violence from responsible employees in accordance with subsection B.

B. Any responsible employee who in the course of his employment obtains information that an act of sexual violence may have been committed against a student attending the institution or may have occurred on campus, in or on a noncampus building or property, or on public property shall report such information to the Title IX coordinator as soon as practicable after addressing the immediate needs of the victim.

C. Upon receipt of information pursuant to subsection B, the Title IX coordinator or his designee shall promptly report the information, including any personally identifiable information, to a review committee established pursuant to subsection D. Nothing in this section shall prevent the Title IX coordinator or any other responsible employee from providing any information to law enforcement with the consent of the victim.

D. Each public institution of higher education or private nonprofit institution of higher education shall establish a review committee for the purposes of reviewing information related to acts of sexual violence, including information reported pursuant to subsection C. Such review committee shall consist of three or more persons and shall include the Title IX coordinator or his designee, a representative of law enforcement, and a student affairs representative. If the institution has established a campus police department pursuant to Chapter 17 (§ 23-232 et seq.) of this title, the representative of law enforcement shall be a member of such department, otherwise the representative of law enforcement shall be a representative of campus security. The review committee may be the threat assessment team established under § 23-9.2:10 or a separate body. The review committee may obtain law-enforcement records, criminal history record information as provided in §§ 19.2-389 and 19.2-389.1, health records as provided in § 32.1-127.1:03, available institutional conduct or personnel records, and known facts and circumstances of the information reported pursuant to subsection C or information or evidence known to the institution or to law enforcement. The review committee shall be considered to be a threat assessment team established pursuant to § 23-9.2:10 for purposes of (i) obtaining criminal history record information and health records and (ii) the Virginia Freedom of Information Act (§ 2.2-3700 et seq.). The review committee shall conduct its review in compliance with federal privacy law.

E. Upon receipt of information of an alleged act of sexual violence reported pursuant to subsection C, the review committee shall meet within 72 hours to review the information and shall meet again as necessary as new information becomes available.

F. If, based on consideration of all factors, the review committee, or if the committee cannot reach a consensus, the representative of law enforcement on the review committee, determines that the disclosure of the information, including personally identifiable information, is necessary to protect the health or safety of the student or other individuals as set forth in 34 C.F.R. § 99.36, the representative of law enforcement on the review committee shall immediately disclose such information to the law-enforcement agency that would be responsible for investigating the alleged act of sexual violence. Such disclosure shall be for the purposes of investigation and other actions by law enforcement. Upon such disclosure, the Title IX coordinator or his designee shall notify the victim that such disclosure is being made. The provisions of this subsection shall not apply if the law-enforcement agency responsible for investigating the alleged act of sexual violence is located outside the United States.

G. In cases in which the alleged act of sexual violence would constitute a felony violation of Article 7 (§ 18.2-61 et seq.) of Chapter 4 of Title 18.2, the representative of law enforcement on the review committee shall inform the other members of the review committee and shall within 24 hours consult with the attorney for the Commonwealth or other prosecutor responsible for prosecuting the alleged act of sexual violence and provide to him the information received by the review committee without disclosing personally identifiable information, unless such information was disclosed pursuant to subsection F. In addition, if such consultation does not occur and any other member of the review committee individually concludes that the alleged act of sexual violence would constitute a felony violation of Article 7 (§ 18.2-61 et seq.) of Chapter 4 of Title 18.2, that member shall within 24 hours consult with the attorney for the Commonwealth or other prosecutor responsible for prosecuting the alleged act of sexual violence and provide to him the information received by the review committee without disclosing personally identifiable information, unless such information was disclosed pursuant to subsection F.

H. At the conclusion of the review, the Title IX coordinator and the law-enforcement representative shall each retain (i) the authority to proceed with any further investigation or adjudication allowed under state or federal law and (ii) independent records of the review team's considerations, which shall be maintained under applicable state and federal law.

I. No responsible employee shall be required to make a report pursuant to subsection B if:

1. The responsible employee obtained the information through any communication considered privileged under state or federal law or the responsible employee obtained the information in the course of providing services as a licensed health care professional, an employee providing administrative support for such health care professionals, a professional counselor, an accredited rape crisis or domestic violence counselor, a campus victim support personnel, a member of clergy, or an attorney; or

2. The responsible employee has actual knowledge that the same matter has already been reported to the Title IX coordinator or to the attorney for the Commonwealth or the law-enforcement agency responsible for investigating the alleged act of sexual violence.

J. Any responsible employee who makes a report required by this section or testifies in a judicial or administrative proceeding as a result of such report shall be immune from any civil liability alleged to have resulted therefrom unless such person acted in bad faith or with malicious intent.

K. The provisions of this section shall not require a person who is the victim of an alleged act of sexual violence to report such violation.

L. The institution shall ensure that a victim of an alleged act of sexual violence is informed of (i) the available law-enforcement options for investigation and prosecution; (ii) the importance of collection and preservation of evidence; (iii) the available options for a protective order; (iv) the available campus options for investigation and adjudication under the institution's policies; (v) the victim's rights to participate or decline to participate in any investigation to the extent permitted under state or federal law; (vi) the applicable federal or state confidentiality provisions that govern information provided by a victim; (vii) the available on-campus resources and any unaffiliated community resources, including sexual assault crisis centers, domestic violence crisis centers, or other victim support services; and (viii) the importance of seeking appropriate medical attention.

History.
2015, cc. 737, 745.

§ 23-9.2:16. (Repealed effective October 1, 2016) Sexual assault; memoranda of understanding; policies.

A. Each public institution of higher education or private nonprofit institution of higher education shall establish and the State Board for Community Colleges shall adopt a policy requiring each community college to establish a written memorandum of understanding with a sexual assault crisis center or other victim support service in order to provide sexual assault victims with immediate access to a confidential, independent advocate who can provide a trauma-informed response that includes an explanation of options for moving forward.

B. Each public institution of higher education or private nonprofit institution of higher education shall adopt policies to provide to sexual assault victims information on contacting such sexual assault crisis center or other victim support service.

C. Each public institution of higher education or nonprofit private institution of higher education may request the cooperation of the primary law-enforcement agency of the locality in which the institution is located to establish a written memorandum of understanding with such law-enforcement agency to address the prevention of and response to criminal sexual assault as set forth in Article 7 (§ 18.2-61 et seq.) of Chapter 4 of Title 18.2.

History.
2015, cc. 737, 745; 2016, c. 481.

§ 23-9.2:17. (Repealed effective October 1, 2016) Sexual violence policy review.

By October 31 of each year, each public institution of higher education or private nonprofit institution of higher education and the State Board for Community Colleges shall certify to the State Council of Higher Education for Virginia that it has reviewed its sexual violence policy and updated it as appropriate. The State Council of Higher Education for Virginia and the Department of Criminal Justice Services shall establish criteria for the certification process and may request information relating to the policies for the purposes of sharing best practices and improving campus safety. The State Council of Higher Education for Virginia and the Department of Criminal Justice Services shall report to the Secretary of Education on the certification status of each institution and the Virginia Community College System by November 30 of each year.

History.
2015, cc. 737, 745.

CHAPTER 6.2.

VIRGINIA COMMONWEALTH UNIVERSITY HEALTH SYSTEM AUTHORITY.

Section

§ 23-50.16:4. (Repealed effective October 1, 2016) Definitions.

As used in this chapter, the following terms have the following meanings, unless the context requires otherwise:

"Authority" means the Virginia Commonwealth University Health System Authority.

"Board" means the Board of Directors of the Authority.

"Bonds" means bonds, notes, revenue certificates, lease participation certificates or other evidences of indebtedness or deferred purchase financing arrangements.

"Costs" means costs of construction, reconstruction, renovation, site work and acquisition of lands, structures, rights-of-way, franchises, easements and other property rights and interests; costs of demolition, removal or relocation of buildings or structures; costs of labor, materials, machinery and all other kinds of equipment; financing charges; costs of engineering and inspections; costs of financial, legal and accounting services; costs of plans, specifications, studies, and surveys; estimates of costs and of revenues; feasibility studies and administrative expenses, including administrative expenses during the start-up of any project; costs of issuance of bonds, including printing, engraving, advertising, legal and other similar expenses; credit enhancement and liquidity facility fees; fees for interest rate caps, collars, swaps or other financial derivative products; interest on bonds in connection with a project prior to and during construction or acquisition thereof and for a period not exceeding one year thereafter; provisions for working capital to be used in connection with any project; redemption premiums, obligations purchased to provide for the payment of bonds being refunded and other costs necessary or incident to refunding of bonds; operating and maintenance reserve funds, debt reserve funds and other reserves for the payment of principal and interest on bonds; and all other expenses necessary, desirable or incidental to the operation of the Authority's facilities or the construction, reconstruction, renovation, acquisition or financing of projects or other facilities or equipment appropriate for carrying out the purposes of this chapter and the placing of the same in operation; or the refunding of bonds.

"Chief executive officer" means the chief executive officer of the Virginia Commonwealth University Health System Authority.

"Hospital facilities" means all property or rights in property, real and personal, tangible and intangible, including all facilities suitable for providing hospital and health care services and including any and all structures, buildings, improvements, additions, extensions, replacements, appurtenances, lands, rights in land, furnishings, landscaping, approaches, roadways and other related and supporting facilities, now or hereafter owned, leased, operated or used, in whole or in part, by Virginia Commonwealth University as part of, or in connection with, the Medical College of Virginia Hospitals in the normal course of its operations as a teaching, research and medical treatment facility.

"Hospital obligations" means all debts or other obligations, contingent or certain, owing to any person or other entity on the transfer date, arising out of the operation of the Medical College of Virginia Hospitals as a medical treatment facility or arising out of the financing or refinancing of hospital facilities, and including all bonds and other debts for the purchase of goods and services, whether or not delivered, and obligations for the delivery of services, whether or not performed.

"Project" means any health care, research or educational facility or equipment necessary or convenient to or consistent with the purposes of the Authority, whether or not owned by the Authority, including, without limitation, hospitals; nursing homes; continuing care facilities; self-care facilities; wellness and health maintenance centers; medical office facilities; clinics; out-patient clinics; surgical centers; alcohol, substance abuse, and drug treatment centers; laboratories; sanitariums; hospices; facilities for the residence or care of the elderly, the handicapped, or the chronically ill; residential facilities for nurses, interns, and physicians; other kinds of facilities for the treatment of sick, disturbed, or infirm persons or the prevention of disease or maintenance of health; colleges, schools or divisions offering undergraduate or graduate programs for the health professions and sciences and such other branches of learning as may be appropriate, together with research, training, and teaching facilities; all related and supporting facilities and equipment necessary or desirable in connection therewith or incidental thereto; or equipment alone, including, without limitation, parking, kitchen, laundry, laboratory, wellness, pharmaceutical, administrative, communications, computer, and recreational facilities; power plants and equipment; storage space; mobile medical facilities; vehicles; air transport equipment and other equipment necessary or desirable for the transportation of medical equipment, medical personnel or patients; and all lands, buildings, improvements, approaches and appurtenances necessary or desirable in connection with or incidental to any project.

"Transfer date" means a date or dates agreed to by the Board of Visitors of Virginia Commonwealth University and the Authority for the transfer of employees to the Authority and for the transfer of hospital facilities, or any parts thereof, to and the assumption, directly or indirectly, of hospital obligations by the Authority, which dates for the various transfers and the various assumptions may be different, but in no event shall any date be later than June 30, 1997.

"University" means Virginia Commonwealth University.

History.

1996, cc. 905, 1046; 2000, c. 720.

CHAPTER 17.
CAMPUS POLICE DEPARTMENTS.

§ 23-232. (Repealed effective October 1, 2016) Establishment authorized; employment of officers.

A. The governing board of each public institution of higher learning named in § 23-14, hereafter sometimes referred to in this chapter as "institution," is authorized to establish a campus police department and to employ campus police officers and auxiliary forces upon appointment as provided in §§ 23-233 and 23-233.1. Such employment shall be governed by the Virginia Personnel Act, as set forth in Chapter 29 (§ 2.2-2900 et seq.) of Title 2.2, except that the governing body of a public institution of higher education may direct that the employment of the chief of the campus police department is not governed by the Virginia Personnel Act.

B. The Virginia Commonwealth University Health System Authority shall be authorized to employ police officers and auxiliary forces as provided in this chapter and in § 23-50.16:10, except that the employment of such officers and forces shall not be governed by the Virginia Personnel Act.

History.
1977, c. 79; 1991, c. 711; 1996, cc. 905, 1046; 2000, c. 720; 2009, c. 596.

§ 23-232.1. (Repealed effective October 1, 2016) Authorization for campus police departments in private institutions of higher education.

The governing board of each private institution of higher education is authorized to establish, in compliance with the provisions of this chapter, a campus police department and to employ campus police officers upon appointment as provided in § 23-233. Except as such provisions apply exclusively to public institutions or employees, the provisions of this chapter shall apply to the appointment and employment of officers, operation, powers, duties and jurisdiction of private campus police departments, and such departments shall be subject to and enjoy the benefits of this chapter. However, to be qualified to use the word "police" to describe the department or its officers, any private college or university which establishes a campus police department shall require that each officer comply with the training or other requirements for law-enforcement officers established by the Department of Criminal Justice Services pursuant to Chapter 1 (§ 9.1-100 et seq.) of Title 9.1.

History.
1992, c. 187.

§ 23-232.2. (Repealed effective October 1, 2016) Inspection of criminal incident information.

A. Criminal incident information, as described in subsection B, of any campus police department established pursuant to § 23-232.1, shall be open to inspection and copying by any (i) citizen of the Commonwealth, (ii) currently registered student of the institution, or (iii) parent of a registered student, during the regular office hours of the custodian of such information.

B. Criminal incident information shall include (i) the date, time, and general location of the alleged crime; (ii) a general description of injuries suffered or property damaged or stolen; and (iii) the name and address of any individual arrested as a result of felonies committed against persons or property or misdemeanors involving assault, battery, or moral turpitude reported to the campus police, except where disclosure is prohibited by law; however, where the release of such information is likely to jeopardize an ongoing criminal investigation or the safety of an individual, cause a suspect to flee or evade detection, or result in the destruction of evidence, such information may be withheld until the above-referenced damage is no longer likely to occur from the release of such information.

History.
1994, c. 457.

§ 23-233. (Repealed effective October 1, 2016) Appointment of officers.

Upon application of the governing board of an institution, the circuit court of the county or city wherein the institution is located, in its discretion, may, by order, appoint the persons named in the application to be campus police officers at such institution.

History.
1977, c. 79.

§ 23-233.1. (Repealed effective October 1, 2016) Establishment of auxiliary police forces; powers, authority and immunities generally.

The governing boards, for the further preservation of public peace, safety and good order of the campus community, shall have the power to establish, equip, and maintain auxiliary police forces. When called into service pursuant to procedures established by the governing board, members of these auxiliary forces shall have all the powers, authority, and immunities of public institutions of higher education campus police officers.

History.
1991, c. 711.

§ 23-234. (Repealed effective October 1, 2016) Powers and duties; jurisdiction; mutual aid agreements; memoranda of understanding.

A. A campus police officer appointed as provided in § 23-233 or appointed and activated pursuant to § 23-233.1 may exercise the powers and duties conferred by law upon police officers of cities, towns, or counties, and shall be so deemed, including but not limited to the provisions of Chapters 5 (§ 19.2-52 et seq.), 7 (§ 19.2-71 et seq.), and 23 (§ 19.2-387 et seq.) of Title 19.2, (i) upon any property owned or controlled by the relevant public or private institution of higher education, or, upon request, any property owned or controlled by another public or private institution of higher education and upon the streets, sidewalks, and highways, immediately adjacent thereto, (ii) pursuant to a mutual aid agreement provided for in § 15.2-1727 between the governing board of a public or private institution and such other institution of higher education, public or private, in the Commonwealth or adjacent political subdivisions, (iii) in close pursuit of a person as provided in § 19.2-77, and (iv) upon approval by the appropriate circuit court of a petition by the local governing body for concurrent jurisdiction in designated areas with the police officers of the county, city, or town in which the institution, its satellite campuses, or other properties are located. The local governing body may petition the circuit court pursuant only to a request by the local law-enforcement agency for concurrent jurisdiction.

B. All public or private institutions of higher education that have campus police forces established in accordance with the provisions of this chapter shall enter into and become a party to mutual aid agreements with one or more of the following: (i) an adjacent local law-enforcement agency or (ii) the Department of State Police, for the use of their joint forces, both regular and auxiliary, equipment, and materials when needed in the investigation of any felony criminal sexual assault or medically unattended death occurring on property owned or controlled by the institution of higher education or any death resulting from an incident occurring on such property. Such mutual aid agreements shall include provisions requiring either the campus police force or the agency with which it has established a mutual aid agreement pursuant to this subsection, in the event that such police force or agency conducts an investigation that involves a felony criminal sexual assault as set forth in Article 7 (§ 18.2-61 et seq.) of Chapter 4 of Title 18.2 occurring on campus, in or on a noncampus building or property, or on public property, to notify the local attorney for the Commonwealth of such investigation within 48 hours of beginning such investigation. Such notification shall not require a campus police force or the agency with which it has established a mutual aid agreement to disclose identifying information about the victim. The provisions of this section shall not prohibit a campus police force from requesting assistance from any appropriate law-enforcement agency of the Commonwealth, even though a mutual aid agreement has not been executed with that agency.

C. All public or nonprofit private institutions of higher education that (i) do not have campus police forces established in accordance with the provisions of this chapter and (ii) have security departments, rely on municipal, county, or state police forces, or contract for security services from private parties pursuant to § 23-238 shall enter into and become a party to a memorandum of understanding with an adjacent local law-enforcement agency or the Department of State Police (the Department) to require either such local law-enforcement agency or the Department, in the event that such agency or the Department conducts an investigation that involves a felony criminal sexual assault as set forth in Article 7 (§ 18.2-61 et seq.) of Chapter 4 of Title 18.2 occurring on campus, in or on a noncampus building or property, or on public property, to notify the local attorney for the Commonwealth of such investigation within 48 hours of beginning such investigation. Such notification shall not require the law-enforcement agency or the Department to disclose identifying information about the victim.

D. All mutual aid agreements and memoranda of understanding entered into pursuant to this section shall specify the procedure for sharing information.

E. For purposes of this section:

"Campus" means (i) any building or property owned or controlled by an institution of higher education located within the same reasonably contiguous geographic area of the institution and used by the institution in direct support of, or in a manner related to, the institution's educational purposes, including residence halls, and (ii) any building or property that is within or reasonably contiguous to the area described in clause (i) that is owned by the

institution but controlled by another person, is frequently used by students, and supports institutional purposes, such as a food or other retail vendor.

"Noncampus building or property" means (i) any building or property owned or controlled by a student organization that is officially recognized by an institution of higher education or (ii) any building or property owned or controlled by an institution of higher education that is used in direct support of, or in relation to, the institution's educational purposes, is frequently used by students, and is not within the same reasonably contiguous geographic area of the institution.

"Public property" means all public property, including thoroughfares, streets, sidewalks, and parking facilities, that is within the campus, or immediately adjacent to and accessible from the campus.

History.

1977, c. 79; 1985, c. 386; 1991, c. 711; 1992, c. 187; 2002, c. 97; 2012, cc. 282, 450; 2015, c. 707; 2016, cc. 513, 571.

§ 23-234.1. (Repealed effective October 1, 2016) Extending police power of public institutions of higher education beyond boundaries thereof; jurisdiction of courts.

A. The governing board of any public institution of higher education that leases, rents, or owns satellite campuses, public buildings, and other property located beyond the limits of such institution shall have and may exercise full police power over these properties and over persons using the same. The governing board may prescribe rules and regulations for the operation and use of these properties and for the conduct of all persons using them and may provide appropriate administrative penalties for the violation of these rules and regulations.

B. The district court for the county, city, or town where violations of law or approved regulations of the institution occurs shall have jurisdiction of all cases arising within the county, city, or town.

It shall be the duty of the attorney for the Commonwealth for the county, city, or town where the offense occurs to prosecute all violators of the laws pertaining to the provisions enumerated in this chapter.

History.

1991, c. 711.

§ 23-235. (Repealed effective October 1, 2016) Officers to comply with requirements of Department of Criminal Justice Services.

All persons appointed and employed as campus police officers or as members of auxiliary forces pursuant to this chapter shall comply with the requirements for law-enforcement officers as established by the Department of Criminal Justice Services pursuant to Chapter 1 (§ 9.1-100 et seq.) of Title 9.1.

History.

1977, c. 79; 1984, c. 779; 1991, c. 711.

§ 23-236. (Repealed effective October 1, 2016) Investigation of prospective officers; terms of employment; uniforms, etc.

A. Prior to appointment as a campus police officer or member of an auxiliary force, each person shall be investigated by the campus police department of the institution applying for the order of appointment or, if none has been established, by the police department of the county, city or town in which such institution is located. Such investigation shall determine whether the person is responsible, honest and in all ways capable of performing the duties of a campus police officer.

B. Each campus police officer and member of an auxiliary force appointed and employed pursuant to this chapter shall be a state employee of the institution named in the order of appointment. Insofar as not inconsistent with the Virginia Personnel Act (§ 2.2-2900 et seq.), the governing board of such institution shall provide for the conditions and terms of employment and compensation and provide a distinctive uniform and badge of office.

History.

1977, c. 79; 1991, c. 711.

§ 23-237. (Repealed effective October 1, 2016) Termination of employment of officers.

A person appointed as a campus police officer shall exercise his powers only as long as he remains employed or activated, as the case may be, by the institution named in the order of the appointment. The appointment order entered by the circuit court shall automatically be revoked upon the termination of the officer's employment at the institution and may be revoked by the court for malfeasance, misfeasance, or nonfeasance. The institution shall notify the court upon termination of the officer's employment at the institution.

History.

1977, c. 79; 1991, c. 711.

§ 23-238. (Repealed effective October 1, 2016) Security departments and other security services.

Nothing in this chapter shall abridge the authority of the governing board of an institution to establish security departments, whose officers and employees shall not have the powers and duties set forth in § 23-234, in place of or supplemental to campus police departments or to rely upon municipal, county or state police forces or to contract for security services from private parties.

History.
1977, c. 79.

TITLE 23.1.
INSTITUTIONS OF HIGHER EDUCATION; OTHER EDUCATIONAL AND CULTURAL INSTITUTIONS.

SUBTITLE II.
STUDENTS AND CAMPUS.

CHAPTER 6.
FINANCIAL ASSISTANCE.

Article 1.

General Provisions.

ARTICLE 1.
GENERAL PROVISIONS.

§ 23.1-602. (Effective October 1, 2016) Payments to institutions of higher education for certain courses taken by law-enforcement officers.

A. The Department of Criminal Justice Services shall enter into contracts to make payments to public institutions of higher education and accredited private institutions of higher education whose primary campus is within the Commonwealth for tuition, books, and mandatory fees for any law-enforcement officer of the Commonwealth or its political subdivisions, departments, or authorities or any locality of the Commonwealth who (i) is enrolled on a full-time or part-time basis in courses included in an undergraduate or graduate program that leads to a degree or certificate in an area relating to law enforcement or suitable for law-enforcement officers and (ii) enters into an agreement to continue to serve as a law-enforcement officer in the Commonwealth upon completion of his course of study for a period at least as long as the length of the course of study undertaken and paid for under the provisions of this section and, in the event that he does not complete such service, to repay the full amount of such payments on the terms and in the manner that the Department of Criminal Justice Services prescribes.

B. Any individual who receives the benefit of funds expended pursuant to this section shall reimburse such funds to the Department of Criminal Justice Services if he fails to satisfactorily complete the course for which the funds were expended.

The Department of Criminal Justice Services shall use such reimbursed funds in accordance with the purposes of this section.

History.
1972, c. 697, § 23-9.2:4; 1974, c. 162; 1977, c. 162; 1982, c. 18; 1986, c. 236; 2016, c. 588.

CHAPTER 8.
HEALTH AND CAMPUS SAFETY.

Article 2.

Campus Safety; General Provisions.

Article 3.

Campus Safety; Campus Police Departments.

ARTICLE 2.
CAMPUS SAFETY; GENERAL PROVISIONS.

§ 23.1-806. (Effective October 1, 2016) Reporting of acts of sexual violence.

A. For purposes of this section:

"Campus" means (i) any building or property owned or controlled by an institution of higher education within the same reasonably contiguous geographic area of the institution and used by the institution in direct support of, or in a manner relating to, the institution's educational purposes, including residence halls, and (ii) any building or property that is within or reasonably contiguous to the area described in clause (i) that is owned by the institution but controlled by another person, is frequently used by students, and supports institutional purposes, such as a food or other retail vendor.

"Noncampus building or property" means (i) any building or property owned or controlled by a student organization officially recognized by an institution of higher education or (ii) any building or property owned or controlled by an institution of higher education that is used in direct support of, or in relation to, the institution's educational purposes, is frequently used by students, and is not within the same reasonably contiguous geographic area of the institution.

"Public property" means all public property, including thoroughfares, streets, sidewalks, and parking facilities, that is within the campus, or immediately adjacent to and accessible from the campus.

"Responsible employee" means a person employed by a public institution of higher education or nonprofit private institution of higher education who has the authority to take action to redress sexual violence, who has been given the duty of reporting acts of sexual violence or any other misconduct by students to the Title IX coordinator or other appropriate institution designee, or whom a student could reasonably believe has this authority or duty.

"Sexual violence" means physical sexual acts perpetrated against a person's will or where a person is incapable of giving consent.

"Title IX coordinator" means an employee designated by a public institution of higher education or nonprofit private institution of higher education to coordinate the institution's efforts to comply with and carry out the institution's responsibilities under Title IX (20 U.S.C. § 1681 et seq.). If no such employee has been designated by the institution, the institution shall designate an employee who will be responsible for receiving information of alleged acts of sexual violence from responsible employees in accordance with subsection B.

B. Any responsible employee who in the course of his employment obtains information that an act of sexual violence may have been committed against a student attending the institution or may have occurred on campus, in or on a noncampus building or property, or on public property shall report such information to the Title IX coordinator as soon as practicable after addressing the immediate needs of the victim.

C. Upon receipt of information pursuant to subsection B, the Title IX coordinator or his designee shall promptly report the information, including any personally identifiable information, to a review committee established pursuant to subsection D. Nothing in this section shall prevent the Title IX coordinator or any other responsible employee from providing any information to law enforcement with the consent of the victim.

D. Each public institution of higher education and nonprofit private institution of higher education shall establish a review committee for the purposes of reviewing information relating to acts of sexual violence, including information reported pursuant to subsection C. Such review committee shall consist of three or more persons and shall include the Title IX coordinator or his designee, a representative of law enforcement, and a student affairs representative. If the institution has established a campus police department pursuant to Article 3 (§ 23.1-809 et seq.), the representative of law enforcement shall be a member of such department; otherwise, the representative of law enforcement shall be a representative of campus security. The review committee may be the threat assessment team established under § 23.1-805 or a separate body. The review committee may obtain law-enforcement records, criminal history record information as provided in §§ 19.2-389 and 19.2-389.1, health records as provided in § 32.1-127.1:03, available institutional conduct or personnel records, and known facts and circumstances of the information reported pursuant to subsection C or information or evidence known to the institution or to law enforcement. The review committee shall be considered to be a threat assessment team established pursuant to § 23.1-805 for purposes of (i) obtaining criminal history record information and health records and (ii) the Virginia Freedom of Information Act (§ 2.2-3700 et seq.). The review committee shall conduct its review in compliance with federal privacy law.

E. Upon receipt of information of an alleged act of sexual violence reported pursuant to subsection C, the review committee shall meet within 72 hours to review the information and shall meet again as necessary as new information becomes available.

F. If, based on consideration of all factors, the review committee, or if the committee cannot reach a consensus, the representative of law enforcement on the review committee, determines that the disclosure of the information, including personally identifiable information, is necessary to protect the health or safety of the student or other individuals as set forth in 34 C.F.R. § 99.36, the representative of law enforcement on the review committee shall immediately disclose such information to the law-enforcement agency that would be responsible for investigating the alleged act of sexual violence. Such disclosure shall be for the purposes of investigation and other actions by law enforcement. Upon such disclosure, the Title IX coordinator or his designee shall notify the victim that such disclosure is being made. The provisions of this subsection shall not apply if the law-enforcement agency responsible for investigating the alleged act of sexual violence is located outside the United States.

G. In cases in which the alleged act of sexual violence would constitute a felony violation of Article 7 (§ 18.2-61 et seq.) of Chapter 4 of Title 18.2, the representative of law enforcement on the review committee shall inform the other members of the review committee and shall within 24 hours consult with the attorney for the Commonwealth or other prosecutor responsible for prosecuting the alleged act of sexual violence and provide to him the information received by the review committee without disclosing personally identifiable information, unless such information was disclosed pursuant to subsection F. In addition, if such consultation does not occur and any other member of the review committee individually concludes that the alleged act of sexual violence would constitute a felony violation of Article 7 (§ 18.2-61 et seq.) of Chapter 4 of Title 18.2, that member shall within 24 hours consult with the attorney for the Commonwealth or other prosecutor responsible for prosecuting the alleged act of sexual violence and provide to him the information received by the review committee without disclosing personally identifiable information, unless such information was disclosed pursuant to subsection F.

H. At the conclusion of the review, the Title IX coordinator and the law-enforcement representative shall each retain (i) the authority to proceed with any further investigation or adjudication allowed under state or federal law and (ii) independent records of the review team's considerations, which shall be maintained under applicable state and federal law.

I. No responsible employee shall be required to make a report pursuant to subsection B if:

1. The responsible employee obtained the information through any communication considered privileged under state or federal law or the responsible employee obtained the information in the course of providing services as a licensed health care professional, an employee providing administrative support for such health care professionals, a professional counselor, an accredited rape crisis or domestic violence counselor, a campus victim support personnel, a member of clergy, or an attorney; or

2. The responsible employee has actual knowledge that the same matter has already been reported to the Title IX coordinator or to the attorney for the Commonwealth or the law-enforcement agency responsible for investigating the alleged act of sexual violence.

J. Any responsible employee who makes a report required by this section or testifies in a judicial or administrative proceeding as a result of such report is immune from any civil liability alleged to have resulted therefrom unless such person acted in bad faith or with malicious intent.

K. The provisions of this section shall not require a person who is the victim of an alleged act of sexual violence to report such violation.

Educational Institutions

L. The institution shall ensure that a victim of an alleged act of sexual violence is informed of (i) the available law-enforcement options for investigation and prosecution; (ii) the importance of collection and preservation of evidence; (iii) the available options for a protective order; (iv) the available campus options for investigation and adjudication under the institution's policies; (v) the victim's rights to participate or decline to participate in any investigation to the extent permitted under state or federal law; (vi) the applicable federal or state confidentiality provisions that govern information provided by a victim; (vii) the available on-campus resources and any unaffiliated community resources, including sexual assault crisis centers, domestic violence crisis centers, or other victim support services; and (viii) the importance of seeking appropriate medical attention.

History.

2015, cc. 737, 745, § 23-9.2:15; 2016, c. 588.

§ 23.1-807. (Effective October 1, 2016) Sexual assault; memoranda of understanding; policies.

A. Richard Bland College and each baccalaureate public institution of higher education and nonprofit private institution of higher education shall establish, and the State Board shall adopt a policy requiring each comprehensive community college to establish, a written memorandum of understanding with a sexual assault crisis center or other victim support service in order to provide sexual assault victims with immediate access to a confidential, independent advocate who can provide a trauma-informed response that includes an explanation of options for moving forward.

B. Each public institution of higher education and nonprofit private institution of higher education shall adopt policies to provide to sexual assault victims information on contacting such sexual assault crisis center or other victim support service.

C. Each public institution of higher education or nonprofit private institution of higher education may request the cooperation of the primary law-enforcement agency of the locality in which the institution is located to establish a written memorandum of understanding with such law-enforcement agency to address the prevention of and response to criminal sexual assault as set forth in Article 7 (§ 18.2-61 et seq.) of Chapter 4 of Title 18.2.

History.

2015, cc. 737, 745, § 23-9.2:16; 2016, cc. 481, 588.

§ 23.1-808. (Effective October 1, 2016) Sexual violence policy review.

By October 31 of each year, the System, Richard Bland College, each baccalaureate public institution of higher education, and each nonprofit private institution of higher education shall certify to the Council that it has reviewed its sexual violence policy and updated it as appropriate. The Council and the Department of Criminal Justice Services shall establish criteria for the certification process and may request information relating to the policies for the purposes of sharing best practices and improving campus safety. The Council and the Department of Criminal Justice Services shall report to the Secretary of Education on the certification status of each such institution by November 30 of each year.

History.
2015, cc. 737, 745, § 23-9.2:17; 2016, c. 588.

ARTICLE 3.

CAMPUS SAFETY; CAMPUS POLICE DEPARTMENTS.

§ 23.1-809. (Effective October 1, 2016) Public institutions of higher education; establishment of campus police departments authorized; employment of officers.

A. The governing board of each public institution of higher education may establish a campus police department and employ campus police officers and auxiliary police forces upon appointment as provided in §§ 23.1-811 and 23.1-812. Such employment is governed by the Virginia Personnel Act (§ 2.2-2900 et seq.), except that the governing board of a public institution of higher education may direct that the employment of the chief of the campus police department is not governed by the Virginia Personnel Act.

B. The Virginia Commonwealth University Health System Authority and Eastern Virginia Medical School may employ police officers and auxiliary police forces as provided in this article and, in the case of the Authority, in § 23.1-2406, except that the employment of such officers and forces is not governed by the Virginia Personnel Act (§ 2.2-2900 et seq.).

History.
1977, c. 79, § 23-232; 1991, c. 711; 1996, cc. 905, 1046; 2000, c. 720; 2009, c. 596; 2016, c. 588.

§ 23.1-810. (Effective October 1, 2016) Authorization for campus police departments in private institutions of higher education.

The governing board of each private institution of higher education may establish, in compliance with the provisions of this article, a campus police department and employ campus police officers upon appointment as provided in § 23.1-812. Except as such provisions apply exclusively to public institutions of higher education or employees, the provisions of this article shall apply to the appointment and employment of officers and the operation, powers, duties, and jurisdiction of campus police departments at private institutions of higher education, and such departments are subject to and shall enjoy the benefits of this article. However, to be qualified to use the word "police" to describe the department or its officers, any private institution of higher education that establishes a campus police department shall require each officer to comply with the training or other requirements for law-enforcement officers established by the Department of Criminal Justice Services pursuant to Chapter 1 (§ 9.1-100 et seq.) of Title 9.1.

History.
1992, c. 187, § 23-232.1; 2016, c. 588.

§ 23.1-811. (Effective October 1, 2016) Establishment of auxiliary police forces.

The governing board of each public institution of higher education and private institution of higher education, for the further preservation of public peace, safety, and good order of the campus community, may establish, equip, and maintain an auxiliary police force. When called into service pursuant to procedures established by the governing board, members of such auxiliary police forces have all the powers, authority, and immunities of campus police officers at public institutions of higher education.

History.
1991, c. 711, § 23-233.1; 2016, c. 588.

§ 23.1-812. (Effective October 1, 2016) Appointment of campus police officers and members of an auxiliary police force.

A. Prior to appointment as a campus police officer or member of an auxiliary police force, each individual shall be investigated by the campus police department of the institution applying for the order of appointment or, if none has been established, by the police department of the locality in which such institution is located. Such investigation shall determine whether the individual is responsible, honest, and in all ways capable of performing the duties of a campus police officer.

B. Upon application of the governing board of a public institution of higher education or private institution of higher education, the circuit court of the locality in which the institution is located may, by order, appoint the individuals named in the application to be campus police officers or members of an auxiliary police force at such institution.

C. Each campus police officer and member of an auxiliary police force appointed and employed pursuant to this article is a state employee of the institution named in the order of appointment. Insofar as it is not inconsistent with the Virginia Personnel Act (§ 2.2-2900 et seq.), the governing board of such institution shall provide for the conditions and terms of employment and compensation and a distinctive uniform and badge of office for such officers and members of an auxiliary police force.

History.
1977, c. 79, §§ 23-233, 23-236; 1991, c. 711; 2016, c. 588.

§ 23.1-813. (Effective October 1, 2016) Officers and members to comply with requirements of Department of Criminal Justice Services.

All individuals appointed and employed as campus police officers or members of an auxiliary police force pursuant to this article shall comply with the requirements for law-enforcement officers as established by the Department of Criminal Justice Services pursuant to Chapter 1 (§ 9.1-100 et seq.) of Title 9.1.

History.
1977, c. 79, § 23-235; 1984, c. 779; 1991, c. 711; 2016, c. 588.

§ 23.1-814. (Effective October 1, 2016) Termination of employment of campus police officers and members of auxiliary police forces.

An individual appointed as a campus police officer or a member of an auxiliary police force shall exercise his powers only as long as he remains employed or activated by the institution named in the order of the appointment. The appointment order entered by the circuit court shall automatically be revoked upon the termination of the employment of the officer or member at the institution and may be revoked by the court for malfeasance, misfeasance, or nonfeasance. The institution shall notify the court upon termination of the employment of the officer or member at the institution.

History.
1977, c. 79, § 23-237; 1991, c. 711; 2016, c. 588.

§ 23.1-815. (Effective October 1, 2016) Campus police forces and auxiliary police forces; powers and duties; jurisdiction.

A. As used in this section:

"Campus" means (i) any building or property owned or controlled by an institution of higher education located within the same reasonably contiguous geographic area of the institution and used by the institution in direct support of, or in a manner relating to, the institution's educational purposes, including residence halls, and (ii) any building or property that is within or reasonably contiguous to the area described in clause (i) that is owned by the institution but controlled by another person, is frequently used by students, and supports institutional purposes, such as a food or other retail vendor.

"Noncampus building or property" means (i) any building or property owned or controlled by a student organization that is officially recognized by an institution of higher education or (ii) any building or property owned or controlled by an institution of higher education that is used in direct support of, or in relation to, the institution's educational purposes, is frequently used by students, and is not within the same reasonably contiguous geographic area of the institution.

"Public property" means all public property, including thoroughfares, streets, sidewalks, and parking facilities, that is within the campus, or immediately adjacent to and accessible from the campus.

B. A campus police officer appointed as provided in § 23.1-812 or a member of an auxiliary police force appointed and activated pursuant to §§ 23.1-811 and 23.1-812 shall be deemed police officers of localities who may exercise the powers and duties conferred by law upon such police officers, including the provisions of Chapters 5 (§ 19.2-52 et seq.), 7 (§ 19.2-71 et seq.), and 23 (§ 19.2-387 et seq.) of Title 19.2, (i) upon any property owned or controlled by the public institution of higher education or private institution of higher education, or, upon request, any property owned or controlled by another public institution of higher education or private institution of higher education, and upon the streets, sidewalks, and highways immediately adjacent to any such property; (ii) pursuant to a mutual aid agreement (a) as provided for in § 15.2-1727 or (b) between the governing board of a public institution of higher education or private institution of higher education and another public institution of higher education or private institution of higher education in the Commonwealth or an adjacent political subdivision; (iii) in close pursuit of a person as provided in § 19.2-77; and (iv) upon approval by the appropriate circuit court of a petition by the local governing body for concurrent jurisdiction in designated areas with the police officers of the locality in which the institution, its satellite campuses, or other properties are located. The local governing body may only petition the circuit court for such concurrent jurisdiction pursuant to a request by the local law-enforcement agency.

C. Each public institution of higher education and private institution of higher education that establishes a campus police force pursuant to this article shall enter into and become a party to a mutual aid agreement with an adjacent local law-enforcement agency or the Department of State Police for the use of their regular and auxiliary joint forces, equipment, and materials when needed in the investigation of any felony criminal sexual assault or medically unattended death occurring on property owned or controlled by such institution or any death resulting from an incident occurring on such property. Such mutual aid agreements shall include provisions requiring either the campus police force or the agency with which it has established a mutual aid agreement pursuant to this subsection, in the event that such police force or agency conducts an investigation that involves a felony criminal sexual assault as set forth in Article 7 (§ 18.2-61 et seq.) of Chapter 4 of Title 18.2 occurring on campus, in or on a noncampus building or property, or on public property, to notify the local attorney for the Commonwealth of such investigation within 48 hours of beginning such investigation. No such notification provision shall require a campus police force or the agency with which it has established a mutual aid agreement to disclose identifying information about the victim. Nothing in this section prohibits a campus police force or auxiliary police force from requesting assistance from any appropriate law-enforcement agency of the Commonwealth with which the institution has not entered into a mutual aid agreement.

D. Each public institution of higher education and nonprofit private institution of higher education that (i) has not established a campus police force or auxiliary police force pursuant to this article and (ii) has a security department, relies on local or state police forces, or contracts for security services from private parties pursuant to § 23.1-818 shall enter into and become a party to a memorandum of understanding with an adjacent local law-enforcement agency or the Department of State Police (the Department) to require either such local law-enforcement agency or the Department, in the event that such agency or the Department conducts an investigation that involves a felony criminal sexual assault as set forth in Article 7 (§ 18.2-61 et seq.) of Chapter 4 of Title 18.2 occurring on campus, in or on a noncampus building or property, or on public property, to notify the local attorney for the Commonwealth of such investigation within 48 hours of beginning such investigation. No such notification provision shall require the law-enforcement agency or the Department to disclose identifying information about the victim.

E. All mutual aid agreements and memoranda of understanding entered into pursuant to this section shall specify the procedure for sharing information.

History.

1977, c. 79, § 23-234; 1985, c. 386; 1991, c. 711; 1992, c. 187; 2002, c. 97; 2012, cc. 282, 450; 2015, c. 707; 2016, cc. 513, 571, 588.

§ 23.1-816. (Effective October 1, 2016) Extending police power of public institutions of higher education beyond boundaries; jurisdiction of general district courts; duty of attorneys for the Commonwealth.

A. The governing board of any public institution of higher education that leases, rents, or owns satellite campuses, public buildings, and other property located beyond the limits of such institution has and may exercise full police power over such property and individuals using such property. The governing board may prescribe policies and regulations for the operation and use of such properties and the conduct of individuals using such property and may provide appropriate administrative penalties for the violation of such policies and regulations.

B. The general district court for the locality in which violations of law or policies or regulations established by the governing board of the institution pursuant to subsection A occurs has jurisdiction over all cases involving such violations.

C. It is the duty of each local attorney for the Commonwealth to prosecute all violators of the laws pertaining to the provisions enumerated in this article that occur in such locality.

History.

1991, c. 711, § 23-234.1; 2016, c. 588.

§ 23.1-817. (Effective October 1, 2016) Inspection of criminal incident information.

Criminal incident information of any campus police department established pursuant to § 23.1-810, including (i) the date, time, and general location of the alleged crime; (ii) a general description of injuries suffered or property damaged or stolen; and (iii) the name and address of any individual arrested as a result of felonies committed against persons or property or misdemeanors involving assault, battery, or moral turpitude reported to the campus police, shall be open to inspection and copying by any citizen of the Commonwealth, currently registered student of the institution, or parent of a registered student during the regular office hours of the custodian of such information unless such disclosure is prohibited by law. If the release of such information is likely to jeopardize an ongoing criminal investigation or the safety of an individual, cause a suspect to flee or evade detection, or result in the destruction of evidence, such information may be withheld until such damage is no longer likely to occur from the release of such information.

History.

1994, c. 457, § 23-232.2; 2016, c. 588.

§ 23.1-818. (Effective October 1, 2016) Security departments and other security services.

Nothing in this article shall abridge the authority of the governing board of a public institution of higher education or private institution of higher education to establish security departments, whose officers and employees shall not have the powers and duties set forth in § 23.1-815, in place of or in addition to campus police departments, rely upon local or state police forces, or contract for security services from private parties.

History.
1977, c. 79, § 23-238; 2016, c. 588.

SUBTITLE IV.
PUBLIC INSTITUTIONS OF HIGHER EDUCATION.

CHAPTER 24.
VIRGINIA COMMONWEALTH UNIVERSITY HEALTH SYSTEM AUTHORITY.

§ 23.1-2400. (Effective October 1, 2016) Definitions.

As used in this chapter, unless the context requires a different meaning:

"Authority" means the Virginia Commonwealth University Health System Authority.

"Board" means the board of directors of the Authority.

"Bonds" means bonds, notes, revenue certificates, lease participation certificates, or other evidences of indebtedness or deferred purchase financing arrangements.

"Chief executive officer" means the chief executive officer of the Virginia Commonwealth University Health System Authority.

"Costs" means (i) costs of (a) construction, reconstruction, renovation, site work, and acquisition of lands, structures, rights-of-way, franchises, easements, and other property rights and interests; (b) demolition, removal, or relocation of buildings or structures; (c) labor, materials, machinery, and all other kinds of equipment; (d) engineering and inspections; (e) financial, legal, and accounting services; (f) plans, specifications, studies, and surveys; (g) estimates of costs and of revenues; (h) feasibility studies; and (i) issuance of bonds, including printing, engraving, advertising, legal, and other similar expenses; (ii) financing charges; (iii) administrative expenses, including administrative expenses during the start-up of any project; (iv) credit enhancement and liquidity facility fees; (v) fees for interest rate caps, collars, swaps, or other financial derivative products; (vi) interest on bonds in connection with a project prior to and during construction or acquisition thereof and for a period not exceeding one year thereafter; (vii) provisions for working capital to be used in connection with any project; (viii) redemption premiums, obligations purchased to provide for the payment of bonds being refunded, and other costs necessary or incident to refunding of bonds; (ix) operating and maintenance reserve funds, debt reserve funds, and other reserves for the payment of principal and interest on bonds; (x) all other expenses necessary, desirable, or incidental to the operation of the Authority's facilities or the construction, reconstruction, renovation, acquisition, or financing of projects, other facilities, or equipment appropriate for carrying out the purposes of this chapter and the placing of the same in operation; or (xi) the refunding of bonds.

"Hospital facilities" means all property or rights in property, real and personal, tangible and intangible, including all facilities suitable for providing hospital and health care services and all structures, buildings, improvements, additions, extensions, replacements, appurtenances, lands, rights in land, furnishings, landscaping, approaches, roadways, and other related and supporting facilities owned, leased, operated, or used, in whole or in part, by Virginia Commonwealth University as part of, or in connection with, MCV Hospitals in the normal course of its operations as a teaching, research, and medical treatment facility.

"Hospital obligations" means all debts or other obligations, contingent or certain, owing to any person or other entity on the transfer date, arising out of the operation of MCV Hospitals as a medical treatment facility or the financing or refinancing of hospital facilities and including all bonds and other debts for the purchase of goods and services, whether or not delivered, and obligations for the delivery of services, whether or not performed.

"Project" means any health care, research, or educational facility or equipment necessary or convenient to or consistent with the purposes of the Authority, whether owned by the Authority, including hospitals; nursing homes; continuing care facilities; self-care facilities; wellness and health maintenance centers; medical office facilities; clinics; outpatient clinics; surgical centers; alcohol, substance abuse, and drug treatment centers; laboratories; sanitariums; hospices; facilities for the residence or care of the elderly, the handicapped, or the chronically ill; residential facilities for nurses, interns, and physicians; other kinds of facilities for the treatment of sick, disturbed, or infirm individuals, the prevention of disease, or maintenance of health; colleges, schools, or divisions offering undergraduate or graduate programs for the health professions and sciences and such other courses of study as may be appropriate, together with research, training, and teaching facilities; all necessary or desirable related and supporting facilities and equipment or equipment alone, including (i) parking, kitchen, laundry, laboratory, wellness, pharmaceutical, administrative, communications, computer, and recreational facilities; (ii) power plants and equipment; (iii) storage space; (iv) mobile medical facilities; (v) vehicles; (vi) air transport equipment; and (vii) other equipment necessary or desirable for the transportation of medical equipment, medical personnel, or

patients; and all lands, buildings, improvements, approaches, and appurtenances necessary or desirable in connection with or incidental to any project.

"Transfer date" means a date or dates agreed to by the board of visitors of Virginia Commonwealth University and the Authority for the transfer of employees to the Authority and for the transfer of hospital facilities, or any parts thereof, to and the assumption, directly or indirectly, of hospital obligations by the Authority, which dates for the various transfers and the various assumptions may be different, but in no event shall any date be later than June 30, 1997.

"University" means Virginia Commonwealth University.

History.
1996, cc. 905, 1046, § 23-50.16:4; 2000, c. 720; 2016, c. 588.

TITLE 27.
FIRE PROTECTION.

CHAPTER 2.
FIRE/EMS DEPARTMENTS AND FIRE/EMS COMPANIES.

Article 1.

Provisions Applicable to Counties, Cities and Towns.

ARTICLE 1.
PROVISIONS APPLICABLE TO COUNTIES, CITIES AND TOWNS.

§ 27-15.1:1. Penalty for refusing or neglecting to obey order of chief or other officer in command.

If any person at a fire refuses or neglects to obey any order duly given by the chief or other officer in command, he shall be fined a civil penalty not to exceed $100.

History.
2015, cc. 502, 503.

§ 27-17. Entry of buildings on fire and premises adjoining.

The chief of any fire department or fire company or other authorized officer in command at a fire or medical emergency, and his subordinates, upon his order or direction, shall have the right at any time of the day or night to enter any building or upon any premises where a fire is in progress, or any building or premises adjacent thereto for the purpose of extinguishing the fire.

History.
Code 1919, § 3130; 1970, c. 187; 2001, c. 142; 2015, cc. 502, 503.

§ 27-19: Repealed by Acts 2015, cc. 502 and 503, cl. 2.

CHAPTER 3.
LOCAL FIRE MARSHALS.

§ 27-30. Appointment of fire marshal.

An officer, who shall be called a "fire marshal," may be appointed for each county, city or town, by the governing body thereof, whenever, in the opinion of such body, the appointment shall be deemed expedient. The term "fire marshal" as used in this chapter may include the local fire official and local arson investigator when appointed pursuant to this section.

History.
Code 1919, § 3137; 1970, c. 187; 1977, c. 334; 1984, c. 644.

§ 27-31. Investigation of fires and explosions.

Such fire marshal shall make an investigation into the origin and cause of every fire and explosion occurring within the limits for which he was appointed, and for any such service he shall receive such compensation as the governing body may allow.

History.
Code 1919, § 3138; 1997, c. 436.

§ 27-32. Summoning witnesses and taking evidence.

In making investigations pursuant to § 27-31, the fire marshal may issue a summons directed to a sheriff or sergeant of any county, city or town commanding the officer to summon witnesses to attend before him at such time and place as he may direct. Any such officer to whom the summons is delivered, shall forthwith execute it, and make return thereof to the fire marshal at the time and place named therein.

Witnesses, on whom the summons before mentioned is served, may be compelled by the fire marshal to attend and give evidence, and shall be liable in like manner as if the summons had been issued by a magistrate in a criminal case. They shall be sworn by the fire marshal before giving evidence, and their evidence shall be reduced to writing by him, or under his direction, and subscribed by them respectively.

History.
Code 1919, §§ 3138, 4808, 4810; 1970, c. 187; 1997, c. 436; 2008, cc. 551, 691.

§ 27-32.1. Right of entry to investigate cause of fire or explosion.

If in making such an investigation, the fire marshal shall make complaint under oath that there is good cause of suspicion or belief that the burning of or explosion on any land, building or vessel or of any object was caused by any act constituting a crime as defined in Article 1 (§ 18.2-77 et seq.) of Chapter 5 of Title 18.2 and that he has been refused admittance to the land, building or vessel or to examine the object in or on which any fire or explosion occurred within fifteen days after the extinguishment of such, any magistrate serving the city or county where the land, building, vessel or object is located may issue a warrant to the sheriff of the county or the sergeant of the city requiring him to enter such land, building or vessel or the premises upon which the object is located in the company of the fire marshal for the purposes of conducting a search for evidence showing that such fire or explosion was caused by any act defined in Article 1 of Chapter 5, of Title 18.2.

History.
1970, c. 187; 2008, cc. 551, 691.

§ 27-32.2. Issuance of fire investigation warrant.

A. If, in undertaking such an investigation, the fire marshal or investigator appointed pursuant to § 27-56 makes an affidavit under oath that the origin or cause of any fire or explosion on any land, building, or vessel, or of any object is undetermined and that he has been refused admittance thereto, or is unable to gain permission to enter such land, building, or vessel, or to examine such object, within 15 days after the extinguishing of such, any magistrate serving the city or county where the land, building, vessel, or object is located may issue a fire investigation warrant to the fire marshal or investigator appointed pursuant to § 27-56 authorizing him to enter such land, building, vessel, or the premises upon which the object is located for the purpose of determining the origin and source of such fire or explosion. After issuing a warrant under this section, the magistrate shall file the affidavit in the manner prescribed by § 19.2-54. After executing the warrant, the fire marshal, or investigator appointed pursuant to § 27-56, shall return the warrant to the clerk of the circuit court of the city or county wherein the investigation was made.

B. If the fire marshal or investigator appointed pursuant to § 27-56, after gaining access to any land, building, vessel, or other premises pursuant to such a fire investigation warrant, has probable cause to believe that the burning or explosion was caused by any act constituting a criminal offense, he shall discontinue the investigation until a search warrant has been obtained pursuant to § 27-32.1, or consent to conduct the search has otherwise been given.

History.
1987, c. 701; 2008, cc. 551, 691; 2012, cc. 279, 330; 2014, c. 354.

§ 27-33. Report of investigation.

The fire marshal shall make report to the governing body by whom he was appointed of any investigation made by him as soon thereafter as practicable, returning therewith the evidence taken by him and submitting such recommendations therein as he may think the public interest demands.

History.
Code 1919, § 3138.

§ 27-34. Duties and powers at fires.

Whenever any fire occurs, it shall be the duty of such fire marshal or his designated representative to be present at the same and advise and act in concert with such officers of police as may be present; and, for preserving order at and during the existence of such fire, and for the protection of property, he shall have concurrent powers with the officers of police, and the chief, director, or other officer in charge, but shall not exercise any authority which will conflict with the powers of any chief, director, or other officer in command of any fire department in the discharge of his special duties as such.

History.
Code 1919, § 3139; 1970, c. 187; 2008, c. 410.

§ 27-34.1. Power of fire marshal or fire chief to take property found at scene of fire or explosion; restitution of such property.

The fire chief, fire marshal or his designated representative is authorized to take and preserve any property found at the scene of a fire or explosion during his presence there while in the act of extinguishing such or found later with the consent of the owner or pursuant to § 27-32.1, which property indicates the fire or explosion was intentionally caused. Any person whose property is so taken and held may petition the circuit court of the county or city in which the property was taken or judge in vacation, for return of the property, and the court may order restitution upon such conditions as are appropriate for preservation of evidence, including the posting of bond.

History.
1970, c. 187; 1979, c. 189.

§ 27-34.2. Power to arrest, to procure and serve warrants and to issue summons; limitation on authority.

In addition to such other duties as may be prescribed by law, the local fire marshal and his assistants appointed pursuant to § 27-36 shall, if authorized by the governing body of the county, city or town appointing the local fire marshal, have the authority to arrest, to procure and serve warrants of arrest and to issue summons in the manner authorized by general law for violation of fire prevention and fire safety laws and related ordinances. The authority granted in this section shall not be exercised by any local fire marshal or assistant until such person has satisfactorily completed a training course designed specifically for local fire marshals and their assistants, which course shall be approved by the Virginia Fire Services Board.

The Department of Fire Programs in cooperation with the Department of Criminal Justice Services shall have the authority to design, establish and maintain the required courses of instruction through such agencies and institutions as the Departments jointly may deem appropriate and to approve such other courses as such Departments determine appropriate.

The authority granted in this section shall not be construed to authorize a fire marshal or his assistants to wear or carry firearms.

History.
1974, c. 334; 1975, c. 173; 1979, c. 402; 1984, c. 779; 1986, c. 60; 1988, c. 65; 1997, c. 436.

§ 27-34.2:1. Police powers of fire marshals.

In addition to such other duties as may be prescribed by law, the local fire marshal and those assistants appointed pursuant to § 27-36 designated by the fire marshal shall, if authorized by the governing body of the county, city or town appointing the local fire marshal, have the same police powers as a sheriff, police officer or law-enforcement officer. The investigation and prosecution of all offenses involving hazardous materials, fires, fire bombings, bombings, attempts or threats to commit such offenses, false alarms relating to such offenses, possession and manufacture of explosive devices, substances and fire bombs shall be the responsibility of the fire marshal or his designee, if authorized by the governing body of the county, city or town appointing the local fire marshal. The police powers granted in this section shall not be exercised by any local fire marshal or assistant until such person has satisfactorily completed a course for fire marshals with police powers, designed by the Department of Fire Programs in cooperation with the Department of Criminal Justice Services, which course shall be approved by the Virginia Fire Services Board.

In addition, fire marshals with police powers shall continue to exercise those powers only upon satisfactory participation in in-service and advanced courses and programs designed by the Department of Fire Programs in cooperation with the Department of Criminal Justice Services, which courses shall be approved by the Virginia Fire Services Board.

History.
1977, c. 209; 1979, c. 446; 1984, c. 779; 1986, c. 60; 1988, c. 65; 2000, cc. 39, 390.

§ 27-34.3. Power to order immediate compliance with law, etc., or prohibit use of building or equipment.

The local fire marshal shall, if authorized by the governing body of the county, city or town appointing him, have the authority to exercise the powers authorized by the Fire Prevention Code. However, an order prohibiting the use of a building or equipment issued pursuant to this section shall not be effective beyond the date of a determination made by the authorities identified in and pursuant to § 27-97, regardless of whether or not said determination overrules, modifies or affirms the order of the local fire marshal. If an order of the local fire marshal issued pursuant to this section conflicts to any degree with an order previously issued by an authority identified in and pursuant to § 27-97, the latter order shall prevail. The local fire marshal shall immediately report to the authorities identified in § 27-97 on the issuance and content of any order issued pursuant to this section.

History.
1975, c. 216; 1988, c. 199.

§ 27-34.4. Inspection and review of plans of buildings under construction.

Inspection of buildings other than state-owned buildings under construction and the review and approval of building plans for these structures for enforcement of the Uniform Statewide Building Code shall be the sole responsibility of the appropriate local building inspectors. Upon completion of such structures, responsibility for fire safety protection shall pass to the local fire marshal or official designated by the locality to enforce the Statewide Fire Prevention Code (§ 27-94 et seq.) in those localities which enforce the Statewide Fire Prevention Code.

History.
1980, c. 498; 1989, c. 258.

§ 27-35. Penalty for failure to discharge duty.

For his failure to discharge any duty required of him by law the fire marshal shall be liable for each offense to a fine not exceeding $100, to be imposed by the governing body and to be collected as other fines are collected.

History.
Code 1919, § 3138.

§ 27-36. Appointment, powers and duties of assistant fire marshals.

The governing body of any county, city or town, or its designee may appoint one or more assistants, who, in the absence of the fire marshal, shall have the powers and perform the duties of the fire marshal.

History.
Code 1919, § 3140; 1970, c. 187; 1984, c. 644; 1998, c. 236.

§ 27-37. Oath of fire marshal and assistants.

The fire marshal and his assistants, before entering upon their duties, shall respectively take an oath, before any officer authorized to administer oaths, faithfully to discharge the duties of such office; the certificate of the oath shall be returned to and preserved by such governing body.

History.
Code 1919, § 3140.

§ 27-37.1. Right of entry to investigate releases of hazardous material, hazardous waste, or regulated substances.

A. The fire marshal shall have the right, if authorized by the governing body of the county, city, or town appointing the fire marshal, to enter upon any property from which a release of any hazardous material, hazardous waste, or regulated substance, as defined in § 10.1-1400 or 62.1-44.34:8, has occurred or is reasonably suspected to have occurred and which has entered into the ground water, surface water or soils of the county, city or town in order to investigate the extent and cause of any such release.

B. If, in undertaking such an investigation, the fire marshal makes an affidavit under oath that the origin or cause of any such release is undetermined and that he has been refused admittance to the property, or is unable to gain permission to enter the property, any magistrate serving the city or county where the property is located may issue an investigation warrant to the fire marshal authorizing him to enter such property for the purpose of determining the origin and source of the release. After issuing a warrant under this section, the magistrate shall file the affidavit in the manner prescribed by § 19.2-54. After executing the warrant, the fire marshal shall return the warrant to the clerk of the circuit court of the city or county wherein the investigation was made.

C. If the fire marshal, after gaining access to any property pursuant to such investigation warrant, has probable cause to believe that the release was caused by any act constituting a criminal offense, he shall discontinue the investigation until a search warrant has been obtained or consent to conduct the search has otherwise been given.

History.
1992, c. 712; 2008, cc. 551, 691; 2014, c. 354.

CHAPTER 5.
SAFETY PROVISIONS GENERALLY.

Article 1.

Generally.

Section

ARTICLE 1.
GENERALLY.

§ 27-51. Exits from public halls, theaters and opera houses.

All owners or lessees of public halls, theaters or opera houses situated in any city or town, or in any county which has elected to come under the provisions of Article 1 (§ 27-6.1 et seq.) of Chapter 2 of this title, shall provide suitable and sufficient exits from such buildings. The doors to the exits shall remain unlocked during all performances or public gatherings in the buildings, and shall in all cases open outwardly, and not inwardly.

History.
Code 1919, § 3142; R. P. 1948, § 27-36.

§ 27-52. Inspection of buildings designated in preceding section.

In cities and towns having police and fire departments or having a fire inspector employed by such city or town, the respective heads of such departments and the mayor of such city or town shall, as a committee of three, or the fire inspector of such city or town, inspect at least semiannually, all buildings mentioned in § 27-51 which are located in their city or town, and see that the provisions thereof are complied with.

In cities and towns which do not possess police and fire departments or a fire inspector, the mayor and two members of the council to be selected by the mayor shall, as a committee of three, inspect all such buildings located in their city or town semiannually, and see that the provisions of § 27-51 are complied with. Any such building as to which such provisions have not been complied with, may be closed by order of the mayor of the city or town until the provisions are complied with.

History.
Code 1919, § 3143; R. P. 1948, § 27-37; 1974, c. 41.

§ 27-53. Penalty for violating § 27-51; separate offenses.

Any owner or lessee of any such building, who shall violate any of the provisions of § 27-51, shall be punishable by a fine of not less than $100 nor more than $500, or by confinement in jail not less than 6 nor more than 12 months, or by both. The continuation of any failure to comply with the provisions of such section for each week after notice has been given the owner or lessee of the buildings that the exits are unsafe or insufficient shall be deemed a separate offense.

History.
Code 1919, § 3144; R. P. 1948, § 27-38.

§ 27-54. Governing body to make additional safety provisions.

The governing body of any city or town, or of any such county, shall make such further provisions insuring the safety of the public using such buildings as is mentioned in § 27-51 as such governing body may see proper to make, not in conflict with such section.

History.
Code 1919, § 3145; R. P. 1948, § 27-39.

CHAPTER 6.

DEPARTMENT OF STATE POLICE; PUBLIC BUILDING SAFETY LAW; ARSON REPORTING IMMUNITY ACT.

Article 1.

General Provisions.

Section

Article 3.

Arson Reporting Immunity Act.

ARTICLE 1.

GENERAL PROVISIONS.

§ 27-55. Department of State Police or successor agency to keep record of fires and explosions; when open to public inspection.

The Department of State Police or its successor agency shall keep in its office a record of all fires occurring in the Commonwealth, investigation of which is provided for in this article, together with all facts, statistics and circumstances concerning the same, including the origin of the fires. Such records shall not be open to public inspection, except insofar as the Department shall permit otherwise. Whenever the word "Department" appears in this article it shall be deemed to mean the Department of State Police or its successor agency in the Office of Public Safety.

History.
Code 1919, § 4148; 1918, p. 123; 1936, p. 259; 1948, p. 487; 1977, c. 613.

Fire Protection

§ 27-56. Department to examine into origin of fires; appointment of arson investigators.

The Department shall examine, or cause examination to be made, into the origin and circumstances of all fires occurring in this Commonwealth, which may be brought to its attention by official report, or otherwise, and for that purpose shall have authority to call for and demand of the chief or other head officer of the fire department, and the chief or other head officer of the police department, of any city or town, and the sheriff of any county, for any information or assistance it may require in making or furthering such examination.

The Department shall appoint a chief arson investigator and assistant arson investigators, who shall have the same police powers as a sheriff in the investigation and prosecution of all offenses involving fires, fire bombings, bombings, attempts, threats to commit such offense, false alarms relating to any such offense, possession and manufacture of explosive devices, substances and firebombs.

History.
Code 1919, § 4186; 1977, c. 613.

§ 27-57. When insurance company to pay expenses of examination.

When such examination is made on the application of any fire insurance company, the necessary expenses attending the same shall be paid by such company.

History.
Code 1919, § 4186.

§ 27-58. Right to examine buildings or premises.

The Department, and such person or persons as it may appoint, shall have authority at all times of the day, in the performance of the duties imposed by the provisions of § 27-56, to enter upon and examine any building or premises where any fire has occurred, and any other buildings or premises immediately adjoining the same; provided, that such adjoining building is not at the time occupied and used as a dwelling house.

History.
Code 1919, § 4187; 1977, c. 613.

§ 27-59. Criminal prosecutions.

If the Department shall be of opinion, after investigation as to the cause or origin of any fire, that there is sufficient evidence to charge any person with the crime of arson, or with incendiary burning of property, it shall furnish to the attorney for the Commonwealth of the city or county all such evidence, together with the names of witnesses, and all information obtained by it, including a copy of all pertinent and material testimony taken by it touching such offense.

History.
Code 1919, § 4188; 1918, p. 123; 1977, c. 613.

§ 27-60. Department to conduct investigations in certain cases; investigations may be private.

The Department may petition an appropriate judicial officer to summons and compel the attendance of witnesses to testify in relation to any matter which is, by the provisions of this chapter, a subject of inquiry and investigation. It may also administer oaths and affirmations to such witnesses, and false swearing in any such matter shall be deemed perjury, and shall be punished as such. It may in its discretion take or cause to be taken the testimony on oath of all persons supposed to be cognizant of any facts or to have means of knowledge in relation to the matters as to which any examination is, in this chapter, required to be made, and shall cause the same to be reduced to writing. Investigations in relation to such matters may, in the discretion of the Department, be private, and persons other than those required to be present by the provisions of this chapter may be excluded from that place where such examination is held, and witnesses may be kept separate and apart from each other, and not allowed to communicate with each other until they have been examined.

History.
Code 1919, § 4189; 1977, c. 613.

§ 27-61. When Department or fire chief may remedy inflammable or unsafe conditions.

The Department of Fire Programs, by its representative, or the chief or other head of the fire department of any county, city or town or district thereof, shall have the right, at all reasonable hours, for the purpose of examination, to enter into and upon any public school building or any other building or premises not at the time occupied and used as a dwelling house, within their respective jurisdictions, for examination as to combustible materials or inflammable or unsafe conditions in any such building or upon any such premises. Upon complaint of any person having an interest in any building or premises or property adjacent thereto, in his jurisdiction, an officer shall make an immediate investigation as to the presence of any combustible materials or the existence of inflammable or unsafe conditions in such buildings or upon such premises. Whenever any officer finds in any building or upon any premises combustible, inflammable or unsafe conditions, dangerous to the safety of the building or premises, or other property, he shall order the same

Fire Protection

to be removed or remedied, and the order shall, within a reasonable time to be fixed in the order, be complied with by the owner or occupant of the building or premises.

Any owner or occupant aggrieved by such order may within five days after notice of such order, appeal to the Department of Fire Programs, and the cause of his complaint shall be at once investigated by the Executive Director of the Department of Fire Programs, and unless by its authority such order is revoked, the order shall remain in force and the owner or occupant shall comply with the order.

Any owner or occupant of any building or premises failing to comply with any final order made or given under the authority of this section, shall be deemed guilty of a misdemeanor, and punished by a fine of not less than $5 nor more than $100 for each offense.

History.
Code 1919, § 4190; 1936, p. 776; 1977, c. 613; 1988, c. 199; 2007, cc. 647, 741.

§ 27-62. Penalty on local officers for violating law.

Any city, town or county officer referred to in this article who willfully neglects or refuses to comply with any of the requirements of this article shall be deemed guilty of a misdemeanor, and upon conviction thereof, be punished by a fine of not less than $5, nor more than $100.

History.
Code 1919, § 4192.

ARTICLE 3.
ARSON REPORTING IMMUNITY ACT.

§ 27-85.3. Short title.

This article shall be known as the Arson Reporting Immunity Act.

History.
1979, c. 279.

§ 27-85.4. Definitions.

For the purposes of this article:

"Action" includes nonaction or the failure to take action.

"Authorized agencies" means:

i. The chief or director of any municipal or county fire or police department or the sheriff of any county;

ii. The arson investigator of the State Police Department; the Alcohol, Tobacco and Firearms Division of the United States Department of the Treasury; or

iii. The attorney for the Commonwealth or other person responsible for prosecutions in the jurisdiction where the fire occurred.

"Insurance company" includes the Virginia Property Insurance Association.

History.
1979, c. 279; 1985, c. 58; 2008, c. 410.

§ 27-85.5. Disclosure of information.

A. Any authorized agency may, in writing, require an insurance company to release to the requesting agency any or all relevant information or evidence deemed material by the requesting agency in the insurance company's possession relating to the fire loss in question. Relevant information may include, but shall not be limited to:

1. Pertinent insurance policy information relevant to a fire loss under investigation and any application for such a policy;

2. Policy premium payment records;

3. History of previous claims made by the insured;

4. Material relating to the investigation of the loss, including statements of any person, proof of loss, and any other evidence relevant to the investigation.

B. 1. When an insurance company has reason to believe that a fire loss in which it has an interest may be of other than accidental cause, then, for the purpose of notification and for having such fire loss investigated, the company shall, in writing, notify an authorized agency and provide it with any or all material developed from the company's inquiry into the fire loss.

2. When an insurance company provides any one of the authorized agencies with notice of a fire loss, it shall be sufficient notice for the purpose of this article.

C. The authorized agency provided with information pursuant to subsections A or B of this section and in furtherance of its own purposes, may release or provide such information to any of the other authorized agencies.

D. Any insurance company providing information to an authorized agency or agencies pursuant to subsections A or B of this section shall have the right to request relevant information and receive, within a reasonable time, not to exceed thirty days, the information requested.

E. Any insurance company, or person acting in its behalf or authorized agency who releases information, whether oral or written, pursuant to subsections A or B of this section shall be immune from any liability arising out of a civil action, or penalty resulting from a criminal prosecution unless actual malice on the part of the insurance company or authorized agency is present.

History.
1979, c. 279.

§ 27-85.6. Evidence.

Any authorized agency and insurance company described in § 27-85.4 or § 27-85.5 who receives any information furnished pursuant to this article, shall hold the information in confidence until such time as its release is required pursuant to a criminal or civil proceeding, except release in accordance with subsection C of § 27-85.5.

History.
1979, c. 279.

CHAPTER 9.
STATEWIDE FIRE PREVENTION CODE ACT.

§ 27-96. Statewide standards.

The purposes of this chapter are to provide for statewide standards for optional local enforcement to safeguard life and property from the hazards of fire or explosion arising from the improper maintenance of life safety and fire prevention and protection materials, devices, systems and structures, and the unsafe storage, handling, and use of substances, materials and devices, including fireworks, explosives and blasting agents, wherever located.

History.
1986, c. 429; 1988, c. 340; 2002, c. 856.

§ 27-96.1. Chapter inapplicable to certain uses of fireworks.

Unless prohibited by a local ordinance, the provisions of this chapter pertaining to fireworks shall not apply to the sale of or to any person using, igniting or exploding permissible fireworks on private property with the consent of the owner of such property.

History.
2002, c. 856.

§ 27-96.2. Exemptions generally.

The provisions of this chapter concerning fireworks shall have no application to any officer or member of the armed forces of this Commonwealth, or of the United States, while acting within the scope of his authority and duties as such, nor to any offer of sale or sale of fireworks to any authorized agent of such armed forces; nor shall it be applicable to the sale or use of materials or equipment, otherwise prohibited by this chapter, when such materials or equipment is used or to be used by any person for signaling or other emergency use in the operation of any boat, railroad train or other vehicle for the transportation of persons or property.

History.
2002, c. 856.

§ 27-98.2. Issuance of warrant.

Search warrants for inspections or reinspection of buildings, structures, property, or premises subject to inspections pursuant to the Code, to determine compliance with regulations or standards set forth in the Code, shall be based upon a demonstration of probable cause and supported by affidavit. Such inspection warrants may be issued by any judge or magistrate having authority to issue criminal warrants whose territorial jurisdiction encompasses the building, structure, property or premises to be inspected or entered, if he is satisfied from the affidavit that there is probable cause for the issuance of an inspection warrant. No inspection warrant shall be issued pursuant to this chapter except upon probable cause, supported by affidavit, particularly describing the place, thing or property to be inspected, examined or tested and the purpose for which the inspection, examination, testing or collection of samples for testing is to be made. Probable cause shall be deemed to exist if such inspection, examination, testing or collection of samples for testing are necessary to ensure compliance with the Fire Prevention Code for the protection of life and property from the hazards of fire or explosion. The supporting affidavit shall contain either a statement that consent to inspect, examine, test or collect samples for testing has been sought and refused or facts or circumstances reasonably justifying the failure to seek such consent in order to enforce effectively the fire safety laws, regulations or standards of the Commonwealth which authorize such inspection, examination, testing or collection of samples for testing. In the case of an inspection warrant based upon legislative or administrative standards for selecting buildings, structures, property or premises for inspections, the affidavit shall contain factual allegations sufficient to justify an independent determination by the judge or magistrate that the inspection program is based on reasonable standards and that the standards are being applied to a particular place in a neutral and fair manner. The issuing judge or magistrate may examine the affiant under oath or affirmation to verify the accuracy of any matter in the affidavit. After issuing the warrant, the judge or magistrate shall file the affidavit in the manner prescribed by § 19.2-54.

History.
1988, c. 549; 2014, c. 354.

§ 27-98.3. Duration of warrant.

An inspection warrant shall be effective for the time specified therein, for a period of not more than seven days, unless extended or renewed by the judicial officer who signed and issued the original warrant. The judicial officer may extend or renew the inspection warrant upon application for extension or renewal setting forth the results which have been obtained or a reasonable explanation of the failure to obtain such results. The extension or renewal period of the warrant shall not exceed seven days. The warrant shall be executed and returned to the clerk of the circuit court of the city or county wherein the inspection was made. The return shall list any samples taken pursuant to the warrant. After the expiration of such time, the warrant, unless executed, shall be void.

History.
1988, c. 549; 2014, c. 354.

§ 27-100. Violation a misdemeanor.

It shall be unlawful for any owner or any other person, firm, or corporation, on or after the effective date of any Code provisions, to violate any provisions of the Fire Prevention Code. Any such violation shall be deemed a Class 1 misdemeanor, and any owner, or any other person, firm, or corporation convicted of such violation shall be punished in accordance with the provisions of § 18.2-11.

History.
1986, c. 429.

§ 27-100.1. Seizure and destruction of certain fireworks.

Any law-enforcement officer arresting any person for a violation of this chapter related to fireworks shall seize any article of fireworks in the possession or under the control of the person so arrested and shall hold the same until final disposition of any criminal proceedings against such person. If a judgment of conviction be entered against such person, the court shall order destruction of such articles upon expiration of the time allowed for appeal of such judgment of conviction.

History.
2002, c. 856.

TITLE 28.2.

FISHERIES AND HABITAT OF THE TIDAL WATERS.

SUBTITLE I.

GENERAL PROVISIONS RELATING TO MARINE RESOURCES COMMISSION.

CHAPTER 1.

ADMINISTRATION.

Article 1.

Commission; Commissioner.

Article 2.

Support Activities.

ARTICLE 1.

COMMISSION; COMMISSIONER.

§ 28.2-100. Definitions.

As used in this title, unless the context requires a different meaning:

"Commission" means the Marine Resources Commission.

"Commissioner" means the Commissioner of Marine Resources.

"Fish" or *"marine fish"* means those finfish species which spend a major portion of their lives in marine or estuarine waters. Sunfish, crappies, and carp are not considered to be marine fish.

"Fishing", "fisheries" or *"to fish"* means all operations involved in (i) taking or catching, (ii) using, setting or operating apparatus employed in killing, taking or catching, or (iii) transporting or preparing for market marine fish, shellfish, and marine organisms.

"Habitat" means those state-owned bottomlands, tidal wetlands and coastal primary sand dunes which are subject to regulation under Subtitle III of this title.

"Marine organisms" means those species other than marine finfish or marine shellfish which inhabit marine or estuarine waters. Terrapin and marine mammals are considered to be marine organisms.

"Marine shellfish" or *"shellfish"* means such species of mollusca as oysters and clams, and such species of crustacea as crabs.

"Officer" means a member of the Virginia Marine Police.

"Territorial sea" means the waters within the belt, three nautical miles wide, that is adjacent to Virginia's coast and seaward of the mean low-water mark.

"Tidewater Virginia" means the following counties: Accomack, Arlington, Caroline, Charles City, Chesterfield, Essex, Fairfax, Gloucester, Hanover, Henrico, Isle of Wight, James City, King and Queen, King George, King William, Lancaster, Mathews, Middlesex, New Kent, Northampton, Northumberland, Prince George, Prince William, Richmond, Spotsylvania, Stafford, Surry, Westmoreland, and York; and the Cities of Alexandria, Chesapeake, Colonial Heights, Fairfax, Falls Church, Fredericksburg, Hampton, Hopewell, Newport News, Norfolk, Petersburg, Poquoson, Portsmouth, Richmond, Suffolk, Virginia Beach, and Williamsburg.

History.

Code 1950, § 28-1; 1962, c. 406, § 28.1-1; 1968, c. 746; 1972, c. 472; 1992, c. 836; 2002, c. 789.

Tidal Waters

ARTICLE 2.
SUPPORT ACTIVITIES.

§ 28.2-106. Virginia Marine Police; law-enforcement responsibilities; qualifications; oath.

A. The law-enforcement division of the Commission shall be designated as the Virginia Marine Police. It shall exercise such powers and duties as the General Assembly may confer upon it by law and as provided in regulations adopted pursuant to law, including but not limited to:

1. Patrolling the tidal waters and shoreline of the Chesapeake Bay, its tidal tributaries, and territorial sea;
2. Enforcing marine fishery and habitat conservation laws and regulations;
3. Enforcing health laws pertaining to the harvesting of seafood from condemned areas;
4. Enforcing or assisting other agencies in enforcing laws pertaining to the removal of obstructions and abandoned vessels from the water, to boating operation and navigation, and to larceny on the water;
5. Providing for water-borne safety;
6. Conducting search and rescue activities; and
7. Protecting from terrorist attack federal and state water-related installations and other water-related locations within the tidal waters of the Commonwealth as may be designated by federal or state officials as important to national security.

B. Officers of the Virginia Marine Police shall have the same powers as (i) sheriffs and other law-enforcement officers to enforce all of the criminal laws of the Commonwealth, and (ii) regular conservation police officers appointed pursuant to Chapter 2 (§ 29.1-200 et seq.) of Title 29.1.

C. A person shall be (i) at least twenty-one years old and (ii) a high school graduate or equivalent to qualify for appointment as an officer.

D. Each officer shall qualify before the clerk of the circuit court of the county or city in which he resides, or in which his district may be, by taking the oaths prescribed by law.

History.

Code 1950, § 28-36; 1962, c. 406, §§ 28.1-41, 28.1-42; 1964, c. 115; 1972, c. 824; 1973, c. 19; 1990, c. 521, § 28.1-45.1; 1991, c. 338, § 28.1-45.2; 1992, c. 836; 2001, c. 232; 2002, c. 789.

§ 28.2-106.2. Establishment, patrol, and enforcement of state water safety zones and restricted areas; penalty.

A. The Commission is authorized, following consultation with the U.S. Coast Guard and the U.S. Army Corps of Engineers, to establish, by regulation, state water safety zones and restricted areas within the tidal waters of the Commonwealth wherein public access shall be restricted or prohibited in the interest of public safety. Such zones or areas shall be consistent with federal law and made effective immediately upon establishment by the Commission. When, in the judgment of the Commissioner, time is of the essence and circumstances require action before a meeting of the Commission may be convened, the Commissioner is authorized, following consultation with the U.S. Coast Guard and the U.S. Army Corps of Engineers, to establish state water safety zones or restricted areas, subject to ratification by the Commission at its next regularly scheduled meeting. The provisions of the Administrative Process Act (§ 2.2-4000 et seq.) and §§ 28.2-209 through 28.2-215 shall not apply to regulations promulgated under this section. The Commission shall publicize the establishment and location of state water safety zones and restricted areas.

B. The Virginia Marine Police shall patrol and enforce all state water safety zones and restricted areas.

C. In times of officially declared national or state emergency, the Governor may adjust the boundaries of state water safety zones or restricted areas by executive order. Upon termination of emergency status, the boundaries shall return to those set forth in regulations.

D. A violation of any regulation promulgated under this section is a Class 1 misdemeanor.

History.
2003, c. 389.

SUBTITLE II.
TIDAL FISHERIES.

CHAPTER 2.
GENERAL PROVISIONS.

ARTICLE 1.
POWERS AND DUTIES.

§ 28.2-200. Definitions.

As used in this subtitle, unless the context requires a different meaning:

"Cultured hard-shell clams" means hard-shell clams (Mercenaria mercenaria) that have been spawned in a hatchery or controlled setting for the purpose of producing seed clams (juveniles), and planted on leased grounds, floating structures, or other privately controlled growing areas, and covered with netting or otherwise protected from predators until harvested.

"Haul seine" means a net made of mesh webbing which may include a pocket and a wing net, set vertically in water and pulled by hand or power to capture and confine fish by encirclement.

"James River seed area" means that area in the James River and its tributaries above a line drawn from Cooper's Creek in Isle of Wight County on the south side of the James River to a line in a northeasterly direction across the James River to the Newport News municipal water tank located on Warwick Boulevard between 59th Street and 60th Street in the City of Newport News.

"Mouth of the Rappahannock River" means the area beginning at Stingray Point, Middlesex County, at the United States Army Corps of Engineers survey station "Bird," an aluminum disk set in the top of a concrete monument, being located at coordinates 453,785.17 North, 2,638,116.66 East, 1927 North American Datum — Virginia South Zone; thence 12 degrees 52' 35" (grid azimuth) 20,846.73 feet to a point on the Eastern side of Windmill Point, Lancaster County, designated as Virginia Marine Resources Commission survey station "Windmill," a one and one-half inch iron pipe driven flush with the ground, being located at coordinates 474,107.68 North, 2,642,762.29 East, 1927 North American Datum — Virginia South Zone.

"Pound net" means any net having a funnel mouth, round mouth or square mouth with the head exposed above the water.

"Resident" means any person who maintains his principal place of abode in Virginia with the intent to make Virginia his domicile.

"Shoals" means subaqueous elevations covered by water less than four feet deep at mean low water.

History.
Code 1950, §§ 28-1, 28-46, 28-93, 28-93.1, 28-93.2, 28-112, 28-201.4; 1954, c. 38; 1958, cc. 182, 476; 1960, c. 517; 1962, c. 406, §§ 28.1-1, 28.1-51, 28.1-98, 28.1-148; 1966, c. 684; 1968, cc. 746, 747; 1972, c. 472; 1978, c. 208; 1980, c. 325; 1981, c. 52; 1986, c. 254; 1992, c. 836; 1994, c. 124; 2003, c. 604.

Tidal Waters

§ 28.2-201. Authority of Commission to make regulations, establish licenses, and prepare fishery management plans; accept federal grants; enforcement; penalty for violation of regulation.

The Commission may:

1. Promulgate regulations, including those for taking seafood, necessary to promote the general welfare of the seafood industry and to conserve and promote the seafood and marine resources of the Commonwealth. The Commission may also promulgate regulations necessary for the conservation and reasonable use of surf clams.

2. Establish new licenses and fees commensurate with other licenses in an amount not to exceed $100 for any device used for taking or catching seafood in the tidal waters of the Commonwealth when the device (i) is not otherwise licensed in this title and (ii) is used for commercial purposes. The Commission may specify, when issuing such licenses, any restrictions or control over the devices or the persons operating the device.

3. Establish fees for permits required for delayed or limited entry fisheries, shellfish relaying, scientific collections, and for the administrative transfer of these permits among fisherman, where applicable.

4. Beginning July 1, 2004, and not more frequently than every three years thereafter, increase fees for tidal fisheries licenses and permits that are authorized under this title or by regulation promulgated pursuant to Article 2 (§ 28.2-209 et seq.) of this chapter. Any fee increase for such licenses and permits shall be capped at $5 or a percentage equal to the increase in the Consumer Price Index calculated from the time the fee was last set or adjusted, whichever is greater. Beginning July 1, 2004, any amounts generated from the increases in commercial fishing licenses and permits shall be paid into the Marine Fishing Improvement Fund for the purposes authorized by § 28.2-208, and any amounts generated from the increases in recreational fishing licenses shall be paid into the Virginia Saltwater Recreational Fishing Development Fund for the purposes authorized by § 28.2-302.3. The Commission may charge nonresidents a higher fee than residents for purchase of any of the fishing licenses issued pursuant to §§ 28.2-302.2, 28.2-302.2:1, 28.2-302.6, 28.2-302.7, 28.2-302.8, 28.2-302.10, and 28.2-302.10:1. The fee charged to a nonresident shall be no greater than twice the Virginia resident fee. The Commission may prohibit the sale of the private boat license established by § 28.2-302.7 to a nonresident whose boat is not registered in Virginia.

5. The Commission shall ensure that increases in licenses and fees are equitably distributed among resource user groups.

6. Prepare fishery management plans containing evaluations of regulatory management options, based upon scientific, economic, biological, and sociological information, and use them in the development of regulations. The Commissioner may appoint a fisheries advisory committee and its chairman, consisting of representatives of the various fishery user groups, to assist in the preparation and implementation of the fishery management plans. The Commission may expend funds to compensate the members of the committee pursuant to § 2.2-2825.

7. Provide for enforcement of any regulation governing surf clams by any law-enforcement officer of any agency of the Commonwealth or its political subdivisions or by any law-enforcement officer of any agency of the federal government. Enforcement agreements with other agencies or political subdivisions shall be stated in the regulation.

8. The Commonwealth hereby assents to the provisions of the Federal Aid in Sport Fish Restoration Act of August 9, 1950 (16 U.S.C. §§ 777-777k), as amended. The Commission is authorized to perform all such acts as may be necessary for the establishment and implementation of cooperative fish restoration and management projects as defined by these federal statutes and the implementing regulations promulgated thereunder.

History.

Code 1950, § 28-43; 1960, c. 517; 1962, c. 406, §§ 28.1-23, 28.1-48; 1966, c. 684; 1968, cc. 748, 749; 1972, c. 833; 1973, cc. 21, 411, § 28.1-120.1; 1976, c. 392; 1979, c. 274; 1981, c. 61; 1983, cc. 307, 318; 1984, c. 463; 1990, c. 445; 1992, c. 836; 1995, c. 136; 2004, c. 860; 2006, c. 5; 2009, c. 371.

§ 28.2-205. Scientific collection permits; penalty.

A. Except as provided for in § 28.2-1101, it is unlawful for any person to remove from the waters of the Commonwealth under the jurisdiction of the Commission any marine fish, marine shellfish, or marine organisms for technical research, scientific, educational or museum purposes without having first obtained from the Commissioner a collection permit.

A violation of this subsection is a Class 3 misdemeanor.

B. Application for a permit shall be made in writing to the Commissioner. There shall be no charge for a permit, and the permit shall not be transferable. The issuance of the permit shall be governed by applicable Commission regulations and shall be subject to any reasonable terms and conditions imposed by the Commissioner. The Commissioner may, with the approval of the Commission, require an applicant for such permit to submit to the Commissioner any data or results acquired through the use of the permit.

C. Any person who has been issued a scientific collection permit shall be exempt from any licensing provision of this subtitle relating to the taking or catching of fish, shellfish, or marine organisms.

History.

1977, c. 33, § 28.1-3.1; 1992, c. 836.

ARTICLE 5.
LICENSING GENERALLY.

§ 28.2-225. Fishing license required; penalty.

It shall be unlawful to fish in the tidal waters of the Commonwealth or those waters under the joint jurisdiction of the Commonwealth without first obtaining the required license, subject to the exemptions set out in § 28.2-226.

Any person who violates this section is guilty of a Class 1 misdemeanor.

History.

Code 1950, §§ 28-42, 28-43, 28-61, 28-66; 1960, c. 517; 1962, c. 406, §§ 28.1-47, 28.1-48, 28.1-59, 28.1-64; 1966, cc. 684, 695; 1968, c. 748; 1972, c. 833; 1973, c. 21; 1974, c. 313; 1976, c. 392; 1978, cc. 347, 358; 1979, c. 274; 1980, c. 605; 1981, cc. 61, 525; 1982, c. 461; 1983, c. 307; 1988, c. 710; 1990, c. 445; 1992, cc. 493, 503, 836, 895.

§ 28.2-227. Special nonresident harvester's license; fee and oath; revocation; penalty.

A. Any nonresident desiring to take or catch marine fish, crabs or any other seafood, except oysters, clams or other mollusks, from the tidal waters of the Commonwealth for which a license is required shall pay to any officer or agent a fee for a nonresident harvester's license. The fee, to be established by the Commission, shall be no less than $350 or more than $1,150 or as subsequently revised by the Commission pursuant to § 28.2-201. Three hundred fifty dollars of each fee shall be credited to the Virginia Marine Products Fund as provided under § 3.2-2705. The remainder of the fee shall be credited to the Marine Fishing Improvement Fund, as established pursuant to § 28.2-208.

B. The license shall be required of each boat used in Virginia's tidal waters and shall be in addition to any other licenses required for the activity involved.

C. The nonresident shall state under oath his true name and address, the name and number of the boat being licensed, and that he will not violate any of the laws of the Commonwealth governing the taking and catching of seafood.

D. A nonresident harvester's license shall be required prior to the purchase of any other license for the harvesting of seafood. Revocation of this license in accordance with § 28.2-232 shall constitute revocation of any other license held by the nonresident under the provisions of this subtitle. No commercial fishing license or permit shall be sold to a nonresident whose state of residence does not offer for sale the same or substantially similar license or permit to a resident of the Commonwealth.

E. Any Virginia resident who enters into a partnership or other agreement with the intent to defeat the object of this section is guilty of a Class 1 misdemeanor.

History.

1983, c. 299, § 28.1-47.1; 1991, c. 411; 1992, c. 836; 1993, c. 245; 1994, c. 155; 2009, c. 9; 2010, cc. 12, 144.

§ 28.2-228. Licenses for purchase of fish, shellfish, or marine organisms from the catcher; fee.

A. Any person purchasing from the catcher clams, crabs, fish, or other seafood, except oysters, caught from the waters of the Commonwealth or the Potomac River, shall pay a license fee of (i) $50 for each place of business and (ii) $25 for each boat or motor vehicle used for buying. The Commission may subsequently revise the cost of licenses pursuant to § 28.2-201.

B. Any person purchasing from the catcher oysters caught from the public grounds of the Commonwealth or the Potomac River shall pay a license fee of (i) $50 for a single place of business with one boat or motor vehicle used for buying oysters and (ii) $100 for a single place of business with multiple boats or motor vehicles used for buying oysters. The Commission may subsequently revise the cost of licenses pursuant to § 28.2-201.

C. No license shall be required of any person purchasing seafood for personal consumption, any place of business which is solely a restaurant, or any person who operates a business which is subject to local license taxes under § 58.1-3703 and who has in his possession no more than one bushel of peeler crabs to be sold as bait.

History.

1970, c. 726, § 28.1-119.1; 1979, c. 274; 1980, c. 218; 1984, c. 316; 1988, c. 27; 1992, c. 836; 2009, c. 9; 2013, c. 38.

§ 28.2-228.1. Seafood landing licenses.

A. The Commission may by regulation establish licenses for the landing of seafood in Virginia, the fee for which shall not exceed $150 or as subsequently revised by the Commission pursuant to § 28.2-201. The regulations may limit the number of such licenses that may be issued and may establish eligibility criteria. Fees collected from the sale of seafood landing licenses shall be deposited to the Marine Fishing Improvement Fund established in § 28.2-208.

B. The Commission may grant exceptions to the license requirement established in subsection A to any person registered as a commercial fisherman under the provisions of § 28.2-241.

C. The following shall be Class 3 misdemeanors: (i) landing seafood without the license that may be required under this section and (ii) failure to produce or have available for inspection the license that may be required under this section when requested by any officer. Failure to produce the license is prima facie evidence that the person is landing seafood without a license.

History.
1996, c. 214; 2009, c. 9.

§ 28.2-229. When licenses terminate; proration and refund not permitted.

A. The Commission shall issue all licenses on an annual basis. All licenses shall be valid from January 1 of each year or their later date of purchase and expire on December 31 of the year in which issued.

B. Refunds shall not be made or prorated if the fishing effort is reduced, or seasons are closed (i) in order to promote conservation of the fisheries or (ii) due to natural conditions. Refunds shall not be made for any license that is suspended or revoked. However, if the license is no longer for sale due to fisheries management purposes, refunds shall be made to the license holder on a prorated basis.

History.
Code 1950, §§ 28-10.1, 28-61, 28-71; 1952, c. 653; 1954, c. 179; 1960, c. 517; 1962, c. 406, §§ 28.1-21, 28.1-59, 28.1-70; 1966, c. 695; 1974, cc. 85, 313; 1978, cc. 347, 358; 1979, cc. 18, 274; 1980, c. 605; 1982, c. 461; 1983, c. 299, §§ 28.1-47, 28.1-47.1; 1988, c. 710; 1991, c. 411; 1992, c. 836; 2009, c. 384.

§ 28.2-230. Penalty for false statements or altering a fishing license; penalty.

It shall be unlawful for any person to (i) subscribe to a materially false statement in applying to secure a license to fish or (ii) alter or change such license.

A violation of this section shall be a Class 1 misdemeanor.

History.
Code 1950, § 28-66; 1962, c. 406, § 28.1-64; 1981, c. 525; 1992, c. 836.

§ 28.2-231. Exhibition of license; display to officers; penalty.

Any person engaged in fishing shall have the required license available for inspection and shall present such license when requested by an officer. Failure to present the license upon request of any officer is a Class 1 misdemeanor and prima facie evidence that the person is fishing without a license.

History.
Code 1950, §§ 28-137, 28-157; 1960, c. 517; 1962, c. 406, §§ 28.1-120, 28.1-133; 1964, c. 393; 1966, c. 684; 1970, c. 726; 1979, c. 274; 1991, c. 285; 1992, c. 836.

§ 28.2-232. Revocation of licenses.

A. The Commission may revoke the fishing privileges within the Commonwealth's tidal waters and revoke, prohibit the issuance, reissuance, or renewal of any licenses if, after a hearing held after 10 days' notice to the applicant or licensee, it finds that the person has violated any provision of this subtitle.

B. The duration of the revocation and prohibition shall be fixed by the Commission up to a maximum of five years with the withdrawal of all fishing privileges conferred by this title during that period, taking into account (i) evidence of repeated or habitual disregard for conservation, health and safety laws and regulations; (ii) abusive conduct and behavior toward officers; and (iii) the severity of any damage that has occurred, or might have occurred, to the natural resources, the public health, or the seafood industry.

C. The Commission may assess a civil penalty of up to $10,000 against a person if it finds, after a hearing held after 10 days' notice, that the person has engaged in fishing, other than for recreational purposes as defined in § 28.2-226.1, while the person's licenses and fishing privileges have been revoked pursuant to this section or § 28.2-528. In setting the amount of the civil penalty, the Commission shall consider the person's history of violating the conservation, health, and safety laws and regulations of the Commonwealth.

D. If the person fails to pay the civil penalty within 180 days of the assessment of the civil penalty by the Commission, the Commissioner may transmit a true copy of the order assessing such civil penalty to the clerk of the court of any county or city wherein it is ascertained that the person owing the penalty has any estate, and the clerk to whom such copy is so sent shall record it, as a judgment is required by law to be recorded, and shall index the same as well in the name of the Commonwealth as of the person owing the penalty, and thereupon there shall be a lien in favor of the Commonwealth on the property of the person within such county or city in the amount of the civil penalty.

E. Civil penalties collected pursuant to this section shall be deposited into the Virginia Marine Products Fund established in § 3.2-2705.

An appeal from the Commission's decision may be taken to the courts as provided in Article 3 (§ 28.2-216 et seq.) of this chapter.

History.
1962, c. 406, § 28.1-36; 1970, c. 610; 1989, c. 2; 1992, c. 836; 2013, c. 50; 2015, c. 468.

ARTICLE 6.

MARKING OF BOATS, NETS AND OTHER DEVICES.

§ 28.2-233. License tags or identification generally.

The Commission shall provide metal license tags or identification numbers to licensees in a form and manner prescribed by the Commission.

History.
Code 1950, § 28-76; 1962, c. 406, §§ 28.1-73, 28.1-74; 1966, c. 684; 1992, c. 836.

§ 28.2-234. License tags and identification numbers to be fastened; penalty.

A. License tags or identification numbers shall be attached and displayed in the following manner:

1. License tags for fixed fishery devices, including pound nets, fyke nets, crab traps, and staked gill nets, shall be fastened to one of the offshore stakes.
2. License tags for anchored gill nets and drift gill nets shall be fastened to a flagstaff or a buoy that is visible from the surface.
3. License tags for vessels using haul seines, purse nets, trawl nets, crab pots, trotlines, and crab scrapes shall be fastened at a conspicuous place on the starboard side or the mast of the vessel.
4. License tags issued for businesses purchasing seafood shall be affixed in a conspicuous place on the business establishment, boat or motor vehicle.
5. Identification numbers when issued for particular devices shall be applied by the license holder and shall be in place at all times when the gear is deployed.

B. Any such licensee who fails to properly attach or display such a license tag or identification number is guilty of a Class 1 misdemeanor.

History.
Code 1950, §§ 28-43, 28-77, 28-78, 28-175; 1960, c. 517; 1962, c. 406, §§ 28.1-48, 28.1-74, 28.1-76, 28.1-171; 1966, c. 684; 1968, cc. 748, 750, § 28.1-173.2; 1970, c. 726, § 28.1-119.1; 1972, c. 833; 1973, c. 21; 1976, c. 392; 1979, c. 274; 1980, c. 218; 1981, c. 61; 1983, c. 307; 1984, c. 316; 1988, c. 27; 1990, c. 445; 1992, c. 836.

§ 28.2-235. Duty to apply for new tag in case of loss; penalty.

Should the metal tag required by § 28.2-234 be removed or destroyed by accident, by the force of the sea, or in any other casual manner, the licensee shall apply for a new tag within twenty-four hours after the discovery of the destruction or loss of the original tag. Failure to do so is a Class 3 misdemeanor.

History.
Code 1950, § 28-79; 1962, c. 406, § 28.1-77; 1992, c. 836.

§ 28.2-236. Seizure of unmarked devices.

Any fishing device not marked, tagged or identified in the required manner may be seized by an officer and held for any forthcoming legal proceeding.

History.
Code 1950, § 28-77; 1962, c. 406, § 28.1-74; 1964, c. 393; 1966, c. 684; 1992, c. 836.

§ 28.2-237. Removal of abandoned pole or stake; revocation of licenses for failure to remove stakes.

A. Any person fishing a pound net or any other type of fishing device requiring the use of fixed poles or stakes shall remove all such abandoned poles or stakes; however, one pole or stake may be left standing at least four feet above mean high water at old stands as an identification marker.

Abandoned poles or stakes are considered to be poles or stakes which are not used for fishing.

B. The Commission may revoke any fishing licenses issued to such person, as set forth in § 28.2-232, if abandoned poles or stakes are not promptly removed. Failure to remove such poles or stakes is a Class 1 misdemeanor. The most recent licensee for the fishing device is responsible for removing the poles or stakes.

History.
1962, c. 406, § 28.1-79; 1964, c. 393; 1992, c. 836.

§ 28.2-238. Concealing name or number of vessel; penalty.

Any captain or owner who covers or conceals the name, registration number, or fishing license tag of any boat licensed and engaged in the fisheries under this subtitle is guilty of a Class 1 misdemeanor.

History.
Code 1950, §§ 28-49, 28-214; 1962, c. 406, §§ 28.1-54, 28.1-190; 1992, c. 836.

§ 28.2-239. Exemptions from article.

Nothing in this article applies to boats used purely for recreation, or for taking fish or shellfish by rod and line or with hand lines, for family use only.

History.
Code 1950, § 28-80; 1962, c. 406, § 28.1-78; 1992, c. 836.

ARTICLE 7.
REGISTRATION OF COMMERCIAL FISHERMEN.

§ 28.2-241. Registration of commercial fishermen required; exemption; penalty.

A. On and after January 1, 1993, holders of gear licenses, except those issued pursuant to § 28.2-402, issued January 1, 1992, through December 31, 1992, shall register as commercial fishermen as provided for in regulation.

B. [Repealed.]

C. On and after January 1, 1993, fishermen not registered as commercial fishermen but who desire to sell their catch shall apply to the Commission for registration as commercial fishermen. The effective date of status as a commercial fisherman shall be two years from the date the application is approved by the Commission. A person whose registration as a commercial fisherman is not effective shall not sell, trade or barter his catch or give his catch to another in order that it may be sold, traded or bartered.

D. For purposes of this section and §§ 28.2-242, 28.2-243 and 28.2-244, "commercial fisherman" means any person who fishes in tidal waters using any gear and who sells, trades or barters his catch or gives his catch to another in order that it may be sold, traded or bartered. The Commission shall provide, by regulation, for exemptions from the definition of "commercial fisherman" those persons who independently sell, trade or barter minnows and who are not part of, hired by, or engaged in a continuing business enterprise as may be defined by the Commission. Such regulation may include, but is not limited to, limits on the quantity of minnows that may be sold, traded or bartered by a person that may be exempted from the definition of commercial fisherman.

E. The cost of registration as a commercial fisherman shall be $150 annually, due no later than the effective date of registration; however, the cost of registration for a person seventy years of age or older shall be seventy-five dollars. All fees collected from the registration of commercial fishermen shall be deposited in the state treasury and credited to the Marine Fishing Improvement Fund as established in § 28.2-208. The Commission may subsequently revise the cost of licenses in this section pursuant to § 28.2-201.

F. Registrations of commercial fishermen shall not be transferable.

G. Whenever a court finds that a defendant has violated any of the provisions of this section, the court shall assess a civil penalty of $500. All civil penalties assessed pursuant to this section shall be paid into the Marine Fishing Improvement Fund as established in § 28.2-208.

H. Only commercial fishermen with valid registrations may purchase licenses pursuant to §§ 28.2-301, 28.2-501 and 28.2-702.

I. Persons who have obtained a recreational gear license pursuant to § 28.2-226.1 or § 28.2-302.1 are exempt from the provisions of this section.

History.

1992, cc. 493, 503; 1993, c. 219; 1994, c. 121; 1996, c. 277; 2009, c. 9.

§ 28.2-244. Purchase of shellfish or finfish; penalty.

A person shall not purchase shellfish or finfish from any fisherman who is known by such person to have not registered as a commercial fisherman as required by § 28.2-241. Whenever a court finds that a defendant has violated the provisions of this section, the court shall assess a civil penalty of $500. All civil penalties assessed pursuant to this section shall be paid into the Marine Fishing Improvement Fund as established in § 28.2-208.

History.

1992, cc. 493, 503.

CHAPTER 8.

HEALTH AND SANITATION PROVISIONS.

Article 2.

Control of Crustacea, Finfish and Shellfish; Violations and Penalties.

ARTICLE 2.

CONTROL OF CRUSTACEA, FINFISH AND SHELLFISH; VIOLATIONS AND PENALTIES.

§ 28.2-810. Removal, transportation, etc., from polluted ground; penalty.

A. It is unlawful for any person to take, catch, transport, sell, offer for sale, remove, receive, keep or store shellfish from condemned areas, or relay shellfish taken from such areas, until the Commissioner of Marine Resources or his designee has issued a special permit. The permittee shall carry the permit when engaged in such operation.

B. It is unlawful for any person to take or remove shellfish from private grounds in condemned areas without written authority in his possession from the owner or lessee, in addition to the permit required by subsection A of this section.

C. It is unlawful for any person to transport, relay, or move shellfish from condemned areas after sunset or before sunrise, except by motor vehicle properly sealed as required by § 28.2-812. It is unlawful to mix clean shellfish and shellfish from condemned areas in the same cargo.

History.

Code 1950, § 28-162.1; 1960, c. 517; 1962, c. 406, § 28.1-179; 1966, c. 684; 1968, c. 745; 1979, c. 274; 1981, c. 52; 1986, c. 184; 1988, c. 600; 1992, c. 836.

§ 28.2-821. Violations; penalty.

A. It is unlawful for any person to have in his possession, to store, to sell, or to offer for sale any shellfish which have been removed or taken from a condemned area other than as provided in § 28.2-810. Any person who violates this section or any provision of this chapter is guilty of a Class 1 misdemeanor.

B. Upon conviction of violating any provision of this chapter any boat, vessel, motor vehicle or equipment used in committing the violation may be forfeited as provided by Chapter 22.1 (§ 19.2-386.1 et seq.) of Title 19.2.

History.

Code 1950, § 28-165; 1962, c. 406, § 28.1-181; 1992, c. 836; 2012, cc. 283, 756.

§ 28.2-825. Importing fish, shellfish or crustacea for introduction into waters of the Commonwealth; penalty.

A. It shall be unlawful for any person to import any fish, shellfish or crustacea into the Commonwealth with the intent of placing such fish, shellfish or crustacea into the waters of the Commonwealth unless one of the following conditions exists:

1. The fish, shellfish or crustacea are coming from within the continental United States from a state or waters which are on the Marine Resources Commission's list of approved states and waters, and are species which are on the Marine Resources Commission's list of approved species; or

2. The person has notified the Commissioner of Marine Resources of such intent and has received written permission from the Commissioner of Marine Resources.

The list of approved states and waters shall be published by the Commissioner of Marine Resources, and a state or water shall be placed on or removed from such list only with the concurrence of the Director of the Virginia Institute of Marine Science. The Commissioner of Marine Resources, with the concurrence of the Director of the Virginia Institute of Marine Science, is authorized to change the list when he determines that it is necessary for the protection of the waters of the Commonwealth.

The list of approved species shall be published by the Commissioner of Marine Resources, and a species shall be placed on or removed from such list only with the concurrence of the Director of the Virginia Institute of Marine Science. The Commissioner of Marine Resources, with the concurrence of the Director of the Virginia Institute of Marine Science, is authorized to change the list when he determines that it is necessary for the protection of the waters of the Commonwealth.

B. The notification of intent to import shall be in writing and submitted to the Commissioner of Marine Resources at least thirty days prior to the date of importation. The notice shall state: (i) the specific fish, shellfish or crustacea to be imported, (ii) from what waters the fish, shellfish or crustacea are being taken, (iii) the period of time over which importation is to be accomplished, (iv) the quantities involved, and (v) into what waters the fish, shellfish or crustacea are to be placed.

A violation of this section is a Class 1 misdemeanor.

History.

1974, c. 327, § 28.1-183.2; 1992, c. 836.

CHAPTER 9.

ENFORCEMENT OF SUBTITLE II; JURISDICTION.

Section

§ 28.2-900. Arrest with or without warrant; larceny; violations of boating laws and Title 62.1.

A. Officers may, with or without warrant, (i) arrest any person violating any provision of this subtitle, (ii) seize any net, pot, or other fishing device or gear used in violating such laws and (iii) seize fish, shellfish or marine organisms taken or handled in violation of this subtitle. Each seized property shall be forfeited to the Commonwealth. The forfeiture shall be enforced as provided in Chapter 22.1 (§ 19.2-386.1 et seq.) of Title 19.2. The officer seizing the property to be forfeited shall immediately give notice to the attorney for the Commonwealth.

B. All officers may arrest, with or without a warrant, any person who commits in his presence (i) any larceny committed upon or adjacent to the waters of the Commonwealth, (ii) any violation of the provisions of Chapter 7 of Title 29.1, or any regulations promulgated thereunder, or (iii) any violation of the provisions of Chapter 18 (§ 62.1-187 et seq.) or 20 (§ 62.1-194 et seq.) of Title 62.1.

History.

Code 1950, §§ 28-206, 28-208; 1962, c. 406, § 28.1-185; 1980, c. 567, § 28.1-185.1; 1981, c. 525; 1987, c. 84; 1992, c. 836; 2012, cc. 283, 756.

§ 28.2-901. Summons issued instead of being taken into custody; failure to appear.

A. Whenever any person is detained by or is in the custody of an arresting officer for any violation of the laws enforceable pursuant to § 28.2-900, the arresting officer shall take the name and address of each person detained and issue a summons or otherwise notify him in writing to appear at a time and court to be specified in the summons or notice. When the person gives his written promise to appear at the designated time and place, the officer shall immediately release him from custody.

B. If the arresting officer (i) believes a detained person is likely to disregard a summons issued under the provisions of this section or (ii) reasonably believes a detained person is likely to harm himself or another, or if the person refuses to give his written promise to appear, the officer may take the offender, vessel and property into custody. The person shall be brought before the nearest or most accessible judicial officer or other person qualified to admit bail having jurisdiction.

C. The failure of any person to appear as required by a summons issued under the provisions of this section shall suspend all licenses issued to the person pursuant to this subtitle until such time as he appears to answer the charges against him. Failure to appear shall bar the issuance of any further license to the person until he appears.

History.

1983, c. 591, § 28.1-185.2; 1992, c. 836.

§ 28.2-902. Procedure after arrest and seizure.

Any person arrested may be (i) taken before a court of competent jurisdiction for trial, (ii) committed to jail pending trial, (iii) admitted to bail or released on recognizance as provided by general law, or (iv) issued a summons requiring him to appear for trial. The time specified in the summons shall not be less than five days from the date of arrest unless such person requests an earlier hearing. Any person failing to appear as directed in the summons shall be guilty of a Class 1 misdemeanor, regardless of the disposition of, and in addition to, the charge upon which he was originally arrested. If the person fails to appear, a warrant for his arrest may be issued.

Any property seized under the provisions of subsection A of § 28.2-900 may be held by the officer or other official who made the seizure, pending final outcome of the legal proceedings.

History.

Code 1950, § 28-209; 1950, p. 978; 1962, c. 406, § 28.1-186; 1992, c. 836.

§ 28.2-903. Violations constitute misdemeanor.

A violation of any provision of this subtitle or regulation promulgated thereunder, unless otherwise specifically provided, is a Class 3 misdemeanor. A second or subsequent violation of any provision of this subtitle or regulation promulgated thereunder committed by the same person within twelve months of a prior violation is a Class 1 misdemeanor.

History.

1962, c. 406, § 28.1-187; 1989, c. 421; 1992, c. 836.

§ 28.2-903.1. Impeding lawful fishing in tidal waters; penalty.

A. It is unlawful for any person to willfully and intentionally impede the lawful fishing of any species of fish or shellfish. "Fishing" means those activities defined in § 28.2-100 as "fishing," "fisheries" or "to fish."

B. Notwithstanding any other provision of law, any person convicted of a violation of this section shall be guilty of a Class 3 misdemeanor.

History.

1997, c. 703.

§ 28.2-904. Pursuit and detention across the Maryland-Virginia line.

When, in the opinion of the legally constituted authorities of the Commonwealth, there has occurred on the waters of Virginia a violation of the laws of the Commonwealth enforceable pursuant to § 28.2-900, or when, in the opinion of the legally constituted authorities of Maryland, there has occurred on the waters of Maryland a violation of any provision of the Natural Resources Article, Annotated Code of Maryland, the offender may be pursued by the legally constituted authorities of the state where the offense was committed up to and across the Maryland-Virginia boundary into the state where the offender flees. If a capture is made in continuous pursuit, the offender, vessel and property shall be dealt with as authorized by the laws of the state where the offense was committed.

The provisions of this section shall be effective as long as the State of Maryland has in force similar provisions authorizing legally constituted authorities of Virginia to make pursuit and arrests in Maryland for violations of the laws of Virginia.

History.

1983, c. 323, § 28.1-188.1; 1992, c. 836.

§ 28.2-905. Resistance to officer or authorized person, etc.; penalty.

Any person found guilty of resisting or impeding an officer or other person authorized to make arrests, seizures, examinations or other performances of duties under this subtitle, shall be guilty of a Class 1 misdemeanor.

History.

Code 1950, § 28-215; 1962, c. 406, § 28.1-191; 1992, c. 836.

§ 28.2-906. Failure to perform duty; penalty.

The failure of any officer or other person to perform any duty required of him by any provision of this subtitle is a Class 1 misdemeanor.

History.

Code 1950, § 28-216; 1962, c. 406, § 28.1-192; 1992, c. 836.

§ 28.2-907. Jurisdiction of courts.

Any proceeding under any section of this subtitle shall be before a court of competent jurisdiction in the county or city (i) in which the offense was committed or (ii) adjacent to the waters in which the offense was committed.

History.
Code 1950, § 28-218; 1962, c. 406, § 28.1-193; 1992, c. 836.

TITLE 29.1.

GAME, INLAND FISHERIES AND BOATING.

CHAPTER 1.

ADMINISTRATION OF GAME AND INLAND FISHERIES.

Article 1.

General Provisions.

ARTICLE 1. GENERAL PROVISIONS.

§ 29.1-100. Definitions.

As used in and for the purposes of this title only, or in any of the regulations of the Board, unless the context clearly requires a different meaning:

"Bag or creel limit" means the quantity of game, fish or fur-bearing animals that may be taken, caught, or possessed during a period fixed by the Board.

"Board" means the Board of Game and Inland Fisheries.

"Closed season" means that period of time fixed by the Board during which wild animals, birds or fish may not be taken, captured, killed, pursued, hunted, trapped or possessed.

"Conservation police officers" means supervising officers, and regular and special conservation police officers.

"Department" means the Department of Game and Inland Fisheries.

"Director" means the Director of the Department of Game and Inland Fisheries.

"Firearm" means any weapon that will or is designed to or may readily be converted to expel single or multiple projectiles by the action of an explosion of a combustible material.

"Fishing" means taking, capturing, killing, or attempting to take, capture or kill any fish in and upon the inland waters of this Commonwealth.

"Fur-bearing animals" includes beaver, bobcat, fisher, fox, mink, muskrat, opossum, otter, raccoon, skunk, and weasel.

"Game" means wild animals and wild birds that are commonly hunted for sport or food.

"Game animals" means deer (including all Cervidae), bear, rabbit, fox, squirrel, bobcat and raccoon.

"Game fish" means trout (including all Salmonidae), all of the sunfish family (including largemouth bass, smallmouth bass and spotted bass, rock bass, bream, bluegill and crappie), walleye or pike perch, white bass, chain pickerel or jackfish, muskellunge, and northern pike, wherever such fish are found in the waters of this Commonwealth and rockfish or striped bass where found above tidewaters or in streams which are blocked from access from tidewaters by dams.

"Hunting and trapping" includes the act of or the attempted act of taking, hunting, trapping, pursuing, chasing, shooting, snaring or netting birds or animals, and assisting any person who is hunting, trapping or attempting to do so regardless of whether birds or animals are actually taken; however, when hunting and trapping are allowed, reference is made to such acts as being conducted by lawful means and in a lawful manner. The Board of Game and Inland Fisheries may authorize by regulation the pursuing or chasing of wild birds or wild animals during any closed hunting season where persons have no intent to take such birds or animals.

"Lawful," "by law," or *"law"* means the statutes of this Commonwealth or regulations adopted by the Board which the Director is empowered to enforce.

"Migratory game birds" means doves, ducks, brant, geese, swan, coot, gallinules, sora and other rails, snipe, woodcock and other species of birds on which open hunting seasons are set by federal regulations.

"Muzzleloading pistol" means a firearm originally designed, made or intended to fire a projectile (bullet) from one or more barrels when held in one hand and that is loaded from the muzzle or forward end of the cylinder.

"Muzzleloading rifle" means a firearm firing a single projectile that is loaded along with the propellant from the muzzle of the gun.

"Muzzleloading shotgun" means a firearm with a smooth bore firing multiple projectiles that are loaded along with the propellant from the muzzle of the gun.

"Nonmigratory game birds" means grouse, bobwhite quail, turkey and all species of birds introduced into the Commonwealth by the Board.

"Nuisance species" means blackbirds, coyotes, crows, cowbirds, feral swine, grackles, English sparrows, starlings, or those species designated as such by regulations of the Board, and those species found committing or about to commit depredation upon ornamental or shade trees, agricultural crops, wildlife, livestock or other property or when concentrated in numbers and manners as to constitute a health hazard or other nuisance. However, the term nuisance does not include (i) animals designated as

endangered or threatened pursuant to §§ 29.1-563, 29.1-564, and 29.1-566, (ii) animals classified as game or fur-bearing animals, and (iii) those species protected by state or federal law.

"Open season" means that period of time fixed by the Board during which wild animals, wild birds and fish may be taken, captured, killed, pursued, trapped or possessed.

"Pistol" means a weapon originally designed, made, and intended to fire a projectile (bullet) from one or more barrels when held in one hand, and having one or more chambers as an integral part of or permanently aligned with the bore and a short stock at an angle to and extending below the line of the bore that is designed to be gripped by one hand.

"Possession" means the exercise of control of any wild animal, wild bird, fish or fur-bearing animal, or any part of the carcass thereof.

"Properly licensed person" means a person who, while engaged in hunting, fishing or trapping, or in any other activity permitted under this title, in and upon the lands and inland waters of this Commonwealth, has upon his person all the licenses, permits and stamps required by law.

"Regulation" means a regulation duly adopted by the Board pursuant to the authority vested by the provisions of this title.

"Revolver" means a projectile weapon of the pistol type, having a breechloading chambered cylinder arranged so that the cocking of the hammer or movement of the trigger rotates it and brings the next cartridge in line with the barrel for firing.

"Rifle" means a weapon designed or redesigned, made or remade, and intended to be fired from the shoulder, and designed or redesigned and made or remade to use the energy of the explosive in a fixed metallic cartridge to fire only a single projectile through a rifled bore for each single pull of the trigger.

"Shotgun" means a weapon designed or redesigned, made or remade, and intended to be fired from the shoulder, and designed or redesigned and made or remade to use the energy of the explosive in a fixed shotgun shell to fire through a smooth bore or rifled shotgun barrel either a number of ball shot or a single projectile for each single pull of the trigger.

"Transportation" means the transportation, either upon the person or by any other means, of any wild animal or wild bird or fish.

"Wildlife" means all species of wild animals, wild birds and freshwater fish in the public waters of this Commonwealth.

History.
1952, c. 573, § 29-131; 1952, c. 608, § 29-2.1; 1962, c. 469; 1974, c. 302; 1979, c. 264; 1984, c. 199; 1987, cc. 134, 488; 1990, c. 371; 2002, c. 157; 2012, cc. 247, 603; 2015, c. 618.

CHAPTER 2.

CONSERVATION POLICE OFFICERS.

Section

§ 29.1-202. Ex officio conservation police officers.

All sheriffs, police officers or other peace officers of this Commonwealth shall be ex officio conservation police officers.

History.
Code 1950, § 29-29; 1987, c. 488.

§ 29.1-203. Jurisdiction; power to serve process.

A. Conservation police officers shall have jurisdiction throughout the Commonwealth to enforce the hunting, trapping and inland fish laws and may serve process in all matters arising from violations of such laws.

B. Conservation police officers shall enforce the State Water Control Board's regulations designating Smith Mountain Lake as a no-discharge zone for boat sewage.

History.
Code 1950, § 29-30; 1979, c. 264; 1987, c. 488; 2001, cc. 93, 123.

§ 29.1-205. Power to make arrests.

All conservation police officers are vested with the authority, upon displaying a badge or other credential of office, to issue a summons or to arrest any person found in the act of violating any of the provisions of the hunting, trapping, inland fish and boating laws.

Regular conservation police officers are vested with the same authority as sheriffs and other law-enforcement officers to enforce all of the criminal laws of the Commonwealth.

Any special conservation police officer shall have general police power while performing his duty on properties owned or controlled by the Board.

Any commissioned, warrant or petty officers of the United States Coast Guard and of the United States Coast Guard Reserve while engaged on active duty, in the conduct of their official duties in uniform, and any officers of the customs as defined by 19 U.S.C. § 1709(b), in the conduct of their official duties in uniform, shall have the same power to make arrests under Chapter 7 (§ 29.1-700 et seq.) of Title 29.1 as conservation police officers.

History.
Code 1950, § 29-32; 1960, c. 540; 1979, c. 264; 1982, c. 64; 1987, c. 488; 1988, c. 605; 2007, c. 87.

§ 29.1-207. Impeding conservation police officer, etc., in discharge of his duty.

If any person, by threats or force, attempts to intimidate or impede any law-enforcement officer enforcing the game, inland fish and boating laws, he shall be guilty of a Class 2 misdemeanor and shall be subject to arrest by the officer and to the procedures set forth in § 29.1-210.

History.
1974, c. 299, § 29-32.2; 1987, c. 488; 2007, c. 87.

§ 29.1-208. Searches and seizures.

All conservation police officers are vested with the authority to search any person arrested as provided in § 29.1-205 together with any box, can, package, barrel or other container, hunting bag, coat, suit, trunk, grip, satchel or fish basket carried by, in the possession of, or belonging to such person. Conservation police officers shall also have the authority, immediately subsequent to such arrest, to enter and search any refrigerator, building, vehicle, or other place in which the officer making the search has reasonable ground to believe that the person arrested has concealed or placed any wild bird, wild animal or fish, which will furnish evidence of a violation of the hunting, trapping and inland fish laws. Such a search may be made without a warrant, except that a dwelling may not be searched without a warrant. Should any container as described in this section reveal any wild bird, wild animal or fish, or any part thereof, which has been illegally taken, possessed, sold, purchased or transported, the conservation police officer shall seize and hold as evidence the container, together with such wild bird, wild animal or fish, and any unlawful gun, net, or other device of any kind for taking wild birds, wild animals or fish which he may find.

History.
Code 1950, § 29-33; 1987, c. 488; 2007, c. 87.

§ 29.1-209. Inspection of game and fish without arrest.

In order to see that bag or creel limits are being observed, conservation police officers shall also have the power to inspect game, fur-bearing animals and fish taken by any person found hunting, trapping or fishing without arresting the person.

History.
Code 1950, § 29-34; 1962, c. 469; 1987, c. 488.

§ 29.1-210. Person arrested may be committed to jail, bailed, recognized or summoned.

Any person arrested for a violation of the game, inland fish and boating laws may be committed to jail pending trial or admitted to bail or released on recognizance as provided by general law; or the arresting officer may issue a summons requiring the person to appear for trial at a time and place specified therein before a court having jurisdiction to try such offenses if the person gives his written promise to appear at the specified time. Such time shall not, however, be less than five days from the date of arrest unless the person requests an earlier hearing.

Any person refusing to give the written promise to appear shall be taken immediately by the arresting or other police officer before the nearest or most accessible judicial officer.

Any person who willfully violates his written promise to appear, given in accordance with this section, shall be guilty of a Class 2 misdemeanor.

History.
1952, c. 608, § 29-34.1; 1974, c. 58; 1987, c. 488.

CHAPTER 3.

LICENSES.

Article 1.

Hunting, Trapping and Fishing Licenses.

Section

ARTICLE 1.

HUNTING, TRAPPING AND FISHING LICENSES.

§ 29.1-300. Unlawful to hunt, trap or fish without license.

It shall be unlawful to hunt, trap or fish in or on the lands or inland waters of this Commonwealth without first obtaining a license, subject to the exceptions set out in § 29.1-301.

History.

Code 1950, § 29-51; 1987, c. 488.

§ 29.1-301. Exemptions from license requirements.

A. No license shall be required of landowners, their spouses, their children and grandchildren and the spouses of such children and grandchildren, or the landowner's parents, resident or nonresident, to hunt, trap and fish within the boundaries of their own lands and inland waters or while within such boundaries or upon any private permanent extension therefrom, to fish in any abutting public waters.

B. No license shall be required of any stockholder owning 50 percent or more of the stock of any domestic corporation owning land in this Commonwealth, his or her spouse and children and minor grandchildren, resident or nonresident, to hunt, trap and fish within the boundaries of lands and inland waters owned by the domestic corporation.

C. No license shall be required of bona fide tenants, renters or lessees to hunt, trap or fish within the boundaries of the lands or waters on which they reside or while within such boundaries or upon any private permanent extension therefrom, to fish in any abutting public waters if such individuals have the written consent of the landlord upon their person. A guest of the owner of a private fish pond shall not be required to have a fishing license to fish in such pond.

D. No license shall be required of resident persons under 16 years old to fish.

D1. No license shall be required of resident persons under 12 years old to hunt, provided such person is accompanied and directly supervised by an adult who has, on his person, a valid Virginia hunting license as described in subsection B of § 29.1-300.1.

E. No license shall be required of a resident person 65 years of age or over to hunt or trap on private property in the county or city in which he resides. An annual license at a fee of $1 shall be required of a resident person 65 years of age or older to fish in any inland waters of the Commonwealth, which shall be in addition to a license to fish for trout as specified in subsection B of § 29.1-310 or a special lifetime trout fishing license as specified in § 29.1-302.4. A resident 65 years of age or older may, upon proof of age satisfactory to the Department and the payment of a $1 fee, apply for and receive from any authorized agent of the Department a nontransferable annual license permitting such person to hunt or an annual license permitting such person to trap in all cities and counties of the Commonwealth. Any lifetime license issued pursuant to this article prior to July 1, 1988, shall remain valid for the lifetime of the person to whom it was issued. Any license issued pursuant to this section includes any damage stamp required pursuant to Article 3 (§ 29.1-352 et seq.) of this chapter.

F. No license to fish, except for trout as provided in § 29.1-302.4 or subsection B of § 29.1-310, shall be required of nonresident persons under 12 years of age when accompanied by a person possessing a valid license to fish in Virginia.

G. No license shall be required to trap rabbits with box traps.

H. No license shall be required of resident persons under 16 years of age to trap when accompanied by any person 18 years of age or older who possesses a valid state license to trap in this Commonwealth.

I. No license to hunt, trap or fish shall be required of any Indian who habitually resides on an Indian reservation or of a member of the Virginia recognized tribes who resides in the Commonwealth; however, such Indian must have on his person an identification card or paper signed by the chief of his tribe, a valid tribal identification card, written confirmation through a central tribal registry, or certification from a tribal office. Such card, paper, confirmation, or certification shall set forth that the person named is an actual resident upon such reservation or member of the recognized tribes in the Commonwealth, and such card, paper, confirmation or certification shall create a presumption of residence, which may be rebutted by proof of actual residence elsewhere.

J. No license to fish shall be required of legally blind persons.

K. No fishing license shall be required in any inland waters of the Commonwealth on free fishing days. The Board shall designate no more than three free fishing days in any calendar year.

L. No license to fish, except for trout as provided in § 29.1-302.4 or subsection B of § 29.1-310, in Laurel Lake and Beaver Pond at Breaks Interstate Park shall be required of a resident of the State of Kentucky who (i) possesses a valid license to fish in Kentucky or (ii) is exempt under Kentucky law from the requirement of possessing a valid fishing license.

M. No license to fish, except for trout as provided in subsection B of § 29.1-310, shall be required of a member of the armed forces of the United States, on active duty, who is a resident of the Commonwealth while such person is on official leave, provided that person presents a copy of his leave papers upon request.

N. No license to hunt or fish shall be required of any person who is not hunting or fishing but is aiding a disabled person to hunt or fish when such disabled person possesses a valid Virginia hunting or fishing license under § 29.1-302, 29.1-302.1, or 29.1-302.2.

History.

Code 1950, § 29-52; 1950, pp. 619, 627; 1954, c. 623; 1962, c. 526; 1964, c. 445; 1968, c. 673; 1974, c. 363; 1977, c. 392; 1980, cc. 494, 500; 1981, c. 16; 1985, c. 154; 1987, cc. 126, 488, 507; 1988, cc. 180, 488; 1992, c. 262; 1996, cc. 118, 151; 1997, c. 267; 2000, cc. 110, 142;

2001, cc. 49, 597; 2002, c. 67; 2004, c. 846; 2008, c. 279; 2010, c. 345; 2016, c. 63.

§ 29.1-305. Special license for hunting bear, deer and turkey; authority of Board to create bear license.

A. A special license is required for hunting bear, deer and turkey in this Commonwealth, which shall be in addition to the license required to hunt other game. The fee for the special license shall be $12 for a resident age 16 or older, $7.50 for a resident under the age of 16, and $60 for a nonresident 16 years of age or older, $15 for a nonresident 12 years of age to 15 years of age, and $12 for a nonresident younger than 12 years of age.

B. The Board may create a separate special license for the hunting of bear in this Commonwealth. The fee for such a special license shall be $25 for residents and $150 for nonresidents. A person who obtains a special license for hunting bear shall also be required to obtain the state resident license or state nonresident license pursuant to § 29.1-303. If a special license to hunt bear is established by the Board, the special license required in subsection A shall authorize the hunting of deer and turkey only.

The license to hunt bear, deer and turkey or, if authorized by the Board, the license to hunt bear may be obtained from the clerk or agent of any county or city whose duty it is to sell hunting licenses.

C. The Board may subsequently revise the cost of licenses set forth in this section pursuant to § 29.1-103.

History.

Code 1950, § 29-122; 1958, c. 318; 1960, c. 568; 1966, c. 493; 1972, c. 509; 1974, c. 363; 1980, c. 494; 1987, c. 488; 1988, c. 250; 2001, c. 55; 2004, c. 269; 2009, c. 9.

§ 29.1-310.1. Sportsman's hunting and fishing license established.

A. Upon implementation of an automated point-of-sale licensing system, any resident individual may apply for and receive from the Department, after payment of the appropriate fee, a sportsman's hunting and fishing license. This license shall serve in lieu of any person having to obtain hunting or fishing licenses provided for under subdivision 2 of § 29.1-303 and §§ 29.1-305, 29.1-306, and 29.1-307, and subdivisions A 2 and B 1 of § 29.1-310.

B. Applications for the license authorized by this section shall be made to the Department. The license shall be valid for the seasons as established by the Board. The form and issuance of the license shall conform to the provisions of this chapter for all licenses.

C. The Board shall establish the fee for this license, which shall not exceed the total cost of purchasing each license separately.

History.

2000, c. 12; 2007, c. 40; 2014, c. 136.

§ 29.1-310.2. Special combined individual sportfishing licenses.

A. Residents and nonresidents of the Commonwealth may obtain a special combined sportfishing license to fish in all inland waters and the tidal waters of the Commonwealth during the open season. For residents, this license shall be in lieu of the state resident freshwater fishing license required by subdivision A 2 of § 29.1-310, and the saltwater recreational license required by § 28.2-302.1. The cost of this license for residents shall be the sum of the costs of the two component resident licenses. For nonresidents, this license shall be in lieu of the state nonresident freshwater fishing license required by subdivision A 3 of § 29.1-310 and the saltwater recreational license required by § 28.2-302.1. The cost of this license for nonresidents shall be the sum of the costs of the two component nonresident licenses.

Of the funds collected under this subsection, (i) the cost of the component saltwater license shall be paid into the state treasury to the credit of the Virginia Saltwater Recreational Fishing Development Fund, as established in § 28.2-302.3, and (ii) the cost of the component freshwater fishing license shall be paid into the state treasury to the credit of the Game Protection Fund, as established in § 29.1-101.

The two component licenses shall be independently priced by their respective agencies. The freshwater fishing license shall be priced by the Board pursuant to § 29.1-103. The saltwater recreational license shall be priced by the Marine Resources Commission pursuant to § 28.2-201.

B. Residents and nonresidents of the Commonwealth may obtain a special combined sportfishing license to fish in all the tidal waters of the Commonwealth during the open season that covers the owner of a recreational boat not carrying anglers for hire, in any registered boat owned and operated by him, and his passengers. For residents, this license shall be in lieu of the state resident fishing license required by subdivision A 2 of § 29.1-310, the saltwater recreational license required by § 28.2-302.1, and the saltwater recreational boat license established by § 28.2-302.7. The cost of this license for residents shall be $125. For nonresidents, this license shall be in lieu of the state nonresident fishing license required by subdivision A 3 of § 29.1-310 and the saltwater recreational license required by § 28.2-302.1. The cost of this license for nonresidents shall be $200.

Of the funds collected under this subsection, (i) $48 per resident license sold and $76 per nonresident license sold shall be paid into the state treasury to the credit of the Virginia Saltwater Recreational Fishing Development Fund, as established in § 28.2-302.3, and (ii) $77 per resident license sold and $124 per nonresident sold shall be paid into the state treasury to the credit of the Game Protection Fund, as established in § 29.1-101.

C. The Board may subsequently revise the cost of licenses set forth in this section pursuant to § 29.1-103.

History.
2004, c. 486; 2009, c. 9; 2011, c. 287; 2012, c. 579.

§ 29.1-311. Trip fishing license for residents and nonresidents; trout stocked waters.

A. Residents and nonresidents of the Commonwealth may obtain trip fishing licenses to fish in the freshwater creeks, bays, inlets, and streams of the Commonwealth, or in any of the impounded waters of the Commonwealth during the open season for game fish. These licenses shall be in lieu of the regular season state or county fishing license required under subsection A of § 29.1-310. The duration for which trip fishing licenses shall be valid shall be established by the Board. The fee for the trip fishing license shall be established by the Board and may be revised pursuant to § 29.1-103.

B. Residents and nonresidents of the Commonwealth may obtain a special combined sportfishing trip license to fish in all inland waters and tidal waters of the Commonwealth during the open season. This license shall be in lieu of the trip fishing license specified in subsection A and the saltwater recreational license required by § 28.2-302.1. The cost of the license shall be $10 for residents and $15 for nonresidents. The license shall be valid for five successive days as specified on the face of the license. Of the funds collected under this subsection, (i) $5 per license sold shall be paid into the state treasury to the credit of the Virginia Saltwater Recreational Fishing Development Fund as established in § 28.2-302.3 and (ii) $5 per resident license sold and $10 per nonresident license sold shall be paid into the state treasury to the credit of the Game Protection Fund as established in § 29.1-101.

C. Possession of a trip fishing license by a nonresident shall not entitle him to fish in designated waters stocked with trout by the Department or other public body unless he also possesses the trout license required under subsection B of § 29.1-310 or has obtained the special lifetime trout fishing license pursuant to § 29.1-302.4.

D. Possession of a trip fishing license by a resident shall not entitle him to fish in designated waters stocked with trout by the Department or other public body. Residents shall only be entitled to fish in such waters if they possess (i) a regular season state or county fishing license and (ii) a trout license, as required by § 29.1-310, or a special lifetime trout fishing license pursuant to § 29.1-302.4.

E. The Board may subsequently revise the cost of licenses set forth in this section pursuant to § 29.1-103.

History.
1954, c. 567, § 29-55.1; 1956, c. 51; 1958, c. 443; 1974, c. 363; 1987, c. 488; 1988, c. 250; 1991, c. 242; 2002, c. 67; 2004, c. 486; 2009, c. 9; 2013, c. 351.

§ 29.1-335. Hunting, trapping or fishing without a license.

No person shall hunt, trap, or fish without having obtained a license when such a license is required. For the purposes of this article, the term "license" shall include any temporary license issued by a clerk or agent to a buyer and authorized to be used in a manner prescribed by the Director. Any person who violates this section shall be guilty of a Class 3 misdemeanor and shall pay to the clerk a fee equal to the cost of the required license to be paid into the state treasury and credited to the game protection fund.

The purchase of a license subsequent to an arrest or notice of summons to appear in court for hunting, trapping or fishing without a license shall not relieve the person from the penalties specified in this section.

History.
Code 1950, § 29-75; 1987, c. 488; 1989, c. 421; 1993, c. 839; 2000, c. 132.

§ 29.1-336. Carrying licenses and certificates; penalty.

A. Every person who is issued a hunting, trapping, or fishing license shall carry the license on his person while hunting, trapping, or fishing. Persons who have been issued such licenses and fail to carry them when required shall be guilty of a Class 4 misdemeanor.

B. Any person who is 16 years of age or older and who is (i) required to present a certificate of completion in hunter education to obtain a hunting license pursuant to § 29.1-300.1, and (ii) issued a hunting license by telephone, the Internet, or other electronic or computerized means, shall also carry such certificate on his person while hunting.

C. Any person who is 12 years of age through 15 years of age, and is issued a hunting license by telephone, the Internet, or other electronic or computerized means, shall carry his certificate of completion in hunter education on his person while hunting, unless he is accompanied and directly supervised by an adult who has, on his person, a valid Virginia hunting license and certificate if required under subsection B.

D. For purposes of this section and § 29.1-337, "carry" means possess a hard copy or electronic copy of the license or certificate, except that any license for bear, deer, or turkey required by § 29.1-305 shall be possessed in hard copy.

History.
Code 1950, § 29-75; 1987, c. 488; 2005, c. 145; 2015, c. 479.

§ 29.1-337. Displaying license upon request.

A. Every person who is issued a hunting, trapping or fishing license and is carrying such a license when hunting, trapping or fishing shall present it immediately upon demand of any officer whose duty it is to enforce the game and inland fish laws. Refusing to exhibit the license upon demand of any conservation police officer or other officer shall be a Class 3 misdemeanor.

B. In accordance with § 18.2-133, the hunting, trapping or fishing license shall also be shown upon the demand of any owner or lessee, or of any employee or representative of such owner or lessee, upon whose lands or waters the person may be hunting, fishing or trapping.

C. The Director may supply buttons or license holders and require the license or button to be displayed in a manner he may determine.

History.
Code 1950, § 29-76; 1987, c. 488; 1989, c. 421; 2007, c. 87.

§ 29.1-337.1. Penalty for false statements; altering, borrowing or lending license.

It shall be unlawful for any person to make a false statement in order to secure a license or to alter, change, borrow, or lend or attempt to use, borrow or lend a license. Any person violating this provision shall be guilty of a Class 2 misdemeanor.

History.
Code 1950, § 29-76; 1987, c. 488.

§ 29.1-338. Revocation of license and privileges; penalties.

If any person is found guilty of violating (i) any of the provisions of the hunting, trapping, or inland fish laws, any provisions of §§ 15.2-915.2, 15.2-1209.1, 18.2-131 through 18.2-136 and §§ 18.2-285 through 18.2-286.1, or any regulations adopted by the Board pursuant thereto, a second time within three years of a previous conviction of violating any such law or regulation, or (ii) any provisions of law or ordinance governing the dumping of refuse, trash or other litter, while engaged in hunting, trapping or fishing, such license and privileges shall be revoked by the court trying the case and that person shall not apply for a new license or exercise such privileges until 12 months succeeding the date of conviction. The court may also prohibit the convicted person from hunting, fishing, or trapping in the Commonwealth for a period of one to five years. If found hunting, trapping or fishing during this prohibited period, the person shall be guilty of a Class 2 misdemeanor. Licenses revoked shall be sent to the Director.

History.
Code 1950, § 29-77; 1962, c. 469; 1970, c. 274; 1983, c. 272; 1987, c. 488; 1989, c. 213; 2004, c. 462; 2010, c. 183.

CHAPTER 4.
PERMITS REQUIRED.

Article 1.

Dealing in Furs.

Article 2.

National Forests.

ARTICLE 1.
DEALING IN FURS.

§ 29.1-400. Unlawful to deal in furs without a permit.

It shall be unlawful to buy, sell, barter, exchange, traffic or trade in, bargain for, solicit for purchase, or possess the hides, furs or pelts of wild animals, or otherwise deal in fur as a business, without having first obtained a permit, subject to the exemptions in § 29.1-401.

History.
Code 1950, § 29-93; 1987, c. 488.

§ 29.1-406. Penalty for violations.

The violation of any of the terms of this article shall constitute a Class 3 misdemeanor. Furthermore, the trial court shall revoke the permit of the fur dealer, and he shall not have a similar permit for that season or for the succeeding season. He may, however, be eligible for a permit thereafter.

History.
Code 1950, § 29-101; 1980, c. 494; 1987, c. 488.

ARTICLE 2.
NATIONAL FORESTS.

§ 29.1-408. Permit required; exceptions.

No person shall hunt, fish, or trap on any lands in the national forests in this Commonwealth without first obtaining, in addition to the regular resident or nonresident license, a special permit to hunt, fish, or trap on such areas in the national forests as the Board and the Forest Service may agree upon. However, no such permit shall be required of (i) residents under the age of sixteen to fish or trap; (ii) residents over the age of sixty-five to fish; (iii) nonresidents under the age of twelve to fish, except for trout, when accompanied by a person possessing a valid license to fish therein; (iv) residents possessing a license as provided by subsection E of § 29.1-301; and (v) persons holding a license as provided by § 29.1-339.

The violation of any of the terms of this article shall constitute a Class 3 misdemeanor.

History.

Code 1950, § 29-117; 1972, c. 381; 1977, c. 377; 1987, c. 488.

§ 29.1-409. From whom permits obtained; fee.

The special national forest permit may be obtained from the clerk or agent of any county or city whose duty it is to sell hunting, fishing, and trapping licenses. The fee for the special permit shall be three dollars.

History.

Code 1950, § 29-118; 1980, c. 494; 1987, c. 488; 1988, c. 250.

CHAPTER 5.

WILDLIFE AND FISH LAWS.

Article 1.

General Provisions.

Article 2.

Hunting and Trapping.

Article 2.1.

Wildlife Violator Compact.

Article 3.

Fishing Laws.

Article 4.

Possession, Transportation, and Sale of Game and Fish.

Article 5.

Penalties in General.

Article 6.

Endangered Species.

Article 7.

Nonindigenous Aquatic Nuisance Species Act.

ARTICLE 1.

GENERAL PROVISIONS.

§ 29.1-500: Reserved.

§ 29.1-501. Promulgation of regulations; publication of proposed regulations or change therein; validation; evidentiary nature of publication.

A. The Board may promulgate regulations pertaining to the hunting, taking, capture, killing, possession, sale, purchase, and transportation of any wild bird, wild animal, or inland water fish, and the feeding of any game, game animals, or furbearing animals as defined in § 29.1-100, or the feeding of any wildlife that results in property damage, endangers any person or wildlife, or creates a public health concern.

B. The full text or an informative summary of any proposed regulation or change in the regulations shall be published not less than fifteen nor more than thirty days before it may be acted upon. The publication shall name the time and place that the specified matters will be taken up, at which time any interested citizen shall be heard. If the proposed regulation or change in the regulations is of local application, the publication shall appear in a newspaper published in or within reasonable proximity to the affected locality. However, if the proposed regulation or change in the regulations is of statewide application, the publication shall be made in a sufficient number of newspapers having a general circulation throughout the entire Commonwealth.

C. A copy of proposed regulations or a change in the regulations, of either local application or statewide application, shall be published in the Virginia Register of Regulations pursuant to § 2.2-4031.

D. Prima facie evidence of any regulation may be given in all courts and proceedings by the production of a copy of the regulation, which shall be certified by the Director or his deputy.

History.
Code 1950, § 29-126; 1956, c. 178; 1960, c. 539; 1962, c. 478; 1974, c. 56; 1987, c. 488; 2010, c. 184.

§ 29.1-502. Adoption of regulations.

The board may adopt regulations and amendments to regulations upon completion of all applicable hearing and notice requirements. The Board shall file the regulations with the Registrar of Regulations pursuant to § 2.2-4103.

History.
Code 1950, § 29-127; 1974, c. 56; 1979, c. 264; 1987, c. 488.

§ 29.1-503: Repealed by Acts 1996, c. 9.

§ 29.1-504. Annual publication of laws and regulations.

All laws relating to hunting, fishing and trapping, together with the regulations of the Board, of both general and local application, shall be published annually by the Department in a handbook or pamphlet. The courts of the Commonwealth shall take judicial notice of all laws and regulations contained in such publication.

History.
1952, c. 608, § 29-128.1; 1979, c. 264; 1987, c. 488.

§ 29.1-505. Penalty for violation of regulations.

It shall be a misdemeanor to violate any regulation promulgated pursuant to this title. Any person violating such a regulation shall be guilty of a Class 3 misdemeanor unless another penalty is specified.

History.
Code 1950, § 29-129; 1987, c. 488; 1988, c. 19.

§ 29.1-505.1. Conspiracy; penalty.

If any person conspires with another to commit any offense defined in this title or any of the regulations of the Board of Game and Inland Fisheries, and one or more such persons does any act to effect the object of the conspiracy, he shall be guilty of conspiracy to commit the underlying offense and shall be subject to the same punishment prescribed for the offense the commission of which was the object of the conspiracy.

History.
1989, c. 362.

§ 29.1-506. Prescribing seasons and bag limits for taking fish and game.

After careful study of each species of wild bird, animal and fish within the jurisdiction of the Board in cities and counties of the Commonwealth, the Board shall have the power to prescribe the seasons and bag limits for hunting, fishing, trapping or otherwise taking such wild birds, animals and fish by regulation adopted as provided in this article.

History.
Code 1950, § 29-129.1; 1950, p. 411; 1952, c. 619; 1960, c. 537; 1970, c. 239; 1987, c. 488.

§ 29.1-507. Closing or shortening open season.

The Board may close or shorten the open season in any county or city (i) whenever extreme weather threatens the welfare of wild birds, wild animals or fish; (ii) whenever such wild birds, wild animals or fish have been seriously affected by adverse weather conditions; (iii) when investigation of the Board shows that there is an unusual scarcity of any species or; (iv) when there is substantial demand from any county or city. The Board shall immediately give notice of any closing or shortening of an open season by publishing the announcement in one or more newspapers having a general circulation in the county or city affected. The notice shall be published at least three days before the action becomes effective.

History.
Code 1950, § 29-130; 1987, c. 488.

§ 29.1-508. Board to prescribe seasons, bag limits and methods of taking and killing fish and game on lands and waters owned or controlled by Board.

The Board is hereby authorized to adopt rules and regulations to prescribe and enforce the seasons, bag limits and methods of taking fish and game on lands and waters owned by the Board and on lands owned by others but controlled by the Board.

History.
1960, c. 538, § 29-130.1; 1987, c. 488.

§ 29.1-508.1. Use of drugs on vertebrate wildlife.

A. Without written authorization from the Director or his designee, it is unlawful to administer any drug to any vertebrate wildlife, except in accordance with a permit issued under the provisions of this title or regulations adopted by the Board. This prohibition shall include, but not be limited to, drugs used for fertility control, disease prevention or treatment, immobilization, or growth stimulation. Nothing in this section shall prohibit the treatment of sick or injured wild animals by licensed veterinarians or permitted wildlife rehabilitators. This section shall not limit employees of agencies of the Commonwealth, the United States, or local animal control officers in the performance of their official duties related to public health, wildlife management, or wildlife removal. For the purposes of this section, the term "drug" means any chemical substance, other than food, that affects the structure or biological function of wildlife species.

B. The Department may take possession and dispose of any vertebrate wildlife if it believes that drugs have been administered to such wildlife in violation of this section.

C. Any person violating this section is guilty of a Class 2 misdemeanor.

History.
2004, c. 171.

§ 29.1-509. Duty of care and liability for damages of landowners to hunters, fishermen, sightseers, etc.

A. For the purpose of this section:

"Fee" means any payment or payments of money to a landowner for use of the premises or in order to engage in any activity described in subsections B and C, but does not include license fees, insurance fees, handling fees, transaction fees, administrative fees, rentals or similar fees received by a landowner from governmental, not-for-profit, or private sources, or payments received by a landowner for rights of ingress and egress or from incidental sales of forest products to an individual for his personal use, or any action taken by another to improve the land or access to the land for the purposes set forth in subsections B and C or remedying damage caused by such uses.

"Land" or *"premises"* means real property or right-of-way, whether rural or urban, waters, boats, private ways, natural growth, trees, railroad property, railroad right-of-way, utility corridor, and any build-

Game and Inland Fisheries

ing or structure which might be located on such real property, waters, boats, private ways and natural growth.

"Landowner" means the legal title holder, any easement holder, lessee, occupant or any other person in control of land or premises, including railroad rights-of-way.

"Low-head dam" means a dam that is built across a river or stream for the purpose of impounding water where the impoundment, at normal flow levels, is completely within the banks, and all flow passes directly over the entire dam structure within the banks, excluding abutments, to a natural channel downstream.

B. A landowner shall owe no duty of care to keep land or premises safe for entry or use by others for hunting, fishing, trapping, camping, participation in water sports, boating, hiking, rock climbing, sightseeing, hang gliding, skydiving, horseback riding, foxhunting, racing, bicycle riding or collecting, gathering, cutting or removing firewood, for any other recreational use, for ingress and egress over such premises to permit passage to other property used for recreational purposes or for use of an easement granted to the Commonwealth or any agency thereof or any not-for-profit organization granted tax-exempt status under § 501(c)(3) of the Internal Revenue Code to permit public passage across such land for access to a public park, historic site, or other public recreational area. No landowner shall be required to give any warning of hazardous conditions or uses of, structures on, or activities on such land or premises to any person entering on the land or premises for such purposes, except as provided in subsection D. The provisions of this subsection apply without regard to whether the landowner has given permission to a person to use their land for recreational purposes.

C. Any landowner who gives permission, express or implied, to another person to hunt, fish, launch and retrieve boats, swim, ride, foxhunt, trap, camp, hike, bicycle, rock climb, hang glide, skydive, sightsee, engage in races, to collect, gather, cut or remove forest products upon land or premises for the personal use of such person, or for the use of an easement or license as set forth in subsection B does not thereby:

1. Impliedly or expressly represent that the premises are safe for such purposes; or

2. Constitute the person to whom such permission has been granted an invitee or licensee to whom a duty of care is owed; or

3. Assume responsibility for or incur liability for any intentional or negligent acts of such person or any other person, except as provided in subsection D.

D. Nothing contained in this section, except as provided in subsection E, shall limit the liability of a landowner which may otherwise arise or exist by reason of his gross negligence or willful or malicious failure to guard or warn against a dangerous condition, use, structure, or activity. The provisions of this section shall not limit the liability of a landowner which may otherwise arise or exist when the landowner receives a fee for use of the premises or to engage in any activity described in subsections B and C. Nothing contained in this section shall relieve any sponsor or operator of any sporting event or competition including but not limited to a race or triathlon of the duty to exercise ordinary care in such events. Nothing contained in this section shall limit the liability of an owner of a low-head dam who fails to implement safety measures described in subsection F.

E. For purposes of this section, whenever any person enters into an agreement with, or grants an easement or license to, the Commonwealth or any agency thereof, any locality, any not-for-profit organization granted tax-exempt status under § 501(c)(3) of the Internal Revenue Code, or any local or regional authority created by law for public park, historic site or recreational purposes, concerning the use of, or access over, his land by the public for any of the purposes enumerated in subsections B and C, the government, agency locality, not-for-profit organization, or authority with which the agreement is made shall indemnify and hold the landowner harmless from all liability and be responsible for providing, or for paying the cost of, all reasonable legal services required by any person entitled to the benefit of this section as the result of a claim or suit attempting to impose liability. Any action against the Commonwealth, or any agency thereof, for negligence arising out of a use of land or railroad rights-of-way covered by this section shall be subject to the provisions of the Virginia Tort Claims Act (§ 8.01-195.1 et seq.). Any provisions in a lease or other agreement which purports to waive the benefits of this section shall be invalid, and any action against any county, city, town, or local or regional authority shall be subject to the provisions of § 15.2-1809, where applicable.

F. Any owner of a low-head dam may mark the areas above and below the dam and on the banks immediately adjacent to the dam with signs and buoys of a design and content, in accordance with the regulations of the Board, to warn the swimming, fishing, and boating public of the hazards posed by the dam. Any owner of a low-head dam who marks a low-head dam in accordance with this subsection shall be deemed to have met the duty of care for warning the public of the hazards posed by the dam. Any owner of a low-head dam who fails to mark a low-head dam in accordance with this subsection shall be presumed not to have met the duty of care for warning the public of the hazards posed by the dam.

History.

Code 1950, §§ 8-654.2, 29-130.2; 1962, c. 545; 1964, c. 435; 1977, c. 624; 1979, c. 276; 1980, c. 560; 1982, c. 29; 1983, c. 283; 1987, c. 488; 1988, c. 191; 1989, cc. 26, 500, 505; 1990, cc. 799, 808; 1991, c. 305; 1992, c. 285; 1994, c. 544; 2007, c. 664; 2010, c. 43.

ARTICLE 2.
HUNTING AND TRAPPING.

§ 29.1-510. Big game; small game.

For the purpose of the hunting and trapping laws of the Commonwealth, big game shall include bear and deer and small game shall include other game animals and all game birds.

History.
Code 1950, § 29-132; 1954, c. 228; 1958, c. 165; 1960, c. 537; 1962, c. 469; 1974, c. 302; 1987, c. 488; 1988, c. 158.

§ 29.1-511. Open season on nuisance species.

There shall be a continuous open season for killing nuisance species of wild birds and wild animals as defined in § 29.1-100.

History.
Code 1950, § 29-133; 1958, c. 165; 1974, c. 302; 1987, c. 488.

§ 29.1-512. Closed season on other species.

There shall be a continuous closed hunting season on all birds and wild animals which are not nuisance species as defined in § 29.1-100, except as provided by law.

History.
Code 1950, § 29-134; 1974, c. 302; 1987, c. 488.

§ 29.1-513. Daily and season bag limits as promulgated by Board regulations.

It shall be lawful to hunt wild birds and wild animals specified in this article within any applicable daily and season bag limits during the open seasons as may be provided by Board regulations.

History.
Code 1950, § 29-135; 1960, c. 590; 1987, c. 488.

§ 29.1-514. Nonmigratory game birds.

A. The following nonmigratory game birds may be hunted during prescribed open seasons:
Birds introduced by the Board.
Bobwhite quail.
Grouse.
Pheasants.
Turkey.

B. The following provisions shall also be applicable to the raising and hunting of the particular nonmigratory game bird species listed:

1. The Board may issue a permit to raise or purchase pheasants which shall entitle the permittee to release pheasants raised or purchased by him on land owned or leased by him, and such pheasants may be hunted under rules and regulations promulgated by the Board.

2. The Board may open the season, including Sunday operation, on pen-raised game birds on controlled shooting areas licensed under Chapter 6 (§ 29.1-600 et seq.) of this title under regulations as may be promulgated by the Board. However, the regulations promulgated by the Board shall not allow Sunday operation in Augusta County, or in any county or city which prohibits Sunday operation by ordinance.

Prior to obtaining a license from the Board to operate a commercially operated controlled shooting area, an applicant shall (i) notify adjoining landowners of the proposed use and (ii) obtain approval from the governing body of the county, city or town that such activity is permitted under existing ordinances. The requirements of clauses (i) and (ii) shall only apply to applications filed on or after July 1, 1993, for commercially operated controlled shooting area licenses issued under Chapter 6 of this title and shall not apply to existing preserve licenses or renewals issued for the shooting of pen raised game birds.

History.
Code 1950, § 29-136; 1954, c. 228; 1956, c. 375; 1960, c. 590; 1987, c. 488; 1993, c. 87; 2007, c. 813.

§ 29.1-515. Migratory game birds.

Migratory game birds may be hunted in accordance with regulations of the Board. Board regulations shall conform to the regulations of the United States government insofar as open seasons and bag limits are concerned.

History.
Code 1950, § 29-137; 1987, c. 488.

§ 29.1-516. Game animals.

The following provisions shall apply to the killing and hunting of the particular game animals listed:

Black bear. — A black bear may be killed by any person when (i) it is inflicting or attempting to inflict injury to a person or (ii) when a person is in pursuit of the bear commenced immediately after the commission of such offense. Any person killing a bear under this provision shall immediately report the killing to a state conservation police officer.

Deer. — It is unlawful for a person to kill or attempt to kill a deer in the water of any stream, lake, or pond. It is unlawful to hunt deer with dogs in the counties west of the Blue Ridge Mountains.

Fox. — There is a continuous open season for hunting with dogs only. The hunting or pursuit of foxes shall mean the actual following of the dogs while in pursuit of a fox or foxes or the managing of the dog or dogs, including by the use of a Global Positioning System (GPS) or other electronic tracking device, while the fox or foxes are being hunted or pursued. Nothing in this section shall preclude the managing of dogs by the use of a GPS or other

Game and Inland Fisheries

electronic tracking device by hunters when hunting other game animals. Foxes may be killed at any time by the owner or tenant of any land when such animals are doing damage to domestic stock or fowl.

Rabbits and squirrels. — It is unlawful to kill rabbits or squirrels during the closed season; however, the following persons may kill rabbits or squirrels for their own use during the closed season:

1. A landowner and members of his immediate family;
2. Resident members of hunt clubs who own the land in fee, either jointly or through a holding company;
3. Tenants residing on the premises, with the written permission of the landowner.

When such animals are committing substantial damage to fruit trees, gardens, crops, or other property, the owner of the premises may kill the animals or have them killed under a permit obtained from the conservation police officer.

History.

Code 1950, § 29-138; 1960, c. 590; 1962, c. 469; 1977, c. 377; 1980, c. 271; 1984, c. 6; 1987, c. 488; 2007, c. 87; 2013, c. 345.

§ 29.1-516.1. Using tracking dogs to retrieve bears or deer.

Tracking dogs maintained and controlled on a lead may be used to find a wounded or dead bear or deer statewide during any archery, muzzleloader, or firearm bear or deer hunting season, or within 24 hours of the end of such season, provided that those who are involved in the retrieval effort have permission to hunt on or to access the land being searched and do not have any weapons in their possession.

History.

2011, c. 459.

§ 29.1-517. Trapping and shooting of fur-bearing animals during closed season.

A landowner may trap or shoot fur-bearing animals upon his own land during closed season when these animals are causing damage to crops or property, or are posing a threat to human health or safety, or are otherwise causing a nuisance.

History.

Code 1950, § 29-139; 1964, c. 207; 1987, c. 488; 2004, c. 421; 2007, c. 87; 2013, c. 349.

§ 29.1-518. When killing of beaver permitted.

When beaver are damaging crops or lands, the owner of the premises, his agent or tenant, may kill the animals, or have them killed.

History.

1958, c. 147, § 29-139.1; 1987, c. 488; 2004, c. 421.

§ 29.1-519. Guns, pistols, revolvers, etc., which may be used; penalty.

A. All wild birds and wild animals may be hunted with the following weapons unless shooting is expressly prohibited:

1. A shotgun or muzzleloading shotgun not larger than 10 gauge;
2. An automatic-loading or hand-operated repeating shotgun capable of holding not more than three shells the magazine of which has been cut off or plugged with a one-piece filler incapable of removal through the loading end, so as to reduce the capacity of the gun to not more than three shells at one time in the magazine and chamber combined, unless otherwise allowed by Board regulations;
3. A rifle, a muzzleloading rifle, or an air rifle;
4. A bow and arrow;
5. [Expired.]
6. A crossbow, which is a type of bow and arrow, in accordance with the provisions of § 29.1-306; and
7. A slingshot, except when hunting deer, bear, elk, or turkey.

B. A pistol, muzzleloading pistol, or revolver may be used to hunt nuisance species of birds and animals.

C. In the counties west of the Blue Ridge Mountains, and counties east of the Blue Ridge where rifles of a caliber larger than.22 caliber may be used for hunting wild birds and animals, game birds and animals may be hunted with pistols or revolvers firing cartridges rated in manufacturers' tables at 350 foot pounds of energy or greater and under the same restrictions and conditions as apply to rifles, provided that no cartridge shall be used with a bullet of less than.23 caliber. In no event shall pistols or revolvers firing cartridges rated in manufacturers' tables at 350 foot pounds of energy or greater be used if rifles of a caliber larger than.22 caliber are not authorized for hunting purposes.

D. The use of muzzleloading pistols and.22 caliber rimfire handguns is permitted for hunting small game where.22 caliber rifles are permitted.

E. The use of muzzleloading pistols of.45 caliber or larger is permitted for hunting big game where and in those seasons when the use of muzzleloading rifles is permitted. The Board may adopt regulations that specify the types of muzzleloading pistols and the projectiles and propellants that shall be permitted.

F. The hunting of wild birds and wild animals with fully automatic firearms, defined as a machine gun in § 18.2-288, is prohibited.

G. The hunting of wild birds or wild animals with (i) weapons other than those authorized by this section or (ii) weapons that have been prohibited by this section is punishable as a Class 3 misdemeanor.

History.

Code 1950, § 29-140; 1962, c. 469; 1964, c. 441; 1974, cc. 108, 302; 1977, c. 377; 1983, c. 166; 1987, c. 488; 1988, c. 162; 1989, c. 421;

1993, c. 684; 1998, c. 144; 2002, c. 157; 2005, c. 8; 2007, c. 643; 2014, cc. 117, 136; 2016, c. 486.

§ 29.1-520. Times for hunting.

A. Nonmigratory game birds and game animals may be hunted from one-half hour before sunrise to one-half hour after sunset. Bears may be hunted without capturing or taking from 4:00 a.m. until 10:00 p.m. during bear hound training season.

B. Fur-bearing animals and nuisance species of birds and animals may be hunted by day or by night, except that muskrats may be hunted by day only.

C. A violation of this section shall be punishable as a Class 3 misdemeanor.

History.

Code 1950, §§ 29-141, 29-142; 1962, c. 469; 1974, c. 302; 1987, c. 488; 1989, c. 421; 2008, c. 31; 2012, cc. 69, 226.

§ 29.1-521. (Effective until July 1, 2017) Unlawful to hunt, trap, possess, sell, or transport wild birds and wild animals except as permitted; exception; penalty.

A. The following shall be unlawful:

1. To hunt or kill any wild bird or wild animal, including any nuisance species, with a gun, firearm, or other weapon, or to hunt or kill any deer or bear with a gun, firearm, or other weapon with the aid or assistance of dogs, on Sunday. The provision of this subdivision that prohibits the hunting or killing of any wild bird or wild animal, including nuisance species, on Sunday shall not apply to (i) any person who hunts or kills raccoons, which may be hunted until 2:00 a.m. on Sunday mornings; (ii) any person who hunts or kills birds in the family Rallidae or waterfowl, subject to geographical limitations established by the Director and except within 200 yards of a place of worship or any accessory structure thereof; or (iii) any landowner or member of his family or any person with written permission from the landowner who hunts or kills any wild bird or wild animal, including any nuisance species, on the landowner's property, except within 200 yards of a place of worship or any accessory structure thereof. However, a person lawfully carrying a gun, firearm, or other weapon on Sunday in an area that could be used for hunting shall not be presumed to be hunting on Sunday, absent evidence to the contrary.

2. To destroy or molest the nest, eggs, dens, or young of any wild bird or wild animal, except nuisance species, at any time without a permit as required by law.

3. To hunt or attempt to kill or trap any species of wild bird or wild animal after having obtained the daily bag or season limit during such day or season. However, any properly licensed person, or a person exempt from having to obtain a license, who has obtained such daily bag or season limit while hunting may assist others who are hunting game by calling game, retrieving game, handling dogs, or conducting drives if the weapon in his possession is an unloaded firearm, a bow without a nocked arrow, or an unloaded crossbow. Any properly licensed person, or person exempt from having to obtain a license, who has obtained such season limit prior to commencement of the hunt may assist others who are hunting game by calling game, retrieving game, handling dogs, or conducting drives, provided he does not have a firearm, bow, or crossbow in his possession.

4. To knowingly occupy any baited blind or other baited place for the purpose of taking or attempting to take any wild bird or wild animal or to put out bait or salt for any wild bird or wild animal for the purpose of taking or killing it. There shall be a rebuttable presumption that a person charged with violating this subdivision knows that he is occupying a baited blind or other baited place for the purpose of taking or attempting to take any wild bird or wild animal. However, this shall not apply to baiting nuisance species of animals and birds, or to baiting traps for the purpose of taking fur-bearing animals that may be lawfully trapped.

5. To kill or capture any wild bird or wild animal adjacent to any area while a field or forest fire is in progress.

6. To shoot or attempt to take any wild bird or wild animal from an automobile or other vehicle, except as provided in § 29.1-521.3.

7. To set a trap of any kind on the lands or waters of another without attaching to the trap: (i) the name and address of the trapper; or (ii) an identification number issued by the Department.

8. To set a trap where it would be likely to injure persons, dogs, stock, or fowl.

9. To fail to visit all traps once each day and remove all animals caught, and immediately report to the landowner as to stock, dogs, or fowl that are caught and the date. However, the Director or his designee may authorize employees of federal, state, and local government agencies, and persons holding a valid Commercial Nuisance Animal Permit issued by the Department, to visit body-gripping traps that are completely submerged at least once every 72 hours, and the Board may adopt regulations permitting trappers to visit traps less frequently under specified conditions. The Board shall adopt regulations permitting trappers to use remote trap-checking technology to check traps under specified conditions.

10. To hunt, trap, take, capture, kill, attempt to take, capture, or kill, possess, deliver for transportation, transport, cause to be transported, by any means whatever, receive for transportation or export, or import, at any time or in any manner, any wild bird or wild animal or the carcass or any part thereof, except as specifically permitted by law and only by the manner or means and within the numbers stated. However, the provisions of this section shall not be construed to prohibit (i) the use or

transportation of legally taken turkey carcasses, or portions thereof, for the purposes of making or selling turkey callers or using turkey feathers or toes for making tools or utensils or selling such tools or utensils; (ii) the manufacture or sale of implements, including tools or utensils made from legally harvested deer skeletal parts, including antlers; (iii) the possession of shed antlers; or (iv) the possession, manufacture, or sale of other parts or implements authorized by regulations adopted by the Board.

11. To offer for sale, sell, offer to purchase, or purchase, at any time or in any manner, any wild bird or wild animal or the carcass or any part thereof, except as specifically permitted by law, including subsection D of § 29.1-553. However, any nonprofit organization exempt from taxation under § 501(c)(3) of the Internal Revenue Code that is (i) organized to provide wild game as food to the hungry and (ii) authorized by the Department to possess, transport, and distribute donated or unclaimed meat to the hungry may pay a processing fee in order to obtain such meat. Such fee shall not exceed the actual cost for processing the meat. In addition, any nonprofit organization exempt from taxation under § 501(c)(3) of the Internal Revenue Code that is (a) organized to support wildlife habitat conservation and (b) approved by the Department shall be allowed to offer wildlife mounts that have undergone the taxidermy process for sale in conjunction with fundraising activities. A violation of this subdivision shall be punishable as provided in § 29.1-553.

B. Notwithstanding any other provision of this article, any American Indian who produces verification that he is an enrolled member of a tribe recognized by the Commonwealth, another state, or the U.S. government, may possess, offer for sale, or sell to another American Indian, or offer to purchase or purchase from another American Indian, parts of legally obtained fur-bearing animals, nonmigratory game birds, and game animals, except bear. Such legally obtained parts shall include antlers, hooves, feathers, claws, and bones.

"Verification" as used in this subsection shall include (i) display of a valid tribal identification card, (ii) confirmation through a central tribal registry, (iii) a letter from a tribal chief or council, or (iv) certification from a tribal office that the person is an enrolled member of the tribe.

C. Notwithstanding any other provision of this chapter, the Department may authorize the use of snake exclusion devices by public utilities at their transmission or distribution facilities and the incidental taking of snakes resulting from the use of such devices.

D. A violation of subdivisions A 1 through 10 shall be punishable as a Class 3 misdemeanor.

History.

Code 1950, § 29-143; 1962, c. 469; 1974, c. 302; 1979, c. 264; 1987, c. 488; 1988, c. 175; 1989, c. 421; 1990, c. 237; 1994, cc. 244, 436; 1997, c. 249; 1998, c. 415; 2000, c. 13; 2001, cc. 26, 60; 2004, c. 862; 2005, cc. 170, 533, 534; 2006, cc. 20, 215; 2008, cc. 160, 161; 2010, c. 10; 2014, cc. 152, 482; 2015, c. 47; 2016, cc. 10, 62, 121, 372.

§ 29.1-521. (Effective July 1, 2017) Unlawful to hunt, trap, possess, sell, or transport wild birds and wild animals except as permitted; exception; penalty.

A. The following shall be unlawful:

1. To hunt or kill any wild bird or wild animal, including any nuisance species, with a gun, firearm, or other weapon, or to hunt or kill any deer or bear with a gun, firearm, or other weapon with the aid or assistance of dogs, on Sunday. The provision of this subdivision that prohibits the hunting or killing of any wild bird or wild animal, including nuisance species, on Sunday shall not apply to (i) any person who hunts or kills raccoons, which may be hunted until 2:00 a.m. on Sunday mornings; (ii) any person who hunts or kills birds in the family Rallidae or waterfowl, subject to geographical limitations established by the Director and except within 200 yards of a place of worship or any accessory structure thereof; or (iii) any landowner or member of his family or any person with written permission from the landowner who hunts or kills any wild bird or wild animal, including any nuisance species, on the landowner's property, except within 200 yards of a place of worship or any accessory structure thereof. However, a person lawfully carrying a gun, firearm, or other weapon on Sunday in an area that could be used for hunting shall not be presumed to be hunting on Sunday, absent evidence to the contrary.

2. To destroy or molest the nest, eggs, dens, or young of any wild bird or wild animal, except nuisance species, at any time without a permit as required by law.

3. To hunt or attempt to kill or trap any species of wild bird or wild animal after having obtained the daily bag or season limit during such day or season. However, any properly licensed person, or a person exempt from having to obtain a license, who has obtained such daily bag or season limit while hunting may assist others who are hunting game by calling game, retrieving game, handling dogs, or conducting drives if the weapon in his possession is an unloaded firearm, a bow without a nocked arrow, or an unloaded crossbow. Any properly licensed person, or person exempt from having to obtain a license, who has obtained such season limit prior to commencement of the hunt may assist others who are hunting game by calling game, retrieving game, handling dogs, or conducting drives, provided he does not have a firearm, bow, or crossbow in his possession.

4. To knowingly occupy any baited blind or other baited place for the purpose of taking or attempting to take any wild bird or wild animal or to put out bait or salt for any wild bird or wild animal for the purpose of taking or killing it. There shall be a rebuttable presumption that a person charged with

violating this subdivision knows that he is occupying a baited blind or other baited place for the purpose of taking or attempting to take any wild bird or wild animal. However, this shall not apply to baiting nuisance species of animals and birds, or to baiting traps for the purpose of taking fur-bearing animals that may be lawfully trapped.

5. To kill or capture any wild bird or wild animal adjacent to any area while a field or forest fire is in progress.

6. To shoot or attempt to take any wild bird or wild animal from an automobile or other vehicle, except as provided in § 29.1-521.3.

7. To set a trap of any kind on the lands or waters of another without attaching to the trap: (i) the name and address of the trapper; or (ii) an identification number issued by the Department.

8. To set a trap where it would be likely to injure persons, dogs, stock, or fowl.

9. To fail to visit all traps once each day and remove all animals caught, and immediately report to the landowner as to stock, dogs, or fowl that are caught and the date. However, the Director or his designee may authorize employees of federal, state, and local government agencies, and persons holding a valid Commercial Nuisance Animal Permit issued by the Department, to visit body-gripping traps that are completely submerged at least once every 72 hours, and the Board may adopt regulations permitting trappers to visit traps less frequently under specified conditions. The Board shall adopt regulations permitting trappers to use remote trap-checking technology to check traps under specified conditions.

10. To hunt, trap, take, capture, kill, attempt to take, capture, or kill, possess, deliver for transportation, transport, cause to be transported, by any means whatever, receive for transportation or export, or import, at any time or in any manner, any wild bird or wild animal or the carcass or any part thereof, except as specifically permitted by law and only by the manner or means and within the numbers stated. However, the provisions of this section shall not be construed to prohibit the (i) use or transportation of legally taken turkey carcasses, or portions thereof, for the purposes of making or selling turkey callers; (ii) the manufacture or sale of implements, including tools or utensils made from legally harvested deer skeletal parts, including antlers; (iii) the possession of shed antlers; or (iv) the possession, manufacture, or sale of other parts or implements authorized by regulations adopted by the Board.

11. To offer for sale, sell, offer to purchase, or purchase, at any time or in any manner, any wild bird or wild animal or the carcass or any part thereof, except as specifically permitted by law, including subsection D of § 29.1-553. However, any nonprofit organization exempt from taxation under § 501(c)(3) of the Internal Revenue Code that is (i) organized to provide wild game as food to the hungry and (ii) authorized by the Department to possess, transport, and distribute donated or unclaimed meat to the hungry may pay a processing fee in order to obtain such meat. Such fee shall not exceed the actual cost for processing the meat. In addition, any nonprofit organization exempt from taxation under § 501(c)(3) of the Internal Revenue Code that is (a) organized to support wildlife habitat conservation and (b) approved by the Department shall be allowed to offer wildlife mounts that have undergone the taxidermy process for sale in conjunction with fundraising activities. A violation of this subdivision shall be punishable as provided in § 29.1-553.

B. Notwithstanding any other provision of this article, any American Indian who produces verification that he is an enrolled member of a tribe recognized by the Commonwealth, another state, or the U.S. government, may possess, offer for sale, or sell to another American Indian, or offer to purchase or purchase from another American Indian, parts of legally obtained fur-bearing animals, nonmigratory game birds, and game animals, except bear. Such legally obtained parts shall include antlers, hooves, feathers, claws, and bones.

"Verification" as used in this section shall include (i) display of a valid tribal identification card, (ii) confirmation through a central tribal registry, (iii) a letter from a tribal chief or council, or (iv) certification from a tribal office that the person is an enrolled member of the tribe.

C. Notwithstanding any other provision of this chapter, the Department may authorize the use of snake exclusion devices by public utilities at their transmission or distribution facilities and the incidental taking of snakes resulting from the use of such devices.

D. A violation of subdivisions A 1 through 10 shall be punishable as a Class 3 misdemeanor.

History.

Code 1950, § 29-143; 1962, c. 469; 1974, c. 302; 1979, c. 264; 1987, c. 488; 1988, c. 175; 1989, c. 421; 1990, c. 237; 1994, cc. 244, 436; 1997, c. 249; 1998, c. 415; 2000, c. 13; 2001, cc. 26, 60; 2004, c. 862; 2005, cc. 170, 533, 534; 2006, cc. 20, 215; 2008, cc. 160, 161; 2010, c. 10; 2014, cc. 152, 482; 2015, c. 47; 2016, cc. 10, 62, 372.

§ 29.1-521.1. Willfully impeding hunting or trapping; penalty.

A. It is unlawful to willfully and intentionally impede the lawful hunting or trapping of wild birds or wild animals.

B. It is unlawful for any person or his agent to knowingly and intentionally facilitate or attempt to cause a violation of subdivision A 4 of § 29.1-521 by putting out bait or salt for any wildlife in any place used or occupied by hunters to hunt wild birds or wild animals.

C. Any person convicted of a violation of this section is guilty of a Class 3 misdemeanor.

History.

1988, c. 584; 2010, c. 626.

§ 29.1-521.2. Violation of § 18.2-286 while hunting; revocation of license and privileges.

A. Any firearm, crossbow or bow and arrow used by any person to hunt any game bird or game animal in a manner which violates § 18.2-286 may, upon conviction of such person violating § 18.2-286, be forfeited to the Commonwealth by order of the court trying the case. The forfeiture shall be enforced as provided in Chapter 22.1 (§ 19.2-386.1 et seq.) of Title 19.2. The officer or other person seizing the property shall immediately give notice to the attorney for the Commonwealth.

B. The court may revoke the current hunting license and privileges of a person hunting any game bird or game animal in a manner that constitutes a violation of § 18.2-286. The court may prohibit that person from hunting for a period of one to five years. If found hunting during this prohibited period, the person shall be guilty of a Class 2 misdemeanor. Notification of such revocation or prohibition shall be forwarded to the Department pursuant to subsection C of § 18.2-56.1.

History.
1993, c. 322; 1994, c. 18; 2010, c. 183; 2012, cc. 283, 756.

§ 29.1-521.3. Shooting wild birds and wild animals from stationary vehicles by disabled persons.

Any person, upon application to a conservation police officer and the presentation of a medical doctor's written statement based on a physical examination that such person is permanently unable to walk due to impaired mobility, may, in the discretion of the conservation police officer, be issued a permit to shoot wild birds and wild animals from a stationary automobile or other vehicle during established open hunting seasons and in accordance with other laws and regulations. Permits issued pursuant to this section shall (i) be issued on a form provided by the Department, (ii) not authorize shooting from a stationary vehicle less than 50 feet from nor in or across any public road or highway subject to the provisions of § 29.1-526, (iii) be issued for the lifetime of the permittee and be issued only to those persons who are properly licensed to hunt, and (iv) be nontransferable. Any permit found in the possession of any person not entitled to such permit shall be subject to confiscation by a conservation police officer.

History.
1994, c. 244; 2007, c. 87.

§ 29.1-522. Unlawful to kill male deer unless antlers visible above hair.

Unless the Board declares otherwise by regulation, it shall be unlawful to kill male deer in any county or city of the Commonwealth unless the deer has antlers visible above the hair.

History.
Code 1950, § 29-144; 1952, c. 608; 1958, c. 444; 1975, c. 529; 1987, c. 488.

§ 29.1-523. Killing deer by use of certain lights; acts raising presumption of attempt to kill.

Any person who kills or attempts to kill any deer between a half hour after sunset and a half hour before sunrise by use of a light attached to any vehicle or a spotlight or flashlight shall be guilty of a Class 2 misdemeanor. The flashing of a light attached to any vehicle or a spotlight or flashlight from any vehicle between a half hour after sunset and half hour before sunrise by any person or persons, then in possession of a firearm, crossbow, or bow and arrow or speargun, without good cause, shall raise a presumption of an attempt to kill deer in violation of this section. Every person in or on any such vehicle shall be deemed a principal in the second degree and subject to the same punishment as a principal in the first degree. Every person who, in any manner, aids, abets or acts in concert with any person or persons violating this section shall be deemed a principal in the second degree and subject to the same punishment as a principal in the first degree.

In addition to the penalty prescribed herein, the court shall revoke the current hunting license and privileges of the person convicted of violating this section and prohibit that person from hunting for a period of one to five years. If found hunting during this prohibited period, the person shall be guilty of a Class 2 misdemeanor. Notification of such revocation or prohibition shall be forwarded to the Department pursuant to subsections C and D of § 18.2-56.1.

This section shall not apply to persons duly authorized to kill deer according to the provisions of § 29.1-529.

History.
1962, c. 520, § 29-144.2; 1970, c. 79; 1973, c. 369; 1980, cc. 602, 607, § 29-144.4:1; 1987, c. 488; 1994, c. 113; 2002, c. 157; 2010, c. 183.

§ 29.1-523.1. Hunting deer with sights after dark; forfeiture of weapon and sighting device.

A. Any person who kills or attempts to kill any deer between one hour after sunset and one hour before sunrise using a firearm equipped with any sighting device other than iron or open sights shall be guilty of a Class 2 misdemeanor. In addition to this penalty, the court shall revoke the current hunting license and privileges of the person convicted of violating this section and prohibit that person from hunting for a period of one to five years.

Notification of such revocation or prohibition shall be forwarded to the Department pursuant to subsections C and D of § 18.2-56.1.

B. Every firearm equipped with any sighting device other than iron or open sights used with the knowledge or consent of the owner in violation of this section shall be forfeited to the Commonwealth. Upon being condemned as forfeited in proceedings under Chapter 22.1 (§ 19.2-386.1 et seq.) of Title 19.2, the proceeds of the sale shall be disposed of according to law.

This section shall not apply to persons duly authorized to kill deer according to the provisions of § 29.1-529.

History.

2001, c. 112; 2010, c. 183; 2012, cc. 283, 756.

§ 29.1-524. Forfeiture of vehicles and weapons used for killing or attempt to kill.

Every vehicle, firearm, crossbow, bow and arrow, or speargun used with the knowledge or consent of the owner or lienholder thereof, in killing or attempting to kill deer between a half hour after sunset and a half hour before sunrise in violation of § 29.1-523, and every vehicle used in the transportation of the carcass, or any part thereof, of a deer so killed shall be forfeited to the Commonwealth. Upon being condemned as forfeited in proceedings under Chapter 22.1 (§ 19.2-386.1 et seq.) of Title 19.2, the proceeds of sale shall be disposed of according to law.

History.

1962, c. 520, § 29-144.3; 1978, c. 199; 1987, c. 488; 2002, c. 157; 2012, cc. 283, 756.

§ 29.1-525. Employment of lights under certain circumstances upon places used by deer.

A. Any person in any vehicle and then in possession of any firearm, crossbow, bow and arrow or speargun who employs a light attached to the vehicle or a spotlight or flashlight to cast a light beyond the water or surface of the roadway upon any place used by deer shall be guilty of a Class 2 misdemeanor. Every person in or on any such vehicle shall be deemed prima facie a principal in the second degree and subject to the same punishment as a principal in the first degree. This subsection shall not apply to a landowner in possession of a weapon when he is on his own land and is making a bona fide effort to protect his property from damage by deer and not for the purpose of killing deer unless the landowner is in possession of a permit to do so pursuant to the provisions of § 29.1-529.

B. Any person in any motor vehicle who deliberately employs a light attached to such vehicle or a spotlight or flashlight to cast a light beyond the surface of the roadway upon any place used by deer, except upon his own land or upon land on which he has an easement or permission for such purpose, shall be guilty of a Class 4 misdemeanor. Every person in or on any such vehicle shall be deemed prima facie a principal in the second degree and subject to the same punishment as a principal in the first degree.

C. The provisions of subsections A and B shall not apply to activities conducted by a locality pursuant to a permit or written authorization issued by the Department.

D. In addition to the penalties prescribed in subsection A, the court shall revoke the current hunting license and privileges of the person convicted of a violation of subsection A and prohibit the person from hunting for a period of one to five years. In addition to the penalties prescribed in subsection B, the court may revoke the current hunting license and privileges of the person convicted of a violation of subsection B and prohibit that person from hunting for one to five years. If a person convicted of a violation of subsection A or B is found hunting during the prohibited period, the person shall be guilty of a Class 2 misdemeanor. Notification of such revocation or prohibition shall be forwarded to the Department pursuant to subsections C and D of § 18.2-56.1.

History.

1962, c. 520, § 29-144.4; 1973, c. 369; 1974, c. 101; 1980, cc. 602, 607, § 29-144.4:1; 1981, c. 60; 1987, c. 488; 1988, c. 450; 1994, c. 113; 2002, c. 157; 2010, c. 183; 2014, c. 126.

§ 29.1-525.1. Deer enclosures prohibited; exceptions; penalty.

A. It is unlawful to erect a fence that prevents or impedes the free egress of deer from the enclosed area with the intent to confine deer.

B. It is unlawful to hunt deer inside a fenced area that prevents or impedes the free egress of deer.

C. The provisions of subsection A shall not apply to:

1. Local, state or federal public lands on which fences are erected to protect public health or safety;
2. Enclosures permitted by the Department as fallow deer farms or permitted exhibitors holding native deer for educational purposes;
3. Enclosures permitted by the U.S. Department of Agriculture as exhibitors, breeders, or dealers; or
4. Zoos accredited by the American Zoological Association.

D. The provisions of subsection B shall not apply to (i) local, state or federal public lands on which fences are erected to protect public health or safety, or (ii) any person hunting in an enclosure or facility that (a) was constructed prior to July 1, 2001, (b) has been registered with the Department not later than August 1, 2001, and annually thereafter, and (c) has been modified not later than 90 days following registration in a manner approved by the Director or his designee to allow the free egress of deer. Such registration shall not be transferable. The Department shall place information of the initial registration requirement in newspapers of general circulation throughout the Commonwealth. Such enclosures or facilities shall operate using acceptable hunting and wildlife management practices determined by the Director or his designee, including, but not limited to, methods of take, use of dogs, and supplemental feeding. The Director or his designee shall provide the owner of the enclosure or facility with information on what constitutes acceptable hunting and wildlife management practices.

E. Any registered enclosure or facility within which the owners or persons hunting have not followed acceptable hunting wildlife management practices shall have its registration revoked by the Department. Upon revocation of the registration, any person hunting within the enclosure or facility shall be subject to the provisions of subsection B and the penalties imposed under subsection F.

F. Any person who violates this section is guilty of a Class 1 misdemeanor. Any person who is convicted of violating this section shall have his hunting license and privileges suspended by the court for a period of one to five years. In addition, the court may order compensation for replacement for any deer killed be paid to the Department as provided for in § 29.1-551, and may order the owner of the fence to modify the fence to allow the free egress by deer.

History.

2001, c. 856; 2010, c. 183.

§ 29.1-525.2. Fox and coyote enclosures prohibited; penalty.

A. It is unlawful to erect, maintain, or operate an enclosure for the purpose of pursuing, hunting, or killing or attempting to pursue, hunt, or kill any fox or coyote with a dog. For purposes of this section, "enclosure" means a fence or other barrier that is used to prevent or impede the natural egress by any fox or coyote. A person who violates any provision of this subsection is guilty of a Class 1 misdemeanor. This subsection shall not be construed to limit the authority of the Department to enforce other available penalties.

B. This section shall not preclude the pursuing, hunting, or killing of any fox or coyote by a dog in the absence of an enclosure, or the killing of any fox or coyote by a landowner or tenant when the fox or coyote is damaging domestic stock or fowl on the owned or leased land.

C. Until July 1, 2054, the provisions of subsection A shall not apply to any location at which, as of January 1, 2014, a foxhound training preserve existed and was operating under a permit issued by the Department. The Department shall continue to issue or renew permits to existing locations in accordance with this section notwithstanding changes in the identity of the person or entity holding the permit.

D. The regulations governing foxhound training preserves in effect as of January 1, 2014, shall continue in full force and effect, provided, however, that the Department shall adopt regulations by October 1, 2014, to limit the total number of foxes stocked annually in all permitted preserves to 900. The Department shall specify a proportional number of foxes that may be stocked in each permitted preserve based upon the number of acres of the preserve as a percentage of the total acreage of permitted foxhound training preserves. If a preserve ceases to operate, its allocation of foxes from the previous year shall be deducted from the total number of foxes that may be stocked in foxhound training preserves in the Commonwealth.

E. The Department shall not deny a permit to an existing location solely due to recordkeeping failures or other technical violations of the regulations governing foxhound training preserves.

F. The Department shall deny a permit to an existing location if the location voluntarily ceases operation of its foxhound training preserve for a period of 12 consecutive months or longer.

G. Notwithstanding the provisions of § 2.2-4002, the denial of a permit to operate a foxhound training preserve by the Department shall constitute a case decision subject to the Administrative Process Act (§ 2.2-4000 et seq.). If a permittee or owner of a location subject to a permit files a notice of appeal with the Department, the Department shall continue to permit the location until any such appeals have been exhausted and the Department's determination upheld.

History.

2014, c. 605.

§ 29.1-526. Counties and cities may prohibit hunting or trapping near primary and secondary highways.

The governing body of any county or city may prohibit by ordinance the hunting, with a firearm, of any game bird or game animal while the hunting is on or within 100 yards of any primary or secondary highway in such county or city and may provide that any violation of the ordinance shall be a Class 3 misdemeanor. In addition, the governing body of any county or city may prohibit by ordinance the trapping of any game animal or furbearer within fifty feet of the shoulder of any primary or secondary highway in the county or city and may provide that any violation of the ordinance shall be a Class 3 misdemeanor. No such ordinance shall prohibit such trapping where the written permission of the landowner is obtained. It shall be the duty of the governing body enacting an ordinance under the provisions of this section to notify the Director by registered mail no later than May 1 of the year in which the ordinance is to take effect. If the governing body fails to make such notice, the ordinance shall be unenforceable.

For the purpose of this section, the terms "hunt" and "trap" shall not include the necessary crossing of highways for the bona fide purpose of going into or leaving a lawful hunting or trapping area.

History.

1962, c. 141, § 29-144.5; 1964, c. 549; 1977, c. 377; 1982, c. 194; 1987, c. 488; 1989, c. 421.

§ 29.1-527. Counties, cities or towns may prohibit hunting near public schools and county, city, town or regional parks.

The governing body of any county, city or town may prohibit by ordinance, shooting or hunting with a firearm, or prohibit hunters from traversing an area while in possession of a loaded firearm, within 100 yards of any property line of a public school or a county, city, town or regional park. The governing body may, in such ordinance, provide that any violation thereof shall be a Class 4 misdemeanor. Nothing in this section shall give any county, city or town the authority to enforce such an ordinance on lands within a national or state park or forest, or wildlife management area.

History.

1985, c. 485, § 29-144.5:1; 1987, c. 488.

§ 29.1-527.1. Localities may prohibit feeding of migratory and nonmigratory waterfowl.

Upon notice to the Department, any locality may prohibit by ordinance the feeding of migratory and nonmigratory waterfowl in any subdivision or other area of such locality which, in the opinion of the governing body, is so heavily populated as to make the feeding of such waterfowl a threat to public health or the environment. The terms "migratory" and "nonmigratory" waterfowl shall include those waterfowl defined as such in a listing as provided by the Department. The Department shall make available to localities a model ordinance suggested for use by localities. The locality shall post the appropriate signage that designates an area where the ordinance is applicable and shall be solely responsible for enforcement of the ordinance. The penalty for violating such an ordinance shall be a civil fine not to exceed $50.

A locality shall not enact such an ordinance on lands within a national or state park or forest, or wildlife management area.

History.

2004, c. 386.

§ 29.1-527.2. Localities may prohibit feeding of deer.

Any city or town may, by ordinance, prohibit the feeding of deer within its jurisdiction. The Department shall make available to localities a model ordinance suggested for use by localities. The penalty for violating such an ordinance shall be a civil fine not to exceed $50. It shall be the duty of the governing body enacting an ordinance under this section to notify the Director by registered mail of the adoption of such an ordinance.

Any such ordinance shall not apply to agricultural, commercial, noncommercial, or residential plantings; distribution of food to livestock; or wildlife management activities conducted or authorized by the Department. The ordinance shall not limit the authority of the Board to regulate feeding of wildlife consistent with this chapter.

History.

2016, c. 376.

§ 29.1-528. Board to develop model ordinances for hunting with firearms; counties or cities may adopt.

A. The Board shall adopt regulations establishing model ordinances for hunting with firearms that may be adopted by counties or cities. Such model ordinances shall address items including firearm caliber; type of firearm, including rifle, shotgun, or muzzleloader; type of ammunition; and the hunting of groundhogs or coyotes.

B. The governing body of any county or city may, by ordinance, (i) prohibit hunting in such county or city with a shotgun loaded with slugs, or with a rifle of a caliber larger than .22 rimfire; (ii) permit the hunting of groundhogs with a rifle of a caliber larger than .22 rimfire between March 1 and August 31; (iii) permit the use of muzzle-loading rifles during the prescribed open seasons for the hunting of game species; (iv) specify permissible types of ammunition to be used for hunting in the county or city; or (v) permit the hunting of coyotes with a rifle of a caliber larger than .22 rimfire.

C. No such ordinance shall be enforceable unless the governing body notifies the Director by registered mail prior to May 1 of the year in which the ordinance is to take effect.

D. In adopting an ordinance pursuant to the provisions of this section, the governing body of any county or city may provide that any person who violates the provisions of the ordinance is guilty of a Class 3 misdemeanor.

History.

1976, c. 443, § 29-144.6; 1977, cc. 20, 377; 1978, c. 303; 1986, c. 342; 1987, c. 488; 1989, c. 421; 2007, c. 642; 2016, c. 64.

§ 29.1-528.1. Board to develop model ordinances for hunting with bow and arrow; counties or cities may adopt.

A. The Board shall adopt regulations establishing model ordinances for hunting deer with bow and

Game and Inland Fisheries

arrow and crossbows in those counties and cities where there is an overabundance of the deer population, which is creating conflicts between humans and deer, including safety hazards to motorists. The model ordinances shall include (i) the times at which such hunting shall commence and end each day and (ii) the number of deer that can be taken based on analysis performed by the Department.

B. No such ordinance shall be enforceable unless the governing body notifies the Director by registered mail prior to May 1 of the year in which the ordinance is to take effect. Any change jurisdictions may seek in the model ordinance shall be approved by the Board prior to its adoption.

C. In adopting an ordinance pursuant to the provisions of this section, the governing body of any locality may provide that any person who violates the provisions of the ordinance shall be guilty of a Class 3 misdemeanor.

History.
2010, c. 512.

§ 29.1-529. Killing of deer, elk or bear damaging fruit trees, crops, livestock, or personal property; wildlife creating a hazard to aircraft or motor vehicles.

A. Whenever deer, elk or bear are damaging fruit trees, crops, livestock or personal property utilized for commercial agricultural production in the Commonwealth, the owner or lessee of the lands on which such damage is done shall immediately report the damage to the Director or his designee for investigation. If after investigation the Director or his designee finds that deer or bear are responsible for the damage, he shall authorize in writing the owner, lessee or any other person designated by the Director or his designee to kill such deer or bear when they are found upon the land upon which the damages occurred. However, the Director or his designee shall have the option of authorizing nonlethal control measures rather than authorizing the killing of elk or bear, provided that such measures occur within a reasonable period of time; and whenever deer cause damage on parcels of land of five acres or less, except when such acreage is used for commercial agricultural production, the Director or his designee shall have discretion as to whether to issue a written authorization to kill the deer. The Director or his designee may limit such authorization by specifying in writing the number of animals to be killed and duration for which the authorization is effective and may in proximity to residential areas and under other appropriate circumstances limit or prohibit the authorization between 11:00 p.m. and one-half hour before sunrise of the following day. The Director or his designees issuing these authorizations shall specify in writing that only antlerless deer shall be killed, unless the Director or his designee determines that there is clear and convincing evidence that the damage was done by deer with antlers. Any owner or lessee of land who has been issued a written authorization shall not be issued an authorization in subsequent years unless he can demonstrate to the satisfaction of the Director or his designee that during the period following the prior authorization, the owner or his designee has hunted bear or deer on the land for which he received a previous authorization.

B. Subject to the provisions of subsection A, the Director or his designee may issue a written authorization to kill deer causing damage to residential plants, whether ornamental, noncommercial agricultural, or other types of residential plants. The Director may charge a fee not to exceed actual costs. The holder of this written authorization shall be subject to local ordinances, including those regulating the discharge of firearms.

C. Whenever wildlife is creating a hazard to the operation of any aircraft or to the facilities connected with the operation of aircraft, the person or persons responsible for the safe operation of the aircraft or facilities shall report such fact to the Director or his designee for investigation. If after investigation the Director or his designee finds that wildlife is creating a hazard, he shall authorize such person or persons or their representatives to kill wildlife when the wildlife is found to be creating such a hazard. As used in this subsection, the term "wildlife" shall not include any federally protected species.

D. Whenever deer are creating a hazard to the operation of motor vehicle traffic within the corporate limits of any city or town, the operator of a motor vehicle or chief law-enforcement officer of the city or town may report such fact to the Director or his designee for investigation. If after investigation the Director or his designee finds that deer are creating a hazard within such city or town, he may authorize responsible persons, or their representatives, to kill the deer when they are found to be creating such a hazard.

E. Whenever deer are damaging property in a locality in which deer herd population reduction has been recommended in the current Deer Management Plan adopted by the Board, the owner or lessee of the lands on which such damage is being done may report such damage to the Director or his designee for investigation. If after investigation the Director or his designee finds that deer are responsible for the damage, he may authorize in writing the owner, lessee or any other person designated by the Director or his designee to kill such deer when they are found upon the land upon which the damages occurred. The Director or his designee also may limit such authorization by specifying in writing the number of animals to be killed and the period of time for which the authorization is effective. The requirement in subsection A of this section, that an owner or lessee of land demonstrate that during the period following the prior authorization deer or bear have been hunted on his land, shall not apply to any locality that conducts a deer population control program authorized by the Department.

F. The Director or his designee may revoke or refuse to reissue any authorization granted under this section when it has been shown by a preponderance of the evidence that an abuse of the authorization has occurred. Such evidence may include a complaint filed by any person with the Department alleging that an abuse of the written authorization has occurred. Any person aggrieved by the issuance, denial or revocation of a written authorization can appeal the decision to the Department of Game and Inland Fisheries. Any person convicted of violating any provision of the hunting and trapping laws and regulations shall be entitled to receive written authorization to kill deer or bear. However, such person shall not (i) be designated as a shooter nor (ii) carry out the authorized activity for a person who has received such written authorization for a period of at least two years and up to five years following his most recent conviction for violating any provision of the hunting and trapping laws and regulations. In determining the appropriate length of this restriction, the Director shall take into account the nature and severity of the most recent violation and of any past violations of the hunting and trapping laws and regulations by the applicant. No person shall be designated as a shooter under this section during a period when such person's hunting license or privileges to hunt have been suspended or revoked.

G. The Director or his designee may authorize, subject to the provisions of this section, the killing of deer over bait within the political boundaries of any city or town, or any county with a special late antlerless season, in the Commonwealth when requested by a certified letter from the governing body of such locality.

H. The parts of any deer or bear killed pursuant to this section or wildlife killed pursuant to subsection C shall not be used for the purposes of taxidermy, mounts, or any public display unless authorized by the Director or his designee. However, the meat of any such animal may be used for human consumption. The carcass and any unused meat of any such animal shall be disposed of within 24 hours of being killed. Any person who violates any provision of this subsection is guilty of a Class 3 misdemeanor.

I. It is unlawful to willfully and intentionally impede any person who is engaged in the lawful killing of a bear or deer pursuant to written authorization issued under this section. Any person convicted of a violation of this subsection is guilty of a Class 3 misdemeanor.

History.

Code 1950, § 29-145.1; 1954, c. 686; 1956, c. 684; 1958, cc. 315, 609; 1960, c. 129; 1962, c. 229; 1970, c. 79; 1980, c. 271; 1987, cc. 48, 488; 1991, c. 99; 1993, cc. 204, 273; 1994, c. 571; 1996, c. 314; 1998, c. 179; 1999, c. 563; 2000, c. 6; 2002, c. 174; 2003, cc. 123, 135; 2004, c. 447; 2008, cc. 17, 260; 2009, cc. 8, 305; 2010, c. 5; 2012, c. 247; 2013, c. 346.

§ 29.1-530. Open and closed season for trapping, bag limits, etc.

A. There shall be a continuous open season for trapping nuisance species and a continuous closed trapping season on all other species of wild birds and wild animals, except as provided by Board regulations. However, a landowner or his agent may trap and dispose of, except by sale, squirrels creating a nuisance on his property at any time in any area where the use of firearms for such purpose is prohibited by law or local ordinance.

B. In addition, the following general rules shall be applicable to any person trapping in the Commonwealth:

1. The trapper shall be responsible for all damage done by an illegally set trap, and any person finding a trap set contrary to law may report it to the landowner upon whose land the trap is located or to any conservation police officer who may destroy or otherwise make the trap inoperable.

2. Licensed trappers may shoot wild animals caught in traps on any day of the week during the seasons prescribed in subsection A in order to dispatch such animal. No additional licenses are required other than a valid Virginia trapping license.

3. It is lawful to trap wild animals within the daily bag and season limits, if any, during the open season provided by Board regulations.

History.

Code 1950, § 29-146; 1958, c. 495; 1974, c. 302; 1982, c. 335; 1987, c. 488; 2006, c. 20; 2007, c. 87; 2013, c. 349.

§ 29.1-530.1. Blaze orange clothing required at certain times.

During any firearms deer season, except during the special season for hunting deer with a muzzleloading rifle only, in counties and cities designated by the Board, every hunter and every person accompanying a hunter shall wear a blaze orange hat, except that the bill or brim of the hat may be a color or design other than solid blaze orange, or blaze orange upper body clothing, that is visible from 360 degrees or display at least 100 square inches of solid blaze orange material at shoulder level within body reach visible from 360 degrees.

During the special season for hunting deer with a muzzle-loading rifle only, in counties and cities designated by the Board, every muzzleloader deer hunter and every person accompanying a muzzleloader deer hunter shall wear a blaze orange hat, except that the bill or brim of the hat may be a color or design other than solid blaze orange, or blaze orange upper body clothing, that is visible from 360 degrees, except when any such person is physically located in a tree stand or other stationary hunting location.

Any person violating the provisions of this section shall, upon conviction, pay a fine of $25.

Violations of this section shall not be admissible in any civil action for personal injury or death as evidence of negligence, contributory negligence or assumption of the risk.

This section shall not apply when (i) hunting waterfowl from stationary or floating blinds, (ii) hunting waterfowl over decoys, (iii) hunting waterfowl in wetlands as defined in § 28.2-1300, (iv) hunting waterfowl from a boat or other floating conveyance, (v) hunting doves, (vi) participating in hunting dog field trials permitted by the Board of Game and Inland Fisheries, (vii) on horseback while hunting foxes with hounds but without firearms, or (viii) hunting with a bow and arrow in areas where the discharge of firearms is prohibited by state law or local ordinance.

History.
1987, c. 319, § 29-147.2; 1988, cc. 474, 715; 2002, c. 39; 2005, c. 167; 2009, c. 11; 2014, c. 140.

§ 29.1-530.2. Unlawfully killing bear; penalty.

Any person who kills or attempts to kill a bear in violation of any provision of this article or of a regulation adopted thereunder shall be guilty of a Class 1 misdemeanor.

History.
1988, c. 19.

§ 29.1-530.3. Remote hunting prohibited; penalty.

A. It is unlawful for any person to engage in computer-assisted remote hunting or provide or operate a facility that allows others to engage in computer-assisted remote hunting if the wild animal or wild bird being hunted or shot is located in the Commonwealth.

B. Any person who violates this section is guilty of a Class 1 misdemeanor. In addition to the penalty prescribed herein, the court shall revoke all current hunting licenses and privileges of the person convicted of violating this section and prohibit that person from hunting for a period of one to five years. Notification of the revocation or prohibition shall be forwarded to the Department pursuant to subsections C and D of § 18.2-56.1.

C. For the purposes of this section "computer-assisted remote hunting" means the use of a computer or other device, equipment, or software, to remotely control the aiming and discharge of a firearm or other weapon, that allows a person, not physically present, to hunt or shoot any wild animal or wild bird.

History.
2005, cc. 172, 226; 2010, c. 183.

§ 29.1-530.4. Duty of certain entities to report hunting incidents.

Any law-enforcement agency or emergency medical services provider that receives a report that a person engaged in hunting as defined in § 29.1-100 has suffered serious bodily injury or death shall immediately give notice of the incident to the Department of Game and Inland Fisheries.

History.
2005, c. 688; 2015, cc. 502, 503.

ARTICLE 2.1. WILDLIFE VIOLATOR COMPACT.

§ 29.1-530.5. Wildlife Violator Compact.

ARTICLE I

Findings, Declaration of Policy, and Purpose

(a) The participating states find that:

(1) Wildlife resources are managed in trust by the respective states for the benefit of all residents and visitors;

(2) The protection of the wildlife resources of a state is materially affected by the degree of compliance with state statutes, laws, regulations, rules, and ordinances relating to the management of those resources;

(3) The preservation, protection, management, and restoration of wildlife contributes immeasurably to the aesthetic, recreational, and economic aspects of such natural resources;

(4) Wildlife resources are valuable without regard to political boundaries; therefore, every person should be required to comply with wildlife preservation, protection, management, and restoration statutes, laws, rules, regulations, and ordinances of the participating states as a condition precedent to the continuance or issuance of any license to hunt, fish, trap, or possess wildlife;

(5) Violation of wildlife laws interferes with the management of wildlife resources and may endanger the safety of persons and property;

(6) The mobility of many wildlife law violators necessitates the maintenance of channels of communication among the various states;

(7) In most instances, a person who is cited for a wildlife violation in a state other than the person's home state:

(i) Is required to post collateral or a bond to secure an appearance for a trial at a later date;

(ii) Is taken into custody until the collateral or bond is posted; or

(iii) Is taken directly to court for an immediate appearance;

(8) The purpose of the enforcement practices set forth in paragraph (7) of this subsection is to ensure compliance with the terms of a wildlife citation by the cited person who, if permitted to continue on the

person's way after receiving the citation, could return to the person's home state and disregard any duty under the terms of the citation;

(9) In most instances, a person receiving a wildlife citation in the person's home state is permitted to accept the citation from the officer at the scene of the violation and immediately continue on the person's way after agreeing or being instructed to comply with the terms of the citation;

(10) The practices described in paragraph (7) of this subsection cause unnecessary inconvenience and, at times, a hardship for the person who is unable at the time to post collateral, furnish a bond, stand trial, or pay a fine, and thus is compelled to remain in custody until some alternative arrangement is made; and

(11) The enforcement practices described in paragraph (7) of this subsection consume an undue amount of law-enforcement time.

(b) It is the policy of the participating states to:

(1) Promote compliance with the statutes, laws, regulations, rules, and ordinancces rclating to management of wildlife resources in their respective states;

(2) Recognize a suspension of wildlife license privileges of any person whose license privileges have been suspended by a participating state and treat that suspension as if it had occurred in each respective state;

(3) Allow a violator, except as provided in Article III, subsection (b) of this compact, to accept a wildlife citation and, without delay, proceed on the person's way, regardless of the violator's home state, if that state is a party to this compact;

(4) Report to the appropriate participating state, as provided in the compact manual, any conviction recorded against a person whose home state was not the issuing state;

(5) Allow the home state to recognize and treat convictions recorded against its residents, which convictions occurred in a participating state, as though they had occurred in the home state;

(6) Extend cooperation to its fullest extent among the participating states for enforcing compliance with the terms of a wildlife citation issued in one participating state to a resident of another participating state;

(7) Maximize the effective use of law-enforcement personnel and information; and

(8) Assist court systems in the efficient disposition of wildlife violations.

(c) The purpose of this compact is to:

(1) Provide a means through which participating states may join in a reciprocal program to effectuate the policies enumerated in subsection (b) of this article in a uniform and orderly manner; and

(2) Provide for the fair and impartial treatment of wildlife violators operating within participating states in recognition of the violator's right to due process and the sovereign status of a participating state.

ARTICLE II
Definitions

As used in this compact, unless the context requires otherwise, the following words have the meanings indicated:

(a) *"Citation"* means any summons, complaint, summons and complaint, ticket, penalty assessment, or other official document issued to a person by a wildlife officer or other law-enforcement officer for a wildlife violation that contains an order requiring the person to respond.

(b) *"Collateral"* means any cash or other security deposited to secure an appearance for trial in connection with the issuance by a wildlife officer or other law-enforcement officer of a citation for a wildlife violation.

(c) *"Compliance"* with respect to a citation means the act of answering a citation through an appearance in a court or tribunal, or through the payment of fines, costs, and surcharges, if any.

(d) *"Conviction"* means a conviction that results in suspension or revocation of a license, including any court conviction, for an offense related to the preservation, protection, management, or restoration of wildlife that is prohibited by state statute, law, regulation, rule, or ordinance. The term also includes the forfeiture of any bail, bond, or other security deposited to secure the appearance of a person charged with having committed the offense, the payment of a penalty assessment, a plea of nolo contendere, or the imposition of a deferred or suspended sentence by the court.

(e) *"Court"* means a court of law, including magistrate's court and the justice of the peace court.

(f) *"Home state"* means the state of primary residence of a person.

(g) *"Issuing state"* means the participating state that issues a wildlife citation to the violator.

(h) *"License"* means a license, permit, or other public document that conveys to the person to whom it was issued the privilege of pursuing, possessing, or taking any wildlife regulated by statute, law, regulation, rule, or ordinance of a participating state.

(i) *"Licensing authority"* means the governmental unit in each participating state that is authorized by law to issue or approve licenses or permits to hunt, fish, trap, or possess wildlife.

(j) *"Participating state"* means a state that enacts legislation to become a member of this Wildlife Violator Compact.

(k) *"Personal recognizance"* means an agreement by a person made at the time of issuance of the wildlife citation that such person will comply with the terms of the citation.

(*l*) *"State"* means any state, territory, or possession of the United States, the District of Columbia, the Commonwealth of Puerto Rico, the provinces of Canada, and other countries.

(m) *"Suspension"* means any revocation, denial,

or withdrawal of any or all license privileges, including the privilege to apply for, purchase, or exercise the benefits conferred by a license.

(n) *"Terms of the citation"* means the conditions and options expressly stated upon the citation.

(o) *"Wildlife"* means all species of animals including, but not limited to, mammals, birds, fish, reptiles, amphibians, mollusks, and crustaceans, that are defined as "wildlife" and are protected or otherwise regulated by statute, law, rule, regulation, or ordinance in a participating state. Species included in the definition of "wildlife" vary from state to state and the determination of whether a species is "wildlife" for the purposes of this Compact shall be based on the law of the issuing state.

(p) *"Wildlife law"* means a statute, law, regulation, rule, or ordinance developed and enacted for the management of wildlife resources and the uses thereof.

(q) *"Wildlife officer"* means any individual authorized by a participating state to issue a citation for a wildlife violation.

(r) *"Wildlife violation"* means any cited violation of a statute, law, regulation, rule, or ordinance developed and enacted for the management of wildlife resources and the uses thereof.

ARTICLE III
Procedures for Issuing State

(a) When issuing a citation for a wildlife violation, a wildlife officer shall issue a citation to any person whose primary residence is in a participating state in the same manner as though the person were a resident of the issuing state and shall not require such person to post collateral to secure appearance, subject to the exceptions noted in subsection (b) of this article, if the officer receives the recognizance of such person that he will comply with the terms of the citation.

(b) Personal recognizance is acceptable if not prohibited by local law; by policy, procedure, or regulation of the issuing agency; or by the compact manual and if the violator provides adequate proof of identification to the wildlife officer.

(c) Upon conviction or failure of a person to comply with the terms of a wildlife citation, the appropriate official shall report the conviction or failure to comply to the licensing authority of the participating state in which the wildlife citation was issued. The report shall be made in accordance with procedures specified by the issuing state and must contain information as specified in the compact manual as minimum requirements for effective processing by the home state.

(d) Upon receiving the report of conviction or noncompliance pursuant to subsection (c) of this article, the licensing authority of the issuing state shall transmit to the licensing authority of the home state of the violator the information in the form and content prescribed in the compact manual.

ARTICLE IV
Procedure for Home State

(a) Upon receipt of a report from the licensing authority of the issuing state reporting the failure of a violator to comply with the terms of a citation, the licensing authority of the home state shall notify the violator and shall initiate a suspension action in accordance with the home state's suspension procedures and shall suspend the violator's license privileges until satisfactory evidence of compliance with the terms of the wildlife citation has been furnished by the issuing state to the home state licensing authority. Due process safeguards shall be accorded to the violator.

(b) Upon receipt of a report of conviction from the licensing authority of the issuing state, the licensing authority of the home state shall enter such conviction in its records and shall treat such conviction as though the conviction had occurred in the home state for the purposes of the suspension of license privileges.

(c) The licensing authority of the home state shall maintain a record of actions taken and shall make reports to issuing states as provided in the compact manual.

ARTICLE V
Reciprocal Recognition of Suspension

(a) All participating states shall recognize the suspension of license privileges of a person by a participating state as though the violation resulting in the suspension had occurred in their state and could have been the basis for suspension of license privileges in their state.

(b) Each participating state shall communicate suspension information to other participating states in a form and content prescribed in the compact manual.

ARTICLE VI
Applicability of Other Laws

Except as expressly required by provisions of this compact, nothing in this compact may be construed to affect the right of a participating state to apply any of its laws relating to license privileges to any person or circumstance or to invalidate or prevent any agreement or other cooperative arrangement between a participating state and a nonparticipating state concerning the enforcement of wildlife laws.

ARTICLE VII
Compact Administrator Procedures

(a) For the purpose of administering the provisions of this compact and to serve as a governing body for the resolution of all matters relating to the operation of this compact, a Board of Compact Administrators is established. The board shall be composed of one representative from each of the participating states to be known as the compact administrator. The compact administrator shall be appointed by the head of the licensing authority of each participating state and shall serve and be subject to removal in accordance with the laws of the state he or she represents. A compact administrator may provide for an alternate for the discharge of his or her duties and the performance of his or her functions as a board member. An alternate is not entitled to serve unless written notification of the alternate's identity has been given to the board.

(b) Each member of the Board of Compact Administrators shall be entitled to one vote. No action of the board shall be binding unless taken at a meeting at which a majority of the total number of the board's votes are cast in favor thereof. Action by the board shall be only at a meeting at which a majority of the participating states are represented.

(c) The board shall elect annually from its membership a chairman and vice chairman.

(d) The board shall adopt bylaws not inconsistent with the provisions of this compact or the laws of a participating state for the conduct of its business and shall have the power to amend and rescind its bylaws.

(e) The board may accept for any of its purposes and functions under this compact any and all donations and grants of moneys, equipment, supplies, materials, and services, conditional or otherwise, from any state, the United States, or any governmental unit, and may receive, utilize, and dispose of those grants and donations.

(f) The board may contract with, or accept services or personnel from, any governmental or intergovernmental unit, individual, firm, or corporation, or any private nonprofit organization or institution.

(g) The board shall formulate all necessary procedures and develop uniform forms and documents for administering the provisions of this compact. All procedures and forms adopted pursuant to board action shall be contained in a compact manual.

ARTICLE VIII
Entry into Compact and Withdrawal

(a) This compact shall become effective at such time as it is adopted in substantially similar form by two or more states.

(b) Entry into the compact shall be made by resolution of ratification executed by the authorized officials of the applying state and submitted to the chairman of the board. The resolution shall substantially be in the form and content as provided in the compact manual and shall include the following:

(1) A citation of the authority from which the state is empowered to become a party to this compact;

(2) An agreement of compliance with the terms and provisions of this compact; and

(3) An agreement that compact entry is with all states participating in the compact and with all additional states legally becoming a party to the compact.

(c) The effective date of entry shall be specified by the applying state, but may not be less than 60 days after notice has been given by the chairman of the Board of Compact Administrators or by the secretariat of the board to each participating state that the resolution from the applying state has been received.

(d) A participating state may withdraw from this compact by official written notice to each participating state, but withdrawal shall not become effective until 90 days after the notice of withdrawal is given. The notice shall be directed to the compact administrator of each member state. The withdrawal of any state does not affect the validity of this compact as to the remaining participating states.

ARTICLE IX
Amendments to the Compact

(a) This Compact may be amended from time to time. Amendments shall be presented in resolution form to the chairman of the Board of Compact Administrators and shall be initiated by one or more participating states.

(b) Adoption of an amendment shall require endorsement by all participating states and shall become effective 30 days after the date of the last endorsement.

(c) Failure of a participating state to respond to the compact chairman within 120 days after receipt of a proposed amendment shall constitute endorsement of the proposed amendment.

ARTICLE X
Construction and Severability

This compact shall be liberally construed so as to effectuate the purposes stated herein. The provisions of this compact shall be severable and if any phrase, clause, sentence, or provision of this compact is declared to be contrary to the constitution of a participating state or of the United States, or if the applicability thereof to any government, unit, individual, or circumstance is held invalid, the validity of the remainder of this compact shall not be affected thereby. If this compact is held contrary to the constitution of a participating state, the compact shall remain in full force and effect as to the remaining states and in full force and effect as to the participating state affected as to all severable matters.

ARTICLE XI
Title

This compact shall be known as the "Wildlife Violator Compact."

History.
2009, c. 648.

ARTICLE 3.
FISHING LAWS.

§ 29.1-531. Unlawful to take or attempt to take, possess, sell or transport fish except as permitted.

A. Unless otherwise provided by a regulation of the Board, it shall be unlawful for any person to take or attempt to take any fish in inland waters other than shad, herring or mullet, except by fishing with a hook and line or rod and reel, held in the hand.

B. It shall be unlawful to catch, trap, take, capture, kill, or attempt to take, capture or kill, possess, deliver for transportation, transport, cause to be transported, receive for transport, export, or import at any time or in any manner any species of game fish, or the carcass or any part thereof, except as specifically permitted by law and only by the means and within the numbers stated.

C. In Mecklenburg, Pittsylvania, Prince Edward, Charlotte, Campbell, Halifax, Amelia (except between Vaughn's Pond and Meadsville Dam), Caroline and King George Counties, in the City of Danville, and in the Meherrin River in Lunenburg County, it shall be lawful to fish with fish traps, fish pots or haul seines in any streams and waters, provided that no person shall catch fish with fish traps or fish pots or haul seines for commercial purposes. However, it shall be unlawful in such localities to remove from the waters thereof any game fish caught with fish pots, fish traps or haul seines, and any person doing so shall immediately return them to the waters. The Board shall have the authority to close any streams or rivers or parts of streams or rivers in such localities when the waters are stocked with fish by the Department.

D. It shall be lawful to sell or offer to sell trout which have been lawfully acquired, provided such trout have been propagated and raised in a hatchery or by other artificial means. The Board shall by appropriate regulation establish a practical system of identification of trout so offered for sale for table or other uses as directed by the Board.

E. It shall be unlawful to offer for sale, sell, offer to purchase, or purchase at any time or in any manner any species of game fish, or the carcass or any part thereof, except as specifically permitted by law and only by the means and within the numbers stated. A violation of the provisions of this subsection shall be punishable as provided in § 29.1-553.

F. A violation of the provisions of subsections A through D shall constitute a Class 2 misdemeanor.

History.

Code 1950, § 29-148; 1956, c. 490; 1958, c. 514; 1960, c. 126; 1962, c. 469; 1966, c. 413; 1987, c. 488; 1994, cc. 413, 848; 2000, cc. 403, 447.

§ 29.1-532. Dams and fishways.

Any dam or other object in a watercourse, which obstructs navigation or the passage of fish, shall be deemed a nuisance, unless it is used to work a mill, factory or other machine or engine useful to the public, and is allowed by law or order of court. Any person owning or having control of any dam or other obstruction in the streams of the Commonwealth which may interfere with the free passage of anadromous and other migratory fish, shall provide every such dam or other obstruction with a suitable fishway unless the Board considers it unnecessary. The purpose of such a fishway is for anadromous and other migratory fish to have free passage up and down the streams during March, April, May and June, and down the streams throughout the remaining months. "Suitable fishway" means a fishway which passes significant numbers of the target fishes, as determined by the Board.

Owners of such dams or other authorized obstructions shall maintain and keep fishways operational, in good repair, and restore them in case of destruction.

Owners of dams or other obstructions which are not authorized by law must have the obstacles removed at their expense when the Board determines that the obstacles interfere with the free passage of anadromous and other migratory fish within the streams of the Commonwealth.

The circuit court of the county or city in which the dam is situated, after reasonable notice to the parties or party interested and upon satisfactory proof of the failure to comply, may order any necessary construction or destruction to be initiated or put in good repair at the expense of the owner of the dam or other obstruction. All such construction or destruction must be initiated within one year of the court order and completed within three years of the court order.

Any person failing to comply with this section shall pay as a penalty a percentage of the estimated cost of construction or destruction equal to the percentage specified on the judgment rate of interest pursuant to § 6.2-302, and the Board shall provide construction or destruction cost estimates.

Penalties collected pursuant to this section shall be directed to the Department of Game and Inland Fisheries.

This section shall not apply to the Meherrin River within the Counties of Brunswick and Greensville, nor to the Meherrin River within or between the Counties of Lunenburg and Mecklenburg, nor to the Nottoway River between the Counties of Lunenburg and Nottoway, nor to Abram's Creek in Shawnee district, Frederick County, nor to the James River between the City of Lynchburg and the County of Amherst, nor to the James River within the City of Richmond and between the City of Richmond and Henrico County, except that the exemption for those dams west of Virginia Route 161 which are located on the James River within the City of Richmond and between the City of Richmond and Henrico County shall expire on January 1, 1990, nor any streams within the Counties of Augusta, Lunenburg, Mecklenburg, Louisa, Buckingham, Halifax, Montgomery, Pulaski, Franklin, Russell, Tazewell, Giles, Bland, Craig, Wythe, Carroll and Grayson, nor to that part of any stream that forms a part of the boundary of Halifax and Franklin Counties. Furthermore, no fish ladders shall be required on dams twenty feet or more in height. The City of Richmond shall continue to work with the Department of Game and Inland Fisheries toward implementing and funding a plan for breaching dams to provide fishways for the passage of anadromous and other migratory fish.

History.
Code 1950, § 29-151; 1950, p. 891; 1958, c. 607; 1987, c. 488; 1988, c. 487.

§ 29.1-533. Prohibition against use of substances injurious to fish.

It shall be unlawful to use any explosive for the destruction of fish, or knowingly cast any noxious substance or matter into any watercourse of the Commonwealth where fish or fish spawn may be destroyed, or to place or to allow to pass into the watercourses of the Commonwealth any sawdust, ashes, lime, gas, tar, or refuse of gas works, injurious to fish. Any person violating any of the provisions of this section shall be guilty of a Class 3 misdemeanor, except that any person convicted of destroying fish by means of explosives shall be guilty of a Class 1 misdemeanor.

The owner or lessee of any property on which fish are destroyed by means of explosives shall be entitled to recover liquidated damages in an amount deemed appropriate by the court from any person convicted of destroying fish by such means.

History.
Code 1950, § 29-153; 1956, c. 709; 1962, c. 469; 1987, c. 488; 1988, c. 158.

Game and Inland Fisheries

§ 29.1-534. Right to fish in interjurisdictional inland waters.

A Virginia resident or a resident of an adjoining jurisdiction which has inland water lying adjacent to Virginia land or water may take fish with hook and line after complying with the requirements of the laws of the jurisdiction where the fishing occurs. For purposes of this section and § 29.1-535, the term "jurisdiction" shall include the District of Columbia.

History.
1952, c. 484, § 29-153.1; 1964, c. 74; 1970, c. 194; 1987, c. 488; 1991, c. 200; 2011, cc. 93, 179.

§ 29.1-535. Reciprocal agreement as to fishing in such waters.

The Board shall have the necessary authority to enter into a reciprocal agreement with an adjoining jurisdiction having inland waters lying adjacent to Virginia land or water relating to the following:

1. A sport fishing license acquired in an adjoining jurisdiction shall be recognized when it is used by the person whose name appears on the face of such license, when such licensee is fishing in that portion of inland waters lying in either Virginia or the other jurisdiction or partly in each of the jurisdictions. Such recognition shall be contingent upon a reciprocal recognition by the adjoining jurisdiction to a licensee of Virginia who is fishing in the same waters.

2. Creel limits, open seasons for fishing and all other laws and regulations of the jurisdiction entering into the agreement shall be strictly observed, and any person failing to comply with the regulations set up under the agreement shall be guilty of a Class 2 misdemeanor and punished accordingly.

History.
1952, c. 484, § 29-153.2; 1964, c. 74; 1970, c. 194; 1980, c. 28; 1987, c. 488; 1991, c. 200.

ARTICLE 4.

POSSESSION, TRANSPORTATION, AND SALE OF GAME AND FISH.

§ 29.1-536. Sale.

When taken in accordance with the provisions of law or regulation, muskrat, opossum, rabbits, raccoon and squirrels may be bought and sold during the open hunting season only, but the hides, furs or pelts of fur-bearing animals legally taken and possessed, and the carcass of any fur-bearing animal may be sold at any time in accordance with §§ 29.1-400 through 29.1-407.

History.
Code 1950, § 29-154; 1977, c. 377; 1980, c. 494; 1987, c. 488; 1994, c. 436; 1999, c. 204.

§ 29.1-537. Possession.

When taken in accordance with the provisions of this title, each species of wild bird, wild animal or fish may be possessed at any time.

History.
Code 1950, § 29-155; 1987, c. 488.

§ 29.1-538: Reserved.

§ 29.1-539. Keeping deer or bear struck by motor vehicle; procedure to be followed by driver.

Any person driving a motor vehicle who collides with a deer or bear may, upon compliance with the provisions of this section, keep the deer or bear for his own use as if the animal had been killed by that person during hunting season for the animal.

Any person so killing any deer or bear shall immediately report the accident to the conservation police officer or other law-enforcement officer of the county or city where the accident occurred. The conservation police officer or other law-enforcement officer shall view the deer or bear and if he believes that the deer or bear was killed by the collision with the motor vehicle or injured to such an extent as to require its death, he shall award the animal to the person claiming the deer or bear, and shall give the person a certificate to that effect on forms furnished by the Department.

History.
1950, pp. 441, 442, §§ 29-155.2 to 29-155.4; 1980, c. 271; 1987, c. 488; 2007, c. 87.

§ 29.1-540. Carriage and shipment.

When taken in accordance with the provisions of this title, wild birds, wild animals or fish may be transported as follows:

1. By any person properly licensed, for lawful use in or out of the county or city where taken to another county or city in the Commonwealth or to another state during the open season in the county or city where taken.
2. By any properly licensed person via freight, express, parcel post or airplane mail, as a gift and not for market or sale, and so stating on the shipping tag. The wild bird, wild animal or fish may be transported in or out of the county or city where taken to another county or city in this Commonwealth, or to another state, during the open season in the county or city where taken. Any package in which birds, animals or fish are transported shall have the name and address of the shipper and consignee and a statement of the numbers and kinds of birds, animals or fish being transported clearly and conspicuously marked on the outside of the container.

Any such birds, animals or fish in transit during the open season may continue in transit, not to exceed five days, in order to reach their destination.

For the purposes of this section the terms "wild birds," "wild animals" and "fish" shall mean all or any part of the carcasses of any such birds, animals or fish.

History.
Code 1950, § 29-156; 1987, c. 488.

§ 29.1-541. Storage.

It shall be unlawful for any person to store any wild birds, wild animals or fish if selling them is prohibited by law, except persons may store them in a bona fide domicile or in a licensed cold storage establishment. Any licensed cold storage establishment which receives any wild birds, wild animals or fish, where selling them is prohibited by law, shall attach a ticket to each lot of wild birds, wild animals or fish. The ticket shall show the number of each kind of wild bird, wild animal or fish, the date upon which they are brought for storage and the name and address of the person storing them. Every such licensed cold storage establishment shall keep a record of all deliveries of game and fish so stored, the dates they are delivered, the number of each species delivered and the name of each person to whom any such delivery is made. Possession of any wild birds, wild animals or fish which are prohibited by law to be sold, in any place of business, except in a licensed cold storage establishment, shall be unlawful.

Any person who violates any provision of this section shall be guilty of a Class 2 misdemeanor.

For the purposes of this section the terms "wild birds," "wild animals" and "fish" shall mean all or any part of the carcasses of any such birds, animals or fish.

History.
Code 1950, § 29-157; 1987, c. 488.

§ 29.1-542. Importation.

Live wolves or coyotes, or birds and animals otherwise classed as predatory or undesirable, may not be imported into the Commonwealth or liberated therein, or possessed therein, except under a special permit of the Board. Nonpredatory birds, animals or fish may be imported, but upon arrival in the Commonwealth, shall be subject to the laws governing the possession of such birds, animals and fish in Virginia. Any person may bring into the Commonwealth, either in his personal possession or as his baggage, on the same conveyance with him and plainly labeled or tagged with his name and address, game and fish legally taken in another state or foreign country, but in no greater quantity than he could legally possess while in such other state or foreign country. Nothing in this section shall be construed as applying to birds, animals and fish being transported in unbroken packages from beyond the confines of Virginia through the Commonwealth to another state.

History.
Code 1950, § 29-158; 1977, c. 377; 1982, c. 73; 1987, c. 488.

§ 29.1-543. Game and fish taken and packaged outside the Commonwealth.

It shall be lawful to possess, store, transport, offer for sale, sell, offer to purchase, purchase and otherwise deal in any wild animal, bird, fish or any part thereof, which has been taken and packaged in a can, tin, pot or other receptacle outside the Commonwealth by any person, company or corporation duly licensed by the state in which such cannery or processing plant is located and recognized by the Board. Such packages may be transported into the Commonwealth, so long as the original package remains unbroken, unopened and intact.

History.
1958, c. 153, § 29-158.1; 1987, c. 488.

§ 29.1-543.1. Introduction, stocking, and release of blue catfish; penalty.

A. It is unlawful for any person to introduce into or stock in waters of the Commonwealth, including private ponds or lakes, the blue catfish or its hybrids or to release any blue catfish or any such hybrid into any water body other than that in which it was caught.

B. Any person who violates any provision of this section is guilty of a Class 2 misdemeanor.

History.
2015, c. 470.

§ 29.1-544. Dressing, packing and selling bobwhite quail.

A. It shall be lawful for the licensee of a shooting preserve or his designated agents to dress, pack and sell bobwhite quail raised by him for use as food, under rules or regulations to be prescribed by the Board.

B. It shall be lawful to sell mounted bobwhite quail in the Commonwealth that have been legally raised captively and mounted outside of the Commonwealth.

History.
1960, c. 131, § 29-158.2; 1987, c. 488; 1998, c. 179.

§ 29.1-545. Possession, sale, offering for sale or liberation of live nutria.

It shall be unlawful for any person, firm, association or corporation to possess, sell, offer for sale, or liberate in the Commonwealth any live fur-bearing animal commonly referred to as nutria.

History.
1962, c. 106, § 29-158.3; 1987, c. 488.

ARTICLE 5.

PENALTIES IN GENERAL.

§ 29.1-546. General penalty.

Any person convicted of violating any of the provisions of this title shall, unless otherwise specified, be guilty of a Class 2 misdemeanor.

History.
Code 1950, § 29-161; 1954, c. 694; 1962, c. 469; 1979, c. 264; 1987, c. 488.

§ 29.1-547. Trapping, selling, purchasing, etc., migratory game birds.

Notwithstanding the provisions of §§ 29.1-546 and 29.1-553, any person convicted of trapping or attempting to trap any migratory game bird, as defined in § 29.1-100, or convicted of possessing any such migratory game bird taken by means of a trap, shall be guilty of a Class 1 misdemeanor. Any person convicted of offering for sale, selling, offering to purchase, or purchasing any migratory game bird shall be subject to penalties as provided in § 29.1-553.

History.
1960, c. 173, § 29-161.1; 1987, c. 488; 1994, c. 848.

§ 29.1-548. Killing deer illegally.

Any person killing a deer in violation of Board regulations, or who exceeds the bag limit for deer, or who kills a deer during the closed season shall be guilty of a Class 2 misdemeanor. However, any person who kills a deer illegally during the open season shall be guilty of a Class 3 misdemeanor if such person immediately delivers the complete carcass in good condition to the conservation police officer of the county or city in which it was killed. At that time it shall be confiscated and disposed of by the conservation police officer or as otherwise provided. Any such person delivering such carcass to the conservation police officer shall be exempt from replacement cost as provided in § 29.1-551.

History.
Code 1950, § 29-162; 1956, c. 466; 1958, c. 444; 1962, c. 469; 1987, c. 488; 1988, c. 19; 2007, c. 87.

§ 29.1-549. Hunting deer from watercraft.

A. Any person who kills or attempts to kill any deer while the person is in a boat or other type watercraft shall be guilty of a Class 4 misdemeanor.

B. Every boat or other watercraft and their motors, and any firearm, crossbow, bow and arrow, or speargun used with the knowledge or consent of the owner or lienholder thereof, in killing or attempting to kill deer in violation of this section, shall be forfeited to the Commonwealth, and upon being condemned as forfeited in proceedings under Chapter 22.1 (§ 19.2-386.1 et seq.) of Title 19.2 the proceeds of sale shall be disposed of according to law.

History.
1973, c. 120, §§ 29-162.1, 29-162.2; 1987, c. 488; 2002, c. 157; 2012, cc. 283, 756.

§ 29.1-550. Taking game or fish during closed season or exceeding bag limit.

It shall be unlawful for any person to (i) take, or attempt to take, any wild bird, wild animal or fish during the closed season, (ii) exceed the bag or creel limit for any wild bird, wild animal or fish, or (iii) possess over the daily bag or creel limit for any wild bird, wild animals or fish while in the forests, fields or waters of the Commonwealth. Any person convicted of violating any provisions of this section shall be guilty of a Class 2 misdemeanor.

Game and Inland Fisheries

History.

Code 1950, § 29-163; 1950, p. 936; 1952, c. 78; 1958, c. 444; 1962, c. 469; 1987, c. 488; 1988, c. 19.

§ 29.1-551. Assessment of value of game or fish unlawfully taken.

The judge or court, upon convicting any person of a violation of §§ 29.1-523, 29.1-525.1, 29.1-530.2, 29.1-548, 29.1-550 or § 29.1-552 shall, in addition to imposition of the punishment prescribed in those sections, ascertain the approximate replacement value of animals, birds or fish taken in violation of those sections and shall assess the value against the person convicted. The assessment shall be paid by the person so convicted within the time prescribed in the judgment of the judge or court, not exceeding sixty days, and the collecting officer shall forward such payments to the Board for payment into the state treasury. The Comptroller shall credit such payments to the game protection fund.

History.

Code 1950, § 29-163.2; 1950, p. 936; 1952, c. 78; 1962, c. 469; 1976, c. 660; 1987, c. 488; 1994, c. 412; 2001, c. 856.

§ 29.1-552. Killing wild turkey during closed season.

Any person who kills a wild turkey during the closed season, or who kills a beardless turkey during an open hunting season prescribed by the Board for bearded turkeys only, shall be guilty of a Class 2 misdemeanor for each such turkey killed. However, if a person kills a beardless turkey when only the hunting of bearded turkeys is permitted, and immediately delivers the complete carcass in good condition to a conservation police officer or game checking station authorized by the Board, it shall be confiscated and disposed of as otherwise provided, and the person delivering the carcass shall be exempt from replacement cost provided in § 29.1-551.

History.

1968, c. 309, § 29-163.2; 1974, c. 60; 1977, c. 377; 1987, c. 488; 1988, c. 19; 2007, c. 87.

§ 29.1-553. Selling or offering for sale; penalty.

A. Any person who offers for sale, sells, offers to purchase, or purchases any wild bird or wild animal, or any part thereof, or any freshwater fish, except as provided by law, shall be guilty of a Class 1 misdemeanor. However, when the aggregate of such sales or purchases or any combination thereof, by any person totals $200 or more during any 90-day period, that person shall be guilty of a Class 6 felony.

B. Whether or not criminal charges have been placed, when any property is taken possession of by a conservation police officer for the purpose of being used as evidence of a violation of this section or for confiscation, the conservation police officer making such seizure shall immediately report the seizure to the Attorney for the Commonwealth.

C. In any prosecution for a violation of this section, photographs of the wild bird, wild animal, or any freshwater fish, or any part thereof shall be deemed competent evidence of such wild bird, wild animal, or freshwater fish, or part thereof and shall be admissible in any proceeding, hearing, or trial of the case to the same extent as if such wild bird, wild animal, or any freshwater fish, or part thereof had been introduced as evidence. Such photographs shall bear a written description of the wild bird, wild animal, or freshwater fish, or parts thereof, the name of the place where the alleged offense occurred, the date on which the alleged offense occurred, the name of the accused, the name of the arresting officer or investigating officer, the date of the photograph, and the name of the photographer. The photographs shall be identified by the signature of the photographer.

D. Any licensed Virginia auctioneer or licensed auction firm that sells, as a legitimate item of an auction sale, wildlife mounts that have undergone the taxidermy process, shall be exempt from the provisions of this section and subdivision A 11 of § 29.1-521.

History.

Code 1950, § 29-164; 1962, c. 469; 1986, c. 182; 1987, c. 488; 1989, c. 203; 1994, c. 848; 1997, c. 172; 2005, c. 170; 2007, c. 87.

§ 29.1-554. Violation of sanctuaries, refuges, preserves and water used for propagation.

It shall be unlawful for any person, including a property owner, to commit the following acts, the violation of which shall constitute a Class 3 misdemeanor:

1. To violate any regulation of the Board concerning refuges, sanctuaries and public shooting or fishing preserves in impounded waters or in forest and watershed areas owned by the United States government;
2. To damage the boundary enclosure of or enter a game refuge owned, leased or operated by the Board for the purpose of molesting any bird or animal, or permit his dog or livestock to go thereon;
3. To fish or trespass with intent to fish upon any waters or lands being utilized for fish propagation, or damage or destroy any pond, pool, flume, dam, pipeline, property or appliance belonging to or being utilized by the Board; or
4. To interfere with, obstruct, pollute, or diminish the natural flow of water into or through a fish hatchery.

History.

Code 1950, § 29-171; 1987, c. 488.

§ 29.1-554.1. Impeding lawful fishing in inland waters; penalty.

A. It is unlawful for any person to willfully and intentionally impede the lawful fishing of any species of fish. "Fishing" means those activities defined in § 29.1-100 as "fishing."

B. Any person convicted of a violation of this section shall be guilty of a Class 3 misdemeanor.

History.
1997, c. 703.

§ 29.1-555: Reserved.

§ 29.1-556. Unlawful devices to be destroyed.

Any firearm, trap, net, or other device of any kind or nature for taking wild birds, wild animals, or fish, except as specifically permitted by law, shall be considered unlawful. Any person who violates the provisions of this section shall be guilty of a Class 3 misdemeanor, and the device shall be forfeited to the Commonwealth. Nets, traps or other such devices, excluding firearms, shall be destroyed by the conservation police officer if the owner or user of the device cannot be located within thirty days. Unlawful fixed devices may be destroyed by the conservation police officer at the place where the devices are found.

History.
Code 1950, § 29-172; 1962, c. 469; 1979, c. 264; 1987, c. 488; 2007, c. 87.

§ 29.1-556.1. Release of certain balloons prohibited; civil penalty.

A. It shall be unlawful for any person to knowingly release or cause to be released into the atmosphere within a one-hour period fifty or more balloons which are (i) made of a nonbiodegradable or nonphotodegradable material or any material which requires more than five minutes' contact with air or water to degrade and (ii) inflated with a substance which is lighter than air. Any person who violates this section shall be liable for a civil penalty not to exceed five dollars per balloon released above the allowable limit, which shall be paid into the Lifetime Hunting and Fishing Endowment Fund established pursuant to § 29.1-101.1.

B. The provisions of this section shall not apply to (i) balloons released by or on behalf of any agency of the Commonwealth, or the United States or pursuant to a contract with the Commonwealth, the United States, or any other state, territory or government for scientific or meteorological purposes or (ii) hot air balloons that are recovered after launch.

History.
1991, c. 607.

§ 29.1-557. Confiscation of wild birds and animals under certain circumstances; disposition.

Wild birds, wild animals and fish are the property of the Commonwealth and may be reduced to personal possession only in accordance with law. Any wild bird, wild animal or fish which is illegally taken, possessed, sold, purchased, transported or imported shall be forfeited to the Commonwealth.

History.
Code 1950, § 29-173; 1987, c. 488.

§§ 29.1-558 through 29.1-560: Reserved.

§ 29.1-561. Self-incrimination.

No person shall be excused from testifying for the Commonwealth as to any offense committed by another under the provisions of the game, inland fish and boating laws by reason of his testimony tending to incriminate himself, but the testimony given by any such person on behalf of the Commonwealth when called as witness for the prosecution shall in no case be used against him, nor shall he be prosecuted as to the offense to which he has testified.

History.
Code 1950, § 29-181; 1987, c. 488.

§ 29.1-562: Reserved.

ARTICLE 6. ENDANGERED SPECIES.

§ 29.1-563. Definitions.

For the purposes of this article:

"Conservation plan" means a document developed by the Department and approved by the Director that describes the Department's approach to managing and, if possible, recovering an endangered or threatened species of fish or wildlife.

"Endangered species" means any species which is in danger of extinction throughout all or a significant portion of its range.

"Experimental population" means any population of an endangered or threatened species of fish or wildlife, excluding those species appearing on the federal list specified in § 29.1-564, that is (i) established through deliberate introduction by humans; (ii) designated by regulation of the Board; and (iii) explicitly delineated in a conservation plan.

"Fish or wildlife" means any member of the animal kingdom, vertebrate or invertebrate, except for the class Insecta, and includes any part, products, egg, or the dead body or parts thereof.

"Incidental take" means any taking of an endangered or threatened species of fish or wildlife, excluding those species appearing on the federal list specified in § 29.1-564, that otherwise would be prohibited by this article or by regulation, if such taking is incidental to but not the purpose of an otherwise lawful activity allowed in accordance with regulations adopted pursuant to § 29.1-568.

"Person" means any individual, firm, corporation, association or partnership.

"Threatened species" means any species which is likely to become an endangered species within the foreseeable future throughout all or a significant portion of its range.

History.

1972, c. 329, § 29-231; 1977, c. 377; 1987, c. 488; 1990, c. 369; 2011, c. 47.

§ 29.1-564. Taking, transportation, sale, etc., of endangered species prohibited.

The taking, transportation, possession, sale, or offer for sale within the Commonwealth of any fish or wildlife appearing on any list of threatened or endangered species published by the United States Secretary of the Interior pursuant to the provisions of the federal Endangered Species Act of 1973 (P.L. 93-205), or any modifications or amendments thereto, is prohibited except as provided in § 29.1-568.

History.

1972, c. 329, § 29-232; 1977, c. 377; 1987, c. 488.

§ 29.1-565: Reserved.

§ 29.1-566. Regulations.

The Board is authorized to adopt the federal list, as well as modifications and amendments thereto by regulations; to declare by regulation, after consideration of recommendations from the Director of the Department of Conservation and Recreation and from other reliable data sources, that species not appearing on the federal lists are endangered or threatened species in Virginia; and to prohibit by regulation the taking, transportation, processing, sale, or offer for sale within the Commonwealth of any threatened or endangered species of fish or wildlife.

History.

1972, c. 329, §§ 29-233, 29-234; 1977, c. 377; 1987, c. 488; 1989, c. 553.

§ 29.1-567. Penalties; authority of conservation police officers and police officers; disposition of property seized.

A. Any person who violates the provisions of § 29.1-564 or § 29.1-566, or any regulations issued pursuant to these sections, or whoever violates any regulation or permit issued under § 29.1-568 shall be guilty of a Class 1 misdemeanor; however, the sale, offering for sale, purchasing or offering to purchase within the Commonwealth of any fish or wildlife appearing on a list of threatened or endangered species as prohibited by § 29.1-564 shall be punishable as provided in § 29.1-553.

B. Any judicial officer or other officer authorized to issue criminal warrants shall have authority to issue a warrant for the search and seizure of any goods, business records, merchandise or fish or wildlife taken, employed or used in connection with a violation of any provision of this article. All such search warrants shall be issued and executed pursuant to Chapter 5 (§ 19.2-52 et seq.) of Title 19.2.

C. Goods, merchandise, fish or wildlife or records seized under the provisions of subsection B of this section shall be held by an officer or agent of the Department at the direction of the judge or court pending disposition of court proceedings, and thereafter be forfeited to the Commonwealth for destruction or disposition as the Director may deem appropriate. However, prior to forfeiture, the Director may direct the transfer of fish or wildlife so seized to a qualified zoological, educational, or scientific institution for safekeeping, with costs assessable to the defendant. The Board is authorized to issue regulations to implement this section.

History.

1972, c. 329, § 29-235; 1987, c. 488; 1990, c. 123; 1994, c. 848.

§ 29.1-568. When Board may permit taking of endangered or threatened species; designated experimental populations.

A. The Board may permit the taking, exportation, transportation, or possession of any fish or wildlife which is listed by the provisions of this article, for zoological, educational, or scientific purposes and for propagation of such fish or wildlife in captivity for preservation purposes. Any person may, in accordance with all applicable federal and state laws, possess, breed, sell, and transport any nonnative wildlife included on any list of threatened or endangered species published by the United States Secretary of the Interior pursuant to provisions of the federal Endangered Species Act of 1973 (P.L. 93-205), as amended, when (i) the federal designation does not specifically prohibit such possession, breeding, selling, or transporting and (ii) the nonnative wildlife is not included on the list of predatory or undesirable animals specified by regulations of the Board adopted pursuant to § 29.1-542.

B. The Board may adopt regulations that:

1. Allow the taking, possession, exportation, transportation, or release of fish or wildlife within or among designated experimental populations of a specific species, within the context of an approved conservation plan for the species. Any regulation designating an experimental population shall (i) specify the circumstances under which taking of an individual member of an experimental population will be exempt from the prohibitions and penalties authorized under this article and (ii) describe the geographic extent of the experimental population, which shall be distinct from naturally occurring

populations continuing to be subject to the prohibitions and penalties authorized under this article.

2. Allow incidental take provided such regulations shall (i) describe the allowable circumstances; (ii) include provisions that ensure offsets through the implementation of conservation actions specified by the Department to enhance the long-term survival of the species or population; and (iii) require any actual taking to be at a minimum.

History.
1972, c. 329, § 29-236; 1987, c. 488; 2011, c. 47; 2014, c. 481.

§ 29.1-569. Keeping of reptiles generally; penalty.

It shall be unlawful for the owner or keeper of any exotic reptile or type of reptile not native to the Commonwealth of Virginia, including but not limited to the American alligator, to keep the reptile in any manner that will permit its escape or to knowingly permit the reptile to run at large. Any violation of this section shall constitute a Class 2 misdemeanor.

History.
1980, c. 202, § 29-213.35; 1987, c. 488; 1999, c. 85.

§ 29.1-570. Cooperation of state agencies.

All departments, commissions, boards, authorities, agencies, offices and institutions within any branch of the state government shall cooperate with the Board in carrying out the purposes of this article.

History.
1978, c. 835, § 29-248; 1987, c. 488.

ARTICLE 7. NONINDIGENOUS AQUATIC NUISANCE SPECIES ACT.

§ 29.1-571. Definition.

"Nonindigenous aquatic nuisance species" means a nonindigenous aquatic freshwater animal species whose presence in state waters poses or is likely to pose a significant threat of harm to (i) the diversity or abundance of any species indigenous to state waters; (ii) the ecological stability of state waters; or (iii) the commercial, industrial, agricultural, municipal, recreational, aquacultural, or other beneficial uses of state waters. Nonindigenous aquatic nuisance species shall include the zebra mussel, quagga mussel, and all species of snakehead fishes of the family Channidae.

History.
2003, c. 446.

§ 29.1-572. Authority of Board; regulations.

The Board may promulgate regulations necessary to carry out the provisions of this article including, but not limited to, the designation of other nonindigenous aquatic nuisance species.

History.
2003, c. 446.

§ 29.1-573. Department; powers.

A. The Department may conduct operations and measures to suppress, control, eradicate, prevent, or retard the spread of any nonindigenous aquatic nuisance species. The maximum effort shall be made to utilize the best available scientific technology that is specific to the targeted nonindigenous aquatic nuisance species, environmentally sound, practical, and cost effective.

B. Such operations and measures shall be conducted subject to the appropriation of general funds authorized for the purpose of suppressing, controlling, eradicating, preventing, or retarding the spread of any nonindigenous aquatic nuisance species, or the receipt of funds designated for this purpose from private entities, local governments, political subdivisions, or federal grants. If such funds are not available to carry out the purposes of this chapter, then the Secretary of Natural Resources shall seek and accept all possible funds from other sources, including federal, state, local, and private grants, loans, and donations.

C. In carrying out its powers, the Department may cooperate with any federal agencies, any agency of an adjacent state, any other state agencies, local governments, political subdivisions, and authorities within the Commonwealth. Other state agencies shall cooperate and provide assistance as requested by the Director in carrying out the purposes of this article.

History.
2003, c. 446; 2004, c. 467.

§ 29.1-574. Prohibitions.

A. No person shall knowingly import, possess, transport, sell, purchase, give, receive, or introduce into the Commonwealth any member of a species designated as a nonindigenous aquatic nuisance species without a permit from the Director issued pursuant to § 29.1-575.

B. Subsection A shall not apply to any person who (i) lawfully catches a snakehead fish of the family *Channidae*, (ii) subsequently kills such fish, and (iii) notifies the Department, as soon as practicable, of his actions.

History.
2003, c. 446; 2005, c. 916.

§ 29.1-575. Permits.

The Director shall permit the importation, possession, purchase, receipt, or transportation of a nonindigenous aquatic nuisance species for purposes of research by recognized academic institutions or government agencies upon receiving satisfactory assurance that adequate safeguards will be maintained to prevent the escape or introduction of any such species into the Commonwealth.

History.
2003, c. 446.

§ 29.1-576. Authority for inspection; warrants.

To carry out the purposes of this article, the Director may obtain a warrant pursuant to § 19.2-52, or with the consent of the owner enter upon and conduct reasonable inspections of any property in the Commonwealth to determine if a nonindigenous aquatic nuisance species is present and to seize or eradicate any nonindigenous aquatic nuisance species found on such property.

History.
2003, c. 446.

§ 29.1-576.1. Zebra mussels; education program.

The Director shall establish an education program that instructs boaters and other members of the public in methods of preventing or slowing the infestation of the waters of the Commonwealth by zebra mussels, quagga mussels, or other nonindigenous aquatic nuisance species as defined in § 29.1-571. The education program may be delivered through the boating safety education program required by § 29.1-735.2, by posting on the Department's website, or by other means, and shall include cleaning and draining guidelines, designated dry times for watercraft and other recreational equipment, and public outreach, including published instructions and training videos.

History.
2016, c. 540.

§ 29.1-577. Penalties.

Any person who violates any provision of this article or who knowingly obstructs the Director or his designee in carrying out his lawful duties under this article shall upon such finding by a court of proper jurisdiction (i) be subject to a civil penalty of not more than $25,000, which shall be paid into the Game Protection Fund established pursuant to § 29.1-101, and (ii) be liable for the costs of investigation, control, and eradication incurred by any state agency, local government, political subdivision, or authority as a result of such unlawful conduct.

History.
2003, c. 446.

CHAPTER 7.
BOATING LAWS.

Article 1.
Boat Registration and Identification.

Article 2.
Watercraft Titling Certificates.

Article 2.1.
Virginia Uniform Certificate of Title for Watercraft Act.

ARTICLE 1.

BOAT REGISTRATION AND IDENTIFICATION.

§ 29.1-700. Definitions.

As used in this chapter, unless the context clearly requires a different meaning:

"Motorboat" means any vessel propelled by machinery whether or not the machinery is the principal source of propulsion.

"No wake" means operation of a motorboat at the slowest possible speed required to maintain steerage and headway.

"Operate" means to navigate or otherwise control the movement of a motorboat or a vessel.

"Owner" means a person, other than a lien holder, having the property in or title to a motorboat. The term includes a person entitled to the use or possession of a motorboat subject to an interest in another person, reserved or created by agreement and securing payment of performance of an obligation, but the term excludes a lessee under a lease not intended as security.

"Personal watercraft" means a motorboat less than sixteen feet in length which uses an inboard motor powering a jet pump, as its primary motive power and which is designed to be operated by a person sitting, standing, or kneeling on, rather than in the conventional manner of sitting or standing inside, the vessel.

"Vessel" means every description of watercraft, other than a seaplane on the water, used or capable of being used as a means of transportation on water.

"Waters of the Commonwealth" means any public waters within the territorial limits of the Commonwealth, the adjacent marginal sea and the high seas when navigated as a part of a journey or ride to or from the Virginia shore.

History.

Code 1960, c. 500, § 62-174.2; 1962, c. 626; 1968, c. 659, § 62.1-167; 1972, c. 412; 1987, c. 488; 1998, cc. 84, 443, 512, 514, 515, 533, 537, 563.

§ 29.1-701. Department to administer chapter; Motorboat Committee; funds for administration; records; rules and regulations.

A. It shall be the duty of the Department to enforce and administer the provisions of this chapter.

B. The chairman of the Board shall designate from among the members of the Board three members who shall serve as the Motorboat Committee. This committee shall place special emphasis on the administration and enforcement of this chapter.

C. All expenses required for administration and enforcement of this chapter shall be paid from the funds collected pursuant to the numbering and certificate of title provisions of this chapter. All moneys collected pursuant to the numbering and certificate of title provisions of this chapter shall be deposited into the state treasury credited to a special fund, known as the game protection fund, and accounted for as a separate part to be designated as the motorboat and water safety fund. Such moneys shall be made available to the Department solely for the administration and enforcement of this chapter, for educational activities relating to boating safety and for other activities and purposes of direct benefit to the boating public. Moneys from the motorboat and water safety fund shall not be diverted to any other state agency. The motorboat and water safety fund and moneys otherwise provided for in this chapter shall be made available to carry out the intent and purposes as set forth in this chapter in accordance with plans approved by the Board. All such funds are hereby reserved until expended for the enforcement, administration and other provisions of this chapter. However, the Board is authorized to adopt a plan or formula for the use of these moneys for employing and equipping any additional personnel necessary to carry out the provisions of this chapter and for paying a proportionate share of the salaries, expense, and operational costs of existing personnel according to the time and effort expended by them in carrying out the provisions of this chapter. Such plan or formula may be altered or amended from time to time by the Board as existing conditions may warrant. No funds derived from the sale of hunting licenses or fishing licenses shall be expended or diverted for carrying out the provisions of this chapter.

D. The Department shall maintain a record of all certificates of title it issues. The certificates of title may be located (i) under a distinctive title number assigned to each watercraft, (ii) under the hull identification number of each watercraft, (iii) under the registration number, (iv) alphabetically under the name of the owner, and (v) at the discretion of the Board by any additional methods it determines.

E. The Board shall make such rules and regulations as it deems necessary and proper for the effective administration of this chapter. The proposal and adoption of rules and regulations shall take place as prescribed in Article 1 (§ 29.1-500 et seq.) of Chapter 5 of this title and all rules and regulations shall be published by the Board in a convenient form. The Board shall cooperate with the Department of Taxation in issuing titles and collecting tax thereon.

History.

1960, c. 500, § 62-174.3; 1968, c. 659, § 62.1-168; 1972, c. 412; 1981, c. 405; 1987, cc. 101, 488.

§ 29.1-701.1. Authority of Board to set fees.

Notwithstanding any other provision of this title, the Board may by regulation adopt revisions in the fees, as it deems appropriate, charged for motorboat registration certificates and certificates of title under this chapter. Such license fees may be increased or decreased beginning July 1, 2004; however, no fee shall be increased or decreased more frequently than once every three years thereafter and no fee shall be increased or decreased more than $5 during such period.

History.

2004, c. 1027.

§ 29.1-702. Registration requirements; display of numbers; cancellation of certificate; exemption.

A. 1. The owner of each motorboat requiring numbering by the Commonwealth shall file an application for a number with the Department on forms approved by it. The owner of the motorboat or the owner's agent shall sign the application and pay the following boat registration fee:

a. For a motorboat under 16 feet, $18;

b. For a motorboat 16 feet to less than 20 feet, $22;

c. For a motorboat 20 feet to less than 40 feet, $28;

d. For a motorboat 40 feet and over, $36.

2. Owners, other than manufacturers or dealers, of more than 10 motorboats numbered by the Commonwealth, shall pay $18 each for the first 10 such boats and $12 for each additional boat.

3. Upon receipt of the application in approved form, the Department shall have the application entered upon the records of its office and issue to the applicant a certificate of number stating the identification number awarded to the motorboat and the name, address and a social security number or numbers, or federal tax identification number of the owner or owners. Any certificate issued in accordance with this chapter shall expire three years from the last day of the month in which it was issued. Upon proper application and payment of fee, and in the discretion of the Director, the certificate may be renewed.

B. The owner shall paint on or attach to each side of the bow of the motorboat the identification number in the manner prescribed by rules and regulations of the Board. The number shall be maintained in legible condition. The certificate of number shall be pocket-size and shall be available for inspection on the motorboat for which issued whenever such motorboat is in operation. However, the certificate of number for any vessel less than 26 feet in length, and leased or rented to another for the lessee's noncommercial use for less than 24 hours, may be retained on shore by the vessel's owner or his representative at the place at which the vessel departs and returns to the possession of the owner or his representative, provided the vessel is appropriately identified as to its owner while in use under such lease or rental.

C. No number other than the number awarded to a motorboat or granted reciprocity pursuant to this chapter shall be displayed on either side of the bow of the motorboat.

D. The Department is authorized to cancel and recall any certificate of number issued by the Department when it appears proper payment has not been made for the certificate of number or when the certificate has been improperly or erroneously issued.

E. Any motorboat purchased and used by a nonprofit volunteer emergency medical services agency or volunteer fire department shall be exempt from the registration fees imposed by subsection A.

History.
1960, c. 500, § 62-174.5; 1962, c. 626; 1964, c. 654; 1968, c. 659, § 62.1-170; 1970, c. 240; 1972, c. 412; 1980, c. 256; 1983, c. 126; 1986, c. 125; 1987, c. 488; 1990, c. 321; 1991, c. 82; 1992, c. 250; 2012, c. 233; 2015, cc. 502, 503.

§ 29.1-702.1. Making false affidavit or swearing falsely, perjury; penalty.

Any person who knowingly makes any false affidavit or knowingly swears to or affirms falsely any matter or thing required by this chapter or Chapter 8 (§ 29.1-800 et seq.) of this title or by the Director incidental to his administration of the boating laws shall, upon conviction, be guilty of perjury.

History.
1990, c. 321.

§ 29.1-703. Identification numbers required; decals.

Every motorboat on the waters of this Commonwealth shall be numbered except those specifically exempt in § 29.1-710. No person shall operate or give permission for the operation of any motorboat on such waters unless the motorboat is numbered in accordance with this chapter, federal law, or a federally approved numbering system of another state, or has been issued a temporary registration certificate pursuant to the provisions of § 29.1-703.1. In addition to the numbering requirements, (i) the certificate of number awarded or temporary registration certificate issued to the motorboat must be in effect, (ii) the identifying number set forth in the certificate of number must be displayed on each side of the bow of the motorboat, and (iii) decals signifying the last month and year during which the certificate of number is valid must be displayed on each side of the motorboat within six inches of the registration number so as to be visible while the motorboat is being operated. Decals will be furnished with each certificate of number issued or reissued by the Department. Expired decals must be removed from the vessel. Upon written request and for good cause, the Board may allow exceptions to the requirement to display decals. If a decal becomes defaced, lost or destroyed, application for replacement shall be made to the Board within fifteen days. A fee of one dollar shall be charged for each decal or set of decals replaced. Decals must be displayed upon the watercraft for which they were purchased and are not transferable.

History.
1960, c. 500, § 62-174.4; 1962, c. 626; 1968, c. 659, § 62.1-169; 1984, c. 3; 1987, c. 488; 1995, c. 241.

§ 29.1-703.1. Temporary registration certificate; fee; application.

A. An owner may obtain a temporary registration certificate from the Department or an authorized agent of the Department. The fee for the temporary registration certificate shall be ten dollars. Each temporary registration certificate issued shall be valid for a period of thirty days from the date of issuance. To qualify for a temporary registration certificate, the owner shall provide his name and address (including zip code), sufficient proof of ownership as determined by the Department and a description of the motorboat to include the: present number on the boat (if any); make and model; type of propulsion; year of manufacture; length as measured along the centerline; hull identification number; state of principal use; and required fee. Application for the permanent certificate of number and certificate of title (if applicable) with applicable fees shall be submitted to the Department immediately upon receipt of a temporary registration certificate.

B. A temporary registration certificate shall not be valid as proof of ownership for any vessel.

History.
1995, c. 241.

§ 29.1-703.2. Designation of agents; compensation to agents; deposit of temporary registration certificate moneys.

A. The Director may authorize any person to act as an agent to issue temporary registration certificates. Persons accepting such authorization may be issued temporary registration certificates which upon issuance, in conformity with this chapter and with any rules and regulations of the Board, shall be valid as if issued directly by the Director.

B. Notwithstanding the provisions of § 2.2-1802, the money received for temporary registration certificates issued pursuant to § 29.1-703.1 shall be paid by each agent to the Department for payment into the state treasury. All moneys collected by the Department from the issuance of temporary registration certificates shall be deposited into the game protection fund and credited to the motorboat and water safety fund.

C. As compensation for such service, agents shall add and retain an amount equal to the fee provided to agents for the sale of hunting and fishing licenses as provided in § 29.1-332.

D. Remittance to the Department shall be made by each agent as required by the Department.

History.
1995, c. 241.

§ 29.1-704. Recording previously awarded numbers.

The owner of any motorboat already covered by a number in effect which has been awarded to it pursuant to then operative federal law or pursuant to a federally approved numbering system of another state shall record the number prior to operating the motorboat on the waters of this Commonwealth in excess of the ninety-day reciprocity period provided for in § 29.1-710. Such recordation shall be in the manner and pursuant to the procedure required for the award of a number under § 29.1-702, except that no additional or substitute number shall be issued.

History.
1960, c. 500, § 62-174.5; 1962, c. 626; 1964, c. 654; 1968, c. 659, § 62.1-170; 1970, c. 240; 1972, c. 412; 1980, c. 256; 1983, c. 126; 1986, c. 125; 1987, c. 488.

§ 29.1-705. Change of ownership of motorboat; lost certificates.

Should the ownership of a numbered motorboat change, a new application form with the appropriate fee as provided in § 29.1-702 shall be filed with the Department, and a new certificate bearing the same number shall be awarded in the manner as provided for in an original award of number. If the registration of the former owner is valid and the new owner has in his possession the dated bill of sale and the valid registration card of the former owner, the new owner may operate the vessel for thirty days from the date of purchase. If a certificate is lost, a new certificate bearing the same number shall be issued upon payment of a fee of fifty cents. Possession of the certificate shall in cases involving prosecution for violation of any provision of this chapter be prima facie evidence that the person whose name appears thereon is the owner of the boat.

History.
1960, c. 500, § 62-174.5; 1962, c. 626; 1964, c. 654; 1968, c. 659, § 62.1-170; 1970, c. 240; 1972, c. 412; 1980, c. 256; 1983, c. 126; 1986, c. 125; 1987, c. 488.

§ 29.1-706. Agents awarding numbers.

The Director may award any certificate of number directly or may authorize any person to act as an agent to make award. Persons accepting such authorization may be assigned a block of numbers and certificates which upon award, in conformity with this chapter and with any rules and regulations of the Board, shall be valid as if awarded directly by the Director.

History.
1960, c. 500, § 62-174.5; 1962, c. 626; 1964, c. 654; 1968, c. 659, § 62.1-170; 1970, c. 240; 1972, c. 412; 1980, c. 256; 1983, c. 126; 1986, c. 125; 1987, c. 488.

§ 29.1-707. Records.

All records of the Department made or kept pursuant to this section shall be public records and shall be open for inspection subject to conditions the Board may prescribe. The Director shall furnish, without cost, the annual lists of boat registrations, as of January 1, to the commissioners of revenue of each county or city, except that the Director shall not send the lists to any commissioner who requests that he not receive them.

History.
1960, c. 500, § 62-174.5; 1962, c. 626; 1964, c. 654; 1968, c. 659, § 62.1-170; 1970, c. 240; 1972, c. 412; 1980, c. 256; 1983, c. 126; 1986, c. 125; 1987, c. 488.

§ 29.1-708. Transfer, destruction or abandonment of motorboat.

The owner shall furnish the Department with notice of (i) the transfer of all or any part of his interest other than the creation of a security interest in a motorboat numbered in Virginia pursuant to § 29.1-702 or § 29.1-704 or (ii) the destruction or abandonment of such motorboat, within fifteen days thereof. Such transfer, destruction, or abandonment shall terminate the certificate of number for the motorboat except that, in the case of a transfer of a part interest which does not affect the owner's right to operate such motorboat, the transfer shall not terminate the certificate of number.

History.
1960, c. 500, § 62-174.5; 1962, c. 626; 1964, c. 654; 1968, c. 659, § 62.1-170; 1970, c. 240; 1972, c. 412; 1980, c. 256; 1983, c. 126; 1986, c. 125; 1987, c. 488.

§ 29.1-709. Change of address of certificate holder.

Any holder of a certificate of number shall notify the Department within fifteen days if his address appearing on the certificate changes, and he shall furnish the Department with his new address. The Board may provide in its rules and regulations for the surrender of the certificate bearing the former address and for certificate replacements or alterations bearing the new address.

History.
1960, c. 500, § 62-174.5; 1962, c. 626; 1964, c. 654; 1968, c. 659, § 62.1-170; 1970, c. 240; 1972, c. 412; 1980, c. 256; 1983, c. 126; 1986, c. 125; 1987, c. 488.

§ 29.1-710. Exemption from numbering requirements.

A motorboat shall not be required to be numbered under this chapter if it is:

1. A motorboat which has been awarded a number pursuant to federal law or a federally approved numbering system of another state if the boat has been within the Commonwealth for less than ninety consecutive days.

2. A motorboat from a country other than the United States temporarily using the waters of the Commonwealth.

3. A motorboat which is used in a governmental function by the United States, a state or a subdivision of the state.

4. A ship's lifeboat.

5. A vessel which has a valid marine document issued by the Bureau of Customs of the United States government or any federal agency successor thereto.

6. A racing boat used during an authorized race and during a twenty-four-hour period before and after the race.

7. A motorboat belonging to a class of vessels which has been exempted from numbering by a regulation adopted by the Board after the Board has found that applicable federal law or federal regulation has exempted, or permitted the exemption of, such class of vessels.

8. A motorboat for which (i) a valid temporary registration certificate has been issued by the Department or an authorized agent of the Department, and (ii) an application has been made for a permanent registration and title (if applicable).

History.

1960, c. 500, § 62-174.7; 1962, c. 626; 1964, c. 654; 1968, c. 659, § 62.1-173; 1972, c. 412; 1987, c. 488; 1995, c. 241.

§ 29.1-711. Dealers and manufacturers of motorboats.

The following shall apply to dealers and manufacturers:

1. The registering and numbering requirements of this chapter shall apply to dealers and manufacturers of motorboats.

2. Applications for certificates of number shall be made on the approved application form prescribed in this chapter. Dealers and manufacturers shall certify that they are dealers or manufacturers.

3. Applications shall be accompanied by a fee of twenty-five dollars for dealers and forty dollars for manufacturers, by check or money order, and shall be forwarded to the Department.

4. Upon receipt by the Department of a properly completed application and fee, it shall issue to the applicant a dealer's or manufacturer's certificate of number, as appropriate, which may be used in connection with the operation of any motorboat in the possession of the dealer or manufacturer when the boat is being used for demonstration purposes.

5. Additional dealer's or manufacturer's certificates of number may be obtained by applying in the same manner as prescribed for the initial certificate with payment of an additional fee of twelve dollars for each additional certificate.

6. Manufacturers or dealers may have the number or numbers awarded to them printed upon or attached to a removable sign or signs to be temporarily but firmly mounted upon or attached to the boat being demonstrated, so long as the display meets the requirements of this chapter.

History.

1960, c. 500, § 62-174.5; 1962, c. 626; 1964, c. 654; 1968, c. 659, § 62.1-170; 1970, c. 240; 1972, c. 412; 1980, c. 256; 1983, c. 126; 1986, c. 125; 1987, c. 488; 1990, c. 321.

ARTICLE 2.
WATERCRAFT TITLING CERTIFICATES.

§§ 29.1-712 through 29.1-733.1: Repealed by Acts 2013, c. 787, cl. 2, effective July 1, 2014.

History.

1981, c. 405, § 62.1-186.1; 1984, c. 418; 1987, c. 488; 1997, c. 877.

Cross references.

For provisions of Virginia Uniform Certificate of Title for Watercraft Act, see Article 2.1 (§ 29.1-733.2 et seq.).

ARTICLE 2.1.
VIRGINIA UNIFORM CERTIFICATE OF TITLE FOR WATERCRAFT ACT.

§ 29.1-733.2. Definitions.

The definitions in this section do not apply to any Virginia or federal law governing licensing, numbering, or registration if the same term is used in that law. As used in this article, unless the context requires a different meaning:

"Abandoned watercraft" means a watercraft that is left unattended on private property for more than 10 days without the consent of the property's owner, regardless of whether it was brought onto the private property with the consent of the owner or person in control of the private property.

"Agreement" means the same as that term is defined in subdivision (b)(3) of § 8.1A-201.

"Barge" means a watercraft that is not self-propelled or fitted for propulsion by sail, paddle, oar, or similar device.

"Builder's certificate" means a certificate of the facts of the build of a vessel described in 46 C.F.R. § 67.99, as amended.

"Buyer" means a person that buys or contracts to buy a watercraft.

"Buyer in ordinary course of business" means the same as that term is defined in subdivision (b)(9) of § 8.1A-201.

"Cancel," with respect to a certificate of title, means to make the certificate ineffective.

Game and Inland Fisheries

"Certificate of origin" means a record created by a manufacturer or importer as the manufacturer's or importer's proof of identity of a watercraft. The term includes a manufacturer's certificate or statement of origin and an importer's certificate or statement of origin. The term does not include a builder's certificate.

"Certificate of title" means a record, created by the Department under this article or by a governmental agency of another jurisdiction under the law of that jurisdiction that is designated as a certificate of title by the Department or agency and is evidence of ownership of a watercraft.

"Conspicuous" means the same as that term is defined in subdivision (b)(10) of § 8.1A-201.

"Consumer goods" means the same as that term is defined in subdivision (a)(23) of § 8.9A-102.

"Dealer" means any watercraft dealer as defined in § 29.1-801.

"Debtor" means the same as that term is defined in subdivision (a)(28) of § 8.9A-102.

"Documented vessel" means a watercraft covered by a certificate of documentation issued pursuant to 46 U.S.C. § 12105, as amended. The term does not include a foreign-documented vessel.

"Electronic" means relating to technology having electrical, digital, magnetic, wireless, optical, electromagnetic, or similar capabilities.

"Electronic certificate of title" means a certificate of title consisting of information that is stored solely in an electronic medium and is retrievable in perceivable form.

"Foreign-documented vessel" means a watercraft whose ownership is recorded in a registry maintained by a country other than the United States that identifies each person that has an ownership interest in a watercraft and includes a unique alphanumeric designation for the watercraft.

"Good faith" means honesty in fact and the observance of reasonable commercial standards of fair dealing.

"Hull damaged" means compromised with respect to the integrity of a watercraft's hull by a collision, allision, lightning strike, fire, explosion, running aground, or similar occurrence, or the sinking of a watercraft in a manner that creates a significant risk to the integrity of the watercraft's hull.

"Hull identification number" means the alphanumeric designation assigned to a watercraft pursuant to 33 C.F.R. Part 181, as amended.

"Knowledge" means the same as that term is defined in § 8.1A-202.

"Lease" means the same as that term is defined in subdivision (1)(j) of § 8.2A-103.

"Lessor" means the same as that term is defined in subdivision (1)(p) of § 8.2A-103.

"Lien creditor," with respect to a watercraft, means:

1. A creditor that has acquired a lien on the watercraft by attachment, levy, or the like;

2. An assignee for benefit of creditors from the time of assignment;

3. A trustee in bankruptcy from the date of the filing of the petition; or

4. A receiver in equity from the time of appointment.

"Notice" means the same as that term is defined in § 8.1A-202.

"Owner" means a person that has legal title to a watercraft.

"Owner of record" means the owner indicated in the files of the Department or, if the files indicate more than one owner, the one first indicated.

"Person" means an individual, corporation, business trust, estate, trust, statutory trust, partnership, limited liability company, association, joint venture, public corporation, government or governmental subdivision, agency or instrumentality, or any other legal or commercial entity.

"Purchase" means to take by sale, lease, mortgage, pledge, consensual lien, security interest, gift, or any other voluntary transaction that creates an interest in a watercraft.

"Purchaser" means a person that takes by purchase.

"Record" means information that is inscribed on a tangible medium or that is stored in an electronic or other medium and is retrievable in perceivable form.

"Registration number" means the alphanumeric designation for a vessel issued pursuant to 46 U.S.C. § 12301, as amended.

"Representative" means the same as that term is defined in subdivision (b)(33) of § 8.1A-201.

"Sale" means the same as that term is defined in § 8.2-106.

"Secured party," with respect to a watercraft, means a person:

1. In whose favor a security interest is created or provided for under a security agreement, whether or not any obligation to be secured is outstanding;

2. That is a consignor under Title 8.9A; or

3. That holds a security interest arising under § 8.2-401 or 8.2-505, subsection (3) of § 8.2-711, or subsection (5) of § 8.2A-508.

"Secured party of record" means the secured party whose name is indicated as the name of the secured party in the files of the Department or, if the files indicate more than one secured party, the one first indicated.

"Security agreement" means the same as that term is defined in subdivision (a)(74) of § 8.9A-102.

"Security interest" means an interest in a watercraft that secures payment or performance of an obligation if the interest is created by contract or arises under § 8.2-401 or 8.2-505, subsection (3) of § 8.2-711, or subsection (5) of § 8.2A-508. The term includes any interest of a consignor in a watercraft in a transaction that is subject to Title 8.9A. The term does not include the special property interest of a buyer of a watercraft on identification of that watercraft to a contract for sale under § 8.2-401, but a buyer also may acquire a security interest by complying with Title 8.9A. Except as otherwise

provided in § 8.2-505, the right of a seller or lessor of a watercraft under Title 8.2 or Title 8.2A to retain or acquire possession of the watercraft is not a security interest, but a seller or lessor also may acquire a security interest by complying with Title 8.9A. The retention or reservation of title by a seller of a watercraft notwithstanding shipment or delivery to the buyer under § 8.2-401 is limited in effect to a reservation of a security interest. Whether a transaction in the form of a lease creates a security interest is determined by § 8.1A-304.

"Seller" means the same as that term is defined in subdivision (1)(o) of § 8.2A-103.

"Send" means the same as that term is defined in subdivision (b)(36) of § 8.1A-201.

"Sign" means, with present intent to authenticate or adopt a record, to:

1. Make or adopt a tangible symbol; or
2. Attach to or logically associate with the record an electronic symbol, sound, or process.

"State" means a state of the United States, the District of Columbia, Puerto Rico, the United States Virgin Islands, or any territory or insular possession subject to the jurisdiction of the United States.

"State of principal use" means the state on whose waters a watercraft is or will be used, operated, navigated, or employed more than on the waters of any other state during a calendar year.

"Title brand" means a designation of previous damage, use, or condition that shall be indicated on a certificate of title.

"Transfer of ownership" means a voluntary or involuntary conveyance of an interest in a watercraft.

"Value" means the same as that term is defined in § 8.1A-204.

"Watercraft" means any vessel that is used or capable of being used as a means of transportation on water and is propelled by machinery, whether or not the machinery is the principal source of propulsion, except:

1. A seaplane;
2. An amphibious vehicle for which a certificate of title is issued pursuant to Chapter 6 (§ 46.2-600 et seq.) of Title 46.2 or a similar statute of another state;
3. A vessel that measures 18 feet or less in length along the centerline and is propelled by sail;
4. A vessel that operates only on a permanently fixed, manufactured course and whose movement is restricted to or guided by means of a mechanical device to which the vessel is attached or by which the vessel is controlled;
5. A stationary floating structure that:

a. Does not have and is not designed to have a mode of propulsion of its own;

b. Is dependent for utilities upon a continuous utility hookup to a source originating on shore; and

c. Has a permanent, continuous hookup to a shoreside sewage system;

6. A vessel owned by the United States, a state, or a foreign government or a political subdivision of any of them;
7. A vessel used solely as a lifeboat on another vessel; or
8. A vessel that has a valid marine document issued by the United States Coast Guard.

"Written certificate of title" means a certificate of title consisting of information inscribed on a tangible medium.

History.
2013, c. 787; 2014, c. 371.

§ 29.1-733.3. Applicability.

Subject to § 29.1-733.29, this article applies to any transaction, certificate of title, or record relating to a watercraft, even if the transaction, certificate of title, or record was entered into or created before July 1, 2014.

History.
2013, c. 787.

§ 29.1-733.4. Supplemental principles of law and equity.

Unless displaced by a provision of this article, the principles of law and equity supplement its provisions.

History.
2013, c. 787.

§ 29.1-733.5. Law governing watercraft covered by certificate of title.

A. The law of the state or other jurisdiction under whose certificate of title a watercraft is covered governs all issues relating to the certificate from the time the watercraft becomes covered by the certificate until the watercraft becomes covered by another certificate or becomes a documented watercraft, even if no other relationship exists between the jurisdiction and the watercraft or its owner.

B. A watercraft becomes covered by a certificate of title when an application for the certificate and the applicable fee are delivered to the Department in accordance with this article or to the governmental agency that creates a certificate in another jurisdiction in accordance with the law of that jurisdiction.

History.
2013, c. 787.

§ 29.1-733.6. Certificate of title required.

A. No person shall operate a watercraft subject to titling under this chapter unless the owner has applied to the Department for a certificate of title for the watercraft or has been issued a valid temporary registration certificate as provided for in § 29.1-703.1. Except as otherwise provided in subsections B through E, the owner of a watercraft for which Virginia is the state of principal use shall deliver to the Department an application for a certificate of title for the watercraft, with the applicable fee, not later than 20 days after the later of:

1. The date of a transfer of ownership; or

2. The date Virginia becomes the state of principal use.

B. An application for a certificate of title is not required for:

1. A documented vessel;

2. A foreign-documented vessel;

3. A barge;

4. A watercraft before delivery if the watercraft is under construction or completed pursuant to contract; or

5. A watercraft held by a dealer for sale or lease.

C. A dealer transferring a watercraft required to be titled under this article shall assign the title to the new owner or, in the case of a new watercraft, assign the certificate of origin. The dealer shall forward all fees and applications to the Department within 20 days of sale. Each dealer shall maintain a record for six years of any watercraft he bought, sold, exchanged, or received for sale or exchange. This record shall be available for inspection by Department representatives during reasonable business hours.

D. No dealer shall purchase or acquire a new watercraft without obtaining from the seller a certificate of origin. No manufacturer, importer, dealer, or other person shall sell or otherwise dispose of a new watercraft to a dealer for purposes of display and resale without delivering to the dealer a certificate of origin. The certificate of origin shall be a uniform or standardized form prescribed by the Department and shall contain:

1. On the front, a description of the watercraft including its trade name, if any, year, series or model, body type, and manufacturer's serial number; certification of date of transfer of watercraft and name and address of transferee; certification that this was the transfer of watercraft in ordinary trade and commerce; and the signature and address of a representative of the transferor; and

2. On the reverse side, an assignment form, including the name and address of the transferee, a certification that the watercraft is new, and a warranty that the title at the time of delivery is subject only to such liens and encumbrances as set forth and described in full in the assignment.

E. The Department shall not issue, transfer, or renew pursuant to the requirements of 46 U.S.C. § 12301, as amended, a certificate of number for a watercraft unless the Department has created a certificate of title for the watercraft or an application for a certificate for the watercraft and the applicable fee have been delivered to the Department. Any owner of a watercraft that was not previously required to be titled and whose certificate of number expires after January 1, 1998, shall apply for a certificate of title at the time of renewal of the certificate of number.

History.
2013, c. 787.

§ 29.1-733.7. Application for certificate of title.

A. Except as otherwise provided in § 29.1-733.10, 29.1-733.15, 29.1-733.19, 29.1-733.20, 29.1-733.21, or 29.1-733.22, only an owner may apply for a certificate of title.

B. An application for a certificate of title shall be signed by the applicant and contain:

1. The applicant's name, the street address of the applicant's principal residence, and, if different, the applicant's mailing address;

2. The name and mailing address of each other owner of the watercraft at the time of application;

3. The motor vehicle driver's license number, social security number, or taxpayer identification number of each owner;

4. The hull identification number for the watercraft or, if none, an application for the issuance of a hull identification number for the watercraft;

5. If numbering is required pursuant to § 29.1-703, the registration number for the watercraft or, if none has been issued by the Department, an application for a registration number pursuant to § 29.1-702;

6. A description of the watercraft as required by the Department, which shall include:

a. The official number for the watercraft, if any, assigned by the U.S. Coast Guard;

b. The name of the manufacturer, builder, or maker;

c. The model year or the year in which the manufacture or build of the watercraft was completed;

d. The overall length of the watercraft;

e. The watercraft type;

f. The hull material;

g. The propulsion type;

h. The engine drive type, if any;

i. The motor identification, including manufacturer's name and serial number, except on motors of 25 horsepower or less; and

j. The fuel type, if any;

7. An indication of all security interests in the watercraft known to the applicant and the name and mailing address of each secured party;

8. A statement that the watercraft is not a documented vessel or a foreign-documented vessel;

9. Any title brand known to the applicant and, if known, the jurisdiction under whose law the title brand was created;

10. If the applicant knows that the watercraft is hull damaged, a statement that the watercraft is hull damaged;

11. If the application is made in connection with a transfer of ownership, the transferor's name, street address and, if different, mailing address, the sales price, if any, and the date of the transfer; and

12. If the watercraft previously was registered or titled in another jurisdiction, a statement identify-

ing each jurisdiction known to the applicant in which the watercraft was registered or titled.

C. In addition to the information required by subsection B, an application for a certificate of title may contain an electronic communication address of the owner, transferor, or secured party.

D. Except as otherwise provided in § 29.1-733.19, 29.1-733.20, 29.1-733.21, or 29.1-733.22, an application for a certificate of title shall be accompanied by:

1. A certificate of title that is signed by the owner shown on the certificate and that:

a. Identifies the applicant as the owner of the watercraft; or

b. Is accompanied by a record that identifies the applicant as the owner; or

2. If there is no certificate of title:

a. If the watercraft was a documented vessel, a record issued by the U.S. Coast Guard that shows that the watercraft is no longer a documented vessel and identifies the applicant as the owner;

b. If the watercraft was a foreign-documented vessel, a record issued by the foreign country that shows that the watercraft is no longer a foreign-documented vessel and identifies the applicant as the owner; or

c. In all other cases, a certificate of origin, bill of sale, or other record that to the satisfaction of the Department identifies the applicant as the owner. Issuance of registration under the provisions of § 29.1-702 is prima facie evidence of ownership of a watercraft and entitlement to a certificate of title under the provisions of this article.

E. A record submitted in connection with an application is part of the application. The Department shall maintain the record in its files.

F. The Department shall require that an application for a certificate of title be accompanied by payment or evidence of payment of all fees and taxes payable by the applicant under law of the Commonwealth other than this article in connection with the application or the acquisition or use of the watercraft. The Department shall charge $7 for issue of each certificate of title, transfer of title, or for the recording of a supplemental lien. The Department shall charge $2 for the issuance of each duplicate title or for changes to a previously issued certificate of title that are made necessary by a change of the motor on the watercraft. Any watercraft purchased and used by a nonprofit volunteer emergency medical services agency shall be exempt from the fees imposed under this section.

G. The application shall be on forms prescribed and furnished by the Department and shall contain any other information required by the Director.

H. Whenever any person, after applying for or obtaining the certificate of title of a watercraft, moves from the address shown in the application or upon the certificate of title, he shall, within 30 days, notify the Department in writing of his change of address. A fee of $7 shall be imposed upon anyone failing to comply with this subsection within the time prescribed.

History.

2013, c. 787; 2014, c. 371; 2015, cc. 502, 503.

§ 29.1-733.8. Creation and cancellation of certificate of title.

A. Unless an application for a certificate of title is rejected under subsection C or D, the Department shall create a certificate for the watercraft in accordance with subsection B not later than 20 days after delivery to it of an application that complies with § 29.1-733.7.

B. If the Department creates electronic certificates of title, the Department shall create an electronic certificate unless in the application the secured party of record or, if none, the owner of record, requests that the Department create a written certificate.

C. Except as otherwise provided in subsection D, the Department shall reject an application for a certificate of title only if:

1. The application does not comply with § 29.1-733.7;

2. The application does not contain documentation sufficient for the Department to determine whether the applicant is entitled to a certificate;

3. There is a reasonable basis for concluding that the application is fraudulent or issuance of a certificate would facilitate a fraudulent or illegal act; or

4. The application does not comply with the law of the Commonwealth other than this article.

D. The Department shall reject an application for a certificate of title for a watercraft that is a documented vessel or a foreign-documented vessel.

E. The Department shall cancel a certificate of title created by it only if the Department:

1. Could have rejected the application for the certificate under subsection C;

2. Is required to cancel the certificate under another provision of this article; or

3. Receives satisfactory evidence that the watercraft is a documented vessel or a foreign-documented vessel.

F. The Department shall provide an opportunity for an informal fact-finding proceeding at which the owner and any other interested party may present evidence in support of or opposition to cancellation of a certificate of title. The Department shall serve all owners and secured parties indicated in the files of the Department with notice of the opportunity for an informal fact-finding proceeding. Service shall be made personally or by mail through the U.S. Postal Service, properly addressed, postage paid, return receipt requested. Service by mail is complete on deposit with the U.S. Postal Service. The Department by rule may authorize service by electronic transmission if a copy is sent on the same day by first-class mail or by a commercial delivery company. If not later than 30 days after the notice was served, the Department receives a request for an informal fact-finding proceeding from an interested party, the Department shall hold the proceeding not later than 20 days after receiving the request.

History.
2013, c. 787.

§ 29.1-733.9. Content of certificate of title.

A. A certificate of title shall contain:

1. The date the certificate was created;

2. The name of the owner of record and, if not all owners are listed, an indication that there are additional owners indicated in the files of the Department;

3. The mailing address of the owner of record;

4. The hull identification number;

5. The information listed in subdivision B 6 of § 29.1-733.7;

6. Except as otherwise provided in subsection B of § 29.1-733.15, the name and mailing address of the secured party of record, if any, and if not all secured parties are listed, an indication that there are other security interests indicated in the files of the Department; and

7. All title brands indicated in the files of the Department covering the watercraft, including brands indicated on a certificate created by a governmental agency of another jurisdiction and delivered to the Department.

B. The Department may note on a certificate of title the name and mailing address of a secured party that is not a secured party of record.

C. For each title brand indicated on a certificate of title, the certificate shall identify the jurisdiction under whose law the title brand was created or the jurisdiction that created the certificate on which the title brand was indicated. If the meaning of a title brand is not easily ascertainable or cannot be accommodated on the certificate, the certificate may state: "Previously branded in (insert the jurisdiction under whose law the title brand was created or whose certificate of title previously indicated the title brand)."

D. If the files of the Department indicate that a watercraft previously was registered or titled in a foreign country, the Department shall indicate on the certificate of title that the watercraft was registered or titled in that country.

E. A written certificate of title shall contain a form that all owners indicated on the certificate may sign to evidence consent to a transfer of an ownership interest to another person. The form shall include a certification, signed under penalty of perjury, that the statements made are true and correct to the best of each owner's knowledge, information, and belief.

F. A written certificate of title shall contain a form for the owner of record to indicate, in connection with a transfer of an ownership interest, that the watercraft is hull damaged.

History.
2013, c. 787.

§ 29.1-733.10. Title brand.

A. Unless subsection C applies, at or before the time the owner of record transfers an ownership interest in a hull-damaged watercraft that is covered by a certificate of title created by the Department, if the damage occurred while that person was an owner of the watercraft and the person has notice of the damage at the time of the transfer, the owner shall:

1. Deliver to the Department an application for a new certificate that complies with § 29.1-733.7 and includes the title brand designation "Hull Damaged"; or

2. Indicate on the certificate in the place designated for that purpose that the watercraft is hull damaged and deliver the certificate to the transferee.

B. Not later than 20 days after delivery to the Department of the application under subdivision A 1 or the certificate of title under subdivision A 2, the Department shall create a new certificate that indicates that the watercraft is branded "Hull Damaged."

C. Before an insurer transfers an ownership interest in a hull-damaged watercraft that is covered by a certificate of title created by the Department, the insurer shall deliver to the Department an application for a new certificate that complies with § 29.1-733.7 and includes the title brand designation "Hull Damaged." Not later than 20 days after delivery of the application to the Department, the Department shall create a new certificate that indicates that the watercraft is branded "Hull Damaged."

D. An owner of record that fails to comply with subsection A, a person that solicits or colludes in a failure by an owner of record to comply with subsection A, or an insurer that fails to comply with subsection C is subject to a civil penalty of $1,000.

History.
2013, c. 787.

§ 29.1-733.11. Maintenance of and access to files.

A. For each record relating to a certificate of title submitted to the Department, the Department shall:

1. Ascertain or assign the hull identification number for the watercraft;

2. Maintain the hull identification number and all the information submitted with the application pursuant to subsection B of § 29.1-733.7 to which the record relates, including the date and time the record was delivered to the Department;

3. Maintain the files for public inspection subject to subsection E; and

4. Index the files of the Department as required by subsection B.

B. The Department shall maintain in its files the information contained in all certificates of title created under this article. The information in the files of the Department shall be searchable by the hull identification number of the watercraft, the registration number, the name of the owner of record, and any other method used by the Department.

C. The Department shall maintain in its files, for each watercraft for which it has created a certificate of title, all title brands known to the Department, the name of each secured party known to the Department, the name of each person known to the Department to be claiming an ownership interest, and all stolen-property reports the Department has received.

D. Upon request, for safety, security, or law-enforcement purposes, the Department shall provide to federal, state, or local government the information in its files relating to any watercraft for which the Department has issued a certificate of title.

E. Except as otherwise provided by the law of the Commonwealth other than this article, the information required under § 29.1-733.9 is a public record. The information provided under subdivision B 3 of § 29.1-733.7 is not a public record.

History.
2013, c. 787.

§ 29.1-733.12. Action required on creation of certificate of title.

A. On creation of a written certificate of title, the Department promptly shall send the certificate to the secured party of record or, if none, to the owner of record at the address indicated for that person in the files of the Department. On creation of an electronic certificate of title, the Department promptly shall send a record evidencing the certificate to the owner of record and, if there is one, to the secured party of record at the address indicated for that person in the files of the Department. The Department shall send the record to the person's mailing address or, if indicated in the files of the Department, an electronic address.

B. If the Department creates a written certificate of title, any electronic certificate of title for the watercraft is canceled and replaced by the written certificate. The Department shall maintain in the files of the Department the date and time of cancellation.

C. Before the Department creates an electronic certificate of title, any written certificate for the watercraft shall be surrendered to the Department. If the Department creates an electronic certificate, the Department shall destroy or otherwise cancel the written certificate for the watercraft that has been surrendered to the Department and maintain in the files of the Department the date and time of destruction or other cancellation. If a written certificate being canceled is not destroyed, the Department shall indicate on the face of the certificate that it has been canceled.

History.
2013, c. 787.

§ 29.1-733.13. Effect of certificate of title.

A certificate of title is prima facie evidence of the accuracy of the information in the record that constitutes the certificate.

History.
2013, c. 787.

§ 29.1-733.14. Effect of possession of certificate of title; judicial process; levy; penalty.

A. Possession of a certificate of title does not by itself provide a right to obtain possession of a watercraft. Garnishment, attachment, levy, replevin, or other judicial process against the certificate is not effective to determine possessory rights to the watercraft. This article does not prohibit enforcement under law of the Commonwealth other than this article of a security interest in, levy on, or foreclosure of a statutory or common-law lien on a watercraft. Absence of an indication of a statutory or common-law lien on a certificate does not invalidate the lien.

B. A levy made by virtue of an execution, fieri facias, or other proper court order, upon a watercraft for which a certificate of title has been issued by the Department, shall constitute a lien, when the officer making the levy reports to the Department at its principal office, on forms provided by the Department, that the levy has been made and that the vessel levied upon is in the custody of the officer. Should the lien thereafter be satisfied or should the vessel levied upon and seized thereafter be released by the officer, he shall immediately report that fact to the Department at its principal office. Any owner who, after such levy and seizure by an officer and before the report is made by the officer to the Department, fraudulently assigns or transfers his title to or interest in the watercraft, or causes the certificate of title to be assigned or transferred, or causes a security interest to be shown upon such certificate of title, is guilty of a Class 1 misdemeanor.

History.
2013, c. 787.

§ 29.1-733.15. Perfection of security interest.

A. Except as otherwise provided in this section or § 29.1-733.29, a security interest in a watercraft shall be perfected only by delivery to the Department of an application for a certificate of title that identifies the secured party and otherwise complies with § 29.1-733.7. The security interest is perfected on the later of delivery to the Department of the application and the applicable fee or attachment of the security interest under § 8.9A-203.

B. If the interest of a person named as owner, lessor, consignor, or bailor in an application for a certificate of title delivered to the Department is a security interest, the application sufficiently identifies the person as a secured party. Identification on the application for a certificate of a person as owner, lessor, consignor, or bailor is not by itself a factor in determining whether the person's interest is a security interest.

C. If the Department has created a certificate of title for a watercraft, a security interest in the watercraft shall be perfected by delivery to the Department of an application, on a form the Department shall require, to have the security interest added to the certificate. The application shall be signed by an owner of the watercraft or by the secured party and shall include:

1. The name of the owner of record;

2. The name and mailing address of the secured party;

3. The hull identification number for the watercraft; and

4. If the Department has created a written certificate of title for the watercraft, the certificate.

D. A security interest perfected under subsection C is perfected on the later of delivery to the Department of the application and all applicable fees or attachment of the security interest under § 8.9A-203.

E. On delivery of an application that complies with subsection C and payment of all applicable fees, the Department shall create a new certificate of title pursuant to § 29.1-733.8 and deliver the new certificate or a record evidencing an electronic certificate pursuant to subsection A of § 29.1-733.12. The Department shall maintain in the files of the Department the date and time of delivery of the application to the Department.

F. If a secured party assigns a perfected security interest in a watercraft, the receipt by the Department of a statement providing the name of the assignee as secured party is not required to continue the perfected status of the security interest against creditors of and transferees from the original debtor. A purchaser of a watercraft subject to a security interest that obtains a release from the secured party indicated in the files of the Department or on the certificate takes free of the security interest and of the rights of a transferee unless the transfer is indicated in the files of the Department or on the certificate.

G. This section does not apply to a security interest:

1. In a watercraft by a person during any period in which the watercraft is inventory held for sale or lease by the person or is leased by the person as lessor if the person is in the business of selling watercraft;

2. In a barge for which no application for a certificate of title has been delivered to the Department; or

3. In a watercraft before delivery if the watercraft is under construction, or completed, pursuant to contract and for which no application for a certificate has been delivered to the Department.

H. This subsection applies if a certificate of documentation for a documented vessel is deleted or canceled. If a security interest in the watercraft was valid immediately before deletion or cancellation against a third party as a result of compliance with 46 U.S.C. § 31321, the security interest is and remains perfected until the earlier of four months after cancellation of the certificate or the time the security interest becomes perfected under this article.

I. A security interest in a watercraft arising under § 8.2-401 or 8.2-505, subsection (3) of § 8.2-711, or subsection (5) of § 8.2A-508 is perfected when it attaches but becomes unperfected when the debtor obtains possession of the watercraft, unless before the debtor obtains possession the security interest is perfected pursuant to subsection A or C.

J. A security interest in a watercraft as proceeds of other collateral is perfected to the extent provided in § 8.9A-315.

K. A security interest in a watercraft perfected under the law of another jurisdiction is perfected to the extent provided in subsection (d) of § 8.9A-316.

History.
2013, c. 787.

§ 29.1-733.16. Termination statement; delivery of certificate of title; penalty.

A. A secured party indicated in the files of the Department as having a security interest in a watercraft shall deliver a termination statement to the Department and, on the debtor's request, to the debtor by the earlier of:

1. Twenty days after the secured party receives a signed demand from an owner for a termination statement and there is no obligation secured by the watercraft subject to the security interest and no commitment to make an advance, incur an obligation, or otherwise give value secured by the watercraft; or

2. If the watercraft is consumer goods, 30 days after there is no obligation secured by the watercraft and no commitment to make an advance, incur an obligation, or otherwise give value secured by the watercraft.

B. If a written certificate of title has been created and delivered to a secured party and a termination statement is required under subsection A, the secured party, not later than the date required by subsection A, shall deliver the certificate to the debtor or to the Department with the statement. An owner, upon securing the release of any security interest upon a vessel shown upon the certificate of title issued for the watercraft, may exhibit the documents evidencing the release, signed by the person or persons making such release, and the certificate of title to the Department. If the certificate is lost, stolen, mutilated, destroyed, or is otherwise unavailable or illegible, the secured party shall deliver with the statement, not later than the date required by subsection A, an application for a replacement certificate meeting the requirements of § 29.1-733.22.

C. On delivery to the Department of a termination statement authorized by the secured party, the security interest to which the statement relates ceases to be perfected. If the security interest to which the statement relates was indicated on the certificate of title, the Department shall create a new certificate and deliver the new certificate or a record evidencing an electronic certificate. The Department shall maintain in its files the date and time of delivery to the Department of the statement.

D. A secured party that fails to deliver a required termination statement is liable for any loss that the secured party had reason to know might result from its failure to comply and that could not reasonably have been prevented and for the cost of an application for a certificate of title under § 29.1-733.7 or 29.1-733.22.

E. It shall constitute a Class 1 misdemeanor for a secured party who holds a certificate of title to refuse or fail to surrender the certificate to the owner or his agent within 10 days after the security interest has been paid and satisfied.

History.
2013, c. 787.

§ 29.1-733.17. Transfer of ownership.

A. On voluntary transfer of an ownership interest in a watercraft covered by a certificate of title, the following rules apply:

1. If the certificate is a written certificate of title and the transferor's interest is noted on the certificate, the transferor promptly shall sign the certificate and deliver it to the transferee. If the transferor does not have possession of the certificate, the person in possession of the certificate has a duty to facilitate the transferor's compliance with this subdivision. A secured party does not have a duty to facilitate the transferor's compliance with this subdivision if the proposed transfer is prohibited by the security agreement.

2. If the certificate of title is an electronic certificate of title, the transferor promptly shall sign and deliver to the transferee a record evidencing the transfer of ownership to the transferee.

3. The transferee has a right enforceable by specific performance to require the transferor comply with subdivision 1 or 2.

B. The creation of a certificate of title identifying the transferee as owner of record satisfies subsection A.

C. A failure to comply with subsection A or to apply for a new certificate of title does not render a transfer of ownership of a watercraft ineffective between the parties. Except as otherwise provided in § 29.1-733.18, 29.1-733.19, 29.1-733.23, or 29.1-733.24, a transfer of ownership without compliance with subsection A is not effective against another person claiming an interest in the watercraft.

D. A transferor that complies with subsection A is not liable as owner of the watercraft for an event occurring after the transfer, regardless of whether the transferee applies for a new certificate of title.

History.
2013, c. 787.

§ 29.1-733.18. Effect of missing or incorrect information.

Except as otherwise provided in § 8.9A-337, a certificate of title or other record required or authorized by this article is effective even if it contains incorrect information or does not contain required information.

History.
2013, c. 787.

§ 29.1-733.19. Transfer of ownership by secured party's transfer statement.

A. For the purpose of this section, "secured party's transfer statement" means a record signed by the secured party of record stating:

1. A default on an obligation secured by the watercraft has occurred;

2. The secured party of record is exercising or has exercised post-default remedies with respect to the watercraft;

3. By reason of the exercise, the secured party of record has the right to transfer the ownership interest of an owner, and the name of the owner;

4. The name and last-known mailing address of the owner of record and the secured party of record;

5. The name of the transferee;

6. All other information required by subsection B of § 29.1-733.7; and

7. One of the following:

a. The certificate of title is an electronic certificate;

b. The secured party does not have possession of the written certificate of title created in the name of the owner of record; or

c. The secured party is delivering the written certificate of title to the Department with the secured party's transfer statement.

B. Unless the Department rejects a secured party's transfer statement for a reason stated in subsection C of § 29.1-733.8, not later than 20 days after delivery to the Department of the statement and payment of fees and taxes payable under the law of the Commonwealth other than this article in connection with the statement or the acquisition or use of the watercraft, the Department shall:

1. Accept the statement;

2. Amend the files of the Department to reflect the transfer; and

3. If the name of the owner whose ownership interest is being transferred is indicated on the certificate of title:

a. Cancel the certificate even if the certificate has not been delivered to the Department;

b. Create a new certificate indicating the transferee as owner; and

c. Deliver the new certificate or a record evidencing an electronic certificate.

C. An application under subsection A or the creation of a certificate of title under subsection B is not by itself a disposition of the watercraft and does not by itself relieve the secured party of its duties under Title 8.9A.

History.
2013, c. 787.

§ 29.1-733.20. Transfer by operation of law.

A. As used in this section, unless the context requires a different meaning:

"By operation of law" means pursuant to a law or judicial order affecting ownership of a watercraft:

1. Because of death, such as in the case of a legatee, distributee, or surviving joint owner;

2. Because of divorce or other family law proceeding;

3. Because of any written agreement ratified or incorporated in a decree or order of a court of record;

4. Because of merger, consolidation, dissolution, insolvency, or bankruptcy;

5. Because of an execution sale;

6. Through the exercise of the rights of a lien creditor or a person having a lien created by statute or rule of law, including a lien provided for in § 43-34; or

7. Through other legal process.

"Transfer-by-law statement" means a record signed by a transferee stating that by operation of law the transferee has acquired or has the right to acquire an ownership interest in a watercraft.

B. A transfer-by-law statement shall contain:

1. The name and last-known mailing address of the owner of record and the transferee and the other information required by subsection B of § 29.1-733.7;

2. Documentation sufficient to establish the transferee's ownership interest or right to acquire the ownership interest;

3. A statement that:

a. The certificate of title is an electronic certificate of title;

b. The transferee does not have possession of the written certificate of title created in the name of the owner of record; or

c. The transferee is delivering the written certificate to the Department with the transfer-by-law statement;

4. Except for a transfer described in subdivision 1 of the definition of "by operation of law," evidence that notification of the transfer and the intent to file the transfer-by-law statement has been sent to all persons indicated in the files of the Department as having an interest, including a security interest, in the watercraft; and

5. If the owner is dead and no fiduciary has qualified for his estate, an estate statement to the effect that no qualification for the estate has been made, that no qualification is expected, and that the decedent's debts have been paid or that the proceeds from the sale of the watercraft will be applied against his debts. The estate statement shall contain the name, residence at the time of death, and date of death of the decedent and the names of any other persons having an interest in the watercraft for which the transfer of title is sought. If these persons are of legal age, they shall signify in writing their consent to the transfer.

C. Unless the Department rejects a transfer-by-law statement for a reason stated in subsection C of § 29.1-733.8 or because the statement does not include documentation or an estate statement satisfactory to the Department as to the transferee's ownership interest or right to acquire the ownership interest, not later than 20 days after delivery to the Department of the transfer-by-law statement and payment of fees and taxes payable under the law of the Commonwealth other than this article in connection with the statement or with the acquisition or use of the watercraft, the Department shall:

1. Accept the statement;

2. Amend the files of the Department to reflect the transfer; and

3. If the name of the owner whose ownership interest is being transferred is indicated on the certificate of title:

a. Cancel the certificate even if the certificate has not been delivered to the Department;

b. Create a new certificate indicating the transferee as owner;

c. Indicate on the new certificate any security interest indicated on the canceled certificate, unless a court order provides otherwise; and

d. Deliver the new certificate or a record evidencing an electronic certificate.

D. This section does not apply to a transfer of an interest in a watercraft by a secured party under Part 6 (§ 8.9A-601 et seq.) of Title 8.9A.

History.
2013, c. 787.

§ 29.1-733.21. Application for transfer of ownership or termination of security interest without certificate of title.

A. Except as otherwise provided in § 29.1-733.19 or 29.1-733.20, if the Department receives, unaccompanied by a signed certificate of title, an application for a new certificate that includes an indication of a transfer of ownership or a termination statement, the Department shall create a new certificate under this section only if:

1. All other requirements under §§ 29.1-733.7 and 29.1-733.8 are met;

2. The applicant provides an affidavit stating facts showing the applicant is entitled to a transfer of ownership or termination statement;

3. The applicant provides the Department with satisfactory evidence that notification of the application has been sent to the owner of record and all persons indicated in the files of the Department as having an interest, including a security interest, in the watercraft, at least 45 days have passed since the notification was sent, and the Department has not received an objection from any of those persons; and

4. The applicant submits any other information required by the Department as evidence of the applicant's ownership or right to terminate the security interest, and the Department has no credible information indicating theft, fraud, or an undisclosed or unsatisfied security interest, lien, or other claim to an interest in the watercraft.

B. The Department shall indicate in a certificate of title created under subsection A that the certificate was created without submission of a signed certificate or termination statement. Unless credible information indicating theft, fraud, or an undisclosed or unsatisfied security interest, lien, or other claim to an interest in the watercraft is delivered to the Department not later than one year after creation of the certificate, on request in a form and manner required by the Department, the Department shall remove the indication from the certificate.

C. Unless the Department determines that the value of a watercraft is less than $5,000, before the Department creates a certificate of title under subsection A, the Department shall require the applicant to post a bond or provide an equivalent source of indemnity or security. The bond, indemnity, or other security shall not exceed twice the value of the watercraft as determined by the Department. The bond, indemnity, or other security shall be in a form required by the Department and provide for indemnification of any owner, purchaser, or other claimant for any expense, loss, delay, or damage, including reasonable attorney fees and costs, but not including incidental or consequential damages, resulting from creation or amendment of the certificate.

D. Unless the Department receives a claim for indemnity not later than one year after creation of a certificate of title under subsection A, on request in a form and manner required by the Department, the Department shall release any bond, indemnity, or other security.

History.
2013, c. 787.

§ 29.1-733.22. Replacement certificate of title.

A. If a written certificate of title is lost, stolen, mutilated, destroyed, or otherwise becomes unavailable or illegible, the secured party of record or, if no secured party is indicated in the files of the Department, the owner of record may apply for and, by furnishing information satisfactory to the Department, obtain a replacement certificate in the name of the owner of record.

B. An applicant for a replacement certificate of title shall sign the application and, except as otherwise permitted by the Department, the application shall comply with § 29.1-733.7. The application shall include the existing certificate unless the certificate is lost, stolen, mutilated, destroyed, or otherwise unavailable.

C. A replacement certificate of title created by the Department shall comply with § 29.1-733.9 and indicate on the face of the certificate that it is a replacement certificate.

D. If a person receiving a replacement certificate of title subsequently obtains possession of the original written certificate, the person promptly shall destroy the original certificate of title.

History.
2013, c. 787.

§ 29.1-733.23. Rights of purchaser other than secured party.

A. A buyer in ordinary course of business has the protections afforded by subsection (2) of § 8.2-403 and subsection (a) of § 8.9A-320 even if an existing certificate of title was not signed and delivered to the buyer or a new certificate listing the buyer as owner of record was not created.

B. Except as otherwise provided in §§ 29.1-733.17 and 29.1-733.24, the rights of a purchaser of a watercraft that is not a buyer in ordinary course of business or a lien creditor are governed by the Uniform Commercial Code.

History.
2013, c. 787.

§ 29.1-733.24. Rights of secured party.

A. Subject to subsection B or C, the effect of perfection and nonperfection of a security interest and the priority of a perfected or unperfected security interest with respect to the rights of a purchaser or creditor, including a lien creditor, is governed by Titles 8.1A through 8.10.

B. A security interest perfected under this article has priority over any statutory lien on the watercraft, except for a mechanics lien for repairs to the extent of $150 given by § 43-33 if the requirements are met, provided the mechanic furnishes the holder of any such recorded lien who requests it with an itemized sworn statement of the work done and materials supplied for which the lien is claimed.

C. If, while a security interest in a watercraft is perfected by any method under this article, the Department creates a certificate of title that does not indicate that the watercraft is subject to the security interest or contain a statement that it may be subject to security interests not indicated on the certificate:

1. A buyer of the watercraft, other than a person in the business of selling or leasing watercraft of that kind, takes free of the security interest if the buyer, acting in good faith and without knowledge of the security interest, gives value and receives possession of the watercraft; and

2. The security interest is subordinate to a conflicting security interest in the watercraft that is perfected under § 29.1-733.15 after creation of the certificate and without the conflicting secured party's knowledge of the security interest.

History.
2013, c. 787.

§ 29.1-733.25. Acquiring title to an abandoned watercraft.

A. Any watercraft abandoned for a period exceeding 60 days is subject to the provisions of this section.

B. A landowner, his lessee, or his agent may acquire title to any watercraft abandoned on his land or the water immediately adjacent to his land. Acquisition of title, under the provisions of this section, divests any other person of any interest in the watercraft.

C. If a watercraft has a registration number assigned by the Commonwealth or any other state, or if there are other means of identifying the owner, the person desiring to acquire title shall make a good faith effort to secure the last-known address of all owners and lien holders. He shall notify each owner and lien holder by registered letter that if ownership is not claimed and the watercraft not removed within 30 days, he will apply for title to the watercraft in his name.

D. The person desiring to acquire title also shall place a notice, to appear for three consecutive issues, in a newspaper of general circulation in the county or city where the watercraft is located. The notice shall describe the watercraft, its location, and any identifying number or numbers. The notice shall state that if the watercraft is not claimed and removed within 30 days after the first day the notice was published, the person who has placed the notice shall apply to the Department for title to the watercraft.

E. At the end of the 30-day period, the person seeking to acquire the watercraft shall apply to the Department for title. The application shall be accompanied by the following: (i) an affidavit stating that to the best of the applicant's knowledge the watercraft has been abandoned for a period of at least 60 days; (ii) proof that the registered letter required by the Department was mailed at least 30 days prior to application or a detailed explanation of the steps taken to identify the owner and lien holder; and (iii) proof that a notice was printed in a newspaper as required in subsection D.

F. Upon receipt by the Department of all items required by subsection E, and after all fees and taxes due have been paid, the Department shall then issue title to the watercraft to the applicant.

G. All costs incurred in obtaining title to a watercraft under this section shall be borne by the applicant.

History.
2013, c. 787.

§ 29.1-733.26. Duties and operation of the Department.

A. The Department shall retain the evidence used to establish the accuracy of the information in its files relating to the current ownership of a watercraft and the information on the certificate of title.

B. The Department shall retain in its files all information regarding a security interest in a watercraft for at least 10 years after the Department receives a termination statement regarding the security interest. The information shall be accessible by the hull identification number for the watercraft and any other methods provided by the Department.

C. If a person submits a record to the Department, or submits information that is accepted by the Department, and requests an acknowledgment of the filing or submission, the Department shall send to the person an acknowledgment showing the hull identification number of the watercraft to which the record or submission relates, the information in the filed record or submission, and the date and time the record was received or the submission accepted. A request under this section shall contain the hull identification number and be delivered by means authorized by the Department.

D. The Department shall send or otherwise make available in a record the following information to any person that requests it and pays the applicable fee:

1. Whether the files of the Department indicate, as of a date and time specified by the Department, but not a date earlier than three days before the Department received the request, any certificate of title, security interest, termination statement, or title brand that relates to a watercraft:

a. Identified by a hull identification number designated in the request;

b. Identified by a registration number designated in the request; or

c. Owned by a person designated in the request;

2. With respect to the watercraft:

a. The name and address of any owner as indicated in the files of the Department or on the certificate of title;

b. The name and address of any secured party as indicated in the files of the Department or on the certificate, and the effective date of the information; and

c. A copy of any termination statement indicated in the files of the Department and the effective date of the termination statement; and

3. With respect to the watercraft, a copy of any certificate of origin, secured party transfer statement, transfer by law statement under § 29.1-733.20, and other evidence of previous or current transfers of ownership.

E. In responding to a request under this section, the Department shall provide the requested information in any medium. On request, the Department shall send the requested information in a record that is self-authenticating.

F. Employees of the Department are authorized to administer oaths and take acknowledgments and affidavits incidental to the administration and enforcement of this article. They shall receive no compensation for these services.

History.
2013, c. 787.

§ 29.1-733.27. Uniformity of application and construction.

In applying and construing this uniform act, consideration shall be given to the need to promote uniformity of the law with respect to its subject matter among states that enact it.

History.
2013, c. 787.

§ 29.1-733.28. Relationship to Electronic Signatures in Global and National Commerce Act.

This article modifies, limits, and supersedes the federal Electronic Signatures in Global and National Commerce Act, 15 U.S.C. § 7001, et seq., but does not modify, limit, or supersede § 101(c) of that act (15 U.S.C. § 7001(c)), or authorize electronic delivery of any of the notices described in § 103(b) of that act (15 U.S.C. § 7003(b)).

History.
2013, c. 787.

§ 29.1-733.29. Savings clause.

A. The rights, duties, and interests flowing from a transaction, certificate of title, or record shall remain valid on and after July 1, 2014, if the transaction, certificate of title, or record:

1. Relates to a watercraft;

2. Was validly entered into or created before July 1, 2014; and

3. Would be subject to this article if it had been entered into or created on or after July 1, 2014.

B. This article does not affect an action or proceeding commenced before July 1, 2014.

C. Except as otherwise provided in subsection D, a security interest that is enforceable immediately before July 1, 2014, and would have priority over the rights of a person that becomes a lien creditor at that time is a perfected security interest under this article.

D. A security interest perfected immediately before July 1, 2014, remains perfected until the earlier of:

1. The time perfection would have ceased under the law under which the security interest was perfected; or

2. Three years after July 1, 2014.

E. This article does not affect the priority of a security interest in a watercraft if immediately before July 1, 2014, the security interest is enforceable and perfected, and that priority is established.

History.
2013, c. 787.

ARTICLE 3.

BOATING SAFETY.

§ 29.1-734. Authorization for and placing of markers in waters of the Commonwealth used for public swimming areas; no motorboating, waterskiing in marked area.

A. Any owner of real estate which touches any of the waters of this Commonwealth or the agent of the owner may petition the Board to authorize the placing of markers approved by the Board around a public swimming or bathing area.

B. The Department, upon receiving the petition and sufficient proof that the water adjacent to the real estate is used in whole or in part as a public swimming or bathing area, may authorize the placement of the markers to designate the area as a swimming or bathing area.

C. The cost of the purchase and placement of the markers shall be borne by the party requesting the placement of the markers.

D. No person shall operate a motorboat or manipulate skis within the area of the waters of the Commonwealth marked under this section. Persons violating this subsection shall be guilty of a Class 4 misdemeanor.

History.
1964, c. 654, § 62-174.5:1; 1968, c. 659, § 62.1-171; 1983, c. 475; 1987, c. 488.

§ 29.1-734.1. Skin and scuba divers.

A. No person shall engage in skin diving or scuba diving from a boat in the waters of this Commonwealth which are open to boating, or assist in such diving, without displaying a diver's flag from a mast, buoy, or other structure at the place of diving; and no person shall display such flag except when diving operations are under way or in preparation or display a diver's flag in a location which will unreasonably obstruct vessels from making legitimate navigational use of the water.

B. The diver's flag shall be square, not less than twelve inches on a side, and shall be of red background with a diagonal white stripe, of a width equal to one fifth of the flag's height, running from the upper corner adjacent to the mast downward to the opposite outside corner.

C. No operator of a vessel under way in the waters of this Commonwealth shall permit such vessel to approach closer than twenty-five yards to any structure from which a diver's flag is then being displayed.

History.
1987, c. 488.

§ 29.1-735. Regulations for vessel operation and equipment.

A. The Board shall adopt such regulations as it deems appropriate: (i) to provide rules for the safe and reasonable operation of vessels so as to reduce the risks of collision, personal injury and property damage as a result of such operation; and (ii) to govern the number, type, condition, performance capabilities, use, and stowage on board, of lifesaving (personal flotation) devices and other safety equipment to be carried on vessels or classes of vessels operated on waters within the territorial limits of this Commonwealth.

B. The Board is hereby authorized to make regulations to the extent necessary to keep these requirements generally in conformity with the provisions of the federal navigation laws, or with the rules promulgated by the United States Coast Guard or the United States Secretary of Transportation.

C. No person shall operate or give permission for the operation of a vessel which is not equipped as required by Board regulations.

History.
1984, c. 417, § 62.1-172.1; 1987, c. 488.

§ 29.1-735.1. Board authorized to promulgate regulations for seaplanes.

The Board may promulgate regulations governing the takeoff, landing and taxi of seaplanes on impoundments located in the inland waters of the Commonwealth, so as to reduce the risks of collision, personal injury and property damage as a result of such operation. Such regulations shall not be inconsistent with regulations of the Federal Aviation Administration. Conservation police officers shall report any alleged violations of federal or state regulations regarding the operation of seaplanes or aircraft to the appropriate federal authorities responsible for regulating the operation of seaplanes and aircraft.

History.
1994, c. 414.

§ 29.1-735.2. Boating safety education required; Board to promulgate regulations.

A. No person shall operate a motorboat with a motor of 10 horsepower or greater or personal watercraft on the public waters of the Commonwealth, unless the operator has met the requirements for boating safety education in accordance with the age provisions established in subsection D.

B. A person shall be considered in compliance with the requirements for boating safety education if the person meets one of the following:

1. Completes and passes a boating safety course approved by the National Association of State Boating Law Administrators (NASBLA) and accepted by the Department;

2. Passes a proctored equivalency examination that tests the knowledge of information included in the curriculum of an approved course;

3. Possesses a valid license to operate a vessel issued to maritime personnel by the United States Coast Guard or a marine certificate issued by the Canadian government;

4. Possesses a state-approved nonrenewable temporary operator's certificate to operate a motorboat for 90 days that was issued with the certificate of number for the motorboat, if the boat is new or was sold with a transfer of ownership;

5. Possesses a rental or lease agreement from a motorboat rental or leasing business, which lists the person as the authorized operator of the motorboat;

6. Operates the motorboat under onboard direct supervision of a person who meets the requirements of this section;

7. Demonstrates that he is not a resident, is temporarily using the waters of Virginia for a period not to exceed 90 days, and meets any applicable boating safety education requirements of the state of residency, or possesses a Canadian Pleasure Craft Operator's Card;

8. Has assumed operation of the motorboat due to the illness or physical impairment of the initial operator, and is returning the motorboat to shore in order to provide assistance or care for the operator;

9. Is registered as a commercial fisherman pursuant to § 28.2-241 or a person who is under the onboard direct supervision of the commercial fisherman while operating the commercial fisherman's boat;

10. Provides documentation that he is serving or has qualified as a surface warfare officer or enlisted surface warfare specialist in the United States Navy; or

11. Provides documentation that he is serving or has qualified as an Officer of the Deck Underway, boat coxswain, boat officer, boat operator, watercraft operator, or Marine Deck Officer in any branch of the Armed Forces of the United States, United States Coast Guard, or Merchant Marine.

C. The Board shall promulgate regulations by July 1, 2008, to implement a boating safety education program for all motorboat and personal watercraft operators to meet boating safety education requirements.

D. Such regulations shall include provisions that phase-in the requirements for boating safety education according to the following:

1. Personal watercraft operators 20 years of age or younger to meet the requirements by July 1, 2009;
2. Personal watercraft operators 35 years of age or younger to meet the requirements by July 1, 2010;
3. Personal watercraft operators 50 years of age or younger to meet the requirements by July 1, 2011;
4. All personal watercraft operators, regardless of age, to meet the requirements by July 1, 2012;
5. Motorboat operators 20 years of age or younger to meet the requirements by July 1, 2011;
6. Motorboat operators 30 years of age or younger to meet the requirements by July 1, 2012;
7. Motorboat operators 40 years of age or younger to meet the requirements by July 1, 2013;
8. Motorboat operators 45 years of age or younger to meet the requirements by July 1, 2014;
9. Motorboat operators 50 years of age or younger to meet the requirements by July 1, 2015; and
10. All motorboat operators, regardless of age, to meet the requirements by July 1, 2016.

E. Such regulations may include, but not be limited to, provisions for compliance, statewide availability of NASBLA-approved courses including through the Internet, the issuance of certificates to document successful course completion, duplicate certificates, recordkeeping, requirements for course providers, instructor certification, student name and address changes, equivalency exam criteria, provisions for an open-book test for classroom based courses, requirements for motorboat rental and leasing businesses, issuance of a temporary operator's certificate, and the establishment of fees (not to exceed the cost of giving such instruction for each person participating in and receiving the instruction) for boating safety courses and certificates.

F. The Board shall consult and coordinate with the boating public, professional organizations for recreational boating safety, and the boating retail, leasing, and dealer business community in the promulgation of such regulations.

G. Any person who operates a motorboat on the waters of the Commonwealth shall, upon the request of a law-enforcement officer, present to the officer evidence that he has complied with subsection B.

H. Any person who violates any provision of this section or any regulation promulgated hereunder shall be subject to a civil penalty of $100. All civil penalties assessed under this section shall be deposited in the Motorboat and Water Safety Fund of the Game Protection Fund and used as provided for in § 29.1-701.

I. The provisions of this section shall not apply to law-enforcement officers while they are engaged in the performance of their official duties.

History.
2007, cc. 615, 732; 2013, c. 48; 2015, c. 160.

§ 29.1-735.3. Regulation of parasail operators.

The Board of Game and Inland Fisheries shall promulgate regulations applicable to the commercial operations of parasail operators on waters of the Commonwealth. Such regulations shall take into consideration the operating standards and guidelines of the Professional Association of Parasail Operators.

History.
2007, c. 625.

§ 29.1-736. Boat rentals; equipment; safety course.

A. It shall be unlawful to rent a motorboat to any person unless the provisions of this chapter have been complied with. It shall be the duty of persons renting motorboats to equip them as required by this chapter.

B. It shall be unlawful for any person to regularly offer a boat or boats, other than a motorboat, for rent for use on the public waters of the Commonwealth unless such person provides, for the use of each passenger in the boat, a life preserver of the sort prescribed by the regulations of the Board.

C. It shall be unlawful for any person, without first successfully completing a basic boating safety education course approved by the Director, to rent a personal watercraft to another person.

History.
1960, c. 500, § 62-174.8; 1962, c. 626; 1968, c. 659, § 62.1-174; 1987, c. 488; 1998, c. 515.

§ 29.1-737. Muffling devices.

The exhaust of every internal combustion engine used on any motorboat shall be effectively muffled by equipment so constructed and used as to muffle the noise of the exhaust in a reasonable manner. The muffling device shall exhaust at or below the water line or it shall be equipped with mechanical baffles. The use of cutouts is prohibited, except as approved by the Department or the U.S. Coast Guard.

History.
1960, c. 500, § 62-174.9; 1968, c. 659, § 62.1-175; 1987, c. 488; 1997, c. 108.

§ 29.1-738. Operating boat or manipulating water skis, etc., in reckless manner or while intoxicated, etc.

A. No person shall operate any motorboat or vessel, or manipulate any skis, surfboard, or similar device, or engage in any spearfishing while skin diving or scuba diving in a reckless manner so as to endanger the life, limb, or property of any person.

B. No person shall operate any watercraft, as defined in § 29.1-733.2, or motorboat which is underway (i) while such person has a blood alcohol concentration at or greater than the blood alcohol concentration at which it is unlawful to drive or operate a motor vehicle as provided in § 18.2-266 as indicated by a chemical test administered in accordance with § 29.1-738.2, (ii) while such person is under the influence of alcohol, (iii) while such person is under the influence of any narcotic drug or any other self-administered intoxicant or drug of whatsoever nature, or any combination of such drugs, to a degree which impairs his ability to operate the watercraft or motorboat safely, (iv) while such person is under the combined influence of alcohol and any drug or drugs to a degree which impairs his ability to operate the watercraft or motorboat safely, or (v) while such person has a blood concentration of any of the following substances at a level that is equal to or greater than (a) 0.02 milligrams of cocaine per liter of blood, (b) 0.1 milligrams of methamphetamine per liter of blood, (c) 0.01 milligrams of phencyclidine per liter of blood, or (d) 0.1 milligrams of 3,4-methylenedioxymethamphetamine per liter of blood.

C. For purposes of this article, the word "operate" includes being in actual physical control of a watercraft or motorboat and "underway" means that a vessel is not at anchor, or made fast to the shore, or aground.

Any person who violates any provision of this section is guilty of a Class 1 misdemeanor.

History.
1960, c. 500, § 62-174.10; 1962, c. 626; 1968, c. 659, § 62.1-176; 1987, c. 488; 1988, c. 176; 1989, c. 726; 1994, c. 587; 1996, cc. 929, 1015; 1997, c. 703; 2005, c. 616; 2013, c. 787.

§ 29.1-738.01. Operating boat in an improper manner; penalty.

Notwithstanding the provisions of § 29.1-738, upon the trial of any person charged with reckless boating where the degree of culpability is slight, the court in its discretion may find the accused not guilty of reckless boating but guilty of improper boating. Improper boating shall be punishable as a Class 3 misdemeanor.

History.
1991, c. 404.

§ 29.1-738.02. Persons under age twenty-one operating watercraft after illegally consuming alcohol; penalty.

A. It shall be unlawful for any person under the age of twenty-one to operate any watercraft or motorboat upon the waters of the Commonwealth after consuming alcohol. Any such person with a blood alcohol concentration of 0.02 percent or more by weight by volume or 0.02 grams or more per 210 liters of breath but less than 0.08 by weight by volume or less than 0.08 grams per 210 liters of breath as indicated by a chemical test administered as provided in Article 2 (§ 18.2-266 et seq.) of Chapter 7 of Title 18.2 shall be in violation of this section.

B. A violation of this section shall be punishable by denial by the court of such person's privilege to operate a watercraft or motorboat for a period of six months from the date of conviction and by a fine of not more than $500. Any person convicted of a violation of this section shall be eligible to attend an Alcohol Safety Action Program under the provisions of § 29.1-738.5.

History.
1996, c. 631.

§ 29.1-738.03. Reckless operation of a personal watercraft.

A person shall be guilty of reckless operation of a motorboat or vessel who operates any personal watercraft recklessly or at a speed or in such a manner so as to endanger the life, limb or property of any person, which shall include, but not be limited to:

1. Weaving through vessels which are underway, stopped, moored or at anchor while exceeding a reasonable speed under the circumstances and traffic conditions existing at the time;
2. Following another vessel or person on water skis or other similar device, crossing the path of another vessel, or jumping the wake of another vessel more closely than is reasonable and prudent, having due regard to the speed of both vessels and the traffic on and the condition of the waters at the time;
3. Crossing between the towing vessel and a person on water skis or other device; or
4. Steering toward an object or person and turning sharply in close proximity to such object or person in order to spray or attempt to spray the object or person with the wash or jet spray of the personal watercraft.

A person who violates this section shall be guilty of a Class 1 misdemeanor, and for a second or subsequent offense, the court shall order the person not to operate a personal watercraft which is underway upon the waters of the Commonwealth for a period of twelve months.

History.
1998, c. 514.

Cross references.

As to punishment for Class 1 misdemeanors, see § 18.2-11.

§ 29.1-738.1. Analysis of breath to determine alcohol content of blood.

Any person who is suspected of a violation of subsection B of § 29.1-738 or § 29.1-738.02 shall be entitled, if such equipment is available, to have a preliminary breath analysis for the purpose of obtaining an analysis of the probable alcohol content of his blood. The procedures and requirements of § 18.2-267 shall apply, mutatis mutandis.

History.

1989, c. 726; 1996, c. 631.

§ 29.1-738.2. Consent to blood or breath test.

A. Any person who operates a watercraft or motorboat which is underway upon waters of the Commonwealth shall be deemed thereby, as a condition of such operation, to have consented to have samples of his blood, breath, or both blood and breath taken for a chemical test to determine the alcohol, drug, or both alcohol and drug content of his blood, if such person is arrested for operating a watercraft or motorboat which is underway in violation of subsection B of § 29.1-738, § 29.1-738.02, or of a similar ordinance of any county, city or town, within three hours of the alleged offense. Any person so arrested for a violation of clause (i) or (ii), or both, of subsection B of § 29.1-738, § 29.1-738.02, or of a similar ordinance, shall submit to a breath test. If the breath test is not available, or the person is physically unable to submit to the breath test, a blood test shall be given. The accused shall, prior to administration of the test, be advised by the person administering the test that he has the right to observe the process of analysis and to see the blood-alcohol reading on the equipment used to perform the breath test. If such equipment automatically produces a written printout of the breath test result, this written printout, or a copy thereof, shall be given to the accused in each case.

B. Any person, after having been arrested for a violation of clause (iii), (iv), or (v) of subsection B of § 29.1-738, § 29.1-738.02, or of a similar ordinance, may be required to submit to a blood test to determine the drug or both drug and alcohol content of his blood. When a person, after having been arrested for a violation of clause (i) or (ii), or both, of subsection B of § 29.1-738, submits to a breath test, in accordance with subsection A of this section, or refuses to take or is incapable of taking such a breath test, he may be required to submit to tests to determine the drug or both drug and alcohol content of his blood if the law-enforcement officer has reasonable cause to believe the person was operating a watercraft or motorboat under the influence of any drug or combination of drugs, or the combined influence of alcohol and drugs.

C. If a person, after being arrested for a violation of subsection B of § 29.1-738, § 29.1-738.02, or of a similar ordinance of any county, city or town and after having been advised by the arresting officer that a person who operates a watercraft or motorboat which is underway upon the waters of the Commonwealth shall be deemed thereby, as a condition of such operation, to have consented to have a sample of his blood and breath taken for a chemical test to determine the alcohol or drug content of his blood, and that the unreasonable refusal to do so constitutes grounds for a court to order him not to operate a watercraft or motorboat which is underway upon the waters of the Commonwealth, then refuses to permit the taking of a sample of his blood or breath or both blood and breath samples for such tests, the arresting officer shall take the person arrested before a committing magistrate. If the person is unable to be taken before a magistrate because the person is taken to a medical facility for treatment or evaluation of his medical condition, the arresting officer at a medical facility, in the presence of a witness other than a law-enforcement officer, shall again advise the person, at the medical facility, of the law requiring blood or breath samples to be taken and the penalty for refusal. If he again so refuses after having been further advised by such magistrate or by the arresting officer at a medical facility of the law requiring a blood or breath sample to be taken and the penalty for refusal, and so declares again his refusal in writing upon a form provided by the Supreme Court of Virginia, or refuses or fails to so declare in writing and such fact is certified as prescribed in § 18.2-268.3, then no blood or breath sample shall be taken even though he may thereafter request same.

D. When any person is arrested for operating a watercraft or motorboat which is underway in violation of subsection B of § 29.1-738 or § 29.1-738.02, the procedures and requirements of §§ 18.2-268.1 through 18.2-268.11 shall apply, mutatis mutandis, to this section.

E. If the court or jury finds the defendant guilty of unreasonably refusing to permit a blood or breath sample to be taken, the court shall order such person not to operate a watercraft or motorboat which is underway for a period of 12 months for a first offense and for 24 months for a second or subsequent offense of refusal within five years of the first or other such refusal. However, if the defendant pleads guilty to a violation of subsection B of § 29.1-738, the court may dismiss the refusal warrant.

History.

1989, c. 726; 1990, cc. 825, 929; 1992, c. 830; 1995, c. 130; 1996, c. 631; 2001, c. 779; 2005, c. 616; 2007, c. 168.

§ 29.1-738.3. Presumptions from alcohol or drug content.

In any prosecution for operating a watercraft or motorboat which is underway in violation of clause (ii), (iii) or (iv) of subsection B of § 29.1-738, or of a similar ordinance of any county, city or town, the amount of alcohol or drugs in the blood of the accused at the time of the alleged offense as indicated by a chemical analysis of a sample of the accused's blood or breath to determine the alcohol or drug content of his blood in accordance with the provisions of § 29.1-738.2 shall give rise to the rebuttable presumptions of subdivisions (1) through (4) of subsection A of § 18.2-269.

History.
1989, c. 726; 1995, c. 130; 2005, c. 616.

§ 29.1-738.4. Additional penalty for reckless or intoxicated operation of a watercraft or motorboat.

In addition to any other penalties authorized by law, upon conviction of any person for violation of any provision of § 29.1-738, the court shall order such person not to operate a watercraft or motorboat which is underway upon the waters of the Commonwealth for a period of twelve months from the date of a first conviction or for a period of three years from the date of a second or subsequent conviction within ten years of a first conviction. The period specified in any such order prohibiting operation of a watercraft or motorboat which is underway imposed pursuant to this section shall run consecutively with any such order imposed for refusal to permit a blood or breath sample to be taken.

A first offense of violating this section shall constitute a Class 2 misdemeanor. A second or subsequent offense shall constitute a Class 1 misdemeanor. In addition, the court shall suspend the person's privilege to operate a motorboat or watercraft for the same period for which it had been suspended or revoked when such person violated this section.

The period specified in any such order prohibiting operation of a watercraft or motorboat which is underway imposed pursuant to this section may be suspended by the court only as authorized in § 29.1-738.5.

History.
1989, c. 726; 1996, cc. 929, 1015.

§ 29.1-738.5. Participation in rehabilitation program.

A. Any person convicted of a violation of subsection B of § 29.1-738, or any ordinance of a county, city or town similar to the provisions thereof, or any second offense thereunder, shall, with leave of court or upon court order, enter into an alcohol safety action program certified by the Commission on the Virginia Alcohol Safety Action Program (VASAP) in the judicial district in which the charge is brought or in any other judicial district upon such terms and conditions as the court may set forth. In the determination of the eligibility of such person to enter a program, the court shall consider his prior record of participation in any other rehabilitation program. Suspension of the penalties imposed pursuant to § 29.1-738.4 shall be conditioned upon successful completion of such a program.

B. The court shall require the person entering such program under the provisions of subsection A to pay a fee of no less than $250 but no more than $300. A reasonable portion of such fee, as may be determined by the Commission on VASAP, but not to exceed ten percent, shall be forwarded quarterly to be deposited with the State Treasurer for expenditure by the Commission on VASAP, and the balance shall be held in a separate fund for local administration of alcohol rehabilitation programs. Upon a finding that the defendant is indigent, the court may reduce or waive the fee. In addition to the costs of the proceeding, fees as may reasonably be required of defendants referred for extended treatment under such program may be charged.

C. Upon such conviction, the court shall impose the sentence authorized. Upon a finding that a person so convicted is eligible for participation in an alcohol rehabilitation program, the court shall enter the conviction on the warrant, and shall note that the person so convicted has been referred to a program. If the court finds that a person is not eligible for a program or subsequently that the person has violated, without good cause, any of the conditions set forth by the court in entering the program, the court shall dispose of the case as if no program had been entered. Appeals from any such disposition shall be allowed as provided by law.

The court shall have jurisdiction over any person entering a program under the provisions of this section until such time as the case has been disposed of by either successful completion of the program, or final imposition of sentence upon ineligibility or violation of a condition imposed by the court, whichever occurs first.

D. The Commission on VASAP shall establish standards and criteria for the implementation and operation of water safety alcohol rehabilitation programs. The Commission on VASAP shall also establish criteria for the modalities of administration of such programs, as well as public information, accounting procedures and allocation of funds.

History.
1989, c. 726.

§ 29.1-738.6. When arrested person operating a vessel; how vessel removed from scene of arrest.

In any case in which a law-enforcement officer arrests the operator of a vessel, and there is no legal cause for the retention of the vessel by the officer, the officer shall allow the person arrested to designate another person who is present at the scene of the arrest to operate the vessel from the scene to a place designated by the person arrested. If such a designation is not made, the officer may cause the vessel to be taken to the nearest appropriate place for safekeeping.

History.
1997, c. 152.

§ 29.1-739. Duty of operator involved in collision, accident or other casualty; immunity from liability; report of collision, etc.; summons in lieu of arrest.

A. It shall be the duty of the operator of a vessel involved in a collision, accident, or other casualty, so far as he can do so without serious danger to his own vessel, crew, and passengers (if any), to render persons affected by the collision, accident, or other casualty such assistance as may be practicable and as may be necessary in order to minimize any danger caused by the collision, accident, or other casualty, and also give his name, address, and identification of his vessel in writing to any person injured and to the owner of any property damaged in the collision, accident, or other casualty. Any person who complies with this subsection or who gratuitously and in good faith renders assistance at the scene of a vessel collision, accident, or other casualty without objection of any person assisted, shall not be held liable for any civil damages as a result of the rendering of assistance or for any act or omission in providing or arranging salvage, towage, medical treatment or other assistance where the assisting person acts as an ordinary, reasonably prudent person would have acted under the same or similar circumstances.

B. In case of collision, accident, or other casualty involving a vessel, the operator of the vessel, if the collision, accident, or other casualty is of such a nature as to be reportable pursuant to regulations adopted by the Board, shall notify within a reasonable time a law-enforcement officer of the Commonwealth, conservation police officer, or Marine Resources Commission inspector.

The operator shall file with the Department a full report of the collision, accident, or other casualty, as the regulations of the Board may require. The report shall be without prejudice, shall be for the information of the Department only, and shall not be open to public inspection. The fact that such a report has been made shall be admissible in evidence solely to show compliance with this section and applicable regulations, but no such report nor any statement contained in the report shall be admissible as evidence for any other purpose in any trial.

C. Any officer investigating any collision, accident or other casualty shall have authority, in lieu of arresting any person charged with violating any of the provisions of this chapter, to issue a written summons to the person (stating name, address, boat number, offense charged, etc.) to appear in court as in § 46.2-936.

History.
1960, c. 500, § 62-174.11; 1962, c. 626; 1968, c. 659, § 62.1-177; 1972, c. 412; 1973, c. 381; 1987, c. 488; 1991, c. 336; 2007, c. 87.

§ 29.1-739.1. Disregarding signal by law-enforcement officer to stop; attempts to elude; penalty.

A. Any person who, having received a visible or audible signal of a flashing light or siren from any conservation police officer or other law-enforcement officer to bring his motorboat or other vessel, or seaplane to a stop, fails to do so promptly shall be guilty of a Class 3 misdemeanor.

B. Any person who, having received a visible or audible signal of a flashing light or siren from any conservation police officer or other law-enforcement officer to bring his motorboat or other vessel, or seaplane to a stop, (i) operates or navigates such motorboat or other vessel, or seaplane in willful or wanton disregard of such signal so as to endanger the life of the law-enforcement officer or other persons or to interfere with the operation of a law-enforcement vessel, or (ii) increases his speed and attempts to escape or elude a law-enforcement officer shall be guilty of a Class 1 misdemeanor.

History.
1993, c. 243; 1994, c. 414; 2007, c. 87.

§ 29.1-739.2. Conservation police officers to patrol lakes.

The Department shall have an enhanced enforcement effort that is commensurate with the level of boating activity from Memorial Day through Labor Day in the waters of those Virginia lakes that (i) are of a size comparable to or greater than Smith Mountain Lake and (ii) have a comparable number of reported boating accidents during the last five years as Smith Mountain Lake.

History.
2005, c. 233; 2007, c. 87; 2008, c. 535.

§ 29.1-740. Duty to stop and render assistance; penalties for violations.

It shall be the duty of every operator of a vessel involved in a collision to stop and render assistance as required by § 29.1-739. If any person knowingly fails to comply with the provisions of § 29.1-739 when the collision, accident or other casualty results in serious bodily injury to, or the death of, any person, he shall be guilty of a Class 6 felony. If any person knowingly fails to comply with the provisions of § 29.1-739, when the collision, accident or other casualty results only in damage to property, he shall be guilty of a Class 1 misdemeanor. However, if the vessel struck is unattended and the damage is less than fifty dollars, such person shall be punished only by a fine not exceeding fifty dollars.

History.
1975, c. 429, § 62.1-177.1; 1987, c. 488.

§ 29.1-741. Furnishing information to agency of United States.

In accordance with any request duly made by an authorized official or agency of the United States, any information compiled or otherwise available to the Department pursuant to subsection B of § 29.1-739 shall be transmitted to the official or agency of the United States.

History.
1960, c. 500, § 62-174.12; 1968, c. 659, § 62.1-178; 1987, c. 488.

§ 29.1-742. Towing water skis, surfboards, etc.

A. No person shall operate a vessel on any waters of the Commonwealth for towing a person or persons on water skis, a surfboard, or a similar device unless there is in the vessel a person, in addition to the operator, in a position to observe the progress of the person or persons being towed or unless the skier or skiers wear life preservers.

B. No person shall operate a vessel on any water of the Commonwealth towing a person or persons on water skis, a surfboard, or a similar device, nor shall any person engage in water skiing or a similar activity at any time between the hours from one-half hour after sunset to one-half hour before sunrise. The provisions of this subsection shall not constitute a defense to any provision of § 29.1-738.

C. The provisions of subsections A and B of this section do not apply to a performer engaged in a professional exhibition.

D. No person shall operate or manipulate any vessel, towrope, or other device by which the direction or location of water skis, a surfboard, or a similar device may be affected or controlled in such a way as to cause the water skis, surfboard, or similar device, or any person upon the device to collide with any object or person.

History.
1960, c. 500, § 62-174.13; 1962, c. 626; 1968, c. 659, § 62.1-179; 1982, c. 236; 1987, c. 488; 1988, c. 265; 1993, c. 275; 1997, c. 108.

§ 29.1-743: Repealed by Acts 1997, c. 108.

§ 29.1-744. Local regulation; application for placement or removal of "no wake" buoys, etc.

A. Any political subdivision of this Commonwealth may, at any time, but only after public notice, formally apply to the Board for special rules and regulations with reference to the safe and reasonable operation of vessels on any water within its territorial limits and shall specify in the application the reasons which make the special rules or regulations necessary or appropriate.

B. The Board is authorized upon application by a political subdivision or its own motion to make special or general rules and regulations with reference to the safe and reasonable operation of vessels on any waters within the territorial limits of any political subdivision of this Commonwealth. Without limiting the generality of the grant of such power, a system of regulatory or navigational markers may be adopted by the Board. Nothing in this section shall be construed to affect the application of any general law concerning the tidal waters of this Commonwealth.

C. Any county, city or town of this Commonwealth may enact ordinances which parallel general law regulating the operation of vessels on any waters within its territorial limits, including the marginal adjacent ocean, and the conduct and activity of any person using such waters. The locality may also provide for enforcement and penalties for the violation of the ordinances, provided the penalties do not exceed the penalties provided in this chapter for similar offenses.

D. After notice to the Department, any county, city or town may, by ordinance, establish "no wake" zones along the waterways within the locality in order to protect public safety and prevent erosion damage to adjacent property. However, any county that is adjacent to an inland lake (i) more than 500 feet above sea level and (ii) of 20,000 acres or more and wholly located within the Commonwealth may, by ordinance, establish "no wake" zones along such lake within the locality in order to protect public safety or prevent erosion damage to adjacent property. The markers and buoys designating a no wake zone shall conform to the requirements established by the Board. Any marker or buoy which is not placed in conformance with the regulations of the Board or which is not properly maintained shall be removed by the locality. The locality may provide for enforcement and penalties for the violation of the ordinance.

E. Any person who desires to place or remove "no wake" buoys or other markers relating to the safe and efficient operation of vessels pursuant to any local ordinance shall apply to the local governing body. The local governing body shall approve, disapprove or approve with modifications the application and forward it to the Director, who shall approve, disapprove or approve with modifications within thirty days the placement and type of marker to be used or the removal of "no wake" buoys or other markers. The cost of the purchase and placement or the removal of the buoys or markers shall be borne by the person requesting the placement or removal of the buoys or markers. Any marker or buoy which is not placed in conformance with the regulations of the Board or which is not properly maintained may be removed by the Department. "No wake" buoys or other markers placed prior to July 1, 2001, shall only be removed when no longer required for the safe and efficient operation of vessels pursuant to any local ordinance.

History.
1960, c. 500, § 62-174.15; 1964, cc. 346, 654; 1968, c. 659, § 62.1-182; 1978, c. 598; 1982, c. 232; 1987, c. 488; 1997, c. 522; 1999, c. 489; 2001, c. 649.

§ **29.1-744.1:** Repealed by Acts 1998, c. 537, effective January 1, 1999.

§ **29.1-744.2:** Repealed by Acts 1998, c. 857, effective January 1, 1999.

§ 29.1-744.3. Slacken speed and control wakes near structures.

It shall be unlawful to operate any motorboat, except personal watercraft, at a speed greater than the slowest possible speed required to maintain steerage and headway when within 50 feet or less of docks, piers, boathouses, boat ramps, or a person in the water, unless such person in the water (i) is being towed by the motorboat or (ii) is accompanying the motorboat, provided that such motorboat is propelled by an inboard motor.

History.
1998, c. 857; 2012, c. 700.

§ 29.1-744.4. "Pass-through" zones; local ordinances; penalties.

After providing notice to the Department, any locality may, by ordinance, establish "pass-through" zones in any portion of a waterway within its territorial limits where congestion of watercraft traffic routinely poses a significant safety risk to persons in such designated area. The ordinance shall provide that while in a pass-through zone, operators of watercraft shall maintain a reasonable and safe speed and shall be prohibited from stopping, anchoring, loitering, or otherwise engaging in recreational activity. The locality shall clearly identify pass-through zones by buoys or other markers that conform to the general requirements as established by the Board for similar buoys or markers. The locality may provide for enforcement and penalties, not to exceed a Class 4 misdemeanor, for the violation of the ordinance.

History.
2003, c. 780.

§ 29.1-745. Enforcement of chapter; vessels displaying Coast Guard inspection decal.

A. Every conservation police officer, officer of the Virginia Marine Police, and other law-enforcement officer of the Commonwealth and its subdivisions shall have the authority to enforce the provisions of this chapter and shall have authority to stop, board, and inspect any vessel subject to this chapter after having identified himself in his official capacity. Except for enforcement of § 29.1-738 and the requirement of having the registration certificate on board, the provisions of this subsection shall not apply to any vessel of 26 feet or more in length on which is displayed a current valid United States Coast Guard or United States Coast Guard Auxiliary inspection decal.

B. Notwithstanding the provisions of subsection A, no conservation police officer, officer of the Virginia Marine Police, or other law-enforcement officer shall, without the consent of the owner, stop, board, or inspect any noncommercial vessel subject to this chapter unless such officer has reasonable suspicion that a violation of law or regulation exists, except that conservation police officers and officers of the Virginia Marine Police may conduct lawful stops or boardings to inspect hunting, fishing, and trapping licenses pursuant to §§ 28.2-231 and 29.1-337 or to inspect creel and bag limits pursuant to § 29.1-209 and may conduct lawful boating safety checkpoints in accordance with established agency policy.

History.
1960, c. 500, § 62-174.17; 1964, c. 654; 1968, c. 659, § 62.1-184; 1980, c. 567; 1987, c. 488; 2007, c. 87; 2015, c. 484.

§ 29.1-746. Penalties.

A. Unless specified otherwise, any person who violates any provision of this chapter or any regulation adopted under this chapter shall be guilty of a Class 4 misdemeanor for each such violation.

B. Upon the conviction of any person for the violation of any provision of this chapter or any regulation adopted thereunder for which the criminal penalty is a Class 3 misdemeanor or greater, the court shall order the person to complete and pass a boating safety course approved by the National Association of State Boating Law Administrators and accepted by the Department. A list of such courses shall be made available by the Department. Any person who has been ordered by the court to complete and pass a boating safety course shall submit to the court, in a form approved by the Department, proof of completion and passage of the course within six months of the time of his conviction. If the person who has been required to complete and pass a boating safety course is under 18 years of age, the court may require the person to obtain parental consent to enroll in the course. If the person does not complete and pass the boating safety course within the prescribed time period, the court may, for good cause, extend the period for completion; however, absent good cause, the court shall impose a fine not to exceed $250.

History.
1960, c. 500, § 62-174.18; 1962, c. 626; 1964, c. 654; 1968, c. 659, § 62.1-185; 1984, c. 417; 1987, c. 488; 2006, c. 23.

ARTICLE 4.
PERSONAL WATERCRAFT.

§ 29.1-747: Repealed by Acts 1998, cc. 84 and 563, and repealed by Acts 1998, cc. 443, 512, 514, 515, 537, effective January 1, 1999.

§ 29.1-748. Restrictions on operation; penalty.

A. It is unlawful for any person to:

1. Operate a personal watercraft unless he is at least sixteen years of age, except any person fourteen or fifteen years of age shall be allowed to operate a personal watercraft if he (i) has successfully completed a boating safety education course approved by the Director and (ii) carries on his person, while operating a personal watercraft, proof of successful completion of such course. Upon the request of a law-enforcement officer, such person shall provide proof of having successfully completed an approved course;

2. Operate a personal watercraft unless he has complied with the provisions of § 29.1-735.2, regarding board regulations for boating safety education;

3. Operate a personal watercraft unless each person riding on the personal watercraft is wearing a type I, type II, type III, or type V personal flotation device approved by the United States Coast Guard;

4. Fail to attach the lanyard to his person, clothing, or personal flotation device, if the personal watercraft is equipped with a lanyard-type engine cut-off switch;

5. Operate a personal watercraft on the waters of the Commonwealth between sunset and sunrise;

6. Operate a personal watercraft while carrying a number of passengers in excess of the number for which the craft was designed by the manufacturer; or

7. Operate a personal watercraft in excess of the slowest possible speed required to maintain steerage and headway within fifty feet of docks, piers, boathouses, boat ramps, people in the water, and vessels other than personal watercraft. Nothing in this section shall prohibit a personal watercraft from towing a person with a rope less than fifty feet in length.

B. A violation of any provision of this section shall constitute a Class 4 misdemeanor, except that any person who violates subdivision A 2 shall be subject to the penalty provided in § 29.1-735.2.

C. A violation of this section shall not constitute negligence, be considered in mitigation of damages of whatever nature, be admissible in evidence or be the subject of comment by counsel in any action for the recovery of damages arising out of the operation, ownership, or maintenance of a personal watercraft, nor shall anything in this section change any existing law, rule, or procedure pertaining to any such civil action, nor shall this section bar any claim which otherwise exists.

History.
1991, c. 320; 1998, cc. 443, 537; 2007, cc. 615, 732.

§ 29.1-748.1. Minimum distance from shoreline; local ordinances; penalty.

The City of Virginia Beach may, by ordinance, regulate in any portion of a waterway located solely within its territorial limits, the minimum distance that personal watercraft may be operated from the shoreline in excess of the slowest possible speed required to maintain steerage and headway. Such ordinance shall provide for distances of 100 feet from the shoreline and 200 feet from swimmers in ocean waters, and shall provide for local enforcement and penalties not exceeding those applicable to Class 4 misdemeanors. Nothing in this section prohibits access to and from waters where operation is not otherwise restricted.

History.
2003, c. 117; 2007, c. 813.

§ 29.1-749. Owner of personal watercraft permitting violation; penalty.

A. It shall be unlawful for the owner of or any person having control of a personal watercraft to authorize or knowingly permit a person under the age of sixteen to operate the personal watercraft, unless the person fourteen or fifteen years of age has successfully completed a boating safety education course as required under subdivision A 1 of § 29.1-748.

B. A violation of any provision of this section shall constitute a Class 4 misdemeanor.

History.
1991, c. 320; 1998, c. 443.

Cross references.
As to punishment for Class 4 misdemeanors, see § 18.2-11.

§ 29.1-749.1. Identification of personal watercraft rentals.

Every business located in a city with a population greater than 390,000 that provides personal watercraft for rent shall place the letter "R," at least eleven inches in height and eight and one-half inches in width, on both sides of each personal watercraft rental, in either red or black, whichever color represents the clearest contrast from the basic color of the rental unit.

History.
1998, c. 84.

§ 29.1-749.2. Local regulation of personal watercraft rentals; penalty.

A. The City of Virginia Beach may by ordinance regulate personal watercraft as provided in this section. Any ordinance enacted pursuant to this section may include any of the following provisions:

1. Any business which offers personal watercraft for rent shall (i) require any person to whom a personal watercraft is rented to present, prior to such rental, a government-issued identification card containing his photograph and (ii) retain such identification card, or a copy thereof, during the time the personal watercraft is being rented.

2. No person who rents or leases a personal watercraft shall knowingly misrepresent any material fact or falsify any information requested on the rental agreement or application.

3. Any business which offers personal watercraft for hourly short-term rental shall have at least one motorboat of at least fifty horsepower operated by an employee or agent of the business, in order to monitor and ensure the safe operation of the personal watercraft.

4. No business which offers personal watercraft for rent shall rent a personal watercraft that has an engine displacement which exceeds 800 cubic centimeters.

5. Any business which offers personal watercraft for rent shall have at least two marine VHF radios in operation during the time that a personal watercraft rental is being operated. The radios shall monitor channel 16 whenever they are not being actively used on a working channel.

B. Any locality may by ordinance establish standards for insurance coverage for any business which offers personal watercraft for rent.

C. Any ordinance adopted by a locality pursuant to this section may provide for a penalty for violation of the ordinance not to exceed the penalty applicable to a Class 3 misdemeanor.

History.
1998, c. 563; 1999, c. 536; 2007, c. 813.

§ 29.1-749.3. Personal watercraft instruction; rental agents.

Any person who is in the business of renting personal watercraft to the public shall provide to any person who rents a personal watercraft instruction on the laws of the Commonwealth governing motorboat operation, specific operating requirements of the personal watercraft being rented, motorboat safety equipment requirements, requirements in the case of a reportable accident, and such other information as the Director may require. The content and methods of instruction shall be approved by the Director.

Any attorney for the county, city or town in which an alleged violation of this section occurred may enforce this section by a civil action to recover a civil penalty not to exceed $250. The civil penalty shall be paid into the local treasury. No filing fee or other fee or cost shall be charged to the county, city or town which instituted the action.

The fact of a violation of this section shall not constitute negligence per se, be considered in mitigation of damages of whatever nature, be admissible in evidence or be the subject of comment by counsel in any action for the recovery of damages arising out of the operation, ownership or maintenance of a personal watercraft. This section shall not change any existing law, rule or procedure pertaining to any such civil action, nor shall this section bar any claim which otherwise exists.

History.
1998, c. 512.

§ 29.1-750. Exemptions.

The provisions of this article shall not apply to participants in regattas, races, marine parades, tournaments, or exhibitions approved by the Board or United States Coast Guard.

History.
1991, c. 320.

TITLE 30.
GENERAL ASSEMBLY.

CHAPTER 3.1.
LEGISLATIVE SUPPORT COMMISSION.

Section

§ 30-34.2:1. Powers, duties and functions of Capitol Police.

The Capitol Police may exercise within the limits of the Capitol Square, when assigned to any other property owned, leased, or controlled by the Commonwealth or any agency, department, institution, or commission thereof, and pursuant to the provisions of §§ 15.2-1724, 15.2-1726, and 15.2-1728 all the powers, duties, and functions that are exercised by the police of the city or the police or sheriff of the county within which such property is located. The jurisdiction of the Capitol Police shall further extend 300 feet beyond the boundary of any property they are required to protect, such jurisdiction to be concurrent with that of other law-enforcement officers of the locality in which such property is located. Additionally, the Capitol Police shall have concurrent jurisdiction with law-enforcement officers of the City of Richmond and of any county contiguous thereto in any case involving the theft or misappropriation of the personal property of any member or employee of the General Assembly. Members of the Capitol Police when assigned to accompany the Governor or Governor-elect, members of the Governor's family, the Lieutenant Governor or Lieutenant Governor-elect, the Attorney General or Attorney General-elect, members of the General Assembly, or members of the Supreme Court or Court of Appeals of Virginia, or when directed to serve a summons issued by the Clerk of the Senate or the Clerk of the House of Delegates, a joint committee or commission thereof, or any committee of either house, shall be vested with all the powers and authority of a law-enforcement officer of any city or county in which they are required to be. All members of the Capitol Police shall be subject to the provisions of § 2.2-1201.1 and Chapter 5 (§ 9.1-500 et seq.) of Title 9.1.

The assignment of jurisdiction to any property pursuant to this section shall be approved by the Legislative Support Commission.

The Division of Capitol Police shall have the authority to enter into contracts or agreements necessary or incidental to the performance of its duties.

History.
1982, c. 243; 1984, c. 149; 1988, c. 329; 1995, cc. 770, 818; 2003, cc. 231, 588; 2008, c. 437; 2012, cc. 803, 835; 2015, cc. 448, 455.

§ 30-34.2:2. Disposal of unclaimed firearms or other weapons in possession of the Division of Capitol Police.

Subject to the provisions of § 19.2-386.29, the Division of Capitol Police may destroy unclaimed firearms and other weapons that have been in the possession of the Division for a period of more than 120 days. For the purposes of this section, "unclaimed firearms and other weapons" means any firearm or other weapon belonging to another that has been acquired by a law-enforcement officer pursuant to his duties, that is not needed in any criminal prosecution, that has not been claimed by its rightful owner, and that the State Treasurer has indicated will be declined if remitted under the Uniform Disposition of Unclaimed Property Act (§ 55-210.1 et seq.).

At the discretion of the chief of police or his designee, unclaimed firearms or other weapons may be destroyed by any means that renders the firearms or other weapons permanently inoperable. Prior to the destruction of such firearms or other weapons, the chief of police or his designee shall (i) make reasonable attempts to notify by mail the rightful owner of the property and (ii) obtain from the attorney for the Commonwealth of the jurisdiction from which the unclaimed item came into the possession of the Division of Capitol Police in writing a statement advising that the item is not needed in any criminal prosecution.

In lieu of destroying any such unclaimed firearm, the chief of police or his designee may donate the firearm to the Department of Forensic Science, upon agreement of the Department.

History.
2012, c. 209; 2015, c. 220.

TITLE 32.1.
HEALTH.

CHAPTER 2.
DISEASE PREVENTION AND CONTROL.

Article 3.

Disease Control Measures.

ARTICLE 3.
DISEASE CONTROL MEASURES.

§ 32.1-45.1. Deemed consent to testing and release of test results related to infection with human immunodeficiency virus or hepatitis B or C viruses.

A. Whenever any health care provider, or any person employed by or under the direction and control of a health care provider, is directly exposed to body fluids of a patient in a manner that may, according to the then current guidelines of the Centers for Disease Control and Prevention, transmit human immunodeficiency virus or hepatitis B or C viruses, the patient whose body fluids were involved in the exposure shall be deemed to have consented to testing for infection with human immunodeficiency virus or hepatitis B or C viruses. Such patient shall also be deemed to have consented to the release of such test results to the person who was exposed. In other than emergency situations, it shall be the responsibility of the health care provider to inform patients of this provision prior to providing them with health care services which create a risk of such exposure.

B. Whenever any patient is directly exposed to body fluids of a health care provider, or of any person employed by or under the direction and control of a health care provider, in a manner that may, according to the then current guidelines of the Centers for

Disease Control and Prevention, transmit human immunodeficiency virus or hepatitis B or C viruses, the person whose body fluids were involved in the exposure shall be deemed to have consented to testing for infection with human immunodeficiency virus or hepatitis B or C viruses. Such person shall also be deemed to have consented to the release of such test results to the patient who was exposed.

C. For the purposes of this section, "health care provider" means any person, facility or agency licensed or certified to provide care or treatment by the Department of Health, Department of Behavioral Health and Developmental Services, Department of Rehabilitative Services, or the Department of Social Services, any person licensed or certified by a health regulatory board within the Department of Health Professions except for the Boards of Funeral Directors and Embalmers and Veterinary Medicine or any personal care agency contracting with the Department of Medical Assistance Services.

D. "Health care provider," as defined in subsection C, shall be deemed to include any person who renders emergency care or assistance, without compensation and in good faith, at the scene of an accident, fire, or any life-threatening emergency, or while en route therefrom to any hospital, medical clinic or doctor's office during the period while rendering such emergency care or assistance. The Department of Health shall provide appropriate counseling and opportunity for face-to-face disclosure of any test results to any such person.

E. Whenever any law-enforcement officer, salaried or volunteer firefighter, or salaried or volunteer emergency medical services provider is directly exposed to body fluids of a person in a manner that may, according to the then current guidelines of the Centers for Disease Control and Prevention, transmit human immunodeficiency virus or hepatitis B or C viruses, the person whose body fluids were involved in the exposure shall be deemed to have consented to testing for infection with human immunodeficiency virus or hepatitis B or C viruses. Such person shall also be deemed to have consented to the release of such test results to the person who was exposed.

F. Whenever a person is directly exposed to the body fluids of a law-enforcement officer, salaried or volunteer firefighter, or salaried or volunteer emergency medical services provider in a manner that may, according to the then current guidelines of the Centers for Disease Control and Prevention, transmit human immunodeficiency virus or hepatitis B or C viruses, the person whose body fluids were involved in the exposure shall be deemed to have consented to testing for infection with human immunodeficiency virus or hepatitis B or C viruses. The law-enforcement officer, salaried or volunteer firefighter, or salaried or volunteer emergency medical services provider shall also be deemed to have consented to the release of such test results to the person who was exposed.

G. For the purposes of this section, "law-enforcement officer" means a person who is both (i) engaged in his public duty at the time of such exposure and (ii) employed by any sheriff's office, any adult or youth correctional facility, or any state or local law-enforcement agency, or any agency or department under the direction and control of the Commonwealth or any local governing body that employs persons who have law-enforcement authority.

H. Whenever any school board employee is directly exposed to body fluids of any person in a manner that may, according to the then current guidelines of the Centers for Disease Control and Prevention, transmit human immunodeficiency virus or hepatitis B or C viruses, the person whose body fluids were involved in the exposure shall be deemed to have consented to testing for infection with human immunodeficiency virus or hepatitis B or C viruses. Such person shall also be deemed to have consented to the release of such test results to the school board employee who was exposed. If the person whose blood specimen is sought for testing is a minor, the parent, guardian, or person standing in loco parentis of such minor shall be notified prior to initiating such testing. In other than emergency situations, it shall be the responsibility of the school board employee to inform the person of this provision prior to the contact that creates a risk of such exposure.

I. Whenever any person is directly exposed to the body fluids of a school board employee in a manner that may, according to the then current guidelines of the Centers for Disease Control and Prevention, transmit human immunodeficiency virus or hepatitis B or C viruses, the school board employee whose body fluids were involved in the exposure shall be deemed to have consented to testing for infection with human immunodeficiency virus or hepatitis B or C viruses. The school board employee shall also be deemed to have consented to the release of such test results to the person.

J. For the purposes of this section, "school board employee" means a person who is both (i) acting in the course of employment at the time of such exposure and (ii) employed by any local school board in the Commonwealth.

K. For purposes of this section, if the person whose blood specimen is sought for testing is a minor, and that minor refuses to provide such specimen, consent for obtaining such specimen shall be obtained from the parent, guardian, or person standing in loco parentis of such minor prior to initiating such testing. If the parent or guardian or person standing in loco parentis withholds such consent, or is not reasonably available, the person potentially exposed to the human immunodeficiency virus or hepatitis B or C viruses, or the employer of such person, may petition the juvenile and domestic relations district court in the county or city where the minor resides or resided, or, in the case of a nonresident, the county or city where the health care provider, law-enforcement agency or school board has its principal office or, in the case of a health care provider rendering emergency care pursuant to subsection D, the county or city where the exposure occurred, for an order requiring the minor to provide a blood specimen or to submit to testing and to disclose the test results in accordance with this section.

L. Except as provided in subsection K, if the person whose blood specimen is sought for testing refuses to provide such specimen, any person potentially exposed to the human immunodeficiency virus or hepatitis B or C viruses, or the employer of such person, may petition the general district court of the county or city in which the person whose specimen is sought resides or resided, or, in the case of a nonresident, the county or city where the health care provider, law-enforcement agency or school board has its principal office or, in the case of a health care provider rendering emergency care pursuant to subsection D, the county or city where the exposure occurred, for an order requiring the person to provide a blood specimen or to submit to testing and to disclose the test results in accordance with this section. At any hearing before the court, the person whose specimen is sought or his counsel may appear. The court shall be advised by the Commissioner or his designee prior to entering any testing order. If a testing order is issued, both the petitioner and the person from whom the blood specimen is sought shall receive counseling and opportunity for face-to-face disclosure of any test results by a licensed practitioner or trained counselor.

History.

1989, c. 613; 1993, c. 315; 1994, cc. 230, 236; 1997, c. 869; 2003, c. 1; 2008, cc. 191, 339; 2009, cc. 96, 478, 552, 813, 840; 2015, cc. 51, 502, 503.

§ 32.1-45.2. Public safety employees; testing for blood-borne pathogens; procedure available for certain citizens; definitions.

A. If, in the course of employment, an employee of a public safety agency is involved in a possible exposure prone incident, the employee shall immediately, or as soon thereafter as practicable, notify the agency of the incident in accordance with the agency's procedures for reporting workplace accidents.

B. If, after reviewing the facts of the possible exposure prone incident with the employee and after medical consultation, the agency concludes that it is reasonable to believe that an exposure prone incident may have occurred, (i) the agency shall request the person whose body fluids were involved to submit to testing for hepatitis B or C virus and human immunodeficiency virus as provided in § 32.1-37.2 and to authorize disclosure of the test results or (ii) if the person is deceased, the agency shall request the custodian of the remains to preserve a specimen of blood and shall request the decedent's next of kin to consent, as provided in § 32.1-37.2, to such testing and to authorize disclosure of the test results.

C. If a person is involved in a possible exposure prone incident involving the body fluids of an employee of a public safety agency, the person may request the agency to review the facts of the possible exposure prone incident for purposes of obtaining the employee's consent to test for hepatitis B or C virus and human immunodeficiency virus as provided in § 32.1-37.2 and to authorize disclosure of the test results. If, after reviewing the facts and after medical consultation, the agency concludes it is reasonable to believe an exposure prone incident involving the person and the employee may have occurred, (i) the agency shall request the employee whose body fluids were involved to give consent to submit to testing for hepatitis B or C virus and human immunodeficiency virus and to authorize disclosure of the test results or (ii) if the employee is deceased, the agency shall request the custodian of the remains to preserve a specimen of blood and shall request the decedent's next of kin to provide consent, as provided in § 32.1-37.2, to such testing and to authorize disclosure of the test results.

D. If consent is refused under subsection B of this section, the public safety agency or the employee may petition the general district court of the city or county in which the person resides or resided, or in the case of a nonresident, the city or county of the public safety agency's principal office, to determine whether an exposure prone incident has occurred and to order testing and disclosure of the test results.

If consent is refused under subsection C of this section, the person involved in the possible exposure prone incident may petition the general district court of the city or county of the public safety agency's principal office to determine whether an exposure prone incident has occurred and to order testing and disclosure of the test results.

E. If the court finds by a preponderance of the evidence that an exposure prone incident has occurred, it shall order testing for hepatitis B or C virus and human immunodeficiency virus and disclosure of the test results. The court shall be advised by the Commissioner or his designee in making this finding. The hearing shall be held in camera as soon as practicable after the petition is filed. The record shall be sealed.

F. A party may appeal an order of the general district court to the circuit court of the same jurisdiction within ten days from the date of the order. Any such appeal shall be de novo, in camera, and shall be heard as soon as possible by the circuit court. The circuit court shall be advised by the Commissioner or his designee. The record shall be sealed. The order of the circuit court shall be final and nonappealable.

G. Disclosure of any test results provided by this section shall be made to the district health director of the jurisdiction in which the petition was brought or the district in which the person or employee was tested. The district health director or his designee shall inform the parties of the test results and counsel them in accordance with subsection B of § 32.1-37.2.

H. The results of the tests shall be confidential as provided in § 32.1-36.1.

I. No person known or suspected to be positive for infection with hepatitis B or C virus or human immunodeficiency virus shall be refused services for that reason by any public safety agency personnel.

J. For the purpose of this section and for no other purpose, the term "employee" shall include: (i) any person providing assistance to a person employed by a public safety agency who is directly affected by a possible exposure prone incident as a result of the specific crime or specific circumstances involved in the assistance and (ii) any victim of or witness to a crime who is directly affected by a possible exposure prone incident as a result of the specific crime.

K. This section shall not be deemed to create any duty on the part of any person where none exists otherwise, and a cause of action shall not arise from any failure to request consent or to consent to testing under this section. The remedies available under this section shall be exclusive.

L. For the purposes of this section, the following terms shall apply:

"Exposure prone incident" means a direct exposure to body fluids of another person in a manner which may, according to the then current guidelines of the Centers for Disease Control and Prevention, transmit hepatitis B or C virus or human immunodeficiency virus and which occurred during the commission of a criminal act, during the performance of emergency procedures, care or assistance, or in the course of public safety or law-enforcement duties.

"Public safety agency" means any sheriff's office; any adult or youth correctional, law-enforcement, or fire safety organization; the Department of Forensic Science; or any agency or department that employs persons who have law-enforcement authority and which is under the direction and control of the Commonwealth or any local governing body.

History.

1992, c. 711; 1994, c. 146; 1997, cc. 722, 804; 2008, c. 641; 2014, c. 275.

CHAPTER 4.

HEALTH CARE PLANNING.

Article 2.1.

Statewide Emergency Medical Services System and Services.

ARTICLE 2.1.

STATEWIDE EMERGENCY MEDICAL SERVICES SYSTEM AND SERVICES.

§ 32.1-111.14:5. Authority of emergency medical services agency incident commander when operating at an emergency incident; penalty for refusal to obey orders.

Except as provided in § 32.1-111.14:6, while any emergency medical services personnel are in the process of operating at an emergency incident where there is imminent danger and when emergency medical services personnel are returning to the emergency medical services agency, the incident commander of such emergency medical services agency at that time shall have the authority to (i) maintain order at such emergency incident or its vicinity, (ii) direct the actions of emergency medical services personnel at the incident, (iii) notwithstanding the provisions of §§ 46.2-888 through 46.2-891, keep bystanders or other persons at a safe distance from the incident and emergency equipment, (iv) facilitate the speedy movement and operation of emergency equipment and emergency medical services personnel, and (v) until the arrival of a police officer, direct and control traffic in person or by deputy and facilitate the movement of traffic. The emergency medical services agency incident commander shall display his emergency medical services personnel's badge or other proper means of identification. Notwithstanding any other provision of law, this authority shall extend to the activation of traffic control signals designed to facilitate the safe egress and ingress of emergency equipment at an emergency medical services agency. Any person refusing to obey the orders of the emergency medical services incident commander at that time is guilty of a Class 4 misdemeanor. The authority granted under the provisions of this section may not be exercised to inhibit or obstruct members of law-enforcement agencies or fire departments or fire companies from performing their normal duties when operating at such emergency incident, nor to conflict with or diminish the lawful authority, duties, and responsibilities of forest wardens, including but not limited to the provisions of Chapter 11 (§ 10.1-1100 et seq.) of Title 10.1. Personnel from the news media, such as the press, radio, and television, when gathering the news may enter at their own risk into the incident area only when the incident commander has deemed the area safe and only into those areas of the incident that do not, in the opinion of the incident commander, interfere with the emergency medical services personnel dealing with such emergencies, in which case the emergency medical services incident commander may order such person from the scene of the emergency incident.

History.
2015, cc. 502, 503.

§ 32.1-111.14:7. Penalty for disobeying emergency medical services agency chief or other officer in command.

If any person at a fire or medical emergency refuses or neglects to obey any order duly given by the individual having command of the incident in accordance with § 32.1-111.14:5 or 32.1-111.14:6, he shall, upon conviction of such offense, be fined not to exceed $100.

History.
2015, cc. 502, 503.

CHAPTER 8.

POSTMORTEM EXAMINATIONS AND SERVICES.

Article 1.

Chief Medical Examiner and Postmortem Examinations.

§ 32.1-282.1. Per diem medicolegal death investigators.

The Chief Medical Examiner may appoint per diem medicolegal death investigators, who shall have knowledge of standards and procedures for medicolegal death investigations, to assist the Office of the Chief Medical Examiner with medicolegal death investigations. Per diem medicolegal death investigators shall be agents of the Commonwealth.

History.
2015, c. 53.

TITLE 33.1.

HIGHWAYS, BRIDGES AND FERRIES.

[Repealed.]

§§ 33.1-1 through 33.1-476: Repealed by Acts 2014, c. 805, cl. 11, effective October 1, 2014.

Cross references.
For note regarding the recodification of Title 33.1 as new Title 33.2, and accompanying revisions of other material, see Editor's note under § 33.2-100.

TITLE 33.2.

HIGHWAYS AND OTHER SURFACE TRANSPORTATION SYSTEMS.

SUBTITLE I.

GENERAL PROVISIONS AND TRANSPORTATION ENTITIES.

CHAPTER 2.

TRANSPORTATION ENTITIES.

Article 3.

Commissioner of Highways.

Article 4.

Department of Transportation.

ARTICLE 3.

COMMISSIONER OF HIGHWAYS.

§ 33.2-238. Closing highways for safety of public or proper completion of construction; injury to barriers, signs, etc.

If it appears to the Commissioner of Highways necessary for the safety of the traveling public or for proper completion of work that is being performed to close any highway under his jurisdiction to all traffic or any class of traffic, the Commissioner of Highways may close, or cause to be closed, the whole or any portion of such highway deemed necessary to be excluded from public travel and may exclude all or any class of traffic from such closed portion. While any such highway or portion thereof is so closed, or while any such highway or portion thereof is in process of construction or maintenance, the Commissioner of Highways, or contractor under authority from the Commissioner of Highways, may erect, or cause to be erected, suitable barriers or obstructions thereon, may post, or cause to be posted, conspicuous notices to the effect that the highway or portion thereof is closed and may place warning signs, lights, and lanterns on such highway or portion thereof. When such highway is closed for the safety of the traveling public or in process of construction or maintenance as provided in this section, any person who willfully breaks down, drives into new construction work, removes, injures, or destroys any such barrier or barriers or obstructions, tears down, removes, or destroys any such notices, or extinguishes, removes, injures, or destroys any such warning lights or lanterns so erected, posted, or placed is guilty of a Class 1 misdemeanor.

History.

Code 1950, § 33-109; 1958, c. 547; 1968, c. 162; 1970, c. 322, § 33.1-193; 2014, c. 805.

§ 33.2-246. Recreational waysides; regulations; penalties.

A. To promote the safety, convenience, and enjoyment of travel on, and protection of the public investment in, highways of the Commonwealth and for the restoration, preservation, and enhancement of scenic beauty within and adjoining such highways, it is hereby declared to be in the public interest to acquire and establish recreational waysides and areas of scenic beauty adjoining the highways of the Commonwealth.

B. The Commissioner of Highways may, whenever in his opinion it is in the best interest of the Commonwealth, accept from the United States, or any authorized agency thereof, a grant or grants of any recreational waysides established and constructed by the United States, or any such agency thereof, or a grant or grants of funds for landscaping and scenic enhancement of highways, and the Commissioner of Highways may, on behalf of the Commonwealth, enter into a contract or contracts with the United States, or any such agency thereof, to maintain and operate any such recreational waysides that may be so granted to the Commonwealth and may do all things necessary to receive and expend federal funds for landscaping and scenic enhancement.

C. The Commissioner of Highways may, whenever it is in the best interest of the operation of the Interstate System or the primary or secondary state highway system, establish, construct, maintain, and operate appropriate recreational waysides and areas of scenic beauty adjoining such highways.

D. The Commissioner of Highways may acquire by purchase, gift, or the power of eminent domain such land or interest in land as may be necessary to carry out the provisions of this section, provided that in exercising the power of eminent domain for areas of scenic beauty, such areas adjoin and lie within 100 feet of the right-of-way of the highway, and the procedure shall be, mutatis mutandis, as provided for the acquisition of land by the Commissioner of Highways in Article 1 (§ 33.2-1000 et seq.) of Chapter 10.

E. The Board may establish regulations for the use of recreational waysides, including regulations relating to (i) the time, place, and manner of parking of vehicles; (ii) activities that may be conducted within such waysides; (iii) solicitation and selling within the waysides; and (iv) such other matters as may be necessary or expedient in the interest of the motoring public.

The regulations when adopted by the Board shall be posted in a conspicuous place at each wayside, along with such other signs as the Commissioner of Highways deems necessary to advise the public.

Any person violating any regulation adopted under this section is guilty of a misdemeanor punishable by a fine of not less than $5 nor more than $100 for each offense.

F. Recreational waysides and areas of scenic beauty when acquired, established, maintained, and operated in accordance with this section shall be deemed to be a part of the Interstate System or primary or secondary state highway system but land acquired for areas of scenic beauty shall not be deemed a part of the right-of-way for the purpose of future acquisition of areas of scenic beauty under the provisions of subsections A through D.

History.

Code 1950, §§ 33-133, 33-133.1, 33-134; 1966, c. 470; 1968, c. 566; 1970, c. 322, §§ 33.1-217, 33.1-218, 33.1-219; 2014, c. 805.

ARTICLE 4.

DEPARTMENT OF TRANSPORTATION.

§ 33.2-267. Family restrooms.

The Department shall provide family restrooms at all rest areas along Interstate System highways in the Commonwealth. All such family restrooms shall be constructed in accordance with federal law. The provisions of this section shall apply only to rest stops constructed on or after July 1, 2003.

History.

2003, c. 279, § 33.1-223.2:7; 2014, c. 805.

SUBTITLE II.

MODES OF TRANSPORTATION: HIGHWAYS, BRIDGES, FERRIES, RAIL, AND PUBLIC TRANSPORTATION.

CHAPTER 5.

HIGH-OCCUPANCY VEHICLE LANES AND HIGH-OCCUPANCY TOLL LANES.

Section

Highways

§ 33.2-500. Definitions.

As used in this chapter, unless the context requires a different meaning:

"High-occupancy requirement" means the number of persons required to be traveling in a vehicle for the vehicle to use HOT lanes without the payment of a toll. Emergency vehicles, law-enforcement vehicles being used in HOT lanes in the performance of law-enforcement duties, which shall not include the use of such vehicles for commuting to and from the workplace or for any purpose other than responding to an emergency incident, patrolling HOT lanes pursuant to an agreement by a state agency with the HOT lanes operator, or the time-sensitive investigation, active surveillance, or actual pursuit of persons known or suspected to be engaged in or with knowledge of criminal activity, and mass transit vehicles and commuter buses shall meet the high-occupancy requirement for HOT lanes, regardless of the number of occupants in the vehicle.

"High-occupancy toll lanes" or *"HOT lanes"* means a highway or portion of a highway containing one or more travel lanes separated from other lanes that (i) has an electronic toll collection system; (ii) provides for free passage by vehicles that meet the high-occupancy requirement, including mass transit vehicles and commuter buses; and (iii) contains a photo-enforcement system for use in such electronic toll collection. HOT lanes shall not be a "toll facility" or "HOV lanes" for the purposes of any other provision of law or regulation.

"High-occupancy vehicle lanes" or *"HOV lanes"* means a highway or portion of a highway containing one or more travel lanes for the travel of high-occupancy vehicles or buses as designated pursuant to § 33.2-501.

"HOT lanes operator" means the operator of the facility containing HOT lanes, which may include the Department of Transportation or some other entity.

"Mass transit vehicles" and *"commuter buses"* means vehicles providing a scheduled transportation service to the general public. Such vehicles shall comprise nonprofit, publicly or privately owned or operated transportation services, programs, or systems that may be funded pursuant to § 58.1-638.

"Owner" means the registered owner of a vehicle on record with the Department of Motor Vehicles or with the equivalent agency in another state. "Owner" does not include a vehicle rental or vehicle leasing company.

"Photo-enforcement system" means a sensor installed in conjunction with a toll collection device to detect the presence of a vehicle that automatically produces one or more photographs, one or more microphotographs, a videotape, or other recorded images of each vehicle's license plate at the time it is detected by the toll collection device.

"Unauthorized vehicle" means a motor vehicle that is restricted from use of the HOT lanes pursuant to subdivision 4 a of § 33.2-503 or does not meet the high-occupancy requirement and indicates with its electronic toll collection device that it meets the applicable high-occupancy requirements.

History.

2004, c. 783, § 33.1-56.1; 2008, cc. 167, 280; 2013, c. 195; 2014, c. 805; 2015, c. 73; 2016, c. 753.

§ 33.2-501. Designation of HOV lanes; use of such lanes; penalties.

A. In order to facilitate the rapid and orderly movement of traffic to and from urban areas during peak traffic periods, the Board may designate one or more lanes of any highway in the Interstate System, primary state highway system, or secondary state highway system as HOV lanes. When lanes have been so designated and have been appropriately marked with signs or other markers as the Board may prescribe, they shall be reserved during periods designated by the Board for the exclusive use of buses and high-occupancy vehicles. Any local governing body may also, with respect to highways under its exclusive jurisdiction, designate HOV lanes and impose and enforce restrictions on the use of such lanes. Any highway for which the locality receives highway maintenance funds pursuant to § 33.2-319 shall be deemed to be within the exclusive jurisdiction of the local governing body for the purposes of this section. HOV lanes shall be reserved for high-occupancy vehicles of a specified number of occupants as determined by the Board or, for HOV lanes designated by a local governing body, by that local governing body. However, no designation of any lane or lanes of any highway as HOV lanes shall apply to the use of any such lanes by:

1. Emergency vehicles such as firefighting vehicles and emergency medical services vehicles;

2. Law-enforcement vehicles;

3. Motorcycles;

4. a. Transit and commuter buses designed to transport 16 or more passengers, including the driver;

b. Any vehicle operating under a certificate issued under § 46.2-2075, 46.2-2080, 46.2-2096, 46.2-2099.4, or 46.2-2099.44;

5. Vehicles of public utility companies operating in response to an emergency call;

6. Vehicles bearing clean special fuel vehicle license plates issued pursuant to § 46.2-749.3, provided such use is in compliance with federal law;

7. Taxicabs having two or more occupants, including the driver; or

8. **(Contingent effective date)** Any active duty military member in uniform who is utilizing Interstate 264 and Interstate 64 for the purposes of

traveling to or from a military facility in the Hampton Roads Planning District.

In the Hampton Roads Planning District, HOV restrictions may be temporarily lifted and HOV lanes opened to use by all vehicles when restricting use of HOV lanes becomes impossible or undesirable and the temporary lifting of HOV limitations is indicated by signs along or above the affected portion of highway.

The Commissioner of Highways shall implement a program of the HOV facilities in the Hampton Roads Planning District beginning not later than May 1, 2000. This program shall include the temporary lifting of HOV restrictions and the opening of HOV lanes to all traffic when an incident resulting from nonrecurring causes within the general lanes occurs such that a lane of traffic is blocked or is expected to be blocked for 10 minutes or longer. The HOV restrictions for the facility shall be reinstated when the general lane is no longer blocked and is available for use.

The Commissioner of Highways shall maintain necessary records to evaluate the effects of such openings on the operation of the general lanes and the HOV lanes. This program will terminate if the Federal Highway Administration requires repayment of any federal highway construction funds because of the program's impact on the HOV facilities in Hampton Roads.

B. In designating any lane or lanes of any highway as HOV lanes, the Board or local governing body shall specify the hour or hours of each day of the week during which the lanes shall be so reserved, and the hour or hours shall be plainly posted at whatever intervals along the lanes the Board or local governing body deems appropriate. Any person driving a motor vehicle in a designated HOV lane in violation of this section is guilty of a traffic infraction, which shall not be a moving violation, and on conviction shall be fined $100. However, violations committed within the boundaries of Planning District 8 shall be punishable as follows:

1. For a first offense, by a fine of $125;

2. For a second offense within a period of five years from a first offense, by a fine of $250;

3. For a third offense within a period of five years from a first offense, by a fine of $500; and

4. For a fourth or subsequent offense within a period of five years from a first offense, by a fine of $1,000.

Upon a conviction under this section, the court shall furnish to the Commissioner of the Department of Motor Vehicles in accordance with § 46.2-383 an abstract of the record of such conviction, which shall become a part of the person's driving record. Notwithstanding the provisions of § 46.2-492, no driver demerit points shall be assessed for any violation of this section, except that persons convicted of second, third, fourth, or subsequent violations within five years of a first offense committed in Planning District 8 shall be assessed three demerit points for each such violation.

C. In the prosecution of an offense, committed in the presence of a law-enforcement officer, of failure to obey a road sign restricting a highway, or portion thereof, to the use of high-occupancy vehicles, proof that the vehicle described in the HOV violation summons was operated in violation of this section, together with proof that the defendant was at the time of such violation the registered owner of the vehicle, shall constitute in evidence a rebuttable presumption that such registered owner of the vehicle was the person who committed the violation. Such presumption shall be rebutted if the registered owner of the vehicle testifies in open court under oath that he was not the operator of the vehicle at the time of the violation. A summons for a violation of this section may be executed in accordance with § 19.2-76.2. Such rebuttable presumption shall not arise when the registered owner of the vehicle is a rental or leasing company.

D. Notwithstanding the provisions of § 19.2-76, whenever a summons for a violation of this section is served in any locality, it may be executed by mailing by first-class mail a copy thereof to the address of the owner of the vehicle as shown on the records of the Department of Motor Vehicles. If the summoned person fails to appear on the date of return set out in the summons mailed pursuant to this section, the summons shall be executed in the manner set out in § 19.2-76.3.

No proceedings for contempt or arrest of a person summoned by mailing shall be instituted for his failure to appear on the return date of the summons.

E. Notwithstanding § 33.2-613, high-occupancy vehicles having three or more occupants (HOV-3) may be permitted to use the Omer L. Hirst-Adelard L. Brault Expressway (Dulles Toll Road) without paying a toll.

F. **(Effective until July 1, 2017)** Notwithstanding the contrary provisions of this section, the following conditions shall be met before the HOV-2 designation of Interstate Route 66 outside the Capital Beltway can be changed to HOV-3 or any more restrictive designation:

1. The Department of Transportation shall publish a notice of its intent to change the existing designation and also immediately provide similar notice of its intent to all members of the General Assembly representing districts that touch or are directly impacted by traffic on Interstate Route 66.

2. The Department of Transportation shall hold public hearings in the corridor to receive comments from the public.

3. The Department of Transportation shall make a finding of the need for a change in such designation, based on public hearings and its internal data, and present this finding to the Board for approval.

4. The Board shall make written findings and a decision based upon the following criteria:

a. Is changing the HOV-2 designation to HOV-3 in the public interest?

b. Is there quantitative and qualitative evidence that supports the argument that HOV-3 will facilitate the flow of traffic on Interstate Route 66?

c. Is changing the HOV-2 designation beneficial to comply with the federal Clean Air Act Amendments of 1990?

F. **(Effective July 1, 2017, until January 1, 2020)** Notwithstanding the contrary provisions of this section, the HOV-2 designation of Interstate 66 shall not be changed to HOV-3 or any more restrictive designation.

F. **(Effective January 1, 2020)** Notwithstanding the contrary provisions of this section, the following conditions shall be met before the HOV-2 designation of Interstate 66 can be changed to HOV-3 or any more restrictive designation:

1. The Department of Transportation shall publish a notice of its intent to change the existing designation and also immediately provide similar notice of its intent to all members of the General Assembly representing districts that touch or are directly impacted by traffic on Interstate 66.

2. The Department of Transportation shall hold public hearings in the corridor to receive comments from the public.

3. The Department of Transportation shall make a finding of the need for a change in such designation, based on public hearings and its internal data, and present this finding to the Board for approval.

4. The Board shall make written findings and a decision based upon the following criteria:

a. Is changing the HOV-2 designation to HOV-3 in the public interest?

b. Is there quantitative and qualitative evidence that supports the argument that HOV-3 will facilitate the flow of traffic on Interstate 66?

c. Is changing the HOV-2 designation beneficial to comply with the federal Clean Air Act Amendments of 1990?

d. Has the change in designation been screened and evaluated by the Department of Transportation according to the process established pursuant to § 33.2-257?

History.

1973, c. 197, § 33.1-46.2; 1983, c. 339; 1988, c. 637; 1989, cc. 573, 744; 1993, cc. 82, 587; 1994, cc. 212, 426, 439; 1995, c. 55; 1996, cc. 34, 187, 191, 695, 921, 1037; 1997, c. 504; 1998, c. 321; 1999, cc. 914, 960; 2000, c. 322; 2002, cc. 89, 757; 2003, c. 324; 2004, c. 704; 2006, cc. 600, 873, 908; 2007, c. 317; 2008, c. 511; 2009, c. 676; 2010, cc. 111, 133, 390, 485; 2011, cc. 735, 881, 889; 2012, cc. 681, 743; 2014, c. 805; 2015, cc. 256, 502, 503; 2016, cc. 699, 715.

Contingent effective date for subdivision A 8. — Acts 2010, cc. 133 and 485, which added subdivision A 8 of former § 33.1-46.2, in cl. 2 provided that: "The provisions of this act shall only become effective upon approval by the Federal Highway Administration."

Editor's note. — Acts 2016, c. 699, cl. 2 provides: "That the provisions of this act shall become effective on July 1, 2017."

Acts 2016, c. 699, cl. 3 provides: "That the provisions of this act shall expire on January 1, 2020."

Acts 2016, c. 715, cl. 2 provides: "That the provisions of this act shall become effective on January 1, 2020."

§ 33.2-502. Designation of HOT lanes.

The Board may designate one or more lanes of any highway, including lanes that may previously have been designated HOV lanes under § 33.2-501, in the Interstate System, primary state highway system, or National Highway System, or any portion thereof, as HOT lanes. In making HOT lanes designations, the Board shall also specify the high-occupancy requirement and conditions for use of such HOT lanes or may authorize the Commissioner of Highways to make such determination consistent with the terms of a comprehensive agreement executed pursuant to § 33.2-1808. The high-occupancy requirement for a HOT lanes facility constructed or operated as a result of the Public-Private Transportation Act (§ 33.2-1800 et seq.) shall not be less than three.

History.

2004, c. 783, § 33.1-56.2; 2014, c. 805.

§ 33.2-503. HOT lanes enforcement.

Any person operating a motor vehicle on designated HOT lanes shall make arrangements with the HOT lanes operator for payment of the required toll prior to entering such HOT lanes. The operator of a vehicle who enters the HOT lanes in an unauthorized vehicle, in violation of the conditions for use of such HOT lanes established pursuant to § 33.2-502, without payment of the required toll or without having made arrangements with the HOT lanes operator for payment of the required toll shall have committed a violation of this section, which may be enforced in the following manner:

1. On a form prescribed by the Supreme Court, a summons for a violation of this section may be executed by a law-enforcement officer, when such violation is observed by such officer. The form shall contain the option for the operator of the vehicle to prepay the unpaid toll and all penalties, administrative fees, and costs.

2. a. A HOT lanes operator shall install and operate, or cause to be installed or operated, a photo-enforcement system at locations where tolls are collected for the use of such HOT lanes.

b. A summons for a violation of this section may be executed when such violation is evidenced by information obtained from a photo-enforcement system as defined in this chapter. A certificate, sworn to or affirmed by a technician employed or authorized by the HOT lanes operator, or a facsimile of such a certificate, based on inspection of photographs, microphotographs, videotapes, or other recorded images produced by a photo-enforcement system, shall be prima facie evidence of the facts contained therein. Any photographs, microphotographs, videotape, or other recorded images evidencing such a violation shall be available for inspection in any proceeding to adjudicate the liability for such violation under this subdivision 2. Any vehicle rental or vehicle leasing company, if named in a summons, shall be released as a party to the action if it provides to the HOT lanes operator a copy of the vehicle rental agreement or lease or an affidavit identifying the renter or lessee prior to the date of hearing set forth in the summons. Upon receipt of such rental agreement, lease, or affidavit, a summons shall be issued for the renter or lessee identified therein. Release of this information shall not be deemed a violation of any provision of the Government Data Collection and Dissemination Practices Act (§ 2.2-3800 et seq.) or the Insurance Information and Privacy Protection Act (§ 38.2-600 et seq.).

c. On a form prescribed by the Supreme Court, a summons issued under this subdivision 2 may be executed as provided in § 19.2-76.2. Such form shall contain the option for the owner or operator to prepay the unpaid toll and all penalties, administrative fees, and costs. A summons for a violation of this section may set forth multiple violations occurring within one jurisdiction. Notwithstanding the provisions of § 19.2-76, a summons for a violation of this section may be executed by mailing by first-class mail a copy thereof to the address of the owner or, if the owner has named and provided a valid address for the operator of the vehicle at the time of the violation in an affidavit executed pursuant to subdivision e, such named operator of the vehicle. Such summons shall be signed either originally or by electronic signature. If the summoned person fails to appear on the date of return set out in the summons mailed pursuant to this section, the summons shall be executed in the manner set out in § 19.2-76.3.

d. No summons may be issued by a HOT lanes operator for a violation of this section unless the HOT lanes operator can demonstrate that (i) there was an attempt to collect the unpaid tolls and applicable administrative fees through debt collection not less than 30 days prior to issuance of the summons and (ii) 120 days have elapsed since the unpaid toll or, in a summons for multiple violations, 120 days have elapsed since the most recent unpaid toll noticed on the summons. For purposes of this subdivision, "debt collection" means the collection of unpaid tolls and applicable administrative fees by (a) retention of a third-party debt collector or (b) collection practices undertaken by employees of a HOT lanes operator that are materially similar to a third-party debt collector.

e. The owner of such vehicle shall be given reasonable notice by way of a summons as provided in this subdivision 2 that his vehicle had been used in violation of this section, and such owner shall be given notice of the time and place of the hearing and notice of the civil penalty and costs for such offense.

It shall be prima facie evidence that the vehicle described in the summons issued pursuant to subdivision 2 was operated in violation of this section. Records obtained from the Department of Motor Vehicles pursuant to § 33.2-504 and certified in accordance with § 46.2-215 or from the equivalent agency in another state and certified as true and correct copies by the head of such agency or his designee identifying the owner of such vehicle shall give rise to a rebuttable presumption that the owner of the vehicle is the person named in the summons.

Upon the filing of an affidavit with the court at least 14 days prior to the hearing date by the owner of the vehicle stating that he was not the operator of the vehicle on the date of the violation and providing the legal name and address of the operator of the vehicle at the time of the violation, a summons will also be issued to the alleged operator of the vehicle at the time of the offense. The affidavit shall constitute prima facie evidence that the person named in the affidavit was driving the vehicle at all the relevant times relating to the matter named in the affidavit.

If the owner of the vehicle produces a certified copy of a police report showing that the vehicle had been reported to the police as stolen prior to the time of the alleged offense and remained stolen at the time of the alleged offense, then the court shall dismiss the summons issued to the owner of the vehicle.

3. a. The HOT lanes operator may impose and collect an administrative fee in addition to the unpaid toll so as to recover the expenses of collecting the unpaid toll, which administrative fee shall be reasonably related to the actual cost of collecting the unpaid toll and not exceed $100 per violation. The operator of the vehicle shall pay the unpaid tolls and any administrative fee detailed in a notice or invoice issued by a HOT lanes operator. If paid within 60 days of notification, the administrative fee shall not exceed $25. The HOT lanes operator shall notify the owner of the vehicle of any unpaid tolls and administrative fees by mailing an invoice pursuant to § 46.2-819.6.

b. Upon a finding by a court of competent jurisdiction that the operator of the vehicle observed by a law-enforcement officer under subdivision 1 or the vehicle described in the summons for a violation issued pursuant to evidence obtained by a photo-enforcement system under subdivision 2 was in violation of this section, the court shall impose a civil penalty upon the operator of such vehicle issued a summons under subdivision 1, or upon the operator or owner of such vehicle issued a summons under subdivision 2, payable to the HOT lanes operator as follows: for a first offense, $50; for a second offense, $100; for a third offense within a period of two years of the second offense, $250; and for a fourth and subsequent offense within a period of three years of the second offense, $500, together with, in each case, the unpaid toll, all accrued administrative fees imposed by the HOT lanes operator as authorized by this section, and applicable court costs. The court shall remand penalties, the unpaid toll, and administrative fees assessed for violation of this section to the treasurer or director of finance of the county or city in which the violation occurred for payment to the HOT lanes operator for expenses associated with operation of the HOT lanes and payments against any bonds or other liens issued as a result of the construction of the HOT lanes. No person shall be subject to prosecution under both subdivisions 1 and

2 for actions arising out of the same transaction or occurrence.

c. Notwithstanding subdivisions a and b, for a first conviction of an operator or owner of a vehicle under this section, the total amount for the first conviction shall not exceed $2,200, including civil penalties and administrative fees regardless of the total number of offenses the operator or owner of a vehicle is convicted of on that date.

d. Upon a finding by a court that a resident of the Commonwealth has violated this section, in the event such person fails to pay the required penalties, fees, and costs, the court shall notify the Commissioner of the Department of Motor Vehicles, who shall suspend all of the registration certificates and license plates issued for any motor vehicles registered solely in the name of such person and shall not issue any registration certificate or license plate for any other vehicle that such person seeks to register solely in his name until the court has notified the Commissioner of the Department of Motor Vehicles that such penalties, fees, and costs have been paid. Upon a finding by a court that a nonresident of the Commonwealth has violated this section, in the event that such person fails to pay the required penalties, fees, and costs, the court shall notify the Commissioner of the Department of Motor Vehicles, who shall, when the vehicle is registered in a state with which the Commonwealth has entered into an agreement to enforce tolling violations pursuant to § 46.2-819.9, provide to the entity authorized to issue vehicle registration certificates or license plates in the state in which the vehicle is registered sufficient evidence of the court's finding to take action against the vehicle registration certificate or license plates in accordance with the terms of the agreement, until the court has notified the Commissioner of the Department of Motor Vehicles that such penalties, fees, and costs have been paid. Upon receipt of such notification from the court, the Commissioner of the Department of Motor Vehicles shall notify the state where the vehicle is registered of such payment. The HOT lanes operator and the Commissioner of the Department of Motor Vehicles may enter into an agreement whereby the HOT lanes operator may reimburse the Department of Motor Vehicles for its reasonable costs to develop, implement, and maintain this enforcement mechanism, and that specifies that the Commissioner of the Department of Motor Vehicles shall have an obligation to suspend such registration certificates or to provide notice to such entities in other states so long as the HOT lanes operator makes the required reimbursements in a timely manner in accordance with the agreement.

e. An action brought under subdivision 1 or 2 shall be commenced within two years of the commission of the offense and shall be considered a traffic infraction. Except as provided in subdivisions 4 and 5, imposition of a civil penalty pursuant to this section shall not be deemed a conviction as an operator of a motor vehicle under Title 46.2 and shall not be made part of the driving record of the person upon whom such civil penalty is imposed, nor shall it be used for insurance purposes in the provision of motor vehicle insurance coverage. The provisions of § 46.2-395 shall not be applicable to any civil penalty, fee, unpaid toll, fine, or cost imposed or ordered paid under this section for a violation of subdivision 1 or 2.

4. a. The HOT lanes operator may restrict the usage of the HOT lanes to designated vehicle classifications pursuant to an interim or final comprehensive agreement executed pursuant to § 33.2-1808 or 33.2-1809. Notice of any such vehicle classification restrictions shall be provided through the placement of signs or other markers prior to and at all HOT lanes entrances.

b. Any person driving an unauthorized vehicle on the designated HOT lanes is guilty of a traffic infraction, which shall not be a moving violation, and shall be punishable as follows: for a first offense, by a fine of $125; for a second offense within a period of five years from a first offense, by a fine of $250; for a third offense within a period of five years from a first offense, by a fine of $500; and for a fourth and subsequent offense within a period of five years from a first offense, by a fine of $1,000. No person shall be subject to prosecution under both this subdivision and subdivision 1 or 2 for actions arising out of the same transaction or occurrence.

Upon a conviction under this subdivision, the court shall furnish to the Commissioner of the Department of Motor Vehicles, in accordance with § 46.2-383, an abstract of the record of such conviction, which shall become a part of the person's driving record. Notwithstanding the provisions of § 46.2-492, no driver demerit points shall be assessed for any violation of this subdivision, except that persons convicted of a second, third, fourth, or subsequent violation within five years of a first offense shall be assessed three demerit points for each such violation.

5. The operator of a vehicle who enters the HOT lanes by crossing through any barrier, buffer, or other area separating the HOT lanes from other lanes of travel is guilty of a violation of § 46.2-852, unless the vehicle is a state or local law-enforcement vehicle, firefighting truck, or emergency medical services vehicle used in the performance of its official duties. No person shall be subject to prosecution both under this subdivision and under subdivision 1, 2, or 4 for actions arising out of the same transaction or occurrence.

Upon a conviction under this subdivision, the court shall furnish to the Commissioner of the Department of Motor Vehicles in accordance with § 46.2-383 an abstract of the record of such conviction, which shall become a part of the convicted person's driving record.

6. No person shall be subject to prosecution both under this section and under § 33.2-501, 46.2-819,

or 46.2-819.1 for actions arising out of the same transaction or occurrence.

7. Any action under this section shall be brought in the general district court of the county or city in which the violation occurred.

History.

2004, c. 783, § 33.1-56.3; 2008, cc. 167, 280; 2013, cc. 85, 101; 2014, c. 805; 2015, cc. 502, 503; 2016, c. 753.

§ 33.2-504. Release of personal information to or by HOT lanes operators; penalty.

A. The HOT lanes operator may enter into an agreement with the Department of Motor Vehicles, in accordance with the provisions of subdivision B 21 of § 46.2-208, to obtain vehicle owner information regarding the owners of vehicles that use HOT lanes and with the Department of Transportation to obtain any information that is necessary to conduct electronic toll collection and otherwise operate HOT lanes. Such agreement may include any information that may be obtained by the Department of Motor Vehicles in accordance with any agreement entered into pursuant to § 46.2-819.9. No HOT lanes operator shall disclose or release any personal information received from the Department of Motor Vehicles or the Department of Transportation to any third party, except in the issuance of a summons and institution of court proceedings in accordance with § 33.2-503. Information in the possession of a HOT lanes operator under this section shall be exempt from disclosure under the Virginia Freedom of Information Act (§ 2.2-3700 et seq.).

B. Information collected by a photo-enforcement system shall be limited exclusively to that information that is necessary for the collection of unpaid tolls. Notwithstanding any other provision of law, all photographs, microphotographs, electronic images, or other data collected by a photo-enforcement system shall be used exclusively for the collection of unpaid tolls and shall not be (i) open to the public; (ii) sold or used for sales, solicitation, or marketing purposes; (iii) disclosed to any other entity except as may be necessary for the collection of unpaid tolls or to a vehicle owner or operator as part of a challenge to the imposition of a toll; or (iv) used in a court in a pending action or proceeding unless the action or proceeding relates to a violation of § 33.2-503 or upon order from a court of competent jurisdiction. Information collected under this section shall be purged and not retained later than 30 days after the collection and reconciliation of any unpaid tolls, administrative fees, or civil penalties. Any entity operating a photo-enforcement system shall annually certify compliance with this section and make all records pertaining to such system available for inspection and audit by the Commissioner of Highways or the Commissioner of the Department of Motor Vehicles or their designee. Any violation of this subsection constitutes a Class 1 misdemeanor. In addition to any fines or other penalties provided for by law, any money or other thing of value obtained as a result of a violation of this section shall be forfeited to the Commonwealth.

History.

2004, c. 783, § 33.1-56.4; 2006, c. 859; 2014, c. 805; 2016, c. 753.

§ 33.2-505. Exclusion of HOT lanes from certain other laws.

Notwithstanding any other provision of law, the provisions of §§ 22.1-187, 33.2-501, 33.2-613, 46.2-819, and 46.2-819.1 shall not apply to HOT lanes.

History.

2004, c. 783, § 33.1-56.5; 2014, c. 805.

CHAPTER 8.

OFFENSES CONCERNING HIGHWAYS.

§ 33.2-800. Definition.

As used in this chapter, *"highway"* means a state or county highway.

History.

Code 1950, § 33-278; 1970, c. 322, § 33.1-344; 2014, c. 805.

§ 33.2-801. Cutting or damaging trees; damaging bridges; damaging markers; obstructing highways; penalty.

Any person is guilty of a Class 1 misdemeanor who:

1. Cuts or damages a tree within 50 feet of a highway so as to render it liable to fall and leaves it standing;

2. Knowingly and willfully, without lawful authority, breaks down, destroys, or damages any bridge or log placed across a stream for the accommodation of pedestrians;

3. Obstructs any highway or any ditch made for the purpose of draining the highway;

4. Willfully or maliciously displaces, removes, destroys, or damages any highway sign or historical marker or any inscription thereon that is lawfully within a highway; or

5. Puts or casts into any public highway any glass, bottles, glassware, crockery, porcelain or pieces thereof, caltrops or any pieces of iron or hard or sharp metal, or any nails, tacks, or sharp-pointed instruments of any kind, likely in their nature to cut

Highways

or puncture any tire of any vehicle or injure any animal traveling thereon. This subdivision shall not apply to the use of any tire deflation device by a law-enforcement officer while in the discharge of his official duties, provided the device was approved for use by the Division of Purchase and Supply.

History.
Code 1950, § 33-279; 1956, c. 676; 1970, c. 322, § 33.1-345; 1972, c. 65; 1980, c. 141; 1981, c. 19; 1988, c. 79; 1989, c. 727; 1997, c. 136; 2014, c. 805.

§ 33.2-802. Dumping trash; penalty.

A. It shall be unlawful for any person to dump or otherwise dispose of trash, garbage, refuse, litter, a companion animal as defined in § 3.2-6500 for the purpose of disposal, or other unsightly matter on public property, including a public highway, right-of-way, or property adjacent to such highway or right-of-way, or on private property without the written consent of the owner or his agent.

B. When any person is arrested for a violation of this section, and the matter alleged to have been illegally dumped or disposed of has been ejected from a motor vehicle or transported to the disposal site in a motor vehicle, the arresting officer may comply with the provisions of § 46.2-936 in making an arrest.

When a violation of the provisions of this section has been observed by any person, and the matter illegally dumped or disposed of has been ejected or removed from a motor vehicle, the owner or operator of the motor vehicle shall be presumed to be the person ejecting or disposing of the matter. However, such presumption shall be rebuttable by competent evidence.

C. Any person convicted of a violation of this section is guilty of a misdemeanor punishable by confinement in jail for not more than 12 months and a fine of not less than $250 or more than $2,500, either or both. In lieu of the imposition of confinement in jail, the court may order the defendant to perform a mandatory minimum of 10 hours of community service in litter abatement activities.

D. The governing bodies of localities may adopt ordinances not in conflict with the provisions of this section and may repeal or amend such ordinances.

E. The provisions of this section shall not apply to the lawful disposal of such matter in landfills.

History.
Code 1950, § 33-279.1; 1950, p. 453; 1970, c. 264, § 33.1-346; 1972, c. 65; 1976, c. 773; 1978, c. 226; 1981, c. 340; 1988, c. 805; 1995, c. 657; 2000, c. 20; 2003, cc. 113, 787; 2013, c. 156; 2014, c. 805.

§ 33.2-803. Dump creating fire hazard to public bridge; penalty.

It shall be unlawful for any person to establish or maintain a public or private dump containing flammable articles within 500 feet of any public bridge constructed wholly or partly of wood so as to create a fire hazard to such bridge. Any person violating this section is guilty of a Class 1 misdemeanor. Each day of operation in violation of this section shall constitute a separate offense. An offense in violation of this section may be enjoined in the manner provided by law for the abatement of public nuisances.

History.
Code 1950, § 33-279.2; 1958, c. 91; 1970, c. 322, § 33.1-347; 2014, c. 805.

CHAPTER 12.

OUTDOOR ADVERTISING IN SIGHT OF PUBLIC HIGHWAYS.

ARTICLE 1.

GENERAL POLICIES AND REGULATIONS.

§ 33.2-1231. Construction of article.

This article shall be liberally construed with a view to the effective accomplishment of its purposes.

History.
2013, cc. 603, 611, § 33.1-378; 2014, c. 805.

ARTICLE 2.

FALSE AND MISLEADING SIGNS.

§ 33.2-1232. Prohibition of false and misleading signs.

It shall be unlawful for any person to erect or maintain alongside, or in plain view of, any public highway any false or misleading sign of any kind or character purporting to furnish travel information relating to place or direction. It shall be unlawful for any person to erect or maintain alongside, or in plain view of, any public highway any sign of any kind or character purporting to furnish travel information relating to merchandise or services unless the design of such sign, the information thereon, and the location thereof are approved in writing by the Commissioner of Highways, provided that the provisions of this section as to merchandise and service shall not:

1. Apply to or restrict the right of any person to post, display, erect, or maintain on any store, dwelling house, or other building, together with so much land therewith as shall be necessary for the convenience, use, and enjoyment thereof, or on any mercantile appliances, contrivances, or machinery annexed or immediately adjacent thereto, any sign advertising goods, merchandise, real or personal property, business services, entertainment, or amusements actually and in good faith manufactured, produced, bought, sold, conducted, furnished, or dealt in on the premises;

2. Limit or restrict the publication of official notices by or under the direction of any public or court officer in the performance of his official or directed duties;

3. Limit or restrict notice of sale by a trustee under a deed of trust, deed of assignment, or other similar instrument; or

4. Apply to or restrict the right of any property owner or his agent, lessee, or tenant to maintain any sign offering to the public farm products, including livestock of every kind, or board or lodging or similar entertainment, or the sale, rental, or lease of the property.

Nothing in this section shall limit the right of any person, firm, or corporation to erect signs that advertise natural scenic attractions in the Commonwealth.

History.
Code 1950, § 33-324; 1970, c. 322, § 33.1-379; 2014, c. 805.

§ 33.2-1233. Penalty for violation of § 33.2-1232.

Any person who violates any of the provisions of § 33.2-1232 shall be subject to a fine not to exceed $10 for each offense, and it shall be deemed a separate offense for the same person to erect, or permit to be erected, a similar sign at each of two or more places.

History.
Code 1950, § 33-325; 1970, c. 322, § 33.1-380; 2014, c. 805.

Behavioral Health

TITLE 37.1.

INSTITUTIONS FOR THE MENTALLY ILL; MENTAL HEALTH GENERALLY.

[Repealed.]

§§ 37.1-1 through 37.1-260: Repealed by Acts 2005, c. 716, cl. 9, effective October 1, 2005.

Cross references.
As to behavioral health and developmental services, see now Title 37.2.

TITLE 37.2.

BEHAVIORAL HEALTH AND DEVELOPMENTAL SERVICES.

SUBTITLE I.

GENERAL PROVISIONS.

CHAPTER 4.

PROTECTION OF CONSUMERS.

Article 2.

Licensing Providers of Behavioral Health and Developmental Services.

Article 4.

Miscellaneous and Penal Provisions.

ARTICLE 2.

LICENSING PROVIDERS OF BEHAVIORAL HEALTH AND DEVELOPMENTAL SERVICES.

§ 37.2-413. Necessity for supervision by licensed provider.

No person shall maintain or operate any service unless such service is under the direct supervision of a provider licensed under this article.

History.
Code 1950, § 37-258; 1950, p. 936; 1968, c. 477, § 37.1-184; 1976, c. 671; 1979, c. 54; 2001, cc. 486, 506; 2005, c. 716.

§ 37.2-422. Penalty.

Any person violating any provision of this article or any applicable regulation made under such provisions shall be guilty of a Class 3 misdemeanor, and each day, or part thereof, of continuation of any such violation shall constitute a separate offense.

History.
Code 1950, § 37-260; 1960, c. 496; 1968, c. 477, § 37.1-189; 1976, c. 671; 2005, c. 716.

ARTICLE 4.

MISCELLANEOUS AND PENAL PROVISIONS.

§ 37.2-426. Officers may be appointed conservators of the peace; regulation of traffic.

Pursuant to § 19.2-13, the director, resident officers, policemen, and fire fighters of any hospital or training center may be appointed conservators of the peace on the hospital or training center property and shall have, in addition to the powers of conservators of the peace, authority to patrol and regulate traffic on all roadways and roads through hospital or training center property and to issue summons for violations thereof.

History.
Code 1950, § 37-15; 1964, c. 298; 1968, c. 477, § 37.1-148; 1972, c. 639; 1976, c. 671; 1977, c. 326; 2005, c. 716.

§ 37.2-427. Mistreatment of individuals receiving services in hospital or training center.

It shall be unlawful for any officer or employee of any hospital or training center or other person to maltreat or misuse any individual who is receiving services in any hospital or training center or who is on a day pass, family visit, or trial visit from a hospital or training center. Any officer or employee of any hospital or training center or other person who maltreats or misuses any individual who is receiving services in any hospital or training center or who is on a day pass, family visit, or trial visit from a hospital or training center is guilty of a Class 1 misdemeanor.

History.
Code 1950, § 37-16; 1950, p. 901; 1968, c. 477, § 37.1-150; 2005, c. 716; 2012, cc. 476, 507.

§ 37.2-428. Aiding and abetting in escapes.

It shall be unlawful for any officer or employee of any hospital or training center or any other person to aid or abet in the escape or secretion of any lawfully admitted individual receiving services in any hospital or training center, while the individual is in the hospital or training center or on a day pass, family visit, trial visit, bond or escapement, or to willfully fail or refuse to return an individual on a day pass, family visit, or trial visit under his care and custody to any hospital or training center in which he is receiving services, having given written obligation to do so, when directed in writing to do so by the director of the hospital or training center. Any such officer or employee of any hospital or training center or any other person is guilty of a Class 1 misdemeanor.

History.
Code 1950, § 37-228; 1968, c. 477, § 37.1-151; 2005, c. 716; 2012, cc. 476, 507.

§ 37.2-429. Disorderly conduct on grounds and interference with officers.

It shall be unlawful for any person to conduct himself in an insulting or disorderly manner on the grounds of any hospital or training center or in any way to resist or interfere with any officer or employee of any hospital or training center in discharge of his duty. Any person who conducts himself in an insulting or disorderly manner on the grounds of any hospital or training center or in any way resists or interferes with any officer or employee of any hospital or training center in discharge of his duty is guilty of a Class 1 misdemeanor.

History.
Code 1950, § 37-229; 1968, c. 477, § 37.1-152; 1976, c. 671; 2005, c. 716.

§ 37.2-430. Providing alcoholic beverages to individuals receiving services.

It shall be unlawful for any person to sell or give alcoholic beverages to any individual receiving services in any hospital or training center, bring alcoholic beverages onto the premises of the hospital or training center, administer alcoholic beverages to any individual receiving services, or place alcoholic beverages or cause them to be placed where any individual receiving services may access them, except if the alcoholic beverages are prescribed by the director or physicians of the hospital or training center. Any such person is guilty of a Class 1 misdemeanor.

History.
Code 1950, § 37-230; 1968, c. 477, § 37.1-153; 1972, c. 639; 1976, c. 671; 2005, c. 716; 2012, cc. 476, 507.

§ 37.2-431. Contriving or conspiring to maliciously obtain admission of person.

It shall be unlawful for any person to knowingly and maliciously contrive or conspire to obtain without reasonable cause the admission of any person to any hospital or training center. Any person who knowingly and maliciously contrives or conspires to obtain without reasonable cause the admission of any person to any hospital or training center is guilty of a Class 1 misdemeanor.

History.

Code 1950, § 37-230.2; 1964, c. 640; 1968, c. 477, § 37.1-154; 2005, c. 716.

SUBTITLE III.

ADMISSIONS AND DISPOSITIONS.

CHAPTER 8.

EMERGENCY CUSTODY AND VOLUNTARY AND INVOLUNTARY CIVIL ADMISSIONS.

ARTICLE 1.

GENERAL PROVISIONS.

§ 37.2-800. Applicability of chapter.

For the purposes of this chapter, whenever the term mental illness appears, it shall include substance abuse. Whenever the term responsible person appears, it shall include a family member as that term is defined in § 37.2-100, a community services board or behavioral health authority, any treating physician of the person, or a law-enforcement officer. Whenever the term community services board or board appears, it shall include behavioral health authority.

History.

1968, c. 477, § 37.1-63; 1976, c. 671; 2005, c. 716; 2008, cc. 850, 870.

§ 37.2-802. Interpreters in admission or certification proceedings.

A. In any proceeding pursuant to § 37.2-806 or §§ 37.2-809 through 37.2-820 in which a person who is deaf is alleged to have intellectual disability or mental illness, an interpreter for the person shall be appointed by the district court judge or special justice before whom the proceeding is pending from a list of qualified interpreters provided by the Department for the Deaf and Hard-of-Hearing. The interpreter shall be compensated as provided for in § 37.2-804.

B. In any proceeding pursuant to § 37.2-806 or §§ 37.2-809 through 37.2-820 in which a non-English-speaking person is alleged to have intellectual disability or mental illness or is a witness in such proceeding, an interpreter for the person shall be appointed by the district court judge or special justice, or in the case of §§ 37.2-809 through 37.2-813 a magistrate, before whom the proceeding is pending. Failure to appoint an interpreter when an interpreter is not reasonably available or when the person's level of English fluency cannot be determined shall not be a basis to dismiss the petition or void the order entered at the proceeding. The compensation for the interpreter shall be fixed by the court in accordance with the guidelines set by the Judicial Council of Virginia and shall be paid out of the state treasury.

History.

1976, c. 671, § 37.1-67.5; 1979, c. 204; 2004, c. 243, § 37.1-67.5:01; 2005, c. 716; 2012, cc. 476, 507.

ARTICLE 2.
VOLUNTARY ADMISSION.

§ 37.2-805. Voluntary admission.

Any state facility shall admit any person requesting admission who has been (i) screened by the community services board or behavioral health authority that serves the county or city where the person resides or, if impractical, where the person is located, (ii) examined by a physician on the staff of the state facility, and (iii) deemed by the board or authority and the state facility physician to be in need of treatment, training, or habilitation in a state facility. Upon motion of the treating physician, a family member or personal representative of the person, or the community services board serving the county or city where the facility is located, the county or city where the person resides, or the county or city where the person receives treatment, a hearing shall be held prior to the release date of any person who has been the subject of a temporary detention order and voluntarily admitted himself in accordance with subsection B of § 37.2-814 to determine whether such person should be ordered to mandatory outpatient treatment pursuant to subsection D of § 37.2-817 upon his release if such person, on at least two previous occasions within 36 months preceding the date of the hearing, has been (a) the subject of a temporary detention order and voluntarily admitted himself in accordance with subsection B of § 37.2-814 or (b) involuntarily admitted pursuant to § 37.2-817. A district court judge or special justice shall hold the hearing within 72 hours after receiving the motion for a mandatory outpatient treatment order; however, if the 72-hour period expires on a Saturday, Sunday, or legal holiday, the hearing shall be held by the close of business on the next day that is not a Saturday, Sunday, or legal holiday.

History.

Code 1950, § 37-113; 1950, p. 915; 1964, c. 640; 1968, c. 477, § 37.1-65; 1970, c. 46; 1972, cc. 639, 823; 1976, c. 671; 1980, c. 582; 1998, c. 446; 2005, c. 716; 2012, c. 300; 2013, c. 179.

§ 37.2-805.1. Admission of incapacitated persons pursuant to advance directives or by guardians.

A. An agent for a person who has been determined to be incapable of making an informed decision may consent to the person's admission to a facility for no more than 10 calendar days if (i) prior to admission, a physician on the staff of or designated by the proposed admitting facility examines the person and states, in writing, that the person (a) has a mental illness, (b) is incapable of making an informed decision, as defined in § 54.1-2982, regarding admission, and (c) is in need of treatment in a facility; (ii) the proposed admitting facility is willing to admit the person; and (iii) the person has executed an advance directive in accordance with the Health Care Decisions Act (§ 54.1-2981 et seq.) authorizing his agent to consent to his admission to a facility and, if the person protests the admission, he has included in his advance directive specific authorization for his agent to make health care decisions even in the event of his protest as provided in § 54.1-2986.2. In addition, for admission to a state facility, the person shall first be screened by the community services board that serves the city or county where the person resides or, if impractical, where the person is located.

B. A guardian who has been appointed for an incapacitated person pursuant to Chapter 20 (§ 64.2-2000 et seq.) of Title 64.2 may consent to admission of that person to a facility for no more than 10 calendar days if (i) prior to admission, a physician on the staff of or designated by the proposed admitting facility examines the person and states, in writing, that the person (a) has a mental illness, (b) is incapable of making an informed decision, as defined in § 54.1-2982, regarding admission, and (c) is in need of treatment in a facility; (ii) the proposed admitting facility is willing to admit the person; and (iii) the guardianship order specifically authorizes the guardian to consent to the admission of such person to a facility, pursuant to § 64.2-2009. In addition, for admission to a state facility, the person shall first be screened by the community services board that serves the city or county where the person resides or, if impractical, where the person is located.

C. A person admitted to a facility pursuant to this section shall be discharged no later than 10 calendar days after admission unless, within that time, the person's continued admission is authorized under other provisions of law.

History.
2009, cc. 211, 268.

ARTICLE 3.
ADMISSION TO TRAINING CENTERS.

§ 37.2-806. Judicial certification of eligibility for admission of persons with intellectual disability.

A. Whenever a person alleged to have intellectual disability is not capable of requesting admission to a training center pursuant to § 37.2-805, a parent or guardian of the person or another responsible person may initiate a proceeding to certify the person's eligibility for admission pursuant to this section.

B. Prior to initiating the proceeding, the parent or guardian or other responsible person seeking the person's admission shall first obtain (i) a preadmission screening report that recommends admission to a training center from the community services board or behavioral health authority that serves the city or county where the person who is alleged to have intellectual disability resides and (ii) the approval of the training center to which it is proposed that the person be admitted. The Board shall adopt regulations establishing the procedure and standards for the issuance of such approval. These regulations may include provision for the observation and evaluation of the person in a training center for a period not to exceed 48 hours. No person alleged to have intellectual disability who is the subject of a proceeding under this section shall be detained on that account pending the hearing except for observation and evaluation pursuant to the provisions of this subsection.

C. Upon the filing of a petition in any city or county alleging that the person has intellectual disability, is in need of training or habilitation, and has been approved for admission pursuant to subsection B, a proceeding to certify the person's eligibility for admission to the training center may be commenced. The petition shall be filed with any district court or special justice. A copy of the petition shall be personally served on the person named in the petition, his attorney, and his guardian or conservator. Prior to any hearing under this section, the judge or special justice shall appoint an attorney to represent the person. However, the person shall not be precluded from employing counsel of his choosing and at his expense.

D. The person who is the subject of the hearing shall be allowed sufficient opportunity to prepare his defense, obtain independent evaluations and expert opinion at his own expense, and summons other witnesses. He shall be present at any hearing held under this section, unless his attorney waives his right to be present and the judge or special justice is satisfied by a clear showing and after personal observation that the person's attendance would subject him to substantial risk of physical or emotional injury or would be so disruptive as to prevent the hearing from taking place.

E. Notwithstanding the above, the judge or special justice shall summons either a physician or a clinical psychologist who is licensed in Virginia and is qualified in the assessment of persons with intellectual disability or a person designated by the local community services board or behavioral health authority who meets the qualifications established by the Board. The physician, clinical psychologist, or community services board or behavioral health authority designee may be the one who assessed the person pursuant to subsection B. The judge or special justice also shall summons other witnesses when so requested by the person or his attorney. The physician, clinical psychologist, or community services board or behavioral health authority designee shall certify that he has personally assessed the person and has probable cause to believe that the person (i) does or does not have intellectual disability, (ii) is or is not eligible for a less restrictive service, and (iii) is or is not in need of training or habilitation in a training center. The judge or special justice may accept written certification of a finding of a physician, clinical psychologist, or community services board or behavioral health authority designee, provided such assessment has been personally made within the preceding 30 days and there is no objection to the acceptance of the written certification by the person or his attorney.

F. If the judge or special justice, having observed the person and having obtained the necessary positive certification and other relevant evidence, specifically finds that (i) the person is not capable of requesting his own admission, (ii) the training center has approved the proposed admission pursuant to subsection B, (iii) there is no less restrictive alternative to training center admission, consistent with the best interests of the person who is the subject of the proceeding, and (iv) the person has intellectual disability and is in need of training or habilitation in a training center, the judge or special justice shall by written order certify that the person is eligible for admission to a training center.

G. Certification of eligibility for admission hereunder shall not be construed as a judicial commitment for involuntary admission of the person but shall authorize the parent or guardian or other responsible person to admit the person to a training center and shall authorize the training center to accept the person.

History.
1976, c. 493, § 37.1-65.1; 1979, c. 204; 1980, c. 582; 1984, c. 425; 2005, c. 716; 2012, cc. 476, 507.

ARTICLE 4.
EMERGENCY CUSTODY AND INVOLUNTARY TEMPORARY DETENTION.

§ 37.2-808. Emergency custody; issuance and execution of order.

A. Any magistrate shall issue, upon the sworn petition of any responsible person, treating physician, or upon his own motion, an emergency custody order when he has probable cause to believe that any person (i) has a mental illness and that there exists a substantial likelihood that, as a result of mental illness, the person will, in the near future, (a) cause serious physical harm to himself or others as evidenced by recent behavior causing, attempting, or threatening harm and other relevant information, if any, or (b) suffer serious harm due to his lack of capacity to protect himself from harm or to provide for his basic human needs, (ii) is in need of hospitalization or treatment, and (iii) is unwilling to volunteer or incapable of volunteering for hospitalization or treatment. Any emergency custody order entered pursuant to this section shall provide for the disclosure of medical records pursuant to § 37.2-804.2. This subsection shall not preclude any other disclosures as required or permitted by law.

When considering whether there is probable cause to issue an emergency custody order, the magistrate may, in addition to the petition, consider (1) the recommendations of any treating or examining physician or psychologist licensed in Virginia, if available, (2) any past actions of the person, (3) any past mental health treatment of the person, (4) any relevant hearsay evidence, (5) any medical records available, (6) any affidavits submitted, if the witness is unavailable and it so states in the affidavit, and (7) any other information available that the magistrate considers relevant to the determination of whether probable cause exists to issue an emergency custody order.

B. Any person for whom an emergency custody order is issued shall be taken into custody and transported to a convenient location to be evaluated to determine whether the person meets the criteria for temporary detention pursuant to § 37.2-809 and to assess the need for hospitalization or treatment. The evaluation shall be made by a person designated by the community services board who is skilled in the diagnosis and treatment of mental illness and who has completed a certification program approved by the Department.

C. The magistrate issuing an emergency custody order shall specify the primary law-enforcement agency and jurisdiction to execute the emergency custody order and provide transportation. However, the magistrate shall consider any request to authorize transportation by an alternative transportation provider in accordance with this section, whenever an alternative transportation provider is identified to the magistrate, which may be a person, facility, or agency, including a family member or friend of the person who is the subject of the order, a representative of the community services board, or other transportation provider with personnel trained to provide transportation in a safe manner, upon determining, following consideration of information provided by the petitioner; the community services board or its designee; the local law-enforcement agency, if any; the person's treating physician, if any; or other persons who are available and have knowledge of the person, and, when the magistrate deems appropriate, the proposed alternative transportation provider, either in person or via two-way electronic video and audio or telephone communication system, that the proposed alternative transportation provider is available to provide transportation, willing to provide transportation, and able to provide transportation in a safe manner. When transportation is ordered to be provided by an alternative transportation provider, the magistrate shall order the specified primary law-enforcement agency to execute the order, to take the person into custody, and to transfer custody of the person to the alternative transportation provider identified in the order. In such cases, a copy of the emergency custody order shall accompany the person being transported pursuant to this section at all times and shall be delivered by the alternative transportation provider to the community services board or its designee responsible for conducting the evaluation. The community services board or its designee conducting the evaluation shall return a copy of the emergency custody order to the court designated by the magistrate as soon as is practicable. Delivery of an order to a law-enforcement officer or alternative transportation provider and return of an order to the court may be accomplished electronically or by facsimile.

Transportation under this section shall include transportation to a medical facility as may be necessary to obtain emergency medical evaluation or treatment that shall be conducted immediately in accordance with state and federal law. Transportation under this section shall include transportation to a medical facility for a medical evaluation if a physician at the hospital in which the person subject to the emergency custody order may be detained requires a medical evaluation prior to admission.

D. In specifying the primary law-enforcement agency and jurisdiction for purposes of this section, the magistrate shall order the primary law-enforcement agency from the jurisdiction served by the community services board that designated the person to perform the evaluation required in subsection B to execute the order and, in cases in which transportation is ordered to be provided by the primary law-enforcement agency, provide transportation. If the community services board serves more than one jurisdiction, the magistrate shall designate the primary law-enforcement agency from the particular jurisdiction within the community services board's service area where the person who is the subject of the emergency custody order was taken into custody or, if the person has not yet been taken into custody, the primary law-enforcement agency from the jurisdiction where the person is presently located to execute the order and provide transportation.

E. The law-enforcement agency or alternative transportation provider providing transportation pursuant to this section may transfer custody of the person to the facility or location to which the person is transported for the evaluation required in subsection B, G, or H if the facility or location (i) is licensed to provide the level of security necessary to protect both the person and others from harm, (ii) is actually capable of providing the level of security necessary to protect the person and others from harm, and (iii) in cases in which transportation is provided by a law-enforcement agency, has entered into an agreement or memorandum of understanding with the law-enforcement agency setting forth the terms and conditions under which it will accept a transfer of custody, provided, however, that the facility or location may not require the law-enforcement agency to pay any fees or costs for the transfer of custody.

F. A law-enforcement officer may lawfully go or be sent beyond the territorial limits of the county, city, or town in which he serves to any point in the Commonwealth for the purpose of executing an emergency custody order pursuant to this section.

G. A law-enforcement officer who, based upon his observation or the reliable reports of others, has probable cause to believe that a person meets the criteria for emergency custody as stated in this section may take that person into custody and transport that person to an appropriate location to assess the need for hospitalization or treatment without prior authorization. A law-enforcement officer who takes a person into custody pursuant to this subsection or subsection H may lawfully go or be sent beyond the territorial limits of the county, city, or town in which he serves to any point in the Commonwealth for the purpose of obtaining the assessment. Such evaluation shall be conducted immediately. The period of custody shall not exceed eight hours from the time the law-enforcement officer takes the person into custody.

H. A law-enforcement officer who is transporting a person who has voluntarily consented to be transported to a facility for the purpose of assessment or evaluation and who is beyond the territorial limits of the county, city, or town in which he serves may take such person into custody and transport him to an appropriate location to assess the need for hospitalization or treatment without prior authorization when the law-enforcement officer determines (i) that the person has revoked consent to be transported to a facility for the purpose of assessment or evaluation, and (ii) based upon his observations, that probable cause exists to believe that the person meets the criteria for emergency custody as stated in this section. The period of custody shall not exceed eight hours from the time the law-enforcement officer takes the person into custody.

I. Nothing herein shall preclude a law-enforcement officer or alternative transportation provider from obtaining emergency medical treatment or further medical evaluation at any time for a person in his custody as provided in this section.

J. A representative of the primary law-enforcement agency specified to execute an emergency custody order or a representative of the law-enforcement agency employing a law-enforcement officer who takes a person into custody pursuant to subsection G or H shall notify the community services board responsible for conducting the evaluation required in subsection B, G, or H as soon as practicable after execution of the emergency custody order or after the person has been taken into custody pursuant to subsection G or H.

K. The person shall remain in custody until a temporary detention order is issued, until the person is released, or until the emergency custody order expires. An emergency custody order shall be valid for a period not to exceed eight hours from the time of execution.

L. Nothing in this section shall preclude the issuance of an order for temporary detention for testing, observation, or treatment pursuant to § 37.2-1104 for a person who is also the subject of an emergency custody order issued pursuant to this section. In any case in which an order for temporary detention for testing, observation, or treatment is issued for a person who is also the subject of an emergency custody order, the person may be detained by a hospital emergency room or other appropriate facility for testing, observation, and treatment for a period not to exceed 24 hours, unless extended by the court as part of an order pursuant to § 37.2-1101, in accordance with subsection A of § 37.2-1104. Upon completion of testing, observation, or treatment pursuant to § 37.2-1104, the hospital emergency room or other appropriate facility in which the person is detained shall notify the nearest community services board, and the designee of the community services board shall, as soon as is practicable and prior to the expiration of the order for temporary detention issued pursuant to § 37.2-1104, conduct an evaluation of the person to determine if he meets the criteria for temporary detention pursuant to § 37.2-809.

M. Any person taken into emergency custody pursuant to this section shall be given a written summary of the emergency custody procedures and the statutory protections associated with those procedures.

N. If an emergency custody order is not executed within eight hours of its issuance, the order shall be void and shall be returned unexecuted to the office of the clerk of the issuing court or, if such office is not open, to any magistrate serving the jurisdiction of the issuing court.

O. **(Expires June 30, 2018)** In addition to the eight-hour period of emergency custody set forth in subsection G, H, or K, if the individual is detained in a state facility pursuant to subsection E of § 37.2-809, the state facility and an employee or designee of the community services board as defined in § 37.2-809 may, for an additional four hours, continue to attempt to identify an alternative facility that is able and willing to provide temporary detention and appropriate care to the individual.

P. Payments shall be made pursuant to § 37.2-804 to licensed health care providers for medical screening and assessment services provided to persons with mental illnesses while in emergency custody.

Q. No person who provides alternative transportation pursuant to this section shall be liable to the person being transported for any civil damages for ordinary negligence in acts or omissions that result from providing such alternative transportation.

History.

1995, c. 844, § 37.1-67.01; 1996, c. 893; 1998, c. 611; 2004, c. 737; 2005, c. 716; 2007, c. 7; 2008, cc. 202, 551, 691, 775, 779, 782, 784, 793, 850, 870; 2009, cc. 21, 112, 383, 455, 555, 607, 697, 838; 2010, cc. 778, 825; 2011, c. 249; 2013, c. 371; 2014, cc. 691, 761; 2015, cc. 297, 308, 659.

§ 37.2-809. Involuntary temporary detention; issuance and execution of order.

A. For the purposes of this section:

"Designee of the local community services board" means an examiner designated by the local community services board who (i) is skilled in the assessment and treatment of mental illness, (ii) has completed a certification program approved by the Department, (iii) is able to provide an independent examination of the person, (iv) is not related by blood or marriage to the person being evaluated, (v) has no financial interest in the admission or treatment of the person being evaluated, (vi) has no investment interest in the facility detaining or admitting the person under this article, and (vii) except for employees of state hospitals and of the U.S. Department of Veterans Affairs, is not employed by the facility.

"Employee" means an employee of the local community services board who is skilled in the assessment and treatment of mental illness and has completed a certification program approved by the Department.

"Investment interest" means the ownership or holding of an equity or debt security, including shares of stock in a corporation, interests or units of a partnership, bonds, debentures, notes, or other equity or debt instruments.

B. A magistrate shall issue, upon the sworn petition of any responsible person, treating physician, or upon his own motion and only after an evaluation conducted in-person or by means of a two-way electronic video and audio communication system as authorized in § 37.2-804.1 by an employee or a designee of the local community services board to determine whether the person meets the criteria for temporary detention, a temporary detention order if it appears from all evidence readily available, including any recommendation from a physician or clinical psychologist treating the person, that the person (i) has a mental illness and that there exists a substantial likelihood that, as a result of mental illness, the person will, in the near future, (a) cause serious physical harm to himself or others as evidenced by recent behavior causing, attempting, or threatening harm and other relevant information, if any, or (b) suffer serious harm due to his lack of capacity to protect himself from harm or to provide for his basic human needs; (ii) is in need of hospitalization or treatment; and (iii) is unwilling to volunteer or incapable of volunteering for hospitalization or treatment. The magistrate shall also consider, if available, (a) information provided by the person who initiated emergency custody and (b) the recommendations of any treating or examining physician licensed in Virginia either verbally or in writing prior to rendering a decision. Any temporary detention order entered pursuant to this section shall provide for the disclosure of medical records pursuant to § 37.2-804.2. This subsection shall not preclude any other disclosures as required or permitted by law.

C. When considering whether there is probable cause to issue a temporary detention order, the magistrate may, in addition to the petition, consider (i) the recommendations of any treating or examining physician or psychologist licensed in Virginia, if available, (ii) any past actions of the person, (iii) any past mental health treatment of the person, (iv) any relevant hearsay evidence, (v) any medical records available, (vi) any affidavits submitted, if the witness is unavailable and it so states in the affidavit, and (vii) any other information available that the magistrate considers relevant to the determination of whether probable cause exists to issue a temporary detention order.

D. A magistrate may issue a temporary detention order without an emergency custody order proceeding. A magistrate may issue a temporary detention order without a prior evaluation pursuant to subsection B if (i) the person has been personally examined within the previous 72 hours by an employee or a designee of the local community services board or (ii) there is a significant physical, psychological, or medical risk to the person or to others associated with conducting such evaluation.

E. An employee or a designee of the local community services board shall determine the facility of temporary detention in accordance with the provisions of § 37.2-809.1 for all individuals detained pursuant to this section. An employee or designee of the local community services board may change the facility of temporary detention and may designate an alternative facility for temporary detention at any point during the period of temporary detention if it is determined that the alternative facility is a more appropriate facility for temporary detention of the individual given the specific security, medical, or behavioral health needs of the person. In cases in which the facility of temporary detention is changed following transfer of custody to an initial facility of temporary custody, transportation of the individual to the alternative facility of temporary detention shall be provided in accordance with the provisions of § 37.2-810. The initial facility of temporary detention shall be identified on the preadmission screening report and indicated on the temporary detention order; however, if an employee or designee of the local community services board designates an alternative facility, that employee or designee shall provide written notice forthwith, on a form developed by the Executive Secretary of the Supreme Court of Virginia, to the clerk of the issuing court of the name and address of the alternative facility. Subject to the provisions of § 37.2-809.1, if a facility of temporary detention cannot be identified by the time of the expiration of the period of emergency custody pursuant to § 37.2-808, the individual shall be detained in a state facility for the treatment of individuals with mental illness and such facility shall be indicated on the temporary detention order. Except as provided in § 37.2-811 for inmates requiring hospitalization in accordance with subdivision A 2 of § 19.2-169.6, the person shall not be detained in a jail or other place of confinement for persons charged with criminal offenses and shall remain in the custody of law enforcement until the person is either detained within a secure facility or custody has been accepted by the appropriate personnel designated by either the initial facility of temporary detention identified in the temporary detention order or by the alternative facility of temporary detention designated by the employee or designee of the local community services board pursuant to this subsection. The person detained or in custody pursuant to this section shall be given a written summary of the temporary detention procedures and the statutory protections associated with those procedures.

F. Any facility caring for a person placed with it pursuant to a temporary detention order is authorized to provide emergency medical and psychiatric services within its capabilities when the facility determines that the services are in the best interests of the person within its care. The costs incurred as a result of the hearings and by the facility in providing services during the period of temporary detention shall be paid and recovered pursuant to § 37.2-804. The maximum costs reimbursable by the Commonwealth pursuant to this section shall be established by the State Board of Medical Assistance Services based on reasonable criteria. The State Board of Medical Assistance Services shall, by regulation, establish a reasonable rate per day of inpatient care for temporary detention.

G. The employee or the designee of the local community services board who is conducting the evaluation pursuant to this section shall determine, prior to the issuance of the temporary detention order, the insurance status of the person. Where coverage by a third party payor exists, the facility seeking reimbursement under this section shall first seek reimbursement from the third party payor. The Commonwealth shall reimburse the facility only for the balance of costs remaining after the allowances covered by the third party payor have been received.

H. The duration of temporary detention shall be sufficient to allow for completion of the examination required by § 37.2-815, preparation of the preadmission screening report required by § 37.2-816, and initiation of mental health treatment to stabilize the person's psychiatric condition to avoid involuntary commitment where possible, but shall not exceed 72 hours prior to a hearing. If the 72-hour period herein specified terminates on a Saturday, Sunday, legal holiday, or day on which the court is lawfully closed, the person may be detained, as herein provided, until the close of business on the next day that is not a Saturday, Sunday, legal holiday, or day on which the court is lawfully closed. The person may be released, pursuant to § 37.2-813, before the 72-hour period herein specified has run.

I. If a temporary detention order is not executed within 24 hours of its issuance, or within a shorter period as is specified in the order, the order shall be void and shall be returned unexecuted to the office of the clerk of the issuing court or, if the office is not open, to any magistrate serving the jurisdiction of the issuing court. Subsequent orders may be issued upon the original petition within 96 hours after the petition is filed. However, a magistrate must again obtain the advice of an employee or a designee of the local community services board prior to issuing a subsequent order upon the original petition. Any petition for which no temporary detention order or other process in connection therewith is served on the subject of the petition within 96 hours after the petition is filed shall be void and shall be returned to the office of the clerk of the issuing court.

J. The Executive Secretary of the Supreme Court of Virginia shall establish and require that a magistrate, as provided by this section, be available seven days a week, 24 hours a day, for the purpose of performing the duties established by this section. Each community services board shall provide to each general district court and magistrate's office within its service area a list of its employees and designees who are available to perform the evaluations required herein.

K. For purposes of this section, a health care provider or designee of a local community services board or behavioral health authority shall not be required to encrypt any email containing information or medical records provided to a magistrate unless there is reason to believe that a third party will attempt to intercept the email.

L. If the employee or designee of the community services board who is conducting the evaluation pursuant to this section recommends that the person should not be subject to a temporary detention order, such employee or designee shall (i) inform the petitioner, the person who initiated emergency custody if such person is present, and an onsite treating physician of his recommendation; (ii) promptly inform such person who initiated emergency custody that the community services board will facilitate communication between the person and the magistrate if the person disagrees with recommendations of the employee or designee of the community services board who conducted the evaluation and the person who initiated emergency custody so requests; and (iii) upon prompt request made by the person who initiated emergency custody, arrange for such person who initiated emergency custody to communicate with the magistrate as soon as is practicable and prior to the expiration of the period of emergency custody. The magistrate shall consider any information provided by the person who initiated emergency custody and any recommendations of the treating or examining physician and the employee or designee of the community services board who conducted the evaluation and consider such information and recommendations in accordance with subsection B in making his determination to issue a temporary detention order. The individual who is the subject of emergency custody shall remain in the custody of law enforcement or a designee of law enforcement and shall not be released from emergency custody until communication with the magistrate pursuant to this subsection has concluded and the magistrate has made a determination regarding issuance of a temporary detention order.

M. For purposes of this section, "person who initiated emergency custody" means any person who initiated the issuance of an emergency custody order pursuant to § 37.2-808 or a law-enforcement officer who takes a person into custody pursuant to subsection G of § 37.2-808.

History.

1974, c. 351, § 37.1-67.1; 1975, cc. 237, 433; 1976, c. 671, § 37.1-67.4; 1980, c. 582; 1981, cc. 233, 463; 1982, c. 435; 1986, cc. 134, 478, 629; 1987, c. 96; 1988, c. 98; 1989, c. 716; 1990, cc. 429, 728; 1991, c. 159; 1992, c. 566; 1995, c. 844; 1996, cc. 343, 893; 1998, cc. 37, 594, 611; 2004, c. 737; 2005, c. 716; 2007, c. 526; 2008, cc. 331, 551, 691, 728, 779, 782, 793, 828, 850, 870; 2009, cc. 455, 555; 2010, cc. 340, 406, 778, 825; 2013, cc. 87, 321; 2014, cc. 499, 538, 675, 691, 761, 773; 2016, cc. 569, 693.

§ 37.2-809.1. Facility of temporary detention.

A. In each case in which an employee or designee of the local community services board as defined in § 37.2-809 is required to make an evaluation of an individual pursuant to subsection B, G, or H of § 37.2-808, an employee or designee of the local community services board shall, upon being notified of the need for such evaluation, contact the state facility for the area in which the community services board is located and notify the state facility that the individual will be transported to the facility upon issuance of a temporary detention order if no other facility of temporary detention can be identified by the time of the expiration of the period of emergency custody pursuant to § 37.2-808. Upon completion of the evaluation, the employee or designee of the local community services board shall convey to the state facility information about the individual necessary to allow the state facility to determine the services the individual will require upon admission.

B. A state facility may, following the notice in accordance with subsection A, conduct a search for an alternative facility that is able and willing to provide temporary detention and appropriate care to the individual, which may include another state facility if the state facility notified in accordance with subsection A is unable to provide temporary detention and appropriate care for the individual. Under no circumstances shall a state facility fail or refuse to admit an individual who meets the criteria for temporary detention pursuant to § 37.2-809 unless an alternative facility that is able to provide temporary detention and appropriate care agrees to accept the individual for temporary detention and the individual shall not during the duration of the temporary detention order be released from custody except for purposes of transporting the individual to the state facility or alternative facility in accordance with the provisions of § 37.2-810. If an alternative facility is identified and agrees to accept the individual for temporary detention, the state facility shall notify the community services board, and an employee or designee of the community services board shall designate the alternative facility on the prescreening report.

C. The facility of temporary detention designated in accordance with this section shall be one that has been approved pursuant to regulations of the Board.

History.
2014, cc. 691, 773; 2015, cc. 121, 309.

§ 37.2-810. Transportation of person in the temporary detention process.

A. In specifying the primary law-enforcement agency and jurisdiction for purposes of this section, the magistrate shall specify in the temporary detention order the law-enforcement agency of the jurisdiction in which the person resides, or any other willing law-enforcement agency that has agreed to provide transportation, to execute the order and, in cases in which transportation is ordered to be provided by the primary law-enforcement agency, provide transportation. However, if the nearest boundary of the jurisdiction in which the person resides is more than 50 miles from the nearest boundary of the jurisdiction in which the person is located, the law-enforcement agency of the jurisdiction in which the person is located shall execute the order and provide transportation.

B. The magistrate issuing the temporary detention order shall specify the law-enforcement agency to execute the order and provide transportation. However, the magistrate shall consider any request to authorize transportation by an alternative transportation provider in accordance with this section, whenever an alternative transportation provider is identified to the magistrate, which may be a person, facility, or agency, including a family member or friend of the person who is the subject of the temporary detention order, a representative of the community services board, or other transportation provider with personnel trained to provide transportation in a safe manner upon determining, following consideration of information provided by the petitioner; the community services board or its designee; the local law-enforcement agency, if any; the person's treating physician, if any; or other persons who are available and have knowledge of the person, and, when the magistrate deems appropriate, the proposed alternative transportation provider, either in person or via two-way electronic video and audio or telephone communication system, that the proposed alternative transportation provider is available to provide transportation, willing to provide transportation, and able to provide transportation in a safe manner. When transportation is ordered to be provided by an alternative transportation provider, the magistrate shall order the specified law-enforcement agency to execute the order, to take the person into custody, and to transfer custody of the person to the alternative transportation provider identified in the order. In such cases, a copy of the temporary detention order shall accompany the person being transported pursuant to this section at all times and shall be delivered by the alternative transportation provider to the temporary detention facility. The temporary detention facility shall return a copy of the temporary detention order to the court designated by the magistrate as soon as is practicable. Delivery of an order to a law-enforcement officer or alternative transportation provider and return of an order to the court may be accomplished electronically or by facsimile.

The order may include transportation of the person to such other medical facility as may be necessary to obtain further medical evaluation or treatment prior to placement as required by a physician at the admitting temporary detention facility. Nothing herein shall preclude a law-enforcement officer or alternative transportation provider from obtaining emergency medical treatment or further medical evaluation at any time for a person in his custody as provided in this section. Such medical evaluation or treatment shall be conducted immediately in accordance with state and federal law.

C. In cases in which an alternative facility of temporary detention is identified and the law-enforcement agency or alternative transportation provider identified to provide transportation in accordance with subsection B continues to have custody of the person, the local law-enforcement agency or alternative transportation provider shall transport the person to the alternative facility of temporary detention identified by the employee or designee of the community services board. In cases in which an alternative facility of temporary detention is identified and custody of the individual has been transferred from the law-enforcement agency or alternative transportation provider that provided transportation in accordance with subsection B to the initial facility of temporary detention, the employee or designee of the community services board shall request, and a magistrate may enter an order specifying, an alternative transportation provider or, if no alternative transportation provider is available, willing, and able to provide transportation in a safe manner, the local law-enforcement agency for the jurisdiction in which the person resides or, if the nearest boundary of the jurisdiction in which the person resides is more than 50 miles from the nearest boundary of the jurisdiction in which the person is located, the law-enforcement agency of the jurisdiction in which the person is located, to provide transportation.

D. A law-enforcement officer may lawfully go to or be sent beyond the territorial limits of the county, city, or town in which he serves to any point in the Commonwealth for the purpose of executing any temporary detention order pursuant to this section. Law-enforcement agencies may enter into agreements to facilitate the execution of temporary detention orders and provide transportation.

E. No person who provides alternative transportation pursuant to this section shall be liable to the person being transported for any civil damages for ordinary negligence in acts or omissions that result from providing such alternative transportation.

History.
1974, c. 351, § 37.1-67.1; 1975, cc. 237, 433; 1976, c. 671; 1980, c. 582; 1981, c. 463; 1986, cc. 478, 629; 1987, c. 96; 1988, c. 98; 1989,

Behavioral Health

c. 716; 1990, cc. 429, 728; 1991, c. 159; 1992, c. 566; 1995, c. 844; 1996, cc. 343, 893; 1998, cc. 37, 594, 611; 2004, c. 737; 2005, c. 716; 2007, c. 7; 2009, cc. 112, 697; 2013, c. 371; 2014, cc. 317, 675; 2015, cc. 297, 308.

§ 37.2-811. Emergency treatment of inmates in the custody of local correctional facilities.

A. In any case in which temporary detention is ordered pursuant to § 37.2-809 upon petition of a person having custody of an inmate in accordance with subdivision A 2 of § 19.2-169.6, the magistrate executing the temporary detention order shall place the person in a hospital designated by the Commissioner as appropriate for treatment and evaluation of persons under a criminal charge or, if such facility is not available, the inmate shall be detained in a local correctional facility or other place of confinement for persons charged with criminal offenses and shall be transferred to such hospital as soon as possible thereafter.

B. The hearing shall be held, upon notice to the attorney for the inmate, either (i) before the court having jurisdiction over the inmate's case or (ii) before a district court judge or special justice in accordance with the provisions of § 37.2-820, in which case the inmate shall be represented by counsel as specified in § 37.2-814.

History.
1974, c. 351, § 37.1-67.1; 1975, cc. 237, 433; 1976, c. 671; 1980, c. 582; 1981, c. 463; 1986, cc. 478, 629; 1987, c. 96; 1988, c. 98; 1989, c. 716; 1990, cc. 429, 728; 1991, c. 159; 1992, c. 566; 1995, c. 844; 1996, cc. 343, 893; 1998, cc. 37, 594, 611; 2004, c. 737; 2005, c. 716; 2010, cc. 340, 406.

§ 37.2-812: Repealed by Acts 2010, cc. 778 and 825, cl. 2.

§ 37.2-813. Release of person prior to commitment hearing for involuntary admission.

Prior to a hearing as authorized in §§ 37.2-814 through 37.2-819, the district court judge or special justice may release the person on his personal recognizance or bond set by the district court judge or special justice if it appears from all evidence readily available that the person does not meet the commitment criteria specified in subsection D of § 37.2-817. The director of any facility in which the person is detained may release the person prior to a hearing as authorized in §§ 37.2-814 through 37.2-819 if it appears, based on an evaluation conducted by the psychiatrist or clinical psychologist treating the person, that the person would not meet the commitment criteria specified in subsection D of § 37.2-817 if released.

History.
1974, c. 351, § 37.1-67.1; 1975, cc. 237, 433; 1976, c. 671; 1980, c. 582; 1981, c. 463; 1986, cc. 478, 629; 1987, c. 96; 1988, c. 98; 1989, c. 716; 1990, cc. 429, 728; 1991, c. 159; 1992, c. 566; 1995, c. 844; 1996, cc. 343, 893; 1998, cc. 37, 594, 611; 2004, c. 737; 2005, c. 716; 2008, cc. 779, 850, 870; 2010, cc. 778, 825.

ARTICLE 5.

INVOLUNTARY ADMISSIONS.

§ 37.2-814. Commitment hearing for involuntary admission; written explanation; right to counsel; rights of petitioner.

A. The commitment hearing for involuntary admission shall be held after a sufficient period of time has passed to allow for completion of the examination required by § 37.2-815, preparation of the preadmission screening report required by § 37.2-816, and initiation of mental health treatment to stabilize the person's psychiatric condition to avoid involuntary commitment where possible, but shall be held within 72 hours of the execution of the temporary detention order as provided for in § 37.2-809; however, if the 72-hour period herein specified terminates on a Saturday, Sunday, legal holiday, or day on which the court is lawfully closed, the person may be detained, as herein provided, until the close of business on the next day that is not a Saturday, Sunday, legal holiday, or day on which the court is lawfully closed.

B. At the commencement of the commitment hearing, the district court judge or special justice shall inform the person whose involuntary admission is being sought of his right to apply for voluntary admission for inpatient treatment as provided for in § 37.2-805 and shall afford the person an opportunity for voluntary admission. The district court judge or special justice shall advise the person whose involuntary admission is being sought that if the person chooses to be voluntarily admitted pursuant to § 37.2-805, such person will be prohibited from possessing, purchasing, or transporting a firearm pursuant to § 18.2-308.1:3. The judge or special justice shall ascertain if the person is then willing and capable of seeking voluntary admission for inpatient treatment. In determining whether a person is capable of consenting to voluntary admission, the judge or special justice may consider evidence regarding the person's past compliance or noncompliance with treatment. If the judge or special justice finds that the person is capable and willingly accepts voluntary admission for inpatient treatment, the judge or special justice shall require him to accept voluntary admission for a minimum period of treatment not to exceed 72 hours. After such minimum period of treatment, the person shall give the facility 48 hours' notice prior to leaving the facility. During this notice period, the person shall not be discharged except as provided in § 37.2-837, 37.2-838, or 37.2-840. The person shall be subject to the transportation provisions as provided in § 37.2-829 and the requirement for preadmission screening by a community services board as provided in § 37.2-805.

C. If a person is incapable of accepting or unwilling to accept voluntary admission and treatment, the judge or special justice shall inform the person of his right to a commitment hearing and right to counsel. The judge or special justice shall ascertain if the person whose admission is sought is represented by counsel, and, if he is not represented by counsel, the judge or special justice shall appoint an attorney to represent him. However, if the person requests an opportunity to employ counsel, the judge or special justice shall give him a reasonable opportunity to employ counsel at his own expense.

D. A written explanation of the involuntary admission process and the statutory protections associated with the process shall be given to the person, and its contents shall be explained by an attorney prior to the commitment hearing. The written explanation shall describe, at a minimum, the person's rights to (i) retain private counsel or be represented by a court-appointed attorney, (ii) present any defenses including independent evaluation and expert testimony or the testimony of other witnesses, (iii) be present during the hearing and testify, (iv) appeal any order for involuntary admission to the circuit court, and (v) have a jury trial on appeal. The judge or special justice shall ascertain whether the person whose involuntary admission is sought has been given the written explanation required herein.

E. To the extent possible, during or before the commitment hearing, the attorney for the person whose involuntary admission is sought shall interview his client, the petitioner, the examiner described in § 37.2-815, the community services board staff, and any other material witnesses. He also shall examine all relevant diagnostic and other reports, present evidence and witnesses, if any, on his client's behalf, and otherwise actively represent his client in the proceedings. A health care provider shall disclose or make available all such reports, treatment information, and records concerning his client to the attorney, upon request. The role of the attorney shall be to represent the wishes of his client, to the extent possible.

F. The petitioner shall be given adequate notice of the place, date, and time of the commitment hearing. The petitioner shall be entitled to retain counsel at his own expense, to be present during the hearing, and to testify and present evidence. The petitioner shall be encouraged but shall not be required to testify at the hearing, and the person whose involuntary admission is sought shall not be released solely on the basis of the petitioner's failure to attend or testify during the hearing.

History.

1976, c. 671, § 37.1-67.3; 1979, c. 426; 1980, cc. 166, 582; 1982, c. 471; 1984, c. 277; 1985, c. 261; 1986, cc. 349, 609; 1988, c. 225; 1989, c. 716; 1990, cc. 59, 60, 728, 798; 1991, c. 636; 1992, c. 752; 1994, cc. 736, 907; 1995, cc. 489, 668, 844; 1996, cc. 343, 893; 1997, cc. 558, 921; 1998, c. 446; 2001, cc. 478, 479, 507, 658, 837; 2004, cc. 66, 1014; 2005, c. 716; 2008, cc. 751, 788, 850, 870; 2009, c. 647; 2014, cc. 499, 538, 691.

§ 37.2-815. Commitment hearing for involuntary admission; examination required.

A. Notwithstanding § 37.2-814, the district court judge or special justice shall require an examination of the person who is the subject of the hearing by a psychiatrist or a psychologist who is licensed in Virginia by the Board of Medicine or the Board of Psychology and is qualified in the diagnosis of mental illness or, if such a psychiatrist or psychologist is not available, a mental health professional who (i) is licensed in Virginia through the Department of Health Professions as a clinical social worker, professional counselor, marriage and family therapist, psychiatric nurse practitioner, or clinical nurse specialist, (ii) is qualified in the assessment of mental illness, and (iii) has completed a certification program approved by the Department. The examiner chosen shall be able to provide an independent clinical evaluation of the person and recommendations for his placement, care, and treatment. The examiner shall (a) not be related by blood or marriage to the person, (b) not be responsible for treating the person, (c) have no financial interest in the admission or treatment of the person, (d) have no investment interest in the facility detaining or admitting the person under this chapter, and (e) except for employees of state hospitals, the U.S. Department of Veterans Affairs, and community service boards, not be employed by the facility. For purposes of this section, the term "investment interest" shall be as defined in § 37.2-809.

B. The examination conducted pursuant to this section shall be a comprehensive evaluation of the person conducted in-person or, if that is not practicable, by two-way electronic video and audio communication system as authorized in § 37.2-804.1. Translation or interpreter services shall be provided during the evaluation where necessary. The examination shall consist of (i) a clinical assessment that includes a mental status examination; determination of current use of psychotropic and other medications; a medical and psychiatric history; a substance use, abuse, or dependency determination; and a determination of the likelihood that, as a result of mental illness, the person will, in the near future, suffer serious harm due to his lack of capacity to protect himself from harm or to provide for his basic human needs; (ii) a substance abuse screening, when indicated; (iii) a risk assessment that includes an evaluation of the likelihood that, as a result of mental illness, the person will, in the near future, cause serious physical harm to himself or others as evidenced by recent behavior causing, attempting, or threatening harm and other relevant information, if any; (iv) an assessment of the person's capacity to consent to treatment, including his ability to maintain and communicate choice, understand relevant information, and comprehend the situation and its consequences; (v) a review of the temporary detention facility's records for the person, including the treating physician's evaluation, any collateral information, reports of any laboratory or toxicology tests conducted, and all admission forms and nurses' notes; (vi) a discussion of treatment preferences expressed by the person or contained in a document provided by the person in support of recovery; (vii) an assessment of whether the person meets the criteria for an order authorizing discharge to mandatory outpatient treatment following a period of inpatient treatment pursuant to subsection C1 of § 37.2-817; (viii) an assessment of alternatives to involuntary inpatient treatment; and (ix) recommendations for the placement, care, and treatment of the person.

C. All such examinations shall be conducted in private. The judge or special justice shall summons the examiner who shall certify that he has personally examined the person and state whether he has probable cause to believe that the person (i) has a mental illness and there is a substantial likelihood that, as a result of mental illness, the person will, in the near future, (a) cause serious physical harm to himself or others as evidenced by recent behavior causing, attempting, or threatening harm and other relevant information, if any, or (b) suffer serious harm due to his lack of capacity to protect himself from harm or to provide for his basic human needs, and (ii) requires involuntary inpatient treatment. The judge or special justice shall not render any decision on the petition until the examiner has presented his report. The examiner may report orally at the hearing, but he shall provide a written report of his examination prior to the hearing. The examiner's written certification may be accepted into evidence unless objected to by the person or his attorney, in which case the examiner shall attend in person or by electronic communication. When the examiner attends the hearing in person or by electronic communication, the examiner shall not be excluded from the hearing pursuant to an order of sequestration of witnesses.

History.

1976, c. 671, § 37.1-67.3; 1979, c. 426; 1980, cc. 166, 582; 1982, c. 471; 1984, c. 277; 1985, c. 261; 1986, cc. 349, 609; 1988, c. 225; 1989, c. 716; 1990, cc. 59, 60, 728, 798; 1991, c. 636; 1992, c. 752; 1994, cc. 736, 907; 1995, cc. 489, 668, 844; 1996, cc. 343, 893; 1997, cc. 558, 921; 1998, c. 446; 2001, cc. 478, 479, 507, 658, 837; 2004, cc. 66, 1014; 2005, c. 716; 2007, c. 400; 2008, cc. 779, 850, 870; 2009, cc. 21, 132, 838; 2010, cc. 330, 461.

§ 37.2-816. Commitment hearing for involuntary admission; preadmission screening report.

The district court judge or special justice shall require a preadmission screening report from the community services board that serves the county or city where the person resides or, if impractical, where the person is located. The report shall be admitted as evidence of the facts stated therein and shall state (i) whether the person has a mental illness and whether there exists a substantial likelihood that, as a result of mental illness, the person will, in the near future, (a) cause serious physical harm to himself or others as evidenced by recent behavior causing, attempting, or threatening harm and other relevant information, if any, or (b) suffer serious harm due to his lack of capacity to protect himself from harm or to provide for his basic human needs, (ii) whether the person is in need of involuntary inpatient treatment, (iii) whether there is no less restrictive alternative to inpatient treatment, and (iv) the recommendations for that person's placement, care, and treatment including, where appropriate, recommendations for mandatory outpatient treatment. The board shall provide the preadmission screening report to the court prior to the hearing, and the report shall be admitted into evidence and made part of the record of the case. In the case of a person who has been sentenced and committed to the Department of Corrections and who has been examined by a psychiatrist or clinical psychologist, the judge or special justice may proceed to adjudicate whether the person has mental illness and should be involuntarily admitted without requesting a preadmission screening report from the community services board.

History.

1976, c. 671, § 37.1-67.3; 1979, c. 426; 1980, cc. 166, 582; 1982, c. 471; 1984, c. 277; 1985, c. 261; 1986, cc. 349, 609; 1988, c. 225; 1989, c. 716; 1990, cc. 59, 60, 728, 798; 1991, c. 636; 1992, c. 752; 1994, cc. 736, 907; 1995, cc. 489, 668, 844; 1996, cc. 343, 893; 1997, cc. 558, 921; 1998, c. 446; 2001, cc. 478, 479, 507, 658, 837; 2004, cc. 66, 1014; 2005, c. 716; 2008, cc. 779, 850, 870; 2009, cc. 21, 838.

§ 37.2-817. Involuntary admission and mandatory outpatient treatment orders.

A. The district court judge or special justice shall render a decision on the petition for involuntary admission after the appointed examiner has presented the report required by § 37.2-815, and after the community services board that serves the county or city where the person resides or, if impractical, where the person is located has presented a preadmission screening report with recommendations for that person's placement, care, and treatment pursuant to § 37.2-816. These reports, if not contested, may constitute sufficient evidence upon which the district court judge or special justice may base his decision. The examiner, if not physically present at the hearing, and the treating physician at the facility of temporary detention shall be available whenever possible for questioning during the hearing through a two-way electronic video and audio or telephonic communication system as authorized in § 37.2-804.1.

B. Any employee or designee of the local community services board, as defined in § 37.2-809, representing the community services board that prepared the preadmission screening report shall attend the hearing in person or, if physical attendance is not practicable, shall participate in the hearing through a two-way electronic video and audio or telephonic communication system as authorized in § 37.2-804.1. Where a hearing is held outside of the service area of the community services board that prepared the preadmission screening report, and it is not practicable for a representative of the board to attend or participate in the hearing, arrangements shall be made by the board for an employee or designee of the board serving the area in which the hearing is held to attend or participate on behalf of the board that prepared the preadmission screening report. The employee or designee of the local community services board, as defined in § 37.2-809, representing the community services board that prepared the preadmission screening report or attending or participating on behalf of the board that prepared the preadmission screening report shall not be excluded from the hearing pursuant to an order of sequestration of witnesses. The community services board that prepared the preadmission screening report shall remain responsible for the person subject to the hearing and, prior to the hearing, shall send the preadmission screening report through certified mail, personal delivery, facsimile with return receipt acknowledged, or other electronic means to the community services board attending the hearing. Where a community services board attends the hearing on behalf of the community services board that prepared the preadmission screening report, the attending community services board shall inform the community services board that prepared the preadmission screening report of the disposition of the matter upon the conclusion of the hearing. In addition, the attending community services board shall transmit the disposition through certified mail, personal delivery, facsimile with return receipt acknowledged, or other electronic means.

At least 12 hours prior to the hearing, the court shall provide to the community services board that prepared the preadmission screening report the time and location of the hearing. If the representative of the community services board will be present by telephonic means, the court shall provide the telephone number to the board.

C. After observing the person and considering (i) the recommendations of any treating or examining physician or psychologist licensed in Virginia, if available, (ii) any past actions of the person, (iii) any past mental health treatment of the person, (iv) any examiner's certification, (v) any health records available, (vi) the preadmission screening report, and (vii) any other relevant evidence that may have been admitted, including whether the person recently has been found unrestorably incompetent to stand trial after a hearing held pursuant to subsection E of § 19.2-169.1, if the judge or special justice finds by clear and convincing evidence that (a) the person has a mental illness and there is a substantial likelihood that, as a result of mental illness, the person will, in the near future, (1) cause serious physical harm to himself or others as evidenced by recent behavior causing, attempting, or threatening harm and other relevant information, if any, or (2) suffer serious harm due to his lack of capacity to protect himself from harm or to provide for his basic human needs, and (b) all available less restrictive treatment alternatives to involuntary inpatient treatment, pursuant to subsection D, that would offer an opportunity for the improvement of the person's condition have been investigated and determined to be inappropriate, the judge or special justice shall by written order and specific findings so certify and order that the person be admitted involuntarily to a facility for a period of treatment not to exceed 30 days from the date of the court order. Such involuntary admission shall be to a facility designated by the community services board that serves the county or city in which the person was examined as provided in § 37.2-816. If the community services board does not designate a facility at the commitment hearing, the person shall be involuntarily admitted to a facility designated by the Commissioner. Upon the expiration of an order for involuntary admission, the person shall be released unless he is involuntarily admitted by further petition and order of a court, which shall be for a period not to exceed 180 days from the date of the subsequent court order, or such person makes application for treatment on a voluntary basis as provided for in § 37.2-805 or is ordered to mandatory outpatient treatment pursuant to subsection D. Upon motion of the treating physician, a family member or personal representative of the person, or the community services board serving the county or city where the facility is located, the county or city where the person resides, or the county or city where the person receives treatment, a hearing shall be held prior to the release date of any involuntarily admitted person to determine whether such person should be ordered to mandatory outpatient treatment pursuant to subsection D upon his release if such person, on at least two previous occasions within 36 months preceding the date of the hearing, has been (A) involuntarily admitted pursuant to this section or (B) the subject of a temporary detention order and voluntarily admitted himself in accordance with subsection B of § 37.2-814. A district court judge or special justice shall hold the hearing within 72 hours after receiving the motion for a mandatory outpatient treatment order; however, if the 72-hour period expires on a Saturday, Sunday, or legal holiday, the hearing shall be held by the close of business on the next day that is not a Saturday, Sunday, or legal holiday.

C1. In the order for involuntary admission, the judge or special justice may authorize the treating physician to discharge the person to mandatory outpatient treatment under a discharge plan developed pursuant to subsection C2, if the judge or special justice further finds by clear and convincing evidence that (i) the person has a history of lack of compliance with treatment for mental illness that at least twice within the past 36 months has resulted in the person being subject to an order for involuntary admission pursuant to subsection C; (ii) in view of the person's treatment history and current behavior, the person is in need of mandatory outpatient treatment following inpatient treatment in order to prevent a relapse or deterioration that would be likely to result in the person meeting the criteria for involuntary inpatient treatment; (iii) as a result of mental illness, the person is unlikely to voluntarily participate in outpatient treatment unless the court enters an order authorizing discharge to mandatory outpatient treatment following inpatient treatment; and (iv) the person is likely to benefit from mandatory outpatient treatment. The duration of mandatory outpatient treatment shall be determined by the court based on recommendations of the community services board, but shall not exceed 90 days. Upon expiration of the order for mandatory outpatient treatment, the person shall be released unless the order is continued in accordance with § 37.2-817.4.

C2. Prior to discharging the person to mandatory outpatient treatment under a discharge plan as authorized pursuant to subsection C1, the treating physician shall determine, based upon his professional judgment, that (i) the person (a) in view of the person's treatment history and current behavior, no longer needs inpatient hospitalization, (b) requires mandatory outpatient treatment at the time of discharge to prevent relapse or deterioration of his condition that would likely result in his meeting the criteria for involuntary inpatient treatment, and (c) has agreed to abide by his discharge plan and has the ability to do so; and (ii) the ordered treatment will be delivered on an outpatient basis by the community services board or designated provider to the person. Prior to discharging a person to mandatory outpatient treatment under a discharge plan who has not executed an advance directive, the treating physician or his designee shall give to the person a written explanation of the procedures for executing an advance directive in accordance with the Health Care Decisions Act (§ 54.1-2981 et seq.) and an advance directive form, which may be the form set forth in § 54.1-2984. In no event shall the treating physician discharge a person to mandatory outpatient treatment under a discharge plan as authorized pursuant to subsection C1 if the person meets the criteria for involuntary commitment set forth in subsection C. The discharge plan developed by the treating physician and facility staff in conjunction with the community services board and the person shall serve as and shall contain all the components of the comprehensive mandatory outpatient treatment plan set forth in subsection G, and no initial mandatory outpatient treatment plan set forth in subsection F shall be required. The discharge plan shall be submitted to the court for approval and, upon approval by the court, shall be filed and incorporated into the order entered pursuant to subsection C1. The discharge plan shall be provided to the person by the community services board at the time of the person's discharge from the inpatient facility. The community services board where the person resides upon discharge shall monitor the person's compliance with the discharge plan and report any material noncompliance to the court in accordance with § 37.2-817.1.

D. After observing the person and considering (i) the recommendations of any treating or examining physician or psychologist licensed in Virginia, if available, (ii) any past actions of the person, (iii) any past mental health treatment of the person, (iv) any examiner's certification, (v) any health records available, (vi) the preadmission screening report, and (vii) any other relevant evidence that may have been admitted, if the judge or special justice finds by clear and convincing evidence that (a) the person has a mental illness and that there exists a substantial likelihood that, as a result of mental illness, the person will, in the near future, (1) cause serious physical harm to himself or others as evidenced by recent behavior causing, attempting, or threatening harm and other relevant information, if any, or (2) suffer serious harm due to his lack of capacity to protect himself from harm or to provide for his basic human needs; (b) less restrictive alternatives to involuntary inpatient treatment that would offer an opportunity for improvement of his condition have been investigated and are determined to be appropriate; (c) the person has agreed to abide by his treatment plan and has the ability to do so; and (d) the ordered treatment will be delivered on an outpatient basis by the community services board or designated provider to the person, the judge or special justice shall by written order and specific findings so certify and order that the person be admitted involuntarily to mandatory outpatient treatment. Less restrictive alternatives shall not be determined to be appropriate unless the services are actually available in the community.

E. Mandatory outpatient treatment may include day treatment in a hospital, night treatment in a hospital, outpatient involuntary treatment with anti-psychotic medication pursuant to Chapter 11 (§ 37.2-1100 et seq.), or other appropriate course of treatment as may be necessary to meet the needs of the person. Mandatory outpatient treatment shall not include the use of restraints or physical force of any kind in the provision of the medication. The community services board that serves the county or city in which the person resides shall recommend a specific course of treatment and programs for the provision of mandatory outpatient treatment. The duration of mandatory outpatient treatment shall be determined by the court based on recommendations of the community services board, but shall not exceed 90 days. Upon expiration of an order for mandatory outpatient treatment, the person shall be released from the requirements of the order unless the order is continued in accordance with § 37.2-817.4.

F. Any order for mandatory outpatient treatment entered pursuant to subsection D shall include an initial mandatory outpatient treatment plan developed by the community services board that completed the preadmission screening report. The plan shall, at a minimum, (i) identify the specific services to be provided, (ii) identify the provider who has agreed to provide each service, (iii) describe the arrangements made for the initial in-person appointment or contact with each service provider, and (iv) include any other relevant information that may be available regarding the mandatory outpatient treatment ordered. The order shall require the community services board to monitor the implementation of the mandatory outpatient treatment plan and report any material noncompliance to the court.

G. No later than five days, excluding Saturdays, Sundays, or legal holidays, after an order for mandatory outpatient treatment has been entered pursuant to subsection D, the community services board where the person resides that is responsible for monitoring compliance with the order shall file a comprehensive mandatory outpatient treatment plan. The comprehensive mandatory outpatient treatment plan shall (i) identify the specific type, amount, duration, and frequency of each service to be provided to the person, (ii) identify the provider that has agreed to provide each service included in the plan, (iii) certify that the services are the most appropriate and least restrictive treatment available for the person, (iv) certify that each provider has complied and continues to comply with applicable provisions of the Department's licensing regulations, (v) be developed with the fullest possible involvement and participation of the person and his family, with the person's consent, and reflect his preferences to the greatest extent possible to support his recovery and self-determination, (vi) specify the particular conditions with which the person shall be required to comply, and (vii) describe how the community services board shall monitor the person's compliance with the plan and report any material noncompliance with the plan. The community services board shall submit the comprehensive mandatory outpatient treatment plan to the court for approval. Upon approval by the court, the comprehensive mandatory outpatient treatment plan shall be filed with the court and incorporated into the order of mandatory outpatient treatment. Any subsequent substantive modifications to the plan shall be filed with the court for review and attached to any order for mandatory outpatient treatment.

H. If the community services board responsible for developing the comprehensive mandatory outpatient treatment plan determines that the services necessary for the treatment of the person's mental illness are not available or cannot be provided to the person in accordance with the order for mandatory outpatient treatment, it shall notify the court within five business days of the entry of the order for mandatory outpatient treatment. Within two business days of receiving such notice, the judge or special justice, after notice to the person, the person's attorney, and the community services board responsible for developing the comprehensive mandatory outpatient treatment plan shall hold a hearing pursuant to § 37.2-817.2.

I. Upon entry of any order for mandatory outpatient treatment entered pursuant to subsection D, the clerk of the court shall provide a copy of the order to the person who is the subject of the order, to his attorney, and to the community services board required to monitor compliance with the plan. The community services board shall acknowledge receipt of the order to the clerk of the court on a form established by the Office of the Executive Secretary of the Supreme Court and provided by the court for this purpose within five business days.

J. The court may transfer jurisdiction of the case to the district court where the person resides at any time after the entry of the mandatory outpatient treatment order. The community services board responsible for monitoring compliance with the mandatory outpatient treatment plan or discharge plan shall remain responsible for monitoring the person's compliance with the plan until the community services board serving the locality to which jurisdiction of the case has been transferred acknowledges the transfer and receipt of the order to the clerk of the court on a form established by the Office of the Executive Secretary of the Supreme Court and provided by the court for this purpose. The community services board serving the locality to which jurisdiction of the case has been transferred shall acknowledge the transfer and receipt of the order within five business days.

K. Any order entered pursuant to this section shall provide for the disclosure of medical records pursuant to § 37.2-804.2. This subsection shall not preclude any other disclosures as required or permitted by law.

History.

1976, c. 671, § 37.1-67.3; 1979, c. 426; 1980, cc. 166, 582; 1982, c. 471; 1984, c. 277; 1985, c. 261; 1986, cc. 349, 609; 1988, c. 225; 1989, c. 716; 1990, cc. 59, 60, 728, 798; 1991, c. 636; 1992, c. 752; 1994, cc. 736, 907; 1995, cc. 489, 668, 844; 1996, cc. 343, 893; 1997, cc. 558, 921; 1998, c. 446; 2001, cc. 478, 479, 507, 658, 837; 2004, cc. 66, 1014; 2005, cc. 458, 716; 2008, cc. 779, 780, 782, 793, 850, 870; 2009, cc. 21, 838; 2010, cc. 330, 461; 2012, cc. 300, 451, 501; 2013, c. 179; 2014, cc. 499, 538; 2016, c. 688.

§ 37.2-817.1. Monitoring mandatory outpatient treatment; petition for hearing.

A. The community services board where the person resides shall monitor the person's compliance with the mandatory outpatient treatment plan or discharge plan ordered by the court pursuant to § 37.2-817. Monitoring compliance shall include (i) contacting the service providers to determine if the person is complying with the mandatory outpatient treatment order or order authorizing discharge to mandatory outpatient treatment following inpatient treatment and (ii) notifying the court of the person's material noncompliance with the mandatory outpatient treatment order or order authorizing discharge to mandatory outpatient treatment following inpatient treatment. Providers of services identified in the plan shall report any material noncompliance to the community services board.

B. If the community services board determines that the person materially failed to comply with the order, it shall petition the court for a review of the mandatory outpatient treatment order or order authorizing discharge to mandatory outpatient treatment following inpatient treatment as provided in § 37.2-817.2. The community services board shall petition the court for a review of the mandatory outpatient treatment order or order authorizing discharge to mandatory outpatient treatment following inpatient treatment within three days of making that determination, or within 24 hours if the person is being detained under a temporary detention order, and shall recommend an appropriate disposition. Copies of the petition shall be sent to the person and the person's attorney.

C. If the community services board determines that the person is not materially complying with the mandatory outpatient treatment order or order authorizing discharge to mandatory outpatient treatment following inpatient treatment or for any other reason, and there is a substantial likelihood that, as a result of the person's mental illness that the person will, in the near future, (i) cause serious physical harm to himself or others as evidenced by recent behavior causing, attempting or threatening harm and other relevant information, if any, or (ii) suffer serious harm due to his lack of capacity to protect himself from harm or to provide for his basic human needs, it shall immediately request that the magistrate issue an emergency custody order pursuant to § 37.2-808 or a temporary detention order pursuant to § 37.2-809.

History.
2008, cc. 850, 870; 2010, cc. 330, 461.

§ 37.2-817.2. Court review of mandatory outpatient treatment plan or discharge plan.

A. The district court judge or special justice shall hold a hearing within five days after receiving the petition for review of the mandatory outpatient treatment plan or discharge plan; however, if the fifth day is a Saturday, Sunday, legal holiday, or day on which the court is lawfully closed, the hearing shall be held by the close of business on the next day that is not a Saturday, Sunday, legal holiday, or day on which the court is lawfully closed. If the person is being detained under a temporary detention order, the hearing shall be scheduled within the same time frame provided for a commitment hearing under § 37.2-814. The clerk shall provide notice of the hearing to the person, the community services board, all treatment providers listed in the comprehensive mandatory outpatient treatment order or discharge plan, and the original petitioner for the person's involuntary treatment. If the person is not represented by counsel, the court shall appoint an attorney to represent the person in this hearing and any subsequent hearings under §§ 37.2-817.3 and 37.2-817.4, giving consideration to appointing the attorney who represented the person at the proceeding that resulted in the issuance of the mandatory outpatient treatment order or order authorizing discharge to mandatory outpatient treatment following inpatient treatment. The same judge or special justice that presided over the hearing resulting in the mandatory outpatient treatment order or order authorizing discharge to mandatory outpatient treatment following inpatient treatment need not preside at the noncompliance hearing or any subsequent hearings. The community services board shall offer to arrange the person's transportation to the hearing if the person is not detained and has no other source of transportation.

B. If requested by the person, the community services board, a treatment provider listed in the comprehensive mandatory outpatient treatment plan or discharge plan, or the original petitioner for the person's involuntary treatment, the court shall appoint an examiner in accordance with § 37.2-815 who shall personally examine the person and certify to the court whether or not he has probable cause to believe that the person meets the criteria for involuntary inpatient admission or mandatory outpatient treatment as specified in subsections C, C1, C2, and D of § 37.2-817. The examination shall include all applicable requirements of § 37.2-815. The certification of the examiner may be admitted into evidence without the appearance of the examiner at the hearing if not objected to by the person or his attorney. If the person is not detained in an inpatient facility, the community services board shall arrange for the person to be examined at a convenient location and time. The community services board shall offer to arrange for the person's transportation to the examination, if the person has no other source of transportation and resides within the service area or an adjacent service area of the community services board. If the person refuses or fails to appear, the community services board shall notify the court, or a magistrate if the court is not available, and the court or magistrate shall issue a mandatory examination order and capias directing the primary law-enforcement agency in the jurisdiction where the person resides to transport the person to the examination. The person shall remain in custody until a temporary detention order is issued or until the person is released, but in no event shall the period exceed eight hours.

C. If the person fails to appear for the hearing, the court shall, after consideration of any evidence from the person, from the community services board, or from any treatment provider identified in the mandatory outpatient treatment plan or discharge plan regarding why the person failed to appear at the hearing, either (i) reschedule the hearing pursuant to subsection A, (ii) issue an emergency custody order pursuant to § 37.2-808, or (iii) issue a temporary detention order pursuant to § 37.2-809.

D. After hearing the evidence regarding the person's material noncompliance with the mandatory outpatient treatment order or order authorizing discharge to mandatory outpatient treatment following inpatient treatment and the person's current condition, and any other relevant information referenced in subsection C of § 37.2-817, the judge or special justice shall make one of the following dispositions:

1. Upon finding by clear and convincing evidence that the person meets the criteria for involuntary admission and treatment specified in subsection C of § 37.2-817, the judge or special justice shall order the person's involuntary admission to a facility designated by the community services board for a period of treatment not to exceed 30 days;

2. Upon finding that the person continues to meet the criteria for mandatory outpatient treatment specified in subsection C1, C2, or D of § 37.2-817, and that a continued period of mandatory outpatient treatment appears warranted, the judge or special justice shall renew the order for mandatory outpatient treatment, making any necessary modifications that are acceptable to the community services board or treatment provider responsible for the person's treatment. In determining the appropriateness of outpatient treatment, the court may consider the person's material noncompliance with the previous mandatory treatment order; or

3. Upon finding that neither of the above dispositions is appropriate, the judge or special justice shall rescind the order for mandatory outpatient treatment or order authorizing discharge to mandatory outpatient treatment following inpatient treatment.

Upon entry of an order for involuntary inpatient admission, transportation shall be provided in accordance with § 37.2-829.

History.
2008, cc. 850, 870; 2009, cc. 112, 697; 2010, cc. 330, 461; 2014, cc. 691, 761.

§ 37.2-817.3. Rescission of mandatory outpatient treatment order.

A. If the community services board determines at any time prior to the expiration of the mandatory outpatient treatment order or order authorizing discharge to mandatory outpatient treatment following inpatient treatment that the person has complied with the order and no longer meets the criteria for involuntary treatment, or that continued mandatory outpatient treatment is no longer necessary for any other reason, it shall file a petition to rescind the order with the court that entered the order or to which venue has been transferred. If the court agrees with the community services board's determination, the court shall rescind the order. Otherwise, the court shall schedule a hearing and provide notice of the hearing in accordance with subsection A of § 37.2-817.2.

B. At any time after 30 days from entry of the mandatory outpatient treatment order or from the discharge of the person from involuntary inpatient treatment pursuant to an order authorizing discharge to mandatory outpatient treatment following inpatient treatment, the person may petition the court to rescind the order on the grounds that he no longer meets the criteria for mandatory outpatient treatment as specified in subsection C1 or D of § 37.2-817. The court shall schedule a hearing and provide notice of the hearing in accordance with subsection A of § 37.2-817.2. The community services board required to monitor the person's compliance with the mandatory outpatient treatment order or order authorizing discharge to mandatory outpatient treatment following inpatient treatment shall provide a preadmission screening report as required in § 37.2-816. After observing the person, and considering the person's current condition, any material noncompliance with the mandatory outpatient treatment order or order authorizing discharge to mandatory outpatient treatment following inpatient treatment on the part of the person, and any other relevant evidence referred to in subsection C of § 37.2-817, shall make one of the dispositions specified in subsection D of § 37.2-817.2. The person may not file a petition to rescind the order more than once during a 90-day period.

History.
2008, cc. 850, 870; 2010, cc. 330, 461.

§ 37.2-817.4. Continuation of mandatory outpatient treatment order.

A. At any time within 30 days prior to the expiration of a mandatory outpatient treatment order or order authorizing discharge to mandatory outpatient treatment following inpatient treatment, the community services board that is required to monitor the person's compliance with the order, the treating physician, or other responsible person may petition the court to continue the order for a period not to exceed 180 days.

B. If the person who is the subject of the order and the monitoring community services board, if it did not initiate the petition, join the petition, the court shall grant the petition and enter an appropriate order without further hearing. If either the person or the monitoring community services board does not join the petition, the court shall schedule a hearing and provide notice of the hearing in accordance with subsection A of § 37.2-817.2.

C. Upon receipt of the petition, the court shall appoint an examiner who shall personally examine the person pursuant to subsection B of § 37.2-815.

The community services board required to monitor the person's compliance with the mandatory outpatient treatment order or order authorizing discharge to mandatory outpatient treatment following inpatient treatment shall provide a preadmission screening report as required in § 37.2-816.

D. If, after observing the person, reviewing the preadmission screening report and considering the appointed examiner's certification and any other relevant evidence, including any relevant evidence referenced in subsection D of § 37.2-817, the court shall make one of the dispositions specified in subsection D of § 37.2-817.2. If the court finds that a continued period of mandatory outpatient treatment is warranted, it may continue the order for a period not to exceed 180 days. Any order of mandatory outpatient treatment that is in effect at the time a petition for continuation of the order is filed shall remain in effect until the disposition of the hearing.

History.
2008, cc. 850, 870; 2010, cc. 330, 461.

§ 37.2-818. Commitment hearing for involuntary admission; recordings and records.

A. The district court judge or special justice shall make or cause to be made a tape or other audio recording of any hearings held under this chapter, with no more than one hearing recorded per tape, and shall submit the recording to the clerk of the district court in the locality in which the hearing is held to be retained in a confidential file. The person who was the subject of the hearing shall be entitled, upon request, to obtain a copy of the tape or other audio recording of such hearing. These recordings shall be retained for at least three years from the date of the commitment hearing.

B. Except as provided in this section and § 37.2-819, the court shall keep its copies of recordings made pursuant to this section, relevant medical records, reports, and court documents pertaining to the hearings provided for in this chapter confidential. The person who is the subject of the hearing may, in writing, waive the confidentiality provided herein. In the absence of such waiver, access to the dispositional order only may be provided upon court order. Any person seeking access to the dispositional order may file a written motion setting forth why such access is needed. The court may issue an order to disclose the dispositional order if it finds that such disclosure is in the best interest of the person who is the subject of the hearing or of the public. The Executive Secretary of the Supreme Court and anyone acting on his behalf shall be provided access to the court's records upon request. Such recordings, records, reports, and documents shall not be subject to the Virginia Freedom of Information Act (§ 2.2-3700 et seq.).

C. After entering an order for involuntary admission or mandatory outpatient treatment, the judge or special justice shall order that copies of the relevant records of the person be released to (i) the facility in which he is placed, (ii) the community services board of the jurisdiction where the person resides, (iii) any treatment providers identified in a treatment plan incorporated into any mandatory outpatient treatment order, and (iv) any other treatment providers or entities.

History.
1976, c. 671, § 37.1-67.3; 1979, c. 426; 1980, cc. 166, 582; 1982, c. 471; 1984, c. 277; 1985, c. 261; 1986, cc. 349, 609; 1988, c. 225; 1989, c. 716; 1990, cc. 59, 60, 728, 798; 1991, c. 636; 1992, c. 752; 1994, cc. 736, 907; 1995, cc. 489, 668, 844; 1996, cc. 343, 893; 1997, cc. 558, 921; 1998, c. 446; 2001, cc. 478, 479, 507, 658, 837; 2004, cc. 66, 1014; 2005, c. 716; 2008, cc. 806, 850, 870.

§ 37.2-819. Order of involuntary admission or mandatory outpatient treatment forwarded to CCRE; certain voluntary admissions forwarded to CCRE; firearm background check.

A. The order from a commitment hearing issued pursuant to this chapter for involuntary admission or mandatory outpatient treatment and the certification of any person who has been the subject of a temporary detention order pursuant to § 37.2-809 and who, after being advised by the judge or special justice that he will be prohibited from possessing a firearm pursuant to § 18.2-308.1:3, subsequently agreed to voluntary admission pursuant to § 37.2-805 shall be filed by the judge or special justice with the clerk of the district court for the county or city where the hearing took place as soon as practicable but no later than the close of business on the next business day following the completion of the hearing.

B. Upon receipt of any order from a commitment hearing issued pursuant to this chapter for involuntary admission to a facility, the clerk of court shall, as soon as practicable but not later than the close of business on the next following business day, certify and forward to the Central Criminal Records Exchange, on a form provided by the Exchange, a copy of the order. Upon receipt of any order from a commitment hearing issued pursuant to this chapter for mandatory outpatient treatment, the clerk of court shall, prior to the close of that business day, certify and forward to the Central Criminal Records Exchange, on a form provided by the Exchange, a copy of the order.

C. The clerk of court shall also, as soon as practicable but no later than the close of business on the next following business day, forward upon receipt to the Central Criminal Records Exchange, on a form provided by the Exchange, certification of any person who has been the subject of a temporary detention order pursuant to § 37.2-809, and who, after being advised by the judge or special justice that he will be prohibited from possessing a firearm pursuant to § 18.2-308.1:3, subsequently agreed to voluntary admission pursuant to § 37.2-805.

D. Except as provided in subdivision A 1 of § 19.2-389, the copy of the forms and orders sent to the Central Criminal Records Exchange pursuant to subsection B, and the forms and certifications sent to the Central Criminal Records Exchange regarding voluntary admission pursuant to subsection C, shall be kept confidential in a separate file and used only to determine a person's eligibility to possess, purchase, or transfer a firearm. No medical records shall be forwarded to the Central Criminal Records Exchange with any form, order, or certification required by subsection B or C. The Department of State Police shall forward only a person's eligibility to possess, purchase, or transfer a firearm to the National Instant Criminal Background Check System.

History.

1976, c. 671, § 37.1-67.3; 1979, c. 426; 1980, cc. 166, 582; 1982, c. 471; 1984, c. 277; 1985, c. 261; 1986, cc. 349, 609; 1988, c. 225; 1989, c. 716; 1990, cc. 59, 60, 728, 798; 1991, c. 636; 1992, c. 752; 1994, cc. 736, 907; 1995, cc. 489, 668, 844; 1996, cc. 343, 893; 1997, cc. 558, 921; 1998, c. 446; 2001, cc. 478, 479, 507, 658, 837; 2004, cc. 66, 1014; 2005, c. 716; 2008, cc. 751, 788; 2009, cc. 21, 838; 2014, cc. 336, 374; 2015, c. 540.

§ 37.2-820. Place of hearing.

The hearing provided for pursuant to §§ 37.2-814 through 37.2-819 may be conducted by the district court judge or a special justice at the convenient facility or other place open to the public provided for in § 37.2-809, if he deems it advisable, even though the facility or place is located in a county or city other than his own. In conducting such hearings in a county or city other than his own, the judge or special justice shall have all of the authority and power that he would have in his own county or city. A district court judge or special justice of the county or city in which the facility or place is located may conduct the hearing provided for in §§ 37.2-814 through 37.2-819.

History.

1976, c. 671, § 37.1-67.4; 1981, c. 233; 1982, c. 435; 1986, c. 134; 1995, c. 844; 2005, c. 716.

§ 37.2-821. Appeal of involuntary admission or certification order.

A. Any person involuntarily admitted to an inpatient facility or ordered to mandatory outpatient treatment pursuant to §§ 37.2-814 through 37.2-819 or certified as eligible for admission pursuant to § 37.2-806 shall have the right to appeal the order to the circuit court in the jurisdiction where he was involuntarily admitted or ordered to mandatory outpatient treatment or certified or where the facility to which he was admitted is located. Choice of venue shall rest with such person. The court may transfer the case upon a finding that the other forum is more convenient. An appeal shall be filed within 10 days from the date of the order and shall be given priority over all other pending matters before the court and heard as soon as possible, notwithstanding § 19.2-241 regarding the time within which the court shall set criminal cases for trial. A petition for or the pendency of an appeal shall not suspend any order unless so ordered by a judge or special justice; however, a person may be released after a petition for or during the pendency of an appeal pursuant to § 37.2-837 or 37.2-838. The clerk of the court from which an appeal is taken shall immediately transmit the record to the clerk of the appellate court. The clerk of the circuit court shall provide written notification of the appeal to the petitioner in the case in accordance with procedures set forth in § 16.1-112. No appeal bond or writ tax shall be required, and the appeal shall proceed without the payment of costs or other fees. Costs may be recovered as provided for in § 37.2-804.

B. The appeal shall be heard de novo in accordance with the provisions set forth in §§ 37.2-802, 37.2-804, 37.2-804.1, 37.2-804.2, and 37.2-805, and (i) § 37.2-806 or (ii) §§ 37.2-814 through 37.2-819, except that the court in its discretion may rely upon the evaluation report in the commitment hearing from which the appeal is taken instead of requiring a new evaluation pursuant to § 37.2-815. Any order of the circuit court shall not extend the period of involuntary admission or mandatory outpatient treatment set forth in the order appealed from. An order continuing the involuntary admission shall be entered only if the criteria in § 37.2-817 are met at the time the appeal is heard. The person so admitted or certified shall be entitled to trial by jury. Seven persons from a panel of 13 shall constitute a jury.

C. If the person is not represented by counsel, the judge shall appoint an attorney to represent him. Counsel so appointed shall be paid a fee of $75 and his necessary expenses. The order of the court from which the appeal is taken shall be defended by the attorney for the Commonwealth.

History.

1977, c. 355, § 37.1-67.6; 1979, c. 204; 1980, c. 176; 1985, c. 106; 1990, c. 274; 2005, c. 716; 2006, c. 486; 2008, cc. 850, 870; 2010, cc. 544, 591.

§ 37.2-822. Treatment of person admitted while appeal is pending.

Whenever the director of any facility reasonably believes that treatment is necessary to protect the life, health, or safety of a person, treatment may be given during the period allowed for any appeal unless prohibited by order of a circuit court in the county or city wherein the appeal is pending.

History.

Code 1950, §§ 37-71.2, 37-204.1; 1964, c. 322; 1968, c. 477, § 37.1-85; 1972, c. 639; 2005, c. 716.

§ 37.2-823. Examination of admission papers by director; examination of persons admitted.

A. Upon the receipt of any order for admission of any person, the director of the facility shall immediately examine the admission papers and, if they are found to be in substantial compliance with the law, he shall forthwith admit the person to the facility.

B. Any person presented for admission to a facility shall be examined within 24 hours after arrival by one or more of the physicians on the facility's staff. If the examination reveals that there is sufficient cause to believe that the person has mental illness, he shall be retained at the facility; but if the examination reveals insufficient cause, the person shall be returned to the locality in which the petition was initiated or in which the person resides.

C. The Board shall adopt regulations to institute preadmission screening to prevent inappropriate admissions to state facilities.

History.
Code 1950, §§ 37-86.2, 37-90; 1950, pp. 908, 910; 1968, c. 477, §§ 37.1-68, 37.1-70; 1970, c. 673; 1972, c. 639; 1976, c. 671; 1980, c. 582; 2005, c. 716.

§ 37.2-824. Periodic review of all persons for purposes of retention.

The director of a state facility shall conduct a review of the progress of each person admitted to the facility at intervals of 30, 60, and 90 days after admission of the person, and every six months thereafter to determine whether the person should be retained at the state facility. A record shall be kept of the findings of each review in the state facility's file on the person.

History.
1974, c. 66, § 37.1-84.2; 1976, c. 671; 2005, c. 716.

§ 37.2-825. Admission raises no presumption of legal incapacity.

The admission of any person to a facility shall not, of itself, create a presumption of legal incapacity.

History.
1968, c. 477, § 37.1-87; 1997, c. 801; 2005, c. 716.

§ 37.2-826. Disposition of nonresidents.

If it appears that the person examined has a mental illness and is not a resident of the Commonwealth, the same proceedings shall be had with regard to him as if he were a resident of the Commonwealth, and, if he is admitted to a state facility under these proceedings, a statement of the fact of his nonresidence and of the place of his domicile or residence or from where he came, as far as known, shall accompany any petition respecting him. The Commissioner shall, as soon as practicable, cause him to be returned to his family or friends, if known, or the proper authorities of the state or country from which he came, if ascertained and such return is deemed expedient by the Commissioner.

History.
Code 1950, § 37-91; 1950, p. 910; 1968, c. 477, § 37.1-91; 1976, c. 671; 2005, c. 716.

§ 37.2-827. Admission of aliens.

Whenever any person is admitted to a state facility, the Commissioner shall inquire forthwith into the nationality of the person. If it shall appear that the person is an alien, the Commissioner shall notify immediately the United States immigration officer in charge of the district in which the state facility is located.

Upon the official request of the United States immigration officer in charge of the territory or district in which is located any district court judge or special justice certifying or ordering the admission of any alien to a state facility, the clerk of the court shall furnish, without charge, a certified copy in duplicate of any record pertaining to the case of the admitted alien. This information shall be deemed confidential.

History.
Code 1950, § 37-91.1; 1950, p. 911; 1968, c. 477, § 37.1-92; 2005, c. 716.

§ 37.2-828. Receiving and maintaining federal prisoners in state facilities.

The Commissioner is authorized to enter into a contract with the United States, through the Director of the United States Bureau of Prisons or other authorized agent of the United States, for the reception, maintenance, care, and observation in state facilities, or in those designated by the Commissioner for the purpose, of any persons charged with a crime in the courts of the United States sitting in Virginia and committed by the courts to the state facilities for those purposes. All persons so admitted shall remain subject to the jurisdiction of the court by whom they were committed, and they may be returned to that court at any time for hearing or trial.

Any such contract shall require that the United States remit to the State Treasurer for each prisoner admitted specified per diem or other payments, or both, with such payments fixed by the contract.

The director of any state facility to which a prisoner of the United States is admitted shall observe the person and, as soon as possible, report in writing to the court by which he is certified or committed as to his mental condition or other matters as the court may direct.

No contract made pursuant to this section shall obligate the Commonwealth or the Commissioner to receive a federal prisoner into any state facility in which all available beds are needed for persons otherwise admitted, or in any other case where, in the opinion of the director, the admission of the prisoner would interfere with the care and treatment of other persons admitted or with the proper administration of the state facility.

History.

Code 1950, § 37-98; 1950, p. 913; 1968, c. 477, § 37.1-95; 1972, c. 639; 1980, c. 582; 2005, c. 716.

ARTICLE 6.

TRANSPORTATION OF ADMITTED PERSONS; DETENTION BY SHERIFF; ESCAPE; TRANSFERS.

§ 37.2-829. Transportation of person in civil admission process.

When a person has volunteered for admission pursuant to § 37.2-814 or been ordered to be admitted to a facility under §§ 37.2-815 through 37.2-821, the judge or special justice shall determine after consideration of information provided by the person's treating mental health professional and any involved community services board or behavioral health authority staff regarding the person's dangerousness, whether transportation shall be provided by the sheriff or may be provided by an alternative transportation provider, including a family member or friend of the person, a representative of the community services board, a representative of the facility at which the person was detained pursuant to a temporary detention order, or other alternative transportation provider with personnel trained to provide transportation in a safe manner. If the judge or special justice determines that transportation may be provided by an alternative transportation provider, the judge or special justice may consult with the proposed alternative transportation provider either in person or via two-way electronic video and audio or telephone communication system to determine whether the proposed alternative transportation provider is available to provide transportation, willing to provide transportation, and able to provide transportation in a safe manner. If the judge or special justice finds that the proposed alternative transportation provider is available to provide transportation, willing to provide transportation, and able to provide transportation in a safe manner, the judge or special justice may order transportation by the proposed alternative transportation provider. In all other cases, the judge or special justice shall order transportation by the sheriff of the jurisdiction where the person is a resident unless the sheriff's office of that jurisdiction is located more than 100 road miles from the nearest boundary of the jurisdiction in which the proceedings took place. In cases where the sheriff of the jurisdiction of which the person is a resident is more than 100 road miles from the nearest boundary of the jurisdiction in which the proceedings took place, it shall be the responsibility of the sheriff of the latter jurisdiction to transport the person.

If the judge or special justice determines that the person requires transportation by the sheriff, the person may be delivered to the care of the sheriff, as specified in this section, who shall transport the person to the proper facility. In no event shall transport commence later than six hours after notification to the sheriff or alternative transportation provider of the judge's or special justice's order.

If any state hospital has become too crowded to admit any such person, the Commissioner shall give notice of the fact to all community services boards and shall designate the facility to which sheriffs or alternative transportation providers shall transport such persons.

No person who provides alternative transportation pursuant to this section shall be liable to the person being transported for any civil damages for ordinary negligence in acts or omissions that result from providing such alternative transportation.

History.

Code 1950, §§ 37-71, 37-79, 37-116; 1950, pp. 904, 907; 1964, c. 640; 1968, c. 477, § 37.1-71; 1970, c. 673; 1971, Ex. Sess., c. 155; 1972, c. 639; 1976, c. 671; 1980, c. 582; 1987, c. 719; 1989, cc. 334, 534; 1990, c. 94; 1992, c. 419; 1995, c. 844; 1996, c. 184; 2003, c. 151; 2004, c. 737; 2005, c. 716; 2009, cc. 112, 697; 2015, cc. 297, 308.

§ 37.2-830: Repealed by Acts 2009, cc. 112 and 697, cl. 2.

Cross references.

Former § 37.2-830, pertaining to custody of person ordered to be admitted for purpose of transportation, derived from Code 1950, § 37-79; 1950, p. 907; 1964, c. 640; 1968, c. 477, § 37.1-72; 1976, c. 671; 1995, c. 844; 2005, c. 716.

§ 37.2-831. Detention in jail after order of admission.

It shall be unlawful for any sheriff, sergeant, or other officer to use any jail or other place of confinement for criminals as a place of detention for any person in his custody for transportation to a facility in accordance with this chapter, unless the person's detention therein, for a period not to exceed 24 hours, is specifically authorized by the judge or special justice who ordered the admission, except that such authority shall not be given by any judge or special justice for the Counties of Augusta, Arlington, and Fairfax and the Cities of Alexandria, Fairfax, Falls Church, Waynesboro, and Staunton.

History.

Code 1950, § 37-78; 1950, p. 907; 1964, c. 640; 1968, c. 477, § 37.1-73; 1971, Ex. Sess., c. 155; 1972, c. 751; 1976, c. 671; 1979, c. 707; 2005, c. 716.

Behavioral Health

§ 37.2-832. Persons with mental illness not to be confined in cells with criminals.

In no case shall any sheriff or jailer confine any person with mental illness in a cell or room with prisoners charged with or convicted of crimes.

History.
Code 1950, § 37-81; 1950, p. 908; 1968, c. 477, § 37.1-74; 1971, Ex. Sess., c. 155; 2005, c. 716.

§ 37.2-833. Escape, sickness, death, or discharge of a person ordered to be involuntarily admitted while in custody; warrant for person escaping.

If any person who has been ordered to be involuntarily admitted to a facility escapes, becomes too sick to travel, dies, or is discharged by due process of law while in the custody of a sheriff or other person, the sheriff or other person shall immediately notify the facility of that fact. If any person in the custody of a sheriff or other person pursuant to the provisions of this chapter escapes, the sheriff or other person having that person in custody shall immediately secure a warrant from any officer authorized to issue warrants charging the individual with escape from lawful custody, directing his apprehension, and stating what disposition shall be made of the person upon arrest.

History.
Code 1950, § 37-85; 1950, p. 908; 1954, c. 668; 1968, c. 477, § 37.1-75; 1971, Ex. Sess., c. 155; 2005, c. 716.

§ 37.2-834. Arrest of certain persons involuntarily admitted.

If a person involuntarily admitted to a facility escapes, the director may forthwith issue a warrant directed to any officer authorized to make arrests, who shall arrest the person and carry him back to the facility or to an appropriate state facility that is in close proximity to the jurisdictions served by the arresting officer. The officer to whom the warrant is directed may execute the same in any part of the Commonwealth.

History.
Code 1950, § 37-97; 1950, p. 39; 1968, c. 477, § 37.1-76; 1972, c. 639; 1976, c. 671; 1981, c. 242; 2005, c. 716.

§ 37.2-835. Arrest without warrant.

Any officer authorized to make arrests is authorized to make an arrest under a warrant issued under the provisions of § 37.2-833 or 37.2-834, without having the warrant in his possession, provided the warrant has been issued and the arresting officer has been advised of the issuance of the warrant by printed message or any form of wire or wireless communication containing the name of the person wanted, directing the disposition to be made of the person when apprehended, and stating the basis of the issuance of the warrant.

History.
Code 1950, § 37-97.1; 1954, c. 668; 1968, c. 477, § 37.1-77; 2005, c. 716.

§ 37.2-836. Employees to accompany persons admitted voluntarily to facilities.

When application is made to the director of a facility for admission pursuant to § 37.2-805, he may send an employee from the facility to accompany the person to the facility. If for any reason it is impracticable for an employee to do so, then the director may appoint some suitable person for the purpose, or may request the sheriff of the county or city in which the person resides to convey him to the facility. The sheriff or other person appointed for the purpose shall receive only his necessary expenses for conveying any person admitted to the facility. Expenses authorized herein shall be paid by the Department.

History.
Code 1950, § 37-87; 1950, p. 909; 1968, c. 477, § 37.1-78; 1971, Ex. Sess., c. 155; 1972, c. 639; 1976, c. 671; 1980, c. 582; 2005, c. 716.

ARTICLE 7.
DISCHARGE AND TRANSFERS.

§ 37.2-837. Discharge from state hospitals or training centers, conditional release, and trial or home visits for individuals.

A. Except for an individual receiving services in a state hospital who is held upon an order of a court for a criminal proceeding, the director of a state hospital or training center may discharge, after the preparation of a discharge plan:

1. Any individual in a state hospital who, in his judgment, (a) is recovered, (b) does not have a mental illness, or (c) is impaired or not recovered but whose discharge will not be detrimental to the public welfare or injurious to the individual;

2. Any individual in a state hospital who is not a proper case for treatment within the purview of this chapter; or

3. Any individual in a training center who chooses to be discharged or, if the individual lacks the mental capacity to choose, whose legally authorized representative chooses for him to be discharged. Pursuant to regulations of the Centers for Medicare & Medicaid Services and the Department of Medical Assistance Services, no individual at a training center who is enrolled in Medicaid shall be discharged if the individual or his legally authorized representative on his behalf chooses to continue receiving services in a training center.

For all individuals discharged, the discharge plan shall be formulated in accordance with the provisions of § 37.2-505 by the community services board or behavioral health authority that serves the city or county where the individual resided prior to admission or by the board or authority that serves the city or county where the individual or his legally authorized representative on his behalf chooses to reside immediately following the discharge. The discharge plan shall be contained in a uniform discharge document developed by the Department and used by all state hospitals, training centers, and community services boards or behavioral health authorities, and shall identify (i) the services, including mental health, developmental, substance abuse, social, educational, medical, employment, housing, legal, advocacy, transportation, and other services that the individual will require upon discharge into the community and (ii) the public or private agencies that have agreed to provide these services. If the individual will be housed in an assisted living facility, as defined in § 63.2-100, the discharge plan shall identify the facility, document its appropriateness for housing and capacity to care for the individual, contain evidence of the facility's agreement to admit and care for the individual, and describe how the community services board or behavioral health authority will monitor the individual's care in the facility. Prior to discharging an individual pursuant to subdivision A 1 or 2 who has not executed an advance directive, the director of a state hospital or his designee shall give to the individual a written explanation of the procedures for executing an advance directive in accordance with the Health Care Decisions Act (§ 54.1-2981 et seq.) and an advance directive form, which may be the form set forth in § 54.1-2984.

B. The director may grant a trial or home visit to an individual receiving services in accordance with regulations adopted by the Board. The state facility granting a trial or home visit to an individual shall not be liable for his expenses during the period of that visit. Such liability shall devolve upon the relative, conservator, person to whose care the individual is entrusted while on the trial or home visit, or the appropriate local department of social services of the county or city in which the individual resided at the time of admission pursuant to regulations adopted by the State Board of Social Services.

C. Any individual who is discharged pursuant to subdivision A 2 shall, if necessary for his welfare, be received and cared for by the appropriate local department of social services. The provision of public assistance or social services to the individual shall be the responsibility of the appropriate local department of social services as determined by regulations adopted by the State Board of Social Services. Expenses incurred for the provision of public assistance to the individual who is receiving 24-hour care while in an assisted living facility licensed pursuant to Chapters 17 (§ 63.2-1700 et seq.) and 18 (§ 63.2-1800 et seq.) of Title 63.2 shall be the responsibility of the appropriate local department of social services of the county or city in which the individual resided at the time of admission.

History.

Code 1950, § 37-94; 1950, p. 912; 1968, c. 477, § 37.1-98; 1972, c. 639; 1976, c. 671; 1977, c. 189; 1980, c. 582; 1985, c. 87; 1986, cc. 256, 309; 1993, cc. 957, 993; 1998, c. 680; 2002, cc. 62, 557, 747; 2005, c. 716; 2008, c. 263; 2012, cc. 476, 507; 2016, c. 688.

§ 37.2-838. Discharge of individuals from a licensed hospital.

The person in charge of a licensed hospital may discharge any individual involuntarily admitted who is recovered or, if not recovered, whose discharge will not be detrimental to the public welfare or injurious to the individual, or who meets other criteria as specified in § 37.2-837. Prior to discharging any individual who has not executed an advance directive, the person in charge of a licensed hospital or his designee shall give to the individual a written explanation of the procedures for executing an advance directive in accordance with the Health Care Decisions Act (§ 54.1-2981 et seq.) and an advance directive form, which may be the form set forth in § 54.1-2984. The person in charge of the licensed hospital may refuse to discharge any individual involuntarily admitted, if, in his judgment, the discharge will be detrimental to the public welfare or injurious to the individual. The person in charge of a licensed hospital may grant a trial or home visit to an individual in accordance with regulations adopted by the Board.

History.

1968, c. 477, § 37.1-99; 1976, c. 671; 1980, cc. 582, 583; 2005, c. 716; 2012, cc. 476, 507; 2016, c. 688.

§ 37.2-839. Exchange of information between community services boards or behavioral health authorities and state facilities.

Community services boards or behavioral health authorities and state facilities may, when the individual has refused authorization, exchange the information required to prepare and implement a comprehensive individualized treatment plan, including a discharge plan as specified in subsection A of § 37.2-837. This section shall apply to all individuals receiving services from community services boards, behavioral health authorities, and state facilities.

When an individual who is deemed suitable for discharge pursuant to subsection A of § 37.2-837 or his guardian or conservator refuses to authorize the release of information that is required to formulate and implement a discharge plan as specified in subsection A of § 37.2-837, then the community services board or behavioral health authority may release without authorization to those service providers and human service agencies identified in the discharge plan only the information needed to secure those services specified in the plan.

The release of any other information about an individual receiving services to any agency or person not affiliated directly or by contract with community services boards, behavioral health authorities, or state facilities shall be subject to all regulations adopted by the Board or by agencies of the United States government that govern confidentiality of patient information.

History.

1985, c. 87, § 37.1-98.2; 1999, c. 764; 2005, c. 716; 2012, cc. 476, 507.

§ 37.2-840. Transfer of individuals receiving services.

A. The Commissioner may order the transfer of an individual receiving services from one state hospital to another or from one training center to another. When so transferred, in accordance with appropriate admission, certification, or involuntary admission criteria as provided in this chapter, the individual is hereby declared to be lawfully admitted to the state facility to which he is transferred.

B. If the guardian, conservator, or relative of an individual receiving services in a licensed hospital refuses or is otherwise unable to provide properly for his care and treatment, the person in charge of the licensed hospital may:

1. Apply to the Commissioner for the transfer of the individual to a state hospital, or

2. Apply to the Director of the United States Veterans Affairs Medical Center for the transfer of the individual to the center.

Upon the transfer, the state hospital or Veterans Affairs Medical Center may admit the individual under the authority of the admission or order applicable to the licensed hospital from which the individual was transferred. The transfer shall not alter any right of an individual under the provisions of Chapter 8 (§ 37.2-800 et seq.) of Title 37.2 nor shall the transfer divest a judge or special justice before whom a hearing or request therefor is pending of jurisdiction to conduct a hearing. Prior to accepting the transfer of any individual from a licensed hospital, the Commissioner shall receive from that hospital a report that indicates that the individual is in need of further hospitalization. Upon admission of an individual to a state hospital pursuant to this section, the director of the state hospital shall notify the community services board or behavioral health authority that serves the city or county where the admitted individual resides of the individual's name and local address and of the location of the state hospital to which the individual has been admitted, provided that the individual or his guardian has authorized the release of the information.

C. Whenever an individual is admitted by a state hospital or training center, the Commissioner, upon a recommendation by the community services board or behavioral health authority serving the individual's county or city of residence prior to his admission to the hospital or training center, may order the transfer of the individual to any other hospital, training center, or Veterans Affairs hospital, center, or other facility or installation. Such other hospital, training center, or Veterans Affairs hospital, center, or other facility or installation may admit the individual under the authority of the admission or order applicable to the hospital or training center from which the individual was transferred. The transfer shall not alter any right of the individual under the provisions of this chapter nor shall the transfer divest a judge or special justice before whom a hearing or request therefor is pending of jurisdiction to conduct such hearing.

History.

Code 1950, §§ 37-7, 37-126.1; 1950, pp. 900, 918; 1968, c. 477, §§ 37.1-48, 37.1-86, 37.1-99; 1970, c. 673, § 37.1-78.1; 1976, c. 671; 1980, cc. 582, 583; 1984, c. 174; 1986, c. 349; 2005, c. 716; 2012, cc. 476, 507.

§ 37.2-841. Admission of veteran to, or transfer to or from, a Veterans Affairs hospital, center, or other facility or installation.

Whenever it appears that a person with mental illness is a veteran eligible for treatment in a Veterans' Affairs hospital, center, or other facility or installation, the district court judge or special justice may, upon receipt of a certificate of eligibility from that hospital, center, or other facility or installation, order the person to that hospital, center, or other facility or installation, regardless of whether the person resides in Virginia. Any veteran who has been or is in a state hospital and is eligible for treatment in a Veterans Affairs hospital, center, or other facility or installation may be transferred to a Veterans Affairs hospital, center, or other facility or installation with the written consent of its manager. Any veteran admitted to a Veterans Affairs hospital, center, or other facility or installation, if he resided in Virginia prior to his admission and meets the criteria for admission to a state hospital, may be transferred to a state hospital with the written authorization of the Commissioner.

History.

Code 1950, § 37-73; 1950, p. 905; 1968, c. 477, § 37.1-93; 2005, c. 716.

§ 37.2-842. Veterans admitted or transferred to Veterans Affairs hospital, center, or other facility or installation subject to rules; power and authority of medical officer in charge.

Every veteran, after admission to a Veterans Affairs hospital, center, or other facility or installation, either upon initial admission or transfer, shall be subject to the regulations of the Veterans Affairs hospital, center, or other facility or installation, and the medical officer in charge of the Veterans Affairs hospital, center, or other facility or installation to which the veteran is admitted or transferred is vested with the same powers authorized by law to be exercised by the director of a state hospital with reference to retention, custody, trial or home visit, and discharge of the veteran so admitted or transferred.

History.

Code 1950, § 37-74; 1950, p. 905; 1968, c. 477, § 37.1-94; 1972, c. 639; 2005, c. 716.

§ 37.2-843. Providing drugs or medicines for certain individuals discharged from state facilities.

When any individual is discharged from a state facility and he or the person liable for his care and treatment is financially unable to pay for or otherwise access drugs or medicines that are prescribed for him by a member of the medical staff of the state facility in order to mitigate or prevent a recurrence of the condition for which he has received care and treatment in the state facility, the Department or the community services board or behavioral health authority serving the individual's county or city of residence may, from funds appropriated to the Department for that purpose, provide the individual with such drugs and medicines, which shall be dispensed only in accordance with law.

History.

Code 1950, § 37-92.1; 1958, c. 158; 1968, c. 477, § 37.1-101; 1986, c. 349; 2005, c. 716; 2012, cc. 476, 507.

ARTICLE 8.

TESTING LEGALITY OF DETENTION.

§ 37.2-844. Habeas corpus as means.

A. Any person held in custody because of his mental illness may by petition for a writ of habeas corpus have the question of the legality of his detention determined by a court of competent jurisdiction. Upon the petition, after notice to the authorities of the facility or other institution in which the person is confined, the court shall determine in a courtroom of the county or city or in some other convenient public place in that county or city, whether the person has a mental illness and whether he should be detained.

B. Any proceeding to challenge the continued secure inpatient treatment of a person held in custody as a sexually violent predator under Chapter 9 (§ 37.2-900 et seq.) of this title shall be conducted in accordance with § 37.2-910.

History.

Code 1950, §§ 37-122, 37-123; 1950, p. 916; 1968, c. 477, § 37.1-103; 1976, c. 671; 2003, cc. 989, 1018; 2005, c. 716.

§ 37.2-845. Procedure when person confined in facility or other institution.

A. If the person referenced in § 37.2-844 is held in custody and actually confined in any facility or other institution, he may file his petition in the circuit court of the county or the city in which the facility or other institution is located or in the circuit court of the county or the city adjoining the county or city in which the facility or other institution is located.

B. Any proceeding to challenge the continued secure inpatient treatment of any person held in custody as a sexually violent predator under Chapter 9 (§ 37.2-900 et seq.) of this title shall be conducted in the circuit court wherein the person was last convicted of a sexually violent offense or wherein the defendant was deemed unrestorably incompetent and referred for commitment pursuant to § 19.2-169.3.

History.

Code 1950, § 37-123; 1950, p. 916; 1968, c. 477, § 37.1-104; 1976, c. 671; 2003, cc. 989, 1018; 2005, c. 716.

§ 37.2-846. Procedure when person not confined in facility or other institution.

A. In all cases, other than those provided for in § 37.2-845, the person may file his petition in the circuit court of the county or the city in which he resides or in which he was found to have a mental illness or in which an order was entered authorizing his continued involuntary inpatient treatment, pursuant to Article 5 (§ 37.2-814 et seq.) of Chapter 8 of this title.

B. Any proceeding to challenge the continued secure inpatient treatment of any person held in custody as a sexually violent predator under Chapter 9 (§ 37.2-900 et seq.) of this title shall be conducted in the circuit court wherein the person was last convicted of a sexually violent offense or wherein the defendant was deemed unrestorably incompetent and referred for commitment pursuant to § 19.2-169.3.

History.

Code 1950, § 37-124; 1950, p. 916; 1968, c. 477, § 37.1-104.1; 1976, c. 671; 2003, cc. 989, 1018; 2005, c. 716.

§ 37.2-847. Duty of attorney for Commonwealth.

In any case to test the legality of the detention of a person pursuant to this article, whether by habeas corpus or otherwise, the attorney for the Commonwealth of the county or city in which the hearing is held shall, on request of the director of the facility or other institution having or claiming custody of the person, represent the Commonwealth in opposition to any such petition, appeal, or procedure for the discharge of the person from custody.

History.

Code 1950, § 37-125; 1950, p. 916; 1968, c. 477, § 37.1-104.2; 1972, c. 639; 2005, c. 716.

CHAPTER 9.

CIVIL COMMITMENT OF SEXUALLY VIOLENT PREDATORS.

Section

§ 37.2-900. Definitions.

As used in this chapter, unless the context requires a different meaning:

"Commissioner" means the Commissioner of Behavioral Health and Developmental Services.

"Defendant" means any person charged with a sexually violent offense who is deemed to be an unrestorably incompetent defendant pursuant to § 19.2-169.3 and is referred for commitment review pursuant to this chapter.

"Department" means the Department of Behavioral Health and Developmental Services.

"Director" means the Director of the Department of Corrections.

"Mental abnormality" or *"personality disorder"* means a congenital or acquired condition that affects a person's emotional or volitional capacity and renders the person so likely to commit sexually violent offenses that he constitutes a menace to the health and safety of others.

"Respondent" means the person who is subject of a petition filed under this chapter.

"Sexually violent offense" means a felony under (i) former § 18-54, former § 18.1-44, subdivision 5 of § 18.2-31, § 18.2-61, 18.2-67.1, or 18.2-67.2; (ii) § 18.2-48 (ii), 18.2-48 (iii), 18.2-63, 18.2-64.1, or 18.2-67.3; (iii) subdivision 1 of § 18.2-31 where the abduction was committed with intent to defile the victim; (iv) § 18.2-32 when the killing was in the commission of, or attempt to commit rape, forcible sodomy, or inanimate or animate object sexual penetration; (v) the laws of the Commonwealth for a forcible sexual offense committed prior to July 1, 1981, where the criminal behavior is set forth in § 18.2-67.1 or 18.2-67.2, or is set forth in § 18.2-67.3; or (vi) conspiracy to commit or attempt to commit any of the above offenses.

"Sexually violent predator" means any person who (i) has been convicted of a sexually violent offense, or has been charged with a sexually violent offense and is unrestorably incompetent to stand trial pursuant to § 19.2-169.3; and (ii) because of a mental abnormality or personality disorder, finds it difficult to control his predatory behavior, which makes him likely to engage in sexually violent acts.

History.

1999, cc. 946, 985, § 37.1-70.1; 2001, c. 776; 2003, cc. 989, 1018; 2005, cc. 716, 914; 2006, cc. 863, 914; 2007, c. 876; 2009, cc. 740, 813, 840.

§ 37.2-900.1. Office of Sexually Violent Predator Services.

There is hereby established within the Department of Behavioral Health and Developmental Services, the Office of Sexually Violent Predator Services for the purpose of administering the duties of the Department under this chapter.

History.

2006, cc. 681, 914; 2009, cc. 813, 840.

§ 37.2-901. Civil proceeding; rights of respondents; discovery.

In hearings and trials held pursuant to this chapter, respondents shall have the following rights:

1. To receive adequate notice of the proceeding.
2. To be represented by counsel.

3. To remain silent or to testify.
4. To be present during the hearing or trial.
5. To present evidence and to cross-examine witnesses.
6. To view and copy all petitions and reports in the court file.

In no event shall a respondent be permitted, as a part of any proceedings under this chapter, to raise challenges to the validity of his prior criminal or institutional convictions, charges, or sentences, or the computation of his term of confinement.

In no event shall a respondent be permitted to raise defenses or objections based on defects in the institution of proceedings under this chapter unless such defenses or objections have been raised in a written motion to dismiss, stating the legal and factual grounds therefor, filed with the court at least 14 days before the hearing or trial.

All proceedings conducted hereunder are civil proceedings. However, no discovery shall be allowed prior to the probable cause hearing. After the probable cause hearing, no discovery other than that provided in this section shall be allowed without prior leave of the court. Counsel for the respondent and any expert employed or appointed pursuant to this chapter may possess and copy the victim impact statement or presentence or postsentence report. In no event shall the respondent be permitted to retain or copy a victim impact statement or presentence or postsentence report.

History.

1999, cc. 946, 985, § 37.1-70.2; 2001, c. 776; 2003, cc. 989, 1018; 2005, cc. 716, 914; 2007, c. 876; 2009, c. 740; 2011, cc. 446, 448.

§ 37.2-902. Commitment Review Committee; membership.

A. The Director shall establish a Commitment Review Committee (CRC) to screen, evaluate, and make recommendations regarding prisoners and defendants for the purposes of this chapter. The CRC shall be under the supervision of the Department of Corrections. Members of the CRC and any licensed psychiatrists or licensed clinical psychologists providing examinations under subsection B of § 37.2-904 shall be immune from personal liability while acting within the scope of their duties except for gross negligence or intentional misconduct.

B. The CRC shall consist of seven members to be appointed as follows: (i) three full-time employees of the Department of Corrections, appointed by the Director; (ii) three full-time employees of the Department, appointed by the Commissioner, at least one of whom shall be a psychiatrist or psychologist licensed to practice in the Commonwealth who is skilled in the diagnosis and risk assessment of sex offenders and knowledgeable about the treatment of sex offenders; and (iii) one assistant or deputy attorney general, appointed by the Attorney General. Initial appointments by the Director and the Commissioner shall be for terms as follows: one member each for two years, one member each for three years, and one member each for four years. The initial appointment by the Attorney General shall be for a term of four years. Thereafter, all appointments to the CRC shall be for terms of four years, and vacancies shall be filled for the unexpired terms. Four members shall constitute a quorum.

C. The CRC shall meet at least monthly and at other times as it deems appropriate. The CRC shall elect a chairman from its membership to preside during meetings.

History.

1999, cc. 946, 985, § 37.1-70.3; 2001, c. 776; 2003, cc. 989, 1018; 2005, c. 716; 2007, c. 876; 2009, c. 740; 2011, c. 42.

§ 37.2-903. Database of prisoners convicted of sexually violent offenses; maintained by Department of Corrections; notice of pending release to CRC.

A. The Director shall establish and maintain a database of each prisoner in his custody who is (i) incarcerated for a sexually violent offense or (ii) serving or will serve concurrent or consecutive time for another offense in addition to time for a sexually violent offense. The database shall include the following information regarding each prisoner: (a) the prisoner's criminal record and (b) the prisoner's sentences and scheduled date of release. A prisoner who is serving or will serve concurrent or consecutive time for other offenses in addition to his time for a sexually violent offense shall remain in the database until such time as he is released from the custody or supervision of the Department of Corrections or Virginia Parole Board for all of his charges. Prior to the initial assessment of a prisoner under subsection C, the Director shall order a national criminal history records check to be conducted on the prisoner.

B. Each month, the Director shall review the database and identify all such prisoners who are scheduled for release from prison within 10 months from the date of such review or have been referred to the Director by the Virginia Parole Board under rules adopted by the Board (i) who receive a score of five or more on the Static-99 or a similar score on a comparable, scientifically validated instrument designated by the Commissioner, (ii) who receive a score of four on the Static-99 or a similar score on a comparable, scientifically validated instrument if the sexually violent offense mandating the prisoner's evaluation under this section was a violation of § 18.2-61, 18.2-67.1, 18.2-67.2, or 18.2-67.3 where the victim was under the age of 13, or (iii) whose records reflect such aggravating circumstances that the Director determines the offender appears to meet the definition of a sexually violent predator. The Director may exclude from referral prisoners who are so incapacitated by a permanent and debilitating medical condition or a terminal illness so as to represent no threat to public safety.

C. If the Director and the Commissioner agree that no specific scientifically validated instrument exists to measure the risk assessment of a prisoner, the prisoner may instead be screened by a licensed psychiatrist, licensed clinical psychologist, or a licensed mental health professional certified by the Board of Psychology as a sex offender treatment provider pursuant to § 54.1-3600 for an initial determination of whether or not the prisoner may meet the definition of a sexually violent predator.

D. The Commissioner shall forward to the Director the records of all defendants who have been charged with a sexually violent offense and found unrestorably incompetent to stand trial, and ordered to be screened pursuant to § 19.2-169.3. The Director, applying the procedure identified in subsection B, shall identify those defendants who shall be referred to the CRC for assessment.

E. Upon the identification of such prisoners and defendants screened pursuant to subsections B, C, and D, the Director shall forward their names, their scheduled dates of release, court orders finding the defendants unrestorably incompetent, and copies of their files to the CRC for assessment.

History.

1999, cc. 946, 985, § 37.1-70.4; 2001, c. 776; 2003, cc. 989, 1018; 2005, cc. 716, 914; 2006, cc. 863, 914; 2007, c. 876; 2009, c. 740; 2010, c. 389; 2012, cc. 668, 800.

§ 37.2-904. CRC assessment of prisoners or defendants eligible for commitment as sexually violent predators; mental health examination; recommendation.

A. Within 180 days of receiving from the Director the name of a prisoner or defendant who has been assessed by the Director pursuant to § 37.2-903, the CRC shall (i) complete its assessment of the prisoner or defendant for possible commitment pursuant to subsection B and (ii) forward its written recommendation regarding the prisoner or defendant to the Attorney General pursuant to subsection C.

B. CRC assessments of eligible prisoners or defendants shall include a mental health examination, including a personal interview, of the prisoner or defendant by a licensed psychiatrist or a licensed clinical psychologist who is designated by the Commissioner, skilled in the diagnosis and risk assessment of sex offenders, knowledgeable about the treatment of sex offenders, and not a member of the CRC. If the prisoner's or defendant's name was forwarded to the CRC based upon an evaluation by a licensed psychiatrist or licensed clinical psychologist, a different licensed psychiatrist or licensed clinical psychologist shall perform the examination for the CRC. The licensed psychiatrist or licensed clinical psychologist shall determine whether the prisoner or defendant is a sexually violent predator, as defined in § 37.2-900, and forward the results of this evaluation and any supporting documents to the CRC for its review.

The CRC assessment may be based on:

An actuarial evaluation, clinical evaluation, or any other information or evaluation determined by the CRC to be relevant, including but not limited to a review of (i) the prisoner's or defendant's institutional history and treatment record, if any; (ii) his criminal background; and (iii) any other factor that is relevant to the determination of whether he is a sexually violent predator.

C. Following the examination and review conducted pursuant to subsection B, the CRC shall recommend that the prisoner or defendant (i) be committed as a sexually violent predator pursuant to this chapter; (ii) not be committed, but be placed in a conditional release program as a less restrictive alternative; or (iii) not be committed because he does not meet the definition of a sexually violent predator. To assist the Attorney General in his review, the Department of Corrections, the CRC, and the psychiatrist or psychologist who conducts the mental health examination pursuant to this section shall provide the Attorney General with all evaluation reports, prisoner records, criminal records, medical files, and any other documentation relevant to determining whether a prisoner or defendant is a sexually violent predator.

D. Pursuant to clause (ii) of subsection C, the CRC may recommend that a prisoner or defendant enter a conditional release program if it finds that (i) he does not need inpatient treatment, but needs outpatient treatment and monitoring to prevent his condition from deteriorating to a degree that he would need inpatient treatment; (ii) appropriate outpatient supervision and treatment are reasonably available; (iii) there is significant reason to believe that, if conditionally released, he would comply with the conditions specified; and (iv) conditional release will not present an undue risk to public safety.

E. Notwithstanding any other provision of law, any mental health professional employed or appointed pursuant to subsection B or § 37.2-907 shall be permitted to copy and possess any presentence or postsentence reports and victim impact statements. The mental health professional shall not disseminate the contents of the reports or the actual reports to any person or entity and shall only utilize the reports for use in examinations, creating reports, and testifying in any proceedings pursuant to this article.

F. If the CRC deems it necessary to have the services of additional experts in order to complete its review of the prisoner or defendant, the Commissioner shall appoint such qualified experts as are needed.

History.

1999, cc. 946, 985, § 37.1-70.5; 2001, c. 776; 2003, cc. 989, 1018; 2004, c. 764; 2005, cc. 716, 914; 2006, cc. 863, 914; 2007, c. 876; 2009, c. 740; 2011, c. 42; 2012, cc. 668, 800.

§ 37.2-905. Review of prisoners convicted of a sexually violent offense; review of unrestorably incompetent defendants charged with sexually violent offenses; petition for commitment; notice to Department of Corrections or referring court regarding disposition of review.

A. Upon receipt of a recommendation by the CRC regarding an eligible prisoner or an unrestorably incompetent defendant for review pursuant to § 19.2-169.3, the Attorney General shall have 90 days to conduct a review of the prisoner or defendant and (i) file a petition for the civil commitment of the prisoner or defendant as a sexually violent predator and stating sufficient facts to support such allegation or (ii) notify the Director and Commissioner, in the case of a prisoner, or the referring court and the Commissioner, in the case of an unrestorably incompetent defendant, that he will not file a petition for commitment. Petitions for commitment shall be filed in the circuit court for the judicial circuit or district in which the prisoner was last convicted of a sexually violent offense or in the circuit court for the judicial circuit or district in which the defendant was deemed unrestorably incompetent and referred for commitment review pursuant to § 19.2-169.3.

B. If the Attorney General decides not to file a petition for the civil commitment of a prisoner or defendant, or if a petition is filed but is dismissed for any reason, the Attorney General and the Director may share any relevant information with the probation and parole officer who is to supervise the prisoner and with the Department to the extent allowed by state and federal law.

History.
1999, cc. 946, 985, § 37.1-70.6; 2001, c. 776; 2003, cc. 989, 1018; 2004, c. 764; 2005, cc. 716, 914; 2006, cc. 863, 914; 2007, c. 876; 2009, c. 740.

§ 37.2-905.1. Substantial compliance.

The provisions of §§ 37.2-903, 37.2-904, and 37.2-905 are procedural and not substantive or jurisdictional. Absent a showing of failure to follow these provisions as a result of gross negligence or willful misconduct, it shall be presumed that there has been substantial compliance with these provisions.

History.
2007, c. 876; 2009, c. 740.

§ 37.2-905.2. Access to records.

A. Notwithstanding any other provision of law and for the purpose of performing their duties and obligations under this chapter, the Department of Corrections, the Commitment Review Committee, the Department, and the Office of the Attorney General are authorized to possess, copy, and use all records, including records under seal, from all state and local courts, clerks, departments, agencies, boards, and commissions, including but not limited to: offices of attorneys for the Commonwealth, Virginia State Police, local police and sheriffs' departments, local schools, colleges and universities, Department of Juvenile Justice, court services units, community services boards, Department, state and local departments of social services and probation and parole districts. Upon request, the records, documents, notes, recordings or other information of any kind shall be provided to the Department of Corrections, the Commitment Review Committee, the Department, or the Office of the Attorney General within 20 days of receiving such request.

B. Notwithstanding any other provision of law, the Department of Corrections, the Commitment Review Committee, the Department, and the Office of the Attorney General may possess, copy and use presentence reports, postsentence reports, and victim impact statements, including records under seal, for all lawful purposes under this chapter.

History.
2007, c. 876; 2009, c. 740.

§ 37.2-906. Probable cause hearing; procedures.

A. Upon the filing of a petition alleging that the respondent is a sexually violent predator, the circuit court shall (i) forthwith order that until a final order is entered in the proceeding, in the case of a prisoner, he remain in the secure custody of the Department of Corrections or, in the case of a defendant, he remain in the secure custody of the Department and (ii) schedule a hearing within 90 days to determine whether probable cause exists to believe that the respondent is a sexually violent predator. The respondent may waive his right to a hearing under this section. A continuance extending the case beyond the 90 days may be granted to either the Attorney General or the respondent upon good cause shown or by agreement of the parties. The clerk shall mail a copy of the petition to the attorney appointed or retained for the respondent and to the person in charge of the facility in which the respondent is then confined. The person in charge of the facility shall cause the petition to be delivered to the respondent and shall certify the delivery to the clerk. In addition, a written explanation of the sexually violent predator involuntary commitment process and the statutory protections associated with the process shall be given to the respondent at the time the petition is delivered.

B. Any hearing or proceeding under this section may be conducted using a two-way electronic video and audio communication system to provide for the appearance of any parties and witnesses. Any two-way electronic video and audio communication system shall meet the standards set forth in subsection B of § 19.2-3.1.

C. Prior to any hearing under this section, the judge shall ascertain if the respondent is represented by counsel and, if he is not represented by counsel, the judge shall appoint an attorney to represent him. However, if the respondent requests an opportunity to employ counsel, the court shall give him a reasonable opportunity to employ counsel at his own expense.

D. A respondent who has refused to cooperate with a mental health examination required pursuant to § 37.2-904 may, within 21 days of the retention of counsel or appointment of counsel, rescind his refusal and elect to cooperate with the mental health examination. Counsel for the respondent shall provide written notice of the respondent's election to cooperate with the mental health examination to the court and the attorney for the Commonwealth within 30 days of the retention or appointment of counsel, and the probable cause hearing shall be stayed until 30 days after receipt of the mental health examiner's report. The mental health examination shall be conducted in accordance with subsection B of § 37.2-904. Results of the evaluation shall be filed with the court and copies of the results shall be provided to counsel for the parties. The mental health examiner's itemized account of expenses, duly sworn to, shall be presented to the court and, when allowed, shall be certified to the Supreme Court for payment out of the state treasury and shall be charged against the appropriations made to pay criminal charges.

In the event that a respondent refuses to cooperate with the mental health examination required by § 37.2-904 or fails or refuses to cooperate with the mental health examination following rescission of his refusal pursuant to this subsection, the court shall admit evidence of such failure or refusal and shall bar the respondent from introducing his own expert psychiatric and psychological evidence.

E. At the probable cause hearing, the judge shall (i) verify the respondent's identity and (ii) determine whether probable cause exists to believe that he is a sexually violent predator. The existence of any prior convictions or charges may be shown with affidavits or documentary evidence. The details underlying the commission of an offense or behavior that led to a prior conviction or charge may be shown by affidavits or documentary evidence, including but not limited to, hearing and/or trial transcripts, probation and parole and sentencing reports, police and sheriffs' reports, and mental health evaluations. If he meets the qualifications set forth in subsection B of § 37.2-904, the expert witness may be permitted to testify at the probable cause hearing as to his diagnosis, his opinion as to whether the respondent meets the definition of a sexually violent predator, his recommendations as to treatment, and the basis for his opinions. Such opinions shall not be dispositive of whether the respondent is a sexually violent predator.

F. In the case of a prisoner in the custody of the Department of Corrections, if the judge finds that there is not probable cause to believe that the respondent is a sexually violent predator, the judge shall dismiss the petition, and the respondent shall remain in the custody of the Department of Corrections until his scheduled date of release from prison. In the case of a defendant, if the judge finds that there is not probable cause to believe the respondent is a sexually violent predator, the judge shall dismiss the petition and order that the respondent be discharged, involuntarily admitted pursuant to §§ 37.2-814 through 37.2-819, or certified for admission pursuant to § 37.2-806.

History.

1999, cc. 946, 985, § 37.1-70.7; 2001, c. 776; 2004, c. 764; 2005, c. 716; 2006, cc. 863, 914; 2007, c. 876; 2009, c. 740; 2011, cc. 446, 448; 2012, cc. 121, 246.

§ 37.2-907. Right to assistance of experts; compensation.

A. Upon a finding of probable cause the judge shall ascertain if the respondent is requesting expert assistance. If the respondent requests expert assistance and has not employed an expert at his own expense, the judge shall appoint such experts as he deems necessary. However, if the respondent refused to cooperate with the mental health examination required pursuant to § 37.2-904 or failed or refused to cooperate with a mental health examination following rescission of a refusal pursuant to § 37.2-906, any expert appointed to assist the respondent shall not be permitted to testify at trial nor shall any report of any such expert be admissible. Any expert employed or appointed pursuant to this section shall be a licensed psychiatrist or licensed clinical psychologist who is skilled in the diagnosis and risk assessment of sex offenders and knowledgeable about the treatment of sex offenders, and who is not a member of the CRC. Any expert employed or appointed pursuant to this section shall have reasonable access to all relevant medical and psychological records and reports pertaining to the respondent. No such expert shall be permitted to testify as a witness on behalf of the respondent unless that expert has prepared a written report detailing his findings and conclusions and has submitted his report, along with all supporting data, to the court, the Attorney General, and counsel for the respondent. Such report shall be submitted no less than 45 days prior to the trial of the matter unless a different time period is agreed to by the parties.

B. Each psychiatrist, psychologist, or other expert appointed by the court to render professional service pursuant to this chapter who is not regularly employed by the Commonwealth, except by the University of Virginia School of Medicine and the Virginia Commonwealth University School of Medicine, shall receive a reasonable fee for such service. The fee shall be determined in each instance by the court that appointed the expert, in accordance with guidelines established by the Supreme Court after consultation with the Department. The fee shall not exceed $5,000. However, in addition, if any such expert is required to appear as a witness in any hearing held pursuant to this chapter, he shall receive mileage and a fee of $750 for each day during which he is required to serve. An itemized account of expenses, duly sworn to, shall be presented to the court, and, when allowed, shall be certified to the Supreme Court for payment out of the state treasury, and shall be charged against the appropriations made to pay criminal charges. Allowance for the fee and for the per diem authorized shall also be made by order of the court, duly certified to the Supreme Court, for payment out of the appropriation to pay criminal charges.

History.

1999, cc. 946, 985, § 37.1-70.8; 2001, c. 776; 2004, c. 764; 2005, c. 716; 2006, cc. 863, 914; 2007, c. 876; 2009, c. 740; 2011, cc. 42, 446, 448.

§ 37.2-908. Trial; right to trial by jury; standard of proof; discovery.

A. Within 120 days after the completion of the probable cause hearing held pursuant to § 37.2-906, the court shall conduct a trial to determine whether the respondent is a sexually violent predator. A continuance extending the case beyond the 120 days may be granted to either the Attorney General or the respondent upon good cause shown or by agreement of the parties.

B. The Attorney General or the respondent shall have the right to a trial by jury. Seven persons from a panel of 13 shall constitute a jury in such cases. If a jury determines that the respondent is a sexually violent predator, a unanimous verdict shall be required. If no demand is made by either party for a trial by jury, the trial shall be before the court.

C. The court or jury shall determine whether, by clear and convincing evidence, the respondent is a sexually violent predator. If the court or jury does not find clear and convincing evidence that the respondent is a sexually violent predator, the court shall, in the case of a prisoner, direct that he be returned to the custody of the Department of Corrections. The Department of Corrections shall immediately release him if his scheduled release date has passed, or hold him until his scheduled release date. In the case of a defendant, if the court or jury does not find by clear and convincing evidence that he is a sexually violent predator, the court shall order that he be discharged, involuntarily admitted pursuant to §§ 37.2-814 through 37.2-819, or certified for admission pursuant to § 37.2-806.

If he meets the qualifications set forth in subsection B of § 37.2-904 or 37.2-907, any expert witness may be permitted to testify at the trial as to his diagnosis, his opinion as to whether the respondent meets the definition of a sexually violent predator, his recommendation as to treatment, and the basis for his opinions. Such opinions shall not be dispositive of whether the respondent is a sexually violent predator.

D. If the court or jury finds the respondent to be a sexually violent predator, the court shall then determine that the respondent shall be committed or continue the trial for not less than 45 days nor more than 60 days pursuant to subsection E. A continuance extending the case beyond the 60 days may be granted to either the Attorney General or the respondent upon good cause shown or by agreement of the parties. In making its determination, the court may consider (i) the nature and circumstances of the sexually violent offense for which the respondent was charged or convicted, including the age and maturity of the victim; (ii) the results of any actuarial test, including the likelihood of recidivism; (iii) the results of any diagnostic tests previously administered to the respondent under this chapter; (iv) the respondent's mental history, including treatments for mental illness or mental disorders, participation in and response to therapy or treatment, and any history of previous hospitalizations; (v) the respondent's present mental condition; (vi) the respondent's disciplinary record and types of infractions he may have committed while incarcerated or hospitalized; (vii) the respondent's living arrangements and potential employment if he were to be placed on conditional release; (viii) the availability of transportation and appropriate supervision to ensure participation by the respondent in necessary treatment; and (ix) any other factors that the court deems relevant. If after considering the factors listed in § 37.2-912, the court finds that there is no suitable less restrictive alternative to involuntary secure inpatient treatment, the judge shall by written order and specific findings so certify and order that the respondent be committed to the custody of the Department for appropriate inpatient treatment in a secure facility designated by the Commissioner. Respondents committed pursuant to this chapter are subject to the provisions of § 19.2-174.1 and Chapter 11 (§ 37.2-1100 et seq.).

E. If the court determines to continue the trial to receive additional evidence on possible alternatives to commitment, the court shall require the Commissioner to submit a report to the court, the Attorney General, and counsel for the respondent suggesting possible alternatives to commitment. The court shall then reconvene the trial and receive testimony on the possible alternatives to commitment. At the conclusion of testimony on the possible alternatives to commitment, the court shall consider: (i) the treatment needs of the respondent; (ii) whether less restrictive alternatives to commitment have been investigated and deemed suitable; (iii) whether any such alternatives will accommodate needed and appropriate supervision and treatment plans for the respondent, including but not limited to, therapy or counseling, access to medications, availability of travel, and location of proposed residence; and (iv) whether any such alternatives will accommodate needed and appropriate regular psychological or physiological testing, including but not limited to, penile plethysmograph testing or sexual interest testing. If the court finds these criteria are adequately addressed and the court finds that the respondent meets the criteria for conditional release set forth in § 37.2-912, the court shall order that the respondent be returned to the custody of the Department of Corrections to be processed for conditional release as a sexually violent predator pursuant to his conditional release plan. The court shall also order the respondent to be subject to electronic monitoring of his location by means of a GPS (Global Positioning System) tracking device, or other similar device, at all times while he is on conditional release. Access to anti-androgen medications or other medication prescribed to lower blood serum testosterone shall not be used as a primary reason for determining that less restrictive alternatives are appropriate pursuant to this chapter.

F. The Department shall recommend a specific course of treatment and programs for provision of such treatment and shall monitor the respondent's compliance with such treatment as may be ordered by the court under this section, unless the respondent is on parole or probation, in which case the parole or probation officer shall monitor his compliance.

G. In the event of a mistrial, the court shall direct that the prisoner remain in the secure custody of the Department of Corrections or the defendant remain in the secure custody of the Department until another trial is conducted. Any subsequent trial following a mistrial shall be held within 90 days of the previous trial.

History.

1999, cc. 946, 985, § 37.1-70.9; 2001, c. 776; 2003, cc. 989, 1018; 2004, c. 764; 2005, cc. 716, 914; 2006, cc. 863, 914; 2007, c. 876; 2009, c. 740.

§ 37.2-909. Placement of committed respondents.

A. Any respondent committed pursuant to this chapter shall be placed in the custody of the Department for control, care, and treatment until such time as the respondent's mental abnormality or personality disorder has so changed that the respondent will not present an undue risk to public safety. The Department shall provide such control, care, and treatment at a secure facility operated by it or may contract with private or public entities, in or outside of the Commonwealth, or with other states to provide comparable control, care, or treatment. At all times, respondents committed for control, care, and treatment by the Department pursuant to this chapter shall be kept in a secure facility. Respondents committed under this chapter shall be segregated by sight and sound at all times from prisoners in the custody of a correctional facility. The Commissioner may make treatment and management decisions regarding committed respondents in his custody without obtaining prior approval of or review by the committing court.

B. Prior to the siting of a new facility or the designation of an existing facility to be operated by the Department for the control, care, and treatment of committed respondents, the Commissioner shall notify the state elected officials for and the local governing body of the jurisdiction of the proposed location, designation, or expansion of the facility. Upon receiving such notice, the local governing body of the jurisdiction of the proposed site or where the existing facility is located may publish a descriptive notice concerning the proposed site or existing facility in a newspaper of general circulation in the jurisdiction.

The Commissioner also shall establish an advisory committee relating to any facility for which notice is required by this subsection or any facility being operated for the purpose of the control, care, and treatment of committed respondents. The advisory committee shall consist of state and local elected officials and representatives of community organizations serving the jurisdiction in which the facility is proposed to be or is located. Upon request, the members of the appropriate advisory committee shall be notified whenever the Department increases the number of beds in the relevant facility.

C. Notwithstanding any other provision of law, when any respondent is committed under this article, the Department of Corrections and the Office of the Attorney General shall provide to the Department of Behavioral Health and Developmental Services, a copy of all relevant criminal history information, medical and mental health records, presentence or postsentence reports and victim impact statements, and the mental health evaluations performed pursuant to subsection B of § 37.2-904 and § 37.2-907, for use in the treatment and evaluation of the committed respondent.

History.

1999, cc. 946, 985, § 37.1-70.10; 2001, c. 776; 2003, cc. 989, 1018; 2004, c. 707; 2005, cc. 716, 914; 2009, cc. 740, 813, 840.

§ 37.2-910. Review of continuation of secure inpatient treatment hearing; procedure and reports; disposition.

A. The committing court shall conduct a hearing 12 months after the date of commitment to assess each respondent's need for secure inpatient treatment. A hearing for assessment shall be conducted at yearly intervals for five years and at biennial intervals thereafter. The court shall schedule the matter for hearing as soon as possible after it becomes due, giving the matter priority over all pending matters before the court. A continuance extending the review may be granted to either the Attorney General or the respondent upon good cause shown or by agreement of the parties. Whenever practicable, the hearing for assessment shall be conducted using a two-way electronic video and audio communication system that meets the standards set forth in subsection B of § 19.2-3.1.

B. Prior to the hearing, the Commissioner shall provide to the court a report reevaluating the respondent's condition and recommending treatment. The report shall be prepared by a licensed psychiatrist or a licensed clinical psychologist skilled in the diagnosis and risk assessment of sex offenders and knowledgeable about the treatment of sex offenders. If the Commissioner's report recommends discharge or the respondent requests discharge, the respondent's condition and need for secure inpatient treatment shall be evaluated by a second person with such credentials who is not currently treating the respondent. Any professional person who conducts a second evaluation of a respondent shall submit a report of his findings to the court and the Commissioner. A copy of any report submitted pursuant to this subsection shall be sent to the Attorney General and to any attorney appointed or retained for the respondent.

C. The burden of proof at the hearing shall be upon the Commonwealth to prove to the court by clear and convincing evidence that the respondent remains a sexually violent predator.

D. If the court finds, based upon the report and other evidence provided at the hearing, that the respondent is no longer a sexually violent predator, the court shall release the respondent from secure inpatient treatment. If the court finds that the respondent remains a sexually violent predator, it shall order that he remain in the custody of the Commissioner for secure inpatient hospitalization and treatment or that he be conditionally released. To determine if the respondent shall be conditionally released, the court shall determine if the respondent meets the criteria for conditional release set forth in § 37.2-912. If the court orders that the respondent be conditionally released, the court shall allow the Department no less than 30 days and no more than 60 days to prepare a conditional release plan. Any such plan must be able to accommodate needed and appropriate supervision and treatment plans for the respondent, including but not limited to, therapy or counseling, access to medications, availability of travel, location of residence, and regular psychological monitoring of the respondent if called for, including polygraph examinations, penile plethysmograph testing, or sexual interest testing, if necessary. Access to anti-androgen medications or other medication prescribed to lower blood serum testosterone shall not be used as a primary reason for determining that less restrictive alternatives are appropriate pursuant to this chapter. In preparing the conditional release plan, the Department shall notify the attorney for the Commonwealth, the chief law-enforcement officer, and the governing body for the locality that is the proposed location of the respondent's residence upon his conditional release.

If the court places the respondent on conditional release, the court shall order the respondent to be subject to electronic monitoring of his location by means of a GPS (Global Positioning System) tracking device, or other similar device, at all times while he is on conditional release.

History.

1999, cc. 946, 985, § 37.1-70.11; 2001, c. 776; 2003, cc. 989, 1018; 2005, c. 716; 2006, cc. 698, 730, 863, 914; 2007, c. 876; 2011, cc. 42, 446, 448; 2013, c. 258; 2015, c. 662.

§ 37.2-911. Petition for release; hearing; procedures.

A. The Commissioner may petition the committing court for conditional release of the committed respondent at any time he believes the committed respondent's condition has so changed that he is no longer in need of secure inpatient treatment. The Commissioner may petition the committing court for unconditional release of the committed respondent at any time he believes the committed respondent's condition has so changed that he is no longer a sexually violent predator. The petition shall be accompanied by a report of clinical findings supporting the petition and by a conditional release or discharge plan, as applicable, prepared by the Department. The committed respondent may petition the committing court for release only once in each year in which no annual judicial review is required pursuant to § 37.2-910. The party petitioning for release shall transmit a copy of the petition to the Attorney General, the Commissioner, and the attorney for the Commonwealth for the locality that is the proposed location of the respondent's residence upon his conditional release.

B. Upon the submission of a petition pursuant to this section, the committing court shall conduct the proceedings according to the procedures set forth in § 37.2-910.

History.

1999, cc. 946, 985, § 37.1-70.12; 2001, c. 776; 2003, cc. 989, 1018; 2005, c. 716; 2009, c. 740; 2015, c. 662.

§ 37.2-912. Conditional release; criteria; conditions; reports.

A. At any time the court considers the respondent's need for secure inpatient treatment pursuant to this chapter, it shall place the respondent on conditional release if it finds that (i) he does not need secure inpatient treatment but needs outpatient treatment or monitoring to prevent his condition from deteriorating to a degree that he would need secure inpatient treatment; (ii) appropriate outpatient supervision and treatment are reasonably available; (iii) there is significant reason to believe that the respondent, if conditionally released, would comply with the conditions specified; and (iv) conditional release will not present an undue risk to public safety. In making its determination, the court may consider (i) the nature and circumstances of the sexually violent offense for which the respondent was charged or convicted, including the age and maturity of the victim; (ii) the results of any actuarial test, including the likelihood of recidivism; (iii) the results of any diagnostic tests previously administered to the respondent under this chapter; (iv) the respondent's mental history, including treatments for mental illness or mental disorders, participation in and response to therapy or treatment, and any history of previous hospitalizations; (v) the respondent's present mental condition; (vi) the respondent's response to treatment while in secure inpatient treatment or on conditional release, including his disciplinary record and any infractions; (vii) the respondent's living arrangements and potential employment if he were to be placed on conditional release; (viii) the availability of transportation and appropriate supervision to ensure participation by the respondent in necessary treatment; and (ix) any other factors that the court deems relevant. The court shall subject the respondent to the orders and conditions it deems will best meet his need for treatment and supervision and best serve the interests of justice and society. In all cases of conditional release, the court shall order the respondent to be subject to electronic monitoring of his location by means of a GPS (Global Positioning System) tracking device, or other similar device, at all times while he is on conditional release.

The Department or, if the respondent is on parole or probation, the respondent's parole or probation officer shall implement the court's conditional release orders and shall submit written reports to the court on the respondent's progress and adjustment in the community no less frequently than every six months. The Department of Behavioral Health and Developmental Services is authorized to contract with the Department of Corrections to provide services for the monitoring and supervision of sexually violent predators who are on conditional release.

The Department or, if the respondent is on parole or probation, the respondent's parole or probation officer shall send a copy of each written report submitted to the court and copies of all correspondence with the court pursuant to this section to the Attorney General and the Commissioner.

B. Notwithstanding any other provision of law, when any respondent is placed on conditional release under this article, the Department of Corrections and the Office of the Attorney General shall provide to the Department, or if the respondent is on parole or probation, the respondent's parole or probation officer, all relevant criminal history information, medical and mental health records, presentence and postsentence reports and victim impact statements, and the mental health evaluations performed pursuant to this chapter, for use in the management and treatment of the respondent placed on conditional release. Any information or document provided pursuant to this subsection shall not be subject to disclosure under the Virginia Freedom of Information Act (§ 2.2-3700 et seq.).

History.

1999, cc. 946, 985, § 37.1-70.13; 2001, c. 776; 2003, cc. 989, 1018; 2005, cc. 716, 914; 2006, cc. 698, 730, 863, 914; 2007, c. 876; 2009, cc. 740, 813, 840.

§ 37.2-913. Emergency custody of conditionally released respondents; revocation of conditional release.

A. A judicial officer may issue an emergency custody order, upon the sworn petition of any responsible person or upon his own motion, based upon probable cause to believe that a respondent on conditional release within his judicial district has violated the conditions of his release and is no longer a proper subject for conditional release. The judicial officer shall forward a copy of the petition and the emergency custody order to the circuit court that conditionally released the respondent, the Attorney General, the Department, and the attorney for the Commonwealth for the locality that is the location of the respondent's residence. Petitions and orders for emergency custody of conditionally released respondents pursuant to this section may be filed, issued, served, or executed by electronic means, with or without the use of two-way electronic video and audio communication, and returned in the same manner with the same force, effect, and authority as an original document. All signatures thereon shall be treated as original signatures.

B. The emergency custody order shall require a law-enforcement officer to take the respondent into custody immediately. A law-enforcement officer may lawfully go to or be sent beyond the territorial limits of the county, city, or town in which he serves to any point in the Commonwealth for the purpose of executing an emergency custody order pursuant to this section. The respondent shall be transported to a secure facility specified by the Department where a person designated by the Department who is skilled in the diagnosis and risk assessment of sex offenders and knowledgeable about the treatment of sex offenders shall, as soon as practicable, perform a mental health examination of the respondent, including a personal interview. The mental health evaluator shall consider the criteria in § 37.2-912 and shall opine whether the respondent remains suitable for conditional release. The evaluator shall report his findings and conclusions in writing to the Department, the Office of the Attorney General, counsel for the respondent, and the court in which the petition was filed. The evaluator's report shall become part of the record in the case.

C. The respondent on conditional release shall remain in custody until a hearing is held in the circuit court that conditionally released the respondent on the motion or petition to determine if he should be returned to the custody of the Commissioner. The hearing shall be given priority on the court's docket.

D. The respondent's failure to comply with the conditions of release, including outpatient treatment, may be admitted into evidence. The evaluator designated in subsection B may be permitted to testify at the hearing as to his diagnosis, his opinion as to whether the respondent remains suitable for conditional release, his recommendation as to treatment and supervision, and the basis for his opinions. If upon hearing the evidence, the court finds that the respondent on conditional release has violated the conditions of his release and that the violation of conditions was sufficient to render him no longer suitable for conditional release, the court shall revoke his conditional release and order him returned to the custody of the Commissioner for secure inpatient treatment. The respondent may petition the court for re-release pursuant to the conditions set forth in § 37.2-911 no sooner than six months from his return to custody. The respondent petitioning for re-release shall transmit a copy of the petition to the Attorney General, the Commissioner, and the attorney for the Commonwealth for the locality that is the proposed location of the respondent's residence.

History.

1999, cc. 946, 985, § 37.1-70.14; 2001, c. 776; 2003, cc. 989, 1018; 2005, cc. 51, 716; 2009, c. 740; 2011, c. 42; 2015, c. 662.

§ 37.2-914. Modification or removal of conditions; notice; objections; review.

A. The court that placed the person on conditional release may modify conditions of release or remove conditions placed on release pursuant to § 37.2-912, upon petition of the Department, the supervising parole or probation officer, the Attorney General, or the person on conditional release or upon its own motion based on reports of the Department or the supervising parole or probation officer. However, the person on conditional release may petition only annually commencing six months after the conditional release order is issued. Upon petition, the court shall require the Department or, if the person is on parole or probation, the person's parole or probation officer to provide a report on the person's progress while on conditional release. The party petitioning for release shall transmit a copy of the petition to the Attorney General, the Commissioner, and the attorney for the Commonwealth for the locality that is the location of the respondent's residence.

B. As it deems appropriate based on the Department's or parole or probation officer's report and any other evidence provided to it, the court may issue a proposed order for modification or removal of conditions. The court shall provide notice of the order and their right to object to it within 21 days of its issuance to the person, the Department or parole or probation officer, the Attorney General, and the attorney for the Commonwealth for the locality that is the location of the respondent's residence. The proposed order shall become final if no objection is filed within 21 days of its issuance. If an objection is so filed, the court shall conduct a hearing at which the person on conditional release, the Attorney General, the Department or the parole or probation officer, and the attorney for the Commonwealth for the locality that is the location of the respondent's residence shall have an opportunity to present evidence challenging the proposed order. At the conclusion of the hearing, the court shall issue an order specifying conditions of release or removing existing conditions of release.

History.

1999, cc. 946, 985, § 37.1-70.15; 2001, c. 776; 2003, cc. 989, 1018; 2005, c. 716; 2009, c. 740; 2015, c. 662.

§ 37.2-915. Representation of Commonwealth and person subject to commitment; nature of proceedings.

The Attorney General shall represent the Commonwealth in all proceedings held pursuant to this chapter. The Attorney General shall receive prior written notice of all proceedings held under this chapter in which he is to represent the Commonwealth.

The court shall appoint counsel for the person subject to commitment or conditional release pursuant to subsection C of § 37.2-906 unless the person waives his right to counsel. The court shall consider appointment of the person who represented the person in previous proceedings.

All proceedings held under this chapter shall be civil proceedings.

History.

1999, cc. 946, 985, § 37.1-70.16; 2001, c. 776; 2003, cc. 989, 1018; 2005, c. 716; 2012, cc. 121, 246.

§ 37.2-916. Authority of Commissioner; delegation to board; liability.

For the purposes of carrying out the duties of this chapter, the Commissioner may appoint an advisory board composed of persons with demonstrated expertise in such matters. The Department shall assist the board in its administrative and technical duties. The membership of the board shall include (i) a citizen appointed by the Commissioner, (ii) a psychiatrist or psychologist licensed to practice in the Commonwealth who is skilled in the diagnosis of mental abnormalities and personality disorders associated with violent sex offenders and who is a full-time employee of the Department of Corrections, to be appointed by its director, (iii) a member of the Department of State Police, and (iv) such other members as deemed appropriate by the Commissioner. Members of the board shall exercise their powers and duties without compensation, except that members of the board who are not state employees shall be reimbursed by the Department for their approved travel expenses to the meetings of this board at the approved state rate. Members of the board shall be immune from personal liability while acting within the scope of their duties except for intentional misconduct.

History.
1999, cc. 946, 985, § 37.1-70.17; 2001, c. 776; 2005, c. 716.

§ 37.2-917. Escape of persons committed; penalty.

Any person committed to the custody of the Commissioner pursuant to this chapter who escapes from custody shall be guilty of a Class 6 felony.

History.
1999, cc. 946, 985, § 37.1-70.18; 2001, c. 776; 2005, c. 716.

§ 37.2-918. Persons on conditional release leaving Commonwealth; penalty.

Any person placed on conditional release pursuant to this chapter who leaves the Commonwealth without permission from the court that conditionally released the person or fails to return to the Commonwealth in violation of a court order shall be guilty of a Class 6 felony.

History.
1999, cc. 946, 985, § 37.1-70.19; 2001, c. 776; 2005, c. 716; 2009, c. 740.

§ 37.2-919. Postrelease supervision of Department; commission of new criminal offense by person committed to Department.

A. If a person committed to the Department of Behavioral Health and Developmental Services, whether in involuntary secure inpatient treatment or on conditional release, who is also on probation, parole, or postrelease supervision, fails to comply with any conditions established by the Department, or fails to comply with the terms of a treatment plan, the Department shall so notify the Department of Corrections or the person's probation and parole officer.

B. If a person committed to the Department of Behavioral Health and Developmental Services is arrested for a felony or Class 1 or 2 misdemeanor offense, he shall be transported to a judicial officer forthwith for a bond determination in accordance with the provisions of § 19.2-80. If the judicial officer admits the accused to bail, he shall, upon his admission to bail, be immediately transported back into the custody of the Department of Behavioral Health and Developmental Services. If, after trial for this offense, no active period of incarceration is imposed, or if the person is acquitted or the charges are withdrawn or dismissed, he shall be returned to the Department of Behavioral Health and Developmental Services pursuant to his commitment. If a period of active incarceration of 12 months or longer is imposed or any suspended sentence is revoked resulting in the person being returned to the Department of Corrections for a period of active incarceration of 12 months or longer, the person shall not be entitled to an annual or biennial review hearing pursuant to § 37.2-910 until 12 months after he has been returned to the custody of the Commissioner. Such reincarceration shall toll the provisions of § 37.2-910.

History.
2005, cc. 716, 914; 2006, cc. 863, 914; 2009, cc. 813, 840.

§ 37.2-920. Appeal by Attorney General; emergency custody order.

In any case in which the Attorney General successfully appeals the trial court's denial of probable cause, denial of civil commitment or conditional release, or discharge or placement on conditional release after an annual review hearing, upon the issuance of the mandate by the Supreme Court of Virginia, the trial court shall immediately issue an emergency custody order to any local law-enforcement official to have the person taken into custody and held in the local correctional facility, pending further appropriate proceedings.

History.
2006, cc. 863, 914.

§ 37.2-921. Department to give notice of Sex Offender and Crimes Against Minors Registry requirements to certain persons.

A. Prior to the release or discharge of any committed respondent for whom registration with the Sex Offender and Crimes Against Minors Registry is required pursuant to Chapter 9 (§ 9.1-900 et seq.) of Title 9.1, the Department shall give notice to the committed respondent of his duty to register with the State Police. A person required to register shall register, submit to be photographed as part of the registration, and provide information regarding place of employment, if available, to the Department. The Department shall also obtain from that person all necessary registration information, including fingerprints and photographs of a type and kind approved by the Department of State Police, inform the person of his duties regarding reregistration and change of address, and inform the person of his duty to register. The Department shall forward the registration information to the Department of State Police on the date of the committed respondent's release or discharge.

B. Whenever a person required to register has failed to comply with the provisions of subsection A, the Department shall promptly investigate or request the State Police promptly investigate and, if there is probable cause to believe a violation has occurred, obtain a warrant or assist in obtaining an indictment charging a violation of § 18.2-472.1 in the jurisdiction in which the person was released or discharged. The Department shall notify the State Police forthwith of such actions taken pursuant to this section.

C. The Department shall notify the State Police immediately upon discovering the escape of any committed respondent for whom registration with the Sex Offender and Crimes Against Minors Registry is required pursuant to Chapter 9 (§ 9.1-900 et seq.) of Title 9.1.

History.
2010, c. 858.

TITLE 38.2.
INSURANCE.

CHAPTER 22.
LIABILITY INSURANCE POLICIES.

Section

§ 38.2-2204. Liability insurance on motor vehicles, aircraft and watercraft; standard provisions; "omnibus clause."

A. No policy or contract of bodily injury or property damage liability insurance, covering liability arising from the ownership, maintenance, or use of any motor vehicle, aircraft, or private pleasure watercraft, shall be issued or delivered in this Commonwealth to the owner of such vehicle, aircraft or watercraft, or shall be issued or delivered by any insurer licensed in this Commonwealth upon any motor vehicle, aircraft, or private pleasure watercraft that is principally garaged, docked, or used in this Commonwealth, unless the policy contains a provision insuring the named insured, and any other person using or responsible for the use of the motor vehicle, aircraft, or private pleasure watercraft with the expressed or implied consent of the named insured, against liability for death or injury sustained, or loss or damage incurred within the coverage of the policy or contract as a result of negligence in the operation or use of such vehicle, aircraft, or watercraft by the named insured or by any such person; however, nothing contained in this section shall be deemed to prohibit an insurer from limiting its liability under any one policy for bodily injury or property damage resulting from any one accident or occurrence to the liability limits for such coverage set forth in the policy for any such accident or occurrence or for any one person, regardless of the number of insureds under that policy. Provided that, when one accident or occurrence involves more than one defendant who is covered by the policy, the plaintiff may recover the per person limit of the policy against each such defendant, subject to the per accident or occurrence limit of the policy. Each such policy or contract of liability insurance, or endorsement to the policy or contract, insuring private passenger automobiles, aircraft, or private pleasure watercraft principally garaged, docked, or used in this Commonwealth, that has as the named insured an individual or husband and wife and that includes, with respect to any liability insurance provided by the policy, contract or endorsement for use of a nonowned automobile, aircraft or private pleasure watercraft, any provision requiring permission or consent of the owner of such automobile, aircraft, or private pleasure watercraft for the insurance to apply, shall be construed to include permission or consent of the custodian in the provision requiring permission or consent of the owner.

B. Notwithstanding any requirements in this section to the contrary, an insurer may exclude any person from coverage under a personal umbrella or excess policy, if the exclusion is requested in writing by the first named insured and is acknowledged in writing by the excluded driver.

C. For aircraft liability insurance, such policy or contract may contain the exclusions listed in § 38.2-2227. Notwithstanding the provisions of this section or any other provisions of law, no policy or contract shall require pilot experience greater than that prescribed by the Federal Aviation Administration, except for pilots operating air taxis, or pilots operating aircraft applying chemicals, seed, or fertilizer.

D. No policy or contract of bodily injury or property damage liability insurance relating to the ownership, maintenance, or use of a motor vehicle shall be issued or delivered in this Commonwealth to the owner of such vehicle or shall be issued or delivered by an insurer licensed in this Commonwealth upon any motor vehicle principally garaged or used in this Commonwealth without an endorsement or provision insuring the named insured, and any other person using or responsible for the use of the motor vehicle with the expressed or implied consent of the named insured, against liability for death or injury sustained, or loss or damage incurred within the coverage of the policy or contract as a result of negligence in the operation or use of the motor vehicle by the named insured or by any other such person; however, nothing contained in this section shall be deemed to prohibit an insurer from limiting its liability under any one policy for bodily injury or property damage resulting from any one accident or occurrence to the liability limits for such coverage set forth in the policy for any such accident or occurrence or for any one person regardless of the number of insureds under that policy. Provided that, when one accident or occurrence involves more than one defendant who is covered by the policy, the plaintiff may recover the per person limit of the policy against each such defendant, subject to the per accident or occurrence limit of the policy. This provision shall apply notwithstanding the failure or refusal of the named insured or such other person to cooperate with the insurer under the terms of the policy. If the failure or refusal to cooperate prejudices the insurer in the defense of an action for damages arising from the operation or use of such insured motor vehicle, then the endorsement or provision shall be void. If an insurer has actual notice of a motion for judgment or complaint having been served on an insured, the mere failure of the insured to turn the motion or complaint over to the insurer shall not be a defense to the insurer, nor void the endorsement or provision, nor in any way relieve the insurer of its obligations to the insured, provided the insured otherwise cooperates and in no way prejudices the insurer.

Where the insurer has elected to provide a defense to its insured under such circumstances and files responsive pleadings in the name of its insured, the insured shall not be subject to sanctions for failure to comply with discovery pursuant to Part Four of the Rules of the Supreme Court of Virginia unless it can be shown that the suit papers actually reached the insured, and that the insurer has failed after exercising due diligence to locate its insured, and as long as the insurer provides such information in response to discovery as it can without the assistance of the insured.

E. Any endorsement, provision or rider attached to or included in any such policy of insurance which purports or seeks to limit or reduce the coverage afforded by the provisions required by this section shall be void, except an insurer may exclude such coverage as is afforded by this section, where such coverage would inure to the benefit of the United States Government or any agency or subdivision thereof under the provisions of the Federal Tort Claims Act, the Federal Drivers Act and Public Law 86-654 District of Columbia Employee Non-Liability Act, or to the benefit of the Commonwealth under the provisions of the Virginia Tort Claims Act (§ 8.01-195.1 et seq.) and the self-insurance plan established by the Department of General Services pursuant to § 2.2-1837 for any state employee who, in the regular course of his employment, transports patients in his own personal vehicle.

History.

Code 1950, § 38-238; 1952, c. 317, § 38.1-381; 1958, c. 282; 1959, Ex. Sess., cc. 42, 70; 1970, c. 462; 1962, c. 457; 1964, c. 477; 1966, cc. 182, 459; 1968, cc. 199, 721; 1970, c. 494; 1971, Ex. Sess., c. 216; 1973, cc. 225, 390; 1974, c. 87; 1976, cc. 121, 122; 1977, c. 78; 1979, c. 113; 1980, cc. 326, 331; 1981, Sp. Sess., c. 6; 1982, cc. 638, 642; 1984, c. 541; 1985, cc. 39, 325; 1986, cc. 544, 562; 1992, c. 140; 1995, c. 652; 1999, c. 4; 2003, cc. 756, 761; 2005, c. 771.

§ 38.2-2205. Liability insurance on motor vehicles; standard provisions; applicability of other valid and collectible insurance.

A. 1. Each policy or contract of bodily injury or property damage liability insurance which provides insurance to a named insured in connection with the business of selling, leasing, repairing, servicing, storing or parking motor vehicles, against liability arising from the ownership, maintenance, or use of any motor vehicle incident thereto shall contain a provision that the insurance coverage applicable to those motor vehicles shall not be applicable to a person other than the named insured and his employees in the course of their employment if there is any other valid and collectible insurance applicable to the same loss covering the other person under a policy with limits at least equal to the financial responsibility requirements specified in § 46.2-472. Such provision shall apply to motor vehicles which are either for the purpose of demonstrating to the other person as a prospective purchaser, or which are loaned or leased to the other person as a convenience during the repairing or servicing of a motor vehicle for the other person, or leased to the other person for a period of six months or more. This provision shall apply whether such repair or service is performed by the owner of the vehicle being loaned or leased or by some other person or business.

2. If the other valid and collectible insurance has limits less than the financial responsibility requirements specified in § 46.2-472, then the coverage afforded a person other than the named insured and his employees in the course of their employment shall be applicable to the extent necessary to equal the financial responsibility requirements specified in § 46.2-472.

3. If there is no other valid and collectible insurance available, the coverage under such policy afforded a person, other than the named insured and his employees in the course of their employment, shall be applicable, but the amount recoverable in such case shall not exceed the financial responsibility requirements specified in § 46.2-472. If there is no other valid and collectible collision or upset insurance available and if such policy provides insurance to the named insured for collision or upset, it shall include any such other person as an additional insured, unless in the case of a leased vehicle such other person receives a conspicuous written disclosure at the commencement of the lease, warning such person that he is not an additional insured under the owner's policy for collision or upset coverage.

B. 1. Any policy or contract of bodily injury or property damage liability insurance relating to the ownership, maintenance, or use of a motor vehicle shall exclude coverage to persons other than (i) the named insured, or (ii) directors, stockholders, partners, agents, or employees of the named insured, or (iii) residents of the household of either (i) or (ii), while those persons are employed or otherwise engaged in the business of selling, repairing, servicing, storing, or parking motor vehicles if there is any other valid or collectible insurance applicable to the same loss covering the persons under a policy with limits at least equal to the financial responsibility requirements specified in § 46.2-472.

2. If the other valid and collectible insurance has limits less than the financial responsibility requirements specified in § 46.2-472, then the coverage afforded a person other than the named insured while that person is employed or otherwise engaged in the business of selling, repairing, servicing, storing, or parking motor vehicles shall be applicable to the extent necessary to equal the financial responsibility requirements specified in § 46.2-472.

3. If there is no other valid and collectible insurance available, the coverage afforded a person other than the named insured while that person is employed or otherwise engaged in the business of selling, repairing, servicing, storing, or parking motor vehicles shall apply, but the amount recoverable shall not exceed the financial responsibility requirements specified in § 46.2-472.

History.

Code 1950, § 38-238; 1952, c. 317, § 38.1-381; 1958, c. 282; 1959, Ex. Sess., cc. 42, 70; 1970, c. 462; 1962, c. 457; 1964, c. 477; 1966, cc. 182, 459; 1968, cc. 199, 721; 1970, c. 494; 1971, Ex. Sess., c. 216; 1973, cc. 225, 390; 1974, c. 87; 1976, cc. 121, 122; 1977, c. 78; 1979, c. 113; 1980, cc. 326, 331; 1981, Sp. Sess., c. 6; 1982, cc. 638, 642; 1984, c. 541; 1985, cc. 39, 325; 1986, c. 562; 1987, c. 685; 1992, c. 474.

§ 38.2-2205.1. Suspension of liability coverage at insured's request.

A. Each insurer issuing or delivering a policy or contract of motor vehicle insurance that includes coverage for bodily injury or property damage liability arising from the ownership, maintenance or use of any motor vehicle as provided in this chapter, shall suspend any coverage for any motor vehicle at the request of a named insured ordered to military duty outside this Commonwealth, or his personal representative, during any period that the motor vehicle is impounded in a motor vehicle impound lot on a military base of the United States Armed Forces, the Reserves of the United States Armed Forces or the National Guard. However, an insurer may decline to suspend such coverage (i) unless satisfactory evidence of such impoundment is furnished to it, or (ii) if the period for which coverage suspension is requested is less than thirty days. The suspended coverage shall be reinstated upon request of the named insured, or his personal representative, effective not earlier than the receipt of such request by the insurer or any of its authorized representatives.

B. Any insurer suspending coverage pursuant to this section shall refund any unearned premium to the named insured, or his personal representative, on a pro rata basis.

C. The provisions of this section shall not alter or limit the insured's obligations under Article 8 (§ 46.2-705 et seq.) of Chapter 6 of Title 46.2.

History.

1991, c. 699.

§ 38.2-2206. Uninsured motorist insurance coverage.

A. Except as provided in subsection J of this section, no policy or contract of bodily injury or property damage liability insurance relating to the ownership, maintenance, or use of a motor vehicle shall be issued or delivered in this Commonwealth to the owner of such vehicle or shall be issued or delivered by any insurer licensed in this Commonwealth upon any motor vehicle principally garaged or used in this Commonwealth unless it contains an endorsement or provisions undertaking to pay the insured all sums that he is legally entitled to recover as damages from the owner or operator of an uninsured motor vehicle, within limits not less than the requirements of § 46.2-472. Those limits shall equal but not exceed the limits of the liability insurance provided by the policy, unless any one named insured rejects the additional uninsured motorist insurance coverage by notifying the insurer as provided in subsection B of § 38.2-2202. This rejection of the additional uninsured motorist insurance coverage by any one named insured shall be binding upon all insureds under such policy as defined in subsection B of this section. The endorsement or provisions shall also obligate the insurer to make payment for bodily injury or property damage caused by the operation or use of an underinsured motor vehicle to the extent the vehicle is underinsured, as defined in subsection B of this section. The endorsement or provisions shall also provide for at least $20,000 coverage for damage or destruction of the property of the insured in any one accident but may provide an exclusion of the first $200 of the loss or damage where the loss or damage is a result of any one accident involving an unidentifiable owner or operator of an uninsured motor vehicle.

B. As used in this section, the term "bodily injury" includes death resulting from bodily injury.

"Insured" as used in subsections A, D, G, and H of this section means the named insured and, while resident of the same household, the spouse of the named insured, and relatives, wards or foster children of either, while in a motor vehicle or otherwise, and any person who uses the motor vehicle to which the policy applies, with the expressed or implied consent of the named insured, and a guest in the motor vehicle to which the policy applies or the personal representative of any of the above.

"Uninsured motor vehicle" means a motor vehicle for which (i) there is no bodily injury liability insurance and property damage liability insurance in the amounts specified by § 46.2-472, (ii) there is such insurance but the insurer writing the insurance denies coverage for any reason whatsoever, including failure or refusal of the insured to cooperate with the insurer, (iii) there is no bond or deposit of money or securities in lieu of such insurance, (iv) the owner of the motor vehicle has not qualified as a self-insurer under the provisions of § 46.2-368, or (v) the owner or operator of the motor vehicle is immune from liability for negligence under the laws of the Commonwealth or the United States, in which case the provisions of subsection F shall apply and the action shall continue against the insurer. A motor vehicle shall be deemed uninsured if its owner or operator is unknown.

A motor vehicle is "underinsured" when, and to the extent that, the total amount of bodily injury and property damage coverage applicable to the operation or use of the motor vehicle and available for payment for such bodily injury or property damage, including all bonds or deposits of money or securities made pursuant to Article 15 (§ 46.2-435 et seq.) of Chapter 3 of Title 46.2, is less than the total amount of uninsured motorist coverage afforded any person injured as a result of the operation or use of the vehicle.

"Available for payment" means the amount of liability insurance coverage applicable to the claim of the injured person for bodily injury or property damage reduced by the payment of any other claims arising out of the same occurrence.

If an injured person is entitled to underinsured motorist coverage under more than one policy, the following order of priority of policies applies and any amount available for payment shall be credited against such policies in the following order of priority:

1. The policy covering a motor vehicle occupied by the injured person at the time of the accident;
2. The policy covering a motor vehicle not involved in the accident under which the injured person is a named insured;
3. The policy covering a motor vehicle not involved in the accident under which the injured person is an insured other than a named insured.

Where there is more than one insurer providing coverage under one of the payment priorities set forth, their liability shall be proportioned as to their respective underinsured motorist coverages.

Recovery under the endorsement or provisions shall be subject to the conditions set forth in this section.

C. There shall be a rebuttable presumption that a motor vehicle is uninsured if the Commissioner of the Department of Motor Vehicles certifies that, from the records of the Department of Motor Vehicles, it appears that: (i) there is no bodily injury liability insurance and property damage liability insurance in the amounts specified by § 46.2-472 covering the owner or operator of the motor vehicle; or (ii) no bond has been given or cash or securities delivered in lieu of the insurance; or (iii) the owner or operator of the motor vehicle has not qualified as a self-insurer in accordance with the provisions of § 46.2-368.

D. If the owner or operator of any motor vehicle that causes bodily injury or property damage to the insured is unknown, and if the damage or injury results from an accident where there has been no contact between that motor vehicle and the motor vehicle occupied by the insured, or where there has been no contact with the person of the insured if the insured was not occupying a motor vehicle, then for the insured to recover under the endorsement required by subsection A of this section, the accident shall be reported promptly to either (i) the insurer or (ii) a law-enforcement officer having jurisdiction in the county or city in which the accident occurred. If it is not reasonably practicable to make the report promptly, the report shall be made as soon as reasonably practicable under the circumstances.

E. If the owner or operator of any vehicle causing injury or damages is unknown, an action may be instituted against the unknown defendant as "John Doe" and service of process may be made by delivering a copy of the motion for judgment or other pleadings to the clerk of the court in which the action is brought. Service upon the insurer issuing the policy shall be made as prescribed by law as though the insurer were a party defendant. The provisions of § 8.01-288 shall not be applicable to the service of process required in this subsection. The insurer shall have the right to file pleadings and take other action allowable by law in the name of John Doe.

F. If any action is instituted against the owner or operator of an uninsured or underinsured motor vehicle by any insured intending to rely on the uninsured or underinsured coverage provision or endorsement of this policy under which the insured is making a claim, then the insured shall serve a copy of the process upon this insurer in the manner prescribed by law, as though the insurer were a party defendant. The provisions of § 8.01-288 shall not be applicable to the service of process required in this subsection. The insurer shall then have the right to file pleadings and take other action allowable by law in the name of the owner or operator of the uninsured or underinsured motor vehicle or in its own name. Notwithstanding the provisions of subsection A, the immunity from liability for negligence of the owner or operator of a motor vehicle shall not be a bar to the insured obtaining a judgment enforceable against the insurer for the negligence of the immune owner or operator, and shall not be a defense available to the insurer to the action brought by the insured, which shall proceed against the named defendant although any judgment obtained against an immune defendant shall be entered in the name of "Immune Defendant" and shall be enforceable against the insurer and any other nonimmune defendant as though it were entered in the actual name of the named immune defendant. Nothing in this subsection shall prevent the owner or operator of the uninsured motor vehicle from employing counsel of his own choice and taking any action in his own interest in connection with the proceeding.

G. Any insurer paying a claim under the endorsement or provisions required by subsection A of this section shall be subrogated to the rights of the insured to whom the claim was paid against the person causing the injury, death, or damage and that person's insurer, although it may deny coverage for any reason, to the extent that payment was made. The bringing of an action against the unknown owner or operator as John Doe or the conclusion of such an action shall not bar the insured from bringing an action against the owner or operator proceeded against as John Doe, or against the owner's or operator's insurer denying coverage for any reason, if the identity of the owner or operator who caused the injury or damages becomes known. The bringing of an action against an unknown owner or operator as John Doe shall toll the statute of limitations for purposes of bringing an action against the owner or operator who caused the injury or damages until his identity becomes known. In no event shall an action be brought against an owner or operator who caused the injury or damages, previously filed against as John Doe, more than three years from the commencement of the action against the unknown owner or operator as John Doe in a court of competent jurisdiction. Any recovery against the owner or operator, or the insurer of the owner or operator shall be paid to the insurer of the injured party to the extent that the insurer paid the named insured in the action brought against the owner or operator as John Doe. However, the insurer shall pay its proportionate part of all reasonable costs and expenses incurred in connection with the action, including reasonable attorney's fees. Nothing in an endorsement or provisions made under this subsection nor any other provision of law shall prevent the joining in an action against John Doe of the owner or operator of the motor vehicle causing the injury as a party defendant, and the joinder is hereby specifically authorized. No action, verdict or release arising out of a suit brought under this subsection shall give rise to any defenses in any other action brought in the subrogated party's name, including res judicata and collateral estoppel.

H. No endorsement or provisions providing the coverage required by subsection A of this section shall require arbitration of any claim arising under the endorsement or provisions, nor may anything be required of the insured except the establishment of legal liability, nor shall the insured be restricted or prevented in any manner from employing legal counsel or instituting legal proceedings.

I. Except as provided in § 65.2-309.1, the provisions of subsections A and B of § 38.2-2204 and the provisions of subsection A of this section shall not apply to any policy of insurance to the extent that it covers the liability of an employer under any workers' compensation law, or to the extent that it covers liability to which the Federal Tort Claims Act applies. No provision or application of this section shall limit the liability of an insurer of motor vehicles to an employee or other insured under this section who is injured by an uninsured motor vehicle; provided that in the event an employee of a self-insured employer receives a workers' compensation award for injuries resulting from an accident with an uninsured motor vehicle, such award shall be set off against any judgment for damages awarded pursuant to this section for personal injuries resulting from such accident.

J. Policies of insurance whose primary purpose is to provide coverage in excess of other valid and collectible insurance or qualified self-insurance may include uninsured motorist coverage as provided in subsection A of this section. Insurers issuing or providing liability policies that are of an excess or umbrella type or which provide liability coverage incidental to a policy and not related to a specifically insured motor vehicle, shall not be required to offer, provide or make available to those policies uninsured or underinsured motor vehicle coverage as defined in subsection A of this section.

K. An injured person, or in the case of death or disability his personal representative, may settle a claim with (i) a liability insurer or insurers, including any insurer providing liability coverage through an excess or umbrella insurance policy or contract and (ii) the liability insurer's or insurers' insured for the available limits of the liability insurer's coverage. Upon settlement with the liability insurer or insurers, the injured party or personal representative shall proceed to execute a full release in favor of the underinsured motorist's liability insurer and its insured and finalize the proposed settlement without prejudice to any underinsured motorist benefits or claim. Upon payment of the liability insurer's available limits to the injured person or personal representative or his attorney, the liability insurer shall thereafter have no further duties to its insured, including the duty to defend its insured if an action has been or is brought against the liability insurer's insured, and the insurer providing applicable underinsured motorist coverage shall have no right of subrogation or claim against the underinsured motorist. However, if the underinsured motorist unreasonably fails to cooperate with the underinsured motorist benefits insurer in the defense of any lawsuit brought by the injured person or his personal representative, he may again be subjected to a claim for subrogation by the underinsured motorist benefits insurer pursuant to § 8.01-66.1:1. This section provides an alternative means by which the parties may resolve claims and does not eliminate or restrict any other available means.

L. Any settlement between the injured person or his personal representative, any insurer providing liability coverage applicable to the claim, and the underinsured motorist described in subsection K shall be in writing, signed by both the injured person or his personal representative and the underinsured motorist, and shall include the following notice to the underinsured motorist, which must be initialed by the underinsured motorist:

"NOTICE TO RELEASED PARTY: Your insurance company has agreed to pay the available limits of its insurance to settle certain claims on your behalf. This settlement secures a full release of you for all claims the claimant/plaintiff has against you arising out of the subject accident, as well as ensures that no judgment can ever be entered against you by the claimant/plaintiff. In order to protect yourself from subrogation by any underinsured motorist insurer, you are agreeing to cooperate with the underinsured motorist benefits insurer(s).

Under this manner of settlement, the underinsured motorist benefits insurer(s) that is/are involved in this case has/have no right of subrogation against you unless you fail to reasonably cooperate in its/their defense of the claim by not (i) attending your deposition and trial, if subpoenaed, (ii) assisting in responding to discovery, (iii) meeting with defense counsel at reasonable times after commencement of this suit and before your testimony at a deposition and/or trial, and (iv) notifying defense counsel of any change in your address.

Upon payment of the agreed settlement amount by your insurance company(ies), such company shall no longer owe you any duties, including the duty to hire and pay for an attorney for you. You are not required to consent to settlement in this manner. If you do not consent to settlement in this manner, your insurance company will still defend you in any lawsuit brought against you by the claimant/plaintiff, but you will not have the protections of a full release from the claimant/plaintiff, judgment could be entered against you and may exceed your available insurance coverage, and any underinsured motorist benefits insurer would have a right of subrogation against you to recover any moneys it pays to the claimant/plaintiff.

You are encouraged to discuss your rights and obligations related to settlement in this manner with your insurance company and/or an attorney. By signing this document, you agree to consent to this settlement and to reasonably cooperate with the underinsured motorist benefits insurer in the defense of any lawsuit brought by the claimant/plaintiff.

____________ (initial)"

In the alternative, the liability insurer may send the notice to the released party by certified mail return receipt requested to the underinsured motorist at his last known address.

M. Any action brought by the injured person or his personal representative to recover underinsured motorist benefits after payment of the liability insurer's available limits pursuant to subsection K shall be brought against the released defendant or defendants, and a copy of the complaint shall be served on any insurer providing underinsured motorist benefits. If an action is pending at the time the liability insurer's available limits are paid to the injured person or personal representative or his attorney, then the action shall remain pending against the named defendant or defendants who have been released. If such action results in a verdict in favor of the injured person or his personal representative against a released defendant, then judgment as to that defendant shall be entered in the name of "Released Defendant" and shall be enforceable against the underinsured motorist benefits insurer or insurers, not to exceed the underinsured motorist benefits limits, and against any unreleased defendant, as though it were entered in the actual name of the released defendant.

N. Any proposed settlement between a liability insurer and a person under a disability or a personal representative as permitted in subsection K that compromises in part a claim for personal injuries by the person under a disability or for death by wrongful act pursuant to § 8.01-50 may be, but is not required to be, approved pursuant to § 8.01-424 or 8.01-55, as applicable. If the personal representative elects not to have the settlement with the liability insurer approved pursuant to § 8.01-55, then any payment made to the personal representative by the liability insurer shall be made payable to the personal representative's attorney, to be held in trust, or paid into the court pursuant to § 8.01-600 if the personal representative is not represented by an attorney, with no disbursements made therefrom until the compromise is approved by the court pursuant to § 8.01-55. Approval by the court of a settlement between the liability insurer and a person under a disability or the personal representative pursuant to this subsection shall not prejudice the person's or personal representative's claim for underinsured motorist benefits.

History.

Code 1950, § 38-238; 1952, c. 317, § 38.1-381; 1958, c. 282; 1959, Ex. Sess., cc. 42, 70; 1960, c. 462; 1962, c. 457; 1964, c. 477; 1966, cc. 182, 459; 1968, cc. 199, 721; 1970, c. 494; 1971, Ex. Sess., c. 216; 1973, cc. 225, 390; 1974, c. 87; 1976, cc. 121, 122; 1977, c. 78; 1979, c. 113; 1980, cc. 326, 331; 1981, Sp. Sess., c. 6; 1982, cc. 638, 642; 1984, c. 541; 1985, cc. 39, 325; 1986, c. 562; 1987, c. 519; 1988, cc. 565, 578, 585, 586, 594; 1989, c. 621; 1993, c. 381; 1995, cc. 189, 267, 476; 1997, cc. 170, 191; 1999, c. 992; 2001, c. 218; 2003, c. 283; 2010, c. 492; 2011, c. 107; 2015, cc. 584, 585.

§ 38.2-2207. No policy to exclude coverage to employee.

No policy or contract of bodily injury or property damage liability insurance relating to the ownership, maintenance, or use of a motor vehicle, aircraft or watercraft shall exclude coverage to an employee of the insured in any controversy arising between employees even though one employee shall be awarded compensation as provided in Title 65.2.

History.

Code 1950, § 38-238; 1952, c. 317, § 38.1-381; 1958, c. 282; 1959, Ex. Sess., cc. 42, 70; 1970, c. 462; 1962, c. 457; 1964, c. 477; 1966, cc. 182, 459; 1968, cc. 199, 721; 1970, c. 494; 1971, Ex. Sess., c. 216; 1973, cc. 225, 390; 1974, c. 87; 1976, cc. 121, 122; 1977, c. 78; 1979, c. 113; 1980, cc. 326, 331; 1981, Sp. Sess., c. 6; 1982, cc. 638, 642; 1984, c. 541; 1985, cc. 39, 325; 1986, c. 562; 1987, c. 519.

§ 38.2-2212. Grounds and procedure for cancellation of or refusal to renew motor vehicle insurance policies; review by Commissioner.

A. The following definitions shall apply to this section:

"Cancellation" or *"to cancel"* means a termination of a policy during the policy period.

"Insurer" means any insurance company, association, or exchange licensed to transact motor vehicle insurance in this Commonwealth.

"Policy of motor vehicle insurance" or *"policy"* means a policy or contract for bodily injury or property damage liability insurance issued or delivered in this Commonwealth covering liability arising from the ownership, maintenance, or use of any motor vehicle, insuring as the named insured one individual or husband and wife who are residents of the same household, and under which the insured vehicle designated in the policy is either:

a. A motor vehicle of a private passenger, station wagon, or motorcycle type that is not used commercially, rented to others, or used as a public or livery conveyance where the term "public or livery conveyance" does not include car pools, or

b. Any other four-wheel motor vehicle which is not used in the occupation, profession, or business, other than farming, of the insured, or as a public or livery conveyance, or rented to others. The term "policy of motor vehicle insurance" or "policy" does not include (i) any policy issued through the Virginia Automobile Insurance Plan, (ii) any policy covering the operation of a garage, sales agency, repair shop, service station, or public parking place, (iii) any policy providing insurance only on an excess basis, or (iv) any other contract providing insurance to the named insured even though the contract may incidentally provide insurance on motor vehicles.

"Renewal" or *"to renew"* means (i) the issuance and delivery by an insurer of a policy superseding at the end of the policy period a policy previously issued and delivered by the same insurer, providing types and limits of coverage at least equal to those contained in the policy being superseded, or (ii) the issuance and delivery of a certificate or notice extending the term of a policy beyond its policy period or term with types and limits of coverage at least equal to those contained in the policy. Each renewal shall conform with the requirements of the manual rules and rating program currently filed by the insurer with the Commission. Except as provided in subsection K of this section, any policy with a policy period or term of less than 12 months or any policy with no fixed expiration date shall for the purpose of this section be considered as if written for successive policy periods or terms of six months from the original effective date.

B. This section shall apply only to that portion of a policy of motor vehicle insurance providing the coverage required by §§ 38.2-2204, 38.2-2205, and 38.2-2206.

C. 1. No insurer shall refuse to renew a motor vehicle insurance policy solely because of any one or more of the following factors:

a. Age;

b. Sex;

c. Residence;

d. Race;

e. Color;

f. Creed;

g. National origin;

h. Ancestry;

i. Marital status;

j. Lawful occupation, including the military service;

k. Lack of driving experience, or number of years driving experience;

l. Lack of supporting business or lack of the potential for acquiring such business;

m. One or more accidents or violations that occurred more than 48 months immediately preceding the upcoming anniversary date;

n. One or more claims submitted under the uninsured motorists coverage of the policy where the uninsured motorist is known or there is physical evidence of contact;

o. A single claim by a single insured submitted under the medical expense coverage due to an accident for which the insured was neither wholly nor partially at fault;

p. One or more claims submitted under the comprehensive or towing coverages. However, nothing in this section shall prohibit an insurer from modifying or refusing to renew the comprehensive or towing coverages at the time of renewal of the policy on the basis of one or more claims submitted by an insured under those coverages, provided that the insurer shall mail or deliver to the insured at the address shown in the policy, or deliver electronically to the address provided by the named insured, written notice of any such change in coverage at least 45 days prior to the renewal;

q. Two or fewer motor vehicle accidents within a three-year period unless the accident was caused either wholly or partially by the named insured, a resident of the same household, or other customary operator;

r. Credit information contained in a "consumer report," as defined in the federal Fair Credit Reporting Act, 15 U.S.C. § 1681 et seq., bearing on a natural person's creditworthiness, credit standing or credit capacity. If credit information is used, in part,

Insurance

as the basis for the nonrenewal, such credit information shall be based on a consumer report procured within 120 days from the effective date of the nonrenewal. The provisions of this subdivision shall apply only to insurance purchased primarily for personal, family, or household purposes; or

s. The refusal of a motor vehicle owner as defined in § 46.2-1088.6 to provide access to recorded data from a recording device as defined in § 46.2-1088.6.

2. Nothing in this section shall require any insurer to renew a policy for an insured where the insured's occupation has changed so as to materially increase the risk. Nothing contained in subdivisions C 1 n, 1 o, and 1 p of this subsection shall prohibit an insurer from refusing to renew a policy where a claim is false or fraudulent. Nothing in this section prohibits any insurer from setting rates in accordance with relevant actuarial data.

D. No insurer shall cancel a policy except for one or more of the following reasons:

1. The named insured or any other operator who either resides in the same household or customarily operates a motor vehicle insured under the policy has had his driver's license suspended or revoked during the policy period or, if the policy is a renewal, during its policy period or the 90 days immediately preceding the last effective date.

2. The named insured fails to pay the premium for the policy or any installment of the premium, whether payable to the insurer or its agent either directly or indirectly under any premium finance plan or extension of credit.

3. The named insured or his duly constituted attorney-in-fact has notified the insurer of a change in the insured's legal residence to a state other than Virginia and the insured vehicle will be principally garaged in the new state of legal residence.

E. No cancellation or refusal to renew by an insurer of a policy of motor vehicle insurance shall be effective unless the insurer delivers or mails to the named insured at the address shown in the policy a written notice of the cancellation or refusal to renew, or the insurer delivers such notice electronically to the address provided by the named insured. The notice shall:

1. Be in a type size authorized under § 38.2-311.

2. State the effective date of the cancellation or refusal to renew. The effective date of cancellation or refusal to renew shall be at least 45 days after mailing or delivering to the insured the notice of cancellation or notice of refusal to renew. However, when the policy is being canceled or not renewed for the reason set forth in subdivision 2 of subsection D of this section the effective date may be less than 45 days but at least 15 days from the date of mailing or delivery.

3. State the specific reason of the insurer for cancellation or refusal to renew and provide for the notification required by §§ 38.2-608, 38.2-609, and subsection B of § 38.2-610. However, those notification requirements shall not apply when the policy is being canceled or not renewed for the reason set forth in subdivision 2 of subsection D of this section.

4. Inform the insured of his right to request in writing within 15 days of the receipt of the notice that the Commissioner review the action of the insurer.

The notice of cancellation or refusal to renew shall contain the following statement to inform the insured of such right:

IMPORTANT NOTICE

Within 15 days of receiving this notice, you or your attorney may request in writing that the Commissioner of Insurance review this action to determine whether the insurer has complied with Virginia laws in canceling or nonrenewing your policy. If this insurer has failed to comply with the cancellation or nonrenewal laws, the Commissioner may require that your policy be reinstated. However, the Commissioner is prohibited from making underwriting judgments. If this insurer has complied with the cancellation or nonrenewal laws, the Commissioner does not have the authority to overturn this action.

5. Inform the insured of the possible availability of other insurance which may be obtained through his agent, through another insurer, or through the Virginia Automobile Insurance Plan.

6. If sent by mail or delivered electronically, comply with the provisions of § 38.2-2208.

Nothing in this subsection prohibits any insurer or agent from including in the notice of cancellation or refusal to renew, any additional disclosure statements required by state or federal laws, or any additional information relating to the availability of other insurance.

F. Nothing in this section shall apply:

1. If the insurer or its agent acting on behalf of the insurer has manifested its willingness to renew by issuing or offering to issue a renewal policy, certificate, or other evidence of renewal, or has manifested its willingness to renew in writing to the insured. The written manifestation shall include the name of a proposed insurer, the expiration date of the policy, the type of insurance coverage, and information regarding the estimated renewal premium. The insurer shall retain a copy of each written manifestation for a period of at least one year from the expiration date of any policy that is not renewed;

2. If the named insured, or his duly constituted attorney-in-fact, has notified the insurer or its agent orally, or in writing, if the insurer requires such notification to be in writing, that he wishes the policy to be canceled or that he does not wish the policy to be renewed, or if prior to the date of expiration he fails to accept the offer of the insurer to renew the policy;

3. To any motor vehicle insurance policy which has been in effect less than 60 days when the termination notice is mailed or delivered to the insured, unless it is a renewal policy; or

4. If an affiliated insurer has manifested its willingness to provide coverage at a lower premium than would have been charged for the same exposures on the expiring policy. The affiliated insurer shall manifest its willingness to provide coverage by issuing a policy with the types and limits of coverage at least equal to those contained in the expiring policy unless the named insured has requested a change in coverage or limits. When such offer is made by an affiliated insurer, an offer of renewal shall not be required of the insurer of the expiring policy, and the policy issued by the affiliated insurer shall be deemed to be a renewal policy.

G. There shall be no liability on the part of and no cause of action of any nature shall arise against the Commissioner or his subordinates; any insurer, its authorized representatives, its agents, or its employees; or any person furnishing to the insurer information as to reasons for cancellation or refusal to renew, for any statement made by any of them in complying with this section or for providing information pertaining to the cancellation or refusal to renew. For the purposes of this section, no insurer shall be required to furnish a notice of cancellation or refusal to renew to anyone other than the named insured, any person designated by the named insured, or any other person to whom such notice is required to be given by the terms of the policy and the Commissioner.

H. Within 15 days of receipt of the notice of cancellation or refusal to renew, any insured or his attorney shall be entitled to request in writing to the Commissioner that he review the action of the insurer in canceling or refusing to renew the policy of the insured. Upon receipt of the request, the Commissioner shall promptly begin a review to determine whether the insurer's cancellation or refusal to renew complies with the requirements of this section and of § 38.2-2208 if the notice was sent by mail or delivered electronically. The policy shall remain in full force and effect during the pendency of the review by the Commissioner except where the cancellation or refusal to renew is for the reason set forth in subdivision 2 of subsection D of this section, in which case the policy shall terminate as of the effective date stated in the notice. Where the Commissioner finds from the review that the cancellation or refusal to renew has not complied with the requirements of this section or of § 38.2-2208, he shall immediately notify the insurer, the insured and any other person to whom such notice was required to be given by the terms of the policy that the cancellation or refusal to renew is not effective. Nothing in this section authorizes the Commissioner to substitute his judgment as to underwriting for that of the insurer. Where the Commissioner finds in favor of the insured, the Commission in its discretion may award the insured reasonable attorneys' fees.

I. Each insurer shall maintain for at least one year, records of cancellation and refusal to renew and copies of every notice or statement referred to in subsection E of this section that it sends to any of its insureds.

J. The provisions of this section shall not apply to any insurer that limits the issuance of policies of motor vehicle liability insurance to one class or group of persons engaged in any one particular profession, trade, occupation, or business. Nothing in this section requires an insurer to renew a policy of motor vehicle insurance if the insured does not conform to the occupational or membership requirements of an insurer who limits its writings to an occupation or membership of an organization. No insurer is required to renew a policy if the insured becomes a nonresident of Virginia.

K. Notwithstanding any other provision of this section, a motor vehicle insurance policy with a policy period or term of five months or less may expire at its expiration date when the insurer has manifested in writing its willingness to renew the policy for at least 30 days and has mailed or delivered the written manifestation to the insured at least 15 days before the expiration date of the policy. The written manifestation shall include the name of the proposed insurer, the expiration date of the policy, the type of insurance coverage, and the estimated renewal premium. The insurer shall retain a copy of the written manifestation for at least one year from the expiration date of any policy that is not renewed.

History.

1970, c. 564, § 38.1-381.5; 1972, c. 273; 1975, cc. 63, 319; 1978, c. 441; 1982, c. 482; 1983, cc. 125, 371; 1984, c. 340; 1986, c. 562; 1988, c. 655; 1990, c. 960; 1991, c. 116; 1995, c. 3; 1996, cc. 206, 239; 1998, cc. 141, 142; 2003, cc. 543, 553; 2006, cc. 851, 889; 2008, cc. 58, 221; 2009, c. 215; 2013, c. 257.

§ 38.2-2212.1. Powers of Commission; replacement policies.

Upon the verified petition of an insurer, where the petitioning insurer proposes to replace all or substantially all of its policies in another insurer, the Commission may relieve the insurer of the requirements of subsection E of § 38.2-2212 and of the mailing requirements of § 38.2-2208, provided the insurer demonstrates to the satisfaction of the Commission that (i) the replacement policy is underwritten by an affiliate insurer under common control with the petitioning insurer; (ii) the replacement policy is substantially similar to the existing policy with the petitioning insurer; (iii) the premium charged for the replacement policy is no greater than that charged by the petitioning insurer for the existing policy; and (iv) the replacement insurer is duly licensed to transact the business of insurance in the Commonwealth of Virginia. The replacement insurer shall retain a copy of any offer of replacement for a period of one year from the expiration of any existing policy that is not replaced. The Commission may further condition any such relief to protect the best interests of the policyholder.

History.
1991, c. 215.

CHAPTER 30.
UNINSURED MOTORISTS FUND.

§ 38.2-3000. Supervision and control of Fund by Commission; payments from Fund.

The Uninsured Motorists Fund, referred to in this chapter as the Fund, shall be under the supervision and control of the Commission. Payments from the Fund shall be made on warrants of the Comptroller issued on vouchers signed by a person designated by the Commission. The purpose of the Fund is to reduce the cost of the insurance required by subsection A of § 38.2-2206.

History.
Code 1950, § 12-65; 1958, c. 455, § 38.1-379.1; 1962, c. 253; 1971, Ex. Sess., c. 44; 1986, c. 562.

§ 38.2-3001. Distribution to insurers; records of loss experience as prerequisite to payment.

The Commission shall distribute moneys annually from the Fund among the several insurers writing motor vehicle bodily injury and property damage liability insurance on motor vehicles registered in this Commonwealth. Moneys shall be distributed in the proportion that each insurer's reported written car years bear to the total number of written car years reported for the preceding year by all insurers in this Commonwealth who have elected to participate in the distribution of the Fund. For purposes of this section, *"written car years"* means the number of motor vehicles insured by policies providing uninsured motorist coverage as required by subsection A of § 38.2-2206 during a twelve-month period. Only insurers that maintain records satisfactory to the Commission shall receive any payment from the Fund.

History.
Code 1950, § 12-66; 1958, c. 455, § 38.1-379.2; 1962, c. 253; 1971, Ex. Sess., c. 44; 1986, c. 562; 2002, c. 145.

TITLE 42.1.
LIBRARIES.

CHAPTER 5.
OFFENSES.

§ 42.1-72. Injuring or destroying books and other property of libraries.

Any person who willfully, maliciously or wantonly writes upon, injures, defaces, tears, cuts, mutilates, or destroys any book or other library property belonging to or in the custody of any public, county or regional library, The Library of Virginia, other repository of public records, museums or any library or collection belonging to or in the custody of any educational, eleemosynary, benevolent, hereditary, historical library or patriotic institution, organization or society, shall be guilty of a Class 1 misdemeanor.

History.
Code 1950, § 42-20; 1970, c. 606; 1975, c. 318; 1994, c. 64.

§ 42.1-73. Concealment of book or other property while on premises of library; removal of book or other property from library.

Whoever, without authority, with the intention of converting to his own or another's use, willfully conceals a book or other library property, while still on the premises of such library, or willfully or without authority removes any book or other property from any of the above libraries or collections shall be deemed guilty of larceny thereof, and upon conviction thereof shall be punished as provided by law. Proof of the willful concealment of such book or other library property while still on the premises of such library shall be prima facie evidence of intent to commit larceny thereof.

History.
Code 1950, § 42-21; 1970, c. 606; 1975, c. 318.

§ 42.1-73.1. Exemption from liability for arrest of suspected person; electronic article surveillance devices.

A library or agent or employee of the library causing the arrest of any person pursuant to the provisions of § 42.1-73, shall not be held civilly liable for unlawful detention, slander, malicious prosecution, false imprisonment, false arrest, or assault and battery of the person so arrested, whether such arrest takes place on the premises of the library or after close pursuit from such premises by such agent or employee, if, in causing the arrest of such person, the library or agent or employee of the library had at the time of such arrest probable cause to believe that the person committed willful concealment of books or other library property.

The activation of an electronic article surveillance device as a result of a person exiting the premises or an area within the premises of a library where an electronic article surveillance device is located shall constitute probable cause for the detention of such person by such library or agent or employee of the library, provided that such person is detained only in a reasonable manner and only for such time as is necessary for an inquiry into the circumstances surrounding the activation of the device, and provided that clear and visible notice is posted at each exit and location within the premises where such device is located indicating the presence of an antitheft device. For purposes of this section, "electronic article surveillance device" means an electronic device designed and operated for the purpose of detecting the removal from the premises or a protected area within such premises, of any specially marked or tagged book or other library property.

History.
1975, c. 318; 1986, c. 33.

Mechanics' Liens

§ 42.1-74. Failure to return book or other library property.

Any person having in his possession any book or other property of any of the above libraries or collections, which he shall fail to return within thirty days after receiving notice in writing from the custodian, shall be guilty of a misdemeanor and punished according to law; provided, however, that if such book should be lost or destroyed, such person may, within thirty days after being so notified, pay to the custodian the value of such book, the value to be determined by the governing board having jurisdiction.

History.
Code 1950, § 42-22; 1970, c. 606.

§ 42.1-74.1. "Book or other library property" defined.

The terms *"book or other library property"* as used in this chapter shall include any book, plate, picture, photograph, engraving, painting, drawing, map, newspaper, magazine, pamphlet, broadside, manuscript, document, letter, public record, microform, sound recording, audiovisual materials in any format, magnetic or other tapes, electronic data processing records, artifacts, or other documentary, written, or printed material, regardless of physical form or characteristics, belonging to, on loan to, or otherwise in the custody of any library, museum, repository of public or other records institution as specified in § 42.1-72.

History.
1975, c. 318.

TITLE 43.

MECHANICS' AND CERTAIN OTHER LIENS.

CHAPTER 4.

LIENS OF INNKEEPERS, LIVERY STABLE, GARAGE AND MARINA KEEPERS, MECHANICS AND BAILEES.

§ 43-32. Lien of keeper of livery stable, marina, etc.

A. Every keeper of a livery stable, hangar, tie-down, or marina, and every person pasturing or keeping any horses or other animals, boats, aircraft, or harness, shall have a lien upon such horses and other animals, boats, aircraft, and harness, for the amount that may be due him for the towing, storage, recovery, keeping, supporting, and care thereof, until such amount is paid.

B. In the case of any boat or aircraft subject to a chattel mortgage, security agreement, deed of trust, or other instrument securing money, the keeper of the marina, hangar, or tie-down shall have a lien thereon for his reasonable charges for storage under this section not to exceed $500 and for alteration and repair under § 43-33 not to exceed $1,000. However, in the case of a storage lien, to obtain the priority for an amount in excess of $300, the person asserting the lien shall make a reasonable attempt to notify any secured party of record at the Department of Game and Inland Fisheries by telephonic means and shall give written notice by certified mail, return receipt requested, to any secured party of record at the Department of Game and Inland Fisheries within seven business days of taking possession of the boat or aircraft. If the secured party does not, within seven business days of receipt of the notice, take or refuse redelivery to it or its designee, the lienor shall be entitled to priority for the full amount of storage charges, not to exceed $500. Notwithstanding a redelivery, the watercraft shall be subject to subsection D.

C. In addition, any person furnishing services involving the towing and recovery of a boat or aircraft shall have a lien for all normal costs incident thereto, if the person asserting the lien gives written notice within seven days of receipt of the boat or aircraft by certified mail, return receipt requested, to all secured parties of record at the Department of Game and Inland Fisheries.

D. In addition, any keeper shall be entitled to a lien against any proceeds remaining after the satisfaction of all prior security interests or liens and may retain possession of such property until such charges are paid.

History.

Code 1919, § 6445; 1968, c. 320; 1970, c. 56; 1976, c. 77; 1977, c. 382; 1981, c. 453; 1984, c. 396; 1988, c. 120; 1990, c. 665; 1992, c. 403; 1999, c. 533; 2004, c. 215; 2005, c. 98; 2006, cc. 874, 891; 2009, c. 664; 2016, c. 397.

§ 43-33. Lien of mechanic for repairs.

Every mechanic who shall alter or repair any article of personal property at the request of the owner of such property shall have a lien thereon for his just and reasonable charges therefor and may retain possession of such property until such charges are paid.

And every mechanic who shall make necessary alterations or repairs on any article of personal property which from its character requires the making of ordinary repairs thereto as a reasonable incident to its reasonable and customary use, at the request of any person legally in possession thereof under a reservation of title contract, chattel mortgage, deed of trust, or other instrument securing money, the person so in possession having authority to use such property, shall have a lien thereon for his just and reasonable charges therefor to the extent of $1,000. In addition, such mechanic shall be entitled to a lien against the proceeds, if any, remaining after the satisfaction of all prior security interests or liens and may retain possession of such property until such charges are paid. In any action to enforce the lien hereby given all persons having an interest in the property sought to be subjected shall be made parties defendant.

If the owner of the property held by the mechanic shall desire to obtain possession thereof, he shall make the mechanic defendant in proceeding in the county or municipal court to recover the property.

The owner may give a bond payable to the court, in a penalty of the amount equal to the lien claimed by the mechanic and court costs, with security to be approved by the clerk, and conditioned for the performance of the final judgment of the court on the trial of the proceeding, and with a further condition to the effect that, if upon the hearing, the judgment of the court be that the lien of the mechanic on such property, or any part thereof, be enforced, judgment may thereupon be entered against the obligors on such bond for the amount due the mechanic and court costs, if assessed against the owner, without further or other proceedings against them thereon. Upon giving of the bond, the property shall be delivered to the owner.

History.

Code 1919, § 6443; 1924, p. 638; 1956, c. 558; 1966, c. 458; 1968, c. 395; 1973, c. 492; 1974, c. 166; 1980, c. 598; 1984, c. 396; 1999, c. 533; 2005, c. 280; 2016, c. 397.

§ 43-34. Enforcement of liens acquired under §§ 43-31 through 43-33 and of liens of bailees.

Any person having a lien under §§ 43-31 through 43-33 and any bailee, except where otherwise provided, having a lien as such at common law on personal property in his possession that he has no power to sell for the satisfaction of the lien, if the debt for which the lien exists is not paid within 10 days after it is due and the value of the property affected by the lien does not exceed $10,000, may sell such property or so much thereof as may be necessary, by public auction, for cash. The proceeds shall be applied to the satisfaction of the debt and expenses of sale, and the surplus, if any, shall be paid within 30 days of the sale to any lienholder, and then to the owner of the property. A seller who fails to remit the surplus as provided shall be liable to the person entitled to the surplus in an amount equal to $50 for each day beyond 30 days that the failure continues.

Before making the sale, the seller shall advertise the time, place, and terms thereof in a public place. In the case of property other than a motor vehicle required to be registered in Virginia having a value in excess of $600, 10 days' prior notice shall be given to any secured party who has filed a financing statement against the property, and written notice shall be given to the owner as hereinafter provided.

If the value of the property is more than $10,000 but does not exceed $25,000, the party having the lien, after giving notice as herein provided, may apply by petition to any general district court of the county or city wherein the property is, or, if the value of the property exceeds $25,000, to the circuit court of the county or city, for the sale of the property. If, on the hearing of the case on the petition, the defense, if any made thereto, and such evidence as may be adduced by the parties respectively, the court is satisfied that the debt and lien are established and the property should be sold to pay the debt, the court shall order the sale to be made by the sheriff of the county or city. The sheriff shall make the same and apply and dispose of the proceeds in the same manner as if the sale were made under a writ of fieri facias.

If the owner of the property is a resident of the Commonwealth, any notice required by this section may be served as provided in § 8.01-296 or, if the sale is to be made without resort to the courts, by personal delivery or by certified or registered mail delivered to the present owner of the property to be sold at his last known address at least 10 days prior to the date of sale. If the owner of the property is a nonresident or if his address is unknown, any notice required by this section may be served by posting a copy thereof in three of any of the following places in any combination: (i) one or more public places in the county or city where the property is located; (ii) one or more websites operated by the Commonwealth, the county or city where the property is located, or a political subdivision of either; or (iii) one or more newspapers of general circulation in the county or city where the property is located, either in print or on their websites. For purposes of this section, "public place" means a premises owned by the Commonwealth or a political subdivision thereof, or an agency of either, that is open to the general public.

History.

Code 1919, § 6449; 1960, c. 571; 1968, c. 605; 1971, Ex. Sess., c. 155; 1978, c. 59; 1980, c. 598; 1987, c. 37; 1988, c. 227; 1992, c. 111; 1993, c. 759; 1998, c. 868; 2002, c. 401; 2004, c. 369; 2006, cc. 874, 891; 2008, c. 171; 2009, c. 664; 2011, cc. 14, 702; 2014, c. 339; 2016, c. 397.

§ 43-34.1. Lien of keeper of hangar or tie-down on aircraft subject to a chattel mortgage.

In the case of any aircraft subject to a chattel mortgage, security agreement, deed of trust or other instrument securing money, the keeper of the hangar or tie-down shall have a lien thereon for his usual and reasonable charges for storage, alteration or repair from the time such lien is perfected as provided herein. Such lien is nonpossessory and shall be deemed a conveyance. To perfect such lien, the following shall be required:

1. The claim of lien shall be signed, under oath, by the claimant, his agent or attorney;

2. The claim of lien shall also be filed within 120 days after completion of alterations or repair or accrual of storage charges, as personal property security interests or liens are recorded, with the State Corporation Commission in accordance with the applicable provisions of Part 5 (§ 8.9A-501 et seq.) of Title 8.9A; and

3. The claim of lien shall also be filed within such 120-day period with the Aircraft Registration Branch of the Federal Aviation Administration.

History.

1993, c. 854.

TITLE 44. MILITARY AND EMERGENCY LAWS.

CHAPTER 3.2. EMERGENCY SERVICES AND DISASTER LAW.

§ 44-146.16. Definitions.

As used in this chapter unless the context requires a different meaning:

"Communicable disease of public health threat" means an illness of public health significance, as determined by the State Health Commissioner in accordance with regulations of the Board of Health, caused by a specific or suspected infectious agent that may be reasonably expected or is known to be readily transmitted directly or indirectly from one individual to another and has been found to create a risk of death or significant injury or impairment; this definition shall not, however, be construed to include human immunodeficiency viruses or tuberculosis, unless used as a bioterrorism weapon. "Individual" shall include any companion animal. Further, whenever "person or persons" is used in Article 3.02 (§ 32.1-48.05 et seq.) of Chapter 2 of Title 32.1, it shall be deemed, when the context requires it, to include any individual;

"Disaster" means (i) any man-made disaster including any condition following an attack by any enemy or foreign nation upon the United States resulting in substantial damage of property or injury to persons in the United States and may be by use of bombs, missiles, shell fire, nuclear, radiological, chemical, or biological means or other weapons or by overt paramilitary actions; terrorism, foreign and domestic; also any industrial, nuclear, or transportation accident, explosion, conflagration, power failure, resources shortage, or other condition such as sabotage, oil spills, and other injurious environmental contaminations that threaten or cause damage to property, human suffering, hardship, or loss of life; and (ii) any natural disaster including any

hurricane, tornado, storm, flood, high water, wind-driven water, tidal wave, earthquake, drought, fire, communicable disease of public health threat, or other natural catastrophe resulting in damage, hardship, suffering, or possible loss of life;

"Discharge" means spillage, leakage, pumping, pouring, seepage, emitting, dumping, emptying, injecting, escaping, leaching, fire, explosion, or other releases;

"Emergency" means any occurrence, or threat thereof, whether natural or man-made, which results or may result in substantial injury or harm to the population or substantial damage to or loss of property or natural resources and may involve governmental action beyond that authorized or contemplated by existing law because governmental inaction for the period required to amend the law to meet the exigency would work immediate and irrevocable harm upon the citizens or the environment of the Commonwealth or some clearly defined portion or portions thereof;

"Emergency services" means the preparation for and the carrying out of functions, other than functions for which military forces are primarily responsible, to prevent, minimize and repair injury and damage resulting from disasters, together with all other activities necessary or incidental to the preparation for and carrying out of the foregoing functions. These functions include, without limitation, fire-fighting services, police services, medical and health services, rescue, engineering, warning services, communications, radiological, chemical and other special weapons defense, evacuation of persons from stricken areas, emergency welfare services, emergency transportation, emergency resource management, existing or properly assigned functions of plant protection, temporary restoration of public utility services, and other functions related to civilian protection. These functions also include the administration of approved state and federal disaster recovery and assistance programs;

"Hazard mitigation" means any action taken to reduce or eliminate the long-term risk to human life and property from natural hazards;

"Hazardous substances" means all materials or substances which now or hereafter are designated, defined, or characterized as hazardous by law or regulation of the Commonwealth or regulation of the United States government;

"Interjurisdictional agency for emergency management" is any organization established between contiguous political subdivisions to facilitate the cooperation and protection of the subdivisions in the work of disaster prevention, preparedness, response, and recovery;

"Local emergency" means the condition declared by the local governing body when in its judgment the threat or actual occurrence of an emergency or disaster is or threatens to be of sufficient severity and magnitude to warrant coordinated local government action to prevent or alleviate the damage, loss, hardship or suffering threatened or caused thereby; provided, however, that a local emergency arising wholly or substantially out of a resource shortage may be declared only by the Governor, upon petition of the local governing body, when he deems the threat or actual occurrence of such an emergency or disaster to be of sufficient severity and magnitude to warrant coordinated local government action to prevent or alleviate the damage, loss, hardship or suffering threatened or caused thereby; provided, however, nothing in this chapter shall be construed as prohibiting a local governing body from the prudent management of its water supply to prevent or manage a water shortage;

"Local emergency management organization" means an organization created in accordance with the provisions of this chapter by local authority to perform local emergency service functions;

"Major disaster" means any natural catastrophe, including any: hurricane, tornado, storm, high water, wind-driven water, tidal wave, tsunami, earthquake, volcanic eruption, landslide, mudslide, snowstorm or drought, or regardless of cause, any fire, flood, or explosion, in any part of the United States, which, in the determination of the President of the United States is, or thereafter determined to be, of sufficient severity and magnitude to warrant major disaster assistance under the Stafford Act (P.L. 93-288 as amended) to supplement the efforts and available resources of states, local governments, and disaster relief organizations in alleviating the damage, loss, hardship, or suffering caused thereby and is so declared by him;

"Political subdivision" means any city or county in the Commonwealth and for the purposes of this chapter, the Town of Chincoteague and any town of more than 5,000 population that chooses to have an emergency management program separate from that of the county in which such town is located;

"Resource shortage" means the absence, unavailability or reduced supply of any raw or processed natural resource, or any commodities, goods or services of any kind that bear a substantial relationship to the health, safety, welfare and economic well-being of the citizens of the Commonwealth;

"State of emergency" means the condition declared by the Governor when in his judgment, the threat or actual occurrence of an emergency or a disaster in any part of the Commonwealth is of sufficient severity and magnitude to warrant disaster assistance by the Commonwealth to supplement the efforts and available resources of the several localities, and relief organizations in preventing or alleviating the damage, loss, hardship, or suffering threatened or caused thereby and is so declared by him.

History.

1973, c. 260; 1974, c. 4; 1975, c. 11; 1978, c. 60; 1979, c. 193; 1981, c. 116; 1984, c. 743; 1993, c. 671; 2000, c. 309; 2004, cc. 773, 1021; 2008, cc. 121, 157.

§ 44-146.17. Powers and duties of Governor.

The Governor shall be Director of Emergency Management. He shall take such action from time to time as is necessary for the adequate promotion and coordination of state and local emergency services activities relating to the safety and welfare of the Commonwealth in time of disasters.

The Governor shall have, in addition to his powers hereinafter or elsewhere prescribed by law, the following powers and duties:

(1) To proclaim and publish such rules and regulations and to issue such orders as may, in his judgment, be necessary to accomplish the purposes of this chapter including, but not limited to such measures as are in his judgment required to control, restrict, allocate or regulate the use, sale, production and distribution of food, fuel, clothing and other commodities, materials, goods, services and resources under any state or federal emergency services programs.

He may adopt and implement the Commonwealth of Virginia Emergency Operations Plan, which provides for state-level emergency operations in response to any type of disaster or large-scale emergency affecting Virginia and that provides the needed framework within which more detailed emergency plans and procedures can be developed and maintained by state agencies, local governments and other organizations.

He may direct and compel evacuation of all or part of the populace from any stricken or threatened area if this action is deemed necessary for the preservation of life, implement emergency mitigation, preparedness, response or recovery actions; prescribe routes, modes of transportation and destination in connection with evacuation; and control ingress and egress at an emergency area, including the movement of persons within the area and the occupancy of premises therein.

Executive orders, to include those declaring a state of emergency and directing evacuation, shall have the force and effect of law and the violation thereof shall be punishable as a Class 1 misdemeanor in every case where the executive order declares that its violation shall have such force and effect.

Such executive orders declaring a state of emergency may address exceptional circumstances that exist relating to an order of quarantine or an order of isolation concerning a communicable disease of public health threat that is issued by the State Health Commissioner for an affected area of the Commonwealth pursuant to Article 3.02 (§ 32.1-48.05 et seq.) of Chapter 2 of Title 32.1.

Except as to emergency plans issued to prescribe actions to be taken in the event of disasters and emergencies, no rule, regulation, or order issued under this section shall have any effect beyond June 30 next following the next adjournment of the regular session of the General Assembly but the same or a similar rule, regulation, or order may thereafter be issued again if not contrary to law;

(2) To appoint a State Coordinator of Emergency Management and authorize the appointment or employment of other personnel as is necessary to carry out the provisions of this chapter, and to remove, in his discretion, any and all persons serving hereunder;

(3) To procure supplies and equipment, to institute training and public information programs relative to emergency management and to take other preparatory steps including the partial or full mobilization of emergency management organizations in advance of actual disaster, to insure the furnishing of adequately trained and equipped forces in time of need;

(4) To make such studies and surveys of industries, resources, and facilities in the Commonwealth as may be necessary to ascertain the capabilities of the Commonwealth and to plan for the most efficient emergency use thereof;

(5) On behalf of the Commonwealth enter into mutual aid arrangements with other states and to coordinate mutual aid plans between political subdivisions of the Commonwealth. After a state of emergency is declared in another state and the Governor receives a written request for assistance from the executive authority of that state, the Governor may authorize the use in the other state of personnel, equipment, supplies, and materials of the Commonwealth, or of a political subdivision, with the consent of the chief executive officer or governing body of the political subdivision;

(6) To delegate any administrative authority vested in him under this chapter, and to provide for the further delegation of any such authority, as needed;

(7) Whenever, in the opinion of the Governor, the safety and welfare of the people of the Commonwealth require the exercise of emergency measures due to a threatened or actual disaster, he may declare a state of emergency to exist;

(8) To request a major disaster declaration from the President, thereby certifying the need for federal disaster assistance and ensuring the expenditure of a reasonable amount of funds of the Commonwealth, its local governments, or other agencies for alleviating the damage, loss, hardship, or suffering resulting from the disaster;

(9) To provide incident command system guidelines for state agencies and local emergency response organizations; and

(10) Whenever, in the opinion of the Governor or his designee, an employee of a state or local public safety agency responding to a disaster has suffered an extreme personal or family hardship in the affected area, such as the destruction of a personal residence or the existence of living conditions that imperil the health and safety of an immediate family member of the employee, the Governor may direct the Comptroller of the Commonwealth to issue war-

rants not to exceed $2,500 per month, for up to three calendar months, to the employee to assist the employee with the hardship.

History.
1973, c. 260; 1974, c. 4; 1975, c. 11; 1981, c. 116; 1990, c. 95; 1997, c. 893; 2000, c. 309; 2004, cc. 773, 1021; 2006, c. 140; 2007, cc. 729, 742; 2008, cc. 121, 157.

§ 44-146.17:1. Transmittal to General Assembly of rules, regulations, and orders.

The Governor shall cause copies of any order, rule, or regulation proclaimed and published by him pursuant to § 44-146.17 to be transmitted forthwith to each member of the General Assembly.

History.
1981, c. 160.

§ 44-146.17:2. Annual statewide drill.

The Governor shall conduct an annual statewide drill on response to a large-scale disaster including, but not limited to, electrical power outages. Such drill shall include the participation of local governments, affected state agencies, public utilities, law-enforcement agencies, and other entities as determined by the Governor. The Governor shall submit a report to the General Assembly on the results of the drill by November 30 of each year. The report shall be delivered to the chairs of the House Committee on Militia, Police and Public Safety and the Senate Committee on General Laws.

History.
2004, c. 430.

§ 44-146.18. Department of Emergency Services continued as Department of Emergency Management; administration and operational control; coordinator and other personnel; powers and duties.

A. The State Office of Emergency Services is continued and shall hereafter be known as the Department of Emergency Management. Wherever the words "State Department of Emergency Services" are used in any law of the Commonwealth, they shall mean the Department of Emergency Management. During a declared emergency this Department shall revert to the operational control of the Governor. The Department shall have a coordinator who shall be appointed by and serve at the pleasure of the Governor and also serve as State Emergency Planning Director. The Department shall employ the professional, technical, secretarial, and clerical employees necessary for the performance of its functions.

B. The Department of Emergency Management shall in the administration of emergency services and disaster preparedness programs:

1. In coordination with political subdivisions and state agencies, ensure that the Commonwealth has up-to-date assessments and preparedness plans to prevent, respond to and recover from all disasters including acts of terrorism;

2. Conduct a statewide emergency management assessment in cooperation with political subdivisions, private industry and other public and private entities deemed vital to preparedness, public safety and security. The assessment shall include a review of emergency response plans, which include the variety of hazards, natural and man-made. The assessment shall be updated annually;

3. Submit to the Governor and to the General Assembly, no later than the first day of each regular session of the General Assembly, an annual executive summary and report on the status of emergency management response plans throughout the Commonwealth and other measures taken or recommended to prevent, respond to and recover from disasters, including acts of terrorism. This report shall be made available to the Division of Legislative Automated Systems for the processing of legislative documents and reports. Information submitted in accordance with the procedures set forth in subdivision 4 of § 2.2-3705.2 shall not be disclosed unless:

a. It is requested by law-enforcement authorities in furtherance of an official investigation or the prosecution of a criminal act;

b. The agency holding the record is served with a proper judicial order; or

c. The agency holding the record has obtained written consent to release the information from the Department of Emergency Management;

4. Promulgate plans and programs that are conducive to adequate disaster mitigation preparedness, response and recovery programs;

5. Prepare and maintain a State Emergency Operations Plan for disaster response and recovery operations that assigns primary and support responsibilities for basic emergency services functions to state agencies, organizations and personnel as appropriate;

6. Coordinate and administer disaster mitigation, preparedness, response and recovery plans and programs with the proponent federal, state and local government agencies and related groups;

7. Provide guidance and assistance to state agencies and units of local government in developing and maintaining emergency management and continuity of operations (COOP) programs, plans and systems;

8. Make necessary recommendations to agencies of the federal, state, or local governments on preventive and preparedness measures designed to eliminate or reduce disasters and their impact;

9. Determine requirements of the Commonwealth and its political subdivisions for those necessities needed in the event of a declared emergency which are not otherwise readily available;

10. Assist state agencies and political subdivisions in establishing and operating training pro-

grams and programs of public information and education regarding emergency services and disaster preparedness activities;

11. Consult with the Board of Education regarding the development and revision of a model school crisis and emergency management plan for the purpose of assisting public schools in establishing, operating, and maintaining emergency services and disaster preparedness activities;

12. **(Effective until October 1, 2016)** Consult with the State Council of Higher Education in the development and revision of a model institutional crisis and emergency management plan for the purpose of assisting public and private two-year and four-year institutions of higher education in establishing, operating, and maintaining emergency services and disaster preparedness activities and, as needed, in developing an institutional crisis and emergency management plan pursuant to § 23-9.2:9;

12. **(Effective October 1, 2016)** Consult with the State Council of Higher Education in the development and revision of a model institutional crisis and emergency management plan for the purpose of assisting public and private two-year and four-year institutions of higher education in establishing, operating, and maintaining emergency services and disaster preparedness activities and, as needed, in developing an institutional crisis and emergency management plan pursuant to § 23.1-804;

13. Develop standards, provide guidance and encourage the maintenance of local and state agency emergency operations plans, which shall include the requirement for a provision that the Department of Criminal Justice Services and the Virginia Criminal Injuries Compensation Fund be contacted immediately to deploy assistance in the event of an emergency as defined in the emergency response plan when there are victims as defined in § 19.2-11.01. The Department of Criminal Justice Services and the Virginia Criminal Injuries Compensation Fund shall be the lead coordinating agencies for those individuals determined to be victims, and the plan shall also contain current contact information for both agencies;

14. Prepare, maintain, coordinate or implement emergency resource management plans and programs with federal, state and local government agencies and related groups, and make such surveys of industries, resources, and facilities within the Commonwealth, both public and private, as are necessary to carry out the purposes of this chapter;

15. Coordinate with the federal government and any public or private agency or entity in achieving any purpose of this chapter and in implementing programs for disaster prevention, mitigation, preparation, response, and recovery;

16. Establish guidelines pursuant to § 44-146.28, and administer payments to eligible applicants as authorized by the Governor;

17. Coordinate and be responsible for the receipt, evaluation, and dissemination of emergency services intelligence pertaining to all probable hazards affecting the Commonwealth;

18. Coordinate intelligence activities relating to terrorism with the Department of State Police; and

19. Develop an emergency response plan to address the needs of individuals with household pets and service animals in the event of a disaster and assist and coordinate with local agencies in developing an emergency response plan for household pets and service animals.

The Department of Emergency Management shall ensure that all such plans, assessments, and programs required by this subsection include specific preparedness for, and response to, disasters resulting from electromagnetic pulses and geomagnetic disturbances.

C. The Department of Emergency Management shall during a period of impending emergency or declared emergency be responsible for:

1. The receipt, evaluation, and dissemination of intelligence pertaining to an impending or actual disaster;

2. Providing facilities from which state agencies and supporting organizations may conduct emergency operations;

3. Providing an adequate communications and warning system capable of notifying all political subdivisions in the Commonwealth of an impending disaster within a reasonable time;

4. Establishing and maintaining liaison with affected political subdivisions;

5. Determining requirements for disaster relief and recovery assistance;

6. Coordinating disaster response actions of federal, state and volunteer relief agencies;

7. Coordinating and providing guidance and assistance to affected political subdivisions to ensure orderly and timely response to and recovery from disaster effects.

D. The Department of Emergency Management shall be provided the necessary facilities and equipment needed to perform its normal day-to-day activities and coordinate disaster-related activities of the various federal, state, and other agencies during a state of emergency declaration by the Governor or following a major disaster declaration by the President.

E. The Department of Emergency Management is authorized to enter into all contracts and agreements necessary or incidental to performance of any of its duties stated in this section or otherwise assigned to it by law, including contracts with the United States, other states, agencies and government subdivisions of the Commonwealth, and other appropriate public and private entities.

F. The Department of Emergency Management shall encourage private industries whose goods and services are deemed vital to the public good to provide annually updated preparedness assessments to the local coordinator of emergency management on or before April 1 of each year, to facilitate overall Commonwealth preparedness. For the purposes of this section, "private industry" means companies, private hospitals, and other businesses or organizations deemed by the State Coordinator of Emergency Management to be essential to the public safety and well-being of the citizens of the Commonwealth.

G. The Department of Emergency Management shall establish a Coordinator of Search and Rescue. Powers and duties of the Coordinator shall include:

1. Coordinating the search and rescue function of the Department of Emergency Management;

2. Coordinating with local, state, and federal agencies involved in search and rescue;

3. Coordinating the activities of search and rescue organizations involved in search and rescue;

4. Maintaining a register of search and rescue certifications, training, and responses;

5. Establishing a memorandum of understanding with the Virginia Search and Rescue Council and its respective member agencies regarding search and rescue efforts;

6. Providing on-scene search and rescue coordination when requested by an authorized person;

7. Providing specialized search and rescue training to police, fire-rescue, EMS, emergency managers, volunteer search and rescue responders, and others who might have a duty to respond to a search and rescue emergency;

8. Gathering and maintaining statistics on search and rescue in the Commonwealth;

9. Compiling, maintaining, and making available an inventory of search and rescue resources available in the Commonwealth;

10. Periodically reviewing search and rescue cases and developing best professional practices; and

11. Providing an annual report to the Secretary of Public Safety and Homeland Security on the current readiness of Virginia's search and rescue efforts.

Nothing in this chapter shall be construed as authorizing the Department of Emergency Management to take direct operational responsibilities from local, state, or federal law enforcement in the course of search and rescue or missing person cases.

History.

1973, c. 260; 1974, c. 4; 1975, c. 11; 1979, c. 193; 1984, c. 720; 1985, cc. 443, 447; 1997, c. 893; 2000, c. 309; 2001, c. 841; 2003, c. 622; 2004, c. 690; 2005, cc. 165, 490; 2007, c. 902; 2008, cc. 450, 526; 2009, cc. 222, 269; 2012, c. 418; 2015, cc. 97, 205, 223.

§ 44-146.18:1. Virginia Disaster Response Funds disbursements; reimbursements.

There is hereby created a nonlapsing revolving fund which shall be maintained as a separate special fund account within the state treasury, and administered by the Coordinator of Emergency Management, consistent with the purposes of this chapter. All expenses, costs, and judgments recovered pursuant to this section, and all moneys received as reimbursement in accordance with applicable provisions of federal law, shall be paid into the fund. Additionally, an annual appropriation to the fund from the general fund or other unrestricted nongeneral fund, in an amount determined by the Governor, may be authorized to carry out the purposes of this chapter. All recoveries from occurrences prior to March 10, 1983, and otherwise qualifying under this section, received subsequent to March 10, 1983, shall be paid into the fund. No moneys shall be credited to the balance in the fund until they have been received by the fund. An accounting of moneys received and disbursed shall be kept and furnished to the Governor or the General Assembly upon request.

Disbursements from the fund may be made for the following purposes and no others:

1. For costs and expenses, including, but not limited to personnel, administrative, and equipment costs and expenses directly incurred by the Department of Emergency Management or by any other state agency or political subdivision or other entity, acting at the direction of the Coordinator of Emergency Management, in and for preventing or alleviating damage, loss, hardship, or suffering caused by emergencies, resource shortages, or disasters; and

2. For procurement, maintenance, and replenishment of materials, equipment, and supplies, in such quantities and at such location as the Coordinator of Emergency Management may deem necessary to protect the public peace, health, and safety and to preserve the lives and property and economic well-being of the people of the Commonwealth; and

3. For costs and expenses incurred by the Department of Emergency Management or by any other state agency or political subdivision or other entity, acting at the direction of the Coordinator of Emergency Management, in the recovery from the effects of a disaster or in the restoration of public property or facilities.

The Coordinator of Emergency Management shall promptly seek reimbursement from any person causing or contributing to an emergency or disaster for all sums disbursed from the fund for the protection, relief and recovery from loss or damage caused by such person. In the event a request for reimbursement is not paid within 60 days of receipt of a written demand, the claim shall be referred to the Attorney General for collection. The Coordinator of Emergency Management shall be allowed to recover all legal and court costs and other expenses incident to such actions for collection. The Coordinator is authorized to recover any sums incurred by any other state agency or political subdivision acting at the direction of the Coordinator as provided in this paragraph.

History.

1983, c. 48; 2000, c. 309; 2008, cc. 121, 157.

§ 44-146.18:2. Authority of Coordinator of Emergency Management in undeclared emergency.

In an emergency which does not warrant a gubernatorial declaration of a state of emergency, the Coordinator of Emergency Management, after consultation with and approval of the Secretary of Public Safety and Homeland Security, may enter into contracts and incur obligations necessary to prevent or alleviate damage, loss, hardship, or suffering caused by such emergency and to protect the health and safety of persons and property. In exercising the powers vested by this section, the Coordinator may proceed without regard to normal procedures pertaining to entering into contracts, incurring of obligations, rental of equipment, purchase of supplies and materials, and expenditure of public funds; however, mandatory constitutional requirements shall not be disregarded.

History.
1985, c. 443; 1990, cc. 1, 317; 2000, c. 309; 2014, cc. 115, 490.

§ 44-146.18:3. First informer broadcasters; coordination with Department of Emergency Management.

A. For purposes of this section, unless the context requires otherwise, "first informer" means the critical radio or television personnel of a radio or television broadcast station engaged in (i) the process of broadcasting; (ii) the maintenance or repair of broadcast station equipment, transmitters, and generators; or (iii) the transportation of fuel for generators of broadcast stations.

B. Unless it is shown to endanger public safety or inhibit recovery efforts, or is otherwise prohibited by state or federal law, state and local government agencies shall permit first informer radio or television personnel with proper identification cards to access their broadcasting station within any area declared a state emergency area by the Governor for the purpose of provision of news, public service and public safety information and repairing or resupplying their facility or equipment.

First informer identification cards shall be issued by the Virginia Association of Broadcasters. A list of those first informers who have been issued identification cards shall be furnished to the Virginia Department of Emergency Management and the Secretary of Veterans and Defense Affairs by the Virginia Association of Broadcasters prior to December 30 of each year.

C. Nothing in this section shall be construed to limit or impair the right or ability of any news organization or its personnel to gather and report the news.

History.
2014, c. 561.

§ 44-146.19. Powers and duties of political subdivisions.

A. Each political subdivision within the Commonwealth shall be within the jurisdiction of and served by the Department of Emergency Management and be responsible for local disaster mitigation, preparedness, response and recovery. Each political subdivision shall maintain in accordance with state disaster preparedness plans and programs an agency of emergency management which, except as otherwise provided under this chapter, has jurisdiction over and services the entire political subdivision.

B. Each political subdivision shall have a director of emergency management who, after the term of the person presently serving in this capacity has expired and in the absence of an executive order by the Governor, shall be the following:

1. In the case of a city, the mayor or city manager, who shall appoint a coordinator of emergency management with consent of council;

2. In the case of a county, a member of the board of supervisors selected by the board or the chief administrative officer for the county, who shall appoint a coordinator of emergency management with the consent of the governing body;

3. A coordinator of emergency management shall be appointed by the council of any town to ensure integration of its organization into the county emergency management organization;

4. In the case of the Town of Chincoteague and of towns with a population in excess of 5,000 having an emergency management organization separate from that of the county, the mayor or town manager shall appoint a coordinator of emergency services with consent of council;

5. In Smyth County and in York County, the chief administrative officer for the county shall appoint a director of emergency management, with the consent of the governing body, who shall appoint a coordinator of emergency management with the consent of the governing body.

C. Whenever the Governor has declared a state of emergency, each political subdivision within the disaster area may, under the supervision and control of the Governor or his designated representative, control, restrict, allocate or regulate the use, sale, production and distribution of food, fuel, clothing and other commodities, materials, goods, services and resource systems which fall only within the boundaries of that jurisdiction and which do not impact systems affecting adjoining or other political subdivisions, enter into contracts and incur obligations necessary to combat such threatened or actual disaster, protect the health and safety of persons and property and provide emergency assistance to the victims of such disaster. In exercising the powers vested under this section, under the supervision and control of the Governor, the political subdivision may proceed without regard to time-consuming procedures and formalities prescribed by law (except mandatory constitutional requirements) pertaining to the performance of public work, entering into contracts, incurring of obligations, employment of temporary workers, rental of equipment, purchase of supplies and materials, levying of taxes, and appropriation and expenditure of public funds.

D. The director of each local organization for emergency management may, in collaboration with (i) other public and private agencies within the Commonwealth or (ii) other states or localities within other states, develop or cause to be developed mutual aid arrangements for reciprocal assistance in case of a disaster too great to be dealt with unassisted. Such arrangements shall be consistent with state plans and programs and it shall be the duty of each local organization for emergency management to render assistance in accordance with the provisions of such mutual aid arrangements.

E. Each local and interjurisdictional agency shall prepare and keep current a local or interjurisdictional emergency operations plan for its area. The plan shall include, but not be limited to, responsibilities of all local agencies and shall establish a chain of command, and a provision that the Department of Criminal Justice Services and the Virginia Criminal Injuries Compensation Fund shall be contacted immediately to deploy assistance in the event of an emergency as defined in the emergency response plan when there are victims as defined in § 19.2-11.01. The Department of Criminal Justice Services and the Virginia Criminal Injuries Compensation Fund shall be the lead coordinating agencies for those individuals determined to be victims, and the plan shall also contain current contact information for both agencies. Every four years, each local and interjurisdictional agency shall conduct a comprehensive review and revision of its emergency operations plan to ensure that the plan remains current, and the revised plan shall be formally adopted by the locality's governing body. In the case of an interjurisdictional agency, the plan shall be formally adopted by the governing body of each of the localities encompassed by the agency. Each political subdivision having a nuclear power station or other nuclear facility within 10 miles of its boundaries shall, if so directed by the Department of Emergency Management, prepare and keep current an appropriate emergency plan for its area for response to nuclear accidents at such station or facility.

F. All political subdivisions shall provide an annually updated emergency management assessment to the State Coordinator of Emergency Management on or before July 1 of each year.

G. By July 1, 2005, all localities with a population greater than 50,000 shall establish an alert and warning plan for the dissemination of adequate and timely warning to the public in the event of an emergency or threatened disaster. The governing body of the locality, in consultation with its local emergency management organization, shall amend its local emergency operations plan that may include rules for the operation of its alert and warning system, to include sirens, Emergency Alert System (EAS), NOAA Weather Radios, or other personal notification systems, amateur radio operators, or any combination thereof.

H. Localities that have established an agency of emergency management shall have authority to require the review of, and suggest amendments to, the emergency plans of nursing homes, assisted living facilities, adult day care centers, and child day care centers that are located within the locality.

History.

1973, c. 260; 1974, c. 4; 1975, c. 11; 1978, c. 495; 1982, c. 5; 1990, cc. 404, 945; 1993, cc. 621, 671, 781; 2000, c. 309; 2003, c. 622; 2004, c. 302; 2005, cc. 6, 205; 2006, c. 138; 2007, cc. 97, 129, 138; 2009, cc. 222, 269; 2012, c. 418.

TITLE 46.2.

MOTOR VEHICLES.

SUBTITLE I. GENERAL PROVISIONS; DEPARTMENT OF MOTOR VEHICLES.

CHAPTER 1. GENERAL PROVISIONS.

§ 46.2-100. Definitions.

As used in this title, unless the context requires a different meaning:

"All-terrain vehicle" means a motor vehicle having three or more wheels that is powered by a motor and is manufactured for off-highway use. "All-terrain vehicle" does not include four-wheeled vehicles commonly known as "go-carts" that have low centers of gravity and are typically used in racing on relatively level surfaces, nor does the term include any riding lawn mower.

"Antique motor vehicle" means every motor vehicle, as defined in this section, which was actually manufactured or designated by the manufacturer as a model manufactured in a calendar year not less than 25 years prior to January 1 of each calendar year and is owned solely as a collector's item.

"Antique trailer" means every trailer or semitrailer, as defined in this section, that was actually manufactured or designated by the manufacturer as a model manufactured in a calendar year not less than 25 years prior to January 1 of each calendar year and is owned solely as a collector's item.

"Autocycle" means a three-wheeled motor vehicle that has a steering wheel and seating that does not require the operator to straddle or sit astride and is

manufactured to comply with federal safety requirements for motorcycles. Except as otherwise provided, an autocycle shall not be deemed to be a motorcycle.

"Automobile or watercraft transporters" means any tractor truck, lowboy, vehicle, or combination, including vehicles or combinations that transport motor vehicles or watercraft on their power unit, designed and used exclusively for the transportation of motor vehicles or watercraft.

"Bicycle" means a device propelled solely by human power, upon which a person may ride either on or astride a regular seat attached thereto, having two or more wheels in tandem, including children's bicycles, except a toy vehicle intended for use by young children. For purposes of Chapter 8 (§ 46.2-800 et seq.), a bicycle shall be a vehicle while operated on the highway.

"Bicycle lane" means that portion of a roadway designated by signs and/or pavement markings for the preferential use of bicycles, electric power-assisted bicycles, and mopeds.

"Business district" means the territory contiguous to a highway where 75 percent or more of the property contiguous to a highway, on either side of the highway, for a distance of 300 feet or more along the highway, is occupied by land and buildings actually in use for business purposes.

"Camping trailer" means every vehicle that has collapsible sides and contains sleeping quarters but may or may not contain bathing and cooking facilities and is designed to be drawn by a motor vehicle.

"Cancel" or *"cancellation"* means that the document or privilege cancelled has been annulled or terminated because of some error, defect, or ineligibility, but the cancellation is without prejudice and reapplication may be made at any time after cancellation.

"Chauffeur" means every person employed for the principal purpose of driving a motor vehicle and every person who drives a motor vehicle while in use as a public or common carrier of persons or property.

"Circular intersection" means an intersection that has an island, generally circular in design, located in the center of the intersection, where all vehicles pass to the right of the island. Circular intersections include roundabouts, rotaries, and traffic circles.

"Commission" means the State Corporation Commission.

"Commissioner" means the Commissioner of the Department of Motor Vehicles of the Commonwealth.

"Converted electric vehicle" means any motor vehicle, other than a motorcycle or autocycle, that has been modified subsequent to its manufacture to replace an internal combustion engine with an electric propulsion system. Such vehicles shall retain their original vehicle identification number, line-make, and model year. A converted electric vehicle shall not be deemed a "reconstructed vehicle" as defined in this section unless it has been materially altered from its original construction by the removal, addition, or substitution of new or used essential parts other than those required for the conversion to electric propulsion.

"Crosswalk" means that part of a roadway at an intersection included within the connections of the lateral lines of the sidewalks on opposite sides of the highway measured from the curbs or, in the absence of curbs, from the edges of the traversable roadway; or any portion of a roadway at an intersection or elsewhere distinctly indicated for pedestrian crossing by lines or other markings on the surface.

"Decal" means a device to be attached to a license plate that validates the license plate for a predetermined registration period.

"Department" means the Department of Motor Vehicles of the Commonwealth.

"Disabled parking license plate" means a license plate that displays the international symbol of access in the same size as the numbers and letters on the plate and in a color that contrasts with the background.

"Disabled veteran" means a veteran who (i) has either lost, or lost the use of, a leg, arm, or hand; (ii) is blind; or (iii) is permanently and totally disabled as certified by the U.S. Department of Veterans Affairs. A veteran shall be considered blind if he has a permanent impairment of both eyes to the following extent: central visual acuity of 20/200 or less in the better eye, with corrective lenses, or central visual acuity of more than 20/200, if there is a field defect in which the peripheral field has contracted to such an extent that the widest diameter of visual field subtends an angular distance no greater than 20 degrees in the better eye.

"Driver's license" means any license, including a commercial driver's license as defined in the Virginia Commercial Driver's License Act (§ 46.2-341.1 et seq.), issued under the laws of the Commonwealth authorizing the operation of a motor vehicle.

"Electric personal assistive mobility device" means a self-balancing two-nontandem-wheeled device that is designed to transport only one person and powered by an electric propulsion system that limits the device's maximum speed to 15 miles per hour or less. For purposes of Chapter 8 (§ 46.2-800 et seq.), an electric personal assistive mobility device shall be a vehicle when operated on a highway.

"Electric power-assisted bicycle" means a vehicle that travels on not more than three wheels in contact with the ground and is equipped with (i) pedals that allow propulsion by human power and (ii) an electric motor with an input of no more than 1,000 watts that reduces the pedal effort required of the rider. For the purposes of Chapter 8 (§ 46.2-800 et seq.), an electric power-assisted bicycle shall be a vehicle when operated on a highway.

"Essential parts" means all integral parts and body parts, the removal, alteration, or substitution of which will tend to conceal the identity of a vehicle.

"Farm tractor" means every motor vehicle designed and used as a farm, agricultural, or horticul-

tural implement for drawing plows, mowing machines, and other farm, agricultural, or horticultural machinery and implements, including self-propelled mowers designed and used for mowing lawns.

"Farm utility vehicle" means a vehicle that is powered by a motor and is designed for off-road use and is used as a farm, agricultural, or horticultural service vehicle, generally having four or more wheels, bench seating for the operator and a passenger, a steering wheel for control, and a cargo bed. "Farm utility vehicle" does not include pickup or panel trucks, golf carts, low-speed vehicles, or riding lawn mowers.

"Federal safety requirements" means applicable provisions of 49 U.S.C. § 30101 et seq. and all administrative regulations and policies adopted pursuant thereto.

"Financial responsibility" means the ability to respond in damages for liability thereafter incurred arising out of the ownership, maintenance, use, or operation of a motor vehicle, in the amounts provided for in § 46.2-472.

"Foreign market vehicle" means any motor vehicle originally manufactured outside the United States, which was not manufactured in accordance with 49 U.S.C. § 30101 et seq. and the policies and regulations adopted pursuant to that Act, and for which a Virginia title or registration is sought.

"Foreign vehicle" means every motor vehicle, trailer, or semitrailer that is brought into the Commonwealth otherwise than in the ordinary course of business by or through a manufacturer or dealer and that has not been registered in the Commonwealth.

"Golf cart" means a self-propelled vehicle that is designed to transport persons playing golf and their equipment on a golf course.

"Governing body" means the board of supervisors of a county, council of a city, or council of a town, as context may require.

"Gross weight" means the aggregate weight of a vehicle or combination of vehicles and the load thereon.

"Highway" means the entire width between the boundary lines of every way or place open to the use of the public for purposes of vehicular travel in the Commonwealth, including the streets and alleys, and, for law-enforcement purposes, (i) the entire width between the boundary lines of all private roads or private streets that have been specifically designated "highways" by an ordinance adopted by the governing body of the county, city, or town in which such private roads or streets are located and (ii) the entire width between the boundary lines of every way or place used for purposes of vehicular travel on any property owned, leased, or controlled by the United States government and located in the Commonwealth.

"Intersection" means (i) the area embraced within the prolongation or connection of the lateral curblines or, if none, then the lateral boundary lines of the roadways of two highways that join one another at, or approximately at, right angles, or the area within which vehicles traveling on different highways joining at any other angle may come in conflict; (ii) where a highway includes two roadways 30 feet or more apart, then every crossing of each roadway of such divided highway by an intersecting highway shall be regarded as a separate intersection, in the event such intersecting highway also includes two roadways 30 feet or more apart, then every crossing of two roadways of such highways shall be regarded as a separate intersection; or (iii) for purposes only of authorizing installation of traffic-control devices, every crossing of a highway or street at grade by a pedestrian crosswalk.

"Lane-use control signal" means a signal face displaying indications to permit or prohibit the use of specific lanes of a roadway or to indicate the impending prohibition of such use.

"Law-enforcement officer" means any officer authorized to direct or regulate traffic or to make arrests for violations of this title or local ordinances authorized by law. For the purposes of access to law-enforcement databases regarding motor vehicle registration and ownership only, "law-enforcement officer" also includes city and county commissioners of the revenue and treasurers, together with their duly designated deputies and employees, when such officials are actually engaged in the enforcement of §§ 46.2-752, 46.2-753, and 46.2-754 and local ordinances enacted thereunder.

"License plate" means a device containing letters, numerals, or a combination of both, attached to a motor vehicle, trailer, or semitrailer to indicate that the vehicle is properly registered with the Department.

"Light" means a device for producing illumination or the illumination produced by the device.

"Low-speed vehicle" means any four-wheeled electrically powered or gas-powered vehicle, except a motor vehicle or low-speed vehicle that is used exclusively for agricultural or horticultural purposes or a golf cart, whose maximum speed is greater than 20 miles per hour but not greater than 25 miles per hour and is manufactured to comply with safety standards contained in Title 49 of the Code of Federal Regulations, § 571.500.

"Manufactured home" means a structure subject to federal regulation, transportable in one or more sections, which in the traveling mode is eight body feet or more in width or 40 body feet or more in length, or, when erected on site, is 320 or more square feet, and which is built on a permanent chassis and designed to be used as a dwelling with or without a permanent foundation when connected to the required utilities, and includes the plumbing, heating, air conditioning, and electrical systems contained therein.

"Moped" means every vehicle that travels on not more than three wheels in contact with the ground that (i) has a seat that is no less than 24 inches in height, measured from the middle of the seat per-

pendicular to the ground; (ii) has a gasoline, electric, or hybrid motor that (a) displaces 50 cubic centimeters or less or (b) has an input of 1500 watts or less; (iii) is power-driven, with or without pedals that allow propulsion by human power; and (iv) is not operated at speeds in excess of 35 miles per hour. For purposes of this title, a moped shall be a motorcycle when operated at speeds in excess of 35 miles per hour. For purposes of Chapter 8 (§ 46.2-800 et seq.), a moped shall be a vehicle while operated on a highway.

"Motor-driven cycle" means every motorcycle that has a gasoline engine that (i) displaces less than 150 cubic centimeters; (ii) has a seat less than 24 inches in height, measured from the middle of the seat perpendicular to the ground; and (iii) has no manufacturer-issued vehicle identification number.

"Motor home" means every private motor vehicle with a normal seating capacity of not more than 10 persons, including the driver, designed primarily for use as living quarters for human beings.

"Motor vehicle" means every vehicle as defined in this section that is self-propelled or designed for self-propulsion except as otherwise provided in this title. Any structure designed, used, or maintained primarily to be loaded on or affixed to a motor vehicle to provide a mobile dwelling, sleeping place, office, or commercial space shall be considered a part of a motor vehicle. Except as otherwise provided, for the purposes of this title, any device herein defined as a bicycle, electric personal assistive mobility device, electric power-assisted bicycle, or moped shall be deemed not to be a motor vehicle.

"Motorcycle" means every motor vehicle designed to travel on not more than three wheels in contact with the ground and is capable of traveling at speeds in excess of 35 miles per hour. "Motorcycle" does not include any "autocycle," "electric personal assistive mobility device," "electric power-assisted bicycle," "farm tractor," "golf cart," "moped," "motorized skateboard or foot-scooter," "utility vehicle," or "wheelchair or wheelchair conveyance" as defined in this section.

"Motorized skateboard or foot-scooter" means every vehicle, regardless of the number of its wheels in contact with the ground, that (i) has no seat, but is designed to be stood upon by the operator, (ii) has no manufacturer-issued vehicle identification number, and (iii) is powered by an electric motor having an input of no more than 1,000 watts or a gasoline engine that displaces less than 36 cubic centimeters. "Motorized skateboard or foot-scooter" includes vehicles with or without handlebars but does not include "electric personal assistive mobility devices."

"Nonresident" means every person who is not domiciled in the Commonwealth, except: (i) any foreign corporation that is authorized to do business in the Commonwealth by the State Corporation Commission shall be a resident of the Commonwealth for the purpose of this title; in the case of corporations incorporated in the Commonwealth but doing business outside the Commonwealth, only such principal place of business or branches located within the Commonwealth shall be dealt with as residents of the Commonwealth; (ii) a person who becomes engaged in a gainful occupation in the Commonwealth for a period exceeding 60 days shall be a resident for the purposes of this title except for the purposes of Chapter 3 (§ 46.2-300 et seq.); (iii) a person, other than (a) a nonresident student as defined in this section or (b) a person who is serving a full-time church service or proselyting mission of not more than 36 months and who is not gainfully employed, who has actually resided in the Commonwealth for a period of six months, whether employed or not, or who has registered a motor vehicle, listing an address in the Commonwealth in the application for registration, shall be deemed a resident for the purposes of this title, except for the purposes of the Virginia Commercial Driver's License Act (§ 46.2-341.1 et seq.).

"Nonresident student" means every nonresident person who is enrolled as a full-time student in an accredited institution of learning in the Commonwealth and who is not gainfully employed.

"Off-road motorcycle" means every motorcycle designed exclusively for off-road use by an individual rider with not more than two wheels in contact with the ground. Except as otherwise provided in this chapter, for the purposes of this chapter off-road motorcycles shall be deemed to be "motorcycles."

"Operation or use for rent or for hire, for the transportation of passengers, or as a property carrier for compensation," and *"business of transporting persons or property"* mean any owner or operator of any motor vehicle, trailer, or semitrailer operating over the highways in the Commonwealth who accepts or receives compensation for the service, directly or indirectly; but these terms do not mean a "truck lessor" as defined in this section and do not include persons or businesses that receive compensation for delivering a product that they themselves sell or produce, where a separate charge is made for delivery of the product or the cost of delivery is included in the sale price of the product, but where the person or business does not derive all or a substantial portion of its income from the transportation of persons or property except as part of a sales transaction.

"Operator" or *"driver"* means every person who either (i) drives or is in actual physical control of a motor vehicle on a highway or (ii) is exercising control over or steering a vehicle being towed by a motor vehicle.

"Owner" means a person who holds the legal title to a vehicle; however, if a vehicle is the subject of an agreement for its conditional sale or lease with the right of purchase on performance of the conditions stated in the agreement and with an immediate right of possession vested in the conditional vendee or lessee or if a mortgagor of a vehicle is entitled to possession, then the conditional vendee or lessee or

mortgagor shall be the owner for the purpose of this title. In all such instances when the rent paid by the lessee includes charges for services of any nature or when the lease does not provide that title shall pass to the lessee on payment of the rent stipulated, the lessor shall be regarded as the owner of the vehicle, and the vehicle shall be subject to such requirements of this title as are applicable to vehicles operated for compensation. A "truck lessor" as defined in this section shall be regarded as the owner, and his vehicles shall be subject to such requirements of this title as are applicable to vehicles of private carriers.

"Passenger car" means every motor vehicle other than a motorcycle or autocycle designed and used primarily for the transportation of no more than 10 persons, including the driver.

"Payment device" means any credit card as defined in 15 U.S.C. § 1602 (k) or any "accepted card or other means of access" set forth in 15 U.S.C. § 1693a (1). For the purposes of this title, this definition shall also include a card that enables a person to pay for transactions through the use of value stored on the card itself.

"Pickup or panel truck" means (i) every motor vehicle designed for the transportation of property and having a registered gross weight of 7,500 pounds or less or (ii) every motor vehicle registered for personal use, designed to transport property on its own structure independent of any other vehicle, and having a registered gross weight in excess of 7,500 pounds but not in excess of 10,000 pounds.

"Private road or driveway" means every way in private ownership and used for vehicular travel by the owner and those having express or implied permission from the owner, but not by other persons.

"Reconstructed vehicle" means every vehicle of a type required to be registered under this title materially altered from its original construction by the removal, addition, or substitution of new or used essential parts. Such vehicles, at the discretion of the Department, shall retain their original vehicle identification number, line-make, and model year. Except as otherwise provided in this title, this definition shall not include a "converted electric vehicle" as defined in this section.

"Replica vehicle" means every vehicle of a type required to be registered under this title not fully constructed by a licensed manufacturer but either constructed or assembled from components. Such components may be from a single vehicle, multiple vehicles, a kit, parts, or fabricated components. The kit may be made up of "major components" as defined in § 46.2-1600, a full body, or a full chassis, or a combination of these parts. The vehicle shall resemble a vehicle of distinctive name, line-make, model, or type as produced by a licensed manufacturer or manufacturer no longer in business and is not a reconstructed or specially constructed vehicle as herein defined.

"Residence district" means the territory contiguous to a highway, not comprising a business district, where 75 percent or more of the property abutting such highway, on either side of the highway, for a distance of 300 feet or more along the highway consists of land improved for dwelling purposes, or is occupied by dwellings, or consists of land or buildings in use for business purposes, or consists of territory zoned residential or territory in residential subdivisions created under Chapter 22 (§ 15.2-2200 et seq.) of Title 15.2.

"Revoke" or *"revocation"* means that the document or privilege revoked is not subject to renewal or restoration except through reapplication after the expiration of the period of revocation.

"Roadway" means that portion of a highway improved, designed, or ordinarily used for vehicular travel, exclusive of the shoulder. A highway may include two or more roadways if divided by a physical barrier or barriers or an unpaved area.

"Safety zone" means the area officially set apart within a roadway for the exclusive use of pedestrians and that is protected or is so marked or indicated by plainly visible signs.

"School bus" means any motor vehicle, other than a station wagon, automobile, truck, or commercial bus, which is: (i) designed and used primarily for the transportation of pupils to and from public, private or religious schools, or used for the transportation of the mentally or physically handicapped to and from a sheltered workshop; (ii) painted yellow and bears the words "School Bus" in black letters of a specified size on front and rear; and (iii) is equipped with warning devices prescribed in § 46.2-1090. A yellow school bus may have a white roof provided such vehicle is painted in accordance with regulations promulgated by the Department of Education.

"Semitrailer" means every vehicle of the trailer type so designed and used in conjunction with a motor vehicle that some part of its own weight and that of its own load rests on or is carried by another vehicle.

"Shared-use path" means a bikeway that is physically separated from motorized vehicular traffic by an open space or barrier and is located either within the highway right-of-way or within a separate right-of-way. Shared-use paths may also be used by pedestrians, skaters, users of wheel chairs or wheel chair conveyances, joggers, and other nonmotorized users.

"Shoulder" means that part of a highway between the portion regularly traveled by vehicular traffic and the lateral curbline or ditch.

"Sidewalk" means the portion of a street between the curb lines, or the lateral lines of a roadway, and the adjacent property lines, intended for use by pedestrians.

"Snowmobile" means a self-propelled vehicle designed to travel on snow or ice, steered by skis or runners, and supported in whole or in part by one or more skis, belts, or cleats.

"Special construction and forestry equipment" means any vehicle which is designed primarily for highway construction, highway maintenance, earth

moving, timber harvesting or other construction or forestry work and which is not designed for the transportation of persons or property on a public highway.

"Specially constructed vehicle" means any vehicle that was not originally constructed under a distinctive name, make, model, or type by a generally recognized manufacturer of vehicles and not a reconstructed vehicle as herein defined.

"Stinger-steered automobile or watercraft transporter" means an automobile or watercraft transporter configured as a semitrailer combination wherein the fifth wheel is located on a drop frame behind and below the rearmost axle of the power unit.

"Superintendent" means the Superintendent of the Department of State Police of the Commonwealth.

"Suspend" or *"suspension"* means that the document or privilege suspended has been temporarily withdrawn, but may be reinstated following the period of suspension unless it has expired prior to the end of the period of suspension.

"Tow truck" means a motor vehicle for hire (i) designed to lift, pull, or carry another vehicle by means of a hoist or other mechanical apparatus and (ii) having a manufacturer's gross vehicle weight rating of at least 10,000 pounds. "Tow truck" also includes vehicles designed with a ramp on wheels and a hydraulic lift with a capacity to haul or tow another vehicle, commonly referred to as "rollbacks." "Tow truck" does not include any "automobile or watercraft transporter," "stinger-steered automobile or watercraft transporter," or "tractor truck" as those terms are defined in this section.

"Towing and recovery operator" means a person engaged in the business of (i) removing disabled vehicles, parts of vehicles, their cargoes, and other objects to facilities for repair or safekeeping and (ii) restoring to the highway or other location where they either can be operated or removed to other locations for repair or safekeeping vehicles that have come to rest in places where they cannot be operated.

"Toy vehicle" means any motorized or propellant-driven device that has no manufacturer-issued vehicle identification number that is designed or used to carry any person or persons, on any number of wheels, bearings, glides, blades, runners, or a cushion of air. "Toy vehicle" does not include electric personal assistive mobility devices, electric power-assisted bicycles, mopeds, or motorcycles, nor does it include any nonmotorized or nonpropellant-driven devices such as bicycles, roller skates, or skateboards.

"Tractor truck" means every motor vehicle designed and used primarily for drawing other vehicles and not so constructed as to carry a load other than a part of the load and weight of the vehicle attached thereto.

"Traffic control device" means a sign, signal, marking, or other device used to regulate, warn, or guide traffic placed on, over, or adjacent to a street, highway, private road open to public travel, pedestrian facility, or shared-use path by authority of a public agency or official having jurisdiction, or in the case of a private road open to public travel, by authority of the private owner or private official having jurisdiction.

"Traffic infraction" means a violation of law punishable as provided in § 46.2-113, which is neither a felony nor a misdemeanor.

"Traffic lane" or *"lane"* means that portion of a roadway designed or designated to accommodate the forward movement of a single line of vehicles.

"Trailer" means every vehicle without motive power designed for carrying property or passengers wholly on its own structure and for being drawn by a motor vehicle, including manufactured homes.

"Truck" means every motor vehicle designed to transport property on its own structure independent of any other vehicle and having a registered gross weight in excess of 7,500 pounds. "Truck" does not include any pickup or panel truck.

"Truck lessor" means a person who holds the legal title to any motor vehicle, trailer, or semitrailer that is the subject of a bona fide written lease for a term of one year or more to another person, provided that: (i) neither the lessor nor the lessee is a common carrier by motor vehicle or restricted common carrier by motor vehicle or contract carrier by motor vehicle as defined in § 46.2-2000; (ii) the leased motor vehicle, trailer, or semitrailer is used exclusively for the transportation of property of the lessee; (iii) the lessor is not employed in any capacity by the lessee; (iv) the operator of the leased motor vehicle is a bona fide employee of the lessee and is not employed in any capacity by the lessor; and (v) a true copy of the lease, verified by affidavit of the lessor, is filed with the Commissioner.

"Utility vehicle" means a motor vehicle that is (i) designed for off-road use, (ii) powered by a motor, and (iii) used for general maintenance, security, agricultural, or horticultural purposes. "Utility vehicle" does not include riding lawn mowers.

"Vehicle" means every device in, on or by which any person or property is or may be transported or drawn on a highway, except devices moved by human power or used exclusively on stationary rails or tracks. For the purposes of Chapter 8 (§ 46.2-800 et seq.), bicycles, electric personal assistive mobility devices, electric power-assisted bicycles, and mopeds shall be vehicles while operated on a highway.

"Wheel chair or wheel chair conveyance" means a chair or seat equipped with wheels, typically used to provide mobility for persons who, by reason of physical disability, are otherwise unable to move about as pedestrians. "Wheel chair or wheel chair conveyance" includes both three-wheeled and four-wheeled devices. So long as it is operated only as provided in § 46.2-677, a self-propelled wheel chair or self-propelled wheel chair conveyance shall not be considered a motor vehicle.

History.

Code 1950, §§ 46-1, 46-169, 46-185, 46-186, 46-343; 1954, c. 59; 1958, cc. 501, 541, §§ 46.1-1, 46.1-161; 1964, c. 618; 1966, c. 643; 1968, cc. 285, 641, 653, 685; 1972, cc. 433, 609; 1974, c. 347; 1975, cc. 382, 426; 1976, c. 372; 1977, cc. 252, 585; 1978, cc. 36, 550, 605; 1979, c. 100; 1980, c. 51; 1981, c. 585; 1983, c. 386; 1984, cc. 404, 780; 1985, c. 447; 1986, cc. 72, 613; 1987, c. 151; 1988, cc. 107, 452, 865; 1989, cc. 645, 705, 727; 1990, cc. 45, 418; 1992, c. 98; 1993, c. 133; 1994, c. 866; 1996, cc. 943, 994; 1997, cc. 9, 186, 486, 783, 904; 1998, c. 888; 1999, cc. 67, 77; 2001, c. 834; 2002, cc. 214, 234, 254; 2003, cc. 29, 46; 2004, cc. 746, 796; 2005, cc. 310, 928; 2006, cc. 529, 538, 540, 874, 891, 896; 2007, cc. 209, 325, 366, 393; 2010, c. 135; 2011, c. 128; 2012, c. 177; 2013, cc. 128, 400, 783; 2014, cc. 53, 256; 2016, cc. 428, 500, 764.

§ 46.2-100.1. Certified mail; subsequent mail or notices may be sent by regular mail.

Whenever in this title the Commissioner or the Department is required to send any mail or notice by certified mail and such mail or notice is sent certified mail, return receipt requested, then any subsequent, identical mail or notice that is sent by the Commissioner or the Department may be sent by regular mail.

History.

2011, c. 566.

§ 46.2-101. Applicability of title to vehicles on certain toll roads and parking facilities.

This title shall apply to any vehicle and any person operating or owning a vehicle operated on any toll facility controlled by the Department of Transportation or any political subdivision of the Commonwealth.

This title shall also apply to any vehicle and any person operating or owning a vehicle operated on or in parking lots, parking garages, or other parking facilities owned, controlled, or leased by the Commonwealth or any of its agencies, instrumentalities, or political subdivisions.

History.

1958, c. 541, § 46.1-21; 1989, c. 727.

§ 46.2-102. Enforcement by law-enforcement officers; officers to be uniformed; officers to be paid fixed salaries.

State police officers and law-enforcement officers of every county, city, town, or other political subdivision of the Commonwealth shall enforce the provisions of this title punishable as felonies, misdemeanors, or traffic infractions. Additionally, notwithstanding § 52-22, state police officers may enforce local ordinances, adopted under subsection G of § 46.2-752, requiring the obtaining and displaying of local motor vehicle licenses. Fifty percent of the revenue collected from such enforcement shall be remitted by the locality to the Department of State Police and disposed of by the Department to cover its costs of operation. Every law-enforcement officer shall be uniformed at the time of the enforcement or shall display his badge or other sign of authority. All officers making arrests incident to the enforcement of this title shall be paid fixed salaries for their services and shall have no interest in, nor be permitted by law to accept the benefit of, any fine or fee resulting from the arrest or conviction of an offender against any provision of this title.

With the consent of the landowner, any such officer or other uniformed employee of the local law-enforcement agency may patrol the landowner's property to enforce state, county, city, or town motor vehicle registration and licensing requirements.

Any law-enforcement officer may patrol the streets and roads within subdivisions of real property or within land submitted to a horizontal property regime pursuant to Chapter 4.1 (§ 55-79.1 et seq.) or 4.2 (§ 55-79.39 et seq.) of Title 55, which streets and roads are maintained by the owners of the lots or parcels of land within the subdivision or the owners of condominium units within any horizontal property regime or any association of owners, on the request or with the consent of the owners or association of owners, to enforce the provisions of this title punishable as felonies, misdemeanors, or traffic infractions.

History.

Code 1950, § 46-14; 1958, c. 541, § 46.1-6; 1972, c. 700; 1975, c. 516; 1980, c. 523; 1989, c. 727; 1995, c. 132.

§ 46.2-103. Stopping vehicles for inspection or to secure information.

Except as prohibited by § 19.2-59, on his request or signal, any law-enforcement officer who is in uniform or displays his badge or other sign of authority may:

1. Stop any motor vehicle, trailer, or semitrailer to inspect its equipment, operation, manufacturer's serial or engine number; or
2. Stop any property-carrying motor vehicle, trailer, or semitrailer to inspect its contents or load or to obtain other necessary information.

Nothing in this section, however, shall be construed to authorize the establishment on any highway of police check-points where the only vehicles subject to inspection are motorcycles.

History.

Code 1950, § 46-16; 1958, c. 541, § 46.1-8; 1989, c. 727; 2012, c. 11.

§ 46.2-104. Possession of registration cards; exhibiting registration card and licenses; failure to carry license or registration card.

The operator of any motor vehicle, trailer, or semitrailer being operated on the highways in the Commonwealth, shall have in his possession: (i) the registration card issued by the Department or the registration card issued by the state or country in which the motor vehicle, trailer, or semitrailer is registered, and (ii) his driver's license, learner's permit, or temporary driver's permit.

The owner or operator of any motor vehicle, trailer, or semitrailer shall stop on the signal of any law-enforcement officer who is in uniform or shows his badge or other sign of authority and shall, on the officer's request, exhibit his registration card, driver's license, learner's permit, or temporary driver's permit and write his name in the presence of the officer, if so required, for the purpose of establishing his identity.

Every person licensed by the Department as a driver or issued a learner's or temporary driver's permit who fails to carry his license or permit, and the registration card for the vehicle which he operates, shall be guilty of a traffic infraction and upon conviction punished by a fine of ten dollars. However, if any person summoned to appear before a court for failure to display his license, permit, or registration card presents, before the return date of the summons, to the court a license or permit issued to him prior to the time the summons was issued or a registration card, as the case may be, or appears pursuant to the summons and produces before the court a license or permit issued to him prior to the time the summons was issued or a registration card, as the case may be, he shall, upon payment of all applicable court costs, have complied with the provisions of this section.

History.

Code 1950, §§ 46-15, 46-80; 1958, c. 541, § 46.1-7; 1964, c. 205; 1972, c. 362; 1978, cc. 500, 605; 1984, c. 780; 1988, c. 74; 1989, c. 727; 2008, cc. 551, 691; 2009, c. 756.

§ 46.2-105. Making false affidavit or swearing falsely, perjury.

Any person who knowingly makes any false affidavit or knowingly swears or affirms falsely to any matter or thing required by this title or the Commissioner incidental to his administration of this title to be sworn to or affirmed shall be guilty of perjury.

History.

Code 1950, § 46-66; 1958, c. 541, § 46.1-15; 1989, c. 727.

§ 46.2-105.1. Unlawful procurement of certificate, license, or permit; unauthorized possession of examination or answers; unlawful distribution of false operator's license; penalty.

A. It shall be unlawful:

1. For any person to procure, or assist another to procure, through theft, fraud, or other illegal means, a certificate, license, or permit, from the Department of Motor Vehicles;

2. For any person, other than an authorized agent of the Department of Motor Vehicles, to procure or have in his possession or furnish to another person, prior to the beginning of an examination, any question intended to be used by the Department of Motor Vehicles in conducting an examination;

3. For any person to receive or furnish to any person taking an examination, prior to or during an examination, any written or printed material purporting to be answers to questions intended to be used by the Department of Motor Vehicles in conducting an examination;

4. For any person to communicate by any means to any person taking an examination, during an examination, any information purporting to be answers to questions intended to be used by the Department of Motor Vehicles in conducting an examination;

5. For any person to attempt to procure, through theft, fraud or other illegal means, any questions intended to be used by the Department of Motor Vehicles in conducting an examination, or the answers to the questions; or

6. To promise or offer any valuable or other consideration to a person having access to the questions or answers as an inducement to procure for delivery to the promisor, or any other person, a copy or copies of any questions or answers.

B. If an examination is divided into separate parts, each of the parts shall be deemed an examination for the purposes of this section.

C. Any violation of any provision of subsection A of this section shall be punishable as a Class 2 misdemeanor.

D. Any person or entity other than the Department of Motor Vehicles that sells, gives, or distributes, or attempts to sell, give or distribute any document purporting to be a license to operate a motor vehicle in the Commonwealth is guilty of a Class 1 misdemeanor.

History.

1990, c. 964; 2006, c. 871; 2015, c. 464.

§ 46.2-105.2. Obtaining documents from the Department when not entitled thereto; penalty.

A. It shall be unlawful for any person to obtain a Virginia driver's license, special identification card, vehicle registration, certificate of title, or other document issued by the Department if such person has not satisfied all legal and procedural requirements for the issuance thereof, or is otherwise not legally entitled thereto, including obtaining any document issued by the Department through the use of counterfeit, forged, or altered documents.

B. It shall be unlawful to aid any person to obtain any driver's license, special identification card, vehicle registration, certificate of title, or other document in violation of the provisions of subsection A.

C. It shall be unlawful to knowingly possess or use for any purpose any driver's license, special identification card, vehicle registration, certificate of title, or other document obtained in violation of the provisions of subsection A.

D. A violation of any provision of this section shall constitute a Class 2 misdemeanor if a person is charged and convicted of a violation of this section that involved the unlawful obtaining or possession of any document issued by the Department for the purpose of engaging in any age-limited activity, including but not limited to obtaining, possessing, or consuming alcoholic beverages. However, if a person is charged and convicted of any other violation of this section, such offense shall constitute a Class 6 felony.

E. Whenever it appears to the satisfaction of the Commissioner that any driver's license, special identification card, vehicle registration, certificate of title, or other document issued by the Department has been obtained in violation of this section, it may be cancelled by the Commissioner, who shall mail notice of the cancellation to the address of record maintained by the Department.

History.

1992, c. 99; 2002, cc. 767, 834; 2003, cc. 817, 819.

§ 46.2-106. Reciprocal agreements entered into by Governor.

The Governor may enter into reciprocal agreements on behalf of the Commonwealth with the appropriate authorities of any state of the United States with respect to all taxes imposed by the Commonwealth and by any other state of the United States on motor vehicles, the operation of motor vehicles, or any transaction incident to the operation of motor vehicles.

Except as provided in this section, all agreements entered into by the Governor with respect to any subject of reciprocity as to which provision is expressly made by statute shall conform to the provisions of that statute. As to any other subject of reciprocity appropriate to the powers vested in the Governor by this section, the Governor may agree to whatever terms and conditions as in his judgment are best calculated to promote the interests of the Commonwealth. Except as provided in this section, it is the policy of the Commonwealth to grant reciprocity to the residents of another state when that state grants reciprocity to the residents of the Commonwealth.

All agreements entered into by the Governor pursuant to this section shall be reduced to writing, and a copy shall be furnished to the Secretary of the Commonwealth and the Superintendent of State Police.

History.

Code 1950, §§ 46-21, 46-22; 1956, c. 354; 1958, c. 541, §§ 46.1-19, 46.1-20; 1964, c. 253; 1989, c. 727; 1995, cc. 744, 803; 2003, c. 299.

§ 46.2-107. Lists of vehicles used for rent or hire, or by contract carriers.

Every person engaged in hiring or renting motor vehicles for the transportation of passengers or property and every contract carrier by motor vehicle of passengers or property who operates, or who should operate, under a permit issued by the State Corporation Commission or by the Interstate Commerce Commission, as provided by law, shall furnish to the Commissioner, whenever required to do so, a list and description of motor vehicles used in his business.

History.

Code 1950, § 46-157; 1958, c. 541, § 46.1-151; 1989, c. 727.

§ 46.2-108. Records required of persons renting motor vehicles without drivers; inspections; insurance.

A. Every person engaged in the business of renting motor vehicles without drivers who rents any vehicle without a driver, otherwise than as a part of a bona fide transaction involving the sale of the motor vehicle, shall maintain a record of the identity of the person to whom the vehicle is rented and the exact time the vehicle is the subject of the rental or in possession of the person renting and having the use of the vehicle. These records shall be public records and open to inspection by any person damaged as to his person or property by the operation of the vehicle or by law-enforcement personnel in the discharge of their duties. Any person who has been damaged as to his person or property may require a production of the written record in person or by his authorized agent or attorney.

B. It shall be unlawful for any person who rents a motor vehicle as provided in this section to fail to make or have in possession or to refuse an inspection of the record required in this section.

C. The Commissioner shall prescribe and the owner shall use the form for the keeping of the record provided in this section.

D. No person engaged in the business of renting automobiles and trucks without drivers shall rent any vehicle without a driver unless the vehicle is an insured motor vehicle as defined in § 46.2-705. A violation of this subsection shall constitute a Class 1 misdemeanor.

History.

Code 1950, § 46-191; 1958, c. 541, § 46.1-14; 1960, c. 141; 1972, c. 373; 1978, c. 605; 1980, c. 9; 1989, c. 727.

§ 46.2-109. Reports by persons in charge of garages and repair shops; vehicles equipped with bullet-proof glass or smoke projectors or struck by bullets.

The person in charge of any garage or repair shop to which is brought any motor vehicle equipped with bullet-proof glass or any smoke screen device or that shows evidence of having been struck by a bullet shall report in writing, on forms furnished by the Superintendent of State Police, to the nearest police station or to the State Police, within twenty-four hours after the motor vehicle is received, the engine number, registration number, serial number or identification number, and the name and address of the owner or operator of the vehicle if known.

History.
Code 1950, §§ 46-17.1, 46-17.3; 1952, c. 538; 1958, c. 541, §§ 46.1-10, 46.1-12; 1960, c. 119; 1989, c. 727.

§ 46.2-110. Right to inspect vehicles in garages.

Any law-enforcement officer or Department officer or employee who is in uniform or exhibits a badge or other sign of authority shall have the right to inspect any motor vehicle, trailer, or semitrailer in any public garage or repair shop for the purpose of locating stolen motor vehicles, trailers, and semitrailers and for investigating the title and registration of motor vehicles, trailers, and semitrailers. For this purpose the owner of any garage or repair shop shall permit any law-enforcement officer or Department officer or employee freely to make investigation as authorized in this section.

History.
Code 1950, § 46-17; 1958, c. 541, § 46.1-9; 1989, c. 727.

§ 46.2-111. Flares and other signals relating to stopped commercial motor vehicles.

A. Whenever any commercial motor vehicle as defined in § 46.2-341.4 is stopped on any roadway or on the shoulder of any highway in the Commonwealth at any time for any cause other than stops necessary to comply with traffic control devices, lawfully installed signs, or signals of law-enforcement officers, the operator of such vehicle shall immediately activate the vehicular hazard warning signal flashers and as soon as possible, but in any event within 10 minutes of stopping, place or cause to be placed on the roadway or shoulder three red reflectorized triangular warning devices of a type approved by the Superintendent. One of the red reflectorized triangular warning devices shall be placed in the center of the lane of traffic or shoulder occupied by the stopped vehicle and not less than 100 feet therefrom in the direction of traffic approaching in that lane, a second not less than 100 feet from such vehicle in the opposite direction and a third at the traffic side of such vehicle not closer than 10 feet from its front or rear. However, if such vehicle is stopped within 500 feet of a curve or crest of a hill, or other obstruction to view, the red reflectorized triangular warning devices in that direction shall be so placed as to afford ample warning to other users of the highway, but in no case less than 500 feet from the stopped vehicle. Vehicular hazard warning signal flashers shall continue to flash until the operator has placed the three red reflectorized triangular warning devices required in this subsection. The placement of red reflectorized triangular warning devices is not required within the corporate limits of cities unless, during the time which lights are required to be illuminated on motor vehicles by § 46.2-1030, the street or highway lighting is insufficient to make such vehicle clearly discernable at a distance of 500 feet to a person on the highway. Flares or torches of a type approved by the Superintendent may be used in lieu of red reflectorized warning devices. In the event that the operator of the stopped vehicle elects to use flares or torches in lieu of red reflectorized triangular warning devices, the operator shall ensure that at least one flare or torch remains lighted at each of the prescribed locations as long as the vehicle is stopped. If gasoline or any other flammable liquid or combustible liquid or gas seeps or leaks from a fuel container or a commercial motor vehicle stopped upon a highway, no emergency warning signal producing a flame shall be lighted or placed except at such a distance from any such liquid or gas as will ensure the prevention of a fire or explosion.

The exception provided in this subsection with respect to highways within the corporate limits of cities shall not apply to any portion of any interstate highway within the corporate limits of any city. The provisions of this section shall not apply to any vehicle in a work zone protected by flagmen or approved temporary traffic control channeling devices, as required by the Virginia Work Area Protection Manual or to any vehicle displaying a flashing amber light authorized by § 46.2-1025 when such vehicle is (i) used for the principal purpose of towing or servicing disabled vehicles, or (ii) engaged in road or utility construction or maintenance.

B. If any such vehicle is used for the transportation of flammable liquids in bulk, whether loaded or empty, or for transporting inflammable gases, red reflectorized triangular warning devices or red electric lanterns of a type approved by the Superintendent of State Police shall be used. Such reflectors or lanterns shall be lighted and placed on the roadway in the manner provided in subsection A of this section.

C. [Repealed.]

History.
Code 1950, §§ 46-260, 46-261, 46-262; 1950, p. 698; 1956, c. 56; 1958, c. 541, §§ 46.1-255 to 46.1-257; 1960, c. 156; 1966, c. 122; 1968, c. 155; 1970, c. 190; 1989, c. 727; 1999, c. 77; 2003, c. 971.

§ 46.2-112. Tampering with odometer; penalty; civil liability.

A. It shall be unlawful to knowingly cause, either personally or through an agent, the changing, tampering with, disconnection, or nonconnection of any odometer or similar device designed to show by numbers or words the distance which a motor vehicle has traveled or the use it has sustained.

B. It shall be unlawful for any person to sell a motor vehicle if he knows or should reasonably know that the odometer or similar device of the motor vehicle has been changed, tampered with, or disconnected to reflect a lesser mileage or use, unless he gives clear and unequivocal notice of such tampering, etc., or of his reasonable belief thereof, to the purchaser in writing prior to the sale. In a prosecution under this subsection, evidence that a person or his agent has changed, tampered with, disconnected, or failed to connect an odometer or similar device of a motor vehicle shall constitute prima facie evidence of knowledge thereof.

C. It shall be unlawful for any person to advertise for sale, sell, or use any device designed primarily for the purpose of resetting the odometer or similar device of a motor vehicle in any manner.

D. The provisions of this section shall not apply to the following:

1. The changing of odometer or similar device readings registered in the course of predelivery testing of any motor vehicle by its manufacturer prior to its delivery to a dealer.

2. Any necessary repair or replacement of an odometer or similar device, provided that the repaired or replaced odometer or similar device is forthwith set at a reading determined by the reading on the device immediately prior to repair or replacement plus a bona fide estimate of the use of the vehicle sustained between the period when the device ceased to accurately record that use and the time of repair or replacement. Compliance with the requirements of 49 USC § 32704 of the Federal Odometer Act in the service, repair, or replacement of an odometer shall be deemed compliance with this subdivision.

3. Passenger vehicles having a capacity in excess of 15 persons.

4. Trucks having a net weight in excess of 10,000 pounds.

E. Any person convicted of a violation of the provisions of subsections A through D shall, for a first offense, be fined not more than $10,000 and sentenced to a term of confinement in jail for not more than 12 months, either or both. Any person convicted of a subsequent offense under this section shall be fined not more than $50,000 and sentenced to a term of confinement in a state correctional facility for not less than one year nor more than five years, either or both, for each offense if the offense is committed with the intent thereby to defraud another. Each violation of this section shall constitute a separate offense.

F. Any person who with intent to defraud violates subsection A or B shall be liable in a civil action in an amount equal to three times the amount of actual damages sustained or $3,000, whichever is greater. In the case of a successful action to enforce the foregoing liability, the costs of the action, together with reasonable attorney fees as determined by the court, shall be assessed against the person committing the violation. An action under this subsection shall be brought within two years from the date on which liability arises. For the purpose of this subsection, liability arises when the injured party discovers, or with due diligence should have discovered, the violation.

History.

1972, c. 851, §§ 46.1-15.1 to 46.1-15.3; 1978, c. 294; 1986, c. 490; 1989, c. 727; 2012, cc. 32, 122.

§ 46.2-113. Violations of this title; penalties.

It shall be unlawful for any person to violate any of the provisions of this title, or any regulation adopted pursuant to this title, or local ordinances adopted pursuant to the authority granted in § 46.2-1300. Unless otherwise stated, these violations shall constitute traffic infractions punishable by a fine of not more than that provided for a Class 4 misdemeanor under § 18.2-11.

If it is found by the judge of a court of proper jurisdiction that the violation of any provision of this title (i) was a serious traffic violation as defined in § 46.2-341.20 and (ii) that such violation was committed while operating a vehicle or combination of vehicles used to transport property that either: (a) has a gross vehicle weight rating of 26,001 or more pounds or (b) has a gross combination weight rating of 26,001 or more pounds inclusive of a towed vehicle with a gross vehicle weight rating of more than 10,000 pounds, the judge may assess, in addition to any other penalty assessed, a further monetary penalty not exceeding $500.

History.

1976, c. 135, § 46.1-16.01; 1977, c. 585; 1982, c. 681; 1989, c. 727; 1992, c. 533; 1997, c. 637; 2003, c. 844.

§ 46.2-114. Disposition of fines and forfeitures.

All fines or forfeitures collected on conviction of any person charged with a violation of any of the provisions of this title punishable as felonies, misdemeanors, or traffic infractions shall be paid into the state treasury to be credited to the Literary Fund unless a different form of payment is required specifically by this title.

History.

Code 1950, § 46-20; 1958, c. 541, § 46.1-18; 1989, c. 727; 2012, c. 408.

§ 46.2-115. Inapplicability of title on Tangier Island; adoption of local ordinances; penalties.

Except for this section, no provisions of this title shall apply in the Town of Tangier.

The council of the Town of Tangier may adopt such ordinances paralleling any provision of this title and adapt their provisions to suit the Town's unique situation. No penalty for any violation of any such ordinance, however, shall exceed the penalty imposed for a violation of the parallel provision of this title.

History.
1995, c. 670.

§ 46.2-116. Registration with Department of Criminal Justice Services required for tow truck drivers; penalty.

A. As used in this section and §§ 46.2-117, 46.2-118, and 46.2-119:

"Consumer" means a person who (i) has vested ownership, dominion, or title to the vehicle; (ii) is the authorized agent of the owner as defined in clause (i); or (iii) is an employee, agent, or representative of an insurance company representing any party involved in a collision that resulted in a police-requested tow who represents in writing that the insurance company had obtained the oral or written consent of the title owner or his agent or the lessee of the vehicle to obtain possession of the vehicle.

"Department" means the Department of Criminal Justice Services.

"Tow truck driver" means an individual who drives a tow truck as defined in § 46.2-100.

"Towing and recovery operator" means any person engaging in the business of providing or offering to provide services involving the use of a tow truck and services incidental to use of a tow truck. "Towing and recovery operator" shall not include a franchised motor vehicle dealer as defined in § 46.2-1500 using a tow truck owned by a dealer when transporting a vehicle to or from a repair facility owned by the dealer when the dealer does not receive compensation from the vehicle owner for towing of the vehicle or when transporting a vehicle in which the dealer has an ownership or security interest.

B. On and after January 1, 2013, no tow truck driver shall drive any tow truck without being registered with the Department, except that this requirement shall not apply to any holder of a tow truck driver authorization document issued pursuant to former § 46.2-2814 until the expiration date of such document. Every applicant for an initial registration or renewal of registration pursuant to this section shall submit his registration application, fingerprints, and personal descriptive information to the Department and a nonrefundable application fee of $100. The Department shall forward the personal descriptive information along with the applicant's fingerprints through the Central Criminal Records Exchange to the Federal Bureau of Investigation for the purpose of obtaining a national criminal history record check regarding such applicant. The cost of the fingerprinting and criminal history record check shall be paid by the applicant.

The Central Criminal Records Exchange, upon receipt of an applicant's record or notification that no record exists, shall make a report to the Department. If an applicant is denied registration as a tow truck driver because of the information appearing in his criminal history record, the Department shall notify the applicant that information obtained from the Central Criminal Records Exchange contributed to such denial. The information shall not be disseminated except as provided in this section.

C. No registration shall be issued to any person who (i) is required to register as a sex offender as provided in § 9.1-901 or in a substantially similar law of any other state, the United States, or any foreign jurisdiction; (ii) has been convicted of a violent crime as defined in subsection C of § 17.1-805 unless such person held a valid tow truck driver authorization document on January 1, 2013, issued by the Board of Towing and Recovery Operators pursuant to former Chapter 28 (§ 46.2-2800 et seq.), and has not been convicted of a violent crime as defined in subsection C of § 17.1-805 subsequent to the abolition of the Board; or (iii) has been convicted of any crime involving the driving of a tow truck, including drug or alcohol offenses, but not traffic infraction convictions. Any person registered pursuant to this section shall report to the Department within 10 days of conviction any convictions for felonies or misdemeanors that occur while he is registered with the Department.

D. Any tow truck driver failing to register with the Department as required by this section is guilty of a Class 3 misdemeanor. A tow truck driver registered with the Department shall have such registration in his possession whenever driving a tow truck on the highways.

E. Registrations issued by the Department pursuant to this section shall be valid for a period not to exceed 24 months, unless revoked or suspended by the Department in accordance with § 46.2-117.

History.
2012, cc. 803, 835; 2014, cc. 59, 441.

§ 46.2-117. Revocation and suspension of registration of tow truck driver; notice and hearing; assessment of costs.

A. Upon receipt of written notice from the Division of Consumer Counsel of the Office of the Attorney General that it has obtained a civil judgment against a tow truck driver for a violation of subsection A of § 46.2-118 or § 46.2-1217, 46.2-1231, or 46.2-1233.1 or upon the failure of a tow truck driver to report to the Department within 10 days any conviction for a felony or misdemeanor that occurred while he is registered in accordance with § 46.2-116, the Department may revoke or suspend the registration of a tow truck driver after notice and hearing as provided in subsection C.

B. Furthermore, the Department shall, after notice and hearing as provided in subsection C, revoke or suspend the registration of a tow truck driver for:

1. Conviction of any crime for which a person must register as a sex offender as provided in § 9.1-901 or in a substantially similar law of any other state, the United States, or any foreign jurisdiction;

2. Conviction of a violent crime as defined in subsection C of § 17.1-805; or

3. Conviction of any crime involving the driving of a tow truck, including drug or alcohol offenses, but not traffic infraction convictions.

C. Before suspending or revoking any registration, reasonable notice of such proposed action shall be given to the tow truck driver by the Department in accordance with the provisions of § 2.2-4020 of the Administrative Process Act. In suspending or revoking the registration of a tow truck driver, the Department may assess the tow truck driver the cost of conducting the hearing unless the Department determines that the violation was inadvertent or done in a good faith belief that such act did not violate a statute. Any costs assessed by the Department shall be limited to (i) the reasonable hourly rate of the hearing officer and (ii) the actual cost of recording the hearing.

History.
2012, cc. 803, 835.

§ 46.2-118. Prohibited acts by tow truck drivers and towing and recovery operators.

A. No tow truck driver shall:

1. Use fraud or deceit in the offering or delivering of towing and recovery services;

2. Conduct his business or offer services in such a manner as to endanger the health and welfare of the public;

3. Use alcohol or drugs to the extent such use renders him unsafe to provide towing and recovery services;

4. Obtain any fee by fraud or misrepresentation;

5. Remove or tow a trespassing vehicle, as provided in § 46.2-1231, or a vehicle towed or removed at the request of a law-enforcement officer to any location outside the Commonwealth; or

6. Violate, or assist, induce, or cooperate with others to violate, any provision of law related to the offering or delivery of towing and recovery services.

B. No towing and recovery operator shall:

1. Use fraud or deceit in the offering or delivering of towing and recovery services;

2. Conduct his business or offer services in such a manner as to endanger the health and welfare of the public;

3. Use alcohol or drugs to the extent such use renders him unsafe to provide towing and recovery services;

4. Neglect to maintain on record at the towing and recovery operator's principal office a list of all drivers employed by the towing and recovery operator;

5. Obtain any fee by fraud or misrepresentation;

6. Advertise services in any manner that deceives, misleads, or defrauds the public;

7. Advertise or offer services under a name other than one's own name;

8. Fail to accept for payment cash, insurance company check, certified check, money order, or at least one of two commonly used, nationally recognized credit cards, except those towing and recovery operators who have an annual gross income of less than $10,000 derived from the performance of towing and recovery services shall not be required to accept credit cards, other than when providing police-requested towing as defined in § 46.2-1217, but shall be required to accept personal checks;

9. Fail to display at the towing and recovery operator's principal office in a conspicuous place a listing of all towing, recovery, and processing fees for vehicles;

10. Fail to have readily available at the towing and recovery operator's principal office, at the customer's request, the maximum fees normally charged by the towing and recovery operator for basic services for towing and initial hookup of vehicles;

11. Knowingly charge excessive fees for towing, storage, or administrative services or charge fees for services not rendered;

12. Fail to maintain all towing records, which shall include itemized fees, for a period of one year from the date of service;

13. Willfully invoice payment for any services not stipulated or otherwise incorporated in a contract for services rendered between the towing and recovery operator and any locality or political subdivision of the Commonwealth;

14. Employ a driver required to register as a sex offender as provided in § 9.1-901;

15. Remove or tow a trespassing vehicle, as provided in § 46.2-1231, or a vehicle towed or removed at the request of a law-enforcement officer to any location outside the Commonwealth;

16. Refuse, at the towing and recovery operator's place of business, to make change, up to $100, for the owner of the vehicle towed without the owner's consent if the owner pays in cash for charges for towing and storage of the vehicle;

17. Violate, or assist, induce, or cooperate with others to violate, any provision of law related to the offering or delivery of towing and recovery services; or

18. Fail to provide the owner of a stolen vehicle written notice of his right under law to be reimbursed for towing and storage of his vehicle out of the state treasury from the appropriation for criminal charges as required in § 46.2-1209.

C. No tow truck driver as defined in § 46.2-116 or towing and recovery operator as defined in § 46.2-100 shall knowingly permit another person to occupy a motor vehicle as defined in § 46.2-100 while such motor vehicle is being towed.

History.
2012, cc. 803, 835; 2015, c. 217.

§ 46.2-119. Complaints against tow truck drivers or towing and recovery operators; enforcement by the Office of the Attorney General.

A. Any consumer aggrieved by the actions of a (i) tow truck driver for an alleged violation of subsection A of § 46.2-118 or § 46.2-1217, 46.2-1231, or 46.2-1233.1 or (ii) towing and recovery operator for an alleged violation of subsection B of § 46.2-118 or § 46.2-1217, 46.2-1231, or 46.2-1233.1 may file a complaint with the Division of Consumer Counsel of the Office of the Attorney General for appropriate action in accordance with this section and any other applicable law.

B. The Attorney General may cause an action to be brought in the appropriate circuit court in the name of the Commonwealth to enjoin any violation of § 46.2-118, 46.2-1217, 46.2-1231, or 46.2-1233.1. The circuit court having jurisdiction may enjoin such violations notwithstanding the existence of an adequate remedy at law. In any action under this section, it shall not be necessary that damages or intent be proved to establish a violation. The standard of proof at trial shall be a preponderance of the evidence. The circuit court may issue temporary or permanent injunctions to restrain and prevent violations of § 46.2-118, 46.2-1217, 46.2-1231, or 46.2-1233.1.

C. In any action brought under this section, the Attorney General may recover damages and such other relief allowed by law, including restitution on behalf of consumers injured by violations of § 46.2-118, 46.2-1217, 46.2-1231, or 46.2-1233.1, as well as costs and reasonable expenses incurred by the Commonwealth in investigating and preparing the case, including attorney fees.

History.
2012, cc. 803, 835.

CHAPTER 2.

DEPARTMENT OF MOTOR VEHICLES.

Article 1.

Powers and Duties of Department, Generally.

Article 2.

Powers and Duties of Department Related to Transportation Safety.

ARTICLE 1.
POWERS AND DUTIES OF DEPARTMENT, GENERALLY.

§ 46.2-200. Department of Motor Vehicles.

There shall be a Department of Motor Vehicles in the executive department, responsible to the Secretary of Transportation. The Department shall be under the supervision and management of the Commissioner of the Department of Motor Vehicles.

The Department shall be responsible for the administration of the motor vehicle license, registration and title laws; the issuance, suspension, and revocation of driver's licenses; the examination of applicants for and holders of driver's licenses; the administration, training, disciplining, and assignment of examiners of applicants for driver's licenses; the administration of the safety responsibility laws, fuel tax laws, the provisions of this title relating to transportation safety, and dealer licensing laws; the registration of carriers of passengers or property and vehicles that may be required to be registered under the International Registration Plan or pay road tax as described under Chapter 27 (§ 58.1-2700 et seq.) of Title 58.1 under the International Fuel Tax Agreement; the audit of carriers of passengers or property for compliance with registration and road tax requirements; proof of financial responsibility; and any other services that may be required to create a single point of contact for motor carriers operating within and without the Commonwealth, including the operation of permanent and mobile motor carrier service centers.

History.
Code 1950, § 46-26; 1958, c. 541, § 46.1-25; 1984, cc. 778, 780; 1989, c. 727; 1990, cc. 1, 317; 1995, cc. 744, 803; 1997, c. 283; 2001, cc. 70, 82.

§ 46.2-201. Appointment of Commissioner; term; vacancies.

The Commissioner shall be appointed by the Governor, subject to confirmation by the General Assembly, if in session when such appointment is made and if not in session, then at its next succeeding session. He shall hold his office at the pleasure of the Governor for a term coincident with that of each Governor making the appointment or until his successor shall be appointed and qualified. Vacancies shall be filled for the unexpired term in the same manner as original appointments are made.

History.
Code 1950, § 46-24; 1958, c. 541, § 46.1-23; 1989, c. 727.

§ 46.2-202. Oath and bond; salary.

The Commissioner, before entering on the discharge of his duties, shall take an oath that he will faithfully and impartially discharge all the duties of his office and he shall give bond in such penalty as may be fixed by the Governor, conditioned on the faithful discharge of his duties. The premium on the bond shall be paid out of the funds available for the maintenance and operation of his office. The Commissioner shall receive the salary appropriated for the purpose.

History.
Code 1950, § 46-25; 1958, c. 541, § 46.1-24; 1989, c. 727.

§ 46.2-203. Regulations; violation; forms for applications, certificates, licenses, etc.

Subject to the provisions of Chapter 40 (§ 2.2-4000 et seq.) of Title 2.2, the Commissioner may adopt reasonable administrative regulations necessary to carry out the laws administered by the Department and may enforce these regulations and laws through the agencies of the Commonwealth he may designate. A violation of any such regulation shall constitute a Class 4 misdemeanor. He shall also provide suitable forms for applications, certificates of title, registration cards, license plates, and driver's licenses. Unless otherwise required in this title, he shall provide all other forms requisite for the purpose of this title.

History.
Code 1950, § 46-27; 1958, c. 541, § 46.1-26; 1984, c. 780; 1989, c. 727.

§ 46.2-203.1. Provision of updated addresses by persons completing forms; acknowledgment of future receipt of official notices.

Whenever any person completes a form for an application, certificate of title, registration card, license plate, driver's license, and any other form requisite for the purpose of this title, or whenever any person is issued a summons for a violation of the motor vehicle laws of the Commonwealth, he shall provide his current address on the form or summons. By signing the form or summons, the person acknowledges that (i) the address is correct, (ii) any official notice, including an order of suspension, will be sent by prepaid first class mail to the address on the signed form with the most current date, and (iii) the notice shall be deemed to have been accepted by the person at that address. In addition, upon signing a summons for a violation of the motor vehicle laws, the person shall acknowledge that his failure to appear in court and pay fines and costs could result in suspension of his operator's license.

History.
1993, c. 24.

§ 46.2-203.2. Emergency contact information program.

A. As used in this section, "emergency contact" means a person 18 years of age or older whom the customer may designate to be contacted by a law-enforcement officer in an emergency situation.

B. The Department may establish an emergency contact information program to assist law-enforcement personnel in emergency situations. To establish such a program, a person who currently holds a learner's permit, temporary driver's license, driver's license, commercial driver's license, or special identification card issued by the Department or completes an application for the same may voluntarily submit emergency contact information for inclusion in his customer record with the Department. Such emergency contact information may include the name, relationship to the customer, address, and telephone number for an individual the customer designates as a contact in the event of an emergency situation.

C. Any person voluntarily submitting emergency contact information to the Department for inclusion in the applicant's customer record is responsible for maintaining current emergency contact information with the Department. Each applicant submitting emergency contact information to the Department shall certify in his application that he has notified the person he has designated as an emergency contact that such information will be supplied to the Department. The Department shall provide a method by which applicants submitting emergency contact information to the Department may submit such information electronically pursuant to § 46.2-216.1. Customers may add, modify, or delete information at any time. Such modifications or deletions will overwrite all previously provided information.

D. In the event of an emergency situation, the Department shall make emergency contact information in customer records electronically available to a law-enforcement officer who in the exercise of his official duties requires assistance in reaching a customer's emergency contact. Emergency contact information provided to the Department by the customer shall only be disclosed as permitted in this section and shall not be considered a public record subject to disclosure under the Freedom of Information Act and shall not be subject to disclosure by court order or other means of discovery.

E. In the absence of gross negligence or willful misconduct, the Department, its employees, and law-enforcement officers shall be immune from any civil or criminal liability in connection with the maintenance and use of emergency contact information voluntarily provided by customers for use in an emergency situation.

History.
2015, c. 162.

§ 46.2-204. Medical Advisory Board.

For the purpose of enabling the Department of Motor Vehicles to comply with its responsibilities under this title, there is hereby created a Medical Advisory Board for the Department. The Board shall consist of seven licensed physicians currently practicing medicine in Virginia appointed by the Governor. Appointments to the Board shall be for four-year terms and vacancies shall be filled by appointment for the unexpired portion of a term. The Governor shall designate the chairman of the Board.

The Commissioner may refer to the Board for an advisory opinion the case of any person applying for a driver's license or renewal thereof, or of any person whose license has been suspended or revoked, or of any person being examined under the provisions of § 46.2-322, when he has cause to believe that such person suffers from a physical or mental disability or disease which will prevent his exercising reasonable and ordinary control over a motor vehicle while driving it on the highways. In addition, the Board shall assist the Commissioner through the development of medical and health standards for use in the issuance of driver's licenses by the Department to avoid the issuance of licenses to persons suffering from any physical or mental disability or disease that will prevent their exercising reasonable and ordinary control over a motor vehicle while driving it on the highways.

The Board shall meet at the pleasure of the Commissioner. Each member shall serve without compensation but shall be reimbursed for his necessary expenses from funds appropriated to the Department of Motor Vehicles.

History.
1968, c. 168, § 46.1-26.1; 1974, c. 453; 1980, c. 728; 1984, c. 780; 1989, c. 727.

§ 46.2-205. Department offices and agencies; agreements with dealers.

A. The Commissioner shall maintain his office in the Commonwealth at a location which he determines to be appropriate. He may appoint agents and maintain branch offices in the Commonwealth in whatever locations he determines to be necessary to carry out this title.

The personnel of each branch office and each agency shall be appointed by the Commissioner and shall be bonded in an amount fixed by the Commissioner. The person in charge of the branch office and each agency shall deposit daily in the local bank, or at such other intervals as may be designated by the

Commissioner, to the account of the State Treasurer, all moneys collected, and shall submit daily to the Commissioner, or at such other intervals as may be designated by the Commissioner, a complete record of what each deposit is intended to cover. The Commissioner shall not be held liable in the event of the loss of any moneys collected by such agents resulting from their failure to deposit such money to the account of the State Treasurer.

The compensation of the personnel of each branch office and each agency is to be fixed by the Commissioner. The compensation fixed for each nonautomated agency for the purpose of maintaining adequate annual service to the public shall be three and one-half percent of the first $500,000 of gross collections made by the agency, two percent of the next $500,000 of gross collections made by the agency, and one percent of all gross collections in excess of $1,000,000 made by the agency during each fiscal year.

The compensation fixed for each automated agency for the purpose of maintaining adequate annual service to the public shall be three and one-half percent of gross collections made by the agency during each fiscal year.

The compensation awarded shall belong to the agents for their services under this section, and the Commissioner shall cause to be paid all freight, cartage, premium on bond and postage, but not any extra clerk hire or other expenses occasioned by their duties.

B. The Commissioner may enter into an agreement with any Virginia-licensed motor vehicle dealer, recreational vehicle dealer, trailer dealer, or motorcycle dealer to act as an agent of the Commissioner as provided in subsection A. Motor vehicle dealers, recreational vehicle dealers, trailer dealers, and motorcycle dealers who act as agents of the Commissioner of the Department of Motor Vehicles as authorized in this subsection shall be compensated as provided in subsection A.

History.

Code 1950, §§ 46-29, 46-31; 1950, p. 299; 1954, c. 585; 1958, c. 541, §§ 46.1-28, 46.1-30; 1970, c. 754; 1972, c. 408, 609; 1974, c. 48; 1979, c. 20; 1989, c. 727; 1999, c. 308; 2002, c. 110; 2003, c. 991; 2015, c. 615.

§ 46.2-205.1: Expired.

Editor's note.

This section was enacted by Acts 2003, c. 1023, and expired July 1, 2005, pursuant to Acts 2003, c. 1023, cl. 3.

§ 46.2-205.2. Agreements with other agencies or contractors for other agencies; collection of fees.

The Commissioner may enter into an agreement with an agency of the Commonwealth, any other state, or the federal government, or where the underlying contract permits, a contractor for such state or federal agency, to conduct customer service transactions on behalf of that agency for the benefit of Virginia residents. For each such transaction conducted, the Department shall collect from the customer any transaction fee required by the responsible agency or contractor and remit the same to that agency or contractor in accordance with the terms of the agreement. However, the Department may receive a portion of the transaction fee required by the responsible agency or contractor in accordance with the terms of the agreement in order to defray the costs of the transaction to the Department. The Department may also impose and collect a processing fee to be used to defray the costs of the transaction to the Department. The amount of the processing fee, if imposed, shall be $2, unless otherwise specified by law. Any transaction fees received from the responsible agency or contractor or processing fees imposed and collected by the Department from the agency, contractor, or customer under this section shall be paid into the state treasury and set aside as a special fund to be used to meet the expenses of the Department.

For purposes of this section, "state," when applied to a part of the United States, means any of the 50 states, the District of Columbia, the Commonwealth of Puerto Rico, Guam, the Northern Mariana Islands, and the United States Virgin Islands.

History.

2012, cc. 215, 222; 2016, c. 368.

§ 46.2-206. Disposition of fees.

Except as otherwise provided in this title, all fees and moneys collected pursuant to the provisions of Chapters 1, 2, 3, 6, 8, 10, 12, and 16 through 26 of this title shall be paid into the state treasury, and warrants for the expenditure of funds necessary for the proper enforcement of this title shall be issued by the Comptroller on certificates of the Commissioner or his representatives, designated by him and bonded, that the parties are entitled thereto, and shall be paid by the State Treasurer out of such funds, not exceeding the amount appropriated in the general appropriation bill.

These funds, except as is otherwise provided in this section, shall constitute special funds within the Commonwealth Transportation Fund to be expended (i) under the direction of the Commissioner of Highways for the construction, reconstruction, and maintenance of roads and bridges in the primary state highway system, interstate system, and secondary state highway system and (ii) as authorized by the Commissioner for the expenses incident to the maintenance of the Department, including its customer service centers, and for other expenses incurred in the enforcement of this title. Any funds available for construction or reconstruction under the provisions of this section shall be, as nearly as possible, equitably apportioned by the Commonwealth Transportation Commission among the several construction districts. Beginning July 1, 1998, any balances remaining in these funds at the end of the fiscal year shall be available for use in subsequent years for the purposes set forth in this section, and any interest income on such funds shall accrue to the respective individual special funds.

There may be paid out of these funds such sums as may be provided by law for (i) contributions toward the construction, reconstruction, and maintenance of streets in cities or towns and (ii) the operation and maintenance of the Department of Transportation, the Department of Rail and Public Transportation, the Department of Aviation, the Virginia Port Authority, the Department of State Police, and the Department of Motor Vehicles.

History.

Code 1950, § 46-179; 1958, cc. 541, 626, § 46.1-167; 1983, c. 566; 1987, c. 696; 1989, c. 727; 1997, c. 423.

§ 46.2-206.1: Repealed by Acts 2008, cc. 656 and 657, cl. 1, effective March 27, 2008.

§ 46.2-207. Uncollected checks and electronic payments tendered for license fees or taxes; penalty.

The penalty set forth in subsection C of § 2.2-614.1, or ten percent of the amount of the check or electronic payment, whichever is greater, shall be in addition to any other penalties imposed by the Motor Vehicle Laws of Virginia, except in a case where there is a specific penalty set forth by statute for the nonpayment or late payment of fees or taxes, in which case subsection C of § 2.2-614.1 shall apply only in the amount it exceeds the specific penalty. All moneys collected by the Commissioner from the penalties imposed under this section and § 2.2-614.1 shall be paid into the state treasury and set aside as a special fund to be used to meet the expenses of the Department of Motor Vehicles.

History.

1972, c. 67, § 46.1-35.1; 1974, c. 210; 1976, c. 20; 1982, c. 671; 1987, c. 696; 1989, c. 727; 2001, c. 800; 2002, c. 719.

§ 46.2-208. Records of Department; when open for inspection; release of privileged information.

A. All records in the office of the Department containing the specific classes of information outlined below shall be considered privileged records:

1. Personal information, including all data defined as "personal information" in § 2.2-3801;

2. Driver information, including all data that relates to driver's license status and driver activity; and

3. Vehicle information, including all descriptive vehicle data and title, registration, and vehicle activity data.

B. The Commissioner shall release such information only under the following conditions:

1. Notwithstanding other provisions of this section, medical data included in personal data shall be released only to a physician, physician assistant, or nurse practitioner as provided in § 46.2-322.

2. Insurance data may be released as specified in §§ 46.2-372, 46.2-380, and 46.2-706.

3. Notwithstanding other provisions of this section, information disclosed or furnished shall be assessed a fee as specified in § 46.2-214.

4. When the person requesting the information is (i) the subject of the information, (ii) the parent or guardian of the subject of the information, (iii) the authorized representative of the subject of the information, or (iv) the owner of the vehicle that is the subject of the information, the Commissioner shall provide him with the requested information and a complete explanation of it. Requests for such information need not be made in writing or in person and may be made orally or by telephone, provided that the Department is satisfied that there is adequate verification of the requester's identity. When so requested in writing by (a) the subject of the information, (b) the parent or guardian of the subject of the information, (c) the authorized representative of the subject of the information, or (d) the owner of the vehicle that is the subject of the information, the Commissioner shall verify and, if necessary, correct the personal information provided and furnish driver and vehicle information in the form of an abstract of the record.

5. On the written request of any insurance carrier, surety, or representative of an insurance carrier or surety, the Commissioner shall furnish such insurance carrier, surety, or representative an abstract of the record of any person subject to the provisions of this title. The abstract shall include any record of any conviction of a violation of any provision of any statute or ordinance relating to the operation or ownership of a motor vehicle or of any injury or damage in which he was involved and a report of which is required by § 46.2-372. No such report of any conviction or accident shall be made after 60 months from the date of the conviction or accident unless the Commissioner or court used the conviction or accident as a reason for the suspension or revocation of a driver's license or driving privilege, in which case the revocation or suspension and any conviction or accident pertaining thereto shall not be reported after 60 months from the date that the driver's license or driving privilege has been reinstated. This abstract shall not be admissible in evidence in any court proceedings.

6. On the written request of any business organization or its agent, in the conduct of its business, the Commissioner shall compare personal information supplied by the business organization or agent with that contained in the Department's records and, when the information supplied by the business organization or agent is different from that contained in the Department's records, provide the business organization or agent with correct information as

contained in the Department's records. Personal information provided under this subdivision shall be used solely for the purpose of pursuing remedies that require locating an individual.

7. The Commissioner shall provide vehicle information to any business organization or agent on such business' or agent's written request. Disclosures made under this subdivision shall not include any personal information and shall not be subject to the limitations contained in subdivision 6.

8. On the written request of any motor vehicle rental or leasing company or its designated agent, the Commissioner shall (i) compare personal information supplied by the company or agent with that contained in the Department's records and, when the information supplied by the company or agent is different from that contained in the Department's records, provide the company or agent with correct information as contained in the Department's records and (ii) provide the company or agent with driver information in the form of an abstract of any person subject to the provisions of this title. Such abstract shall include any record of any conviction of a violation of any provision of any statute or ordinance relating to the operation or ownership of a motor vehicle or of any injury or damage in which the subject of the abstract was involved and a report of which is required by § 46.2-372. No such abstract shall include any record of any conviction or accident more than 60 months after the date of such conviction or accident unless the Commissioner or court used the conviction or accident as a reason for the suspension or revocation of a driver's license or driving privilege, in which case the revocation or suspension and any conviction or accident pertaining thereto shall cease to be included in such abstract after 60 months from the date on which the driver's license or driving privilege was reinstated. No abstract released under this subdivision shall be admissible in evidence in any court proceedings.

9. On the request of any federal, state, or local governmental entity, local government group self-insurance pool, law-enforcement officer, attorney for the Commonwealth, court, or the authorized agent of any of the foregoing, the Commissioner shall (i) compare personal information supplied by the governmental entity, local government group self-insurance pool, law-enforcement officer, attorney for the Commonwealth, court, or the authorized agent of any of the foregoing, with that contained in the Department's records and, when the information supplied by the governmental entity, local government group self-insurance pool, law-enforcement officer, attorney for the Commonwealth, court, or the authorized agent of any of the foregoing, is different from that contained in the Department's records, provide the governmental entity, local government group self-insurance pool, law-enforcement officer, attorney for the Commonwealth, court, or the authorized agent of any of the foregoing, with correct information as contained in the Department's records and (ii) provide driver and vehicle information in the form of an abstract of the record showing all convictions, accidents, driver's license suspensions or revocations, and other appropriate information as the governmental entity, local government group self-insurance pool, law-enforcement officer, attorney for the Commonwealth, court, or the authorized agent of any of the foregoing, may require in order to carry out its official functions. The abstract shall be provided free of charge.

10. On request of the driver licensing authority in any other state or foreign country, the Commissioner shall provide whatever classes of information the requesting authority shall require in order to carry out its official functions. The information shall be provided free of charge.

11. On the written request of any employer, prospective employer, or authorized agent of either, and with the written consent of the individual concerned, the Commissioner shall (i) compare personal information supplied by the employer, prospective employer, or agent with that contained in the Department's records and, when the information supplied by the employer, prospective employer, or agent is different from that contained in the Department's records, provide the employer, prospective employer, or agent with correct information as contained in the Department's records and (ii) provide the employer, prospective employer, or agent with driver information in the form of an abstract of an individual's record showing all convictions, accidents, driver's license suspensions or revocations, and any type of driver's license that the individual currently possesses, provided that the individual's position or the position that the individual is being considered for involves the operation of a motor vehicle.

12. On the written request of any member of or applicant for membership in a volunteer fire company or any volunteer emergency medical services personnel or applicant to serve as volunteer emergency medical services personnel, the Commissioner shall (i) compare personal information supplied by the volunteer fire company or volunteer emergency medical services agency with that contained in the Department's records and, when the information supplied by the volunteer fire company or volunteer emergency medical services agency is different from that contained in the Department's records, provide the volunteer fire company or volunteer emergency medical services agency with correct information as contained in the Department's records and (ii) provide driver information in the form of an abstract of the member's, personnel, or applicant's record showing all convictions, accidents, license suspensions or revocations, and any type of driver's license that the individual currently possesses. Such abstract shall be provided free of charge if the request is accompanied by appropriate written evidence that the person is a member of or applicant for membership in a volunteer fire company or a volunteer emergency

medical services agency to serve as a member of a volunteer emergency medical services agency and the abstract is needed by a volunteer fire company or volunteer emergency medical services agency to establish the qualifications of the member, volunteer, or applicant to operate equipment owned by the volunteer fire company or volunteer emergency medical services agency.

13. On the written request of any person who has applied to be a volunteer with a Virginia affiliate of Big Brothers/Big Sisters of America, the Commissioner shall (i) compare personal information supplied by a Virginia affiliate of Big Brothers/Big Sisters of America with that contained in the Department's records and, when the information supplied by a Virginia affiliate of Big Brothers/Big Sisters of America is different from that contained in the Department's records, provide the Virginia affiliate of Big Brothers/Big Sisters of America with correct information as contained in the Department's records and (ii) provide driver information in the form of an abstract of the applicant's record showing all convictions, accidents, license suspensions or revocations, and any type of driver's license that the individual currently possesses. Such abstract shall be provided at a fee that is one-half the normal charge if the request is accompanied by appropriate written evidence that the person has applied to be a volunteer with a Virginia affiliate of Big Brothers/Big Sisters of America.

14. On the written request of any person who has applied to be a volunteer with a court-appointed special advocate program pursuant to § 9.1-153, the Commissioner shall provide an abstract of the applicant's record showing all convictions, accidents, license suspensions or revocations, and any type of driver's license that the individual currently possesses. Such abstract shall be provided free of charge if the request is accompanied by appropriate written evidence that the person has applied to be a volunteer with a court-appointed special advocate program pursuant to § 9.1-153.

15. Upon the request of any employer, prospective employer, or authorized representative of either, the Commissioner shall (i) compare personal information supplied by the employer, prospective employer, or agent with that contained in the Department's records and, when the information supplied by the employer, prospective employer, or agent is different from that contained in the Department's records, provide the employer, prospective employer, or agent with correct information as contained in the Department's records and (ii) provide driver information in the form of an abstract of the driving record of any individual who has been issued a commercial driver's license, provided that the individual's position or the position that the individual is being considered for involves the operation of a commercial motor vehicle. Such abstract shall show all convictions, accidents, license suspensions, revocations, or disqualifications, and any type of driver's license that the individual currently possesses.

16. Upon the receipt of a completed application and payment of applicable processing fees, the Commissioner may enter into an agreement with any governmental authority or business to exchange information specified in this section by electronic or other means.

17. Upon the request of an attorney representing a person in a motor vehicle accident, the Commissioner shall provide vehicle information, including the owner's name and address, to the attorney.

18. Upon the request, in the course of business, of any authorized representative of an insurance company or of any not-for-profit entity organized to prevent and detect insurance fraud, or perform rating and underwriting activities, the Commissioner shall provide to such person (i) all vehicle information, including the owner's name and address, descriptive data and title, registration, and vehicle activity data as requested or (ii) all driver information including name, license number and classification, date of birth, and address information for each driver under the age of 22 licensed in the Commonwealth of Virginia meeting the request criteria designated by such person, with such request criteria consisting of driver's license number or address information. No such information shall be used for solicitation of sales, marketing, or other commercial purposes.

19. Upon the request of an officer authorized to issue criminal warrants, for the purpose of issuing a warrant for arrest for unlawful disposal of trash or refuse in violation of § 33.2-802 the Commissioner shall provide vehicle information, including the owner's name and address.

20. Upon written request of the compliance agent of a private security services business, as defined in § 9.1-138, which is licensed by the Department of Criminal Justice Services, the Commissioner shall provide the name and address of the owner of the vehicle under procedures determined by the Commissioner.

21. Upon the request of the operator of a toll facility or traffic light photo-monitoring system acting on behalf of a government entity, or of the Dulles Access Highway, or an authorized agent or employee of a toll facility operator or traffic light photo-monitoring system operator acting on behalf of a government entity or the Dulles Access Highway, for the purpose of obtaining vehicle owner data under subsection M of § 46.2-819.1 or subsection H of § 15.2-968.1 or subsection N of § 46.2-819.5. Information released pursuant to this subdivision shall be limited to the name and address of the owner of the vehicle having failed to pay a toll or having failed to comply with a traffic light signal or having improperly used the Dulles Access Highway and the vehicle information, including all descriptive vehicle data and title and registration data of the same vehicle.

22. On the written request of any person who has applied to be a volunteer with a Virginia affiliate of

Compeer, the Commissioner shall (i) compare personal information supplied by a Virginia affiliate of Compeer with that contained in the Department's records and, when the information supplied by a Virginia affiliate of Compeer is different from that contained in the Department's records, provide the Virginia affiliate of Compeer with correct information as contained in the Department's records and (ii) provide driver information in the form of an abstract of the applicant's record showing all convictions, accidents, license suspensions or revocations, and any type of driver's license that the individual currently possesses. Such abstract shall be provided at a fee that is one-half the normal charge if the request is accompanied by appropriate written evidence that the person has applied to be a volunteer with a Virginia affiliate of Compeer.

23. Upon the request of the Department of Environmental Quality for the purpose of obtaining vehicle owner data in connection with enforcement actions involving on-road testing of motor vehicles, pursuant to § 46.2-1178.1.

24. On the written request of any person who has applied to be a volunteer vehicle operator with a Virginia chapter of the American Red Cross, the Commissioner shall (i) compare personal information supplied by a Virginia chapter of the American Red Cross with that contained in the Department's records and, when the information supplied by a Virginia chapter of the American Red Cross is different from that contained in the Department's records, provide the Virginia chapter of the American Red Cross with correct information as contained in the Department's records and (ii) provide driver information in the form of an abstract of the applicant's record showing all convictions, accidents, license suspensions or revocations, and any type of driver's license that the individual currently possesses. Such abstract shall be provided at a fee that is one-half the normal charge if the request is accompanied by appropriate written evidence that the person has applied to be a volunteer vehicle operator with a Virginia chapter of the American Red Cross.

25. On the written request of any person who has applied to be a volunteer vehicle operator with a Virginia chapter of the Civil Air Patrol, the Commissioner shall (i) compare personal information supplied by a Virginia chapter of the Civil Air Patrol with that contained in the Department's records and, when the information supplied by a Virginia chapter of the Civil Air Patrol is different from that contained in the Department's records, provide the Virginia chapter of the Civil Air Patrol with correct information as contained in the Department's records and (ii) provide driver information in the form of an abstract of the applicant's record showing all convictions, accidents, license suspensions or revocations, and any type of driver's license that the individual currently possesses. Such abstract shall be provided at a fee that is one-half the normal charge if the request is accompanied by appropriate written evidence that the person has applied to be a volunteer vehicle operator with a Virginia chapter of the Civil Air Patrol.

26. On the written request of any person who has applied to be a volunteer vehicle operator with Faith in Action, the Commissioner shall (i) compare personal information supplied by Faith in Action with that contained in the Department's records and, when the information supplied by Faith in Action is different from that contained in the Department's records, provide Faith in Action with correct information as contained in the Department's records and (ii) provide driver information in the form of an abstract of the applicant's record showing all convictions, accidents, license suspensions or revocations, and any type of driver's license that the individual currently possesses. Such abstract shall be provided at a fee that is one-half the normal charge if the request is accompanied by appropriate written evidence that the person has applied to be a volunteer vehicle operator with Faith in Action.

27. On the written request of the surviving spouse or child of a deceased person or the executor or administrator of a deceased person's estate, the Department shall, if the deceased person had been issued a driver's license or special identification card by the Department, supply the requestor with a hard copy image of any photograph of the deceased person kept in the Department's records.

28. On the written request of any person who has applied to be a volunteer with a Virginia Council of the Girl Scouts of the USA, the Commissioner shall (i) compare personal information supplied by a Virginia Council of the Girl Scouts of the USA with that contained in the Department's records and, when the information supplied by a Virginia Council of the Girl Scouts of the USA is different from that contained in the Department's records, provide a Virginia Council of the Girl Scouts of the USA with correct information as contained in the Department's records and (ii) provide driver information in the form of an abstract of the applicant's record showing all convictions, accidents, license suspensions or revocations, and any type of driver's license that the individual currently possesses. Such abstract shall be provided at a fee that is one-half the normal charge if the request is accompanied by appropriate written evidence that the person has applied to be a volunteer with the Virginia Council of the Girl Scouts of the USA.

C. Whenever the Commissioner issues an order to suspend or revoke the driver's license or driving privilege of any individual, he may notify the National Driver Register Service operated by the United States Department of Transportation and any similar national driver information system and provide whatever classes of information the authority may require.

D. Accident reports may be inspected under the provisions of §§ 46.2-379 and 46.2-380.

E. Whenever the Commissioner takes any licensing action pursuant to the provisions of the Virginia Commercial Driver's License Act (§ 46.2-341.1 et seq.), he may provide information to the Commercial Driver License Information System, or any similar national commercial driver information system, regarding such action.

F. In addition to the foregoing provisions of this section, vehicle information may also be inspected under the provisions of §§ 46.2-633, 46.2-644.02, 46.2-644.03, and §§ 46.2-1200.1 through 46.2-1237.

G. The Department may promulgate regulations to govern the means by which personal, vehicle, and driver information is requested and disseminated.

H. Driving records of any person accused of an offense involving the operation of a motor vehicle shall be provided by the Commissioner upon request to any person acting as counsel for the accused. If such counsel is from the public defender's office or has been appointed by the court, such records shall be provided free of charge.

I. The Department shall maintain the records of persons convicted of violations of § 18.2-36.2, subsection B of § 29.1-738, and §§ 29.1-738.02, 29.1-738.2, and 29.1-738.4 which shall be forwarded by every general district court or circuit court or the clerk thereof, pursuant to § 46.2-383. Such records shall be electronically available to any law-enforcement officer as provided for under clause (ii) of subdivision B 9.

J. Whenever the Commissioner issues a certificate of title for a motor vehicle, he may notify the National Motor Vehicle Title Information System, or any other nationally recognized system providing similar information, or any entity contracted to collect information for such system, and may provide whatever classes of information are required by such system.

History.

Code 1950, § 46-32; 1958, c. 541, § 46.1-31; 1964, c. 42; 1976, c. 505; 1979, c. 611; 1980, c. 23; 1982, c. 226; 1986, c. 607; 1989, cc. 705, 727; 1991, c. 307; 1993, cc. 48, 348; 1994, cc. 304, 700, 830, 959; 1995, cc. 118, 657, 676, 686; 1998, cc. 147, 802; 1998, Sp. Sess. I, c. 2; 2002, cc. 131, 710; 2003, c. 768; 2004, cc. 811, 855; 2005, cc. 376, 443; 2006, cc. 396, 846, 859; 2007, cc. 79, 156, 188, 447; 2009, c. 664; 2010, cc. 15, 175, 813, 865; 2011, c. 321; 2013, cc. 673, 789; 2015, cc. 502, 503; 2016, c. 753.

Editor's note.

References in this section were updated at the direction of the Virginia Code Commission to conform to the recodification of Title 33.2 by Acts 2014, c. 805, effective October 1, 2014.

§ 46.2-208.1. Electronic transfer of information in Department records for voter registration purposes.

Notwithstanding the provisions of § 46.2-208, the Commissioner shall provide for the electronic transfer of information from the Department's records to the State Board of Elections and the general registrars for the purpose of voter registration as required by Chapter 4 of Title 24.2, including but not limited to the purposes of § 24.2-410.1. Except as provided in §§ 24.2-404 and 24.2-444, the State Board of Elections and the general registrars shall not make information provided by the Department available to the public and shall not provide such information to any third party.

History.

1999, c. 118; 2006, cc. 926, 940; 2011, c. 528.

§ 46.2-208.2. Delinquent accounts; publication thereof.

Upon the failure of any owner, operator, or other person to timely deliver to the Department either payment in full of uncontested civil penalties, liquidated damages, weighing fees, processing fees, delinquent taxes, debts, and levies such as the Department may be authorized to collect, the Department at the direction of the Commissioner shall be permitted to publish on a website available to the public the name of such owner, operator, or the person, along with the county or city of his residence or incorporation, and the amount owed and the type of assessment.

The Department shall remove such name, county or city of residence or incorporation, amount owed, and type of assessment from such website immediately upon receipt of payment in full of the amount owed.

History.

2011, cc. 881, 889.

§ 46.2-209. Release of information in Department records for motor vehicle research purposes.

Notwithstanding the provisions of § 46.2-208, the Commissioner may furnish information for motor vehicle research purposes when the information is furnished in such a manner that individuals cannot be identified by social security or license number or in other cases wherein, in his opinion, highway safety or the general welfare of the public will be promoted by furnishing the information, and the recipient of the information has agreed in writing with the Commissioner or his designee that the information furnished will be used for no purpose other than the purpose for which it was furnished. No such information shall be used for solicitation of sales.

History.

1976, c. 505, § 46.1-31.1; 1989, c. 727; 1994, c. 959; 1995, c. 118.

§ 46.2-209.1. Release of vehicle information by Department to prospective vehicle purchasers.

Notwithstanding the provisions of § 46.2-208, the Commissioner may furnish vehicle information to a prospective purchaser of that vehicle, if the prospective purchaser completes an application therefor, including the vehicle's make, model, year, and vehicle identification number, and pays the fee prescribed by the Commissioner. Such information furnished by the Commissioner may be provided from the Department's own records, or may be obtained by the Commissioner through the National Motor Vehicle Title Information System or any other nationally recognized system providing similar information.

Nothing in this section shall be construed to authorize the release of any personal information as defined in § 2.2-3801.

History.
2000, cc. 87, 92, 235, 257.

§ 46.2-210. List of registrations and titles.

The Commissioner shall have prepared a list of registrations and titles and furnish it to the commissioner of the revenue of each county and city without cost. The Commissioner shall not make such list available to the public, nor shall any commissioner of the revenue make such list available to any third party.

History.
Code 1950, § 46-33; 1958, c. 541, § 46.1-32; 1989, c. 727; 1994, c. 959.

§ 46.2-211. Commissioner to advise local commissioners of revenue of situs of certain vehicles.

Before issuing any registration or certificate of title for any tractor truck, or any three-axle truck, trailer, or semitrailer with a registered gross weight in excess of 26,000 pounds, the Commissioner shall determine the county, city, or town in which the vehicle is or will be normally garaged or parked, and shall advise each commissioner of the revenue of the situs of such vehicles as may be in his jurisdiction. The provisions of this section shall not apply to motor vehicles and rolling stock of certificated intrastate common carriers, or electric power, gas, pipeline transmission, railroad, telegraph, telephone, and water companies.

History.
1974, c. 47, § 46.1-32.1; 1989, c. 727.

§ 46.2-212. Notice given for records supplied.

Whenever any records held by the Department are supplied to third persons, the third persons shall notify the subject of the records that the records have been supplied and shall send to the subject a copy of the records.

As used in this section "records supplied to third persons" means all abstracts of operating records held by the Department in which the person who is the subject of the records is identified or identifiable, where the records are made available, in any way, to a person who is not the subject of the records.

This section shall not apply to records supplied to any officials, including court and police officials of the Commonwealth and of any of the counties, cities, and towns of the Commonwealth, and court and law-enforcement officials of other states and of the federal government, provided the records or information supplied is for official use; nor shall this section apply to any records supplied to any insurer or its agents unless insurance is denied or the premium charged therefor is increased either wholly or in part because of information contained in such records.

History.
1976, c. 505, § 46.1-33.1; 1989, c. 727.

§ 46.2-212.1. Payments by payment devices.

The Commissioner may authorize the acceptance of payment devices in lieu of money for payment of any fees, fines, penalties, and taxes collected by the Department of Motor Vehicles or agents acting on behalf of the Department. The Department may add to such payment an amount of no more than four percent of the payment as a service charge for the acceptance of a payment device.

The Commissioner may authorize a Department transaction receipt to be used with existing Department documents as evidence that the holder has complied with Department payment requirements, provided the transaction is completed before the document's expiration date. Any such transaction receipt shall include detailed information as to length of time by which the document's period of validity will be extended and how the transaction receipt is to be verified.

History.
1989, c. 62, § 46.1-33.2; 1996, cc. 943, 994; 2000, c. 122.

§ 46.2-212.2. Automatic payments.

Upon application of any person, the Commissioner may (i) include in that person's records with the Department such credit card or automated clearing house transfer information as is necessary to enable automatic payments of fees, fines, penalties, and taxes payable by that person to the Department, and (ii) authorize the automatic payment by credit card or electronic funds transfer of any such fees, fines, penalties, and taxes. The Commissioner may procure the services of a third-party vendor for the secure storage of information collected under this section. Prior to the completion of any automatic payment transaction, the Commissioner shall provide notice to the person who has requested automatic payments, which notice shall state the reason for the charge and the amount to be charged, and shall provide the person an opportunity to cancel the transaction.

History.
2013, cc. 673, 789.

§ 46.2-213. Certificate of license plate number; prima facie evidence of ownership.

The Commissioner, on request of any person, shall furnish a certificate, under seal of the Department, setting forth a distinguishing number or license plate of a motor vehicle, trailer, or semitrailer, together with the name and address of its owner. The certificate shall be prima facie evidence in any court in the Commonwealth of the ownership of the vehicle to which the distinguishing number or license plate has been assigned by the Department. Certificates furnished under this section shall be provided free of charge to law-enforcement officers of the Commonwealth, any other state, or the federal government, but the Commissioner may charge a reasonable fee for certificates furnished under this section to other persons.

History.
Code 1950, § 46-35; 1958, c. 541, § 46.1-34; 1989, c. 727.

§ 46.2-214. Charges for information supplied by Department.

The Commissioner may make a reasonable charge for furnishing information under this title, but no fee shall be charged to any official of the Commonwealth, including court and police officials; officials of counties, cities, or towns; local government group self-insurance pools; or court, police, or licensing officials of other states or of the federal government, provided that the information requested is for official use and such officials do not charge the Commonwealth a fee for the provision of the same or substantially similar information. The fees received by the Commissioner under this section shall be paid into the state treasury and shall be set aside as a special fund to be used to meet the expenses of the Department.

History.
1976, c. 505, § 46.1-31.2; 1989, c. 727; 1991, c. 167; 2006, c. 846; 2007, cc. 156, 447; 2016, c. 368.

§ 46.2-214.1. Additional charge for information supplied by Department.

Beginning July 1, 2002, in addition to the fee charged pursuant to § 46.2-214, the Commissioner shall charge $2 for furnishing information under this title, but no fee shall be charged to any official, including court and police officials, of the Commonwealth or any county, city or town of the Commonwealth, or to court, police, and licensing officials of other states or of the federal government, provided that the information requested is for official use.

History.
2003, c. 1042, cl. 9.

§ 46.2-214.2. Waiver of certain fees by Department.

The Department may waive the fee for a duplicate driver's license that would have otherwise been imposed by the Department under this title if the person subject to the fee is on active duty with the armed forces of the United States outside the boundaries of the United States.

History.
2008, c. 502.

§ 46.2-214.3. Service charge to be imposed and collected by the Department; discount for multiyear registration.

A. In addition to any other fee imposed and collected by the Department, the Department shall impose and collect a service charge upon each person who carries out the registration renewal of a vehicle in any of the Department's Customer Service Centers if such registration can be conducted (i) by mail or telephone or by using an electronic medium using a format prescribed by the Commissioner, or (ii) through an agent of the Department that has entered into an agreement with the Department to perform certain services as described in subsection B of § 46.2-205. The service charge shall not apply (a) if concurrently with the registration of the vehicle, the person undertakes another transaction at a Customer Service Center, which other transaction cannot be conducted through a means described in clause (i) or (ii), (b) to the registration of any vehicle for which no registration fee is otherwise required by law, or (c) to any registration conducted by a motor vehicle dealer subject to the provisions of § 46.2-1530.2.

B. The service charge shall equal $5 per vehicle registration renewal that is carried out in any Customer Service Center of the Department. The Department shall include information regarding such service charge in all vehicle registration renewal notices sent to vehicle owners.

C. All service charges imposed and collected by the Commissioner under this section shall be paid into the state treasury and shall be set aside as a special fund to be used to meet the expenses of the Department.

D. Pursuant to subsection C of § 46.2-646, for each motor vehicle, trailer, or semitrailer registered, the Commissioner may offer, at his discretion, a discount for multiyear registrations of such vehicles. The discount shall be equal to $1 for each year of the multiyear registration or fraction thereof. The discount shall not be applicable to any motor vehicle, trailer, or semitrailer registered (i) under the International Registration Plan or (ii) as an uninsured motor vehicle. When this option is offered and chosen by the registrant, all annual and 12-month fees due at the time of registration shall be multiplied by the number of years or fraction thereof that the vehicle will be registered.

E. In addition to the discount authorized in subsection D, for the renewal of registration of each motor vehicle, trailer, or semitrailer pursuant to § 46.2-646, the Commissioner shall offer a discount for renewal when such registration renewal is conducted using the Internet. The discount shall be equal to $1. The discount shall not apply to any motor vehicle, trailer, or semitrailer registered (i) under the International Registration Plan or (ii) as an uninsured motor vehicle.

History.
2008, c. 866.

§ 46.2-214.4. Discount for online transactions.

The Department may offer a $1 discount for the following transactions if conducted using the Internet: (i) a driver's license renewal pursuant to § 46.2-330, (ii) a driver's license duplicate or reissue pursuant to § 46.2-343, (iii) an identification card renewal pursuant to § 46.2-345, (iv) an identification card duplicate or reissue pursuant to § 46.2-345, or (v) a certificate of title replacement pursuant to § 46.2-607.

History.
2016, c. 368.

§ 46.2-215. Certification of certain records and admissibility in evidence.

Whenever any record, including records maintained by electronic media, by photographic processes, or paper, in the office of the Department is admissible in evidence, a copy, a machine-produced transcript, or a photograph of the record or paper attested by the Commissioner or his designee may be admitted as evidence in lieu of the original. In any case in which the records are transmitted by electronic means a machine imprint of the Commissioner's name purporting to authenticate the record shall be the equivalent of attestation or certification by the Commissioner.

Any copy, transcript, photograph, or any certification purporting to be sealed or sealed and signed by the Commissioner or his designee or imprinted with the Commissioner's name may be admitted as evidence without any proof of the seal or signature or of the official character of the person whose name is signed thereto. If an issue as to the authenticity of any information transmitted by electronic means is raised, the court shall require that a record attested by the Commissioner or his designee be submitted for admission into evidence.

History.
1962, c. 368, § 46.1-34.1; 1966, c. 196; 1986, c. 607; 1988, c. 427; 1989, c. 727.

§ 46.2-216. Destruction of records.

In accordance with the provisions of Chapter 7 (§ 42.1-76 et seq.) of Title 42.1, the Commissioner may establish standards for the disposal of any paper or record which need not be preserved as a permanent record.

History.
Code 1950, § 46-37; 1958, c. 541, § 46.1-36; 1960, c. 121; 1989, c. 727.

§ 46.2-216.1. Electronic filings or submissions to Department; provision of electronic documents by Department.

A. Whenever this title or Title 58.1 provides that applications, certificates, fees, letters of credit, notices, penalties, records, reports, surety bonds, tariffs, taxes, time schedules, or any other documents or payments be filed or submitted to the Department in written form or otherwise, the Commissioner may, after providing 12-months' written notification to impacted applicants, licensees, or any other person or entity, require that all or certain applicants, licensees, or any other person or entity engaged in business with the Department, make such filings or submissions electronically in a format prescribed by the Commissioner. Any such requirement shall not apply to an individual application for a driver's license, commercial driver's license, special identification card, or the titling or registration of 12 or fewer vehicles during a period of one year. The Commissioner shall develop a method to ensure that the electronic filing is received and stored accurately and that it is readily available to satisfy the requirements of the statutes which call for a written document. Notwithstanding the provisions of this section, the Commissioner may accept, in lieu of paper documents, a filing or submission made by electronic means for any document not required to be filed or submitted electronically pursuant to the provisions of this title or Title 58.1.

B. Whenever this title or Title 58.1 provides that a written certificate or other document is to be delivered to an owner, registrant, licensee, lien holder, or any other person or entity by the Department or the Commissioner, the Commissioner may provide the written certificate or other document by electronic means. The electronic document may consist of all of the information included in the paper certificate or document or it may be an abstract or listing of the information held in electronic form by the Department. Whenever a certificate or other document is provided by electronic means, the Department will not be required to produce a written certificate or document until requested to do so by the owner, registrant, licensee, lien holder, or other party.

History.
1991, c. 115; 2009, c. 419.

§ 46.2-216.2 : Repealed by Acts 2009, c. 419, cl. 3.

§ 46.2-216.3: Repealed by Acts 2003, c. 1042, cl. 12, effective May 1, 2003.

§ 46.2-216.4. Department to provide self-service options to customers.

The Department may provide, at its offices, self-service options that will provide customers with access to the Department's Internet transactions for persons who would prefer to transact their business with the Department accordingly. In determining the form and number of such options, and whether any option will be made available at a location, the Department shall consider the volume of business and the cost effectiveness of implementing any such option at the location.

History.
2003, c. 320.

§ 46.2-216.5. Partnership of Department and The Library of Virginia to promote use of public library Internet access terminals to complete on-line transactions with the Department.

The Department shall enter into a partnership with The Library of Virginia to promote the use of public library Internet access terminals to complete on-line transactions with the Department.

History.
2003, c. 336.

§ 46.2-217. Enforcement of laws by Commissioner; authority of officers.

The Commissioner, his several assistants, including those who are full-time sworn members of the enforcement division of the Department of Motor Vehicles, and police officers appointed by him are vested with the powers of sheriffs for the purpose of enforcing the laws of the Commonwealth which the Commissioner is required to enforce. Such full-time sworn members of the enforcement division of the Department of Motor Vehicles are hereby authorized to enforce the criminal laws of the Commonwealth.

The Commissioner may also appoint or designate any of his staff to be "size and weight compliance agents" who shall thereby have the authority to (i) enforce the requirements for the use of dyed diesel fuel in §§ 58.1-2265 and 58.1-2267; (ii) enforce the requirements of Article 17 (§ 46.2-1122 et seq.) of Chapter 10; (iii) issue citations for violations of license, registration, and tax requirements and vehicle size limits pursuant to § 46.2-613.1; and (iv) carry out the vehicle seizure provisions of §§ 46.2-613.4, 46.2-613.5, 46.2-703, 46.2-1134, and 46.2-1136 at any permanent weighing station. For the purposes of this section, a permanent weighing station shall include any location equipped with fixed, permanent scales for weighing motor vehicles.

Nothing in this title shall relieve any law-enforcement officer, commissioner of the revenue, or any other official invested with police powers and duties, state or local, of the duty of assisting in the enforcement of such laws within the scope of his respective authority and duty.

All law-enforcement officers appointed by the Commissioner may administer oaths and take acknowledgments and affidavits incidental to the administration and enforcement of this title and all other laws relating to the operation of motor vehicles, applications for driver's licenses, and the collection and refunding of taxes levied on gasoline. They shall receive no compensation for administering oaths or taking acknowledgments.

History.
Code 1950, § 46-38; 1958, c. 541, § 46.1-37; 1984, c. 780; 1989, c. 727; 1993, c. 533; 2008, c. 460; 2011, cc. 62, 73; 2012, cc. 22, 111.

§ 46.2-218. Fees not allowed law-enforcement officers.

No court in the Commonwealth shall, in any case in which a fine is assessed for the violation of any law of the Commonwealth or any subdivision thereof, assess as a part of the cost of the case any fee for arrest, or as a witness, for the benefit of any law-enforcement officer of the Department; nor shall any Department law-enforcement officer receive any such fee. Any Department law-enforcement officer who accepts or receives any such fee shall be guilty of a Class 4 misdemeanor and, in addition, the Commissioner may remove him therefor. Department law-enforcement officers are not prohibited, however, from accepting or receiving rewards.

History.
Code 1950, § 46-39; 1958, c. 541, § 46.1-38; 1980, c. 29; 1989, c. 727.

§ 46.2-219. Bonds of Commissioner, Deputy Commissioners, assistants, administrators, and law-enforcement officers; liability insurance policies.

The Commissioner, the Deputy Commissioners, the assistant commissioners, the administrators, and law-enforcement officers appointed by the Commissioner and engaged in the enforcement of criminal laws and the laws relating to the operation of motor vehicles on the highways in the Commonwealth shall, before entering on or continuing in their duties, enter into bond with some solvent guaranty, indemnity, fidelity, or casualty company authorized to do business in the Commonwealth as surety, in the penalty of $100,000 and with condition for the faithful and lawful performance of their duties. These bonds shall be filed in the office of the Department and the premiums thereon shall be paid out of the fund appropriated for the enforcement of the laws concerning motor vehicles. All persons injured or damaged in any manner by the unlawful, negligent, or improper conduct of any such officer while on duty may maintain an action on the bond.

In lieu of posting bond as provided in this section, any assistant or law-enforcement officer may furnish an adequate liability insurance policy as proof of his ability to respond in damages which may be adjudged against him in favor of any person or persons injured or damaged in any manner resulting from his unlawful, negligent, or improper conduct while on official duty, to the amount of $100,000. The premiums on any such insurance policy or policies shall be paid out of the funds appropriated for the enforcement of the laws concerning motor vehicles.

All such bonds and insurance policies shall be approved by the Commissioner.

History.

Code 1950, § 46-40; 1950, p. 221; 1958, c. 541, § 46.1-39; 1976, c. 78; 1989, c. 727.

§ 46.2-220. Special counsel for defense of law-enforcement officers.

If any law-enforcement officer appointed by the Commissioner is arrested, indicted, or prosecuted on any charge arising out of any act committed in the discharge of his official duties, the Commissioner may employ special counsel approved by the Attorney General to defend him. The compensation for special counsel employed pursuant to this section shall, subject to approval of the Attorney General, be paid out of the funds appropriated for the administration of the Department.

History.

Code 1950, § 46-41; 1958, c. 541, § 46.1-40; 1989, c. 727.

§ 46.2-221. Certain state agencies to report to Department concerning the blind and nearly blind; use of such information by Department; Department to report names of persons refused licenses for defective vision; reports to law-enforcement agencies concerning certain blind or visually impaired persons who operate motor vehicles.

Every state agency having knowledge of the blind or visually handicapped, maintaining any register of the blind, or administering either tax deductions or exemptions for or aid to the blind or visually handicapped shall report in January of each year to the Department the names of all persons so known, registered or benefiting from such deductions or exemptions, for aid to the blind or visually handicapped. This information shall be used by the Department only for the purpose of determining qualifications of these persons for licensure under Chapter 3 (§ 46.2-300 et seq.). If any such state agency has knowledge that any person so reported continues to operate a motor vehicle, such agency may provide this information to appropriate law-enforcement agencies as otherwise permitted by law.

The Department shall report to the Virginia Department for the Blind and Vision Impaired and the Department for Aging and Rehabilitative Services at least annually the name and address of every person who has been refused a driver's license solely or partly because of failure to pass the Department's visual examination.

If any employee of the Virginia Department for the Blind and Vision Impaired makes a report to the Department of Motor Vehicles or provides information to an appropriate law-enforcement agency as required or permitted by this section concerning any client of the agency, it shall not be deemed to have been made in violation of the client-agency relationship.

History.

1968, c. 98, §§ 46.1-40.1, 46.1-40.1:1; 1977, c. 340; 1984, c. 780; 1988, c. 798; 1989, c. 727; 2003, c. 301; 2012, cc. 803, 835.

§ 46.2-221.1. Registration with Selective Service required for issuance of learner's permits, driver's licenses, commercial driver's licenses, and special identification cards to certain applicants.

A. Every male applicant for a learner's permit, driver's license, commercial driver's license, special identification card, or renewal of any such permit, license, or card who is less than twenty-six years old and is either a citizen of the United States or an immigrant shall, at the time of his application, be registered in compliance with the requirement of section 3 of the Military Selective Service Act, 50 U.S.C. Appx. § 3801 et seq. The application for a learner's permit, driver's license, commercial driver's license, special identification card, or renewal of any such permit, license, or card submitted by any such person shall indicate either (i) that he is already registered with the Selective Service or (ii) that he authorizes the Department to forward to the Selective Service System the personal information necessary for such registration. This personal information shall be forwarded by the Department to the Selective Service System in an electronic format. The Department shall include on its application forms notice to affected persons that their submission of the application grants their consent to be registered with the Selective Service System, if required to so register by federal law.

Data received by the Selective Service System under this subsection that pertains to any persons less than eighteen years old shall not be used to register that person with the Selective Service until that person is eighteen years old.

B. If the applicant for a learner's permit, driver's license, commercial driver's license, special identification card, or renewal of any such permit, license, or card is a male less than eighteen years old, his application shall be signed by his parent or by the guardian having custody of him. If he has no parent or guardian, then no learner's permit, driver's license, commercial driver's license, or special identification card shall be issued to him or renewed by the Department unless his application is signed by the judge of the juvenile and domestic relations district court of the city or county in which he resides. If the minor making the application is married or otherwise emancipated, in lieu of any parent's, guardian's or judge's signature, the minor may present proper evidence of the solemnization of the marriage or the order of emancipation and sign the application himself. By signing the application as required in this subsection, the parent, guardian, or judge, or emancipated minor shall be deemed to authorize the Department to register the applicant with the Selective Service System as provided in subsection A.

C. If any male applicant for a learner's permit, driver's license, commercial driver's license, special identification card, or renewal of any such permit, license, or card who is required by subsection A to be registered with the Selective Service System declines, refuses, or fails to do so, his application shall be denied.

History.
2002, c. 118.

§ 46.2-221.2. Extension of expiration of driver's licenses issued to certain persons in service to the United States government.

Notwithstanding any contrary provision of law, any driver's license that is issued by the Department under Chapter 3 (§ 46.2-300 et seq.) to (i) a person serving outside the Commonwealth in the armed services of the United States, (ii) a person serving outside the Commonwealth as a member of the diplomatic service of the United States appointed under the Foreign Service Act of 1946, (iii) a civilian employee of the United States government or any agency or contractor thereof serving outside the United States on behalf of the United States government, or (iv) a spouse or dependent accompanying any such member of the armed services or diplomatic service serving outside the Commonwealth or civilian employee of the United States government or any agency or contractor thereof serving outside the United States on behalf of the United States government shall be held not to have expired during the period of the licensee's service outside the Commonwealth in the armed services of the United States or as a member of the diplomatic service of the United States appointed under the Foreign Service Act of 1946 or as a civilian employee of the United States government or any agency or contractor thereof serving outside the United States on behalf of the United States government and 180 days thereafter. However, no extension granted under this section shall exceed three years from the date of expiration shown on the individual's driver's license. The Department shall furnish any person whose driver's license is extended under this section documentary or other proof, when operating any motor vehicle, that he is entitled to the benefits of this section.

For the purposes of this section "service in the armed services of the United States" includes active duty service with the regular Armed Forces of the United States or the National Guard or other reserve component.

History.
2004, c. 975; 2006, c. 85; 2007, cc. 249, 589; 2008, c. 591; 2012, c. 384.

§ 46.2-221.3. Grace period for business credentialing for armed forces personnel returning from duty outside the United States.

Owners or operators of businesses and other persons licensed or credentialed in the Commonwealth by the Department who have served outside of the United States in the armed services of the United States shall have a 60-day grace period, beginning on the date they are no longer serving outside the United States, during which they may reopen the business or again perform credentialed activities prior to complying with the business license, certificate, permit, or other such business and professional credential requirements of this title.

To be eligible for the grace period, persons qualifying under this section shall:

1. Have held a valid license, permit, certificate, or other such business or professional credential issued by the Department at the time the person began service in the armed forces outside of the United States; and

2. Not operate the business or perform credentialed activities during the period of the person's military service.

Prior to reopening the business or again performing credentialed activities during the 60-day grace period, persons qualifying under this section shall notify the Department of their intentions and verify that they are in compliance with all other requirements established by the Department and set forth in this title relating to their business or profession. Such persons shall have in their possession, while operating the business or performing credentialed activities, (i) orders or other military documentation demonstrating that they are entitled to the benefits of this section, and (ii) the latest license, certificate, permit, or other such business or professional credential issued to them by the Department.

For the purposes of this section "service in the armed services" includes active duty service with the regular Armed Forces of the United States or the National Guard or other reserve component.

History.
2004, c. 975.

§ 46.2-221.4. Grace period for replacement of license plates or decals and registrations for certain persons in service to the United States government.

Owners or lessees of vehicles registered in the Commonwealth who (i) have served outside of the United States in the armed services of the United States, (ii) have served outside the United States as a member of the diplomatic service of the United States appointed under the Foreign Service Act of 1946, (iii) have been a civilian employee of the United States government or any agency or contractor thereof serving outside the United States on behalf of the United States government, or (iv) are a spouse or dependent accompanying any such member of the armed services or diplomatic service serving outside the United States or civilian employee of the United States government or any agency or contractor thereof serving outside the United States on behalf of the United States government shall have a 90-day grace period, beginning on the date that such person is no longer serving outside the United States, in which to comply with the vehicle registration requirements of this title.

To be eligible for the grace period, the vehicle shall:

1. Be owned or leased by a person or persons qualifying under this section;

2. Have had valid registration issued by the Department at the time the member of the armed services of the United States, member of the diplomatic service, civilian employee of the United States government, or any agency or contractor thereof began service outside of the United States;

3. Comply with the financial responsibility requirements of this title;

4. Display the latest license plates and decals issued by the Department for the vehicle; and

5. Be operated only by persons qualifying under this section while possessing:

a. Orders or other military documentation demonstrating that they are entitled to the benefits of this section; and

b. The latest registration card issued by the Department for the vehicle.

Nothing in this section shall be construed to prohibit any person or persons who own or lease vehicles registered in the Commonwealth and are currently serving outside of the United States in the armed services of the United States from complying, when possible and as necessary, with the vehicle registration requirements of this title during the period of service outside the United States or while on leave in Virginia.

For the purposes of this section "the armed services of the United States" includes active duty service with the regular Armed Forces of the United States or the National Guard or other reserve component.

The provisions of this section shall not apply to special license plates issued to members of the National Guard under § 46.2-744.

History.
2004, c. 975; 2008, c. 591; 2012, c. 385.

ARTICLE 2.
POWERS AND DUTIES OF DEPARTMENT RELATED TO TRANSPORTATION SAFETY.

§ 46.2-222. General powers of Commissioner with respect to transportation safety.

The Commissioner shall have the following general powers to carry out the purposes of this article:

1. To employ required personnel.

2. To enter into all contracts and agreements necessary or incidental to the performance of the Department's duties and the execution of its powers under this article, including, but not limited to, contracts with the United States, other states, and agencies and governmental subdivisions of the Commonwealth.

3. To accept grants from the United States government and its agencies and instrumentalities and any other source. To these ends, the Department shall have the power to comply with conditions and execute agreements necessary, convenient or desirable.

4. To do all acts necessary or convenient to carry out the purposes of this article.

History.
1984, c. 778, § 46.1-40.3; 1989, c. 727.

§ 46.2-223. Additional powers and duties of Commissioner.

The Commissioner shall have the following powers and duties related to transportation safety:

1. To evaluate safety measures currently in use by all transport operators in all modes which operate in or through the Commonwealth, with particular attention to the safety of equipment and appliances and methods and procedures of operation;

2. To engage in training and educational activities aimed at enhancing the safe transport of passengers and property in and through the Commonwealth;

3. To cooperate with all relevant entities of the federal government, including, but not limited to,

the Department of Transportation, the Federal Railway Administration, the Federal Aviation Administration, the Coast Guard, and the Independent Transportation Safety Board in matters concerning transportation safety;

4. To initiate, conduct, and issue special studies on matters pertaining to transportation safety;

5. To evaluate transportation safety efforts, practices, and procedures of the agencies or other entities of the government of the Commonwealth and make recommendations to the Secretary of Transportation, the Governor, and the General Assembly on ways to increase transportation safety consciousness or improve safety practices;

6. To assist entities of state government and political subdivisions of the Commonwealth in enhancing their efforts to ensure safe transportation, including the dissemination of relevant materials and the rendering of technical or other advice;

7. To collect, tabulate, correlate, analyze, evaluate, and review the data gathered by various entities of the state government in regard to transportation operations, management, and accidents, especially the information gathered by the Department of Motor Vehicles, the Department of State Police, and the State Corporation Commission;

8. To develop, implement, and review, in conjunction with relevant state and federal entities, a comprehensive highway safety program for the Commonwealth, and to inform the public about it;

9. To assist towns, counties and other political subdivisions of the Commonwealth in the development, implementation, and review of local highway safety programs as part of the state program;

10. To review the activities, role, and contribution of various state entities to the Commonwealth's highway safety program and to report annually and in writing to the Governor and General Assembly on the status, progress, and prospects of highway safety in the Commonwealth;

11. To recommend to the Secretary of Transportation, the Governor, and the General Assembly any corrective measures, policies, procedures, plans, and programs which are needed to make the movement of passengers and property on the highways of the Commonwealth as safe as practicable;

12. To design, implement, administer, and review special programs or projects needed to promote highway safety in the Commonwealth;

13. To integrate highway safety activities into the framework of transportation safety in general; and

14. To administer the Traffic Safety Fund established pursuant to § 46.2-749.2:10 and to accept grants, gifts, bequests, and other moneys contributed to, deposited in, or designated for deposit in the Fund.

History.

1984, c. 778, § 46.1-40.4; 1989, c. 727; 1990, cc. 1, 317; 1998, c. 743.

§ 46.2-224: Repealed by Acts 2012, cc. 803 and 835, cl. 105.

SUBTITLE II.

TITLING, REGISTRATION AND LICENSURE.

CHAPTER 3.

LICENSURE OF DRIVERS.

Article 1.

Unlicensed Driving Prohibited.

Article 2.

When License Not Required.

Article 3.

Persons Not to Be Licensed.

Article 4.

Obtaining Licenses, Generally.

Article 5.

Licensure of Minors, Student Drivers, School Bus Drivers, and Motorcyclists.

Article 6.

Licensure of Commercial Vehicle Drivers.

Article 6.1.

Commercial Driver's Licenses.

Article 7.

Form of Licenses; Identity Documents Issued by Department.

Article 8.

Prohibited Uses of Driver's Licenses.

Article 9.

Habitual Offenders.

Article 10.

Driver Responsibilities, Generally.

Article 11.

Accident Reports.

Article 12.

Suspension and Revocation of Licenses, Generally; Additional Penalties.

Article 13.

Suspension of Licenses for Unsatisfied Judgments and After Certain Accidents.

Article 14.

Suspension of Licenses of Nonresidents or for Accidents in Other States.

Article 15.

Proof of Financial Responsibility.

ARTICLE 1.

UNLICENSED DRIVING PROHIBITED.

§ 46.2-300. Driving without license prohibited; penalties.

No person, except those expressly exempted in §§ 46.2-303 through 46.2-308, shall drive any motor vehicle on any highway in the Commonwealth until such person has applied for a driver's license, as provided in this article, satisfactorily passed the examination required by § 46.2-325, and obtained a driver's license, nor unless the license is valid.

A violation of this section is a Class 2 misdemeanor. A second or subsequent violation of this section is a Class 1 misdemeanor.

Upon conviction under this section, the court may suspend the person's privilege to drive for a period not to exceed 90 days.

History.

Code 1950, § 46-347; 1958, c. 541, § 46.1-349; 1968, c. 494; 1970, c. 347; 1984, c. 780; 1989, c. 727; 2005, c. 245; 2007, c. 532; 2008, c. 684.

§ 46.2-301. Driving while license, permit, or privilege to drive suspended or revoked.

A. In addition to any other penalty provided by this section, any motor vehicle administratively impounded or immobilized under the provisions of § 46.2-301.1 may, in the discretion of the court, be impounded or immobilized for an additional period of up to 90 days upon conviction of an offender for driving while his driver's license, learner's permit, or privilege to drive a motor vehicle has been suspended or revoked for (i) a violation of § 18.2-36.1, 18.2-51.4, 18.2-266, 18.2-272, or 46.2-341.24 or a substantially similar ordinance or law in any other jurisdiction or (ii) driving after adjudication as an habitual offender, where such adjudication was based in whole or in part on an alcohol-related offense, or where such person's license has been administratively suspended under the provisions of § 46.2-391.2. However, if, at the time of the violation, the offender was driving a motor vehicle owned by another person, the court shall have no jurisdiction over such motor vehicle but may order the impoundment or immobilization of a motor vehicle owned solely by the offender at the time of arrest. All costs of impoundment or immobilization, including removal or storage expenses, shall be paid by the offender prior to the release of his motor vehicle.

B. Except as provided in §§ 46.2-304 and 46.2-357, no resident or nonresident (i) whose driver's license, learner's permit, or privilege to drive a motor vehicle has been suspended or revoked or (ii) who has been directed not to drive by any court or by the Commissioner, or (iii) who has been forbidden, as prescribed by operation of any statute of the Commonwealth or a substantially similar ordinance of any county, city or town, to operate a motor vehicle in the Commonwealth shall thereafter drive any motor vehicle or any self-propelled machinery or equipment on any highway in the Commonwealth until the period of such suspension or revocation has terminated or the privilege has been reinstated or a restricted license is issued pursuant to subsection E. A clerk's notice of suspension of license for failure to pay fines or costs given in accordance with § 46.2-395 shall be sufficient notice for the purpose of maintaining a conviction under this section. For the purposes of this section, the phrase "motor vehicle or any self-propelled machinery or equipment" shall not include mopeds.

C. A violation of subsection B is a Class 1 misdemeanor. A third or subsequent offense occurring within a 10-year period shall include a mandatory minimum term of confinement in jail of 10 days. However, the court shall not be required to impose a mandatory minimum term of confinement in any case where a motor vehicle is operated in violation of this section in a situation of apparent extreme emergency which requires such operation to save life or limb.

D. Upon a violation of subsection B, the court shall suspend the person's license or privilege to drive a motor vehicle for the same period for which it had been previously suspended or revoked. In the event the person violated subsection B by driving during a period of suspension or revocation which was not for a definite period of time, the court shall suspend the person's license, permit or privilege to drive for an additional period not to exceed 90 days, to commence upon the expiration of the previous suspension or revocation or to commence immediately if the previous suspension or revocation has expired.

E. Any person who is otherwise eligible for a restricted license may petition each court that suspended his license pursuant to subsection D for authorization for a restricted license, provided that the period of time for which the license was suspended by the court pursuant to subsection D, if measured from the date of conviction, has expired, even though the suspension itself has not expired. A court may, for good cause shown, authorize the Department of Motor Vehicles to issue a restricted license for any of the purposes set forth in subsection E of § 18.2-271.1. No restricted license shall be issued unless each court that issued a suspension of the person's license pursuant to subsection D authorizes the Department to issue a restricted license. Any restricted license issued pursuant to this subsection shall be in effect until the expiration of any and all suspensions issued pursuant to subsection D, except that it shall automatically terminate upon the expiration, cancellation, suspension, or revocation of the person's license or privilege to drive for any other cause. No restricted license issued pursuant to this subsection shall permit a person to operate a commercial motor vehicle as defined in the Commercial Driver's License Act (§ 46.2-341.1 et seq.). The court shall forward to the Commissioner a copy of its authorization entered pursuant to this subsection, which shall specifically enumerate the restrictions imposed and contain such information regarding the person to whom such a license is issued as is reasonably necessary to identify the person. The court shall also provide a copy of its authorization to the person, who may not operate a motor vehicle until receipt from the Commissioner of a restricted license. A copy of the restricted license issued by the Commissioner shall be carried at all times while operating a motor vehicle.

F. Any person who operates a motor vehicle or any self-propelled machinery or equipment in violation of the terms of a restricted license issued pursuant to subsection E of § 18.2-271.1 is not guilty of a violation of this section but is guilty of a violation of § 18.2-272.

History.

Code 1950, § 46-347.1; 1952, c. 666; 1958, c. 541, § 46.1-350; 1960, c. 364; 1962, c. 302; 1964, c. 239; 1966, cc. 546, 589; 1968, c. 494; 1970, c. 507; 1984, c. 780; 1985, c. 232; 1988, c. 859; 1989, c. 727; 1991, c. 64; 1992, c. 273; 1993, c. 24; 1994, cc. 359, 363; 1997, c. 691; 2000, cc. 956, 982; 2004, cc. 461, 801, 948; 2009, cc. 390, 764; 2010, c. 519.

§ 46.2-301.1. Administrative impoundment of motor vehicle for certain driving while license suspended or revoked offenses; judicial impoundment upon conviction; penalty for permitting violation with one's vehicle.

A. The motor vehicle being driven by any person (i) whose driver's license, learner's permit or privilege to drive a motor vehicle has been suspended or revoked for a violation of § 18.2-51.4 or 18.2-272 or driving while under the influence in violation of § 18.2-266, 46.2-341.24 or a substantially similar ordinance or law in any other jurisdiction; (ii) driving after adjudication as an habitual offender, where such adjudication was based in whole or in part on an alcohol-related offense, or where such person's license has been administratively suspended under the provisions of § 46.2-391.2; (iii) driving after such person's driver's license, learner's permit or privilege to drive a motor vehicle has been suspended or revoked for unreasonable refusal of tests in violation of § 18.2-268.3, 46.2-341.26:3 or a substantially similar ordinance or law in any other jurisdiction; or (iv) driving without an operator's license in violation of § 46.2-300 having been previously convicted of such offense or a substantially similar ordinance of any county, city, or town or law in any other jurisdiction shall be impounded or immobilized by the arresting law-enforcement officer at the time the person is arrested for driving after his driver's license, learner's permit or privilege to drive has been so revoked or suspended or for driving without an operator's license in violation of § 46.2-300 having been previously convicted of such offense or a substantially similar ordinance of any county, city, or town or law in any other jurisdiction. The impoundment or immobilization for a violation of clauses (i) through (iii) shall be for a period of 30 days. The period of impoundment or immobilization for a violation of clause (iv) shall be until the offender obtains a valid operator's license pursuant to § 46.2-300 or three days, whichever is less. In the event that the offender obtains a valid operator's license at any time during the three-day impoundment period and presents such license to the court, the court shall authorize the release of the vehicle upon payment of all reasonable costs of impoundment or immobilization to the person holding the vehicle.

The provisions of this section as to the offense described in clause (iv) of this subsection shall not apply to a person who drives a motor vehicle with no operator's license (i) whose license has been expired for less than one year prior to the offense or (ii) who is under 18 years of age at the time of the offense. The arresting officer, acting on behalf of the Commonwealth, shall serve notice of the impoundment upon the arrested person. The notice shall include information on the person's right to petition for review of the impoundment pursuant to subsection B. A copy of the notice of impoundment shall be delivered to the magistrate and thereafter promptly forwarded to the clerk of the general district court of the jurisdiction where the arrest was made. Transmission of the notice may be by electronic means.

At least five days prior to the expiration of the period of impoundment imposed pursuant to this section or § 46.2-301, the clerk shall provide the offender with information on the location of the motor vehicle and how and when the vehicle will be released; however, for a violation of clause (iv) above, such information shall be provided at the time of arrest.

All reasonable costs of impoundment or immobilization, including removal and storage expenses, shall be paid by the offender prior to the release of his motor vehicle. Notwithstanding the above, where the arresting law-enforcement officer discovers that the vehicle was being rented or leased from a vehicle renting or leasing company, the officer shall not impound the vehicle or continue the impoundment but shall notify the rental or leasing company that the vehicle is available for pickup and shall notify the clerk if the clerk has previously been notified of the impoundment.

B. Any driver who is the owner of the motor vehicle that is impounded or immobilized under subsection A may, during the period of the impoundment, petition the general district court of the jurisdiction in which the arrest was made to review that impoundment. The court shall review the impoundment within the same time period as the court hears an appeal from an order denying bail or fixing terms of bail or terms of recognizance, giving this matter precedence over all other matters on its docket. If the person proves to the court by a preponderance of the evidence that the arresting law-enforcement officer did not have probable cause for the arrest, or that the magistrate did not have probable cause to issue the warrant, the court shall rescind the impoundment. Upon rescission, the motor vehicle shall be released and the Commonwealth shall pay or reimburse the person for all reasonable costs of impoundment or immobilization, including removal or storage costs paid or incurred by him. Otherwise, the court shall affirm the impoundment. If the person requesting the review fails to appear without just cause, his right to review shall be waived.

The court's findings are without prejudice to the person contesting the impoundment or to any other potential party as to any proceedings, civil or criminal, and shall not be evidence in any proceedings, civil or criminal.

C. The owner or co-owner of any motor vehicle impounded or immobilized under subsection A who was not the driver at the time of the violation may petition the general district court in the jurisdiction where the violation occurred for the release of his motor vehicle. The motor vehicle shall be released if the owner or co-owner proves by a preponderance of the evidence that he (i) did not know that the offender's driver's license was suspended or revoked when he authorized the offender to drive such motor vehicle; (ii) did not know that the offender had no operator's license and that the operator had been previously convicted of driving a motor vehicle without an operator's license in violation of § 46.2-300 or a substantially similar ordinance of any county, city, or town or law in any other jurisdiction when he authorized the offender to drive such motor vehicle; or (iii) did not consent to the operation of the motor vehicle by the offender. If the owner proves by a preponderance of the evidence that his immediate family has only one motor vehicle and will suffer a substantial hardship if that motor vehicle is impounded or immobilized for the period of impoundment that otherwise would be imposed pursuant to this section, the court, in its discretion, may release the vehicle after some period of less than such impoundment period.

D. Notwithstanding any provision of this section, a subsequent dismissal or acquittal of the charge of driving without an operator's license or of driving on a suspended or revoked license shall result in an immediate rescission of the impoundment or immobilization provided in subsection A. Upon rescission, the motor vehicle shall be released and the Commonwealth shall pay or reimburse the person for all reasonable costs of impoundment or immobilization, including removal or storage costs, incurred or paid by him.

E. Any person who knowingly authorizes the operation of a motor vehicle by (i) a person he knows has had his driver's license, learner's permit or privilege to drive a motor vehicle suspended or revoked for any of the reasons set forth in subsection A or (ii) a person who he knows has no operator's license and who he knows has been previously convicted of driving a motor vehicle without an operator's license in violation of § 46.2-300 or a substantially similar ordinance of any county, city, or town or law in any other jurisdiction shall be guilty of a Class 1 misdemeanor.

F. Notwithstanding the provisions of this section or § 46.2-301, nothing in this section shall impede or infringe upon a valid lienholder's rights to cure a default under an existing security agreement. Furthermore, such lienholder shall not be liable for any cost of impoundment or immobilization, including removal or storage expenses which may accrue pursuant to the provisions of this section or § 46.2-301. In the event a lienholder repossesses or removes a vehicle from storage pursuant to an existing security agreement, the Commonwealth shall pay all reasonable costs of impoundment or immobilization, including removal and storage expenses, to any person or entity providing such services to the Commonwealth, except to the extent such costs or expenses have already been paid by the offender to such person or entity. Such payment shall be made within seven calendar days after a request is made by such person or entity to the Commonwealth for payment. Nothing herein, however, shall relieve the offender from liability to the Commonwealth for reimbursement or payment of all such reasonable costs and expenses.

History.

1994, cc. 359, 363; 1994, 1st Sp. Sess., c. 10; 1995, cc. 426, 435; 1997, cc. 378, 478, 691; 2005, c. 312; 2010, cc. 519, 829.

§ 46.2-302. Driving while restoration of license is contingent on furnishing proof of financial responsibility.

No resident or nonresident (i) whose driver's license or learner's permit has been suspended or revoked by any court or by the Commissioner or by operation of law, pursuant to the provisions of this title or of § 18.2-271, or who has been disqualified pursuant to the provisions of the Virginia Commercial Driver's License Act (§ 46.2-341.1 et seq.), or (ii) who has been forbidden as prescribed by law by the Commissioner, the State Corporation Commission, the Commissioner of Highways, or the Superintendent of State Police, to drive a motor vehicle in the Commonwealth shall drive any motor vehicle in the Commonwealth during any period wherein the restoration of license or privilege is contingent upon the furnishing of proof of financial responsibility, unless he has given proof of financial responsibility in the manner provided in Article 15 (§ 46.2-435 et seq.) of Chapter 3 of this title. Any person who drives a motor vehicle on the roads of the Commonwealth and has furnished proof of financial responsibility but who has failed to pay a reinstatement fee, shall be tried under § 46.2-300.

A first offense violation of this section shall constitute a Class 2 misdemeanor. A second or subsequent violation of this section shall constitute a Class 1 misdemeanor.

History.

Code 1950, § 46-484; 1958, c. 541, § 46.1-351; 1960, cc. 157, 364; 1962, c. 302; 1980, c. 29; 1984, c. 780; 1989, cc. 705, 727; 1991, c. 118.

ARTICLE 2. WHEN LICENSE NOT REQUIRED.

§ 46.2-303. Licenses not required for operating road roller or farm tractor.

No person shall be required to obtain a driver's license to operate a road roller or road machinery used under the supervision and control of the Department of Transportation for construction or maintenance purposes. No person shall be required to obtain a driver's license for the purpose of operating any farm tractor, farm machinery, or vehicle defined in §§ 46.2-663 through 46.2-674, temporarily drawn, moved, or propelled on the highways. The term "road machinery" shall not include motor ve-

Motor Vehicles

hicles required to be licensed by the Department of Motor Vehicles.

History.
Code 1950, § 46-348; 1952, c. 498; 1958, c. 541, § 46.1-352; 1972, c. 346; 1984, c. 780; 1989, c. 727.

§ 46.2-304. Limited operation of farm tractor by persons convicted of driving under influence of intoxicants or drugs.

The conviction of a person for driving under the influence of intoxicants or some other self-administered drug in violation of any state law or local ordinance shall not prohibit the person from operating a farm tractor on the highways when it is necessary to move the tractor from one tract of land used for agricultural purposes to another tract of land used for the same purposes, provided that the distance between the said tracts of land does not exceed five miles.

History.
1958, c. 489, § 46.1-352.1; 1989, c. 727.

§ 46.2-305. Exemption of persons in armed services.

Every person in the armed services of the United States, when furnished with a driver's license, and when operating an official motor vehicle in such service, shall be exempt from licensure under this chapter.

History.
Code 1950, § 46-350; 1958, c. 541, § 46.1-354; 1984, c. 780; 1989, c. 727.

§ 46.2-306. Exemption of armed services personnel and spouses and dependent children of armed services personnel.

Notwithstanding § 46.2-100, a person on active duty with the armed services of the United States or a spouse or a dependent child not less than sixteen years of age of a person on active duty with the armed services of the United States who has been licensed as a driver under a law requiring the licensing of drivers in his home state or country and who has in his immediate possession a valid driver's license issued to him in his home state or country shall be permitted without examination or license under this chapter to drive a motor vehicle on the highways in the Commonwealth. The provisions of this section shall not be affected by the person's, spouse's, or dependent child's ownership of a motor vehicle registered in Virginia.

History.
1970, c. 269, § 46.1-354.1; 1975, c. 240; 1984, c. 780; 1988, c. 107; 1989, c. 727.

§ 46.2-307. Nonresidents licensed under laws of home state or country; extension of reciprocal privileges.

A. A nonresident over the age of sixteen years and three months who has been duly licensed as a driver under a law requiring the licensing of drivers in his home state or country and who has in his immediate possession a driver's license issued to him in his home state or country shall be permitted, without a Virginia license, to drive a motor vehicle on the highways of the Commonwealth.

B. Notwithstanding any other provisions of this chapter, the Commissioner, with the consent of the Governor, may extend to nonresidents from foreign countries the same driver's licensing privileges which are granted by the foreign country, or political subdivision wherein such nonresidents are residents, to residents of this Commonwealth residing in such foreign country or political subdivision.

C. Driver's license privileges may be extended to nonresidents from foreign countries or political subdivisions who are over the age of sixteen years and three months, have been duly licensed as drivers under a law requiring the licensing of drivers in their home country or political subdivision, and have in their immediate possession a driver's license issued to them in their home country or political subdivision.

History.
Code 1950, § 46-351; 1958, c. 541, § 46.1-355; 1984, c. 780; 1989, cc. 705, 727; 1997, c. 486; 2002, c. 755.

§ 46.2-308. Temporary exemption for new resident licensed under laws of another state; privately owned vehicle driver's licenses.

A resident over the age of sixteen years and three months who has been duly licensed as a driver under a law of another state or country requiring the licensing of drivers shall, for the first sixty days of his residency in the Commonwealth, be permitted, without a Virginia license, to drive a motor vehicle on the highways of the Commonwealth.

Persons to whom military privately-owned vehicle driver's licenses have been issued by the Department of Defense shall, for the first sixty days of their residency in the Commonwealth, be permitted, without a Virginia license, to drive motor vehicles on the highways of the Commonwealth.

History.
1976, c. 17, § 46.1-355.1; 1989, cc. 705, 727; 1994, c. 356; 2002, cc. 755, 767, 834.

§ 46.2-309: Repealed by Acts 2005, c. 245, cl. 2.

§ 46.2-310. Localities may not require license except for taxicabs; prosecutions for operation of vehicle without license or while suspended.

Counties, cities, and towns shall not require any local permit to drive, except as provided in this section. Counties, cities, and towns may adopt regulations for the licensing of drivers of taxicabs and similar for-hire passenger vehicles and for the control of the operation of such for-hire vehicles. This section shall not preclude any county, city, or town from prosecuting, under a warrant issued by such county, city, or town, a person charged with violation of a local ordinance prohibiting operation of a motor vehicle without a driver's license or while his driver's license or privilege to drive is suspended or revoked.

History.

Code 1950, § 46-349; 1958, c. 541, § 46.1-353; 1964, c. 455; 1984, c. 780; 1989, c. 727.

ARTICLE 3.

PERSONS NOT TO BE LICENSED.

§ 46.2-311. Persons having defective vision; minimum standards of visual acuity and field of vision; tests of vision.

A. The Department shall not issue a driver's license or learner's permit (i) to any person unless he demonstrates a visual acuity of at least 20/40 in one or both eyes with or without corrective lenses or (ii) to any such person unless he demonstrates at least a field of 100 degrees of horizontal vision in one or both eyes or a comparable measurement that demonstrates a visual field within this range. However, a license permitting the driving of motor vehicles during a period beginning one-half hour after sunrise and ending one-half hour before sunset, may be issued to a person who demonstrates a visual acuity of at least 20/70 in one or both eyes without or with corrective lenses provided he demonstrates at least a field of 70 degrees of horizontal vision or a comparable measurement that demonstrates a visual field within this range, and further provided that if such person has vision in one eye only, he demonstrates at least a field of 40 degrees temporal and 30 degrees nasal horizontal vision or a comparable measurement that demonstrates a visual field within this range.

B. The Department shall not issue a driver's license or learner's permit to any person authorizing the driving of a commercial motor vehicle as defined in the Virginia Commercial Driver's License Act (§ 46.2-341.1 et seq.) unless he demonstrates a visual acuity of at least 20/40 in each eye and at least a field of 140 degrees of horizontal vision or a comparable measurement that demonstrates a visual field within this range.

C. Every person applying to renew a driver's license and required to be reexamined as a prerequisite to the renewal of the license, shall:

1. Appear before a license examiner of the Department to demonstrate his visual acuity and horizontal field of vision, or

2. Accompany his application with a report of such examination made within 90 days prior thereto by an ophthalmologist or optometrist.

D. The test of horizontal visual fields made by license examiners of the Department shall be performed at thirty-three and one-third centimeters with a 10 millimeter round white test object or may, at the discretion of the Commissioner, be performed with electronic or other devices designed for the purpose of testing visual acuity and horizontal field of vision. The report of examination of visual acuity and horizontal field of vision made by an ophthalmologist or optometrist shall have precedence over an examination made by a license examiner of the Department in administrative determination as to the issuance of a license to drive. Any such report may, in the discretion of the Commissioner, be referred to a medical advisory board or to the State Health Commissioner for evaluation.

E. Notwithstanding the provisions of subsection B of this section, any person who is licensed to drive any motor vehicle may, on special application to the Department, be licensed to drive any vehicle, provided the operation of the vehicle would not unduly endanger the public safety, as determined by the Commissioner.

The Commissioner may waive the vision requirements of subsection B for any commercial driver's license applicant who either (i) is subject to the Federal Motor Carrier Safety Regulations but is exempt from the vision standards of 49 C.F.R. Part 391 or (ii) is not required to meet the vision standards specified in 49 C.F.R. § 391.41 of the regulations.

In order to determine whether such a waiver would unduly endanger the public safety, the Commissioner shall require such commercial driver's license applicant to submit a special waiver application and to provide all medical information relating to his vision that may be requested by the Department. The Department may require such commercial driver's license applicant to take a road test administered by the Department before determining whether to grant a waiver. If a waiver is granted, the Department may subject the applicant's use of a commercial motor vehicle to reasonable restrictions, which shall be noted on the commercial driver's license. If a waiver is granted, the Department may also limit the validity period of the commercial driver's license, and the expiration date shall be noted on the commercial driver's license.

History.

1968, c. 642, § 46.1-357.2; 1972, c. 502; 1980, c. 118; 1981, c. 194; 1984, c. 780; 1989, cc. 705, 727; 2010, c. 18; 2013, cc. 165, 582.

§ 46.2-312. Persons using bioptic telescopic lenses.

A. Persons using bioptic telescopic lenses shall be eligible for driver's licenses if they:

1. Demonstrate a visual acuity of at least 20/200 in one or both eyes and a field of seventy degrees horizontal vision without or with corrective carrier lenses or a comparable measurement that demonstrates a visual field within this range, or if these persons have vision in one eye only, they demonstrate a field of at least forty degrees temporal and thirty degrees nasal horizontal vision or a comparable measurement that demonstrates a visual field within this range;
2. Demonstrate a visual acuity of at least 20/70 in one or both eyes with the bioptic telescopic lenses and without the use of field expanders;
3. Meet all other criteria for licensure;
4. Accompany the license application with a report of examination by an ophthalmologist or optometrist on a form prescribed by the Department for evaluation by the Medical Advisory Board.

B. Persons using bioptic telescopic lenses shall be eligible for learner's permits issued under § 46.2-335 provided they first meet the requirements of subsection A of this section, except for that part of the examination requiring the applicant to drive a motor vehicle.

C. Persons using bioptic telescopic lenses shall be subject to the following restrictions:

1. They shall not be eligible for any of the driver's license endorsements provided for in § 46.2-328;
2. Their driver's licenses shall permit the operation of motor vehicles only during the period beginning one-half hour after sunrise and ending one-half hour before sunset.

D. Notwithstanding the provisions of subdivision C 2 of this section, persons using bioptic telescopic lenses may be licensed to drive motor vehicles between one-half hour before sunset and one-half hour after sunrise if they:

1. Demonstrate a visual acuity of at least 20/40 in one or both eyes with the bioptic telescopic lenses and without the use of field expanders;
2. Have been licensed under subsection C of this section for at least one year; and
3. Pass a skills test taken at night.

History.

1986, c. 115, § 46.1-357.3; 1989, cc. 147, 727; 2010, c. 18.

§ 46.2-313. Persons with suspended or revoked licenses.

The Department shall not issue a driver's license to any person whose license has been suspended, during the period of the suspension; nor to any person whose license has been revoked, or should have been revoked, under the provisions of this title, until the expiration of one year after the license was revoked, unless otherwise permitted by the provisions of this title.

History.

Code 1950, § 46-354; 1958, c. 541, § 46.1-358; 1984, c. 780; 1989, c. 727.

§ 46.2-314. Mental incapacity.

No driver's license shall be issued to any applicant who has previously been adjudged incapacitated and who has not, at the time of such application, been (i) adjudged restored to capacity by judicial decree or (ii) released from a hospital for individuals with mental illness on a certificate of the superintendent of the hospital that the person is capable. In either case, no driver's license shall be issued to him unless the Department is satisfied that he is competent to drive a motor vehicle with safety to persons and property.

History.

Code 1950, § 46-356; 1958, c. 541, § 46.1-360; 1976, c. 368; 1984, c. 780; 1989, c. 727; 1997, c. 801; 2012, cc. 476, 507.

§ 46.2-315. Disabled persons.

The Department shall not issue a driver's license to any person when, in the opinion of the Department, the person is suffering from a physical or mental disability or disease which will prevent his exercising reasonable and ordinary control over a motor vehicle while driving it on the highways, nor shall a license be issued to any person who is unable to understand highway warning or direction signs.

The words "disability or disease" shall not mean inability of a person to hear or to speak, or both, when he has good vision and can satisfactorily demonstrate his ability to drive a motor vehicle and has sufficient knowledge of traffic rules and regulations.

History.

Code 1950, § 46-357; 1958, c. 541, § 46.1-361; 1984, c. 780; 1989, c. 727.

§ 46.2-316. Persons convicted or found not innocent of certain offenses; requirement of proof of financial responsibility for certain offenses.

A. The Department shall not issue a driver's license or learner's permit to any resident or nonresident person while his license or other privilege to drive is suspended or revoked because of his conviction, or finding of not innocent in the case of a juvenile, or forfeiture of bail upon the following charges of offenses committed in violation of either a law of the Commonwealth or a valid local ordinance or of any federal law or law of any other state or any valid local ordinance of any other state:

1. Voluntary or involuntary manslaughter resulting from the operation of a motor vehicle.

2. Perjury, the making of a false affidavit to the Department under any law requiring the registration of motor vehicles or regulating their operation on the highways, or the making of a false statement in any application for a driver's license.

3. Any crime punishable as a felony under the motor vehicle laws or any felony in the commission of which a motor vehicle is used.

4. Violation of the provisions of § 18.2-51.4, pertaining to maiming while under the influence, § 18.2-266, pertaining to driving while under the influence of intoxicants or drugs, or of § 18.2-272, pertaining to driving while the driver's license has been forfeited for a conviction, or finding of not innocent in the case of a juvenile, under §§ 18.2-51.4, 18.2-266 or § 18.2-272, or for violation of the provisions of any federal law or law of any other state or any valid local ordinance similar to §§ 18.2-51.4, 18.2-266 or § 18.2-272.

5. Failure of a driver of a motor vehicle, involved in an accident resulting in death or injury to another person, to stop and disclose his identity at the scene of the accident.

6. On a charge of operating or permitting the operation, for the second time, of a passenger automobile for the transportation of passengers for rent or for hire, without having first obtained a license for the privilege as provided in § 46.2-694.

B. Except as provided in subsection C, the Department shall not issue a driver's license or learner's permit to any person convicted of a crime mentioned in subsection A of this section for a further period of three years after he otherwise becomes entitled to a license or permit until he proves to the Commissioner his ability to respond in damages as provided in Article 15 (§ 46.2-435 et seq.) of Chapter 3 of this title or any other law of the Commonwealth requiring proof of financial responsibility.

C. In addition to the prohibition on licensure set forth in subsection A, the Department shall not issue or reinstate a driver's license or learner's permit to any person convicted of a violation set forth in subdivision A 4 for a period of three years after he otherwise becomes entitled to a license or permit until he furnishes proof of financial responsibility in the future under a motor vehicle liability insurance policy that satisfies the requirements of § 46.2-472 except that the limits of coverage exclusive of interest and costs, with respect to each motor vehicle insured under the policy, shall be not less than double the minimum limits set forth in subdivision 3 of § 46.2-472 for bodily injury or death of one person in any one accident, for bodily injury to or death of two or more persons in any one accident, and for injury to or destruction of property of others in any one accident.

Motor Vehicles

History.

Code 1950, § 46-358; 1958, c. 541, § 46.1-362; 1960, c. 364; 1966, c. 549; 1974, c. 453; 1980, c. 29; 1984, c. 780; 1989, c. 727; 1997, c. 691; 2007, c. 496.

§ 46.2-317. Persons making false statement in application.

The Department shall not issue, for a period of one year, a driver's license or learner's permit when the records of the Department clearly show to the satisfaction of the Commissioner that the person has made a willful material false statement on any application for a driver's license.

History.

Code 1950, § 46-358.1; 1958, c. 541, § 46.1-363; 1984, c. 780; 1989, c. 727.

§ 46.2-318. Cancellation or revocation of license where application is false in material particular.

The Commissioner may cancel or revoke any license or permit issued pursuant to this title when it appears that the information set forth in the application for the license or permit is false in any material particular.

History.

1958, c. 541, § 46.1-364; 1989, c. 727.

§ 46.2-319. Refusal or revocation of license for certain fraudulent acts in obtaining a driver's license.

The Department shall not issue any permit or license under this title to any person who has been convicted, or found not innocent in the case of a juvenile, of violating § 46.2-348, when the violation was based on the taking of any examination under §§ 46.2-311, 46.2-322, 46.2-325 or the provisions of the Virginia Commercial Driver's License Act (§ 46.2-341.1 et seq.) for another person, or the appearance for another for renewal of a license under this chapter, for a period of ten years from the date of conviction, or finding of not innocent in the case of a juvenile. If the person has a license or permit issued pursuant to this title, the Commissioner shall revoke the license or permit for a period of ten years from the date of the conviction, or finding of not innocent in the case of a juvenile.

History.

1968, c. 642, § 46.1-365; 1974, c. 453; 1989, cc. 705, 727.

§ 46.2-320. Other grounds for refusal or suspension.

The Department may refuse to grant an application for a driver's license in any of the circumstances set forth in § 46.2-608 as circumstances justifying the refusal of an application for the registration of a motor vehicle. The Department may refuse to issue or reissue a driver's license for the willful failure or refusal to pay any taxes or fees required to be collected or authorized to be collected by the Department.

History.

Code 1950, § 46-359; 1958, c. 541, § 46.1-366; 1982, c. 147; 1984, c. 780; 1989, c. 727; 1995, c. 595; 1996, cc. 785, 1013; 1997, cc. 473, 794, 857, 898; 1999, c. 615; 2001, cc. 645, 779; 2010, c. 682; 2011, c. 773; 2012, c. 829.

§ 46.2-320.1. Other grounds for suspension; nonpayment of child support.

A. The Commissioner may enter into an agreement with the Department of Social Services whereby the Department may suspend or refuse to renew the driver's license of any person upon receipt of notice from the Department of Social Services that the person (i) is delinquent in the payment of child support by 90 days or more or in an amount of $5,000 or more or (ii) has failed to comply with a subpoena, summons, or warrant relating to paternity or child support proceedings. A suspension or refusal to renew authorized pursuant to this section shall not be effective until 30 days after service on the delinquent obligor of notice of intent to suspend or refusal to renew. The notice of intent shall be served on the obligor by the Department of Social Services (a) by certified mail, return receipt requested, or by electronic means, sent to the obligor's last known addresses as shown in the records of the Department or the Department of Social Services or (b) pursuant to § 8.01-296, or service may be waived by the obligor in accordance with procedures established by the Department of Social Services. The obligor shall be entitled to a judicial hearing if a request for a hearing is made, in writing, to the Department of Social Services within 10 days from service of the notice of intent. Upon receipt of the request for a hearing, the Department of Social Services shall petition the court that entered or is enforcing the order, requesting a hearing on the proposed suspension or refusal to renew. The court shall authorize the suspension or refusal to renew only if it finds that the obligor's noncompliance with the child support order was willful. Upon a showing by the Department of Social Services that the obligor is delinquent in the payment of child support by 90 days or more or in an amount of $5,000 or more, the burden of proving that the delinquency was not willful shall rest upon the obligor. The Department shall not suspend or refuse to renew the driver's license until a final determination is made by the court.

B. At any time after service of a notice of intent, the person may petition the juvenile and domestic relations district court in the jurisdiction where he resides for the issuance of a restricted license to be used if the suspension or refusal to renew becomes effective. Upon such petition and a finding of good cause, the court may provide that such person be issued a restricted permit to operate a motor vehicle for any of the purposes set forth in subsection E of § 18.2-271.1. A restricted license issued pursuant to this subsection shall not permit any person to operate a commercial motor vehicle as defined in § 46.2-341.4. The court shall order the surrender of the person's license to operate a motor vehicle, to be disposed of in accordance with the provisions of § 46.2-398, and shall forward to the Commissioner a copy of its order entered pursuant to this subsection. The order shall specifically enumerate the restrictions imposed and contain such information regarding the person to whom such a permit is issued as is reasonably necessary to identify him.

C. The Department shall not renew a driver's license or terminate a license suspension imposed pursuant to this section until it has received from the Department of Social Services a certification that the person has (i) paid the delinquency in full; (ii) reached an agreement with the Department of Social Services to satisfy the delinquency within a period not to exceed 10 years, and at least one payment representing at least five percent of the total delinquency or $600, whichever is greater, has been made pursuant to the agreement; (iii) complied with a subpoena, summons, or warrant relating to a paternity or child support proceeding; or (iv) completed or is successfully participating in an intensive case monitoring program for child support as ordered by a juvenile and domestic relations district court or as administered by the Department of Social Services. Certification by the Department of Social Services shall be made by electronic or telephonic communication and shall be made on the same work day that payment required by clause (i) or (ii) is made.

D. If a person who has entered into an agreement with the Department of Social Services pursuant to clause (ii) of subsection C fails to comply with the requirements of the agreement, the Department of Social Services shall notify the Department of the person's noncompliance and the Department shall suspend or refuse to renew the driver's license of the person until it has received from the Department of Social Services a certification that the person has paid the delinquency in full or has entered into a subsequent agreement with the Department of Social Services to satisfy the delinquency within a period not to exceed seven years and has made at least one payment of $1,200 or five percent of the total delinquency, whichever is greater, pursuant to the agreement. If the person fails to comply with the terms of a subsequent agreement reached with the Department of Social Services pursuant to this section, without further notice to the person as provided in the subsequent agreement, the Department of Social Services shall notify the Department of the person's noncompliance, and the Department shall suspend or refuse to renew the driver's license of the person. A person who has failed to comply with the terms of a second or subsequent agreement pursuant to this subsection may be granted a new agreement with the Department of Social Services if the person has made at least one payment of $1,800 or five percent of the total delinquency, whichever is greater, and agrees to a repayment schedule of not more than seven years. Upon receipt of certification from the Department of Social Services of the person's satisfaction of these conditions, the Department shall issue a driver's license to the person or reinstate the person's driver's license. Certification by the Department of Social Services shall be made by electronic or telephonic communication and shall be made on the same work day that payment required by this subsection is made.

History.
2012, c. 829; 2015, c. 506; 2016, c. 29.

§ 46.2-320.2. Other grounds for suspension; nonpayment of fees owed to local correctional facilities or regional jails.

A. The Commissioner may enter into an agreement with a local correctional facility or regional jail whereby the Department shall suspend or refuse to renew the driver's license of any person upon receipt of notice from the local correctional facility or regional jail that (i) the person is delinquent in payment of fees imposed under § 53.1-131.3, (ii) a judgment for such fees has been issued by a court of competent jurisdiction, and (iii) a court of competent jurisdiction has, for good cause, ordered the suspension or nonrenewal of the driver's license of the person in accordance with the provisions of this section. A suspension or refusal to renew authorized pursuant to this section shall be effective upon notice to the Department by the local correctional facility or regional jail. Notification to the Department by the local correctional facility or regional jail shall be made by electronic communication, which shall include copies of the judgment and court order for suspension or nonrenewal of the person's driver's license and provide the person's most current mailing address.

B. The Department shall not renew a driver's license or terminate a license suspension imposed pursuant to this section until it has received from the local correctional facility or regional jail a notification that the person has (i) paid the delinquency in full or (ii) reached an agreement with the local correctional facility or regional jail to satisfy the delinquency within an acceptable period. Notification to the Department by the local correctional facility or regional jail shall be made by electronic communication and shall be made on the same work day that the payment or agreement required by clause (i) or (ii) is made.

C. Any person whose license is suspended pursuant to subsection A may petition the district court of the jurisdiction where he resides or wherein the jail or correctional facility is located for the issuance of a restricted driver's license for a period not to exceed one year for any of the purposes set forth in subsection E of § 18.2-271.1. The district court may, for good cause shown, issue such a restricted permit.

History.
2012, c. 829.

§ 46.2-321. Appeal from denial, suspension, or revocation of license; operation of vehicle pending appeal.

Any person denied a license or whose license has been revoked, suspended, or cancelled under this article may appeal in accordance with the provisions of the Administrative Process Act (§ 2.2-4000 et seq.). From the final judgment of the court, either the petitioner or the Commonwealth shall have an appeal as a matter of right to the Court of Appeals.

While an appeal is pending from the action of the Department denying a license or from the court affirming the action of the Department, the person aggrieved shall not drive a motor vehicle on the highways of the Commonwealth.

History.
Code 1950, § 46-360; 1958, c. 541, § 46.1-367; 1960, c. 511; 1973, c. 544; 1984, c. 703; 1986, c. 615; 1989, c. 727; 1990, c. 418.

§ 46.2-322. Examination of licensee believed incompetent; suspension or restriction of license; license application to include questions as to physical or mental conditions of applicant; false answers; examination of applicant; physician's, nurse practitioner's, or physician assistant's statement.

A. If the Department has good cause to believe that a driver is incapacitated and therefore unable to drive a motor vehicle safely, after written notice of at least 15 days to the person, it may require him to submit to an examination to determine his fitness to drive a motor vehicle. If the driver so requests in writing, the Department shall give the Department's reasons for the examination, including the identity of all persons who have supplied information to the Department regarding the driver's fitness to drive a motor vehicle. However, the Department shall not supply the reasons or information if its source is a relative of the driver or a physician, physician assistant, nurse practitioner, pharmacist, or other licensed medical professional as defined in § 38.2-602 treating, or prescribing medications for, the driver.

B. As a part of its examination, the Department may require a physical examination by a licensed physician, licensed nurse practitioner, or licensed physician assistant and a report on the results thereof. When it has completed its examination, the Department shall take whatever action may be appropriate and may suspend the license or privilege to drive a motor vehicle in the Commonwealth of the person or permit him to retain his license or privilege to drive a motor vehicle in the Commonwealth, or may issue a license subject to the restrictions authorized by § 46.2-329. Refusal or neglect of the person to submit to the examination or comply with restrictions imposed by the Department shall be grounds for suspension of his license or privilege to drive a motor vehicle in the Commonwealth.

C. The Commissioner shall include, as a part of the application for an original driver's license, or renewal thereof, questions as to the existence of physical or mental conditions that impair the ability of the applicant to drive a motor vehicle safely. Any person knowingly giving a false answer to any such question shall be guilty of a Class 2 misdemeanor. If the answer to any such question indicates the existence of such condition, the Commissioner shall require an examination of the applicant by a licensed physician, licensed physician assistant, or licensed nurse practitioner as a prerequisite to the issuance of the driver's license. The report of the examination shall contain a statement that, in the opinion of the physician, physician assistant, or nurse practitioner, the applicant's physical or mental condition at the time of the examination does or does not preclude his safe driving of motor vehicles.

History.

Code 1950, § 46-378; 1952, c. 666; 1958, c. 541, § 46.1-383; 1960, c. 201; 1966, c. 631; 1968, c. 167; 1972, c. 419; 1974, c. 453; 1978, c. 353; 1984, c. 780; 1988, c. 798; 1989, c. 727; 1997, c. 801; 2004, cc. 351, 855; 2006, c. 396; 2011, c. 441.

ARTICLE 4.

OBTAINING LICENSES, GENERALLY.

§ 46.2-323. Application for driver's license; proof of completion of driver education program; penalty.

A. Every application for a driver's license, temporary driver's permit, learner's permit, or motorcycle learner's permit shall be made on a form prescribed by the Department and the applicant shall write his usual signature in ink in the space provided on the form. The form shall include notice to the applicant of the duty to register with the Department of State Police as provided in Chapter 9 (§ 9.1-900 et seq.) of Title 9.1, if the applicant has been convicted of an offense for which registration with the Sex Offender and Crimes Against Minors Registry is required.

B. Every application shall state the full legal name, year, month, and date of birth, social security number, sex, and residence address of the applicant; whether or not the applicant has previously been licensed as a driver and, if so, when and by what state, and whether or not his license has ever been suspended or revoked and, if so, the date of and reason for such suspension or revocation. The Department, as a condition for the issuance of any driver's license, temporary driver's permit, learner's permit, or motorcycle learner's permit shall require the surrender of any driver's license or, in the case of a motorcycle learner's permit, a motorcycle license issued by another state and held by the applicant. The applicant shall also answer any questions on the application form or otherwise propounded by the Department incidental to the examination. The applicant may also be required to present proof of identity, residency, and social security number or non-work authorized status, if required to appear in person before the Department to apply.

The Commissioner shall require that each application include a certification statement to be signed by the applicant under penalty of perjury, certifying that the information presented on the application is true and correct.

If the applicant fails or refuses to sign the certification statement, the Department shall not issue the applicant a driver's license, temporary driver's permit, learner's permit or motorcycle learner's permit.

Any applicant who knowingly makes a false certification or supplies false or fictitious evidence shall be punished as provided in § 46.2-348.

C. Every application for a driver's license shall include a photograph of the applicant supplied under arrangements made by the Department. The photograph shall be processed by the Department so that the photograph can be made part of the issued license.

D. Notwithstanding the provisions of § 46.2-334, every applicant for a driver's license who is under 18 years of age shall furnish the Department with satisfactory proof of his successful completion of a driver education program approved by the State Department of Education.

E. Every application for a driver's license submitted by a person less than 18 years old and attending a public school in the Commonwealth shall be accompanied by a document, signed by the applicant's parent or legal guardian, authorizing the principal, or his designee, of the school attended by the applicant to notify the juvenile and domestic relations district court within whose jurisdiction the minor resides when the applicant has had 10 or more unexcused absences from school on consecutive school days.

F. The Department shall electronically transmit application information to the Department of State Police, in a format approved by the State Police, for comparison with information contained in the Virginia Criminal Information Network and National Crime Information Center Convicted Sexual Offender Registry Files, at the time of issuance of a driver's license, temporary driver's permit, learner's permit, or motorcycle learner's permit. Whenever it appears from the records of the State Police that a person has failed to comply with the duty to register or reregister pursuant to Chapter 9 (§ 9.1-900 et seq.) of Title 9.1, the State Police shall promptly investigate and, if there is probable cause to believe a violation has occurred, obtain a warrant or assist in obtaining an indictment charging a violation of § 18.2-472.1 in the jurisdiction in which the person made application of licensure.

History.

Code 1950, § 46-362; 1958, c. 541, § 46.1-368; 1962, c. 368; 1968, c. 642; 1974, c. 605; 1982, c. 180; 1983, c. 608; 1984, cc. 778, 780; 1988, c. 105; 1989, cc. 705, 727; 1993, cc. 471, 501; 1994, c. 362; 1998, c. 322; 2002, cc. 535, 867; 2003, c. 584; 2005, cc. 259, 828; 2006, cc. 857, 914; 2009, cc. 439, 872; 2016, c. 488.

§ 46.2-323.01. Issuance of documents; relationship with federal law.

A. The Department shall establish a process for persons who, for reasons beyond their control, are unable to provide all necessary documents required for driver's licenses, permits, and special identification cards and must rely on alternate documents to establish identity or date of birth. Alternative documents to demonstrate legal presence will only be allowed to demonstrate United States citizenship.

B. The Department shall not comply with any federal law or regulation that would require the Department to use any type of computer chip or radio-frequency identification tag or other similar device on or in a driver's license or special identification card.

History.

2009, c. 872.

§ 46.2-323.1. Certification of Virginia residency; nonresidents not to be issued driver's licenses, commercial driver's licenses, learner's permits, or special identification card; penalty.

No driver's license, commercial driver's license, temporary driver's permit, learner's permit, motorcycle learner's permit, or special identification card shall be issued to any person who is not a Virginia resident. Every person applying for a driver's license, commercial driver's license, temporary driver's permit, learner's permit, motorcycle learner's permit, or special identification card shall execute and furnish to the Commissioner his certificate that he is a resident of Virginia. The Commissioner or his duly authorized agent may require any such applicant to supply, along with his application, such evidence of his Virginia residency as the Commissioner may deem appropriate and adequate, provided that neither an immigration visa nor a signed written statement, whether or not such statement is notarized, wherein the maker of the statement vouches for the Virginia residency of the applicant, shall be acceptable proof of Virginia residency. If the applicant is less than nineteen years old and cannot otherwise provide proof of Virginia residency, the Commissioner may accept proof of the applicant's parent's or guardian's Virginia residency. Any minor providing proper evidence of the solemnization of his marriage or a certified copy of a court order of emancipation shall not be required to provide the parent's certification of residency. It shall be unlawful for any applicant knowingly to make a false certification of Virginia residency or supply false or fictitious evidence of Virginia residency. Any violation of this section shall be punished as provided in § 46.2-348.

History.

1993, c. 444; 2002, cc. 767, 834.

§ 46.2-324. Applicants and license holders to notify Department of change of address; fee.

A. Whenever any person, after applying for or obtaining a driver's license or special identification card shall move from the address shown in the application or on the license or special identification card, he shall, within 30 days, notify the Department of his change of address. If the Department receives notification from the person or any court or law-enforcement agency that a person's residential address has changed to a non-Virginia address, unless the person (i) is on active duty with the armed forces of the United States, (ii) provides proof that he is a U.S. citizen and resides outside the United States because of his employment or the employment of a spouse or parent, or (iii) provides proof satisfactory to the Commissioner that he is a bona fide resident of Virginia, the Department shall (i) mail, by first-class mail, no later than three days after the notice of address change is received by the Department, notice to the person that his license and/or special identification card will be cancelled by the Department and (ii) cancel the driver's license and/or special identification card 30 days after notice of cancellation has been mailed.

B. The Department may contract with the United States Postal Service or an authorized agent to use the National Change of Address System for the purpose of obtaining current address information for a person whose name appears in customer records maintained by the Department. If the Department receives information from the National Change of Address System indicating that a person whose name appears in a Department record has submitted a permanent change of address to the Postal Service, the Department may then update its records with the mailing address obtained from the National Change of Address System.

C. There may be imposed upon anyone failing to notify the Department of his change of address as required by this section a fee of $5, which fee shall be used to defray the expenses incurred by the Department. Notwithstanding the foregoing provision of this subsection, no fee shall be imposed on any person whose address is obtained from the National Change of Address System.

D. The Department shall electronically transmit change of address information to the Department of State Police, in a format approved by the State Police, for comparison with information contained in the Virginia Criminal Information Network and National Crime Information Center Convicted Sexual Offender Registry Files, at the time of the change of address. Whenever it appears from the records of the State Police that a person has failed to comply with the duty to register or reregister pursuant to Chapter 9 (§ 9.1-900 et seq.) of Title 9.1, the State Police shall promptly investigate and, if there is probable cause to believe a violation has occurred, obtain a warrant or assist in obtaining an indictment charging a violation of § 18.2-472.1 in the jurisdiction in which the person last registered or reregistered or in the jurisdiction where the person made application for change of address.

History.

1974, c. 347, § 46.1-368.1; 1989, c. 727; 1996, cc. 943, 994; 2002, cc. 767, 834; 2006, cc. 857, 914; 2010, cc. 25, 55.

§ 46.2-324.1. Requirements for initial licensure of certain applicants.

A. No driver's license shall be issued to any applicant unless he either (i) provides written evidence of having satisfactorily completed a course of driver instruction at a driver training school licensed under Chapter 17 (§ 46.2-1700 et seq.) or a comparable course approved by the Department or Department of Education or (ii) has held a learner's permit issued by the Department for at least 60 days prior to his first behind-the-wheel examination by the Department when applying for a noncommercial driver's license.

The provisions of this section shall only apply to persons who are at least 18 years old and who either (a) have never held a driver's license issued by Virginia or any other state or territory of the United States or foreign country or (b) have never been licensed or held the license endorsement or classification required to operate the type of vehicle which they now propose to operate. Completion of a course of driver instruction approved by the Department or the Department of Education at a driver training school may include the final behind-the-wheel examination for a driver's license; however, a driver training school shall not administer the behind-the-wheel examination to any applicant who is under medical control pursuant to § 46.2-322. Applicants completing a course of driver instruction approved by the Department or the Department of Education at a driver training school retain the option of having the behind-the-wheel examination administered by the Department.

B. No commercial driver's license shall be issued to any applicant unless he is 18 years old or older and has complied with the requirements of subsection A of § 46.2-341.9. Applicants for a commercial driver's license who have never before held a commercial driver's license shall apply for a commercial learner's permit and either (i) provide written evidence of having satisfactorily completed a course of driver instruction at a driver training school licensed under Chapter 17 (§ 46.2-1700 et seq.) or a comparable course approved by the Department or Department of Education and hold the commercial learner's permit for a minimum of 14 days prior to taking the behind-the-wheel examination for the commercial driver's license or (ii) hold the commercial learner's permit for a minimum of 30 days before taking the behind-the-wheel examination for the commercial driver's license.

Holders of a commercial driver's license who have never held the license endorsement or classification required to operate the type of commercial motor vehicle which they now propose to operate must apply for a commercial learner's permit if the upgrade requires a skills test and hold the permit for a minimum of 14 days prior to taking the behind-the-wheel examination for the commercial driver's license.

C. Nothing in this section shall be construed to prohibit the Department from requiring any person to complete the skills examination as prescribed in § 46.2-325 and the written or automated examinations as prescribed in § 46.2-335.

D. Notwithstanding the provisions of subsection B, applicants for a commercial driver's license who have never before held a commercial driver's license who are members of the active duty military, military reserves, National Guard, active duty United States Coast Guard, or Coast Guard Auxiliary and provide written evidence of having satisfactorily completed a military commercial driver training program shall hold the commercial learner's permit for a minimum of 14 days prior to taking the behind-the-wheel examination for the commercial driver's license.

E. Notwithstanding the provisions of subsection B, applicants for a commercial driver's license who have never before held a commercial driver's license who are employed by a public school division as a bus driver and provide written evidence of having satisfactorily completed a commercial driver training program with a public school division shall hold the commercial learner's permit for a minimum of 14 days prior to taking the behind-the-wheel examination for the commercial driver's license.

History.

2000, c. 685; 2005, cc. 245, 513; 2012, cc. 215, 222; 2013, cc. 165, 582; 2014, c. 685; 2015, c. 258; 2016, c. 488.

§ 46.2-325. Examination of applicants; waiver of Department's examination under certain circumstances; behind-the-wheel and knowledge examinations.

A. The Department shall examine every applicant for a driver's license before issuing any license to determine (i) his physical and mental qualifications and his ability to drive a motor vehicle without jeopardizing the safety of persons or property and (ii) if any facts exist which would bar the issuance of a license under §§ 46.2-311 through 46.2-316, 46.2-334, or 46.2-335. The examination, however, shall not include investigation of any facts other than those directly pertaining to the ability of the applicant to drive a motor vehicle with safety, or other than those facts declared to be prerequisite to the issuance of a license under this chapter. No applicant otherwise competent shall be required to demonstrate ability to park any motor vehicle except in an adequate parking space between horizontal markers, and not between flags or sticks simulating parked vehicles. Except as provided for in § 46.2-337, applicants for licensure to drive motor vehicles of the classifications referred to in § 46.2-328 shall submit to examinations which relate to the operation of those vehicles. The motor vehicle to be used by the applicant for the behind-the-wheel examination shall meet the safety and equipment requirements specified in Chapter 10 (§ 46.2-1000 et seq.) and possess a valid inspection sticker as required pursuant to § 46.2-1157. An autocycle shall not be used by the applicant for a behind-the-wheel examination.

Prior to taking the examination, the applicant shall either (a) present evidence that the applicant has completed a state-approved driver education class pursuant to the provisions of § 46.2-324.1 or 46.2-334 or (b) submit to the examiner a behind-the-wheel maneuvers checklist, on a form provided by the Department, that describes the vehicle maneuvers the applicant may be expected to perform while taking the behind-the-wheel examination, that has been signed by a licensed driver, certifying that the applicant has practiced the driving maneuvers contained and described therein, and that has been signed by the applicant certifying that, at all times while holding a learner's permit, the applicant has complied with the provisions of § 46.2-335 while operating a motor vehicle.

Except for applicants subject to § 46.2-312, if the Commissioner is satisfied that an applicant has demonstrated the same proficiency as required by the Department's examination through successful completion of either (1) the driver education course approved by the Department of Education or (2) a driver training course offered by a driver training school licensed under Chapter 17 (§ 46.2-1700 et seq.), he may waive those parts of the Department's examination provided for in this section that require the applicant to drive and park a motor vehicle.

B. Any person who fails the behind-the-wheel examination for a driver's license administered by the Department shall wait two days before being permitted to take another such examination. No person who fails the behind-the-wheel examination for a driver's license administered by the Department three times shall be permitted to take such examination a fourth time until he successfully completes, subsequent to the third examination failure, the in-vehicle component of driver instruction at a driver training school licensed under Chapter 17 (§ 46.2-1700 et seq.) or a comparable course approved by the Department or the Department of Education. In addition, no person who fails the driver knowledge examination for a driver's license administered by the Department three times shall be permitted to take such examination a fourth time until he successfully completes, subsequent to the third examination failure, the classroom component of driver instruction at a driver training school licensed under Chapter 17 (§ 46.2-1700 et seq.) or, for (i) persons at least 19 years old or (ii) persons less than 19 years old who have previously completed the classroom component of driver instruction at a driver training school licensed under Chapter 17 (§ 46.2-1700 et seq.), a course of instruction based on the Virginia Driver's Manual offered by a driver training school licensed under Chapter 17 (§ 46.2-1700 et seq.) and approved by the Department or the Department of Education. All persons required to attend a driver training school pursuant to this section shall be required after successful completion of the necessary courses to have the applicable examination administered by the Department.

The provisions of this subsection shall not apply to persons placed under medical control by the Department pursuant to § 46.2-322.

History.

Code 1950, § 46-365; 1954, c. 454; 1958, c. 541, § 46.1-369; 1966, cc. 375, 595; 1968, c. 176; 1976, c. 8; 1984, c. 780; 1989, c. 727; 1995, c. 847; 1997, c. 841; 2007, c. 190; 2008, c. 735; 2012, cc. 215, 222; 2013, c. 272; 2014, cc. 53, 256, 685; 2016, c. 381.

§ 46.2-326. Designation of examiners; conduct of examination; reports.

The Commissioner shall designate persons within the Commonwealth to act for the Department in examining driver's license applicants. Any person so designated shall conduct examinations of driver's license applicants under this title and report his findings and recommendations to the Department.

History.

Code 1950, § 46-366; 1958, c. 541, § 46.1-371; 1984, c. 780; 1989, cc. 705, 727.

§ 46.2-327. Copies of applications; record of licenses and learner's permits issued, suspended, or revoked.

The Department shall retain a copy of every application for a driver's license or learner's permit. The Department shall index and maintain a record of all licenses and learner's permits issued, suspended, or revoked.

History.

Code 1950, § 46-367; 1958, c. 541, § 46.1-372; 1984, c. 780; 1989, c. 727.

§ 46.2-328. Department to issue licenses; endorsements, classifications, and restrictions authorizing operation of certain vehicles.

A. The Department shall issue to every person licensed as a driver a driver's license. Every driver's license shall contain all appropriate endorsements, classifications, and restrictions, where applicable, if the licensee has been licensed:

1. To operate a motorcycle as defined in § 46.2-100;

2. To operate a school bus as defined in § 46.2-100;

3. To operate a commercial motor vehicle pursuant to the provisions of the Virginia Commercial Driver's License Act (§ 46.2-341.1 et seq.); or

4. To operate a passenger car as defined in § 46.2-100.

B. Every applicant intending to operate one or more of the motor vehicles described in subsection A, when applying for a driver's license, shall state in his application the classification of each vehicle that he intends to operate and for which he seeks to be licensed and submit to and pass the examination provided for in § 46.2-325 and, if applicable, §§ 46.2-337 and 46.2-341.14, using the type of each vehicle for which he seeks to be licensed.

C. Every applicant intending to drive a motorcycle, when applying for a classification to authorize the driving of a motorcycle, shall submit to and pass the examination provided for in § 46.2-337. A classification on any license to drive a motorcycle shall indicate that the license is classified for the purpose of authorizing the licensee to drive only motorcycles and shall indicate as applicable a further restriction to a two-wheeled motorcycle only or a three-wheeled motorcycle only. However, if the applicant has a valid license at the time of application for a classification to drive a motorcycle, or if the applicant, at the time of such application, applies for a regular driver's license and submits to and passes the examination provided for in § 46.2-325, he shall be granted a classification on his license to drive motorcycles based on the applicable restrictions, in addition to any other vehicles his driver's license or commercial driver's license may authorize him to operate.

A valid Virginia driver's license issued to a person 19 years of age or older shall constitute a driver's license with a temporary motorcycle classification for the purposes of driving a motorcycle if the driver's license is accompanied by either (i) documentation verifying his successful completion of a motorcycle rider safety training course offered by a provider licensed under Article 23 (§ 46.2-1188 et seq.) of Chapter 10 or (ii) documentation that the license holder is a member, the spouse of a member, or a dependent of a member of the United States Armed Services and that the license holder has successfully completed a basic motorcycle rider course approved by the United States Armed Services. The temporary motorcycle classification shall only be valid for 30 days from the date of successful completion of the motorcycle rider safety training course as shown on the documentation evidencing completion of such course. The temporary motorcycle classification shall indicate whether the license holder is authorized to operate any motorcycle or is restricted to either a two-wheeled motorcycle only or a three-wheeled motorcycle only.

Any person who holds a valid Virginia driver's license and is a member, the spouse of a member, or a dependent of a member of the United States Armed Services shall be issued a motorcycle classification by mail upon documentation of (a) successful completion of a basic motorcycle rider course approved by the United States Armed Services and (b) documentation of his assignment outside the Commonwealth.

D. The Department may make any changes in the classifications and endorsements during the validity of the license as may be appropriate.

E. The provisions of this section shall be applicable to persons applying for learner's permits as otherwise provided for in this title.

F. Every person issued a driver's license or commercial driver's license who drives any motor vehicle of the classifications in this section and whose driver's license does not carry an endorsement or indication that the licensee is licensed as provided in this section is guilty of a Class 1 misdemeanor.

History.

Code 1950, § 46-368; 1958, c. 541, § 46.1-373; 1964, c. 239; 1968, c. 642; 1970, c. 696; 1984, cc. 73, 476, 780; 1989, cc. 705, 727; 2000, c. 269; 2007, c. 190; 2009, c. 77; 2013, cc. 673, 783, 789; 2016, c. 368.

§ 46.2-328.1. Licenses, permits and special identification cards to be issued only to United States citizens, legal permanent resident aliens, or holders of valid unexpired nonimmigrant visas; exceptions; renewal, duplication, or reissuance.

A. Notwithstanding any other provision of this title, except as provided in subsection G of § 46.2-345, the Department shall not issue an original license, permit, or special identification card to any applicant who has not presented to the Department, with the application, valid documentary evidence that the applicant is either (i) a citizen of the United States, (ii) a legal permanent resident of the United States, or (iii) a conditional resident alien of the United States.

B. Notwithstanding the provisions of subsection A and the provisions of §§ 46.2-330 and 46.2-345, an applicant who presents in person valid documentary evidence of (i) a valid, unexpired nonimmigrant visa or nonimmigrant visa status for entry into the United States, (ii) a pending or approved application for asylum in the United States, (iii) entry into the United States in refugee status, (iv) a pending or approved application for temporary protected status in the United States, (v) approved deferred action status, or (vi) a pending application for adjustment of status to legal permanent residence status or conditional resident status, may be issued a temporary license, permit, or special identification card. Such temporary license, permit, or special identification card shall be valid only during the period of time of the applicant's authorized stay in the United States or if there is no definite end to the period of authorized stay a period of one year. No license, permit, or special identification card shall be issued if an applicant's authorized stay in the United States is less than 30 days from the date of application. Any temporary license, permit, or special identification card issued pursuant to this subsection shall clearly indicate that it is temporary and shall state the date that it expires. Such a temporary license, permit or identification card may be renewed only upon presentation of valid documentary evidence that the status by which the applicant qualified for the temporary license, permit or special identification has been extended by the United States Immigration and Naturalization Service or the Bureau of Citizenship and Immigration Services of the Department of Homeland Security.

C. Any license or special identification card for which an application has been made for renewal, duplication or reissuance shall be presumed to have been issued in accordance with the provisions of subsection A, provided that, at the time the application is made, (i) the license or special identification card has not expired or been cancelled, suspended or revoked or (ii) the license or special identification card has been canceled or suspended as a result of the applicant having been placed under medical review by the Department pursuant to § 46.2-322. The requirements of subsection A shall apply, however, to a renewal, duplication or reissuance if the Department is notified by a local, state or federal government agency that the individual seeking such renewal, duplication or reissuance is neither a citizen of the United States nor legally in the United States.

D. The Department shall cancel any license, permit, or special identification card that it has issued to an individual if it is notified by a federal government agency that the individual is neither a citizen of the United States nor legally present in the United States.

E. For any applicant who presents a document pursuant to this section proving legal presence other than citizenship, the Department shall record and provide to the State Board of Elections monthly the applicant's document number, if any, issued by an agency or court of the United States government.

History.

2003, cc. 817, 819; 2005, c. 260; 2007, c. 493; 2009, c. 872; 2010, c. 129; 2011, c. 396; 2013, c. 686.

§ 46.2-329. Special restrictions on particular licensees.

The Department, on issuing a driver's license may, whenever good cause appears, impose restrictions suitable to the licensee's driving ability with respect to the type of, or special mechanical control devices required on, a motor vehicle which the licensee may drive, or any other restrictions applicable to the licensee as the Department may determine. When it appears from the records of the Department that the licensee has failed or refused to comply with the restrictions imposed on the licensee's driving of a motor vehicle, the Department may, after 10 days' written notice to the address indicated in the records of the Department, suspend the person's driver's license and the suspension shall remain in effect until this section has been complied with.

Any person issued a driver's license on which there are printed or stamped restrictions as provided by this section, and who drives a motor vehicle in violation of these restrictions shall be guilty of a Class 2 misdemeanor.

Any person who operates a motor vehicle or any self-propelled machinery or equipment in violation of the terms of a restricted license issued pursuant to subsection E of § 18.2-271.1 is not guilty of a violation of this section but is guilty of a violation of § 18.2-272.

History.

Code 1950, § 46-373; 1958, c. 541, § 46.1-378; 1960, c. 177; 1962, c. 368; 1984, c. 780; 1989, c. 727; 2004, c. 948.

§ 46.2-330. Expiration and renewal of licenses; examinations required.

A. Every driver's license shall expire on the applicant's birthday at the end of the period of years for which a driver's license has been issued. At no time shall any driver's license be issued for more than eight years. Thereafter the driver's license shall be renewed on or before the birthday of the licensee and shall be valid for a period not to exceed eight years except as otherwise provided by law. Any driver's license issued to a person age 75 or older shall be issued for a period not to exceed five years. Notwithstanding these limitations, the Commissioner may extend the validity period of an expiring license if (i) the Department is unable to process an application for renewal due to circumstances beyond its control, (ii) the extension has been authorized under a directive from the Governor, and (iii) the license was not issued as a temporary driver's license under the provisions of subsection B of § 46.2-328.1. However, in no event shall the validity period be extended more than 90 days per occurrence of such conditions. In determining the number of years for which a driver's license shall be renewed, the Commissioner shall take into consideration the examinations, conditions, requirements, and other criteria provided under this title that relate to the issuance of a license to operate a vehicle. Any driver's license issued to a person required to register pursuant to Chapter 9 (§ 9.1-900 et seq.) of Title 9.1 shall expire on the applicant's birthday in years which the applicant attains an age equally divisible by five.

B. Within one year prior to the date shown on the driver's license as the date of expiration, the Department shall send notice, to the holder thereof, at the address shown on the records of the Department in its driver's license file, that his license will expire on a date specified therein, whether he must be reexamined, and when he may be reexamined. Nonreceipt of the notice shall not extend the period of validity of the driver's license beyond its expiration date. The license holder may request the Department to send such renewal notice to an email or other electronic address, upon provision of such address to the Department.

Any driver's license may be renewed by application after the applicant has taken and successfully completed those parts of the examination provided for in §§ 46.2-311, 46.2-325, and the Virginia Commercial Driver's License Act (§ 46.2-341.1 et seq.), including vision and written tests, other than the parts of the examination requiring the applicant to drive a motor vehicle. All drivers applying in person for renewal of a license shall take and successfully complete the examination each renewal year. Every applicant for a renewal shall appear in person before the Department, unless specifically notified by the Department that renewal may be accomplished in another manner as provided in the notice. Applicants who are required to appear in person before the Department to apply for a renewal may also be required to present proof of identity, legal presence, residency, and social security number or non-work authorized status.

C. Notwithstanding any other provision of this section, the Commissioner, in his discretion, may require any applicant for renewal to be fully examined as provided in §§ 46.2-311 and 46.2-325 and the Virginia Commercial Driver's License Act (§ 46.2-341.1 et seq.). Furthermore, if the applicant is less than 75 years old, the Commissioner may waive the vision examination for any applicant for renewal of a driver's license that is not a commercial driver's license and the requirement for the taking of the written test as provided in subsection B of this section, § 46.2-325, and the Virginia Commercial Driver's License Act (§ 46.2-341.1 et seq.). However, in no case shall there be any waiver of the vision examination for applicants for renewal of a commercial driver's license or of the knowledge test required by the Virginia Commercial Driver's License Act for the hazardous materials endorsement on a commercial driver's license. No driver's license or learner's permit issued to any person who is 75 years old or older shall be renewed unless the applicant for renewal appears in person and either (i) passes a vision examination or (ii) presents a report of a vision examination, made within 90 days prior thereto by an ophthalmologist or optometrist, indicating that the applicant's vision meets or exceeds the standards contained in § 46.2-311.

D. Every applicant for renewal of a driver's license, whether renewal shall or shall not be dependent on any examination of the applicant, shall appear in person before the Department to apply for renewal, unless specifically notified by the Department that renewal may be accomplished in another manner as provided in the notice.

E. This section shall not modify the provisions of § 46.2-221.2.

F. 1. The Department shall electronically transmit application information, including a photograph, to the Department of State Police, in a format approved by the State Police, for comparison with information contained in the Virginia Criminal Information Network and National Crime Information Center Convicted Sexual Offender Registry files, at the time of the renewal of a driver's license. Whenever it appears from the records of the State Police that a person has failed to comply with the duty to register or reregister pursuant to Chapter 9 (§ 9.1-900 et seq.) of Title 9.1, the State Police shall promptly investigate and, if there is probable cause to believe a violation has occurred, obtain a warrant or assist in obtaining an indictment charging a violation of § 18.2-472.1 in the jurisdiction in which the person last registered or reregistered or in the jurisdiction where the person made application for licensure. The Department of State Police shall electronically transmit to the Department, in a format approved by the Department, for each person required to register pursuant to Chapter 9 of Title 9.1, registry information consisting of the person's name, all aliases that he has used or under which he may have been known, his date of birth, and his social security number as set out in § 9.1-903.

2. For each person required to register pursuant to Chapter 9 of Title 9.1, the Department may not waive the requirement that each such person shall appear for each renewal or the requirement to obtain a photograph in accordance with subsection C of § 46.2-323.

History.

1968, c. 642, § 46.1-380.1; 1975, c. 24; 1976, c. 48; 1984, c. 780; 1989, cc. 705, 727; 1993, cc. 471, 501; 1997, c. 486; 2001, cc. 659, 665; 2003, c. 333; 2004, cc. 112, 218, 975; 2005, c. 302; 2006, cc. 857, 914; 2008, cc. 487, 866; 2009, c. 872; 2011, cc. 57, 70; 2012, cc. 215, 222; 2014, c. 282; 2016, c. 368.

§ 46.2-331: Repealed by Acts 2004, c. 975.

Cross references.

For current provisions concerning extension of driver's licenses issued to persons in armed services and foreign services, see § 46.2-221.2.

§ 46.2-332. Fees.

On and after January 1, 1990, the fee for each driver's license other than a commercial driver's license shall be $2.40 per year. If the license is a commercial driver's license or seasonal restricted commercial driver's license, the fee shall be $6 per year. Persons 21 years old or older may be issued a scenic driver's license, learner's permit, or commercial driver's license for an additional fee of $5. For any one or more driver's license endorsements or classifications, except a motorcycle classification, there shall be an additional fee of $1 per year; for a motorcycle classification, there shall be an additional fee of $2 per year. For any and all driver's license classifications, there shall be an additional fee of $1 per year. For any revalidation of a seasonal restricted commercial driver's license, the fee shall be $5.

In addition to any other fee imposed and collected by the Department, the Department shall impose and collect a service charge of $5 upon each person who carries out the renewal of a driver's license or special identification card in any of the Department's Customer Service Centers if such renewal can be conducted by mail or telephone or by using an electronic medium in a format prescribed by the Commissioner. Such service charge shall not apply if, concurrently with the renewal of the driver's license or special identification card, the person undertakes another transaction at a Customer Service Center that cannot be conducted by mail or telephone or by using an electronic medium in a format prescribed by the Commissioner. Such service charge shall be paid by the Commissioner into the state treasury and shall be set aside as a special fund to be used to meet the expenses of the Department.

A reexamination fee of $2 shall be charged for each administration of the knowledge portion of the driver's license examination taken by an applicant who is 18 years of age or older if taken more than once within a 15-day period. The reexamination fee shall be charged each time the examination is administered until the applicant successfully completes the examination, if taken prior to the fifteenth day.

An applicant who is less than 18 years of age who does not successfully complete the knowledge portion of the driver's license examination shall not be permitted to take the knowledge portion more than once in 15 days.

A fee of $50 shall be charged each time an applicant for a commercial driver's license fails to keep a scheduled skills test appointment, unless such applicant cancels his appointment with the assigned driver's license examiner at least 24 hours in advance of the scheduled appointment. The Commissioner may, on a case-by-case basis, waive such fee for good cause shown. All such fees shall be paid by the Commissioner into the state treasury and set aside as a special fund to be used to meet the necessary expenses incurred by the Department.

If the applicant for a driver's license is an employee of the Commonwealth, or of any county, city, or town who drives a motorcycle or a commercial motor vehicle solely in the line of his duty, he shall be exempt from the additional fee otherwise assessable for a motorcycle classification or a commercial motor vehicle endorsement. The Commissioner may prescribe the forms as may be requisite for completion by persons claiming exemption from additional fees imposed by this section.

No additional fee above $2.40 per year shall be assessed for the driver's license or commercial driver's license required for the operation of a school bus.

Excluding the $2 reexamination fee, $1.50 of all fees collected for each original or renewal driver's license shall be paid into the driver education fund of the state treasury and expended as provided by law. Unexpended funds from the driver education fund shall be retained in the fund and be available for expenditure in ensuing years as provided therein.

All fees for motorcycle classifications shall be distributed as provided in § 46.2-1191.

This section shall supersede conflicting provisions of this chapter.

History.

1968, c. 642, § 46.1-380.2; 1970, cc. 35, 548, 696; 1972, c. 490; 1973, c. 396; 1974, c. 212; 1976, c. 48; 1980, c. 559; 1984, c. 780; 1989, cc. 705, 727; 1993, c. 70; 1996, cc. 943, 994; 1997, cc. 104, 493; 1999, c. 593; 2007, cc. 190, 223; 2011, cc. 57, 70.

§ 46.2-333. Disposition of fees; expenses.

Except as otherwise provided in this chapter, all fees accruing under the provisions of this chapter shall be paid to, and received by the Commissioner, and by him forthwith paid into the state treasury and set aside as a special fund to be used to meet the necessary expenses incurred by the Department.

History.

Code 1950, § 46-346; 1958, c. 541, § 46.1-381; 1987, c. 696; 1989, c. 727.

§ 46.2-333.1. Surcharges on certain fees of Department; disposition of proceeds.

Notwithstanding any contrary provision of this chapter, beginning May 1, 2003, there are hereby imposed, in addition to other fees imposed by this chapter, the following surcharges in the following amounts:

1. For the issuance of any driver's license other than a commercial driver's license, $1.60 per year of validity of the license;
2. For the issuance of any commercial driver's license, $1 per year of validity of the license;
3. For the reissuance or replacement of any driver's license, $5;
4. For the issuance of any special identification card, $5; and
5. For the reinstatement of any driver's license, $15.

All surcharges collected by the Department under this section shall be paid into the state treasury and shall be set aside as a special fund to be used to support the operation and activities of the Department's customer service centers.

History.
2003, c. 1042, cl. 9.

ARTICLE 5.

LICENSURE OF MINORS, STUDENT DRIVERS, SCHOOL BUS DRIVERS, AND MOTORCYCLISTS.

§ 46.2-334. Conditions and requirements for licensure of persons under 18.

A. Minors at least 16 years and three months old may be issued driver's licenses under the following conditions:

1. The minor shall submit a proper application and satisfactory evidence that he (i) is a resident of the Commonwealth; (ii) has successfully completed a driver education course approved by either the State Department of Education or, in the case of a course offered by a driver training school licensed under Chapter 17 (§ 46.2-1700 et seq.) of this title, by the Department of Motor Vehicles; and (iii) is mentally, physically, and otherwise qualified to drive a motor vehicle safely.

2. The minor's application for a driver's license must be signed by a parent of the applicant, otherwise by the guardian having custody of him. However, in the event a minor has no parent or guardian, then a driver's license shall not be issued to him unless his application is signed by the judge of the juvenile and domestic relations district court of the city or county in which he resides. If the minor making the application is married or otherwise emancipated, in lieu of any parent's, guardian's or judge's signature, the minor may present proper evidence of the solemnization of the marriage or the order of emancipation.

3. The minor shall be required to state in his application whether or not he has been convicted of an offense triable by, or tried in, a juvenile and domestic relations district court or found by such court to be a child in need of supervision, as defined in § 16.1-228. If it appears that the minor has been adjudged not innocent of the offense alleged or has been found to be a child in need of supervision, the Department shall not issue a license without the written approval of the judge of the juvenile and domestic relations district court making an adjudication as to the minor or the like approval of a similar court of the county or city in which the parent or guardian, respectively, of the minor resides.

4. The application for a permanent driver's license by a minor of the age of persons required to attend school pursuant to § 22.1-254 shall be accompanied by evidence of compliance with the compulsory school attendance law set forth in Article 1 (§ 22.1-254 et seq.) of Chapter 14 of Title 22.1. This evidence shall be provided in writing by the minor's parent. If the minor is unable to provide such evidence, he shall not be granted a driver's license until he reaches the age of 18 or presents proper evidence of the solemnization of his marriage or an order of emancipation, or the parent, as defined in § 22.1-1, or other person standing in loco parentis has provided written authorization for the minor to obtain a driver's license.

A minor may, however, present a high school diploma or its equivalent or a certificate indicating completion of a prescribed course of study as defined by the local school board pursuant to § 22.1-253.13:4 as evidence of compulsory school attendance compliance.

5. The minor applicant shall certify in writing, on a form prescribed by the Commissioner, that he is a resident of the Commonwealth. The applicant's parent or guardian shall also certify that the applicant is a resident by signing the certification. Any minor providing proper evidence of the solemnization of his marriage or a certified copy of a court order of emancipation shall not be required to provide the parent's certification of residence.

B. Any custodial parent or guardian of an unmarried or unemancipated minor may, after the issuance of a permanent driver's license to such minor, file with the Department a written request that the license of the minor be canceled. When such request is filed, the Department shall cancel the license of the minor and the license shall not thereafter be reissued by the Department until a period of six months has elapsed from the date of cancellation or the minor reaches his eighteenth birthday, whichever shall occur sooner. Notwithstanding the foregoing provisions of this subsection, in the case of a minor whose parents have been awarded joint legal custody, a request that the license of the minor be cancelled must be signed by both legal custodians. In the event one parent is not reasonably available or the parents do not agree, one parent may petition the juvenile and domestic relations district court to make a determination that the license of the minor be cancelled.

C. The provisions of subsection A of this section requiring that an application for a driver's license be signed by the parent or guardian shall be waived by the Commissioner if the application is accompanied by proper evidence of the solemnization of the minor's marriage or a certified copy of a court order, issued under the provisions of Article 15 (§ 16.1-331 et seq.) of Chapter 11 of Title 16.1, declaring the applicant to be an emancipated minor.

D. A learner's permit accompanied by documentation verifying the minor's successful completion of an approved driver education course, signed by the minor's parent, guardian, legal custodian or other person standing in loco parentis, shall constitute a temporary driver's license for purposes of driving unaccompanied by a licensed driver as required in § 46.2-335, if all other requirements of this chapter have been met. The temporary license shall only be valid until the permanent license is presented as provided in § 46.2-336.

E. Notwithstanding the provisions of subsection A requiring the successful completion of a driver education course approved by the State Department of Education, the Commissioner, on application therefor by a person at least 16 years and three months old but less than 18 years old, shall issue to the applicant a temporary driver's license valid for six months if he (i) certifies by signing, together with his parent or guardian, if applicable, on a form prescribed by the Commissioner that he is a resident of the Commonwealth; (ii) is the holder of a valid driver's license from another U.S. state, U.S. territory, Canadian province, or Canadian territory; and (iii) has not been found guilty of or otherwise responsible for an offense involving the operation of a motor vehicle. No temporary license issued under this subsection shall be renewed, nor shall any second or subsequent temporary license under this subsection be issued to the same applicant. Any such minor providing proper evidence of the solemnization of his marriage or a certified copy of a court order of emancipation shall not be required to obtain the signature of his parent or guardian for the temporary driver's license.

In order to obtain a permanent driver's license, applicants who transfer to Virginia from another U.S. state or any U.S. territory, Canadian province, or Canadian territory must have documentation of at least 30 hours of classroom instruction and six hours of in-car instruction from a government-approved program in the other U.S. state, U.S. territory, or Canadian province or Canadian territory. If a transfer applicant successfully completes a government-approved classroom and in-car driver education program from another state or any U.S. territory, Canadian province, or Canadian territory, the applicant must present the certificate of completion, specifying the number of instructional hours, to the Department.

F. For persons qualifying for a driver's license through driver education courses approved by the Department of Education or courses offered by driver training schools licensed by the Department, the application for the learner's permit shall be used as the application for the driver's license pursuant to § 46.2-335.

G. Driver's licenses shall be issued by the Department to students successfully completing driver education courses approved by the Department of Education (i) when the Department receives from the school proper certification that the student (a) has successfully completed such course, including a road skills examination and (b) is regularly attending school and is in good academic standing or, if not in such standing or submitting evidence thereof, whose parent or guardian, having custody of such minor, provides written authorization for the minor to obtain a driver's license, which written authorization shall be obtained on forms provided by the Department and indicating the Commonwealth's interest in the good academic standing and regular school attendance of such minors; and (ii) upon payment of a fee of $2.40 per year, based on the period of the license's validity. For applicants attending public schools, good academic standing may be certified by the public school principal or any of his designees. For applicants attending nonpublic schools, such certification shall be made by the private school principal or any of his designees; for students receiving home schooling, such certification shall be made by the home schooling parent or tutor. Any minor providing proper evidence of the solemnization of his marriage or a certified copy of a court order of emancipation shall not be required to provide the certification of good academic standing or any written authorization from his parent or guardian to obtain a driver's license.

H. For those home schooled students completing driver education courses approved by the Board of Education and instructed by his own parent or guardian, no driver's license shall be issued until the student has successfully completed the driver's license examination administered by the Department. Furthermore, the Commissioner shall not issue a driver's license for those home schooled students completing driver education courses approved by the Board of Education and instructed by his own parent or guardian if it is determined by the Commissioner that, at the time of such instruction, such parent or guardian had accumulated six or more driver demerit points in the most recently preceding 12 months, had been convicted within the most recent 11 preceding years of driving while intoxicated in violation of § 18.2-266 or a substantially similar law in another state, or had ever been convicted of voluntary or involuntary manslaughter in violation of § 18.2-35 or 18.2-36 or a substantially similar law in another state.

I. The Commissioner, on application therefor by a person from another U.S. state or any U.S. territory, Canadian province, or Canadian territory who is at least 16 years and three months old but less than 18 years old, shall issue a Virginia driver's license to the applicant if the applicant (i) certifies by signing, together with his parent or guardian, if applicable, on a form prescribed by the Commissioner that he is now a resident of the Commonwealth; (ii) has completed a government-approved classroom and in-car driver education program from another U.S. state or any U.S. territory, Canadian province, or Canadian territory, which shall not be required to meet the 30 hours of classroom instruction and six hours of in-car instruction requirement in subsection E; (iii) is the holder of a valid driver's license from another U.S. state or any U.S. territory, Canadian province, or Canadian territory; (iv) has held the valid driver's license for the 12 months immediately prior to applying for a Virginia license; (v) has not been found guilty of or otherwise responsible for an offense involving the operation of a motor vehicle; and (vi) successfully completes behind-the-wheel and driver knowledge examinations administered by the Department.

The applicant must present the certificate of completion specifying the number of classroom and in-car driver education program instructional hours for the government-approved classroom and in-car driver education program from another U.S. state or any U.S. territory, Canadian province, or Canadian territory to the Department.

History.
Code 1950, §§ 46-353, 46-361, 46-363, 46-364; 1950, p. 249; 1952, c. 396; 1954, c. 123; 1956, c. 665; 1958, c. 541, § 46.1-357; 1960, cc. 110, 424; 1962, cc. 254, 482; 1964, c. 617; 1966, c. 36; 1968, c. 642; 1970, c. 41; 1972, c. 823; 1973, c. 1; 1974, cc. 223, 542; 1976, c. 8; 1977, cc. 548, 552; 1980, c. 165; 1982, c. 287; 1984, c. 780; 1987, cc. 154, 632; 1989, cc. 392, 705, 727; 1991, c. 214; 1993, cc. 471, 501; 1995, c. 535; 1996, cc. 943, 994, 1011, 1022; 1997, c. 841; 1999, cc. 459, 462, 887; 2001, cc. 659, 665, 851; 2003, c. 951; 2014, cc. 286, 685; 2016, c. 488.

§ 46.2-334.001. Court to suspend driver's license issued to certain minors.

A. Upon receipt by the juvenile and domestic relations district court within whose jurisdiction the minor resides of a petition from the principal, or his designee, of any public school in the Commonwealth that any person who is less than 18 years old and attending that public school has had 10 or more unexcused absences from school on consecutive school days, the court shall give notice and opportunity for the minor to show cause why his driver's license should not be suspended. Upon failure to show cause for the license not to be suspended, the court may suspend the minor's driver's license for any period of time, until the minor is 18 years old.

B. The foregoing provisions of this section shall not apply in cases where the student has withdrawn from school for a reason or reasons beyond the control of the student, for the purpose of transferring to another school as confirmed in writing by the student's parent or guardian, or when the student's parent or guardian expresses in open court his desire to allow the student to retain his license. The juvenile and domestic relations district court judge shall be the sole authority as to whether the licensee's withdrawal from school is due to circumstances beyond the control of the student.

C. Any person whose driver's license is suspended as provided in this section may apply to a juvenile and domestic relations district court for issuance of a restricted driver's license for any of the purposes set forth in subsection E of § 18.2-271.1. No restricted license shall be issued pursuant to this section unless the licensee (i) is employed at least four hours per day and at least 20 hours per week, (ii) has a medical condition that requires him to be able to drive a motor vehicle, or (iii) is the only licensee in his household. The court shall order the surrender of such person's license and shall forward to the Commissioner a copy of its order entered pursuant to this subsection. This order shall specifically enumerate the restrictions imposed and contain such information regarding the person to whom such a restricted license is issued as is reasonably necessary to identify such person. The court shall also provide a copy of its order to such person, who may operate a motor vehicle on the order until receipt from the Commissioner of the Department of Motor Vehicles of a restricted driver's license, but only if the order provides for a restricted driver's license for that period. Any person who operates a motor vehicle in violation of any restriction imposed pursuant to this section shall be guilty of a violation of § 46.2-301.

History.
2009, c. 439.

§ 46.2-334.01. Licenses issued to persons less than 18 years old subject to certain restrictions.

A. Any learner's permit or driver's license issued to any person less than 18 years old shall be subject to the following:

1. Notwithstanding the provisions of § 46.2-498, whenever the driving record of a person less than 19 years old shows that he has been convicted of committing, when he was less than 18 years old, (i) an offense for which demerit points have been assessed or are assessable under Article 19 (§ 46.2-489 et seq.) or (ii) a violation of any provision of Article 12 (§ 46.2-1091 et seq.) or Article 13 (§ 46.2-1095 et seq.) of Chapter 10, the Commissioner shall direct such person to attend a driver improvement clinic. No safe driving points shall be awarded for such clinic attendance, nor shall any safe driving points be awarded for voluntary or court-assigned clinic attendance. Such person's parent, guardian, legal custodian, or other person standing in loco parentis may attend such clinic and receive a reduction in demerit points and/or an award of safe driving points pursuant to § 46.2-498. The provisions of this subdivision shall not be construed to prohibit awarding of safe driving points to a person less than 18 years old who attends and successfully completes a driver improvement clinic without having been directed to do so by the Commissioner or required to do so by a court.

2. If any person less than 19 years old is convicted a second time of committing, when he was less than 18 years old, (i) an offense for which demerit points have been assessed or are assessable under Article 19 (§ 46.2-489 et seq.) or (ii) a violation of any provision of Article 12 (§ 46.2-1091 et seq.) or Article 13 (§ 46.2-1095 et seq.) of Chapter 10, the Commissioner shall suspend such person's driver's license or

privilege to operate a motor vehicle for 90 days. Such suspension shall be consecutive to, and not concurrent with, any other period of license suspension, revocation, or denial. Any person who has had his driver's license or privilege to operate a motor vehicle suspended in accordance with this subdivision may petition the juvenile and domestic relations district court of his residence for a restricted license to authorize such person to drive a motor vehicle in the Commonwealth to and from his home, his place of employment, or an institution of higher learning where he is enrolled, provided there is no other means of transportation by which such person may travel between his home and his place of employment or the institution of higher learning where he is enrolled. On such petition the court may, in its discretion, authorize the issuance of a restricted license for a period not to exceed the term of the suspension of the person's license or privilege to operate a motor vehicle in the Commonwealth. Such restricted license shall be valid solely for operation of a motor vehicle between such person's home and his place of employment or the institution of higher learning where he is enrolled.

3. If any person is convicted a third time of committing, when he was less than 18 years old, (i) an offense for which demerit points have been assessed or are assessable under Article 19 (§ 46.2-489 et seq.) or (ii) a violation of any provision of Article 12 (§ 46.2-1091 et seq.) or Article 13 (§ 46.2-1095 et seq.) of Chapter 10, the Commissioner shall revoke such person's driver's license or privilege to operate a motor vehicle for one year or until such person reaches the age of 18 years, whichever is longer. Such revocation shall be consecutive to, and not concurrent with, any other period of license suspension, revocation, or denial.

4. In no event shall any person subject to the provisions of this section be subject to the suspension or revocation provisions of subdivision 2 or 3 for multiple convictions arising out of the same transaction or occurrence.

B. The initial license issued to any person younger than 18 years of age shall be deemed a provisional driver's license. Until the holder is 18 years old, a provisional driver's license shall not authorize its holder to operate a motor vehicle with more than one passenger who is less than 21 years old. After the first year the provisional license is issued, the holder may operate a motor vehicle with up to three passengers who are less than 21 years old (i) when the holder is driving to or from a school-sponsored activity, (ii) when a licensed driver who is at least 21 years old is occupying the seat beside the driver, or (iii) in cases of emergency. These passenger limitations, however, shall not apply to members of the driver's family or household. For the purposes of this subsection, "a member of the driver's family or household" means any of the following: (a) the driver's spouse, children, stepchildren, brothers, sisters, half-brothers, half-sisters, first cousins, and any individual who has a child in common with the driver, whether or not they reside in the same home with the driver; (b) the driver's brothers-in-law and sisters-in-law who reside in the same home with the driver; and (c) any individual who cohabits with the driver, and any children of such individual residing in the same home with the driver.

C. The holder of a provisional driver's license shall not operate a motor vehicle on the highways of the Commonwealth between the hours of midnight and 4:00 a.m. except when driving (i) to or from a place of business where he is employed; (ii) to or from an activity that is supervised by an adult and is sponsored by a school or by a civic, religious, or public organization; (iii) accompanied by a parent, a person acting in loco parentis, or by a spouse who is 18 years old or older, provided that such person accompanying the driver is actually occupying a seat beside the driver and is lawfully permitted to operate a motor vehicle at the time; or (iv) in cases of emergency, including response by volunteer firefighters and volunteer emergency medical services personnel to emergency calls.

C1. Except in a driver emergency or when the vehicle is lawfully parked or stopped, the holder of a provisional driver's license shall not operate a motor vehicle on the highways of the Commonwealth while using any cellular telephone or any other wireless telecommunications device, regardless of whether such device is or is not hand-held.

D. The provisional driver's license restrictions in subsections B, C, and C1 shall expire on the holder's eighteenth birthday. A violation of the provisional driver's license restrictions in subsection B, C, or C1 shall constitute a traffic infraction. For a second or subsequent violation of the provisional driver's license restrictions in subsection B, C, or C1, in addition to any other penalties that may be imposed pursuant to § 16.1-278.10, the court may suspend the juvenile's privilege to drive for a period not to exceed six months.

E. A violation of subsection B, C, or C1 shall not constitute negligence, be considered in mitigation of damages of whatever nature, be admissible in evidence, or be the subject of comment by counsel in any action for the recovery of damages arising out of the operation, ownership, or maintenance of a motor vehicle, nor shall anything in this subsection change any existing law, rule, or procedure pertaining to any such civil action.

F. No citation for a violation of this section shall be issued unless the officer issuing such citation has cause to stop or arrest the driver of such motor vehicle for the violation of some other provision of this Code or local ordinance relating to the operation, ownership, or maintenance of a motor vehicle or any criminal statute.

History.

1998, cc. 124, 792; 2001, cc. 655, 659, 665; 2002, cc. 61, 807; 2003, cc. 308, 323, 771; 2007, c. 777; 2009, c. 54; 2013, cc. 397, 579; 2015, cc. 502, 503; 2016, c. 488.

§ 46.2-334.02. Licenses issued to persons less than twenty years old subject to certain restrictions.

Notwithstanding the provisions of § 46.2-498, whenever the driving record of a person who is at least eighteen years old but less than twenty years old shows that he has been convicted of (i) an offense for which demerit points have been assessed or are assessable under Article 19 (§ 46.2-489 et seq.) of this chapter or (ii) a violation of any provision of Article 12 (§ 46.2-1091 et seq.) or Article 13 (§ 46.2-1095 et seq.) of Chapter 10 of this title, the Commissioner shall direct such person to attend a driver improvement clinic.

History.
2001, cc. 659, 665.

§ 46.2-334.1. Knowledge test; waiting period prior to reexamination.

Any person under the age of eighteen who applies for a driver's license under § 46.2-334 and fails the motor vehicle knowledge test administered pursuant to that section shall not be eligible for retesting for at least fifteen days.

History.
1996, c. 1035.

§ 46.2-335. Learner's permits; fees; certification required.

A. The Department, on receiving from any Virginia resident over the age of 15 years and six months an application for a learner's permit or motorcycle learner's permit, may, subject to the applicant's satisfactory documentation of meeting the requirements of this chapter and successful completion of the written or automated knowledge and vision examinations and, in the case of a motorcycle learner's permit applicant, the automated motorcycle test, issue a permit entitling the applicant, while having the permit in his immediate possession, to drive a motor vehicle or, if the application is made for a motorcycle learner's permit, a motorcycle, on the highways, when accompanied by any licensed driver 21 years of age or older or by his parent or legal guardian, or by a brother, sister, half-brother, half-sister, step-brother, or step-sister 18 years of age or older. The accompanying person shall be (i) alert, able to assist the driver, and actually occupying a seat beside the driver or, for motorcycle instruction, providing immediate supervision from a separate accompanying motor vehicle and (ii) lawfully permitted to operate the motor vehicle or accompanying motorcycle at that time.

The Department shall not, however, issue a learner's permit or motorcycle learner's permit to any minor applicant required to provide evidence of compliance with the compulsory school attendance law set forth in Article 1 (§ 22.1-254 et seq.) of Chapter 14 of Title 22.1, unless such applicant is in good academic standing or, if not in such standing or submitting evidence thereof, whose parent or guardian, having custody of such minor, provides written authorization for the minor to obtain a learner's permit or motorcycle learner's permit, which written authorization shall be obtained on forms provided by the Department and indicating the Commonwealth's interest in the good academic standing and regular school attendance of such minors. Any minor providing proper evidence of the solemnization of his marriage or a certified copy of a court order of emancipation shall not be required to provide the certification of good academic standing or any written authorization from his parent or guardian to obtain a learner's permit or motorcycle learner's permit.

Such permit, except a motorcycle learner's permit, shall be valid until the holder thereof either is issued a driver's license as provided for in this chapter or no longer meets the qualifications for issuance of a learner's permit as provided in this section. Motorcycle learner's permits shall be valid for 12 months. When a motorcycle learner's permit expires, the permittee may, upon submission of an application, payment of the application fee, and successful completion of the examinations, be issued another motorcycle learner's permit valid for 12 months.

Any person 25 years of age or older who is eligible to receive an operator's license in Virginia, but who is required, pursuant to § 46.2-324.1, to be issued a learner's permit for 60 days prior to his first behind-the-wheel exam, may be issued such learner's permit even though restrictions on his driving privilege have been ordered by a court. Any such learner's permit shall be subject to the restrictions ordered by the court.

B. No driver's license shall be issued to any such person who is less than 18 years old unless, while holding a learner's permit, he has driven a motor vehicle for at least 45 hours, at least 15 of which were after sunset, as certified by his parent, foster parent, or legal guardian unless the person is married or otherwise emancipated. Such certification shall be on a form provided by the Commissioner and shall contain the following statement:

"It is illegal for anyone to give false information in connection with obtaining a driver's license. This certification is considered part of the driver's license application, and anyone who certifies to a false statement may be prosecuted. I certify that the statements made and the information submitted by me regarding this certification are true and correct."

Such form shall also include the driver's license or Department of Motor Vehicles-issued identification card number of the person making the certification.

C. No learner's permit shall authorize its holder to operate a motor vehicle with more than one passenger who is less than 21 years old, except when participating in a driver education program approved by the Department of Education or a course offered by a driver training school licensed by the Department. This passenger limitation, however, shall not apply to the members of the driver's family or household as defined in subsection B of § 46.2-334.01.

D. No learner's permit shall authorize its holder to operate a motor vehicle between midnight and four o'clock a.m.

E. Except in a driver emergency or when the vehicle is lawfully parked or stopped, no holder of a learner's permit shall operate a motor vehicle on the highways of the Commonwealth while using any cellular telephone or any other wireless telecommunications device, regardless of whether or not such device is handheld. No citation for a violation of this subsection shall be issued unless the officer issuing such citation has cause to stop or arrest the driver of such motor vehicle for the violation of some other provision of this Code or local ordinance relating to the operation, ownership, or maintenance of a motor vehicle or any criminal statute.

F. A violation of subsection C, D, or E shall not constitute negligence, be considered in mitigation of damages of whatever nature, be admissible in evidence or be the subject of comment by counsel in any action for the recovery of damages arising out of the operation, ownership, or maintenance of a motor vehicle, nor shall anything in this subsection change any existing law, rule, or procedure pertaining to any such civil action.

G. The provisions of §§ 46.2-323 and 46.2-334 relating to evidence and certification of Virginia residence and, in the case of persons of school age, compliance with the compulsory school attendance law shall apply, mutatis mutandis, to applications for learner's permits and motorcycle learner's permits issued under this section.

H. For persons qualifying for a driver's license through driver education courses approved by the Department of Education or courses offered by driver training schools licensed by the Department, the application for the learner's permit shall be used as the application for the driver's license.

I. The Department shall charge a fee of $3 for each learner's permit and motorcycle learner's permit issued under this section. Fees for issuance of learner's permits shall be paid into the driver education fund of the state treasury; fees for issuance of motorcycle learner's permits shall be paid into the state treasury and credited to the Motorcycle Rider Safety Training Program Fund created pursuant to § 46.2-1191. It shall be unlawful for any person, after having received a learner's permit, to drive a motor vehicle without being accompanied by a licensed driver as provided in the foregoing provisions of this section; however, a learner's permit other than a motorcycle learner's permit, accompanied by documentation verifying that the driver is at least 16 years and three months old and has successfully completed an approved driver's education course, signed by the minor's parent, guardian, legal custodian or other person standing in loco parentis, shall constitute a temporary driver's license for the purpose of driving unaccompanied by a licensed driver 18 years of age or older, if all other requirements of this chapter have been met. Such temporary driver's license shall only be valid until the driver has received his permanent license pursuant to § 46.2-336.

J. Nothing in this section shall be construed to permit the issuance of a learner's permit entitling a person to drive a commercial motor vehicle, except as provided by the Virginia Commercial Driver's License Act (§ 46.2-341.1 et seq.).

K. The following limitations shall apply to operation of motorcycles by all persons holding motorcycle learner's permits:

1. The operator shall wear an approved safety helmet as provided in § 46.2-910.

2. Operation shall be under the immediate supervision of a person licensed to operate a motorcycle who is 21 years of age or older.

3. No person other than the operator shall occupy the motorcycle.

L. Any violation of this section shall be punishable as a Class 2 misdemeanor.

History.

Code 1950, §§ 46-353, 46-361, 46-363, 46-364; 1950, p. 249; 1952, c. 396; 1954, c. 123; 1956, c. 665; 1958, c. 541, § 46.1-357; 1960, cc. 110, 424; 1962, cc. 254, 482; 1964, c. 617; 1966, c. 36; 1968, c. 642; 1970, c. 41; 1972, c. 823; 1973, c. 1; 1974, cc. 223, 542; 1976, c. 8; 1977, cc. 548, 552; 1980, c. 165; 1982, c. 287; 1984, c. 780; 1987, cc. 154, 632; 1989, cc. 392, 705, 727; 1993, cc. 471, 501; 1995, cc. 254, 337, 535, 847; 1996, cc. 892, 894, 918, 943, 994, 1011, 1022, 1035; 1997, c. 841; 1998, c. 322; 1999, cc. 459, 462; 2000, c. 686; 2001, cc. 659, 665; 2004, cc. 733, 805; 2008, cc. 493, 735; 2010, cc. 541, 593; 2012, cc. 215, 222; 2016, c. 488.

§ 46.2-335.1. Knowledge test; waiting period prior to reexamination.

Any person under the age of eighteen who applies for a learner's permit under § 46.2-335 and fails the motor vehicle knowledge test administered pursuant to that section shall not be eligible for retesting for at least fifteen days.

History.

1996, c. 1035.

§ 46.2-335.2. Learner's permits; required before driver's license; minimum holding period.

A. No person under the age of 18 years shall be eligible to receive a driver's license pursuant to § 46.2-334 unless the Department has previously issued such person a learner's permit pursuant to § 46.2-335 and such person has satisfied the minimum holding period requirements set forth in subsection B, or unless such person is the holder of a valid driver's license from another state and qualifies for a temporary license under subsection E of § 46.2-334.

B. Any person under the age of 18 years issued a learner's permit pursuant to § 46.2-335 shall hold such permit for a minimum period of nine months or until he reaches the age of 18 years, whichever occurs first.

History.

1996, c. 1035; 2001, cc. 659, 665; 2002, c. 535; 2016, c. 488.

§ 46.2-336. Manner of issuing original driver's licenses to minors.

The Department shall forward all original driver's licenses issued to persons under the age of 18 years to the judge of the juvenile and domestic relations court in the city or county in which the licensee resides. The judge or a substitute judge shall issue to each person to be licensed the license so forwarded, and shall, at the time of issuance, conduct a formal, appropriate ceremony, in which he shall illustrate to the licensee the responsibility attendant on the privilege of driving a motor vehicle. The attorney for the Commonwealth who serves the jurisdiction in which the ceremony is to be conducted may request in writing in advance of such ceremony an opportunity to participate in the ceremony. Any judge who presides over such ceremony shall, upon request, afford the attorney for the Commonwealth the opportunity to participate in such ceremony and to address the prospective licensees and the persons enumerated below who may be accompanying the prospective licensees as to matters of enforcement, prosecutions, applicable punishments, and the responsibility of drivers generally. If the licensee is under the age of 18 years at the time his ceremony is held, he shall be accompanied at the ceremony by a parent, his guardian, spouse, or other person in loco parentis. However, the judge, for good cause shown, may mail or otherwise deliver the driver's license to any person who is a student at any educational institution outside of the Commonwealth of Virginia at the time such license is received by the judge as prescribed in this section.

The provisions of this section shall not apply to the issuance of Virginia driver's licenses to persons who hold valid driver's licenses issued by other states.

History.

1962, c. 261, § 46.1-375.1; 1964, c. 185; 1984, c. 780; 1989, c. 727; 1993, c. 53; 1998, c. 472; 2012, cc. 30, 100; 2014, c. 352.

§ 46.2-337. Examination and road test required for license to operate motorcycle; regulations.

No person shall drive any motorcycle on a highway in the Commonwealth unless he has passed a special examination, including written material and a road test, pertaining to his ability to drive a motorcycle with reasonable competence and with safety to other persons using the highways. The Department may adopt regulations as may be necessary to provide for the special examination under § 46.2-325 of persons desiring to qualify to drive motorcycles in the Commonwealth and for the granting of licenses or permits suitably endorsed for qualified applicants. The road test for two-wheeled motorcycles and the road test for three-wheeled motorcycles shall be separate and distinct examinations emphasizing the skills and maneuvers necessary to operate each type of motorcycle.

No person applying for a classification to authorize the driving of a motorcycle who fails the road test portion of the special examination two times shall be eligible for such classification until he successfully completes a motorcycle rider safety training course offered by a provider licensed under Article 23 (§ 46.2-1188 et seq.) of Chapter 10.

If the Commissioner is satisfied that a person intending to operate a motorcycle has demonstrated the same proficiency as required by the special examination through successful completion of a motorcycle rider safety training course offered by a provider licensed under Article 23 (§ 46.2-1188 et seq.) of Chapter 10, he may waive the written material or road test portion or both portions of the special examination. The Commissioner may also waive the written material or road test portion or both portions of the special examination if the person intending to operate a motorcycle holds a valid Virginia driver's license and is a member, the spouse of a member, or a dependent of a member of the United States Armed Services, and the license holder has successfully completed a basic motorcycle rider course approved by the United States Armed Services.

History.

1968, c. 642, § 46.1-370.1; 1989, c. 727; 2007, c. 190; 2013, cc. 673, 783, 789.

§ 46.2-338: Repealed by Acts 1989, c. 705.

§ 46.2-339. Qualifications of school bus driver; examination.

No person shall drive any school bus on a highway in the Commonwealth unless he has had a reasonable amount of experience in driving motor vehicles, and has passed a special examination pertaining to his ability to drive a school bus with safety to its passengers and to other persons using the highways. Such person shall obtain a commercial driver's license with the applicable classifications and endorsements, issued pursuant to the Virginia Commercial Driver's License Act (§ 46.2-341.1 et seq.), if the school bus he drives is a commercial motor vehicle as defined in the Virginia Commercial Driver's License Act. For the purpose of preparing for the examination required by this section, any person holding a valid driver's license issued under Article 4 of this chapter, may drive, under the direct supervision of a person holding a valid school bus license endorsement, a school bus which contains no other passengers, provided that, on and after April 1, 1992, only persons holding a valid commercial driver's license or instruction permit issued under the provisions of the Virginia Commercial Driver's License Act, may operate, under the direct supervision of a person holding a valid commercial driver's license with a school bus endorsement, a school bus which is a commercial motor vehicle as defined in the Virginia Commercial Driver's License Act and which contains no pupil passengers. The Department may adopt regulations necessary to provide for the examination of persons desiring to qualify to drive school buses in the Commonwealth and for the granting of permits to qualified applicants. Notwithstanding the provisions of this section otherwise, no person shall drive any school bus on a highway in the Commonwealth during any period in which he is a person for whom registration with the Sex Offender and Crimes Against Minors Registry is required pursuant to Chapter 9 (§ 9.1-900 et seq.) of Title 9.1.

History.

Code 1950, § 22-278; 1958, c. 541, § 46.1-370; 1978, c. 263; 1984, c. 780; 1989, cc. 705, 727; 2011, c. 477.

§ 46.2-340. Information concerning school bus drivers and driver education instructors.

A. At the beginning of each school year, and whenever changes need to be made, each local school division shall furnish to the Department of Motor Vehicles the name, driver's license number, and commercial driver's license number of all persons driving school buses for that school division. Whenever any commercial driver's license with a school bus driver's endorsement is suspended or revoked, or the holder of a driver's license with a school bus driver's endorsement or commercial driver's license with a school bus driver's endorsement is convicted in any court of reckless driving or driving while intoxicated, the Department shall notify the affected local school division of the name and driver's license number or commercial driver's license number of the driver involved.

B. At the beginning of each school year, and whenever changes need to be made, each local school division and private school providing a driver education program approved by the Department of Education shall furnish to the Department of Motor Vehicles the name and driver's license number of all persons providing instruction in driver education for that school division or private school. Whenever a driver's license of a person providing such instruction is suspended or revoked, or such person is convicted in any court of reckless driving or driving while intoxicated, the Department shall notify the affected local school division or private school of the name and driver's license number of the driver involved.

If the driving record of such driver education instructor accumulates more than six demerit points based on convictions occurring in any calendar year, the Department shall notify the relevant local school division or private school of the name and driver's license number of the driver. Safe driving points shall not be used to reduce the six demerit points. No driver education program in a public school division or a private school shall retain its approval by the Department of Education unless such a person who has accumulated such six demerit points is removed from providing behind-the-wheel driver education instruction in the private school or public school division for a period of twenty-four months.

C. The provisions of the Government Data Collection and Dissemination Practices Act (Chapter 38 of Title 2.2, § 2.2-3800 et seq.) shall not apply to the exchange of information under this section.

History.

1986, c. 287, § 46.1-370.01; 1989, c. 727; 1993, c. 52; 1999, c. 463.

ARTICLE 6.
LICENSURE OF COMMERCIAL VEHICLE DRIVERS.

§ **46.2-341:** Repealed by Acts 1989, c. 705.

ARTICLE 6.1.
COMMERCIAL DRIVER'S LICENSES.

§ 46.2-341.1. Title.

This Act may be cited as the "Virginia Commercial Driver's License Act."

History.

1989, c. 705, § 46.1-372.1.

§ **46.2-341.2:** Statement of intent and purpose [Not set out.] (1989, c. 705.)

Editor's note.

This section, relating to statement of intent and purpose, was enacted by Acts 1989, c. 705. In furtherance of the general policy of the Virginia Code Commission to include in the Code only provisions having general and permanent application, this section, which is limited in its purpose and scope, is not set out here, but attention is called to it by this reference.

The section catchline was inserted at the direction of the Virginia Code Commission.

§ 46.2-341.3. Conflicts; supplement to driver licensing statutes.

This article is intended to supplement, not supplant, the laws of the Commonwealth relating to drivers, driver licensing, vehicles and vehicle operations, which laws shall continue to apply to persons required to be licensed pursuant to this article, unless the context clearly indicates otherwise. To the extent that any provisions of this article conflict with such other laws of the Commonwealth, the provisions of this article shall prevail. Where this article is silent, such other laws shall apply.

Notwithstanding the provisions of § 46.2-1300, the governing bodies of counties, cities or towns shall not be authorized to adopt ordinances that are substantially similar to the provisions of this article.

History.

1989, c. 705, § 46.1-372.3.

§ 46.2-341.4. Definitions.

The following definitions shall apply to this article, unless a different meaning is clearly required by the context:

"Air brake" means any braking system operating fully or partially on the air brake principle.

"Applicant" means an individual who applies to obtain, transfer, upgrade, or renew a commercial driver's license or to obtain or renew a commercial learner's permit.

"Automatic transmission" means, for the purposes of the skills test and the restriction, any transmission other than a manual transmission.

"CDLIS driver record" means the electronic record of the individual commercial driver's status and history stored by the State of Record as part of the Commercial Driver's License Information System (CDLIS).

"Commercial driver's license" means any driver's license issued to a person in accordance with the provisions of this article, or if the license is issued by another state, any license issued to a person in accordance with the federal Commercial Motor Vehicle Safety Act, which authorizes such person to drive a commercial motor vehicle of the class and type and with the restrictions indicated on the license.

"Commercial driver's license information system" (CDLIS) means the CDLIS established by the Federal Motor Carrier Safety Administration pursuant to § 12007 of the Commercial Motor Vehicle Safety Act of 1986.

"Commercial learner's permit" means a permit issued to an individual in accordance with the provisions of this article or, if issued by another state, a permit issued in accordance with the standards contained in the Federal Motor Carrier Safety Regulations, which, when carried with a valid driver's license issued by the same state or jurisdiction, authorizes the individual to operate a class of commercial motor vehicle when accompanied by a holder of a valid commercial driver's license for purposes of behind-the-wheel training. When issued to a commercial driver's license holder, a commercial learner's permit serves as authorization for accompanied behind-the-wheel training in a commercial motor vehicle for which the holder's current commercial driver's license is not valid.

"Commercial motor vehicle" means, except for those vehicles specifically excluded in this definition, every motor vehicle, vehicle or combination of vehicles used to transport passengers or property which either: (i) has a gross vehicle weight rating of 26,001 or more pounds; or (ii) has a gross combination weight rating of 26,001 or more pounds inclusive of a towed vehicle with a gross vehicle weight rating of more than 10,000 pounds; or (iii) is designed to transport 16 or more passengers including the driver; or (iv) is of any size and is used in the transportation of hazardous materials as defined in this section. Every such motor vehicle or combination of vehicles shall be considered a commercial motor vehicle whether or not it is used in a commercial or profit-making activity.

The following shall be excluded from the definition of commercial motor vehicle: any vehicle when used by an individual solely for his own personal purposes, such as personal recreational activities; or any vehicle which (i) is controlled and operated by a farmer, whether or not it is owned by the farmer, and which is used exclusively for farm use, as provided in §§ 46.2-649.3 and 46.2-698, (ii) is used to transport either agricultural products, farm machinery or farm supplies to or from a farm, (iii) is not used in the operation of a common or contract motor carrier, and (iv) is used within 150 miles of the farmer's farm; or any vehicle operated for military purposes by (a) active duty military personnel, (b) members of the military reserves, (c) members of the national guard on active duty, including personnel on full-time national guard duty, personnel on part-time national guard training, and national guard military technicians (civilians who are required to wear military uniforms), but not U.S. Reserve technicians, and (d) active duty U.S. Coast Guard personnel; or emergency equipment operated by a member of a firefighting, rescue, or emergency entity in the performance of his official duties.

"Commercial Motor Vehicle Safety Act" means the federal Commercial Motor Vehicle Safety Act of 1986, Title XII of Public Law 99-570, as amended.

"Conviction" means an unvacated adjudication of guilt, or a determination that a person has violated or failed to comply with the law in a court of original jurisdiction, an unvacated forfeiture of bond, bail or collateral deposited to secure the person's appearance in court, a plea of guilty or nolo contendere accepted by the court, the payment of a fine or court costs in lieu of trial, a violation of a condition of release without bail, regardless of whether the penalty is rebated, suspended or probated, or, for the purposes of alcohol or drug-related offenses involving the operation of a motor vehicle, a civil or an administrative determination of a violation. For the purposes of this definition, an administrative determination shall include an unvacated certification or

finding by an administrative or authorized law-enforcement official that a person has violated a provision of law.

"Disqualification" means a prohibition against driving, operating or being in physical control of a commercial motor vehicle for a specified period of time, imposed by a court or a magistrate, or by an authorized administrative or law-enforcement official or body.

"Domicile" means a person's true, fixed and permanent home and principal residence, to which he intends to return whenever he is absent.

"Employee" means a payroll employee or person employed under lease or contract, or a person who has applied for employment and whose employment is contingent upon obtaining a commercial driver's license.

"Employer" means a person who owns or leases commercial motor vehicles and assigns employees to drive such vehicles.

"Endorsement" means an authorization to an individual's commercial driver's license or commercial learner's permit required to permit the individual to operate certain types of commercial motor vehicles.

"FMCSA" means the Federal Motor Carrier Safety Administration.

"Full air brake" means any braking system operating fully on the air brake principle.

"Gross combination weight rating" means the value specified by the manufacturers of an articulated vehicle or combination of vehicles as the maximum loaded weight of such vehicles. In the absence of such a value specified by the manufacturer, for law-enforcement purposes, the gross combination weight rating shall be the greater of (i) the gross vehicle weight rating of the power units of the combination vehicle plus the total weight of the towed units, including any loads thereon, or (ii) the gross weight at which the articulated vehicle or combination of vehicles is registered in its state of registration; however, the registered gross weight shall not be applicable for determining the classification of an articulated vehicle or combination of vehicles for purposes of skills testing pursuant to § 46.2-341.14 or 46.2-341.16.

"Gross vehicle weight rating" means the value specified by the manufacturer of the vehicle as the maximum loaded weight of a single vehicle. In the absence of such a value specified by the manufacturer, for law-enforcement purposes, the gross vehicle weight rating shall be the greater of (i) the actual gross weight of the vehicle, including any load thereon; or (ii) the gross weight at which the vehicle is registered in its state of registration; however, the registered gross weight of the vehicle shall not be applicable for determining the classification of a vehicle for purposes of skills testing pursuant to § 46.2-341.14 or 46.2-341.16.

"Hazardous materials" means materials designated to be hazardous in accordance with § 103 of the federal Hazardous Materials Transportation Act, as amended, (49 U.S.C. § 5101 et seq.) and which require placarding when transported by motor vehicle as provided in the federal Hazardous Materials Regulations (49 C.F.R. Part 172, Subpart F); it also includes any quantity of any material listed as a select agent or toxin in federal Public Health Service Regulations at 42 C.F.R. Part 73.

"Manual transmission" (also known as a stick shift, stick, straight drive, or standard transmission) means a transmission utilizing a driver-operated clutch that is activated by a pedal or lever and a gear-shift mechanism operated by either hand or foot.

"Non-commercial driver's license" means any other type of motor vehicle license, such as an automobile driver's license, a chauffeur's license, or a motorcycle license.

"Nondomiciled commercial learner's permit" or *"nondomiciled commercial driver's license"* means a commercial learner's permit or commercial driver's license, respectively, issued to a person in accordance with the provisions of this article or, if issued by another state, under either of the following two conditions: (i) to an individual domiciled in a foreign jurisdiction that does not test drivers and issue commercial driver's licenses in accordance with, or under standards similar to, the standards contained in subparts F, G, and H of Part 383 of the Federal Motor Carrier Safety Regulations or (ii) to an individual domiciled in another state while that state is prohibited from issuing commercial driver's licenses in accordance with decertification requirements of 49 C.F.R. § 384.405.

"Out-of-service order" or *"out-of-service declaration"* means an order by a judicial officer pursuant to § 46.2-341.26:2 or 46.2-341.26:3 or an order or declaration by an authorized law-enforcement officer under § 46.2-1001 or regulations promulgated pursuant to § 52-8.4 relating to Motor Carrier Safety, and including similar actions by authorized judicial officers or enforcement officers acting pursuant to similar laws of other states, the United States, the Canadian Provinces, Canada, Mexico, and localities within them, and also including actions by federal or other jurisdictions' officers pursuant to Federal Motor Carrier Safety Regulations, that a driver, a commercial motor vehicle, or a motor carrier is out of service. Such order or declaration as to a driver means that the driver is prohibited from operating a commercial motor vehicle for the duration of the out-of-service period. Such order or declaration as to a vehicle means that such vehicle cannot be operated until the hazardous condition that resulted in the order or declaration has been removed and the vehicle has been cleared for further operation. Such order or declaration as to a motor carrier means that no vehicle may be operated for or on behalf of such carrier until the out-of-service order or declaration has been lifted. For purposes of this article, the provisions of the Federal Motor Carrier Safety Regulations (49 C.F.R. Parts 390 through 397), including

such regulations or any substantially similar regulations as may have been adopted by any state of the United States, the Provinces of Canada, Canada, Mexico, or any locality shall be considered laws similar to the laws of the Commonwealth referenced herein.

"Person" means a natural person, firm, partnership, association, corporation, or a governmental entity including a school board.

"Restriction" means a prohibition on a commercial driver's license or commercial learner's permit that prohibits the holder from operating certain commercial motor vehicles.

"Seasonal restricted commercial driver's license" means a commercial driver's license issued, under the authority of the waiver promulgated by the federal Department of Transportation (49 C.F.R. § 383.3) by the Commonwealth or any other jurisdiction, to an individual who has not passed the knowledge or skills tests required of other commercial driver's license holders. This license authorizes operation of a commercial motor vehicle only on a seasonal basis, stated on the license, by a seasonal employee of a farm service business, within 150 miles of the place of business or the farm currently being served.

"State" means one of the 50 states of the United States or the District of Columbia.

"Tank vehicle" means any commercial motor vehicle that is designed to transport any liquid or gaseous materials within a tank or tanks having an individual rated capacity of more than 119 gallons and an aggregate rated capacity of 1,000 gallons or more that is either permanently or temporarily attached to the vehicle or the chassis. Such vehicles include, but are not limited to, cargo tanks and portable tanks, as defined in 49 C.F.R. Part 171. However, this definition does not include portable tanks having a rated capacity under 1,000 gallons as provided in 49 C.F.R. Part 383. A commercial motor vehicle transporting an empty storage container tank, not designed for transportation, with a rated capacity of 1,000 gallons or more that is temporarily attached to a flatbed trailer is not considered a tank vehicle.

"Third party examiner" means an individual who is an employee of a third party tester and who is certified by the Department to administer tests required for a commercial driver's license.

(Effective until October 1, 2016) *"Third party tester"* means a person (including another state, a motor carrier, a private institution, the military, a government entity, including each comprehensive community college in the Virginia Community College System established by the State Board for Community Colleges pursuant to Chapter 16 (§ 23-192 et seq.) of Title 23, or a department, agency, or instrumentality of a local government) certified by the Department to employ third party examiners to administer a test program for testing commercial driver's license applicants in accordance with this article.

(Effective October 1, 2016) *"Third party tester"* means a person (including another state, a motor carrier, a private institution, the military, a government entity, including each comprehensive community college in the Virginia Community College System established by the State Board for Community Colleges pursuant to Chapter 29 (§ 23.1-2900 et seq.) of Title 23.1, or a department, agency, or instrumentality of a local government) certified by the Department to employ third party examiners to administer a test program for testing commercial driver's license applicants in accordance with this article.

"VAMCSR" means the Virginia Motor Carrier Safety Regulations (19VAC30-20) adopted by the Department of State Police pursuant to § 52-8.4.

History.

1989, c. 705, § 46.1-372.4; 1990, c. 218; 1993, c. 70; 1998, c. 883; 2005, c. 513; 2008, c. 190; 2013, cc. 165, 582; 2014, cc. 77, 803; 2015, c. 258; 2016, c. 429.

§ 46.2-341.5. Regulations consistent with Commercial Motor Vehicle Safety Act.

The Department is authorized to promulgate regulations and establish procedures to enable it to issue commercial driver's licenses, maintain and exchange driver records, and impose licensing sanctions consistent with the provisions of this article and with the minimum standards of the federal Commercial Motor Vehicle Safety Act and the federal regulations promulgated thereunder.

History.

1989, c. 705, § 46.1-372.5.

§ 46.2-341.6. Limitation on number of driver's licenses.

No person who drives a commercial motor vehicle shall have more than one driver's license.

History.

1989, c. 705, § 46.1-372.6.

§ 46.2-341.7. Commercial driver's license required; penalty.

A. No person shall drive a commercial motor vehicle in the Commonwealth unless he has been issued a commercial driver's license or commercial learner's permit and unless such license or permit authorizes the operation of the type and class of vehicle so driven, and unless such license or permit is valid.

B. Every driver of a commercial motor vehicle, while driving such vehicle in the Commonwealth, shall have in his immediate possession the commercial driver's license or commercial learner's permit authorizing the operation of such vehicle and shall make it available to any law-enforcement officer upon request. Failure to comply with this subsection shall be punishable as provided in § 46.2-104.

C. No person shall drive a commercial vehicle in Virginia in violation of any of the restrictions or limitations stated on his commercial driver's license or commercial learner's permit. A violation of the subsection shall constitute a Class 2 misdemeanor.

History.

1989, c. 705, § 46.1-372.7; 1993, c. 70; 2013, cc. 165, 582; 2015, c. 258.

§ 46.2-341.8. Nonresidents and new residents.

A. Any person who is not domiciled in the Commonwealth, who has been duly issued a commercial driver's license or commercial learner's permit by his state of domicile, who has such license or permit in his immediate possession, whose privilege or license to drive any motor vehicle is not suspended, revoked, or cancelled, and who has not been disqualified from driving a commercial motor vehicle, shall be permitted without further examination or licensure by the Commonwealth, to drive a commercial motor vehicle in the Commonwealth.

Within 30 days after becoming domiciled in this Commonwealth, any person who has been issued a commercial driver's license by another state and who intends to drive a commercial motor vehicle shall apply to the Department for a Virginia commercial driver's license. If the Commissioner determines that such applicant is otherwise eligible for a commercial driver's license, the Department will issue him a Virginia commercial driver's license with the same classification and endorsements as his commercial driver's license from another state, without requiring him to take the knowledge or skills test required for such commercial driver's license in accordance with § 46.2-330. However, any such applicant seeking to transfer his commercial driver's license and to retain a hazardous materials endorsement shall have, within the two-year period preceding his application for a Virginia commercial driver's license, either (i) passed the required test for such endorsement specified in 49 C.F.R. § 383.121 or (ii) successfully completed a hazardous materials test or training that is given by a third party and that is deemed to substantially cover the same knowledge base as described in 49 C.F.R. § 383.121.

B. Any person who is (i) domiciled in a foreign jurisdiction that does not test drivers and issue commercial driver's licenses in accordance with, or under standards similar to, the standards contained in subparts F, G, and H of Part 383 of the Federal Motor Carrier Safety Regulations or (ii) domiciled in another state while that state is prohibited from issuing commercial driver's licenses in accordance with decertification requirements of 49 C.F.R. § 384.405 may apply to the Department for a nondomiciled commercial learner's permit or nondomiciled commercial driver's license.

An applicant for a nondomiciled commercial learner's permit or nondomiciled commercial driver's license shall be required to meet all requirements for a commercial learner's permit or commercial driver's license, respectively.

An applicant domiciled in a foreign jurisdiction shall provide an unexpired employment authorization document (EAD) issued by the U.S. Citizenship and Immigration Services (USCIS) or an unexpired foreign passport accompanied by an approved Form I-94 documenting the applicant's most recent admittance into the United States.

An applicant for a nondomiciled commercial driver's license or nondomiciled commercial learner's permit shall not be required to surrender his foreign license.

After receipt of a nondomiciled commercial driver's license or nondomiciled commercial learner's permit and for as long as it is valid, holders of such licenses or permits shall be required to notify the Department of any adverse action taken by any jurisdiction or governmental agency, foreign or domestic, against his driving privileges. Such notification shall be made before the end of the business day following the day the driver receives notice of the suspension, revocation, cancellation, lost privilege, or disqualification.

History.

1989, c. 705, § 46.1-372.8; 2013, cc. 165, 582; 2014, cc. 77, 803; 2015, c. 258.

§ 46.2-341.9. Eligibility for commercial driver's license or commercial learner's permit.

A. A Virginia commercial driver's license or commercial learner's permit shall be issued only to a person who drives or intends to drive a commercial motor vehicle, who is domiciled in the Commonwealth, and who is eligible for a commercial driver's license or commercial learner's permit under such terms and conditions as the Department may require.

No person shall be eligible for a Virginia commercial driver's license or commercial learner's permit until he has applied for such license or permit and has passed the applicable vision, knowledge and skills tests required by this article, and has satisfied all other applicable licensing requirements imposed by the laws of the Commonwealth. Such requirements shall include meeting the standards contained in subparts F, G, and H, of Part 383 of the FMCSA regulations.

No person shall be eligible for a Virginia commercial driver's license or commercial learner's permit during any period in which he is disqualified from driving a commercial motor vehicle, or his driver's license or privilege to drive is suspended, revoked or cancelled in any state, or during any period wherein the restoration of his license or privilege is contingent upon the furnishing of proof of financial responsibility.

No person shall be eligible for a Virginia commercial driver's license until he surrenders all other driver's licenses issued to him by any state.

No person shall be eligible for a Virginia commercial learner's permit until he surrenders all other driver's licenses and permits issued to him by any other state. The applicant for a commercial learner's permit is not required to surrender his Virginia noncommercial driver's license.

No person under the age of 21 years shall be eligible for a commercial driver's license, except that a person who is at least 18 years of age may be issued a commercial driver's license or commercial learner's permit, provided that such person is exempt from or is not subject to the age requirements of the Federal Motor Carrier Safety Regulations contained in 49 C.F.R. Part 391, and is not prohibited from operating a commercial motor vehicle by the Virginia Motor Carrier Safety Regulations, and has so certified. No person under the age of 21 years shall be issued a hazardous materials endorsement.

No person shall be eligible for a Virginia commercial driver's license to drive a Type S vehicle, as defined in subsection B of § 46.2-341.16, during any period in which he is a person for whom registration with the Sex Offender and Crimes Against Minors Registry is required pursuant to Chapter 9 (§ 9.1-900 et seq.) of Title 9.1.

In determining the eligibility of any applicant for a Virginia commercial driver's license, the Department shall consider, to the extent not inconsistent with federal law, the applicant's military training and experience.

A person for whom registration with the Sex Offender and Crimes Against Minors Registry is required pursuant to Chapter 9 (§ 9.1-900 et seq.) of Title 9.1 may be issued a Virginia commercial driver's license to drive a Type P vehicle, as defined in subsection B of § 46.2-341.16, provided the commercial driver's license includes a restriction prohibiting the license holder from operating a commercial vehicle to transport children to or from activities sponsored by a school or by a child day care facility licensed, regulated, or approved by the Virginia Department of Social Services.

B. Notwithstanding the provisions of subsection A, pursuant to 49 U.S.C. 31311(a)(12) a commercial driver's license or commercial learner's permit may be issued to an individual who (i) operates or will operate a commercial motor vehicle; (ii) is a member of the active duty military, military reserves, National Guard, active duty United States Coast Guard, or Coast Guard Auxiliary; and (iii) is not domiciled in the Commonwealth, but whose temporary or permanent duty station is located in the Commonwealth.

History.
1989, c. 705, § 46.1-372.9; 2011, c. 477; 2012, cc. 12, 153; 2013, cc. 165, 582; 2015, c. 258.

§ 46.2-341.9:1. Commissioner to grant variances for commercial drivers transporting hazardous wastes.

The Commissioner may, to the extent allowed by federal law, grant variances from the regulations with respect to the physical qualifications for drivers of commercial motor vehicles transporting hazardous materials if:

1. The driver is regularly employed in a job requiring the operation of a commercial motor vehicle transporting hazardous materials;
2. The driver is at least twenty-one years of age;
3. A physician licensed in Virginia certifies that, in his professional opinion, the driver is capable of safely operating a commercial motor vehicle transporting hazardous materials; and
4. In the opinion of the Commissioner, the driver is able to perform the normal tasks associated with operating a commercial motor vehicle and comply with the applicable regulations authorized by § 10.1-1450.

The Commissioner may promulgate regulations addressing such variances.

History.
1997, c. 260.

§ 46.2-341.10. Special provisions relating to commercial learner's permit.

A. The Department, upon receiving an application on forms prescribed by the Commissioner and upon the applicant's satisfactory completion of the vision and knowledge tests required for the class and type of commercial motor vehicle to be driven by the applicant may, in its discretion, issue to such applicant a commercial learner's permit. Such permit shall be valid for no more than 180 days from the date of issuance. The Department may renew the commercial learner's permit for an additional 180 days without requiring the commercial learner's permit holder to retake the general and endorsement knowledge tests. No additional renewals are permitted. A commercial learner's permit shall entitle the applicant to drive a commercial motor vehicle of the class and type designated on the permit, but only when accompanied by a person licensed to drive the class and type of commercial motor vehicle driven by the applicant. The person accompanying the permit holder shall occupy the seat closest to the driver's seat for the purpose of giving instruction to the permit holder in driving the commercial motor vehicle.

B. No person shall be issued a commercial learner's permit unless he possesses a valid Virginia driver's license or has satisfied all the requirements necessary to obtain such a license.

C. A commercial learner's permit holder with a passenger (P) endorsement (i) must have taken and passed the P endorsement knowledge test and (ii) is prohibited from operating a commercial motor vehicle carrying passengers, other than federal or state auditors and inspectors, test examiners, other trainees, and the commercial driver's license holder accompanying the commercial learner's permit holder. The P endorsement must be class specific.

D. A commercial learner's permit holder with a school bus (S) endorsement (i) must have taken and passed the S endorsement knowledge test and (ii) is prohibited from operating a school bus with passengers other than federal or state auditors and inspectors, test examiners, other trainees, and the commercial driver's license holder accompanying the commercial learner's permit holder. No person shall be issued a commercial learner's permit to drive school buses or to drive any commercial vehicle to transport children to or from activities sponsored by a school or by a child day care facility licensed, regulated, or approved by the Virginia Department of Social Services during any period in which he is a person for whom registration with the Sex Offender and Crimes Against Minors Registry is required pursuant to Chapter 9 (§ 9.1-900 et seq.) of Title 9.1.

E. A commercial learner's permit holder with a tank vehicle (N) endorsement (i) must have taken and passed the N endorsement knowledge test and (ii) may only operate an empty tank vehicle and is prohibited from operating any tank vehicle that previously contained hazardous materials that has not been purged of any residue.

F. The issuance of a commercial learner's permit is a precondition to the initial issuance of a commercial driver's license and to the upgrade of a commercial driver's license if the upgrade requires a skills test. The commercial learner's permit holder is not eligible to take the commercial driver's license skills test until he has held the permit for the required period of time specified in § 46.2-324.1.

G. Any commercial learner's permit holder who operates a commercial motor vehicle without being accompanied by a licensed driver as provided in this section is guilty of a Class 2 misdemeanor.

H. The Department shall charge a fee of $3 for each commercial learner's permit issued under the provisions of this section.

History.

1989, c. 705, § 46.1-372.10; 2011, c. 477; 2012, c. 153; 2013, cc. 165, 582; 2014, cc. 77, 803; 2015, c. 258.

§ 46.2-341.10:1. Seasonal restricted commercial drivers' licenses.

A. The Commissioner may, in his discretion, issue seasonal restricted commercial drivers' licenses in accordance with this section.

B. A Virginia seasonal restricted commercial driver's license shall be issued only to a person who (i) is a seasonal employee of a farm retail outlet or supplier, a custom harvester, a livestock feeder, or an agri-chemical business, (ii) is a Virginia-licensed driver with at least one year of driving experience as a licensed driver, and (iii) has satisfied every requirement for issuance of a commercial driver's license except successful completion of the knowledge and skills tests.

C. The Department shall not issue or renew a seasonal restricted commercial driver's license and shall not revalidate the seasonal period for which such license authorizes operation of a commercial motor vehicle, unless:

1. The applicant has not, and certifies that he has not, at any time during the two years immediately preceding the date of application:

a. Had more than one driver's license;

b. Had any driver's license or driving privilege suspended, revoked, or canceled;

c. Had any convictions involving any kind of motor vehicle for any of the offenses listed in §§ 46.2-341.18, 46.2-341.19, or § 46.2-341.20;

d. Been convicted of a violation of state or local laws relating to motor vehicle traffic control, other than a parking violation, which violation arose in connection with any reportable traffic accident;

e. Been convicted of any serious traffic violation, as defined in § 46.2-341.20, whether or not committed in a commercial motor vehicle; and

2. The applicant certifies and provides evidence satisfactory to the Commissioner that he is employed on a seasonal basis by a farm retail outlet or supplier, custom harvester, livestock feeder, or agrichemical business in a job requiring the operation of a commercial motor vehicle.

D. Such seasonal restricted license shall entitle the licensee to drive a commercial motor vehicle of the class and type designated on the license, but shall not authorize operation of a Class A vehicle.

E. Such seasonal restricted license shall authorize operation of a commercial motor vehicle only during the seasonal period or periods prescribed by the Commissioner and stated on the license, provided the total number of calendar days in any twelve-month period for which the seasonal restricted license authorizes operation of a commercial motor vehicle shall not exceed 180. The license is valid for operation of a commercial motor vehicle during the seasonal period or periods for which it has been validated and must be revalidated annually by the Department for each successive seasonal period or periods for which commercial vehicle operation is sought; such license shall authorize operation of noncommercial motor vehicles at any time, unless it has been suspended, revoked, or canceled, or has expired.

F. Such seasonal restricted license shall not authorize operation of a commercial motor vehicle during any period during which the licensee is not employed by an entity described in subdivision B hereof, nor if such operation is not directly related to such employment.

G. Such seasonal restricted license shall not authorize the licensee to operate any vehicle transporting hazardous materials as defined in this article, except that a seasonal restricted licensee may drive a vehicle transporting:

1. Diesel fuel in quantities of 1,000 gallons or less;

2. Liquid fertilizers to be used as plant nutrients, in a vehicle or implement of husbandry with a total capacity of 3,000 gallons or less; or

3. Solid plant nutrients that are not transported with any organic substance.

H. Such seasonal restricted license shall authorize the operation of a commercial motor vehicle only within 150 miles of the place of business of the licensee's employer or the farm being served.

History.

1993, c. 70.

§ 46.2-341.11. Commercial drivers required to notify the Department of change of address.

A. If any person who is licensed by the Department to drive a commercial motor vehicle changes the mailing or residential address he most recently submitted to the Department, such person shall notify the Department in writing within thirty days after his change of address. If the Department receives notification from the person or any court or law-enforcement agency that a person's residential address has changed to a non-Virginia address, the Department shall (i) mail, by first-class mail, no later than three days after the notice of address change is received by the Department, notice to the person that his commercial driver's license will be cancelled by the Department and (ii) cancel the commercial driver's license thirty days after notice of cancellation has been mailed.

B. Any person who fails to notify the Department of his change of address in accord with the provisions of this subsection shall be guilty of a traffic infraction.

History.

1989, c. 705, § 46.1-372.11; 2002, cc. 767, 834.

§ 46.2-341.12. Application for commercial driver's license or commercial learner's permit.

A. Every application to the Department for a commercial driver's license or commercial learner's permit shall be made upon a form approved and furnished by the Department, and the applicant shall write his usual signature in ink in the space provided. The applicant shall provide the following information:

1. Full legal name;

2. Current mailing and residential addresses;

3. Physical description including sex, height, weight and eye and hair color;

4. Year, month and date of birth;

5. Social security number;

6. Domicile or, if not domiciled in the Commonwealth, proof of status as a member of the active duty military, military reserves, National Guard, active duty United States Coast Guard, or Coast Guard Auxiliary pursuant to 49 U.S.C. § 31311(a)(12); and

7. Any other information required on the application form.

The applicant's social security number shall be provided to the Commercial Driver's License Information System as required by 49 C.F.R. § 383.153.

B. Every applicant for a commercial driver's license or commercial learner's permit shall also submit to the Department the following:

1. A consent to release driving record information;

2. Certifications that:

a. He either meets the federal qualification requirements of 49 C.F.R. Parts 383 and 391, or he is exempt from or is not subject to such federal requirements;

b. He either meets the state qualification requirements established pursuant to § 52-8.4, or he is exempt from or is not subject to such requirements;

c. The motor vehicle in which the applicant takes the skills test is representative of the class and, if applicable, the type of motor vehicle for which the applicant seeks to be licensed;

d. He is not subject to any disqualification, suspension, revocation or cancellation of his driving privileges;

e. He does not have more than one driver's license;

3. Other certifications required by the Department;

4. Any evidence required by the Department to establish proof of identity, citizenship or lawful permanent residency, domicile, and social security number notwithstanding the provisions of § 46.2-328.1 and pursuant to 49 C.F.R. Part 383;

5. A statement indicating whether (i) the applicant has previously been licensed to drive any type of motor vehicle during the previous 10 years and, if so, all states that licensed the applicant and the dates he was licensed, and (ii) whether or not he has ever been disqualified, or his license suspended, revoked or cancelled and, if so, the date of and reason therefor; and

6. An unexpired employment authorization document (EAD) issued by the U.S. Citizenship and Immigration Services (USCIS) or an unexpired foreign passport accompanied by an approved Form I-94 documenting the applicant's most recent admittance into the United States for persons applying for a nondomiciled commercial driver's license or nondomiciled commercial learner's permit.

C. Every application for a commercial driver's license shall include a photograph of the applicant supplied under arrangements made therefor by the Department in accordance with § 46.2-323.

D. The Department shall disqualify any commercial driver for a period of one year when the records of the Department clearly show to the satisfaction of the Commissioner that such person has made a material false statement on any application or certification made for a commercial driver's license or commercial learner's permit. The Department shall take such action within 30 days after discovering such falsification.

E. The Department shall review the driving record of any person who applies for a Virginia commercial driver's license or commercial learner's permit, for the renewal or reinstatement of such license or permit or for an additional commercial classification or endorsement, including the driving record from all jurisdictions where, during the previous 10 years, the applicant was licensed to drive any type of motor vehicle. Such review shall include checking the photograph on record whenever the applicant or holder appears in person to renew, upgrade, transfer, reinstate, or obtain a duplicate commercial driver's license or to renew, upgrade, reinstate, or obtain a duplicate commercial learner's permit. If appropriate, the Department shall incorporate information from such other jurisdictions' records into the applicant's Virginia driving record, and shall make a notation on the applicant's driving record confirming that such review has been completed and the date it was completed. The Department's review shall include research through the Commercial Driver License Information System established pursuant to the Commercial Motor Vehicle Safety Act and the National Driver Register Problem Driver Pointer System in addition to the driver record maintained by the applicant's previous jurisdictions of licensure. This research shall be completed prior to the issuance, renewal, transfer, or reinstatement of a commercial driver's license or additional commercial classification or endorsement.

The Department shall verify the name, date of birth, and Social Security number provided by the applicant with the information on file with the Social Security Administration for initial issuance of a commercial learner's permit or transfer of a commercial driver's license from another state. The Department shall make a notation in the driver's record confirming that the necessary verification has been completed and noting the date it was done. The Department shall also make a notation confirming that proof of citizenship or lawful permanent residency has been presented and the date it was done.

F. Every new applicant for a commercial driver's license or commercial learner's permit, including any person applying for a commercial driver's license or permit after revocation of his driving privileges, who certifies that he will operate a commercial motor vehicle in non-excepted interstate or intrastate commerce shall provide the Department with an original or certified copy of a medical examiner's certificate prepared by a medical examiner as defined in 49 C.F.R. § 390.5. Upon receipt of an appropriate medical examiner's certificate, the Department shall post a certification status of "certified" on the record of the driver on the Commercial Driver's License Information System. Any new applicant for a commercial driver's license or commercial learner's permit who fails to comply with the requirements of this subsection shall be denied the issuance of a commercial driver's license or commercial learner's permit by the Department.

G. Every existing holder of a commercial driver's license or commercial learner's permit who certifies that he will operate a commercial motor vehicle in non-excepted interstate or intrastate commerce shall provide the Department with an original or certified copy of a medical examiner's certificate prepared by a medical examiner as defined in 49 C.F.R. § 390.5. Upon receipt of an appropriate medical examiner's certificate, the Department shall post a certification status of "certified" and any other necessary information on the record of the driver on the Commercial Driver's License Information System. If an existing holder of a commercial driver's license fails to provide the Department with a medical certificate as required by this subsection, the Department shall post a certification status of "noncertified" on the record of the driver on the Commercial Driver's License Information System and initiate a downgrade of his commercial driver's license as defined in 49 C.F.R. § 383.5.

H. Any person who provides a medical certificate to the Department pursuant to the requirements of subsections F and G shall keep the medical certificate information current and shall notify the Department of any change in the status of the medical certificate. If the Department determines that the medical certificate is no longer valid, the Department shall initiate a downgrade of the driver's commercial driver's license as defined in 49 C.F.R. § 383.5.

I. If the Department receives notice that the holder of a commercial driver's license has been issued a medical variance as defined in 49 C.F.R. § 390.5, the Department shall indicate the existence of such medical variance on the commercial driver's license document of the driver and on the record of the driver on the Commercial Driver's License Information System using the restriction code "V."

J. Any holder of a commercial driver's license who has been issued a medical variance shall keep the medical variance information current and shall notify the Department of any change in the status of the medical variance. If the Department determines that the medical variance is no longer valid, the Department shall initiate a downgrade of the driver's commercial driver's license as defined in 49 C.F.R. § 383.5.

K. Any applicant applying for a hazardous materials endorsement must comply with Transportation Security Administration requirements in 49 C.F.R. Part 1572. A lawful permanent resident of the United States requesting a hazardous materials endorsement must additionally provide his U.S. Citizenship and Immigration Services (USCIS) alien registration number.

History.
1989, c. 705, § 46.1-372.12; 2005, c. 513; 2009, c. 872; 2011, cc. 881, 889; 2013, cc. 165, 582; 2014, cc. 77, 803; 2015, c. 258.

§ 46.2-341.13. Disposition of fees.

Except as otherwise provided, all fees accruing under the provisions of this chapter shall be paid to and received by the Commissioner, and by him forthwith paid into the state treasury and shall be set aside as a special fund in the state treasury to be used to meet the necessary additional expenses incurred by the Department of Motor Vehicles and the Commissioner in the performance of the duties required by this article.

History.
1989, c. 705, § 46.1-372.13.

§ 46.2-341.14. Testing requirements for commercial driver's license; behind-the-wheel and knowledge examinations.

A. The Department shall conduct an examination of every applicant for a commercial driver's license, which examination shall comply with the minimum federal standards established pursuant to the federal Commercial Motor Vehicle Safety Act. The examination shall be designed to test the vision, knowledge, and skills required for the safe operation of the class and type of commercial motor vehicle for which the applicant seeks a license.

B. An applicant's skills test shall be conducted in a vehicle that is representative of or meets the description of the class of vehicle for which the applicant seeks to be licensed. In addition, applicants who seek to be licensed to drive vehicles with air brakes, passenger-carrying vehicles, or school buses must take the skills test in a vehicle that is representative of such vehicle type. Such vehicle shall be furnished by the applicant and shall be properly licensed, inspected and insured.

C. The Commissioner may designate such persons as he deems fit, including private or governmental entities, including comprehensive community colleges in the Virginia Community College System, to administer the knowledge and skills tests required of applicants for a commercial driver's license. Any person so designated shall comply with all statutes and regulations with respect to the administration of such tests.

The Commissioner shall require all state and third party test examiners to successfully complete a formal commercial driver's license test examiner training course and examination before certifying them to administer commercial driver's license knowledge and skills tests. All state and third party test examiners shall complete a refresher training course and examination every four years to maintain their commercial driver's license test examiner certification. The refresher training course shall comply with 49 C.F.R. § 384.228. At least once every two years, the Department shall conduct covert and overt monitoring of examinations performed by state and third party commercial driver's license test examiners.

The Commissioner shall require a nationwide criminal background check of all test examiners at the time of hiring or prior to certifying them to administer commercial driver's license testing. The Commissioner shall complete a nationwide criminal background check for any state or third party test examiners who are current examiners and who have not had a nationwide criminal background check.

The Commissioner shall revoke the certification to administer commercial driver's license tests for any test examiner who (i) does not successfully complete the required refresher training every four years or (ii) does not pass the required nationwide criminal background check. Criteria for not passing the criminal background check include but are not limited to having a felony conviction within the past 10 years or any conviction involving fraudulent activities.

D. Every applicant for a commercial driver's license who is required by the Commissioner to take a vision test shall either (i) appear before a license examiner of the Department of Motor Vehicles to demonstrate his visual acuity and horizontal field of vision; or (ii) submit with his application a copy of the vision examination report which was used as the basis for such examination made within 90 days of the application date by an ophthalmologist or optometrist. The Commissioner may, by regulation, determine whether any other visual tests will satisfy the requirements of this title for commercial drivers.

E. No person who fails the behind-the-wheel examination for a commercial driver's license administered by the Department three times shall be permitted to take such examination a fourth time until he successfully completes, subsequent to the third examination failure, the in-vehicle component of driver instruction at a driver training school licensed under Chapter 17 (§ 46.2-1700 et seq.) or a comparable course approved by the Department or the Department of Education. In addition, no person who fails the general knowledge examination for a commercial driver's license administered by the Department three times shall be permitted to take such examination a fourth time until he successfully completes, subsequent to the third examination failure, the knowledge component of driver instruction at a driver training school licensed under Chapter 17 (§ 46.2-1700 et seq.) or a comparable course approved by the Department or the Department of Education.

The provisions of this subsection shall not apply to persons placed under medical control pursuant to § 46.2-322.

F. Knowledge tests may be administered in written form, verbally, or in automated format and can be administered in a foreign language, provided no interpreter is used in administering the test.

G. Interpreters are prohibited during the administration of the skills tests. Applicants must be able to understand and respond to verbal commands and instructions in English by a skills test examiner. Neither the applicant nor the examiner may communicate in a language other than English during the skills test.

H. Skills tests may be administered to an applicant who has taken training in the Commonwealth and is to be licensed in another state. Such test results shall be electronically transmitted directly from the Commonwealth to the licensing state in an efficient and secure manner. The Department may charge a fee of not more than $85 to any such applicant.

I. The Department shall accept the results of skills tests administered to applicants by any other state in fulfillment of the applicant's testing requirements for commercial licensure in the Commonwealth.

History.
1989, c. 705, § 46.1-372.14; 2008, c. 735; 2013, cc. 165, 582; 2014, cc. 77, 803; 2015, c. 258; 2016, c. 429.

§ 46.2-341.14:01. Military third party testers and military third party examiners; substitute for driving skills tests for drivers with military commercial motor vehicle experience.

A. Pursuant to § 46.2-341.14, the Commissioner shall permit military bases that have entered into an agreement with the Department to serve as third party testers in administering state knowledge and skills tests for issuing commercial driver's licenses. Military third party testers and military third party examiners shall comply with the requirements set forth in §§ 46.2-341.14:1 through 46.2-341.14:9 with respect to knowledge and skills tests.

B. Pursuant to 49 C.F.R. § 383.77, the Commissioner may waive the driving skills test as specified in 49 C.F.R. § 383.113 for a commercial motor vehicle driver with military commercial motor vehicle experience who is currently licensed at the time of his application for a commercial driver's license and substitute an applicant's driving record in combination with certain driving experience for the skills test.

C. To obtain a skills test waiver, the following conditions and limitations must be met:

1. An applicant must certify that, during the two-year period immediately prior to applying for a commercial driver's license, he:

a. Has not had more than one license except for a military license;

b. Has not had any license suspended, revoked, canceled, or disqualified;

c. Has not had any convictions for any type of motor vehicle for the disqualifying offenses contained in this article;

d. Has not had more than one conviction for any type of motor vehicle for serious traffic violations contained in this article; and

e. Has not had any conviction for a violation of military, state, or local law relating to motor vehicle traffic control, other than a parking violation, arising in connection with any traffic crash and has no record of a crash in which he was at fault; and

2. An applicant must provide evidence and certify that he:

a. Is regularly employed or was regularly employed within the last 90 days or any other period authorized by the FMCSA in a military position requiring operation of a commercial motor vehicle;

b. Was exempted from the commercial driver's license requirements in 49 C.F.R. § 383.3(c); and

c. Was operating a vehicle representative of the commercial motor vehicle the driver applicant operates, or expects to operate, for at least the two years immediately preceding discharge from the military.

History.
2014, cc. 77, 803.

§ 46.2-341.14:1. Requirements for third party testers.

A. Pursuant to § 46.2-341.14, third party testers will be authorized to issue skills test certificates, which will be accepted by the Department as evidence of satisfaction of the skills test component of the commercial driver's license examination. Authority to issue skills test certificates will be granted only to third party testers certified by the Department.

B. To qualify for certification, a third party tester shall:

1. Make application to and enter into an agreement with the Department as provided in § 46.2-341.14:3;

2. Maintain a place of business in the Commonwealth;

3. Have at least one certified third party examiner in his employ;

4. Ensure that all third party examiners in his employ are certified and comply with the requirements of §§ 46.2-341.14:2 and 46.2-341.14:7;

5. Permit the Department and the FMCSA of the U.S. Department of Transportation to conduct random examinations, inspections, and audits of its records, facilities, and operations that relate to the third party testing program without prior notice;

6. Maintain at the principal place of business a copy of the state certificate authorizing the third party tester to administer a commercial driver's license testing program and current third party agreement;

7. Maintain at a location in the Commonwealth, for a minimum of two years after a skills test is conducted, a record of each driver for whom the third party tester conducts a skills test, whether the

driver passes or fails the test. Each such record shall include:

a. The complete name of the driver;

b. The driver's Social Security number or other driver's license number and the name of the state or jurisdiction that issued the license held by the driver at the time of the test;

c. The date the driver took the skills test;

d. The test score sheet or sheets showing the results of the skills test and a copy of the skills test certificate, if issued;

e. The name and certification number of the third party examiner conducting the skills test;

f. Evidence of the driver's employment with the third party tester at the time the test was taken. If the third party tester is a school board that tests drivers who are trained but not employed by the school board, evidence that (i) the driver was employed by a school board at the time of the test and (ii) the third party tester trained the driver in accordance with the Virginia School Bus Driver Training Curriculum Guide; and

g. Notwithstanding the provisions of subdivision f, evidence of the student's enrollment in a commercial driver training course offered by a community college at the time the test was taken if the third party tester is a comprehensive community college in the Virginia Community College System.

8. Maintain at a location in the Commonwealth a record of each third party examiner in the employ of the third party tester. Each record shall include:

a. Name and Social Security number;

b. Evidence of the third party examiner's certification by the Department;

c. A copy of the third party examiner's current training and driving record, which must be updated annually;

d. Evidence that the third party examiner is an employee of the third party tester; and

e. If the third party tester is a school board, a copy of the third party examiner's certification of instruction issued by the Department of Education;

9. Retain the records required in subdivision 8 for at least two years after the third party examiner leaves the employ of the third party tester;

10. Ensure that skills tests are conducted, and that skills test certificates are issued in accordance with the requirements of §§ 46.2-341.14:8 and 46.2-341.14:9 and the instructions provided by the Department;

11. Maintain compliance with all applicable provisions of this article and the third party tester agreement executed pursuant to § 46.2-341.14:3; and

12. Maintain a copy of the third party tester's road test route or routes approved by the Department.

C. In addition to the requirements listed in subsection B, all third party testers who are not governmental entities, including a comprehensive community college in the Virginia Community College System, shall:

1. Be engaged in a business involving the use of commercial motor vehicles, which business has been in operation in the Commonwealth for a minimum of one year;

2. Employ at least 75 drivers of commercial motor vehicles licensed in the Commonwealth, during the 12-month period preceding the application, including part-time and seasonal drivers. This requirement may be waived by the Department pursuant to § 46.2-341.14:10;

3. If subject to the FMCSA regulations and rated by the U.S. Department of Transportation, maintain a rating of "satisfactory";

4. Comply with the Virginia Motor Carrier Safety Regulations; and

5. Initiate and maintain a bond in the amount of $5,000 to pay for retesting drivers in the event that the third-party tester or one or more of its examiners are involved in fraudulent activities related to conducting knowledge or skills testing for applicants.

History.

2013, cc. 165, 582; 2014, cc. 77, 803; 2015, c. 258; 2016, c. 429.

§ 46.2-341.14:2. Requirements for third party examiners.

A. Third party examiners may be certified to conduct skills tests on behalf of only one third party tester at any given time. If a third party examiner leaves the employ of a third party tester, he must be recertified in order to conduct skills tests on behalf of a new third party tester.

B. To qualify for certification as a third party examiner, an individual must:

1. Make application to the Department as provided in § 46.2-341.14:3 and pass the required nationwide criminal background check;

2. Be an employee of the third party tester;

3. Possess a valid Virginia commercial driver's license with the classification and endorsements required for operation of the class and type of commercial motor vehicle used in skills tests conducted by the examiner;

4. Satisfactorily complete any third party examiner training course required by the Department;

5. Within three years prior to application, have had no driver's license suspensions, revocations, or disqualifications;

6. At the time of application, have no more than six demerit points on his driving record and not be on probation under the Virginia Driver Improvement Program;

7. Within three years prior to application, have had no conviction for any offense listed in § 46.2-341.18 or 46.2-341.19, whether or not such offense was committed in a commercial motor vehicle;

8. If the examiner is employed by a school board, be certified by the Virginia Department of Education as a school bus training instructor;

9. Conduct skills tests on behalf of the third party tester in accordance with this article and in accor-

dance with current instructions provided by the Department; and

10. Successfully complete a training course and examination every four years to maintain the commercial driver's license test examiner certification.

History.

2013, cc. 165, 582; 2014, cc. 77, 803.

§ 46.2-341.14:3. Application for certification by the Department.

A. Application for third party tester certification.

1. An applicant for certification shall provide the following information in a format prescribed by the Department:

a. Name, address, and telephone number of principal office or headquarters;

b. Name, title, address, and telephone number of an individual in the Commonwealth who has been designated to be the applicant's contact person with the Department;

c. Description of the vehicle fleet owned or leased by the applicant, including the number of commercial motor vehicles by class and type;

d. Classes and types of commercial motor vehicles for which the applicant seeks to be certified as a third party tester;

e. Total number of drivers licensed in the Commonwealth employed during the preceding 12 months to operate commercial motor vehicles and the number of such drivers who are full time, part time, and seasonal. However, this provision shall not apply to a comprehensive community college in the Virginia Community College System certified as a third party tester for the purposes of administering tests to students enrolled in a commercial driver training course offered by such community college;

f. Name, driver's license number, and home address of each employee who is to be certified as a third party examiner. If any employee has previously been certified as an examiner by the Department, the examiner's certification number;

g. The address of each location in the Commonwealth where the third party tester intends to conduct skills tests and a map, drawing, or written description of each driving course that satisfies the Department's requirements for a skills test course;

h. If the applicant is not a governmental entity, including a comprehensive community college in the Virginia Community College System, it shall also provide: (i) a description of the applicant's business and length of time in business in the Commonwealth; (ii) if subject to the FMCSA regulations, the applicant's Interstate Commerce Commission number or U.S. Department of Transportation number and rating; and (iii) the applicant's State Corporation Commission number; and

i. Any other relevant information required by the Department.

2. An applicant for certification shall also execute an agreement in a format prescribed by the Department in which the applicant agrees, at a minimum, to comply with the regulations and instructions of the Department for third party testers, including audit procedures, and agrees to hold the Department harmless from liability resulting from the third party tester's administration of its commercial driver's license skills test program.

B. Application for third party examiner certification.

1. An applicant for certification shall provide the following information in a format prescribed by the Department:

a. Name, home, and business addresses and telephone numbers;

b. Driver's license number;

c. Name, address, and telephone number of the principal office or headquarters of the applicant's employer, who has applied for and received certification as a third party tester;

d. Job title and description of duties and responsibilities;

e. Length of time employed by present employer. If less than two years, list previous employer, address, and telephone number;

f. Present employer's recommendation of the applicant for certification;

g. A list of the classes and types of vehicles for which the applicant seeks certification to conduct skills tests; and

h. Any other relevant information required by the Department.

C. Evaluation of applicant by the Department.

1. The Department will evaluate the materials submitted by the third party tester applicant, and, if the application materials are satisfactory, the Department will schedule an onsite inspection and audit of the applicant's third party testing program to complete the evaluation.

2. The Department will evaluate the materials submitted by the third party examiner applicant as well as the applicant's driving record. If the application materials and driving record are satisfactory, the Department will schedule the applicant for third party examiner training. Training may be waived if the applicant is seeking recertification only because he has changed employers.

3. No more than two applications will be accepted from any one third party tester or examiner applicant in any 12-month period, excluding applications for recertification because of a change in employers.

History.

2013, cc. 165, 582; 2016, c. 429.

§ 46.2-341.14:4. Certification by the Department.

A. Upon successful application and evaluation, a third party tester will be issued a letter or certificate that will evidence his authority to administer a third party testing program and issue skills test certificates for the classes and types of vehicles listed.

B. Upon successful application, evaluation, and training, a third party examiner will be issued a letter or certificate that will evidence his authority to conduct skills tests for the classes and types of commercial motor vehicles listed.

C. Certification will remain valid until canceled by the Department or voluntarily relinquished by the third party tester or examiner.

History.
2013, cc. 165, 582.

§ 46.2-341.14:5. Terminating certification of third party tester or examiner.

A. Any third party tester or examiner may relinquish certification upon 30 days' notice to the Department. Relinquishment of certification by a third party tester or examiner shall not release such tester or examiner from any responsibility or liability that arises from his activities as a third party tester or examiner.

B. The Department reserves the right to cancel the third party testing program established by this article, in its entirety.

C. The Department shall revoke the skills testing certification of any examiner:

1. Who does not conduct skills test examinations of at least 10 different applicants per calendar year. However, examiners who do not meet the 10-test minimum must either take a refresher commercial driver's license training that complies with 49 C.F.R. § 384.228 or have a Department examiner ride along to observe the third party examiner successfully administer at least one skills test; or

2. Who does not successfully complete the required refresher training every four years pursuant to 49 C.F.R. § 384.228.

D. The Department may cancel the certification of an individual third party tester or examiner upon the following grounds:

1. Failure to comply with or satisfy any of the provisions of this article, federal standards for the commercial driver's license testing program, the Department's instructions, or the third party tester agreement;

2. Falsification of any record or information relating to the third party testing program;

3. Commission of any act that compromises the integrity of the third party testing program; or

4. Failure to pass the required nationwide criminal background check. Criteria for not passing the criminal background check include but are not limited to having a felony conviction within the past 10 years or any conviction involving fraudulent activities.

E. If the Department determines that grounds for cancellation exist for failure to comply with or satisfy any of the requirements of this chapter or the third party tester agreement, the Department may postpone cancellation and allow the third party tester or examiner 30 days to correct the deficiency.

History.
2013, cc. 165, 582; 2014, cc. 77, 803.

§ 46.2-341.14:6. Onsite inspections and audits.

A. Each applicant for certification as a third party tester shall permit the Department or FMCSA to conduct random examinations, inspections, and audits of its operations, facilities, and records as they relate to its third party testing program, for the purpose of determining whether the applicant is qualified for certification. Each person who has been certified as a third party tester shall permit the Department to periodically inspect and audit his third party testing program to determine whether it remains in compliance with certification requirements.

B. The Department or FMCSA will perform its random examinations, inspections, and audits of third party testers during regular business hours with or without prior notice to the third party tester.

C. Inspections and audits of third party testers will occur at a minimum once every two years and include, at a minimum, an examination of:

1. Records relating to the third party testing program;

2. Evidence of compliance with the FMCSA regulations and Virginia Motor Carrier Safety Regulations;

3. Skills testing procedures, practices, and operations;

4. Vehicles used for testing;

5. Qualifications of third party examiners;

6. Effectiveness of the skills test program by either (i) testing a sample of drivers who have been issued skills test certificates by the third party tester to compare pass/fail results, (ii) having Department employees covertly take the skills tests from a third party examiner, or (iii) having Department employees co-score along with the third party examiner during commercial driver's license applicant's skills tests to compare pass/fail results;

7. A comparison of the commercial driver's license skills test results of applicants who are issued commercial driver's licenses with the commercial driver's license scoring sheets that are maintained in the third party testers' files; and

8. Any other aspect of the third party tester's operation that the Department determines is necessary to verify that the third party tester meets or continues to meet the requirements for certification.

D. The Department will prepare a written report of the results of each inspection and audit of third party testers. A copy of the report will be provided to the third party tester.

History.
2013, cc. 165, 582; 2014, cc. 77, 803.

§ 46.2-341.14:7. Notification requirements.

A. Every third party tester shall:

1. Notify the Department in a format prescribed by the Department within 10 days of any change in:

a. The third party tester's name or address; or

b. The third party examiners who are employed by the third party tester.

2. Notify the Department in a format prescribed by the Department within 10 days of any of the following occurrences:

a. The third party tester ceases business operations in Virginia;

b. The third party tester fails to comply with any of the requirements set forth in this article; or

c. Any third party examiner fails to comply with any of the requirements set forth in this article.

3. Notify the Department of any proposed change in the skills test route at least 30 days before the third party tester plans to change the route.

B. Every third party examiner shall notify the Department, within 10 days after leaving the employ of the third party tester, of his change in employment.

History.
2013, cc. 165, 582.

§ 46.2-341.14:8. Test administration.

A. Skills tests shall be conducted strictly in accordance with the provisions of this article and with current test instructions provided from time to time by the Department. Such instructions will include test forms and directions for completing such forms.

B. Skills tests shall be conducted:

1. On test routes that are located at least in part in Virginia and have been approved by the Department;

2. In a vehicle that is representative of the class and type of vehicle for which the commercial driver's license applicant seeks to be licensed and for which the third party tester and third party examiner are certified to test; and

3. In vehicles that are inspected, licensed, and insured, as required by law.

C. All third party testers shall submit a skills test schedule of commercial driver's license skills testing appointments to the Department no later than two business days prior to each test.

D. All third party testers shall notify the Department through secure electronic means when a driver applicant passes skills tests.

History.
2013, cc. 165, 582.

§ 46.2-341.14:9. The skills test certificate.

A. The Department will accept a skills test certificate issued in accordance with this section as satisfaction of the skills test component of the commercial driver's license examination.

B. Skills test certificates may be issued only to drivers who are employees of the third party tester who issues the certificate, except as otherwise provided herein. In the case of school boards certified as third party testers, certificates may be issued to employees and to other drivers who have been trained by the school board in accordance with the Virginia School Bus Driver Training Curriculum Guide. For comprehensive community colleges in the Virginia Community College System that are certified as third party testers, certificates may be issued to students who are enrolled in a commercial driver training course offered by such community college at the time of the test.

C. Skills test certificates may be issued only to drivers who have passed the skills test conducted in accordance with this chapter and the instructions issued by the Department.

D. A skills test certificate will be accepted by the Department only if it is:

1. Issued by a third party tester certified by the Department in accordance with this article;

2. In a format prescribed by the Department, completed in its entirety, without alteration;

3. Submitted to the Department within 60 days of the date of the skills test; and

4. Signed by the third party examiner who conducted the skills test.

History.
2013, cc. 165, 582; 2016, c. 429.

§ 46.2-341.14:10. Waiver of requirement that third party tester applicant employ 75 drivers.

A. Any applicant for certification as third party tester may submit with his application a request for a waiver of the requirement that the third party tester employ at least 75 drivers within the 12-month period preceding the application.

Such request shall include the following:

1. A statement of need. This statement should explain why the applicant should be certified as a third party tester. The statement should also include reasons why the testing facilities or programs offered by the Department will not meet the applicant's business requirements.

2. An estimate of the number of employees per year who will require commercial driver's license skills testing after April 1, 1992. If the waiver request is filed prior to April 1, 1992, the request should also include an estimate of the number of employees who will require skills testing prior to that date.

B. The Department will review the applicant's waiver request and will evaluate the Department's testing and third party monitoring resources. The Department will decide whether to grant the waiver request after balancing the stated needs of the applicant and the available resources of the Department. The Department will notify the applicant in writing of its decision.

History.

2013, cc. 165, 582.

§ 46.2-341.15. Commercial driver's license and commercial learner's permit document.

A. The commercial driver's license issued by the Department shall be identified as a Virginia commercial driver's license and shall include at least the following:

1. Full name, a Virginia address, and signature of the licensee;

2. A photograph of the licensee;

3. A physical description of the licensee, including sex and height;

4. The licensee's date of birth and license number that shall be assigned by the Department to the licensee and shall not be the same as the licensee's Social Security number;

5. A designation of the class and type of commercial motor vehicle or vehicles which the licensee is authorized to drive, together with any restrictions; and

6. The date of license issuance and expiration.

B. The commercial learner's permit shall be identified as such but shall in all other respects conform to subsection A of this section. A commercial learner's permit shall also contain a statement that the permit is invalid unless accompanied by the underlying driver's license.

C. A nondomiciled commercial driver's license or a nondomiciled commercial learner's permit shall contain the word "nondomiciled" on the face of the document.

History.

1989, c. 705, § 46.1-372.15; 2002, cc. 767, 834; 2008, c. 190; 2009, c. 872; 2013, cc. 165, 582; 2015, c. 258.

§ 46.2-341.16. Vehicle classifications, restrictions, and endorsements.

A. A commercial driver's license or commercial learner's permit shall authorize the licensee or permit holder to operate only the classes and types of commercial motor vehicles designated thereon. The classes of commercial motor vehicles for which such license may be issued are:

1. Class A-Combination heavy vehicle. — Any combination of vehicles with a gross combination weight rating of 26,001 or more pounds, provided the gross vehicle weight rating of the vehicles being towed is in excess of 10,000 pounds;

2. Class B-Heavy straight vehicle or other combination. — Any single motor vehicle with a gross vehicle weight rating of 26,001 or more pounds, or any such vehicle towing a vehicle with a gross vehicle weight rating that is not in excess of 10,000 pounds; and

3. Class C-Small vehicle. — Any vehicle that does not fit the definition of a Class A or Class B vehicle and is either (i) designed to transport 16 or more passengers including the driver or (ii) is used in the transportation of hazardous materials.

B. Commercial driver's licenses shall be issued with endorsements authorizing the driver to operate the types of vehicles identified as follows:

1. Type T-Vehicles with double or triple trailers;

2. Type P-Vehicles carrying passengers;

3. Type N-Vehicles with cargo tanks;

4. Type H-Vehicles required to be placarded for hazardous materials;

5. Type S-School buses carrying 16 or more passengers, including the driver;

6. Type X-combination of tank vehicle and hazardous materials endorsements for commercial driver's licenses issued on or after July 1, 2014; and

7. At the discretion of the Department, any additional codes for groupings of endorsements with an explanation of such code appearing on the front or back of the license.

C. Commercial driver's licenses shall be issued with restrictions limiting the driver to the types of vehicles identified as follows:

1. L for no air brake equipped commercial motor vehicles for licenses issued on or after July 1, 2014. An applicant is restricted from operating a commercial motor vehicle with any type of air brake if he does not take or fails the air brake component of the knowledge test or performs the skills test in a vehicle not equipped with air brakes;

2. Z for no full air brake equipped commercial motor vehicles. If an applicant performs the skills test in a vehicle equipped with air over hydraulic brakes, the applicant is restricted from operating a commercial motor vehicle equipped with any braking system operating fully on the air brake principle;

3. E for no manual transmission equipped commercial motor vehicles for commercial driver's licenses issued on or after July 1, 2014;

4. O for no tractor-trailer commercial motor vehicles;

5. M for no class A passenger vehicles;

6. N for no class A and B passenger vehicles;

7. K for vehicles not equipped with air brakes for commercial driver's licenses issued before July 1, 2014. An applicant is restricted from operating a commercial motor vehicle with any type of air brakes if he does not take or fails the air brake component of the knowledge test or performs the skills test in a vehicle not equipped with air brakes;

8. K for intrastate only for commercial driver's licenses issued on or after July 1, 2014;

9. V for medical variance; and

10. At the discretion of the Department, any additional codes for groupings of restrictions with an explanation of such code appearing on the front or back of the license.

D. Commercial learner's permits shall be issued with endorsements authorizing the driver to operate the types of vehicles identified as follows:

1. Type P-Vehicles carrying passengers as provided in § 46.2-341.10;

2. Type N-Vehicles with cargo tanks as provided in § 46.2-341.10; and

3. Type S-School buses carrying 16 or more passengers, including the driver as provided in § 46.2-341.10.

E. Commercial learner's permits shall be issued with restrictions limiting the driver to the types of vehicles identified as follows:

1. P for no passengers in commercial motor vehicles bus;

2. X for no cargo in commercial motor vehicles tank vehicle;

3. L for no air brake equipped commercial motor vehicles for commercial learner's permits issued on or after July 1, 2014. An applicant is restricted from operating a commercial motor vehicle with any type of air brake if he does not take or fails the air brake component of the knowledge test;

4. M for no class A passenger vehicles;

5. N for no class A and B passenger vehicles;

6. K for vehicles not equipped with air brakes for commercial learner's permits issued before July 1, 2014. An applicant is restricted from operating a commercial motor vehicle with any type of air brake if he does not take or fails the air brake component of the knowledge test;

7. K for intrastate only for commercial learner's permits issued on or after July 1, 2014;

8. V for medical variance; and

9. Any additional jurisdictional restrictions that apply to the commercial learner's permit.

F. Persons authorized to drive Class A vehicles are also authorized to drive Classes B and C vehicles, provided such persons possess the requisite endorsements for the type of vehicle driven.

G. Persons authorized to drive Class B vehicles are also authorized to drive Class C vehicles, provided such persons possess the requisite endorsements for the type of vehicle driven.

H. Any licensee who seeks to add a classification or endorsement to his commercial driver's license must submit the application forms, certifications and other updated information required by the Department and shall take and successfully complete the tests required for such classification or endorsement.

I. If any endorsement to a commercial driver's license is canceled by the Department and the licensee does not appear in person at the Department to have such endorsement removed from the license, then the Department may cancel the commercial driver's license of the licensee.

History.

1989, c. 705, § 46.1-372.15:1; 1990, c. 218; 2006, c. 226; 2012, cc. 22, 111; 2013, cc. 165, 582; 2014, cc. 77, 803; 2015, c. 258.

§ 46.2-341.16:1. Conformance with requirements of U.S.A. Patriot Act of 2001.

A. Notwithstanding any other provision of this title, no endorsement authorizing the driver to operate a vehicle transporting hazardous materials shall be issued, renewed, or reissued by the Department unless the endorsement is issued, renewed, or reissued in conformance with the requirements of § 1012 of the U.S.A. Patriot Act of 2001, including all amendments thereto, and the federal regulation promulgated thereunder, for the issuance by the states of licenses to operate motor vehicles transporting hazardous materials, and the Department has received notification from the U.S. Secretary of Transportation or the U.S. Transportation Security Administration, if required by the U.S.A. Patriot Act 2001 (49 U.S.C. § 5103a et seq.) and federal regulations, that the applicant does not pose a security threat warranting denial of such endorsement. Further, the Department shall cancel any existing endorsement authorizing a driver to operate a vehicle transporting hazardous materials if it has received notification that the holder of such endorsement does not meet the standards for security threat assessment established by the U.S. Transportation Security Administration.

B. Notwithstanding the provisions of § 46.2-330, a Virginia commercial driver's license with a hazardous materials endorsement shall be issued so that it expires no later than five years from its date of issuance, and it may be issued for a period of less than three years if a shorter period is necessary in order to put the license into a five-year renewal cycle as provided in § 46.2-330.

C. Notwithstanding the provisions of § 46.2-332, the Commissioner or his agent may collect an additional nonrefundable fee in conjunction with an application for a hazardous materials endorsement to offset the additional costs of collecting and processing fingerprints and other information required in conjunction with the security threat assessment program established through the U.S. Transportation Security Administration for hazardous materials endorsement applicants, which fee shall include a pass-through of the fees assessed by the Transportation Security Administration or other federal agencies as well as an additional amount, not to exceed $100, to cover additional costs incurred by the Commonwealth in issuing commercial driver's licenses pursuant to the provisions of this section, and there shall be no exemption from such additional fee for any applicant who is an employee of the Commonwealth or any county, city, or town. In addition, any local law-enforcement agency that provided fingerprinting services in conjunction with the security threat assessment program may assess a fee from the applicant in an amount set by local ordinance, not to exceed $25. Such amount shall be collected by the local law-enforcement agency and remitted to the treasurer of the appropriate locality to be used solely for the purpose of defraying the costs of operating the law-enforcement agency and shall not be used to supplant existing local funds for the operation of the law-enforcement agency.

History.

2003, cc. 913, 920; 2004, c. 109.

§ 46.2-341.17. Penalty for violation of this article.

Unless otherwise provided in this article or by the laws of the Commonwealth, any person who violates any provision of this article shall be guilty of a Class 2 misdemeanor.

History.

1989, c. 705, § 46.1-372.16.

§ 46.2-341.18. Disqualification for certain offenses.

A. Except as otherwise provided in this section and in § 46.2-341.18:01, the Commissioner shall disqualify for a period of one year any person whose record, as maintained by the Department of Motor Vehicles, shows that he has been convicted of any of the following offenses, if such offense was committed while operating a commercial motor vehicle:

1. A violation of any provision of § 46.2-341.21 or a violation of any federal law or the law of another jurisdiction substantially similar to § 46.2-341.21;
2. A violation of any provision of § 46.2-341.24 or a violation of any federal law or the law of another state substantially similar to § 46.2-341.24;
3. A violation of any provision of § 18.2-51.4 or 18.2-266 or a violation of a local ordinance paralleling or substantially similar to § 18.2-51.4 or 18.2-266, or a violation of any federal, state or local law or ordinance substantially similar to § 18.2-51.4 or 18.2-266;
4. Refusal to submit to a chemical test to determine the alcohol or drug content of the person's blood or breath in accordance with §§ 18.2-268.1 through 18.2-268.12 or this article, or the comparable laws of any other state or jurisdiction;
5. Failure of the driver whose vehicle is involved in an accident to stop and disclose his identity at the scene of the accident; or
6. Commission of any crime punishable as a felony in the commission of which a motor vehicle is used, other than a felony described in § 46.2-341.19.

B. The Commissioner shall disqualify any such person for a period of three years if any offense listed in subsection A of this section was committed while driving a commercial motor vehicle used in the transportation of hazardous materials required to be placarded under federal Hazardous Materials Regulations (49 C.F.R. Part 172, Subpart F).

C. Beginning September 30, 2005, the Commissioner shall disqualify for a period of one year any person whose record, as maintained by the Department, shows that he has been convicted of any of the following offenses committed while operating a noncommercial motor vehicle, provided that the person was, at the time of the offense, the holder of a commercial driver's license, and provided further that the offense was committed on or after September 30, 2005:

1. A violation of any provision of § 18.2-51.4, 18.2-266, or a violation of a local ordinance paralleling or substantially similar to § 18.2-51.4 or 18.2-266, or a violation of any federal, state, or local law or ordinance, or law of any other jurisdiction, substantially similar to § 18.2-51.4 or 18.2-266;
2. Refusal to submit to a chemical test to determine the alcohol or drug content of the person's blood or breath in accordance with §§ 18.2-268.1 through 18.2-268.12, or the comparable laws of any other state or jurisdiction;
3. Failure of the driver whose vehicle is involved in an accident to stop and disclose his identity at the scene of the accident; or
4. Commission of any crime punishable as a felony in the commission of which a motor vehicle is used.

D. The Commissioner shall disqualify for life any person whose record, as maintained by the Department, shows that he has been convicted of two or more violations of any of the offenses listed in subsection A or C of this section, if each offense arose from a separate incident, except that if all of the offenses are for violation of an out-of-service order, the disqualification shall be for five years. If two or more such disqualification offenses arise from the same incident, the disqualification periods imposed pursuant to subsection A, B, or C of this section shall run consecutively and not concurrently.

E. The Commissioner shall disqualify for a period of five years a person who is convicted of voluntary or involuntary manslaughter, where the death occurred as a direct result of the operation of a commercial motor vehicle.

F. The Department may issue, if permitted by federal law, regulations establishing guidelines, including conditions, under which a disqualification for life under subsection D may be reduced to a period of not less than 10 years.

History.

1989, c. 705, § 46.1-372.17; 1992, c. 830; 1997, c. 691; 2005, c. 513; 2008, c. 190; 2010, c. 424.

§ 46.2-341.18:01. Disqualification for violation of out-of-service order; commercial motor vehicle designed to transport 16 or more passengers; commercial motor vehicle used to transport hazardous materials.

The Commissioner shall disqualify, for a period of two years, any person convicted of violating an out-of-service order while operating (i) a commercial motor vehicle designed to transport 16 or more passengers, including the driver, or (ii) notwithstanding the provisions of § 46.2-341.18, a commercial motor vehicle while used in the transport of hazardous materials required to be placarded under federal Hazardous Materials Regulations (49 C.F.R. Part 172, Subpart F). If the person is convicted of two or more violations of this section, and each offense arose from a separate incident committed within a period of 10 years, the disqualification shall be for five years.

History.
2008, c. 190; 2009, c. 102.

§ 46.2-341.18:1. Disqualification for certain alcohol-related offenses committed in other jurisdictions whose laws provide for disqualification for such offenses without a conviction.

A. Notwithstanding the provisions of § 46.2-341.18 that require the Commissioner act to disqualify only on the basis of conviction records for certain offenses committed while operating a commercial motor vehicle, the Commissioner shall also act to disqualify, as provided in § 46.2-341.18, where he has received a record from another jurisdiction indicating that a Virginia licensee has been disqualified in that jurisdiction, solely as a result of his violation in that jurisdiction, of either of the two offenses listed in subdivisions 1 and 2, committed while operating a commercial motor vehicle, even though the disqualification was imposed as the result of an administrative or civil action and there was no court proceeding that could result in a conviction for such offense. The two offenses for which such action shall be taken are:

1. Operation of a commercial motor vehicle with a blood alcohol content of 0.04 percent or more, or

2. Refusal to submit to a chemical test to determine the alcohol or drug content of blood or breath of the operator of a commercial motor vehicle under the implied consent laws of that jurisdiction.

B. The Commissioner shall treat such a record of disqualification as though it were a conviction record from that jurisdiction under a law substantially similar to subsection B of § 46.2-341.24 or § 46.2-341.26:4, respectively, for purposes of implementing the disqualification provisions of § 46.2-341.18. Such treatment as a conviction for purposes of § 46.2-341.18 shall be applicable only if the disqualification action is final and unappealable or has been appealed and the appeal dismissed or the action affirmed and no further appeals are possible under the laws of the jurisdiction wherein the offense was committed, and only if the disqualification period imposed by that jurisdiction is at least as long as the periods set out in § 46.2-341.18 for such an offense. If the Commissioner receives notice from a jurisdiction that a Virginia licensee has been subject to an administrative action or civil judgment resulting from a violation of subdivision A 1 or A 2, committed while operating a commercial motor vehicle, the Commissioner shall treat such notice as a conviction for the purposes of this article.

C. In no case shall the Commissioner act more than once to disqualify a Virginia licensee for any single violation committed in another jurisdiction, even though such violation may be reported by that jurisdiction as both an administrative or civil disqualification action and as a conviction from a court in that jurisdiction. Moreover, the Commissioner shall rescind a disqualification imposed pursuant to this section if the disqualification has been vacated or rescinded by the other jurisdiction as a result of the licensee's acquittal in the court proceedings, or the dismissal of those proceedings, in that jurisdiction.

History.
2002, c. 724; 2005, c. 513.

§ 46.2-341.18:2. Disqualification for use of urine-masking agent or device.

The Commissioner shall disqualify for a period of one year any person who has been convicted of a violation of § 18.2-251.4.

History.
2007, c. 422.

§ 46.2-341.18:3. Cancellation of commercial driver's license endorsement for certain offenders.

The Commissioner shall cancel the Type S school bus endorsement for any person holding a commercial driver's license or commercial learner's permit who is convicted of an offense for which registration is required in the Sex Offender and Crimes Against Minors Registry pursuant to Chapter 9 (§ 9.1-900 et seq.) of Title 9.1.

Any person holding a commercial driver's license or commercial learner's permit with a Type P passenger endorsement who is convicted of an offense for which registration is required in the Sex Offender and Crimes Against Minors Registry pursuant to Chapter 9 (§ 9.1-900 et seq.) of Title 9.1 shall surrender such license or permit to the Department, and shall be issued a license or permit that includes a restriction prohibiting the license or permit holder from operating a vehicle to transport children to or from activities sponsored by a school or by a child day care facility licensed, regulated, or approved by the Virginia Department of Social Services.

If the holder of a commercial driver's license or commercial learner's permit fails to surrender the license or permit as required under this section, the Department shall cancel the license or permit.

History.
2011, c. 477; 2012, c. 153; 2015, c. 258.

§ 46.2-341.19. Controlled substance felony; disqualification.

No person shall use a commercial motor vehicle in the commission of any felony involving manufacturing, distributing or dispensing a controlled substance or possession with intent to manufacture, distribute or dispense such controlled substance. For the purpose of this section, a controlled substance shall be defined as provided in § 102 (6) of the federal Controlled Substances Act (21 U.S.C. § 802 (6)) and includes all substances listed on Schedules I through V of 21 C.F.R. Part 1308 as they may be revised from time to time.

Violation of this section shall constitute a separate and distinct offense and any person violating this section shall be guilty of a Class 1 misdemeanor. Punishment for a violation of this section shall be separate and apart from any punishment received from the commission of the primary felony.

The Commissioner shall, upon receiving a record of a conviction of a violation of this section, disqualify for life any person who is convicted of such violation.

History.
1989, c. 705, § 46.1-372.18.

§ 46.2-341.20. Disqualification for multiple serious traffic violations.

A. For the purposes of this section, the following offenses, if committed in a commercial motor vehicle, are serious traffic violations:

1. Driving at a speed 15 or more miles per hour in excess of the posted speed limits;
2. Reckless driving;
3. A violation of a state law or local ordinance relating to motor vehicle traffic control arising in connection with a fatal traffic accident;
4. Improper or erratic traffic lane change;
5. Following the vehicle ahead too closely;
6. Driving a commercial motor vehicle without obtaining a commercial driver's license or commercial learner's permit;
7. Driving a commercial motor vehicle without a commercial driver's license or commercial learner's permit in the driver's immediate possession;
8. Driving a commercial motor vehicle without the proper class of commercial driver's license and/or endorsements for the specific vehicle group being operated or for the passengers or type of cargo being transported;
9. A violation of a state law, including §§ 46.2-341.20:5 and 46.2-919.1 or a local ordinance relating to motor vehicle traffic control prohibiting texting while driving; and
10. A violation of a state law, including §§ 46.2-341.20:5 and 46.2-919.1, or a local ordinance relating to motor vehicle traffic control restricting or prohibiting the use of a handheld mobile telephone while driving a commercial motor vehicle.

For the purposes of this section, parking, vehicle weight, and vehicle defect violations shall not be considered traffic violations.

B. Beginning September 30, 2005, the following offenses shall be treated as serious traffic violations if committed while operating a noncommercial motor vehicle, but only if (i) the person convicted of the offense was, at the time of the offense, the holder of a commercial driver's license or commercial learner's permit; (ii) the offense was committed on or after September 30, 2005; and (iii) the conviction, by itself or in conjunction with other convictions that satisfy the requirements of this section, resulted in the revocation, cancellation, or suspension of such person's driver's license or privilege to drive.

1. Driving at a speed 15 or more miles per hour in excess of the posted speed limits;
2. Reckless driving;
3. A violation of a state law or local ordinance relating to motor vehicle traffic control arising in connection with a fatal traffic accident;
4. Improper or erratic traffic lane change; or
5. Following the vehicle ahead too closely.

C. The Department shall disqualify for the following periods of time, any person whose record as maintained by the Department shows that he has committed, within any three-year period, the requisite number of serious traffic violations:

1. A 60-day disqualification period for any person convicted of two serious traffic violations; or
2. A 120-day disqualification period for any person convicted of three serious traffic violations.

D. Any disqualification period imposed pursuant to this section shall run consecutively, and not concurrently, with any other disqualification period imposed hereunder.

History.
1989, c. 705, § 46.1-372.19; 1990, c. 218; 2005, c. 513; 2011, cc. 881, 889; 2013, cc. 165, 582; 2014, cc. 77, 803; 2015, c. 258.

§ 46.2-341.20:1. Disqualification for railroad/highway grade crossing violations.

A. Except as otherwise provided in subsection B, the Commissioner shall disqualify for a period of sixty days any person whose record, as maintained by the Department, shows that he has been convicted of any offense committed while operating a commercial motor vehicle in violation of any law relating to the operation of a motor vehicle at a railroad/highway grade crossing, including but not limited to the provisions of Article 9 (§ 46.2-884 et seq.) of Chapter 8 of this title and the provisions of the Virginia and Federal Motor Carrier Safety Regulations, and any similar law of any other state or any locality.

B. The period of disqualification shall be for 120 days if the conviction was for an offense described in subsection A, committed within three years of a prior such offense, or for one year if for a third or subsequent such offense committed within three years, provided each offense arose from separate incidents.

History.
2002, c. 724.

§ 46.2-341.20:2. Employer penalty; railroad/highway grade crossing violations; out-of-service order violation.

Any employer who knowingly allows, permits, authorizes, or requires an employee to operate a commercial motor vehicle in violation of any law or regulation pertaining to railroad/highway grade crossings, or in violation of an out-of-service order, shall be subject to a civil penalty for each violation pursuant to 49 C.F.R. Part 383, which shall be imposed by the Commissioner upon receipt of notification from federal or state motor carrier officials that an employer may have violated this provision, and upon notice to the employer of the charge and a hearing conducted as provided under the Administrative Process Act (§ 2.2-4000 et seq.), to determine whether such employer has violated this provision. Civil penalties collected under this section shall be deposited into the Transportation Trust Fund established pursuant to § 33.2- 1524.

History.
2002, c. 724; 2005, c. 513; 2008, c. 190; 2014, cc. 77, 803.

§ 46.2-341.20:3. Disqualification for determination of imminent hazard.

If the Department receives notification from the Federal Motor Carrier Safety Administration that a driver determined to constitute an imminent hazard has been disqualified from operating a commercial motor vehicle pursuant to 49 C.F.R. Part 383.52, the Department shall make a notation of such disqualification on the driver record maintained by the Department and any disqualification imposed by the Department on the driver shall run concurrently with the period of disqualification imposed pursuant to 49 CFR 383.52.

History.
2005, c. 513; 2008, c. 190.

§ 46.2-341.20:4. Disqualification of driver convicted of fraud related to the testing and issuance of a commercial learner's permit or commercial driver's license.

A person who has been convicted of fraud pursuant to § 46.2-348 related to the issuance of a commercial learner's permit or commercial driver's license shall be disqualified for a period of one year. The application of a person so convicted who seeks to renew, transfer, or upgrade the fraudulently obtained commercial driver's license or seeks to renew or upgrade the fraudulently obtained commercial learner's permit must also, at a minimum, be disqualified. Any disqualification must be recorded in the person's driving record. The person may not reapply for a new commercial driver's license for at least one year.

If the Department receives credible information that a commercial learner's permit holder or commercial driver's license holder is suspected, but has not been convicted, of fraud related to the issuance of his commercial learner's permit or commercial driver's license, the Department shall require the driver to retake the skills test or knowledge test, or both. Within 30 days of receiving notification from the Department that retesting is necessary, the affected commercial learner's permit holder or commercial driver's license holder must make an appointment or otherwise schedule to take the next available test. If the commercial learner's permit holder or commercial driver's license holder fails to make an appointment within 30 days, the Department shall disqualify his commercial learner's permit or commercial driver's license. If the driver fails either the knowledge or skills test or does not take the test, the Department shall disqualify his commercial learner's permit or commercial driver's license. Once a commercial learner's permit holder's or commercial driver's license holder's commercial learner's permit or commercial driver's license has been disqualified, he must reapply for a commercial learner's permit or commercial driver's license under Department procedures applicable to all commercial learner's permit and commercial driver's license applicants.

History.
2013, cc. 165, 582; 2014, cc. 77, 803; 2015, c. 258.

§ 46.2-341.20:5. Prohibition on texting and use of handheld mobile telephone; penalties.

A. No person driving a commercial motor vehicle shall text or use a handheld mobile telephone while driving such vehicle. A driver who violates this section is subject to a civil penalty not to exceed $2,750. Civil penalties collected under this section shall be deposited into the Transportation Trust Fund established pursuant to § 33.2-1524. Pursuant to 49 C.F.R. § 386.81, the determination of the actual civil penalties assessed is based on consideration of information available at the time the claim is made concerning the nature and gravity of the violation and, with respect to the violator, the degree of culpability, history of prior offenses, ability to pay, effect on ability to continue to do business, and such other matters as justice and public safety may require.

B. Notwithstanding the definition of commercial motor vehicle in § 46.2-341.4, this section shall apply to any driver who drives a vehicle designed or used to transport between nine and 15 passengers, including the driver, not for direct compensation.

C. The provisions of this section shall not apply to drivers who are texting or using a handheld mobile telephone when necessary to communicate with law-enforcement officials or other emergency services.

D. The following words and phrases when used in this section only shall have the meanings respectively ascribed to them in this section except in those instances where the context clearly indicates a different meaning:

"Driving" means operating a commercial motor vehicle on a highway, including while temporarily stationary because of traffic, a traffic control device, or other momentary delays. Driving does not include operating a commercial motor vehicle when the driver has moved the vehicle to the side of or off a highway and has halted in a location where the vehicle can safely remain stationary.

"Mobile telephone" means a mobile communication device that falls under or uses any commercial mobile radio service, as defined in regulations of the Federal Communications Commission, 47 C.F.R. § 20.3. "Mobile telephone" does not include two-way or citizens band radio services.

"Texting" means manually entering alphanumeric text into, or reading text from, an electronic device. This action includes, but is not limited to, short message service, emailing, instant messaging, a command or request to access a website, pressing more than a single button to initiate or terminate a voice communication using a mobile telephone, or engaging in any other form of electronic text retrieval or entry for present or future communication. "Texting" does not include inputting, selecting, or reading information on a global positioning system or navigation system; pressing a single button to initiate or terminate a voice communication using a telephone; or using a device capable of performing multiple functions (e.g., fleet management systems, dispatching devices, smartphones, citizens band radios, music players, etc.) for a purpose that is not otherwise prohibited in this section.

"Use a handheld mobile telephone" means using at least one hand to hold a mobile telephone to conduct a voice communication; dialing or answering a mobile telephone by pressing more than a single button; or reaching for a mobile telephone in a manner that requires a driver to maneuver so that he is no longer in a seated driving position, restrained by a seat belt that is installed in accordance with 49 C.F.R. § 393.93 and adjusted in accordance with the vehicle manufacturer's instructions.

History.

2013, cc. 165, 582; 2014, cc. 77, 803.

§ 46.2-341.20:6. Prohibition on requiring use of handheld mobile telephone or texting; motor carrier penalty.

No motor carrier shall allow or require its drivers to use a handheld mobile telephone or to text while driving a commercial motor vehicle. Motor carriers violating this section are subject to a civil penalty not to exceed $11,000. Civil penalties collected under this section shall be deposited into the Transportation Trust Fund established pursuant to § 33.2-1524. Pursuant to 49 C.F.R. § 386.81, the determination of the actual civil penalties assessed is based on consideration of information available at the time the claim is made concerning the nature and gravity of the violation and, with respect to the violator, the degree of culpability, history of prior offenses, ability to pay, effect on ability to continue to do business, and such other matters as justice and public safety may require. "Driving," "mobile telephone," "texting," and "use a handheld mobile telephone" have the same meanings as assigned to them in § 46.2-341.20:5.

History.

2014, cc. 77, 803.

§ 46.2-341.21. Driving while disqualified; penalties.

No person whose privilege to drive a commercial motor vehicle has been suspended or revoked or who has been disqualified from operating a commercial motor vehicle or who has been ordered out of service, and who has been given notice of, or reasonably should know of the suspension, revocation, disqualification, or out-of-service order shall operate a commercial motor vehicle anywhere in the Commonwealth until the period of such suspension, revocation, disqualification, or out-of-service order has terminated, nor shall any person operate on any highway any vehicle that has been declared out of service until such time as the out-of-service declaration has been lifted.

Any person who violates this section shall, for the first offense, be guilty of a Class 2 misdemeanor, and for the second or any subsequent offense, be guilty of a Class 1 misdemeanor; however, if the offense is the violation of an out-of-service order, the minimum mandatory fine shall be $2,500 for any person so convicted of a first offense and $5,000 for a person convicted of a second or subsequent offense. Upon receipt of a record of a violation of this section, the Commissioner shall impose an additional disqualification in accordance with the provisions of §§ 46.2-341.18 and 46.2-341.18:01.

History.

1989, c. 705, § 46.1-372.20; 1990, c. 218; 1995, cc. 145, 151; 2005, c. 513; 2008, c. 190.

§ 46.2-341.22. Requirements upon disqualification.

Any person who has been disqualified pursuant to any provision of this Act shall be subject to the provisions of §§ 46.2-370 and 46.2-414, and shall be required to comply with the provisions of §§ 46.2-370 and 46.2-411 as conditions to the reinstatement of his privilege to drive a commercial motor vehicle.

Any person who has been disqualified pursuant to the provisions of § 46.2-341.18 or § 46.2-341.19 shall be required as further conditions to reinstatement of his privilege to operate a commercial motor vehicle, to (i) apply for such license; (ii) pass the knowledge and skills tests required for the class and type of commercial motor vehicle for which he seeks to be licensed; and (iii) satisfy all other applicable licensing requirements, including the payment of licensing fees, imposed by the laws of the Commonwealth.

The provisions of this section shall not apply to out-of-service orders issued pursuant to §§ 46.2-341.26:2 and 46.2-341.26:3.

History.

1989, c. 705, § 46.1-372.21; 1992, c. 830.

§ 46.2-341.23. Offenses under substantially similar laws.

Except as otherwise provided, whenever in this Act reference is made to an offense which is a violation of a provision of this Code, such reference shall be deemed to include offenses under any local ordinance, any federal law, any law of another state or any local ordinance of another state, substantially similar to such provision of this Code.

History.

1989, c. 705, § 46.1-372.22.

§ 46.2-341.24. Driving a commercial motor vehicle while intoxicated, etc.

A. It shall be unlawful for any person to drive or operate any commercial motor vehicle (i) while such person has a blood alcohol concentration of 0.08 percent or more by weight by volume or 0.08 grams per 210 liters of breath as indicated by a chemical test administered as provided in this article; (ii) while such person is under the influence of alcohol; (iii) while such person is under the influence of any narcotic drug or any other self-administered intoxicant or drug of whatsoever nature, or any combination of such drugs, to a degree which impairs his ability to drive or operate any commercial motor vehicle safely; (iv) while such person is under the combined influence of alcohol and any drug or drugs to a degree which impairs his ability to drive or operate any commercial motor vehicle safely; or (v) while such person has a blood concentration of any of the following substances at a level that is equal to or greater than: (a) 0.02 milligrams of cocaine per liter of blood, (b) 0.1 milligrams of methamphetamine per liter of blood, (c) 0.01 milligrams of phencyclidine per liter of blood, or (d) 0.1 milligrams of 3,4-methylenedioxymethamphetamine per liter of blood.

B. It shall be unlawful and a lesser included offense of an offense under provision (i), (ii), or (iv) of subsection A of this section for a person to drive or operate a commercial motor vehicle while such person has a blood alcohol concentration of 0.04 percent or more by weight by volume or 0.04 grams or more per 210 liters of breath as indicated by a chemical test administered in accordance with the provisions of this article.

History.

1989, c. 705, § 46.1-372.23; 1992, c. 830; 1994, cc. 359, 363; 2005, c. 616.

§ 46.2-341.25. Preliminary analysis of breath of commercial drivers to determine alcohol content of blood.

A. Any person who is reasonably suspected of a violation of § 46.2-341.24 or of having any alcohol in his blood while driving or operating a commercial motor vehicle may be required by any law-enforcement officer to provide a sample of such person's breath for a preliminary screening to determine the probable alcohol content of his blood. Such person shall be entitled, upon request, to observe the process of analysis and to see the blood-alcohol reading on the equipment used to perform the breath test. Such breath may be analyzed by any police officer of the Commonwealth, or of any county, city, or town, or by any member of a sheriff's department in the normal discharge of his duties.

B. The Department of Forensic Science shall determine the proper method and equipment to be used in analyzing breath samples taken pursuant to this section and shall advise the respective police and sheriff's departments of the same.

C. If the breath sample analysis indicates that there is alcohol present in the person's blood, or if the person refuses to provide a sample of his breath for a preliminary screening, such person shall then be subject to the provisions of §§ 46.2-341.26:1 through 46.2-341.26:11.

D. The results of a breath analysis conducted pursuant to this section shall not be admitted into evidence in any prosecution under § 46.2-341.24 or 46.2-341.31, but may be used as a basis for charging a person for a violation of the provisions of § 46.2-341.24 or 46.2-341.31.

E. The law-enforcement officer requiring the preliminary screening test shall advise the person of his obligations under this section and of the provisions of subsection C of this section.

History.

1989, c. 705, § 46.1-372.24; 1990, cc. 218, 825; 1992, c. 830; 1996, cc. 154, 952; 2005, cc. 868, 881.

§ 46.2-341.26: Repealed by Acts 1992, c. 830.

Cross references.

For present provisions as to use of chemical tests to determine alcohol or drug content of blood of a commercial driver, see § 46.2-341.26:1 et seq.

§ 46.2-341.26:1. Use of chemical tests to determine alcohol or drug content of blood of commercial driver; definitions.

As used in §§ 46.2-341.26:2 through 46.2-341.26:11, unless the context clearly indicates otherwise:

The phrase *"alcohol or drug"* means alcohol, drug or drugs, or any combination of alcohol and a drug or drugs.

The phrase *"blood or breath"* means either or both.

"Chief police officer" means the sheriff in any county not having a chief of police, the chief of police of any county having a chief of police, the chief of police of the city, or the sergeant or chief of police of the town in which the charge will be heard, or their authorized representatives.

"Department" means the Department of Forensic Science.

"Director" means the Director of the Department of Forensic Science.

History.

1992, c. 830; 2005, cc. 868, 881.

§ 46.2-341.26:2. Implied consent to post-arrest chemical test to determine alcohol or drug content of blood of commercial driver.

A. Any person, whether licensed by Virginia or not, who operates a commercial motor vehicle upon a highway as defined in § 46.2-100 in the Commonwealth shall be deemed thereby, as a condition of such operation, to have consented to have samples of his blood, breath, or both blood and breath taken for a chemical test to determine the alcohol, drug or both alcohol and drug content of his blood, if he is arrested for violation of § 46.2-341.24 or 46.2-341.31 within two hours of the alleged offense.

B. Such person shall be required to have a breath sample taken and shall be entitled, upon request, to observe the process of analysis and to see the blood-alcohol reading on the equipment used to perform the breath test. If the equipment automatically produces a written printout of the breath test result, the printout or a copy shall be given to the suspect. If a breath test is not available, then a blood test shall be required.

C. The person may be required to submit to blood tests to determine the drug content of his blood if he has been arrested pursuant to provision (iii), (iv), or (v) of subsection A of § 46.2-341.24, or if he has taken the breath test required pursuant to subsection B and the law-enforcement officer has reasonable cause to believe the person was driving under the influence of any drug or combination of drugs, or the combined influence of alcohol and drugs.

D. If the certificate of analysis referred to in § 46.2-341.26:9 indicates the presence of alcohol in the suspect's blood, the suspect shall be taken before a magistrate to determine whether the magistrate should issue an out-of-service order prohibiting the suspect from driving any commercial motor vehicle for a 24-hour period. If the magistrate finds that there is probable cause to believe that the suspect was driving a commercial motor vehicle with any measurable amount of alcohol in his blood, the magistrate shall issue an out-of-service order prohibiting the suspect from driving any commercial motor vehicle for a period of 24 hours. The magistrate shall forward a copy of the out-of-service order to the Department within seven days after issuing the order. The order shall be in addition to any other action or sanction permitted or required by law to be taken against or imposed upon the suspect.

History.

1992, c. 830; 1993, c. 673; 2005, c. 616.

§ 46.2-341.26:3. Refusal of tests; issuance of out-of-service orders; disqualification.

A. If a person arrested for a violation of § 46.2-341.24 or § 46.2-341.31, after having been advised by a law-enforcement officer (i) that a person who operates a commercial motor vehicle on a public highway in the Commonwealth is deemed thereby, as a condition of such operation, to have consented to have samples of his blood or breath taken for chemical tests to determine the alcohol or drug content of his blood, (ii) that a finding of unreasonable refusal to consent may be admitted as evidence at a criminal trial, and (iii) that the unreasonable refusal to do so constitutes grounds for the issuance of an out-of-service order and for the disqualification of such person from operating a commercial motor vehicle, then refuses to permit blood or breath samples to be taken for such tests, the law-enforcement officer shall take the person before a magistrate. If he again refuses after having been further advised by the magistrate (i) of the law requiring blood or breath samples to be taken, (ii) that a finding of unreasonable refusal to consent may be admitted as evidence at a criminal trial, and (iii) the sanctions for refusal, and declares again his refusal in writing on a form provided by the Supreme Court, or refuses or fails to so declare in writing and such fact is certified as prescribed below, then no blood or breath samples shall be taken even though he may later request them.

B. The form shall contain a brief statement of the law requiring the taking of blood or breath samples, that a finding of unreasonable refusal to consent may be admitted as evidence at a criminal trial, and the sanctions for refusal; a declaration of refusal; and lines for the signature of the person from whom the blood or breath sample is sought, the date, and the signature of a witness to the signing. If the person refuses or fails to execute the declaration, the magistrate shall certify such fact and that the magistrate advised the person that a refusal to permit a blood or breath sample to be taken, if found to be unreasonable, constitutes grounds for immediate issuance of an out-of-service order prohibiting him from driving a commercial vehicle for a period of twenty-four hours, and for the disqualification of such person from operating a commercial motor vehicle.

C. If the magistrate finds that there was probable cause to believe the refusal was unreasonable, he shall immediately issue an out-of-service order prohibiting the person from operating a commercial motor vehicle for a period of twenty-four hours and shall issue a warrant or summons charging such person with a violation of § 46.2-341.26:2. The warrant or summons shall be executed in the same manner as criminal warrants. Venue for the trial of the warrant or summons shall lie in the court of the county or city in which the criminal offense is to be tried.

D. The executed declaration of refusal or the certificate of the magistrate, as the case may be, shall be attached to the warrant and shall be forwarded by the magistrate to the court.

E. When the court receives the declaration or certificate together with the warrant or summons charging refusal, the court shall fix a date for the trial of the warrant or summons, at such time as the court designates.

F. The declaration of refusal or certificate under § 46.2-341.26:3 shall be prima facie evidence that the defendant refused to allow a blood or breath sample to be taken to determine the alcohol or drug content of his blood. However, this shall not prohibit the defendant from introducing on his behalf evidence of the basis for his refusal. The court shall determine the reasonableness of such refusal.

History.
1992, c. 830; 2001, c. 654.

§ 46.2-341.26:4. Appeal and trial; sanctions for refusal; procedures.

The procedure for appeal and trial shall be the same as provided by law for misdemeanors. If requested by either party on appeal to the circuit court, trial by jury shall be as provided in Article 4 (§ 19.2-260 et seq.) of Chapter 15 of Title 19.2, and the Commonwealth shall be required to prove its case beyond a reasonable doubt.

If the court or jury finds the defendant guilty as charged in the warrant or summons referred to in § 46.2-341.26:3, the defendant shall be disqualified as provided in § 46.2-341.18. However, if the defendant pleads guilty to a violation of § 46.2-341.24, the court may dismiss the warrant or summons.

The court shall notify the Commissioner of any such finding of guilt and shall forward the defendant's license to the Commissioner as in other cases of similar nature for suspension of license unless the defendant appeals his conviction. In such case the court shall return the license to the defendant upon his appeal being perfected.

History.
1992, c. 830.

§ 46.2-341.26:5. Qualifications and liability of persons authorized to take blood samples; procedure for taking samples.

For purposes of this article, only a physician, registered nurse, licensed practical nurse, phlebotomist, graduate laboratory technician or a technician or nurse designated by order of a circuit court acting on the recommendation of a licensed physician, using soap and water, polyvinylpyrrolidone iodine, pvp iodine, povidone iodine or benzalkonium chloride to cleanse the part of the body from which the blood is taken and using instruments sterilized by the accepted steam sterilizer or some other sterilizer which will not affect the accuracy of the test, or using chemically clean sterile disposable syringes, shall withdraw blood for the purpose of determining its alcohol or drug content. It is a Class 3 misdemeanor to reuse single-use-only needles or syringes. No civil liability shall attach to any person authorized by this section to withdraw blood as a result of the act of withdrawing blood from any person submitting thereto, provided the blood was withdrawn according to recognized medical procedures. However, the person shall not be relieved from liability for negligence in the withdrawing of any blood sample.

No person arrested for a violation of § 46.2-341.24 or § 46.2-341.31 shall be required to execute in favor of any person or corporation a waiver or release of liability in connection with the withdrawal of blood or as a condition precedent to the withdrawal of blood as provided for in this section.

History.
1992, c. 830; 2004, cc. 150, 440.

§ 46.2-341.26:6. Transmission of blood samples.

The blood sample withdrawn pursuant to § 46.2-341.26:5 shall be placed in vials provided or approved by the Department of Forensic Science. The vials shall be sealed by the person taking the sample or at his direction. The person who seals the vials shall complete the prenumbered certificate of blood withdrawal forms and attach one form to each vial. The completed withdrawal certificate for each vial shall show the name of the suspect, the name of the person taking the blood sample, the date and time the blood sample was taken and information identifying the arresting or accompanying officer. The vials shall be placed in a container provided by the Department, and the container shall be sealed to prevent tampering with the vials. A law-enforcement officer shall take possession of the container as soon as the vials are placed in such container and sealed, and shall promptly transport or mail the container to the Department.

History.

1992, c. 830; 2003, cc. 933, 936; 2005, cc. 868, 881.

§ 46.2-341.26:7. Transmission of samples.

A. Upon receipt of a blood sample forwarded to the Department for analysis pursuant to § 46.2-341.26:6, the Department shall have it examined for its alcohol or drug content, and the Director shall execute a certificate of analysis indicating the name of the suspect; the date, time, and by whom the blood sample was received and examined; a statement that the seal on the vial had not been broken or otherwise tampered with; a statement that the container and vial were provided or approved by the Department and that the vial was one to which the completed withdrawal certificate was attached; and a statement of the sample's alcohol or drug content. The Director or his representative shall remove the withdrawal certificate from the vial and either (i) attach it to the certificate of analysis and state in the certificate of analysis that it was so removed and attached or (ii) electronically scan it into the Department's Laboratory Information Management System and place the original withdrawal certificate in its case-specific file. The certificate of analysis and the withdrawal certificate shall be returned or electronically transmitted to the clerk of the court in which the charge will be heard. After completion of the analysis, the Department shall preserve the remainder of the blood until at least 90 days have lapsed from the date the blood was drawn. During this 90-day period, the accused may, by motion filed before the court in which the charge will be heard, with notice to the Department, request an order directing the Department to transmit the remainder of the blood sample to an independent laboratory retained by the accused for analysis. The Department shall destroy the remainder of the blood sample if no notice of a motion to transmit the remaining blood sample is received during the 90-day period.

B. When a blood sample taken in accordance with the provisions of §§ 46.2-341.26:2 through 46.2-341.26:6 is forwarded for analysis to the Department, a report of the test results shall be filed in that office. Upon proper identification of the certificate of withdrawal, the certificate of analysis, with the withdrawal certificate attached, shall, when attested by the Director, be admissible in any court as evidence of the facts therein stated and of the results of such analysis (i) in any criminal proceeding, provided that the requirements of subsection A of § 19.2-187.1 have been satisfied and the accused has not objected to the admission of the certificate pursuant to subsection B of § 19.2-187.1, or (ii) in any civil proceeding. On motion of the accused, the report of analysis prepared for the remaining blood sample shall be admissible in evidence provided the report is duly attested by a person performing such analysis and the independent laboratory that performed the analysis is accredited or certified to conduct forensic blood alcohol/drug testing by one or more of the following bodies: American Society of Crime Laboratory Directors/Laboratory Accreditation Board (ASCLD/LAB); College of American Pathologists (CAP); United States Department of Health and Human Services Substance Abuse and Mental Health Services Administration (SAMHSA); or American Board of Forensic Toxicology (ABFT).

Upon request of the person whose blood or breath was analyzed, the test results shall be made available to him.

The Director may delegate or assign these duties to an employee of the Department.

History.

1992, c. 830; 2003, cc. 933, 936; 2005, cc. 868, 881; 2009, Sp. Sess. I, cc. 1, 4; 2014, c. 328.

§ 46.2-341.26:8. Fees.

Payment for withdrawing blood shall not exceed $25, which shall be paid out of the appropriation for criminal charges.

If the person whose blood sample was withdrawn is subsequently convicted for violation of § 46.2-341.24 or § 46.2-341.31, any fees paid by the Commonwealth to the person withdrawing the sample shall be taxed as part of the costs of the criminal case and shall be paid into the general fund of the state treasury.

History.

1992, c. 830; 2003, cc. 933, 936.

§ 46.2-341.26:9. Assurance of breath test validity; use of breath tests as evidence.

To be capable of being considered valid in a prosecution under § 46.2-341.24 or 46.2-341.31, chemical analysis of a person's breath shall be performed by an individual possessing a valid license to conduct such tests, with the type of equipment and in accordance with methods approved by the Department.

Any individual conducting a breath test under the provisions of § 46.2-341.26:2 shall issue a certificate which includes the name of the suspect, the date and time the sample was taken from the suspect, the alcohol content of the sample, and the identity of the person who examined the sample. The certificate will also indicate that the test was conducted in accordance with the Department's specifications.

The certificate of analysis, when attested by the authorized individual conducting the breath test on equipment maintained by the Department, shall be admissible in any court as evidence of the facts therein stated and of the results of such analysis (i) in any criminal proceeding, provided that the requirements of subsection A of § 19.2-187.1 have been satisfied and the accused has not objected to the admission of the certificate pursuant to subsection B of § 19.2-187.1, or (ii) in any civil proceeding. Any such certificate of analysis purporting to be signed by a person authorized by the Department shall be admissible in evidence without proof of seal or signature of the person whose name is signed to it.

A copy of such certificate shall be promptly delivered to the suspect. The law-enforcement officer requiring the test or anyone with such officer at the time if otherwise qualified to conduct such test as provided by this section, may administer the breath test or analyze the results thereof.

History.

1992, c. 830; 2005, cc. 868, 881; 2009, Sp. Sess. I, cc. 1, 4.

§ 46.2-341.26:10. Evidence.

A. In any trial for a violation of § 46.2-341.24, admission of the blood or breath test results shall not limit the introduction of any other relevant evidence bearing upon any question at issue before the court, and the court shall, regardless of the results of the blood or breath tests, consider other relevant admissible evidence of the condition of the accused. If the test results indicate the presence of any drugs other than alcohol, the test results shall be admissible except in a prosecution under clause (v) of subsection A of § 46.2-341.24, only if other competent evidence has been presented to relate the presence of the drug or drugs to the impairment of the accused's ability to drive or operate any commercial motor vehicle safely.

B. The failure of an accused to permit a blood or breath sample to be taken to determine the alcohol or drug content of his blood is not evidence and shall not be subject to any comment by the Commonwealth at the trial of the case, except in rebuttal or pursuant to subsection C; nor shall the fact that a blood or breath test had been offered the accused be evidence or the subject of comment by the Commonwealth, except in rebuttal or pursuant to subsection C.

C. Evidence of a finding against the defendant under § 18.2-268.3 for his unreasonable refusal to permit a blood or breath sample to be taken to determine the alcohol or drug content of his blood shall be admissible into evidence, upon the motion of the Commonwealth or the defendant, for the sole purpose of explaining the absence at trial of a chemical test of such sample. When admitted pursuant to this subsection such evidence shall not be considered evidence of the accused's guilt.

D. The court or jury trying the case involving a violation of clause (ii), (iii) or (iv) of subsection A of § 46.2-341.24 shall determine the innocence or guilt of the defendant from all the evidence concerning his condition at the time of the alleged offense.

Motor Vehicles

History.

1992, c. 830; 2001, c. 654; 2005, c. 616.

§ 46.2-341.26:11. Substantial compliance.

The steps set forth in §§ 46.2-341.26:2 through 46.2-341.26:9 relating to taking, handling, identifying, and disposing of blood or breath samples are procedural and not substantive. Substantial compliance shall be sufficient. Failure to comply with any steps or portions thereof shall not of itself be grounds for finding the defendant not guilty, but shall go to the weight of the evidence and shall be considered with all the evidence in the case; however, the defendant shall have the right to introduce evidence on his own behalf to show noncompliance with the aforesaid procedures or any part thereof, and that as a result his rights were prejudiced.

History.

1992, c. 830; 2003, cc. 933, 936.

§ 46.2-341.27. Presumptions from alcohol and drug content of blood.

In any prosecution for a violation of clause (ii), (iii) or (iv) of subsection A of § 46.2-341.24, the amount of alcohol or drugs in the blood of the accused at the time of the alleged offense as indicated by a chemical analysis of a sample of the suspect's blood or breath to determine the alcohol or drug content of his blood in accordance with the provisions of §§ 46.2-341.26:1 through 46.2-341.26:11 shall give rise to the following rebuttable presumptions:

A. If there was at that time 0.08 percent or more by weight by volume of alcohol in the accused's blood or 0.08 grams or more per 210 liters of the accused's breath, it shall be presumed that the accused was under the influence of alcoholic intoxicants.

B. If there was at that time less than 0.08 percent by weight by volume of alcohol in the accused's blood or 0.08 grams or more per 210 liters of the accused's breath, such fact shall not give rise to any presumption that the accused was or was not under the influence of alcoholic intoxicants, but such fact may be considered with other competent evidence in determining the guilt or innocence of the accused.

C. If there was at that time an amount of the following substances at a level that is equal to or greater than: (a) 0.02 milligrams of cocaine per liter of blood, (b) 0.1 milligrams of methamphetamine per liter of blood, (c) 0.01 milligrams of phencyclidine per liter of blood, or (d) 0.1 milligrams of 3,4-methylenedioxymethamphetamine per liter of blood, it shall be presumed that the accused was under the influence of drugs to a degree which impairs his ability to drive or operate any commercial motor vehicle safely.

History.

1989, c. 705, § 46.1-372.26; 1992, c. 830; 1994, cc. 359, 363; 2005, c. 616.

§ 46.2-341.28. Penalty for driving commercial motor vehicle while intoxicated; subsequent offense; prior conviction.

Any person violating any provision of subsection A of § 46.2-341.24 shall be guilty of a Class 1 misdemeanor.

Any person convicted of a second offense committed within less than five years after a first offense under subsection A of § 46.2-341.24 shall be punishable by a fine of not less than $200 nor more than $2,500 and by confinement in jail for not less than one month nor more than one year. Five days of such confinement shall be a mandatory minimum sentence. Any person convicted of a second offense committed within a period of five to 10 years of a first offense under subsection A of § 46.2-341.24 shall be punishable by a fine of not less than $200 nor more than $2,500 and by confinement in jail for not less than one month nor more than one year. Any person convicted of a third offense or subsequent offense committed within 10 years of an offense under subsection A of § 46.2-341.24 shall be punishable by a fine of not less than $500 nor more than $2,500 and by confinement in jail for not less than two months nor more than one year. Thirty days of such confinement shall be a mandatory minimum sentence if the third or subsequent offense occurs within less than five years. Ten days of such confinement shall be a mandatory minimum sentence if the third or subsequent offense occurs within a period of five to 10 years of a first offense.

For the purposes of this section a conviction or finding of not innocent in the case of a juvenile under (i) § 18.2-51.4 or § 18.2-266, (ii) the ordinance of any county, city or town in this Commonwealth substantially similar to the provisions of § 18.2-51.4 or § 18.2-266, (iii) subsection A of § 46.2-341.24, or (iv) the laws of any other state substantially similar to the provisions of §§ 18.2-51.4, 18.2-266 or subsection A of § 46.2-341.24, shall be considered a prior conviction.

History.

1989, c. 705, § 46.1-372.27; 1993, c. 673; 1997, c. 691; 2000, cc. 958, 980; 2004, c. 461.

§ 46.2-341.29. Penalty for driving commercial motor vehicle with blood alcohol content equal to or greater than 0.04.

Any person violating the provisions of subsection B of § 46.2-341.24 shall be guilty of a Class 3 misdemeanor.

History.

1989, c. 705, § 46.1-372.28.

§ 46.2-341.30. Disqualification for driving commercial motor vehicle while intoxicated, etc.

A. The judgment of conviction under any provision of § 46.2-341.24 shall of itself operate to disqualify the person so convicted from the privilege to drive or operate any commercial motor vehicle as provided in § 46.2-341.18. Notwithstanding any other provision of law, such disqualification shall not be subject to any suspension, reduction, limitation or other modification by the court or the Commissioner.

B. A judgment of conviction under any provision of subsection A of § 46.2-341.24, in addition to causing the disqualification under subsection A of this section, shall also operate to deprive the person so convicted of his privilege to drive or operate any motor vehicle as provided in § 18.2-271.

History.

1989, c. 705, § 46.1-372.29.

§ 46.2-341.31. Driving commercial motor vehicle with any alcohol in blood.

No person shall drive a commercial motor vehicle while having any amount of alcohol in his blood, as measured by a test administered pursuant to the provisions of §§ 46.2-341.26:1 through 46.2-341.26:11. Any person found to have so driven a commercial motor vehicle shall be guilty of a traffic infraction.

History.

1989, c. 705, § 46.1-372.29:1; 1990, c. 218; 1992, c. 830.

§ 46.2-341.32. Authority to enter into agreements.

The Department may procure and enter into agreements or arrangements for the purpose of participating in the Commercial Driver License System or any other similar information system established to implement the requirements of the Commercial Motor Vehicle Safety Act, and may procure and enter into other agreements or arrangements to carry out the provisions of this article.

History.

1989, c. 705, § 46.1-372.30.

§ 46.2-341.33: Repealed by Acts 2015, c. 709, cl. 2.

§ 46.2-341.34. Appeals.

Any person denied a commercial driver's license or who has been disqualified from operating a commercial motor vehicle under the provisions of this article is entitled to judicial review in accordance with the provisions of the Administrative Process Act (§ 2.2-4000 et seq.). No appeal shall lie in any case in which such denial or disqualification was mandatory except to determine the identity of the person concerned when the question of identity is in dispute.

From the final decision of the circuit court, either party shall have an appeal as of right to the Court of Appeals.

While an appeal is pending from the action of the Department disqualifying the person or denying him a license, or from the court affirming the action of the Department, the person aggrieved shall not drive a commercial motor vehicle.

History.

1989, c. 705, § 46.1-372.32.

ARTICLE 7.

FORM OF LICENSES; IDENTITY DOCUMENTS ISSUED BY DEPARTMENT.

§ 46.2-342. What license to contain; organ donor information; Uniform Donor Document.

A. Every license issued under this chapter shall bear:

1. For licenses issued or renewed on or after July 1, 2003, a license number which shall be assigned by the Department to the licensee and shall not be the same as the licensee's social security number;
2. A photograph of the licensee;
3. The licensee's full name, year, month, and date of birth;
4. The licensee's address, subject to the provisions of subsection B;
5. A brief description of the licensee for the purpose of identification;
6. A space for the signature of the licensee; and
7. Any other information deemed necessary by the Commissioner for the administration of this title.

No abbreviated names or nicknames shall be shown on any license.

B. At the option of the licensee, the address shown on the license may be either the post office box, business, or residence address of the licensee, provided such address is located in Virginia. However, regardless of which address is shown on the license, the licensee shall supply the Department with his residence address, which shall be an address in Virginia. This residence address shall be maintained in the Department's records. Whenever the licensee's address shown either on his license or in the Department's records changes, he shall notify the Department of such change as required by § 46.2-324.

C. The Department may contract with the United States Postal Service or an authorized agent to use the National Change of Address System for the purpose of obtaining current address information for a person whose name appears in customer records maintained by the Department. If the Department receives information from the National Change of Address System indicating that a person whose name appears in a Department record has submitted a permanent change of address to the Postal Service, the Department may then update its records with the mailing address obtained from the National Change of Address System.

D. The license shall be made of a material and in a form to be determined by the Commissioner.

E. Licenses issued to persons less than 21 years old shall be immediately and readily distinguishable from those issued to persons 21 years old or older. Distinguishing characteristics shall include unique design elements of the document and descriptors within the photograph area to identify persons who are at least 15 years old but less than 21 years old. These descriptors shall include the month, day, and year when the person will become 21 years old.

F. The Department shall establish a method by which an applicant for a driver's license or an identification card may indicate his consent to make an anatomical gift for transplantation, therapy, research, and education pursuant to § 32.1-291.5, and shall cooperate with the Virginia Transplant Council to ensure that such method is designed to encourage organ, tissue, and eye donation with a minimum of effort on the part of the donor and the Department.

G. If an applicant indicates his consent to be a donor pursuant to subsection F, the Department may make a notation of this designation on his license or card and shall make a notation of this designation in his driver record. The notation shall remain on the individual's license or card until he revokes his consent to make an anatomical gift by requesting removal of the notation from his license or card or otherwise in accordance with § 32.1-291.6. Inclusion of a notation indicating consent to making an organ donation on an applicant's license or card pursuant to this subsection shall be sufficient legal authority for removal, following death, of the subject's organs or tissues without additional authority from the donor or his family or estate, in accordance with the provisions of § 32.1-291.8.

H. A minor may make a donor designation pursuant to subsection F without the consent of a parent or legal guardian as authorized by the Revised Uniform Anatomical Gift Act (§ 32.1-291.1 et seq.).

I. The Department shall provide a method by which an applicant conducting a Department of Motor Vehicles transaction using electronic means may make a voluntary contribution to the Virginia Donor Registry and Public Awareness Fund (Fund) established pursuant to § 32.1-297.1. The Department shall inform the applicant of the existence of the Fund and also that contributing to the Fund is voluntary.

J. The Department shall collect all moneys contributed pursuant to subsection I and transmit the moneys on a regular basis to the Virginia Transplant Council, which shall credit the contributions to the Fund.

K. When requested by the applicant, and upon presentation of a signed statement by a licensed physician confirming the applicant's condition, the Department shall indicate on the applicant's driver's license that the applicant (i) is an insulin-dependent diabetic, (ii) is hearing or speech impaired, or (iii) has an intellectual disability, as defined in § 37.2-100, or autism spectrum disorder, as defined in § 38.2-3418.17.

L. In the absence of gross negligence or willful misconduct, the Department and its employees shall be immune from any civil or criminal liability in connection with the making of or failure to make a notation of donor designation on any license or card or in any person's driver record.

M. The Department shall, in coordination with the Virginia Transplant Council, prepare an organ donor information brochure describing the organ donor program and providing instructions for completion of the uniform donor document information describing the bone marrow donation program and instructions for registration in the National Bone Marrow Registry. The Department shall include a copy of such brochure with every driver's license renewal notice or application mailed to licensed drivers in Virginia.

History.

Code 1950, § 46-370; 1958, c. 541, § 46.1-375; 1962, c. 368; 1968, c. 642; 1972, c. 538; 1976, c. 57; 1979, c. 124; 1982, c. 180; 1983, c. 608; 1984, c. 780; 1989, cc. 139, 705, 727; 1990, c. 159; 1993, cc. 118, 986; 1995, cc. 350, 372; 1997, c. 486; 1998, c. 322; 1999, c. 330; 2000, c. 810; 2001, cc. 148, 157; 2002, cc. 135, 767, 834; 2003, cc. 306, 335; 2005, cc. 259, 828; 2007, cc. 92, 907; 2008, c. 82; 2009, cc. 834, 872; 2010, cc. 25, 55; 2014, c. 702; 2016, cc. 135, 743.

§ 46.2-343. Duplicate driver's license, reissued driver's licenses, learner's permit; fees.

If a driver's license or learner's permit issued under the provisions of this chapter is lost, stolen, or destroyed, the person to whom it was issued may obtain a duplicate or substitute thereof on furnishing proof satisfactory to the Department that his license or permit has been lost, stolen, or destroyed, or that there are good reasons why a duplicate should be issued. Every applicant for a duplicate or reissued driver's license shall appear in person before the Department to apply, unless permitted by the Department to apply for duplicate or reissue in another manner. Applicants who are required to apply in person may be required to present proof of identity, legal presence, residency, and social security number or non-work authorized status.

There shall be a fee of five dollars for each duplicate license and two dollars for each duplicate learner's permit. An additional fee of five dollars shall be charged to add or change the scene on a duplicate license or duplicate learner's permit.

There shall be a fee of five dollars for reissuance of any driver's license upon the termination of driving restrictions imposed upon the licensee by the Department or a court. An additional fee of five dollars shall be charged to add or change the scene on a license upon reissuance.

History.

Code 1950, § 46-374; 1958, c. 541, § 46.1-379; 1968, c. 642; 1976, c. 48; 1982, c. 202; 1984, c. 780; 1989, c. 727; 1995, c. 468; 1997, c. 486; 1999, c. 593; 2009, c. 872.

§ 46.2-344. Temporary driver's permit.

The Department, upon determining, after an examination, that an applicant is mentally, physically, and otherwise qualified to receive a license, may issue to him a temporary driver's permit entitling him, while having the permit in his immediate possession, to drive a motor vehicle on the highways. The temporary driver's permit shall be valid until receipt of the driver's license but in no case shall be valid for more than 90 days from the date of issuance.

History.

Code 1950, § 46-372; 1958, c. 541, § 46.1-377; 1984, c. 780; 1989, c. 727; 2009, c. 872.

§ 46.2-345. Issuance of special identification cards; fee; confidentiality; penalties.

A. On the application of any person who is a resident of the Commonwealth or the parent or legal guardian of any such person who is under the age of 15, the Department shall issue a special identification card to the person provided:

1. Application is made on a form prescribed by the Department and includes the applicant's full legal name; year, month, and date of birth; social security number; sex; and residence address;

2. The applicant presents, when required by the Department, proof of identity, legal presence, residency, and social security number or non-work authorized status;

3. The Department is satisfied that the applicant needs an identification card or the applicant shows he has a bona fide need for such a card; and

4. The applicant does not hold a driver's license, commercial driver's license, temporary driver's permit, learner's permit, or motorcycle learner's permit.

Persons 70 years of age or older may exchange a valid Virginia driver's license for a special identification card at no fee. Special identification cards subsequently issued to such persons shall be subject to the regular fees for special identification cards.

B. The fee for the issuance of an original or renewal special identification card is $5. The fee for the issuance of a duplicate or reissue of a special identification card is $5. Persons 21 years old or older may be issued a scenic special identification card for an additional fee of $5.

C. Every special identification card shall expire on the last day of the month of birth of the applicant in years in which the applicant attains an age exactly divisible by five. At no time shall any special identification card be issued for less than three nor more than seven years, except under the provisions of subsection B of § 46.2-328.1 and except that those cards issued to children under the age of 15 shall expire on the child's sixteenth birthday, thereafter the special identification card may be renewed on or before the last day of the month of birth of the applicant and shall be valid for five years, expiring in the next year in which the applicant's age is exactly divisible by five, except under the provisions of subsection B of § 46.2-328.1. Notwithstanding these limitations, the Commissioner may extend the validity period of an expiring card if (i) the Department is unable to process an application for renewal due to circumstances beyond its control, (ii) the extension has been authorized under a directive from the Governor, and (iii) the card was not issued as a temporary special identification card under the provisions of subsection B of § 46.2-328.1. However, in no event shall the validity period be extended more than 90 days per occurrence of such conditions.

D. A special identification card issued under this section may be similar in size, shape, and design to a driver's license, and include a photograph of its holder, but the card shall be readily distinguishable from a driver's license and shall clearly state that it does not authorize the person to whom it is issued to drive a motor vehicle. Every applicant for a special identification card shall appear in person before the Department to apply for a renewal, duplicate or reissue unless specifically permitted by the Department to apply in another manner.

E. Special identification cards, for persons at least 15 years old but less than 21 years old, shall be immediately and readily distinguishable from those issued to persons 21 years old or older. Distinguishing characteristics shall include unique design elements of the document and descriptors within the photograph area to identify persons who are at least 15 years old but less than 21 years old. These descriptors shall include the month, day, and year when the person will become 21 years old.

F. Special identification cards for persons under age 15 shall bear a full face photograph. The special identification card issued to persons under age 15 shall be readily distinguishable from a driver's license and from other special identification cards issued by the Department. Such cards shall clearly indicate that it does not authorize the person to whom it is issued to drive a motor vehicle.

G. Unless otherwise prohibited by law, a valid Virginia driver's license may be surrendered for a special identification card without the applicant's having to present proof of legal presence as required by § 46.2-328.1 if the Virginia driver's license is unexpired and it has not been revoked, suspended, or cancelled. The special identification card shall be considered a reissue and the expiration date shall be the last day of the month of the surrendered driver's license's month of expiration.

H. Any personal information, as identified in § 2.2-3801, which is retained by the Department from an application for the issuance of a special identification card is confidential and shall not be divulged to any person, association, corporation, or organization, public or private, except to the legal guardian or the attorney of the applicant or to a person, association, corporation, or organization nominated in writing by the applicant, his legal guardian, or his attorney. This subsection shall not prevent the Department from furnishing the application or any information thereon to any law-enforcement agency.

I. Any person who uses a false or fictitious name or gives a false or fictitious address in any application for an identification card or knowingly makes a false statement or conceals a material fact or otherwise commits a fraud in any such application shall be guilty of a Class 2 misdemeanor. However, where the name or address is given, or false statement is made, or fact is concealed, or fraud committed, with the intent to purchase a firearm or where the identification card is obtained for the purpose of committing any offense punishable as a felony, a violation of this section shall constitute a Class 4 felony.

J. The Department may promulgate regulations necessary for the effective implementation of the provisions of this section.

K. The Department shall utilize the various communications media throughout the Commonwealth to inform Virginia residents of the provisions of this section and to promote and encourage the public to take advantage of its provisions.

L. The Department shall electronically transmit application information to the Department of State Police, in a format approved by the State Police, for comparison with information contained in the Virginia Criminal Information Network and National Crime Information Center Convicted Sexual Offender Registry Files, at the time of issuance of a special identification card. Whenever it appears from the records of the State Police that a person has failed to comply with the duty to register or reregister pursuant to Chapter 9 (§ 9.1-900 et seq.) of Title 9.1, the State Police shall promptly investigate and, if there is probable cause to believe a violation has occurred, obtain a warrant or assist in obtaining an indictment charging a violation of § 18.2-472.1 in the jurisdiction in which the person made application for the special identification card.

M. When requested by the applicant, the applicant's parent if the applicant is a minor, or the applicant's guardian, and upon presentation of a signed statement by a licensed physician confirming the applicant's condition, the Department shall indicate on the applicant's special identification card that the applicant has any condition listed in subsection K of § 46.2-342.

History.

1973, c. 214, § 46.1-383.3; 1975, c. 549; 1981, cc. 593, 594; 1982, c. 180; 1983, c. 608; 1984, c. 780; 1989, c. 727; 1993, cc. 471, 501; 1997, c. 486; 1998, c. 322; 1999, c. 593; 2002, cc. 767, 834; 2005, cc. 259, 260, 281, 665, 828; 2006, cc. 857, 914; 2009, c. 872; 2012, cc. 215, 222; 2014, c. 702; 2015, c. 167; 2016, cc. 135, 743.

§ 46.2-345.1. Veterans identification card; fee.

In cooperation with the Department of Veterans Services and the Department of Military Affairs, the Department may issue veterans identification cards. The fee for the issuance or replacement of such cards shall be $10. Veterans identification cards shall not be special identification cards as provided for in § 46.2-345.

For the purposes of this section, "veteran" means (i) a Virginia resident who has served in the active military, naval, or air service and whose final discharge or release therefrom under honorable conditions or (ii) a Virginia resident who has served honorably for greater than 180 days in the Virginia National Guard or the reserves of the United States armed forces.

The veterans identification card shall not be used for determination of any federal benefit.

History.

2013, c. 673; 2015, c. 693.

ARTICLE 8.

PROHIBITED USES OF DRIVER'S LICENSES.

§ 46.2-346. Unlawful acts enumerated.

A. No person shall:

1. Display, cause or permit to be displayed, or have in his possession any driver's license which he knows to be fictitious or to have been cancelled, revoked, suspended, or altered, or photographed for the purpose of evading the intent of this chapter;

2. Lend to, or knowingly permit the use of by one not entitled thereto, any driver's license issued to the person so lending or permitting the use thereof;

3. Display or represent as his own any driver's license not issued to him;

4. Reproduce by photograph or otherwise, any driver's license, temporary driver's permit, learner's permit, or special identification card issued by the Department with the intent to commit an illegal act;

5. Fail or refuse to surrender to the Department, on demand, any driver's license issued in the Commonwealth or any other state when the license has been suspended, cancelled, or revoked by proper authority in the Commonwealth, or any other state as provided by law, or to fail or refuse to surrender the suspended, cancelled, or revoked license to any court in which a driver has been tried and convicted for the violation of any law or ordinance of the Commonwealth or any county, city, or town thereof, regulating or affecting the operation of a motor vehicle.

B. Any law-enforcement officer empowered to enforce the provisions of this title may retain any driver's license held in violation of this section and shall submit the license to the appropriate court for evidentiary purposes.

History.

Code 1950, § 46-380; 1958, c. 541, § 46.1-384; 1962, c. 368; 1984, c. 780; 1988, c. 323; 1989, c. 727; 2004, c. 722.

§ 46.2-347. Fraudulent use of driver's license or Department of Motor Vehicles identification card to obtain alcoholic beverages; penalties.

Any underage person as specified in § 4.1-304 who knowingly uses or attempts to use a forged, deceptive or otherwise nongenuine driver's license issued by any state, territory or possession of the United States, the District of Columbia, the Commonwealth of Puerto Rico or any foreign country or government; United States Armed Forces identification card; United States passport or foreign government visa; Virginia Department of Motor Vehicles special identification card; official identification issued by any other federal, state or foreign government agency; or official university or college student identification card to obtain alcoholic beverages shall be guilty of a Class 3 misdemeanor, and upon conviction of a violation of this section, the court shall revoke such convicted person's driver's license or privilege to drive a motor vehicle for a period of not less than thirty days nor more than one year.

History.

1980, c. 519, § 46.1-384.1; 1981, c. 24; 1983, c. 473; 1984, c. 780; 1985, c. 559; 1989, c. 727; 1992, c. 531; 1993, c. 866.

§ 46.2-348. Fraud or false statements in applications for license; penalties.

Any person who uses a false or fictitious name or gives a false or fictitious address in any application for a driver's license or escort vehicle driver certificate, or any renewal or duplicate thereof, or knowingly makes a false statement or conceals a material fact or otherwise commits a fraud during the driver's license examination, including for a commercial driver's license or commercial learner's permit, or in his application is guilty of a Class 2 misdemeanor. However, where the license is used, or the fact concealed, or fraud is done, with the intent to purchase a firearm or use as proof of residency under § 9.1-903, a violation of this section shall be punishable as a Class 4 felony.

History.

Code 1950, § 46-381; 1958, c. 541, § 46.1-385; 1981, c. 593; 1984,

c. 780; 1989, c. 727; 1993, cc. 471, 501; 2006, cc. 857, 914; 2013, cc. 165, 312, 477, 582; 2014, cc. 77, 803; 2015, c. 258.

§ 46.2-349. Unlawful to permit violations of chapter.

No person shall authorize or knowingly permit a motor vehicle owned by him or under his control to be driven by any person who has no legal right to do so or in violation of any of the provisions of this chapter.

History.
Code 1950, § 46-384; 1958, c. 541, § 46.1-386; 1989, c. 727.

§ 46.2-350. Penalty for violation.

Notwithstanding § 46.2-113, except as otherwise provided any violation of any provision of this chapter not declared to be a felony shall constitute a Class 2 misdemeanor.

History.
Code 1950, § 46-385; 1958, c. 541, § 46.1-387; 1989, c. 727.

ARTICLE 9.
HABITUAL OFFENDERS.

§§ 46.2-351 through 46.2-355: Repealed by Acts 1999, cc. 945, 987.

§ 46.2-355.1. Intervention required for certain offenders; fee; penalty; notice.

A. Upon receiving notification of a second conviction entered on or after July 1, 1999, for driving while the offender's license, permit or privilege to drive is suspended or revoked in violation of § 46.2-301, the Commissioner shall notify such person that he shall report to a Virginia Alcohol Safety Action Program within sixty days of the date of such notice for intervention. Intervention shall be in accordance with § 18.2-271.1. The program shall provide the Commissioner with information of the offender's compliance.

B. An interview shall be conducted by a representative of a Virginia Alcohol Safety Action Program. The representative shall review all applicable laws with the person attending the interview, provide guidance with respect to budgeting for payment of court fines and costs, if applicable, and explain the laws and the consequences of future offenses and may refer the person to any driver improvement clinic. A fee of thirty dollars shall be paid to the Virginia Alcohol Safety Action Program for attendance at a driver intervention interview. All fees collected by a Virginia Alcohol Safety Action Program shall be used to meet its expenses.

C. The Commissioner shall suspend the driving privilege of any person who fails to complete and pay the required fee for an intervention interview within the sixty-day period. The suspension shall continue until such time as the person has completed and paid for the intervention interview.

D. Notice to report for intervention shall be sent by the Department by certified mail, return receipt requested, to the driver at the last known address supplied by the driver and on file with the Department.

E. Failure of the offender to attend as required or failure of the Department to notify the offender upon the second offense shall not prevent conviction for any subsequent offense committed in violation of § 46.2-301.

History.
1999, cc. 945, 987.

§ 46.2-356. Period during which habitual offender not to be licensed to drive motor vehicle.

No license to drive motor vehicles in Virginia shall be issued to any person determined or adjudicated an habitual offender (i) for a period of ten years from the date of any final order of a court entered under this article or if no such order was entered then the notice of the determination by the Commissioner finding the person to be an habitual offender and (ii) until the privilege of the person to drive a motor vehicle in the Commonwealth has been restored by an order of a court entered in a proceeding as provided in this article.

History.
1968, c. 476, § 46.1-387.7; 1989, c. 727; 1995, c. 799; 1999, cc. 945, 987.

§ 46.2-357. Operation of motor vehicle or self-propelled machinery or equipment by habitual offender prohibited; penalty; enforcement of section.

A. It shall be unlawful for any person determined or adjudicated an habitual offender to drive any motor vehicle or self-propelled machinery or equipment on the highways of the Commonwealth while the revocation of the person's driving privilege remains in effect. However, the revocation determination shall not prohibit the person from operating any farm tractor on the highways when it is necessary to move the tractor from one tract of land used for agricultural purposes to another tract of land used for agricultural purposes, provided that the distance between the said tracts of land is no more than five miles.

B. Except as provided in subsection D, any person found to be an habitual offender under this article, who is thereafter convicted of driving a motor vehicle or self-propelled machinery or equipment in the Commonwealth while the revocation determination is in effect, shall be punished as follows:

1. If such driving does not of itself endanger the life, limb, or property of another, such person shall

be guilty of a Class 1 misdemeanor punishable by a mandatory minimum term of confinement in jail of 10 days except in cases wherein such operation is necessitated in situations of apparent extreme emergency that require such operation to save life or limb, the sentence, or any part thereof, may be suspended.

2. If such driving of itself endangers the life, limb, or property of another or takes place while such person is in violation of §§ 18.2-36.1, 18.2-51.4, 18.2-266 or § 46.2-341.24, irrespective of whether the driving of itself endangers the life, limb or property of another and the person has been previously convicted of a violation of §§ 18.2-36.1, 18.2-51.4, 18.2-266 or § 46.2-341.24, such person shall be guilty of a felony punishable by confinement in a state correctional facility for not less than one year nor more than five years, one year of which shall be a mandatory minimum term of confinement or, in the discretion of the jury or the court trying the case without a jury, by mandatory minimum confinement in jail for a period of 12 months. However, in cases wherein such operation is necessitated in situations of apparent extreme emergency that require such operation to save life or limb, the sentence, or any part thereof, may be suspended. For the purposes of this section, an offense in violation of a valid local ordinance, or law of any other jurisdiction, which ordinance or law is substantially similar to any provision of law herein shall be considered an offense in violation of such provision of law.

3. If the offense of driving while a determination as an habitual offender is in effect is a second or subsequent such offense, such person shall be punished as provided in subdivision 2 of this subsection, irrespective of whether the offense, of itself, endangers the life, limb, or property of another.

C. For the purpose of enforcing this section, in any case in which the accused is charged with driving a motor vehicle or self-propelled machinery or equipment while his license, permit, or privilege to drive is suspended or revoked or is charged with driving without a license, the court before hearing the charge shall determine whether the person has been determined an habitual offender and, by reason of this determination, is barred from driving a motor vehicle or self-propelled machinery or equipment on the highways in the Commonwealth. If the court determines the accused has been determined to be an habitual offender and finds there is probable cause that the alleged offense under this section is a felony, it shall certify the case to the circuit court of its jurisdiction for trial.

D. Notwithstanding the provisions of subdivisions 2 and 3 of subsection B, following conviction and prior to imposition of sentence with the consent of the defendant, the court may order the defendant to be evaluated for and to participate in the Boot Camp Incarceration Program pursuant to § 19.2-316.1, or the Detention Center Incarceration Program pursuant to § 19.2-316.2, or the Diversion Center Incarceration Program pursuant to § 19.2-316.3.

History.

1968, c. 476, § 46.1-387.8; 1970, c. 507; 1980, c. 436; 1988, c. 559; 1989, c. 727; 1990, c. 828; 1993, c. 677; 1994, c. 50; 1995, c. 799; 1997, cc. 5, 344; 1998, c. 298; 1999, cc. 945, 987; 2000, cc. 956, 982; 2004, c. 461.

§ 46.2-358. Restoration of privilege of driving motor vehicle; when petition may be brought; terms and conditions.

In any case where the provisions of § 46.2-360 or § 46.2-361 do not apply, five years from the date of any final order of a court entered under this article, or if no such order was entered then the notice of the determination by the Commissioner finding a person to be an habitual offender and revoking his privilege to drive a motor vehicle in the Commonwealth, the person may petition the court in which he was found to be an habitual offender, or any court of record in Virginia having criminal jurisdiction in the political subdivision in which he then resides, for restoration of his privilege to drive a motor vehicle in the Commonwealth. On such petition, and for good cause shown, the court may, upon a finding that such person does not constitute a threat to the safety and welfare of himself or others with regard to the driving of a motor vehicle, (i) restore to the person the privilege to drive a motor vehicle in the Commonwealth on whatever conditions the court may prescribe or (ii) order that the person be issued a restricted license to drive a motor vehicle in the Commonwealth for any of the purposes set forth in and in accordance with the procedures of subsection E of § 18.2-271.1, subject to other provisions of law relating to the issuance of driver's licenses.

History.

1968, c. 476, § 46.1-387.9; 1984, c. 780; 1989, c. 727; 1993, c. 617; 1995, c. 799.

§ 46.2-359. Restoration of driving privilege to certain persons.

Any person eighteen years of age or older who has been adjudged an habitual offender based in whole or in part on findings of not innocent as a juvenile may petition the court in which he was found to be an habitual offender, or any circuit court in Virginia having criminal jurisdiction in the political subdivision in which the person now resides, for restoration of his privilege to operate a motor vehicle in the Commonwealth. On such petition, and for good cause shown, the court may, in its discretion, restore to him the privilege to drive a motor vehicle in the Commonwealth on whatever conditions the court may prescribe, subject to other provisions of law relating to the issuance of driver's licenses.

History.

1968, c. 476, § 46.1-387.2; 1970, cc. 507, 724; 1974, c. 453; 1982, c. 655; 1984, c. 780; 1989, c. 727.

§ 46.2-360. Restoration of privilege of operating motor vehicle; restoration of privilege to persons convicted under certain other provisions of Habitual Offender Act.

Any person who has been found to be an habitual offender where the determination or adjudication was based in part and dependent on a conviction as set out in subdivision 1 b of former § 46.2-351, may petition the court in which he was found to be an habitual offender, or the circuit court in the political subdivision in which he then resides to:

1. Restore his privilege to drive a motor vehicle in the Commonwealth, provided that five years have elapsed from the date of the final order of a court entered under this article, or if no such order was entered then the notice of the determination by the Commissioner. On such petition, and for good cause shown, the court may, in its discretion, restore to the person the privilege to drive a motor vehicle in the Commonwealth on whatever conditions the court may prescribe, subject to other provisions of law relating to the issuance of driver's licenses, if the court is satisfied from the evidence presented that: (i) at the time of the previous convictions, the petitioner was addicted to or psychologically dependent on the use of alcohol or other drugs; (ii) at the time of the hearing on the petition, he is no longer addicted to or psychologically dependent on the use of alcohol or such other drug; and (iii) the person does not constitute a threat to the safety and welfare of himself or others with regard to the driving of a motor vehicle. However, prior to acting on the petition, the court shall order that an evaluation of the person be conducted by a Virginia Alcohol Safety Action Program and recommendations therefrom be submitted to the court, and the court shall give the recommendations such weight as the court deems appropriate. The court may, in lieu of restoring the person's privilege to drive, authorize the issuance of a restricted license for a period not to exceed five years in accordance with the provisions of subsection E of § 18.2-271.1. The local Virginia Alcohol Safety Action Program shall during the term of the restricted license monitor the person's compliance with the terms of the restrictions imposed by the court. Any violation of the restrictions shall be reported to the court, and the court may then modify the restrictions or revoke the license.

2. Issue a restricted permit to authorize such person to drive a motor vehicle in the Commonwealth in the course of his employment, to and from his home to the place of his employment or such other medically necessary travel as the court deems necessary and proper upon written verification of need by a licensed physician, provided that three years have elapsed from the date of the final order, or if no such order was entered then the notice of the determination by the Commissioner. The court may order that a restricted license for such purposes be issued in accordance with the procedures of subsection E of § 18.2-271.1, if the court is satisfied from the evidence presented that (i) at the time of the previous convictions, the petitioner was addicted to or psychologically dependent on the use of alcohol or other drugs, (ii) at the time of the hearing on the petition, he is no longer addicted to or psychologically dependent on the use of alcohol or such other drugs, and (iii) the defendant does not constitute a threat to the safety and welfare of himself and others with regard to the driving of a motor vehicle. The court may prohibit the person to whom a restricted license is issued from operating a motor vehicle that is not equipped with a functioning, certified ignition interlock system during all or any part of the term for which the restricted license is issued, in accordance with the provisions set forth in § 18.2-270.1. However, prior to acting on the petition, the court shall order that an evaluation of the person be conducted by a Virginia Alcohol Safety Action Program and recommendations therefrom be submitted to the court, and the court shall give the recommendations such weight as the court deems appropriate. The local Virginia Alcohol Safety Action Program shall during the term of the restricted license monitor the person's compliance with the terms of the restrictions imposed by the court. Any violation of the restrictions shall be reported to the court, and the court may then modify the restrictions or revoke the license.

In the computation of the five-year and three-year periods under subdivisions 1 and 2 of this section, such person shall be given credit for any period his driver's license was administratively revoked under subsection B of § 46.2-391 prior to the final order or notification by the Commissioner of the habitual offender determination.

A copy of any petition filed hereunder shall be served on the attorney for the Commonwealth for the jurisdiction wherein the petition was filed, and shall also be served on the Commissioner of the Department of Motor Vehicles, who shall provide to the attorney for the Commonwealth a certified copy of the petitioner's driving record. The Commissioner shall also advise the attorney for the Commonwealth whether there is anything in the records maintained by the Department that might make the petitioner ineligible for restoration, and may also provide notice of any potential ineligibility to the Attorney General's Office, which may join in representing the interests of the Commonwealth where it appears that the petitioner is not eligible for restoration. The hearing on a petition filed pursuant to this article shall not be set for a date sooner than thirty days after the petition is filed and served as provided herein.

History.

1976, c. 158, § 46.1-387.9:2; 1977, c. 408; 1987, c. 409; 1989, c. 727; 1990, c. 828; 1993, c. 514; 1994, c. 573; 1995, cc. 486, 799; 1996, c. 374; 1998, c. 749; 1999, cc. 742, 945, 987; 2016, c. 230.

§ 46.2-361. Restoration of privilege after driving while license revoked or suspended for failure to pay fines or costs, furnish proof of financial responsibility or pay uninsured motorist fee.

A. Any person who has been found to be an habitual offender, where the determination or adjudication was based in part and dependent on a conviction as set out in subdivision 1 c of former § 46.2-351, may, after three years from the date of the final order of a court entered under this article, or if no such order was entered then the notice of the determination or adjudication by the Commissioner, petition the court in which he was found to be an habitual offender, or the circuit court in the political subdivision in which he then resides, for restoration of his privilege to drive a motor vehicle in the Commonwealth. In no event, however, shall the provisions of this subsection apply when such person's determination or adjudication was also based in part and dependent on a conviction as set out in subdivision 1 b of former § 46.2-351. In such case license restoration shall be in compliance with the provisions of § 46.2-360.

B. Any person who has been found to be an habitual offender, where the determination or adjudication was based entirely upon a combination of convictions of § 46.2-707 and convictions as set out in subdivision 1 c of former § 46.2-351, may, after payment in full of all outstanding fines, costs and judgments relating to his determination, and furnishing proof of (i) financial responsibility and (ii) compliance with the provisions of Article 8 (§ 46.2-705 et seq.) of Chapter 6 of this title or both, if applicable, petition the court in which he was found to be an habitual offender, or the circuit court in the political subdivision in which he then resides, for restoration of his privilege to drive a motor vehicle in the Commonwealth.

C. This section shall apply only where the conviction or convictions as set out in subdivision 1 c of former § 46.2-351 resulted from a suspension or revocation ordered pursuant to (i) § 46.2-395 for failure to pay fines and costs, (ii) § 46.2-459 for failure to furnish proof of financial responsibility, or (iii) § 46.2-417 for failure to satisfy a judgment, provided the judgment has been paid in full prior to the time of filing the petition or was a conviction under § 46.2-302 or former § 46.1-351.

D. On any such petition, the court, in its discretion, may restore to the person his privilege to drive a motor vehicle, on whatever conditions the court may prescribe, if the court is satisfied from the evidence presented that the petitioner does not constitute a threat to the safety and welfare of himself or others with respect to the operation of a motor vehicle, and that he has satisfied in full all outstanding court costs, court fines and judgments relating to determination as an habitual offender and furnished proof of financial responsibility, if applicable.

E. A copy of any petition filed hereunder shall be served on the attorney for the Commonwealth for the jurisdiction wherein the petition was filed, and shall also be served on the Commissioner of the Department of Motor Vehicles, who shall provide to the attorney for the Commonwealth a certified copy of the petitioner's driving record. The Commissioner shall also advise the attorney for the Commonwealth whether there is anything in the records maintained by the Department that might make the petitioner ineligible for restoration, and may also provide notice of any potential ineligibility to the Attorney General's Office, which may join in representing the interests of the Commonwealth where it appears that the petitioner is not eligible for restoration. The hearing on a petition filed pursuant to this article shall not be set for a date sooner than thirty days after the petition is filed and served as provided herein.

History.

1984, c. 660, § 46.1-387.9:3; 1985, c. 292; 1987, c. 334; 1989, c. 727; 1992, c. 568; 1993, cc. 291, 518, 687; 1995, c. 799; 1998, c. 749; 1999, cc. 945, 987; 2000, c. 792.

§ 46.2-362. Appeals.

An appeal to the circuit court may be taken from any final action or order of the general district court under former § 46.2-355 in the same manner and form as provided in §§ 16.1-106 and 16.1-107. An appeal to the Court of Appeals may be taken from any final action or order of a circuit court entered under this article in the same manner and form as such an appeal would be taken in any criminal case.

History.

1968, c. 476, § 46.1-387.10; 1984, c. 703; 1989, c. 727; 1996, c. 414; 1999, cc. 945, 987.

§ 46.2-363. Construction of article.

Nothing in this article shall be construed as amending, modifying, or repealing any existing law of Virginia or any existing ordinance of any political subdivision relating to the driving or licensing of motor vehicles, the licensing of persons to drive motor vehicles, or providing penalties for violations. Nor shall this article preclude the exercise of the regulatory powers of any division, agency, department, or political subdivision of the Commonwealth having the statutory power to regulate driving and licensing.

History.

1968, c. 476, § 46.1-387.11; 1989, c. 727.

ARTICLE 10. DRIVER RESPONSIBILITIES, GENERALLY.

§ 46.2-364. Definitions.

For the purposes of this chapter, unless a different meaning is clearly required by the context:

"Conviction" means conviction on a plea of guilty or the determination of guilt by a jury or by a court though no sentence has been imposed or, if imposed, has been suspended and includes a forfeiture of bail or collateral deposited to secure appearance in court of the defendant unless the forfeiture has been vacated, in any case of a charge, the conviction of which requires or authorizes the Commissioner to suspend or revoke the license of the defendant;

"Insured" means the person in whose name a motor vehicle liability policy has been issued, as defined in this section, and any other person insured under its terms;

"Judgment" means any judgment for $350 or more arising out of (i) a civil action filed pursuant to § 15.2-1716 or (ii) a motor vehicle accident because of injury to or destruction of property, including loss of its use, or any judgment for damages, including damages for care and loss of services, because of bodily injury to or death of any person arising out of the ownership, use or operation of any motor vehicle, including any judgment for contribution between joint tort-feasors arising out of any motor vehicle accident which occurred within the Commonwealth, except a judgment rendered against the Commonwealth, which has become final by expiration without appeal in the time within which an appeal might be perfected or by final affirmance on appeal rendered by a court of competent jurisdiction of the Commonwealth or any other state or court of the United States or Canada or its provinces;

"Motor vehicle" means every vehicle which is self-propelled or designed for self-propulsion and every vehicle drawn by or designed to be drawn by a motor vehicle and includes every device in, on or by which any person or property is or can be transported or drawn on a highway, except devices moved by human or animal power and devices used exclusively on rails or tracks, and vehicles used in the Commonwealth but not required to be licensed by the Commonwealth;

"Motor vehicle liability policy" means an owner's or a driver's policy of liability insurance certified, as provided in this chapter, by an insurance carrier licensed to do business in the Commonwealth or by an insurance carrier not licensed to do business in the Commonwealth on compliance with the provisions of this chapter, as proof of financial responsibility.

History.
Code 1950, § 46-387; 1958, c. 541, § 46.1-389; 1989, c. 727; 1996, cc. 474, 489; 2002, c. 289; 2010, c. 343.

Motor Vehicles

§ 46.2-365. Plaintiff not prevented from relying upon other legal process.

This article shall not prevent the plaintiff in any action at law from relying upon any other process provided by law.

History.
Code 1950, § 46-389; 1958, c. 541, § 46.1-391; 1989, c. 727.

§ 46.2-366. Partial application to certain motor vehicles.

This chapter, except its provisions as to the requirements of making reports of motor vehicle accidents and as to the filing of proof of financial responsibility by a common carrier for its drivers, shall not apply to any motor vehicle:

1. Operated under a certificate of convenience and necessity issued by the State Corporation Commission, if public liability and property damage insurance for the protection of the public is required to be carried on it, or

2. Owned by the Commonwealth.

History.
Code 1950, § 46-390; 1958, c. 541, § 46.1-392; 1989, cc. 705, 727.

§ 46.2-367. Persons included within scope of chapter.

Persons who have, by any law of the Commonwealth, been required to file proof of financial responsibility are included within the scope of this chapter. Persons who have been convicted of violations of any law of the Commonwealth or law of any other state or county, city, or town ordinance of either or a federal law pertaining to the driver or driving of motor vehicles or of violations of any provisions of this title are also included.

History.
Code 1950, § 46-391; 1958, c. 541, § 46.1-393; 1989, c. 727.

§ 46.2-368. Certificate of self-insurance exempts from chapter.

A. This chapter, except §§ 46.2-371 through 46.2-373, shall not apply to any person who has registered in his name in the Commonwealth more than twenty motor vehicles, nor to any person operating more than twenty vehicles whether as owner or as lessee, if the person seeking exemption under this section obtains from the Commissioner a certificate of self-insurance as provided in subsection B of this section.

B. The Commissioner may, in his discretion and on the application of such a person, issue a certificate of self-insurance when he is reasonably satisfied (i) that the person has and will continue to have financial ability to respond to a judgment as provided in this chapter, obtained against the person, arising out of the ownership, maintenance, use, or operation of his motor vehicles and (ii) that the certificate provides for protection against the uninsured or underinsured motorist to the extent required by § 38.2-2206. However, protection against the uninsured or underinsured motorist required under this section shall not exceed the financial requirements of § 46.2-472 and shall be secondary coverage to any other valid and collectible insurance providing the same protection which is available to any person otherwise entitled to assert a claim to such protection by virtue of this section.

C. No holder of a certificate of self-insurance shall be liable to pay any judgment arising out of the use or operation of any motor vehicle covered by such certificate by a person who used or operated the vehicle without the permission of the owner of such vehicle; nor shall any holder of a certificate of self-insurance be liable to pay any judgment arising out of the use or operation of any motor vehicle covered by such certificate by a permissive user of such vehicle, where the permissive user has prejudicially failed to cooperate in the defense of the claim which resulted in the judgment. This subsection shall only apply to a holder of a certificate of self-insurance who has provided notice of its intention to rely on the provisions of this subsection as set forth in § 38.2-2226.

D. On due notice and hearing, the Commissioner may, in his discretion and on reasonable grounds, cancel a certificate of self-insurance.

History.

Code 1950, § 46-393; 1958, c. 541, § 46.1-395; 1972, c. 463; 1989, c. 727; 1991, c. 374; 1995, c. 85; 1997, c. 553.

§ 46.2-369. Commissioner to administer and enforce chapter; regulations; summoning witnesses and taking testimony.

The Commissioner shall administer and enforce the provisions of this chapter and he may adopt regulations for its administration. He may issue subpoenas for witnesses to attend, administer oaths, and take testimony in, the hearings provided in this chapter for the purpose of finding whether driver's licenses, license plates, or registrations should be suspended or revoked. If any person fails or refuses to obey the subpoena, or to give testimony, the Commissioner shall notify the circuit or district court of the county or city in which the hearing is or was to have been held. On receipt of the notice, the court shall, by appropriate process, compel his attendance or testimony or both, to the same extent that it could be required in a proceeding in the court.

History.

Code 1950, § 46-394; 1952, c. 670; 1958, c. 541, § 46.1-396; 1984, c. 780; 1989, c. 727.

§ 46.2-370. Revoked driver's licenses, special identification cards, certificates of title, license plates, registration cards to be returned; Commissioner may take possession of them.

A. Any person whose driver's license, special identification card, certificate of title, registration card, or license plates have been suspended, cancelled, or revoked as provided in this title or in Title 18.2 and have not been reinstated, shall immediately return every such license, unless it has been surrendered to the court as required by law, special identification card, certificate of title, registration card, and set of license plates or decals held by him to the Commissioner.

B. The Commissioner may take possession of any driver's license, special identification card, certificate of title, registration card, or set of license plates or decals on their suspension, cancellation, or revocation under the provisions of this title or in Title 18.2 or may direct any law-enforcement officer to take possession of and return them to the office of the Commissioner. Whenever any person fails or refuses to surrender a driver's license, special identification card, certificate of title, registration card, license plates, or decals requiring a representative of the Department designated by the Commissioner to serve the order of suspension, cancellation, or revocation, or whenever the Department directs a sheriff to effect service of a decision, order, or notice pursuant to § 46.2-416, the person sought to be served shall, in addition to any other required statutory fees, pay a fee of ten dollars to partially defray the cost of administration incurred by the Department and the Commissioner. No such revoked, cancelled, or suspended license, special identification card, certificate of title, or registration items shall be reinstated before the ten-dollar fee is paid. All fees collected under the provisions of this section shall be paid by the Commissioner into the state treasury and shall be set aside as a special fund to be used to meet the expenses of the Department.

History.

Code 1950, § 46-395; 1958, cc. 322, 541, § 46.1-397; 1976, c. 156; 1981, c. 619; 1984, c. 780; 1987, c. 696; 1989, c. 727; 1992, c. 99.

ARTICLE 11.

ACCIDENT REPORTS.

§ 46.2-371. Driver to give immediate notice of certain accidents.

The driver of any vehicle involved in any accident resulting in injury to or death of any person, or some person acting for him, shall immediately give notice of the accident to a law-enforcement officer. A willful failure to make the report required in this section shall constitute a Class 4 misdemeanor.

History.

Code 1950, § 46-397; 1958, c. 541, § 46.1-399; 1989, c. 727.

§ 46.2-372. Driver to report certain accidents in writing; certification of financial responsibility to Department; supplemental reports; reports by witnesses.

A. Any person involved in an accident (i) resulting in injury to or death of any person or property damage, or (ii) when there is reason to believe a motor vehicle involved in the accident was uninsured at the time of the accident, may make a written report of it to the Commissioner, on a form prescribed by the Department.

B. If any accident report filed pursuant to the provisions of this article is alleged to be false or inaccurate, the Commissioner shall withhold any action under this section or imposition of any penalty and shall investigate and determine the true circumstances of the accident, including a determination of the identity of the parties involved.

C. For the purposes of this article the definitions provided in subsection B of § 38.2-2206 shall apply.

D. The Commissioner shall require the owner of a motor vehicle involved in any accident of which report is made pursuant to this section to provide information relating to certification of insurance or bond if there was in effect at the time of the accident with respect to the motor vehicle involved:

1. A standard provisions automobile liability policy in form approved by the State Corporation Commission and issued by an insurance carrier authorized to do business in the Commonwealth or, if the motor vehicle was not registered in the Commonwealth or was a motor vehicle which was registered elsewhere than in the Commonwealth at the effective date of the policy, or at its most recent renewal, an automobile liability policy acceptable to that Commission as substantially the equivalent of a standard provisions automobile liability policy; in either event, every automobile liability policy is subject to the limits provided in § 46.2-472.

2. Any other form of liability insurance policy issued by an insurance carrier authorized to do business in the Commonwealth or by a bond; provided that every such policy or bond mentioned herein is subject to limits set out in § 46.2-472.

E. The Commissioner shall forward the certification of insurance or bond to the insurance company or surety company, whichever is applicable, for verification as to whether or not the policy or bond certified was applicable to any liability that may arise out of the accident as to the named insured. A copy of the certification of insurance or bond shall be retained by the Commissioner and shall be disclosed pursuant to § 46.2-380.

History.

Code 1950, § 46-398; 1958, c. 541, § 46.1-400; 1966, c. 130; 1972, c. 442; 1974, c. 453; 1975, c. 553; 1978, c. 205; 1979, c. 228; 1982, c. 221; 1986, c. 639; 1989, c. 727.

§ 46.2-373. Report by law-enforcement officer investigating accident.

A. Every law-enforcement officer who in the course of duty investigates a motor vehicle accident resulting in injury to or death of any person or total property damage to an apparent extent of $1,500 or more, either at the time of and at the scene of the accident or thereafter and elsewhere, by interviewing participants or witnesses shall, within twenty-four hours after completing the investigation, forward a written report of the accident to the Department. The report shall include the name or names of the insurance carrier or of the insurance agent of the automobile liability policy on each vehicle involved in the accident.

B. Any report filed pursuant to subsection A of this section shall include information as to (i) the speed of each vehicle involved in the accident and (ii) the type of vehicles involved in all accidents between passenger vehicles and vehicles or combinations of vehicles used to transport property, and (iii) whether any trucks involved in such accidents were covered or uncovered.

C. The Department shall supply copies of accident reports received under this section to the Commissioner of Highways who shall exercise the authority granted to him under §§ 46.2-870 through 46.2-878 to reduce speed limits where accident frequency or severity or other factors may indicate the course of action to be warranted.

History.

Code 1950, § 46-399; 1958, c. 541, § 46.1-401; 1975, c. 553; 1986, c. 639; 1988, cc. 662, 897; 1989, c. 727; 1992, cc. 149, 413; 2009, c. 1.

§ 46.2-374. Department to prepare and supply forms for reports.

The Department shall prepare and, on request, supply to police departments, medical examiners or other officials exercising like functions, sheriffs, and other suitable agencies forms for accident reports and other reports required to be made to the Department, appropriate with respect to the persons required to make the reports and the purpose to be served. The forms for accident reports shall include suitable spaces for the name or names of the insurance carrier of the automobile liability policy of each vehicle involved in the accidents as required to be reported by § 46.2-373.

History.

Code 1950, § 46-401; 1958, c. 541, § 46.1-403; 1975, c. 553; 1986, c. 639; 1989, c. 727.

§ 46.2-375. Reports by medical examiners of deaths resulting from accidents.

Every person holding the office of medical examiner shall report to the Commissioner: (i) the death of a person in his jurisdiction as a result of a motor vehicle accident, immediately after learning of the death; (ii) on or before the tenth day of each month, all deaths resulting from motor vehicle accidents during the preceding calendar month. These reports shall be made in the form prescribed by the Commissioner.

History.
Code 1950, §§ 46-402, 46-404; 1958, c. 541, § 46.1-404; 1985, c. 10; 1989, c. 727.

§ 46.2-376. Report required of person in charge of garage or repair shop.

The person in charge of any garage or repair shop to which is brought any motor vehicle (i) that shows evidence of having been involved in a serious motor vehicle accident or (ii) with evidence of bloodstains shall report to the nearest police station or to the State Police, within twenty-four hours after the motor vehicle is received, giving the engine number, registration number and the name and address of the owner or operator of the vehicle if known. Reports required by this section shall be made upon forms furnished by the Superintendent of State Police.

History.
Code 1950, §§ 46-405, 46-406; 1958, c. 541, § 46.1-406; 1989, c. 727.

§ 46.2-377. Reports made by garages to be without prejudice and confidential; exceptions.

All accident reports made by garages pursuant to this article shall be without prejudice to the individual so reporting and shall be for the confidential use of the State Police, local law-enforcement agencies, or by agencies having use for the records for accident prevention purposes.

History.
Code 1950, § 46-407; 1958, c. 541, § 46.1-407; 1986, c. 639; 1989, c. 727.

§ 46.2-378. Extent to which reports may be used as evidence.

No report submitted pursuant to this article shall be used as evidence in any trial, civil or criminal, arising out of an accident, except that the Department shall furnish, on demand of any person who has or claims to have made such a report, or upon demand of any court, a certificate showing that a specified accident report has or has not been made to the Department, solely to prove compliance or noncompliance with the requirement that the report be made to the Department.

History.
Code 1950, § 46-408; 1958, c. 541, § 46.1-408; 1989, c. 727.

§ 46.2-379. Use of crash reports made by investigating officers.

All crash reports made by investigating officers shall be for the confidential use of the Department and of other state agencies for accident prevention purposes and shall not be used as evidence in any trial, civil or criminal, arising out of any accident. If otherwise authorized by law, the Department may disclose from the reports, on request of any person, the date, time, and location of the accident and the names and addresses of the drivers, the owners of the vehicles involved, the injured persons, the witnesses, and one investigating officer.

History.
Code 1950, § 46-409; 1952, c. 544; 1958, c. 541, § 46.1-409; 1986, c. 639; 1989, c. 727; 2014, cc. 77, 803.

§ 46.2-380. Reports made under certain sections open to inspection by certain persons; copies; maintenance of reports and photographs for three-year period.

A. Any report of an accident made pursuant to § 46.2-372, 46.2-373, 46.2-375, or 46.2-377 shall be maintained by the Department in either hard copy or electronic form for a period of at least 36 months from the date of the accident and shall be open to the inspection of any person involved or injured in the accident or as a result thereof, or his attorney or any authorized representative of any insurance carrier reasonably anticipating exposure to civil liability as a consequence of the accident or to which the person has applied for issuance or renewal of a policy of automobile insurance. The Commissioner shall on written request of the person or attorney or any authorized representative of any insurance carrier reasonably anticipating exposure to civil liability as a consequence of the accident or to which the person has applied for issuance or renewal of a policy of automobile insurance, furnish a copy of the report, in either hard copy or electronic form, at the expense of the person, attorney, or representative. Any such report shall also be open to inspection by the personal representative of any person injured or killed in the accident, including his guardian, conservator, executor, committee, next of kin as defined in § 54.1-2800, or administrator, or, if the person injured or killed is under 18 years of age, his parent or guardian. The Commissioner shall only be required to furnish under this section copies of reports required by the provisions of this article to be made directly to the Commissioner. The Commissioner may set a reasonable fee for furnishing a copy of any report, provide to whom payment shall be made, and establish a procedure for payment.

B. The Commissioner or Superintendent of State Police having a copy of any photograph taken by a law-enforcement officer relating to a nonfatal accident, shall maintain the negatives for such photographs in their records for at least 36 months from the date of the accident.

History.

Code 1950, § 46-410; 1956, c. 648; 1958, c. 541, § 46.1-410; 1975, c. 21; 1976, c. 40; 1978, c. 829; 1986, c. 639; 1989, cc. 302, 727; 1997, c. 801; 1998, c. 522; 2013, cc. 80, 104; 2015, c. 171.

§ 46.2-381. Accident reports required by county or municipal ordinance; copies.

Any county, city, or town may, by ordinance, require that the driver of a vehicle involved in an accident file with a designated department a report of the accident. These reports shall be for the confidential use of the department and subject to the provisions of this article. The county, city, or town may, by ordinance, require the designated department to make the reports, including the report of the law-enforcement officer, and including any photographs taken by law-enforcement officers, available for inspection by any person involved or injured in the accident or his attorney or any authorized representative of any insurance carrier reasonably anticipating exposure to civil liability as a consequence of the accident. The county, city, or town may, by ordinance, prescribe fees to be charged for copies of the reports and photographs and require the designated department to furnish copies of the reports and photographs, after payment of the prescribed fees, to any such person, attorney, or authorized representative.

History.

Code 1950, § 46-413; 1954, c. 393; 1956, c. 703; 1958, c. 541, § 46.1-411; 1962, c. 458; 1986, c. 639; 1989, c. 727.

§ 46.2-382. Courts to keep full records of certain cases.

Every general district court or circuit court or the clerk thereof shall keep a full record of every case in which:

1. A person is charged with (i) a violation of any law of the Commonwealth pertaining to the operator or operation of a motor vehicle; (ii) a violation of any ordinance of any county, city, or town pertaining to the operator or operation of any motor vehicles, except parking regulations; (iii) any theft of a motor vehicle or unauthorized use thereof or theft of any part attached to it; or (iv) a violation of § 18.2-36.2, subsection B of § 29.1-738, or § 29.1-738.02, 29.1-738.2, or 29.1-738.4;

2. A person is charged with manslaughter or any other felony in the commission of which a motor vehicle was used; or

3. There is rendered a judgment for damages, the rendering and nonpayment of which under the terms of this title require the Commissioner to suspend the driver's license and registration in the name of the judgment debtor.

History.

Code 1950, §§ 46-195, 46-414; 1952, c. 188; 1954, c. 168; 1958, c. 541, § 46.1-412; 1966, c. 533; 1984, c. 780; 1989, c. 727; 1998, c. 147; 2005, c. 376.

§ 46.2-382.1. Courts to make findings relating to commercial motor vehicles.

For the purpose of enforcing the Virginia Commercial Driver's License Act (§ 46.2-341.1 et seq.), in any case in which a person is charged with a violation of any law of the Commonwealth or of any ordinance of any county, city or town pertaining to the operator or operation of a motor vehicle, except parking violations, and the warrant or summons indicates that the motor vehicle so operated was a commercial motor vehicle as defined in the Virginia Commercial Driver's License Act, or that it was a commercial motor vehicle carrying hazardous materials as defined by the Virginia Commercial Driver's License Act, the court hearing such case shall make a finding, which shall be noted on the record, as to whether such vehicle was in fact a commercial motor vehicle and, if applicable, whether such vehicle was carrying hazardous materials.

If the offense charged is one in which operation of a commercial motor vehicle is an element of the offense, the conviction of the offense shall constitute the court's finding that the vehicle was a commercial motor vehicle, but a separate finding shall be made as to whether such vehicle was carrying hazardous materials, if applicable. If the offense charged is one in which operation of a commercial motor vehicle is not an element of the offense, then the court, after convicting the person charged, shall make a separate finding as to whether the vehicle was a commercial motor vehicle and, if applicable, whether it was carrying hazardous materials. The separate findings required by this section shall be noted on the conviction record, and the following procedures shall apply to such separate findings:

1. If the person charged prepays fines and costs pursuant to § 19.2-254.1, he shall be deemed to have admitted that such motor vehicle was a commercial motor vehicle and, if applicable, that it carried hazardous materials at the time of the violation, as indicated on the warrant or summons, and such admission or admissions shall be noted on the conviction record as the court's finding.

2. In all other cases, the Commonwealth shall have the burden of proving by a preponderance of the evidence that the vehicle was a commercial motor vehicle and, if applicable, that it carried hazardous materials.

History.

1989, c. 705, § 46.1-412.1.

§ 46.2-383. Courts to forward abstracts of records or furnish abstract data of conviction by electronic means in certain cases; records in office of Department; inspection; clerk's fee for reports.

A. In the event (i) a person is convicted of a charge described in subdivision 1 or 2 of § 46.2-382 or § 46.2-382.1 or (ii) a person fails or refuses to pay any fine, costs, forfeiture, restitution or penalty, or any installment thereof, imposed in any traffic case, or (iii) a person forfeits bail or collateral or other deposit to secure the defendant's appearance on the charges, unless the conviction has been set aside or the forfeiture vacated, or (iv) a court assigns a defendant to a driver education program or alcohol treatment or rehabilitation program, or both such programs, as authorized by § 18.2-271.1, or (v) compliance with the court's probation order is accepted by the court in lieu of a conviction under § 18.2-266 or the requirements specified in § 18.2-271 as provided in § 18.2-271.1, or (vi) there is rendered a judgment for damages against a person as described in § 46.2-382, every district court or clerk of a circuit court shall forward an abstract of the record to the Commissioner within 18 days after such conviction, failure or refusal to pay, forfeiture, assignment, or acceptance, and in the case of civil judgments, on the request of the judgment creditor or his attorney, within 30 days after judgment has become final. No abstract of the record in a district court shall be forwarded to the Commissioner unless the period allowed for an appeal has elapsed and no appeal has been perfected. On or after July 1, 2013, in the event that a conviction or adjudication has been nullified by separate order of the court, the clerk shall forward to the Commissioner an abstract of that record.

B. Abstract data of conviction may be furnished to the Commissioner by electronic means provided that the content of the abstract and the certification complies with the requirements of § 46.2-386. In cases where the abstract data is furnished by electronic means, the paper abstract shall not be required to be forwarded to the Commissioner. The Commissioner shall develop a method to ensure that all data is received accurately. The Commissioner, with the approval of the Governor, may destroy the record of any conviction, forfeiture, assignment, acceptance, or judgment, when three years has elapsed from the date thereof, except records of conviction or forfeiture on charges of reckless driving and speeding, which records may be destroyed when five years has elapsed from the date thereof, and further excepting those records that alone, or in connection with other records, will require suspension or revocation or disqualification of a license or registration under any applicable provisions of this title.

C. The records required to be kept may, in the discretion of the Commissioner, be kept by electronic media or by photographic processes and when so done the abstract of the record may be destroyed.

D. The Code section and description of an offense referenced in an abstract for any juvenile adjudication obtained from a district court or clerk of circuit court pursuant to subdivision A 9 of § 16.1-278.8, § 16.1-278.9, clause (iii) of subdivision 1 of § 46.2-382, or any other provision of law that does not involve an offense referenced in subsection A or an offense involving the operation of a motor vehicle shall be available only to the person himself, his parent or guardian, law-enforcement officers, attorneys for the Commonwealth, and courts.

History.

Code 1950, §§ 46-195, 46-414; 1952, c. 188; 1954, c. 168; 1958, c. 541, § 46.1-413; 1960, c. 179; 1966, c. 376; 1968, c. 335; 1972, c. 406; 1976, cc. 28, 336, 505; 1978, c. 134; 1979, c. 594; 1988, cc. 770, 852; 1989, cc. 705, 727; 2002, c. 258; 2013, c. 263; 2015, c. 478.

§ 46.2-384. Law-enforcement officers arresting drivers for certain offenses to request abstracts or transcripts of drivers' conviction records.

Every law-enforcement officer who has arrested any person for (i) driving while under the influence of intoxicants or drugs in violation of § 18.2-51.4 or § 18.2-266 or a parallel local ordinance, or § 46.2-341.24, (ii) reckless driving in violation of §§ 46.2-852 through 46.2-865 or a parallel local ordinance, (iii) failure to stop at the scene of an accident in violation of §§ 46.2-894 through 46.2-899 or a parallel local ordinance or (iv) driving without a license or while his license has been suspended or revoked in violation of § 18.2-51.4 or § 18.2-272, or §§ 46.2-300 through 46.2-302 or a parallel local ordinance or while he is disqualified in violation of § 46.2-341.21 of the Commercial Vehicle Driver's License Act (§ 46.2-341.1 et seq.), shall request from the Department an abstract or transcript of the person's driver's conviction record on file at the Department. The Department shall furnish the abstract or transcript to the attorney for the Commonwealth of the jurisdiction in which the case will be heard, to be held available for the court in which the person is to be tried for the violation or charge. However, the failure of the attorney for the Commonwealth to receive the abstract or transcript in any case shall not constitute grounds for the granting of a continuance of such case. In any such prosecution wherein a necessary element of the offense charged is that the defendant was previously convicted of the same or similar offense, a copy, certified as provided in § 46.2-215, of (1) the abstract of the relevant prior conviction, certified as provided in § 46.2-386, or (2) that portion of the transcript relating to the relevant prior conviction, shall be prima facie evidence of the facts stated therein with respect to the prior offense.

History.

1968, c. 335, § 46.1-413.1; 1976, c. 148; 1984, c. 780; 1988, c. 413; 1989, cc. 705, 727; 1992, c. 838; 1997, c. 691.

§ 46.2-385. Prosecuting attorneys to appear in certain cases.

If requested by the judge trying the case, attorneys for the Commonwealth and all city and town attorneys whose general duties include the prosecution of offenses which are reportable by the courts to the Department under § 46.2-383, shall appear on behalf of the Commonwealth or the locality in any contested criminal case wherein a resulting conviction is required to be reported to the Department under § 46.2-383.

The failure of the attorney to appear shall, in no case, affect the validity of any conviction.

History.

1968, c. 640, § 46.1-413.2; 1989, c. 727.

§ 46.2-386. Forms for and information to be contained in abstracts; certification.

Abstracts required by § 46.2-383 shall be made on forms prepared by or approved by the Department and the Department of State Police. They shall include all information as to the parties to the case. In the event the abstract relates to a person convicted or found not innocent of a charge described in subdivision 1 or 2 of § 46.2-382, it shall include the nature and date of the offense, the date of conviction or finding of not innocent, the plea, the judgment, the penalty or forfeiture as the case may be, and the driver's license number if any, the month, day and year of birth, the sex and the residence address or whereabouts of the defendant and shall indicate whether the defendant appeared and was represented by or waived counsel. Every such abstract shall be certified by the general district court or juvenile and domestic relations district court judge or clerk of the general district court or juvenile and domestic relations district court or clerk of a circuit court as a true abstract of the records of the court as it relates to the charge, judgment and penalty.

Abstracts transmitted to the Department by electronic means may be certified by machine imprint of the name of the general district court or juvenile and domestic relations district court judge or the clerk's name of the general district court or juvenile and domestic relations district court or the name of the clerk of the circuit court that furnished the record as a true abstract of the records of the court as it relates to the charge, judgment, and penalty.

History.

Code 1950, § 46-196; 1958, c. 541, § 46.1-414; 1968, c. 151; 1984, c. 780; 1986, c. 607; 1989, c. 727; 1992, c. 838.

§ 46.2-387. Penalty for failure to forward record of conviction or of judgment for damages.

Any person required to forward to the Commissioner a record of a conviction or of a judgment for damages as provided in this chapter who fails, refuses, or neglects so to do without reasonable cause shall be guilty of a Class 4 misdemeanor and may be suspended or removed from office or otherwise disciplined for dereliction of duty.

The Commissioner shall call every such failure to the attention of the person guilty of the dereliction and to the judge of the court of which he is an officer in cases of dereliction on the part of officers of courts and also to the appropriate attorney for the Commonwealth.

Discipline for dereliction of the duties provided by this chapter is cumulative to the other penalties prescribed and may be imposed by the court having jurisdiction over the official whose negligence is complained of.

History.

Code 1950, § 46-415; 1958, c. 541, § 46.1-416; 1989, c. 727.

§ 46.2-388. Uniform summons to be used for reportable motor vehicle law violations; citations.

A. The Attorney General, after consultation with the Committee on District Courts, the Superintendent of State Police and the Commissioner, shall approve a form for the summons to be issued in either an electronic or paper format and all revisions to the form to be used by all law-enforcement officers throughout the Commonwealth in cases of motor vehicle law violations reportable to the Department under the provisions of §§ 46.2-382 and 46.2-383 and for other offenses charged on a summons pursuant to § 19.2-74. The commencement and termination date for the use of the form and each revised version of the form shall be made by the Attorney General after consultation with the Committee on District Courts, the Superintendent of State Police and the Commissioner. The law-enforcement agency issuing the summons shall determine whether to use an electronic or paper format.

The form of the summons shall include multiple copies with the original to be used for court records and other copies in sufficient number to permit the use of one copy by the courts for purposes of filing abstracts of records with the Department as required by § 46.2-383 and shall be a form prepared by the Department within the meaning of § 46.2-386. The form of the summons shall also include appropriate space for use in cases of violation of either state laws or local ordinances.

B. A separate citation which has been approved in the manner prescribed in subsection A shall be used for violations of §§ 46.2-1122 through 46.2-1127 and 46.2-1130. The citation shall be directed to the owner, operator or other person responsible for the overweight violation, and shall advise him of:

1. The nature of the violation charged against him;

2. The amount of monetary fees, penalties, and damages that may be assessed for violations;

3. The requirement that he either pay the fees, penalties, and damages in full or deliver a notice of his intent to contest the charge to the Department;

4. The procedures and time limits for making the payments or contesting such charge, which shall include the trial date, which shall in no event be earlier than 60 days after the violation; and

5. The consequences of a failure to timely pay or contest the charge.

C. A separate citation that has been approved in the manner prescribed in subsection A shall be used for violations of § 46.2-613.1. The citation shall be directed to the owner, operator, or other person responsible for the violation and shall advise him of:

1. The nature of the violation charged against him;

2. The amount of monetary fees and penalties that may be assessed for violations;

3. The requirement that he either pay the fee and penalties in full or deliver a notice of his intent to contest the charge to the Department;

4. The procedures and time limits for making the payments or contesting such charge which shall include the trial date, which shall in no event be earlier than 60 days after the violation; and

5. The consequences of a failure to timely pay or contest the charge.

History.

1968, c. 712, § 46.1-416.1; 1977, cc. 81, 585; 1984, c. 24; 1986, c. 588; 1989, c. 727; 2005, c. 589; 2011, cc. 62, 73.

ARTICLE 12.

SUSPENSION AND REVOCATION OF LICENSES, GENERALLY; ADDITIONAL PENALTIES.

§ 46.2-389. Required revocation for one year upon conviction or finding of guilty of certain offenses; exceptions.

A. The Commissioner shall forthwith revoke, and not thereafter reissue for a period of time specified in subsection B, except as provided in § 18.2-271 or § 18.2-271.1, the driver's license of any resident or nonresident on receiving a record of his conviction or a record of his having been found guilty in the case of a juvenile of any of the following crimes, committed in violation of a state law or a valid county, city, or town ordinance or law of the United States, or a law of any other state, substantially paralleling and substantially conforming to a like state law and to all changes and amendments of it:

1. Voluntary or involuntary manslaughter resulting from the driving of a motor vehicle;

2. Violation of § 18.2-266 or § 18.2-272, or subsection A of § 46.2-341.24 or violation of a substantially similar local ordinance;

3. Perjury or the making of a false affidavit to the Department under this chapter or any other law of the Commonwealth requiring the registration of motor vehicles or regulating their operation on the highways;

4. The making of a false statement to the Department on any application for a driver's license;

5. Any crime punishable as a felony under the motor vehicle laws of the Commonwealth or any other felony in the commission of which a motor vehicle is used;

6. Failure to stop and disclose his identity at the scene of the accident, on the part of a driver of a motor vehicle involved in an accident resulting in the death of or injury to another person; or

7. Violation of § 18.2-36.1 or § 18.2-51.4.

B. Upon conviction of an offense set forth in subsection A, the person's driver's license shall be revoked for one year; however, for a violation of subdivision A 1 or A 7, the driver's license shall be revoked as provided in subsection B of § 46.2-391. However, in no such event shall the Commissioner reinstate the driver's license of any person convicted of a violation of § 18.2-266, or of a substantially similar valid local ordinance or law of another jurisdiction, until receipt of notification that such person has successfully completed an alcohol safety action program if such person was required by a court to do so unless the requirement for completion of the program has been waived by the court for good cause shown.

History.

Code 1950, § 46-416; 1958, cc. 496, 541, § 46.1-417; 1960, c. 364; 1966, c. 238; 1974, c. 453; 1976, cc. 612, 691; 1982, c. 301; 1984, c. 780; 1988, c. 860; 1989, cc. 705, 727; 1990, c. 949; 1992, cc. 109, 891; 1997, cc. 486, 691; 1999, cc. 945, 987; 2000, cc. 956, 959, 982, 985.

§ 46.2-390. Required suspension for conviction of theft or unauthorized use of a motor vehicle.

When any person is convicted, or found guilty in the case of a juvenile, of any theft of a motor vehicle or its unauthorized use, or the theft of any of its parts, whether the motor vehicle is used in the commission of a theft or not, then in addition to any penalties provided by law, the driver's license of the person shall be suspended by the court for a period of not less than sixty days nor more than six months. In case of conviction the court shall order the surrender of the license to the court where it shall be disposed of in accordance with § 46.2-398. If the conviction is a second or subsequent offense, the license shall be suspended at least sixty days and not more than one year, and the court shall transmit the license to the Department as provided by law. If the person has not obtained a license as required by this chapter, or is a nonresident, the court shall direct in the judgment of conviction that the person shall not drive any motor vehicle in the Commonwealth for a period to coincide with the judgment of the court. This section shall not apply in the event that the theft is one in which the revocation of the license of any person is required under the provisions of subdivision 5 of § 46.2-389. Sections 46.2-391.1 and 46.2-411 shall not apply to any person whose license is suspended under this section.

History.

1966, c. 533, § 46.1-417.1; 1984, c. 780; 1988, c. 860; 1989, c. 727; 1992, c. 109.

§ 46.2-390.1. Required revocation for conviction of drug offenses or deferral of proceedings.

A. Except as otherwise ordered pursuant to § 18.2-259.1, the Commissioner shall forthwith revoke, and not thereafter reissue for six months from the later of (i) the date of conviction or deferral of proceedings under § 18.2-251 or (ii) the next date of eligibility to be licensed, the driver's license, registration card, and license plates of any resident or nonresident on receiving notification of (i) his conviction, (ii) his having been found guilty in the case of a juvenile or (iii) the deferral of further proceedings against him under § 18.2-251 for any violation of any provisions of Article 1 (§ 18.2-247 et seq.) of Chapter 7 of Title 18.2, or of any state or federal law or valid county, city or town ordinance, or a law of any other state substantially similar to provisions of such Virginia laws. Such license revocation shall be in addition to and shall run consecutively with any other license suspension, revocation or forfeiture in effect against such person.

B. Any person whose license has been revoked pursuant to this section and § 18.2-259.1 shall be subject to the provisions of §§ 46.2-370 and 46.2-414 and shall be required to pay a reinstatement fee as provided in § 46.2-411 in order to have his license restored.

History.

1992, cc. 58, 833; 1993, c. 920; 1997, c. 486; 2001, c. 790.

§ 46.2-391. Revocation of license for multiple convictions of driving while intoxicated; exception; petition for restoration of privilege.

A. The Commissioner shall forthwith revoke and not thereafter reissue for three years the driver's license of any person on receiving a record of the conviction of any person who (i) is adjudged to be a second offender in violation of the provisions of subsection A of § 46.2-341.24 (driving a commercial motor vehicle under the influence of drugs or intoxicants), or § 18.2-266 (driving under the influence of drugs or intoxicants), if the subsequent violation occurred within 10 years of the prior violation, or (ii) is convicted of any two or more offenses of § 18.2-272 (driving while the driver's license has been forfeited for a conviction under § 18.2-266) if the second or subsequent violation occurred within 10 years of the prior offense. However, if the Commissioner has received a copy of a court order authorizing issuance of a restricted license as provided in subsection E of § 18.2-271.1, he shall proceed as provided in the order of the court. For the purposes of this subsection, an offense in violation of a valid local ordinance, or law of any other jurisdiction, which ordinance or law is substantially similar to any provision of Virginia law herein shall be considered an offense in violation of such provision of Virginia law. Additionally, in no event shall the Commissioner reinstate the driver's license of any person convicted of a violation of § 18.2-266, or of a substantially similar valid local ordinance or law of another jurisdiction, until receipt of notification that such person has successfully completed an alcohol safety action program if such person was required by court order to do so unless the requirement for completion of the program has been waived by the court for good cause shown. A conviction includes a finding of not innocent in the case of a juvenile.

B. The Commissioner shall forthwith revoke and not thereafter reissue the driver's license of any person after receiving a record of the conviction of any person (i) convicted of a violation of § 18.2-36.1 or 18.2-51.4 or a felony violation of § 18.2-266 or (ii) convicted of three offenses arising out of separate incidents or occurrences within a period of 10 years in violation of the provisions of subsection A of § 46.2-341.24 or 18.2-266, or a substantially similar ordinance or law of any other jurisdiction, or any combination of three such offenses. A conviction includes a finding of not innocent in the case of a juvenile.

C. Any person who has had his driver's license revoked in accordance with subsection B of this section may petition the circuit court of his residence, or, if a nonresident of Virginia, any circuit court:

1. For restoration of his privilege to drive a motor vehicle in the Commonwealth after the expiration of five years from the date of his last conviction. On such petition, and for good cause shown, the court may, in its discretion, restore to the person the privilege to drive a motor vehicle in the Commonwealth on condition that such person install an ignition interlock system in accordance with § 18.2-270.1 on all motor vehicles, as defined in § 46.2-100, owned by or registered to him, in whole or in part, for a period of at least six months, and upon whatever other conditions the court may prescribe, subject to the provisions of law relating to issuance of driver's licenses, if the court is satisfied from the evidence presented that: (i) at the time of his previous convictions, the petitioner was addicted to or psychologically dependent on the use of alcohol or other drugs; (ii) at the time of the hearing on the petition, he is no longer addicted to or psychologically dependent on the use of alcohol or other drugs; and (iii) the defendant does not constitute a threat to the safety and welfare of himself or others with regard to the driving of a motor vehicle. However,

prior to acting on the petition, the court shall order that an evaluation of the person, to include an assessment of his degree of alcohol abuse and the appropriate treatment therefor, if any, be conducted by a Virginia Alcohol Safety Action Program and recommendations therefrom be submitted to the court, and the court shall give the recommendations such weight as the court deems appropriate. The court may, in lieu of restoring the person's privilege to drive, authorize the issuance of a restricted license for a period not to exceed five years in accordance with the provisions of § 18.2-270.1 and subsection E of § 18.2-271.1. The court shall notify the Virginia Alcohol Safety Action Program which shall during the term of the restricted license monitor the person's compliance with the terms of the restrictions imposed by the court. Any violation of the restrictions shall be reported to the court, and the court may then modify the restrictions or revoke the license.

2. For a restricted license to authorize such person to drive a motor vehicle in the Commonwealth in the course of his employment and to drive a motor vehicle to and from his home to the place of his employment after the expiration of three years from the date of his last conviction. The court may order that a restricted license for such purposes be issued in accordance with the procedures of subsection E of § 18.2-271.1, if the court is satisfied from the evidence presented that (i) at the time of the previous convictions, the petitioner was addicted to or psychologically dependent on the use of alcohol or other drugs; (ii) at the time of the hearing on the petition, he is no longer addicted to or psychologically dependent on the use of alcohol or such other drugs; and (iii) the defendant does not constitute a threat to the safety and welfare of himself and others with regard to the driving of a motor vehicle. The court shall prohibit the person to whom a restricted license is issued from operating a motor vehicle that is not equipped with a functioning, certified ignition interlock system during all or any part of the term for which the restricted license is issued, in accordance with the provisions set forth in § 18.2-270.1. However, prior to acting on the petition, the court shall order that an evaluation of the person, to include an assessment of his degree of alcohol abuse and the appropriate treatment therefor, if any, be conducted by a Virginia Alcohol Safety Action Program and recommendations therefrom be submitted to the court, and the court shall give the recommendations such weight as the court deems appropriate. The Virginia Alcohol Safety Action Program shall during the term of the restricted license monitor the person's compliance with the terms of the restrictions imposed by the court. Any violation of the restrictions shall be reported to the court, and the court may then modify the restrictions or revoke the license.

The ignition interlock system installation requirement under subdivisions 1 and 2 of this subsection need only be satisfied once as to any single revocation under subsection B of this section for any person seeking restoration under subdivision 1 following the granting of a restricted license under subdivision 1 or 2.

D. Any person convicted of driving a motor vehicle or any self-propelled machinery or equipment (i) while his license is revoked pursuant to subsection A or B or (ii) in violation of the terms of a restricted license issued pursuant to subsection C shall, provided such revocation was based on at least one conviction for an offense committed after July 1, 1999, be punished as follows:

1. If such driving does not of itself endanger the life, limb, or property of another, such person shall be guilty of a Class 1 misdemeanor punishable by a mandatory minimum term of confinement in jail of 10 days except in cases wherein such operation is necessitated in situations of apparent extreme emergency that require such operation to save life or limb, the sentence, or any part thereof, may be suspended.

2. a. If such driving (i) of itself endangers the life, limb, or property of another or (ii) takes place while such person is in violation of §§ 18.2-36.1, 18.2-51.4, 18.2-266, subsection A of § 46.2-341.24, or a substantially similar law or ordinance of another jurisdiction, irrespective of whether the driving of itself endangers the life, limb or property of another and the person has been previously convicted of a violation of §§ 18.2-36.1, 18.2-51.4, 18.2-266, subsection A of § 46.2-341.24, or a substantially similar local ordinance, or law of another jurisdiction, such person shall be guilty of a felony punishable by confinement in a state correctional facility for not less than one year nor more than five years, one year of which shall be a mandatory minimum term of confinement or, in the discretion of the jury or the court trying the case without a jury, by mandatory minimum confinement in jail for a period of 12 months and no portion of such sentence shall be suspended or run concurrently with any other sentence.

b. However, in cases wherein such operation is necessitated in situations of apparent extreme emergency that require such operation to save life or limb, the sentence, or any part thereof, may be suspended.

3. If any such offense of driving is a second or subsequent violation, such person shall be punished as provided in subdivision 2 of this subsection, irrespective of whether the offense, of itself, endangers the life, limb, or property of another.

E. Notwithstanding the provisions of subdivisions 2 and 3 of subsection D, following conviction and prior to imposition of sentence with the consent of the defendant, the court may order the defendant to be evaluated for and to participate in the Boot Camp Incarceration Program pursuant to § 19.2-316.1, or the Detention Center Incarceration Program pursuant to § 19.2-316.2, or the Diversion Center Incarceration Program pursuant to § 19.2-316.3.

F. Any period of driver's license revocation imposed pursuant to this section shall not begin to expire until the person convicted has surrendered his license to the court or to the Department of Motor Vehicles.

G. Nothing in this section shall prohibit a person from operating any farm tractor on the highways when it is necessary to move the tractor from one tract of land used for agricultural purposes to another such tract of land when the distance between the tracts is no more than five miles.

H. Any person who operates a motor vehicle or any self-propelled machinery or equipment (i) while his license is revoked pursuant to subsection A or B, or (ii) in violation of the terms of a restricted license issued pursuant to subsection C, where the provisions of subsection D do not apply, shall be guilty of a violation of § 18.2-272.

History.
Code 1950, § 46-417; 1958, c. 541, § 46.1-421; 1960, c. 364; 1964, c. 194; 1968, c. 561; 1976, cc. 359, 612, 691; 1983, c. 504; 1984, cc. 658, 673, 780; 1987, c. 409; 1989, cc. 705, 727; 1990, c. 949; 1994, c. 573; 1995, c. 486; 1997, cc. 691, 706; 1999, cc. 945, 987; 2000, cc. 243, 956, 958, 959, 980, 982, 985; 2001, c. 739; 2004, cc. 461, 937, 951; 2013, cc. 415, 655; 2016, c. 230.

§ 46.2-391.01. Administrative enforcement of ignition interlock requirements.

If the court, as a condition of license restoration or as a condition of a restricted license under subsection C or D of § 18.2-271.1 or § 46.2-391, or when required by § 18.2-270.1, fails to prohibit an offender from operating a motor vehicle that is not equipped with a functioning, certified ignition interlock system, the Commissioner shall enforce the requirements relating to installation of such systems in accordance with the provisions of § 18.2-270.1.

History.
2001, c. 739; 2002, c. 811; 2014, c. 707; 2015, c. 729.

§ 46.2-391.1. Suspension of registration certificates and plates upon suspension or revocation of driver's license.

Whenever the Commissioner, under the authority of law of the Commonwealth, suspends or revokes the driver's license of any person upon receiving record of that person's conviction, or whenever the Commissioner is notified that a court has suspended a person's driving privilege pursuant to § 46.2-395, the Commissioner shall also suspend all of the registration certificates and license plates issued for any motor vehicles registered solely in the name of such person and shall not issue any registration certificate or license plate for any other vehicle that such person seeks to register solely in his name. Except for persons whose privileges have been suspended by a court pursuant to § 46.2-395, the Commissioner shall not suspend such registration certificates or license plates in the event such person has previously given or gives and thereafter maintains proof of his financial responsibility in the future, in the manner specified in this chapter, with respect to each and every motor vehicle owned and registered by such person. In this event it shall be lawful for said vehicle or vehicles to be operated during this period of suspension by any duly licensed driver when so authorized by the owner.

History.
1992, c. 109; 1994, cc. 841, 945.

§ 46.2-391.2. Administrative suspension of license or privilege to operate a motor vehicle.

A. If a breath test is taken pursuant to § 18.2-268.2 or any similar ordinance and (i) the results show a blood alcohol content of 0.08 percent or more by weight by volume or 0.08 grams or more per 210 liters of breath, or (ii) the results, for persons under 21 years of age, show a blood alcohol concentration of 0.02 percent or more by weight by volume or 0.02 grams or more per 210 liters of breath or (iii) the person refuses to submit to the breath or blood test in violation of § 18.2-268.3 or any similar ordinance, and upon issuance of a petition or summons, or upon issuance of a warrant by the magistrate, for a violation of § 18.2-51.4, 18.2-266, or 18.2-266.1, or any similar ordinance, or upon the issuance of a warrant or summons by the magistrate or by the arresting officer at a medical facility for a violation of § 18.2-268.3, or any similar ordinance, the person's license shall be suspended immediately or in the case of (i) an unlicensed person, (ii) a person whose license is otherwise suspended or revoked, or (iii) a person whose driver's license is from a jurisdiction other than the Commonwealth, such person's privilege to operate a motor vehicle in the Commonwealth shall be suspended immediately. The period of suspension of the person's license or privilege to drive shall be seven days, unless the petition, summons or warrant issued charges the person with a second or subsequent offense. If the person is charged with a second offense the suspension shall be for 60 days. If not already expired, the period of suspension shall expire on the day and time of trial of the offense charged on the petition, summons or warrant, except that it shall not so expire during the first seven days of the suspension. If the person is charged with a third or subsequent offense, the suspension shall be until the day and time of trial of the offense charged on the petition, summons or warrant.

A law-enforcement officer, acting on behalf of the Commonwealth, shall serve a notice of suspension personally on the arrested person. When notice is served, the arresting officer shall promptly take possession of any driver's license held by the person and issued by the Commonwealth and shall promptly deliver it to the magistrate. Any driver's license taken into possession under this section shall be forwarded promptly by the magistrate to the clerk of the general district court or, as appropriate, the court with jurisdiction over juveniles of the jurisdiction in which the arrest was made together with any petition, summons or warrant, the results of the breath test, if any, and the report required by subsection B. A copy of the notice of suspension shall be forwarded forthwith to both (a) the general district court or, as appropriate, the court with jurisdiction over juveniles of the jurisdiction in which the arrest was made and (b) the Commissioner. Transmission of this information may be made by electronic means.

The clerk shall promptly return the suspended license to the person at the expiration of the suspension. Whenever a suspended license is to be returned under this section or § 46.2-391.4, the person may elect to have the license returned in person at the clerk's office or by mail to the address on the person's license or to such other address as he may request.

B. Promptly after arrest and service of the notice of suspension, the arresting officer shall forward to the magistrate a sworn report of the arrest that shall include (i) information which adequately identifies the person arrested and (ii) a statement setting forth the arresting officer's grounds for belief that the person violated § 18.2-51.4, 18.2-266, or 18.2-266.1, or a similar ordinance or refused to submit to a breath or blood test in violation of § 18.2-268.3 or a similar ordinance. The report required by this subsection shall be submitted on forms supplied by the Supreme Court.

C. Any person whose license or privilege to operate a motor vehicle has been suspended under subsection A may, during the period of the suspension, request the general district court or, as appropriate, the court with jurisdiction over juveniles of the jurisdiction in which the arrest was made to review that suspension. The court shall review the suspension within the same time period as the court hears an appeal from an order denying bail or fixing terms of bail or terms of recognizance, giving this matter precedence over all other matters on its docket. If the person proves to the court by a preponderance of the evidence that the arresting officer did not have probable cause for the arrest, that the magistrate did not have probable cause to issue the warrant, or that there was not probable cause for issuance of the petition, the court shall rescind the suspension, or that portion of it that exceeds seven days if there was not probable cause to charge a second offense or 60 days if there was not probable cause to charge a third or subsequent offense, and the clerk of the court shall forthwith, or at the expiration of the reduced suspension time, (i) return the suspended license, if any, to the person unless the license has been otherwise suspended or revoked, (ii) deliver to the person a notice that the suspension under § 46.2-391.2 has been rescinded or reduced, and (iii) forward to the Commissioner a copy of the notice that the suspension under § 46.2-391.2 has been rescinded or reduced. Otherwise, the court shall affirm the suspension. If the person requesting the review fails to appear without just cause, his right to review shall be waived.

The court's findings are without prejudice to the person contesting the suspension or to any other potential party as to any proceedings, civil or criminal, and shall not be evidence in any proceedings, civil or criminal.

D. If a person whose license or privilege to operate a motor vehicle is suspended under subsection A is convicted under § 18.2-36.1, 18.2-51.4, 18.2-266, or 18.2-266.1, or any similar ordinance during the suspension imposed by subsection A, and if the court decides to issue the person a restricted permit under subsection E of § 18.2-271.1, such restricted permit shall not be issued to the person before the expiration of the first seven days of the suspension imposed under subsection A.

History.
1994, cc. 359, 363; 1996, cc. 865, 1007; 1997, c. 691; 2001, c. 779; 2003, c. 605; 2004, cc. 937, 960; 2005, cc. 757, 840; 2014, c. 707.

§ 46.2-391.3. Content of notice of suspension.

A notice of suspension issued pursuant to § 46.2-391.2 shall clearly specify (i) the reason and statutory grounds for the suspension, (ii) the effective date and duration of the suspension, (iii) the right of the offender to request a review of that suspension by the appropriate district court of the jurisdiction in which the arrest was made, and (iv) the procedures for requesting such a review.

History.
1994, cc. 359, 363.

§ 46.2-391.4. When suspension to be rescinded.

Notwithstanding any other provision of § 46.2-391.2, a subsequent dismissal or acquittal of all the charges under §§ 18.2-36.1, 18.2-51.4, 18.2-266, and 18.2-268.3 or any similar ordinances, for the same offense for which a person's driver's license or privilege to operate a motor vehicle was suspended under § 46.2-391.2 shall result in the immediate rescission of the suspension. In any such case, the clerk of the court shall forthwith (i) return the suspended license, if any, to the person unless the license has been otherwise suspended or revoked, (ii) deliver to the person a notice that the suspension under § 46.2-391.2 has been rescinded and (iii) forward to the Commissioner a copy of the notice that the suspension under § 46.2-391.2 has been rescinded.

History.
1994, cc. 359, 363; 1997, c. 691; 2005, cc. 757, 840.

§ 46.2-391.5. Preparation and distribution of forms.

The Supreme Court shall develop policies and regulations pertaining to the notice of suspension under subsection A of § 46.2-391.2 and the notice that the suspension has been rescinded under subsection C of § 46.2-391.2 and § 46.2-391.4, and shall furnish appropriate forms to all law-enforcement officers and district courts, respectively.

History.

1994, cc. 359, 363.

§ 46.2-392. Suspension of license or issuance of a restricted license on conviction of reckless or aggressive driving; probationary conditions required; generally.

In addition to the penalties for reckless driving prescribed in § 46.2-868 and the penalties for aggressive driving prescribed in § 46.2-868.1, the court may suspend the driver's license issued to a person convicted of reckless driving or aggressive driving for a period of not less than 10 days nor more than six months and the court shall require the convicted person to surrender his license so suspended to the court where it will be disposed of in accordance with § 46.2-398.

Additionally, any person convicted of a reckless driving offense which the court has reason to believe is alcohol-related or drug-related may be required as a condition of probation or otherwise to enter into and successfully complete an alcohol safety action program. If the court suspends a person's driver's license for reckless driving and requires the person to enter into and successfully complete an alcohol safety action program, the Commissioner shall not reinstate the driver's license of the person until receipt of certification that the person has enrolled in an alcohol safety action program.

If a person so convicted has not obtained the license required by this chapter, or is a nonresident, the court may direct in the judgment of conviction that he shall not, for a period of not less than 10 days or more than six months as may be prescribed in the judgment, drive any motor vehicle in the Commonwealth. The court or the clerk of court shall transmit the license to the Commissioner along with the report of the conviction required to be sent to the Department.

The court may, in its discretion and for good cause shown, provide that such person be issued a restricted permit to operate a motor vehicle during the period of suspension for any of the purposes set forth in subsection E of § 18.2-271.1. The court shall order the surrender of such person's license to operate a motor vehicle to be disposed of in accordance with the provisions of § 46.2-398 and shall forward to the Commissioner a copy of its order entered pursuant to this subsection, which shall specifically enumerate the restrictions imposed and contain such information regarding the person to whom such a permit is issued as is reasonably necessary to identify such person. The court shall also provide a copy of its order to the person who may operate a motor vehicle on the order until receipt from the Commissioner of a restricted license. A copy of such order and, after receipt thereof, the restricted license shall be carried at all times while operating a motor vehicle. Any person who operates a motor vehicle in violation of any restrictions imposed pursuant to this section shall be punished as provided in subsection C of § 46.2-301. No restricted license issued pursuant to this section shall permit any person to operate a commercial motor vehicle as defined in the Virginia Commercial Driver's License Act (§ 46.2-341.1 et seq.).

History.

Code 1950, § 46-210; 1950, p. 691; 1952, Ex. Sess., c. 16; 1958, c. 541, § 46.1-422; 1981, c. 237; 1989, c. 727; 1996, c. 615; 2000, c. 342; 2001, cc. 645, 779; 2004, c. 361; 2007, c. 432.

§ 46.2-393. Suspension of license on conviction of certain reckless offenses; restricted licenses.

A. When any person is convicted of reckless driving as provided in §§ 46.2-853 through 46.2-864, in addition to any penalties provided by law, the driver's license of the person may be suspended by the court for a period of not less than 60 days nor more than six months. In case of conviction the court shall order the surrender of the license to the court where it shall be disposed of in accordance with the provisions of § 46.2-398. If the person so convicted has not obtained a license required by this chapter or is a nonresident, the court shall direct in the judgment of conviction that the person shall not drive any motor vehicle in the Commonwealth for a period of not less than 60 days nor more than six months.

B. The court may, in its discretion and for good cause shown, provide that such person be issued a restricted permit to operate a motor vehicle during the period of suspension for any of the purposes set forth in subsection E of § 18.2-271.1. The court shall forward to the Commissioner a copy of its order entered pursuant to this section, which shall specifically enumerate the restrictions imposed and contain such information regarding the person to whom such a permit is issued as is reasonably necessary to identify such person. The court shall also provide a copy of its order to the person who may operate a motor vehicle on the order until receipt from the Commissioner of a restricted license. A copy of such order and, after receipt thereof, the restricted license shall be carried at all times while operating a motor vehicle. Any person who operates a motor vehicle in violation of any restrictions imposed pursuant to this section shall be punished as provided in subsection C of § 46.2-301. No restricted license issued pursuant to this section shall permit any person to operate a commercial motor vehicle as defined in the Virginia Commercial Driver's License Act (§ 46.2-341.1 et seq.).

History.

Code 1950, § 46-209.1; 1954, c. 401; 1958, c. 541, § 46.1-423; 1960, c. 200; 1966, c. 694; 1974, c. 453; 1984, c. 780; 1989, c. 727; 2004, c. 115; 2005, c. 152.

§ 46.2-394. Revocation of license for fourth conviction of certain offenses.

If any person is convicted four times of a violation of §§ 46.2-865, 46.2-894, or § 46.2-895, or any substantially similar ordinance or law of any other jurisdiction, the court shall revoke his driver's license for five years.

History.

1962, c. 424, § 46.1-423.2; 1984, c. 780; 1989, c. 727; 1997, c. 691; 2000, cc. 956, 982.

§ 46.2-395. Suspension of license for failure or refusal to pay fines or costs.

A. Any person, whether licensed by Virginia or not, who drives a motor vehicle on the highways in the Commonwealth shall thereby, as a condition of such driving, consent to pay all lawful fines, court costs, forfeitures, restitution, and penalties assessed against him for violations of the laws of the Commonwealth; of any county, city, or town; or of the United States. For the purpose of this section, such fines and costs shall be deemed to include any fee assessed by the court under the provisions of § 18.2-271.1 for entry by a person convicted of a violation of § 18.2-51.4 or 18.2-266 into an alcohol safety action program.

B. In addition to any penalty provided by law and subject to the limitations on collection under §§ 19.2-340 and 19.2-341, when any person is convicted of any violation of the law of the Commonwealth or of the United States or of any valid local ordinance and fails or refuses to provide for immediate payment in full of any fine, costs, forfeitures, restitution, or penalty lawfully assessed against him, or fails to make deferred payments or installment payments as ordered by the court, the court shall forthwith suspend the person's privilege to drive a motor vehicle on the highways in the Commonwealth. The driver's license of the person shall continue suspended until the fine, costs, forfeiture, restitution, or penalty has been paid in full. However, if the defendant, after having his license suspended, pays the reinstatement fee to the Department of Motor Vehicles and enters into an agreement under § 19.2-354 that is acceptable to the court to make deferred payments or installment payments of unpaid fines, costs, forfeitures, restitution, or penalties as ordered by the court, the defendant's driver's license shall thereby be restored. If the person has not obtained a license as provided in this chapter, or is a nonresident, the court may direct in the judgment of conviction that the person shall not drive any motor vehicle in Virginia for a period to coincide with the nonpayment of the amounts due.

C. Before transmitting to the Commissioner a record of the person's failure or refusal to pay all or part of any fine, costs, forfeiture, restitution, or penalty or a failure to comply with an order issued pursuant to § 19.2-354, the clerk of the court that convicted the person shall provide or cause to be sent to the person written notice of the suspension of his license or privilege to drive a motor vehicle in Virginia, effective 30 days from the date of conviction, if the fine, costs, forfeiture, restitution, or penalty is not paid prior to the effective date of the suspension as stated on the notice. Notice shall be provided to the person at the time of trial or shall be mailed by first-class mail to the address certified on the summons or bail recognizance document as the person's current mailing address, or to such mailing address as the person has subsequently provided to the court as a change of address. If so mailed on the date of conviction or within five business days thereof, or if delivered to the person at the time of trial, such notice shall be adequate notice of the license suspension and of the person's ability to avoid suspension by paying the fine, costs, forfeiture, restitution, or penalty prior to the effective date. No other notice shall be required to make the suspension effective. A record of the person's failure or refusal and of the license suspension shall be sent to the Commissioner if the fine, costs, forfeiture, restitution, or penalty remains unpaid on the effective date of the suspension specified in the notice or on the failure to make a scheduled payment.

C1. Whenever a person provides for payment of a fine, costs, forfeiture, restitution or penalty other than by cash and such provision for payment fails, the clerk of the court that convicted the person shall cause to be sent to the person written notice of the failure and of the suspension of his license or privilege to drive in Virginia. The license suspension shall be effective 10 days from the date of the notice. The notice shall be effective notice of the suspension and of the person's ability to avoid the suspension by paying the full amount owed by cash, cashier's check or certified check prior to the effective date of the suspension if the notice is mailed by first class mail to the address provided by the person to the court pursuant to subsection C or § 19.2-354. Upon such a failure of payment and notice, the fine, costs, forfeiture, restitution or penalty due shall be paid only in cash, cashier's check or certified check, unless otherwise ordered by the court, for good cause shown.

D. If the person pays the amounts assessed against him subsequent to the time the suspended license has been transmitted to the Department, and his license is not under suspension or revocation for any other lawful reason, except pursuant to this section, then the Commissioner shall return the license to the person on presentation of the official report of the court evidencing the payment of the fine, costs, forfeiture, restitution, or penalty.

E. Any person otherwise eligible for a restricted license may petition each court that suspended his license pursuant to this section for authorization for a restricted license. A court may, upon written verification of employment and for good cause shown, authorize the Department of Motor Vehicles to issue a restricted license to operate a motor vehicle for any of the purposes set forth in subsection E of § 18.2-271.1. No restricted license may be issued unless each court which suspended the person's license pursuant to this section provides authorization for a restricted license. Such restricted license shall not be issued for more than a six-month period. No restricted license issued pursuant to this subsection shall permit a person to operate a commercial motor vehicle as defined in the Commercial Driver's License Act (§ 46.2-341.1 et seq.).

The court shall forward to the Commissioner a copy of its authorization entered pursuant to this section, which shall specifically enumerate the restrictions imposed and contain such information regarding the person to whom such a license is issued as is reasonably necessary to identify the person. The court shall also provide a copy of its authorization to the person, who may not operate a motor vehicle until receipt from the Commissioner of a restricted license. A copy of the restricted license issued by the Commissioner shall be carried at all times while operating a motor vehicle. Any person who operates a motor vehicle in violation of any restrictions imposed pursuant to this section shall be punished as provided in subsection C of § 46.2-301.

History.

1971, Ex. Sess., c. 249, § 46.1-423.3; 1975, c. 134; 1977, c. 585; 1982, c. 673; 1983, c. 279; 1984, c. 780; 1988, cc. 770, 852; 1989, cc. 444, 727; 1992, c. 891; 1993, c. 24; 1994, cc. 841, 945; 1997, c. 691; 1998, c. 831; 2000, cc. 956, 982; 2001, cc. 278, 414; 2002, c. 246; 2003, c. 218; 2007, c. 327; 2008, c. 861; 2012, c. 615; 2016, c. 282.

§ 46.2-396. Suspension of license for reckless driving resulting in death of any person.

When any person is convicted of reckless driving as provided for in §§ 46.2-853 through 46.2-864 and the reckless driving was the cause of the death of any person, then in addition to any other penalties provided by law, the driver's license of the person may be suspended by the court for no more than twelve months. In case of conviction the court may order the surrender of the license to the court where it shall be disposed of in accordance with the provisions of § 46.2-398. If the person so convicted has not obtained a license required by this chapter or is a nonresident, the court may direct in the judgment of conviction that the person shall not drive any motor vehicle in the Commonwealth for a period not to exceed twelve months. The fact of the suspension shall not be admissible as evidence in any related civil proceeding.

History.

1976, c. 320, § 46.1-423.4; 1984, c. 780; 1989, c. 727.

§ 46.2-396.1. Conviction of serious driving offense.

Upon the conviction of a traffic offense that causes the death of any person and which (i) the Commissioner has designated a serious traffic offense, a relatively serious traffic offense, or a traffic offense of a less serious nature under § 46.2-492 or (ii) constitutes any criminal offense in this title, the court may suspend the driver's license of the person convicted for not more than twelve months, in addition to any other penalties provided by law and may order the surrender of his license to the court to be disposed of in accordance with § 46.2-398. In those cases where the court determines it is appropriate, the court may provide that any individual whose license is suspended pursuant to this section be issued a restricted license to operate a motor vehicle for any of the purposes set forth in subsection E of § 18.2-271.1 during the term of suspension. If the convicted driver does not have a driver's license, as defined in § 46.2-100, or is a nonresident, the court may order the driver not to drive any motor vehicle in the Commonwealth for not more than twelve months.

History.

2002, c. 849.

§ 46.2-397. Suspension of license for certain violations while transporting explosives, inflammable gas or liquid.

When the driver of any motor vehicle is convicted of any violation of §§ 46.2-816, 46.2-820 through 46.2-823, 46.2-825, 46.2-826 or §§ 46.2-852 through 46.2-864, or of any of the applicable speed limits prescribed in §§ 46.2-870 through 46.2-878 and the violation was committed while driving a motor vehicle, tractor truck, trailer, or semitrailer, transporting explosives or any inflammable gas or liquid, in addition to any penalty imposed, the court may suspend the driver's license of the convicted person for a period of ninety days from the date of conviction.

History.

Code 1950, § 46-197.2; 1954, c. 377; 1958, c. 541, § 46.1-424; 1984, c. 780; 1989, c. 727.

§ 46.2-398. Disposition of surrendered licenses on revocation or suspension.

In any case in which the accused is convicted of an offense, on the conviction of which the law requires or permits revocation or suspension of the driver's license of the person so convicted, the court shall order the surrender of such license, which shall remain in the custody of the court during the period of revocation or suspension if the period does not exceed 30 days.

If the revocation or suspension period exceeds 30 days, and the conviction was obtained in a court not of record, the license shall remain in the custody of that court (i) until the time allowed by law for an appeal to the circuit court has elapsed, when it shall be forwarded to the Commissioner, or (ii) until an appeal to the circuit court is noted, at which time it shall be returned to the accused.

If the revocation or suspension period exceeds 30 days, and the conviction was obtained in the circuit court, the circuit court shall forward the license to the Commissioner forthwith upon the conviction.

For any revocation or suspension of a privilege to drive in Virginia of a person who does not have a Virginia driver's license but who does have a valid driver's license from another jurisdiction, the court shall not order the physical surrender of such license.

History.
Code 1950, § 46-195.1; 1952, c. 66; 1958, c. 541, § 46.1-425; 1973, c. 164; 1977, c. 585; 1982, c. 673; 1984, c. 780; 1989, c. 727; 2005, c. 943; 2011, c. 271.

§ 46.2-398.1. Issuance of restricted driver's privilege to out-of-state licensees.

When the operator of any motor vehicle who is not licensed to drive in Virginia, but who has a valid driver's license from another jurisdiction, is convicted in Virginia of any violation for which license suspension and issuance of a restricted license to a Virginia driver is authorized, the court may issue him a restricted driving privilege in Virginia upon the same conditions as if the person held a valid Virginia license. The court order, and any writing or communication setting forth the person's restricted privilege, shall include clear language indicating that the person is not a licensed Virginia driver.

History.
2010, c. 493.

§ 46.2-399. Revocation of license for improper use or failure to pay certain taxes.

The Department shall revoke a driver's license whenever the person to whom the license has been issued makes or permits to be made an unlawful use of it or permits the use of it by a person not entitled to it or fails or refuses to pay within the time prescribed by law, any lawful taxes due the Commonwealth imposed under Chapter 27 of Title 58.1.

History.
Code 1950, § 46-379; 1958, c. 541, § 46.1-426; 1984, c. 780; 1989, c. 727.

§ 46.2-400. Suspension of license of person incompetent because of mental illness, intellectual disability, alcoholism, or drug addiction; return of license; duty of clerk of court.

The Commissioner, on receipt of notice that any person has been legally adjudged to be incapacitated in accordance with Article 1 (§ 64.2-2000 et seq.) of Chapter 20 of Title 64.2 or that a person discharged from a facility operated or licensed by the Department of Behavioral Health and Developmental Services is, in the opinion of the authorities of the facility, not competent because of mental illness, intellectual disability, alcoholism, or drug addiction to drive a motor vehicle with safety to persons or property, shall forthwith suspend his license; but he shall not suspend the license if the person has been adjudged competent by judicial order or decree.

In any case in which the person's license has been suspended prior to his discharge it shall not be returned to him unless the Commissioner is satisfied, after an examination such as is required of applicants by § 46.2-325, that the person is competent to drive a motor vehicle with safety to persons and property.

The clerk of the court in which the adjudication is made shall forthwith send a certified copy or abstract of such adjudication to the Commissioner.

History.
Code 1950, § 46-418; 1950, p. 949; 1954, c. 213; 1958, cc. 154, 541, § 46.1-427; 1964, c. 230; 1987, c. 413; 1988, c. 78; 1989, c. 727; 1997, c. 921; 2009, cc. 813, 840; 2012, cc. 476, 507.

§ 46.2-401. Reports to Commissioner of discharge of individuals from state facilities.

Whenever practicable, at least 10 days prior to the time when any individual is to be discharged from any facility operated or licensed by the Department of Behavioral Health and Developmental Services, if the mental condition of the individual is, because of mental illness, intellectual disability, alcoholism, or drug addiction, in the judgment of the director or chief medical officer of the facility such as to prevent him from being competent to drive a motor vehicle with safety to persons and property, the director or chief medical officer shall forthwith report to the Commissioner, in sufficient detail for accurate identification, the date of discharge of the individual, together with a statement concerning his ability to drive a motor vehicle.

History.
Code 1950, § 46-419; 1954, c. 293; 1958, c. 541, § 46.1-429; 1964,

c. 230; 1987, c. 413; 1989, c. 727; 2009, cc. 813, 840; 2012, cc. 476, 507.

§ 46.2-402. When Commissioner may suspend or revoke license for not more than one year after hearing.

A. The Commissioner may, after due hearing, after giving not less than five days' written notice by registered letter to the most recent address of the driver on file at the Department, suspend or revoke for not more than one year and not thereafter reissue during the period of suspension or revocation the Virginia driver's license issued to any person whenever it is satisfactorily proved at the hearing conducted by the Commissioner or other personnel of the Department designated by him, that the licensee under charges:

1. Has, by reckless or unlawful operation of a motor vehicle, caused or contributed to an accident resulting in death or injury to any other person or in serious property damage,
2. Is incompetent to drive a motor vehicle,
3. Suffers from mental or physical infirmities or disabilities rendering it unsafe for him to drive a motor vehicle on the highways,
4. Is habitually a reckless or negligent driver of a motor vehicle, or
5. Has committed a serious violation of the motor vehicle laws of this Commonwealth.

B. The Commissioner, in determining the propriety of suspending or revoking a license as provided in this section, may take into consideration facts and conditions antedating the issuance of the current license.

History.

Code 1950, § 46-420; 1958, c. 541, § 46.1-430; 1984, c. 780; 1989, c. 727; 1996, cc. 943, 994.

§ 46.2-403. Contents of notice of hearing.

A. The notice of a hearing when mailed to any person, as provided in § 46.2-402 shall contain:

1. A specific statement of the alleged offense or offenses or other grounds for suspension or revocation of the license, including the date, time and place thereof when applicable;
2. The date, time and place of the hearing;
3. The names and addresses of all known witnesses whose testimony is proposed to be taken at the hearing;
4. As to any record of conviction of any offense which is to be offered as evidence, the date of the conviction and the court in which the same was had.

B. If these requirements are complied with it shall be sufficient regardless of whether the licensee appeared and regardless of whether the notice was ever received.

History.

Code 1950, § 46-421; 1952, c. 544; 1958, c. 541, § 46.1-431; 1989, c. 727.

§ 46.2-404. Where and before whom hearing held.

The hearing shall be in the county or city where the licensee resides or in the county or city in which the licensee works or, with the consent of the licensee, in any other county or city to which the county or city of his residence is contiguous. The hearing shall be before the Commissioner or any of the personnel of the Department designated by him.

History.

Code 1950, § 46-422; 1958, c. 541, § 46.1-432; 1978, c. 563; 1980, c. 10; 1989, c. 727.

§ 46.2-405. How hearings to be conducted.

A. In any such hearing all relevant and material evidence shall be received, except that: (i) the rules relating to privileged communications and privileged topics shall be observed; (ii) hearsay evidence shall be received only according to the rules of evidence prevailing in courts of record; and (iii) secondary evidence of the contents of a document shall be received only if the original is not readily available.

B. All reports of inspectors and subordinates of the Department and other records and documents in the possession of the Department bearing on the case subject to the provisions of subsection A of this section shall be introduced at the hearing. Any certified copy of any conviction forwarded to the Commissioner under the provisions of § 46.2-383, shall be prima facie evidence of the conviction, and may be introduced in evidence.

C. Subject to the provisions of subsection A of this section, every party shall have the right to cross-examine adverse witnesses and any inspector or subordinate of the Department whose report is in evidence, and to submit rebuttal evidence.

D. The decision shall be based only on evidence received at the hearing and matters of which a court of record could take judicial notice.

History.

Code 1950, § 46-422.1; 1952, c. 544; 1958, c. 541, § 46.1-433; 1989, c. 727.

§ 46.2-406. Appointment and authority of hearing officers.

The Commissioner may appoint one or more persons to conduct the hearings provided for in this title. The hearing officers are hereby authorized to administer oaths, take acknowledgments and affidavits, take testimony and depositions, and perform other duties which are incidental to conducting the hearings.

History.

1958, c. 541, § 46.1-434; 1989, c. 727.

§ 46.2-407. Form and contents of decision; copies.

Any decision or order of the Commissioner to be valid must be reduced to writing and contain the explicit findings of fact and conclusions of law upon which the decision or order of the Commissioner is based. Certified copies of the decision or order shall be delivered to any party affected by it.

History.

Code 1950, § 46-422.2; 1952, c. 544; 1958, c. 541, § 46.1-435; 1989, c. 727.

§ 46.2-408. When Commissioner may suspend or revoke license for no more than five years.

On any reasonable ground appearing in the records of the Department, the Commissioner may, when he deems it necessary for the safety of the public on the highways in the Commonwealth and after notice as provided in § 46.2-403 and hearing as provided in §§ 46.2-404, 46.2-405, 46.2-406 and 46.2-407 suspend or revoke for no more than five years, and not reissue during the period of suspension or revocation, the driver's license of any person who is a violator of any of the provisions of this title punishable as felonies, misdemeanors, or traffic infractions and he may suspend or revoke for a like period, and not reissue during the period of suspension or revocation, any or all of his registration cards and license plates for any motor vehicle.

History.

Code 1950, § 46-423; 1952, c. 544; 1958, c. 541, § 46.1-436; 1974, c. 453; 1984, c. 780; 1989, c. 727.

§ 46.2-409. Certain abstracts of conviction to be prima facie evidence of conviction.

In any administrative hearing conducted by the Commissioner or his designee pursuant to this article, an abstract showing a conviction of the violation of any of the provisions of this title, submitted as provided by § 46.2-383 by the court in which the conviction was had, shall be prima facie evidence that the person named in the abstract was duly convicted of the violation, and the burden shall be on any person challenging the propriety of the conviction to show that the conviction was improper.

History.

1966, c. 183, § 46.1-436.1; 1989, c. 727.

§ 46.2-410. Appeals from order suspending or revoking license or registration.

Any person aggrieved by an order or act of the Commissioner requiring suspension or revocation of a license or registration under the provisions of this chapter is entitled to judicial review in accordance with the provisions of the Administrative Process Act (§ 2.2-4000 et seq.). No appeal shall lie in any case in which the suspension or revocation of the license or registration was mandatory except to determine the identity of the person concerned when the question of identity is in dispute.

From the final decision of the circuit court, either the person who petitioned the court for an appeal or the Commissioner shall have an appeal as of right to the Court of Appeals.

History.

Code 1950, § 46-424; 1952, c. 544; 1958, c. 541, § 46.1-437; 1960, c. 511; 1984, cc. 673, 703; 1986, c. 615; 1989, c. 727.

§ 46.2-410.1. Judicial review of revocation or suspension by Commissioner.

A. Notwithstanding the provisions of § 46.2-410, when the Commissioner orders a revocation or suspension of a person's driver's license under the provisions of this chapter, unless such revocation or suspension is required under § 46.2-390.1, the person so aggrieved may, in cases of manifest injustice, within sixty days of receipt of notice of the suspension or revocation, petition the circuit court of the jurisdiction wherein he resides for a hearing to review the Commissioner's order. Manifest injustice is defined as those instances where the Commissioner's order was the result of an error or was issued without authority or jurisdiction. The person shall provide notice of his petition to the attorney for the Commonwealth of that jurisdiction.

B. At the hearing on the petition, if the court finds that the Commissioner's order is manifestly unjust the court may, notwithstanding any other provision of law, order the Commissioner to modify the order or issue the person a restricted license in accordance with the provisions of § 18.2-271.1. For any action under this section, no appeal shall lie from the determination of the circuit court.

C. This section shall not apply to any disqualification of eligibility to operate a commercial motor vehicle imposed by the Commissioner pursuant to Article 6.1 (§ 46.2-341.1 et seq.) of this chapter.

History.

2001, cc. 739, 749; 2002, c. 811.

§ 46.2-411. Reinstatement of suspended or revoked license or other privilege to operate or register a motor vehicle; proof of financial responsibility; reinstatement fee.

A. The Commissioner may refuse, after a hearing if demanded, to issue to any person whose license has been suspended or revoked any new or renewal license, or to register any motor vehicle in the name of the person, whenever he deems or in case of a hearing finds it necessary for the safety of the public on the highways in the Commonwealth.

B. Before granting or restoring a license or registration to any person whose driver's license or other privilege to drive motor vehicles or privilege to register a motor vehicle has been revoked or suspended pursuant to § 46.2-389, 46.2-391, 46.2-391.1, or 46.2-417, the Commissioner shall require proof of financial responsibility in the future as provided in Article 15 (§ 46.2-435 et seq.), but no person shall be licensed who may not be licensed under the provisions of §§ 46.2-389 through 46.2-431.

C. Whenever the driver's license or registration cards, license plates and decals, or other privilege to drive or to register motor vehicles of any resident or nonresident person is suspended or revoked by the Commissioner or by a district court or circuit court pursuant to the provisions of Title 18.2 or this title, or any valid local ordinance, the order of suspension or revocation shall remain in effect and the driver's license, registration cards, license plates and decals, or other privilege to drive or register motor vehicles shall not be reinstated and no new driver's license, registration cards, license plates and decals, or other privilege to drive or register motor vehicles shall be issued or granted unless such person, in addition to complying with all other provisions of law, pays to the Commissioner a reinstatement fee of $30. The reinstatement fee shall be increased by $30 whenever such suspension or revocation results from conviction of involuntary manslaughter in violation of § 18.2-36.1; conviction of maiming resulting from driving while intoxicated in violation of § 18.2-51.4; conviction of driving while intoxicated in violation of § 18.2-266 or 46.2-341.24; conviction of driving after illegally consuming alcohol in violation of § 18.2-266.1 or failure to comply with court imposed conditions pursuant to subsection D of § 18.2-271.1; unreasonable refusal to submit to drug or alcohol testing in violation of § 18.2-268.2; conviction of driving while a license, permit or privilege to drive was suspended or revoked in violation of § 46.2-301 or 46.2-341.21; disqualification pursuant to § 46.2-341.20; violation of driver's license probation pursuant to § 46.2-499; failure to attend a driver improvement clinic pursuant to § 46.2-503 or habitual offender interventions pursuant to former § 46.2-351.1; conviction of eluding police in violation of § 46.2-817; conviction of hit and run in violation of § 46.2-894; conviction of reckless driving in violation of Article 7 (§ 46.2-852 et seq.) of Chapter 8 of Title 46.2 or a conviction, finding or adjudication under any similar local ordinance, federal law or law of any other state. Five dollars of the additional amount shall be retained by the Department as provided in this section and $25 shall be transferred to the Commonwealth Neurotrauma Initiative Trust Fund established pursuant to Article 12 (§ 51.5-178 et seq.) of Chapter 14 of Title 51.5. When three years have elapsed from the termination date of the order of suspension or revocation and the person has complied with all other provisions of law, the Commissioner may relieve him of paying the reinstatement fee.

D. No reinstatement fee shall be required when the suspension or revocation of license results from the person's suffering from mental or physical infirmities or disabilities from natural causes not related to the use of self-administered intoxicants or drugs. No reinstatement fee shall be collected from any person whose license is suspended by a court of competent jurisdiction for any reason, other than a cause for mandatory suspension as provided in this title, provided the court ordering the suspension is not required by § 46.2-398 to forward the license to the Department during the suspended period.

E. Except as otherwise provided in this section and § 18.2-271.1, reinstatement fees collected under the provisions of this section shall be paid by the Commissioner into the state treasury and shall be set aside as a special fund to be used to meet the expenses of the Department.

F. Before granting or restoring a license or registration to any person whose driver's license or other privilege to drive motor vehicles or privilege to register a motor vehicle has been revoked or suspended, the Commissioner shall collect from such person, in addition to all other fees provided for in this section, an additional fee of $40. The Commissioner shall pay all fees collected pursuant to this subsection into the Trauma Center Fund, created pursuant to § 18.2-270.01, for the purpose of defraying the costs of providing emergency medical care to victims of automobile accidents attributable to alcohol or drug use.

G. Whenever any person is required to pay a reinstatement fee pursuant to subsection C or pursuant to subsection E of § 18.2-271.1 and such person has more than one suspension or revocation on his record for which reinstatement is required, then such person shall be required to pay one reinstatement fee, the amount of which shall equal the full reinstatement fee attributable to the one of his revocations or suspensions that would trigger the highest reinstatement fee, plus an additional $5 fee for administrative costs associated with compliance for each additional suspension or revocation. Fees collected pursuant to this subsection shall be set aside as a special fund to be used to meet the expenses of the Department.

History.

Code 1950, § 46-425; 1958, c. 541, § 46.1-438; 1973, c. 396; 1980, c. 29; 1982, c. 671; 1984, c. 780; 1987, c. 696; 1988, c. 860; 1989, c. 727; 1992, c. 109; 1998, c. 703; 1999, cc. 945, 987; 2002, c. 60; 2005, c. 886; 2011, cc. 54, 71; 2012, cc. 803, 835.

§ 46.2-411.1. Reinstatement of driver's license suspended or revoked for a conviction of driving while intoxicated.

A. Before restoring a driver's license to any person (i) whose license to drive a motor vehicle has been suspended or revoked as a result of a conviction for driving while intoxicated in violation of § 18.2-266, or of any substantially similar valid local ordinance or law of another jurisdiction, or of subsection A of § 46.2-341.24 and (ii) who has been required by a court order to successfully complete an alcohol safety action program pursuant to § 18.2-271.1 because of that conviction, the Commissioner shall require written confirmation that the person has successfully completed such program unless the requirement for completion of the program has been waived by the court for good cause shown.

B. Any person who drives a motor vehicle in the Commonwealth after the period of license suspension has expired and after all requirements for reinstatement have been satisfied except for successful completion of such program shall be guilty of a violation of § 46.2-300.

History.

2000, cc. 959, 985; 2001, cc. 133, 160.

§ 46.2-412. Time suspension or revocation.

Every suspension or revocation shall remain in effect and the Commissioner shall not issue any new or renewal license or register in his name any motor vehicle, until permitted under the provisions of this chapter. When three years shall have elapsed from the date of the termination of the revocation provided by § 46.2-389 or § 46.2-391, or in the case of a suspension pursuant to the provisions of § 46.2-417, when three years has elapsed from the date of satisfaction of the judgment or judgments, the person may be relieved of giving proof of his financial responsibility in the future, provided he is not required to furnish or maintain proof of financial responsibility under any other provision of this chapter. The requirement of this section for giving and maintaining proof of financial responsibility shall not, however, apply in the case of a person whose license has been suspended under § 46.2-400.

History.

Code 1950, § 46-426; 1958, cc. 154, 541, § 46.1-439; 1966, c. 377; 1989, c. 727.

§ 46.2-413. Effect of reversal of conviction.

Reversal on appeal of any conviction because of which conviction any license or registration has been suspended or revoked pursuant to the provisions of this chapter shall entitle the holder to the restoration of his license or registration forthwith without proof of financial responsibility.

History.

Code 1950, § 46-427; 1958, c. 541, § 46.1-440; 1989, c. 727.

§ 46.2-414. Commencement of periods for suspension or revocation of licenses, registration cards, or license plates.

Wherever it is provided in this title that the driver's license, registration cards, or license plates of any person be suspended or revoked for a period of time on conviction of certain offenses, or after a hearing before the Commissioner as provided by law, the period shall be counted from the date the conviction becomes final or after the order of the Commissioner, as a result of the hearing, becomes final. However, the provisions of this section shall not apply in any case where the person whose license is subject to suspension or revocation gives a false name or otherwise conceals his identity.

History.

Code 1950, § 46-427.1; 1954, c. 222; 1958, c. 541, § 46.1-441; 1984, c. 780; 1989, c. 727; 2005, c. 565.

§ 46.2-415. United States magistrates and judges of district courts authorized to revoke or suspend driver's license under certain conditions.

When any person is found guilty of a violation of any traffic regulation by a United States magistrate or a judge of a district court of the United States, which violation occurred on a federal reservation, and, for which, if the violation had occurred on the highways in the Commonwealth, revocation or suspension of the person's driver's license would be mandatory or discretionary with a court of the Commonwealth, the magistrate or judge is authorized to revoke or suspend the person's driver's license, provided it is forwarded to the Commissioner as is provided by law as to courts of the Commonwealth.

History.

1966, c. 591, § 46.1-441.1; 1976, c. 62; 1984, c. 780; 1985, c. 90; 1989, c. 727.

§ 46.2-416. Notice of suspension or revocation of license.

A. Whenever it is provided in this title that a driver's license may or shall be suspended or revoked either by the Commissioner or by a court, notice of the suspension or revocation or any certified copy of the decision or order of the Commissioner may be sent by the Department by certified mail to the driver at the most recent address of the driver on file at the Department. If the driver has previously been notified by mail or in person of the suspension or revocation or of an impending suspension for failure to pay fines and costs pursuant to § 46.2-395, whether notice is given by the court or law-enforcement officials as provided by law, and the Department has been notified by the court that notice was so given and the fines and costs were not paid within 30 days, no notice of suspension shall be sent by the Department to the driver. If the certificate of the Commissioner or someone designated by him for that purpose shows that the notice or copy has been so sent or provided, it shall be deemed prima facie evidence that the notice or copy has been sent and delivered or otherwise provided to the driver for all purposes involving the application of the provisions of this title. In the discretion of the Commissioner, service may be made as provided in § 8.01-296, which service on the driver shall be made by delivery in writing to the driver in person in accordance with subdivision 1 of § 8.01-296 by a sheriff or deputy sheriff in the county or city in which the address is located, who shall, as directed by the Commissioner, take possession of any suspended or revoked license, registration card, or set of license plates or decals and return them to the office of the Commissioner. No such service shall be made if, prior to service, the driver has complied with the requirement which caused the issuance of the decision or order. In any such case, return shall be made to the Commissioner.

B. In lieu of making a direct payment to sheriffs as a fee for delivery of the Department's processes, the Commissioner shall effect a transfer of funds, on a monthly basis, to the Compensation Board to be used to provide additional support to sheriffs' departments. The amount of funds so transferred shall be as provided in the general appropriation act.

C. The Department may contract with the United States Postal Service or an authorized agent to use the National Change of Address System for the purpose of obtaining current address information for a person whose name appears in customer records maintained by the Department. If the Department receives information from the National Change of Address System indicating that a person whose name appears in a Department record has submitted a permanent change of address to the Postal Service, the Department may then update its records with the mailing address obtained from the National Change of Address System.

History.

1968, c. 144, § 46.1-441.2; 1980, c. 704; 1981, c. 619; 1984, c. 780; 1985, c. 231; 1989, cc. 439, 727; 1993, c. 24; 1994, c. 345; 1996, cc. 943, 994; 2001, c. 414; 2010, cc. 25, 55; 2012, c. 615.

§ 46.2-416.1. Suspension for failure to comply with traffic citation issued under federal law.

On receipt of a notice from a United States District Court in Virginia that a person licensed to drive in Virginia has failed to comply with a traffic citation issued under the laws of the United States for a violation occurring in Virginia, the Commissioner may suspend the driving privileges of such person, if the person has been provided written notice mailed to his last known address that his license or privilege to drive a motor vehicle in Virginia will be suspended if he has not complied with the terms of the citation within ten days, and if the person has not so complied.

History.

1992, c. 891.

ARTICLE 13.

SUSPENSION OF LICENSES FOR UNSATISFIED JUDGMENTS AND AFTER CERTAIN ACCIDENTS.

§ 46.2-417. Suspension for failure to satisfy motor vehicle accident judgment; exceptions; insurance in liquidated company; insurer obligated to pay judgment.

A. Upon the application of any judgment creditor, the Commissioner shall suspend the driver's license and all of the registration certificates and license plates of any person who has failed for 30 days to satisfy any judgment (i) in an amount and on a cause of action as hereinafter stated in this subsection or (ii) in an amount and on a cause of action pursuant to § 15.2-1716 or 15.2-1716.1, immediately upon receiving an authenticated judgment order or abstract thereof in an action for damages in a motor vehicle accident or pursuant to § 15.2-1716 or 15.2-1716.1, if the order or abstract is received by the Commissioner within 10 years of the date of judgment or if the judgment has been revived. However, if judgment is marked satisfied on the court records on or before the Commissioner's issuance of suspension, the order of suspension shall be invalid.

B. The Commissioner shall not, however, suspend the license of an owner or driver if the insurance carried by him was in a company which was authorized to transact business in this Commonwealth and which subsequent to an accident involving the owner or driver and prior to settlement of the claim therefor went into liquidation, so that the owner or driver is thereby unable to satisfy the judgment arising out of the accident.

C. The Commissioner shall not suspend the driver's license or driving privilege or any registration certificate, license plates, or decals under clause (i) of subsection A or § 46.2-418, if the Commissioner finds that an insurer authorized to do business in the Commonwealth was obligated to pay the judgment upon which suspension is based, or that a policy of the insurer covers the person subject to the suspension, if the insurer's obligation or the limits of the policy are in an amount sufficient to meet the minimum amounts required by § 46.2-472, even though the insurer has not paid the judgment for any reason. A finding by the Commissioner that an insurer is obligated to pay a judgment, or that a policy of an insurer covers the person, shall not be binding upon the insurer and shall have no legal effect whatever except for the purpose of administering this article. Whenever in any judicial proceeding it is determined by any final judgment, decree, or order that an insurer is not obligated to pay the judgment, the Commissioner, notwithstanding any contrary finding made by him, forthwith shall suspend the driver's license or driving privilege, or any registration card, license plates or decals of any person against whom the judgment was rendered, as provided in subsection A.

D. Any suspensions timely requested by any judgment creditor under subsection A and issued by the Commissioner shall not extend (i) beyond 10 years from the date of judgment for any civil judgment obtained in a general district court, unless the judgment creditor notifies the Commissioner that an extension has been granted as provided in subdivision B 4 of § 16.1-69.55 or (ii) beyond 20 years from the date of judgment for any civil judgment obtained in a circuit court, unless the judgment creditor notifies the Commissioner that an extension has been granted as provided in § 8.01-251. The expiration of such suspension shall not relieve the judgment debtor of complying with the requirements of proof of financial responsibility pursuant to subsection B of § 46.2-411 and the reinstatement fees pursuant to subsections C and F of § 46.2-411 after the judgment debtor becomes eligible for restoration of his driving privileges.

History.

Code 1950, § 46-430; 1958, c. 541, § 46.1-442; 1973, c. 394; 1974, cc. 49, 360; 1984, c. 780; 1988, c. 860; 1989, c. 727; 1992, c. 109; 2004, c. 998; 2013, c. 598.

§ 46.2-418. Nonpayment of judgments of Virginia and other states.

The Commissioner shall take action as required in § 46.2-417 on receiving proper evidence that the person has failed for a period of thirty days to satisfy any judgment, in amount and on a cause of action as stated in §§ 46.2-364 and 46.2-417, rendered by a court of competent jurisdiction of the Commonwealth, any other state of the United States, the United States, Canada or its provinces.

History.

Code 1950, § 46-430; 1958, c. 541, § 46.1-443; 1989, c. 727.

§ 46.2-419. When judgment satisfied.

A. Every judgment for damages in any motor vehicle accident referred to in this chapter shall, for the purpose of this chapter, be satisfied:

1. When paid in full or when $25,000 has been credited upon any judgment or judgments rendered in excess of that amount because of bodily injury to or death of one person as the result of any one accident;

2. When, subject to the limit of $25,000 because of bodily injury to or death of one person, the judgment has been paid in full or when the sum of $50,000 has been credited upon any judgment or judgments rendered in excess of that amount because of bodily injury to or death of two or more persons as the result of any one accident;

3. When the judgment has been paid in full or when $20,000 has been credited upon any judgment or judgments rendered in excess of that amount because of injury to or destruction of property of others as a result of any one accident; or

4. When the judgment has been discharged in bankruptcy.

B. Payments made in settlement of any claims because of bodily injury, death or property damage arising from a motor vehicle accident shall be credited in reduction of the amount provided in this section.

History.

Code 1950, § 46-431; 1954, c. 378; 1958, cc. 501, 541, § 46.1-444; 1968, c. 685; 1970, c. 272; 1972, cc. 47, 433; 1975, c. 382; 1978, c. 550; 1989, cc. 621, 727.

§ 46.2-420. Order for payment of judgment in installments.

A judgment debtor, on five days' notice to the judgment creditor, may apply to the court in which the judgment was obtained for the privilege of paying it in installments. The court, without prejudice to other legal remedies which the judgment creditor may have, may so order, fixing the amounts and times of payment of the installments.

History.

Code 1950, § 46-432; 1958, c. 541, § 46.1-445; 1989, c. 727.

§ 46.2-421. Effect of order for such payment and proof of financial responsibility.

The Commissioner shall not suspend a license or registration of a motor vehicle and shall restore any license or registration suspended following nonpayment of a judgment, if the judgment debtor obtains an order from the court in which the judgment was rendered permitting payment of the judgment in installments and if the judgment debtor gives proof of his financial responsibility in the future as provided in this chapter.

History.

Code 1950, § 46-433; 1958, c. 541, § 46.1-446; 1989, c. 727.

§ 46.2-422. Suspension on failure to pay installments.

If the judgment debtor fails to pay any installment as permitted by the order of the court, then on notice of default, the Commissioner shall forthwith suspend the driver's license, registration cards, and license plates of the judgment debtor until the judgment is satisfied as provided in this chapter. The judgment debtor may apply, after due notice to the judgment creditor, to the court which allowed installment payment of the judgment, within thirty days after the default, for resumption of the privilege of paying the judgment in installments, if past-due installments are first paid.

History.

Code 1950, § 46-434; 1958, c. 541, § 46.1-447; 1989, c. 727.

§ 46.2-423. Creditor's consent to license notwithstanding default in payment.

If the judgment creditor consents in writing, in whatever form the Commissioner prescribes, that the judgment debtor be allowed a driver's license and motor vehicle registration, the Commissioner may allow the same, notwithstanding default in the payment of the judgment or any installment thereof, for six months from the date of consent and thereafter until it is revoked in writing, if the judgment debtor furnishes proof of his financial responsibility in the future as provided in this chapter.

History.

Code 1950, § 46-435; 1958, c. 541, § 46.1-448; 1989, c. 727.

§ 46.2-424. Duty of insurance carrier after notice of accident; report of omissions by insurers to State Corporation Commission; investigation and assessment for omissions.

On receipt of the certificate of insurance, the insurance carrier or surety company named in the certificate of insurance shall determine whether the policy or bond was applicable to liability, if any, as to the named insured. Thereupon and not later than thirty days following receipt of the certificate of insurance, the insurance company or surety company shall cause to be filed with the Commissioner a written notice if the policy or bond was not applicable to liability, if any, as to the named insured resulting from the accident. The Commissioner shall prescribe the manner in which the written notice shall be made.

When the insurance company or surety company notifies the Commissioner that the policy or bond named in the certificate of insurance was not applicable to liability resulting from the accident, the Department shall determine, under § 46.2-708, whether suspension of the driver's license, registration cards, and license plates issued to the owner of the motor vehicle involved in the accident is required.

If the records of the Department reasonably indicate that any insurance carrier or surety company does not cause to be filed the notice herein required, the Commissioner shall report every such omission to the State Corporation Commission.

The State Corporation Commission shall investigate every such report of omission. If the Commission finds that any insurance carrier or surety company licensed to transact business in the Commonwealth, has failed, without good reason, to cause to be filed the notice required hereunder, the State Corporation Commission may assess the carrier or company fifty dollars for each omission.

Motor Vehicles

History.

Code 1950, § 46-438; 1958, c. 541, § 46.1-451; 1972, c. 442; 1989, c. 727.

§ 46.2-425. Driver or owner having no license issued by Department.

In case a driver or owner has no driver's license issued by the Department or no motor vehicle registered in his name in the Commonwealth, he shall not be allowed a driver's license or motor vehicle registration until he has complied with this chapter to the same extent as would be necessary if he had held a driver's license or a motor vehicle registration at the time of the accident in which he was involved or at the time of the commission of the offense resulting in a conviction as is mentioned in §§ 46.2-389 and 46.2-391.

History.

Code 1950, § 46-439; 1958, c. 541, § 46.1-452; 1984, c. 780; 1989, c. 727.

§ 46.2-426. Custody and application of cash or securities deposited; limitation of actions; assignment.

Cash or securities furnished in compliance with the requirements of this chapter shall be placed by the Commissioner in the custody of the State Treasurer and shall be applicable only to the payment of any judgment against the depositor for damages arising out of the accident in question in an action at law in a court in the Commonwealth begun not later than one year after the date of the accident. The cash or securities may be assigned by the depositor for the benefit of the person or persons damaged or injured in the accident as the result of which the cash or securities were filed or deposited without the damaged or injured person being required to institute legal proceedings. The Commissioner shall accept the assignment if, in his opinion, the rights of any other person or persons shall not be prejudiced thereby.

History.

Code 1950, § 46-441; 1958, c. 541, § 46.1-454; 1989, c. 727.

§ 46.2-427. When suspensions to remain effective; relief from furnishing proof of financial responsibility; prohibition against registration in name of another person.

The suspension required by the provisions of § 46.2-417 shall continue except as otherwise provided by §§ 46.2-421 and 46.2-423 until the person satisfies the judgment or judgments as prescribed in § 46.2-419 and gives proof of his financial responsibility in the future. However, the judgment debtor whose driving privileges, registration certificates, and license plates have been so suspended may petition the court that entered the judgment for reinstatement of his driving privileges, registration certificates, and license plates and the court may order reinstatement if the judgment has not been satisfied, provided the judgment debtor proves by a preponderance of the evidence that the judgment debtor (i) is unable, after examination of the records of the Department and the court reflecting that suspension and the exercise of due diligence, to locate the person to whom payment is due or, if the person to whom payment is due is dead, the judgment debtor is unable to identify either who are his heirs and assignees, or where they are located, and (ii) has paid into the court an amount equal to the judgment, court costs, and all interest that has accrued up to the date payment was made to the court. Any payment made to the court under this section shall be held for one year and, if unclaimed by the judgment creditor during that period, shall be transmitted by the court to the State Treasurer or his designee to be disposed of pursuant to Chapter 11.1 (§ 55-210.1 et seq.) of Title 55.

Upon receipt of such an order, the Commissioner shall reinstate the driving privileges, registration certificates, and license plates of the judgment debtor, provided the judgment debtor has given proof of his financial responsibility in the future and satisfied all other reinstatement requirements as provided in this chapter.

The motor vehicle involved in the accident on which the suspension under § 46.2-417 is based shall not be registered in the name of any other person when the Commissioner has reasonable grounds to believe that the registration of the vehicle will have the effect of defeating the purpose of the chapter and no other motor vehicle shall be registered, and no driver's license or learner's permit shall be issued in the name of the person suspended, except as prescribed in § 46.2-437 until the suspension is terminated.

This section shall not relieve any person from giving or maintaining proof of his financial responsibility when he is required so to do for some reason rather than having been involved in a motor vehicle accident.

History.

Code 1950, §§ 46-446, 46-447, 46-477.1; 1950, p. 639; 1958, c. 541, § 46.1-459; 1972, c. 638; 1984, c. 780; 1989, c. 727; 2003, c. 316; 2013, c. 598.

§ 46.2-428. Commonwealth responsible for deposits.

The Commonwealth shall be responsible for the safekeeping of all bonds, cash, and securities deposited with the State Treasurer under the provisions of this chapter, and if the deposit or any part of the deposit is lost, destroyed, or misappropriated the Commonwealth shall make good the loss to any person entitled thereto.

History.

Code 1950, § 46-448; 1958, c. 541, § 46.1-460; 1989, c. 727.

§ 46.2-429. Release of deposits only upon consent of Commissioner.

Bonds, cash, or securities deposited with the State Treasurer pursuant to this chapter shall only be released by the State Treasurer upon consent of the Commissioner given in conformity with this chapter.

History.

Code 1950, § 46-449; 1958, c. 541, § 46.1-461; 1989, c. 727.

ARTICLE 14.

SUSPENSION OF LICENSES OF NONRESIDENTS OR FOR ACCIDENTS IN OTHER STATES.

§ 46.2-430. Power over nonresidents.

Whenever by the laws of the Commonwealth the Commissioner may suspend or revoke: (i) the license of a resident driver, or (ii) the registration cards and license plates of a resident owner, he may:

1. Suspend or revoke the privilege of operating a motor vehicle in the Commonwealth by a nonresident driver, and
2. Suspend the privilege of driving a vehicle owned by a nonresident regardless of whether the vehicle is registered in the Commonwealth.

History.

Code 1950, § 46-450; 1958, c. 541, § 46.1-462; 1984, c. 780; 1989, c. 727.

§ 46.2-431. Chapter applies to nonresidents.

Every provision of this chapter applies to any person who is not a resident of the Commonwealth under the same circumstances as it would apply to a resident. No nonresident may drive any motor vehicle in the Commonwealth and no motor vehicle owned by him may be driven in the Commonwealth, unless the nonresident has complied with the requirements of this chapter with respect to giving proof of financial responsibility in the future.

History.

Code 1950, § 46-451; 1958, c. 541, § 46.1-463; 1972, c. 638; 1989, c. 727.

§ 46.2-432. Failure of nonresident to report accident.

The failure of a nonresident to report an accident as required in this title shall constitute sufficient ground for suspension or revocation of his privileges of driving a motor vehicle in the Commonwealth and of driving within the Commonwealth of any motor vehicle owned by him.

History.

Code 1950, § 46-452; 1958, c. 541, § 46.1-464; 1989, c. 727.

§ 46.2-433. Notification of officers in nonresident's home state.

On conviction of a nonresident or in case any unsatisfied judgment results in suspension of a nonresident's driving privileges in the Commonwealth and the prohibition of driving within the Commonwealth of any motor vehicle, or on suspension of a nonresident's driving privileges in the Commonwealth pursuant to any other provision of this chapter, the Commissioner shall transmit a certified copy of the record of the conviction or the unsatisfied judgment, or any other action pursuant to this chapter resulting in suspension of a nonresident's driving privileges of any motor vehicle owned by such nonresident, to the motor vehicle commissioner or officer performing the functions of a commissioner in the state of the United States, or possession under the exclusive control of the United States, Mexico or its states, or Canada or its provinces in which the nonresident resides.

History.
Code 1950, § 46-453; 1958, c. 541, § 46.1-465; 1989, c. 727; 2005, c. 513.

§ 46.2-434. Conviction of or judgment against resident in another jurisdiction.

The Commissioner shall suspend or revoke the license and registration certificate and plates of any resident of the Commonwealth upon receiving notice of his conviction, in a court of competent jurisdiction of the Commonwealth, any other state of the United States, the United States, Canada or its provinces or any territorial subdivision of such state or country, of an offense therein which, if committed in the Commonwealth, would be grounds for the suspension or revocation of the license granted to him or registration of any motor vehicle registered in his name. No suspension or revocation under this subsection shall continue for a longer period than it would have, had the offense been committed in the Commonwealth, provided the person gives proof of his financial responsibility in the future for the period provided in § 46.2-412.

The Commissioner shall take like action upon receipt of notice that a resident of the Commonwealth has failed, for a period of thirty days, to satisfy any final judgment in amount and upon a cause of action as stated herein, rendered against him in a court of competent jurisdiction of any other state of the United States, the United States, Canada or its provinces, or any territorial subdivision of such state or country.

History.
Code 1950, § 46-454; 1950, p. 888; 1958, c. 541, § 46.1-466; 1988, c. 860; 1989, c. 727; 1992, c. 109; 1997, c. 486.

ARTICLE 15. PROOF OF FINANCIAL RESPONSIBILITY.

§ 46.2-435. Proof of financial responsibility to be furnished for each vehicle.

Proof of financial responsibility in the amounts required by this chapter shall be furnished for each motor vehicle registered by the person required to furnish such proof.

History.
Code 1950, § 46-455; 1954, c. 378; 1958, cc. 501, 541, § 46.1-467; 1989, c. 727.

§ 46.2-436. Methods of proving financial responsibility.

Proof of financial responsibility when required under this chapter may be given by proof that:

1. A policy or policies of motor vehicle liability insurance have been obtained and are in full force;
2. A bond has been duly executed;
3. A deposit has been made of money or securities; or
4. A self-insurance certificate has been filed, all as provided in this chapter.

History.
Code 1950, § 46-456; 1958, c. 541, § 46.1-468; 1989, c. 727.

§ 46.2-437. Proof of financial responsibility by owner in lieu of driver.

When the Commissioner finds that any person required to give proof of financial responsibility under this title is or later becomes a driver, however designated, or a member of the immediate family or household, in the employ or home of an owner of a motor vehicle, the Commissioner shall accept proof of financial responsibility given by the owner in lieu of proof of financial responsibility by such person to permit him to operate a motor vehicle for which the owner has given proof of financial responsibility as provided in this chapter. The Commissioner shall designate the restrictions imposed by this section on the face of the person's driver's license.

History.
Code 1950, § 46-457; 1958, c. 541, § 46.1-469; 1972, c. 638; 1984, c. 780; 1989, c. 727.

§ 46.2-438. Proof by owner of vehicles operated under permit or certificate of State Corporation Commission or Department of Motor Vehicles.

If the owner of a motor vehicle is one whose vehicles are operated under a permit or a certificate of convenience and necessity issued by the State Corporation Commission or the Department, proof by the owner on behalf of another as provided by this chapter may be made if there is filed with the Commissioner satisfactory evidence that the owner has complied with the law with respect to his liability for damage caused by the operation of his vehicles by providing the required insurance or other security or has qualified as a self-insurer as described in § 46.2-368.

History.
Code 1950, § 46-458; 1958, c. 541, § 46.1-470; 1989, c. 727; 1997, c. 283.

§ 46.2-439. Certificate of insurance carrier.

Proof of financial responsibility, when requested, shall be made by filing with the Commissioner the written certificate of any insurance carrier authorized to do business in the Commonwealth, certifying that there is in effect a motor vehicle liability policy for the benefit of the person required to furnish proof of financial responsibility. This certificate shall give its effective date and the effective date of the policy.

History.
Code 1950, § 46-459; 1958, c. 541, § 46.1-471; 1972, c. 380; 1976, c. 143; 1988, c. 860; 1989, c. 727.

§ 46.2-440. Certificate for nonresident may be by carrier not qualified in Commonwealth.

A nonresident owner of a vehicle not registered in Virginia may give proof of financial responsibility by filing with the Commissioner a written certificate or certificates of an insurance carrier not authorized to transact business in the Commonwealth but authorized to transact business in any other state, any territory or possession of the United States and under its exclusive control, Canada or its provinces, or the territorial subdivisions of such states or countries, in which any motor vehicle described in the certificate and all replacement vehicles of similar classification are registered or, if the nonresident does not own a motor vehicle, then in the like jurisdiction in which the insured resides and otherwise conforming to the provisions of this chapter. The Commissioner shall accept the same if the insurance carrier, in addition to having complied with all other provisions of this chapter as requisite, shall:

1. Execute a power of attorney authorizing the Commissioner to accept service on its behalf of notice or process in any action arising out of a motor vehicle accident in the Commonwealth;
2. Duly adopt a resolution, which shall be binding upon it, declaring that its policies are to be deemed to be modified to comply with the law of the Commonwealth and the terms of this chapter relating to the terms of motor vehicle liability policies issued herein;
3. Agree to accept as final and binding the judgment of any court of competent jurisdiction in the Commonwealth from which judgment no appeal is or can be taken, duly rendered in any action arising out of a motor vehicle accident;
4. Deposit with the State Treasurer cash or securities as are mentioned in § 46.2-453 or the surety bond of a company authorized to do business in Virginia equal in value to $60,000 for each insurance policy filed as proof of financial responsibility.

History.
Code 1950, § 46-460; 1954, c. 378; 1958, cc. 501, 541, § 46.1-472; 1968, c. 685; 1972, c. 433; 1975, c. 382; 1976, c. 143; 1978, c. 220; 1989, cc. 621, 727; 1993, c. 164; 1995, c. 121.

§ 46.2-441. Nonresident may file proof of future financial responsibility of insurance company or other state-authorized entity providing insurance.

Notwithstanding the requirement of §§ 46.2-439 and 46.2-440, a nonresident required to file proof of future financial responsibility under this chapter may file proof of future financial responsibility of an insurance company or other state-authorized entity providing insurance and authorized or licensed to do business in the nonresident's state of residence as long as such proof of future financial responsibility is in the amounts equal to those required by § 46.2-472.

History.
Code 1950, § 46-461; 1958, c. 541, § 46.1-473; 1989, c. 727; 1995, c. 121.

§ 46.2-442. Default of foreign insurance carrier.

If any insurance carrier not authorized to do business in the Commonwealth which is qualified to furnish proof of financial responsibility defaults in any of its undertakings or agreements, the Commissioner shall not thereafter accept any certificate of that carrier so long as the default continues and shall revoke licenses previously granted on the basis of its policies unless the default is immediately repaired.

History.
Code 1950, § 46-462; 1958, c. 541, § 46.1-474; 1989, c. 727.

§ 46.2-443. Chapter not applicable to certain policies of insurance.

This chapter does not apply to:

1. Policies of automobile insurance against liability which may now or hereafter be required by any other law of the Commonwealth and such policies if endorsed to the requirements of this chapter shall be

accepted as proof of financial responsibility when required under this chapter; or

2. Policies insuring solely the insured named in the policy against liability resulting from the maintenance, use, or operation by persons in the insured's employ or in his behalf of motor vehicles not owned by the insured.

History.

Code 1950, § 46-463; 1958, c. 541, § 46.1-475; 1989, c. 727.

§ 46.2-444. Surety requirements of bond.

The bond mentioned in subdivision 2 of § 46.2-436 shall be duly executed by the person giving proof and by a surety company duly authorized to transact business in the Commonwealth or by the person giving proof and by one or more individual sureties owning real estate within the Commonwealth and having an equity therein in at least the amount of the bond and the real estate shall be scheduled in the bond. But the Commissioner may not accept any real estate bond unless it is first approved by the circuit court of the jurisdiction wherein the real estate is located.

History.

Code 1950, § 46-465; 1958, c. 541, § 46.1-476; 1989, c. 727.

§ 46.2-445. How bond to be conditioned.

The Commissioner shall not accept any bond unless it is conditioned for payments in amounts and under the same circumstances as would be required in a motor vehicle liability policy furnished by the person giving proof.

History.

Code 1950, § 46-466; 1958, c. 541, § 46.1-477; 1989, c. 727.

§ 46.2-446. Notice to Commissioner prerequisite to cancellation of bond; cancellation not to affect rights arising prior thereto.

No bond shall be cancelled unless twenty days' prior written notice of cancellation is given the Commissioner, but cancellation of the bond shall not prevent recovery thereon with respect to any right or cause of action arising prior to the date of cancellation.

History.

Code 1950, § 46-467; 1958, c. 541, § 46.1-478; 1989, c. 727.

§ 46.2-447. Bond to constitute lien on real estate of surety.

A bond with individual sureties shall constitute a lien in favor of the Commonwealth on the real estate of any individual surety. The lien shall exist in favor of any holder of any final judgment against the principal on account of damage to property or injury to or death of any person or persons resulting from the ownership, maintenance, use, or operation of his, or any other, motor vehicle, upon the recording of the bond in the office of the clerk of the court where deeds are admitted to record of the city or county where the real estate is located.

History.

Code 1950, § 46-468; 1958, c. 541, § 46.1-479; 1989, c. 727.

§ 46.2-448. Notice of cancellation; record; fees.

Notice of cancellation is to be signed by the Commissioner or by someone designated by him and the seal of the Department placed thereon. Notwithstanding any other provision of law the clerk shall record the notice in the books kept for the recording of deeds and shall index the same in the indices thereto for grantors and grantees, under the respective names of the individual sureties in the column for grantors, and the Commonwealth of Virginia in the column for grantees, for which he shall receive two dollars and fifty cents to be paid by the principal in full payment of all services in connection with the recordation and release of the bond. The clerk shall place on the notice a statement showing the time of recording and the book and page of recording and return the notice to the Commissioner.

History.

Code 1950, § 46-469; 1958, c. 541, § 46.1-480; 1989, c. 727.

§ 46.2-449. Cancellation of bond with individual sureties; certificates of cancellation.

When a bond with individual sureties filed with the Commissioner is no longer required under this chapter, the Commissioner shall, on request, cancel it as to liability for damage to property or injury to or death of any person or persons thereafter caused and when a bond has been cancelled by the Commissioner or otherwise he shall, on request, furnish a certificate of the cancellation signed by him or by someone designated by him and bearing the seal of the Department. The certificate, notwithstanding any other provision of law, may be recorded in the office of the clerk of the court in which the bond was admitted to record.

History.

Code 1950, § 46-470; 1958, c. 541, § 46.1-481; 1989, c. 727.

§ 46.2-450. Order discharging lien of bond.

On satisfactory proof that the bond filed with the Commissioner as provided for in this chapter has been cancelled and that there are no claims or judgments against the principal in the bond on account of damage to property or injury to or death of any person or persons resulting from the ownership, maintenance, use, or operation of a motor vehicle of the principal caused while the bond was in effect, the court in which the bond was admitted to record may enter an order discharging the lien of the bond on the real estate of the sureties thereon, upon their petition and at their proper cost.

History.
Code 1950, § 46-471; 1958, c. 541, § 46.1-482; 1989, c. 727.

§ 46.2-451. Action or suit on bond.

If a final judgment rendered against the principal on the bond filed with the Commissioner as provided in this chapter is not satisfied within fifteen days after its rendition, the judgment creditor may, for his own use and benefit and at his sole expense, bring an action on the bond in the name of the Commonwealth against the company or persons executing the bond.

History.
Code 1950, § 46-472; 1958, c. 541, § 46.1-483; 1989, c. 727.

§ 46.2-452. Parties to suit on bond with individual sureties.

When the sureties on the bond filed with the Commissioner as provided in this chapter are individuals the judgment creditor may proceed against any or all parties to the bond at law for a judgment or in equity for a decree and foreclosure of the lien on the real estate of the sureties. The proceeding whether at law or in equity may be against one, all, or any intermediate number of the parties to the bond and when less than all are joined other or others may be impleaded in the same proceeding and after final judgment or decree other proceedings may be instituted until full satisfaction is obtained.

History.
Code 1950, § 46-473; 1958, c. 541, § 46.1-484; 1989, c. 727.

§ 46.2-453. Proof of financial responsibility by delivering cash or securities.

A person may give proof of financial responsibility by delivering to the Commissioner cash or securities equal to the sum of the liability coverage required for bodily injury or death of two or more persons in any one accident and injury to or destruction of property of others in any one accident as prescribed by § 46.2-472. Securities so deposited shall be such as public bodies may invest in according to § 2.2-4500.

History.
Code 1950, § 46-474; 1954, c. 378; 1958, cc. 501, 541, § 46.1-485; 1968, c. 685; 1978, c. 220; 1980, c. 484; 1986, c. 16; 1989, c. 727.

§ 46.2-454. Moneys or securities to be deposited with State Treasurer subject to execution.

All moneys or securities delivered to the Commissioner pursuant to this chapter shall be placed by him in the custody of the State Treasurer and shall be subject to execution to satisfy any judgment within the limits on amounts required by this chapter for motor vehicle liability insurance policies. The State Treasurer shall certify the value of such moneys or securities to the Commissioner as soon as practicable after their delivery to him.

History.
Code 1950, § 46-475; 1958, c. 541, § 46.1-486; 1986, c. 16; 1989, c. 727.

§ 46.2-455. Assessment for expense of holding deposits.

For the purpose of defraying the expense of the safekeeping and handling of the cash or securities deposited with him under the provisions of this title, in December of each year the State Treasurer shall levy against each person having cash or securities deposited with him an assessment of not more than one-tenth of one percent of the cash or of the par value of the securities deposited to his account, and shall collect the assessment in January of each year. These funds shall be deposited to the general fund of the state treasury. If any assessment is not paid by January 31 of each year, the State Treasurer shall so notify the Commissioner in writing, attaching thereto a dated copy of the original assessment.

History.
1986, c. 16, § 46.1-486.1; 1989, c. 727.

§ 46.2-456. Additional security if fund impaired by any legal process, or otherwise.

Whenever the moneys or securities are subjected to attachment, garnishment, execution, or other legal process or are otherwise depleted or threatened with depletion or impairment in amount or value the depositor must immediately furnish additional moneys or securities, free from lien, claim, or threat of impairment, in sufficient amount or value fully to comply with the requirements of this chapter.

The Treasurer shall notify the Commissioner promptly of any depletion, impairment, or decrease or of any legal threat of depletion, impairment, or decrease in the value of the securities or in the moneys on deposit with him under the provisions of this chapter.

History.
Code 1950, § 46-476; 1958, c. 541, § 46.1-487; 1989, c. 727.

§ 46.2-457. Substitution of new proof; cancellation or return of old.

The Commissioner may cancel any bond or return any certificate of insurance and on the substitution and acceptance by him of other adequate proof of financial responsibility pursuant to this chapter, and on his direction to such effect the State Treasurer shall return any money or securities on deposit with him to the person entitled to it.

History.
Code 1950, § 46-477; 1958, c. 541, § 46.1-488; 1989, c. 727.

§ 46.2-458. Interpleader to determine rights in deposits; other proceedings.

The Commissioner and the State Treasurer, or either, may proceed in equity by bill of interpleader for the determination of any dispute as to ownership of or rights in any deposit held by the State Treasurer pursuant to this chapter and may have recourse to any other appropriate proceeding for determination of any question that arises as to their rights or liabilities or as to the rights or liabilities of the Commonwealth under this chapter.

History.
Code 1950, § 46-478; 1958, c. 541, § 46.1-489; 1989, c. 727.

§ 46.2-459. When other proof of financial responsibility required; suspension of license pending furnishing of proof required.

Whenever any proof of financial responsibility filed by any person under this chapter no longer fulfills the purpose for which required, the Commissioner shall require other proof of financial responsibility as required by this chapter and shall suspend the person's driver's license, registration cards and license plates pending the furnishing of proof as required.

Nonpayment of the assessment provided for in § 46.2-455 shall also be reason for suspension of the driver's license, registration cards and license plates of a person offering cash or securities as proof of financial responsibility under this chapter. The suspension shall be promptly initiated by the Commissioner on receipt of written notice of nonpayment of the assessment from the State Treasurer and shall take effect ten days from the date of a written notice sent by the Commissioner to the person by first-class mail, the notice to notify the person of the forthcoming suspension if payment is not received within the ten-day period.

History.
Code 1950, § 46-479; 1958, c. 541, § 46.1-490; 1984, c. 780; 1986, c. 16; 1989, c. 727.

§ 46.2-460. When Commissioner to consent to cancellation of bond or policy, or return of money or securities.

The Commissioner, on request and subject to the provisions of § 46.2-461, shall consent to the cancellation of any bond or insurance policy or to the return to the person entitled thereto of any money or securities deposited pursuant to this chapter as proof of financial responsibility or he shall not require proof of financial responsibility in the event:

1. Of the death of the person on whose behalf the proof was filed;
2. Of his permanent incapacity to operate a motor vehicle; or
3. That the person who has given proof of financial responsibility surrenders his driver's license, and all of his registration cards, and license plates to the Commissioner.

History.
Code 1950, § 46-480; 1958, c. 541, § 46.1-491; 1984, c. 780; 1989, c. 727.

§ 46.2-461. When Commissioner not to release proof of financial responsibility; affidavit of nonexistence of facts.

A. Notwithstanding the provisions of § 46.2-460 the Commissioner shall not release the proof in the event:

1. Any action for damages upon a liability included in this chapter is then pending;
2. Any judgment on any liability is then outstanding and unsatisfied; or
3. The Commissioner has received notice that the person involved has within the period of twelve months immediately preceding been involved as a driver in any motor vehicle accident.

B. An affidavit of the applicant of the nonexistence of these facts shall be sufficient evidence thereof in the absence of evidence in the records of the Department tending to indicate the contrary.

History.
Code 1950, § 46-481; 1958, c. 541, § 46.1-492; 1989, c. 727.

§ 46.2-462. New license or registration to person to whom proof surrendered.

Whenever any person to whom proof has been surrendered as provided in § 46.2-460 applies for a driver's license or the registration of a motor vehicle, the application shall be refused unless the applicant reestablishes proof as required by this chapter.

History.
Code 1950, § 46-482; 1958, c. 541, § 46.1-493; 1984, c. 780; 1989, c. 727.

§ 46.2-463. Penalty for forging evidence of financial responsibility.

Any person who forges or without authority signs any evidence of ability to respond in damages or knowingly attempts to employ or use any evidence of ability to respond in damages, as required by the Commissioner in the administration of this chapter shall be guilty of a Class 1 misdemeanor.

History.
Code 1950, § 46-485; 1958, c. 541, § 46.1-496; 1989, c. 727.

ARTICLE 16.

ASSIGNMENT OF INSURANCE RISKS.

§ 46.2-464. Application for assignment of risk to insurance carrier.

Every person who has been unable to obtain a motor vehicle liability policy shall have the right to apply to the State Corporation Commission to have his risk assigned to an insurance carrier licensed to write and writing motor vehicle liability insurance in the Commonwealth and the insurance carrier, whether a stock or mutual company, reciprocal, or interinsurance exchange, or other type or form of insurance organization, as provided in this article shall issue a motor vehicle liability policy which will meet at least the minimum requirements for establishing financial responsibility as provided in this chapter, and in addition shall provide, at the option of the insured, reasonable motor vehicle physical damage and medical payments coverages, (both as defined in § 38.2-124) in the same policy.

Every person who has otherwise obtained a motor vehicle liability insurance policy, or who has been afforded motor vehicle liability insurance under the provisions of § 38.2-2015, but who was not afforded motor vehicle medical payments insurance or motor vehicle physical damage insurance in the same policy, or who was not afforded such coverages under the provisions of that section, shall have the right to apply to the Commission to have his risk assigned to an insurance carrier, as provided above, licensed to write and writing either or both coverages, and the insurance carrier shall issue a policy providing the coverage or coverages applied for.

History.

Code 1950, § 46-486; 1958, c. 541, § 46.1-497; 1972, c. 842; 1974, c. 88; 1989, c. 727.

§ 46.2-465. Optional coverage for persons occupying insured motor vehicle and for named insured and his family.

Once an assigned risk policy has been issued to an insured, every insurer licensed in the Commonwealth issuing or delivering any policy or contract of bodily injury liability insurance, or of property damage liability insurance, covering liability arising from the ownership, maintenance, or use of any motor vehicle shall provide on request of the insured, on payment of premium established by law for the coverage (i) to the named insured and, while resident of the named insured's household, the spouse and relatives of the named insured while occupying a motor vehicle or if struck by a motor vehicle while not occupying a motor vehicle; and (ii) to persons occupying the insured motor vehicle, the following health care and disability benefit for each accident:

1. Medical and chiropractic payments (accident insurance as defined in Article 2, § 38.2-101 et seq. of Chapter 1 of Title 38.2) coverages incurred within two years after the date of the accident, up to $2,000 per person;

2. If the person is usually engaged in a remunerative occupation, an amount equal to the loss of income incurred within one year after the date of the accident resulting from injuries received in the accident up to $100 per week during the period from the first work day lost as a result of the accident up to the date on which the person is able to return to his usual occupation and for a period not to exceed fifty-two weeks or any part thereof; and

3. The insured has the option of purchasing either or both of the coverages set forth in subdivisions 1 and 2 of this section.

History.

1972, c. 859, § 46.1-497.1; 1973, c. 294; 1977, c. 112; 1982, c. 450; 1989, c. 727.

§ 46.2-466. Regulations for assignment, rate classifications, and schedules.

The Commission may make reasonable regulations for the assignment of risks to insurance carriers.

It shall establish rate classifications, rating schedules, rates, and regulations to be used by insurance carriers issuing assigned risk, policies of motor vehicle liability, physical damage, and medical payments insurance in accordance with this chapter as appear to it to be proper.

In the establishment of rate classifications, rating schedules, rates, and regulations, it shall be guided by the principles and practices which have been established under its statutory authority to regulate motor vehicle liability, physical damage, and medical payments insurance rates and it may act in conformity with its statutory discretionary authority in such matters.

History.

Code 1950, § 46-487; 1958, c. 541, § 46.1-498; 1972, c. 842; 1989, c. 727.

§ 46.2-467. Action within power of Commission.

The Commission may, in its discretion, after reviewing all information pertaining to the applicant or policyholder available from its records, the records of the Department or from other sources:

1. Refuse to assign an application;

2. Approve the rejection of an application by an insurance carrier;

3. Approve the cancellation of a policy of motor vehicle liability, physical damage, and medical payments insurance by an insurance carrier; or

4. Refuse to approve the renewal or the reassignment of an expiring policy.

History.

Code 1950, § 46-488; 1958, c. 541, § 46.1-499; 1972, c. 842; 1989, c. 727.

§ 46.2-468. Information filed with Commission by insurance carrier confidential.

Any information filed with the Commission by an insurance carrier in connection with an assigned risk shall be confidential and solely for the information of the Commission and its staff and shall not be disclosed to any person, including an applicant, policyholder, and any other insurance carrier.

History.

Code 1950, § 46-489; 1958, c. 541, § 46.1-500; 1989, c. 727.

§ 46.2-469. Commission not required to disclose reasons for action; liability of Commission for act or omission.

A. The Commission shall not be required to disclose to any person, including the applicant or policyholder, its reasons for:

1. Refusing to assign an application;
2. Approving the rejection of an application by an insurance carrier;
3. Approving the cancellation of a policy of motor vehicle liability, physical damage, and medical payments insurance by an insurance carrier; or
4. Refusing to approve the renewal or the reassignment of an expiring policy.

B. The Commission or anyone acting for it shall not be held liable for any act or omission in connection with the administration of the duties imposed upon it by the provisions of this chapter, except upon proof of actual malfeasance.

History.

Code 1950, § 46-490; 1958, c. 541, § 46.1-501; 1972, c. 842; 1989, c. 727.

§ 46.2-470. Assignment of risks for nonresidents.

The provisions of this chapter relevant to assignment of risks shall be available to nonresidents who are unable to obtain a policy of motor vehicle liability, physical damage, and medical payments insurance with respect only to motor vehicles registered and used in the Commonwealth.

History.

Code 1950, § 46-491; 1958, c. 541, § 46.1-502; 1972, c. 842; 1989, c. 727.

§ 46.2-471. Assignment of risks for certain carriers.

Notwithstanding the provisions of § 46.2-366, the provisions of this chapter relating to assignment of risks shall be available to carriers by motor vehicle who are required by law to carry public liability and property damage insurance for the protection of the public.

History.

Code 1950, § 46-491.1; 1954, c. 345; 1958, c. 541, § 46.1-503; 1989, c. 727.

ARTICLE 17.
MOTOR VEHICLE LIABILITY INSURANCE POLICIES.

§ 46.2-472. Coverage of owner's policy.

Every motor vehicle owner's policy shall:

1. Designate by explicit description or by appropriate reference, all motor vehicles with respect to which coverage is intended to be granted.
2. Insure as insured the person named and any other person using or responsible for the use of the motor vehicle or motor vehicles with the permission of the named insured.
3. Insure the insured or other person against loss from any liability imposed by law for damages, including damages for care and loss of services, because of bodily injury to or death of any person, and injury to or destruction of property caused by accident and arising out of the ownership, use, or operation of such motor vehicle or motor vehicles within the Commonwealth, any other state in the United States, or Canada, subject to a limit exclusive of interest and costs, with respect to each motor vehicle, of $25,000 because of bodily injury to or death of one person in any one accident and, subject to the limit for one person, to a limit of $50,000 because of bodily injury to or death of two or more persons in any one accident, and to a limit of $20,000 because of injury to or destruction of property of others in any one accident.

History.

Code 1950, § 46-492; 1954, c. 378; 1958, cc. 501, 541, § 46.1-504; 1968, c. 685; 1972, c. 433; 1975, c. 382; 1978, c. 550; 1989, cc. 621, 727.

§ 46.2-473. Coverage of driver's policy.

Every driver's policy shall insure the person named therein as insured against loss from the liability imposed upon him by law for damages, including damages for care and loss of services, because of bodily injury to or death of any person, and injury to or destruction of property arising out of the use by him of any motor vehicle not owned by him, within the territorial limits and subject to the limits of liability set forth with respect to a motor vehicle owner's policy.

History.

Code 1950, § 46-493; 1958, c. 541, § 46.1-505; 1989, c. 727.

§ 46.2-474. Policy must contain certain agreement; additional coverage.

Every policy of insurance subject to the provisions of this chapter:

1. Shall contain an agreement that the insurance is provided in accordance with the coverage defined in this chapter as respects bodily injury, death, property damage, and destruction and that it is subject to all the provisions of this chapter and of the laws of the Commonwealth relating to this kind of insurance; and

2. May grant any lawful coverage in excess of or in addition to the coverage herein specified and this excess or additional coverage shall not be subject to the provisions of this chapter but shall be subject to other applicable laws of the Commonwealth.

History.

Code 1950, § 46-494; 1958, c. 541, § 46.1-506; 1989, c. 727.

§ 46.2-475. Policy must comply with law.

No policy required under this chapter shall be issued or delivered in the Commonwealth unless it complies with §§ 38.2-2218 through 38.2-2225, with all other applicable and not inconsistent laws of the Commonwealth, and with the terms and conditions of this chapter.

History.

Code 1950, § 46-495; 1958, c. 541, § 46.1-507; 1989, c. 727.

§ 46.2-476. Liability covered by workers' compensation law.

Policies issued under this chapter shall not insure any liability of the employer on account of bodily injury to, or death of, an employee of the insured for which benefits are payable under any workers' compensation law.

History.

Code 1950, § 46-496; 1958, c. 541, § 46.1-508; 1989, c. 727.

§ 46.2-477. When chapter applicable to policy.

This chapter shall not apply to any policy of insurance except as to liability thereunder incurred after certification thereof as proof of financial responsibility.

History.

Code 1950, § 46-496.1; 1958, c. 541, § 46.1-509; 1989, c. 727.

§ 46.2-478. Several policies together meeting requirements of chapter.

Several policies of one or more insurance carriers which together meet the requirements of this chapter shall be deemed a motor vehicle liability policy within the meaning of this chapter.

History.

Code 1950, § 46-497; 1958, c. 541, § 46.1-510; 1989, c. 727.

§ 46.2-479. Provisions to which every policy shall be subject but need not contain.

Every policy shall be subject to the following provisions which need not be contained therein:

1. The liability of any insurance carrier to the insured under a policy becomes absolute when loss or damage covered by the policy occurs and the satisfaction by the insured of a judgment for the loss or damage shall not be a condition precedent to the right or duty of the carrier to make payment on account of the loss or damage;

2. No policy shall be cancelled or annulled, as respects any loss or damage, by any agreement between the carrier and the insured after the insured has become responsible for the loss or damage and any attempted cancellation or annulment shall be void;

3. If the death of the insured occurs after the insured has become liable, during the policy period, for loss or damage covered by the policy, the policy shall not be terminated by the death with respect to the liability and the insurance carrier shall be liable hereunder as though death had not occurred;

4. On the recovery of a judgment against any person for loss or damage, if the person or the decedent he represents was at the accrual of the cause of action insured against the liability under the policy, the judgment creditor shall be entitled to have the insurance money applied to the satisfaction of the judgment;

5. If the death, insolvency, or bankruptcy of the insured occurs within the policy period, the policy during the unexpired portion of the period shall cover the legal representatives of the insured; and

6. No statement made by the insured or on his behalf and no violation of the terms of the policy shall operate to defeat or avoid the policy so as to bar recovery within the limits provided in this chapter.

History.

Code 1950, § 46-498; 1958, c. 541, § 46.1-511; 1989, c. 727.

§ 46.2-480. Reimbursement of carrier and proration of insurance.

Any policy may provide:

1. That the insured, or any other person covered by the policy, shall reimburse the insurance carrier for payments made on account of any accident, claim, or suit involving a breach of the terms, provisions, or conditions of the policy; or

2. For proration of the insurance with other applicable valid and collectible insurance.

History.

Code 1950, § 46-499; 1958, c. 541, § 46.1-512; 1989, c. 727.

§ 46.2-481. Binder or endorsement in lieu of policy.

Insurance carriers authorized to issue policies as provided in this chapter may, pending the issuance of the policy, execute an agreement to be known as a binder, which shall not be valid beyond sixty days from the date it becomes effective, or may, in lieu of a policy, issue an endorsement to an existing policy, each of which shall be construed to provide indemnity or protection in like manner and to the same extent as a formal policy. The provisions of this chapter apply to these binders and endorsements.

History.
Code 1950, § 46-500; 1958, c. 541, § 46.1-513; 1989, c. 727.

§ 46.2-482. Notification of cancellation or termination of certified policy.

When any insurance policy certified under this chapter is cancelled or terminated, the insurer shall report the fact to the Commissioner within fifteen days after the cancellation on a form prescribed by the Commissioner.

History.
1976, c. 259, § 46.1-513.2; 1989, c. 727.

ARTICLE 18.

DRIVER LICENSE COMPACT.

§ 46.2-483. Compact enacted into law; terms.

The Driver License Compact is hereby enacted into law and entered into with all other jurisdictions legally joining therein in the form substantially as follows:

THE DRIVER LICENSE COMPACT

Article I

Findings and Declaration of Policy

(a) The party states find that:

(1) The safety of their streets and highways is materially affected by the degree of compliance with state and local ordinances relating to the operation of motor vehicles.

(2) Violation of such a law or ordinance is evidence that the violator engages in conduct which is likely to endanger the safety of persons and property.

(3) The continuance in force of a license to drive is predicated upon compliance with laws and ordinances relating to the operation of motor vehicles, in whichever jurisdiction the vehicle is operated.

(b) It is the policy of each of the party states to:

(1) Promote compliance with the laws, ordinances, and administrative rules and regulations relating to the operation of motor vehicles by their operators in each of the jurisdictions where such operators drive motor vehicles.

(2) Make the reciprocal recognition of licenses to drive and eligibility therefor more just and equitable by considering the overall compliance with motor vehicle laws, ordinances and administrative rules and regulations as a condition precedent to the continuance or issuance of any license by reason of which the licensee is authorized or permitted to operate a motor vehicle in any of the party states.

Article II

Definitions

As used in this compact:

(a) *"State"* means a state, territory or possession of the United States, the District of Columbia, or the Commonwealth of Puerto Rico.

(b) *"Home state"* means the state which has issued and has the power to suspend or revoke the use of the license or permit to operate a motor vehicle.

(c) *"Conviction"* means a conviction of any offense related to the use or operation of a motor vehicle which is prohibited by state law, municipal ordinance or administrative rule or regulation, or a forfeiture of bail, bond, or other security deposited to secure appearance by a person charged with having committed any such offense, and which conviction or forfeiture is required to be reported to the licensing authority.

Article III

Reports of Conviction

The licensing authority of a party state shall report each conviction of a person from another party state occurring within its jurisdiction to the licensing authority of the home state of the licensee. Such report shall clearly identify the person convicted; describe the violation specifying the section of the statute, code or ordinance violated; identify the court in which action was taken; indicate whether a plea of guilty or not guilty was entered, or the conviction was a result of the forfeiture of bail, bond or other security; and shall include any special findings made in connection therewith.

Article IV

Effect of Conviction

(a) The licensing authority in the home state, for the purposes of suspension, revocation or limitation of the license to operate a motor vehicle, shall give the same effect to the conduct reported, pursuant to Article III of this compact, as it would if such conduct had occurred in the home state, in the case of convictions for:

(1) Manslaughter or negligent homicide resulting from the operation of a motor vehicle;

(2) Driving a motor vehicle while under the influence of intoxicating liquor or a narcotic drug, or under the influence of any other drug to a degree which renders the driver incapable of safely driving a motor vehicle;

(3) Any felony in the commission of which a motor vehicle is used;

(4) Failure to stop and render aid in the event of a motor vehicle accident resulting in the death or personal injury of another.

(b) As to other convictions, reported pursuant to Article III, the licensing authority in the home state shall give such effect to the conduct as is provided by the laws of the home state.

(c) If the laws of a party state do not provide for offenses or violations denominated or described in precisely the words employed in subdivision (a) of this article, such party state shall construe the denominations and descriptions appearing in subdivision (a) hereof as being applicable to and identifying those offenses or violations of a substantially similar nature and the laws of such party state shall contain such provisions as may be necessary to ensure that full force and effect is given to this article.

Article V

Applications for New Licenses

Upon application for a license to drive, the licensing authority in a party state shall ascertain whether the applicant has ever held, or is the holder of a license to drive issued by any other party state. The licensing authority in the state where application is made shall not issue a license to drive to the applicant if:

(1) The applicant has held such a license, but the same has been suspended by reason, in whole or in part, of a violation and if such suspension period has not terminated.

(2) The applicant has held such a license, but the same has been revoked by reason, in whole or in part, of a violation and if such revocation has not terminated, except that after the expiration of one year from the date the license was revoked, such person may make application for a new license if permitted by law. The licensing authority may refuse to issue a license to any such applicant if, after investigation, the licensing authority determines that it will not be safe to grant to such person the privilege of driving a motor vehicle on the public highways.

(3) The applicant is the holder of a license to drive issued by another party state and currently in force unless the applicant surrenders such license.

Article VI

Applicability of Other Laws

Except as expressly required by provisions of this compact, nothing contained herein shall be construed to affect the right of any party state to apply any of its other laws relating to licenses to drive to any person or circumstance, nor to invalidate or prevent any driver license agreement or other cooperative arrangement between a party state and a nonparty state.

Article VII

Compact Administrator and Interchange of Information

(a) The head of the licensing authority of each party state shall be the administrator of this compact for his state. The administrators, acting jointly, shall have the power to formulate all necessary and proper procedures for the exchange of information under this compact.

(b) The administrator of each party state shall furnish to the administrator of each other party state any information or documents reasonably necessary to facilitate the administration of this compact.

Article VIII

Entry Into Force and Withdrawal

(a) This compact shall enter into force and become effective as to any state when it has enacted the same into law.

(b) Any party state may withdraw from this compact by enacting a statute repealing the same, but no such withdrawal shall take effect until six months after the executive head of the withdrawing state has given notice of the withdrawal to the executive heads of all other party states. No withdrawal shall affect the validity or applicability by the licensing authorities of states remaining party to the compact of any report of conviction occurring prior to the withdrawal.

Article IX

Construction and Severability

This compact shall be liberally construed so as to effectuate the purposes thereof. The provisions of this compact shall be severable and if any phrase, clause, sentence or provision of this compact is declared to be contrary to the constitution of any party state or of the United States or the applicability thereof to any government, agency, person or circumstance is held invalid, the validity of the remainder of this compact and the applicability thereof to any government, agency, person or circumstance shall not be affected thereby. If this compact shall be held contrary to the constitution of any state party thereto, the compact shall remain in full force and effect as to the remaining states and in full force and effect as to the state affected as to all severable matters.

History.
1968, c. 166, § 46.1-167.8; 1989, c. 727.

§ 46.2-484. Department of Motor Vehicles to be "licensing authority" within meaning of compact; duties of Department.

As used in the compact, the term "licensing authority" with reference to this Commonwealth shall mean the Department of Motor Vehicles. The Department shall furnish to the appropriate authorities of any other party state any information or documents reasonably necessary to facilitate the administration of Articles III, IV, and V of the compact.

History.
1968, c. 166, § 46.1-167.9; 1989, c. 727.

§ 46.2-485. Compensation and expenses of compact administrator.

The compact administrator provided for in Article VII of the compact shall not be entitled to any additional compensation on account of his service as such administrator, but shall be entitled to expenses incurred in connection with his duties and responsibilities as such administrator, in the same manner as for expenses incurred in connection with any other duties or responsibilities of his office or employment.

History.
1968, c. 166, § 46.1-167.10; 1989, c. 727.

§ 46.2-486. Governor to be "executive head" within meaning of compact.

As used in the compact, with reference to the Commonwealth, the term "executive head" shall mean the Governor.

History.
1968, c. 166, § 46.1-167.11; 1989, c. 727.

§ 46.2-487. Statutes and ordinances deemed to cover offenses specified in subdivision (a) of Article IV of compact.

For the purposes of complying with subdivisions (a) and (c) of Article IV of the compact, the following sections of the Code of Virginia and county, city, or town ordinances substantially paralleling such sections shall be deemed to cover the offenses of subdivision (a) of Article IV: With respect to subdivision (2), §§ 18.2-266 and 46.2-341.24 A; with respect to subdivision (4), §§ 46.2-894 through 46.2-899 subject to the limitation that the accident resulted in the death or personal injury of another; with respect to subdivisions (1) and (3), the Department shall determine which offenses are covered in the same manner as under § 46.2-389.

History.
1968, c. 166, § 46.1-167.12; 1989, c. 727; 1994, c. 255.

§ 46.2-488. Question to be included in application for driver's license; surrender of license issued by another party state.

For the purpose of enforcing subdivision (3) of Article V of this compact, the Department shall include as part of the form for application for a driver's license under § 46.2-323 a question whether the applicant is currently licensed in another state and shall, if the applicant is so licensed, require the surrender of such license prior to the granting of such application in accordance with the provisions of this chapter.

History.
1968, c. 166, § 46.1-167.13; 1984, c. 780; 1989, c. 727.

ARTICLE 19.

DRIVER IMPROVEMENT PROGRAM.

§ 46.2-489. Regulations; appeals.

The Commissioner may, subject to the provisions of § 46.2-203, promulgate regulations which he deems necessary to carry out the provisions of this article.

Any person receiving an order of the Commissioner to suspend or revoke his driver's license or licensing privilege or to require attendance at a driver improvement clinic or placing him on probation may, within thirty days from the date of the order, file a petition of appeal in accordance with § 46.2-410.

History.
1974, c. 453, § 46.1-514.2; 1989, c. 727; 1995, c. 672.

§ 46.2-490. Establishment of driver improvement clinic program; application fees.

A. The Commissioner shall, in his discretion, contract with such entities as the Commissioner deems fit, including private or governmental entities, to develop curricula for a statewide driver improvement clinic program. Such program shall include instruction concerning but not limited to (i) alcohol and drug abuse, (ii) aggressive driving, (iii) distracted driving, (iv) motorcycle awareness, and (v) work zone safety. The driver improvement clinic program shall be established for the purpose of instructing persons identified by the Department and the court system as problem drivers in need of driver improvement education and training and for those drivers interested in improved driving safety. The clinics shall be composed of uniform education and training programs designed for the rehabilitation of problem drivers, and for the purpose of creating a lasting and corrective influence on their driving performance. The clinics shall operate in localities based on their geographical location so as to be reasonably accessible to persons attending these clinics.

B. All businesses, organizations, governmental entities or individuals that want to provide driver improvement clinic instruction as a driver improvement clinic or instructor in the Commonwealth using approved curricula shall apply to the Department to be licensed to do so, based on criteria established by the Department. A nonrefundable annual license application fee of $100 shall be paid to the Department by all such businesses, organizations, governmental entities or individuals. A nonrefundable annual license fee of $25 shall also be paid for each additional clinic location operated by a clinic. A nonrefundable annual license fee of $50 shall be paid to the Department by a person applying for a clinic instructor license. However, neither the annual license fee for each additional clinic location nor the annual license fee for a clinic instructor license shall be required of or collected from the Virginia Association of Volunteer Rescue Squads or its members in connection with clinics that are provided for emergency vehicle operation training. All such application fees collected by the Department shall be paid by the Commissioner into the state treasury and shall be set aside as a special fund to be used to meet the expenses of the Department.

History.

1974, c. 453, § 46.1-514.3; 1989, c. 727; 1995, c. 672; 2002, c. 177; 2004, c. 622; 2007, c. 180.

§ 46.2-490.1. Section 46.2-391.1 not applicable.

The provisions of § 46.2-391.1 shall not apply to any person whose license or other privilege to operate a motor vehicle is suspended or revoked in accordance with the provisions of this article.

History.

1992, c. 109.

§ **46.2-490.2:** Repealed by Acts 2004, c. 622.

§ 46.2-490.3. Definitions.

As used in this chapter, unless the context requires a different meaning:

"Computer-based clinic provider," means any clinic licensed by the Department to conduct driver improvement clinics via the Internet or other electronic means approved by the Department.

"Driver improvement clinic" or *"clinic"* means an individual, partnership or corporation, college or university, or government entity licensed by the Department as prescribed by this chapter for the purpose of instructing persons identified by the Department and the court system as problem drivers; in need of driver improvement education and training; and for drivers interested in improving their own knowledge of highway safety.

"Instructor" means any person, whether acting for himself as operator of a driver training clinic or for such clinic for compensation, who is licensed by the Department as prescribed by this chapter and who teaches, conducts classes, gives demonstrations, or supervises persons undergoing mandatory or voluntary driver improvement training.

History.

2004, c. 622.

§ 46.2-490.4. Action on applications; hearing on denial.

The Commissioner shall act on any application for a clinic or instructor license under this chapter within 30 days after receipt by either granting or denying the application. Any applicant denied a clinic or instructor license shall, on his written request, made within 30 days, be given a hearing at a time and place determined by the Commissioner or his designee. All hearings under this section shall be public and shall be held promptly. The applicant may be represented by counsel. Any applicant denied a license may not apply again for a license for 30 days from the date of denial of the application or outcome of the hearing.

History.

2004, c. 622.

§ 46.2-490.5. Suspension, revocation, cancellation or refusal to renew clinic license or instructor license; imposition of monetary penalties.

A. Except as otherwise provided in this section, no license issued under this chapter shall be suspended, revoked, or cancelled or renewal thereof denied, and no monetary penalty shall be imposed pursuant to § 46.2-490.6, unless the licensee has been furnished a written copy of the complaint against him and the grounds upon which the action is taken and has been offered an opportunity for an administrative hearing to show cause why such action should not be taken.

B. The order suspending, revoking, canceling, or denying renewal of a license, or imposing a monetary penalty, except as otherwise provided in subsection D of this section, shall not become effective until the licensee has had 30 days after notice of the opportunity for a hearing to make a written request for such a hearing. If no hearing has been requested within such 30-day period, the order shall become effective and no hearing shall thereafter be held. Except as provided in subsection D of this section, a timely request for a hearing shall automatically stay operation of the order until after the hearing.

C. Notice of an order suspending, revoking, canceling or denying renewal of a license, or imposing a monetary penalty and advising the licensee of the opportunity for a hearing shall be mailed to the licensee by registered mail to the clinic address as shown in the Department's records and shall be considered served when mailed.

D. Notwithstanding the provisions of subsection B of this section, if the Commissioner makes a finding, after conducting a preliminary investigation, that the conduct of a licensee (i) is in violation of this chapter, regulations adopted pursuant to this chapter, or criteria established by the Department pursuant to this chapter, and (ii) such violation constitutes a danger to public safety, the Commissioner may issue an order suspending, revoking, or denying renewal of the instructor's license, the clinic's license, or both, as deemed appropriate by the Commissioner. Orders suspending, revoking, or denying renewal of such license pursuant to this subsection shall be effective immediately. Notice of the suspension, revocation or denial shall be in writing and mailed in accordance with subsection C of this section. Upon receipt of a request for a hearing appealing the suspension, the licensee shall be afforded the opportunity for a hearing as soon as practicable, but no longer than 30 days of receipt of the hearing request. The suspension shall remain in effect pending the outcome of the hearing.

History.
2004, c. 622.

§ 46.2-490.6. Civil penalties.

In addition to any other sanctions or remedies available to the Commissioner under this chapter, the Commissioner may assess a civil penalty not to exceed $1,000 for any violation of any provision of this chapter, any regulation promulgated thereunder, or any criteria established by the Department pursuant to this chapter. The penalty may be sued for and recovered in the name of the Commonwealth.

History.
2004, c. 622.

§ 46.2-490.7. Acts of owners, operators, officers, directors, partners, and instructors.

If a licensee is a partnership or corporation, it shall be sufficient cause for the denial, suspension, or revocation of a clinic license if any, owner, operator, officer, director, or trustee of the partnership or corporation, or any member in the case of a partnership, has committed any act or omitted any duty which would be cause for refusing, suspending, or revoking a license issued to him as an individual under this chapter. Each licensee shall be responsible for the acts of any of his instructors while acting as his agent, if the clinic approved of those acts or had knowledge of those acts or other similar acts and after such knowledge retained the benefit, proceeds, profits, or advantages accruing from those acts or otherwise ratified those acts.

History.
2004, c. 622.

§ 46.2-490.8. Grounds for denying, suspending, or revoking licenses of clinics and clinic instructors.

A clinic or instructor license may be denied, suspended, or revoked on any one or more of the following grounds:

1. Material misstatement or omission in an application for a driver improvement clinic license or a driver improvement clinic instructor license;
2. Failure to comply subsequent to receipt of a written warning from the Department for any willful failure to comply with any provision of this chapter or any regulation promulgated by the Commissioner under this chapter; or any criteria established by the Department pursuant to this chapter;
3. Defrauding any student in a driver improvement clinic, or any other person in the conduct of a driver improvement clinic's business;
4. Employment of fraudulent devices, methods or practices in connection with compliance with the requirements under the statutes of the Commonwealth;
5. Having used deceptive acts or practices;
6. Knowingly advertising by any means any assertion, representation, or statement of fact which is untrue, misleading, or deceptive in any particular relating to the conduct of a clinic;
7. Having been convicted of any fraudulent act in connection with a driver improvement clinic or driver training school, or any consumer-related fraud;
8. Having been convicted of any criminal act involving the operation of a driver improvement clinic or driver training school;
9. Having been convicted of a felony;
10. Failing or refusing to pay civil penalties imposed by the Department pursuant to § 46.2-490.6.

History.
2004, c. 622.

§ 46.2-490.9. Unlawful acts; prosecution; proceedings in equity.

A. It shall be unlawful for any person to engage in any of the following acts:

1. Operate as a driver improvement clinic or as an instructor without holding a valid license as required by statute or regulation;
2. Make use of any designation provided by statute or regulation to denote a standard of professional or occupational competence without being duly licensed;

3. Perform any act or function that is restricted by statute or regulation to persons holding a driver improvement clinic or instructor license, without being duly licensed;

4. Materially misrepresenting facts in an application for a license;

5. Willfully refusing to furnish the Department information or records required or requested pursuant to statute, regulation, or criteria established by the Department pursuant to § 46.2-490.

B. In addition to the provisions of subsection A of this section, the Department may institute proceedings in equity to enjoin any person from engaging in any unlawful act enumerated in this section. Such proceedings shall be brought in the name of the Commonwealth in the circuit court of the city or county in which the unlawful act occurred or in which the defendant resides.

C. Any person who willfully engages in any unlawful act enumerated in this section shall be guilty of a Class 1 misdemeanor.

History.
2004, c. 622.

§ 46.2-490.10. Changes in form of ownership or name.

Any change in the form of ownership or the addition or deletion of a partner shall require a new application and license. The addition or deletion of a clinic site or change in the name of a clinic shall require immediate notification to the Department and the Department may endorse the change on the license as appropriate. The change of an officer or director of a corporation shall be made at the time of license renewal.

History.
2004, c. 622.

§ 46.2-490.11. Reports, records of licensed computer-based clinic providers.

A. The Department is hereby authorized to require annual, periodical, or special reports from computer-based clinic providers the Department has authorized to conduct clinics; to prescribe the manner and form in which such reports shall be made; and to require from such computer-based clinic providers specific answers to all questions upon which the Department may deem information to be necessary. Such reports shall be under oath whenever the Department so requires. The Department may also require any computer-based clinic provider to file with it a true copy of each or any contract, agreement, or arrangement between such licensees and any person in relation to the provisions of this chapter.

B. The Department may, in its discretion, prescribe (i) the forms of any and all accounts, records, and memoranda to be kept by licensed computer-based clinic providers and (ii) the length of time such accounts, records, and memoranda shall be preserved.

History.
2004, c. 622.

§ 46.2-491. Persons included within scope of article.

This article shall apply to (i) every resident of the Commonwealth, regardless of whether he possesses a driver's license issued by the Department and (ii) every nonresident to whom the Department has issued a driver's license.

History.
1974, c. 453, § 46.1-514.5; 1989, c. 727; 1995, c. 672.

§ 46.2-492. Uniform Demerit Point System.

A. The Commissioner shall assign point values to those convictions, or findings of not innocent in the case of a juvenile, which are required to be reported to the Department in accordance with § 46.2-383 for traffic offenses committed in violation of the laws of the Commonwealth or any county, city, or town ordinance paralleling and substantially conforming to state law, provided that no conviction, or finding of not innocent in the case of a juvenile for any offense, relating to registration, insurance, or equipment shall be included except as otherwise provided by this title.

B. The Commissioner shall assign point values to those convictions received from any other state of the United States, the United States, Canada or its provinces, or any territorial subdivision of any of them, of an offense therein, which if committed in this Commonwealth, would be required to be reported to the Department by § 46.2-383.

C. No point assignment shall be made for any conviction which results from a vehicle having been parked or stopped, in order for the driver to sleep or rest, on the shoulder or other portion of a highway not ordinarily used for vehicular traffic. The court shall make a separate finding on this issue and note such finding on the conviction record.

D. The Uniform Demerit Point System standard for rating convictions of traffic offenses shall be based on the severity of the offense and the potential hazardous exposure to other users of the highways and streets. The Commissioner shall designate the point values assigned to convictions, or findings of not innocent in the case of a juvenile, on a graduated scale not to exceed six demerit points for any single conviction. The Commissioner shall develop point system assignments as follows:

1. Serious traffic offenses such as driving while intoxicated in violation of § 18.2-266, persons under age twenty-one driving after illegally consuming alcohol in violation of § 18.2-266.1, reckless driving in violation of § 46.2-852, speeding twenty or more

miles per hour above the posted speed limit, racing in violation of § 46.2-865, and other serious traffic offenses as the Commissioner may designate, shall be assigned six demerit points.

2. Relatively serious traffic offenses such as failure to yield the right-of-way in violation of §§ 46.2-820 through 46.2-823, speeding between ten and nineteen miles per hour above the posted speed limit, following too closely in violation of § 46.2-816, failure to stop when entering a highway in violation of § 46.2-863, aggressive driving in violation of § 46.2-868.1 and other relatively serious traffic offenses as the Commissioner may designate, shall be assigned four demerit points.

3. Traffic offenses of a less serious nature such as improper driving in violation of § 46.2-869, speeding between one and nine miles per hour above the posted speed limit, improper passing in violation of § 46.2-838, failure to obey a highway sign in violation of § 46.2-830 and other offenses of a less serious nature as the Commissioner may designate, shall be assigned three demerit points.

E. When a person is convicted of two or more traffic offenses committed on a single occasion, he shall be assessed points for one offense only and if the offenses involved have different point values, he shall be assessed points for the offense having the greater point value.

History.
1974, c. 453, § 46.1-514.6; 1976, c. 86; 1989, c. 727; 1992, c. 856; 1998, c. 430; 2002, cc. 752, 782.

§ 46.2-493. Demerit points valid for two years.

Demerit points, assigned to any conviction, or finding of not innocent in the case of a juvenile, shall be valid for a period of two years from the date the offense was committed. Demerit points used prior to the termination of the two-year period as the basis for suspension, revocation, probation, or other action which extends beyond the two-year period shall remain valid until the suspension, revocation, probationary period, or other action has terminated.

History.
1974, c. 453, § 46.1-514.7; 1989, c. 727.

§ 46.2-494. Safe driving point credit.

Every resident or nonresident person holding a valid Virginia driver's license whose driving record does not contain any suspension, revocation, conviction, or finding of not innocent in the case of a juvenile, of a traffic violation, during any calendar year shall be awarded one safe driving point. One safe driving point shall be awarded for each calendar year of safe driving, but no person shall be permitted to accumulate more than five safe driving points. The Commissioner shall apply these points to offset an equivalent number of demerit points, if any, to the chronologically earliest offense conviction, or finding of not innocent in the case of a juvenile, for which demerit points have been assigned and are valid. If subsequent to awarding a safe driving point to any person, the Department receives a conviction, or finding of not innocent in the case of a juvenile, for an offense which occurred during the period for which a safe driving point was awarded for and which requires the Department to assess demerit points, the safe driving point shall be invalidated.

History.
1974, c. 453, § 46.1-514.8; 1978, c. 44; 1989, c. 727.

§ 46.2-495. Advisory letters.

Whenever the driving record of any person who is eighteen years old or older shows an accumulation of at least eight demerit points based on convictions for traffic offenses committed within a period of twelve consecutive months, or at least twelve demerit points based on convictions for traffic offenses committed within a period of twenty-four consecutive months, respectively, the Commissioner may mail, by first-class mail, to the last known address of the person an advisory letter listing his convictions and the demerit points assigned thereto, including his safe driving points, if any, and furnish any other information deemed appropriate and applicable to the rehabilitation of the person, for the purpose of preventing subsequent traffic offenses.

The Department's failure to mail, or the citizen's nonreceipt of the advisory letter shall not be grounds for waiving any other provision of this article.

History.
1974, c. 453, § 46.1-514.9; 1984, c. 673; 1989, c. 727; 1995, c. 672; 1998, cc. 124, 792.

§§ 46.2-496, 46.2-497: Repealed by Acts 1995, c. 672.

§ 46.2-498. Driver improvement clinics; voluntary attendance.

A. Whenever the driving record of any person who is eighteen years old or older shows an accumulation of at least twelve demerit points based on convictions for traffic offenses committed within a period of twelve consecutive months, or at least eighteen demerit points based on convictions for traffic offenses committed within a period of twenty-four consecutive months, respectively, the Commissioner shall direct the person to attend a driver improvement clinic.

B. Except for those persons whose licenses are subject to the restrictions of § 46.2-334.01, whenever the driving record of a person under the age of eighteen years shows an accumulation of (i) at least nine points based on convictions for traffic offenses committed within a period of twelve consecutive months or (ii) at least twelve points based on convictions for traffic offenses committed within a period of twenty-four consecutive months, the Commissioner shall direct the person to attend a driver improvement clinic and such person shall be subject to probation pursuant to § 46.2-499.

C. Except as provided for in subsection D of this section and in §§ 46.2-334.01 and 46.2-505, every person who attends a driver improvement clinic conducted by the Department or those businesses, organizations, governmental entities or individuals certified by the Department to provide driver improvement clinic instruction and who satisfactorily completes the clinic shall have five demerit points subtracted from his total accumulation of demerit points, except in those instances where a person has not accumulated five demerit points, in which case a reduction in demerit points and/or the award of safe driving points will be made. No person shall be allowed to accumulate more than five safe driving points.

Safe driving points shall be awarded or reductions in premium charges, as set forth in § 38.2-2217, shall be received for the completion of a driver improvement clinic only once within a period of two years from the date a person satisfactorily completes the clinic. Persons shall be eligible to voluntarily attend a driver improvement clinic again for either safe driving points or a reduction in premium charges, whichever was not awarded or received previously, one year from the date of satisfactory completion of a driver improvement clinic in which safe driving points or a reduction in premium charges was received or awarded.

D. Any resident or nonresident person holding a valid license to drive a motor vehicle in Virginia, whether or not he has accumulated demerit points, may apply to any business, organization, governmental entity or individual certified by the Department to provide driver improvement clinic instruction for permission to attend a driver improvement clinic on a voluntary basis. Such businesses, organizations, governmental entities or individuals may, when seating space is available, schedule the person to attend a driver improvement clinic.

Persons who voluntarily attend and satisfactorily complete a driver improvement clinic shall be eligible (i) to have five demerit points subtracted from their total accumulation of demerit points, except in those instances where a person has not accumulated five demerit points, in which case a reduction in demerit points and/or the award of safe driving points will be made, or (ii) to receive a reduction in premium charges as set forth under § 38.2-2217, either of which, but not both, shall be awarded or received no more than once in a two-year period, as set forth in subsection C of this section. Such persons shall inform the business, organization or individual providing instruction if they are attending to be awarded safe driving points or to receive a reduction in premium charges as set forth under § 38.2-2217.

History.

1974, c. 453, § 46.1-514.12; 1982, c. 671; 1984, c. 673; 1989, c. 727; 1995, cc. 226, 672; 1996, cc. 307, 1035; 1998, cc. 124, 792.

§ 46.2-499. Driver's license probation.

A. The Commissioner shall place on probation for a period of six months any person who has been directed to attend a driver improvement clinic pursuant to the provisions of § 46.2-498. In addition, the Commissioner shall place any person on probation for a period of six months on receiving a record of a conviction of such person of any offense for which demerit points are assessed and the offense was committed within any driver control period imposed pursuant to § 46.2-500. Whenever a person who has been placed on probation is convicted, or found not innocent in the case of a juvenile, of any offense for which demerit points are assessed, and the offense was committed during the probation period, the Commissioner shall suspend the person's license for a period of ninety days when six demerit points are assigned, for a period of sixty days when four demerit points are assigned, and for a period of forty-five days when three demerit points are assigned. In addition, the Commissioner shall again place the person on probation for a period of six months, effective on termination of the suspension imposed pursuant to this section.

B. Upon request, the Commissioner shall grant a restricted license during the first period of suspension imposed pursuant to subsection A of this section provided the person is otherwise eligible to be licensed. Any person whose driver's license is suspended for a second or subsequent time under subsection A of this section shall be eligible to receive a restricted driver's license only if the violation occurred within a probation period that was immediately preceded by a control period. A restricted license may be issued for any of the purposes set forth in subsection E of § 18.2-271.1. Written verifications of the person's employment, continuing education or medically necessary travel shall also be required and made available to the Commissioner. Whenever a person who has been granted a restricted license pursuant to this subsection is convicted, or found not innocent in the case of a juvenile, of any offense for which demerit points are assessed, and the offense was committed during the restricted license period, the Commissioner shall suspend the person's license using the same demerit point criteria and suspension periods set forth in subsection A of this section. No restricted license issued pursuant to this subsection shall permit any person to operate a commercial motor vehicle as defined in the Virginia Commercial Driver's License Act (§ 46.2-341.1 et seq.).

C. Whenever the Department receives notice from the court that restricted license privileges have been granted to a person who has an existing restricted license issued pursuant to subsection B of this section, the existing restricted license shall be cancelled, and the Commissioner shall suspend the person's license for the period of time remaining on the original order of suspension. No court-granted restricted license shall be issued until the end of the suspension period imposed by the Commissioner.

History.

1974, c. 453, § 46.1-514.13; 1978, c. 221; 1984, c. 673; 1989, c. 727; 1994, c. 849; 1995, c. 672; 1996, cc. 943, 994; 2001, cc. 645, 779.

§ 46.2-500. Driver control period.

Whenever an individual is placed on probation pursuant to §§ 46.2-498, 46.2-499 or § 46.2-506, the Commissioner shall also place the person on driver control status for a period of eighteen months following the termination of the probationary period. If the individual commits any violation during the driver control period for which points are assessed, the Commissioner shall again place the individual on probation for a period of six months and on driver control status for an additional period of eighteen months following the probationary period.

History.

1984, c. 673, § 46.1-514.13:1; 1989, c. 727; 1995, c. 672.

§ 46.2-501. Notice to attend driver improvement clinic.

A. Any notice to attend a driver improvement clinic shall contain:

1. Information on how to schedule a driver improvement clinic.

2. The purpose of the driver improvement clinic, including the consequences of not attending the clinic program.

3. An explanation of the terms of the probationary licensing period.

4. A requirement stating that the clinic must be satisfactorily completed within ninety days from the date of the notice. The Commissioner may for good cause shown, and provided the person provides the Commissioner with satisfactory evidence documenting the need and soonest date of return, extend the time limit otherwise provided for attending such a clinic when the person directed to attend a driver improvement clinic is (i) attending an institution of higher education outside Virginia, and attendance is to coincide with a break in the school year of such institution of higher education, provided that jurisdiction does not offer an approved driver improvement clinic or (ii) in the military or is a military dependent and is stationed outside the United States or outside the Commonwealth in a jurisdiction that does not offer an approved driver improvement clinic.

B. The notice directing any person to attend a driver improvement clinic shall be forwarded by certified mail to the last known address of the person, as shown on the records of the Department.

History.

1974, c. 453, § 46.1-514.14; 1989, c. 727; 1995, c. 672; 2002, c. 385.

§ 46.2-502. Clinic fees.

A. The Department and all businesses, organizations, governmental entities or individuals certified by the Department to provide driver improvement clinic instruction may charge a fee not to exceed $100, which shall include the processing fee set forth in subsection B of this section, to persons notified by the Department to attend a driver improvement clinic. No person shall be permitted to attend a driver improvement clinic unless the person first pays the required attendance fee to the business, organization, governmental entity or individual providing the driver improvement clinic instruction.

B. All businesses, organizations, governmental entities or individuals certified by the Department to provide driver improvement clinic instruction shall collect for the Department a processing fee of $10 from each person attending a driver improvement clinic taught by such businesses, organizations, governmental entities or individuals. Such processing fee payments shall accompany the clinic rosters submitted to the Department by such businesses, organizations, governmental entities or individuals. No such processing fee, however, shall be required or collected from members of volunteer emergency medical services agencies and volunteer fire departments who attend such clinics in order to successfully complete training for emergency vehicle operation. All fees collected by the Department under this subsection shall be paid by the Commissioner into the state treasury and shall be set aside as a special fund to be used to meet the expenses of the Department.

History.

1974, c. 453, § 46.1-514.15; 1984, c. 673; 1987, c. 696; 1989, c. 727; 1992, c. 459; 1995, c. 672; 1996, c. 171; 1998, c. 437; 2013, c. 326; 2015, cc. 502, 503.

§ 46.2-503. Suspension of privilege to operate a motor vehicle for failure to attend clinics.

The Commissioner shall suspend the privilege to operate a motor vehicle of any person who fails to satisfactorily complete a driver improvement clinic. This suspension shall remain in effect until such person satisfactorily completes the driver improvement clinic. This section shall not be applicable to persons attending clinics on a voluntary basis.

History.

1974, c. 453, § 46.1-514.16; 1984, c. 673; 1989, c. 727; 1995, c. 672.

§ 46.2-504. Form and contents of order of probation, suspension or revocation; service.

Whenever the Commissioner issues a probation, suspension or revocation order in accordance with any provision of this chapter, the order shall provide the addressee with a minimum of ten days' notice and shall be served as provided in § 46.2-416.

History.

1974, c. 453, § 46.1-514.17; 1980, c. 704; 1984, c. 673; 1989, c. 727.

§ 46.2-505. Court may direct defendant to attend driver improvement clinic.

A. Any circuit or general district court or juvenile court of the Commonwealth, or any federal court, charged with the duty of hearing traffic cases for offenses committed in violation of any law of the Commonwealth, or any valid local ordinance, or any federal law regulating the movement or operation of a motor vehicle, may require any person found guilty, or in the case of a juvenile found not innocent, of a violation of any state law, local ordinance, or federal law, to attend a driver improvement clinic or a mature driver motor vehicle crash prevention course as provided for in § 38.2-2217. The attendance requirement may be in lieu of or in addition to the penalties prescribed by § 46.2-113, the ordinance, or federal law. The court shall determine if a person is to receive safe driving points upon satisfactory completion of a driver improvement clinic conducted by the Department or by any business, organization, governmental entity or individual certified by the Department to provide driver improvement clinic instruction. In the absence of such notification, no safe driving points shall be awarded by the Department.

B. Notwithstanding the provisions of subsection A, no court shall, as a result of a person's attendance at a driver improvement clinic or a mature driver motor vehicle crash prevention course, reduce, dismiss, or defer the conviction of a person charged with any offense committed while operating a commercial motor vehicle as defined in the Virginia Commercial Driver's License Act (§ 46.2-341.1 et seq.) or any holder of a commercial driver's license charged with any offense committed while operating a noncommercial motor vehicle.

C. Persons required by the court to attend a driver improvement clinic or a mature driver motor vehicle crash prevention course shall notify the court if the driver improvement clinic or mature driver motor vehicle crash prevention course has or has not been attended and satisfactorily completed, in compliance with the court order. Failure of the person to attend and satisfactorily complete a driver improvement clinic or mature driver motor vehicle crash prevention course, in compliance with the court order, may be punished as contempt of such court.

History.

1974, c. 453, § 46.1-514.18; 1989, c. 727; 1995, c. 672; 2002, c. 724; 2008, c. 190; 2014, c. 282.

§ 46.2-506. Formal hearings; suspension for excessive point accumulation.

A. Whenever the operating record of any person shows a continued disregard of the motor vehicle laws subsequent to being placed on probation, he may be charged as a reckless or negligent driver of a motor vehicle, and cited for a formal hearing in accordance with the provisions of §§ 46.2-402 through 46.2-408. If the hearing results in the suspension of a person's driving privilege, the person shall be placed on probation at the end of the suspension period in accordance with the provisions of § 46.2-499.

B. Whenever the operating record of any person shows an accumulation of at least eighteen demerit points based on convictions, or findings of not innocent in the case of a juvenile, for traffic violations committed within any twelve consecutive months, or at least twenty-four demerit points based on convictions, or findings of not innocent in the case of a juvenile, for traffic violations committed within any twenty-four consecutive months, respectively, the Commissioner shall suspend the person's license or licenses for a period of ninety days and thereafter until he attends and satisfactorily completes a driver improvement clinic. At the end of this suspension period, the person shall be placed on probation in accordance with the provisions of § 46.2-499.

History.

1974, c. 453, § 46.1-514.19; 1984, c. 673; 1989, c. 727; 1995, c. 672.

CHAPTER 4.

RESERVED.

CHAPTER 5.

RESERVED.

CHAPTER 6.

TITLING AND REGISTRATION OF MOTOR VEHICLES.

Article 1.

Titling and Registration, Generally.

Article 2.

Titling Vehicles.

Article 2.1.

All-Terrain Vehicle and Off-Road Motorcycle Certificates of Title.

Article 3.

Registration of Vehicles.

Article 4.

Temporary Registration.

Article 5.

Reciprocity for Nonresidents.

Article 6.

Exemptions from Registration.

Article 7.

Fees for Registration.

Article 8.

Registration of Uninsured Motor Vehicles.

Article 9.

License Plates, Generally.

Article 10.

Special License Plates.

Article 11.

State and Local Motor Vehicle Registration.

Article 12.

Insurance Requirements for Motor Carriers.

ARTICLE 1.

TITLING AND REGISTRATION, GENERALLY.

§ 46.2-600. Owner to secure registration and certificate of title or certificate of ownership.

Except as otherwise provided, for the purposes of this chapter, a moped shall be deemed a motor vehicle.

Except as otherwise provided in this chapter every person who owns a motor vehicle, trailer or semitrailer, or his authorized attorney-in-fact, shall, before it is operated on any highway in the Commonwealth, register with the Department and obtain from the Department the registration card and certificate of title for the vehicle. Individuals applying for registration shall provide the Department with the residence address of the owner of the vehicle being registered. A business applying for registration shall provide the Department with the street address of the owner or lessee of the vehicle being registered.

At the option of the applicant for registration, the address shown on the title and registration card may be either a post office box or the business or residence address of the applicant.

Unless he has previously applied for registration and a certificate of title or he is exempted under §§ 46.2-619, 46.2-626.1, 46.2-631, and 46.2-1206, every person residing in the Commonwealth who owns a motor vehicle, trailer, or semitrailer, or his duly authorized attorney-in-fact, shall, within 30 days of the purchase or transfer, apply to the Department for a certificate of ownership.

Nothing in this chapter shall be construed to require titling or registration in the Commonwealth of any farm tractor or special construction and forestry equipment, as defined in § 46.2-100.

Notwithstanding the foregoing provisions of this section, provided such vehicle is registered and titled elsewhere in the United States, nothing in this chapter shall be construed to require titling or registration in the Commonwealth of any vehicle located in the Commonwealth if that vehicle is registered to a non-Virginia resident active duty military service member, activated reserve or national guard member, mobilized reserve or national guard member living in the Commonwealth, or person who is serving a full-time church service or proselyting mission of not more than 36 months and who is not gainfully employed.

History.

Code 1950, § 46-42; 1958, c. 541, § 46.1-41; 1972, c. 301; 1978, c. 402; 1980, c. 469; 1986, c. 228; 1988, c. 363; 1989, c. 727; 2003, c. 297; 2007, c. 934; 2010, c. 135; 2013, cc. 244, 367, 783; 2016, c. 428.

§ 46.2-601. Appointment of Commissioner agent for service of process.

Each nonresident owner of a motor vehicle, trailer, or semitrailer applying for the registration thereof in the Commonwealth shall file with the application a duly executed instrument, constituting the Commissioner and his successors in office his attorney on whom all lawful process against and notice to the owner may be served in any action or legal proceeding brought as the result of the operation or use of any motor vehicle, trailer, or semitrailer registered by or for him, in the Commonwealth; and therein shall agree that any process against or notice to the owner shall have the same effect as if served on the owner within the Commonwealth. The service of the process or notice shall be made by leaving a copy of it in the office of the Commissioner with a service fee of three dollars to be taxed as a part of the costs of the suit. The Commissioner shall forthwith notify the owner of the service by letter.

History.

Code 1950, § 46-125; 1958, c. 541, § 46.1-139; 1989, c. 727.

§ 46.2-602. Titling and registration of foreign market vehicles.

A. The Department shall not issue a permanent certificate of title or registration for a foreign market vehicle until the applicant submits proof that the vehicle complies with federal safety requirements.

B. The Department shall accept as proof that a foreign market vehicle complies with federal safety requirements documents from either the United States Department of Transportation or the United States Customs Service stating that the vehicle conforms or has been brought into conformity with federal safety requirements.

C. The certificate of title of any foreign market vehicle titled under this section shall contain an appropriate notation that the owner has submitted proof that it complies with federal safety requirements.

D. Any foreign market vehicle previously titled in the Commonwealth shall be titled and registered without further proof of compliance with federal safety requirements. If, however, proof of compliance is not submitted to the Department, the certificate of title shall contain an appropriate notation that the owner of the foreign market vehicle has not submitted proof that the vehicle complies with federal safety requirements.

E. No foreign market vehicle manufactured prior to 1968 shall be subject to this section.

F. Notwithstanding the provisions of subsection A of this section, the Department shall issue a nonnegotiable title for a foreign market vehicle on submission of a complete application for a title including all necessary documents of ownership. A negotiable title will be issued on proof of compliance as provided in subsection A of this section. The Department shall show on the face of any title issued under this section any negotiable security interests in the motor vehicle as provided in §§ 46.2-636 through 46.2-643.

G. The Department shall not transfer the title to a foreign market vehicle if ownership of the vehicle is evidenced by a nonnegotiable title, unless the nonnegotiable title owner is deceased. If the nonnegotiable title owner is deceased, a new, nonnegotiable title may be issued to the legatee or distributee in accordance with §§ 46.2-633 and 46.2-634.

H. A nonnegotiable title may be issued for the purpose of recording a lien. A negotiable certificate of title shall be issued on proof of compliance with all regulations prescribed in this section.

I. Notwithstanding other provisions of this section, the Department shall issue, on application, a temporary, nonrenewable 180-day registration to a foreign market vehicle upon:

1. Proof that the vehicle has been brought into compliance with all federal safety requirements and that the applicant is merely waiting for documentary releases from the Federal Department of Transportation;

2. Proof of satisfactory passage of a Virginia safety inspection; and

3. Submission of a complete application for a title, including all necessary documents of ownership.

J. The Department shall withhold delivery of the certificate of title during the 180-day period of conditional registration and shall not issue the permanent title until the requirements of subsection A of this section have been met.

K. Upon application, the Department shall issue a temporary one-trip permit for the purpose of transporting a foreign market vehicle from the port of entry to the applicant's home or to a conversion facility. The one-trip permit shall be issued in accordance with § 46.2-651.

History.

1986, c. 613, § 46.1-41.2; 1989, c. 727.

§ 46.2-602.1. Titling and registration of replica vehicles.

Notwithstanding any other provision of this chapter, the model year of vehicles constructed or assembled by multiple manufacturers or assemblers shall be the model year of which the vehicle is a replica. No vehicle titled under this section shall be driven more than 5,000 miles per year as shown by the vehicle's odometer. No vehicle titled under this section shall be automatically eligible for antique motor vehicle license plates provided for in § 46.2-730.

Any vehicle registered under this section shall be subject to vehicle safety inspections as provided for in Article 21 (§ 46.2-1157 et seq.) of Chapter 10 and emissions inspections as provided for in Article 22 (§ 46.2-1176 et seq.) of Chapter 10. Such vehicles shall meet such safety and emission requirements as established for the model year of which the vehicle is a replica.

The Department shall assign each such vehicle a new vehicle identification number, line-make, and model year, if required.

History.

2007, cc. 325, 393.

§ 46.2-602.2. Titling and registration of company vehicles of automotive manufacturers.

For the purpose of this section:

"Automotive manufacturer" means the entire worldwide affiliated group as defined in § 58.1-3700.1, as of July 31, 2007, if at least one member of the worldwide affiliated group is an automotive manufacturer, as classified under the 2007 North American Industry Classification System Codes 3361, 3362, and 3363 in effect as of December 31, 2007.

"Company vehicles" means the following vehicles owned or operated by an automotive manufacturer having its headquarters in Virginia:

1. Vehicles used for sales or service training, advertising, public relations, quality control, and emissions or other testing and/or evaluation purposes;

2. Vehicles used for headquarters-related purposes, including but not necessarily limited to use by visiting executives or employees;

3. Vehicles provided for use by eligible headquarters employees or their eligible family members in compliance with established corporate policies as may from time to time be in effect, but not more than four vehicles may be leased for the benefit of any eligible headquarters employee at any one time; and

4. All other vehicles deemed by the automotive manufacturer to serve a headquarters function, but excluding any vehicles provided for use by eligible headquarters employees or their eligible family members in compliance with established corporate policies.

"Family members" means the spouse of an employee, and the children and parents of an employee or an employee's spouse.

"Headquarters" means a facility at which company employees are physically employed and at which the majority of the company's financial, personnel, legal, or planning functions are handled either on a regional or national basis.

Each automotive manufacturer having its headquarters in the Commonwealth shall be issued a motor vehicle dealer license or equivalent permit by the Commissioner. Such license or permit shall authorize the automotive manufacturer to dispose of company vehicles using a manufacturer's certificate of origin, but if disposed of within the Commonwealth of Virginia, such vehicles may only be transferred to a new motor vehicle dealer holding a franchise for the automotive manufacturer's line-make, provided each vehicle is transferred with a designation indicating that it is not a new motor vehicle as defined in § 46.2-1500. The automotive manufacturer and its affiliates may sell used motor vehicles directly to its lessees.

An automotive manufacturer having its headquarters in the Commonwealth may obtain a title for any company vehicle, but issuance of any such title shall be exempt from all fees except for the fee for issuance of a certificate of title as provided in § 46.2-627.

All company vehicles used as provided in this section may be driven using license plates issued and affixed as provided in Article 5 (§ 46.2-1545.1 et seq.) of Chapter 15. All such vehicles shall be classified as merchants' capital and subject to merchants' capital tax pursuant to Article 3 (§ 58.1-3509 et seq.) of Chapter 35 of Title 58.1.

History.

2008, cc. 304, 753; 2015, c. 615.

§ 46.2-602.3. Titling and registration of converted electric vehicles.

A. Upon receipt of an application and such evidence of ownership as required by the Commissioner pursuant to § 46.2-625, the Department shall issue a certificate of title for a converted electric vehicle. The first certificate of title issued for a converted electric vehicle shall be an original certificate of title, regardless of the submission of a Virginia certificate of title issued for the vehicle prior to conversion.

B. 1. No converted electric vehicle shall be registered or operated on the highways of the Commonwealth until the owner submits to the Department a certification by a certified Virginia safety inspector that the conversion to electric propulsion is complete and proof that the vehicle has passed a Virginia safety inspection subsequent to the certification. Such certification shall be on a form approved by the Commissioner and the Superintendent and shall state that the inspector has verified that (i) the internal combustion engine has been removed; (ii) the fuel tank has been removed and not replaced; (iii) a traction battery pack has been installed that is distinct from the vehicle's original auxiliary battery system; and (iv) an electric motor has been installed to drive the wheels of the vehicle. The safety inspector may charge a fee not to exceed $40 to complete a certification pursuant to this subsection, but no such charge shall be mandatory. Any fee charged for such certification shall be in addition to any fee imposed pursuant to § 46.2-1167 for the completion of a Virginia safety inspection.

2. The completion of the certification required by this section shall not impose any liability on the safety inspector for the quality of the conversion process; however, nothing in this section shall be construed so as to relieve the safety inspector of any liability that may be imposed pursuant to Article 21 (§ 46.2-1157 et seq.) of Chapter 10 or under any regulation promulgated pursuant to § 46.2-1165, relating to the safety inspection of the converted electric vehicle.

3. The submission of a certification pursuant to this section shall be sufficient documentation to exempt the converted electric vehicle for which it is submitted from the emissions inspection program required by Article 22 (§ 46.2-1176 et seq.) of Chapter 10.

4. When necessary and upon application, the Department shall issue temporary trip permits in accordance with § 46.2-651 for the purpose of transporting the converted electric vehicle to and from an official Virginia safety inspection station.

C. The provisions of this section need only be satisfied once for each converted electric vehicle.

History.

2012, c. 177; 2013, c. 216.

§ 46.2-602.4. Titling and registration of off-road motorcycle converted to on-road use.

A. For the purpose of this section:

"Converter" means a person who, through the act of conversion, alters an off-road motorcycle for on-road use on the highways by the addition, substitution, or removal of motor vehicle equipment, creating a motor vehicle to which Federal Motor Vehicle Safety Standards for new motorcycles will become applicable at the time of the conversion. A converter shall be considered a manufacturer responsible under 49 U.S.C. § 30112 for compliance of the motorcycle with Federal Motor Vehicle Safety Standards and the certification of compliance required by those standards.

"Federal Motor Vehicle Safety Standards" means the standards prescribed by 49 C.F.R. Part 571.

"Manufacturer" means a person manufacturing or assembling motor vehicles or motor vehicle equipment.

"Motor vehicle equipment" means (i) any system, part, or component of a motor vehicle as originally manufactured or (ii) any similar part or component manufactured or sold for replacement or improvement of a system, part, or component, or as an accessory or addition to a motor vehicle.

"Off-road motorcycle converted to on-road use" means every off-road motorcycle that has been converted for use on the public highways with the addition of such necessary equipment to meet all applicable Federal Motor Vehicle Safety Standards for new motorcycles for the year in which it is converted.

B. Each converter shall certify in accordance with the requirements of subsection E that the off-road motorcycle converted to on-road use meets all applicable Federal Motor Vehicle Safety Standards for new motorcycles for the year in which it is converted. If the converter is unavailable or unknown, the owner shall certify that the converter is unavailable or unknown and that he assumes responsibility for all duties and corresponding liabilities under the Federal Motor Vehicle Safety Act. If a converter or owner fails or refuses to provide the required certification, the vehicle shall remain an off-road motorcycle.

C. Each converter, or owner if the converter is unavailable or unknown, shall permanently affix to each vehicle a label containing the following: (i) the name of manufacturer, (ii) the month and year of manufacture, (iii) the gross vehicle weight rating, (iv) the gross axle weight rating, (v) certification that the vehicle conforms to all applicable Federal Motor Vehicle Safety Standards in effect on the date of manufacture in the year in which it is converted, (vi) the vehicle identification number, and (vii) the motorcycle vehicle classification. Such label shall meet the requirements set forth in 49 C.F.R. § 567.4.

D. Upon receipt of an application and such evidence of ownership as required by the Commissioner pursuant to § 46.2-625, the Department shall issue a certificate of title for an off-road motorcycle converted to on-road use. The first certificate of title issued for an off-road motorcycle converted to on-road use shall be an original certificate of title, regardless of the submission of a Virginia certificate of title issued for the off-road motorcycle prior to conversion.

E. No off-road motorcycle converted to on-road use shall be registered or operated on the highways of the Commonwealth until the owner submits to the Department, upon a form approved and furnished by the Department, (i) certification that the motor vehicle has passed the motor vehicle safety inspection subsequent to the conversion; (ii) certification from the converter, or owner if the converter is unavailable or unknown, that the motor vehicle meets all applicable Federal Motor Vehicle Safety Standards; and (iii) certification that the motor vehicle has been labeled in accordance with subsection C.

F. When necessary and upon application, the Department shall issue temporary trip permits in accordance with § 46.2-651 for the purpose of transporting the off-road motorcycle converted to on-road use to and from an official motor vehicle safety inspection station.

G. Notwithstanding §§ 46.2-105 and 46.2-605, any certification required by this section found to be knowingly given falsely is punishable as a Class 1 misdemeanor.

History.
2015, c. 259.

§ 46.2-603. Issuance of certificate of title and registration card.

A. The Department, on receiving an application for a certificate of title for a motor vehicle, trailer, or semitrailer, shall issue to the owner a certificate of title and a registration card as separate documents.

B. Subject to all applicable federal laws, the Department may refrain from issuing a certificate of title in paper form and, instead, shall create only the electronic record of such title to be retained by the Department in its existing electronic title record system with a notation that no certificate of title has been printed on paper. The owner of a vehicle will be deemed to have obtained and the Department will be deemed to have issued a certificate of title when such title record has been created electronically as provided in this subsection. An owner or lienholder listed on a title record so created may at any time request and the Department shall provide a paper certificate of title for the vehicle. Except as provided in § 46.2-603.1, all transfers of vehicle ownership shall require a paper certificate of title in accordance with, and subject to, all applicable federal laws.

History.
Code 1950, § 46-68; 1958, c. 541, § 46.1-68; 1989, c. 727; 2005, c. 305; 2012, c. 650.

§ 46.2-603.1. Electronic titling program.

The Department may establish an electronic titling program for any "new motor vehicle" as that term is defined in § 46.2-1500. Participants in the electronic titling program shall submit electronic applications for original motor vehicle titles in a form and format prescribed by the Department. Participants must provide all documentation or information required by the Department to process the electronic title application, including an electronic manufacturer's certificate of origin and any information required by the Department in accordance with § 46.2-623. The records of a nationally recognized motor vehicle title database shall be searched prior to transfer of vehicle ownership. Participants shall collect from the purchaser of the new motor vehicle any fee charged for the search of the nationally recognized motor vehicle title database. Upon receipt of a completed electronic application, the Department shall refrain from issuing a certificate of title in paper form and, instead, shall create only the electronic record of such title to be retained by the Department in its existing electronic title record system with a notation that no certificate of title has been printed on paper. The owner of a motor vehicle will be deemed to have obtained and the Department will be deemed to have issued a certificate of title when such title record has been created electronically as provided in this section. An owner listed on a title record so created may at any time request and the Department shall provide a paper certificate of title for the vehicle.

History.
2012, c. 650.

§ 46.2-604. Contents of registration card and certificate; vehicle color data; notation of certain disabled owners.

The registration card and the certificate of title shall each contain the date issued, the registration number assigned to the motor vehicle, trailer, or semitrailer, the name and address of the owner, a description of the registered motor vehicle, trailer, or semitrailer, and other statement of facts as may be determined by the Department. Every applicant for registration or renewal of registration shall indicate on his application the color that best describes the predominant color of the vehicle. In so doing, the applicant shall select a color from a list of standard, primary colors, developed by the Commissioner. Such color information shall be maintained in the Department's records and made available to law-enforcement agencies for their official use and may, in the discretion of the Commissioner, be indicated on the registration card and the certificate of title.

Whenever disabled parking license plates are issued under § 46.2-731 to the parent or legal guardian of a person with a disability that limits or impairs his ability to walk or that creates a concern for his safety while walking, the registration card for such vehicle shall so note.

Whenever (i) disabled parking license plates are issued under § 46.2-731 or DV disabled parking license plates are issued under subsection B of § 46.2-739 and (ii) the vehicle for which such license plates are issued is registered in the name of more than one owner, the registration card for such vehicle shall include a notation indicating which owner or owners of the vehicle is a "person with a disability that limits or impairs his ability to walk" as defined in § 46.2-1240. However, no vehicle owned and used by an organization for the transportation of disabled persons shall be subject to the notation requirement imposed by this paragraph.

The registration card shall contain forms for providing notice to the Department of a transfer of the ownership of the motor vehicle, trailer, or semitrailer. Whenever a Virginia-registered motor vehicle is sold or its ownership otherwise transferred, the seller or transferor shall notify the Department of the sale or transfer by completing the appropriate portion of the registration card. Section 46.2-113 shall not apply to failures to provide such notification.

The certificate of title shall contain a statement of the owner's title and of all liens or encumbrances on the motor vehicle, trailer, or semitrailer described in the certificate and whether possession is held by the owner under a lease, contract, or conditional sale or other like agreement. The certificate of title shall also contain forms of assignment of title or interest and warranty of title with space for notation of liens and encumbrances on the motor vehicle, trailer, or semitrailer at the time of a transfer.

History.
Code 1950, § 46-79; 1958, c. 541, § 46.1-79; 1988, c. 363; 1989, c. 727; 1990, c. 79; 1998, cc. 285, 302; 2000, c. 667; 2004, c. 692.

§ 46.2-605. Altering or forging certificate of title, salvage/nonrepairable certificate, or registration card; penalty.

Any person who (i) with fraudulent intent alters any certificate of title, salvage/nonrepairable certificate, or registration card issued by the Department or by any other state, (ii) with fraudulent intent, makes a false statement on any application for a certificate of title, salvage/nonrepairable certificate, or registration card issued by the Department or any other state, (iii) forges or counterfeits any certificate of title, salvage/nonrepairable certificate, or registration card purporting to have been issued by the Department under the provisions of this title or by any other state under a similar law or laws or, with fraudulent intent, alters or falsifies, or forges any assignment of title, or salvage/nonrepairable certificate, (iv) holds or uses any certificate, registration card, or assignment, knowing the same to have been altered, forged, or falsified, shall be guilty of a Class 6 felony.

It shall be unlawful for any person to conspire with any other person to violate the provisions of this section.

History.
Code 1950, § 46-12; 1958, c. 541, § 46.1-85; 1986, c. 490; 1989, c. 727; 1996, cc. 591, 917.

§ 46.2-606. Notice of change of address.

A. Whenever any person who has applied for or obtained the registration or title to a vehicle moves from the address shown in his application, registration card or certificate of title, he shall notify the Department of his change of address within 30 days.

B. The Department may contract with the United States Postal Service or an authorized agent to use the National Change of Address System for the purpose of obtaining current address information for a person whose name appears in customer records maintained by the Department. If the Department receives information from the National Change of Address System indicating that a person whose name appears in a Department record has submitted a permanent change of address to the Postal Service, the Department may then update its records with the mailing address obtained from the National Change of Address System.

C. Anyone failing to comply with this section may be charged a fee of $5, to be used to cover the Department's expenses. Notwithstanding the foregoing provision of this subsection, no fee shall be imposed on any person whose address is obtained from the National Change of Address System.

History.

1974, c. 347, § 46.1-52.1; 1989, c. 727; 1996, cc. 943, 994; 2010, cc. 25, 55.

§ 46.2-607. Duplicates for lost or mutilated indicia of titling and registration.

If any license plate, decal, registration card, or certificate of title is lost, mutilated, or has become illegible, the person who is entitled to the certificate shall immediately apply for and obtain a replacement after furnishing information of the fact satisfactory to the Department and after payment of the required fees.

A person who has twice obtained a replacement set of license plates or decals shall not be entitled to obtain another set of license plates or decals during the license period for which the original set of plates was issued unless the Commissioner finds that the replacement license plates or decals have been lost or mutilated without the fault of the person entitled to them.

History.

Code 1950, § 46-53; 1958, c. 541, § 46.1-55; 1968, c. 334; 1972, c. 609; 1982, c. 671; 1986, c. 165; 1989, c. 727.

§ 46.2-608. When application for registration or certificate of title rejected.

The Department may reject an application for the registration of a motor vehicle, trailer, or semitrailer or certificate of title when:

1. The applicant for registration is not entitled to it under the provisions of this title or Title 43;
2. The applicant has neglected or refused to furnish the Department with the information required on the appropriate official form or other information required by the Department;
3. The required fees have not been paid;
4. The vehicle is not equipped with equipment required by this title or the vehicle is equipped with equipment prohibited by this title;
5. The applicant, if not a resident of the Commonwealth, has not filed with the Commissioner a power of attorney appointing him the applicant's authorized agent or attorney-in-fact upon whom process or notice may be served as required in § 46.2-601;
6. There is reason to believe that the application or accompanying documents have been altered or contain any false statement;
7. The vehicle is a commercial motor vehicle and is being operated by a motor carrier that has been prohibited to operate by a federal agency;
8. The vehicle is a commercial motor vehicle and the vehicle has been assigned for safety to a motor carrier that has been prohibited from operating by a federal agency or a motor carrier whose business is operated, managed, or otherwise controlled or affiliated with a person who is ineligible for registration, including the owner or a relative, family member, corporate officer, or shareholder; or
9. The vehicle is a commercial motor vehicle and the applicant has applied on behalf of or for the benefit of the real party in interest who has been issued a federal out of service order or if the applicant's business is operated, managed, or otherwise controlled or affiliated with a person who is ineligible for registration, including the applicant or an entity, relative, family member, corporate officer, or shareholder.

For purposes of this section, the terms "commercial motor vehicle" and "motor carrier" shall be as defined in § 52-8.4.

History.

Code 1950, § 46-54; 1958, c. 541, § 46.1-56; 1968, c. 605; 1986, c. 490; 1989, c. 727; 2011, c. 61.

§ 46.2-609. When registration may be suspended or revoked.

A. The Department may revoke the registration of a motor vehicle, trailer, or semitrailer and may revoke the registration card, license plates, or decals whenever the person to whom the registration card, license plates, or decals have been issued makes or permits to be made an unlawful use of any of them or permits their use by a person not entitled to them, or fails or refuses to pay, within the time prescribed by law, any fuel taxes or other taxes or fees required to be collected or authorized to be collected by the Department regardless of whether the fee applies to that particular vehicle.

B. The Department may suspend or revoke the registration card, license plates, or decals issued to a commercial motor vehicle if the motor carrier responsible for safety of the vehicle has been prohibited from operating by a federal agency. For purposes of this subsection, the terms "commercial motor vehicle" and "motor carrier" shall be as defined in § 52-8.4.

History.

Code 1950, § 46-57; 1958, c. 541, § 46.1-59; 1962, c. 368; 1972, c. 609; 1974, c. 171; 1989, c. 727; 2011, c. 61.

§ 46.2-610. Suspension of registration on theft or embezzlement of vehicle; notices.

Whenever the owner of any motor vehicle, trailer, or semitrailer which is stolen or embezzled notifies the Department directly or through law-enforcement authorities of the theft or embezzlement, the Department shall immediately suspend the registration of that motor vehicle, trailer, or semitrailer until such time as it shall be notified that the owner has recovered his motor vehicle, trailer, or semitrailer. In the event of an embezzlement the owner shall obtain a warrant for the arrest of the person charged with the embezzlement before the Department shall suspend the registration. Any such suspension shall be effective only for the current registration period in which the notice was given. If during that period the motor vehicle, trailer, or semitrailer is not recovered, a new notice may be given with like effect during the ensuing period. Every owner who has given a notice of theft or embezzlement shall immediately notify the Department of the recovery of his motor vehicle, trailer, or semitrailer.

History.

Code 1950, § 46-4; 1958, c. 541, § 46.1-60; 1989, c. 727.

§ 46.2-611. Appeal.

From any action by the Department under this title suspending or revoking, rescinding or cancelling the registration of any motor vehicle, trailer, or semitrailer or suspending, revoking, cancelling, or repossessing any registration card, license plates, or decals or denying an application for transfer of title, an appeal shall lie in accordance with the Administrative Process Act (§ 2.2-4000 et seq.).

History.

Code 1950, § 46-60; 1958, c. 541, § 46.1-61; 1972, c. 609; 1979, c. 478; 1986, c. 615; 1989, c. 727.

§ 46.2-612. Failure to surrender revoked certificate of title, registration card, license plates or decals.

It shall be unlawful for the owner of any motor vehicle, trailer, or semitrailer, for which license plates, decals, or registration cards have been revoked pursuant to this article, to fail or refuse to surrender to the Department, on demand, a certificate of title if it is incorrect in any material particular, or a revoked registration card, license plates, and decals. Violation of this section shall constitute a Class 2 misdemeanor.

History.

Code 1950, § 46-61; 1958, c. 541, § 46.1-62; 1962, c. 302; 1972, c. 609; 1989, c. 727.

§ 46.2-613. Offenses relating to registration, licensing, and certificates of title; penalty.

No person shall:

1. Operate or permit the operation of a motor vehicle, trailer, or semitrailer owned, leased, or otherwise controlled by him to be operated on a highway unless (i) it is registered, (ii) a certificate of title therefor has been issued, and (iii) it has displayed on it the license plate or plates and decal or decals, if any, assigned to it by the Department for the current registration period, subject to the exemptions mentioned in Article 5 (§ 46.2-655 et seq.) and Article 6 (§ 46.2-662 et seq.) of this chapter. The provisions of this subdivision shall apply to the registration, licensing, and titling of mopeds on or after July 1, 2014.

2. Display, cause or permit to be displayed, any registration card, certificate of title, or license plate or decal which he knows is fictitious or which he knows has been cancelled, revoked, suspended, or altered; or display or cause or permit to be displayed on any motor vehicle, trailer, or semitrailer any license plate or decal that he knows is currently issued for another vehicle. Violation of this subdivision shall constitute a Class 2 misdemeanor.

3. Possess or lend or knowingly permit the use of any registration card, license plate, or decal by anyone not entitled to it.

4. Fail or refuse to surrender to the Department or the Department of State Police, on demand, any certificate of title, registration card, or license plate or decal which has been suspended, cancelled, or revoked. Violation of this subdivision shall constitute a Class 2 misdemeanor.

5. Use a false name or address in any application for the registration of any motor vehicle, trailer, or semitrailer or for a certificate of title or for any renewal or duplicate certificate, or knowingly to make a false statement of a material fact or to conceal a material fact or otherwise commit a fraud in any registration application. Violation of this subdivision shall constitute a Class 1 misdemeanor.

History.

Code 1950, § 46-63; 1950, p. 251; 1958, c. 541, § 46.1-64; 1960, c. 79; 1972, c. 609; 1974, c. 400; 1975, c. 124; 1979, c. 620; 1989, c. 727; 1997, c. 283; 1999, c. 212; 2002, c. 93; 2006, cc. 444, 472; 2013, c. 783.

§ 46.2-613.1. Civil penalty for violation of license, registration, and tax requirements and vehicle size limitations.

A. A civil penalty of $250 and a processing fee of $20 shall be levied against any person who while at a permanent weighing station:

1. Operates or permits the operation of a truck or tractor truck with a gross weight greater than 7,500 pounds, a trailer, or a semitrailer owned, leased, or otherwise controlled by him on any highway in the Commonwealth unless (i) it is registered, (ii) a certificate of title therefor has been issued, and (iii) it has displayed on it the license plate or plates and decal or decals required by this title.

2. Operates or causes to be operated on any highway in the Commonwealth any motor vehicle that is not in compliance with the Unified Carrier Registration System authorized under 49 U.S.C. § 14504a, enacted pursuant to the Unified Carrier Registration Act of 2005, and the federal regulations promulgated thereunder.

3. Operates or permits the operation of any truck or tractor truck for which the fee for registration is

prescribed by § 46.2-697 on any highway in the Commonwealth (i) without first having paid the registration fee hereinabove prescribed or (ii) if at the time of operation the gross weight of the vehicle or of the combination of vehicles of which it is a part is in excess of the gross weight on the basis of which it is registered. In any case where a pickup truck is used in combination with another vehicle, the civil penalty and processing fee shall be assessed only if the combined gross weight exceeds the combined gross weight on the basis of which each vehicle is registered.

4. (i) Fails to obtain a proper registration card, identification marker, or other evidence of registration as required by Chapter 21 (§ 46.2-2100 et seq.); (ii) operates or causes to be operated on any highway in the Commonwealth any motor vehicle that does not carry the proper registration and identification marker required by Chapter 21 (§ 46.2-2100 et seq.) or any motor vehicle that does not display an identification marker or other identifying information as prescribed by the Department or required by this Title; or (iii) operates or causes to be operated on any highway in the Commonwealth any motor vehicle requiring registration cards or identification markers from the Department after such registration cards or identification markers have been revoked, canceled, or suspended.

5. (i) Fails to obtain a proper registration card, identification marker, or other evidence of registration required by Chapter 27 (§ 58.1-2700 et seq.) of Title 58.1 or the terms and provisions of the International Fuel Tax Agreement, as amended by the International Fuel Tax Association, Inc.; (ii) operates or causes to be operated on any highway in the Commonwealth any motor vehicle that does not carry the proper registration and identification marker required by Chapter 27 (§ 58.1-2700 et seq.) of Title 58.1 or the terms and provisions of the International Fuel Tax Agreement, as amended by the International Fuel Tax Association, Inc., or any motor vehicle that does not display an identification marker or other identifying information as prescribed by the Department or required by Title 58.1 or the terms of the International Fuel Tax Agreement, as amended by the International Fuel Tax Association, Inc.; or (iii) operates or causes to be operated on any highway in the Commonwealth any motor vehicle requiring registration cards or identification markers from the Department after such registration cards or identification markers have been revoked, canceled, or suspended.

6. Operates or causes to be operated on any highway in the Commonwealth any truck or tractor truck or combination of vehicles exceeding the size limitations of Articles 14 (§ 46.2-1101 et seq.), 15 (§ 46.2-1105 et seq.), 16 (§ 46.2-1112 et seq.), and 18 (§ 46.2-1139 et seq.) of Chapter 10.

B. Upon collection by the Department, civil penalties levied pursuant to subdivisions A 1 and A 3 through A 5 shall be paid into the Commonwealth Transportation Fund, but civil penalties levied pursuant to subdivisions A 2 and A 6 and all processing fees levied pursuant to this section shall be paid into the state treasury and shall be set aside as a special fund to meet the expenses of the Department of Motor Vehicles.

C. The penalties and fees specified in this section shall be in addition to any other penalty, fee, tax, or liability that may be imposed by law.

History.

2011, cc. 62, 73; 2012, cc. 22, 111.

§ 46.2-613.2. Service of process in civil penalty cases for violation of license, registration, and tax requirements and vehicle size limitations.

Any person, whether resident or nonresident, who permits the operation of a motor vehicle in the Commonwealth by his agent or employee shall be deemed to have appointed the operator of such motor vehicle his statutory agent for the purpose of service of process in any proceeding against such person growing out of any violation under § 46.2-613.1. Acceptance by a nonresident of the rights and privileges conferred by Article 5 (§ 46.2-655 et seq.) of Chapter 6 shall have the same effect under this section as operation of such motor vehicle by such nonresident, his agent, or his employee.

History.

2011, cc. 62, 73.

§ 46.2-613.3. Special processing provisions for civil penalties levied for violation of license, registration, and tax requirements and vehicle size limitations.

Notwithstanding any other provision of law, all civil penalties levied pursuant to § 46.2-613.1 shall be processed in the following manner:

1. The size and weight compliance agent charging the violation shall serve a citation on the operator of the vehicle. The citation shall be directed to the owner, operator, or other person responsible for the violation as determined by the size and weight compliance agent. Service of the citation on the vehicle operator shall constitute service of process upon the owner, operator, or other person charged with the violation as provided in § 46.2-613.5.

2. The size and weight compliance agent charging the violation shall cause the citation to be delivered or sent by first-class mail to the Department within 24 hours after it is served.

3. The owner, operator, or other person charged with the violation shall, within 21 days after the citation is served upon the vehicle operator, either make full payment to the Department of the civil penalty and processing fee as stated on the citation or deliver to the Department a written notice of his election to contest the charges in court.

4. Failure of the owner, operator, or other person charged with the violation to timely deliver to the Department either payment in full of the uncontested civil penalty and processing fee or a notice of contest of the violation shall cause the Department to issue an administrative order of assessment against such person. A copy of the order shall be sent by first-class mail to the person charged with the violation. Any such administrative order shall have the same effect as a judgment entered by a general district court.

5. Upon timely receipt of a notice of contest of a violation under § 46.2-613.1, the Department shall:

a. Forward the citation to the general district court named in the citation; and

b. Send by first-class mail to the person charged with the violation and to the size and weight compliance agent who issued the citation confirmation that the citation has been forwarded to the court for trial.

6. Notices and pleadings may be served by first-class mail to the address shown on the citation as the address of the person charged with the weight violation or, if none is shown, to the address of record for the person to whom the vehicle is registered.

7. An alleged violation that is contested shall be tried as a civil case. The attorney for the Commonwealth shall represent the interests of the Commonwealth. The disposition of the case shall be recorded in an appropriate order, a copy of which shall be sent to the Department in lieu of any record that may be otherwise required by § 46.2-383. If judgment is for the Commonwealth, payment shall be made to the Department.

8. Notwithstanding any other provisions of this section, any and all citations and notices required by this section to be provided to the person charged with a violation or received from the person charged with a violation, with the exclusion of the citation as set out in subdivision 1, may be served or provided in an electronic manner if the Department and the person charged with the violation have agreed to utilize electronic notification.

History.

2011, cc. 62, 73.

§ 46.2-613.4. Special seizure provisions for unpaid fees and penalties.

Any size and weight compliance agent authorized to serve process under the provisions of this chapter may hold a vehicle without an attachment summons or court order, but only for such time as is reasonably necessary to promptly petition for an attachment summons to attach the vehicle.

After finding reasonable cause for the issuance of an attachment summons, the judicial officer conducting the hearing shall inform the operator of the vehicle of his option to either pay the previously assessed fees and penalties due the Commonwealth or contest the charge through the attachment proceeding. If the operator chooses to make payment, he shall do so to the judicial officer, who shall transmit the citation along with the fees and penalties to the Department for distribution in accordance with subsection B of § 46.2-613.1.

The Commonwealth shall not be required to post bond in order to attach a vehicle pursuant to this section. The size and weight compliance agent authorized to hold the vehicle pending a hearing on the attachment petition shall also be empowered to execute the attachment summons if issued. Any bond for the retention of the vehicle or for release of the attachment shall be given in accordance with § 8.01-553 except that the bond shall be taken by a judicial officer. The judicial officer shall return the bond to the clerk of the appropriate court in place of the officer serving the attachment as otherwise provided in § 8.01-554.

In the event the fees and penalties are not paid in full, or no bond is given by, or for the person responsible for paying the fees and penalties, the vehicle shall be stored in a secure place, as may be designated by the owner or operator of the vehicle. If no place is designated, the officer or size and weight compliance agent executing the attachment summons shall designate the place of storage. The owner or operator shall be afforded the right of unloading and removing the cargo from the vehicle. The risk and cost of the storage shall be borne by the owner or operator of the vehicle.

Whenever an attachment summons is issued for unpaid fees and penalties the court shall forward to the Department both a copy of the order disposing of the case and the citation prepared by the size and weight compliance agent but not served.

Upon notification of the judgment or administrative order entered for such unpaid fees and penalties and notification of the failure of such person to satisfy the judgment or order, the Department, the Department of State Police, or any law-enforcement officer or size and weight compliance agent shall thereafter deny the offending person the right to operate a motor vehicle or vehicles on any highway of the Commonwealth until the judgment or order has been satisfied and a reinstatement fee of $50 has been paid to the Department. Reinstatement fees collected under the provisions of this section shall be paid by the Commissioner into the state treasury and shall be set aside as a special fund to be used to meet the expenses of the Department.

When informed that the right to operate the motor vehicle has been denied, the driver shall drive the motor vehicle to a nearby location off the public highways and not move it or permit it to be moved until such judgment or order has been satisfied. Failure by the driver to comply with this provision shall constitute a Class 4 misdemeanor.

All costs incurred by the Commonwealth and all judgments, if any, against the Commonwealth due to action taken pursuant to this section shall be paid from the fund into which the civil penalties levied pursuant to § 46.2-613.1 are paid.

Officers of the Department of State Police and all other law-enforcement officers are vested with the same powers with respect to the enforcement of this chapter as they have with respect to the enforcement of the criminal laws of the Commonwealth.

History.
2011, cc. 62, 73; 2012, cc. 22, 111.

§ 46.2-613.5. Procedures for issuing and serving process in civil penalty cases.

Any size and weight compliance agent authorized to enforce the provisions of § 46.2-613.1 may issue a citation for a violation of such provisions. Such size and weight compliance agent may also serve an attachment summons issued by a judge or magistrate in connection with a violation of § 46.2-613.1.

Service of any such citation shall be made upon the driver of the motor vehicle involved in the violation. Such service on the driver shall have the same legal force and validity as if served within the Commonwealth personally upon the owner, operator, or other person charged with the violation, whether such owner, operator, or other person charged is a resident or nonresident.

History.
2011, cc. 62, 73.

§ 46.2-614. Right to recover damages not affected.

Nothing contained in this chapter shall affect the right of any person injured in his person or property by the negligent operation of any motor vehicle, trailer, semitrailer, or locomotive to sue and recover damages.

History.
Code 1950, § 46-67; 1958, c. 541, § 46.1-67; 1989, c. 727.

§ 46.2-615. Registration effective after death of owner.

Upon the death of an owner of a registered motor vehicle, trailer, or semitrailer, its registration shall continue in force as a valid registration until (i) the end of the registration period for which the license plates or decals are issued or (ii) the ownership of the motor vehicle, trailer, or semitrailer is transferred before the end of the registration period by the executor or administrator of the estate of the deceased owner or by a legatee or distributee of the estate, as provided in § 46.2-632 or 46.2-633, (iii) its ownership is transferred to a new owner before the end of the registration period by the survivor of its two joint owners, or (iv) its ownership is transferred pursuant to § 46.2-633.2.

History.
Code 1950, § 46-92; 1958, c. 541, § 46.1-96; 1968, c. 187; 1972, c. 609; 1989, c. 727; 2013, c. 318.

ARTICLE 2.
TITLING VEHICLES.

§ 46.2-616. Acquiring vehicle from vendor who does not have certificate of title.

Except as otherwise provided in this title, no person shall purchase, trade, exchange, or barter for a motor vehicle, trailer, or semitrailer in the Commonwealth, knowing or having reason to believe that its seller has not secured a certificate of title, or knowing or having reason to believe that its seller does not legally have in his possession a certificate of title to the vehicle issued to its owner. Except as otherwise provided in this title, for the purposes of this article, off-road motorcycles and all-terrain vehicles shall be deemed motor vehicles.

History.
Code 1950, § 46-7; 1958, c. 541, § 46.1-5; 1978, c. 605; 1989, c. 727; 2006, c. 896.

§ 46.2-617. Sale of vehicle without certificate of title.

Except as provided in §§ 46.2-644.03 and 58.1-3942, any person who sells, trades, exchanges, or barters a motor vehicle, trailer, or semitrailer in the Commonwealth without first having secured a certificate of title for it or without legally having in his possession a certificate of title for the vehicle issued to its owner, except as otherwise provided in this title, shall be guilty of a Class 3 misdemeanor.

History.
Code 1950, § 46-7; 1958, c. 541, § 46.1-88; 1968, c. 605; 1978, c. 605; 1988, c. 363; 1989, c. 727; 2009, c. 664; 2012, c. 623.

§ 46.2-618. When unlawful to have in possession certificate of title issued to another; remedy of purchaser against persons in possession of title of vehicle purchased from dealer.

A. It shall constitute a Class 1 misdemeanor for any person in the Commonwealth to possess a certificate of title issued by the Commissioner to a person other than the holder thereof, unless the certificate of title has been assigned to the holder as provided in this title. This section, however, shall apply neither to secured parties who legally hold certificates of title as provided in this title nor to the spouse of the person to whom the certificate of title was issued.

B. When a purchaser of a motor vehicle is unable to obtain the title for such vehicle because the motor vehicle dealer who sold the vehicle to the purchaser is no longer engaged in business in the Commonwealth as a dealer as defined in § 46.2-1500 and the purchaser must petition a court of competent jurisdiction to direct that a person other than the dealer holding the title to release the title to the purchaser, the Court may order the title be released to the buyer if the court finds that the purchaser has a right to the title superior to that of the person holding the title under the laws of the Commonwealth. The court may also, upon finding that the person holding the title must release it, award reasonable attorney fees, expenses, and costs incurred by the purchaser in making the petition to the court.

History.

Code 1950, § 46-81; 1958, c. 541, § 46.1-80; 1966, c. 558; 1972, c. 208; 1982, c. 205; 1989, c. 727; 2012, c. 119; 2015, c. 615.

§ 46.2-619. New indicia of title; procedure as to leased vehicles.

When the Department receives a certificate of title properly assigned and acknowledged, accompanied by an application for registration, it shall register the motor vehicle, trailer, or semitrailer described in the application and shall issue to the person entitled to it by reason of the transfer a new registration card, license plate, or plates and certificate of title in the manner and form and for the fees provided in this chapter for original registration. For leased vehicles, such application shall include (i) if the lessee is an individual, the name and residence street address of the lessee and the name of the locality in which the leased vehicle will be principally garaged or parked and (ii) if the lessee is a business, the name of the business, its street address, and the name of the locality in which the leased vehicle will be principally garaged or parked. The Department shall also make this information available to the commissioner of the revenue or other assessing officer of the locality in which the leased vehicle is to be principally garaged or parked. Nothing in this section shall permit the registration of all-terrain vehicles or off-road motorcycles titled pursuant to this title.

History.

Code 1950, § 46-87; 1958, c. 541, § 46.1-91; 1989, c. 727; 1996, c. 761; 2006, c. 896; 2012, c. 135.

§ 46.2-620. Period of validity of certificate of title.

Every certificate of title issued under this chapter shall be valid for the life of the motor vehicle, trailer, or semitrailer so long as the owner to whom it is issued shall retain legal title or right of possession of or to the vehicle. Such certificates need not be renewed except on a transfer of title or interest of the owner.

History.

Code 1950, § 46-83; 1958, c. 541, § 46.1-86; 1989, c. 727; 2002, c. 93.

§ 46.2-621. Application for certificate of title.

The owner of a vehicle, or his duly authorized attorney-in-fact, shall apply for a certificate of title in the name of the owner on appropriate forms prescribed and furnished by the Commissioner. Officers and employees of the Department are vested with the authority to administer oaths and take acknowledgments and affidavits incidental to the administration and enforcement of this section and all other laws relating to the operation of motor vehicles, the collection and refunding of taxes levied on motor fuels and sales and use tax, for which services they shall receive no compensation.

History.

Code 1950, § 46-49; 1958, c. 541, § 46.1-51; 1972, cc. 301, 378; 1989, c. 727.

§ 46.2-621.1. Correcting errors in titling.

If the owner of a vehicle or his duly authorized attorney-in-fact make a sufficient showing by providing an affidavit stating that the vehicle identification information provided on the application for certificate of title, the certificate of origin, manufacturer's statement of origin, or title, as the case may be, forwarded to the Commissioner by any means generally allowed, was incorrect, the Commissioner may take all actions necessary to correct the error.

History.

2005, c. 283.

§ 46.2-622. Issuance of certificate of title in names of joint owners.

When the Department receives an application for a certificate of title for a motor vehicle, trailer, or semitrailer, to be issued in the names of two natural persons, jointly with right of survivorship, the Department shall issue to its owners a certificate of title accordingly. Any certificate issued in the name of two persons may contain an expression such as "or the survivor of them," which shall be deemed sufficient to create joint ownership during the lives of the two owners, and individual ownership in the survivor. A certificate issued in the names of two persons, with their names separated only by "or," shall create joint ownership during the lives of the owners, and individual ownership in the survivor of them.

Nothing herein shall (i) prohibit the issuance of a certificate of title in the names of two or more persons as owners in common which shall be sufficient evidence of ownership of undivided interests in the vehicle; (ii) grant immunity from enforcement of any liability of any person owning the vehicle, as one of two joint owners, to the extent of his interest in the vehicle, during the lives of its owners; (iii) permit the issuance of a certificate of title in the names of two persons as tenants by the entireties; or (iv) be used by one of the joint owners as a defense to the secured party's enforcement of a security interest in the vehicle that was granted by one or both of the joint owners of the vehicle on the same date or prior to the issuance of the certificate of title.

History.

1968, c. 188, § 46.1-68.1; 1983, c. 586; 1989, c. 727; 2002, c. 432.

§ 46.2-623. Statements in application.

A. Every application for a certificate of title shall contain (i) a statement of the applicant's title and of all liens or encumbrances on the vehicle and the names and addresses of all persons having any interest in the vehicle and the nature of every interest in the vehicle; (ii) the Social Security number, if any, of the owner and, if the application is in the name of an employer for a business vehicle, the employer's identification number assigned by the United States Internal Revenue Service; and (iii) a brief description of the vehicle to be titled or registered, including the name of the maker, the vehicle identification or serial number and, when titling or registering a new vehicle, the date of sale by the manufacturer or dealer to the person first operating the vehicle.

B. The lessor of a qualifying vehicle, as defined in § 58.1-3523, shall send a report to the Department for each such qualifying vehicle containing (i) the name and address of the lessee as it appears in the lease contract; (ii) the social security number of the lessee; and (iii) the registration number of the vehicle as described under Article 1 (§ 46.2-600 et seq.) of Chapter 6.

C. Such lessor shall send a monthly report to the Department, by the fifteenth day of the month or such later day as may be prescribed in the guidelines promulgated under § 58.1-3532, listing any changes, additions or deletions to the information provided under subsection B as of the last day of the preceding month.

D. The application for title or registration shall contain such additional information as may be required by the Department.

E. The Department may require that an applicant present proof reasonably acceptable to the Department of the accuracy of information provided on the application, including proof of identity, and may refuse to issue a certificate of title until such proof has been provided.

History.

Code 1950, § 46-50; 1958, c. 541, § 46.1-52; 1972, c. 230; 1989, c. 727; 1998, Sp. Sess. I, c. 2; 2005, c. 305; 2006, c. 896; 2008, c. 171; 2012, c. 650.

§ 46.2-624. Information required on transfer of titles of taxicabs or vehicles damaged by water.

A. Unless there is attached to the certificate of title of the vehicle a statement signed by the owner to the effect that the vehicle has been used as a taxicab, it shall be unlawful for any person knowingly to sell, transfer, or otherwise dispose of any motor vehicle that has been used as a taxicab.

B. Violation of subsection A shall constitute a Class 1 misdemeanor.

C. When a vehicle has been damaged by water to such an extent that the insurance company insuring it has paid a claim of $3,500 or more because of this water damage, the insurance company shall report the payment of such claim to the Department.

D. On receipt of a certificate of title to which the information required in subsection A is attached or upon receipt of information from an insurance company pursuant to subsection C, the Commissioner shall, on issuing a new certificate of title, place an appropriate indicator upon such certificate in order to convey that information to the new owner of the motor vehicle.

History.

1966, c. 550, § 46.1-64.1; 1989, c. 727; 2011, cc. 652, 678.

§ 46.2-625. Specially constructed, reconstructed, replica, converted electric, or foreign vehicles.

If a vehicle for which the registration or a certificate of title is applied is (i) a specially constructed, reconstructed, replica, converted electric, or foreign vehicle or (ii) off-road motorcycle converted to on-road use, the fact shall be stated in the application and, in the case of any foreign vehicle registered outside the Commonwealth, the owner shall present to the Department the certificate of title and registration card or other evidence of registration as he may have. The Commissioner may require such other evidence of ownership as he may deem advisable and promulgate regulations establishing what additional evidence of ownership, if any, shall be required for titling and registration of (i) specially constructed, reconstructed, replica, converted electric, or foreign vehicles or (ii) off-road motorcycles converted to on-road use. All titles and registrations for specially constructed, reconstructed, replica, and converted electric vehicles and off-road motorcycles converted to on-road use shall be branded with the words "specially constructed," "reconstructed," "replica," "converted electric," or "off-road motorcycle converted to on-road use," as appropriate. Titles for vehicles that are both converted electric vehicles and reconstructed vehicles shall be branded with the words "reconstructed" and "converted electric."

History.

Code 1950, § 46-51; 1958, c. 541, § 46.1-53; 1970, c. 632; 1989, c. 727; 2007, cc. 325, 393; 2012, c. 177; 2015, c. 259.

§ 46.2-626: Repealed by Acts 1996, cc. 591 and 917.

§ 46.2-626.1. Motorcycle purchased by manufacturer for parts; documentation required for sale of parts.

For the purposes of this section, "certificate of origin," "line-make," "manufacturer," and "new motorcycle" have the meanings ascribed to them in § 46.2-1500.

A licensed motorcycle manufacturer shall not be required to obtain a certificate of title for a new motorcycle of a different line-make purchased by the manufacturer for the purpose of obtaining parts used in the production of another new motorcycle or an autocycle, provided such manufacturer obtains a salvage dealer license in accordance with § 46.2-1601. The manufacturer shall not be required to obtain a nonrepairable certificate for the purchased motorcycle, as required by § 46.2-1603.1, but shall stamp the words "Va. Code § 46.2-626.1: DISASSEMBLED FOR PARTS" in a minimum font size of 14 point across the face of the original manufacturer's certificate of origin. The certificate of origin shall be forwarded to the Department, which shall make a record of the disassembly of the motorcycle. The manufacturer shall retain a photocopy of the stamped certificate of origin for its records.

Any parts remaining from the purchased motorcycle and sold as parts by the manufacturer shall be accompanied by documentation of how such parts were obtained. Documentation accompanying the frame of the purchased motorcycle shall include a photocopy of the stamped manufacturer's certificate of origin and certification from the manufacturer that the original certificate of origin has been forwarded to the Department.

History.

2013, cc. 244, 367; 2014, cc. 53, 256; 2015, c. 615.

§ 46.2-627. Fee for certificate of title; use in special fund.

The fee to be paid to the Department for the issuance of each original certificate of title shall be ten dollars. The fee to record a supplemental lien and issue a new title shall be six dollars. All fees collected under the provisions of this section shall be paid into the state treasury and set aside as a special fund to be used to meet the expenses of the Department.

History.

Code 1950, § 46-78; 1958, c. 541, § 46.1-78; 1962, c. 368; 1964, c. 218; 1974, c. 454; 1982, c. 671; 1986, c. 553; 1987, c. 696; 1989, c. 727.

§ 46.2-628. How certificate of title transferred.

The owner of a motor vehicle, trailer, or semitrailer registered under this chapter, when transferring or assigning his title or interest thereto, shall fully and correctly endorse the assignment and warranty of title on the certificate of title of the motor vehicle, trailer, or semitrailer to its purchaser, with a statement of all security interests on it, and shall deliver the certificate to the purchaser or transferee at the time of delivering the motor vehicle, trailer, or semitrailer. Any owner who willfully fails fully and correctly to endorse the assignment and warranty of title shall be guilty of a Class 3 misdemeanor.

History.

Code 1950, § 46-84; 1958, c. 541, § 46.1-87; 1966, c. 558; 1972, c. 378; 1988, c. 363; 1989, c. 727.

§ 46.2-629. Odometer reading to be reported on certificate of title, application, or power of attorney.

A. Every owner or transferor of any motor vehicle, including a dealer, shall, at the time of transfer of ownership of any motor vehicle by him, record on the certificate of title, if one is currently issued on the vehicle in the Commonwealth, and on any application for certificate of title the reading on the odometer or similar device plus any known additional distance traveled not shown by the odometer or similar device of the motor vehicle at the time of transfer. If, however, a transferor gives his power of attorney to a dealer or other person for the purpose of assigning the transferor's interest in a motor vehicle, the transferor shall conspicuously record on the power of attorney the reading on the odometer or similar device at the time of the assignment. The owner or transferor of a motor vehicle may electronically provide, in a form and format prescribed by the Commissioner, the reading on the odometer or similar device at the time of transfer if a paper certificate of title was not issued by the Department in accordance with § 46.2-603.1 and electronic provision of odometer readings is permitted under the Federal Odometer Act (49 U.S.C. § 32701 et seq.) or any federal regulations promulgated thereunder.

B. The Department shall not issue to any transferee any new certificate of title to a motor vehicle unless subsection A has been complied with.

C. It shall be unlawful for any person knowingly to record an incorrect odometer or similar device reading plus any known additional distance not shown by the odometer or similar device on any certificate of title or application for a title, or on any power of attorney as described in subsection A.

D. Notwithstanding other provisions of this section, an owner or transferor, including a dealer, of any of the following types of motor vehicles need not disclose the vehicle's odometer reading:

1. Vehicles having gross vehicle weight ratings of more than 16,000 pounds; and

2. Vehicles that were manufactured for a model year at least 10 years earlier than the calendar year in which the sale or transfer occurs and were previously exempt from recording an odometer reading on the certificate of title in another state, provided that

the Department shall brand the titles of all such vehicles to indicate this exemption.

E. Violation of this section shall constitute a Class 1 misdemeanor.

F. The provisions of subsections A and B shall not apply to transfers under § 46.2-633.

G. This section shall not apply to transfers or application for certificates of title of all-terrain vehicles, mopeds, or off-road motorcycles as defined in § 46.2-100.

History.

1972, c. 851, § 46.1-89.1; 1978, c. 294; 1986, c. 490; 1989, c. 727; 2004, c. 724; 2006, c. 896; 2007, c. 225; 2012, c. 650; 2013, c. 783.

§ 46.2-630. Transfer and application for certificate of title forwarded to Department.

The transferee shall write his name and address in ink on the certificate of title and, except as provided in §§ 46.2-619 and 46.2-631, shall within thirty days forward the certificate to the Department with an application for the registration of the motor vehicle, trailer, or semitrailer and for a certificate of title.

History.

Code 1950, § 46-85; 1958, c. 541, § 46.1-89; 1988, c. 363; 1989, c. 727.

§ 46.2-631. When transferred certificate of title need not be forwarded.

When the transferee of a motor vehicle, trailer, or semitrailer is a dealer who holds it for resale and operates it only for sales purposes under a dealer's license plate, the transferee shall not be required to register it nor forward the certificate of title to the Department, as provided in § 46.2-630, but the transferee, on transferring his title or interest to another person, shall notify the Department of the transfer and shall endorse and acknowledge an assignment and warranty of title on the certificate and deliver it to the person to whom the transfer is made.

History.

Code 1950, § 46-86; 1958, c. 541, § 46.1-90; 1988, c. 363; 1989, c. 727.

§ 46.2-632. Transfer when certificate of title lost.

A. Whenever the applicant for the registration of a motor vehicle, manufactured home, trailer, or semitrailer or a new certificate of title is unable to present a certificate of title because the certificate has been lost or unlawfully detained by one in possession of it or whenever the certificate of title is otherwise not available, the Department may receive the application and investigate the circumstances of the case and may require the filing of affidavits or other information. When the Department is satisfied that the applicant is entitled to the title, it may register the motor vehicle, manufactured home, trailer, or semitrailer and issue a new registration card, license plate, or plates and certificate of title to the person entitled to it.

B. Whenever the insurance company or its agent makes application for a certificate of title to a vehicle that is not a salvage vehicle as defined in § 46.2-1600 and is unable to present a certificate of title, the Department may receive the application along with an affidavit indicating that the vehicle was acquired as the result of the claims process and describing the efforts made by the insurance company or its agent to obtain the certificate of title from the previous owner. When the Department is satisfied that the applicant is entitled to the title, it may issue a certificate of title to the person entitled to it. The Commissioner may charge a fee of $25 for the expense of processing an application under this subsection that is accompanied by an affidavit. Such fee shall be in addition to any other fees and taxes required. All fees collected under the provisions of this subsection shall be paid into the state treasury and set aside as a special fund to be used to meet the expenses of the Department.

History.

Code 1950, § 46-88; 1958, c. 541, § 46.1-92; 1989, c. 727; 2009, c. 171; 2014, c. 624.

§ 46.2-633. Transfer of title by operation of law.

A. Except as otherwise provided in § 46.2-615 in the event of the transfer by operation of law of the title or interest of an owner in and to a motor vehicle, trailer, or semitrailer registered under the provisions of this chapter to anyone as legatee or distributee or as surviving joint owner or by an order in bankruptcy or insolvency, execution sale, sales as provided for in § 46.2-644.03, repossession on default in the performing of the terms of a lease or executory sales contract or of any written agreement ratified or incorporated in a decree or order of a court of record, or otherwise than by the voluntary act of the person whose title or interest is so transferred, the transferee or his legal representative shall apply to the Department for a certificate of title, giving the name and address of the person entitled to it, and accompany his application with the registration card and certificate of title previously issued for the motor vehicle, trailer, or semitrailer, if available, together with whatever instruments or documents of authority, or certified copies of them, are required by law to evidence or effect a transfer of title or interest in or to chattels in the case. The Department shall cancel the registration of the motor vehicle, trailer, or semitrailer and issue a new certificate of title to the person entitled to it.

B. Notwithstanding the provisions of subsection A, if a title is presented from a state other than the

Commonwealth, the Department shall, upon presentation of the title and a form prescribed by the Commissioner attesting to the lawful repossession of the vehicle and the intent to offer the vehicle for sale in the Commonwealth, issue a new certificate of title to the person entitled to it and request the state in which the vehicle is titled to cancel the title. Nothing in this subsection, however, shall be construed to require the presentation of a title from a state other than the Commonwealth if the vehicle is not required to be titled by the laws of that other state.

History.
Code 1950, § 46-89; 1958, c. 541, § 46.1-93; 1964, c. 142; 1968, cc. 187, 605; 1970, c. 287; 1989, c. 727; 2005, cc. 766, 849; 2008, Sp. Sess. II, c. 7; 2009, c. 664.

§ 46.2-633.1. Sale in Virginia of vehicle repossessed in another state.

Any motor vehicle dealer who purchases a vehicle titled in another state and that was repossessed may sell that vehicle in Virginia without obtaining a Virginia title for the vehicle from Virginia or the state in which the vehicle is titled, provided the motor vehicle dealer has an affidavit of repossession or similar document showing the lawful repossession, which affidavit or document would be sufficient to allow the sale of the repossessed vehicle in the state where it is titled without titling the vehicle in the name of the seller.

History.
2009, cc. 185, 691.

§ 46.2-633.2. Transfer of title on death.

A. A motor vehicle, trailer, or semitrailer may include in the certificate of title a designation of a beneficiary to whom the motor vehicle, trailer, or semitrailer shall be transferred after the death of the owner.

B. A motor vehicle, trailer, or semitrailer may be titled with a designated beneficiary by applying to the Department for a certificate of title on which is stated the name of the sole owner followed by "transfer on death" or "TOD" and the name of the beneficiary.

C. A certificate of title with a designated beneficiary shall not be issued if (i) the owner is not a natural person; (ii) the motor vehicle, trailer, or semitrailer is encumbered by a lien or security interest; or (iii) the owner holds an interest in the motor vehicle, trailer, or semitrailer with another person.

D. During the lifetime of the owner:

1. The beneficiary shall have no interest in the motor vehicle, trailer, or semitrailer and the signature or consent of the beneficiary shall not be required for any transaction; and

2. The certificate of title with the designated beneficiary shall not be issued by the Department or shall be canceled if:

a. The owner files an application for a certificate of title under subsection B to remove or change the beneficiary;

b. The owner sells the motor vehicle, trailer, or semitrailer and delivers the certificate of title to another person; or

c. An application for the recording of a lien or security interest has been filed with the Department for the motor vehicle, trailer, or semitrailer prior to the death of the owner or filed within the time limits in § 46.2-639.

E. Except as provided in this section, the designated beneficiary shall not be changed or revoked by will or any other instrument, by a change in circumstances, or in any other manner.

F. A certificate of title with a designated beneficiary shall not be required to be supported by consideration and need not be delivered to the beneficiary to be effective.

G. Upon the death of the owner and application by the beneficiary, the Department shall issue a new certificate of title in accordance with § 46.2-600 for the motor vehicle, trailer, or semitrailer to the beneficiary. The beneficiary must apply for a certificate of title upon submitting proof of the death of the owner and such other documents and information as the Department may reasonably require. If the beneficiary does not survive the owner or does not apply for a certificate of title within 120 days of the death of the owner, the beneficiary or his estate shall have no right to obtain title to the motor vehicle, trailer, or semitrailer under this section. Upon transfer of title to the beneficiary, the Department shall cancel the registration of the deceased owner.

H. Any transfer pursuant to this section shall be subject to any lien or security interest authorized under § 46.2-644, 46.2-644.01, or 46.2-644.02.

I. Any transfer pursuant to this section is not testamentary and shall not be subject to the provisions of Title 64.2.

History.
2013, c. 318.

§ 46.2-634. Transfer of title when no qualification on estate.

If the holder of a certificate of title is dead and there has been no qualification on his estate, a transfer may be made by a legatee or distributee if there is presented to the Department a statement made by a legatee or distributee to the effect that there has not been and there is not expected to be a qualification on the estate and that the decedent's debts have been paid or that the proceeds from the sale of the motor vehicle will be applied against his debts. The statement shall contain the name, residence at the time of death, date of death, and the names of any other persons having an interest in the motor vehicle which is sought to be transferred and, if these persons are of legal age, they shall signify in writing their consent to the transfer of the title.

History.

Code 1950, § 46-90; 1958, c. 541, § 46.1-94; 1964, c. 574; 1972, c. 211; 1989, c. 727.

§ 46.2-635. Surrender of certificates for vehicles to be demolished; securing new title certificates.

Every person disposing of a motor vehicle, trailer, or semitrailer which is to be demolished shall make an assignment of title to the transferee as provided in § 46.2-628. The assigned certificate of title, when available, however, shall be delivered to the Department, accompanied by a form provided by the Commissioner, stating that the vehicle is to be demolished. On receipt of this form and the assigned title, the Commissioner shall forward to the transferee a receipt for them.

If the person, in lieu of demolishing the vehicle, sells, transfers, or operates the motor vehicle, trailer, or semitrailer, he shall first secure a certificate of title from the Department. Before issuing the new certificate of title, the Department shall inspect, or have inspected, the reconstructed vehicle.

If a motor vehicle, trailer, or semitrailer obtained for use or resale, is subsequently demolished, the owner shall immediately surrender its certificate of title to the Department.

History.

1968, c. 156, § 46.1-98.1; 1978, c. 605; 1989, c. 727; 2006, cc. 16, 163.

§ 46.2-636. Certificate to show security interests.

When the Department receives an application for a certificate of title to a motor vehicle, trailer, or semitrailer showing security interests on the motor vehicle, trailer, or semitrailer, the certificate of title issued by the Department to the owner of the vehicle shall show all security interests disclosed by the application. All security interests shown on the certificate of title shall be shown in the order of their priority according to the information contained in the application.

History.

Code 1950, § 46-69; 1958, c. 541, § 46.1-69; 1966, c. 558; 1989, c. 727.

§ 46.2-636.1. Security interests in farm tractors and special construction and forestry equipment.

A financing statement, as defined in § 8.9A-102, must be filed to perfect all security interests in farm tractors and special construction and forestry equipment, as defined in § 46.2-100. No other provisions of this chapter pertaining to security interests shall apply to these motor vehicles.

History.

2010, c. 135.

§ 46.2-637. Security interests subsequently created.

Security interests, other than those in inventory held for sale, in motor vehicles, trailers, or semitrailers created by the voluntary act of the owner after the original issue of a certificate of title to the owner must be shown on the certificate of title. In such cases, the owner shall file an application with the Department on a form furnished for that purpose, setting forth the security interests and whatever additional information the Department may deem necessary. If satisfied that it is proper for the security interest to be recorded, when the certificate of title covering the motor vehicle, trailer, or semitrailer, is surrendered, the Department shall issue a new certificate of title, showing security interests in the order of their priority according to the date of the filing of the application. For the purpose of recording a subsequent security interest, the Commissioner may require any secured party to deliver to him the certificate of title. The new certificate shall be sent or delivered to the secured party from whom the prior certificate was obtained. Notwithstanding any other provision of law, a security interest in a motor vehicle, trailer, or semitrailer which is inventory held for sale shall be perfected only as provided in §§ 8.9A-301 through 8.9A-527.

History.

Code 1950, § 46-70; 1958, c. 541, § 46.1-70; 1966, c. 558; 1989, c. 727; 2006, c. 896.

§ 46.2-638. Certificate as notice of security interest.

A certificate of title, when issued by the Department showing a security interest, shall be adequate notice to the Commonwealth, creditors, and purchasers that a security interest in the motor vehicle exists and the recording or filing of such creation or reservation of a security interest in the county or city wherein the purchaser or debtor resides or elsewhere is not necessary and shall not be required. Motor vehicles, trailers or semitrailers, other than those which are inventory held for sale, registered or for which a certificate of title shall have been issued under this title shall not be subjected to, but shall be exempt from the provisions of §§ 8.9A-301 through 8.9A-527 and § 55-96, nor shall recordation or filing of such security interest, except a security interest in inventory held for sale, in any other place for any other purpose, be required or have any effect.

History.

Code 1950, § 46-71; 1958, c. 541, § 46.1-71; 1966, c. 558; 1989, c. 727; 2006, c. 896; 2010, c. 135.

§ 46.2-639. Security interest may be filed within thirty days after purchase.

If application for the registration or recordation of a security interest to be placed on a motor vehicle, trailer, or semitrailer is filed with the Department, it shall be deemed perfected as of the date of filing, and, if the date of filing is within thirty days from the date of an applicant's purchase of the motor vehicle, trailer, or semitrailer, it shall be as valid as to all persons, including the Commonwealth, as if that registration had been accomplished on the day the security interest was acquired.

History.
Code 1950, § 46-72; 1958, c. 541, § 46.1-72; 1966, c. 558; 1972, cc. 300, 408; 1989, c. 727; 2000, c. 71.

§ 46.2-640. Priority of security interests shown on certificates of title.

The security interests, except security interests in motor vehicles, trailers and semitrailers which are inventory held for sale and are perfected under §§ 8.9A-401 through 8.9A-527, shown upon such certificates of title issued by the Department pursuant to applications for same shall have priority over any other liens or security interests against such motor vehicle, trailer, or semitrailer, however created and recorded. The foregoing provisions of this section shall not apply to liens for taxes as provided in § 58.1-3942, liens of keepers of garages to the extent given by § 46.2-644.01 and liens of mechanics for repairs to the extent given by § 46.2-644.02 if the requirements therefor exist, provided the garage keeper or mechanic furnishes the holder of any recorded lien who may request it with an itemized sworn statement of the storage charges, work done, and materials supplied for which the lien is claimed.

History.
Code 1950, § 46-73; 1958, c. 541, § 46.1-73; 1966, c. 558; 1977, c. 382; 1983, c. 397; 1984, c. 396; 1989, c. 727; 1999, c. 299; 2009, c. 664.

§ 46.2-640.1. Vehicle leases that are not sales or security interests.

Notwithstanding any other provision of law, in the case of motor vehicles, trailers or semi-trailers, a transaction does not create a sale or security interest merely because it provides that the rental price is permitted or required to be adjusted under the agreement either upward or downward by reference to the amount realized upon sale or other disposition of the motor vehicle or trailer.

History.
1991, c. 536.

§ 46.2-641. Who to hold certificate of title subject to security interest.

The certificate of title of a motor vehicle, trailer, or semitrailer shall be delivered to the person holding the security interest having first priority on the motor vehicle, trailer, or semitrailer and retained by him until the entire amount of his security interest is fully paid by the owner. When the security interest is fully paid, the certificate of title shall be delivered to the secured party next in order of priority or, if none, then to the owner.

History.
Code 1950, § 46-74; 1958, c. 541, § 46.1-74; 1966, c. 558; 1989, c. 727.

§ 46.2-642. Release of security interest shown on certificate of title.

When an owner secures the release of any security interest on a motor vehicle, trailer, or semitrailer shown on its certificate of title, he may exhibit the documents evidencing the release, signed by the person or persons making the release, and the certificate of title to the Department. However, when it is impossible to secure the release from the secured party, the owner may exhibit to the Department whatever evidence may be available showing that the debt secured has been satisfied, together with a statement by the owner under oath that the debt has been paid. The Department, when satisfied as to the genuineness and regularity of the release, shall issue to the owner either a new certificate of title or an endorsement or rider showing the release of the security interest, which the Department shall attach to the outstanding certificate of title.

History.
Code 1950, § 46-75; 1958, c. 541, § 46.1-75; 1966, c. 558; 1972, c. 249; 1989, c. 727.

§ 46.2-643. Surrender of certificate of title required when security interest paid.

It shall constitute a Class 3 misdemeanor for a secured party who holds a certificate of title as provided in this title to refuse or fail to mark satisfied and surrender it to the person legally entitled thereto within ten days after his security interest is satisfied.

History.
Code 1950, § 46-76; 1958, c. 541, § 46.1-76; 1966, c. 558; 1978, c. 605; 1989, c. 727.

§ 46.2-644. Levy of execution.

A levy made by virtue of an execution, fieri facias, or other court order, on a motor vehicle, trailer, or semitrailer for which a certificate of title has been issued by the Department, shall constitute a lien, subsequent to security interests previously recorded by the Department and subsequent to security interests in inventory held for sale and perfected as otherwise permitted by law, when the officer making the levy reports to the Department on forms provided by the Department, that the levy has been made and that the motor vehicle, trailer, or semitrailer levied on has been seized by him. If the lien is

Motor Vehicles

thereafter satisfied or should the motor vehicle, trailer, or semitrailer thus levied on and seized thereafter be released by the officer, he shall immediately report that fact to the Department. Any owner who, after the levy and seizure by an officer and before the officer reports the levy and seizure to the Department, shall fraudulently assign or transfer his title to or interest in a motor vehicle, trailer, or semitrailer or cause its certificate of title to be assigned or transferred or cause a security interest to be shown on its certificate of title shall be guilty of a Class 1 misdemeanor.

History.

Code 1950, § 46-77; 1958, c. 541, § 46.1-77; 1966, c. 558; 1972, c. 408; 1989, c. 727.

§ 46.2-644.01. Lien of keeper of garage.

A. Every keeper of a garage and every person keeping any vehicles shall have a lien upon such vehicles for the amount that may be due him for the towing, storage, recovery, and care thereof, until such amount is paid.

B. In the case of any vehicle subject to a chattel mortgage, security agreement, deed of trust, or other instrument securing money, the keeper of the garage shall have a lien thereon for his reasonable charges for storage under this section not to exceed $500 and for alteration and repair under § 46.2-644.02 not to exceed $1,000. However, in the case of a storage lien, to obtain the priority for an amount in excess of $300, the person asserting the lien shall make a reasonable attempt to notify any secured party of record at the Department of Motor Vehicles by telephonic means and shall give written notice by certified mail, return receipt requested, to any secured party of record at the Department of Motor Vehicles within seven business days of taking possession of the vehicle. If the secured party does not, within seven business days of receipt of the notice, take or refuse redelivery to it or its designee, the lienor shall be entitled to priority for the full amount of storage charges, not to exceed $500. Notwithstanding a redelivery, the vehicle shall be subject to subsection D.

C. In addition, any person furnishing services involving the towing and recovery of a vehicle shall have a lien for all normal costs incident thereto, if the person asserting the lien gives written notice within seven days of receipt of the vehicle by certified mail, return receipt requested, to all secured parties of record at the Department of Motor Vehicles.

D. In addition, any keeper shall be entitled to a lien against any proceeds remaining after the satisfaction of all prior security interests or liens and may retain possession of such property until such charges are paid.

E. Any lien created under this section shall not extend to any personal property that is not attached to or considered to be necessary for the proper operation of any motor vehicle, and it shall be the duty of any keeper of such personal property to return it to the owner if the owner claims the items prior to auction.

F. For the purposes of this section, in the case of a truck or combination of vehicles, the owner, or in the case of a rented or leased vehicle, the lessee of the truck or tractor truck, shall be liable for the costs of the towing, recovery, and storage of the cargo and of any trailer or semitrailer in the combination. Nothing in this subsection, however, shall bar the owner of the truck or tractor truck from subsequently seeking to recover from the owner of any trailer, semitrailer, or cargo all or any portion of these towing, recovery, and storage costs.

History.

2009, c. 664; 2016, c. 397.

§ 46.2-644.02. Lien of mechanic for repairs.

Every mechanic who shall alter or repair any article of personal property at the request of the owner of such property shall have a lien thereon for his just and reasonable charges therefor and may retain possession of such property until such charges are paid.

And every mechanic who shall make necessary alterations or repairs on any article of personal property which from its character requires the making of ordinary repairs thereto as a reasonable incident to its reasonable and customary use, at the request of any person legally in possession thereof under a reservation of title contract, chattel mortgage, deed of trust, or other instrument securing money, the person so in possession having authority to use such property, shall have a lien thereon for his just and reasonable charges therefor to the extent of $1,000. In addition, such mechanic shall be entitled to a lien against the proceeds, if any, remaining after the satisfaction of all prior security interests or liens and may retain possession of such property until such charges are paid. In any action to enforce the lien hereby given all persons having an interest in the property sought to be subjected shall be made parties defendant.

If the owner of the property held by the mechanic shall desire to obtain possession thereof, he shall make the mechanic defendant in proceeding in the county or municipal court to recover the property.

The owner may give a bond payable to the court, in a penalty of the amount equal to the lien claimed by the mechanic and court costs, with security to be approved by the clerk, and conditioned for the performance of the final judgment of the court on the trial of the proceeding, and with a further condition to the effect that, if upon the hearing, the judgment of the court be that the lien of the mechanic on such property, or any part thereof, be enforced, judgment may thereupon be entered against the obligors on such bond for the amount due the mechanic and court costs, if assessed against the owner, without further or other proceedings against them thereon. Upon giving of the bond, the property shall be delivered to the owner.

History.
2009, c. 664; 2016, c. 397.

§ 46.2-644.03. Enforcement of liens acquired under §§ 46.2-644.01 and 46.2-644.02 and of liens of bailees.

Any person having a lien under §§ 46.2-644.01 and 46.2-644.02 and any bailee, except where otherwise provided, having a lien as such at common law on personal property in his possession that he has no power to sell for the satisfaction of the lien, if the debt for which the lien exists is not paid within 10 days after it is due and the value of the property affected by the lien does not exceed $12,500, may sell such property or so much thereof as may be necessary, by public auction, for cash. The proceeds shall be applied to the satisfaction of the debt and expenses of sale, and the surplus, if any, shall be paid within 30 days of the sale to any lienholder, and then to the owner of the property. A seller who fails to remit the surplus as provided shall be liable to the person entitled to the surplus in an amount equal to $50 for each day beyond 30 days that the failure continues.

Before making the sale, the seller shall advertise the time, place, and terms thereof in a public place. In the case of property other than a motor vehicle required to be registered in Virginia having a value in excess of $600, 10 days' prior notice shall be given to any secured party who has filed a financing statement against the property, and written notice shall be given to the owner as hereinafter provided. If the property is a motor vehicle required by the motor vehicle laws of Virginia to be registered, the person having the lien shall ascertain from the Commissioner of the Department of Motor Vehicles whether the certificate of title of the motor vehicle shows a lien thereon. At that time, the Commissioner shall also determine the value of the property and shall communicate it to the bailee. If the certificate of title shows a lien, the bailee proposing the sale of the motor vehicle shall notify the lienholder of record, by certified mail, at the address on the certificate of title of the time and place of the proposed sale 10 days prior thereto. If the name of the owner cannot be ascertained, the name of "John Doe" shall be substituted in any proceedings hereunder and no written notice as to him shall be required to be mailed. Whenever a vehicle is shown by the Department of Motor Vehicles records to be owned by a person who has indicated that he is on active military duty or service, the Department shall include such information in response to requests for vehicle information pursuant to the requirements of this chapter.

If the value of the property is more than $12,500 but does not exceed $25,000, the party having the lien, after giving notice as herein provided, may apply by petition to any general district court of the county or city wherein the property is, or, if the value of the property exceeds $25,000, to the circuit court of the county or city, for the sale of the property. If, on the hearing of the case on the petition, the defense, if any made thereto, and such evidence as may be adduced by the parties respectively, the court is satisfied that the debt and lien are established and the property should be sold to pay the debt, the court shall order the sale to be made by the sheriff of the county or city. The sheriff shall make the same and apply and dispose of the proceeds in the same manner as if the sale were made under a writ of fieri facias.

In determining the value of the property as required by this section, the Commissioner shall use a recognized pricing guide and, in using such guide, shall use the trade-in value specified in such guide.

If the owner of the property is a resident of the Commonwealth, any notice required by this section may be served as provided in § 8.01-296 or, if the sale is to be made without resort to the courts, by personal delivery or by certified or registered mail delivered to the present owner of the property to be sold at his last known address at least 10 days prior to the date of sale. If the owner of the property is a nonresident or if his address is unknown, any notice required by this section may be served by posting a copy thereof in three of any of the following places in any combination: (i) one or more public places in the county or city where the property is located; (ii) one or more websites operated by the Commonwealth, the county or city where the property is located, or a political subdivision of either; or (iii) one or more newspapers of general circulation in the county or city where the property is located, either in print or on their websites. For purposes of this section, " public place " means a premises owned by the Commonwealth or a political subdivision thereof, or an agency of either, that is open to the general public.

If the property is a motor vehicle (i) for which neither the owner nor any other lienholder or secured party can be determined by the Department of Motor Vehicles through a diligent search of its records, (ii) manufactured for a model year at least six years prior to the current model year, and (iii) having a value of no more than $3,000 as determined by the provisions of § 8.01-419.1, a person having a lien on such vehicle may, after showing proof that the vehicle has been in his continuous custody for at least 30 days, apply for and receive from the Department of Motor Vehicles title or a nonrepairable certificate to such vehicle, free of all liens and claims of ownership of others, and proceed to sell or otherwise dispose of the vehicle.

Whenever a motor vehicle is sold hereunder, the Department of Motor Vehicles shall issue a certificate of title and registration or a nonrepairable certificate to the purchaser thereof upon his application containing the serial or motor number of the vehicle purchased together with an affidavit of the lienholder that he has complied with the provisions hereof, or by the sheriff conducting a sale that he has complied with said order.

Any garage keeper to whom a motor vehicle has been delivered pursuant to § 46.2-1209, 46.2-1213, or 46.2-1215 may after 30 days from the date of delivery proceed under this section, provided that action has not been taken pursuant to such sections for the sale of such motor vehicle.

Notwithstanding any provisions to the contrary, any person having a lien under § 46.2-644.01 or 46.2-644.02 shall comply with the provisions of the federal Servicemembers Civil Relief Act (50 U.S.C. § 3901 et seq.) when disposing of a vehicle owned by a member of the military duty or service.

History.
2009, c. 664; 2011, cc. 14, 702; 2014, c. 339; 2015, c. 640; 2016, c. 397.

ARTICLE 2.1.

ALL-TERRAIN VEHICLE AND OFF-ROAD MOTORCYCLE CERTIFICATES OF TITLE.

§ 46.2-644.1. Titling of all-terrain vehicles and off-road motorcycles.

A. Every owner, except a dealer licensed under § 46.2-1508, of any all-terrain vehicle or off-road motorcycle powered by a gasoline or diesel engine displacing more than 50 cubic centimeters and purchased as new on or after July 1, 2006, shall apply to the Department for a certificate of title in the name of the owner before the all-terrain vehicle or off-road motorcycle is operated anywhere in the Commonwealth.

B. Any owner of an all-terrain vehicle or off-road motorcycle not required to be titled under this section and not titled elsewhere may apply to the Department for a certificate of title. The Department shall issue the certificate upon reasonable evidence of ownership, such as a buyer's order or other document satisfactory to the Department.

C. Except as otherwise provided in this title, all-terrain vehicles and off-road motorcycles shall comply with the titling requirements of motor vehicles pursuant to Article 2 (§ 46.2-616 et seq.).

History.
2006, c. 896; 2015, c. 615.

§ 46.2-644.2. Department's records; fees; exemption.

The Department shall maintain a record of any certificate of title it issued under this article. Fees to be paid to the Department for issuance of such certificates of title shall be the same as those imposed for the titling of motor vehicles pursuant to § 46.2-627.

Any all-terrain vehicle or off-road motorcycle purchased and used by a nonprofit volunteer emergency medical services agency shall be exempt from fees imposed under this section.

History.
2006, c. 896; 2015, cc. 502, 503.

§ 46.2-644.3. Acquisition of all-terrain vehicle or off-road motorcycle by dealer.

Any dealer licensed under § 46.2-1508 who acquires an all-terrain vehicle or off-road motorcycle for resale shall be exempt from the titling requirements of this title.

Any dealer transferring an all-terrain vehicle or off-road motorcycle titled under this title shall assign the title to the new owner or, in the case of a new all-terrain vehicle or off-road motorcycle, assign the certificate of origin.

History.
2006, c. 896; 2015, c. 615.

ARTICLE 3.

REGISTRATION OF VEHICLES.

§ 46.2-645. Registration of vehicles.

The Department shall file each motor vehicle registration application received and, when satisfied that the applicant is entitled to register the vehicle, shall register the vehicle.

History.
Code 1950, § 46-52; 1952, c. 536; 1958, c. 541, § 46.1-54; 1989, c. 727.

§ 46.2-646. Expiration and renewal of registration.

A. Every registration under this title, unless otherwise provided, shall expire on the last day of the twelfth month next succeeding the date of registration. Every registration, unless otherwise provided, shall be renewed annually on application by the owner and by payment of the fees required by law, the renewal to take effect on the first day of the month succeeding the date of expiration. Notwithstanding these limitations, the Commissioner may extend the validity period of an expiring registration if (i) the Department is unable to process an application for renewal due to circumstances beyond its control, and (ii) the extension has been authorized under a directive from the Governor. However, in no event shall the validity period be extended more than 90 days per occurrence of such conditions.

B. All motor vehicles, trailers, and semitrailers registered in the Commonwealth shall, at the discretion of the Commissioner, be placed in a system of registration on a monthly basis to distribute the work of registering motor vehicles as uniformly as practicable throughout the twelve months of the year. All such motor vehicles, trailers, and semitrailers, unless otherwise provided, shall be registered for a period of twelve months. The registration shall be extended, at the discretion of the Commissioner, on receipt of appropriate prorated fees, as required by law, for a period of not less than one month nor more than eleven months as is necessary to distribute the registrations as equally as practicable on a monthly basis. The Commissioner shall, on request, assign to any owner or owners of two or more motor vehicles, trailers, or semitrailers the same registration period. The expiration date shall be the last day of the twelfth month or the last day of the designated month. Except for motor vehicles, trailers, and semitrailers registered for more than one year under subsection C of this section, every registration shall be renewed annually on application by the owner and by payment of fees required by law, the renewal to take effect on the first day of the succeeding month.

C. The Commissioner may offer, at his discretion, an optional multi-year registration for all motor vehicles, trailers, and semitrailers except for (i) those registered under the International Registration Plan and (ii) those registered as uninsured motor vehicles. When this option is offered and chosen by the registrant, all annual and twelve-month fees due at the time of registration shall be multiplied by the number of years or fraction thereof that the vehicle will be registered.

History.

Code 1950, § 46-62; 1958, c. 541, § 46.1-63; 1972, c. 609; 1974, c. 170; 1988, cc. 701, 704; 1989, c. 727; 2013, c. 337.

§ 46.2-646.1. Deactivation and reactivation of registration; fees.

A. The owner of a motor vehicle that has been registered in the Commonwealth may apply to the Commissioner to deactivate the registration of such vehicle. The owner of a motor vehicle who has voluntarily deactivated the vehicle's registration pursuant to this section shall not be required, with respect to such vehicle, to carry bodily injury liability insurance or property damage insurance, or to pay the uninsured motor vehicle fee as provided under § 46.2-706.

It shall be unlawful to operate any motor vehicle whose registration has been deactivated on any highway in the Commonwealth.

B. Any person having a motor vehicle for which registration has been deactivated under subsection A may apply to the Commissioner to reactivate the registration of such vehicle. Every applicant for reactivation of registration shall furnish the Commissioner with such evidence as is required under § 46.2-649 and shall either (i) execute and furnish to the Commissioner his certificate that the motor vehicle for which registration is to be reactivated is an insured motor vehicle as defined in § 46.2-705, or that the Commissioner has issued to its owner, in accordance with § 46.2-368, a certificate of self-insurance applicable to the vehicle or (ii) pay the uninsured motor vehicle fee required by § 46.2-706, which shall be disposed of as provided by § 46.2-710. The fee to be paid to the Department for the reactivation of a motor vehicle's registration shall be $10 unless the vehicle's registration has expired or the vehicle is registered under the International Registration Plan.

History.

2013, cc. 673, 789.

§ 46.2-647. Grace period for replacement of license plates or decals and renewal of registrations.

The Commissioner may, on finding either that the Department is unable to efficiently handle the replacement of license plates or decals or the renewal of registrations scheduled to expire during a specific month, or that persons seeking to secure license plates, decals, or registration renewals are, as a group, unable to do so without being substantially inconvenienced, declare a grace period for the replacement of license plates or decals and the renewal of registrations. The declaration of a grace period shall have the effect of postponing the expiration of those license plates, decals, and registrations scheduled to expire on the last day of that month to the fifteenth day of the succeeding month.

History.

1975, c. 17, § 46.1-63.1; 1989, c. 727.

§ 46.2-648. Registration of logging vehicles.

On receipt of an application on a form prescribed by him, the Commissioner shall register in a separate category trucks, tractor trucks, trailers, and semitrailers used exclusively in connection with logging operations. For the purposes of this section, the term "logging" shall mean the harvesting of timber and transportation from forested sites to places of sale.

Fees for the registration of vehicles under this section shall be the same as those ordinarily charged for the type of vehicle being registered.

History.

1985, c. 185, § 46.1-105.12; 1989, c. 727.

§ 46.2-648.1. Optional registration of tow dolly and converter gear.

The Department may, upon request, register any tow dolly or converter gear as defined in § 46.2-1119. For the purpose of determining the applicable fee for any such registration, the tow dolly or converter gear shall be considered a trailer and the registration fee determined in accordance with § 46.2-694.1. The fee for reserved numbers or letters on license plates for any tow dolly or converter gear shall be determined in accordance with § 46.2-726.

History.

1999, c. 593.

§ 46.2-649. Certain vehicles required to show evidence of payment of taxes and of registration or exemption from registration with Department of Motor Vehicles.

A. Before the Commissioner registers or reregisters any motor vehicle, trailer, or semitrailer under § 46.2-697, 46.2-698, 46.2-700, or 46.2-703, the applicant shall furnish evidence satisfactory to the Commissioner that all state, local, and federal taxes levied on that motor vehicle, trailer, or semitrailer have been paid and that the motor vehicle, trailer, or semitrailer either (i) is registered with the Department as required by law, or (ii) is not required so to register.

B. The Commissioner, in consultation with local commissioners of the revenue and directors of finance, and with appropriate federal officials, shall provide for the kinds of evidence required to satisfy the provisions of subsection A.

C. The provisions of this section shall not apply to (i) pickup trucks, (ii) panel trucks, or (iii) trucks having a registered gross weight less than 33,000 pounds.

D. The State Corporation Commission may notify the Department that a motor carrier (i) has not filed an annual report as required by § 58.1-2654 or (ii) has not paid taxes due as required by the State Corporation Commission. Upon receiving the notice, the Department shall not register or reregister motor vehicles, trailers, or semitrailers owned by the motor carrier until such requirements have been met.

History.

1983, c. 515, § 46.1-153.1; 1989, c. 727; 1997, c. 283; 2002, c. 47; 2013, c. 226.

§ 46.2-649.1. Registration of tow trucks; fees.

A. No tow truck registered under this section shall be subject to registration under the international registration plan or subject to any other state registration requirements under this chapter. Registration under this section shall not prohibit the use of "rollbacks" to transport storage sheds, similar structures, or other cargoes.

B. Vehicles registered under this section shall be subject to the following annual fees, based upon their manufacturer's gross vehicle weight ratings:

less than 15,000 pounds	$100
15,000 to 22,999 pounds	$200
23,000 to 29,499 pounds	$300
more than 29,499 pounds	$400

C. No vehicle shall be registered under this section unless there is in force as to such vehicle at the time of its registration commercial liability insurance coverage for those classes of insurance defined in §§ 38.2-117 and 38.2-118 in the amount of at least $750,000.

History.

1993, c. 120; 2006, cc. 874, 891.

§ 46.2-649.1:1. Registration of vehicles owned and used by volunteer fire departments or volunteer, commercial, or private emergency medical services agencies.

Upon application therefor, the Commissioner shall register and issue permanent license plates without year or month decals for display on any (i) firefighting truck, trailer, and semitrailer on which firefighting apparatus is permanently attached when any such vehicle is owned or under exclusive control of a volunteer fire department; (ii) emergency medical services vehicle or other vehicle owned or used exclusively by a volunteer fire department or volunteer emergency medical services agency if any such vehicle is used exclusively as an emergency medical services vehicle and is not rented, leased, or lent to any private individual, firm, or corporation, and no charge is made by the organization for the use of the vehicle; or (iii) emergency medical services vehicle owned or under exclusive control of a commercial or privately owned emergency medical services agency, as defined in § 32.1-111.1, if any such vehicle is not rented, leased, or lent to any private individual, firm, or corporation that is not another emergency medical services agency. The equipment shall be painted a distinguishing color and conspicuously display in letters and figures not less than three inches in height the identity of the emergency medical services agency, volunteer fire department, or volunteer emergency medical services agency having control of its operation.

No fee shall be charged for any vehicle registration or license plate issuance under clause (i) or (ii). The fees charged for vehicle registration under clause (iii) shall be as provided in § 46.2-694.

History.

1999, c. 329; 2015, cc. 502, 503; 2016, cc. 125, 133.

§ 46.2-649.2. Certain vehicles to comply with clean alternative fuel fleet standards prior to registration; penalty.

The Commissioner shall not register a motor vehicle subject to § 46.2-1179.1 which does not comply with the requirements of that section. Upon a determination that a motor vehicle is exempt from the requirements of § 46.2-1179.1, it shall forever be exempt, and the exemption shall be noted on its title. Whoever, through fraud or misrepresentation, procures or attempts to procure the registration of a motor vehicle in violation of the provisions of this section shall be guilty of a Class 1 misdemeanor.

History.
1993, cc. 234, 571.

§ 46.2-649.3. Registration of covered farm vehicles.

A. For the purposes of this section, a covered farm vehicle shall be registered pursuant to the provisions of § 46.2-698.

B. As defined in regulations promulgated by the Federal Motor Carrier Safety Administration (49 C.F.R. Part 390.5), a "covered farm vehicle" means a straight truck or articulated vehicle that is:

1. a. Registered in Virginia pursuant to the provisions of § 46.2-698; or

b. Registered in another state with a license plate or other designation issued by the state of registration that allows law enforcement to identify it as a farm vehicle;

2. Operated by the owner or operator of a farm or ranch or by an employee or family member of an owner or operator of a farm or ranch;

3. Used to transport agricultural commodities, livestock, machinery, or supplies to or from a farm or ranch;

4. Not used in for-hire motor carrier operations; however, for-hire motor carrier operations do not include the operation of a vehicle meeting the requirements of subdivisions 1, 2, and 3 by a tenant pursuant to a crop share farm lease agreement to transport the landlord's portion of the crops under that agreement; and

5. Not used in transporting material found by the U.S. Secretary of Transportation to be hazardous under 49 U.S.C. § 5103 and transported in a quantity requiring placarding under regulations prescribed by the Secretary under 49 C.F.R., subtitle B, chapter I, subchapter C.

C. A straight truck or articulated vehicle meeting the requirements of subsection B and having (i) a gross vehicle weight or gross vehicle weight rating, whichever is greater, of 26,001 pounds or less may utilize the exemptions provided in § 46.2-649.4 without mileage limitations or (ii) a gross vehicle weight or gross vehicle weight rating, whichever is greater, of more than 26,001 pounds may utilize the exemptions defined in § 46.2-649.4 anywhere in the Commonwealth or across state lines within 150 air miles (176.2 miles) of the farm or ranch with respect to which the vehicle is being operated.

D. For the purposes of this section, "agricultural commodities" means any horticultural plants and crops, cultivated plants and crops, poultry, dairy, and farm products, livestock and livestock products, and products derived from bees and beekeeping, primarily for sale, consumption, propagation, or other use by man or animals.

History.
2015, c. 258.

§ 46.2-649.4. Covered farm vehicles; exemptions.

A covered farm vehicle as defined in § 46.2-649.3, including the operator of that vehicle, is exempt from the following:

1. Any requirement relating to commercial driver's licenses in Federal Motor Carrier Safety Regulations 49 C.F.R. Part 383;

2. Any requirement relating to controlled substances and alcohol use and testing in Federal Motor Carrier Safety Regulations 49 C.F.R. Part 382;

3. Any requirement in Federal Motor Carrier Safety Regulations 49 C.F.R. Part 391, Subpart E, Physical Qualifications and Examinations;

4. Any requirement in Federal Motor Carrier Safety Regulations 49 C.F.R. Part 395, Hours of Service of Drivers; and

5. Any requirement in Federal Motor Carrier Safety Regulations 49 C.F.R. Part 396, Inspection, Repair, and Maintenance.

History.
2015, c. 258.

ARTICLE 4.

TEMPORARY REGISTRATION.

§ 46.2-650. Temporary permits or duplicate applications.

The Department may promulgate regulations providing that on application for a certificate of title and registration of a vehicle, either new or after a transfer, the vehicle may be operated on the highway under (i) a temporary permit issued by the Department or (ii) a duplicate application carried in the vehicle.

History.
Code 1950, § 46-43; 1958, c. 541, § 46.1-42; 1989, c. 727.

§ 46.2-651. Trip permits; regulations; fees.

A. The Department may, on application on forms provided by the Department, issue a trip permit to any owner of a motor vehicle, trailer, or semitrailer which would otherwise be subject to registration plates but is not currently registered. If the vehicle operating under the permit is a vehicle designed as a property-carrying vehicle, it shall be unladen at the time of operation under the permit. The permit shall be valid for three days and shall show the registration or permit number, the date of issue, the date of expiration, the make of vehicle, the vehicle identification number, the beginning point and the point of destination. The fee for the permit shall be five dollars.

B. For vehicles to be purchased by a Virginia resident and registered in Virginia, the Department shall issue to the prospective purchaser, upon his application therefor, trip permits as provided in subsection A of this section, except that permits issued under this subsection shall not be valid unless and until the prospective purchaser receives an original bill of sale pertaining to the vehicle purchased. Permits issued under this subsection shall be valid for three days, beginning on the date of the original bill of sale, and shall be kept with the original bill of sale in the purchased vehicle at all times during the trip until the vehicle is properly registered with the Department. The Commissioner may charge a reasonable fee, adequate to recover the Department's costs, for the issuance of permits under this subsection, and may promulgate such regulations as he deems necessary or convenient in carrying out the provisions of this subsection.

History.

1974, c. 215, § 46.1-42.1; 1976, c. 59; 1989, c. 727; 2000, c. 144; 2001, c. 192.

§ 46.2-652. Temporary registration or permit for oversize vehicles; fees.

The Commissioner may grant a temporary registration or permit for the operation of a vehicle or equipment that cannot be licensed because the vehicle, excluding any load thereon, exceeds statutory size limits on the highways in the Commonwealth from one point to another within the Commonwealth, or from the Commonwealth to a point or points outside the Commonwealth, or from outside the Commonwealth to a point or points within the Commonwealth. Any temporary registration or permit issued under this section shall show the registration or permit number, the date of issue, the date of expiration, the vehicle to which it refers, and the route to be traveled or other restrictions and shall be carried in the vehicle.

For a single-trip temporary registration or permit issued under this section, the applicant shall pay a fee of 10 cents ($0.10) per mile for every mile to be traveled, in addition to any administrative fee required by the Department. In lieu of a single-trip permit, an annual multi-trip permit may be issued for a fee of $40, in addition to any administrative fee required by the Department.

For any vehicle that is both overweight and oversize, the permit fees under § 46.2-652.1 shall apply.

History.

Code 1950, § 46-44; 1958, c. 541, § 46.1-43; 1962, c. 535; 1989, c. 727; 1997, c. 283; 2003, c. 314; 2012, c. 443.

§ 46.2-652.1. Temporary registration or permit for overweight vehicles; fees.

A. The Commissioner may grant a temporary registration or permit for the operation of (i) a vehicle or equipment that cannot be licensed because the vehicle, excluding any load thereon, is overweight or (ii) a licensed vehicle that exceeds statutory weight limits on the highways in the Commonwealth from one point to another within the Commonwealth, or from the Commonwealth to a point or points outside the Commonwealth, or from outside the Commonwealth to a point or points within the Commonwealth. Any temporary registration or permit issued under this section shall show the registration or permit number, the date of issue, the date of expiration, the vehicle to which it refers, and the route to be traveled or other restrictions and shall be carried in the vehicle.

B. For a single-trip temporary registration or permit issued under this section, the applicant shall pay (i) a fee of 30 cents ($0.30) per mile for every mile to be traveled, to be allocated as follows: (a) 20 cents ($0.20) per mile deposited into the Highway Maintenance and Operating Fund established pursuant to § 33.2-1530 to be used to assist in funding needed highway pavement and bridge maintenance and rehabilitation and (b) 10 cents ($0.10) per mile to the Department and (ii) one of the following fees, depending on gross weight:

1. For a single-trip overweight permit issued for gross weights of 115,000 pounds or less, a $20 administrative fee to the Department, plus, if needed, an additional $10 to cover extra research and analysis;

2. For a single-trip overweight permit issued for gross weights of 115,001 to 150,000 pounds, a fee of $80, to be allocated as follows: (i) $50 deposited into the Highway Maintenance and Operating Fund to be used to assist in funding needed highway pavement and bridge maintenance and rehabilitation and (ii) a $30 administrative fee to the Department;

3. For a single-trip overweight permit issued for gross weights of 150,001 to 200,000 pounds, a fee of $190, to be allocated as follows: (i) $160 deposited into the Highway Maintenance and Operating Fund to be used to assist in funding needed highway pavement and bridge maintenance and rehabilitation and (ii) a $30 administrative fee to the Department;

4. For a single-trip overweight permit issued for gross weights of 200,001 to 500,000 pounds, a fee of $280, to be allocated as follows: (i) $250 deposited into the Highway Maintenance and Operating Fund to be used to assist in funding needed highway pavement and bridge maintenance and rehabilitation and (ii) a $30 administrative fee to the Department; or

5. For a single-trip overweight permit issued for gross weights in excess of 500,000 pounds, a fee of $1,450, to be allocated as follows: (i) $1,420 deposited into the Highway Maintenance and Operating

Fund to be used to assist in funding needed highway pavement and bridge maintenance and rehabilitation and (ii) a $30 administrative fee to the Department.

C. In lieu of a single-trip permit, an annual multi-trip overweight permit may be issued for the following fee:

1. For an annual multi-trip overweight permit issued for gross weights of 115,000 pounds and below, a fee of $500, to be allocated as follows: (i) $360 deposited into the Highway Maintenance and Operating Fund to be used to assist in funding needed highway pavement and bridge maintenance and rehabilitation and (ii) $140 to the Department; or

2. For an annual multi-trip overweight permit issued for gross weights in excess of 115,000 pounds, a fee of $560, to be allocated as follows: (i) $420 deposited into the Highway Maintenance and Operating Fund to be used to assist in funding needed highway pavement and bridge maintenance and rehabilitation and (ii) $140 to the Department.

D. In lieu of an annual permit, a three-month overweight permit may be issued for a fee of $220, to be allocated as follows: (i) $110 deposited into the Highway Maintenance and Operating Fund to be used to assist in funding needed highway pavement and bridge maintenance and rehabilitation and (ii) $110 to the Department.

E. For any vehicle that is both overweight and oversize, the permit fees under this section shall apply.

History.
2012, c. 443.

§ 46.2-653. Temporary registration or permit for transportation of manufactured homes exceeding the size permitted by law.

The Commissioner may grant a temporary registration or permit for the transportation of manufactured homes, which exceed the size permitted by law, on the highways in the Commonwealth from one point to another within the Commonwealth, or from the Commonwealth to a point or points outside the Commonwealth, or from outside the Commonwealth to a point or points within the Commonwealth. Such temporary registration or permit shall show the registration or permit number, the date of issue, the date of expiration, and the route to be traveled or other restrictions and shall be displayed in a prominent place on the vehicle. The owner of every manufactured home of this sort purchased in the Commonwealth for use within the Commonwealth or brought into the Commonwealth for use within the Commonwealth shall apply within 30 days to the Department for title in the name of the owner. This requirement shall not apply to inventory held by licensed Virginia dealers for the purpose of resale.

The authorities in cities and towns regulating the movement of traffic may prescribe the route or routes over which these manufactured homes may be transported, and no manufactured home of this sort shall be transported through any city or town except along a prescribed route or routes.

For each temporary single-trip registration or permit issued hereunder, the applicant shall pay a fee of $1, in addition to any administrative fee required by the Department. In lieu of a single-trip permit, an annual multi-trip permit may be issued for a fee of $40, in addition to any administrative fee required by the Department.

No permit, as provided in this section, shall be issued covering any manufactured home that is subject to a license plate.

History.
Code 1950, § 46-44.1; 1956, c. 85; 1958, c. 541, § 46.1-44; 1973, c. 207; 1977, c. 587; 1989, c. 727; 1997, c. 283; 1999, c. 77; 2003, c. 314; 2006, c. 202; 2008, c. 178; 2014, c. 624.

§ 46.2-653.1. Conversion of manufactured home to real property.

A. After a manufactured home has been titled in the Commonwealth and at such time as the wheels and other equipment previously used for mobility have been removed and the unit has been attached to real property owned by the manufactured home owner, the owner may convert the home to real property in accordance with the provisions of subsection B. Except as provided in §§ 58.1-3219.5 and 58.1-3219.9, and for the purposes stated in §§ 58.1-3219.5 and 58.1-3219.9, the provisions of this section constitute the only manner by which a manufactured home owner may convert a manufactured home to real property.

B. A manufactured home owner who wishes to convert the home to real property shall submit a sworn affidavit to the Department that the wheels and other equipment previously used for mobility have been removed from the manufactured home and the unit has been attached to real property owned by the manufactured home owner.

The affidavit must be in a form approved by the Commissioner. Upon compliance by the owner with the procedure for surrender of title, the Department shall rescind and cancel the Virginia title. The Department shall not cancel the title if a security interest has been recorded on the title and not released by the secured party. After canceling the title, the Department shall provide written confirmation to the owner that the title has been surrendered and has been canceled by the Department.

Upon receipt of confirmation that the title has been surrendered and has been canceled by the Department, the owner shall file a sworn affidavit of affixation with the circuit court of the locality where the real property is located. The affidavit shall include all of the following information:

1. The manufacturer and, if applicable, the model name of the manufactured home.

2. The vehicle identification number and serial number of the manufactured home.

3. The legal description of the real property on which the manufactured home is placed, including the property address, stating that the owner of the manufactured home also owns the real property.

4. Certification that there are no security interests in the manufactured home that have not been released by the secured party.

5. The homeowner's statement that the title has been surrendered and has been canceled by the Department and that the home is intended to be a permanent fixture and improvement to the land, to the same extent as any site-built home, and assessed and taxed with the land as real property.

In addition, a copy of the confirmation provided by the Department that the title has been surrendered and canceled by the Department shall be attached to and filed with the affidavit.

Upon filing the affidavit of affixation, the manufactured home shall then be deemed to be real estate and shall thereafter be conveyed and encumbered only as real estate is conveyed and encumbered, except when the home is thereafter physically severed from the real property and a new title issued in accordance with subsection C.

A security interest in a manufactured home is perfected against the rights of judicial lien creditors, execution creditors, and purchasers for value on and after the date such security interest attaches. The Commissioner shall have prepared a list of all titles canceled pursuant to this section and furnish it, in conjunction with the reports submitted pursuant to § 46.2-210, to the commissioner of the revenue of each county and city without cost.

C. If the owner of a manufactured home whose certificate of title has been canceled under this section subsequently seeks to sever the manufactured home from the real property, the owner may apply for a new certificate of title in accordance with the provisions of this section.

1. The owner shall file with the circuit court where the real property is located an affidavit that includes or provides for all of the following information:

a. The manufacturer and, if applicable, the model name of the manufactured home.

b. The vehicle identification number and serial number of the manufactured home.

c. The legal description of the real property on which the manufactured home is or was placed, stating that the owner of the manufactured home also owns the real property.

d. Certification that there are no security interests in the manufactured home that have not been released by the secured party.

e. The homeowner's statement that the home has been or will be physically severed from the real property.

2. The owner must submit the following to the Department:

a. A copy of the affidavit filed in accordance with subdivision C 1.

b. Verification that the manufactured home has been severed from the real property. Confirmation of severance by the commissioner of the revenue where the real property is located shall constitute acceptable evidence that the unit has been severed from the real property.

Upon receipt of the information required in subdivision C 2, together with a title application and required fee, the Department is authorized to issue a new title for the manufactured home. The initial title issued under the provisions of this subsection shall contain no security interests, provided however, that nothing contained herein shall be construed to prevent a subsequent security interest from being recorded on the title.

History.
2014, c. 624; 2016, cc. 349, 393.

§ 46.2-654. Issuance of temporary registration certificates by motor vehicle auctions.

In addition to the provisions of § 46.2-1542, businesses licensed by the Department to conduct sales of motor vehicles by auction may issue to persons who purchase motor vehicles through auctions conducted by these businesses temporary certificates of registration.

Issuance of certificates under this section shall be subject to regulations promulgated by the Commissioner.

History.
1988, c. 739, § 46.1-90.2; 1989, c. 727.

§ 46.2-654.1. Temporary registration issued for purchasers of motor vehicles from motor vehicle dealers who are no longer engaged in business and title is held by person other than dealer.

The Department may issue a temporary registration to any purchaser of a motor vehicle who is unable to obtain the title for such vehicle because the motor vehicle dealer who sold the vehicle to the purchaser is no longer engaged in business in the Commonwealth as a dealer as defined in § 46.2-1500 and the title is held by a person other than such dealer.

History.
2012, c. 119; 2015, c. 615.

ARTICLE 5.
RECIPROCITY FOR NONRESIDENTS.

§ 46.2-655. Reciprocity required.

The privileges extended under this article to nonresident owners of foreign motor vehicles, trailers, and semitrailers operated in the Commonwealth are extended only on condition that the same privileges are granted by the state of the United States or foreign country wherein such nonresident owners are residents to residents of the Commonwealth operating motor vehicles, trailers, or semitrailers in such state of the United States or foreign country.

History.
Code 1950, § 46-110; 1958, c. 541, § 46.1-131; 1989, c. 727.

§ 46.2-656. Nonresident may operate temporarily without registration.

Except as otherwise provided in this article, a nonresident owner of a passenger car which has been registered for the current calendar year in the state or country of which the owner is a resident and which at all times when operated in the Commonwealth displays the license plate or plates issued for such vehicle in the place of residence of such owner, may operate or permit the operation of such passenger car within or partly within this Commonwealth for a period of six months without registering the passenger car or paying any fees to the Commonwealth. If, however, at the expiration of such six months the passenger car is still in the Commonwealth, its owner shall apply for registration of the vehicle and shall pay a fee for such registration based on the time operation of the vehicle in the Commonwealth commenced.

History.
Code 1950, § 46-111; 1958, c. 541, § 46.1-132; 1989, c. 727.

§ 46.2-657. When registration by nonresident not required.

Notwithstanding other provisions of this article, any nonresident from a state that does not require the registration of a vehicle like that owned by such nonresident when such vehicle is owned and operated by a resident of Virginia in the state in which the foreign vehicle owned or operated by such nonresident is registered, shall not be required to register such vehicle in the Commonwealth. This section, however, shall not permit the operation of any truck, trailer, or semitrailer the weight, length, width, or height of which vehicle or combination of vehicles is in violation of the provisions of this title or at a speed in violation of this title; nor shall the privileges provided in this section apply to common carriers or passenger cars.

History.
Code 1950, § 46-116; 1958, c. 541, § 46.1-133; 1989, c. 727.

§ 46.2-658. Regular operation other than for pleasure.

Except as provided in § 46.2-657, a nonresident owner of a foreign motor vehicle, trailer, or semitrailer which is regularly operated in the Commonwealth, or from a point or points outside the Commonwealth to a point or points within the Commonwealth, or from a point or points within the Commonwealth to a point or points outside the Commonwealth, or through the Commonwealth, for purposes other than purposes of pleasure, shall, unless otherwise provided in this chapter, register such vehicle and pay the same fees therefor as are required with reference to like vehicles owned by residents of the Commonwealth. Any owner who operates or permits to be operated one or more of these vehicles either simultaneously or alternately as often as four times in any one month shall be considered to be regularly operating them in the Commonwealth.

History.
Code 1950, § 46-117; 1958, c. 541, § 46.1-134; 1989, c. 727.

§ 46.2-659: Repealed by Acts 1997, c. 283.

§ 46.2-660. Operating vehicles in business in Commonwealth.

Every nonresident, including any foreign corporation, conducting business in the Commonwealth and owning and regularly operating in such business any motor vehicle, trailer, or semitrailer in the Commonwealth shall be required to register the vehicle and pay the same fees required for registration of similar vehicles owned by residents of the Commonwealth.

History.
Code 1950, § 46-121; 1958, c. 541, § 46.1-136; 1989, c. 727.

§ 46.2-661. Extension of reciprocal privileges.

Notwithstanding the other provisions of this chapter, the Commissioner, with the consent of the Governor, may extend to the owners of foreign vehicles operated in the Commonwealth the same privileges which are granted by the state of the United States or foreign country wherein the owners of the foreign vehicles are residents to residents of this Commonwealth operating vehicles in such state of the United States or foreign country.

History.
Code 1950, § 46-122; 1958, c. 541, § 46.1-137; 1989, c. 727.

ARTICLE 6.

EXEMPTIONS FROM REGISTRATION.

§ 46.2-662. Temporary exemption for new resident operating vehicle registered in another state or country.

A. A resident owner of any passenger car, pickup or panel truck, moped, autocycle, or motorcycle, other than those provided for in § 46.2-652, that has been duly registered for the current calendar year in another state or country and that at all times when operated in the Commonwealth displays the license plate or plates issued for the vehicle in the other state or country, may operate or permit the operation of the passenger car, pickup or panel truck, moped, autocycle, or motorcycle within or partly within the Commonwealth for the first 30 days of his residency in the Commonwealth without registering the passenger car, pickup or panel truck, moped, autocycle, or motorcycle or paying any fees to the Commonwealth.

B. In addition to any penalty authorized under this title, any locality may adopt an ordinance imposing a penalty of up to $250 upon the resident owner of any motor vehicle that, following the end of the 30-day period provided in subsection A, is required to be registered in Virginia but has not been so registered. The locality may impose the penalty upon the resident owner annually for as long as the motor vehicle remains unregistered in Virginia. The ordinance shall set forth a reasonable method for assessing and collecting the penalty, whether by civil, criminal, or administrative process, and shall identify the employees or agents of the locality who are to execute such assessment and collection.

History.
1976, c. 17, § 46.1-41.1; 1980, c. 53; 1989, c. 727; 2013, cc. 347, 783; 2014, cc. 53, 256; 2016, c. 131.

§ 46.2-663. Backhoes.

No person shall be required to obtain the registration certificate, license plates, or decals for or pay a registration fee for any backhoe operated on any highway for a distance of no more than twenty miles from its operating base.

History.
Code 1950, § 46-45; 1950, p. 693; 1952, c. 498; 1956, cc. 292, 568; 1958, c. 541, § 46.1-45; 1962, cc. 214, 535; 1964, c. 611; 1966, c. 654; 1968, c. 46; 1970, c. 192; 1972, c. 609; 1973, c. 495; 1978, c. 307; 1988, cc. 76, 568; 1989, c. 727; 2016, c. 142.

§ 46.2-664. Vehicles used for spraying fruit trees and other plants.

No person shall be required to obtain the registration certificate, license plates, or decals for or pay a registration fee for any vehicle on which is securely attached a machine for spraying fruit trees and other plants of the owner or lessee of the truck.

History.
Code 1950, § 46-45; 1950, p. 693; 1952, c. 498; 1956, cc. 292, 568; 1958, c. 541, § 46.1-45; 1962, cc. 214, 535; 1964, c. 611; 1966, c. 654; 1968, c. 46; 1970, c. 192; 1972, c. 609; 1973, c. 495; 1978, c. 307; 1988, cc. 76, 568; 1989, c. 727; 2016, c. 142.

§ 46.2-665. Vehicles used for agricultural or horticultural purposes.

A. No person shall be required to obtain the registration certificate, license plates, or decals for or pay a registration fee for any motor vehicle, trailer, or semitrailer used exclusively for agricultural or horticultural purposes on lands owned or leased by the vehicle's owner.

B. This exemption shall only apply to (i) pickup or panel trucks, (ii) sport utility vehicles, (iii) vehicles having a gross vehicle weight rating greater than 7,500 pounds, and (iv) trailers and semitrailers that are not operated on or over any public highway in the Commonwealth for any purpose other than:

1. Crossing a highway;
2. Operating along a highway for a distance of no more than 50 miles from one part of the owner's land to another, irrespective of whether the tracts adjoin;
3. Taking the vehicle or attached fixtures to and from a repair shop for repairs;
4. Taking another vehicle exempt from registration under any provision of §§ 46.2-664 through 46.2-668 or 46.2-672, or any part or subcomponent of such a vehicle, to or from a repair shop for repairs, including return trips;
5. Operating along a highway to and from a refuse disposal facility for the purpose of disposing of trash and garbage generated on a farm; or
6. Operating along a highway for a distance of no more than 50 miles for the purpose of obtaining supplies for agricultural or horticultural purposes, seeds, fertilizers, chemicals, or animal feed and returning.

History.
Code 1950, § 46-45; 1950, p. 693; 1952, c. 498; 1956, cc. 292, 568; 1958, c. 541, § 46.1-45; 1962, cc. 214, 535; 1964, c. 611; 1966, c. 654; 1968, c. 46; 1970, c. 192; 1972, c. 609; 1973, c. 495; 1978, c. 307; 1988, cc. 76, 568; 1989, c. 727; 1994, c. 253; 2000, c. 318; 2001, c. 327; 2010, c. 293; 2012, c. 174; 2013, c. 776; 2016, c. 142.

§ 46.2-666. Vehicles used for seasonal transportation of farm produce and livestock.

No person shall be required to obtain the registration certificate, license plates, or decals for or pay a registration fee prescribed for any motor vehicle, trailer, or semitrailer owned by the owner or lessee of a farm and used by him on a seasonal basis in transporting farm produce and livestock along public highways for a distance of no more than 50 miles including the distance to the nearest storage house, packing plant, or market. The provisions of this section shall only apply to (i) pickup or panel trucks, (ii) sport utility vehicles, (iii) vehicles having a gross vehicle weight rating greater than 7,500 pounds, and (iv) trailers and semitrailers.

History.
Code 1950, § 46-45; 1950, p. 693; 1952, c. 498; 1956, cc. 292, 568; 1958, c. 541, § 46.1-45; 1962, cc. 214, 535; 1964, c. 611; 1966, c. 654; 1968, c. 46; 1970, c. 192; 1972, c. 609; 1973, c. 495; 1978, c. 307; 1988, cc. 76, 568; 1989, c. 727; 1995, c. 126; 1998, c. 323; 2010, c. 293; 2012, c. 174; 2013, c. 776; 2016, c. 142.

§ 46.2-667. Farm machinery and tractors.

No person shall be required to obtain the registration certificate, license plates, or decals for or pay the prescribed fee for any farm machinery or tractor when operated on a highway (i) between one tract of land and another regardless of whether the land is owned by the same person or (ii) to and from a repair shop for repairs.

History.
Code 1950, § 46-45; 1950, p. 693; 1952, c. 498; 1956, cc. 292, 568; 1958, c. 541, § 46.1-45; 1962, cc. 214, 535; 1964, c. 611; 1966, c. 654; 1968, c. 46; 1970, c. 192; 1972, c. 609; 1973, c. 495; 1978, c. 307; 1988, cc. 76, 568; 1989, c. 727; 1996, c. 55; 2000, c. 318; 2016, c. 142.

§ 46.2-668. Vehicles validly registered in other states and used in conjunction with harvesting operations.

A. No person shall be required to obtain the registration certificate, license plates, or decals for or pay a registration fee for any motor vehicle, trailer, or semitrailer which is validly registered in another state and bears valid license plates issued by that state when the use of the vehicle has been contracted for by the owner or lessee of a farm as an incidental part of the harvesting of a crop from his farm. This exemption shall only be valid while the vehicle is engaged principally in transporting farm produce from the farm:

1. As an incidental part of harvesting operations;
2. Along a public highway for a distance of not more than 20 miles to a storage house, packing plant, market, or transportation terminal;
3. When the use is a seasonal operation; and
4. When the owner of the vehicle has secured from the Commissioner an exemption permit for each vehicle.

B. The Commissioner, upon receipt of an application certifying that a vehicle is entitled to the exemption set forth in this subsection and, if the vehicle is a qualified highway vehicle under § 58.1-2700, payment of $150, shall issue an exemption permit on a form prescribed by him. The exemption permit shall be carried at all times by the operator of the vehicle for which it is issued or displayed in a conspicuous place on the vehicle. The exemption permit shall be valid for a period of 90 days from date of issue and shall be renewable by the procedure set forth in the foregoing provisions of this section.

History.
Code 1950, § 46-45; 1950, p. 693; 1952, c. 498; 1956, cc. 292, 568; 1958, c. 541, § 46.1-45; 1962, cc. 214, 535; 1964, c. 611; 1966, c. 654; 1968, c. 46; 1970, c. 192; 1972, c. 609; 1973, c. 495; 1978, c. 307; 1988, cc. 76, 568; 1989, c. 727; 2003, c. 896; 2011, cc. 881, 889; 2016, c. 142.

§ 46.2-669. Tractors and similar vehicles owned by sawmill operators.

No person shall be required to obtain the registration certificate, license plates, or decals for or pay a registration fee for any tractor, trailer, log cart, or similar vehicle owned by a sawmill operator when the vehicle is operated or moved:

1. Along a highway from one sawmill or sawmill site to another;
2. To or from a repair shop for repairs; or
3. Across a highway from one contiguous tract of land to another.

History.
Code 1950, § 46-45; 1950, p. 693; 1952, c. 498; 1956, cc. 292, 568; 1958, c. 541, § 46.1-45; 1962, cc. 214, 535; 1964, c. 611; 1966, c. 654; 1968, c. 46; 1970, c. 192; 1972, c. 609; 1973, c. 495; 1978, c. 307; 1988, cc. 76, 568; 1989, c. 727; 2016, c. 142.

§ 46.2-670. Vehicles owned by farmers and used to transport certain wood products.

No person shall be required to obtain the registration certificate, license plates, or decals for or pay a registration fee for any motor vehicle, trailer, or semitrailer owned by a farm owner when the vehicle is operated or moved along a highway for no more than twenty miles between a sawmill or sawmill site and his farm to transport sawdust, wood shavings, slab wood, and other wood wastes. The provisions of this section shall only apply to (i) pickup or panel trucks, (ii) sport utility vehicles, (iii) vehicles having a gross vehicle weight rating greater than 7,500 pounds, and (iv) trailers and semitrailers.

History.
Code 1950, § 46-45; 1950, p. 693; 1952, c. 498; 1956, cc. 292, 568; 1958, c. 541, § 46.1-45; 1962, cc. 214, 535; 1964, c. 611; 1966, c. 654; 1968, c. 46; 1970, c. 192; 1972, c. 609; 1973, c. 495; 1978, c. 307; 1988, cc. 76, 568; 1989, c. 727; 2010, c. 293; 2012, c. 174; 2013, c. 776; 2016, c. 142.

§ 46.2-670.1. Vehicles owned by maritime cargo terminal operators.

No person shall be required to obtain the registration certificate, certificate of title, license plates, or decals for or to pay a registration fee for any motor vehicle owned or leased by a maritime cargo terminal owner or operator and used to transport a seagoing container and operated along a highway on a route of no more than one mile approved by the Department.

History.
2016, c. 379.

§ 46.2-671. Vehicles used at mines.

No person shall be required to obtain the registration certificate, license plates, or decals for or pay a registration fee for any motor vehicle, trailer, or semitrailer used at mines when operated on the highway for no more than twenty miles between mines or to or from a repair shop for repairs.

History.
Code 1950, § 46-45; 1950, p. 693; 1952, c. 498; 1956, cc. 292, 568; 1958, c. 541, § 46.1-45; 1962, cc. 214, 535; 1964, c. 611; 1966, c. 654; 1968, c. 46; 1970, c. 192; 1972, c. 609; 1973, c. 495; 1978, c. 307; 1988, cc. 76, 568; 1989, c. 727; 2016, c. 142.

§ 46.2-672. Certain vehicles transporting fertilizer, cotton, or peanuts.

No person shall be required to obtain the registration certificate, license plates, or decals for or pay a registration fee for any motor vehicle or trailer, semitrailer, or fertilizer spreader drawn by a farm tractor used by a farmer, his tenant, agent or employee or a cotton ginner, peanut buyer, or fertilizer distributor to transport unginned cotton, peanuts, or fertilizer owned by the farmer, cotton ginner, peanut buyer, or fertilizer distributor from one farm to another, from farm to gin, from farm to dryer, from farm to market, or from fertilizer distributor to farm and on return to the distributor.

The provisions of this section shall not apply to vehicles operated on a for-hire basis.

History.
Code 1950, § 46-45; 1950, p. 693; 1952, c. 498; 1956, cc. 292, 568; 1958, c. 541, § 46.1-45; 1962, cc. 214, 535; 1964, c. 611; 1966, c. 654; 1968, c. 46; 1970, c. 192; 1972, c. 609; 1973, c. 495; 1978, c. 307; 1988, cc. 76, 568; 1989, c. 727; 2016, c. 142.

§ 46.2-673. Return trips of exempted farm vehicles.

No person shall be required to obtain the registration certificate, license plates, or decals for or pay a registration fee for any farm vehicle exempted from registration under the provisions of this article when that vehicle is:

1. Making a return trip from any marketplace;
2. Transporting back to a farm ordinary and essential food and other products for home and farm use; or
3. Transporting supplies to the farm.

History.
Code 1950, § 46-45; 1950, p. 693; 1952, c. 498; 1956, cc. 292, 568; 1958, c. 541, § 46.1-45; 1962, cc. 214, 535; 1964, c. 611; 1966, c. 654; 1968, c. 46; 1970, c. 192; 1972, c. 609; 1973, c. 495; 1978, c. 307; 1988, cc. 76, 568; 1989, c. 727; 2016, c. 142.

§ 46.2-674. Vehicles used by commercial fishermen.

No person shall be required to obtain the registration certificate, license plates, or decals for or pay a registration fee for any motor vehicle, trailer, boat trailer, or semitrailer, or any combination thereof not having a gross vehicle weight exceeding 12,000 pounds used by commercial fishermen, their agents, or employees for the purpose of:

1. Transporting boats or other equipment used in commercial fishing no more than 50 miles between his place of residence or business and the waters within the territorial limits of the Commonwealth or the adjacent marginal seas;
2. Any return trip to his place of residence or business; or
3. Transporting harvested seafood no more than 50 miles between the place where the seafood is first brought ashore and the transporter's place of business or the location of the seafood's first point of sale.

History.
Code 1950, § 46-45; 1950, p. 693; 1952, c. 498; 1956, cc. 292, 568; 1958, c. 541, § 46.1-45; 1962, cc. 214, 535; 1964, c. 611; 1966, c. 654; 1968, c. 46; 1970, c. 192; 1972, c. 609; 1973, c. 495; 1978, c. 307; 1988, cc. 76, 568; 1989, c. 727; 1997, c. 500; 2013, c. 777; 2016, c. 142.

§ 46.2-675. Certain vehicles engaged in mining or quarrying operations; permit when such vehicle required to cross public highways.

No person shall be required to obtain the registration certificate, license plates, or decals for or pay a registration fee prescribed for any motor vehicle engaged in coal mining operations or other types of mining and quarrying operations, if the sole function of the motor vehicle is to haul coal from mine to tipple or to haul other mined or quarried products from mine or quarry to a processing plant. The owner of the vehicle, however, shall first obtain, without charge, a permit from the Commissioner of Highways in any case in which the motor vehicle is required to cross the public highways. The Commissioner of Highways shall not issue the permit unless he is satisfied that the owner of the motor vehicle has, at his own expense, strengthened the highway crossing so that it will adequately bear the load and has provided adequate signs, lights, or flagmen as may be required for the protection of the public. Any damage done to the highways as a result of this operation shall be repaired in a manner satisfactory to the Commissioner of Highways at the expense of the vehicle's owner.

History.
1970, c. 604, § 46.1-45.1; 1972, c. 609; 1989, c. 727; 2016, c. 142.

§ 46.2-676. Registration certificate, license plates, or decals for any golf carts and utility vehicles; fees.

No person shall be required to obtain the registration certificate, license plates, or decals for or pay any registration fee for any golf cart or utility vehicle that either (i) is not operated on or over any public highway in the Commonwealth or (ii) is operated on or over a public highway as authorized by Article 13.1 (§ 46.2-916.1 et seq.) of Chapter 8.

History.
1973, c. 194, § 46.1-45.2; 1980, c. 37; 1986, c. 220; 1987, cc. 151, 342, 388; 1989, c. 727; 1995, c. 670; 1996, c. 920; 1997, cc. 485, 783, 904; 1999, c. 211; 2002, cc. 44, 98; 2003, c. 105; 2004, c. 746; 2016, c. 142.

§ 46.2-677. Self-propelled wheelchairs.

No person shall be required to obtain the registration certificate, license plates, or decals for or pay any registration fee for any self-propelled wheelchair or self-propelled wheelchair conveyance provided it is:

1. Operated by a person who is capable of operating it properly and safely but who, by reason of physical disability, is otherwise unable to move about as a pedestrian; and

2. Not operated on a public highway in this Commonwealth except to the extent necessary to cross the highway.

History.
1973, c. 194, § 46.1-45.2; 1980, c. 37; 1986, c. 220; 1987, cc. 151, 342, 388; 1989, c. 727; 2016, c. 142.

§ 46.2-678. Forklift trucks.

A. No person shall be required to obtain the registration certificate, license plates, or decals for or pay a registration fee for any forklift truck provided it is:

1. Operated by a person holding a valid Virginia driver's license;

2. Operated along or across highways only in traveling from one plant, factory, or job site to another by the most direct route;

3. Not carrying or transporting any object or person, other than the driver;

4. Displaying a slow-moving vehicle emblem in conformity with § 46.2-1081;

5. In compliance with requirements of the federal Occupational Safety and Health Administration;

6. Not operated on or along any limited access highway; and

7. Not operated for a distance of more than ten miles.

B. For the purposes of this section, "forklift truck" means a self-propelled machine used for hoisting and transporting heavy objects by means of steel fingers inserted under the load.

History.
1973, c. 194, § 46.1-45.2; 1980, c. 37; 1986, c. 220; 1987, cc. 151, 342, 388; 1989, c. 727; 2016, c. 142.

§ 46.2-679. Snowmobiles.

No person shall be required to obtain the registration certificate, license plates, or decals for or pay a registration fee for any snowmobile.

History.
1973, c. 194, § 46.1-45.2; 1980, c. 37; 1986, c. 220; 1987, cc. 151, 342, 388; 1989, c. 727; 2016, c. 142.

§ 46.2-679.1. All-terrain vehicles.

No person shall be required to obtain the registration certificate, license plate, or decals for or pay a registration fee for any all-terrain vehicle.

History.
2006, c. 896; 2016, c. 142.

§ 46.2-679.2. Off-road motorcycles.

No person shall be required to obtain the registration certificate, license plate, or decals for or pay a registration fee for any off-road motorcycle.

History.
2006, c. 896; 2016, c. 142.

§ 46.2-680. Vehicles transporting oyster shells.

No person shall be required to obtain the registration certificate, license plates, or decals for or pay a registration fee for any motor vehicle properly registered in Maryland and used for the purpose of hauling oyster shells for a distance of less than three miles on a public highway of this Commonwealth to navigable waters to be further transported by water to Maryland.

History.
1974, c. 359, § 46.1-45.3; 1989, c. 727; 2016, c. 142.

§ 46.2-681: Repealed by Acts 1999, c. 329.

§ 46.2-682. Tractors, rollers, and other machinery used for highway purposes.

Tractors, rollers, and other machinery used for highway purposes need not be registered under this chapter.

History.
Code 1950, § 46-46; 1958, c. 541, § 46.1-47; 1989, c. 727.

§ 46.2-683. Traction engines; vehicles operating on rails.

Nothing in this chapter shall apply to machines known as traction engines or to any locomotives or electric cars operating on rails.

History.
Code 1950, § 46-47; 1958, c. 541, § 46.1-48; 1989, c. 727.

§ 46.2-684. Nocturnal use of highways by exempted vehicles.

It shall be unlawful for any vehicle exempted under this article from registration under this chapter to use the highways between sunset and sunrise unless it is equipped with lights as required by law.

History.
1989, c. 727.

§ 46.2-684.1. Insurance coverage for exempted motor vehicles.

If a motor vehicle, trailer, or semi-trailer that is exempt from motor vehicle registration requirements pursuant to this article is insured under a policy other than a policy of motor vehicle insurance as defined in § 38.2-124, such insurance policy shall not be required to comply with the provisions of Chapter 22 (§ 38.2-2200 et seq.) of Title 38.2 of the Code of Virginia that relate to the ownership, maintenance, or use of the exempt motor vehicle, trailer, or semi-trailer.

History.
2005, c. 445.

ARTICLE 7.

FEES FOR REGISTRATION.

§ 46.2-685. Payment of fees into special fund.

Except as otherwise provided, all fees collected by the Commissioner under §§ 46.2-651 through 46.2-653 shall be paid into the state treasury and set aside as a special fund to be used to meet the expenses of the Department.

History.
1987, c. 696, § 46.1-44.2; 1989, c. 727; 2012, c. 443.

§ 46.2-686. Portion of certain fees to be paid into special fund.

Except as provided in subdivision 13 of subsection A of § 46.2-694 and § 46.2-703, an amount equal to twenty percent of the fees collected, after refunds, from the registration of motor vehicles, trailers, and semitrailers pursuant to this chapter, calculated at the rates in effect on December 31, 1986, shall be transferred from the special fund established by the provisions of § 46.2-206 to a special fund in the state treasury to be used to meet the expenses of the Department.

History.
1987, c. 696, § 46.1-157.2; 1989, c. 727.

§ 46.2-687. Failure to pay certain fees; penalty.

Any person who operates or permits the operation over any highway in the Commonwealth of any motor vehicle, trailer, or semitrailer for the transportation of passengers without first having paid to the Commissioner the fee prescribed by § 46.2-694 shall be guilty of a Class 2 misdemeanor.

History.
Code 1950, § 46-161; 1958, c. 541, § 46.1-152; 1989, c. 727; 1990, c. 418.

§ 46.2-688. Refund of fees paid.

Any person holding a registration card and license plate or license plates with decal who disposes of, elects not to use the vehicle for which it was issued on the highways in the Commonwealth, or transfers another valid license plate to the vehicle, may surrender, prior to the beginning of the registration period, the license plates or license plates with decals and registration card or provide other evidence of registration of the vehicle to the Commissioner with a statement that the vehicle for which the license plate or license plate with decal was issued has been disposed of, election has been made not to use the vehicle on the highways in the Commonwealth, or another valid license plate has been transferred to the vehicle and request a refund of the fee paid. The Commissioner shall retain five dollars of the fee to cover the costs incurred in issuing the plates and processing the refund.

The Commissioner shall refund to the applicant a proration, in six-month increments, of the total cost of the registration and license plates or license plates with decals if application for the refund is made when there are six or more months remaining in the registration period. No charge or deduction shall be assessed for any refund made under this subsection.

History.
Code 1950, § 46-94; 1958, c. 541, § 46.1-97; 1972, c. 609; 1976, c. 339; 1977, c. 236; 1988, c. 704; 1989, c. 727.

§ 46.2-689. Refund of certain registration fees.

Upon application on a form prescribed by the Commissioner, any person registering any vehicle whose fees are set under § 46.2-697 shall be refunded that portion of the registration fee for a gross weight in excess of that set forth § 46.2-1126.

History.
1984, c. 342, § 46.1-154.01; 1989, c. 727.

§ 46.2-690. Refund for certain for-hire vehicles.

Notwithstanding any other provision of law, the owner of any motor vehicle which is required to be licensed under § 46.2-697 as a for-hire vehicle, may apply for a refund of that portion of the license fee paid in excess of the fee required if it were licensed not for-hire, subject to the conditions and limitations set forth in this section.

If the motor vehicle, while licensed as a for-hire vehicle, is used exclusively in seasonal operation for the transportation of agricultural, horticultural, or forest products and seed and fertilizer therefor to and from the land of the producer, for compensation, the owner may surrender the for-hire license plates issued at any times prior to the expiration of an accumulated total of not more than ninety days. A refund may be obtained for seventy-five percent of that portion of the fee paid in excess of the license fee required for private carrier license plates. The Commissioner shall refund this surcharge on application on forms prescribed by him and submitted to the Department within thirty days of the registration expiration date of the license plates.

History.
1958, c. 541, § 46.1-154.1; 1974, c. 170; 1989, c. 727.

§ 46.2-691. Credit to truck owner inducted into armed forces.

The owner of any truck who secured and paid for a license therefor but was prevented from operating the truck for the full license year by induction into the armed forces of the United States and who, after his discharge from the service, resumes his trucking operations, shall be entitled to a pro rata credit on any new license purchased by him, in the proportion that the part of the year for which he had paid the license and during which part the truck was not in operation bears to the full license year.

The application for a credit shall be made during the license year for which credit is sought and each application shall be accompanied by the registration card and license plate issued the owner for the year for which credit is sought and an affidavit that the owner has been or will be inducted into the armed forces.

All such affidavits shall set forth that the vehicle cannot be operated due to the owner's service in the armed forces.

The Commissioner, when the owner is entitled to a refund, shall issue to him a credit to be applied on the purchase of a new license, in the proportion that the part of the year for which the license fee was paid and during which the truck will not be operated bears to the full license year.

History.
Code 1950, § 46-178; 1958, c. 541, § 46.1-166; 1989, c. 727.

§ 46.2-692. Fee for replacement of lost, mutilated, or illegible indicia of titling and registration.

The fee for the replacement of license plates, decals, registration cards, or certificates of title which are lost, mutilated or illegible shall be as follows:

1. For any type of replacement or duplication of vehicle registration cards, International Registration Plan cab cards, registration cards for overload permits, or dealer registration cards, $2, except that no fee shall be charged for the replacement or duplication of a vehicle registration card or registration card for overload permit that is conducted using the Internet;
2. For a certificate of title, $5;
3. For license plates or license plates with decals, $10;
4. For a license plate with decals issued for trailers, $5; and
5. For one or two decals, $1.

History.
Code 1950, § 46-53; 1958, c. 541, § 46.1-55; 1968, c. 334; 1972, c. 609; 1982, c. 671; 1986, c. 165; 1989, c. 727; 1992, c. 631; 1997, c. 486; 2000, c. 579; 2012, cc. 215, 222.

§ 46.2-692.1. Sample license plates; fee; use.

Upon application therefor, the Commissioner may issue samples of authorized license plates currently issued by the Department. Sample license plates may display, as requested by the applicant and approved by the Commissioner, a combination of up to seven numbers or letters, when feasible. Notwithstanding the provisions of this section, every such license plate shall display the word "SAMPLE" on its face, in a manner prescribed by the Commissioner.

The fee for sample license plates not displaying numbers or letters requested by the applicant shall be ten dollars for each license plate. The fee for sample license plates displaying numbers or letters requested by the applicant shall be twenty dollars for each license plate. Sample license plates shall not be valid for registration purposes and shall not be mounted or displayed on any motor vehicle.

History.
1996, c. 1026; 1997, cc. 774, 816.

§ 46.2-692.2. Fee for exchange of license plates.

The fee for the exchange of license plates shall be the greater of the total of any statutory fees required for the requested license plates, as calculated under the provisions of subsection B of § 46.2-694, or $10.

As used in this section, an "exchange of license plates" means a transaction that occurs within the registration period of a vehicle in which the vehicle owner voluntarily returns the license plates assigned to the vehicle and requests for the same vehicle new license plates with a different design or alphanumeric combination or both.

A request for new license plates made as part of the vehicle registration renewal process shall not be considered an exchange of license plates for purposes of this section.

The provisions of this section shall apply to a replacement request made under the provisions of § 46.2-607 for license plates that are not duplicates or otherwise equivalent to the lost, mutilated, or illegible plates required to be replaced under that section. Such a request shall be considered both a replacement for purposes of §§ 46.2-607 and 46.2-692 and an exchange for purposes of this section.

History.
2011, cc. 57, 70.

§ 46.2-693. Use of old plates and registration number on another vehicle.

Upon receipt of a proper application, an owner who sells or transfers a registered vehicle may have the license plates and registration number assigned to another vehicle titled in the name of the owner. If the vehicle requires identical registration fees, the transfer fee shall be two dollars. If the license fee required for the second vehicle requires a greater registration fee, the fee shall be two dollars plus the difference in registration fees between the two vehicles. All fees collected under the provisions of this section shall be paid by the Commissioner into the state treasury and shall be set aside as a special fund to meet the expenses of the Department.

History.
1989, c. 727.

§ 46.2-694. (Contingent expiration date) Fees for vehicles designed and used for transportation of passengers; weights used for computing fees; burden of proof.

A. The annual registration fees for motor vehicles, trailers, and semitrailers designed and used for the transportation of passengers on the highways in the Commonwealth are:

1. Thirty-three dollars for each private passenger car or motor home if the passenger car or motor home weighs 4,000 pounds or less, provided that it is not used for the transportation of passengers for compensation and is not kept or used for rent or for hire, or is not operated under a lease without a chauffeur; however, the fee provided under this subdivision shall apply to a private passenger car or motor home that weighs 4,000 pounds or less and is used as a TNC partner vehicle as defined in § 46.2-2000.

2. Thirty-eight dollars for each private passenger car or motor home that weighs more than 4,000 pounds, provided that it is not used for the transportation of passengers for compensation and is not kept or used for rent or for hire, or is not operated under a lease without a chauffeur; however, the fee provided under this subdivision shall apply to a private passenger car or motor home that weighs more than 4,000 pounds and is used as a TNC partner vehicle as defined in § 46.2-2000.

3. Thirty cents per 100 pounds or major fraction thereof for a private motor vehicle other than a motorcycle with a normal seating capacity of more than 10 adults, including the driver, if the private motor vehicle is not used for the transportation of passengers for compensation and is not kept or used for rent or for hire or is not operated under a lease without a chauffeur. In no case shall the fee be less than $23 if the vehicle weighs 4,000 pounds or less or $28 if the vehicle weighs more than 4,000 pounds.

4. Thirty cents per 100 pounds or major fraction thereof for a school bus. In no case shall the fee be less than $23 if the vehicle weighs 4,000 pounds or less or $28 if the vehicle weighs more than 4,000 pounds.

5. Twenty-three dollars for each trailer or semitrailer designed for use as living quarters for human beings.

6. Thirteen dollars plus $0.30 per 100 pounds or major fraction thereof for each motor vehicle, trailer, or semitrailer used as a common carrier of passengers, operating either intrastate or interstate. Interstate common carriers of interstate passengers may elect to be licensed and pay the fees prescribed in subdivision 7 on submission to the Commissioner of a declaration of operations and equipment as he may prescribe. An additional $5 shall be charged if the motor vehicle weighs more than 4,000 pounds.

7. Thirteen dollars plus $0.70 per 100 pounds or major fraction thereof for each motor vehicle, trailer, or semitrailer used as a common carrier of interstate passengers if election is made to be licensed under this subsection. An additional $5 shall be charged if the motor vehicle weighs more than 4,000 pounds. In lieu of the foregoing fee of $0.70 per 100 pounds, a motor carrier of passengers, operating two or more vehicles both within and outside the Commonwealth and registered for insurance purposes with the Surface Transportation Board of the U.S. Department of Transportation, Federal Highway Administration, may apply to the Commissioner for prorated registration. Upon the filing of such application, in such form as the Commissioner may prescribe, the Commissioner shall apportion the registration fees provided in this subsection so that the total registration fees to be paid for such vehicles of such carrier shall be that proportion of the total fees, if there were no apportionment, that the total number of miles traveled by such vehicles of such carrier within the Commonwealth bears to the total number of miles traveled by such vehicles within and outside the Commonwealth. Such total mileage in each instance is the estimated total mileage to be traveled by such vehicles during the license year for which such fees are paid, subject to the adjustment in accordance with an audit to be made by representatives of the Commissioner at the end of such license year, the expense of such audit to be borne by the carrier being audited. Each vehicle passing into or through Virginia shall be registered and licensed in Virginia and the annual registration fee to be paid for each

such vehicle shall not be less than $33. For the purpose of determining such apportioned registration fees, only those motor vehicles, trailers, or semitrailers operated both within and outside the Commonwealth shall be subject to inclusion in determining the apportionment provided for herein.

8. Thirteen dollars plus $0.80 per 100 pounds or major fraction thereof for each motor vehicle, trailer or semitrailer kept or used for rent or for hire or operated under a lease without a chauffeur for the transportation of passengers. An additional fee of $5 shall be charged if the vehicle weighs more than 4,000 pounds. This subdivision does not apply to vehicles used as common carriers or as TNC partner vehicles as defined in § 46.2-2000.

9. Twenty-three dollars for a taxicab or other vehicle which is kept for rent or hire operated with a chauffeur for the transportation of passengers, and which operates or should operate under permits issued by the Department as required by law. An additional fee of $5 shall be charged if the vehicle weighs more than 4,000 pounds. This subdivision does not apply to vehicles used as common carriers or as TNC partner vehicles as defined in § 46.2-2000.

10. Eighteen dollars for a motorcycle, with or without a sidecar. To this fee shall be added a surcharge of $3 which shall be distributed as provided in § 46.2-1191.

10a. Fourteen dollars for a moped, to be paid into the state treasury and set aside as a special fund to be used to meet the expenses of the Department.

10b. Eighteen dollars for an autocycle.

11. Twenty-three dollars for a bus used exclusively for transportation to and from church school, for the purpose of religious instruction, or church, for the purpose of divine worship. If the empty weight of the vehicle exceeds 4,000 pounds, the fee shall be $28.

12. Thirteen dollars plus $0.70 per 100 pounds or major fraction thereof for other passenger-carrying vehicles.

13. An additional fee of $4.25 per year shall be charged and collected at the time of registration of each pickup or panel truck and each motor vehicle under subdivisions 1 through 12. All funds collected from $4 of the $4.25 fee shall be paid into the state treasury and shall be set aside as a special fund to be used only for emergency medical services purposes. The moneys in the special emergency medical services fund shall be distributed as follows:

a. Two percent shall be distributed to the State Department of Health to provide funding to the Virginia Association of Volunteer Rescue Squads to be used solely for the purpose of conducting volunteer recruitment, retention, and training activities;

b. Thirty percent shall be distributed to the State Department of Health to support (i) emergency medical services training programs (excluding advanced life support classes); (ii) advanced life support training; (iii) recruitment and retention programs (all funds for such support shall be used to recruit and retain volunteer emergency medical services personnel only, including public awareness campaigns, technical assistance programs, and similar activities); (iv) emergency medical services system development, initiatives, and priorities based on needs identified by the State Emergency Medical Services Advisory Board; (v) local, regional, and statewide performance contracts for emergency medical services to meet the objectives stipulated in § 32.1-111.3; (vi) technology and radio communication enhancements; and (vii) improved emergency preparedness and response. Any funds set aside for distribution under this provision and remaining undistributed at the end of any fiscal year shall revert to the Rescue Squad Assistance Fund;

c. Thirty-two percent shall be distributed to the Rescue Squad Assistance Fund;

d. Ten percent shall be available to the State Department of Health's Office of Emergency Medical Services for use in emergency medical services; and

e. Twenty-six percent shall be returned by the Comptroller to the locality wherein such vehicle is registered, to provide funding for training of volunteer or salaried emergency medical services personnel of nonprofit emergency medical services agencies that hold a valid license issued by the Commissioner of Health and for the purchase of necessary equipment and supplies for use in such locality for emergency medical services provided by nonprofit emergency medical services agencies that hold a valid license issued by the Commissioner of Health.

All revenues generated by the remaining $0.25 of the $4.25 fee approved by the 2008 Session of the General Assembly shall be deposited into the Rescue Squad Assistance Fund and used only to pay for the costs associated with the certification and recertification training of emergency medical services personnel.

The Comptroller shall clearly designate on the warrant, check, or other means of transmitting these funds that such moneys are only to be used for purposes set forth in this subdivision. Such funds shall be in addition to any local appropriations and local governing bodies shall not use these funds to supplant local funds. Each local governing body shall report annually to the Board of Health on the use of the funds returned to it pursuant to this section. In any case in which the local governing body grants the funds to a regional emergency medical services council to be distributed to the nonprofit emergency medical services agency that holds a valid license issued by the Commissioner of Health, the local governing body shall remain responsible for the proper use of the funds. If, at the end of any fiscal year, a report on the use of the funds returned to the locality pursuant to this section for that year has not been received from a local governing body, any funds due to that local governing body for the next fiscal year shall be retained until such time as the report has been submitted to the Board.

B. All motor vehicles, trailers, and semitrailers registered as provided in subsection B of § 46.2-646 shall pay a registration fee equal to one-twelfth of all fees required by subsection A of this section or § 46.2-697 for such motor vehicle, trailer, or semitrailer, computed to the nearest cent, multiplied by the number of months in the registration period for such motor vehicles, trailers, and semitrailers.

C. The manufacturer's shipping weight or scale weight shall be used for computing all fees required by this section to be based upon the weight of the vehicle.

D. The applicant for registration bears the burden of proof that the vehicle for which registration is sought is entitled by weight, design, and use to be registered at the fee tendered by the applicant to the Commissioner or to his authorized agent.

History.

Code 1950, §§ 46-154 through 46-156, 46-158.1, 46-159, 46-163.1, 46-166.1; 1950, p. 621; 1952, cc. 224, 418; 1956, cc. 132, 597, 705; 1958, c. 541, § 46.1-149; 1960, c. 243; 1964, c. 218; 1972, c. 609; 1974, c. 170; 1978, c. 708; 1980, c. 25; 1982, c. 671; 1983, c. 566; 1984, cc. 476, 545; 1985, c. 333; 1986, Sp. Sess., c. 11; 1988, cc. 701, 704; 1989, c. 727; 1990, c. 508; 1991, c. 472; 1994, c. 279; 1997, c. 283; 2002, c. 794; 2004, c. 194; 2005, c. 928; 2007, c. 896; 2008, c. 182; 2013, c. 783; 2014, cc. 53, 256; 2015, cc. 2, 3, 502, 503.

Section set out twice.

The section above is effective until December 31 of any year revenues designated for the Highway Maintenance and Operating Fund or the Transportation Trust Fund are appropriated for any non-transportation related purposes. For this section as in effect after that date, see the following section, also numbered 46.2-694.

Editor's note.

Acts 2007, c. 896, cl. 22 provides: "That the provisions of this act which generate additional revenue for the Transportation Trust Fund, established under § 33.1-23.03:1 [see now § 33.2-1524] of the Code of Virginia, or the Highway Maintenance and Operating Fund shall expire on December 31 of any year in which the General Assembly appropriates any of the revenues designated under general law to the Highway Maintenance and Operating Fund or the Transportation Trust Fund for any non-transportation related purpose."

Acts 2010, c. 874, cl. 8 provides: "That the provisions of the first enactment of this act shall expire at midnight on June 30, 2012. The provisions of the second, third, fourth, fifth, sixth, and seventh enactments of this act shall have no expiration date."

Acts 2016, c. 780, § 3-6.02, effective for the biennium ending June 30, 2018, provides: "Notwithstanding § 46.2-694 paragraph 13 of the Code of Virginia, the additional fee that shall be charged and collected at the time of registration of each pickup or panel truck and each motor vehicle shall be $6.25."

§ 46.2-694. (Contingent effective date) Fees for vehicles designed and used for transportation of passengers; weights used for computing fees; burden of proof.

A. The annual registration fees for motor vehicles, trailers, and semitrailers designed and used for the transportation of passengers on the highways in the Commonwealth are:

1. Twenty-three dollars for each private passenger car or motor home if the passenger car or motor home weighs 4,000 pounds or less, provided that it is not used for the transportation of passengers for compensation and is not kept or used for rent or for hire, or is not operated under a lease without a chauffeur; however, the fee provided under this subdivision shall apply to a private passenger car or motor home that weighs 4,000 pounds or less and is used as a TNC partner vehicle as defined in § 46.2-2000.

2. Twenty-eight dollars for each private passenger car or motor home that weighs more than 4,000 pounds, provided that it is not used for the transportation of passengers for compensation and is not kept or used for rent or for hire, or is not operated under a lease without a chauffeur; however, the fee provided under this subdivision shall apply to a private passenger car or motor home that weighs more than 4,000 pounds and is used as a TNC partner vehicle as defined in § 46.2-2000.

3. Thirty cents per 100 pounds or major fraction thereof for a private motor vehicle other than a motorcycle with a normal seating capacity of more than 10 adults, including the driver, if the private motor vehicle is not used for the transportation of passengers for compensation and is not kept or used for rent or for hire or is not operated under a lease without a chauffeur. In no case shall the fee be less than $23 if the vehicle weighs 4,000 pounds or less or $28 if the vehicle weighs more than 4,000 pounds.

4. Thirty cents per 100 pounds or major fraction thereof for a school bus. In no case shall the fee be less than $23 if the vehicle weighs 4,000 pounds or less or $28 if the vehicle weighs more than 4,000 pounds.

5. Twenty-three dollars for each trailer or semitrailer designed for use as living quarters for human beings.

6. Thirteen dollars plus $0.30 per 100 pounds or major fraction thereof for each motor vehicle, trailer, or semitrailer used as a common carrier of passengers, operating either intrastate or interstate. Interstate common carriers of interstate passengers may elect to be licensed and pay the fees prescribed in subdivision 7 on submission to the Commissioner of a declaration of operations and equipment as he may prescribe. An additional $5 shall be charged if the motor vehicle weighs more than 4,000 pounds.

7. Thirteen dollars plus $0.70 per 100 pounds or major fraction thereof for each motor vehicle, trailer, or semitrailer used as a common carrier of interstate passengers if election is made to be licensed under this subsection. An additional $5 shall be charged if the motor vehicle weighs more than 4,000 pounds. In lieu of the foregoing fee of $0.70 per 100 pounds, a motor carrier of passengers, operating two or more vehicles both within and outside the Commonwealth and registered for insurance purposes with the Surface Transportation Board of the U.S. Department of Transportation, Federal Highway Administration, may apply to the Commissioner for prorated registration. Upon the filing of such application, in such form as the Commissioner may prescribe, the Commissioner shall apportion the registration fees pro-

vided in this subsection so that the total registration fees to be paid for such vehicles of such carrier shall be that proportion of the total fees, if there were no apportionment, that the total number of miles traveled by such vehicles of such carrier within the Commonwealth bears to the total number of miles traveled by such vehicles within and outside the Commonwealth. Such total mileage in each instance is the estimated total mileage to be traveled by such vehicles during the license year for which such fees are paid, subject to the adjustment in accordance with an audit to be made by representatives of the Commissioner at the end of such license year, the expense of such audit to be borne by the carrier being audited. Each vehicle passing into or through Virginia shall be registered and licensed in Virginia and the annual registration fee to be paid for each such vehicle shall not be less than $33. For the purpose of determining such apportioned registration fees, only those motor vehicles, trailers, or semitrailers operated both within and outside the Commonwealth shall be subject to inclusion in determining the apportionment provided for herein.

8. Thirteen dollars plus $0.80 per 100 pounds or major fraction thereof for each motor vehicle, trailer or semitrailer kept or used for rent or for hire or operated under a lease without a chauffeur for the transportation of passengers. An additional fee of $5 shall be charged if the vehicle weighs more than 4,000 pounds. This subdivision does not apply to vehicles used as common carriers or as TNC partner vehicles as defined in § 46.2-2000.

9. Twenty-three dollars for a taxicab or other vehicle which is kept for rent or hire operated with a chauffeur for the transportation of passengers, and which operates or should operate under permits issued by the Department as required by law. An additional fee of $5 shall be charged if the vehicle weighs more than 4,000 pounds. This subdivision does not apply to vehicles used as common carriers or as TNC partner vehicles as defined in § 46.2-2000.

10. Eighteen dollars for a motorcycle, with or without a sidecar. To this fee shall be added a surcharge of $3, which shall be distributed as provided in § 46.2-1191.

10a. Fourteen dollars for a moped, to be paid into the state treasury and set aside as a special fund to be used to meet the expenses of the Department.

10b. Eighteen dollars for an autocycle.

11. Twenty-three dollars for a bus used exclusively for transportation to and from church school, for the purpose of religious instruction, or church, for the purpose of divine worship. If the empty weight of the vehicle exceeds 4,000 pounds, the fee shall be $28.

12. Thirteen dollars plus $0.70 per 100 pounds or major fraction thereof for other passenger-carrying vehicles.

13. An additional fee of $4.25 per year shall be charged and collected at the time of registration of each pickup or panel truck and each motor vehicle under subdivisions 1 through 12. All funds collected from $4 of the $4.25 fee shall be paid into the state treasury and shall be set aside as a special fund to be used only for emergency medical services purposes. The moneys in the special emergency medical services fund shall be distributed as follows:

a. Two percent shall be distributed to the State Department of Health to provide funding to the Virginia Association of Volunteer Rescue Squads to be used solely for the purpose of conducting volunteer recruitment, retention and training activities;

b. Thirty percent shall be distributed to the State Department of Health to support (i) emergency medical services training programs (excluding advanced life support classes); (ii) advanced life support training; (iii) recruitment and retention programs (all funds for such support shall be used to recruit and retain volunteer emergency medical services personnel only, including public awareness campaigns, technical assistance programs, and similar activities); (iv) emergency medical services system development, initiatives, and priorities based on needs identified by the State Emergency Medical Services Advisory Board; (v) local, regional, and statewide performance contracts for emergency medical services to meet the objectives stipulated in § 32.1-111.3; (vi) technology and radio communication enhancements; and (vii) improved emergency preparedness and response. Any funds set aside for distribution under this provision and remaining undistributed at the end of any fiscal year shall revert to the Rescue Squad Assistance Fund;

c. Thirty-two percent shall be distributed to the Rescue Squad Assistance Fund;

d. Ten percent shall be available to the State Department of Health's Office of Emergency Medical Services for use in emergency medical services; and

e. Twenty-six percent shall be returned by the Comptroller to the locality wherein such vehicle is registered, to provide funding for training of volunteer or salaried emergency medical services personnel of nonprofit emergency medical services agencies that hold a valid license issued by the Commissioner of Health and for the purchase of necessary equipment and supplies for use in such locality for emergency medical services provided by nonprofit or volunteer emergency medical services agencies that hold a valid license issued by the Commissioner of Health.

All revenues generated by the remaining $0.25 of the $4.25 fee approved by the 2008 Session of the General Assembly shall be deposited into the Rescue Squad Assistance Fund and used only to pay for the costs associated with the certification and recertification training of emergency medical services personnel.

The Comptroller shall clearly designate on the warrant, check, or other means of transmitting these funds that such moneys are only to be used for purposes set forth in this subdivision. Such funds shall be in addition to any local appropriations and local governing bodies shall not use these funds to supplant local funds. Each local governing body shall report annually to the Board of Health on the use of the funds returned to it pursuant to this section. In any case in which the local governing body grants the funds to a regional emergency medical services council to be distributed to the emergency medical services agency that holds a valid license issued by the Commissioner of Health, the local governing body shall remain responsible for the proper use of the funds. If, at the end of any fiscal year, a report on the use of the funds returned to the locality pursuant to this section for that year has not been received from a local governing body, any funds due to that local governing body for the next fiscal year shall be retained until such time as the report has been submitted to the Board.

B. All motor vehicles, trailers, and semitrailers registered as provided in subsection B of § 46.2-646 shall pay a registration fee equal to one-twelfth of all fees required by subsection A of this section or § 46.2-697 for such motor vehicle, trailer, or semitrailer, computed to the nearest cent, multiplied by the number of months in the registration period for such motor vehicles, trailers, and semitrailers.

C. The manufacturer's shipping weight or scale weight shall be used for computing all fees required by this section to be based upon the weight of the vehicle.

D. The applicant for registration bears the burden of proof that the vehicle for which registration is sought is entitled by weight, design, and use to be registered at the fee tendered by the applicant to the Commissioner or to his authorized agent.

History.

Code 1950, §§ 46-154 through 46-156, 46-158.1, 46-159, 46-163.1, 46-166.1; 1950, p. 621; 1952, cc. 224, 418; 1956, cc. 132, 597, 705; 1958, c. 541, § 46.1-149; 1960, c. 243; 1964, c. 218; 1972, c. 609; 1974, c. 170; 1978, c. 708; 1980, c. 25; 1982, c. 671; 1983, c. 566; 1984, cc. 476, 545; 1985, c. 333; 1986, Sp. Sess., c. 11; 1988, cc. 701, 704; 1989, c. 727; 1990, c. 508; 1991, c. 472; 1994, c. 279; 1997, c. 283; 2002, c. 794; 2004, c. 194; 2005, c. 928; 2008, c. 182; 2013, c. 783; 2014, cc. 53, 256; 2015, cc. 2, 3, 502, 503.

Section set out twice.

The section above is effective December 31 of any year revenues designated for the Highway Maintenance and Operating Fund or the Transportation Trust Fund are appropriated for any non-transportation related purposes. For this section as in effect until that date, see the preceding section, also numbered 46.2-694.

Editor's note.

Acts 2007, c. 896, cl. 22 provides: "That the provisions of this act which generate additional revenue for the Transportation Trust Fund, established under § 33.1-23.03:1 [see now § 33.2-1524] of the Code of Virginia, or the Highway Maintenance and Operating Fund shall expire on December 31 of any year in which the General Assembly appropriates any of the revenues designated under general law to the Highway Maintenance and Operating Fund or the Transportation Trust Fund for any non-transportation related purpose."

Acts 2016, c. 780, § 3-6.02, effective for the biennium ending June 30, 2018, provides: "Notwithstanding § 46.2-694 paragraph 13 of the Code of Virginia, the additional fee that shall be charged and collected at the time of registration of each pickup or panel truck and each motor vehicle shall be $6.25."

§ 46.2-694.1. (Contingent expiration date — see Editor's note) Fees for trailers and semitrailers not designed and used for transportation of passengers.

Unless otherwise specified in this title, the registration fees for trailers and semitrailers not designed and used for the transportation of passengers on the highways in the Commonwealth shall be as follows:

Registered Gross Weight	*1-Year Fee*	*2-Year Fee*	*Permanent Fee*
0-1,500 lbs	$18.00	$36.00	$70.00
1,501-4,000 lbs	$28.50	$57.00	$75.00
4,001 lbs & above	$40.00	$80.00	$100.00

From the foregoing registration fees, the following amounts, regardless of weight category, shall be paid by the Department into the state treasury and set aside for the payment of the administrative costs of the safety inspection program provided for in Article 21 (§ 46.2-1157 et seq.) of Chapter 10 of this title: (i) from each one-year registration fee, one dollar and fifty cents; (ii) from each two-year registration fee, three dollars; and (iii) from each permanent registration fee, four dollars.

History.

1997, c. 283; 2007, c. 896.

Section set out twice.

The section above is effective until December 31 of any year revenues designated for the Highway Maintenance and Operating Fund or the Transportation Trust Fund are appropriated for any non-transportation related purposes. For this section effective until that time, see the following section, also numbered 46.2-694.1.

Editor's note.

Acts 2007, c. 896, cl. 22 provides: "That the provisions of this act which generate additional revenue for the Transportation Trust Fund, established under § 33.1-23.03:1 [see now § 33.2-1524] of the Code of Virginia, or the Highway Maintenance and Operating Fund shall expire on December 31 of any year in which the General Assembly appropriates any of the revenues designated under general law to the Highway Maintenance and Operating Fund or the Transportation Trust Fund for any non-transportation related purpose."

Acts 2010, c. 874, cl. 8 provides: "That the provisions of the first enactment of this act shall expire at midnight on June 30, 2012. The provisions of the second, third, fourth, fifth, sixth, and seventh enactments of this act shall have no expiration date."

§ 46.2-694.1. (Contingent effective date — see Editor's note) Fees for trailers and semitrailers not designed and used for transportation of passengers.

Unless otherwise specified in this title, the registration fees for trailers and semitrailers not designed and used for the transportation of passengers on the highways in the Commonwealth shall be as follows:

Registered Gross Weight	*1-Year Fee*	*2-Year Fee*	*Permanent Fee*
0-1,500 lbs	$8.00	$16.00	$50.00

Registered Gross Weight	*1-Year Fee*	*2-Year Fee*	*Permanent Fee*
1,501-4,000 lbs	$18.50	$37.00	$50.00
4,001 lbs & above	$23.50	$47.00	$50.00

From the foregoing registration fees, the following amounts, regardless of weight category, shall be paid by the Department into the state treasury and set aside for the payment of the administrative costs of the safety inspection program provided for in Article 21 (§ 46.2-1157 et seq.) of Chapter 10 of this title: (i) from each one-year registration fee, one dollar and fifty cents; (ii) from each two-year registration fee, three dollars; and (iii) from each permanent registration fee, four dollars.

History.

1997, c. 283.

Section set out twice.

The section above is effective December 31 of any year revenues designated for the Highway Maintenance and Operating Fund or the Transportation Trust Fund are appropriated for any non-transportation related purposes. For this section in effect until that time, see the preceding section, also numbered 46.2-694.1.

§ 46.2-695. Small rented ridesharing vehicles.

The fees required by subdivisions A 8 and A 9 of § 46.2-694 to be paid for registration of motor vehicles used for rent or hire shall not be required for the operation of any motor vehicle with a normal seating capacity of not more than fifteen adults including the driver while used (i) not for profit in transporting persons in a ridesharing arrangement, as defined in § 46.2-1400, or (ii) by a lessee renting or hiring such vehicle for such purpose for a period of twelve months or longer under a written lease or agreement. For the purposes of § 46.2-694, the fee for the annual registration card and license plates for such vehicle shall be the same as for a private passenger car of the same weight.

History.

Code 1950, § 46-158; 1952, c. 415; 1958, c. 541, § 46.1-150; 1964, c. 218; 1966, c. 608; 1976, c. 60; 1989, c. 727; 2002, c. 337.

§ 46.2-696: Repealed by Acts 2011, cc. 881 and 889, cl. 2.

§ 46.2-697. (Contingent expiration date — see Editor's note) Fees for vehicles not designed or used for transportation of passengers.

A. Except as otherwise provided in this section, the fee for registration of all motor vehicles not designed and used for the transportation of passengers shall be $23 plus an amount determined by the gross weight of the vehicle or combination of vehicles of which it is a part, when loaded to the maximum capacity for which it is registered and licensed, according to the schedule of fees set forth in this section. For each 1,000 pounds of gross weight, or major fraction thereof, for which any such vehicle is registered, there shall be paid to the Commissioner the fee indicated in the following schedule immediately opposite the weight group and under the classification established by the provisions of subsection B of § 46.2-711 into which such vehicle, or any combination of vehicles of which it is a part, falls when loaded to the maximum capacity for which it is registered and licensed. The fee for a pickup or panel truck shall be $33 if its gross weight is 4,000 pounds or less, and $38 if its gross weight is 4,001 pounds through 6,500 pounds. The fee shall be $39 for any motor vehicle with a gross weight of 6,501 pounds through 10,000 pounds.

Fee Per Thousand Pounds of Gross Weight

Gross Weight Groups (pounds)		Private Carriers	For Rent or For Hire Carriers
10,001 — 11,000	......	$3.17	$4.75
11,001 — 12,000	......	3.42	4.90
12,001 — 13,000	......	3.66	5.15
13,001 — 14,000	......	3.90	5.40
14,001 — 15,000	......	4.15	5.65
15,001 — 16,000	......	4.39	5.90
16,001 — 17,000	......	4.88	6.15
17,001 — 18,000	......	5.37	6.40
18,001 — 19,000	......	5.86	7.50
19,001 — 20,000	......	6.34	7.70
20,001 — 21,000	......	6.83	7.90
21,001 — 22,000	......	7.32	8.10
22,001 — 23,000	......	7.81	8.30
23,001 — 24,000	......	8.30	8.50
24,001 — 25,000	......	8.42	8.70
25,001 — 26,000	......	8.48	8.90
26,001 — 27,000	......	10.07	10.35
27,001 — 28,000	......	10.13	10.55
28,001 — 29,000	......	10.18	10.75
29,001 — 40,000	......	10.31	10.95
40,001 — 45,000	......	10.43	11.15
45,001 — 50,000	......	10.68	11.25
50,001 — 55,000	......	11.29	13.25
55,001 — 76,000	......	13.73	15.25
76,001 — 80,000	......	16.17	16.25

For all such motor vehicles exceeding a gross weight of 6,500 pounds, an additional fee of five dollars shall be imposed.

B. In lieu of registering any motor vehicle referred to in this section for an entire licensing year, the owner may elect to register the vehicle only for one or more quarters of a licensing year, and in such case, the fee shall be twenty-five percent of the annual fee plus five dollars for each quarter that the vehicle is registered.

C. When an owner elects to register and license a motor vehicle under subsection B of this section, the provisions of §§ 46.2-646 and 46.2-688 shall not apply.

D. Notwithstanding any other provision of law, no vehicle designed, equipped, and used to tow disabled or inoperable motor vehicles shall be required to register in accordance with any gross weight other than the gross weight of the towing vehicle itself, exclusive of any vehicle being towed.

E. All registrations and licenses issued for less than a full year shall expire on the date shown on the license and registration.

History.

Code 1950, § 46-162; 1956, c. 477; 1958, c. 541, § 46.1-154; 1962, c. 86; 1964, c. 218; 1964, Ex. Sess., c. 22; 1973, c. 517; 1974, c. 150; 1979, c. 244; 1982, c. 671; 1984, c. 144; 1986 Sp. Sess., c. 11; 1989, c. 727; 1997, c. 283; 2007, c. 896.

Section set out twice.

The section above is effective until December 31 of any year revenues designated for the Highway Maintenance and Operating Fund or the Transportation Trust Fund are appropriated for any non-transportation related purposes. For this section as in effect until that time, see the following section, also numbered 46.2-697.

Editor's note.

Acts 2007, c. 896, cl. 22 provides: "That the provisions of this act which generate additional revenue for the Transportation Trust Fund, established under § 33.1-23.03:1 [see now § 33.2-1524] of the Code of Virginia, or the Highway Maintenance and Operating Fund shall expire on December 31 of any year in which the General Assembly appropriates any of the revenues designated under general law to the Highway Maintenance and Operating Fund or the Transportation Trust Fund for any non-transportation related purpose."

Acts 2010, c. 874, cl. 2 provides: "That no provision of this act shall be construed or interpreted to cause the expiration of any provision of Chapter 896 of the Acts of Assembly of 2007 pursuant to the 22nd enactment of such Chapter."

Acts 2010, c. 874, cl. 8 provides: "That the provisions of the first enactment of this act shall expire at midnight on June 30, 2012. The provisions of the second, third, fourth, fifth, sixth, and seventh enactments of this act shall have no expiration date."

§ 46.2-697. (Contingent effective date — see Editor's note) Fees for vehicles not designed or used for transportation of passengers.

A. Except as otherwise provided in this section, the fee for registration of all motor vehicles not designed and used for the transportation of passengers shall be thirteen dollars plus an amount determined by the gross weight of the vehicle or combination of vehicles of which it is a part, when loaded to the maximum capacity for which it is registered and licensed, according to the schedule of fees set forth in this section. For each 1,000 pounds of gross weight, or major fraction thereof, for which any such vehicle is registered, there shall be paid to the Commissioner the fee indicated in the following schedule immediately opposite the weight group and under the classification established by the provisions of subsection B of § 46.2-711 into which such vehicle, or any combination of vehicles of which it is a part, falls when loaded to the maximum capacity for which it is registered and licensed. The fee for a pickup or panel truck shall be twenty-three dollars if its gross weight is 4,000 pounds or less, and twenty-eight dollars if its gross weight is 4,001 pounds through 6,500 pounds. The fee shall be twenty-nine dollars for any motor vehicle with a gross weight of 6,501 pounds through 10,000 pounds.

Fee Per Thousand Pounds of Gross Weight

Gross Weight Groups (pounds)		Private Carriers	For Rent or For Hire Carriers
10,001 — 11,000	......	$2.60	$4.75
11,001 — 12,000	......	2.80	4.90
12,001 — 13,000	......	3.00	5.15
13,001 — 14,000	......	3.20	5.40
14,001 — 15,000	......	3.40	5.65
15,001 — 16,000	......	3.60	5.90
16,001 — 17,000	......	4.00	6.15
17,001 — 18,000	......	4.40	6.40
18,001 — 19,000	......	4.80	7.50
19,001 — 20,000	......	5.20	7.70
20,001 — 21,000	......	5.60	7.90
21,001 — 22,000	......	6.00	8.10
22,001 — 23,000	......	6.40	8.30
23,001 — 24,000	......	6.80	8.50
24,001 — 25,000	......	6.90	8.70
25,001 — 26,000	......	6.95	8.90
26,001 — 27,000	......	8.25	10.35
27,001 — 28,000	......	8.30	10.55
28,001 — 29,000	......	8.35	10.75
29,001 — 40,000	......	8.45	10.95
40,001 — 45,000	......	8.55	11.15
45,001 — 50,000	......	8.75	11.25
50,001 — 55,000	......	8.25	13.25
55,001 — 76,000	......	11.25	15.25
76,001 — 80,000	......	13.25	16.25

For all such motor vehicles exceeding a gross weight of 6,500 pounds, an additional fee of five dollars shall be imposed.

B. In lieu of registering any motor vehicle referred to in this section for an entire licensing year, the owner may elect to register the vehicle only for one or more quarters of a licensing year, and in such case, the fee shall be twenty-five percent of the annual fee plus five dollars for each quarter that the vehicle is registered.

C. When an owner elects to register and license a motor vehicle under subsection B of this section, the provisions of §§ 46.2-646 and 46.2-688 shall not apply.

D. Notwithstanding any other provision of law, no vehicle designed, equipped, and used to tow disabled or inoperable motor vehicles shall be required to register in accordance with any gross weight other than the gross weight of the towing vehicle itself, exclusive of any vehicle being towed.

E. All registrations and licenses issued for less than a full year shall expire on the date shown on the license and registration.

History.

Code 1950, § 46-162; 1956, c. 477; 1958, c. 541, § 46.1-154; 1962, c. 86; 1964, c. 218; 1964, Ex. Sess., c. 22; 1973, c. 517; 1974, c. 150; 1979, c. 244; 1982, c. 671; 1984, c. 144; 1986 Sp. Sess., c. 11; 1989, c. 727; 1997, c. 283.

Section set out twice.

The section above is effective December 31 of any year revenues designated for the Highway Maintenance and Operating Fund or the Transportation Trust Fund are appropriated for any non-transportation related purposes. For this section as in effect until that time, see the preceding section, also numbered 46.2-697.

Editor's note.

Acts 2007, c. 896, cl. 22 provides: "That the provisions of this act which generate additional revenue for the Transportation Trust Fund, established under § 33.1-23.03:1 [see now § 33.2-1524] of the Code of Virginia, or the Highway Maintenance and Operating Fund shall expire on December 31 of any year in which the General Assembly appropriates any of the revenues designated under general law to the Highway Maintenance and Operating Fund or the Transportation Trust Fund for any non-transportation related purpose."

§ **46.2-697.1:** Repealed by Acts 2003, c. 1042, cl. 12, effective May 1, 2003.

§ 46.2-698. Fees for farm vehicles.

A. The fees for registration of farm motor vehicles having gross weights of 7,500 pounds or more, when such vehicles are used exclusively for farm use as defined in this section, shall be one-half of the fee per 1,000 pounds of gross weight for private carriers as calculated under the provisions of § 46.2-697 and one-half of the fee for overload permits under § 46.2-1128, but the annual registration fee to be paid for each farm vehicle shall not be less than $15.

B. A farm motor vehicle is used exclusively for farm use:

1. When owned by a person who is engaged either as an owner, renter, or operator of a farm of a size reasonably requiring the use of such vehicle or vehicles and when such vehicle is:

a. Used in the transportation of agricultural products of the farm he is working to market, or to other points for sale or processing, or when used to transport materials, tools, equipment, or supplies which are to be used or consumed on the farm he is working, or when used for any other transportation incidental to the regular operation of such farm;

b. Used in transporting forest products, including forest materials originating on a farm or incident to the regular operation of a farm, to the farm he is working or transporting for any purpose forest products which originate on the farm he is working; or

c. Used in the transportation of farm produce, supplies, equipment, or materials to a farm not worked by him, pursuant to a mutual cooperative agreement.

2. When the nonfarm use of such motor vehicle is limited to the personal use of the owner and his immediate family in attending church or school, securing medical treatment or supplies, or securing other household or family necessities.

C. As used in this section, the term "farm" means one or more areas of land used for the production, cultivation, growing, or harvesting of agricultural products, but does not include a tree farm that is not also a nursery or Christmas tree farm, unless it is part of what otherwise is a farm. As used in this section, the term "agricultural products" means any nursery plants; Christmas trees; horticultural, viticultural, and other cultivated plants and crops; aquaculture; dairy; livestock; poultry; bee; or other farm products.

D. The first application for registration of a vehicle under this section shall be made on forms provided by the Department and shall include:

1. The location and acreage of each farm on which the vehicle to be registered is to be used;

2. The type of agricultural commodities, poultry, dairy products or livestock produced on such farms and the approximate amounts produced annually;

3. A statement, signed by the vehicle's owner, that the vehicle to be registered will only be used for one or more of the purposes specified in subsection B; and

4. Other information required by the Department.

The above information is not required for the renewal of a vehicle's registration under this section.

E. The Department shall issue appropriately designated license plates for those motor vehicles registered under this section. The manner in which such license plates are designated shall be at the discretion of the Commissioner.

F. The owner of a farm vehicle shall inform the Commissioner within 30 days or at the time of his next registration renewal, whichever comes first, when such vehicle is no longer used exclusively for farm use as defined in this section, and shall pay the appropriate registration fee for the vehicle based on its type of operation. It shall constitute a Class 2 misdemeanor to: (i) operate or to permit the operation of any farm motor vehicle for which the fee for registration and license plates is herein prescribed on any highway in the Commonwealth without first having paid the prescribed registration fee; or (ii) operate or permit the operation of any motor vehicle, registered under this section, for purposes other than as provided under subsection B; or (iii) operate as a for-hire vehicle.

G. Nothing in this section shall affect the exemptions of agricultural and horticultural vehicles under §§ 46.2-664 through 46.2-670.

H. Notwithstanding other provisions of this section, vehicles licensed under this section may be used by volunteer emergency medical services personnel and volunteer firefighters in responding to emergency calls, in reporting for regular duty, and in attending emergency medical services agency or fire company meetings and drills.

History.

1976, c. 323, § 46.1-154.3; 1978, c. 29; 1985, c. 424; 1989, cc. 402, 727; 1996, cc. 943, 994; 1997, cc. 774, 816; 2004, c. 663; 2015, cc. 502, 503.

§ **46.2-699:** Repealed by Acts 1997, c. 283.

§ 46.2-700. Fees for vehicles for transporting well-drilling machinery and specialized mobile equipment.

A. The fee for registration of any motor vehicle, trailer, or semitrailer on which well-drilling machinery is attached and which is permanently used solely for transporting the machinery shall be $15.

B. The fee for the registration of specialized mobile equipment shall be $15. "Specialized mobile equipment" shall mean any self-propelled motor vehicle manufactured for a specific purpose, other than for the transportation of passengers or property, which is used on a job site and whose movement on any highway is incidental to the purpose for which it was designed and manufactured. The vehicle must be constructed to fall within all size and weight requirements as contained in §§ 46.2-1105, 46.2-1110, 46.2-1113 and Article 17 (§ 46.2-1122 et seq.) of Chapter 10 and must be capable of maintaining sustained highway speeds of 40 miles per hour or more. Nothing in this subsection shall be construed as prohibiting the transportation on specialized mobile equipment of safety equipment, including but not limited to highway traffic safety cones, to be used on a job site.

C. Specialized mobile equipment which cannot maintain a sustained highway speed in excess of 40 miles per hour, and trailers or semitrailers which are designed and manufactured for a specific purpose and whose movement on the highway is incidental to the purpose for which it was manufactured and which are not designed or used to transport persons or property, shall not be required to be registered under this chapter.

History.

Code 1950, § 46-164; 1958, c. 541, § 46.1-156; 1964, c. 218; 1979, c. 244; 1989, c. 727; 2004, c. 478; 2011, c. 283.

§ 46.2-701. Combinations of tractor trucks and semitrailers; five-year registration of certain trailer fleets.

A. Each vehicle of a combination of a truck or tractor truck and a trailer or semitrailer shall be registered as a separate vehicle, and separate vehicle license plates shall be issued for each vehicle, but, for the purpose of determining the gross weight group into which any vehicle falls pursuant to § 46.2-697, the combination of vehicles of which such vehicle constitutes a part shall be considered a unit, and the aggregate gross weight of the entire combination shall determine the gross weight group. The fee for the registration card and license plates for a trailer or semitrailer constituting a part of the combination shall be as provided in § 46.2-694.1.

B. In determining the fee to be paid for the registration of a truck or tractor truck constituting a part of such combination the fee shall be assessed on the total gross weight and the fee per 1,000 pounds applicable to the gross weight of the combination when loaded to the maximum capacity for which it is registered and licensed.

C. Existing five-year registrations for fleets of fifty or more trailers previously issued under this section shall remain valid through the five-year period, but shall not be renewable.

History.

Code 1950, § 46-165; 1950, p. 249; 1956, c. 477; 1958, c. 541, § 46.1-157; 1964, c. 218; 1979, cc. 61, 244; 1982, c. 157; 1989, c. 727; 1997, c. 283.

§ 46.2-702. Fees for service or wrecking vehicles.

For the purpose of determining the registration and license fees paid by the owners of motor vehicles used as service or wrecking cranes, these motor vehicles, when used in connection with the business of any person engaged in selling motor vehicles or repairing the same, shall be treated as private motor vehicles and not as motor vehicles operated for compensation or for hire.

History.

Code 1950, § 46-174; 1958, c. 541, § 46.1-163; 1960, c. 123; 1989, c. 727.

§ 46.2-702.1. (Contingent expiration — see Editor's note) Distribution of certain revenue.

A. Except as provided in subsection B, the net additional revenues generated by increases in the registration fees under §§ 46.2-694, 46.2-694.1, and 46.2-697 pursuant to enactments of the 2007 Session of the General Assembly, shall be deposited into the Highway Maintenance and Operating Fund established pursuant to § 33.2-1530.

B. In the case of vehicles registered under the International Registration Plan, an amount that is approximately equal to the net additional revenues generated by increases in the registration fees under §§ 46.2-694, 46.2-694.1, and 46.2-697 that are in regard to such vehicles pursuant to enactments of the 2007 Session of the General Assembly shall be deposited into the Highway and Maintenance Operating Fund.

C. For purposes of this title, "net additional revenues" shall mean the additional revenues provided pursuant to enactments of the 2007 Session of the General Assembly minus any refunds or remittances required to be paid.

History.

2007, c. 896.

Editor's note.

Acts 2007, c. 896, cl. 22 provides: "That the provisions of this act which generate additional revenue for the Transportation Trust Fund, established under § 33.1-23.03:1 [see now § 33.2-1524] of the Code of Virginia, or the Highway Maintenance and Operating Fund shall expire on December 31 of any year in which the General Assembly appropriates any of the revenues designated under general law to the Highway Maintenance and Operating Fund or the Transportation Trust Fund for any non-transportation related purpose."

Acts 2010, c. 874, cl. 2 provides: "That no provision of this act shall be construed or interpreted to cause the expiration of any provision of Chapter 896 of the Acts of Assembly of 2007 pursuant to the 22nd enactment of such Chapter."

Acts 2010, c. 874, cl. 8 provides: "That the provisions of the first enactment of this act shall expire at midnight on June 30, 2012.

The provisions of the second, third, fourth, fifth, sixth, and seventh enactments of this act shall have no expiration date."

§ 46.2-702.2. Fees for registration of vehicles specially equipped to accommodate persons with disabilities.

In determining the fee to be charged for registration of any vehicle specially equipped to be driven by or to transport persons with disabilities, the weight of the vehicle upon which such fee is based shall be the weight of the vehicle prior to the installation of such special equipment for the accommodation of persons with disabilities.

History.
2008, c. 130.

§ 46.2-703. Reciprocal agreement with other states; assessment and collection of fees on an apportionment or allocation basis; registration of vehicles and reporting of road tax; violations; vehicle seizures; penalties.

A. Notwithstanding any other provision of this title, the Governor may, on the advice of the Department, enter into reciprocal agreements on behalf of the Commonwealth with the appropriate authorities of any state of the United States or a state or province of a country providing for the assessing and collecting of license fees for motor vehicles, tractor trucks, trucks, trailers, and semitrailers on an apportionment or allocation basis, as outlined in the International Registration Plan developed by the International Registration Plan, Inc.

The Commissioner is authorized to audit the records of any owner, lessor, or lessee to verify the accuracy of any information required by any jurisdiction to determine the registration fees due. Based on this audit, the Commissioner may assess any owner, lessor, or lessee for any license fees due this Commonwealth, including interest and penalties as provided in this section. In addition to any other penalties prescribed by law, the Commissioner or the Reciprocity Board may deny the owner, lessor, or lessee the right to operate any motor vehicle on the highways in the Commonwealth until the assessment has been paid.

Trip permit registration may be issued for any vehicle or combination of vehicles that could be lawfully operated in the jurisdiction if full registration or proportional registration were obtained. The fee for this permit shall be $15 and the permit shall be valid for 10 days.

Any person who operates or permits the operation of any motor vehicle, trailer, or semitrailer over any highway in the Commonwealth without first having paid to the Commissioner the fees prescribed and payable under this section shall be guilty of a Class 2 misdemeanor. Failure to display a license plate indicating that the vehicle is registered on an apportionment or allocation basis or carry a trip permit, as outlined in the International Registration Plan, shall constitute prima facie evidence the apportioned or allocated fee has not been paid.

If the Commissioner ascertains that any fees that he is authorized to assess any owner, lessor, or lessee for any license year have not been assessed or have been assessed for less than the law required for the year because of failure or refusal of any owner, lessor, or lessee to make his records available for audit as provided herein, or if any owner, lessor, or lessee misrepresents, falsifies, or conceals any of these records, the Commissioner shall determine from any information obtainable the lawful fees at the rate prescribed for that year, plus a penalty of five percent and interest at the rate of six percent per year, which shall be computed on the fees and penalty from the date the fees became due to the date of assessment, and is authorized to make an assessment therefor against the owner, lessor, or lessee. If the assessment is not paid within 30 days after its date, interest at the rate of six percent per year shall accrue thereon from the date of such assessment until the fees and penalty are paid. The notice of the assessment shall be forthwith sent to the owner, lessor, or lessee by registered or certified mail to the address of the owner, lessor, or lessee as it appears on the records in the office of the Department. The notice, when sent in accordance with these requirements, shall be sufficient regardless of whether it was received.

If any owner, lessor, or lessee fails to pay the fees, penalty, and interest, or any portion thereof, assessed pursuant to this section, in addition to any other provision of law, the Attorney General or the Commissioner shall bring an appropriate action before the Circuit Court of the City of Richmond for the recovery of the fees, penalty, and interest, and judgment shall be rendered for the amount found to be due together with costs. If it is found that the failure to pay was willful on the part of the owner, lessor or lessee, judgment shall be rendered for double the amount of the fees found to be due, plus costs.

B. Notwithstanding any other provision of this title or Chapter 27 (§ 58.1-2700 et seq.) of Title 58.1, the Governor, on the advice of the Department, may enter into reciprocal agreements on behalf of the Commonwealth with the duly authorized representatives of other jurisdictions providing for the road tax registration of vehicles, establishing periodic road tax reporting and road tax payment requirements from owners of such vehicles, and disbursement of funds collected due to other jurisdictions based on mileage traveled and fuel used in those jurisdictions as outlined in the International Fuels Tax Agreement.

Notwithstanding any statute contrary to the provisions of any reciprocal agreement entered into by the Governor or his duly authorized representative as authorized by this title, the provisions of the reciprocal agreement shall govern and apply to all matters relating to administration and enforcement of the road tax. In the event the language of any reciprocal agreement entered into by the Governor as authorized by this title is later amended so that it conflicts with or is contrary to any statute, the Department shall consider the amended language of the reciprocal agreement controlling and shall administer and enforce the road tax in accordance with the amended language of the reciprocal agreement.

An agreement may provide for determining the base state for motor carriers, records requirements, audit procedures, exchange of information, persons eligible for tax licensing, defining qualified motor vehicles, determining if bonding is required, specifying reporting requirements and periods, including defining uniform penalties and interest rates for late reporting, determining methods for collecting and forwarding of motor fuel taxes and penalties to another jurisdiction, and other provisions as will facilitate the administration of the agreement.

The Governor may, as required by the terms of the agreement, forward to officers of another member jurisdiction any information in the Department's possession relative to the use of motor fuels by any motor carrier. The Department may disclose to officers of another state the location of offices, motor vehicles, and other real and personal property of motor carriers.

An agreement may provide for each state to audit the records of motor carriers based in the state to determine if the road taxes due each member jurisdiction are properly reported and paid. Each member jurisdiction shall forward the findings of the audits performed on motor carriers based in the member jurisdiction to each jurisdiction in which the carrier has taxable use of motor fuels. For motor carriers not based in the Commonwealth and which have taxable use of motor fuel in the Commonwealth, the Department may serve the audit findings received from another jurisdiction, in the form of an assessment, on the carrier as though an audit had been conducted by the Department.

Any agreement entered into pursuant to this chapter does not preclude the Department from auditing the records of any motor carrier covered by the provisions of this chapter.

The Department shall not enter into any agreement that would affect the motor fuel road tax rate.

The Department may adopt and promulgate such rules, regulations, and procedures as may be necessary to effectuate and administer this title. Nothing in this title shall be construed to affect the tax rate provisions found in Chapter 27 (§ 58.1-2700 et seq.) of Title 58.1.

C. Notwithstanding any other provision in this title or Title 56, the Governor, on the advice of the Department, may participate in the single state registration system as authorized under 49 U.S.C. § 14504 and 49 C.F.R. Part 367, and the Unified Carrier Registration System authorized under 49 U.S.C. § 14504a, enacted pursuant to the Unified Carrier Registration Act of 2005, and the federal regulations promulgated thereunder.

D. Notwithstanding any other provision of this title or Title 58.1, the following violations of laws shall be punished as follows:

1. Any person who operates or causes to be operated on any highway in the Commonwealth any motor vehicle that is not in compliance with the Unified Carrier Registration System authorized under 49 U.S.C. § 14504a, enacted pursuant to the Unified Carrier Registration Act of 2005, and the federal regulations promulgated thereunder shall be guilty of a Class 4 misdemeanor.

2. Any person who operates or causes to be operated on any highway in the Commonwealth any motor vehicle that is not in compliance with Chapter 27 (§ 58.1-2700 et seq.) of Title 58.1 or the terms and provisions of the International Fuel Tax Agreement, as amended by the International Fuel Tax Association, Inc., shall be guilty of a Class 4 misdemeanor.

3. Any person who knowingly displays or uses on any vehicle operated by him any registration, license, identification marker or other identification or credential authorized to be issued pursuant to this title, Chapter 27 (§ 58.1-2700 et seq.) of Title 58.1, or the reciprocal agreements entered into pursuant to this chapter that has not been issued to the owner or operator thereof for such vehicle and any person who knowingly assists him to do so shall be guilty of a Class 3 misdemeanor.

E. An officer charging a violation under subsection D shall serve a citation on the operator of the vehicle in violation. Such citation shall be directed to the owner, operator or other person responsible for the violation as determined by the officer. Service of the citation on the vehicle operator shall constitute service of process upon the owner, operator, or other person charged with the violation under this article, and shall have the same legal force as if served within the Commonwealth personally upon the owner, operator, or other person charged with the violation, whether such owner, operator, or other person charged is a resident or nonresident.

F. Any police officer or size and weight compliance agent of the Commonwealth authorized to serve process may hold a motor vehicle owned or operated by a person against whom an order or penalty has been entered pursuant to this section, §§ 46.2-613.3 and 46.2-1133, the International Registration Plan, the International Fuel Tax Agreement, or the Unified Carrier Registration System authorized under 49 U.S.C. § 14504a, enacted pursuant to the Unified Carrier Registration Act of 2005, and the federal regulations promulgated thereunder, but only for such time as is reasonably necessary to promptly petition for a writ of fieri facias. The Commonwealth shall not be required to post bond in order to hold and levy upon any vehicle held pursuant to this section. Upon notification of the order, judgment, or penalty entered against the offending person and notice to such person of the failure to satisfy the order, judgment or penalty, any investigator, special agent, officer, or size and weight compliance agent of the Commonwealth shall thereafter deny the offending person the right to operate a motor vehicle or vehicles on the highways of the Commonwealth until the order, judgment, or penalty has been satisfied and a reinstatement fee of $50 has been paid to the Department. Reinstatement fees collected under the provisions of this section shall be paid by the Commissioner into the state treasury and shall be set aside as a special fund to be used to meet the expenses of the Department.

History.

1974, c. 326, § 46.1-157.1; 1978, c. 294; 1989, c. 727; 1995, cc. 744, 803; 2002, c. 239; 2004, c. 376; 2006, c. 208; 2009, c. 563; 2011, cc. 62, 73; 2012, cc. 22, 111.

§ 46.2-703.1. Additional fee for fleets of vehicles registered under § 46.2-703.

In addition to any other fees required to be paid for vehicles registered under the provisions of § 46.2-703, the Department shall charge an administrative fee of one dollar per year per fleet for each application processed. All fees collected under this section shall be used exclusively for the administration and support of reciprocity activities described in § 46.2-703.

History.

1993, c. 83.

§ 46.2-704. Prohibited operations; checking on weights; penalties.

A. No person shall operate or permit the operation of any motor vehicle, trailer, or semitrailer for which the fee for registration is prescribed by § 46.2-697 on any highway in the Commonwealth, under any of the following circumstances:

1. Without first having paid the registration fee hereinabove prescribed.

2. If, at the time of the operation, the gross weight of the vehicle or of the combination of vehicles of which it is a part, is in excess of the gross weight on the basis of which it is registered. In any case where a pickup truck is used in combination with another vehicle, operation shall be unlawful only if the combined gross weight exceeds the combined gross weight on the basis of which each vehicle is registered.

B. Any officer authorized to enforce the motor vehicle laws, having reason to believe that the gross weight of any motor vehicle, trailer, or semitrailer being operated on any highway in the Commonwealth exceeds that on the basis of which the vehicle is registered, may weigh the vehicle by whatever means the Superintendent may prescribe and the operator, or other person in possession of the vehicle, shall permit this weighing whenever requested by the officer.

C. Any person who violates any provision of this section or who operates or permits the operation of a trailer or semitrailer designed for the use of human beings as living quarters, on the highways in the Commonwealth without having first paid to the Commissioner the fee prescribed in subdivision 5 of subsection A of § 46.2-694 is guilty of a Class 2 misdemeanor.

History.

Code 1950, § 46-167; 1958, c. 541, § 46.1-159; 1962, c. 92; 1975, c. 18; 1982, c. 681; 1989, c. 727.

ARTICLE 8.
REGISTRATION OF UNINSURED MOTOR VEHICLES.

§ 46.2-705. Definitions.

For the purposes of this article, the following terms shall have the meanings respectively ascribed to them in this section:

"Motor vehicle" means a vehicle capable of self-propulsion which is either (i) required to be titled and licensed and for which a license fee is required to be paid by its owner, or (ii) owned by or assigned to a motor vehicle manufacturer, distributor, or dealer licensed in the Commonwealth. For the purposes of this article, "motor vehicle" does not include "moped" as defined in § 46.2-100.

"Insured motor vehicle" means a motor vehicle as to which there is bodily injury liability insurance and property damage liability insurance, both in the amounts specified in § 46.2-472, issued by an insurance carrier authorized to do business in the Commonwealth, or as to which a bond has been given or cash or securities delivered in lieu of the insurance; or as to which the owner has qualified as a self-insurer in accordance with the provisions of § 46.2-368.

"Uninsured motor vehicle" means a motor vehicle as to which there is no such bodily injury liability insurance and property damage liability insurance, or no such bond has been given or cash or securities delivered in lieu thereof, or the owner of which has not so qualified as a self-insurer.

History.

1958, c. 407, § 46.1-167.2; 1960, c. 188; 1982, c. 638; 1988, c. 865; 1989, c. 727; 2013, c. 783.

§ 46.2-706. Additional fee; proof of insurance required of applicants for registration of insured motor vehicles; verification of insurance; suspension of driver's license, registration certificates, and license plates for certain violations.

In addition to any other fees prescribed by law, every person registering an uninsured motor vehicle, as defined in § 46.2-705, at the time of registering or reregistering the uninsured vehicle, shall pay a fee of $500; however, if the uninsured motor vehicle is being registered or reregistered for a period of less than a full year, the uninsured motor vehicle fee shall be prorated for the unexpired portion of the registration period. If the vehicle is a motor vehicle being registered or reregistered as provided in subsection B of § 46.2-697, the fee shall be one-fourth of the annual uninsured motor vehicle fee for each quarter for which the vehicle is registered.

If the owner of a motor vehicle registered under this article as an uninsured motor vehicle, during the period for which such vehicle is registered, obtains insurance coverage adequate to permit such vehicle's registration as an insured motor vehicle and presents evidence satisfactory to the Commissioner of the existence of such insurance coverage, the Commissioner shall amend the Department's records to show such vehicle to be registered as an insured motor vehicle and shall refund to the owner a prorated portion of the additional fee required by this section for registration of an uninsured motor vehicle. Such proration shall be on a monthly basis, except that no such refund shall be made (i) as to any registration during the last three months of its validity or (ii) on any portion of any such fee required to be paid resulting from a determination by the Department or any court that a vehicle was uninsured and no fee had been paid.

Every person applying for registration of a motor vehicle and declaring it to be an insured motor vehicle shall, under the penalties set forth in § 46.2-707, execute and furnish to the Commissioner his certificate that the motor vehicle is an insured motor vehicle as defined in § 46.2-705, or that the Commissioner has issued to its owner, in accordance with § 46.2-368, a certificate of self-insurance applicable to the vehicle sought to be registered. The Commissioner, or his duly authorized agent, may verify that the motor vehicle is properly insured by comparing owner and vehicle identification information on file at the Department of Motor Vehicles with liability information on the owner and vehicle transmitted to the Department by any insurance company licensed to do business in the Commonwealth as provided in § 46.2-706.1. If no record of liability insurance is found, the Department may require the motor vehicle owner to verify insurance in a method prescribed by the Commissioner.

The refusal or neglect of any owner within 30 days to submit the liability insurance information when required by the Commissioner or his duly authorized agent, or the electronic notification by the insurance company or surety company that the policy or bond named in the certificate of insurance is not in effect, shall require the Commissioner to suspend any driver's license and all registration certificates and license plates issued to the owner of the motor vehicle until the person (i) has paid to the Commissioner a fee of $500 to be disposed of as provided for in § 46.2-710 with respect to the motor vehicle determined to be uninsured and (ii) furnishes proof of financial responsibility for the future in the manner prescribed in Article 15 (§ 46.2-435 et seq.) of Chapter 3. No order of suspension required by this section shall become effective until the Commissioner has offered the person an opportunity for an administrative hearing to show cause why the order should not be enforced. Notice of the opportunity for an administrative hearing may be included in the order of suspension. Any request for an administrative hearing made by such person must be received by the Department within 180 days of the issuance date of the order of suspension unless the person presents to the Department evidence of military service as defined by the federal Servicemembers Civil Relief Act (50 U.S.C. § 3901 et seq.), incarceration, commitment, hospitalization, or physical presence outside the United States at the time the order of suspension was issued. When three years have elapsed from the effective date of the suspension required in this section, the Commissioner may relieve the person of the requirement of furnishing proof of future financial responsibility.

The Commissioner shall suspend the driver's license and all registration certificates and license plates of any person on receiving a record of his conviction of a violation of any provisions of § 46.2-707, but the Commissioner shall dispense with the suspension when the person is convicted for a violation of § 46.2-707 and the Department's records show conclusively that the motor vehicle was insured or that the fee applicable to the registration of an uninsured motor vehicle has been paid by the owner prior to the date and time of the alleged offense.

History.

1958, c. 407, § 46.1-167.1; 1960, c. 188; 1966, c. 181; 1972, cc. 552, 609, 638; 1973, c. 25; 1974, c. 170; 1975, c. 16; 1976, c. 27; 1978, c. 563; 1981, c. 193; 1984, c. 399; 1986, c. 527; 1988, c. 470; 1989, c. 727; 1993, c. 127; 1996, cc. 474, 489; 1998, c. 404; 2012, cc. 151, 471.

§ 46.2-706.1. Insurance and surety companies to furnish certain insurance information.

Any liability insurance information relating to individually identified vehicles or persons, received from such companies under this section, shall be considered privileged information and not subject to the Virginia Freedom of Information Act (§ 2.2-3700 et seq.).

Such information shall be used in conjunction with information supplied under § 46.2-706 to verify insurance for motor vehicles certified by their owners to be insured.

Insurance companies licensed to do business in Virginia shall provide to the Department monthly electronic updates of insured information and vehicle descriptions required by the Commissioner when they (i) cancel liability insurance for vehicles registered in Virginia, (ii) add liability insurance for vehicles registered in Virginia, or (iii) provide liability insurance for vehicles registered in Virginia newly satisfying financial responsibility requirements.

History.
1993, c. 949; 1996, cc. 474, 489; 2009, c. 419.

§ 46.2-707. Operating uninsured motor vehicle without payment of fee; verification of insurance; false evidence of insurance.

Any person who owns an uninsured motor vehicle (i) licensed in the Commonwealth, (ii) subject to registration in the Commonwealth, or (iii) displaying temporary license plates provided for in § 46.2-1558 who operates or permits the operation of that motor vehicle without first having paid to the Commissioner the uninsured motor vehicle fee required by § 46.2-706, to be disposed of as provided by § 46.2-710, shall be guilty of a Class 3 misdemeanor.

Any person who is the operator of such an uninsured motor vehicle and not the titled owner, who knows that the required fee has not been paid to the Commissioner, shall be guilty of a Class 3 misdemeanor.

The Commissioner or his duly authorized agent, having reason to believe that a motor vehicle is being operated or has been operated on any specified date, may require the owner of such motor vehicle to verify insurance in a method prescribed by the Commissioner as provided for by § 46.2-706. The refusal or neglect of the owner who has not, prior to the date of operation, paid the uninsured motor vehicle fee required by § 46.2-706 as to such motor vehicle, to provide such verification shall be prima facie evidence that the motor vehicle was an uninsured motor vehicle at the time of such operation.

Any person who falsely verifies insurance to the Commissioner or gives false evidence that a motor vehicle sought to be registered is an insured motor vehicle, shall be guilty of a Class 3 misdemeanor.

However, the foregoing portions of this section shall not be applicable if it is established that the owner had good cause to believe and did believe that such motor vehicle was an insured motor vehicle, in which event the provisions of § 46.2-609 shall be applicable.

Any person who owns an uninsured motor vehicle (i) licensed in the Commonwealth, (ii) subject to registration in the Commonwealth, or (iii) displaying temporary license plates provided for in § 46.2-1558, and who has not paid the uninsured motor vehicle fee required by § 46.2-706, shall immediately surrender the vehicle's license plates to the Department, unless the vehicle's registration has been deactivated as provided by § 46.2-646.1. Any person who fails to immediately surrender his vehicle's license plates as required by this section is guilty of a Class 3 misdemeanor.

Abstracts of records of conviction, as defined in this title, of any violation of any of the provisions of this section shall be forwarded to the Commissioner as prescribed by § 46.2-383.

The Commissioner shall suspend the driver's license and all registration certificates and license plates of any titled owner of an uninsured motor vehicle upon receiving a record of his conviction of a violation of any provisions of this section, and he shall not thereafter reissue the driver's license and the registration certificates and license plates issued in the name of such person until such person pays the fee applicable to the registration of an uninsured motor vehicle as prescribed in § 46.2-706 and furnishes proof of future financial responsibility as prescribed by Article 15 (§ 46.2-435 et seq.) of Chapter 3 of this title. However, when three years have elapsed from the date of the suspension herein required, the Commissioner may relieve such person of the requirement of furnishing proof of future financial responsibility. When such suspension results from a conviction for presenting or causing to be presented to the Commissioner false verification as to whether a motor vehicle is an insured motor vehicle or false evidence that any motor vehicle sought to be registered is insured, then the Commissioner shall not thereafter reissue the driver's license and the registration certificates and license plates issued in the name of such person so convicted for a period of 180 days from the date of such order of suspension, and only then when all other provisions of law have been complied with by such person.

The Commissioner shall suspend the driver's license of any person who is the operator but not the titled owner of a motor vehicle upon receiving a record of his conviction of a violation of any provisions of this section and he shall not thereafter reissue the driver's license until 30 days from the date of such order of suspension.

History.
1958, c. 407, § 46.1-167.3; 1960, c. 188; 1966, cc. 181, 568; 1972, c. 552; 1973, c. 25; 1977, c. 196; 1978, c. 605; 1984, cc. 399, 780; 1986, c. 527; 1989, c. 727; 1996, cc. 474, 489; 2013, cc. 673, 789.

§ 46.2-707.1. (Effective January 1, 2017) Uninsured motor vehicle fee payment plan.

A. The Department may establish an uninsured motor vehicle fee payment plan to allow individuals to pay the fees for a motor vehicle determined to be uninsured as prescribed in § 46.2-706, 46.2-707, or 46.2-708. Notwithstanding §§ 46.2-706, 46.2-707, and 46.2-708, a Virginia resident 18 years of age or older whose driver's license and vehicle registration have been suspended pursuant to § 46.2-706, 46.2-707, or 46.2-708 may apply to the Department to enter into a payment plan agreement with a duration of no more than three years from the agreement date, referred to in this section as the "payment plan period."

B. To be eligible to enter into the payment plan, the individual must (i) have one or more outstanding suspensions of driving privileges pursuant to the provisions of § 46.2-706, 46.2-707, or 46.2-708 and have no other outstanding suspensions or revocations; (ii) meet all other conditions for reinstatement of driving privileges; and (iii) have never defaulted on a prior uninsured motor vehicle payment plan agreement.

C. An eligible individual who enters into a payment plan agreement with the Department, pays a $25 administrative fee, and pays the reinstatement fee pursuant to §§ 46.2-333.1 and 46.2-411, if required, shall be eligible to have his driving privileges reinstated by the Department.

D. The amount and frequency of each payment and the duration of the payment plan shall be described in the payment plan agreement signed by the Department and the individual. Payments may be made in person, online, or by mail. The full fee must be paid in no more than three years from the agreement date; however, an individual may repay the balance of the fee at any time during the payment plan period with no penalty.

E. If an individual defaults on the payment plan agreement, the Commissioner shall suspend the driver's license and all registration certificates and license plates issued to the owner of the motor vehicle determined to be uninsured. Such driver's license, registration certificates, and license plates shall remain suspended until the individual pays the balance of the fee applicable to the registration of an uninsured motor vehicle as prescribed in § 46.2-706, 46.2-707, or 46.2-708 and furnishes proof of future financial responsibility as prescribed by Article 15 (§ 46.2-435 et seq.) of Chapter 3. An individual is in default if he (i) pays an installment payment late as defined in the payment plan agreement or (ii) fails to make an installment payment as agreed to in the payment plan agreement. If an individual is in default, full payment of the balance of the fee shall be due as agreed to in the payment plan agreement.

F. When all fees are paid, the individual shall continue to furnish proof of financial responsibility pursuant to Article 15 (§ 46.2-435 et seq.) of Chapter 3 and § 46.2-709.

G. Installment payments of the fee with respect to the motor vehicle determined to be uninsured shall be disposed of pursuant to § 46.2-710. The administrative fee shall be paid to the Commissioner and deposited into the state treasury account set aside in a special fund to be used to meet the necessary expenses incurred by the Department.

History.

2016, c. 590.

§ 46.2-708. Suspension of driver's license and registration when uninsured motor vehicle is involved in reportable accident; hearing prior to suspension.

When it appears to the Commissioner from the records of his office that an uninsured motor vehicle as defined in § 46.2-705, subject to registration in the Commonwealth, is involved in a reportable accident in the Commonwealth resulting in death, injury or property damage with respect to which motor vehicle the owner thereof has not paid the uninsured motor vehicle fee as prescribed in § 46.2-706, the Commissioner shall, in addition to enforcing the applicable provisions of Article 13 (§ 46.2-417 et seq.) of Chapter 3, suspend such owner's driver's license and all of his license plates and registration certificates until such person has complied with Article 13 of Chapter 3 and has paid to the Commissioner a fee of $500, to be disposed of as provided by § 46.2-710, with respect to the motor vehicle involved in the accident and furnishes proof of future financial responsibility in the manner prescribed in Article 15 (§ 46.2-435 et seq.) of Chapter 3. However, no order of suspension required by this section shall become effective until the Commissioner has offered the person an opportunity for an administrative hearing to show cause why the order should not be enforced. Notice of the opportunity for an administrative hearing may be included in the order of suspension. Any request for an administrative hearing made by such person must be received by the Department within 180 days of the issuance date of the order of suspension unless the person presents to the Department evidence of military service as defined by the federal Servicemembers Civil Relief Act (50 U.S.C. § 3901 et seq.), incarceration, commitment, hospitalization, or physical presence outside the United States at the time the order of suspension was issued.

However, when three years have elapsed from the effective date of the suspension herein required, the Commissioner may relieve such person of the requirement of furnishing proof of future financial responsibility. The presentation by a person subject to the provisions of this section of a certificate of insurance, executed by an agent or representative of an insurance company qualified to do business in this Commonwealth, showing that on the date and at the time of the accident the vehicle was an insured motor vehicle as herein defined, or, presentation by such person of evidence that the additional fee applicable to the registration of an uninsured motor vehicle had been paid to the Department prior to the date and time of the accident, shall be sufficient bar to the suspension provided for in this section.

History.

1958, c. 407, § 46.1-167.4; 1960, c. 188; 1966, cc. 181, 548; 1970, c. 68; 1972, cc. 552, 638, 729; 1973, c. 25; 1974, c. 604; 1978, c. 563;

1981, c. 193; 1984, cc. 399, 780; 1988, c. 470; 1989, c. 727; 1998, c. 404; 2012, cc. 151, 471.

§ 46.2-709. Requiring other proof of financial responsibility; suspended driver's license, registration certificate and license plates to be returned to Commissioner; Commissioner may take possession thereof.

Whenever any proof of financial responsibility filed by any person as required by this article no longer fulfills the purpose for which required, the Commissioner shall require other proof of financial responsibility as required by this article and shall suspend such person's driver's license, registration certificates, and license plates and decals pending the furnishing of proof as required.

Any person whose driver's license or registration certificates, or license plates and decals have been suspended as provided in this article and have not been reinstated shall immediately return every such license, registration certificate, and set of license plates and decals held by him to the Commissioner. Any person failing to comply with this requirement shall be guilty of a traffic infraction and upon conviction thereof shall be punished as provided in § 46.2-113.

The Commissioner is authorized to take possession of any license, registration certificate, or set of license plates and decals on their suspension under the provisions of this chapter or to direct any police officer to take possession of and return them to the office of the Commissioner.

History.

1958, c. 407, § 46.1-167.5; 1960, c. 188; 1972, cc. 435, 609; 1976, c. 156; 1978, c. 605; 1984, c. 780; 1989, cc. 705, 727.

§ 46.2-710. Disposition of funds collected.

All funds collected by the Commissioner under the provisions of this article shall be paid into the state treasury and held in a special fund to be known as the Uninsured Motorists Fund to be disbursed as provided by law. The Commissioner may expend monies from such funds, for the administration of this article, in accordance with the General Appropriations Act.

History.

1958, c. 407, § 46.1-167.6; 1989, c. 727.

ARTICLE 9.

LICENSE PLATES, GENERALLY.

§ 46.2-711. Furnishing number and design of plates; displaying on vehicles required.

A. The Department shall furnish one license plate for every registered moped, motorcycle, autocycle, tractor truck, semitrailer, or trailer, and two license plates for every other registered motor vehicle, except to licensed motor vehicle dealers and persons delivering unladen vehicles who shall be furnished one license plate. The license plates for trailers, semitrailers, commercial vehicles, and trucks, other than license plates for dealers, may be of such design as to prevent removal without mutilating some part of the indicia forming a part of the license plate, when secured to the bracket.

B. The Department shall issue appropriately designated license plates for:

1. Passenger-carrying vehicles for rent or hire for the transportation of passengers for private trips, other than TNC partner vehicles as defined in § 46.2-2000 and emergency medical services vehicles pursuant to clause (iii) of § 46.2-649.1:1;
2. Taxicabs;
3. Passenger-carrying vehicles operated by common carriers or restricted common carriers;
4. Property-carrying motor vehicles to applicants who operate as private carriers only;
5. Applicants, other than TNC partners as defined in § 46.2-2000 and emergency medical services vehicles pursuant to clause (iii) of § 46.2-649.1:1, who operate motor vehicles as carriers for rent or hire;
6. Vehicles operated by nonemergency medical transportation carriers as defined in § 46.2-2000; and
7. Trailers and semitrailers.

C. The Department shall issue appropriately designated license plates for motor vehicles held for rental as defined in § 58.1-1735.

D. The Department shall issue appropriately designated license plates for low-speed vehicles.

E. No vehicles shall be operated on the highways in the Commonwealth without displaying the license plates required by this chapter. The provisions of this subsection shall not apply to vehicles used to collect and deliver the Unites States mail to the extent that their rear license plates may be covered by the "CAUTION, FREQUENT STOPS, U.S. MAIL" sign when the vehicle is engaged in the collection and delivery of the United States mail.

F. Pickup or panel trucks are exempt from the provisions of subsection B with reference to displaying for-hire license plates when operated as a carrier for rent or hire. However, this exemption shall not apply to pickup or panel trucks subject to regulation under Chapter 21 (§ 46.2-2100 et seq.).

History.

Code 1950, §§ 46-96, 46-160; 1950, p. 625; 1954, c. 211; 1958, c. 541, § 46.1-99; 1974, cc. 150, 477; 1989, c. 727; 1993, c. 290; 1995, c. 46; 1997, cc. 774, 816; 2001, c. 596; 2005, c. 140; 2011, cc. 405, 639, 881, 889; 2013, c. 783; 2014, cc. 53, 256; 2015, cc. 2, 3; 2016, cc. 125, 133.

§ 46.2-712. Requirements of license plates and decals.

A. Every license plate shall display the registration number assigned to the motor vehicle, trailer, or semitrailer and to the owner thereof, the name of the Commonwealth, which may be abbreviated, and the year or the month and year, which may be abbreviated and in the form of decals, for which it is issued. Subject to the need for legibility, the size of the plate, the letters, numerals, and decals thereon, and the color of the plate, letters, numerals, and decals shall be in the discretion of the Commissioner. Decals shall be placed on the license plates in the manner prescribed by the Commissioner, and shall indicate the month and year of expiration. On the issuance of the decals, a new registration card shall be issued with the same date of expiration as the decals.

B. Notwithstanding any other provision of this title, the Department may issue permanent license plates without decals and without a month and year of expiration for all trailers and semitrailers, regardless of weight; trucks and tractor trucks with a gross vehicle weight rating or gross combination weight rating of more than 26,000 pounds; taxicabs or other motor vehicles performing a taxicab service; and common carrier vehicles operated for hire, both of the latter as defined in § 46.2-2000 that are in compliance with the requirements of Chapter 20 (§ 46.2-2000 et seq.) of this title. In addition, the Department may issue permanent license plates without decals and without a month and year of expiration for trucks and tractor trucks with gross vehicle weight ratings or gross combination weight ratings of at least 7,501 pounds but not more than 26,000 pounds, provided that such vehicles are for business use only, and for farm vehicles registered with the Department pursuant to § 46.2-698.

C. Notwithstanding any contrary provision of this section, any person who, pursuant to former § 56-304.3, repealed by Chapters 744 and 803 of the Acts of Assembly of 1995, obtained from the State Corporation Commission an exemption from the marker or decal requirements of former § 56-304, 56-304.1 or 56-304.2, and who has painted or, in the case of newly acquired vehicles, who paints an identifying number on the sides of any vehicle with respect to which such exemption applies and, in all other respects, continues to comply with the requirements of former § 56-304.3, shall be deemed to be in compliance with § 46.2-2011.23 and subdivision 18 of § 46.2-2011.24.

History.

Code 1950, § 46-97; 1958, c. 541, § 46.1-101; 1972, c. 609; 1974, c. 170; 1988, c. 701; 1989, c. 727; 1997, c. 283; 1999, c. 593; 2000, c. 133; 2005, c. 301.

§ 46.2-713. License plates and decals remain property of Department.

Every license plate and decal issued by the Department shall remain the property of the Department and shall be subject to be revoked, cancelled, and repossessed by the Department at any time as provided in this title.

History.

Code 1950, § 46-98; 1958, c. 541, § 46.1-102; 1972, c. 609; 1989, c. 727.

§ 46.2-714. Permanent license plates.

Notwithstanding the provisions of §§ 46.2-711 and 46.2-712 the Department may, in its discretion, issue a type of license plate suitable for permanent use on motor vehicles, trailers, semitrailers, and motorcycles, together with decals, unless decals are not required under § 46.2-712, to be attached to the license plates to indicate the registration period for which such vehicles have been properly licensed. The design of the license plates and decals, when required, shall be determined by the Commissioner.

Every permanent license plate and decal, when required, shall be returned to the Department whenever the owner of a vehicle disposes of it by sale or otherwise and when not actually in use on a motor vehicle, except dealer's plates temporarily not in use. The person in whose name the license plate is registered may apply, during the registration period for which it is issued, for the return thereof if the license plate is intended to be used on a subsequently acquired motor vehicle.

Every permanent license plate and decal, when issued, shall be returned to the Department whenever the owner of a vehicle elects to garage the vehicle and discontinue the use of it on the highway. The person in whose name the license plate is registered may apply, during the registration period for which it is issued, for the return thereof if the vehicle is to be returned to use on the highway.

For the purposes of this section, the term "motor vehicle" does not include a "moped" as defined in § 46.2-100.

History.

Code 1950, § 46-99; 1958, c. 541, § 46.1-103; 1972, c. 609; 1989, c. 727; 1997, c. 283; 2013, c. 783.

§ 46.2-715. Display of license plates.

License plates assigned to a motor vehicle, other than a moped, motorcycle, autocycle, tractor truck, trailer, or semitrailer, or to persons licensed as motor vehicle dealers or transporters of unladen vehicles, shall be attached to the front and the rear of the vehicle. The license plate assigned to a moped, motorcycle, autocycle, trailer, or semitrailer shall be attached to the rear of the vehicle. The license plate assigned to a tractor truck shall be attached to the front of the vehicle. The license plates issued to licensed motor vehicle dealers and to persons licensed as transporters of unladen vehicles shall consist of one plate for each set issued and shall be attached to the rear of the vehicle to which it is assigned.

History.

Code 1950, § 46-101; 1954, c. 210; 1958, c. 541, § 46.1-106; 1972, c. 609; 1974, c. 150; 1989, c. 727; 2013, c. 783; 2014, cc. 53, 256.

§ 46.2-716. How license plates fastened to vehicle; altering appearance of license plates.

A. Every license plate shall be securely fastened to the motor vehicle, trailer, or semitrailer to which it is assigned:

1. So as to prevent the plate from swinging,
2. In a position to be clearly visible, and
3. In a condition to be clearly legible.

B. No colored glass, colored plastic, bracket, holder, mounting, frame, or any other type of covering shall be placed, mounted, or installed on, around, or over any license plate if such glass, plastic, bracket, holder, mounting, frame, or other type of covering in any way alters or obscures (i) the alpha-numeric information, (ii) the color of the license plate, (iii) the name or abbreviated name of the state wherein the vehicle is registered, or (iv) any character or characters, decal, stamp, or other device indicating the month or year in which the vehicle's registration expires. No insignia, emblems, or trailer hitches or couplings shall be mounted in such a way as to hide or obscure any portion of the license plate or render any portion of the license plate illegible.

C. The Superintendent may make such regulations as he may deem advisable to enforce the proper mounting and securing of the license plate on the vehicle.

History.
Code 1950, § 46-102; 1958, c. 541, § 46.1-107; 1960, c. 119; 1986, c. 186; 1989, c. 727; 2000, c. 258; 2001, c. 19; 2006, c. 549.

§ 46.2-717: Repealed by Acts 1997, c. 486.

§ 46.2-718. Use of old license plates or decals after application for new.

An owner who has applied for renewal of registration of a motor vehicle, trailer, or semitrailer fifteen days prior to the day the registration period begins, but who has not received the license plates, decals, or registration card for the ensuing registration period shall be entitled to operate or permit the operation of the vehicle on the highways on displaying on the vehicle the license plates or decals issued for the preceding registration period for such time to be prescribed by the Department as it may find necessary to issue new license plates or decals.

History.
Code 1950, § 46-104; 1958, c. 541, § 46.1-109; 1972, c. 609; 1989, c. 727.

§ 46.2-719. Permit for emergency use of license plates.

A. The Commissioner may, in his discretion, grant a special permit for the use of license plates on a vehicle other than the vehicle for which the license plates were issued, when the vehicle for which the license plates were issued is undergoing repairs in a licensed motor vehicle dealer's repair shop and when the license plates are being used on a vehicle owned by the dealer in whose repair shop the vehicle is being repaired.

B. Application for the permit shall be made jointly by the dealer and the person whose vehicle is being repaired, on forms provided by the Department and shall show, in addition to whatever other information may be required by the Commissioner, that an emergency exists which would warrant the issuance of the permit.

C. The permit shall be evidenced by a certificate, issued by the Commissioner, which shall show the date of issuance, the person to whom issued, the motor number, serial number or identification number of the vehicle on which the license plates are to be used, and shall be in the immediate possession of the person operating the vehicle at all times while operating it. The certificate shall be valid for a period of five days from its issuance. On its expiration, application may be made for a renewal permit in the manner provided for the original permit, but only one renewal permit shall be issued to cover any one emergency.

D. The Commissioner may, subject to the limitations and conditions set forth in this section, authorize a motor vehicle dealer licensed in the Commonwealth to issue such permit on behalf of the Commissioner in accordance with the provisions of subsections A, B, and C of this section provided such permits are issued only with regard to the transfer in an emergency situation of license plates from a vehicle undergoing repairs in that dealer's repair shop. Any dealer to whom the authority is delegated by the Commissioner shall use the forms provided by the Commissioner and shall maintain in permanent form a record of all permits issued by him and any other relevant information that may be required by the Commissioner. Each record shall be kept by the dealer for not less than three years from the date of entry. The dealer shall allow full access to these records, during regular business hours, to duly authorized representatives of the Department and to law-enforcement officers. One copy of any permit of this kind issued by a dealer and the application form submitted for the permit shall be filed promptly by the dealer with the Department. The Commissioner, on determining that the provisions of this section or the directions of the Department are not being complied with by a dealer, may suspend the right of such dealer to issue license plate transfer permits.

History.
Code 1950, § 46-104.1; 1952, c. 537; 1958, c. 541, § 46.1-110; 1978, c. 289; 1989, c. 727.

§ 46.2-720. Use of license plates from another vehicle in certain circumstances.

The owner of a motor vehicle to which license plates have been assigned by the Department may remove the license plates from the motor vehicle and use them on another motor vehicle owned by a person operating a garage or owned by a motor vehicle dealer provided such use does not extend for more than five days and provided the use is limited to the time during which the first motor vehicle is being repaired or while the second motor vehicle is loaned to him for demonstration, as provided by § 46.2-719.

For the purposes of this section, the term "motor vehicle" does not include a "moped" as defined in § 46.2-100.

History.
1960, c. 457, § 46.1-110.1; 1989, c. 727; 2013, c. 783.

§ 46.2-721. Application of liability insurance policy to vehicle carrying plates from insured vehicle.

The policy of liability insurance issued to the owner of a motor vehicle and covering the operation thereof shall extend to and be the primary insurance applicable to his operation of a motor vehicle on which he has placed license tags from another motor vehicle as provided in § 46.2-720.

For the purposes of this section, the term "motor vehicle" does not include a "moped" as defined in § 46.2-100.

History.
1960, c. 457, § 46.1-110.2; 1989, c. 727; 2013, c. 783.

§ 46.2-722. Altered or forged license plates or decals; use as evidence of knowledge.

Any person who, with fraudulent intent, alters any license plate or decal issued by the Department or by any other state, forges or counterfeits any license plate or decal purporting to have been issued by the Department under the provisions of this title or by any other state under a similar law or who, with fraudulent intent, alters, falsifies, or forges any assignment thereof, or who holds or uses any license plate or decal knowing it to have been altered, forged, or falsified, shall be guilty of a Class 1 misdemeanor.

The owner of a vehicle who operates it while it displays altered or forged license plates or decals shall be presumed to have knowledge of the alteration or forgery.

History.
Code 1950, § 46-12; 1958, c. 541, § 46.1-112; 1972, c. 609; 1982, c. 247; 1989, c. 727.

§ 46.2-723. License plates for transporting mobile homes used as temporary offices at construction sites.

The Department shall issue to persons engaged in the business of transporting from one construction site to another mobile homes or house trailers used on those sites as temporary offices, license plates to be affixed to such mobile homes or house trailers while being transported. The plates shall not be issued or used to transport mobile homes or house trailers which exceed normally permissible load dimensions. The fee for each plate issued under this section shall be twenty-two dollars per year.

History.
1986, c. 226, § 46.1-44.1; 1989, c. 727.

§ 46.2-724. Operation for hire of certain vehicles registered as not-for-hire; penalty.

If a motor vehicle of over 10,000 pounds registered gross weight that is registered to be operated exclusively not-for-hire is operated for-hire, the licensee shall be guilty of a traffic infraction. This penalty shall be in addition to the penalty prescribed by § 46.2-704.

History.
Code 1950, § 46-168; 1950, p. 625; 1956, c. 477; 1958, c. 541, § 46.1-160; 1978, c. 605; 1982, c. 672; 1989, c. 727; 1995, c. 46; 1997, cc. 774, 816.

ARTICLE 10.
SPECIAL LICENSE PLATES.

§ 46.2-725. Special license plates, generally.

A. No series of special license plates shall be created or issued by the Commissioner or the Department except as authorized pursuant to this article. No special license plates in any series not provided for pursuant to this article and no registration decal for any such license plate shall be issued, reissued, or renewed on or after July 1, 1995. However, subject to the limitations contained in subdivisions 1 and 2 of subsection B of this section, the Commissioner may issue, when feasible, special license plates that are combinations of no more than two series of special license plates authorized pursuant to this article and currently issued by the Department; in addition to the state registration fee, the fee for any such combination shall be equal to the sum of the fees for the two series plus the fee for reserved numbers and letters, if applicable. The provisions of subdivisions 1 and 2 of subsection B of this section shall not apply to special license plates that are combinations of two series of special license plates authorized pursuant to this article and currently issued by the Department if one of the two combined designs, when feasible, incorporates or includes the international symbol of access.

B. Except as otherwise provided in this article:

1. No special license plates shall be considered for authorization by the General Assembly unless and until the individual, group, entity, organization, or

other entity seeking the authorization of such special license plates shall have demonstrated to the satisfaction of the General Assembly that they meet the issuance requirements set forth in this subdivision. For the purposes of this article, each prepaid application shall be on a form prescribed by the Department and, excluding the vehicle registration fee, shall include the proposed or authorized fee for the issuance of the proposed or authorized special license plates and, if applicable, the annual fee for reserved numbers or letters prescribed under § 46.2-726. Once authorized by the General Assembly, no license plates provided for in this article shall be developed and issued by the Department until the Commissioner receives at least 450 prepaid applications therefor within 30 days of the effective date of the authorization associated with the applications. If the end of the 30-day period falls on a Saturday, Sunday, or holiday, the 30-day period shall end on the following business day.

2. No additional license plates shall be issued or reissued in any series that, after five or more years of issuance, has fewer than 200 active sets of plates. No such license plates shall be issued or reissued unless reauthorized by the General Assembly. Such reauthorized license plates shall remain subject to the provisions of this article.

3. The annual fee for the issuance of any license plates issued pursuant to this article shall be $10 plus the prescribed fee for state license plates. Applications for all special license plates issued pursuant to this article shall be on forms prescribed by the Commissioner. All special license plates issued pursuant to this article shall be of designs prescribed by the Commissioner and shall bear unique letters and numerals, clearly distinguishable from any other license plate designs, and be readily identifiable by law-enforcement personnel.

No other state license plates shall be required on any vehicles bearing special license plates issued under the provisions of this article.

All fees collected by the Department under this article shall be paid by the Commissioner into the state treasury and shall be set aside as a special fund to be used to meet the expenses of the Department.

C. The provisions of this article relating to registration fees shall apply only to those vehicles registered as passenger cars, motor homes, and pick-up or panel trucks, as defined in § 46.2-100. All other vehicle types registered with special license plates shall be subject to the appropriate special license plate fees, registration fees and other fees prescribed by law for such vehicle types.

D. For special license plates that generate revenues that are shared with entities other than the Department, hereinafter referred to as "revenue sharing special license plates," the General Assembly shall review all proposed revenue sharing special license plate authorizations to determine whether the revenues are to be shared with entities or organizations that (i) provide to the Commonwealth or its citizens a broad public service that is to be funded, in whole or in part, by the proposed revenue sharing special license plate authorization and (ii) are at least one of the following:

1. A nonprofit corporation as defined in § 501(c)(3) of the United States Internal Revenue Code;

2. An agency, board, commission, or other entity established or operated by the Commonwealth;

3. A political subdivision of the Commonwealth; or

4. An institution of higher education whose main campus is located in Virginia.

No revenue sharing special license plate authorization shall be approved if, as determined by the General Assembly, it does not meet the criteria set forth in this subsection.

E. No special license plates authorized pursuant to this article shall be issued to or renewed for any owner or co-owner of a vehicle who is registered pursuant to the Sex Offender and Crimes Against Minors Registry Act (§ 9.1-900 et seq.) if the design of such special license plates, including any logo, emblem, seal, or symbol therein, references children or children's programs or if any revenue-sharing provision authorized for such special license plates contributes, directly or indirectly, to any fund or program established for the benefit of children.

History.

1989, c. 727; 1995, c. 747; 1996, cc. 922, 1026; 1997, cc. 774, 816; 2003, c. 923; 2004, c. 747; 2005, c. 294; 2006, c. 550; 2011, c. 115; 2016, cc. 143, 430.

§ 46.2-725.1: Repealed by Acts 1995, c. 747.

§ 46.2-725.2. Special license plates for certain business entities with fleets of vehicles registered in the Commonwealth.

A. Notwithstanding the provisions of §§ 46.2-725 and 46.2-726, upon application by certain business entities with vehicle fleets registered in the Commonwealth, the Commissioner may develop and issue special license plates bearing the logos of such businesses in accordance with policies and procedures established by the Commissioner for the issuance of license plates and in accordance with the following provisions:

1. Any business wishing to obtain these special license plates must (i) have a fleet of at least 100 vehicles registered in the Commonwealth, (ii) utilize one of the Department's online electronic fleet titling and registration systems to obtain title and registration documents for its vehicles, and (iii) enter into an agreement with the Department for the use of the business's logo.

2. Any business that enters into an agreement with the Department for the issuance of license plates under this section thereby waives any royalty

fees to which it might otherwise be entitled for use of its logo.

3. Any initial request for license plates under this section shall be accompanied by an administrative fee as follows: (i) for 100-199 vehicles in a fleet, a fee of $4,500; (ii) for 200-349 vehicles in a fleet, a fee of $4,200; or (iii) for more than 349 vehicles in a fleet, a fee of $4,000.

4. For each set of license plates issued under this section without reserved numbers or letters, the Commissioner shall charge, in addition to the prescribed fee for state license plates, a one-time fee of $5. The fee for a replacement set of license plates issued under this section without reserved numbers or letters shall be $5.

5. For each set of license plates issued under this section with reserved letters or numbers as provided for in § 46.2-726, in lieu of the fees prescribed by that section, the Commissioner shall charge, in addition to the prescribed fee for state license plates, a one-time fee of $15. The fee for a replacement set of license plates issued under this section with reserved numbers or letters shall be $15.

B. License plates may be issued under this section to vehicles of any type registered by the Department, including those registered under the International Registration Plan.

C. 1. Subsequent to the development of license plates for a business pursuant to subsection A, a business may agree to permit the use of such plates on vehicles not in the company fleet. Written authorization from the business shall be required to obtain or retain any license plates issued pursuant to this subsection. The business may withdraw any such authorization at any time.

2. Upon receipt of written authorization and an application, the Commissioner shall issue to the applicant license plates bearing the logo of the business. The annual fee for each set of license plates issued under this subsection shall be $10 plus the prescribed fee for state license plates. For each set of license plates issued under this subsection bearing reserved numbers or letters, the annual fee shall be the same as for those issued under § 46.2-726.

3. The fee for a replacement set of license plates issued under this subsection shall be as required by § 46.2-692.

4. License plates issued under this subsection shall not be issued through one of the Department's online electronic fleet titling and registration systems.

5. The provisions of subdivisions B 1 and 2 of § 46.2-725 shall not apply to license plates issued under this subsection.

History.

2011, c. 56; 2012, cc. 22, 111.

§ 46.2-726. License plates with reserved numbers or letters; fees.

The Commissioner may, in his discretion, reserve license plates with certain registration numbers or letters or combinations thereof for issuance to persons requesting license plates so numbered and lettered. However, no such reserved license plates shall be issued to or renewed for any owner or co-owner of a vehicle who is registered pursuant to the Sex Offender and Crimes Against Minors Registry Act (§ 9.1-900 et seq.) if the requested registration numbers or letters or combination thereof could be read, interpreted, or understood to be a reference to children.

License plates with reserved numbers or letters may be issued for and displayed on emergency medical services vehicles operated by emergency medical services agencies.

The annual fee or, in the case of permanent license plates for trailers and semitrailers, the one-time fee, for the issuance of any license plates with reserved numbers or letters shall be $10 plus the prescribed fee for state license plates. If those license plates with reserved numbers or letters are subject to an additional fee beyond the prescribed fee for state license plates, the fee for such special license plates with reserved numbers or letters shall be $10 plus the additional fee for the special license plates plus the prescribed fee for state license plates.

The annual fee for reissuing license plates with the same combination of letters and numbers as license plates that were previously issued but not renewed shall be $10 plus the prescribed fee for state license plates. If those license plates are special license plates subject to an additional fee beyond the prescribed fee for state license plates, the fee shall be $10 plus the additional fee for the special license plates plus the prescribed fee for state license plates.

History.

1972, c. 427, § 46.1-105.2; 1987, c. 696; 1989, c. 727; 1992, c. 141; 1995, c. 747; 1997, cc. 94, 283; 2000, c. 126; 2001, c. 20; 2015, cc. 502, 503; 2016, cc. 143, 430.

§ 46.2-727. Bicentennial license plates and decals; fees.

Bicentennial license plates and decals issued to any properly registered passenger motor vehicle from January 1, 1976, through December 31, 1981, may continue in use for a period determined by the Commissioner if the proper fee is paid as required in § 46.2-694.

History.

1975, c. 206, § 46.1-105.5; 1980, c. 24; 1989, c. 727.

§ 46.2-728. Special license plates incorporating the Great Seal of Virginia; fees.

On receipt of an application, the Commissioner shall issue license plates incorporating the Great Seal of Virginia. These license plates shall be valid for whatever period the Commissioner determines.

For each set of license plates issued under this section the Commissioner shall charge, in addition to the prescribed cost of state license plates, a one-time fee of twenty-five dollars.

History.
1985, c. 547, § 46.1-105.14; 1987, c. 696; 1989, c. 727.

§ 46.2-728.1. Special license plates incorporating the official bird and the floral emblem of the Commonwealth; fee.

On receipt of an application, the Commissioner shall issue license plates incorporating the official bird and the floral emblem of the Commonwealth. These license plates shall be valid for whatever period the Commissioner determines.

For each set of license plates issued under this section the Commissioner shall charge, in addition to the prescribed cost of state license plates, a one-time fee of ten dollars at the time the plates are issued.

History.
1992, cc. 142, 631.

§ 46.2-728.2. Special license plates displaying a scenic design of Virginia; fees.

On receipt of an application, the Commissioner shall issue license plates displaying a scenic design of Virginia. These license plates shall be valid for whatever period the Commissioner determines.

For each set of license plates issued under this section the Commissioner shall charge, in addition to the prescribed cost of state license plates, a one-time fee of ten dollars at the time the plates are issued.

History.
1992, cc. 142, 631.

§ 46.2-728.3. Special license plates displaying the official insect of the Commonwealth; fees.

On receipt of an application, the Commissioner shall issue license plates displaying the official insect of the Commonwealth as designated by § 1-510.

History.
1994, c. 183; 1995, c. 747; 2005, c. 839.

§ 46.2-729: Repealed by Acts 1995, c. 747.

§ 46.2-729.1. Presidential inauguration license plates.

Notwithstanding any other provisions of law, presidential inauguration license plates duly issued by the District of Columbia may be displayed on any motor vehicle duly registered and licensed in Virginia in lieu of license plates assigned to that motor vehicle. Such presidential license plates shall not be displayed except for the period beginning January 1 through the last day of March in the year of such inauguration.

History.
1997, cc. 774, 816.

§ 46.2-730. License plates for antique motor vehicles and antique trailers; fee.

A. On receipt of an application and evidence that the applicant owns or has regular use of another passenger car, autocycle, or motorcycle, the Commissioner shall issue appropriately designed license plates to owners of antique motor vehicles and antique trailers. These license plates shall be valid so long as title to the vehicle is vested in the applicant. The fee for the registration card and license plates of any of these vehicles shall be a one-time fee of $50.

B. On receipt of an application and evidence that the applicant owns or has regular use of another passenger car, autocycle, or motorcycle, the Commissioner may authorize for use on antique motor vehicles and antique trailers Virginia license plates manufactured prior to 1976 and designed for use without decals, if such license plates are embossed with or are of the same year of issue as the model year of the antique motor vehicle or antique trailer on which they are to be displayed. Original metal year tabs issued in place of license plates for years 1943 and 1952 and used with license plates issued in 1942 and 1951, respectively, also may be authorized by the Commissioner for use on antique motor vehicles and antique trailers that are of the same model year as the year the metal tab was originally issued. These license plates and metal tabs shall remain valid so long as title to the vehicle is vested in the applicant. The fee for the registration card and permission to use the license plates and metal tabs on any of these vehicles shall be a one-time fee of $50. If more than one request is made for use, as provided in this section, of license plates having the same number, the Department shall accept only the first such application.

C. Notwithstanding the provisions of §§ 46.2-711 and 46.2-715, antique motor vehicles may display single license plates if the original manufacturer's design of the antique motor vehicles allows for the use of only single license plates or if the license plate was originally issued in one of the following years and is displayed in accordance with the provisions of subsection B: 1906, 1907, 1908, 1909, 1945, or 1946.

D. Antique motor vehicles and antique trailers registered with license plates issued or authorized for use under this section shall not be used for general transportation purposes, including, but not limited to, daily travel to and from the owner's place of employment, but shall only be used:

1. For participation in club activities, exhibits, tours, parades, and similar events;

2. On the highways of the Commonwealth for the purpose of testing their operation or selling the vehicle or trailer, obtaining repairs or maintenance, transportation to and from events as described in subdivision 1, and for occasional pleasure driving not exceeding 250 miles from the residence of the owner; and

3. To carry or transport (i) passengers in the antique motor vehicles, (ii) personal effects in the antique motor vehicles and antique trailers, or (iii) other antique motor vehicles being transported for show purposes.

The registration card issued to an antique motor vehicle or an antique trailer registered pursuant to subsections A, B, and C shall indicate such vehicle or trailer is for limited use.

E. Owners of motor vehicles and trailers applying for registration pursuant to subsections A, B and C shall submit to the Department, in the manner prescribed by the Department, certifications that such vehicles or trailers are capable of being safely operated on the highways of the Commonwealth.

Pursuant to § 46.2-1000, the Department shall suspend the registration of any vehicle or trailer registered with license plates issued under this section that the Department or the Department of State Police determines is not properly equipped or otherwise unsafe to operate. Any law-enforcement officer shall take possession of the license plates, registration card and decals, if any, of any vehicle or trailer registered with license plates issued under this section when he observes any defect in such vehicle or trailer as set forth in § 46.2-1000.

F. Antique motor vehicles and antique trailers displaying license plates issued or authorized for use pursuant to subsections B and C may be used for general transportation purposes if the following conditions are met:

1. The physical condition of the vehicle's license plate or plates has been inspected and approved by the Department;

2. The license plate or plates are registered to the specific vehicle by the Department;

3. The owner of the vehicle periodically registers the vehicle with the Department and pays a registration fee for the vehicle equal to that which would be charged to obtain regular state license plates for that vehicle;

4. The vehicle passes a periodic safety inspection as provided in Article 21 (§ 46.2-1157 et seq.) of Chapter 10;

5. The vehicle displays current decals attached to the license plate, issued by the Department, indicating the valid registration period for the vehicle; and

6. When applicable, the vehicle meets the requirement of Article 22 (§ 46.2-1176 et seq.) of Chapter 10.

If more than one request is made for use, as provided in this subsection, of license plates having the same number, the Department shall accept only the first such application. Only vehicles titled to the person seeking to use license plates as provided in this subsection shall be eligible to use license plates as provided in this subsection.

G. Nothing in this section shall be construed as prohibiting the use of an antique motor vehicle to tow a trailer or semitrailer.

H. Any owner of an antique motor vehicle or antique trailer registered with license plates pursuant to this section who is convicted of a violation of this section is guilty of a Class 4 misdemeanor. Upon receiving a record of conviction of a violation of this section, the Department shall revoke and not reinstate the owner's privilege to register the vehicle operated in violation of this section with license plates issued or authorized for use pursuant to this section for a period of five years from the date of conviction.

I. Except for the one-time $50 registration fee prescribed in subsections A and B, the provisions of this section shall apply to all owners of vehicles and trailers registered with license plates issued under this section prior to July 1, 2007. Such owners shall, based on a schedule and a manner prescribed by the Department, (i) provide evidence that they own or have regular use of another passenger car or motorcycle, as required under subsections A and B, and (ii) comply with the certification provisions of subsection E. The Department shall cancel the registrations of vehicles owned by persons that, prior to January 1, 2008, do not provide the Department (i) evidence of owning or having regular use of another autocycle, passenger car, or motorcycle as required under subsections A and B, and (ii) the certification required pursuant to subsection E.

History.

Code 1950, § 46-99.1; 1954, c. 60; 1958, c. 541, § 46.1-104; 1980, c. 359; 1986, c. 8; 1989, cc. 338, 727; 1999, c. 292; 2000, c. 259; 2004, c. 796; 2007, c. 492; 2008, c. 159; 2014, cc. 53, 256.

§ 46.2-731. Disabled parking license plates; owners of vehicles specially equipped and used to transport persons with disabilities; fees.

On receipt of an application, the Commissioner shall issue appropriately designed disabled parking license plates to persons with physical disabilities that limit or impair their ability to walk or that create a concern for his safety while walking or to the parents or legal guardians of such persons. The Commissioner shall request that the application be accompanied by a certification signed by a licensed physician, licensed podiatrist, licensed chiropractor, licensed nurse practitioner, or licensed physician assistant that the applicant meets the definition of "person with a disability that limits or impairs his ability to walk" contained in § 46.2-1240. The issuance of a disabled parking license plate shall not preclude the issuance of a permanent removable windshield placard.

On application of an organization, the Commissioner shall issue disabled parking license plates for vehicles registered in the applicant's name if the vehicles are primarily used to transport persons with disabilities. The application shall include a certification by the applicant, under criteria determined by the Commissioner, that the vehicle is primarily used to transport persons with disabilities that limit or impair their ability to walk, as defined in § 46.2-1240.

The fee for the issuance of a disabled parking license plate under this section may not exceed the fee charged for a similar license plate for the same class vehicle.

History.

1972, c. 473, § 46.1-104.1; 1973, c. 182; 1974, cc. 46, 410; 1976, cc. 410, 460; 1978, cc. 185, 605; 1982, c. 88; 1983, c. 38; 1986, c. 144; 1989, c. 727; 1993, c. 566; 1994, cc. 225, 866; 1995, cc. 776, 805; 1997, cc. 783, 904; 2004, c. 692; 2007, c. 715.

§ 46.2-732. Special license plates and decals for the deaf; fees.

On receipt of an application, the Commissioner shall issue appropriately designed license plates to deaf persons. For purposes of this section, a deaf person shall be defined as a person who cannot hear and understand normal speech. The fee for these license plates shall be as provided in § 46.2-694.

The Commissioner shall also issue to any deaf person a removable decal, to be used on any passenger car, pickup or panel truck operated by such person. The decals shall be of a design determined by the Commissioner and shall be displayed in a manner determined by the Superintendent of State Police. A reasonable fee to be determined by the Commissioner shall be charged each person issued a decal under this section, but no fee shall be charged any person exempted from fees by § 46.2-739.

It shall be unlawful for any person who is not a person described in this section to willfully and falsely represent himself as having the qualifications to obtain the special plates or decal.

The provisions of subdivisions 1 and 2 of subsection B of § 46.2-725 shall not apply to license plates issued under this section.

History.

1979, c. 74, § 46.1-104.2; 1989, c. 727; 1995, c. 747.

§ 46.2-733. License plates for persons delivering unladen vehicles; fees.

A. On receipt of an application, the Commissioner shall issue appropriately designed license plates to persons engaged in the business of delivering unladen motor vehicles under their own power from points of assembly or distribution.

B. Every applicant for license plates to be issued under this section shall, before he begins delivery of any of these vehicles, apply to the Commissioner for a registration card and license plates. On the payment of a fee of $75, a registration card and license plates shall be issued to the applicant in a form prescribed by the Commissioner. The Commissioner shall issue to the applicant two license plates. For each additional license plate, a fee of $20 per plate shall be paid by the applicant.

C. It shall be unlawful for any person to use these license plates other than on unladen motor vehicles, trailers, and semitrailers which are being delivered from points of assembly or distribution in the usual course of his delivery business or which are used as provided in subsection D of this section. The operators of such vehicles being delivered, bearing license plates issued under this section, shall at all times during their operation have in their possession a proper bill of lading showing the point of origin and destination of the vehicle being delivered and describing it. It shall be unlawful for any person to use these license plates unless either the origin or the destination of the vehicle being delivered is within the Commonwealth.

D. License plates issued under this section may be used by any financial institutions specifically excluded from the definition of "motor vehicle dealer" in subdivision 5 of § 46.2-1500 for the purpose of using them in the normal course of business in taking, repossessing, or otherwise transporting vehicles for the purpose of preservation, sale, allowing a prospective buyer to test-drive the vehicle if the prospective buyer is accompanied by an employee of the financial institution or has the written permission of the financial institution on a form provided by the Department, or otherwise in connection with repossession or foreclosure of the vehicle on which there is a security interest securing a loan to a financial institution.

E. License plates issued under this section may be issued to any business engaged in automobile auctions or the mounting, installing, servicing, or repairing of equipment on or in a vehicle. The use of license plates issued under this section shall be limited to (i) the pick up and delivery of a vehicle or (ii) driving on the highway in order to test the installation, service, or repairs at a distance of not more than five miles from the place of business and shall not be used on vehicles employed for general transportation.

History.

Code 1950, § 46-170; 1958, c. 541, § 46.1-162; 1964, c. 218; 1977, c. 260; 1982, c. 161; 1984, c. 464; 1989, c. 727; 1998, c. 370; 2004, c. 788; 2011, c. 103.

§ 46.2-734. Reconstructed and specially constructed vehicles; inspection requirements; storage of unlicensed vehicles; use.

A. On receipt of an application therefor and written evidence that the applicant is a hobbyist and is registering a reconstructed or specially constructed vehicle built, reconstructed, restored, preserved, and maintained for historic or hobby interest, the Commissioner shall issue to the applicant one special license plate, which shall be mounted on the rear of the vehicle.

For the purposes of this section, "hobbyist" means the owner of one or more reconstructed or specially constructed vehicles who collects, purchases, acquires, trades, or disposes of reconstructed or specially constructed vehicles or parts thereof for his own use in order to build, reconstruct, restore, preserve, and maintain a reconstructed or specially constructed vehicle for historic or hobby interest.

B. These vehicles shall be titled according to their chassis numbers or, if no chassis number exists, then by their motor serial numbers. The vehicles shall meet inspection requirements applicable to the model year shown on the registration certificate.

C. A hobbyist may store unlicensed, operable or inoperable, vehicles on his property provided the vehicles and the outdoor storage area are maintained in such a manner that they do not constitute a health hazard and are screened from ordinary public view by a fence, rapidly growing trees, shrubbery, billboards or other appropriate means. The hobbyist shall, however, not be exempt from local zoning ordinances governing the storage of these vehicles.

D. Vehicles registered under this section shall not be used for general transportation purposes, including but not limited to daily travel to and from the owner's place of employment, but shall only be used (i) for participation in hobbyist vehicle exhibits and similar limited-use events and (ii) on the highways of the Commonwealth for the purpose of testing their operation, obtaining repairs or maintenance, and transportation to and from events as described in this subsection.

History.

1979, c. 159, § 46.1-53.1; 1989, c. 727; 2004, c. 678.

§ 46.2-734.1: Repealed by Acts 2002, c. 90, cl. 2.

§ 46.2-735. Special license plates for members of volunteer emergency medical services agencies and members of volunteer emergency medical services agency auxiliaries; fees.

The Commissioner, on application, shall supply members of volunteer emergency medical services agencies and members of volunteer emergency medical services agency auxiliaries special license plates bearing the letters "R S" followed by numbers or letters or any combination thereof.

Only one application shall be required from each volunteer emergency medical services agency or volunteer emergency medical services agency auxiliary. The application shall contain the names and residence addresses of all members of the volunteer emergency medical services agency and members of the volunteer emergency medical services agency auxiliary who request license plates. The Commissioner shall charge the prescribed cost of state license plates for each set of license plates issued under this section.

History.

1972, c. 605, § 46.1-105.3; 1978, c. 201; 1987, c. 696; 1989, c. 727; 1996, c. 1026; 2015, cc. 502, 503.

§ 46.2-736. Special license plates for professional or volunteer fire fighters and members of volunteer fire department auxiliaries; fees.

The Commissioner, on application, shall supply professional fire fighters, members of volunteer fire departments, members of volunteer fire department auxiliaries, and volunteer members of any fire department license plates bearing the letters "F D" followed by numbers or letters or any combination thereof.

An application shall be required from each professional fire fighter, volunteer fire fighter, or member of a volunteer fire department auxiliary. The application shall be approved by the chief or head of the fire department and shall contain the name and residence address of the applicant. The Commissioner shall charge each professional fire fighter a fee of one dollar in addition to the prescribed cost of state license plates, for each set of license plates issued under this section. No additional fee shall be charged to members of volunteer fire departments, members of volunteer fire department auxiliaries, or volunteer members of any fire department.

History.

1973, c. 190, § 46.1-105.4; 1975, c. 25; 1976, cc. 460, 500; 1978, c. 201; 1987, c. 696; 1989, c. 727; 1996, c. 1026.

§§ 46.2-736.01, 46.2-736.02: Repealed by Acts 2004, c. 717.

§ 46.2-736.1. Special license plates for certain officials; fees.

On request, the Commissioner shall issue special license plates to the following officials: the Speaker of the House of Delegates, members of the House of Delegates, members of the Virginia Senate, the Clerk of the House of Delegates, the Clerk of the Virginia Senate, the Governor of Virginia, the Lieutenant Governor of Virginia, the Attorney General of Virginia, United States Congressmen, and United States Senators.

The annual fee for license plates issued pursuant to this section shall be $25 plus the prescribed fees for (i) vehicle registration and (ii) license plates with reserved numbers or letters.

The provisions of subdivisions 1 and 2 of subsection B of § 46.2-725 shall not apply to license plates issued under this section.

History.

1995, c. 747; 2005, c. 300.

§ 46.2-736.2. Special license plates for certain elected or appointed officials.

The Commissioner, on application, shall issue to honorary consuls, upon receipt of written evidence from the United States Department of State that the applicant is an honorary consul on active status, and members of county boards of supervisors, city councils, town councils, state commissions and boards and to other state officials appointed by the Governor special license plates bearing decals or stickers bearing the legend "HONORARY CONSUL" or identifying the commission, board, or office to which the applicant has been elected or appointed.

For the purposes of subdivision B 2 of § 46.2-725, the total number of active plates issued under this section shall be used to determine whether the plates authorized under this section shall continue to be issued.

History.

1995, c. 747; 1996, c. 1026; 2003, c. 921; 2004, c. 747.

§ 46.2-737. Special license plates for certain constitutional officers; fees.

The Commissioner, on application, shall issue to sheriffs, county and city treasurers and commissioners of the revenue, attorneys for the Commonwealth, circuit court clerks, and general registrars special license plates identifying the office held by the applicant.

The annual fee for license plates issued pursuant to this section shall be $25 plus the prescribed fees for (i) vehicle registration and (ii) license plates with reserved numbers or letters.

The provisions of subdivisions 1 and 2 of subsection B of § 46.2-725 shall not apply to license plates issued under this section.

History.

1976, c. 147, § 46.1-105.6; 1987, c. 696; 1989, c. 727; 1995, c. 747; 2004, c. 984; 2005, c. 300.

§ 46.2-738. Special license plates for amateur radio operators.

The Commissioner, on request, may supply any amateur radio operator licensed by the federal government or an agency thereof with license plates bearing his official call letters.

If more than one request is made for use, as provided in this section, of license plates having the same alpha-numeric, the Department shall accept the first such application. Persons receiving amateur radio operator special license plates shall affix such plates only to vehicles to which they are the titled owner.

The Commissioner shall charge a fee of one dollar in addition to the prescribed cost of state license plates for each set of license plates issued under the provisions of this section.

History.

Code 1950, § 46-22.1; 1952, c. 675; 1954, c. 630; 1958, c. 541, § 46.1-105; 1987, c. 696; 1989, c. 727; 1996, cc. 943, 994; 2014, c. 331.

§ 46.2-738.1: Repealed by Acts 2002, c. 90, cl. 2.

§ 46.2-739. Special license plates for certain disabled veterans; fees.

A. On receipt of an application, the Commissioner shall issue special license plates to applicants who are veterans who have been certified by the U.S. Department of Veterans Affairs to have a service-connected disability or unremarried surviving spouses of disabled veterans as defined in § 46.2-100. These license plates shall be special permanent red, white, and blue license plates bearing the letters "DV." The application shall be accompanied by a certification from the U.S. Department of Veterans Affairs that the veteran's disability is service-connected. License plates issued under this subsection shall not permit the vehicles upon which they are displayed to use parking spaces reserved for persons with disabilities that limit or impair their ability to walk.

B. On receipt of an application, the Commissioner shall issue special DV disabled parking license plates displaying the international symbol of access in the same size as the numbers and letters on the plate and in a color that contrasts to the background to veterans who are also persons with disabilities that limit or impair their ability to walk as defined in § 46.2-100. The Commissioner shall require that such application be accompanied by a certification signed by a licensed physician, licensed podiatrist, licensed chiropractor, licensed nurse practitioner, or licensed physician assistant to that effect. Special DV disabled parking license plates issued under this subsection shall authorize the vehicles upon which they are displayed to use parking spaces reserved for persons with disabilities that limit or impair their ability to walk.

C. No annual registration fee, as prescribed in § 46.2-694, and no annual fee, as set forth in subdivision B 3 of § 46.2-725, shall be required for any one motor vehicle owned and used personally by any disabled veteran as defined in § 46.2-100 or the unremarried surviving spouse of such disabled veteran, provided that such vehicle displays license plates issued under this section.

D. The provisions of subdivisions B 1 and 2 of § 46.2-725 shall not apply to license plates issued under this section.

History.

1972, c. 80, § 46.1-149.1; 1976, c. 410; 1977, c. 167; 1989, c. 727; 1994, c. 866; 1995, c. 747; 1997, cc. 774, 816; 2007, c. 715; 2015, c. 457.

§ 46.2-740. Special license plates for survivors of Battle of Chosin Reservoir.

On receipt of an application and written evidence that the applicant is a survivor of the Battle of Chosin Reservoir, the Commissioner shall issue special license plates to the applicant.

The provisions of subdivisions 1 and 2 of subsection B of § 46.2-725 shall not apply to license plates issued under this section.

History.

1987, c. 669, § 46.1-105.17; 1989, c. 727; 1995, c. 747.

§ 46.2-741. Special license plates for survivors of attack on Pearl Harbor; fees.

On receipt of an application and written evidence that the applicant is an honorably discharged former member of one of the armed forces of the United States and, while serving in the armed forces of the United States, was present during the attack on the island of Oahu, Territory of Hawaii, on December 7, 1941, between the hours of 7:55 a.m. and 9:45 a.m., Hawaii time, the Commissioner shall issue to the applicant special license plates identifying the vehicle as registered to a Pearl Harbor survivor.

For each set of license plates issued under this section, the Commissioner shall charge, in addition to the prescribed cost of state license plates, a one-time fee of ten dollars at the time the plates are issued.

The provisions of subdivisions 1 and 2 of subsection B of § 46.2-725 shall not apply to license plates issued under this section.

History.

1987, c. 467, § 46.1-105.16; 1989, c. 727; 1995, c. 747; 1997, cc. 774, 816.

§ 46.2-742. Special license plates for persons awarded Purple Heart; fee.

On receipt of an application and written evidence that the applicant has been awarded the Purple Heart, the Commissioner shall issue to the applicant special license plates.

No fee shall be charged for license plates issued under this section to any one motor vehicle owned and used personally by any applicant. For each additional set of license plates issued to an applicant under this section, the Commissioner shall charge the prescribed fee for state license plates.

Unremarried surviving spouses of persons eligible to receive special license plates under this section may also be issued special license plates under this section.

The provisions of subdivisions 1 and 2 of subsection B of § 46.2-725 shall not apply to license plates issued under this section.

The design of license plates issued under this section to persons who have been awarded multiple decorations shall reflect the number of such decorations.

History.

1987, cc. 466, 472, § 46.1-105.15; 1989, c. 727; 1994, c. 914; 1995, c. 747; 1996, cc. 922, 1026; 2004, c. 747; 2008, c. 614; 2011, c. 436.

§ 46.2-742.1. Special license plates for persons awarded the Bronze Star, Bronze Star with a "V" for valor, or the Silver Star; fee.

On receipt of an application and written evidence that the applicant has been awarded a Bronze Star, Bronze Star with a "V" for valor, or Silver Star Medal, the Commissioner shall issue to the applicant special license plates.

For each set of license plates issued under this section, the Commissioner shall charge, in addition to the prescribed cost of state license plates, a one-time fee of $10 at the time the plates are issued.

The provisions of subdivisions 1 and 2 of subsection B of § 46.2-725 shall not apply to license plates issued under this section.

The design of license plates issued under this section to persons who have been awarded multiple decorations shall reflect the number of such decorations.

Unremarried surviving spouses of persons eligible to receive special license plates under this section may also be issued special license plates under this section.

History.

1992, c. 577; 1995, c. 747; 1996, c. 1026; 1999, c. 907; 2002, c. 864; 2004, c. 747.

§ 46.2-742.1:1: Repealed by Acts 2011, c. 21.

§ 46.2-742.2. Special license plates for persons awarded the Navy Cross, the Distinguished Service Cross, the Air Force Cross, or the Distinguished Flying Cross.

On receipt of an application and written evidence that the applicant has been awarded the Navy Cross, the Distinguished Service Cross, the Air Force Cross, or the Distinguished Flying Cross, the Commissioner shall issue to the applicant special license plates.

The provisions of subdivisions 1 and 2 of subsection B of § 46.2-725 shall not apply to license plates issued under this section.

Unremarried surviving spouses of persons eligible to receive special license plates under this section may also be issued special license plates under this section.

The design of license plates issued under this section to persons who have been awarded multiple decorations shall reflect the number of such decorations.

For each set of license plates issued under this section the Commissioner shall charge, in addition to the prescribed cost of state license plates, a one-time fee of $10 at the time the plates are issued.

History.

1994, cc. 228, 301; 1995, c. 747; 1996, c. 1026; 1997, cc. 774, 816; 2004, c. 747.

§ **46.2-742.3:** Repealed by Acts 2004, c. 984.

Cross references.

For current provisions concerning special license plates for persons awarded the Combat Infantryman Badge, see § 46.2-742.4.

§ 46.2-742.4. Special license plates for persons awarded the Combat Infantryman Badge.

On receipt of an application and written evidence that the applicant has been awarded the Combat Infantryman Badge, the Commissioner shall issue to the applicant special license plates.

History.

2004, c. 984.

§ **46.2-742.5:** Repealed by Acts 2006, c. 437, cl. 2.

§ **46.2-742.6:** Repealed by Acts 2008, c. 114, cl. 1.

§ 46.2-743. Special license plates for active duty members of the armed forces of the United States and certain veterans; fees.

A. On receipt of an application and written evidence that the applicant is an honorably discharged former member of one of the armed forces of the United States, the Commissioner shall issue to the applicant special license plates.

B. On receipt of an application and written evidence that the applicant is on active duty with, has been honorably discharged after at least six months of active duty service in, or has retired from the United States Marine Corps, the Commissioner shall issue to the applicant special license plates whose design incorporates an emblem of the United States Marine Corps. Unremarried surviving spouses of persons eligible to receive special license plates under this subsection may also be issued special license plates under this subsection.

C. On receipt of an application and written evidence that the applicant is on active duty with, has been honorably discharged after at least six months of active duty service in, or has retired from the United States Army, the Commissioner shall issue to the applicant special license plates whose design incorporates an emblem of the United States Army.

D. On receipt of an application and written evidence that the applicant is on active duty with, has been honorably discharged after at least six months of active duty service in, or has retired from the United States Coast Guard, the Commissioner shall issue to the applicant special license plates whose design incorporates an emblem of the United States Coast Guard. Unremarried surviving spouses of persons eligible to receive special license plates under this subsection may also be issued special license plates under this subsection.

E. All special license plates that have been developed and issued pursuant to subsection B, C, or D shall also be issued to applicants who can provide documentation from the U.S. Department of Veterans Affairs indicating that the applicant has been designated disabled, and that his disability is service-connected, and that he has been honorably discharged from a branch of the armed forces of the United States.

F. On receipt of an application and written evidence that the applicant is a veteran of World War II, the Commissioner shall issue special license plates to veterans of World War II. For each set of license plates issued under this subsection, the Commissioner shall charge, in addition to the prescribed cost of state license plates, a one-time fee of $10 at the time the plates are issued.

G. On receipt of an application and written evidence that the applicant is a veteran of the Korean War, the Commissioner shall issue special license plates to veterans of the Korean War.

H. On receipt of an application and written evidence that the applicant is a veteran of the Vietnam War, the Commissioner shall issue special license plates to veterans of the Vietnam War.

I. On receipt of an application and written evidence that the applicant is a veteran of the Asiatic-Pacific Campaign, the Commissioner shall issue special license plates to veterans of that campaign. For each set of license plates issued under this subsection, the Commissioner shall charge, in addition to the prescribed cost of state license plates, a one-time fee of $10 at the time the plates are issued.

J. On receipt of an application and written evidence that the applicant is a veteran of Operation Iraqi Freedom, the Commissioner shall issue special license plates to veterans of Operation Iraqi Freedom.

K. On receipt of an application and written evidence that the applicant is a veteran of Operation Enduring Freedom, the Commissioner shall issue special license plates to veterans of Operation Enduring Freedom.

L. On receipt of an application and written evidence that the applicant is a member of the Virginia

Defense Force, the Commissioner shall issue special license plates to members of the Virginia Defense Force.

M. On receipt of an application and written evidence that the applicant is a veteran of Operation Desert Shield or Operation Desert Storm, the Commissioner shall issue special license plates to veterans of those military operations.

N. The provisions of subdivisions B 1 and B 2 of § 46.2-725 shall not apply to license plates issued under subsections F, G, H, J, K, L, and M.

History.

1985, c. 162, § 46.1-105.11; 1987, c. 696; 1989, c. 727; 1995, c. 747; 1996, c. 1026; 1997, cc. 774, 816; 1999, cc. 883, 907; 2000, cc. 75, 190; 2002, cc. 90, 864; 2005, cc. 264, 273, 929; 2006, c. 437; 2008, Sp. Sess. II, c. 4; 2009, c. 679; 2011, cc. 572, 586; 2012, c. 379; 2013, c. 478; 2014, cc. 270, 483.

§ 46.2-744. Special license plates for members of National Guard; fees.

On receipt of an application and written confirmation that the applicant is a member of the National Guard, the Commissioner shall issue to the applicant special license plates.

The fee for license plates issued under this section to members of the National Guard units shall be one-half the fee prescribed in § 46.2-694, unless the plates bear reserved numbers or letters as provided for in § 46.2-726. In this latter case, the fee for the issuance of license plates shall be the same as for those issued under § 46.2-726.

The fee for members of non-Virginia National Guard units shall be ten dollars per year plus the prescribed cost for state license plates, unless the plates bear reserved numbers or letters as provided for in § 46.2-726. In this latter case, such license plates shall be subject to an additional charge of ten dollars per year for the reserved numbers or letters.

The provisions of subdivisions 1 and 2 of subsection B of § 46.2-725 shall not apply to license plates issued under this section.

History.

1981, c. 355, § 46.1-105.9; 1982, c. 85; 1989, c. 727; 1995, cc. 252, 747.

§ 46.2-744.1: Repealed by Acts 2006, c. 437, cl. 2.

§ 46.2-745. Special license plates for persons awarded the Medal of Honor; fees.

On receipt of an application and written confirmation from one of the armed services that the applicant has been awarded the Medal of Honor, the Commissioner shall issue special license plates to such persons and to unremarried surviving spouses of such persons. No fee shall be charged for the issuance of these license plates.

It shall be unlawful for any person who is not a person described in this section to willfully and falsely represent himself as having the qualifications to obtain the special license plates herein provided for.

The provisions of subdivisions 1 and 2 of subsection B of § 46.2-725 shall not apply to license plates issued under this section.

The design of license plates issued under this section to persons who have been awarded multiple decorations shall reflect the number of such decorations.

Unremarried surviving spouses of persons eligible to receive special license plates under this section may also be issued special license plates under this section.

History.

1980, c. 55, § 46.1-105.8; 1989, c. 727; 1995, c. 747; 2004, c. 747.

§ 46.2-746. Special license plates for former prisoners of war; fees.

On receipt of an application and written evidence from one of the armed forces that the applicant was a prisoner of war and was honorably discharged, if not currently a member of the armed forces, the Commissioner shall issue special license plates to persons who have been prisoners of the enemy in any war. No fee shall be charged for license plates issued under the provisions of this section.

It shall be unlawful for any person to willfully and falsely represent himself as having the qualifications to obtain the special plates provided for in this section.

No individual shall be issued special license plates under this section for more than one vehicle.

On presentation of appropriate written evidence from the Foreign Claims Settlement Commission of the United States, special license plates provided for in this section shall also be issued by the Commissioner to persons who were not members of the armed forces.

Unremarried surviving spouses of persons eligible to receive special license plates under this section may also be issued special license plates under this section.

The provisions of subdivisions 1 and 2 of subsection B of § 46.2-725 shall not apply to license plates issued under this section.

History.

1977, c. 164, § 46.1-105.7; 1978, c. 605; 1981, c. 125; 1982, c. 199; 1987, c. 146; 1989, c. 727; 1994, c. 127; 1995, c. 747.

§ 46.2-746.01: Repealed by Acts 2002, c. 90, cl. 2.

§ 46.2-746.1. Special license plates for members of military assault forces.

On receipt of an application and written evidence that the applicant is or has been, while serving in the armed forces of the United States, a member of a military assault force, the Commissioner shall issue to the applicant special license plates. For the purposes of this section, a military assault force is a unit or element of the armed forces of the United States engaged in or charged with the invasion or capture of territory under the control of enemy forces.

The provisions of subdivisions 1 and 2 of subsection B of § 46.2-725 shall not apply to license plates issued under this section.

History.
1991, c. 108; 1995, c. 747.

§ **46.2-746.2:** Repealed by Acts 1999, c. 907.

§ **46.2-746.2:1:** Repealed by Acts 2003, c. 295.

§ 46.2-746.2:2. Special license plates; members and former members of the 173rd Airborne Brigade.

On receipt of an application therefor and presentation of written evidence that the applicant is a member or former member of the 173rd Airborne Brigade, the Commissioner shall issue to the applicant special license plates.

The provisions of subdivisions 1 and 2 of subsection B of § 46.2-725 shall not apply to license plates issued under this section.

No license plates shall be issued under this section unless and until a one-time fee of $3,500 shall have been paid to the Commissioner.

History.
1999, c. 907; 2002, c. 864.

§ **46.2-746.2:2.1:** Repealed by Acts 2004, cc. 717 and 984.

§ **46.2-746.2:2.2:** Repealed by Acts 2005, c. 908, cl. 2.

§ 46.2-746.2:3. Members and former members of the 3rd Infantry Regiment (Old Guard).

On receipt of an application therefor and presentation of written evidence that the applicant is a member or former member of the 3rd Infantry Regiment (Old Guard), the Commissioner shall issue special license plates to members and former members of the 3rd Infantry Regiment (Old Guard).

History.
2003, c. 921.

§ **46.2-746.2:3.1:** Repealed by Acts 2006, c. 437, cl. 2.

§ 46.2-746.2:4. Members of the Special Forces Association; fee.

On receipt of an application therefor and presentation of written evidence that the applicant is a member of the Special Forces Association, the Commissioner shall issue to the applicant special license plates.

The provisions of subdivisions B 1 and 2 of § 46.2-725 shall not apply to license plates issued under this section.

No license plates provided for in this section shall be issued unless and until the Commissioner receives at least 50 prepaid applications therefor and payment of a one-time fee of $3,500, less the total amount of $10 annual fees collected from the prepaid applications received.

History.
2003, cc. 921, 932.

§ **46.2-746.2:5:** Repealed by Acts 2005, c. 908, cl. 2.

§ 46.2-746.2:6. Special license plates; members of the Veterans of Foreign Wars of the United States organization.

On receipt of an application therefor and presentation of written evidence that the applicant is a member of the Veterans of Foreign Wars of the United States organization, the Commissioner shall issue special license plates to the applicant.

History.
2005, c. 273.

§ 46.2-746.3. Special license plates for members of certain military reserve organizations.

The Commissioner, on application therefor, shall issue special license plates to members of the Air Force Reserve, the Army Reserve, the Coast Guard Reserve, the Marine Reserve, and the Naval Reserve. Such special license plates may, when feasible, bear decals or stickers identifying the reserve organization of which the applicant is a member.

The provisions of subdivision B 2 of § 46.2-725 shall not apply to license plates issued under this section.

History.
1995, c. 747; 1996, c. 1026; 2004, c. 747.

§ 46.2-746.4. Special license plates for members of certain military veterans' organizations.

On receipt of an application and written evidence that the applicant is a member of any of the following military veterans' organizations, the Commissioner shall issue special license plates to the members of the following organizations: the Legion of Valor of the USA, the Marine Corps League, the Retired Officers Association, the Veterans of the Battle of Iwo Jima, and the Vietnam Veterans of America.

The provisions of subdivisions 1 and 2 of subsection B of § 46.2-725 shall not apply to license plates issued to members of the Legion of Valor of the USA under this section.

History.
1995, c. 747; 1996, c. 1026; 1997, cc. 774, 816; 2000, cc. 75, 111; 2002, c. 90; 2003, c. 921; 2004, c. 984.

§ **46.2-746.4:01:** Repealed by Acts 2005, c. 908, cl. 2.

§ **46.2-746.4:1:** Repealed by Acts 2000, c. 766.

§ **46.2-746.4:2:** Expired.

Editor's note.
This section was enacted by Acts 2000, c. 145, and expired on July 1, 2005, according to its own terms.

§ **46.2-746.4:3:** Repealed by Acts 2004, c. 717.

§ 46.2-746.5. Special license plates for National Guard retirees; fees.

On receipt of an application and written evidence that the applicant is a retired member of the National Guard, the Commissioner shall issue special license plates to National Guard retirees.

The fee for license plates issued under this section to retired members of the Virginia National Guard shall be the fee prescribed in § 46.2-694, unless the plates bear reserved numbers or letters as provided for in § 46.2-726. In this latter case, the fee for the issuance of license plates shall be the same as for those issued under § 46.2-726.

The fee for non-Virginia National Guard retirees shall be ten dollars per year plus the prescribed cost for state license plates, unless the plates bear reserved numbers or letters as provided for in § 46.2-726. In this latter case, such license plates shall be subject to an additional charge of ten dollars per year for the reserved numbers or letters.

History.
1995, c. 747; 1997, cc. 774, 816.

§ 46.2-746.6. Special license plates for members of certain volunteer search and rescue organizations.

On receipt of an application and written evidence that the applicant is a member, the Commissioner shall issue special license plates to members of the following organizations: the Civil Air Patrol, the Coast Guard Auxiliary, and any other volunteer search and rescue organization.

History.
1995, c. 747.

§ **46.2-746.6:1:** Repealed by Acts 2000, cc. 75, 766.

§ **46.2-746.6:2:** Repealed by Acts 2004, c. 717.

§ 46.2-746.7. Special license plates for members of certain civic and fraternal organizations.

On receipt of an application and written evidence that the applicant is a member of such organization, the Commissioner shall issue special license plates to members of the following organizations: the Exchange Club, the Jaycees, the Kiwanis, the Lions of Virginia, Rotary International, Ruritan National, the Freemasons, the Shriners, the Most Worshipful Prince Hall Grand Lodge of Virginia, the Order of the Eastern Star, the Knights of Columbus, and college and university fraternities and sororities.

No license plates shall be developed and issued for college or university fraternities or sororities until the Commissioner receives 350 or more prepaid applications and a design for each new series. All other license plates authorized under this section shall be subject to the development and issuance provisions of subdivision B 1 of § 46.2-725.

History.
1995, c. 747; 1996, c. 1026; 1998, c. 175; 1999, c. 907; 2000, c. 75; 2002, cc. 90, 864; 2003, c. 925; 2004, cc. 717, 747; 2005, c. 908.

§ 46.2-746.8. Special license plates for members of certain occupational associations.

On receipt of an application and written evidence that the applicant is a member of such organization, the Commissioner shall issue special license plates to members of the following organizations: the International Association of Firefighters, the Association of Realtors, and the Society of Certified Public Accountants.

History.
1995, c. 747; 1997, cc. 774, 816; 1999, c. 907; 2000, c. 75; 2002, c. 90; 2003, cc. 295, 925; 2004, c. 717; 2007, cc. 172, 181.

§ **46.2-746.8:1:** Repealed by Acts 2004, c. 717.

§ **46.2-746.8:2:** Repealed by Acts 2005, c. 908, cl. 2.

§ 46.2-746.9. Special license plates for certain occupations.

On receipt of an application and written evidence that the applicant is a magistrate, pharmacist, or postmaster, the Commissioner shall issue special license plates to the applicant.

History.
1995, c. 747; 2000, c. 148; 2002, c. 864; 2003, c. 925; 2004, cc. 717, 984; 2005, c. 908.

§ 46.2-746.10. Special license plates for supporters of the AFL-CIO.

On receipt of an application therefor, the Commissioner shall issue special license plates to supporters of the AFL-CIO.

History.
1997, cc. 774, 816.

§ 46.2-746.11. Special license plates for supporters of certain aviation education facilities; fees.

A. On receipt of an application and payment of the fee prescribed by this section, the Commissioner shall issue special license plates bearing the following legend: NATIONAL AIR AND SPACE MUSEUM.

B. The annual fee for plates issued pursuant to this section shall be twenty-five dollars in addition to the prescribed fee for state license plates. For each such twenty-five-dollar fee collected in excess of 1,000 registrations pursuant to this section, fifteen dollars shall be paid into the state treasury and credited to the special nonreverting fund known as the Aviation Education Facilities Fund, established within the Department of Accounts, for use by the Department of Aviation to support aviation education facilities located in the Commonwealth that are annexes of or affiliated with similar national facilities located in the nation's capital.

History.
1998, cc. 286, 295.

§ 46.2-746.12. Special license plates for supporters of credit unions.

On receipt of an application therefor, the Commissioner shall issue special license plates to supporters of credit unions.

History.
1998, c. 288.

§ **46.2-746.13:** Repealed by Acts 2002, c. 90, cl. 2.

§ 46.2-746.14. Special license plates; aviation enthusiasts.

On receipt of an application therefor, the Commissioner shall issue special license plates to aviation enthusiasts.

History.
1998, c. 294.

§§ **46.2-746.15 through 46.2-746.20:** Repealed by Acts 2002, c. 90, cl. 2.

§ **46.2-746.21:** Expired.

Editor's note.
This section, relating to special license plates for the tercentenary of the City of Williamsburg, expired by its own terms on July 1, 2003.

§ 46.2-746.22. Special license plates; members of the Sons of Confederate Veterans.

On receipt of an application therefor and written evidence that the applicant is a member of the Sons of Confederate Veterans, the Commissioner shall issue special license plates to members of the Sons of Confederate Veterans. No logo or emblem of any description shall be displayed or incorporated into the design of license plates issued under this section.

History.
1999, c. 902.

§ **46.2-746.23:** Repealed by Acts 2006, c. 437, cl. 2.

§ 46.2-747. Special license plates for street rods.

On receipt of an application, the Commissioner shall issue special license plates to owners of street rods. For the purposes of this section, "street rods" shall mean modernized private passenger motor vehicles either manufactured prior to 1949 or designed or manufactured to resemble vehicles manufactured prior to 1949.

History.
1985, c. 452, § 46.1-105.13; 1987, c. 696; 1989, c. 727.

§ **46.2-747.1:** Repealed by Acts 2002, c. 90, cl. 2.

§ 46.2-748. Special license plates for members of "REACT."

On receipt of an application, the Commissioner shall issue special license plates to members of Radio Emergency Associated Communications Teams (REACT).

The provisions of subdivisions 1 and 2 of subsection B of § 46.2-725 shall not apply to license plates issued under this section prior to July 1, 1997.

History.
1983, c. 494, § 46.1-105.10; 1987, c. 696; 1989, c. 727; 1996, c. 1026.

§ **46.2-748.1:** Repealed by Acts 2000, c. 75.

§ **46.2-748.2:** Repealed by Acts 2002, c. 90, cl. 2.

§ 46.2-749. (Effective until October 1, 2016) Issuance of license plates bearing seal, symbol, emblem, or logotype of certain institutions of higher education; fees.

A. On receipt of an application, the Commissioner may develop and issue for any accredited college or university located in Virginia, in accordance with policies and procedures established by the Commissioner and in accordance with an agreement between the institution and the Department, special license plates bearing the seal, symbol, emblem, or logotype of that institution of higher education.

On receipt of a minimum of 350 prepaid applications and a design therefor, the Commissioner may develop and issue special license plates bearing the seal, symbol, emblem or logotype of such institutions that are located outside Virginia, in accordance with policies and procedures established by the Commissioner and in accordance with an agreement between the institution and the Department.

For each set of license plates issued hereunder, the Commissioner shall charge, in addition to the prescribed cost of state license plates, an annual fee of $25.

B. Any institution of higher education that enters into an agreement with the Department pursuant to this section thereby waives any royalty fees to which it might otherwise be entitled for use of its seal, symbol, emblem, or logotype as provided in this section. However, any such institution located in Virginia shall annually receive an allocation of $15 for each set of license plates in excess of 1,000 registrations pursuant to the institution's agreement with the Department during the term of the agreement. The allocated funds shall be deposited by the Department into the state treasury and credited to the relevant institution to be used to support scholarships for eligible undergraduate students enrolled in the institution. Only students who (i) are bona fide domiciliaries of Virginia as defined in § 23-7.4 and (ii) are enrolled in educational programs whose primary purpose is not to provide religious training or theological education shall be eligible to receive such scholarships.

The State Council of Higher Education for Virginia shall review and approve plans for each participating institution for the implementation of these scholarship programs. These plans shall include, but need not be limited to, criteria for the awarding of the scholarships and procedures for determining the recipients.

The provisions of subdivisions 1 and 2 of subsection B of § 46.2-725 shall not apply to license plates issued under this section for any institution of higher education located in Virginia. The provisions of subdivision B 1 of § 46.2-725 shall not apply to license plates issued under this section for any institution of higher education located outside Virginia.

History.

1988, c. 656, § 46.1-105.18; 1989, c. 727; 1990, c. 319; 1995, c. 747; 1996, c. 1026; 2004, c. 747.

§ 46.2-749. (Effective October 1, 2016) Issuance of license plates bearing seal, symbol, emblem, or logotype of certain institutions of higher education; fees.

A. On receipt of an application, the Commissioner may develop and issue for any accredited college or university located in Virginia, in accordance with policies and procedures established by the Commissioner and in accordance with an agreement between the institution and the Department, special license plates bearing the seal, symbol, emblem, or logotype of that institution of higher education.

On receipt of a minimum of 350 prepaid applications and a design therefor, the Commissioner may develop and issue special license plates bearing the seal, symbol, emblem or logotype of such institutions that are located outside Virginia, in accordance with policies and procedures established by the Commissioner and in accordance with an agreement between the institution and the Department.

For each set of license plates issued hereunder, the Commissioner shall charge, in addition to the prescribed cost of state license plates, an annual fee of $25.

B. Any institution of higher education that enters into an agreement with the Department pursuant to this section thereby waives any royalty fees to which it might otherwise be entitled for use of its seal, symbol, emblem, or logotype as provided in this section. However, any such institution located in Virginia shall annually receive an allocation of $15 for each set of license plates in excess of 1,000 registrations pursuant to the institution's agreement with the Department during the term of the agreement. The allocated funds shall be deposited by the Department into the state treasury and credited to the relevant institution to be used to support scholarships for eligible undergraduate students enrolled in the institution. Only students who (i) are bona fide domiciliaries of Virginia as defined in § 23.1-502 and (ii) are enrolled in educational programs whose primary purpose is not to provide religious training or theological education shall be eligible to receive such scholarships.

The State Council of Higher Education for Virginia shall review and approve plans for each participating institution for the implementation of these scholarship programs. These plans shall include, but need not be limited to, criteria for the awarding of the scholarships and procedures for determining the recipients.

The provisions of subdivisions 1 and 2 of subsection B of § 46.2-725 shall not apply to license plates issued under this section for any institution of higher education located in Virginia. The provisions of subdivision B 1 of § 46.2-725 shall not apply to license plates issued under this section for any institution of higher education located outside Virginia.

History.
1988, c. 656, § 46.1-105.18; 1989, c. 727; 1990, c. 319; 1995, c. 747; 1996, c. 1026; 2004, c. 747.

§ 46.2-749.1. Special wildlife conservation plates.

A. On receipt of an application and payment of the fee prescribed by this section, the Commissioner shall issue special license plates bearing the following legend: WILDLIFE CONSERVATIONIST.

B. The annual fee for plates issued pursuant to this section shall be twenty-five dollars plus the prescribed fee for state license plates. For each such twenty-five-dollar fee collected in excess of 1,000 registrations pursuant to this section, fifteen dollars shall be paid into the state treasury and credited to the special fund known as the game protection fund.

History.
1991, c. 113; 1995, c. 747.

§ 46.2-749.2. Special Chesapeake Bay preservation plates.

A. On receipt of an application and payment of the fee prescribed by this section, the Commissioner shall issue special license plates bearing the following legend: FRIEND OF THE CHESAPEAKE.

B. The annual fee for plates issued pursuant to this section shall be twenty-five dollars in addition to the prescribed fee for state license plates. For each such twenty-five dollar fee collected in excess of 1,000 registrations pursuant to this section, fifteen dollars shall be paid into the state treasury and credited to the special nonreverting fund known as the Chesapeake Bay Restoration Fund, established within the Department of Accounts, for use by the Commonwealth of Virginia for environmental education and restoration projects relating to the Chesapeake Bay and its tributaries. Interest earned on the Fund will accrue to the Fund.

History.
1992, cc. 227, 323; 1995, cc. 747, 749, 823.

§ 46.2-749.2:1. Special license plates for supporters of certain children's programs; fees.

On receipt of an application and payment of the fee prescribed by this section, the Commissioner shall issue special license plates bearing, at the applicant's option, either (i) a heart, (ii) a five-pointed star, (iii) a child's handprint, or (iv) another design or device approved by the Commissioner.

The annual fee for plates issued pursuant to this section shall be twenty-five dollars plus the prescribed fee for state license plates. For each such twenty-five-dollar fee collected in excess of 1,000 registrations pursuant to this section, fifteen dollars shall be paid into the state treasury and credited to the special fund known as the Children's Programs Support Fund for use as follows: one-half shall be paid into the Family and Children's Trust Fund and one-half shall be paid to the Department of Health for use by the Safe Kids Coalition.

History.
1994, c. 914; 1995, c. 747; 1996, c. 922.

§ 46.2-749.2:2. Special license plates for Virginians for the Arts; fees.

A. On receipt of an application and payment of the fee prescribed by this section, the Commissioner shall issue special license plates bearing the following legend: VIRGINIANS FOR THE ARTS.

B. The annual fee for plates issued pursuant to this section shall be twenty-five dollars in addition to the prescribed fee for state license plates. For each such twenty-five-dollar fee collected in excess of 1,000 registrations pursuant to this section, fifteen dollars shall be paid into the state treasury and credited to the special nonreverting fund known as the Virginia Arts Foundation Fund established within the Department of Accounts, for use by the Virginia Arts Foundation.

History.
1996, cc. 922, 1026; 1997, c. 878.

§§ 46.2-749.2:3 through 46.2-749.2:6: Repealed by Acts 2000, c. 75.

§ 46.2-749.2:7. Special license plates for supporters of dog and cat sterilization programs; fees.

A. On receipt of an application and payment of the fee prescribed by this section, the Commissioner shall issue special license plates to supporters of dog and cat sterilization programs.

B. The annual fee for plates issued pursuant to this section shall be twenty-five dollars in addition to the prescribed fee for state license plates. For each such twenty-five-dollar fee collected in excess of 1,000 registrations pursuant to this section, fifteen dollars shall be paid into the state treasury and credited to a special nonreverting fund known as the Dog and Cat Sterilization Fund, established within the Department of Accounts. These funds shall be paid annually to the locality in which the vehicle is registered and shall be used by the localities to which they are paid to support sterilization programs for dogs and cats.

Each affected locality shall annually certify in a manner prescribed by the Commissioner that these funds have been or are being used to support sterilization programs for dogs and cats. If an affected locality does not have such a sterilization program, it shall (i) make the funds available to any private, nonprofit sterilization program for dogs and cats in that locality; (ii) return the funds to the Commissioner; or (iii) refuse the funds. Any funds refused, returned to the Commissioner, or otherwise not paid to an affected locality shall be distributed to other affected localities on a pro rata basis.

History.
1996, c. 922.

§§ **46.2-749.2:8, 46.2-749.2:9:** Repealed by Acts 2002, c. 90, cl. 2.

§ 46.2-749.2:10. Special license plates for supporters of community traffic safety programs in the Commonwealth; fees.

A. On receipt of an application and payment of the fee prescribed by this section, the Commissioner shall issue special license plates bearing the following legend: DRIVE SMART.

B. The annual fee for plates issued pursuant to this section shall be $25 in addition to the prescribed fee for state license plates. For each such $25 fee collected in excess of 1,000 registrations pursuant to this section, $15 shall be paid into the state treasury and credited to the special nonreverting fund known as the Drive Smart Virginia Fund, established within the Department of Accounts, for use by Drive Smart Virginia to support its programs and activities in the Commonwealth.

History.
1997, cc. 774, 816; 2005, cc. 244, 273.

§§ **46.2-749.2:11, 46.2-749.2:12:** Repealed by Acts 2002, c. 90, cl. 2. 2

§ **46.2-749.2:13:** Expired.

Editor's note.
Acts 1998, c. 763, which amended this section, provides in cl. 2: "That the provisions of this act shall expire on January 1, 2013."

§ **46.2-749.2:14:** Expired.

Editor's note.
This section, relating to special license plates commemorating the 1999 Bicentennial of George Washington, expired pursuant to Acts 1998, cc. 174 and 181, cl. 2, on July 1, 2003.

§ **46.2-749.2:15:** Expired.

Editor's note.
This section, relating to special license plates commemorating the 250th anniversary of the City of Alexandria, expired pursuant to Acts 1998, c. 284, cl. 2, on July 1, 2003.

§ **46.2-749.2:16:** Expired.

Editor's note.
This section, relating to special license plates commemorating the 250th anniversary of the County of Chesterfield, expired pursuant to Acts 1998, c. 284, cl. 2, on July 1, 2003.

§ **46.2-749.2:17:** Repealed by Acts 2002, c. 90, cl. 2.

§ 46.2-749.3. Special license plates for clean special fuel vehicles.

A. The owner of any motor vehicle, except a motorcycle, that may utilize clean special fuel may purchase special license plates indicating the motor vehicle utilizes clean special fuels. Upon receipt of an application, the Commissioner shall issue special license plates to the owners of such vehicles.

As used in this section, "clean special fuel" means any product or energy source used to propel a highway vehicle, the use of which, compared to conventional gasoline or reformulated gasoline, results in lower emissions of oxides of nitrogen, volatile organic compounds, carbon monoxide or particulates or any combination thereof. The term includes compressed natural gas, liquefied natural gas, liquefied petroleum gas, hydrogen, hythane (a combination of compressed natural gas and hydrogen), and electricity.

On and after July 1, 2006, license plates provided for in this section shall be issued with a new design distinctively different from the design of license plates issued to owners of vehicles that qualify for license plates under this section whose applications are received by the Department prior to July 1, 2006, hereinafter referred to as "the FY 2007 design." The distinctively different design shall be developed by the Department in consultation with the Department of State Police.

On and after July 1, 2011, license plates provided for in this section shall be issued with a new design distinctively different from the design of license plates issued to owners of vehicles that qualify for license plates under this section whose applications are received by the Department prior to July 1, 2011 (hereinafter referred to as the FY 2012 design). The distinctively different design shall be developed by the Department in consultation with the Department of State Police. Thereafter, only "the FY 2012 design" plate shall be issued to owners of vehicles that qualify for license plates under this section.

1. For the purposes of subdivision A 6 of § 33.2-501, on HOV lanes serving the I-95/395 corridor, only vehicles registered with and displaying special license plates issued under this section prior to July 1, 2006, shall be treated as vehicles displaying special license plates issued under this section.

2. For the purposes of subdivision A 6 of § 33.2-501, on HOV lanes serving the Interstate Route 66 corridor, only vehicles registered with and displaying special license plates issued under this section prior to July 1, 2011, shall be treated as vehicles displaying special license plates issued under this section.

3. The Commissioner of Highways shall provide annually to the Chairmen of the Senate and House of Delegates Committees on Transportation traffic volumes on the HOV facilities that result in a degraded condition as identified in SAFETEA-LU or other applicable federal law and reported to the Federal Highway Administration. This report shall be used by the Chairmen of their respective committees to recommend further restriction on use of HOV facilities by clean special fuel vehicles.

4. The Commissioner of the Department of Motor Vehicles, in consultation with the Motor Vehicle Dealer Board, shall develop procedures to ensure that all potential purchasers of clean special fuel vehicles receive adequate notice of the benefits, risks and timelines required for the issuance of clean special fuel vehicle license plates.

B. With the exception of plates issued to government-use vehicles, the annual fee for plates issued pursuant to this section shall be $25 in addition to the prescribed fee for state license plates. For each such $25 fee collected in excess of 1,000 registrations pursuant to this section, $15 shall be paid to the State Treasury and credited to a special nonreverting fund known as the HOV Enforcement Fund, established within the Department of Accounts, for use by the Virginia State Police for enhanced HOV enforcement. The fee for plates issued pursuant to this section to government-use vehicles shall be as prescribed in subsection A of § 46.2-750.

History.

1993, cc. 255, 625; 1995, c. 134; 1999, c. 883; 2000, cc. 729, 758; 2006, cc. 873, 908; 2010, cc. 351, 390; 2012, cc. 681, 743.

Editor's note.

References in this section were updated at the direction of the Virginia Code Commission to conform to the recodification of Title 33.2 by Acts 2014, c. 805, effective October 1, 2014.

§ 46.2-749.4. Special license plates bearing the seal, symbol, emblem, or logotype of counties, cities, and towns.

A. On receipt of a minimum of 350 paid applications and a design therefor, the Commissioner may develop and issue special license plates whose design incorporates the seal, symbol, emblem, or logotype of any county, city or town. If all affected localities agree as to its design, the Commissioner may develop and issue special license plates jointly for more than one locality. Each local governing body of the counties, cities, or towns involved in the design of the license plates shall agree as to the issuance fee, and shall indicate to the Commissioner in writing, whether the license plates issued shall be revenue sharing or nonrevenue sharing license plates.

B. The annual fee for plates issued pursuant to this section that are nonrevenue sharing license plates shall be $10 plus the prescribed fee for state license plates.

C. The annual fee for plates issued pursuant to this section that are revenue sharing license plates shall be $25 plus the prescribed fee for state license plates. For each such $25 fee collected in excess of 1,000 registrations pursuant to this section, $15 shall be paid to the locality whose seal, symbol, emblem, or logotype appears on the plate. These funds shall be paid to the affected localities annually and may be used as provided by the local governing body. For license plates issued jointly for more than one locality, these funds shall be apportioned among the affected localities as agreed to with the Commissioner prior to issue.

The provisions of subdivision B 1 of § 46.2-725 shall not apply to license plates issued under this section.

History.

1993, c. 560; 1995, c. 747; 1996, c. 1026; 1999, cc. 883, 907; 2003, c. 925; 2004, c. 747; 2005, c. 273.

§§ 46.2-749.4:1 through 46.2-749.4:3: Repealed by Acts 2002, c. 90, cl. 2.

§ 46.2-749.4:4. Commemorative license plates for counties, cities, and towns.

On receipt of a minimum of 350 prepaid applications and a proposed design therefor, the Commissioner may develop and issue special license plates commemorating the twenty-fifth or subsequent anniversary, in increments of 25 years, of the establishment of any county, city, or town in the Commonwealth.

The provisions of subdivision B 1 of § 46.2-725 shall not apply to license plates issued under this section.

The authority to issue each commemorative license plate under this section shall be valid for a period of five years from the date each such commemorative license plate is first issued.

History.

2005, c. 294.

§ 46.2-749.5. Special license plates celebrating Virginia's tobacco heritage.

A. On receipt of an application, the Commissioner shall issue special license plates celebrating Virginia's tobacco heritage. For each set of license plates issued under this section, the Commissioner shall charge, in addition to the prescribed cost of state license plates, an annual fee of $10.

B. License plates may be issued under this section for display on vehicles registered as trucks, as that term is defined in § 46.2-100, provided that no license plates are issued pursuant to this section for (i) vehicles operated for hire, except TNC partner vehicles as defined in § 46.2-2000; (ii) vehicles registered under the International Registration Plan; or (iii) vehicles registered as tow trucks or tractor trucks as defined in § 46.2-100. No permanent license plates without decals as authorized in subsection B of § 46.2-712 may be issued under this section. For each set of truck license plates issued under this subsection, the Commissioner shall charge, in addition to the prescribed cost of state license plates, an annual fee of $25.

History.
1994, c. 914; 2009, c. 679; 2015, cc. 2, 3.

§ **46.2-749.5:1:** Repealed by Acts 2004, c. 717.

§ 46.2-749.6. Special license plates for supporters of the National Rifle Association.

On receipt of an application therefor, the Commissioner shall issue special license plates to supporters of the National Rifle Association.

History.
1995, c. 747.

§§ **46.2-749.6:1, 46.2-749.6:1.1:** Repealed by Acts 2002, c. 90, cl. 2. .1

§ 46.2-749.7. Special license plates for supporters of Ducks Unlimited.

On receipt of an application therefor, the Commissioner shall issue special license plates to supporters of Ducks Unlimited.

History.
1995, c. 747.

§ **46.2-749.7:1:** Repealed by Acts 2000, c. 75.

§ **46.2-749.7:2:** Repealed by Acts 2002, c. 90, cl. 2.

§ 46.2-749.7:3. Special license plates supporting education, charity, and scientific study for Virginia's Eastern Shore business community; fees.

A. On receipt of an application therefor and payment of the fee prescribed by this section, and following the provisions of § 46.2-725, other than those relating to the fee for the plates and its disposition, the Commissioner shall issue to the applicant special license plates promoting tourism on Virginia's Eastern Shore.

B. The annual fee for plates issued pursuant to this section shall be $25 in addition to the prescribed fee for state license plates. For each such $25 fee collected in excess of 1,000 registrations pursuant to this section, $15 shall be paid into the state treasury and credited to a special nonreverting fund known as the Eastern Shore Foundation Fund, established within the Department of Accounts. These funds shall be paid annually to the Eastern Shore of Virginia Chamber of Commerce Foundation and used to support education, charity, and scientific study for Virginia's Eastern Shore business community. All other fees imposed under the provisions of this section shall be paid to, and received by, the Commissioner of the Department of Motor Vehicles and paid by him into the state treasury and set aside as a special fund to be used to meet the necessary expenses incurred by the Department of Motor Vehicles.

History.
1998, c. 381; 2014, c. 662.

§ 46.2-749.8. Special license plates for Harley-Davidson motor vehicle owners.

On receipt of an application therefor, the Commissioner shall issue special license plates to owners of Harley-Davidson motor vehicles.

History.
1995, c. 747.

§ 46.2-749.9. Special license plates; Virginia Bowler.

On receipt of an application therefor, the Commissioner shall issue to the applicant special license plates bearing the legend: Virginia Bowler.

History.
1995, c. 747.

§ 46.2-749.10. Special license plates for ridesharing vehicles.

On receipt of an application therefor, the Commissioner shall issue special license plates for display on ridesharing vehicles. License plates shall be issued under this section only for privately owned or leased motor vehicles (i) with seating for no more than fifteen adult persons including the driver and (ii) participating in ridesharing arrangements. The cost for such special license plates shall be the same as for the regular license plates for vehicles described in § 46.2-695.

History.
1995, c. 747; 2002, c. 337.

§ **46.2-749.11:** Repealed by Acts 2000, c. 75.

§ **46.2-749.12:** Repealed by Acts 2003, c. 295, cl. 2.

§ 46.2-749.13. Special license plates; Internet commerce industry.

On receipt of an application therefor, the Commissioner shall issue to the applicant special license plates designed to represent the Internet commerce industry.

History.
1999, c. 907.

§ 46.2-749.14. Special license plates; supporters of greyhound adoption programs.

On receipt of an application therefor, the Commissioner shall issue special license plates to supporters of greyhound adoption programs.

History.
1999, c. 907.

§§ 46.2-749.15, 46.2-749.16: Repealed by Acts 2003, c. 295, cl. 2.

§ 46.2-749.16:1: Repealed by Acts 2011, c. 21.

§ 46.2-749.17: Repealed by Acts 2003, c. 295, cl. 2.

§ 46.2-749.18. Special license plates; horse enthusiasts.

On receipt of an application therefor, the Commissioner shall issue special license plates to horse enthusiasts.

History.
1999, c. 907.

§§ 46.2-749.19 through 46.2-749.23: Repealed by Acts 2003, c. 295, cl. 2.

§ 46.2-749.23:1: Repealed by Acts 2004, c. 717.

§§ 46.2-749.24, 46.2-749.25: Repealed by Acts 2003, c. 295, cl. 2.

§ 46.2-749.26. Special license plates; Natural Bridge of Virginia.

On receipt of an application therefor, the Commissioner shall issue to the applicant special license plates celebrating the Natural Bridge of Virginia.

History.
1999, c. 907.

§ 46.2-749.27: Repealed by Acts 2003, c. 295, cl. 2.

§ 46.2-749.28. Special license plates; Oceana Naval Air Station.

On receipt of an application therefor, the Commissioner shall issue to the applicant special license plates bearing the legend: OCEANA NAVAL AIR STATION.

History.
1999, c. 883.

§ 46.2-749.28:1: Repealed by Acts 2004, cc. 717 and 984.

§ 46.2-749.28:2: Repealed by Acts 2005, c. 908, cl. 2.

§ 46.2-749.29. Special license plates; supporters of Operation Wildflower; fees.

A. On receipt of an application and payment of the fee prescribed by this section, the Commissioner shall issue special license plates to supporters of Operation Wildflower.

B. The annual fee for plates issued pursuant to this section shall be twenty-five dollars in addition to the prescribed fee for state license plates. For each such twenty-five-dollar fee collected in excess of 1,000 registrations pursuant to this section, fifteen dollars shall be paid into the state treasury and credited to a special nonreverting fund known as the Operation Wildflower Fund, established within the Department of Accounts. These funds shall be paid annually to the Virginia Department of Transportation and used to support its Operation Wildflower program.

History.
1999, c. 883.

§ 46.2-749.30: Repealed by Acts 2003, c. 295, cl. 2.

§§ 46.2-749.30:1, 46.2-749.30:2: Repealed by Acts 2005, c. 908, cl. 2.

§ 46.2-749.31. Special license plates; Virginia lighthouses.

On receipt of an application therefor, the Commissioner shall issue to the applicant special license plates celebrating Virginia lighthouses.

History.
1999, c. 883.

§§ 46.2-749.32 through 46.2-749.36: Repealed by Acts 2004, c. 717.

§ 46.2-749.36:1: Repealed by Acts 2005, c. 908, cl. 2.

§ 46.2-749.37: Expired.

Editor's note.
This section was enacted by Acts 2000, c. 85, and expired July 1, 2005, according to its own terms.

§ 46.2-749.38: Expired.

Editor's note.
This section was enacted by Acts 2000, c. 124, and expired July 1, 2005, according to its own terms.

§ 46.2-749.39: Repealed by Acts 2004, c. 717.

§ 46.2-749.40. Special license plates; Class-J No. 611 steam locomotive.

On receipt of an application therefor, the Commissioner shall issue to the applicant special license plates commemorating the Class-J No. 611 steam locomotive.

History.
2000, c. 143.

§§ 46.2-749.41, 46.2-749.42: Repealed by Acts 2004, c. 717.

§ 46.2-749.43: Repealed by Acts 2004, cc. 653 and 717.

§§ 46.2-749.43:1, 46.2-749.44: Repealed by Acts 2005, c. 908, cl. 2.

§ 46.2-749.45. Special license plates; supporters of the Virginia Breast Cancer Foundation.

A. On receipt of an application and payment of the fee prescribed by this section, the Commissioner shall issue to the applicant special license plates bearing the legend: Virginia Breast Cancer Foundation.

B. The annual fee for plates issued pursuant to this section shall be twenty-five dollars in addition to the prescribed fee for state license plates. For each such twenty-five-dollar fee collected in excess of 1,000 registrations pursuant to this section, fifteen dollars shall be paid into the state treasury and credited to a special nonreverting fund known as the Virginia Breast Cancer Foundation Fund, established within the Department of Accounts. These funds shall be paid annually to the Virginia Breast Cancer Foundation and used to support statewide breast cancer educational programs.

History.
2000, c. 319.

§ 46.2-749.46. Special license plates; naval aviators.

On receipt of an application and written evidence that the applicant is or has been a naval aviator, the Commissioner shall issue to the applicant special license plates.

History.
2000, c. 766.

§ 46.2-749.47: Repealed by Acts 2004, c. 717.

§ 46.2-749.48. Special license plates for supporters of Family and Children's Trust Fund; fees.

On receipt of an application and payment of the fee prescribed by this section, the Commissioner shall issue special license plates for supporters of the Family and Children's Trust Fund.

The annual fee for plates issued pursuant to this section shall be twenty-five dollars plus the prescribed fee for state license plates. For each such twenty-five-dollar fee collected in excess of 1,000 registrations pursuant to this section, fifteen dollars shall be paid into the state treasury and credited to the Family and Children's Trust Fund.

History.
2000, c. 766.

§ 46.2-749.49: Repealed by Acts 2005, cc. 273 and 908, cl. 2.

§ 46.2-749.49:1: Repealed by Acts 2009, c. 755, cl. 2.

Editor's note.
Acts 2009, c. 755, cl. 3 provides: "That, notwithstanding the foregoing provisions of this act, special license plates issued to supporters of the Shenandoah National Park Association pursuant to § 46.2-749.49:1 of the Code of Virginia prior to July 1, 2009, shall remain valid until their expiration date, but shall be renewed thereafter under the provisions of subsection B of § 2 of this act [Acts 2009, c. 755, cl. 1, § 2 is noted under § 46.2-725]."

§§ 46.2-749.50 through 46.2-749.53: Repealed by Acts 2005, c. 908, cl. 2.

§ 46.2-749.54. Special license plates; BoatU.S.

On receipt of an application therefor, the Commissioner shall issue to members of BoatU.S. special license plates bearing the legend: BoatU.S. Member.

History.
2002, c. 864.

§ 46.2-749.55: Repealed by Acts 2005, c. 908.

§ 46.2-749.56: Repealed by Acts 2005, cc. 273 and 908, cl. 2.

§ 46.2-749.56:1: Repealed by Acts 2006, c. 437, cl. 2.

§ 46.2-749.57: Repealed by Acts 2005, c. 908, cl. 2.

§ 46.2-749.58. Special license plates bearing the legend: FOX HUNTING.

On receipt of an application therefor, the Commissioner shall issue special license plates bearing the legend: FOX HUNTING.

History.
2002, c. 864.

§ 46.2-749.59: Repealed by Acts 2005, c. 908, cl. 2.

§ 46.2-749.60. Special license plates bearing the legend: UNLOCKING AUTISM.

On receipt of an application therefor, the Commissioner shall issue special license plates bearing the legend: UNLOCKING AUTISM.

History.
2002, c. 864.

§ **46.2-749.61:** Repealed by Acts 2011, c. 21.

§ 46.2-749.62. Special license plates whose design incorporates the flag of the United States.

A. On receipt of an application therefor, the Commissioner shall issue special license plates whose design incorporates the flag of the United States and the legend: FIGHT TERRORISM.

B. On receipt of an application therefor from a member of the Senate or House of Delegates, the Commissioner shall issue to the applicant special license plates combining the designs of special license plates issued under subsection A of this section and special license plates issued to members of the Senate or House of Delegates, as the case may be, under § 46.2-736.1.

History.
2002, c. 864; 2004, c. 984.

§§ **46.2-749.63 through 46.2-749.65:** Repealed by Acts 2005, c. 908, cl. 2.

§ 46.2-749.66. Special license plates; victims of attack on USS Cole.

On receipt of an application therefor, the Commissioner shall issue to the applicant special license plates honoring the persons injured or killed in the attack on the USS Cole (DDG 67) during its refueling in Aden, Yemen, on October 12, 2000.

History.
2002, c. 864.

§ **46.2-749.67:** Repealed by Acts 2005, c. 908, cl. 2.

§ 46.2-749.68. Special license plates; Parrothead Club.

On receipt of an application therefor, the Commissioner shall issue special license plates to members and supporters of the Parrothead Club.

History.
2002, c. 864.

§ **46.2-749.69:** Repealed by Acts 2004, c. 984.

§ 46.2-749.69:1. Special license plates bearing the names, numbers, and color schemes used by professional stock car drivers; fees.

A. On receipt of an application and payment of the fee prescribed by this section, the Commissioner shall issue special license plates to supporters of the Virginia Motor Sports Initiative.

B. The Commissioner may enter into agreements for the purchase of distinctive license plates bearing the name of a specific professional stock car driver and the race car number and color scheme used by that driver, or for distinctive general motor sports-themed license plates, for issuance as provided in this section. The design of such license plates shall be as mutually agreed by the Commissioner and the supplier of such license plates. The purchase price of such plates shall be as agreed between the Commissioner and the supplier or other entity, but shall in no case exceed a total, one-time cost of $15 for each set of license plates. In the event that a race car number, color scheme, or both, change for a driver with a currently issued series, a new series for that driver may be issued subject to the requirements of this section.

The provisions of subdivision B 1 of § 46.2-725 shall not apply to license plates issued under this section.

C. The annual fee for plates issued pursuant to this section shall be $25 in addition to the prescribed fee for state license plates. For each such $25 fee collected in excess of 1,000 registrations pursuant to this section, $15 shall be paid into the state treasury and credited to the special nonreverting fund known as the Virginia Motor Sports Initiative Fund established within the Department of Accounts and paid annually in equal amounts to the Virginia Economic Development Partnership Authority and the Virginia Department of Small Business and Supplier Diversity and used to support their programs related to the Virginia Motor Sports Initiative.

In calculating the amount to be paid into such fund each year, however, there shall be deducted an amount equal to the amount paid in that year by the Department for the purchase of license plates for which the additional $25 fees have been collected for that year.

History.
2004, c. 984; 2005, c. 554; 2013, c. 482.

§§ **46.2-749.70 through 46.2-749.72:** Repealed by Acts 2005, c. 908, cl. 2.

§ 46.2-749.73. Special license plates; supporters of the Washington Redskins football team; fees.

A. On receipt of an application and payment of the fee prescribed by this section, the Commissioner shall issue special license plates to supporters of the Washington Redskins football team.

B. The annual fee for plates issued pursuant to this section shall be twenty-five dollars in addition to the prescribed fee for state license plates. For each such twenty-five-dollar fee collected in excess of 1,000 registrations pursuant to this section, fifteen dollars shall be paid into the state treasury and credited to a special nonreverting fund known as the Washington Redskins Leadership Council Fund established within the Department of Accounts. These funds shall be paid annually to the Washington Redskins Leadership Council for its use in community programs in Virginia.

History.
2002, c. 864.

§ **46.2-749.73:1:** Repealed by Acts 2004, c. 717.

§§ **46.2-749.74 through 46.2-749.77:** Repealed by Acts 2005, c. 908, cl. 2.

§ 46.2-749.78. Special license plates; United We Stand.

On receipt of an application and payment of the fee prescribed by this section, the Commissioner shall issue special license plates whose design incorporates the flag of the United States of America and the legend: United We Stand.

History.
2002, c. 893; 2006, c. 852.

§ **46.2-749.79:** Repealed by Acts 2005, c. 908, cl. 2.

§ 46.2-749.80. Special license plates bearing the legend: EDUCATION BEGINS AT HOME.

On receipt of an application therefor, the Commissioner shall issue special license plates bearing the legend: EDUCATION BEGINS AT HOME.

History.
2002, c. 893.

§ 46.2-749.81. Special license plates; supporters of the NASA Langley Research Center.

On receipt of an application therefor, the Commissioner shall issue special license plates to supporters of the NASA Langley Research Center.

History.
2002, c. 893.

§§ **46.2-749.82, 46.2-749.83:** Repealed by Acts 2005, c. 908, cl. 2.

§§ **46.2-749.84, 46.2-749.85:** Repealed by Acts 2004, c. 717.

§ 46.2-749.86. Special license plates; members and supporters of the Urban League of Hampton Roads.

On receipt of an application therefor, the Commissioner shall issue special license plates to members and supporters of the Urban League of Hampton Roads.

History.
2003, c. 921.

§§ **46.2-749.87, 46.2-749.88:** Repealed by Acts 2004, c. 717.

§ 46.2-749.89. Special license plates bearing the legend FRIENDS OF TIBET; fees.

A. On receipt of an application and payment of the fee prescribed by this section, the Commissioner shall issue special license plates bearing the legend FRIENDS OF TIBET.

B. The annual fee for plates issued pursuant to this section shall be $25 in addition to the prescribed fee for state license plates. For each such $25 fee collected in excess of 1,000 registrations pursuant to this section, $15 shall be paid into the state treasury and credited to a special nonreverting fund known as the Conservancy for Tibetan Art and Culture Fund, established within the Department of Accounts. These funds shall be paid annually to the Conservancy for Tibetan Art and Culture and used to assist in its programs and activities in Virginia.

History.
2003, c. 921.

§§ **46.2-749.90 through 46.2-749.92:** Repealed by Acts 2006, c. 437, cl. 2.

§ **46.2-749.93:** Repealed by Acts 2004, c. 717.

§ **46.2-749.94:** Repealed by Acts 2006, c. 437, cl. 2.

§§ **46.2-749.95 through 46.2-749.97:** Repealed by Acts 2004, c. 717.

§ **46.2-749.98:** Repealed by Acts 2004, cc. 717 and 984.

§ **46.2-749.98:1:** Repealed by Acts 2005, c. 908, cl. 2.

§§ **46.2-749.99, 46.2-749.100:** Repealed by Acts 2004, c. 717.

§ **46.2-749.101:** Repealed by Acts 2005, c. 908, cl. 2.

§ 46.2-749.102. Special license plates; supporters of Virginia agriculture; fees.

A. On receipt of an application and payment of the fee prescribed by this section, the Commissioner shall issue special license plates to supporters of Virginia agriculture.

B. The annual fee for plates issued pursuant to this section shall be $25 in addition to the prescribed fee for state license plates. For each such $25 fee collected in excess of 1,000 registrations pursuant to this section, $15 shall be paid into the state treasury and credited to a special nonreverting fund known as the Virginia Agricultural Vitality Program Fund, established within the Department of Accounts. These funds shall be paid annually to the Office of Farm Land Preservation and used to support the Virginia Agricultural Vitality Program.

History.
2004, c. 653.

§ 46.2-749.103: Expired.

Editor's note.
This section, Special license plates; 275th anniversary of the County of Prince William, enacted by Acts 2004, cc. 653 and 984, expired by its own terms on July 1, 2009.

§ 46.2-749.104: Repealed by Acts 2005, c. 908, cl. 2.

§ 46.2-749.105. Special license plates to encourage participation in the organ donor program.

On receipt of an application therefor, the Commissioner shall issue special license plates that encourage participation by Virginia-licensed drivers in the organ donor program.

History.
2004, c. 653.

§§ 46.2-749.106, 46.2-749.107: Repealed by Acts 2005, c. 908, cl. 2.

§ 46.2-749.108: Repealed by Acts 2011, c. 21.

§ 46.2-749.109: Repealed by Acts 2005, cc. 248 and 908, cl. 2.

§ 46.2-749.109:1: Repealed by Acts 2006, c. 437, cl. 2.

§ 46.2-749.110. Special license plates; supporters of the Virginia Sheriffs' Institute; fees.

A. On receipt of an application and payment of the fee prescribed by this section, the Commissioner shall issue special license plates to supporters of the Virginia Sheriffs' Institute.

B. The annual fee for plates issued pursuant to this section shall be $25 in addition to the prescribed fee for state license plates. For each such $25 fee collected in excess of 1,000 registrations pursuant to this section, $15 shall be paid into the state treasury and credited to a special nonreverting fund known as the Virginia Sheriffs' Institute Fund, established within the Department of Accounts. These funds shall be paid annually to the Virginia Sheriffs' Institute and used exclusively to memorialize and honor Virginia law-enforcement officers killed in the line of duty.

History.
2004, c. 700.

§ 46.2-749.111. Special license plates for bicycle enthusiasts.

On receipt of an application therefor, the Commissioner shall issue special license plates to bicycle enthusiasts.

History.
2004, c. 984.

§ 46.2-749.112: Repealed by Acts 2011, c. 21.

§§ 46.2-749.113, 46.2-749.114: Repealed by Acts 2005, c. 908, cl. 2.

§ 46.2-749.115. Special license plates; Juvenile Diabetes Research Foundation; fees.

A. On receipt of an application and payment of the fee prescribed by this section, the Commissioner shall issue to the applicant special license plates for supporters of the Juvenile Diabetes Research Foundation.

B. The annual fee for plates issued pursuant to this section shall be $25 in addition to the prescribed fee for state license plates. For each such $25 fee collected in excess of 1,000 registrations pursuant to this section, $15 shall be paid into the state treasury and credited to a special nonreverting fund known as the Juvenile Diabetes Research Foundation Fund, established within the Department of Accounts. These funds shall be paid annually to the Juvenile Diabetes Research Foundation and used to support its programs and activities in Virginia.

History.
2004, c. 984.

§§ 46.2-749.116, 46.2-749.117: Repealed by Acts 2005, c. 908, cl. 2.

§ 46.2-749.118: Repealed by Acts 2006, c. 437, cl. 2.

§ 46.2-749.119. Special license plates; members and supporters of the Virginia Association for Community Conflict Resolution; fees.

A. On receipt of an application and payment of the fee prescribed by this section, the Commissioner shall issue to the applicant special license plates for members and supporters of the Virginia Association for Community Conflict Resolution.

B. The annual fee for plates issued pursuant to this section shall be $25 in addition to the prescribed fee for state license plates. For each such $25 fee collected in excess of 1,000 registrations pursuant to this section, $15 shall be paid into the state treasury and credited to a special nonreverting fund known as the Virginia Association for Community Conflict Resolution Fund, established within the Department of Accounts. These funds shall be paid annually to the Virginia Association for Community Conflict Resolution and used to support its programs and activities in Virginia.

History.
2005, c. 248.

§§ 46.2-749.120, 46.2-749.121: Repealed by Acts 2006, c. 437, cl. 2.

§§ 46.2-749.122 through 46.2-749.125: Repealed by Acts 2008, c. 114, cl. 1.

§§ 46.2-749.126 through 46.2-749.128: Repealed by Acts 2006, c. 437, cl. 2.

§ 46.2-749.129: Repealed by Acts 2008, c. 114, cl. 1.

§ 46.2-749.130. Special license plates for supporters of the Surfrider Foundation; fees.

A. On receipt of an application therefor and payment of the fee prescribed by this section, and following the provisions of § 46.2-725, other than those relating to the fee for the plates and its disposition, the Commissioner shall issue to the applicant special license plates for supporters of the Surfrider Foundation.

B. The annual fee for plates issued pursuant to this section shall be $25 in addition to the prescribed fee for state license plates. For each such $25 fee collected in excess of 1,000 registrations pursuant to this section, $15 shall be paid into the state treasury and credited to a special nonreverting fund known as the Surfrider Foundation Fund, established within the Department of Accounts. These funds shall be paid annually to the Surfrider Foundation and used by its Virginia Beach chapter to support the protection and enjoyment of oceans, waves, and beaches in Virginia. All other fees imposed under the provisions of this section shall be paid to, and received by, the Commissioner and paid by him into the state treasury and set aside as a special fund to be used to meet the necessary expenses incurred by the Department of Motor Vehicles.

History.
2005, c. 273; 2014, c. 556.

§§ 46.2-749.131 through 46.2-749.133: Repealed by Acts 2006, c. 437, cl. 2.

§§ 46.2-749.134, 46.2-749.135: Repealed by Acts 2008, c. 114, cl. 1.

ARTICLE 11.

STATE AND LOCAL MOTOR VEHICLE REGISTRATION.

§ 46.2-750. Vehicles of Commonwealth, its political subdivisions, and regional jail authorities.

A. Motor vehicles, trailers, and semitrailers owned by the Commonwealth, political subdivisions of the Commonwealth, and regional jail authorities created pursuant to Article 3.1 (§ 53.1-95.2 et seq.) of Chapter 3 of Title 53.1 and used solely for governmental purposes shall be registered and shall display license plates as provided in this section. The fee for such license plates shall be equal to the cost incurred by the Department in the purchase or manufacture of such license plates. The fees received by the Commissioner under this section shall be paid into the state treasury and shall be set aside as a special fund to be used to meet the expenses of the Department of Motor Vehicles.

License plates issued for vehicles owned by the Commonwealth, except plates issued to be used on vehicles (i) devoted solely to police work, (ii) used by the Virginia Economic Development Partnership to the extent approved by the Governor, (iii) used by an institution of higher education solely for purposes of vehicle technology research, or (iv) used by the Governor and the Attorney General, shall have conspicuously and legibly inscribed, stamped, or printed thereon words stating that the vehicle is for official state use only. The Commissioner shall reserve a unique series of numbers for use on such license plates and shall provide for a design and combination of colors which distinguish such license plates from those issued for vehicles owned by the political subdivisions of the Commonwealth.

License plates issued for vehicles owned by political subdivisions of the Commonwealth and regional jail authorities, except such plates issued to be used (i) on vehicles used by any local or regional economic development authority, agency, instrumentality, or organization, upon the request of the chief administrative officer of the affected locality (or, in the case of regional organizations, the chief administrative officer of any of the affected localities) or (ii) on vehicles devoted solely to police work, shall have conspicuously and legibly inscribed, stamped, or printed thereon words stating that the vehicle is for official local government use only. The Commissioner shall reserve a unique series of numbers for use on such license plates and shall provide for a design and combination of colors which distinguish such license plates from those issued for vehicles owned by the Commonwealth.

No other license plates shall be used on vehicles for which official use plates have been issued, except for vehicles used solely for police work and as provided in subsection B of this section.

B. In addition to any other license plate authorized by this section, the Commissioner may issue permanent or temporary license plates for use on vehicles owned by the Commonwealth or any of its departments, institutions, boards, or agencies and used for security or transportation purposes in conjunction with conferences, meetings, or other events involving the Governor or members of the General Assembly. No state agency shall use government funds to cover the costs of any license plates issued under this subsection. The design of these license plates shall be at the discretion of the Commissioner. These license plates shall be issued under the following conditions:

1. For each set of permanent license plates issued, the Commissioner shall charge a fee of $100. The Commissioner shall limit the validity of any set of license plates issued under this subdivision to no more than 30 consecutive days. The Commissioner's written authorization for use of any set of license plates issued under this subdivision shall be kept in the vehicle on which the license plates are displayed until expiration of the authorization.

2. The Commissioner shall limit the validity of each set of temporary license plates to no more than 14 consecutive days. For each set of temporary license plates, the Commissioner shall charge a fee of $25 for the first set and $2 for each additional set. The Commissioner's written authorization for use of any set of license plates issued under this subdivision shall be kept in the vehicle on which the license plates are displayed until expiration of the authorization.

History.

Code 1950, § 46-48; 1958, c. 541, § 46.1-49; 1970, c. 66; 1974, c. 129; 1982, c. 317; 1989, cc. 110, 727; 1994, 1st Sp. Sess., c. 6; 1995, cc. 432, 747; 1996, cc. 590, 598, 1026; 2004, c. 721; 2016, cc. 302, 707.

§ 46.2-750.1. Vehicles used for police work.

Motor vehicles, trailers, and semitrailers owned by the Commonwealth and the counties, cities, and towns thereof and used solely for police work may be issued the same license plates as those issued in registration of vehicles owned by private citizens. The head of a state agency, the chief of police of a city, county, or town having a police department, or the sheriff of a city or county, shall certify under oath and the law-enforcement agencies of the federal government shall certify to the Commissioner of Motor Vehicles the vehicles to be used solely for police work.

History.

1989, cc. 48, 110, §§ 46.1-49, 46.1-49.1.

§ 46.2-751. State-owned passenger vehicles.

Except as provided in subsection B of § 46.2-750, the Commissioner shall not issue any license plates for use on vehicles owned by the Commonwealth or any of its departments, institutions, boards, or agencies and used for passenger transportation unless written application has been filed with the Governor showing the necessity for the use and unless the Governor has directed the Commissioner to issue the license plates.

History.

Code 1950, § 46-55; 1958, c. 541, § 46.1-57; 1972, c. 723; 1989, c. 727; 1994, 1st Sp. Sess., c. 6.

§ 46.2-752. Taxes and license fees imposed by counties, cities, and towns; limitations on amounts; disposition of revenues; requiring evidence of payment of personal property taxes and certain fines; prohibiting display of licenses after expiration; failure to display valid local license required by other localities; penalty.

A. Except as provided in § 46.2-755, counties, cities, and towns may levy and assess taxes and charge license fees on motor vehicles, trailers, and semitrailers. However, none of these taxes and license fees shall be assessed or charged by any county on vehicles owned by residents of any town located in the county when such town constitutes a separate school district if the vehicles are already subject to town license fees and taxes, nor shall a town charge a license fee to any new resident of the town, previously a resident of a county within which all or part of the town is situated, who has previously paid a license fee for the same tax year to such county. The amount of the license fee or tax imposed by any county, city, or town on any motor vehicle, trailer, or semitrailer shall not be greater than the annual or one-year fee imposed by the Commonwealth on the motor vehicle, trailer, or semitrailer. The license fees and taxes shall be imposed in such manner, on such basis, for such periods, and subject to proration for fractional periods of years, as the proper local authorities may determine.

Owners or lessees of motor vehicles, trailers, and semitrailers who have served outside of the United States in the armed services of the United States

Motor Vehicles

shall have a 90-day grace period, beginning on the date they are no longer serving outside the United States, in which to comply with the requirements of this section. For purposes of this section, "the armed services of the United States" includes active duty service with the regular Armed Forces of the United States or the National Guard or other reserve component.

Local licenses may be issued free of charge for any or all of the following:

1. Vehicles powered by clean special fuels as defined in § 46.2-749.3, including dual-fuel and bi-fuel vehicles,

2. Vehicles owned by volunteer emergency medical services agencies,

3. Vehicles owned by volunteer fire departments,

4. Vehicles owned or leased by active members or active auxiliary members of volunteer emergency medical services agencies,

5. Vehicles owned or leased by active members or active auxiliary members of volunteer fire departments,

6. Vehicles owned or leased by auxiliary police officers,

7. Vehicles owned or leased by volunteer police chaplains,

8. Vehicles owned by surviving spouses of persons qualified to receive special license plates under § 46.2-739,

9. Vehicles owned or leased by auxiliary deputy sheriffs or volunteer deputy sheriffs,

10. Vehicles owned by persons qualified to receive special license plates under § 46.2-739,

11. Vehicles owned by any of the following who served at least 10 years in the locality: former members of volunteer emergency medical services agencies, former members of volunteer fire departments, former auxiliary police officers, members and former members of authorized police volunteer citizen support units, members and former members of authorized sheriff's volunteer citizen support units, former volunteer police chaplains, and former volunteer special police officers appointed under former § 15.2-1737. In the case of active members of volunteer emergency medical services agencies and active members of volunteer fire departments, applications for such licenses shall be accompanied by written evidence, in a form acceptable to the locality, of their active affiliation or membership, and no member of an emergency medical services agency or member of a volunteer fire department shall be issued more than one such license free of charge,

12. All vehicles having a situs for the imposition of licensing fees under this section in the locality,

13. Vehicles owned or leased by deputy sheriffs; however, no deputy sheriff shall be issued more than one such license free of charge,

14. Vehicles owned or leased by police officers; however, no police officer shall be issued more than one such license free of charge,

15. Vehicles owned or leased by officers of the State Police; however, no officer of the State Police shall be issued more than one such license free of charge,

16. Vehicles owned or leased by salaried firefighters; however, no salaried firefighter shall be issued more than one such license free of charge,

17. Vehicles owned or leased by salaried emergency medical services personnel; however, no salaried emergency medical services personnel shall be issued more than one such license free of charge,

18. Vehicles with a gross weight exceeding 10,000 pounds owned by museums officially designated by the Commonwealth,

19. Vehicles owned by persons, or their surviving spouses, qualified to receive special license plates under subsection A of § 46.2-743, and

20. Vehicles owned or leased by members of the Virginia Defense Force; however, no member of the Virginia Defense Force shall be issued more than one such license free of charge.

The governing body of any county, city, or town issuing licenses under this section may by ordinance provide for a 50 percent reduction in the fee charged for the issuance of any such license issued for any vehicle owned or leased by any person who is 65 years old or older. No such discount, however, shall be available for more than one vehicle owned or leased by the same person.

The governing body of any county, city, or town issuing licenses free of charge under this subsection may by ordinance provide for (i) the limitation, restriction, or denial of such free issuance to an otherwise qualified applicant, including without limitation the denial of free issuance to a taxpayer who has failed to timely pay personal property taxes due with respect to the vehicle and (ii) the grounds for such limitation, restriction, or denial.

The situs for the imposition of licensing fees under this section shall in all cases, except as hereinafter provided, be the county, city, or town in which the motor vehicle, trailer, or semitrailer is normally garaged, stored, or parked. If it cannot be determined where the personal property is normally garaged, stored, or parked, the situs shall be the domicile of its owner. In the event the owner of the motor vehicle is a full-time student attending an institution of higher education, the situs shall be the domicile of such student, provided the student has presented sufficient evidence that he has paid a personal property tax on the motor vehicle in his domicile.

B. The revenue derived from all county, city, or town taxes and license fees imposed on motor vehicles, trailers, or semitrailers shall be applied to general county, city, or town purposes.

C. A county, city, or town may require that no motor vehicle, trailer, or semitrailer shall be locally licensed until the applicant has produced satisfactory evidence that all personal property taxes on the motor vehicle, trailer, or semitrailer to be licensed have been paid and satisfactory evidence that any delinquent motor vehicle, trailer, or semitrailer personal property taxes owing have been paid which have been properly assessed or are assessable against the applicant by the county, city, or town. A county, city, or town may also provide that no motor vehicle license shall be issued unless the tangible personal property taxes properly assessed or assessable by that locality on any tangible personal property used or usable as a dwelling titled by the Department of Motor Vehicles and owned by the taxpayer have been paid. Any county and any town within any such county may by agreement require that all personal property taxes assessed by either the county or the town on any vehicle be paid before licensure of such vehicle by either the county or the town.

C1. The Counties of Dinwiddie, Lee, and Wise may, by ordinance or resolution adopted after public notice and hearing and, with the consent of the treasurer, require that no license may be issued under this section unless the applicant has produced satisfactory evidence that all fees, including delinquent fees, payable to such county or local solid waste authority, for the disposal of solid waste pursuant to the Virginia Water and Waste Authorities Act (§ 15.2-5100 et seq.), or pursuant to § 15.2-2159, have been paid in full. For purposes of this subsection, all fees, including delinquent fees, payable to a county for waste disposal services described herein, shall be paid to the treasurer of such county; however, in Wise County, the fee shall be paid to the county or its agent.

D. The Counties of Arlington, Fairfax, Loudoun, and Prince William and towns within them and any city may require that no motor vehicle, trailer, or semitrailer shall be licensed by that jurisdiction unless all fines owed to the jurisdiction by the owner of the vehicle, trailer, or semitrailer for violation of the jurisdiction's ordinances governing parking of vehicles have been paid. The provisions of this subsection shall not apply to vehicles owned by firms or companies in the business of renting motor vehicles.

E. If in any county imposing license fees and taxes under this section, a town therein imposes like fees and taxes on vehicles of owners resident in the town, the owner of any vehicle subject to the fees or taxes shall be entitled, on the owner's displaying evidence that he has paid the fees or taxes, to receive a credit on the fees or taxes imposed by the county to the extent of the fees or taxes he has paid to the town. Nothing in this section shall deprive any town now imposing these licenses and taxes from increasing them or deprive any town not now imposing them from hereafter doing so, but subject to the limitations provided in subsection D. The governing body of any county and the governing body of any town in that county wherein each imposes the license tax herein provided may provide mutual agreements so that not more than one license plate or decal in addition to the state plate shall be required.

F. Notwithstanding the provisions of subsection E, in a consolidated county wherein a tier-city exists, the tier-city may, in accordance with the provisions of the agreement or plan of consolidation, impose license fees and taxes under this section in addition to those fees and taxes imposed by the county, provided that the combined county and tier-city rates do not exceed the maximum provided in subsection A. No credit shall be allowed on the fees or taxes imposed by the county for fees or taxes paid to the tier-city, except as may be provided by the consolidation agreement or plan. The governing body of any county and the governing body of any tier-city in such county wherein each imposes the license tax herein may provide by mutual agreement that no more than one license plate or decal in addition to the state license plate shall be required.

G. Any county, city, or town may by ordinance provide that it shall be unlawful for any owner or operator of a motor vehicle, trailer, or semitrailer (i) to fail to obtain and, if any required by such ordinance, to display the local license required by any ordinance of the county, city or town in which the vehicle is registered, or (ii) to display upon a motor vehicle, trailer, or semitrailer any such local license, required by ordinance to be displayed, after its expiration date. The ordinance may provide that a violation shall constitute a misdemeanor the penalty for which shall not exceed that of a Class 4 misdemeanor and may, in the case of a motor vehicle registered to a resident of the locality where such vehicle is registered, authorize the issuance by local law-enforcement officers of citations, summonses, parking tickets, or uniform traffic summonses for violations. Any such ordinance may also provide that a violation of the ordinance by the registered owner of the vehicle may not be discharged by payment of a fine except upon presentation of satisfactory evidence that the required license has been obtained. Nothing in this section shall be construed to require a county, city, or town to issue a decal or any other tangible evidence of a local license to be displayed on the licensed vehicle if the county's, city's, or town's ordinance does not require display of a decal or other evidence of payment. No ordinance adopted pursuant to this section shall require the display of any local license, decal, or sticker on any vehicle owned by a public service company, as defined in § 56-76, having a fleet of at least 2,500 vehicles garaged in the Commonwealth.

H. Except as provided by subsections E and F, no vehicle shall be subject to taxation under the provisions of this section in more than one jurisdiction. Furthermore, no person who has purchased a local vehicle license, decal, or sticker for a vehicle in one county, city, or town and then moves to and garages his vehicle in another county, city, or town shall be required to purchase another local license, decal, or sticker from the county, city, or town to which he has moved and wherein his vehicle is now garaged until the expiration date of the local license, decal, or sticker issued by the county, city, or town from which he moved.

I. Purchasers of new or used motor vehicles shall be allowed at least a 10-day grace period, beginning with the date of purchase, during which to pay license fees charged by local governments under authority of this section.

J. The treasurer or director of finance of any county, city, or town may enter into an agreement with the Commissioner whereby the Commissioner will refuse to issue or renew any vehicle registration of any applicant therefor who owes to such county, city or town any local vehicle license fees or delinquent tangible personal property tax or parking citations. Before being issued any vehicle registration or renewal of such license or registration by the Commissioner, the applicant shall first satisfy all such local vehicle license fees and delinquent taxes or parking citations and present evidence satisfactory to the Commissioner that all such local vehicle license fees and delinquent taxes or parking citations have been paid in full. The Commissioner shall charge a reasonable fee to cover the costs of such enforcement action, and the treasurer or director of finance may add the cost of this fee to the delinquent tax bill or the amount of the parking citation. The treasurer or director of finance of any county, city, or town seeking to collect delinquent taxes or parking citations through the withholding of registration or renewal thereof by the Commissioner as provided for in this subsection shall notify the Commissioner in the manner provided for in his agreement with the Commissioner and supply to the Commissioner information necessary to identify the debtor whose registration or renewal is to be denied. Any agreement entered into pursuant to the provisions of this subsection shall provide the debtor notice of the intent to deny renewal of registration at least 30 days prior to the expiration date of a current vehicle registration. For the purposes of this subsection, notice by first-class mail to the registrant's address as maintained in the records of the Department of Motor Vehicles shall be deemed sufficient. In the case of parking violations, the Commissioner shall only refuse to issue or renew the vehicle registration of any applicant therefor pursuant to this subsection for the vehicle that incurred the parking violations. The provisions of this subsection shall not apply to vehicles owned by firms or companies in the business of renting motor vehicles.

K. The governing bodies of any two or more counties, cities, or towns may enter into compacts for the regional enforcement of local motor vehicle license requirements. The governing body of each participating jurisdiction may by ordinance require the owner or operator of any motor vehicle, trailer, or semitrailer to display on his vehicle a valid local license issued by another county, city, or town that is a party to the regional compact, provided that the owner or operator is required by the jurisdiction of situs, as provided in § 58.1-3511, to obtain and display such license. The ordinance may also provide that no motor vehicle, trailer, or semitrailer shall be locally licensed until the applicant has produced satisfactory evidence that (i) all personal property taxes on the motor vehicle, trailer, or semitrailer to be licensed have been paid to all participating jurisdictions and (ii) any delinquent motor vehicle, trailer, or semitrailer personal property taxes that have been properly assessed or are assessable by any participating jurisdiction against the applicant have been paid. Any city and any county having the urban county executive form of government, the counties adjacent to such county and towns within them may require that no motor vehicle, trailer, or semitrailer shall be licensed by that jurisdiction or any other jurisdiction in the compact unless all fines owed to any participating jurisdiction by the owner of the vehicle for violation of any participating jurisdiction's ordinances governing parking of vehicles have been paid. The ordinance may further provide that a violation shall constitute a misdemeanor the penalty for which shall not exceed that of a Class 4 misdemeanor. Any such ordinance may also provide that a violation of the ordinance by the owner of the vehicle may not be discharged by payment of a fine and applicable court costs except upon presentation of satisfactory evidence that the required license has been obtained. The provisions of this subsection shall not apply to vehicles owned by firms or companies in the business of renting motor vehicles.

L. In addition to the taxes and license fees permitted in subsection A, counties, cities, and towns may charge a license fee of no more than $1 per motor vehicle, trailer, and semitrailer. Except for the provisions of subsection B, such fee shall be subject to all other provisions of this section. All funds collected pursuant to this subsection shall be paid pursuant to § 51.1-1204 to the Volunteer Firefighters' and Rescue Squad Workers' Service Award Fund to the accounts of all members of the Fund who are volunteers for fire departments or emergency medical services agencies within the jurisdiction of the particular county, city, or town.

M. In any county, the county treasurer or comparable officer and the treasurer of any town located wholly or partially within such county may enter into a reciprocal agreement, with the approval of the respective local governing bodies, that provides for the town treasurer to collect current, non-delinquent license fees or taxes on any motor vehicle, trailer, or semitrailer owed to the county or for the county treasurer to collect current, non-delinquent license fees or taxes owed to the town. A treasurer or comparable officer collecting any such license fee or tax pursuant to an agreement entered into under this subsection shall account for and pay over such amounts to the locality owed such license fee or tax in the same manner as provided by law. As used in this subsection, with regard to towns, "treasurer" means the town officer or employee vested with authority by the charter, statute, or governing body to collect local taxes.

History.
Code 1950, § 46-64; 1950, p. 240; 1952, c. 169; 1954, cc. 491, 594; 1956, cc. 66, 549, 570; 1958, c. 541, § 46.1-65; 1959, Ex. Sess., cc. 22, 55; 1962, c. 574; 1964, c. 218; 1972, c. 200; 1974, c. 621; 1975, c. 105; 1977, c. 166; 1979, c. 185; 1980, c. 105; 1982, c. 85; 1984, cc. 308, 630, 695; 1986, c. 123; 1987, cc. 208, 243; 1989, cc. 321, 706, 727; 1990, cc. 181, 187, 188, 455; 1991, c. 622; 1992, cc. 226, 355, 794, 806; 1993, cc. 50, 63, 175, 565; 1994, cc. 528, 962; 1995, cc. 91, 412, 449, 460, 479, 659; 1996, cc. 89, 562; 1997, cc. 246, 499, 905, 911; 1998, c. 649; 1999, c. 236; 2000, c. 303; 2001, cc. 338, 471, 605, 606; 2002, cc. 206, 553; 2003, c. 326; 2004, cc. 689, 723; 2005, c. 317; 2006, c. 148; 2007, cc. 213, 230, 813, 865; 2008, cc. 163, 457, 591; 2009, cc. 366, 756, 843; 2010, cc. 125, 131; 2013, c. 82; 2014, c. 543; 2015, cc. 69, 502, 503.

§ 46.2-752.1. One-time, one-month registration extension to allow for satisfaction of requirements of counties, cities, and towns.

A. On request of an applicant, the Commissioner may grant a one-month extension of the registration period of a vehicle if the vehicle registration has been withheld pursuant to § 46.2-752 and the current registration period will expire within the calendar month. No extension may be granted for an expired vehicle registration and only one extension may be granted for any one vehicle registration period.

For each extension granted, the Commissioner shall collect (i) a $10 administrative fee and (ii) a fee sufficient for a one-month registration period for the vehicle, as calculated under subsection B of § 46.2-694. Neither fee shall apply, however, if the applicant has been granted an extension under § 46.2-1183.1 with respect to the same registration period and has paid the fees pursuant to that section.

On receipt of such fees, the Commissioner shall issue a registration card and, if applicable, decals indicating the month of expiration of the vehicle registration. Upon satisfaction of the requirements of § 46.2-752, the applicant may elect to renew the vehicle registration. For such renewal, the Commissioner shall collect the appropriate registration renewal fee and issue a registration card and, if applicable, decals. The renewal shall take effect the first day succeeding the month in which the registration extension expires. When offered by the Commissioner, the applicant may elect to renew the vehicle registration for multiple years, pursuant to § 46.2-646.

B. All administrative fees imposed and collected by the Commissioner under this section shall be paid into the state treasury and set aside as a special fund to be used to meet the expenses of the Department.

History.
2012, cc. 215, 222; 2013, cc. 673, 789.

§ 46.2-753. Additional license fees in certain localities.

Notwithstanding any other provision of law, the governing bodies of Alexandria, Arlington, Fairfax County, Fairfax City, and Falls Church are authorized to charge annual license fees, in addition to those specified in § 46.2-752, on passenger cars, including passenger cars that are used as TNC partner vehicles as defined in § 46.2-2000, but not on passenger cars that are otherwise used for the transportation of passengers for compensation. The additional fee shall be no more than $5. The total local license fee shall be no more than $25 on any vehicle, and this license fee shall not be imposed on any motor vehicle exempted under § 46.2-739.

The governing bodies are also authorized to charge additional annual license fees on the motor vehicles, trailers, and semitrailers as specified in § 46.2-697 in an amount of no more than $5 for each such vehicle. This authorization shall not increase the maximum chargeable by more than $5 or affect any existing exemption.

Any funds acquired in excess of those allowed by § 46.2-752, shall be allocated to the Northern Virginia Transportation Commission to be a credit to that locality making the payment for its share of any operating deficit assigned to it by the Washington Metropolitan Area Transit Authority.

History.
1974, c. 487; 1977, c. 258, § 46.1-65.1; 1989, c. 727; 2015, cc. 2, 3.

§ 46.2-754. Local motor vehicle licenses in Arlington County.

Arlington County may by ordinance require the owner of any motor vehicle, trailer, or semitrailer to obtain and display a license from the county licensing authority designated by the ordinance. The ordinance may also require that the license be obtained only after showing satisfactory evidence that all personal property taxes on the motor vehicle, trailer, or semitrailer have been paid, and that any delinquent personal property taxes assessed or assessable against the vehicle have been paid. The ordinance may also prohibit the display of the license after its expiration date and may prescribe the form of the license. This license requirement shall be imposed in such manner, on such basis, for such period, and subject to proration for fractional periods of years as the governing body requires.

The situs for the imposition of the license requirement under the ordinance shall be the locality in which the vehicle is normally garaged, stored, or parked. If it cannot be determined where it is normally garaged, stored, or parked, the situs shall be the domicile of its owner.

The ordinance may provide that no motor vehicle, trailer, or semitrailer may be licensed by the county unless all fines owed by the owner of the vehicle for violation of the county's parking ordinances have been paid.

The ordinance may provide that a violation of such ordinance constitutes a misdemeanor the penalty for which shall not exceed that of a Class 4 misdemeanor.

History.

1988, c. 451, § 46.1-65.2; 1989, c. 727.

§ 46.2-755. Limitations on imposition of motor vehicle license taxes and fees.

A. No locality shall impose any motor vehicle license tax or fee on any motor vehicle, trailer, or semitrailer when:

1. A similar tax or fee is imposed by the locality wherein the vehicle is normally garaged, stored, or parked;

2. The vehicle is owned by a nonresident of such locality and is used exclusively for pleasure or personal transportation or as a TNC partner vehicle as defined in § 46.2-2000 and not otherwise for hire or for the conduct of any business or occupation other than that set forth in subdivision 3;

3. The vehicle is (i) owned by a nonresident and (ii) used for transporting into and within the locality, for sale in person or by his employees, wood, meats, poultry, fruits, flowers, vegetables, milk, butter, cream, or eggs produced or grown by him, and not purchased by him for sale;

4. The motor vehicle, trailer, or semitrailer is owned by an officer or employee of the Commonwealth who is a nonresident of such locality and who uses the vehicle in the performance of his duties for the Commonwealth under an agreement for such use;

5. The motor vehicle, trailer, or semitrailer is kept by a dealer or manufacturer for sale or for sales demonstration;

6. The motor vehicle, trailer, or semitrailer is operated by a common carrier of persons or property operating between cities and towns in the Commonwealth and not in intracity transportation or between cities and towns on the one hand and points and places outside cities and towns on the other and not in intracity transportation; or

7. The motor vehicle, trailer, or semitrailer is inoperable and unlicensed pursuant to § 46.2-734.

B. No locality shall impose a license fee for any one motor vehicle owned and used personally by any veteran who holds a current state motor vehicle registration card establishing that he has received a disabled veteran's exemption from the Department and has been issued a disabled veteran's motor vehicle license plate as prescribed in § 46.2-739.

C. No locality shall impose any license tax or license fee or the requirement of a license tag, sticker or decal upon any daily rental vehicle, as defined in § 58.1-1735, the rental of which is subject to the tax imposed by subdivision A 2 of § 58.1-1736.

D. In the rental agreement between a motor vehicle renting company and a renter, the motor vehicle renting company may separately itemize and charge daily fees or transaction fees to the renter, provided that the amounts of such fees are disclosed at the time of reservation and rental as part of any estimated pricing provided to the renter. Such fees include a vehicle license fee to recover the company's incurred costs in licensing, titling, and registering its rental fleet, concession recovery fees actually charged the company by an airport, or other governmentally owned or operated facility, and consolidated facility charges actually charged by an airport, or other governmentally owned or operated facility for improvements to or construction of facilities at such facility where the motor vehicle rental company operates. The vehicle license fee shall represent the company's good faith estimate of the average per day per vehicle portion of the company's total annual vehicle licensing, titling, and registration costs.

No motor vehicle renting company charging a vehicle license fee, concession recovery fee, or consolidated facility charge may make an advertisement in the Commonwealth that includes a statement of the rental rate for a vehicle available for rent in the Commonwealth unless such advertisement includes a statement that the customer will be required to pay a vehicle license fee, concession recovery fee, or consolidated facility charge. The vehicle license fee, concession recovery fee, or consolidated facility charge shall be shown as a separately itemized charge on the rental agreement. The vehicle license fee shall be described in either the terms and conditions of the rental agreement as the "estimated average per day per vehicle portion of the company's total annual vehicle licensing, titling, and registration costs" or, for renters participating in an extended rental program pursuant to a master rental agreement, by posting such statement on the rental company website.

Any amounts collected by the motor vehicle renting company in excess of the actual amount of its costs incurred relating to its vehicle license fees shall be retained by the motor vehicle renting company and applied toward the recovery of its next calendar year's costs relating to such fees. In such event, the good faith estimate of any vehicle license fee to be charged by the company for the next calendar year shall be reduced to take into account the excess amount collected from the prior year.

E. As used in this section, common carrier of persons or property includes any person who undertakes, whether directly or by lease or any other arrangement, to transport passengers or household goods for the general public by motor vehicle for compensation over the highways of the Commonwealth, whether over regular or irregular routes, that has obtained the required certificate from the Department of Motor Vehicles pursuant to § 46.2-2075 or 46.2-2150.

History.

Code 1950, § 46-65; 1950, p. 407; 1954, c. 575; 1958, c. 541, § 46.1-66; 1959, Ex. Sess., c. 22; 1976, cc. 5, 339; 1978, c. 188; 1984, c. 156; 1985, c. 123; 1989, c. 727; 1997, cc. 283, 496, 853; 2006, c. 515; 2007, c. 296; 2011, cc. 405, 639, 881, 889; 2015, cc. 2, 3.

§§ 46.2-755.1, 46.2-755.2: Repealed by Acts 2009, cc. 864 and 871, cl. 5.

§ 46.2-756. Collection by Department of certain license fees.

The Department shall develop and implement standardized procedures and fees whereby, upon the written request of the governing body of any county, city, or town, the Department may collect motor vehicle, trailer, and semitrailer license fees, or portions thereof, provided the portions are for the identical period as the state license plate, levied by such county, city, or town. The Department shall make such charge as may be proper to defray the cost of handling such fees, and such monies as may be received shall be used by the Commissioner to defray the expenses of the Department incurred hereunder. All receipts from the local fees collected shall be deposited in a fiduciary account, and any interest that may accrue shall be credited to such account for the benefit of the participating counties, cities, and towns. However, before a registration or certificate of title is issued under the requirements of § 46.2-600 the owner of the motor vehicle, trailer, or semitrailer shall advise the Department of the situs, as provided in subsection A of § 46.2-752, of the motor vehicle, trailer, or semitrailer. The Department of Motor Vehicles shall not collect the motor vehicle, trailer, or semitrailer license fee of a county, city, or town on motor vehicles or vehicles falling within the provisions of § 46.2-755.

History.

Code 1950, § 46-104.2; 1952, c. 395; 1958, c. 541, § 46.1-111; 1975, c. 533; 1977, c. 388; 1982, c. 160; 1984, c. 47; 1989, c. 727; 2003, c. 293; 2006, c. 418.

ARTICLE 12.

INSURANCE REQUIREMENTS FOR MOTOR CARRIERS.

§§ 46.2-757 through 46.2-768: Repealed by Acts 2001, c. 596, cl. 2, effective July 1, 2002.

Cross references.

For present provisions relating to the regulation of motor carriers, see § 46.2-2000 et seq.

§ 46.2-769: Repealed by Acts 1997, c. 283.

CHAPTER 7.

[RESERVED.]

SUBTITLE III.

OPERATION.

CHAPTER 8.

REGULATION OF TRAFFIC.

Article 1.

General and Miscellaneous.

Article 1.1.

Toll Violations and Enforcement.

Article 2.

Right-of-Way.

Article 3.

Traffic Signs, Lights, and Markings.

Article 4.

Passing.

Article 5.

Turning.

Article 6.

Signals by Drivers.

Article 7.

Reckless Driving and Improper Driving.

Article 8.

Speed.

Article 9.

Railroad Crossings.

Article 10.

Stopping on Highways.

Article 11.

Accidents.

Article 12.

Bicycles.

Article 12.1.

Low-Speed Vehicles.

Article 13.

Motorcycles and Mopeds and All-Terrain Vehicles.

Article 13.1.

Golf Cart and Utility Vehicle Operation.

Article 14.

School Buses.

ARTICLE 1.

GENERAL AND MISCELLANEOUS.

§ 46.2-800. Riding bicycles, electric personal assistive mobility devices, electric power-assisted bicycles, or mopeds; riding or driving animals.

Every person riding a bicycle, electric personal assistive mobility device, electric power-assisted bicycle, moped, or an animal or driving an animal on a highway shall be subject to the provisions of this chapter and shall have all of the rights and duties applicable to the driver of a vehicle, unless the context of the provision clearly indicates otherwise.

The provisions of subsections A and C of § 46.2-920 applicable to operation of emergency vehicles under emergency conditions shall also apply, mutatis mutandis, to bicycles, electric personal assistive mobility devices, electric power-assisted bicycles, and mopeds operated under similar emergency conditions by law-enforcement officers.

History.

Code 1950, § 46-183; 1958, c. 541, § 46.1-171; 1980, c. 456; 1981, c. 585; 1989, c. 727; 1994, c. 176; 2001, c. 834; 2002, c. 254.

§ 46.2-800.1. Riding animals on highways after sunset.

A. No person riding upon any animal on a highway between sunset and sunrise shall ride the animal on the roadway unless the rider:

1. Wears a hat made of or coated with reflectorized material; or

2. Wears upper body clothing made of or coated with reflectorized material visible from 360 degrees; or

3. Displays at least 100 square inches of solid reflectorized material at shoulder level visible from 360 degrees; or

4. Carries a light visible in clear weather from a distance of 500 feet.

B. The requirements of subsection A of this section shall only apply to the riders of the first and last animals in a group riding one behind the other.

C. A violation of this section shall not be construed as negligence per se in any civil action.

History.

1989, c. 295, § 46.1-171.01.

§ 46.2-800.2. Operation of off-road recreational vehicles in localities embraced by the Southwest Regional Recreation Authority.

A. The governing body of any county, city, or town embraced by the Southwest Regional Recreation Authority may by ordinance authorize the operation of any off-road recreational vehicles (i) on highways within its boundaries that have a maximum speed limit of no more than 25 miles per hour and (ii) for a distance of no more than five miles on any highway within its boundaries that has a maximum speed limit of more than 25 miles per hour. Any such ordinance shall define "off-road recreational vehicle." Any such operation shall be subject to the following conditions, and such additional restrictions and limitations as the county, city, or town by ordinance may impose:

1. Signs whose design, number, and location are approved by the Virginia Department of Transportation shall have been posted by the county, city, town, or Southwest Regional Recreation Authority warning motorists that off-road recreational vehicles may be operating on the highway;

2. Such off-road recreational vehicles shall be operated only during daylight hours;

3. Off-road recreational vehicle operators shall, when operating on the highway, obey all rules of the road applicable to other motor vehicles;

4. Riders of such off-road recreational vehicles shall wear helmets of a type approved by the Superintendent of State Police; and

5. Operators shall be licensed drivers or accompanied by a licensed driver who is either occupying the same vehicle or occupying another vehicle within a prudent distance; however, no person shall operate any off-road recreational vehicle as provided in this section if his driver's license, whether issued in the Commonwealth or in another jurisdiction, has been suspended or revoked.

B. The governing body of any county, city, or town that enacts any ordinance under subsection A shall notify in writing the Virginia State Police and all law-enforcement agencies within the county, city, or town of its action, together with a copy of such ordinance.

C. Operation of any off-road recreational vehicle as provided in the foregoing provisions of this section shall be subject to the issuance of a permit by the Southwest Regional Recreation Authority pursuant to § 15.2-6020. Any such permit shall be valid for such period of time and subject to the payment of such fee as the Authority shall provide.

History.
2010, cc. 332, 463.

§ 46.2-800.3. Driving in flooded areas prohibited.

The governing body of any locality may by ordinance prohibit any person from operating a motor vehicle or watercraft on a flooded highway, street, alley, or parking lot, regardless of whether such highway, street, alley, or parking lot is publicly or privately owned in such a manner as to increase the level of floodwaters to a level that causes or could reasonably be expected to cause damage to any real or personal property.

Such ordinance shall not apply to any law-enforcement officer, firefighter, or emergency medical services personnel engaged in the performance of his duties nor to the operator of any vehicle owned or controlled by the Department of Transportation or a public utility company as defined in § 56-265.1. Any locality adopting such an ordinance shall provide for adequate notice, including signs that, at a minimum, warn operators of motor vehicles and watercraft of the prohibition and penalties.

A violation of such ordinance shall constitute a Class 4 misdemeanor.

History.
2016, c. 249.

§ 46.2-801. Chapter applicable to drivers of all vehicles regardless of ownership.

The provisions of this chapter applicable to the drivers of vehicles on the highways shall apply to the drivers of all vehicles regardless of their ownership, subject to such exceptions as are set forth in this chapter.

History.
Code 1950, § 46-181; 1958, c. 541, § 46.1-168; 1989, c. 727.

§ 46.2-802. Drive on right side of highways.

Except as otherwise provided by law, on all highways of sufficient width, the driver of a vehicle shall drive on the right half of the highway, unless it is impracticable to travel on such side of the highway and except when overtaking and passing another vehicle, subject to the provisions applicable to overtaking and passing set forth in Article 4 (§ 46.2-837 et seq.) of this chapter.

History.
Code 1950, § 46-220; 1952, c. 671; 1958, c. 541, § 46.1-203; 1989, c. 727.

§ 46.2-803. Keep to the right in crossing intersections or railroads.

Except as otherwise provided by law, when crossing an intersection of highways or the intersection of a highway by a railroad right-of-way, the driver of a vehicle shall drive on the right half of the roadway unless it is obstructed or impassable. When crossing an intersection of highways, however, the driver of a vehicle may overtake or pass another vehicle in the intersection if such intersection is designated and marked as a passing zone.

History.

Code 1950, § 46-221; 1958, c. 541, § 46.1-205; 1972, c. 369; 1978, c. 27; 1989, c. 727.

§ 46.2-803.1. Commercial motor vehicles limited to use of certain lanes of certain interstate highways.

Except where the posted speed limit is less than 65 miles per hour, no person shall drive any commercial motor vehicle, as defined in § 46.2-341.4, on the left-most lane of any interstate highway having more than two lanes in each direction.

Furthermore, within the Eighth Planning District and on Interstate Route 81, no person shall drive any commercial motor vehicle, as defined in § 46.2-341.4, on the left-most lane of any interstate highway having more than two lanes in each direction, regardless of the posted speed limit. Every commercial motor vehicle shall keep to the right-most lane when operating at a speed of 15 miles per hour or more below the posted speed limit on an interstate highway with no more than two lanes in each direction.

The provisions of this section shall not apply to (i) buses or school buses or (ii) other commercial vehicles when (a) preparing to exit a highway via a left exit or (b) being used to perform maintenance or construction work on an interstate highway.

History.

1997, c. 733; 1998, c. 555; 2000, cc. 60, 306, 407; 2004, c. 809.

§ 46.2-804. Special regulations applicable on highways laned for traffic.

For the purposes of this section, "traffic lines" includes any temporary traffic control devices used to emulate the lines and markings in subdivisions 6 and 7.

Whenever any roadway has been divided into clearly marked lanes for traffic, drivers of vehicles shall obey the following:

1. Any vehicle proceeding at less than the normal speed of traffic at the time and place and under the conditions existing, shall be driven in the lane nearest the right edge or right curb of the highway when such lane is available for travel except when overtaking and passing another vehicle or in preparation for a left turn or where right lanes are reserved for slow-moving traffic as permitted in this section;

2. A vehicle shall be driven as nearly as is practicable entirely within a single lane and shall not be moved from that lane until the driver has ascertained that such movement can be made safely;

3. Except as otherwise provided in subdivision 5, on a highway which is divided into three lanes, no vehicle shall be driven in the center lane except when overtaking and passing another vehicle or in preparation for a left turn or unless such center lane is at the time allocated exclusively to traffic moving in the direction the vehicle is proceeding and is signed or marked to give notice of such allocation. Traffic-control devices may be erected directing specified traffic to use a designated lane or designating those lanes to be used by traffic moving in a particular direction regardless of the center of the roadway and drivers of vehicles shall obey the directions of every such device;

4. The Commissioner of Highways, or local authorities in their respective jurisdictions, may designate right lanes for slow-moving vehicles and the Virginia Department of Transportation shall post signs requiring trucks and combination vehicles to keep to the right on Interstate Highway System components with no more than two travel lanes in each direction where terrain is likely to slow the speed of such vehicles climbing hills and inclines to a speed that is less than the posted speed limit;

5. Wherever a highway is marked with double traffic lines consisting of a solid line immediately adjacent to a broken line, no vehicle shall be driven to the left of such line if the solid line is on the right of the broken line, except (i) when turning left for the purpose of entering or leaving a public, private, or commercial road or entrance or (ii) in order to pass a pedestrian or a device moved by human power, including a bicycle, skateboard, or foot-scooter, provided such movement can be made safely. Where the middle lane of a highway is marked on both sides with a solid line immediately adjacent to a broken line, such middle lane shall be considered a left-turn or holding lane and it shall be lawful to drive to the left of such line if the solid line is on the right of the broken line for the purpose of turning left into any road or entrance, provided that the vehicle may not travel in such lane further than 150 feet;

6. Wherever a highway is marked with double traffic lines consisting of two immediately adjacent solid yellow lines, no vehicle shall be driven to the left of such lines, except (i) when turning left or (ii) in order to pass a pedestrian or a device moved by human power, including a bicycle, skateboard, or foot-scooter, provided such movement can be made safely; and

7. Whenever a highway is marked with double traffic lines consisting of two immediately adjacent solid white lines, no vehicle shall cross such lines.

History.

Code 1950, § 46-222; 1952, c. 671; 1958, c. 541, § 46.1-206; 1962, c. 87; 1979, c. 25; 1985, c. 481; 1989, c. 727; 2007, c. 501; 2013, cc. 128, 400, 585, 646; 2015, c. 416.

§ 46.2-805. Lane-use control signals.

A. When lane-use control signals are placed over the individual lanes of a highway, vehicular traffic may travel in any lane over which a green signal is shown, but shall not enter or travel in any lane over which a red signal is shown and shall vacate as soon as possible any lane over which an amber signal is shown.

B. Vehicular traffic shall not enter or travel in a lane over which a one-way or two-way left turn white arrow lane-use control signal is shown, except to make the turning movement indicated by the signal. Such turning traffic shall yield the right-of-way to pedestrians lawfully within a crosswalk and to other traffic using the intersection.

History.
1974, c. 347, § 46.1-206.1; 1989, c. 727; 2013, cc. 128, 400.

§ 46.2-806. One-way roadways and highways.

The Commissioner of Highways may designate any highway or any separate roadway under his jurisdiction for one-way traffic and shall erect appropriate signs. Traffic thereon shall move only in the direction designated.

History.
Code 1950, § 46-220.1; 1952, c. 671; 1958, c. 541, § 46.1-204; 1989, c. 727; 2013, cc. 585, 646.

§ 46.2-807. Path of travel at circular intersections.

A vehicle passing through a circular intersection shall be driven only to the right of the central island, unless otherwise directed by traffic control devices.

History.
Code 1950, § 46-220.1; 1952, c. 671; 1958, c. 541, § 46.1-204; 1989, c. 727; 2013, cc. 128, 400.

§ 46.2-808. Commonwealth Transportation Board may prohibit certain uses of controlled access highways; penalty.

A. The Commonwealth Transportation Board may, when necessary to promote safety, prohibit the use of controlled access highways or any part thereof by any or all of the following:

1. Pedestrians,
2. Persons riding bicycles, electric power-assisted bicycles, electric personal assistive mobility devices, or mopeds,
3. Animal-drawn vehicles,
4. Self-propelled machinery or equipment, and
5. Animals led, ridden or driven on the hoof.

B. The termini of any section of controlled access highways, use of which is restricted under the provisions of this section, shall be clearly indicated by a conspicuous marker.

C. This section shall not apply to any vehicle or equipment owned or controlled by the Virginia Department of Transportation, while actually engaged in the construction, reconstruction, or maintenance of highways or to any vehicle or equipment for which a permit has been obtained for operation on such highway.

Any person violating a restriction or prohibition imposed pursuant to this section shall be guilty of a traffic infraction.

History.
1964, c. 239, § 46.1-171.1; 1966, c. 365; 1981, c. 585; 1983, c. 262; 1989, c. 727; 1991, c. 55; 2004, cc. 947, 973; 2006, cc. 529, 538; 2007, cc. 209, 366.

§ 46.2-808.1. Use of crossovers on controlled access highways; penalty.

It shall be unlawful for the driver of any vehicle other than an authorized vehicle to use or attempt to use any crossover posted for authorized vehicles only on any controlled access highway.

For the purposes of this section, "authorized vehicle" means (i) Department of Transportation vehicles, (ii) law-enforcement vehicles, (iii) emergency vehicles as defined in § 46.2-920, (iv) towing and recovery vehicles operating under the direction of a law-enforcement agency, (v) vehicles for which permits authorizing use of such crossovers have been issued by the Department of Transportation, and (vi) other vehicles operating in medical emergency situations.

Violation of any provision of this section shall constitute a traffic infraction punishable by a fine of no more than $250.

History.
1997, c. 881; 2008, cc. 470, 647.

§ 46.2-809. Regulation of truck traffic on primary and secondary highways.

The Commonwealth Transportation Board, or its designee, in response to a formal request by a local governing body, after such body has held public hearings, may, after due notice and a proper hearing, prohibit or restrict the use by through traffic of any part of a primary or secondary highway if a reasonable alternate route is provided. The Board, or its designee, shall act upon any such formal request within nine months of its receipt, unless good cause is shown. Such restriction may apply to any truck or truck and trailer or semitrailer combination, except a pickup or panel truck, as may be necessary to promote the health, safety, and welfare of the citizens of the Commonwealth. Nothing in this section shall affect the validity of any city charter provision or city ordinance heretofore adopted.

The provisions of this section shall not apply in (i) cities, (ii) any town which maintains its own system of streets, and (iii) in any county which owns, operates, and maintains its own system of roads and streets.

History.
1973, c. 67, § 46.1-171.2; 1989, c. 727; 2003, c. 300.

§ 46.2-809.1. Regulation of residential cut-through traffic by Board.

The Commonwealth Transportation Board may develop a residential cut-through traffic policy and procedure for the control of residential cut-through traffic on designated secondary highways.

For the purposes of this section, "residential cut-through traffic" means vehicular traffic passing through a residential area without stopping or without at least an origin or destination within the area.

The provisions of this section shall not apply in (i) cities, (ii) any town that maintains its own system of streets, and (iii) any county that owns, operates, and maintains its own system of highways.

History.
1995, c. 556.

§ 46.2-810. Age limits for drivers of public passenger-carrying vehicles.

No person, whether licensed or not, under the age of eighteen years shall drive a motor vehicle while in use as a public passenger-carrying vehicle.

History.
Code 1950, § 46-182; 1958, c. 541, § 46.1-170; 1970, c. 481; 1972, cc. 386, 823; 1989, c. 727.

§ 46.2-810.1. Smoking in vehicle with a minor present; civil penalty.

A. For the purposes of this section, "smoke" means to carry or hold any lighted pipe, cigar, or cigarette of any kind or any other lighted smoking equipment or to light or inhale or exhale smoke from a pipe, cigar, or cigarette of any kind or any other lighted smoking equipment.

B. It is unlawful for a person to smoke in a motor vehicle, whether in motion or at rest, when a minor under the age of eight is present in the motor vehicle. A violation of this section is punishable by a civil penalty of $100 to be paid into the state treasury and credited to the Literary Fund. No demerit points shall be assigned under Article 19 (§ 46.2-489 et seq.) of Chapter 3 and no court costs shall be assessed for a violation of this section. A violation of this section may be charged on the uniform traffic summons form.

C. No citation for a violation of this section shall be issued unless the officer issuing such citation has cause to stop or arrest the driver of such motor vehicle for the violation of some other provision of this Code or local ordinance relating to the operation, ownership, or maintenance of a motor vehicle or any criminal statute.

History.
2016, c. 515.

§ 46.2-811. Coasting prohibited.

The driver of any motor vehicle traveling on a downgrade on any highway shall not coast with the gears of the vehicle in neutral.

History.
Code 1950, § 46-218; 1958, c. 541, § 46.1-200; 1989, c. 727.

§ 46.2-812. Driving more than thirteen hours in twenty-four prohibited.

No person shall drive any motor vehicle on the highways of the Commonwealth for more than thirteen hours in any period of twenty-four hours or for a period which, when added to the time such person may have driven in any other state, would make an aggregate of more than thirteen hours in any twenty-four-hour period. The provisions of this section, however, shall not apply to the operation of motor vehicles used in snow or ice control or removal operations or similar emergency situations.

No person shall drive any motor vehicle on the highways of the Commonwealth for more than thirteen hours in any period of twenty-four hours or for a period which, when added to the time such person may have driven in any other state, would make an aggregate of more than thirteen hours in any twenty-four-hour period. The provisions of this section, however, shall not apply to the operation of motor vehicles used in snow or ice control or removal operations or similar emergency situations.

History.
Code 1950, § 46-218; 1958, c. 541, § 46.1-200; 1989, c. 727.

§ 46.2-813. Occupation of trailer being towed on highways.

No person shall occupy a house trailer or camping trailer while it is being towed on a public highway in this Commonwealth. No operator of a towing vehicle shall knowingly permit another person to occupy a house trailer or camping trailer as defined in § 46.2-100 while it is being towed.

In any civil proceeding, the violation of this section shall not constitute negligence per se.

History.
1970, c. 103, § 46.1-172.1; 1978, c. 605; 1989, c. 727.

§ 46.2-814. Driving through safety zone prohibited.

No driver of a vehicle shall drive through or over a safety zone.

History.
Code 1950, § 46-252; 1958, c. 541, § 46.1-242; 1989, c. 727.

§ 46.2-815. Hauling certain cargoes through tunnels in violation of posted signs; penalty.

The hauling of any explosive, flammable, or other hazardous cargo, as prohibited by the Department of Transportation under the authority of §§ 33.2-210 and 33.2-300, through any tunnel on any highway in the Commonwealth in violation of any lawfully posted sign shall constitute a Class 1 misdemeanor.

History.
1984, c. 488, § 46.1-228.1; 1989, c. 727.

Editor's note.

References in this section were updated at the direction of the Virginia Code Commission to conform to the recodification of Title 33.2 by Acts 2014, c. 805, effective October 1, 2014.

§ 46.2-816. Following too closely.

The driver of a motor vehicle shall not follow another vehicle, trailer, or semitrailer more closely than is reasonable and prudent, having due regard to the speed of both vehicles and the traffic on, and conditions of, the highway at the time.

History.

Code 1950, § 46-229; 1958, c. 541, § 46.1-213; 1983, c. 248; 1989, c. 727; 2015, cc. 31, 188.

§ 46.2-817. Disregarding signal by law-enforcement officer to stop; eluding police; penalties.

A. Any person who, having received a visible or audible signal from any law-enforcement officer to bring his motor vehicle to a stop, drives such motor vehicle in a willful and wanton disregard of such signal or who attempts to escape or elude such law-enforcement officer whether on foot, in the vehicle, or by any other means, is guilty of a Class 2 misdemeanor. It shall be an affirmative defense to a charge of a violation of this subsection if the defendant shows he reasonably believed he was being pursued by a person other than a law-enforcement officer.

B. Any person who, having received a visible or audible signal from any law-enforcement officer to bring his motor vehicle to a stop, drives such motor vehicle in a willful and wanton disregard of such signal so as to interfere with or endanger the operation of the law-enforcement vehicle or endanger a person is guilty of a Class 6 felony. It shall be an affirmative defense to a charge of a violation of this subsection if the defendant shows he reasonably believed he was being pursued by a person other than a law-enforcement officer.

C. If a law-enforcement officer pursues a person as a result of a violation of subsection B and the law-enforcement officer is killed as a direct and proximate result of the pursuit, the person who violated subsection B is guilty of a Class 4 felony.

D. When any person is convicted of an offense under this section, in addition to the other penalties provided in this section, the driver's license of such person shall be suspended by the court for a period of not less than thirty days nor more than one year. However, in any case where the speed of such person is determined to have exceeded the maximum allowed by twenty miles per hour, his driver's license shall be suspended by the court trying the case for a period of not less than ninety days. In case of conviction and suspension, the court or judge shall order the surrender of the license to the court, which shall dispose of it in accordance with the provisions of § 46.2-398.

E. Violation of this section shall constitute a separate and distinct offense. If the acts or activities violating this section also violate another provision of law, a prosecution under this section shall not prohibit or bar any prosecution or proceeding under such other provision or the imposition of any penalties provided for thereby.

History.

1964, c. 614, § 46.1-192.1; 1984, cc. 544, 780; 1988, c. 307; 1989, c. 727; 1993, c. 796; 1996, cc. 577, 817; 1999, c. 720; 2000, c. 315; 2002, c. 505; 2008, cc. 773, 811; 2010, c. 655.

§ 46.2-818. Stopping vehicle of another; blocking access to premises; damaging or threatening commercial vehicle or operator thereof; penalties.

No person shall intentionally and willfully:

1. Stop the vehicle of another for the sole purpose of impeding its progress on the highways, except in the case of an emergency or mechanical breakdown;
2. Block the access to or egress from any premises of any service facility operated for the purposes of (i) selling fuel for motor vehicles, (ii) performing repair services on motor vehicles, or (iii) furnishing food, rest, or any other convenience for the use of persons operating motor vehicles engaged in intrastate and interstate commerce on the highways of the Commonwealth;
3. Damage any vehicle engaged in commerce on the highways of the Commonwealth, or threaten, assault, or otherwise harm the person of any operator of a motor vehicle being used for the transportation of property for hire.

Any person violating any provision of this section is guilty of a Class 1 misdemeanor, and in addition, his driver's license may be suspended by the court for a period of not more than one year. The court shall forward such license to the Department as provided by § 46.2-398.

The provisions of this section shall not apply to any law-enforcement officer, school guard, firefighter, or emergency medical services personnel engaged in the performance of his duties nor to any vehicle owned or controlled by the Virginia Department of Transportation while engaged in the construction, reconstruction, or maintenance of highways.

History.

1974, c. 457, § 46.1-250.1; 1977, c. 326; 1984, c. 780; 1989, c. 727; 2015, cc. 502, 503.

§ 46.2-818.1. Opening and closing motor vehicle doors; penalty.

No operator shall open the door of a parked motor vehicle on the side adjacent to moving vehicular traffic unless it is reasonably safe to do so.

A violation of this section shall constitute a traffic infraction punishable by a fine of not more than $50.

No demerit points shall be awarded by the Commissioner for a violation of this section.

The provisions of this section shall not apply to any law-enforcement officer, firefighter, or emergency medical services personnel engaged in the performance of his duties.

History.

2016, c. 607.

ARTICLE 1.1.
TOLL VIOLATIONS AND ENFORCEMENT.

§ 46.2-819. Use of toll facility without payment of toll; circumstances to be considered in assessing penalty.

Except for those permitted free use of toll facilities under § 33.2-613, it is unlawful for the operator of a motor vehicle to use a toll facility without payment of the specified toll.

However, in considering the case of anyone accused of violating this section, the court shall take into consideration (i) except for lanes equipped for payment of tolls through an automatic vehicle identification system, whether the toll booth or collection facility at which the defendant failed to pay the toll was manned at the time; (ii) whether the defendant was required to pay the toll with the exact amount in change; (iii) whether the defendant had the exact change to make the payment; and (iv) whether the defendant had been afforded appropriate advance notice, by signs or other means, that he would be required to pay a toll and pay it with the exact change. No person shall be subject to both prosecution under this section and to the provisions of § 46.2-819.1 or 46.2-819.3 for actions arising out of the same transaction or occurrence.

History.

1988, c. 79, § 46.1-229.4; 1989, c. 727; 1998, c. 802; 2004, c. 924; 2016, c. 753.

Editor's note.

References in this section were updated at the direction of the Virginia Code Commission to conform to the recodification of Title 33.2 by Acts 2014, c. 805, effective October 1, 2014.

§ 46.2-819.1. Installation and use of photo-monitoring system or automatic vehicle identification system in conjunction with electronic or manual toll facilities; penalty.

A. For purposes of this section:

"Automatic vehicle identification device" means an electronic device that communicates by wireless transmission with an automatic vehicle identification system.

"Automatic vehicle identification system" means an electronic vehicle identification system installed to work in conjunction with a toll collection device that automatically produces an electronic record of each vehicle equipped with an automatic vehicle identification device that uses a toll facility.

"Debt collection" means the collection of unpaid tolls and applicable administrative fees by (i) retention of a third-party debt collector or (ii) collection practices undertaken by employees of a toll facility operator that are materially similar to a third-party debt collector.

"Operator of a toll facility other than the Department of Transportation" means any agency, political subdivision, authority, or other entity that operates a toll facility.

"Owner" means the registered owner of a vehicle on record with the Department of Motor Vehicles or with the equivalent agency in another state. "Owner" does not include a vehicle rental or vehicle leasing company.

"Photo-monitoring system" means a vehicle sensor installed to work in conjunction with a toll collection device that automatically produces one or more photographs, one or more microphotographs, a videotape, or other recorded images of each vehicle at the time it is used or operated in violation of this section.

B. The operator of any toll facility or the locality within which such toll facility is located may install and operate or cause to be installed and operated a photo-monitoring system or automatic vehicle identification system, or both, at locations where tolls are collected for the use of such toll facility. The operator of a toll facility shall send an invoice or bill for unpaid tolls to the owner of a vehicle as part of an electronic or manual toll collection process pursuant to § 46.2-819.6 prior to seeking remedies under this section.

C. Information collected by a photo-monitoring system or automatic vehicle identification system installed and operated pursuant to subsection B shall be limited exclusively to that information that is necessary for the collection of unpaid tolls. Notwithstanding any other provision of law, all photographs, microphotographs, electronic images, or other data collected by a photo-monitoring system or automatic vehicle identification system shall be used exclusively for the collection of unpaid tolls and shall not (i) be open to the public; (ii) be sold and/or used for sales, solicitation, or marketing purposes; (iii) be disclosed to any other entity except as may be necessary for the collection of unpaid tolls or to a vehicle owner or operator as part of a challenge to the imposition of a toll; and (iv) be used in a court in a pending action or proceeding unless the action or proceeding relates to a violation of this section or upon order from a court of competent jurisdiction. Information collected under this section shall be purged and not retained later than 30 days after the collection and reconciliation of any unpaid tolls, administrative fees, and/or civil penalties. Any entity operating a photo-monitoring system or automatic vehicle identification system shall annually certify compliance with this section and make all records pertaining to such system available for inspection and audit by the Commissioner of Highways or the Commissioner of the Department of Motor Vehicles or their designee. Any violation of this subsection shall constitute a Class 1 misdemeanor. In addition to any fines or other penalties provided for by law, any money or other thing of value obtained as a result of a violation of this section shall be forfeited to the Commonwealth.

The toll facility operator may impose and collect an administrative fee in addition to the unpaid toll so as to recover the expenses of collecting the unpaid toll, which administrative fee shall be reasonably related to the actual cost of collecting the unpaid toll and not exceed $100 per violation. Such fee may be levied upon the operator of the vehicle after the first unpaid toll has been documented. The operator of the vehicle shall pay the unpaid toll and any administrative fee detailed in an invoice for the unpaid toll issued by a toll facility operator. If paid within 60 days of notification, the administrative fee shall not exceed $25.

D. If the matter proceeds to court, the owner or operator of a vehicle shall be liable for a civil penalty as follows: for a first offense, $50; for a second offense within one year from the first offense, $100; for a third offense within two years from the second offense, $250; and for a fourth and any subsequent offense within three years from the second offense, $500 plus, in each case, the unpaid toll, all accrued administrative fees imposed by the toll facility operator, and applicable court costs if the vehicle is found, as evidenced by information obtained from a photo-monitoring system or automatic vehicle identification system as provided in this section, to have used such a toll facility without payment of the required toll.

E. Notwithstanding subsections C and D, for a first conviction of an operator or owner of a vehicle under this section, the total amount for the first conviction shall not exceed $2,200, including civil penalties and administrative fees regardless of the total number of offenses the operator or owner of a vehicle is convicted of on that date.

F. No summons may be issued by a toll facility operator for a violation of this section unless the toll facility operator can demonstrate that (i) there was an attempt to collect the unpaid tolls and applicable administrative fees through debt collection not less than 30 days prior to issuance of the summons and (ii) 120 days have elapsed since the unpaid toll or, in a summons for multiple violations, 120 days have elapsed since the most recent unpaid toll noticed on the summons.

G. Any action under this section shall be brought in the general district court of the county or city in which the toll facility is located and shall be commenced within two years of the commission of the offense. Such action shall be considered a traffic infraction. The attorney for the Commonwealth may represent the interests of the toll facility operator. Any authorized agent or employee of a toll facility operator acting on behalf of a governmental entity shall be allowed the privileges accorded by § 16.1-88.03 in such cases.

H. Proof of a violation of this section shall be evidenced by information obtained from a photo-monitoring system or automatic vehicle identification system as provided in this section. A certificate, sworn to or affirmed by a technician employed or authorized by the operator of a toll facility or by the locality wherein the toll facility is located, or a facsimile of such a certificate, based on inspection of photographs, microphotographs, videotapes, or other recorded images produced by a photo-monitoring system, or of electronic data collected by an automatic vehicle identification system, shall be prima facie evidence of the facts contained therein. Any photographs, microphotographs, videotape, or other recorded images or electronic data evidencing such a violation shall be available for inspection in any proceeding to adjudicate the liability for such violation under this section. A record of communication by an automatic vehicle identification device with the automatic vehicle identification system at the time of a violation of this section shall be prima facie evidence that the automatic vehicle identification device was located in the vehicle registered to use such device in the records of the Department of Transportation.

I. On a form prescribed by the Supreme Court, a summons for a violation of this section may be executed as provided in § 19.2-76.2. A summons for a violation of this section may set forth multiple violations occurring within one jurisdiction. Notwithstanding the provisions of § 19.2-76, a summons for a violation of this section may be executed by mailing by first-class mail a copy thereof to the address of the owner or, if the owner has named and provided a valid address for the operator of the vehicle at the time of the violation in an affidavit executed pursuant to this subsection, such named operator of the vehicle. Such summons shall be signed either originally or by electronic signature. If the summoned person fails to appear on the date of return set out in the summons mailed pursuant to this section, the summons shall be executed in the manner set out in § 19.2-76.3.

Upon a finding by a court of competent jurisdiction that the vehicle described in the summons issued pursuant to this subsection was in violation of this section, the court shall impose a civil penalty upon the owner or operator of such vehicle in accordance with the amounts specified in subsection D, together with applicable court costs, the operator's administrative fee, and the toll due. Penalties assessed as the result of action initiated by the Department of Transportation shall be remanded by the clerk of the court that adjudicated the action to the Department of Transportation's Toll Facilities

Revolving Account. Penalties assessed as the result of action initiated by an operator of a toll facility other than the Department of Transportation shall be remanded by the clerk of the court that adjudicated the action to the treasurer or director of finance of the county or city in which the violation occurred for payment to the toll facility operator.

The owner of such vehicle shall be given reasonable notice by way of a summons as provided in this subsection that his vehicle had been used in violation of this section, and such owner shall be given notice of the time and place of the hearing as well as the civil penalty and costs for such offense. The toll facility operator may offer to the owner an option to pay the unpaid toll and fees plus a reduced civil penalty of $25 for a first or second offense or $50 for a third, fourth, or subsequent offense, as specified on the summons, provided the owner actually pays to the toll facility operator the entire amount so calculated at least 14 days prior to the hearing date specified on the summons. If the owner accepts such offer and such amount is actually received by the toll facility operator at least 14 days prior to the hearing date specified on the summons, the toll facility operator shall move the court at least five business days prior to the date set for trial to dismiss the summons issued to the owner of the vehicle, and the court shall dismiss upon such motion.

It shall be prima facie evidence that the vehicle described in the summons issued pursuant to this subsection was operated in violation of this section. Records obtained from the Department of Motor Vehicles pursuant to § 46.2-208 and certified in accordance with § 46.2-215 or from the equivalent agency in another state and certified as true and correct copies by the head of such agency or his designee identifying the owner of such vehicle shall give rise to a rebuttable presumption that the owner of the vehicle is the person named in the summons.

Upon either (i) the filing of an affidavit with the toll facility operator within 14 days of receipt of an invoice for an unpaid toll from the toll facility operator or (ii) the filing of an affidavit with the court at least 14 days prior to the hearing date by the owner of the vehicle stating that he was not the operator of the vehicle on the date of the violation and providing the legal name and address of the operator of the vehicle at the time of the violation, an invoice and/or summons, as appropriate, will also be issued to the alleged operator of the vehicle at the time of the offense.

In any action against a vehicle operator, an affidavit made by the owner providing the name and address of the vehicle operator at the time of the violation shall constitute prima facie evidence that the person named in the affidavit was operating the vehicle at all the relevant times relating to the matter named in the affidavit.

If the owner of the vehicle produces for the toll facility operator or the court a certified copy of a police report showing that the vehicle had been reported to the police as stolen prior to the time of the alleged offense and remained stolen at the time of the alleged offense, then the toll facility operator shall not pursue the owner for the unpaid toll and, if a summons has been issued, the court shall dismiss the summons issued to the owner of the vehicle.

J. Upon a finding by a court that a person has two or more unpaid tolls and such person fails to pay the required penalties, fees, and unpaid tolls, the court shall notify the Commissioner of the Department of Motor Vehicles, who shall refuse to issue or renew any vehicle registration certificate of any applicant or the license plate issued for the vehicle driven in the commission of the offense or, when the vehicle is registered in a state with which the Commonwealth has entered into an agreement to enforce tolling violations pursuant to § 46.2-819.9, who shall provide to the entity authorized to issue vehicle registration certificates or license plates in the state in which the vehicle is registered sufficient evidence of the court's finding to take action against the vehicle registration certificate or license plates in accordance with the terms of the agreement, until the court has notified the Commissioner that such penalties, fees, and unpaid tolls have been paid. Upon receipt of such notification from the court, the Commissioner of the Department of Motor Vehicles shall notify the state where the vehicle is registered of such payment. If it is proven that the vehicle owner was not the operator at the time of the offense and upon a finding by a court that the person identified in an affidavit pursuant to subsection I as the operator violated this section and such person fails to pay the required penalties, fees, and unpaid tolls, the court shall notify the Commissioner, who shall refuse to issue or renew any vehicle registration certificate of any applicant or the license plate issued for any vehicle owned or co-owned by such person or, when such vehicle is registered in a state with which the Commonwealth has entered into an agreement to enforce tolling violations pursuant to § 46.2-819.9, who shall provide to the entity authorized to issue vehicle registration certificates or license plates in the state in which the vehicle is registered sufficient evidence of the court's finding to take action against the vehicle registration certificate or license plates in accordance with the terms of the agreement, until the court has notified the Commissioner that such penalties, fees, and unpaid tolls have been paid. Upon receipt of such notification from the court, the Commissioner of the Department of Motor Vehicles shall notify the state where the vehicle is registered of such payment. Such funds representing payment of unpaid tolls and all administrative fees of the toll facility operator shall be transferred from the court to the Department of Transportation's Toll Facilities Revolving Account or, in the case of an action initiated by an operator of a toll facility other than the Department of Transportation, to the treasurer or director of finance of the county or city in which the violation occurred for payment to the toll facility operator. The Commissioner shall collect a $40 administrative fee from the owner or operator of the vehicle to defray the cost of processing and removing an order to deny registration or registration renewal.

K. Any vehicle rental or vehicle leasing company, if it receives an invoice or is named in a summons, shall be released as a party to the action if it provides the operator of the toll facility a copy of the vehicle rental agreement or lease or an affidavit identifying the renter or lessee within 30 days of receipt of the invoice or at least 14 days prior to the date of hearing set forth in the summons. Upon receipt of such rental agreement, lease, or affidavit, a notice shall be mailed to the renter or lessee identified therein. Release of this information shall not be deemed a violation of any provision of the Government Data Collection and Dissemination Practices Act (§ 2.2-3800 et seq.) or the Insurance Information and Privacy Protection Act (§ 38.2-600 et seq.). The toll facility operator shall allow at least 30 days from the date of such mailing before pursuing other remedies under this section. In any action against the vehicle operator, a copy of the vehicle rental agreement, lease, or affidavit identifying the renter or lessee of the vehicle at the time of the violation is prima facie evidence that the person named in the rental agreement, lease, or affidavit was operating the vehicle at all the relevant times relating to the matter named in the summons.

L. Imposition of a civil penalty pursuant to this section shall not be deemed a conviction as an operator and shall not be made part of the driving record of the person upon whom such civil penalty is imposed nor shall it be used for insurance purposes in the provision of motor vehicle insurance coverage. The provisions of § 46.2-395 shall not be applicable to any civil penalty, fee, unpaid toll, fine, or cost imposed or ordered paid under this section for a violation of this section.

M. The operator of a toll facility may enter into an agreement with the Department of Motor Vehicles, in accordance with the provisions of subdivision B 21 of § 46.2-208, to obtain vehicle owner information regarding the owners of vehicles that fail to pay tolls required for the use of toll facilities and with the Department of Transportation to obtain any information that is necessary to conduct electronic toll collection. Such agreement may include any information that may be obtained by the Department of Motor Vehicles in accordance with any agreement entered into pursuant to § 46.2-819.9. Information provided to the operator of a toll facility shall only be used for the collection of unpaid tolls and the operator of the toll facility shall be subject to the same conditions and penalties regarding release of the information as contained in subsection C.

N. No person shall be subject to both the provisions of this section and to prosecution under § 46.2-819 for actions arising out of the same transaction or occurrence.

History.
1998, c. 802; 2001, cc. 803, 852; 2003, c. 768; 2004, c. 924; 2005, c. 862; 2006, c. 859; 2007, cc. 78, 200; 2010, c. 839; 2011, c. 736; 2016, c. 753.

§ 46.2-819.2. Driving a motor vehicle from establishment where motor fuel offered for sale; suspension of license; penalty.

A. No person shall drive a motor vehicle off the premises of an establishment at which motor fuel offered for retail sale was dispensed into the fuel tank of such motor vehicle unless payment for such fuel has been made.

B. Any person who violates this section shall be liable for a civil penalty not to exceed $250 and applicable court costs if the matter proceeds to court.

C. The driver's license of any person found to have violated this section (i) may be suspended, for the first offense, for a period of up to 30 days and (ii) shall be suspended for a period of 30 days for the second and subsequent offenses.

D. Nothing herein shall preclude a prosecution for larceny.

History.
2000, cc. 729, 758; 2004, c. 795; 2005, c. 208; 2006, c. 487.

§ 46.2-819.3. Use of toll facility without payment of toll; enforcement; penalty.

A. For purposes of this section:

"Debt collection" means the collection of unpaid tolls and applicable administrative fees by (i) retention of a third-party debt collector or (ii) collection practices undertaken by employees of a toll facility operator that are materially similar to a third-party debt collector.

"Operator of a toll facility other than the Department of Transportation" means any agency, political subdivision, authority, or other entity that operates a toll facility.

"Owner" means the registered owner of a vehicle on record with the Department of Motor Vehicles or with the equivalent agency in another state. "Owner" does not include a vehicle rental or vehicle leasing company.

B. The toll facility operator may impose and collect an administrative fee in addition to the unpaid toll so as to recover the expenses of collecting the unpaid toll, which administrative fee shall be reasonably related to the actual cost of collecting the unpaid toll and not exceed $100 per violation. Such fee shall not be levied on a first unpaid toll unless the written promise to pay executed pursuant to subsection F remains unpaid after 30 days. The person who executed the written promise to pay pursuant to subsection F shall pay the unpaid toll and any administrative fee detailed in an invoice or bill issued by a toll facility operator. If paid within 60 days of notification, the administrative fee shall not exceed $25.

C. If the matter proceeds to court, the owner or operator of the vehicle shall be liable for a civil penalty as follows: for a first offense, $50; for a second offense within one year from the first offense, $100; for a third offense within two years from the second offense, $250; and for a fourth and any subsequent offense within three years from the second offense, $500 plus, in each case, the unpaid toll, all accrued administrative fees imposed by the toll facility operator and applicable court costs if the vehicle operator is found, as evidenced by information obtained from the toll facility operator, to have used such a toll facility without payment of the required toll.

D. Notwithstanding subsections B and C, for a first conviction of an operator or owner of a vehicle under this section, the total amount for the first conviction shall not exceed $2,200, including civil penalties and administrative fees regardless of the total number of offenses the operator or owner of a vehicle is convicted of on that date.

E. No summons may be issued by a toll facility operator for a violation of this section unless the toll facility operator can demonstrate that (i) there was an attempt to collect the unpaid tolls and applicable administrative fees through debt collection not less than 30 days prior to issuance of the summons and (ii) 120 days have elapsed since the unpaid toll or, in a summons for multiple violations, 120 days have elapsed since the most recent unpaid toll noticed on the summons.

F. A written promise to pay an unpaid toll within a specified period of time executed by the operator of a motor vehicle, accompanied by a certificate sworn to or affirmed by an authorized agent of the toll facility that the unpaid toll was not paid within such specified period, shall be prima facie evidence of the facts contained therein.

G. The operator of a toll facility shall send an invoice or bill to the owner of a motor vehicle using a toll facility without payment of the specified toll as part of an electronic or manual toll collection process pursuant to § 46.2-819.6, prior to seeking remedies under this section. Any action under this section shall be brought in the general district court of the county or city in which the toll facility is located and shall be commenced within two years of the commission of the offense. Such an action shall be considered a traffic infraction. The attorney for the Commonwealth may represent the interests of the toll facility operator. Any authorized agent or employee of a toll facility operator acting on behalf of a governmental entity shall be allowed the privileges accorded by § 16.1-88.03 in such cases.

H. Upon a finding by a court of competent jurisdiction that the operator of a motor vehicle identified in the summons issued pursuant to subsection J was in violation of this section, the court shall impose a civil penalty upon the operator of a motor vehicle in accordance with the amounts specified in subsection C, together with applicable court costs, the operator's administrative fee, and the toll due. Penalties assessed as the result of action initiated by the Department of Transportation shall be remanded by the clerk of the court that adjudicated the action to the Department of Transportation's Toll Facilities Revolving Account. Penalties assessed as the result of action initiated by an operator of a toll facility other than the Department of Transportation shall be remanded by the clerk of the court that adjudicated the action to the treasurer or director of finance of the county or city in which the violation occurred for payment to the toll facility operator.

I. The toll facility operator may offer to the owner an option to pay the unpaid toll and fees plus a reduced civil penalty of not more than $25 for a first or second offense or not more than $50 for a third, fourth, or subsequent offense, as specified on the summons, provided the owner actually pays to the toll facility operator the entire amount so calculated at least 14 days prior to the hearing date specified on the summons. If the owner accepts such offer and such amount is actually received by the toll facility operator at least 14 days prior to the hearing date specified on the summons, the toll facility operator shall move the court at least five business days prior to the date set for trial to dismiss the summons issued to the owner of the vehicle, and the court shall dismiss upon such motion.

J. A summons for a violation of this section may be executed as provided in § 19.2-76.2. A summons for a violation of this section may set forth multiple violations occurring within one jurisdiction. Notwithstanding the provisions of § 19.2-76, a summons for a violation of this section may be executed by mailing by first-class mail a copy thereof to the address of the operator of a motor vehicle as shown on the written promise to pay executed pursuant to subsection F or records of the Department of Motor Vehicles. Such summons shall be signed either originally or by electronic signature. If the summoned person fails to appear on the date of return set out in the summons mailed pursuant to this subsection, the summons shall be executed in the manner set out in § 19.2-76.3.

K. Upon a finding by a court that a person has three or more unpaid tolls and such person fails to pay the required penalties, fees, and unpaid tolls, the court shall notify the Commissioner of the Department of Motor Vehicles, who shall refuse to issue or renew any vehicle registration certificate of any applicant or the license plate issued for any vehicle owned or co-owned by the offender or, when the vehicle is registered in a state with which the Commonwealth has entered into an agreement to enforce tolling violations pursuant to § 46.2-819.9, who shall provide to the entity authorized to issue vehicle registration certificates or license plates in the state in which the vehicle is registered sufficient evidence of the court's finding to take action against the vehicle registration certificate or license plates in accordance with the terms of the agreement.

Upon receipt of such notification from the court, the Commissioner of the Department of Motor Vehicles shall notify the state where the vehicle is registered of such payment. The Commissioner shall collect a $40 administrative fee from the owner or operator of the vehicle to defray the cost of processing and removing an order to deny registration or registration renewal.

L. Imposition of a civil penalty pursuant to this section shall not be deemed a conviction as an operator and shall not be made part of the driving record of the person upon whom such civil penalty is imposed nor shall it be used for insurance purposes in the provision of motor vehicle insurance coverage. The provisions of § 46.2-395 shall not be applicable to any civil penalty, fee, unpaid toll, fine, or cost imposed or ordered paid under this section for a violation of this section.

M. No person shall be subject to both the provisions of this section and to prosecution under § 46.2-819 for actions arising out of the same transaction or occurrence.

History.

2004, c. 924; 2006, c. 859; 2007, cc. 78, 200; 2011, c. 736; 2016, c. 753.

§ 46.2-819.3:1. Installation and use of video-monitoring system and automatic vehicle identification system in conjunction with all-electronic toll facilities; penalty.

A. For purposes of this section:

"Automatic vehicle identification device" means an electronic device that communicates by wireless transmission with an automatic vehicle identification system.

"Automatic vehicle identification system" means an electronic vehicle identification system installed to work in conjunction with a toll collection device that automatically produces an electronic record of each vehicle equipped with an automatic vehicle identification device that uses a toll facility.

"Debt collection" means the collection of unpaid tolls and applicable administrative fees by (i) retention of a third-party debt collector or (ii) collection practices undertaken by employees of a toll facility operator that are materially similar to a third-party debt collector.

"Operator" means a person who was driving a vehicle that was the subject of a toll violation but who is not the owner of the vehicle.

"Operator of a toll facility other than the Department of Transportation" means any agency, political subdivision, authority, or other entity that operates a toll facility.

"Owner" means the registered owner of a vehicle on record with the Department of Motor Vehicles or with the equivalent agency in another state. "Owner" does not mean a vehicle rental or vehicle leasing company.

"Video-monitoring system" means a vehicle sensor installed to work in conjunction with a toll collection device that automatically produces one or more photographs, one or more microphotographs, a videotape, or other recorded images of each vehicle at the time it is used or operated in violation of this section.

B. The operator of any toll facility or the locality within which such toll facility is located may install and operate or cause to be installed and operated a video-monitoring system in conjunction with an automatic vehicle identification system on facilities for which tolls are collected for the use of such toll facility and that do not offer manual toll collection. A video-monitoring system shall include, but not be limited to, electronic systems that monitor and capture images of vehicles using a toll facility to enable toll collection for vehicles that do not pay using a toll collection device. The operator of a toll facility shall send an invoice for unpaid tolls in accordance with the requirements of § 46.2-819.6 to the owner of a vehicle as part of a video-monitoring toll collection process, prior to seeking remedies under this section.

C. Information collected by a video-monitoring system in conjunction with an automatic vehicle identification system installed and operated pursuant to subsection B shall be limited exclusively to that information that is necessary for the collection of unpaid tolls and establishing when violations occur, including use in any proceeding to determine whether a violation occurred. Notwithstanding any other provision of law, all images or other data collected by a video-monitoring system in conjunction with an automatic vehicle identification system shall be protected in a database with security comparable to that of the Department of Motor Vehicles' system and used exclusively for the collection of unpaid tolls and for efforts to pursue violators of this section and shall not (i) be open to the public; (ii) be sold and/or used for sales, solicitation, or marketing purposes other than those of the toll facility operator to facilitate toll payment; (iii) be disclosed to any other entity except as may be necessary for the collection of unpaid tolls or to a vehicle owner or operator as part of a challenge to the imposition of a toll; and/or (iv) be used in a court in a pending action or proceeding unless the action or proceeding relates to a violation of this section or upon order from a court of competent jurisdiction. Except as provided above, information collected under this section shall be purged and not retained later than 30 days after the collection and reconciliation of any unpaid tolls, administrative fees, and/or civil penalties. Any entity operating a video-monitoring system in conjunction with an automatic vehicle identification system shall annually certify compliance with this section and make all records pertaining to such system available for inspection and audit by the Commissioner of Highways or the Commissioner of the Department of Motor Vehicles or their designee. Any violation of this subsection shall constitute a Class 1 misdemeanor. In addition to any fines or other penalties provided for by law, any money or other thing of value obtained as a result of a violation of this section shall be forfeited to the Commonwealth.

If a vehicle uses a toll facility without paying the toll, the owner or operator shall be in violation of this section if he refuses to pay the toll within 30 days of notification. The toll facility operator may impose and collect an administrative fee in addition to the unpaid toll so as to recover the expenses of collecting the unpaid toll, which administrative fee shall be reasonably related to the actual cost of collecting the unpaid toll and not exceed $100 per violation. Such fee shall not be levied upon the owner or operator of the vehicle unless the toll has not been paid by the owner or operator within 30 days after receipt of the invoice for the unpaid toll, which nonpayment for 30 days shall constitute the violation of this section. Once such a violation has occurred, the owner or operator of the vehicle shall pay the unpaid tolls and any administrative fee detailed in the invoice for the unpaid toll issued by a toll facility operator. If paid within 60 days of the toll violation, the administrative fee shall not exceed $25.

The toll facility operator may levy charges for the direct cost of use of and processing for a video-monitoring system and to cover the cost of the invoice, which are in addition to the toll and may not exceed double the amount of the base toll, provided that potential toll facility users are provided notice before entering the facility by conspicuous signs that clearly indicate that the toll for use of the facility could be tripled for any vehicle that does not have an active, functioning automatic vehicle identification device registered for and in use in the vehicle using the toll facility, and such signs are posted at a location where the operator can still choose to avoid the use of the toll facility if he chooses not to pay the toll.

A person receiving an invoice for an unpaid toll under this section may (a) pay the toll and administrative fees directly to the toll facility operator or (b) file with the toll facility operator a notice, on a form provided by the toll facility operator as required under subsection B of § 46.2-819.6, to contest liability for a toll violation. The notice to contest liability for a toll violation may be filed by any person receiving an invoice for an unpaid toll by mailing or delivering the notice to the toll facility operator within 60 days of receiving such invoice for an unpaid toll. Upon receipt of such notice, the toll facility operator may issue a summons pursuant to subsection I and may not seek withholding of registration or renewal thereof under subsection L until a court of competent jurisdiction has found the alleged violator liable for tolls under this section.

D. If the matter proceeds to court, the owner or operator of a vehicle shall be liable for a civil penalty as follows: for a first offense, $50; for a second offense within one year from the first offense, $100; for a third offense within two years from the second offense, $250; and for a fourth and any subsequent offense within three years from the second offense, $500; plus, in each case, the unpaid toll, all accrued administrative fees imposed by the toll facility operator, and applicable court costs if the vehicle is found, as evidenced by information obtained from a video-monitoring system in conjunction with an automatic vehicle identification system as provided in this section, to have used such a toll facility without payment of the required toll within 30 days of receipt of the invoice for the toll.

E. Notwithstanding subsections C and D, for a first conviction of an operator or owner of a vehicle under this section the total amount for the first conviction shall not exceed $2,200, including civil penalties and administrative fees regardless of the total number of offenses the operator or owner of a vehicle is convicted of on that date.

F. No summons may be issued by a toll facility operator for a violation of this section unless the toll facility operator can demonstrate that (i) there was an attempt to collect the unpaid tolls and applicable administrative fees through debt collection not less than 30 days prior to issuance of the summons and (ii) 120 days have elapsed since the unpaid toll or, in a summons for multiple violations, 120 days have elapsed since the most recent unpaid toll noticed on the summons.

G. Any action under this section shall be brought in the general district court of the county or city in which the toll facility is located and shall be commenced within two years of the commission of the offense. Such action shall be considered a traffic infraction. The attorney for the Commonwealth may represent the interests of the toll facility operator. Any authorized agent or employee of a toll facility operator acting on behalf of a governmental entity shall be allowed the privileges accorded by § 16.1-88.03 in such cases.

H. Proof of a violation of this section shall be evidenced by information obtained from a video-monitoring system or automatic vehicle identification system as provided in this section. A certificate, sworn to or affirmed by a technician employed or authorized by the operator of a toll facility or by the locality wherein the toll facility is located, or a facsimile of such a certificate, based on inspection of photographs, microphotographs, videotapes, or other recorded images produced by a video-monitoring system or of electronic data collected by an automatic vehicle identification system, shall be prima facie evidence of the facts contained therein. Any photographs, microphotographs, videotape, or other recorded images or electronic data evidencing such a violation shall be available for inspection in any proceeding to adjudicate the liability for such violation under this section. A record of communication by an automatic vehicle identification device with the automatic vehicle identification system at the time of a violation of this section shall be prima facie evidence that the automatic vehicle identification device was located in the vehicle registered to use such device in the records of the Department of Transportation.

I. On a form prescribed by the Supreme Court, a summons for a violation of this section may be executed as provided in § 19.2-76.2. A summons for a violation of this section may set forth multiple violations occurring within one jurisdiction. Notwithstanding the provisions of § 19.2-76, a summons for a violation of unpaid tolls may be executed by mailing by first-class mail a copy thereof to the address of the owner or, if the owner has named and provided a valid address for the operator of the vehicle at the time of the violation in an affidavit executed pursuant to subsection J, such named operator of the vehicle. Such summons shall be signed either originally or by electronic signature. If the summoned person fails to appear on the date of return set out in the summons mailed pursuant to this section, the summons shall be executed in the manner set out in § 19.2-76.3.

J. Upon a finding by a court of competent jurisdiction that the vehicle described in the summons issued pursuant to subsection I was in violation of this section, the court shall impose a civil penalty upon the owner or operator of such vehicle in accordance with the amounts specified in subsection D, together with applicable court costs, the operator's administrative fee, and the toll due. Penalties assessed as the result of action initiated by the Department of Transportation shall be remanded by the clerk of the court that adjudicated the action to the Department of Transportation's Toll Facilities Revolving Account. Penalties assessed as the result of action initiated by an operator of a toll facility other than the Department of Transportation shall be remanded by the clerk of the court that adjudicated the action to the treasurer or director of finance of the county or city in which the violation occurred for payment to the toll facility operator.

The owner of such vehicle shall be given reasonable notice by way of a summons as provided in subsection I that his vehicle had been used in violation of this section, and such owner shall be given notice of the time and place of the hearing as well as the civil penalty and costs for such offense.

It shall be prima facie evidence that the vehicle described in the summons issued pursuant to subsection I was operated in violation of this section. Records obtained from the Department of Motor Vehicles pursuant to subsection P and certified in accordance with § 46.2-215 or from the equivalent agency in another state and certified as true and correct copies by the head of such agency or his designee identifying the owner of such vehicle shall give rise to a rebuttable presumption that the owner of the vehicle is the person named in the summons.

Upon the filing of an affidavit by the owner of the vehicle with the toll facility operator within 14 days of receipt of an invoice for unpaid toll or a summons stating that such owner was not the operator of the vehicle on the date of the violation and providing the legal name and address of the operator of the vehicle at the time of the violation, an invoice for unpaid toll or summons, whichever the case may be, will also be issued to the alleged operator of the vehicle at the time of the offense.

In any action against a vehicle operator, an affidavit made by the owner providing the name and address of the vehicle operator at the time of the violation shall constitute prima facie evidence that the person named in the affidavit was operating the vehicle at all the relevant times relating to the matter named in the affidavit.

If the owner of the vehicle produces for the toll facility operator or the court a certified copy of a police report showing that the vehicle had been reported to the police as stolen prior to the time of the alleged offense and remained stolen at the time of the alleged offense, then the toll facility operator shall not pursue the owner for the unpaid toll contained in the invoice for unpaid toll or the court shall dismiss the summons issued to the owner of the vehicle.

K. Upon a finding by a court that a person has two or more unpaid tolls and such person fails to pay the required penalties, fees, and unpaid tolls, then the court or toll facility operator shall notify the Commissioner of the Department of Motor Vehicles, who shall refuse to issue or renew any vehicle registration certificate of any applicant or the license plate issued for the vehicle driven in the commission of the offense or, when the vehicle is registered in a state with which the Commonwealth has entered into an agreement to enforce tolling violations pursuant to § 46.2-819.9, who shall provide to the entity authorized to issue vehicle registration certificates or license plates in the state in which the vehicle is registered sufficient evidence of the court's finding to take action against the vehicle registration certificate or license plates in accordance with the terms of the agreement, until the court has notified the Commissioner that such penalties, fees, and unpaid tolls have been paid. Upon receipt of such notification from the court, the Commissioner of the Department of Motor Vehicles shall notify the state where the vehicle is registered of such payment. If it is proven that the vehicle owner was not the operator at the time of the offense and upon a finding by a court that the person identified in an affidavit pursuant to subsection J as the operator violated this section and such person fails to pay the required penalties, fees, and unpaid tolls, the court shall notify the Commissioner, who shall refuse to issue or renew any vehicle registration certificate of any applicant or the license plate issued for any vehicle owned or co-owned by such person or, when such vehicle is registered in a state with which the Commonwealth has entered into an agreement to enforce tolling violations pursuant to

§ 46.2-819.9, who shall provide to the entity authorized to issue vehicle registration certificates or license plates in the state in which the vehicle is registered sufficient evidence of the court's finding to take action against the vehicle registration certificate or license plates in accordance with the terms of the agreement, until the court has notified the Commissioner that such penalties, fees, and unpaid tolls have been paid. Upon receipt of such notification from the court, the Commissioner of the Department of Motor Vehicles shall notify the state where the vehicle is registered of such payment. Such funds representing payment of unpaid tolls and all administrative fees of the toll facility operator shall be transferred from the court to the Department of Transportation's Toll Facilities Revolving Account or, in the case of an action initiated by an operator of a toll facility other than the Department of Transportation, to the treasurer or director of finance of the county or city in which the violation occurred for payment to the toll facility operator. The Commissioner shall collect a $40 administrative fee from the owner or operator of the vehicle to defray the cost of processing and removing an order to deny registration or registration renewal.

L. If an owner of a vehicle has received at least one invoice for two or more unpaid tolls in accordance with § 46.2-819.6 by certified mail and has (i) failed to pay the unpaid tolls and administrative fees and (ii) failed to file a notice to contest liability for a toll violation, then the toll facility operator may notify the Commissioner, who shall, if no form contesting liability has been timely filed with the toll facility operator pursuant to this section, refuse to issue or renew the vehicle registration certificate of any applicant therefor or the license plate issued for any vehicle driven in the commission of the offense until the toll facility operator has notified the Commissioner that such fees and unpaid tolls have been paid.

If the vehicle owner was not the operator at the time of the offense and the person identified in an affidavit pursuant to subsection J as the operator has received at least one invoice for two or more unpaid tolls in accordance with § 46.2-819.6 by certified mail and such person has (a) failed to pay the unpaid tolls and administrative fees and (b) failed to file a notice to contest liability for a toll violation, then the toll facility operator may notify the Commissioner, who shall, if no form contesting liability has been timely filed with the toll facility operator pursuant to this section, refuse to issue or renew any vehicle registration certificate of any applicant therefor or the license plate issued for any vehicle owned or co-owned by such person until the toll facility operator has notified the Commissioner that such fees and unpaid tolls have been paid.

The Commissioner may only refuse to issue or renew any vehicle registration pursuant to this subsection upon the request of a toll facility operator if such toll facility operator has entered into an agreement with the Commissioner whereby the Commissioner will refuse to issue or renew any vehicle registration of any applicant therefor who owes unpaid tolls and administrative fees to the toll facility operator. The toll facility operator seeking to collect unpaid tolls and administrative fees through the withholding of registration or renewal thereof by the Commissioner as provided for in this subsection shall notify the Commissioner in the manner provided for in his agreement with the Commissioner and supply to the Commissioner information necessary to identify the violator whose registration or renewal is to be denied. The Commissioner shall charge a $40 fee to defray the cost of processing and withholding the registration or registration renewal, and the toll facility operator may add this fee to the amount of the unpaid tolls and administrative fees. Any agreement entered into pursuant to the provisions of this subsection shall provide for the Department to send the violator notice of the intent to deny renewal of registration at least 30 days prior to the expiration date of a current vehicle registration and such notice shall include a form, as required under subsection B of § 46.2-819.6, to contest liability of the underlying toll violation. The notice provided by the Commissioner shall include instructions for filing the form to contest liability with the toll facility operator within 21 days after the date of mailing of the Commissioner's notice. Upon timely receipt of the form, the toll facility operator shall notify the Commissioner, who shall refrain from withholding the registration or renewal thereof, after which the toll facility operator may proceed to issue a summons for unpaid toll. For the purposes of this subsection, notice by first-class mail to the registrant's address as maintained in the records of the Department shall be deemed sufficient.

M. Any vehicle rental or vehicle leasing company, if it receives an invoice for unpaid toll or is named in a summons, shall be released as a party to the action if it provides the operator of the toll facility a copy of the vehicle rental agreement or lease or an affidavit identifying the renter or lessee within 30 days of receipt of the invoice or summons. Upon receipt of such rental agreement, lease, or affidavit, an invoice for unpaid toll shall be mailed to the renter or lessee identified therein. Release of this information shall not be deemed a violation of any provision of the Government Data Collection and Dissemination Practices Act (§ 2.2-3800 et seq.) or the Insurance Information and Privacy Protection Act (§ 38.2-600 et seq.). The toll facility operator shall allow at least 30 days from the date of such mailing before pursuing other remedies under this section. In any action against the vehicle operator, a copy of the vehicle rental agreement, lease, or affidavit identifying the renter or lessee of the vehicle at the time of the violation is prima facie evidence that the person named in the rental agreement, lease, or affidavit was operating the vehicle at all the relevant times relating to the matter named in the summons.

N. Imposition of a civil penalty pursuant to this section shall not be deemed a conviction as an operator and shall not be made part of the driving record of the person upon whom such civil penalty is imposed, nor shall it be used for insurance purposes in the provision of motor vehicle insurance coverage. The provisions of § 46.2-395 shall not be applicable to any civil penalty, fee, unpaid toll, fine, or cost imposed or ordered paid under this section for a violation of this section.

O. The toll facility operator may offer to the owner an option to pay the unpaid toll and fees plus a reduced civil penalty of $25 for a first or second offense or $50 for a third, fourth, or subsequent offense, as specified on the summons, provided the owner actually pays to the toll facility operator the entire amount so calculated at least 14 days prior to the hearing date specified on the summons. If the owner accepts such offer and such amount is actually received by the toll facility operator at least 14 days prior to the hearing date specified on the summons, the toll facility operator shall move the court at least five business days prior to the date set for trial to dismiss the summons issued to the owner of the vehicle, and the court shall dismiss upon such motion.

P. The operator of a toll facility may enter into an agreement with the Department, in accordance with the provisions of subdivision B 21 of § 46.2-208, to obtain vehicle owner information regarding the owners of vehicles that fail to pay tolls required for the use of toll facilities and with the Department of Transportation to obtain any information that is necessary to conduct electronic toll collection. Such agreement may include any information that may be obtained by the Department of Motor Vehicles in accordance with any agreement entered into pursuant to § 46.2-819.9. Information provided to the operator of a toll facility shall be used only for the collection of unpaid tolls, and the operator of the toll facility shall be subject to the same conditions and penalties regarding release of the information as contained in subsection C.

Q. No person shall be subject to both the provisions of this section and to prosecution under § 46.2-819 for actions arising out of the same transaction or occurrence.

History.
2010, c. 839; 2011, c. 736; 2016, c. 753.

§ 46.2-819.4. Smoking in proximity to gas pumps; penalty.

Any person who smokes or uses an open flame within 20 feet of a pump used to fuel motor vehicles or a fueling tanker being used to deliver gasoline to a gasoline station is guilty of a Class 3 misdemeanor if smoking or the use of an open flame is prohibited by a sign at the pump. Any person who causes a fire or explosion as a result of a violation of this section is guilty of a Class 1 misdemeanor.

History.
2007, c. 848.

§ 46.2-819.5. Enforcement through use of photo-monitoring system or automatic vehicle identification system in conjunction with usage of Dulles Access Highway.

A. A photo-monitoring system or automatic vehicle identification system established at locations along the Dulles Access Highway, in order to identify vehicles that are using the Dulles Access Highway in violation of the Metropolitan Washington Airports Authority (Authority) regulation regarding usage, which makes violations of the regulation subject to civil penalties, shall be administered in accordance with this section. The civil penalties for violations of such regulation may not exceed the following: $50 for the first violation; $100 for a second violation within one year from the first violation; $250 for a third violation within two years from the second violation; and $500 for a fourth and any subsequent violation within three years from the second violation. In the event a violation of the Authority regulation is identified via the photo-monitoring system or automatic vehicle identification system, the operator of the Dulles Access Highway shall send a notice of the violation, of the applicable civil penalty and of any administrative fee calculated in accordance with subsection C to the registered owner of the vehicle identified by the system prior to seeking further remedies under this section. Upon receipt of the notice, the registered owner of the vehicle may elect to avoid any action by the operator to enforce the violation in court by waiving his right to a court hearing, pleading guilty to the violation, and paying a reduced civil penalty along with any applicable administrative fee to the operator. Should the recipient of the notice make such an election, the amount of the reduced civil penalty shall be as follows: $30 for the first violation; $50 for a second violation within one year from the first violation; $125 for a third violation within two years from the second violation; and $250 for a fourth and any subsequent violations within three years from the second violation.

B. Information collected by the photo-monitoring system or automatic vehicle identification system referenced in subsection A shall be limited exclusively to that information that is necessary for identifying those drivers who improperly use the Dulles Access Highway in violation of the Authority regulation. Notwithstanding any other provision of law, all photographs, microphotographs, electronic images, or other data collected by a photo-monitoring system or automatic vehicle identification system shall be used exclusively for the identification of violators and shall not (i) be open to the public; (ii) be sold or used for sales, solicitation, or marketing purposes; (iii) be disclosed to any other entity except as may be necessary for the identification of viola-

Motor Vehicles

tors or to a vehicle owner or operator as part of a challenge to the imposition of a civil penalty; or (iv) be used in a court in a pending action or proceeding unless the action or proceeding relates to a violation of the Authority regulation governing usage of the Dulles Access Highway or upon order from a court of competent jurisdiction. Information collected by the system shall be protected in a database with security comparable to that of the Department of Motor Vehicles' system, and be purged and not retained later than 30 days after the collection and reconciliation of any civil penalties and administrative fees. The operator of the Dulles Access Highway shall annually certify compliance with this subsection and make all records pertaining to such system available for inspection and audit by the Commissioner of Highways or the Commissioner of the Department of Motor Vehicles or their designee. Any violation of this subsection shall constitute a Class 1 misdemeanor. In addition to any fines or other penalties provided for by law, any money or other thing of value obtained as a result of a violation of this subsection shall be forfeited to the Commonwealth.

C. The operator of the Dulles Access Highway may impose and collect an administrative fee, in addition to the civil penalty established by regulation, so as to recover the expenses of collecting the civil penalty, which administrative fee shall be reasonably related to the actual cost of collecting the civil penalty and shall not exceed $100 per violation. Such fee shall not be levied upon the operator of the vehicle until a second violation has been documented within 12 months of an initial violation, in which case the fee shall apply to such second violation and to any additional violation occurring thereafter. If the recipient of the notice referenced in subsection A makes the election provided by that subsection, the administrative fee shall not exceed $25.

D. If the election provided for in subsection A is not made, the operator of the Dulles Access Highway may proceed to enforce the violation in court. If the matter proceeds to court, the registered owner or operator of a vehicle shall be liable for the civil penalty set out in the Authority regulation governing usage of the Dulles Access Highway, any applicable administrative fees calculated in accordance with subsection C and applicable court costs if the vehicle is found, as evidenced by information obtained from a photo-monitoring system or automatic vehicle identification system as provided in this section, to have used the Dulles Access Highway in violation of the Authority regulation; provided, that the civil penalty may not exceed the amount of the penalty identified in subsection A.

E. Any action under this section shall be brought in the General District Court of the county in which the violation occurred.

F. Proof of a violation of the Authority regulation governing the use of the Dulles Access Highway shall be evidenced by information obtained from the photo-monitoring system or automatic vehicle identification system referenced in subsection A. A certificate, sworn to or affirmed by a technician employed or authorized by the operator of the Dulles Access Highway, or a facsimile of such a certificate, that is based on inspection of photographs, microphotographs, videotapes, or other recorded images or electronic data produced by the photo-monitoring system shall be prima facie evidence of the facts contained therein. Any photographs, microphotographs, videotape, or other recorded images or electronic data evidencing such a violation shall be available for inspection in any proceeding to adjudicate the liability for such violation under this section.

G. A summons issued under this section, which describes a vehicle that, on the basis of a certificate referenced in subsection F, is alleged to have been operated in violation of the Authority regulation governing usage of the Dulles Access Highway, shall be prima facie evidence that such vehicle was operated in violation of the Authority regulation.

H. Upon a finding by a court that the vehicle described in the summons issued under this section was in violation of the Authority regulation, the court shall impose a civil penalty upon the registered owner or operator of such vehicle in accordance with the penalty amounts specified in subsection D, together with any applicable court costs and applicable administrative fees calculated in accordance with subsection C. Civil penalties and administrative fees assessed as a result of an action initiated under this section and collected by the court shall be remanded by the clerk of the court that adjudicated the action to the treasurer or director of finance of the county or city in which the violation occurred for payment to the operator of the Dulles Access Highway.

The registered owner of a vehicle shall be given reasonable notice of an enforcement action in court by way of a summons that informs the owner that his vehicle has been used in violation of the Authority regulation governing the use of the Dulles Access Highway and of the time and place of the court hearing, as well as of the civil penalty and court costs for the violation. Upon the filing of an affidavit with the court at least 14 days prior to the hearing date by the registered owner of the vehicle stating that he was not the driver of the vehicle on the date of the violation and providing the legal name and address of the operator of the vehicle at the time of the violation, a summons shall be issued to such alleged operator of the vehicle.

In any action against such a vehicle operator, an affidavit made by the registered owner providing the name and address of the vehicle operator at the time of the violation shall constitute prima facie evidence that the person named in the affidavit was operating the vehicle at all the relevant times relating to the matter addressed in the affidavit.

If the registered owner of the vehicle produces a certified copy of a police report showing that the vehicle had been reported to the police as stolen prior to the time of the alleged offense and remained stolen at the time of the alleged offense, then the court shall dismiss the summons issued to the registered owner of the vehicle.

I. Upon a finding by a court that a person has three or more violations of the Authority regulation governing the use of the Dulles Access Highway and has failed to pay the required civil penalties, administrative fees and court costs into the court, the court shall notify the Commissioner of the Department of Motor Vehicles, who shall refuse to issue or renew any vehicle registration certificate to or for such person or the license plate for the vehicle owned by such person until the court has notified the Commissioner that such civil penalties, fees, and costs have been paid. The Commissioner shall collect a $40 administrative fee from such person to defray the cost of responding to court notices given pursuant to this subsection.

J. For purposes of this section, "operator of the Dulles Access Highway" means the Metropolitan Washington Airports Authority; "owner" means the registered owner of a vehicle on record with the Department of Motor Vehicles; "photo-monitoring system" means equipment that produces one or more photographs, microphotographs, videotapes, or other recorded images of vehicles at the time they are used or operated in violation of the Authority regulation governing the use of the Dulles Access Highway; "automatic vehicle identification system" means an electronic vehicle identification system that automatically produces an electronic record of each vehicle equipped with an automatic vehicle identification device that uses monitored portions of the Dulles Access Highway; and "automatic vehicle identification device" means an electronic device that communicates by wireless transmission with an automatic vehicle identification system.

K. Any vehicle rental or vehicle leasing company, if named in a summons, shall be released as a party to the action if it provides the operator of the Dulles Access Highway with a copy of the vehicle rental agreement or lease, or an affidavit that identifies the renter or lessee, prior to the date of hearing set forth in the summons. Upon receipt of such rental agreement, lease, or affidavit, a summons shall be issued to such renter or lessee. Release of this information shall not be deemed a violation of any provision of the Government Data Collection and Dissemination Practices Act (§ 2.2-3800 et seq.) or the Insurance Information and Privacy Protection Act (§ 38.2-600 et seq.). In any action against the renter or lessee, a copy of the vehicle rental agreement, lease, or affidavit identifying the renter or lessee of the vehicle at the time of the violation shall be prima facie evidence that the person named in the rental agreement, lease, or affidavit was operating the vehicle at all the relevant times relating to the matter named in the summons.

L. Imposition of a civil penalty pursuant to this section shall not be deemed a conviction as an operator and shall not be made a part of the driving record of the person upon whom such civil penalty is imposed, nor shall it be used for insurance purposes in the provision of motor vehicle insurance coverage. The provisions of § 46.2-395 shall not be applicable to any civil penalty, administrative fee, or cost imposed or ordered paid under this section.

M. On a form prescribed by the Supreme Court, a summons for a violation of the Authority regulation governing the use of the Dulles Access Highway may be executed pursuant to § 19.2-76.2. The operator of the Dulles Access Highway or its personnel or agents mailing such summons shall be considered conservators of the peace for the sole and limited purpose of mailing such summons. Pursuant to § 19.2-76.2, the summons for a violation of the Authority regulation governing usage of the Dulles Access Highway may be executed by mailing by first-class mail a copy thereof to the address of the owner of the vehicle as shown on the records of the Department of Motor Vehicles or, if the registered owner or rental or leasing company has named and provided a valid address for the operator of the vehicle at the time of the violation as provided in this section, to the address of such named operator of the vehicle. If the summoned person fails to appear on the date of return set out in the summons mailed pursuant to this section, the summons shall be executed in the manner set out in § 19.2-76.3.

N. The operator of the Dulles Access Highway may enter into an agreement with the Department of Motor Vehicles, in accordance with the provisions of subdivision B 21 of § 46.2-208, to obtain vehicle owner information regarding the registered owners of vehicles that improperly use the Dulles Access Highway. Information provided to the operator of the Dulles Access Highway shall only be used in the enforcement of the Authority regulation governing use of the Dulles Access Highway, and the operator shall be subject to the same conditions and penalties regarding release of the information as contained in subsection B.

O. Should other vehicle recognition technology become available that is appropriate to be used for the purpose of monitoring improper usage of the Dulles Access Highway, the operator of the Dulles Access Highway shall be permitted to use any such technology that has been approved for use by the Virginia State Police, the Commonwealth of Virginia, or any of its localities.

P. All civil penalties paid to the operator of the Dulles Access Highway pursuant to this section shall be used by the operator of the Dulles Access Highway only for the operation and improvement of the Dulles Corridor, including the Dulles Toll Road.

History.
2010, cc. 813, 865.

§ 46.2-819.6. Invoice for unpaid toll.

A. The operator of a toll facility shall send an invoice for the unpaid toll pursuant to subsection C to the registered owner of the vehicle. An invoice for the unpaid toll shall contain the following:

1. The name and address of the registered owner alleged to be liable under this section;

2. The registration number of the motor vehicle involved in such violation or information obtained from an automatic vehicle identification system if the vehicle is identified by an automatic vehicle identification system for the purpose of violation detection;

3. The location where such violation took place;

4. The date and time of such violation;

5. The amount of the toll not paid;

6. The amount of the administrative fee;

7. The date by which the toll and administrative fee must be paid;

8. The statutory defenses available under this chapter, including a notice of (i) the summoned person's ability to provide the name and address of the vehicle operator at the time of the violation through the filing of an affidavit as provided in § 33.2-503, 46.2-819.1, or 46.2-819.3:1 and (ii) instructions for filing such affidavit, including the address to which the affidavit is to be sent;

9. A warning describing the penalties for nonpayment of the invoice for the unpaid toll or failure to file a notice to contest liability for the unpaid toll; and

10. The procedures and time limits for filing a notice to contest liability for an unpaid toll as provided in subsection C of § 46.2-819.3:1.

B. The toll facility operator shall include with the invoice a form to be used by the registered owner or operator of the vehicle to contest liability for an unpaid toll. This form shall include the mailing address to which it should be sent.

C. Whenever an invoice for an unpaid toll is to be provided to any person by the toll facility operator, it may be executed by mailing by first-class mail a copy of the invoice to the address of the owner of the vehicle as shown on the records of the Department.

History.
2011, c. 736; 2016, c. 753.

§ 46.2-819.7: Repealed by Acts 2016, c. 753, cl. 3.

Cross references.
For current similar provisions, see § 46.2-819.6.

§ 46.2-819.8. Toll grace period.

When a vehicle has been operated in violation of § 33.2-503, 46.2-819.1, 46.2-819.3, or 46.2-819.3:1, no holder of an account for an electronic toll collection device that is property of the Commonwealth when (i) such device is detected by the toll operator or (ii) such device is not detected by the toll operator but such vehicle is associated with such an account shall owe any penalties, fees, or costs in addition to the unpaid toll, unless and until the toll operator or HOT lanes operator has attempted to process the collection of the toll through the Commonwealth's electronic toll account system at least twice and at least 10 days have elapsed since the unpaid toll. A toll operator shall make an attempt to process and collect an unpaid toll on the sixth day after the unpaid toll and shall make an additional attempt on the tenth day after the unpaid toll if earlier attempts to process and collect the unpaid toll were unsuccessful.

History.
2016, c. 753.

§ 46.2-819.9. Agreements for enforcement of tolling violations against nonresidents.

A. The Governor or his designee may enter into an agreement on behalf of the Commonwealth with another state that provides for reciprocal enforcement of HOT lanes violations or toll violations, in accordance with this article and Chapter 5 (§ 33.2-500 et seq.) of Title 33.2, between the Commonwealth and the other state.

B. Any agreement made under this section shall provide that drivers and vehicles licensed or registered in the Commonwealth, while operating on the highways and bridges of another state, shall receive benefits, privileges, and exemptions of a similar kind with regard to toll enforcement as are extended to the drivers and vehicles licensed or registered in the other state while they are operating on the highways and bridges of the Commonwealth.

C. Any agreement made under this section shall provide for enforcement of HOT lanes violations or toll violations by refusal or suspension of the registration of the owner's or operator's motor vehicle in accordance with the provisions of this article and Chapter 5 (§ 33.2-500 et seq.) of Title 33.2 for Virginia residents and enforcement of HOT lanes violations or toll violations in accordance with the laws of the state in which the vehicle is registered for nonresidents. Furthermore, such agreement shall provide that any notice required to be sent between the Commonwealth and the other state for enforcement under the provisions of the agreement shall be sent via electronic means.

D. Any agreement made under this section shall provide that any vehicle owner or operator identified as a violator pursuant to the terms of the agreement shall be afforded the opportunity to challenge or otherwise contest liability for the unpaid toll in accordance with the laws or regulations of the state in which the violation occurred.

History.
2016, c. 753.

§ 46.2-819.10. Withholding of vehicle registration for enforcement of out-of-state toll violations.

A. Upon receipt of notice from a state that has entered into an agreement with the Commonwealth pursuant to § 46.2-819.9 that a resident of Virginia owes unpaid tolls, administrative fees, or penalties to that state, the Commissioner shall refuse to issue or renew the vehicle registration certificate or the license plate issued for a vehicle or vehicles owned by such resident in accordance with this section until such state has notified the Commissioner that such tolls, fees, or penalties have been paid.

If the resident is the owner and operator of the vehicle used in the commission of the offense, the Commissioner shall refuse to issue or renew the vehicle registration certificate or the license plate issued for that vehicle. If the resident was the operator of the vehicle, but not the owner, the Commissioner shall refuse to issue or renew any vehicle registration certificate or license plates for any vehicle owned by the resident.

B. The Department shall send each resident identified pursuant to subsection A notice of the intent to deny renewal of registration at least 30 days prior to the expiration date of a current vehicle registration. Such notice shall include instructions for contacting the state to which the unpaid tolls, administrative fees, or penalties are owed by the resident and indicate that such contact information is provided for the purpose of payment of the amounts owed.

C. Upon receipt of notice from the applicable state that the resident has satisfied all outstanding obligations to that state, the Commissioner shall release the hold on the vehicle registrations and permit the same to be issued or renewed.

D. The Commissioner shall charge a $40 fee to defray the cost of processing and withholding the registration or registration renewal under this section.

History.
2016, c. 753.

ARTICLE 2.

RIGHT-OF-WAY.

§ 46.2-820. Right-of-way at uncontrolled intersections, generally.

Except as otherwise provided in this article, when two vehicles approach or enter an uncontrolled intersection at approximately the same time, the driver of the vehicle on the left shall yield the right-of-way to the vehicle on the right.

History.
Code 1950, § 46-238; 1952, c. 666; 1956, c. 533; 1958, c. 541, § 46.1-221; 1985, c. 218; 1989, c. 727.

§ 46.2-821. Vehicles before entering certain highways shall stop or yield right-of-way.

The driver of a vehicle approaching an intersection on a highway controlled by a stop sign shall, immediately before entering such intersection, stop at a clearly marked stop line, or, in the absence of a stop line, stop before entering the crosswalk on the near side of the intersection, or, in the absence of a marked crosswalk, stop at the point nearest the intersecting roadway where the driver has a view of approaching traffic on the intersecting roadway. Before proceeding, he shall yield the right-of-way to the driver of any vehicle approaching on such other highway from either direction.

Where a "Yield Right-of-Way" sign is posted, the driver of a vehicle approaching or entering such intersection shall slow down to a speed reasonable for the existing conditions, yield the right-of-way to the driver of another vehicle approaching or entering such intersection from another direction, and, if required for safety, shall stop at a clearly marked stop or yield line, or, in the absence of a stop or yield line, stop before entering the crosswalk on the near side of the intersecting roadway where the driver has a view of approaching traffic on the intersecting roadway, and shall yield the right-of-way to the driver of any vehicle approaching on such other highway from either direction.

History.
Code 1950, §§ 46-238, 46-255; 1952, c. 666; 1954, c. 137; 1956, c. 533; 1958, c. 541, §§ 46.1-221, 46.1-247; 1972, c. 489; 1974, c. 347; 1976, c. 314; 1985, c. 218; 1989, c. 727; 2013, cc. 128, 400.

§ 46.2-822. Right-of-way at circular intersections.

At circular intersections, vehicles already in the circle shall have the right-of-way over vehicles approaching and entering the circle, unless otherwise directed by traffic control devices.

History.
Code 1950, § 46-238; 1952, c. 666; 1956, c. 533; 1958, c. 541, § 46.1-221; 1985, c. 218; 1989, c. 727; 2013, cc. 128, 400.

§ 46.2-823. Unlawful speed forfeits right-of-way.

The driver of any vehicle traveling at an unlawful speed shall forfeit any right-of-way which he might otherwise have under this article.

History.
Code 1950, § 46-238; 1952, c. 666; 1956, c. 533; 1958, c. 541, § 46.1-221; 1985, c. 218; 1989, c. 727.

§ 46.2-824. Right-of-way at uncontrolled "T" intersections.

When vehicles arrive at approximately the same time at an uncontrolled "T" intersection, the driver of the vehicle on the highway that intersects but does not cross the other highway shall yield the right-of-way to any vehicle traveling on the other highway.

History.
1985, c. 218, § 46.1-221.1; 1989, c. 727.

§ 46.2-825. Left turn traffic to yield right-of-way.

The driver of a vehicle, intending to turn left within an intersection or into an alley, private road, or driveway shall yield the right-of-way to any vehicle approaching from the opposite direction if it is so close as to constitute a hazard. At intersections controlled by traffic lights with separate left-turn signals, any vehicle making a left turn when so indicated by the signal shall have the right-of-way over all other vehicles approaching the intersection.

History.

Code 1950, § 46-239; 1958, c. 541, § 46.1-222; 1974, c. 347; 1989, c. 727.

§ 46.2-826. Stop before entering public highway or sidewalk from private road, etc.; yielding right-of-way.

The driver of a vehicle entering a public highway or sidewalk from a private road, driveway, alley, or building shall stop immediately before entering such highway or sidewalk and yield the right-of-way to vehicles approaching on such public highway and to pedestrians or vehicles approaching on such public sidewalk.

The provisions of this section shall not apply at an intersection of public and private roads controlled by a traffic control device. At any such intersection, all movement of traffic into and through the intersection shall be controlled by the traffic control device.

History.

Code 1950, § 46-240; 1958, c. 541, § 46.1-223; 1987, c. 346; 1989, c. 727; 2013, cc. 128, 400.

§ 46.2-827. Right-of-way of United States forces, troops, National Guard, etc.

United States forces or troops, or any portion of the Virginia National Guard, parading or performing any duty according to law, or any civil defense personnel performing any duty according to law, shall have the right-of-way in any highway through which they may pass. Such passage, however, shall not interfere with the carrying of the United States mails and the legitimate functions of police and fire fighters or with the passage of emergency vehicles as defined in § 46.2-920.

History.

Code 1950, § 44-101; 1958, c. 541, § 46.1-224; 1989, c. 727; 2015, c. 221.

§ 46.2-828. Right-of-way for funeral processions under police or sheriff's escort; improper joining of, passing through, or interfering with processions prohibited; use of high beam headlights and hazard lights by vehicles traveling in funeral processions.

Funeral processions traveling under police or sheriff's escort shall have the right-of-way in any highway through which they may pass. Localities may, by ordinance, provide for such escort service and provide for the imposition of reasonable fees to defray the cost of such service.

The sheriff or police department in any locality may provide traffic control for funeral processions when equipment and personnel are not otherwise engaged in law-enforcement activities.

Vehicles traveling as part of any funeral procession, whether escorted or unescorted, may display high beam headlights and flash all four turn signals or hazard lights to identify themselves as part of the procession.

No vehicle that is not properly part of a funeral procession shall join, pass through, or interfere with the passage of any funeral procession under escort as provided in this section.

History.

1976, c. 361, § 46.1-224.1; 1981, c. 542; 1989, c. 727; 1994, c. 54; 2001, c. 359; 2003, c. 853; 2012, c. 26.

§ 46.2-828.1. Impeding or disrupting certain funeral processions; penalty.

A. It shall be unlawful for the operator of any motor vehicle intentionally to impede or disrupt a funeral procession. Any person convicted of violating this subsection shall be guilty of a traffic infraction and shall, in addition to a penalty assessed pursuant to § 46.2-113, be assessed four driver demerit points.

B. This section shall apply only to funeral processions that are either (i) travelling under police or sheriff's escort as provided in § 46.2-828 or (ii) escorted or led by vehicles displaying warning lights as provided in § 46.2-1025.

History.

2000, c. 274.

§ 46.2-828.2. Impeding or disrupting vehicles operating under a valid highway hauling permit.

A. It shall be unlawful for the operator of any motor vehicle intentionally to impede or disrupt any vehicle or vehicles being operated under a valid highway hauling permit, issued under the provisions of § 46.2-1139, that requires an escort vehicle or vehicles. Any person convicted of violating this subsection is guilty of a traffic infraction and shall, in addition to a penalty assessed pursuant to § 46.2-113, be assessed four driver demerit points.

B. This section shall apply only to vehicles being operated under a valid highway hauling permit issued under the provisions of § 46.2-1139 that are either (i) traveling under police or sheriff's escort or (ii) being escorted or led by an escort vehicle driver operating an escort vehicle required by the highway hauling permit.

History.
2013, cc. 312, 477.

§ 46.2-829. Approach of law-enforcement or fire-fighting vehicles, rescue vehicles, or ambulances; violation as failure to yield right-of-way.

Upon the approach of any emergency vehicle as defined in § 46.2-920 giving audible signal by siren, exhaust whistle, or air horn designed to give automatically intermittent signals, and displaying a flashing, blinking, or alternating emergency light or lights as provided in §§ 46.2-1022 through 46.2-1024, the driver of every other vehicle shall, as quickly as traffic and other highway conditions permit, drive to the nearest edge of the roadway, clear of any intersection of highways, and stop and remain there, unless otherwise directed by a law-enforcement officer, until the emergency vehicle has passed. This provision shall not relieve the driver of any such vehicle to which the right-of-way is to be yielded of the duty to drive with due regard for the safety of all persons using the highway, nor shall it protect the driver of any such vehicle from the consequences of an arbitrary exercise of such right-of-way.

Violation of this section shall constitute failure to yield the right-of-way; however, any violation of this section that involves overtaking or passing a moving emergency vehicle giving an audible signal and displaying activated warning lights as provided for in this section shall constitute reckless driving, punishable as provided in § 46.2-868.

History.
Code 1950, § 46-241; 1958, c. 541, § 46.1-225; 1960, c. 570; 1966, cc. 613, 699; 1968, c. 89; 1976, c. 754; 1984, c. 539; 1985, c. 462; 1989, c. 727; 1993, c. 579.

ARTICLE 3.

TRAFFIC SIGNS, LIGHTS, AND MARKINGS.

§ 46.2-830. Uniform traffic control devices on highways; drivers to obey traffic control devices; enforcement of section.

The Commissioner of Highways may classify, designate, and mark state highways and provide a uniform system of traffic control devices for such highways under the jurisdiction of the Commonwealth. Such system of traffic control devices shall correlate with and, so far as possible, conform to the system adopted in other states.

All drivers of vehicles shall obey lawfully erected traffic control devices.

No provision of this section relating to the prohibition of disobeying traffic control devices or violating local traffic control devices shall be enforced against an alleged violator if, at the time and place of the alleged violation, any such traffic control device is not in proper position and sufficiently legible to be seen by an ordinarily observant person.

History.
Code 1950, § 46-184; 1958, c. 541, § 46.1-173; 1970, c. 163; 1976, c. 184; 1979, c. 604; 1981, c. 585; 1989, c. 727; 1994, c. 280; 1997, c. 881; 2013, cc. 128, 400, 585, 646.

§ 46.2-830.1. Failure to obey highway sign where driver sleeping or resting.

Upon the trial of a person charged with failure to obey a highway sign in violation of § 46.2-830 where the court finds that the violation resulted from the vehicle having been parked or stopped by the driver on the shoulder or other portion of the highway not ordinarily used for vehicular traffic in order for the driver to sleep or rest, the court may, in lieu of convicting under § 46.2-830, find the driver guilty of violating this section, which shall be a lesser-included offense of § 46.2-830. No demerit points shall be assigned pursuant to the Uniform Demerit Point System for convictions pursuant to this section.

History.
1992, c. 856.

§ 46.2-831. Unofficial traffic control devices prohibited; penalties.

No unauthorized person shall erect or maintain on any highway any warning or direction sign, signal, or light in imitation of any official traffic control device erected as provided by law. No person shall erect or maintain on any highway any traffic control device bearing any commercial advertising.

Nothing in this section shall prohibit the erection or maintenance of signs or signals bearing the name of an organization authorized to erect it by the Commonwealth Transportation Board, the Department of Transportation, or local authorities of counties, cities, and towns as provided by law. Nor shall this section be construed to prohibit the erection by contractors or public utility companies of temporary signs approved by the Virginia Department of Transportation warning motorists that work is in progress on or adjacent to the highway.

Any violation of this section shall constitute a Class 4 misdemeanor.

History.

Code 1950, § 46-187; 1958, c. 541, § 46.1-174; 1982, c. 681; 1989, c. 727; 2013, cc. 128, 400, 585, 646.

§ 46.2-832. Damaging or removing traffic control devices or street address signs.

Any person who intentionally defaces, damages, knocks down, or without authorization interferes with the effective operation of, or removes any traffic control device or a street address sign posted to assist in address identification in connection with enhanced 9-1-1 service as defined in § 56-484.12 is guilty of a Class 1 misdemeanor.

History.

Code 1950, § 46-188; 1958, c. 541, § 46.1-175; 1989, c. 727; 2003, c. 134; 2004, c. 291; 2013, cc. 128, 400.

§ 46.2-833. Traffic lights; penalty.

A. Signals by traffic lights shall be as follows:

Steady red indicates that moving traffic shall stop and remain stopped as long as the red signal is shown, except in the direction indicated by a steady green arrow.

Green indicates the traffic shall move in the direction of the signal and remain in motion as long as the green signal is given, except that such traffic shall yield to other vehicles and pedestrians lawfully within the intersection.

Steady amber indicates that a change is about to be made in the direction of the moving of traffic. When the amber signal is shown, traffic which has not already entered the intersection, including the crosswalks, shall stop if it is not reasonably safe to continue, but traffic which has already entered the intersection shall continue to move until the intersection has been cleared.

Flashing circular red indicates that traffic shall stop before entering an intersection. Such traffic shall yield the right-of-way to pedestrian and vehicular traffic lawfully within the intersection.

Flashing red arrow indicates that traffic shall stop before entering an intersection. After stopping, traffic may cautiously enter the intersection to turn in the direction of the signal. Such traffic shall yield the right-of-way to pedestrian and vehicular traffic lawfully within the intersection.

Flashing circular amber indicates that traffic may proceed through the intersection or past such signal with reasonable care under the circumstances. Such traffic shall yield the right-of-way to pedestrian and vehicular traffic lawfully within the intersection.

Flashing amber arrow indicates that traffic may turn in the direction of such signal with reasonable care under the circumstances. Such traffic shall yield the right-of-way to pedestrian and vehicular traffic lawfully within the intersection.

B. Notwithstanding any other provision of law, if a driver of a motorcycle or moped or a bicycle rider approaches an intersection that is controlled by a traffic light, the driver or rider may proceed through the intersection on a steady red light only if the driver or rider (i) comes to a full and complete stop at the intersection for two complete cycles of the traffic light or for two minutes, whichever is shorter, (ii) exercises due care as provided by law, (iii) otherwise treats the traffic control device as a stop sign, (iv) determines that it is safe to proceed, and (v) yields the right of way to the driver of any vehicle approaching on such other highway from either direction.

C. If the traffic lights controlling an intersection are out of service because of a power failure or other event that prevents the giving of signals by the traffic lights, the drivers of vehicles approaching such an intersection shall proceed as though such intersection were controlled by a stop sign on all approaches. The provisions of this subsection shall not apply to: intersections controlled by portable stop signs, intersections with law-enforcement officers or other authorized persons directing traffic, or intersections controlled by traffic lights displaying flashing red or flashing amber lights as provided in subsection A.

D. The driver of any motor vehicle may be detained or arrested for a violation of this section if the detaining law-enforcement officer is in uniform, displays his badge of authority, and (i) has observed the violation or (ii) has received a message by radio or other wireless telecommunication device from another law-enforcement officer who observed the violation. In the case of a person being detained or arrested based on a radio message, the message shall be sent immediately after the violation is observed, and the observing officer shall furnish the license number or other positive identification of the vehicle to the detaining officer.

Violation of any provision of this section shall constitute a traffic infraction punishable by a fine of no more than $350.

History.

Code 1950, § 46-203; 1952, c. 671; 1954, c. 381; 1958, c. 541, § 46.1-184; 1964, c. 613; 1966, c. 607; 1970, cc. 515, 736; 1972, cc. 4, 234, 454; 1974, c. 347; 1976, cc. 30, 31; 1977, c. 9; 1978, c. 300; 1981,

c. 163; 1989, c. 727; 2000, c. 834; 2004, cc. 252, 743; 2006, c. 928; 2011, c. 471; 2013, cc. 128, 400.

§ 46.2-833.01: Expired.

Editor's note.
This section was enacted by Acts 1995, c. 492, and amended by Acts 1996, c. 392; 1998, cc. 663 and 685; 1999, c. 884; 2000, c. 575, and expired July 1, 2005, according to its own terms.

§ 46.2-833.1. Evasion of traffic control devices.

It shall be unlawful for the driver of any motor vehicle to drive off the roadway and onto or across any public or private property in order to evade any stop sign, yield sign, traffic light, or other traffic control device.

History.
1993, c. 117.

§ 46.2-834. Signals by law-enforcement officers, crossing guards, and flaggers.

A. Law-enforcement officers may assume control of traffic at any intersection, regardless of whether such intersection is controlled by lights, controlled by other traffic control devices, or uncontrolled. Whenever any law-enforcement officer so assumes control of traffic, all drivers of vehicles shall obey his signals.

B. Law-enforcement officers and uniformed school crossing guards may assume control of traffic otherwise controlled by lights, and in such event, signals by such officers and uniformed crossing guards shall take precedence over such traffic control devices.

C. Uniformed school crossing guards may control traffic at any marked school crossing, whether such crossing is at an intersection or another location. Uniformed school crossing guards who are supplied by their local school division with hand-held stop signs shall use such signs whenever controlling traffic as authorized in this subsection.

D. Whenever an authorized flagger assumes control of vehicular traffic into or through a temporary traffic control zone using hand-signaling devices or an automated flagger assistance device, all drivers of vehicles shall obey his signals.

History.
Code 1950, § 46-203; 1952, c. 671; 1954, c. 381; 1958, c. 541, § 46.1-184; 1964, c. 613; 1966, c. 607; 1970, cc. 515, 736; 1972, cc. 4, 234, 454; 1974, c. 347; 1976, cc. 30, 31; 1977, c. 9; 1978, c. 300; 1981, c. 163; 1989, c. 727; 1994, c. 469; 2001, cc. 56, 71; 2004, c. 575; 2013, cc. 128, 400.

§ 46.2-835. Right turn on steady red light after stopping.

Notwithstanding the provisions of § 46.2-833, except where a traffic control device is placed prohibiting turns on steady red, vehicular traffic facing a steady red circular signal, after coming to a full stop, may cautiously enter the intersection and make a right turn.

Notwithstanding the provisions of § 46.2-833, except where a traffic control device is placed permitting turns on a steady red, vehicular traffic facing a steady red arrow, after coming to a full stop, shall remain standing until a signal to proceed is shown.

Such turning traffic shall yield the right-of-way to pedestrians lawfully within an adjacent crosswalk and to other traffic using the intersection.

History.
Code 1950, § 46-203; 1952, c. 671; 1954, c. 381; 1958, c. 541, § 46.1-184; 1964, c. 613; 1966, c. 607; 1970, cc. 515, 736; 1972, cc. 4, 234, 454; 1974, c. 347; 1976, cc. 30, 31; 1977, c. 9; 1978, c. 300; 1981, c. 163; 1989, c. 727; 2013, cc. 128, 400.

§ 46.2-836. Left turn on steady red after stopping.

Notwithstanding the provisions of § 46.2-833, except where a traffic control device is placed prohibiting turns on steady red, vehicular traffic facing a steady red circular signal on a one-way highway, after coming to a full stop, may cautiously enter the intersection and make a left turn onto another one-way highway.

Notwithstanding the provisions of § 46.2-833, except where a traffic control device is placed permitting turns on a steady red, vehicular traffic facing a steady red arrow signal, after coming to a full stop, shall remain standing until a signal to proceed is shown.

Such turning traffic shall yield the right-of-way to pedestrians lawfully within an adjacent crosswalk and to other traffic using the intersection.

History.
Code 1950, § 46-203; 1952, c. 671; 1954, c. 381; 1958, c. 541, § 46.1-184; 1964, c. 613; 1966, c. 607; 1970, cc. 515, 736; 1972, cc. 4, 234, 454; 1974, c. 347; 1976, cc. 30, 31; 1977, c. 9; 1978, c. 300; 1981, c. 163; 1989, c. 727; 2013, cc. 128, 400.

ARTICLE 4.
PASSING.

§ 46.2-837. Passing vehicles proceeding in opposite directions.

Drivers of vehicles proceeding in opposite directions on highways not marked to indicate traffic lanes shall pass each other to the right, each giving to the other, as nearly as possible, one-half of the main traveled portion of the roadway.

History.
Code 1950, § 46-223; 1958, c. 541, § 46.1-207; 1989, c. 727.

§ 46.2-838. Passing when overtaking a vehicle.

A. The driver of any vehicle overtaking another vehicle proceeding in the same direction shall pass at least two feet to the left of the overtaken vehicle and shall not again drive to the right side of the highway until safely clear of such overtaken vehicle, except as otherwise provided in this article.

B. The driver of any motor vehicle, upon overtaking a stationary vehicle that is displaying a flashing, blinking, or alternating amber light as provided in § 46.2-892 or subdivision A 10 of § 46.2-1025, shall proceed with due caution and maintain a safe speed for highway conditions.

C. The driver of any motor vehicle, upon overtaking a stationary vehicle in the process of refuse collection operations, shall (i) on a highway having at least four lanes, at least two of which are intended for traffic proceeding in the same direction as the approaching vehicle, proceed with caution and, if reasonable, with due regard for safety and traffic conditions, yield the right-of-way by making a lane change into a lane not adjacent to the stationary vehicle or (ii) if changing lanes would be unreasonable or unsafe or on highways having fewer than four lanes, proceed with due caution and decrease speed to 10 miles per hour below the posted speed limit and pass at least two feet to the left of the vehicle.

History.

Code 1950, § 46-224; 1958, c. 541, § 46.1-208; 1989, c. 727; 1999, c. 999; 2004, cc. 947, 973; 2015, cc. 189, 197.

§ 46.2-839. Passing bicycle, electric personal assistive mobility device, electric power-assisted bicycle, moped, animal, or animal-drawn vehicle.

Any driver of any vehicle overtaking a bicycle, electric personal assistive mobility device, electric power-assisted bicycle, moped, animal, or animal-drawn vehicle proceeding in the same direction shall pass at a reasonable speed at least three feet to the left of the overtaken bicycle, electric personal assistive mobility device, electric power-assisted bicycle, moped, animal, or animal-drawn vehicle and shall not again proceed to the right side of the highway until safely clear of such overtaken bicycle, electric personal assistive mobility device, electric power-assisted bicycle, moped, animal, or animal-drawn vehicle.

History.

1981, c. 585, § 46.1-208.1; 1989, c. 727; 1999, c. 999; 2001, c. 834; 2002, c. 254; 2004, cc. 947, 973; 2014, c. 358.

§ 46.2-840: Repealed by Acts 1996, c. 147.

§ 46.2-841. When overtaking vehicle may pass on right.

A. The driver of a vehicle may overtake and pass to the right of another vehicle only:

1. When the overtaken vehicle is making or about to make a left turn, and its driver has given the required signal;

2. On a highway with unobstructed pavement, not occupied by parked vehicles, of sufficient width for two or more lines of moving vehicles in each direction;

3. On a one-way street or on any one-way roadway when the roadway is free from obstructions and of sufficient width for two or more lines of moving vehicles.

B. The driver of a vehicle may overtake and pass another vehicle on the right only under conditions permitting such movement in safety. Except where driving on paved shoulders is permitted by lawfully placed signs, no such movement shall be made by driving on the shoulder of the highway or off the pavement or main traveled portion of the roadway.

History.

Code 1950, § 46-226; 1952, c. 666; 1958, c. 541, § 46.1-210; 1985, c. 481; 1989, c. 727.

§ 46.2-842. Driver to give way to overtaking vehicle.

Except when overtaking and passing on the right is permitted, the driver of an overtaken vehicle shall give way to the right in favor of the overtaking vehicle on audible signal and shall not increase the speed of his vehicle until completely passed by the overtaking vehicle. Any over-width, or slow-moving vehicle as defined by § 46.2-1081 shall be removed from the roadway at the nearest suitable location when necessary to allow traffic to pass.

History.

Code 1950, § 46-227; 1958, c. 541, § 46.1-211; 1979, c. 361; 1989, c. 727.

§ 46.2-842.1. Drivers to give way to certain overtaking vehicles on divided highways.

It shall be unlawful to fail to give way to overtaking traffic when driving a motor vehicle to the left and abreast of another motor vehicle on a divided highway. On audible or light signal, the driver of the overtaken vehicle shall move to the right to allow the overtaking vehicle to pass as soon as the overtaken vehicle can safely do so. A violation of this section shall not be construed as negligence per se in any civil action.

History.

1989, c. 708, § 46.1-211.1.

§ 46.2-843. Limitations on overtaking and passing.

The driver of a vehicle shall not drive to the left side of the center line of a highway in overtaking and passing another vehicle proceeding in the same direction unless such left side is clearly visible and is free of oncoming traffic for a sufficient distance ahead to permit such overtaking and passing to be made safely.

No person operating a truck or combination of vehicles shall pass or attempt to pass any truck or combination of vehicles going in the same direction on an upgrade if such passing will impede the passage of following traffic.

History.

Code 1950, § 46-228; 1958, c. 541, § 46.1-212; 1989, c. 727.

§ 46.2-844. Passing stopped school buses; penalty; prima facie evidence.

A. The driver of a motor vehicle approaching from any direction a clearly marked school bus that is stopped on any highway, private road, or school driveway for the purpose of taking on or discharging children, the elderly, or mentally or physically handicapped persons, who, in violation of § 46.2-859, fails to stop and remain stopped until all such persons are clear of the highway, private road, or school driveway is subject to a civil penalty of $250, and any prosecution shall be instituted and conducted in the same manner as prosecutions for traffic infractions.

A prosecution or proceeding under § 46.2-859 is a bar to a prosecution or proceeding under this section for the same act, and a prosecution or proceeding under this section is a bar to a prosecution or proceeding under § 46.2-859 for the same act.

In any prosecution for which a summons charging a violation of this section was issued within 10 days of the alleged violation, proof that the motor vehicle described in the summons was operated in violation of this section, together with proof that the defendant was at the time of such violation the registered owner of the vehicle, as required by Chapter 6 (§ 46.2-600 et seq.) shall give rise to a rebuttable presumption that the registered owner of the vehicle was the person who operated the vehicle at the place where, and for the time during which, the violation occurred. Such presumption shall be rebutted if (i) the owner of the vehicle files an affidavit by regular mail with the clerk of the general district court that he was not the operator of the vehicle at the time of the alleged violation, (ii) the owner testifies in open court under oath that he was not the operator of the vehicle at the time of the alleged violation, or (iii) a certified copy of a police report showing that the vehicle had been reported to the police as stolen prior to the time of the alleged violation of this section is presented prior to the return date established on the summons issued pursuant to this section to the court adjudicating the alleged violation. Nothing herein shall limit the admission of otherwise admissible evidence.

The testimony of the school bus driver, the supervisor of school buses, or a law-enforcement officer that the vehicle was yellow, conspicuously marked as a school bus, and equipped with warning devices as prescribed in § 46.2-1090 is prima facie evidence that the vehicle is a school bus.

B. A locality may, by ordinance, authorize the school division of the locality to install and operate a video-monitoring system in or on the school buses operated by the division or to contract with a private vendor to do so on behalf of the school division for the purpose of recording violations of subsection A. Such ordinance may direct that any civil penalty levied for a violation of subsection A shall be payable to the local school division. In any locality that has adopted such an ordinance, a summons for a violation of subsection A may be executed as provided in § 19.2-76.2 and, notwithstanding the provisions of § 19.2-76, the summons may be executed by mailing by first-class mail a copy thereof to the address of the owner of the vehicle contained in the records of the Department. Every such mailing shall include, in addition to the summons, a notice of (i) the summoned person's ability to rebut the presumption that he was the operator of the vehicle at the time of the alleged violation through the filing of an affidavit as provided in subsection A and (ii) instructions for filing such an affidavit, including the address to which the affidavit is to be sent. If the summoned person fails to appear on the date of return set out in the summons mailed pursuant to this section, the summons shall be executed in the manner set out in § 19.2-76.3. No proceedings for contempt or arrest of a person summoned by mailing shall be instituted for failure to appear on the return date of the summons. Any summons executed for violation of this section shall provide to the person summoned at least 30 business days from the mailing of the summons to inspect information collected by a video-monitoring system in connection with the violation.

For purposes of this subsection, "video-monitoring system" means a system with one or more camera sensors and computers installed and operated on a school bus that produces live digital and recorded video of motor vehicles being operated in violation of § 46.2-859. All such systems installed shall, at a minimum, produce a recorded image of the license plate and shall record the activation status of at least one warning device as prescribed in § 46.2-1090 and the time, date, and location of the vehicle when the image is recorded.

History.

1985, c. 511, § 46.1-212.1; 1987, c. 106; 1989, c. 727; 1997, cc. 622, 800, 908; 2001, c. 126; 2002, c. 541; 2011, cc. 787, 838; 2016, cc. 637, 700.

ARTICLE 5.

TURNING.

§ 46.2-845. Limitation on U-turns.

The driver of a vehicle within cities, towns or business districts of counties shall not turn his vehicle so as to proceed in the opposite direction except at an intersection.

No vehicle shall be turned so as to proceed in the opposite direction on any curve, or on the approach to or near the crest of a grade, where the vehicle cannot be seen by the driver of any other vehicle approaching from any direction within 500 feet.

History.
Code 1950, § 46-230; 1958, c. 541, § 46.1-214; 1989, c. 727.

§ 46.2-846. Required position and method of turning at intersections; local regulations.

A. Except where turning is prohibited, a driver intending to turn at an intersection or other location on any highway shall execute the turn as provided in this section.

1. Right turns: Both the approach for a right turn and a right turn shall be made as close as practicable to the right curb or edge of the roadway.

2. Left turns on two-way roadways: At any intersection where traffic is permitted to move in both directions on each roadway entering the intersection, an approach for a left turn shall be made from the right half of the roadway and as close as possible to the roadway's center line, passing to the right of the center line where it enters the intersection. After entering the intersection, the left turn shall be made so as to leave the intersection to the right of the center line of the roadway being entered. Whenever practicable, the left turn shall be made to the left of the center of the intersection.

3. Left turns on other than two-way roadways: At any intersection where traffic is restricted to one direction on one or more of the roadways, and at any crossover from one roadway of a divided highway to another roadway thereof on which traffic moves in the opposite direction, the driver intending to turn left at any such intersection or crossover shall approach the intersection or crossover in the extreme left lane lawfully available to traffic moving in the direction of travel of such vehicle and after entering the intersection or crossover the left turn shall be made so as to leave the intersection or crossover, as nearly as practicable, in the left lane lawfully available to traffic moving in such direction upon the roadway being entered.

B. Local authorities having the power to regulate traffic in their respective jurisdictions may cause traffic control devices to be placed within or adjacent to intersections and thereby direct that a different course from that specified in this section be traveled by vehicles turning at any intersection. When traffic control devices are so placed, no driver shall turn a vehicle at an intersection other than as directed by such traffic control devices.

History.
Code 1950, § 46-231; 1952, c. 666; 1958, c. 541, § 46.1-215; 1966, c. 128; 1989, c. 727; 2013, cc. 128, 400.

§ 46.2-847. Left turns by bicycles, electric personal assistive mobility devices, electric power-assisted bicycles, and mopeds.

A person riding a bicycle, electric personal assistive mobility device, electric power-assisted bicycle, or moped and intending to turn left shall either follow a course described in § 46.2-846 or make the turn as provided in this section.

A person riding a bicycle, electric personal assistive mobility device, electric power-assisted bicycle, or moped and intending to turn left shall approach the turn as close as practicable to the right curb or edge of the roadway. After proceeding across the intersecting roadway, the rider shall comply with traffic signs or signals and continue his turn as close as practicable to the right curb or edge of the roadway being entered.

Notwithstanding the foregoing provisions of this section, the Commissioner of Highways and local authorities, in their respective jurisdictions, may cause official traffic control devices to be placed at intersections to direct that a specific course be traveled by turning bicycles, electric personal assistive mobility devices, electric power-assisted bicycles, and mopeds. When such devices are so placed, no person shall turn a bicycle, electric personal assistive mobility device, electric power-assisted bicycle, or moped other than as directed by such devices.

History.
1981, c. 585, § 46.1-215.1; 1989, c. 727; 2001, c. 834; 2002, c. 254; 2013, cc. 585, 646.

ARTICLE 6.

SIGNALS BY DRIVERS.

§ 46.2-848. Signals required on backing, stopping, or turning.

Every driver who intends to back, stop, turn, or partly turn from a direct line shall first see that such movement can be made safely and, whenever the operation of any other vehicle may be affected by such movement, shall give the signals required in this article, plainly visible to the driver of such other vehicle, of his intention to make such movement.

History.
Code 1950, § 46-233; 1958, c. 541, § 46.1-216; 1960, c. 113; 1989, c. 727.

§ 46.2-849. How signals given.

A. Signals required by § 46.2-848 shall be given by means of the hand and arm or by some mechanical or electrical device approved by the Superintendent, in the manner specified in this section. Whenever the signal is given by means of the hand and arm, the driver shall indicate his intention to start, stop, turn, or partly turn by extending the hand and arm beyond the left side of the vehicle in the manner following:

1. For left turn or to pull to the left, the arm shall be extended in a horizontal position straight from and level with the shoulder;

2. For right turn or to pull to the right, the arm shall be extended upward;

3. For slowing down or stopping, the arm shall be extended downward.

B. Wherever the lawful speed is more than 35 miles per hour, such signals shall be given continuously for a distance of at least 100 feet, and in all other cases at least 50 feet, before slowing down, stopping, turning, or partly turning.

C. A person riding a bicycle, electric personal assistive mobility device, electric power-assisted bicycle, or moped shall signal his intention to stop or turn. Such signals, however, need not be given continuously if both hands are needed in the control or operation of the bicycle, electric personal assistive mobility device, electric power-assisted bicycle, or moped.

D. Notwithstanding the foregoing provisions of this section, a person operating a bicycle, electric personal assistive mobility device, electric power-assisted bicycle, or moped may signal a right turn or pull to the right by extending the right hand and arm in a horizontal position straight from and level with the shoulder beyond the right side of the bicycle, electric personal assistive mobility device, electric power-assisted bicycle, or moped, and may signal slowing down or stopping by extending the right arm downward.

History.

Code 1950, § 46-234; 1954, c. 15; 1958, c. 541, § 46.1-217; 1981, c. 585; 1989, c. 727; 2001, c. 834; 2002, c. 254; 2004, cc. 947, 973.

§ 46.2-850. Change of course after giving signal.

Drivers having once given a hand or light signal shall continue the course thus indicated, unless they alter the original signal.

History.

Code 1950, § 46-235; 1958, c. 541, § 46.1-218; 1989, c. 727.

§ 46.2-851. Signals prior to moving standing vehicles into traffic.

Drivers of vehicles stopped at the curb or edge of a highway, before moving such vehicles, shall signal their intentions to move into traffic, as provided in this article, before turning in the direction the vehicle will proceed from the curb.

History.

Code 1950, § 46-237; 1958, c. 541, § 46.1-220; 1989, c. 727.

Motor Vehicles

ARTICLE 7.

RECKLESS DRIVING AND IMPROPER DRIVING.

§ 46.2-852. Reckless driving; general rule.

Irrespective of the maximum speeds permitted by law, any person who drives a vehicle on any highway recklessly or at a speed or in a manner so as to endanger the life, limb, or property of any person shall be guilty of reckless driving.

History.

Code 1950, § 46-208; 1958, c. 541, § 46.1-189; 1983, c. 380; 1989, c. 727.

§ 46.2-853. Driving vehicle which is not under control; faulty brakes.

A person shall be guilty of reckless driving who drives a vehicle which is not under proper control or which has inadequate or improperly adjusted brakes on any highway in the Commonwealth.

History.

Code 1950, §§ 46-209, 46-209.1; 1950, p. 880; 1952, c. 671; 1954, cc. 225, 401, 458; 1958, c. 541, § 46.1-190; 1960, c. 510; 1964, c. 266; 1966, c. 694; 1968, c. 575; 1970, c. 521; 1974, cc. 222, 455; 1975, c. 633; 1978, c. 27; 1979, c. 86; 1981, cc. 333, 585; 1985, c. 148; 1989, c. 727; 1991, c. 119.

§ 46.2-854. Passing on or at the crest of a grade or on a curve.

A person shall be guilty of reckless driving who, while driving a vehicle, overtakes and passes another vehicle proceeding in the same direction, on or approaching the crest of a grade or on or approaching a curve in the highway, where the driver's view along the highway is obstructed, except where the overtaking vehicle is being operated on a highway having two or more designated lanes of roadway for each direction of travel or on a designated one-way roadway or highway.

History.

Code 1950, §§ 46-209, 46-209.1; 1950, p. 880; 1952, c. 671; 1954, cc. 225, 401, 458; 1958, c. 541, § 46.1-190; 1960, c. 510; 1964, c. 266; 1966, c. 694; 1968, c. 575; 1970, c. 521; 1974, cc. 222, 455; 1975, c. 633; 1978, c. 27; 1979, c. 86; 1981, cc. 333, 585; 1985, c. 148; 1989, c. 727.

§ 46.2-855. Driving with driver's view obstructed or control impaired.

A person shall be guilty of reckless driving who drives a vehicle when it is so loaded, or when there are in the front seat such number of persons, as to obstruct the view of the driver to the front or sides of the vehicle or to interfere with the driver's control over the driving mechanism of the vehicle.

History.

Code 1950, §§ 46-209, 46-209.1; 1950, p. 880; 1952, c. 671; 1954, cc. 225, 401, 458; 1958, c. 541, § 46.1-190; 1960, c. 510; 1964, c. 266; 1966, c. 694; 1968, c. 575; 1970, c. 521; 1974, cc. 222, 455; 1975, c. 633; 1978, c. 27; 1979, c. 86; 1981, cc. 333, 585; 1985, c. 148; 1989, c. 727.

§ 46.2-856. Passing two vehicles abreast.

A person shall be guilty of reckless driving who passes or attempts to pass two other vehicles abreast, moving in the same direction, except on highways having separate roadways of three or more lanes for each direction of travel, or on designated one-way streets or highways. This section shall not apply, however, to a motor vehicle passing two other vehicles when one or both of such other vehicles is a bicycle, electric personal assistive mobility device, electric power-assisted bicycle, or moped; nor shall this section apply to a bicycle, electric personal assistive mobility device, electric power-assisted bicycle, or moped passing two other vehicles.

History.

Code 1950, §§ 46-209, 46-209.1; 1950, p. 880; 1952, c. 671; 1954, cc. 225, 401, 458; 1958, c. 541, § 46.1-190; 1960, c. 510; 1964, c. 266; 1966, c. 694; 1968, c. 575; 1970, c. 521; 1974, cc. 222, 455; 1975, c. 633; 1978, c. 27; 1979, c. 86; 1981, cc. 333, 585; 1985, c. 148; 1989, c. 727; 2001, c. 834; 2002, c. 254.

§ 46.2-857. Driving two abreast in a single lane.

A person shall be guilty of reckless driving who drives any motor vehicle so as to be abreast of another vehicle in a lane designed for one vehicle, or drives any motor vehicle so as to travel abreast of any other vehicle traveling in a lane designed for one vehicle. Nothing in this section shall be construed to prohibit two two-wheeled motorcycles from traveling abreast while traveling in a lane designated for one vehicle. In addition, this section shall not apply to (i) any validly authorized parade, motorcade, or motorcycle escort; (ii) a motor vehicle traveling in the same lane of traffic as a bicycle, electric personal assistive mobility device, electric power-assisted bicycle, or moped; nor shall it apply to (iii) any vehicle when lawfully overtaking and passing one or more vehicles traveling in the same direction in a separate lane.

History.

Code 1950, §§ 46-209, 46-209.1; 1950, p. 880; 1952, c. 671; 1954, cc. 225, 401, 458; 1958, c. 541, § 46.1-190; 1960, c. 510; 1964, c. 266; 1966, c. 694; 1968, c. 575; 1970, c. 521; 1974, cc. 222, 455; 1975, c. 633; 1978, c. 27; 1979, c. 86; 1981, cc. 333, 585; 1985, c. 148; 1989, c. 727; 2001, c. 834; 2002, c. 254; 2010, cc. 52, 110; 2012, c. 7.

§ 46.2-858. Passing at a railroad grade crossing.

A person shall be guilty of reckless driving who overtakes or passes any other vehicle proceeding in the same direction at any railroad grade crossing or at any intersection of highways unless such vehicles are being operated on a highway having two or more designated lanes of roadway for each direction of travel or unless such intersection is designated and marked as a passing zone or on a designated one-way street or highway, or while pedestrians are passing or about to pass in front of either of such vehicles, unless permitted so to do by a traffic light or law-enforcement officer.

History.

Code 1950, §§ 46-209, 46-209.1; 1950, p. 880; 1952, c. 671; 1954, cc. 225, 401, 458; 1958, c. 541, § 46.1-190; 1960, c. 510; 1964, c. 266; 1966, c. 694; 1968, c. 575; 1970, c. 521; 1974, cc. 222, 455; 1975, c. 633; 1978, c. 27; 1979, c. 86; 1981, cc. 333, 585; 1985, c. 148; 1989, c. 727.

§ 46.2-859. Passing a stopped school bus; prima facie evidence.

A person driving a motor vehicle shall stop such vehicle when approaching, from any direction, any school bus which is stopped on any highway, private road or school driveway for the purpose of taking on or discharging children, the elderly, or mentally or physically handicapped persons, and shall remain stopped until all the persons are clear of the highway, private road or school driveway and the bus is put in motion; any person violating the foregoing is guilty of reckless driving. The driver of a vehicle, however, need not stop when approaching a school bus if the school bus is stopped on the other roadway of a divided highway, on an access road, or on a driveway when the other roadway, access road, or driveway is separated from the roadway on which he is driving by a physical barrier or an unpaved area. The driver of a vehicle also need not stop when approaching a school bus which is loading or discharging passengers from or onto property immediately adjacent to a school if the driver is directed by a law-enforcement officer or other duly authorized uniformed school crossing guard to pass the school bus. This section shall apply to school buses which are equipped with warning devices prescribed in § 46.2-1090 and are painted yellow with the words "School Bus" in black letters at least eight inches high on the front and rear thereof. Only school buses which are painted yellow and equipped with the required lettering and warning devices shall be identified as school buses.

The testimony of the school bus driver, the supervisor of school buses or a law-enforcement officer that the vehicle was yellow, conspicuously marked as a school bus, and equipped with warning devices as prescribed in § 46.2-1090 is prima facie evidence that the vehicle is a school bus.

History.

Code 1950, §§ 46-209, 46-209.1; 1950, p. 880; 1952, c. 671; 1954, cc. 225, 401, 458; 1958, c. 541, § 46.1-190; 1960, c. 510; 1964, c. 266; 1966, c. 694; 1968, c. 575; 1970, c. 521; 1974, cc. 222, 455; 1975, c. 633; 1978, c. 27; 1979, c. 86; 1981, cc. 333, 585; 1985, c. 148; 1989, c. 727; 2001, c. 126; 2002, c. 541; 2011, cc. 325, 326.

§ 46.2-860. Failing to give proper signals.

A person shall be guilty of reckless driving who fails to give adequate and timely signals of intention to turn, partly turn, slow down, or stop, as required by Article 6 (§ 46.2-848 et seq.) of this chapter.

History.

Code 1950, §§ 46-209, 46-209.1; 1950, p. 880; 1952, c. 671; 1954, cc. 225, 401, 458; 1958, c. 541, § 46.1-190; 1960, c. 510; 1964, c. 266; 1966, c. 694; 1968, c. 575; 1970, c. 521; 1974, cc. 222, 455; 1975, c. 633; 1978, c. 27; 1979, c. 86; 1981, cc. 333, 585; 1985, c. 148; 1989, c. 727.

§ 46.2-861. Driving too fast for highway and traffic conditions.

A person shall be guilty of reckless driving who exceeds a reasonable speed under the circumstances and traffic conditions existing at the time, regardless of any posted speed limit.

History.

Code 1950, §§ 46-209, 46-209.1; 1950, p. 880; 1952, c. 671; 1954, cc. 225, 401, 458; 1958, c. 541, § 46.1-190; 1960, c. 510; 1964, c. 266; 1966, c. 694; 1968, c. 575; 1970, c. 521; 1974, cc. 222, 455; 1975, c. 633; 1978, c. 27; 1979, c. 86; 1981, cc. 333, 585; 1985, c. 148; 1989, c. 727.

§ 46.2-862. Exceeding speed limit.

A person shall be guilty of reckless driving who drives a motor vehicle on the highways in the Commonwealth (i) at a speed of twenty miles per hour or more in excess of the applicable maximum speed limit or (ii) in excess of eighty miles per hour regardless of the applicable maximum speed limit.

History.

Code 1950, §§ 46-209, 46-209.1; 1950, p. 880; 1952, c. 671; 1954, cc. 225, 401, 458; 1958, c. 541, § 46.1-190; 1960, c. 510; 1964, c. 266; 1966, c. 694; 1968, c. 575; 1970, c. 521; 1974, cc. 222, 455; 1975, c. 633; 1978, c. 27; 1979, c. 86; 1981, cc. 333, 585; 1985, c. 148; 1989, c. 727; 1992, c. 608; 2006, c. 301.

§ 46.2-863. Failure to yield right-of-way.

A person shall be guilty of reckless driving who fails to bring his vehicle to a stop immediately before entering a highway from a side road when there is traffic approaching on such highway within 500 feet of such point of entrance, unless (i) a "Yield Right-of-Way" sign is posted or (ii) where such sign is posted, fails, upon entering such highway, to yield the right-of-way to the driver of a vehicle approaching on such highway from either direction.

History.

Code 1950, §§ 46-209, 46-209.1; 1950, p. 880; 1952, c. 671; 1954, cc. 225, 401, 458; 1958, c. 541, § 46.1-190; 1960, c. 510; 1964, c. 266; 1966, c. 694; 1968, c. 575; 1970, c. 521; 1974, cc. 222, 455; 1975, c. 633; 1978, c. 27; 1979, c. 86; 1981, cc. 333, 585; 1985, c. 148; 1989, c. 727.

§ 46.2-864. Reckless driving on parking lots, etc.

A person is guilty of reckless driving who operates any motor vehicle at a speed or in a manner so as to endanger the life, limb, or property of any person:

1. On any driveway or premises of a church, school, recreational facility, or business or governmental property open to the public; or
2. On the premises of any industrial establishment providing parking space for customers, patrons, or employees; or
3. On any highway under construction or not yet open to the public.

History.

Code 1950, §§ 46-209, 46-209.1; 1950, p. 880; 1952, c. 671; 1954, cc. 225, 401, 458; 1958, c. 541, § 46.1-190; 1960, c. 510; 1964, c. 266; 1966, c. 694; 1968, c. 575; 1970, c. 521; 1974, cc. 222, 455; 1975, c. 633; 1978, c. 27; 1979, c. 86; 1981, cc. 333, 585; 1985, c. 148; 1989, c. 727; 2011, c. 280.

§ 46.2-865. Racing; penalty.

Any person who engages in a race between two or more motor vehicles on the highways in the Commonwealth or on any driveway or premises of a church, school, recreational facility, or business property open to the public in the Commonwealth shall be guilty of reckless driving, unless authorized by the owner of the property or his agent. When any person is convicted of reckless driving under this section, in addition to any other penalties provided by law the driver's license of such person shall be suspended by the court for a period of not less than six months nor more than two years. In case of conviction the court shall order the surrender of the license to the court where it shall be disposed of in accordance with the provisions of § 46.2-398.

History.

Code 1950, § 46-209.2; 1956, c. 686; 1958, c. 541, § 46.1-191; 1972, c. 33; 1984, c. 780; 1989, c. 727.

§ 46.2-865.1. Injuring another or causing the death of another while engaging in a race; penalties.

A. Any person who, while engaging in a race in violation of § 46.2-865 in a manner so gross, wanton and culpable as to show a reckless disregard for human life:

1. Causes serious bodily injury to another person who is not involved in the violation of § 46.2-865 is guilty of a Class 6 felony; or
2. Causes the death of another person is guilty of a felony punishable by a term of imprisonment of not less than one nor more than 20 years, one year of which shall be a mandatory minimum term of imprisonment.

B. Upon conviction, the court shall suspend the driver's license of such person for a period of not less than one year nor more than three years, and shall order the surrender of the license to be disposed of in accordance with the provisions of § 46.2-398.

History.

2004, c. 859; 2006, c. 348.

§ 46.2-866. Racing; aiders or abettors.

Any person, although not engaged in a race as defined in § 46.2-865, who aids or abets any such race, shall be guilty of a Class 1 misdemeanor.

History.
1968, c. 575, § 46.1-191.1; 1989, c. 727.

§ 46.2-867. Racing; seizure of motor vehicle.

If the owner of a motor vehicle (i) is convicted of racing such vehicle in a prearranged, organized, and planned speed competition in violation of § 46.2-865, (ii) is present in the vehicle which is being operated by another in violation of § 46.2-865, and knowingly consents to the racing, or (iii) is convicted of a violation of § 46.2-865.1, the vehicle shall be seized and shall be forfeited to the Commonwealth, and upon being condemned as forfeited in proceedings under Chapter 22.1 (§ 19.2-386.1 et seq.) of Title 19.2, the proceeds of sale shall be disposed of according to law. Such sections shall apply mutatis mutandis.

The penalties imposed by these sections are in addition to any other penalty imposed by law.

History.
1972, c. 702, § 46.1-191.2; 1989, c. 727; 1993, c. 866; 2004, c. 859; 2012, cc. 283, 756.

§ 46.2-868. Reckless driving; penalties.

A. Every person convicted of reckless driving under the provisions of this article is guilty of a Class 1 misdemeanor.

B. Every person convicted of reckless driving under the provisions of this article who, when he committed the offense, (i) was driving without a valid operator's license due to a suspension or revocation for a moving violation and, (ii) as the sole and proximate result of his reckless driving, caused the death of another, is guilty of a Class 6 felony.

C. The punishment for every person convicted of reckless driving under the provisions of this article who, when he committed the offense, was in violation of § 46.2-1078.1 shall include a mandatory minimum fine of $250.

History.
Code 1950, § 46-210; 1950, p. 691; 1952, Ex. Sess., c. 16; 1958, c. 541, § 46.1-192; 1962, c. 302; 1970, c. 337; 1980, cc. 29, 221; 1989, c. 727; 2004, c. 349; 2013, cc. 752, 790.

§ 46.2-868.1. Aggressive driving; penalties.

A. A person is guilty of aggressive driving if (i) the person violates one or more of the following: § 46.2-802 (Drive on right side of highways), § 46.2-804 (Failure to observe lanes marked for traffic), § 46.2-816 (Following too closely), § 46.2-821 (Vehicles before entering certain highways shall stop or yield right-of-way), § 46.2-833.1 (Evasion of traffic control devices), § 46.2-838 (Passing when overtaking a vehicle), § 46.2-841 (When overtaking vehicle may pass on right), § 46.2-842 (Driver to give way to overtaking vehicle), § 46.2-842.1 (Driver to give way to certain overtaking vehicles on divided highway), § 46.2-843 (Limitations on overtaking and passing), any provision of Article 8 (§ 46.2-870 et seq.) of Chapter 8 of Title 46.2 (Speed), or § 46.2-888 (Stopping on highways); and (ii) that person is a hazard to another person or commits an offense in clause (i) with the intent to harass, intimidate, injure or obstruct another person.

B. Aggressive driving shall be punished as a Class 2 misdemeanor. However, aggressive driving with the intent to injure another person shall be punished as a Class 1 misdemeanor. In addition to the penalties described in this subsection, the court may require successful completion of an aggressive driving program.

History.
2002, cc. 752, 782.

§ 46.2-869. Improper driving; penalty.

Notwithstanding the foregoing provisions of this article, upon the trial of any person charged with reckless driving where the degree of culpability is slight, the court in its discretion may find the accused not guilty of reckless driving but guilty of improper driving. However, an attorney for the Commonwealth may reduce a charge of reckless driving to improper driving at any time prior to the court's decision and shall notify the court of such change. Improper driving shall be punishable as a traffic infraction punishable by a fine of not more than $500.

History.
1966, c. 511, § 46.1-192.2; 1972, c. 278; 1989, c. 727; 1990, c. 770; 2000, c. 340.

ARTICLE 8.
SPEED.

§ 46.2-870. Maximum speed limits generally.

Except as otherwise provided in this article, the maximum speed limit shall be 55 miles per hour on interstate highways or other limited access highways with divided roadways, nonlimited access highways having four or more lanes, and all state primary highways.

The maximum speed limit on all other highways shall be 55 miles per hour if the vehicle is a passenger motor vehicle, bus, pickup or panel truck, or a motorcycle, but 45 miles per hour on such highways if the vehicle is a truck, tractor truck, or combination of vehicles designed to transport property, or is a motor vehicle being used to tow a vehicle designed for self-propulsion, or a house trailer.

Notwithstanding the foregoing provisions of this section, the maximum speed limit shall be 70 miles per hour where indicated by lawfully placed signs, erected subsequent to a traffic engineering study and analysis of available and appropriate accident and law-enforcement data, on: (i) interstate highways, (ii) multilane, divided, limited access highways, and (iii) high-occupancy vehicle lanes if such lanes are physically separated from regular travel lanes. The maximum speed limit shall be 60 miles per hour where indicated by lawfully placed signs, erected subsequent to a traffic engineering study and analysis of available and appropriate accident and law-enforcement data, on U.S. Route 23, U.S. Route 29, U.S. Route 58, U.S. Alternate Route 58, U.S. Route 360, U.S. Route 460, and on U.S. Route 17 between the Town of Port Royal and Saluda where they are nonlimited access, multilane, divided highways.

History.

Code 1950, § 46-212; 1950, p. 881; 1952, c. 666; 1954, c. 244; 1956, c. 364; 1958, c. 541, §§ 46.1-193, 46.1-401; 1960, c. 153; 1962, c. 307; 1964, cc. 118, 408; 1966, c. 85; 1968, c. 641; 1972, cc. 89, 546, 553, 608; 1974, c. 528; 1975, c. 533; 1977, c. 577; 1978, c. 605; 1980, c. 347; 1986, c. 639; 1988, cc. 662, 897; 1989, cc. 276, 526, 727; 1992, c. 598; 1994, c. 423; 1996, c. 1; 1998, cc. 546, 560; 1999, c. 142; 2001, c. 298; 2002, c. 872; 2003, c. 838; 2004, c. 696; 2005, cc. 266, 267, 268; 2006, c. 213; 2007, cc. 222, 544; 2010, cc. 26, 56; 2014, c. 91.

§ 46.2-871. Maximum speed limit for school buses.

The maximum speed limit for school buses shall be 45 miles per hour or the minimum speed allowable, whichever is greater, on any highway where the maximum speed limit is 55 miles per hour or less, and 60 miles per hour on all interstate highways and on other highways where the maximum speed limit is more than 55 miles per hour.

History.

Code 1950, § 46-212; 1950, p. 881; 1952, c. 666; 1954, c. 244; 1956, c. 364; 1958, c. 541, § 46.1-193; 1960, c. 153; 1962, c. 307; 1964, cc. 118, 408; 1966, c. 85; 1968, c. 641; 1972, cc. 89, 546, 553, 608; 1974, c. 528; 1977, c. 577; 1978, c. 605; 1980, c. 347; 1989, c. 727; 1993, c. 278; 1994, c. 676; 1999, c. 166; 2006, c. 416; 2007, c. 98.

§ 46.2-872. Maximum speed limits for vehicles operating under special permits.

The maximum speed limit shall be fifty-five miles per hour on any highway having a posted speed limit of fifty-five miles or more per hour if the vehicle or combination of vehicles is operating under a special permit issued by the Commissioner in accordance with § 46.2-1139 or § 46.2-1149.2. The Commissioner may, however, further reduce the speed limit on any permit issued in accordance with § 46.2-1139.

History.

Code 1950, § 46-212; 1950, p. 881; 1952, c. 666; 1954, c. 244; 1956, c. 364; 1958, c. 541, § 46.1-193; 1960, c. 153; 1962, c. 307; 1964, cc. 118, 408; 1966, c. 85; 1968, c. 641; 1972, cc. 89, 546, 553, 608; 1974, c. 528; 1977, c. 577; 1978, c. 605; 1980, c. 347; 1989, c. 727; 1995, c. 113; 1996, cc. 36, 87; 1998, c. 439.

§ 46.2-873. Maximum speed limits at school crossings; penalty.

A. For the purposes of this section, "school crossing zone" means an area located within the vicinity of a school at or near a highway where the presence of children on such school property or going to and from school reasonably requires a special warning to motorists. Such zones are marked and operated in accordance with the requirements of this section with appropriate warning signs or other traffic control devices indicating that a school crossing is in progress.

B. The maximum speed limit shall be twenty-five miles per hour between portable signs, tilt-over signs, or fixed blinking signs placed in or along any highway and bearing the word "school" or "school crossing." Any signs erected under this section shall be placed not more than 600 feet from the limits of the school property or crossing in the vicinity of the school. However, "school crossing" signs may be placed in any location if the Department of Transportation or the council of the city or town or the board of supervisors of a county maintaining its own system of secondary roads approves the crossing for such signs. If the portion of the highway to be posted is within the limits of a city or town, such portable signs shall be furnished and delivered by such city or town. If the portion of highway to be posted is outside the limits of a city or town, such portable signs shall be furnished and delivered by the Department of Transportation. The principal or chief administrative officer of each school or a school board designee, preferably not a classroom teacher, shall place such portable signs in the highway at a point not more than 600 feet from the limits of the school property and remove such signs when their presence is no longer required by this section. Such portable signs, tilt-over signs, or fixed blinking signs shall be placed in a position plainly visible to vehicular traffic approaching from either direction, but shall not be placed so as to obstruct the roadway.

C. Such portable signs, tilt-over signs, or blinking signs shall be in a position, or be turned on, for thirty minutes preceding regular school hours, for thirty minutes thereafter, and during such other times as the presence of children on such school property or going to and from school reasonably requires a special warning to motorists. The governing body of any county, city, or town may, however, decrease the period of time preceding and following regular school hours during which such portable signs, tilt-over signs, or blinking signs shall be in position or lit if it determines that no children will be going to or from school during the period of time that it subtracts from the thirty-minute period.

D. The governing body of any city or town may, if the portion of the highway to be posted is within the limits of such city or town, increase or decrease the speed limit provided in this section only after justification for such increase or decrease has been shown by an engineering and traffic investigation, and no such increase or decrease in speed limit shall be effective unless such increased or decreased speed limit is conspicuously posted on the portable signs, tilt-over signs, or fixed blinking signs required by this section.

E. The governing body of a county within Planning District 8 may, if the portion of the highway to be posted is within the limits of such county, increase or decrease the speed limit provided in this section only after justification for such increase or decrease has been shown by an engineering and traffic investigation, and no such increase or decrease in speed limit shall be effective unless such increased or decreased speed limit is conspicuously posted on the portable signs, tilt-over signs, or fixed blinking signs required by this section.

F. The City of Virginia Beach may establish school zones as provided in this section and mark such zones with flashing warning lights as provided in this section on and along all highways adjacent to Route 58.

G. Any person operating any motor vehicle in excess of a maximum speed limit established specifically for a school crossing zone, when such school crossing zone is (i) indicated by appropriately placed signs displaying the maximum speed limit and (ii) in operation pursuant to subsection B of this section shall be guilty of a traffic infraction punishable by a fine of not more than $250, in addition to other penalties provided by law.

H. Notwithstanding the foregoing provisions of this section, the maximum speed limit in school zones in residential areas may be decreased to fifteen miles per hour if (i) the school board having jurisdiction over the school nearest to the affected school zone passes a resolution requesting the reduction of the maximum speed limit for such school zone from twenty-five miles per hour to fifteen miles per hour and (ii) the local governing body of the jurisdiction in which such school is located enacts an ordinance establishing the speed-limit reduction requested by the school board.

History.

Code 1950, § 46-212; 1950, p. 881; 1952, c. 666; 1954, c. 244; 1956, c. 364; 1958, c. 541, § 46.1-193; 1960, c. 153; 1962, c. 307; 1964, cc. 118, 408; 1966, c. 85; 1968, c. 641; 1972, cc. 89, 546, 553, 608; 1974, c. 528; 1977, c. 577; 1978, c. 605; 1980, c. 347; 1989, c. 727; 1990, c. 928; 1994, c. 157; 1997, cc. 629, 781; 2007, c. 813; 2015, cc. 459, 460.

§ 46.2-873.1. Maximum speed limit on nonsurface-treated highways.

The maximum speed limit on nonsurface-treated highways, which are roads that are comprised of an earth-aggregate or aggregate surface (i.e., dirt and gravel) that have not been stabilized with a bituminous or cementitious material, shall be 35 miles per hour. The maximum speed limit upon such highways may be increased or decreased by the Commissioner of Highways or other authority having jurisdiction over highways. However, such increased or decreased maximum speed limit shall be effective only when indicated by sign on the highway. For such highways upon which maximum speed limit is not indicated by sign, the maximum speed limit shall be 35 miles per hour.

History.

2000, c. 262; 2004, c. 719; 2005, cc. 239, 804; 2009, c. 74; 2010, cc. 19, 48; 2011, c. 29; 2012, c. 207; 2014, cc. 80, 261.

§ 46.2-873.2. Maximum speed limit on rural rustic roads.

The maximum speed limit on any highway designated a rural rustic road pursuant to § 33.2-332 shall be 35 miles per hour; however, all speed limits on rural rustic roads in effect on July 1, 2008, shall remain in effect unless and until changed subsequent to a traffic engineering study.

History.

2008, c. 165.

Editor's note.

A reference in this section was updated at the direction of the Virginia Code Commission to conform to the recodification of Title 33.2 by Acts 2014, c. 805, effective October 1, 2014.

§ 46.2-874. Maximum speed limit in business and residence districts.

The maximum speed shall be 25 miles per hour on highways in business or residence districts, except on interstate or other limited access highways with divided roadways or nonlimited access highways having four or more lanes and all state primary highways. The speed limit on all nonlimited access highways having four or more lanes and all state primary highways shall remain as indicated by signs posted prior to July 1, 2005, unless changed as provided by law.

History.

Code 1950, § 46-212; 1950, p. 881; 1952, c. 666; 1954, c. 244; 1956, c. 364; 1958, c. 541, § 46.1-193; 1960, c. 153; 1962, c. 307; 1964, cc. 118, 408; 1966, c. 85; 1968, c. 641; 1972, cc. 89, 546, 553, 608; 1974, c. 528; 1977, c. 577; 1978, c. 605; 1980, c. 347; 1989, c. 727; 2005, c. 310.

§ 46.2-874.1. Exceptions to maximum speed limits in residence districts; penalty.

A. The governing body of any town with a population between 14,000 and 15,000 may by ordinance (i) prohibit the operation of a motor vehicle at a speed of twenty miles per hour or more in excess of the applicable maximum speed limit in a residence district and (ii) provide that any person who violates the prohibition shall be subject to a mandatory civil penalty of $100, not subject to suspension.

B. The governing body of the City of Falls Church, or the City of Manassas may by ordinance (i) prohibit the operation of a motor vehicle at a speed of fifteen miles per hour or more in excess of the applicable maximum speed limit in a residence district, as defined in § 46.2-100 of the Code of Virginia, when indicated by appropriately placed signs displaying the maximum speed limit and the penalty for violations, and (ii) provide that any person who violates the prohibition shall be subject to a civil penalty of $100, in addition to other penalty provided by law.

History.
1999, c. 865; 2000, c. 957; 2007, c. 813.

§ 46.2-875. Maximum speed limit on certain other highways in cities and towns.

The maximum speed limit shall be 35 miles per hour on highways in any city or town, except on interstate or other limited access highways with divided roadways and in business or residence districts. However, municipalities that maintain their own roads may increase or decrease speed limits on highways over which they have jurisdiction following appropriate traffic engineering investigation.

History.
Code 1950, § 46-212; 1950, p. 881; 1952, c. 666; 1954, c. 244; 1956, c. 364; 1958, c. 541, § 46.1-193; 1960, c. 153; 1962, c. 307; 1964, cc. 118, 408; 1966, c. 85; 1968, c. 641; 1972, cc. 89, 546, 553, 608; 1974, c. 528; 1977, c. 577; 1978, c. 605; 1980, c. 347; 1989, c. 727; 2011, c. 182.

§ 46.2-876. Maximum speed limit for passenger vehicles towing certain trailers.

The maximum speed limit for passenger motor vehicles while towing utility, camping, or boat trailers not exceeding an actual gross weight of 2,500 pounds shall be the same as that for passenger motor vehicles.

History.
Code 1950, § 46-212; 1950, p. 881; 1952, c. 666; 1954, c. 244; 1956, c. 364; 1958, c. 541, § 46.1-193; 1960, c. 153; 1962, c. 307; 1964, cc. 118, 408; 1966, c. 85; 1968, c. 641; 1972, cc. 89, 546, 553, 608; 1974, c. 528; 1977, c. 577; 1978, c. 605; 1980, c. 347; 1989, c. 727.

§ 46.2-877. Minimum speed limits.

No person shall drive a motor vehicle at such a slow speed as to impede the normal and reasonable movement of traffic except when reduced speed is necessary for safe operation or in compliance with law.

Whenever the Commissioner of Highways or local authorities within their respective jurisdictions determine on the basis of a traffic engineering and traffic investigation that slow speeds on any part of a highway consistently impede the normal and reasonable movement of traffic, the Commissioner or such local authority may determine and declare a minimum speed limit to be set forth on signs posted on such highway below which no person shall drive a vehicle except when necessary for safe operation or in compliance with law.

History.
Code 1950, § 46-212; 1950, p. 881; 1952, c. 666; 1954, c. 244; 1956, c. 364; 1958, c. 541, § 46.1-193; 1960, c. 153; 1962, c. 307; 1964, cc. 118, 408; 1966, c. 85; 1968, c. 641; 1972, cc. 89, 546, 553, 608; 1974, c. 528; 1977, c. 577; 1978, c. 605; 1980, c. 347; 1989, c. 727.

§ 46.2-878. Authority to change speed limits.

A. Notwithstanding the other provisions of this article, the Commissioner of Highways or other authority having jurisdiction over highways may decrease the speed limits set forth in § 46.2-870 and may increase or decrease the speed limits set forth in §§ 46.2-873 through 46.2-875 on any highway under its jurisdiction; and may establish differentiated speed limits for daytime and nighttime by decreasing for nighttime driving the speed limits set forth in § 46.2-870 and by increasing for daytime or decreasing for nighttime the speed limits set forth in §§ 46.2-873 through 46.2-875 on any highway under his jurisdiction. Such increased or decreased speed limits and such differentiated speed limits for daytime and nighttime driving shall be effective only when prescribed after a traffic engineering investigation and when indicated on the highway by signs. It shall be unlawful to operate any motor vehicle in excess of speed limits established and posted as provided in this section. The increased or decreased speed limits over highways under the control of the Commissioner of Highways shall be effective only when prescribed in writing by the Commissioner of Highways and kept on file in the Central Office of the Department of Transportation. Whenever the speed limit on any highway has been increased or decreased or a differential speed limit has been established and such speed limit is properly posted, there shall be a rebuttable presumption that the change in speed was properly established in accordance with the provisions of this section.

B. Notwithstanding any other provision of this article, including the provisions of subsection A, the governing body of any town located entirely within the confines of a United States military base may by ordinance reduce the speed limit to less than 25 miles per hour on any highway within its boundaries, provided such reduced speed limit is indicated by lawfully placed signs.

History.
Code 1950, § 46-212; 1950, p. 881; 1952, c. 666; 1954, c. 244; 1956, c. 364; 1958, c. 541, § 46.1-193; 1960, c. 153; 1962, c. 307; 1964, cc. 118, 408; 1966, c. 85; 1968, c. 641; 1972, cc. 89, 546, 553, 608; 1974, c. 528; 1977, c. 577; 1978, c. 605; 1980, c. 347; 1989, c. 727; 1990, c. 779; 1993, c. 98; 2013, c. 303.

§ 46.2-878.1. Maximum speed limits in highway work zones; penalty.

Operation of any motor vehicle in excess of a maximum speed limit established specifically for a highway work zone, when workers are present and when such highway work zone is indicated by appropriately placed signs displaying the maximum speed limit and the penalty for violations, shall be unlawful and constitute a traffic infraction punishable by a fine of not more than $500.

For the purposes of this section, "highway work zone" means a construction or maintenance area that is located on or beside a highway and marked by appropriate warning signs and, for projects covered by contracts entered into on or after July 1, 2012, with attached flashing lights or other traffic control devices indicating that work is in progress.

Nothing in this section shall preclude the prosecution or conviction for reckless driving of any motor vehicle operator whose operation of any motor vehicle in a highway work zone, apart from speed, demonstrates a reckless disregard for life, limb, or property.

History.

1992, c. 462; 1995, c. 54; 2003, c. 839; 2012, c. 397.

§ 46.2-878.2. Maximum speed limits in certain residence districts of counties, cities, and towns; penalty.

Operation of any motor vehicle in excess of a maximum speed limit established for a highway in a residence district of a county, city, or town, when indicated by appropriately placed signs displaying the maximum speed limit and the penalty for violations, shall be unlawful and constitute a traffic infraction punishable by a fine of $200, in addition to other penalties provided by law. No portion of the fine shall be suspended unless the court orders 20 hours of community service. The Commissioner of Highways or any local governing body having jurisdiction over highways shall develop criteria for the overall applicability for the installation of signs. Such criteria shall not exclude highways, functionally classified as minor arterials, serving areas that either (i) were built as residential developments or (ii) have grown to resemble residential developments, provided, in either case, (a) such highways are experiencing documented speeding problems and (b) the local governing body requests the application of this section to such highway. Such signs may be installed in any town and shall not require the approval of the county within which such town is located. Any such signs installed in any town shall be paid for by the town requesting the installation of the signs, or out of the county's secondary system construction allocation.

History.

1996, c. 172; 1999, c. 87; 2002, c. 882; 2004, c. 350; 2006, c. 547; 2013, cc. 585, 646.

§ 46.2-878.3. Prepayment of fines for violations of speed limits.

Except as otherwise provided in this section, the Traffic Infractions and Uniform Fine Schedule adopted by the Supreme Court for prepayment of fines shall, in all instances where prepayment of a fine is permitted, include a fine of $6 per mile-per-hour in excess of posted speed limits provided for in this article. However, such Traffic Infractions and Uniform Fine Schedule shall include a fine of $7 per mile-per-hour in excess of posted speed limits for a violation of §§ 46.2-873 and 46.2-878.1 and $8 per mile-per-hour in excess of posted speed limits for a violation of § 46.2-878.2.

History.

2003, c. 838; 2010, c. 874; 2011, c. 890.

§ 46.2-879. No conviction for speeding in certain areas unless markers installed.

No person shall be convicted of a violation of a statute or an ordinance enacted by local authorities pursuant to the provisions of § 46.2-1300 decreasing the speed limit established in this article when such person has exceeded the speed limit in an area where the speed limit has been decreased unless such area is clearly indicated by a conspicuous marker at the termini of such area.

History.

Code 1950, § 46-212.1; 1954, c. 643; 1958, c. 541, § 46.1-194; 1962, c. 307; 1989, c. 727.

§ 46.2-880. Tables of speed and stopping distances.

All courts shall take notice of the following tables of speed and stopping distances of motor vehicles, which shall not raise a presumption, in actions in which inquiry thereon is pertinent to the issues:

SPEED IN		AVERAGE STOPPING DISTANCES			TOTAL STOPPING DISTANCES: DRIVER AND	
Miles Per Hour	Feet Per Second	Automobile Brakes (In Feet)	Truck Brakes Brakes on All Wheels (In Feet)	Average Driver Perception-Reaction Time (1.5 Seconds) (In Feet)	Automobiles (In Feet)	Trucks (In Feet)
10	14.7	5	6	22	27	28
15	22.0	11	14	33	44	47
20	29.3	19	25	44	63	69
25	36.7	30	40	55	85	95
30	44.0	43	57	66	109	123
35	51.3	58	78	77	135	155
40	58.7	76	102	88	164	190
45	66.0	96	129	99	195	228
50	73.3	119	159	110	229	269
55	80.7	144	192	121	265	313
60	88.0	171	229	132	303	361
65	95.3	201	268	143	344	411
70	102.7	233	311	154	387	465
75	110.0	268	357	165	433	522
80	117.3	305	406	176	481	582
85	124.7	344	459	187	531	646
90	132.0	386	514	198	584	712
95	139.3	430	573	209	639	782
100	146.7	476	635	220	696	855

The courts shall further take notice that the above table has been constructed, using scientific reasoning, to provide factfinders with an average baseline for motor vehicle stopping distances: (1) for a vehicle in good condition and (2) on a level, dry stretch of highway, free from loose material.

Deviations from these circumstances do not negate the usefulness of the table, but rather call for additional site-specific examination and/or explanation.

Site-specific research may be utilized under any circumstances.

History.

Code 1950, § 46-212.2; 1956, c. 600; 1958, c. 541, § 46.1-195; 1989, c. 727; 2001, c. 145; 2003, c. 277.

§ 46.2-881. Special speed limitation on bridges, tunnels and interstates.

It shall be unlawful to drive any motor vehicle, trailer, or semitrailer on any public bridge, causeway, viaduct, or in any tunnel, or on any interstate at a speed exceeding that indicated as a maximum by signs posted thereon or at its approach by or on the authority of the Commissioner of Highways.

The Commissioner of Highways, on request or on his own initiative, may conduct an investigation of any public bridge, causeway, viaduct, tunnel, or interstate and, on the basis of his findings, may set the maximum speed of vehicles which such structure or roadway can withstand or which is necessitated in consideration of the benefit and safety of the traveling public and the safety of the structure or roadway. The Commissioner of Highways is expressly authorized to establish and indicate variable speed limits on such structures or roadways to be effective under such conditions as would in his judgment, warrant such variable limits, including but not limited to darkness, traffic conditions, atmospheric conditions, weather, emergencies, and like conditions which may affect driving safety. Any speed limits, whether fixed or variable, shall be prominently posted in such proximity to such structure or roadway as deemed appropriate by the Commissioner of Highways. The findings of the Commissioner shall be conclusive evidence of the maximum safe speed which can be maintained on such structure or roadway.

History.

Code 1950, § 46-215; 1958, c. 541, § 46.1-196; 1966, c. 85; 1977, c. 259; 1989, c. 727; 2006, c. 139.

§ 46.2-882. Determining speed with various devices; certificate as to accuracy of device; arrest without warrant.

The speed of any motor vehicle may be determined by the use of (i) a laser speed determination device,

Motor Vehicles

(ii) radar, (iii) a microcomputer device that is physically connected to an odometer cable and both measures and records distance traveled and elapsed time to determine the average speed of a motor vehicle, or (iv) a microcomputer device that is located aboard an airplane or helicopter and measures and records distance traveled and elapsed time to determine the average speed of a motor vehicle being operated on highways within the Interstate System of highways as defined in § 33.2-100. The results of such determinations shall be accepted as prima facie evidence of the speed of such motor vehicle in any court or legal proceeding where the speed of the motor vehicle is at issue.

In any court or legal proceeding in which any question arises about the calibration or accuracy of any laser speed determination device, radar, or microcomputer device as described in this section used to determine the speed of any motor vehicle, a certificate, or a true copy thereof, showing the calibration or accuracy of (i) the speedometer of any vehicle, (ii) any tuning fork employed in calibrating or testing the radar or other speed determination device or (iii) any other method employed in calibrating or testing any laser speed determination device, and when and by whom the calibration was made, shall be admissible as evidence of the facts therein stated. No calibration or testing of such device shall be valid for longer than six months.

The driver of any such motor vehicle may be arrested without a warrant under this section if the arresting officer is in uniform and displays his badge of authority and if the officer has observed the registration of the speed of such motor vehicle by the laser speed determination device, radar, or microcomputer device as described in this section, or has received a radio message from the officer who observed the speed of the motor vehicle registered by the laser speed determination device, radar, or microcomputer device as described in this section. However, in case of an arrest based on such a message, such radio message shall have been dispatched immediately after the speed of the motor vehicle was registered and furnished the license number or other positive identification of the vehicle and the registered speed to the arresting officer.

Neither State Police officers nor local law-enforcement officers shall use laser speed determination devices or radar, as described herein in airplanes or helicopters for the purpose of determining the speed of motor vehicles.

State Police officers may use laser speed determination devices, radar, and/or microcomputer devices as described in this section. All localities may use radar and laser speed determination devices to measure speed. The Cities of Alexandria, Fairfax, Falls Church, Manassas, and Manassas Park and the Counties of Arlington, Fairfax, Loudoun, and Prince William and towns within such counties may use microcomputer devices as described in this section.

The Division of Purchases and Supply, pursuant to § 2.2-1112, shall determine the proper equipment used to determine the speed of motor vehicles and shall advise the respective law-enforcement officials of the same. Police chiefs and sheriffs shall ensure that all such equipment and devices purchased on or after July 1, 1986, meet or exceed the standards established by the Division.

History.

Code 1950, § 46-215.2; 1954, c. 313; 1956, c. 216; 1958, c. 541, § 46.1-198; 1966, c. 585; 1968, c. 497; 1974, c. 554; 1984, c. 357; 1986, c. 530; 1988, c. 712; 1989, c. 727; 1990, cc. 691, 974; 1991, c. 345; 1994, c. 734; 1997, c. 33; 1998, c. 423; 1999, cc. 693, 694, 698, 724, 729, 733; 2000, cc. 354, 357, 365; 2002, c. 109; 2003, cc. 608, 965; 2006, c. 930; 2007, c. 231.

Editor's note.

References in this section were updated at the direction of the Virginia Code Commission to conform to the recodification of Title 33.2 by Acts 2014, c. 805, effective October 1, 2014.

§ 46.2-883. Signs indicating legal rate of speed and measurement of speed by radar.

Signs to indicate the legal rate of speed and that the speed of motor vehicles may be measured by radar or other electrical devices shall be placed at or near the State boundary on those interstate and primary highways which connect the Commonwealth to other jurisdictions at such locations as the Commissioner of Highways, in his discretion, may select. There shall be a prima facie presumption that such signs were placed at the time of the commission of the offense of exceeding the legal rate of speed, and a certificate by the Commissioner of Highways as to the placing of such signs shall be admissible in evidence to support or rebut the presumption. Such legal rate of speed and notice of measurement of speed by radar or other electrical devices may be posted on different signs and need not be posted on the same sign.

History.

1968, c. 497, § 46.1-198.2; 1989, c. 727.

ARTICLE 9.
RAILROAD CROSSINGS.

§ 46.2-884. Railroad warning signals must be obeyed.

No person driving a vehicle shall disobey a clearly visible or audible crossing signal which gives warning of the immediate approach of a train at a railroad grade crossing.

History.

Code 1950, § 46-253; 1958, c. 541, § 46.1-243; 1989, c. 727.

§ 46.2-885. When vehicles to stop at railroad grade crossings.

A. Except in cities or towns, whenever any person driving a vehicle approaches a railroad grade crossing under any of the circumstances stated in this section, the driver of the vehicle shall stop within 50 feet but not less than 15 feet from the nearest rail of such railroad, and shall not proceed until he can do so safely. The foregoing requirements shall apply when:

1. A clearly visible electric or mechanical signal device gives warning of the immediate approach of a train;

2. A crossing gate is lowered or a flagman gives or continues to give a signal of the approach or passage of a train;

3. A train approaching such crossing gives the signals required by § 56-414;

4. An approaching train or any self-propelled machinery or automobile type vehicle traveling on a railroad track is plainly visible and is in hazardous proximity to such crossing, regardless of whether a clearly visible electric or mechanical signal device or flagman gives warning.

B. No person shall drive any vehicle through, around, or under any crossing gate or barrier at a railroad crossing while such gate or barrier is closed or is being opened or closed.

History.

Code 1950, § 46-254; 1956, c. 164; 1958, c. 541, § 46.1-244; 1989, c. 727; 2012, c. 828.

§ 46.2-886. When drivers of certain vehicles to stop, look, and listen at railroad crossings; crossing tracks without shifting gears.

Except in cities or towns, the driver of any motor vehicle carrying passengers for hire, or of any vehicle carrying explosive substances or flammable liquids as a cargo or part of a cargo, before crossing at grade any railroad track, shall stop such vehicle within fifty feet but not less than fifteen feet from the nearest rail of such railroad and while stopped shall listen and look in both directions along the track for any approaching train, and for signals indicating the approach of a train, except as hereinafter provided in this section, and shall not proceed until he can do so safely. After stopping and upon proceeding when it is safe to do so, the driver of any vehicle shall cross only in such gear of the vehicle that there will be no necessity for changing gears while traversing the crossing.

Before crossing any railroad tracks at grade, the driver of any school bus shall stop the school bus within fifty feet but not less than fifteen feet from the nearest rail of such railroad and while stopped shall listen and look in both directions along the track for any approaching train, except as hereinafter provided in this section, and shall not proceed until he can do so safely. After stopping and upon proceeding when it is safe to do so, the driver of any school bus shall cross only in such gear of the vehicle that there will be no necessity for changing gears while traversing the crossing.

Notwithstanding the foregoing provisions of this section, no stop need be made at any such crossing where a law-enforcement officer or a traffic-control signal directs traffic to proceed.

History.

Code 1950, § 46-254.1; 1956, c. 164; 1958, c. 541, § 46.1-245; 1989, c. 727.

§ 46.2-887. Moving crawler-type tractors, steam shovels, derricks, rollers, etc., over railroad grade crossings.

Except in cities or towns, no person shall move any crawler-type tractor, steam shovel, derrick, roller, or any equipment or structure having a normal operating speed of ten or less miles per hour or a vertical body or load clearance of less than one-half inch per foot of the distance between any two adjacent axles or in any event of less than nine inches, measured above the level surface of a roadway, on or across any tracks at a railroad grade crossing without first complying with this section.

Notice of any intended crossing shall be given to a station agent of the railroad and a reasonable time shall be given to the railroad to provide proper protection at the crossing.

Before making any such crossing, the person moving any such vehicle or equipment shall first stop it not less than fifteen feet nor more than fifty feet from the nearest rail of the railroad and while so stopped shall listen and look in both directions along such track for any approaching train and for signals indicating the approach of a train, and shall not proceed until the crossing can be made safely.

No such crossing shall be made when warning is given by automatic signal, crossing gates, a flagman, or otherwise of the immediate approach of a train. If a flagman is provided by the railroad, movement over the crossing shall be under his direction.

History.

Code 1950, § 46-254.2; 1956, c. 164; 1958, c. 541, § 46.1-246; 1989, c. 727.

ARTICLE 10.

STOPPING ON HIGHWAYS.

§ 46.2-888. Stopping on highways; general rule.

No person shall stop a vehicle in such manner as to impede or render dangerous the use of the highway by others, except in the case of an emergency, an accident, or a mechanical breakdown. In the event of such an emergency, accident, or breakdown, the emergency flashing lights of such vehicle shall be turned on if the vehicle is equipped with such lights and such lights are in working order. If the driver is capable of safely doing so and the vehicle is movable, the driver may move the vehicle from the roadway to prevent obstructing the regular flow of traffic; provided, however, that the movement of the vehicle to prevent the obstruction of traffic shall not relieve the law-enforcement officer of his duty pursuant to § 46.2-373. A report of the vehicle's location shall be made to the nearest law-enforcement officer as soon as practicable, and the vehicle shall be moved from the roadway to the shoulder as soon as possible and removed from the shoulder without unnecessary delay. If the vehicle is not promptly removed, such removal may be ordered by a law-enforcement officer at the expense of the owner if the disabled vehicle creates a traffic hazard.

History.
Code 1950, § 46-256; 1952, c. 671; 1958, c. 541, § 46.1-248; 1962, c. 175; 1972, c. 63; 1974, c. 230; 1977, cc. 284, 326; 1985, c. 93; 1989, c. 727; 1997, c. 431; 2008, c. 737.

§ 46.2-889. Location of parked vehicles.

No vehicle shall be stopped except close to and parallel to the right edge of the curb or roadway, except that a vehicle may be stopped close to and parallel to the left curb or edge of the roadway on one-way streets or may be parked at an angle where permitted by the Commonwealth Transportation Board, the Department, or local authorities with respect to highways under their jurisdiction.

History.
Code 1950, § 46-256; 1952, c. 671; 1958, c. 541, § 46.1-248; 1962, c. 175; 1972, c. 63; 1974, c. 230; 1977, cc. 284, 326; 1985, c. 93; 1989, c. 727; 2013, cc. 585, 646.

§ 46.2-890. Stopping in vicinity of fire or emergency.

No vehicle shall be stopped at or in the vicinity of a fire, vehicle or airplane accident, or other area of emergency, in such a manner as to create a traffic hazard or interfere with law-enforcement officers, fire fighters, rescue workers, or others whose duty it is to deal with such emergencies. Any vehicle found unlawfully parked in the vicinity of a fire, accident, or area of emergency may be removed by order of a law-enforcement officer or, in the absence of a law-enforcement officer, by order of the uniformed fire or rescue officer in charge, at the risk and expense of the owner if such vehicle creates a traffic hazard or interferes with the necessary procedures of law-enforcement officers, fire fighters, rescue workers, or others whose assigned duty it is to deal with such emergencies. The charge for such removal shall not exceed the actual and necessary cost. Vehicles being used by accredited information services, such as press, radio, and television, when being used for the gathering of news, shall be exempt from the provisions of this section, except when actually obstructing the law-enforcement officers, fire fighters, and rescue workers dealing with such emergencies.

History.
Code 1950, § 46-256; 1952, c. 671; 1958, c. 541, § 46.1-248; 1962, c. 175; 1972, c. 63; 1974, c. 230; 1977, cc. 284, 326; 1985, c. 93; 1989, c. 727.

§ 46.2-891. Exemption for highway construction and maintenance vehicles.

The provisions of this article shall not apply to any vehicle owned or controlled by the Virginia Department of Transportation or counties, cities or towns, while actually engaged in the construction, reconstruction, maintenance, or emergency road clearance of highways.

History.
Code 1950, § 46-256; 1952, c. 671; 1958, c. 541, § 46.1-248; 1962, c. 175; 1972, c. 63; 1974, c. 230; 1977, cc. 284, 326; 1985, c. 93; 1989, c. 727; 2007, cc. 189, 918.

§ 46.2-892. Rural mail carriers stopping on highways.

The provisions of § 46.2-888 shall not apply to any rural mail carrier stopping on the highway while collecting or delivering the United States mail at a mailbox, provided there is lettered on the back of the vehicle operated by such rural mail carrier, or lettered on a sign securely attached to and displayed at the rear of such vehicle, in letters at least four inches in height the following words and groups of words, which may be in any order:

CAUTION

FREQUENT STOPS

U.S. MAIL

Additionally, the provisions of § 46.2-888 shall not apply to such rural mail carrier so stopping if, in lieu of such sign, the vehicle has, and is using, supplemental turn signals mounted at each side of the roof of the vehicle. Between the lights on the assembly shall be mounted a sign with the words "U.S. Mail", or at least one flashing amber warning light, mounted on the roof or rear of the vehicle, to be used in conjunction with a rear-mounted "U.S. Mail" sign.

The roof-mounted "U.S. Mail" sign required by the foregoing provisions of this section shall be yellow with black letters at least four inches in height, and the lights shall be of the type approved by the Superintendent of State Police. The lettered sign shall be displayed only when the vehicle is engaged in the collection or delivery of the United States mail.

Nothing in this section shall be construed to relieve any such mail carrier from civil liability for such stopping on any highway if he is negligent in so doing, and if the negligence proximately contributes to any personal injury or property damage resulting therefrom.

History.
Code 1950, § 46-256.1; 1954, c. 433; 1958, c. 541, § 46.1-249; 1962, c. 382; 1989, c. 727; 1998, c. 411; 2004, c. 359; 2005, c. 140.

§ 46.2-893. Stopping on highways to discharge cargo or passengers; school buses.

No truck or bus, except a school bus, shall be stopped wholly or partially on the traveled portion of any highway outside of cities and towns for the purpose of taking on or discharging cargo or passengers unless the operator cannot leave the traveled portion of the highway with safety. A school bus may be stopped on the traveled portion of the highway when taking on or discharging school children, but these stops shall be made only at points where the bus can be clearly seen for a safe distance from both directions.

History.
Code 1950, § 46-257; 1950, p. 941; 1956, c. 505; 1958, c. 541, § 46.1-250; 1960, c. 256; 1989, c. 727.

ARTICLE 11.

ACCIDENTS.

§ 46.2-894. Duty of driver to stop, etc., in event of accident involving injury or death or damage to attended property; penalty.

The driver of any vehicle involved in an accident in which a person is killed or injured or in which an attended vehicle or other attended property is damaged shall immediately stop as close to the scene of the accident as possible without obstructing traffic, as provided in § 46.2-888, and report his name, address, driver's license number, and vehicle registration number forthwith to the State Police or local law-enforcement agency, to the person struck and injured if such person appears to be capable of understanding and retaining the information, or to the driver or some other occupant of the vehicle collided with or to the custodian of other damaged property. The driver shall also render reasonable assistance to any person injured in such accident, including taking such injured person to a physician, surgeon, or hospital if it is apparent that medical treatment is necessary or is requested by the injured person.

Where, because of injuries sustained in the accident, the driver is prevented from complying with the foregoing provisions of this section, the driver shall, as soon as reasonably possible, make the required report to the State Police or local law-enforcement agency and make a reasonable effort to locate the person struck, or the driver or some other occupant of the vehicle collided with, or the custodian of the damaged property, and report to such person or persons his name, address, driver's license number, and vehicle registration number.

Any person convicted of a violation of this section is guilty of (i) a Class 5 felony if the accident results in injury to or the death of any person, or if the accident results in more than $1000 of damage to property or (ii) a Class 1 misdemeanor if the accident results in damage of $1000 or less to property.

History.
Code 1950, § 46-189; 1958, c. 541, § 46.1-176; 1970, c. 59; 1977, c. 267; 1982, c. 503; 1984, c. 780; 1989, c. 727; 1997, c. 431; 2001, c. 808; 2002, c. 115; 2005, c. 131.

§ 46.2-895. Duty of certain persons accompanying driver to report accidents involving injury, death, or damage to attended property.

If the driver fails to stop and make the report required by § 46.2-894, every person sixteen years of age or older in the vehicle with the driver at the time of the accident, who has knowledge of the accident, shall have a duty to ensure that a report is made within twenty-four hours from the time of the accident to the State Police or, if the accident occurs in a city or town, to the local law-enforcement agency. The report shall include his name, address, and such other information within his knowledge as the driver is required to report pursuant to § 46.2-894.

History.
Code 1950, § 46-189; 1958, c. 541, § 46.1-176; 1970, c. 59; 1977, c. 267; 1982, c. 503; 1984, c. 780; 1989, c. 727.

§ 46.2-896. Duties of driver in event of accident involving damage only to unattended property.

The driver of any vehicle involved in an accident in which no person is killed or injured, but in which an unattended vehicle or other unattended property is damaged, shall make a reasonable effort to find the owner or custodian of such property and shall report to the owner or custodian the information which the driver is required to report pursuant to § 46.2-894 if such owner or custodian is found. If the owner or custodian of such damaged vehicle or property cannot be found, the driver shall leave a note or other sufficient information including driver identification and contact information in a conspicuous place at the scene of the accident and shall report the accident in writing within 24 hours to the State Police or the local law-enforcement agency. Such note or other information and written report shall contain the information that the driver is required to report pursuant to § 46.2-894. The written report shall, in addition, state the date, time, and place of the accident and the driver's description of the property damage.

Where, because of injuries sustained in the accident, the driver is prevented from complying with the foregoing provisions of this section, the driver shall, as soon as reasonably possible, make the required report to the State Police or local law-enforcement agency and make a reasonable effort to locate the owner or custodian of the unattended vehicle or property and report to him the information required by § 46.2-894.

History.

Code 1950, § 46-189; 1958, c. 541, § 46.1-176; 1970, c. 59; 1977, c. 267; 1982, c. 503; 1984, c. 780; 1989, c. 727; 1997, c. 431; 2005, c. 137.

§ 46.2-897. Duty of certain persons accompanying driver to report accidents involving damage only to unattended property.

If the driver fails to stop and make a reasonable search for the owner or custodian of an unattended vehicle or property or to leave a note for such owner or custodian as required by § 46.2-896, every person sixteen years of age or older in the vehicle with the driver at the time of the accident who has knowledge of the accident shall have a duty to ensure that a report is made within twenty-four hours from the time of the accident to the State Police or, if the accident occurs in a city or town, to the local law-enforcement agency. The report shall include his name, address, and such other facts within his knowledge as are required by § 46.2-896 to be reported by the driver.

History.

Code 1950, § 46-189; 1958, c. 541, § 46.1-176; 1970, c. 59; 1977, c. 267; 1982, c. 503; 1984, c. 780; 1989, c. 727.

§ 46.2-898. Reports are in addition to others.

The reports required by §§ 46.2-894 through 46.2-897 are in addition to other accident reports required by this title and shall be made irrespective of the amount of property damage involved.

History.

Code 1950, § 46-189; 1958, c. 541, § 46.1-176; 1970, c. 59; 1977, c. 267; 1982, c. 503; 1984, c. 780; 1989, c. 727.

§ 46.2-899. Article applies to accidents on private or public property.

The provisions of this article shall apply irrespective of whether such accident occurs on the public streets or highways or on private property.

History.

Code 1950, § 46-189; 1958, c. 541, § 46.1-176; 1970, c. 59; 1977, c. 267; 1982, c. 503; 1984, c. 780; 1989, c. 727.

§ 46.2-900. Penalty for violation of §§ 46.2-895 through 46.2-897.

Any person convicted of violating the provisions of §§ 46.2-895 through 46.2-897 shall, if such accident results in injury to or the death of any person, be guilty of a Class 6 felony. If such accident results only in damage to property, the person so convicted shall be guilty of a Class 1 misdemeanor; however, if the vehicle or other property struck is unattended and such damage is less than $250, such person shall be guilty of a Class 4 misdemeanor. A motor vehicle operator convicted of a Class 4 misdemeanor under this section shall be assigned three demerit points by the Commissioner of the Department of Motor Vehicles.

History.

Code 1950, § 46-190; 1958, c. 541, § 46.1-177; 1962, c. 302; 1973, c. 8; 1979, c. 653; 1989, c. 727; 1992, c. 279; 2001, c. 808.

§ 46.2-901. Suspension of driver's license for failure to report certain accidents.

Any person convicted of violating the provisions of §§ 46.2-894 through 46.2-897 may be punished, in addition to the penalties provided in §§ 46.2-894 and 46.2-900, if such accident resulted only in damage to property and such damage exceeded $500, by suspension of his license or privilege to operate a motor vehicle on the highways of the Commonwealth for a period not to exceed six months by the court. This section shall in no case be construed to limit the authority or duty of the Commissioner with respect to revocation of licenses for violation of §§ 46.2-894 through 46.2-897 as provided in Article 10 (§ 46.2-364 et seq.) of Chapter 3 of this title. Any license revoked under the provisions of this section shall be surrendered to the court to be disposed of in accordance with the provisions of § 46.2-398.

History.

1968, c. 493, § 46.1-177.1; 1984, c. 780; 1989, c. 727; 2001, c. 808.

§ 46.2-902. Leaving scene of accident when directed to do so by officer.

A person shall leave the scene of a traffic accident when directed to do so by a law-enforcement officer.

History.

Code 1950, § 46-258; 1958, c. 541, § 46.1-251; 1989, c. 727.

§ 46.2-902.1. Officer may require certain motorists to furnish proof of insurance or payment of fee for registration of an uninsured motor vehicle; penalty.

Any law-enforcement officer present at the scene of a motor vehicle accident as to which a law-enforcement officer is required by § 46.2-373 to file an accident report with the Department may require the operator of any motor vehicle involved in such accident to furnish proof that the vehicle he was operating at the time of such accident was either (i) an insured motor vehicle as defined in § 46.2-705 or (ii) a vehicle for which the fee required by § 46.2-706 for registration of an uninsured vehicle had been paid as to that vehicle. Failure to furnish proof of insurance or payment of the uninsured vehicle registration fee when required by a law-enforcement officer as provided in this section within thirty days shall constitute a Class 2 misdemeanor.

History.
2002, c. 450.

ARTICLE 12.

BICYCLES.

§ 46.2-903. Riding or driving vehicles other than bicycles, electric power-assisted bicycles, or electric personal assistive mobility devices on sidewalks.

No person shall ride or drive any vehicle other than (i) an emergency vehicle, as defined in § 46.2-920, (ii) a vehicle engaged in snow or ice removal and control operations, (iii) a wheel chair or wheel chair conveyance, whether self-propelled or otherwise, (iv) a bicycle, (v) an electric personal assistive mobility device, or (vi) an electric power-assisted bicycle on the sidewalks of any county, city, or town of the Commonwealth.

History.
Code 1950, § 33-283; 1958, c. 541, § 46.1-229; 1964, c. 522; 1973, c. 158; 1974, c. 541; 1975, c. 187; 1978, c. 605; 1981, c. 585; 1989, c. 727; 1994, c. 116; 2001, c. 834; 2002, c. 254.

§ 46.2-904. Use of roller skates and skateboards on sidewalks and shared-use paths; operation of bicycles, motorized skateboards or foot-scooters, motor-driven cycles, electric power-assisted bicycles, and electric personal assistive mobility devices on sidewalks and crosswalks and shared-use paths; local ordinances.

The governing body of any county, city, or town may by ordinance prohibit the use of roller skates and skateboards and/or the riding of bicycles, electric personal assistive mobility devices, motorized skateboards or foot-scooters, motor-driven cycles, or electric power-assisted bicycles on designated sidewalks or crosswalks, including those of any church, school, recreational facility, or any business property open to the public where such activity is prohibited. Signs indicating such prohibition shall be conspicuously posted in general areas where use of roller skates and skateboards, and/or bicycle, electric personal assistive mobility devices, motorized skateboards or foot-scooters, motor-driven cycles, or electric power-assisted bicycle riding is prohibited.

A person riding a bicycle, electric personal assistive mobility device, motorized skateboard or foot-scooter, motor-driven cycle, or an electric power-assisted bicycle on a sidewalk, shared-use path, or across a roadway on a crosswalk, shall yield the right-of-way to any pedestrian and shall give an audible signal before overtaking and passing any pedestrian.

No person shall ride a bicycle, electric personal assistive mobility device, motorized skateboard or foot-scooter, motor-driven cycle, or an electric power-assisted bicycle on a sidewalk, or across a roadway on a crosswalk, where such use of bicycles, electric personal assistive mobility devices, motorized skateboards or foot-scooters, motor-driven cycles, or electric power-assisted bicycles is prohibited by official traffic control devices.

A person riding a bicycle, electric personal assistive mobility device, motorized skateboard or foot-scooter, motor-driven cycle, or an electric power-assisted bicycle on a sidewalk, shared-use path, or across a roadway on a crosswalk, shall have all the rights and duties of a pedestrian under the same circumstances.

A violation of any ordinance adopted pursuant to this section shall be punishable by a civil penalty of not more than $50.

History.
1981, c. 585, § 46.1-229.01; 1984, c. 124; 1989, c. 727; 1999, c. 943; 2001, c. 834; 2002, c. 254; 2003, cc. 29, 46; 2006, cc. 529, 538; 2013, c. 783.

§ 46.2-905. Riding bicycles, electric personal assistive mobility devices, electric power-assisted bicycles, and mopeds on roadways and bicycle paths.

Any person operating a bicycle, electric personal assistive mobility device, electric power-assisted bicycle, or moped on a roadway at less than the normal speed of traffic at the time and place under conditions then existing shall ride as close as safely practicable to the right curb or edge of the roadway, except under any of the following circumstances:

1. When overtaking and passing another vehicle proceeding in the same direction;
2. When preparing for a left turn at an intersection or into a private road or driveway;
3. When reasonably necessary to avoid conditions including, but not limited to, fixed or moving objects, parked or moving vehicles, pedestrians, animals, surface hazards, or substandard width lanes that make it unsafe to continue along the right curb or edge;
4. When avoiding riding in a lane that must turn or diverge to the right; and
5. When riding upon a one-way road or highway, a person may also ride as near the left-hand curb or edge of such roadway as safely practicable.

For purposes of this section, a "substandard width lane" is a lane too narrow for a bicycle, electric personal assistive mobility device, electric power-assisted bicycle, motorized skateboard or foot-scooter, or moped and another vehicle to pass safely side by side within the lane.

Persons riding bicycles, electric personal assistive mobility devices, or electric power-assisted bicycles on a highway shall not ride more than two abreast. Persons riding two abreast shall not impede the normal and reasonable movement of traffic, shall move into a single file formation as quickly as is practicable when being overtaken from the rear by a faster moving vehicle, and, on a laned roadway, shall ride in a single lane.

Notwithstanding any other provision of law to the contrary, the Department of Conservation and Recreation shall permit the operation of electric personal assistive mobility devices on any bicycle path or trail designated by the Department for such use.

History.
1974, c. 347, § 46.1-229.1; 1980, c. 130; 1981, c. 585; 1989, c. 727; 2001, c. 834; 2002, c. 254; 2003, cc. 29, 46; 2004, cc. 947, 973; 2006, cc. 529, 538; 2007, cc. 209, 366; 2013, c. 783.

§ 46.2-906. Carrying articles or passengers on bicycles, electric personal assistive mobility devices, electric power-assisted bicycles, and mopeds.

No person operating a bicycle, electric personal assistive mobility device, electric power-assisted bicycle, or moped on a highway shall carry any package, bundle, or article that prevents the driver from keeping at least one hand on the handlebars.

No bicycle or moped shall be used to carry more persons at one time than the number of persons for which it was designed or is equipped, except that an adult bicycle rider may carry a child less than six years old if such child is securely attached to the bicycle in a seat or trailer designed for carrying children.

History.
1974, c. 347, § 46.1-229.2; 1981, c. 585; 1989, c. 727; 2001, c. 834; 2002, c. 254; 2003, cc. 29, 46; 2006, cc. 529, 538; 2007, cc. 209, 366.

§ 46.2-906.1. Local ordinances may require riders of bicycles, electric personal assistive mobility devices, and electric power-assisted bicycles to wear helmets.

The governing body of any county, city or town may, by ordinance, provide that every person 14 years of age or younger shall wear a protective helmet that at least meets the Consumer Product Safety Commission standard whenever riding or being carried on a bicycle, an electric personal assistive mobility device, a toy vehicle, or an electric power-assisted bicycle on any highway as defined in § 46.2-100, sidewalk, or public bicycle path.

Violation of any such ordinance shall be punishable by a fine of $25. However, such fine shall be suspended (i) for first-time violators and (ii) for violators who, subsequent to the violation but prior to imposition of the fine, purchase helmets of the type required by the ordinance.

Violation of any such ordinance shall not constitute negligence, or assumption of risk, be considered in mitigation of damages of whatever nature, be admissible in evidence, or be the subject of comment by counsel in any action for the recovery of damages arising out of the operation of any bicycle, electric personal assistive mobility device, toy vehicle, or electric power-assisted bicycle, nor shall anything in this section change any existing law, rule, or procedure pertaining to any civil action.

History.
1993, c. 924; 1994, c. 56; 1995, cc. 42, 671; 2001, c. 834; 2002, c. 254; 2004, cc. 947, 973; 2006, cc. 529, 538; 2007, cc. 209, 366.

§ 46.2-907. Overtaking and passing vehicles.

A person riding a bicycle, electric personal assistive mobility device, electric power-assisted bicycle, motorized skateboard or foot-scooter, or moped may overtake and pass another vehicle on either the left or right side, staying in the same lane as the overtaken vehicle, or changing to a different lane, or riding off the roadway as necessary to pass with safety.

A person riding a bicycle, electric personal assistive mobility device, electric power-assisted bicycle, motorized skateboard or foot-scooter, or moped may overtake and pass another vehicle only under conditions that permit the movement to be made with safety.

A person riding a bicycle, electric personal assistive mobility device, electric power-assisted bicycle, motorized skateboard or foot-scooter, or moped shall not travel between two lanes of traffic moving in the same direction, except where one lane is a separate turn lane or a mandatory turn lane.

Except as otherwise provided in this section, a person riding a bicycle, electric personal assistive mobility device, electric power-assisted bicycle, motorized skateboard or foot-scooter, or moped shall comply with all rules applicable to the driver of a motor vehicle when overtaking and passing.

History.
1981, c. 585, § 46.1-229.2:1; 1989, c. 727; 2001, c. 834; 2002, c. 254; 2006, cc. 529, 538; 2013, c. 783.

§ 46.2-908. Registration of bicycle, electric personal assistive mobility device, and electric power-assisted bicycle serial numbers.

Any person who owns a bicycle, electric personal assistive mobility device, or electric power-assisted bicycle may register its serial number with the local law-enforcement agency of the political subdivision in which such person resides.

History.
1975, c. 171, § 46.1-66.1; 1989, c. 727; 2001, c. 834; 2002, c. 254.

§ 46.2-908.1. Electric personal assistive mobility devices, electrically powered toy vehicles, and electric power-assisted bicycles.

All electric personal assistive mobility devices, electrically powered toy vehicles, and electric power-assisted bicycles shall be equipped with spill-proof, sealed, or gelled electrolyte batteries. No person shall at any time or at any location drive an electric personal assistive mobility device, or an electric power-assisted bicycle faster than twenty-five miles per hour. No person less than fourteen years old shall drive any electric personal assistive mobility device, motorized skateboard or foot-scooter, or electric power-assisted bicycle unless under the immediate supervision of a person who is at least eighteen years old.

An electric personal assistive mobility device or motorized skateboard or foot-scooter may be operated on any highway with a maximum speed limit of twenty-five miles per hour or less. An electric personal assistive mobility device shall only operate on any highway authorized by this section if a sidewalk is not provided along such highway or if operation of the electric personal assistive mobility device on such sidewalk is prohibited pursuant to § 46.2-904. Nothing in this section shall prohibit the operation of an electric personal assistive mobility device or motorized skateboard or foot-scooter in the crosswalk of any highway where the use of such crosswalk is authorized for pedestrians, bicycles, or electric power-assisted bicycles.

Operation of electric personal assistive mobility devices, electrically powered toy vehicles, bicycles and electric power-assisted bicycles is prohibited on any Interstate Highway System component except as provided by the section.

The Commonwealth Transportation Board may authorize the use of bicycles on an Interstate Highway System Component provided the operation is limited to bicycle or pedestrian facilities that are barrier separated from the roadway and automobile traffic and such component meets all applicable safety requirements established by federal and state law.

History.
2001, c. 834; 2002, c. 254; 2006, cc. 529, 538; 2007, cc. 209, 366; 2009, c. 795; 2013, c. 783.

ARTICLE 12.1.

LOW-SPEED VEHICLES.

§ 46.2-908.2. Low-speed vehicles; required equipment.

Every low-speed vehicle operated upon a highway shall be equipped with head lights, brake lights, tail lights, reflex reflectors, an emergency or parking brake, an externally mounted rearview mirror, an internally mounted rearview mirror, a windshield, one or more windshield wipers, a speedometer, an odometer, braking for each wheel, a safety belt system, and a vehicle identification number.

History.
2002, cc. 214, 234.

§ 46.2-908.3. Low-speed vehicles; operation on highways; license required; registration required; safety and emissions inspections not required.

Low-speed vehicles may be operated on public highways where the maximum speed limit is no greater than 35 miles per hour, but this limitation shall not prohibit the operation of low-speed vehicles across intersections with highways whose maximum speed limits are greater than 35 miles per hour. Operation of low-speed vehicles shall be prohibited on any highway where the Department of Transportation or the local governing body of the locality having control of the highway, as the case may be, has prohibited their operation in the interest of safety and such prohibition is indicated by conspicuously posted signs.

Low-speed vehicles shall be operated on public highways only by persons who hold driver's licenses or learner's permits issued as provided in Chapter 3 (§ 46.2-300 et seq.).

Low-speed vehicles shall be titled and registered as provided in Chapter 6 (§ 46.2-600 et seq.) and shall be subject to the same requirements as to insurance applicable to other motor vehicles under that chapter.

On or after October 1, 2013, low-speed vehicles titled and registered as provided in Chapter 6 (§ 46.2-600 et seq.) shall display license plates as provided in subsection D of § 46.2-711.

The operator of any low-speed vehicle being operated on the highways in the Commonwealth shall have in his possession: (i) the registration card issued by the Department or the registration card issued by the state or country in which the low-speed vehicle is registered, and (ii) his driver's license, learner's permit, or temporary driver's permit.

The provisions of Article 22 (§ 46.2-1176 et seq.) of Chapter 10 of this title shall not apply to low-speed vehicles.

History.
2002, cc. 214, 234; 2011, c. 283; 2013, c. 783.

ARTICLE 13.

MOTORCYCLES AND MOPEDS AND ALL-TERRAIN VEHICLES.

§ 46.2-909. Riding on motorcycles, generally.

Every person operating a motorcycle, as defined in § 46.2-100, excluding three-wheeled vehicles, shall ride only upon the permanent seat attached to the motorcycle, unless safety dictates standing on both footpegs for no longer than is necessary. Such operator shall not carry any other person, unless the motorcycle is designed to carry more than one person, in which event a passenger may ride on the permanent seat if designed for two persons, or on another seat firmly attached to the rear or side of the seat for the operator. If the motorcycle is designed to carry more than one person, it shall also be equipped with a footrest for the use of such passenger.

History.

Code 1950, §§ 46-183.1, 46-183.2; 1954, c. 204; 1958, c. 541, § 46.1-172; 1968, c. 498; 1970, cc. 29, 99; 1982, cc. 390, 681; 1989, cc. 6, 727; 2015, c. 218.

§ 46.2-910. Motorcycle and autocycle operators to wear helmets, etc.; certain sales prohibited; penalty.

A. Every person operating a motorcycle or autocycle shall wear a face shield, safety glasses or goggles, or have his motorcycle or autocycle equipped with safety glass or a windshield at all times while operating the vehicle, and operators and any passengers thereon shall wear protective helmets. Operators and passengers riding on motorcycles with wheels of eight inches or less in diameter or in three-wheeled motorcycles or autocycles that have nonremovable roofs, windshields, and enclosed bodies shall not be required to wear protective helmets. The windshields, face shields, glasses or goggles, and protective helmets required by this section shall meet or exceed the standards and specifications of the Snell Memorial Foundation, the American National Standards Institute, Inc., or the federal Department of Transportation. Failure to wear a face shield, safety glasses or goggles, or protective helmets shall not constitute negligence per se in any civil proceeding. The provisions of this section requiring the wearing of protective helmets shall not apply to operators of or passengers on motorcycles or autocycles being operated (i) as part of an organized parade authorized by the Department of Transportation or the locality in which the parade is being conducted and escorted, accompanied, or participated in by law-enforcement officers of the jurisdiction wherein the parade is held and (ii) at speeds of no more than 15 miles per hour.

No motorcycle or autocycle operator shall use any face shield, safety glasses, or goggles, or have his motorcycle or autocycle equipped with safety glass or a windshield, unless of a type either (i) approved by the Superintendent prior to July 1, 1996, or (ii) that meets or exceeds the standards and specifications of the Snell Memorial Foundation, the American National Standards Institute, Inc., or the federal Department of Transportation and is marked in accordance with such standards.

B. It shall be unlawful to sell or offer for sale, for highway use in Virginia, any protective helmet that fails to meet or exceed any standard as provided in the foregoing provisions of this section. Any violation of this subsection is a Class 4 misdemeanor.

History.

Code 1950, §§ 46-183.1, 46-183.2; 1954, c. 204; 1958, c. 541, § 46.1-172; 1968, c. 498; 1970, cc. 29, 99; 1982, cc. 390, 681; 1989, cc. 6, 727; 1996, c. 690; 1998, c. 789; 2014, cc. 53, 256.

§ 46.2-911: Repealed by Acts 1994, c. 51.

§ 46.2-911.1. Operation of motor-driven cycles on public highways prohibited.

No person shall operate a motor-driven cycle on or over any public highway in the Commonwealth.

History.

2006, cc. 529, 538.

§ 46.2-912. Operating motorcycle without headlight, horn or rearview mirror.

A. Notwithstanding any other provision of law, motorcycles may be operated without headlights, horns, or rearview mirrors on public highways if all the following conditions are met:

1. The motorcycles are designed for use in trail riding and endurance runs;
2. The motorcycles are being driven by duly licensed persons;
3. The motorcycles are being operated between sunrise and sunset; and
4. The motorcycles are being operated during endurance runs sanctioned by the American Motorcycle Association.

B. No person shall operate motorcycles without such equipment on the public highways of the Commonwealth other than at the times and under the circumstances set forth in this section.

History.

1970, c. 300, § 46.1-172.01; 1978, c. 605; 1989, c. 727.

§ 46.2-913. Vendors of certain motorcycles to furnish statements of registration and licensing requirements.

Every retailer of motorcycles having a rating of seven horsepower or less, shall provide written statements to every vendee regarding registration and licensing of such vehicles and the requirement of a motor vehicle driver's license.

History.

1973, c. 72, § 46.1-172.02; 1978, c. 605; 1984, c. 780; 1989, c. 727.

§ 46.2-914. Limitations on operation of mopeds.

A. No moped shall be driven on any highway or public vehicular area faster than 35 miles per hour.

Any person who operates a moped faster than 35 miles per hour shall be deemed, for all the purposes of this title, to be operating a motorcycle.

B. No moped shall be driven on any highway by any person under the age of 16, and every person driving a moped shall carry with him a government-issued form of photo identification that includes his name, address, and date of birth.

C. Operation of mopeds is prohibited on any Interstate Highway System component.

Violation of any provision of this section shall constitute a traffic infraction punishable by a fine of no more than $50.

History.

Code 1950, §§ 46-1, 46-185, 46-186, 46-343; 1954, c. 59; 1958, cc. 501, 541, § 46.1-1; 1964, c. 618; 1966, c. 643; 1968, cc. 285, 641, 653, 685; 1972, cc. 433, 609; 1974, c. 347; 1975, cc. 382, 426; 1976, c. 372; 1977, cc. 252, 585; 1978, cc. 36, 550, 605; 1979, c. 100; 1980, c. 51; 1981, c. 585; 1983, c. 386; 1984, cc. 404, 780; 1985, c. 447; 1986, cc. 72, 613; 1987, c. 151; 1988, cc. 107, 452, 865; 1989, c. 727; 2004, c. 758; 2006, cc. 529, 538; 2008, c. 525; 2009, c. 795; 2013, c. 783.

§ 46.2-915. Stickers required on mopeds.

Any dealer who sells any moped at retail shall affix to any such moped, or verify that there is affixed thereto a permanent decal or sticker which states (i) that the operation of mopeds on highways and public vehicular areas by persons under the age of sixteen is prohibited by Virginia law, (ii) the maximum engine displacement or wattage of the moped, and (iii) the maximum speed at which the moped may be ridden.

Any dealer who sells any such moped which does not have affixed thereto such a permanent decal or sticker shall be guilty of a Class 1 misdemeanor.

History.

1976, c. 264, § 46.1-172.03; 1981, c. 585; 1987, c. 344; 1989, c. 727; 2007, c. 111; 2013, c. 783.

§ 46.2-915.1. All-terrain vehicles and off-road motorcycles; penalty.

A. No all-terrain vehicle shall be operated:

1. On any public highway, or other public property, except (i) as authorized by proper authorities, (ii) to the extent necessary to cross a public highway by the most direct route, or (iii) by law-enforcement officers, firefighters, or emergency medical services personnel responding to emergencies;

2. By any person under the age of 16, except that (i) children between the ages of 12 and 16 may operate all-terrain vehicles powered by engines of no more than 90 cubic centimeters displacement and (ii) children less than 12 years old may operate all-terrain vehicles powered by engines of no more than 70 cubic centimeters displacement;

3. By any person unless he is wearing a protective helmet of a type approved by the Superintendent of State Police for use by motorcycle operators;

4. On another person's property without the written consent of the owner of the property or as explicitly authorized by law; or

5. With a passenger at any time, unless such all-terrain vehicle is designed and equipped to be operated with more than one rider.

B. Notwithstanding subsection A, all-terrain vehicles may be operated on the highways in Buchanan County and Tazewell County if the following conditions are met:

1. Such operation is approved by action of the Buchanan County Board of Supervisors for operation along the Pocahontas Trail on Bill Young Mountain and across Virginia Route 635 in Buchanan County and approved by action of the Tazewell County Board of Supervisors for operation along the Pocahontas Trail in and between the Town of Pocahontas and Boissevain; across Virginia Routes 644, 663, 659, 627, 734, and 747; within the corporate limits of the Town of Pocahontas in Tazewell County; and across property of the Virginia Department of Corrections in Tazewell County, provided that permission is granted for such operation pursuant to § 2.2-1150;

2. Signs, whose design, number, and location are approved by the Virginia Department of Transportation, have been posted warning motorists that all-terrain vehicles may be operating on the highway;

3. Such all-terrain vehicles are operated during daylight hours on the highway for no more than one mile between one off-road trail and another;

4. Signs required by this subsection are purchased and installed by the person or club requesting the Board of Supervisors' approval for such over-the-road operation of all-terrain vehicles;

5. All-terrain vehicles operators shall, when operating on the highway, obey all rules of the road applicable to other motor vehicles;

6. Riders of such all-terrain vehicles shall wear approved helmets; and

7. Such all-terrain vehicles shall operate at speeds of no more than 25 miles per hour.

No provision of this subsection shall be construed to require all-terrain vehicles operated on a highway as provided in this subsection to comply with lighting requirements contained in this title.

C. Any retailer selling any all-terrain vehicle shall affix thereto, or verify that there is affixed thereto, a decal or sticker, approved by the Superintendent of State Police, which clearly and completely states the prohibition contained in subsection A.

D. A violation of this section shall not constitute negligence, be considered in mitigation of damages of whatever nature, be admissible in evidence or be the subject of comment by counsel in any action for the recovery of damages arising out of the operation, ownership, or maintenance of an all-terrain vehicle or off-road motorcycle, nor shall anything in this section change any existing law, rule, or procedure pertaining to any such civil action, nor shall this section bar any claim which otherwise exists.

E. Violation of any provision of this section shall be punishable by a civil penalty of not more than $500.

F. The provisions of this section shall not apply:

1. To any all-terrain vehicle being used in conjunction with farming activities; or

2. To members of the household or employees of the owner or lessee of private property on which the all-terrain vehicle is operated.

G. For the purposes of this section, "all-terrain vehicle" shall have the meaning ascribed in § 46.2-100.

History.
1989, c. 290, § 46.1-172.04; 1995, c. 670; 2001, c. 147; 2003, c. 313; 2006, c. 896; 2011, c. 822; 2015, cc. 502, 503.

§ 46.2-915.2. Safety equipment for mopeds; effect of violation; penalty.

Every person operating a moped, as defined in § 46.2-100, on a public street or highway shall wear a face shield, safety glasses, or goggles of a type approved by the Superintendent or have his moped equipped with safety glass or a windshield at all times while operating such vehicle, and operators and passengers thereon, if any, shall wear protective helmets of a type approved by the Superintendent. A violation of this section shall not constitute negligence, be considered in mitigation of damages of whatever nature, be admissible in evidence or be the subject of comment by counsel in any action for the recovery of damages arising out of the operation, ownership, or maintenance of a moped or motor vehicle, nor shall anything in this section change any existing law, rule, or procedure pertaining to any such civil action. Any person who knowingly violates this section shall be guilty of a traffic infraction and be subject to a fine of not more than fifty dollars.

History.
1989, c. 6, § 46.1-172; 2013, c. 783.

§ 46.2-916. Ordinances providing for the disposition of unregistered or unlicensed motorcycles.

The governing bodies of counties, cities, and towns may by ordinance provide for the lawful seizure, impounding and disposition of unlicensed or unregistered motorcycles operated either on the highways or on private property without the consent of the private property owner.

History.
1974, c. 540; 1978, c. 17, § 46.1-229.3; 1989, c. 727.

ARTICLE 13.1.

GOLF CART AND UTILITY VEHICLE OPERATION.

§ 46.2-916.1. Golf cart and utility vehicle operations on public highways not otherwise designated for such operation.

No person shall operate a golf cart or utility vehicle on or over any public highway in the Commonwealth except as provided in this article.

History.
2004, c. 746.

§ 46.2-916.2. Designation of public highways for golf cart and utility vehicle operations.

A. No portion of the public highways may be designated for use by golf carts and utility vehicles unless the governing body of the county, city, or town in which that portion of the highway is located has reviewed and approved such highway usage.

B. The governing body of any county, city or town may by ordinance authorize the operation of golf carts and utility vehicles on designated public highways within its boundaries after (i) considering the speed, volume, and character of motor vehicle traffic using such highways and (ii) determining that golf cart and utility vehicle operation on particular highways is compatible with state and local transportation plans and consistent with the Commonwealth's Statewide Pedestrian Policy provided for in § 33.2-354.

C. Notwithstanding the other provisions of this section, no town that has not established its own police department, as defined in § 9.1-165, may authorize the operation of golf carts or utility vehicles. The provision of this subsection shall not apply to the Towns of Claremont, Clifton, Irvington, Saxis, Urbanna, or Wachapreague.

D. No public highway shall be designated for use by golf carts and utility vehicles if such golf cart and utility vehicle operations will impede the safe and efficient flow of motor vehicle traffic.

E. The county, city or town that has authorized the operation of golf carts or utility vehicles shall be responsible for the installation and continuing maintenance of any signs pertaining to the operation of golf carts or utility vehicles. Such county, city or town may include in its ordinance for designating highways the ability to recover its costs of the signs and maintenance pertaining thereto from organizations, individuals or entities requesting the designations. The cost of installation and continuing maintenance of any signs pertaining to the operation of golf carts or utility vehicles shall not be paid by the Virginia Department of Transportation.

F. Notwithstanding the other provisions of this section, employees of the Department of Conservation and Recreation may operate golf carts and utility vehicles on those portions of public highways located within Department of Conservation and Recreation property and on Virginia Department of Transportation-maintained highways that are adjacent to Department of Conservation and Recreation property, provided the golf cart or utility vehicle is being operated on highways with speed limits of no more than 35 miles per hour.

History.

2004, c. 746; 2006, c. 728; 2008, c. 196; 2009, cc. 68, 504; 2011, c. 469; 2012, c. 9; 2013, c. 64; 2014, c. 69.

Editor's note.

References in this section were updated at the direction of the Virginia Code Commission to conform to the recodification of Title 33.2 by Acts 2014, c. 805, effective October 1, 2014.

§ 46.2-916.3. Limitations on golf cart and utility vehicle operations on designated public highways.

A. Golf cart and utility vehicle operations on designated public highways shall be in accordance with the following limitations:

1. A golf cart or utility vehicle may be operated only on designated public highways where the posted speed limit is 25 miles per hour or less. However, a golf cart or utility vehicle may cross a highway at an intersection controlled by a traffic light if the highway has a posted speed limit of no more than 35 miles per hour and in the Town of Colonial Beach may cross any highway at an intersection marked as a golf cart crossing by signs posted by the Virginia Department of Transportation;

2. In towns with a population of 2,000 or less, a golf cart or utility vehicle may cross a highway at an intersection conspicuously marked as a golf cart crossing by signs posted by the Virginia Department of Transportation if the highway has a posted speed limit of no more than 35 miles per hour and the crossing is required as the only means to provide golf cart access from one part of the town to another part of the town;

3. No person shall operate any golf cart or utility vehicle on any public highway unless he has in his possession a valid driver's license;

4. Every golf cart or utility vehicle, whenever operated on a public highway, shall display a slow-moving vehicle emblem in conformity with § 46.2-1081; and

5. Golf carts and utility vehicles shall be operated upon the public highways only between sunrise and sunset, unless equipped with such lights as are required in Article 3 (§ 46.2-1010 et seq.) of Chapter 10 for different classes of vehicles.

B. The limitations of subdivision A 1 shall not apply to golf carts and utility vehicles being operated as follows:

1. To cross a highway from one portion of a golf course to another portion thereof or to another adjacent golf course or to travel between a person's home and golf course if (i) the trip would not be longer than one-half mile in either direction and (ii) the speed limit on the road is no more than 35 miles per hour;

2. To the extent necessary for local government employees, operating only upon highways located within the locality, to fulfill a governmental purpose, provided the golf cart or utility vehicle is being operated on highways with speed limits of 35 miles per hour or less;

3. As necessary by employees of public or private two-year or four-year institutions of higher education if operating on highways within the property limits of such institutions, provided the golf cart or utility vehicle is being operated on highways with speed limits of 35 miles per hour or less;

4. On a secondary highway system component that has a posted speed limit of no more than 35 miles per hour and is within three miles of a motor speedway with a seating capacity of at least 25,000 but less than 90,000 on the same day as any race or race-related event conducted on that speedway; and

5. To the extent necessary for employees of the Department of Conservation and Recreation, operating only on highways located within Department of Conservation and Recreation property or upon Virginia Department of Transportation-maintained highways that are adjacent to Department of Conservation and Recreation property, to fulfill a governmental purpose, provided that the golf cart or utility vehicle is being operated on highways with speed limits of no more than 35 miles per hour.

C. The governing body of any county, city, or town may by ordinance impose additional restrictions or limitations on operations of golf carts, utility vehicles, or both, on public highways within its boundaries, provided that the restrictions or limitations imposed by any such ordinance are no less stringent than the restrictions and limitations contained in this article. In the event that any provision of any such ordinance conflicts with any provision of this section other than subdivision B 5, the provision of the ordinance shall be controlling.

History.

2004, c. 746; 2008, c. 456; 2009, cc. 743, 835; 2010, c. 112; 2011, cc. 68, 140, 469.

ARTICLE 14.

SCHOOL BUSES.

§ 46.2-917. Operation of yellow motor vehicles of certain seating capacity on state highways prohibited; exceptions; penalty.

It shall be unlawful for any motor vehicle licensed in Virginia having a seating capacity of more than 15 persons to be operated on the highways of the Commonwealth if it is yellow, unless it is used in transporting students who attend public, private, or religious schools or used in transporting the elderly or mentally or physically handicapped persons.

Any violation of this section shall constitute a Class 1 misdemeanor.

History.

1966, c. 586, § 46.1-169.1; 1968, c. 756; 1970, c. 521; 1989, c. 727; 2005, c. 928.

§ 46.2-917.1. School buses hired to transport children.

Notwithstanding § 46.2-917, any person may contract to hire school buses for the purpose of transporting students to or from school, camp, or any other place during any part of the year. All provisions of this title applicable to school buses shall also apply to any school bus hired under the provisions of this section.

History.

1989, c. 727.

§ 46.2-917.2. School buses operating under State Corporation Commission or Department certificate.

Notwithstanding § 46.2-917, any person holding a special or charter party certificate issued by the State Corporation Commission or the Department pursuant to Chapter 23 (§ 46.2-2300 et seq.) of this title may transport special or charter parties in school buses provided all lettering required by § 46.2-1089 and warning devices required by § 46.2-1090 are covered with some opaque detachable material.

History.

1989, c. 727; 1997, c. 283.

§ 46.2-918. School buses to be routed so as to avoid necessity of pupils' crossing divided highways.

All school buses transporting pupils to and from all public, private, or religious schools or in connection with such schools, operating on any highway in the Commonwealth which has two or more roadways separated by a physical barrier or barriers or an unpaved area, or which have five or more lanes the center lane of which is a flush median marked for use by turning traffic only, shall be routed so that no pupil shall be picked up or discharged at any point which will require any pupil to cross such highway as described in this section, in order for such pupil to reach such bus or to return to his residence. Any violation of this section shall constitute a Class 1 misdemeanor.

History.

Code 1950, § 46-216; 1950, p. 84; 1958, c. 541, §§ 46.1-169.2, 46.1-199; 1964, c. 15; 1966, c. 699; 1972, c. 86; 1974, c. 365; 1976, c. 24; 1981, c. 395; 1984, c. 539; 1985, cc. 209, 250, 462; 1989, cc. 712, 727; 2005, c. 928.

§ 46.2-919. Age limit for drivers of school buses.

It shall be unlawful for any person, whether licensed or not, who is under the age of eighteen years to drive a motor vehicle while in use as a school bus for the transportation of pupils.

History.

Code 1950, § 46-182; 1958, c. 541, § 46.1-169; 1989, c. 727.

§ 46.2-919.1. Use of wireless telecommunications devices by persons driving school buses.

No person shall use any wireless telecommunications device, whether handheld or otherwise, while driving a school bus, except in case of an emergency, or when the vehicle is lawfully parked and for the purposes of dispatching. Nothing in this section shall be construed to prohibit the use of two-way radio devices authorized by the owner of the school bus.

History.

2008, cc. 234, 447.

ARTICLE 15.

EMERGENCY VEHICLES.

§ 46.2-920. Certain vehicles exempt from regulations in certain situations; exceptions and additional requirements.

A. The driver of any emergency vehicle, when such vehicle is being used in the performance of public services, and when such vehicle is operated under emergency conditions, may, without subjecting himself to criminal prosecution:

1. Disregard speed limits, while having due regard for safety of persons and property;

2. Proceed past any steady or flashing red signal, traffic light, stop sign, or device indicating moving traffic shall stop if the speed of the vehicle is sufficiently reduced to enable it to pass a signal,

traffic light, or device with due regard to the safety of persons and property;

3. Park or stop notwithstanding the other provisions of this chapter;

4. Disregard regulations governing a direction of movement of vehicles turning in specified directions so long as the operator does not endanger life or property;

5. Pass or overtake, with due regard to the safety of persons and property, another vehicle at any intersection;

6. Pass or overtake with due regard to the safety of persons and property, while en route to an emergency, stopped or slow-moving vehicles, by going to the left of the stopped or slow-moving vehicle either in a no-passing zone or by crossing the highway centerline; or

7. Pass or overtake with due regard to the safety of persons and property, while en route to an emergency, stopped or slow-moving vehicles, by going off the paved or main traveled portion of the roadway on the right. Notwithstanding other provisions of this section, vehicles exempted in this instance will not be required to sound a siren or any device to give automatically intermittent signals.

B. The exemptions granted to emergency vehicles by subsection A in subdivisions A1, A3, A4, A5, and A6 shall apply only when the operator of such vehicle displays a flashing, blinking, or alternating emergency light or lights as provided in §§ 46.2-1022 and 46.2-1023 and sounds a siren, exhaust whistle, or air horn designed to give automatically intermittent signals, as may be reasonably necessary. The exemption granted under subdivision A 2 shall apply only when the operator of such emergency vehicle displays a flashing, blinking, or alternating emergency light or lights as provided in §§ 46.2-1022 and 46.2-1023 and either (a) sounds a siren, exhaust whistle, or air horn designed to give automatically intermittent signals or (b) slows the vehicle down to a speed reasonable for the existing conditions, yields right-of-way to the driver of another vehicle approaching or entering the intersection from another direction or, if required for safety, brings the vehicle to a complete stop before proceeding with due regard for the safety of persons and property. In addition, the exemptions granted to emergency vehicles by subsection A shall apply only when there is in force and effect for such vehicle either (i) standard motor vehicle liability insurance covering injury or death to any person in the sum of at least $100,000 because of bodily injury to or death of one person in any one accident and, subject to the limit for one person, to a limit of $300,000 because of bodily injury to or death of two or more persons in any one accident, and to a limit of $20,000 because of injury to or destruction of property of others in any one accident or (ii) a certificate of self-insurance issued pursuant to § 46.2-368. Such exemptions shall not, however, protect the operator of any such vehicle from criminal prosecution for conduct constituting reckless disregard of the safety of persons and property. Nothing in this section shall release the operator of any such vehicle from civil liability for failure to use reasonable care in such operation.

C. For the purposes of this section, the term "emergency vehicle" shall mean:

1. Any law-enforcement vehicle operated by or under the direction of a federal, state, or local law-enforcement officer (i) in the chase or apprehension of violators of the law or persons charged with or suspected of any such violation or (ii) in response to an emergency call;

2. Any regional detention center vehicle operated by or under the direction of a correctional officer responding to an emergency call or operating in an emergency situation;

3. Any vehicle used to fight fire, including publicly owned state forest warden vehicles, when traveling in response to a fire alarm or emergency call;

4. Any emergency medical services vehicle designed or used for the principal purpose of providing emergency medical services where human life is endangered;

5. Any Department of Emergency Management vehicle or Office of Emergency Medical Services vehicle, when responding to an emergency call or operating in an emergency situation;

6. Any Department of Corrections vehicle designated by the Director of the Department of Corrections, when (i) responding to an emergency call at a correctional facility, (ii) participating in a drug-related investigation, (iii) pursuing escapees from a correctional facility, or (iv) responding to a request for assistance from a law-enforcement officer;

7. Any vehicle authorized to be equipped with alternating, blinking, or flashing red or red and white secondary warning lights under the provisions of § 46.2-1029.2; and

8. Any Virginia National Guard Civil Support Team vehicle when responding to an emergency.

D. Any law-enforcement vehicle operated by or under the direction of a federal, state, or local law-enforcement officer may disregard speed limits, while having due regard for safety of persons and property, (i) in testing the accuracy of speedometers of such vehicles, (ii) in testing the accuracy of speed measuring devices specified in § 46.2-882, or (iii) in following another vehicle for the purpose of determining its speed.

E. A Department of Environmental Quality vehicle, while en route to an emergency and with due regard to the safety of persons and property, may overtake and pass stopped or slow-moving vehicles by going off the paved or main traveled portion of the highway on the right or on the left. These Department of Environmental Quality vehicles shall not be required to sound a siren or any device to give automatically intermittent signals, but shall display red or red and white warning lights when performing such maneuvers.

F. Any law-enforcement vehicle operated by or under the direction of a federal, state, or local law-enforcement officer while conducting a funeral escort, wide-load escort, dignitary escort, or any other escort necessary for the safe movement of vehicles and pedestrians may, without subjecting himself to criminal prosecution:

1. Disregard speed limits, while having due regard for safety of persons and property;

2. Proceed past any steady or flashing red signal, traffic light, stop sign, or device indicating moving traffic shall stop if the speed of the vehicle is sufficiently reduced to enable it to pass a signal, traffic light, or device with due regard for the safety of persons and property;

3. Park or stop notwithstanding the other provisions of this chapter;

4. Disregard regulations governing a direction of movement of vehicles turning in specified directions so long as the operator does not endanger life or property; or

5. Pass or overtake, with due regard for the safety of persons and property, another vehicle.

Notwithstanding other provisions of this section, vehicles exempted in this subsection may sound a siren or any device to give automatically intermittent signals.

History.

Code 1950, § 46-241.1; 1954, c. 356; 1956, c. 192; 1958, c. 541, § 46.1-226; 1966, cc. 350, 699; 1968, c. 89; 1974, c. 365; 1976, c. 24; 1977, c. 549; 1980, cc. 30, 354; 1981, c. 395; 1984, c. 539; 1985, cc. 209, 462; 1989, c. 727; 1992, cc. 33, 96; 1994, c. 69; 1995, c. 92; 2000, c. 120; 2002, c. 134; 2003, c. 115; 2005, c. 583; 2007, cc. 860, 908; 2011, c. 629; 2014, cc. 171, 800; 2015, cc. 502, 503.

§ 46.2-920.1. Operation of tow trucks or vehicles owned or controlled by the Virginia Department of Transportation under certain circumstances; incident management.

A. When operating at or en route to or from the scene of a traffic accident or similar emergency and when specifically directed by a law-enforcement officer present at the scene of a motor vehicle crash or similar incident, tow truck operators or vehicles owned or controlled by the Virginia Department of Transportation may:

1. Operate on a highway in a direction opposite that otherwise permitted for traffic;

2. Cross medians of divided highways;

3. Use cross-overs and turn-arounds otherwise reserved for use only by authorized vehicles;

4. Drive on a portion of the highway other than the roadway;

5. Stop or stand on any portion of the highway; and

6. Operate in any other manner as directed by a law-enforcement officer at the scene.

B. When operating at, en route to, or from the scene of a traffic accident or similar emergency, a vehicle operated pursuant to a Virginia Department of Transportation safety service patrol program, with due regard to the safety of persons and property and without direction of law enforcement, may overtake and pass stopped or slow-moving vehicles by going off the paved or main traveled portion of the highway on the right or on the left. For purposes of this subsection, "safety service patrol program" means a program sponsored or operated by the Virginia Department of Transportation that assists stranded motorists and provides traffic control during traffic incidents, including traffic accidents and road work.

C. Nothing in this section, however, shall (i) immunize the driver of any such vehicle from criminal prosecution for conduct constituting reckless disregard of the safety of persons and property or (ii) release the driver of any such vehicle from any civil liability for failure to use reasonable care in operations permitted in this section. However, drivers of vehicles owned or operated by the Virginia Department of Transportation and employees of the Commonwealth of Virginia are immune for acts of simple negligence for claims of civil liability arising from the operation of such vehicles pursuant to this section.

History.

1990, c. 470; 2007, cc. 189, 918; 2012, cc. 27, 108.

§ 46.2-920.2. Operation of vehicles owned or controlled by the Wildlife Center of Virginia.

When specifically requested by a law-enforcement agency to rescue or euthanize injured wildlife, vehicles owned or controlled by the Wildlife Center of Virginia may:

1. Cross medians of divided highways;

2. Use cross-overs and turn-arounds otherwise reserved for use only by authorized vehicles;

3. Drive on a portion of the highway other than the roadway;

4. Stop or stand on any portion of the highway; and

5. Operate in any other manner as directed by a law-enforcement officer at the scene.

Nothing in this section, however, shall (i) immunize the driver of any vehicle owned or controlled by the Wildlife Center of Virginia from criminal prosecution for conduct constituting reckless disregard of the safety of persons and property or (ii) release the driver of any vehicle owned or controlled by the Wildlife Center of Virginia from any civil liability for failure to use reasonable care in operations permitted in this section.

History.

2007, c. 139.

§ 46.2-921. Following or parking near fire apparatus or emergency medical services vehicle.

It shall be unlawful, in any county, city, or town for the driver of any vehicle, other than one on official business, to follow any fire apparatus or emergency medical services vehicle traveling in response to a fire alarm or emergency call at any distance closer than 500 feet to such apparatus or emergency medical services vehicle or to park such vehicle within 500 feet of where fire apparatus has stopped in answer to a fire alarm.

History.

Code 1950, § 46-242; 1958, c. 541, § 46.1-227; 1981, c. 394; 1989, c. 727; 2015, cc. 502, 503.

§ 46.2-921.1. Drivers to yield right-of-way or reduce speed when approaching stationary emergency vehicles on highways; penalties.

A. The driver of any motor vehicle, upon approaching a stationary vehicle that is displaying a flashing, blinking, or alternating blue, red, or amber light or lights as provided in § 46.2-1022, 46.2-1023, or 46.2-1024 or subdivision A 1 or A 2 of § 46.2-1025 shall (i) on a highway having at least four lanes, at least two of which are intended for traffic proceeding as the approaching vehicle, proceed with caution and, if reasonable, with due regard for safety and traffic conditions, yield the right-of-way by making a lane change into a lane not adjacent to the stationary vehicle or (ii) if changing lanes would be unreasonable or unsafe, proceed with due caution and maintain a safe speed for highway conditions.

B. A violation of any provision of this section shall be punishable as a traffic infraction, except that a second or subsequent violation of any provision of this section, when such violation involved a vehicle with flashing, blinking, or alternating blue or red lights, shall be punishable as a Class 1 misdemeanor.

C. If the violation resulted in damage to property of another person, the court may, in addition, order the suspension of the driver's privilege to operate a motor vehicle for not more than one year. If the violation resulted in injury to another person, the court may, in addition to any other penalty imposed, order the suspension of the driver's privilege to operate a motor vehicle for not more than two years. If the violation resulted in the death of another person, the court may, in addition to any other penalty imposed, order the suspension of the driver's privilege to operate a motor vehicle for two years.

D. The provisions of this section shall not apply in highway work zones as defined in § 46.2-878.1.

History.

2002, cc. 163, 341; 2008, c. 818; 2010, c. 289.

§ 46.2-922. Driving over fire hose.

It shall be unlawful, without the consent of the fire department official in command, for the driver of any vehicle to drive over any unprotected hose of a fire department laid down for use at any fire or alarm of fire.

History.

Code 1950, § 46-242.1; 1954, c. 13; 1958, c. 541, § 46.1-228; 1989, c. 727.

ARTICLE 16. PEDESTRIANS.

§ 46.2-923. How and where pedestrians to cross highways.

When crossing highways, pedestrians shall not carelessly or maliciously interfere with the orderly passage of vehicles. They shall cross, wherever possible, only at intersections or marked crosswalks. Where intersections contain no marked crosswalks, pedestrians shall not be guilty of negligence as a matter of law for crossing at any such intersection or between intersections when crossing by the most direct route.

The governing body of any town or city or the governing body of a county authorized by law to regulate traffic may by ordinance permit pedestrians to cross an intersection diagonally when all traffic entering the intersection has been halted by lights, other traffic control devices, or by a law-enforcement officer.

History.

Code 1950, § 46-243; 1958, c. 541, § 46.1-230; 1966, c. 706; 1976, c. 322; 1981, c. 163; 1989, c. 727.

§ 46.2-924. Drivers to stop for pedestrians; installation of certain signs; penalty.

A. The driver of any vehicle on a highway shall yield the right-of-way to any pedestrian crossing such highway:

1. At any clearly marked crosswalk, whether at mid-block or at the end of any block;
2. At any regular pedestrian crossing included in the prolongation of the lateral boundary lines of the adjacent sidewalk at the end of a block;
3. At any intersection when the driver is approaching on a highway or street where the legal maximum speed does not exceed 35 miles per hour.

B. Notwithstanding the provisions of subsection A, at intersections or crosswalks where the movement of traffic is being regulated by law-enforcement officers or traffic control devices, the driver shall yield according to the direction of the law-enforcement officer or device.

No pedestrian shall enter or cross an intersection in disregard of approaching traffic.

The drivers of vehicles entering, crossing, or turning at intersections shall change their course, slow down, or stop if necessary to permit pedestrians to cross such intersections safely and expeditiously.

Pedestrians crossing highways at intersections shall at all times have the right-of-way over vehicles

Motor Vehicles

making turns into the highways being crossed by the pedestrians.

C. The governing body of Arlington County, Fairfax County, Loudoun County and any town therein, the City of Alexandria, the City of Fairfax, and the City of Falls Church may by ordinance provide for the installation and maintenance of highway signs at marked crosswalks specifically requiring operators of motor vehicles, at the locations where such signs are installed, to yield the right-of-way to pedestrians crossing or attempting to cross the highway. Any operator of a motor vehicle who fails at such locations to yield the right-of-way to pedestrians as required by such signs shall be guilty of a traffic infraction punishable by a fine of no less than $100 or more than $500. The Department of Transportation shall develop criteria for the design, location, and installation of such signs. The provisions of this section shall not apply to any limited access highway.

D. Where a shared-use path crosses a highway at a clearly marked crosswalk and there are no traffic control signals at such crossing, the local governing body may by ordinance require pedestrians, cyclists, and any other users of such shared-used path to come to a complete stop prior to entering such crosswalk. Such local ordinance may provide for a fine not to exceed $100 for violations. Any locality adopting such an ordinance shall install and maintain stop signs, consistent with standards adopted by the Commonwealth Transportation Board and to the extent necessary in coordination with the Department of Transportation. At such crosswalks, no user of such shared-use path shall enter the crosswalk in disregard of approaching traffic.

E. A locality adopting an ordinance under subsection D shall coordinate the enforcement and placement of any stop signs affecting a shared-use path owned and operated by a park authority formed under Chapter 57 (§ 15.2-5700 et seq.) of Title 15.2 with such authority.

History.
Code 1950, §§ 46-243, 46-244; 1958, c. 541, § 46.1-231; 1962, c. 471; 1968, c. 165; 1972, c. 576; 1976, c. 322; 1989, c. 727; 2000, c. 323; 2002, c. 327; 2004, c. 658; 2007, c. 813; 2012, c. 339; 2013, cc. 507, 585, 646, 681.

§ 46.2-925. Pedestrian control signals.

Whenever pedestrian control signals exhibiting the words, numbers, or symbols meaning "Walk" or "Don't Walk" are in place such signals shall indicate and apply to pedestrians as follows:

Walk. — Pedestrians facing such signal may proceed across the highway in the direction of the signal and shall be given the right-of-way by the drivers of all vehicles.

Don't Walk. — No pedestrian shall start to cross the highway in the direction of such signal, but any pedestrian who has partially completed his crossing on the Walk signal shall proceed to a sidewalk or safety island and remain there while the Don't Walk signal is showing.

History.
1974, c. 347, § 46.1-231.1; 1989, c. 727; 2008, c. 451.

§ 46.2-926. Pedestrians stepping into highway where they cannot be seen.

No pedestrian shall step into a highway open to moving vehicular traffic at any point between intersections where his presence would be obscured from the vision of drivers of approaching vehicles by a vehicle or other obstruction at the curb or side. The foregoing prohibition shall not apply to a pedestrian stepping into a highway to board a bus or to enter a safety zone, in which event he shall cross the highway only at right angles.

History.
Code 1950, § 46-245; 1958, c. 541, § 46.1-232; 1989, c. 727.

§ 46.2-927. Boarding or alighting from buses.

When actually boarding or alighting from buses, pedestrians shall have the right-of-way over vehicles, but shall not, in order to board or alight from buses, step into the highway sooner or remain there longer than is absolutely necessary.

History.
Code 1950, § 46-246; 1958, c. 541, § 46.1-233; 1989, c. 727.

§ 46.2-928. Pedestrians not to use roadway except when necessary; keeping to left.

Pedestrians shall not use the roadways for travel, except when necessary to do so because of the absence of sidewalks which are reasonably suitable and passable for their use. If they walk on the hard surface, or the main travelled portion of the roadway, they shall keep to the extreme left side or edge thereof, or where the shoulders of the highway are of sufficient width to permit, they may walk on either shoulder thereof.

History.
Code 1950, § 46-247; 1950, p. 850; 1958, c. 541, § 46.1-234; 1968, c. 165; 1989, c. 727.

§ 46.2-929. Pedestrians soliciting rides.

Pedestrians shall not stand or stop in any roadway for the purpose of soliciting rides.

History.
Code 1950, § 46-247; 1950, p. 850; 1958, c. 541, § 46.1-234; 1968, c. 165; 1989, c. 727.

§ 46.2-930. Loitering on bridges or highway rights-of-way.

Pedestrians shall not loiter on any bridge or in any portion of the right-of-way of any highway where loitering has been determined by the Commissioner of Highways or the local governing body of any county, city, or town to present a public safety hazard and on which the Commissioner of Highways or the governing body of any county, city, or town has posted signs prohibiting such action. Local jurisdictions shall obtain concurrence from the Commissioner of Highways on the placements of signs on the right-of-way of any bridge or highway under the jurisdiction and control of the Commissioner of Highways or the Virginia Department of Transportation; however, the local jurisdiction shall be responsible for all costs of the production, installation, and maintenance of the signs. Any person violating the provisions of this section shall be guilty of a traffic infraction.

History.

1966, c. 469, § 46.1-234.1; 1978, c. 605; 1989, c. 727; 2008, c. 503; 2009, c. 432.

§ 46.2-931. Localities may prohibit or regulate distribution of handbills, etc., solicitation of contributions, and sale of merchandise or services on highways within their boundaries or on public roadways and medians.

A. Any county, city, or town is hereby authorized to adopt an ordinance prohibiting or regulating:

1. The distribution of handbills, leaflets, bulletins, literature, advertisements, or similar material to the occupants of motor vehicles on highways located within its boundaries or on public roadways and medians;

2. The solicitation of contributions of any nature from the occupants of motor vehicles on highways located within its boundaries or on public roadways and medians; and

3. The sale of merchandise or services or the attempted sale of merchandise or services to the occupants of motor vehicles on highways located within its boundaries or on public roadways and medians.

B. Ordinances adopted pursuant to this section may provide that any person violating the provisions of such ordinances shall be guilty of a traffic infraction.

C. The Virginia Department of Transportation may regulate activities within such streets and highways under its jurisdiction, subject to regulations promulgated by the Commonwealth Transportation Board. Nothing in this section shall be construed to allow any locality to permit activities within any highway under the maintenance and operational jurisdiction of the Virginia Department of Transportation.

History.

1980, c. 113; 1989, c. 727; 2005, cc. 488, 541; 2008, cc. 120, 235, 310; 2009, cc. 422, 656, 722; 2010, cc. 378, 589.

§ 46.2-932. Playing on highways; use of toy vehicle on highways, persons riding bicycles, electric personal assistive mobility devices, electric power-assisted bicycles, mopeds, etc., not to attach to vehicles; exception.

A. No person shall play on a highway, other than on the sidewalks thereof, within a city or town or on any part of a highway outside the limits of a city or town designated by the Commissioner of Highways exclusively for vehicular travel. No person shall use any toy vehicle on the roadway of any highway that (i) has a speed limit greater than 25 miles per hour, (ii) has more than two travel lanes, or (iii) is located outside a residence district as defined in § 46.2-100. The governing bodies of counties, cities, and towns may designate areas on highways under their control where play is permitted and may impose reasonable restrictions on play on such highways. Persons using such devices, except bicycles, electric personal assistive mobility devices, electric power-assisted bicycles, mopeds, and motorcycles, shall keep as near as safely practicable to the far right side or edge of the right traffic lane so that they will be proceeding in the same direction as other traffic.

No person riding on any bicycle, electric personal assistive mobility device, electric power-assisted bicycle, moped, roller skates, skateboards or other devices on wheels or runners, shall attach the same or himself to any vehicle on a highway.

B. Notwithstanding the provisions of subsection A of this section, the governing body of Arlington County may by ordinance permit the use of devices on wheels or runners on highways under such county's control, subject to such limitations and conditions as the governing body may deem necessary and reasonable.

History.

Code 1950, § 46-248; 1958, c. 541, § 46.1-235; 1972, c. 817; 1973, c. 288; 1981, c. 585; 1989, c. 727; 2001, cc. 170, 834; 2002, c. 254; 2004, cc. 947, 973; 2006, cc. 529, 538; 2007, cc. 209, 366, 813.

§ 46.2-932.1. Duty of driver approaching blind pedestrian; effect of failure of blind person to carry white cane or use dog guide.

The driver of a vehicle approaching a totally or partially blind pedestrian who is carrying a cane predominantly white or metallic in color (with or without a red tip) or using a dog guide shall take all necessary precautions to avoid injury to such blind pedestrian and dog guide, and any driver who fails to take such precautions shall be liable in damages for any injury caused such pedestrian and dog guide; provided that a totally or partially blind pedestrian not carrying such a cane or using a dog guide in any of the places, accommodations or conveyances listed in § 51.5-44, shall have all of the rights and privileges conferred by law upon other persons, and the failure of a totally or partially blind pedestrian to carry such a cane or to use a dog guide in any such places, accommodations or conveyances shall not be held to constitute nor be evidence of contributory negligence; provided, that nothing in this section shall be construed to limit the application of § 46.2-933 or § 46.2-934.

History.
1972, c. 156, § 63.1-171.3; 1975, c. 473; 2002, c. 747.

§ 46.2-933. When vehicles to stop for pedestrian guided by dog or carrying white, red-tipped white, or metallic cane.

Whenever a totally or partially blind pedestrian crossing or attempting to cross a highway in accordance with the provisions of § 46.2-923 is guided by a dog guide or carrying a cane which is predominantly metallic or white in color, with or without a red tip, the driver of every vehicle approaching the intersection or place of crossing shall bring his vehicle to a full stop before arriving at such intersection or place of crossing, unless such intersection or place of crossing is controlled by a law-enforcement officer or traffic light. Any person violating any provision of this section shall be guilty of a Class 3 misdemeanor.

History.
Code 1950, § 46-249.1; 1950, p. 1520; 1958, c. 541, § 46.1-237; 1964, c. 20; 1975, c. 117; 1982, c. 681; 1989, c. 727; 1990, c. 555.

§ 46.2-934. Failure to use cane or guide dog not contributory negligence.

Nothing contained in § 46.2-933 shall be construed to deprive any totally or partially blind or otherwise incapacitated person not carrying such a cane or walking stick or not being guided by a dog, of the rights and privileges conferred by law upon pedestrians crossing highways. Nor shall the failure of such totally or partially blind or otherwise incapacitated person to carry a cane or walking stick, or to be guided by a guide dog on the highways or sidewalks of the Commonwealth, be held to constitute nor be evidence of contributory negligence.

History.
Code 1950, § 46-249.3; 1950, p. 1521; 1958, c. 541, § 46.1-240; 1975, c. 117; 1989, c. 727.

§ 46.2-935. Regulation by ordinance in counties, cities, and towns.

The governing bodies of counties, cities, and towns may enact ordinances requiring pedestrians to obey signs and signals erected on highways therein for the direction and control of traffic, to obey the orders of law-enforcement officers engaged in directing traffic on such highways, and may provide penalties not exceeding those of a traffic infraction.

History.
Code 1950, § 46-250; 1950, p. 942; 1958, c. 541, § 46.1-241; 1968, c. 165; 1989, c. 727.

ARTICLE 17.

LEGAL PROCEDURES AND REQUIREMENTS.

§ 46.2-936. Arrest for misdemeanor; release on summons and promise to appear; right to demand hearing immediately or within twenty-four hours; issuance of warrant on request of officer for violations of §§ 46.2-301 and 46.2-302; refusal to promise to appear; violations.

Whenever any person is detained by or in the custody of an arresting officer, including an arrest on a warrant, for a violation of any provision of this title punishable as a misdemeanor, the arresting officer shall, except as otherwise provided in § 46.2-940, take the name and address of such person and the license number of his motor vehicle and issue a summons or otherwise notify him in writing to appear at a time and place to be specified in such summons or notice. Such time shall be at least five days after such arrest unless the person arrested demands an earlier hearing. Such person shall, if he so desires, have a right to an immediate hearing, or a hearing within twenty-four hours at a convenient hour, before a court having jurisdiction under this title within the county, city, or town wherein such offense was committed. Upon the giving by such person of his written promise to appear at such time and place, the officer shall forthwith release him from custody.

Notwithstanding the foregoing provisions of this section, if prior general approval has been granted by order of the general district court for the use of this section in cases involving violations of §§ 46.2-301 and 46.2-302, the arresting officer may take the person before the appropriate judicial officer of the county or city in which the violation occurred and make oath as to the offense and request issuance of a warrant. If a warrant is issued, the judicial officer shall proceed in accordance with the provisions of Article 1 (§ 19.2-119 et seq.) of Chapter 9 of Title 19.2.

Notwithstanding any other provision of this section, in cases involving a violation of § 46.2-341.24 or § 46.2-341.31, the arresting officer shall take the person before a magistrate as provided in §§ 46.2-341.26:2 and 46.2-341.26:3. The magistrate may issue either a summons or a warrant as he shall deem proper.

Any person refusing to give such written promise to appear under the provisions of this section shall be taken immediately by the arresting officer before a magistrate or other issuing officer having jurisdiction who shall proceed according to the provisions of § 46.2-940.

Any person who willfully violates his written promise to appear, given in accordance with this section, shall be treated in accordance with the provisions of § 46.2-938.

Any officer violating any of the provisions of this section shall be guilty of misconduct in office and subject to removal therefrom upon complaint filed by any person in a court of competent jurisdiction. This section shall not be construed to limit the removal of a law-enforcement officer for other misconduct in office.

History.
Code 1950, § 46-193; 1950, p. 94; 1954, c. 174; 1958, c. 541, § 46.1-178; 1972, c. 477; 1975, c. 191; 1981, c. 382; 1983, c. 458; 1989, c. 727; 1990, c. 218; 1992, c. 830; 1999, cc. 829, 846.

§ 46.2-937. Traffic infractions treated as misdemeanors for arrest purposes.

For purposes of arrest, traffic infractions shall be treated as misdemeanors. Except as otherwise provided by this title, the authority and duties of arresting officers shall be the same for traffic infractions as for misdemeanors.

History.
1977, c. 585, § 46.1-178.01; 1989, c. 727.

§ 46.2-938. Issuance of warrant upon failure to comply with summons; penalties; suspension of licenses for failure to appear.

Upon the failure of any person to comply with the terms of a summons or notice as provided in § 46.2-936, such person shall be guilty of a Class 1 misdemeanor and the court may order a warrant for his arrest. The warrant shall be returnable to the court having jurisdiction of the offense and shall be accompanied by a report by the arresting officer which shall clearly identify the person arrested, specifying the section of the Code of Virginia or ordinance violated, the location of the offense, a description of the motor vehicle and its registration or license number.

If the warrant is returned to the court with the notation "not found" or the person named in the warrant does not appear on the return date thereof, the court shall forward a certificate of the fact of nonservice or nonappearance, with a copy of the report specified in the foregoing provisions of this section, to the Commissioner of the Department of Motor Vehicles, who shall forthwith suspend the driver's license of such person. The order of suspension shall specify the reason for the suspension. Such suspension shall continue until such time as the court has notified the Commissioner that the defendant has appeared before the court under the terms of the summons or notice and the warrant.

History.
1974, c. 372, § 46.1-178.1; 1975, c. 201; 1981, c. 382; 1984, c. 780; 1989, c. 727.

§ 46.2-939. Authority of law-enforcement officers to issue subpoenas.

Local law-enforcement officers and state police officers, in the course of their duties in the investigation of any accident involving a motor vehicle or vehicles, may, at the scene of any such accident, issue a subpoena to any witness to appear in court and testify with respect to any criminal charge brought against any person as a result of such accident. State police officers, additionally, may issue such subpoenas at any other location within seventy-two hours of the time of such accident, with the return of service thereof made to the appropriate court clerk within forty-eight hours after such service. A subpoena so issued shall have the same force and effect as if issued by the court.

Any person failing to appear in response to a subpoena issued as provided in this section shall be punished as provided by law.

History.
1975, c. 138, § 46.1-178.2; 1986, c. 40; 1989, c. 727.

§ 46.2-940. When arresting officer shall take person before issuing authority.

If any person is: (i) believed by the arresting officer to have committed a felony; (ii) believed by the arresting officer to be likely to disregard a summons issued under § 46.2-936; or (iii) refuses to give a written promise to appear under the provisions of § 46.2-936 or § 46.2-945, the arresting officer shall promptly take him before a magistrate or other issuing authority having jurisdiction and proceed in accordance with the provisions of § 19.2-82. The magistrate or other authority may issue either a summons or warrant as he shall determine proper.

History.
Code 1950, § 46-194; 1958, c. 541, § 46.1-179; 1966, c. 639; 1972, c. 474; 1981, c. 382; 1989, c. 727; 2006, c. 276.

§ 46.2-941. Conditions precedent to issuance of summons for violation of parking ordinance; notice.

Before any summons shall be issued for the prosecution of a violation of an ordinance of any county, city, or town regulating parking, the violator shall have been first notified by mail at his last known address or at the address shown for such violator on the records of the Department of Motor Vehicles, that he may pay the fine provided by law for such violation, within five days of receipt of such notice, and the authorized person issuing such summons shall be notified that the violator has failed to pay such fine within such time. The notice to the violator, required by the provisions of this section, shall be contained in an envelope bearing the words "Law-Enforcement Notice" stamped or printed on the face thereof in all capital letters, bold face type, no smaller than the print type size used for the primary address on the envelope. If "window" envelopes are used, the words "Law-Enforcement Notice" shall be clearly visible through the window of the envelope.

History.

1968, c. 388, § 46.1-179.01; 1970, c. 510; 1978, c. 194; 1983, c. 329; 1989, c. 727; 1999, cc. 291, 323; 2002, c. 102.

§ 46.2-942. Admissibility of results of speedometer test in prosecution for exceeding speed limit.

In the trial of any person charged with exceeding any maximum speed limit in the Commonwealth, the court shall receive as evidence a sworn report of the results of a calibration test of the accuracy of the speedometer in the motor vehicle operated by the defendant or the arresting officer at the time of the alleged offense. The report shall be considered by the court or jury in both determining guilt or innocence and in fixing punishment.

History.

1966, c. 687, § 46.1-193.1; 1970, c. 11; 1975, c. 202; 1989, c. 727.

§ 46.2-943. Court or jury may consider defendant's prior traffic record before sentencing.

The term "traffic offense" when used in this section shall mean any moving traffic violation described or enumerated in subdivisions 1 and 2 of § 46.2-382, whether such violation was committed within or outside the Commonwealth according to the records of the Department of Motor Vehicles.

The term "prior traffic record" when used in this section shall mean the record of prior suspensions and revocations of a driver's license, and the record of prior convictions of traffic offenses described in the foregoing provisions of this section.

When any person is found guilty of a traffic offense, the court or jury trying the case may consider the prior traffic record of the defendant before imposing sentence as provided by law. After the prior traffic record of the defendant has been introduced, the defendant shall be afforded an opportunity to present evidence limited to showing the nature of his prior convictions, suspensions, and revocations.

History.

1975, c. 577, §§ 46.1-347.1, 46.1-347.2; 1984, c. 780; 1989, c. 727.

ARTICLE 18. ARREST OF NONRESIDENTS.

§ 46.2-944. Definitions.

As used in this article:

"Jurisdiction" means a state, territory, or possession of the United States, the District of Columbia, or the Commonwealth of Puerto Rico.

"Home jurisdiction" means the jurisdiction that issued the driver's license of the traffic violator.

"Issuing jurisdiction" means the jurisdiction in which the traffic citation was issued to the motorist.

"Party jurisdiction" means any jurisdiction which by its laws or by written agreement with the Commonwealth extends to residents of Virginia substantially the rights and privileges provided by this article.

"Court" means a court of law or traffic tribunal.

"Citation" means any summons, ticket, or other official document issued by a police officer for a traffic violation containing an order which requires the motorist to respond.

"Terms of the citation" means those options expressly stated upon the citation.

"Compliance" means the motorist must appear for a hearing and/or pay court fines and costs.

"Driver's license" means any license or privilege to operate a motor vehicle issued under the laws of the home jurisdiction.

"Collateral" or *"bond"* means any cash or other security deposited to secure an appearance for trial, following the issuance by a police officer of a citation for a traffic violation.

"Personal recognizance" means a signed agreement by a motorist made at the time of issuance of the traffic citation that he will comply with the terms of that traffic citation.

"Motorist" means a driver of a motor vehicle operating in a party jurisdiction other than the home jurisdiction.

"Police officer" means any individual authorized by the party jurisdiction to issue a citation for a traffic violation.

History.

1964, c. 247, § 46.1-179.1; 1974, c. 559; 1975, c. 205; 1980, c. 366; 1989, c. 727.

§ 46.2-945. Issuance of citation to motorist; party jurisdiction; police officer to report noncompliance with citation.

A. When issuing a citation for a traffic violation, a police officer shall issue the citation to a motorist who is a resident of or holds a driver's license issued by a party jurisdiction and shall not, subject to the exceptions noted in subsection C of this section, require such motorist to post collateral or bond to secure appearance for trial, but shall accept such motorist's written promise that he will comply with the terms of such citation; provided, however, the motorist shall have the right upon his request to post collateral or bond in a manner provided by law and, in such case, the provisions of this article shall not apply.

B. In the absence of the motorist's written promise, the officer shall proceed according to the provisions of § 46.2-940.

C. No motorist shall be entitled to receive a citation under the terms of subsection A of this section nor shall any police officer issue such citation under the same in the event the offense for which the citation is issued shall be one of the following: (i) an offense for which the issuance of a citation in lieu of a hearing or the posting of collateral or bond is prohibited by the laws of this Commonwealth; or (ii) an offense, the conviction of or the forfeiture of collateral for which requires the revocation of the motorist's license.

D. Upon the failure of any motorist to comply with the terms of a traffic citation, the police officer or the appropriate official shall report this fact to the Department of Motor Vehicles. Such report shall clearly identify the motorist; describe the violation, specifying the section of the statute, code or ordinance violated; shall indicate the location of the offense, give description of vehicle involved, and show the registration or license number of the vehicle. Such report shall be signed by the police officer or appropriate official.

History.

1964, c. 247, § 46.1-179.2; 1972, c. 474; 1976, c. 7; 1980, c. 366; 1981, c. 382; 1989, c. 727.

§ 46.2-946. Department to transmit officer's report to party jurisdiction; suspension of resident's license for noncompliance with citation issued by party jurisdiction.

Upon receipt of the report as described in § 46.2-945, the Department of Motor Vehicles shall transmit a certified copy of such report to the official in charge of the issuance of driver's licenses in the home jurisdiction in which the motorist resides or by which he is licensed.

Upon receipt from the issuing jurisdiction of a certification of noncompliance with a citation by a motorist holding a driver's license issued by this Commonwealth, the Commissioner of the Department of Motor Vehicles forthwith shall suspend such motorist's driver's license. The order of suspension shall indicate the reason for the order, and shall notify the motorist that his license shall remain suspended until he has furnished evidence satisfactory to the Commissioner that he has fully complied with the terms of the citation which was the basis for the suspension order.

The licensing authority of the issuing jurisdiction may suspend the privilege of a motorist for whom a report has been transmitted.

It shall be the duty of the Commissioner of Motor Vehicles to ascertain and remain informed as to which jurisdictions are party jurisdictions hereunder and, accordingly, to maintain a current listing of such jurisdictions, which listing he shall from time to time cause to be disseminated among the appropriate departments, divisions, bureaus and agencies of this Commonwealth, the principal executive officers of the several counties, cities and towns of this Commonwealth and the licensing authorities in all other jurisdictions which are, have been, or claim to be a party jurisdiction pursuant hereto.

Consistent with the terms of the applicable Nonresident Violator Compact, the home jurisdiction shall take no action regarding any report transmitted by the issuing jurisdiction, which is transmitted more than six months after the date on which the traffic citation was issued.

Consistent with the terms of the applicable Nonresident Violator Compact, the home jurisdiction shall take no action regarding any report on any violation where the date of issuance of the citation predates the entry into the compact for the two party jurisdictions affected.

History.

1964, c. 247, § 46.1-179.3; 1980, c. 366; 1989, c. 727.

§ 46.2-947. Violations committed within highway safety corridor; report on benefits.

Notwithstanding any other provision of law, the fine for any moving violation of any provision of this chapter while operating a motor vehicle in a designated highway safety corridor pursuant to § 33.2-253 shall be no more than $500 for any violation which is a traffic infraction and not less than $200 for any violation which is a criminal offense. The otherwise applicable fines set forth in Rule 3B:2 of the Rules of the Supreme Court shall be doubled in the case of a waiver of appearance and a plea of guilty under § 16.1-69.40:1 or § 19.2-254.2 for a violation of a provision of this chapter while operating a motor vehicle in a designated highway safety corridor pursuant to § 33.2-253. The Commissioner shall report, on an annual basis, statistical data related to benefits derived from the designation of such highway safety corridors. This information may be posted on the Virginia Department of Transportation's official website. Notwithstanding the provisions of § 46.2-1300, the governing bodies of counties, cities and towns may not adopt ordinances providing for penalties under this section.

History.

2003, c. 877.

Editor's note.

References in this section were updated at the direction of the

Virginia Code Commission to conform to the recodification of Title 33.2 by Acts 2014, c. 805, effective October 1, 2014.

CHAPTER 9.

[RESERVED.]

CHAPTER 10.

MOTOR VEHICLE AND EQUIPMENT SAFETY.

Article 1.

Vehicle and Equipment Safety, Generally.

Article 2.

Testing, Evaluation, and Approval of Equipment.

Article 3.

Lights and Turn Signals.

Article 4.

Tires.

Article 5.

Exhaust System.

Article 6.

Windshields and Windows.

Article 7.

Horns, Sirens, and Whistles.

Article 8.

Steering and Suspension Systems.

Article 9.

Brakes.

Article 10.

Miscellaneous Equipment.

Article 11.

Paint, Lettering, and Special Equipment for School Buses.

Article 12.

Safety Belts.

Article 13.

Child Restraints.

Article 14.

Maximum Vehicle Size, Generally.

Article 15.

Maximum Vehicle Widths and Heights.

Article 16.

Maximum Vehicle Lengths.

Article 17.

Maximum Vehicle Weights.

Article 18.

Permits for Excessive Size and Weight.

Article 19.

Towing and Towed Vehicles.

Article 20.

Loads and Cargoes.

Article 21.

Safety Inspections.

ARTICLE 1. VEHICLE AND EQUIPMENT SAFETY, GENERALLY.

§ 46.2-1000. Department to suspend registration of vehicles lacking certain equipment; officer to take possession of registration card, license plates and decals when observing defect in motor vehicle; when to be returned.

The Department shall suspend the registration of any motor vehicle, trailer, or semitrailer which the Department or the Department of State Police determines is not equipped with proper (i) brakes, (ii) lights, (iii) horn or warning device, (iv) turn signals, (v) safety glass when required by law, (vi) mirror, (vii) muffler, (viii) windshield wiper, (ix) steering gear adequate to ensure the safe movement of the vehicle as required by this title or when such vehicle is equipped with a smoke screen device or cutout or when such motor vehicle, trailer, or semitrailer is otherwise unsafe to be operated.

Any law-enforcement officer shall, when he observes any defect in a motor vehicle as described above, take possession of the registration card, license plates, and decals of any such vehicle and retain the same in his possession for a period of fifteen days unless the owner of the vehicle corrects the defects or obtains a new safety inspection sticker from an authorized safety inspection station. When the defect or defects are corrected as indicated above the registration card, license plates, and decals shall be returned to the owner.

History.

Code 1950, § 46-56; 1958, c. 541, § 46.1-58; 1960, c. 119; 1964, c. 414; 1972, c. 609; 1989, c. 727.

§ 46.2-1001. Removal of unsafe vehicles; penalty.

Any motor vehicle, trailer, or semitrailer examined by a law-enforcement officer certified to perform vehicle safety inspections and found to be operating with defective brakes, tires, wheels, steering mechanism, or any other condition which is likely to cause an accident or a breakdown of the motor vehicle, trailer, or semitrailer may be removed from the highway and not permitted to operate again on the highway until the defects have been corrected and the law-enforcement officer has found the corrections to be satisfactory. Such law-enforcement officer may allow any motor vehicle, trailer, or semitrailer discovered to be in such an unsafe condition while being operated on the highway to continue in operation only to the nearest place where repairs can be safely effected and only if such operation is less hazardous to the public than to permit the motor vehicle, trailer, or semitrailer to remain on the highway.

No person shall operate a motor vehicle, trailer, or semitrailer which has been removed from service as provided in the foregoing provisions of this section prior to correction and proper authorization by a law-enforcement officer certified to perform vehicle safety inspection procedures.

For the purpose of this section, the term "law-enforcement officer certified to perform vehicle safety inspections" means those law-enforcement officers who have satisfactorily met the requirements for initial certification and maintenance of certification of driver/vehicle inspectors as prescribed by the U.S. Department of Transportation, Federal Motor Carrier Safety Administration. Those law-enforcement officers certified to place vehicles out of service must receive annual in-service training in current federal motor carrier safety regulations, safety inspection procedures, and out-of-service criteria. The Superintendent of State Police shall be responsible for coordinating the annual in-service training. The agency administrator of the law-enforcement agencies employing law-enforcement officers certified to perform vehicle safety inspections shall provide the Department of Criminal Justice Services with verification that law-enforcement officers certified to perform vehicle safety inspections have met the requirements for initial certification and maintenance of certification of driver/vehicle inspectors prescribed by the U.S. Department of Transportation, Federal Motor Carrier Safety Administration and satisfactorily completed the annual in-service training required by this section.

Every vehicle inspected by a local law-enforcement officer pursuant to this section and found to be free of defects which would constitute grounds for removal of the vehicle from service shall be issued a sticker as evidence of such inspection and freedom from defects. Such stickers shall be valid for 90 days. Any vehicle displaying a valid sticker shall be exempt from local or State Police inspections under this section. However, the fact that a vehicle displays a valid sticker shall not prevent any local or State Police officer from stopping and inspecting the vehicle if he observes an obvious safety defect. The Superintendent of State Police shall work cooperatively with local law-enforcement agencies of localities whose officers are authorized to perform inspections pursuant to this section to develop a standard sticker as provided for in this section and uniform policies and procedures for issuance and display of such stickers.

However, notwithstanding the foregoing provisions of this section, before placing any vehicle out of service, the vehicle operator shall be allowed two hours to effect repairs to his vehicle. Such repairs may be performed at the site where the vehicle was inspected and found to be unsafe, provided the vehicle requiring repair is off the highway, where the repairs can be effected safely. If such repairs remedy the condition or conditions that would have caused it to be taken out of service, it shall not be taken out of service, but allowed to resume its operations. No such repairs, however, shall be allowed if the vehicle's load consists of hazardous material as defined in § 10.1-1400.

History.

1982, c. 90, § 46.1-279.01; 1985, c. 561; 1988, c. 77; 1989, c. 727; 1990, cc. 20, 167; 1991, cc. 284, 416; 1993, c. 409; 1995, cc. 39, 458; 1996, cc. 24, 91, 144, 525; 1997, c. 35; 1999, cc. 68, 279; 2000, cc. 59, 112; 2002, cc. 142, 223, 263; 2003, cc. 82, 85.

§ 46.2-1001.1. Special equipment required for converted electric vehicles.

In addition to any other equipment required by this chapter, no converted electric vehicle may be registered in or operated on the highways of the Commonwealth without the following:

1. Orange-colored high voltage cables and high voltage markings on all conduit containing high voltage cables. No high voltage cables may be attached to the chassis of the vehicle in such a way as to cause the chassis to be used to ground the electric current;
2. A breaker or fuse in the high voltage circuit that contains the traction battery pack and the motor controller. Such breaker or fuse must be rated to interrupt the expected maximum current at or above the battery pack voltage;
3. An externally mounted switch to open the high voltage circuit in case of an emergency. Such switch must be located where the fuel tank filler cap was located prior to conversion. Any cover protecting the switch must be able to be opened from the outside of the vehicle;
4. Traction batteries mounted in secure nonconductive enclosures that provide for limited access. Multiple enclosures may be used but must be connected by high voltage cables encased in conduit made of metal, composite, or other materials of comparable strength, crush, and abrasion resistance to metal or composite;
5. If batteries other than lead acid batteries are used as traction batteries, a temperature monitoring system that monitors the temperature of at least one battery in each battery enclosure. Such system must warn the driver of the vehicle if the temperature of the battery is rising rapidly or is above safe levels;
6. Conduit made of metal, composite, or other materials of comparable strength, crush, and abrasion resistance to metal or composite, encasing any high voltage cables running under or outside of the vehicle. Such conduit must be secured to the vehicle chassis and must not violate the ground clearance provisions of § 46.2-1063;
7. A vacuum system and pump, or comparable equipment, to maintain proper brake function and capacity, as required by this chapter; and
8. Labeling on three sides of the vehicle identifying such vehicle as "CONVERTED ELECTRIC." Each label shall be at least six inches long and consist of lettering at least three inches tall.

At such time as the federal government establishes minimum equipment and safety standards, including any related to synthetic vehicle sounds, for converted electric vehicles, to the extent that such standards are different from the standards established by this section, the federal standards shall apply to converted electric vehicles in the Commonwealth. If any federal standard conflicts with a standard set forth by this section, the stricter standard shall prevail.

History.
2012, c. 177.

§ 46.2-1002. Illegal possession or sale of certain unapproved equipment.

It shall be unlawful for any person to possess with intent to sell or offer for sale, either separately or as a part of the equipment of a motor vehicle, or to use or have as equipment on a motor vehicle operated on a highway any lighting device, warning device, signal device, safety glass, or other equipment for which approval is required by any provision of this chapter or any part or parts tending to change or alter the operation of such device, glass, or other equipment unless of a type that has been submitted to and approved by the Superintendent or meets or exceeds the standards and specifications of the Society of Automotive Engineers, the American National Standards Institute, Incorporated or the federal Department of Transportation.

History.
Code 1950, § 46-311; 1958, c. 541, § 46.1-308; 1960, c. 125; 1968, c. 172; 1970, c. 26; 1984, c. 426; 1989, c. 727.

§ 46.2-1003. Illegal use of defective or unsafe equipment.

It shall be unlawful for any person to use or have as equipment on a motor vehicle operated on a highway any device or equipment mentioned in § 46.2-1002 which is defective or in unsafe condition.

History.
1960, c. 125, § 46.1-308.1; 1989, c. 727.

§ 46.2-1004. Trademark or name and instructions required.

Each device or other equipment mentioned in § 46.2-1002 and offered for sale in the Commonwealth shall bear a trademark or name or be identified in keeping with the Superintendent's regulations and shall be accompanied by printed instructions as to the proper mounting, use, and candlepower of any bulbs to be used therewith and any particular methods of mounting or adjustments necessary to meet the requirements of this title and any regulation of the Superintendent.

History.
Code 1950, § 46-312; 1958, c. 541, § 46.1-309; 1989, c. 727.

ARTICLE 2.

TESTING, EVALUATION, AND APPROVAL OF EQUIPMENT.

§ 46.2-1005. Procedure for approval of equipment.

The Superintendent may establish a procedure for the approval of equipment required to be approved by him. Such procedure shall include the submission of a sample of the device for test and record purposes, submission of evidence that the device complies with this title and with recognized testing standards which the Superintendent is hereby authorized to adopt, and payment of the fee as provided by § 46.2-1008. The Superintendent shall then, within a reasonable time, either disapprove the device or issue a certificate of approval therefor.

The Superintendent may waive such approval and the issuance of a certificate of approval when the device or equipment required to be approved by this title is identified as complying with the standards and specifications of the Society of Automotive Engineers, the American National Standards Institute, Incorporated, or the regulations of the federal Department of Transportation.

History.
Code 1950, § 46-313; 1954, c. 364; 1958, c. 541, § 46.1-311; 1960, c. 125; 1968, c. 172; 1970, c. 27; 1989, c. 727.

§ 46.2-1005.1. Auxiliary lights on motorcycles.

The Superintendent of State Police shall establish guidelines setting forth a procedure pursuant to § 46.2-1005 to allow for the submission and approval of auxiliary lights on motorcycles that are not approved by the Society of Automotive Engineers and shall publish such procedure on the Department of State Police's website by January 1, 2017. The approval of any lights or equipment shall also be published on the Department's website and the Department shall notify official safety inspection stations of such approved equipment.

History.
2016, c. 701.

§ 46.2-1006. Approval of brake and head light testing methods and equipment.

The Superintendent shall approve methods of brake testing and head light testing. Approval of the use of mechanical brake and light testing equipment may be given by the Superintendent. When necessary, the Superintendent may call upon the United States Bureau of Standards or some other recognized testing agency to assist him in determining

Motor Vehicles

whether such mechanical testing equipment shall be approved for the purpose set forth in this chapter.

History.

Code 1950, § 46-314; 1958, c. 541, § 46.1-312; 1989, c. 727.

§ 46.2-1007. Retesting of devices and revocation of approval certificates.

The Superintendent, when having reason to believe that an approved device or equipment for which a certificate of approval has been issued and which is being sold commercially does not, under ordinary conditions of use, comply with the requirements of this chapter, may, after notice to the manufacturer thereof, suspend or revoke the certificate of approval issued therefor, until or unless the device is resubmitted to and retested by an authorized testing agency and is found to meet the requirements of this chapter. If the certificate of approval for such device or equipment has been waived by the Superintendent as provided in § 46.2-1005, the notice to the manufacturer as provided in this section shall have the effect of making further sales of such device or equipment unlawful in the Commonwealth until such device or equipment has been submitted to the Superintendent and a certificate of approval has been issued in accordance with the procedure established pursuant to § 46.2-1005. The Superintendent may, at the time of retest, purchase in the open market and submit to the testing agency one or more sets of the approved device, and if the device fails to meet the requirements of this title, the Superintendent may permanently revoke the certificate of approval of the device. In the discretion of the Superintendent, an approval for the sale and use of any such device may be amended to permit the continued use of such devices already sold but to prohibit further sales of the device.

History.

Code 1950, § 46-315; 1958, c. 541, § 46.1-313; 1960, c. 125; 1962, c. 146; 1989, c. 727.

§ 46.2-1008. Fees for approval certificates.

Any person who applies to the Superintendent for a certificate of approval required by this article shall pay a fee not to exceed the following amounts:

1. For approval and recordation of headlights, warning devices, safety glass, signal devices, and other devices required by this title to be approved by the Superintendent and not provided for elsewhere in this section, $150.
2. For approval and recordation of taillights, spot lights or any other lighting devices, seventy-five dollars.
3. For approval and recordation of brake-testing and light-testing machines, $100 for each type approved.
4. For approval and recordation of safety lap belts and shoulder straps or harnesses or any combination lap belt and shoulder strap or harness, fifty dollars.
5. For approval and recordation of safety glasses, face shields, or goggles for motorcycle operators, fifty dollars.

Fees collected under this section shall be used by the Superintendent in examining and testing devices to be approved and for maintaining and publishing necessary records.

History.

Code 1950, § 46-316; 1956, c. 36; 1958, c. 541, § 46.1-314; 1962, c. 146; 1966, c. 37; 1968, c. 171; 1970, c. 25; 1989, c. 727.

§ 46.2-1009. Exemptions for certain electrically powered vehicles; standards and permits for such vehicles.

The provisions of §§ 46.2-1002 through 46.2-1008 shall not apply to vehicles which are powered solely by electricity, capable of speeds of no more than fifteen miles per hour. The Superintendent may establish standards for safety equipment to be used on such vehicles. Upon the establishment of such standards, permits to use such vehicles may be issued to persons owning vehicles meeting such standards by the officer in charge of the division of the Department of State Police having jurisdiction in the county, city, or town in which such person resides.

History.

1973, c. 455, § 46.1-314.1; 1989, c. 727.

ARTICLE 3.

LIGHTS AND TURN SIGNALS.

§ 46.2-1010. Equipment required.

Every vehicle driven or moved on a highway within the Commonwealth shall at all times be equipped with such lights as are required in this chapter for different classes of vehicles. The lights shall at all times be capable of being lighted, except as otherwise provided. This section shall not apply, however, to any vehicle for transporting well-drilling machinery licensed under § 46.2-700 when operated only between the hours of sunrise and sunset.

History.

Code 1950, § 46-264; 1950, p. 690; 1958, c. 541, § 46.1-259; 1989, c. 727.

§ 46.2-1011. Headlights on motor vehicles.

Every motor vehicle other than a motorcycle, autocycle, road roller, road machinery, or tractor used on a highway shall be equipped with at least two headlights as approved by the Superintendent, at the front of and on opposite sides of the motor vehicle.

History.

Code 1950, § 46-265; 1956, c. 639; 1958, c. 541, § 46.1-260; 1989, c. 727; 2014, cc. 53, 256.

§ 46.2-1012. Headlights, auxiliary headlights, tail lights, brake lights, and illumination of license plates on motorcycles or autocycles.

Every motorcycle or autocycle shall be equipped with at least one headlight which shall be of a type that has been approved by the Superintendent and shall be capable of projecting sufficient light to the front of such motorcycle or autocycle to render discernible a person or object at a distance of 200 feet. However, the lights shall not project a glaring or dazzling light to persons approaching such motorcycles or autocycles. In addition, each motorcycle or autocycle may be equipped with not more than two auxiliary headlights of a type approved by the Superintendent.

Motorcycles or autocycles may be equipped with means of modulating the high beam of their headlights between high and low beam at a rate of 200 to 280 flashes per minute. Such headlights shall not be so modulated during periods when headlights would ordinarily be required to be lighted under § 46.2-1030.

Every motorcycle or autocycle registered in the Commonwealth and operated on the highways of the Commonwealth shall be equipped with at least one brake light of a type approved by the Superintendent. Motorcycles or autocycles may be equipped with one or more auxiliary brake lights of a type approved by the Superintendent. The Superintendent may by regulation prescribe or limit the size, number, location, and configuration of such auxiliary brake lights.

Every motorcycle or autocycle shall carry at the rear at least one or more red lights plainly visible in clear weather from a distance of 500 feet to the rear of such vehicle. Such tail lights shall be constructed and so mounted in their relation to the rear license plate as to illuminate the license plate with a white light so that the same may be read from a distance of 50 feet to the rear of such vehicle. Alternatively, a separate white light shall be so mounted as to illuminate the rear license plate from a distance of 50 feet to the rear of such vehicle. Any such tail lights or special white light shall be of a type approved by the Superintendent.

Motorcycles or autocycles may be equipped with a means of varying the brightness of the vehicle's brake light upon application of the vehicle's brakes.

History.

Code 1950, § 46-266; 1958, c. 541, § 46.1-261; 1983, c. 132; 1989, c. 727; 1991, c. 165; 2003, c. 964; 2009, c. 79; 2014, cc. 53, 256; 2015, c. 405.

§ 46.2-1013. Tail lights.

Every motor vehicle and every trailer or semitrailer being drawn at the end of one or more other vehicles shall carry at the rear two red lights plainly visible in clear weather from a distance of 500 feet to the rear of such vehicle. Such tail lights shall be constructed and so mounted in their relation to the rear license plate as to illuminate the license plate with a white light so that the same may be read from a distance of 50 feet to the rear of such vehicle. Alternatively, a separate white light shall be so mounted as to illuminate the rear license plate from a distance of 50 feet to the rear of such vehicle. Any such tail lights or special white light shall be of a type approved by the Superintendent.

In any instance where the tail light is to be installed on a boat trailer and the boat extends beyond the end of the trailer or to the end of the trailer, an approved portable light assembly or assemblies may be attached to the exposed rear of the boat, provided such installation complies with the visibility requirements of this section. The provisions of this section shall not apply to motorcycles.

History.

Code 1950, § 46-267; 1952, c. 652; 1958, c. 541, § 46.1-262; 1964, c. 16; 1989, c. 727; 2003, c. 964.

§ 46.2-1014. Brake lights.

Every motor vehicle, trailer, or semitrailer, except an antique vehicle not originally equipped with a brake light, registered in the Commonwealth and operated on the highways in the Commonwealth shall be equipped with at least two brake lights of a type approved by the Superintendent. Such brake lights shall automatically exhibit a red or amber light plainly visible in clear weather from a distance of 500 feet to the rear of such vehicle when the brake is applied.

The provisions of this section shall not apply to motorcycles or autocycles equipped with brake lights as required by § 46.2-1012.

History.

1970, c. 17, § 46.1-262.1; 1972, c. 6; 1989, c. 727; 2000, cc. 54, 63; 2003, c. 964; 2014, cc. 53, 256.

§ 46.2-1014.1. Supplemental high mount stop light.

Whenever operated on the highways, every Virginia-registered passenger car manufactured for the 1986 or subsequent model year shall be equipped with a supplemental center high mount stop light of a type approved by the Superintendent or which meets the standards adopted by the United States Department of Transportation. The light shall be mounted as near the vertical center line of the vehicle as possible. The light shall be actuated only in conjunction with the vehicle's brake lights and hazard lights. Any supplemental high mount stop light installed on any other vehicle shall comply with those requirements.

History.

1990, c. 955.

§ 46.2-1015. Lights on bicycles, electric personal assistive mobility devices, electric power-assisted bicycles, and mopeds.

A. Every bicycle, electric personal assistive mobility device, electric power-assisted bicycle, and moped when in use between sunset and sunrise shall be equipped with a headlight on the front emitting a white light visible in clear weather from a distance of at least 500 feet to the front and a red reflector visible from a distance of at least 600 feet to the rear when directly in front of lawful lower beams of headlights on a motor vehicle. Such lights and reflector shall be of types approved by the Superintendent.

In addition to the foregoing provisions of this section, a bicycle or its rider may be equipped with lights or reflectors. These lights may be steady burning or blinking.

B. Every bicycle, or its rider, shall be equipped with a taillight on the rear emitting a red light plainly visible in clear weather from a distance of at least 500 feet to the rear when in use between sunset and sunrise and operating on any highway with a speed limit of 35 mph or greater. Any such taillight shall be of a type approved by the Superintendent.

History.

Code 1950, §§ 46-268, 46-270; 1958, c. 541, § 46.1-263; 1981, c. 585; 1989, c. 727; 2001, c. 834; 2002, c. 254; 2004, cc. 947, 973; 2005, c. 381.

§ 46.2-1016. Lights on other vehicles; reflectors.

All vehicles or other mobile equipment not otherwise in this article required to be equipped with specified lights shall carry at least one or more white lights to the front and a red light to the rear visible in clear weather from a distance of not less than 500 feet to the front and rear of such vehicles.

In lieu of or in addition to the lights, a reflector of a type, size, and color approved by the Superintendent may be permanently affixed to the rear and front of such vehicle.

History.

Code 1950, §§ 46-269, 46-270; 1952, c. 652; 1958, c. 541, § 46.1-264; 1989, c. 727.

§ 46.2-1017. Dimension or marker lights and reflectors, generally.

All motor vehicles, trailers, or semitrailers exceeding seven feet in width or the widest portion of which extends four inches beyond the front fender extremes shall be equipped with amber lights mounted at the extreme right and left front top corners of such vehicle. Each such light shall be visible in clear weather for a distance of at least 500 feet to the front of such vehicle. Such vehicles shall also be equipped with red lights mounted at the extreme right and left rear top corners of such vehicle. Each such light shall be visible in clear weather for at least 500 feet to the rear of such vehicle. Any tractor truck, however, need not be equipped with rear red dimension or marker lights. If the front or the rear of such vehicle is not the widest portion of the vehicle, the dimension or marker lights required in this section shall be mounted on the widest portions of the vehicle with the amber lights herein required visible from the front as herein required and the red lights herein required visible from the rear as herein required. The lights herein required shall be of a type approved by the Superintendent.

In addition to the lights required in this section, each such vehicle shall be equipped with amber reflectors located on each side thereof, at or near the front. Red reflectors shall be used on the rear of each such vehicle. Such reflectors shall be securely fastened to the vehicle not less than fifteen inches and not more than sixty inches from the ground. For a vehicle that is less than fifteen inches tall, however, such reflectors shall be securely fastened thereto at the highest point the structure of a vehicle will permit. The reflectors shall be of a type approved by the Superintendent.

If any vehicle is so constructed as to make compliance with the requirements of this section impractical, the lights and reflectors shall be placed on the vehicle in accordance with the Superintendent's regulations.

If any vehicle required by this section to be equipped with dimension or marker lights has installed on its rear, as close as practicable to the top of the vehicle and as close as practicable to the vertical centerline of the vehicle, three red identification lights of a type approved by the Superintendent, with the light centers spaced not less than six inches or more than twelve inches apart, the rear dimension or marker lights may be mounted at any height but must indicate as nearly as practicable the extreme width of the vehicle.

History.

Code 1950, § 46-271; 1952, c. 652; 1958, c. 541, § 46.1-265; 1960, c. 156; 1974, c. 218; 1977, c. 383; 1989, c. 727; 1997, c. 23.

§ 46.2-1018. Marker lights on vehicles or loads exceeding thirty-five feet.

Whenever any motor vehicle or combination of vehicles whose actual length, including its load, exceeds thirty-five feet and is not subject to the provisions of § 46.2-1017, such vehicle shall be equipped with reflectors of a type approved by the Superintendent when operated between sunset and sunrise. Such reflectors shall be mounted on the widest part of the vehicle or its load so as to be visible from the front and sides of the vehicle.

History.

1958, c. 541, § 46.1-265.1; 1989, c. 727.

§ 46.2-1019. Spotlights.

Any motor vehicle or motorcycle may be equipped with one or two spotlights which, when lighted, shall be aimed and used so that no portion of the beam will be directed to the left of the center of the highway at any time or more than 100 feet ahead of the vehicle. Any such lights shall be of a type approved by the Superintendent. No such spotlights shall be used in conjunction with or as a substitute for required head lights, except in case of emergency.

History.

Code 1950, § 46-272; 1954, c. 58; 1958, c. 541, § 46.1-266; 1989, c. 727.

§ 46.2-1020. Other permissible lights.

Any motor vehicle may be equipped with fog lights, not more than two of which can be illuminated at any time, one or two auxiliary driving lights if so equipped by the manufacturer, two daytime running lights, two side lights of not more than six candlepower, an interior light or lights of not more than 15 candlepower each, and signal lights.

The provision of this section limiting interior lights to no more than 15 candlepower shall not apply to (i) alternating, blinking, or flashing colored emergency lights mounted inside law-enforcement motor vehicles which may otherwise legally be equipped with such colored emergency lights, or (ii) flashing shielded red or red and white lights, authorized under § 46.2-1024, mounted inside vehicles owned or used by (a) members of volunteer fire companies or volunteer emergency medical services agencies, (b) professional firefighters, or (c) police chaplains. A vehicle equipped with lighting devices as authorized in this section shall be operated by a police chaplain only if he has successfully completed a course of training in the safe operation of a motor vehicle under emergency conditions and a certificate attesting to such successful completion, signed by the course instructor, is carried at all times in the vehicle when operated by the police chaplain to whom the certificate applies.

Unless such lighting device is both covered and unlit, no motor vehicle which is equipped with any lighting device other than lights required or permitted in this article, required or approved by the Superintendent, or required by the federal Department of Transportation shall be operated on any highway in the Commonwealth. Nothing in this section shall permit any vehicle, not otherwise authorized, to be equipped with colored emergency lights, whether blinking or steady-burning.

History.

Code 1950, § 46-273; 1954, c. 310; 1958, c. 541, § 46.1-267; 1960, cc. 156, 391; 1962, c. 512; 1966, cc. 655, 664; 1968, c. 89; 1972, c. 7; 1974, c. 537; 1976, c. 6; 1977, c. 72; 1978, cc. 311, 357; 1980, c. 337; 1981, c. 338; 1984, cc. 440, 539; 1985, cc. 248, 269, 287, 462; 1986, cc. 124, 127, 229; 1987, cc. 347, 370; 1988, cc. 339, 351; 1989, c. 727; 1991, c. 516; 1995, c. 122; 2003, c. 153; 2006, c. 122; 2015, cc. 502, 503.

§ 46.2-1021. Additional lights permitted on certain commercial vehicles.

In addition to other lights permitted in this article, buses operated as public carriers, taxicabs as defined in § 46.2-2000, and commercial motor vehicles as defined in § 52-8.4 may be equipped with (i) illuminated vacant or destination signs and (ii) single steady-burning white lights, emitting a diffused light of such intensity as not to project a glaring or dazzling light, for the nighttime illumination of exterior advertising.

In addition to other lights authorized by this article, buses operated as public carriers may be equipped with flashing white warning lights of types authorized by the Superintendent of State Police. These warning lights shall be installed in a manner authorized by the Superintendent and shall be lighted while the bus is transporting passengers during periods of reduced visibility caused by atmospheric conditions other than darkness. These warning lights may also be lighted at other times while the bus is transporting passengers.

History.

Code 1950, § 46-273; 1954, c. 310; 1958, c. 541, § 46.1-267; 1960, cc. 156, 391; 1962, c. 512; 1966, cc. 655, 664; 1968, c. 89; 1972, c. 7; 1974, c. 537; 1976, c. 6; 1977, c. 72; 1978, cc. 311, 357; 1980, c. 337; 1981, c. 338; 1984, cc. 440, 539; 1985, cc. 248, 269, 287, 462; 1986, cc. 124, 127, 229; 1987, cc. 347, 370; 1988, cc. 339, 351; 1989, c. 727; 1998, c. 419.

§ 46.2-1021.1. Additional lights permitted on certain privately owned cars.

Privately owned passenger cars used for home delivery of commercially prepared food may be equipped with one steady-burning white light for the nighttime illumination of a sign identifying the business delivering the food. Such sign shall not utilize primarily green, red or blue colors. Such sign shall not exceed eighteen inches in height nor have more than four sides, no side of which shall exceed fifteen by twenty-four inches. Such light shall emit diffused illumination of such an intensity as not to project a glaring or dazzling light. Such light may only be illuminated during delivery.

History.

1989, c. 262, § 46.1-267.

§ 46.2-1022. Flashing blue, red and blue, blue and white, or red, white and blue warning lights.

Certain Department of Military Affairs vehicles and certain Virginia National Guard vehicles designated by the Adjutant General, when used in state active duty to perform particular law-enforcement functions, Department of Corrections vehicles designated by the Director of the Department of Corrections, and law-enforcement vehicles may be equipped with flashing, blinking, or alternating blue, blue and red, blue and white, or red, white, and blue combination warning lights of types approved by the Superintendent. Such warning lights may be of types constructed within turn signal housings or motorcycle headlight housings, subject to approval by the Superintendent.

History.

Code 1950, § 46-273; 1954, c. 310; 1958, c. 541, § 46.1-267; 1960, cc. 156, 391; 1962, c. 512; 1966, cc. 655, 664; 1968, c. 89; 1972, c. 7; 1974, c. 537; 1976, c. 6; 1977, c. 72; 1978, cc. 311, 357; 1980, c. 337; 1981, c. 338; 1984, cc. 440, 539; 1985, cc. 248, 269, 287, 462; 1986, cc. 124, 127, 229; 1987, cc. 347, 370; 1988, cc. 339, 351; 1989, c. 727; 1992, c. 96; 1996, cc. 141, 347; 2004, c. 323; 2008, c. 181.

§ 46.2-1023. Flashing red or red and white warning lights.

Fire apparatus, forest warden vehicles, emergency medical services vehicles, vehicles of the Department of Emergency Management, vehicles of the Department of Environmental Quality, vehicles of the Virginia National Guard Civil Support Team when responding to an emergency, vehicles of county, city, or town Departments of Emergency Management, vehicles of the Office of Emergency Medical Services, animal warden vehicles, and vehicles used by security personnel of the Huntington Ingalls Industries, Bassett-Walker, Inc., the Winchester Medical Center, the National Aeronautics and Space Administration's Wallops Flight Facility, and, within those areas specified in their orders of appointment, by special conservators of the peace and policemen for certain places appointed pursuant to §§ 19.2-13 and 19.2-17 may be equipped with flashing, blinking, or alternating red or red and white combination warning lights of types approved by the Superintendent. Such warning lights may be of types constructed within turn signal housings or motorcycle headlight housings, subject to approval by the Superintendent.

History.

Code 1950, § 46-273; 1954, c. 310; 1958, c. 541, § 46.1-267; 1960, cc. 156, 391; 1962, c. 512; 1966, cc. 655, 664; 1968, c. 89; 1972, c. 7; 1974, c. 537; 1976, c. 6; 1977, c. 72; 1978, cc. 311, 357; 1980, c. 337; 1981, c. 338; 1984, cc. 440, 539; 1985, cc. 248, 269, 287, 462; 1986, cc. 124, 127, 229; 1987, cc. 347, 370; 1988, cc. 339, 351; 1989, c. 727; 1991, c. 105; 1992, c. 34; 1994, c. 178; 1995, c. 92; 2003, cc. 152, 217; 2005, c. 583; 2006, c. 86; 2008, c. 181; 2009, c. 595; 2014, cc. 171, 800; 2015, cc. 502, 503.

§ 46.2-1024. Flashing or steady-burning red or red and white warning lights.

Any member of a fire department, volunteer fire company, or volunteer emergency medical services agency and any police chaplain may equip one vehicle owned by him with no more than two flashing or steady-burning red or red and white combination warning lights of types approved by the Superintendent. Warning lights permitted by this section shall be lit only when answering emergency calls. A vehicle equipped with lighting devices as authorized in this section shall be operated by a police chaplain only if he has successfully completed a course of training in the safe operation of a motor vehicle under emergency conditions and a certificate attesting to such successful completion, signed by the course instructor, is carried at all times in the vehicle when operated by the police chaplain to whom the certificate applies.

History.

Code 1950, § 46-273; 1954, c. 310; 1958, c. 541, § 46.1-267; 1960, cc. 156, 391; 1962, c. 512; 1966, cc. 655, 664; 1968, c. 89; 1972, c. 7; 1974, c. 537; 1976, c. 6; 1977, c. 72; 1978, cc. 311, 357; 1980, c. 337; 1981, c. 338; 1984, cc. 440, 539; 1985, cc. 248, 269, 287, 462; 1986, cc. 124, 127, 229; 1987, cc. 347, 370; 1988, cc. 339, 351; 1989, c. 727; 1992, c. 379; 2003, c. 153; 2015, cc. 502, 503.

§ 46.2-1025. Flashing amber, purple, or green warning lights.

A. The following vehicles may be equipped with flashing, blinking, or alternating amber warning lights of types approved by the Superintendent:

1. Vehicles used for the principal purpose of towing or servicing disabled vehicles;
2. Vehicles used in constructing, maintaining, and repairing highways or utilities on or along public highways, or in assisting with the management of roadside and traffic incidents, or performing traffic management services along public highways;
3. Vehicles used for the principal purpose of removing hazardous or polluting substances from state waters and drainage areas on or along public highways, or state vehicles used to perform other state-required environmental activities, provided that the amber lights are not lit while the vehicle is in motion;
4. Vehicles used for servicing automatic teller machines, provided the amber lights are not lit while the vehicle is in motion;
5. Vehicles used in refuse collection, provided the amber lights are lit only when the vehicles are engaged in refuse collection operations;
6. Vehicles used by individuals for emergency snow-removal purposes;
7. Hi-rail vehicles, provided the amber lights are lit only when the vehicles are operated on railroad rails;
8. Fire apparatus and emergency medical services vehicles, provided the amber lights are used in addition to lights permitted under § 46.2-1023 and are so mounted or installed as to be visible from behind the vehicle;
9. Vehicles owned and used by businesses providing security services, provided the amber lights are not lit while the vehicle is being operated on a public highway;
10. Vehicles used to collect and deliver the United States mail, provided the amber lights are lit only when the vehicle is actually engaged in such collection or delivery;
11. Vehicles used to transport petroleum or propane products, provided the amber light is mounted

on the rear of the vehicle and is lit when parked while making a delivery of petroleum or propane products, or when the vehicle's back-up lights are lit and its device producing an audible signal when the vehicle is operated in reverse gear, as provided for in § 46.2-1175.1, is in operation;

12. Vehicles used by law-enforcement agency personnel in the enforcement of laws governing motor vehicle parking;

13. Government-owned law-enforcement vehicles, provided the lights are used for the purpose of giving directional warning to vehicular traffic to move one direction or another and are not lit while the vehicle is in motion;

14. Chase vehicles when used to unload a hot air balloon or used to load a hot air balloon after landing, provided the amber lights are not lit while the vehicle is in motion;

15. Vehicles used for farm, agricultural, or horticultural purposes, or any farm tractor;

16. Vehicles owned and used by construction companies operating under Virginia contractors licenses;

17. Vehicles used to lead or provide escorts for bicycle races authorized by the Department of Transportation or the locality in which the race is being conducted;

18. Vehicles used by radio or television stations for remote broadcasts, provided that the amber lights are not lit while the vehicle is in motion;

19. Vehicles used by municipal safety officers in the performance of their official duties. For the purpose of this subdivision, "municipal safety officers" means municipal employees responsible for managing municipal safety programs and ensuring municipal compliance with safety and environmental regulatory mandates;

20. Vehicles used as pace cars, security vehicles, or firefighting vehicles by any speedway or motor vehicle race track, provided that the amber lights are not lit while the vehicle is being operated on a public highway;

21. Vehicles used in patrol work by members of neighborhood watch groups approved by the chief law-enforcement officer of the locality in their assigned neighborhood watch program area, provided that the vehicles are clearly identified as neighborhood watch vehicles, and the amber lights are not lit while the vehicle is in motion;

22. Vehicles that are not tow trucks as defined in § 46.2-100, but are owned or controlled by a towing and recovery business, provided that the amber lights are lit only when the vehicle is being used at a towing and recovery site; and

23. Publicly owned or operated transit buses.

B. Except as otherwise provided in this section, such amber lights shall be lit only when performing the functions which qualify them to be equipped with such lights.

C. Vehicles used to lead or provide escorts for funeral processions may use either amber warning lights or purple warning lights, but amber warning lights and purple warning lights shall not simultaneously be used on the same vehicle. The Superintendent of State Police shall develop standards and specifications for purple lights authorized in this subsection.

D. Vehicles used by police, firefighting, or emergency medical services personnel as command centers at the scene of incidents may be equipped with and use green warning lights of a type approved by the Superintendent. Such lights shall not be activated while the vehicle is operating upon the highway.

History.

Code 1950, § 46-273; 1954, c. 310; 1958, c. 541, § 46.1-267; 1960, cc. 156, 391; 1962, c. 512; 1966, cc. 655, 664; 1968, c. 89; 1972, c. 7; 1974, c. 537; 1976, c. 6; 1977, c. 72; 1978, cc. 311, 357; 1980, c. 337; 1981, c. 338; 1984, cc. 440, 539; 1985, cc. 248, 269, 287, 462; 1986, cc. 124, 127, 229; 1987, cc. 347, 370; 1988, cc. 339, 351; 1989, c. 727; 1991, c. 465; 1992, cc. 93, 410, 805; 1995, c. 727; 1997, c. 149; 1998, cc. 134, 417; 1999, cc. 18, 72, 232; 2000, cc. 84, 121, 278; 2003, c. 93; 2005, c. 574; 2010, c. 127; 2011, c. 268; 2014, c. 54; 2015, cc. 41, 502, 503; 2016, cc. 198, 226.

§ 46.2-1026. Flashing high-intensity amber warning lights.

High-intensity flashing, blinking, or alternating amber warning lights visible for at least 500 feet, of types approved by the Superintendent, shall be used on any vehicle engaged in either escorting or towing over-dimensional materials, equipment, boats, or manufactured housing units by authority of a highway hauling permit issued pursuant to § 46.2-1139. Such lights shall be mounted on the top of the escort and tow vehicles and on the upper rear end of the over-dimensional vehicles or loads for maximum visibility, front and rear. However, any vehicles operating under a permit issued pursuant to § 46.2-1139 shall be deemed to be in compliance with the requirements of this section if accompanied by escort vehicles.

The provisions of this section shall apply only to vehicles or loads which are either (i) more than twelve feet wide or (ii) more than seventy-five feet long.

History.

Code 1950, § 46-273; 1954, c. 310; 1958, c. 541, § 46.1-267; 1960, cc. 156, 391; 1962, c. 512; 1966, cc. 655, 664; 1968, c. 89; 1972, c. 7; 1974, c. 537; 1976, c. 6; 1977, c. 72; 1978, cc. 311, 357; 1980, c. 337; 1981, c. 338; 1984, cc. 440, 539; 1985, cc. 248, 269, 287, 462; 1986, cc. 124, 127, 229; 1987, cc. 347, 370; 1988, cc. 339, 351; 1989, c. 727.

§ 46.2-1027. Warning lights on certain demonstrator vehicles.

Dealers or businesses engaged in the sale of fire, emergency medical services, or law-enforcement vehicles may, for demonstration purposes, equip such vehicles with colored warning lights.

History.

Code 1950, § 46-273; 1954, c. 310; 1958, c. 541, § 46.1-267; 1960, cc. 156, 391; 1962, c. 512; 1966, cc. 655, 664; 1968, c. 89; 1972, c. 7;

1974, c. 537; 1976, c. 6; 1977, c. 72; 1978, cc. 311, 357; 1980, c. 337; 1981, c. 338; 1984, cc. 440, 539; 1985, cc. 248, 269, 287, 462; 1986, cc. 124, 127, 229; 1987, cc. 347, 370; 1988, cc. 339, 351; 1989, c. 727; 2015, cc. 502, 503.

§ 46.2-1028. Auxiliary lights on firefighting, Virginia Department of Transportation, and other emergency vehicles.

Any firefighting vehicle, emergency medical services vehicle, Virginia Department of Transportation vehicle, or tow truck may be equipped with clear auxiliary lights, which shall be used exclusively for lighting emergency scenes. Such lights shall be of a type approved by the Superintendent and shall not be used in a manner that may blind or interfere with the vision of the drivers of approaching vehicles. In no event shall such lights be lighted while the vehicle is in motion.

History.
1972, c. 385, § 46.1-267.1; 1989, c. 727; 1996, c. 403; 2006, cc. 874, 891; 2015, cc. 502, 503.

§ 46.2-1028.1. Illuminated identification systems on certain emergency vehicles.

Any firefighting vehicle, ambulance, rescue or life-saving vehicle, or vehicle used by police, firefighting, or rescue personnel as a command center at the scene of incidents may be equipped with and use an illuminated identification system of a type approved by the Superintendent to enable aircraft more easily to read number decals and other identifying markings on the roofs of such vehicle. Any such illuminated identification system may be used when the vehicle is in motion or stationary.

History.
2015, c. 333.

§ 46.2-1028.2. Auxiliary lights on public utility vehicles.

Any electrical service utility vehicle owned and operated by a public utility, as defined in § 56-265.1, and having a gross vehicle weight rating greater than 15,000 pounds may be equipped with clear auxiliary lights that shall be mounted on the lower portion of the vehicle and aimed downward for the exclusive use of ground lighting. Such lights shall be of a type approved by the Superintendent and shall not be used in a manner that may blind or interfere with the vision of the drivers of approaching vehicles. In no event shall such lights be lighted while the vehicle is in motion.

History.
2015, c. 341.

§ 46.2-1029. Auxiliary lights on law-enforcement vehicles.

Notwithstanding any other provision of this article, any government-owned law-enforcement vehicle may be equipped with clear auxiliary lights of a type approved by the Superintendent. Such lights may be used to light emergency scenes and other areas for the purpose of detecting offenders, apprehending violators of law, and in performing other reasonably necessary law-enforcement functions. Such lights may be used when the vehicle on which they are mounted is standing or proceeding at a speed of no more than fifteen miles per hour. Such lights shall not be used in a manner which may blind or interfere with the vision of the operators of approaching vehicles.

Any law-enforcement officer may also use spotlights, as authorized in § 46.2-1019, for the purpose and in the manner described herein.

History.
1975, c. 291, § 46.1-267.2; 1980, c. 14; 1989, c. 727.

§ 46.2-1029.1. Flashing of headlights on certain vehicles.

Emergency vehicles as defined in subsection C of § 46.2-920 may be equipped with the means to flash their headlights when their warning lights are activated if (i) the headlights are wired to allow either the high beam or low beam to flash, but not both, and (ii) the headlight system includes a switch or device which prevents flashing of headlights when headlights are required to be lighted under § 46.2-1030.

The provisions of clause (ii) above shall not apply in the City of Chesapeake, the City of Portsmouth, the City of Poquoson, or the County of York.

History.
1989, c. 47; 1994, c. 69; 2003, c. 121; 2005, c. 209.

§ 46.2-1029.2. Certain vehicles may be equipped with secondary warning lights.

In addition to other lights authorized by this article, any (i) fire apparatus, (ii) government-owned vehicle operated on official business by a local fire chief or other local fire official, and (iii) emergency medical services vehicle may be equipped with alternating, blinking, or flashing red or red and white secondary warning lights mounted inside the vehicle's taillights or marker lights of a type approved by the Superintendent of State Police.

History.
2003, c. 115; 2015, cc. 502, 503.

§ 46.2-1030. When lights to be lighted; number of lights to be lighted at any time; use of warning lights.

A. Every vehicle in operation on a highway in the Commonwealth shall display lighted headlights and illuminating devices as required by this article (i) from sunset to sunrise; (ii) during any other time when, because of rain, smoke, fog, snow, sleet, insufficient light, or other unfavorable atmospheric conditions, visibility is reduced to a degree whereby persons or vehicles on the highway are not clearly discernible at a distance of 500 feet; and (iii) whenever windshield wipers are in use as a result of fog, rain, sleet, or snow. The provisions of this subsection, however, shall not apply to instances when windshield wipers are used intermittently in misting rain, sleet, or snow.

B. Not more than four lights used to provide general illumination ahead of the vehicle, including at least two headlights and any other combination of fog lights or other auxiliary lights approved by the Superintendent, shall be lighted at any time. However, motorcycles may be equipped with and use not more than five approved lights in order to provide general illumination ahead of the motorcycle. These limitations shall not preclude the display of warning lights authorized in §§ 46.2-1020 through 46.2-1027, or other lights as may be authorized by the Superintendent.

C. Vehicles equipped with warning lights authorized in §§ 46.2-1020 through 46.2-1027 shall display lighted warning lights as authorized in such sections at all times when responding to emergency calls, towing disabled vehicles, or constructing, repairing, and maintaining public highways or utilities on or along public highways, except that amber lights on vehicles designed with a ramp on wheels and a hydraulic lift with a capacity to haul or tow another vehicle, commonly referred to as "rollbacks," need not be lit while the vehicle is in motion unless it is actually towing a vehicle.

D. The failure to display lighted headlights and illuminating devices under the conditions set forth in clause (iii) of subsection A shall not constitute negligence per se, nor shall violation of clause (iii) of subsection A constitute a defense to any claim for personal injury or recovery of medical expenses for injuries sustained in a motor vehicle accident.

E. No demerit points shall be assessed for failure to display lighted headlights and illuminating devices during periods of fog, rain, sleet, or snow in violation of clause (iii) of subsection A.

F. No citation for a violation of clause (iii) of subsection A shall be issued unless the officer issuing such citation has cause to stop or arrest the driver of such motor vehicle for the violation of some other provision of this Code or local ordinance relating to the operation, ownership, or maintenance of a motor vehicle or any criminal statute.

History.

Code 1950, § 46-275; 1956, c. 640; 1958, c. 541, § 46.1-268; 1960, c. 156; 1970, c. 165; 1983, c. 132; 1987, c. 381; 1989, c. 727; 1992, c. 364; 1997, cc. 25, 589; 2016, cc. 195, 206.

§ 46.2-1031. Requirements as to single-beam head lights.

Approved single-beam head lights shall be aimed in accordance with regulations promulgated by the Superintendent so as not to project a glaring or dazzling light to persons approaching such head lights and shall be of sufficient intensity to reveal persons and objects at a distance of at least 200 feet.

History.

Code 1950, § 46-276; 1958, c. 541, § 46.1-269; 1989, c. 727.

§ 46.2-1032. Requirements as to multiple-beam headlights.

Approved multiple-beam headlights shall be aimed in accordance with regulations promulgated by the Superintendent, based on recommendations of the Society of Automotive Engineers. The high beam of any such lights shall be of sufficient intensity to reveal persons and objects at least 350 feet ahead. At least one nonglaring low beam shall be provided and shall be of such intensity as to reveal persons and objects at least 100 feet ahead.

History.

Code 1950, § 46-277; 1958, c. 541, § 46.1-270; 1989, c. 727.

§ 46.2-1033. Indicator light required.

Every motor vehicle operated on a highway shall be equipped with a working indicator light that indicates to the driver when the high beam of the headlights is being used.

History.

Code 1950, § 46-278; 1958, c. 541, § 46.1-271; 1989, c. 727.

§ 46.2-1034. When dimming headlights required.

Whenever a vehicle is being driven on a highway or a portion thereof which is sufficiently lighted to reveal any person or object upon such highway at a distance of 350 feet ahead, the operator of such vehicle shall use the low beam of his vehicle's headlights or shall dim the headlights if the vehicle has single-beam lights. Whenever a vehicle approaches an oncoming vehicle within 500 feet, the driver of such vehicle shall use the low beam of his vehicle's headlights so aimed that glaring rays are not projected into the eyes of the oncoming driver or dim the headlights, if the vehicle has single-beam lights. Whenever the driver of any motor vehicle approaches from the rear or follows within 200 feet of another vehicle proceeding in the same direction, the driver shall use the low beam of his vehicle's headlights or shall dim the headlights if the vehicle has single-beam lights.

History.
Code 1950, § 46-279; 1954, c. 114; 1958, c. 541, § 46.1-272; 1989, c. 727.

§ 46.2-1035. Dimming headlights on parked vehicles.

Whenever a vehicle is parked so that the beam from its headlights will glare into the eyes of the driver of a vehicle approaching on a highway, the operator of the parked vehicle shall dim or use the low beam of such lights so that glaring rays are not projected into the eyes of an approaching driver.

History.
Code 1950, § 46-279.1; 1950, p. 54; 1958, c. 541, § 46.1-273; 1989, c. 727.

§ 46.2-1036. Acetylene lights on antique motor vehicles.

Antique motor vehicles as defined in § 46.2-100 may be equipped with acetylene headlights, taillights, and lights to illuminate their rear license plates as provided in regulations promulgated by the Superintendent.

History.
Code 1950, § 46-280; 1958, c. 541, § 46.1-274; 1989, c. 727.

§ 46.2-1037. Lights on parked vehicles.

Any vehicle parked or stopped on a highway, whether attended or unattended, between sunset and sunrise shall display at least one light projecting a white or amber light visible in clear weather from a distance of 500 feet to the front of such vehicle and projecting a red light visible under like conditions from a distance of 500 feet to the rear. No lights, however, need be displayed upon any such vehicle when legally parked.

History.
Code 1950, § 46-282; 1958, c. 541, § 46.1-276; 1959, Ex. Sess., c. 86; 1989, c. 727.

§ 46.2-1038. When turn signals required; exceptions.

A. Any motor vehicle, trailer, or semitrailer which is so constructed or carries a load in such a manner as to prevent a hand and arm signal required in § 46.2-849 from being visible both to the front and rear of such motor vehicle, trailer, or semitrailer or any vehicle the driver of which is incapable of giving the required hand and arm signals, shall be equipped with electrical turn signals which meet the requirements of this title and are of a type that has been approved by the Superintendent. A tractor truck, however, need not be equipped with electrical turn signals on the rear if it is equipped with double faced signal lights mounted on the front fenders or on the sides near the front of the vehicle clearly visible to the rear.

B. It shall be unlawful for any person to drive on any highway a motor vehicle registered in the Commonwealth and manufactured or assembled after January 1, 1955, unless such vehicle is equipped with such turn signals on both front and rear.

C. Any such turn signal may be used in lieu of the hand and arm signal required by § 46.2-849.

D. Subsections A and B of this section shall not apply to any motorcycle. The provisions of this section shall not apply to motor vehicles, trailers, or semitrailers used for agricultural or horticultural purposes and exempted from registration under Article 6 (§ 46.2-662 et seq.) of Chapter 6 of this title.

History.
Code 1950, § 46-302; 1954, c. 44; 1958, c. 541, § 46.1-298; 1962, c. 255; 1974, c. 217; 1989, c. 727.

§ 46.2-1039. Requirements of turn signals; regulations.

Every turn signal used to give a signal of intention to turn a vehicle shall be so constructed and so installed as to give a signal plainly visible in clear weather and under normal traffic conditions from a distance of at least 100 feet to the rear and 100 feet to the front of the vehicle. No front turn signal, however, shall be required on vehicles manufactured before January 1, 1943.

The Superintendent may promulgate regulations not inconsistent with this section and § 46.2-1038 governing the construction, location, and operation of turn signals and the color of lights which may be used in any such signal device. Nothing contained herein, however, shall prohibit the requiring of turn signals on any vehicle whose driver is prevented by any reason from giving the hand and arm signal required in § 46.2-849.

History.
Code 1950, § 46-303; 1958, c. 541, § 46.1-299; 1962, c. 89; 1968, c. 99; 1972, c. 445; 1974, c. 347; 1979, c. 44; 1989, c. 727.

§ 46.2-1040. Hazard lights.

Motor vehicles, trailers, and semitrailers, when temporarily stopped on the traveled or paved portion of the highway so as to create a traffic hazard, shall flash all four turn signals simultaneously to signal approaching motorists of the existing hazard whenever such vehicle is equipped with a device which will cause the four turn signals to flash simultaneously. All four turn signals may be flashed simultaneously on a vehicle slowed or stopped at the scene of a traffic hazard, when traveling as part of a funeral procession, or when traveling at a speed of thirty miles per hour or less. Except for vehicles traveling as part of a funeral procession, all four turn signals shall not be flashed simultaneously while the vehicle is traveling faster than thirty miles per hour.

School buses shall flash all four turn signals when approaching and stopping at railroad grade crossings.

History.
Code 1950, § 46-303; 1958, c. 541, § 46.1-299; 1962, c. 89; 1968, c. 99; 1972, c. 445; 1974, c. 347; 1979, c. 44; 1989, c. 727; 2001, c. 359.

ARTICLE 4.
TIRES.

§ 46.2-1041. Restrictions as to solid rubber tires.

Every tire, other than a pneumatic tire, made of rubber on a vehicle moved on any highway shall have rubber on its entire traction surface at least one inch thick above the edge of the flange of the entire periphery. No vehicle equipped with such tires shall be operated on any highway in the Commonwealth unless a permit therefor is first secured from the Department of Transportation.

History.
Code 1950, § 46-299; 1958, c. 541, § 46.1-295; 1989, c. 727; 2013, cc. 585, 646.

§ 46.2-1042. Standard for vehicle tire; sale of certain tires prohibited; penalty.

No person shall sell or offer for sale, or have in his possession with intent to sell any motor vehicle tire unless that tire (i) meets or exceeds standards established by the Society of Automotive Engineers, the American National Standards Institute, Inc., or the federal Department of Transportation and (ii) is marked in accordance with those standards.

No person shall knowingly operate on any highway in the Commonwealth a Virginia registered motor vehicle equipped with any regrooved or recut tire unless that tire (i) meets or exceeds standards established by the Society of Automotive Engineers, the American National Standards Institute, Inc., or the federal Department of Transportation and (ii) is marked in accordance with those standards.

Any person violating the provisions of this section shall be guilty of a Class 1 misdemeanor.

History.
1966, c. 490, § 46.1-295.2; 1989, c. 727; 1996, c. 92.

§ 46.2-1043. Tire tread depth.

A. No person shall operate a motor vehicle, trailer, or semitrailer on any highway in the Commonwealth if it is equipped with one or more tires which:

1. When measured in any two adjacent major tread grooves where the tread is thinnest, at three equally spaced intervals around the circumference of the tire and exclusive of "tiebars" by a tread depth gauge calibrated in thirty-seconds of an inch, are found to have tread depth of less than two thirty-seconds of an inch at such locations; or

2. When equipped with tread wear indicators, are found to have such indicators in contact with pavement at any two adjacent grooves at three equally spaced intervals around the circumference of the tire.

B. No motor vehicle, trailer, or semitrailer shall be issued a safety inspection approval sticker if equipped with any tire whose use is prohibited under the provisions of this section.

C. This section shall not apply to tires mounted on dual wheels installed on motor vehicles which have seats for more than seven passengers and are (i) operated wholly within a municipality, or (ii) operated by urban and suburban bus lines. For purposes of this section, "urban and suburban bus lines" are defined as bus lines operating over regular scheduled routes the majority of whose passengers use the buses for traveling one-way distances not exceeding forty miles on the same day between their residence and their place of work, shopping areas, or schools.

D. The foregoing exemptions shall not apply to buses owned or operated by any public school district, private school, or contract operator of school buses.

E. The provisions of this section shall not apply to any vehicle not required to be registered or licensed.

History.
1968, c. 145, § 46.1-295.3; 1973, c. 162; 1983, c. 281; 1984, c. 125; 1989, c. 727.

§ 46.2-1043.1. Tire loading.

No person shall operate for a commercial purpose a truck, trailer, or semitrailer with tires on any highway in the Commonwealth if any officer authorized to enforce overweight vehicle laws determines upon weighing such truck, trailer, or semitrailer that any such tire carries a weight greater than 125 percent of that marked on the sidewall of the tire.

The provisions of this section shall not apply to:

1. Any vehicle that is being operated under the terms of a permit issued under Article 18 (§ 46.2-1139 et seq.) and is being operated at a reduced speed as required by the permit to compensate for the tire loading in excess of the manufacturer's rated capacity for the tire;
2. Any vehicle having a gross vehicle weight rating of 26,001 pounds or more;
3. Any manufactured home; or
4. Any vehicle not required to be registered.

History.
2013, c. 430.

§ 46.2-1044. Cleats, etc., on tires; chains; tires with studs.

No tire on a vehicle moved on a highway shall have on its periphery any block, stud, flange, cleat, spike, or any other protuberance of any material other than rubber which projects beyond the tread of the traction surface of the tire. It shall be permissible, however, to use on the highways farm machinery having protuberances which will not injure the highway and to use tire chains of reasonable proportions when required for safety because of snow, ice, or other conditions tending to cause a vehicle to slide or skid. It shall also be permissible to use on any vehicle whose gross weight does not exceed 10,000 pounds tires with studs which project no more than one-sixteenth of an inch beyond the tread of the traction surface of the tire when compressed if the studs cover no more than three percent of the traction surface of the tire.

The use of studded tires shall be permissible only from October 15 to April 15.

The provisions of this section shall not apply to any (i) law-enforcement vehicle operated by or under the direction of a federal, state, or local law-enforcement officer; (ii) vehicle used to fight fire, including publicly owned state forest warden vehicles; (iii) emergency medical services vehicle; or (iv) vehicle owned or operated by the Virginia Department of Transportation or its contractors in maintenance and emergency response operations.

History.

Code 1950, § 46-300; 1958, c. 541, § 46.1-296; 1968, c. 1; 1970, c. 263; 1972, c. 39; 1974, c. 368; 1976, c. 315; 1978, c. 259; 1989, c. 727; 2009, c. 118; 2015, cc. 502, 503.

§ 46.2-1045. Sale of tires having cleats, etc., prohibited; studded tires excepted.

No person shall sell to any resident of the Commonwealth a tire which shall have on its periphery any block, stud, flange, cleat, spike, or any other protuberance of any material other than rubber which projects beyond the tread of the traction surface of the tire. Farm machinery having protuberances which will not injure the highway and tire chains of reasonable proportions may, however, be sold. It shall also be permissible to sell studded tires whose use is permitted under the provisions of this article. Violation of this section shall constitute a Class 1 misdemeanor.

History.

1966, c. 592, § 46.1-296.1; 1968, c. 1; 1970, c. 263; 1989, c. 727.

§ 46.2-1046. Traction engines and tractors.

The Commissioner of Highways and local authorities in their respective jurisdictions may, in their discretion, issue special permits authorizing the operation on a highway of traction engines or tractors having movable tracks with transverse corrugations upon the periphery of such movable tracks.

History.

Code 1950, § 46-301; 1958, c. 541, § 46.1-297; 1989, c. 727; 2013, cc. 585, 646.

ARTICLE 5. EXHAUST SYSTEM.

§ 46.2-1047. Muffler cutout, etc., illegal.

It shall be unlawful to sell or offer for sale any (i) muffler without interior baffle plates or other effective muffling device or (ii) gutted muffler, muffler cutout, or straight exhaust. It shall be unlawful for any person to operate on the highways in the Commonwealth a motor vehicle, moped, or motorized skateboard or foot-scooter equipped with a gutted muffler, muffler cutout, or straight exhaust.

History.

Code 1950, § 46-306; 1950, p. 54; 1958, c. 541, § 46.1-302; 1964, c. 628; 1989, c. 727; 2006, cc. 529, 538; 2013, c. 783.

§ 46.2-1048. Pollution control systems or devices.

No motor vehicle registered in the Commonwealth and manufactured for the model year 1973 or for subsequent model years shall be operated on the highways in the Commonwealth unless it is equipped with an air pollution control system, device, or combination of such systems or devices installed in accordance with federal laws and regulations.

It shall be unlawful for any person to operate a motor vehicle, as herein described, on the highways in the Commonwealth with its pollution control system or device removed or otherwise rendered inoperable.

It shall be unlawful for any person to operate on the highways in the Commonwealth a motor vehicle, as described in this section, equipped with any emission control system or device unless it is of a type installed as standard factory equipment, or comparable to that designed for use upon the particular vehicle as standard factory equipment.

No motor vehicle, as described in this section, shall be issued a safety inspection approval sticker unless it is equipped as provided under the foregoing provisions of this section or if it violates this section.

The provisions of this section shall not prohibit or prevent shop adjustments or replacements of equipment for maintenance or repair or the conversion of engines to low polluting fuels, such as, but not limited to, natural gas or propane, so long as such action does not degrade the antipollution capabilities of the vehicle power system.

The provisions of this section shall not apply to converted electric vehicles.

History.

1972, c. 640, § 46.1-301.1; 1973, c. 5; 1989, c. 727; 2012, c. 177.

§ 46.2-1049. Exhaust system in good working order.

No person shall drive and no owner of a vehicle shall permit or allow the operation of any such vehicle on a highway unless it is equipped with an exhaust system in good working order and in constant operation to prevent excessive or unusual levels of noise; provided however, that for motor vehicles, such exhaust system shall be of a type installed as standard factory equipment, or comparable to that designed for use on the particular vehicle as standard factory equipment. An exhaust system shall not be deemed to prevent excessive or unusual noise if it permits the escape of noise in excess of that permitted by the standard factory equipment exhaust system of private passenger motor vehicles or trucks of standard make.

The term "exhaust system," as used in this section, means all the parts of a vehicle through which the exhaust passes after leaving the engine block, including mufflers and other sound dissipative devices.

Chambered pipes are not an effective muffling device to prevent excessive or unusual noise, and any vehicle equipped with chambered pipes shall be deemed in violation of this section.

The provisions of this section shall not apply to (i) any antique motor vehicle manufactured prior to 1950, provided the engine is comparable to that designed as standard factory equipment for use on that particular vehicle, and the exhaust system is in good working order, or (ii) converted electric vehicles.

History.

Code 1950, § 46-305; 1952, c. 455; 1956, c. 651; 1958, c. 541, § 46.1-301; 1960, c. 120; 1970, c. 266; 1972, c. 66; 1989, c. 727; 2006, cc. 529, 538; 2012, c. 177; 2015, cc. 77, 165.

§ 46.2-1050. Mufflers on motorcycles.

It shall be unlawful for any person to operate or cause to be operated any motorcycle not equipped with a muffler or other sound dissipative device in good working order and in constant operation.

No person shall remove or render inoperative, or cause to be removed or rendered inoperative, other than for purposes of maintenance, repair or replacement, any muffler or sound dissipative device on a motorcycle.

History.

1976, c. 65, § 46.1-302.3; 1989, c. 727.

§ 46.2-1051. Certain local governments may impose restrictions on operations of certain vehicles.

The governing body of any county, city, or town which is located within the Northern Virginia Planning District may provide by ordinance that no person shall operate and no owner shall permit the operation of, either on a highway or on public or private property within 500 feet of any residential district, any motorcycle, moped, all-terrain vehicle as defined in § 46.2-100, not being used for agriculture or silviculture production as defined in § 3.2-300, electric power-assisted bicycle, motorcycle-like device commonly known as a trail-bike or mini-bike, off-road motorcycle, or motorized cart commonly known as a go-cart unless it is equipped with an exhaust system of a type installed as standard equipment, or comparable to that designed for use on that particular vehicle or device as standard factory equipment, in good working order and in constant operation to prevent excessive noise.

History.

1983, c. 211, § 46.1-302.4; 1989, c. 727; 2004, cc. 947, 973; 2006, cc. 830, 896.

ARTICLE 6.

WINDSHIELDS AND WINDOWS.

§ 46.2-1052. Tinting films, signs, decals, and stickers on windshields, etc.; penalties.

A. Except as otherwise provided in this article or permitted by federal law, it shall be unlawful for any person to operate any motor vehicle on a highway with any sign, poster, colored or tinted film, sun-shading material, or other colored material on the windshield, front or rear side windows, or rear windows of such motor vehicle. This provision, however, shall not apply to any certificate or other paper required by law or permitted by the Superintendent to be placed on a motor vehicle's windshield or window.

The size of stickers or decals used by counties, cities, and towns in lieu of license plates shall be in compliance with regulations promulgated by the Superintendent. Such stickers shall be affixed on the windshield at a location designated by the Superintendent.

B. Notwithstanding the foregoing provisions of this section, whenever a motor vehicle is equipped with a mirror on each side of such vehicle, so located as to reflect to the driver of such vehicle a view of the highway for at least 200 feet to the rear of such vehicle, any or all of the following shall be lawful:

1. To drive a motor vehicle equipped with one optically grooved clear plastic right-angle rear view lens attached to one rear window of such motor vehicle, not exceeding 18 inches in diameter in the case of a circular lens or not exceeding 11 inches by 14 inches in the case of a rectangular lens, which enables the driver of the motor vehicle to view below the line of sight as viewed through the rear window;

2. To have affixed to the rear side windows, rear window or windows of a motor vehicle any sticker or stickers, regardless of size; or

3. To drive a motor vehicle when the driver's clear view of the highway through the rear window or windows is otherwise obstructed.

C. Except as provided in § 46.2-1053, but notwithstanding the foregoing provisions of this section, no sun-shading or tinting film may be applied or affixed to any window of a motor vehicle unless such motor vehicle is equipped with a mirror on each side of such motor vehicle, so located as to reflect to the driver of the vehicle a view of the highway for at least 200 feet to the rear of such vehicle, and the sun-shading or tinting film is applied or affixed in accordance with the following:

1. No sun-shading or tinting films may be applied or affixed to the rear side windows or rear window or windows of any motor vehicle operated on the highways of the Commonwealth that reduce the total light transmittance of such window to less than 35 percent;

2. No sun-shading or tinting films may be applied or affixed to the front side windows of any motor vehicle operated on the highways of the Commonwealth that reduce total light transmittance of such window to less than 50 percent;

3. No sun-shading or tinting films shall be applied or affixed to any window of a motor vehicle that (i) have a reflectance of light exceeding 20 percent or (ii) produce a holographic or prism effect.

Any person who operates a motor vehicle on the highways of the Commonwealth with sun-shading or tinting films that (i) have a total light transmittance less than that required by subdivisions 1 and 2, (ii) have a reflectance of light exceeding 20 percent, or (iii) produce holographic or prism effects is guilty of a traffic infraction but shall not be awarded any demerit points by the Commissioner for the violation.

Any person or firm who applies or affixes to the windows of any motor vehicle in Virginia sun-shading or tinting films that (i) reduce the light transmittance to levels less than that allowed in subdivisions 1 and 2, (ii) have a reflectance of light exceeding 20 percent, or (iii) produce holographic or prism effects is guilty of a Class 3 misdemeanor for the first offense and of a Class 2 misdemeanor for any subsequent offense.

D. The Division of Purchases and Supply, pursuant to § 2.2-1112, shall determine the proper standards for equipment or devices used to measure light transmittance through windows of motor vehicles. Law-enforcement officers shall use only such equipment or devices to measure light transmittance through windows that meet the standards established by the Division. Such measurements made by law-enforcement officers shall be given a tolerance of minus seven percentage points.

E. No film or darkening material may be applied on the windshield except to replace the sunshield in the uppermost area as installed by the manufacturer of the vehicle.

F. Nothing in this section shall prohibit the affixing to the rear window of a motor vehicle of a single sticker no larger than 20 square inches if such sticker is totally contained within the lower five inches of the glass of the rear window, nor shall subsection B apply to a motor vehicle to which but one such sticker is so affixed.

G. Nothing in this section shall prohibit applying to the rear side windows or rear window of any multipurpose passenger vehicle or pickup truck sun-shading or tinting films that reduce the total light transmittance of such window or windows below 35 percent.

H. As used in this article:

"Front side windows" means those windows located adjacent to and forward of the driver's seat;

"Holographic effect" means a picture or image that may remain constant or change as the viewing angle is changed;

"Multipurpose passenger vehicle" means any motor vehicle that is (i) designed to carry no more than 10 persons and (ii) constructed either on a truck chassis or with special features for occasional off-road use;

"Prism effect" means a visual, iridescent, or rainbow-like effect that separates light into various colored components that may change depending on viewing angle;

"Rear side windows" means those windows located to the rear of the driver's seat;

"Rear window" or *"rear windows"* means those windows which are located to the rear of the passenger compartment of a motor vehicle and which are approximately parallel to the windshield.

I. Notwithstanding the foregoing provisions of this section, sun-shading material which was applied or installed prior to July 1, 1987, in a manner and on which windows not then in violation of Virginia law, shall continue to be lawful, provided that it can be shown by appropriate receipts that such material was installed prior to July 1, 1987.

J. Where a person is convicted within one year of a second or subsequent violation of this section involving the operation of the same vehicle having a tinted or smoked windshield, the court, in addition to any other penalty, may order the person so convicted to remove such tinted or smoked windshield from the vehicle.

K. The provisions of this section shall not apply to law-enforcement vehicles.

L. The provisions of this section shall not apply to the rear windows or rear side windows of any emergency medical services vehicle used to transport patients.

M. The provisions of subdivision C 1 shall not apply to sight-seeing carriers as defined in § 46.2-2000 and contract passenger carriers as defined in § 46.2-2000.

History.

Code 1950, § 46-295; 1958, c. 541, § 46.1-291; 1970, c. 16; 1978, c. 233; 1981, cc. 17, 626; 1985, c. 160; 1987, cc. 298, 315; 1988, c. 751; 1989, c. 727; 1991, cc. 100, 328; 1993, c. 808; 1994, c. 118; 1997, cc.

744, 880; 1998, c. 133; 1999, c. 75; 2004, c. 613; 2008, c. 189; 2015, cc. 502, 503.

§ 46.2-1053. Equipping certain motor vehicles with sun-shading or tinting films or applications.

Notwithstanding the provisions of § 46.2-1052, a motor vehicle operated by or regularly used to transport any person with a medical condition which renders him susceptible to harm or injury from exposure to sunlight or bright artificial light may be equipped, on its windshield and any or all of its windows, with sun-shading or tinting films or applications which reduce the transmission of light into the vehicle to levels not less than thirty-five percent. Such sun-shading or tinting film when applied to the windshield of a motor vehicle shall not cause the total light transmittance to be reduced to any level less than seventy percent except for the upper five inches of such windshield or the AS-1 line, whichever is closer to the top of the windshield. Vehicles equipped with such sun-shading or tinting films shall not be operated on any highway unless, while being so operated, the driver or an occupant of the vehicle has in his possession a written authorization issued by the Commissioner of the Department of Motor Vehicles authorizing such operation. The Commissioner shall issue such written authorization only upon receipt of a signed statement from a licensed physician or licensed optometrist (i) identifying with reasonable specificity the person seeking the written authorization and (ii) stating that, in the physician's or optometrist's professional opinion, the equipping of a vehicle with sun-shading or tinting films or applications is necessary to safeguard the health of the person seeking the written authorization. Written authorizations issued by the Commissioner under this section shall be valid so long as the condition requiring the use of sun-shading or tinting films or applications persists or until the vehicle is sold, whichever first occurs. Such written authorizations shall permit the approval of any such vehicle upon its safety inspection as required by this chapter if such vehicle otherwise qualifies for inspection approval. In the discretion of the Commissioner, one or more written authorizations may be issued to an individual or a family. The Division of Purchases and Supply, pursuant to § 2.2-1112, shall determine the proper standards for equipment or devices used to measure light transmittance through windows of motor vehicles. Law-enforcement officers shall use only such equipment or devices to measure light transmittance through windows that meet the standards established by the Division. Such measurements made by law-enforcement officers shall be given a tolerance of minus seven percentage points.

History.
1986, c. 67, § 46.1-291.01; 1987, c. 391; 1989, cc. 65, 727; 1990, c. 161; 1993, cc. 800, 808; 1996, cc. 943, 994.

§ 46.2-1054. Suspension of objects or alteration of vehicle so as to obstruct driver's view.

It shall be unlawful for any person to drive a motor vehicle on a highway in the Commonwealth with any object or objects, other than a rear view mirror, sun visor, or other equipment of the motor vehicle approved by the Superintendent, suspended from any part of the motor vehicle in such a manner as to obstruct the driver's clear view of the highway through the windshield, the front side windows, or the rear window, or to alter a passenger-carrying vehicle in such a manner as to obstruct the driver's view through the windshield. However, this section shall not apply (i) when the driver's clear view of the highway through the rear window is obstructed if such motor vehicle is equipped with a mirror on each side, so located as to reflect to the driver a view of the highway for at least 200 feet to the rear of such vehicle, (ii) to safety devices installed on the windshields of vehicles owned by private waste haulers or local governments and used to transport solid waste, or (iii) to bicycle racks installed on the front of any bus operated by any city, county, transit authority, or transit or transportation district.

History.
1960, c. 122, § 46.1-291.1; 1972, cc. 8, 844; 1987, c. 135; 1989, c. 727; 2003, c. 273.

§ 46.2-1055. Windshield wipers.

Every permanent windshield on a motor vehicle shall be equipped with a device for cleaning snow, rain, moisture, or other matter from the windshield directly in front of the driver. The device shall be so constructed as to be controlled or operated by the driver of the vehicle. Every such device on a school bus or a vehicle designed or used to carry passengers for compensation or hire or as a public conveyance shall be of a mechanically or electrically operated type. The device or devices on any motor vehicle manufactured or assembled after January 1, 1943, shall clean both the right and left sides of the windshield and shall be of a mechanically or electrically operated type.

History.
Code 1950, § 46-296; 1958, c. 541, § 46.1-292; 1989, c. 727.

§ 46.2-1055.1. Windshield defroster or defogger.

Every Virginia-registered motor vehicle manufactured for the 1969 or subsequent model years and required to be equipped with a windshield shall be equipped with a windshield defroster or defogger. The defroster or defogger shall be in good working order at all times when the vehicle is operated on the highways.

History.
1990, c. 955.

§ 46.2-1056. When safety glass required.

It shall be unlawful for any person to drive on any highway a motor vehicle registered in the Commonwealth and manufactured or assembled after January 1, 1935, and designed or used for the purpose of carrying persons for compensation or hire or as a public conveyance to transport school children and others, unless such vehicle is equipped with safety glass wherever glass is used in doors, windows, and windshields.

It shall be unlawful to drive on any highway any motor vehicle registered in the Commonwealth, manufactured or assembled after January 1, 1936, unless the vehicle is equipped with safety glass approved by the Superintendent, or meets the standards and specifications of the American National Standards Institute, Incorporated, or the regulations of the federal Department of Transportation whenever glass is used in doors, windows, and windshields.

The term "safety glass" as used in this section shall mean any product composed of glass so manufactured, fabricated or treated as substantially to prevent shattering and flying of the glass when struck or broken. The Commissioner shall maintain a list of types of glass approved by the Superintendent as conforming to the specifications and requirements for safety glass as set forth in this section and shall not issue a license for or relicense any motor vehicle subject to the provisions herein stated unless such motor vehicle is equipped as herein provided with the approved type of glass.

No glazing material other than safety glass shall be used in any motor vehicle registered in the Commonwealth, except that the Superintendent may permit safety glazing materials other than glass to be used in lieu of safety glass in portions of motor vehicles, trailers, and semitrailers designated by him, provided any such material bears a trade name or identifying mark, and has been submitted to and approved by the Superintendent.

If any person drives any vehicle in violation of this section while under a certificate issued by the State Corporation Commission, in addition to the penalty provided in § 46.2-113, the certificate of such person may, in the discretion of the State Corporation Commission, be suspended until this section is satisfactorily complied with.

Replacement safety glass installed in any part of a vehicle other than the windshield need not bear a trademark or name, provided (i) the glass consists of two or more sheets of glass separated by a glazing material, (ii) the glass is cut from a piece of approved safety glass, and (iii) the edge of the glass can be observed.

History.

Code 1950, § 46-297; 1950, p. 698; 1958, c. 541, § 46.1-293; 1960, c. 125; 1968, c. 172; 1970, c. 18; 1989, c. 727.

§ 46.2-1057. Windshields.

It shall be unlawful for any person to drive on a highway in the Commonwealth any motor vehicle or reconstructed motor vehicle, other than a motorcycle or autocycle, registered in the Commonwealth that was manufactured, assembled, or reconstructed after July 1, 1970, unless the motor vehicle is equipped with a windshield.

History.

1970, c. 22, § 46.1-293.1; 1989, c. 727; 2014, cc. 53, 256.

§ 46.2-1058. Replacement of glass in vehicle.

It shall be unlawful for any person to replace any glass in any vehicle with any material other than an approved type of safety glass. Safety glazing materials other than glass approved by the Superintendent as provided in § 46.2-1056 may, however, be used to replace safety glass in any portion of a motor vehicle which has been designated for such use by the Superintendent.

History.

Code 1950, § 46-298; 1950, p. 699; 1958, c. 541, § 46.1-294; 1989, c. 727.

ARTICLE 7.
HORNS, SIRENS, AND WHISTLES.

§ 46.2-1059. Horns.

Every motor vehicle driven on a highway shall be equipped with a working horn capable of emitting sound audible under normal conditions for at least 200 feet.

History.

Code 1950, § 46-289; 1958, c. 541, § 46.1-283; 1989, c. 727.

§ 46.2-1060. Illegal sirens, whistles, etc.; unlawful use of warning devices; exceptions.

It shall be unlawful for any vehicle to be equipped with or for any person to use on any vehicle any siren or exhaust, compression or spark plug whistle, or horn except as may be authorized in this title. It shall be unlawful for any vehicle operated on a public highway to be equipped with any warning device that is not of a type that has been approved by the Superintendent. It shall further be unlawful for any person at any time to use a horn otherwise than as a reasonable warning or to make any unnecessary or unreasonably loud or harsh sound by means of a horn or other warning device. However, vehicles of common carriers or extraordinarily large and heavy vehicles may be equipped with such type of warning device as the Superintendent may require or permit.

Notwithstanding the provisions of this article, a siren, bell, or supplemental horn may be used on a vehicle as a noisemaker for an alarm system if the device is installed so as to prohibit actuation of the system by the driver while the vehicle is in motion.

History.
Code 1950, § 46-290; 1958, c. 541, § 46.1-284; 1962, c. 146; 1970, c. 283; 1989, c. 727.

§ 46.2-1061. Sirens or exhaust whistles on emergency vehicles.

Every law-enforcement vehicle, every vehicle authorized to be equipped with warning lights pursuant to §§ 46.2-1022 and 46.2-1023 shall be equipped with a siren, exhaust whistle, or air horn designed to give automatically intermittent signals. Such devices shall be of types not prohibited by the Superintendent.

History.
Code 1950, § 46-291; 1958, c. 541, § 46.1-285; 1960, c. 391; 1966, cc. 655, 664, 699; 1968, c. 89; 1980, c. 337; 1989, c. 727; 1990, c. 418.

§ 46.2-1062. Approval of warning devices.

The Superintendent may promulgate regulations relating to the construction, mounting, use, and number of warning devices for which there shall be an approval fee as prescribed in § 46.2-1008.

History.
Code 1950, § 46-293; 1958, c. 541, § 46.1-286; 1989, c. 727.

ARTICLE 8.
STEERING AND SUSPENSION SYSTEMS.

§ 46.2-1063. Alteration of suspension system; bumper height limits; raising body above frame rail.

No person shall drive on a public highway any motor vehicle registered as a passenger motor vehicle if it has been modified by alteration of its altitude from the ground to the extent that its bumpers, measured to any point on the lower edge of the main horizontal bumper bar, exclusive of any bumper guards, are not within the range of fourteen inches to twenty-two inches above the ground. Notwithstanding the foregoing provisions of this section, the range of bumper heights for motor vehicles bearing street rod license plates issued pursuant to § 46.2-747 shall be nine to twenty-two inches.

No vehicle shall be modified to cause the vehicle body or chassis to come in contact with the ground, expose the fuel tank to damage from collision, or cause the wheels to come in contact with the body under normal operation. No part of the original suspension system of a motor vehicle shall be disconnected to defeat the safe operation of its suspension system. However, nothing contained in this section shall prevent the installation of heavy duty equipment, including shock absorbers and overload springs. Nothing contained in this section shall prohibit the driving on a public highway of a motor vehicle with normal wear to the suspension system if such normal wear does not adversely affect the control of the vehicle.

No person shall drive on a public highway any motor vehicle registered as a truck if it has been modified by alteration of its altitude from the ground to the extent that its bumpers, measured to any point on the lower edge of the main horizontal bumper bar, exclusive of any bumper guards, do not fall within the limits specified herein for its gross vehicle weight rating category. The front bumper height of trucks whose gross vehicle weight ratings are 4,500 pounds or less shall be no less than 14 inches and no more than 28 inches, and their rear bumper height shall be no less than 14 inches and no more than 28 inches. The front bumper height of trucks whose gross vehicle weight ratings are 4,501 pounds to 7,500 pounds shall be no less than 14 inches and no more than 29 inches, and their rear bumper height shall be no less than 14 inches and no more than 30 inches. The front bumper height of trucks whose gross vehicle weight ratings are 7,501 pounds to 15,000 pounds shall be no less than 14 inches and no more than 30 inches, and their rear bumper height shall be no less than 14 inches and no more than 31 inches. Bumper height limitations contained in this section shall not apply to trucks with gross vehicle weight ratings in excess of 15,000 pounds. For the purpose of this section, "truck" includes pickup and panel trucks, and "gross vehicle weight ratings" means manufacturer's gross vehicle weight ratings established for that vehicle as indicated by a number, plate, sticker, decal, or other device affixed to the vehicle by its manufacturer.

In the absence of bumpers, and in cases where bumper heights have been lowered, height measurements under the foregoing provisions of this section shall be made to the bottom of the frame rail. However, if bumper heights have been raised, height measurements under the foregoing provisions of this section shall be made to the bottom of the main horizontal bumper bar.

No vehicle shall be operated on a public highway if it has been modified by any means so as to raise its body more than three inches, in addition to any manufacturer's spacers and bushings, above the vehicle's frame rail or manufacturer's attachment points on the frame rail.

This section shall not apply to specially designed or modified motor vehicles when driven off the public highways in races and similar events. Such motor vehicles may be lawfully towed on the highways of the Commonwealth.

History.
1973, c. 498, § 46.1-282.1; 1978, c. 605; 1980, c. 342; 1986, c. 570; 1989, c. 727; 1991, c. 688; 1992, c. 864; 1993, c. 73.

§ 46.2-1064. Modification of front-end suspension by use of lift blocks.

No motor vehicle whose front-end suspension has been modified by the use of lift blocks shall be driven on any highway in the Commonwealth.

History.

1985, c. 11, § 46.1-282.2; 1989, c. 727.

§ 46.2-1065. Steering gear; installation, sale, etc., of repair kit or preventive maintenance kit for use on part of steering gear prohibited.

Every motor vehicle driven on a highway shall be equipped with steering gear adequate to ensure the safe control of the vehicle. Such steering gear shall not show signs of weakness or breaking under ordinary conditions. The Superintendent may promulgate regulations establishing standards of adequacy of steering gear, which shall be the current standard specifications of steering gear adopted by the United States Bureau of Standards or the Society of Automotive Engineers, or the regulations of the federal Department of Transportation, for determining whether or not any motor vehicle operated on any highway conforms to the requirements of the Department of State Police.

No Virginia-registered motor vehicle shall be issued a safety inspection approval sticker or be operated on a highway in the Commonwealth if equipped with a repair kit or preventive maintenance kit installed on a tie rod end, idler arm, ball joint or any other part of the vehicle's steering gear.

It shall be unlawful for any person to sell or offer for sale any repair kit or preventive maintenance kit for use on a tie rod end, idler arm, ball joint, or any other part of a vehicle's steering gear to prevent wear or to repair or remove play or looseness in the steering gear components.

Nothing contained in this section shall prohibit or prevent shop adjustments or the replacement of parts or complete components of a motor vehicle's steering gear that meet Society of Automotive Engineers standards of excellence, in order to correct deficiencies in the steering gear.

History.

Code 1950, § 46-288; 1958, c. 541, § 46.1-282; 1968, c. 172; 1970, c. 23; 1983, c. 226; 1989, c. 727.

ARTICLE 9.

BRAKES.

§ 46.2-1066. Brakes.

Every motor vehicle when driven on a highway shall be equipped with brakes adequate to control the movements of and to stop and hold such vehicle. The brakes shall be maintained in good working order and shall conform to the provisions of this article.

Every bicycle, electric power-assisted bicycle, and moped, when operated on a highway, shall be equipped with a brake that will enable the operator to make the braked wheels skid on dry, level, clean pavement. Every electric personal assistive mobility device, when operated on a highway, shall be equipped with a system that, when activated or engaged, will enable the operator to bring the device to a controlled stop.

History.

Code 1950, § 46-283; 1958, c. 541, § 46.1-277; 1974, c. 347; 1981, c. 585; 1989, c. 727; 2001, c. 834; 2002, c. 254.

§ 46.2-1067. Within what distances brakes should stop vehicle.

On a dry, hard, approximately level stretch of highway free from loose material, the service braking system shall be capable of stopping a motor vehicle or combination of vehicles at all times and under all conditions of loading at a speed of 20 miles per hour within the following distances:

1. Passenger motor vehicles, except buses and antique vehicles, 25 feet.
2. Buses, trucks, and tractor trucks, 40 feet.
3. Motor vehicles registered or qualified to be registered as antique vehicles, when equipped with two-wheel brakes, 45 feet; four-wheel brakes, 25 feet.
4. All combinations of vehicles, 40 feet.
5. Motorcycles or autocycles, 30 feet.

History.

Code 1950, § 46-284; 1958, c. 541, § 46.1-278; 1968, c. 164; 1970, c. 28; 1972, c. 3; 1989, c. 727; 2014, cc. 53, 256.

§ 46.2-1068. Emergency or parking brakes.

Every motor vehicle and combination of vehicles, except motorcycles or autocycles, shall be equipped with emergency or parking brakes adequate to hold the vehicle or vehicles on any grade on which it is operated, under all conditions of loading on a surface free from snow, ice, or loose material.

History.

1968, c. 164, § 46.1-278.1; 1989, c. 727; 2014, cc. 53, 256.

§ 46.2-1069. Brakes on motorcycles.

Every motorcycle manufactured after July 1, 1974, and driven on a highway in the Commonwealth shall be equipped with either a split-service brake system or two independently actuated brake systems which shall act on the front as well as the rear wheel or wheels.

It shall be unlawful for any person to drive on a highway in the Commonwealth a motorcycle which was originally equipped with a brake system on both the front or rear wheel or wheels if the brake system has been altered by removing or disconnecting any of the brake-system components from any of the wheels.

History.
1974, c. 219, § 46.1-279.1; 1989, c. 727.

§ 46.2-1070. Brakes on trailers.

Every semitrailer, trailer, or separate vehicle attached by a drawbar, chain, or coupling to a towing vehicle other than a farm tractor or a vehicle not required to obtain a registration certificate and having an actual gross weight of 3,000 pounds or more, shall be equipped with brakes controlled or operated by the driver of the towing vehicle, which shall conform to the specifications set forth in § 46.2-1067 and shall be of a type approved by the Superintendent. Farm trailers used exclusively for hauling raw agricultural produce from farm to farm or farm to packing shed or processing plant within the normal growing area of thc packing shed or processing plant and trailers or semitrailers drawn by a properly licensed motor vehicle but exempt from registration, shall be exempt from the requirements of this section.

"Gross weight" for the purpose of this section includes weight of the vehicle and the load upon such semitrailer, trailer, or separate vehicle.

This section shall not apply to any vehicle being towed for repairs, repossession, in an emergency, or being moved by a tow truck when two wheels of the towed vehicle are off the ground.

History.
Code 1950, § 46-286; 1958, c. 541, § 46.1-280; 1959, Ex. Sess., cc. 21, 90; 1962, c. 313; 1966, c. 654; 1968, c. 164; 1970, c. 169; 1989, c. 727; 2006, cc. 874, 891.

§ 46.2-1071. Requirements for parking.

No person having control of a motor vehicle shall allow such vehicle to stand on any highway unattended without first effectively setting the emergency or parking brake thereon, stopping the motor, and turning the front wheels into the curb or side of the roadway.

History.
Code 1950, § 46-287; 1958, c. 541, § 46.1-281; 1989, c. 727.

ARTICLE 10.

MISCELLANEOUS EQUIPMENT.

§ 46.2-1072. Operation of vehicle without serial or identification number; requirements for stamping, cutting, or embossing numbers; regulations.

It shall be unlawful to sell or to drive on any highway in the Commonwealth any motor vehicle which does not have stamped on or cut into its motor its motor number or which does not bear a permanent serial or other identification number assigned by the manufacturer or by the Commissioner, or any trailer or semitrailer which does not bear a permanent serial or other identification number assigned by its manufacturer or the Commissioner. The number shall be stamped, cut, embossed, or attached in such a manner that it cannot be changed, altered, or removed without plainly showing evidence which would be readily detectable or which would destroy the attached plate. The number shall be die stamped, cut, or embossed into or attached to a permanent part of the vehicle which is easily accessible for verification. However, nonresident owners who are permitted to operate motor vehicles, trailers, or semitrailers without registration, under the registration provision relating to nonresidents contained in §§ 46.2-655 through 46.2-661 shall not be required to comply with this section before operating a motor vehicle, trailer, or semitrailer on the highways in the Commonwealth.

The Commissioner may adopt regulations to carry out the provisions of this section.

History.
Code 1950, § 46-11; 1952, c. 545; 1958, c. 541, § 46.1-84; 1978, c. 294; 1989, c. 727; 1997, c. 96.

§ 46.2-1072.1. Fees.

The Commissioner may charge a fee of $125 per vehicle, for the examination, verification, or identification of the serial or identification number of any vehicle, motor vehicle, trailer, or semitrailer. The Commissioner may also receive applications for the issuance of an identification number and investigate the circumstances of the application. When the Commissioner is satisfied that the applicant is entitled to the identification number, the fee for the issuance of such identification number shall be five dollars. If any inspection under this provision is done at the same time as an inspection under § 46.2-1605, then only one $125 fee shall be charged for both inspections. All fees collected under this section shall be paid by the Commissioner into the state treasury and set aside as a special fund to be used to meet the expenses of the vehicle identification number and salvage vehicle inspection program.

History.
1997, c. 96; 2006, c. 615.

§ 46.2-1073. Engine or serial number illegible, removed, or obliterated.

The owner of a motor vehicle, trailer, or semitrailer on which the engine, serial, or other identification number has become illegible or has been removed or obliterated shall immediately apply to the Department for a new identification number for such motor vehicle, trailer, or semitrailer. The Department, when satisfied that the applicant is the lawful owner or possessor of the motor vehicle, trailer, or semitrailer may assign a new identification number and shall require that such number, together with the name of the Commonwealth or a symbol indicating the Commonwealth and the date of such assignment, be stamped, inscribed or affixed upon such portion of the motor vehicle, trailer, or semitrailer as shall be designated by the Department. Whenever a new identification number has been assigned to and stamped, inscribed or affixed on a motor vehicle, trailer, or semitrailer as provided in this section, the Department shall insert the number on the registration card and certificate of title or salvage/nonrepairable certificate issued the motor vehicle, trailer, or semitrailer.

History.
Code 1950, § 46-6; 1958, c. 541, § 46.1-4; 1989, c. 727; 1996, cc. 591, 917.

§ 46.2-1074. Removing or altering serial or identification numbers, decals and devices without consent of Department.

Any person who, individually or in association with one or more others, knowingly removes, changes, alters, or conceals any motor number, serial, or other identification number, decal or device affixed to a motor vehicle, trailer, semitrailer or motor vehicle part as required by federal law without the consent of the Department, shall be guilty of a Class 6 felony.

History.
Code 1950, § 46-9; 1958, cc. 391, 541, § 46.1-82; 1978, cc. 294, 605; 1979, c. 428; 1989, c. 727; 1996, cc. 591, 917.

§ 46.2-1075. Possession of vehicles with serial numbers removed or altered.

Any person who shall knowingly have in his possession a motor vehicle, motor vehicle part, trailer, or semitrailer whose motor number, serial number, identification number, decal or device as required by federal law has been removed, changed, or altered without the consent of the Department shall be guilty of a Class 6 felony.

History.
Code 1950, § 46-10; 1958, c. 541, § 46.1-83; 1978, cc. 294, 605; 1979, c. 428; 1989, c. 727; 1996, cc. 591, 917.

§ 46.2-1075.1. Tampering with gross vehicle weight ratings; penalty.

It shall be unlawful for any person willfully to remove, alter, deface, or tamper with any number, plate, bracket, sticker, decal, indication, or other device indicating the manufacturer's gross vehicle weight rating of any vehicle which (i) has a manufacturer's gross vehicle weight rating of 15,000 pounds or less and (ii) has been modified by alteration of its height from the ground. Violation of this section shall constitute a Class 3 misdemeanor.

History.
1991, c. 193.

§ 46.2-1076. Lettering on certain vehicles.

A. No person shall drive, cause to be driven, or permit the driving of a "for hire" motor vehicle on the highways in the Commonwealth unless the legal name or trade name of the motor carrier as defined in Chapter 20 (§ 46.2-2000 et seq.) or Chapter 21 (§ 46.2-2100 et seq.) operating the vehicle is plainly displayed on both sides of the vehicle. The letters and numerals in the display shall be of such size, shape, and color as to be readily legible during daylight hours from a distance of 50 feet while the vehicle is not in motion. The display shall be kept legible and may take the form of a removable device which meets the identification and legibility requirements of this section.

B. This section shall not apply to any motor vehicle:

1. Having a registered gross weight of less than 10,000 pounds;

2. Which is used exclusively for weddings or funeral services;

3. Which is rented without chauffeur and operated under a valid lease which gives the lessee exclusive control of the vehicle; or

4. Which is used exclusively as an emergency medical services vehicle.

C. Subsection A shall also apply to tow trucks used in providing service to the public for hire. For the purposes of this section, "tow truck" means any motor vehicle which is constructed and used primarily for towing, lifting, or otherwise moving disabled vehicles.

D. No person shall drive on the highways in the Commonwealth a pickup or panel truck, tractor truck, trailer, or semitrailer bearing any name other than that of the vehicle's owner or lessee. However, the provisions of this subsection shall not apply to advertising material for another, displayed pursuant to a valid contract.

History.
Code 1950, § 46-63; 1950, p. 251; 1958, c. 541, §§ 46.1-64, 46.1-158.1; 1960, c. 79; 1972, cc. 77, 609; 1974, c. 400; 1975, c. 124; 1979, c. 620; 1989, c. 727; 2013, cc. 165, 582; 2015, cc. 502, 503.

§ 46.2-1077. Motor vehicles not to be equipped with television within view of driver; viewing motion pictures or similar displays while driving.

A. No motor vehicle registered in the Commonwealth shall be equipped with, nor shall there be used therein, a television receiver when the moving images are visible to the driver while the vehicle is in motion. The operator of a motor vehicle that is not required to be registered in the Commonwealth shall not operate a television receiver that violates the provisions of this section while driving in the Commonwealth.

The prohibitions contained in this subsection shall not, however, include:

1. Electronic displays used in conjunction with vehicle navigation and mapping systems, or as part of a digital dispatch system;

2. Closed circuit video monitors designed to operate only in conjunction with dedicated video cameras and used in rear-view systems on trucks, motor homes, and other motor vehicles;

3. Television receivers or monitors used in government-owned vehicles by law-enforcement officers and employees of the Department of Transportation in the course of their official duties;

4. Visual displays used to enhance or supplement the driver's view forward, behind, or to the sides of a motor vehicle for the purpose of maneuvering the vehicle;

5. A vehicle information display;

6. A visual display used to enhance or supplement a driver's view of vehicle occupants;

7. Television-type receiving equipment used exclusively for safety or traffic engineering information; or

8. A television receiver, video monitor, television or video screen, or any other similar means of visually displaying a moving image, if that equipment is factory-installed and has an interlock device that, when the motor vehicle operator is performing one or more of the driving tasks, disables the equipment so that such moving images are not visible to the motor vehicle operator except as a visual display described in subdivisions 1 through 7. For the purposes of this subdivision, "driving task" means all of the real-time functions required to operate a vehicle in on-road traffic, excluding the selection of destinations and waypoints, and including steering, turning, lane keeping and lane changing, accelerating, and decelerating.

B. Except for displays explicitly authorized in subsection A, no driver of any motor vehicle shall view any motion picture or similar video display while driving.

History.

Code 1950, § 46-219.1; 1950, p. 882; 1958, c. 541, § 46.1-202; 1989, c. 727; 1994, c. 117; 2005, cc. 210, 913; 2007, c. 110; 2011, c. 275; 2016, cc. 302, 707.

§ 46.2-1077.01. Display of certain visual material in motor vehicles prohibited; penalty.

It shall be unlawful for the operator of any motor vehicle on a public highway to display or permit the display within the vehicle of any image, motion picture, or video display that is obscene as defined in § 18.2-372 if such image, motion picture, or video display can be seen by persons outside the vehicle. Violation of this section shall constitute a Class 4 misdemeanor.

History.

2005, c. 669.

§ 46.2-1077.1. Mobile infrared transmitters; demerit points not to be awarded.

A. It shall be unlawful for any person to operate a motor vehicle on the highways of the Commonwealth when such vehicle is equipped with a mobile infrared transmitter or any other device or mechanism, passive or active, used to preempt or change the signal given by a traffic light so as to give the right-of-way to the vehicle equipped with such device. It shall be unlawful to use any such device or mechanism on any such motor vehicle on the highways. It shall be unlawful to sell any such device or mechanism in the Commonwealth, except for uses permitted under this section. In addition, the provisions of this section shall not apply to any law-enforcement, firefighting, or emergency medical services vehicle responding to an emergency call or operating in an emergency situation or any vehicle providing public transportation service in a corridor approved for public transportation priority by the Virginia Department of Transportation or the governing body of any county, city, or town having control of the highways within its boundaries.

This section shall not be construed to authorize the forfeiture to the Commonwealth of any such device or mechanism. Any such device or mechanism may be taken by the arresting officer if needed as evidence, and, when no longer needed, shall be returned to the person charged with a violation of this section, or at that person's request and his expense, mailed to an address specified by him. Any unclaimed devices may be destroyed on court order after six months have elapsed from the final date for filing an appeal.

Except as provided in subsection B, the presence of any such prohibited device or mechanism in or on a motor vehicle on the highways of the Commonwealth shall constitute prima facie evidence of the violation of this section. The Commonwealth need not prove that the device or mechanism in question was in an operative condition or being operated.

B. A person shall not be guilty of a violation of this section when the device or mechanism in question, at the time of the alleged offense, had no power source and was not readily accessible for use by the driver or any passenger in the vehicle.

C. No demerit points shall be awarded by the Commissioner for violations of this section.

History.

2004, c. 268; 2015, cc. 502, 503.

§ 46.2-1078. Unlawful to operate motor vehicle, bicycle, electric personal assistive mobility device, electric power-assisted bicycle, or moped while using earphones.

It shall be unlawful for any person to operate a motor vehicle, bicycle, electric personal assistive mobility device, electric power-assisted bicycle, or moped on the highways in the Commonwealth while using earphones on or in both ears.

For the purpose of this section, "earphones" shall mean any device worn on or in both ears that converts electrical energy to sound waves or which impairs or hinders the person's ability to hear, but shall not include (i) any prosthetic device that aids the hard of hearing, (ii) earphones installed in helmets worn by motorcycle operators and riders and used as part of a communications system, or (iii) nonprosthetic, closed-ear, open-back, electronic noise-cancellation devices designed and used to enhance the hearing ability of persons who operate vehicles in high-noise environments, provided any such device is being worn by the operator of a vehicle with a gross vehicle weight rating of 26,000 pounds or more. The provisions of this section shall not apply to the driver of any emergency vehicle as defined in § 46.2-920.

History.

Code 1950, § 46-219.1; 1950, p. 882; 1958, c. 541, § 46.1-202.1; 1989, c. 727; 1993, c. 126; 1997, c. 36; 2001, c. 834; 2002, c. 254.

§ 46.2-1078.1. Use of handheld personal communications devices in certain motor vehicles; exceptions; penalty.

A. It is unlawful for any person to operate a moving motor vehicle on the highways in the Commonwealth while using any handheld personal communications device to:

1. Manually enter multiple letters or text in the device as a means of communicating with another person; or

2. Read any email or text message transmitted to the device or stored within the device, provided that this prohibition shall not apply to any name or number stored within the device nor to any caller identification information.

B. The provisions of this section shall not apply to:

1. The operator of any emergency vehicle while he is engaged in the performance of his official duties;

2. An operator who is lawfully parked or stopped;

3. The use of factory-installed or aftermarket global positioning systems (GPS) or wireless communications devices used to transmit or receive data as part of a digital dispatch system; or

4. Any person using a handheld personal communications device to report an emergency.

C. A violation of this section is a traffic infraction punishable, for a first offense, by a fine of $125 and, for a second or subsequent offense, by a fine of $250.

For the purposes of this section, "emergency vehicle" means:

1. Any law-enforcement vehicle operated by or under the direction of a federal, state, or local law-enforcement officer;

2. Any regional detention center vehicle operated by or under the direction of a correctional officer responding to an emergency call or operating in an emergency situation;

3. Any vehicle used to fight fire, including publicly owned state forest warden vehicles, when traveling in response to a fire alarm or emergency call;

4. Any emergency medical services vehicle designed or used for the principal purpose of emergency medical services where human life is endangered;

5. Any Department of Emergency Management vehicle or Office of Emergency Medical Services vehicle, when responding to an emergency call or operating in an emergency situation;

6. Any Department of Corrections vehicle designated by the Director of the Department of Corrections, when (i) responding to an emergency call at a correctional facility, (ii) participating in a drug-related investigation, (iii) pursuing escapees from a correctional facility, or (iv) responding to a request for assistance from a law-enforcement officer; and

7. Any vehicle authorized to be equipped with alternating, blinking, or flashing red or red and white secondary warning lights pursuant to § 46.2-1029.2.

D. Distracted driving shall be included as a part of the driver's license knowledge examination.

History.

2009, c. 661; 2013, cc. 752, 790; 2014, cc. 77, 803; 2015, cc. 502, 503.

§ 46.2-1079. Radar detectors; demerit points not to be awarded.

A. It shall be unlawful for any person to operate a motor vehicle on the highways of the Commonwealth when such vehicle is equipped with any device or mechanism, passive or active, to detect or purposefully interfere with or diminish the measurement capabilities of any radar, laser, or other device or mechanism employed by law-enforcement personnel to measure the speed of motor vehicles on the highways of the Commonwealth for law-enforcement purposes. It shall be unlawful to use any such device or mechanism on any such motor vehicle on the highways. It shall be unlawful to sell any such device or mechanism in the Commonwealth. However, provisions of this section shall not apply to any receiver of radio waves utilized for lawful purposes to receive any signal from a frequency lawfully licensed by any state or federal agency.

This section shall not be construed to authorize the forfeiture to the Commonwealth of any such device or mechanism. Any such device or mechanism may be taken by the arresting officer if needed as evidence, and, when no longer needed, shall be returned to the person charged with a violation of this section, or at that person's request, and his expense, mailed to an address specified by him. Any unclaimed devices may be destroyed on court order after six months have elapsed from the final date for filing an appeal.

Except as provided in subsection B of this section, the presence of any such prohibited device or mechanism in or on a motor vehicle on the highways of the Commonwealth shall constitute prima facie evidence of the violation of this section. The Commonwealth need not prove that the device or mechanism in question was in an operative condition or being operated.

B. A person shall not be guilty of a violation of this section when the device or mechanism in question, at the time of the alleged offense, had no power source and was not readily accessible for use by the driver or any passenger in the vehicle.

C. This section shall not apply to motor vehicles owned by the Commonwealth or any political subdivision thereof and used by law-enforcement officers in their official duties, nor to the sale of any such device or mechanism to law-enforcement agencies for use in their official duties.

D. No demerit points shall be awarded by the Commissioner for violations of this section. Any demerit points awarded by the Commissioner prior to July 1, 1992, for any violation of this section shall be rescinded and the driving record of any person awarded demerit points for a violation of this section shall be amended to reflect such rescission.

History.

1962, c. 125, § 46.1-198.1; 1975, c. 108; 1976, c. 90; 1978, cc. 87, 91; 1981, c. 303; 1989, c. 727; 1992, c. 825; 1998, c. 300.

§ 46.2-1080. Speedometer in good working order.

It shall be unlawful for any person to possess with intent to sell or offer for sale, either separately or as a part of the equipment of a motor vehicle, or to use or have as a part of the equipment of a motor vehicle, or to use or have as equipment on a motor vehicle operated on a highway any speedometer which is not in good working order.

History.

Code 1950, § 46-311; 1958, c. 541, § 46.1-308; 1960, c. 125; 1968, c. 172; 1970, c. 26; 1984, c. 426; 1989, c. 727.

§ 46.2-1081. Slow-moving vehicle emblems.

A. Every farm tractor, self-propelled unit of farm equipment or implement of husbandry, and any other vehicle designed for operation at speeds not in excess of 25 miles per hour or normally operated at speeds not in excess of 25 miles per hour, shall display a triangular slow-moving vehicle emblem on the rear of the vehicle when traveling on a public highway at any time of the day or night.

B. Should a slow-moving vehicle tow a unit on a public highway, then the towing vehicle or the towed unit shall be equipped with the slow-moving vehicle emblem as follows:

1. If the towed unit or any load thereon obscures the slow-moving vehicle emblem on the towing vehicle, the towed unit shall be equipped with a slow-moving vehicle emblem, in which case the towing vehicle need not display such emblem.

2. If the slow-moving vehicle emblem on the towing vehicle is not obscured by the towed unit or any load thereon, then either or both such vehicles may be equipped with such emblem.

C. The standards and specifications for the slow-moving vehicle emblem and the position of mounting of the emblem shall conform to standards and specifications adopted by the American Society of Agricultural Engineers, the Society of Automotive Engineers, the American National Standards Institute, Inc., or the federal Department of Transportation.

D. The use of the slow-moving vehicle emblem shall be restricted to the uses specified in this title.

E. The provisions of this section shall not apply to bicycles, electric power-assisted bicycles, or mopeds. Display of a slow-moving vehicle emblem on a bicycle, electric power-assisted bicycle, or moped shall not be deemed a violation of this section.

History.

1970, c. 301, § 46.1-264.1; 1972, c. 146; 1978, c. 605; 1989, c. 727; 1996, c. 82; 2003, cc. 29, 46.

§ 46.2-1082. Mirrors.

No person shall drive a motor vehicle on a highway in the Commonwealth if the vehicle is not equipped with a mirror which reflects to the driver a view of the highway for a distance of not less than 200 feet to the rear of such vehicle.

No motor vehicle registered in the Commonwealth, designed and licensed primarily for passenger vehicular transportation on the public highways and manufactured after 1968 shall be driven on the highways in the Commonwealth unless equipped with at least one outside and at least one inside rear view mirror meeting the requirements of this section.

Notwithstanding the other provisions of this section, no motor vehicle which either has no rear window, or which has a rear window so obstructed as to prevent rearward vision by means of an inside rear view mirror, shall be required to be equipped with an inside rear view mirror if such motor vehicle has horizontally and vertically adjustable outside rear view mirrors installed on both sides of such motor vehicle in such a manner as to provide the driver of such motor vehicle a rearward view along both sides of such motor vehicle for at least 200 feet.

History.

Code 1950, § 46-294; 1958, c. 541, § 46.1-289; 1968, c. 730; 1980, c. 13; 1989, c. 727.

§ 46.2-1083. Rear fenders, flaps, or guards required for certain motor vehicles.

No person shall operate on a highway any motor vehicle or combination of vehicles having a licensed gross weight in excess of 40,000 pounds unless the motor vehicle or combination of vehicles is equipped with rear fenders, flaps, or guards of sufficient size to substantially prevent the projection of rocks, dirt, water, or other substances to the rear. Vehicles used exclusively for hauling logs and tractor trucks shall be exempt from the provisions of this section.

History.

Code 1950, § 46-294.1; 1954, c. 403; 1958, c. 541, § 46.1-290; 1960, c. 120; 1981, c. 304; 1989, c. 727.

§ 46.2-1084. Vehicle to have securely affixed seat for driver; location of such seat.

It shall be unlawful for any person to drive any motor vehicle on a highway in the Commonwealth unless it is equipped with a securely affixed seat for the driver. The seat shall be so located as to permit the driver to adequately control the steering and braking mechanisms and other instruments necessary for the safe operation of the motor vehicle.

History.

1973, c. 56, § 46.1-302.1; 1989, c. 727.

§ 46.2-1085: Repealed by Acts 2003, c. 686.

§ 46.2-1086. Devices for emission of smoke screens, gas projectors or flame throwers; prohibited.

It shall be a Class 6 felony to install or to aid or abet in installing, in any manner, in or on any motor vehicle any device, appliance, equipment, or instrument of any kind, character, or description, or any part of such device, appliance, equipment, or instrument, designed for generating or emitting smoke, thereby creating what is commonly known as a "smoke screen," or of emitting any gas or flame which may be a hindrance or obstruction to traffic. It shall also be a Class 6 felony to knowingly possess or drive on the highways any motor vehicle so equipped.

Additionally, the driver's license of any person convicted of a violation of this section shall be suspended for six months from the date of conviction.

The provisions of this section shall not apply to vehicles used in applying herbicides, insecticides, or pesticides.

History.

Code 1950, § 46-309; 1958, c. 541, § 46.1-305; 1962, c. 302; 1989, c. 727.

§ 46.2-1087. Forfeiture of vehicles equipped with smoke projectors, etc.

Any motor vehicle found to be equipped with any device, appliance, equipment, or instrument, as mentioned in § 46.2-1086, or equipped for the installation or attachment of any "smoke screen" or gas or flame emitting device, appliance, equipment, or instrument, as so mentioned, shall be forfeited to the Commonwealth, and upon being condemned as forfeited in proceedings under Chapter 22.1 (§ 19.2-386.1 et seq.) of Title 19.2, the proceeds of sale shall be disposed of according to law. No such forfeiture, however, shall take place unless the owner or operator knows that such vehicle is so equipped.

History.

Code 1950, § 46-310; 1958, c. 541, § 46.1-306; 1989, c. 727; 2012, cc. 283, 756.

§ 46.2-1088. Air conditioning units.

No motor vehicle operated on any highway shall be equipped with any air conditioning unit unless such device is of a type approved as to safety by the Superintendent. The Superintendent is authorized to promulgate regulations setting specifications relating to the design, construction, installation, maintenance, and use of such air conditioning units. No refrigerant used in such unit shall be explosive, flammable, or toxic, unless the refrigerant is included in the list published by the United States Environmental Protection Agency as a safe alternative motor vehicle air conditioning substitute for chloroflourocarbon-12, pursuant to 42 U.S.C. 7671 k (c).

History.

Code 1950, § 46-310.1; 1954, c. 217; 1958, c. 541, § 46.1-307; 1989, c. 727; 2008, c. 443.

§ 46.2-1088.1. Hood scoops.

No motor vehicle shall be operated on a public highway in the Commonwealth if any hood scoop installed thereon exceeds any of the following dimensions:

1. For any hood scoop installed on any motor vehicle manufactured for the 1990 or earlier model year: thirty-eight inches wide at its widest point, two and one-quarter inches high at its highest point measured from the junction of the dashboard and the windshield, and fifty-two and one-quarter inches long at its longest point.

2. For any hood scoop installed on any motor vehicle manufactured for the 1991 or subsequent model year: thirty-eight inches wide at its widest point, one and one-eighth inches high at its highest point measured from the junction of the dashboard and the windshield, and fifty and one-half inches long at its longest point.

History.

1991, c. 494.

§ 46.2-1088.2. Warning devices required on certain vehicles.

Any self-propelled vehicle used to sell ice cream, snacks and similar products at retail directly from the vehicle in residential neighborhoods shall be equipped with a device or devices, of a type approved by the Superintendent of State Police, in good working order, that, whenever the vehicle is operated in reverse gear, automatically display a light signal and emit an audible alarm signal. The provisions of this section shall not be construed to authorize such vehicles to be equipped with red, blue, or amber warning lights unless authorized under Article 3 (§ 46.2-1010 et seq.) of this chapter.

The provisions of this section shall not apply to vehicles commonly known as "concession trailers," "special events trailers" and similar equipment used to sell or dispense food, soft drinks, bottled water, fruit drinks, wine or malt beverages directly to consumers.

History.
2001, c. 200.

§ 46.2-1088.3. Air bags; installation of other object in lieu of air bag prohibited; notice of installation of previously installed air bag required; penalty.

Any person who, without the knowledge of the vehicle's owner or the person requesting the installation, reinstallation, or replacement of a motor vehicle air bag, installs or reinstalls any air bag or other component of the vehicle's inflatable restraint system knowing that the air bag installation is not in accordance with federal safety regulations applicable to that specific line-make, model, and model year vehicle is guilty of a Class 1 misdemeanor.

Any person who, without the knowledge of the vehicle's owner or the person requesting the installation, reinstallation, or replacement of a motor vehicle air bag, installs, reinstalls, or replaces a motor vehicle air bag or other component of the vehicle's inflatable restraint system with an air bag or other component of a vehicle's inflatable restraint system knowing that the air bag was previously installed in another motor vehicle is guilty of a Class 2 misdemeanor.

History.
2002, c. 402.

§ 46.2-1088.4. Devices used to supply nitrous oxide to the engines of motor vehicles.

It shall be unlawful for any person to operate any motor vehicle on the highways of the Commonwealth if such vehicle is equipped with any device that supplies the vehicle's engine with nitrous oxide, unless the device has been disabled such that the supply of nitrous oxide is disconnected and not readily accessible to the source of delivery.

Violation of any provision of this section shall constitute a Class 3 misdemeanor.

History.
2004, c. 282.

§ 46.2-1088.5. Reflectors or reflectorized material required on rear end of certain trailers.

There shall be affixed to the rear end of every utility trailer that does not require state inspection either two or more reflectors of a type approved by the Superintendent or at least 100 square inches of solid reflectorized material. The reflectors or reflective material shall be applied so as to outline the rear end of the trailer. For the purposes of this section, "utility trailer" means a trailer whose body and tailgate consist largely or exclusively of a metal mesh.

History.
2004, c. 785; 2005, c. 563.

§ 46.2-1088.6. Motor vehicle recording devices.

A. As used in this section:

"Accessed" means downloaded, extracted, scanned, read, or otherwise retrieved.

"Owner" means a person having all the incidents of ownership, including the legal title of a vehicle whether or not such person lends, rents, or creates a security interest in the vehicle; a person entitled to the possession of a vehicle as the purchaser under a security agreement; or a person entitled to possession of the vehicle as the lessee pursuant to a written lease agreement, provided such agreement at inception is for a period in excess of three months.

"Recorded data" means the data stored or preserved electronically in a recording device identifying performance or operation information about the motor vehicle including, but not limited to:

1. Speed of the motor vehicle or the direction in which the vehicle is traveling, or both;
2. Vehicle location data;
3. Vehicle steering performance;
4. Vehicle brake performance including, but not limited to, whether brakes were applied before a crash;
5. The driver's seatbelt status; and
6. Information concerning a crash in which the motor vehicle has been involved, including the ability to transmit such information to a central communications system.

"Recording device" means an electronic system, and the physical device or mechanism containing the electronic system, that primarily, or incidental to its primary function, preserves or records, in electronic form, data collected by sensors or provided by

other systems within the vehicle. "Recording device" includes event data recorders (EDRs), sensing and diagnostic modules (SDMs), electronic control modules (ECMs), automatic crash notification (ACN) systems, geographic information systems (GIS), and any other device that records and preserves data that can be accessed related to that vehicle.

B. Recorded data may only be accessed by the motor vehicle owner or with the consent of the motor vehicle owner or the owner's agent or legal representative; except under the following circumstances:

1. The owner of the motor vehicle or the owner's agent or legal representative has a contract with a third-party subscription service that requires access to a recording device or recorded data in order to perform the contract, so long as the recorded data is only accessed and used in accordance with the contract;

2. A licensed new motor vehicle dealer, or a technician or mechanic at a motor vehicle repair or servicing facility requires access to recorded data in order to carry out his normal and ordinary diagnosing, servicing, and repair duties and such recorded data is used only to perform such duties;

3. The recorded data is accessed by an emergency response provider and is used only for the purpose of determining the need for or facilitating an emergency response. Such persons are authorized to receive data transmitted or communicated by any electronic system of a motor vehicle that constitutes an automatic crash notification system and utilizes or reports data provided by or recorded by recording devices installed on or attached to a motor vehicle to assist them in performing their duties as emergency response providers;

4. Upon authority of a court of competent jurisdiction; or

5. The recorded data is accessed by law enforcement in the course of an investigation where constitutionally permissible and in accordance with any applicable law regarding searches and seizures upon probable cause to believe that the recording device contains evidence relating to a violation of the laws of the Commonwealth or the United States.

C. The consent of the motor vehicle owner or the owner's agent or legal representative for use of recorded data for purposes of investigating a motor vehicle accident or insurance claim shall not be requested or obtained until after the event giving rise to the claim has occurred, and shall not be made a condition of the defense, payment or settlement of an obligation or claim. For underwriting and rating purposes, the motor vehicle owner may provide his consent either directly to the insurer or through and as certified by a named insured.

D. If a person or entity accesses recorded data pursuant to subdivisions B 2 or B 3, such entity or person shall not transmit or otherwise convey the recorded data to a third party unless necessary to carry out their duties thereunder.

E. When the recording device and recorded data are not removed or separated from the motor vehicle, the ownership of the recording device and recorded data survives the sale of the motor vehicle to any nonbeneficial owner such as an insurer, salvage yard, or other person who does not possess and use the motor vehicle for normal transportation purposes.

F. The failure of an insurer to obtain access to the recorded data shall not create, nor shall it be construed to create, an independent or private cause of action in favor of any person.

History.
2006, cc. 851, 889.

ARTICLE 11.

PAINT, LETTERING, AND SPECIAL EQUIPMENT FOR SCHOOL BUSES.

§ 46.2-1089. Paint and lettering on school bus.

School buses shall be painted yellow with the words "School Bus" on the front and rear in letters at least eight inches high. All school buses shall be equipped with warning devices prescribed in § 46.2-1090. Only school buses as defined in § 46.2-100 may be painted yellow, identified by lettering as provided in this section, and equipped with the specified warning devices. A vehicle which merely transports pupils or residents at a school from one point to another without intermittent stops for the purpose of picking up or discharging pupils need not comply with the requirements of this section.

History.
1968, c. 653, § 46.1-286.1; 1974, c. 455; 1989, c. 727.

§ 46.2-1089.1. Signs and markings on school buses using alternative fuels.

The State Board of Education may provide by regulation for the display of appropriate signs or other markings on school buses using alternative fuels. Such signs or markings shall conspicuously identify the vehicle as an alternatively fueled vehicle and indicate the type of alternative fuel used. No such sign or marking shall be more than 4 3/4 inches long or more than 3 1/4 inches high.

For the purposes of this section: (i) "alternative fuel" means a motor fuel used as an alternative to gasoline or diesel fuel; (ii) alcohol/gasoline blended fuels which contain less than eighty-five percent ethanol or methanol shall not be considered alternative fuels; and (iii) dual-fuel and bi-fuel vehicles equipped to operate on both a conventional fuel and an alternative fuel shall be considered alternatively fueled vehicles.

Signs and markings provided for under this section shall be in addition to other markings permitted or required by this title.

History.
1993, c. 172.

§ 46.2-1090. Warning devices on school buses; other buses; use thereof; penalties.

Every bus used for the principal purpose of transporting school children shall be equipped with a warning device of such type as may be prescribed by the State Board of Education after consultation with the Superintendent of State Police. Such a warning device shall indicate when such bus is either (i) stopped or about to stop to take on or discharge children, the elderly, or mentally or physically handicapped persons or (ii) stopped or about to stop for another such bus, when approaching from any direction, that is stopped or about to stop to take on or discharge any such persons. Such warning device shall be used and in operation for at least 100 feet before any proposed stop of such bus if the lawful speed limit is less than thirty-five miles per hour, and for at least 200 feet before any proposed stop of such bus if the lawful speed limit is thirty-five miles per hour or more.

For any new bus placed into service on or after July 1, 2007, such warning devices, at a minimum, shall include a nonsequential system of red traffic warning lights, a warning sign with flashing lights, and a crossing control arm such that when the bus door is opened, the red warning lights, warning sign with flashing lights, and crossing control arm are automatically activated.

Failure of a warning device to function on any school bus shall not relieve any person operating a motor vehicle from his duty to stop as provided in §§ 46.2-844 and 46.2-859.

Any person operating such bus who fails or refuses to equip such vehicle being driven by him with such equipment, or who fails to use such warning devices in the operation of such vehicle shall be guilty of a Class 3 misdemeanor.

Transit buses used to transport school children in the City of Hampton may be equipped with an advisory sign that extends from the left side of the bus and displays the words: "CAUTION-STUDENTS." Such sign may be equipped with not more than two warning lights of a type approved for use by the Superintendent of State Police.

History.

Code 1950, § 22-280; 1956, c. 213; 1958, c. 541, § 46.1-287; 1960, c. 156; 1970, c. 521; 1975, c. 633; 1982, c. 681; 1989, c. 727; 1995, c. 106; 1996, c. 512; 2007, c. 421.

§ 46.2-1090.1. Warning lights on school buses.

In addition to other lights authorized by law, school buses may be equipped with flashing white or amber warning lights of types authorized by the Board of Education after consultation with the Superintendent of State Police. These warning lights shall be installed in a manner authorized by the Board after consultation with the Superintendent and shall be lighted while the bus is transporting school children during periods of reduced visibility caused by atmospheric conditions other than darkness. These warning lights may also be lighted at other times while the bus is transporting school children. Drivers of motor vehicles approaching school buses displaying lighted warning lights authorized in this section shall not be required to stop except as required in §§ 46.2-844 and 46.2-859.

History.

1992, c. 159; 1997, c. 65.

ARTICLE 12.

SAFETY BELTS.

§ 46.2-1091. Safety belts to be worn by certain bus drivers.

Any person operating a school bus shall wear the appropriate safety belt system when the bus is in motion.

Violation of this section shall constitute a Class 3 misdemeanor.

History.

1973, c. 66, § 46.1-287.2; 1989, c. 727; 1994, c. 104.

§ 46.2-1092. Safety lap belts or a combination of lap belts and shoulder harnesses to be installed in certain motor vehicles.

No passenger car or autocycle registered in the Commonwealth and manufactured for the year 1963 or for subsequent years shall be operated on the highways in the Commonwealth unless the front seats thereof are equipped with adult safety lap belts or a combination of lap belts and shoulder harnesses of types approved by the Superintendent.

Failure to use the safety lap belts or a combination of lap belts and shoulder harnesses after installation shall not be deemed to be negligence. Nor shall evidence of such nonuse of such devices be considered in mitigation of damages of whatever nature.

No motor vehicle registered in the Commonwealth and manufactured after January 1, 1968, shall be issued a safety inspection approval sticker if any lap belt, combination of lap belt and shoulder harness, or passive belt systems required to be installed at the time of manufacture by the federal Department of Transportation have been either removed from the motor vehicle or rendered inoperable.

No autocycle registered in the Commonwealth shall be issued a safety inspection sticker if any lap belt, combination of lap belt and shoulder harness, or passive belt systems required to be installed under this section have been either removed from the autocycle or rendered inoperable.

No passenger car, except convertibles, registered in the Commonwealth and manufactured on or after September 1, 1990, shall be operated on the highways in the Commonwealth unless the forward-facing rear outboard seats thereof are equipped with rear seat lap/shoulder belts of types required to be installed at the time of manufacture by the federal Department of Transportation.

No passenger car, including convertibles, registered in the Commonwealth and manufactured on or after September 1, 1991, shall be operated on the highways in the Commonwealth unless the forward-facing rear outboard seats thereof are equipped with rear seat lap/shoulder belts of types required to be installed at the time of manufacture by the federal Department of Transportation.

No truck, multi-purpose vehicle, or bus, except school buses and motor homes, with a gross vehicle weight rating of 10,000 pounds or less, registered in the Commonwealth and manufactured on or after September 1, 1991, shall be operated on the highways in the Commonwealth unless the forward-facing rear outboard seats thereof are equipped with rear seat lap/shoulder belts of types required to be installed at the time of manufacture by the federal Department of Transportation.

Passenger cars, trucks, multipurpose vehicles, and buses, except school buses and motor homes, registered in the Commonwealth and manufactured on or after September 1, 1992, shall not be operated on the highways of the Commonwealth unless equipped with rear seat lap/shoulder belts of types required to be installed at the time of manufacture by the federal Department of Transportation for each forward-facing rear outboard seating position on a readily removable seat.

For the purposes of this section, forward-facing rear outboard seats are defined as those designated seating positions for passengers in outside front facing seats behind the driver and front passenger seats, except any designated seating position adjacent to a walkway that is located between the seat and the near side of the vehicle and is designed to allow access to a more rearward seating position.

The Superintendent of State Police shall include in the Official Motor Vehicle Inspection Regulations a section which identifies each classification of motor vehicle required to be equipped with any of the devices described in the foregoing provisions of this section.

Such regulations shall also include a listing of the exact devices which are required to be installed in each motor vehicle classification and the model year of each motor vehicle classification on which the standards of the federal Department of Transportation first became applicable.

History.

1962, c. 357, § 46.1-309.1; 1964, c. 334; 1966, c. 37; 1968, c. 171; 1970, c. 19; 1980, c. 486; 1982, c. 434; 1989, c. 727; 1992, c. 553; 2014, cc. 53, 256.

§ 46.2-1093. Requirements for safety lap belts, shoulder harnesses and combinations thereof.

Any safety lap belt or shoulder harness or any combination of lap belt and shoulder harness installed in a vehicle shall be designed and installed in such manner as to prevent or materially reduce movement of any person using the same in the event of collision or upset of the vehicle.

The Superintendent shall establish specifications or requirements for approved type safety lap belts and shoulder harnesses or any combination of lap belt and shoulder harness, attachments, and installation, in accordance with the provisions of this section. Such specifications or requirements may be the same as those specifications or requirements for safety lap belts or shoulder harnesses or any combination of lap belt and shoulder harness established by the Civil Aeronautics Administration Technical Standard Orders or regulations established by the Society of Automotive Engineers or the standards of the federal Department of Transportation, for safety lap belts and shoulder harnesses or combination of lap belts and shoulder harnesses.

No person shall sell or offer for sale any safety lap belt, shoulder harness, or any combination of lap belt and shoulder harness or attachments thereto for use in a vehicle, unless of a type which has been approved by the Superintendent.

History.

Code 1950, § 46-312.1; 1956, c. 36; 1958, c. 541, § 46.1-310; 1966, c. 37; 1968, c. 171; 1970, c. 20; 1989, c. 727.

§ 46.2-1094. Occupants of front seats of motor vehicles required to use safety lap belts and shoulder harnesses; penalty.

A. Any driver, and any other person at least 18 years of age and occupying the front seat, of a motor vehicle equipped or required by the provisions of this title to be equipped with a safety belt system, consisting of lap belts, shoulder harnesses, combinations thereof or similar devices, shall wear the appropriate safety belt system at all times while the motor vehicle is in motion on any public highway. A passenger under the age of 18 years, however, shall be protected as required by the provisions of Article 13 (§ 46.2-1095 et seq.) of this chapter.

B. This section shall not apply to:

1. Any person for whom a licensed physician determines that the use of such safety belt system would be impractical by reason of such person's physical condition or other medical reason, provided the person so exempted carries on his person or in the vehicle a signed written statement of the physician identifying the exempted person and stating the grounds for the exemption; or

2. Any law-enforcement officer transporting persons in custody or traveling in circumstances which render the wearing of such safety belt system impractical; or

3. Any person while driving a motor vehicle and performing the duties of a rural mail carrier for the United States Postal Service; or

4. Any person driving a motor vehicle and performing the duties of a rural newspaper route carrier, newspaper bundle hauler or newspaper rack carrier; or

5. Drivers of and passengers in taxicabs; or

6. Personnel of commercial or municipal vehicles while actually engaged in the collection or delivery of goods or services, including but not limited to solid waste, where such collection or delivery requires the personnel to exit and enter the cab of the vehicle with such frequency and regularity so as to render the use of safety belt systems impractical and the safety benefits derived therefrom insignificant. Such personnel shall resume the use of safety belt systems when actual collection or delivery has ceased or when the vehicle is in transit to or from a point of final disposition or disposal, including but not limited to solid waste facilities, terminals, or other location where the vehicle may be principally garaged; or

7. Any person driving a motor vehicle and performing the duties of a utility meter reader; or

8. Law-enforcement agency personnel driving motor vehicles to enforce laws governing motor vehicle parking.

C. Any person who violates this section shall be subject to a civil penalty of twenty-five dollars to be paid into the state treasury and credited to the Literary Fund. No assignment of demerit points shall be made under Article 19 of Chapter 3 (§ 46.2-489 et seq.) of this title and no court costs shall be assessed for violations of this section.

D. A violation of this section shall not constitute negligence, be considered in mitigation of damages of whatever nature, be admissible in evidence or be the subject of comment by counsel in any action for the recovery of damages arising out of the operation, ownership, or maintenance of a motor vehicle, nor shall anything in this section change any existing law, rule, or procedure pertaining to any such civil action.

E. A violation of this section may be charged on the uniform traffic summons form.

F. No citation for a violation of this section shall be issued unless the officer issuing such citation has cause to stop or arrest the driver of such motor vehicle for the violation of some other provision of this Code or local ordinance relating to the operation, ownership, or maintenance of a motor vehicle or any criminal statute.

G. The governing body of the City of Lynchburg may adopt an ordinance not inconsistent with the provisions of this section, requiring the use of safety belt systems. The penalty for violating any such ordinance shall not exceed a fine or civil penalty of twenty-five dollars.

History.

1987, c. 538, § 46.1-309.2; 1988, cc. 326, 344; 1989, c. 727; 1993, c. 591; 1997, c. 793; 2007, c. 813; 2010, c. 661.

ARTICLE 13.
CHILD RESTRAINTS.

§ 46.2-1095. Child restraint devices required when transporting certain children; safety belts for passengers less than eighteen years old required; penalty.

A. Any person who drives on the highways of Virginia any motor vehicle manufactured after January 1, 1968, shall ensure that any child, up to age eight, whom he transports therein is provided with and properly secured in a child restraint device of a type which meets the standards adopted by the United States Department of Transportation. Further, rear-facing child restraint devices shall be placed in the back seat of a vehicle. In the event the vehicle does not have a back seat, the child restraint device may be placed in the front passenger seat only if the vehicle is either not equipped with a passenger side airbag or the passenger side airbag has been deactivated.

B. Any person transporting another person less than 18 years old, except for those required pursuant to subsection A to be secured in a child restraint device, shall ensure that such person is provided with and properly secured by an appropriate safety belt system when driving on the highways of Virginia in any motor vehicle manufactured after January 1, 1968, equipped or required by the provisions of this title to be equipped with a safety belt system, consisting of lap belts, shoulder harnesses, combinations thereof or similar devices.

C. A violation of this section shall not constitute negligence, be considered in mitigation of damages of whatever nature, be admissible in evidence or be the subject of comment by counsel in any action for the recovery of damages in a civil action.

D. A violation of this section may be charged on the uniform traffic summons form.

E. Nothing in this section shall apply to taxicabs, school buses, executive sedans, or limousines.

History.

1982, c. 634, § 46.1-314.2; 1984, c. 280; 1986, c. 283; 1989, c. 727; 1992, cc. 119, 405; 1997, c. 793; 2000, c. 736; 2002, cc. 358, 616, 660; 2007, cc. 91, 935; 2010, c. 661.

§ 46.2-1096. Exceptions for certain children.

Whenever any physician licensed to practice medicine in the Commonwealth or any other state determines, through accepted medical procedures, that use of a child restraint system by a particular child would be impractical by reason of the child's weight, physical unfitness, or other medical reason, the child shall be exempt from the provisions of this article. Any person transporting a child so exempted shall carry on his or her person or in the vehicle a signed written statement of the physician identifying the child so exempted and stating the grounds therefor.

History.
1982, c. 634, § 46.1-314.3; 1983, c. 296; 1989, c. 727.

§ 46.2-1097. Child restraint devices; special fund created.

The Department of Health shall operate a program to promote, purchase, and distribute child restraint devices to applicants who need a child restraint device but are unable to acquire one because of financial inability. A special fund, known as the Child Restraint Device Special Fund, shall fund the program. The Department of Health shall determine the number of child restraint devices that can be purchased by the program, based upon the amount of funds in the Child Restraint Device Special Fund, provided, however, that the requirements of the Virginia Public Procurement Act (§ 2.2-4300 et seq.) shall not apply to child restraint device purchases by the Department of Health pursuant to this section. The Child Restraint Device Special Fund shall consist of all civil penalties that are collected pursuant to § 46.2-1098 and other funds that may be appropriated for that purpose.

History.
1982, c. 634, § 46.1-314.4; 1984, c. 778; 1986, c. 283; 1989, c. 727; 1996, c. 145.

§ 46.2-1098. Penalties; violations not negligence per se.

Any person, including those subject to jurisdiction of a juvenile and domestic relations district court, found guilty of violating this article shall be subject to a civil penalty of $50, which shall not be suspended in whole or in part, for a violation of § 46.2-1095; however, any person found guilty of violating § 46.2-1095 a second or subsequent time when the violations occurred on different dates shall be subject to a civil penalty of up to $500. An additional civil penalty of $20 shall be imposed for failure to carry a statement as required by § 46.2-1096. Notwithstanding the foregoing provisions of § 46.2-1095, the court may waive or suspend the imposition of the penalty for a violation of § 46.2-1095 if it finds that the failure of the defendant to comply with the section was due to his financial inability to acquire a child restraint system. All civil penalties collected pursuant to this section shall be paid into the Child Restraint Device Special Fund as provided for in § 46.2-1097.

No assignment of demerit points shall be made under Article 19 (§ 46.2-489 et seq.) of Chapter 3 of this title and no court costs shall be assessed for violation of § 46.2-1095.

Violations of this article shall not constitute negligence per se; nor shall violation of this article constitute a defense to any claim for personal injuries to a child or recovery of medical expenses for injuries sustained in any motor vehicle accident.

History.
1982, c. 634, § 46.1-314.5; 1989, c. 727; 1992, cc. 119, 405; 2002, c. 358; 2008, c. 714.

§ 46.2-1099. Further exemptions.

This article shall not apply to:

The transporting of any child in a vehicle having an interior design which makes the use of such device impractical; or

The transporting of children by public transportation, bus, school bus, or farm vehicle.

For the purposes of this section, "farm vehicle" means a vehicle which is either (i) exempt from registration pursuant to §§ 46.2-664, 46.2-665, 46.2-666, 46.2-667, 46.2-670, or § 46.2-672, (ii) registered as a farm vehicle pursuant to § 46.2-698, or (iii) owned by a resident of another state under whose laws the vehicle is either registered as a farm vehicle or exempt from registration by virtue of its use as a farm vehicle.

History.
1982, c. 634, § 46.1-314.6; 1989, c. 727; 1992, cc. 119, 405; 1993, c. 181.

§ 46.2-1100. Use of standard seat belts permitted for certain children.

The use of a seat belt of the type which is standard equipment shall not violate this article if (i) the affected child is at least four years old but less than eight years old and (ii) any physician licensed to practice medicine in the Commonwealth or any other state determines that use of a child restraint system by a particular child would be impractical by reason of the child's weight, physical fitness, or other medical reason, provided that any person transporting a child so exempted shall carry on his person or in the vehicle a signed written statement of the physician identifying the child so exempted and stating the grounds for the determination.

History.
1982, c. 634, § 46.1-314.7; 1989, c. 727; 2002, cc. 616, 660; 2007, cc. 91, 935.

ARTICLE 14. MAXIMUM VEHICLE SIZE, GENERALLY.

§ 46.2-1101. Limitations applicable throughout Commonwealth; alteration by local authorities.

The maximum size and weight of vehicles specified in Articles 14 through 17 (§ 46.2-1101 et seq.) of this chapter shall apply throughout the Commonwealth. Local authorities shall not alter such limitations except as expressly authorized in this title.

History.

Code 1950, § 46-325; 1958, c. 541, § 46.1-327; 1989, c. 727.

§ 46.2-1102. Size and weight limitations inapplicable to farm machinery, agricultural multipurpose drying units, and fire-fighting equipment; amber warning lights.

A. Except when restricted by bridge capacity in § 46.2-1104, the vehicle size and weight limitations contained in Articles 14 through 17 (§ 46.2-1101 et seq.) of this chapter shall not apply to any farm machinery or agricultural multipurpose drying unit when such farm machinery or agricultural multipurpose drying unit is temporarily propelled, hauled, transported, or moved on the highway by a farm machinery distributor or dealer, fertilizer distributor, or farmer in the ordinary course of business. Nor shall those limitations apply to fire-fighting equipment of any county, city, town, or fire-fighting company or association. Any farm tractor or agricultural multipurpose drying unit wider than 108 inches, however, which is so propelled, hauled, transported, or moved on the highway shall be equipped with a safety light of a type approved by the Superintendent of State Police. The light shall be plainly visible from the rear of the tractor or agricultural multipurpose drying unit.

No overweight farm machinery or agricultural multipurpose drying unit under this section shall be operated on any Interstate Highway System component if the vehicle has:

1. A single axle weight in excess of 20,000 pounds;
2. A tandem axle weight in excess of 34,000 pounds;
3. A gross weight, based on axle spacing, greater than that permitted in § 46.2-1126; or
4. A gross weight, regardless of axle spacing, in excess of 80,000 pounds.

B. Notwithstanding subsection A, any farm tractor or other farm, agricultural, or horticultural vehicle wider than 108 inches may be equipped with an amber flashing, blinking, or alternating warning light as provided in § 46.2-1025. Any such light may be installed in lieu of or in addition to the safety light described in subsection A. The absence of amber flashing, blinking, or alternating warning lights on any farm tractor or other farm, agricultural, or horticultural vehicle, as authorized under this subsection, shall not constitute negligence, be considered in mitigation of damages of whatever nature, be admissible in evidence or be the subject of comment by counsel in any action for the recovery of damages arising out of the operation, ownership, or maintenance of any motor vehicle or farm tractor, nor shall anything in this section change any existing law, rule, or procedure pertaining to any such civil action.

History.

Code 1950, § 46-326; 1950, p. 982; 1952, c. 403; 1956, c. 483; 1958, c. 541, § 46.1-332; 1962, c. 197; 1973, c. 183; 1974, c. 361; 1989, c. 727; 1993, c. 151; 1997, c. 149; 2011, c. 331.

§ 46.2-1103. Greater size, weight, and load limits permitted by interstate commerce regulations.

If a federal regulation of interstate commerce permits the use in interstate commerce over the highways of Virginia or any of them, of a greater size, weight, or load limit than prescribed in this title, the Board shall prescribe a similar size, weight, and load limit for vehicles in intrastate commerce operated over the same highways.

History.

1958, c. 541, § 46.1-344; 1989, c. 727.

§ 46.2-1104. Reduction of limits by Commissioner of Highways and local authorities; penalties.

The Commissioner of Highways, acting through employees of the Department of Transportation, may prescribe the weight, width, height, length, or speed of any vehicle or combination of vehicles passing over any highway or section of highway or bridge constituting a part of the interstate, primary, or secondary system of highways. Any limitations thus prescribed may be less than those prescribed in this title whenever an engineering study discloses that it would promote the safety of travel or is necessary for the protection of any such highway.

If the reduction of limits as provided in this section is to be effective for more than 90 days, a written record of this reduction shall be kept on file at the central office of the Department of Transportation. In instances where the limits, including speed limits, are to be temporarily reduced, the representative of the Department of Transportation in the county wherein such highway is located shall immediately notify the Chief Engineer for the Department of Transportation of such reduction. The Chief Engineer shall either affirm or rescind the action of reducing such limits within five days from the date the limits have been posted as hereinafter provided. A list of all highways on which there has been a reduction of limits as herein provided shall be kept on file at the central office of the Department of Transportation. Anyone aggrieved by such reduction of limits may appeal directly to the Commissioner of Highways for redress, and if he affirms the action of reducing such limits, the Commonwealth Transportation Board shall afford any such aggrieved person the opportunity of being heard at its next regular meeting.

The local authorities of counties, cities, and towns, where the highways are under their jurisdiction, may adopt regulations or pass ordinances decreasing the weight limits prescribed in this title for a total period of no more than 90 days in any calendar year, when an engineering study discloses that operation over such highways or streets by reason of deterioration, rain, snow, or other climatic conditions will seriously damage such highways unless such weights are reduced.

In all instances where the limits for weight, size, or speed have been reduced by the Commissioner of Highways or the weights have been reduced by local authorities pursuant to this section, signs stating the weight, height, width, length, or speed permitted on such highway shall be erected at each end of the section of highway affected and no such reduced limits shall be effective until such signs have been posted.

Notwithstanding any other provision of law to the contrary, it shall be unlawful to operate a vehicle or combination of vehicles on any public highway or section thereof when the weight, size, or speed thereof exceeds the maximum posted by authority of the Commissioner of Highways or local authorities pursuant to this section.

Any violation of any provision of this section shall constitute a Class 2 misdemeanor. Furthermore, the vehicle or combination of vehicles involved in such violation may be held upon an order of the court until all fines and costs have been satisfied.

History.

Code 1950, §§ 46-340, 46-341; 1952, cc. 137, 237; 1958, c. 600, § 46.1-345; 1966, c. 85; 1968, c. 218; 1989, c. 727; 2005, c. 645; 2013, c. 118.

ARTICLE 15.

MAXIMUM VEHICLE WIDTHS AND HEIGHTS.

§ 46.2-1105. Width of vehicles generally; exceptions.

A. No vehicle, including any load thereon, but excluding the mirror required by § 46.2-1082 and any warning device installed on a school bus pursuant to § 46.2-1090, shall exceed a total outside width as follows:

1. Passenger bus operated in an incorporated city or town when authorized under § 46.2-1300 — 102 inches;
2. School buses — 100 inches;
3. Vehicles hauling boats or other watercraft — 102 inches;
4. Other vehicles — 102 inches.

B. Notwithstanding subsection A, a travel trailer as defined in § 46.2-1500 or a motor home may exceed 102 inches if such excess width is attributable to an appurtenance that extends no more than six inches beyond the body of the vehicle. For the purposes of this subsection, "appurtenance" includes (i) an awning and its support hardware and (ii) any appendage that is installed by the manufacturer or dealer intended to be an integral part of a motor home or travel trailer, but does not include any item that is temporarily attached to the exterior of the vehicle by the vehicle's owner for the purposes of transporting the item from one location to another.

History.

Code 1950, § 46-326; 1950, p. 982; 1952, c. 403; 1956, c. 483; 1958, c. 541, § 46.1-328; 1960, c. 591; 1968, c. 333; 1973, c. 183; 1979, c. 70; 1983, c. 515; 1985, c. 426; 1986, c. 72; 1989, c. 727; 1994, c. 819; 1996, cc. 446, 506; 2001, c. 151; 2015, c. 615.

§ 46.2-1106: Bus widths in Arlington County [Not set out.] (1989, c. 727.)

Editor's note.

This section, relating to bus widths in Arlington County, was enacted by Acts 1989, c. 727. In furtherance of the general policy of the Commission to include in the Code only provisions having general and permanent application, this section, which is limited in its purpose and scope, is not set out here, but attention is called to it by this reference.

The section catchline was inserted at the direction of the Virginia Code Commission.

§ 46.2-1107. Bus widths in certain counties.

Upon application by the governing body of any county, the Commissioner of Highways may permit within that county the operation of passenger buses wider than 96 inches but no wider than 102 inches.

History.

Code 1950, § 46-326; 1950, p. 982; 1952, c. 403; 1956, c. 483; 1958, c. 541, § 46.1-328; 1960, c. 591; 1968, c. 333; 1973, c. 183; 1979, c. 70; 1983, c. 515; 1985, c. 426; 1986, c. 72; 1989, c. 727; 2013, cc. 585, 646.

§ 46.2-1108. Bus widths to comply with federal law.

If federal law permits the operation of passenger buses wider than 96 inches on the interstate highway system, the Commissioner of Highways may permit the operation of passenger buses of a total outside width, excluding the mirror required by § 46.2-1082, of more than 96 inches, but not exceeding more than 102 inches, on interstate and defense highways or any other four lane divided highways under the jurisdiction of the Commonwealth Transportation Board. The use of any other state highways between the aforesaid highways and the passenger bus terminals may be permitted upon application to the Commissioner of Highways by the governing body of any county, city, or town in which such other highways are located. Any such increase in width of passenger buses or designation of highways to be used by them shall not exceed the federal law which may hereafter be adopted, or jeopardize the Commonwealth's allotment of or qualification for federal aid highway funds.

History.

Code 1950, § 46-326; 1950, p. 982; 1952, c. 403; 1956, c. 483; 1958, c. 541, § 46.1-328; 1960, c. 591; 1968, c. 333; 1973, c. 183; 1979, c. 70; 1983, c. 515; 1985, c. 426; 1986, c. 72; 1989, c. 727; 2013, cc. 585, 646.

§ 46.2-1109. Widths of commercial vehicles.

No commercial vehicle shall exceed 102 inches in width when operating on any interstate highway or on any highway designated by the Commonwealth Transportation Board. The width limitation in this section shall not include rear view mirrors, turn signal lights, handholds for cab entry and egress, splash suppressant devices, and load-induced tire bulge. Safety devices, with the exception of rear view mirrors, shall not extend more than three inches on each side of a vehicle. The Commissioner of Highways shall designate reasonable access to terminals, facilities for food, fuel, repairs, and rest. Household goods carriers and any tractor truck semitrailer combination in which the semitrailer has a length of no more than twenty-eight and one-half feet shall not be denied reasonable access to points of loading and unloading, except as designated, based on safety considerations, by the Commissioner of Highways. No reasonable access designation shall be made, however, until notice of any proposed designation has been provided by the Commissioner of Highways to the governing body of every locality wherein any highway affected by the proposed designation is located.

For the purposes of this section, a commercial vehicle is defined as a loaded or empty motor vehicle, trailer, or semitrailer designed or regularly used for carrying freight, merchandise, or more than ten passengers, including buses, but not including vehicles used for vanpools.

History.

1986, c. 72, § 46.1-328.1; 1989, cc. 645, 727; 1994, c. 456; 1997, c. 773; 2013, cc. 585, 646.

§ 46.2-1110. Height of vehicles; damage to overhead obstruction; penalty.

No loaded or unloaded vehicle shall exceed a height of 13 feet, six inches.

Nothing contained in this section shall require either the public authorities or railroad companies to provide vertical clearances of overhead bridges or structures in excess of 12 feet, six inches, or to make any changes in the vertical clearances of existing overhead bridges or structures crossing highways. The driver or owner of vehicles on highways shall be held financially responsible for any damage to overhead bridges or structures that results from collisions therewith.

The driver or owner of any vehicle colliding with an overhead bridge or structure shall immediately notify, either in person or by telephone, a law-enforcement officer or the public authority or railroad company, owning or maintaining such overhead bridge or structure of the fact of such collision, and his name, address, driver's license number, and the registration number of his vehicle. Failure to give such notice immediately, either in person or by telephone, shall constitute a Class 1 misdemeanor.

On any highway maintained by the Department of Transportation over which there is a bridge or structure having a vertical clearance of less than 14 feet, the Commissioner of Highways shall have at least two signs erected setting forth the height of the bridge or structure. Such signs shall be located at least 1,500 feet ahead of the bridge or structure.

On any highway maintained by a county, city, or town over which a bridge or structure has a vertical clearance of less than 14 feet, the local governing body shall have at least two signs erected setting forth the height of the bridge or structure. Such signs shall be located at least 1,500 feet ahead of the bridge or structure.

The Department of Transportation may install and use overheight vehicle optical detection systems to identify vehicles that exceed the overhead clearance of the westbound tunnel of the Hampton Roads Bridge Tunnel on Interstate 64. When the optical system sensor located closest to the westbound tunnel entrance is used in identifying such vehicles, the system shall be installed at the specified height as determined by measurement standards that have been certified by the Commissioner of the Department of Agriculture and Consumer Services, and are traceable to national standards of measurement. Such identification by such system shall, for all purposes of law, be equivalent to having measured the height of the vehicle with a tape measure or other measuring device. When an employee of the Department of Transportation or the Department of State Police identifies a vehicle whose height exceeds 13 feet, six inches and whose driver is driving or attempting to drive through the westbound tunnel of the Hampton Roads Bridge Tunnel on Interstate 64, the driver of such vehicle may elect to wait until the end of peak traffic periods, as determined by the Department of Transportation, so that the Department of Transportation or Department of State Police may safely stop traffic and allow such vehicle to proceed in the opposite direction. If the driver does not elect to wait, he shall be subject to the penalties under this section.

Any person who drives or attempts to drive any vehicle or combination of vehicles into or through any tunnel when the height of such vehicle, any vehicle in a combination of vehicles, or any load on any such vehicle exceeds that permitted for such tunnel, shall be guilty of a misdemeanor and, in addition, shall be assessed three driver demerit points. In addition, the driver of any such vehicle shall be fined $1,000, of which $1,000 shall be a mandatory minimum. For subsequent offenses, the owner of any such vehicle shall be fined $2,500, of which $2,500 shall be a mandatory minimum.

A violation of this section shall be deemed for all purposes a moving violation.

History.

Code 1950, § 46-327; 1950, p. 480; 1958, c. 541, § 46.1-329; 1962, c. 85; 1984, c. 780; 1989, c. 727; 2001, c. 94; 2005, cc. 542, 543; 2006, Sp. Sess. I, c. 6; 2011, c. 620; 2015, c. 181.

§ 46.2-1111. Extension of loads beyond line of fender or body.

No vehicle shall carry any load extending more than six inches beyond the line of the fender or body. Nor shall such load exceed a total outside width as prescribed by §§ 46.2-1105 through 46.2-1109.

Notwithstanding the foregoing provisions of this section, watercraft carried on vehicles may extend more than six inches beyond the line of the fender or body of such vehicle if the total width of watercraft and the carrier upon which it is carried does not exceed seventy-six inches.

History.

Code 1950, § 46-330; 1958, c. 541, § 46.1-334; 1960, c. 280; 1979, c. 526; 1989, c. 727.

ARTICLE 16.

MAXIMUM VEHICLE LENGTHS.

§ 46.2-1112. Length of vehicles, generally; special permits; vehicle combinations, etc., operating on certain highways; penalty.

No motor vehicle longer than 40 feet shall be operated on any highway in the Commonwealth except for buses and motor homes. The actual length of any combination of vehicles, including motor homes and buses, coupled together including any load thereon shall not exceed a total of 65 feet. However, the length of a tractor truck semitrailer combination may exceed 65 feet in length, provided the semitrailer does not exceed 53 feet in length and the distance between the kingpin of the semitrailer and the rearmost axle or a point midway between the rear tandem axles does not exceed 41 feet. The Commissioner of Highways may impose restrictions on the operation of vehicles exceeding 65 feet in length on certain roads, based on a safety and engineering analysis. No bus or motor home longer than 45 feet shall be operated on any highway in the Commonwealth. No tolerance shall be allowed that exceeds 12 inches.

The Commissioner, however, when good cause is shown, may issue a special permit for combinations either in excess of 65 feet, including any load thereon, or where the object or objects to be carried cannot be moved otherwise. Such permits may also be issued by the Department when the total number of otherwise overdimensional loads of modular housing of no more than two units may be reduced by permitting the use of an overlength trailer not exceeding 54 feet. No permit shall be issued by the Commissioner until an engineering analysis of a proposed routing has been conducted by the Commissioner of Highways to assess the ability of the roadway to be traversed to sustain the vehicle's size.

No overall length restrictions, however, shall be imposed on any tractor truck semitrailer combinations drawing one trailer or any tractor truck semitrailer combinations when operated on any interstate highway or on any highway as designated by the Commonwealth Transportation Board. No such designation shall be made, however, until notice of any proposed designation has been provided by the Commissioner of Highways to the governing body of every locality wherein any highway affected by the proposed designation is located.

No individual semitrailer or trailer being drawn in a tractor truck semitrailer trailer combination, however, shall exceed 28 ½ feet in length, and no semitrailer being operated in a tractor truck semitrailer combination shall exceed 48 feet in length, except when semitrailers have a distance of not more than 41 feet between the kingpin of the semitrailer and the rearmost axle or a point midway between the rear tandem axles, such semitrailer shall be allowed not more than 53 feet in length.

The length limitations on semitrailers and trailers in the foregoing provisions of this section shall be exclusive of safety and energy conservation devices, steps and handholds for entry and egress, rubber dock guards, flexible fender extensions, mudflaps, refrigeration units, and air compressors. The Commissioner of Highways shall designate reasonable access to terminals, facilities for food, fuel, repairs and rest. Household goods carriers and any tractor truck semitrailer combination in which the semitrailer has a length of no more than 28 ½ feet shall not be denied reasonable access to points of loading and unloading, except as designated, based on safety considerations, by the Commissioner of Highways.

Any person operating a vehicle whose length is not in conformity with the provisions of this chapter on a two-lane highway where passing is permitted shall be guilty of a traffic infraction and fined $250.

History.

Code 1950, § 46-328; 1950, p. 665; 1952, c. 342; 1956, cc. 476, 483; 1958, c. 541, § 46.1-330; 1962, c. 113; 1966, c. 59; 1972, c. 446; 1974, c. 664; 1975, c. 104; 1978, c. 254; 1983, c. 515; 1985, c. 426; 1986, c. 417; 1989, cc. 644, 645, 727; 1993, c. 984; 1994, c. 456; 1995, c. 71; 1997, c. 773; 2001, c. 151; 2003, c. 314; 2005, c. 262; 2006, cc. 210, 232; 2013, cc. 585, 646; 2016, c. 122.

§ 46.2-1113. Length exceptions for certain passenger buses and motor homes.

Passenger buses and motor homes longer than thirty-five feet, but not longer than forty-five feet, may be operated on the streets of cities and towns when authorized pursuant to § 46.2-1300. Passenger buses and motor homes may exceed the forty-five-foot limitation when such excess length is caused by the projection of a front or rear safety bumper or both. Such safety bumper shall not cause the length of the bus to exceed the maximum legal limit by more than one foot in the front and one foot in the rear. "Safety bumper" means any device which may be fitted on an existing bumper or which replaces the bumper and is so constructed, treated, or manufactured to absorb energy upon impact.

History.
Code 1950, § 46-328; 1950, p. 665; 1952, c. 342; 1956, cc. 476, 483; 1958, c. 541, § 46.1-330; 1962, c. 113; 1966, c. 59; 1972, c. 446; 1974, c. 664; 1975, c. 104; 1978, c. 254; 1983, c. 515; 1985, c. 426; 1986, c. 417; 1989, c. 727; 1993, c. 984; 2001, c. 151.

§ 46.2-1114. Length of automobile or watercraft transporters; operation on certain highways.

Automobile or watercraft transporters shall not exceed a length of 65 feet when operated on any interstate highway or on any highway as designated by the Commonwealth Transportation Board. Stinger-steered automobile or watercraft transporters shall not exceed a length of 75 feet when operated on any interstate highway or on any highway designated by the Commonwealth Transportation Board. In addition, watercraft may be transported on a truck/trailer combination no more than 65 feet long when operated on any interstate highway or on any highway designated by the Commonwealth Transportation Board. Any such vehicle shall display a sign of a size and type approved by the Commissioner of Highways warning that the vehicle is an over-length vehicle. However, an additional three-foot overhang shall be allowed beyond the front and a four-foot overhang shall be allowed beyond the rear of the vehicle. Such combinations shall have reasonable access to terminals, facilities for food, fuel, repairs, and rest as designated by the Commissioner of Highways.

History.
1986, c. 72, § 46.1-330.1; 1989, cc. 645, 727; 1994, c. 456; 2013, cc. 585, 646.

§ 46.2-1115. Lengths of manufactured homes or house trailers.

The actual length of any combination of a towing vehicle and any manufactured home or house trailer, coupled together, shall not exceed a total length of sixty-five feet, including coupling.

History.
Code 1950, § 46-328.1; 1956, c. 86; 1958, c. 541, § 46.1-331; 1985, c. 426; 1989, c. 727; 1996, cc. 39, 146; 1999, c. 77.

§ 46.2-1116. Vehicles having more than one trailer, etc., attached thereto; exceptions.

Except as provided in this section and § 46.2-1117, no motor vehicle shall be driven on a highway while drawing or having attached thereto more than one motor vehicle, trailer, or semitrailer unless such vehicle is being operated under a special permit from the Commissioner of Highways. This limitation, however, shall not apply between sunrise and sunset to farm trailers or semitrailers being moved from one farm to another farm owned or operated by the same person within a radius of 10 miles. This limitation also shall not apply to a combination of vehicles coupled together by a saddle mount device used to transport motor vehicles in a drive-away service when not more than two saddle mounts are used. Vehicles coupled together by not more than three saddle mounts shall not exceed 75 feet when operated on any primary highway as designated by the Commonwealth Transportation Board and shall not exceed 97 feet when operated on the National Network of interstate and primary highways as designated under 23 CFR 658.5, as amended. Use of saddle mounts as provided in this section shall be in conformity with safety regulations adopted by the federal Department of Transportation.

The Commissioner of Highways shall designate reasonable access to terminals and facilities for food, fuel, repairs, and rest.

The governing body of any city may by ordinance permit motor vehicles to be driven on the highways of their respective cities while drawing or having attached thereto more than one other vehicle, trailer, or semitrailer.

History.
Code 1950, § 46-331; 1958, c. 541, § 46.1-335; 1962, c. 575; 1964, c. 286; 1966, c. 373; 1974, c. 580; 1978, c. 254; 1983, c. 515; 1985, c. 426; 1986, c. 72; 1989, c. 727; 1994, c. 456; 1996, c. 340; 2010, c. 24; 2013, cc. 585, 646.

§ 46.2-1117. Tractor truck semitrailer combinations operating on certain highways; access to certain facilities.

A tractor truck semitrailer combination may draw one trailer when operating on any interstate highway and any highway as designated by the Commonwealth Transportation Board. The Commissioner of Highways shall designate reasonable access to terminals, facilities for food, fuel, repairs, and rest, and points of loading and unloading for carriers of household goods.

History.
1983, c. 515, § 46.1-335.1; 1989, c. 727; 1994, c. 456; 2013, cc. 585, 646.

§ 46.2-1118. Connection between vehicles; tow trucks towing vehicles by means of a wheel lift apparatus.

The connection between any two vehicles, one of which is towing or drawing the other on a highway, shall consist of a fifth wheel, drawbar, trailer hitch, or other similar device not to exceed 15 feet in length from one vehicle to the other. Any such two vehicles shall, in addition to such drawbar or other similar device, be equipped at all times when so operated on the highway with an emergency chain or cable that is structurally adequate to securely stop and hold the trailer being towed.

The fifth wheel, drawbar, trailer hitch, or similar device must (i) be structurally adequate for the weight being drawn, (ii) be properly and securely mounted, (iii) provide for adequate articulation at the connection without excessive slack at that location, and (iv) be provided with a locking device that prevents accidental separation of the towed and towing vehicles. The mounting of the fifth wheel, drawbar, trailer hitch, or similar device on the towing vehicle must include reinforcement or bracing of the frame sufficient to produce strength and rigidity of the frame to prevent its undue distortion.

The foregoing provisions of this section shall not apply to (i) any farm tractor, as defined in § 46.2-100, when such farm tractor is towing any farm implement or farm machinery by means of a drawbar coupled with a safety hitch pin or manufacturer's coupling device or (ii) any tow truck towing a vehicle by means of a wheel lift apparatus that employs a safety strap to hold two of the towed vehicle's wheels within a wheel lift cradle in a manner consistent with instructions of the manufacturer of such wheel lift apparatus.

For the purposes of this section, "tow truck" means any motor vehicle that is constructed and used primarily for towing, lifting, or otherwise moving illegally parked or disabled vehicles.

History.

Code 1950, § 46-332; 1958, c. 541, § 46.1-336; 1982, c. 189; 1985, c. 426; 1989, c. 727; 2003, c. 414; 2010, c. 614.

§ 46.2-1119. Tow dolly and converter gear.

No axle-like device, commonly called a "tow dolly," used to support the front or rear wheels of a passenger vehicle or pick-up or panel truck for towing purposes, and no axle-like device, commonly called "converter gear," on which is mounted a fifth wheel used to convert a semitrailer to a full trailer, shall be considered vehicles. Either such device, when used on the public highways, shall be equipped with a safety chain or chains of a strength to restrain the device and vehicle being towed, should the connection fail. In addition, either device, when moved on the public highway, shall be equipped with rear marker lights or reflectors when towed without a load. When a tow dolly or converter gear is used to tow a vehicle, the towed vehicle must comply with all requirements of law pertaining to towed vehicles.

History.

1984, c. 182, § 46.1-336.1; 1989, c. 727.

§ 46.2-1120. Extension of loads beyond front of vehicles.

A. As used in this section, "self-propelled pole carrier" means a motor vehicle that is (i) operated by a public utility company as defined in § 56-265.1, or its agents, (ii) designed to carry a pole at a height of at least five feet when measured from the bottom of the brace used to carry the pole, and (iii) carrying no more than two utility poles.

B. Except as provided in subsection C, no vehicle shall carry any load extending more than three feet beyond the front of such vehicle.

C. Any utility pole carried by a self-propelled pole carrier may extend beyond the front overhang limit set by this section if the pole is no more than 55 feet in length, the pole cannot be dismembered and does not extend more than 10 feet beyond the front bumper of the vehicle, and either:

1. Between sunrise and sunset, the front of the pole is marked by a flag of the type required under § 46.2-1121 on the rear of certain loads; or

2. Between sunset and sunrise, operation of the vehicle is required to make emergency repairs to utility service, and the front of the pole is marked by a light of the type required under § 46.2-1121 on the rear of certain loads.

History.

Code 1950, § 46-329; 1958, c. 541, § 46.1-333; 1989, c. 727; 2013, cc. 242, 385.

§ 46.2-1121. Flag or light at end of load.

Whenever the load on any vehicle extends more than four feet beyond the rear of the bed or body thereof, there shall be displayed at the end of the load, in such a position as to be clearly visible at all times from the rear of the load, a red flag, not less than twelve inches, both in length and width. Between sunset and sunrise, however, there shall be displayed at the end of the load a red light plainly visible in clear weather at least 500 feet to the sides and rear of the vehicle.

History.

Code 1950, § 46-304; 1958, c. 541, § 46.1-300; 1989, c. 727.

ARTICLE 17.
MAXIMUM VEHICLE WEIGHTS.

§ 46.2-1122. Definitions.

For the purposes of this article the following terms shall have the following meanings, unless the context clearly indicates otherwise:

"Single axle" means an assembly of two or more wheels whose centers are in one transverse vertical plane or may be included between two parallel transverse vertical planes forty inches apart, extending across the full width of the vehicle.

"Tandem axle" means any two or more consecutive axles whose centers are more than forty inches but not more than ninety-six inches apart, and are individually attached to and/or articulated from a common attachment to the vehicle including a connecting mechanism designed to equalize the load between axles.

"Single axle weight" means the total weight transmitted to the highway by all wheels whose centers may be included between two parallel transverse vertical planes forty inches apart, extending across the full width of the vehicle.

"Tandem axle weight" means the total weight transmitted to the highway by two or more consecu-

tive axles whose centers may be included between parallel transverse vertical planes spaced more than forty inches and not more than ninety-six inches apart, extending across the full width of the vehicle.

"Group of axles" means any two or more consecutive axles located under a vehicle or combination.

History.

Code 1950, § 46-334; 1952, c. 454; 1956, cc. 141, 476; 1958, c. 541, § 46.1-339; 1962, c. 84; 1964, c. 354; 1974, c. 145; 1981, c. 187; 1982, c. 671; 1983, c. 515; 1987, c. 695; 1989, c. 727.

§ 46.2-1123. Weight of vehicles and loads.

The maximum gross weight and axle weight to be permitted on the road surface of any highway shall be in accordance with the provisions of this article. Any notice by the Department of Transportation to truckers as to the provisions of this article shall include all limits as provided in this article.

History.

Code 1950, § 46-334; 1952, c. 454; 1956, cc. 141, 476; 1958, c. 541, § 46.1-339; 1962, c. 84; 1964, c. 354; 1974, c. 145; 1981, c. 187; 1982, c. 671; 1983, c. 515; 1987, c. 695; 1989, c. 727.

§ 46.2-1124. Maximum single axle weight, generally; maximum weight per inch of tire width.

The single axle weight of any vehicle or combination shall not exceed 20,000 pounds, nor shall it exceed 650 pounds per inch, width of tire, measured in contact with the surface of the highway.

History.

Code 1950, § 46-334; 1952, c. 454; 1956, cc. 141, 476; 1958, c. 541, § 46.1-339; 1962, c. 84; 1964, c. 354; 1974, c. 145; 1981, c. 187; 1982, c. 671; 1983, c. 515; 1987, c. 695; 1989, c. 727.

§ 46.2-1125. Maximum tandem axle weight, generally.

The tandem axle weight of any vehicle or combination shall not exceed 34,000 pounds, and no one axle of such tandem unit shall exceed the weight permitted for a single axle. Furthermore, the weight imposed on the highway by two or more consecutive axles, individually attached to the vehicle and spaced not less than forty inches nor more than ninety-six inches apart, shall not exceed 34,000 pounds and no one axle of such unit shall exceed the weight permitted for a single axle.

History.

Code 1950, § 46-334; 1952, c. 454; 1956, cc. 141, 476; 1958, c. 541, § 46.1-339; 1962, c. 84; 1964, c. 354; 1974, c. 145; 1981, c. 187; 1982, c. 671; 1983, c. 515; 1987, c. 695; 1989, c. 727.

§ 46.2-1126. Maximum gross weight, generally.

Except as provided in § 46.2-1128, the gross weight imposed on the highway by a vehicle or combination shall not exceed the maximum weight given for the respective distance between the first and last axle of the vehicle or combination, nor shall any two or more consecutive axles exceed the maximum weight given, when measured longitudinally with any fraction of a foot rounded to the next highest as set forth in the following table:

Distance in feet between the extremes of any group of two or more consecutive axles	or Maximum weight in pounds on any group of axles					
	2 axles	3 axles	4 axles	5 axles	6 axles	7 axles
4	34,000	...	...	...	...	...
5	34,000	...	...	...	...	...
6	34,000	...	...	...	...	...
7	34,000	...	...	...	...	...
8	34,000	34,000	...	...	...	...
9	39,000	42,500	...	...	...	...
10	40,000	43,500	...	...	...	...
11	...	44,000	...	...	...	...
12	...	45,000	50,000	...	...	...
13	...	45,000	50,500	...	...	...
14	...	46,500	51,500	...	...	...
15	...	47,000	52,000	...	...	...
16	...	48,000	52,500	58,000	...	...
17	...	48,500	53,500	58,500	...	...
18	...	49,500	54,000	59,000	...	...
19	...	50,000	54,500	60,000	...	...
20	...	51,000	55,500	60,500	66,000	...
21	...	51,500	56,000	61,000	66,500	...
22	...	52,500	56,500	61,500	67,000	...

Motor Vehicles

Distance in feet between the extremes of any group of two or more consecutive axles			or Maximum weight in pounds on any group of axles			
	2 axles	3 axles	4 axles	5 axles	6 axles	7 axles
23	...	53,000	57,500	62,500	68,000	...
24	...	54,000	58,000	63,000	68,500	74,000
25	...	54,500	58,500	63,500	69,000	74,500
26	...	55,500	59,500	64,000	69,500	75,000
27	...	56,000	60,000	65,000	70,000	75,500
28	...	57,000	60,500	65,500	71,000	76,500
29	...	57,500	61,500	66,000	71,500	77,000
30	...	58,500	62,000	66,500	72,000	77,500
31	...	59,000	62,500	67,500	72,500	78,000
32	...	60,000	63,500	68,000	73,000	78,500
33	...	...	64,000	68,500	74,000	79,000
34	...	...	64,500	69,000	74,500	80,000
35	...	...	65,500	70,000	75,000	...
36	...	...	66,000	70,500	75,500	...
37	...	...	66,500	71,000	76,000	...
38	...	...	67,500	72,000	77,000	...
39	...	...	68,000	72,500	77,500	...
40	...	...	68,500	73,000	78,000	...
41	...	...	69,500	73,500	78,500	...
42	...	...	70,000	74,000	79,000	...
43	...	...	70,500	75,000	80,000	...
44	...	...	71,500	75,500	...	...
45	...	...	72,000	76,000	...	...
46	...	...	72,500	76,500	...	...
47	...	...	73,500	77,500	...	...
48	...	...	74,000	78,000	...	...
49	...	...	74,500	78,500	...	...
50	...	...	75,500	79,000	...	...
51	...	...	76,000	80,000	...	...

History.

Code 1950, § 46-334; 1952, c. 454; 1956, cc. 141, 476; 1958, c. 541, § 46.1-339; 1962, c. 84; 1964, c. 354; 1974, c. 145; 1981, c. 187; 1982, c. 671; 1983, c. 515; 1987, c. 695; 1989, c. 727; 1994, c. 456.

§ 46.2-1127. Weight limits for vehicles using interstate highways.

No motor vehicle or combination of vehicles shall travel on an interstate highway in the Commonwealth with (i) a single axle weight in excess of 20,000 pounds, or (ii) a tandem axle weight in excess of 34,000 pounds, or (iii) a gross weight, based on axle spacing, greater than that permitted in § 46.2-1126, or (iv) a gross weight, regardless of axle spacing, in excess of 80,000 pounds, unless otherwise permitted by the proper authority. If such weights on interstate highways are increased, the Governor, upon recommendation of the Department of Transportation, may authorize the axle and gross weights set forth in this section to be used on interstate highways in the Commonwealth.

History.

Code 1950, § 46-334; 1952, c. 454; 1956, cc. 141, 476; 1958, c. 541, § 46.1-339; 1962, c. 84; 1964, c. 354; 1974, c. 145; 1981, c. 187; 1982, c. 671; 1983, c. 515; 1987, c. 695; 1989, c. 727.

§ 46.2-1128. Extensions of weight limits; fees.

The owner of any motor vehicle may obtain an extension of single axle, tandem axle, and gross weight set forth in this article by purchasing an overload permit for such vehicle. The permit shall extend the single axle weight limit of 20,000 pounds, tandem axle weight limit of 34,000 pounds, and gross weight limit based on axle spacing and number of axles on such vehicle by a maximum of five percent. However, no such permit shall authorize the operation of a motor vehicle whose gross weight exceeds 84,000 pounds, nor shall any such permit authorize any extension of the limitations provided in § 46.2-1127 for interstate highways.

Permits under this section shall be valid for one year and the fee shall be $250.

Such fee shall be allocated as follows: (i) $245 deposited into the Highway Maintenance and Operating Fund established pursuant to § 33.2-1530 to be used to assist in funding needed highway pavement and bridge maintenance and rehabilitation and (ii) a $5 administrative fee paid into the state treasury and set aside as a special fund to be used to meet the expenses of the Department.

The Commissioner shall make the permit available to vehicles registered outside the Commonwealth under the same conditions and restrictions which are applicable to vehicles registered within the Commonwealth. The Commissioner may promulgate regulations governing such permits. Except as provided in this section and § 46.2-1129, no weights in excess of those authorized by law shall be tolerated.

Vehicles that are registered as farm use vehicles as provided in § 46.2-698 may operate as authorized under this section without a permit or the payment of any fee; provided, however, that should such vehicle violate the weight limits permitted by this section and § 46.2-1129, such vehicle shall be required to apply for and receive a permit and pay the permit fee to operate as authorized in this section.

History.

1987, c. 695, § 46.1-339.01; 1988, c. 669; 1989, c. 727; 1997, c. 283; 2002, c. 265; 2006, c. 534; 2012, c. 443.

§ 46.2-1129. Further extensions of weight limits for certain vehicles hauling Virginia-grown farm or forest products.

The owner of any motor vehicle used for hauling Virginia-grown forest or farm products, as defined in § 3.2-4709, from the place where they are first produced, cut, harvested, or felled to the location where they are first processed may obtain from the Commissioner an extension for such vehicle of the single axle, tandem axle, and gross weight limits set forth in this title. The permit shall extend the single axle, tandem axle, and gross weight limits set forth in this title. The permit shall extend the single axle, tandem axle, and gross weight limits based on axle spacing and number of axles on such vehicle by five percent, respectively. However, no such permit shall authorize the operation of a motor vehicle whose gross weight exceeds 84,000 pounds.

No permit issued under this section shall permit the operation on an interstate highway of any vehicle with (i) a single axle weight in excess of 20,000 pounds, or (ii) a tandem axle weight in excess of 34,000 pounds, or (iii) a gross weight, based on axle spacing, greater than that permitted in § 46.2-1126, or (iv) a gross weight, regardless of axle spacing, in excess of 80,000 pounds. The Commissioner may promulgate regulations governing such permits.

Weight extensions provided in this section shall be in addition to those provided in § 46.2-1128, but no weights beyond those permitted by the combination of the extensions provided in this section and § 46.2-1128 shall be tolerated.

Vehicles that are registered as farm use vehicles as provided in § 46.2-698 may operate as authorized under this section; provided, however, that should such vehicle violate the weight limits permitted by this section and § 46.2-1128, such vehicle shall no longer be permitted to operate as authorized in this section.

History.

1988, c. 669, § 46.1-339.02; 1989, c. 727; 1997, c. 283; 2006, c. 534; 2012, c. 443.

§ 46.2-1129.1. Further extension of weight limits for certain vehicles utilizing an auxiliary power unit or other idle reduction technology.

Any motor vehicle that utilizes an auxiliary power unit or other idle reduction technology in order to promote reduction of fuel use and emissions due to engine idling shall be allowed up to an additional 550 pounds total in gross, single axle, tandem axle, or bridge formula weight limits.

To be eligible for this exception, the operator of the vehicle must be able to prove (i) by written certification, the weight of the auxiliary power unit or other idle reduction technology unit and (ii) by demonstration or written certification, that such idle reduction technology is fully functional at all times.

Certification of the weight of the auxiliary power unit must be available to law-enforcement officials if the vehicle is found in violation of applicable weight laws. The additional weight allowed cannot exceed 550 pounds or the weight certified, whichever is less.

For purposes of this section, "auxiliary power unit" means a mechanical or electrical device affixed to a motor vehicle that is designed to be used to generate an alternative source of power for any of the motor vehicle's systems other than the primary propulsion engine, and "idle reduction technology" refers to a technology that allows engine operators to refrain from long-duration idling of the main propulsion engine by using an alternative technology.

History.

2009, c. 92; 2013, c. 118.

§ 46.2-1129.2. Further extension of weight limits for vehicles fueled by natural gas.

Any motor vehicle that is fueled, wholly or partially, by natural gas shall be allowed up to an additional 2,000 pounds total in gross, single axle, tandem axle, or bridge formula weight limits.

To be eligible for this exception, the operator of the vehicle must be able to demonstrate that the vehicle is a natural gas vehicle, a bi-fuel vehicle using natural gas, or a vehicle that has been converted to a natural gas vehicle. No such allowance shall authorize any extension of the limitations provided in § 46.2-1127 for Interstate highways.

History.

2014, c. 64.

§ 46.2-1130. Crossing bridge or culvert by vehicle heavier than allowed; where weight signs to be erected.

No vehicle shall cross any bridge or culvert in the Commonwealth if the gross weight of such vehicle is greater than the amount posted for the bridge or culvert as its carrying capacity.

Signs stating the carrying capacity shall be erected and maintained near each end of the bridge or culvert on the approaches to such bridge or culvert. Whenever the weight capacity of any structure on the interstate or primary system is reduced below the weight limit permitted on the road of which it is a part, a sign indicating that there is a restricted structure shall be placed in advance of the last alternate route on the road upon which there is a restricted structure. Whenever the weight capacity of any structure is reduced below the weight limit permitted on the road of which it is a part, a sign indicating that there is a restricted structure, shall be placed in advance of the last alternate route on the road upon which there is a restricted structure.

History.

Code 1950, § 46-335; 1958, c. 541, § 46.1-340; 1974, c. 347; 1989, c. 727.

§ 46.2-1130.1. Overweight permits granted to cross bridges and culverts by certain emergency response vehicles responding to an emergency call.

Notwithstanding the provisions of §§ 46.2-1104 and 46.2-1130, emergency response vehicles, including fire and emergency medical apparatus responding to and returning from an emergency call, may be permitted to exceed the gross weight limit posted on a bridge or culvert, except those maintained by a railroad, provided that a determination has been made by a licensed professional engineer, qualified in the appropriate discipline, that the emergency response vehicle can safely cross that bridge or culvert and that determination has been documented by the issuance of a written permit or letter of authorization by the agency or entity responsible for the maintenance of that bridge or culvert.

The permitting agency or entity shall not be held liable for any damage or injury caused as a result of an emergency response vehicle crossing a bridge or culvert while responding to or returning from an emergency call under the conditions specified in the overweight permit pursuant to this section.

History.

2007, cc. 177, 540.

§ 46.2-1131. Penalty for violation of weight limits.

Any person violating any weight limit as provided in this chapter or any permit issued by the Department or its designee or by local authorities pursuant to this article shall be subject to a civil penalty of $25 and a processing fee of $20 in addition to any liquidated damages and weighing fees imposed by this article. Upon collection by the Department, except as provided in § 46.2-1138, civil penalties shall be paid to the Literary Fund, but processing fees shall be paid to the state treasury and, beginning July 1, 1990, shall be set aside as a special fund to be used to meet the expenses of the Department of Motor Vehicles. In addition, liquidated damages and weighing fees shall be distributed as provided in §§ 46.2-1135 and 46.2-1137, respectively, except as provided in § 46.2-1138.

The penalties, damages, and fees specified in this section shall be in addition to any other liability which may be legally fixed against the owner, operator, or other person charged with the weight violation for damage to a highway or bridge attributable to such weight violation.

History.

Code 1950, § 46-335.1; 1956, c. 215; 1958, c. 541, § 46.1-341; 1972, c. 439; 1978, cc. 294, 605; 1986, c. 588; 1987, c. 372; 1988, c. 11; 1989, c. 727; 1990, c. 418; 2003, c. 314.

§ 46.2-1132. Service of process in weight violation cases.

Any person, whether resident or nonresident, who permits the operation of a motor vehicle in the Commonwealth by his agent or employee shall be deemed to have appointed the operator of such motor vehicle his statutory agent for the purpose of service of process in any proceeding against such person growing out of any weight violation involving such motor vehicle. Acceptance by a nonresident of the rights and privileges conferred by §§ 46.2-655 through 46.2-661 shall have the same effect under this section as operation of such motor vehicle by such nonresident, his agent, or his employee.

History.

1986, c. 588, § 46.1-341.01; 1989, c. 727.

§ 46.2-1133. Special processing provisions for overweight violations.

Notwithstanding any other provision of law, all violations of any weight limit as provided in this article or any permit issued by either the Department or its designee or by local authorities pursuant to this chapter shall be processed in the following manner:

1. The officer or size and weight compliance agent charging the violation shall serve a citation on the operator of the overweight vehicle. The citation shall be directed to the owner, operator, or other person responsible for the overweight violation as determined by the officer or size and weight compliance agent. Service of the citation on the vehicle operator shall constitute service of process upon the owner, operator, or other person charged with the weight violation as provided in § 46.2-1136.

2. The officer or size and weight compliance agent charging the violation shall cause the citation to be delivered or mailed by first-class mail to the Department within 24 hours after it is served.

3. The owner, operator, or other person charged with the weight violation shall, within 21 days after the citation is served upon the vehicle operator, either make full payment to the Department of the civil penalty, liquidated damages, weighing fee, and processing fee as stated on the citation, or deliver to the Department a written notice of his election to contest the overweight charge in court.

4. Failure of the owner, operator, or other person charged with the weight violation to timely deliver to the Department either payment in full of the uncontested civil penalty, liquidated damages, weighing fee, and processing fee or a notice of contest of the weight violation shall cause the Department to issue an administrative order of assessment against such person. A copy of the order shall be sent by first-class mail to the person charged with the weight violation. Any such administrative order shall have the same effect as a judgment for liquidated damages entered by a general district court.

5. Upon timely receipt of a notice of contest of an overweight charge, the Department shall:

a. Forward the citation to the general district court named in the citation, and

b. Send by first-class mail to the person charged with the weight violation, and to the officer or size and weight compliance agent who issued the citation, confirmation that the citation has been forwarded to the court for trial.

6. Notices and pleadings may be served by first-class mail sent to the address shown on the citation as the address of the person charged with the weight violation or, if none is shown, to the address of record for the person to whom the vehicle is registered.

7. An alleged weight violation which is contested shall be tried as a civil case. The attorney for the Commonwealth shall represent the interests of the Commonwealth. The disposition of the case shall be recorded in an appropriate order, a copy of which shall be sent to the Department in lieu of any record which may be otherwise required by § 46.2-383. If judgment is for the Commonwealth, payment shall be made to the Department.

8. Notwithstanding any other provisions of this section, any and all citations and notices required by this section to be provided to the person charged with a violation or received from the person charged with a violation, with the exclusion of the citation as set out in subdivision 1, may be served or provided in an electronic manner if the Department and the person charged with the violation have agreed to utilize electronic notification.

History.

1986, c. 588, § 46.1-341.02; 1987, c. 372; 1989, c. 727; 2003, c. 314; 2011, cc. 62, 73.

§ 46.2-1134. Special overweight seizure provisions; penalty.

Any officer or size and weight compliance agent authorized to serve process or weigh vehicles under the provisions of this chapter may hold an overweight vehicle without an attachment summons or court order, but only for such time as is reasonably necessary to promptly petition for an attachment summons to attach the vehicle.

After finding reasonable cause for the issuance of an attachment summons, the judicial officer conducting the hearing shall inform the operator of the vehicle of his option to either pay the liquidated damages, civil penalty, weighing fee, and processing fee, or contest the charge through the attachment proceeding. If the operator chooses to make payment, he shall do so to the judicial officer who shall transmit the citation, liquidated damages, civil penalty, weighing fee, and processing fee to the Department for distribution in accordance with § 46.2-1131.

The Commonwealth shall not be required to post bond in order to attach a vehicle pursuant to this section. The officer or size and weight compliance agent authorized to hold the overweight vehicle pending a hearing on the attachment petition shall also be empowered to execute the attachment summons if issued. Any bond for the retention of the vehicle or for release of the attachment shall be given in accordance with § 8.01-553 except that the bond shall be taken by a judicial officer. The judicial officer shall return the bond to the clerk of the appropriate court in place of the officer serving the attachment as otherwise provided in § 8.01-554.

In the event the civil penalty, liquidated damages, weighing fee, and processing fee are not paid in full, or no bond is given by or for the person charged with the weight violation, the vehicle involved in the weight violation shall be stored in a secure place, as may be designated by the owner or operator of the vehicle. If no place is designated, the officer or size and weight compliance agent executing the attachment summons shall designate the place of storage. The owner or operator shall be afforded the right of unloading and removing the cargo from the vehicle. The risk and cost of the storage shall be borne by the owner or operator of the vehicle.

Whenever an attachment summons is issued for a weight violation, the court shall forward to the Department both a copy of the order disposing of the case and the weight violation citation prepared by the officer or size and weight compliance agent but not served.

Upon notification of the judgment or administrative order entered for such weight violation and notification of the failure of such person to satisfy the judgment or order, the Department or the Department of State Police or any law-enforcement officer or size and weight compliance agent shall thereafter deny the offending person the right to operate a motor vehicle or vehicles upon the highways of the Commonwealth until the judgment or order has been satisfied and a reinstatement fee of $50 has been paid to the Department. Reinstatement fees collected under the provisions of this section shall be paid by the Commissioner into the state treasury and shall be set aside as a special fund to be used to meet the expenses of the Department.

When informed that the right to operate the motor vehicle has been denied, the driver shall drive the motor vehicle to a nearby location off the public highways and not move it or permit it to be moved until such judgment or order has been satisfied. Failure by the driver to comply with this provision shall constitute a Class 4 misdemeanor.

All costs incurred by the Commonwealth and all judgments, if any, against the Commonwealth due to action taken pursuant to this section shall be paid from the fund into which liquidated damages are paid.

Police officers of the Department of State Police and all other law-enforcement officers are vested with the same powers with respect to the enforcement of this chapter as they have with respect to the enforcement of the criminal laws of the Commonwealth.

History.

1986, c. 588, § 46.1-341.03; 1987, c. 372; 1989, c. 727; 2011, cc. 62, 73.

§ 46.2-1135. (Contingent expiration date — see Editor's notes) Liquidated damages for violation of weight limits.

A. Any person violating any weight limit as provided in this chapter or in any permit issued pursuant to Article 18 (§ 46.2-1139 et seq.) of this chapter by the Department or its designee or by local authorities pursuant to this chapter shall be assessed liquidated damages. The amount of those damages shall be:

Excess weight over the prescribed or permitted axle weight limits	Assessed amount per pound
2,000 pounds or less	1¢ per pound
2,001 to 4,000 pounds	3¢ per pound
4,001 to 8,000 pounds	12¢ per pound
8,001 to 12,000 pounds	22¢ per pound
12,001 pounds or more	35¢ per pound

Excess weight over the prescribed gross weight limit	Assessed amount per pound
2,000 pounds or less	1¢ per pound
2,001 to 4,000 pounds	3¢ per pound
4,001 to 8,000 pounds	7¢ per pound
8,001 to 12,000 pounds	12¢ per pound
12,001 pounds or more	20¢ per pound

All gross permit violations shall be assessed $.20 per pound over the permitted weight limit.

In addition to all damages assessed herein, for every violation of any weight limit as provided in this chapter or in any permit issued pursuant to Article 18 (§ 46.2-1139 et seq.) of this chapter, there shall be assessed additional liquidated damages of $20.

If a person has no prior violations under the motor vehicle weight laws, and the excess weight does not exceed 1,500 pounds, the general district court may waive the liquidated damages against such person. Except as provided by § 46.2-1138, such assessment shall be entered by the court or by the Department as a judgment for the Commonwealth, the entry of which shall constitute a lien upon the overweight vehicle. Except as provided by § 46.2-1138, such sums shall be paid to the Department or collected by the attorney for the Commonwealth and forwarded to the State Treasurer and allocated to the fund appropriated for the construction and maintenance of state highways.

B. If the gross weight of the vehicle exceeds lawful limits by at least 25 percent but no more than 50 percent, the amount of the liquidated damages shall be two times the amount provided for in the foregoing provisions of this section; if the gross weight of the vehicle exceeds lawful limits by more than 50 percent, the amount of the liquidated damages shall be three times the amount provided for in the foregoing provisions of this section. The provisions of this subsection shall not apply to pickup or panel trucks.

C. The increases in the liquidated damages under subsection A pursuant to enactments of the 2007 Session of the General Assembly shall not be applicable to any motor vehicle hauling forest or farm products from the place where such products are first produced, cut, harvested, or felled to the location where they are first processed. The amount of liquidated damages assessed against such motor vehicles shall be:

Excess weight over the prescribed or permitted axle weight limits	Assessed amount per pound
4,000 pounds or less	1¢ per pound
4,001 to 8,000 pounds	10¢ per pound
8,001 to 12,000 pounds	20¢ per pound
12,001 pounds or more	30¢ per pound

Excess weight over the prescribed gross weight limit	Assessed amount per pound
4,000 pounds or less	1¢ per pound
4,001 to 8,000 pounds	5¢ per pound
8,001 to 12,000 pounds	10¢ per pound
12,001 pounds or more	15¢ per pound

History.

Code 1950, § 46-338.2; 1956, c. 215; 1958, cc. 541, 612, § 46.1-342; 1968, c. 184; 1974, c. 331; 1977, c. 644; 1981, c. 187; 1986, c. 588; 1987, c. 372; 1989, c. 727; 1994, c. 922; 1997, c. 479; 2001, cc. 411, 433; 2003, c. 314; 2007, c. 896.

Section set out twice.

The section above is effective until December 31 of any year revenues designated for the Highway Maintenance and Operating Fund or the Transportation Trust Fund are appropriated for any non-transportation related purposes. For this section as in effect after that date, see the following section, also numbered 46.2-1135.

Editor's note.

Acts 2007, c. 896, cl. 22 provides: "That the provisions of this act which generate additional revenue for the Transportation Trust Fund, established under § 33.1-23.03:1 [see now § 33.2-1524] of the Code of Virginia, or the Highway Maintenance and Operating Fund shall expire on December 31 of any year in which the General Assembly appropriates any of the revenues designated under general law to the Highway Maintenance and Operating Fund or the Transportation Trust Fund for any non-transportation related purpose."

Acts 2010, c. 874, cl. 2 provides: "That no provision of this act shall be construed or interpreted to cause the expiration of any provision of Chapter 896 of the Acts of Assembly of 2007 pursuant to the 22nd enactment of such Chapter."

Acts 2010, c. 874, cl. 8 provides: "That the provisions of the first enactment of this act shall expire at midnight on June 30, 2012. The provisions of the second, third, fourth, fifth, sixth, and seventh enactments of this act shall have no expiration date."

§ 46.2-1135. (Contingent effective date — see Editor's notes) Liquidated damages for violation of weight limits.

A. Any person violating any weight limit as provided in this chapter or in any permit issued pursuant to Article 18 (§ 46.2-1139 et seq.) of this chapter by the Department or its designee or by local authorities pursuant to this chapter shall be assessed liquidated damages. The amount of those damages shall be:

Excess weight over the prescribed or permitted axle weight limits	Assessed amount per pound
4,000 pounds or less	1¢ per pound
4,001 to 8,000 pounds	10¢ per pound
8,001 to 12,000 pounds	20¢ per pound
12,001 pounds or more	30¢ per pound

Excess weight over the prescribed gross weight limit	Assessed amount per pound
4,000 pounds or less	1¢ per pound
4,001 to 8,000 pounds	5¢ per pound
8,001 to 12,000 pounds	10¢ per pound
12,001 pounds or more	15¢ per pound

All gross permit violations shall be assessed $.20 per pound over the permitted weight limit.

If a person has no prior violations under the motor vehicle weight laws, and the excess weight does not exceed 2,500 pounds, the general district court may waive the liquidated damages against such person. Except as provided by § 46.2-1138, such assessment shall be entered by the court or by the Department as a judgment for the Commonwealth, the entry of which shall constitute a lien upon the overweight vehicle. Except as provided by § 46.2-1138, such sums shall be paid to the Department or collected by the attorney for the Commonwealth and forwarded to the State Treasurer and allocated to the fund appropriated for the construction and maintenance of state highways.

B. If the gross weight of the vehicle exceeds lawful limits by at least 25 percent but no more than 50 percent, the amount of the liquidated damages shall be two times the amount provided for in the foregoing provisions of this section; if the gross weight of the vehicle exceeds lawful limits by more than 50 percent, the amount of the liquidated damages shall be three times the amount provided for in the foregoing provisions of this section. The provisions of this subsection shall not apply to pickup or panel trucks.

History.

Code 1950, § 46-338.2; 1956, c. 215; 1958, cc. 541, 612, § 46.1-342; 1968, c. 184; 1974, c. 331; 1977, c. 644; 1981, c. 187; 1986, c. 588; 1987, c. 372; 1989, c. 727; 1994, c. 922; 1997, c. 479; 2001, cc. 411, 433; 2003, c. 314.

Section set out twice.

The section above is effective December 31 of any year revenues designated for the Highway Maintenance and Operating Fund or the Transportation Trust Fund are appropriated for any non-transportation related purposes. For this section as in effect until that time, see the preceding section, also numbered 46.2-1135.

Editor's note.

Acts 2007, c. 896, cl. 22 provides: "That the provisions of this act which generate additional revenue for the Transportation Trust Fund, established under § 33.1-23.03:1 [see now § 33.2-1524] of the Code of Virginia, or the Highway Maintenance and Operating Fund shall expire on December 31 of any year in which the General Assembly appropriates any of the revenues designated under general law to the Highway Maintenance and Operating Fund or the Transportation Trust Fund for any non-transportation related purpose."

§ 46.2-1136. Procedures for issuing and serving process in overweight vehicle cases.

Any officer or size and weight compliance agent authorized to enforce overweight vehicle laws may issue a citation for a violation of such laws. Such officer may also serve an attachment summons issued by a judge or magistrate in connection with a weight violation.

Service of any such citation shall be made upon the driver of the motor vehicle involved in the violation. Such service on the driver shall have the same legal force and validity as if served within the Commonwealth personally upon the owner, operator, or other person charged with the weight violation, whether such owner, operator, or other person charged is a resident or nonresident.

History.

1986, c. 588, § 46.1-179.02; 1989, c. 727; 2011, cc. 62, 73.

§ 46.2-1137. Weighing vehicles; procedure; shifting loads; unloading excess load; weighing fee; certificate as to accuracy of scales admissible in evidence; penalties.

Any officer or size and weight compliance agent authorized to enforce the law under this title, having reason to believe that the weight of a vehicle and load is unlawful, is authorized to weigh the load and the vehicle. If the place where the vehicle is stopped is 10 road miles or less from a permanent weighing station, the officer may, and upon demand of the driver shall, require the vehicle to proceed to such station. If the distance to the nearest permanent weighing station is more than 10 road miles such vehicle may be weighed by wheel load weighers. Any driver who fails or unreasonably refuses to drive his vehicle to such permanent weighing station or such scales or wheel load weighers upon the request and direction of the officer to do so shall be guilty of a Class 4 misdemeanor. The penalty for such violation shall be in addition to any other penalties prescribed for exceeding the maximum weight permitted or for any other violation.

In the event of such failure or unreasonable refusal, where the officer has reason to believe the vehicle is overweight, the officer may use whatever reasonable means are available to have the vehicle weighed, including the employment of a tow truck to move the vehicle to the weighing area. He may also use whatever means are necessary to reload the vehicle if the load is intentionally dumped. In such a case, any expenses incurred in having the vehicle weighed may be taxed as costs to be imposed upon the operator who failed or unreasonably refused to drive his vehicle to such weighing area, when he has been convicted of such failure or refusal and an overweight violation. In all cases where such failure or refusal or overweight charges are dismissed, payment shall be made from highway funds.

Should the officer or size and weight compliance agent find that the weight of any vehicle and its load is greater than that permitted by this title or that the weight of the load carried in or on such vehicle is greater than that which the vehicle is licensed to carry under the provisions of this title, he may require the driver to unload, at the nearest place where the property unloaded may be stored or transferred to another vehicle, such portion of the load as may be necessary to decrease the gross weight of the vehicle to the maximum therefor permitted by this title. Any property so unloaded shall be stored or cared for by the owner or operator of the overweight vehicle at the risk of such owner or operator.

However, notwithstanding the provisions of §§ 46.2-1122 through 46.2-1127, should the officer or size and weight compliance agent find that the gross weight of the vehicle and its load is within limits permitted under this title and does not exceed the limit for which the vehicle is registered, but that the axle weight of any axle or axles of the vehicle exceeds that permitted under this title, the driver shall be allowed one hour to shift his load within or on that same vehicle in order to bring the axle weight or axle weights within proper limits. However, liquidated damages shall be assessed under § 46.2-1135 based on the weight prior to shifting the load, unless the load can be successfully shifted to bring the vehicle's axle weight within limits permitted under this title by (i) sliding the axle or axles of the semitrailer or the fifth wheel of the tractor truck, (ii) repositioning the load if the motor vehicle is transporting off-the-road mobile construction equipment, or (iii) adjusting the load if the vehicle is operating on non-interstate highways and qualifies for weight extensions pursuant to § 46.2-1129. Such load shifting shall be performed at the site where the vehicle was weighed and found to exceed allowable axle weight limits. No such load shifting shall be allowed if such load is required to be placarded as defined in § 10.1-1450 and consists of hazardous material as defined in § 10.1-1400.

If the driver of an overloaded vehicle is convicted, forfeits bail, or purchases an increased license as a result of such weighing, the court in addition to all other penalties shall assess and collect a weighing fee of two dollars from the owner or operator of the vehicle and shall forward such fee to the State Treasurer. Upon receipt of the fee, the State Treasurer shall allocate the same to the fund appropriated for the administration and maintenance of the Department of State Police.

In any court or legal proceedings in which any question arises as to the calibration or accuracy of any such scales at permanent weighing stations or wheel load weighers, a certificate, executed and signed under oath by the inspector calibrating or testing such device as to its accuracy as well as to the accuracy of the test weights used in such test, and stating the date of such test, type of test and results of testing, shall be admissible when attested by one such inspector who executed and signed it as evidence of the facts therein stated and the results of such testing.

History.

Code 1950, § 46-342; 1954, c. 312; 1956, c. 698; 1958, c. 541, § 46.1-347; 1972, c. 292; 1981, c. 187; 1982, c. 681; 1983, c. 577; 1986, c. 589; 1989, c. 727; 1996, c. 422; 2001, cc. 411, 433; 2002, cc. 99, 431; 2011, cc. 62, 73.

§ 46.2-1138: County ordinances fixing weight limits on roads which have been withdrawn from secondary system [Not set out.] (1989, c. 727.)

Editor's note.

This section, relating to adoption of Ordinances by Arlington and Henrico Counties fixing weight limits on roads which have been withdrawn from the secondary system, was enacted by Acts 1989, c. 727. In furtherance of the general policy of the Commission to include in the Code only provisions having general and permanent application, this section, which is limited in its purpose and scope, is not set out here, but attention is called to it by this reference.

The section catchline was inserted at the direction of the Virginia Code Commission.

§ 46.2-1138.1. City ordinances fixing weight limits on certain roads.

The governing body of any city may adopt ordinances providing weight limits in accordance with the weight limits established by §§ 46.2-1123 through 46.2-1127 for any vehicle or combination of vehicles passing over any such roads under the jurisdiction of such city, and providing further for the assessment of liquidated damages as to overweight vehicles at rates and amounts not exceeding those applicable to the liquidated damages under § 46.2-1135. Such ordinances may provide:

Upon a finding of a violation of any weight limit prescribed therein, the court shall assess the owner, operator or other person causing the operation of such overweight vehicle at such rate and amount as may be provided in such ordinance;

The assessment shall be entered by the court as a judgment for such city;

The entry of such judgment shall constitute a lien upon the overweight vehicles;

Such sums shall be paid into the treasury of such city, and allocated to the fund appropriated by such city for the construction and maintenance of such roads under its jurisdiction.

Such ordinances may include additional provisions relating to payment of such assessment and enforcement powers applicable to such city and corresponding to the provisions of §§ 46.2-1131, 46.2-1133, 46.2-1134 and 46.2-1135, except that civil penalties, liquidated damages and weighing fees collected pursuant to such ordinances shall be paid to the city, and the city attorney or his designee shall represent the city in any court proceeding.

History.

1960, c. 218, § 46.1-342.1; 1986, c. 588; 1987, c. 372; 1989, cc. 685, 727.

§ 46.2-1138.2. Town ordinances concerning weight limits on certain roads.

A. The governing body of any town that provided, on January 1, 1993, town-owned and -maintained weight scales for the purpose of enforcing the weight limits established by §§ 46.2-1123 through 46.2-1127 for any vehicle or combination of vehicles passing over any roads in the town may adopt ordinances for the assessment of liquidated damages as to overweight vehicles in accordance with the liquidated damages under § 46.2-1135. Such ordinances may provide that:

1. Upon a finding of a violation of any weight limit prescribed therein, the court shall assess the owner, operator or other person causing the operation of such overweight vehicle at such rate and amount as may be provided in such ordinance;
2. The assessment shall be entered by the court as a judgment for such town;
3. The entry of such judgment shall constitute a lien upon the overweight vehicle; and
4. Such sum shall be paid into the treasury of the town and allocated to the fund appropriated by the town for the construction and maintenance of roads under its jurisdiction.

B. Such ordinances may include additional provisions relating to the payment of such assessment and the enforcement powers applicable to such town and corresponding to the provisions of §§ 46.2-1131, 46.2-1133, 46.2-1134 and 46.2-1135, except that civil penalties, liquidated damages and weighing fees collected pursuant to such ordinances shall be paid to the town, and the town attorney or his designee shall represent the town in any court proceeding.

History.

1993, c. 511.

ARTICLE 18.

PERMITS FOR EXCESSIVE SIZE AND WEIGHT.

§ 46.2-1139. Permits for excessive size and weight generally; penalty.

A. The Commissioner and, unless otherwise indicated in this article, local authorities of cities and towns, in their respective jurisdictions, may, upon written application and good cause being shown, and pursuant to the requirements of subsection A1, issue a permit authorizing the applicant to operate on a highway a vehicle of a size or weight exceeding the maximum specified in this title. Any such permit may designate the route to be traversed and contain any other restrictions or conditions deemed necessary by the body granting the permit.

A1. Any city or town, as authorized under subsection A, or any county that has withdrawn its roads from the secondary system of state highways that opts to issue permits under this article shall enter into a memorandum of understanding with the Commissioner that:

1. Allows the Commissioner to issue permits on behalf of that locality; and

2. Provides that the locality shall satisfy the following requirements prior to issuing such permits:

a. The locality shall have applications for each permit type available online.

b. The locality shall have designated telephone and fax lines to address permit requests and inquiries.

c. The locality shall have at least one staff member whose primary function is to issue permits.

d. The locality shall have one or more engineers on staff or contracted to perform bridge inspections and provide analysis for overweight vehicles.

e. The locality shall maintain maps indicating up-to-date vertical and horizontal clearance locations and limitations.

f. The locality shall provide to the Department an emergency contact phone number and assign a staff person who is authorized to issue the permit or authorized to make a decision regarding the permit request at all times (24 hours a day, seven days a week).

g. The locality shall process a "standard permit" for a "standard vehicle" by the next business day after receiving the completed permit application. Each locality shall define "standard vehicle" and "standard permit" and provide the Department with those definitions. All other requests for permits shall be processed within 10 business days.

h. The locality shall retain for at least 36 months all permit data it collects.

i. The locality shall maintain an updated list of all maintenance and construction projects within that locality. The list shall provide starting and ending locations and dates for each project, and shall be updated as those dates change.

j. The locality shall maintain a list of restricted streets. This list shall indicate all times of travel restrictions, oversize restrictions, and weight restrictions for streets within the locality's jurisdiction.

If the locality satisfies the requirements in the memorandum of understanding, the locality may issue permits under this article.

B. Except for permits issued under § 46.2-1141 for overweight vehicles transporting containerized freight and permits issued for overweight vehicles transporting irreducible loads, no overweight permit issued by the Commissioner or any local authority under any provision of this article shall be valid for the operation of any vehicle on an interstate highway if the vehicle has:

1. A single axle weight in excess of 20,000 pounds; or

2. A tandem axle weight in excess of 34,000 pounds; or

3. A gross weight, based on axle spacing, greater than that permitted in § 46.2-1127; or

4. A gross weight, regardless of axle spacing, in excess of 80,000 pounds.

C. The Commissioner may issue permits to operate or tow one or more travel trailers as defined in § 46.2-1500 or motor homes when any of such vehicles exceed the maximum width specified by law, provided the movement of the vehicle is prior to its retail sale and it complies with the provisions of § 46.2-1105. A copy of each such permit shall be carried in the vehicle for which it is issued.

D. 1. Every permit issued under this article for the operation of oversize or overweight vehicles shall be carried in the vehicle to which it refers and may be inspected by any officer or size and weight compliance agent. Violation of any term of any permit issued under this article shall constitute a Class 1 misdemeanor. Violation of terms and conditions of any permit issued under this article shall not invalidate the weight allowed on such permit unless (i) the permit vehicle is operating off the route listed on the permit, (ii) the vehicle has fewer axles than required by the permit, (iii) the vehicle has less axle spacing than required by the permit when measured longitudinally from the center of the axle to center axle with any fraction of a foot rounded to the next highest foot, or (iv) the vehicle is transporting multiple items not allowed by the permit.

2. Any multi-trip permit authorizing the applicant to operate on a highway a vehicle of a size or weight exceeding the maximum specified in this title may be transferred to another vehicle no more than two times in a 12-month period, provided that the vehicle to which the permit is transferred is subject to all the limitations set forth in the permit as originally issued. The applicant shall pay the Department an administrative fee of $10 for each transfer.

E. Any permit issued by the Commissioner or local authorities pursuant to state law may be restricted so as to prevent travel on any federal-aid highway if the continuation of travel on such highway would result in a loss of federal-aid funds. Before any such permit is restricted by the Commissioner, or local authority, written notice shall be given to the permittee.

F. When application is made for permits issued by the Commissioner as well as local authorities, any fees imposed therefor by the Commissioner as well as all affected local authorities may be paid by the applicant, at the applicant's option, to the Commissioner, who shall promptly transmit the local portion of the total fee to the appropriate locality or localities.

G. Engineering analysis, performed by the Department of Transportation or local authority, shall be conducted of a proposed routing before the Commissioner or local authority issues any permit under this section when such analysis is required to promote safety and preserve the capacity and structural integrity of highways and bridges. The Commissioner or local authority shall not issue a permit when the Department of Transportation or local authority determines that the roadway and bridges to be traversed cannot sustain a vehicle's size and weight.

History.
Code 1950, § 46-339; 1956, c. 476; 1958, c. 541, §§ 46.1-343, 46.1-343.2; 1959, Ex. Sess., c. 91; 1960, c. 223; 1962, cc. 35, 162; 1966, c. 502; 1968, c. 203; 1972, c. 521; 1974, cc. 145, 252, 556; 1975, c. 599; 1976, c. 744; 1977, c. 632; 1979, c. 263; 1980, c. 328; 1981, c. 187; 1982, c. 256; 1983, cc. 170, 515; 1985, c. 7; 1987, cc. 321, 406, 420, 721; 1988, c. 82; 1989, c. 727; 1993, c. 68; 1996, cc. 36, 87; 1997, c. 70; 2001, c. 151; 2003, c. 314; 2009, c. 456; 2011, cc. 62, 73; 2012, c. 443; 2013, c. 118; 2015, c. 615.

§ 46.2-1139.1. Delegation of permitting authority.

The Commissioner may authorize an agent, including a state agency, to issue designated permits pursuant to this article.

History.
2002, c. 265; 2003, c. 314.

§ 46.2-1140. Authority to use certain streets and highways in cities and towns.

When the Commissioner issues a permit to a person to move a vehicle of excessive size and weight along specified highways in Virginia, the Commissioner may also include within such permit, after coordinating with or notifying the authorities of a city or town, the authority to use specified highways at specified times within any such city or town which highways constitute extensions of any part of the primary highway system. No city or town otherwise having jurisdiction over its highways, shall have authority to prohibit the use of its highways to a person holding a permit issued by the Commissioner so long as such person travels upon the highways specified in the permit.

History.
1973, c. 62, § 46.1-343.3; 1989, c. 727; 1996, cc. 36, 87; 2003, c. 314; 2012, c. 443.

§ 46.2-1140.1. Annual overweight permits; fees.

Except as otherwise provided, the annual fee for overweight permits issued under §§ 46.2-1141 through 46.2-1149.5 shall be $130, to be allocated as follows: (i) $120 to the Highway Maintenance and Operating Fund established pursuant to § 33.2-1530, with a portion equal to the percentage of the Commonwealth's total lane miles represented by the lane miles eligible for maintenance payments pursuant to §§ 33.2-319 and 33.2-366 being redistributed on the basis of lane miles to the applicable localities pursuant to §§ 33.2-319 and 33.2-366, to be used to assist in funding needed highway pavement and bridge maintenance and rehabilitation and (ii) a $10 administrative fee to the Department.

Unless otherwise prohibited, overweight permits issued under §§ 46.2-1141 through 46.2-1149.5 shall be valid on all unrestricted state and local highways.

History.
2012, c. 443.

Editor's note.
References in this section were updated at the direction of the Virginia Code Commission to conform to the recodification of Title 33.2 by Acts 2014, c. 805, effective October 1, 2014.

§ 46.2-1141. Overweight permits for containerized freight.

Permits to operate on the highways a vehicle exceeding the maximum weight specified in this title shall be granted if the vehicle is hauling containerized cargo in a sealed, seagoing container bound to or from a seaport and has been or will be transported by marine shipment. In order to qualify for such a permit the contents of such seagoing container shall not be changed from the time it is loaded by the consignor or his agents to the time it is delivered to the consignee or his agents. Cargo moving in vehicles conforming to specifications shown in this section shall be considered irreducible and eligible for permits under regulations of the Commissioner.

The fee for a permit issued under this section shall be as provided in § 46.2-1140.1. Only the Commissioner may issue a permit under this section.

History.
1973, c. 62, § 46.1-343.3; 1989, c. 727; 1991, 1st Sp. Sess., c. 17; 1995, c. 146; 1996, cc. 36, 87; 2003, c. 314; 2012, c. 443.

§ 46.2-1142. Overweight permits for concrete haulers.

The Commissioner, upon written application made by the owner or operator, shall issue overweight permits for operation of certain vehicles used to haul concrete. Permits under this section shall be issued only for vehicles that are used exclusively for the mixing of concrete in transit or at a project site or for transporting necessary components in a compartmentalized vehicle to produce concrete immediately upon arrival at a project site and either have (i) four axles with more than 22 feet between the first and last axle of the vehicle or (ii) three axles. Any vehicle operating under a permit issued pursuant to this section shall have a gross weight of no more than 60,000 pounds for three-axle vehicles and 70,000 pounds for four-axle vehicles, a single axle weight of no more than 20,000 pounds, tandem axle weight of no more than 40,000 pounds, and a tri-axle grouping weight of no more than 50,000 pounds, with no single axle of such tri-axle grouping exceeding the weight permitted for a single axle. The fee for such permits shall be as provided in § 46.2-1140.1. Such permit shall not designate the route to be traversed nor contain restrictions or conditions not applicable to other vehicles in their general use of the highways.

Each vehicle, when loaded according to the provisions of a permit issued under this section, shall be operated at a reduced speed. The reduced speed limit is to be 10 miles per hour slower than the legal speed limit in 55, 45, and 35 miles per hour speed limit zones.

History.

1973, c. 62, § 46.1-343.3; 1989, c. 727; 1994, c. 154; 1996, cc. 36, 87; 2000, c. 265; 2003, c. 314; 2012, c. 443.

§ 46.2-1142.1. Extensions of overweight limits authorized under § 46.2-1142 for vehicles used to haul concrete; fees.

Owners or operators of vehicles used exclusively to haul concrete may apply for permits to extend the single axle weight limit of 20,000 pounds, the tandem axle weight limit of 40,000 pounds, the four axle weight of 70,000 pounds, the tri-axle grouping weight of 50,000 pounds, and the three-axle weight of 60,000 pounds provided for in § 46.2-1142, by a maximum of five percent. The fee for such permits shall be $250, to be allocated as follows: (i) $245 deposited into the Highway Maintenance and Operating Fund established pursuant to § 33.2-1530 to be used to assist in funding needed highway pavement and bridge maintenance and rehabilitation and (ii) a $5 administrative fee to the Department.

Permits issued under this section shall be valid for one year from the date of issuance. No permit issued under this section shall authorize violation of any weight limitation, promulgated and posted in accordance with § 46.2-1130, applicable to bridges or culverts. Permits issued under this section shall authorize extensions of the limitation provided for in § 46.2-1128 for vehicles operating on interstate highways only to the extent that any such extension (i) is not inconsistent with federal law and (ii) will not jeopardize or require the withholding or reduction of federal transportation funding otherwise available to the Commonwealth or any of its political subdivisions.

The Commissioner shall make the permit available to vehicles registered outside the Commonwealth under the same conditions and restrictions which are applicable to vehicles registered within the Commonwealth. The Commissioner may promulgate regulations governing such permits. Except as provided in this section and § 46.2-1142, no weights in excess of those authorized by law shall be tolerated.

History.

1990, c. 195; 1997, c. 283; 2000, c. 265; 2001, cc. 822, 857; 2012, c. 443.

§ 46.2-1143. Overweight permits for coal haulers; trucks hauling gravel, sand, crushed stone, or liquids produced from gas or oil wells in certain counties; penalties.

A. The Commissioner upon written application by the owner or operator of vehicles used exclusively for hauling coal or coal byproducts from a mine or other place of production to a preparation plant, electricity-generation facility, loading dock, or railroad shall issue, without a fee, a permit authorizing those vehicles to operate with gross weights in excess of those established in § 46.2-1126 on the conditions set forth in this section.

B. Vehicles with three axles may have a maximum gross weight, when loaded, of no more than 60,000 pounds, a single axle weight of not more than 24,000 pounds and a tandem axle weight of no more than 45,000 pounds. Vehicles with four axles may have a maximum gross weight, when loaded, of no more than 70,000 pounds, a single axle weight of no more than 24,000 pounds, and a tri-axle weight of no more than 50,000 pounds. Vehicles with five axles having no less than 35 feet of axle space between extreme axles may have a maximum gross weight, when loaded, of no more than 90,000 pounds, a single axle weight of no more than 20,000 pounds, and a tandem axle weight of no more than 40,000 pounds. Vehicles with six axles may have a maximum gross weight, when loaded, of no more than 110,000 pounds, a single axle weight of no more than 24,000 pounds, a tandem axle weight of no more than 44,000 pounds, and a tri-axle weight of no more than 54,500 pounds.

C. No load of any vehicle operating under a permit issued according to this section shall rise above the top of the bed of such vehicle, not including extensions of the bed. Three-axle vehicles shall not carry loads in excess of the maximum bed size in cubic feet for such vehicle which shall be computed by a formula of 60,000 pounds minus the weight of the empty truck divided by the average weight of coal. For the purposes of this section, the average weight of coal shall be 52 pounds per cubic foot. Four-axle vehicles shall not carry loads in excess of the maximum bed size for such vehicle which shall be computed by a formula of 70,000 pounds minus the weight of the truck empty divided by the average weight of coal. Five-axle vehicles shall not carry loads in excess of the maximum bed size for such vehicle, which shall be computed by a formula of

90,000 pounds minus the weight of the truck empty divided by the average weight of coal. Six-axle vehicles shall not carry loads in excess of the maximum bed size for such vehicle, which shall be computed by a formula of 110,000 pounds minus the weight of the truck empty divided by the average weight of coal.

D. For the purposes of this section, "bed" means that part of the vehicle used to haul coal. Bed size shall be based on its interior dimensions, which may be determined by measuring the exterior of the bed, with volume expressed in cubic feet. In order to ensure compliance with this section by visual inspection, if the actual bed size of the vehicle exceeds the maximum as provided above, the owner or operator shall be required to paint a horizontal line two inches wide on the sides of the outside of the bed of the vehicle, clearly visible to indicate the uppermost limit of the maximum bed size applicable to the vehicle as provided in this section. In addition, one hole two inches high and six inches long on each side of the bed shall be cut in the center of the bed and at the top of the painted line. Any vehicle in violation of this section shall subject the vehicle's owner or operator or both to a penalty of $250 for a first offense, $500 for a second offense within a 12-month period, and $1,000 and revocation of the permit for a third offense within a 12-month period from the first offense.

E. If the bed of any vehicle is enlarged beyond the maximum bed size for which its permit was granted, or if the line or holes required are altered so that the vehicle exceeds the bed size for which its permit was granted, the owner, operator, or both shall be subject to a penalty of $1,000 for each offense and revocation of the permit. Upon revocation, a permit shall not be reissued for six months. The penalties provided in this section shall be in lieu of those imposed under § 46.2-1135.

F. For any vehicle with a valid permit issued pursuant to the conditions required by this section, when carrying loads which do not rise above the top of the bed or the line indicating the bed's maximum size, if applicable, it shall be, in the absence of proof to the contrary, prima facie evidence that the load is within the applicable weight limits. If any vehicle is stopped by enforcement officials for carrying a load rising above the top of the bed or the line indicating the bed's maximum size, the operator of the vehicle shall be permitted to shift his load within the bed to determine whether the load can be contained in the bed without rising above its top or above the line.

G. No such permit shall be valid for the operation of any such vehicle for a distance of more than 85 miles within the Commonwealth of Virginia from the preparation plant, loading dock, or railroad.

H. In counties that impose a severance tax on gases as authorized by § 58.1-3712 or a severance license tax on coal producers as authorized by § 58.1-3741, the Commissioner, upon written application by the owner or operator of vehicles used exclusively for hauling gravel, sand, or crushed stone no more than 50 miles from origin to destination, shall issue a permit authorizing those vehicles to operate with the weight limits prescribed in subsection B. Nothing contained in this subsection shall authorize any extension of weight limits provided in § 46.2-1127 for operation on interstate highways. Any weight violation hauling sand, gravel, or crushed stone under this subsection shall be subject to the penalties authorized by § 46.2-1135.

The fee for a permit issued under this subsection shall be $70, to be allocated as follows: (i) $65 to the Highway Maintenance and Operating Fund established pursuant to § 33.2-1530, with a portion equal to the percentage of the Commonwealth's total lane miles represented by the lane miles eligible for maintenance payments pursuant to §§ 33.2-319 and 33.2-366 being redistributed on the basis of lane miles to the applicable localities pursuant to §§ 33.2-319 and 33.2-366, to be used to assist in funding needed highway pavement and bridge maintenance and rehabilitation and (ii) a $5 administrative fee to the Department.

I. In counties that impose a severance tax on gases as authorized by § 58.1-3712 or a severance license tax on coal producers as authorized by § 58.1-3741, the weight limits prescribed in subsection B shall also apply to motor vehicles hauling liquids produced from a gas or oil well and water used for drilling and completion of a gas or oil well no more than 50 miles from origin to destination. Nothing contained in this subsection shall authorize any extension of weight limits provided in § 46.2-1127 for operation on interstate highways. Any weight violation involving hauling liquids produced from a gas or oil well and water used for drilling and completion of a gas or oil well under this subsection shall be subject to the penalties authorized by § 46.2-1135.

History.

1973, c. 62, § 46.1-343.3; 1989, c. 727; 1996, cc. 36, 87; 1999, c. 915; 2001, c. 417; 2002, c. 264; 2003, cc. 314, 315; 2005, c. 556; 2007, c. 523; 2008, c. 716; 2009, c. 188; 2010, c. 361; 2011, c. 131; 2012, cc. 443, 569; 2013, cc. 305, 618.

Editor's note.

References in this section were updated at the direction of the Virginia Code Commission to conform to the recodification of Title 33.2 by Acts 2014, c. 805, effective October 1, 2014.

§ 46.2-1143.1. Overweight permits for haulers of excavated material.

The Commissioner, upon written application made by the owner or operator, shall issue overweight permits for operation of certain vehicles hauling excavated material from construction-related land-clearing operations. Permits shall be issued under this section only for vehicles that have either (i) four axles with more than 22 feet between the first and last axle of the vehicle or (ii) three axles. Any vehicle operating under a permit issued pursuant to this section shall have a gross weight of no more than 60,000 pounds for three-axle vehicles and 70,000 pounds for four-axle vehicles, a single axle weight of no more than 20,000 pounds, tandem axle weight of no more than 40,000 pounds, and a tri-axle grouping weight of no more than 50,000 pounds, with no single axle of such tri-axle grouping exceeding the weight permitted for a single axle. The fee for such permits shall be as provided in § 46.2-1140.1.

No permit issued under this section shall authorize the operation of any vehicle hauling excavated material for a distance of more than 25 miles from the land-clearing operation. However, such permit shall not designate the route to be traversed nor contain restrictions or conditions not applicable to other vehicles in their general use of the highways. Each vehicle, when loaded according to the provisions of a permit issued under this section, shall be operated at a reduced speed of 10 miles per hour slower than the legal speed limit in 55, 45, and 35 miles per hour speed limit zones.

For purposes of this section, the term "excavated material" shall mean natural earth materials, which includes stumps, brush, leaves, soil, and rocks, removed by any mechanized means.

History.

2002, c. 265; 2003, c. 314; 2012, c. 443.

§ 46.2-1144. Overweight permits for solid waste haulers.

The Commissioner, upon written application by the owner or operator of vehicles used exclusively for hauling solid waste other than hazardous waste, shall issue a permit authorizing the operation on the highway of such vehicles at gross weights in excess of those set forth in § 46.2-1126.

No permit issued under this section shall authorize a single axle weight of more than 20,000 pounds or a tandem axle weight of more than 40,000 pounds. No such permit shall be issued for a total gross weight in excess of 40,000 pounds for a two-axle vehicle, or of more than 60,000 pounds for a three-axle vehicle. Such permit shall be obtained annually at the time the vehicle is registered. The Commissioner may promulgate regulations governing such permits.

No such permit shall authorize the operation of any vehicle enumerated in this section beyond the boundary of the county or city where it is principally garaged or for a distance of more than 25 miles from the place where it is principally garaged, whichever is greater. However, the permit shall not designate the route to be traversed nor contain restrictions or conditions not applicable to other vehicles in their general use of the highways. Each vehicle, when loaded according to the provisions of a permit issued under this section, shall be operated at a reduced speed of 10 miles per hour slower than the legal speed limit in 55, 45, and 35 miles per hour speed limit zones.

The fee for a permit issued under this section shall be as provided in § 46.2-1140.1.

For the purposes of this section, the terms "solid waste" and "hazardous waste" shall have the meanings provided in § 10.1-1400.

History.

1973, c. 62, § 46.1-343.3; 1989, c. 727; 1996, cc. 36, 87; 2003, c. 314; 2012, c. 443.

§ 46.2-1144.1. Overweight permits for tank wagons.

The Commissioner, upon written application and payment of a fee by the owner of tank wagon vehicles as defined in § 58.1-2201, shall issue overweight permits for operation of said vehicles.

The fee for such permit shall be as provided in § 46.2-1140.1.

No permit issued under this section shall authorize a single axle weight of more than 24,000 pounds and a total gross weight in excess of 40,000 pounds. Permits issued under this section shall be valid for one year from the date of issuance. No permit issued under this section shall authorize violation of any weight limitation, promulgated and posted in accordance with § 46.2-1130, applicable to bridges or culverts. This permit shall not be combined with any other overweight permit or extension of weight limits.

History.

2007, c. 738; 2008, c. 33; 2012, c. 443.

§ 46.2-1144.2. Overweight permits for haulers of farm animal feed.

The Commissioner, upon written application by the owner or operator of certain vehicles used exclusively for hauling farm animal feed, shall issue overweight permits for operation of such vehicle. Permits shall be issued under this section only for specially designed five-axle semi-trailer combinations with bulk feed compartments and at least 51 feet of axle spacing between the first and last axle. Such permits shall not be combined with any other overweight permits or extension of weight limits.

No permits issued under this section shall authorize a tandem axle weight of more than 37,400 pounds or a total gross weight in excess of 84,000 pounds. Permits issued under this section shall be valid for one year from the date of issuance. No permit issued under this section shall designate the route to be traversed or contain restrictions or conditions not applicable to other vehicles in their general use of the highways. However, no such permit shall authorize violation of any weight limitation applicable to bridges or culverts, as promulgated and posted in accordance with § 46.2-1130. Nothing contained in this section shall authorize any extension of weight limits provided in § 46.2-1127 for operation on interstate highways.

The fee for a permit issued under this section shall be as provided in § 46.2-1140.1.

History.

2012, c. 443.

§ 46.2-1145. Overweight permits for certain trucks operated by Arlington County.

The Commissioner, upon written application by Arlington County, shall issue without a fee to such county a permit authorizing the county's operation of vehicles used for hauling household waste and vehicles used for highway or utility construction, operation, or maintenance upon the highways of such county at gross weights exceeding those set forth in § 46.2-1126. Permits issued hereunder shall specify that vehicles with two axles may have a maximum gross weight of no more than 48,000 pounds and a single axle weight of not more than 24,000 pounds and that vehicles with three axles may have a maximum gross weight of not more than 60,000 pounds and a single axle weight of not more than 24,000 pounds and a tandem axle weight of not more than 40,000 pounds.

The permit shall not designate the route to be traversed nor contain restrictions or conditions not applicable to other vehicles in their general use of the highways. Each vehicle, when loaded according to the provisions of a permit issued under this section shall be operated at a reduced speed of 10 miles per hour slower than the legal speed limit in 55, 45, and 35 miles per hour speed limit zones.

History.

1973, c. 62, § 46.1-343.3; 1989, c. 727; 1996, cc. 36, 87; 2012, c. 443.

§ 46.2-1146. Excess height and length permits for haulers of certain imported goods.

The Commissioner and local authorities of cities and towns in their respective jurisdictions, upon written application by the owners or operators of motor vehicles used to transport items arriving at a Virginia port by ship from overseas points of origin and consigned to an assembly plant in this Commonwealth, shall issue without cost permits for the operation of such motor vehicles on the highways if those vehicles do not exceed the height limitation set forth in § 46.2-1110 by more than one and one-half feet and not exceeding the length limitation as set forth in §§ 46.2-1112 and 46.2-1113 by more than three feet. The Commissioner and local authorities may designate the routes such permittees shall use from the port to the assembly plant.

History.

1973, c. 62, § 46.1-343.3; 1989, c. 727; 1996, cc. 36, 87; 2003, c. 314.

§ 46.2-1147. Permits for excessive size and weight for articulated buses.

The Commissioner, upon written application by the owner or operator of passenger buses having three or more axles consisting of two sections joined together by an articulated joint with the trailer being equipped with a mechanically steered rear axle, and having a gross weight of no more than 60,000 pounds, a single axle weight of no more than 25,000 pounds, and a width of no more than 102 inches, shall issue to such owner or operator a written permit authorizing the operation of such vehicles on the highways. The fee for such permit shall be as provided in § 46.2-1140.1.

History.

1973, c. 62, § 46.1-343.3; 1989, c. 727; 1996, cc. 36, 87; 2003, c. 314; 2012, c. 443.

§ 46.2-1148. Overweight permit for hauling Virginia-grown farm produce.

In addition to other permits provided for in this article, the Commissioner, upon written application by the owner or operator of any vehicle hauling farm produce grown in Virginia, shall issue permits for overweight operation of such vehicles as provided in this section. Such permits shall allow the vehicles to have a single axle weight of no more than 24,000 pounds, a tandem axle weight of no more than 40,000 pounds, and a tri-axle grouping weight of no more than 50,000 pounds. Additionally, any five-axle combination may have a gross weight of no more than 90,000 pounds, any four-axle combination, may have a gross weight of not more than 70,000 pounds, any three-axle combination may have a gross weight of no more than 60,000 pounds, and any two-axle combination may have a gross weight of no more than 40,000 pounds.

Except as otherwise provided in this section, no such permit shall designate the route to be traversed nor contain restrictions or conditions not applicable to other vehicles in their general use of the highways.

No permit issued under this section shall authorize any vehicle whose axle weights or axle spacing would not be permissible under §§ 46.2-1122 through 46.2-1127 to cross any bridge constituting a part of any public road.

The fee for a permit issued under this section shall be $45, to be allocated as follows: (i) $40 to the Highway Maintenance and Operating Fund established pursuant to § 33.2-1530, with a portion equal to the percentage of the Commonwealth's total lane miles represented by the lane miles eligible for maintenance payments pursuant to §§ 33.2-319 and 33.2-366 being redistributed on the basis of lane miles to the applicable localities pursuant to §§ 33.2-319 and 33.2-366, to be used to assist in funding needed highway pavement and bridge maintenance and rehabilitation and (ii) a $5 administrative fee to the Department. Such permits shall be valid only in Accomack and Northampton Counties.

History.

1962, c. 192, § 46.1-343.1; 1974, c. 145; 1983, c. 169; 1987, c. 372; 1989, c. 727; 1996, cc. 36, 87; 2003, c. 314; 2012, c. 443; 2013, c. 118.

Editor's note.

References in this section were updated at the direction of the Virginia Code Commission to conform to the recodification of Title 33.2 by Acts 2014, c. 805, effective October 1, 2014.

§ 46.2-1148.1. Overweight permit for hauling forest products.

A. For purposes of this section, "forest products" means raw logs to market and wood residuals, including wood chips, sawdust, mulch, and tree bark.

B. In addition to other permits provided for in this article, the Commissioner, upon written application by the owner or operator of any vehicle hauling forest products transported from the place where they are first produced, cut, harvested, or felled to the location where they are first processed, shall issue permits for overweight operation of such vehicles as provided in this section. Such permits shall allow the vehicles to have a single-axle weight of no more than 24,000 pounds, a tandem-axle weight of no more than 40,000 pounds, and a tri-axle grouping weight of no more than 50,000 pounds. Additionally, any five-axle combination having a minimum of 48 feet between the first and last axle may have a gross weight of no more than 90,000 pounds, any four-axle combination may have a gross weight of no more than 70,000 pounds, any three-axle combination may have a gross weight of no more than 60,000 pounds, and any two-axle combination may have a gross weight of no more than 40,000 pounds.

C. No permit issued under this section shall designate the route to be traversed or contain restrictions or conditions not applicable to other vehicles in their general use of the highways. However, no such permit shall authorize violation of the length limitations in § 46.2-1149.2 or any weight limitation applicable to bridges or culverts, as promulgated and posted in accordance with § 46.2-1130. Nothing contained in this section shall authorize any extension of weight limits provided in § 46.2-1127 for operation on interstate highways.

D. The fee for a permit issued under this section shall be as provided in § 46.2-1140.1. Only the Commissioner may issue a permit under this section.

E. Each vehicle when loaded according to the provisions of a permit issued under this section shall be operated at a reduced speed as provided in § 46.2-872.

History.

2015, cc. 40, 72.

§ 46.2-1149. Unladen, oversize and overweight, rubber-tired, self-propelled haulers and loaders; permits; engineering analysis; costs.

The Commissioner and local authorities of cities and towns in their respective jurisdictions, upon written application by the owner or operator of any empty, oversize and overweight, rubber-tired, self-propelled hauler or loader used in the construction and coal mining industries, may issue to such owner or operator a permit authorizing operation upon the highways of such equipment with gross empty weights in excess of those established in §§ 46.2-1122 through 46.2-1127 and sizes in excess of those established in §§ 46.2-1105 through 46.2-1108. The permits shall be issued only after an engineering analysis of a proposed routing has been conducted by the Virginia Department of Transportation or local authorities of counties, cities, and towns in their respective jurisdictions to assess the ability of the roadway and bridges to be traversed to sustain the vehicles' size and weight. The fee for a permit issued under this section shall be based on the costs assessed against the applicant to cover engineering analysis, not to exceed three hours.

No permit issued under this section shall be valid for the operation of the equipment for a distance of more than 75 miles.

History.

1983, c. 311, § 46.1-343.4; 1989, c. 727; 1996, cc. 36, 87; 2000, c. 129; 2003, c. 314; 2012, c. 443; 2013, c. 354.

§ 46.2-1149.1. Excess tandem axle weight permits for cotton module haulers.

The Commissioner, upon application made by the owner or operator of vehicles used exclusively to transport seed cotton modules, shall issue a permit authorizing the operation on the highway of such vehicles, from September 1 through December 31 of each year, at tandem axle weights in excess of that authorized in § 46.2-1125. The Commissioner may promulgate regulations governing such permits. Such permits shall allow the vehicles to have tandem axle weights of no more than 44,000 pounds. No permit issued under this section shall authorize a single axle weight in excess of that authorized in § 46.2-1124 or a gross weight in excess of 56,000 pounds.

The fee for a permit issued under this section shall be $45, to be allocated as follows: (i) $40 to the Highway Maintenance and Operating Fund established pursuant to § 33.2-1530, with a portion equal to the percentage of the Commonwealth's total lane miles represented by the lane miles eligible for maintenance payments pursuant to §§ 33.2-319 and 33.2-366 being redistributed on the basis of lane miles to the applicable localities pursuant to §§ 33.2-319 and 33.2-366, to be used to assist in funding needed highway pavement and bridge maintenance and rehabilitation and (ii) a $5 administrative fee to the Department.

History.

1995, c. 419; 1996, cc. 29, 36, 87; 2003, c. 314; 2012, c. 443.

Editor's note.

References in this section were updated at the direction of the Virginia Code Commission to conform to the recodification of Title 33.2 by Acts 2014, c. 805, effective October 1, 2014.

§ 46.2-1149.2. Permit authorizing transportation of tree-length logs.

The Commissioner, upon application made by the owner or operator of vehicles used to transport tree-length logs, shall issue a permit authorizing the operation on the highways of such vehicles in excess of lengths authorized in Article 16 (§ 46.2-1112 et seq.) of this chapter. Such permit shall be issued in accordance with regulations promulgated as provided in Chapter 40 (§ 2.2-4000 et seq.) of Title 2.2, and §§ 33.2-210 and 33.2-300.

History.

1997, c. 283; 2003, c. 314.

Editor's note.

References in this section were updated at the direction of the Virginia Code Commission to conform to the recodification of Title 33.2 by Acts 2014, c. 805, effective October 1, 2014.

§ 46.2-1149.3. Payment of fees into special fund.

Except as otherwise provided, all fees collected by the Commissioner under this article shall be paid into the state treasury and set aside as a special fund to be used to meet the expenses of the Department.

History.

2003, c. 314; 2007, c. 738; 2012, c. 443.

§ 46.2-1149.4. Overweight permits for specialized mobile equipment.

The Commissioner, upon written application made by the owner or operator, shall issue an overweight permit for the operation of specialized mobile equipment. Any vehicle operating under a permit issued pursuant to this section shall have a gross weight of no more than 64,000 pounds, a single axle weight of no more than 20,000 pounds, and a tandem axle weight of no more than 44,000 pounds. Such permit shall not designate the route to be traversed nor contain restrictions or conditions not applicable to other vehicles in their general use of the highways. The fee for such permit shall be as provided in § 46.2-1140.1.

For purposes of this section, "specialized mobile equipment" means a self-propelled motor vehicle manufactured for the specific purpose of supporting well-drilling machinery on the job site and whose movement on any highway is incidental to the purpose for which it was designed and manufactured.

History.

2003, c. 1002; 2012, c. 443.

§ 46.2-1149.5. Overweight permits for underground pipe cleaning, hydroexcavating, and water blasting equipment.

The Commissioner, upon written application made by the owner or operator, shall issue an overweight permit for the operation of underground pipe cleaning, hydroexcavating, and water blasting equipment. Any vehicle operating under a permit issued pursuant to this section shall have a gross weight of no more than 64,000 pounds, a single axle weight of no more than 20,000 pounds, and a tandem axle weight of no more than 44,000 pounds. Such permit shall not designate the route to be traversed nor contain restrictions or conditions not applicable to other vehicles in their general use of the highways. The fee for such permit shall be as provided in § 46.2-1140.1.

For purposes of this section, "underground pipe cleaning equipment" means a self-propelled motor vehicle manufactured for the specific purpose of vacuuming and cleaning underground sanitary and storm pipe. "Hydroexcavating equipment" means a self-propelled motor vehicle manufactured for the specific purpose of digging with water and vacuuming of debris. "Water blasting equipment" means a self-propelled motor vehicle manufactured for the specific purpose of waterblasting flat concrete surfaces and vacuuming spent water for reuse.

History.

2007, c. 429; 2012, c. 443.

§ 46.2-1149.6. Permits for truck cranes.

The Commissioner and local authorities of cities and towns, in their respective jurisdictions, may, upon written application made by an owner or operator and subject to the requirements of § 46.2-1139, issue permits authorizing the operation over the highways of truck cranes that exceed the maximum weight specified in this title. Truck cranes that have been mounted with counterweights and other manufactured equipment that enable a single person to assemble and operate the truck crane shall be considered irreducible, and no application for a permit under this section shall be denied because of the applicant's refusal to remove such counterweights or other manufactured equipment.

History.

2014, cc. 68, 258.

§ 46.2-1149.7. Specialized construction equipment; permits; engineering analysis; costs.

A. For the purpose of this section, "specialized construction equipment" means (i) rubber-tracked, or tracked when protective matting is used, self-propelled equipment being used in highway maintenance and construction projects and (ii) tracked, self-propelled equipment being used in emergency operations, including snow removal.

B. The Commissioner of Highways, upon written application made by the owner or operator of specialized construction equipment, may issue a single trip or multi-trip permit allowing such equipment to be driven across structures maintained by the Department of Transportation within, or to gain access to, a highway construction or maintenance work zone of the Department of Transportation, as defined in the most recent version of the Department of Transportation's Virginia Work Area Protection Manual, or to access any road or structure maintained by the Department of Transportation when needed by the Department for snow removal or other emergency operations. The permits shall be issued only after an engineering analysis of a proposed routing has been conducted by the Department of Transportation to assess the ability of the roads and structures to be traversed to sustain the equipment's size and weight. Such permit shall designate the route to be traversed and contain restrictions or conditions regarding the specialized construction equipment's operation across structures. The fee for a permit issued under this section shall be based on the costs assessed against the applicant to cover engineering analysis, not to exceed three hours.

History.
2014, c. 70.

§ 46.2-1149.8. Excess width permits for vehicles transporting watercraft.

The Commissioner shall issue a permit authorizing the operation of vehicles hauling boats or other watercraft that exceed a total outside width of 102 inches but do not exceed a total outside width of 108 inches upon application by the owner of such vehicle. Such permit shall authorize the operation of such vehicle on all unrestricted state and local highways. The annual fee for a permit issued pursuant to this section and the allocation of such fee shall be the same as provided for overweight permits in § 46.2-1140.1.

History.
2016, cc. 115, 533.

ARTICLE 19.

TOWING AND TOWED VEHICLES.

§ 46.2-1150. Towing certain unlicensed or uninspected vehicles.

Nothing in this title shall prohibit towing an unlicensed motor vehicle or motor vehicle which has not been inspected pursuant to Article 21 (§ 46.2-1157 et seq.) or 22 (§ 46.2-1176 et seq.) of Chapter 10 of this title.

Nothing in this title shall prohibit the towing of an unlicensed trailer or semitrailer used on a construction site as an office or for storage or a trailer or semitrailer which has been used on a construction site as an office or for storage, but which has not been inspected pursuant to Article 21 of Chapter 10 of this title, provided that any such unlicensed or uninspected trailer or semitrailer (i) is towed by a tow truck or other vehicle designed and equipped for the towing of inoperable or disabled vehicles; (ii) is operated only in intrastate commerce; (iii) has an actual gross weight, including contents, of no more than 15,000 pounds; (iv) is secured to the towing vehicle by means of safety chains; and (v) is equipped with rear-mounted bar lights which function as tail lights, brake lights, and turn signals as provided in Article 3 (§ 46.2-1010 et seq.) of Chapter 10 of this title. However, nothing in this section shall authorize the towing or drawing of an unlicensed or uninspected trailer or semitrailer by means of a tractor truck except for the purpose of having such trailer or semitrailer inspected as provided in § 46.2-1157.

History.
Code 1950, § 46-333.1; 1956, c. 47; 1958, c. 541, § 46.1-338; 1989, c. 727; 1991, c. 106; 2006, cc. 874, 891.

§ 46.2-1151. Weight limit exception as to vehicles designed for towing disabled vehicles.

The provisions of §§ 46.2-1122 through 46.2-1127 shall not apply to a vehicle designed for towing disabled vehicles, when towing such vehicle in an emergency in such manner that a part of the combined weight of the two vehicles rests upon an axle or axles of the towing vehicle, provided the towed and towing vehicles each are within the weight limits prescribed in §§ 46.2-1122 through 46.2-1127. This section shall not permit the violation of any lawfully established load limit on any bridge. For the purpose of this section, "emergency" includes towing disabled inoperative vehicles to places designated by owners.

History.
1958, c. 541, § 46.1-339.1; 1977, c. 472; 1989, c. 727.

§ 46.2-1152. Certain tow trucks need not be weighed.

Notwithstanding any other provision of law, no truck designed and equipped for the towing of inoperative or disabled motor vehicles shall be required to be weighed at state-operated permanent weighing stations when not actually engaged in towing another vehicle.

History.
1984, c. 98, § 46.1-339.2; 1989, c. 727.

§ 46.2-1153. Permissible lengths of combination vehicles being towed in emergencies.

In an emergency as provided in § 46.2-1149, the towing of disabled vehicles which cannot be separated for safety, physical, or mechanical reasons and which exceed length limits established in Article 16 (§ 46.2-1112 et seq.) of this chapter, shall be permissible for the purpose of towing any such vehicle to the nearest facility which can make the necessary repairs but not more than fifty miles from the point such vehicle was disabled.

History.
Code 1950, §§ 46-328, 46-331; 1950, p. 665; 1952, c. 342; 1956, cc. 476, 483; 1958, c. 541, §§ 46.1-330, 46.1-335; 1962, cc. 113, 575; 1964, c. 286; 1966, cc. 59, 373; 1972, c. 446; 1974, cc. 580, 664; 1975, c. 104; 1978, c. 254; 1983, c. 515; 1985, c. 426; 1986, cc. 72, 417; 1989, c. 727.

§ 46.2-1154. Length of vehicles; exceptions in case of breakdown.

The provisions of § 46.2-1118 shall not apply to vehicles which, because of a mechanical breakdown or an accident, are towed to the nearest repair facility which can furnish the required service. In any such case such connection may consist solely of a chain, rope, or cable of no more than fifteen feet long. A licensed driver shall be at the controls of the towed vehicle to brake, steer and control its lights.

History.
Code 1950, § 46-333; 1958, c. 541, § 46.1-337; 1989, c. 727.

ARTICLE 20.

LOADS AND CARGOES.

§ 46.2-1155. Fastening load of logs, barrels, etc.

No vehicle which is designed or used for the purpose of hauling logs, poles, lumber, barrels, hogsheads, or other materials or containers which by their nature may shift or roll, shall be operated or moved on any highway unless its load is securely fastened by adequate log chains, metal cables, nylon webbing, steel straps or other restraining devices so as to prevent the load from shifting or falling from the vehicle. Tobacco hogsheads may, however, be secured by manila or hemp rope, at least five-eighths inch in diameter, of sufficient strength securely to fasten the hogshead against shifting, falling, or rolling.

Nothing in this section shall release the owner or operator from liability for failure to use reasonable care to prevent the load from shifting or falling.

History.
Code 1950, § 46-308; 1954, c. 34; 1958, c. 541, § 46.1-304; 1972, c. 64; 1989, c. 727.

§ 46.2-1156. Construction, maintenance and loading must prevent escape of contents; load covers; exemptions.

A. No vehicle shall be operated or moved on any highway unless it is so constructed, maintained, and loaded as to prevent its contents from dropping, sifting, leaking, or otherwise escaping. No provision of this section, however, shall apply to any (i) motor vehicle that is used exclusively for agricultural purposes as provided in § 46.2-698 and is not licensed in any other state; (ii) agricultural vehicle, tractor, or other vehicle exempted from registration and licensing requirements pursuant to Article 6 (§ 46.2-662 et seq.) of Chapter 6 of this title; or (iii) motor vehicle transporting forest products, poultry, or livestock.

B. The loads of all trucks, trailers and semitrailers carrying gravel, sand, coal or other nonagricultural and nonforestry products on interstate, primary, or secondary highways or roads maintained by cities, counties or incorporated towns shall be either (i) secured to the vehicle in which they are being transported or (ii) covered. Covers used to prevent the escape of material from commercial vehicles used to transport solid waste shall be of such design, installation, and construction as to contain the vehicle's cargo within the vehicle, regardless of the vehicle's speed or weather conditions. Public service company vehicles, pickup trucks, and emergency snow removal equipment while engaged in snow removal operations shall be excluded from the provisions of this subsection.

History.
Code 1950, § 46-307; 1958, c. 541, §§ 46.1-303, 46.1-401; 1975, c. 553; 1979, c. 213; 1980, c. 21; 1986, c. 639; 1988, cc. 662, 897; 1989, cc. 526, 727; 1992, c. 149; 1997, c. 283; 2001, c. 180.

§ 46.2-1156.1. Transportation of persons less than sixteen years old in pickup truck beds prohibited; exception.

No person under sixteen years of age shall be transported in the rear cargo area of any pickup truck on the highways of Virginia. The provisions of this section shall not apply to transportation of persons in the bed of any pickup truck being operated (i) as part of an organized parade authorized by the Department of Transportation or the locality in which the parade is being conducted or (ii) on or across a highway from one field or parcel of land to another field or parcel of land in connection with farming operations.

History.

2000, c. 736.

ARTICLE 21.
SAFETY INSPECTIONS.

§ 46.2-1157. Inspection of motor vehicles required.

A. The owner or operator of any motor vehicle, trailer, or semitrailer registered in Virginia and operated or parked on a highway within the Commonwealth shall submit his vehicle to an inspection of its mechanism and equipment by an official inspection station, designated for that purpose, in accordance with § 46.2-1158. No owner or operator shall fail to submit a motor vehicle, trailer, or semitrailer operated or parked on the highways in the Commonwealth to such inspection or fail or refuse to correct or have corrected in accordance with the requirements of this title any mechanical defects found by such inspection to exist.

B. The provisions of this section requiring safety inspections of motor vehicles shall also apply to vehicles used for firefighting; inspections of firefighting vehicles shall be conducted pursuant to regulations promulgated by the Superintendent of State Police, taking into consideration the special purpose of such vehicles and the conditions under which they operate.

C. Each day during which such motor vehicle, trailer, or semitrailer is operated or parked on any highway in the Commonwealth after failure to comply with this law shall constitute a separate offense.

D. Except as otherwise provided, autocycles shall be inspected as motorcycles under this article.

History.

Code 1950, § 46-317; 1950, p. 691; 1958, c. 541, § 46.1-315; 1962, c. 246; 1978, cc. 275, 605; 1982, c. 646; 1989, c. 727; 1991, cc. 107, 717; 1993, c. 134; 1995, c. 670; 1997, c. 283; 2004, cc. 267, 796; 2007, cc. 75, 137; 2009, cc. 115, 514, 756; 2011, c. 283; 2014, cc. 53, 256.

§ 46.2-1158. Frequency of inspection; scope of inspection.

Motor vehicles, trailers, and semitrailers required to be inspected pursuant to the provisions of § 46.2-1157 shall be reinspected within 12 months of the month of the first inspection and at least once every 12 months thereafter.

Each inspection shall be a complete inspection. A reinspection of a rejected vehicle by the same station during the period of validity of the rejection sticker on such vehicle, however, need only include an inspection of the item or items previously found defective unless there is found an obvious defect that would warrant further rejection of the vehicle.

A rejection sticker shall be valid for 15 calendar days beyond the day of issuance. A complete inspection shall be performed on any vehicle bearing an expired rejection sticker.

The completion of the conversion process for a converted electric vehicle shall invalidate any inspection of such vehicle conducted in accordance with this section prior to the conversion. Following the initial inspection of a converted electric vehicle, as required under § 46.2-602.3 and the provisions of this chapter, such vehicle shall be reinspected in accordance with this section.

History.

1977, c. 655, § 46.1-315.2; 1978, cc. 302, 748; 1982, c. 646; 1989, c. 727; 2012, c. 177.

§ 46.2-1158.01. Exceptions to motor vehicle inspection requirement.

A. The following shall be exempt from inspection as required by § 46.2-1157:

1. Four-wheel vehicles weighing less than 500 pounds and having less than 6 horsepower;

2. Boat, utility, or travel trailers that are not equipped with brakes;

3. Antique motor vehicles or antique trailers as defined in § 46.2-100 and licensed pursuant to § 46.2-730;

4. Any motor vehicle, trailer, or semitrailer that is outside the Commonwealth at the time its inspection expires when operated by the most direct route to the owner's or operator's place of residence or the owner's legal place of business in the Commonwealth;

5. A truck, tractor truck, trailer, or semitrailer for which the period fixed for inspection has expired while the vehicle was outside the Commonwealth (i) from a point outside the Commonwealth to the place where such vehicle is kept or garaged within the Commonwealth or (ii) to a destination within the Commonwealth where such vehicle will be (a) unloaded within 24 hours of entering the Commonwealth, (b) inspected within such 24-hour period, and (c) operated, after being unloaded, only to an inspection station or to the place where it is kept or garaged within the Commonwealth;

6. New motor vehicles, new trailers, or new semitrailers operated upon the highways of the Commonwealth for the purpose of delivery from the place of manufacture to the dealer's or distributor's designated place of business or between places of business if such manufacturer, dealer, or distributor has more than one place of business; dealers or distributors may take delivery and operate upon the highways of the Commonwealth new motor vehicles, new trailers, or new semitrailers from another dealer or distributor provided a motor vehicle, trailer, or semi-

trailer shall not be considered new if driven upon the highways for any purpose other than the delivery of the vehicle;

7. New motor vehicles, new trailers, or new semitrailers bearing a manufacturer's license operated for test purposes by the manufacturer;

8. Motor vehicles, trailers, or semitrailers operated for test purposes by a certified inspector during the performance of an official inspection;

9. New motor vehicles, new trailers, or new semitrailers operated upon the highways of the Commonwealth over the most direct route to a location for installation of a permanent body;

10. Motor vehicles, trailers, or semitrailers purchased outside the Commonwealth driven to the purchaser's place of residence or the dealer's or distributor's designated place of business;

11. Prior to purchase from auto auctions, motor vehicles, trailers, or semitrailers operated upon the highways not to exceed a five-mile radius of such auction by prospective purchasers only for the purpose of road testing and motor vehicles, trailers, or semitrailers purchased from auto auctions operated upon the highways from such auction to (i) an official safety inspection station provided that (a) the inspection station is located between the auto auction and the purchaser's residence or place of business or within a five-mile radius of such residence or business and (b) the vehicle is taken to the inspection station on the same day the purchaser removes the vehicle from the auto auction or (ii) the purchaser's place of residence or business;

12. Motor vehicles, trailers, or semitrailers, after the expiration of a period fixed for the inspection thereof, (i) operated over the most direct route between the place where such vehicle is kept or garaged and an official inspection station or (ii) parked on a highway and that have been submitted for a motor vehicle safety inspection to an official inspection station, for the purpose of having the same inspected pursuant to a prior appointment with such station;

13. Any vehicle for transporting well-drilling machinery and mobile equipment as defined in § 46.2-700;

14. Motor vehicles being towed in a legal manner as exempted under § 46.2-1150;

15. Logtrailers as exempted under § 46.2-1159;

16. Motor vehicles designed or altered and used exclusively for racing or other exhibition purposes as exempted under § 46.2-1160;

17. Any tow dolly or converter gear as defined in § 46.2-1119;

18. A new motor vehicle, as defined in § 46.2-1500, that has been inspected in accordance with an inspection requirement of the manufacturer or distributor of the new motor vehicle by an employee who customarily performs such inspection on behalf of a motor vehicle dealer licensed pursuant to § 46.2-1508. Such inspection shall be deemed to be the first inspection for the purpose of § 46.2-1158, and an inspection approval sticker furnished by the Department of State Police at the uniform price paid by all official inspection stations to the Department of State Police for an inspection approval sticker may be affixed to the vehicle as required by § 46.2-1163;

19. Mopeds;

20. Low-speed vehicles; and

21. Vehicles exempt from registration pursuant to Article 6 (§ 46.2-662 et seq.) of Chapter 6.

B. The following shall be exempt from inspection as required by § 46.2-1157 provided (i) the commercial motor vehicle operates in interstate commerce; (ii) the commercial motor vehicle is found to meet the federal requirements for annual inspection through a self-inspection, a third-party inspection, a Commercial Vehicle Safety Alliance inspection, or a periodic inspection performed by any state with a program; (iii) the inspection has been determined by the Federal Motor Carrier Safety Administration to be comparable to or as effective as the requirements of 49 C.F.R. Part 396 § 396.3(a); and (iv) documentation of such determination as provided for in 49 C.F.R. Part 396 § 396.3(b) is available for review by law-enforcement officials to verify that the inspection is current:

1. Any commercial motor vehicle operating in interstate commerce that is subject to the Federal Motor Carrier Safety Regulations;

2. Any trailer or semitrailer being operated in interstate commerce that is subject to the Federal Motor Carrier Safety Regulations.

History.

2011, c. 283; 2016, cc. 128, 702.

§ 46.2-1158.02. Penalty for failure to have motor vehicle inspection.

Notwithstanding the penalty provisions of § 46.2-1171, a violation of § 46.2-1158 constitutes a traffic infraction. The court may, in its discretion, dismiss a summons issued under § 46.2-1158 where correction of vehicle or safety equipment defects or proof of compliance with § 46.2-1158 is provided to the court subsequent to the issuance of the summons.

History.

2011, c. 283.

§ 46.2-1158.1. Extension of validity of vehicle safety inspection approval stickers issued for vehicles whose registered owners are persons in the armed services of the United States.

Notwithstanding any contrary provision of law, any vehicle safety inspection approval sticker issued for any vehicle that is principally garaged outside the Commonwealth while its registered owner is a person in the armed services of the United States shall be held not to have expired during the period of the owner's official absence from the Commonwealth in the armed services of the United States, regardless of whether such vehicle is operated in or through the Commonwealth during the owner's official absence from the Commonwealth in the armed services of the United States. Should the armed services member be domiciled in another state of the United States, nothing in this section shall be construed to absolve such person from obtaining a current inspection sticker from his state of domicile, if required by such state. In cases where a vehicle's owner has been officially absent from the Commonwealth because of service in the armed services of the United States but returns to Virginia following such official absence and the vehicle becomes operational in the Commonwealth, the vehicle's owner will have 14 calendar days following such return, Sundays and holidays excepted, to have the vehicle inspected. Furthermore, no penalty shall be imposed on any such owner or operator for operation of a motor vehicle, trailer, or semitrailer after the expiration of a period fixed for the inspection thereof, over the most direct route between the place where such vehicle is kept or garaged and an official inspection station for the purpose of having it inspected pursuant to an appointment with such station.

Motor vehicles owned and operated by persons on active duty with the United States armed forces who are Virginia residents stationed outside the Commonwealth at the time the inspection expires may be operated on the highways of the Commonwealth while persons on active duty are on leave, provided such vehicle displays a valid inspection sticker issued by another state.

For the purposes of this section, "service in the armed services of the United States" includes active duty service with the regular armed forces of the United States or the National Guard or other reserve component.

History.
2005, c. 582; 2008, c. 722; 2009, c. 523; 2011, c. 283; 2014, cc. 67, 250.

§ 46.2-1159. Logtrailers defined; exempt from inspection under certain conditions.

For the purpose of this section, a "logtrailer" shall be any vehicle designed and used solely as an implement for hauling logs, lumber, or other forest products from the forest to the mill or loading platform. Log trailers shall be exempt from the requirements of § 46.2-1157 if operation on the highways in the Commonwealth does not exceed two miles and is made during daylight hours.

History.
Code 1950, § 46-317.1; 1954, c. 436; 1958, c. 541, § 46.1-316; 1989, c. 727.

§ 46.2-1160. Towed vehicle defined; exempt from inspection requirement.

For the purpose of this section a towed vehicle shall be any motor vehicle designed or altered and used exclusively for racing or other exhibition purposes at places other than the highways in the Commonwealth where such vehicle does not operate under its own power on the highways in the Commonwealth in going to or from such places. A towed vehicle as defined in this section shall be exempt from the requirements of § 46.2-1157.

History.
Code 1950, § 46-317.2; 1956, c. 128; 1958, c. 541, § 46.1-317; 1989, c. 727.

§ 46.2-1161: Repealed by Acts 2011, c. 283, cl. 2.

§ 46.2-1161.1. Inspections of trailers and semitrailers equipped with heating or cooking appliances.

If any trailer or semitrailer subject to the periodic safety inspections required by this article is equipped with a heating or cooking appliance, the safety inspection of such trailer or semitrailer shall include a visual inspection of the venting of such cooking or heating appliance to the outside of the trailer or semitrailer. No safety inspection approval sticker shall be issued to any such trailer or semitrailer unless any such heating or cooking appliance is adequately vented to prevent the asphyxiation of occupants of any such trailer or semitrailer by the operation of the heating or cooking appliance.

History.
1991, c. 169.

§ 46.2-1162. Inspection of certain trailers.

Any trailer required to be inspected under the provisions of this article may, only if the size or configuration of the trailer and the size and configuration of the facilities of the inspection station prevent the trailer from being inspected inside the inspection station, be inspected outside the inspection station. The provisions of this section shall apply only to trailers as defined in § 46.2-100 and shall not apply to recreational vehicles commonly known as "motor homes" or to any vehicle required to be equipped with head lights.

History.
1982, c. 159, § 46.1-317.2; 1989, c. 727.

§ 46.2-1163. Official inspection stations; safety inspection approval stickers; actions of Superintendent subject to the Administrative Process Act.

The Superintendent may designate, furnish instructions to, and supervise official inspection stations for the inspection of motor vehicles, trailers, and semitrailers and for adjusting and correcting equipment enumerated in this chapter in such a manner as to conform to specifications hereinbefore set forth. The Superintendent shall adopt and furnish to such official inspection stations regulations governing the making of inspections required by this chapter. The Superintendent may at any time, after five days' written notice, revoke the designation of any official inspection station designated by him.

If no defects are discovered or when the equipment has been corrected in accordance with this title, the official inspection station shall issue to the operator or owner of the vehicle, on forms furnished by the Department of State Police, a duplicate of which is retained by such station, a certificate showing the date of correction, registration number of the vehicle, and the official designation of such station. On or before December 1, 2010, any information an official inspection station is required to provide to the Department of State Police shall be accepted by the Department in electronic form. There also shall be placed on the windshield of the vehicle at a place to be designated by the Superintendent an approval sticker furnished by the Department of State Police. If any vehicle is not equipped with a windshield, the approval sticker shall be placed on the vehicle in a location designated by the Superintendent. If the vehicle is a motorcycle, the approval sticker may be placed on a plate securely fastened to the motorcycle for the purpose of displaying the sticker or in any other location designated by the Superintendent. This sticker shall be displayed on the windshield of such vehicle or at such other designated place upon the vehicle at all times when it is operated or parked on the highways in the Commonwealth and until such time as a new inspection period shall be designated and a new inspection sticker issued. Common carriers, operating under certificate from the State Corporation Commission or the Department of Motor Vehicles, who desire to do so may use with the approval of the Superintendent private inspection stations for the inspection and correction of their equipment.

Actions of the Superintendent relating to official inspection stations shall be governed by the provisions of the Administrative Process Act (§ 2.2-4000 et seq.).

History.
Code 1950, § 46-318; 1954, c. 57; 1956, c. 381; 1958, c. 541, § 46.1-318; 1989, c. 727; 1996, c. 573; 2003, c. 138; 2006, c. 620; 2007, cc. 75, 137; 2009, c. 241.

§ 46.2-1164. Reinspection not required when windshield replaced; transfer of inspection sticker to new windshield; replacement of lost or damaged stickers.

When any vehicle requires the replacement of a windshield pursuant to § 46.2-1058, it shall not be necessary to inspect such vehicle at the time of replacement if a valid state inspection sticker is displayed on the windshield being replaced.

The sticker found on the broken windshield may be removed and placed on the new windshield.

The Superintendent may designate certain State Police officers to issue safety inspection approval stickers to vehicles from which the original valid safety inspection approval sticker has been lost, stolen or damaged without causing the vehicle to be reinspected, provided the vehicle owner or operator produces the original safety inspection approval sticker receipt issued to the vehicle within the past eleven months. Such replacement safety inspection approval stickers shall be issued in accordance with regulations promulgated by the Superintendent.

History.
1978, c. 266, § 46.1-294.1; 1989, c. 727; 1993, c. 94; 1994, c. 396.

§ 46.2-1165. Regulations for inspection of vehicles; posting.

The Superintendent shall promulgate regulations for the inspection of motor vehicles under this title and shall furnish each official inspection station with a printed set of such regulations suitable for posting. Such station shall post the regulations in a conspicuous place in the portion of its premises where inspections are made and shall cause its employees making official inspections to be conversant with such regulations.

History.
Code 1950, § 46-323; 1958, c. 541, § 46.1-319; 1960, c. 391; 1970, c. 21; 1989, c. 727.

§ 46.2-1166. Minimum standards required for inspection stations.

The Superintendent shall not designate any person, firm, or corporation as an official inspection station unless and until such person, firm or corporation satisfies the Superintendent, under such regulations as the Superintendent shall prescribe, that such person, firm, or corporation has met and will continue to meet the following standards:

1. The station has sufficient mechanical equipment and skilled and competent mechanics to make a complete inspection in accordance with the provisions of this article;

2. Adequate means are provided by the station to test the brakes, headlights, and steering mechanism of motor vehicles and to ascertain that motor vehicles inspected by the station meet the safety standards prescribed by the Superintendent under the terms of this title;

3. The person making the actual inspection or under whose immediate supervision such inspection is made shall have at least one year's practical experience as an automotive mechanic, or has satisfactorily completed a training program in automo-

tive mechanics approved by the Superintendent of State Police;

4. No person shall be designated by such station to make such inspections unless the person has been approved for that purpose by the Department of State Police;

5. The Superintendent of State Police may, at his discretion, waive the experience and training requirements of this section for inspections of motorcycles and trailers when, in the Superintendent's opinion, the person performing such inspections is otherwise qualified to perform such inspections; and

6. The station has garage liability insurance in the amount of at least $500,000 with an approved surplus lines carrier or insurance company licensed to write such insurance in this Commonwealth, provided this requirement shall not apply to inspection stations that inspect only their company-owned or leased or government-owned or leased vehicles.

History.

Code 1950, § 46-319; 1958, c. 541, § 46.1-320; 1962, c. 246; 1980, cc. 31, 168; 1989, c. 727; 2004, c. 383; 2005, c. 179.

§ 46.2-1167. Charges for inspection and reinspection; exemption.

A. Each official safety inspection station may charge no more than:

1. Fifty-one dollars for each inspection of any (i) tractor truck, (ii) truck that has a gross vehicle weight rating of 26,000 pounds or more, or (iii) motor vehicle that is used to transport passengers and has a seating capacity of more than 15 passengers, including the driver, $0.50 of which shall be transmitted to the Department of State Police to support the Department's costs in administering the motor vehicle safety inspection program;

2. Twelve dollars for each inspection of any motorcycle, $10 of which shall be retained by the inspection station and $2 of which shall be transmitted to the Department of State Police who shall retain $0.50 to support the Department's costs in administering the motor vehicle safety inspection program and deposit the remaining $1.50 into the Motorcycle Rider Safety Training Program Fund created pursuant to § 46.2-1191;

3. Twelve dollars for each inspection of any autocycle, $10 of which shall be retained by the inspection station and $2 of which shall be transmitted to the Department of State Police to be used to support the Department's costs in administering the motor vehicle safety inspection program; and

4. Sixteen dollars for each inspection of any other vehicle, $0.50 of which shall be transmitted to the Department of State Police to support the Department's costs in administering the motor vehicle safety inspection program.

No such charge shall be mandatory, however, and no such charge shall be made unless the station has previously contracted therefor.

B. Each official safety inspection station may charge $1 for each reinspection of a vehicle rejected by the station, as provided in § 46.2-1158, if the vehicle is submitted for reinspection within the validity period of the rejection sticker. If a rejected vehicle is not submitted to the same station within the validity period of the rejection sticker or is submitted to another official safety inspection station, an amount no greater than that permitted under subsection A may be charged for the inspection.

History.

Code 1950, § 46-320; 1958, c. 541, § 46.1-321; 1968, c. 163; 1973, c. 386; 1976, c. 501; 1982, c. 646; 1985, c. 450; 1989, c. 727; 1990, c. 39; 2001, c. 791; 2002, cc. 322, 337; 2005, c. 628; 2006, c. 620; 2014, cc. 53, 256.

§ 46.2-1167.1: Repealed by Acts 2009, cc. 864 and 871, cl. 5.

§ 46.2-1168. Additional registration fee.

In addition to any other fees imposed, at the time of registration the owner of every motor vehicle, trailer, or semitrailer required to be registered in this Commonwealth shall pay to the Department of Motor Vehicles one dollar and fifty cents per year of registration or, in the case of trailers and semitrailers, such other fee as is provided in § 46.2-694.1, to be paid into the state treasury and set aside for the payment of the administrative costs of the official motor vehicle safety inspection program as appropriated by the General Assembly.

History.

1985, c. 450, § 46.1-321.2; 1988, c. 704; 1989, c. 727; 1990, cc. 418, 496; 1992, c. 597; 1997, c. 283.

§ 46.2-1169. Inspection defined; making of repairs or adjustments.

The term "inspection" as herein used shall not include repairs or adjustments. Repairs or adjustments necessary to bring the vehicle into conformity with this title may be made by agreement between the owner and such station or whatever repair station the owner may select. If such adjustments or repairs are made by anyone other than an official inspection station, such vehicle shall again be inspected by an official inspection station.

History.

Code 1950, § 46-321; 1958, c. 541, § 46.1-322; 1989, c. 727.

§ 46.2-1170. Advertising, etc., of official inspection station when not authorized.

No person, firm, or corporation, unless designated as such in accordance with the provisions of this article, shall, either directly or indirectly, display, advertise, or represent that such person, firm or corporation is an official inspection station.

History.
Code 1950, § 46-321; 1958, c. 541, § 46.1-323; 1989, c. 727.

§ 46.2-1171. Penalties for violation of article.

Any person violating this article shall be guilty of a Class 3 misdemeanor for the first offense and guilty of a Class 1 misdemeanor for each subsequent offense except as otherwise provided in this article. If the violation of this article or regulations of the Superintendent made pursuant thereto is by an official inspection station in addition to or in lieu of such fine imposed by a court the Superintendent may, whether or not the violation is a first offense against this article or regulation of the Superintendent, suspend the appointment of the inspection station or, if in his opinion after a hearing, the facts warrant such action, the Superintendent may revoke the designation of such inspection station.

History.
Code 1950, § 46-322; 1958, c. 541, § 46.1-324; 1989, c. 727.

§ 46.2-1172. Unauthorized taking, possession, or use of inspection stickers, etc.; penalty.

No person shall remove any inspection sticker or any paper issued by the Superintendent in connection with vehicle safety inspections from the custody of any person to whom the same has been issued by or under the authority of the Superintendent of State Police. Nor shall any person have any such sticker or paper in his possession or use otherwise than as authorized by the Superintendent. In any case where the Superintendent has suspended or revoked the designation of any official inspection station designated by him, such station shall surrender possession to the Superintendent or his duly authorized representative all inspection stickers and other forms and papers used in connection with safety inspection of vehicles on or before the effective date of such suspension or revocation. Any person violating the provisions of this section shall be guilty of a Class 1 misdemeanor.

History.
Code 1950, § 46-322.1; 1956, c. 35; 1958, c. 541, § 46.1-325; 1989, c. 727; 1998, c. 299.

§ 46.2-1173. Imitation or counterfeit inspection stickers.

No person shall make, issue, or knowingly use any imitation or counterfeit of an official safety inspection sticker.

No person shall display or cause or permit to be displayed upon any vehicle any safety inspection sticker knowing it to be fictitious or issued for another vehicle.

History.
Code 1950, § 46-322.2; 1952, c. 466; 1958, c. 541, § 46.1-326; 1989, c. 727.

§ 46.2-1174. Superintendent authorized to enter into Uniform Vehicle Inspection Reciprocity Agreement.

The Superintendent is authorized to enter into the Uniform Vehicle Inspection Reciprocity Agreement, adopted by the American Association of Motor Vehicles Administrators on January 1, 1967.

History.
1968, c. 148, § 46.1-326.1; 1989, c. 727.

§ 46.2-1175. Operators of certain commuter buses to maintain certain records; inspection of records and buses by employees of Department of State Police; penalty.

Persons, firms, corporations, and other business entities operating commuter buses for compensation in intrastate commerce shall maintain records of all maintenance performed on such buses. Such records shall include the dates of service, the odometer reading of the bus on that date, the maintenance performed, and the name of the person or persons performing the maintenance. Such records shall be open to inspection during the operator's normal business hours by employees of the Department of State Police specifically designated by the Superintendent. Employees of the Department of State Police designated for that purpose by the Superintendent shall also be authorized with the consent of the owner, operator, or agent in charge or with an appropriate warrant obtained under the procedure prescribed in Chapter 24 (§ 19.2-393 et seq.) of Title 19.2 to go onto the property of business entities operating commuter buses for compensation in intrastate commerce to inspect buses directly on such property or on the property where such buses are principally garaged at any time during normal business hours. Such inspections may be either for the purpose of determining the safe condition of the buses or to verify the accuracy of the maintenance logs or for both purposes.

A violation of any provision of this section shall constitute a Class 3 misdemeanor.

The provisions of this section shall not apply to local or regional governments, to authorities created to provide local or regional mass transit service, or to buses which those governments or authorities own or operate.

For the purpose of this section, "commuter bus" means a motor vehicle which has a seating capacity of more than seventeen passengers, is used primarily to transport workers directly to and from factories, plants, offices, or other places where they work, and is registered with the Department for such operation.

History.
1983, c. 203, § 46.1-326.1:1; 1989, c. 727; 1997, c. 283.

§ 46.2-1175.1. Inspection of certain refuse collection and highway maintenance vehicles.

No safety inspection approval sticker shall be issued under this article to any publicly or privately owned vehicle (i) used for garbage and refuse collection and disposal or (ii) having a manufacturer's gross vehicle weight rating of 10,001 pounds or more and used primarily for highway repair or maintenance unless any such vehicle is equipped with a device, in good working order, which automatically emits an audible alarm signal when the vehicle is operated in reverse gear. Any such device shall be of a type approved by the Superintendent of State Police.

History.
1989, cc. 297, 317, § 46.1-326.1:2.

ARTICLE 22. EMISSIONS INSPECTIONS.

§ 46.2-1176. Definitions.

The following words and phrases when used in this article shall have the following meanings except where the context clearly indicates a different meaning:

"Basic, test and repair program" means a motor vehicle emissions inspection system established by regulations of the Board which shall designate the use of an OBD-II (on-board diagnostic system) with wireless capability, and a two-speed idle analyzer as the only authorized testing equipment. Only those computer software programs and emissions testing procedures necessary to comply with the applicable provisions of Title I of the federal Clean Air Act shall be included. Such testing equipment shall be approvable for motor vehicle manufacturers' warranty repairs.

"Board" means the State Air Pollution Control Board.

"Certificate of emissions inspection" means a document, device, or symbol, prescribed by the Director and issued pursuant to this article, which indicates that (i) a motor vehicle has satisfactorily complied with the emissions standards and passed the emissions inspection provided for in this article; (ii) the requirement of compliance with such emissions standards has been waived; or (iii) the motor vehicle has failed such emissions inspection.

"Director" means the Director of the Department of Environmental Quality.

"Emissions inspection station" means any facility or portion of a facility that has obtained an emissions inspection station permit from the Director authorizing the facility to perform emissions inspections in accordance with this article.

"Enhanced emissions inspection program" means a motor vehicle emissions inspection system established by regulations of the Board that shall designate, as the only authorized testing equipment for emissions inspection stations, (i) the use of the ASM 50-15 (acceleration simulation mode or method) together with an OBD-II (on-board diagnostic system) with wireless capability, (ii) the use of the ASM 50-15 together with the use of a dynamometer, and (iii) two-speed tailpipe testing equipment. Possession and availability of a dynamometer shall be required for enhanced emissions inspection stations. Only those computer software programs and emissions testing procedures necessary to comply with applicable provisions of Title I of the federal Clean Air Act shall be included. Such testing equipment shall be approvable for motor vehicle manufacturers' warranty repairs. An enhanced emissions inspection program shall include remote sensing and an on-road clean screen program as provided in this article.

"Fleet emissions inspection station" means any inspection facility operated under a permit issued to a qualified fleet owner or lessee as determined by the Director.

"Motor vehicle" means any vehicle that:

1. Is designed for the transportation of persons or property; and

2. Is powered by an internal combustion engine.

"On-road clean screen program" means a program that allows a motor vehicle owner to voluntarily certify compliance with emissions standards by means of on-road remote sensing.

"On-road emissions inspector" means the entity or entities authorized by the Department of Environmental Quality to perform on-road testing, including on-road testing in accordance with the on-road clean screen program.

"On-road testing" means tests of motor vehicle emissions or emissions control devices by means of roadside pullovers or remote sensing devices.

"Program coordinator" means any person or corporation that has entered into a contract with the Director to provide services in accordance with this article.

"Qualified hybrid motor vehicle" means a motor vehicle that (i) meets or exceeds all applicable regulatory requirements, (ii) meets or exceeds the applicable federal motor vehicle emissions standards for gasoline-powered passenger cars, and (iii) can draw propulsion energy both from gasoline or diesel fuel and a rechargeable energy storage system.

"Referee station" means an inspection facility operated or used by the Department of Environmental Quality (i) to determine program effectiveness, (ii) to resolve emissions inspection conflicts between motor vehicle owners and emissions inspection stations, and (iii) to provide such other technical support and information, as appropriate, to emissions inspection stations and vehicle owners.

"Remote sensing" means the measurement of motor vehicle emissions through electronic or light-sensing equipment from a remote location such as

the roadside. Remote sensing equipment may include devices to detect and record the vehicle's registration or other identification numbers.

"Test and repair" means motor vehicle emissions inspection facilities that perform official motor vehicle emissions inspections and may also perform vehicle repairs. No regulation of the Board pertaining to test and repair shall bar inspection facilities from also performing vehicle repairs. Emissions inspections and vehicle safety inspections may be performed in the same service bay, provided that the facility is both an emissions inspection station and an official safety inspection station pursuant to §§ 46.2-1163 and 46.2-1166. Emissions inspections may be performed in any service bay of the emissions inspection station or, if by wireless means, in any other area on the premises of the emissions inspection station.

"Validation program" or *"program validation"* means a program approved by the Director by which vehicles are randomly identified and provided a free emissions inspection for the purpose of monitoring the effectiveness of the emissions inspection program. A "validation program" may be conducted at an emissions inspection station, as defined by § 46.2-1176, in conjunction with a state safety inspection or using on-road testing.

History.

1980, c. 469, § 46.1-326.2; 1982, c. 92; 1984, c. 256; 1988, cc. 81, 806; 1989, c. 727; 1993, cc. 995, 998; 1993, Sp. Sess., c. 2; 1994, c. 838; 1995, cc. 836, 851; 2000, c. 311; 2002, c. 710; 2004, c. 915; 2012, cc. 216, 824.

§ 46.2-1177. Emissions inspection program.

The Director shall administer an emissions inspection program. Such program shall require biennial inspections of motor vehicles at official emissions inspection stations in accordance with this article and may require additional inspections of motor vehicles that have been shown by on-road testing to exceed emissions standards established by the Board.

The emissions inspections required in § 46.2-1178 shall not apply to any:

1. Vehicle powered by a clean special fuel as defined in § 46.2-749.3, provided provisions of the federal Clean Air Act permit such exemption for vehicles powered by a clean special fuel;
2. Motorcycle or autocycle, unless such autocycle has been emissions certified with an on-board diagnostic system by the U.S. Environmental Protection Agency;
3. Vehicle which, at the time of its manufacture was not designed to meet emissions standards set or approved by the federal government;
4. Antique motor vehicle as defined in § 46.2-100 and licensed pursuant to § 46.2-730;
5. Vehicle for which no testing standards have been adopted by the Board; or
6. Vehicle manufactured for the current model year or any of the three immediately preceding model years unless identified by the remote sensing program as violating the emissions standards established for that program.

History.

1980, c. 469, § 46.1-326.3; 1981, c. 624; 1988, c. 806; 1989, c. 727; 1993, cc. 995, 998; 1993, Sp. Sess., c. 2; 1995, cc. 836, 851; 2006, c. 729; 2015, cc. 95, 161.

§ 46.2-1177.1. Inspection program coordinator; agreement for services.

The Director may enter into an agreement to designate a program coordinator for all inspection programs pursuant to this article, except that no on-road clean screen program or any program or inspection process that utilizes remote sensing shall be included in the agreement. The Director shall determine the services to be provided by the program coordinator and the amount to be paid to the program coordinator for such services by the Department. Such agreement shall include a provision that the program coordinator shall provide and maintain inspection stations as defined in § 46.2-1176 with equipment, as set forth in this article, as required for a station to provide inspections. In addition to the amount the Director agrees for the Department to pay the program coordinator, the agreement shall permit the program coordinator to be paid up to $3,500 per year from each inspection station for each set of required equipment for the provision and maintenance of such equipment by the program coordinator.

History.

2012, cc. 216, 824.

§ 46.2-1178. Administration and scope of emissions inspection program.

A. Except as otherwise provided in this section, the emissions inspection program provided for in this article shall apply to motor vehicles having actual gross weights of 8,500 pounds or less that are registered in the Counties of Arlington, Fairfax, and Prince William, and the Cities of Alexandria, Fairfax, Falls Church, Manassas, and Manassas Park. The provisions of this subsection shall expire when the provisions of subsection C of this section become effective.

B. An emissions inspection program as required by regulations adopted by the Board under this article shall apply to motor vehicles that have actual gross weights of 8,500 pounds or less and are registered or operated primarily, as defined by the Board in accordance with the provisions of the Administrative Process Act (§ 2.2-4000 et seq.), in the Counties of Chesterfield, Hanover, and Henrico and the Cities of Colonial Heights, Hopewell, and Richmond. Such emissions inspection program shall be a basic, test and repair program with the greatest number of inspection facilities consistent with the consumer

Motor Vehicles

protection and fee provisions herein as consistent with the federal Clean Air Act.

The provisions of this subsection shall apply but not necessarily be limited to (i) motor vehicles owned by governmental entities, (ii) motor vehicles owned by military personnel residing in those localities, (iii) motor vehicles owned by leasing or rental companies, and (iv) motor vehicles owned or leased by employees of the federal government and operated on a federal installation. The provisions of this subsection shall become effective July 1, 1995. The Board may promulgate regulations to implement the provisions of this article, but such regulations shall not require inspections in the localities mentioned in this subsection prior to the later of: (i) July 1, 1996; or (ii) the date on which the U.S. Environmental Protection Agency, pursuant to the federal Clean Air Act, formally and in writing approves this program for such localities or on such later date as may be provided by regulations of the Board.

B1. The emissions inspection program provided for in this article shall not apply to any qualified hybrid motor vehicle if such vehicle obtains a rating from the U.S. Environmental Protection Agency of at least (i) 50 miles per gallon during city fuel economy tests or (ii) 48 miles per gallon during city fuel economy tests for hybrid vehicles with a model year of 2008 or 2009, unless remote sensing devices indicate the hybrid vehicle may not meet current emissions standards. The Board shall adopt such regulations as may be required to implement this exemption.

C. The emissions inspection program provided for in this subsection shall be a test and repair enhanced emissions inspection program with the greatest number of inspection facilities consistent with the consumer protection and fee provisions herein and shall include on-road testing, remote sensing devices, and an on-road clean screen program. Any enhanced emissions inspection program provided for in this article shall apply to motor vehicles that have actual gross weights of 10,000 pounds or less that were actually manufactured or designated by the manufacturer as a model manufactured in a calendar year less than 25 calendar years prior to January 1 of the present calendar year and are registered or operated primarily, as defined by the Board in accordance with the provisions of the Administrative Process Act (§ 2.2-4000 et seq.) in the Counties of Arlington, Fairfax, Loudoun, Prince William, and Stafford and the Cities of Alexandria, Fairfax, Falls Church, Manassas, and Manassas Park. On and after July 1, 2012, and before July 1, 2013, an on-road clean screen program shall be limited to no more than 10 percent of the motor vehicles described in this subsection which are eligible for emissions inspection during the applicable 12-month period. On and after July 1, 2013, and before July 1, 2014, an on-road clean screen program shall be limited to no more than 20 percent of the motor vehicles described in this subsection which are eligible for emissions inspection during the applicable 12-month period. On and after July 1, 2014, an on-road clean screen program shall be limited to no more than 30 percent of the motor vehicles described in this subsection which are eligible for emissions inspection during the applicable 12-month period. An on-road clean screen program or a validation program utilizing remote sensing equipment shall not be considered emissions inspection stations. The Board may reduce the percentage of vehicles eligible to participate in the on-road clean screen program as is necessary to meet applicable air quality requirements under the federal Clean Air Act, 42 U.S.C. § 7401 et seq., as amended. Notwithstanding the provisions of § 46.2-1176, the Board shall designate remote sensing equipment as authorized testing equipment pursuant to this section.

The provisions of this subsection shall apply but not necessarily be limited to (i) motor vehicles owned by governmental entities, (ii) motor vehicles owned by military personnel residing in those localities, (iii) vehicles owned by leasing or rental companies, and (iv) motor vehicles owned or leased by employees of the federal government and operated on a federal installation.

The provisions of this subsection shall be effective January 1, 1996, or on such later date as may be provided by regulations of the Board. However, the provisions of this subsection may become effective immediately provided that (a) the U.S. Environmental Protection Agency, pursuant to the federal Clean Air Act, formally and in writing approves the program for such localities; (b) the Governor determines in writing that expedited promulgation of such regulations is in the best interest of the Commonwealth, determining that such shall constitute an "emergency situation" pursuant to § 2.2-4011; and (c) the Governor authorizes the Board to promulgate the regulations as emergency regulations in accordance with this section.

D. Any emissions inspection program regulations in effect at the time amendments to this section become effective shall remain in effect until the Board promulgates new regulations or amends or repeals existing regulations in accordance with this section.

History.

1980, c. 469, § 46.1-326.4; 1988, c. 806; 1989, c. 727; 1993, cc. 995, 998; 1993, Sp. Sess., c. 2; 1994, c. 838; 1995, cc. 836, 851; 1997, c. 507; 2002, c. 710; 2004, c. 915; 2012, cc. 216, 824; 2013, c. 634.

§ 46.2-1178.1. On-road testing of motor vehicle emissions; authority to adopt regulations; civil charges.

A. The emissions inspection program authorized by § 46.2-1177 and provided for in § 46.2-1178 shall include on-road testing of motor vehicle emissions and an on-road clean screen program. The Board shall promulgate regulations establishing on-road testing and on-road clean screen program requirements including, but not limited to, collecting data and information necessary to comply with or determine compliance with applicable laws and regulations, random testing of motor vehicle emissions, procedures to notify owners of test results, assessment of civil charges for noncompliance with emissions standards adopted by the Board, and standards for operating the on-road clean screen program, including provisions for the suspension or revocation of any on-road emissions inspection program for failure to act in accordance with the provisions of this article and regulations adopted by the Board.

B. If an emissions test performed pursuant to this section indicates that a motor vehicle does not meet emissions standards established by the Board, the Board may collect from the owner of the vehicle a civil charge based on actual emissions. The Board shall establish a schedule of civil charges to be collected pursuant to this section. Such civil penalties shall not exceed $450 using 1990 as the base year and adjusted annually by the Consumer Price Index. The schedule of charges and their assessment shall be established by regulations promulgated to be in accordance with the provisions of the Administrative Process Act (§ 2.2-4000 et seq.).

C. Civil charges assessed pursuant to this section shall be waived by the Board if, within 30 calendar days of notice of the violation, the vehicle's owner provides proof that the vehicle (i) since the date of the violation, has passed a vehicle emissions test as provided in § 46.2-1178, (ii) qualifies for an emissions inspection waiver as provided in § 46.2-1181, or (iii) has qualified for an emissions inspection waiver as provided in § 46.2-1181 within the 12 months prior to the violation.

D. Civil charges collected pursuant to this section shall be paid into the state treasury and deposited by the State Treasurer into the Vehicle Emissions Inspection Program Fund pursuant to § 46.2-1182.2.

E. If the on-road clean screen program indicates that a motor vehicle does not exceed emissions standards adopted by the Board for on-road testing pursuant to § 46.2-1179, then such testing may be considered proof of compliance for the purposes of § 46.2-1183 and may be considered to satisfy the requirements of § 46.2-1177 for a biennial inspection. The Board shall establish criteria under which such testing shall satisfy the requirements of § 46.2-1183.

History.

1995, cc. 836, 851; 1996, cc. 35, 100; 2002, c. 710; 2012, cc. 216, 824.

§ 46.2-1178.2. Repair of certain vehicles not in compliance with standards established by the Board; payment of repairs from Vehicle Emissions Inspection Program Fund.

The Department of Environmental Quality shall operate a program to subsidize repairs of vehicles identified by on-road testing pursuant to § 46.2-1178.1 that fail to meet emissions standards established by the Board when the owner of the vehicle is financially unable to have the vehicle repaired. The costs of implementing and operating such program shall be borne by the Vehicle Emissions Inspection Program Fund. The Board shall, in connection with such program, establish by regulation such standards, criteria, and procedures as the Board shall deem necessary or convenient.

History.

2002, c. 710.

§ 46.2-1179. Board to adopt emissions standards.

A. The Board shall adopt emissions standards necessary to implement the emissions inspection program provided for in this article. Such standards shall include specifications and criteria that will enable the identification of vehicles whose emissions so far exceed those permissible under this article as to qualify them as "gross violators," and enable the expedited identification of such vehicles through on-road testing pursuant to § 46.2-1178.1.

B. The Board shall establish separate and distinct emissions standards applicable to on-road testing of motor vehicles pursuant to § 46.2-1178.1. Notwithstanding any contrary provision of this article, except for any motor vehicle registered as an antique motor vehicle, such criteria shall be applicable to all motor vehicles manufactured for the 1968 model year or any more recent model year, with criteria for each model year being appropriate to that model year.

History.

1980, c. 469, § 46.1-326.5; 1989, c. 727; 1993, cc. 995, 998; 1993, Sp. Sess., c. 2; 1995, cc. 836, 851; 2002, c. 710.

§ 46.2-1179.1. Board to adopt clean alternative fuel fleet standards for motor vehicles; penalty.

A. For purposes of this section:

"Clean alternative fuel" means any fuel, including methanol, ethanol, other alcohols, reformulated gasoline, diesel, natural gases, liquified petroleum gas, hydrogen, and electricity or other power source used in a clean fuel vehicle that complies with the standards applicable to such vehicle under the federal Clean Air Act when using such fuel or other power source. In the case of a flexible fuel vehicle or dual fuel vehicle, "clean alternative fuel" means only a fuel for which the vehicle was certified when operating on clean alternative fuel.

"Fleet" means any centrally fueled fleet of ten or more motor vehicles owned or operated by a single entity. "Fleet" does not include motor vehicles held for lease or rental to the general public, motor vehicles held for sale by motor vehicle dealers, motor

vehicles used for manufacturer product tests, law-enforcement and other emergency vehicles, or nonroad vehicles, including farm and construction vehicles.

B. The Board may adopt by regulation motor vehicle clean alternative fuel fleet standards consistent with the provisions of Part C of Title II of the federal Clean Air Act for model years beginning with the model year 1998 or the first succeeding model year for which adoption of such standards is practicable. If adoption and implementation by the Board of an equivalent air pollution reduction program is approved by the federal Environmental Protection Agency, the regulation and program authorized by this section shall not become effective. Such regulations shall contain the minimum phase-in schedule contained in § 246 (b) of Part C of Title II of the Clean Air Act. However, nothing in this section shall preclude affected fleet owners from exceeding the minimum requirements of the federal Clean Air Act. Beginning in 1995 and upon adoption of the standards by the Board, the Board shall require the fleet owned by the federal government to meet the clean alternative fuel fleet standard and phase-in schedule established by the Board. If necessary to meet the Board's standards and phase-in schedule, the Board shall require fleets owned by the federal government to convert a portion of existing fleet vehicles to the use of clean alternative fuels as defined by the federal Clean Air Act. The standards specified in this subsection shall apply only to (i) motor vehicles registered in localities designated by the federal Environmental Protection Agency, pursuant to the federal Clean Air Act, as serious, severe, or extreme air quality nonattainment areas, or as maintenance areas formerly designated serious, severe, or extreme and (ii) motor vehicles not registered in the above-mentioned localities, but having either (a) a base of operations or (b) a majority of their annual travel in one or more of those localities.

C. An owner of a covered fleet shall not use any motor vehicle or motor vehicle engine which is manufactured during or after the first model year to which the standards specified in subsection A of this section are applicable, if such vehicle or engine is registered or has its base of operations in the localities specified in subsection B of this section and has not been certified in accordance with regulations promulgated by the Board. The Board may promulgate regulations providing for reasonable exemptions consistent with the provisions of Part C of Title II of the federal Clean Air Act. Motor vehicles exempted from the provisions of this section shall forever be exempt.

D. Any person that violates the requirements of this section or any regulation adopted hereunder shall be subject to the penalties in §§ 46.2-1187 and 46.2-1187.2. Each day of violation shall be a separate offense, and each motor vehicle shall be treated separately in assessing violations.

E. In order to limit adverse economic and administrative impacts on covered fleets operating both in Virginia and in neighboring states, the Department of Environmental Quality shall, to the maximum extent practicable, coordinate the provisions of its regulations promulgated under this section with neighboring states' statutes and regulations relating to use of clean alternative fuels by motor vehicle fleets.

F. The State Corporation Commission, as to matters within its jurisdiction, and the Department of Environmental Quality, as to other matters, may, should they deem such action necessary, promulgate regulations necessary or convenient to ensure the availability of clean alternative fuels to operators of fleets covered by the provisions of this section. The State Air Pollution Control Board may delegate to the Commissioner of Agriculture its authority under the Air Pollution Control Law of Virginia, Chapter 13 (§ 10.1-1300 et seq.) of Title 10.1, to implement and enforce any provisions of its regulations covering the availability of clean alternative fuels. Upon receiving such delegation, the authority to implement and enforce the regulations under the Air Pollution Control Law of Virginia shall be vested solely in the Commissioner, notwithstanding any provision of law contained in Title 10.1, except as provided in this section. The State Air Pollution Control Board, in delegating its authority under this section, may make the delegation subject to any conditions it deems appropriate to ensure effective implementation of the regulations according to the policies of the State Air Pollution Control Board.

History.
1993, cc. 234, 571; 1995, c. 141; 1998, cc. 401, 421.

§ 46.2-1180. Board to adopt regulations; exemption of certain motor vehicles.

A. The Board is authorized to adopt such regulations for purposes of implementation, administration, and regulation as may be necessary to carry out the provisions of this article. Such regulations shall include but not necessarily be limited to requirements for the following:

1. The collection of data and maintenance of records of emissions inspection test results and vehicle repairs under this article and the inspection results of the air pollution control systems or devices in accordance with § 46.2-1048 and regulations of the Board.

2. The calibration of emissions testing equipment by emissions inspection stations to ensure conformance with the standards adopted by the Board.

3. The establishment of appropriate referee stations.

4. The permitting of emissions inspection stations and fleet emissions inspection stations and the licensing of emissions inspectors, including the suspension or revocation of such permit or license.

5. The protection of consumer interests in accordance with regulations of the Board concerning, but not limited to: (i) the number of inspection facilities

and inspection lanes relative to population density, (ii) the proximity of inspection facilities to motor vehicle owners, (iii) the time spent waiting for inspections, and (iv) the days and hours of operation of inspection facilities.

6. The prohibition of any manufacturer or distributor of emissions testing equipment from directly or indirectly owning or operating any emissions testing facility or having any direct or indirect financial interest in any such facility other than the leasing of or providing financing for equipment related to emissions testing.

7. The certification of motor vehicle emissions repair technicians and emissions repair facilities, including the suspension or revocation of such certification. The regulations shall apply to emissions repair technicians and emissions repair facilities that conduct emissions-related repairs for vehicles that have failed a motor vehicle emissions test according to regulations adopted by the Board.

The Director shall administer these regulations and seek compliance with conditions of any contractual arrangements which the Commonwealth may make for inspection services related to air pollution control and may include entering into an agreement with a program coordinator to implement provisions of this subsection.

B. Motor vehicles being titled for the first time may be registered for up to four years without being subject to an emissions inspection, and the four immediately preceding model years being held in a motor vehicle dealer's inventory for resale may be registered in the localities mentioned in subsection C of § 46.2-1178 for up to one year without being subject to an emissions inspection, provided that the dealer states in writing that the emissions equipment on the motor vehicle was operating in accordance with the manufacturer's or distributor's warranty at the time of resale.

C. No motor vehicle for which the Board has not adopted emissions inspection standards shall be subject to an emissions inspection.

D. The Director may enter into bilateral agreements with other states providing for assistance in enforcing each state's statutes and regulations relating to motor vehicle emissions and motor vehicle emissions programs as to vehicles registered in one state and operated in another. Subject to such bilateral agreement, owners of motor vehicles registered in other states and operated in Virginia shall be subject to the on-road testing provisions of § 46.2-1178.1, and shall be notified of test results and assessment of civil charges for noncompliance with emissions standards adopted by the Board. Such notification shall also be provided to the appropriate motor vehicle agency in the state of registration.

History.

1980, c. 469, § 46.1-326.6; 1982, c. 92; 1988, c. 806; 1989, c. 727; 1993, cc. 995, 998; 1993, Sp. Sess., c. 2; 1994, c. 838; 1995, cc. 836, 851; 1997, c. 559; 2006, c. 729; 2012, cc. 216, 824.

§ 46.2-1181. Emissions inspection; cost of repairs; waivers.

A. A motor vehicle shall qualify for an emissions inspection waiver in the event that such vehicle has failed an initial inspection and subsequently failed a reinspection if the owner provides written proof that (i) at least the amount specified in this section has been spent by the owner on the maintenance and repair of the vehicle's engine and emission control system and related equipment and (ii) any emission control system or part thereof which has been removed, damaged, or rendered inoperable by any act enumerated in § 46.2-1048 has been replaced and restored to operating condition.

B. The Director shall establish and revise, as necessary, specifications and procedures for motor vehicle maintenance and repair of pollution control devices and systems.

C. For the purposes of subsection A:

For motor vehicles subject to basic emissions inspections under subsection A of § 46.2-1178, cost limitations on repairs under the emissions inspection program, including parts and labor, but excluding costs of repairs covered by warranties, shall be $175 for pre-1980 model vehicles and $200 for 1980 and newer vehicles, using 2012, or a later date if allowed by federal regulations and approved by the Board, as the base year and annually adjusted by the Consumer Price Index. The Board may phase in waiver amounts.

For motor vehicles subject to emissions inspections under subsection C of § 46.2-1178, the cost limitations on repairs shall be a base amount of $450 per vehicle using 1990, or a later date if allowed by federal regulations and approved by the Board, as the base year and annually adjusted by the Consumer Price Index. The Board may phase in waiver amounts.

Repairs credited toward this waiver must be done by a repair technician certified in accordance with § 46.2-1180. Repairs shall include parts and labor.

D. For the purposes of subsection A of this section, for motor vehicles subject to emissions inspections under subsection B of § 46.2-1178, the cost limitations on repairs under the emissions inspection program, including parts and labor but excluding costs of repairs covered by warranties, shall be:

1. $75 for pre-1981 vehicles; and
2. $200 for 1981 and newer vehicles.

History.

1980, c. 469, § 46.1-326.7; 1988, c. 806; 1989, cc. 722, 727; 1993, cc. 995, 998; 1993, Sp. Sess., c. 2; 1995, cc. 836, 851; 2012, cc. 216, 824.

§ 46.2-1182. Emissions inspection fees; exemption.

Emissions inspection stations performing emissions inspections under subsection A of § 46.2-1178 may charge $11.40 for each emissions inspection, but such charge shall not be mandatory. Any such fee shall be paid to the emissions inspection station.

Each emissions inspection station performing emissions inspections under subsection B of § 46.2-1178 may charge for each emissions inspection an amount not to exceed $17. Any such fee shall be paid to and retained by the emissions inspection station.

Beginning at such date upon which the program becomes an enhanced emissions program, each emissions inspection station performing emissions inspections under subsection C of § 46.2-1178 may charge an amount not to exceed $28 for each emissions inspection. Any such fee shall be paid to and retained by the emissions inspection station.

Within 14 days of an initial failure of an emissions inspection performed at an emissions inspection station, the vehicle's owner shall be entitled to one free reinspection at the station or facility that conducted the original inspection.

The on-road emissions inspector performing emissions inspections under subsection C of § 46.2-1178 may charge each motor vehicle owner who elects to participate in the on-road clean screen program an amount not to exceed $28 for each emissions inspection. Any such fee shall be paid to the on-road emissions inspector. From each emissions inspection fee received by the on-road emissions inspector, a minimum of $4.50 shall be appropriated to the Highway Maintenance and Operating Fund established pursuant to § 33.2-1530.

History.

1980, c. 469, § 46.1-326.8; 1982, c. 646; 1983, c. 85; 1984, c. 263; 1988, c. 806; 1989, c. 727; 1990, c. 522; 1993, cc. 995, 998; 1993, Sp. Sess., c. 2; 1995, cc. 836, 851; 2002, c. 322; 2012, cc. 216, 824.

§ 46.2-1182.1. Additional registration fee; exemption.

Beginning July 1, 1994, in addition to any other fees imposed, at the time of registration by the Department of Motor Vehicles, the owner of any motor vehicle subject to registration in Virginia and subject to the program provided for in this article by virtue of the locality in which it is registered shall pay two dollars per year.

Beginning July 1, 1995, or later if required by regulation of the Board, owners of motor vehicles which are subject to the program by virtue of the location of their base of operation or the location where they are primarily operated shall remit a fee of two dollars per vehicle per year to the Department of Environmental Quality. Payment shall be made according to procedures and on a schedule prescribed by the Department of Environmental Quality. State and local governmental units and agencies shall be exempt from the payment of fees under this subsection.

History.

1993, cc. 995, 998; 1993, Sp. Sess., c. 2; 1995, cc. 836, 851.

§ 46.2-1182.2. Vehicle Emissions Inspection Program Fund established; use of moneys.

A special nonreverting fund known as the Vehicle Emissions Inspection Program Fund is hereby established in the state treasury.

Notwithstanding the provisions of § 2.2-1802, all moneys collected pursuant to § 46.2-1182.1 shall be paid into the treasury and credited to the Vehicle Emissions Inspection Program Fund.

No moneys remaining in the Fund at the end of each fiscal year shall revert to the general fund, but shall remain in the Fund. Interest earned on such moneys shall remain in the Fund and be credited to it.

The Department of Environmental Quality may release moneys from the Fund, on warrants issued by the State Comptroller, for covering the costs of the emissions inspection program, including payment to the program coordinator for contracted services. The moneys in this Fund may also be released for the purpose of long-term maintenance of air quality and the correction and prevention of nonattainment status for National Ambient Air Quality Standards through air quality programs under the direction of the Director. Any remaining funds shall be remitted for use in transportation maintenance projects so that such funds generated from localities required to have emissions inspections pursuant to subsection B of § 46.2-1178 shall have such remaining funds generated pursuant to § 46.2-1182.1 transferred on an annual basis to the Northern Virginia Transportation District. Such funds shall be used for transportation maintenance in the respective locality.

History.

1993, cc. 995, 998; 1993, Sp. Sess., c. 2; 2012, cc. 216, 824.

§ 46.2-1183. Emissions inspection required prior to registration of certain vehicles; records.

No vehicle subject to the provisions of this article shall be registered or reregistered until it has passed an emissions inspection or has been issued an emissions inspection waiver. Any (i) proof of compliance with emissions standards and emissions inspection requirements and (ii) emissions inspection waiver issued for any motor vehicle shall be valid for two years from the end of the month in which it is issued, regardless of any sale or trade of the motor vehicle for which either document was issued during that time, unless such motor vehicle has failed on-road testing pursuant to § 46.2-1178.1 and has not subsequently passed an emissions inspection or received a waiver. Motor vehicles being titled for the first time shall be considered to have valid emissions inspection certificates for a period of four years from the month of first titling. The Commissioner of Motor Vehicles may enter into an agreement with the Director whereby the Department of Motor Vehicles may refuse to register or reregister those motor vehicles subject to emissions inspection programs set forth in this article if the registration period for such vehicles exceeds the valid emissions inspection period by a period of time to be determined by the Director in consultation with the Department of Motor Vehicles and the Commissioner.

Owners of motor vehicles that are not registered with the Department of Motor Vehicles shall maintain such records pertaining to all vehicles located or operated in the areas specified in § 46.2-1178 as the Board may by regulation require. Such records shall contain proof of compliance with this article and be made available to the Department of Environmental Quality upon the Department's request.

History.
1980, c. 469, § 46.1-326.9; 1981, c. 624; 1988, c. 806; 1989, c. 727; 1993, cc. 995, 998; 1993, Sp. Sess., c. 2; 1995, cc. 836, 851; 1996, cc. 35, 100; 2006, c. 729.

§ 46.2-1183.1. Registration extension for satisfaction of emissions inspection requirements.

A. Upon request by an applicant, the Commissioner may grant a one-month extension of the registration period of a vehicle if the vehicle registration has been withheld pursuant to § 46.2-1183 and the current registration period will expire within the calendar month. No extension may be granted for an expired vehicle registration and only one extension may be granted for any one vehicle registration period.

If an applicant who is granted an extension under this section also requests and is granted an extension under § 46.2-752.1, the extension granted under this section shall run concurrently with the extension granted under § 46.2-752.1. No combination of extensions granted under this section and under § 46.2-752.1 shall extend a vehicle's registration period for more than one month for any one vehicle registration period.

For each extension granted, the Commissioner shall collect (i) a $10 administrative fee and (ii) a fee sufficient for a one-month registration period for the vehicle, as calculated under subsection B of § 46.2-694. Neither fee shall apply, however, if the applicant has been granted an extension under § 46.2-752.1 with respect to the same registration period and has paid the fees provided under that section.

On receipt of such fees, the Commissioner shall issue a registration card and, if applicable, decals indicating the month of expiration of the vehicle registration. Upon passing an emissions inspection or being issued an emissions inspection waiver, the applicant may elect to renew the vehicle registration. For such renewal, the Commissioner shall collect the appropriate registration renewal fee and issue a registration card and, if applicable, decals. The renewal shall take effect the first day succeeding the month in which the registration extension expires. When offered by the Commissioner, the applicant may elect to renew the vehicle registration for multiple years, pursuant to § 46.2-646.

B. All administrative fees imposed and collected by the Commissioner under this section shall be paid into the state treasury and set aside as a special fund to be used to meet the expenses of the Department.

History.
2013, cc. 673, 789.

§ 46.2-1184. Fleet emissions inspection stations.

Any registered owner or lessee of a fleet of at least twenty vehicles may apply to the Director for a permit to establish a fleet emissions inspection station consistent with federal requirements. The Director shall not issue any fleet emissions inspection station permit until he has found that the applicant:

1. Maintains an established place of business for the applicant's fleet of vehicles;
2. Has obtained approved machinery, tools, and equipment to adequately conduct the required emissions inspection in the manner prescribed by regulations of the Board;
3. Employs properly trained and licensed personnel to perform the necessary labor; and
4. Agrees to provide test records and data as may be prescribed by the Director.

Upon issuance of a permit by the Director, the owner or lessee of the motor vehicle fleet may conduct emissions inspections of the vehicles in his fleet. No emissions inspection approval shall be issued to any fleet vehicle until it has been inspected and found to comply with applicable regulations.

No holder of a fleet emissions inspection station permit shall inspect any vehicle for which such permittee is not the registered owner or lessee.

History.
1980, c. 469, § 46.1-326.10; 1988, c. 806; 1989, c. 727; 1993, cc. 995, 998; 1993, Sp. Sess., c. 2.

§ 46.2-1185. Investigation of inspection stations; revocation or suspension of permits for emissions inspection stations.

The Director shall investigate the operation of each emissions inspection station and fleet emissions inspection station as the conditions and circumstances of such operation indicate. He may require the holder of any permit to submit such documentation required concerning the operation of such inspection station. The Director may suspend or revoke and require the forfeiture of any emissions inspection station permit if he finds that such station is not operated in accordance with the provisions of this article and the regulations adopted by the Board or the holder of such permit has failed or refused to submit records or documentation required.

If the Director finds that any permit holder has violated any provision of this article or any order or regulation of the Board, after notice or a reasonable attempt to give notice to the permit holder, the Director may, without a hearing, suspend the permit of the emissions inspection station and require the permit holder immediately to cease performing emissions inspections. Within ten days of such action, the Director shall, after reasonable notice to the permit holder as to the time and place thereof, hold a hearing to affirm, modify, amend, or cancel the suspension and the requirement to cease performing emissions inspections. With the consent of the permit holder, the Director may forego such hearing and allow the suspension and requirement to cease performing emissions inspections to stand. If the Director finds that a permit holder is not complying with any such suspension or requirement to cease performing emissions inspections, the Director may proceed in accordance with § 46.2-1187 or § 46.2-1187.2.

Nothing in this section shall limit the Director's authority to proceed against the permit holder directly under § 46.2-1187 or § 46.2-1187.2.

History.
1980, c. 469, § 46.1-326.11; 1988, c. 806; 1989, c. 727; 1991, c. 531; 1993, cc. 995, 998; 1993, Sp. Sess., c. 2.

§ 46.2-1186. False certificate.

No person shall make, issue, or knowingly use any imitation or otherwise counterfeit official certificate of emissions inspection.

No person shall issue or cause or permit to be issued any certificate of inspection knowing it to be fictitious or knowing it to have been issued for a vehicle other than the vehicle identified on the certificate.

History.
1980, c. 469, § 46.1-326.12; 1989, c. 727; 1993, cc. 995, 998; 1993, Sp. Sess., c. 2.

§ 46.2-1187. Penalties.

Any person violating this article shall be guilty of a Class 3 misdemeanor for the first offense and fined not less than $100 nor more than $1,000 for each subsequent offense except as otherwise provided in this article. If any official emissions inspection station violates this article or regulations of the Director made pursuant hereto, the Director, in addition to or in lieu of such fine imposed by a court, may suspend the permit of the emissions inspection station or if, in the opinion of the Director, the facts warrant such action, the Director may revoke the authority and cancel the permit of such inspection station, whether or not the violation is a first offense against this article.

History.
1980, c. 469, § 46.1-326.13; 1988, c. 806; 1989, c. 727; 1991, c. 531; 1993, cc. 995, 998; 1993, Sp. Sess., c. 2.

§ 46.2-1187.1. Right of entry.

Whenever it is necessary for the purposes of this article, the Executive Director or his duly authorized agent or employee at reasonable times may enter any establishment or upon any public or private property to obtain information or conduct surveys, audits, or investigations.

History.
1991, c. 531.

§ 46.2-1187.2. Compelling compliance with regulations and order of Board; penalty.

Any emissions inspection station owner violating or failing, neglecting, or refusing to obey any regulation or order of the Board may be compelled to comply by injunction, mandamus, or other appropriate remedy.

Without limiting the remedies which may be obtained under the foregoing provisions of this section, any emissions inspection station owner violating or failing, neglecting, or refusing to obey any regulation or order of the Board or any provision of this article, shall, in the discretion of the court, be subject to a civil penalty of no more than $25,000 for each violation. Each day of violation shall constitute a separate offense. In determining the amount of any civil penalty to be assessed, the court shall consider, in addition to such other factors as it may deem appropriate, the size of the emissions inspection station owner's business, the severity of the economic impact of the penalty on that business, and the seriousness of the violation. Such civil penalties may, in the discretion of the court, be directed to be paid into the treasury of the county, city, or town in which the violation occurred to be used to abate environmental pollution in whatever manner the court, by order, may direct. However, where the emissions inspection station owner is the county, city, or town or an agent thereof, the court shall direct the penalty to be paid into the state treasury.

With the consent of the emissions inspection station owner who has violated or failed, neglected, or refused to obey any regulation or order of the Board or any provision of this article, the Board may, in any order issued by the Board against such owner, provide for the payment of civil charges in specific sums, not to exceed the limit in the foregoing provisions of this section. Such civil charges shall be in lieu of any civil penalty which could be imposed under the foregoing provisions of this section.

Any penalty provided for in this section to which an emissions inspection station owner is subject shall apply to any emissions inspector or certified emissions repair mechanic employed by or at that station.

As to emissions inspection station owners, emissions inspectors, and certified emissions repair mechanics, minor violations as set forth in Board regulations may be punishable by letters of reprimand from the Department. Major violations as set forth in Board regulations may be punishable by probation, suspension and/or license or certificate revocation, depending on the nature and type of violation. Civil penalties may be imposed only for major types of violations.

The Board shall provide by regulation a process whereby emissions inspection station owners, emissions inspectors and certified emissions repair mechanics may appeal penalties for violations. Such regulations regarding the process to appeal penalties for violations shall provide that the appeal process shall be handled by a person other than the Program Manager for the applicable emissions program or one of his regional employees.

History.
1991, c. 531; 1995, cc. 836, 851.

§ 46.2-1187.3. Vehicles used for investigations.

Motor vehicles owned by the Commonwealth and used solely for investigations pursuant to this article may be issued the same license plates as those issued for vehicles owned by private citizens. The Executive Director shall certify under oath to the Commissioner of the Department of Motor Vehicles the vehicles to be used solely for such investigations.

History.
1991, c. 531.

ARTICLE 23.
MOTORCYCLE RIDER SAFETY.

§ 46.2-1188. Motorcycle rider safety training courses.

"Motorcycle rider safety training courses" means courses of instruction in the operation of motorcycles, including instruction in the safe on-road operation of motorcycles, the rules of the road, and the laws of the Commonwealth relating to motor vehicles, for the purposes of obtaining a waiver pursuant to § 46.2-337 for (i) both two-wheeled and three-wheeled motorcycles, (ii) two-wheeled motorcycles, or (iii) three-wheeled motorcycles. Courses shall meet the requirements of this article and be approved by the Department of Motor Vehicles. Qualifying providers of such courses shall either be reimbursed for eligible costs or not be reimbursed as provided in § 46.2-1192.

History.
1984, c. 476, § 46.1-566; 1989, c. 727; 2001, cc. 21, 27; 2004, c. 734; 2016, c. 380.

§ 46.2-1189. Authority of the Department of Motor Vehicles.

The Department of Motor Vehicles may do all things necessary to carry out the purposes of this article, including entering into contracts for administrative and other operational support for motorcycle rider safety training centers.

History.
1984, c. 476, § 46.1-567; 1989, c. 727; 2004, c. 734.

§ 46.2-1190. Regional motorcycle rider safety training centers; requirements.

A. Any public or private agency, organization, school, institution of higher education, partnership, corporation, or individual that meets the program requirements set forth in this article shall be eligible for participation in the program and may organize a regional motorcycle rider safety training center and offer motorcycle rider safety training courses.

B. No such agency, organization, business or individual shall operate a motorcycle rider safety training center without a license. Such agencies, organizations, businesses and individuals shall apply to the Department for a license pursuant to § 46.2-1192. The applications for training center licenses shall include, but not be limited to:

1. The address and detailed description of the facility or facilities where the course shall be conducted;
2. The name, address, federal identification number, and telephone number of the agency, organization, school, institution of higher education, partnership, or corporation organized as a training center;
3. The name, address, social security number, and telephone number of the individual who is authorized to obligate the training center;
4. The names, addresses, social security numbers, and telephone numbers of the administrator and the instructors;
5. For those agencies, organizations, businesses, and individuals that apply to receive reimbursement, the names, addresses, social security numbers, and telephone numbers of all individuals who are to receive reimbursement;
6. A planned course schedule including course type, dates, and hours of course conduct;
7. The projected number of students to be trained in the program during the calendar year;
8. Detailed specifications of the curricula intended for use;
9. For those agencies, organizations, businesses, and individuals that apply to receive reimbursement, a planned course budget to include all estimated costs for course operation, administration, instructors' salaries, insurance, advertising, purchase of test books, equipment and materials, and other course-related expenses;
10. For those agencies, organizations, businesses, and individuals that apply to receive reimburse-

ment, estimated course fees to be charged to participants;

11. Verification of adequate insurance coverage to protect both the Commonwealth and the training center and all instructors, aides, and participants in any course conducted under the program, including the following:

a. Minimum employers liability — $100,000;

b. Minimum commercial general liability — $500,000 combined single limit;

c. Minimum automobile liability — $500,000 combined single limit; and

d. Workers' compensation insurance in accordance with § 2.2-4332 and Chapter 8 (§ 65.2-800 et seq.) of Title 65;

12. Verification of proper safety equipment and a sufficient number of training motorcycles for novice rider courses;

13. Verification that the designated classrooms, ranges, and motorcycle and equipment storage areas are available for all training courses offered by the training center at that site and that they comply with all necessary zoning, health, and safety codes;

14. Criminal background checks on all corporate officers, owners, administrators, and all individuals authorized to obligate the training center; and

15. A statement as to the ability and willingness to meet all requirements set forth in this article.

The Department shall issue licenses to applicants whose curricula, facilities, equipment, corporate officers, administrators, instructors, and all individuals authorized to obligate the training center meet the requirements set forth in this article, subject to the provisions of § 46.2-1192.

C. The Commissioner shall act on any application for a license under this article within 30 days after receipt by either granting or denying the application. The Commissioner may, as may be necessary during the initial review and evaluation of an application, request additional information from an applicant, thereby extending the period for granting or denying a license by not more than 30 days from the receipt of such additional information. Any applicant denied a license shall, on his written request made within 30 days of the Commissioner's action, be given a hearing at a time and place determined by the Commissioner or his designee. All hearings under this section shall be public and shall be held as soon as practicable, but in no case later than 30 days from receipt of the hearing request. The applicant may be represented by counsel. Any applicant denied a license may not apply again for the same type of license for 180 calendar days from the date of denial of the application.

D. The facilities, equipment, curriculum, accreditation, and geographic areas in which each training center may offer courses shall be approved by the Department. The location of the training centers shall be in accordance with the Department's administrative districts. No training center shall change its location without the approval of the Department. Training centers shall provide courses for either novice, experienced or sidecar and three-wheeled motorcyclists or any of the three, depending upon the curricula used. Training centers shall maintain such records and provide such reports as determined by the Department. Training centers shall submit all reports required by the Department for evaluation. The Department shall monitor and evaluate the performance of the training centers and the effectiveness of the program in training motorcyclists.

E. Training centers shall ensure that instructors maintain the minimum qualifications and meet any other instructor requirements established in this article. The Department may, pursuant to subsection C of § 46.2-1190.5, terminate a training course if it finds an instructor in violation of any provision of this article.

Instructors shall meet the requirements of this article, the Department and the public or private agency, organization, school, institution of higher education, partnership, corporation or individual offering the program.

History.

1984, c. 476, § 46.1-568; 1989, c. 727; 2001, cc. 21, 27; 2004, c. 734; 2013, c. 226.

§ 46.2-1190.1. Curricula requirements.

A. The curriculum used in a novice rider-training course to train novice riders shall be approved by the Department. Each participant enrolled in a novice rider-training course shall receive no less than the minimum number of hours of classroom and on-cycle instruction as specified in the current approved curriculum.

All novice rider courses shall include a module on the effects of alcohol and other drugs on motorcycle operation, and a thorough review of Virginia laws and rules of the road applicable to motorcycles. All novice rider course participants shall be provided one copy of the course textbook and one copy of the Virginia Motorcycle Operator Manual. During the on-cycle instruction no more than six students may be under the supervision of any one instructor at any one time. No more than 12 students may operate motorcycles on the same range at the same time.

B. The curriculum used to train experienced riders shall be approved by the Department. Each participant enrolled in an experienced rider course shall receive no less than the minimum number of hours of classroom and on-cycle instruction as specified in the current approved curriculum.

All experienced rider courses shall include a module on the effects of alcohol and other drugs on motorcycle operation, and a review of Virginia laws and rules of the road applicable to motorcycles. During on-cycle instruction no more than six students may be under the supervision of any one instructor at any one time, and no more than 12 students may operate motorcycles on the same range at the same time.

C. The curriculum used to train sidecar and three-wheeled motorcycle riders shall be approved by the Department. Each participant enrolled in a sidecar and three-wheeled motorcycle course shall receive no less than the minimum number of hours of classroom and on-cycle instruction as specified in the current curriculum.

All sidecar and three-wheeled motorcycle course participants shall include a module on the effects of alcohol and other drugs on motorcycle operation, and a thorough review of Virginia laws and rules of the road applicable to motorcycles. During on-cycle instruction no more than six students may be under the supervision of any one instructor at any one time, and no more than six students may operate sidecars or three-wheeled motorcycles on the same range at the same time.

D. All course participants shall be required to wear the following protective gear during on-cycle instruction:

1. A minimum three-quarter shell motorcycle helmet that meets U.S. Department of Transportation Safety standards;

2. Eye protection;

3. A pair of boots or shoes that cover and protect the ankles and feet;

4. A long sleeved jacket or long sleeved shirt and long pants of denim or other material of equivalent durability; and

5. A pair of full-fingered gloves of leather or other material with resistance to abrasion.

History.
2004, c. 734.

§ 46.2-1190.2. Facilities and equipment; requirements and approval.

A. A training center shall possess or have access to the use of all classroom, range, storage facilities, and equipment. A training center's facilities and equipment shall be approved by the Department and include, but not be limited to:

1. A classroom for the presentation of the off-cycle instructional portion of the novice, experienced, and sidecar and three-wheeled motorcycle rider courses;

2. A paved range area for the on-cycle portion of the novice, experienced rider, and sidecar and three-wheeled motorcycle courses consistent with the minimum range requirements established by the Department-approved curriculum used in the course;

3. For those agencies, organizations, businesses and individuals that apply to receive reimbursement, adequate storage to protect motorcycles and equipment from vandalism, theft, and environmental damage;

4. Audio-visual equipment; and

5. Fire extinguisher and first aid kit.

B. The training center shall be responsible for procuring and providing a minimum of one motorcycle per student. Each such motorcycle shall be of a type that may lawfully be operated on the highways of the Commonwealth and, subject to the provisions of subsection D, meets two of the following three criteria: (i) an engine displacement of no more than 500 cubic centimeters, (ii) a weight of less than 400 pounds, and (iii) a seat height of 30 inches or less. Each participant in the experienced rider course shall provide a motorcycle for use in the course. One sidecar rig or three-wheeled motorcycle, provided by either a participant or the training center, shall be required for use by every two students in the sidecar and three-wheeled motorcycle course.

C. The training center shall be responsible for the normal maintenance and repair of all motorcycles it provides for each novice rider and sidecar and three-wheeled motorcycle course participant. All motorcycles used in course instruction shall pass a safety inspection performed by the instructors prior to use in any motorcycle rider-training course.

D. The Department, or its authorized agent, shall inspect and approve each training center's facilities and equipment prior to issuance or renewal of a license. Even if a motorcycle meets the criteria under subsection B, the Department or its authorized agent may deny its use by motorcycle rider safety training centers if it is deemed unsafe by the Department. A motorcycle may be deemed unsafe because of modification, damage, lack of maintenance, nonstandard configuration, or any other substantial safety reason.

History.
2004, c. 734; 2007, c. 190; 2013, c. 111.

§ 46.2-1190.3. Instructor qualifications.

A. Training centers shall employ only motorcycle safety instructors who meet the following minimum qualifications:

1. Have a current, valid driver's license, endorsed for motorcycle operation, that is neither suspended, revoked, cancelled, nor under probation, with less than six demerit points in a 12-month period and no conviction for any of the offenses enumerated in subsection E of § 18.2-270;

2. Be a valid training course instructor, as approved by the Department, which includes:

a. Having instructor certification to teach the current curriculum approved by the Department;

b. Attending all required program clinics offered by the Department that provide continuously updated course instructor and motorcycle safety education; and

c. Avoiding putting course participants or others associated with course instruction in physical danger during periods of instruction through the use of appropriate instruction techniques and methods;

3. Conduct themselves in a professional manner, including, but not limited to, using appropriate

language and having interactions with participants and others involved in the course that are free from threat and intimidation; and

4. Comply with other requirements specified in this article.

B. The requirements of subsection A of this section shall not apply to those persons who are valid training course instructors prior to being stationed outside the United States, during the period of such person's service, if any, in the armed services of the United States, and 60 days thereafter. However, no such temporary exemption granted under this section shall exceed five years. Any person who receives a temporary exemption under this section shall provide documentary or other proof that he is entitled to the benefits of this section, and shall be required to meet the requirements of subsection A of this section prior to being eligible to provide course instruction.

History.
2004, c. 734; 2013, c. 226.

§ 46.2-1190.4. Administrative and reporting requirements.

A. Training centers shall be responsible for verifying that all participants are eligible for enrollment in a course under the program, based on the following:

1. Persons enrolling in a novice rider course shall (i) possess a valid learner's permit or valid driver's license; (ii) have written parental or guardian permission if under the age of 18 years of age; and (iii) be physically able to balance and operate a motorcycle.

2. Persons enrolling in an experienced rider course shall (i) possess a valid driver's license endorsed for motorcycle operation; (ii) have written parental or guardian permission if under the age of 18; (iii) use a motorcycle that may lawfully be operated on the highways of the Commonwealth during course training; and (iv) have valid proof of ownership of such motorcycle, or have its owner's written permission to use it and valid proof of insurance.

3. Persons enrolling in a sidecar and three-wheeled motorcycle course shall (i) possess a valid learner's permit or a valid driver's license; (ii) have written parental or guardian permission if under the age of 18; (iii) use a sidecar rig or three-wheeled motorcycle that may lawfully be operated on the highways of the Commonwealth during course training; and (iv) if providing their own sidecar rig or three-wheeled motorcycle, have valid proof of ownership of such sidecar rig or three-wheeled motorcycle, or have its owner's written permission to use it and valid proof of insurance.

B. Training centers shall provide the following information to the Department on each course within 20 business days of course completion, on forms provided by the Department:

1. The type of course and date of completion;

2. The name, address, social security number, and certification number of each instructor;

3. The name, address, driver's license number, and date of birth of all participants enrolled in each course; and

4. The course completion status of each participant.

C. The training center shall issue a Department-approved certificate of completion to each participant who successfully completes a course in the program.

D. Training centers shall (i) retain a copy of each participant's waiver form and original course evaluation form and (ii) establish and maintain records of course administration, including the information outlined in subsection B of this section, for a three-year period following the course completion. The Department may audit course records, and monitor and evaluate any and all aspects of a training center's operation.

History.
2004, c. 734.

§ 46.2-1190.5. Penalties and remedies for violations of article.

A. The Department shall impose the following penalties on any training center for violations of the requirements of this article:

1. Limit the type of instruction provided by the training center;

2. Suspend or revoke the license of the training center;

3. Impose a civil penalty as set forth in § 46.2-1190.7; or

4. Impose any combination of the penalties set forth in this subsection.

B. When violations occur that are not found by the Department to pose a threat to the health, safety or welfare of the public or the course participants, instructors or others associated with the course, the Department shall (i) notify the training center of the violations that have occurred, (ii) direct corrective action to be completed by the training center within 30 calendar days, and (iii) require a formal written response documenting that corrections have been made as directed. Such violations shall typically be associated with, but not limited to, training center administration and operations. If corrections are not completed as directed, the Department shall notify the training center and may impose any or all of the sanctions set forth in subsection A of this section. Such penalties shall continue until all required corrections are made and the Department receives formal documentation confirming compliance.

The Department shall suspend the license of any training center that receives three or more notices under this subsection within any 12-month period. Such suspensions shall be for an initial 90-day period and shall continue until all required corrections are made and the Department receives formal documentation confirming compliance.

C. When violations occur that are found by the Department to pose a threat to the health, safety or welfare of the public or the course participants, instructors or others associated with the course, the Department shall (i) notify the training center of the violations that have occurred and immediately limit all types of instruction provided by the training center, (ii) direct corrective action to be completed by the training center within 30 calendar days of receipt of notice of such violations and (iii) shall require a formal written response documenting that corrections have been made as directed. If corrections are not completed as directed, the Department shall suspend the license of the training center and impose a civil penalty as set forth in § 46.2-1190.7. The period of such license suspension shall continue until all required corrections are made and the Department receives formal documentation confirming compliance. If the required corrections are not made within 30 calendar days of the suspension, the Department shall revoke the license.

D. Once a training center license is revoked, the Department shall not renew or reissue the license until (i) it receives formal documentation confirming compliance with the required corrective actions, and (ii) the training center applies for renewal or reissuance. Such training centers shall not be eligible to apply for a license again until 180 calendar days after the Department receives formal documentation confirming compliance with the required corrective actions.

E. Notice of an order suspending or revoking a license, imposing a limitation on training center operations or imposing a civil penalty, and advising the licensee of the opportunity for a hearing as a result of such order, shall be in writing and mailed to the licensee by registered mail to the training center address as shown on the most recent licensee's application for license and shall be considered served when mailed.

Upon receipt of a request for a hearing appealing the order, the licensee shall be afforded the opportunity for a hearing as soon as practicable, but in no case later than 30 days from receipt of the hearing request. The order shall remain in effect pending the outcome of the hearing.

History.
2004, c. 734; 2013, c. 226.

§ 46.2-1190.6. Other grounds for denying, suspending, or revoking licenses.

A license issued pursuant to this article may be denied, suspended, or revoked on any one or more of the following grounds, where applicable:

1. Material misstatement or omission in application for license;
2. Failure to comply subsequent to receipt of a written notice from the Department or any willful failure to comply with a lawful order, any provision of this article, or any term, condition, or restriction of a license;
3. Failure to comply with zoning or other land use regulations, ordinances, or statutes;
4. Use of deceptive business acts or practices;
5. Knowingly advertising by any means any assertion, representation, or statement of fact that is untrue, misleading, or deceptive relating to the conduct of the business for which a license is held or sought;
6. Having been found, through a judicial or administrative hearing, to have committed fraudulent or deceptive acts in connection with the training center for which a license is held or sought, or any consumer-related fraud;
7. Having been convicted of any criminal act involving the training center for which a license is held or sought;
8. Improper assignment, lending, or otherwise allowing the improper use of a license;
9. Any corporate officer, owner, administrator and any individual authorized to obligate the training center having been convicted of a felony;
10. Any corporate officer, owner, administrator and any individual authorized to obligate the training center having been convicted of any misdemeanor involving lying, cheating, stealing, or moral turpitude;
11. Failure to furnish the Department information, documentation, or records required or requested pursuant to this article;
12. Knowingly and willfully filing any false report, account, record, or memorandum;
13. Willfully altering or changing the appearance or wording of a training center license or a course completion certificate;
14. Failure to provide services in accordance with the terms, limitations, conditions, or requirements of the license; or
15. Failure to comply with other state and federal requirements relating to training center operations.

History.
2004, c. 734.

§ 46.2-1190.7. Civil penalties.

In addition to any other penalties or remedies available to the Commissioner under this article, the Commissioner may assess a civil penalty for any violation of any provision of this article not to exceed (i) $5,000 for training centers that are not reimbursed or (ii) the amount of funds disbursed to a training center for eligible costs, as set forth in § 46.2-1192. The penalty may be sued for and recovered in the name of the Commonwealth.

Any business, individual or entity operating a training center without a valid license issued by the Department after its license was suspended or revoked shall be subject to a civil penalty of $10,000.

History.
2004, c. 734.

§ 46.2-1191. Motorcycle Rider Safety Training Program Fund.

To finance the cost of the Motorcycle Rider Safety Training Program, the Department of Motor Vehicles shall deposit the fee collected for the issuance of each motorcycle learner's permit and $3 of the fee collected for the issuance of each motorcycle registration and all motorcycle driver's license endorsement fees into a special fund to be known as the Motorcycle Rider Safety Training Program Fund. The Department shall use the Fund as necessary for: (i) the costs of the Department of Motor Vehicles incurred in the administration of this article, (ii) the funding of licensed, approved regional cycle rider safety training centers for the conducting of courses, as set forth in § 46.2-1192 and (iii) any other purposes related to the administration of this article, including contractual costs related to administrative and other operational support for the reimbursed training centers.

History.
1984, c. 476, § 46.1-569; 1989, c. 727; 1997, cc. 104, 493; 1998, c. 322; 2004, c. 734.

§ 46.2-1192. Issuance and renewal of licenses by Department; payments to regional training centers.

The Department of Motor Vehicles is authorized to issue or renew licenses for regional motorcycle rider safety training centers for the conducting of motorcycle rider safety training courses, and to make payments in fulfillment of those licenses requiring reimbursement from funds appropriated from the Motorcycle Rider Safety Training Program Fund. The Department shall determine the number of such reimbursed licenses issued or renewed based on (i) the training centers meeting the requirements set forth in this article, (ii) regional demand for such training, and (iii) availability of funding. Costs eligible for reimbursement, method of payment, and required documentation associated with such payment shall be specified by the Department at the time the license is issued or renewed. Such licenses shall be valid for the period specified, but shall not exceed three years.

Those licenses issued or renewed for providers of such training courses that do not require reimbursement shall be awarded based on the training centers meeting the requirements set forth in this article. Such licenses shall be valid for the period specified, but shall not exceed three years.

No license shall be transferred or assigned as a result of any change in (i) the individual who is authorized to obligate the training center, (ii) ownership or (iii) officers in a corporation or other business entity without the approval of the Department. Such approval shall be based on the licensing requirements set forth in this article.

History.
1984, c. 476, § 46.1-570; 1989, c. 727; 2004, c. 734; 2013, c. 226.

CHAPTER 11.

[RESERVED.]

CHAPTER 12.

ABANDONED, IMMOBILIZED, UNATTENDED AND TRESPASSING VEHICLES; PARKING.

Article 1.

Abandoned Vehicles.

Article 2.

Immobilized and Unattended Vehicles.

Article 3.

Trespassing Vehicles, Parking, and Towing.

Article 4.

Potomac River Bridge Towing Compact of 1991.

ARTICLE 1.

ABANDONED VEHICLES.

§ 46.2-1200. Definitions.

As used in this article:

"Abandoned motor vehicle" means a motor vehicle, trailer, or semitrailer that:

1. Is left unattended on public property for more than 48 hours in violation of a state law or local ordinance, or

2. Has remained for more than 48 hours on private property without the consent of the property's owner, regardless of whether it was brought onto the private property with the consent of the owner or person in control of the private property, or

3. Is left unattended on the shoulder of a primary highway.

"Scrap metal processor" means any person who is engaged in the business of processing motor vehicles into scrap for remelting purposes who, from a fixed location, utilizes machinery and equipment for processing and manufacturing ferrous and nonferrous metallic scrap into prepared grades, and whose principal product is metallic scrap.

"Vehicle removal certificate" means a transferable document issued by the Department for any abandoned motor vehicle that authorizes the removal and destruction of the vehicle.

History.

1968, c. 421, § 46.1-555.1; 1978, c. 348; 1989, c. 727; 1997, c. 431; 2009, c. 664; 2011, cc. 487, 824.

§ 46.2-1200.1. Abandoning motor vehicles prohibited; penalty.

No person shall cause any motor vehicle to become an abandoned motor vehicle as defined in § 46.2-1200. In any prosecution for a violation of this section, proof that the defendant was, at the time that the vehicle was found abandoned, the owner of the vehicle shall constitute in evidence a rebuttable presumption that the owner was the person who committed the violation. Such presumption, however, shall not arise if the owner of the vehicle provided notice to the Department, as provided in § 46.2-604, that he had sold or otherwise transferred the ownership of the vehicle.

A summons for a violation of this section shall be executed by mailing a copy of the summons by first-class mail to the address of the owner of the vehicle as shown on the records of the Department of Motor Vehicles. If the person fails to appear on the date of return set out in the summons, a new summons shall be issued and delivered to the sheriff of the county, city, or town for service on the accused personally. If the person so served then fails to appear on the date of return set out in the summons, proceedings for contempt shall be instituted.

Any person convicted of a violation of this section shall be subject to a civil penalty of no more than $500. If any person fails to pay any such penalty, his privilege to drive a motor vehicle on the highways of the Commonwealth shall be suspended as provided in § 46.2-395.

All penalties collected under this section shall be paid into the state treasury to be credited to the Literary Fund as provided in § 46.2-114.

History.
1990, c. 725.

§ 46.2-1200.2. Vehicles registered to active duty military personnel.

Whenever a vehicle is shown by the Department of Motor Vehicles records to be owned by a person who has indicated that he is on active military duty or service, the Department shall include such information in response to requests for vehicle information pursuant to the requirements of this chapter.

Notwithstanding any provisions of this chapter, any person having a lien under the provisions of this chapter shall comply with the provisions of the federal Servicemembers Civil Relief Act (50 U.S.C. § 3901 et seq.) when disposing of a vehicle owned by a member of the military on active duty or service.

History.
2008, c. 171.

§ 46.2-1201. Ordinances.

The governing body of any county, city, or town may provide by ordinance for taking abandoned vehicles into custody and disposing of them in accordance with this article.

Any county, city, or town may take any abandoned motor vehicle into custody. The locality may employ its own personnel, equipment, and facilities or hire persons, equipment, and facilities, or firms or corporations that may be independent contractors for removing, preserving, storing, and selling at public auction abandoned motor vehicles.

History.
1968, c. 421, §§ 46.1-555.2, 46.1-555.3; 1989, c. 727; 1997, c. 150.

§ 46.2-1202. Search for owner and secured party; notice.

A. Any person in possession of an abandoned motor vehicle shall initiate with the Department, in a manner prescribed by the Commissioner, a search for the owner and/or lienholder of record of the vehicle, requesting the name and address of the owner of record of the motor vehicle and all persons having security interests in the motor vehicle on record in the office of the Department, describing, if ascertainable, the motor vehicle by year, make, model, and vehicle identification number. A fee of $25 shall be paid to the Department at the time of application. Those fees shall be paid into the state treasury and set aside as a special, nonreverting fund to be used to meet the expenses of the Department. A local government agency with a written agreement with the Department shall be exempt from this fee.

The Department shall check: (i) its own records, (ii) the records of a nationally recognized crime database, and (iii) records of a nationally recognized motor vehicle title database for owner and lienholder information. If a vehicle has been reported as stolen, the Department shall notify the appropriate law-enforcement agency of that fact. If a vehicle has been found to have been titled in another jurisdiction, the Department shall notify the applicant of that jurisdiction. In cases of motor vehicles titled in other jurisdictions, the Commissioner shall issue certificates of title on proof satisfactory to the Commissioner that the persons required to be notified by registered or certified mail have received actual notice fully containing the information required by this section.

B. If the Department confirms owner or lienholder information, the Department shall notify the owner, at the last known address of record, and lienholder, at the last known address of record, of the notice of interest in their vehicle, by certified mail, return receipt requested, and advise them to reclaim and remove the vehicle within 15 days, or, if the vehicle is a manufactured home or a mobile home, 120 days, from the date of notice. Such notice, when sent in accordance with these requirements, shall be sufficient regardless of whether or not it was ever received. Following the notice required in this subsection, if the motor vehicle remains unclaimed, the owner and all persons having security interests in the motor vehicle shall have waived all right, title, and interest in the motor vehicle.

Whenever a vehicle is shown by the Department's records to be owned by a person who has indicated that he is on active military duty or service, the Department shall notify the requestor of such information. Any person having an interest in such vehicle under the provisions of this article shall comply with the provisions of the federal Servicemembers Civil Relief Act (50 U.S.C. § 3901 et seq.).

C. If records of the Department contain no address for the owner or no address of any person shown by the Department's records to have a security interest, or if the identity and addresses of the owner and all persons having security interests cannot be determined with reasonable certainty, the person in possession of the abandoned motor vehicle shall obtain from the Department in a manner prescribed by the Commissioner, a Vehicle Removal Certificate. The vehicle may be sold or transferred to a licensee or a scrap metal processor, as defined in § 46.2-1600.

History.
1968, c. 421, § 46.1-555.4; 1989, c. 727; 1997, c. 150; 2009, c. 664.

§ 46.2-1202.1. Vehicle Removal Certificates.

The person in possession of an abandoned motor vehicle shall obtain from the Department in a manner prescribed by the Commissioner, a Vehicle Removal Certificate at no fee. The vehicle may be sold or transferred to a licensee or a scrap metal processor, as defined in § 46.2-1600.

If the person in possession of an abandoned motor vehicle desires to obtain title to the vehicle, that person shall post notice for at least 21 days of his intent to auction the motor vehicle. Postings of intent shall be in an electronic manner prescribed by the Commissioner who shall also ensure that written notice of intent is provided in public locations throughout the Commonwealth. If the Department confirms a lien, the person proposing the sale of the motor vehicle shall notify the lienholder of record, by certified mail, at the address on the certificate of title of the time and place of the proposed sale 10 days prior thereto.

A purchaser of the motor vehicle may apply for a title upon payment of the applicable fees and taxes, and by supplying the Department with the completed Vehicle Removal Certificate and the transcript from the Department that indicates that the Department has no record of the abandoned motor vehicle.

History.
2009, c. 664.

§ 46.2-1203. Sale of vehicle at public auction; disposition of proceeds.

If an abandoned motor vehicle is not reclaimed as provided for in § 46.2-1202, the locality or its authorized agent shall, notwithstanding the provisions of § 46.2-617, sell it at public auction. For the purposes of this article, the term "public auction," when conducted by any county, city, or town, shall include an Internet sale by auction. The purchaser of the motor vehicle shall take title to the motor vehicle free of all liens and claims of ownership of others, shall receive a sales receipt from the sale, and shall be entitled to apply to and receive from the Department a certificate of title and registration card for the vehicle. The sales receipt from the sale shall be sufficient title only for purposes of transferring the vehicle to a demolisher for demolition, wrecking, or dismantling, and in that case no further titling of the vehicle shall be necessary; however, such demolisher shall provide the Department acceptable documentation indicating that the vehicle has been demolished. From the proceeds of the sale of an abandoned motor vehicle the locality or its authorized agent shall reimburse itself for the expenses of the auction, the cost of towing, preserving, and storing the vehicle which resulted from placing the abandoned motor vehicle in custody, and all notice and publication costs incurred pursuant to § 46.2-1202. Any remainder from the proceeds of a sale shall be held for the owner of the abandoned motor vehicle or any person having security interests in the vehicle, as their interests may appear, for 60 days, and then be deposited into the treasury of the locality in which the abandoned motor vehicle was abandoned.

History.
1968, c. 421, § 46.1-555.5; 1989, c. 727; 2004, c. 369; 2013, c. 241.

§ 46.2-1204: Repealed by Acts 2009, c. 664, cl. 2, effective October 1, 2009.

§ 46.2-1205. Disposition of inoperable abandoned vehicles.

A. For the purposes of this section, "demolisher" has the meaning ascribed to it in § 46.2-1600.

B. Notwithstanding any other provisions of this article, any inoperable motor vehicle, trailer, semitrailer, or part of a motor vehicle, trailer, or semitrailer which has been taken into custody pursuant to other provisions of this article may be disposed of to a demolisher, without the title and without the notification procedures, by the person or locality on whose property or in whose possession the motor vehicle, trailer, or semitrailer is found. Such demolisher shall be properly licensed under the provisions of Chapter 16 (§ 46.2-1600 et seq.). The demolisher, on taking custody of the inoperable abandoned motor vehicle, shall notify the Department on forms and in the manner prescribed by the Commissioner. Notwithstanding any other provision of law, no other report or notice shall be required in this instance.

History.
1968, c. 421, § 46.1-555.7; 1972, c. 375; 1974, c. 454; 1989, c. 727; 2014, c. 58.

§ 46.2-1206. Surrender of certificate of title, etc., where motor vehicle acquired for demolition; records to be kept by demolisher or scrap metal processor.

No demolisher or scrap metal processor who purchases or otherwise acquires a motor vehicle for wrecking, dismantling, or demolition shall be required to obtain a certificate of title for the motor vehicle in his own name. After the motor vehicle has been demolished, processed, or changed so that it physically is no longer a motor vehicle, the demolisher or scrap metal processor shall surrender to the Department for cancellation the certificate of title, Vehicle Removal Certificate, properly executed vehicle disposition history, or sales receipt from a foreign jurisdiction for the vehicle. The Department shall issue the appropriate forms for the surrender of sales receipts, certificates of title, vehicle disposition histories, and vehicle removal certificates.

Demolishers and scrap metal processors shall keep accurate and complete records, in accordance with § 46.2-1608, of all motor vehicles purchased or received by them in the course of their business. Demolishers and scrap metal processors shall also collect and verify:

1. The towing company's name;

2. One of the ownership or possession documents set out in this section following verification of its accuracy;

3. The driver's license of the person delivering the motor vehicle; and

4. The license plate number of the vehicle that delivered the motor vehicle or scrap.

In addition, a photocopy or electronic copy of the appropriate ownership document or a Vehicle Removal Certificate presented by the customer shall be maintained. Ownership documents shall consist of either a motor vehicle title or a sales receipt from a foreign jurisdiction or a vehicle disposition history. These records shall be maintained in a permanent ledger in a manner acceptable to the Department at the place of business or at another readily accessible and secure location within the Commonwealth for at least five years. The personal identifying information contained within these records shall be protected from unauthorized disclosure through the ultimate destruction of the information. Disclosure of personal identifying information by anyone other than the Department is subject to the Driver's Privacy Protection Act (18 U.S.C. § 2721 et seq.).

If requested by a law-enforcement officer, a licensee shall make available, during regular business hours, a report of all the purchases of motor vehicles. Each report shall include the information set out in this chapter and be available electronically or in an agreed-upon format. Any person who violates any provision of this chapter or who falsifies any of the information required to be maintained by this article shall be guilty of a Class 3 misdemeanor for the first offense. Any licensee or scrap metal processor who is found guilty of second or subsequent violations shall be guilty of a Class 1 misdemeanor. The Department shall also assess a civil penalty not to exceed $500 for the first offense and $1,000 for the second and subsequent offenses. Those penalties shall be paid into the state treasury and set aside as a special fund to be used to meet the expenses of the Department.

If the vehicle identification number has been altered, is missing, or appears to have been otherwise tampered with, the demolisher or scrap metal processor shall take no further action with regard to the vehicle except to safeguard it in its then-existing condition and shall promptly notify the Department. The Department shall, after an investigation has been made, notify the demolisher or scrap metal processor whether the motor vehicle can be freed from this limitation. In no event shall the motor vehicle be disassembled, demolished, processed, or otherwise modified or removed prior to authorization by the Department. If the vehicle is a motorcycle, the demolisher or scrap metal processor shall cause to be noted on the title or salvage certificate, certifying on the face of the document, in addition to the above requirements, the frame number of the motorcycle and motor number, if available.

History.

1968, c. 421, § 46.1-555.8; 1989, c. 727; 2009, c. 664; 2012, cc. 803, 835.

§ 46.2-1207. Certification of disposal; reimbursement of locality by Commissioner.

On certification by a locality on forms provided by the Department that an inoperable abandoned motor vehicle left on property within the locality has been disposed of as provided in § 46.2-1205 or that an inoperable motor vehicle has been removed from the vehicle owner's property and disposed of by the locality or its authorized agent, the Commissioner shall reimburse the locality fifty dollars for each such motor vehicle disposed of at the expense of the locality. These reimbursements shall be made from appropriations made in the general appropriations act. In the event the appropriation is insufficient to satisfy requests for reimbursement, payments shall be made in chronological order on the basis of the date on which the requests were received. No payments, however, shall be made for requests received on any date until adequate funds are available to pay all requests received on that date. The Commissioner may promulgate regulations necessary to carry out the provisions of this section. These regulations shall include the requirement of the identification number or motor number of the vehicle for which reimbursement is applied, or an acceptable reason why that number is not furnished.

No reimbursement shall be made to any locality for vehicles which it acquires from sources outside its jurisdiction nor for vehicles it receives from dealers engaged in the business of dismantling used automobiles.

History.

1974, c. 454, § 46.1-555.9; 1976, c. 196; 1986, cc. 10, 553; 1989, c. 727; 1990, c. 207; 2006, c. 603.

§ 46.2-1208: Repealed by Acts 2009, c. 664, cl. 2, effective October 1, 2009.

ARTICLE 2.

IMMOBILIZED AND UNATTENDED VEHICLES.

§ 46.2-1209. Unattended or immobile vehicles, generally.

No person shall leave any motor vehicle, trailer, semitrailer, or part or combination thereof immobilized or unattended on or adjacent to any roadway if it constitutes a hazard in the use of the highway. No person shall leave any immobilized or unattended motor vehicle, trailer, semitrailer, or part or combination thereof longer than 24 hours on or adjacent to any roadway outside the corporate limits of any city or town, or on an interstate highway or limited access highway, expressway, or parkway inside the corporate limits of any city or town. Any law-enforcement officer or other uniformed employee of the local law-enforcement agency who specifically is authorized to do so by the chief law-enforcement officer or his designee may remove it or have it removed to a storage area for safekeeping and shall report the removal to the Department and to the owner of the motor vehicle, trailer, semitrailer, or combination as promptly as possible. Before obtaining possession of the motor vehicle, trailer, semitrailer, or combination, its owner or successor in interest to ownership shall pay to the parties entitled thereto all costs incidental to its removal or storage. In any violation of this section the owner of such motor vehicle, trailer, semitrailer or part or combination of a motor vehicle, trailer, or semitrailer, shall be presumed to be the person committing the violation; however, this presumption shall be rebuttable by competent evidence.

When a motor vehicle, trailer, semitrailer, or part or combination of a motor vehicle, trailer, or semitrailer was stolen or illegally used by a person other than the owner of the vehicle at the time of the theft or used without his authorization, express or implied, it shall be forthwith returned to its owner or the owner's successor in interest, other than an insurance company, who shall be relieved of the payment of any costs charged by the towing operator or storage facility for its daily storage, towing, and recovery fees, provided that the owner removes the vehicle within five business days following the owner's receipt of written notice by certified mail, return receipt requested. If the vehicle's owner fails to remove the vehicle within five days of receipt of such notice, the vehicle shall be released to the owner upon payment of the full costs of storage, towing, and recovery fees, and the owner shall then be entitled to seek reimbursement from the state treasury from the appropriation for criminal charges. The owner shall produce a valid motor vehicle registration or other proof of ownership to the employees of the facility wherein the motor vehicle, trailer, semitrailer or part or combination thereof is being stored. In any case in which the identity of the violator cannot be determined, or where it is found by a court that this section was not violated, the costs of daily storage, towing, and recovery fees of the vehicle shall be reimbursed to the towing and recovery operator and paid out of the state treasury from the appropriation for criminal charges. Payment from the treasury shall be made no later than 45 days from the application for such payment. In all cases where an insurance company is the stolen vehicle owner's successor in interest, the motor vehicle, trailer, semitrailer, or part or combination thereof shall be released to the insurance company upon presentation of a valid motor vehicle registration and payment by the insurance company to the towing operator or storage facility for its daily storage, towing, and recovery fees. The insurance company shall be entitled to seek reimbursement for the costs of the daily storage, towing, and recovery fees through the state treasury from the appropriation for criminal charges. If any person convicted of violating this section fails or refuses to pay these costs or if the identity or whereabouts of the owner is unknown and unascertainable after a diligent search has been made or after notice to the owner at his address as indicated by the records of the Department and to the holder of any lien of record with the Department, against the motor vehicle, trailer, semitrailer, or combination, the Commissioner may, after 30 days and after having the value of such motor vehicle, trailer, semitrailer, or combination determined by three disinterested dealers dispose of it by public or private sale. The proceeds from the sale shall be forthwith paid by him into the state treasury and shall be set aside as a special fund to be used to meet the expenses of the Department in carrying out the duties required by this section and to reimburse the owner of such motor vehicle, trailer, semitrailer, or combination as hereafter provided in this section.

If after the sale or other disposition of the motor vehicle, trailer, semitrailer, or combination the ownership of a motor vehicle, trailer, or semitrailer at the time of its removal is established satisfactorily to the Commissioner by the person claiming its ownership, the Commissioner shall pay him so much of the proceeds from the sale or other disposition of the motor vehicle, trailer, semitrailer, or combination as remains after paying the costs of daily storage, towing, and recovery fees, investigation of ownership, appraisal, and sale.

History.

Code 1950, § 46-5; 1952, c. 508; 1958, c. 541, § 46.1-2; 1964, c. 103; 1972, cc. 267, 402, 408; 1976, c. 454; 1978, cc. 47, 605; 1988, c. 293; 1989, cc. 256, 727; 2006, cc. 874, 891; 2012, c. 474.

§ 46.2-1210. Motor vehicles immobilized by weather conditions or emergencies.

Whenever any motor vehicle, trailer, semitrailer, or combination or part of a motor vehicle, trailer, or semitrailer is immobilized on any roadway by weather conditions or other emergency situations, the Department of Transportation may move or have the vehicle removed to some reasonably accessible portion of the adjacent right-of-way. Disposition thereafter shall be effected as provided by § 46.2-1209.

History.

Code 1950, § 46-5; 1952, c. 508; 1958, c. 541, § 46.1-2; 1964, c. 103; 1972, cc. 267, 402, 408; 1976, c. 454; 1978, cc. 47, 605; 1988, c. 293; 1989, cc. 256, 727.

§ 46.2-1211. Removal of motor vehicles obstructing movement; storage; payment of costs.

Whenever any motor vehicle, trailer, semitrailer, or part of a motor vehicle, trailer, or semitrailer interferes with the free ingress, egress, or movement on any premises, driveway, or parking area, without the permission of the owner of that property, any law-enforcement officer or other uniformed employee of the local law-enforcement agency who specifically is authorized to do so by the chief law-enforcement officer or his designee may remove it or have it removed to a storage area for safekeeping and shall report the removal to the Department and to the owner of the motor vehicle, trailer, semitrailer, or other vehicle as promptly as possible. Before obtaining the possession of his property, the owner shall pay to the parties entitled thereto all costs incidental to its removal or storage.

History.
1974, c. 589, § 46.1-2.1; 1989, c. 727; 2012, c. 474.

§ 46.2-1212. Authority to provide for temporary removal and disposition of vehicles involved in accidents.

The governing body of any county, city, or town may provide by ordinance that whenever a motor vehicle, trailer, or semitrailer involved in an accident is so located as to impede the orderly flow of traffic, the police or other uniformed employee of the local law-enforcement agency who specifically is authorized to do so by the chief law-enforcement officer or his designee may (i) at no cost to the owner or operator remove the motor vehicle, trailer, or semitrailer to some point in the vicinity where it will not impede the flow of traffic or (ii) have the vehicle removed to a storage area for safekeeping and shall report the removal to the Department and to the owner of the vehicle as promptly as possible. If the vehicle is removed to a storage area under clause (ii), the owner shall pay to the parties entitled thereto all costs incidental to its removal and storage.

History.
1964, c. 349, § 46.1-3.1; 1989, c. 727; 1992, c. 269; 2012, c. 474.

§ 46.2-1212.1. Authority to provide for removal and disposition of vehicles and cargoes of vehicles involved in accidents.

A. As a result of a motor vehicle accident or incident, the Department of State Police and/or local law-enforcement agency in conjunction with other public safety agencies may, without the consent of the owner or carrier, remove:

1. A vehicle, cargo, or other personal property that has been (i) damaged or spilled within the right-of-way or any portion of a roadway in the primary state highway system and (ii) is blocking the roadway or may otherwise be endangering public safety; or

2. Cargo or personal property that the Department of Transportation, Department of Emergency Management, or the fire officer in charge has reason to believe is a hazardous material, hazardous waste or regulated substance as defined by the Virginia Waste Management Act (§ 10.1-1400 et seq.), the Hazardous Materials Transportation Act (49 U.S.C. § 1808 et seq.) or the State Water Control Law (§ 62.1-44.2 et seq.), if the Department of Transportation or applicable person complies with the applicable procedures and instructions defined either by the Department of Emergency Management or the fire officer in charge.

B. The Department of Transportation, Department of State Police, Department of Emergency Management, local law-enforcement agency and other local public safety agencies and their officers, employees and agents, shall not be held responsible for any damages or claims that may result from the failure to exercise any authority granted under this section provided they are acting in good faith.

C. The owner and carrier, if any, of the vehicle, cargo or personal property removed or disposed of under the authority of this section shall reimburse the Department of Transportation, Department of State Police, Department of Emergency Management, local law-enforcement agency, and local public safety agencies for all costs incurred in the removal and subsequent disposition of such property.

History.
1997, c. 431.

§ 46.2-1213. Removal and disposition of unattended, or immobile vehicles; ordinances in counties, cities, and towns.

A. The governing body of any county, city, or town may by ordinance provide for the removal for safekeeping of motor vehicles, trailers, semitrailers, or parts thereof to a storage area if:

1. It is left unattended on a public highway or other public property and constitutes a traffic hazard;

2. It is illegally parked;

3. It is left unattended for more than 10 days either on public property or on private property without the permission of the property owner, lessee, or occupant;

4. It is immobilized on a public roadway by weather conditions or other emergency situation.

B. Removal shall be carried out by or under the direction of a law-enforcement officer or other uniformed employee of the local law-enforcement agency who specifically is authorized to do so by the chief law-enforcement officer or his designee. The ordinance, however, shall not authorize removal of motor vehicles, trailers, semitrailers, and parts thereof from private property without the written request of the owner, lessee, or occupant of the premises. The ordinance may also provide that the person at whose request the motor vehicle, trailer, semitrailer, or part of a motor vehicle, trailer, or semitrailer is removed from private property shall indemnify the county, city, or town against any loss or expense incurred by reason of removal, storage, or sale thereof. Any such ordinance may also provide that it shall be presumed that such motor vehicle, trailer, semitrailer, or part thereof is abandoned if it (i) lacks either a current license plate; or a current county, city or town license plate or sticker; or a valid state safety inspection certificate or sticker; and (ii) it has been in a specific location for four days without being moved. As promptly as possible, each removal shall be reported to a local governmental office to be designated in the ordinance and to the owner of the motor vehicle, trailer, or semitrailer. Before obtaining possession of the motor vehicle, trailer, semitrailer, or part thereof, the owner shall pay to the parties entitled thereto all costs incidental to its removal and storage and locating the owner. If the owner fails or refuses to pay the cost or if his identity or whereabouts is unknown and unascertainable after a diligent search has been made, and after notice to him at his last known address and to the holder of any lien of record with the office of the Department against the motor vehicle, trailer, semitrailer, or part of a motor vehicle, trailer, or semitrailer, the vehicle shall be treated as an abandoned vehicle under the provisions of Article 1 (§ 46.2-1200 et seq.).

History.

Code 1950, § 46-5.1; 1956, c. 114; 1958, c. 541, § 46.1-3; 1960, cc. 75, 204; 1966, c. 297; 1972, c. 267; 1974, c. 142; 1980, c. 551; 1984, cc. 190, 381; 1985, c. 91; 1989, c. 727; 2012, c. 474.

§ 46.2-1214. Sale of personal property found in unattended or abandoned vehicles.

Any personal property found in any unattended or abandoned motor vehicle, trailer, or semitrailer may be sold incident to the sale of the vehicle as authorized in this article.

History.

1970, c. 160, § 46.1-3.01; 1989, c. 727.

§ 46.2-1215. Leaving vehicles on private property prohibited; authority of counties, cities, and towns to provide for removal and disposition; notice of disposition.

No person shall leave any motor vehicle, trailer, semitrailer, or part of a motor vehicle, trailer, or semitrailer on the private property of any other person without his consent. The governing body of any county, city, or town may by ordinance provide, that on complaint of the owner of the property on which such motor vehicle, trailer, semitrailer, or part thereof has been left for more than 72 hours, that such motor vehicle, trailer, semitrailer, or part thereof, may be removed by or under the direction of a law-enforcement officer or other uniformed employee of the local law-enforcement agency who specifically is authorized to do so by the chief law-enforcement officer or his designee to a storage area. The ordinance shall require the owners of private property which is normally open to the public for parking to post or cause to be posted signs warning that vehicles left on the property for more than 72 hours will be towed or removed at their owners' expense. The ordinance may also provide that the person at whose request the vehicle, trailer, semitrailer, or part thereof is so removed shall indemnify the county, city, or town against any loss or expense incurred by reason of removal, storage, or sale thereof.

In the case of the removal of a motor vehicle, trailer, semitrailer, or part of a motor vehicle, trailer, or semitrailer from private property, when it cannot be readily sold, the motor vehicle, trailer, semitrailer, or part may be disposed of in whatever manner the governing body of the county, city, or town may provide.

In all other respects, the provisions of §§ 46.2-1213 and 46.2-1217 shall apply to these removals. Disposal of a motor vehicle, trailer, or semitrailer may at the option of the governing body of the county, city, or town be carried out under either the provisions of § 46.2-1213, or under the provisions of this section after a diligent search for the owner, after notice to him at his last known address and to the holder of any lien of record in the office of the Department against the motor vehicle, trailer, or semitrailer, and after the motor vehicle, trailer, or semitrailer has been held at least 60 days.

The Department shall be notified of the disposition of any motor vehicle, trailer, or semitrailer under § 46.2-1213 or the provisions of this section.

History.

1964, c. 391, § 46.1-3.2; 1966, c. 615; 1984, c. 158; 1987, cc. 152, 202; 1989, c. 727; 2012, c. 474.

ARTICLE 3.

TRESPASSING VEHICLES, PARKING, AND TOWING.

§ 46.2-1216. Removal or immobilization of motor vehicles, vehicles, and trailers against which there are outstanding parking violations; ordinances.

The governing body of any county, city, or town may provide by ordinance that any motor vehicle, vehicle, or trailer parked on the public highways or public grounds against which there are three or more unpaid or otherwise unsettled parking violation notices may be removed to a place within such county, city, or town or in an adjacent locality designated by the chief law-enforcement officer for the temporary storage of the motor vehicle, vehicle, or trailer, or the motor vehicle, vehicle, or trailer may be immobilized in a manner which will prevent its removal or operation except by authorized law-enforcement personnel. The governing body of Fairfax County, and any town adjacent to such county, Loudoun County, Prince William County, and the Cities of Alexandria, Fairfax, Falls Church, Manassas, Manassas Park, and Virginia Beach may also provide by ordinance that whenever any motor vehicle, vehicle, or trailer against which there are three or more outstanding unpaid or otherwise unsettled parking violation notices is found parked upon private property, including privately owned streets and roads, the motor vehicle, vehicle, or trailer may, by towing or otherwise, be removed or immobilized in the manner provided above; provided that no motor vehicle, vehicle, or trailer may be removed or immobilized from property which is owned or occupied as a single family residence. Any such ordinance shall further provide that no such motor vehicle, vehicle, or trailer parked on private property may be removed or immobilized unless written authorization to enforce this section has been given by the owner of the property or an association of owners formed pursuant to Chapter 4.1 (§ 55-79.1 et seq.) or Chapter 4.2 (§ 55-79.39 et seq.) of Title 55 and that the local governing body has provided written assurance to the owner of the property that he will be held harmless from all loss, damage, or expense, including costs and attorney fees, that may be incurred as a result of the towing or otherwise of any motor vehicle, vehicle, or trailer pursuant to this section. The ordinance shall provide that the removal or immobilization of the motor vehicle, vehicle, or trailer shall be by or under the direction of, an officer or employee of the police department or sheriff's office.

Any ordinance shall provide that it shall be the duty of the law-enforcement personnel removing or immobilizing the motor vehicle, vehicle, or trailer or under whose direction such motor vehicle, vehicle, or trailer is removed or immobilized, to inform as soon as practicable the owner of the removed or immobilized motor vehicle, vehicle, or trailer of the nature and circumstances of the prior unsettled parking violation notices for which the motor vehicle, vehicle, or trailer was removed or immobilized. In any case involving immobilization of a motor vehicle, vehicle, or trailer pursuant to this section, there shall be placed on the motor vehicle, vehicle, or trailer, in a conspicuous manner, a notice warning that the motor vehicle, vehicle, or trailer has been immobilized and that any attempt to move the motor vehicle, vehicle, or trailer might damage it.

Any ordinance shall provide that the owner of an immobilized motor vehicle, vehicle, or trailer, or other person acting on his behalf, shall be allowed at least 24 hours from the time of immobilization to repossess or secure the release of the motor vehicle, vehicle, or trailer. Failure to repossess or secure the release of the motor vehicle, vehicle, or trailer within that time period may result in the removal of the motor vehicle, vehicle, or trailer to a storage area for safekeeping under the direction of law-enforcement personnel.

Any ordinance shall provide that the owner of the removed or immobilized motor vehicle, vehicle, or trailer or other person acting on his behalf, shall be permitted to repossess or to secure the release of the motor vehicle, vehicle, or trailer by payment of the outstanding parking violation notices for which the motor vehicle, vehicle, or trailer was removed or immobilized and by payment of all costs incidental to the immobilization, removal, and storage of the motor vehicle, vehicle, or trailer and the efforts to locate the owner of the motor vehicle, vehicle, or trailer. Should the owner fail or refuse to pay such fines and costs, or should the identity or whereabouts of the owner be unknown and unascertainable, the ordinance may provide for the sale of the motor vehicle, vehicle, or trailer in accordance with the procedures set forth in § 46.2-1213.

History.

1977, c. 666, § 46.1-3.02; 1978, c. 282; 1984, c. 64; 1988, c. 520; 1989, c. 727; 1990, c. 686; 2007, c. 813; 2010, c. 23; 2012, cc. 104, 150.

§ 46.2-1217. Local governing body may regulate certain towing.

The governing body of any county, city, or town by ordinance may regulate services rendered pursuant to police towing requests by any business engaged in the towing or storage of unattended, abandoned, or immobile vehicles. The ordinance may include delineation of service areas for towing services, the limitation of the number of persons engaged in towing services in any area, including the creation of one or more exclusive service areas, and the specification of equipment to be used for providing towing service. The governing body of any county, city, or town may contract for services rendered pursuant to a police towing request with one or more businesses engaged in the towing or storage of unattended, abandoned, or immobile vehicles. The contract may specify the fees or charges to be paid by the owner or operator of a towed vehicle to the person undertaking its towing or storage and may prescribe the geographical area to be served by each person providing towing services. The county, city, or town may establish criteria for eligibility of persons to enter into towing services contracts and, in its discretion, may itself provide exclusive towing and storage service for police-requested towing of unattended, abandoned, or immobile vehicles.

Prior to adopting an ordinance or entering into a contract pursuant to this section, the local governing body shall appoint an advisory board to advise the governing body with regard to the appropriate provisions of the ordinance or terms of the contract. The advisory board shall include representatives of local law-enforcement agencies, towing and recovery operators, and the general public.

"Police-requested towing" or "police towing request," as used in this section, includes all requests made by a law-enforcement officer of the county, city, or town or by a State Police officer within the county, city, or town pursuant to this article or Article 2 (§ 46.2-1209 et seq.) and towing requests made by a law-enforcement officer at the request of the owner or operator of an unattended, abandoned, or immobile vehicle, when no specific service provider is requested by such owner or operator.

If an unattended, abandoned, or immobile vehicle is located so as to impede the free flow of traffic on a highway declared by resolution of the Commonwealth Transportation Board to be a portion of the interstate highway system and a law-enforcement officer determines, in his discretion, that the business or businesses authorized to undertake the towing or storage of the vehicle pursuant to an ordinance or contract adopted pursuant to this section cannot respond in a timely manner, the law-enforcement officer may request towing or storage service from a towing or storage business other than those authorized by such ordinance or contract.

If an unattended, abandoned, or immobile vehicle is towed as the result of a police-towing request, the owner or person having control of the business or property to which the vehicle is towed shall allow the owner of the vehicle or any other towing and recovery business, upon presentation of a written request therefor from the owner of the vehicle, to have access to the vehicle for the purpose of inspecting or towing the vehicle to another location for the purpose of repair, storage, or disposal. For the purpose of this section, "owner of the vehicle" means a person who (i) has vested ownership, dominion, or title to the vehicle; (ii) is the authorized agent of the owner as defined in clause (i); or (iii) is an employee, agent, or representative of an insurance company representing any party involved in a collision that resulted in a police-requested tow who represents in writing that the insurance company has obtained the oral or written consent of the title owner or his agent or the lessee of the vehicle to obtain possession of the vehicle. It shall be unlawful for any towing and recovery business to refuse to release a vehicle to the owner as defined in this section upon tender of full payment for all lawful charges by cash, insurance company check, certified check, money order, at least one of two commonly used, nationally recognized credit cards, or additional methods of payment approved by the Commonwealth Transportation Board. Thereafter, if a towing and recovery business refuses to release the vehicle, future charges related to storage or handling of the vehicle by such towing and recovery business shall be suspended and no longer payable.

The vehicle owner who has vested ownership, dominion, or title to the vehicle shall indemnify and hold harmless the towing and recovery operator from any and all liability for releasing the vehicle to any vehicle owner as defined in this section for inspecting or towing the vehicle to another location for the purpose of repair, storage, or disposal.

Motor Vehicles

History.

Code 1950, § 46-5.1; 1956, c. 114; 1958, c. 541, §§ 46.1-3, 46.1-3.02; 1960, cc. 75, 204; 1966, c. 297; 1972, c. 267; 1974, c. 142; 1977, c. 666; 1980, c. 551; 1978, c. 282; 1984, cc. 64, 190, 381; 1985, c. 91; 1988, c. 520; 1989, c. 727; 1993, c. 405; 1999, c. 78; 2006, cc. 874, 891; 2008, cc. 470, 647; 2012, cc. 803, 835.

§ 46.2-1218. Reports by persons in charge of garages, parking places, etc.; unclaimed vehicles.

The person in charge of any garage, repair shop, or automotive service, storage, or parking place shall report on forms furnished by the Superintendent of State Police, to the nearest police station or to the State Police any motor vehicle left unclaimed in his place of business for more than two weeks when he does not know the name of the owner and the reason for the storage.

History.

Code 1950, § 46-17.2; 1958, c. 541, § 46.1-11; 1989, c. 727.

§ 46.2-1219. Regulation of vehicular and pedestrian traffic on certain parking lots.

The governing body of any county, city, or town may by ordinance regulate the flow of vehicular and pedestrian traffic, the parking of vehicles, and speed limits on parking lots which are open to the public and designed to accommodate fifty or more vehicles, but no such ordinance shall conflict with state law.

History.

1970, c. 338, § 46.1-181.1; 1989, c. 727.

§ 46.2-1219.1. Regulation or prohibition of vehicular traffic on certain privately owned public parking areas and driveways; penalties.

The governing body of any county, city, or town may adopt an ordinance not in conflict with state law regulating or prohibiting the stopping, standing, parking, or flow of vehicles in parking areas or driveways of shopping centers and commercial office and apartment complexes. The ordinance shall be applied to and enforced in a specific center or commercial area upon application in writing by the owner or person in general charge of the operation of such area to the chief law-enforcement officer or other official designated by the ordinance for that purpose.

The provisions of any such ordinance shall be substantially as follows:

Cruising Ordinance.

No person shall drive or permit a motor vehicle under his care, custody, or control to be driven past a traffic control point three or more times within a two-hour period from 6:00 p.m. to 4:00 a.m. Monday through Sunday, in or around a posted no cruising area so as to contribute to traffic congestion; obstruction of streets, sidewalks, parking lots, or public vehicular areas; impediment of access to shopping centers or other buildings open to the public; or interference with the use of property or conduct of business in the area adjacent thereto.

At every point where a public street or alley becomes or provides ingress to a no-cruising area, there shall be posted a sign which designates "No-Cruising" areas and times.

"Traffic control point," as used in this section, means any point or points within the no-cruising area established by the local law-enforcement agency for the purpose of monitoring cruising.

No violations shall occur except upon the third passage past the same traffic control point within a two-hour period.

No area shall be designated or posted as a no-cruising area except upon the passage of a resolution by the local governing body specifically requiring such designation and posting for a particular area.

This ordinance shall not apply to in-service emergency vehicles, taxicabs for hire, buses, and other vehicles being used for business purposes.

Where there is a violation of any provision of this ordinance, a law-enforcement officer shall charge such violation on the uniform traffic summons form. The ordinance may further provide that any person violating the ordinance shall, upon conviction, be subject to a fine of twenty-five dollars.

Any person convicted of a second or subsequent violation of the ordinance may be punished by a fine of not less than $50 nor more than $100 for each succeeding violation. No assignment of demerit points shall be made under Article 19 (§ 46.2-489 et seq.) of this title for any violation of the ordinance.

History.

1990, c. 891; 1993, c. 574.

§ 46.2-1219.2. Parking of vehicles in commuter parking lots owned by the Virginia Department of Transportation.

A. It shall constitute a traffic infraction for any person to park any vehicle in any commuter parking lot owned by the Virginia Department of Transportation in any manner not in conformance with posted signs and pavement markings. In Planning District 8, such signs shall clearly indicate that before 10:00 a.m. Monday through Friday except holidays parking is only for commuters using mass transit or who are car pool or bicycle riders.

B. In the prosecution of an offense established under this section, prima facie evidence that the vehicle described in the summons issued pursuant to this section was parked in violation of this section, together with proof that the defendant was at the time of such violation the owner, lessee, or renter of the vehicle, shall constitute in evidence a rebuttable presumption that such owner, lessee, or renter of the vehicle was the person who committed the violation. Such presumption shall be rebutted if the owner, lessee, or renter of the vehicle (i) files an affidavit by regular mail with the clerk of the general district court that he was not the operator of the vehicle at the time of the alleged violation or (ii) testifies in open court under oath that he was not the operator of the vehicle at the time of the alleged violation. Such presumption shall also be rebutted if a certified copy of a police report, showing that the vehicle had been reported to the police as stolen prior to the time of the alleged violation of this section, is presented, prior to the return date established on the summons issued pursuant to this section, to the court adjudicating the alleged violation. A violation of this section may be charged on the uniform traffic summons form.

C. Notwithstanding the provisions of § 19.2-76, whenever a summons for a violation of this section is served in any county, city, or town, it may be executed by mailing by first-class mail a copy thereof to the address of the owner of the vehicle as shown on the records of the Department of Motor Vehicles. If the summoned person fails to appear on the date of return set out in the summons mailed pursuant to this section, the summons shall be executed in the manner set out in § 19.2-76.3.

Enforcement of the provisions of this section may be enforced by any law-enforcement officer as defined in § 9.1-101.

History.

2007, c. 263; 2016, c. 708.

§ 46.2-1220. Parking, stopping, and standing regulations in counties, cities, or towns; parking meters; presumption as to violation of ordinances; penalty.

The governing body of any county, city, or town may by ordinance provide for the regulation of parking, stopping, and standing of vehicles within its limits, including, but not limited to, the regulation of any vehicle blocking access to and preventing use of curb ramps, fire hydrants, and mailboxes on public or private property. Such ordinances may also include the installation and maintenance of parking meters. The ordinance may require the deposit of a coin of a prescribed denomination, determine the length of time a vehicle may be parked, and designate a department, official, or employee of the local government to administer the provisions of the ordinance. The ordinance may delegate to that department, official, or employee the authority to make and enforce any additional regulations concerning parking that may be required, including, but not limited to, penalties for violations, deadlines for the payment of fines, and late payment penalties for fines not paid when due. In a city having a population of at least 90,000, the ordinance may also provide that a summons or parking ticket for the violation of the ordinance or regulations may be issued by law-enforcement officers, other uniformed city employees, or by uniformed personnel serving under contract with the city. Notwithstanding the foregoing provisions of this section, the governing bodies of Augusta, Bath, and Rockingham Counties may by ordinance provide for the regulation of parking, stopping, and standing of vehicles within their limits, but no such ordinance shall authorize or provide for the installation and maintenance of parking meters.

No ordinance adopted under the provisions of this section shall prohibit the parking of two motorcycles in single parking spaces designated, marked, and sized for four-wheel vehicles. The governing body of any county, city, or town may, by ordinance, permit the parking of three or more motorcycles in single parking spaces designated, marked, and sized for four-wheel vehicles.

If any ordinance regulates parking on an interstate highway or any arterial highway or any extension of an arterial highway, it shall be subject to the approval of the Commissioner of Highways.

In any prosecution charging a violation of the ordinance or regulation, proof that the vehicle described in the complaint, summons, parking ticket citation, or warrant was parked in violation of the ordinance or regulation, together with proof that the defendant was at the time the registered owner of the vehicle, as required by Chapter 6 (§ 46.2-600 et seq.) of this title, shall constitute in evidence a prima facie presumption that the registered owner of the vehicle was the person who committed the violation. Violators of local ordinances adopted by Chesterfield County or James City County pursuant to this section shall be subject to a civil penalty not to exceed $75, the proceeds from which shall be paid into the locality's general fund.

History.

Code 1950, §§ 46-259, 46-259.1; 1958, c. 541, §§ 46.1-252, 46.1-252.1, 46.1-253; 1962, c. 121; 1966, c. 712; 1968, c. 583; 1975, c. 560; 1976, c. 74; 1978, cc. 182, 202, 424; 1985, c. 244; 1989, c. 727; 1990, cc. 121, 418; 1991, c. 372; 1992, c. 268; 1993, cc. 86, 125; 1994, cc. 218, 417; 1995, c. 144; 1996, c. 348; 1997, cc. 506, 780, 912; 1998, c. 545; 1999, c. 71; 2001, cc. 128, 141, 143, 156; 2002, cc. 48, 132, 266; 2003, cc. 32, 773; 2008, c. 193; 2014, cc. 505, 563.

§ 46.2-1221. Authority of county to regulate parking on county-owned or leased property or on county highways; parking meters; presumption as to violation of ordinances.

The governing body of any county may, by ordinance, provide for the regulation of parking on county-owned or leased property and may prohibit parking within fifteen feet of any fire hydrant or in any way obstructing a fire hydrant.

In any prosecution charging a violation of the ordinance or regulation, proof that the vehicle described in the complaint, summons, parking ticket citation, or warrant was parked in violation of the ordinance or regulation, together with proof that the defendant was at the time the registered owner of the vehicle, as required by Chapter 6 (§ 46.2-600 et seq.) of this title, shall constitute in evidence a prima facie presumption that the registered owner of the vehicle was the person who committed the violation.

History.

1962, c. 121, § 46.1-252.1; 1966, c. 712; 1975, c. 560; 1976, c. 74; 1978, cc. 182, 202, 424; 1985, c. 244; 1989, c. 727; 1991, c. 219; 1994, c. 218; 1995, c. 66.

§ 46.2-1222. Regulation of parking on secondary highways by certain counties.

Notwithstanding any other provision of law, the governing bodies of Fairfax, James City, Loudoun, Montgomery, Prince George, Prince William, and York Counties by ordinance may (i) restrict or prohibit parking on any part of the state secondary system of highways within their respective boundaries, (ii) provide for the classification of vehicles for the purpose of these restrictions and prohibitions, and (iii) provide that the violation of the ordinance shall constitute a traffic infraction and prescribe penalties therefor.

All signs and other markings designating the areas where parking is prohibited or restricted shall be installed by the county at its expense under permit from the Virginia Department of Transportation.

In any prosecution charging a violation of the ordinance, proof that the vehicle described in the complaint, summons, or warrant was parked in violation of such ordinance, together with proof that the defendant was at the time the registered owner of the vehicle, as required by Chapter 6 of this title, shall give rise to a prima facie presumption that the registered owner of the vehicle was the person who committed the violation.

Any ordinance adopted pursuant to this section shall require (i) that uncontested payments of penalties for violations of the ordinance shall be collected and accounted for by a county officer or employee, (ii) that the officer or employee shall report on a proper form to the appropriate district court any person's contesting of any citation for violation of the ordinance, and (iii) that the officer or employee shall cause warrants to be issued for delinquent parking citations.

History.

1989, c. 727; 1990, c. 78; 1998, c. 422; 2004, c. 797.

§ 46.2-1222.1. Regulation or prohibition of parking of certain vehicles in certain counties and towns.

A. The Counties of Arlington, Fairfax, Hanover, Stafford, and Prince William and the Towns of

Blackstone, Clifton, Herndon, and Vienna may by ordinance regulate or prohibit the parking on any public highway in such county or town of any or all of the following: (i) watercraft; (ii) boat trailers; (iii) motor homes, as defined in § 46.2-100; and (iv) camping trailers, as defined in § 46.2-100.

B. In addition to commercial vehicles defined in § 46.2-1224, any such county or town may also, by ordinance, regulate or prohibit the parking on any public highway in any residence district as defined in § 46.2-100 any or all of the following: (i) any trailer or semitrailer, regardless of whether such trailer or semitrailer is attached to another vehicle; (ii) any vehicle with three or more axles; (iii) any vehicle that has a gross vehicle weight rating of 12,000 or more pounds; (iv) any vehicle designed to transport 16 or more passengers including the driver; and (v) any vehicle of any size that is being used in the transportation of hazardous materials as defined in § 46.2-341.4. The provisions of any such ordinance shall not apply to (i) any commercial vehicle when taking on or discharging passengers or when temporarily parked pursuant to the performance of work or service at a particular location or (ii) utility generators located on trailers and being used to power network facilities during a loss of commercial power.

History.

2000, cc. 72, 270; 2001, c. 144; 2003, cc. 122, 470; 2004, cc. 108, 225, 702; 2009, c. 535; 2011, c. 201; 2014, cc. 49, 680.

§ 46.2-1222.2. Local ordinances prohibiting parking of certain vehicles.

The governing body of any county, city, or town may by ordinance limit to no more than two hours the length of time of parking on streets, adjacent to commercial business areas, of vehicles with gross weights in excess of 12,000 pounds or lengths of 30 feet or more, unless such vehicles are actively engaged in loading or unloading operations or waiting to be loaded or unloaded or are engaged in or preparing to engage in utility or similar service work.

History.

2007, c. 487.

§ 46.2-1223. Authority of Commissioner to regulate parking on certain parts of primary state highway system.

Except as otherwise provided in this article, the Commissioner of Highways may, by regulation, regulate parking on any part of the primary and secondary systems of state highways.

History.

1970, c. 257, § 46.1-252.2; 1989, c. 727.

§ 46.2-1224. County ordinances prohibiting certain parking in streets and highways.

A. The governing body of any county may, by ordinance, prohibit any person from parking any motor vehicle, trailer, or semitrailer on or adjacent to the highways in the county when such person parks any such motor vehicle, trailer, or semitrailer for commercial purposes. The provisions of any such ordinance shall not apply to motor vehicle carriers when picking up or discharging passengers.

B. The governing bodies of (i) counties with populations greater than 500,000 and of towns located therein and (ii) counties with populations of at least 210,000 but less than 217,000 may, by ordinance, prohibit any person from parking any commercial vehicle, as defined in this section, on the highways within their respective jurisdiction in areas zoned for residential use. For the purposes of this section, the term "commercial vehicle" may include: (i) any solid waste collection vehicle, tractor truck or tractor truck/semitrailer or tractor truck/trailer combination, dump truck, concrete mixer truck, tow truck with a registered gross weight of 12,000 pounds or more, and any heavy construction equipment, whether located on the highway or on a truck, trailer, or semitrailer; (ii) any trailer, semitrailer, or other vehicle in which food or beverages are stored or sold; (iii) any trailer or semitrailer used for transporting landscaping or lawn-care equipment whether or not such trailer or semitrailer is attached to another vehicle; (iv) any vehicle licensed by the Commonwealth for use as a common or contract carrier or as a limousine; (v) any truck more than 20 feet in length, other than commercial vehicles used by a public service company as defined in § 56-1 or by others working on its behalf, or commercial vehicles used in the provision of cable television service as defined in § 15.2-2108.2, or commercial vehicles used in the provision of propane gas service; and (vi) any vehicle carrying commercial freight in plain view. Such ordinance shall permit, however, one resident of each single-family dwelling unit zoned for residential use to park one vehicle licensed as a taxicab or limousine on such highways, provided other vehicles are permitted to park thereon. The provisions of any such ordinance shall not apply to a commercial vehicle when picking up or discharging passengers or when temporarily parked pursuant to the performance of work or service at a particular location.

C. The governing bodies of counties with populations greater than 500,000 and the governing bodies of towns within such counties' boundaries may by ordinance prohibit any person from parking any of the following vehicles on the highways within their respective jurisdictions in areas zoned for commercial or industrial use if such highways do not comply with the current geometric design standards of the

Virginia Department of Transportation Road Design Manual or Subdivision Street Requirements that would apply had the highways been constructed at the time of adoption of such ordinance: (i) any solid waste collection vehicle, tractor truck, or tractor truck/semitrailer or tractor truck/trailer combination, dump truck, concrete mixer truck, tow truck with a registered gross weight of 12,000 pounds or more, and any heavy construction equipment, whether located on the highway or on a truck, trailer, or semitrailer; (ii) any trailer, semitrailer, or other vehicle in which food or beverages are stored or sold; or (iii) any trailer or semitrailer used for transporting landscaping or lawn care equipment whether or not such trailer or semitrailer is attached to another vehicle. The provisions of any such ordinance shall not apply to any commercial vehicle when picking up or discharging passengers or when temporarily parked pursuant to the delivery of goods or the performance of work or service at a particular location.

Any violation of the provisions of any such ordinance shall be a traffic infraction.

History.

Code 1950, § 46-259.2; 1952, c. 602; 1958, cc. 10, 541, § 46.1-254; 1989, c. 727; 1996, c. 770; 1997, c. 19; 1998, cc. 391, 403, 424; 2005, c. 293; 2006, cc. 874, 891; 2009, c. 183.

§ 46.2-1224.1. Local ordinances regulating certain parking; penalty.

The governing body of any county having the county manager plan of government may by ordinance prohibit idling the engine of a bus for more than 10 minutes when the bus is parked, left unattended, or is stopped for other than traffic or maintenance reasons. The governing body of any other county, city, or town may by ordinance prohibit idling the engine of a bus for more than 15 minutes when the bus is parked, left unattended, or is stopped for any reason other than traffic, maintenance, or loading or unloading a disabled passenger.

Violators of such ordinance shall be subject to a civil penalty not to exceed $50, the proceeds from which shall be paid into the locality's general fund.

The provisions of this section shall not apply to school buses or public transit buses.

History.

1996, c. 389; 2008, c. 587.

§ 46.2-1225. Enforcement provisions in city or county parking ordinances.

Any city or county ordinance regulating parking under this article shall require:

1. That uncontested payment of parking citation penalties be collected and accounted for by a local administrative official or officials who shall be compensated by the locality or by a private management company under contract with the locality;

2. That contest by any person of any parking citation shall be certified on an appropriate form, to the appropriate district court, by such official or officials; and

3. That the local administrative official or officials shall cause complaints, summons, or warrants to be issued for delinquent parking citations.

Every action to collect unpaid parking citation penalties imposed for violation of a city or county ordinance regulating parking under this article shall be commenced within three years of the date upon which such penalty became delinquent.

History.

1974, c. 403, § 46.1-254.1; 1975, c. 440; 1977, c. 671; 1980, c. 355; 1989, c. 727; 1995, c. 459; 2014, c. 563.

§ 46.2-1226. Enforcement of regulations governing parking in Capitol Square.

Any regulation adopted pursuant to § 2.2-1172 and relating to parking in Capitol Square shall provide:

That uncontested citations issued under those regulations shall be paid to the administrative official or officials appointed under the provisions of this section in the City of Richmond, who shall promptly pay these sums into the general fund of the state treasury; and

That contested or delinquent citations shall be certified or complaint, summons, or warrant shall be issued as provided in § 46.2-1225 to the general district court of the City of Richmond. Any sums collected by the court, minus court costs, shall be promptly paid by the clerk to the general fund of the state treasury.

History.

1974, c. 403, § 46.1-254.1; 1975, c. 440; 1977, c. 671; 1980, c. 355; 1989, c. 727.

§ 46.2-1227. Enforcement of state regulations governing parking on primary and secondary highways.

Any regulation of the Commissioner under the provisions of § 46.2-1223 relating to parking on any primary or secondary highway shall provide:

1. That uncontested citations issued under the regulation shall be paid to the administrative official or officials appointed under the provisions of this section in the locality in which the part of the highway lies, or in the locality where there is no appointed administrative official the citations shall be paid to the local treasurer, who shall promptly pay them into the general fund of the state treasury; and

2. That contested or delinquent citations shall be certified or complaint, summons, or warrant shall be issued as provided in § 46.2-1225 to the general district court in whose jurisdiction the part of the highway lies. Any sums collected by such court,

minus court costs, shall be promptly paid by the clerk into the general fund of the state treasury.

History.
1974, c. 403, § 46.1-254.1; 1975, c. 440; 1977, c. 671; 1980, c. 355; 1989, c. 727.

§ 46.2-1228. (Effective until October 1, 2016) Enforcement of parking regulations of boards of visitors of educational institutions.

Any regulation of any board of visitors or other governing body of an educational institution pursuant to the provisions of § 23-9.2:3 relating to parking on property owned by the institution shall provide:

1. That uncontested citations issued thereunder shall be paid to the administrative official or officials appointed under the provisions of this section in the city or county in which the property of the institution lies, who shall promptly deposit such sums into the state treasury as a special revenue of the institution; and

2. That contested or delinquent citations shall be certified or complaint, summons, or warrant shall be issued as provided in § 46.2-1225 to the general district court in whose jurisdiction the institution lies. Any sum collected by the court, minus court costs, shall be promptly deposited by the clerk into the state treasury as a special revenue of the institution. However, nothing in this section shall prevent any educational institution which adopts, or has adopted, regulations pursuant to § 23-9.2:3 providing for administrative disposition of contested, uncontested, or delinquent citations from disposing of those citations in accordance with those regulations, and all moneys collected under those regulations shall be deposited promptly into the state treasury as a special revenue of the institution.

History.
1974, c. 403, § 46.1-254.1; 1975, c. 440; 1977, c. 671; 1980, c. 355; 1989, c. 727.

§ 46.2-1228. (Effective October 1, 2016) Enforcement of parking regulations of boards of visitors of educational institutions.

Any regulation of any board of visitors or other governing body of an educational institution pursuant to the provisions of § 23.1-1301 relating to parking on property owned by the institution shall provide:

1. That uncontested citations issued thereunder shall be paid to the administrative official or officials appointed under the provisions of this section in the city or county in which the property of the institution lies, who shall promptly deposit such sums into the state treasury as a special revenue of the institution; and

2. That contested or delinquent citations shall be certified or complaint, summons, or warrant shall be issued as provided in § 46.2-1225 to the general district court in whose jurisdiction the institution lies. Any sum collected by the court, minus court costs, shall be promptly deposited by the clerk into the state treasury as a special revenue of the institution. However, nothing in this section shall prevent any educational institution which adopts, or has adopted, regulations pursuant to § 23.1-1301 providing for administrative disposition of contested, uncontested, or delinquent citations from disposing of those citations in accordance with those regulations, and all moneys collected under those regulations shall be deposited promptly into the state treasury as a special revenue of the institution.

History.
1974, c. 403, § 46.1-254.1; 1975, c. 440; 1977, c. 671; 1980, c. 355; 1989, c. 727.

§ 46.2-1229. Enforcement of parking regulations of State Board of Behavioral Health and Developmental Services.

Any regulations of the State Board of Behavioral Health and Developmental Services pursuant to the provisions of § 37.2-203 relating to parking on property owned or controlled by the Department of Behavioral Health and Developmental Services shall provide:

1. That uncontested citations issued thereunder shall be paid to the administrative official or officials appointed under the provisions of this section in the locality in which the part of the state facility lies, who shall promptly deposit the sums into the state treasury as a special revenue of the Department of Behavioral Health and Developmental Services; and

2. That contested or delinquent citations shall be certified or complaint, summons, or warrant shall be issued as provided in § 46.2-1225 to the general district court in whose jurisdiction the state facility lies. Any sum collected by the court, minus court costs, shall be promptly deposited by the clerk into the state treasury as a special revenue of the Department of Behavioral Health and Developmental Services.

History.
1974, c. 403, § 46.1-254.1; 1975, c. 440; 1977, c. 671; 1980, c. 355; 1989, c. 727; 2009, cc. 813, 840.

§ 46.2-1230. Authority of counties, cities, and towns to issue parking permits.

The governing body of any county, city, or town may by ordinance provide for the issuance of permits for motor vehicles parking on public streets, to set the rates for the permits, and to set the term of validity of the permits. In setting the rates, the governing body may differentiate between motor vehicles registered in the political subdivision issuing the permit and other motor vehicles.

History.

1972, c. 819, § 46.1-252.01; 1989, c. 727.

§ 46.2-1231. Ticketing, removal, or immobilization of trespassing vehicles by owner or operator of parking or other lot or building; charges.

The owner, operator, or lessee of any parking lot, parking area, or parking space in a parking lot or area or any part of a parking lot or area, or of any other lot or building, including any county, city, or town, or authorized agent of the person having control of such premises may have any vehicle occupying the lot, area, space, or building without the permission of its owner, operator, lessee, or authorized agent of the one having the control of the premises, removed by towing or otherwise to a licensed garage for storage until called for by the owner or his agent if there are posted at all entrances to the parking lot or area signs clearly and conspicuously disclosing that such vehicle, if parked without permission, will be removed, towed, or immobilized. Such signs shall, at a minimum, include the nonemergency telephone number of the local law-enforcement agency or the telephone number of the responsible towing and recovery operator to contact for information related to the location of vehicles towed from that location. The requirements of this section relating to the posting of signs by an owner, operator, or lessee of any parking lot, parking area or space shall not apply to localities in which the local governing body has adopted an ordinance pursuant to § 46.2-1232.

Whenever a trespassing vehicle is removed or towed as permitted by this section, notice of this action shall forthwith be given by the tow truck operator to the State Police or the local law-enforcement agency of the jurisdiction from which the vehicle was towed. It shall be unlawful to fail to report such tow as required by this section and violation of the reporting requirement of this section shall constitute a traffic infraction punishable by a fine of not more than $100. Such failure to report shall limit the amount which may be charged for the storage and safekeeping of the towed vehicle to an amount no greater than that charged for one day of storage and safekeeping. If the vehicle is removed and stored, the vehicle owner may be charged and the vehicle may be held for a reasonable fee for the removal and storage.

All businesses engaged in towing vehicles without the consent of their owners shall prominently display (i) at their main place of business and (ii) at any other location where towed vehicles may be reclaimed a comprehensive list of all their fees for towing, recovery, and storage services, or the basis of such charges. This requirement to display a list of fees may also be satisfied by providing, when the towed vehicle is reclaimed, a written list of such fees, either as part of a receipt or separately, to the person who reclaims the vehicle. Charges in excess of those posted shall not be collectable from any motor vehicle owner whose vehicle is towed, recovered, or stored without his consent.

Notwithstanding the foregoing provisions of this section, if the owner or representative or agent of the owner of the trespassing vehicle is present and removes the trespassing vehicle from the premises before it is actually towed, the trespassing vehicle shall not be towed, but the owner or representative or agent of the owner of the trespassing vehicle shall be liable for a reasonable fee, not to exceed $25 or such other limit as the governing body of the county, city, or town may set by ordinance, in lieu of towing.

In lieu of having a trespassing vehicle removed by towing or otherwise, the owner, operator, lessee or authorized agent of the premises on which the trespassing vehicle is parked may cause the vehicle to be immobilized by a boot or other device that prevents a vehicle from being moved by preventing a wheel from turning, provided that the boot or other device does not damage the vehicle or wheel. The charge for the removal of any boot or device shall not exceed $25 or such other limit as the governing body of the county, city, or town may set by ordinance. In lieu of having the vehicle removed by towing or otherwise, or in lieu of causing the vehicle to be immobilized, the owner, operator, lessee or authorized agent of the premises on which the trespassing vehicle is parked may cause to have an authorized local government official or law-enforcement officer issue, on the premises, a notice of the violation of a parking ordinance or regulation created pursuant to § 46.2-1220 or § 46.2-1221 to the registered owner of the vehicle.

This section shall not apply to police, fire, or public health vehicles or where a vehicle, because of a wreck or other emergency, is parked or left temporarily on the property of another. The governing body of every county, city, and town may by ordinance set limits on fees and charges provided for in this section.

History.

Code 1950, § 46-541; 1952, c. 352; 1954, c. 435; 1958, c. 541, § 46.1-551; 1978, cc. 202, 335; 1979, c. 132; 1983, c. 34; 1985, c. 375; 1987, cc. 147, 152, 332; 1988, cc. 471, 701; 1989, c. 727; 1990, c. 502; 1991, c. 221; 1993, c. 394; 1994, c. 619; 2003, c. 305; 2006, cc. 874, 891.

§ 46.2-1231.1. Immunity from liability for certain towing.

No towing and recovery operator shall be liable for damages in any civil action for responding in good faith to the lawful direction of a law-enforcement or, in the case that life, limb, or property is endangered, a fire or rescue agency to tow, recover, or store any vehicle, combination of vehicles, their contents, or any other object. The immunity provided by this section shall not extend to the liability for negligence in the towing, recovery, or storage carried out by the towing and recovery operator. For the purposes of this section, any towing, recovery, or storage carried out in compliance with a contract between a towing business and a local law-enforcement agency or local government shall be deemed to have been performed at the lawful direction of a law-enforcement agency.

History.
1990, c. 604; 2007, c. 376.

§ 46.2-1232. Localities may regulate removal or immobilization of trespassing vehicles.

A. The governing body of any county, city, or town may by ordinance regulate the removal of trespassing vehicles from property by or at the direction of the owner, operator, lessee, or authorized agent in charge of the property. In the event that a vehicle is towed from one locality and stored in or released from a location in another locality, the local ordinance, if any, of the locality from which the vehicle was towed shall apply.

B. No local ordinance adopted under authority of this section shall require that any towing and recovery business also operate as or provide services as a vehicle repair facility or body shop, filling station, or any business other than a towing and recovery business.

C. Any such local ordinance may also require towing and recovery operators to (i) obtain and retain photographs or other documentary evidence substantiating the reason for the removal; (ii) post signs at their main place of business and at any other location where towed vehicles may be reclaimed conspicuously indicating (a) the maximum charges allowed by local ordinance, if any, for all their fees for towing, recovery, and storage services and (b) the name and business telephone number of the local official, if any, responsible for handling consumer complaints; (iii) obtain at the time the vehicle is towed, verbal approval of an agent designated in the local ordinance who is available at all times; and (iv) obtain, at the time the vehicle is towed, if such towing is performed during the normal business hours of the owner of the property from which the vehicle is being towed, the written authorization of the owner of the property from which the vehicle is towed, or his agent. Such written authorization, if required, shall be in addition to any written contract between the towing and recovery operator and the owner of the property or his agent. For the purposes of this subsection, "agent" shall not include any person who either (a) is related by blood or marriage to the towing and recovery operator or (b) has a financial interest in the towing and recovery operator's business.

D. Any such ordinance adopted by a locality within Planning District 8 may require towing companies that tow vehicles from the county, city, or town adopting the ordinance to other localities, provided that the stored or released location is within the Commonwealth of Virginia and within 10 miles of the point of origin of the actual towing, (i) to obtain from the locality from which such vehicles are towed a permit to do so and (ii) to submit to an inspection of such towing company's facilities to ensure that the company meets all the locality's requirements, regardless of whether such facilities are located within the locality or elsewhere. The locality may impose and collect reasonable fees for the issuance and administration of permits as provided for in this subsection. Such ordinance may also provide grounds for revocation, suspension, or modification of any permit issued under this subsection, subject to notice to the permittee of the revocation, suspension, or modification and an opportunity for the permittee to have a hearing before the governing body of the locality or its designated agent to challenge the revocation, suspension, or modification. Nothing in this subsection shall be applicable to public safety towing.

History.
Code 1950, § 46-541; 1952, c. 352; 1954, c. 435; 1958, c. 541, § 46.1-551; 1978, cc. 202, 335; 1979, c. 132; 1983, c. 34; 1985, c. 375; 1989, cc. 17, 727; 1990, cc. 502, 573; 2006, cc. 874, 891; 2009, cc. 186, 544; 2012, cc. 149, 812.

§ 46.2-1233. Localities may regulate towing fees.

The governing body of any locality may by ordinance set reasonable limits on fees charged for the removal of motor vehicles, trailers, and parts thereof left on private property in violation of § 46.2-1231, and for the removal of trespassing vehicles under § 46.2-1215, taking into consideration the fair market value of such removal.

Localities in Planning District 8 shall establish by ordinance (i) a hookup and initial towing fee of $135 and (ii) for towing a vehicle between seven o'clock p.m. and eight o'clock a.m. or on any Saturday, Sunday, or holiday, an additional fee of $25 per instance; however, such ordinance shall also provide that in no event shall more than two such additional fees be charged for towing any vehicle.

History.
Code 1950, § 46-541; 1952, c. 352; 1954, c. 435; 1958, c. 541, § 46.1-551; 1978, cc. 202, 335; 1979, c. 132; 1983, c. 34; 1985, c. 375; 1989, cc. 17, 727; 1990, cc. 502, 571, 573; 2016, c. 476.

§ 46.2-1233.1. Limitation on charges for towing and storage of certain vehicles.

A. Unless different limits are established by ordinance of the local governing body pursuant to § 46.2-1233, as to vehicles towed or removed from private property, no charges imposed for the towing, storage, and safekeeping of any passenger car removed, towed, or stored without the consent of its owner shall be in excess of the maximum charges provided for in this section. No hookup and initial towing fee shall exceed $135. For towing a vehicle between seven o'clock p.m. and eight o'clock a.m. or on any Saturday, Sunday, or holiday, an additional fee of no more than $25 per instance may be charged; however, in no event shall more than two such fees be charged for towing any such vehicle. No charge shall be made for storage and safekeeping for a period of twenty-four hours or less. Except for fees or charges imposed by this section or a local ordinance adopted pursuant to § 46.2-1233, no other fees or charges shall be imposed during the first 24-hour period.

B. The governing body of any county, city, or town may by ordinance, with the advice of an advisory board established pursuant to § 46.2-1233.2, (i) provide that no towing and recovery business having custody of a vehicle towed without the consent of its owner impose storage charges for that vehicle for any period during which the owner of the vehicle was prevented from recovering the vehicle because the towing and recovery business was closed and (ii) place limits on the amount of fees charged by towing and recovery operators. Any such ordinance limiting fees shall also provide for periodic review of and timely adjustment of such limitations.

History.

1990, c. 266; 1993, c. 598; 2006, cc. 874, 891; 2013, c. 592.

§ 46.2-1233.2. Advisory board.

Prior to adopting or amending any ordinance pursuant to § 46.2-1232 or § 46.2-1233, the local governing body shall appoint an advisory board to advise the governing body with regard to the appropriate provisions of the ordinance. Voting members of the advisory board shall consist of an equal number of representatives of local law-enforcement agencies and representatives of licensed towing and recovery operators, and one member of the general public. Any such advisory board shall meet at least once per year at the call of the chairman of the advisory board, who shall be elected annually from among the voting members of the advisory board by a majority vote.

History.

1993, c. 405; 2006, cc. 874, 891.

§ 46.2-1234. Liability of persons furnishing free parking accommodations as to motor vehicles and property left therein.

No action shall lie or proceeding be brought against any person conducting any business and maintaining a parking lot at which free parking accommodations are provided for customers or employees of such business, when a motor vehicle is parked in such parking lot, for the total or partial loss of any motor vehicle because of theft or damage by any person other than an employee or for the total or partial loss of property left in the motor vehicle because of theft or damage by any person other than an employee.

As used in this section, "free parking accommodations" means parking accommodations for which no specific charge is made and the patronage of the business by customers and the performance of the regular services for the business by employees shall not constitute the payment of any consideration for the use of the parking accommodations.

Nothing in this section shall relieve any person of liability resulting from his own wrongdoing.

History.

Code 1950, § 46-542; 1952, c. 357; 1958, c. 541, § 46.1-552; 1989, c. 727.

§ 46.2-1235: Authority of Chesterfield County law-enforcement personnel to issue tickets [Not set out.] (1989, c. 727.)

Editor's note.

This section, relating to the authority of Chesterfield County law-enforcement personnel to issue tickets, was enacted by Acts 1989, c. 727. In furtherance of the general policy of the Commission to include in the Code only provisions having general and permanent application, this section, which is limited in its purpose and scope, is not set out here, but attention is called to it by this reference.

The section catchline was inserted at the direction of the Virginia Code Commission.

§ 46.2-1236: Repealed by Acts 1994, c. 866.

§ 46.2-1237: Repealed by Acts 1997, cc. 783 and 904.

§ 46.2-1238: Repealed by Acts 1994, c. 866.

§ 46.2-1239. Parking in certain locations; penalty.

No person shall park a vehicle or permit it to stand, whether attended or unattended, on a highway in front of a private driveway, within 15 feet of a fire hydrant or the entrance to a fire station, within 15 feet of the entrance to a plainly designated emergency medical services agency, or within 20 feet from the intersection of curb lines or, if none, then within 15 feet of the intersection of property lines at any highway intersection.

History.

Code 1950, § 46-263; 1958, c. 541, § 46.1-258; 1972, c. 528; 1984, c. 126; 1989, c. 727; 2015, cc. 502, 503.

ARTICLE 4.
POTOMAC RIVER BRIDGE TOWING COMPACT OF 1991.

§ 46.2-1239.1. Potomac River Bridge Towing Compact.

Article I.

Parties and Titles.

The Parties to this Compact are the Commonwealth of Virginia, the State of Maryland and the District of Columbia. This agreement shall be known as the Potomac River Bridge Towing Compact.

Article II.

Findings and Purpose.

The Woodrow Wilson Memorial Bridge, Rochambeau Memorial Bridge, George Mason Memorial Bridge, Theodore Roosevelt Memorial Bridge, Francis Scott Key Bridge, Chain Bridge and American Legion Memorial Bridge all pass through the territorial jurisdiction of two or more of the three Parties. Experience has shown that traffic back-ups often prevent state troopers or police officers of the appropriate jurisdiction from arriving at the scene of a disabled or abandoned vehicle to take corrective action. The purpose of this Compact is to facilitate the prompt and orderly removal of disabled and abandoned vehicles from the bridges by giving all three Parties jurisdiction to exercise appropriate authority anywhere on the bridges.

Article III.

Authority to Direct Traffic and Authorize Removal of Vehicles.

The Parties hereby give one another all necessary power and authority to have their respective state troopers or local law-enforcement officers direct traffic and authorize the removal of disabled or abandoned vehicles, trailers, semitrailers or the parts or contents thereof, from any part of the Potomac River bridges, to the same extent and in the same manner that such troopers and local law-enforcement officers may exercise such authority in their own jurisdictions. However, no Party, acting through its troopers or local law-enforcement officers, shall have the authority to direct or authorize the towing or removal of any vehicle or other thing to a destination outside its own jurisdiction, unless the consent of an officer or trooper of the destination jurisdiction has been obtained.

Article IV.

Disposition of Towed Vehicles.

All vehicles and their contents towed or removed from the Potomac River bridges pursuant to this Compact shall be subject to the exclusive jurisdiction of the place to which such vehicle and its contents are taken, and the handling and disposition of such vehicle and its contents shall be governed by the laws and procedures of that jurisdiction.

Article V.

No Agency.

Each of the Parties shall act solely on its own authority within the jurisdiction granted. This Compact shall not be construed as creating any agency relationship between the Parties.

Article VI.

Effective Date.

The provisions of this Compact shall take effect thirty days after the legislative bodies of the Parties having jurisdiction over one or several of the bridges identified in Article II have enacted Compacts substantially identical to this Compact.

Article VII.

Termination.

The Governor of the Commonwealth of Virginia or State of Maryland, or the Mayor of the District of Columbia may withdraw from this Compact at any time upon thirty days' written notice to the other Parties.

History.
1991, c. 452.

CHAPTER 12.1.
PARKING FOR PERSONS WITH DISABILITIES.

Section

§ 46.2-1240. Definitions.

"Disabled parking sign" means any sign used to identify parking spaces for use by vehicles bearing valid organizational, permanent, or temporary removable windshield placards, disabled parking license plates, or disabled parking license plates issued under § 46.2-739. All disabled parking signs shall be erected and maintained in accordance with signage requirements specified in § 36-99.11.

"Organizational removable windshield placard" means a two-sided, hooked placard which includes on each side: (i) the international symbol of access at least three inches in height, centered on the placard, and shown in white on a green background; (ii) the name of the institution or organization; (iii) an identification number; (iv) an expiration date imprinted on the placard and indicated by a month and year hole-punch system or an alternative system designed by the Department; (v) a misuse hotline number designated by the Department; (vi) a warning of the penalties for placard misuse; and (vii) the seal or identifying symbol of the issuing authority.

"Permanent removable windshield placard" means a two-sided, hooked placard which includes on each side: (i) the international symbol of access at least three inches in height, centered on the placard, and shown in white on a blue background; (ii) an identification number; (iii) an expiration date imprinted on the placard and indicated by a month and year hole-punch system or an alternative system designed by the Department; (iv) a misuse hotline number designated by the Department; (v) a warning of the penalties for placard misuse; and (vi) the seal or other identifying symbol of the issuing authority. All holders of permanent removable windshield placards shall be required to carry the Disabled Parking Placard Identification Card issued with the placard by the Department and present it to law-enforcement officials upon request.

"Person with a disability that limits or impairs his ability to walk or that creates a concern for his safety while walking" means a person who, as determined by a licensed physician, podiatrist, or chiropractor: (i) cannot walk 200 feet without stopping to rest; (ii) cannot walk without the use of or assistance from a brace, cane, crutch, another person, prosthetic device, wheelchair, or other assistive device; (iii) is restricted by lung disease to such an extent that his forced (respiratory) expiratory volume for one second, when measured by spirometry, is less than one liter, or when at rest, his arterial oxygen tension is less than 60 millimeters of mercury on room air; (iv) uses portable oxygen; (v) has a cardiac condition to the extent that his functional limitations are classified in severity as Class III or Class IV according to standards set by the American Heart Association; (vi) is severely limited in his ability to walk due to an arthritic, neurological, or orthopedic condition; (vii) has some other debilitating condition that, in the view of a licensed physician, podiatrist, or chiropractor, limits or impairs his ability to walk; (viii) has been diagnosed with a mental or developmental amentia or delay that impairs judgment including, but not limited to, an autism spectrum disorder; (ix) has been diagnosed with Alzheimer's disease or another form of dementia; (x) is legally blind or deaf; or (xi) has some other condition that, in the view of a licensed physician creates a safety concern while walking because of impaired judgment or other physical, developmental, or mental limitation. For the purposes of this definition, a determination of a disability by a podiatrist or chiropractor shall be limited to those conditions specified in items (i), (ii), (vi) or (vii) of this definition.

Any licensed physician, nurse practitioner, physician assistant, podiatrist, or chiropractor who signs a certification that states that an applicant is disabled under clause (vii) of this definition shall specify, in a space provided on the certification form, the medical condition that limits or impairs the applicant's ability to walk. Any licensed physician, licensed nurse practitioner, or licensed physician assistant who signs a certification that states that an applicant is disabled under clause (xi) of this definition shall specify, in a space provided on the certification form, the physical, developmental, or mental condition that creates the safety concern.

"Temporary removable windshield placard" means a two-sided, hooked placard which includes on each side: (i) the international symbol of access at least three inches in height, centered on the placard, and shown in white on a red background; (ii) an identification number; (iii) an expiration date imprinted on the placard and indicated by a month and year hole-punch system or an alternative system designed by the Department; (iv) a misuse hotline number; (v) a warning of the penalties for placard misuse; and (vi) the seal or other identifying symbol of the issuing authority.

History.

1997, cc. 783, 904; 1999, c. 188; 2002, c. 108; 2003, c. 992; 2005, c. 276; 2007, c. 715; 2010, c. 47.

§ 46.2-1241. Issuance of disabled parking placards.

A. Upon application of a person with a disability that limits or impairs his ability to walk or that creates a concern for his safety while walking, the Commissioner shall issue a permanent removable windshield placard for use on a passenger car or pickup or panel truck. The Commissioner shall require that each original application be accompanied by a certification signed by a licensed physician, licensed podiatrist, licensed chiropractor, licensed nurse practitioner, or licensed physician assistant on forms prescribed by the Commissioner that the applicant meets the definition of "person with a disability that limits or impairs his ability to walk or that creates a concern for his safety while walking" contained in § 46.2-1240.

1. The Commissioner shall provide for the renewal of such placards every five years. Applications for renewals may require the applicant to certify that his disability is a permanent disability, but renewal applications need not be accompanied by a physician's, podiatrist's, chiropractor's, nurse practitioner's, or physician assistant's certification of the applicant's disability. The Commissioner shall work in consultation with the Medical Advisory Board for the Department to develop a definition of "permanent disability" as used in this subdivision. Notwithstanding any contrary provision of this chapter, no physician's, podiatrist's, chiropractor's, nurse practitioner's, or physician assistant's certification of an applicant's disability shall be required for the renewal of any disabled parking placard of an applicant to whom disabled parking license plates have been issued under § 46.2-731.

2. The Commissioner shall charge a reasonable fee for each placard, but no fee shall be charged any person exempted from fees in § 46.2-739.

3. The placards shall be of a design approved by the Commissioner pursuant to the specifications and definitions contained in § 46.2-1240.

B. Upon the application of a person with a disability that limits or impairs his ability to walk and whose disability is temporary, the Commissioner shall issue a temporary removable windshield placard. The application for a temporary removable windshield placard shall be accompanied by a certification signed by a licensed physician, nurse practitioner, physician assistant, podiatrist, or chiropractor on forms prescribed by the Commissioner that the applicant meets the definition of "person with a condition that limits or impairs his ability to walk" contained in § 46.2-1240 and shall also include the period of time that the physician, podiatrist, or chiropractor determines the applicant will have the disability, not to exceed six months.

1. A licensed physician, nurse practitioner, physician assistant, podiatrist, or chiropractor may certify up to 15 days in advance of an applicant's medical procedure that an applicant will meet the definition of "person with a condition that limits or impairs his ability to walk" and that the disability will be temporary. Any licensed physician, nurse practitioner, physician assistant, podiatrist, or chiropractor who certifies an applicant's disability in advance of a medical procedure shall provide the period of time for which the physician, nurse practitioner, physician assistant, podiatrist, or chiropractor has determined that the applicant will have the disability, not to exceed six months. The Commissioner will mail the temporary placard to the applicant.

2. The temporary removable windshield placard shall be valid for the period of time for which the physician, podiatrist, or chiropractor has determined that the applicant will have the disability, not to exceed six months from the date of issuance.

3. The Commissioner shall provide for a reasonable fee to be charged for the placard. The placards shall be of a design approved by the Commissioner pursuant to the specifications and definitions contained in § 46.2-1240.

C. On application, the Commissioner shall issue to hospitals, hospices, nursing homes, and other institutions and organizations meeting criteria determined by the Commissioner organizational removable windshield placards, as provided for in the foregoing provisions of this section, for use by volunteers when transporting disabled persons in passenger vehicles and pickup or panel trucks owned by such volunteers. The provisions of this section relating to other windshield placards issued under this section shall also apply, mutatis mutandis, to windshield placards issued to these institutions and organizations, except that windshield placards issued to institutions and agencies, in addition to their expiration date, shall bear the name of the institution or organization whose volunteers will be using the windshield placards rather than the name, age, and sex of the person to whom issued.

1. The Commissioner shall provide for the renewal of such placards every five years.

2. The placards shall be of a design approved by the Commissioner pursuant to the specifications and definitions contained in § 46.2-1240.

D. No person shall use or display an organizational removable windshield placard, permanent removable windshield placard or temporary removable windshield placard beyond its expiration date.

E. Organizational removable windshield placards, permanent removable windshield placards and temporary removable windshield placards shall be displayed in such a manner that they may be viewed from the front and rear of the vehicle and be hanging from the rearview mirror of a vehicle utilizing a parking space reserved for persons with disabilities that limit or impair their ability to walk. When there is no rearview mirror, the placard shall be displayed on the vehicle's dashboard. No placard shall be displayed from the rearview mirror while a vehicle is in motion.

History.

1997, cc. 783, 904; 2001, c. 136; 2002, c. 133; 2003, c. 992; 2005, c. 276; 2007, c. 715; 2013, c. 137.

§ 46.2-1242. Parking in spaces reserved for persons with disabilities; local ordinances; penalty.

A. No vehicles other than those displaying disabled parking license plates, organizational removable windshield placards, permanent removable windshield placards, or temporary removable windshield placards issued under § 46.2-1241, or DV disabled parking license plates issued under subsection B of § 46.2-739, shall be parked in any parking spaces reserved for persons with disabilities.

1. No person without a disability that limits or impairs his ability to walk shall park a vehicle with disabled parking license plates, organizational removable windshield placards, permanent removable windshield placards, temporary removable windshield placards, or DV disabled parking license plates issued under subsection B of § 46.2-739 in a parking space reserved for persons with disabilities that limit or impair their ability to walk except when transporting a disabled person in the vehicle.

2. A summons or parking ticket for the offense may be issued by law-enforcement officers, uniformed law-enforcement department employees, or volunteers acting pursuant to § 46.2-1244 without the necessity of a warrant's being obtained by the owner of any private parking area.

3. Parking a vehicle in a space reserved for persons with disabilities in violation of this section shall be punishable by a fine of not less than $100 nor more than $500.

B. The governing body of any county, city, or town may, by ordinance, provide that it shall be unlawful for a vehicle not displaying disabled parking license plates, an organizational removable windshield placard, a permanent removable windshield placard, or a temporary removable windshield placard issued under § 46.2-1241, or DV disabled parking license plates issued under subsection B of § 46.2-739, to be parked in a parking space reserved for persons with disabilities that limit or impair their ability to walk or for a person who is not limited or impaired in his ability to walk to park a vehicle in a parking space so designated except when transporting a person with such a disability in the vehicle. If there is a placard within a vehicle utilizing a parking space reserved for persons with disabilities, but that placard is not displayed as required pursuant to subsection E of § 46.2-1241, such ordinance may provide for a fine less than that imposed under this section.

1. Any local governing body, by such ordinance, may assess and retain a fine of not less than $100 nor more than $500 for its violation.

2. The ordinance may further provide that a summons or parking ticket for the offense may be issued by law-enforcement officers, volunteers serving in units established pursuant to § 46.2-1244, and other uniformed personnel employed by the locality to enforce parking regulations without the necessity of a warrant's being obtained by the owner of the private parking area.

C. In any prosecution charging a violation of this section or an ordinance adopted pursuant to this section, proof that the vehicle described in the complaint, summons, parking ticket, citation, or warrant was parked in violation of this section or the ordinance, together with proof that the defendant was at the time the registered owner of the vehicle, as required by Chapter 6 (§ 46.2-600 et seq.) of this title, shall constitute prima facie evidence that the registered owner of the vehicle was the person who committed the violation.

D. No violation of this section or an ordinance adopted pursuant to this section shall be dismissed for a property owner's failure to comply strictly with the requirements for disabled parking signs set forth in § 36-99.11, provided the space is clearly distinguishable as a parking space reserved for persons with disabilities that limit or impair their ability to walk.

History.
1997, cc. 783, 904; 2008, c. 715.

§ 46.2-1243. Enforcement by private security guards in certain localities.

The local governing bodies of Franklin County, Henry County, and the Cities of Danville and Martinsville may by ordinance provide that, in privately owned parking areas open to the public, a summons for violation of an ordinance promulgated under § 46.2-1242 may be issued by (i) private security guards licensed under the provisions of Article 4 (§ 9.1-138 et seq.) of Chapter 1 of Title 9.1 and deputized to issue a summons for the offense by the chief law-enforcement officer of the county or city in which the private parking area is located or (ii) any owner of the private parking area of a nursing home, as defined in § 32.1-123, or agent or employee thereof, provided that such owner has registered in writing on his own behalf or on behalf of his agent or employee with the chief law-enforcement officer of the locality his intention to issue summonses pursuant to this section.

History.
1997, cc. 783, 904; 2002, c. 390.

§ 46.2-1244. Volunteer disabled parking enforcement units.

A. The governing body of any county, city, or town may by ordinance provide that its law-enforcement agency establish and supervise volunteers to enforce violations of § 46.2-1242.

B. Excluding § 46.2-1242, volunteers acting pursuant to this section shall not have the power or duty to enforce any other traffic or criminal laws of the state or any county, city, or town.

C. No volunteer acting pursuant to this section shall carry a firearm or other weapon during the course of his volunteer enforcement duties.

History.
1997, cc. 783, 904.

§ 46.2-1245. Four hours' free parking in time-restricted or metered spaces; local option.

A. The disabled person, vehicle owner, or volunteer for an institution or organization to which disabled parking license plates, organizational removable windshield placards, permanent windshield placards, or temporary removable windshield placards are issued or any person to whom disabled parking license plates have been issued under subsection B of § 46.2-739 shall be allowed to park the vehicle on which such license plates or placards are displayed for up to four hours in metered or unmetered parking zones restricted as to length of parking time permitted and shall be exempted from paying parking meter fees of any county, city, or town.

B. This section shall not apply to any local ordinance which creates zones where stopping, standing, or parking is prohibited, or which creates parking zones for special types of vehicles, nor shall it apply to any local ordinance which prohibits parking during heavy traffic periods, during specified rush hours, or where parking would clearly present a traffic hazard.

C. The governing body of any county, city, or town may by ordinance provide that this section shall not apply within the boundaries or within any designated portion of such county, city, or town. Any county, city, or town adopting an ordinance pursuant to this subsection shall indicate by signs or other reasonable notice that the provisions of this section do not apply in such county, city, or town or designated portion thereof.

History.
1997, cc. 783, 904; 2012, cc. 17, 286.

§ 46.2-1246. Towing of unauthorized vehicles.

A. The owner or duly authorized agent of the owner of a parking space properly designated and clearly marked as reserved for use by persons with disabilities that limit or impair their ability to walk may have any vehicle not displaying disabled parking license plates, organizational removable windshield placards, permanent removable windshield placards, temporary removable windshield placards, or DV disabled parking license plates removed from the parking space and stored.

B. The owner of a vehicle which has been removed and stored may regain possession of his vehicle on payment to the person or persons who removed and stored the vehicle all reasonable costs incidental to the removal and storage. The owner of the vehicle, on notice to the owner or duly authorized agent of the owner of the parking space, may also petition the general district court having jurisdiction over the location where the parking occurred for an immediate determination as to whether the removal of the vehicle was lawful. If the court finds that the removal was unlawful, the court shall direct the owner of the parking space to pay the costs incidental to the removal and storage of the vehicle and return the vehicle to its owner.

History.
1997, cc. 783, 904.

§ 46.2-1247. Counterfeiting disabled parking license plates or placards; penalty.

A. Any person who creates a counterfeit or unauthorized replica of a disabled parking license plate, DV disabled parking license plate which has been issued under subsection B of § 46.2-739, organizational removable windshield placard, permanent removable windshield placard, or temporary removable windshield placard, shall be guilty of a Class 2 misdemeanor.

B. The local governing body of any county, city, or town may by ordinance incorporate this provision by reference.

History.
1997, cc. 783, 904.

§ 46.2-1248. Use of counterfeit disabled parking license plates or placards; penalty.

A. Any person who displays a counterfeit or unauthorized replica of a disabled parking license plate, DV disabled parking license plate which has been issued under subsection B of § 46.2-739, organizational removable windshield placard, permanent removable windshield placard, or temporary removable windshield placard and parks in a disabled parking space or attempts to use the parking privileges afforded by § 46.2-1245, shall be guilty of a Class 2 misdemeanor.

B. The local governing body of any county, city, or town may by ordinance incorporate this provision by reference.

History.
1997, cc. 783, 904.

§ 46.2-1249. Alteration of disabled parking license plates or placards; penalty.

A. Any person who alters a disabled parking license plate, DV disabled parking license plate which has been issued under subsection B of § 46.2-739, organizational removable windshield placard, permanent removable windshield placard, or temporary removable windshield placard shall be guilty of a Class 2 misdemeanor.

B. The local governing body of any county, city, or town may by ordinance incorporate this provision by reference.

History.
1997, cc. 783, 904.

§ 46.2-1250. Unauthorized use of disabled parking license plates or placards; penalty.

A. Any person who parks in a space reserved for persons with disabilities that limit or impair their ability to walk or attempts to use the parking privileges afforded by § 46.2-1245 and displays a disabled parking license plate, DV disabled parking license plate which has been issued under subsection B of § 46.2-739, organizational removable windshield placard, permanent removable windshield placard, or temporary removable windshield placard which has been issued to another person, and is not transporting a person with a disability which limits or impairs his ability to walk, shall be guilty of a Class 2 misdemeanor.

B. The local governing body of any county, city, or town may by ordinance incorporate this provision by reference.

History.

1997, cc. 783, 904.

§ 46.2-1251. Fraudulently obtaining a disabled parking license plate or placard; penalty.

A. Any person who makes a false statement of material fact to obtain or assist an individual in obtaining a disabled parking license plate, DV disabled parking license plate which has been issued under subsection B of § 46.2-739, organizational removable windshield placard, permanent removable windshield placard, or temporary removable windshield placard shall be guilty of a Class 2 misdemeanor.

B. The local governing body of any county, city, or town may by ordinance incorporate this provision by reference.

History.

1997, cc. 783, 904.

§ 46.2-1252. Selling or exchanging a disabled parking license plate or placard; penalty.

A. Any person who sells or exchanges for consideration any valid, altered, or counterfeit disabled parking license plate, DV disabled parking license plate which has been issued under subsection B of § 46.2-739, organizational removable windshield placard, permanent removable windshield placard, or temporary removable windshield placard shall be guilty of a Class 2 misdemeanor.

B. The local governing body of any county, city, or town may by ordinance incorporate this provision by reference.

History.

1997, cc. 783, 904.

§ 46.2-1253. Providing a disabled parking license plate or placard; penalty.

A. Any person who knowingly provides to another person, without sale or exchange of consideration, any valid, altered, or counterfeit disabled parking license plate, DV disabled parking license plate which has been issued under subsection B of § 46.2-739, permanent removable windshield placard, temporary removable windshield placard, or organizational removable windshield placard, shall be guilty of a Class 3 misdemeanor.

B. The local governing body of any county, city, or town may by ordinance incorporate this provision by reference.

History.

1997, cc. 783, 904.

§ 46.2-1254. Photo identification.

Any law-enforcement officer or private security guard acting pursuant to § 46.2-1243 may request to examine the driver's license, state identification card, or other form of photo identification of any person using disabled parking privileges afforded by this chapter.

History.

1997, cc. 783, 904.

§ 46.2-1255. Confiscation of disabled parking placards.

A. Any law-enforcement officer or private security guard acting pursuant to § 46.2-1243 who issues a summons to or arrests an individual for any violation of §§ 46.2-1247 through 46.2-1249 and §§ 46.2-1251 through 46.2-1253 may confiscate the defendant's permanent, temporary, or organizational removable windshield placard and shall notify, by mail or facsimile, the Department of Motor Vehicles of such confiscation and the number of the placard involved.

B. After receiving notice specified in subsection A of this section, the Department may prohibit the issuance of any form of disabled parking license plate or placard to the defendant until the defendant's charge under §§ 46.2-1247 through 46.2-1249 and §§ 46.2-1251 through 46.2-1253 reaches final disposition, including appeals.

C. Upon the defendant's acquittal for any violation of §§ 46.2-1247 through 46.2-1249 and §§ 46.2-1251 through 46.2-1253, the law-enforcement officer or private security guard shall return the confiscated placard to the defendant and the court shall notify the Department of such acquittal by electronic or other means. Upon the defendant's conviction for any violation of §§ 46.2-1247 through 46.2-1249 and §§ 46.2-1251 through 46.2-1253, the law-enforcement officer or private security guard shall send the confiscated placard to the Department and the court shall notify the Department pursuant to § 46.2-1256.

History.
1997, cc. 783, 904.

§ 46.2-1256. Notice of convictions; revocation of disabled parking placards and license plates.

A. Upon the entry of a conviction under §§ 46.2-1247 through 46.2-1253, or under any ordinance which incorporates any of those sections by reference, the court shall send notice of the conviction and the number of the license plate or placard involved to the Commissioner. Such notice may be transmitted by electronic means.

B. Upon receiving notice pursuant to subsection A of this section, the Commissioner may revoke any disabled parking license plate, DV disabled parking license plate, organizational, permanent, or temporary placard of an individual or organization found guilty under §§ 46.2-1247 through 46.2-1253 if he finds, after a hearing if requested by the person to whom the license plate or placard is issued, that such person (i) is not a person with a disability that limits or impairs his ability to walk and is not otherwise eligible to be issued a license plate or a placard pursuant to §§ 46.2-731, 46.2-739, or § 46.2-1241, or (ii) is authorized to have such license plate or placard but has allowed the abuse or misuse of the privilege granted thereby so that revocation appears appropriate to remedy the abuse or misuse.

History.
1997, cc. 783, 904.

§ 46.2-1257: Repealed by Acts 2010, c. 47, cl. 3.

§ 46.2-1258. Reciprocity.

Disabled parking license plates, permanent removable windshield placards, temporary removable windshield placards, and DV disabled parking license plates issued by other states and countries for the purpose of identifying vehicles permitted to use parking spaces reserved for persons with disabilities that limit or impair their ability to walk shall be accorded all rights and privileges accorded vehicles displaying such devices issued in Virginia.

History.
1997, cc. 783, 904.

§ 46.2-1259. Placard issuance; additional requirements.

In developing and issuing organizational, permanent, and temporary removable windshield placards pursuant to the requirements of § 46.2-1240, the Commissioner shall, in consultation with representatives of law-enforcement and disability services boards, develop and issue placards that are (i) resistant to tampering, alteration, and counterfeiting, (ii) clear and legible, and (iii) protective of the privacy rights of the placard user to the extent the requirements of § 46.2-1240 allow.

History.
1997, cc. 783, 904; 2010, c. 47.

CHAPTER 13.

POWERS OF LOCAL GOVERNMENTS.

Section

§ 46.2-1300. Powers of local authorities generally; erection of signs and markers; maximum penalties.

A. The governing bodies of counties, cities, and towns may adopt ordinances not in conflict with the provisions of this title to regulate the operation of vehicles on the highways in such counties, cities, and towns. They may also repeal, amend, or modify such ordinances and may erect appropriate signs or markers on the highway showing the general regulations applicable to the operation of vehicles on such highways. The governing body of any county, city, or town may by ordinance, or may by ordinance authorize its chief administrative officer to:

1. Increase or decrease the speed limit within its boundaries, provided such increase or decrease in

speed shall be based upon an engineering and traffic investigation by such county, city or town and provided such speed area or zone is clearly indicated by markers or signs;

2. Authorize the city or town manager or such officer thereof as it may designate, to reduce for a temporary period not to exceed sixty days, without such engineering and traffic investigation, the speed limit on any portion of any highway of the city or town on which work is being done or where the highway is under construction or repair;

3. Require vehicles to come to a full stop or yield the right-of-way at a street intersection if one or more of the intersecting streets has been designated as a part of the primary state highway system in a town which has a population of less than 3,500.

B. No such ordinance shall be violated if at the time of the alleged violation the sign or marker placed in conformity with this section is missing, substantially defaced, or obscured so that an ordinarily observant person under the same circumstances would not be aware of the existence of the ordinance.

C. No governing body of a county, city, or town may provide penalties for violating a provision of an ordinance adopted pursuant to this section which is greater than the penalty imposed for a similar offense under the provisions of this title.

D. No county whose roads are under the jurisdiction of the Department of Transportation shall designate, in terms of distance from a school, the placement of flashing warning lights unless the authority to do so has been expressly delegated to such county by the Department of Transportation, in its discretion.

History.

Code 1950, §§ 46-198, 46-200; 1956, c. 134; 1958, c. 541, § 46.1-180; 1960, c. 172; 1972, c. 522; 1984, c. 345; 1989, c. 727.

§ 46.2-1301. Designation of stop and yield right-of-way intersections.

The governing body of any county, city, or town operating its own system of roads may by ordinance authorize the city or town manager or some other local officer to designate intersections, other than intersections at which one or more of the intersecting streets have been designated as a part of the primary state highway system in a town which has a population of less than 3,500, at which vehicles shall come to a full stop or yield the right-of-way. No such ordinance shall be violated if, at the time of the alleged violation the sign or marker placed in conformity with this section is missing or is defaced so that an ordinarily observant person under the same circumstances would not be aware of the existence of the regulation.

History.

1958, c. 541, § 46.1-180.1; 1989, c. 727.

§ 46.2-1302. Regulation of operation of vehicles in snow, sleet, etc.; designation of play areas; penalties.

The governing body of any county, city, or town may by ordinance regulate the operation of vehicles on the highways in such county, city, or town in the event of snow, sleet, hail, freezing rain, ice, water, flood, high wind, storm or the threat thereof. In addition to the general powers granted by this section, and any other provisions of this title notwithstanding, any such ordinance may:

1. Prohibit vehicles from parking or operating on designated highways;

2. Authorize the designation and posting of highways as snow routes and prohibit any person to obstruct or impede traffic on a highway designated and posted as a snow route through his failure to have the vehicle operated by him equipped with snow tires or chains;

3. Prohibit the abandoning of vehicles on designated highways;

4. Authorize the removal of vehicles that are stalled, stuck, parked, or abandoned on designated highways;

5. Authorize the storing of removed vehicles and the imposition of reasonable charges for removal and storage;

6. Authorize the designation of certain highways, or portions thereof, as play areas for sledding and similar recreational activities. No city or town shall be liable in any civil action or proceeding for damages resulting from any injury to the person or property of any person caused by an act or omission constituting simple or ordinary negligence on the part of any officer or agent of any such city or town in the designation or operation of any such play area. Every such city or town may be liable in damages for the gross or wanton negligence of any of its officers or agents in the operation of any such play area;

7. Authorize and regulate the operation of snowmobiles on or across streets and highways during periods of snow or ice or at the direction of any law-enforcement officer during an emergency;

8. Set fines for violations. Such fines may be in place of or in addition to the removal and storage of the vehicle and charges therefor, but no such fine shall exceed fifty dollars for each such offense.

History.

1962, c. 431, § 46.1-180.2; 1980, c. 37; 1989, c. 727; 1997, c. 47.

§ 46.2-1303. Issuance of permits to perform construction or repair work within right-of-way lines of public roadways.

The governing body of any county, city, or town having jurisdiction over and responsibility for the construction and maintenance of public roadways within its boundaries may by ordinance authorize an officer or agency of such political subdivision to issue a permit prior to the performance by any person, firm, partnership or corporation of construction and repair work within the right-of-way lines of any public highways under the jurisdiction of the political subdivision. Such authority, however, shall not extend to any railroad crossings or to any highways under the jurisdiction of the Virginia Department of Transportation. Such ordinance may provide that:

1. No person, firm, partnership or corporation shall enter into any repair, alteration, construction, or reconstruction of any type whatever, other than emergency repairs to or maintenance of public utility facilities within the right-of-way lines of any public highway without first having obtained a permit for such work from the agency or officer designated by such ordinance.

2. Such permit may require the notification of all emergency services likely to be affected by such repair, alteration, construction or reconstruction; the types of traffic control devices necessary to properly warn the motoring public and provide for reinspection by the appropriate authority from time to time and at the conclusion of such repair, alteration, construction, or reconstruction.

3. The owner or owners of any such firm, partnership or corporation shall be subject to arrest for a violation of this section or his representative on the site, if the owner is not present.

4. The person, firm, partnership, or corporation requesting such permit shall be responsible for furnishing and maintaining the required traffic control devices in accord with the Virginia Manual of Uniform Traffic Control Devices for Streets and Highways.

5. The penalty for violation of such ordinance shall be a fine of not less than $25 nor more than $100 for the first offense and not less than $100 nor more than $500 for the second and subsequent offenses.

History.

1972, c. 105, § 46.1-180.3; 1989, c. 727.

§ 46.2-1304. Local regulation of trucks and buses.

The governing bodies of counties, cities, and towns may by ordinance, whenever in their judgment conditions so require:

1. Prohibit the use of trucks, except for the purpose of receiving loads or making deliveries on certain designated streets under their jurisdiction;

2. Restrict the use of trucks passing through the city or town to such street or streets under their jurisdiction as may be designated in such ordinance.

The Cities of Poquoson and Williamsburg may restrict the operation of nonscheduled buses, other than school buses, over designated streets under its jurisdiction.

History.

Code 1950, § 46-206; 1958, c. 541, § 46.1-181; 1968, c. 463; 1989, c. 727; 1998, cc. 547, 574; 2007, c. 813.

§ 46.2-1304.1. Localities may regulate construction and parking of commercial motor vehicles used to transport municipal solid waste; penalty.

The governing body of any county, city, or town may by ordinance provide that:

1. No commercial motor vehicle used to transport municipal solid waste shall be parked anywhere within the county, city, or town, except at locations zoned or otherwise authorized for such use by applicable ordinance, special exception, or variance;

2. Any such commercial motor vehicle found parked at a nonauthorized location may be towed or removed from that location as provided in § 46.2-1231; and

3. The cargo compartment of every commercial motor vehicle that is used to transport municipal solid waste shall be so constructed so as to prevent the escape of municipal solid waste therefrom. Such ordinances shall exclude from their provisions vehicles owned or operated by persons transporting municipal solid waste from their residences to a permitted transfer or disposal facility.

No such ordinance shall impose, for any violation of any of its provisions, a penalty greater than provided for a traffic infraction as provided in § 46.2-113. Any such penalty shall be in addition to any vehicle towing and storage charges.

For the purposes of this section, "municipal solid waste" shall have the meaning prescribed by the Virginia Waste Management Board by regulation (9VAC20-80-10).

For the purposes of this section and local ordinances adopted under this section, "commercial motor vehicle" shall have the meaning prescribed in § 46.2-341.4.

History.

2001, c. 356.

§ 46.2-1305. Regulation of vehicular and pedestrian traffic on roadways and parking areas in residential subdivisions.

The governing body of any county, city, or town which has adopted ordinances under the provisions of Chapter 22 (§ 15.2-2200 et seq.) of Title 15.2, may require as a part of such land use regulations for residential subdivisions employing roadways and parking areas not in public ownership, the posting and maintenance of signs or other appropriate markings regulating the operation and parking of motor vehicles and pedestrian traffic, and may adopt ordinances applying the regulations to existing and future residential subdivisions.

History.
1972, c. 471, § 46.1-181.2; 1989, c. 727; 2003, c. 418.

§§ 46.2-1306, 46.2-1306.1: Repealed by Acts 2014, c. 505, cl. 2.

Cross references.
For current provisions allowing ordinances prohibiting parking near fire hydrants and parking so as to prevent the use of curb ramps, see § 46.2-1220.

§ 46.2-1307. Designation of private roads as highways for law-enforcement purposes.

The governing body of any county, city, or town may adopt ordinances designating the private roads, within any residential development containing 100 or more lots or residential dwelling units, as highways for law-enforcement purposes. Such ordinance may also provide for certification of road signs and speed limits by private licensed professional engineers using criteria developed by the Commissioner of Highways, and, for law-enforcement purposes, such certification shall have the same effect as if certified by the Commissioner of Highways.

History.
1979, c. 100, § 46.1-181.5; 1987, c. 152; 1989, c. 727; 2007, cc. 74, 187, 310.

§ 46.2-1307.1. Designation of private roads as highways for law-enforcement purposes in certain counties.

Notwithstanding the provisions of § 46.2-1307, the governing body of Warren County may adopt ordinances designating the private roads within any residential development containing 50 or more lots as highways for law-enforcement purposes, and the governing body of Greene County, upon receipt of a petition therefore by a majority of property owners within a residential development containing 25 or more lots, may adopt ordinances designating the private roads within any such development as highways for law-enforcement purposes. Such ordinance may also provide for certification of road signs and speed limits by private licensed professional engineers using criteria developed by the Commissioner of Highways, and for law-enforcement purposes, such certification shall have the same effect as if certified by the Commissioner of Highways.

History.
2006, c. 870; 2007, c. 187; 2014, c. 90.

§ 46.2-1308. Disposition of fines in traffic cases; failure or neglect to comply with section.

In counties, cities, and towns whose governing bodies adopt the ordinances authorized by §§ 46.2-1300 and 46.2-1304, all fines imposed for violations of such ordinances shall be paid into the county, city or town treasury. Fees shall be disposed of according to law.

In all cases, however, in which the arrest is made or the summons is issued by an officer of the Department of State Police or of any other division of the state government, for violation of the motor vehicle laws of the Commonwealth, the person arrested or summoned shall be charged with and tried for a violation of some provision of this title and all fines and forfeitures collected upon convictions of any person so arrested or summoned shall be credited to the Literary Fund.

Willful failure, refusal or neglect to comply with this provision shall constitute a Class 4 misdemeanor and may be grounds for removal of the guilty person from office. Charges for dereliction of the duties here imposed shall be tried by the circuit court of the jurisdiction served by the officer charged with the violation.

History.
Code 1950, § 46-199; 1952, c. 251; 1958, c. 541, § 46.1-182; 1989, c. 727; 2012, c. 408.

§ 46.2-1309. Officers may direct traffic; signals.

Law-enforcement officers and uniformed school crossing guards may direct traffic by signals. Such signals other than by voice shall be as follows:

1. To stop traffic by hand. — Stand with shoulders parallel to moving traffic. Raise arms forty-five degrees above shoulder with hand extended, palm towards moving traffic to be stopped.
2. To move traffic by hand. — Stand with shoulders parallel to traffic to be moved. Extend right arm and hand full length at height of shoulders towards such traffic, fingers extended and joined, palm down. Bring hand sharply in direction traffic is to move. Repeat movement with left arm and hand to start traffic from opposite direction.
3. To stop and start traffic by whistle. — One blast, moving traffic to stop; two blasts, traffic in opposite direction to move.
4. Emergency stop of traffic by whistle. — Three or more short blasts, all traffic shall immediately clear the intersection and stop.

Such law-enforcement officers and uniformed school crossing guards may also use supplemental traffic direction devices, including but not limited to hand-held stop or go signs, in directing traffic as provided in this section.

History.
Code 1950, §§ 46-201, 46-202; 1954, c. 380; 1958, c. 541, § 46.1-183; 1966, c. 607; 1989, c. 727; 1995, c. 473.

§ 46.2-1310. Authority to deputize persons to direct traffic in certain circumstances.

The chief of police of any county, city, or town, or the sheriff of any county which does not have a chief of police, may deputize persons over the age of eighteen years for the limited purpose of directing traffic in accordance with § 46.2-1309 during periods of heavy traffic or congestion. Such persons shall first receive training as the chief of police or sheriff determines necessary to fully acquaint such persons with the techniques of traffic control. They shall not have arrest powers.

Any person who is deputized as provided in the foregoing provisions of this section, shall at all times while engaged in traffic control wear a distinctive uniform, safety vest, or a white reflectorized belt which crosses both the chest and back above the waist.

History.
1973, c. 371, § 46.1-183.1; 1989, c. 727.

§ 46.2-1311. Applicability of county ordinances within towns.

Any traffic ordinance adopted by the governing body of a county shall not apply within the limits of any town in which the traffic is regulated by town ordinances.

History.
1958, c. 541, § 46.1-185; 1989, c. 727.

§ 46.2-1312. Size, design, and color of signs, signals, and markings erected by local authorities.

Traffic signs and traffic signals and markings placed or erected by local authorities pursuant to this title shall conform in size, design, and color to those erected for the same purpose by the Department of Transportation.

History.
1958, c. 541, § 46.1-187; 1964, c. 319; 1968, c. 146; 1989, c. 727.

§ 46.2-1313. Incorporation of provisions of this title, Article 9 (§ 16.1-278 et seq.) of Chapter 11 of Title 16.1 and Article 2 (§ 18.2-266 et seq.) of Chapter 7 of Title 18.2 in ordinances.

Ordinances enacted by local authorities pursuant to this chapter may incorporate appropriate provisions of this title, of Article 9 (§ 16.1-278 et seq.) of Chapter 11 of Title 16.1, and of Article 2 (§ 18.2-266 et seq.) of Chapter 7 of Title 18.2 into such ordinances by reference. Nothing contained in this title shall require the readoption of ordinances heretofore validly adopted. Local authorities may adopt ordinances incorporating by reference the appropriate provisions of state law before the effective date of such state law; provided that such local ordinances do not become effective before the effective date of the state law. The provisions of this section are declaratory of existing law.

History.
1958, c. 541, § 46.1-188; 1968, c. 243; 1972, c. 286; 1976, c. 396; 1989, c. 727; 1991, c. 224; 1993, c. 302; 1994, c. 264; 2000, c. 48.

§ 46.2-1314. Traffic schools; requiring attendance by persons convicted of certain violations.

The governing body of any county or city may by ordinance provide for the establishment of a traffic school in the locality, at which instruction concerning laws and ordinances for the regulation of vehicular traffic, safe operation of vehicles, and such other subjects as may be prescribed shall be given. The ordinance shall provide for the supervision of the school, the days and hours of its operation, and its personnel. In the discretion of the governing body, the ordinance establishing a traffic school may vest the direction and conduct of the school in the general district court charged with hearing traffic cases.

The governing body of any county or city may, alternatively, by ordinance provide for the designation of an existing traffic school or course operated as part of a county or city adult education program as a traffic school for the purposes of this section.

Any court in a county or city which provides for a traffic school under this section may require any person found guilty of a violation of any provision of Chapter 8 (§ 46.2-800 et seq.) of this title or local ordinance governing the operation of motor vehicles to attend a traffic school in the county or city where the person is a resident or any traffic school that has been established in any jurisdiction contiguous to the county or city of residence of the convicted violator for a period specified in the order requiring the attendance if the governing body of that contiguous jurisdiction consents thereto. The requirement for attendance may be in lieu of or in addition to the penalties prescribed by § 46.2-113 or any such ordinance. Failure to comply with the order of the court shall be punishable as contempt.

History.
1964, c. 267, § 46.1-16.1; 1968, c. 47; 1973, c. 389; 1989, c. 727; 1993, c. 72.

CHAPTER 14.
RIDESHARING.

Section

§ 46.2-1400. "Ridesharing arrangement" defined.

"Ridesharing arrangement" means the transportation of persons in a motor vehicle when such transportation is incidental to the principal purpose of the driver, which is to reach a destination and not to transport persons for profit. The term includes ridesharing arrangements known as carpools, vanpools, and bus pools. "Ridesharing arrangement" does not include a prearranged ride as defined in § 46.2-2000.

History.
1981, c. 218, § 46.1-556; 1989, c. 727; 2015, cc. 2, 3.

§ 46.2-1401. Motor carrier laws do not apply.

The following laws and regulations of the Commonwealth shall not apply to any ridesharing arrangement using a motor vehicle with a seating capacity for not more than fifteen persons, including the driver:

1. Laws and regulations containing insurance requirements that are specifically applicable to motor carriers or commercial vehicles;
2. Laws imposing a greater standard of care on motor carriers or commercial vehicles than that imposed on other drivers or owners of motor vehicles;
3. Laws and regulations with equipment requirements and special accident reporting requirements that are specifically applicable to motor carriers or commercial vehicles; and
4. Laws imposing a tax on fuel purchased in another state by a motor carrier or road user taxes on commercial buses.

History.
1981, c. 218, § 46.1-557; 1989, c. 727; 2002, c. 337.

§ 46.2-1402. Workers' compensation law does not apply.

Title 65.2, providing compensation for workers injured during the course of their employment, shall not apply to a person injured while participating in a ridesharing arrangement between his place of residence and place of employment or termini near such places; however, if the employer owns, leases, or contracts for the motor vehicle used in such arrangement, Title 65.2 shall apply.

History.
1981, c. 218, § 46.1-558; 1989, c. 727.

Motor Vehicles

§ 46.2-1403. Liability of employer.

An employer shall not be liable for injuries to passengers and other persons resulting from the operation or use of a motor vehicle, not owned, leased or contracted for by the employer, in a ridesharing arrangement.

An employer shall not be liable for injuries to passengers and other persons because he provides information or incentives or otherwise encourages his employees to participate in ridesharing arrangements.

History.
1981, c. 218, § 46.1-559; 1989, c. 727.

§ 46.2-1404. Ridesharing payments or transit reduced fares are not income.

Money and other benefits, other than salary, received by a driver in a ridesharing arrangement using a motor vehicle with a seating capacity for not more than fifteen persons, including the driver, shall not constitute income for the purpose of Chapter 3 (§ 58.1-300 et seq.) of Title 58.1 imposing taxes on income. Regular payments by riders toward a capital recovery fund not exceeding the cost of the vehicle or used to pay for leasing the vehicle shall be considered reimbursement for eligible expenses of operation. Neither shall the difference in the amount between discount and full transit fares constitute income for the purpose of Chapter 3 of Title 58.1 imposing taxes on income.

History.
1981, c. 218, § 46.1-560; 1989, c. 727; 2002, c. 337.

§ 46.2-1405. Municipal licenses and taxes.

No county, city, or town may impose a tax on or require a license, including business licenses or gross receipts taxes, for a ridesharing arrangement using a motor vehicle with a seating capacity for not more than fifteen persons, including the driver.

History.
1981, c. 218, § 46.1-561; 1989, c. 727; 2002, c. 337.

§ 46.2-1406. Overtime compensation and minimum wage laws.

The participation of an employee in any kind of ridesharing arrangement shall not result in the application of Title 40.1.

History.
1981, c. 218, § 46.1-562; 1989, c. 727.

§ 46.2-1407. Certain ridesharing vehicles are not commercial vehicles or buses.

A motor vehicle used in a ridesharing arrangement that has a seating capacity for not more than fifteen persons, including the driver, shall not be a "bus" under those portions of this title relating to equipment requirements or rules of the road.

A motor vehicle used in a ridesharing arrangement that has a seating capacity for not more than fifteen persons, including the driver, shall not be a "bus" or "commercial vehicle" under the portions of this title relating to registration.

History.

1981, c. 218, § 46.1-563; 1989, cc. 705, 727; 2002, c. 337.

SUBTITLE IV. DEALERS AND DRIVER TRAINING SCHOOLS.

CHAPTER 15. MOTOR VEHICLE DEALERS.

Article 1.

Motor Vehicle Dealers, Generally.

Article 2.

Motor Vehicle Dealer Licenses.

Article 3.

Motor Vehicle Transaction Recovery Fund.

Article 3.1.

Motor Vehicle Transaction Recovery Fund.

Article 3.2.

Bonding Requirements for Dealers Not Participating in Motor Vehicle Transaction Recovery Fund.

Article 4.

Conduct of Business.

Article 5.

Dealer's License Plates.

Article 6.

Issuance of Temporary License Plates by Dealers.

Article 7.

Franchises.

Article 7.1.

Late Model and Factory Repurchase Franchises.

Article 7.2.

Recreational Vehicle Franchises.

Article 7.3.

Trailer Franchises.

Article 7.4.

Motorcycle Franchises.

ARTICLE 1.
MOTOR VEHICLE DEALERS, GENERALLY.

§ 46.2-1500. Definitions.

As used in this chapter, unless the context requires a different meaning:

"Affiliate" means any entity in which a manufacturer, factory branch, distributor, or distributor branch has voting control or owns at least 51 percent of the ownership equity, or any entity in which another entity has voting control or owns at least 51 percent of the ownership equity and also has voting control and owns at least 51 percent of the ownership of a manufacturer, factory branch, distributor, or distributor branch. An entity that provides vehicle purchase or lease financing that uses the name of the manufacturer or distributor, or the name of any line make of the manufacturer or distributor, in the name of the entity under which it transacts business with a consumer, other than in the name of an individual product offered by the entity, shall be considered an "affiliate."

"Board" means the Motor Vehicle Dealer Board.

"Camping trailer" means a recreational vehicle constructed with collapsible partial side walls that fold for towing by a consumer-owned tow vehicle and unfold at the campsite to provide temporary living quarters for recreational, camping, or travel use.

"Certificate of origin" means the document provided by the manufacturer of a new motor vehicle, or its distributor, which is the only valid indication of ownership between the manufacturer, its distributor, its franchised motor vehicle dealers, and the original purchaser not for resale.

"Dealer-operator" means the individual who works at the established place of business of a dealer and who is responsible for and in charge of day-to-day operations of that place of business.

"Demonstrator" means a new motor vehicle having a gross vehicle weight rating of less than 16,000 pounds that (i) has more than 750 miles accumulated on its odometer that has been driven by dealer personnel or by prospective purchasers during the course of selling, displaying, demonstrating, showing, or exhibiting it and (ii) may be sold as a new motor vehicle, provided the dealer complies with the provisions of subsection D of § 46.2-1530.

"Distributor" means a person who is licensed by the Department under this chapter and who sells or distributes new motor vehicles pursuant to a written agreement with the manufacturer to franchised motor vehicle dealers in the Commonwealth.

"Distributor branch" means a branch office licensed by the Department under this chapter and maintained by a distributor for the sale of motor vehicles to motor vehicle dealers or for directing or supervising, in whole or in part, its representatives in the Commonwealth.

"Distributor representative" means a person who is licensed by the Department under this chapter and employed by a distributor or by a distributor branch, for the purpose of making or promoting the sale of motor vehicles or for supervising or contacting its dealers, prospective dealers, or representatives in the Commonwealth.

"Factory branch" means a branch office maintained by a person for the sale of motor vehicles to distributors or for the sale of motor vehicles to motor vehicle dealers, or for directing or supervising, in whole or in part, its representatives in the Commonwealth.

"Factory representative" means a person who is licensed by the Department under this chapter and employed by a person who manufactures or assembles motor vehicles or by a factory branch for the purpose of making or promoting the sale of its motor vehicles or for supervising or contacting its dealers, prospective dealers, or representatives in the Commonwealth.

"Factory repurchase motor vehicle" means a motor vehicle sold, leased, rented, consigned, or otherwise transferred to a person under an agreement that the motor vehicle will be resold or otherwise retransferred only to the manufacturer or distributor of the motor vehicle, and which is reacquired by the manufacturer or distributor, or its agents.

"Family member" means a person who either (i) is the spouse, child, grandchild, spouse of a child, spouse of a grandchild, brother, sister, or parent of the dealer or owner or (ii) has been employed continuously by the dealer for at least five years.

"Franchise" means a written contract or agreement between two or more persons whereby one person, the franchisee, is granted the right to engage in the business of offering and selling, offering and delivering pursuant to a lease, servicing, or offering, selling, and servicing new motor vehicles of a particular line-make or late model or used motor vehicles of a particular line-make manufactured or

distributed by the grantor of the right, the franchisor, and where the operation of the franchisee's business is substantially associated with the franchisor's trademark, trade name, advertising, or other commercial symbol designating the franchisor, the motor vehicle or its manufacturer or distributor. "Franchise" includes any severable part or parts of a franchise agreement which separately provides for selling and servicing different line-makes of the franchisor.

"Franchised late model or franchised used motor vehicle dealer" means a dealer selling used motor vehicles, including vehicles purchased from the franchisor, under the trademark of a manufacturer or distributor that has a franchise agreement with a manufacturer or distributor.

"Franchised motor vehicle dealer" or *"franchised dealer"* means a dealer in new motor vehicles that has a franchise agreement with a manufacturer or distributor of new motor vehicles to sell new motor vehicles or to sell used motor vehicles under the trademark of a manufacturer or distributor regardless of the age of the motor vehicles.

"Fund" means the Motor Vehicle Dealer Board Fund.

"Independent motor vehicle dealer" means a dealer in used motor vehicles.

"Late model motor vehicle" means a motor vehicle of the current model year and the immediately preceding model year.

"Line-make" means the name of the motor vehicle manufacturer or distributor and a brand or name plate marketed by the manufacturer or distributor. The line-make of a motorcycle manufacturer, factory branch, distributor, or distributor branch includes every brand of all-terrain vehicle, autocycle, and off-road motorcycle manufactured or distributed bearing the name of the motorcycle manufacturer or distributer.

"Manufactured home dealer" means any person licensed as a manufactured home dealer under Chapter 4.2 (§ 36-85.16 et seq.) of Title 36.

"Manufacturer" means a person who is licensed by the Department under this chapter and engaged in the business of constructing or assembling new motor vehicles and, in the case of trucks, recreational vehicles, and motor homes, also means a person engaged in the business of manufacturing engines, transmissions, power trains, or rear axles, when such engines, transmissions, power trains, or rear axles are not warranted by the final manufacturer or assembler of the truck, recreational vehicle, or motor home.

"Motorcycle" means every motor vehicle designed to travel on not more than three wheels in contact with the ground, except any vehicle within the term "farm tractor" or "moped" as defined in § 46.2-100. Except as otherwise provided, for the purposes of this chapter, all-terrain vehicles, autocycles, and off-road motorcycles are deemed to be motorcycles.

"Motor home" means a motorized recreational vehicle designed to provide temporary living quarters for recreational, camping, or travel use that contains at least four of the following permanently installed independent life support systems that meet the National Fire Protection Association standards for recreational vehicles: (i) a cooking facility with an onboard fuel source; (ii) a potable water supply system that includes at least a sink, a faucet, and a water tank with an exterior service supply connection; (iii) a toilet with exterior evacuation; (iv) a gas or electric refrigerator; (v) a heating or air conditioning system with an onboard power or fuel source separate from the vehicle engine; or (vi) a 110-125 volt electric power supply.

"Motor vehicle" means the same as provided in § 46.2-100, except, for the purposes of this chapter, "motor vehicle" does not include (i) manufactured homes, sales of which are regulated under Chapter 4.2 (§ 36-85.16 et seq.) of Title 36; (ii) nonrepairable vehicles, as defined in § 46.2-1600; (iii) salvage vehicles, as defined in § 46.2-1600; or (iv) mobile cranes that exceed the size or weight limitations as set forth in § 46.2-1105, 46.2-1110, or 46.2-1113 or Article 17 (§ 46.2-1122 et seq.) of Chapter 10.

"Motor vehicle dealer" or *"dealer"* means any person who:

1. For commission, money, or other thing of value, buys, sells, exchanges, either outright or on conditional sale, bailment lease, chattel mortgage, or otherwise or arranges or offers or attempts to solicit or negotiate on behalf of others a sale, purchase, or exchange of an interest in new motor vehicles, new and used motor vehicles, or used motor vehicles alone, whether or not the motor vehicles are owned by him; or

2. Is wholly or partly engaged in the business of selling new motor vehicles, new and used motor vehicles, or used motor vehicles only, whether or not the motor vehicles are owned by him; or

3. Offers to sell, sells, displays, or permits the display for sale, of five or more motor vehicles within any 12 consecutive months.

For the purposes of Article 7.2 (§ 46.2-1573.2 et seq.), "dealer" means recreational vehicle dealer. For the purposes of Article 7.3 (§ 46.2-1573.13 et seq.), "dealer" means trailer dealer and watercraft trailer dealer. For the purposes of Article 7.4 (§ 46.2-1573.25 et seq.), "dealer" means motorcycle dealer.

"Motor vehicle dealer" or "dealer" does not include:

1. Receivers, trustees, administrators, executors, guardians, conservators or other persons appointed by or acting under judgment or order of any court or their employees when engaged in the specific performance of their duties as employees.

2. Public officers, their deputies, assistants, or employees, while performing their official duties.

3. Persons other than business entities primarily engaged in the leasing or renting of motor vehicles to others when selling or offering such vehicles for sale at retail, disposing of motor vehicles acquired for their own use and actually so used, when the vehicles have been so acquired and used in good faith

and not for the purpose of avoiding the provisions of this chapter.

4. Persons dealing solely in the sale and distribution of funeral vehicles, including motor vehicles adapted therefor; however, this exemption shall not exempt any person from the provisions of §§ 46.2-1519, 46.2-1520, and 46.2-1548.

5. Any financial institution chartered or authorized to do business under the laws of the Commonwealth or the United States which may have received title to a motor vehicle in the normal course of its business by reason of a foreclosure, other taking, repossession, or voluntary reconveyance to that institution occurring as a result of any loan secured by a lien on the vehicle.

6. An employee of an organization arranging for the purchase or lease by the organization of vehicles for use in the organization's business.

7. Any person licensed to sell real estate who sells a manufactured home or similar vehicle in conjunction with the sale of the parcel of land on which the manufactured home or similar vehicle is located.

8. Any person who permits the operation of a motor vehicle show or permits the display of motor vehicles for sale by any motor vehicle dealer licensed under this chapter.

9. An insurance company authorized to do business in the Commonwealth that sells or disposes of vehicles under a contract with its insured in the regular course of business.

10. Any publication, broadcast, or other communications media when engaged in the business of advertising, but not otherwise arranging for the sale of vehicles owned by others.

11. Any person dealing solely in the sale or lease of vehicles designed exclusively for off-road use.

12. Any credit union authorized to do business in Virginia, provided the credit union does not receive a commission, money, or other thing of value directly from a motor vehicle dealer.

13. Any person licensed as a manufactured home dealer, broker, manufacturer, or salesperson under Chapter 4.2 (§ 36-85.16 et seq.) of Title 36.

14. The State Department of Social Services or local departments of social services.

15. Any person dealing solely in the sale and distribution of utility or cargo trailers that have unloaded weights of 3,000 pounds or less; however, this exemption shall not exempt any person who deals in stock trailers or watercraft trailers.

For the purposes of Article 7 (§ 46.2-1566 et seq.), "dealer" does not include recreational vehicle dealers, trailer dealers, watercraft trailer dealers, or motorcycle dealers.

"Motor vehicle salesperson" or *"salesperson"* means (i) any person who is hired as an employee by a motor vehicle dealer to sell or exchange motor vehicles and who receives or expects to receive a commission, fee, or any other consideration from the dealer; (ii) any person who supervises salespersons employed by a motor vehicle dealer, whether compensated by salary or by commission; (iii) any person, compensated by salary or commission by a motor vehicle dealer, who negotiates with or induces a customer to enter into a security agreement on behalf of a dealer; or (iv) any person who is licensed as a motor vehicle dealer and who sells or exchanges motor vehicles. For purposes of this section, any person who is an independent contractor as defined by the United States Internal Revenue Code shall be deemed not to be a motor vehicle salesperson.

"Motor vehicle show" means a display of motor vehicles to the general public at a location other than a dealer's location licensed under this chapter where the vehicles are not being offered for sale or exchange during or as part of the display.

"New motor vehicle" means any vehicle, excluding trailers, that is in the possession of the manufacturer, factory branch, distributor, distributor branch, or motor vehicle dealer and for which an original title has not been issued by the Department or by the issuing agency of any other state and has less than 7,500 miles accumulated on its odometer.

"New trailer" means any trailer that (i) has not been previously sold except in good faith for the purpose of resale; (ii) has not been used as a rental, driver education, or demonstration trailer or for the personal or business transportation of the manufacturer, distributor, dealer, or any of its employees; (iii) has not been used except for limited use necessary in moving or road testing the trailer prior to delivery to a customer; (iv) is transferred by a certificate of origin; and (v) has the manufacturer's certification that it conforms to all applicable federal trailer safety and emission standards. Notwithstanding clauses (i) and (iii), a trailer that has been previously sold but not titled shall be deemed a new trailer if it meets the requirements of clauses (ii), (iv), and (v).

"Original license" means a motor vehicle dealer license issued to an applicant who has never been licensed as a motor vehicle dealer in Virginia or whose Virginia motor vehicle dealer license has been expired for more than 30 days.

"Recreational vehicle" or *"RV"* means a vehicle that (i) is either self-propelled or towed by a consumer-owned tow vehicle, (ii) is primarily designed to provide temporary living quarters for recreational, camping, or travel use; and (iii) complies with all applicable federal vehicle regulations and does not require a special movement permit to legally use the highways. Recreational vehicle includes motor homes, travel trailers, and camping trailers.

"Relevant market area" means as follows:

1. For motor vehicle dealers except motorcycle dealers, in metropolitan localities the relevant market area shall be a circular area around an existing franchised dealer with a population of 250,000, not to exceed a radius of 10 miles, but in no case less than seven miles.

2. For motor vehicle dealers except motorcycle dealers, if the population in a circular area within a

radius of 10 miles around an existing franchised dealer is less than 250,000, but the population in an area within a radius of 15 miles around an existing franchised dealer is 150,000 or more, the relevant market area shall be that circular area within the 15-mile radius.

3. For motor vehicle dealers except motorcycle dealers, in all other cases the relevant market area shall be a circular area within a radius of 20 miles around an existing franchised dealer or the area of responsibility defined in the franchise, whichever is greater. In any case where the franchise agreement is silent as to area of responsibility, the relevant market area shall be the greater of a circular area within a radius of 20 miles around an existing franchised dealer or that area in which the franchisor otherwise requires the franchisee to make significant retail sales or sales efforts.

4. For motorcycle dealers, the relevant market area shall be a circular area within a radius of 20 miles around an existing franchised dealer location with a population of one million or more. If the population within a 20-mile radius is less than one million but greater than 750,000, the relevant market area shall be a circular area within a radius of 30 miles. If the population within a 30-mile radius is less than 750,000, the relevant market area shall be a circular area within a radius of 40 miles.

Notwithstanding the foregoing provision of this section, in the case of dealers in motor vehicles with gross vehicle weight ratings of 26,000 pounds or greater, excluding recreational vehicles, the relevant market area with respect to the dealer's franchise for all such vehicles shall be a circular area around an existing franchised dealer with a radius of 25 miles, except where the population in such circular area is less than 250,000, in which case the relevant market area shall be a circular area around an existing franchised dealer with a radius of 50 miles, or the area of responsibility defined in the franchise, whichever is greater.

In determining population for relevant market areas, the most recent census by the U.S. Bureau of the Census or the most recent population update, either from the National Planning Data Corporation or other similar recognized source, shall be accumulated for all census tracts either wholly or partially within the relevant market area.

"Retail installment sale" means every sale of one or more motor vehicles to a buyer for his use and not for resale, in which the price of the vehicle is payable in one or more installments and in which the seller has either retained title to the goods or has taken or retained a security interest in the goods under form of contract designated either as a security agreement, conditional sale, bailment lease, chattel mortgage, or otherwise.

"Sale at retail" or *"retail sale"* means the act or attempted act of selling, bartering, exchanging, or otherwise disposing of a motor vehicle to a buyer for his personal use and not for resale.

"Sale at wholesale" or *"wholesale"* means a sale to motor vehicle dealers or wholesalers other than to consumers; a sale to one who intends to resell.

"Semitrailer" means every vehicle of the trailer type so designed and used in conjunction with another motor vehicle that some part of its own weight and that of its own load rests on or is carried by another vehicle.

"Tractor truck" means every motor vehicle designed and used primarily for drawing other vehicles and not so constructed as to carry a load other than a part of the load and weight of the vehicle attached thereto.

"Trailer" means every vehicle without motive power designed for carrying property or passengers wholly on its own structure and for being drawn by another motor vehicle, including semitrailers but not manufactured homes, watercraft trailers, camping trailers, or travel trailers.

"Travel trailer" means a vehicle designed to provide temporary living quarters for recreational, camping, or travel use of such size or weight so as not to require a special highway movement permit when towed by a consumer-owned tow vehicle.

"Used motor vehicle" means any vehicle other than a new motor vehicle as defined in this section.

"Watercraft trailer" means any new or used trailer specifically designed to carry a watercraft or a motorboat and purchased, sold, or offered for sale by a watercraft dealer licensed under Chapter 8 (§ 29.1-800 et seq.) of Title 29.1.

"Watercraft trailer dealer" means any watercraft dealer licensed under Chapter 8 (§ 29.1-800 et seq.) of Title 29.1.

"Wholesale auction" means an auction of motor vehicles restricted to sales at wholesale.

History.

Code 1950, § 46-503; 1950, p. 1604; 1956, c. 120; 1958, c. 541, § 46.1-516; 1962, c. 368; 1964, c. 375; 1974, c. 189; 1975, c. 304; 1976, c. 362; 1980, c. 161; 1982, c. 394; 1983, c. 234; 1986, c. 630; 1988, c. 865; 1989, cc. 15, 148, 727; 1992, cc. 134, 148, 572; 1993, c. 124; 1994, c. 888; 1995, cc. 767, 816; 1996, c. 1053; 1997, cc. 801, 848; 1999, cc. 77, 910; 2004, cc. 111, 788; 2005, c. 456; 2006, c. 441; 2010, cc. 284, 292, 318, 459; 2014, cc. 53, 75, 256; 2015, cc. 236, 615.

§ 46.2-1501. General powers of Commissioner.

The Commissioner shall promote the interest of the retail buyers of motor vehicles and endeavor to prevent unfair methods of competition and unfair or deceptive acts or practices.

History.

Code 1950, § 46-504; 1958, c. 541, § 46.1-517; 1988, c. 865; 1989, c. 727.

§ 46.2-1502: Repealed by Acts 1995, cc. 767 and 816.

§ 46.2-1503. Motor Vehicle Dealer Board.

A. **(Effective until October 1, 2016)** The Motor Vehicle Dealer Board is hereby created. The Board shall consist of 19 members appointed by the Governor, subject to confirmation by the General Assembly. Every member appointed by the Governor shall be a citizen of the United States and a resident of Virginia. The Governor may remove any member as provided in subsection B of § 2.2-108. The members shall be at-large members and, insofar as practical, should reflect fair and equitable statewide representation.

A. **(Effective October 1, 2016)** The Motor Vehicle Dealer Board is hereby created. The Board shall consist of 19 members appointed by the Governor, subject to confirmation by the General Assembly. Every member appointed by the Governor shall be a citizen of the United States and a resident of Virginia. The Governor may remove any member as provided in subsection A of § 2.2-108. The members shall be at-large members and, insofar as practical, should reflect fair and equitable statewide representation.

B. Ten members shall be licensed franchised motor vehicle dealers who have been licensed as such for at least two years prior to being appointed by the Governor and seven members shall be licensed independent motor vehicle dealers who (i) have been licensed as such for at least two years prior to being appointed by the Governor and (ii) are not also franchised motor vehicle dealers. One of the franchised dealers appointed to the Board shall be a licensed franchised motorcycle dealer who is primarily engaged in the sale of new motorcycles. One of the independent dealers appointed to the Board shall be a licensed independent motorcycle dealer, and one shall be a licensed independent dealer who is also an independent trailer or recreational vehicle dealer or engaged in the rental vehicle business. One member shall be an individual who has no direct or indirect interest, other than as a consumer, in or relating to the motor vehicle industry.

C. Appointments shall be for terms of four years, and no person other than the Commissioner or his designee shall be eligible to serve more than two successive four-year terms. The Commissioner shall serve as chairman of the Board. Vacancies shall be filled by appointment by the Governor for the unexpired term and shall be effective until 30 days after the next meeting of the ensuing General Assembly and, if confirmed, thereafter for the remainder of the term. Any person appointed to fill a vacancy may serve two additional successive terms.

D. The Commissioner or his designee shall be an ex officio voting member of the Board.

E. Members of the Board shall be reimbursed their actual and necessary expenses incurred in carrying out their duties, such reimbursement to be paid from the special fund referred to in § 46.2-1520.

History.

1988, c. 865, § 46.1-517.2; 1989, c. 727; 1992, c. 95; 1995, cc. 767, 816; 2011, c. 791; 2014, c. 695; 2015, c. 615.

§ 46.2-1503.1. Board to employ Executive Director.

The Board shall employ an executive director who shall serve at the pleasure of the Board. He shall direct the affairs of the Board and keep records of all proceedings, transactions, communications, and official acts of the Board. He shall be custodian of all records of the Board and perform such duties as the Board may require. The Executive Director shall call a meeting of the Board at the direction of the chairman or upon written request of three or more Board members. The Executive Director, with approval of the Board, may employ such additional staff as needed. The annual salary of the Executive Director shall be at Level II of the Executive Compensation Plan contained in the Appropriation Act.

History.

1995, cc. 767, 816.

§ 46.2-1503.2. State Personnel and Public Procurement Acts not applicable.

A. The Executive Director and all staff employed by the Board shall be exempt from the Virginia Personnel Act (§ 2.2-2900 et seq.) of Title 2.2. Personnel actions under this exemption shall be taken without regard to race, sex, color, national origin, religion, age, handicap or political affiliation.

B. The Board and the Executive Director shall be exempt from the Virginia Public Procurement Act (§ 2.2-4300 et seq.) of Title 2.2.

History.

1995, cc. 767, 816.

§ 46.2-1503.3. Motor Vehicle Dealer Board Fund; receipts; disbursements.

The Motor Vehicle Dealer Board Fund is established as a special fund in the state treasury. Except as otherwise provided in this chapter, all fees collected as provided in this chapter and by regulations promulgated by the Board, shall be paid into the state treasury immediately upon collection and credited to the Motor Vehicle Dealer Board Fund. Any interest income shall accrue to the Motor Vehicle Dealer Board Fund. All disbursements from the Fund shall be made by the State Treasurer upon warrants of the Comptroller issued upon vouchers signed by an authorized officer of the Board or the Executive Director as authorized by the Board.

History.

1995, cc. 767, 816; 1998, c. 325.

§ 46.2-1503.4. General powers and duties of Board.

The powers and duties of the Board shall include, but not be limited to the following:

1. To establish the qualifications of applicants for certification or licensure, provided that all qualifications shall be necessary to ensure competence and integrity.

2. To examine, or cause to be examined, the qualifications of each applicant for certification or licensure, including the preparation, administration and grading of examinations.

3. To certify or license qualified applicants as motor vehicle dealers and motor vehicle salespersons.

4. To levy and collect fees for certification or licensure and renewal that are sufficient to cover all expenses for the administration and operation of the Board.

5. To levy on licensees special assessments necessary to cover expenses of the Board.

6. To revoke, suspend, or fail to renew a certificate or license for just cause as set out in Articles 2 (§ 46.2-1508 et seq.), 3.1 (§ 46.2-1527.1 et seq.), 4 (§ 46.2-1528 et seq.), 8 (§ 46.2-1574 et seq.), and 9 (§ 46.2-1580 et seq.) of this chapter or enumerated in regulations promulgated by the Board.

7. To ensure that inspections are conducted relating to the motor vehicle sales industry and to ensure that all licensed dealers and salespersons are conducting business in a professional manner, not in violation of any provision of Articles 2 (§ 46.2-1508 et seq.), 3.1 (§ 46.2-1527.1 et seq.), 4 (§ 46.2-1528 et seq.), 7 (§ 46.2-1566 et seq.), 8 (§ 46.2-1574 et seq.), and 9 (§ 46.2-1580 et seq.) of this chapter and within the lawful regulations promulgated by the Board.

8. To receive complaints concerning the conduct of persons and businesses licensed by the Board and to take appropriate disciplinary action if warranted.

9. To enter into contracts necessary or convenient for carrying out the provisions of this chapter or the functions of the Board.

10. To establish committees of the Board, appoint persons to such committees, and to promulgate regulations establishing the responsibilities of these committees. Each of these committees shall include at least one Board member and the Advertising, Dealer Practices and Transaction Recovery Fund committees shall include at least one citizen member who is not licensed or certified by the Board. The Board may establish one of each committee in each DMV District. Committees to be established shall include, but not be limited to the following:

a. Advertising;

b. Licensing;

c. Dealer Practices;

d. Franchise Review and Advisory Committee; and

e. Transaction Recovery Fund.

11. To do all things necessary and convenient for carrying into effect Articles 2, 3.1, 4, 8 and 9 of this chapter or as enumerated in regulations promulgated by the Board.

History.

1995, cc. 767, 816.

§ 46.2-1503.5. Biennial report.

The Board shall submit a biennial report to the Governor and General Assembly on or before November 1 of each even-numbered year. The biennial report shall contain, at a minimum, the following information: (i) a summary of the Board's fiscal affairs, (ii) a description of the Board's activities, (iii) statistical information regarding the administrative hearings and decisions of the Board, and (iv) a general summary of all complaints received against licensees and the procedures used to resolve the complaints.

History.

1995, cc. 767, 816; 2004, c. 650.

§ 46.2-1504. Board's powers with respect to hearings under this chapter.

The Board may, in hearings arising under this chapter, except as provided for in Articles 7 (§ 46.2-1566 et seq.), 7.2 (§ 46.2-1573.2 et seq.), 7.3 (§ 46.2-1573.13 et seq.), and 7.4 (§ 46.2-1573.25 et seq.), determine the place in the Commonwealth where they shall be held; subpoena witnesses; take depositions of witnesses residing outside the Commonwealth in the manner provided for in civil actions in courts of record; pay these witnesses the fees and mileage for their attendance as is provided for witnesses in civil actions in courts of record; and administer oaths.

History.

Code 1950, § 46-505; 1958, c. 541, § 46.1-518; 1989, c. 727; 1995, cc. 767, 816; 2015, c. 615.

§ 46.2-1505. Suit to enjoin violations.

A. The Board, whenever it believes from evidence submitted to the Board that any person has been violating, is violating, or is about to violate any provision of this chapter, in addition to any other remedy, may bring an action in the name of the Commonwealth to enjoin any violation of this chapter.

B. Any manufacturer, factory branch, distributor, distributor branch, or factory or distributor representative who obtains a license under this chapter is engaged in business in the Commonwealth and is subject to the jurisdiction of the courts of the Commonwealth. Any manufacturer, factory branch, distributor, distributor branch, or factory or distributor representative of motorcycles of a recognized line-make that are sold or leased in the Commonwealth pursuant to a plan, system, or channel of distribution established, approved, authorized, or known to the manufacturer shall be subject to the jurisdiction of the courts of the Commonwealth in any action seeking relief under or to enforce any of the remedies or penalties provided for in this chapter.

History.

Code 1950, § 46-506; 1958, c. 541, § 46.1-519; 1989, c. 727; 1995, cc. 767, 816; 2015, c. 615.

§ 46.2-1506. Regulations.

The Board may promulgate regulations requiring persons licensed under this chapter to keep and maintain records reasonably required for the enforcement of §§ 46.2-112 and 46.2-629, and any other regulations, not inconsistent with the provisions of this chapter, as it shall consider necessary for the effective administration and enforcement of this chapter. A copy of any regulation promulgated under this section shall be mailed to each motor vehicle dealer licensee thirty days prior to its effective date.

History.
Code 1950, § 46-507; 1958, c. 541, § 46.1-520; 1986, c. 490; 1988, c. 865; 1989, c. 727; 1995, cc. 767, 816.

§ 46.2-1506.1. Additional training.

The Board may promulgate regulations specifying additional training or conditions for individuals seeking certification, licensure, or renewal of certificates or licenses.

History.
1995, cc. 767, 816.

§ 46.2-1507. Penalties.

Except as otherwise provided in this chapter, any person violating any of the provisions of this chapter may be assessed a civil penalty by the Board. No such civil penalty shall exceed $1,000 for any single violation. Civil penalties collected under this chapter shall be deposited in the Transportation Trust Fund established pursuant to § 33.2-1524.

History.
Code 1950, § 46-509; 1958, c. 541, § 46.1-522; 1988, c. 865; 1989, c. 727; 1995, cc. 767, 816.

ARTICLE 2.
MOTOR VEHICLE DEALER LICENSES.

§ 46.2-1508. Licenses required; penalty.

It shall be unlawful for any person to engage in business in the Commonwealth as a motor vehicle dealer or salesperson without first obtaining a license as provided in this chapter. It shall be unlawful for any person to engage in business in the Commonwealth as a manufacturer, factory branch, distributor, distributor branch, or factory or distributor representative without first obtaining a license from the Department. Every person licensed as a manufactured home dealer under Chapter 4.2 (§ 36-85.16 et seq.) of Title 36 shall obtain a certificate of dealer registration as provided in this chapter. Every person licensed as a watercraft dealer under Chapter 8 (§ 29.1-800 et seq.) of Title 29.1 and who offers for sale watercraft trailers shall obtain a certificate of dealer registration as provided in this chapter but shall not be required to obtain a dealer license unless he also sells other types of trailers. Any nonprofit organization exempt from taxation under § 501(c)(3) of the Internal Revenue Code, after having obtained a nonprofit organization certificate as provided in this chapter, may consign donated motor vehicles to licensed Virginia motor vehicle dealers. Any person licensed in another state as a motor vehicle dealer may sell motor vehicles at wholesale auctions in the Commonwealth after having obtained a certificate of dealer registration as provided in this chapter. The offering or granting of a motor vehicle dealer franchise in the Commonwealth shall constitute engaging in business in the Commonwealth for purposes of this section, and no new motor vehicle may be sold or offered for sale in the Commonwealth unless the franchisor of motor vehicle dealer franchises for that line-make in the Commonwealth, whether such franchisor is a manufacturer, factory branch, distributor, distributor branch, or otherwise, is licensed under this chapter. In the event a license issued to a franchisor of motor vehicle dealer franchises is suspended, revoked, or not renewed, nothing in this section shall prevent the sale of any new motor vehicle of such franchisor's line-make manufactured in or brought into the Commonwealth for sale prior to the suspension, revocation or expiration of the license.

Violation of any provision of this section shall constitute a Class 1 misdemeanor.

Notwithstanding the provisions of subsection A, a manufacturer, factory branch, distributor, distributor branch, or factory or distributor representative engaged in the manufacture or distribution of all-terrain vehicles or off-road motorcycles that does not also manufacture or distribute in the Commonwealth any motorcycle designed for lawful use on the public highways shall not be required to obtain a license from the Department.

History.
Code 1950, § 46-514; 1958, c. 541, § 46.1-523; 1974, c. 189; 1976, c. 362; 1988, c. 865; 1989, c. 727; 1993, c. 123; 1995, cc. 767, 816; 1997, c. 848; 2000, c. 180; 2014, c. 695; 2015, c. 615.

§ 46.2-1508.1. Licensure of certain nonprofit organizations.

A. Any nonprofit organization exempt from taxation under § 501 (c) (3) of the Internal Revenue Code that (i) receives title to motor vehicles as qualified charitable gifts to the organization, (ii) provides no more than twelve of these donated vehicles in any twelve-month period to low-income persons, as defined in § 2.2-5400, in need of transportation, and (iii) receives from the recipients of the vehicles only reimbursement for the costs of repairs, towing, titles, taxes, license fees and inspection fees shall be required to obtain a dealer's license. However, such nonprofit organization shall be exempt from the requirements of § 46.2-1510, Article 3.1 (§ 46.2-1527.1 et seq.) of Chapter 15 of this title, §§ 46.2-1533, and 46.2-1534. Transactions of such nonprofit organization shall not be subject to recovery from the Motor Vehicle Transaction Recovery Fund.

B. Upon application to and approval by the Board, any nonprofit organization exempt from taxation under § 501 (c) (3) of the Internal Revenue Code may be issued a nonprofit organization certificate authorizing it to consign donated motor vehicles to licensed Virginia motor vehicle dealers when the nonprofit organization receives title to such motor vehicles as qualified charitable gifts and titles the vehicles in the name of the nonprofit organization.

History.
1998, c. 393; 2000, c. 180.

§ 46.2-1508.2. Display, parking, selling, advertising sale of certain used motor vehicles prohibited.

No owner or lessee of any real property shall permit the display or parking of more than five used motor vehicles within any 12-month period on such real property for the purpose of selling or advertising the sale of such used motor vehicles by the owner or lessee of such vehicles unless exempted pursuant to this section.

No owner or lessee of any used motor vehicle shall display or park such used motor vehicle on the real property of another for the purpose of selling or advertising the sale of such used motor vehicle if the display or parking of such vehicle will cause the owner or lessee of the real property to be in violation of the provisions of this section.

No owner or lessee of any used motor vehicle shall display or park such used motor vehicle on the real property of another for the purpose of selling or advertising the sale of such used motor vehicle unless the owner or lessee of such vehicle has the right to occupy such property pursuant to a lease or other occupancy document or prior written permission of the owner or lessee of the real property. Copies of such written permission shall be posted on the inside of a side window of the motor vehicle and must be retained by both the property owner or lessee and by the vehicle owner for at least 12 months and shall be made available to law-enforcement officers or agencies, the Board, and local zoning officials upon request.

The provisions of this section shall not apply if (i) the owner or lessee of the vehicle displayed or parked is employed by the owner or lessee of the real property on which the vehicle is displayed or parked; (ii) the owner or lessee of the vehicle displayed or parked is conducting business with the owner or lessee of the real property on which the vehicle is parked or displayed at the time such vehicle is displayed or parked; (iii) the real property on which a vehicle is parked is a parking lot for which a fee is charged for the use of such parking lot, the owner or lessee of the parked vehicle has paid the fee for the use of such parking lot, and such vehicle is legitimately parked on the property for purposes other than displaying, selling, or advertising the sale of such vehicle; or (iv) the vehicle displays a dealer's license plate pursuant to § 46.2-1550 and the licensed dealer is not displaying for sale or selling a motor vehicle at a location other than his specific business location without first meeting the requirements of § 46.2-1516.

The provisions of this section shall also not apply to (i) any motor vehicle dealer licensed under this chapter, or (ii) any owner or lessee of real property who permits the display or parking of five or more used motor vehicles on such real property by a licensed motor vehicle dealer within any 12-month period for the purpose of selling or advertising the sale of such used motor vehicles.

Except as permitted in § 46.2-631 and except as permitted in this section, no owner or lessee of any real property shall permit any used motor vehicle to be displayed or parked on such real property for the purpose of selling or advertising the sale of such used motor vehicle if such vehicle is not lawfully titled and registered in the name of the individual or entity offering such vehicle for sale as provided in Chapter 6 (§ 46.2-600 et seq.) of this title. However, this limitation shall not apply if the individual offering the vehicle for sale is an immediate family member of the owner or lessee of the real property on which the motor vehicle is displayed or parked for the purpose of selling or advertising the sale of such vehicle.

Except as permitted in § 46.2-631, no person shall advertise, display, sell, or offer for sale any used motor vehicle unless such vehicle is lawfully titled and registered in such person's name as provided in Chapter 6 (§ 46.2-600 et seq.) of this title. However, this limitation shall not apply if the person offering the vehicle for sale is a motor vehicle dealer licensed under this chapter or has the authority pursuant to law to advertise, display, sell, or offer for sale the used motor vehicle.

Notwithstanding any other provision of law, any law-enforcement officer or agency, local zoning official, or the owner or lessee of any real property upon which a vehicle is displayed or parked in violation of this section for longer than 48 consecutive hours after a notice on a form approved by the Board has been affixed or placed on the vehicle by a law-enforcement officer or agency, Board representative, local zoning official, or the owner or lessee of the real property upon which the vehicle is displayed or parked, may have any such vehicle towed from such real property and stored at the expense of the owner or lessee of such vehicle and may then dispose of such vehicle as provided in § 46.2-1203.

The provisions of this section shall not be deemed to eliminate, change, or supersede the requirement for any person to obtain a license under this chapter if such person engages in any conduct or activity for which a license is required under this chapter.

History.

2008, c. 168.

§ 46.2-1509. Application for license or certificate of dealer registration.

Application for license or certificate of dealer registration under this chapter shall be made to the Board and contain such information as the Board shall require. Such information shall include whether the applicant will be seeking a license to sell cars, trucks, motorcycles, recreational vehicles, or trailers and whether such vehicles will be new or used. The Board shall maintain a record of this information and place the appropriate endorsement on any license issued under this chapter. The application shall be accompanied by the fee as required by the Board.

The Board shall also require, in the application or otherwise, information relating to the matters set forth in § 46.2-1575 as grounds for refusing licenses, certificates of dealer registration, and to other pertinent matters requisite for the safeguarding of the public interest, including, if the applicant is a dealer in new motor vehicles with factory warranties, a copy of a current service agreement with the manufacturer or with the distributor, requiring the applicant to perform within a reasonable distance of his established place of business, the service, repair, and replacement work required of the manufacturer or distributor by such vehicle warranty. All of these matters shall be considered by the Board in determining the fitness of the applicant to engage in the business for which he seeks a license or certificate of dealer registration.

History.

Code 1950, § 46-514; 1958, c. 541, § 46.1-525; 1974, c. 189; 1976, c. 362; 1988, c. 865; 1989, c. 727; 1995, cc. 767, 816; 2015, c. 615.

§ 46.2-1510. Dealers required to have established place of business.

No license shall be issued to any motor vehicle dealer unless he has an established place of business, owned or leased by him, where a substantial portion of the sales activity of the business is routinely conducted and which:

1. Satisfies all local zoning regulations;
2. Has sales, service, and office space devoted exclusively to the dealership of at least 250 square feet in a permanent, enclosed building not used as a residence;
3. Houses all records the dealer is required to maintain by § 46.2-1529;
4. Is equipped with a desk, chairs, filing space, a working telephone listed in the name of the dealership, working utilities including electricity and provisions for space heating, and an Internet connection and email address;
5. Displays a sign and business hours as required by this chapter; and
6. Has contiguous space designated for the exclusive use of the dealer adequate to permit the display of at least 10 vehicles.

Any dealer licensed on or before July 1, 1995, shall be considered in compliance with subdivisions 2 and 6 of this section for that licensee.

History.

1988, c. 865, § 46.1-525.01; 1989, c. 727; 1995, cc. 767, 816; 1998, c. 418; 2011, c. 791; 2015, c. 615.

§ 46.2-1511. Dealer-operator to have certificate of qualification.

A. No license shall be issued to any franchised motor vehicle dealer or any independent motor vehicle dealer owned by a franchised motor vehicle dealer or its dealer-operator and operated by the dealer-operator of a franchised motor vehicle dealer unless the dealer-operator holds a valid certificate of qualification issued by the Board. Such certificate shall be issued only on application to the Board, payment of an application fee of no more than $50 as determined by the Board, the successful completion of an examination prepared and administered by the Board, and other prerequisites as set forth in this subsection. However, any individual who is the dealer-operator of a licensed dealer on July 1, 1995, shall be entitled to such a certificate without examination on application to the Board made on or before January 1, 1996.

The Board may establish minimum qualifications for applicants and require applicants to satisfactorily complete courses of study or other prerequisites prior to taking the examination.

B. No license shall be issued to any independent motor vehicle dealer, except as permitted in subsection A, unless the dealer-operator holds a valid certificate of qualification issued by the Board. Such certificate shall be issued only on application to the Board, payment of an application fee of no more than $50, as determined by the Board, the successful completion of an examination approved by the Board, and other prerequisites as set forth in this subsection. The Board may establish minimum qualifications for applicants and shall require applicants for an original independent dealer-operator certificate of qualification to be issued pursuant to this subsection to satisfactorily complete a course of study prior to taking the examination. The Board shall develop the course curriculum and set course fees and may approve qualified persons to prepare and present such courses and to administer the examination. This subsection shall not be subject to the provisions of the Administrative Process Act (§ 2.2-4000 et seq.).

History.

1988, c. 865, § 46.1-525.02; 1989, c. 727; 1995, cc. 767, 816; 2005, c. 321; 2015, c. 615.

§ 46.2-1512. Salesperson to have certificate of qualification.

No license shall be issued to any motor vehicle salesperson unless he holds a valid certificate of qualification issued by the Board. A certificate shall be issued only on application to the Board, payment of the required application fee of no more than $50 as determined by the Board, the successful completion of an examination prepared and administered by the Board, and other prerequisites as set forth in this section. Any individual who is licensed as a salesperson on July 1, 1995, shall be entitled to such a certificate without examination on application to the Board made on or before January 1, 1996.

The Board may establish minimum qualifications for applicants and require applicants to satisfactorily complete courses of study or other prerequisites prior to taking the examination.

History.

1988, c. 865, § 46.1-525.03; 1989, c. 727; 1995, cc. 767, 816; 2015, c. 615.

§ 46.2-1513. Continued operation on loss of a dealer-operator holding certificate of qualification.

Each dealer shall notify the Board in writing immediately when a dealer-operator who holds a certificate of qualification dies, becomes disabled, retires, is removed, or for any other cause ceases to act as dealer-operator. The dealer may continue to operate for 120 days thereafter without a dealer-operator and may be granted approval by the Board to operate for an additional 60 days on application and good cause shown for such delay.

History.

1988, c. 865, § 46.1-525.04; 1989, c. 727; 1995, cc. 767, 816.

§ 46.2-1514. Action on applications; hearing on denial; denial for failure to have established place of business.

The Board shall act on all applications for a license or certificate of dealer registration under this chapter within sixty days after receipt by either granting or refusing the application. Any applicant denied a license or certificate shall, on his written request filed within thirty days, be given a hearing at a time and place determined by the Board or a person designated by the Board. All hearings under this section shall be public and shall be held promptly. The applicant may be represented by counsel.

Any applicant denied a license for failure to have an established place of business as provided in § 46.2-1510 may not, nor shall anyone, apply for a license for premises for which a license was denied for thirty days from the date of the rejection of the application.

History.

1988, c. 865, § 46.1-525.05; 1989, c. 727; 1995, cc. 767, 816.

§ 46.2-1515. Location to be specified; display of license; change of location.

The licenses of motor vehicle dealers, manufacturers, factory branches, distributors, and distributor branches shall specify the location of each place of business, branch, or other location occupied or to be occupied by the licensee in conducting his business, and the license issued therefor shall be conspicuously displayed at each of the premises. In the event any licensee intends to change a licensed location, he shall provide the Department, or in the case of motor vehicle dealers, the Board, 30 days' advance written notice and a successful inspection of the new location shall be required prior to approval of a change of location. The Department or Board shall endorse the change of location on the license, without charge, if the new location is within the same county or city. A change in location to another county or city shall require a new license and fee.

History.

1988, c. 865, § 46.1-525.06; 1989, c. 727; 1995, cc. 767, 816; 2015, c. 615.

§ 46.2-1516. Supplemental sales locations.

The Board may issue a license for a licensed motor vehicle dealer to display for sale or sell vehicles at locations other than his established place of business, subject to compliance with local ordinances and requirements. A license issued pursuant to this section shall not be required for a licensed motor vehicle dealer to display for sale or sell vehicles at wholesale auction; placing vehicles for sale at a wholesale auction shall not be considered a consignment.

A permanent supplemental license may be issued for premises less than 500 yards from the dealer's established place of business, provided a sign is displayed as required for the established place of business. A supplemental license shall not be required for premises otherwise contiguous to the established place of business except for a public thoroughfare.

A temporary supplemental license may be issued for a period not to exceed seven days, or 14 days for trailers and motorcycles, provided that the application is made 15 days prior to the sale. The Board shall not issue a temporary supplemental license (i) for the same jurisdiction for a consecutive seven-day period or (ii) for motorcycles for a consecutive 14-day period. The Board shall not issue more than eight supplemental licenses per year to any licensed motor vehicle dealer.

A temporary supplemental license for the sale of new motor vehicles may be issued only for locations within the dealer's area of responsibility, as defined in his franchise or sales agreement, unless proof is provided that all dealers in the same line-make in whose areas of responsibility, as defined in their franchise or sales agreements, where the temporary supplemental license is sought do not oppose the issuance of the temporary license.

A temporary supplemental license for sale of used motor vehicles may be issued only for the county, city, or town in which the dealer is licensed pursuant to § 46.2-1510, or for a contiguous county, city, or town. Temporary licenses may be issued without regard to the foregoing geographic restrictions where the dealer operating under a temporary license provides notice by certified mail, at least 30 days before any proposed sale under a temporary license, to all other dealers licensed in the jurisdiction in which the sale will occur of the intent to conduct a sale and permits any locally licensed dealer who wishes to do so to participate in the sale on the same terms as the dealer operating under the temporary license. Any locally licensed dealer who chooses to participate in the sale must obtain a temporary supplemental license for the sale pursuant to this section. The dealer operating under a temporary license shall provide to the Board a copy of the notice required under this section and a list of the dealers to whom the notice was distributed.

A temporary supplemental license may be issued for the sale of boat trailers at a boat show. Any such license shall be valid for no more than 14 days. Application for such a license shall be made and such license obtained prior to the opening of the show. Temporary supplemental licenses for sale of boat trailers at boat shows may be issued for any boat show located anywhere in the Commonwealth without notification of or approval by other boat trailer dealers.

History.
1988, c. 865, § 46.1-525.07; 1989, c. 727; 1990, c. 940; 1993, c. 69; 1995, cc. 767, 816; 2012, c. 13; 2013, c. 247; 2015, c. 615.

§ 46.2-1517. Changes in form of ownership, make, name.

Any change in the form of ownership or the addition or deletion of a partner shall require a new application, license, and fee.

Any addition or deletion of a franchise or change in the name of a dealer shall require immediate notification to the Department and the Board, and the Board shall endorse the change on the license without a fee. The change of an officer or director of a corporation shall be made at the time of license renewal.

History.
1988, c. 865, § 46.1-525.08; 1989, c. 727; 1995, cc. 767, 816.

§ 46.2-1518. Display of salesperson's license; notice on termination.

No salesperson shall be employed by more than one dealer, unless the dealers are owned by the same person.

Each dealer shall post and maintain in a place conspicuous to the public a list of salespersons employed.

Each salesperson, factory representative, and distributor representative shall carry his license when engaged in his business and shall display it on request.

Each dealer shall notify the Board in writing not later than the tenth day following the month of the termination of any licensed salesperson's employment. In lieu of written notification, the license of the terminated salesperson may be returned to the Board annotated "terminated" on the face of the license and signed and dated by the dealer-operator, owner, or officer.

History.
1988, c. 865, § 46.1-525.09; 1989, c. 727; 1995, cc. 767, 816; 2015, c. 615.

§ 46.2-1519. License and registration fees; additional to other licenses and fees required by law.

A. The fee for each license and registration year or part thereof shall be determined by the Board, subject to the following:

1. For motor vehicle dealers, not more than $300 for each principal place of business, plus not more than $40 for each supplemental license.
2. For motor vehicle salespersons, not more than $50.
3. For motor vehicle dealers licensed in other states, but not in the Commonwealth, who sell motor vehicles at wholesale auctions, not more than $100.
4. For manufactured home dealers, not more than $100.
5. For watercraft trailer dealers, not more than $100.

The determination of fees by the Board under this subsection shall not be subject to the provisions of the Administrative Process Act (§ 2.2-4000 et seq.).

B. The licenses, registrations, and fees required by this chapter are in addition to licenses, taxes, and fees imposed by other provisions of law and nothing contained in this chapter shall exempt any person from any license, tax, or fee imposed by any other provision of law.

C. The fee for issuance to a nonprofit organization of a certificate pursuant to subsection B of § 46.2-1508.1 shall be $25 per year or any part thereof.

D. No nonprofit organization granted a certificate pursuant to subsection B of § 46.2-1508.1 shall, either orally or in writing, assign a value to any donated vehicle for the purpose of establishing tax deduction amounts on any federal or state income tax return.

E. The Board may authorize discounts and other incentives to encourage licensees to conduct transactions with the Board (i) by means of electronic technologies and (ii) for multi-year periods.

F. The fee for reprinting licenses, certificates, and registrations shall be $10 for each reprint.

G. The fee for reinstating a license, certificate, or registration that has been suspended shall be $50.

H. The fee for each license and registration year or part thereof for each motor vehicle manufacturer, factory branch, distributor, and distributor branch shall be $100 and shall be paid to the Department.

History.

1988, c. 865, § 46.1-525.010; 1989, c. 727; 1992, c. 148; 1993, c. 122; 1995, cc. 767, 816; 2000, c. 180; 2001, c. 23; 2011, c. 791; 2014, c. 695; 2015, c. 615.

§ 46.2-1520. Collection of license and registration fees; payments from fund.

All licensing and registration fees provided for in this chapter, except as identified in Article 3.1 (§ 46.2-1527.1 et seq.) of this chapter shall be collected by the Board and paid into the state treasury and set aside as a special fund to meet the expenses of the Board.

History.

1988, c. 865, § 46.1-525.011; 1989, c. 727; 1995, cc. 767, 816.

§ 46.2-1521. Issuance, expiration, and renewal of licenses and certificates of registration.

A. All licenses and certificates of registration issued under this chapter shall be issued for a period of 12 consecutive months except, at the discretion of the issuing agency, the periods may be adjusted as is necessary to distribute the licenses and certificates as equally as practicable on a monthly basis. The expiration date shall be the last day of the twelfth month of validity or the last day of the designated month. Every license and certificate of registration shall be renewed annually on application by the licensee or registrant and by payment of fees required by law, the renewal to take effect on the first day of the succeeding month.

B. Licenses and certificates of registration issued under this chapter shall be deemed not to have expired if the renewal application and required fees as set forth in this subsection are received by the issuing agency or postmarked not more than 30 days after the expiration date of such license or certificate of registration. Whenever the renewal application is received by the issuing agency or postmarked no more than 30 days after the expiration date of such license or certificate of registration, the license fees shall be 150 percent of the fees provided for in § 46.2-1519.

C. For dealers and salespersons who have served outside of the United States in the armed services of the United States, licenses and certificates issued under this chapter shall be deemed not to have expired if the renewal application and required fees as set forth in § 46.2-1519 are received by the issuing agency or postmarked not more than 60 days from the date they are no longer serving outside the United States and they have:

1. Held a valid license or certificate issued by the issuing agency at the time the person began service in the armed forces outside of the United States;
2. Not performed sales activities during the period of the person's military service; and
3. Submitted to the issuing agency orders or other military documentation demonstrating that they have served outside of the United States in the armed services of the United States and it has been less than 61 days from the date they are no longer serving outside the United States.

Prior to renewing a license or certificate under this subsection, the applicant shall notify the issuing agency of their intentions and verify that they are in compliance with all other requirements established by the issuing agency and set forth in this title.

D. The issuing agency may offer an optional multiyear license. When such option is offered and chosen by the licensee, all annual and 12-month fees due at the time of licensing shall be multiplied by the number of years or fraction thereof for which the license will be issued.

E. The Board may issue a salesperson's license to an applicant, as required by § 46.2-1508, even though the applicant is not employed by a motor vehicle dealer if (i) the applicant has been certified pursuant to § 46.2-1512 and is employed by a person that has contracted in writing with a dealer or dealers to provide temporary personnel for the sale of products and services to include but not be limited to providing payment, financing and leasing alternatives; and offering and selling extended service agreements, prepaid maintenance agreements, and similar products and services that are sold in connection with the sale of a vehicle; provided, however, that such persons do not negotiate for the sale of the vehicle but may complete the required paperwork for the sale of the vehicle in addition to the other products and services being offered or to provide training to salespersons employed by a dealer, and (ii) the applicant meets the other qualifications to be licensed as a salesperson under this chapter. The requirements of §§ 46.2-1518 and 46.2-1537 shall not apply to any such salesperson so licensed, provided that any salesperson so licensed:

1. May only act as a salesperson for a dealer who has a contract with the salesperson's employer as provided in this subsection;
2. Shall carry his license when engaged in business and shall display it upon request; and
3. Need not be the person who signs the buyer's order on behalf of the dealer, but the name of that salesperson shall be listed on the buyer's order in any transaction in which the salesperson engages.

History.

1988, c. 865, § 46.1-525.012; 1989, c. 727; 1990, c. 197; 1995, cc. 767, 816; 1997, c. 848; 1998, c. 325; 2004, c. 975; 2007, c. 828; 2015, c. 615.

ARTICLE 3.

MOTOR VEHICLE TRANSACTION RECOVERY FUND.

§§ 46.2-1522 through 46.2-1527: Repealed by Acts 1994, c. 478, effective April 8, 1994.

ARTICLE 3.1.

MOTOR VEHICLE TRANSACTION RECOVERY FUND.

§ 46.2-1527.1. Motor Vehicle Transaction Recovery Fund established.

A. All fees in this article shall be deposited in the Motor Vehicle Transaction Recovery Fund, referred to in this article as "the Fund." The Fund shall be a special fund in the state treasury to pay claims against the Fund and for no other purpose, provided that any such payment does not result in a negative balance of the Fund, except the Board may expend moneys for the administration of this article up to the maximum amount authorized for consumer assistance in the general appropriation act, provided the amount expended for administration does not result in a balance of the Fund of less than $250,000. The Fund shall be used to satisfy unpaid judgments, as provided for in § 46.2-1527.3. Any interest income shall accrue to the Fund. The Board shall maintain an accurate record of all transactions involving the Fund. The Board may levy a special assessment on all dealers participating in the Fund to pay claims against the Fund and to maintain a minimum Fund balance that is in its judgment adequate. The Board may choose to await a positive balance in the Fund to pay claims ready for payment in chronological order, provided such claims do not go unpaid for more than 60 days.

B. Every applicant renewing a motor vehicle dealer's license shall pay, in addition to other license fees, an annual Fund fee of $100, and every applicant for a motor vehicle salesperson's license shall pay, in addition to other license fees, an annual Fund fee of $10, prior to license issue. However, annual Fund renewal fees from salespersons shall not exceed $100 per year from an individual dealer. These fees shall be deposited in the Motor Vehicle Transaction Recovery Fund. Any salesperson licensed by the Department and having never paid such a fee prior to July 1, 2015, shall be exempt from this subsection.

C. Applicants for an original motor vehicle dealer's license shall pay an annual Fund fee of $350 each year for three consecutive years. During this period, the $350 Fund fee will take the place of the annual $100 Fund fee.

D. In addition to the $350 annual fee, applicants for an original dealer's license shall have a $50,000 bond pursuant to § 46.2-1527.2 for three consecutive years. Only those renewing licensees who have not been the subject of a claim against their bond or against the Fund for three consecutive years shall pay the annual $100 fee and will no longer be required to pay the $350 annual fee or hold the $50,000 bond. Any salesperson licensed by the Department and having never paid such fee prior to July 1, 2015, shall be exempt from this subsection.

E. In addition to other license fees, applicants for an original Certificate of Dealer Registration or its renewal shall pay a Fund fee of $60.

F. The Board may suspend or reinstate collection of Fund fees.

G. The provisions of this section shall not apply to manufactured home dealers or nonprofit organizations issued certificates pursuant to subsection B of § 46.2-1508.1.

H. The provisions of this section shall not apply to applicants for the renewal of a motor vehicle dealer's license where such applicants have not been the subject of a claim against a bond issued pursuant to § 46.2-1527.2 or against the Fund for three years and such applicants elect to maintain continuous bonding pursuant to Article 3.2 (§ 46.2-1527.9 et seq.). Such applicants shall not participate in the Fund and shall be exempt from the payment of any Fund fees.

I. The provisions of this article shall not apply to any recreational vehicle, trailer, or motorcycle dealer licensed by the Department prior to July 1, 2015.

History.

1994, cc. 478, 671; 1995, cc. 767, 816; 1998, c. 325; 2000, c. 180; 2003, c. 331; 2006, c. 172; 2011, c. 407; 2012, cc. 10, 119; 2014, c. 695; 2015, c. 615.

§ 46.2-1527.2. Bonding requirements for applicants for an original license.

Before the Board shall issue to an applicant an original license, the applicant shall obtain and file with the Board a bond in the amount of $50,000. The bond shall come from a corporate surety licensed to do business in the Commonwealth and approved by the Attorney General. The bond shall be conditioned on a statement by the applicant that the applicant will not practice fraud, make any fraudulent representation, or violate any provision of this chapter in the conduct of the applicant's business. The Board may, without holding a hearing, suspend the dealer's license during the period that the dealer does not have a sufficient bond on file.

If a person suffers any of the following: (i) loss or damage in connection with the purchase or lease of a motor vehicle by reason of fraud practiced on him or fraudulent representation made to him by a licensed motor vehicle dealer or one of the dealer's salespersons acting within his scope of employment, (ii) loss or damage by reason of the violation by a dealer or salesperson of any provision of this chapter in connection with the purchase or lease of a motor vehicle, or (iii) loss or damage resulting from a breach of an extended service contract as defined by § 59.1-435 entered into on or after April 8, 1994, that person shall have a claim against the dealer and the dealer's bond, and may recover such damages as may be awarded to such person by final judgment of a court of competent jurisdiction against the dealer as a proximate result of such loss or damage up to but not exceeding $25,000, from such surety, who shall be subrogated to the rights of such person against the dealer or salesperson. The liability of such surety shall be limited to actual damages and attorney fees and shall not include any punitive damages assessed against the dealer or salesperson. On January 1 of each year, the amount that may be awarded against such bond to any person as a result of loss or damage to that person as provided in this section shall be increased by the percentage increase over the most recently available unadjusted 12-month period in the Consumer Price Index for used motor vehicles, as published by the U.S. Bureau of Labor Statistics or any successor index. In the event that this index decreases over any such 12-month period, there shall be no change in the amount that may be awarded.

In those cases in which a dealer's surety shall be liable pursuant to this section, the surety shall be liable only for the first $50,000 in claims against the dealer. Thereafter, the Fund shall be liable for amounts in excess of the bond up to the amount that may be paid out of the Fund, less the amount of the bond, in those cases in which the Fund itself may be liable. The aggregate liability of the dealer's surety to any and all persons, regardless of the number of claims made against the bond or the number of years the bond remains in force, shall in no event exceed $50,000.

The dealer's surety shall notify the Board when a claim is made against a dealer's bond, when a claim is paid and when the bond is cancelled. Such notification shall include the amount of a claim and the circumstances surrounding the claim. Notification of cancellation shall include the effective date and reason for cancellation. The bond may be cancelled as to future liability by the dealer's surety upon 30 days' notice to the Board.

History.

1994, c. 478; 1995, cc. 767, 816; 1998, c. 325; 2001, c. 194; 2006, c. 172; 2011, c. 407; 2012, cc. 10, 119; 2015, c. 615.

§ 46.2-1527.3. Recovery from Fund, generally.

Except as otherwise provided in this chapter, whenever any person is awarded a final judgment in a court of competent jurisdiction in the Commonwealth for (i) any loss or damage in connection with the purchase or lease of a motor vehicle by reason of any fraud practiced on him or fraudulent representation made to him by a licensed or registered motor vehicle dealer participating in the Motor Vehicle Transaction Recovery Fund or one of a dealer's salespersons acting for the dealer or within the scope of his employment or (ii) any loss or damage by reason of the violation by a dealer or salesperson participating in the Motor Vehicle Transaction Recovery Fund of any of the provisions of this chapter, the judgment creditor may file a verified claim with the Board, requesting payment from the Fund of the amount unpaid on the judgment subject to the following conditions:

1. The claim shall be filed with the Board no sooner than 30 days and no later than 12 months after the judgment becomes final along with the evidence of compliance with subdivision 3 below.

2. The Board shall consider for payment claims submitted by retail purchasers of motor vehicles, and for purchases of motor vehicles by licensed or registered motor vehicle dealers who contribute to the Fund. The Board shall also consider for payment claims submitted by lessees of motor vehicles leased from licensed or registered motor vehicle dealers who contribute to the Fund.

3. If the final judgment from a court of competent jurisdiction includes, as part of the judgment, an award of attorney fees and court costs, the Fund may include those in its payment of the claim if (i) the claimant had previously submitted to the trial court a detailed and itemized affidavit by counsel for the judgment creditor seeking such fees and costs, including a breakdown of the hours worked and the subject matter of those hours; (ii) said itemized affidavit formed the basis of the court's award of such fees; and (iii) a copy of such affidavit is provided to the Board with the judgment creditor's claim. If the award of attorney fees and costs by the trial court was not based on a detailed and itemized affidavit from counsel for the judgment creditor with a breakdown of the hours worked, then the Board may review and limit any claim for attorney fees to those attorney fees directly attributable to that portion of the final judgment that is determined to be a compensable claim by the Board against the Fund, and the Board may require a detailed itemization from counsel before considering such claim for attorney fees.

History.

1994, c. 478; 1995, cc. 767, 816; 1998, c. 325; 2003, c. 331; 2007, c. 826; 2015, c. 615.

§ 46.2-1527.4. Opportunity to intervene.

Any action instituted by a person against a licensed or registered dealer or a salesperson, which may become a claim against the Fund, shall be served to the Board in the manner prescribed by law. All subsequent pleadings and documents shall also be served to the Board. Included in such service shall be an affidavit stating all acts constituting fraud or violations of this chapter. Upon service of process, the Board, or duly authorized representative, shall have the right to request leave of the court to intervene. The person shall submit such pleadings or documents to the Board by certified mail or the equivalent.

History.

1994, c. 478; 1995, cc. 767, 816.

§ 46.2-1527.5. Limitations on recovery from Fund.

The maximum claim of one judgment creditor against the Fund based on an unpaid final judgment arising out of any loss or damage by reason of a claim submitted under § 46.2-1527.2 or 46.2-1527.3 involving a single transaction shall be limited to $25,000, including any amount paid from the dealer's surety bond, regardless of the amount of the unpaid final judgment of one judgment creditor. On January 1 of each year, the amount that may be awarded to any person as a result of loss or damage to that person as provided in this section shall be increased by the percentage increase over the most recently available unadjusted 12-month period in the Consumer Price Index for used motor vehicles, as published by the U.S. Bureau of Labor Statistics or any successor index. In the event that this index decreases over any such 12-month period, there shall be no change in the amount which may be awarded.

The aggregate of claims against the Fund based on unpaid final judgments arising out of any loss or damage by reason of a claim submitted under § 46.2-1527.3 involving more than one transaction shall be limited to four times the amount that may be awarded to a single judgment creditor, regardless of the total amounts of the unpaid final judgments of judgment creditors.

However, aggregate claims against the Fund under § 46.2-1527.2 shall be limited to the amount that may be paid out of the Fund under the preceding paragraph less the amount of the dealer's bond and then only after the dealer's bond has been exhausted.

If a claim has been made against the Fund, and the Board has reason to believe that there may be additional claims against the Fund from other transactions involving the same licensee or registrant, the Board may withhold any payment from the Fund involving the licensee or registrant for a period not to exceed the end of the relevant license or registration period. After this period, if the aggregate of claims against the licensee or registrant exceeds the aggregate amount that may be paid from the Fund under this section, then such amount shall be prorated among the claimants and paid from the Fund in proportion to the amounts of their unpaid final judgments against the licensee or registrant.

However, claims against motor vehicle dealers and salespersons participating in the Motor Vehicle Transaction Recovery Fund pursuant to § 46.2-1527.2 shall be prorated when the aggregate exceeds $50,000. Claims shall be prorated only after the dealer's $50,000 bond has been exhausted.

On receipt of a verified claim filed against the Fund, the Board shall forthwith notify the licensee or registrant who is the subject of the unpaid judgment that a verified claim has been filed and that the licensee or registrant should satisfy the judgment debt. If the judgment debt is not fully satisfied 30 days following the date of the notification by the Board, the Board shall make payment from the Fund subject to the other limitations contained in this article.

Excluded from the amount of any unpaid final judgment on which a claim against the Fund is based shall be any sums representing interest and punitive damages. Awards from the Fund shall be limited to reimbursement of costs paid to the dealer for all charges related to the vehicle including without limitation, the sales price, taxes, insurance, and repairs; other out of pocket costs related to the purchase, insuring and registration of the vehicle, and to the loss of use of the vehicle by the purchaser.

If at any time the Fund is insufficient to fully satisfy any claims or claim filed with the Board and authorized by this article, the Board shall pay such claims, claim, or portion thereof to the claimants in the order that the claims were filed with the Board. However, claims by retail purchasers shall take precedence over other claims.

History.

1994, c. 478; 1995, cc. 767, 816; 1998, c. 325; 2001, c. 194; 2003, c. 331; 2006, c. 172; 2007, c. 826; 2011, c. 407; 2012, c. 119; 2015, cc. 615, 710.

§ 46.2-1527.6. Assignment of claimant's rights to the Board; payment of claims.

Subject to the provisions of this article and on the claimant's execution and delivery to the Board of an assignment to the Board of his rights against the licensee or registrant, to the extent he received satisfaction from the Fund, the Board shall pay the claimant from the Fund the amount of the unpaid final judgment.

History.

1994, c. 478; 1995, cc. 767, 816.

§ 46.2-1527.7. Revocation of license or certificate of registration on payment from the Fund.

On payment by the Board to a claimant from the Fund as provided in this article, the Board shall immediately notify the licensee or registrant in writing of the Board's payment to the claimant and request full reimbursement be made to the Board within thirty days of the notification. Failure to reimburse the Board in full within the specified period shall cause the Board to immediately revoke the license or certificate of the dealer or the license of a salesperson whose fraud, fraudulent representation, or violation of this chapter resulted in this payment. Any person whose license or certificate is revoked shall not be eligible to apply for a license or certificate as a motor vehicle dealer or a license as a salesperson until the person has repaid in full the amount paid from the Fund on his account, plus interest at the rate of eight percent per year from the date of payment.

History.
1994, c. 478; 1995, cc. 767, 816.

§ 46.2-1527.8. No waiver by the Board of disciplinary action against licensee or registrant.

Nothing contained in this article shall limit the authority of the Board to take disciplinary action against any licensee or registrant for any violation of this chapter or any regulation promulgated thereunder, nor shall full repayment of the amount paid from the Fund on a licensee's or registrant's account nullify or modify the effect of any disciplinary action against that licensee or registrant for any violation.

History.
1994, c. 478; 1995, cc. 767, 816.

ARTICLE 3.2.

BONDING REQUIREMENTS FOR DEALERS NOT PARTICIPATING IN MOTOR VEHICLE TRANSACTION RECOVERY FUND.

§ 46.2-1527.9. Continuous bonding requirements for Fund nonparticipants.

Applicants for a renewal of a motor vehicle dealer's license may elect to obtain and continuously maintain a bond in the amount of $100,000 in lieu of participation in the Motor Vehicle Transaction Recovery Fund, provided that such applicants have not been the subject of a claim against a bond issued pursuant to § 46.2-1527.2, or against the Fund for three consecutive years. The bond shall come from a corporate surety licensed to do business in the Commonwealth and approved by the Attorney General and shall be filed with the Board. The bond shall be conditioned on a statement by the applicant that the applicant will not practice fraud, make any fraudulent representation, or violate any provision of this chapter in the conduct of the applicant's business. In those cases in which the surety of a dealer electing continuous bonding under this section shall be liable pursuant to this section, the maximum liability to one claimant against the surety by reason of a claim involving a single transaction shall be limited to $20,000 regardless of the amount of the claim by one claimant, and the aggregate liability of the dealer's surety to any and all persons, regardless of the number of claims made against the bond or the number of years the bond remains in effect shall in no event exceed $100,000.

An applicant for a renewal of a motor vehicle dealer's license who is a member of a nonprofit organization established under 26 U.S.C. § 501(c)(6) that provides on behalf of its membership a blanket or umbrella bond in the amount of $1 million satisfies the bonding requirements of this section. When posted, a blanket or umbrella bond shall be considered a dealer bond for the purposes of § 46.2-1527.10. The bond shall come from a corporate surety licensed to do business in the Commonwealth and approved by the Attorney General and shall be filed with the Board. In those cases in which the nonprofit organization's surety shall be liable pursuant to § 46.2-1527.10, the maximum liability to one claimant against the surety by reason of a claim involving a single transaction shall be limited to $20,000, regardless of the amount of the claim by one claimant, and the aggregate liability of the nonprofit organization's surety to any and all persons for claims against a single dealer shall in no event exceed $100,000. In those cases in which the nonprofit organization's surety shall be liable pursuant to § 46.2-1527.10, the maximum liability to any and all persons, regardless of the number of claims made against the bond or the number of years the bond remains in force shall in no event exceed $1 million.

The Board may, without holding a hearing, suspend the dealer's license during the period that the dealer does not have a sufficient bond on file. Dealers bonded under this article and those salespersons employed by such dealers shall be exempt from the Fund fees specified in § 46.2-1527.1.

History.
2003, c. 331.

§ 46.2-1527.10. Recovery on bond.

With respect to a motor vehicle dealer electing continuous bonding under § 46.2-1527.9, whenever any person is awarded a final judgment in a court of competent jurisdiction in the Commonwealth against the dealer for (i) any loss or damage in connection with the purchase or lease of a motor vehicle by reason of fraud practiced on him or fraudulent representation made to him by the dealer or one of the dealer's salespersons acting within the scope of his employment, (ii) any loss or damage by reason of the violation by the dealer or salesperson of any provision of this chapter in connection with the purchase or lease of a motor vehicle, or (iii) any loss or damage resulting from a breach of an extended service contract, as defined in § 59.1-435, entered into on or after July 1, 2003, the judgment creditor shall have a claim against the dealer bond for such damages as may be awarded such person in final judgment and unpaid by the dealer, and may recover such unpaid damages up to but not exceeding the maximum liability of the surety as set forth in § 46.2-1527.9 from the surety who shall be subrogated to the rights of such person against the dealer or salesperson. The liability of such surety shall be limited to actual damages and attorney fees assessed against the dealer or salesperson as part of the underlying judgment but this section does not authorize the award of attorney fees in the underlying judgment. The liability of such surety shall not include any sums representing interest or punitive damages assessed against the dealer or salesperson.

The dealer's surety shall notify the Board when a claim is made against a dealer's bond, when a claim is paid, and when the bond is cancelled. Such notification shall include the amount of claim and the circumstances surrounding the claim. Notification of cancellation shall include the effective date and reason for cancellation. The bond may be cancelled as to future liability by the dealer's surety upon 30 days' notice to the Board.

History.
2003, c. 331; 2015, cc. 615, 710.

§ 46.2-1527.11. No waiver by the Board of disciplinary action against licensee or registrant.

Nothing contained in this article shall limit the authority of the Board to take disciplinary action against any licensee or registrant for any violation of this chapter or any regulation promulgated under this chapter.

History.
2003, c. 331.

ARTICLE 4.
CONDUCT OF BUSINESS.

§ 46.2-1528. Examination or audit of licensee; costs.

The Board or authorized representatives of the Board may examine, during the posted business hours, the records required to be maintained by this chapter. If a licensee is found to have violated this chapter or any order of the Board, the actual cost of the examination shall be paid by the licensee so examined within thirty days after demand therefor by the Board. The Board may maintain an action for the recovery of these costs in any court of competent jurisdiction.

History.
1988, c. 865, § 46.1-547.3; 1989, c. 727; 1995, cc. 767, 816.

§ 46.2-1529. Dealer records.

All dealer records regarding employees; lists of vehicles in inventory for sale, resale, or on consignment; vehicle purchases, sales, trades, and transfers of ownership; collections of taxes; titling, uninsured motor vehicle, and registration fees; odometer disclosure statements; records of permanent dealer registration plates assigned to the dealer and temporary transport plates and temporary certificates of registration; proof of safety inspections performed on vehicles sold at retail; and other records required by the Department or the Board shall be maintained on the premises of the licensed location. The Board may, on written request by a dealer, permit his records to be maintained at a location other than the premises of the licensed location for good cause shown. All dealer records shall be preserved in original form or in film, magnetic, or optical media, including microfilm, microfiche, or other electronic media, for a period of five years in a manner that permits systematic retrieval. Certain records may be maintained on a computerized record-keeping system with the prior approval of the Board.

History.
1988, c. 865, § 46.1-547.4; 1989, c. 727; 1991, c. 712; 1995, cc. 767, 816; 2000, c. 128; 2011, c. 791; 2015, c. 615.

§ 46.2-1529.1. Sales of used motor vehicles by dealers; disclosures; penalty.

A. If, in any retail sale by a dealer of a used motor vehicle of under 6,000 pounds gross vehicle weight for use on the public highways, and normally used for personal, family or household use, the dealer offers an express warranty, the dealer shall provide the buyer a written disclosure of this warranty. The written disclosure shall be the Buyer's Guide required by federal law, shall be completely filled out and, in addition, signed and dated by the buyer and incorporated as part of the buyer's order.

B. A dealer may sell a used motor vehicle at retail "AS IS" and exclude all warranties only if the dealer provides the buyer, prior to sale, a separate written disclosure as to the effect of an "AS IS" sale. The written disclosure shall be conspicuous and contained on the front of the buyer's order and printed in not less than bold, 10-point type and signed by the buyer: "I understand that this vehicle is being sold "AS IS' with all faults and is not covered by any dealer warranty. I understand that the dealer is not required to make any repairs after I buy this vehicle. I will have to pay for any repairs this vehicle will need." A fully completed Buyer's Guide, as required by federal law, shall be signed and dated by the buyer and incorporated as part of the buyer's order.

C. Failure to provide the applicable disclosure required by subsection A or B shall be punishable by a civil penalty of no more than $1,000. Any such civil penalty shall be paid into the general fund of the state treasury. Furthermore, if the applicable disclosure required by subsection A or B is not provided as required in this section, the buyer may cancel the sale within 30 days. In this case, the buyer shall have the right to return the vehicle to the dealer and obtain a full refund of all payments made toward the purchase of the vehicle, less any damage to the vehicle incurred while ownership was vested in the purchaser, and less a reasonable amount for the use not to exceed one-half the amount allowed per mile by the Internal Revenue Service, as provided by regulation, revenue procedure, or revenue ruling promulgated pursuant to § 162 of the Internal Revenue Code, for use of a personal vehicle for business purposes. Notice of the provisions of this subsection shall be included as part of every disclosure made under subsection A or B.

D. The provisions of this section shall not apply to motorcycles, trailers, or travel trailers.

History.

1995, c. 849; 2015, c. 615.

§ 46.2-1530. Buyer's order.

A. Every motor vehicle dealer shall complete, in duplicate, a buyer's order for each sale or exchange of a motor vehicle. A copy of the buyer's order form shall be made available to a prospective buyer during the negotiating phase of a sale and prior to any sales agreement. The completed original shall be retained for a period of five years in accordance with § 46.2-1529, and a duplicate copy shall be delivered to the purchaser at the time of sale or exchange. A buyer's order shall include:

1. The name and address of the person to whom the vehicle was sold or traded.

2. The date of the sale or trade.

3. The name and address of the motor vehicle dealer selling or trading the vehicle.

4. The make, model year, vehicle identification number and body style of the vehicle.

5. The sale price of the vehicle.

6. The amount of any cash deposit made by the buyer.

7. A description of any vehicle used as a trade-in and the amount credited the buyer for the trade-in. The description of the trade-in shall be the same as outlined in subdivision 4.

8. The amount of any sales and use tax, title fee, uninsured motor vehicle fee, registration fee, purchaser's online systems filing fee, or other fee required by law for which the buyer is responsible and the dealer has collected. Each tax and fee shall be individually listed and identified.

9. The net balance due at settlement.

10. Any item designated as "processing fee," and the amount charged by the dealer, if any, for processing the transaction. As used in this section, processing includes obtaining title and license plates for the purchaser, but does not include any "purchaser's online systems filing fee, " as defined in § 46.2-1530.1, or any "dealer's manual transaction fee, " as defined in § 46.2-1530.2.

11. Any item designated as "dealer's business license tax," and the amount charged by the dealer, if any.

12. If the dealer delivers to the customer a vehicle purchased by the customer on or after July 1, 2010, that is conditional on dealer-arranged financing, the following notice, printed in bold type no less than 10 point: "IF YOU ARE FINANCING THIS VEHICLE, PLEASE READ THIS NOTICE: YOU ARE PROPOSING TO ENTER INTO A RETAIL INSTALLMENT SALES CONTRACT WITH THE DEALER. PART OF YOUR CONTRACT INVOLVES FINANCING THE PURCHASE OF YOUR VEHICLE. IF YOU ARE FINANCING THIS VEHICLE AND THE DEALER INTENDS TO TRANSFER YOUR FINANCING TO A FINANCE PROVIDER SUCH AS A BANK, CREDIT UNION OR OTHER LENDER, YOUR VEHICLE PURCHASE DEPENDS ON THE FINANCE PROVIDER'S APPROVAL OF YOUR PROPOSED RETAIL INSTALLMENT SALES CONTRACT. IF YOUR RETAIL INSTALLMENT SALES CONTRACT IS APPROVED WITHOUT A CHANGE THAT INCREASES THE COST OR RISK TO YOU OR THE DEALER, YOUR PURCHASE CANNOT BE CANCELLED. IF YOUR RETAIL INSTALLMENT SALES CONTRACT IS NOT APPROVED, THE DEALER WILL NOTIFY YOU VERBALLY OR IN WRITING. YOU CAN THEN DECIDE TO PAY FOR THE VEHICLE IN SOME OTHER WAY OR YOU OR THE DEALER CAN CANCEL YOUR PURCHASE. IF THE SALE IS CANCELLED, YOU NEED TO RETURN THE VEHICLE TO THE DEALER WITHIN 24 HOURS OF VERBAL OR WRITTEN NOTICE IN THE SAME CONDITION IT WAS GIVEN TO YOU, EXCEPT FOR NORMAL WEAR AND TEAR. ANY DOWN PAYMENT OR TRADE-IN YOU GAVE THE DEALER WILL BE RETURNED TO YOU. IF YOU DO NOT RETURN THE VEHICLE WITHIN 24 HOURS OF VERBAL OR WRITTEN NOTICE OF CANCELLATION, THE DEALER MAY LOCATE THE VEHICLE AND TAKE IT BACK WITHOUT FURTHER NOTICE TO YOU AS LONG AS THE DEALER FOLLOWS THE LAW AND DOES NOT CAUSE A BREACH OF THE PEACE WHEN TAKING THE VEHICLE BACK. IF THE DEALER DOES NOT RETURN YOUR DOWN PAYMENT AND ANY TRADE-IN WHEN THE DEALER GETS THE VEHICLE BACK IN THE SAME CONDITION IT WAS GIVEN TO YOU, EXCEPT FOR NORMAL WEAR AND TEAR, THE DEALER MAY BE LIABLE TO YOU UNDER THE VIRGINIA CONSUMER PROTECTION ACT."

13. For sales of used motor vehicles, the disclosure required by § 46.2-1529.1.

Except for trailers and travel trailers, if the transaction does not include a policy of motor vehicle liability insurance, the seller shall stamp or mark on the face of the bill of sale in boldface letters no smaller than 18-point type the following words: "No Liability Insurance Included."

A completed buyer's order when signed by both buyer and seller may constitute a bill of sale.

B. The Board shall approve a buyer's order form and each dealer shall file with each original license application its buyer's order form, on which the processing fee amount is stated.

C. If a processing fee is charged, that fact and the amount of the processing fee shall be disclosed by the dealer. Disclosure shall be by placing a clear and conspicuous sign in the public sales area of the dealership. The sign shall be no smaller than eight and one-half inches by 11 inches and the print shall be no smaller than one-half inch, and in a form as approved by the Board.

D. Except for trailers, if the buyer's order is for a new motor vehicle that had accumulated, at the time of the sale, mileage in excess of 750 miles as a demonstrator or as a result of delivery to a prospective purchaser who never took title to the new motor vehicle and returned it, the vehicle may be sold as new, provided the dealer delivers this disclosure in writing on the buyer's order containing type of no smaller than 10 point or in a separate document containing only the disclosure in type of no smaller than 14 point: "Notice: This new motor vehicle has accumulated mileage in excess of 750 miles as the result of use as a demonstrator and/or as the result of delivery to a prior prospective purchaser who never took title to it and who returned it." When delivered as a separate document, this disclosure shall also contain the actual odometer reading for the vehicle and shall be signed by the purchaser.

E. The provisions of this section shall not apply to the sale or exchange of (i) a tractor truck, (ii) a truck having a gross vehicle weight rating of 16,000 pounds or more, or (iii) a semitrailer.

History.

1988, c. 865, § 46.1-547.5; 1989, c. 727; 1990, c. 900; 1993, c. 586; 1995, cc. 767, 816, 849; 2000, c. 116; 2003, c. 997; 2009, c. 783; 2010, cc. 292, 359, 459; 2011, c. 791; 2015, cc. 615, 682.

§ 46.2-1530.1. Purchaser's on-line systems filing fee; collection and remittance.

Any dealer licensed under this chapter who uses a Department-approved system of remote electronic filing of documentation necessary to obtain a certificate of title or registration for the purchaser of a vehicle shall collect from the purchaser and remit to the Department-approved electronic systems provider any fees charged for the transaction by the systems provider. Any such fee shall be listed separately on the buyer's order and identified as "on-line systems filing fee."

History.

2003, c. 997.

§ 46.2-1530.2. Dealer's manual transaction fee; use in special fund.

Every dealer licensed under this chapter shall pay to the Department a fee of $15 for each manual transaction in excess of 20 transactions per month. For purposes of this section, a "manual transaction" shall be any transaction that is not conducted electronically or at a location run by an agent authorized to act on behalf of the Department pursuant to subsection B of § 46.2-205. Such fee shall be in addition to any fees charged by the Department pursuant to this title for the processing of an application for a new certificate of title or registration of a vehicle. The dealer's manual transaction fee authorized by this section shall not apply to any transaction for which there is no Department-approved remote electronic filing option available. Any dealer who has been charged a dealer's manual transaction fee shall not collect such transaction fee from the purchaser of the vehicle. All fees collected under the provisions of this section shall be paid into the state treasury and set aside as a special fund to meet the expenses of the Department.

History.

2003, c. 997; 2006, c. 536.

§ 46.2-1531. Consignment vehicles; contract.

Any motor vehicle dealer offering a vehicle for sale on consignment shall have in his possession a consignment contract for the vehicle, executed and signed by the dealer and the consignor. The consignment contract shall include:

1. The complete name, address, and the telephone number of the owners.

2. The name, address, and dealer certificate number of the selling dealer.

3. A complete description of the vehicle on consignment, including the make, model year, vehicle identification number, and body style, except that trailers shall not be subject to the requirement for vehicle identification number or body style.

4. The beginning and termination dates of the contract.

5. The percentage of commission, the amount of the commission, or the net amount the owner is to receive, if the vehicle is sold.

6. Any fees for which the owner is responsible.

7. A disclosure of all unsatisfied liens on the vehicle and the location of the certificate of title to the vehicle.

8. A requirement that the motor vehicle pass a safety inspection prior to sale or, if the motor vehicle is found not to be in compliance with any safety inspection requirement after having been inspected, the dealer shall either take steps to bring it into compliance or furnish any buyer intending to use that vehicle on the public highways a written disclosure, prior to sale, that the vehicle did not pass a safety inspection.

Any dealer offering a vehicle for sale on consignment shall inform any prospective customer that the vehicle is on consignment.

Dealer license plates shall not be used to demonstrate a vehicle on consignment except on (i) motor vehicles with gross vehicle weight of 15,000 pounds or more, excluding RVs, (ii) vehicles on consignment from another licensed motor vehicle dealer, and (iii) vehicles on consignment from a nonprofit organization certified pursuant to subsection B of § 46.2-1508.1. The owner's license plates may be used if liability insurance coverage is in effect in the amounts prescribed by § 46.2-472.

No vehicles except motorcycles shall be sold on consignment by motorcycle dealers.

No vehicles except recreational vehicles shall be sold on consignment by recreational vehicle dealers.

No vehicles other than trailers shall be sold on consignment by trailer dealers.

The provisions of this section shall also apply to watercraft trailers and watercraft trailer dealers.

History.

1988, c. 865, § 46.1-547.6; 1989, cc. 187, 727; 1993, c. 289; 2000, c. 180; 2013, c. 247; 2015, c. 615.

§ 46.2-1532. Odometer disclosure; penalty.

Every motor vehicle dealer shall comply with all requirements of the Federal Odometer Act and § 46.2-629 by completing the appropriate odometer mileage statement form for each vehicle purchased, sold or transferred, or in any other way acquired or disposed of. Odometer disclosure statements shall be maintained by the dealer in a manner that permits systematic retrieval. Any person found guilty of violating any of the provisions of this section is guilty of a Class 1 misdemeanor.

The provisions of this section shall not apply to trailers, travel trailers, all-terrain vehicles, or off-road motorcycles.

History.

1988, c. 865, § 46.1-547.7; 1989, c. 727; 1995, cc. 767, 816; 2015, c. 615.

§ 46.2-1532.1. Certain disclosures required by manufacturers and distributors.

Motor vehicle manufacturers and distributors shall affix or cause to be affixed in a conspicuous place to every motor vehicle offered for sale as a new vehicle a statement disclosing the place of assembly or manufacture of the vehicle. For disclosures of place of assembly, the assembly plant shall be the same as that designated by the vehicle identification number.

The provisions of this section shall apply only to motor vehicles manufactured for the 1991 or subsequent model years.

History.

1990, c. 786; 1994, c. 72.

§ 46.2-1532.2. Certain disclosures required by motor vehicle manufacturers; motor vehicle recording devices.

A. A manufacturer of a new vehicle sold or leased in the Commonwealth that is equipped with one or more recording devices, as defined in § 46.2-1088.6, installed by the manufacturer shall disclose that fact in the owner's manual for the vehicle.

B. The provisions of this section shall apply only to vehicles manufactured for 2008 and subsequent model years.

History.

2006, cc. 851, 888, 889.

§ 46.2-1533. Business hours.

Each motor vehicle dealer shall be open for business a minimum of 20 hours per week, at least 10 of which shall be between the hours of 9:00 a.m. and 5:00 p.m. Monday through Friday, except that the Board, on written request by a dealer, may modify these requirements for good cause. The dealer's hours shall be posted and maintained conspicuously on or near the main entrance of each place of business.

Each dealer shall include his business hours on the original and every renewal application for a license, and changes to these hours shall be immediately filed with the Department.

History.

1988, c. 865, § 46.1-547.8; 1989, c. 727; 1995, cc. 767, 816; 2015, c. 615.

§ 46.2-1534. Signs.

Each retail motor vehicle dealer's place of business shall be identified by a permanent sign visible from the front of the business office so that the public may quickly and easily identify the dealership. The sign shall contain the dealer's trade name in letters no less than six inches in height unless otherwise restricted by law or contract.

History.

1988, c. 865, § 46.1-547.9; 1989, c. 727; 2015, c. 615.

§ 46.2-1535. Advertisements.

Unless the dealer is clearly identified by name, whenever any licensee places an advertisement in any newspaper or publication, the abbreviations "VA DLR," denoting a Virginia licensed dealer, shall appear therein.

History.

1988, c. 865, § 46.1-547.10; 1989, c. 727; 1991, c. 117.

§ 46.2-1536. Coercing purchaser to provide insurance coverage on motor vehicle; penalty.

It shall be unlawful for any dealer or salesperson or any employee of a dealer or representative of either to coerce or offer anything of value to any purchaser of a motor vehicle to provide any type of insurance coverage on the motor vehicle.

Nothing in this section shall prohibit a dealer from requiring that a retail customer obtain automobile physical damage insurance to protect collateral secured by an installment sales contract. Any person found guilty of violating any of the provisions of this section is guilty of a Class 1 misdemeanor.

Nothing in this section shall prohibit a dealer from informing the retail customer of the Commonwealth's insurance requirements.

History.

Code 1950, § 46-536; 1958, c. 541, § 46.1-548; 1988, c. 865; 1989, c. 727; 1995, cc. 767, 816; 2015, c. 615.

§ 46.2-1537. Prohibited solicitation and compensation.

It shall be unlawful for any motor vehicle dealer or salesperson licensed under this chapter, directly or indirectly, to solicit the sale of a motor vehicle through a pecuniarily interested person, or to pay, or cause to be paid, any commission or compensation in any form whatsoever to any person in connection with the sale of a motor vehicle, unless the person is duly licensed as a salesperson employed by the dealer. It shall also be unlawful for any motor vehicle dealer to compensate, in any form whatsoever, any person acting in the capacity of a salesperson as defined in § 46.2-1500 unless that person is licensed as required by this chapter.

History.

Code 1950, § 46-538; 1958, c. 541, § 46.1-549; 1988, c. 865; 1989, c. 727; 2006, c. 441.

§ 46.2-1538. Salesman selling for other than his employer prohibited.

It shall be unlawful for any motor vehicle salesman licensed under this chapter to sell or exchange or offer or attempt to sell or exchange any motor vehicle except for the licensed motor vehicle dealer by whom he is employed, or to offer, transfer, or assign any sale or exchange that he may have negotiated to any other dealer or salesman.

History.

Code 1950, § 46-539; 1958, c. 541, § 46.1-550; 1976, c. 362; 1989, c. 727.

§ 46.2-1539. Inspection of vehicles required; penalty.

No person required to be licensed as a dealer under this chapter shall sell at retail any motor vehicle which is intended by the buyer for use on the public highways, and which is required to comply with the safety inspection requirements provided in Article 21 (§ 46.2-1157 et seq.) of Chapter 10 unless between the time the vehicle comes into the possession of the dealer and the time it is sold at retail it is inspected by an official safety inspection station. In the event the vehicle is found not to be in compliance with all safety inspection requirements, the dealer shall either take steps to bring it into compliance or shall furnish any buyer intending it for use on the public highway a written disclosure, prior to sale, that the vehicle did not pass a safety inspection. Any person found guilty of violating any of the provisions of this section is guilty of a Class 1 misdemeanor.

The provisions of this section shall also apply to watercraft trailers and watercraft trailer dealers.

History.

1973, c. 420, § 46.1-550.3; 1978, c. 203; 1989, c. 727; 1995, cc. 767, 816; 2015, c. 615.

§ 46.2-1539.1. Safety inspections or disclosure required before sale of certain trailers; penalty.

Any trailer required by any provision of this title to undergo periodic safety inspections shall be inspected by an official inspection station between the time it comes into the possession of a retail dealer and the time the trailer is sold by the dealer or, in lieu of an inspection, the dealer shall present to the purchaser, prior to purchase of the trailer, a written itemization of all the trailer's deficiencies relative to applicable safety inspection requirements. The provisions of this section shall not apply to (i) sales of trailers or watercraft trailers by individuals not ordinarily engaged in the business of selling trailers or watercraft trailers or (ii) the retail sale of five or more trailers to the same buyer. Any person found guilty of violating any provision of this section is guilty of a Class 1 misdemeanor.

History.

2015, c. 615.

§ 46.2-1540. Inspections prior to sale not required of certain sellers.

The provisions of §§ 46.2-1158 and 46.2-1539 requiring inspection of any motor vehicle prior to sale at retail shall not apply to any person conducting a public auction for the sale of motor vehicles at retail, provided that the individual, firm, or business conducting the auction shall not have taken title to the vehicle, but is acting as an agent for the sale of the vehicle. Nor shall the provisions of §§ 46.2-1158 and 46.2-1539 requiring inspection of any motor vehicle prior to sale at retail apply to any new motor vehicle or vehicles sold on the basis of a special order placed by a dealer with a manufacturer outside the Commonwealth on behalf of a customer who is a nonresident of the Commonwealth and takes delivery outside the Commonwealth. Nor shall the provisions of §§ 46.2-1158 and 46.2-1539 requiring inspection of any trailer prior to sale at retail apply to the sale of five or more used trailers with a gross weight of more than 10,000 pounds to the same buyer, provided that the trailers have a valid safety inspection.

The provisions of this section shall also apply to watercraft trailers.

History.

1982, c. 321, § 46.1-550.3:1; 1984, c. 129; 1985, c. 235; 1989, c. 727; 2015, c. 615.

§ 46.2-1541: Repealed by Acts 1995, cc. 767 and 816.

§ 46.2-1542. Temporary registration.

A. Notwithstanding §§ 46.2-617 and 46.2-628, whenever a dealer licensed by the Board sells or conditionally sells and delivers to a purchaser a motor vehicle, the dealer may issue temporary license plates and a certificate of temporary registration. The temporary license plates and the certificates for temporary registration shall be obtained from the Commissioner or may be printed according to terms set by the Commissioner and may be issued if (i) the dealer has the title or the certificate of origin for the vehicle or (ii) is unable at the time of the sale to deliver to the purchaser the certificate of title or certificate of origin for the vehicle because the certificate of title or certificate of origin is lost or is being detained by another in possession or for any other reason beyond the dealer's control. The temporary registration certificate shall bear its date of issuance, the name and address of the purchaser, the identification number of the vehicle, the registration number to be used temporarily on the vehicle, the name of the state in which the vehicle is to be registered, the name and address of the person from whom the dealer acquired the vehicle, and whatever other information may be required by the Commissioner. A copy of the temporary registration certificate and a bona fide buyer's order shall be delivered to the purchaser and shall be in the possession of the purchaser at all times when operating the vehicle. One copy of the certificate shall be retained by the dealer, which copy may be retained in electronic format under terms set by the Commissioner, and shall be subject to inspection at any time by the Department's agents. The original of the certificate shall be forwarded by the dealer to the Department directly on issuance to the purchaser if the vehicle is to be titled outside the Commonwealth, along with the physical or electronic application for title. The issuance of a temporary certificate of registration to a purchaser pursuant to this section shall have the effect of vesting sufficient interest in the vehicle in the purchaser for the period that the certificate remains effective for purposes of allowing the purchaser (a) to obtain and provide insurance coverage for the vehicle, including insurance indemnifying the purchaser against liability or providing for recovery for damage to or loss of the vehicle and (b) to operate the vehicle as if the purchaser had full rights of ownership, all subject to cancellation by applicable law or agreement between the dealer and the purchaser prior to the time the dealer submits an application for title along with all required fees. If the dealer or purchaser exercises the statutory or contractual rights to cancel a purchaser's contract to buy a vehicle before application for title to the vehicle has been submitted to the Department in the name of the purchaser, the dealer shall have the right to possession of the vehicle without claim of possession by the purchaser within 24 hours of written or oral notice to the purchaser and without regard to the provision of Title 8.9A, provided the dealer's right to possession is enforced otherwise in accordance with law and without breach of the peace. In the event the dealer regains possession of the vehicle, in the same condition, normal wear and tear excepted, as delivered to the purchaser, the purchaser shall have the right to possession of any trade-in and return of any down payment, and if the dealer fails to return the trade-in and/or down payment the dealer may be held liable under § 59.1-200 of the Virginia Consumer Protection Act (§ 59.1-196), in addition to any other rights and remedies available by statute or contract.

B. A temporary certificate of registration issued by a dealer to a purchaser pursuant to this section shall expire when the certificate of title to the vehicle is issued by the Department in the name of the purchaser or vehicle ownership is transferred in accordance with § 46.2-603.1 and the permanent license plates have been affixed to the vehicle, but in no event shall any temporary certificate of registration issued under this section be effective for more than 30 days from the date of its issuance. In the event that the dealer fails to produce the old certificate of title or certificate of origin to the vehicle, fails to transfer vehicle ownership in accordance with § 46.2-603.1, or fails to apply for a replacement certificate of title pursuant to § 46.2-632, thereby preventing delivery to the Department or purchaser before the expiration of the temporary certificate of registration, the purchaser's temporary rights may terminate and the purchaser shall have the right to return the vehicle to the dealer and obtain a full refund of all payments made toward the purchase of the vehicle, provided the purchaser provides notice to the dealer of a decision to return the vehicle before issuance of a title for the vehicle by the Department, less any damage to the vehicle incurred while ownership was vested in the purchaser, and less a reasonable amount for use not to exceed one-half the amount allowed per mile by the Internal Revenue Service, as provided by regulation, revenue procedure, or revenue ruling promulgated pursuant to § 162 of the Internal Revenue Code, for use of a personal vehicle for business purposes.

C. Notwithstanding subsection B, if the dealer fails to deliver the certificate of title or certificate of origin to the purchaser or fails to transfer vehicle ownership in accordance with § 46.2-603.1 within 30 days, a second temporary certificate of registration may be issued. However, the dealer shall, not later than the expiration of the first temporary certificate, deliver to the Department an application for title, copy of the bill of sale, all required fees and a written statement of facts describing the dealer's efforts to secure the certificate of title or certificate of origin to the vehicle. On receipt of the title application with attachments as described herein, the Department shall record the purchaser's rights hereunder to the vehicle and may authorize the dealer to issue a second 30-day temporary certificate of registration. If the dealer does not produce the certificate of title or certificate of origin to the vehicle before the expiration of the second temporary certificate, the purchaser's rights to the vehicle under this section may terminate and he shall have the right to return the vehicle as provided in subsection B.

D. If the dealer is unable to produce the certificate of title or certificate of origin to the vehicle or transfer vehicle ownership in accordance with § 46.2-603.1 within the 60-day period from the date of issuance of the first temporary certificate, the Department may extend temporary registration for an additional period of up to 90 days, provided the dealer makes application in the format required by the Department. If the dealer does not produce the certificate of title or certificate of origin to the vehicle or transfer vehicle ownership in accordance with § 46.2-603.1 before the expiration of the additional 90-day period, the purchaser's rights hereunder to the vehicle may terminate and he shall have the right to return the vehicle as provided in subsection B.

E. The Commissioner, on determining that the provisions of this section or the directions of the Department are not being complied with by a dealer, may suspend, after a hearing, the right of the dealer to issue temporary certificates of registration.

The provisions of this section shall also apply to watercraft trailers and watercraft trailer dealers but shall not apply to all-terrain vehicles and off-road motorcycles.

History.

1988, c. 865, § 46.1-550.5:1; 1989, cc. 364, 727; 1995, cc. 767, 816; 2006, cc. 835, 897; 2009, c. 783; 2012, c. 650; 2015, c. 615.

§ 46.2-1543. Use of old license plates and registration number on another vehicle.

An owner who sells or transfers a registered motor vehicle may have the license plates and the registration number transferred to another vehicle titled in the owner's name according to the provisions of Chapter 6 (§ 46.2-600 et seq.), which is in a like vehicle category as specified in § 46.2-694 and requires an identical registration fee, on application to the Department accompanied by a fee of $2 or, if the other vehicle requires a greater registration fee than that for which the license plates were assigned, on the payment of a fee of $2 and the amount of the difference in registration fees between the two vehicles, all such transfers to be in accordance with the regulations of the Department. All fees collected under this section shall be paid by the Commissioner into the state treasury and shall be set aside as a special fund to be used to meet the expenses of the Department. For purposes of this section, a motor vehicle dealer licensed by the Board may be authorized to act as an agent of the Department for the purpose of receiving, processing, and approving applications from its customers for assignment of license plates and registration numbers pursuant to this section, using the forms and following the procedures prescribed by the Department. The Commissioner, on determining that the provisions of this section or the directions of the Department are not being complied with by a dealer, may suspend, after a hearing, the authority of the dealer to receive, process, and approve the assignment of license plates and registration numbers pursuant to this section.

The provisions of this section shall also apply to watercraft trailers and watercraft trailer dealers.

History.

1988, c. 865, § 46.1-550.5:1.1; 1989, c. 727; 1995, cc. 767, 816; 2015, c. 615.

§ 46.2-1544. Certificate of title for dealers; penalty.

Except as otherwise provided in this chapter, every dealer shall obtain, on the purchase of each vehicle, a certificate of title issued to the dealer or shall obtain an assignment or reassignment of a certificate of title for each vehicle purchased, except that a certificate of title shall not be required for any new vehicle to be sold as such. Any person found guilty of violating any of the provisions of this section is guilty of a Class 1 misdemeanor.

The provisions of this section shall also apply to watercraft trailers and watercraft trailer dealers.

History.

1988, c. 865, § 46.1-550.5:2; 1989, c. 727; 1995, cc. 767, 816; 2015, c. 615.

§ 46.2-1545. Termination of business.

No dealer, unless his license has been suspended, revoked, or canceled, shall cease business without a 30-day prior notification to the Department and the Board. On cessation of the business, the dealer shall immediately surrender to the Board the dealer's certificate of license, all salespersons' licenses, and any other materials furnished by the Board. The dealer shall also immediately surrender to the Department all dealer and temporary license plates, all fees and taxes collected, and any other materials furnished by the Department. After cessation of business, the former licensee shall continue to maintain and make available to the Department and the Board dealer records as set forth in this chapter.

The provisions of this section shall also apply to watercraft trailers and watercraft trailer dealers.

History.

1988, c. 865, § 46.1-550.5:3; 1989, c. 727; 1995, cc. 767, 816; 2015, c. 615.

ARTICLE 5.
DEALER'S LICENSE PLATES.

§ 46.2-1545.1. Watercraft trailer dealers and watercraft trailers.

For the purposes of this article:

"Dealer" and *"trailer dealer"* includes watercraft trailer dealers.

"Trailer" includes watercraft trailers.

History.
2015, c. 615.

§ 46.2-1545.2. Exclusion of all-terrain vehicles and off-road motorcycles.

Nothing in this article shall apply to all-terrain vehicles or off-road motorcycles.

History.
2015, c. 615.

§ 46.2-1546. Registration of dealers; fees.

Every manufacturer, distributor, or dealer, before he commences to operate vehicles in his inventory for sale or resale, shall apply to the Commissioner for a dealer's certificate of vehicle registration and license plates. For the purposes of this article, a vehicle is in inventory when it is owned by or assigned to a dealer and is offered and available for sale or resale. All dealer's certificates of vehicle registration and license plates issued under this section may, at the discretion of the Commissioner, be placed in a system of staggered issue to distribute the work of issuing vehicle registration certificates and license plates as uniformly as practicable throughout the year. Dealerships which sold fewer than twenty-five vehicles during the last twelve months of the preceding license year shall be eligible to receive no more than two dealer's license plates; dealerships which sold at least twenty-five but fewer than fifty vehicles during the last twelve months of the preceding license year shall be eligible to receive no more than four dealer's license plates. However, dealerships which sold fifty or more vehicles during their current license year may apply for additional license plates not to exceed four times the number of licensed salespersons employed by that dealership. Dealerships which sold fifty or more vehicles during the last twelve months of the preceding license year shall be eligible to receive a number of dealer's license plates not to exceed four times the number of licensed salespersons employed by that dealership. A new applicant for a dealership shall be eligible to receive a number of dealer's license plates not to exceed four times the number of licensed salespersons employed by that dealership. For the purposes of this article, a salesperson or employee shall be considered to be employed only if he (i) works for the dealership at least twenty-five hours each week on a regular basis and (ii) is compensated for this work. All salespersons' or employees' employment records shall be retained in accordance with the provisions of § 46.2-1529. A salesperson shall not be considered employed, within the meaning of this section, if he is an independent contractor as defined by the United States Internal Revenue Code. The fee for the issuance of dealer's license plates shall be determined by the Board, but not more than $30 per license plate; however, the fee for the first two dealer's plates shall not be less than twenty-four dollars and the fee for additional dealer's license plates shall not be less than ten dollars and forty cents each. For the first two dealer's license plates issued by the Department to a dealer, twenty-four dollars shall be deposited into the Transportation Trust Fund established pursuant to § 33.2-1524 and the remainder shall be deposited into the Motor Vehicle Dealer Fund. For each additional dealer's license plate issued to a dealer, ten dollars and forty cents shall be deposited into the Transportation Trust Fund and the remainder shall be deposited into the Motor Vehicle Dealer Fund.

History.
1988, c. 865, § 46.1-550.5:4; 1989, c. 727; 1990, c. 197; 1991, c. 712; 1995, cc. 767, 816.

§ 46.2-1547. License under this chapter prerequisite to receiving dealer's license plates; insurance required; Commissioner may revoke plates.

No motor vehicle manufacturer, distributor, or dealer, unless licensed under this chapter, shall be entitled to receive or maintain any dealer's license plates. It shall be unlawful to use or permit the use of any dealer's license plates for which there is no automobile liability insurance coverage or a certificate of self-insurance as defined in § 46.2-368 on any motor vehicle. No dealer's license plates shall be issued unless the dealer certifies to the Department that there is automobile liability insurance coverage or a certificate of self-insurance with respect to each dealer's license plate to be issued. Such automobile liability insurance or a certificate of self-insurance shall be maintained as to each dealer's license plate for so long as the registration for the dealer's license plate remains valid without regard to whether the plate is actually being used on a vehicle. If insurance or a certificate of self-insurance is not so maintained, the dealer's license plate shall be surrendered to the Department. The Commissioner shall revoke any dealer's license plate as to which there is no insurance or a certificate of self-insurance. The Commissioner may also revoke any dealer's license plate that has been used in any way not authorized by the provisions of this title.

The requirements relating to insurance in this article shall not apply to trailers or watercraft trailers.

History.

1988, c. 865, § 46.1-550.5:5; 1989, c. 727; 1990, c. 954; 1995, cc. 767, 816; 2015, c. 615.

§ 46.2-1548. Transferable license plates.

In lieu of registering each vehicle of a type described in this section, a manufacturer, distributor, or dealer owning and operating any motor vehicle on any highway may obtain a license plate bearing the legend provided in § 46.2-1549 from the Department, on application therefor on the prescribed form and on payment of the fees required by law. These license plates shall be attached to each vehicle as required by subsection A of § 46.2-711. Each plate shall bear a distinctive number, and the name of the Commonwealth, which may be abbreviated, together with the word "dealer" or a distinguishing symbol indicating that the plate is issued to a manufacturer, distributor, or dealer. Month and year decals indicating the date of expiration shall be affixed to each license plate. Any license plates so issued may, during the calendar year or years for which they have been issued, be transferred from one motor vehicle to another, used or operated by the manufacturer, distributor, or dealer, who shall keep a written record of the motor vehicle on which the dealer's license plates are used. This record shall be in a format approved by the Commissioner and shall be open to inspection by any law-enforcement officer or any officer or employee of the Department.

Display of a transferable manufacturer's, distributor's, or dealer's license plate or plates on a motor vehicle shall subject the vehicle to the requirements of §§ 46.2-1038 and 46.2-1056.

All manufacturer's, distributor's, and dealer's license plates shall be issued for a period of twelve consecutive months except, at the discretion of the Commissioner, the periods may be adjusted as may be necessary to distribute the registrations as equally as practicable on a monthly basis. The expiration date shall be the last day of the twelfth month of validity or the last day of the designated month. Every license plate shall be renewed annually on application by the owner and by payment of fees required by law, such renewal to take effect on the first day of the succeeding month.

The Commissioner may offer an optional multi-year license plate registration to manufacturers, distributors, and dealers licensed pursuant to this chapter provided that he has chosen to offer optional multi-year licensing to such persons pursuant to § 46.2-1521. When such option is offered and chosen by the licensee, all annual and twelve-month fees due at the time of registration shall be multiplied by the number of years or fraction thereof the licensee will be licensed pursuant to § 46.2-1521.

History.

1988, c. 865, § 46.1-550.5:6; 1989, c. 727; 1990, c. 197; 1991, c. 712; 1995, cc. 767, 816; 2008, cc. 304, 753.

§ 46.2-1549. Dealer's, manufacturer's, and distributor's license plates to distinguish between various types of dealers.

The Commissioner shall provide for the issuance of appropriate franchised or independent dealer's license plates. License plates for manufacturers shall bear the appropriate legend.

History.

1988, c. 865, § 46.1-550.5:7; 1989, c. 727; 1991, c. 712; 1995, cc. 767, 816; 2008, cc. 304, 753.

§ 46.2-1549.1. Dealer's promotional license plates.

In addition to any other license plate authorized by this article, the Commissioner may issue permanent or temporary dealer's promotional license plates to a dealer for use on vehicles held for sale or resale in the dealer's inventory. The design of these license plates shall be at the discretion of the Commissioner. These license plates shall be for use as authorized by the Commissioner. These plates shall be issued under the following conditions:

1. For each permanent promotional license plate issued or renewed, the Commissioner shall charge an annual fee of $100. Issuance of license plates pursuant to this subdivision shall be subject to the insurance requirement contained in § 46.2-1547. The Commissioner shall limit the validity of any license plate issued under this subdivision to no more than thirty consecutive days. Upon written request from the dealership, the Commissioner may consider an extended use of a license plate issued under this subdivision. The Commissioner's authorization for use of any license plate issued under this subdivision shall be kept in the vehicle on which the license plate is displayed until expiration of the authorization. These license plates shall be included in the number of dealer's license plates authorized under § 46.2-1546 and not in addition thereto.

2. The Commissioner shall limit the validity of each temporary promotional license plate to no more than fourteen consecutive days. For each request, the Commissioner shall charge a fee of twenty-five dollars for the first plate and two dollars for each additional plate. Issuance of license plates pursuant to this subdivision shall be subject to the insurance requirement contained in § 46.2-1547. The Commissioner's authorization for use of any license plate issued under this subdivision shall be kept in the vehicle on which the license plate is displayed until expiration of the authorization. License plates issued under this subdivision shall not be included in the number of dealer's license plates authorized under § 46.2-1546.

History.

1991, c. 712; 1994, 1st Sp. Sess., c. 6.

§ 46.2-1550. Use of dealer's and manufacturer's license plates, generally.

A. Dealer's license plates may be used on vehicles in the inventory of licensed motor vehicle manufacturers, distributors, and dealers in the Commonwealth when operated on the highways of Virginia by dealers or dealer-operators, their spouses, or employees of manufacturers, distributors, and dealers as permitted in this article, which shall include business, personal, and family purposes. Except as otherwise explicitly permitted in this article, it shall be unlawful for any dealer to cause or permit: (i) use of dealer's license plates on vehicles other than those held in inventory for sale or resale; (ii) dealer's license plates to be lent, leased, rented, or placed at the disposal of any persons other than those permitted by this article to use dealer's license plates; and (iii) use of dealer's license plates on any vehicle of a type for which their use is not authorized by this article. Manufacturer's license plates may be used on company vehicles as defined in § 46.2-602.2 operated on the highways of Virginia as provided in § 46.2-602.2 and as permitted by this article. It shall be unlawful for any dealer to cause or permit dealer's license plates to be used on:

1. Motor vehicles such as tow trucks, wrecking cranes, or other service motor vehicles;
2. Vehicles used to deliver or transport (i) other vehicles; (ii) portions of vehicles; (iii) vehicle components, parts, or accessories; or (iv) fuel;
3. Courtesy vehicles; or
4. Vehicles used in conjunction with any other business.

B. A dealer may permit his license plates to be used in the operation of a motor vehicle:

1. By any person whom the dealer reasonably believes to be a bona fide prospective purchaser who is either accompanied by a licensed salesperson or has the written permission of the dealer;
2. When the plates are being used by a customer on a vehicle owned by the dealer in whose repair shop the customer's vehicle is being repaired; or
3. By a person authorized by the dealer on a vehicle that is being driven to or from (i) a point of sale, (ii) an auction, (iii) a repair facility for the purpose of mechanical repairs, painting, or installation of parts or accessories, or (iv) a dealer exchange.

The dealer shall issue to the prospective purchaser, customer whose vehicle is being repaired, or other person authorized under subdivision 3 of this subsection, a certificate on forms provided by the Department, a copy of which shall be retained by the dealer and open at all times to the inspection of the Commissioner or any of the officers or agents of the Department. The certificate shall be in the immediate possession of the person operating or authorized to operate the vehicle. The certificate shall entitle a person to operate with dealer's license plates under (i) subdivision 1 or 2 of this subsection for a specific period of no more than five days or (ii) subdivision 3 of this subsection for no more than twenty-four hours. No more than two certificates may be issued by a dealer to the same person under subdivision 1 or 2 of this subsection for successive periods.

History.

1988, c. 865, § 46.1-550.5:8; 1989, c. 727; 1991, c. 712; 1993, c. 504; 1995, cc. 767, 816; 1998, c. 827; 2008, cc. 304, 753.

§ 46.2-1550.1. Use of dealer's license plates and temporary transport plates on certain vehicles.

Notwithstanding the provisions of § 46.2-1550, dealer's license plates or dealer's temporary transport plates may be used on vehicles being transported (i) from a motor vehicle auction or other point of purchase or sale, (ii) between properties owned or controlled by the same dealership, or (iii) for repairs, painting, or installation of parts or accessories. This section shall also apply to return trips by such vehicles.

History.

1991, c. 712.

§ 46.2-1550.2. Issuance and use of temporary transport plates, generally.

The Department, subject to the limitations and conditions set forth in this section and the insurance requirements contained in § 46.2-1547, may provide for the issuance of temporary transport plates designed by the Department to any dealer licensed under this chapter who applies for at least 10 plates and who encloses with his application a fee of $1.50 for each plate. The application shall be made on a form prescribed and furnished by the Department. Temporary transport plates may be used for those purposes outlined in § 46.2-1550.1. Every dealer who has applied for temporary transport plates shall maintain a record of (i) all temporary transport plates delivered to him, (ii) all temporary transport plates issued by him, and (iii) any other information pertaining to the receipt or the issuance of temporary transport plates which may be required by the Department.

Every dealer who issues temporary transport plates shall insert clearly and indelibly on the face of the temporary transport plates the name of the issuing dealer, the date of issuance and expiration, and the make and identification number of the vehicle for which issued.

The dealer shall issue to the operator of the specified vehicle a certificate on forms provided by the Department, a copy of which shall be retained by the dealer and open at all times to the inspection of the Commissioner or any of the officers or agents of the Department. The certificate shall be in the immediate possession of the person operating or authorized to operate the vehicle. The certificate shall entitle the person to operate with the dealer's temporary transport plate for a period of no more than five days. Temporary transport plates may also be used by the dealer to demonstrate types of vehicles taken in trade but for which he has not been issued dealer's license plates.

History.
1991, c. 712; 2012, cc. 215, 222.

§ 46.2-1550.3. Alternative print-on-demand program for issuance of temporary transport license plates to dealers and vehicle owners.

A. Notwithstanding the provisions of § 46.2-1550.2, the Department may develop and implement procedures and requirements necessary for delivery of temporary transport license plates to dealers and issuance of temporary transport license plates by dealers to vehicle owners, using print-on-demand technology.

B. In the event the Department implements a print-on-demand temporary license plate program pursuant to this section, all dealers licensed on or after the effective date of the program shall be required to purchase and issue only print-on-demand temporary license plates.

C. The Commissioner shall not impose a requirement relating to the minimum number of sets of temporary plates that must be purchased by a dealer pursuant to a print-on-demand temporary license plate program implemented under this section.

D. Except as otherwise provided in this section, temporary license plates delivered and issued pursuant to this section shall be subject to all conditions and limitations set forth in this article.

History.
2011, c. 786.

§ 46.2-1551. Use of dealer's license plates or temporary transport plates on certain vehicles traveling from one establishment to another for purpose of having special equipment installed.

Notwithstanding the provisions of § 46.2-1550, dealer's license plates or temporary transport plates may be used on tractor trucks or trucks for the purpose of delivering these vehicles to another establishment for the purpose of having a fifth wheel, body, or any special permanently mounted equipment installed on the vehicles, and for the purpose of returning the vehicle to the dealer whose plates are attached to the tractor truck or truck whether or not the title to the vehicle has been retained by the dealer, and no other license, permit, warrant, exemption card, or classification plate from any other agency of the Commonwealth shall be required under these circumstances. No other statute or regulation in conflict with the provisions of this section shall be applicable to the extent of the conflict. This section shall also apply to trips into the Commonwealth by a vehicle owned and operated outside the Commonwealth to an establishment within the Commonwealth and to the return trip of that vehicle from the Commonwealth to another state, provided the operator of the vehicle carries on his person when so operating a bill of sale for the fifth wheel, body, or special equipment.

History.
1988, c. 865, § 46.1-550.5:9; 1989, c. 727; 1991, c. 712; 1995, cc. 767, 816.

§ 46.2-1552. Use of dealer's license plates on newly purchased vehicles.

Notwithstanding the provisions of § 46.2-1550, any dealer who sells and delivers to a purchaser a motor vehicle at a time when the main offices of the Department, its branch offices, or offices of its local agents, are not open for business and the purchaser is therefore unable to register the vehicle, may permit the purchaser to use, for a period not exceeding five days, on the newly purchased vehicle, license plates which have been issued to the dealer, provided that, at the time of the purchase, the dealer executes in duplicate, on forms provided by the Commissioner, a certificate bearing the date of issuance, the name and address of the purchaser, the identification number of the vehicle, the registration number to be used temporarily on the vehicle, the name of the state in which the vehicle is to be registered, and whatever other information may be required by the Commissioner. The original of the certificate and a bona fide bill of sale shall be delivered to the purchaser and shall be in the possession of the purchaser at all times when operating the vehicle under dealer plates. One copy of the certificate shall be retained by the dealer, filed by him, and shall be subject to inspection at any time by the Department's agents. If the vehicle is to be titled and registered in the Commonwealth, application for title and registration shall be made by the purchaser on the first business day following issuance of the certificate and a copy of the certificate shall accompany the applications.

License plates temporarily used by the purchaser shall be returned to the dealer by the purchaser not later than five days after the issuance of the certificate.

History.
1988, c. 865, § 46.1-550.5:10; 1989, c. 727; 1991, c. 712.

§ 46.2-1552.1. Use of dealer's license plates or temporary transport plates for demonstrating trucks or tractor trucks.

Notwithstanding any other provision of this chapter, dealer's license plates issued under § 46.2-1548 and temporary transport plates issued under § 46.2-1550.2 may be used on trucks or tractor trucks in the inventory of licensed motor vehicle dealers for the purpose of demonstrating trucks or tractor trucks in the inventory of a licensed dealer by a bona fide prospective purchaser. Any such demonstration vehicle may be loaded in a manner consistent with the prospective purchaser's usual commercial activities. Such use of dealer's license plates on demonstration trucks or tractor trucks in a prospective purchaser's commercial activities shall be for not more than three days or 750 miles, whichever comes first, and shall not thereafter be used on the same truck or tractor truck by the same prospective purchaser for a period of sixty days. The dealer shall issue to the prospective purchaser, or to his authorized agent, a certificate on forms provided by the Department, a copy of which shall be retained by the dealer and open at all times to the inspection of the Commissioner or any of the officers or agents of the Department. The certificate shall be in the immediate possession of the person operating or authorized to operate the truck or tractor truck. The certificate shall entitle the person to operate with the dealer's license plate or temporary transport plate for a specific period of no more than three days. This certificate shall be in lieu of any other registration, permit, and motor fuel road tax identification otherwise required by law.

History.
1993, c. 503; 1997, c. 283.

§ 46.2-1553. Operation without license plate prohibited.

No manufacturer or distributor of or dealer in motor vehicles shall cause or permit any motor vehicle owned by him to be operated or moved on a public highway without there being displayed on the motor vehicle a license plate or plates issued to him, either under § 46.2-711 or under § 46.2-1548, except as otherwise authorized in §§ 46.2-733, 46.2-1554 and 46.2-1555.

History.
1988, c. 865, § 46.1-550.5:11; 1989, c. 727; 1995, cc. 767, 816.

§ 46.2-1554. Movement by manufacturer to place of shipment or delivery.

Any manufacturer of motor vehicles may operate or move or cause to be moved or operated on the highways for a distance of no more than twenty-five miles motor vehicles from the factory where manufactured or assembled to a railway depot, vessel, or place of shipment or delivery, without registering them and without license plates attached thereto, under a written permit first obtained from the local law-enforcement authorities having jurisdiction over the highways and on displaying in plain sight on each motor vehicle a placard bearing the name and address of the manufacturer authorizing or directing the movement.

History.
1988, c. 865, § 46.1-550.5:12; 1989, c. 727; 1995, cc. 767, 816.

§ 46.2-1555. Movement by dealers to salesrooms.

Any dealer in motor vehicles may operate or move, or cause to be operated or moved, any motor vehicle on the highways for a distance of no more than twenty-five miles from a vessel, railway depot, warehouse, or any place of shipment or from a factory where manufactured or assembled to a salesroom, warehouse, or place of shipment or transshipment without registering them and without license plates attached thereto, under a written permit first obtained from the local law-enforcement authorities having jurisdiction over the highways and on displaying in plain sight on each motor vehicle a placard bearing the name and address of the dealer authorizing or directing the movement.

History.
1988, c. 865, § 46.1-550.5:13; 1989, c. 727; 1995, cc. 767, 816.

§ 46.2-1556. Operation under foreign dealer's license.

It shall be unlawful, except as provided for by reciprocal agreement, for any person to operate a motor vehicle or for the owner thereof to permit a motor vehicle to be operated in the Commonwealth on a foreign dealer's license, unless the operation of the motor vehicle on the license is specifically authorized by the Commissioner.

History.
1988, c. 865, § 46.1-550.5:14; 1989, c. 727; 1995, cc. 767, 816.

§ 46.2-1557. Use of certain foreign-registered motor vehicles in driver education programs.

Dealer's license plates may be displayed on motor vehicles used by Virginia school systems in connection with driver education programs approved by the State Board of Education. In the event of such use of a motor vehicle or vehicles by a school system, any dealer, his employees and agents furnishing the motor vehicle or vehicles shall be immune from liability in any suit, claim, action, or cause of action, including but not limited to, actions or claims for injury to persons or property arising out of such use. Nothing in this section shall authorize the sale of any motor vehicle or vehicles so used in such driver education program as a demonstrator vehicle.

Notwithstanding the provisions of §§ 46.2-1500 and 46.2-1556, school divisions either (i) bordering on Kentucky, Maryland, North Carolina, Tennessee, or West Virginia, or (ii) located in Accomack or

Northampton County may use motor vehicles bearing foreign motor vehicle dealer's license plates in connection with their driver education programs.

History.
1988, c. 865, §§ 46.1-550.5:8, 46.1-550.5:15; 1989, c. 727.

§ 46.2-1557.1. Removal of plates by Department of Motor Vehicles investigators; cancellation; reissuance.

If any Department of Motor Vehicles investigator finds that a vehicle bearing license plates or temporary transport plates issued under this article is being operated in a manner inconsistent with (i) the requirements of this article or (ii) the Commissioner's authorization provided for in this article, the Department of Motor Vehicles investigator may remove the license plate for cancellation. Once a license plate has been cancelled, the dealership may reapply for the license plate. Reissuance of the license plate shall be subject to the approval of the Commissioner and the payment of the fee prescribed for issuance of license plates under this article.

History.
1991, c. 712.

§ 46.2-1557.2. Penalties for violations of article; service of summons.

Notwithstanding § 46.2-1507, any person violating any of the provisions of this article shall be guilty of a Class 3 misdemeanor. Any summons issued for any violation of any provision of this article relating to use or misuse of dealer's license plates shall be served upon the dealership to whom the plates were issued or to the person expressly permitting the unlawful use, or upon the operator of the motor vehicle if the plates are used contrary to the use authorized by the certificate issued pursuant to § 46.2-1550.

History.
1993, c. 504.

ARTICLE 6.

ISSUANCE OF TEMPORARY LICENSE PLATES BY DEALERS.

§ 46.2-1557.3. Exclusion of all-terrain vehicles and off-road motorcycles.

Nothing in this article shall apply to all-terrain vehicles or off-road motorcycles.

History.
2015, c. 615.

§ 46.2-1557.4. Watercraft trailer dealers and watercraft trailers.

For the purposes of this article:

"Dealer" and *"trailer dealer"* includes watercraft trailer dealers.

"Trailer" includes watercraft trailers.

History.
2015, c. 615.

§ 46.2-1558. Issuance of temporary license plates to dealers and vehicle owners.

The Department may, subject to the limitations and conditions set forth in this article, deliver temporary license plates designed by the Department to any dealer licensed under this chapter who applies for at least 10 sets of plates and who encloses with his application a fee of $3 for each set applied for. The application shall be made on a form prescribed and furnished by the Department. Dealers, subject to the limitations and conditions set forth in this article, may issue temporary license plates to owners of vehicles. The owners shall comply with the provisions of this article and §§ 46.2-705, 46.2-706 and 46.2-707. Dealers issuing temporary license plates may do so free of charge, but if they charge a fee for issuing temporary plates, the fee shall be no more than the fee charged the dealer by the Department under this section.

Display of a temporary license plate or plates on a motor vehicle shall subject the vehicle to the requirements of §§ 46.2-1038 and 46.2-1056.

History.
1988, c. 865, § 46.1-550.5:16; 1989, c. 727; 1992, c. 631; 2012, cc. 215, 222; 2015, c. 615.

§ 46.2-1558.1. Alternative print-on-demand program for issuance of temporary license plates to dealers and vehicle owners.

A. Notwithstanding the provisions of § 46.2-1558, the Department may develop and implement procedures and requirements necessary for delivery of temporary license plates to dealers and issuance of temporary license plates by dealers to vehicle owners, using print-on-demand technology.

B. In the event the Department implements a print-on-demand temporary license plate program pursuant to this section, all dealers licensed on or after the effective date of the program shall be required to purchase and issue only print-on-demand temporary license plates.

C. The Commissioner shall not impose a requirement relating to the minimum number of sets of temporary plates that must be purchased by a dealer pursuant to a print-on-demand temporary license plate program implemented under this section.

D. Except as otherwise provided in this section, temporary license plates delivered and issued pursuant to this section shall be subject to all conditions and limitations set forth in this article.

History.
2006, c. 545.

§ 46.2-1559. Records to be kept by dealers; inspection.

Every dealer who has applied for temporary license plates shall maintain a permanent record of (i) all temporary license plates delivered to him, (ii) all temporary license plates issued by him, and (iii) any other information pertaining to the receipt or the issuance of temporary license plates which may be required by the Department. Each record shall be kept for at least one year from the date of entry. Every dealer shall allow full access to these records during regular business hours to authorized representatives of the Department and to law-enforcement officers.

History.
1988, c. 865, § 46.1-550.5:17; 1989, c. 727.

§ 46.2-1560. Application for temporary license plate.

No dealer shall issue a temporary license plate except on written application by the person entitled to receive the license plate, which application shall be forwarded by the dealer to the Department as provided in § 46.2-1542.

History.
1988, c. 865, § 46.1-550.5:18; 1989, c. 727.

§ 46.2-1561. To whom temporary plates shall not be issued; dealer to forward application for current titling and registration; misstatements and false information.

No dealer shall issue, assign, transfer, or deliver temporary license plates to other than the bona fide purchaser or owner of a vehicle, whether or not the vehicle is to be registered in the Commonwealth. If the vehicle is to be registered in the Commonwealth, the dealer shall submit to the Department a written application for the current titling and registration of the purchased vehicle, accompanied by the prescribed fees. Any dealer who issues temporary license plates to a purchaser who fails or declines to request that his application be forwarded promptly to the Department forthwith shall notify the Department of the issuance in the manner provided in this article. No dealer shall lend temporary license plates to any person for use on any vehicle. If the dealer does not have in his possession the certificate of title or certificate of origin he may issue temporary license plates even though the purchaser has current license plates to be transferred. The dealer shall present the title or certificate of origin to the customer or transfer vehicle ownership in accordance with § 46.2-603.1 within 30 days of purchase and after this transaction is completed the customer shall transfer his current license plates to the vehicle. If the title or certificate of origin cannot be produced for a vehicle or the dealer fails to transfer vehicle ownership in accordance with § 46.2-603.1 within 30 days, a second set of temporary license plates may be issued provided that a temporary certificate of registration is issued as provided in § 46.2-1542. It shall be unlawful for any person to issue any temporary license plates containing any misstatement of fact, or for any person issuing or using temporary license plates knowingly to insert any false information on their face.

History.
1988, c. 865, § 46.1-550.5:19; 1989, c. 727; 2005, c. 558; 2012, c. 650; 2015, c. 615.

§ 46.2-1562. Dealer to insert his name, date of issuance and expiration, make and identification number of vehicle.

Every dealer who issues temporary license plates shall insert clearly and indelibly on the face of each temporary license plate the name of the issuing dealer, the date of issuance and expiration, and the make and identification number of the vehicle for which issued.

History.
1988, c. 865, § 46.1-550.5:20; 1989, c. 727.

§ 46.2-1563. Suspension of right of dealer to issue.

The Commissioner, on determining that the provisions of this chapter or the directions of the Department are not being complied with by any dealer, may suspend, after a hearing, the right of a dealer to issue temporary license plates.

History.
1988, c. 865, § 46.1-550.5:21; 1989, c. 727.

§ 46.2-1564. Plates to be destroyed on expiration.

Every person to whom temporary license plates have been issued shall destroy them on the thirtieth day after issue or immediately on receipt of the permanent license plates from the Department, whichever occurs first.

History.
1988, c. 865, § 46.1-550.5:22; 1989, c. 727.

§ 46.2-1565. When plates to expire; refunds or credit.

Temporary license plates shall expire on the receipt of the permanent license plates from the Department, or on the rescission of a contract to purchase a motor vehicle, or on the expiration of thirty days from the date of issuance, whichever occurs first. No refund or credit of fees paid by dealers to the Department for temporary license plates shall be allowed, except that when the Department discontinues the right of a dealer to issue temporary license plates, the dealer, on returning temporary license plates to the Department, may receive a refund or a credit for them.

History.

1988, c. 865, § 46.1-550.5:23; 1989, c. 727.

§ 46.2-1565.1. Penalties.

Any person violating any of the provisions of this article is guilty of a Class 1 misdemeanor. Any summons issued for any violation of any provision of this article relating to use or misuse of temporary license plates shall be served upon the dealership to whom the plates were issued or to the person expressly permitting the unlawful use, or upon the operator of the motor vehicle if the plates are used contrary to the use authorized pursuant to § 46.2-1561.

History.

1995, cc. 767, 816; 2015, c. 615.

ARTICLE 7.
FRANCHISES.

§ 46.2-1566. Filing of franchises.

A. It shall be the responsibility of each motor vehicle manufacturer, factory branch, distributor, distributor branch, or subsidiary thereof to file with the Commissioner by certified mail a true copy of each new, amended, modified, or different form or addendum offered to more than one dealer which affects the rights, responsibilities, or obligations of the parties of a franchise or sales, service, or sales and service agreement to be offered to a motor vehicle dealer or prospective motor vehicle dealer in the Commonwealth no later than 60 days prior to the date the franchise or sales agreement is offered. In no event shall a new, amended, modified, or different form of franchise or sales, service, or sales and service agreement be offered a motor vehicle dealer in the Commonwealth until the form has been determined by the Commissioner as not containing terms inconsistent with the provisions of this chapter. At the time a filing is made with the Commissioner pursuant to this section, the manufacturer, factory branch, distributor, distributor branch, or subsidiary shall also give written notice together with a copy of the papers so filed to the affected dealer or dealers.

B. The Department shall inform the manufacturer, factory branch, distributor, distributor branch, or subsidiary and the dealer or dealers or other parties named in the agreement of a preliminary recommendation as to the consistency of the agreement with the provisions of this chapter. If any of the parties involved have comments on the preliminary recommendation, they must be submitted to the Commissioner within 30 days of receiving the preliminary recommendation. The Commissioner shall render his decision within 15 days of receiving comments from the parties involved. If the Commissioner does not receive comments within the 30-day time period, he shall make the final determination as to the consistency of the agreement with the provisions of this chapter.

C. Any form or addendum that is not filed as required by this section may not be the basis for (i) any reduction in compensation due to a dealer from the franchisor, (ii) any franchisor demand or requirement by which a dealer must abide, or (iii) any penalty or detriment a franchisor imposes or attempts to impose on a motor vehicle dealer. This section shall not apply to any dealer program or dealer incentive that is not inconsistent with any form or addendum already on file by the manufacturer with the state or that expires within 12 months of its start date, or the continuation, renewal, or modification of any dealer program or dealer incentive that was in place as of July 1, 2015. This section shall not apply to any consumer program or consumer incentive, including discount pricing programs.

History.

1988, c. 865, § 46.1-550.5:24; 1989, c. 727; 1994, c. 537; 1995, cc. 767, 816; 2015, c. 236.

§ 46.2-1567. Exemption of franchises from Retail Franchising Act.

Franchises subject to the provisions of this chapter shall not be subject to any requirement contained in Chapter 8 (§ 13.1-557 et seq.) of Title 13.1.

History.

1988, c. 865, § 46.1-550.5:25; 1989, c. 727.

§ 46.2-1568. Coercion of retail dealer by manufacturer or distributor with respect to retail installment sales contracts, extended service contracts or extended maintenance plans, financing, or leasing prohibited; penalty.

A. It shall be unlawful for any manufacturer or distributor, or any officer, agent, representative, or affiliate of either to coerce or attempt to coerce any retail motor vehicle dealer or prospective retail motor vehicle dealer in the Commonwealth to (i) offer to sell or sell any extended service contract or extended maintenance plan offered, sold, backed by, or sponsored by the manufacturer or distributor or affiliate of either or (ii) sell, assign, or transfer any retail installment sales contract or lease obtained by the dealer in connection with the sale or lease by him in the Commonwealth of motor vehicles manufactured or sold by the manufacturer or distributor, to a specified finance company or class of finance companies, affiliate, leasing company or class of leasing companies, or any other specified persons by any of the following:

1. By any statement, suggestion, promise, or threat that the manufacturer or distributor will in any manner benefit or injure the dealer, whether the statement, suggestion, threat, or promise is express or implied or made directly or indirectly.

2. By any act that will benefit or injure the dealer.

3. By any contract, or any express or implied offer of contract, made directly or indirectly to the dealer, for handling the motor vehicle on the condition that the dealer shall offer to sell or sell any extended service contract or extended maintenance plan offered, sold, backed by, or sponsored by the manufacturer or distributor or that the dealer sell, assign, or transfer his retail installment sales contract on or lease of the vehicle, in the Commonwealth, to a specified finance company or class of finance companies, leasing company or class of leasing companies, or any other specified person.

4. By any express or implied statement or representation made directly or indirectly that the dealer is under any obligation whatsoever to offer to sell or sell any extended service contract or extended maintenance plan offered, sold, backed by, or sponsored by the manufacturer or distributor or to sell, assign, or transfer any of his retail sales contracts or leases in the Commonwealth on motor vehicles manufactured or sold by the manufacturer or distributor to a finance company or class of finance companies, leasing company or class of leasing companies, or other specified person, because of any relationship or affiliation between the manufacturer or distributor and the finance company or companies, leasing company or leasing companies, or the specified person or persons.

B. Any such statements, threats, promises, acts, contracts, or offers of contracts, when their effect may be to lessen or eliminate competition or tend to create a monopoly, are declared unfair trade practices and unfair methods of competition and are prohibited.

C. To further avoid any acts or practices, the effect of which may be to lessen or eliminate competition, it shall be unlawful for any manufacturer or distributor, or any officer, agent, or representative thereof, or any person or company affiliated therewith, to condition the provision of lead information to a dealer upon the agreement of the dealer to sell or lease a vehicle to the prospective customer only if the financing or leasing connected with the transaction is effected through a specified finance company or class of finance companies or leasing company or class of leasing companies. For the purposes of this section, "lead information" means information concerning a prospective customer who contacts or is contacted by the manufacturer or distributor or any person or company affiliated therewith concerning the manufacturer's or distributor's products. The provisions of this subsection, however, shall not prohibit a manufacturer or distributor from so conditioning the provision of lead information concerning any prospective customer who qualifies for any manufacturer-sponsored or distributor-sponsored factory employee, factory retiree, or factory vendor new vehicle purchase program.

D. It shall be unlawful for any manufacturer or distributor or any affiliate thereof to coerce or require a dealer that is a franchisee of the manufacturer or distributor to sell products sponsored, sold, or offered by the manufacturer, distributor, or affiliate in connection with sales of vehicles whether or not in connection with any retail installment sales contract or lease; however, this subsection shall not apply to used motor vehicles sold under a manufacturer used vehicle certification program. For purposes of this section, the refusal by an affiliate of a manufacturer or distributor to accept assignment of a retail installment sales contract or lease solely because it includes a product in connection with the sale of the vehicle not sponsored, sold, or offered by the manufacturer or distributor, or any affiliate thereof, shall be unlawful; but an affiliate of a manufacturer or distributor may establish standards for products in connection with a sale of a vehicle to be included in retail installment sales contracts or leases it will accept, provided the standards, including the establishment of maximum prices for products, are equally enforceable and enforced with respect to products in connection with the sale of a vehicle sponsored, sold, or offered by the manufacturer, distributor, or affiliate and products that are not. Nothing in this section prohibits a manufacturer, distributor, or affiliate from offering dealer or consumer incentive programs directly related to the sale of products sponsored, sold, or offered by the manufacturer, distributor, or affiliate whether or not in connection with any retail installment sales contract or lease. A dealer that chooses not to participate in these programs shall not be penalized as a result. Non-payment of the incentive due to non-participation in the incentive programs directly related to the sale of products sponsored, sold, or offered by the manufacturer, distributor, or affiliate by the dealer shall not qualify as a penalty.

E. Any person aggrieved by an action prohibited by this section may seek a hearing, pursuant to § 46.2-1573, against any manufacturer or distributor licensed under this title.

F. Nothing contained in this section shall prohibit a manufacturer or distributor from offering or providing incentive benefits or bonus programs to a retail motor vehicle dealer or prospective retail motor vehicle dealer in the Commonwealth who makes the voluntary decision to offer to sell or sell any extended service contract or extended maintenance plan offered, sold, backed, or sponsored by the manufacturer or distributor or to sell, assign, or transfer any retail installment sale or lease by him in the Commonwealth of motor vehicles manufactured or sold by the manufacturer or distributor to a specified finance company or leasing company controlled by or affiliated with the manufacturer or distributor.

History.

1988, c. 865, § 46.1-550.5:26; 1989, c. 727; 1995, cc. 767, 816; 2001, c. 149; 2005, c. 906; 2015, c. 236.

§ 46.2-1568.1. Discrimination by manufacturers or distributors prohibited.

No manufacturer or distributor, or any officer, agent, or representative of either, shall discriminate against a dealer holding a franchise of the manufacturer or distributor in favor of another dealer or other dealers of the same line-make in the Commonwealth by:

1. Selling or offering to sell a new motor vehicle to a dealer at a lower actual price, including the price for vehicle transportation, than the actual price at which the same model similarly equipped is offered to or is available to another dealer in the Commonwealth during a similar time period;

2. Using a promotional program or device or an incentive, payment, or other benefit, whether paid at the time of the sale of the new motor vehicle to the dealer or later, that results in the sale or offer to sell a new motor vehicle to a dealer at a lower price, including the price for vehicle transportation, than the price at which the same model similarly equipped is offered or is available to another dealer in the Commonwealth during a similar time period. This subdivision shall not prohibit a promotional or incentive program that is functionally available to competing dealers of the same line-make in the Commonwealth on substantially comparable terms;

3. Providing lead information to a dealer when the address provided by the prospective customer (or the preferred contact address, if more than one address is provided) is in the relevant market area of another dealer or other dealers of the same line-make without providing or offering to provide the same information on equal terms to the dealer or dealers of the same line-make in whose relevant market area the prospective customer's address (or preferred contact address, if more than one address is provided) is located. The foregoing requirement of this subdivision shall not apply if (i) the lead information is generated under any program administered by an entity in which one or more dealers, together with the manufacturer or distributor, hold an ownership interest, where the program is designed to facilitate sales of motor vehicles through dealers participating in the program, provided that ownership or the right to participate in the entity has been made available to all dealers of the same line-make in the Commonwealth on substantially comparable terms or (ii) the prospective customer requests that the lead information be forwarded to a particular dealer or (iii) the lead information is the result of the prospective customer's request for a specific type of vehicle when the specific type of vehicle in the color and with the equipment desired by the prospective customer is not available at a dealer or dealers of the same line-make in whose relevant market area the prospective customer's address (or preferred contact address, if more than one address is provided) is located. For purposes of this subsection, "lead information" is information concerning a prospective customer (i) who contacts the manufacturer or distributor in response to an advertisement, a solicitation, or a message broadcast, distributed, or made available to the public by the manufacturer or distributor or (ii) who is contacted by the manufacturer or distributor, and (iii) such contact is in relation to the sale of, service on, or parts or accessories for new or used motor vehicles. This subdivision shall not be construed to permit provision of or access to customer information that is otherwise protected from disclosure by law or by agreement between a dealer and a manufacturer or distributor.

History.

2001, cc. 817, 849.

§ 46.2-1569. Other coercion of dealers; transfer, grant, succession to and cancellation of dealer franchises; delivery of vehicles, parts, and accessories.

Notwithstanding the terms of any franchise agreement, it shall be unlawful for any manufacturer, factory branch, distributor, distributor branch, or affiliate, or any field representative, officer, agent, or their representatives to do any of the following. It shall further be unlawful for any manufacturer, factory branch, distributor, distributor branch, or any field representative, officer, agent, or their representatives to engage in conduct prohibited under this section through an affiliate.

1. To coerce or attempt to coerce any dealer to accept delivery of any motor vehicle or vehicles, parts or accessories therefor, or any other commodities, which have not been ordered by the dealer.

2. To coerce or attempt to coerce any dealer to enter into an agreement with the manufacturer, factory branch, distributor, or distributor branch, or representative thereof by threat to take or by taking any action in violation of the chapter, or by any other act unfair or injurious to the dealer. If a manufacturer, factory branch, distributor, or distributor branch conditions the grant of a new franchise to a dealer on the dealer's consent (i) to provide a site control agreement as defined in subdivision 10, (ii) to provide a written agreement containing an option to purchase the franchise of the dealer, provided, however, that agreements pursuant to § 46.2-1569.1 shall be permitted, or (iii) to provide a termination agreement to be held by the manufacturer,

factory branch, distributor, or distributor branch for subsequent use, it shall be considered coercion and an act that is unfair and injurious to the dealer; provided, however, that the provisions of § 46.2-1572.3 related to the good faith settlement of disputes shall apply to the agreements described in clauses (i), (ii), and (iii) of this subdivision, mutatis mutandis. This subdivision shall not apply to any agreement the enforcement of which is subject to the jurisdiction of a United States Bankruptcy Court.

2a. To coerce or attempt to coerce any dealer to join, contribute to, or affiliate with any advertising association.

2b. To coerce or require any dealer to establish in connection with the sale of a motor vehicle prices at which the dealer shall sell products or services not manufactured or distributed by the manufacturer, factory branch, distributor, or distributor branch, whether by agreement, program, incentive provision, or otherwise.

2c. To coerce or require any dealer, whether by agreement, program, incentive provision, or otherwise, to construct improvements to its facilities or to install new signs or other franchisor image elements that replace or substantially alter those improvements, signs, or franchisor image elements completed within the preceding 10 years that were required or approved by the manufacturer, factory branch, distributor, or distributor branch or one of its affiliates. If a manufacturer, factory branch, distributor, or distributor branch offers incentives, or other payments under a program offered after the effective date of this subdivision and available to more than one dealer in the Commonwealth that are premised wholly or in part on dealer facility improvements or installation of franchisor signs or other franchisor image elements, a dealer that constructed improvements or installed signs or other franchisor image elements required by or approved by the manufacturer, factory branch, distributor, or distributor branch and completed within the 10 years preceding the program shall be deemed to be in compliance with the program requirements pertaining to construction of facilities or installation of signs or other franchisor image elements that would replace or substantially alter those previously constructed or installed within that 10-year period. This subdivision shall not apply to a program that provides lump sum payments to assist dealers in making facility improvements or to pay for signs or franchisor image elements when such payments are not dependent on the dealer selling or purchasing specific numbers of new vehicles and shall not apply to a program that is in effect with more than one dealer in the Commonwealth on the effective date of this subdivision, nor to any renewal or modification of such a program.

2d. To coerce or require any dealer, whether by agreement, program, incentive provision, or provision for loss of incentive payments or other benefits, to refrain from selling any used motor vehicle subject to (i) recall, (ii) stop sale directive, (iii) technical service bulletin, or (iv) other manufacturer, factory branch, distributor, or distributor branch notification to perform work on such used motor vehicle, unless the manufacturer, factory branch, distributor, or distributor branch has a remedy and parts available to the dealer to remediate the basis for the coercion or requirement of the dealer to refrain from selling each affected used motor vehicle. If there is no remedy or there are no parts available from the manufacturer, factory branch, distributor, or distributor branch to remediate each affected used motor vehicle in the inventory of the dealer, the manufacturer, factory branch, distributor, or distributor branch shall (a) compensate the dealer for any affected used motor vehicle in the inventory of the dealer that it cannot sell because of such coercion or requirement at least one percent a month or any part thereof of the cost of such used motor vehicle, including repairs and reconditioning expenses based on the financial records of the dealer, and (b) establish a written procedure to compensate dealers under this subdivision that it shall provide to dealers subject to its coercion or requirement and file with the Commissioner as a franchise document pursuant to § 46.2-1566.

Any claim for compensation by a dealer shall be submitted on a monthly basis for the amount owed pursuant to this subdivision. The manufacturer, factory branch, distributor, or distributor branch shall process and pay the claim in the same manner as a claim for warranty reimbursements as provided in § 46.2-1571. This subdivision shall not prevent a manufacturer, factory branch, distributor, or distributor branch from (1) requiring that a motor vehicle not be subject to an open recall or stop sale directive in order to be qualified, remain qualified, or be sold as a certified pre-owned vehicle or similar designation; (2) paying incentives for selling used vehicles with no unremedied recalls; or (3) paying incentives for performing recall repairs on a vehicle in the dealer's inventory.

Nothing in this subdivision shall prevent a manufacturer, factory branch, distributor, or distributor branch from instructing that a dealer repair used vehicles of the line-make for which the dealer holds a franchise with an open recall, provided that the instruction does not involve coercion that imposes a penalty or provision of loss of benefits on the dealer.

3. To prevent or refuse to approve the sale or transfer of the ownership of a dealership by the sale of the business, stock transfer, or otherwise, or the transfer, sale, or assignment of a dealer franchise, or a change in the executive management or principal operator of the dealership, unless the franchisor provides written notice to the dealer of its objection and the reasons therefor by certified mail or overnight delivery or other method designed to ensure delivery to the dealer at least 30 days prior to the proposed effective date of the transfer, sale, assignment, or change. No such objection shall be suffi-

cient unless the failure to approve is reasonable. Notwithstanding the provisions of subsection D of § 46.2-1573, the only grounds that may be considered reasonable for a failure to approve are that an individual who is the applicant or is in control of an entity that is an applicant (i) lacks good moral character, (ii) lacks reasonable motor vehicle dealership management experience and qualifications, (iii) lacks financial ability to be the dealer, or (iv) fails to meet the standards otherwise established by this title to be a dealer. No such objection shall be effective to prevent the sale, transfer, assignment, or change if the Commissioner has determined, if requested in writing by the dealer within 30 days after receipt of an objection to the proposed sale, transfer, or change, and after a hearing on the matter, that the failure to permit or honor the sale, transfer, assignment, or change is unreasonable under the circumstances. No franchise may be sold, assigned, or transferred unless (a) the franchisor has been given at least 90 days' prior written notice by the dealer as to the identity, financial ability, and qualifications of the proposed transferee on forms generally utilized by the franchisor to conduct its review, as well as the full agreement for the proposed transaction, and (b) the sale or transfer of the franchise and business will not involve, without the franchisor's consent, a relocation of the business.

3a. To impose a condition on the approval of the sale or transfer of the ownership of a dealership by the sale of the business, stock transfer, or otherwise if the condition would violate the provisions of this title if imposed on the existing dealer.

In the event the manufacturer, factory branch, distributor or distributor branch takes action to prevent or refuse to approve the sale or transfer of the ownership of a dealership by the sale of the business, stock transfer, or otherwise, or the transfer, sale or assignment of a dealer franchise, or a change in the executive management or principal operator of the dealership, without a statement of specific grounds for doing so that is consistent with subdivision 3 hereof or imposes a condition in violation of subdivision 3a hereof, that shall constitute a violation of this section. The existing dealer may request review of the action or imposition of the condition in a hearing by the Commissioner. If the Commissioner finds that the action or the imposition of the condition was a violation of this section, the Commissioner may order that the sale or transfer be approved by the manufacturer, factory branch, distributor, or distributor branch, without imposition of the condition. If the existing dealer does not request a hearing by the Commissioner concerning the action or the condition imposed by the manufacturer, factory branch, distributor, or distributor branch, and the action or condition was the proximate cause of the failure of the contract for the sale or transfer of ownership of the dealership, the applicant for approval of the sale or transfer or the existing dealer, or both, may commence an action at law for violation of this section. The action may be commenced in the circuit court of the city or county in which the dealer is located, or in any other circuit court with permissible venue, within two years following the action or the imposition of the condition by the manufacturer, factory branch, distributor, or distributor branch for the damages suffered by the applicant or the dealer as a result of the violation of this section by the manufacturer, factory branch, distributor, or distributor branch, plus the applicant's or dealer's reasonable attorney fees and costs of litigation. Notwithstanding the foregoing, an exercise of the right of first refusal by the manufacturer, factory branch, distributor, or distributor branch pursuant to § 46.2-1569.1 shall not be considered the imposition of a condition prohibited by this section.

4. To grant an additional franchise for a particular line-make of motor vehicle in a relevant market area in which a dealer or dealers in that line-make are already located unless the franchisor has first advised in writing all other dealers in the line-make in the relevant market area. No such additional franchise may be established at the proposed site unless the Commissioner has determined, if requested by a dealer of the same line-make in the relevant market area within 30 days after receipt of the franchisor's notice of intention to establish the additional franchise, and after a hearing on the matter, that the franchisor can show by a preponderance of the evidence that after the grant of the new franchise, the relevant market area will support all of the dealers in that line-make in the relevant market area. Establishing a franchised dealer in a relevant market area to replace a franchised dealer that has not been in operation for more than two years shall constitute the establishment of a new franchise subject to the terms of this subdivision. The two-year period for replacing a franchised dealer shall begin on the day the franchise was terminated, or, if a termination hearing was held, on the day the franchisor was legally permitted finally to terminate the franchise. The relocation of a franchise in a relevant market area, whether by an existing dealer or by a dealer who is acquiring the franchise, shall constitute the establishment of a new franchise subject to the terms of this subdivision. This subdivision shall not apply to (i) the relocation of an existing dealer within that dealer's relevant market area if the relocation site is to be more than 10 miles distant from any other dealer for the same line-make; (ii) the relocation of an existing dealer within that dealer's relevant market area if the relocation site is to be more distant than the existing site from all other dealers of the same line-make in that relevant market area; or (iii) the relocation of an existing new motor vehicle dealer within two miles of the existing site of the relocating dealer.

5. Except as otherwise provided in this subdivision and notwithstanding the terms of any fran-

chise, to terminate, cancel, or refuse to renew the franchise of any dealer without good cause and unless (i) the dealer and the Commissioner have received written notice of the franchisor's intentions at least 60 days prior to the effective date of such termination, cancellation, or the expiration date of the franchise, setting forth the specific grounds for the action, and (ii) the Commissioner has determined, if requested in writing by the dealer within the 60-day period prior to the effective date of such termination, cancellation, or the expiration date of the franchise and, after a hearing on the matter, that the franchisor has shown by a preponderance of the evidence that there is good cause for the termination, cancellation, or nonrenewal of the franchise. If any manufacturer, factory branch, distributor, or distributor branch takes action that will have the effect of terminating, canceling, or refusing to renew the franchise of any dealer (a) by use of a termination agreement executed by the dealer and obtained more than 90 days before the purported date of use, (b) by exercise of rights under a written option to purchase the franchise of a dealer, or (c) by exercise of rights under a site control agreement as defined in subdivision 10, that action shall be considered a termination, cancellation, or refusal to renew pursuant to the terms of this subdivision and subject to the rights, provisions, and procedures provided herein. In any case where a petition is made to the Commissioner for a determination as to good cause for the termination, cancellation, or nonrenewal of a franchise, the franchise in question shall continue in effect pending the Commissioner's decision or, if that decision is appealed to the circuit court, pending the decision of the circuit court. Where the termination, cancellation, or nonrenewal of a franchise will result from use of a termination agreement executed by the dealer and obtained more than 90 days before the purported date of use, exercise of rights under a written option to purchase the franchise of a dealer, or exercise of rights under a site control agreement as defined in subdivision 10, such use or exercise shall be stayed pending the Commissioner's decision or, if that decision is appealed to the circuit court, pending the decision of the circuit court, and its use or exercise will be allowed only where the franchisor has shown by a preponderance of the evidence that there is good cause for the termination, cancellation, or nonrenewal of the franchise. In any case in which a franchisor neither advises a dealer that it does not intend to renew a franchise nor takes any action to renew a franchise beyond its expiration date, the franchise in question shall continue in effect on the terms last agreed to by the parties. Notwithstanding the other provisions of this subdivision notice of termination, cancellation, or nonrenewal may be provided to a dealer by a franchisor not less than 15 days prior to the effective date of such termination, cancellation, or nonrenewal when the grounds for such action are any of the following:

a. Insolvency of the franchised motor vehicle dealer or filing of any petition by or against the franchised motor vehicle dealer, under any bankruptcy or receivership law, leading to liquidation or which is intended to lead to liquidation of the franchisee's business.

b. Failure of the franchised motor vehicle dealer to conduct its customary sales and service operations during its posted business hours for seven consecutive business days, except where the failure results from acts of God or circumstances beyond the direct control of the franchised motor vehicle dealer.

c. Revocation of any license which the franchised motor vehicle dealer is required to have to operate a dealership.

d. Conviction of the dealer or any principal of the dealer of a felony.

The change or discontinuance of a marketing or distribution system of a particular line-make product by a manufacturer or distributor, while the name identification of the product is continued in substantial form by the same or a different manufacturer or distributor, may be considered to be a franchise termination, cancellation, or nonrenewal. The provisions of this paragraph shall apply to changes and discontinuances made after January 1, 1989, but they shall not be considered by any court in any case in which such a change or discontinuance occurring prior to that date has been challenged as constituting a termination, cancellation or nonrenewal.

5a. To fail to provide continued parts and service support to a dealer which holds a franchise in a discontinued line-make for at least five years from the date of such discontinuance. This requirement shall not apply to a line-make which was discontinued prior to January 1, 1989.

5b. Upon the involuntary or voluntary termination, nonrenewal, or cancellation of the franchise of any dealer, by either the manufacturer, distributor, or factory branch or by the dealer, notwithstanding the terms of any franchise whether entered into before or after the enactment of this section, to fail to pay the dealer for at least the following:

(1) The dealer cost plus any charges by the franchisor for distribution, delivery, and taxes paid by the dealer, less all allowances paid to the dealer by the franchisor, for new and undamaged motor vehicles in the dealer's inventory acquired from the franchisor or from another dealer of the same line — make in the ordinary course of business within 18 months of termination;

(2) The dealer cost as shown in the price catalog of the franchisor current at the time of repurchase of each new, unused, undamaged, and unsold part or accessory if such part or accessory is in the current parts catalog and is still in the original, resalable merchandising package and in unbroken lots, except that in the case of sheet metal, a comparable substitute for the original package may be used;

(3) The fair market value of each undamaged sign owned by the dealer that bears a trademark, trade name or commercial symbol used or claimed by the franchisor if such sign was purchased from or at the request of the franchisor;

(4) The fair market value of all special tools and automotive service equipment owned by the dealer that were recommended and designated as special tools or equipment by the franchisor, if the tools and equipment are in usable and good condition, normal wear and tear excepted; and

(5) The reasonable cost of transporting, handling, packing, and loading of motor vehicles, parts, signs, tools, and special equipment subject to repurchase hereunder.

The provisions of this subdivision do not apply to a dealer who is unable to convey clear title to the property identified in this subdivision.

For purposes of this subdivision, a voluntary termination shall not include the transfer of the terminating dealer's franchised business in connection with a transfer of that business by means of sale of the equity ownership or assets thereof to another dealer.

5c. If the termination, cancellation, or nonrenewal of the dealer's franchise is the result of the termination, elimination, or cessation of a line-make by the manufacturer, distributor, or factory branch, then, in addition to the payments to the dealer pursuant to subdivision 5b, the manufacturer, distributor, or factory branch shall be liable to the dealer for the following:

(1) An amount at least equivalent to the fair market value of the franchise for the line-make, which shall be the greater of that value determined as of (i) the date the franchisor announces the action that results in termination, cancellation, or nonrenewal, (ii) the date the action that resulted in the termination, cancellation, or nonrenewal first became general knowledge, or (iii) the day 12 months prior to the date on which the notice of termination, cancellation, or nonrenewal is issued. In determining the fair market value of a franchise for a line-make, if the line-make is not the only line-make for which the dealer holds a franchise in the dealership facilities, the dealer shall also be entitled to compensation for the contribution of the line-make to payment of the rent or to covering obligation for the fair rental value of the dealership facilities for the period set forth in subdivision 5c (2). Fair market value of the franchise for the line-make shall only include the goodwill value of the dealer's franchise for that line-make in the dealer's relevant market area.

(2) If the line-make is the only line-make for which the dealer holds a franchise in the dealership facilities, the manufacturer, distributor, or factory branch shall also pay assistance with respect to the dealership facilities leased or owned by the dealer as follows: (i) the manufacturer, distributor, or factory branch shall pay the dealer a sum equivalent to the rent for the unexpired term of the lease or three years' rent, whichever is the lesser, or (ii) if the dealer owns the dealership facilities, the manufacturer, distributor, or factory branch shall pay the dealer a sum equivalent to the reasonable rental value of the dealership facilities for three years.

To be entitled to facilities assistance from the manufacturer, distributor, or factory branch, the dealer shall have the obligation to mitigate damages by listing the dealership facilities for lease or sublease with a licensed real estate agent within 30 days after the effective date of the termination of the franchise and thereafter by reasonably cooperating with such real estate agent in the performance of the agent's duties and responsibilities. If the dealer is able to lease or sublease the dealership facilities on terms that are consistent with local zoning requirements to preserve the right to sell motor vehicles from the dealership facilities and the terms of the dealer's lease, the dealer shall be obligated to pay the manufacturer the net revenue received from such mitigation, but only following receipt of facilities assistance payments pursuant to clause (i) or (ii) of subdivision 5c (2), and only up to the total amount of facilities assistance payments that the dealer has received.

6. To fail to allow a dealer the right at any time to designate a member of his family as a successor to the dealership in the event of the death or incapacity of the dealer. Such designation may be made by the dealer or, in the event of the death or incapacity of the dealer, by the qualified executor or personal representative of the dealer. It shall be unlawful to prevent or refuse to honor the succession to a dealership by a member of the family of a deceased or incapacitated dealer if the franchisor has not provided to the member of the family designated the dealer's successor written notice of its objections to the succession and of such person's right to seek a hearing on the matter before the Commissioner pursuant to this article, and the Commissioner determines, if requested in writing by such member of the family within 30 days of receipt of such notice from the franchisor, and after a hearing on the matter before the Commissioner pursuant to this article, that the failure to permit or honor the succession is unreasonable under the circumstances. No member of the family may succeed to a franchise unless (i) the franchisor has been given written notice as to the identity, financial ability, and qualifications of the member of the family in question, and (ii) the succession to the franchise will not involve, without the franchisor's consent, a relocation of the business.

7. To delay, refuse, or fail to deliver to any dealer, if ordered by the dealer, in reasonable quantities and within a reasonable time, any new vehicles of each series and model sold or distributed by the franchisor as covered by such franchise and which are publicly advertised by the manufacturer, factory branch, distributor, or distributor branch in the Commonwealth to be available for immediate delivery, provided, however, that the failure to deliver any motor vehicle shall not be considered a violation of this chapter if such failure is due to an act of God, a work stoppage or delay due to a strike or labor difficulty, a shortage of materials, a lack of available

manufacturing capacity, a freight embargo, or other cause over which the manufacturer, factory branch, distributor, or distributor branch shall have no control. If ordered by a dealer, a franchisor shall deliver an equitable supply of new vehicles during the model year of each series and model under the dealer's franchise in proportion to the sales objectives or goals established by the franchisor for the dealer compared to the sales objectives or goals established by the other same line-make dealers in the Commonwealth, provided, however, that the failure to deliver any motor vehicle shall not be considered a violation of this chapter if such failure is due to a cause over which the manufacturer, factory branch, distributer, or distributer branch shall have no control. Upon the written request of any dealer holding its sales or sales and service franchise, the manufacturer or distributor shall disclose to the dealer in writing the basis upon which new motor vehicles of the same line-make are allocated, scheduled, and delivered to dealers in the Commonwealth, and the basis upon which the current allocation or distribution is being made or will be made to such dealer. In the event that allocation is at issue in a request for a hearing, the dealer may demand the Commissioner to direct that the manufacturer or distributor provide to the dealer, within 30 days of such demand, all records of sales and all records of distribution of all motor vehicles to the same line-make dealers who compete with the dealer requesting the hearing.

7a. To fail or refuse to offer to its same line-make franchised dealers all models manufactured for the line-make, or require a dealer to pay any extra fee, or remodel, renovate, or recondition the dealer's existing facilities, or purchase unreasonable advertising displays or other materials as a prerequisite to receiving a model or a series of vehicles.

7b. To require or otherwise coerce a dealer to underutilize the dealer's facilities by requiring or otherwise coercing a dealer to exclude or remove from the dealer's facilities operations for selling or servicing of a line-make of vehicles for which the dealer has a franchise agreement to utilize the facilities.

7c. To require a dealer to purchase goods or services from a vendor selected, identified, or designated by a manufacturer, factory branch, distributor, distributor branch, or one of its affiliates by agreement, program, incentive provision, or otherwise without making available to the dealer the option to obtain the goods or services of substantially similar quality from a vendor chosen by the dealer. For purposes of this subdivision, the term "goods" does not include moveable displays, brochures, and promotional materials containing material subject to intellectual property rights of, or special tools and training as required by the manufacturer, or parts to be used in repairs under warranty obligations of, a manufacturer, factory branch, distributor, or distributor branch.

7d. To fail to provide a notice to a dealer when notifying it of the requirement to purchase goods or services from a vendor selected, identified, or designated by a manufacturer, factory branch, distributor, or distributor branch of the dealer's rights pursuant to subdivision 7c.

7e. To fail to provide to a dealer, when the manufacturer, factory branch, distributor, or distributor branch claims that a vendor chosen by the dealer cannot supply goods and services of substantially similar quality, a disclosure concerning the vendor selected, identified, or designated by the franchisor stating (i) whether the manufacturer, factory branch, distributor, distributor branch, or one of its affiliates, or any officer, director, or employee of the same, has an ownership interest, actual or beneficial, in the vendor and, if so, the percentage of the ownership interest and (ii) whether the manufacturer, factory branch, distributor, distributor branch, or one of its affiliates has an agreement or arrangement by which the vendor pays to the manufacturer, factory branch, distributor, distributor branch, or one of its affiliates, or any officer, director, or employee of the same, any compensation and, if so, the basis and amount of the compensation to be paid as a result of any purchases by the dealer, whether it is to be paid by direct payment by the vendor or by credit from the vendor for the benefit of the recipient.

7f. To fail to provide to a dealer, if the goods and services to be supplied to the dealer by a vendor selected, identified, or designated by the manufacturer, factory branch, distributor, or distributor branch are signs or other franchisor image elements to be leased to the dealer, the right to purchase the signs or other franchisor image elements of like kind and quality from a vendor selected by the dealer. If the vendor selected by the manufacturer, factory branch, distributor, or distributor branch is the only available vendor, the dealer must be given the opportunity to purchase the signs or other franchisor image elements at a price substantially similar to the capitalized lease costs thereof. This subdivision shall not be construed to allow a dealer to impair or eliminate the intellectual property rights of the manufacturer, factory branch, distributor, or distributor branch, nor to permit a dealer to erect or maintain signs that do not conform to the intellectual property usage guidelines of the manufacturer, factory branch, distributor, or distributor branch.

8. To include in any franchise with a motor vehicle dealer terms that are contrary to, prohibited by, or otherwise inconsistent with the requirements of this chapter.

8a. For any franchise agreement, to require a motor vehicle dealer to pay the attorney fees of the manufacturer or distributor related to hearings and appeals brought under this article.

9. To fail to include in any franchise with a motor vehicle dealer the following language: "If any provision herein contravenes the laws or regulations of

any state or other jurisdiction wherein this agreement is to be performed, or denies access to the procedures, forums, or remedies provided for by such laws or regulations, such provision shall be deemed to be modified to conform to such laws or regulations, and all other terms and provisions shall remain in full force," or words to that effect.

10. To enter into any agreement with a motor vehicle dealer in which the manufacturer, factory branch, distributor, distributor branch, or one of its affiliates is given site control over the premises of a dealer that does not terminate upon the occurrence of any of the following events: (i) the right of the franchisor to manufacture or distribute the line-make of vehicles covered by the dealer's franchise is sold, assigned, or otherwise transferred by the manufacturer, factory branch, distributor, or distributor branch to another; (ii) the final termination of the dealer's franchise for any reason; or (iii) the manufacturer, factory branch, distributor, or distributor branch of its affiliate fails for any reason to exercise its right of first refusal to purchase the assets or ownership of the business of the dealer when given the opportunity to do so by virtue of its franchise agreement, another agreement, or as set forth in § 46.2-1569. For purposes of this subdivision, the term "site control" shall mean the contractual right to control in any way the commercial use and development of the premises upon which a dealer's business operations are located, including the right to approve of additional or different uses for the property beyond those of its franchise, the right to lease or sublease the dealer's property, or the right or option to purchase the dealer's property.

11. To require or coerce a motor vehicle dealer, whether by agreement, program, incentive provision, or otherwise, to submit or to provide a manufacturer, factory branch, distributor, or distributor branch access to consumer data maintained by the dealer (i) by any method that violates or would violate the dealer's chosen policies and processes for complying with obligations to protect consumer data under laws of the United States or the Commonwealth or (ii) through franchisor access to the computer database of the dealer if the dealer chooses to submit data specified by the franchisor.

The manufacturer, factory branch, distributor, or distributor branch shall provide a dealer the right to cancel the dealer's participation in a program under which the dealer provides consumer data or access to data to the manufacturer, factory branch, distributor, or distributor branch, provided that a manufacturer, factory branch, distributor, or distributor branch may require notice of up to 60 days of the dealer's decision to cancel the dealer's participation.

If a manufacturer, factory branch, distributor, or distributor branch offers incentives or other payments under a program offered after July 1, 2015, excluding any continuation, renewal, or modification of any existing program, and available to more than one dealer in the Commonwealth that are premised wholly or in part on dealer participation in manufacturer, factory branch, distributor, or distributor branch programs under which consumer data is provided to or accessed by the manufacturer, factory branch, distributor, or distributor branch, a dealer that exercises its rights under this subdivision shall be deemed to be in compliance with the program requirements pertaining to providing consumer data, provided that the dealer has otherwise met program requirements to the extent of providing any consumer data that is not nonpublic personal information.

It shall not constitute a violation of this subdivision for a manufacturer, factory branch, distributor, or distributor branch to require a motor vehicle dealer to provide data (a) concerning a new motor vehicle sale or used motor vehicle sale under a manufacturer certification program, (b) to validate a customer or dealer incentive, (c) to calculate dealer or market sales or evaluate service performance or customer satisfaction to facilitate analysis of product quality and market feedback, (d) to facilitate warranty service work on a vehicle, (e) concerning information with respect to recall repairs or information about a recalled vehicle, (f) pursuant to a mutual agreement between a manufacturer, factory branch, distributor, or distributor branch and a dealer, or (g) where consumer data is reasonably necessary to enable a manufacturer, factory branch, distributor, or distributor branch to provide programs, products, or services to a dealer.

A dealer that elects to submit or push data or information to the manufacturer, factory branch, distributor, or distributor branch through any method other than that provided by the manufacturer, factory branch, distributor, or distributor branch shall timely obtain and furnish the requested data in a widely accepted electronic file format. A manufacturer, factory branch, distributor, or distributor branch shall not impose a fee, surcharge, or charge of any type on a dealer that chooses to submit data specified by the manufacturer, factory branch, distributor, or distributor branch rather than provide the manufacturer, factory branch, distributor, or distributor branch access to the dealer's computer database.

History.

1988, c. 865, § 46.1-550.5:27; 1989, cc. 363, 686, 727; 1990, c. 83; 1992, c. 116; 1994, c. 385; 1995, cc. 767, 816; 1998, c. 682; 2007, cc. 827, 837; 2009, cc. 173, 176; 2010, cc. 284, 318; 2011, cc. 774, 856; 2015, cc. 155, 236; 2016, cc. 432, 534.

§ 46.2-1569.1. Manufacturer or distributor right of first refusal.

Notwithstanding the terms of any franchise agreement, in the event of a proposed sale or transfer of a dealership, the manufacturer or distributor shall be permitted to exercise a right of first refusal to acquire the new vehicle dealer's assets or ownership, if such sale or transfer is conditioned upon the manufacturer's or dealer's entering into a dealer agreement with the proposed new owner or transferee, only if all the following requirements are met:

1. To exercise its right of first refusal, the manufacturer or distributor must notify the dealer in writing within 45 days of its receipt of the completed proposal for the proposed sale or transfer;

2. The exercise of the right of first refusal will result in the dealer's and dealer's owner's receiving the same or greater consideration as they have contracted to receive in connection with the proposed change of ownership or transfer;

3. The proposed sale or transfer of the dealership's assets does not involve the transfer or sale to a member or members of the family of one or more dealer owners, or to a qualified manager or a partnership, limited liability company, corporation, or other entity controlled by such persons; and

4. The manufacturer or distributor agrees to pay the reasonable expenses, including attorney's fees which do not exceed the usual, customary, and reasonable fees charged for similar work done for other clients, incurred by the proposed new owner and transferee prior to the manufacturer's or distributor's exercise of its right of first refusal in negotiating and implementing the contract for the proposed sale or transfer of the dealership or dealership assets. Notwithstanding the foregoing, no payment of such expenses and attorney's fees shall be required if the dealer has not submitted or caused to be submitted an accounting of those expenses within 30 days of the dealer's receipt of the manufacturer's or distributor's written request for such an accounting. Such accounting may be requested by a manufacturer or distributor before exercising its right of first refusal.

History.
1994, c. 809; 2003, c. 298.

§ 46.2-1570. Discontinuation of distributors.

If the contract between a distributor and a manufacturer or importer is terminated or otherwise discontinued, all franchises granted to motor vehicle dealers in Virginia by that distributor shall continue in full force and shall not be affected by the discontinuance, except that the manufacturer, factory branch, distributor, representative, or other person who undertakes to distribute motor vehicles of the same line-make or the same motor vehicles of a re-named line-make shall be substituted for the discontinued distributor under the existing motor vehicle dealer franchises and those franchises shall be modified accordingly.

History.
1988, c. 865, § 46.1-550.5:29; 1989, c. 727.

§ 46.2-1571. Recall, warranty, and sales incentive obligations.

A. Each motor vehicle manufacturer, factory branch, distributor, or distributor branch shall (i) specify in writing to each of its motor vehicle dealers licensed in the Commonwealth the dealer's obligations for preparation, delivery, recall, and warranty service on its products and (ii) compensate the dealer for recall or warranty parts, service, and diagnostic work required of the dealer by the manufacturer or distributor as follows:

1. Compensation of a dealer for recall or warranty parts, service, and diagnostic work shall not be less than the amounts charged by the dealer for the manufacturer's or distributor's original parts, service, and diagnostic work to retail customers for nonwarranty service, parts, and diagnostic work installed or performed in the dealer's service department unless the amounts are not reasonable. Recall or warranty parts compensation shall be stated as a percentage of markup, which shall be an agreed reasonable approximation of retail markup and which shall be uniformly applied to all of the manufacturer's or distributor's parts unless otherwise provided for in this section. If the dealer and manufacturer or distributor cannot agree on the recall or warranty parts compensation markup to be paid to the dealer, the markup shall be determined by an average of the dealer's retail markup on all of the manufacturer's or distributor's parts as described in subdivisions 2 and 3.

2. For purposes of determining recall or warranty parts and service compensation paid to a dealer by the manufacturer or distributor, menu-priced parts or services, group discounts, special event discounts, and special event promotions shall not be considered in determining amounts charged by the dealer to retail customers. For purposes of determining labor compensation for recall or warranty body shop repairs paid to a dealer by the manufacturer or distributor, internal and insurance-paid repairs shall not be considered in determining amounts charged by the dealer to retail customers.

3. Increases in dealer recall or warranty parts and service compensation and diagnostic work compensation, pursuant to this section, shall be requested by the dealer in writing, shall be based on 100 consecutive repair orders or all repair orders over a 90-day period, whichever occurs first, and, in the case of parts, shall be stated as a percentage of markup that shall be uniformly applied to all the manufacturer's or distributor's parts.

4. In the case of recall or warranty parts compensation, the provisions of this subsection shall be effective only for model year 1992 and succeeding model years.

5. If a manufacturer or distributor furnishes a part to a dealer at no cost for use by the dealer in

performing work for which the manufacturer or distributor is required to compensate the dealer under this section, the manufacturer or distributor shall compensate the dealer for the part in the same manner as recall or warranty parts compensation, less the wholesale costs, for such part as listed in the manufacturer's current price schedules. A manufacturer or distributor may pay the dealer a reasonable handling fee instead of the compensation otherwise required by this subsection for special high-performance complete engine assemblies in limited production motor vehicles that constitute less than five percent of model production furnished to the dealer at no cost, if the manufacturer or distributor excludes such special high-performance complete engine assemblies in determining whether the amounts requested by the dealer for recall or warranty compensation are consistent with the amounts that the dealer charges its other retail service customers for parts used by the dealer to perform similar work.

6. In the case of service work, manufacturer original parts or parts otherwise specified by the manufacturer or distributor, and parts provided by a dealer either pursuant to an adjustment program as defined in § 59.1-207.34 or as otherwise requested by the manufacturer or distributor, the dealer shall be compensated in the same manner as for recall or warranty service or parts.

This section does not apply to compensation for parts such as components, systems, fixtures, appliances, furnishings, accessories, and features that are designed, used, and maintained primarily for nonvehicular, residential purposes. Recall, warranty, and sales incentive audits of dealer records may be conducted by the manufacturer, factory branch, distributor, or distributor branch on a reasonable basis, and dealer claims for recall, warranty, or sales incentive compensation shall not be denied except for good cause, such as performance of nonwarranty repairs, lack of material documentation, fraud, or misrepresentation. A dealer's failure to comply with the specific requirements of the manufacturer or distributor for processing the claim shall not constitute grounds for the denial of the claim or reduction of the amount of compensation to the dealer as long as reasonable documentation or other evidence has been presented to substantiate the claim. The manufacturer, factory branch, distributor, or distributor branch shall not deny a claim or reduce the amount of compensation to the dealer for recall or warranty repairs to resolve a condition discovered by the dealer during the course of a separate repair requested by the customer or to resolve a condition on the basis of advice or recommendation by the dealer. Claims for dealer compensation shall be paid within 30 days of dealer submission or within 30 days of the end of an incentive program or rejected in writing for stated reasons. The manufacturer, factory branch, distributor, or distributor branch shall reserve the right to reasonable periodic audits to determine the validity of all such paid claims for dealer compensation. Any chargebacks for recall or warranty parts or service compensation and service incentives shall only be for the six-month period immediately following the date of the claim and, in the case of chargebacks for sales compensation only, for the six-month period immediately following the date of claim. However, such limitations shall not be effective if a manufacturer, factory branch, distributor, or distributor branch has reasonable cause to believe that a claim submitted by a dealer is intentionally false or fraudulent. For purposes of this section, "reasonable cause" means a bona fide belief based upon evidence that the material issues of fact are such that a person of ordinary caution, prudence, and judgment could believe that a claim was intentionally false or fraudulent. A dealer shall not be charged back or otherwise liable for sales incentives or charges related to a motor vehicle sold by the dealer to a purchaser other than a licensed, franchised motor vehicle dealer and subsequently exported or resold, unless the manufacturer, factory branch, distributor, or distributor branch can demonstrate by a preponderance of the evidence that the dealer should have known of and did not exercise due diligence in discovering the purchaser's intention to export or resell the motor vehicle.

B. It shall be unlawful for any motor vehicle manufacturer, factory branch, distributor, or distributor branch to:

1. Fail to perform any of its recall or warranty obligations, including tires, with respect to a motor vehicle;

2. Fail to assume all responsibility for any liability resulting from structural or production defects;

3. Fail to include in written notices of factory recalls to vehicle owners and dealers the expected date by which necessary parts and equipment will be available to dealers for the correction of defects;

4. Fail to compensate any of the motor vehicle dealers licensed in the Commonwealth for repairs effected by the dealer of merchandise damaged in manufacture or transit to the dealer where the carrier is designated by the manufacturer, factory branch, distributor, or distributor branch;

5. Fail to fully compensate its motor vehicle dealers licensed in the Commonwealth for recall or warranty parts, work, and service pursuant to subsection A either by reduction in the amount due to the dealer or by separate charge, surcharge, or other imposition by which the motor vehicle manufacturer, factory branch, distributor, or distributor branch seeks to recover its costs of complying with subsection A, or for legal costs and expenses incurred by such dealers in connection with recall or warranty obligations for which the manufacturer, factory branch, distributor, or distributor branch is legally responsible or which the manufacturer, factory branch, distributor, or distributor branch imposes upon the dealer;

6. Misrepresent in any way to purchasers of motor vehicles that warranties with respect to the manufacture, performance, or design of the vehicle are made by the dealer, either as warrantor or co-warrantor;

7. Require the dealer to make warranties to customers in any manner related to the manufacture, performance, or design of the vehicle;

8. Shift or attempt to shift to the motor vehicle dealer, directly or indirectly, any liabilities of the manufacturer, factory branch, distributor or distributor branch under the Virginia Motor Vehicle Warranty Enforcement Act (§ 59.1-207.9 et seq.), unless such liability results from the act or omission by the dealer; or

9. Deny any dealer the right to return any part or accessory that the dealer has not sold within 12 months where the part or accessory was not obtained through a specific order initiated by the dealer but instead was specified for, sold to and shipped to the dealer pursuant to an automated ordering system, provided that such part or accessory is in the condition required for return to the manufacturer, factory branch, distributor, or distributor branch, and the dealer returns the part within 30 days of it becoming eligible under this subdivision. For purposes of this subdivision, an "automated ordering system" shall be a computerized system that automatically specifies parts and accessories for sale and shipment to the dealer without specific order thereof initiated by the dealer. The manufacturer, factory branch, distributor, or distributor branch shall not charge a restocking or handling fee for any part or accessory being returned under this subdivision. This subdivision shall not apply if the manufacturer, factory branch, distributor, or distributor branch has available to the dealer an alternate system for ordering parts and accessories that provides for shipment of ordered parts and accessories to the dealer within the same time frame as the dealer would receive them when ordered through the automated ordering system.

C. Notwithstanding the terms of any franchise, it shall be unlawful for any motor vehicle manufacturer, factory branch, distributor, or distributor branch to fail to indemnify and hold harmless its motor vehicle dealers against any losses or damages arising out of complaints, claims, or suits relating to the manufacture, assembly, or design of motor vehicles, parts, or accessories, or other functions by the manufacturer, factory branch, distributor, or distributor branch beyond the control of the dealer, including, without limitation, the selection by the manufacturer, factory branch, distributor, or distributor branch of parts or components for the vehicle or any damages to merchandise occurring in transit to the dealer where the carrier is designated by the manufacturer, factory branch, distributor, or distributor branch. The dealer shall notify the manufacturer of pending suits in which allegations are made that come within this subsection whenever reasonably practicable to do so. Every motor vehicle dealer franchise issued to, amended, or renewed for motor vehicle dealers in Virginia shall be construed to incorporate provisions consistent with the requirements of this subsection.

D. On any new motor vehicle, any uncorrected damage or any corrected damage exceeding three percent of the manufacturer's or distributor's suggested retail price as defined in 15 U.S.C. §§ 1231 -1233, as measured by retail repair costs, must be disclosed to the dealer in writing prior to delivery. Factory mechanical repair and damage to glass, tires, and bumpers are excluded from the three percent rule when properly replaced by identical manufacturer's or distributor's original equipment or parts. Whenever a new motor vehicle is damaged in transit, when the carrier or means of transportation is determined by the manufacturer or distributor, or whenever a motor vehicle is otherwise damaged prior to delivery to the new motor vehicle dealer, the new motor vehicle dealer shall:

1. Notify the manufacturer or distributor of the damage within three business days from the date of delivery of the new motor vehicle to the new motor vehicle dealership or within the additional time specified in the franchise; and

2. Request from the manufacturer or distributor authorization to replace the components, parts, and accessories damaged or otherwise correct the damage, unless the damage to the vehicle exceeds the three percent rule, in which case the dealer may reject the vehicle within three business days.

E. If the manufacturer or distributor refuses or fails to authorize correction of such damage within 10 days after receipt of notification, or if the dealer rejects the vehicle because damage exceeds the three percent rule, ownership of the new motor vehicle shall revert to the manufacturer or distributor, and the new motor vehicle dealer shall have no obligation, financial or otherwise, with respect to such motor vehicle. Should either the manufacturer, distributor, or the dealer elect to correct the damage or any other damage exceeding the three percent rule, full disclosure shall be made by the dealer in writing to the buyer and an acknowledgement by the buyer is required. If there is less than three percent damage, no disclosure is required, provided the damage has been corrected. Predelivery mechanical work shall not require a disclosure. Failure to disclose any corrected damage within the knowledge of the selling dealer to a new motor vehicle in excess of the three percent rule shall constitute grounds for revocation of the buyer order, provided that, within 30 days of purchase, the motor vehicle is returned to the dealer with an accompanying written notice of the grounds for revocation. In case of revocation pursuant to this section, the dealer shall accept the vehicle and refund any payments made to the dealer in connection with the transaction, less a reasonable allowance for the consumer's use of the vehicle as defined in § 59.1-207.11. Nothing in this section shall be construed to exempt from the provisions of this section damage to a new motor vehicle that occurs following delivery of the vehicle to the dealer.

F. If there is a dispute between the manufacturer, factory branch, distributor, or distributor branch and the dealer with respect to any matter referred to in subsection A, B, or C, either party may petition the Commissioner in writing, within 30 days after either party has given written notice of the dispute to the other, for a hearing. The decision of the Commissioner shall be binding on the parties, subject to rights of judicial review and appeal as provided in Chapter 40 (§ 2.2-4000 et seq.) of Title 2.2. However, nothing contained in this section shall give the Commissioner any authority as to the content or interpretation of any manufacturer's or distributor's warranty. A manufacturer, factory branch, distributor, or distributor branch may not collect chargebacks, fully or in part, either through direct payment or by charge to the dealer's account, for recall or warranty parts or service compensation, including service incentives, sales incentives, other sales compensation, surcharges, fees, penalties, or any financial imposition of any type arising from an alleged failure of the dealer to comply with a policy of, directive from, or agreement with the manufacturer, factory branch, distributor, or distributor branch until 40 days following final notice of the amount charged to the dealer following all internal processes of the manufacturer, factory, factory branch, distributor, or distributor branch. Within 30 days following receipt of such final notice, the dealer may petition the Commissioner, in writing, for a hearing. If a dealer requests such a hearing, the manufacturer, factory branch, distributor, or distributor branch may not collect the chargeback, fully or in part, either through direct payment or by charge to the dealer's account, until the completion of the hearing and a final decision of the Commissioner concerning the validity of the chargeback.

History.

1988, c. 865, § 46.1-550.5:30; 1989, cc. 365, 727; 1990, c. 250; 1991, c. 92; 1992, c. 135; 1993, c. 90; 1994, c. 783; 1995, cc. 421, 477; 1997, c. 484; 1998, c. 681; 2001, cc. 80, 89; 2006, cc. 809, 818; 2007, c. 830; 2009, cc. 173, 176; 2010, cc. 284, 318; 2013, cc. 260, 630; 2016, cc. 432, 534.

§ 46.2-1572. Operation of dealership by manufacturer.

It shall be unlawful for any motor vehicle manufacturer, factory branch, distributor, distributor branch, or subsidiary thereof, to own, operate, or control any motor vehicle dealership in the Commonwealth. However, this section shall not prohibit:

1. The operation by a manufacturer, factory branch, distributor, distributor branch, or subsidiary thereof, of a dealership for a temporary period, not to exceed one year, during the transition from one owner or operator to another;

2. The ownership or control of a dealership by a manufacturer, factory branch, distributor, distributor branch, or subsidiary thereof, while the dealership is being sold under a bona fide contract or purchase option to the operator of the dealership;

3. The ownership, operation, or control of a dealership by a manufacturer, factory branch, distributor, distributor branch, or subsidiary thereof, if the manufacturer, factory branch, distributor, distributor branch, or subsidiary has been engaged in the retail sale of motor vehicles through the dealership for a continuous period of three years prior to July 1, 1972, and if the Commissioner determines, after a hearing on the matter at the request of any party, that there is no dealer independent of the manufacturer or distributor, factory branch or distributor branch, or subsidiary thereof available in the community to own and operate the franchise in a manner consistent with the public interest;

4. The ownership, operation, or control of a dealership by a manufacturer, factory branch, distributor, distributor branch, or subsidiary thereof if the Commissioner determines, after a hearing at the request of any party, that there is no dealer independent of the manufacturer or distributor, factory branch or distributor branch, or subsidiary thereof available in the community or trade area to own and operate the franchise in a manner consistent with the public interest;

5. The ownership, operation, or control of a dealership dealing exclusively with school buses by a school bus manufacturer or school bus parts manufacturer or a person who assembles school buses; or

6. The ownership, operation, or control of a dealership dealing exclusively with refined fuels truck tanks by a manufacturer of refined fuels truck tanks or by a person who assembles refined fuels truck tanks. Notwithstanding any contrary provision of this chapter, any manufacturer of fire-fighting equipment who, on or before December 31, 2004, had requested a hearing before the Department or the Commissioner in accordance with subdivision 4 for licensure as a dealer in fire-fighting equipment and/or ambulances may be licensed as a dealer in fire-fighting equipment and/or ambulances.

History.

1988, c. 865, § 46.1-550.5:31; 1989, c. 727; 1990, c. 41; 2005, c. 456.

§ 46.2-1572.1. Ownership of service facilities.

A. It shall be unlawful for any motor vehicle manufacturer, factory branch, distributor, distributor branch, or subsidiary thereof, to own, operate, or control, either directly or indirectly, any motor vehicle warranty or service facility located in the Commonwealth. Nothing in this section shall prohibit any motor vehicle manufacturer, factory branch, distributor, distributor branch, or subsidiary thereof, from owning, operating, or controlling any warranty or service facility for warranty or service of motor vehicles owned or operated by the manufacturer, factory branch, distributor, distributor branch, or subsidiary thereof. Nothing contained in this section shall prohibit a motor vehicle manufacturer, factory branch, distributor, or distributor branch from performing service for reasons of compliance with an order of a court of competent jurisdiction or of warranty under Chapter 17.3 (§ 59.1-207.9 et seq.) of Title 59.1.

B. Subsection A shall not apply to the following:

1. Manufacturers of refined fuels truck tanks, persons who assemble refined fuels truck tanks, or persons who exclusively manufacture or assemble school buses or school bus parts; or

2. Manufacturers of engines for trucks having a gross vehicle weight rating of more than 7,500 pounds that owned, operated, or controlled a warranty or service facility in the Commonwealth as of January 1, 2016, provided that the manufacturer:

a. Does not own, operate, or control more than five such facilities in the Commonwealth;

b. Does not otherwise manufacture, distribute, or sell motor vehicles, as defined in § 46.2-1500; and

c. Provides to dealers on substantially equal terms access to all support for completing repairs, including parts and assemblies, training, and technical service bulletins and other information concerning repairs, that the manufacturer provides to facilities owned, operated, or controlled by the manufacturer.

History.
1990, c. 329; 2016, c. 427.

§ 46.2-1572.2. Mediation of disputes.

At any time before a hearing under this article is commenced before the Commissioner, either party to a franchise agreement for the sale or service of passenger cars, pickup trucks or trucks may demand that a dispute be submitted to nonbinding mediation as a condition precedent to the right to a hearing before the Commissioner.

A demand for mediation may be served on the other party and shall be filed with the Commissioner at any time before a hearing is commenced by the Commissioner. The service of the demand for mediation shall, of itself, toll the time required to file requests for hearings and for the time for commencing and completing hearings under this article until mediation is concluded.

A demand for mediation shall be in writing and shall be served upon the other party by certified mail at an address designated in the franchise agreement or in the records of the Department. The demand for mediation shall contain a brief statement of the dispute and the relief sought by the party filing the demand.

Within ten days after the date on which the demand for mediation is served, the Commissioner shall select one mediator from his approved list of mediators or from the lists of hearing officers as set forth in § 2.2-4024. Within twenty-five days of the date of demand, the parties shall meet with the mediator for the purpose of attempting to resolve the dispute. The meeting place shall be within the Commonwealth at a location selected by the mediator. The mediator may extend the date of the meeting for good cause shown by either party or upon the stipulation of both parties.

History.
1994, c. 418.

§ 46.2-1572.3. Waiver prohibited.

No motor vehicle manufacturer, factory branch, distributor, distributor branch, or subsidiary thereof shall obtain from a motor vehicle dealer a waiver of the dealer's rights by threatening to impose a detriment upon the dealer's business or threatening to withhold from the dealer any entitlement, benefit, or service to which the dealer is entitled by virtue of any franchise agreement, contract, statute, regulation, or law of any kind or which has been granted to more than one other franchisee of the manufacturer, factory branch, distributor, or distributor branch in the Commonwealth. This section shall not apply to good faith settlement of disputes, including disputes pertaining to contract negotiations, in which a waiver is granted in exchange for fair consideration in the form of a benefit conferred upon the dealer; however, this section shall apply to a dispute as to whether a waiver of such rights by a motor vehicle dealer has been obtained in violation of this section.

History.
2001, cc. 135, 150; 2010, cc. 284, 318.

§ 46.2-1572.4. Manufacturer or distributor use of performance standards.

A. Any performance standard or program that is used by a manufacturer or distributor for measuring dealership performance and may have a material effect on a dealer, and the application of any such standard or program by a manufacturer or distributor, shall be fair, reasonable and equitable, and if based upon a survey, shall be based upon a statistically valid sample. Upon the request of any dealer, a manufacturer or distributor shall disclose in writing to the dealer a description of how a performance standard or program is designed and all relevant information used in the application of the performance standard or program to that dealer.

B. A manufacturer or distributor shall not use any data, calculations, or statistical determinations of the sales performance of a dealer for any purpose, including (i) loss of incentive payments or other benefits, (ii) claim of breach or threats thereof, or (iii) notice of termination or threats thereof for the period of time the manufacturer, factory branch, distributor, or distributor branch has established an agreement, program, incentive program, or provision for loss of incentive payments or other benefits that causes a dealer to refrain from selling any used motor vehicle subject to (a) recall, (b) stop sale directive, (c) technical service bulletin, or (d) other manufacturer, factory branch, distributor, or distributor branch notification to perform work on a dealer's used motor vehicles in its inventory when there is no remedy or there are no parts to remediate each such affected used motor vehicle from the manufacturer, factory branch, distributor, or distributor branch and for 90 days after the termination of such agreement, program, incentive program, or provision for loss of incentive payments or other benefits.

The data on which the manufacturer or distributor seeks to rely under this subsection shall only be for a period or periods not excluded under this subsection. For any performance standard or program that is used by a manufacturer or distributor for measuring dealership performance during the period or periods excluded under this subsection, a dealer shall be deemed in compliance with any such program requirements related to sales performance or sales or service customer satisfaction performance of a dealer.

This subsection shall not prevent a manufacturer, factory branch, distributor, or distributor branch from (1) requiring that a motor vehicle not be subject to an open recall or stop sale directive in order to be qualified, remain qualified, or be sold as a certified pre-owned vehicle or similar designation; (2) paying incentives for selling used vehicles with no unremedied recalls; (3) paying incentives for performing recall repairs on a vehicle in the dealer's inventory; or (4) instructing that a dealer repair used vehicles of the line-make for which the dealer holds a franchise with an open recall, provided that the instruction does not involve coercion that imposes a penalty or provision of loss of benefits on the dealer.

C. A dealer may apply to the manufacturer, factory branch, distributor, or distributor branch for adjustment to data, calculations, or statistical determinations of sales performance or sales and service customer satisfaction performance for any period of time that such dealer has at least five percent of its new motor vehicle inventory subject to a recall or stop sale directive and for 90 days after the end of such period of time. Within 30 days of application for adjustment, the manufacturer, factory branch, distributor, or distributor branch shall use reasonable efforts to review and adjust the data, calculations, or other statistical determinations back to the date that the dealer was prevented from selling the new motor vehicles. A dealer applying for adjustment shall have the burden of showing that the prevention of sale had a material, adverse impact on such dealer's new vehicle sales performance or sales and service customer satisfaction performance, and the adjustments by the manufacturer, factory branch, distributor, or distributor branch shall use reasonable efforts to remediate the effect of the impact shown on the data, calculations, or statistical determinations of sales performance or sales and service customer satisfaction performance.

The manufacturer shall take into consideration any adjustments to a dealer's new vehicle sales performance or sales and service customer satisfaction performance made by the manufacturer under this subsection in determining a dealer's compliance with a manufacturer performance standard or program.

History.
2001, cc. 165, 173; 2016, cc. 432, 534.

§ 46.2-1573. Hearings and other remedies; civil penalties.

A. In every case of a hearing before the Commissioner authorized under this article, the Commissioner shall give reasonable notice of each hearing to all interested parties, and the Commissioner's decision shall be binding on the parties, subject to the rights of judicial review and appeal as provided in Chapter 40 (§ 2.2-4000 et seq.) of Title 2.2. In every case of a hearing before the Commissioner authorized under this article based on a request or petition of a motor vehicle dealer, the manufacturer, factory branch, distributor, or distributor branch shall have the burden of proving by a preponderance of the evidence that the manufacturer, factory branch, distributor, or distributor branch has good cause to take the action or actions for which the dealer has filed the petition for a hearing or that such actions are reasonable if required under the relevant provision.

B. The hearing process before the Commissioner under this article shall commence within 90 days of the request for a hearing by prehearing conference between the hearing officer and the parties in person, by telephone, or by other electronic means designated by the Commissioner. The hearing officer will set the hearing on a date or dates consistent with the rights of due process of the parties. The Commissioner's decision shall be rendered within 60 days from the receipt of the hearing officer's recommendation. Hearings authorized under this article shall be presided over by a hearing officer selected from a list prepared by the Executive Secretary of the Supreme Court of Virginia within 60 days following the request for a hearing. Reasonable efforts shall be made to ensure that a hearing officer shall have at least five years of experience as a hearing officer in administrative hearings in the Commonwealth, shall have telephone and email capability, and shall be an active member of the Virginia State Bar. On request of the Commissioner, the Executive Secretary will name a hearing officer from the list, selected on a rotation system administered by the Executive Secretary. The hearing officer shall provide recommendations to the Commissioner within 90 days of the conclusion of the hearing.

C. Notwithstanding any contrary provision of this article, the Commissioner shall initiate investigations, conduct hearings, and determine the rights of parties under this article whenever he is provided information by the Motor Vehicle Dealer Board or any other person indicating a possible violation of any provision of this article.

D. For purposes of any matter brought to the Commissioner under subdivisions 3, 4, 5, 6 and 7b of § 46.2-1569 with respect to which the Commissioner is to determine whether there is good cause for a proposed action or whether it would be unreasonable under the circumstances, the Commissioner shall consider:

1. The volume of the affected dealer's business in the relevant market area;

2. The nature and extent of the dealer's investment in its business;

3. The adequacy of the dealer's capitalization to the franchisor's standards and the adequacy of the dealer's facilities, equipment, parts, supplies, and personnel;

4. The effect of the proposed action on the community;

5. The extent and quality of the dealer's service under motor vehicle warranties;

6. The dealer's performance under the terms of its franchise;

7. Other economic and geographical factors reasonably associated with the proposed action; and

8. The recommendations, if any, from a three-member panel composed of members of the Board who are franchised dealers not of the same line-make involved in the hearing and who are appointed to the panel by the Commissioner.

E. An interested party in a hearing held pursuant to subsection A of this section shall comply with the effective date of compliance established by the Commissioner in his decision in such hearing, unless a stay or extension of such date is granted by the Commissioner or the Commissioner's decision is under judicial review and appeal as provided in subsection A of this section. If, after notice to such interested party and an opportunity to comment, the Commissioner finds an interested party has not complied with his decision by the designated date of compliance, unless a stay or extension of such date has been granted by the Commissioner or the Commissioner's decision is under judicial review and appeal, the Commissioner may assess such interested party a civil penalty not to exceed $1,000 per day of noncompliance. Civil penalties collected under this subsection shall be deposited into the Transportation Trust Fund established pursuant to § 33.2-1524.

F. During the hearing process, parties may obtain documents and materials by discovery pursuant to Rules 4:9 and 4:9A of the Supreme Court of Virginia. The parties shall exchange reports of experts, which shall meet the standard of Rule 4:1 of the Supreme Court of Virginia, at times to be established by the hearing officer. The parties may utilize any other form of discovery provided under the Rules of Supreme Court of Virginia if allowed by the hearing officer based on good cause shown. For discovery permitted under the Rules of Supreme Court of Virginia, a party may object to the discovery sought or seek to limit the discovery sought on any grounds permitted by the Rules or applicable law.

History.

1988, c. 865, § 46.1-550.5:32; 1989, c. 727; 1992, c. 115; 1994, c. 702; 1995, cc. 767, 816; 2000, c. 106; 2001, cc. 165, 173; 2009, cc. 173, 176; 2010, cc. 284, 318; 2011, c. 650; 2015, c. 557.

§ 46.2-1573.01. Recovery of attorney's fees.

Any party to a proceeding under § 46.2-1573 who is found to have violated any provision of this article may be ordered by the circuit court before which an application therefor is pending to pay the reasonable attorney's fees and costs incurred by the complaining party, including those attorney's fees and costs incurred as a result of any appeal. Following issuance of the Commissioner's case decision finding that such violation has occurred, the complaining party may make application to an appropriate circuit court for entry of an order awarding it reasonable attorney's fees and costs. Notice of an initial application for entry of such order shall be served in the manner provided by law for the service of a summons in an action. The court shall take such evidence thereon as it deems necessary. Entry of a judgment in conformity with any order awarding such fees and costs shall be stayed pending any appeal of such order or pending any appeal of the Commissioner's underlying decision on the merits. Such application shall be made within sixty days following the date of the Commissioner's order. Venue for the application shall be the circuit court before which any appeal of the Commissioner's decision is pending, and the application may be considered concurrently with consideration of the appeal; otherwise, venue shall be as provided in § 2.2-4003.

History.

2001, cc. 812, 843.

§ 46.2-1573.02. Limited right of dealers to sell new motor vehicles following termination of franchise.

Notwithstanding any provision of this title to the contrary, a motor vehicle dealer shall have the right, for 180 days following the termination of its franchise, to continue to sell and advertise as new any existing new motor vehicle inventory of the line-make of the terminated franchise, under the following circumstances:

1. The vehicle was acquired in the ordinary course of business as a new vehicle by a dealer franchised to sell that vehicle;

2. The franchise agreement of the dealer is terminated, canceled, or rejected by the manufacturer, factory branch, distributor, or distributor branch and the termination, cancellation, or rejection is not a result of the revocation of the dealer's license to operate as a dealer or the dealer's conviction of a crime; and

3. The vehicle was held in the inventory of the dealer on the date of the franchise agreement's termination.

This provision does not entitle a dealer whose franchise agreement has been terminated, canceled, or rejected to continue to perform warranty service repairs or continue to be eligible to offer or receive consumer or dealer incentives offered by the manufacturer, factory branch, distributor, or distributor branch, except as earned by the dealer prior to termination of the franchise agreement.

History.
2010, cc. 284, 318.

ARTICLE 7.1.
LATE MODEL AND FACTORY REPURCHASE FRANCHISES.

§ 46.2-1573.1. Late model and factory repurchase franchises.

Franchised late model or factory repurchase motor vehicle dealers shall have the same rights and obligations as provided for franchised new motor vehicle dealers in Article 7 (§ 46.2-1566 et seq.) of this chapter, mutatis mutandis.

History.
1992, c. 572.

ARTICLE 7.2.
RECREATIONAL VEHICLE FRANCHISES.

§ 46.2-1573.2. Filing of franchises.

Each recreational vehicle manufacturer, factory branch, distributor, distributor branch, or subsidiary thereof shall file with the Commissioner a true copy of each new, amended, modified, or different form or addendum offered to more than one dealer that affects the rights, responsibilities, or obligations of the parties of a franchise or sales, service, or sales and service agreement to be offered to a recreational vehicle dealer or prospective recreational vehicle dealer in the Commonwealth no later than 60 days prior to the date the franchise or sales agreement is offered. In no event shall a new, amended, modified, or different form of franchise or sales, service, or sales and service agreement be offered a recreational vehicle dealer in the Commonwealth until the form has been determined by the Commissioner as not containing terms inconsistent with the provisions of this chapter. At the time a filing is made with the Commissioner pursuant to this section, the manufacturer, factory branch, distributor, distributor branch, or subsidiary shall also give written notice together with a copy of the papers so filed to the affected dealer or dealers.

History.
1995, cc. 767, 816, § 46.2-1973; 2015, c. 615.

§ 46.2-1573.3. Exemption of franchises from Retail Franchising Act.

Franchises subject to the provisions of this chapter shall not be subject to any requirement contained in Chapter 8 (§ 13.1-557 et seq.) of Title 13.1.

History.
1995, cc. 767, 816, § 46.2-1974; 2015, c. 615.

§ 46.2-1573.4. Coercion of retail dealer by manufacturer or distributor with respect to retail installment sales contracts prohibited; penalty.

A. It shall be unlawful for any manufacturer or distributor, or any officer, agent, or representative of either, to coerce or attempt to coerce any retail recreational vehicle dealer or prospective retail recreational vehicle dealer in the Commonwealth to sell, assign, or transfer any retail installment sales contract, obtained by the dealer in connection with the sale by him in the Commonwealth of recreational vehicles manufactured or sold by the manufacturer or distributor, to a specified finance company or class of finance companies or to any other specified persons by any of the following:

1. Any statement, suggestion, promise, or threat that the manufacturer or distributor will in any manner benefit or injure the dealer, whether the statement, suggestion, threat, or promise is expressed or implied or made directly or indirectly.

2. Any act that will benefit or injure the dealer.

3. Any contract, or any expressed or implied offer of contract, made directly or indirectly to the dealer, for handling the recreational vehicle on the condition that the dealer sell, assign, or transfer his retail installment sales contract on the recreational vehicle, in the Commonwealth, to a specified finance company or class of finance companies or to any other specified person.

4. Any expressed or implied statement or representation made directly or indirectly that the dealer is under any obligation whatsoever to sell, assign, or transfer any of his retail sales contracts in the Commonwealth on recreational vehicles manufactured or sold by the manufacturer or distributor to a finance company, class of finance companies, or other specified person, because of any relationship or affiliation between the manufacturer or distributor and the finance company or companies or the specified person.

B. Any such statements, threats, promises, acts, contracts, or offers of contracts, when their effect may be to lessen or eliminate competition or tend to create a monopoly, are declared unfair trade practices and unfair methods of competition and are prohibited.

C. Any person violating any of the provisions of this section is guilty of a Class 1 misdemeanor.

History.

1995, cc. 767, 816, § 46.2-1975; 1996, cc. 1043, 1052; 2015, c. 615.

§ 46.2-1573.5. Other coercion of dealers; transfer, grant, succession to and cancellation of dealer franchises; delivery of recreational vehicles, parts, and accessories.

It shall be unlawful for any manufacturer, factory branch, distributor, or distributor branch, or any field representative, officer, agent, or their representatives:

1. To coerce or attempt to coerce any dealer to accept delivery of any recreational vehicle or recreational vehicles, parts or accessories therefor, or any other commodities that have not been ordered by the dealer.

2. To coerce or attempt to coerce any dealer to enter into an agreement with the manufacturer, factory branch, distributor, or distributor branch, or representative thereof, or do any other act unfair to the dealer, by threatening to cancel any franchise existing between the manufacturer, factory branch, distributor, distributor branch, or representative thereof and the dealer.

3. To coerce or attempt to coerce any dealer to join, contribute to, or affiliate with any advertising association.

4. To prevent or refuse to approve the sale or transfer of the ownership of a dealership by the sale of the business, stock transfer, or otherwise, or the transfer, sale, or assignment of a dealer franchise, or a change in the executive management or principal operator of the dealership, unless the franchisor provides written notice to the dealer of its objection and the reasons therefor at least 30 days prior to the proposed effective date of the transfer, sale, assignment, or change. No such objection shall be effective to prevent the sale, transfer, assignment, or change if the Commissioner has determined, if requested in writing by the dealer within 30 days after receipt of an objection to the proposed sale, transfer, or change, and after a hearing on the matter, that the failure to permit or honor the sale, transfer, assignment, or change is unreasonable under the circumstances. No franchise may be sold, assigned, or transferred unless (i) the franchisor has been given at least 90 days' prior written notice by the dealer as to the identity, financial ability, and qualifications of the proposed transferee and (ii) the sale or transfer of the franchise and business will not involve, without the franchisor's consent, a relocation of the business.

5. To grant an additional franchise for a particular line-make of recreational vehicle in a relevant market area in which a dealer or dealers in that line-make are already located unless the franchisor has first advised in writing all other dealers in the line-make in the relevant market area. No such additional franchise may be established at the proposed site unless the Commissioner has determined, if requested by a dealer of the same line-make in the relevant market area within 30 days after receipt of the franchisor's notice of intention to establish the additional franchise, and after a hearing on the matter, that there is reasonable evidence that after the grant of the new franchise, the market will support all of the dealers in that line-make in the relevant market area. Establishing a franchised dealer in a relevant market area to replace a franchised dealer that has not been in operation for more than two years shall constitute the establishment of a new franchise subject to the terms of this subdivision. The two-year period for replacing a franchised dealer shall begin on the day the franchise was terminated or, if a termination hearing was held, on the day the franchisor was legally permitted finally to terminate the franchise. This subdivision shall not apply to (i) the relocation of an existing dealer within that dealer's relevant market area if the relocation site is to be more than 10 miles distant from any other dealer for the same line-make; (ii) the relocation of an existing dealer within that dealer's relevant market area if the relocation site is to be more distant than the existing site from all other dealers of the same line-make in that relevant market area; or (iii) the relocation of an existing new recreational vehicle dealer within two miles of the existing site of the relocating dealer.

6. Except as otherwise provided in this subdivision and notwithstanding the terms of any franchise, to terminate, cancel, or refuse to renew the franchise of any dealer without good cause and unless (i) the dealer and the Commissioner have received written notice of the franchisor's intentions at least 60 days prior to the effective date of such termination, cancellation, or the expiration date of the franchise, setting forth the specific grounds for the action, and (ii) the Commissioner has determined, if requested in writing by the dealer within the 60-day period and, after a hearing on the matter, that there is good cause for the termination, cancellation, or nonrenewal of the franchise. In any case where a petition is made to the Commissioner for a determination as to good cause for the termination, cancellation, or nonrenewal of a franchise, the franchise in question shall continue in effect pending the Commissioner's decision or, if that decision is appealed to the circuit court, pending the decision of the circuit court. In any case in which a franchisor neither advises a dealer that it does not intend to renew a franchise nor takes any action to renew a

franchise beyond its expiration date, the franchise in question shall continue in effect on the terms last agreed to by the parties. Notwithstanding the other provisions of this subdivision, notice of termination, cancellation, or nonrenewal may be provided to a dealer by a franchisor not less than 15 days prior to the effective date of such termination, cancellation, or nonrenewal when the grounds for such action are any of the following:

a. Insolvency of the franchised recreational vehicle dealer or filing of any petition by or against the franchised recreational vehicle dealer, under any bankruptcy or receivership law, leading to liquidation or that is intended to lead to liquidation of the franchisee's business;

b. Failure of the franchised recreational vehicle dealer to conduct its customary sales and service operations during its posted business hours for seven consecutive business days, except where the failure results from acts of God or circumstances beyond the direct control of the franchised recreational vehicle dealer;

c. Revocation of any license that the franchised recreational vehicle dealer is required to have to operate a dealership; or

d. Conviction of the dealer or any principal of the dealer of a felony.

The change or discontinuance of a marketing or distribution system of a particular line-make product by a manufacturer or distributor, while the name identification of the product is continued in substantial form by the same or different manufacturer or distributor, may be considered to be a franchise termination, cancellation, or nonrenewal.

7. To fail to provide continued parts and service support to a dealer that holds a franchise in a discontinued line-make for at least five years from the date of such discontinuance.

8. To fail to allow a dealer the right at any time to designate a member of his family as a successor to the dealership in the event of the death or incapacity of the dealer. It shall be unlawful to prevent or refuse to honor the succession to a dealership by a member of the family of a deceased or incapacitated dealer if the franchisor has not provided to the member of the family previously designated by the dealer as his successor written notice of its objections to the succession and of such person's right to seek a hearing on the matter before the Commissioner pursuant to this article, and the Commissioner determines, if requested in writing by such member of the family within 30 days of receipt of such notice from the franchisor, and after a hearing on the matter before the Commissioner pursuant to this article, that the failure to permit or honor the succession is unreasonable under the circumstances. No member of the family may succeed to a franchise unless (i) the franchisor has been given written notice as to the identity, financial ability, and qualifications of the member of the family in question and (ii) the succession to the franchise will not involve, without the franchisor's consent, a relocation of the business.

9. To fail to ship monthly to any dealer, if ordered by the dealer, the number of new recreational vehicles of each make, series, and model needed by the dealer to receive a percentage of total new recreational vehicle sales of each make, series, and model equitably related to the total new recreational vehicle production or importation currently being achieved nationally by each make, series, and model covered under the franchise. Upon the written request of any dealer holding its sales or sales and service franchise, the manufacturer or distributor shall disclose to the dealer in writing the basis upon which new recreational vehicles are allocated, scheduled, and delivered to the dealers of the same line-make. If allocation is at issue in a request for a hearing, the dealer may demand the Commissioner to direct that the manufacturer or distributor provide to the dealer, within 30 days of such demand, all records of sales and all records of distribution of all recreational vehicles to the same line-make dealers who compete with the dealer requesting the hearing.

10. To require or otherwise coerce a dealer to underutilize the dealer's facilities.

11. To include in any franchise with a recreational vehicle dealer terms that are contrary to, prohibited by, or otherwise inconsistent with the requirements of this chapter.

12. To require under any franchise agreement a recreational vehicle dealer to pay the attorney fees of the manufacturer or distributor related to hearings and appeals brought under this article.

13. To fail to include in any franchise with a recreational vehicle dealer the following language: "If any provision herein contravenes the laws or regulations of any state or other jurisdiction wherein this agreement is to be performed, or denies access to the procedures, forums, or remedies provided for by such laws or regulations, such provision shall be deemed to be modified to conform to such laws or regulations, and all other terms and provisions shall remain in full force," or words to that effect.

History.

1995, cc. 767, 816, § 46.2-1976; 1996, cc. 1043, 1052; 2015, c. 615.

§ 46.2-1573.6. Manufacturer or distributor right of first refusal.

Notwithstanding the terms of any franchise agreement, in the event of a proposed sale or transfer of a dealership, the manufacturer or distributor shall be permitted to exercise a right of first refusal to acquire the new recreational vehicle dealer's assets or ownership, if such sale or transfer is conditioned upon the manufacturer's or dealer's entering into a dealer agreement with the proposed new owner or transferee, only if all the following requirements are met:

1. To exercise its right of first refusal, the manufacturer or distributor must notify the dealer in writing within 45 days of its receipt of the completed proposal for the proposed sale or transfer;

2. The exercise of the right of first refusal will result in the dealer's and dealer owner's receiving the same or greater consideration as they have contracted to receive in connection with the proposed change of ownership or transfer;

3. The proposed sale or transfer of the dealership's assets does not involve the transfer or sale to a member or members of the family of one or more dealer owners, or to a qualified manager or a partnership or corporation controlled by such persons; and

4. The manufacturer or distributor agrees to pay the reasonable expenses, including attorney fees that do not exceed the usual, customary, and reasonable fees charged for similar work done for other clients, incurred by the proposed new owner and transferee prior to the manufacturer's or distributor's exercise of its right of first refusal in negotiating and implementing the contract for the proposed sale or transfer of the dealership or dealership assets. Notwithstanding the foregoing, no payment of such expenses and attorney fees shall be required if the dealer has not submitted or caused to be submitted an accounting of those expenses within 30 days of the dealer's receipt of the manufacturer's or distributor's written request for such an accounting. Such accounting may be requested by a manufacturer or distributor before exercising its right of first refusal.

History.

1995, cc. 767, 816, § 46.2-1977; 1996, cc. 1043, 1052; 2015, c. 615.

§ 46.2-1573.7. Discontinuation of distributors.

If the contract between a distributor and a manufacturer or importer is terminated or otherwise discontinued, all franchises granted to recreational vehicle dealers in the Commonwealth by that distributor shall continue in full force and shall not be affected by the discontinuance, except that the manufacturer, factory branch, distributor, representative, or other person who undertakes to distribute recreational vehicles of the same line-make or the same recreational vehicles of a renamed line-make shall be substituted for the discontinued distributor under the existing recreational vehicle dealer franchises, and those franchises shall be modified accordingly.

History.

1995, cc. 767, 816, § 46.2-1978; 2015, c. 615.

§ 46.2-1573.8. Warranty obligations.

A. Each recreational vehicle manufacturer, factory branch, distributor, or distributor branch shall (i) specify in writing to each of its recreational vehicle dealers licensed in the Commonwealth the dealer's obligations for preparation, delivery, and warranty service on its products and (ii) compensate the dealer for warranty parts, service, and diagnostic work required of the dealer by the manufacturer or distributor as follows:

1. Compensation of a dealer for warranty parts, service, and diagnostic work shall not be less than the amounts charged by the dealer for the manufacturer's or distributor's original parts, service, and diagnostic work to retail customers for nonwarranty service, parts, and diagnostic work installed or performed in the dealer's service department unless the amounts are not reasonable;

2. For purposes of determining warranty parts and service compensation, menu-priced parts or services, group discounts, special event discounts, and special event promotions shall not be considered in determining amounts charged by the dealer to retail customers;

3. Increases in dealer warranty parts and service compensation and diagnostic work compensation, pursuant to this section, shall be requested by the dealer in writing, shall be based on 100 consecutive repair orders or all repair orders over a 90-day period, whichever occurs first, and, in the case of parts, shall be stated as a percentage of markup that shall be uniformly applied to all the manufacturer's or distributor's parts;

4. In the case of warranty parts compensation, the provisions of this subsection shall be effective only for model year 1992 and succeeding model years;

5. If a manufacturer or distributor furnishes a part to a dealer at no cost for use by the dealer in performing work for which the manufacturer or distributor is required to compensate the dealer under this section, the manufacturer or distributor shall compensate the dealer for the part in the same manner as warranty parts compensation, less the wholesale costs, for such part as listed in the manufacturer's current price schedules. A manufacturer or distributor may pay the dealer a reasonable handling fee instead of the compensation otherwise required by this subsection for special high-performance complete engine assemblies in limited production recreational vehicles that constitute less than five percent of model production furnished to the dealer at no cost, if the manufacturer or distributor excludes such special high-performance complete engine assemblies in determining whether the amounts requested by the dealer for warranty compensation are consistent with the amounts that the dealer charges its other retail service customers for parts used by the dealer to perform similar work; or

6. In the case of service work, manufacturer original parts or parts otherwise specified by the manufacturer or distributor, and parts provided by a dealer either pursuant to an adjustment program as defined in § 59.1-207.34 or as otherwise requested by the manufacturer or distributor, the dealer shall

be compensated in the same manner as for warranty service or parts.

This section does not apply to compensation for parts such as components, systems, fixtures, appliances, furnishings, accessories, and features that are designed, used, and maintained primarily for nonvehicular, residential purposes. Warranty audits of dealer records may be conducted by the manufacturer, factory branch, distributor, or distributor branch on a reasonable basis, and dealer claims for warranty compensation shall not be denied except for good cause, such as performance of nonwarranty repairs, lack of material documentation, fraud, or misrepresentation. Claims for dealer compensation shall be paid within 30 days of dealer submission or within 30 days of the end of an incentive program or rejected in writing for stated reasons. The manufacturer, factory branch, distributor, or distributor branch shall reserve the right to reasonable periodic audits to determine the validity of all such paid claims for dealer compensation. Any chargebacks for warranty parts or service compensation and service incentives shall only be for the 12-month period immediately following the date of the claim and, in the case of chargebacks for sales compensation only, for the 18-month period immediately following the date of claim. However, such limitations shall not be effective in the case of intentionally false or fraudulent claims.

B. It shall be unlawful for any recreational vehicle manufacturer, factory branch, distributor, or distributor branch to:

1. Fail to perform any of its warranty obligations, including tires, with respect to a recreational vehicle;

2. Fail to assume all responsibility for any liability resulting from structural or production defects;

3. Fail to include in written notices of factory recalls to recreational vehicle owners and dealers the expected date by which necessary parts and equipment will be available to dealers for the correction of defects;

4. Fail to compensate any of the recreational vehicle dealers licensed in the Commonwealth for repairs effected by the dealer of merchandise damaged in manufacture or transit to the dealer where the carrier is designated by the manufacturer, factory branch, distributor, or distributor branch;

5. Fail to compensate its recreational vehicle dealers licensed in the Commonwealth for warranty parts, work, and service pursuant to subsection A or for legal costs and expenses incurred by such dealers in connection with warranty obligations for which the manufacturer, factory branch, distributor, or distributor branch is legally responsible or that the manufacturer, factory branch, distributor, or distributor branch imposes upon the dealer;

6. Misrepresent in any way to purchasers of recreational vehicles that warranties with respect to the manufacture, performance, or design of the recreational vehicle are made by the dealer, either as warrantor or co-warrantor;

7. Require the dealer to make warranties to customers in any manner related to the manufacture, performance, or design of the recreational vehicle; or

8. Shift or attempt to shift to the recreational vehicle dealer, directly or indirectly, any liabilities of the manufacturer, factory branch, distributor, or distributor branch under the Virginia Motor Vehicle Warranty Enforcement Act (§ 59.1-207.9 et seq.), unless such liability results from the act or omission by the dealer.

C. Notwithstanding the terms of any franchise, it shall be unlawful for any recreational vehicle manufacturer, factory branch, distributor, or distributor branch to fail to indemnify and hold harmless its recreational vehicle dealers against any losses or damages arising out of complaints, claims, or suits relating to the manufacture, assembly, or design of recreational vehicles, parts, or accessories, or other functions by the manufacturer, factory branch, distributor, or distributor branch beyond the control of the dealer, including, without limitation, the selection by the manufacturer, factory branch, distributor, or distributor branch of parts or components for the recreational vehicle or any damages to merchandise occurring in transit to the dealer where the carrier is designated by the manufacturer, factory branch, distributor, or distributor branch. The dealer shall notify the manufacturer of pending suits in which allegations are made that come within this subsection whenever reasonably practicable to do so. Every recreational vehicle dealer franchise issued to, amended, or renewed for recreational vehicle dealers in the Commonwealth shall be construed to incorporate provisions consistent with the requirements of this subsection.

D. On any new recreational vehicle, any uncorrected damage or any corrected damage exceeding three percent of the manufacturer's or distributor's suggested retail price as defined in 15 U.S.C. §§ 1231-1233, as measured by retail repair costs, must be disclosed to the dealer in writing prior to delivery. Factory mechanical repair and damage to glass, tires, and bumpers are excluded from the three percent rule when properly replaced by identical manufacturer's or distributor's original equipment or parts. Whenever a new recreational vehicle is damaged in transit, when the carrier or means of transportation is determined by the manufacturer or distributor, or whenever a recreational vehicle is otherwise damaged prior to delivery to the new recreational vehicle dealer, the new recreational vehicle dealer shall:

1. Notify the manufacturer or distributor of the damage within three business days from the date of delivery of the new recreational vehicle to the new recreational vehicle dealership or within the additional time specified in the franchise; and

2. Request from the manufacturer or distributor authorization to replace the components, parts, and accessories damaged or otherwise correct the damage, unless the damage to the recreational vehicle

exceeds the three percent rule, in which case the dealer may reject the vehicle within three business days.

E. If the manufacturer or distributor refuses or fails to authorize correction of such damage within 10 days after receipt of notification, or if the dealer rejects the recreational vehicle because damage exceeds the three percent rule, ownership of the new recreational vehicle shall revert to the manufacturer or distributor, and the new recreational vehicle dealer shall have no obligation, financial or otherwise, with respect to such recreational vehicle. Should either the manufacturer, distributor, or the dealer elect to correct the damage or any other damage exceeding the three percent rule, full disclosure shall be made by the dealer in writing to the buyer and an acknowledgment by the buyer is required. If there is less than three percent damage, no disclosure is required, provided that the damage has been corrected. Predelivery mechanical work shall not require a disclosure. Failure to disclose any corrected damage within the knowledge of the selling dealer to a new recreational vehicle in excess of the three percent rule shall constitute grounds for revocation of the buyer order, provided that, within 30 days of purchase, the recreational vehicle is returned to the dealer with an accompanying written notice of the grounds for revocation. In case of revocation pursuant to this section, the dealer shall accept the recreational vehicle and refund any payments made to the dealer in connection with the transaction, less a reasonable allowance for the consumer's use of the vehicle as defined in § 59.1-207.11.

F. If there is a dispute between the manufacturer, factory branch, distributor, or distributor branch and the dealer with respect to any matter referred to in subsection A, B, or C, either party may petition the Commissioner in writing, within 30 days after either party has given written notice of the dispute to the other, for a hearing. The decision of the Commissioner shall be binding on the parties, subject to rights of judicial review and appeal as provided in the Administrative Process Act (§ 2.2-4000 et seq.). However, nothing contained in this section shall give the Commissioner any authority as to the content or interpretation of any manufacturer's or distributor's warranty.

History.

1995, cc. 767, 816, § 46.2-1979; 1996, cc. 453, 1043, 1052; 2015, c. 615.

§ 46.2-1573.9. Operation of dealership by manufacturer.

It shall be unlawful for any recreational vehicle manufacturer, factory branch, distributor, distributor branch, or subsidiary thereof to own, operate, or control any recreational vehicle dealership in the Commonwealth. However, this section shall not prohibit:

1. The operation by a manufacturer, factory branch, distributor, distributor branch, or subsidiary thereof, of a dealership for a temporary period, not to exceed one year, during the transition from one owner or operator to another;
2. The ownership or control of a dealership by a manufacturer, factory branch, distributor, distributor branch, or subsidiary thereof, while the dealership is being sold under a bona fide contract or purchase option to the operator of the dealership;
3. The ownership, operation, or control of a dealership by a manufacturer, factory branch, distributor, distributor branch, or subsidiary thereof if the Commissioner determines, after a hearing at the request of any party, that there is no dealer independent of the manufacturer or distributor, factory branch or distributor branch, or subsidiary thereof available in the community or trade area to own and operate the franchise in a manner consistent with the public interest;
4. The ownership, operation, or control of a dealership dealing exclusively with school buses by a school bus manufacturer or school bus parts manufacturer or a person who assembles school buses; or
5. The ownership, operation, or control of a dealership dealing exclusively with refined fuels truck tanks by a manufacturer of refined fuels truck tanks or by a person who assembles refined fuels truck tanks.

History.

1995, cc. 767, 816, § 46.2-1980; 2015, c. 615.

§ 46.2-1573.10. Ownership of service facilities.

It shall be unlawful for any recreational vehicle manufacturer, factory branch, distributor, distributor branch, or subsidiary thereof to own, operate, or control, either directly or indirectly, any recreational vehicle warranty or service facility located in the Commonwealth. Nothing in this section shall prohibit any recreational vehicle manufacturer, factory branch, distributor, distributor branch, or subsidiary thereof from owning, operating, or controlling any warranty or service facility for warranty or service of recreational vehicles owned or operated by the manufacturer, factory branch, distributor, distributor branch, or subsidiary thereof. Nothing contained in this section shall prohibit a recreational vehicle manufacturer, factory branch, distributor, or distributor branch from performing service for reasons of compliance with an order of a court of competent jurisdiction or of warranty under Chapter 17.3 (§ 59.1-207.9 et seq.) of Title 59.1.

The preceding provisions of this section shall not apply to manufacturers of refined fuels truck tanks or to persons who assemble refined fuels truck tanks or to persons who exclusively manufacture or assemble school buses or school bus parts.

History.

1995, cc. 767, 816, § 46.2-1981; 2015, c. 615.

§ 46.2-1573.11. Hearings and other remedies; civil penalties.

A. In every case of a hearing before the Commissioner authorized under this article, the Commissioner shall give reasonable notice of each hearing to all interested parties, and the Commissioner's decision shall be binding on the parties, subject to the rights of judicial review and appeal as provided in the Administrative Process Act (§ 2.2-4000 et seq.).

B. Hearings before the Commissioner under this article shall commence within 90 days of the request for a hearing, and the Commissioner's decision shall be rendered within 60 days from the receipt of the hearing officer's recommendation. Hearings authorized under this article shall be presided over by a hearing officer selected from a list prepared by the Executive Secretary of the Supreme Court. On request of the Commissioner, the Executive Secretary will name a hearing officer from the list, selected on a rotation system administered by the Executive Secretary. The hearing officer shall provide recommendations to the Commissioner within 90 days of the conclusion of the hearing.

C. Notwithstanding any contrary provision of this article, the Commissioner shall initiate investigations, conduct hearings, and determine the rights of parties under this article whenever he is provided information indicating a possible violation of any provision of this article.

D. For purposes of any matter brought to the Commissioner under subdivisions 3, 4, 5, 6, and 9 of § 46.2-1573.5 with respect to which the Commissioner is to determine whether there is good cause for a proposed action or whether it would be unreasonable under the circumstances, the Commissioner shall consider:

1. The volume of the affected dealer's business in the relevant market area;

2. The nature and extent of the dealer's investment in its business;

3. The adequacy of the dealer's service facilities, equipment, parts, supplies, and personnel;

4. The effect of the proposed action on the community;

5. The extent and quality of the dealer's service under recreational vehicle warranties;

6. The dealer's performance under the terms of its franchise; and

7. Other economic and geographical factors reasonably associated with the proposed action.

With respect to subdivision 6, any performance standard or program for measuring dealership performance that may have a material effect on a dealer, and the application of any such standard or program by a manufacturer or distributor, shall be fair, reasonable, and equitable and, if based upon a survey, shall be based upon a statistically valid sample. Upon the request of any dealer, a manufacturer or distributor shall disclose in writing to the dealer a description of how a performance standard or program is designed and all relevant information used in the application of the performance standard or program to that dealer.

E. An interested party in a hearing held pursuant to subsection A shall comply with the effective date of compliance established by the Commissioner in his decision in such hearing, unless a stay or extension of such date is granted by the Commissioner or the Commissioner's decision is under judicial review and appeal as provided in subsection A. If, after notice to such interested party and an opportunity to comment, the Commissioner finds an interested party has not complied with his decision by the designated date of compliance, unless a stay or extension of such date has been granted by the Commissioner or the Commissioner's decision is under judicial review and appeal, the Commissioner may assess such interested party a civil penalty not to exceed $1,000 per day of noncompliance. Civil penalties collected under this subsection shall be deposited into the Transportation Trust Fund established pursuant to § 33.2-1524.

History.
1995, cc. 767, 816, § 46.2-1982; 2000, c. 106; 2015, c. 615.

§ 46.2-1573.12. Late model and factory repurchase franchises.

Franchised late model or factory repurchase recreational vehicle dealers shall have the same rights and obligations as provided for franchised new recreational vehicle dealers in this article, mutatis mutandis.

History.
1995, cc. 767, 816, § 46.2-1983; 2015, c. 615.

ARTICLE 7.3.

TRAILER FRANCHISES.

§ 46.2-1573.13. Watercraft trailer dealers and watercraft trailers.

For the purposes of this article:

"Dealer" and *"trailer dealer"* includes watercraft trailer dealers.

"Trailer" includes watercraft trailers.

History.
2015, c. 615.

§ 46.2-1573.14. Trailer dealers filing of franchises.

Each trailer manufacturer, factory branch, distributor, distributor branch, or subsidiary thereof shall file with the Commissioner a true copy of each new, amended, modified, or different form or addendum offered to more than one dealer that affects the rights, responsibilities, or obligations of the parties of a franchise or sales, service, or sales and service agreement to be offered to a trailer dealer or prospective trailer dealer in the Commonwealth no later than 60 days prior to the date the franchise or sales agreement is offered. In no event shall a new, amended, modified, or different form of franchise or sales, service, or sales and service agreement be offered a trailer dealer in the Commonwealth until the form has been determined by the Commissioner as not containing terms inconsistent with the provisions of this chapter. At the time a filing is made with the Commissioner pursuant to this section, the manufacturer, factory branch, distributor, distributor branch, or subsidiary shall also give written notice together with a copy of the papers so filed to the affected dealer or dealers.

History.
1996, cc. 1043, 1052, § 46.2-1992.66; 2015, c. 615.

§ 46.2-1573.15. Exemption of franchises from Retail Franchising Act.

Franchises subject to the provisions of this chapter shall not be subject to any requirement contained in Chapter 8 (§ 13.1-557 et seq.) of Title 13.1.

History.
1996, cc. 1043, 1052, § 46.2-1992.67; 2015, c. 615.

§ 46.2-1573.16. Coercion of retail dealer by manufacturer or distributor with respect to retail installment sales contracts prohibited; penalty.

A. It shall be unlawful for any manufacturer or distributor, or any officer, agent, or representative of either, to coerce or attempt to coerce any retail trailer dealer or prospective retail trailer dealer in the Commonwealth to sell, assign, or transfer any retail installment sales contract obtained by the dealer in connection with the sale by him in the Commonwealth of trailers manufactured or sold by the manufacturer or distributor, to a specified finance company or class of finance companies or to any other specified persons by any of the following:

1. Any statement, suggestion, promise, or threat that the manufacturer or distributor will in any manner benefit or injure the dealer, whether the statement, suggestion, threat, or promise is expressed or implied or made directly or indirectly.

2. Any act that will benefit or injure the dealer.

3. Any contract, or any expressed or implied offer of contract, made directly or indirectly to the dealer, for handling the trailer on the condition that the dealer sell, assign, or transfer his retail installment sales contract on the trailer, in the Commonwealth, to a specified finance company or class of finance companies or to any other specified person.

4. Any expressed or implied statement or representation made directly or indirectly that the dealer is under any obligation whatsoever to sell, assign, or transfer any of his retail sales contracts in the Commonwealth on trailers manufactured or sold by the manufacturer or distributor to a finance company, or class of finance companies, or other specified person, because of any relationship or affiliation between the manufacturer or distributor and the finance company or companies or the specified person.

B. Any such statements, threats, promises, acts, contracts, or offers of contracts, when their effect may be to lessen or eliminate competition or tend to create a monopoly, are declared unfair trade practices and unfair methods of competition and are prohibited.

C. Any person violating any of the provisions of this section is guilty of a Class 1 misdemeanor.

History.
1996, cc. 1043, 1052, § 46.2-1992.68; 2015, c. 615.

§ 46.2-1573.17. Other coercion of dealers; transfer, grant, succession to and cancellation of dealer franchises; delivery of trailers, parts, and accessories.

It shall be unlawful for any manufacturer, factory branch, distributor, or distributor branch, or any field representative, officer, agent, or their representatives:

1. To coerce or attempt to coerce any dealer to accept delivery of any trailer or trailers, parts or accessories therefor, or any other commodities that have not been ordered by the dealer.

2. To coerce or attempt to coerce any dealer to enter into an agreement with the manufacturer, factory branch, distributor, or distributor branch, or representative thereof, or do any other act unfair to the dealer, by threatening to cancel any franchise existing between the manufacturer, factory branch, distributor, distributor branch, or representative thereof and the dealer.

3. To coerce or attempt to coerce any dealer to join, contribute to, or affiliate with any advertising association.

4. To prevent or refuse to approve the sale or transfer of the ownership of a dealership by the sale of the business, stock transfer, or otherwise, or the transfer, sale, or assignment of a dealer franchise, or a change in the executive management or principal operator of the dealership, unless the franchisor provides written notice to the dealer of its objection and the reasons therefor at least 30 days prior to the proposed effective date of the transfer, sale, assignment, or change. No such objection shall be effective to prevent the sale, transfer, assignment, or change if the Commissioner has determined, if requested in writing by the dealer within 30 days after receipt of an objection to the proposed sale, transfer, or change, and after a hearing on the matter, that the failure to permit or honor the sale, transfer, assignment, or change is unreasonable under the circumstances. No franchise may be sold, assigned, or

transferred unless (i) the franchisor has been given at least 90 days' prior written notice by the dealer as to the identity, financial ability, and qualifications of the proposed transferee and (ii) the sale or transfer of the franchise and business will not involve, without the franchisor's consent, a relocation of the business.

5. To grant an additional franchise for a particular line-make of trailer in a relevant market area in which a dealer or dealers in that line-make are already located unless the franchisor has first advised in writing all other dealers in the line-make in the relevant market area. No such additional franchise may be established at the proposed site unless the Commissioner has determined, if requested by a dealer of the same line-make in the relevant market area within 30 days after receipt of the franchisor's notice of intention to establish the additional franchise, and after a hearing on the matter, that there is reasonable evidence that after the grant of the new franchise, the market will support all of the dealers in that line-make in the relevant market area. Establishing a franchised dealer in a relevant market area to replace a franchised dealer that has not been in operation for more than two years shall constitute the establishment of a new franchise subject to the terms of this subdivision. The two-year period for replacing a franchised dealer shall begin on the day the franchise was terminated or, if a termination hearing was held, on the day the franchisor was legally permitted finally to terminate the franchise. This subdivision shall not apply to (i) the relocation of an existing dealer within that dealer's relevant market area if the relocation site is to be more than 10 miles distant from any other dealer for the same line-make; (ii) the relocation of an existing dealer within that dealer's relevant market area if the relocation site is to be more distant than the existing site from all other dealers of the same line-make in that relevant market area; or (iii) the relocation of an existing new trailer dealer within two miles of the existing site of the relocating dealer.

6. Except as otherwise provided in this subdivision and notwithstanding the terms of any franchise, to terminate, cancel, or refuse to renew the franchise of any dealer without good cause and unless (i) the dealer and the Commissioner have received written notice of the franchisor's intentions at least 60 days prior to the effective date of such termination, cancellation, or the expiration date of the franchise, setting forth the specific grounds for the action, and (ii) the Commissioner has determined, if requested in writing by the dealer within the 60-day period, and after a hearing on the matter, that there is good cause for the termination, cancellation, or nonrenewal of the franchise. In any case where a petition is made to the Commissioner for a determination as to good cause for the termination, cancellation, or nonrenewal of a franchise, the franchise in question shall continue in effect pending the Commissioner's decision or, if that decision is appealed to the circuit court, pending the decision of the circuit court. In any case in which a franchisor neither advises a dealer that it does not intend to renew a franchise nor takes any action to renew a franchise beyond its expiration date, the franchise in question shall continue in effect on the terms last agreed to by the parties. Notwithstanding the other provisions of this subdivision, notice of termination, cancellation, or nonrenewal may be provided to a dealer by a franchisor not less than 15 days prior to the effective date of such termination, cancellation, or nonrenewal when the grounds for such action are any of the following:

a. Insolvency of the franchised trailer dealer or filing of any petition by or against the franchised trailer dealer, under any bankruptcy or receivership law, leading to liquidation or that is intended to lead to liquidation of the franchisee's business;

b. Failure of the franchised trailer dealer to conduct its customary sales and service operations during its posted business hours for seven consecutive business days, except where the failure results from acts of God or circumstances beyond the direct control of the franchised trailer dealer;

c. Revocation of any license that the franchised trailer dealer is required to have to operate a dealership; or

d. Conviction of the dealer or any principal of the dealer of a felony.

The change or discontinuance of a marketing or distribution system of a particular line-make product by a manufacturer or distributor, while the name identification of the product is continued in substantial form by the same or different manufacturer or distributor, may be considered to be a franchise termination, cancellation, or nonrenewal.

7. To fail to provide continued parts and service support to a dealer that holds a franchise in a discontinued line-make for at least five years from the date of such discontinuance.

8. To fail to allow a dealer the right at any time to designate a member of his family as a successor to the dealership in the event of the death or incapacity of the dealer. It shall be unlawful to prevent or refuse to honor the succession to a dealership by a member of the family of a deceased or incapacitated dealer if the franchisor has not provided to the member of the family previously designated by the dealer as his successor written notice of its objections to the succession and of such person's right to seek a hearing on the matter before the Commissioner pursuant to this article, and the Commissioner determines, if requested in writing by such member of the family within 30 days of receipt of such notice from the franchisor, and after a hearing on the matter before the Commissioner pursuant to this article, that the failure to permit or honor the succession is unreasonable under the circumstances. No member of the family may succeed to a franchise unless (i) the franchisor has been given written

notice as to the identity, financial ability, and qualifications of the member of the family in question and (ii) the succession to the franchise will not involve, without the franchisor's consent, a relocation of the business.

9. To fail to ship monthly to any dealer, if ordered by the dealer, the number of new trailers of each make, series, and model needed by the dealer to receive a percentage of total new trailer sales of each make, series, and model equitably related to the total new trailer production or importation currently being achieved nationally by each make, series, and model covered under the franchise. Upon the written request of any dealer holding its sales or sales and service franchise, the manufacturer or distributor shall disclose to the dealer in writing the basis upon which new trailers are allocated, scheduled, and delivered to the dealers of the same line-make. If allocation is at issue in a request for a hearing, the dealer may demand the Commissioner to direct that the manufacturer or distributor provide to the dealer, within 30 days of such demand, all records of sales and all records of distribution of all trailers to the same line-make dealers who compete with the dealer requesting the hearing.

10. To require or otherwise coerce a dealer to underutilize the dealer's facilities.

11. To include in any franchise with a trailer dealer terms that are contrary to, prohibited by, or otherwise inconsistent with the requirements of this chapter.

12. To require under any franchise agreement a trailer dealer to pay the attorney fees of the manufacturer or distributor related to hearings and appeals brought under this article.

13. To fail to include in any franchise with a trailer dealer the following language: "If any provision herein contravenes the laws or regulations of any state or other jurisdiction wherein this agreement is to be performed, or denies access to the procedures, forums, or remedies provided for by such laws or regulations, such provision shall be deemed to be modified to conform to such laws or regulations, and all other terms and provisions shall remain in full force," or words to that effect.

History.

1996, cc. 1043, 1052, § 46.2-1992.69; 2015, c. 615.

§ 46.2-1573.18. Manufacturer or distributor right of first refusal.

Notwithstanding the terms of any franchise agreement, in the event of a proposed sale or transfer of a dealership, the manufacturer or distributor shall be permitted to exercise a right of first refusal to acquire the new trailer dealer's assets or ownership, if such sale or transfer is conditioned upon the manufacturer's or dealer's entering into a dealer agreement with the proposed new owner or transferee, only if all the following requirements are met:

1. To exercise its right of first refusal, the manufacturer or distributor must notify the dealer in writing within 45 days of its receipt of the completed proposal for the proposed sale or transfer;

2. The exercise of the right of first refusal will result in the dealer's and dealer owner's receiving the same or greater consideration as they have contracted to receive in connection with the proposed change of ownership or transfer;

3. The proposed sale or transfer of the dealership's assets does not involve the transfer or sale to a member or members of the family of one or more dealer owners, or to a qualified manager or a partnership or corporation controlled by such persons; and

4. The manufacturer or distributor agrees to pay the reasonable expenses, including attorney fees that do not exceed the usual, customary, and reasonable fees charged for similar work done for other clients, incurred by the proposed new owner and transferee prior to the manufacturer's or distributor's exercise of its right of first refusal in negotiating and implementing the contract for the proposed sale or transfer of the dealership or dealership assets. Notwithstanding the foregoing, no payment of such expenses and attorney fees shall be required if the dealer has not submitted or caused to be submitted an accounting of those expenses within 30 days of the dealer's receipt of the manufacturer's or distributor's written request for such an accounting. Such accounting may be requested by a manufacturer or distributor before exercising its right of first refusal.

History.

1996, cc. 1043, 1052, § 46.2-1992.70; 2015, c. 615.

§ 46.2-1573.19. Discontinuation of distributors.

If the contract between a distributor and a manufacturer or importer is terminated or otherwise discontinued, all franchises granted to trailer dealers in the Commonwealth by that distributor shall continue in full force and shall not be affected by the discontinuance, except that the manufacturer, factory branch, distributor, representative, or other person who undertakes to distribute trailers of the same line-make or the same trailers of a renamed line-make shall be substituted for the discontinued distributor under the existing trailer dealer franchises, and those franchises shall be modified accordingly.

History.

1996, cc. 1043, 1052, § 46.2-1992.71; 2015, c. 615.

§ 46.2-1573.20. Warranty obligations.

A. Each trailer manufacturer, factory branch, distributor, or distributor branch shall (i) specify in writing to each of its trailer dealers licensed in the

Commonwealth the dealer's obligations for preparation, delivery, and warranty service on its products and (ii) compensate the dealer for warranty parts, service, and diagnostic work required of the dealer by the manufacturer or distributor as follows:

1. Compensation of a dealer for warranty parts, service, and diagnostic work shall not be less than the amounts charged by the dealer for the manufacturer's or distributor's original parts, service, and diagnostic work to retail customers for nonwarranty service, parts, and diagnostic work installed or performed in the dealer's service department unless the amounts are not reasonable;

2. For purposes of determining warranty parts and service compensation, menu-priced parts or services, group discounts, special event discounts, and special event promotions shall not be considered in determining amounts charged by the dealer to retail customers;

3. Increases in dealer warranty parts and service compensation and diagnostic work compensation, pursuant to this section, shall be requested by the dealer in writing, shall be based on 100 consecutive repair orders or all repair orders over a 90-day period, whichever occurs first, and, in the case of parts, shall be stated as a percentage of markup that shall be uniformly applied to all the manufacturer's or distributor's parts;

4. In the case of warranty parts compensation, the provisions of this subsection shall be effective only for model year 1992 and succeeding model years;

5. If a manufacturer or distributor furnishes a part to a dealer at no cost for use by the dealer in performing work for which the manufacturer or distributor is required to compensate the dealer under this section, the manufacturer or distributor shall compensate the dealer for the part in the same manner as warranty parts compensation, less the wholesale costs, for such part as listed in the manufacturer's current price schedules; or

6. In the case of service work, manufacturer original parts or parts otherwise specified by the manufacturer or distributor, and parts provided by a dealer either pursuant to an adjustment program as defined in § 59.1-207.34 or as otherwise requested by the manufacturer or distributor, the dealer shall be compensated in the same manner as for warranty service or parts.

This section does not apply to compensation for parts such as components, systems, fixtures, appliances, furnishings, accessories, and features that are designed, used, and maintained primarily for nonvehicular, residential purposes. Warranty audits of dealer records may be conducted by the manufacturer, factory branch, distributor, or distributor branch on a reasonable basis, and dealer claims for warranty compensation shall not be denied except for good cause, such as performance of nonwarranty repairs, lack of material documentation, fraud, or misrepresentation. Claims for dealer compensation shall be paid within 30 days of dealer submission or within 30 days of the end of an incentive program or rejected in writing for stated reasons. The manufacturer, factory branch, distributor, or distributor branch shall reserve the right to reasonable periodic audits to determine the validity of all such paid claims for dealer compensation. Any chargebacks for warranty parts or service compensation and service incentives shall only be for the 12-month period immediately following the date of the claim and, in the case of chargebacks for sales compensation only, for the 18-month period immediately following the date of claim. However, such limitations shall not be effective in the case of intentionally false or fraudulent claims.

B. It shall be unlawful for any trailer manufacturer, factory branch, distributor, or distributor branch to:

1. Fail to perform any of its warranty obligations, including tires, with respect to a trailer;

2. Fail to assume all responsibility for any liability resulting from structural or production defects;

3. Fail to include in written notices of factory recalls to trailer owners and dealers the expected date by which necessary parts and equipment will be available to dealers for the correction of defects;

4. Fail to compensate any of the trailer dealers licensed in the Commonwealth for repairs effected by the dealer of merchandise damaged in manufacture or transit to the dealer where the carrier is designated by the manufacturer, factory branch, distributor, or distributor branch;

5. Fail to compensate its trailer dealers licensed in the Commonwealth for warranty parts, work, and service pursuant to subsection A or for legal costs and expenses incurred by such dealers in connection with warranty obligations for which the manufacturer, factory branch, distributor, or distributor branch is legally responsible or that the manufacturer, factory branch, distributor, or distributor branch imposes upon the dealer;

6. Misrepresent in any way to purchasers of trailers that warranties with respect to the manufacture, performance, or design of the trailer are made by the dealer, either as warrantor or co-warrantor;

7. Require the dealer to make warranties to customers in any manner related to the manufacture, performance, or design of the trailer; or

8. Shift or attempt to shift to the trailer dealer, directly or indirectly, any liabilities of the manufacturer, factory branch, distributor, or distributor branch under the Virginia Motor Vehicle Warranty Enforcement Act (§ 59.1-207.9 et seq.), unless such liability results from the act or omission by the dealer.

C. Notwithstanding the terms of any franchise, it shall be unlawful for any trailer manufacturer, factory branch, distributor, or distributor branch to fail to indemnify and hold harmless its trailer dealers against any losses or damages arising out of complaints, claims, or suits relating to the manufacture, assembly, or design of trailers, parts, or accessories, or other functions by the manufacturer, factory branch, distributor, or distributor branch beyond the control of the dealer, including, without limitation, the selection by the manufacturer, factory branch, distributor, or distributor branch of parts or components for the trailer or any damages to merchandise occurring in transit to the dealer where the carrier is designated by the manufacturer, factory branch, distributor, or distributor branch. The dealer shall notify the manufacturer of pending suits in which allegations are made that come within this subsection whenever reasonably practicable to do so. Every trailer dealer franchise issued to, amended, or renewed for trailer dealers in the Commonwealth shall be construed to incorporate provisions consistent with the requirements of this subsection.

D. On any new trailer, any uncorrected damage or any corrected damage exceeding three percent of the manufacturer's or distributor's suggested retail price as defined in 15 U.S.C. §§ 1231-1233, as measured by retail repair costs, must be disclosed to the dealer in writing prior to delivery. Factory mechanical repair and damage to glass, tires, and bumpers are excluded from the three percent rule when properly replaced by identical manufacturer's or distributor's original equipment or parts. Whenever a new trailer is damaged in transit, when the carrier or means of transportation is determined by the manufacturer or distributor, or whenever a trailer is otherwise damaged prior to delivery to the new trailer dealer, the new trailer dealer shall:

1. Notify the manufacturer or distributor of the damage within three business days from the date of delivery of the new trailer to the new trailer dealership or within the additional time specified in the franchise; and

2. Request from the manufacturer or distributor authorization to replace the components, parts, and accessories damaged or otherwise correct the damage, unless the damage to the trailer exceeds the three percent rule, in which case the dealer may reject the trailer within three business days.

E. If the manufacturer or distributor refuses or fails to authorize correction of such damage within 10 days after receipt of notification, or if the dealer rejects the trailer because damage exceeds the three percent rule, ownership of the new trailer shall revert to the manufacturer or distributor, and the new trailer dealer shall have no obligation, financial or otherwise, with respect to such trailer. Should either the manufacturer, distributor, or the dealer elect to correct the damage or any other damage exceeding the three percent rule, full disclosure shall be made by the dealer in writing to the buyer and an acknowledgment by the buyer is required. If there is less than three percent damage, no disclosure is required, provided that the damage has been corrected. Predelivery mechanical work shall not require a disclosure. Failure to disclose any corrected damage within the knowledge of the selling dealer to a new trailer in excess of the three percent rule shall constitute grounds for revocation of the buyer order, provided that, within 30 days of purchase, the trailer is returned to the dealer with an accompanying written notice of the grounds for revocation. In case of revocation pursuant to this section, the dealer shall accept the trailer and refund any payments made to the dealer in connection with the transaction, less a reasonable allowance for the consumer's use of the trailer as defined in § 59.1-207.11.

F. If there is a dispute between the manufacturer, factory branch, distributor, or distributor branch and the dealer with respect to any matter referred to in subsection A, B, or C, either party may petition the Commissioner in writing, within 30 days after either party has given written notice of the dispute to the other, for a hearing. The decision of the Commissioner shall be binding on the parties, subject to rights of judicial review and appeal as provided in the Administrative Process Act (§ 2.2-4000 et seq.). However, nothing contained in this section shall give the Commissioner any authority as to the content or interpretation of any manufacturer's or distributor's warranty.

History.

1996, cc. 1043, 1052, § 46.2-1992.72; 2015, c. 615.

§ 46.2-1573.21. Operation of dealership by manufacturer.

It shall be unlawful for any trailer manufacturer, factory branch, distributor, distributor branch, or subsidiary thereof to own, operate, or control any trailer dealership in the Commonwealth. However, this section shall not prohibit:

1. The operation by a manufacturer, factory branch, distributor, distributor branch, or subsidiary thereof, of a dealership for a temporary period, not to exceed one year, during the transition from one owner or operator to another;

2. The ownership or control of a dealership by a manufacturer, factory branch, distributor, distributor branch, or subsidiary thereof, while the dealership is being sold under a bona fide contract or purchase option to the operator of the dealership; or

3. The ownership, operation, or control of a dealership by a manufacturer, factory branch, distributor, distributor branch, or subsidiary thereof if the Commissioner determines, after a hearing at the request of any party, that there is no dealer independent of the manufacturer or distributor, factory branch or distributor branch, or subsidiary thereof available in the community or trade area to own and operate the franchise in a manner consistent with the public interest.

History.

1996, cc. 1043, 1052, § 46.2-1992.73; 2015, c. 615.

§ 46.2-1573.22. Ownership of service facilities.

It shall be unlawful for any trailer manufacturer, factory branch, distributor, distributor branch, or subsidiary thereof to own, operate, or control, either directly or indirectly, any trailer warranty or service facility located in the Commonwealth. Nothing in this section shall prohibit any trailer manufacturer, factory branch, distributor, distributor branch, or subsidiary thereof from owning, operating, or controlling any warranty or service facility for warranty or service of trailers owned or operated by the manufacturer, factory branch, distributor, distributor branch, or subsidiary thereof. Nothing contained in this section shall prohibit a trailer manufacturer, factory branch, distributor, or distributor branch from performing service for reasons of compliance with an order of a court of competent jurisdiction or of warranty under Chapter 17.3 (§ 59.1-207.9 et seq.) of Title 59.1.

History.

1996, cc. 1043, 1052, § 46.2-1992.74; 2015, c. 615.

§ 46.2-1573.23. Hearings and other remedies; civil penalties.

A. In every case of a hearing before the Commissioner authorized under this article, the Commissioner shall give reasonable notice of each hearing to all interested parties, and the Commissioner's decision shall be binding on the parties, subject to the rights of judicial review and appeal as provided in the Administrative Process Act (§ 2.2-4000 et seq.).

B. Hearings before the Commissioner under this article shall commence within 90 days of the request for a hearing, and the Commissioner's decision shall be rendered within 60 days from the receipt of the hearing officer's recommendation. Hearings authorized under this article shall be presided over by a hearing officer selected from a list prepared by the Executive Secretary of the Supreme Court. On request of the Commissioner, the Executive Secretary will name a hearing officer from the list, selected on a rotation system administered by the Executive Secretary. The hearing officer shall provide recommendations to the Commissioner within 90 days of the conclusion of the hearing.

C. Notwithstanding any contrary provision of this article, the Commissioner shall initiate investigations, conduct hearings, and determine the rights of parties under this article whenever he is provided information indicating a possible violation of any provision of this article.

D. For purposes of any matter brought to the Commissioner under subdivisions 3, 4, 5, 6, and 9 of § 46.2-1573.16 with respect to which the Commissioner is to determine whether there is good cause for a proposed action or whether it would be unreasonable under the circumstances, the Commissioner shall consider:

1. The volume of the affected dealer's business in the relevant market area;
2. The nature and extent of the dealer's investment in its business;
3. The adequacy of the dealer's service facilities, equipment, parts, supplies, and personnel;
4. The effect of the proposed action on the community;
5. The extent and quality of the dealer's service under trailer warranties;
6. The dealer's performance under the terms of its franchise; and
7. Other economic and geographical factors reasonably associated with the proposed action.

With respect to subdivision 6, any performance standard or program for measuring dealership performance that may have a material effect on a dealer, and the application of any such standard or program by a manufacturer or distributor, shall be fair, reasonable, and equitable and, if based upon a survey, shall be based upon a statistically valid sample. Upon the request of any dealer, a manufacturer or distributor shall disclose in writing to the dealer a description of how a performance standard or program is designed and all relevant information used in the application of the performance standard or program to that dealer.

E. An interested party in a hearing held pursuant to subsection A shall comply with the effective date of compliance established by the Commissioner in his decision in such hearing, unless a stay or extension of such date is granted by the Commissioner or the Commissioner's decision is under judicial review and appeal as provided in subsection A. If, after notice to such interested party and an opportunity to comment, the Commissioner finds an interested party has not complied with his decision by the designated date of compliance, unless a stay or extension of such date has been granted by the Commissioner or the Commissioner's decision is under judicial review and appeal, the Commissioner may assess such interested party a civil penalty not to exceed $1,000 per day of noncompliance. Civil penalties collected under this subsection shall be deposited into the Transportation Trust Fund established pursuant to § 33.2-1524.

History.

1996, cc. 1043, 1052, § 46.2-1992.75; 2000, c. 106; 2015, c. 615.

§ 46.2-1573.24. Late model and factory repurchase franchises.

Franchised late model or factory repurchase trailer dealers shall have the same rights and obligations as provided for franchised new trailer dealers in this article, mutatis mutandis.

History.

1996, cc. 1043, 1052, § 46.2-1992.76; 2015, c. 615.

ARTICLE 7.4.
MOTORCYCLE FRANCHISES.

§ 46.2-1573.25. Motorcycle dealers filing of franchises.

Except as otherwise provided in this section, each motorcycle manufacturer, factory branch, distributor, distributor branch, or subsidiary thereof shall file with the Commissioner a true copy of each new, amended, modified, or different form or addendum offered to more than one dealer that affects the rights, responsibilities, or obligations of the parties of a franchise or sales, service, or sales and service agreement to be offered to a motorcycle dealer or prospective motorcycle dealer in the Commonwealth no later than 60 days prior to the date the franchise or sales agreement is offered. In no event shall a new, amended, modified, or different form of franchise or sales, service, or sales and service agreement be offered a motorcycle dealer in the Commonwealth until the form has been determined by the Commissioner as not containing terms inconsistent with the provisions of this chapter. At the time a filing is made with the Commissioner pursuant to this section, the manufacturer, factory branch, distributor, distributor branch, or subsidiary shall also give written notice together with a copy of the papers so filed to the affected dealer or dealers.

The provisions of this article shall not apply to a manufacturer, factory branch, distributor, distributor branch, or factory or distributor representative engaged in the manufacture or distribution of all-terrain vehicles or off-road motorcycles that does not also manufacture or does not also distribute in the Commonwealth any motorcycle designed for lawful use on the public highways.

History.

1996, cc. 1043, 1052, § 46.2-1993.64; 2003, c. 334; 2015, c. 615.

§ 46.2-1573.26. Exemption of franchises from Retail Franchising Act.

Franchises subject to the provisions of this chapter shall not be subject to any requirement contained in Chapter 8 (§ 13.1-557 et seq.) of Title 13.1.

History.

1996, cc. 1043, 1052, § 46.2-1993.65; 2015, c. 615.

§ 46.2-1573.27. Coercion of retail dealer by manufacturer or distributor with respect to retail installment sales contracts and extended warranties prohibited; penalty.

A. It shall be unlawful for any manufacturer or distributor, or any officer, agent, or representative of either, to coerce or attempt to coerce any retail motorcycle dealer or prospective retail motorcycle dealer in the Commonwealth to sell or offer to sell extended warranties or to sell, assign, or transfer any retail installment sales contract obtained by the dealer in connection with the sale by him in the Commonwealth of motorcycles manufactured or sold by the manufacturer or distributor, to a specified finance company or class of finance companies or to any other specified persons by any of the following:

1. Any statement, suggestion, promise, or threat that the manufacturer or distributor will in any manner benefit or injure the dealer, whether the statement, suggestion, threat, or promise is expressed or implied or made directly or indirectly.

2. Any act that will benefit or injure the dealer.

3. Any contract, or any expressed or implied offer of contract, made directly or indirectly to the dealer, for handling the motorcycle on the condition that the dealer sell, assign, or transfer his retail installment sales contract on the motorcycle, in the Commonwealth, to a specified finance company or class of finance companies or to any other specified person.

4. Any expressed or implied statement or representation made directly or indirectly that the dealer is under any obligation whatsoever to sell, assign, or transfer any of his retail sales contracts in the Commonwealth on motorcycles manufactured or sold by the manufacturer or distributor to a finance company, or class of finance companies, or other specified person, because of any relationship or affiliation between the manufacturer or distributor and the finance company or companies or the specified person.

B. Any such statements, threats, promises, acts, contracts, or offers of contracts, when their effect may be to lessen or eliminate competition or tend to create a monopoly, are declared unfair trade practices and unfair methods of competition and are prohibited.

C. Any person violating any of the provisions of this section is guilty of a Class 1 misdemeanor.

History.

1996, cc. 1043, 1052, § 46.2-1993.66; 2015, c. 615.

§ 46.2-1573.28. Other coercion of dealers; transfer, grant, succession to and cancellation of dealer franchises; delivery of motorcycles, parts, and accessories.

It shall be unlawful for any manufacturer, factory branch, distributor, or distributor branch, or any field representative, officer, agent, or their representatives:

1. To coerce or attempt to coerce any dealer to accept delivery of any motorcycle or motorcycles, parts or accessories therefor, or any other commodities that have not been ordered by the dealer.

2. To coerce or attempt to coerce any dealer to enter into an agreement with the manufacturer, factory branch, distributor, or distributor branch, or representative thereof, or do any other act unfair to

the dealer, by threatening to cancel any franchise existing between the manufacturer, factory branch, distributor, distributor branch, or representative thereof and the dealer.

3. To coerce or attempt to coerce any dealer to join, contribute to, or affiliate with any advertising association.

4. To prevent or refuse to approve the sale or transfer of the ownership of a dealership by the sale of the business, stock transfer, or otherwise, or the transfer, sale, or assignment of a dealer franchise, or a change in the executive management or principal operator of the dealership, unless the franchisor provides written notice to the dealer of its objection and the reasons therefor at least 30 days prior to the proposed effective date of the transfer, sale, assignment, or change. No such objection shall be effective to prevent the sale, transfer, assignment, or change if the Commissioner has determined, if requested in writing by the dealer within 30 days after receipt of an objection to the proposed sale, transfer, or change, and after a hearing on the matter, that the failure to permit or honor the sale, transfer, assignment, or change is unreasonable under the circumstances. No franchise may be sold, assigned, or transferred unless (i) the franchisor has been given at least 90 days' prior written notice by the dealer as to the identity, financial ability, and qualifications of the proposed transferee and (ii) the sale or transfer of the franchise and business will not involve, without the franchisor's consent, a relocation of the business.

5. To grant an additional franchise for a particular line-make of motorcycle in a relevant market area in which a dealer or dealers in that line-make are already located unless the franchisor has first advised in writing, by certified mail, return receipt requested, all other dealers in the line-make in the relevant market area. No such additional franchise may be established at the proposed site unless the Commissioner has determined, if requested by a dealer of the same line-make in the relevant market area within 30 days after receipt of the franchisor's notice of intention to establish the additional franchise, and after a hearing on the matter, that there is reasonable evidence that after the grant of the new franchise, the market will support all of the dealers in that line-make in the relevant market area. Establishing a franchised dealer in a relevant market area to replace a franchised dealer that has not been in operation for more than two years shall constitute the establishment of a new franchise subject to the terms of this subdivision. The two-year period for replacing a franchised dealer shall begin on the day the franchise was terminated or, if a termination hearing was held, on the day the franchisor was legally permitted finally to terminate the franchise. This subdivision shall not apply to (i) the relocation of an existing dealer within that dealer's relevant market area if the relocation site is to be more than 10 miles distant from any other dealer for the same line-make; (ii) the relocation of an existing dealer within that dealer's relevant market area if the relocation site is to be more distant than the existing site from all other dealers of the same line-make in that relevant market area; or (iii) the relocation of an existing new motorcycle dealer within two miles of the existing site of the relocating dealer.

6. Except as otherwise provided in this subdivision and notwithstanding the terms of any franchise, to terminate, cancel, or refuse to renew the franchise of any dealer without good cause and unless (i) the dealer and the Commissioner have received written notice of the franchisor's intentions at least 60 days prior to the effective date of such termination, cancellation, or the expiration date of the franchise, setting forth the specific grounds for the action, and (ii) the Commissioner has determined, if requested in writing by the dealer within the 60-day period, and after a hearing on the matter, that there is good cause for the termination, cancellation, or nonrenewal of the franchise. In any case where a petition is made to the Commissioner for a determination as to good cause for the termination, cancellation, or nonrenewal of a franchise, the franchise in question shall continue in effect pending the Commissioner's decision or, if that decision is appealed to the circuit court, pending the decision of the circuit court. In any case in which a franchisor neither advises a dealer that it does not intend to renew a franchise nor takes any action to renew a franchise beyond its expiration date, the franchise in question shall continue in effect on the terms last agreed to by the parties. Notwithstanding the other provisions of this subdivision, notice of termination, cancellation, or nonrenewal may be provided to a dealer by a franchisor not less than 15 days prior to the effective date of such termination, cancellation, or nonrenewal when the grounds for such action are any of the following:

a. Insolvency of the franchised motorcycle dealer or filing of any petition by or against the franchised motorcycle dealer, under any bankruptcy or receivership law, leading to liquidation or that is intended to lead to liquidation of the franchisee's business;

b. Failure of the franchised motorcycle dealer to conduct its customary sales and service operations during its posted business hours for seven consecutive business days, except where the failure results from acts of God or circumstances beyond the direct control of the franchised motorcycle dealer;

c. Revocation of any license that the franchised motorcycle dealer is required to have to operate a dealership; or

d. Conviction of the dealer or any principal of the dealer of a felony.

The change or discontinuance of a marketing or distribution system of a particular line-make product by a manufacturer or distributor, while the name identification of the product is continued in substantial form by the same or different manufacturer or distributor, may be considered to be a franchise termination, cancellation, or nonrenewal. The provisions of this paragraph shall apply to changes and discontinuances made after January 1, 1989, but they shall not be considered by any court in any case in which such a change or discontinuance occurring prior to that date has been challenged as constituting a termination, cancellation, or nonrenewal.

7. To fail to provide continued parts and service support to a dealer that holds a franchise in a discontinued line-make for at least five years from the date of such discontinuance. This requirement shall not apply to a line-make that was discontinued prior to January 1, 1989.

8. To fail to allow a dealer the right at any time to designate a member of his family as a successor to the dealership in the event of the death or incapacity of the dealer. It shall be unlawful to prevent or refuse to honor the succession to a dealership by a member of the family of a deceased or incapacitated dealer if the franchisor has not provided to the member of the family previously designated by the dealer as his successor written notice of its objections to the succession and of such person's right to seek a hearing on the matter before the Commissioner pursuant to this article, and the Commissioner determines, if requested in writing by such member of the family within 30 days of receipt of such notice from the franchisor, and after a hearing on the matter before the Commissioner pursuant to this article, that the failure to permit or honor the succession is unreasonable under the circumstances. No member of the family may succeed to a franchise unless (i) the franchisor has been given written notice as to the identity, financial ability, and qualifications of the member of the family in question and (ii) the succession to the franchise will not involve, without the franchisor's consent, a relocation of the business.

9. To fail to ship monthly to any dealer, if ordered by the dealer, the number of new motorcycles of each make, series, and model needed by the dealer to receive a percentage of total new motorcycle sales of each make, series, and model equitably related to the total new motorcycle production or importation currently being achieved nationally by each make, series, and model covered under the franchise. Upon the written request of any dealer holding its sales or sales and service franchise, the manufacturer or distributor shall disclose to the dealer in writing the basis upon which new motorcycles are allocated, scheduled, and delivered to the dealers of the same line-make. If allocation is at issue in a request for a hearing, the dealer may demand the Commissioner to direct that the manufacturer or distributor provide to the dealer, within 30 days of such demand, all records of sales and all records of distribution of all motorcycles to the same line-make dealers who compete with the dealer requesting the hearing.

10. To require or otherwise coerce a dealer to underutilize the dealer's facilities.

11. To include in any franchise with a motorcycle dealer terms that are contrary to, prohibited by, or otherwise inconsistent with the requirements of this chapter.

12. To require under any franchise agreement a motorcycle dealer to pay the attorney fees of the manufacturer or distributor related to hearings and appeals brought under this article.

13. To fail to include in any franchise with a motorcycle dealer the following language: "If any provision herein contravenes the laws or regulations of any state or other jurisdiction wherein this agreement is to be performed, or denies access to the procedures, forums, or remedies provided for by such laws or regulations, such provision shall be deemed to be modified to conform to such laws or regulations, and all other terms and provisions shall remain in full force," or words to that effect.

14. To include in any franchise agreement with a motorcycle dealer terms that prohibit a motorcycle dealer from exercising his right to a trial by jury in any action where such right otherwise exists.

History.

1996, cc. 1043, 1052, § 46.2-1993.67; 1997, c. 802; 2010, c. 610; 2015, c. 615.

§ 46.2-1573.29. When discontinuation, cancellation, or nonrenewal of franchise unfair.

A discontinuation, cancellation, or nonrenewal of a franchise agreement is unfair if it is not clearly permitted by the franchise agreement, is not undertaken in good faith, is not undertaken for good cause, or is based on an alleged breach of the franchise agreement that is not in fact a material and substantial breach.

History.

1997, c. 802, § 46.2-1993.67:1; 2015, c. 615.

§ 46.2-1573.30. Repurchase of vehicles, parts, and equipment in the event of involuntary discontinuation, cancellation, or nonrenewal of franchise agreement.

A. In the event of any involuntary discontinuation, cancellation, or nonrenewal of a franchise agreement, the manufacturer or distributor shall, within 60 days from the effective date of the discontinuation, cancellation, or nonrenewal of a franchise agreement, repurchase at the price equal to the amount paid therefor by the motorcycle dealer, less all incentives and allowances received by the dealer, (i) all new, unused, undamaged, and unaltered motorcycles, all-terrain vehicles, or off-road motorcycles of the current or previous model year that the manufacturer or distributor sold to the dealer and (ii) any other such motorcycle, all-terrain vehicle, or off-road motorcycle that it sold to the dealer not more than 180 days prior to the notice of termination. The foregoing provisions of this subsection shall apply only if the dealer transfers to the manufacturer or distributor full right and legal title to the motorcycles, all-terrain vehicles, and off-road motorcycles prior to their repurchase.

B. In the event of any involuntary discontinuation, cancellation, or nonrenewal of a franchise agreement, the manufacturer or distributor shall, if so requested by the dealer within the same 60-day period, also repurchase all genuine new and unused motorcycle, all-terrain vehicle, and off-road motorcycle parts and accessories that the manufacturer or distributor sold to the dealer so long as such parts and accessories are undamaged, in their original packaging, and listed in the current parts and accessories price list of the manufacturer or distributor. Such parts and accessories shall be repurchased at a price equal to the wholesale price stated in the current parts and accessories price list of the manufacturer or distributor, less all incentives and allowances received by the dealer and without reduction for such repurchase or for processing or handling the repurchase. The foregoing provisions of this subsection shall apply only if the dealer transfers to the manufacturer or distributor full right and legal title to the parts and accessories prior to their repurchase.

C. In the event of any involuntary discontinuation, cancellation, or nonrenewal of a franchise agreement, the manufacturer or distributor shall, if so requested by the dealer within the same 60-day period, repurchase the new and used equipment that the manufacturer or distributor sold to the dealer at its then fair market value, including signs, special tools, and manuals that the manufacturer or distributor required the dealer to purchase. The foregoing provisions of this subsection shall apply only if the dealer transfers to the manufacturer or distributor full right and legal title to the equipment prior to its repurchase.

History.
2004, c. 107, § 46.2-1993.67:2; 2015, c. 615.

§ 46.2-1573.31. Manufacturer or distributor right of first refusal.

Notwithstanding the terms of any franchise agreement, in the event of a proposed sale or transfer of a dealership, the manufacturer or distributor shall be permitted to exercise a right of first refusal to acquire the new motorcycle dealer's assets or ownership, if such sale or transfer is conditioned upon the manufacturer's or dealer's entering into a dealer agreement with the proposed new owner or transferee, only if all the following requirements are met:

1. To exercise its right of first refusal, the manufacturer or distributor must notify the dealer in writing within 45 days of its receipt of the completed proposal for the proposed sale or transfer;

2. The exercise of the right of first refusal will result in the dealer's and dealer owner's receiving the same or greater consideration as they have contracted to receive in connection with the proposed change of ownership or transfer;

3. The proposed sale or transfer of the dealership's assets does not involve the transfer or sale to a member or members of the family of one or more dealer owners, or to a qualified manager or a partnership or corporation controlled by such persons; and

4. The manufacturer or distributor agrees to pay the reasonable expenses, including attorney fees that do not exceed the usual, customary, and reasonable fees charged for similar work done for other clients, incurred by the proposed new owner and transferee prior to the manufacturer's or distributor's exercise of its right of first refusal in negotiating and implementing the contract for the proposed sale or transfer of the dealership or dealership assets. Notwithstanding the foregoing, no payment of such expenses and attorney's fees shall be required if the dealer has not submitted or caused to be submitted an accounting of those expenses within 30 days of the dealer's receipt of the manufacturer's or distributor's written request for such an accounting. Such accounting may be requested by a manufacturer or distributor before exercising its right of first refusal.

History.
1996, cc. 1043, 1052, § 46.2-1993.68; 2015, c. 615.

§ 46.2-1573.32. Discontinuation of distributors.

If the contract between a distributor and a manufacturer or importer is terminated or otherwise discontinued, all franchises granted to motorcycle dealers in the Commonwealth by that distributor shall continue in full force and shall not be affected by the discontinuance, except that the manufacturer, factory branch, distributor, representative, or other person who undertakes to distribute motorcycles of the same line-make or the same motorcycles of a renamed line-make shall be substituted for the discontinued distributor under the existing motorcycle dealer franchises, and those franchises shall be modified accordingly.

History.
1996, cc. 1043, 1052, § 46.2-1993.69; 2015, c. 615.

§ 46.2-1573.33. Warranty obligations.

A. Each motorcycle manufacturer, factory branch, distributor, or distributor branch shall (i) specify in writing to each of its motorcycle dealers licensed in the Commonwealth the dealer's obligations for preparation, delivery, and warranty service on its products and (ii) compensate the dealer for warranty parts, service, and diagnostic work required of the dealer by the manufacturer or distributor as follows:

1. Compensation of a dealer for warranty parts, service, and diagnostic work shall not be less than the amounts charged by the dealer for the manufacturer's or distributor's original parts, service, and diagnostic work to retail customers for nonwarranty service, parts, and diagnostic work installed or performed in the dealer's service department unless the amounts are not reasonable;

2. For purposes of determining warranty parts and service compensation, menu-priced parts or services, group discounts, special event discounts, and special event promotions shall not be considered in determining amounts charged by the dealer to retail customers;

3. Increases in dealer warranty parts and service compensation and diagnostic work compensation, pursuant to this section, shall be requested by the dealer in writing, shall be based on 100 consecutive repair orders or all repair orders over a 90-day period, whichever occurs first, and, in the case of parts, shall be stated as a percentage of markup that shall be uniformly applied to all the manufacturer's or distributor's parts;

4. In the case of warranty parts compensation, the provisions of this subsection shall be effective only for model year 1992 and succeeding model years;

5. If a manufacturer or distributor furnishes a part to a dealer at no cost for use by the dealer in performing work for which the manufacturer or distributor is required to compensate the dealer under this section, the manufacturer or distributor shall compensate the dealer for the part in the same manner as warranty parts compensation, less the wholesale costs, for such part as listed in the manufacturer's current price schedules. A manufacturer or distributor may pay the dealer a reasonable handling fee instead of the compensation otherwise required by this subsection for special high-performance complete engine assemblies in limited production motorcycles that constitute less than five percent of model production furnished to the dealer at no cost, if the manufacturer or distributor excludes such special high-performance complete engine assemblies in determining whether the amounts requested by the dealer for warranty compensation are consistent with the amounts that the dealer charges its other retail service customers for parts used by the dealer to perform similar work; or

6. In the case of service work, manufacturer original parts or parts otherwise specified by the manufacturer or distributor, and parts provided by a dealer either pursuant to an adjustment program as defined in § 59.1-207.34 or as otherwise requested by the manufacturer or distributor, the dealer shall be compensated in the same manner as for warranty service or parts.

Warranty audits of dealer records may be conducted by the manufacturer, factory branch, distributor, or distributor branch on a reasonable basis, and dealer claims for warranty compensation shall not be denied except for good cause, such as performance of nonwarranty repairs, lack of material documentation, fraud, or misrepresentation. Claims for dealer compensation shall be paid within 30 days of dealer submission or within 30 days of the end of an incentive program or rejected in writing for stated reasons. The manufacturer, factory branch, distributor, or distributor branch shall reserve the right to reasonable periodic audits to determine the validity of all such paid claims for dealer compensation. Any chargebacks for warranty parts or service compensation and service incentives shall only be for the 12-month period immediately following the date of the claim and, in the case of chargebacks for sales compensation only, for the 18-month period immediately following the date of claim. However, such limitations shall not be effective in the case of intentionally false or fraudulent claims.

B. It shall be unlawful for any motorcycle manufacturer, factory branch, distributor, or distributor branch to:

1. Fail to perform any of its warranty obligations, including tires, with respect to a motorcycle;

2. Fail to assume all responsibility for any liability resulting from structural or production defects;

3. Fail to include in written notices of factory recalls to motorcycle owners and dealers the expected date by which necessary parts and equipment will be available to dealers for the correction of defects;

4. Fail to compensate any of the motorcycle dealers licensed in the Commonwealth for repairs effected by the dealer of merchandise damaged in manufacture or transit to the dealer where the carrier is designated by the manufacturer, factory branch, distributor, or distributor branch;

5. Fail to compensate its motorcycle dealers licensed in the Commonwealth for warranty parts, work, and service pursuant to subsection A or for legal costs and expenses incurred by such dealers in connection with warranty obligations for which the manufacturer, factory branch, distributor, or distributor branch is legally responsible or that the manufacturer, factory branch, distributor, or distributor branch imposes upon the dealer;

6. Misrepresent in any way to purchasers of motorcycles that warranties with respect to the manufacture, performance, or design of the motorcycle are made by the dealer, either as warrantor or co-warrantor;

7. Require the dealer to make warranties to customers in any manner related to the manufacture, performance, or design of the motorcycle; or

8. Shift or attempt to shift to the motorcycle dealer, directly or indirectly, any liabilities of the manufacturer, factory branch, distributor, or distributor branch under the Virginia Motor Vehicle Warranty Enforcement Act (§ 59.1-207.9 et seq.), unless such liability results from the act or omission by the dealer.

C. Notwithstanding the terms of any franchise, it shall be unlawful for any motorcycle manufacturer, factory branch, distributor, or distributor branch to fail to indemnify and hold harmless its motorcycle dealers against any losses or damages arising out of complaints, claims, or suits relating to the manufacture, assembly, or design of motorcycles, parts, or accessories, or other functions by the manufacturer, factory branch, distributor, or distributor branch beyond the control of the dealer, including, without limitation, the selection by the manufacturer, factory branch, distributor, or distributor branch of parts or components for the motorcycle or any damages to merchandise occurring in transit to the dealer where the carrier is designated by the manufacturer, factory branch, distributor, or distributor branch. The dealer shall notify the manufacturer of pending suits in which allegations are made that come within this subsection whenever reasonably practicable to do so. Every motorcycle dealer franchise issued to, amended, or renewed for motorcycle dealers in the Commonwealth shall be construed to incorporate provisions consistent with the requirements of this subsection.

D. On any new motorcycle, any uncorrected damage or any corrected damage exceeding three percent of the manufacturer's or distributor's suggested retail price as defined in 15 U.S.C. §§ 1231-1233, as measured by retail repair costs, must be disclosed to the dealer in writing prior to delivery. Factory mechanical repair and damage to tires are excluded from the three percent rule when properly replaced by identical manufacturer's or distributor's original equipment or parts. Whenever a new motorcycle is damaged in transit, when the carrier or means of transportation is determined by the manufacturer or distributor, or whenever a motorcycle is otherwise damaged prior to delivery to the new motorcycle dealer, the new motorcycle dealer shall:

1. Notify the manufacturer or distributor of the damage within three business days from the date of delivery of the new motorcycle to the new motorcycle dealership or within the additional time specified in the franchise; and

2. Request from the manufacturer or distributor authorization to replace the components, parts, and accessories damaged or otherwise correct the damage, unless the damage to the motorcycle exceeds the three percent rule, in which case the dealer may reject the motorcycle within three business days.

E. If the manufacturer or distributor refuses or fails to authorize correction of such damage within 10 days after receipt of notification, or if the dealer rejects the motorcycle because damage exceeds the three percent rule, ownership of the new motorcycle shall revert to the manufacturer or distributor, and the new motorcycle dealer shall have no obligation, financial or otherwise, with respect to such motorcycle. Should either the manufacturer, distributor, or the dealer elect to correct the damage or any other damage exceeding the three percent rule, full disclosure shall be made by the dealer in writing to the buyer and an acknowledgment by the buyer is required. If there is less than three percent damage, no disclosure is required, provided the damage has been corrected. Predelivery mechanical work shall not require a disclosure. Failure to disclose any corrected damage within the knowledge of the selling dealer to a new motorcycle in excess of the three percent rule shall constitute grounds for revocation of the buyer order, provided that, within 30 days of purchase, the motorcycle is returned to the dealer with an accompanying written notice of the grounds for revocation. In case of revocation pursuant to this section, the dealer shall accept the motorcycle and refund any payments made to the dealer in connection with the transaction, less a reasonable allowance for the consumer's use of the motorcycle as defined in § 59.1-207.11.

F. If there is a dispute between the manufacturer, factory branch, distributor, or distributor branch and the dealer with respect to any matter referred to in subsection A, B, or C, either party may petition the Commissioner in writing, within 30 days after either party has given written notice of the dispute to the other, for a hearing. The decision of the Commissioner shall be binding on the parties, subject to rights of judicial review and appeal as provided in the Administrative Process Act (§ 2.2-4000 et seq.). However, nothing contained in this section shall give the Commissioner any authority as to the content or interpretation of any manufacturer's or distributor's warranty.

History.

1996, cc. 1043, 1052, § 46.2-1993.70; 2015, c. 615.

§ 46.2-1573.34. Operation of dealership by manufacturer.

It shall be unlawful for any motorcycle manufacturer, factory branch, distributor, distributor branch, or subsidiary thereof to own, operate, or control any motorcycle dealership in the Commonwealth. However, this section shall not prohibit:

1. The operation by a manufacturer, factory branch, distributor, distributor branch, or subsidiary thereof of a dealership for a temporary period, not to exceed one year, during the transition from one owner or operator to another;

2. The ownership or control of a dealership by a manufacturer, factory branch, distributor, distributor branch, or subsidiary thereof, while the dealership is being sold under a bona fide contract or purchase option to the operator of the dealership; or

3. The ownership, operation, or control of a dealership by a manufacturer, factory branch, distributor, distributor branch, or subsidiary thereof if the Commissioner determines, after a hearing at the request of any party, that there is no dealer independent of the manufacturer or distributor, factory branch or distributor branch, or subsidiary thereof available in the community or trade area to own and

operate the franchise in a manner consistent with the public interest.

History.
1996, cc. 1043, 1052, § 46.2-1993.71; 2015, c. 615.

§ 46.2-1573.35. Ownership of service facilities.

It shall be unlawful for any motorcycle manufacturer, factory branch, distributor, distributor branch, or subsidiary thereof to own, operate, or control, either directly or indirectly, any motorcycle warranty or service facility located in the Commonwealth. Nothing in this section shall prohibit any motorcycle manufacturer, factory branch, distributor, distributor branch, or subsidiary thereof from owning, operating, or controlling any warranty or service facility for warranty or service of motorcycles owned or operated by the manufacturer, factory branch, distributor, distributor branch, or subsidiary thereof. Nothing contained in this section shall prohibit a motorcycle manufacturer, factory branch, distributor, or distributor branch from performing service for reasons of compliance with an order of a court of competent jurisdiction or of warranty under Chapter 17.3 (§ 59.1-207.9 et seq.) of Title 59.1.

History.
1996, cc. 1043, 1052, § 46.2-1993.72; 2015, c. 615.

§ 46.2-1573.36. Hearings and other remedies; civil penalties.

A. In every case of a hearing before the Commissioner authorized under this article, the Commissioner shall give reasonable notice of each hearing to all interested parties, and the Commissioner's decision shall be binding on the parties, subject to the rights of judicial review and appeal as provided in the Administrative Process Act (§ 2.2-4000 et seq.).

B. Hearings before the Commissioner under this article shall commence within 90 days of the request for a hearing, and the Commissioner's decision shall be rendered within 60 days from the receipt of the hearing officer's recommendation. Hearings authorized under this article shall be presided over by a hearing officer selected from a list prepared by the Executive Secretary of the Supreme Court. On request of the Commissioner, the Executive Secretary will name a hearing officer from the list, selected on a rotation system administered by the Executive Secretary. The hearing officer shall provide recommendations to the Commissioner within 90 days of the conclusion of the hearing.

C. Notwithstanding any contrary provision of this article, the Commissioner shall initiate investigations, conduct hearings, and determine the rights of parties under this article whenever he is provided information indicating a possible violation of any provision of this article.

D. For purposes of any matter brought to the Commissioner under subdivisions 3, 4, 5, 6, and 9 of § 46.2-1573.28 with respect to which the Commissioner is to determine whether there is good cause for a proposed action or whether it would be unreasonable under the circumstances, the Commissioner shall consider:

1. The volume of the affected dealer's business in the relevant market area;
2. The nature and extent of the dealer's investment in its business;
3. The adequacy of the dealer's service facilities, equipment, parts, supplies, and personnel;
4. The effect of the proposed action on the community;
5. The extent and quality of the dealer's service under motorcycle warranties;
6. The dealer's performance under the terms of its franchise; and
7. Other economic and geographical factors reasonably associated with the proposed action.

With respect to subdivision 6, any performance standard or program for measuring dealership performance that may have a material effect on a dealer, and the application of any such standard or program by a manufacturer or distributor, shall be fair, reasonable, and equitable and, if based upon a survey, shall be based upon a statistically valid sample. Upon the request of any dealer, a manufacturer or distributor shall disclose in writing to the dealer a description of how a performance standard or program is designed and all relevant information used in the application of the performance standard or program to that dealer.

E. An interested party in a hearing held pursuant to subsection A shall comply with the effective date of compliance established by the Commissioner in his decision in such hearing, unless a stay or extension of such date is granted by the Commissioner or the Commissioner's decision is under judicial review and appeal as provided in subsection A. If, after notice to such interested party and an opportunity to comment, the Commissioner finds an interested party has not complied with his decision by the designated date of compliance, unless a stay or extension of such date has been granted by the Commissioner or the Commissioner's decision is under judicial review and appeal, the Commissioner may assess such interested party a civil penalty not to exceed $1,000 per day of noncompliance. Civil penalties collected under this subsection shall be deposited into the Transportation Trust Fund established pursuant to § 33.2-1524.

History.
1996, cc. 1043, 1052, § 46.2-1993.73; 2000, c. 106; 2015, c. 615.

§ 46.2-1573.37. Late model and factory repurchase franchises.

Franchised late model or factory repurchase motorcycle dealers shall have the same rights and obligations as provided for franchised new motorcycle dealers in this article, mutatis mutandis.

History.

1996, cc. 1043, 1052, § 46.2-1993.74; 2015, c. 615.

ARTICLE 8.

DENIAL, SUSPENSION, AND REVOCATION OF DEALER LICENSES.

§ 46.2-1574. Acts of officers, directors, partners, and salespersons.

If a licensee or registrant is a partnership or corporation, it shall be sufficient cause for the denial, suspension, or revocation of a license or certificate of dealer registration that any officer, director, or trustee of the partnership or corporation, or any member in the case of a partnership or the dealer-operator, has committed any act or omitted any duty which would be cause for refusing, suspending, or revoking a license or certificate of dealer registration issued to him as an individual under this chapter. Each licensee or registrant shall be responsible for the acts of any of his salespersons while acting as his agent, if the licensee approved of those acts or had knowledge of those acts or other similar acts and after such knowledge retained the benefit, proceeds, profits, or advantages accruing from those acts or otherwise ratified those acts.

History.

1988, c. 865, § 46.1-550.5:33; 1989, c. 727.

§ 46.2-1575. Grounds for denying, suspending, or revoking licenses or certificates of dealer registration or qualification.

A license or certificate of dealer registration or qualification issued under this subtitle may be denied, suspended, or revoked on any one or more of the following grounds:

1. Material misstatement or omission in application for license, dealer's license plates, certificate of dealer registration, certificate of qualification, or certificate of title;
2. Failure to comply subsequent to receipt of a written warning from the Department or the Board or any willful failure to comply with any provision of this chapter or any regulation promulgated by the Commissioner or the Board under this chapter;
3. Failure to have an established place of business as defined in § 46.2-1510 or failure to have as the dealer-operator an individual who holds a valid certificate of qualification;
4. Defrauding any retail buyer, to the buyer's damage, or any other person in the conduct of the licensee's or registrant's business;
5. Employment of fraudulent devices, methods or practices in connection with compliance with the requirements under the statutes of the Commonwealth with respect to the retaking of vehicles under retail installment contracts and the redemption and resale of those vehicles;
6. Having used deceptive acts or practices;
7. Knowingly advertising by any means any assertion, representation, or statement of fact which is untrue, misleading, or deceptive in any particular relating to the conduct of the business licensed or registered or for which a license or registration is sought;
8. Having been convicted of any fraudulent act in connection with the business of selling vehicles or any consumer-related fraud;
9. Having been convicted of any criminal act involving the business of selling vehicles;
10. Willfully retaining in his possession title to a motor vehicle that has not been completely and legally assigned to him;
11. Failure to comply with any provision of Chapter 4.1 (§ 36-85.2 et seq.) of Title 36 or any regulation promulgated pursuant to that chapter;
12. Leasing, renting, lending, or otherwise allowing the use of a dealer's license plate by persons not specifically authorized under this title;
13. Having been convicted of a felony;
14. Failure to submit to the Department, within thirty days from the date of sale, any application, tax, or fee collected for the Department on behalf of a buyer;
15. Having been convicted of larceny of a vehicle or receipt or sale of a stolen vehicle;
16. Having been convicted of odometer tampering or any related violation;
17. If a salvage dealer, salvage pool, or rebuilder, failing to comply with any provision of Chapter 16 (§ 46.2-1600 et seq.) of this title or any regulation promulgated by the Commissioner under that chapter;
18. Failing to maintain automobile liability insurance, issued by a company licensed to do business in the Commonwealth, or a certificate of self-insurance as defined in § 46.2-368, with respect to each dealer's license plate issued to the dealer by the Department; or
19. Failing or refusing to pay civil penalties imposed by the Board pursuant to § 46.2-1507.

History.

1988, c. 865, § 46.1-550.5:34; 1989, c. 727; 1990, cc. 197, 954; 1995, cc. 767, 816; 1999, c. 217.

§ 46.2-1576. Suspension, revocation, and refusal to renew licenses or certificates of dealer registration or qualification; notice and hearing.

A. Except as provided in § 46.2-1527.7 and subsections B and C of this section, no license or certificate of dealer registration or qualification issued under this subtitle shall be suspended or revoked, or renewal thereof refused, until a written copy of the complaint made has been furnished to the licensee, registrant, or qualifier against whom the same is directed and a public hearing thereon has been had before a hearing officer designated by the Board. At least ten days' written notice of the time and place of the hearing shall be given to the licensee, registrant, or qualifier by registered mail addressed to his last known post office address or as shown on his license or certificate or other record of information in possession of the Board. At the hearing the licensee, registrant, or qualifier shall have the right to be heard personally or by counsel. The hearing officer shall provide recommendations to the Board within ninety days of the conclusion of the hearing. After receiving the recommendations from the hearing officer, the Board may suspend, revoke, or refuse to renew the license or certificate in question. A Board member shall disqualify himself and withdraw from any case in which he cannot accord fair and impartial consideration. Any party may request the disqualification of any Board member by stating with particularity the grounds upon which it is claimed that fair and impartial consideration cannot be accorded. The remaining members of the Board shall determine whether the individual should be disqualified. Immediate notice of any suspension, revocation, or refusal shall be given to the licensee, registrant, or qualifier in the manner provided in this section in the case of notices of hearing.

B. Should a dealer fail to maintain an established place of business, the Board may cancel the license of the dealer without a hearing after notification of the intent to cancel has been sent, by return receipt mail, to the dealer at the dealer's residence and business addresses, and the notices are returned undelivered or the dealer does not respond within twenty days from the date the notices were sent. Any subsequent application for a dealer's license shall be treated as an original application.

C. Should a dealer fail or refuse to pay civil penalties imposed by the Board pursuant to § 46.2-1507, the Board may deny, revoke, or suspend the dealer's license without a hearing after notice of imposition of civil penalties has been sent, by certified mail, return receipt requested, to the dealer at the dealer's business address and such civil penalty is not paid in full within thirty days after receipt of the notice.

History.

1988, c. 865, § 46.1-550.5:35; 1989, c. 727; 1990, c. 197; 1995, cc. 767, 816; 1996, cc. 639, 658; 1999, c. 217.

§ 46.2-1577. Appeals from actions of the Board.

Any person aggrieved by the action of the Board in refusing to grant or renew a license or certificate of dealer registration or qualification issued under this chapter, or by any other action of the Board which is alleged to be improper, unreasonable, or unlawful under the provisions of this chapter is entitled to judicial review in accordance with the provisions of the Administrative Process Act (§ 2.2-4000 et seq.).

History.

1988, c. 865, § 46.1-550.5:36; 1989, c. 727; 1990, c. 197; 1995, cc. 767, 816.

§ 46.2-1578. Appeals to Court of Appeals; bond.

Either party may appeal from the decision of the court under § 46.2-1577 to the Court of Appeals. These appeals shall be taken and prosecuted in the same manner and with like effect as is provided by law in other cases appealed as a matter of right to the Court of Appeals.

History.

1988, c. 865, § 46.1-550.5:37; 1989, c. 727; 1990, c. 197; 1996, c. 573.

§ 46.2-1579. Equitable remedies not impaired.

The remedy at law provided by §§ 46.2-1577 and 46.2-1578 shall not in any manner impair the right to applicable equitable relief. That right to equitable relief is hereby preserved, notwithstanding the provisions of §§ 46.2-1577 and 46.2-1578.

History.

1988, c. 865, § 46.1-550.5:38; 1989, c. 727.

ARTICLE 9. MOTOR VEHICLE DEALER ADVERTISING.

§ 46.2-1580: Legislative findings [Not set out.] (1989, c. 308.)

Editor's note.

This section, relating to legislative findings, was derived from Acts 1989, c. 308. In furtherance of the general policy of the Virginia Code Commission to include in the Code only provisions having general and permanent application, this section is not set out here, but attention is called to it by this reference.

The section catchline was inserted at the direction of the Virginia Code Commission.

§ 46.2-1581. Regulated advertising practices.

For purposes of this chapter, a violation of the following regulated advertising practices shall be an unfair, deceptive, or misleading act or practice.

1. A vehicle shall not be advertised as new, either by word or implication, unless it is one which conforms to the requirements of § 46.2-1500.

2. When advertising any vehicle which does not conform to the definition of "new" as provided in § 46.2-1500, the fact that it is used shall be clearly and unequivocally expressed by the term "used" or by such other term as is commonly understood to mean that the vehicle is used. By way of example but not by limitation, "special purchase" by itself is not a satisfactory disclosure; however, such terms as

"demonstrator" or "former leased vehicles" used alone clearly express that the vehicles are used for advertising purposes.

3. Advertisement of finance charges or other interest rates shall not be used when there is a cost to buy-down said charge or rate which is passed on, in whole or in part, to the purchaser.

4. Terms, conditions, and disclaimers shall be stated clearly and conspicuously. An asterisk or other reference symbol may be used to point to a disclaimer or other information, but shall not be used as a means of contradicting or changing the meaning of an advertised statement.

5. The expiration date of an advertised sale shall be clearly and conspicuously disclosed.

6. The term "list price," "sticker price," or "suggested retail price" and similar terms, shall be used only in reference to the manufacturer's suggested retail price for new vehicles or the dealer's own usual and customary price for used vehicles.

7. Terms such as "at cost," "below cost," "$ off cost" shall not be used in advertisements because of the difficulty in determining a dealer's actual net cost at the time of the sale. Terms such as "invoice price," "$ over invoice," may be used, provided that the invoice referred to is the manufacturer's factory invoice or a bona fide bill of sale and the invoice or bill of sale is available for customer inspection.

"Manufacturer's factory invoice" means that document supplied by the manufacturer to the dealer listing the manufacturer's charge to the dealer before any deduction for holdback, group advertising, factory incentives or rebates, or any governmental charges.

8. When the price or credit terms of a vehicle are advertised, the vehicle shall be fully identified as to year, make, and model. In addition, in advertisements placed by individual dealers and not line-make marketing groups, the advertised price or credit terms shall include all charges which the buyer must pay to the seller, except buyer-selected options, state and local fees and taxes, and manufacturer's or distributor's freight or destination charges, and a processing fee, if any. If a processing fee or freight or destination charges are not included in the advertised price, the amount of any such processing fee and freight or destination charge must be (i) clearly and conspicuously disclosed in not less than eight-point boldface type or (ii) not smaller than the largest typeface within the advertisement. If the processing fee is not included in the advertised price, the amount of the processing fee may be omitted from any advertisement in which the largest type size is less than eight-point typeface, so long as the dealer participates in a media-provided listing of processing fees and the dealer's advertisement includes an asterisk or other such notation to refer the reader to the listing of the fees.

9. Advertisements which set out a policy of matching or bettering competitors' prices shall not be used unless the terms of the offer are specific, verifiable and reasonable.

10. Advertisements of "dealer rebates" shall not be used. This does not affect advertisement of manufacturer rebates.

11. "Free," "at no cost," or other words to that effect shall not be used unless the "free" item, merchandise, or service is available without a purchase. This provision shall not apply to advertising placed by manufacturers, distributors, or line-make marketing groups.

12. "Bait" advertising, in which an advertiser may have no intention to sell at the price or terms advertised, shall not be used. By way of example, but not by limitation:

a. If a specific vehicle is advertised, the seller shall be in possession of a reasonable supply of said vehicles, and they shall be available at the advertised price. If the advertised vehicle is available only in limited numbers or only by order, that shall be stated in the advertisement. For purposes of this subdivision, the listing of a vehicle by stock number or vehicle identification number in the advertisement is one means of satisfactorily disclosing a limitation of availability.

b. Advertising a vehicle at a certain price, including "as low as" statements, but having available for sale only vehicles equipped with dealer added cost "options" which increase the selling price, above the advertised price, shall also be considered "bait" advertising.

c. If a lease payment is advertised, the fact that it is a lease arrangement shall be disclosed.

13. The term "repossessed" shall be used only to describe vehicles that have been sold, registered, titled and then taken back from a purchaser and not yet resold to an ultimate user. Advertisers offering repossessed vehicles for sale shall provide proof of repossession upon request.

14. Words such as "finance" or "loan" shall not be used in a motor vehicle advertiser's firm name or trade name, unless that person is actually engaged in the financing of motor vehicles.

15. Any advertisement which gives the impression a dealer has a special arrangement or relationship with the distributor or manufacturer, as compared to similarly situated dealers, shall not be used.

History.

1989, c. 308, § 46.1-550.5:40; 1990, c. 84; 1991, c. 626; 1996, c. 1027; 1998, c. 325; 2008, c. 166.

§ 46.2-1582. Enforcement; regulations.

The Board may promulgate regulations reasonably necessary for enforcement of this article.

In addition to any other sanctions or remedies available to the Board under this chapter, the Board may assess a civil penalty not to exceed $1,000 for any single violation of this article. Each day that a violation continues shall constitute a separate violation.

History.
1989, c. 308, § 46.1-550.5:41; 1995, cc. 767, 816.

CHAPTER 16.

SALVAGE, NONREPAIRABLE, AND REBUILT VEHICLES.

§ 46.2-1600. Definitions.

The following words, terms, and phrases when used in this chapter shall have the meaning ascribed to them in this section, except where the context indicates otherwise:

"Actual cash value," as applied to a vehicle, means the retail cash value of the vehicle prior to damage as determined, using recognized evaluation sources, either (i) by an insurance company responsible for paying a claim or (ii) if no insurance company is responsible therefor, by the Department.

"Auto recycler" means any person licensed by the Commonwealth to engage in business as a salvage dealer, rebuilder, demolisher, or scrap metal processor.

"Cosmetic damage," as applied to a vehicle, means damage to custom or performance aftermarket equipment, audio-visual accessories, nonfactory-sized tires and wheels, custom paint, and external hail damage. "Cosmetic damage" does not include (i) damage to original equipment and parts installed by the manufacturer or (ii) damage that requires any repair to enable a vehicle to pass a safety inspection pursuant to § 46.2-1157. The cost for cosmetic damage repair shall not be included in the cost to repair the vehicle when determining the calculation for a nonrepairable vehicle.

"Current salvage value," as applied to a vehicle, means (i) the salvage value of the vehicle, as determined by the insurer responsible for paying the claim, or (ii) if no insurance company is responsible therefor, 25 percent of the actual cash value.

"Demolisher" means any person whose business is to crush, flatten, bale, shred, log, or otherwise reduce a vehicle to a state where it can no longer be considered a vehicle.

"Diminished value compensation" means the amount of compensation that an insurance company pays to a third party vehicle owner, in addition to the cost of repairs, for the reduced value of a vehicle due to damage.

"Independent appraisal firm" means any business providing cost estimates for the repair of damaged motor vehicles for insurance purposes and having all required business licenses and zoning approvals. This term shall not include insurance companies that provide the same service, nor shall any such entity be a rebuilder or affiliated with a rebuilder.

"Late model vehicle" means the current-year model of a vehicle and the five preceding model years, or any vehicle whose actual cash value is determined to have been at least $10,000 prior to being damaged.

"Licensee" means any person who is licensed or is required to be licensed under this chapter.

"Major component" means any one of the following subassemblies of a motor vehicle: (i) front clip assembly, consisting of the fenders, grille, hood, bumper, and related parts; (ii) engine; (iii) transmission; (iv) rear clip assembly, consisting of the quarter panels, floor panels, trunk lid, bumper, and related parts; (v) frame; (vi) air bags; and (vii) any door that displays a vehicle identification number.

"Nonrepairable certificate" means a document of ownership issued by the Department for any nonrepairable vehicle upon surrender or cancellation of the vehicle's title and registration or salvage certificate.

"Nonrepairable vehicle" means (i) any late model vehicle that has been damaged and whose estimated cost of repair, excluding the cost to repair cosmetic damages, exceeds 90 percent of its actual cash value prior to damage; (ii) any vehicle that has been determined to be nonrepairable by its insurer or owner, and for which a nonrepairable certificate has been issued or applied for; or (iii) any other vehicle that has been damaged, is inoperable, and has no value except for use as parts and scrap metal.

"Rebuilder" means any person who acquires and repairs, for use on the public highways, two or more salvage vehicles within a 12-month period.

"Rebuilt vehicle" means (i) any salvage vehicle that has been repaired for use on the public highways and the estimated cost of repair did not exceed 90 percent of its actual cash value or (ii) any late

model vehicle that has been repaired and the estimated cost of repair exceeded 75 percent of its actual cash value, excluding the cost to repair damage to the engine, transmission, or drive axle assembly.

"Repairable vehicle" means a late model vehicle that is not a rebuilt vehicle, but is repaired to its pre-loss condition by an insurance company and is not accepted by the owner of said vehicle immediately prior to its acquisition by said insurance company as part of the claims process.

"Salvage certificate" means a document of ownership issued by the Department for any salvage vehicle upon surrender or cancellation of the vehicle's title and registration.

"Salvage dealer" means any person who acquires any vehicle for the purpose of reselling any parts thereof.

"Salvage pool" means any person providing a storage service for salvage vehicles or nonrepairable vehicles who either displays the vehicles for resale or solicits bids for the sale of salvage vehicles or nonrepairable vehicles, but this definition shall not apply to an insurance company that stores and displays fewer than 100 salvage vehicles and nonrepairable vehicles in one location; however, any two or more insurance companies who display salvage and nonrepairable vehicles for resale, using the same facilities, shall be considered a salvage pool.

"Salvage vehicle" means (i) any late model vehicle that has been (a) acquired by an insurance company as a part of the claims process other than a stolen vehicle or (b) damaged as a result of collision, fire, flood, accident, trespass, or any other occurrence to such an extent that its estimated cost of repair, excluding charges for towing, storage, and temporary replacement/rental vehicle or payment for diminished value compensation, would exceed its actual cash value less its current salvage value; (ii) any recovered stolen vehicle acquired by an insurance company as a part of the claims process, whose estimated cost of repair exceeds 75 percent of its actual cash value; or (iii) any other vehicle that is determined to be a salvage vehicle by its owner or an insurance company by applying for a salvage certificate for the vehicle, provided that such vehicle is not a nonrepairable vehicle.

"Scrap metal processor" means any person who acquires one or more whole vehicles to process into scrap for remelting purposes who, from a fixed location, utilizes machinery and equipment for processing and manufacturing ferrous and nonferrous metallic scrap into prepared grades, and whose principal product is metallic scrap.

"Vehicle" shall have the meaning ascribed to it in § 46.2-100. A vehicle that has been demolished or declared to be nonrepairable pursuant to this chapter shall no longer be considered a vehicle. For the purposes of this chapter, a major component shall not be considered a vehicle.

"Vehicle removal operator" means any person who acquires a vehicle for the purpose of reselling it to a demolisher, scrap metal processor, or salvage dealer.

History.

1979, c. 401, § 46.1-550.6; 1988, cc. 842, 865; 1989, c. 727; 1992, c. 148; 1993, c. 376; 2000, cc. 123, 235, 257; 2003, c. 304; 2009, c. 664; 2012, cc. 64, 280; 2015, cc. 33, 177.

§ 46.2-1601. Licensing of dealers of salvage vehicles; fees.

A. It shall be unlawful for any person to engage in business in the Commonwealth as an auto recycler, salvage pool, or vehicle removal operator without first acquiring a license issued by the Commissioner for each such business at each location. The fee for the first such license issued or renewed under this chapter shall be $100 per license year or part thereof. The fee for each additional license issued or renewed under this chapter for the same location shall be $25 per license year or part thereof. However, no fee shall be charged for supplemental locations of a business located within 500 yards of the licensed location.

B. No license shall be issued or renewed for any person unless (i) the licensed business contains at least 600 square feet of enclosed space, (ii) the licensed business is shown to be in compliance with all applicable zoning ordinances, and (iii) the applicant may (a) certify to the Commissioner that the licensed business is permitted under a Virginia Pollutant Discharge Elimination System individual or general permit issued by the State Water Control Board for discharges of storm water associated with industrial activity and provides the permit number(s) from such permit(s) or (b) certify to the Commissioner that the licensed business is otherwise exempt from such permitting requirements. Nothing in this section shall authorize any person to act as a motor vehicle dealer or salesperson without being licensed under Chapter 15 (§ 46.2-1500 et seq.) and meeting all requirements imposed by such chapter.

C. Licenses issued under this section shall be deemed not to have expired if the renewal application and required fees as set forth in subsection A are received by the Commissioner or postmarked not more than 30 days after the expiration date of such license. Whenever the renewal application is received by the Commissioner or postmarked not more than 30 days after the expiration date of such license, the license fees shall be 150 percent of the fees provided for in subsection A.

D. The Commissioner may offer an optional multiyear license for any license set forth in this section. When such option is offered and chosen by the licensee, all fees due at the time of licensing shall be multiplied by the number of years for which the license will be issued.

History.

1988, c. 865, § 46.1-550.7:1; 1989, c. 727; 1990, c. 197; 1992, c. 148; 1999, c. 53; 2009, c. 664; 2014, c. 58; 2015, cc. 33, 177.

§ 46.2-1601.1. Advertising and display of license; business hours.

A. Any license issued under this chapter shall be conspicuously displayed at the licensed place of business.

The licensee shall display his usual business hours at the licensed place of business. The hours shall be posted and maintained conspicuously on or near the main entrance of each place of business. Each licensee shall include his usual business hours on the original and every renewal application for a license issued under this chapter. Changes to these hours shall be immediately filed with the Commissioner.

B. The purchase, sale, transport, delivery, removal, or receipt of a salvage or nonrepairable vehicle or the major component parts of such vehicle shall not be advertised to the public unless the advertiser is a licensee or an individual authorized to dispose of a salvage vehicle under subdivision B 2 of § 46.2-1602. The licensee advertiser shall display in such advertisement its license number issued under this chapter.

C. Advertisements by a licensee, subject to the provisions of subsection B, in a newspaper, on a website, or by any other means of electronic communication for the purchase, sale, transport, delivery, removal, or receipt of any salvage or nonrepairable vehicle or the major component parts of such vehicle shall clearly state the correct company name, physical address, telephone number, and license number issued under this chapter.

History.

2014, c. 58; 2015, cc. 240, 254.

§ 46.2-1601.2. Acts of officers, directors, and partners.

If a licensee is a partnership or corporation, it shall be sufficient cause for the denial, suspension, or revocation of a license that any officer, director, or trustee of the partnership or corporation, or any member in the case of a partnership, has committed any act or omitted any duty which would be cause for refusing, suspending, or revoking a license issued to him as an individual under this chapter.

History.

2014, c. 58.

§ 46.2-1601.3. Grounds for denying, suspending, or revoking licenses.

The Commissioner may deny, suspend, or revoke a license under this chapter on any one or more of the following grounds:

1. Material misstatement or omission in application for license, certificate of title, salvage certificate, or nonrepairable certificate;

2. Failure to comply subsequent to receipt of a written warning from the Commissioner;

3. Failure to comply with the requirements of subsection B of § 46.2-1601;

4. Defrauding any retail buyer, to the buyer's damage, or any other person in the conduct of the licensee's business;

5. Having used deceptive acts or practices;

6. Knowingly advertising by any means any assertion, representation, or statement of fact which is untrue, misleading, or deceptive in any particular relating to the conduct of the business licensed for which a license is sought;

7. Having been convicted of any fraudulent act in connection with the business of selling vehicles, vehicle parts, or major components;

8. Having been convicted of any criminal act involving the business of selling vehicles, vehicle parts, or major components;

9. Willfully retaining in his possession title to a motor vehicle or a salvage certificate that has not been completely and legally assigned to him;

10. Having been convicted of a felony;

11. Having been convicted of larceny of a vehicle or receipt or sale of a stolen vehicle;

12. Having been convicted of odometer tampering or any related violation;

13. Having been convicted of a violation of § 46.2-1074 or 46.2-1075;

14. Failure to comply with federal reporting requirements pursuant to subsection G of § 46.2-1603.1;

15. Failure or refusal to pay civil penalties imposed by the Commissioner pursuant to § 46.2-1609;

16. Failure to comply with the requirements of § 46.2-1205;

17. Failure to comply with the requirements of § 46.2-1608.2; or

18. Failure to comply with any other provision of this chapter.

Suspension or revocation under this section shall only be imposed on the specific business found to be in violation.

History.

2014, c. 58.

§ 46.2-1602. Certain sales prohibited; exceptions.

A. It shall be unlawful:

1. For any scrap metal processor to sell a vehicle or vehicle components or parts;

2. For any salvage pool to sell either in person or through any Internet auction a salvage vehicle stored in the Commonwealth to any person who is not licensed as an auto recycler, motor vehicle dealer, or vehicle removal operator by the Common-

wealth or regulated as a similar business under the laws of another state;

3. For any person to sell a nonrepairable vehicle to any person who is not licensed as an auto recycler or vehicle removal operator by the Commonwealth or regulated as a similar business under the laws of another state; or

4. For any person to sell a rebuilt vehicle without first having disclosed the fact that the vehicle is a rebuilt vehicle to the buyer in writing on a form prescribed by the Commissioner.

B. Notwithstanding the provisions of subsection A of this section, it shall not be unlawful:

1. For a salvage dealer to sell vehicle components or parts to unlicensed persons; or

2. For an individual to dispose of a salvage vehicle acquired or retained for his own use when it has been acquired or retained and used in good faith and not for the purpose of avoiding the provisions of this chapter.

History.

1979, c. 401, § 46.1-550.6; 1988, cc. 842, 865; 1989, c. 727; 1992, c. 148; 2015, cc. 33, 177.

§ 46.2-1602.1. Duties of insurance companies upon acquiring certain vehicles.

Every insurance company which acquires, as a result of the claims process, any late model vehicle titled in the Commonwealth or any recovered stolen vehicle whose estimated cost of repair exceeds seventy-five percent of its actual cash value shall apply to and obtain from the Department either (i) a salvage certificate or certificate of title as provided in § 46.2-1603 or (ii) a nonrepairable certificate as provided in § 46.2-1603.2 for each such vehicle. An insurance company may apply to and obtain from the Department either a salvage certificate as provided in § 46.2-1603 or a nonrepairable certificate as provided in § 46.2-1603.2 for any other vehicle which is determined to be either a salvage vehicle or a nonrepairable vehicle.

History.

1992, c. 148; 1993, c. 376; 2000, cc. 235, 257.

§ 46.2-1602.2. Exemptions.

A repairable vehicle, as defined in § 46.2-1600, shall be exempt from the remaining provisions of this chapter, provided that the insurance company responsible for repair (i) notifies the Department of each late model vehicle declared repairable, and that (ii) upon discovery by the Department that such vehicle was incorrectly designated as a repairable vehicle, the Department may require that vehicle's certificate status be corrected.

History.

2012, cc. 64, 280.

§ 46.2-1603. Obtaining salvage certificate or certificate of title for an unrecovered stolen vehicle.

A. The owner of any vehicle titled in the Commonwealth may declare such vehicle to be a salvage vehicle and apply to the Department and obtain a salvage certificate for that vehicle.

B. Every insurance company or its authorized agent shall apply to the Department and obtain a salvage certificate for each late model vehicle acquired by the insurance company as the result of the claims process if such vehicle is titled in the Commonwealth and is a salvage vehicle. Whenever the insurance company or its agent makes application for a salvage certificate and is unable to present a certificate of title, the Department may receive the application along with an affidavit indicating that the vehicle was acquired as the result of the claims process and describing the efforts made by the insurance company or its agent to obtain the certificate of title from the previous owner. When the Department is satisfied that the applicant is entitled to the title, it may issue a certificate of title to the person entitled to it. The Commissioner may charge a fee of $25 for the expense of processing an application under this subsection that is accompanied by an affidavit. Such fee shall be in addition to any other fees required. All fees collected under the provisions of this subsection shall be paid into the state treasury and set aside as a special fund to be used to meet the expenses of the Department.

C. Every insurance company or its authorized agent shall apply to the Department and obtain a certificate of title for each stolen vehicle acquired by the insurance company as the result of the claims process if such vehicle is titled in the Commonwealth and has not been recovered at the time of application to the Department. For each recovered stolen vehicle, acquired as a result of the claims process, whose estimated cost of repair exceeds seventy-five percent of its actual cash value, the insurance company or its authorized agent shall apply to the Department and obtain a salvage certificate. The application shall be accompanied by the vehicle's title certificate and shall contain a description of the damage to the salvage vehicle and an itemized estimate of the cost of repairs up to the point where a nonrepairable certificate would be issued. Application for the certificate of title shall be made within fifteen days after payment has been made to the owner, lienholder, or both. Application for the salvage certificate shall be made within fifteen days after the stolen vehicle is recovered.

D. Every insurance company or its authorized agent shall notify the Department of each late model vehicle titled in the Commonwealth on which a claim for damage to the vehicle has been paid by the insurance company if (i) the estimated cost of repair exceeds seventy-five percent of actual cash value of the vehicle and (ii) the vehicle is to be retained by its owner. No such notification shall be required for a vehicle when a supplemental claim has been paid for the cost of repairs to the engine, transmission, or drive axle assembly if such components are replaced by components of like kind and quality.

E. Every owner of an uninsured or self-insured late model vehicle which sustains damage to such an extent that the estimated cost of repairs exceeds seventy-five percent of the actual cash value of the vehicle prior to being damaged shall similarly apply for and obtain a salvage certificate. If no estimated cost of repairs is available from an insurance company, the owner of the vehicle may provide an estimate from an independent appraisal firm. Any such estimate from an independent appraisal firm shall be verified by the Department in such a manner as may be provided for by Department regulations.

F. The fee for issuance of the salvage certificate shall be $10. If a salvage vehicle is sold after a salvage certificate has been issued, the owner of the salvage vehicle shall make proper assignment to the purchaser.

G. The Department, upon receipt of an application for a salvage certificate for a vehicle titled in the Commonwealth, or upon receipt of notification from an insurance company or its authorized agent as provided in subsection D of this section, shall cause the title of such vehicle to be cancelled and the appropriate certificate issued to the vehicle's owner.

H. All provisions of this Code applicable to a motor vehicle certificate of title shall apply, mutatis mutandis, to a salvage certificate, except that no registration or license plates shall be issued for the vehicle described in the salvage certificate. A vehicle for which a salvage certificate has been issued may be retitled for use on the highways in accordance with the provisions of § 46.2-1605.

History.

1979, c. 401, § 46.1-550.8; 1982, c. 671; 1989, c. 727; 1992, c. 148; 1993, c. 376; 2000, cc. 235, 257; 2009, c. 171.

§ 46.2-1603.1. Duties of licensees.

A. If a salvage vehicle is purchased by a salvage dealer and the vehicle is sold as a unit to anyone other than a demolisher, rebuilder, vehicle removal operator, or scrap metal processor, the purchaser shall obtain from the Department a salvage certificate. If the sale is to a demolisher or vehicle removal operator, the salvage vehicle shall be assigned in the space provided for such assignments on the existing salvage certificate. If a vehicle is purchased by a salvage dealer and disassembled for parts only or demolished by a demolisher, the salvage dealer shall immediately and conspicuously indicate on the salvage certificate or title that the vehicle was disassembled for parts only or demolished and immediately forward the salvage certificate or title to the Department for cancellation. The Department shall cancel the title or salvage certificate and issue a nonrepairable certificate for the vehicle to the salvage dealer.

1. If a vehicle for which a title or salvage certificate or other ownership document has been issued by a foreign jurisdiction and is purchased by a salvage dealer or demolisher and disassembled for parts only or demolished by a demolisher, the salvage dealer or demolisher shall immediately and conspicuously indicate on the salvage certificate, title, or other ownership document that the vehicle was disassembled for parts only or demolished and immediately forward the salvage certificate, title or other ownership document to the Department for cancellation. The Department shall cancel the title, salvage certificate, or other ownership document and issue a nonrepairable certificate for the vehicle to the salvage dealer.

2. There shall be no fee for the issuance of a nonrepairable certificate.

B. If a licensee acquires any late model vehicle, he shall immediately compare the vehicle identification number assigned by the manufacturer or the Department or the identification number issued or assigned by another state with the title or salvage certificate of the vehicle and shall notify the Department as provided in subsection C. Such comparison and notification shall not be required of a demolisher if the vehicle was acquired from a licensed salvage dealer, rebuilder, salvage pool, or vehicle removal operator and such licensee delivers to the demolisher a title or salvage certificate for the vehicle.

C. If the vehicle identification number has been altered, is missing, or appears to have been otherwise tampered with, the licensee shall take no further action with regard to the vehicle except to safeguard it in its then-existing condition and shall promptly notify the Department. The Department shall, after an investigation has been made, notify the licensee whether the vehicle can be freed from this limitation. In no event shall the vehicle be disassembled, demolished, processed, or otherwise modified or removed prior to authorization by the Department. If the vehicle is a motorcycle, the licensee shall cause to be noted on the title or salvage certificate, certifying on the face of the document, in addition to the above requirements, the frame number of the motorcycle and motor number, if available.

D. Except as provided in § 46.2-1203, after a vehicle has been demolished, the demolisher shall, within five working days, deliver to the Department the salvage certificate or title, certifying on the face of the document that the vehicle has been destroyed.

E. Except as provided in § 46.2-1203, it shall be unlawful for any licensee to purchase, receive, take into inventory, or otherwise accept from any person any late model vehicle unless, as a part of any such transaction, the licensee also receives a title, salvage certificate, nonrepairable certificate, or other ownership documents, issued by an appropriate regulatory agency within or without the Commonwealth, relating to such vehicle. Every licensee shall maintain as a part of his business records a title, salvage certificate, nonrepairable certificate, or other ownership documents, issued by an appropriate regulatory agency within or without the Commonwealth, pertaining to every late model vehicle in his inventory or possession.

F. If a licensee intends to utilize machinery to crush, flatten, or otherwise reduce one or more vehicles to a state where it can no longer be considered a vehicle at a location other than the location specified on the license filed with the Department, the licensee shall apply to the Department for a permit of operation in a manner prescribed by the Commissioner. Each permit shall be valid for a period not to exceed 15 days and shall specify the location of intended operation. The cost of each permit shall be $15.

G. The licensee shall comply with all applicable federal title reporting requirements, including the reporting requirements of the National Motor Vehicle Title Information System pursuant to 28 C.F.R. § 25.56.

History.

1992, c. 148; 1995, cc. 390, 394; 2004, c. 369; 2011, c. 824; 2014, c. 58.

§ 46.2-1603.2. Owner may declare vehicle nonrepairable; insurance company required to obtain a nonrepairable certificate; applicability of certain other laws to nonrepairable certificates; titling and registration of nonrepairable vehicle prohibited.

A. The owner of any vehicle titled in the Commonwealth may declare such vehicle to be a nonrepairable vehicle by applying to the Department for a nonrepairable certificate.

B. Every insurance company or its authorized agent shall apply to the Department and obtain a nonrepairable certificate for each vehicle acquired by the insurance company as a result of the claims process if such vehicle is titled in the Commonwealth and is (i) a late model nonrepairable vehicle or (ii) a stolen vehicle that has been recovered and determined to be a nonrepairable vehicle. The application shall be accompanied by the vehicle's title certificate or salvage certificate. Application for the nonrepairable certificate shall be made within 15 days after payment has been made to the owner, lienholder, or both.

C. Every insurance company or its authorized agent shall notify the Department of each late model vehicle titled in the Commonwealth upon which a claim has been paid if such vehicle is a nonrepairable vehicle that is retained by its owner.

D. The Department, upon receipt of an application for a nonrepairable certificate for a vehicle titled in the Commonwealth, or upon receipt of notification from an insurance company or its authorized agent as provided in subsection C of this section that a vehicle registered in the Commonwealth has become a nonrepairable vehicle, shall cause the title of such vehicle to be cancelled and a nonrepairable certificate issued to the vehicle's owner.

There shall be no fee for the issuance of a nonrepairable certificate. All provisions of this Code applicable to a motor vehicle certificate of title shall apply, mutatis mutandis, to a nonrepairable certificate, except that no registration or license plates shall be issued for the vehicle described in a nonrepairable certificate. No vehicle for which a nonrepairable certificate has been issued shall ever be titled or registered for use on the highways in the Commonwealth.

E. The Department, upon receipt of a title, salvage certificate, or other ownership document from a licensed salvage dealer or demolisher pursuant to subdivision A 1 of § 46.2-1603.1, shall cause the title, salvage certificate, or other ownership document to such vehicle to be cancelled and a nonrepairable certificate issued to the vehicle's owner.

History.

1992, c. 148; 1993, c. 376; 1995, c. 390; 2015, cc. 33, 177.

§ 46.2-1604. Rebuilders required to possess certificate of title.

Each rebuilder shall have in his possession a certificate of title assigned to him for each vehicle in his inventory for resale. If a rebuilder purchases a salvage vehicle to be used or sold for parts only, he shall conspicuously indicate on the salvage certificate that the vehicle will be sold or used as parts only and immediately forward the salvage certificate to the Department for cancellation. The Department shall issue a nonrepairable certificate for that vehicle.

History.

1979, c. 401, § 46.1-550.9; 1989, c. 727; 1992, c. 148.

§ 46.2-1605. Vehicles rebuilt for highway use; examinations; branding of titles.

A. Each salvage vehicle that has been rebuilt for use on the highways shall be submitted for a state safety inspection in accordance with § 46.2-1157. The inspection shall be conducted by an inspector wholly unaffiliated with the person requesting the inspection of the vehicle.

B. Upon passage of a state safety inspection, each rebuilt vehicle shall be examined by the Department prior to the issuance of a title for the vehicle. The examination by the Department shall include a review of video or photographic images of the vehicle prior to being rebuilt, if available; all documentation for the parts and labor used for the repair of the salvage vehicle; and verification of the vehicle's identification number, confidential number, odometer reading, and engine, transmission, or electronic modules, if applicable. This inspection shall serve as an antitheft and antifraud measure and shall not certify the safety or roadworthiness of the vehicle. The Commissioner shall ensure that, in scheduling and performing examinations of salvage vehicles under this section, single vehicles owned by private owner-operators are afforded no lower priority than examinations of vehicles owned by motor vehicle dealers, salvage pools, licensed auto recyclers, or vehicle removal operators. The Commissioner may charge a fee of $125 per vehicle, for the examination of rebuilt vehicles.

C. Any salvage vehicle whose vehicle identification number or confidential number has been altered, is missing, or appears to have been tampered with may be impounded by the Department until completion of an investigation by the Department. The vehicle may not be moved, sold, or tampered with until the completion of this investigation. Upon completion of an investigation by the Department, if the vehicle identification number is found to be missing or altered, a new vehicle identification number may be issued by the Department. If the vehicle is found to be a stolen vehicle and its owner can be determined, the vehicle shall be returned to him. If the owner cannot be determined or located and the person seeking to title the vehicle has been convicted of a violation of § 46.2-1074 or 46.2-1075, the vehicle shall be deemed forfeited to the Commonwealth and said forfeiture shall proceed in accordance with Chapter 22.1 (§ 19.2-386.1 et seq.) of Title 19.2.

D. If the Department's examination of a rebuilt salvage vehicle indicates no irregularities, a title and registration may be issued for the vehicle upon application therefor to the Department by the owner of the salvage vehicle. The title issued by the Department and any subsequent title thereafter issued for the rebuilt vehicle shall be permanently branded to indicate that it is a rebuilt vehicle. All rebuilt vehicles shall be subject to all safety equipment requirements provided by law. No title or registration shall be issued by the Department for any rebuilt vehicle that has not first passed a safety inspection or for any vehicle for which a nonrepairable certificate has ever been issued.

E. If the Department's examination of a rebuilt salvage vehicle reveals irregularities in the required documentation or obvious defects, the Department shall identify to the owner the irregularities and defects that must be corrected before the Department's examination can be completed.

F. When necessary and upon application, the Department shall issue temporary trip permits in accordance with § 46.2-651 for the purpose of transporting the rebuilt salvage vehicle to and from an official Virginia safety inspection station.

History.

1979, c. 401, § 46.1-550.10; 1986, c. 161; 1989, c. 727; 1992, c. 148; 1994, c. 73; 1996, cc. 21, 843; 2003, c. 304; 2006, c. 615; 2011, c. 824; 2012, cc. 283, 756; 2015, cc. 33, 177.

§ 46.2-1606. Certificates of title issued by other states.

The Commissioner may accept certificates of titles for salvage vehicles or other documents deemed appropriate by the Department issued by other states indicating a vehicle has been declared salvage, and shall carry forward all appropriate brands or indicators. If the vehicle has not been rebuilt and the requirements of § 46.2-1605 have not been met, the Department shall issue a salvage certificate for the vehicle.

History.

1979, c. 401, § 46.1-550.11; 1981, c. 9; 1989, c. 727; 1992, c. 148.

§ 46.2-1607. Inspection of records and examination of inventory.

The Commissioner or any person authorized by the Commissioner or any law-enforcement officer, during the usual business hours, may examine any records, books, papers, or other documents required to be maintained by this chapter, and may examine any vehicle or component part of any vehicle located in the yard, garage, or storage area of any salvage dealer, rebuilder, demolisher, salvage pool, scrap metal processor, or vehicle removal operator to ensure compliance with this chapter.

History.

1979, c. 401, § 46.1-550.12; 1987, c. 325; 1989, c. 727; 1992, c. 148.

§ 46.2-1608. Maintenance and contents of records.

A. Each licensee shall maintain a record of the receipt and sale of any vehicle. Such record shall be maintained at the licensee's place of business. The record, at a minimum, shall contain:

1. A description of each vehicle sold, purchased, exchanged, or acquired by the licensee, including, but not limited to, the model, make, year of the vehicle as well as the vehicle's title number with state of issuance and vehicle identification number;
2. The price paid for each vehicle;
3. The name and address of the seller from whom each vehicle is purchased, exchanged, or acquired and the name and address of the buyer to whom the vehicle is sold;
4. The date and hour the sale, purchase, exchange, or acquisition was made;
5. A photocopy of the seller's and buyer's driver's license, state identification card, official United States military identification card, or any other form of personal identification with photograph;
6. For the sale of nonrepairable vehicles, a photocopy of the buyer's business license if the buyer is authorized to purchase a vehicle under § 46.2-1602

or, if the buyer represents a third party authorized to purchase a vehicle under § 46.2-1602, then a photocopy of the third party's business license and documentation that the buyer is authorized to act on behalf of that third party;

7. Digital photographs of the seller, the buyer, and the vehicle that is being sold, purchased, exchanged, or acquired through or from the licensee; and

8. The signature of the licensee, the seller, and the buyer as executed at the time of the sale, purchase, exchange, or acquisition of the vehicle by the licensee.

B. If any major component, as defined in § 46.2-1600, is sold, the salvage dealer shall provide, upon request of any law-enforcement official, the information required by this section as to the vehicle from which the part was taken.

C. The provisions of subdivisions A 5, 6, and 7 shall not apply to vehicles when the licensee maintains a photocopy or electronic copy of one of the documents set out in § 46.2-1206 or this chapter.

D. The provisions of this section shall not apply to salvage pools as defined in § 46.2-1600, except that salvage pools shall maintain a record of the receipt of any vehicle that contains (i) the date of receipt of the vehicle and its make, year, model, and identification number; (ii) the name and address of the person from whom it was acquired; (iii) the name and address of the buyer as well as (a) a photocopy of the buyer's driver's license, state identification card, official United States military identification card, or any other form of personal identification with photograph and (b) a photocopy of the buyer's business license or, if the buyer represents a third party authorized to purchase the vehicle under § 46.2-1602, then a photocopy of the third party's business license and documentation that the buyer is authorized to act on behalf of the third party; and (iv) the vehicle's title number and state of issuance.

History.

1979, c. 401, § 46.1-550.13; 1989, c. 727; 1992, c. 148; 2000, c. 123; 2010, c. 873; 2014, c. 58; 2015, cc. 33, 177.

§ 46.2-1608.1. Reports to police department; local ordinance; holding period; penalty.

A. The governing body of any county, city, or town may by ordinance require each licensee within the jurisdiction to make a written or electronic report of the information required to be maintained by § 46.2-1608, at the request of the police department or sheriff, on a daily basis or such other frequency as requested by the police department or sheriff, of every purchase, exchange or acquisition of any salvage or scrap vehicle. The ordinance may also require that the photocopy of the seller's driver's license, state identification card, official United States military identification card, or any other form of personal identification with photograph and a copy of the digital photograph required by § 46.2-1608 be electronically transmitted to the police department or sheriff on a weekly basis at an electronic address to be provided. Any local governing body, by such ordinance, may assess and retain a fine of not more than $2,500 for its violation.

B. No licensee shall crush, flatten, or otherwise reduce a vehicle to a state where it can no longer be considered a vehicle until it has been in his possession for up to 10 days unless the vehicle is accompanied by proper documentation pursuant to subsection C. This subsection shall not apply to inoperable vehicles. For purposes of this subsection, an "inoperable vehicle" shall mean any vehicle that is physically damaged beyond use or any vehicle that does not contain or have an engine in running condition or does not have any other essential parts required for operation of the vehicle.

C. The provisions of this section shall not apply to vehicles when the licensee maintains a photocopy or electronic copy of one of the documents set out in § 46.2-1206 or this chapter.

D. The provisions of this section shall not apply to scrap metal processors as defined in § 59.1-136.1 or to salvage pools as defined in § 46.2-1600.

History.

2010, c. 873.

§ 46.2-1608.2. Licensees to update records of the Department for motor vehicles that are to be demolished or dismantled.

A. A licensed auto recycler may be exempted from the waiting period in subsection B of § 46.2-1608.1 by:

1. Entering into a contractual agreement with the Department to update records of motor vehicles to be demolished or dismantled if such motor vehicles have either been issued a certificate of title, salvage certificate, or nonrepairable certificate in the Commonwealth or are titled in another state. In addition to the contractual agreement, the licensed auto recycler shall be required to comply with the Department's procedures for securely accessing and updating the Department's records; and

2. Notifying the Department that a motor vehicle is being demolished or dismantled or of the intention to demolish, dismantle, or reduce the motor vehicle to a state where it can no longer be considered a motor vehicle. Licensed auto recyclers shall electronically notify the Department of the demolished or dismantled vehicle's certificate of title, salvage certificate, or nonrepairable certificate number and vehicle identification number.

B. Licensed auto recyclers in possession of the certificate of title, salvage certificate, or nonrepairable certificate from the Commonwealth may demolish or dismantle the subject motor vehicle. Licensed auto recyclers shall electronically notify the Department of the demolished or dismantled vehicle's certificate of title, salvage certificate, or nonrepairable certificate number and vehicle identification number within required time frames pursuant to subsection D of § 46.2-1603.1.

C. Licensed auto recyclers in possession of a certificate of title issued by another state may demolish or dismantle the subject motor vehicle. Licensed auto recyclers shall electronically notify the Department of the demolished or dismantled vehicle's certificate of title number, vehicle identification number, year, make, and model within required time frames pursuant to subsection D of § 46.2-1603.1.

D. Licensed auto recyclers that do not possess a certificate of title, salvage certificate, or nonrepairable certificate may demolish the subject motor vehicle if the motor vehicle is a model year that is at least 10 years older than the current model year. The licensed auto recycler shall provide electronically to the Department the vehicle identification number and the year, make, and model of the motor vehicle and shall remit to the Department the fees set out in § 46.2-627 and an additional $10 transaction fee. Upon receipt of such notification, the Department shall check the records of nationally recognized databases. The licensed auto recycler may not demolish or dismantle the vehicle until the Department has notified the licensed auto recycler of the results of that inquiry. If a licensed auto recycler is not in possession of the certificate of title, salvage certificate, or nonrepairable certificate and the subject motor vehicle is of the current model year or of a model year that is nine years old or less, that vehicle shall be processed in accordance with § 46.2-1202.

E. Nothing in this section shall release a licensed auto recycler from complying with the provisions of §§ 46.2-1603.1, 46.2-1608, and 46.2-1608.1.

History.
2011, c. 279; 2015, cc. 33, 177.

§ 46.2-1609. Penalties.

A. First violations of any provision of this chapter shall constitute a Class 1 misdemeanor, and second and subsequent violations of any provision of this chapter shall constitute a Class 5 felony. Upon receipt of any such conviction, the Commissioner may suspend, revoke, cancel, or refuse to renew the license of any licensee under this chapter, and the Commissioner may also assess a civil penalty against such licensee not to exceed $2,500 for any conviction.

B. Except as otherwise provided in this chapter, any licensee violating any of the provisions of this chapter may be assessed a civil penalty by the Commissioner not to exceed $1,000 for any single violation.

C. Notice of an order suspending, revoking, canceling, or denying renewal of a license, imposing a limitation on operation, or imposing a civil penalty and advising the licensee of the opportunity for a hearing shall be mailed to the licensee by first-class mail to the address as shown on the licensee's most recent application for a license and shall be considered served when mailed. No order required by this section shall become effective until the Commissioner has offered the licensee an opportunity for an administrative hearing to show cause why the order should not be enforced. Notice of the opportunity for an administrative hearing may be included in the order. Any request for an administrative hearing made by such person must be received by the Department within 30 days of the issuance date of the order unless the person presents to the Department evidence of military service as defined by the federal Servicemembers Civil Relief Act (50 U.S.C. § 3901 et seq.), incarceration, commitment, hospitalization, or physical presence outside the United States at the time the order was issued.

D. Upon receipt of a request for a hearing appealing the suspension or imposition of civil penalties, the licensee shall be afforded the opportunity for a hearing as soon as practicable, but in no case later than 30 days from receipt of the hearing request. Any suspension shall remain in effect pending the outcome of the hearing.

History.
1979, c. 401, § 46.1-550.14; 1989, c. 727; 1992, c. 148; 2011, c. 824; 2014, c. 58.

§ 46.2-1610. Disposition of fees.

All fees collected under this chapter shall be paid by the Commissioner into the state treasury and set aside as a special fund to be used to meet the expenses of the vehicle identification number and salvage vehicle inspection programs.

History.
1987, c. 696, § 46.1-550.15; 1989, c. 727; 2006, c. 615.

CHAPTER 17.

DRIVER TRAINING SCHOOLS.

Section

§ 46.2-1700. Definitions.

As used in this chapter, unless the context requires a different meaning:

"Class A licensee" means a driver training school that provides training in the operation of commercial motor vehicles as defined in § 46.2-341.4.

"Class B licensee" means a driver training school that provides training in the operation of any type of motor vehicle other than motorcycles and commercial motor vehicles as defined in § 46.2-341.4.

"Computer-based driver education course" means the classroom portion of driver education offered by a computer-based driver education provider through the Internet or other electronic means approved by the Department whose content and quality is comparable to that of courses offered in the Commonwealth's public schools.

"Computer-based driver education provider" means a driver training school licensed by the Department in accordance with this chapter to conduct computer-based driver education courses.

"Driver training school" or *"school"* means a business enterprise conducted by an individual, association, partnership, or corporation, for the education and training of persons, either practically or theoretically or both, to operate or drive motor vehicles, and charging a consideration or tuition for such services. "Driver training school" or "school" does not mean any college, university, school established pursuant to § 46.2-1314, school maintained or classes conducted by employers for their own employees where no fee or tuition is charged, schools or classes owned and operated by or under the authority of bona fide religious institutions, or by the Commonwealth or any political subdivision thereof, training programs for school bus operators established pursuant to § 22.1-181, driver education programs established pursuant to § 22.1-205, or schools accredited by accrediting associations approved by the Department of Education; however, if any such entity or program excluded from the definition of "driver training school" offers driver education and training through a contractual arrangement with another person for consideration, then that other person shall be considered a driver training school subject to the requirements of this chapter.

"Instructor" means any person, whether acting for himself as operator of a driver training school or for such school for compensation, who teaches, conducts classes, gives demonstrations, or supervises persons learning to operate or drive a motor vehicle.

History.
1990, c. 466; 2004, c. 587; 2016, c. 437.

§ 46.2-1701. Licenses required for school and instructor; fees.

No driver training school shall be established or continue operation unless the school obtains from the Commissioner a license authorizing the school to operate within this Commonwealth.

No instructor shall perform the actions enumerated in the definition of "instructor" in § 46.2-1700 unless he obtains from the Commissioner a license authorizing him to act as driving instructor.

The Commissioner shall have authority to set and collect school and instructor licensing fees. All licensing fees collected by the Commissioner under this chapter shall be paid into the state treasury and set aside as a special fund to meet the expenses of the Department of Motor Vehicles.

Upon application of a driver training school licensed in accordance with this chapter, the Commissioner may license such driver training school using criteria established by the Commissioner pursuant to § 46.2-1702 to provide computer-based driver education courses using curricula approved by the Commissioner. A nonrefundable annual licensing fee of $100 shall be required with each application. Such annual licensing fee shall be in addition to fees permitted under this chapter.

History.
1990, c. 466; 2004, c. 587; 2016, c. 437.

§ 46.2-1701.1. Bond of applicants.

The applicant shall file a surety bond in the amount of $100,000 for a Class A licensee and $5,000 for a Class B licensee. The bond shall be payable to the Commonwealth of Virginia and conditioned to protect the contractual rights of students. The bonding requirement for a Class A license may be reduced, at the discretion of the Department, on a showing by the school that no course of study for which tuition is collected lasts longer than thirty days or that the school collects no advance tuition other than equal monthly installments based on the length of the course of study. The minimum bond for any school shall be $5,000.

History.
1991, c. 214.

§ 46.2-1701.2. Schools required to have established places of business.

No license shall be issued or renewed to any driver training school unless it has an established place of business in the Commonwealth that:

1. Satisfies all local zoning regulations;

2. Has office space in which the driver training school houses all records required to be maintained under § 46.2-1701.3 and which:

a. Is equipped with a desk, chairs, filing space, a working telephone listed in the name of the school, and working utilities;

b. Complies with federal, state, and local health, fire, and building code requirements; and

c. Meets all other place of business and recordkeeping requirements set forth in this chapter and established in regulations promulgated by the Department.

History.
2004, c. 587.

§ 46.2-1701.3. Student records to be maintained.

All student records and other records, as required by the Department, shall be maintained on the premises of the licensed location. The Commissioner may, on written request from a driver training school, permit records to be maintained at a location other than the premises of the licensed location for good cause shown. All records shall be preserved in original form or in film, magnetic, electronic, or optical media, including but not limited to microfilm or microfiche, for a period of three years in a manner that permits systematic retrieval. All records required to be maintained by the provisions of this section or by regulation shall be available to the Commissioner or his agents during regular business hours or at any other reasonable time, as determined by the Commissioner.

History.
2004, c. 587.

§ 46.2-1701.4. Reports and records of licensed computer-based driver education providers.

The Commissioner may require annual, periodic, or special reports from computer-based driver education providers in a manner and form approved by the Commissioner. The Commissioner may require a computer-based driver education provider to file with the Department a true copy of any contract, agreement, or arrangement between such computer-based driver education provider and any person in relation to the provisions of this chapter. The Commissioner may prescribe the forms of any accounts, records, and memoranda to be kept by computer-based driver education providers and the length of time such accounts, records, and memoranda shall be preserved.

History.
2016, c. 437.

§ 46.2-1702. Certification of driver education courses by Commissioner.

Notwithstanding any other provision of law, the Commissioner shall have the authority to approve as a driver education course satisfying the requirements of § 46.2-334 any course which is offered by any driver training school licensed under the provisions of this chapter if he finds that the course is of comparable content and quality to that offered in the Commonwealth's public schools. In making such finding, the Commissioner shall not require that the instructors of any driver training school meet the certification requirements of teachers in the Commonwealth's public schools.

Any community college within the Virginia Community College System shall have the authority to offer the courses required by the Virginia Board of Education to become a certified driver education instructor in Virginia on a not-for-credit basis so long as the courses include the same content and curriculum required by the Department of Education, enabling individuals who complete those courses to then teach driver's education in Virginia driver education training schools upon official certification by the Department of Motor Vehicles. The Virginia Department of Education shall provide the curriculum, content, and other information regarding the courses required to become certified driver education instructors in Virginia to any community college within the Virginia Community College System. The content of each course must be accurate and rigorous and must meet the requirements for the Department of Education's Curriculum and Administrative Guide for Driver's Education, which includes the Board of Education's standards of learning.

Except for schools in the Commonwealth's public school system and providers of correspondence courses approved by the Board of Education pursuant to subsection F of § 22.1-205, only those driver training schools that are licensed as computer-based driver education providers shall be authorized to administer computer-based driver education courses. The content and quality of such computer-based driver education courses shall be comparable to that of courses offered in the Commonwealth's public schools. The Commissioner may establish minimum standards for testing students who have enrolled in computer-based driver education courses. Such standards may include (i) requirements for the test site; (ii) verification that the person taking the test is the person enrolled in the course; (iii) verification of the identity of the student using photo identification approved by the Commissioner; and (iv) maintenance of a log containing the name and title of the licensed instructor monitoring the test, the test date, the name of the student taking the test, and the student's time-in and time-out of the test site. Computer-based driver education providers shall not issue a certificate of completion to a student in Planning District 8 prior to receiving proof of completion of the additional minimum 90-minute parent/student driver education component pursuant to § 22.1-205.

The Commissioner shall have authority to approve any driver education course offered by any Class A licensee if he finds the course meets the requirements for such courses as set forth in this chapter and as otherwise established by the Department. Class A licensees shall not be permitted to administer knowledge or behind-the-wheel examinations. Driver education courses offered by any Class B licensee shall be based on the driver education curriculum currently approved by the Department of Education and the Department.

The Commissioner may accept 20 years' service with the Virginia Department of State Police by a person who retired or resigned while in good standing from such Department in lieu of requirements established by the Department of Education for instructor qualification.

History.
1990, c. 466; 1991, c. 214; 2004, c. 587; 2014, cc. 666, 685, 753; 2016, c. 437.

§ 46.2-1703. Authority to promulgate regulations.

The Commissioner may promulgate regulations necessary to (i) enforce the provisions of this chapter, (ii) provide adequate training for students, (iii) protect student and public safety and (iv) carry out the other provisions of this chapter. These regulations shall include but need not be limited to curriculum requirements, contractual arrangements with students, obligations to students, facilities and equipment, qualifications and other requirements for instructors, school ownership requirements, surety bond requirements, and financial stability of schools.

History.
1990, c. 466; 1991, c. 214; 2004, c. 587.

§ 46.2-1704. Action on applications; hearing on denial.

The Commissioner shall act on any application for a license under this chapter within thirty days after receipt by either granting or denying the application. Any applicant denied a license shall, on his written request made within thirty days, be given a hearing at a time and place determined by the Commissioner or his designee. All hearings under this section shall be public and shall be held promptly. The applicant may be represented by counsel. Any applicant denied a license may not apply again for a license for thirty days from the date of denial of the application.

History.
1991, c. 214.

§ 46.2-1705. Suspension, revocation, cancellation or refusal to renew license; limitations on operations; imposition of monetary penalties.

A. Except as otherwise provided in this section, no license issued under this chapter shall be suspended, revoked, or cancelled or renewal thereof denied, no limitation on operations shall be imposed pursuant to subsection F of this section, and no monetary penalty shall be imposed pursuant to § 46.2-1706, unless the licensee has been furnished a written copy of the complaint against him and the grounds upon which the action is taken and has been offered an opportunity for an administrative hearing to show cause why such action should not be taken.

B. The order suspending, revoking, cancelling, or denying renewal of a license, imposing a limitation on operation, or imposing a monetary penalty, except as otherwise provided in subsection E of this section, shall not become effective until the licensee has had 30 days after notice of the opportunity for a hearing to make a written request for such a hearing. If no hearing has been requested within such 30-day period, the order shall become effective and no hearing shall thereafter be held. A timely request for a hearing shall automatically stay operation of the order until after the hearing.

C. Notice of an order suspending, revoking, cancelling or denying renewal of a license, imposing a limitation on operation, or imposing a monetary penalty and advising the licensee of the opportunity for a hearing shall be mailed to the licensee by registered mail to the school address as shown on the licensee's most recent application for license and shall be considered served when mailed.

D. No licensee whose license has been revoked or cancelled or who has been denied renewal shall apply for a new license within 180 days of such action.

E. Notwithstanding the provisions of subsection B of this section, an order suspending, revoking, cancelling, or denying renewal of an instructor license shall be effective immediately if the order is based upon a finding by the Commissioner (i) that the instructor's driving record is such that he is not presently qualified to act as an instructor or (ii) that he is otherwise a danger to the safety of his students or the public. Such finding by the Commissioner shall be based on records of driver's license suspension or revocation, upon records of conviction of serious motor vehicle related offenses punishable as a misdemeanor or felony including driving under the influence or reckless driving, and upon such other criteria as the Commissioner may establish by regulation.

Notice of the order of suspension, revocation, cancellation, or denial shall be in writing and mailed in accordance with subsection C. Upon receipt of a request for a hearing appealing the suspension, revocation, cancellation, or denial, the licensee shall be afforded the opportunity for a hearing as soon as practicable, but in no case later than 30 days from receipt of the hearing request. The order shall remain in effect pending the outcome of the hearing.

F. If the Commissioner makes a finding that the conduct of a licensee is in violation of this chapter or regulations adopted pursuant to this chapter, he may suspend, revoke, cancel, or refuse to renew the license of such licensee or may order the licensee, in accordance with subsections A, B and C of this section, to limit the types of driver education training provided, restrict the use of the licensee's training vehicles, or both. Whenever the Commissioner takes action limiting operations under this subsection, the Commissioner shall require the licensee to post conspicuous notice of the Commissioner's action under this subsection at the same location as the licensee's license was issued under this chapter, as soon as the Commissioner's order becomes effective. Orders of the Commissioner limiting operations and requiring posting of notices shall remain in effect until (i) the time period for the limitations or restriction has expired and the Commissioner makes a finding that the violations causing the imposition of such limitations or restrictions have been remedied by the licensee or (ii) the Commissioner's order is lifted as the result of an appeal under § 46.2-1704 or by a court of competent jurisdiction.

G. If the Commissioner makes a finding, after conducting a preliminary investigation, that the conduct of a licensee (i) is in violation of this chapter or regulations adopted pursuant to this chapter and (ii) such violation constitutes a danger to public safety, the Commissioner may issue an order suspending the licensee's license to operate a driver training school. Notice of the suspension shall be in writing and mailed in accordance with subsection C of this section. Upon receipt of a request for a hearing appealing the suspension, the licensee shall be afforded the opportunity for a hearing as soon as practicable, but in no case later than 30 days from receipt of the hearing request. The suspension shall remain in effect pending the outcome of the hearing.

History.
1991, c. 214; 2000, c. 179; 2004, c. 587.

§ 46.2-1706. Civil penalties.

In addition to any other sanctions or remedies available to the Commissioner under this chapter, the Commissioner may assess a civil penalty not to exceed $1,000 for any violation of any provision of this chapter or any regulation promulgated thereunder. The penalty may be sued for and recovered in the name of the Commonwealth.

History.
1991, c. 214.

§ 46.2-1707. Unlawful acts; prosecution; proceedings in equity.

A. It shall be unlawful for any person to engage in any of the following acts:

1. Practicing as a driver training school or as an instructor without holding a valid license as required by statute or regulation;

2. Making use of any designation provided by statute or regulation to denote a standard of professional or occupational competence without being duly certified or licensed;

3. Performing any act or function which is restricted by statute or regulation to persons holding a driver training school or instructor license or certification, without being duly certified or licensed;

4. Materially misrepresenting facts in an application for licensure, certification or registration;

5. Willfully refusing to furnish the Department information or records required or requested pursuant to statute or regulation; or

6. Violating any statute or regulation governing the practice of any driver training school or instructor regulated pursuant to this chapter.

Any person who willfully engages in any unlawful act enumerated in this section shall be guilty of a Class 1 misdemeanor. However, the third or any subsequent conviction for violating this section during a 36-month period shall constitute a Class 6 felony.

B. In addition to the provisions of subsection A of this section, the Department may institute proceedings in equity to enjoin any person from engaging in any unlawful act enumerated in this section. Such proceedings shall be brought in the name of the Commonwealth in the circuit court of the city or county in which the unlawful act occurred or in which the defendant resides.

History.
1991, c. 214; 2004, c. 587.

CHAPTER 18.

VIRGINIA MOTOR VEHICLE SCRAPPAGE PROGRAM.

§§ 46.2-1801 through 46.2-1805: Repealed by Acts 1996, cc. 165 and 926.

CHAPTER 19.

T&M VEHICLE DEALERS.

§§ 46.2-1900 through 46.2-1991: Repealed by Acts 2015, c. 615, cl. 9.

Cross references.
For current provisions as to recreational vehicle franchises, see Article 7.2 (§ 46.2-1573.2 et seq.).

CHAPTER 19.1.

TRAILER DEALERS.

§§ 46.2-1992 through 46.2-1992.85: Repealed by Acts 2015, c. 615, cl. 9.

Cross references.

For current provisions as to trailer franchises, see Article 7.3 (§ 46.2-1573.13 et seq.).

CHAPTER 19.2.
MOTORCYCLE DEALERS.

§§ 46.2-1993 through 46.2-1993.82: Repealed by Acts 2015, c. 615, cl. 9.

Cross references.

For current provisions as to motor cycle franchises, see Article 7.4 (§ 46.2-1573.25 et seq.).

SUBTITLE V.
MOTOR CARRIERS.

CHAPTER 20.
REGULATION OF PASSENGER CARRIERS.

Article 1.

Motor Carriers of Passengers — Generally.

Article 2.

Insurance Requirements.

Article 3.

Taxicabs.

Article 4.

Employee Haulers.

Article 5.

Nonprofit/Tax-Exempt Passenger Carriers.

ARTICLE 1.

MOTOR CARRIERS OF PASSENGERS — GENERALLY.

§ 46.2-2000. Definitions.

Whenever used in this chapter unless expressly stated otherwise:

"Authorized insurer" means, in the case of an interstate motor carrier whose operations may or may not include intrastate activity, an insurer authorized to transact business in any one state, or, in the case of a solely intrastate motor carrier, an insurer authorized to transact business in the Commonwealth.

"Broker" means any person not included in the term "motor carrier" and not a bona fide employee or agent of any such carrier, who, as principal or agent, sells or offers for sale any transportation subject to this chapter, or negotiates for, or holds himself out by solicitation, advertisement, or otherwise as one who sells, provides, furnishes, contracts, or arranges for such transportation.

"Carrier by motor launch" means a common carrier, which carrier uses one or more motor launches

operating on the waters within the Commonwealth to transport passengers.

"Certificate" means a certificate of public convenience and necessity or a certificate of fitness.

"Certificate of fitness" means a certificate issued by the Department to a contract passenger carrier, a sight-seeing carrier, a transportation network company, or a nonemergency medical transportation carrier.

"Certificate of public convenience and necessity" means a certificate issued by the Department of Motor Vehicles to certain common carriers, but nothing contained in this chapter shall be construed to mean that the Department can issue any such certificate authorizing intracity transportation.

"Common carrier" means any person who undertakes, whether directly or by a lease or any other arrangement, to transport passengers for the general public by motor vehicle for compensation over the highways of the Commonwealth, whether over regular or irregular routes, including such motor vehicle operations of carriers by rail or water under this chapter. "Common carrier" does not include nonemergency medical transportation carriers, transportation network companies, or TNC partners as defined in this section.

"Contract passenger carrier" means a motor carrier that transports groups of passengers under a single contract made with one person for an agreed charge for such transportation, regardless of the number of passengers transported, and for which transportation no individual or separate fares are solicited, charged, collected, or received by the carrier. "Contract passenger carrier" does not include a transportation network company or TNC partner as defined in this section.

"Department" means the Department of Motor Vehicles.

"Digital platform" means any online-enabled application, software, website, or system offered or utilized by a transportation network company that enables the prearrangement of rides with TNC partners.

"Employee hauler" means a motor carrier operating for compensation and exclusively transporting only bona fide employees directly to and from the factories, plants, office or other places of like nature where the employees are employed and accustomed to work.

"Excursion train" means any steam-powered train that carries passengers for which the primary purpose of the operation of such train is the passengers' experience and enjoyment of this means of transportation, and does not, in the course of operation, carry (i) freight other than the personal luggage of the passengers or crew or supplies and equipment necessary to serve the needs of the passengers and crew, (ii) passengers who are commuting to work, or (iii) passengers who are traveling to their final destination solely for business or commercial purposes.

"Financial responsibility" means the ability to respond in damages for liability thereafter incurred arising out of the ownership, maintenance, use, or operation of a motor vehicle, in the amounts provided for in this chapter.

"Highway" means every public highway or place of whatever nature open to the use of the public for purposes of vehicular travel in the Commonwealth, including the streets and alleys in towns and cities.

"Identification marker" means a decal or other visible identification issued or required by the Department to show one or more of the following: (i) that the operator of the vehicle has registered with the Department for the payment of the road tax imposed under Chapter 27 (§ 58.1-2700 et seq.) of Title 58.1; (ii) proof of the possession of a certificate or permit issued pursuant to Chapter 20 (§ 46.2-2000 et seq.); (iii) proof that the vehicle has been registered with the Department as a TNC partner vehicle under subsection B of § 46.2-2099.50; (iv) proof that the vehicle has been authorized by a transportation network company to be operated as a TNC partner vehicle, in accordance with subsection C of § 46.2-2099.50; or (v) proof of compliance with the insurance requirements of this chapter.

"Interstate" means transportation of passengers between states.

"Intrastate" means transportation of passengers solely within a state.

"License" means a license issued by the Department to a broker.

"Minibus" means any motor vehicle having a seating capacity of not less than seven nor more than 31 passengers, including the driver, and used in the transportation of passengers.

"Motor carrier" means any person who undertakes, whether directly or by lease, to transport passengers for compensation over the highways of the Commonwealth.

"Motor launch" means a motor vessel that meets the requirements of the U.S. Coast Guard for the carriage of passengers for compensation, with a capacity of six or more passengers, but not in excess of 50 passengers. "Motor launch" does not include sight-seeing vessels, special or charter party vessels within the provisions of this chapter. A carrier by motor launch shall not be regarded as a steamship company.

"Nonemergency medical transportation carrier" means a motor carrier that exclusively provides nonemergency medical transportation and provides such transportation only (i) through the Department of Medical Assistance Services; (ii) through a broker operating under a contract with the Department of Medical Assistance Services; or (iii) as a Medicaid Managed Care Organization contracted with the Department of Medical Assistance Services to provide such transportation.

"Nonprofit/tax-exempt passenger carrier" means a bona fide nonprofit corporation organized or existing under Chapter 10 (§ 13.1-801 et seq.) of Title 13.1, or a tax-exempt organization as defined in §§ 501(c)(3) and 501(c)(4) of the Internal Revenue

Code, as amended, who undertakes, whether directly or by lease, to control and operate minibuses exclusively in the transportation, for compensation, of members of such organization if it is a membership corporation, or of elderly, disabled, or economically disadvantaged members of the community if it is not a membership corporation.

"Operation" or *"operations"* includes the operation of all motor vehicles, whether loaded or empty, whether for compensation or not, and whether owned by or leased to the motor carrier who operates them or causes them to be operated.

"Operation of a TNC partner vehicle" means (i) any time a TNC partner is logged into a digital platform and is available to pick up passengers; (ii) any time a passenger is in the TNC partner vehicle; and (iii) any time the TNC partner has accepted a prearranged ride request through the digital platform and is en route to a passenger.

"Operator" means the employer or person actually driving a motor vehicle or combination of vehicles.

"Permit" means a permit issued by the Department to carriers operating as employee haulers or nonprofit/tax-exempt passenger carriers or to operators of taxicabs or other vehicles performing taxicab service under this chapter.

"Person" means any individual, firm, copartnership, corporation, company, association, or joint-stock association, and includes any trustee, receiver, assignee, or personal representative thereof.

"Personal vehicle" means a motor vehicle that is not used to transport passengers for compensation except as a TNC partner vehicle.

"Prearranged ride" means passenger transportation for compensation in a TNC partner vehicle arranged through a digital platform. "Prearranged ride" includes the period of time that begins when a TNC partner accepts a ride requested through a digital platform, continues while the TNC partner transports a passenger in a TNC partner vehicle, and ends when the passenger exits the TNC partner vehicle.

"Restricted common carrier" means any person who undertakes, whether directly or by a lease or other arrangement, to transport passengers for compensation, whereby such transportation service has been restricted. "Restricted common carrier" does not include a transportation network company or TNC partner as defined in this section.

"Route," when used in connection with or with respect to a certificate of public convenience and necessity, means the road or highway, or segment thereof, operated over by the holder of a certificate of public convenience and necessity or proposed to be operated over by an applicant therefor, whether such road or highway is designated by one or more highway numbers.

"Services" and *"transportation"* include the service of, and all transportation by, all vehicles operated by, for, or in the interest of any motor carrier irrespective of ownership or contract, expressed or implied, together with all facilities and property operated or controlled by any such carrier or carriers and used in the transportation of passengers or the performance of any service in connection therewith.

"Sight-seeing carrier" means a restricted common carrier authorized to transport passengers under the provisions of this chapter, whereby the primary purpose of the operation is the passengers' experience and enjoyment or the promotion of tourism.

"Sight-seeing carrier by boat" means a restricted common carrier, which restricted common carrier uses a boat or boats operating on waters within the Commonwealth to transport passengers, and whereby the primary purpose of the operation is the passengers' experience and enjoyment or the promotion of tourism. Sight-seeing carriers by boat shall not be regarded as steamship companies.

"Single state insurance receipt" means any receipt issued pursuant to 49 C.F.R. Part 367 evidencing that the carrier has the required insurance and paid the requisite fees to the Commonwealth and other qualified jurisdictions.

"Special or charter party carrier by boat" means a restricted common carrier which transports groups of persons under a single contract made with one person for an agreed charge for such movement regardless of the number of persons transported. Special or charter party carriers by boat shall not be regarded as steamship companies.

"Taxicab or other motor vehicle performing a taxicab service" means any motor vehicle having a seating capacity of not more than six passengers, excluding the driver, not operating on a regular route or between fixed terminals used in the transportation of passengers for hire or for compensation, and not a common carrier, restricted common carrier, transportation network company, TNC partner, or nonemergency medical transportation carrier as defined in this chapter.

"TNC insurance" means a motor vehicle liability insurance policy that specifically covers liabilities arising from a TNC partner's operation of a TNC partner vehicle.

"TNC partner" means a person authorized by a transportation network company to use a TNC partner vehicle to provide prearranged rides on an intrastate basis in the Commonwealth.

"TNC partner vehicle" means a personal vehicle authorized by a transportation network company and used by a TNC partner to provide prearranged rides on an intrastate basis in the Commonwealth.

"Trade dress" means a logo, insignia, or emblem attached to or visible from the exterior of a TNC partner vehicle that identifies a transportation network company or digital platform with which the TNC partner vehicle is affiliated.

"Transportation network company" means a person who provides prearranged rides using a digital platform that connects passengers with TNC partners.

History.

Code 1950, § 56-273; 1950, p. 368; 1966, c. 543; 1973, cc. 306,

460; 1982, c. 257; 1989, c. 625; 1995, cc. 744, 803; 2001, c. 596; 2002, c. 861; 2004, c. 780; 2011, cc. 881, 889; 2012, cc. 22, 111; 2015, cc. 2, 3.

§ 46.2-2000.1. Vehicles excluded from operation of chapter.

This chapter shall not be construed to include:

1. Motor vehicles employed solely in transporting school children and teachers;

2. Taxicabs, or other motor vehicles performing bona fide taxicab service, having a seating capacity of not more than six passengers, excluding the driver, while operating in a county, city, or town which has or adopts an ordinance regulating and controlling taxicabs and other vehicles performing a bona fide taxicab service, and not operating on a regular route or between fixed termini;

3. Motor vehicles owned or operated by or on behalf of hotels while used exclusively for the transportation of hotel patronage between hotels and local railroad or other common carrier stations;

4. Motor vehicles owned and operated by the United States, the District of Columbia, or any state, or any municipality or any other political subdivision of this Commonwealth, including passenger-carrying motor vehicles while being operated under an exclusive contract with the United States;

5. Any motor vehicle designed with a seating capacity for and used to transport not more than 15 passengers, including the driver, if the driver and the passengers are engaged in a share-the-ride undertaking and if they share not more than the expenses of operation of the vehicle. Regular payments toward a capital recovery fund not exceeding the cost of the vehicle or used to pay for leasing the vehicle are to be considered eligible expenses of operation;

6. Unless otherwise provided, motor vehicles while used exclusively in the transportation of passengers within the corporate limits of incorporated cities or towns, and motor vehicles used exclusively in the regular transportation of passengers within the boundaries of such cities or towns and adjacent counties where such vehicles are being operated by such county or pursuant to a contract with the board of supervisors of such county;

7. Motor vehicles while operated under the exclusive regulatory control of a transportation district commission acting pursuant to the Transportation District Act of 1964 (§ 33.2-1900 et seq.) of Title 33.2;

8. Motor vehicles used for the transportation of passengers by nonprofit, nonstock corporations funded solely by federal, state or local subsidies, the use of which motor vehicles are restricted as to regular and irregular routes to contracts with four or more counties and, at the commencement of the operation, no certificated carrier provides the same or similar services within such counties; and

9. Emergency medical services vehicles as defined in § 32.1-111.1.

History.

Code 1950, § 56-274; 1950, p. 370; 1958, c. 285; 1966, c. 575; 1968, c. 183; 1970, c. 33; 1973, c. 460; 1975, c. 122; 1976, cc. 378, 411; 1977, c. 514; 1978, c. 152; 1979, cc. 608, 618; 1980, c. 230; 1982, c. 257; 1983, c. 112; 1985, c. 88; 1986, c. 420; 1989, c. 625; 1995, cc. 744, 803; 2001, c. 596; 2002, c. 337; 2011, cc. 881, 889; 2015, cc. 502, 503.

Editor's note.

The reference to the Transportation District Act in subdivision 7 was updated at the direction of the Virginia Code Commission to conform to the recodification of Title 33.2 by Acts 2014, c. 805, effective October 1, 2014.

§ 46.2-2000.2: Repealed by Acts 2001, c. 596, cl. 2, effective July 1, 2002.

§ 46.2-2000.3. Disposition of funds collected.

Except as otherwise provided, all fees collected by the Department pursuant to this chapter shall be paid into the state treasury and set aside as a special fund to be used to meet the expenses of the Department.

History.

2001, c. 596.

§ 46.2-2001. Regulation by Department; reports; prevention of discrimination; regulation of leasing of motor vehicles.

The Department shall supervise, regulate and control all motor carriers, carriers by rail, and brokers not exempted under this chapter doing business in the Commonwealth, and all matters relating to the performance of their public duties and their charges therefor as provided by this chapter, and shall correct abuses therein by such carriers; and to that end the Department may prescribe reasonable rules, regulations, forms and reports for such carriers and brokers in furtherance of the administration and operation of this chapter; and the Department shall have the right at all times to require from such motor carriers, carriers by rail, and brokers special reports and statements, under oath, concerning their business.

The Department shall make and enforce such requirements, rules and regulations as may be necessary to prevent unjust or unreasonable discriminations by any carrier or broker in favor of, or against, any person, locality, community or connecting carrier in the matter of service, schedule, efficiency of transportation or otherwise, in connection with the public duties of such carrier or broker. The Department shall administer and enforce all provisions of this chapter, and may prescribe reasonable rules, regulations and procedure looking to that end.

The Department may prescribe and enforce such reasonable requirements, rules and regulations in the matter of leasing of motor vehicles as are necessary to prevent evasion of the Department's regulatory powers.

The Department shall work in conjunction with the Department of State Police and local law-enforcement officials to promote uniform enforcement of the laws pertaining to motor carriers and the rules, regulations, forms, and reports prescribed under the provisions of this chapter.

History.

Code 1950, § 56-276; 1964, c. 571; 1995, cc. 744, 803; 2001, c. 596; 2002, c. 861; 2012, cc. 22, 111.

§ 46.2-2001.1. License, permit, or certificate required.

A. It shall be unlawful for any person to operate, offer, advertise, provide, procure, furnish, or arrange by contract, agreement, or arrangement to transport passengers for compensation as a broker, motor carrier or excursion train operator without first obtaining a license, permit, or certificate, unless otherwise exempted, as provided in this chapter.

B. Beginning July 1, 2014, any person making application for a license, permit, or certificate pursuant to this chapter who has violated § 46.2-2001.1, either as a result of a conviction or as a result of an imposition of a civil penalty, shall be denied such license, permit, or certificate for a period of 12 months from the date the final disposition of the conviction or imposition of the civil penalty has been rendered.

The Department of Motor Vehicles shall require applicants for a license, permit, or certificate to report any conviction or imposition of civil penalties for violations of § 46.2-2001.1.

History.

2001, c. 596; 2002, c. 861; 2013, cc. 165, 582.

§ 46.2-2001.2. Identification marker required.

Each motor carrier shall be issued an identification marker, unless the operation is interstate in nature and the carrier has been issued a single state registration receipt by the Department or other qualified jurisdiction. The identification marker issued by the Department shall be displayed on each vehicle as prescribed by the Department and shall be valid for the period of time prescribed by the Department.

History.

2001, c. 596.

§ 46.2-2001.3. Application; notice requirements.

A. Applications for a license, permit, certificate, identification marker, or TNC partner vehicle registration or renewal of a license, permit, certificate, identification marker, or TNC partner vehicle registration under this chapter shall be made to the Department and contain such information and exhibits as the Department shall require. Such information shall include except in the case of a TNC partner vehicle, in the application or otherwise, the matters set forth in § 46.2-2011.24 as grounds for denying licenses, permits, and certificates, and other pertinent matters requisite for the safeguarding of the public interest.

Notwithstanding any other provision of this chapter, the Commissioner may require all or certain applications for a license, permit, certificate, identification marker, or TNC partner vehicle registration to be filed electronically.

For the purposes of this subsection, "identification marker" does not include trade dress.

B. An applicant for any original certificate of public convenience and necessity issued under this chapter, or any request for a transfer of such certificate, unless otherwise provided, shall cause a notice of such application, on the form and in the manner prescribed by the Department, on every motor carrier holding the same type of certificate issued by the Department and operating or providing service within the area proposed to be served by the applicant.

C. For any application for original certificate or license issued under this chapter, or any request for a transfer of such certificate or license, the Department shall publish a notice of such application on the Department's public website in the form and in the manner prescribed by the Department.

D. An applicant for any original certificate of public convenience and necessity issued under this chapter, or any request for a transfer of such certificate of public convenience and necessity, shall cause a publication of a summary of the application to be made in a newspaper having a general circulation in the proposed area to be served or area where the primary business office is located within such time as the Department may prescribe.

History.

2001, c. 596; 2002, c. 870; 2011, cc. 881, 889; 2012, cc. 22, 111; 2013, cc. 165, 582; 2015, cc. 2, 3.

§§ 46.2-2002 through 46.2-2004: Repealed by Acts 2001, c. 596, cl. 2, effective July 1, 2002.

§ 46.2-2005. Action on applications; hearings on denials and protests.

A. The Department may act upon any application required under this chapter for a certificate of public convenience and necessity without a hearing, unless such application is protested by any aggrieved party, except that no protest shall be heard in such cases whereby the applicant has received a notice of intent to award a contract under the Virginia Public Procurement Act (§ 2.2-4300 et seq.) for irregular route common carrier service to or from a public-use airport located in the City of Norfolk or the County of Henrico. Aggrieved parties may protest an application by submitting written grounds to the Department setting forth (i) a precise statement of the party's interest and how the party could be aggrieved if the application were granted; (ii) a full and clear statement of the facts that the person is prepared to provide by competent evidence; (iii) a statement of the specific relief sought; (iv) the case number assigned to the application; and (v) a certification that a copy of the protest was sent to the applicant.

B. The Department may act upon any application required under this chapter for a license or certificate of fitness without a hearing, unless such application is protested by any party based upon fitness allegations. Parties may protest an application by submitting written grounds to the Department setting forth (i) a precise statement of the party's objections to the application being granted; (ii) a full and clear statement of the facts that the person is prepared to provide by competent evidence; (iii) the case number assigned to the application; and (iv) a certification that a copy of the protest was sent to the applicant. The Department shall have full discretion as to whether a hearing is warranted based on the merits of any protest filed.

C. Any applicant denied without a hearing an original license, permit, or certificate under subsection A or B of this section or subsection B of § 46.2-2001.1, or any request for a transfer of such a license or certificate, shall be given a hearing at a time and place determined by the Commissioner or his designee upon the applicant's written request for such hearing made within 30 days of denial.

History.
Code 1950, § 56-279; 1995, cc. 744, 803; 2001, c. 596; 2002, cc. 681, 734, 870; 2011, cc. 424, 881, 889; 2013, cc. 165, 582.

§ 46.2-2005.1. Determination for issuance for license, permit, or certificate.

If the Department finds the applicant for a license, permit, or certificate has met all the requirements of this chapter, it shall issue a license, permit, or certificate to the applicant, subject to such terms, limitations, and restrictions as the Department may deem proper.

History.
2001, c. 596.

§§ 46.2-2006 through 46.2-2010: Repealed by Acts 2001, c. 596, cl. 2, effective July 1, 2002.

§ 46.2-2011. Considerations for determination of issuance of license or certificate.

In determining whether a license or certificate required by this chapter shall be granted, the Department may, among other things, consider the applicant's experience, qualifications, character, fitness, financial responsibility, and compliance with the requirements of this chapter.

History.
Code 1950, § 56-282; 1979, c. 609; 1995, cc. 744, 803; 2001, c. 596.

§ 46.2-2011.1. Issuance of temporary authority.

To enable the provision of service for which there is an immediate and urgent need to a point or between points in Virginia where certificated carriers are unable to perform the service, or within a territory having no certificated carrier, the Department may, in its discretion and without hearings or other proceedings, grant temporary authority for such service by a carrier that would otherwise be required to obtain a certificate under this chapter. Such temporary authority, unless suspended or revoked in accordance with § 46.2-2011.26, shall be valid for such time as the Department shall specify, but for not more than an aggregate of 180 days, and shall create no presumption that corresponding permanent authority will be granted thereafter.

History.
1996, c. 170; 2001, c. 596.

§ 46.2-2011.2. Temporary emergency operation.

In an emergency, the Department or its agents may, by letter, telegram, or other means, authorize a vehicle to be operated in the Commonwealth without a proper registration card or identification marker for not more than ten days.

History.
2001, c. 596.

§ 46.2-2011.3. Issuance, expiration, and renewal of license, permit, and certificate.

All licenses, permits, and certificates issued under this chapter shall be issued for a period of twelve consecutive months except, at the discretion of the Department, the periods may be adjusted as necessary. Such licenses, permits, and certificates shall expire if not renewed annually. Such expiration shall be effective thirty days after the Department has provided the licensee, permittee, or certificate holder notice of non-renewal. If the license, permit, or certificate is renewed within thirty days after notice of non-renewal, then the license, permit, or certificate shall not expire.

History.
2001, c. 596.

§ 46.2-2011.4. Conversion of contract bus certificates.

All contract bus carriers that hold a certificate issued prior to July 1, 2012, shall be issued a replacement certificate of fitness as a contract passenger carrier. The holder of such certificate shall not be required to apply for a replacement certificate.

History.
2001, c. 596; 2002, c. 861; 2011, cc. 881, 889; 2012, cc. 22, 111.

§ 46.2-2011.5. Filing and application fees.

Unless otherwise provided, every applicant, other than a transportation network company, for an original license, permit, or certificate issued under this chapter and transfer of a license or certificate under the provisions of this chapter shall, upon the filing of an application, deposit with the Department, as a filing fee, a sum in the amount of $50. The fee to accompany an application for an original of the certificate required under § 46.2-2099.45 shall be $100,000, and the annual fee to accompany an application for a renewal thereof shall be $60,000. If the Department does not approve an application for an original of the certificate required under § 46.2-2099.45, the Department shall refund $90,000 of the application fee to the applicant. The Department shall collect a fee of $3 for the issuance of a duplicate license, permit, or certificate.

History.
2001, c. 596; 2015, cc. 2, 3.

§ 46.2-2011.6. Vehicle fees.

Every person, other than a TNC partner, who operates a passenger vehicle for compensation over the highways of the Commonwealth, unless such operation is exempted from this chapter, shall be required to pay an annual fee of $3 for each such vehicle so operated, unless a vehicle identification marker fee has been paid to the Department as to such vehicle for the current year under the provisions of Chapter 27 (§ 58.1-2700 et seq.) of Title 58.1. Such fee shall be paid through the single state registration system established pursuant to 49 U.S.C. § 14504 and 49 C.F.R. Part 367 or through the unified carrier registration system established pursuant to 49 U.S.C. § 14504a and the federal regulations promulgated thereunder for carriers registered pursuant to those provisions. No more than one vehicle fee shall be charged or paid as to any vehicle in any one year under Chapter 27 (§ 58.1-2700 et seq.) of Title 58.1 and this chapter, including payments made pursuant to the single state registration system or the unified carrier registration system.

History.
2001, c. 596; 2003, c. 322; 2006, c. 208; 2015, cc. 2, 3.

§ 46.2-2011.7. Certificate holders must provide services.

Every holder of a certificate of public convenience and necessity shall provide services in accordance with this chapter and any terms, limitations, conditions, or restrictions as the Department may place on such certificate.

History.
2001, c. 596.

§ 46.2-2011.8. Transfers of certificates of public convenience and necessity.

Any certificate of public convenience and necessity issued under this chapter may be transferred, subject to the approval of the Department, and under such reasonable rules and regulations as may be prescribed by the Department. An application for such approval shall be made jointly by the transferor and transferee. The transfer of a certificate of public convenience and necessity can only be made upon a satisfactory showing that such purchaser or transferee can and will comply with the applicable motor carrier or broker laws, rules and regulations of the Department, is fit, willing and able to properly perform the services, and all taxes due the Commonwealth have been paid, or payment guaranteed.

History.
2001, c. 596; 2011, cc. 881, 889; 2012, cc. 22, 111.

§ 46.2-2011.9. Bond and letter of credit requirements.

A. Every applicant for an original certificate under this chapter shall obtain and file with the Department, along with the application, a surety bond or an irrevocable letter of credit, in addition to any other bond or letter of credit required by law, in the amount of $25,000, which shall remain in effect for the first three years of licensure. The bond or letter of credit shall be in a form and content acceptable to the Department. The bond or letter of credit shall be conditioned on a statement by the applicant that the applicant will not practice fraud, make any fraudulent representation, or violate any provision of this chapter in the conduct of the applicant's business. The Department may, without holding a hearing, suspend the certificate during the period that the certificate holder does not have a sufficient bond or letter of credit on file.

B. Every applicant for an original license pursuant to this chapter shall obtain and file with the Department, along with the application, a surety bond or an irrevocable letter of credit, in addition to any other bond or letter of credit required by law, in the amount of $25,000. The bond or letter of credit shall be in a form and content acceptable to the Department. The bond or letter of credit shall be conditioned on a statement by the applicant that the applicant will not practice fraud, make any fraudulent representation, or violate any provision of this chapter in the conduct of the applicant's business. The Department may, without holding a hearing, suspend the license during the period that the licensee does not have a sufficient bond or letter of credit on file.

C. If a person suffers any of the following: (i) loss or damage in connection with the transportation service by reason of fraud practiced on him or fraudulent representation made to him by a licensee or certificate holder or his agent or employee acting within the scope of employment; (ii) loss or damage by reason of a violation by a licensee or certificate holder or his agent or employee of any provision of this chapter in connection with the transportation service; or (iii) loss or damage resulting from a breach of a contract entered into on or after the effective date of this act, that person shall have a claim against the licensee or certificate holder's bond or letter of credit, and may recover from such bond or letter of credit the amount awarded to such person by final judgment of a court of competent jurisdiction against the licensee or certificate holder as a result of such loss or damage up to, but not exceeding, the amount of the bond or letter of credit.

D. The licensee or certificate holder's surety shall notify the Department when a claim is made against a licensee or certificate holder's bond, when a claim is paid and when the bond is canceled. Such notification shall include the amount of a claim and the circumstances surrounding the claim. Notification of cancellation shall include the effective date and reason for cancellation.

E. The surety on any bond filed by a licensee or certificate holder shall be released and discharged from all liability accruing on such bond after the expiration of 60 days from the date on which the surety files with the Department a written request to be released and discharged. Such request shall not operate to relieve, release or discharge the surety from any liability already accrued or which shall accrue before the expiration of the 60-day period.

History.
2001, c. 596; 2013, cc. 165, 582.

§ 46.2-2011.10. Advertisements.

A. No person shall advertise or permit to be advertised by any means a transportation service unless such person first obtains a license, permit, or certificate as provided in this chapter. Whenever any licensee, permittee, or certificate holder places an advertisement in any newspaper or publication advertising a transportation service, there shall appear within such advertisement the license, permit, or certificate number. If multiple licenses, permits, or certificates are held, only one number must appear.

B. It shall be unlawful for any licensee, permittee, or certificate holder to knowingly advertise by any means any assertion, representation, or statement of fact that is untrue, misleading, or deceptive relating to the conduct of the business for which a license, permit, or certificate is held.

C. The requirement of subsection A of this section to include a license, permit, or certificate number in advertisements shall not apply to excursion train operators.

History.
2001, c. 596; 2002, c. 861.

§ 46.2-2011.11. Established place of business.

A. No license or certificate shall be issued to any applicant that does not have an established place of business, owned or leased by the applicant, where a substantial portion of the activity of the motor carrier or broker business will be routinely conducted and that:

1. Satisfies all applicable local zoning regulations;

2. Houses all records that the motor carrier or broker is required to maintain by this chapter or by regulations promulgated pursuant to this chapter; and

3. Is equipped with a working telephone listed or advertised in the name of the motor carrier or broker.

B. Every licensee and certificate holder shall maintain an established place of business in accordance with subsection A of this section and keep on file a physical address with the Department. Every licensee and certificate holder shall inform the Department by certified letter or other manner prescribed by the Department of any changes to the motor carrier or broker's mailing address, physical location, telephone number, and legal status, legal name of company, or trade name of company within 30 days of such change.

C. Any licensee or certificate holder that relocates his established place of business shall confirm to the Department that the new established place of business conforms to the requirements of subsection A.

History.
2001, c. 596; 2012, cc. 22, 111; 2013, cc. 165, 582.

§ 46.2-2011.12. Transportation of baggage with passengers.

A certificate authorizing the transportation of passengers as a motor carrier shall also be deemed to include authority to transport in the same vehicle with passengers the baggage of passengers.

History.
2001, c. 596.

§ 46.2-2011.13. Stowing of baggage, parcels, etc.

Motor carriers transporting baggage or other property of passengers shall do so only when such articles are stowed in a manner to assure:

1. Unrestricted freedom of motion to the driver for proper operation of the vehicle.

2. Unobstructed passage to regular and emergency exits by any person.

3. Adequate protection from personal injury that may result from the displacement or fall of such articles.

History.
2001, c. 596.

§ 46.2-2011.14. Notice of abandonment of service.

Every motor carrier, broker or excursion train operator who ceases operation or abandons his rights under a license, certificate, or permit issued shall notify the Department within thirty days of such cessation or abandonment.

History.
2001, c. 596; 2002, c. 861.

§ 46.2-2011.15. Department may seek judgment for refunds due public and collect and distribute same.

If any motor carrier or broker, upon the final decision of an appeal from the action of the Department prescribing rates, charges, tariffs, or classification of traffic, confirming or modifying the action of the Department, fails to refund in the manner and within the time prescribed in the notice of the Department all amounts that the appealing carrier or broker may have collected, pending the appeal, in excess of that authorized by such final decision, upon notice to such carrier or broker by the Department of such final decision, then the Department, after thirty days' notice to any such carrier or broker, may, unless the amount required by such final decision is paid to the Department, seek judgment in the name of the Commonwealth, for the use of the persons, firms and corporations entitled to the same, against any such carrier or broker for the aggregate amount of such collections and for costs, and may enforce the amount of such judgment and costs by process of execution, as provided by law. The Department shall, upon the collection of such judgment, forthwith distribute the amount thereof among the parties entitled thereto, respectively, in such manner as it may by its rules or regulations prescribe, and shall, upon the payment or collection of any such judgment, mark the same satisfied upon its records, and have the same entered satisfied on the judgment lien docket of the court where the same may have been docketed; the satisfaction of any such judgment shall be a bar to any further action or recovery against any such carrier or broker to the extent of such recovery.

History.
2001, c. 596; 2002, c. 861.

§ 46.2-2011.16. Reports, records, etc.

A. The Department is hereby authorized to require annual, periodical, or special reports from motor carriers, except such as are exempt from the operation of the provisions of this chapter; to prescribe the manner and form in which such reports shall be made; and to require from such carriers specific answers to all questions upon which the Department may deem information to be necessary. Such reports shall be under oath whenever the Department so requires. The Department may also require any motor carrier to file with it a true copy of each or any contract, agreement, or arrangement between such carrier and any other carrier or person in relation to the provisions of this chapter.

B. The Department may, in its discretion, prescribe (i) the forms of any and all accounts, records, and memoranda to be kept by motor carriers and (ii) the length of time such accounts, records, and memoranda shall be preserved, as well as of the receipts and expenditures of money. The Department or its employees shall at all times have access to all lands, buildings, or equipment of motor carriers used in connection with their operations and also all accounts, records, and memoranda, including all documents, papers, and correspondence now or hereafter existing, and kept, or required to be kept, by motor carriers. The Department and its employees shall have authority to inspect and examine any and all such lands, buildings, equipment, accounts, records, and memoranda, including all documents, papers, and correspondence now or hereafter existing and kept or required to be kept by such carriers. These provisions shall apply to receivers of carriers and to operating trustees and, to the extent deemed necessary by the Department, to persons having control, direct or indirect, over or affiliated with any motor carrier.

C. As used in this section the term *"motor carriers"* includes brokers and excursion train operators.

History.
2001, c. 596; 2002, c. 861.

§ 46.2-2011.17. Certificate, license, or permit holder not relieved of liability for negligence.

Nothing in this chapter shall relieve any holder of a certificate, license, or permit issued by and under the authority of the Department from any liability resulting from his negligence, whether or not he has complied with the requirements of this chapter.

History.
2001, c. 596.

§ 46.2-2011.18. Violation by passengers; misdemeanor; ejection.

All persons who fail, while using transportation services of a common carrier or restricted common carrier, to act in an orderly manner so as to permit the safe operation of a vehicle by the driver, or who fail to obey the directions of any such driver, operator, or other person in charge to act in such orderly manner, shall be deemed guilty of a Class 4 misdemeanor. Furthermore, such persons may be ejected from any such vehicle by any driver, operator, or person in charge of such vehicle, or by any police officer or other conservator of the peace; and in case such persons ejected have paid their fares upon such vehicle, they shall not be entitled to the return of any part of the same. For the refusal of any such passenger to abide by the direction of the person in charge of such vehicle as aforesaid, and his consequent ejection from such vehicle, neither the driver, operator, person in charge, owner, manager, nor common carrier or restricted common carrier operating such vehicle shall be liable for damages in any court.

History.
2001, c. 596.

§ 46.2-2011.19. Vehicle seizure; penalty.

A. Any police officer of the Commonwealth authorized to serve process may hold a motor vehicle owned by a person against whom an order or penalty has been entered, but only for such time as is reasonably necessary to promptly petition for a writ of fieri facias. The Commonwealth shall not be required to post bond in order to hold and levy upon any vehicle held pursuant to this section.

B. Upon notification of the judgment or penalty entered against the owner of the vehicle and notice to such person of the failure to satisfy the judgment or penalty, any investigator, special agent, or officer of the Commonwealth shall thereafter deny the offending person the right to operate the motor vehicle on the highways of the Commonwealth.

History.
2001, c. 596.

§ 46.2-2011.20. Unlawful use of registration and identification markers.

It shall be unlawful for any person to operate or cause to be operated on any highway in the Commonwealth any motor vehicle that (i) does not carry the proper registration and identification that this chapter requires, (ii) does not display an identification marker in such manner as is prescribed by the Department, or (iii) bears registration or identification markers of persons whose TNC partner vehicle registration under subsection B of § 46.2-2099.50 or whose license, permit, or certificate issued by the Department has been canceled, revoked, suspended, or renewal thereof denied in accordance with this chapter.

History.
2001, c. 596; 2015, cc. 2, 3.

§ 46.2-2011.21. Registration and identification violations; penalties.

A. The following violations of laws shall be punished as follows:

1. Any person who does not obtain a proper registration card, identification marker, or other evidence of registration as required by this chapter shall be guilty of a Class 4 misdemeanor.

2. Any person who operates or causes to be operated on any highway in the Commonwealth any motor vehicle that does not carry the proper registration and identification that this article requires or any motor vehicle that does not display (i) an identification marker in such manner as is prescribed by the Department or (ii) other identifying information that this article requires it to display shall be guilty of a Class 4 misdemeanor.

3. Any person who knowingly displays or uses on any vehicle operated by him any identification marker or other identification that has not been issued to the owner or operator thereof for such vehicle and any person who knowingly assists him to do so shall be guilty of a Class 3 misdemeanor.

4. Any person who operates or causes to be operated on any highway in the Commonwealth any motor vehicle requiring registration from the Department under this title after such registration cards or identification markers have been revoked, canceled or suspended shall be guilty of a Class 3 misdemeanor.

B. The officer charging the violation under this section shall serve a citation on the operator of the vehicle in violation. Such citation shall be directed to the owner, operator or other person responsible for the violation as determined by the officer. Service of the citation on the vehicle operator shall constitute service of process upon the owner, operator, or other person charged with the violation under this article, and shall have the same legal force as if served within the Commonwealth personally upon the owner, operator, or other person charged with the violation, whether such owner, operator, or other person charged is a resident or nonresident.

History.
2001, c. 596.

§ 46.2-2011.22. Violation; criminal penalties.

A. Any person knowingly and willfully violating any provision of this chapter, or any rule or regulation thereunder, or any term or condition of any certificate, permit, or license, for which a penalty is not otherwise herein provided, is guilty of a misdemeanor and, upon conviction, shall be fined not more than $2,500 for the first offense and not more than $5,000 for any subsequent offense. Each day of such violation shall constitute a separate offense.

B. Any person, whether carrier, broker, or any officer, employee, agent, or representative thereof, or a TNC partner, who knowingly and willfully by any such means or otherwise fraudulently seeks to evade or defeat regulation as in this chapter shall be deemed guilty of a misdemeanor and, upon conviction thereof, be fined not more than $500 for the first offense and not more than $2,000 for any subsequent offense.

C. Any motor carrier, broker, or excursion train operator or any officer, agent, employee, or representative thereof, or a TNC partner, who willfully fails or refuses to make a report to the Department as required by this chapter or to keep accounts, records, and memoranda in the form and manner approved or prescribed by the Department, or knowingly and willfully falsifies, destroys, mutilates, or alters any such report, account, record, or memorandum, or knowingly and willfully files any false report, account, record, or memorandum, is guilty of a misdemeanor and, upon conviction, be subject for each offense to a fine of not less than $100 and not more than $5,000.

History.

2001, c. 596; 2002, c. 861; 2015, cc. 2, 3.

§ 46.2-2011.23. Violations; civil penalties.

The Department may impose a civil penalty not exceeding $1,000 if any person has:

1. Made any misrepresentation of a material fact to obtain proper operating credentials as required by this chapter or other requirements in this Code regulating the operation of motor vehicles;
2. Failed to make any report required in this chapter;
3. Failed to pay any fee or tax properly assessed against him; or
4. Failed to comply with any provision of this chapter or lawful order, rule or regulation of the Department or any term or condition of any certificate, permit, or license.

Any such penalty shall be imposed by order; however, no order issued pursuant to this section shall become effective until the Department has offered the person an opportunity for an administrative hearing to show cause why the order should not be enforced. Instead of or in addition to imposing such penalty, the Department may suspend, revoke, or cancel any license, permit, certificate, registration card or identification marker issued pursuant to this title. If, in any such case, it appears that the defendant owes any fee or tax to the Commonwealth, the Department shall enter order therefor.

For the purposes of this section, each separate violation shall be subject to the civil penalty.

History.

2001, c. 596; 2013, cc. 165, 582.

§ 46.2-2011.24. Grounds for denying, suspending, or revoking licenses, permits, or certificates.

A license, permit, or certificate issued pursuant to this chapter may be denied, suspended, or revoked on any one or more of the following grounds, where applicable:

1. Material misstatement or omission in application for license, certificate, permit, identification marker, or vehicle registration;
2. Failure to comply subsequent to receipt of a written warning from the Department or any willful failure to comply with a lawful order, any provision of this chapter or any regulation promulgated by the Department under this chapter, or any term, condition, or restriction of a license, permit, or certificate;
3. Failure to comply with zoning or other land use regulations, ordinances, or statutes;
4. Use of deceptive business acts or practices;
5. Knowingly advertising by any means any assertion, representation, or statement of fact that is untrue, misleading, or deceptive relating to the conduct of the business for which a license, certificate, permit, identification marker, or vehicle registration is held or sought;
6. Having been found, through a judicial or administrative hearing, to have committed fraudulent or deceptive acts in connection with the business for which a license, permit, or certificate is held or sought or any consumer-related fraud;
7. Having been convicted of any criminal act involving the business for which a license, permit, or certificate is held or sought;
8. Failure to comply with § 46.2-2056 or any regulation promulgated pursuant thereto;
9. Improper leasing, renting, lending, or otherwise allowing the improper use of a license, certificate, permit, identification marker, or vehicle registration;
10. Having been convicted of a felony;
11. Having been convicted of any misdemeanor involving lying, cheating, stealing, or moral turpitude;
12. Failure to submit to the Department any tax, fees, dues, fines, or penalties owed to the Department;
13. Failure to furnish the Department information, documentation, or records required or requested pursuant to statute or regulation;
14. Knowingly and willfully filing any false report, account, record, or memorandum;
15. Failure to meet or maintain application certifications or requirements of public convenience and necessity, character, fitness, and financial responsibility pursuant to this chapter;
16. Willfully altering or changing the appearance or wording of any license, permit, certificate, identi-

fication marker, license plate, or vehicle registration;

17. Failure to provide services in accordance with license, permit, or certificate terms, limitations, conditions, or requirements;

18. Failure to maintain and keep on file with the Department motor carrier liability insurance, issued by a company licensed to do business in the Commonwealth, or a bond, certificate of insurance, certificate of self-insurance, or unconditional letter of credit in accordance with this chapter, with respect to each motor vehicle operated in the Commonwealth;

19. Failure to comply with the Workers' Compensation Act of Title 65.2;

20. Failure to properly register a motor vehicle under this title;

21. Failure to comply with any federal motor carrier statute, rule, or regulation;

22. Failure to comply with the requirements of the Americans with Disabilities Act or the Virginians with Disabilities Act (§ 51.5-1 et seq.);

23. Inactivity of a motor carrier as may be evidenced by the absence of a motor vehicle registered to operate under such certificate or permit for a period of greater than three months; or

24. Failure to comply with any provision regarding the filing and registered agent requirements set forth in Title 13.1.

History.

2001, c. 596; 2013, cc. 165, 582; 2015, cc. 2, 3.

§ 46.2-2011.25. Altering or amending licenses, permits, or certificates.

The Department may alter or amend a license, permit, or certificate at the request of a licensee, permittee, or certificate holder, or upon a finding by the Department that a licensee, permittee, or certificate holder failed to observe any of the provisions within this chapter, or any of the rules or regulations of the Department, or any term, condition, or limitation of such license, permit, or certificate.

History.

2001, c. 596.

§ 46.2-2011.26. Suspension, revocation, and refusal to renew licenses, permits, or certificates; notice and hearing.

A. Except as provided in subsection D of this section, unless otherwise provided in this chapter, no license, permit, or certificate issued under this chapter shall be suspended or revoked, or renewal thereof refused, unless the licensee, permittee, or certificate holder has been furnished a written copy of the complaint against him and the grounds upon which the action is taken and has been offered an opportunity for an administrative hearing to show cause why such action should not be taken.

B. The order suspending, revoking, or denying renewal of a license, permit, or certificate shall not become effective until the licensee, permittee, or certificate holder has, after notice of the opportunity for a hearing, had thirty days to make a written request for such a hearing. If no hearing has been requested within such thirty-day period, the order shall become effective and no hearing shall thereafter be held. A timely request for a hearing shall automatically stay operation of the order until after the hearing.

C. Notice of an order suspending, revoking, or denying renewal of a license, permit, or certificate and an opportunity for a hearing shall be mailed to the licensee, permittee, or certificate holder by registered or certified mail at the address as shown on the license, permit, or certificate or other record of information in possession of the Department and shall be considered served when mailed.

D. If the Department makes a finding, after conducting a preliminary investigation, that the conduct of a licensee, permittee, or certificate holder (i) is in violation of this chapter or regulations adopted pursuant to this chapter and (ii) such violation constitutes a danger to public safety, the Department may issue an order suspending the license, permit, or certificate. Notice of the suspension shall be in writing and mailed in accordance with subsection C of this section. Upon receipt of a request for a hearing appealing the suspension, the licensee, permittee, or certificate holder shall be afforded the opportunity for a hearing within thirty days. The suspension shall remain in effect pending the outcome of the hearing.

History.

2001, c. 596.

§ 46.2-2011.27. Basis for reinstatement of suspended licenses, permits, or certificates; reinstatement fees.

A. The Department shall reinstate any license, permit, or certificate suspended pursuant to this chapter provided the grounds upon which the suspension action was taken have been satisfied and the appropriate reinstatement fee and other applicable fees have been paid to the Department.

B. The reinstatement fee for suspensions issued pursuant to this chapter shall be fifty dollars. In the event multiple credentials have been suspended under this chapter for the same violation, only one reinstatement fee shall be applicable.

C. In addition to a reinstatement fee, a fee of $500 shall be paid for failure of a motor carrier to keep in force at all times insurance, a bond or bonds, in an amount required by this chapter. Any motor carrier who applies for a new license, permit, or certificate because his prior license, permit, or certificate was revoked for failure to keep in force at all times insurance, a bond or bonds, in an amount required by this chapter, shall also be subject to a fee of $500.

History.
2001, c. 596; 2011, cc. 881, 889.

§ 46.2-2011.28. Basis for relicensure after revocation of licenses, permits, or certificates; fees.

The Department shall not accept an application for a license, permit, or certificate from an applicant where such credentials have been revoked pursuant to this chapter until the period of revocation imposed by the Department has passed. The Department shall process such applications under the same provisions, procedures, and requirements as an original application for such license, permit, or certificate. The Department shall issue such license, permit, or certificate provided the applicant has met all the appropriate qualifications and requirements, has satisfied the grounds upon which the revocation action was taken, and has paid the appropriate application or filing fees to the Department.

History.
2001, c. 596.

§ 46.2-2011.29. Surrender of identification marker, license plate, and registration card; removal by law enforcement; operation of vehicle denied.

A. For purposes of this section, "identification marker" does not include trade dress.

B. It shall be unlawful for a licensee, permittee, or certificate holder, or for the registrant or operator of a vehicle registered under subsection B of § 46.2-2099.50, whose license, permit, certificate, or vehicle's registration as a TNC partner vehicle, has expired or been revoked or suspended, canceled, or whose renewal thereof has been denied pursuant to this chapter to fail or refuse to surrender, on demand, to the Department license plates, identification markers, and registration cards issued under this title.

C. It shall be unlawful for a vehicle owner who is not the holder of a valid permit or certificate or whose vehicle is not validly leased to a motor carrier holding an active permit or certificate to fail or refuse to surrender to the Department on demand license plates, identification markers, and registration cards issued under this title.

D. Except as provided in subsection E, if any law-enforcement officer finds that a vehicle bearing Virginia license plates or temporary transport plates is in violation of subsection B or C, such law-enforcement officer may remove the license plate, identification marker, and registration card. If a law-enforcement officer removes a license plate, identification marker, or registration card, he shall forward the same to the Department.

E. If the officer finds that a TNC partner vehicle bearing Virginia license plates is being operated in violation of subsection B, such law-enforcement officer shall direct the operator of the vehicle to promptly remove any identification marker and any registration card issued under subsection B of § 46.2-2099.50 and return the same to the Department. If any law-enforcement officer finds that a TNC partner vehicle not bearing Virginia license plates is being operated in violation of subsection B, such law-enforcement officer shall remove any identification marker and any registration card issued under subsection B of § 46.2-2099.50 and shall forward the same to the Department.

F. When informed that a vehicle is being operated in violation of this section, the driver shall drive the vehicle to a nearby location off the public highways and not remove it or allow it to be moved until the motor carrier is in compliance with all provisions of this chapter.

History.
2001, c. 596; 2015, cc. 2, 3, 258.

§ 46.2-2011.30. No property rights in highways conferred by chapter.

Nothing in this chapter shall confer any proprietary or property rights in the use of the public highways.

History.
2001, c. 596.

§ 46.2-2011.31. Licenses, taxes, etc., not affected.

Nothing in this chapter shall be construed to relieve any person from the payment of any licenses, fees, taxes or levies now or hereafter imposed by law.

History.
2001, c. 596.

§ 46.2-2011.32. Title to plates and markers.

All registration cards and identification markers issued by the Department shall remain the property of the Department.

History.
2001, c. 596.

§§ 46.2-2012 through 46.2-2041: Repealed by Acts 2001, c. 596, cl. 2, effective July 1, 2002.

§ 46.2-2042: Repealed by Acts 2001, c. 137.

§§ 46.2-2043 through 46.2-2050: Repealed by Acts 2001, c. 596, cl. 2, effective July 1, 2002.

ARTICLE 2.
INSURANCE REQUIREMENTS.

§ 46.2-2051. Application of article.

Unless otherwise stated, this article shall apply to all motor carriers except transportation network companies.

History.
2001, c. 596; 2015, cc. 2, 3.

§ 46.2-2052. Bonds or insurance to be kept in force; amounts.

Each motor carrier shall keep in force at all times insurance, a bond, or bonds, in an amount required by this article.

History.
2001, c. 596.

§ 46.2-2053. Surety bonds, insurance, letter of credit, or securities required prior to issuance of registration; amounts.

A. No certificate, permit, identification marker, registration card, or license plate shall be issued by the Department to any vehicle operated by a motor carrier until the motor carrier certifies to the Department that the vehicle is covered by:

1. An insurance policy or bond;

2. A certificate of insurance in lieu of the insurance policy or bond, certifying that such policy or bond covers the liability of such motor carrier in accordance with the provisions of this article, is issued by an authorized insurer, or in the case of bonds, is in an amount approved by the Department. The bonds may be issued by the Commonwealth of Virginia, the United States of America, or any municipality in the Commonwealth. Such bonds shall be deposited with the State Treasurer and the surety shall not be reduced except in accordance with an order of the Department;

3. An unconditional letter of credit, issued by a bank doing business in Virginia, for an amount approved by the Department. The letter of credit shall be in effect so long as the motor carrier operates motor vehicles in the Commonwealth; or

4. In the case of a lessor who acts as a registrant for purposes of consolidating lessees' vehicle registration applications, a statement that the registrant has, before leasing a vehicle, obtained from the lessee an insurance policy, bond, or certificate of insurance in lieu of the insurance policy or bond and can make available said proof of insurance coverage upon demand.

Vehicles operated by carriers who have filed proof of financial responsibility in accordance with the single state registration system authorized by 49 U.S.C. § 14504 or the Unified Carrier Registration System authorized by 49 U.S.C. § 14504a are deemed to have fulfilled the requirements of this article for insurance purposes, provided there is on board the vehicle a copy of an insurance receipt issued pursuant to the federal regulations promulgated pursuant to 49 U.S.C. § 14504 or 14504a. The Department is further authorized to issue single state registration system or unified carrier registration system receipts to any qualified carrier as well as to collect and disperse the fees for and to qualified jurisdictions.

B. All motor carriers shall keep in force at all times insurance, a bond or bonds, in an amount required by this section. Except for taxicabs, the minimum financial responsibility requirements for motor carriers operating intrastate shall be based on the number of passengers a vehicle is designed or manufactured to transport, including the driver, and shall be as follows: one to six passengers — $350,000; seven to 15 passengers — $1,500,000; 16 or more passengers — $5,000,000. All motor carriers operating exclusively taxicabs or other motor vehicles performing a taxicab service shall maintain liability insurance of at least $125,000.

C. The minimum insurance for motor carriers operating in interstate commerce shall equal the minimum required by federal law, rule, or regulation. Any motor carrier that meets the minimum federal financial responsibility requirements and also operates in intrastate commerce may submit, in lieu of a separate filing for its intrastate operation, proof of the minimum federal limits, provided that both interstate and intrastate operations are insured.

History.
2001, c. 596; 2006, c. 208.

§ 46.2-2054. Policies or surety bonds to be filed with the Department and securities with State Treasurer.

A. Each motor carrier shall keep on file with the Department proof of an insurance policy or bond in accordance with this article. Record of the policy or bond shall remain in the files of the Department six months after the certificate, registration card, license plate, identification marker or permit is canceled for any cause. If federal, state, or municipal bonds are deposited with the State Treasurer in lieu of an insurance policy, the bonds shall remain deposited until six months after the registration card, license plate, certificate, permit or identification marker is canceled for any cause unless otherwise ordered by the Department.

B. The Department may, without holding a hearing, suspend a permit or certificate if the permittee or certificate holder fails to comply with the requirements of this section.

History.
2001, c. 596.

§ 46.2-2055. Condition or obligation of security.

The insurance, bond or other security provided for in § 46.2-2054 shall obligate the insurer or surety to pay any final judgment for (i) injury to any passenger or passengers and (ii) any and all injuries to persons and loss of or damage to property resulting from the negligent operation of any motor vehicle.

History.
2001, c. 596.

§ 46.2-2056. Effect of unfair claims settlement practices on self-insured motor carriers.

The provisions of subdivisions 4, 6, 11, and 12 of subsection A of § 38.2-510 shall apply to each holder of a certificate or permit issued by and under the authority of the Department who, in lieu of filing an insurance policy, has deposited with the State Treasurer state, federal or municipal bonds or has filed an unconditional letter of credit issued by a bank. The failure of any such holder of a certificate or permit to comply with the provisions of § 38.2-510 shall be the cause for revocation or suspension of the certificate or permit.

History.
2001, c. 596.

§ 46.2-2057. Taxicab insurance required.

Each operator of a motor vehicle performing a bona fide taxicab service shall file insurance as required under this article unless evidence can be shown to the Department that the operator is a self-insurer under an ordinance of the city or county where the home office of the operator is located.

History.
2001, c. 596.

§ 46.2-2058. When taxicab operator a self-insurer.

If the operator of any taxicab or other motor vehicle performing a taxicab service is a self-insurer under an ordinance of the city or county where the home office of the operator is located, such operator shall not be required to obtain and keep on file with the Department insurance as required by law.

History.
2001, c. 596.

ARTICLE 3.

TAXICABS.

§ 46.2-2059. Permit required for taxicab service.

It shall be unlawful for any taxicab or other motor vehicle performing a taxicab service to operate on an intrastate basis on any public highway in the Commonwealth outside the corporate limits of incorporated cities or towns without first obtaining from the Department a permit in accordance with the provisions of this chapter.

History.
2001, c. 596.

§ 46.2-2059.1. Roof signs and markings for taxicabs.

Every motor vehicle operating in the Commonwealth as a taxicab or performing a taxicab service shall bear (i) the word or words "taxicab," "taxi," or "cab," permanently affixed to its exterior, in letters at least three inches in height, and (ii) a roof sign. Such markings and roof sign, taken together, shall clearly reflect that the motor vehicle is operating as a taxicab or performing a taxicab service.

History.
2010, c. 242; 2011, c. 1.

§ 46.2-2060. Limitations on advertising.

Within the jurisdictions of Planning District Number Eight, no person shall use the term "taxi" or "taxicab" in any advertisement, sign, or trade name, or hold himself out by means of advertising, signs, trade names, or otherwise as an operator of a taxicab or other motor vehicle performing a taxicab service as defined by § 46.2-2000, unless he complies with the requirements of § 46.2-2059 and any county, city, or town ordinance adopted pursuant to § 46.2-2062. This statute, however, shall not preempt, supersede, or affect in any way the authority of the governing body of any county, city, or town to issue local ordinances under §§ 46.2-2062 through 46.2-2067.

History.
2001, c. 596.

§ 46.2-2061. Article does not make taxicab operators common carriers.

Nothing in this article shall be construed to make or constitute operators of taxicabs or other motor vehicles performing a taxicab service common carriers.

History.
2001, c. 596.

§ 46.2-2062. Regulation of taxicab service by localities; rates and charges.

A. The governing body of any county, city or town in the Commonwealth may by ordinance regulate the rates or charges of any motor vehicles used for the transportation of passengers for a consideration on any highway, street, road, lane or alley in such county, city or town, and may prescribe such reasonable regulations as to filing of schedules of rates, charges and the general operation of such vehicles; provided that, notwithstanding anything contained in this chapter to the contrary, such ordinances and regulations shall not prescribe the wages or compensation to be paid to any driver or lessor of any such motor vehicle by the owner or lessee thereof.

B. In considering rates or charges pursuant to this section, or financial responsibility as provided by this chapter, the governing body may require the owner or operator to submit such supporting financial data as may be necessary, including federal or state income tax returns for the two years preceding, provided that the governing body shall not require any owner or operator to submit any audit more extensive than that conducted by such owner or operator in the normal course of business. Such financial data shall be used only for consideration of rates or charges, or to determine financial responsibility, and shall be kept confidential by the governing body to which it has been submitted. Nothing in this subsection shall make confidential any certificate of insurance, bond, letter of credit, or other certification that the owner or operator has met the requirements of this chapter or of any local ordinance with regard to financial responsibility.

History.
2001, c. 596; 2007, c. 238.

§ 46.2-2063. Locality license and payment of locality license tax may be required.

The governing body of any county, city, or town may require a license for and impose upon and collect a license tax from every person, firm, association, or corporation that operates or intends to operate in such county, city, or town any taxicab or other motor vehicle for the transportation of passengers for a consideration. The tax may be upon each such motor vehicle so operated. The governing body of the county, city, or town may by ordinance provide for levying and collecting the tax and may impose penalties for violations of the ordinance and for operating any such vehicle without obtaining the required license. Any person accepting a license issued under authority of this section and operating a taxicab business based in a county, city or town shall be subject to the provision that any complaint relating to taxicab service in the Commonwealth shall be resolved under the license regulations of the county, city, or town from which that person obtained a taxicab license.

History.
2001, c. 596.

§ 46.2-2064. When local license may not be required.

No such county, city or town shall require a license or impose a license tax for the operation of any such motor vehicle for which a similar license is imposed or tax levied by the county, city or town of which the owner or operator of the motor vehicle is a resident, except that such license may be required and such license tax imposed by any such county, city, or town for the operation of any such motor vehicle if the owner, lessee, or operator thereof maintains a taxicab stand or otherwise solicits business within such county, city, or town; nor, except as herein expressly authorized, shall more than one county, city or town impose any such license fee or tax on the same vehicle. This article shall not be construed to apply to common carriers of persons operating as public carriers by authority of the Department of Motor Vehicles or under a franchise granted by any county, city, or town.

History.
2001, c. 596.

§ 46.2-2065. Local regulation of qualifications of operators; stands.

The governing body of any county, city, or town may prescribe such reasonable regulations as to the character and qualifications of operators of any such vehicle as they deem proper and may provide for the designation and allocation, by the sheriff or chief of police, of stands for such vehicles and the persons who may use the same.

History.
2001, c. 596.

§ 46.2-2066. Penalty for violation of provisions of article or regulations.

Every owner or operator of a motor vehicle used as a vehicle for the transportation of persons for a consideration on any highway, street, road, lane or alley in any county, city or town who violates any of the provisions of this article or regulations of a governing body made pursuant to this chapter shall be guilty of a misdemeanor and upon conviction thereof be fined not more than $100 for the first offense and not more than $500 for each subsequent offense.

History.
2001, c. 596.

§ 46.2-2067. Local regulation of number of taxicabs.

A. It is the policy of this Commonwealth, based on the public health, safety and welfare, to assure safe and reliable privately operated taxicab service for the riding public in this Commonwealth; and in furtherance of this policy, it is recognized that it is essential that counties, cities and towns be granted the authority to reasonably regulate such taxicab service as to the number of operators and the number of vehicles that shall provide such service and regulations as to the rates or charges for such taxicab service, even though such regulations may have an anti-competitive effect on such service by limiting the number of operators and vehicles within a particular jurisdiction.

B. The governing body of any county, city, or town in the Commonwealth may regulate by ordinance and limit the number of taxicab operators and the number of taxicabs within its jurisdiction in order to provide safe and reliable privately operated taxicab service on any highway, street, road, lane or alley in such county, city, or town. The governing body may promulgate such reasonable regulations to further the provisions of this section including, but not limited to, minimum liability insurance requirements. However, such ordinances and regulations shall not prescribe the wages or compensation to be paid to any driver or lessor of any such motor vehicle by the owner or lessee thereof; nor shall such ordinances and regulations authorize the governing body to reduce the number of taxicabs permitted to be operated by a taxicab operator or a holder of a certificate issued under such ordinance, other than for non-use of such taxicabs or for cause as defined by such ordinance, including instances where there is a decrease in the demand for taxicab service. Further, such ordinances and regulations shall not impose (i) regulatory requirements concerning claims settlement practices beyond those imposed by § 46.2-2056 or (ii) financial requirements to qualify as a self-insurer beyond those imposed by § 46.2-2053 on any taxicab operator who, in lieu of filing an insurance policy or surety bond, has qualified as a self-insurer pursuant to § 46.2-2053 by depositing with the State Treasurer state, federal or municipal bonds or has filed an unconditional letter of credit issued by a bank. Nothing herein shall be construed to affect or control the authority of counties, cities or towns to set the amount, if any, of locally established liability insurance requirements that may be met by a program of self-insurance.

History.
2001, c. 596; 2012, cc. 35, 105.

ARTICLE 4.

EMPLOYEE HAULERS.

§ 46.2-2068. Required permit.

No employee hauler, unless otherwise exempted, shall transport passengers on any highway within the Commonwealth on an intrastate basis without first having obtained from the Department a permit authorizing such operation.

History.
2001, c. 596.

§ 46.2-2069. Application; requirements.

An applicant for a permit issued pursuant to this article shall furnish, at the time the application is made, a statement in writing signed by the applicant (i) setting forth the names and locations of the factories, plants, offices or other places of like nature to and from which the applicant proposes to operate and (ii) stating that such applicant will transport only bona fide employees of such factories, plants, offices or like places to and from work.

History.
2001, c. 596.

§ 46.2-2070. Permit restrictions.

A permit issued under this article shall authorize the holder named in the permit to transport bona fide employees solely to and from the factories, plants, offices or other places of like nature specified at the time of application.

History.
2001, c. 596.

ARTICLE 5.

NONPROFIT/TAX-EXEMPT PASSENGER CARRIERS.

§ 46.2-2071. Required permit.

No nonprofit/tax-exempt passenger carrier, unless otherwise exempted, shall transport passengers on any highway within the Commonwealth on an intrastate basis without first having obtained from the Department a permit authorizing such operation.

History.
2001, c. 596.

§ 46.2-2072. Operational restrictions.

No nonprofit/tax-exempt passenger carrier shall operate over the same or an adjacent route and on a similar schedule as a public transportation authority or a common carrier holding a certificate of public convenience and necessity issued pursuant to this chapter.

History.
2001, c. 596.

§ 46.2-2073. Exemption from permit filing fees.

The original permit filing fee collected pursuant to this chapter shall not be applicable to non-profit/tax-exempt passenger carriers.

History.
2001, c. 596.

ARTICLE 6.

COMMON CARRIERS.

§ 46.2-2074. Application of article.

Unless otherwise stated, this article shall only apply to common carriers of passengers over the highways of the Commonwealth.

History.
2001, c. 596.

§ 46.2-2075. Required certificates of public convenience and necessity.

No common carrier not otherwise exempted, other than a sight-seeing carrier, shall engage in intrastate operation on any highway within the Commonwealth without first having obtained from the Department a certificate of public convenience and necessity authorizing such operation.

History.
2001, c. 596; 2011, cc. 881, 889.

§ 46.2-2076. Application; notice requirements.

In addition to the requirements of § 46.2-2001.3, an applicant for a common carrier certificate of public convenience and necessity issued under this article shall cause a notice of such application, on the form and in the manner prescribed by the Department, on the mayor or principal officer of any city or town and on the chairman of the board of supervisors of every county into or through which the applicant may desire to provide service.

History.
2001, c. 596.

§ 46.2-2077. Considerations for determination of issuance of certificate.

In addition to the requirements of § 46.2-2011, in determining whether a certificate of public convenience and necessity required by this article shall be granted, the Department may consider the present transportation facilities over the proposed route or within the proposed service area, the volume of traffic over such route or in such service area, and the condition of the highway over the proposed route or service area.

History.
2001, c. 596.

§ 46.2-2078. No certificate to issue when service already adequate.

No certificate of public convenience and necessity shall be granted to an applicant proposing to operate over the route of any certificated common carrier unless it is proved to the satisfaction of the Department that the service rendered by such certificate holder, over such route, is inadequate to the requirements of the public necessity and convenience; and if the Department is of the opinion that the service rendered by such certificate holder over such route is in any respect inadequate to the requirements of the public necessity and convenience, such certificate holder shall be given reasonable time and opportunity to remedy such inadequacy before any certificate shall be granted to an applicant proposing to operate over such route.

For the purpose of this section, the transportation of passengers by an urban-suburban bus line, hereby defined as a bus line, the majority of whose passengers use the buses for traveling a distance no more than forty miles, measured one way, on the same day, between their places of abode and their places of work, shopping areas, or schools, shall not be deemed an operation over the route of any common carrier of passengers holding a certificate of public convenience and necessity.

History.
2001, c. 596.

§ 46.2-2079. Certificates for passenger carriers operating over Interstate Highway System.

Notwithstanding the provisions of § 46.2-2078, upon a showing of public convenience and necessity, the Department may, if it finds from the evidence that the public interest will be promoted thereby, issue to any carrier of passengers by motor vehicle a certificate or certificates authorizing operations in the Commonwealth upon highways that are part of the Interstate Highway System. The foregoing shall be applicable only to issuance of certificates for operations over such System. Except as otherwise indicated, all other applicable provisions of this chapter shall apply to such carriers and to such certificates.

History.
2001, c. 596.

§ 46.2-2080. Irregular route passenger certificates.

Notwithstanding any of the provisions of § 46.2-2078, the Department may grant common carrier certificates to applicants to serve irregular routes on an irregular schedule within a specified geographic area. The Department shall issue no more certificates than the public convenience and necessity require, and shall place such restrictions upon such certificates as may be reasonably necessary to protect any existing regular or irregular route common carrier certificate holders operating within the proposed service area, but shall not deny a certificate solely on the ground that the applicant will operate in the same service area that an existing regular or irregular route common carrier certificate holder is operating. Certificates issued hereunder shall be restricted to operation of vehicles with a passenger-carrying capacity not to exceed 15 persons, including the driver. Certificates hereunder shall also be restricted to prohibit pickup or delivery of passengers at their personal residence in the City of Norfolk, except that this restriction shall not apply to specially equipped vehicles for the transportation of disabled persons.

A motor carrier receiving a notice of intent to award a contract under the Virginia Public Procurement Act (§ 2.2-4300 et seq.) for irregular route common carrier service to or from a public-use airport located in the City of Norfolk or the County of Henrico is entitled to a conclusive presumption of a need for such service.

History.
2001, c. 596; 2002, cc. 681, 734; 2007, c. 813; 2011, c. 424.

§ 46.2-2081. Schedule required.

Every common carrier operating pursuant to this chapter shall file with the Department time schedules. A common carrier shall not deviate from its time schedule and can only amend such schedule in accordance with § 46.2-2082.

History.
2001, c. 596.

§ 46.2-2082. Schedule changes require Department approval; posting notice.

A common carrier operating under a certificate issued by the Department pursuant to this article shall not make any change in schedules or service without having first received the approval of the Department for such change in schedules or service and without first posting a notice of such change in a conspicuous place at each station or ticket agency affected at least ten days before the effective date thereon. Any request for a change in schedules or service shall be received by the Department a minimum of ten days prior to the proposed effective date of such change.

History.
2001, c. 596.

§ 46.2-2083. Schedule title page and content.

A. Title page of time schedules shall contain the following:

1. Time schedules must be numbered consecutively in the upper right hand corner, beginning with No. 1, and show the number of the time schedule cancelled thereby, if any.
2. Name of the motor carrier.
3. The termini or points between which the time schedules apply.
4. Date issued and date effective.
5. The name, title, and address of the officer issuing such time schedule, including street address.

B. Time schedules shall show:

1. The time of departure from all termini.
2. The time of departure from intermediate points between termini.
3. What points, if any, on route of carrier at which service cannot be rendered.

History.
2001, c. 596.

§ 46.2-2084: Repealed by Acts 2011, cc. 881 and 889, cl. 2.

§ 46.2-2085. Abandonment, discontinuance, or deviation of service.

Notwithstanding anything contained in this chapter to the contrary, no common carrier regulated pursuant to this article shall abandon or discontinue any service established under the provisions of this chapter without permission of the Department and on such terms as the Department may prescribe. Common carriers may occasionally deviate from their route or routes when authorized to do so by the Department.

History.
2001, c. 596.

§ 46.2-2086. Interruption of service.

All interruptions of regular service that are likely to continue for more than twenty-four hours shall be promptly reported in writing to the Department with a full statement of cause of such interruption and its probable duration; however, any interruption of regular service that results from an act of God need not be reported to the Department unless it continues for more than seventy-two hours.

All interruptions of regular service shall be promptly reported to the agents of the carrier on the routes involved.

History.
2001, c. 596.

§ 46.2-2087. Refusal of service.

No common carrier regulated pursuant to this chapter shall refuse service without good cause. The Department may, at any time, require an explanation from such carrier for its refusal to provide service.

History.
2001, c. 596.

§ 46.2-2088. Duties of carriers of passengers as to through routes, equipment, rates, regulations, etc.

Every common carrier regulated pursuant to this article shall establish reasonable through routes with other such common carriers and shall provide safe and adequate service, equipment, and facilities for the transportation of passengers; shall establish, observe, and enforce just and reasonable individual and joint rates, fares and charges and just and reasonable regulations and practices relating thereto, and to the issuance, form, and substance of tickets, the carrying of baggage, the facilities for transportation, and all other matters relating to or connected with the transportation of passengers; and in case of such joint rates, fares, and charges, shall establish just, reasonable and equitable divisions thereof as between the carriers participating therein which shall not unduly prefer or prejudice any of such participating carriers.

History.
2001, c. 596.

§ 46.2-2089. Undue preference not permitted.

Except as provided in § 46.2-2091, it shall be unlawful for any common carrier regulated pursuant to this article to make, give, or cause any undue or unreasonable preference or advantage to any particular person, port, gateway, locality, or description of traffic in any respect whatsoever, or to subject any particular person, port, gateway, locality, or description of traffic to any unjust discrimination or any undue or unreasonable prejudice or disadvantage in any respect whatsoever; however, this section shall not be construed to apply to discriminations, prejudice or disadvantage to the traffic of any other carrier of whatever description.

History.
2001, c. 596.

§ 46.2-2090. Tariffs showing rates, fares and charges; available for inspection.

Every common carrier regulated pursuant to this article shall file with the Department at least thirty days before the effective date, and make available for public inspection, tariffs showing all the rates, fares and charges for transportation, and all services in connection therewith, of passengers between points on its own route and points on the route of any other such carrier, or on the route of any common carrier by railroad, air, or water, when a through route and joint rate shall have been established. Such rates, fares, and charges shall be stated in terms of lawful money of the United States. The tariffs required by this section shall be published, filed, and posted in such form and manner, and shall contain such information as the Department may prescribe. The Department is authorized to reject any tariff filed with it that is not in consonance with this section. Any tariff rejected by the Department shall be void, and its use shall be unlawful.

History.
2001, c. 596.

§ 46.2-2091. Unlawful to charge other than published tariff.

No common carrier regulated pursuant to this article shall charge or demand or collect or receive greater compensation for transportation or for any service in connection therewith between the points enumerated in such tariff than the rates, fares, and charges specified in the tariffs in effect at the time.

History.
2001, c. 596.

§ 46.2-2092. Changes in tariffs.

No change shall be made in any rate, fare, charge, or classification, or any rule, regulation, or practice affecting such rate, fare, charge, or classification, or the value of the service thereunder, specified in any effective tariff of a common carrier regulated pursuant to this article, except after thirty days' notice of the proposed change. Such notice shall plainly state the change proposed to be made and the time when such change will take effect. The Department may, in its discretion and for good cause shown, allow such change upon notice less than that herein specified or modify the requirements of this section with respect to posting and filing of tariffs.

History.
2001, c. 596.

§ 46.2-2093. Joint tariffs; power of attorney.

A. A common carrier regulated pursuant to this article may authorize an agent or may join with another carrier or carriers in the publication of a joint tariff, supplement or amendment, and, where such authority is given, shall file with the Department prior to publication power of attorney or notice of concurrence, which shall specifically set out the authority given.

B. Where a carrier issues a power of attorney to an agent or a concurrence to another carrier for the publication of tariffs, such power of attorney or concurrence may not be revoked except upon sixty days' notice to the Department and the agent or carrier to which the power of attorney or concurrence was issued, except upon special permission of the Department.

History.
2001, c. 596.

§ 46.2-2094. No transportation except when rates have been filed and published.

No common carrier regulated pursuant to this article, unless otherwise provided by this chapter, shall engage in the transportation of passengers unless the rates, fares, and charges upon which the same are transported by such carrier have been filed and published in accordance with the provisions of this article.

History.
2001, c. 596.

§ 46.2-2095. Terminals; local license taxes on operation.

Counties, cities and towns may impose license taxes for the privilege of operating or conducting terminals for use by common carriers regulated pursuant to this article. Operation of terminals by such carriers in connection with and incidental to their business as such common carriers, and not for profit, or for such carriers where the local agent receives as his compensation a commission on tickets sold shall not be subject to the imposition of any such taxes. Lots used by such carriers for parking, storage and servicing of motor vehicles used in the business of such carriers and for taking on and discharging passengers shall not be deemed terminals. Nothing herein contained shall be construed to exempt the payment of license taxes on any other business that may be conducted on, at, or in any such terminal or lot.

History.
2001, c. 596.

ARTICLE 7.
CONTRACT PASSENGER CARRIERS.

§ 46.2-2096. Certificates required unless exempted.

Unless otherwise exempted, no person shall engage in the business of a contract passenger carrier by motor vehicle on any highway within the Commonwealth on an intrastate basis unless such person has secured from the Department a certificate of fitness authorizing such business.

History.
2001, c. 596; 2011, cc. 881, 889.

§§ 46.2-2097, 46.2-2097.1: Repealed by Acts 2011, cc. 881 and 889, cl. 2.

§ 46.2-2098. Control, supervision and regulation by Department.

Except as otherwise provided in this chapter, every contract passenger carrier shall be subject to the exclusive control, supervision, and regulation by the Department, except that enforcement of statutes and Department regulations shall be not only by the Department, but also by the Department of State Police and local law-enforcement agencies. Nothing in this section shall be construed as authorizing the adoption of local ordinances providing for local regulation of contract passenger carriers.

History.
2001, c. 596.

§ 46.2-2099. Operation except in accordance with chapter prohibited.

No contract passenger carrier shall operate any motor vehicle for the transportation of passengers for compensation on any highway in the Commonwealth on an intrastate basis except in accordance with the provisions of this chapter. There shall be no commingling of unrelated passengers by use of a contract between a contract passenger carrier and a licensed broker for the transportation of passengers by motor vehicles.

History.
2001, c. 596.

§ 46.2-2099.1. Operational requirements; penalty.

Contract passenger carriers shall provide service on a prearranged basis only for a minimum of one-hour per vehicle trip under a single contract made with one person for an agreed charge for such movement regardless of the number of passengers transported. Contract passenger carriers shall, prior to and at all times when providing compensated service, carry in each motor vehicle a trip sheet, contract order, or wireless text dispatching device identifying the names of the passengers who have arranged for use of the motor vehicle, the date and approximate time of pickup, and the origin and destination. Such trip sheet, contract order, or wireless text dispatching device shall be made available immediately upon request to authorized representatives of the Department, law-enforcement agencies, and airport authorities. Trip sheets, contract orders, or documentation produced by wireless text dispatching devices shall be retained and available for inspection at the carrier's place of business for a period of at least three years. Trip sheets, contract orders, or documentation may be retained (i) in the form of paper records; (ii) by microfilm, microfiche, similar microphotographic process; or (iii) by electronic means. The fact that a contract passenger carrier stations a motor vehicle at an airport, in front of or across the street from a hotel or motel, or within 100 feet of a recognized taxicab stand shall constitute prima facie evidence that the contract passenger carrier is operating in violation of this section, unless the carrier has (i) a completed trip sheet, contract order, or wireless text dispatching device displaying the information required by this section in the vehicle or (ii) a written agreement with an airport authority or hotel or motel owner providing office space devoted to the carrier's business in the airport, hotel, or motel. Any violation of this section shall be punishable as a Class 3 misdemeanor.

History.
2001, c. 596; 2006, c. 449.

ARTICLE 8.
CONTRACT BUS CARRIERS.

§§ 46.2-2099.2, 46.2-2099.3: Repealed by Acts 2012, cc. 22 and 111, cl. 2.

ARTICLE 9.
SIGHT-SEEING CARRIERS.

§ 46.2-2099.4. Required certificate of fitness.

No sight-seeing carrier, unless otherwise exempted, shall transport passengers on any highway within the Commonwealth on an intrastate basis without first having obtained from the Department a certificate of fitness authorizing such operation.

History.
2001, c. 596; 2011, cc. 881, 889.

§ 46.2-2099.5. Specific service and route requirements.

A sight-seeing carrier shall transport passengers from a specific point or points of origin over regular routes to specific points of interest and back to the point or points of origin. Each passenger shall be issued a ticket on which shall be printed the points of interest and the fare charged for the round trip. Passengers shall be transported only on round trips without stopover privileges, and no part of a fare shall be refunded because of a passenger's refusal to complete the round trip.

History.
2001, c. 596; 2011, cc. 881, 889.

§ 46.2-2099.6: Repealed by Acts 2011, cc. 881 and 889, cl. 2.

§§ 46.2-2099.7 through 46.2-2099.10: Repealed by Acts 2012, cc. 22 and 111, cl. 2.

§ 46.2-2099.11. Refusal of service.

No sight-seeing carrier shall refuse service without good cause. The Department may, at any time, require an explanation from such carrier for its refusal to provide service.

History.
2001, c. 596.

§§ 46.2-2099.12 through 46.2-2099.16: Repealed by Acts 2012, cc. 22 and 111, cl. 2.

ARTICLE 10.
BROKERS.

§ 46.2-2099.17. Regulation of brokers.

The Department shall regulate brokers and make and enforce reasonable requirements respecting their licenses, financial responsibility, accounts, records, reports, operations and practices.

History.
2001, c. 596.

§ 46.2-2099.18. Broker's license required.

No person shall for compensation sell or offer for sale transportation subject to this chapter or shall make any contract, agreement, or arrangement to provide, procure, furnish, or arrange for such transportation or shall hold himself out by advertisement, solicitation, or otherwise as one who sells, provides, procures, contracts, or arranges for such transportation, unless such person holds a broker's license issued by the Department to engage in such transactions; however, the provisions of this section shall not apply to any carrier holding a certificate or permit under the provisions of this chapter or to any bona fide employee or agent of such motor carrier, so far as concerns transportation to be furnished wholly by such carrier or jointly with other motor carriers holding like certificates or permits.

History.
2001, c. 596.

§ 46.2-2099.19. Broker's license not substitute for other certificates or permits required.

No person who holds a broker's license under this article shall engage in transportation subject to this chapter unless he holds a certificate or permit as provided in this chapter. In the execution of any contract, agreement, or arrangement to sell, provide, procure, furnish, or arrange for such transportation, it shall be unlawful for such person to employ any carrier by motor vehicle who is not the lawful holder of an effective certificate or permit issued as provided in this chapter or when such certificate or permit does not authorize the carrier to perform the service being acquired.

A person holding a broker's license shall obtain and maintain a copy of the certificate of public convenience and necessity issued to those carriers through which the broker arranges transportation services.

History.
2001, c. 596; 2013, cc. 165, 582.

ARTICLE 11.

SIGHT-SEEING CARRIERS BY BOAT AND SPECIAL OR CHARTER PARTY CARRIERS BY BOAT.

§ **46.2-2099.20:** Repealed by Acts 2002, c. 861.

§ 46.2-2099.21. Exemptions from operation of article.

This article shall not be construed to include:

1. Persons engaged in operating boats exclusively for fishing;

2. Persons engaged in operating boats that have (i) an approved passenger capacity of twenty-five or less persons and (ii) are operated as special or charter parties under this chapter; or

3. The City of Hampton when acting as a sight-seeing carrier by boat or special or charter party carrier by boat.

History.
2001, c. 596; 2007, c. 813.

§§ **46.2-2099.22 through 46.2-2099.29:** Repealed by Acts 2002, c. 861.

§ 46.2-2099.30. Insurance to be kept in force.

Sight-seeing carriers by boat, special or charter party carriers by boat and motor carriers by launch shall keep in force at all times marine protection and indemnity insurance in an amount not less than $500,000 for bodily injury and property damage.

History.
2001, c. 596; 2002, c. 861.

ARTICLE 12.

MOTOR CARRIERS BY LAUNCH.

§§ **46.2-2099.31 through 46.2-2099.40:** Repealed by Acts 2002, c. 861.

ARTICLE 13.

EXCURSION TRAINS.

§ 46.2-2099.41. Certification requirements.

A. A person may apply to the Department for certification as an operator of an excursion train. The Department shall certify an applicant if the Department determines that the applicant will operate a passenger train that:

1. Is primarily used for tourism or public service; and

2. Leads to the promotion of the tourist industry in the Commonwealth.

B. An application for certification shall include:

1. The name and address of each person who owns an interest of at least 10 percent of the excursion train operation;

2. An address in the Commonwealth where the excursion train is based;

3. An operations plan, including the route to be used and a schedule of operations and stops along the route; and

4. Evidence of insurance that meets the requirements of subsection C.

C. The Department shall not certify to a person under subsection A unless the person files with the Department evidence of insurance providing coverage of liability resulting from injury to persons or damages to property in the amount of at least $10 million for the operation of the train.

D. The Department shall not certify an applicant under subsection A if the applicant or any other person owning interest in the excursion train also owns or operates a regularly scheduled passenger train service with interstate connection.

History.
2001, c. 596; 2003, c. 286; 2007, c. 813; 2016, c. 431.

§ 46.2-2099.42. Assignment of liability.

A. The operator of an excursion train shall be liable for personal injury or wrongful death arising from the operation of such excursion train, including operations, maintenance, and signalization of the tracks and facilities upon which the excursion train operates.

B. Any county, city, or town may by resolution determine that the provision of excursion train services within the locality promotes tourism and furthers other public purposes. Any railroad company that authorizes the operator of an excursion train to use its tracks and facilities for the purposes of this article shall not be liable for personal injury or wrongful death arising from the operation of such excursion train, including operations, maintenance, and signalization of the tracks and facilities upon which the excursion train operates.

C. The limitation of liability under subsection B does not apply if:

1. The injury or damages result from intentional misconduct, malice, or gross negligence of the railroad company; or

2. The operator of the excursion train was not operating in accordance with the definition of an excursion train under this chapter and the railroad company had otherwise authorized the operations that were inconsistent with this chapter.

D. Each passenger on the excursion train shall be deemed to have accepted and consented to the limitation of liability under this section. This agreement shall be governed by the laws of the Commonwealth as the place of performance notwithstanding any choice of law rules to the contrary.

E. The railroad company may charge reasonable amounts to the operator of the excursion train for the use of its tracks and facilities as determined by agreement between the railroad company and the operator.

History.
2001, c. 596; 2016, c. 431.

§ 46.2-2099.43. Notice to passengers.

The operator of an excursion train shall:

1. Issue each passenger a ticket with the following statement in twelve point boldface type: "THE RAILROAD COMPANY WHICH OWNS THE TRACKS AND FACILITIES UPON WHICH THIS EXCURSION TRAIN OPERATES SHALL NOT BE LIABLE FOR PERSONAL INJURY OR WRONGFUL DEATH ARISING FROM THE OPERATION OF THE EXCURSION TRAIN, INCLUDING OPERATIONS, MAINTENANCE, AND SIGNALIZATION OF THE TRACKS AND FACILITIES."
2. Post a notice near any passenger boarding area containing the same statement contained in subdivision 1, in letters that are at least two inches high.

History.
2001, c. 596.

ARTICLE 14.
NONEMERGENCY MEDICAL TRANSPORTATION CARRIERS.

§ 46.2-2099.44. Certificate of fitness required.

No nonemergency medical transportation carrier, unless otherwise exempted, shall transport passengers on any highway within the Commonwealth on an intrastate basis without first having obtained from the Department a certificate of fitness authorizing such operation.

History.
2011, cc. 881, 889.

ARTICLE 15.
TRANSPORTATION NETWORK COMPANIES.

§ 46.2-2099.45. Certificates required unless exempted.

Unless otherwise exempted, no person shall engage in the business of a transportation network company on any highway within the Commonwealth on an intrastate basis unless such person has secured from the Department a certificate of fitness authorizing such business.

History.
2015, cc. 2, 3.

§ 46.2-2099.46. Control, supervision, and regulation by Department.

Except as otherwise provided in this chapter, every transportation network company, TNC partner, and TNC partner vehicle shall be subject to exclusive control, supervision, and regulation by the Department, but enforcement of statutes and Department regulations shall be not only by the Department but also by any other law-enforcement officer. Nothing in this section shall be construed as authorizing the adoption of local ordinances providing for local regulation of transportation network companies, TNC partners, or TNC partner vehicles.

History.
2015, cc. 2, 3.

§ 46.2-2099.47. Operation except in accordance with chapter prohibited.

No transportation network company or TNC partner shall transport passengers for compensation on any highway in the Commonwealth on an intrastate basis except in accordance with the provisions of this chapter.

History.
2015, cc. 2, 3.

§ 46.2-2099.48. General operational requirements for transportation network companies and TNC partner.

A. A transportation network company and a TNC partner shall provide passenger transportation only on a prearranged basis and only by means of a digital platform that enables passengers to connect with TNC partners using a TNC partner vehicle. No TNC partner shall transport a passenger unless a transportation network company has matched the TNC partner to that passenger through the digital platform. A TNC partner shall not solicit, accept, arrange, or provide transportation in any other manner.

B. A transportation network company shall authorize collection of fares for transporting passengers solely through a digital platform. A TNC partner shall not accept payment of fares directly from a passenger or any other person prearranging a ride or by any means other than electronically via a digital platform.

C. A transportation network company with knowledge that a TNC partner has violated the provisions of subsection A or B shall remove the TNC partner from the transportation network company's digital platform for at least one year.

D. A transportation network company shall publish the following information on its public website and associated digital platform:

1. The method used to calculate fares or the applicable rates being charged and an option to receive an estimated fare;

2. Information about its TNC partner screening criteria, including a description of the offenses that the transportation network company will regard as grounds for disqualifying an individual from acting as a TNC partner;

3. The means for a passenger or other person to report a TNC partner reasonably suspected of operating a TNC partner vehicle under the influence of drugs or alcohol;

4. Information about the company's training and testing policies for TNC partners;

5. Information about the company's standards for TNC partner vehicles; and

6. A customer support telephone number or email address and instructions regarding any alternative methods for reporting a complaint.

E. A transportation network company shall associate a TNC partner with one or more personal vehicles and shall authorize a TNC partner to transport passengers only in a vehicle specifically associated with a TNC partner by the transportation network company. The transportation network company shall arrange transportation solely for previously associated TNC partners and TNC partner vehicles. A TNC partner shall not transport passengers except in a TNC partner vehicle associated with the TNC partner by the transportation network company.

F. A TNC partner shall carry at all times while operating a TNC partner vehicle proof of coverage under each in-force TNC insurance policy, which may be displayed as part of the digital platform, and each in-force personal automobile insurance policy covering the vehicle. The TNC partner shall present such proof of insurance upon request to the Commissioner, a law-enforcement officer, an airport owner and operator, an official of the Washington Metropolitan Area Transit Commission, or any person involved in an accident that occurs during the operation of a TNC partner vehicle. The transportation network company shall require the TNC partner's compliance with the provisions of this subsection.

G. Prior to a passenger's entering a TNC partner vehicle, a transportation network company shall provide through the digital platform to the person prearranging the ride the first name and a photograph of the TNC partner, the make and model of the TNC partner vehicle, and the license plate number of the TNC partner vehicle.

H. A transportation network company shall provide to each of its TNC partners a credential, which may be displayed as part of the digital platform, that includes the following information:

1. The name or logo of the transportation network company;

2. The name and a photograph of the TNC partner; and

3. The make, model, and license plate number of each TNC partner vehicle associated with the TNC partner and the state issuing each such license plate.

The TNC partner shall carry the credential at all times during the operation of a TNC partner vehicle and shall present the credential upon request to law-enforcement officers, airport owners and operators, officials of the Washington Metropolitan Area Transit Commission, or a passenger. The transportation network company shall require the TNC partner's compliance with this subsection.

I. A transportation network company and its TNC partner shall, at all times during a prearranged ride, make the following information available through its digital platform immediately upon request to representatives of the Department, to law-enforcement officers, to officials of the Washington Metropolitan Area Transit Commission, and to airport owners and operators:

1. The name of the transportation network company;

2. The name of the TNC partner and the identification number issued to the TNC partner by the transportation network company;

3. The license plate number of the TNC partner vehicle and the state issuing such license plate; and

4. The location, date, and approximate time that each passenger was or will be picked up.

J. Upon completion of a prearranged ride, a transportation network company shall transmit to the person who prearranged the ride an electronic receipt that includes:

1. A map of the route taken;

2. The date and the times the trip began and ended;

3. The total fare, including the base fare and any additional charges incurred for distance traveled or duration of the prearranged ride;

4. The TNC partner's first name and photograph; and

5. Contact information by which additional support may be obtained.

K. The transportation network company shall adopt and enforce a policy of nondiscrimination on the basis of a passenger's points of departure and destination and shall notify TNC partners of such policy.

TNC partners shall comply with all applicable laws regarding nondiscrimination against passengers or potential passengers.

A transportation network company shall provide passengers an opportunity to indicate whether they require a wheelchair-accessible vehicle. If a transportation network company cannot arrange wheelchair-accessible service in a TNC partner vehicle in any instance, it shall direct the passenger to an alternate provider of wheelchair-accessible service, if available.

A transportation network company shall not impose additional charges for providing services to persons with disabilities because of those disabilities.

TNC partners shall comply with all applicable laws relating to accommodation of service animals.

A TNC partner may refuse to transport a passenger for any reason not prohibited by law, including any case in which (i) the passenger is acting in an unlawful, disorderly, or endangering manner; (ii) the passenger is unable to care for himself and is not in the charge of a responsible companion; or (iii) the TNC partner has already committed to providing a ride for another passenger.

A TNC partner shall immediately report to the transportation network company any refusal to transport a passenger after accepting a request to transport that passenger.

L. No transportation network company or TNC partner shall conduct any operation on the property of or into any airport unless such operation is authorized by the airport owner and operator and is in compliance with the rules and regulations of that airport. The Department may take action against a transportation network company that violates any regulation of an airport owner and operator, including the suspension or revocation of the transportation network company's certificate.

M. A TNC partner shall access and utilize a digital platform in a manner that is consistent with traffic laws of the Commonwealth.

N. In accordance with § 46.2-812, no TNC partner shall operate a motor vehicle for more than 13 hours in any 24-hour period.

History.
2015, cc. 2, 3.

§ 46.2-2099.49. Requirements for TNC partners; mandatory background screening; drug and alcohol policy; mandatory disclosures to TNC partners; duty of TNC partners to provide updated information to transportation network companies.

A. Before authorizing an individual to act as a TNC partner, a transportation network company shall confirm that the person is at least 21 years old and possesses a valid driver's license.

B. 1. Before authorizing an individual to act as a TNC partner, and at least once every two years after authorizing an individual to act as a TNC partner, a transportation network company shall obtain a national criminal history records check of that person. The background check shall include (i) a Multi-State/Multi-Jurisdiction Criminal Records Database Search or a search of a similar nationwide database with validation (primary source search) and (ii) a search of the Sex Offender and Crimes Against Minors Registry and the U.S. Department of Justice's National Sex Offender Public Website. The person conducting the background check shall be accredited by the National Association of Professional Background Screeners or a comparable entity approved by the Department.

2. Before authorizing an individual to act as a TNC partner, and at least once annually after authorizing an individual to act as a TNC partner, a transportation network company shall obtain and review a driving history research report on that person from the individual's state of licensure.

3. Before authorizing an individual to act as a TNC partner, and at least once every two years after authorizing a person to act as a TNC partner, a transportation network company shall verify that the person is not listed on the Sex Offender and Crimes Against Minors Registry or on the U.S. Department of Justice's National Sex Offender Public Website.

C. A transportation network company shall not authorize an individual to act as a TNC partner if the criminal history records check required under subsection B reveals that the individual:

1. Is a person for whom registration with the Sex Offender and Crimes Against Minors Registry is required pursuant to Chapter 9 (§ 9.1-900 et seq.) of Title 9.1 or is listed on the U.S. Department of Justice's National Sex Offender Public Website;

2. Has ever been convicted of or has ever pled guilty or nolo contendere to a violent felony offense as listed in subsection C of § 17.1-805, or a substantially similar law of another state or of the United States;

3. Within the preceding seven years has been convicted of or has pled guilty or nolo contendere to any of the following offenses, either under Virginia law or a substantially similar law of another state or of the United States: (i) any felony offense other than those included in subdivision 2; (ii) an offense under § 18.2-266, 18.2-266.1, 18.2-272, or 46.2-341.24; or (iii) any offense resulting in revocation of a driver's license pursuant to § 46.2-389 or 46.2-391; or

4. Within the preceding three years has been convicted of or has pled guilty or nolo contendere to any of the following offenses, either under Virginia law or a substantially similar law of another state or of the United States: (i) three or more moving violations; (ii) eluding a law-enforcement officer, as described in § 46.2-817; (iii) reckless driving, as described in Article 7 (§ 46.2-852 et seq.) of Chapter 8; (iv) operating a motor vehicle in violation of § 46.2-301; or (v) refusing to submit to a chemical test to determine the alcohol or drug content of the person's blood or breath, as described in § 18.2-268.3.

D. A transportation network company shall employ a zero-tolerance policy with respect to the use of drugs and alcohol by TNC partners and shall include a notice concerning the policy on its website and associated digital platform.

E. A transportation network company shall make the following disclosures in writing to a TNC partner or prospective TNC partner:

1. The transportation network company shall disclose the liability insurance coverage and limits of liability that the transportation network company provides while the TNC partner uses a vehicle in connection with the transportation network company's digital platform.

2. The transportation network company shall disclose any physical damage coverage provided by the transportation network company for damage to the vehicle used by the TNC partner in connection with the transportation network company's digital platform.

3. The transportation network company shall disclose the uninsured motorist and underinsured motorist coverage and policy limits provided by the transportation network company while the TNC partner uses a vehicle in connection with the transportation network company's digital platform and advise the TNC partner that the TNC partner's personal automobile insurance policy may not provide uninsured motorist and underinsured motorist coverage when the TNC partner uses a vehicle in connection with a transportation network company's digital platform.

4. The transportation network company shall include the following disclosure prominently in writing to a TNC partner or prospective TNC partner: "If the vehicle that you plan to use to transport passengers for our transportation network company has a lien against it, you must notify the lienholder that you will be using the vehicle for transportation services that may violate the terms of your contract with the lienholder."

F. A TNC partner shall inform each transportation network company that has authorized him to act as a TNC partner of any event that may disqualify him from continuing to act as a TNC partner, including any of the following: a change in the registration status of the TNC partner vehicle; the revocation, suspension, cancellation, or restriction of the TNC partner's driver's license; a change in the insurance coverage of the TNC partner vehicle; a motor vehicle moving violation; and a criminal arrest, plea, or conviction.

History.

2015, cc. 2, 3.

§ 46.2-2099.50. Requirements for TNC partner vehicles; registration with and identification markers issued by Department; identification markers issued by transportation network company.

A. A TNC partner vehicle shall:

1. Be a personal vehicle;

2. Have a seating capacity of no more than eight persons, including the driver;

3. Be validly titled and registered in the Commonwealth or in another state;

4. Not have been issued a certificate of title, either in Virginia or in any other state, branding the vehicle as salvage, nonrepairable, rebuilt, or any equivalent classification;

5. Have a valid Virginia safety inspection and carry proof of that inspection in the vehicle;

6. Be covered under a TNC insurance policy meeting the requirements of § 46.2-2099.51 or 46.2-2099.52, as applicable; and

7. Be registered with the Department for use as a TNC partner vehicle and display an identification marker issued by the Department as provided in subsection B.

No TNC partner shall operate a TNC partner vehicle unless that vehicle meets the requirements of this subsection.

B. A vehicle owner, lessee, or TNC partner shall register a personal vehicle for use as a TNC partner vehicle. A TNC partner that is not the vehicle owner or lessee shall, prior to registering any TNC partner vehicle with the Department, secure the consent of each owner, lessor, and lessee of the vehicle as applicable for its registration as a TNC partner vehicle and for its use as a TNC partner vehicle by the TNC partner. A transportation network company shall have the option of registering a TNC partner vehicle on behalf of a TNC partner electronically through a secure portal maintained by the Department provided the TNC partner, if the TNC partner is not the vehicle owner or lessee, certifies that it has secured consent from each owner, lessor, and lessee of the vehicle for its registration as a TNC partner vehicle and for its use as a TNC partner vehicle by the TNC partner.

Prior to registering for use as a TNC partner vehicle any vehicle that has been titled and registered in another state, the vehicle owner or lessee, or a transportation network company on behalf of the owner or lessee, shall provide the Department with such information as the Department requires to establish a customer record for that person and that person's vehicle. A transportation network company shall have the option to submit this information electronically through a secure portal maintained by the Department.

For each TNC partner vehicle a transportation network company authorizes, the transportation network company or TNC partner shall provide to the Department, in a form acceptable to the Department, any information reasonably necessary for the Department to identify the vehicle and register it for use as a TNC partner vehicle.

Upon registering a vehicle for use as a TNC partner vehicle, the Department shall issue a temporary registration, an identification marker to the vehicle owner or lessee, and a registration card indicating the vehicle's registration for use as a TNC partner vehicle.

The Commissioner may deny, suspend, cancel, or revoke the TNC partner vehicle registration and identification marker for any of the following reasons: (i) the vehicle is not properly registered, (ii) the vehicle does not carry insurance as required by this article, (iii) the vehicle is sold, or (iv) the vehicle is used by a TNC partner in a manner not authorized by this chapter.

Registration of a TNC partner vehicle under this subsection shall remain valid until (a) the vehicle is no longer authorized to operate as a TNC partner vehicle by a transportation network company; (b) the TNC partner, vehicle owner, or lessee requests cancellation of the registration; (c) there is a transfer of vehicle ownership, other than a transfer from the lessor of the vehicle to the lessee; (d) the vehicle's lease terminates and ownership is not transferred to the lessee; or (e) the Department suspends, revokes, or cancels the registration of the vehicle for use as a TNC partner vehicle. The fee for the replacement of a lost, mutilated, or illegible identification marker or registration card shall be the same as the fee set forth in § 46.2-692 for the replacement of a decal or vehicle registration card. However, if the TNC partner vehicle is not titled and registered in Virginia, the replacement fee for an identification marker shall be $40.

Any vehicle registered with the Department as a personal vehicle and subject to further registration as a TNC partner vehicle pursuant to this section shall be presumed to be used for nonbusiness purposes for the purpose of determining whether it is a qualifying vehicle under § 58.1-3523 absent clear and convincing evidence to the contrary, and any registration pursuant to this section shall not create any presumption of business or commercial use of the vehicle or of business activity on the part of the TNC partner, for purposes of any state or local requirement.

C. Before authorizing a vehicle to be used as a TNC partner vehicle, a transportation network company shall confirm that the vehicle meets the requirements of subsection A and shall provide each TNC partner with proof of any TNC insurance policy maintained by the transportation network company.

For each TNC partner vehicle it authorizes, a transportation network company shall issue trade dress to the TNC partner associated with that vehicle. The trade dress shall be sufficient to identify the transportation network company or digital platform with which the vehicle is affiliated and shall be displayed in a manner that complies with Virginia law. The trade dress shall be of such size, shape, and color as to be readily identifiable during daylight hours from a distance of 50 feet while the vehicle is not in motion and shall be reflective, illuminated, or otherwise patently visible in darkness. The trade dress may take the form of a removable device that meets the identification and visibility requirements of this subsection.

The transportation network company shall submit to the Department proof that the transportation network company has established the trade dress required under this subsection by filing with the Department an illustration or photograph of the trade dress.

A TNC partner shall keep the trade dress issued under this subsection visible at all times while the vehicle is being operated as a TNC partner vehicle.

No person shall operate a vehicle bearing trade dress issued under this subsection without the authorization of the transportation network company issuing the trade dress.

D. Any information provided to the Department pursuant to this section, whether held by the Department or another public entity, shall not be subject to disclosure under the Virginia Freedom of Information Act (§ 2.2-3700 et seq.). Neither the Department nor any such public entity shall disclose any such information to a nongovernmental entity absent a court order or subpoena. In the event information provided pursuant to this section is sought through a court order or subpoena, the Department or other public entity shall promptly notify the transportation network company prior to disclosure so as to afford the transportation network company the opportunity to take appropriate actions to prevent disclosure. The Department shall not disclose such information to a governmental entity other than to enable that entity to perform its governmental function.

History.

2015, cc. 2, 3.

§ 46.2-2099.51. TNC insurance until January 1, 2016.

A. Until January 1, 2016, at all times during the operation of a TNC partner vehicle, a transportation network company or TNC partner shall keep in force TNC insurance as provided in this section.

B. The following requirements shall apply to TNC insurance from the moment a TNC partner accepts a prearranged ride request on a transportation network company's digital platform until the TNC partner completes the transaction on the digital platform or until the prearranged ride is complete, whichever is later:

1. TNC insurance shall provide motor vehicle liability coverage. Such coverage shall be primary and the minimum amount of liability coverage for death, bodily injury, and property damage shall be $1 million.

2. TNC insurance shall provide uninsured motorist coverage and underinsured motorist coverage. Such coverage shall apply from the moment a passenger enters a TNC partner vehicle until the passenger exits the vehicle. The minimum amount of uninsured motorist coverage and underinsured motorist coverage for death, bodily injury, and property damage shall be $1 million.

3. The requirements of this subsection may be satisfied by any of the following:

a. TNC insurance maintained by a TNC partner;

b. TNC insurance maintained by a transportation network company; or

c. Any combination of subdivisions a and b.

A transportation network company may meet its obligations under this subsection through a policy obtained by a TNC partner under subdivision a or c only if the transportation network company verifies that the policy is maintained by the TNC partner.

4. Insurers providing insurance coverage under this subsection shall have the exclusive duty to defend any liability claim, including any claim against a TNC partner, arising from an accident occurring within the time periods specified in this subsection. Neither the TNC partner's nor the vehicle owner's personal automobile insurance policy shall have the duty to defend or indemnify the TNC partner's activities in connection with the transportation network company, unless the policy expressly provides otherwise for the period of time to which this subsection is applicable or the policy contains an amendment or endorsement to provide that coverage.

5. Coverage under a TNC insurance policy shall not be dependent on a personal automobile insurance policy first denying a claim, nor shall a personal automobile insurance policy be required to first deny a claim.

6. Nothing in this subsection shall be construed to require a personal automobile insurance policy to provide primary or excess coverage. Neither the TNC partner's nor the vehicle owner's personal automobile insurance policy shall provide any coverage to the TNC partner, the vehicle owner, or any third party, unless the policy expressly provides for that coverage during the period of time to which this subsection is applicable or the policy contains an amendment or endorsement to provide that coverage.

C. The following requirements shall apply to TNC insurance (i) from the moment a TNC partner logs on to a transportation network company's associated digital platform until the TNC partner accepts a request to transport a passenger and (ii) from the moment the TNC partner completes the transaction on the digital platform or the prearranged ride is complete, whichever is later, until the TNC partner either accepts another prearranged ride request on the digital platform or logs off the digital platform:

1. TNC insurance shall provide motor vehicle liability coverage. Such coverage shall be secondary and shall provide liability coverage of at least $125,000 per person and $250,000 per incident for death and bodily injury and at least $50,000 for property damage.

2. The requirements for the coverage required by this subsection may be satisfied by any of the following:

a. TNC insurance maintained by a TNC partner;

b. TNC insurance maintained by a transportation network company that provides coverage in the event that a TNC partner's insurance policy under subdivision a has ceased to exist or has been canceled or in the event that the TNC partner does not otherwise maintain TNC insurance; or

c. Any combination of subdivisions a and b.

A transportation network company may meet its obligations under this subsection through a policy obtained by a TNC partner pursuant to subdivision a or c only if the transportation network company verifies that the policy is maintained by the TNC partner and is specifically written to cover the TNC partner's use of a vehicle in connection with a transportation network company's digital platform.

3. If the TNC partner vehicle is insured under a personal automobile insurance policy that does not exclude coverage, then such policy shall provide primary coverage and an insurance policy maintained by the transportation network company under subdivision 2 c shall provide excess coverage up to at least the limits required by subdivision 1.

D. In the event that the digital platform becomes inaccessible due to failure or malfunction while a TNC partner is en route to or transporting a passenger during a prearranged ride described in subsection B, TNC insurance coverage shall be presumed to be that required in subdivision B 1 until the passenger exits the vehicle.

E. In every instance where TNC insurance maintained by a TNC partner to fulfill the insurance obligations of this section has lapsed or ceased to exist, the transportation network company shall provide the coverage required by this section beginning with the first dollar of a claim.

F. This section shall not limit the liability of a transportation network company arising out of an accident involving a TNC partner in any action for damages against a transportation network company for an amount above the required insurance coverage.

G. Any person, or an attorney acting on his behalf, who suffers a loss in an automobile accident with a reasonable belief that the accident involves a TNC partner vehicle driven by a TNC partner in connection with a transportation network company and who provides the transportation network company with the date, approximate time, and location of the accident, and if available the name of the TNC partner and if available the accident report, may request in writing from the transportation network company information relating to the insurance coverage and the company providing the coverage. The transportation network company shall respond electronically or in writing within 30 days. The transportation network company's response shall contain the following information: (i) whether, at the approximate time of the accident, the TNC partner was logged into the transportation network company's digital platform and, if so logged in, whether a trip request had been accepted or a passenger was in the TNC partner vehicle; (ii) the name of the insurance carrier providing primary coverage; and (iii) the identity and last known address of the TNC partner.

H. No contract, receipt, rule, or regulation shall exempt any transportation network company from the liability that would exist had no contract been made or entered into, and no such contract, receipt, rule, or regulation for exemption from liability for injury or loss occasioned by the neglect or misconduct of such transportation network company shall be valid. The liability referred to in this subsection shall mean the liability imposed by law upon a transportation network company for any loss, damage, or injury to passengers in its custody and care as a transportation network company.

I. Any insurance required by this section may be placed with an insurer that has been admitted in Virginia or with an insurer providing surplus lines insurance as defined in § 38.2-4805.2.

J. Any insurance policy required by this section shall satisfy the financial responsibility requirement for a motor vehicle under § 46.2-706 during the period such vehicle is being operated as a TNC partner vehicle.

K. The Department shall not issue the certificate of fitness required under § 46.2-2099.45 to any transportation network company that has not certified to the Department that every TNC partner vehicle it has authorized to operate on its digital platform is covered by an insurance policy that meets the requirements of this section.

L. Each transportation network company shall keep on file with the Department proof of an insurance policy maintained by the transportation network company in accordance with this section. Such proof shall be in a form acceptable to the Commissioner. A record of the policy shall remain in the files of the Department six months after the certificate is suspended or revoked for any cause.

M. The Department may suspend a certificate if the certificate holder fails to comply with the requirements of this section. Any person whose certificate has been suspended pursuant to this subsection may request a hearing as provided in subsection D of § 46.2-2011.26.

N. In a claims coverage investigation, a transportation network company and its insurer shall cooperate with insurers involved in the claims coverage investigation to facilitate the exchange of information, including the dates and times of any accident involving a TNC partner and the precise times that the TNC partner logged in and was logged out of the transportation network company's digital platform.

History.
2015, cc. 2, 3.

§ 46.2-2099.52. TNC insurance.

A. On and after January 1, 2016, at all times during the operation of a TNC partner vehicle, a transportation network company or TNC partner shall keep in force TNC insurance as provided in this section.

B. The following requirements shall apply to TNC insurance from the moment a TNC partner accepts a prearranged ride request on a transportation network company's digital platform until the TNC partner completes the transaction on the digital platform or until the prearranged ride is complete, whichever is later:

1. TNC insurance shall provide motor vehicle liability coverage. Such coverage shall be primary and the minimum amount of liability coverage for death, bodily injury, and property damage shall be $1 million.

2. TNC insurance shall provide uninsured motorist coverage and underinsured motorist coverage. Such coverage shall apply from the moment a passenger enters a TNC partner vehicle until the passenger exits the vehicle. The minimum amount of uninsured motorist coverage and underinsured motorist coverage for death, bodily injury, and property damage shall be $1 million.

3. The requirements of this subsection may be satisfied by any of the following:

a. TNC insurance maintained by a TNC partner;

b. TNC insurance maintained by a transportation network company; or

c. Any combination of subdivisions a and b.

A transportation network company may meet its obligations under this subsection through a policy obtained by a TNC partner under subdivision a or c only if the transportation network company verifies that the policy is maintained by the TNC partner.

4. Insurers providing insurance coverage under this subsection shall have the exclusive duty to defend any liability claim, including any claim against a TNC partner, arising from an accident occurring within the time periods specified in this subsection. Neither the TNC partner's nor the vehicle owner's personal automobile insurance policy shall have the duty to defend or indemnify the TNC partner's activities in connection with the transportation network company, unless the policy expressly provides otherwise for the period of time to which this subsection is applicable or the policy contains an amendment or endorsement to provide that coverage.

5. Coverage under a TNC insurance policy shall not be dependent on a personal automobile insurance policy first denying a claim, nor shall a personal automobile insurance policy be required to first deny a claim.

6. Nothing in this subsection shall be construed to require a personal automobile insurance policy to provide primary or excess coverage. Neither the TNC partner's nor the vehicle owner's personal automobile insurance policy shall provide any coverage to the TNC partner, the vehicle owner, or any third party, unless the policy expressly provides for that coverage during the period of time to which this subsection is applicable or the policy contains an

amendment or endorsement to provide that coverage.

C. The following requirements shall apply to TNC insurance (i) from the moment a TNC partner logs on to a transportation network company's associated digital platform until the TNC partner accepts a request to transport a passenger and (ii) from the moment the TNC partner completes the transaction on the digital platform or the prearranged ride is complete, whichever is later, until the TNC partner either accepts another prearranged ride request on the digital platform or logs off the digital platform:

1. TNC insurance shall provide motor vehicle liability coverage. Such coverage shall be primary and shall provide liability coverage of at least $50,000 per person and $100,000 per incident for death and bodily injury and at least $25,000 for property damage.

2. The requirements for the coverage required by this subsection may be satisfied by any of the following:

a. TNC insurance maintained by a TNC partner;

b. TNC insurance maintained by a transportation network company that provides coverage in the event that a TNC partner's insurance policy under subdivision a has ceased to exist or has been canceled or in the event that the TNC partner does not otherwise maintain TNC insurance; or

c. Any combination of subdivisions a and b.

A transportation network company may meet its obligations under this subsection through a policy obtained by a TNC partner pursuant to subdivision a or c only if the transportation network company verifies that the policy is maintained by the TNC partner and is specifically written to cover the TNC partner's use of a vehicle in connection with a transportation network company's digital platform.

D. In the event that the digital platform becomes inaccessible due to failure or malfunction while a TNC partner is en route to or transporting a passenger during a prearranged ride described in subsection B, TNC insurance coverage shall be presumed to be that required in subdivision B 1 until the passenger exits the vehicle.

E. In every instance where TNC insurance maintained by a TNC partner to fulfill the insurance obligations of this section has lapsed or ceased to exist, the transportation network company shall provide the coverage required by this section beginning with the first dollar of a claim.

F. This section shall not limit the liability of a transportation network company arising out of an accident involving a TNC partner in any action for damages against a transportation network company for an amount above the required insurance coverage.

G. Any person, or an attorney acting on his behalf, who suffers a loss in an automobile accident with a reasonable belief that the accident involves a TNC partner vehicle driven by a TNC partner in connection with a transportation network company and who provides the transportation network company with the date, approximate time, and location of the accident, and if available the name of the TNC partner and if available the accident report, may request in writing from the transportation network company information relating to the insurance coverage and the company providing the coverage. The transportation network company shall respond electronically or in writing within 30 days. The transportation network company's response shall contain the following information: (i) whether, at the approximate time of the accident, the TNC partner was logged into the transportation network company's digital platform and, if so logged in, whether a trip request had been accepted or a passenger was in the TNC partner vehicle; (ii) the name of the insurance carrier providing primary coverage; and (iii) the identity and last known address of the TNC partner.

H. No contract, receipt, rule, or regulation shall exempt any transportation network company from the liability that would exist had no contract been made or entered into, and no such contract, receipt, rule, or regulation for exemption from liability for injury or loss occasioned by the neglect or misconduct of such transportation network company shall be valid. The liability referred to in this subsection shall mean the liability imposed by law upon a transportation network company for any loss, damage, or injury to passengers in its custody and care as a transportation network company.

I. Any insurance required by this section may be placed with an insurer that has been admitted in Virginia or with an insurer providing surplus lines insurance as defined in § 38.2-4805.2.

J. Any insurance policy required by this section shall satisfy the financial responsibility requirement for a motor vehicle under § 46.2-706 during the period such vehicle is being operated as a TNC partner vehicle.

K. The Department shall not issue the certificate of fitness required under § 46.2-2099.45 to any transportation network company that has not certified to the Department that every TNC partner vehicle it has authorized to operate on its digital platform is covered by an insurance policy that meets the requirements of this section.

L. Each transportation network company shall keep on file with the Department proof of an insurance policy maintained by the transportation network company in accordance with this section. Such proof shall be in a form acceptable to the Commissioner. A record of the policy shall remain in the files of the Department six months after the certificate is revoked or suspended for any cause.

M. The Department may suspend a certificate if the certificate holder fails to comply with the requirements of this section. Any person whose certificate has been suspended pursuant to this subsection may request a hearing as provided in subsection D of § 46.2-2011.26.

N. In a claims coverage investigation, a transportation network company and its insurer shall cooperate with insurers involved in the claims coverage investigation to facilitate the exchange of information, including the dates and times of any accident involving a TNC partner and the precise times that the TNC partner logged in and was logged out of the transportation network company's digital platform.

History.
2015, cc. 2, 3.

§ 46.2-2099.53. Recordkeeping and reporting requirements for transportation network companies.

A. Records maintained by a transportation network company shall be adequate to confirm compliance with subsection D of § 46.2-2099.48 and with §§ 46.2-2099.49 and 46.2-2099.50 and shall at a minimum include:

1. True and accurate results of each national criminal history records check for each individual that the transportation network company authorizes to act as a TNC partner;

2. True and accurate results of the driving history research report for each individual that the transportation network company authorizes to act as a TNC partner;

3. Driver's license records of TNC partners, including records associated with participation in a driver record monitoring program;

4. True and accurate results of the sex offender screening for each individual that the transportation network company authorizes to act as a TNC partner;

5. Proof of compliance with the requirements enumerated in subdivisions A 1 and 3 through 6 of § 46.2-2099.50;

6. Proof of compliance with the notice and disclosure requirements of subsection D of § 46.2-2099.48 and subsections D and E of § 46.2-2099.49; and

7. Proof that the transportation network company obtained certification from the TNC partner that the TNC partner secured the consent of each owner, lessor, and lessee of the vehicle for its registration as a TNC partner vehicle and for its use as a TNC partner vehicle by the TNC partner.

A transportation network company shall retain all records required under this subsection for a period of three years. Such records shall be retained in a manner that permits systematic retrieval and shall be made available to the Department in a format acceptable to the Commissioner for the purposes of conducting an audit on no more than an annual basis.

B. A transportation network company shall maintain the following records and make them available, in an acceptable format, on request to the Commissioner, a law-enforcement officer, an official of the Washington Metropolitan Area Transit Commission, or an airport owner and operator to investigate and resolve a complaint or respond to an incident:

1. Data regarding TNC partner activity while logged into the digital platform, including beginning and ending times and locations of each prearranged ride;

2. Records regarding any actions taken against a TNC partner;

3. Contracts or agreements between the transportation network company and its TNC partners;

4. Information identifying each TNC partner, including the TNC partner's name, date of birth, and driver's license number and the state issuing the license; and

5. Information identifying each TNC partner vehicle the transportation network company has authorized, including the vehicle's make, model, model year, vehicle identification number, and license plate number and the state issuing the license plate.

Requests for information pursuant to subdivision 2 or 3 shall be in writing.

C. Information obtained by the Department, law-enforcement officers, officials of the Washington Metropolitan Area Transit Commission, or airport owners and operators pursuant to this section shall be considered privileged information and shall only be used by the Department, law-enforcement officers, officials of the Washington Metropolitan Area Transit Commission, and airport owners and operators for purposes specified in subsection A or B. Such information shall not be subject to disclosure except on the written request of the Commissioner, a law-enforcement officer, an official of the Washington Metropolitan Area Transit Commission, or an airport owner and operator who requires such information for the purposes specified in subsection A or B.

D. Except as provided in subsection C, information obtained by the Department, law-enforcement officers, officials of the Washington Metropolitan Area Transit Commission, or airport owners and operators pursuant to this section shall not be disclosed to anyone without the transportation network company's express written permission and shall not be subject to disclosure through a court order or through a third-party request submitted pursuant to the Virginia Freedom of Information Act (§ 2.2-3700 et seq.). This provision shall not be construed to mean that a person is denied the right to seek such information directly from a transportation network company during a court proceeding.

E. Except as required under this section, a transportation network company shall not disclose any personal information, as defined in § 2.2-3801, about a user of its digital platform unless:

1. The transportation network company obtains the user's consent to disclose the personal information;

2. The disclosure is necessary to comply with a legal obligation; or

3. The disclosure is necessary to protect or defend the terms and conditions for use of the service or to investigate violations of the terms and conditions.

This limitation regarding disclosure does not apply to the disclosure of aggregated user data or to information about the user that is not personal information as defined in § 2.2-3801.

History.
2015, cc. 2, 3.

CHAPTER 21.
REGULATION OF PROPERTY CARRIERS.

Article 1.

Motor Carriers of Property — Generally.

Article 2.

Insurance Requirements.

Article 3.

Property Carriers.

Article 4.

Household Goods Carriers.

Article 5.

Brokers.

ARTICLE 1.
MOTOR CARRIERS OF PROPERTY — GENERALLY.

§ 46.2-2100. Definitions.

Whenever used in this chapter, unless expressly stated otherwise:

"Authorized insurer" means, in the case of an interstate motor carrier whose operations may or may not include intrastate activity, an insurer authorized to transact business in any one state, or, in the case of a solely intrastate motor carrier, an insurer authorized to transact business in the Commonwealth.

"Broker" means any person not included in the term "motor carrier" and not a bona fide employee or agent of any such carrier, who, as principal or agent, sells or offers for sale any transportation subject to this chapter, or negotiates for, or holds himself out by solicitation, advertisement, or otherwise as one who sells, provides, furnishes, contracts, or arranges for such transportation.

"Bulk commodity" means any non-liquid, non-gaseous commodity shipped loose or in mass/aggregate and which in the loading and unloading thereof is ordinarily shoveled, scooped, forked, or mechanically conveyed or which is not in containers or in units of such size to permit piece by piece loading and unloading.

"Bulk property carrier" means any person, not herein exempted, who undertakes either directly or by lease, to transport exclusively bulk commodities, as defined, for compensation including for purposes of this section for-hire tow truck operations.

"Certificate of fitness" means a certificate issued by the Department to certain "household goods carriers" under this chapter.

"Constructive weight" means a measurement of seven pounds per cubic foot of properly loaded van space.

"Courier service" means a motor carrier that engages, directly or by lease, exclusively in the transportation of letters, envelopes, negotiable or nonnegotiable instruments, or other documents or papers for compensation.

"Department" means the Department of Motor Vehicles.

"Financial responsibility" means the ability to respond in damages for liability thereafter incurred arising out of the ownership, maintenance, use, or operation of a motor vehicle, in the amounts provided for in this chapter.

"Gross weight" means the weight of a truck after a shipment has been loaded.

"Highway" means every public highway or place of whatever nature open to the use of the public for purposes of vehicle travel in this Commonwealth, excluding the streets and alleys in towns and cities.

"Household goods" means personal effects and property used or to be used in a dwelling, when a part of the equipment or supplies of such dwelling, and similar property if the transportation of such effects or property is (i) arranged and paid for by the householder, including transportation of the property from a factory or store when the property is purchased by the householder with intent to use it in his dwelling or (ii) arranged and paid for by another party.

"Household goods carrier" means a restricted common carrier who undertakes, whether directly or by a lease or other arrangement, to transport "household goods," as herein defined, by motor vehicle for compensation, on any highway in this Commonwealth, between two or more points in this Commonwealth, whether over regular or irregular routes.

"Identification marker" means a decal or other visible identification issued by the Department to show (i) that the operator of the vehicle has registered with the Department for the payment of the road tax imposed under Chapter 27 (§ 58.1-2700 et seq.) of Title 58.1, (ii) proof of the possession of a certificate or permit issued pursuant to Chapter 21 (§ 46.2-2100 et seq.) of this title, and/or (iii) proof of compliance with the insurance requirements of this chapter.

"Interstate" means the transportation of property between states.

"Intrastate" means the transportation of property solely within a state.

"License" means a license issued by the Department to a broker.

"Motor carrier" means any person who undertakes whether directly or by a lease, to transport property, including household goods, as defined by this chapter, for compensation over the highways of the Commonwealth.

"Motor vehicle" means any vehicle, machine, tractor, trailer, or semitrailer propelled or drawn by mechanical power and used upon the highways in the transportation of property, but does not include any vehicle, locomotive or car operated exclusively on a rail or rails.

"Net weight" means the tare weight subtracted from the gross weight.

"Permit" means a permit issued by the Department authorizing the transportation of property, excluding household goods transported for a distance greater than 30 road miles.

"Person" means any individual, firm, copartnership, corporation, company, association or joint-stock association, and includes any trustee, receiver, assignee, or personal representative thereof.

"Property carrier" means any person, not herein exempted, who undertakes either directly or by a lease, to transport property for compensation.

"Restricted common carrier" means any person who undertakes, whether directly or by a lease or other arrangement, to transport household goods by motor vehicle for compensation whether over regular or irregular routes.

"Services" and *"transportation"* includes the services of, and all transportation by, all vehicles operated by, for, or in the interest of any motor carrier, irrespective of ownership or contract, express or implied, together with all facilities and property operated or controlled by any such carrier or carriers and used in the transportation of property or in the performance of any service in connection therewith.

"Single state insurance receipt" means any receipt issued pursuant to 49 C.F.R. Part 367 evidencing

that the carrier has the required insurance and paid the requisite fees to the Commonwealth and other qualified jurisdictions.

"Tare weight" means the weight of a truck before being loaded at a shipper's residence or place of business, including the pads, dollies, hand-trucks, ramps and other equipment normally used in the transportation of household goods shipments.

History.

Code 1950, § 56-338.1; 1995, cc. 744, 803; 1997, c. 283; 2001, c. 596; 2003, c. 832; 2006, cc. 874, 891; 2011, cc. 881, 889.

§ 46.2-2101. Exemptions from chapter.

The following are exempt from this chapter:

1. Motor vehicles owned and operated by the United States, District of Columbia, any state, municipality, or any other political subdivision of the Commonwealth.

2. Transportation of property between any point in this Commonwealth and any point outside this Commonwealth or between any points wholly within the limits of any city or town in the Commonwealth. This exemption shall not apply to the insurance requirement imposed on motor carriers pursuant to § 46.2-2143.1.

3. Motor vehicles controlled and operated by a bona fide cooperative association as defined in the Federal Marketing Act, approved June 15, 1929, as amended, or organized or existing under Article 2 (§ 13.1-312 et seq.) of Chapter 3 of Title 13.1, while used exclusively in the conduct of the business of such association.

4. Motor vehicles while used exclusively in (i) carrying newspapers, water, livestock, poultry, poultry products, buttermilk, fresh milk and cream, meats, butter and cheese produced on a farm, fish (including shellfish), slate, horticultural or agricultural commodities (not including manufactured products thereof), and forest products, including lumber and staves (but not including manufactured products thereof), (ii) transporting farm supplies to a farm or farms, (iii) hauling for the Department of Transportation, (iv) carrying fertilizer to any warehouse or warehouses for subsequent distribution to a local area farm or farms, or (v) collecting and disposing of trash, garbage and other refuse.

5. Motor vehicles used for transporting property by an air carrier or carrier affiliated with a direct air carrier whether or not such property has had or will have a prior or subsequent air movement.

6. Motor carriers exclusively operating vehicles with a registered gross weight of 7,500 pounds or less for the sole purpose of providing courier service.

History.

Code 1950, § 56-338.2; 1954, c. 344; 1956, c. 697; 1973, c. 305; 1995, cc. 744, 803; 2001, c. 596; 2003, c. 832; 2012, c. 638.

§ 46.2-2102. Compliance with chapter required.

No motor carrier shall operate any motor vehicle for the transportation of property for compensation on any highway in this Commonwealth on an intrastate basis except in accordance with the provisions of this chapter.

History.

Code 1950, § 56-338.3; 1995, cc. 744, 803; 2001, c. 596.

§§ 46.2-2103 through 46.2-2108: Repealed by Acts 2001, c. 596, cl. 2, effective July 1, 2002.

§ 46.2-2108.1. Disposition of funds collected.

Except as otherwise provided, all fees collected by the Commissioner pursuant to this chapter shall be paid into the state treasury and set aside as a special fund to be used to meet the expenses of the Department.

History.

2001, c. 596.

§ 46.2-2108.2. Necessity of a license, permit, or certificate.

It shall be unlawful for any person to operate, offer, advertise, provide, procure, furnish, or arrange by contract, agreement or arrangement to transport property for compensation on an intrastate basis as a motor carrier or broker without first obtaining from the Department a license, permit, or certificate of fitness as required by this chapter.

History.

2001, c. 596; 2011, cc. 881, 889.

§ 46.2-2108.3. Identification marker required.

Each motor carrier shall be issued an identification marker unless the operation is interstate in nature and the carrier has been issued a single state registration receipt by the Department or other qualified jurisdiction. The identification marker shall be displayed on each vehicle as prescribed by the Department and shall be valid for the period of time prescribed by the Department.

History.

2001, c. 596.

§ 46.2-2108.4. Application; notice requirements.

A. Applications for a license, permit, or certificate of fitness or renewal of a license, permit, or certificate of fitness under this chapter shall be made to the Department and contain such information as the Department shall require. Such information shall include, in the application or otherwise, the matters set forth in §§ 46.2-2133 and 46.2-2134 as grounds for denying licenses, permits, and certificates.

B. The applicant for a certificate of fitness issued under this chapter shall cause a notice of such application, on the form and in the manner prescribed by the Department, to be served on every affected person who has requested notification.

History.
2001, c. 596; 2011, cc. 881, 889; 2013, cc. 165, 582.

§ 46.2-2108.5. Registered for fuels tax; business, professional, and occupational license taxes.

License, permit, and certificate of fitness holders shall be licensed and registered in accordance with the road tax requirements of Chapter 27 (§ 58.1-2700 et seq.) of Title 58.1 and licensed for payment of local business, professional, and occupational license taxes of Chapter 37 (§ 58.1-3700 et seq.) of Title 58.1 as required.

History.
2001, c. 596; 2011, cc. 881, 889.

§ 46.2-2108.6. Considerations for determination of issuance of license, permit, or certificate.

In determining whether a license, permit, or certificate of fitness required by this chapter shall be issued, the Department may, among other things, consider compliance with financial responsibility, bonding and other requirements of this chapter.

History.
2001, c. 596; 2011, cc. 881, 889.

§ 46.2-2109. Action on applications; hearings on denials and protests.

A. The Department may act upon any application required under this chapter without a hearing, unless such application is protested by any party based upon fitness allegations. Parties may protest an application by submitting written grounds to the Department setting forth (i) a precise statement of the party's objections to the application being granted; (ii) a full and clear statement of the facts that the person is prepared to provide by competent evidence; (iii) the case number assigned to the application; and (iv) a certification that a copy of the protest was sent to the applicant. The Department shall have full discretion as to whether a hearing is warranted based on the merits of any protest filed.

B. Any applicant denied without a hearing an original license or certificate of fitness under subsection A, or any request for a transfer for such license or certificate, shall be given a hearing at a time and place determined by the Commissioner or his designee upon the applicant's written request for such hearing made within thirty days of denial.

History.
Code 1950, § 56-338.11; 1995, cc. 744, 803; 2001, c. 596; 2002, c. 870; 2011, cc. 881, 889.

§§ 46.2-2110 through 46.2-2114: Repealed by Acts 2001, c. 596, cl. 2, effective July 1, 2002.

§ 46.2-2114.1: Expired.

Editor's note.
This section was enacted by Acts 2001, c. 596, and expired by its own terms on July 1, 2002.

§ 46.2-2115. Determination for issuance of license, permit, or certificate.

If the Department finds the applicant has met all requirements of this chapter, it shall issue a license, permit, or certificate of fitness to the applicant, subject to such terms, limitations and restrictions as the Department may deem proper.

History.
2001, c. 596; 2011, cc. 881, 889.

§ 46.2-2116: Repealed by Acts 2012, cc. 22 and 111, cl. 2.

§ 46.2-2117. Temporary emergency operation.

In an emergency, the Department or its agents may, by letter, telegram, or other means, authorize a vehicle to be operated in the Commonwealth without a proper registration card or identification marker for not more than ten days.

History.
2001, c. 596.

§ 46.2-2118. Issuance, expiration, and renewal of license, permit, and certificate.

All licenses, permits, and certificates of fitness issued under this chapter shall be issued for a period of twelve consecutive months except, at the discretion of the Department, the periods may be adjusted as necessary. Such licenses, permits, and certificates shall expire if not renewed annually. Such expiration shall be effective thirty days after the Department has provided the licensee, permittee, or certificate holder notice of non-renewal. If the license, permit, or certificate is renewed within thirty days after notice of non-renewal, then the license, permit, or certificate shall not expire.

History.
2001, c. 596; 2011, cc. 881, 889.

§ 46.2-2119: Repealed by Acts 2012, cc. 22 and 111, cl. 2.

§ 46.2-2120. Filing and application fees.

Every applicant for an original license or certificate of fitness issued under this chapter and transfer of a license or certificate of fitness under this chapter shall, upon the filing of an application, deposit with the Department, as a filing fee, a sum in the amount of fifty dollars. The Department shall collect a fee of three dollars for the issuance of a duplicate license or certificate of fitness.

History.
2001, c. 596; 2011, cc. 881, 889.

§ 46.2-2121. Vehicle fees.

Every person who operates a property carrying vehicle for compensation over the highways of the Commonwealth, unless such operation is exempted from this chapter, shall be required to pay an annual fee of $10 for each such vehicle so operated, unless a vehicle identification marker fee has been paid to the Department as to such vehicle for the current year under the provisions of Chapter 27 (§ 58.1-2700 et seq.) of Title 58.1. Such fee shall be paid through the single state registration system established pursuant to 49 U.S.C. § 14504 and 49 CFR Part 367 or through the unified carrier registration system established pursuant to 49 U.S.C. § 14504a and the regulations promulgated thereunder for carriers registered pursuant to those provisions. No more than one vehicle fee shall be charged or paid as to any vehicle in any one year under Chapter 27 (§ 58.1-2700 et seq.) of Title 58.1 and this chapter, including payments made pursuant to the single state registration system or the unified carrier registration system.

History.
2001, c. 596; 2003, c. 322; 2006, c. 208.

§ 46.2-2122. Bond and letter of credit requirements of applicants for license and certificate.

A. Every applicant for an original certificate of fitness under this chapter shall obtain and file with the Department, along with the application, a surety bond or an irrevocable letter of credit, in addition to any other bond or letter of credit required by law, in the amount of $50,000, which shall remain in effect for the first five years of licensure. The bond or letter of credit shall be in a form and content acceptable to the Department. The bond or letter of credit shall be conditioned on a statement by the applicant that the applicant will not practice fraud, make any fraudulent representation, or violate any provision of this chapter in the conduct of the applicant's business. The Department may, without holding a hearing, suspend the certificate of fitness during the period that the certificate holder does not have a sufficient bond or letter of credit on file.

B. Every applicant for an original license pursuant to Article 5 (§ 46.2-2174 et seq.) shall obtain and file with the Department, along with the application, a surety bond or an irrevocable letter of credit, in addition to any other bond or letter of credit required by law, in the amount of $25,000. The bond or letter of credit shall be in a form and content acceptable to the Department. The bond or letter of credit shall be conditioned on a statement by the applicant that the applicant will not practice fraud, make any fraudulent representation, or violate any provision of this chapter in the conduct of the applicant's business. The Department may, without holding a hearing, suspend the license during the period that the licensee does not have a sufficient bond or letter of credit on file.

C. If a person suffers any of the following: (i) loss or damage in connection with the transportation service by reason of fraud practiced on him or fraudulent representation made to him by a licensee or certificate holder or his agent or employee acting within the scope of employment; (ii) loss or damage by reason of a violation by a licensee or certificate holder or his agent or employee of any provision of this chapter in connection with the transportation service; or (iii) loss or damage resulting from a breach of a contract entered into on or after the effective date of this act, that person shall have a claim against the licensee or certificate holder's bond or letter of credit, and may recover from such bond or letter of credit the amount awarded to such person by final judgment of a court of competent jurisdiction against the licensee or certificate holder as a result of such loss or damage up to, but not exceeding, the amount of the bond or letter of credit.

D. The licensee or certificate holder's surety shall notify the Department when a claim is made against a licensee or certificate holder's bond, when a claim is paid and/or when the bond is canceled. Such notification shall include the amount of a claim and the circumstances surrounding the claim. Notification of cancellation shall include the effective date and reason for cancellation.

E. The surety on any bond filed by a licensee or certificate holder shall be released and discharged from all liability accruing on such bond after the expiration of 60 days from the date on which the surety files with the Department a written request to be released and discharged. Such request shall not operate to relieve, release, or discharge the surety from any liability already accrued or that shall accrue before the expiration of the 60-day period.

History.
2001, c. 596; 2011, cc. 881, 889; 2013, cc. 165, 582.

§ 46.2-2123: Repealed by Acts 2012, cc. 22 and 111, cl. 2.

§ 46.2-2124. Notice of discontinuance of service.

Every motor carrier or broker who ceases operation or abandons his rights under a license, permit, or certificate of fitness issued shall notify the Department within thirty days of such cessation or abandonment.

History.
2001, c. 596; 2011, cc. 881, 889.

§ 46.2-2125. Reports, records, etc.

A. The Department is hereby authorized to require annual, periodical, or special reports from motor carriers, except such as are exempted from the operation of the provisions of this chapter; to prescribe the manner and form in which such reports shall be made; and to require from such carriers specific answers to all questions upon which the Department may deem information to be necessary. Such reports shall be under oath whenever the Department so requires. The Department may also require any motor carrier to file with it a true copy of each or any contract, agreement, or arrangement between such carrier and any other carrier or person in relation to the provisions of this chapter.

B. The Department may, in its discretion, prescribe (i) the forms of any and all accounts, records, and memoranda to be kept by motor carriers and (ii) the length of time such accounts, records, and memoranda shall be preserved, as well as of the receipts and expenditures of money. The Department or its employees shall at all times have access to all lands, buildings, or equipment of motor carriers used in connection with their operations and also all accounts, records, and memoranda, including all documents, papers, and correspondence now or hereafter existing, and kept, or required to be kept, by motor carriers. The Department and its employees shall have authority to inspect and examine any and all such lands, buildings, equipment, accounts, records, and memoranda, including all documents, papers, and correspondence now or hereafter existing and kept or required to be kept by such carriers. These provisions shall apply to receivers of carriers and to operating trustees and, to the extent deemed necessary by the Department, to persons having control, direct or indirect, over or affiliated with any motor carrier.

C. As used in this section the term “motor carriers” includes brokers.

History.
2001, c. 596.

§ 46.2-2126. Certificate, license, or permit holder not relieved of liability for negligence.

Nothing in this chapter shall relieve any holder of a certificate, license, or permit by and under the authority of the Department from any liability resulting from his negligence, whether or not he has complied with the requirements of this chapter.

History.
2001, c. 596.

§ 46.2-2127. Freight bill violation.

Any motor carrier that consistently submits a freight bill to a shipper for services rendered, which bill is more than ten percent above the written estimate of charges for such services, shall be subject to penalties and/or revocation or suspension of certificate as provided in this chapter.

History.
2001, c. 596.

§ 46.2-2128. Vehicle seizure; penalty.

A. Any police officer of the Commonwealth authorized to serve process may hold a motor vehicle owned by a person against whom an order or penalty has been entered, but only for such time as is reasonably necessary to promptly petition for a writ of fieri facias. The Commonwealth shall not be required to post bond in order to hold and levy upon any vehicle held pursuant to this section.

B. Upon notification of the judgment or penalty entered against the owner of the vehicle and notice to such person of the failure to satisfy the judgment or penalty, any investigator, special agent, or officer of the Commonwealth shall thereafter deny the offending person the right to operate the motor vehicle on the highways of the Commonwealth.

History.
2001, c. 596.

§ 46.2-2129. Unlawful use of registration and identification markers.

It shall be unlawful for any person to operate or cause to be operated on any highway in the Commonwealth any motor vehicle that (i) does not carry the proper registration and identification that this title requires, (ii) does not display an identification marker in such manner as is prescribed by the Department, or (iii) bears registration or identification markers of persons whose license, permit, or certificate issued by the Department has been revoked, suspended, or renewal thereof denied in accordance with this chapter.

History.
2001, c. 596.

§ 46.2-2130. Registration violations; penalties.

A. The following violations of laws shall be punished as follows:

1. Any person who does not obtain a proper registration card, identification marker, or other evidence of registration as required by this chapter shall be guilty of a Class 4 misdemeanor.

2. Any person who operates or causes to be operated on any highway in the Commonwealth any motor vehicle that does not carry the proper registration and identification that this title requires or any motor vehicle that does not display (i) an identification marker in such manner as is prescribed by the Department or (ii) other identifying information that this title requires it to display shall be guilty of a Class 4 misdemeanor.

3. Any person who knowingly displays or uses on any vehicle operated by him any identification marker or other identification that has not been issued to the owner or operator thereof for such vehicle and any person who knowingly assists him to do so shall be guilty of a Class 3 misdemeanor.

4. Any person who operates or causes to be operated on any highway in the Commonwealth any motor vehicle requiring registration from the Department under this article after such registration cards or identification markers have been revoked, canceled or suspended shall be guilty of a Class 3 misdemeanor.

B. The officer charging the violation under this section shall serve a citation on the operator of the vehicle in violation. Such citation shall be directed to the owner, operator or other person responsible for the violation as determined by the officer. Service of the citation on the vehicle operator shall constitute service of process upon the owner, operator, or other person charged with the violation under this article, and shall have the same legal force as if served within the Commonwealth personally upon the owner, operator, or other person charged with the violation, whether such owner, operator, or other person charged is a resident or nonresident.

History.
2001, c. 596.

§ 46.2-2131. Violation; criminal penalties.

A. Any person knowingly and willfully violating any provision of this chapter, or any rule or regulation thereunder, or any term or condition of any certificate, permit, or license, for which a penalty is not otherwise herein provided, shall, upon conviction thereof, be fined not more than $2,500 for the first offense and not more than $5,000 for any subsequent offense. Each day of such violation shall constitute a separate offense.

B. Any person, whether carrier, broker, shipper, consignee, or any officer, employee, agent, or representative thereof, who shall knowingly and willfully by any such means or otherwise fraudulently seek to evade or defeat regulation as in this chapter provided for motor carriers or brokers, shall be deemed guilty of a misdemeanor and, upon conviction thereof, be fined not more than $500 for the first offense and not more than $2,000 for any subsequent offense.

C. Any motor carrier or broker, or any officer, agent, employee, or representative thereof who willfully fails or refuses to make a report to the Department as required by this chapter or to keep accounts, records, and memoranda in the form and manner approved or prescribed by the Department, or knowingly and willfully falsifies, destroys, mutilates, or alters any such report, account, record or memorandum, or knowingly and willfully files any false report, account, record or memorandum, shall be deemed guilty of a misdemeanor and upon conviction thereof be subject for each offense to a fine of not less than $100 and not more than $5,000.

History.
2001, c. 596.

§ 46.2-2132. Violations; civil penalties.

The Department may impose a civil penalty not exceeding $1,000 if any person has:

1. Made any misrepresentation of a material fact to obtain proper operating credentials as required by this chapter or other requirements in this title regulating the operation of motor vehicles;

2. Failed to make any report required in this chapter;

3. Failed to pay any fee or tax properly assessed against him; or

4. Failed to comply with any provision of this chapter or lawful order, rule or regulation of the Department or any term or condition of any certificate, permit, or license.

Any such penalty shall be imposed by order; however, no order issued pursuant to this section shall become effective until the Department has offered the person an opportunity for an administrative hearing to show cause why the order should not be enforced. Instead of or in addition to imposing such penalty, the Department may suspend, revoke, or cancel any license, permit, certificate of fitness, registration card or identification marker issued pursuant to this title. If, in any such case, it appears that the defendant owes any fee or tax to the Commonwealth, the Department shall enter order therefor.

For the purposes of this section, each separate violation shall be subject to the civil penalty.

History.
2001, c. 596; 2011, cc. 881, 889; 2013, cc. 165, 582.

§ 46.2-2133. Grounds for denying, suspending, or revoking licenses or certificates.

A license or certificate of fitness issued under this chapter may be denied, suspended, or revoked on any one or more of the following grounds, where applicable:

1. Material misstatement or omission in application for license or certificate of public convenience

and necessity, identification marker, or vehicle registration;

2. Failure to comply subsequent to receipt of a written warning from the Department or any willful failure to comply with a lawful order, any provision of this chapter or any regulation promulgated by the Department under this chapter, or any term or condition of any license or certificate of fitness;

3. Use of deceptive business acts or practices;

4. Knowingly advertising by any means any assertion, representation, or statement of fact that is untrue, misleading, or deceptive relating to the conduct of the business for which a license, certificate of fitness, identification marker, or vehicle registration is held or sought;

5. Having been found, through a judicial or administrative hearing, to have committed fraudulent or deceptive acts in connection with the business for which a license or certificate of fitness is held or sought or any consumer-related fraud;

6. Having been convicted of any criminal act involving the business for which a license or certificate of fitness is held or sought;

7. Improper leasing, renting, lending, or otherwise allowing the improper use of a license, certificate of fitness, identification marker, or vehicle registration;

8. Having been convicted of a felony;

9. Having been convicted of any misdemeanor involving lying, cheating, stealing, or moral turpitude;

10. Failure to submit to the Department any tax, fees, dues, fines, or penalties owed to the Department;

11. Failure to furnish the Department information, documentation, or records required or requested pursuant to statute or regulation;

12. Knowingly and willfully filing any false report, account, record, or memorandum;

13. Failure to meet or maintain application certifications or requirements of character, fitness, and financial responsibility pursuant to this chapter;

14. Willfully altering or changing the appearance or wording of any license, certificate, identification marker, license plate, or vehicle registration;

15. Failure to provide services in accordance with license or certificate of fitness terms, limitations, conditions, or requirements;

16. Failure to maintain and keep on file with the Department motor carrier liability insurance or cargo insurance, issued by a company licensed to do business in the Commonwealth, or a bond, certificate of insurance, certificate of self-insurance, or unconditional letter of credit in accordance with this chapter, with respect to each motor vehicle operated in the Commonwealth;

17. Failure to comply with the Workers' Compensation Act of Title 65.2;

18. Failure to properly register a motor vehicle under this title;

19. Failure to comply with any federal motor carrier statute, rule, or regulation; or

20. Inactivity of a motor carrier as may be evidenced by the absence of a motor vehicle registered to operate under such certificate or permit for a period of greater than three months.

History.

2001, c. 596; 2011, cc. 881, 889; 2013, cc. 165, 582.

§ 46.2-2134. Grounds for denying, suspending, or revoking permits.

A permit issued under this chapter may be denied, suspended, or revoked on any one or more of the following grounds:

1. Failure to submit to the Department any tax, fees, fines, or penalties owed to the Department.

2. Failure to maintain and keep on file with the Department motor carrier liability insurance or cargo insurance, issued by a company licensed to do business in the Commonwealth, or a bond, certificate of insurance, certificate of self-insurance, or unconditional letter of credit in accordance with this chapter, with respect to each motor vehicle operated in the Commonwealth.

3. Inactivity of a motor carrier as may be evidenced by the absence of a motor vehicle registered to operate under such permit or certificate for a period of greater than three months.

History.

2001, c. 596.

§ 46.2-2135. Altering or amending licenses, permits, or certificates.

The Department may alter or amend a license, permit, or certificate of fitness at the request of a licensee, permittee, or certificate holder, or upon a finding by the Department that a licensee, permittee, or certificate holder failed to observe any of the provisions within this chapter, or any of the rules or regulations of the Department, or any term, condition, or limitation of such license or certificate.

History.

2001, c. 596; 2011, cc. 881, 889.

§ 46.2-2136. Suspension, revocation, and refusal to renew license, permit, or certificate; notice and hearing.

A. Except as provided in subsection D of this section, unless otherwise provided in this chapter, no license, permit, or certificate of fitness issued under this chapter shall be suspended or revoked, or renewal thereof refused, unless the licensee, permittee, or certificate holder has been furnished a written copy of the complaint against him and the grounds upon which the action is taken and has been offered an opportunity for an administrative hearing to show cause why such action should not be taken.

B. The order suspending, revoking, or denying renewal of a license, permit, or certificate of fitness shall not become effective until the licensee, permittee, or certificate holder has, after notice of the opportunity for a hearing, had thirty days to make a written request for such a hearing. If no hearing has been requested within such thirty-day period, the order shall become effective and no hearing shall thereafter be held. A timely request for a hearing shall automatically stay operation of the order until after the hearing.

C. Notice of an order suspending, revoking, or denying renewal of a license, permit, or certificate of fitness and an opportunity for a hearing shall be mailed to the licensee, permittee, or certificate holder by registered or certified mail at the address as shown on the license, permit, or certificate or other record of information in possession of the Department and shall be considered served when mailed.

D. If the Department makes a finding, after conducting a preliminary investigation, that the conduct of a licensee, permittee, or certificate holder (i) is in violation of this chapter or regulations adopted pursuant to this chapter and (ii) such violation constitutes a danger to public safety, the Department may issue an order suspending the license, permit, or certificate. Notice of the suspension shall be in writing and mailed in accordance with subsection C of this section. Upon receipt of a request for a hearing appealing the suspension, the licensee, permittee, or certificate holder shall be afforded the opportunity for a hearing within thirty days. The suspension shall remain in effect pending the outcome of the hearing.

History.
2001, c. 596; 2011, cc. 881, 889.

§ 46.2-2137. Basis for reinstatement of suspended licenses, permits, or certificates; reinstatement fees.

A. The Department shall reinstate any license, permit, or certificate suspended pursuant to this chapter provided the grounds upon which the suspension action was taken have been satisfied and the appropriate reinstatement fee and other applicable fees have been paid to the Department.

B. The reinstatement fee for suspensions issued pursuant to this chapter shall be fifty dollars. In the event multiple credentials have been suspended under this chapter for the same violation only one reinstatement fee shall be applicable.

C. In addition to a reinstatement fee, a fee of $500 shall be paid for failure of a motor carrier to keep in force at all times insurance, a bond or bonds, in an amount required by this chapter. Any motor carrier who applies for a new license, permit, or certificate because his prior license, permit, or certificate was revoked for failure to keep in force at all times insurance, a bond or bonds, in an amount required by this chapter, shall also be subject to a fee of $500.

History.
2001, c. 596; 2011, cc. 881, 889.

§ 46.2-2138. Basis for relicensure after revocation of licenses, permits, or certificates; fees.

The Department shall not accept an application for a license, permit, or certificate from an applicant where such credentials have been revoked pursuant to this chapter until the period of revocation imposed by the Department has passed. The Department shall process such applications under the same provisions, procedures and requirements as an original application for such license, permit, or certificate. The Department shall issue such license, permit, or certificate provided the applicant has met all the appropriate qualifications and requirements, has satisfied the grounds upon which the revocation action was taken, and has paid the appropriate application or filing fees to the Department.

History.
2001, c. 596.

§ 46.2-2139. Surrender of identification marker, license plate, and registration card; removal by law enforcement; operation of vehicle denied.

A. It shall be unlawful for a licensee, permittee, or certificate holder whose license, permit, or certificate has expired or been revoked or suspended or whose renewal thereof has been denied pursuant to this chapter to fail or refuse to surrender, on demand, to the Department license plates, identification markers, and registration cards issued under this title.

B. It shall be unlawful for a vehicle owner who is not the holder of a valid permit or certificate or whose vehicle is not validly leased to a motor carrier holding an active permit or certificate to fail or refuse to surrender to the Department on demand license plates, identification markers, and registration cards issued under this title.

C. If any law-enforcement officer finds that a vehicle bearing Virginia license plates or temporary transport plates is in violation of subsection A or B, such law-enforcement officer may remove the license plate or plates, identification marker, and registration card. If a law-enforcement officer removes a license plate, identification marker, or registration card, he shall forward such license plate, identification marker, and registration card to the Department.

D. When informed that a motor carrier vehicle is being operated in violation of this section, the driver shall drive the vehicle to a nearby location off the public highways and not remove it or allow it to be moved until the motor carrier is in compliance with all provisions of this chapter.

History.
2001, c. 596; 2015, c. 258.

§ 46.2-2140. Title to plates and markers.

All registration cards and identification markers issued by the Department shall remain the property of the Department.

History.
2001, c. 596.

ARTICLE 2.
INSURANCE REQUIREMENTS.

§ 46.2-2141. Application of article.

Unless otherwise stated, this article shall apply to all motor carriers as defined under this chapter.

History.
2001, c. 596.

§ 46.2-2142. Bonds or insurance to be kept in force; amounts.

Each motor carrier shall keep in force at all times insurance, a bond or bonds, in an amount required by this article.

History.
2001, c. 596.

§ 46.2-2143. Surety bonds, insurance, letter of credit or securities required prior to issuance of registration.

No certificate of fitness, permit, identification marker, registration card, or license plate shall be issued by the Department to any vehicle operated by a motor carrier until the motor carrier certifies to the Department that the vehicle is covered by one or more of the following, in the amount or amounts set forth in § 46.2-2143.1:

1. An insurance policy or bond;
2. A certificate of insurance in lieu of the insurance policy or bond, certifying that such policy or bond covers the liability of such motor carrier in accordance with the provisions of this article, is issued by an authorized insurer, or in the case of bonds, is in an amount approved by the Department. The bonds may be issued by the Commonwealth of Virginia, the United States of America, or any municipality in the Commonwealth. Such bonds shall be deposited with the State Treasurer and the surety shall not be reduced except in accordance with an order of the Department;
3. An unconditional letter of credit, issued by a bank doing business in Virginia, for an amount approved by the Department. The letter of credit shall be in effect so long as the motor carrier operates motor vehicles in the Commonwealth; or
4. In the case of a lessor who acts as a registrant for purposes of consolidating lessees' vehicle registration applications, a statement that the registrant has, before leasing a vehicle, obtained from the lessee an insurance policy, bond, or certificate of insurance in lieu of the insurance policy or bond and can make available said proof of insurance coverage upon demand.

Vehicles belonging to carriers who have filed proof of financial responsibility in accordance with the single state registration system authorized by 49 U.S.C. § 14504 or the unified carrier registration system authorized by 49 U.S.C. § 14504a are deemed to have fulfilled the requirements of this article for insurance purposes, provided there is on board the vehicle a copy of an insurance receipt issued pursuant to the federal regulations promulgated pursuant to 49 U.S.C. § 14504 or 14504a. The Department is further authorized to issue single state registration system or unified carrier registration system receipts to any qualified carrier as well as to collect and disperse the fees for and to qualified jurisdictions.

History.
2001, c. 596; 2006, c. 208; 2011, cc. 881, 889; 2012, c. 638.

§ 46.2-2143.1. Insurance requirement for motor carriers.

A. All motor carriers shall keep in force at all times insurance, a bond, or bonds in an amount required by this section.

B. The minimum public liability financial responsibility requirements for motor carriers operating in intrastate commerce shall be $750,000. The minimum insurance for motor carriers operating in interstate commerce shall equal the minimum required by federal law, rule, or regulation.

C. The minimum cargo insurance required for motor carriers operating in intrastate commerce shall be $50,000. Motor carriers engaged exclusively in the transportation of bulk commodities shall not be required to file any cargo insurance, bond, or bonds for cargo liability.

D. Any motor carrier that meets the minimum federal financial responsibility requirements and also operates in intrastate commerce may submit, in lieu of a separate filing for its intrastate operation pursuant to § 46.2-2143, proof of the minimum federal limits, provided that (i) both interstate and intrastate operations are insured, (ii) the public liability filed is at least $750,000, and (iii) any cargo insurance requirements of this section have been met.

History.
2012, c. 638.

§ 46.2-2144. Policies or surety bonds to be filed with the Department and securities with State Treasurer.

A. Each motor carrier shall keep on file with the Department proof of an insurance policy or bond in accordance with this article. Record of the policy or bond shall remain in the files of the Department six months after the certificate of fitness, registration card, license plate, identification marker or permit is canceled for any cause. If federal, state, or municipal bonds are deposited with the State Treasurer in lieu of an insurance policy, the bonds shall remain deposited until six months after the registration card, license plate, certificate, permit or identification marker is canceled for any cause unless otherwise ordered by the Department.

B. The Department may, without holding a hearing, suspend a permit or certificate of fitness if the permittee or certificate holder fails to comply with the requirements of this section.

History.
2001, c. 596; 2011, cc. 881, 889.

§ 46.2-2145. Condition or obligation of security.

The insurance, bond or other security provided for in § 46.2-2144 shall obligate the insurer or surety to pay any final judgment for (i) damages sustained by the shippers or consignees for injury to any passenger or passengers or for loss or damage to property entrusted to such motor carrier when a cargo policy is required and (ii) any and all injuries to persons and loss of or damage to property resulting from the negligent operation of any motor vehicle.

History.
2001, c. 596.

§ 46.2-2146. Effect of unfair claims settlement practices on self-insured motor carriers.

The provisions of subdivisions 4, 6, 11 and 12 of subsection A of § 38.2-510 shall apply to each holder of a certificate of fitness or permit issued by and under the authority of the Department who, in lieu of filing an insurance policy, has deposited with the State Treasurer state, federal or municipal bonds or has filed an unconditional letter of credit issued by a bank. The failure of any such holder of a certificate or permit to comply with the provisions of § 38.2-510 shall be the cause for revocation or suspension of the certificate or permit.

History.
2001, c. 596; 2011, cc. 881, 889.

ARTICLE 3.
PROPERTY CARRIERS.

§ 46.2-2147. Certain household goods carriers exempted from article.

Household goods carriers transporting solely household goods under a certificate of fitness issued pursuant to this chapter are exempt from the provisions of this article.

History.
2001, c. 596; 2011, cc. 881, 889.

§ 46.2-2148. Required permit.

No property carrier, unless otherwise exempted, shall transport property on any highway within the Commonwealth on an intrastate basis without first having obtained from the Department a permit authorizing such operation.

History.
2001, c. 596.

ARTICLE 4.
HOUSEHOLD GOODS CARRIERS.

§ 46.2-2149. Certain household goods carriers exempt from certain provisions of article.

Household goods carriers transporting household goods for a lesser distance than thirty-one road miles are exempt from this article except the provisions of § 46.2-2168.

History.
2001, c. 596.

§ 46.2-2150. Required certificates of fitness.

No household goods carrier, unless otherwise exempted, shall engage in intrastate operations on any highway within the Commonwealth without first having obtained from the Department a certificate of fitness authorizing such operation.

History.
2001, c. 596; 2011, cc. 881, 889.

§ 46.2-2151. Considerations for determination of issuance of certificate.

In determining whether the certificate of fitness required by this article shall be granted, the Department may, among other things, consider the provisions of § 46.2-2108.6, the applicant's character and fitness, and the applicant's compliance with federal, state, and local taxes.

History.
2001, c. 596; 2011, cc. 881, 889.

§ 46.2-2152. Control by Department.

Every household goods carrier is hereby declared to be subject to control, supervision and regulation by the Department.

History.
2001, c. 596.

§ 46.2-2153. Provisions of chapter controlling.

As to household goods carriers, the provisions of this chapter shall be controlling, and no laws in conflict herewith, or inconsistent herewith, shall have any application to such carriers.

History.
2001, c. 596.

§ 46.2-2154. Discontinuance of service.

Notwithstanding anything contained in this chapter to the contrary, no household goods carrier shall abandon or discontinue either temporarily or permanently any service established under the provisions of this chapter without permission of the Department and on such terms as the Department may prescribe.

History.
2001, c. 596.

§ 46.2-2155. Power and duty of Department.

The Department shall regulate and control all household goods carriers not herein exempted, doing business in the Commonwealth, in all matters relating to the performance of their duties as such carriers and their rates and charges therefor, which rates and charges shall be filed with and subject to approval by the Department by individual household goods carriers or by groups of such carriers, and correct abuses by such carriers. To that end the Department may prescribe reasonable rules, regulations, bills of lading, forms and reports for such carriers to administer and enforce the provisions of this chapter. The Department shall have the right at all times to require from such carriers special reports and statements, under oath, concerning their business. It shall make and enforce such requirements, rules, and regulations as may be necessary to prevent unjust or unreasonable discriminations by any such carrier. The Department may prescribe and enforce such reasonable requirements, rules and regulations in the matter of leasing of motor vehicles as are necessary to prevent evasion of the Department's regulatory powers.

The Department shall work in conjunction with the Department of State Police and local law-enforcement officials to promote uniform enforcement of the laws pertaining to motor carriers and the rules, regulations, forms, and reports prescribed under the provisions of this chapter.

History.
2001, c. 596; 2011, cc. 881, 889; 2012, cc. 22, 111.

§ 46.2-2156. Solicitation, booking, registration by other persons prohibited; storage-in-transit.

A. No person except a certificated household goods carrier, its parent, or its wholly owned subsidiary company, or other entity under complete ownership, or an employee of the above certificated carrier may solicit, book or register a shipment of household goods moving intrastate and only in the name of that certificated carrier.

B. No person or employee of a certificated or a noncertificated carrier may act as an employee, representative, or agent for another certificated carrier for purpose of soliciting, booking or registering an intrastate shipment except as provided in subsection A of this section. No person or employee of a certificated carrier who solicits, books or registers intrastate shipments may be employed by a noncertificated carrier.

C. A certificated household goods carrier may utilize the services of another certificated household goods carrier or a permitted property carrier that has complied with the minimum cargo insurance requirements of this chapter for storage and final delivery on storage-in-transit shipments at destination. A property carrier who does not hold a household goods certificate of fitness is prohibited from delivering a shipment for a greater distance than thirty road miles from the warehouse. The shipment must move on the bill of lading of the originating certificated household goods carrier with the delivering certificated household goods carrier or property carrier shown on the bill of lading. The legal liability of the shipment remains the responsibility of the originating certificated household goods carrier.

D. A household goods carrier may interchange or interline shipments with any other certificated household goods carrier provided both carriers hold proper authority to transport the shipment from origin to destination. The shipment must move on the bill of lading of the originating certificated household goods carrier with the delivering certificated household goods carrier shown on the bill of lading. The legal liability of the shipment remains the responsibility of the originating certificated household goods carrier.

History.
2001, c. 596; 2011, cc. 881, 889.

§ 46.2-2157. Estimate of charges; penalties; information booklet for shippers.

A. Household goods carriers may, upon request of a shipper, cause to be given to such shipper an estimate of the charges for proposed services in the manner and form specified in this section:

1. The estimate may be made only after a visual inspection of the goods by the estimator or be based upon information furnished to the carrier by the shipper.

2. If a written estimate is furnished, across the top of each form there shall be imprinted, in bold type, the words "ESTIMATED COST OF SERVICES."

3. The name, address and phone number of the carrier providing the estimate must be shown in a legible manner on each estimate form.

4. Imprinted thereunder in regular type shall be words to the effect "IMPORTANT NOTICE: This estimate covers only the articles and services listed. It is not a guarantee that the actual charges will not exceed the amount of the estimate. However, carriers may bind the estimate and guarantee that charges may not exceed the bound estimate except for any accessorial tariff charges incurred at destination that are not known to the carrier until actual delivery of the shipment and a sight survey reveals that additional charges are necessary to effect delivery as published in the carrier's tariff. Household goods carriers are required by law to collect transportation and other incidental charges computed on the basis of rates shown in their lawfully published tariffs. Charges for additional services will be added to the transportation charges."

5. The original or a true legible copy of each estimate form prepared in accordance with this section may be delivered to the shipper and a copy thereof shall be maintained by the carrier as part of its record of shipment.

B. If the carrier provides a shipper with a written estimate, the carrier will give to the shipper an information booklet that has been approved by the Department and will obtain a receipt therefor from the shipper. Such receipt will become a part of the permanent file of the carrier.

History.
2001, c. 596; 2006, c. 609.

§ 46.2-2158. Bill of lading.

A. A bill of lading shall be issued.

B. A bill of lading shall contain the following information:

1. Name, address and telephone number of the household goods carrier.

2. Agreed pick-up period of time, the actual pick-up date and agreed delivery date or the agreed period of time within which delivery of the shipment is expected at destination.

3. True copies of the gross and tare weight tickets shall be attached to the bill of lading as soon as such weight tickets are obtained. If the shipper is present at the weighing, he shall then be given a copy of the gross and tare weight tickets upon request, otherwise, he shall be given a copy thereof at destination upon request.

4. The number of the vehicle onto which the shipment is loaded.

5. Amount of charges and method of payment of total tariff charges.

6. Total amount required to be paid in cash, postal money order, traveler's check, cashier's check, bank treasurer's check, bank wire transfer, or approved credit card to relinquish possession of a C.O.D. shipment.

History.
2001, c. 596; 2006, c. 609.

§ 46.2-2159. Freight bill or freight bill/bill of lading.

A. There shall be furnished by every household goods carrier at destination to the consignee of every C.O.D. shipment transported by him a freight bill, if a combination freight bill/bill of lading is not used, which bill shall contain the following information: point of origin, point of destination, date of shipment, description of article or commodity, weight of article or commodity rate, or rates applicable for the service rendered, statement of nature and amounts of charges for special services, where charges incurred, and method of payment of total tariff charges.

B. If a carrier uses a uniform household goods bill of lading and freight bill, subsection A of this section shall not apply.

History.
2001, c. 596.

§ 46.2-2160. Bill of lading kept in vehicle; preserved in office.

With every motor vehicle transporting household goods there shall be carried with such property on the same vehicle a copy of the bill of lading of all such property, which shall indicate the consignor, consignee, origin, destination and weight of each shipment on the motor vehicle. The original or a copy of the bill of lading shall be preserved in the office of such carrier for a period of at least three years.

History.
2001, c. 596.

§ 46.2-2161. Payment of tariff charges; payment of specific charges.

A. The carrier will not deliver or relinquish possession of any property transported by it until all tariff rates and charges thereon have been paid in cash, postal money order, traveler's check, cashier's check, bank treasurer's check, bank wire transfer, or approved credit card, except where other satisfactory arrangements have been made between the carrier and the consignor or consignee.

B. Carrier may require prepayment of charges for a specific service in full or in part on or before commencing performance of such services as requested by shipper.

C. Estimated charges may be bound or fixed so that the price estimated may not be exceeded with the exception that any accessorial tariff charges incurred at destination that are not known to the carrier until actual delivery of the shipment and a sight survey reveals that additional charges are necessary to effect delivery as published in the carrier's tariff.

History.

2001, c. 596; 2006, c. 609.

§ 46.2-2162. Carrier liability.

A. No delivery acknowledgement on any shipping document to be signed by the consignee at time of delivery shall contain any language that purports to release or discharge the carrier or its agents from liability, other than a statement that the property has been received in apparent good condition except as noted on the shipping documents.

B. Household goods carriers shall not assume any liability in excess of that for which they are legally liable under their lawful bills of lading and published tariffs.

C. Household goods carriers shall not advertise or represent to the public that "all loads are insured" or other similar wording, unless such carrier has filed tariffs with the Department, assuming complete liability, and has filed evidence of insurance with the Department providing protection covering all shipments to their full value without limitation and insuring against every peril to which any shipment may be exposed.

D. Shipper or his representative will acknowledge that the property has been received in apparent good condition except as noted on the shipping documents at time of delivery.

History.

2001, c. 596.

§ 46.2-2163. Determination of weights by certified scales.

A. Each household goods carrier shall determine the tare weight of each vehicle used by having it weighed prior to, if practicable, the loading of each shipment under the following conditions:

1. By a certified weighmaster or on a certified scale, and

2. The vehicle shall contain all pads, chains, dollies, handtrucks and other equipment needed in the transportation of shipments to be loaded thereon.

B. After the vehicle has been loaded it shall be weighed under the following conditions:

1. At the certified scale nearest to the point of origin of the shipment, if practicable, and

2. The vehicle shall contain all pads, chains, dollies, handtrucks and other equipment needed in the transportation of shipments to be loaded thereon.

C. The net weight of the shipment shall be determined by deducting the tare weight from the gross weight and such weight shall be entered on the bill of lading.

D. Where no certified scale is available at the point of origin, the gross weight shall be obtained at the nearest certified scale either in the direction of the movement of the shipment or in the direction of the next pick-up or delivery in the case of partial loads.

In the transportation of partial loads, this section shall apply in all respects, except that the gross weight of a vehicle containing one or more partial loads shall be used as the tare weight of such vehicle as to partial loads subsequently loaded thereon.

E. The person paying the freight charges, or his representative upon request of either, shall be permitted without charge to accompany, in his own conveyance, the carrier to the weighing station and to observe the weighing of his shipment after loading.

The carrier shall use a certified scale that will permit the shipper to observe the weighing of his shipment without causing delay.

F. The provisions of this section shall not apply to bound or fixed estimates provided in accordance with the provisions of § 46.2-2161.

History.

2001, c. 596; 2006, c. 609.

§ 46.2-2164. Constructive weight.

If no certified scale is available at origin, at any point enroute, or at destination, a constructive weight based upon seven pounds per cubic foot of properly loaded van space may be used.

History.

2001, c. 596.

§ 46.2-2165. Obtaining weight tickets.

The carrier shall obtain a weight ticket signed by the weighmaster or its driver for each weighing required under this section, with tare and gross weights evidenced by separate tickets, and the driver shall enter thereon the number of the bill of lading or shipper's name. No other alterations shall be made on any such ticket.

1. As soon as weight tickets are obtained, true copies thereof shall be attached to the bill of lading

accompanying the shipment and retained in the carrier's file.

2. If a shipper requests, a true copy of each weight ticket pertaining to a shipment shall be given to the shipper at the weighing station if the shipper is present or upon delivery of the shipment if the shipper is not present at the weighing.

3. Any of the following shipments may be weighed on a certified scale or by a certified weighmaster prior to being loaded on the vehicle:

a. A part load for any one shipper not exceeding 1,000 pounds;

b. An automobile or other article weighing in excess of 500 pounds, which is mounted on wheels;

c. A shipment that the carrier containerizes for further transportation, in which case the net weight of the shipment shall be the gross weight of the container less the tare weight of the container. The gross weight of the container shall be as packed and prepared for shipment and the tare weight of the container shall include all of the pads, skins, blocking and bracing used, or to be used, to protect the contents of the container, but not including packing materials used in the preliminary packing of the shipment.

History.
2001, c. 596.

§ 46.2-2166. Minimum weight shipments, notice.

No carrier shall accept an order for a shipment for transportation that appears to be subject to the minimum weight provisions of the carrier's tariff without first having advised the shipper of such minimum weight provisions.

History.
2001, c. 596.

§ 46.2-2167. Reweighing of shipment.

The household goods carrier, upon request of the shipper or his representative made prior to the delivery, shall reweigh the shipment subject to the availability of scales at destination.

1. The household goods carrier shall inform the person requesting the reweigh, within a reasonable time prior to the gross reweighing, of the tariff charges therefor and the location of a certified scale in close proximity to the destination of the shipment that shall be used, and of the right of the shipper, or his representative, to observe the gross and tare reweighing.

2. The household goods carrier, without altering or deleting the initial weights, shall cause to be recorded on the bill of lading the gross, tare and net weights on reweigh, and shall give the shipper, or his representative, original or true copies of the weight tickets on reweigh in the same manner as prescribed in subdivision 2 of § 46.2-2165 for initial weighing.

3. The lower of the two net scale weights shall be used for determining the applicable charges.

4. The household goods carrier may publish in its tariff a reasonable charge for reweighing shipments, which charge shall be applicable when the reweigh develops a net scale weight in excess of the initial net scale weight or if the difference between the initial net scale weight and the reweight net scale weight is less than 100 pounds on a shipment weighing 5,000 pounds or less or two percent or less of the lower net scale weight on shipments in excess of 5,000 pounds.

History.
2001, c. 596.

§ 46.2-2168. Claims.

A. Every household goods carrier that receives a written claim for loss of or damage to property transported by it shall:

1. Acknowledge receipt of such claim in writing to the claimant within thirty calendar days after its receipt by the carrier. The carrier shall, at the time such claim is received, cause the date of receipt to be recorded on the claim;

2. Pay, decline or make a firm compromise settlement offer in writing to the claimant within 120 days after receipt of the claim by the carrier or its agent.

B. If the claim cannot be processed and disposed of within 120 days after the receipt thereof, the carrier shall, at that time and the expiration of each succeeding thirty-day period while the claim remains pending, advise the claimant in writing of the status of the claim and the reasons for the delay in making final disposition thereof.

C. No household goods carrier shall provide by contract or otherwise a shorter period for the filing of loss and damage claims than thirty calendar days, and for the institution of suits than two years, such period for institution of suits to be computed from the day when notice in writing is given by the carrier to the claimant that the carrier has disallowed the claim or any part or parts thereof specified in the notice.

History.
2001, c. 596.

§ 46.2-2169. Tariffs showing rates and charges, etc.

Every household goods carrier by motor vehicle shall file with the Department at least thirty days before the effective date and make available for public inspection, tariffs showing all the rates and charges for transportation, and all services in connection therewith. Such rates and charges shall be stated in terms of lawful money of the United States. The tariffs required by this section shall be published, filed, and posted in such form and manner, and shall contain such information as the Department may prescribe. The Department is authorized to reject any tariff filed with it that is not in consonance with this section and with such regulations. Any tariff so rejected by the Department shall be void, and its use shall be unlawful.

History.
2001, c. 596.

§ 46.2-2170. Unlawful to charge other than published tariff.

No household goods carrier shall charge or demand or collect or receive a greater compensation for transportation or for any service in connection therewith than the rates and charges specified in the tariffs in effect at the time.

History.
2001, c. 596; 2006, c. 609.

§ 46.2-2171. Changes in tariffs.

No change shall be made in any rate or charge, or any rule, regulation, or practice affecting such rate or charge, or the value of the service thereunder, specified in any effective tariff of a household goods carrier, except after thirty days' notice of the proposed change. Such notice shall plainly state the change proposed to be made and the time when such change will take effect. The Department may, in its discretion and for good cause shown, allow such change upon notice less than that herein specified or modify the requirements of this section with respect to posting and filing of tariffs.

History.
2001, c. 596.

§ 46.2-2172. Joint tariffs; power of attorney.

A. A household goods carrier may authorize an agent or may join with another carrier or carriers in the publication of a joint tariff, supplement or amendment, and, where such authority is given, shall file with the Department prior to publication power of attorney or notice of concurrence, which shall specifically set out the authority given.

B. Where a household goods carrier issues a power of attorney to an agent or a concurrence to another carrier for the publication of tariffs, such power of attorney or concurrence may not be revoked except upon sixty days' notice to the Department and the agent or carrier to which the power of attorney or concurrence was issued, except upon special permission of the Department.

History.
2001, c. 596.

§ 46.2-2173. Tariff contents.

Tariff contents shall contain certain information:

1. Table of contents, arranged in alphabetical order, showing the number of the page and/or item number on which each subject may be found. If a tariff contains so small a volume of matter that its title page or interior arrangement plainly discloses its contents, the table of contents may be omitted.

2. A complete list of all carriers participating in the tariff, or reference to the governing publication which participation is shown.

3. A complete index of all commodities on which specific rates are named therein, together with reference to the page and/or items in which they are shown. No index need be shown in tariffs of less than five pages, or if all the rates to each destination are alphabetically arranged by commodities.

4. Explanations of all notes, abbreviations, symbols and reference marks used in tariff.

5. Rules that govern in clear and explicit terms, setting forth all privileges and services covered.

6. Any exceptions to the application of rates named, and non-application of rates named therein.

7. All line haul transportation rates shall be explicitly stated in dollars and cents.

8. Household goods carriers shall establish the charge to be made for each accessorial or terminal service rendered in connection with the shipment. The tariff shall separately state each service to be rendered and the charge therefor.

a. The charges for packing and unpacking shall be stated in amounts per container or per hundred weight.

b. An hourly labor charge may be established to cover miscellaneous labor services performed at the request of the shipper when a rate is not separately stated for the service requested.

9. Tariffs based on distances from point of origin to destination shall show the mileages or indicate a definite method by which such mileages shall be determined.

History.
2001, c. 596; 2006, c. 609.

ARTICLE 5.

BROKERS.

§ 46.2-2174. Regulation of brokers.

The Department shall regulate brokers and make and enforce reasonable requirements respecting their licenses, financial responsibility, accounts, records, reports, operations and practices.

History.
2001, c. 596.

§ 46.2-2175. Broker's license required.

No person shall for compensation sell or offer for sale transportation subject to this chapter or shall make any contract, agreement, or arrangement to provide, procure, furnish, or arrange for such transportation or shall hold himself out by advertisement, solicitation, or otherwise as one who sells, provides, procures, contracts, or arranges for such transportation, unless such person holds a broker's license issued by the Department to engage in such transactions; however, the provisions of this section shall not apply to any carrier holding a certificate or permit under the provisions of this chapter or to any bona fide employee or agent of such motor carrier, so far as concerns transportation to be furnished wholly by such carrier or jointly with other motor carriers holding like certificates or permits.

History.
2001, c. 596.

§ 46.2-2176. Broker's license not substitute for other certificates or permits.

No person who holds a broker's license under this article shall engage in transportation subject to this chapter unless he holds a certificate or permit as provided in this chapter. In the execution of any contract, agreement, or arrangement to sell, provide, procure, furnish, or arrange for such transportation, it shall be unlawful for such person to employ any carrier by motor vehicle who is not the lawful holder of an effective certificate or permit issued as provided in this chapter or when such certificate or permit does not authorize the carrier to perform the service being acquired.

History.
2001, c. 596; 2013, cc. 165, 582.

CHAPTER 22.

REGULATION OF SIGHT-SEEING CARRIERS.

§§ 46.2-2200 through 46.2-2209: Repealed by Acts 2001, c. 596, cl. 2, effective July 1, 2002.

Cross references.
As to present provisions concerning sight-seeing carriers, see § 46.2-2099.4 et seq. and § 46.2-2099.21 et seq.

CHAPTER 23.

REGULATION OF SPECIAL OR CHARTER PARTY CARRIERS.

§§ 46.2-2300 through 46.2-2312: Repealed by Acts 2001, c. 596, cl. 2, effective July 1, 2002.

Cross references.
As to present provisions concerning special or charter carriers by boat, see § 46.2-2099.21 et seq.

CHAPTER 23.1.

EXCURSION TRAINS.

§§ 46.2-2313 through 46.2-2316: Repealed by Acts 2001, c. 596, cl. 2, effective July 1, 2002.

Cross references.
As to present provisions governing excursion trains, see § 46.2-2099.41 et seq.

CHAPTER 24.

REGULATION OF CARRIERS BY MOTOR LAUNCH.

§§ 46.2-2400 through 46.2-2409: Repealed by Acts 2001, c. 596, cl. 2, effective July 1, 2002.

Cross references.
As to present provisions concerning motor carriers by launch, see § 46.2-2099.31 et seq.

CHAPTER 25.

REGULATION OF LIMOUSINES AND EXECUTIVE SEDANS.

§§ 46.2-2500 through 46.2-2519: Repealed by Acts 2001, c. 596, cl. 2, effective July 1, 2002.

CHAPTER 26.

REGULATION OF SIGHT-SEEING CARRIERS BY BOAT.

§§ 46.2-2600 through 46.2-2610: Repealed by Acts 2001, c. 596, cl. 2, effective July 1, 2002.

Cross references.
As to present provisions governing sight-seeing carriers by boat, see § 46.2-2099.21 et seq.

CHAPTER 27.

VIRGINIA MOTOR VEHICLE EMISSIONS REDUCTION PROGRAM.

§§ 46.2-2700 through 46.2-2703: Repealed by Acts 1997, c. 117.

CHAPTER 28.

BOARD OF TOWING AND RECOVERY OPERATORS.

§§ **46.2-2800 through 46.2-2828:** Repealed by Acts 2012, cc. 803 and 835, cl. 107, effective January 1, 2013.

CHAPTER 29.

CERTIFIED ESCORT VEHICLE DRIVERS.

§ 46.2-2900. Definitions.

As used in this chapter, the following words and terms shall have the following meaning unless the context clearly indicates otherwise:

"Certified escort vehicle driver" means a person 18 years of age or older who holds a valid driver's license and a valid escort vehicle driver certificate issued (i) by the Commonwealth or (ii) by a state whose escort vehicle driver certification program has been determined to be substantially similar to the Commonwealth's and to which the Commonwealth has extended reciprocity.

"Escort vehicle driver certificate" means a credential issued under the laws of the Commonwealth or other state authorizing the holder to escort a permitted vehicle or vehicles.

"Permitted vehicle or vehicles" means any vehicle being operated under the provisions of a valid highway hauling permit issued pursuant to § 46.2-1139 that requires that the permitted vehicle or vehicles be accompanied by a certified escort vehicle driver or drivers.

History.
2013, cc. 312, 477; 2015, c. 258.

§ 46.2-2901. Certificate required.

No person shall escort any vehicle that is being moved by authority of a valid highway hauling permit requiring a certified escort vehicle driver and issued pursuant to § 46.2-1139 unless such person holds a valid driver's license and a valid escort vehicle driver certificate issued by the Commonwealth or another state that has a reciprocal agreement with the Commonwealth recognizing escort vehicle driver certificates issued by that state.

An escort vehicle driver certificate shall be deemed invalid if the certificate holder's driver's license has expired or has been suspended, revoked, or canceled.

History.
2013, cc. 312, 477.

§ 46.2-2902. Insurance to be kept in force; amount.

Each person or company providing certified escort vehicle services shall keep in force at all times valid liability insurance coverage for those classes of insurance defined in §§ 38.2-117 and 38.2-118 in the amount of at least $750,000 that has been issued by an insurance carrier authorized to do business in the Commonwealth.

History.
2013, cc. 312, 477.

§ 46.2-2903. Eligibility for escort vehicle driver certificate.

A Virginia escort vehicle driver certificate shall be issued only to a person who intends to provide certified vehicle escort services for a permitted vehicle and who (i) holds a valid Virginia driver's license and who is domiciled in the Commonwealth or (ii) is a nonresident who meets the requirements of § 46.2-2907 or 46.2-2908.

No person shall be eligible for a Virginia escort vehicle driver certificate until he has (i) passed the applicable training course and knowledge test required by this chapter and has satisfied all other applicable requirements imposed by the laws of the Commonwealth or (ii) has met the requirements of § 46.2-2907 or 46.2-2908.

No person shall be eligible for a Virginia escort vehicle driver certificate during any period in which his driver's license or privilege to drive is expired or is suspended, revoked, or canceled in any state or during any period wherein the restoration of his license or privilege is contingent upon the furnishing of proof of financial responsibility.

History.
2013, cc. 312, 477.

§ 46.2-2904. Certified escort vehicle driver training.

Every applicant for a Virginia escort vehicle driver certificate shall undergo and successfully complete an eight-hour training course presented by a business, organization, governmental entity, or individual that has been approved by the Department and that offers a course approved by the Department.

History.
2013, cc. 312, 477.

§ 46.2-2905. Knowledge test; waiting period prior to reexamination.

The Department shall examine every applicant for an escort vehicle driver certificate before issuing a Virginia escort vehicle driver certificate. Every applicant shall be required to take and pass an escort vehicle driver knowledge test. Prior to taking the knowledge test, the applicant shall present evidence that he has completed a state-approved escort vehicle driver certification training course pursuant to the provisions of § 46.2-2904.

Any person who applies for an escort vehicle driver certificate under § 46.2-2906 and fails the knowledge test administered pursuant to that section three times shall not be eligible for retesting for at least 30 days. A reexamination fee of $2 shall be charged for the second and subsequent test in the same manner as provided for driver license testing under the provisions of § 46.2-332.

History.
2013, cc. 312, 477.

§ 46.2-2906. Application for escort vehicle driver certificate; driving record; proof of completion of escort vehicle driver training; fee.

A. Every application for an escort vehicle driver certificate shall be made on a form prescribed by the Department, and the applicant shall write his usual signature in ink in the space provided on the form. A person who applies for an escort vehicle driver certificate must meet the following requirements:

1. Be at least 18 years of age;
2. Hold a valid Virginia driver's license or a valid driver's license for another state;
3. Authorize the Department to review his driving record;
4. Present satisfactory proof of successful completion of an eight-hour escort vehicle driver certification training course, as required by § 46.2-2904;
5. Pass the escort vehicle driver certification knowledge test as required by § 46.2-2905 with a score of 80 percent or higher; and
6. Pay the appropriate fee for certificate issuance.

B. Every application shall state the applicant's full legal name; year, month, and date of birth; social security number; sex; and residence address. The applicant shall also answer any questions on the application form, or otherwise propounded, and provide any other information as required by the Department incidental to the application.

C. The Commissioner shall require that each application include a certification statement, to be signed by the applicant under penalty of perjury, certifying that the information presented on the application is true and correct. If the applicant fails or refuses to sign the certification statement, the Department shall not issue the applicant an escort vehicle driver certificate.

Any applicant who knowingly makes a false certification or supplies false or fictitious evidence shall be punished as provided in § 46.2-348.

History.
2013, cc. 312, 477; 2015, c. 258.

§ 46.2-2907. Nonresident; extensions of reciprocal privileges.

A nonresident age 18 years or older who has been duly licensed as a driver under a law regulating the licensure of drivers in his home state and who has in his immediate possession a valid driver's license and a valid escort vehicle driver certificate issued to him in his home state, where such state's escort vehicle driver certification program has been determined to be substantially similar to the Commonwealth's and to which the Commonwealth has extended reciprocity, shall be permitted without a Virginia license or a Virginia escort vehicle driver certificate to escort a permitted vehicle or vehicles on the highways of the Commonwealth. Such nonresident shall be exempt from the escort vehicle driver certification eligibility, training, and testing requirements of this chapter.

If such nonresident desires to also hold a Virginia escort vehicle driver certificate, in addition to the valid certificate issued to him by his home state, he must then meet all of the Virginia escort vehicle driver certification eligibility, training, and testing requirements of this chapter.

History.
2013, cc. 312, 477; 2015, c. 258.

§ 46.2-2908. Nonresident; issuance of Virginia escort vehicle driver certificate; nonreciprocal state.

A nonresident who has not been issued an escort vehicle driver certificate in his home state but who has in his immediate possession a valid driver's license issued by his home state may be certified through Virginia's Escort Vehicle Driver Certification Program. Such nonresident must meet all escort vehicle driver certification eligibility, training, and testing requirements of this chapter.

A nonresident who has in his immediate possession a valid driver's license and valid escort vehicle driver certificate issued to him by his home state, to which state's escort vehicle driver certification program the Commonwealth has not extended reciprocity, may be certified through Virginia's Escort Vehicle Driver Certification Program. Such nonresident must meet all escort vehicle driver certification eligibility, training, and testing requirements of this chapter.

History.
2013, cc. 312, 477.

§ 46.2-2909. Issuance, expiration and renewal of certificate; fees.

The fee for issuance of an original or renewal escort vehicle driver certificate shall be $5 for each year of validity. The certificate shall be valid for five years and expire on the last day of the month of issuance. Notwithstanding this limitation, the Commissioner may extend the validity period of an expiring certificate if (i) the Department is unable to process an application for renewal due to circumstances beyond its control or (ii) the extension has been authorized under a directive from the Governor. However, in no case shall the validity period be extended more than 90 days per occurrence of such conditions.

Persons who wish to renew an escort vehicle driver certificate shall successfully pass the escort vehicle driver certification knowledge test prior to recertification.

History.
2013, cc. 312, 477.

§ 46.2-2910. Certified escort vehicle drivers; duties and responsibilities.

A. Each certified escort vehicle driver shall have in his possession his escort vehicle driver certificate and proof of insurance while escorting a permitted vehicle. The driver's certificate, driver's license, and proof of insurance must be presented when requested by any Department of Motor Vehicles size and weight compliance agent, law-enforcement officer, or Department of Transportation official. Failure of the certified escort vehicle driver to have the certificate, driver's license, or proof of insurance in his possession while escorting a permitted vehicle or load may cause the movement of the permitted vehicle to be interrupted until properly credentialed escort services can be obtained.

B. The driver of an escort vehicle shall comply with all applicable traffic laws and with the requirements of this chapter when escorting a permitted vehicle or vehicles on all roads within the Commonwealth.

History.
2013, cc. 312, 477.

TITLE 51.5.
PERSONS WITH DISABILITIES.

CHAPTER 9.
RIGHTS OF PERSONS WITH DISABILITIES.

Section

§ 51.5-44.1. Fraudulent representation of a service dog or hearing dog; penalty.

Any person who knowingly and willfully fits a dog with a harness, collar, vest, or sign, or uses an identification card commonly used by a person with a disability, in order to represent that the dog is a service dog or hearing dog to fraudulently gain public access for such dog pursuant to provisions in § 51.5-44 is guilty of a Class 4 misdemeanor.

History.
2016, c. 575.

TITLE 52.
POLICE (STATE).

CHAPTER 4.
ARRESTS BY STATE POLICE.

Section

§ 52-20. Arrests without warrants in certain cases.

Members of the State Police force of the Commonwealth, provided such officers are in uniform, or displaying a badge of office, may, at the scene of any motor vehicle accident, or in the apprehension of any person charged with the theft of any motor vehicle, on any of the highways of the Commonwealth, upon reasonable grounds to believe, based upon personal investigation, including information obtained from eyewitnesses, that a crime has been committed by any person then and there present, apprehend such person without a warrant of arrest; and such officers may arrest, without a warrant, persons duly charged with crime in another jurisdiction upon receipt of a telegram, a radio or teletype message, in which telegram, radio or teletype message shall be given the name or a reasonably accurate description of such person wanted, the crime alleged and an allegation that such person is likely to flee the jurisdiction of the Commonwealth.

History.
1942, p. 481; Michie Code 1942, § 4827a; 1950, p. 888.

§ 52-21. Procedure after arrest without warrant.

Except in the case of a violation of a provision of Title 46.2, in which case the officer making the arrest shall proceed as provided in § 46.2-936, the officer making the arrest shall forthwith bring the person so arrested before an officer authorized to issue criminal warrants in the county or city where the arrest is made. The officer before whom such person is brought shall proceed to examine the officer making the arrest. If the officer before whom such person is brought has reasonable grounds upon which to believe that a criminal offense has been committed, and that the person arrested has committed such offense, he shall issue such a warrant as might have been issued prior to the arrest of such person under the provisions of § 19.2-72. If such a warrant is issued the case shall thereafter be disposed of in like manner as though the warrant had been issued prior to the arrest. If such a warrant be not issued the person so arrested shall be released.

History.
1942, p. 481; Michie Code 1942, § 4827a; 1960, c. 375; 1962, c. 22; 1982, c. 35.

§ 52-22. Arrests for violations of ordinances.

The Superintendent of State Police, his assistants, and the State troopers, patrolmen and police officers appointed by him, shall have authority to execute warrants of arrest for violations of ordinances of counties, cities and towns when requested so to do by the county, city or town authorities. Such arrests may be made upon information transmitted as provided in § 52-20, as well as in cases where the officer is in possession of the warrant.

The execution of any such warrant shall rest entirely in the discretion of the Superintendent and other officers who may be requested to execute the same, and no such officer shall execute the same in any case where it will in any way interfere with, delay or hinder him in the discharge of his official duties.

History.
1947, p. 30; Michie Suppl. 1948, § 4827b.

CHAPTER 6.
UNIFORM CRIME REPORTING PROGRAM.

Section

§ 52-25. Uniform crime reporting system established.

The Superintendent shall establish, organize, equip, staff and maintain within the Department of State Police, at such departmental locations as the Superintendent may direct, a uniform crime reporting system for the purpose of receiving, compiling, classifying, analyzing and publishing crime statistics of offenses known, persons arrested, and persons charged and other information pertaining to the investigation of crime and the apprehension of criminals, as hereinafter provided. The Superintendent shall appoint or designate necessary personnel to carry out the duties and assignments in accordance with rules and regulations pertaining thereto promulgated by the Superintendent.

History.
1974, c. 577.

§ 52-25.1. Reporting and return of firearms confiscated or recovered by law-enforcement agencies.

A. Whenever a law-enforcement agency confiscates a firearm in connection with a criminal investigation or otherwise recovers a firearm, such agency shall immediately take all appropriate steps to identify and trace the history of such firearm.

B. The Superintendent shall establish a procedure within the Department of State Police to obtain information regarding all firearms seized, forfeited, found, or otherwise coming into the possession of any state or local law-enforcement agency of the Commonwealth. All law-enforcement agencies of the Commonwealth and of political subdivisions of the Commonwealth shall share with other Virginia law-enforcement agencies all information regarding firearms seized, forfeited, found, or otherwise coming into the agency's possession that are believed to have been used in the commission of a crime and shall enter such information into a firearms tracing system maintained by the U.S. Department of Justice. The Superintendent shall adopt regulations prescribing the method for reporting this information and the time and manner of submission of the information to a firearms tracing system maintained by the U.S. Department of Justice.

C. Except as provided in § 19.2-386.29, whenever a firearm is identified as stolen, the law-enforcement agency shall return such firearm to the rightful owner thereof, if known, provided the owner is not prohibited from possessing the firearm and the agency does not need to retain the firearm as evidence in a criminal prosecution.

History.
1993, cc. 475, 834; 1994, cc. 394, 502; 2016, c. 214.

§ 52-26. Cooperation with other law-enforcement agencies.

The Superintendent is authorized to maintain liaison and to cooperate with law-enforcement and criminal justice agencies of all counties, cities and towns and all other agencies, departments, and institutions of the Commonwealth, other states and of the United States in order to develop and carry on a comprehensive uniform crime reporting program for the Commonwealth. Uniform crime reports for the Commonwealth shall be published by the Superintendent and distributed in an electronic format to the General Assembly and the office of the Governor, annually. The Superintendent shall publicize the availability of the reports to all law-enforcement agencies, attorneys for the Commonwealth, and the courts.

History.
1974, c. 577; 1979, c. 83; 2007, c. 135.

§ 52-27. Aid to reporting agencies.

The Department shall render all necessary aid and assistance to all reporting agencies in order to fulfill the requirements of the uniform crime reporting program for the Commonwealth.

History.
1974, c. 577.

§ 52-28. Duty of Commonwealth and local agencies to make reports.

All Commonwealth, county and municipal law-enforcement agencies shall submit to the Department all periodic uniform crime reports setting forth their activities in connection with law enforcement. The provisions of this chapter shall not apply to any police agency not paid entirely from public funds.

History.
1974, c. 577; 1979, c. 83.

§ 52-28.1. Reporting of gang-related criminal information; inclusion in annual Crime in Virginia report.

The Department of State Police shall include arrest statistics for violations of §§ 18.2-46.2, 18.2-46.3, 18.2-46.3:1, 18.2-46.3:3, and 18.2-55.1 in the annual Crime in Virginia report.

History.
2008, c. 746.

§ 52-28.2. Reporting of officer-involved shootings; inclusion in annual Crime in Virginia report.

The Department of State Police shall include any officer-involved shooting and whether such shooting was determined to be justified in the annual Crime in Virginia report. Any law-enforcement or public safety officer required to make such report shall receive training concerning such reporting requirement.

For the purposes of this section, "officer-involved shooting" means the discharge of a firearm by a law-enforcement officer, as defined in § 9.1-101, that results in the death or serious bodily injury of another.

History.
2016, c. 333.

§ 52-29. Rules and regulations for form, etc.

The Superintendent shall adopt and promulgate rules and regulations prescribing the form, general content, time and manner of submission of such uniform crime reports of all offenses designated by him, including, but not limited to, part I and part II offenses as set out by the Federal Bureau of Investigation.

History.
1974, c. 577.

§ 52-30. Reports to Federal Bureau of Investigation.

The Department shall correlate reports submitted to it and shall compile and submit reports to the Federal Bureau of Investigation on behalf of all agencies of the Commonwealth, as may be required by the federal standards for the uniform crime reporting program.

History.
1974, c. 577.

CHAPTER 7.
MISSING CHILDREN INFORMATION CLEARINGHOUSE.

§ 52-31. Missing Children Information Clearinghouse established.

The Superintendent shall establish, organize, equip, staff and maintain within the Department of State Police a Missing Children Information Clearinghouse as a central repository of information regarding missing children. Such information shall be collected, processed, maintained and disseminated by the Clearinghouse as accurately and completely as possible to assist in the location of missing children.

History.
1985, c. 259.

§ 52-31.1. Superintendent to establish network.

The Superintendent of State Police shall establish a network to implement reports of the disappearance of children by local law-enforcement agencies to local school division superintendents and the State Registrar of Vital Records. The network shall be designed to establish cooperative arrangements between local law-enforcement agencies and local school divisions concerning reports of missing children, whereby law enforcement shall within 24 hours or the next business day, notify the principal of the school where the missing child is or was most recently enrolled and inform the school official of the report, and notices to law-enforcement agencies of requests for copies of the cumulative records and birth certificates of missing children. Upon notification of a request for a marked school record or other information regarding a missing child, the Superintendent shall immediately initiate an investigation into the circumstances surrounding the request, including a search for any record that may exist showing who has legal custody of the child and for any record that may disclose an allegation of child abuse perpetrated against a member of the child's family. The network shall also establish a mechanism for reporting the identities of all missing children to the State Registrar of Vital Records.

History.
1990, c. 295; 2006, c. 295.

§ 52-32. Definitions.

As used in this chapter, unless the context requires otherwise or it is otherwise specifically provided:

"Missing child" means any person who is under the age of 21 years, whose temporary or permanent residence is in Virginia, or is believed to be in Virginia, whose whereabouts are unknown to any parent, guardian, legal custodian or other person standing in loco parentis of the child, and who has been reported as missing to a law-enforcement agency within the Commonwealth.

"Missing child report" means a report prepared in a format prescribed by the Superintendent for use by law-enforcement agencies to report missing child information to the Missing Children Information Clearinghouse.

History.
1985, c. 259; 1986, c. 330; 2004, c. 248.

§ 52-33. Powers and duties of Clearinghouse.

The Clearinghouse shall have the following powers and duties:

1. To maintain a centralized file for the exchange of information on missing children within the Commonwealth. The Clearinghouse shall accept a missing child report from any law-enforcement officer as defined in § 9.1-101. Any parent, guardian, legal custodian or other person standing in loco parentis of a missing child may contact the Clearinghouse to verify the entry of a missing child report on such child. If the Clearinghouse is requested to verify a missing child report which has not been received, the Clearinghouse shall immediately contact the appropriate law-enforcement agency and take such measures as may be necessary to determine whether a report should be entered in the centralized file.

2. To maintain a system of intrastate communication to receive information relating to the disappearance or sighting of missing children. Such system shall be available twenty-four hours per day, seven days per week.

3. To maintain close liaison with the National Crime Information Center and the National Center for Missing and Exploited Children for the exchange of information on children suspected of interstate or international travel and for assistance in the operation of the Clearinghouse.

4. To circulate a monthly bulletin on missing children to the news media, all law-enforcement agencies, and every school in the Commonwealth.

5. To provide emergency flyers containing physical and situational descriptions of missing children when requested by law-enforcement agencies.

6. To provide for training of public and private organizations regarding the operation of the Clearinghouse.

7. To provide assistance to law-enforcement agencies in planning and implementing programs to fingerprint children.

History.
1985, c. 259; 2011, cc. 818, 852.

§ 52-34. Notification required when missing child located.

Any law-enforcement officer who has reported a missing child to the Clearinghouse shall notify the Clearinghouse immediately upon determining the location of the child.

History.
1985, c. 259.

CHAPTER 7.1.
VIRGINIA AMBER ALERT PROGRAM.

§ 52-34.1. Definitions.

As used in this chapter:

"Abducted child" means a child (i) whose whereabouts are unknown, (ii) who is believed to have been abducted, (iii) who is 17 years of age or younger or is currently enrolled in a secondary school in the Commonwealth, regardless of age, and (iv) whose disappearance poses a credible threat as determined by law enforcement to the safety and health of the child and under such other circumstances as deemed appropriate by the Virginia State Police.

"Amber Agreement" means the voluntary agreement between law-enforcement officials and members of the media whereby a child will be declared abducted, and the public will be notified, and includes all other incidental conditions of the partnership as found appropriate by the Virginia State Police.

"Amber Alert" means the notice of child abduction provided to the public by the media or other methods under an Amber Agreement.

"Amber Alert Program" or *"Program"* means the procedures and Amber Agreements to aid in the identification and location of abducted children.

"Media" means print, radio, television, and Internet-based communication systems or other methods of communicating information to the public.

History.
2003, cc. 83, 86; 2007, c. 198.

§ 52-34.2. Establishment of the Virginia Amber Alert Program.

The Virginia State Police shall develop policies for the establishment of uniform standards for the creation of Amber Alert Programs throughout the Commonwealth. Amber Alert Programs may be local, regional, or statewide. They may include multiple localities or regions and may be expanded or compressed. The Virginia State Police may (i) inform local law-enforcement officials of the policies and procedures for the Amber Alert Programs set by the State Police; (ii) assist in determining the geographic scope of a particular Amber Alert; and (iii) establish procedures and standards by which a local law-enforcement agency may verify a child has been abducted and report such information to the Virginia State Police.

The establishment of an Amber Alert Program by a locality and the media is voluntary and nothing in this chapter shall be construed to be a mandate that local officials or the media establish or participate in an Amber Alert Program. Existing Amber Agreements and Programs shall not be altered by the act of assembly creating this chapter.

History.
2003, cc. 83, 86.

§ 52-34.3. Activation of Amber Alert Program upon an incident of child abduction.

A. Upon receipt of a notice of a child abduction from a law-enforcement agency, the Virginia State Police shall confirm the accuracy of the information and provide assistance in the implementation of the Amber Alert Program as the investigation dictates.

B. Amber Alerts may be local, regional, or statewide. The initial decision to make a local or regional Amber Alert shall be at the discretion of the local or regional law-enforcement officials. Prior to making a local or regional Amber Alert, the local or regional law-enforcement officials shall confer with the Virginia State Police and provide information regarding the abducted child to the Virginia State Police. The initial decision to make a statewide Amber Alert shall be at the discretion of the Virginia State Police. The Missing Children Information Clearinghouse operated by the Virginia State Police shall serve as a central repository for information related to an abduction.

C. In those situations where appropriate, the Virginia State Police shall send the Amber Alert to Virginia's emergency alert system. Participating media are encouraged to issue the alert at designated intervals as specified by the Amber Alert Program.

D. In those situations where appropriate and an existing system is available, the Virginia State Police shall contact the operator of the existing automatic dialing-announcing device system to target residents in the geographic location where the abducted child was most recently seen. For purposes of this section, "automatic dialing-announcing device system" means a device that (i) selects and dials telephone numbers; and (ii) working alone or in conjunction with other equipment, disseminates a prerecorded or synthesized voice message to the telephone number called.

E. The Amber Alert shall include such information as the law-enforcement agency deems appropriate that will assist in the safe recovery of the abducted child.

F. The Amber Alert shall be cancelled under the terms of the Amber Agreement. Any local law-enforcement agency that locates a child who is the subject of an alert shall notify the Virginia State Police immediately that the child has been located.

History.
2003, cc. 83, 86; 2004, c. 270; 2007, c. 130.

CHAPTER 7.2.

VIRGINIA SENIOR ALERT PROGRAM.

§ 52-34.4. Definitions.

As used in this chapter:

"Media" means print, radio, television, and Internet-based communication systems or other methods of communicating information to the public.

"Missing senior adult" means an adult whose whereabouts are unknown and who is over 60 years of age and suffers a cognitive impairment to the extent that he is unable to provide care to himself without assistance from a caregiver, including a diagnosis of Alzheimer's Disease or dementia, and whose disappearance poses a credible threat as determined by a law-enforcement agency to the health and safety of the adult and under such other circumstances as deemed appropriate by the Virginia State Police.

"Senior alert" means the notice of a missing senior adult provided to the public by the media or other methods under a Senior Alert Agreement.

"Senior Alert Agreement" means a voluntary agreement between law-enforcement officials and members of the media whereby a senior adult will be declared missing, and the public will be notified by media outlets, and includes all other incidental conditions of the partnership as found appropriate by the Virginia State Police.

"Senior Alert Program" or *"Program"* means the procedures and Senior Alert Agreements to aid in the identification and location of a missing senior adult.

History.
2007, cc. 486, 723.

§ 52-34.5. Establishment of the Virginia Senior Alert Program.

The Virginia State Police shall develop policies for the establishment of uniform standards for the creation of Senior Alert Programs throughout the Commonwealth. The Virginia State Police shall (i) inform local law-enforcement officials of the policies and procedures to be used for the Senior Alert Programs; (ii) assist in determining the geographic scope of a particular Senior Alert; and (iii) establish procedures and standards by which a local law-enforcement agency shall verify that a senior adult is missing and shall report such information to the Virginia State Police.

The establishment of a Senior Alert Program by a local law-enforcement agency and the media is voluntary, and nothing in this chapter shall be construed to be a mandate that local officials or the media establish or participate in a Senior Alert Program.

History.
2007, cc. 486, 723.

§ 52-34.6. Activation of Senior Alert Program upon an incident of a missing senior adult.

A. Upon receipt of a notice of a missing senior adult from a law-enforcement agency, the Virginia State Police shall confirm the accuracy of the information and provide assistance in the activation of the Senior Alert Program as the investigation dictates.

B. Senior Alerts may be local, regional, or statewide. The initial decision to make a local Senior Alert shall be at the discretion of the local law-enforcement official. Prior to making a local Senior Alert, the local law-enforcement official shall confer with the Virginia State Police and provide information regarding the missing senior adult to the Virginia State Police. The decision to make a regional or statewide Senior Alert shall be at the discretion of the Virginia State Police.

C. The Senior Alert shall include the missing senior adult information as defined in § 15.2-1718.1 and any other such information as the law-enforcement agency deems appropriate that will assist in the safe recovery of the missing senior adult.

D. The Senior Alert shall be cancelled under the terms of the Senior Alert Agreement. Any local law-enforcement agency that locates a missing senior adult who is the subject of an alert shall notify the Virginia State Police immediately that the missing senior adult has been located.

History.
2007, cc. 486, 723.

CHAPTER 7.3. VIRGINIA BLUE ALERT PROGRAM.

Section

§ 52-34.7. Definitions.

As used in this chapter, unless the context requires a different meaning:

"Law-enforcement agency" means a law-enforcement agency with jurisdiction over the search for a suspect in a case involving the death or serious injury of a law-enforcement officer or an agency employing a law-enforcement officer who is missing in the line of duty.

(Effective until October 1, 2016) *"Law-enforcement officer"* means any full-time or part-time employee of the Department of State Police or a police department or sheriff's office that is a part of or administered by the Commonwealth or any political subdivision thereof, and any campus police officer appointed under Chapter 17 (§ 23-232 et seq.) of Title 23, who is responsible for the prevention and detection of crime and the enforcement of the penal, traffic, or highway laws of the Commonwealth.

(Effective October 1, 2016) *"Law-enforcement officer"* means any full-time or part-time employee of the Department of State Police or a police department or sheriff's office that is a part of or administered by the Commonwealth or any political subdivision thereof, and any campus police officer appointed under Article 3 (§ 23.1-809 et seq.) of Chapter 8 of Title 23.1, who is responsible for the prevention and detection of crime and the enforcement of the penal, traffic, or highway laws of the Commonwealth.

History.
2011, c. 669; 2012, c. 776.

§ 52-34.8. Establishment of the Virginia Blue Alert Program.

The Department of State Police shall establish a Blue Alert Program in the Commonwealth and develop policies for its implementation. The Blue Alert Program may be activated when a suspect for a crime involving the death or serious injury of a law-enforcement officer has not been apprehended and may be a serious threat to the public or when a law-enforcement officer is missing while in the line of duty under circumstances warranting concern for the law-enforcement officer's safety. The Department of State Police shall (i) establish procedures and standards by which a local law-enforcement agency may assess whether the conditions for a Blue Alert have been met and report such information to the Department of State Police, (ii) inform local law-enforcement officials of the policies and procedures for the Blue Alert Program set by the Department, and (iii) assist in determining the geographic scope of a particular Blue Alert.

History.
2011, c. 669.

§ 52-34.9. Activation of Blue Alert Program.

A. Upon notification by a law-enforcement agency that a suspect in a case involving the death or serious injury of a law-enforcement officer has not been apprehended and may be a serious threat to the public, the Department of State Police shall confirm that (i) a suspect has not been apprehended, (ii) the suspect may be a serious threat to the public, and (iii) sufficient information is available to disseminate to the public that could assist in locating the suspect.

B. Upon notification by a law-enforcement agency that a law-enforcement officer is missing while in the line of duty under circumstances warranting concern for such law-enforcement officer's safety, the Department of State Police shall confirm this information and determine whether sufficient information is available to disseminate to the public that could assist in locating the missing law-enforcement officer.

C. Upon verification that conditions set forth in subsection A or B have been met, the Department of State Police shall activate the Blue Alert Program.

D. The area of the alert may be less than statewide if the Department of State Police determines that the nature of the event makes it probable that the suspect did not leave a certain geographic location or if the nature of the event makes it probable that the missing law-enforcement officer is within a certain geographic location. The Department of State Police shall assess the appropriate boundaries for the alert based on the nature of the suspect, the circumstances surrounding the crime or the last known location of the missing law-enforcement officer.

E. The Blue Alert shall include such information as the Department of State Police deems appropriate that will assist in the apprehension of the suspect or the locating of the missing law-enforcement officer.

F. A law-enforcement agency shall notify the Department of State Police immediately when the suspect is located or the law-enforcement officer is found or the incident is otherwise resolved.

G. The Department of State Police shall terminate any activation of the Blue Alert Program with respect to a particular incident if (i) the suspect or law-enforcement officer is located or the incident is otherwise resolved or (ii) the Department of State

Police determines that the Blue Alert Program is no longer an effective tool for locating the suspect or law-enforcement officer.

History.
2011, c. 669.

CHAPTER 8.
WITNESS PROTECTION PROGRAM.

§ 52-35. Witness protection program established.

The Superintendent of State Police may establish and maintain within the Department of State Police a witness protection program to temporarily relocate or otherwise protect witnesses and their families who may be in danger because of their cooperation with the investigation and prosecution of serious violent crimes, felony violations of § 18.2-248, and violations of §§ 18.2-57.2, 18.2-67.5:1, 18.2-67.5:2, and 18.2-67.5:3. The Superintendent may make the services of the program available to law-enforcement and criminal justice agencies of all counties, cities, and towns, and of the Commonwealth, pursuant to regulations promulgated by the Superintendent under the Administrative Process Act. (§ 2.2-4000 et seq.).

History.
1994, c. 833; 2002, cc. 810, 818.

CHAPTER 10.
PROTECTIVE ORDER REGISTRY.

§ 52-45. Protective Order Registry established.

The Superintendent shall establish, organize and maintain within the Department of State Police a computerized Protective Order Registry as a central repository of information regarding outstanding, valid protective orders. Such information shall be maintained and disseminated by the registry as accurately and completely as possible to assist in the expedited entry and dissemination of protective order information.

History.
2002, cc. 810, 818.

§ 52-46. Applicant Fingerprint Database; maintenance; dissemination; penalty.

A. The Department of State Police shall keep and maintain an Applicant Fingerprint Database separate and apart from all other records maintained by the Department. The purpose of the database shall be to allow those agencies and entities who require a criminal background check as a condition of licensure, certification, employment, or volunteer service to be advised when an individual subject to such screening is arrested for, or convicted of, a criminal offense which would disqualify that individual from licensure, certification, employment or volunteer service with that entity.

B. As used in this section:

"Participating entity" means an agency or organization that requires a fingerprint background check as a condition of licensure, certification, employment, or volunteer service, and that has elected to participate in the database.

"Individual" means any person who has submitted fingerprints to a participating entity in order to be licensed, certified, employed, or to perform volunteer service with that entity.

C. The Department of State Police shall notify forthwith the participating entity that employs, certifies, licenses, or accepts the volunteer services of an individual whose prints are maintained in the database upon receipt of a report that the individual has been arrested for or convicted of an offense that would disqualify that individual from licensure, certification, employment or volunteer service with that entity. The information contained in the notification shall be used by the entity for purposes of determining the eligibility of the continued service of the individual and shall not be further disseminated.

D. Use of the information contained in the database or received from the database for purposes not authorized by this section is prohibited, and a willful violation of this section with the intent to harass or intimidate another shall be punished as a Class 1 misdemeanor.

E. No liability shall be imposed upon any law-enforcement official who disseminates information or fails to disseminate information in good faith compliance with the requirements of this section, but this provision shall not be construed to grant immunity for gross negligence or willful misconduct.

F. The Department of State Police shall promulgate regulations governing the operation and maintenance of the database and the expungement of records on persons who are deceased, or who are no longer employed, licensed, certified, or in volunteer service for the entity that submitted the fingerprints.

G. The Department of State Police may charge an annual fee not to exceed $10 per individual entered into the database. The fee shall be paid no later than July 15 of each year by the participating entity or entities submitting fingerprints to the database or by the entity or entities requesting notification regarding an individual. An individual whose licensure, certification, employment, or volunteer service moves from one entity to another need not be reprinted. When more than one participating entity licenses, certifies, employs, or accepts the volunteer services of an individual in the database, both entities shall be responsible for paying the full cost for maintenance and notification. Any fees collected shall be deposited in a special account to be used to offset the costs of enhancing and administering the database.

H. The Department of State Police shall make the database available no later than January 1, 2005, unless funds necessary to develop and operate the database are unavailable.

I. No entity authorized to submit fingerprints shall be considered negligent per se in a civil action solely because the entity elected not to submit an individual's fingerprints to the database pursuant to this section.

History.
2004, c. 826.

TITLE 53.1.

PRISONS AND OTHER METHODS OF CORRECTION.

CHAPTER 2.

STATE CORRECTIONAL FACILITIES.

Article 1.

General Provisions.

Section

ARTICLE 1.

GENERAL PROVISIONS.

§ 53.1-20. Commitment of convicted persons to custody of Director.

A. Every person convicted of a felony committed before January 1, 1995, and sentenced to the Department for a total period of more than two years shall be committed by the court to the custody of the Director of the Department. The Director shall receive all such persons into the state corrections system within sixty days of the date on which the final sentencing order is mailed by certified letter or sent by electronic transmission to the Director by the clerk.

B. Persons convicted of felonies committed on or after January 1, 1995, and sentenced to the Department or sentenced to confinement in jail for a year or more shall be placed in the custody of the Department and received by the Director into the state corrections system within sixty days of the date on which the final sentencing order is mailed by certified letter or sent by electronic transmission to the Director by the clerk.

C. If the Governor finds that the number of prisoners in state facilities poses a threat to public safety, it shall be within the discretion of the Director to determine the priority for receiving prisoners into the state corrections system from local correctional facilities.

D. All felons sentenced to a period of incarceration and not placed in an adult state correctional facility pursuant to this section shall serve their sentences in local correctional facilities which shall not include a secure facility or detention home as defined in § 16.1-228.

E. Felons committed to the custody of the Department for a new felony offense shall be received by the Director into the state corrections system in accordance with the provisions of this section without any delay for resolution of (i) issues of alleged parole violations set for hearing before the Parole Board or (ii) any other pending parole-related administrative matter.

History.
Code 1950, §§ 19-270, 19.1-296, 53-21.1; 1960, c. 366; 1966, c. 522; 1970, cc. 67, 648; 1972, c. 145; 1973, c. 330; 1974, cc. 44, 45, 506; 1981, c. 529; 1982, c. 636; 1990, cc. 676, 768; 1993, c. 502; 1994, cc. 128, 859, 949; 1994, 2nd Sp. Sess., cc. 1, 2; 1997, c. 840.

§ 53.1-20.1. Compensation of local jails for cost of incarceration.

If the Director is unable to accommodate in a state correctional facility any convicted felon sentenced to the Department for a felony committed before January 1, 1995, whose sentence totals more than two years or who is convicted of a felony committed on or after January 1, 1995, and who is required to serve a total period of one year or more in a state correctional facility, the Department of Corrections shall compensate local jails for the cost of incarceration as provided for in the general appropriation act beginning on the sixty-first day following the date of mailing by certified letter or electronic transmittal by the clerk of the committing court to the Director of the final order.

History.
1982, c. 680; 1990, cc. 676, 768; 1994, 2nd Sp. Sess., cc. 1, 2; 1997, c. 775.

§ 53.1-21. Transfer of prisoners into and between state and local correctional facilities.

A. Any person who (1) is accused or convicted of an offense (a) in violation of any county, city or town ordinance within the Commonwealth, (b) against the laws of the Commonwealth or (c) against the laws of any other state or country, or (2) is a witness held in any case in which the Commonwealth is a party and who is confined in a state or local correctional facility, may be transferred by the Director, subject to the provisions of § 53.1-20, to any other state or local correctional facility which he may designate.

B. The following limitations shall apply to the transfer of persons into the custody of the Department:

1. No person convicted of violating § 20-61 shall be committed or transferred to the custody of the Department.

2. No person who is convicted of any violation pursuant to Article 9 (§ 46.2-355.1 et seq.) of Chapter 3 of Title 46.2 shall be committed or transferred to the custody of the Department without the consent of the Director.

3. No person who is convicted of a misdemeanor or a felony and receives a jail sentence of twelve months or less shall be committed or transferred to the custody of the Department without the consent of the Director.

4. Beginning July 1, 1991, and subject to the provisions of § 53.1-20, no person, whether convicted of a felony or misdemeanor, shall be transferred to the custody of the Department when the combined length of all sentences to be served totals two years or less, without the consent of the Director.

History.

Code 1950, §§ 19.2-310.1, 53-19.17, 53-84, 53-103, 53-135.1; Code 1950, § 53-8; 1952, c. 557; 1960, c. 432; 1962, c. 326; 1968, c. 357; 1970, c. 648; 1971, Ex. Sess., c. 110; 1972, c. 573; 1973, cc. 330, 342; 1974, cc. 44, 45; 1976, cc. 287, 462; 1982, c. 636; 1990, cc. 676, 768; 1999, cc. 945, 987.

§ 53.1-29. Authority for correctional officers and other employees to carry weapons.

It shall be lawful for any correctional officer and any noncustodial employee who has been designated by the Director of the Department, and who has completed the basic course in firearms for correctional officers as approved by the Department of Criminal Justice Services, to carry and use sufficient weapons to prevent escapes, suppress rebellion, and defend or protect himself or others in the course of his assigned duties.

History.

Code 1950, § 53-39; 1970, c. 648; 1979, c. 642; 1982, c. 636; 1984, c. 720; 1996, cc. 804, 838.

CHAPTER 3.
LOCAL CORRECTIONAL FACILITIES.

Article 3.

Funding Local Correctional Facilities and Programs.

Section

Article 6.

Duties of Sheriffs.

Article 7.

Prisoner Programs and Treatment.

ARTICLE 3.
FUNDING LOCAL CORRECTIONAL FACILITIES AND PROGRAMS.

§ 53.1-93. When sheriffs to summon or employ guards and other persons; allowances therefor; fees charged to prisoner.

Whenever in the discretion of the court it is necessary for the safekeeping of a prisoner under charge of or sentence for a crime, whether the prisoner be in jail, hospital, court or elsewhere, the court may order the sheriff to summon a sufficient guard. Whenever ordered by the court to do so, the sheriff shall summon or employ temporarily such persons as may be needed to preserve proper order or otherwise to aid the court in its proper operation and functioning. For such guard or other service the court may allow so much as it deems proper, not exceeding the hourly equivalent of the minimum annual salary paid a full-time deputy sheriff who performs like services in the same county or city. In addition, mileage and other expenses for rendering the services shall be paid for each such person. A prisoner may be charged reasonable fees for providing him a security escort, supervision and transportation to and from a funeral or graveside service.

History.
Code 1950, §§ 19-283, 19.1-308, 53-183.2; 1956, c. 687; 1960, c. 366; 1972, c. 145; 1973, c. 401; 1976, c. 286; 1981, c. 386; 1982, c. 636; 2002, c. 336.

§ 53.1-94. Same when paid by county or city; same when by Compensation Board.

The circuit court, before certifying any allowance pursuant to § 53.1-93, shall inquire into the condition of the jail. If it appears that a guard was necessary because of the insecurity of the jail, it shall order the allowance to be certified to the governing body of the county or city. If otherwise, and the guard was necessary, the allowance shall be paid out of the budget of the sheriff as approved by the Compensation Board.

History.
Code 1950, §§ 19-284, 19.1-309, 53-183.3; 1960, c. 366; 1972, c. 145; 1982, c. 636; 1985, c. 321.

ARTICLE 6.
DUTIES OF SHERIFFS.

§ 53.1-118. Courts to fine sheriffs for failure to perform duties.

If it appears to the circuit court having jurisdiction that the sheriff or jail superintendent has in any respect failed to perform his duties with respect to the operation of the jail, the court may, after summoning him to show cause against it, summarily fine him not more than fifty dollars.

History.
Code 1950, § 53-161; 1970, c. 648; 1982, c. 636; 1991, c. 383.

§ 53.1-119. Court duties of sheriff.

The sheriff shall provide officers to attend the courts within his jurisdiction while such courts are in session as the respective judges may require. The sheriff, or the superintendent of a regional jail or jail farm, shall receive into the jail facility all persons committed by the order of such courts, or under process issuing therefrom, and all persons committed by any other lawful authority.

History.
Code 1950, § 53-162; 1982, c. 636; 1995, c. 112.

§ 53.1-120. Sheriff to provide for courthouse and courtroom security; designation of deputies for such purpose; assessment.

A. Each sheriff shall ensure that the courthouses and courtrooms within his jurisdiction are secure from violence and disruption and shall designate deputies for this purpose. A list of such designations shall be forwarded to the Director of the Department of Criminal Justice Services.

B. The chief circuit court judge, the chief general district court judge and the chief juvenile and domestic relations district court judge shall be responsible by agreement with the sheriff of the jurisdiction for the designation of courtroom security deputies for their respective courts. If the respective chief judges and sheriff are unable to agree on the number, type and working schedules of courtroom security deputies for the court, the matter shall be referred to the Compensation Board for resolution in accordance with existing budgeted funds and personnel.

C. The sheriff shall have the sole responsibility for the identity of the deputies designated for courtroom security.

D. Any county or city, through its governing body, may assess a sum not in excess of $10 as part of the costs in each criminal or traffic case in its district or circuit court in which the defendant is convicted of a violation of any statute or ordinance. If a town provides court facilities for a county, the governing body of the county shall return to the town a portion of the assessments collected based on the number of criminal and traffic cases originating and heard in the town. The imposition of such assessment shall be by ordinance of the governing body that may provide for different sums in the circuit courts and district courts. The assessment shall be collected by the clerk of the court in which the case is heard, remitted to the treasurer of the appropriate county or city and held by such treasurer to be appropriated by the governing body to the sheriff's office. The assessment shall be used solely for the funding of courthouse security personnel, and, if requested by the sheriff, equipment and other personal property used in connection with courthouse security.

History.
Code 1950, § 53-168.1; 1972, c. 135; 1982, c. 636; 1986, c. 568; 1988, c. 119; 1989, c. 571; 2002, cc. 533, 756; 2003, cc. 26, 44; 2004, cc. 390, 432; 2006, c. 495; 2007, c. 377.

§ 53.1-127. Who may enter interior of local correctional facilities; searches of those entering.

A. Members of the local governing bodies which participate in the funding of a local correctional facility may go into the interior of that facility. Agents of the Board may go into the interior of any local correctional facility. In addition, Department of Corrections staff and state and local health department staff shall, in the performance of their duties, have access to the interior of any local correctional facility subject to the standards promulgated pursuant to § 53.1-68 A and B. Attorneys shall be permitted in the interior of a local correctional facility to confer with prisoners who are their clients and with prisoners who are witnesses in cases in which they are involved. Except for the announced or unannounced inspections authorized pursuant to § 53.1-68 A and B, the sheriff, jail administrator or other person in charge of the facility shall prescribe the time and conditions under which attorneys and other persons may enter the local correctional facility for which he is responsible.

B. Any person seeking to enter the interior of any local correctional facility shall be subject to a search of his person and effects. Such search shall be performed in a manner reasonable under the circumstances and may be a condition precedent to entering a local correctional facility.

History.
1982, c. 636; 1995, c. 797.

§ 53.1-127.1. Establishment of stores in local correctional facilities.

Each sheriff who operates a correctional facility is authorized to provide for the establishment and operation of a store or commissary to deal in such articles and services as he deems proper. The net profits from the operation of such store that are generated from the inmates' accounts shall be used within the facility for educational, recreational or other purposes for the benefit of the inmates as may be prescribed by the sheriff. Any other profits may be used for the general operation of the sheriff's office. The sheriff shall be the purchasing agent in all matters involving the commissary and nonappropriated funds received from inmates. The funds from such operation of a store or commissary and from the inmate telephone services account shall be considered public funds.

History.
1993, cc. 314, 616; 2002, c. 182; 2013, c. 91.

§ 53.1-127.2. Fees for electronic visitation and messaging with prisoners in local correctional facilities.

Each sheriff or jail superintendent who operates a correctional facility that utilizes an electronic visitation system or electronic messaging system, including Voice-over-Internet Protocol technology and web-based communication systems, for communication between prisoners and third parties is authorized to provide for the establishment and collection of a fee for the system utilized. However, no fee shall be charged for communication between prisoners and third parties within any local correctional facility or appurtenance thereto operated or controlled by the sheriff or jail superintendent.

This section does not apply to telephonic communication systems or to electronic video and audio communication systems used in judicial proceedings.

History.
2011, c. 532; 2013, c. 449.

§ 53.1-127.3. Deferred or installment payment agreement for unpaid fees; suspension of privilege to operate a motor vehicle.

If a person is unable to pay in full the fees owed to the local correctional facility or regional jail pursuant to § 53.1-131.3, the sheriff or jail superintendent shall establish a deferred or installment payment agreement subject to the approval of the general district court. As a condition of every such agreement, a person who enters into a deferred or installment payment agreement shall promptly inform the sheriff or jail superintendent of any change of mailing address during the term of the agreement. The sheriff or jail superintendent shall give notice to the person at the time the deferred or installment payment agreement is entered into and the person shall certify on a form prescribed by the local correctional facility or regional jail that he understands that upon his failure or refusal to pay in accordance with a deferred or installment payment agreement, the person's privilege to operate a motor vehicle shall be suspended pursuant to the provisions of § 46.2-320.2.

History.
2012, c. 829.

§ 53.1-127.4. Suspension of privilege to operate motor vehicle for failure to pay fees.

No suspension of driving privileges shall be issued by the Department of Motor Vehicles for failure or refusal to provide for immediate payment in full of fees imposed under § 53.1-131.3 or for failure to make payments under a deferred or installment payment agreement unless the sheriff or jail superintendent has (i) entered into an agreement with the Department of Motor Vehicles pursuant to § 46.2-320.2, (ii) has obtained a judgment and court order for suspension or nonrenewal issued by a court of competent jurisdiction, and (iii) has provided to the

Commissioner of Motor Vehicles electronic notice of such judgment or default and court order and the person's most current mailing address.

The provisions of this section shall apply to all unpaid fees imposed under § 53.1-131.3 provided the sheriff or jail administrator or other entity under a contract pursuant to § 53.1-127.5 informs the person who owes the fees and receives signed certification of understanding at the time the deferred or installment payment agreement is entered into that upon failure or refusal to pay in accordance with the payment agreement the person's privilege to operate a motor vehicle shall be suspended pursuant to the provisions of § 46.2-320.2.

History.
2012, c. 829.

§ 53.1-127.5. Collection of fees owed; contract for collection; duties of Department of Taxation.

The sheriff or jail superintendent may (i) contract with private attorneys or private collection agencies, (ii) enter into an agreement with a local governing body, or (iii) enter into an agreement with the county or city treasurer, upon such terms and conditions as may be established by guidelines promulgated by the Board, to collect fees imposed under § 53.1-131.3. As part of such contract, private attorneys or collection agencies shall be given access to the social security number of the person who owes the fees in order to assist in the collection effort. Any such private attorney or collection agency shall be subject to the penalties and provisions of § 18.2-186.3.

The fees of any private attorney or collection agency shall be paid on a contingency fee basis out of the proceeds of the amounts collected. However, in no event shall such attorney or collection agency receive a fee for amounts collected by the Department of Taxation under the Setoff Debt Collection Act (§ 58.1-520 et seq.). A local treasurer undertaking collection pursuant to an agreement with the sheriff or jail superintendent may collect the administrative fee authorized by § 58.1-3958.

History.
2012, c. 829.

ARTICLE 7.
PRISONER PROGRAMS AND TREATMENT.

§ 53.1-128. Workforces and authorized work places.

The local governing body of any county, city or town may establish workforces in the county, city or town under such conditions as it may prescribe. Such workforces are authorized to work on (i) public property or works owned, leased or operated by the Commonwealth or the county, city or town; (ii) a privately operated national park on federal land; (iii) any property owned by a nonprofit organization that is exempt from taxation under 26 U.S.C. § 501(c)(3) or (c)(4) and that is organized and operated exclusively for charitable or social welfare purposes whether the same is located within such county, city or town, or elsewhere; or (iv) private property (a) owned or occupied by an elderly or indigent person or persons where such property has been identified by a citizens housing advisory committee as needing rehabilitation or repair and the property owner has consented to such work or (b) classified as or used as a cemetery where such property has been abandoned and where on such property exist nuisances that have been identified by a municipal corporation for abatement or removal pursuant to § 15.2-1115 or a similar local ordinance. Every person 18 years of age or older who is convicted and confined for any violation of a local ordinance and who is confined as a punishment or for failure to pay a required fine, shall be liable to work in such workforce. Every person 18 years of age or older who is confined pending disposition of a nonviolent criminal offense or an offense under Chapter 5 (§ 20-61 et seq.) of Title 20 may work in such workforce on a voluntary basis with the approval of and under the supervision of the sheriff.

History.
Code 1950, § 53-163; 1970, c. 648; 1982, c. 636; 1991, c. 580; 1997, cc. 123, 546; 2010, c. 168; 2011, c. 767.

§ 53.1-129. Order permitting prisoners to work on state, county, city, town, certain private property or nonprofit organization property; bond of person in charge of prisoners.

The circuit court of any county or city may, by order entered of record, allow persons confined in the jail of such county or city who are awaiting disposition of, or serving sentences imposed for, misdemeanors or felonies to work on (i) state, county, city or town property, (ii) any property owned by a nonprofit organization that is exempt from taxation under 26 U.S.C. § 501(c)(3) and that is organized and operated exclusively for charitable or social welfare purposes on a voluntary basis with the consent of the county, city, town or state agency or the local public service authority or upon the request of the nonprofit organization involved, (iii) private property that is part of a community improvement project sponsored by a locality or that has structures that are found to be public nuisances pursuant to §§ 15.2-900 and 15.2-906 provided that the court has reviewed and approved the project for the purposes herein and permits the prisoners to work on such project, (iv) any private property utilized by a nonprofit organization that is exempt from taxation under 26 U.S.C. § 501(c)(3), or (v) private property in any locality that meets the criteria under an ordinance adopted by such locality under § 15.2-908. The district court of any county or city may allow persons confined in the jail of such county or city who are awaiting disposition of, or serving sentences imposed for, misdemeanors to work on (a) state, county, city or town property, (b) any property owned by a nonprofit organization that is exempt from taxation under 26 U.S.C. § 501(c)(3) and that is organized and operated exclusively for charitable or social welfare purposes on a voluntary basis with consent of the county, city, town or state agency or the local public service authority or upon the request of the nonprofit organization involved, (c) private property that is part of a community improvement project sponsored by a locality or that has structures that are found to be public nuisances pursuant to §§ 15.2-900 and 15.2-906 provided that the court has reviewed and approved the project for the purposes herein and permits the prisoners to work on such project, (d) any private property utilized by a nonprofit organization that is exempt from taxation under 26 U.S.C. § 501(c)(3), or (e) private property in any locality that meets the criteria under an ordinance adopted by such locality under § 15.2-908. Prisoners performing work as provided in this paragraph may receive credit on their respective sentences for the work done, whether such sentences are imposed prior or subsequent to the work done, as the court orders.

The court may, by order entered of record, require a person convicted of a felony to work on state, county, city or town property, with the consent of the county, city, town or state agency or the local public service authority involved, for such credit on his sentence as the court orders.

In the event that a person other than the sheriff or jail superintendent is designated by the court to have charge of such prisoners while so working, the court shall require a bond of the person, in an amount to be fixed by the court, conditioned upon the faithful discharge of his duties. Neither the sheriff nor the jail superintendent shall be held responsible for any acts of omission or commission on the part of such person.

Any person committed to jail upon a felony offense committed on or after January 1, 1995, who receives credit on his sentence as provided in this section shall not be entitled to good conduct credit, sentence credit, earned sentence credit, other credit, or a combination of any credits in excess of that permissible under Article 4 (§ 53.1-202.2 et seq.) of Chapter 6 of this title. So much of an order of any court contrary to the provisions of Article 4 shall be deemed null and void.

History.

Code 1950, § 53-165; 1976, c. 618; 1978, c. 609; 1982, c. 636; 1984, c. 43; 1991, c. 580; 1994, c. 269; 1997, cc. 134, 546; 1998, c. 311; 1999, cc. 277, 951, 1007; 2001, cc. 185, 196; 2003, cc. 818, 820; 2005, c. 409; 2008, c. 623; 2010, c. 132.

§ 53.1-130. Sheriffs, jail superintendents, etc., not to be interested in property where work performed; penalty.

No sheriff, jail superintendent, deputy or other jail officer shall have any prisoner work on property owned by him or by his relative, or on projects in which he is interested, nor shall any such prisoner be used for the personal gain or convenience of any sheriff or of any other individual. Any person found guilty of a violation of this section shall be guilty of a Class 1 misdemeanor.

History.

Code 1950, § 53-166; 1970, c. 648; 1982, c. 636; 1991, c. 383.

§ 53.1-131. Provision for release of prisoner from confinement for employment, educational or other rehabilitative programs; escape; penalty; disposition of earnings.

A. Any court having jurisdiction for the trial of a person charged with a criminal offense or charged with an offense under Chapter 5 (§ 20-61 et seq.) of Title 20 may, if the defendant is convicted and (i) sentenced to confinement in jail or (ii) being held in jail pending completion of a presentence report pursuant to § 19.2-299, and if it appears to the court that such offender is a suitable candidate for work release, assign the offender to a work release program under the supervision of a probation officer, the sheriff or the administrator of a local or regional jail or a program designated by the court. The court further may authorize the offender to participate in educational or other rehabilitative programs designed to supplement his work release employment. The court shall be notified in writing by the director or administrator of the program to which the offender is assigned of the offender's place of employment and the location of any educational or rehabilitative program in which the offender participates.

Any person who has been sentenced to confinement in jail or who has been convicted of a felony but is confined in jail pursuant to § 53.1-20, in the discretion of the sheriff may be assigned by the sheriff to a work release program under the supervision of the sheriff or the administrator of a local or regional jail. The sheriff may further authorize the offender to participate in educational or other rehabilitative programs as defined in this section designed to supplement his work release employment. The court that sentenced the offender shall be notified in writing by the sheriff or the administrator of a local or regional jail of any such assignment and of the offender's place of employment or other rehabilitative program. The court, in its discretion, may thereafter revoke the authority for such an offender to participate in a work release program.

The sheriff and the Director may enter into agreements whereby persons who are committed to the

Department, whether such persons are housed in a state or local correctional facility, and who have met all standards for such release, may participate in a local work release program or in educational or other rehabilitative programs as defined in this section. The administrator of a regional jail and the Director may also enter into such agreements where such agreements are approved in advance by a majority of the sheriffs on the regional jail board. All persons accepted in accordance with this section shall be governed by all regulations applying to local work release, notwithstanding the provisions of any other section of the Code. Local jails shall qualify for compensation for cost of incarceration of such persons pursuant to § 53.1-20.1, less any payment for room and board collected from the inmate.

If an offender who has been assigned to such a program by the court is in violation of the rules of the jail pursuant to § 53.1-117, the sheriff or jail administrator may remove the offender from the work release program, either temporarily or for the duration of the offender's confinement. Upon removing an offender from the work release program, the sheriff or jail administrator shall notify in writing the court that sentenced the offender and indicate the specific violations that led to the decision.

Any offender assigned to such a program by the court or sheriff who, without proper authority or just cause, leaves the area to which he has been assigned to work or attend educational or other rehabilitative programs, or leaves the vehicle or route of travel involved in his going to or returning from such place, is guilty of a Class 1 misdemeanor. In the event such offender leaves the Commonwealth, the offender may be found guilty of an escape as provided in § 18.2-477. An offender who is found guilty of a Class 1 misdemeanor in accordance with this section shall be ineligible for further participation in a work release program during his current term of confinement.

The Board shall prescribe regulations to govern the work release, educational and other rehabilitative programs authorized by this section.

Any wages earned pursuant to this section by an offender may, upon order of the court, be paid to the director or administrator of the program after standard payroll deductions required by law. Distribution of such wages shall be made for the following purposes:

1. To pay an amount to defray the cost of his keep;
2. To pay travel and other such expenses made necessary by his work release employment or participation in an educational or rehabilitative program;
3. To provide support and maintenance for his dependents or to make payments to the local department of social services or the Commissioner of Social Services, as appropriate, on behalf of dependents who are receiving public assistance or social services as defined in § 63.2-100; or
4. To pay any fines, restitution or costs as ordered by the court.

Any balance at the end of his sentence shall be paid to the offender upon his release.

B. For the purposes of this section:

"Educational program" means a program of learning recognized by the State Council of Higher Education, the State Board of Education or the State Board of Corrections.

"Rehabilitative program" includes an alcohol and drug treatment program, mental health program, family counseling, community service or other community program approved by the court having jurisdiction over the offender.

"Sheriff" means the sheriff of the jurisdiction where the person charged with the criminal offense was convicted and sentenced, provided that the sheriff may designate a deputy sheriff or regional jail administrator to assign offenders to work release programs under this section.

"Work release" means full-time employment or participation in suitable career and technical education programs.

History.

Code 1950, §§ 19-273.1, 53-166.1; 1956, c. 688; Code 1950, § 19.1-300; 1960, c. 366; 1970, c. 121; 1972, c. 145; 1973, c. 38; 1976, c. 295; 1979, c. 706; 1980, c. 566; 1982, c. 636; 1984, c. 516; 1985, c. 301; 1988, c. 397; 1989, c. 586; 1990, cc. 107, 676, 768; 2000, c. 423; 2002, cc. 747, 800; 2006, c. 792.

§ 53.1-131.1. Provision for sentencing of person to nonconsecutive days in jail; payment to defray costs; penalty.

Any court having jurisdiction for the trial of a person charged with a misdemeanor or traffic offense or charged with any offense under Chapter 5 (§ 20-61 et seq.) of Title 20 may, if the defendant is convicted and sentenced to confinement in jail, impose the time to be served on weekends or nonconsecutive days to permit the convicted defendant to retain gainful employment. A person sentenced pursuant to this section shall pay an amount to defray the cost of his keep, which amount shall be the actual cost of incarceration but shall not exceed that amount charged to the Compensation Board for purposes of reimbursement as provided in the general appropriation act. Such amount shall be collected by the sheriff, if he is responsible for operating a jail, or by the regional jail superintendent, and remitted by the sheriff to the treasurer of the appropriate county or city, or by the regional jail superintendent to the regional jail board or authority, solely for the purposes of defraying the costs of such weekend or nonconsecutive incarceration. The funds collected pursuant to this section shall not be used for purposes other than those provided for in this section. The assessment provided for herein shall be in addition to any other fees prescribed by law. If the defendant willfully fails to report at times specified by the court, the sentence imposed pursuant to this section shall be revoked and a straight jail sentence imposed.

If an offender who has been sentenced to nonconsecutive days by the court is in violation of the rules of the jail pursuant to § 53.1-117, the sheriff or jail administrator may require the offender to serve out a portion or the entirety of the remainder of his sentence in consecutive days. Upon revoking the offender's ability to serve his sentence on nonconsecutive days, the sheriff or jail administrator shall notify in writing the court that sentenced the offender and indicate the specific violations that led to the decision.

The time served by a person sentenced for violation of state law in a local jail, regional jail, or local jail farm pursuant to this section shall be included in the count of prisoner days reported by the Department for the purpose of apportioning state funds to local correctional facilities for operating costs in accordance with § 53.1-84.

History.

1983, c. 172; 1984, c. 490; 1994, c. 901; 1999, c. 9; 2002, cc. 805, 831; 2003, c. 1039; 2006, c. 792.

§ 53.1-131.2. Assignment to a home/electronic incarceration program; payment to defray costs; escape; penalty.

A. Any court having jurisdiction for the trial of a person charged with a criminal offense, a traffic offense or an offense under Chapter 5 (§ 20-61 et seq.) of Title 20, or failure to pay child support pursuant to a court order may, if the defendant is convicted and sentenced to confinement in a state or local correctional facility, and if it appears to the court that such an offender is a suitable candidate for home/electronic incarceration, assign the offender to a home/electronic incarceration program as a condition of probation, if such program exists, under the supervision of the sheriff, the administrator of a local or regional jail, or a Department of Corrections probation and parole district office established pursuant to § 53.1-141. However, any offender who is convicted of any of the following violations of Chapter 4 (§ 18.2-30 et seq.) of Title 18.2 shall not be eligible for participation in the home/electronic incarceration program: (i) first and second degree murder and voluntary manslaughter under Article 1 (§ 18.2-30 et seq.); (ii) mob-related felonies under Article 2 (§ 18.2-38 et seq.); (iii) any kidnapping or abduction felony under Article 3 (§ 18.2-47 et seq.); (iv) any malicious felonious assault or malicious bodily wounding under Article 4 (§ 18.2-51 et seq.); (v) robbery under § 18.2-58.1; or (vi) any criminal sexual assault punishable as a felony under Article 7 (§ 18.2-61 et seq.). The court may further authorize the offender's participation in work release employment or educational or other rehabilitative programs as defined in § 53.1-131 or, as appropriate, in a court-ordered intensive case monitoring program for child support. The court shall be notified in writing by the director or administrator of the program to which the offender is assigned of the offender's place of home/electronic incarceration, place of employment, and the location of any educational or rehabilitative program in which the offender participates.

B. In any city or county in which a home/electronic incarceration program established pursuant to this section is available, the court, subject to approval by the sheriff or the jail superintendent of a local or regional jail, may assign the accused to such a program pending trial if it appears to the court that the accused is a suitable candidate for home/electronic incarceration.

C. Any person who has been sentenced to jail or convicted and sentenced to confinement in prison but is actually serving his sentence in jail, after notice to the attorney for the Commonwealth of the convicting jurisdiction, may be assigned by the sheriff to a home/electronic incarceration program under the supervision of the sheriff, the administrator of a local or regional jail, or a Department of Corrections probation and parole office established pursuant to § 53.1-141. However, if the offender violates any provision of the terms of the home/electronic incarceration agreement, the offender may have the assignment revoked and, if revoked, shall be held in the jail facility to which he was originally sentenced. Such person shall be eligible if his term of confinement does not include a sentence for a conviction of a felony violent crime, a felony sexual offense, burglary or manufacturing, selling, giving, distributing or possessing with the intent to manufacture, sell, give or distribute a Schedule I or Schedule II controlled substance. The court shall retain authority to remove the offender from such home/electronic incarceration program. The court which sentenced the offender shall be notified in writing by the sheriff or the administrator of a local or regional jail of the offender's place of home/electronic incarceration and place of employment or other rehabilitative program.

D. The Board may prescribe regulations to govern home/electronic incarceration programs.

E. Any offender or accused assigned to such a program by the court or sheriff who, without proper authority or just cause, leaves his place of home/electronic incarceration, the area to which he has been assigned to work or attend educational or other rehabilitative programs, including a court-ordered intensive case monitoring program for child support, or the vehicle or route of travel involved in his going to or returning from such place, is guilty of a Class 1 misdemeanor. An offender or accused who is found guilty of a violation of this section shall be ineligible for further participation in a home/electronic incarceration program during his current term of confinement.

F. The director or administrator of a home/electronic incarceration program who also operates a residential program may remove an offender from a home/electronic incarceration program and place him in such residential program if the offender commits a noncriminal program violation. The court shall be notified of the violation and of the placement of the offender in the residential program.

G. The director or administrator of a home/electronic incarceration program shall charge the offender or accused a fee for participating in the program to pay for the cost of home/electronic incarceration equipment. The offender or accused shall be required to pay the program for any damage to the equipment which is in his possession or for failure to return the equipment to the program.

H. Any wages earned by an offender or accused assigned to a home/electronic incarceration program and participating in work release shall be paid to the director or administrator after standard payroll deductions required by law. Distribution of the money collected shall be made in the following order of priority to:

1. Meet the obligation of any judicial or administrative order to provide support and such funds shall be disbursed according to the terms of such order;
2. Pay any fines, restitution or costs as ordered by the court;
3. Pay travel and other such expenses made necessary by his work release employment or participation in an education or rehabilitative program, including the sums specified in § 53.1-150; and
4. Defray the offender's keep.

The balance shall be credited to the offender's account or sent to his family in an amount the offender so chooses.

The Board of Corrections shall promulgate regulations governing the receipt of wages paid to persons participating in such programs, the withholding of payments and the disbursement of appropriate funds.

I. For the purposes of this section, "sheriff" means the sheriff of the jurisdiction where the person charged with the criminal offense was convicted and sentenced, provided that the sheriff may designate a deputy sheriff or regional jail administrator to assign offenders to home/electronic incarceration programs pursuant to this section.

History.
1989, c. 476; 1990, c. 209; 1991, cc. 278, 428; 1992, c. 604; 1994, cc. 612, 659, 688, 720, 841, 945; 2000, c. 423; 2002, c. 800; 2010, c. 682.

§ 53.1-131.3. Payment of costs associated with prisoners' keep.

Any sheriff or jail superintendent may establish a program to charge inmates a reasonable fee, not to exceed $3 per day, to defray the costs associated with the prisoners' keep. The Board shall develop a model plan and adopt regulations for such program, and shall provide assistance, if requested, to the sheriff or jail superintendent in the implementation of such program. Such funds shall be retained in the locality where the funds were collected and shall be used for general jail purposes; however, in the event the jail is a regional jail, funds collected from any such fee shall be retained by the regional jail. Any person jailed for an offense they are later acquitted for shall be refunded any such fees paid during their incarceration.

History.
2003, c. 860; 2009, c. 842; 2010, c. 548.

§ 53.1-132. Furloughs from local work release programs; penalty for violations.

The director of any work release program authorized by § 53.1-131 may, subject to rules and regulations prescribed by the Board, extend the limits of confinement of any offender participating in a work release program which is subject to the director's authority, to permit the offender a furlough for the purpose of visiting his home or family. Such furlough shall be for a period to be prescribed by the director, not to exceed three days. The time during which an offender is on furlough shall not be counted as time served against any sentence, and during any furlough, no earned sentence credit as defined in § 53.1-116, good conduct allowance or credits or any other reduction of sentence shall accrue.

Any offender who, without proper authority or without just cause, fails to remain within the limits of confinement set by the director hereunder, or fails to return within the time prescribed to the place designated by the director in granting such authority, shall be guilty of a Class 1 misdemeanor. An offender who is found guilty of a Class 1 misdemeanor in accordance with this section shall be ineligible for further participation in a work release program during his current term of confinement.

History.
Code 1950, § 53-166.2; 1980, c. 566; 1982, c. 636; 2000, c. 423; 2003, c. 846.

§ 53.1-133. Treatment of prisoner with contagious disease.

Upon application of the person in charge of a local correctional facility, if that application is affirmed by the physician serving such facility, a judge of a circuit court is authorized to have removed from any correctional facility within his jurisdiction any person confined therein who has contracted any contagious or infectious disease dangerous to the public health. Such persons shall be removed to some other place designated by the judge. When any person is so removed, he shall be safely kept and receive proper care and attention including medical treatment. As soon as he recovers his health, he shall be returned to the correctional facility from which he was moved, unless the term of his imprisonment has expired, in which event he shall be discharged, but not until all danger of his spreading contagion has passed. Expenses incurred under and by reason of this section shall be paid as provided by law.

History.
Code 1950, § 53-135.2; 1979, c. 109; 1982, c. 636.

§ 53.1-133.01. Medical treatment for prisoners.

Any sheriff or superintendent may establish a medical treatment program for prisoners in which prisoners participate and pay towards a portion of the costs thereof. The Board of Corrections shall develop a model plan and promulgate regulations for such program, and shall provide assistance, if requested, to the sheriff or superintendent in the implementation of a program.

History.
1994, c. 694.

§ 53.1-133.01:1. Payment for bodily injury.

Each jail superintendent or sheriff who operates a correctional facility is authorized to establish administrative procedures according to regulations promulgated by the Board for recovering from an inmate the cost for medical treatment of a physical injury that is inflicted intentionally on any person, including the inmate himself, by the inmate. Such administrative procedures shall ensure that the inmate is afforded due process.

History.
1997, c. 125; 2003, cc. 928, 1019.

§ 53.1-133.02. Notice to be given upon prisoner release, escape, etc.

Prior to the release, including work release, or discharge of any prisoner, and as soon as practicable following his transfer to a prison, a different jail facility, or any other correctional or detention facility, his escape, or the change of his name, the sheriff or superintendent who has custody of the prisoner shall give notice of any such occurrence, delivered by first-class mail or by telephone or both, to any victim of the offense as defined in § 19.2-11.01 who, in writing, requests notice or to any person designated in writing by the victim. The notice shall be given at least 15 days prior to release or discharge and as soon as practicable following a transfer, an escape, or a change of name. Notice shall be given using the address and telephone number provided in writing by the victim. For the purposes of this section, "prisoner" means a person sentenced to serve more than 30 days of incarceration or detention. Such notification may be provided through the Virginia Statewide VINE (Victim Information and Notification Everyday) System or other similar electronic or automated system.

No civil liability shall attach for a failure to give notice as provided in this section.

History.
1995, c. 687; 2007, cc. 94, 109; 2015, c. 101.

§ 53.1-133.03. Exchange of medical and mental health information and records.

Notwithstanding any other provision of law relating to disclosure and confidentiality of patient records maintained by a health care provider, medical and mental health information and records of any person committed to jail, and transferred to another correctional facility, may be exchanged among the following:

1. Administrative personnel of the correctional facilities involved and of the administrative personnel within the holding facility when there is reasonable cause to believe that such information is necessary to maintain the security and safety of the holding facility, its employees, or prisoners. The information exchanged shall continue to be confidential and disclosure shall be limited to that necessary to ensure the safety and security of the facility.
2. Members of the Parole Board or its designees, as specified in § 53.1-138, in order to conduct the investigation required under § 53.1-155.
3. Probation and parole officers for use in parole and probation planning, release and supervision.
4. Officials of the facilities involved and officials within the holding facility for the purpose of formulating recommendations for treatment and rehabilitative programs; classification, security and work assignments; and determining the necessity for medical, dental and mental health care, treatment and other such programs.
5. Medical and mental health hospitals and facilities, both public and private, including community service boards and health departments, for use in treatment while committed to jail or a correctional facility while under supervision of a probation or parole officer.

Substance abuse records subject to federal regulations, Confidentiality of Alcohol and Drug Abuse Patient Records, 42 C.F.R. § 2.11 et seq., shall not be subject to the provisions of this section. The disclosure of results of a test for human immunodeficiency virus shall not be permitted except as provided in §§ 32.1-36.1 and 32.1-116.3.

The release of medical and mental health information and records to any other agency or individual shall be subject to all regulations promulgated by the Board of Corrections which govern confidentiality of such records. Medical and mental health information concerning a prisoner which has been exchanged pursuant to this section may be used only as provided herein and shall otherwise remain confidential and protected from disclosure.

Nothing contained in this section shall prohibit the release of records to the Department of Health Professions or health regulatory boards consistent with Subtitle III (§ 54.1-2400 et seq.) of Title 54.1 of the Code of Virginia.

History.
1997, c. 443.

CHAPTER 4.
PROBATION AND PAROLE.

Article 2.

State Probation and Parole Services.

ARTICLE 2.
STATE PROBATION AND PAROLE SERVICES.

§ 53.1-145. Powers and duties of probation and parole officers.

In addition to other powers and duties prescribed by this article, each probation and parole officer shall:

1. Investigate and report on any case pending in any court or before any judge in his jurisdiction referred to him by the court or judge;

2. Supervise and assist all persons within his territory placed on probation, secure, as appropriate and when available resources permit, placement of such persons in a substance abuse treatment program which may include utilization of acupuncture and other treatment modalities, and furnish every such person with a written statement of the conditions of his probation and instruct him therein; if any such person has been committed to the Department of Behavioral Health and Developmental Services under the provisions of Chapter 9 (§ 37.2-900 et seq.) of Title 37.2, the conditions of probation shall include the requirement that the person comply with all conditions given him by the Department of Behavioral Health and Developmental Services, and that he follow all of the terms of his treatment plan;

3. Supervise and assist all persons within his territory released on parole or postrelease supervision, secure, as appropriate and when available resources permit, placement of such persons in a substance abuse treatment program which may include utilization of acupuncture and other treatment modalities, and, in his discretion, assist any person within his territory who has completed his parole, postrelease supervision, or has been mandatorily released from any correctional facility in the Commonwealth and requests assistance in finding a place to live, finding employment, or in otherwise becoming adjusted to the community;

4. Arrest and recommit to the place of confinement from which he was released, or in which he would have been confined but for the suspension of his sentence or of its imposition, for violation of the terms of probation, post-release supervision pursuant to § 19.2-295.2 or parole, any probationer, person subject to post-release supervision or parolee under his supervision, or as directed by the Chairman, Board member or the court, pending a hearing by the Board or the court, as the case may be;

5. Keep such records, make such reports, and perform other duties as may be required of him by the Director or by regulations prescribed by the Board of Corrections, and the court or judge by whom he was authorized;

6. Order and conduct, in his discretion, drug and alcohol screening tests of any probationer, person subject to post-release supervision pursuant to § 19.2-295.2 or parolee under his supervision who the officer has reason to believe is engaged in the illegal use of controlled substances or marijuana, or the abuse of alcohol. The cost of the test may be charged to the person under supervision. Regulations governing the officer's exercise of this authority shall be promulgated by the Board;

7. Have the power to carry a concealed weapon in accordance with regulations promulgated by the Board and upon the certification of appropriate training and specific authorization by a judge of a circuit court;

8. Provide services in accordance with any contract entered into between the Department of Corrections and the Department of Behavioral Health and Developmental Services pursuant to § 37.2-912;

9. Pursuant to any contract entered into between the Department of Corrections and the Department of Behavioral Health and Developmental Services, probation and parole officers shall have the power to provide intensive supervision services to persons placed on conditional release, regardless of whether the person has any time remaining to serve on any criminal sentence, pursuant to Chapter 9 (§ 37.2-900 et seq.);

10. Determine by reviewing the Local Inmate Data System upon intake and again prior to release whether a blood, saliva, or tissue sample has been taken for DNA analysis for each person placed on probation or parole required to submit a sample pursuant to Article 1.1 (§ 19.2-310.2 et seq.) of Chapter 18 of Title 19.2 and, if no sample has been taken, require a person placed on probation or parole to submit a sample for DNA analysis; and

11. For every offender accepted pursuant to the Interstate Compact for the Supervision of Adult Offenders (§ 53.1-176.1 et seq.) who has been convicted of an offense that, if committed in Virginia, would be considered a felony, take a sample or verify

that a sample has been taken and accepted into the data bank for DNA analysis in the Commonwealth.

Nothing in this article shall require probation and parole officers to investigate or supervise cases before general district or juvenile and domestic relations district courts.

History.

Code 1950, § 53-250; 1970, c. 648; 1973, c. 253; 1974, cc. 44, 45, 240; 1975, c. 630; 1976, c. 39; 1982, c. 636; 1992, cc. 188, 740; 1994, c. 935; 1994, 2nd Sp. Sess., cc. 1, 2; 1995, cc. 502, 574; 1997, c. 526; 2003, c. 944; 2006, cc. 698, 730, 863, 914; 2007, c. 528; 2009, cc. 813, 840; 2011, cc. 384, 410; 2014, cc. 674, 719.

§ 53.1-149. Arrest of probationer without warrant; written statement.

Any probation officer appointed pursuant to this chapter may arrest a probationer without a warrant, or may deputize any other officer with power to arrest to do so, by a written statement setting forth that the probationer has, in the judgment of the probation officer, violated one or more of the terms or conditions upon which the probationer was released on probation. Such a written statement by a probation officer delivered to the officer in charge of any local jail or lockup shall be sufficient warrant for the detention of the probationer. Any officer deputized upon receipt of the written statement shall, in accordance with § 19.2-390, enter, or cause to be entered, the person's name and other appropriate information required by the Department of State Police into the "information systems" known as the Virginia Criminal Information Network (VCIN), established and maintained by the Department pursuant to Chapter 2 (§ 52-12 et seq.) of Title 52. Such information shall be deemed a warrant authorizing the arrest of the person anywhere in the Commonwealth.

History.

Code 1950, § 53-278.5; 1962, c. 327; 1982, c. 636; 2010, c. 273.

§ 53.1-150. Contributions by persons on parole, probation, and work release.

A. Any person who has costs assessed against him pursuant to §§ 17.1-275.1, 17.1-275.2, 17.1-275.7, or § 17.1-275.8, or subsection B or C of § 16.1-69.48:1 shall be required to pay, as specified in those sections, a sentencing/supervision fee to be deposited in the general fund of the state treasury.

All fees assessed pursuant to this section shall be paid to the clerk of the sentencing court.

B. Except when the fee referenced in subsection A has been previously assessed, any person (i) who is granted parole or (ii) who participates in a work release program pursuant to the provisions of §§ 53.1-60 and 53.1-131 shall be required to pay a fee of fifty dollars as a condition of parole or work release.

History.

Code 1950, § 53-19.40; 1981, c. 634; 1982, cc. 492, 636; 1984, c. 668; 1988, c. 824; 1990, cc. 511, 816; 1992, c. 529; 1993, c. 195; 1994, cc. 613, 638; 1994, 2nd Sp. Sess., cc. 1, 2; 1999, c. 9; 2000, c. 1040; 2002, c. 831.

§ 53.1-150.1. Contribution by persons on parole.

Any person who is granted parole and who is required to receive substance abuse treatment as a condition of parole shall contribute towards the cost of such treatment based upon his ability to pay, as established pursuant to regulations promulgated by the Board of Corrections. The regulations shall provide that (i) any fees collected for such treatment shall be paid directly to the service provider and (ii) any person may be exempt from the payment of such fees on the grounds of unreasonable hardship.

History.

1996, c. 807.

ARTICLE 3.

PROCEDURES GOVERNING PAROLE.

§ 53.1-161. Arrest and return of parolee or felon serving a period of postrelease supervision; warrant; release pending adjudication of violation.

The Chairman or any member of the Board may at any time upon information or a showing of a violation or a probable violation by any parolee or felon serving a period of postrelease supervision of any of the terms or conditions upon which he was released on parole or postrelease period of supervision, issue or cause to be issued, a warrant for the arrest and return of the parolee or felon serving a period of postrelease supervision to the institution from which he was paroled, or to any other correctional facility which may be designated by the Chairman or member. However, a determination of whether a parolee or felon serving a period of postrelease supervision returned to a correctional facility pursuant to this section shall be returned to a state or local correctional facility shall be made based on the length of the parolee's original sentence as set forth in § 53.1-20 or the period of postrelease supervision as set at sentencing. Each such warrant shall authorize all officers named therein to arrest and return the parolee to actual custody in the facility from which he was paroled, or to any other facility designated by the Chairman or member.

In any case in which the parolee or felon serving a period of postrelease supervision is charged with the violation of any law, the violation of which caused the issuance of such warrant, upon request of the parolee or his attorney, the Chairman or member shall as soon as practicable consider all the circumstances surrounding the allegations of such violation, including the probability of conviction thereof, and may, after such consideration, release the parolee, pending adjudication of the violation charged.

History.

Code 1950, § 53-258; 1970, c. 648; 1973, c. 253; 1976, c. 45; 1978, c. 227; 1982, c. 636; 1990, cc. 676, 768; 2000, c. 767.

§ 53.1-162. Arrest of parolee or felon serving a period of postrelease supervision without warrant; written statement.

Any probation and parole officer may arrest a parolee or felon serving a period of postrelease supervision without a warrant or may deputize any other officer with power of arrest to do so by a written statement setting forth that the parolee or felon serving a period of postrelease supervision has, in the judgment of the probation and parole officer, violated one or more of the terms or conditions of his parole or postrelease period of supervision. Such a written statement by a probation and parole officer delivered to the officer in charge of any state or local correctional facility shall be sufficient warrant for the detention of the parolee or felon serving a period of postrelease supervision. Any officer deputized upon receipt of the written statement shall, in accordance with § 19.2-390, enter, or cause to be entered, the person's name and other appropriate information required by the Department of State Police into the "information systems" known as the Virginia Criminal Information Network (VCIN), established and maintained by the Department pursuant to Chapter 2 (§ 52-12 et seq.) of Title 52. Such information shall be deemed a warrant authorizing the arrest of the person anywhere in the Commonwealth.

History.

Code 1950, § 53-259; 1982, c. 636; 2000, c. 767; 2010, c. 273.

§ 53.1-163. Parolee considered as escapee after issuance of warrant.

Any parolee for whose arrest a warrant has been issued by the Board or by the Chairman shall after the issuance of the warrant be treated as an escaped prisoner. The time from the issuing of such warrant to the date of his arrest shall not be counted as any part of the time to be served under his sentence.

History.

Code 1950, § 53-260; 1970, c. 648; 1973, c. 253; 1982, c. 636.

CHAPTER 7.

CRIMES AND CRIMINAL PROCEEDINGS INVOLVING PRISONERS.

Article 1.

Crimes by Prisoners.

Section

ARTICLE 1.

CRIMES BY PRISONERS.

§ 53.1-203. Felonies by prisoners; penalties.

It shall be unlawful for a prisoner in a state, local or community correctional facility or in the custody of an employee thereof to:

1. Escape from a correctional facility or from any person in charge of such prisoner;
2. Willfully break, cut or damage any building, furniture, fixture or fastening of such facility or any part thereof for the purpose of escaping, aiding any other prisoner to escape therefrom or rendering such facility less secure as a place of confinement;
3. Make, procure, secrete or have in his possession any instrument, tool or other thing for the purpose of escaping from or aiding another to escape from a correctional facility or employee thereof;
4. Make, procure, secrete or have in his possession a knife, instrument, tool or other thing not authorized by the superintendent or sheriff which is capable of causing death or bodily injury;
5. Procure, sell, secrete or have in his possession any chemical compound which he has not lawfully received;
6. Procure, sell, secrete or have in his possession a controlled substance classified in Schedule III of the Drug Control Act (§ 54.1-3400 et seq.) or marijuana;
7. Introduce into a correctional facility or have in his possession firearms or ammunition for firearms;
8. Willfully burn or destroy by use of any explosive device or substance, in whole or in part, or cause to be burned or destroyed, any personal property, within any correctional facility;
9. Willfully tamper with, damage, destroy, or disable any fire protection or fire suppression system, equipment, or sprinklers within any correctional facility; or

10. Conspire with another prisoner or other prisoners to commit any of the foregoing acts.

For violation of any of the provisions of this section, except subdivision 6, the prisoner shall be guilty of a Class 6 felony. For a violation of subdivision 6, he shall be guilty of a Class 5 felony. If the violation is of subdivision 1 of this section and the escapee is a felon, he shall be sentenced to a mandatory minimum term of confinement of one year, which shall be served consecutively with any other sentence. The prisoner shall, upon conviction of escape, immediately commence to serve such escape sentence, and he shall not be eligible for parole during such period. Any prisoner sentenced to life imprisonment who escapes shall not be eligible for parole. No part of the time served for escape shall be credited for the purpose of parole toward the sentence or sentences, the service of which is interrupted for service of the escape sentence, nor shall it be credited for such purpose toward any other sentence.

History.

Code 1950, § 53-291; 1966, c. 300; 1970, c. 648; 1973, c. 403; 1975, c. 588; 1977, c. 497; 1978, cc. 177, 361; 1982, c. 636; 1985, c. 555; 1988, c. 371; 2004, c. 461; 2006, c. 104; 2011, cc. 384, 410; 2014, cc. 674, 719.

§ 53.1-204. If prisoner commits any other felony, how punished.

If a prisoner in a state, local or community correctional facility or in the custody of an employee thereof commits any felony other than those specified in §§ 18.2-31, 18.2-55 and 53.1-203, which is punishable by confinement in a state correctional facility or by death, such prisoner shall be subject to the same punishment therefor as if he were not a prisoner.

History.

Code 1950, § 53-294; 1970, c. 648; 1975, c. 588; 1982, c. 636.

CHAPTER 10.

COMMITMENT OF ALIENS.

§ 53.1-218. Duty of officer in charge to inquire as to citizenship; notice to federal immigration officer of commitment of alien.

Whenever any person is committed to a correctional facility the director, sheriff or other officer in charge of such facility shall inquire as to whether the person (i) was born in a country other than the United States, and (ii) is a citizen of a country other than the United States. The director, sheriff or other officer in charge of such facility shall make an immigration alien query to the Law Enforcement Support Center of the United States Immigration and Customs Enforcement for any person who (i) was born in a country other than the United States, and (ii) is a citizen of a country other than the United States, or for whom the answer to (i) or (ii) is unknown.

In the case of a jail, the sheriff, or other officer in charge of such facility shall communicate the results of any immigration alien query that confirm that the person is illegally present in the United States to the Local Inmate Data System of the State Compensation Board. The State Compensation Board shall communicate, on a monthly basis, the results of any immigration alien query that results in a confirmation that the person is illegally present in the United States to the Central Criminal Records Exchange of the Department of State Police in a format approved by the Exchange.

In the case of a correctional facility of the Department of Corrections, the director or other officer in charge of such facility shall communicate the results of any immigration alien query that results in a confirmation that the person is illegally present in the United States to the Central Criminal Records Exchange of the Department of State Police in a format approved by the Exchange.

The information received by the Central Criminal Records Exchange concerning the person's immigration status shall be recorded in the person's criminal history record.

However, notification need not be made to the Central Criminal Records Exchange if it is apparent that a report on alien status has previously been made to the Exchange pursuant to § 19.2-83.2 or 19.2-294.2.

History.

Code 1950, §§ 53-313, 53-314; 1970, c. 648; 1982, c. 636; 1985, c. 247; 1994, c. 579; 2008, cc. 180, 415; 2014, c. 641.

CHAPTER 12.

EXECUTIVE CLEMENCY.

§ 53.1-229. Powers vested in Governor.

In accordance with the provisions of Article V, Section 12 of the Constitution of Virginia, the power to commute capital punishment and to grant pardons or reprieves is vested in the Governor.

History.
Code 1950, § 53-228; 1970, c. 648; 1982, c. 636.

§ 53.1-230. Commutation of capital punishment.

In any case in which the Governor shall exercise the power conferred on him to commute capital punishment, he may issue his order to the Director, who shall receive and confine the person whose punishment is commuted according to such order. To carry into effect any commutation of punishment, the Governor may issue his warrant directed to any proper officer, and the same shall be obeyed and executed.

History.
Code 1950, § 53-228.1; 1956, c. 344; 1981, c. 497; 1982, c. 636.

§ 53.1-231. Investigation of cases for executive clemency by Parole Board.

The Virginia Parole Board shall, at the request of the Governor, investigate and report to the Governor on cases in which executive clemency is sought. In any other case in which it believes action on the part of the Governor is proper or in the best interest of the Commonwealth, the Board may investigate and report to the Governor with its recommendations.

History.
Code 1950, § 53-229; 1970, c. 648; 1982, c. 636.

CHAPTER 12.1.
RESTORATION OF CIVIL RIGHTS.

Section

§ 53.1-231.1. Process for notification regarding restoration of civil rights.

The Director of the Department of Corrections shall provide that any person convicted of a felony is notified of the loss of his civil rights and of the processes to apply for restoration of civil rights and of voting rights. The notice shall be given at the time the person has completed service of his sentence, period of probation or parole, or suspension of sentence.

The Director shall assist the Secretary of the Commonwealth in the administration of the process established by the Governor for the review of applications for restoration of civil rights.

To promote the efficient processing of applications to the Governor, the Secretary of the Commonwealth shall maintain a record of the applications for restoration of rights received, the dates such applications are received, and the dates they are either granted or denied by the Governor. The Secretary shall notify each applicant who has filed a complete application that the complete application has been received and the date the complete application was forwarded by the Secretary to the Governor. Such complete application shall be forwarded by the Secretary to the Governor within ninety days after receipt of the application.

History.
2000, c. 969; 2002, c. 344.

§ 53.1-231.2. Restoration of the civil right to be eligible to register to vote to certain persons.

This section shall apply to any person who is not a qualified voter because of a felony conviction, who seeks to have his right to register to vote restored and become eligible to register to vote, and who meets the conditions and requirements set out in this section.

Any person, other than a person (i) convicted of a violent felony as defined in § 19.2-297.1 or in subsection C of § 17.1-805 and any crime ancillary thereto, (ii) convicted of a felony pursuant to §§ 18.2-248, 18.2-248.01, 18.2-248.1, 18.2-255, 18.2-255.2 or § 18.2-258.02, or (iii) convicted of a felony pursuant to § 24.2-1016, may petition the circuit court of the county or city in which he was convicted of a felony, or the circuit court of the county or city in which he presently resides, for restoration of his civil right to be eligible to register to vote through the process set out in this section. On such petition, the court may approve the petition for restoration to the person of his right if the court is satisfied from the evidence presented that the petitioner has completed, five or more years previously, service of any sentence and any modification of sentence including probation, parole, and suspension of sentence; that the petitioner has demonstrated civic responsibility through community or comparable service; and that the petitioner has been free from criminal convictions, excluding traffic infractions, for the same period.

If the court approves the petition, it shall so state in an order, provide a copy of the order to the petitioner, and transmit its order to the Secretary of the Commonwealth. The order shall state that the petitioner's right to be eligible to register to vote may be restored by the date that is 90 days after the date of the order, subject to the approval or denial of restoration of that right by the Governor. The Secretary of the Commonwealth shall transmit the order to the Governor who may grant or deny the petition for restoration of the right to be eligible to register to vote approved by the court order. The Secretary of the Commonwealth shall send, within 90 days of the date of the order, to the petitioner at the address stated on the court's order, a certificate of restoration of that right or notice that the Governor has denied the restoration of that right. The Governor's denial of a petition for the restoration of voting rights shall be a final decision and the petitioner shall have no right of appeal. The Secretary shall notify the court and the State Board of Elections in each case of the restoration of the right or denial of restoration by the Governor.

On receipt of the certificate of restoration of the right to register to vote from the Secretary of the Commonwealth, the petitioner, who is otherwise a qualified voter, shall become eligible to register to vote.

History.
2000, c. 969; 2003, c. 946.

CHAPTER 13.
DEATH SENTENCES.

Section

§ 53.1-232. Procedures for execution of death sentence; subsequent process.

A. Sentence of death shall not be executed sooner than thirty days after the sentence is pronounced. The court shall, in imposing such sentence, fix a day when the execution shall occur.

B. Whenever the day fixed for the execution of a sentence of death shall have passed without the execution of the sentence and it becomes necessary to fix a new date therefor, the circuit court which pronounced the sentence shall fix another day for the execution. The person to be executed need not be present but shall be represented by an attorney when such other day is fixed. A copy of the order fixing the new date of execution shall be promptly furnished by the clerk of the court making the order to the Director. The Director shall cause a copy of the order to be delivered to the person to be executed, and, if he is unable to read it, cause it to be explained to him at least ten days before the date fixed for such execution, and make return thereof to the clerk of the court which issued such order.

C. When the day fixed for the execution of a sentence of death has passed without the execution of the sentence by reason of a reprieve granted by the Governor, it shall not be necessary for the court to resentence the prisoner. The sentence of death shall be executed on the day to which the prisoner has been reprieved.

D. Should the condemned prisoner be granted a reprieve by the Governor, or obtain a writ of error from the Supreme Court of Virginia, or should the execution of the sentence be stayed by any other competent judicial proceeding, notice of such reprieve, writ of error or stay of execution shall be served upon (i) the Director, (ii) the warden or superintendent having actual custody of the prisoner, and (iii) the prisoner himself; the Director shall yield obedience to the same. In any subsequent proceeding, the mandate of the court having regard to the condemned prisoner shall be served upon the Director, the warden or superintendent having actual custody of the prisoner and upon the prisoner. Should the condemned prisoner be resentenced to death by the court, the proceedings shall be as hereinabove provided under the original sentence. Should a new trial be granted, such condemned prisoner shall be conveyed back to the place of trial by such officer or officers as the Director may direct.

History.
Code 1950, §§ 19-274, 19.1-301, 53 316; 1960, c. 366; 1972, c. 145; 1978, c. 667; 1982, c. 636.

§ 53.1-232.1. When execution dates required.

In a criminal case where a sentence of death has been imposed, the trial court shall set an execution date when it is notified in writing by the Attorney General or the attorney for the Commonwealth, and the court finds that: (i) the Supreme Court of Virginia has denied habeas corpus relief or the time for filing a timely habeas corpus petition in that Court has passed without such a petition being filed, (ii) the Supreme Court of the United States has issued a final order disposing of the case after granting a stay to review the judgment of the Supreme Court of Virginia on habeas corpus, (iii) the United States Court of Appeals has affirmed the denial of federal habeas corpus relief or the time for filing a timely appeal in that court has passed without such an appeal being filed, or (iv) the Supreme Court of the United States has issued a final order after granting a stay in order to dispose of the petition for a writ of certiorari to review the judgment of the United States Court of Appeals.

The trial court shall conduct a proceeding to set the date within ten days after receiving the written notice from the Attorney General or the attorney for the Commonwealth. The execution date shall be set by the trial court in accordance with the provisions of §§ 53.1-232 and 53.1-234, but in any event shall be no later than sixty days after the date of the proceeding. Nothing in this provision shall prohibit the trial court from setting an execution date under circumstances other than those specified herein. Once an execution date is scheduled, a stay of execution may be granted by the trial court or the Supreme Court of Virginia only upon a showing of substantial grounds for habeas corpus relief.

History.
1995, c. 503.

§ 53.1-233. Death chamber; who to execute death sentence.

The Director is hereby authorized and directed to provide and maintain a permanent death chamber and necessary appurtenant facilities within the confines of a state correctional facility. The death chamber shall have all the necessary appliances for the proper execution of prisoners by electrocution or by continuous intravenous injection of a substance or combination of substances sufficient to cause death. Any such substance shall be applied until the prisoner is pronounced dead by a physician licensed in the Commonwealth. All prisoners upon whom the death penalty has been imposed shall be executed in the death chamber. Each execution shall be conducted by the Director or one or more assistants designated by him.

The identities of persons designated by the Director to conduct an execution, and any information reasonably calculated to lead to the identities of such persons, including, but not limited to, their names, residential or office addresses, residential or office telephone numbers, and social security numbers, shall be confidential, shall be exempt from the Freedom of Information Act (§ 2.2-3700 et seq.), and shall not be subject to discovery or introduction as evidence in any civil proceeding unless good cause is shown.

History.

Code 1950, §§ 19-275, 19-302, 53-317; 1960, c. 366; 1972, c. 145; 1978, c. 667; 1982, c. 636; 1989, c. 541; 1994, c. 921; 2007, cc. 652, 737.

§ 53.1-234. Transfer of prisoner; how death sentence executed; who to be present.

The clerk of the circuit court in which is pronounced the sentence of death against any person shall, after such judgment becomes final in the circuit court, deliver a certified copy thereof to the Director. Such person so sentenced to death shall be confined prior to the execution of the sentence in a state correctional facility designated by the Director. Prior to the time fixed in the judgment of the court for the execution of the sentence, the Director shall cause the condemned prisoner to be conveyed to the state correctional facility housing the death chamber.

The Director, or the assistants appointed by him, shall at the time named in the sentence, unless a suspension of execution is ordered, cause the prisoner under sentence of death to be electrocuted or injected with a lethal substance, until he is dead. The method of execution shall be chosen by the prisoner. In the event the prisoner refuses to make a choice at least 15 days prior to the scheduled execution, the method of execution shall be by lethal injection. Execution by lethal injection shall be permitted in accordance with procedures developed by the Department. At the execution there shall be present the Director or an assistant, a physician employed by the Department or his assistant, such other employees of the Department as may be required by the Director and, in addition thereto, at least six citizens who shall not be employees of the Department. In addition, the counsel for the prisoner and a clergyman may be present.

The Director may make and enter into contracts with a pharmacy, as defined in § 54.1-3300, or outsourcing facility, as defined in § 54.1-3401, for the compounding of drugs necessary to carry out an execution by lethal injection. Any such drugs provided to the Department pursuant to the terms of such a contract shall be used only for the purpose of carrying out an execution by lethal injection. The compounding of such drugs pursuant to the terms of such a contract (i) shall not constitute the practice of pharmacy as defined in § 54.1-3300; (ii) is not subject to the jurisdiction of the Board of Pharmacy, the Board of Medicine, or the Department of Health Professions; and (iii) is exempt from the provisions of Chapter 33 (§ 54.1-3300 et seq.) of Title 54.1 and the Drug Control Act (§ 54.1-3400 et seq.). The pharmacy or outsourcing facility providing such drugs to the Department pursuant to the terms of such a contract shall label each such drug with the drug name, its quantity, a projected expiration date for the drug, and a statement that the drug shall be used only by the Department for the purpose of carrying out an execution by lethal injection.

The identities of any pharmacy or outsourcing facility that enters into a contract with the Department for the compounding of drugs necessary to carry out an execution by lethal injection, any officer or employee of such pharmacy or outsourcing facility, and any person or entity used by such pharmacy or outsourcing facility to obtain equipment or substances to facilitate the compounding of such drugs and any information reasonably calculated to lead to the identities of such persons or entities, including their names, residential and office addresses, residential and office telephone numbers, social security numbers, and tax identification numbers, shall be confidential, shall be exempt from the Freedom of Information Act (§ 2.2-3700 et seq.), and shall not be subject to discovery or introduction as evidence in any civil proceeding unless good cause is shown.

History.

Code 1950, §§ 19-276, 19.1-303, 53-318; 1960, c. 366; 1972, c. 145; 1978, c. 667; 1982, c. 636; 1989, c. 541; 1994, c. 921; 1996, c. 679; 2007, cc. 652, 737; 2016, c. 747.

§ 53.1-235. Certificate of execution of death sentence.

After execution of the death sentence as provided in this chapter, the physician in attendance shall perform an examination to determine that death has occurred. The Director shall certify the fact of the execution, appending the physician's death certificate thereto, to the clerk of the court by which such sentence was pronounced. The clerk shall file the certificate with the papers of the case and shall enter the same upon the records of the case.

History.
Code 1950, § 53-319.1; 1978, c. 451; 1982, c. 636.

§ 53.1-236. Disposition of remains.

Upon application of the relatives of the person executed, the remains after execution shall be returned to their address and at their cost. If no such application is made within three days of the date of execution, the provisions of § 32.1-298 shall apply.

History.
Code 1950, §§ 19-281, 19.1-307, 53-323; 1960, c. 366; 1972, c. 145; 1978, c. 614; 1982, c. 636.

TITLE 54.1. PROFESSIONS AND OCCUPATIONS.

SUBTITLE I. GENERAL PROVISIONS RELATING TO REGULATORY BOARDS.

CHAPTER 1. GENERAL PROVISIONS.

Section

§ 54.1-102. Unlawful procurement of certificate, license or permit; unauthorized possession of examination or answers; penalty.

A. It shall be unlawful:

1. For any person to procure, or assist another to procure, through theft, fraud or other illegal means, a certificate, license or permit, from any state board, or other body charged by law with the responsibility of examining persons desiring to engage in a regulated business or profession;

2. For any person, other than a member or officer of the board or body, to procure or have in his possession prior to the beginning of an examination, without written authority of a member or officer of the board or body, any question intended to be used by the board or body conducting the examination, or to receive or furnish to any person taking the examination, prior to or during the examination, any written or printed material purporting to be answers to, or aid in answering such questions;

3. For any person to attempt to procure, through theft, fraud or other illegal means, any questions intended to be used by the board or body conducting the examination, or the answers to the questions;

4. For any person to use, disclose or release any questions intended to be used by the board or body conducting the examination, or to release the answers to the questions, beyond the scope specifically authorized by the board or body; or

5. To promise or offer any valuable or other consideration to a person having access to the questions or answers as an inducement to procure for delivery to the promisor, or any other person, a copy or copies of any questions or answers.

If an examination is divided into separate parts, each of the parts shall be deemed an examination for the purposes of this section.

B. Any person violating the provisions of subsection A shall be guilty of a Class 2 misdemeanor.

History.
Code 1950, §§ 54-1.1, 54-1.2; 1988, c. 765; 2012, c. 416.

SUBTITLE II. PROFESSIONS AND OCCUPATIONS REGULATED BY THE DEPARTMENT OF PROFESSIONAL AND OCCUPATIONAL REGULATION AND BOARDS WITHIN THE DEPARTMENT.

CHAPTER 6. AUCTIONEERS.

Section

§ 54.1-606. Unlawful to advertise as an auctioneer.

It shall be unlawful for any person not licensed under the provisions of this chapter to advertise that he is in the auction business or to hold himself out to the public as an auctioneer.

History.
1982, c. 538, § 54-824.19; 1983, c. 522; 1988, c. 765; 1991, c. 299.

CHAPTER 9.

BRANCH PILOTS.

Article 6.

Offenses and Penalties Generally.

ARTICLE 6.

OFFENSES AND PENALTIES GENERALLY.

§ 54.1-924. Piloting, etc., vessel without license; how offenders proceeded against.

No person shall conduct or pilot a vessel to or from sea, or to or from any port or place in Virginia unless he is licensed under this chapter.

Warrants for persons violating this section may be issued by any magistrate, upon the oath of any party complaining, and shall be returnable to the Circuit Court of the City of Norfolk. After a bond hearing held pursuant to Chapter 9 (§ 19.2-119 et seq.) of Title 19.2, the bond shall be returned by the judicial officer to the circuit court of the City of Norfolk, which shall have jurisdiction for trial of such misdemeanor.

History.
Code 1950, § 54-571; 1988, c. 765.

§ 54.1-927. Violation of chapter a misdemeanor.

Any person who violates any of the provisions of this chapter shall be guilty of a Class 1 misdemeanor.

History.
1988, c. 765.

CHAPTER 18.

POLYGRAPH EXAMINERS.

§ 54.1-1800. Definitions.

As used in this chapter, unless the context requires a different meaning:

"Course of instruction" means a formal course of instruction in the detection of deception and the verification of truth in an institution approved by the Director.

"Department" means the Department of Professional and Occupational Regulation.

"Director" means the Director of the Department of Professional and Occupational Regulation.

"Other detection device" or *"device"* means any mechanical or electronic instrument or device, other than a polygraph, used to test or question individuals for the purpose of detecting deception or verifying truthfulness.

"Person" means any natural person, partnership, association, corporation or trust.

"Polygraph" means any mechanical or electronic instrument or device used to test or question individuals for the purpose of determining truthfulness.

"Polygraph examiner" means any person who uses a polygraph to test or question individuals for the purpose of determining truthfulness.

"Polygraph examiner intern" means any person engaged in the study of polygraphy and the administration of polygraph examinations under the personal supervision and control of a polygraph examiner.

History.
1975, c. 522, § 54-916; 1988, c. 765; 1993, c. 499; 2010, c. 625.

§ 54.1-1801. Licenses.

A. All polygraph examiners shall be licensed pursuant to this chapter.

B. All persons who operate any other detection device shall be licensed pursuant to this chapter.

History.
1975, c. 522, § 54-918; 1988, c. 765; 2010, c. 625.

§ 54.1-1802: Repealed by Acts 2010, c. 578, cl. 2.

Cross references.
For current provisions as to the authority of the Department to promulgate regulations, see § 54.1-1802.1.

§ 54.1-1802.1. Powers and duties of the Department.

The Department shall administer and enforce the provisions of this chapter. In addition to the powers and duties otherwise conferred by the law, the Director shall have the powers and duties of a regulatory board as contained in §§ 54.1-201 and 54.1-202 and shall have the power and duty to:

1. Promulgate regulations necessary for the reasonable administration of this chapter in accordance with the Administrative Process Act (§ 2.2-4000 et seq.). Such regulations shall include, but not be

limited to, the establishment of minimum qualifications for the operators of polygraphs and other detection devices;

2. Charge each applicant for licensure and for renewals of licensure a nonrefundable fee subject to the provisions of § 54.1-113 and subdivision A 4 of § 54.1-201; and

3. Conduct investigations to determine the suitability of applicants for licensure and to determine the licensee's compliance with applicable statutes and regulations.

History.
2010, cc. 578, 625; 2012, c. 769.

§ 54.1-1803. Approval of schools to teach courses of instruction.

The Director shall promulgate regulations for the approval of schools in which courses of instruction for polygraph examiners and persons who operate other detection devices approved pursuant to § 54.1-1805 are taught.

History.
1975, c. 522, § 54-920; 1988, c. 765; 2010, c. 625.

§ 54.1-1804. Submission of fingerprints.

Each applicant for licensure as a polygraph examiner, each polygraph examiner intern, and each applicant for licensure to operate any other detection device shall submit his fingerprints to the Department on a form provided by the Department.

History.
1975, c. 522, § 54-921; 1988, c. 765; 2010, c. 625.

§ 54.1-1805. Instrument to be used.

A. Each polygraph examiner shall use an instrument that records permanently and simultaneously the subject's cardiovascular and respiratory patterns as minimum standards, but such an instrument may record additional physiological changes pertinent to the determination of truthfulness.

B. 1. The use of any other detection device that does not meet the instrumentation requirements set forth in subsection A shall be approved by the Director. The Director shall approve such other detection device only when the data collected by such device is deemed to be reliable and valid in detecting deception or verifying truth, based upon the preponderance of available scientific evidence. The voluntary, written consent of any individual to be tested using a detection device approved pursuant to this subsection shall be obtained prior to the administration of any such test or questioning using the device.

2. Any such approved device shall be subject to regulations promulgated by the Director regarding its use in the Commonwealth.

3. The Director shall establish standards of practice related to the use of any such other detection device approved pursuant to this subsection.

History.
1975, c. 522, § 54-922; 1988, c. 765; 2010, c. 625.

§ 54.1-1806. Prohibition of use of certain questions on polygraph tests for employment.

No licensed polygraph operator shall, during a polygraph examination required as a condition of employment, ask any question concerning the sexual activities of the person being examined if the question violates state or federal law. A violation of this section shall constitute grounds for disciplinary action pursuant to § 54.1-1802.1.

History.
1989, c. 693; 2010, c. 578.

SUBTITLE III.

PROFESSIONS AND OCCUPATIONS REGULATED BY BOARDS WITHIN THE DEPARTMENT OF HEALTH PROFESSIONS.

CHAPTER 24.

GENERAL PROVISIONS.

Section

§ 54.1-2400.1. Mental health service providers; duty to protect third parties; immunity.

A. As used in this section:

"Certified substance abuse counselor" means a person certified to provide substance abuse counseling in a state-approved public or private substance abuse program or facility.

"Client" or *"patient"* means any person who is voluntarily or involuntarily receiving mental health services or substance abuse services from any mental health service provider.

"Clinical psychologist" means a person who practices clinical psychology as defined in § 54.1-3600.

"Clinical social worker" means a person who practices social work as defined in § 54.1-3700.

"Licensed practical nurse" means a person licensed to practice practical nursing as defined in § 54.1-3000.

"Licensed substance abuse treatment practitioner" means any person licensed to engage in the practice of substance abuse treatment as defined in § 54.1-3500.

"Marriage and family therapist" means a person licensed to engage in the practice of marriage and family therapy as defined in § 54.1-3500.

"Mental health professional" means a person who by education and experience is professionally qualified and licensed in Virginia to provide counseling interventions designed to facilitate an individual's achievement of human development goals and remediate mental, emotional, or behavioral disorders and associated distresses which interfere with mental health and development.

"Mental health service provider" or *"provider"* refers to any of the following: (i) a person who provides professional services as a certified substance abuse counselor, clinical psychologist, clinical social worker, licensed substance abuse treatment practitioner, licensed practical nurse, marriage and family therapist, mental health professional, physician, professional counselor, psychologist, registered nurse, school psychologist, or social worker; (ii) a professional corporation, all of whose shareholders or members are so licensed; or (iii) a partnership, all of whose partners are so licensed.

"Professional counselor" means a person who practices counseling as defined in § 54.1-3500.

"Psychologist" means a person who practices psychology as defined in § 54.1-3600.

"Registered nurse" means a person licensed to practice professional nursing as defined in § 54.1-3000.

"School psychologist" means a person who practices school psychology as defined in § 54.1-3600.

"Social worker" means a person who practices social work as defined in § 54.1-3700.

B. A mental health service provider has a duty to take precautions to protect third parties from violent behavior or other serious harm only when the client has orally, in writing, or via sign language, communicated to the provider a specific and immediate threat to cause serious bodily injury or death to an identified or readily identifiable person or persons, if the provider reasonably believes, or should believe according to the standards of his profession, that the client has the intent and ability to carry out that threat immediately or imminently. If the third party is a child, in addition to taking precautions to protect the child from the behaviors in the above types of threats, the provider also has a duty to take precautions to protect the child if the client threatens to engage in behaviors that would constitute physical abuse or sexual abuse as defined in § 18.2-67.10. The duty to protect does not attach unless the threat has been communicated to the provider by the threatening client while the provider is engaged in his professional duties.

C. The duty set forth in subsection B is discharged by a mental health service provider who takes one or more of the following actions:

1. Seeks involuntary admission of the client under Article 16 (§ 16.1-335 et seq.) of Chapter 11 of Title 16.1 or Chapter 8 (§ 37.2-800 et seq.) of Title 37.2.

2. Makes reasonable attempts to warn the potential victims or the parent or guardian of the potential victim if the potential victim is under the age of 18.

3. Makes reasonable efforts to notify a law-enforcement official having jurisdiction in the client's or potential victim's place of residence or place of work, or place of work of the parent or guardian if the potential victim is under age 18, or both.

4. Takes steps reasonably available to the provider to prevent the client from using physical violence or other means of harm to others until the appropriate law-enforcement agency can be summoned and takes custody of the client.

5. Provides therapy or counseling to the client or patient in the session in which the threat has been communicated until the mental health service provider reasonably believes that the client no longer has the intent or the ability to carry out the threat.

D. A mental health service provider shall not be held civilly liable to any person for:

1. Breaching confidentiality with the limited purpose of protecting third parties by communicating the threats described in subsection B made by his clients to potential third party victims or law-enforcement agencies or by taking any of the actions specified in subsection C.

2. Failing to predict, in the absence of a threat described in subsection B, that the client would cause the third party serious physical harm.

3. Failing to take precautions other than those enumerated in subsection C to protect a potential third party victim from the client's violent behavior.

History.

1994, c. 958; 1997, c. 901; 2005, c. 716; 2010, cc. 778, 825.

§ 54.1-2400.4. Mental health service providers duty to inform; immunity; civil penalty.

A. Any mental health service provider, as defined in § 54.1-2400.1, shall, upon learning of evidence that indicates a reasonable probability that another mental health provider is or may be guilty of a violation of standards of conduct as defined in statute or regulation, advise his patient of his right to report such misconduct to the Department of Health Professions, hereinafter referred to as the "Department."

B. The mental health service provider shall provide relevant information to the patient, including, but not limited to, the Department's toll-free complaint hotline number for consumer complaints and written information, published by the Department of Health Professions, explaining how to file a report. The mental health service provider shall document in the patient's record the alleged misconduct, the category of licensure or certification, and approximate dates of treatment, if known, of the mental health service provider who will be the subject of the report, and the action taken by the mental health service provider to inform the patient of his right to file a complaint with the Department of Health Professions.

C. Any mental health service provider informing a patient of his right to file a complaint against a regulated person and providing the information required by this section shall be immune from any civil liability or criminal prosecution resulting therefrom unless such person acted in bad faith or with malicious intent.

D. Notwithstanding any other provision of law, any person required to inform a patient of his right to file a complaint against a regulated person pursuant to this section who fails to do so shall be subject to a civil penalty not to exceed $100.

History.
2000, c. 578.

§ 54.1-2409.1. Criminal penalties for practicing certain professions and occupations without appropriate license.

Any person who, without holding a current valid license or multistate licensure privilege, issued by a regulatory board pursuant to this title (i) performs an invasive procedure for which a license or multistate licensure privilege is required; (ii) administers, prescribes, sells, distributes, or dispenses a controlled drug; or (iii) practices a profession or occupation after having his license or multistate licensure privilege to do so suspended or revoked shall be guilty of a Class 6 felony.

History.
1994, c. 722; 2004, c. 49.

CHAPTER 29.
MEDICINE AND OTHER HEALING ARTS.

ARTICLE 1.
GENERAL PROVISIONS.

§ 54.1-2902. Unlawful to practice without license.

It shall be unlawful for any person to practice medicine, osteopathic medicine, chiropractic, podiatry, or as a physician's or podiatrist's assistant in the Commonwealth without a valid unrevoked license issued by the Board of Medicine.

History.
Code 1950, § 54-274; 1950, p. 98; 1958, c. 161; 1962, c. 127; 1966, c. 657; 1970, c. 69; 1973, cc. 105, 514, 529; 1975, c. 508; 1976, c. 15; 1980, c. 157; 1982, c. 220; 1985, cc. 303, 347; 1986, c. 377; 1988, c. 765; 1996, cc. 937, 980; 2000, c. 688.

§ 54.1-2903. What constitutes practice.

Any person shall be regarded as practicing the healing arts who actually engages in such practice as defined in this chapter, or who opens an office for such purpose, or who advertises or announces to the public in any manner a readiness to practice or who uses in connection with his name the words or letters "Doctor," "Dr.," "M.D.," "D.O.," "D.P.M.," "D.C.," "Healer," or any other title, word, letter or designation intending to designate or imply that he is a practitioner of the healing arts or that he is able to heal, cure or relieve those suffering from any injury, deformity or disease. No person regulated under this chapter shall use the title "Doctor" or the abbreviation "Dr." in writing or in advertising in connection with his practice unless he simultaneously uses a clarifying title, initials, abbreviation or designation or language that identifies the type of practice for which he is licensed.

Signing a birth or death certificate, or signing any statement certifying that the person so signing has rendered professional service to the sick or injured, or signing or issuing a prescription for drugs or other remedial agents, shall be prima facie evidence that the person signing or issuing such writing is practicing the healing arts within the meaning of this chapter except where persons other than physicians are required to sign birth certificates.

History.
Code 1950, § 54-275; 1958, c. 161; 1966, c. 657; 1973, c. 529; 1975, c. 508; 1988, c. 765; 1991, c. 102; 1996, cc. 937, 980; 2000, c. 688.

ARTICLE 8.

HEALTH CARE DECISIONS ACT.

§ 54.1-2981. Short title.

The provisions of this article shall be known and may be cited as the "Health Care Decisions Act."

History.
1983, c. 532, § 54-325.8:1; 1988, c. 765; 1992, cc. 748, 772.

§ 54.1-2983. Procedure for making advance directive; notice to physician.

Any adult capable of making an informed decision may, at any time, make a written advance directive to address any or all forms of health care in the event the declarant is later determined to be incapable of making an informed decision. A written advance directive shall be signed by the declarant in the presence of two subscribing witnesses and may (i) specify the health care the declarant does or does not authorize; (ii) appoint an agent to make health care decisions for the declarant; and (iii) specify an anatomical gift, after the declarant's death, of all of the declarant's body or an organ, tissue or eye donation pursuant to Article 2 (§ 32.1-289.2 et seq.) of Chapter 8 of Title 32.1. A written advance directive may be submitted to the Advance Health Care Directive Registry, pursuant to Article 9 (§ 54.1-2994 et seq.).

Further, any adult capable of making an informed decision who has been diagnosed by his attending physician as being in a terminal condition may make an oral advance directive (i) directing the specific health care the declarant does or does not authorize in the event the declarant is incapable of making an informed decision, and (ii) appointing an agent to make health care decisions for the declarant under the circumstances stated in the advance directive if the declarant should be determined to be incapable of making an informed decision. An oral advance directive shall be made in the presence of the attending physician and two witnesses.

An advance directive may authorize an agent to take any lawful actions necessary to carry out the declarant's decisions, including, but not limited to, granting releases of liability to medical providers, releasing medical records, and making decisions regarding who may visit the patient.

It shall be the responsibility of the declarant to provide for notification to his attending physician that an advance directive has been made. If an advance directive has been submitted to the Advance Health Care Directive Registry pursuant to Article 9 (§ 54.1-2994 et seq.), it shall be the responsibility of the declarant to provide his attending physician, legal representative, or other person with the information necessary to access the advance directive. In the event the declarant is comatose, incapacitated or otherwise mentally or physically incapable of communication, any other person may notify the physician of the existence of an advance directive and, if applicable, the fact that it has been submitted to the Advance Health Care Directive Registry. An attending physician who is so notified shall promptly make the advance directive or a copy of the advance directive, if written, or the fact of the advance directive, if oral, a part of the declarant's medical records.

In the event that any portion of an advance directive is invalid or illegal, such invalidity or illegality shall not affect the remaining provisions of the advance directive.

History.
1983, c. 532, § 54-325.8:3; 1988, c. 765; 1992, cc. 748, 772; 1997, c. 801; 2008, cc. 301, 696; 2009, cc. 211, 268; 2010, c. 16.

§ 54.1-2983.1. Participation in health care research.

An advance directive may authorize an agent to approve participation by the declarant in any health care study approved by an institutional review board pursuant to applicable federal regulations, or by a research review committee pursuant to Chapter 5.1 (§ 32.1-162.16 et seq.) of Title 32.1 that offers the prospect of direct therapeutic benefit to the declarant. An advance directive may also authorize an agent to approve participation by the declarant in any health care study approved by an institutional review board pursuant to applicable federal regulations, or by a research review committee pursuant to Chapter 5.1 (§ 32.1-162.16 et seq.) of Title 32.1 that aims to increase scientific understanding of any condition that the declarant may have or otherwise to promote human well-being, even though it offers no prospect of direct benefit to the patient.

History.
2009, cc. 211, 268.

§ 54.1-2983.2. Capacity; required determinations.

A. Every adult shall be presumed to be capable of making an informed decision unless he is determined to be incapable of making an informed decision in accordance with this article. A determination that a patient is incapable of making an informed decision may apply to a particular health care decision, to a specified set of health care decisions, or to all health care decisions. No person shall be deemed incapable of making an informed decision based solely on a particular clinical diagnosis.

B. Prior to providing, continuing, withholding, or withdrawing health care pursuant to an authorization that has been obtained or will be sought pursuant to this article and prior to, or as soon as reasonably practicable after initiating health care for which authorization has been obtained or will be sought pursuant to this article, and no less frequently than every 180 days while the need for health care continues, the attending physician shall certify in writing upon personal examination of the patient that the patient is incapable of making an informed decision regarding health care and shall obtain written certification from a capacity reviewer that, based upon a personal examination of the patient, the patient is incapable of making an informed decision. However, certification by a capacity reviewer shall not be required if the patient is unconscious or experiencing a profound impairment of consciousness due to trauma, stroke, or other acute physiological condition. The capacity reviewer providing written certification that a patient is incapable of making an informed decision, if required, shall not be otherwise currently involved in the treatment of the person assessed, unless an independent capacity reviewer is not reasonably available. The cost of the assessment shall be considered for all purposes a cost of the patient's health care.

C. If, at any time, a patient is determined to be incapable of making an informed decision, the patient shall be notified, as soon as practical and to the extent he is capable of receiving such notice, that such determination has been made before providing, continuing, withholding, or withdrawing health care as authorized by this article. Such notice shall also be provided, as soon as practical, to the patient's agent or person authorized by § 54.1-2986 to make health care decisions on his behalf.

D. A single physician may, at any time, upon personal evaluation, determine that a patient who has previously been determined to be incapable of making an informed decision is now capable of making an informed decision, provided such determination is set forth in writing.

History.
2009, cc. 211, 268; 2010, c. 792.

§ 54.1-2983.3. Exclusions and limitations of advance directives.

A. The absence of an advance directive by an adult patient shall not give rise to any presumption as to his intent to consent to or refuse any particular health care.

B. The provisions of this article shall not apply to authorization of nontherapeutic sterilization, abortion, or psychosurgery.

C. If any provision of a patient's advance directive conflicts with the authority conferred by any emergency custody, temporary detention, involuntary admission, and mandatory outpatient treatment order set forth in Chapter 8 (§ 37.2-800 et seq.) of Title 37.2 or by any other provision of law, the provisions of the patient's advance directive that create the conflict shall have no effect. However, a patient's advance directive shall otherwise be given full effect.

D. The provisions of this article, if otherwise applicable, may be used to authorize admission of a patient to a facility, as defined in § 37.2-100, only if the admission is otherwise authorized under Chapter 8 (§ 37.2-800 et seq.) of Title 37.2.

History.
2009, cc. 211, 268; 2010, c. 792.

§ 54.1-2987.1. Durable Do Not Resuscitate Orders.

A. A Durable Do Not Resuscitate Order may be issued by a physician for his patient with whom he has a bona fide physician/patient relationship as defined in the guidelines of the Board of Medicine, and only with the consent of the patient or, if the patient is a minor or is otherwise incapable of making an informed decision regarding consent for such an order, upon the request of and with the consent of the person authorized to consent on the patient's behalf.

B. If a patient is able to, and does, express to a health care provider or practitioner the desire to be resuscitated in the event of cardiac or respiratory arrest, such expression shall revoke the provider's or practitioner's authority to follow a Durable Do Not Resuscitate Order. In no case shall any person other than the patient have authority to revoke a Durable Do Not Resuscitate Order executed upon the request of and with the consent of the patient himself.

If the patient is a minor or is otherwise incapable of making an informed decision and the Durable Do Not Resuscitate Order was issued upon the request of and with the consent of the person authorized to consent on the patient's behalf, then the expression by said authorized person to a health care provider or practitioner of the desire that the patient be resuscitated shall so revoke the provider's or practitioner's authority to follow a Durable Do Not Resuscitate Order.

When a Durable Do Not Resuscitate Order has been revoked as provided in this section, a new Order may be issued upon consent of the patient or the person authorized to consent on the patient's behalf.

C. Durable Do Not Resuscitate Orders issued in accordance with this section shall remain valid and in effect until revoked as provided in subsection B or until rescinded, in accordance with accepted medical practice, by the provider who issued the Durable Do Not Resuscitate Order. In accordance with this section and regulations promulgated by the Board of Health, (i) qualified emergency medical services personnel as defined in § 32.1-111.1; (ii) licensed health care practitioners in any facility, program or organization operated or licensed by the Board of Health, the Department of Social Services, or the Department of Behavioral Health and Developmental Services or operated, licensed or owned by another state agency; and (iii) licensed health care practitioners at any continuing care retirement community registered with the State Corporation Commission pursuant to Chapter 49 (§ 38.2-4900 et seq.) of Title 38.2 are authorized to follow Durable

Do Not Resuscitate Orders that are available to them in a form approved by the Board of Health.

D. The provisions of this section shall not authorize any qualified emergency medical services personnel or licensed health care provider or practitioner who is attending the patient at the time of cardiac or respiratory arrest to provide, continue, withhold or withdraw health care if such provider or practitioner knows that taking such action is protested by the patient incapable of making an informed decision. No person shall authorize providing, continuing, withholding or withdrawing health care pursuant to this section that such person knows, or upon reasonable inquiry ought to know, is contrary to the religious beliefs or basic values of a patient incapable of making an informed decision or the wishes of such patient fairly expressed when the patient was capable of making an informed decision. Further, this section shall not authorize the withholding of other medical interventions, such as intravenous fluids, oxygen or other therapies deemed necessary to provide comfort care or to alleviate pain.

E. For the purposes of this section:

"Health care provider" includes, but is not limited to, qualified emergency medical services personnel.

"Person authorized to consent on the patient's behalf" means any person authorized by law to consent on behalf of the patient incapable of making an informed decision or, in the case of a minor child, the parent or parents having custody of the child or the child's legal guardian or as otherwise provided by law.

F. This section shall not prevent, prohibit or limit a physician from issuing a written order, other than a Durable Do Not Resuscitate Order, not to resuscitate a patient in the event of cardiac or respiratory arrest in accordance with accepted medical practice.

G. Valid Do Not Resuscitate Orders or Emergency Medical Services Do Not Resuscitate Orders issued before July 1, 1999, pursuant to the then-current law, shall remain valid and shall be given effect as provided in this article.

History.

1992, c. 412; 1994, c. 956; 1998, cc. 564, 628, 630, 803, 854; 1999, c. 814; 2009, cc. 211, 268, 549, 813, 840; 2010, c. 792.

§ 54.1-2988. Immunity from liability; burden of proof; presumption.

A health care facility, physician or other person acting under the direction of a physician shall not be subject to criminal prosecution or civil liability or be deemed to have engaged in unprofessional conduct as a result of issuing a Durable Do Not Resuscitate Order or the providing, continuing, withholding or the withdrawal of health care under authorization or consent obtained in accordance with this article or as the result of the provision, withholding or withdrawal of ongoing health care in accordance with § 54.1-2990. No person or facility providing, continuing, withholding or withdrawing health care or physician issuing a Durable Do Not Resuscitate Order under authorization or consent obtained pursuant to this article or otherwise in accordance with § 54.1-2990 shall incur liability arising out of a claim to the extent the claim is based on lack of authorization or consent for such action.

Any agent or person identified in § 54.1-2986 who authorizes or consents to the providing, continuing, withholding or withdrawal of health care in accordance with this article shall not be subject, solely on the basis of that authorization or consent, to (i) criminal prosecution or civil liability for such action or (ii) liability for the cost of health care.

No individual serving on a facility's patient care consulting committee as defined in this article and no physician rendering a determination or affirmation in cases in which no patient care consulting committee exists shall be subject to criminal prosecution or civil liability for any act or omission done or made in good faith in the performance of such functions.

The provisions of this section shall apply unless it is shown by a preponderance of the evidence that the person authorizing or effectuating the providing, continuing, withholding or withdrawal of health care, or issuing, consenting to, making or following a Durable Do Not Resuscitate Order in accordance with § 54.1-2987.1 did not, in good faith, comply with the provisions of this article.

The distribution to patients of written advance directives in a form meeting the requirements of § 54.1-2984 and assistance to patients in the completion and execution of such forms by health care providers shall not constitute the unauthorized practice of law pursuant to Chapter 39 (§ 54.1-3900 et seq.).

An advance directive or Durable Do Not Resuscitate Order made, consented to or issued in accordance with this article shall be presumed to have been made, consented to, or issued voluntarily and in good faith by an adult who is capable of making an informed decision, physician or person authorized to consent on the patient's behalf.

History.

1983, c. 532, § 54-325.8:8; 1988, c. 765; 1992, cc. 412, 748, 772; 1998, cc. 803, 854; 1999, c. 814; 2000, cc. 590, 598; 2009, cc. 211, 268; 2010, c. 792.

§ 54.1-2989. Willful destruction, concealment, etc., of declaration or revocation; penalties.

A. Any person who willfully (i) conceals, cancels, defaces, obliterates, or damages the advance directive or Durable Do Not Resuscitate Order of another without the declarant's or patient's consent or the consent of the person authorized to consent for the patient; (ii) falsifies or forges the advance directive or Durable Do Not Resuscitate Order of another; or (iii) falsifies or forges a revocation of the advance directive or Durable Do Not Resuscitate Order of another shall be guilty of a Class 1 misdemeanor. If such action causes life-prolonging procedures to be utilized in contravention of the previously expressed intent of the patient or a Durable Do Not Resuscitate Order, the person committing such action shall be guilty of a Class 6 felony.

B. Any person who willfully (i) conceals, cancels, defaces, obliterates, or damages the advance directive or Durable Do Not Resuscitate Order of another without the declarant's or patient's consent or the consent of the person authorized to consent for the patient, (ii) falsifies or forges the advance directive or Durable Do Not Resuscitate Order of another, (iii) falsifies or forges a revocation of the advance directive or Durable Do Not Resuscitate Order of another, or (iv) conceals or withholds personal knowledge of the revocation of an advance directive or Durable Do Not Resuscitate Order, with the intent to cause a withholding or withdrawal of life-prolonging procedures, contrary to the wishes of the declarant or a patient, and thereby, because of such act, directly causes life-prolonging procedures to be withheld or withdrawn and death to be hastened, shall be guilty of a Class 2 felony.

History.
1983, c. 532, § 54-325.8:9; 1988, c. 765; 1992, cc. 412, 748, 772; 1998, cc. 803, 854; 1999, c. 814; 2009, cc. 211, 268.

§ 54.1-2989.1. Failure to deliver advance directive.

An agent in possession of an advance medical directive vesting any power or authority in him shall, when the instrument is otherwise valid, be deemed to possess the powers and authority granted by such instrument notwithstanding any failure by the declarant to deliver the instrument to him, and persons dealing with such agent shall have no obligation to inquire into the manner or circumstances by which such possession was acquired; provided, however, that nothing herein shall preclude the court from considering such manner or circumstances as relevant factors in a proceeding brought to remove the agent or revoke the directive.

History.
2003, c. 269.

§ 54.1-2990. Medically unnecessary health care not required; procedure when physician refuses to comply with an advance directive or a designated person's health care decision; mercy killing or euthanasia prohibited.

A. Nothing in this article shall be construed to require a physician to prescribe or render health care to a patient that the physician determines to be medically or ethically inappropriate. However, in such a case, if the physician's determination is contrary to the request of the patient, the terms of a patient's advance directive, the decision of an agent or person authorized to make decisions pursuant to § 54.1-2986, or a Durable Do Not Resuscitate Order, the physician shall make a reasonable effort to inform the patient or the patient's agent or person with decision-making authority pursuant to § 54.1-2986 of such determination and the reasons for the determination. If the conflict remains unresolved, the physician shall make a reasonable effort to transfer the patient to another physician who is willing to comply with the request of the patient, the terms of the advance directive, the decision of an agent or person authorized to make decisions pursuant to § 54.1-2986, or a Durable Do Not Resuscitate Order. The physician shall provide the patient or his agent or person with decision-making authority pursuant to § 54.1-2986 a reasonable time of not less than fourteen days to effect such transfer. During this period, the physician shall continue to provide any life-sustaining care to the patient which is reasonably available to such physician, as requested by the patient or his agent or person with decision-making authority pursuant to § 54.1-2986.

B. For purposes of this section, "life-sustaining care" means any ongoing health care that utilizes mechanical or other artificial means to sustain, restore or supplant a spontaneous vital function, including hydration, nutrition, maintenance medication, and cardiopulmonary resuscitation.

C. Nothing in this section shall require the provision of health care that the physician is physically or legally unable to provide, or health care that the physician is physically or legally unable to provide without thereby denying the same health care to another patient.

D. Nothing in this article shall be construed to condone, authorize or approve mercy killing or euthanasia, or to permit any affirmative or deliberate act or omission to end life other than to permit the natural process of dying.

History.
1983, c. 532, § 54-325.8:10; 1988, c. 765; 1992, cc. 748, 772; 1999, c. 814; 2000, cc. 590, 598; 2009, cc. 211, 268.

§ 54.1-2991. Effect of declaration; suicide; insurance; declarations executed prior to effective date.

The withholding or withdrawal of life-prolonging procedures in accordance with the provisions of this article shall not, for any purpose, constitute a suicide. Nor shall the making of an advance directive pursuant to this article affect the sale, procurement or issuance of any policy of life insurance, nor shall the making of an advance directive or the issuance of a Durable Do Not Resuscitate Order pursuant to this article be deemed to modify the terms of an existing policy of life insurance. No policy of life insurance shall be legally impaired or invalidated by the withholding or withdrawal of life-prolonging procedures from an insured patient in accordance with this article, notwithstanding any term of the policy to the contrary. A person shall not be required to make an advance directive or consent to a Durable Do Not Resuscitate order as a condition for being insured for, or receiving, health care services.

The declaration of any patient made prior to July 1, 1983, an advance directive made prior to July 1, 1992, or the issuance, in accordance with the then current law, of a Do Not Resuscitate Order or an Emergency Medical Services Do Not Resuscitate Order prior to July 1, 1999, shall be given effect as provided in this article.

History.

1983, c. 532, § 54-325.8:11; 1988, c. 765; 1992, cc. 412, 748, 772; 1999, c. 814; 2009, cc. 211, 268.

CHAPTER 33.

PHARMACY.

Article 1.

General Provisions.

ARTICLE 1.

GENERAL PROVISIONS.

§ 54.1-3303. Prescriptions to be issued and drugs to be dispensed for medical or therapeutic purposes only.

A. A prescription for a controlled substance may be issued only by a practitioner of medicine, osteopathy, podiatry, dentistry or veterinary medicine who is authorized to prescribe controlled substances, or by a licensed nurse practitioner pursuant to § 54.1-2957.01, a licensed physician assistant pursuant to § 54.1-2952.1, or a TPA-certified optometrist pursuant to Article 5 (§ 54.1-3222 et seq.) of Chapter 32. The prescription shall be issued for a medicinal or therapeutic purpose and may be issued only to persons or animals with whom the practitioner has a bona fide practitioner-patient relationship.

For purposes of this section, a bona fide practitioner-patient-pharmacist relationship is one in which a practitioner prescribes, and a pharmacist dispenses, controlled substances in good faith to his patient for a medicinal or therapeutic purpose within the course of his professional practice. In addition, a bona fide practitioner-patient relationship means that the practitioner shall (i) ensure that a medical or drug history is obtained; (ii) provide information to the patient about the benefits and risks of the drug being prescribed; (iii) perform or have performed an appropriate examination of the patient, either physically or by the use of instrumentation and diagnostic equipment through which images and medical records may be transmitted electronically; except for medical emergencies, the examination of the patient shall have been performed by the practitioner himself, within the group in which he practices, or by a consulting practitioner prior to issuing a prescription; and (iv) initiate additional interventions and follow-up care, if necessary, especially if a prescribed drug may have serious side effects.

For the purpose of prescribing a Schedule VI controlled substance to a patient via telemedicine services as defined in § 38.2-3418.16, a prescriber may establish a bona fide practitioner-patient relationship by an examination through face-to-face interactive, two-way, real-time communications services or store-and-forward technologies when all of the following conditions are met: (a) the patient has provided a medical history that is available for review by the prescriber; (b) the prescriber obtains an updated medical history at the time of prescribing; (c) the prescriber makes a diagnosis at the time of prescribing; (d) the prescriber conforms to the standard of care expected of in-person care as appropriate to the patient's age and presenting condition, including when the standard of care requires the use of diagnostic testing and performance of a physical examination, which may be carried out through the use of peripheral devices appropriate to the patient's condition; (e) the prescriber is actively licensed in the Commonwealth and authorized to prescribe; (f) if the patient is a member or enrollee of a health plan or carrier, the prescriber has been credentialed by the health plan or carrier as a participating provider and the diagnosing and prescribing meets the qualifications for reimbursement by the health plan or carrier pursuant to § 38.2-3418.16; and (g) upon request, the prescriber provides patient records in a timely manner in accordance with the provisions of § 32.1-127.1:03 and all other state and federal laws and regulations. Nothing in this paragraph shall permit a prescriber to establish a bona fide practitioner-patient relationship for the purpose of prescribing a Schedule VI controlled substance when the standard of care dictates that an in-person physical examination is necessary for diagnosis. Nothing in this paragraph shall apply to: (1) a prescriber providing on-call coverage per an agreement with another prescriber or his prescriber's professional entity or employer; (2) a prescriber consulting with another prescriber regarding a patient's care; or (3) orders of prescribers for hospital out-patients or in-patients.

Any practitioner who prescribes any controlled substance with the knowledge that the controlled substance will be used otherwise than medicinally or for therapeutic purposes shall be subject to the criminal penalties provided in § 18.2-248 for violations of the provisions of law relating to the distribution or possession of controlled substances.

B. In order to determine whether a prescription that appears questionable to the pharmacist results from a bona fide practitioner-patient relationship, the pharmacist shall contact the prescribing practitioner or his agent and verify the identity of the patient and name and quantity of the drug prescribed. The person knowingly filling an invalid prescription shall be subject to the criminal penalties provided in § 18.2-248 for violations of the provisions of law relating to the sale, distribution or possession of controlled substances.

No prescription shall be filled unless there is a bona fide practitioner-patient-pharmacist relationship. A prescription not issued in the usual course of treatment or for authorized research is not a valid prescription.

C. Notwithstanding any provision of law to the contrary and consistent with recommendations of the Centers for Disease Control and Prevention or the Department of Health, a practitioner may prescribe Schedule VI antibiotics and antiviral agents to other persons in close contact with a diagnosed patient when (i) the practitioner meets all requirements of a bona fide practitioner-patient relationship, as defined in subsection A, with the diagnosed patient; (ii) in the practitioner's professional judgment, the practitioner deems there is urgency to begin treatment to prevent the transmission of a communicable disease; (iii) the practitioner has met all requirements of a bona fide practitioner-patient relationship, as defined in subsection A, for the close contact except for the physical examination required in clause (iii) of subsection A; and (iv) when such emergency treatment is necessary to prevent imminent risk of death, life-threatening illness, or serious disability.

D. A pharmacist may dispense a controlled substance pursuant to a prescription of an out-of-state practitioner of medicine, osteopathy, podiatry, dentistry or veterinary medicine authorized to issue such prescription if the prescription complies with the requirements of this chapter and the Drug Control Act (§ 54.1-3400 et seq.).

E. A licensed nurse practitioner who is authorized to prescribe controlled substances pursuant to § 54.1-2957.01 may issue prescriptions or provide manufacturers' professional samples for controlled substances and devices as set forth in the Drug Control Act (§ 54.1-3400 et seq.) in good faith to his patient for a medicinal or therapeutic purpose within the scope of his professional practice.

F. A licensed physician assistant who is authorized to prescribe controlled substances pursuant to § 54.1-2952.1 may issue prescriptions or provide manufacturers' professional samples for controlled substances and devices as set forth in the Drug Control Act (§ 54.1-3400 et seq.) in good faith to his patient for a medicinal or therapeutic purpose within the scope of his professional practice.

G. A TPA-certified optometrist who is authorized to prescribe controlled substances pursuant to Article 5 (§ 54.1-3222 et seq.) of Chapter 32 may issue prescriptions in good faith or provide manufacturers' professional samples to his patients for medicinal or therapeutic purposes within the scope of his professional practice for the drugs specified on the TPA-Formulary, established pursuant to § 54.1-3223, which shall be limited to (i) analgesics included on Schedule II controlled substances as defined in § 54.1-3448 of the Drug Control Act (§ 54.1-3400 et seq.) consisting of hydrocodone in combination with acetaminophen; (ii) oral analgesics included in Schedules III through VI, as defined in §§ 54.1-3450 and 54.1-3455 of the Drug Control Act (§ 54.1-3400 et seq.), which are appropriate to relieve ocular pain; (iii) other oral Schedule VI controlled substances, as defined in § 54.1-3455 of the Drug Control Act, appropriate to treat diseases and abnormal conditions of the human eye and its adnexa; (iv) topically applied Schedule VI drugs, as defined in § 54.1-3455 of the Drug Control Act; and (v) intramuscular administration of epinephrine for treatment of emergency cases of anaphylactic shock.

H. The requirement for a bona fide practitioner-patient relationship shall be deemed to be satisfied by a member or committee of a hospital's medical staff when approving a standing order or protocol for the administration of influenza vaccinations and pneumococcal vaccinations in a hospital in compliance with § 32.1-126.4.

History.

1983, c. 528, § 54-524.50:1; 1985, c. 336; 1988, c. 765; 1991, cc. 519, 524; 1992, c. 793; 1996, cc. 152, 158, 408; 1997, c. 806; 1998, c. 101; 1999, c. 745; 2000, cc. 882, 924; 2001, c. 465; 2003, c. 639; 2004, c. 744; 2006, c. 432; 2010, c. 74; 2015, cc. 32, 115; 2016, c. 86.

CHAPTER 34.

DRUG CONTROL ACT.

Article 1.

General Provisions.

Section

Article 4.1.

Expanded Access to Investigational Drugs, Biological Products, and Devices.

Article 5.

Standards and Schedules.

Article 6.

Misbranded and Adulterated Drugs and Cosmetics.

Article 7.

Controlled Paraphernalia.

ARTICLE 1.

GENERAL PROVISIONS.

§ 54.1-3400. Citation.

This chapter may be cited as "The Drug Control Act."

History.
1970, c. 650, § 54-524.1; 1988, c. 765.

§ 54.1-3401. Definitions.

As used in this chapter, unless the context requires a different meaning:

"Administer" means the direct application of a controlled substance, whether by injection, inhalation, ingestion, or any other means, to the body of a patient or research subject by (i) a practitioner or by his authorized agent and under his direction or (ii) the patient or research subject at the direction and in the presence of the practitioner.

"Advertisement" means all representations disseminated in any manner or by any means, other than by labeling, for the purpose of inducing, or which are likely to induce, directly or indirectly, the purchase of drugs or devices.

"Agent" means an authorized person who acts on behalf of or at the direction of a manufacturer, distributor, or dispenser. It does not include a common or contract carrier, public warehouseman, or employee of the carrier or warehouseman.

"Anabolic steroid" means any drug or hormonal substance, chemically and pharmacologically related to testosterone, other than estrogens, progestins, corticosteroids, and dehydroepiandrosterone.

"Animal" means any nonhuman animate being endowed with the power of voluntary action.

"Automated drug dispensing system" means a mechanical or electronic system that performs operations or activities, other than compounding or administration, relating to pharmacy services, including the storage, dispensing, or distribution of drugs and the collection, control, and maintenance of all transaction information, to provide security and accountability for such drugs.

"Biological product" means a virus, therapeutic serum, toxin, antitoxin, vaccine, blood, blood component or derivative, allergenic product, protein other than a chemically synthesized polypeptide, or analogous product, or arsphenamine or any derivative of arsphenamine or any other trivalent organic arsenic compound, applicable to the prevention, treatment, or cure of a disease or condition of human beings.

"Biosimilar" means a biological product that is highly similar to a specific reference biological product, notwithstanding minor differences in clinically inactive compounds, such that there are no clinically meaningful differences between the reference biological product and the biological product that has been licensed as a biosimilar pursuant to 42 U.S.C. § 262(k) in terms of safety, purity, and potency of the product.

"Board" means the Board of Pharmacy.

"Bulk drug substance" means any substance that is represented for use, and that, when used in the compounding, manufacturing, processing, or packaging of a drug, becomes an active ingredient or a finished dosage form of the drug; however, "bulk drug substance" shall not include intermediates that are used in the synthesis of such substances.

"Change of ownership" of an existing entity permitted, registered, or licensed by the Board means (i) the sale or transfer of all or substantially all of the assets of the entity or of any corporation that owns or controls the entity; (ii) the creation of a partnership by a sole proprietor, the dissolution of a partnership, or change in partnership composition; (iii) the acquisition or disposal of 50 percent or more of the outstanding shares of voting stock of a corporation owning the entity or of the parent corporation of a wholly owned subsidiary owning the entity, except that this shall not apply to any corporation the voting stock of which is actively traded on any securities exchange or in any over-the-counter market; (iv) the merger of a corporation owning the entity or of the parent corporation of a wholly-owned subsidiary owning the entity with another business or corporation; or (v) the expiration or forfeiture of a corporation's charter.

"Co-licensed partner" means a person who, with at least one other person, has the right to engage in the manufacturing or marketing of a prescription drug, consistent with state and federal law.

"Compounding" means the combining of two or more ingredients to fabricate such ingredients into a single preparation and includes the mixing, assembling, packaging, or labeling of a drug or device (i) by a pharmacist, or within a permitted pharmacy, pursuant to a valid prescription issued for a medicinal or therapeutic purpose in the context of a bona fide practitioner-patient-pharmacist relationship, or in expectation of receiving a valid prescription based on observed historical patterns of prescribing and dispensing; (ii) by a practitioner of medicine, osteopathy, podiatry, dentistry, or veterinary medicine as an incident to his administering or dispensing, if authorized to dispense, a controlled substance in the course of his professional practice; or (iii) for the purpose of, or as incident to, research, teaching, or chemical analysis and not for sale or for dispensing. The mixing, diluting, or reconstituting of a manufacturer's product drugs for the purpose of administration to a patient, when performed by a practitioner of medicine or osteopathy licensed under Chapter 29 (§ 54.1-2900 et seq.), a person supervised by such practitioner pursuant to subdivision A 6 or 19 of § 54.1-2901, or a person supervised by such practitioner or a licensed nurse practitioner or physician assistant pursuant to subdivision A 4 of § 54.1-2901 shall not be considered compounding.

"Controlled substance" means a drug, substance, or immediate precursor in Schedules I through VI of this chapter. The term shall not include distilled spirits, wine, malt beverages, or tobacco as those terms are defined or used in Title 3.2 or Title 4.1. The term "controlled substance" includes a controlled substance analog that has been placed into Schedule I or II by the Board pursuant to the regulatory authority in subsection D of § 54.1-3443.

"Controlled substance analog" means a substance the chemical structure of which is substantially similar to the chemical structure of a controlled substance in Schedule I or II and either (i) which has a stimulant, depressant, or hallucinogenic effect on the central nervous system that is substantially similar to or greater than the stimulant, depressant, or hallucinogenic effect on the central nervous system of a controlled substance in Schedule I or II or (ii) with respect to a particular person, which such person represents or intends to have a stimulant, depressant, or hallucinogenic effect on the central nervous system that is substantially similar to or greater than the stimulant, depressant, or hallucinogenic effect on the central nervous system of a controlled substance in Schedule I or II. "Controlled substance analog" does not include (a) any substance for which there is an approved new drug application as defined under § 505 of the federal Food, Drug,

and Cosmetic Act (21 U.S.C. § 355) or that is generally recognized as safe and effective pursuant to §§ 501, 502, and 503 of the federal Food, Drug, and Cosmetic Act (21 U.S.C. §§ 351, 352, and 353) and 21 C.F.R. Part 330; (b) with respect to a particular person, any substance for which an exemption is in effect for investigational use for that person under § 505 of the federal Food, Drug, and Cosmetic Act to the extent that the conduct with respect to that substance is pursuant to such exemption; or (c) any substance to the extent not intended for human consumption before such an exemption takes effect with respect to that substance.

"DEA" means the Drug Enforcement Administration, U.S. Department of Justice, or its successor agency.

"Deliver" or *"delivery"* means the actual, constructive, or attempted transfer of any item regulated by this chapter, whether or not there exists an agency relationship.

"Device" means instruments, apparatus, and contrivances, including their components, parts, and accessories, intended for use in the diagnosis, cure, mitigation, treatment, or prevention of disease in man or animals or to affect the structure or any function of the body of man or animals.

"Dialysis care technician" or *"dialysis patient care technician"* means an individual who is certified by an organization approved by the Board of Health Professions pursuant to Chapter 27.01 (§ 54.1-2729.1 et seq.) and who, under the supervision of a licensed physician, nurse practitioner, physician assistant, or a registered nurse, assists in the care of patients undergoing renal dialysis treatments in a Medicare-certified renal dialysis facility.

"Dialysis solution" means either the commercially available, unopened, sterile solutions whose purpose is to be instilled into the peritoneal cavity during the medical procedure known as peritoneal dialysis, or commercially available solutions whose purpose is to be used in the performance of hemodialysis not to include any solutions administered to the patient intravenously.

"Dispense" means to deliver a drug to an ultimate user or research subject by or pursuant to the lawful order of a practitioner, including the prescribing and administering, packaging, labeling, or compounding necessary to prepare the substance for that delivery. However, dispensing shall not include the transportation of drugs mixed, diluted, or reconstituted in accordance with this chapter to other sites operated by such practitioner or that practitioner's medical practice for the purpose of administration of such drugs to patients of the practitioner or that practitioner's medical practice at such other sites. For practitioners of medicine or osteopathy, "dispense" shall only include the provision of drugs by a practitioner to patients to take with them away from the practitioner's place of practice.

"Dispenser" means a practitioner who dispenses.

"Distribute" means to deliver other than by administering or dispensing a controlled substance.

"Distributor" means a person who distributes.

"Drug" means (i) articles or substances recognized in the official United States Pharmacopoeia National Formulary or official Homeopathic Pharmacopoeia of the United States, or any supplement to any of them; (ii) articles or substances intended for use in the diagnosis, cure, mitigation, treatment, or prevention of disease in man or animals; (iii) articles or substances, other than food, intended to affect the structure or any function of the body of man or animals; (iv) articles or substances intended for use as a component of any article specified in clause (i), (ii), or (iii); or (v) a biological product. "Drug" does not include devices or their components, parts, or accessories.

"Drug product" means a specific drug in dosage form from a known source of manufacture, whether by brand or therapeutically equivalent drug product name.

"Electronic transmission prescription" means any prescription, other than an oral or written prescription or a prescription transmitted by facsimile machine, that is electronically transmitted directly to a pharmacy without interception or intervention from a third party from a practitioner authorized to prescribe or from one pharmacy to another pharmacy.

"Facsimile (FAX) prescription" means a written prescription or order that is transmitted by an electronic device over telephone lines that sends the exact image to the receiving pharmacy in hard copy form.

"FDA" means the U.S. Food and Drug Administration.

"Hashish oil" means any oily extract containing one or more cannabinoids, but shall not include any such extract with a tetrahydrocannabinol content of less than 12 percent by weight.

"Immediate precursor" means a substance which the Board of Pharmacy has found to be and by regulation designates as being the principal compound commonly used or produced primarily for use, and which is an immediate chemical intermediary used or likely to be used in the manufacture of a controlled substance, the control of which is necessary to prevent, curtail, or limit manufacture.

"Interchangeable" means a biosimilar that meets safety standards for determining interchangeability pursuant to 42 U.S.C. § 262(k)(4).

"Label" means a display of written, printed, or graphic matter upon the immediate container of any article. A requirement made by or under authority of this chapter that any word, statement, or other information appear on the label shall not be considered to be complied with unless such word, statement, or other information also appears on the outside container or wrapper, if any, of the retail package of such article or is easily legible through the outside container or wrapper.

"Labeling" means all labels and other written, printed, or graphic matter on an article or any of its

containers or wrappers, or accompanying such article.

"Manufacture" means the production, preparation, propagation, conversion, or processing of any item regulated by this chapter, either directly or indirectly by extraction from substances of natural origin, or independently by means of chemical synthesis, or by a combination of extraction and chemical synthesis, and includes any packaging or repackaging of the substance or labeling or relabeling of its container. This term does not include compounding.

"Manufacturer" means every person who manufactures, a manufacturer's co-licensed partner, or a repackager.

"Marijuana" means any part of a plant of the genus Cannabis whether growing or not, its seeds, or its resin; and every compound, manufacture, salt, derivative, mixture, or preparation of such plant, its seeds, or its resin. Marijuana shall not include any oily extract containing one or more cannabinoids unless such extract contains less than 12 percent of tetrahydrocannabinol by weight, nor shall marijuana include the mature stalks of such plant, fiber produced from such stalk, or oil or cake made from the seeds of such plant, unless such stalks, fiber, oil, or cake is combined with other parts of plants of the genus Cannabis. Marijuana shall not include industrial hemp as defined in § 3.2-4112 that is possessed, cultivated, or manufactured by a grower licensed pursuant to § 3.2-4115.

"Medical equipment supplier" means any person, as defined in § 1-230, engaged in the delivery to the ultimate consumer, pursuant to the lawful order of a practitioner, of hypodermic syringes and needles, medicinal oxygen, Schedule VI controlled devices, those Schedule VI controlled substances with no medicinal properties that are used for the operation and cleaning of medical equipment, solutions for peritoneal dialysis, and sterile water or saline for irrigation.

"Narcotic drug" means any of the following, whether produced directly or indirectly by extraction from substances of vegetable origin, or independently by means of chemical synthesis, or by a combination of extraction and chemical synthesis: (i) opium, opiates, and any salt, compound, derivative, or preparation of opium or opiates; (ii) any salt, compound, isomer, derivative, or preparation thereof which is chemically equivalent or identical with any of the substances referred to in clause (i), but not including the isoquinoline alkaloids of opium; (iii) opium poppy and poppy straw; (iv) coca leaves and any salt, compound, derivative, or preparation of coca leaves, and any salt, compound, isomer, derivative, or preparation thereof which is chemically equivalent or identical with any of these substances, but not including decocainized coca leaves or extraction of coca leaves which do not contain cocaine or ecgonine.

"New drug" means (i) any drug, except a new animal drug or an animal feed bearing or containing a new animal drug, the composition of which is such that such drug is not generally recognized, among experts qualified by scientific training and experience to evaluate the safety and effectiveness of drugs, as safe and effective for use under the conditions prescribed, recommended, or suggested in the labeling, except that such a drug not so recognized shall not be deemed to be a "new drug" if at any time prior to the enactment of this chapter it was subject to the Food and Drugs Act of June 30, 1906, as amended, and if at such time its labeling contained the same representations concerning the conditions of its use, or (ii) any drug, except a new animal drug or an animal feed bearing or containing a new animal drug, the composition of which is such that such drug, as a result of investigations to determine its safety and effectiveness for use under such conditions, has become so recognized, but which has not, otherwise than in such investigations, been used to a material extent or for a material time under such conditions.

"Nuclear medicine technologist" means an individual who holds a current certification with the American Registry of Radiological Technologists or the Nuclear Medicine Technology Certification Board.

"Official compendium" means the official United States Pharmacopoeia National Formulary, official Homeopathic Pharmacopoeia of the United States, or any supplement to any of them.

"Official written order" means an order written on a form provided for that purpose by the U.S. Drug Enforcement Administration, under any laws of the United States making provision therefor, if such order forms are authorized and required by federal law, and if no such order form is provided then on an official form provided for that purpose by the Board of Pharmacy.

"Opiate" means any substance having an addiction-forming or addiction-sustaining liability similar to morphine or being capable of conversion into a drug having such addiction-forming or addiction-sustaining liability. It does not include, unless specifically designated as controlled under Article 4 (§ 54.1-3437 et seq.), the dextrorotatory isomer of 3-methoxy-n-methylmorphinan and its salts (dextromethorphan). It does include its racemic and levorotatory forms.

"Opium poppy" means the plant of the species Papaver somniferum L., except the seeds thereof.

"Original package" means the unbroken container or wrapping in which any drug or medicine is enclosed together with label and labeling, put up by or for the manufacturer, wholesaler, or distributor for use in the delivery or display of such article.

"Outsourcing facility" means a facility that is engaged in the compounding of sterile drugs and is currently registered as an outsourcing facility with the U.S. Secretary of Health and Human Services and that complies with all applicable requirements of federal and state law, including the Federal Food, Drug, and Cosmetic Act.

"Person" means both the plural and singular, as the case demands, and includes an individual, partnership, corporation, association, governmental agency, trust, or other institution or entity.

"Pharmacist-in-charge" means the person who, being licensed as a pharmacist, signs the application for a pharmacy permit and assumes full legal responsibility for the operation of the relevant pharmacy in a manner complying with the laws and regulations for the practice of pharmacy and the sale and dispensing of controlled substances; the "pharmacist-in-charge" shall personally supervise the pharmacy and the pharmacy's personnel as required by § 54.1-3432.

"Poppy straw" means all parts, except the seeds, of the opium poppy, after mowing.

"Practitioner" means a physician, dentist, licensed nurse practitioner pursuant to § 54.1-2957.01, licensed physician assistant pursuant to § 54.1-2952.1, pharmacist pursuant to § 54.1-3300, TPA-certified optometrist pursuant to Article 5 (§ 54.1-3222 et seq.) of Chapter 32, veterinarian, scientific investigator, or other person licensed, registered, or otherwise permitted to distribute, dispense, prescribe and administer, or conduct research with respect to a controlled substance in the course of professional practice or research in the Commonwealth.

"Prescriber" means a practitioner who is authorized pursuant to §§ 54.1-3303 and 54.1-3408 to issue a prescription.

"Prescription" means an order for drugs or medical supplies, written or signed or transmitted by word of mouth, telephone, telegraph, or other means of communication to a pharmacist by a duly licensed physician, dentist, veterinarian, or other practitioner authorized by law to prescribe and administer such drugs or medical supplies.

"Prescription drug" means any drug required by federal law or regulation to be dispensed only pursuant to a prescription, including finished dosage forms and active ingredients subject to § 503(b) of the Federal Food, Drug, and Cosmetic Act (21 U.S.C. § 353(b)).

"Production" or *"produce"* includes the manufacture, planting, cultivation, growing, or harvesting of a controlled substance or marijuana.

"Proprietary medicine" means a completely compounded nonprescription drug in its unbroken, original package which does not contain any controlled substance or marijuana as defined in this chapter and is not in itself poisonous, and which is sold, offered, promoted, or advertised directly to the general public by or under the authority of the manufacturer or primary distributor, under a trademark, trade name, or other trade symbol privately owned, and the labeling of which conforms to the requirements of this chapter and applicable federal law. However, this definition shall not include a drug that is only advertised or promoted professionally to licensed practitioners, a narcotic or drug containing a narcotic, a drug that may be dispensed only upon prescription or the label of which bears substantially the statement "Warning — may be habit-forming," or a drug intended for injection.

"Radiopharmaceutical" means any drug that exhibits spontaneous disintegration of unstable nuclei with the emission of nuclear particles or photons and includes any non-radioactive reagent kit or radionuclide generator that is intended to be used in the preparation of any such substance, but does not include drugs such as carbon-containing compounds or potassium-containing salts that include trace quantities of naturally occurring radionuclides. The term also includes any biological product that is labeled with a radionuclide or intended solely to be labeled with a radionuclide.

"Reference biological product" means the single biological product licensed pursuant to 42 U.S.C. § 262(a) against which a biological product is evaluated in an application submitted to the U.S. Food and Drug Administration for licensure of biological products as biosimilar or interchangeable pursuant to 42 U.S.C. § 262(k).

"Sale" includes barter, exchange, or gift, or offer therefor, and each such transaction made by any person, whether as an individual, proprietor, agent, servant, or employee.

"Therapeutically equivalent drug products" means drug products that contain the same active ingredients and are identical in strength or concentration, dosage form, and route of administration and that are classified as being therapeutically equivalent by the U.S. Food and Drug Administration pursuant to the definition of "therapeutically equivalent drug products" set forth in the most recent edition of the Approved Drug Products with Therapeutic Equivalence Evaluations, otherwise known as the "Orange Book."

"Third-party logistics provider" means a person that provides or coordinates warehousing of or other logistics services for a drug or device in interstate commerce on behalf of a manufacturer, wholesale distributor, or dispenser of the drug or device but does not take ownership of the product or have responsibility for directing the sale or disposition of the product.

"USP-NF" means the current edition of the United States Pharmacopeia-National Formulary.

"Warehouser" means any person, other than a wholesale distributor, manufacturer, or third-party logistics provider, engaged in the business of selling or otherwise distributing prescription drugs or devices to any person who is not the ultimate user or consumer. No person shall be subject to any state or local tax by reason of this definition.

"Wholesale distribution" means distribution of prescription drugs to persons other than consumers or patients, subject to the exemptions set forth in the federal Drug Supply Chain Security Act.

"Wholesale distributor" means any person other than a manufacturer, a manufacturer's co-licensed

partner, a third-party logistics provider, or a repackager that engages in wholesale distribution.

The words "drugs" and "devices" as used in Chapter 33 (§ 54.1-3300 et seq.) and in this chapter shall not include surgical or dental instruments, physical therapy equipment, X-ray apparatus, or glasses or lenses for the eyes.

The terms "pharmacist," "pharmacy," and "practice of pharmacy" as used in this chapter shall be defined as provided in Chapter 33 (§ 54.1-3300 et seq.) unless the context requires a different meaning.

History.

Code 1950, §§ 54-399, 54-487; 1952, c. 451; 1958, c. 551, § 54-524.2; 1966, c. 193; 1968, c. 582; 1970, c. 650; 1971, Ex. Sess., c. 94; 1972, c. 798; 1975, c. 425; 1976, c. 14; 1977, c. 193; 1978, c. 833; 1979, c. 435; 1980, c. 150; 1988, c. 765; 1991, cc. 519, 524; 1992, cc. 737, 793; 1996, cc. 37, 152, 158, 407, 408; 1997, cc. 20, 677, 806; 1998, c. 470; 1999, cc. 661, 750; 2000, cc. 861, 878, 935; 2003, cc. 509, 639, 995; 2005, cc. 475, 839; 2006, c. 346; 2012, c. 213; 2013, cc. 412, 504, 544, 765; 2014, cc. 674, 719; 2015, cc. 158, 180, 300; 2016, cc. 221, 495.

§ **54.1-3401.1:** Repealed by Acts 2016, c. 221, cl. 2.

§ **54.1-3402:** Repealed by Acts 2003, c. 509.

Cross references.

For present provisions relating to the exemption of certain permitted pharmacies, see § 54.1-3435.02.

§ 54.1-3403. Chapter not applicable to economic poisons.

This chapter shall not be construed to apply (i) to poisons used for the control of insects, animal pests, weeds, fungus diseases or other substances sold for use in agricultural, horticultural or related arts and sciences when such substances which are poisons within the meaning of this chapter are sold in original unbroken packages bearing a label having plainly printed upon it the name of the contents and the word POISON and an effective antidote or (ii) to any person, persons, corporations or associations engaged in the business of selling, making, compounding or manufacturing industrial chemicals for distribution or sale at wholesale or for making, compounding or manufacturing other products.

History.

Code 1950, § 54-403.1; 1958, c. 551; 1970, c. 650, § 54-524.4; 1988, c. 765.

§ 54.1-3404. Inventories of controlled substances required of certain persons; contents and form of record.

A. Except as set forth in subsection G, every person manufacturing, compounding, processing, selling, dispensing or otherwise disposing of drugs in Schedules I, II, III, IV or V shall take a complete and accurate inventory of all stocks of Schedules I through V drugs on the date he first engages in business. If there are no controlled substances on hand at that time, he shall record this fact as part of the inventory. An inventory taken by use of an oral recording device shall be promptly reduced to writing and maintained in a written, typewritten or printed form. Such inventory shall be made either as of the opening of business or as of the close of business on the inventory date.

B. After the initial inventory is taken, every person described herein shall take a new inventory at least every two years of all stocks on hand of Schedules I through V drugs. The biennial inventory shall be taken on any date which is within two years of the previous biennial inventory.

C. The record of such drugs received shall in every case show the date of receipt, the name and address of the person from whom received and the kind and quantity of drugs received, the kind and quantity of drugs produced or removed from process of manufacture, and the date of such production or removal from process of manufacture. The record shall in every case show the proportion of morphine, cocaine, or ecgonine contained in or producible from crude opium or coca leaves received or produced.

D. The record of all drugs sold, administered, dispensed, or otherwise disposed of, shall show the date of selling, administering, or dispensing, the name and address of the person to whom or for whose use, or the owner and species of animal for which the drugs were sold, administered or dispensed, and the kind and quantity of drugs. Any person selling, administering, dispensing or otherwise disposing of such drugs shall make and sign such record at the time of each transaction. The keeping of a record required by or under the federal laws, containing substantially the same information as is specified above, shall constitute compliance with this section, except that every such record shall contain a detailed list of any drugs lost, destroyed or stolen, the kind and quantity of such drugs, and the date of the discovery of such loss, destruction or theft. The form of records shall be prescribed by the Board.

E. Whenever any registrant or licensee discovers a theft or any other unusual loss of any controlled substance, he shall immediately report such theft or loss to the Board. If the registrant or licensee is unable to determine the exact kind and quantity of the drug loss, he shall immediately make a complete inventory of all Schedule I through V drugs.

Within 30 days after the discovery of a loss of drugs, the registrant or licensee shall furnish the Board with a listing of the kind, quantity and strength of such drugs lost.

F. All records required pursuant to this section shall be maintained completely and accurately for two years from the date of the transaction recorded.

G. Each person authorized to conduct chemical analyses using controlled substances in the Department of Forensic Science shall comply with the inventory requirements set forth in subsections A through F; however, the following substances shall not be required to be included in such inventory: (i) controlled substances on hand at the time of the inventory in a quantity of less than one kilogram, other than a hallucinogenic controlled substance listed in Schedule I of this chapter; or (ii) hallucinogenic controlled substances, other than lysergic acid diethylamide, on hand at the time of the inventory in a quantity of less than 20 grams; or (iii) lysergic acid diethylamide on hand at the time of the inventory in a quantity of less than 0.5 grams. Further, no inventory shall be required of known or suspected controlled substances that have been received as evidentiary materials for analyses by the Department of Forensic Science.

History.
1970, c. 650, § 54-524.56; 1972, c. 798; 1978, c. 833; 1979, c. 435; 1980, c. 203; 1982, c. 278; 1988, c. 765; 1998, c. 105; 2004, c. 51; 2005, cc. 868, 881.

§ 54.1-3405. Access to and copies of records; inspections.

Every person required to prepare or obtain, and keep, records, and any carrier maintaining records with respect to any shipment containing any drug, and every person in charge or having custody of such records shall, upon request of an agent designated by the Board, permit such agent at reasonable times to have access to and copy such records.

Any agent designated by the Superintendent of the Department of State Police to conduct drug diversion investigations shall, for the purpose of such investigations, also be permitted access at reasonable times to all such records relevant to a specific investigation and be allowed to inspect and copy such records. However, agents designated by the Superintendent of the Department of State Police to conduct drug diversion investigations shall not copy and remove patient records unless such patient records are relevant to a specific investigation. Any agent designated by the Superintendent of the Department of State Police shall allow the person or carrier maintaining such records, or agent thereof, to examine any copies of records before their removal from the premises. If the agent designated by the Superintendent of State Police copies records on magnetic storage media, he will deliver a duplicate of the magnetic storage media on which the copies are stored to the person or carrier maintaining such records or an agent thereof, prior to removing the copies from the premises. If the original of any record is removed by any agent designated by the Superintendent of State Police, a receipt therefor shall be left with the person or carrier maintaining such records or an agent thereof, and a copy of the removed record shall be provided the person or carrier maintaining such records within a reasonable time thereafter.

For the purposes of verification of such records and of enforcement of this chapter, agents designated by the Board or by the Superintendent are authorized, upon presenting appropriate credentials to the owner, operator, or agent in charge, to enter, at reasonable times, any factory, warehouse, establishment, or vehicle in which any drug is held, manufactured, compounded, processed, sold, delivered, or otherwise disposed of; and to inspect, within reasonable limits and in a reasonable manner, such factory, warehouse, establishment, or vehicle, and all pertinent equipment, finished and unfinished material, containers and labeling, including records, files, papers, processes, controls, and facilities, bearing on violation of this chapter; and to inventory and obtain samples of any stock of any drugs.

If a sample of any drug is obtained, the agent making the inspection shall, upon completion of the inspection and before leaving the premises, give to the owner, operator, or agent in charge a receipt describing the sample. No inspection shall extend to financial data, sales data other than shipment data, pricing data, personnel data or research data.

Any information obtained by a designated State Police agent during an inspection under this section which constitutes evidence of a violation of any provision of this chapter shall be reported to the Department of Health Professions upon its discovery.

Any information obtained by an agent designated by the Board during an inspection under this section which constitutes evidence of a violation of Article 1 (§ 18.2-247 et seq.) of Chapter 7 of Title 18.2 shall be reported to the Department of State Police upon its discovery.

History.
1970, c. 650, § 54-524.57; 1988, cc. 266, 765; 1992, cc. 743, 808.

§ 54.1-3406. Records confidential; disclosure of information about violations of federal law.

A. No agent of the Board or agent designated by the Superintendent of the Department of State Police having knowledge by virtue of his office of any prescriptions, papers, records, or stocks of drugs shall divulge such knowledge, except in connection with a criminal investigation authorized by the Attorney General or attorney for the Commonwealth or with a prosecution or proceeding in court or before a regulatory board or officer, to which investigation, prosecution or proceeding the person to whom such prescriptions, papers or records relate is a subject or party. This section shall not be construed to prohibit the Board president or his designee and the Director of the Department of Health Professions from discharging their duties as provided in this title.

B. Notwithstanding the provisions of § 54.1-2400.2, the Board shall have the authority to submit to the U.S. Secretary of Health and Human Services information resulting from an inspection or an investigation indicating that a compounding pharmacy or outsourcing facility may be in violation of federal law or regulations with the exception of compounding for office-based administration in accordance with § 54.1-3410.2.

History.

Code 1950, § 54-512; 1970, c. 650; 1983, c. 528, § 54-524.58; 1988, cc. 266, 765; 2015, c. 300.

§ 54.1-3407. Analysis of controlled substances.

A licensed physician or pharmacist may receive controlled substances from or on behalf of a patient for qualitative or quantitative analysis purposes only, without an official order form, if within twenty-four hours of its receipt the physician or pharmacist mails or delivers the entire sample to a laboratory operated by the Commonwealth and designated by the Board to receive such substances. If the sample is mailed, it shall be sent by registered or certified mail, postage prepaid, with return receipt requested. If personally delivered, a receipt shall be obtained from such laboratory. All receipts or returns shall be kept on file for three years and shall be available for inspection by the Board at any reasonable time.

History.

1972, c. 798, § 54-524.59:1; 1988, c. 765.

§ 54.1-3408. Professional use by practitioners.

A. A practitioner of medicine, osteopathy, podiatry, dentistry, or veterinary medicine or a licensed nurse practitioner pursuant to § 54.1-2957.01, a licensed physician assistant pursuant to § 54.1-2952.1, or a TPA-certified optometrist pursuant to Article 5 (§ 54.1-3222 et seq.) of Chapter 32 shall only prescribe, dispense, or administer controlled substances in good faith for medicinal or therapeutic purposes within the course of his professional practice.

B. The prescribing practitioner's order may be on a written prescription or pursuant to an oral prescription as authorized by this chapter. The prescriber may administer drugs and devices, or he may cause drugs or devices to be administered by:

1. A nurse, physician assistant, or intern under his direction and supervision;

2. Persons trained to administer drugs and devices to patients in state-owned or state-operated hospitals or facilities licensed as hospitals by the Board of Health or psychiatric hospitals licensed by the Department of Behavioral Health and Developmental Services who administer drugs under the control and supervision of the prescriber or a pharmacist;

3. Emergency medical services personnel certified and authorized to administer drugs and devices pursuant to regulations of the Board of Health who act within the scope of such certification and pursuant to an oral or written order or standing protocol; or

4. A licensed respiratory therapist as defined in § 54.1-2954 who administers by inhalation controlled substances used in inhalation or respiratory therapy.

C. Pursuant to an oral or written order or standing protocol, the prescriber, who is authorized by state or federal law to possess and administer radiopharmaceuticals in the scope of his practice, may authorize a nuclear medicine technologist to administer, under his supervision, radiopharmaceuticals used in the diagnosis or treatment of disease.

D. Pursuant to an oral or written order or standing protocol issued by the prescriber within the course of his professional practice, such prescriber may authorize registered nurses and licensed practical nurses to possess (i) epinephrine and oxygen for administration in treatment of emergency medical conditions and (ii) heparin and sterile normal saline to use for the maintenance of intravenous access lines.

Pursuant to the regulations of the Board of Health, certain emergency medical services technicians may possess and administer epinephrine in emergency cases of anaphylactic shock.

Pursuant to an order or standing protocol issued by the prescriber within the course of his professional practice, any school nurse, school board employee, employee of a local governing body, or employee of a local health department who is authorized by a prescriber and trained in the administration of epinephrine may possess and administer epinephrine.

Pursuant to an order or a standing protocol issued by the prescriber within the course of his professional practice, any employee of a school for students with disabilities, as defined in § 22.1-319 and licensed by the Board of Education, or any employee of a private school that is accredited pursuant to § 22.1-19 as administered by the Virginia Council for Private Education who is authorized by a prescriber and trained in the administration of epinephrine may possess and administer epinephrine.

Pursuant to an order issued by the prescriber within the course of his professional practice, an employee of a provider licensed by the Department of Behavioral Health and Developmental Services or a person providing services pursuant to a contract with a provider licensed by the Department of Behavioral Health and Developmental Services may possess and administer epinephrine, provided such person is authorized and trained in the administration of epinephrine.

Pursuant to an oral or written order or standing protocol issued by the prescriber within the course of his professional practice, such prescriber may authorize pharmacists to possess epinephrine and oxygen for administration in treatment of emergency medical conditions.

E. Pursuant to an oral or written order or standing protocol issued by the prescriber within the course of his professional practice, such prescriber may authorize licensed physical therapists to possess and administer topical corticosteroids, topical lidocaine, and any other Schedule VI topical drug.

F. Pursuant to an oral or written order or standing protocol issued by the prescriber within the course of his professional practice, such prescriber may authorize licensed athletic trainers to possess and administer topical corticosteroids, topical lidocaine, or other Schedule VI topical drugs; oxygen for use in emergency situations; and epinephrine for use in emergency cases of anaphylactic shock.

G. Pursuant to an oral or written order or standing protocol issued by the prescriber within the course of his professional practice, and in accordance with policies and guidelines established by the Department of Health pursuant to § 32.1-50.2, such prescriber may authorize registered nurses or licensed practical nurses under the immediate and direct supervision of a registered nurse to possess and administer tuberculin purified protein derivative (PPD) in the absence of a prescriber. The Department of Health's policies and guidelines shall be consistent with applicable guidelines developed by the Centers for Disease Control and Prevention for preventing transmission of mycobacterium tuberculosis and shall be updated to incorporate any subsequently implemented standards of the Occupational Safety and Health Administration and the Department of Labor and Industry to the extent that they are inconsistent with the Department of Health's policies and guidelines. Such standing protocols shall explicitly describe the categories of persons to whom the tuberculin test is to be administered and shall provide for appropriate medical evaluation of those in whom the test is positive. The prescriber shall ensure that the nurse implementing such standing protocols has received adequate training in the practice and principles underlying tuberculin screening.

The Health Commissioner or his designee may authorize registered nurses, acting as agents of the Department of Health, to possess and administer, at the nurse's discretion, tuberculin purified protein derivative (PPD) to those persons in whom tuberculin skin testing is indicated based on protocols and policies established by the Department of Health.

H. Pursuant to a written order or standing protocol issued by the prescriber within the course of his professional practice, such prescriber may authorize, with the consent of the parents as defined in § 22.1-1, an employee of (i) a school board, (ii) a school for students with disabilities as defined in § 22.1-319 licensed by the Board of Education, or (iii) a private school accredited pursuant to § 22.1-19 as administered by the Virginia Council for Private Education who is trained in the administration of insulin and glucagon to assist with the administration of insulin or administer glucagon to a student diagnosed as having diabetes and who requires insulin injections during the school day or for whom glucagon has been prescribed for the emergency treatment of hypoglycemia. Such authorization shall only be effective when a licensed nurse, nurse practitioner, physician, or physician assistant is not present to perform the administration of the medication.

Pursuant to a written order issued by the prescriber within the course of his professional practice, such prescriber may authorize an employee of a provider licensed by the Department of Behavioral Health and Developmental Services or a person providing services pursuant to a contract with a provider licensed by the Department of Behavioral Health and Developmental Services to assist with the administration of insulin or to administer glucagon to a person diagnosed as having diabetes and who requires insulin injections or for whom glucagon has been prescribed for the emergency treatment of hypoglycemia, provided such employee or person providing services has been trained in the administration of insulin and glucagon.

I. A prescriber may authorize, pursuant to a protocol approved by the Board of Nursing, the administration of vaccines to adults for immunization, when a practitioner with prescriptive authority is not physically present, by (i) licensed pharmacists, (ii) registered nurses, or (iii) licensed practical nurses under the immediate and direct supervision of a registered nurse. A prescriber acting on behalf of and in accordance with established protocols of the Department of Health may authorize the administration of vaccines to any person by a pharmacist, nurse, or designated emergency medical services provider who holds an advanced life support certificate issued by the Commissioner of Health under the direction of an operational medical director when the prescriber is not physically present. The emergency medical services provider shall provide documentation of the vaccines to be recorded in the Virginia Immunization Information System.

J. A dentist may cause Schedule VI topical drugs to be administered under his direction and supervision by either a dental hygienist or by an authorized agent of the dentist.

Further, pursuant to a written order and in accordance with a standing protocol issued by the dentist in the course of his professional practice, a dentist may authorize a dental hygienist under his general supervision, as defined in § 54.1-2722, to possess and administer topical oral fluorides, topical oral anesthetics, topical and directly applied antimicrobial agents for treatment of periodontal pocket lesions, as well as any other Schedule VI topical drug approved by the Board of Dentistry.

In addition, a dentist may authorize a dental hygienist under his direction to administer Schedule VI nitrous oxide and oxygen inhalation analgesia and, to persons 18 years of age or older, Schedule VI local anesthesia.

K. Pursuant to an oral or written order or standing protocol issued by the prescriber within the course of his professional practice, such prescriber may authorize registered professional nurses certified as sexual assault nurse examiners-A (SANE-A) under his supervision and when he is not physically present to possess and administer preventive medications for victims of sexual assault as recommended by the Centers for Disease Control and Prevention.

L. This section shall not prevent the administration of drugs by a person who has satisfactorily completed a training program for this purpose approved by the Board of Nursing and who administers such drugs in accordance with a prescriber's instructions pertaining to dosage, frequency, and manner of administration, and in accordance with regulations promulgated by the Board of Pharmacy relating to security and record keeping, when the drugs administered would be normally self-administered by (i) an individual receiving services in a program licensed by the Department of Behavioral Health and Developmental Services; (ii) a resident of the Virginia Rehabilitation Center for the Blind and Vision Impaired; (iii) a resident of a facility approved by the Board or Department of Juvenile Justice for the placement of children in need of services or delinquent or alleged delinquent youth; (iv) a program participant of an adult day-care center licensed by the Department of Social Services; (v) a resident of any facility authorized or operated by a state or local government whose primary purpose is not to provide health care services; (vi) a resident of a private children's residential facility, as defined in § 63.2-100 and licensed by the Department of Social Services, Department of Education, or Department of Behavioral Health and Developmental Services; or (vii) a student in a school for students with disabilities, as defined in § 22.1-319 and licensed by the Board of Education.

In addition, this section shall not prevent a person who has successfully completed a training program for the administration of drugs via percutaneous gastrostomy tube approved by the Board of Nursing and been evaluated by a registered nurse as having demonstrated competency in administration of drugs via percutaneous gastrostomy tube from administering drugs to a person receiving services from a program licensed by the Department of Behavioral Health and Developmental Services to such person via percutaneous gastrostomy tube. The continued competency of a person to administer drugs via percutaneous gastrostomy tube shall be evaluated semiannually by a registered nurse.

M. Medication aides registered by the Board of Nursing pursuant to Article 7 (§ 54.1-3041 et seq.) of Chapter 30 may administer drugs that would otherwise be self-administered to residents of any assisted living facility licensed by the Department of Social Services. A registered medication aide shall administer drugs pursuant to this section in accordance with the prescriber's instructions pertaining to dosage, frequency, and manner of administration; in accordance with regulations promulgated by the Board of Pharmacy relating to security and recordkeeping; in accordance with the assisted living facility's Medication Management Plan; and in accordance with such other regulations governing their practice promulgated by the Board of Nursing.

N. In addition, this section shall not prevent the administration of drugs by a person who administers such drugs in accordance with a physician's instructions pertaining to dosage, frequency, and manner of administration and with written authorization of a parent, and in accordance with school board regulations relating to training, security and record keeping, when the drugs administered would be normally self-administered by a student of a Virginia public school. Training for such persons shall be accomplished through a program approved by the local school boards, in consultation with the local departments of health.

O. In addition, this section shall not prevent the administration of drugs by a person to (i) a child in a child day program as defined in § 63.2-100 and regulated by the State Board of Social Services or a local government pursuant to § 15.2-914, or (ii) a student of a private school that is accredited pursuant to § 22.1-19 as administered by the Virginia Council for Private Education, provided such person (a) has satisfactorily completed a training program for this purpose approved by the Board of Nursing and taught by a registered nurse, licensed practical nurse, nurse practitioner, physician assistant, doctor of medicine or osteopathic medicine, or pharmacist; (b) has obtained written authorization from a parent or guardian; (c) administers drugs only to the child identified on the prescription label in accordance with the prescriber's instructions pertaining to dosage, frequency, and manner of administration; and (d) administers only those drugs that were dispensed from a pharmacy and maintained in the original, labeled container that would normally be self-administered by the child or student, or administered by a parent or guardian to the child or student.

P. In addition, this section shall not prevent the administration or dispensing of drugs and devices by persons if they are authorized by the State Health Commissioner in accordance with protocols established by the State Health Commissioner pursuant to § 32.1-42.1 when (i) the Governor has declared a disaster or a state of emergency or the United States Secretary of Health and Human Services has issued a declaration of an actual or potential bioterrorism incident or other actual or potential public health emergency; (ii) it is necessary to permit the provision of needed drugs or devices; and (iii) such persons have received the training necessary to safely administer or dispense the needed drugs or devices. Such persons shall administer or dispense all drugs or devices under the direction, control, and supervision of the State Health Commissioner.

Q. Nothing in this title shall prohibit the administration of normally self-administered drugs by unlicensed individuals to a person in his private residence.

R. This section shall not interfere with any prescriber issuing prescriptions in compliance with his authority and scope of practice and the provisions of this section to a Board agent for use pursuant to subsection G of § 18.2-258.1. Such prescriptions issued by such prescriber shall be deemed to be valid prescriptions.

S. Nothing in this title shall prevent or interfere with dialysis care technicians or dialysis patient care technicians who are certified by an organization approved by the Board of Health Professions or persons authorized for provisional practice pursuant to Chapter 27.01 (§ 54.1-2729.1 et seq.), in the ordinary course of their duties in a Medicare-certified renal dialysis facility, from administering heparin, topical needle site anesthetics, dialysis solutions, sterile normal saline solution, and blood volumizers, for the purpose of facilitating renal dialysis treatment, when such administration of medications occurs under the orders of a licensed physician, nurse practitioner, or physician assistant and under the immediate and direct supervision of a licensed registered nurse. Nothing in this chapter shall be construed to prohibit a patient care dialysis technician trainee from performing dialysis care as part of and within the scope of the clinical skills instruction segment of a supervised dialysis technician training program, provided such trainee is identified as a "trainee" while working in a renal dialysis facility.

The dialysis care technician or dialysis patient care technician administering the medications shall have demonstrated competency as evidenced by holding current valid certification from an organization approved by the Board of Health Professions pursuant to Chapter 27.01 (§ 54.1-2729.1 et seq.).

T. Persons who are otherwise authorized to administer controlled substances in hospitals shall be authorized to administer influenza or pneumococcal vaccines pursuant to § 32.1-126.4.

U. Pursuant to a specific order for a patient and under his direct and immediate supervision, a prescriber may authorize the administration of controlled substances by personnel who have been properly trained to assist a doctor of medicine or osteopathic medicine, provided the method does not include intravenous, intrathecal, or epidural administration and the prescriber remains responsible for such administration.

V. A physician assistant, nurse or a dental hygienist may possess and administer topical fluoride varnish to the teeth of children aged six months to three years pursuant to an oral or written order or a standing protocol issued by a doctor of medicine, osteopathic medicine, or dentistry that conforms to standards adopted by the Department of Health.

W. A prescriber, acting in accordance with guidelines developed pursuant to § 32.1-46.02, may authorize the administration of influenza vaccine to minors by a licensed pharmacist, registered nurse, licensed practical nurse under the direction and immediate supervision of a registered nurse, or emergency medical services provider who holds an advanced life support certificate issued by the Commissioner of Health when the prescriber is not physically present.

X. Notwithstanding the provisions of § 54.1-3303, pursuant to an oral, written, or standing order issued by a prescriber, and in accordance with protocols developed by the Board of Pharmacy in consultation with the Board of Medicine and the Department of Health, a pharmacist may dispense naloxone or other opioid antagonist used for overdose reversal and a person may possess and administer naloxone or other opioid antagonist used for overdose reversal to a person who is believed to be experiencing or about to experience a life-threatening opiate overdose. Law-enforcement officers as defined in § 9.1-101 and firefighters who have completed a training program may also possess and administer naloxone in accordance with protocols developed by the Board of Pharmacy in consultation with the Board of Medicine and the Department of Health.

History.

Code 1950, § 54-497; 1956, c. 225; 1970, c. 650, § 54-524.65; 1973, c. 468; 1976, cc. 358, 614; 1977, c. 302; 1978, c. 224; 1980, cc. 270, 287; 1983, cc. 456, 528; 1984, cc. 141, 555; 1986, c. 81; 1987, c. 226; 1988, c. 765; 1990, c. 309; 1991, cc. 141, 519, 524, 532; 1992, cc. 610, 760, 793; 1993, cc. 15, 810, 957, 993; 1994, c. 53; 1995, cc. 88, 529; 1996, cc. 152, 158, 183, 406, 408, 490; 1997, cc. 272, 566, 806, 906; 1998, c. 112; 1999, c. 570; 2000, cc. 135, 498, 861, 881, 935; 2003, cc. 465, 497, 515, 794, 995, 1020; 2005, cc. 113, 610, 924; 2006, cc. 75, 432, 686, 858; 2007, cc. 17, 699, 702, 783; 2008, cc. 85, 694; 2009, cc. 48, 110, 506, 813, 840; 2010, cc. 179, 245, 252; 2011, c. 292; 2012, cc. 787, 803, 833, 835; 2013, cc. 114, 132, 183, 191, 252, 267, 328, 336, 359, 617; 2014, cc. 88, 491; 2015, cc. 302, 387, 502, 503, 514, 725, 732, 752; 2016, c. 144.

§ 54.1-3408.01. Requirements for prescriptions.

A. The written prescription referred to in § 54.1-3408 shall be written with ink or individually typed or printed. The prescription shall contain the name, address, and telephone number of the prescriber. A prescription for a controlled substance other than one controlled in Schedule VI shall also contain the federal controlled substances registration number assigned to the prescriber. The prescriber's information shall be either preprinted upon the prescription blank, electronically printed, typewritten, rubber stamped, or printed by hand.

The written prescription shall contain the first and last name of the patient for whom the drug is prescribed. The address of the patient shall either be placed upon the written prescription by the prescriber or his agent, or by the dispenser of the prescription. If not otherwise prohibited by law, the dispenser may record the address of the patient in an electronic prescription dispensing record for that patient in lieu of recording it on the prescription.

Each written prescription shall be dated as of, and signed by the prescriber on, the day when issued. The prescription may be prepared by an agent for the prescriber's signature.

This section shall not prohibit a prescriber from using preprinted prescriptions for drugs classified in Schedule VI if all requirements concerning dates, signatures, and other information specified above are otherwise fulfilled.

No written prescription order form shall include more than one prescription. However, this provision shall not apply (i) to prescriptions written as chart orders for patients in hospitals and long-term-care facilities, patients receiving home infusion services or hospice patients, or (ii) to a prescription ordered through a pharmacy operated by or for the Department of Corrections or the Department of Juvenile Justice, the central pharmacy of the Department of Health, or the central outpatient pharmacy operated by the Department of Behavioral Health and Developmental Services; or (iii) to prescriptions written for patients residing in adult and juvenile detention centers, local or regional jails, or work release centers operated by the Department of Corrections.

B. Prescribers' orders, whether written as chart orders or prescriptions, for Schedules II, III, IV, and V controlled drugs to be administered to (i) patients or residents of long-term care facilities served by a Virginia pharmacy from a remote location or (ii) patients receiving parenteral, intravenous, intramuscular, subcutaneous or intraspinal infusion therapy and served by a home infusion pharmacy from a remote location, may be transmitted to that remote pharmacy by an electronic communications device over telephone lines which send the exact image to the receiver in hard copy form, and such facsimile copy shall be treated as a valid original prescription order. If the order is for a radiopharmaceutical, a physician authorized by state or federal law to possess and administer medical radioactive materials may authorize a nuclear medicine technologist to transmit a prescriber's verbal or written orders for radiopharmaceuticals.

C. The oral prescription referred to in § 54.1-3408 shall be transmitted to the pharmacy of the patient's choice by the prescriber or his authorized agent. For the purposes of this section, an authorized agent of the prescriber shall be an employee of the prescriber who is under his immediate and personal supervision, or if not an employee, an individual who holds a valid license allowing the administration or dispensing of drugs and who is specifically directed by the prescriber.

History.

2000, cc. 135, 861; 2002, c. 411; 2003, c. 639; 2006, c. 195; 2009, cc. 813, 840.

§ 54.1-3408.02. Transmission of prescriptions.

Consistent with federal law and in accordance with regulations promulgated by the Board, prescriptions may be transmitted to a pharmacy by electronic transmission or by facsimile machine and shall be treated as valid original prescriptions.

History.

2000, c. 878.

§ 54.1-3408.03. Dispensing of therapeutically equivalent drug product permitted.

A. A pharmacist may dispense a therapeutically equivalent drug product for a prescription that is written for a brand-name drug product unless (i) the prescriber indicates such substitution is not authorized by specifying on the prescription, "brand medically necessary" or (ii) the patient insists on the dispensing of the brand-name drug product.

In the case of an oral prescription, the prescriber's oral dispensing instructions regarding substitution shall be followed.

B. Prescribers using prescription blanks printed in compliance with Virginia law in effect on June 30, 2003, having two check boxes and referencing the Virginia Voluntary Formulary, may indicate, until July 1, 2006, that substitution is not authorized by checking the "Dispense as Written" box. If the "Voluntary Formulary Permitted" box is checked on such prescription blanks or if neither box is checked, a pharmacist may dispense a therapeutically equivalent drug product pursuant to such prescriptions.

C. If the pharmacist dispenses a drug product other than the brand name prescribed, he shall so inform the purchaser and shall indicate, unless otherwise directed by the prescriber, on both his permanent record and the prescription label, the brand name or, in the case of a therapeutically equivalent drug product, the name of the manufacturer or the distributor. Whenever a pharmacist dispenses a therapeutically equivalent drug product pursuant to a prescription written for a brand-name product, the pharmacist shall label the drug with the name of the therapeutically equivalent drug product followed by the words "generic for" and the brand name of the drug for which the prescription was written.

D. When a pharmacist dispenses a drug product other than the drug product prescribed, the dispensed drug product shall be at a lower retail price than that of the drug product prescribed. Such retail price shall not exceed the usual and customary retail price charged by the pharmacist for the dispensed therapeutically equivalent drug product.

History.

2003, c. 639.

§ 54.1-3408.04. Dispensing of interchangeable biosimilars permitted.

A. A pharmacist may dispense a biosimilar that has been licensed by the U.S. Food and Drug Administration as interchangeable with the prescribed product unless (i) the prescriber indicates such substitute is not authorized by specifying on the prescription "brand medically necessary" or (ii) the patient insists on the dispensing of the prescribed biological product. In the case of an oral prescription, the prescriber's oral dispensing instructions regarding dispensing of an interchangeable biosimilar shall be followed. No pharmacist shall dispense a biosimilar in place of a prescribed biological product unless the biosimilar has been licensed as interchangeable with the prescribed biological product by the U.S. Food and Drug Administration.

B. When a pharmacist dispenses an interchangeable biosimilar in the place of a prescribed biological product, the pharmacist or his designee shall inform the patient prior to dispensing the interchangeable biosimilar. The pharmacist or his designee shall also indicate, unless otherwise directed by the prescriber, on both the record of dispensing and the prescription label, the brand name or, in the case of an interchangeable biosimilar, the product name and the name of the manufacturer or distributor of the interchangeable biosimilar. Whenever a pharmacist substitutes an interchangeable biosimilar pursuant to a prescription written for a brand-name product, the pharmacist or his designee shall label the drug with the name of the interchangeable biosimilar followed by the words "Substituted for" and the name of the biological product for which the prescription was written. Records of substitutions of interchangeable biosimilars shall be maintained by the pharmacist and the prescriber for a period of not less than two years from the date of dispensing.

C., D. [Expired.]

History.
2013, cc. 412, 544.

§ 54.1-3408.1. Prescription in excess of recommended dosage in certain cases.

In the case of a patient with intractable pain, a physician may prescribe a dosage in excess of the recommended dosage of a pain relieving agent if he certifies the medical necessity for such excess dosage in the patient's medical record. Any person who prescribes, dispenses or administers an excess dosage in accordance with this section shall not be in violation of the provisions of this title because of such excess dosage, if such excess dosage is prescribed, dispensed or administered in good faith for accepted medicinal or therapeutic purposes.

Nothing in this section shall be construed to grant any person immunity from investigation or disciplinary action based on the prescription, dispensing or administration of an excess dosage in violation of this title.

History.
1988, c. 870, § 54-524.65:1; 1990, c. 681; 1995, c. 277.

§ 54.1-3408.2. Failure to report administration or dispensing of or prescription for controlled substances; report required; penalty.

Any person authorized to prescribe, dispense, or administer controlled substances pursuant to § 54.1-3408 who has reason to suspect that a person has obtained or attempted to obtain a controlled substance or prescription for a controlled substance by fraud or deceit, may report the activity to the local law-enforcement agency for investigation. Any person who, in good faith, makes a report or furnishes information or records to a law-enforcement officer or entity pursuant to this section shall not be liable for civil damages in connection with making such report or furnishing such information or records.

History.
2010, c. 185.

§ 54.1-3408.3. Certification for use of cannabidiol oil or THC-A oil to treat intractable epilepsy.

A. As used in this section:

"Cannabidiol oil" means a processed Cannabis plant extract that contains at least 15 percent cannabidiol but no more than five percent tetrahydrocannabinol, or a dilution of the resin of the Cannabis plant that contains at least 50 milligrams of cannabidiol per milliliter but not more than five percent tetrahydrocannabinol.

"THC-A oil" means a processed Cannabis plant extract that contains at least 15 percent tetrahydrocannabinol acid but not more than five percent tetrahydrocannabinol, or a dilution of the resin of the Cannabis plant that contains at least 50 milligrams of tetrahydrocannabinol acid per milliliter but not more than five percent tetrahydrocannabinol.

B. A practitioner of medicine or osteopathy licensed by the Board of Medicine in the course of his professional practice may issue a written certification for the use of cannabidiol oil or THC-A oil for treatment or to alleviate the symptoms of a patient's intractable epilepsy.

C. The written certification shall be on a form provided by the Office of the Executive Secretary of the Supreme Court developed in consultation with the Board of Medicine. Such written certification shall contain the name, address, and telephone number of the practitioner, the name and address of the patient issued the written certification, the date on which the written certification was made, and the signature of the practitioner. Such written certification issued pursuant to subsection B shall expire no later than one year after its issuance unless the practitioner provides in such written certification an earlier expiration.

D. No practitioner shall be prosecuted under § 18.2-248 or 18.2-248.1 for dispensing or distributing cannabidiol oil or THC-A oil for the treatment or to alleviate the symptoms of a patient's intractable epilepsy pursuant to a written certification issued pursuant to subsection B. Nothing in this section shall preclude the Board of Medicine from sanctioning a practitioner for failing to properly evaluate or treat a patient's medical condition or otherwise violating the applicable standard of care for evaluating or treating medical conditions.

History.
2015, cc. 7, 8.

§ 54.1-3409. Professional use by veterinarians.

A veterinarian may not prescribe controlled substances for human use and shall only prescribe, dispense or administer a controlled substance in good faith for use by animals within the course of his professional practice. He may prescribe, on a written prescription or on oral prescription as authorized by § 54.1-3410. He may administer drugs, and he may cause them to be administered by an assistant or orderly under his direction and supervision. Such a prescription shall be dated and signed by the person prescribing on the day when issued, and shall bear the full name and address of the owner of the animal, and the species of the animal for which the drug is prescribed and the full name, address and registry number, under the federal laws of the person prescribing, if he is required by those laws to be so registered.

History.
Code 1950, § 54-498; 1956, c. 225; 1970, c. 650, § 54-524.66; 1983, c. 528; 1988, c. 765.

§ 54.1-3410. When pharmacist may sell and dispense drugs.

A. A pharmacist, acting in good faith, may sell and dispense drugs and devices to any person pursuant to a prescription of a prescriber as follows:

1. A drug listed in Schedule II shall be dispensed only upon receipt of a written prescription that is properly executed, dated and signed by the person prescribing on the day when issued and bearing the full name and address of the patient for whom, or of the owner of the animal for which, the drug is dispensed, and the full name, address, and registry number under the federal laws of the person prescribing, if he is required by those laws to be so registered. If the prescription is for an animal, it shall state the species of animal for which the drug is prescribed;

2. In emergency situations, Schedule II drugs may be dispensed pursuant to an oral prescription in accordance with the Board's regulations;

3. Whenever a pharmacist dispenses any drug listed within Schedule II on a prescription issued by a prescriber, he shall affix to the container in which such drug is dispensed, a label showing the prescription serial number or name of the drug; the date of initial filling; his name and address, or the name and address of the pharmacy; the name of the patient or, if the patient is an animal, the name of the owner of the animal and the species of the animal; the name of the prescriber by whom the prescription was written, except for those drugs dispensed to a patient in a hospital pursuant to a chart order; and such directions as may be stated on the prescription.

B. A drug controlled by Schedules III through VI or a device controlled by Schedule VI shall be dispensed upon receipt of a written or oral prescription as follows:

1. If the prescription is written, it shall be properly executed, dated and signed by the person prescribing on the day when issued and bear the full name and address of the patient for whom, or of the owner of the animal for which, the drug is dispensed, and the full name and address of the person prescribing. If the prescription is for an animal, it shall state the species of animal for which the drug is prescribed.

2. If the prescription is oral, the prescriber shall furnish the pharmacist with the same information as is required by law in the case of a written prescription for drugs and devices, except for the signature of the prescriber.

A pharmacist who dispenses a Schedule III through VI drug or device shall label the drug or device as required in subdivision A 3 of this section.

C. A drug controlled by Schedule VI may be refilled without authorization from the prescriber if, after reasonable effort has been made to contact him, the pharmacist ascertains that he is not available and the patient's health would be in imminent danger without the benefits of the drug. The refill shall be made in compliance with the provisions of § 54.1-3411.

If the written or oral prescription is for a Schedule VI drug or device and does not contain the address or registry number of the prescriber, or the address of the patient, the pharmacist need not reduce such information to writing if such information is readily retrievable within the pharmacy.

D. Pursuant to authorization of the prescriber, an agent of the prescriber on his behalf may orally transmit a prescription for a drug classified in Schedules III through VI if, in such cases, the written record of the prescription required by this subsection specifies the full name of the agent of the prescriber transmitting the prescription.

History.
1970, c. 650, § 54-524.67; 1972, c. 798; 1976, c. 614; 1977, c. 302; 1983, cc. 395, 612; 1988, c. 765; 1996, c. 408; 2003, c. 511.

§ 54.1-3410.1. Requirements for radiopharmaceuticals.

A. A pharmacist who is authorized by the Board and acting in good faith, may sell and dispense radiopharmaceuticals pursuant to the order of a physician who is authorized by state or federal law to possess and administer radiopharmaceuticals for the treatment or diagnosis of disease.

B. When an authorized nuclear pharmacist dispenses a radioactive medical material, he shall assure that the outer container (shield) of the radiopharmaceutical shall bear the following information:

1. The name and address of the nuclear pharmacy;
2. The name of the prescriber (authorized user);
3. The date of dispensing;
4. The serial number assigned to the radiopharmaceutical order;
5. The standard radiation symbol;
6. The name of the diagnostic procedure;
7. The words "Caution: Radioactive Material";
8. The name of the radionuclide;
9. The amount of radioactivity and the calibration date and time;
10. The expiration date and time;
11. In the case of a diagnostic radiopharmaceutical, the patient's name or the words "Per Physician's Order"; and
12. In the case of a therapeutic radiopharmaceutical, the patient's name.

C. Orders for radiopharmaceuticals, whether written or verbal, shall include at least the following information:

1. The name of the institution or facility and the name of the person transmitting the order;
2. The date that the radiopharmaceutical will be needed and the calibration time;
3. The name or generally recognized and accepted abbreviation of the radiopharmaceutical;
4. The dose or activity of the radiopharmaceutical at the time of calibration; and
5. In the case of a therapeutic radiopharmaceutical or a radiopharmaceutical blood product, the name of the patient shall be obtained prior to dispensing.

History.
2000, c. 861.

§ 54.1-3410.2. Compounding; pharmacists' authority to compound under certain conditions; labeling and record maintenance requirements.

A. A pharmacist may engage in compounding of drug products when the dispensing of such compounded products is (i) pursuant to valid prescriptions for specific patients and (ii) consistent with the provisions of § 54.1-3303 relating to the issuance of prescriptions and the dispensing of drugs.

Pharmacists shall label all compounded drug products that are dispensed pursuant to a prescription in accordance with this chapter and the Board's regulations, and shall include on the labeling an appropriate beyond-use date as determined by the pharmacist in compliance with USP-NF standards for pharmacy compounding.

B. A pharmacist may also engage in compounding of drug products in anticipation of receipt of prescriptions based on a routine, regularly observed prescribing pattern.

Pharmacists shall label all products compounded prior to dispensing with (i) the name and strength of the compounded medication or a list of the active ingredients and strengths; (ii) the pharmacy's assigned control number that corresponds with the compounding record; (iii) an appropriate beyond-use date as determined by the pharmacist in compliance with USP-NF standards for pharmacy compounding; and (iv) the quantity.

C. In accordance with the conditions set forth in subsections A and B, pharmacists shall not distribute compounded drug products for subsequent distribution or sale to other persons or to commercial entities, including distribution to pharmacies or other entities under common ownership or control with the facility in which such compounding takes place; however, a pharmacist may distribute to a veterinarian in accordance with federal law.

Compounded products for companion animals, as defined in regulations promulgated by the Board of Veterinary Medicine, and distributed by a pharmacy to a veterinarian for further distribution or sale to his own patients shall be limited to drugs necessary to treat an emergent condition when timely access to a compounding pharmacy is not available as determined by the prescribing veterinarian.

A pharmacist may, however, deliver compounded products dispensed pursuant to valid prescriptions to alternate delivery locations pursuant to § 54.1-3420.2.

A pharmacist may provide a reasonable amount of compounded products to practitioners of medicine, osteopathy, podiatry, or dentistry to administer to their patients, either personally or under their direct and immediate supervision, if there is a critical need to treat an emergency condition, or as allowed by federal law or regulations. A pharmacist may also provide compounded products to practitioners of veterinary medicine for office-based administration to their patients.

Pharmacists who provide compounded products for office-based administration for treatment of an emergency condition or as allowed by federal law or regulations shall label all compounded products distributed to practitioners other than veterinarians for administration to their patients with (i) the statement "For Administering in Prescriber Practice Location Only"; (ii) the name and strength of the compounded medication or list of the active ingredients and strengths; (iii) the facility's control number; (iv) an appropriate beyond-use date as determined by the pharmacist in compliance with USP-NF standards for pharmacy compounding; (v) the name and address of the pharmacy; and (vi) the quantity.

Pharmacists shall label all compounded products for companion animals, as defined in regulations promulgated by the Board of Veterinary Medicine, and distributed to a veterinarian for either further distribution or sale to his own patient or administration to his own patient with (a) the name and strength of the compounded medication or list of the active ingredients and strengths; (b) the facility's control number; (c) an appropriate beyond-use date as determined by the pharmacist in compliance with USP-NF standards for pharmacy compounding; (d) the name and address of the pharmacy; and (e) the quantity.

D. Pharmacists shall personally perform or personally supervise the compounding process, which shall include a final check for accuracy and conformity to the formula of the product being prepared, correct ingredients and calculations, accurate and precise measurements, appropriate conditions and procedures, and appearance of the final product.

E. Pharmacists shall ensure compliance with USP-NF standards for both sterile and non-sterile compounding.

F. Pharmacists may use bulk drug substances in compounding when such bulk drug substances:

1. Comply with the standards of an applicable United States Pharmacopoeia or National Formulary monograph, if such monograph exists, and the United States Pharmacopoeia chapter on pharmacy compounding; or are drug substances that are components of drugs approved by the FDA for use in the United States; or are otherwise approved by the FDA; or are manufactured by an establishment that is registered by the FDA; and

2. Are distributed by a licensed wholesale distributor or registered nonresident wholesale distributor, or are distributed by a supplier otherwise approved by the Board and the FDA to distribute bulk drug substances if the pharmacist can establish purity and safety by reasonable means, such as lot analysis, manufacturer reputation, or reliability of the source.

G. Pharmacists may compound using ingredients that are not considered drug products in accordance with the USP-NF standards and guidance on pharmacy compounding.

H. Pharmacists shall not engage in the following:

1. The compounding for human use of a drug product that has been withdrawn or removed from the market by the FDA because such drug product or a component of such drug product has been found to be unsafe. However, this prohibition shall be limited to the scope of the FDA withdrawal;

2. The regular compounding or the compounding of inordinate amounts of any drug products that are essentially copies of commercially available drug products. However, this prohibition shall not include (i) the compounding of any commercially available product when there is a change in the product ordered by the prescriber for an individual patient, (ii) the compounding of a commercially manufactured drug only during times when the product is not available from the manufacturer or supplier, (iii) the compounding of a commercially manufactured drug whose manufacturer has notified the FDA that the drug is unavailable due to a current drug shortage, (iv) the compounding of a commercially manufactured drug when the prescriber has indicated in the oral or written prescription for an individual patient that there is an emergent need for a drug that is not readily available within the time medically necessary, or (v) the mixing of two or more commercially available products regardless of whether the end product is a commercially available product; or

3. The compounding of inordinate amounts of any preparation in cases in which there is no observed historical pattern of prescriptions and dispensing to support an expectation of receiving a valid prescription for the preparation. The compounding of an inordinate amount of a preparation in such cases shall constitute manufacturing of drugs.

I. Pharmacists shall maintain records of all compounded drug products as part of the prescription, formula record, formula book, or other log or record. Records may be maintained electronically, manually, in a combination of both, or by any other readily retrievable method.

1. In addition to other requirements for prescription records, records for products compounded pursuant to a prescription order for a single patient where only manufacturers' finished products are used as components shall include the name and quantity of all components, the date of compounding and dispensing, the prescription number or other identifier of the prescription order, the total quantity of finished product, the signature or initials of the pharmacist or pharmacy technician performing the compounding, and the signature or initials of the pharmacist responsible for supervising the pharmacy technician and verifying the accuracy and integrity of compounded products.

2. In addition to the requirements of subdivision I 1, records for products compounded in bulk or batch in advance of dispensing or when bulk drug substances are used shall include: the generic name and the name of the manufacturer of each component or the brand name of each component; the manufacturer's lot number and expiration date for each component or when the original manufacturer's lot number and expiration date are unknown, the source of acquisition of the component; the assigned lot number if subdivided, the unit or package size and the number of units or packages prepared; and the beyond-use date. The criteria for establishing the beyond-use date shall be available for inspection by the Board.

3. A complete compounding formula listing all procedures, necessary equipment, necessary environmental considerations, and other factors in detail shall be maintained where such instructions are necessary to replicate a compounded product or where the compounding is difficult or complex and must be done by a certain process in order to ensure the integrity of the finished product.

4. A formal written quality assurance plan shall be maintained that describes specific monitoring and evaluation of compounding activities in accordance with USP-NF standards. Records shall be maintained showing compliance with monitoring and evaluation requirements of the plan to include training and initial and periodic competence assessment of personnel involved in compounding, monitoring of environmental controls and equipment calibration, and any end-product testing, if applicable.

J. Practitioners who may lawfully compound drugs for administering or dispensing to their own patients pursuant to §§ 54.1-3301, 54.1-3304, and 54.1-3304.1 shall comply with all provisions of this section and the relevant Board regulations.

K. Every pharmacist-in-charge or owner of a permitted pharmacy or a registered nonresident pharmacy engaging in sterile compounding shall notify the Board of its intention to dispense or otherwise deliver a sterile compounded drug product into the Commonwealth. Upon renewal of its permit or registration, a pharmacy or nonresident pharmacy shall notify the Board of its intention to continue dispensing or otherwise delivering sterile compounded drug products into the Commonwealth. Failure to provide notification to the Board shall constitute a violation of Chapter 33 (§ 54.1-3300 et seq.) or Chapter 34 (§ 54.1-3400 et seq.). The Board shall maintain this information in a manner that will allow the production of a list identifying all such sterile compounding pharmacies.

History.

2003, c. 509; 2005, c. 200; 2012, c. 173; 2013, c. 765; 2014, c. 147; 2015, c. 300; 2016, c. 221.

§ 54.1-3411. When prescriptions may be refilled.

Prescriptions may be refilled as follows:

1. A prescription for a drug in Schedule II may not be refilled.

2. A prescription for a drug in Schedules III or IV may not be filled or refilled more than six months after the date on which such prescription was issued and no such prescription may be authorized to be refilled, nor be refilled, more than five times, except that any prescription for such a drug after six months from the date of issue, or after being refilled five times, may be renewed by the prescriber issuing it either in writing, or orally, if promptly reduced to writing and filed by the pharmacist filling it.

3. A prescription in Schedule VI may not be refilled, unless authorized by the prescriber either on the face of the original prescription or orally by the prescriber except as provided in subdivision 4 of this section. Oral instructions shall be reduced promptly to writing by the pharmacist and filed on or with the original prescription.

4. A prescription for a drug controlled by Schedule VI may be refilled without authorization from the prescriber if reasonable effort has been made to communicate with the prescriber, and the pharmacist has determined that he is not available and the patient's health would be in imminent danger without the benefits of the drug. The pharmacist shall inform the patient of the prescriber's unavailability and that the refill is being made without his authorization. The pharmacist shall promptly inform the prescriber of such refill. The date and quantity of the refill, the prescriber's unavailability and the rationale for the refill shall be noted on the reverse side of the prescription.

History.

1970, c. 650, § 54-524.68; 1972, c. 798; 1976, c. 614; 1983, c. 395; 1988, c. 765; 1996, c. 408.

§ 54.1-3411.1. Prohibition on returns, exchanges, or re-dispensing of drugs; exceptions.

A. Drugs dispensed to persons pursuant to a prescription shall not be accepted for return or exchange for the purpose of re-dispensing by any pharmacist or pharmacy after such drugs have been removed from the pharmacy premises from which they were dispensed except:

1. In a hospital with an on-site hospital pharmacy wherein drugs may be returned to the pharmacy in accordance with practice standards;

2. In such cases where official compendium storage requirements are assured and the drugs are in manufacturers' original sealed containers or in sealed individual dose or unit dose packaging that meets official compendium class A or B container requirements, or better, and such return or exchange is consistent with federal law; or

3. When a dispensed drug has not been out of the possession of a delivery agent of the pharmacy.

B. The Board of Pharmacy shall promulgate regulations to establish a Prescription Drug Donation Program for accepting unused previously dispensed prescription drugs that meet the criteria set forth in subdivision A 2, for the purpose of re-dispensing such drugs to indigent patients, either through hospitals, or through clinics organized in whole or in part for the delivery of health care services to the indigent. Such program shall not authorize the donation of Schedule II-V controlled substances if so prohibited by federal law. No drugs shall be re-dispensed unless the integrity of the drug can be assured.

C. Unused prescription drugs dispensed for use by persons eligible for coverage under Title XIX or Title XXI of the Social Security Act, as amended, may be donated pursuant to this section unless such donation is prohibited.

D. A pharmaceutical manufacturer shall not be liable for any claim or injury arising from the storage, donation, acceptance, transfer, or dispensing of any drug provided to a patient, or any other activity undertaken in accordance with a drug distribution program established pursuant to this section.

E. Nothing in this section shall be construed to create any new or additional liability, or to abrogate any liability that may exist, applicable to a pharmaceutical manufacturer for its products separately from the storage, donation, acceptance, transfer, or dispensing of any drug provided to a patient in accordance with a drug distribution program established pursuant to this section.

History.
2002, c. 632; 2005, c. 68; 2008, c. 429; 2009, cc. 109, 114.

§ 54.1-3411.2. Prescription drug disposal programs.

A. As used in this section:

"Authorized pharmacy disposal site" means a pharmacy that qualifies as a collection site pursuant to 21 C.F.R § 1317.40.

"Pharmacy drug disposal program" means any voluntary drug disposal program located at or operated in accordance with state and federal law by a pharmacy.

B. A pharmacy may participate in a pharmacy drug disposal program in accordance with state and federal law regarding proper collection, storage, and destruction of prescription drugs, including controlled and noncontrolled substances. A pharmacy that chooses to participate in a pharmacy drug disposal program shall notify the Board, and the Board shall maintain a list of all pharmacies in the Commonwealth that have chosen to participate in a pharmacy drug disposal program on a website maintained by the Board.

C. No person that participates in a pharmacy drug disposal program shall be liable for any theft, robbery, or other criminal act related to its participation in the pharmacy drug disposal program nor shall such person be liable for acts of simple negligence in the collection, storage, or destruction of prescription drugs collected through such pharmacy drug disposal program, provided that the pharmacy practice site is acting in good faith and in accordance with applicable state and federal law and regulations.

History.
2016, c. 95.

§ 54.1-3412. Date of dispensing; initials of pharmacist; automated data processing system.

Pursuant to regulations promulgated by the Board, the pharmacist dispensing any prescription shall record the date of dispensing and his initials on the prescription in (i) an automated data processing system used for the storage and retrieval of dispensing information for prescriptions or (ii) on another record that is accurate from which dispensing information is retrievable and in which the original prescription and any information maintained in such data processing system concerning such prescription can be found.

History.
1970, c. 650, § 54-524.69; 1979, c. 388; 1987, c. 198; 1988, c. 765; 2002, c. 411.

§ 54.1-3413. Manufacturing and administering Schedule I drugs.

It shall be lawful for a person to manufacture, and for a practitioner to administer, Schedule I drugs if:

1. The manufacturer and practitioner are expressly authorized to engage in such activities by the Attorney General of the United States, or pursuant to the federal Food, Drug and Cosmetic Act;
2. The manufacturer or dispenser is registered under all appropriate provisions of this chapter;
3. Any Schedule I drug so manufactured is sold or furnished on an official written order to a practitioner or other authorized person only; and
4. The manufacturer and practitioner comply with all other requirements of this chapter.

History.
1970, c. 650, § 54-524.58:1; 1972, c. 798; 1988, c. 765.

§ 54.1-3414. Official orders for Schedule II drugs.

An official written order for any Schedule II drug shall be signed by the purchasing licensee or by his agent. The original shall be presented to the person who supplies the drug or drugs. If such person accepts the order, each party to the transaction shall preserve his copy of the order for two years in such a way as to be readily accessible for inspection by any public officer or employee engaged in the enforcement of this chapter. It shall be deemed a compliance with this section if the parties to the transaction have complied with the federal laws respecting the requirements governing the use of order forms. Parties ordering Schedule II drugs electronically shall comply with all requirements of federal law and regulation governing such transactions.

History.
Code 1950, § 54-493; 1970, c. 650, § 54-524.60; 1988, c. 765; 2006, c. 346.

§ 54.1-3415. Distribution of drugs in Schedules II through VI by manufacturers and wholesalers.

A. A permitted manufacturer or wholesaler may distribute Schedule II drugs to any of the following persons, but only on official written orders or pursuant to an electronic order in compliance with federal laws and regulations governing the electronic ordering of Schedule II drugs:

1. To a manufacturer or wholesaler who has been issued permits pursuant to this chapter;

2. To a licensed pharmacist, permitted pharmacy or a licensed practitioner of medicine, osteopathy, podiatry, dentistry or veterinary medicine;

3. To a person who has been issued a controlled substance registration certificate pursuant to § 54.1-3422, if the certificate of such person authorizes such purchase;

4. On a special written order accompanied by a certificate of exemption, as required by the federal laws, to a person in the employ of the United States government or of any state, territorial, district, county, municipal, or insular government, purchasing, receiving or possessing drugs by reason of his official duties;

5. To a master of a ship or a person in charge of any aircraft upon which no physician is regularly employed, for the actual medical needs of persons on board such ship or aircraft when not in port. However, such drugs shall be sold to a master of such ship or person in charge of such aircraft pursuant to a special order form approved by a commissioned medical officer or acting assistant surgeon of the United States Public Health Service; and

6. To a person in a foreign country in compliance with the provisions of the relevant federal laws.

B. A permitted manufacturer or wholesaler may distribute drugs classified in Schedule III through Schedule VI and devices to all persons listed in subsection A of this section without an official written order. However, this section shall not be construed to prohibit the distribution of a Schedule VI drug or device to any person who is otherwise authorized by law to administer, prescribe or dispense such drug or device.

History.

Code 1950, § 54-492; 1970, c. 650; 1972, c. 798, § 54-524.59; 1977, c. 302; 1978, c. 833; 1988, c. 765; 1998, c. 490; 2006, c. 346.

§ 54.1-3416. No prescription for preparations listed pursuant to Schedule V.

A preparation listed pursuant to Schedule V may be dispensed without a prescription if:

1. The preparation is dispensed only by a pharmacist directly to the person requesting the preparation;

2. The preparation is dispensed only to a person who is at least eighteen years of age;

3. The pharmacist requires the person requesting the preparation to furnish suitable identification including proof of age when appropriate;

4. The pharmacist does not dispense to any one person, or for the use of any one person or animal, any narcotic drug preparation or preparations, when he knows, or can by reasonable diligence ascertain, that such dispensing will provide the person to whom or for whose use, or the owner of the animal for the use of which, such preparation is dispensed, within 48 consecutive hours, with more than 200 milligrams of opium, or more than 270 milligrams of codeine, or more than 130 milligrams of dihydrocodeinone, or more than 65 milligrams of ethylmorphine, or more than 32 5/10 milligrams of diphenoxylate. In dispensing such a narcotic drug preparation, the pharmacist shall exercise professional discretion to ensure that the preparation is being dispensed for medical purposes only.

Any pharmacist shall, at the time of dispensing, make and keep a record showing the date of dispensing, the name and quantity of the preparation, the name and address of the person to whom the preparation is dispensed, and enter his initials thereon. Such records shall be maintained as set forth in § 54.1-3404 and the regulations of the Board.

History.

1970, c. 650, § 54-524.75; 1972, c. 798; 1988, c. 765.

§ 54.1-3417. Disposing of stocks of Schedules II through V drugs.

The owner of any stocks of drugs included in Schedules II through V obtained in compliance with this chapter, upon discontinuance of dealing in such drugs, may dispose of such stocks only on an official written order as follows:

1. A pharmacy or practitioner or an agent or agents of a pharmacy or practitioner under specific written authorization from the owner of such pharmacy or such practitioner, may dispose of such stocks to a manufacturer or wholesaler holding a valid license to deal in such drugs, or to another pharmacy or practitioner.

2. A manufacturer or wholesaler may dispose of such stocks only to a manufacturer or wholesaler holding a valid permit to deal in such drugs.

History.

1970, c. 650, § 54-524.61; 1976, c. 406; 1988, c. 765.

§ 54.1-3418. Sale of aqueous or oleaginous solutions.

A pharmacist, only upon an official written order, may sell to a physician, dentist, or veterinarian, in quantities not exceeding one ounce at any one time, aqueous or oleaginous solutions compounded by the pharmacist, of which the content of narcotic drugs does not exceed a proportion greater than twenty percent of the complete solution, to be used for medical purposes.

History.

Code 1950, § 54-496; 1956, c. 225; 1970, c. 650, § 54-524.62; 1988, c. 765.

§ 54.1-3419. Dispensing of insulin preparations.

Any insulin preparation shall be dispensed only by or under the supervision of a licensed pharmacist.

History.
1984, c. 723, § 54-524.67:3; 1988, c. 765.

§ 54.1-3420. Distribution of certain drugs; written request or confirmation of receipt.

No manufacturer or distributor of controlled substances shall distribute or dispense any substance listed on Schedules II through V to any person, whether a practitioner of the healing arts or some other profession, except with the written request or confirmation of receipt of the practitioner. Such request or confirmation shall be maintained as required by this chapter.

Subject to the foregoing provisions, no person shall be prohibited from distributing controlled substances listed on Schedules II through V for charitable uses or for use in research or investigations.

History.
1984, c. 724, § 54-524.58:2; 1988, c. 765.

§ 54.1-3420.1. Identification required for filling prescriptions.

A. Before dispensing any drug listed on Schedules III through V, a pharmacist may require proof of identity from any patient presenting a prescription or requesting a refill of a prescription.

B. A pharmacist, or his agent, shall require proof of identity at the time of delivery from any person seeking to take delivery of any drug listed on Schedule II pursuant to a valid prescription, unless such person is known to the pharmacist or to his agent. If the person seeking to take delivery of a drug listed on Schedule II pursuant to a valid prescription is not the patient for whom the drug is prescribed, and the person is not known to the pharmacist or his agent, the pharmacist or his agent shall either make a photocopy or electronic copy of such person's identification or record the full name and address of such person. The pharmacist shall keep records of the names and addresses or copies of proof of identity of persons taking delivery of drugs as required by this subsection for a period of at least one month. For the purposes of this subsection, "proof of identity" means a driver's license, government-issued identification card, or other photo identification along with documentation of the person's current address.

C. Whenever any pharmacist permitted to operate in the Commonwealth or nonresident pharmacist registered to conduct business in the Commonwealth delivers a prescription drug order for any drug listed on Schedule II by mail, common carrier, or delivery service to a Virginia address, the method of delivery employed shall require the signature of the recipient as confirmation of receipt.

History.
1988, c. 400, § 54-524.67:4; 2010, c. 193; 2011, cc. 262, 318.

§ 54.1-3420.2. Delivery of prescription drug order.

A. Whenever any pharmacy permitted to operate in this Commonwealth or nonresident pharmacy registered to conduct business in the Commonwealth delivers a prescription drug order by mail, common carrier, or delivery service, when the drug order is not personally hand delivered directly, to the patient or his agent at the person's residence or other designated location, the following conditions shall be required:

1. Written notice shall be placed in each shipment alerting the consumer that under certain circumstances chemical degradation of drugs may occur; and

2. Written notice shall be placed in each shipment providing a toll-free or local consumer access telephone number which is designed to respond to consumer questions pertaining to chemical degradation of drugs.

B. If a prescription drug order for a Schedule VI controlled substance is not personally hand delivered directly to the patient or the patient's agent, or if the prescription drug order is not delivered to the residence of the patient, the delivery location shall hold a current permit, license, or registration with the Board that authorizes the possession of controlled substances at that location. The Board shall promulgate regulations related to the security, access, required records, accountability, storage, and accuracy of delivery of such drug delivery systems. Schedule II through Schedule V controlled substances shall be delivered to an alternate delivery location only if such delivery is authorized by federal law and regulations of the Board.

C. Prescription drug orders dispensed to a patient and delivered to a community services board or behavioral health authority facility licensed by the Department of Behavioral Health and Developmental Services upon the signed written request of the patient or the patient's legally authorized representative may be stored, retained, and repackaged at the facility on behalf of the patient for subsequent delivery or administration. The repackaging of a dispensed prescription drug order retained by a community services board or behavioral health authority facility for the purpose of assisting a client with self-administration pursuant to this subsection shall only be performed by a pharmacist, pharmacy technician, nurse, or other person who has successfully completed a Board-approved training program for repackaging of prescription drug orders as authorized by this subsection. The Board shall promulgate regulations relating to training, packaging, labeling, and recordkeeping for such repackaging.

D. Prescription drug orders dispensed to a patient and delivered to a Virginia Department of Health or local health department clinic upon the signed written request of a patient, a patient's legally authorized representative, or a Virginia Department of Health district director or his designee may be stored and retained at the clinic on behalf of the patient for subsequent delivery or administration.

E. Prescription drug orders dispensed to a patient and delivered to a program of all-inclusive care for the elderly (PACE) site licensed by the Department of Social Services pursuant to § 63.2-1701 and overseen by the Department of Medical Assistance Services in accordance with § 32.1-330.3 upon the signed written request of the patient or the patient's legally authorized representative may be stored, retained, and repackaged at the site on behalf of the patient for subsequent delivery or administration. The repackaging of a dispensed prescription drug order retained by the PACE site for the purpose of assisting a client with self-administration pursuant to this subsection shall only be performed by a pharmacist, pharmacy technician, nurse, or other person who has successfully completed a Board-approved training program for repackaging of prescription drug orders as authorized by this subsection. The Board shall promulgate regulations relating to training, packaging, labeling, and recordkeeping for such repackaging.

History.
1998, c. 597; 2002, c. 411; 2010, c. 28; 2015, c. 505.

§ 54.1-3421. New drugs.

A. No person shall sell, deliver, offer for sale, hold for sale or give away any new drug unless an application with respect to the drug has been approved and the approval has not been withdrawn under § 505 of the federal Food, Drug, and Cosmetic Act (21 U.S.C. § 355).

B. This section shall not apply to a drug subject to the federal act intended solely for investigational use and for which a notice of claimed investigational exemption for a new drug has been filed with the U.S. Food and Drug Administration in accordance with 21 C.F.R. Part 312.

History.
1970, c. 650, § 54-524.95; 1988, c. 765; 2000, c. 135.

§ 54.1-3422. Controlled substances registration certificate required in addition to other requirements; exemptions.

A. Every person who manufactures, distributes or dispenses any substance that is controlled in Schedules I through V or who proposes to engage in the manufacture, distribution or dispensing of any such controlled substance except permitted pharmacies, those persons who are licensed pharmacists, those persons who are licensed physician assistants, and those persons who are licensed practitioners of medicine, osteopathy, podiatry, dentistry, optometry, nursing, or veterinary medicine shall obtain annually a controlled substances registration certificate issued by the Board. This registration shall be in addition to other licensing or permitting requirements enumerated in this chapter or otherwise required by law.

B. Registration under this section and under all other applicable registration requirements shall entitle the registrant to possess, manufacture, distribute, dispense, or conduct research with those substances to the extent authorized by this registration and in conformity with the other provisions of this chapter.

C. The following persons need not register and may possess controlled substances listed on Schedules I through VI:

1. An agent or employee of any holder of a controlled substance registration certificate or of any practitioner listed in subsection A of this section as exempt from the requirement for registration, if such agent or employee is acting in the usual course of his business or employment;

2. A common or contract carrier or warehouseman, or his employee, whose possession is in the usual course of business or employment; or

3. An ultimate user or a person in possession of any controlled substance pursuant to a lawful order of a prescriber or in lawful possession of a Schedule V substance.

D. A separate registration is required at each principal place of business or professional practice where the applicant manufactures, distributes, or dispenses controlled substances.

History.
1972, c. 798, § 54-524.47:2; 1988, c. 765; 1996, cc. 408, 468, 496; 1998, c. 490; 2001, cc. 243, 465.

§ 54.1-3423. Board to issue registration unless inconsistent with public interest; authorization to conduct research; application and fees.

A. The Board shall register an applicant to manufacture or distribute controlled substances included in Schedules I through V unless it determines that the issuance of that registration would be inconsistent with the public interest. In determining the public interest, the Board shall consider the following factors:

1. Maintenance of effective controls against diversion of controlled substances into other than legitimate medical, scientific, or industrial channels;

2. Compliance with applicable state and local law;

3. Any convictions of the applicant under any federal and state laws relating to any controlled substance;

4. Past experience in the manufacture or distribution of controlled substances, and the existence in the applicant's establishment of effective controls against diversion;

5. Furnishing by the applicant of false or fraudulent material in any application filed under this chapter;

6. Suspension or revocation of the applicant's federal registration to manufacture, distribute, or dispense controlled substances as authorized by federal law; and

7. Any other factors relevant to and consistent with the public health and safety.

B. Registration under subsection A does not entitle a registrant to manufacture and distribute controlled substances in Schedule I or II other than those specified in the registration.

C. Practitioners must be registered to conduct research with controlled substances in Schedules II through VI. Practitioners registered under federal law to conduct research with Schedule I substances may conduct research with Schedule I substances within this Commonwealth upon furnishing the evidence of that federal registration.

D. The Board may register other persons or entities to possess controlled substances listed on Schedules II through VI upon a determination that (i) there is a documented need, (ii) the issuance of the registration is consistent with the public interest, (iii) the possession and subsequent use of the controlled substances complies with applicable state and federal laws and regulations, and (iv) the subsequent storage, use, and recordkeeping of the controlled substances will be under the general supervision of a licensed pharmacist, practitioner of medicine, osteopathy, podiatry, dentistry or veterinary medicine as specified in the Board's regulations. The Board shall consider, at a minimum, the factors listed in subsection A of this section in determining whether the registration shall be issued. Notwithstanding the exceptions listed in § 54.1-3422 A, the Board may mandate a controlled substances registration for sites maintaining certain types and quantities of Schedules II through VI controlled substances as it may specify in its regulations. The Board shall promulgate regulations related to requirements or criteria for the issuance of such controlled substances registration, storage, security, supervision, and recordkeeping.

E. The Board may register a public or private animal shelter as defined in § 3.2-6500 to purchase, possess, and administer certain Schedule II-VI controlled substances approved by the State Veterinarian for the purpose of euthanizing injured, sick, homeless, and unwanted domestic pets and animals; and to purchase, possess, and administer certain Schedule VI controlled substances for the purpose of preventing, controlling, and treating certain communicable diseases that failure to control would result in transmission to the animal population in the shelter. The drugs used for euthanasia shall be administered only in accordance with protocols established by the State Veterinarian and only by persons trained in accordance with instructions by the State Veterinarian. The list of Schedule VI drugs used for treatment and prevention of communicable diseases within the shelter shall be determined by the supervising veterinarian of the shelter and the drugs shall be administered only pursuant to written protocols established or approved by the supervising veterinarian of the shelter and only by persons who have been trained in accordance with instructions established or approved by the supervising veterinarian. The shelter shall maintain a copy of the approved list of drugs, written protocols for administering, and training records of those persons administering drugs on the premises of the shelter.

F. The Board may register a crisis stabilization unit established pursuant to § 37.2-500 or 37.2-601 and licensed by the Department of Behavioral Health and Developmental Services to maintain a stock of Schedule VI controlled substances necessary for immediate treatment of patients admitted to the crisis stabilization unit, which may be accessed and administered by a nurse pursuant to a written or oral order of a prescriber in the absence of a prescriber. Schedule II through Schedule V controlled substances shall only be maintained if so authorized by federal law and Board regulations.

G. Applications for controlled substances registration certificates and renewals thereof shall be made on a form prescribed by the Board and such applications shall be accompanied by a fee in an amount to be determined by the Board.

H. Upon (i) any change in ownership or control of a business, (ii) any change of location of the controlled substances stock, (iii) the termination of authority by or of the person named as the responsible party on a controlled substances registration, or (iv) a change in the supervising practitioner, if applicable, the registrant or responsible party shall immediately surrender the registration. The registrant shall, within 14 days following surrender of a registration, file a new application and, if applicable, name the new responsible party or supervising practitioner.

History.

1972, c. 798, § 54-524.47:3; 1978, c. 833; 1980, c. 288; 1988, c. 765; 1996, cc. 468, 496; 1998, c. 490; 2009, cc. 149, 169; 2010, c. 28; 2014, c. 148.

§ 54.1-3424. Suspension or revocation of registration, license or permit; limitation to particular controlled substance; controlled substances placed under seal; sale of perishables and forfeiture; notification to DEA.

A. A registration to manufacture, distribute, or dispense a controlled substance may be suspended or revoked by the Board upon a finding that the registrant:

1. Has furnished false or fraudulent material information in an application filed under this chapter;

2. Has been convicted of a felony under any state or federal law relating to any controlled substance;

3. Has had his federal registration to manufacture, distribute or dispense controlled substances suspended or revoked;

4. Has violated or cooperated with others in violating any provision of this chapter or regulations of the Board relating to the manufacture, distribution or dispensing of controlled substances.

B. The Board may limit revocation or suspension of a registration to the particular controlled substance with respect to which grounds for revocation or suspension exist.

C. If the Board suspends or revokes a registration, or if the license or permit of a person possessing controlled substances under an exemption in § 54.1-3422 A is suspended or revoked by the issuing board, all controlled substances owned or possessed by the registrant, licensee or permittee at the time of suspension or the effective date of the revocation order may be placed under seal. No disposition may be made of substances under seal until the time for taking an appeal has elapsed or until all appeals have been concluded unless a court orders the sale of perishable substances and the deposit of the proceeds of the sale with the court. Upon a revocation order becoming final, all controlled substances shall be forfeited to the Commonwealth.

D. The Board shall promptly notify the DEA of all orders suspending or revoking registration and all forfeitures of controlled substances.

History.
1972, c. 798, § 54-524.47:4; 1988, c. 765; 1996, cc. 468, 496; 1998, c. 490.

§ 54.1-3425: Repealed by Acts 2009, c. 149, cl. 2, effective March 6, 2009, and c. 169, cl. 2, effective March 23, 2009.

Cross references.
For current provisions as to permits for animal shelters, see subsection E of § 54.1-3423.

§ 54.1-3426. Regulations for special packaging.

A. The Board shall adopt standards for special packaging consistent with those promulgated pursuant to the federal Poison Prevention Packaging Act of 1970 (15 U.S.C. § 1471 et seq.). The Board may exempt any drug from the requirements of special packaging and shall exempt any drug exempted pursuant to the Poison Prevention Packaging Act of 1970.

B. A prescriber or a purchaser may direct that a drug, which is subject to being dispensed in special packaging, be dispensed in other than special packaging.

History.
1978, c. 833, § 54-524.67:1; 1988, c. 765; 1996, c. 408.

§ 54.1-3427. Dispensing drugs without safety closure container.

When a pharmacist receives the request of any person that a drug or drugs for such person to be dispensed by the pharmacist not be placed in a safety closure container, the pharmacist may dispense such drug or drugs in such nonsafety closure container. The delivering pharmacist shall not be civilly liable simply by reason of dispensing a drug or drugs in such a container if the recipient signs a release covering a period of time or a single delivery, which release provides that the recipient releases the pharmacist from civil liability for not using the safety closure container, unless the pharmacist acted with willful and wanton disregard of safety.

History.
1978, c. 839, § 54-524.67:2; 1988, c. 765.

§ 54.1-3428. Dissemination of information.

The Board may disseminate such information regarding drugs, devices, and cosmetics as the Board deems necessary in the interest of public health and the protection of the consumer against fraud. This section shall not be construed to prohibit the Board from collecting, reporting, and illustrating the results of its investigations.

History.
1970, c. 650, § 54-524.100; 1988, c. 765.

§ 54.1-3429. Revocation of permit issued to manufacturer, wholesaler or distributor.

The Board may revoke a permit issued to a manufacturer, wholesaler or distributor for failure to comply with regulations promulgated pursuant to the provisions of this chapter.

History.
1970, c. 650, § 54-524.46; 1988, c. 765.

§ 54.1-3430. Display of permit; permits nontransferable; renewal.

Permits issued under the provisions of this chapter shall be displayed in a conspicuous place in the factory or other place of business for which issued.

Permits shall not be transferable and shall be renewed annually.

History.
Code 1950, §§ 54-449, 54-450; 1970, c. 650, § 54-524.38; 1976, c. 614, § 54-524.39; 1988, c. 765.

§ 54.1-3431. Admission into evidence of certain certificates of analysis.

In any administrative hearing, a certificate of analysis of a chemist, performed in any laboratory operated by the Department of Forensic Science or authorized by such Department to conduct such analysis, when such certificate is attested by such chemist, shall be admissible as evidence. A copy of such certificate shall be delivered to the parties in interest at least seven days prior to the date fixed for the hearing.

Any certificate of analysis purporting to be signed by any chemist shall be admissible as evidence in such hearing without any proof of the seal or signature or of the official character of the chemist whose name is signed to it.

History.

Code 1950, § 54-524.77; 1970, c. 650; 1972, cc. 741, 798, § 54-524.77:1; 1973, c. 479; 1977, c. 633; 1988, c. 765; 1990, c. 825; 2005, cc. 868, 881.

ARTICLE 4.1.

EXPANDED ACCESS TO INVESTIGATIONAL DRUGS, BIOLOGICAL PRODUCTS, AND DEVICES.

§ 54.1-3442.1. Definitions.

As used in this article, unless the context requires a different meaning:

"Investigational drug, biological product, or device" means a drug, biological product, or device that has successfully completed Phase I of a clinical trial but has not been approved for general use by the U.S. Food and Drug Administration and remains under investigation in a clinical trial.

"Terminal condition" means a condition caused by injury, disease, or illness from which, to a reasonable degree of medical probability, a patient cannot recover and (i) the patient's death is imminent or (ii) the patient is in a persistent vegetative state.

"Treating physician" means a physician who is providing or has previously provided medical treatment or evaluation to and has or previously had an ongoing treatment relationship with the person.

History.

2015, cc. 655, 656.

§ 54.1-3442.2. Eligibility for expanded access to investigational drugs, biological products, and devices; written, informed consent to treatment.

A. A person shall be eligible for expanded access to investigational drugs, biological products, or devices if:

1. He has a terminal condition, attested to by his treating physician and confirmed by a second physician not previously involved in the treatment of the person who has conducted an independent examination of the person;

2. He has, in consultation with his treating physician, considered all other treatment options currently approved by the U.S. Food and Drug Administration and the treating physician has determined that no reasonable opportunity exists for him to participate in an ongoing clinical trial for his terminal condition;

3. The potential benefits of use of the investigational drug, biological product, or device to treat his terminal condition are greater than the potential risks of the use of the investigational drug, biological product, or device to treat his terminal condition;

4. He has received a recommendation from his treating physician for use of an investigational drug, biological product, or device for treatment of his terminal condition; and

5. He or, if he is incapable of making an informed decision, his legally authorized representative has given written informed consent to use of the investigational drug, biological product, or device for treatment of his terminal condition or, if the person is a minor or lacks capacity to provide informed consent, his parent or legal guardian has given written informed consent to the use of the investigational drug, biological product, or device for treatment of his terminal condition.

Documentation indicating that the person meets the criteria for eligibility for expanded access to investigational drugs, biological products, or devices shall be provided by the person's treating physician and shall be included in the person's medical record.

B. Written informed consent to use of an investigational drug, biological product, or device shall include:

1. An explanation of the currently approved products and treatments for the person's terminal condition;

2. A statement that the person has, in consultation with his treating physician, considered all other treatment options currently approved by the U.S. Food and Drug Administration and the treating physician has determined that no reasonable opportunity exists for the person to participate in an ongoing clinical trial for his terminal condition;

3. An explanation of the specific investigational drug, biological product, or device proposed for treatment of the person's terminal condition;

4. A description of possible outcomes resulting from use of the investigational drug, biological product, or device to treat the person's terminal condition, including a statement that new, unanticipated, different, or worse symptoms might result from and death could be hastened by the proposed treatment, based on the treating physician's knowledge of the proposed treatment in conjunction with an awareness of the person's terminal condition;

5. A statement that the person may be required to pay any costs associated with use of the investigational drug, biological product, or device; and

6. A statement that the person or, if the person is a minor or lacks capacity to provide informed con-

sent, his parent or legal guardian consents to the use of the investigational drug, biological product, or device for treatment of his terminal condition.

History.
2015, cc. 655, 656.

§ 54.1-3442.3. Expanded access to investigational drugs, biological products, or devices; cost; insurance coverage.

A. A manufacturer of an investigational drug, biological product, or device may make such investigational drug, biological product, or device available to a person who meets the criteria set forth in subsection A of § 54.1-3442.2; however, nothing in this article shall require a manufacturer of an investigational drug, biological product, or device to make such investigational drug, biological product, or device available to such person.

B. A manufacturer that makes an investigational drug, biological product, or device available to a person who meets the criteria set forth in subsection A of § 54.1-3442.2 may provide the investigational drug, biological product, or device to the person free of charge or may require the person to pay the costs of, or the costs associated with, the manufacture of the investigational drug, biological product, or device.

C. An insurer proposing to issue individual or group accident and sickness insurance policies providing hospital, medical and surgical, or major medical coverage on an expense-incurred basis, a corporation providing individual or group accident and sickness subscription contracts, or a health maintenance organization providing a health care plan for health care services may provide coverage for costs related to treatment of a person's terminal condition with an investigational drug, biological product, or device; however, nothing in this article shall require an insurer proposing to issue individual or group accident and sickness insurance policies providing hospital, medical and surgical, or major medical coverage on an expense-incurred basis, a corporation providing individual or group accident and sickness subscription contracts, or a health maintenance organization providing a health care plan for health care services to provide coverage for costs related to treatment of a person's terminal condition with an investigational drug, biological product, or device.

History.
2015, cc. 655, 656.

§ 54.1-3442.4. Limitation of liability.

A. Notwithstanding any other provision of law to the contrary, a health care provider as defined in § 8.01-581.1 who recommends an investigational drug, biological product, or device to a person who meets the criteria set forth in subsection A of § 54.1-3442.2 shall be immune from civil liability for any adverse action, condition, or other outcome resulting from the person's use of the investigational drug, biological product, or device.

B. Notwithstanding any other provision of law to the contrary, a manufacturer, distributor, administrator, health care provider as defined in § 8.01-581.1, sponsor, or physician who manufactures, supplies, distributes, administers, prescribes, or recommends an investigational drug, biological product, or device to a person who meets the criteria set forth in § 54.1-3442.2 shall be immune from suit and liability caused by, arising out of, or relating to the design, development, clinical testing and investigation, manufacture, labeling, distribution, sale, purchase, donation, dispensing, prescription, recommendation, administration, efficacy, or use of such investigational drug, biological product, or device made available to such person.

C. No claim or cause of action against a manufacturer, distributor, administrator, health care provider as defined in § 8.01-581.1, sponsor, or physician who manufactures, supplies, distributes, administers, prescribes, or recommends an investigational drug, biological product, or device to a person who meets the criteria set forth in § 54.1-3442.2 shall exist in any state court for claims of property, personal injury, or death caused by, arising out of, or relating to the design, development, clinical testing and investigation, manufacture, labeling, distribution, sale, purchase, donation, dispensing, prescription, recommendation, administration, efficacy, or use of such investigational drug, biological product, or device made available to such person.

D. No health care provider as defined in § 8.01-581.1 who recommends, prescribes, administers, distributes, or supplies an investigational drug, biological product, or device to a person who meets the criteria set forth in § 54.1-3442.2 shall be deemed to have engaged in unprofessional conduct, or shall be adversely affected in any decision relating to licensure, on such grounds.

E. Nothing in this article shall require a person to violate or act in contravention of any federal or state law as such law relates to the prescribing, dispensing, administration, or use of an investigational drug, biological product, or device.

History.
2015, cc. 655, 656.

ARTICLE 5.
STANDARDS AND SCHEDULES.

§ 54.1-3443. Board to administer article.

A. The Board shall administer this article and may add substances to or deschedule or reschedule all substances enumerated in the schedules in this article pursuant to the procedures of the Administrative Process Act (§ 2.2-4000 et seq.). In making a determination regarding a substance, the Board shall consider the following:

1. The actual or relative potential for abuse;
2. The scientific evidence of its pharmacological effect, if known;
3. The state of current scientific knowledge regarding the substance;
4. The history and current pattern of abuse;
5. The scope, duration, and significance of abuse;
6. The risk to the public health;
7. The potential of the substance to produce psychic or physical dependence; and
8. Whether the substance is an immediate precursor of a substance already controlled under this article.

B. After considering the factors enumerated in subsection A, the Board shall make findings and issue a regulation controlling the substance if it finds the substance has a potential for abuse.

C. If the Board designates a substance as an immediate precursor, substances which are precursors of the controlled precursor shall not be subject to control solely because they are precursors of the controlled precursor.

D. If the Board, in consultation with the Department of Forensic Science, determines the substance shall be placed into Schedule I or II pursuant to § 54.1-3445 or 54.1-3447, the Board may amend its regulations pursuant to Article 2 (§ 2.2-4006 et seq.) of the Administrative Process Act. Prior to making such amendments, the Board shall conduct a public hearing. At least 30 days prior to conducting such hearing, it shall post notice of the hearing on the Virginia Regulatory Town Hall and shall send notice of the hearing to any persons requesting to be notified of a regulatory action. In the notice, the Board shall include a list of all substances it intends to schedule by regulation. The Board shall notify the House Courts of Justice and Senate Courts of Justice Committees of any new substance added to Schedule I or II pursuant to this subsection. Any substance added to Schedule I or II pursuant to this subsection shall remain on Schedule I or II for a period of 18 months. Upon expiration of such 18-month period, such substance shall be descheduled unless a general law is enacted adding such substance to Schedule I or II. Nothing in this subsection shall preclude the Board from adding substances to or descheduling or rescheduling all substances enumerated in the schedules pursuant to the provisions of subsections A, B, and E.

E. If any substance is designated, rescheduled, or descheduled as a controlled substance under federal law and notice of such action is given to the Board, the Board may similarly control the substance under this chapter after the expiration of 120 days from publication in the Federal Register of the final order designating a substance as a controlled substance or rescheduling or descheduling a substance without following the provisions specified in subsections A and B.

F. Authority to control under this section does not extend to distilled spirits, wine, malt beverages, or tobacco as those terms are defined or used in Title 4.1.

G. The Board shall exempt any nonnarcotic substance from a schedule if such substance may, under the provisions of the federal Food, Drug and Cosmetic Act (21 U.S.C. § 301 et seq.) or state law, be lawfully sold over the counter without a prescription.

History.
1972, c. 798, § 54-524.84:1; 1976, c. 614; 1988, c. 765; 1993, c. 866; 1996, c. 408; 2014, cc. 674, 719.

§ 54.1-3444. Controlled substances included by whatever name designated.

The controlled substances listed or to be listed in the schedules in this chapter are included by whatever official, common, usual, chemical, or trade name designated.

History.
1972, c. 798, § 54-524.84:2; 1988, c. 765.

§ 54.1-3445. Placement of substance in Schedule I.

The Board shall place a substance in Schedule I if it finds that the substance:

1. Has high potential for abuse; and
2. Has no accepted medical use in treatment in the United States or lacks accepted safety for use in treatment under medical supervision.

History.
1972, c. 798, § 54-524.84:3; 1988, c. 765.

§ 54.1-3446. Schedule I.

The controlled substances listed in this section are included in Schedule I:

1. Any of the following opiates, including their isomers, esters, ethers, salts, and salts of isomers, esters, and ethers, unless specifically excepted, whenever the existence of these isomers, esters, ethers and salts is possible within the specific chemical designation:

Acetylmethadol;
Allylprodine;
Alphacetylmethadol (except levo-alphacetylmethadol, also known as levo-alpha-acetylmethadol, levomethadyl acetate, or LAAM);
Alphameprodine;
Alphamethadol;
Benzethidine;
Betacetylmethadol;
Betameprodine;
Betamethadol;
Betaprodine;
Clonitazene;
Dextromoramide;

Diampromide;
Diethylthiambutene;
Difenoxin;
Dimenoxadol;
Dimepheptanol;
Dimethylthiambutene;
Dioxaphetylbutyrate;
Dipipanone;
Ethylmethylthiambutene;
Etonitazene;
Etoxeridine;
Furethidine;
Hydroxypethidine;
Ketobemidone;
Levomoramide;
Levophenacylmorphan;
Morpheridine;
Noracymethadol;
Norlevorphanol;
Normethadone;
Norpipanone;
Phenadoxone;
Phenampromide;
Phenomorphan;
Phenoperidine;
Piritramide;
Proheptazine;
Properidine;
Propiram;
Racemoramide;
Tilidine;
Trimeperidine.

2. Any of the following opium derivatives, their salts, isomers and salts of isomers, unless specifically excepted, whenever the existence of these salts, isomers and salts of isomers is possible within the specific chemical designation:

Acetorphine;
Acetyldihydrocodeine;
Benzylmorphine;
Codeine methylbromide;
Codeine-N-Oxide;
Cyprenorphine;
Desomorphine;
Dihydromorphine;
Drotebanol;
Etorphine;
Heroin;
Hydromorphinol;
Methyldesorphine;
Methyldihydromorphine;
Morphine methylbromide;
Morphine methylsulfonate;
Morphine-N-Oxide;
Myrophine;
Nicocodeine;
Nicomorphine;
Normorphine;
Pholcodine;
Thebacon.

3. Unless specifically excepted or unless listed in another schedule, any material, compound, mixture, or preparation, which contains any quantity of the following hallucinogenic substances, or which contains any of its salts, isomers, and salts of isomers, whenever the existence of such salts, isomers, and salts of isomers is possible within the specific chemical designation (for purposes of this subdivision only, the term "isomer" includes the optical, position, and geometric isomers):

Alpha-ethyltryptamine (some trade or other names: Monase;a-ethyl-1H-indole-3-ethanamine; 3-2-aminobutyl] indole; a-ET; AET);

4-Bromo-2,5-dimethoxyphenethylamine (some trade or other names: 2-4-bromo-2,5-dimethoxyphenyl]-1-aminoethane;alpha-desmethyl DOB; 2C-B; Nexus);

3,4-methylenedioxy amphetamine;

5-methoxy-3,4-methylenedioxy amphetamine;

3,4,5-trimethoxy amphetamine;

Alpha-methyltryptamine (other name: AMT);

Bufotenine;

Diethyltryptamine;

Dimethyltryptamine;

4-methyl-2,5-dimethoxyamphetamine;

2,5-dimethoxy-4-ethylamphetamine (DOET);

2,5-dimethoxy-4-(n)-propylthiophenethylamine (other name: 2C-T-7);

Ibogaine;

5-methoxy-N,N-diisopropyltryptamine (other name: 5-MeO-DIPT);

Lysergic acid diethylamide;

Mescaline;

Parahexyl (some trade or other names: 3-Hexyl-1-hydroxy-7, 8, 9, 10-tetrahydro-6, 6, 9-trimethyl-6H-dibenzo -b,d] pyran; Synhexyl);

Peyote;

N-ethyl-3-piperidyl benzilate;

N-methyl-3-piperidyl benzilate;

Psilocybin;

Psilocyn;

Salvinorin A;

Tetrahydrocannabinols, except as present in marijuana and dronabinol in sesame oil and encapsulated in a soft gelatin capsule in a drug product approved by the U.S. Food and Drug Administration;

Hashish oil (some trade or other names: hash oil; liquid marijuana; liquid hashish);

2,5-dimethoxyamphetamine (some trade or other names: 2,5-dimethoxy-a-methylphenethylamine; 2,5-DMA);

3,4-methylenedioxymethamphetamine (MDMA), its optical, positional and geometric isomers, salts and salts of isomers;

3,4-methylenedioxy-N-ethylamphetamine (also known as N-ethyl-alpha-methyl-3,4 (methylenedioxy)phenethylamine, N-ethyl MDA, MDE, MDEA);

N-hydroxy-3,4-methylenedioxyamphetamine (some other names: N-hydroxy-alpha-methyl-3,4(methylenedioxy)phenethylamine, and N-hydroxy MDA);

4-bromo-2,5-dimethoxyamphetamine (some trade or other names: 4-bromo-2,5-dimethoxy-a-methylphenethylamine; 4-bromo-2,5-DMA);

4-methoxyamphetamine (some trade or other names: 4-methoxy-a-methylphenethylamine; para-methoxyamphetamine; PMA);

Ethylamine analog of phencyclidine (some other names: N-ethyl-1-phenylcyclohexylamine, (1-phenylcyclohexyl) ethylamine, N-(1-phenylcyclohexyl) ethylamine, cyclohexamine, PCE);

Pyrrolidine analog of phencyclidine (some other names: 1-(1-phenylcyclohexyl) -pyrrolidine, PCPy, PHP);

Thiophene analog of phencyclidine (some other names: 1-1-(2-thienyl) -cyclohexyl]-piperidine, 2-thienyl analog of phencyclidine, TPCP, TCP);

1-1-(2-thienyl)cyclohexyl]pyrrolidine (other name: TCPy);

3,4-methylenedioxypyrovalerone (other name: MDPV);

4-methylmethcathinone (other names: mephedrone, 4-MMC);

3,4-methylenedioxymethcathinone (other name: methylone);

Naphthylpyrovalerone (other name: naphyrone);

4-fluoromethcathinone (other name: flephedrone, 4-FMC);

4-methoxymethcathinone (other names: methedrone; bk-PMMA);

Ethcathinone (other name: N-ethylcathinone);

3,4-methylenedioxyethcathinone (other name: ethylone);

Beta-keto-N-methyl-3,4-benzodioxyolybutanamine (other name: butylone);

N,N-dimethylcathinone (other name: metamfepramone);

Alpha-pyrrolidinopropiophenone (other name: alpha-PPP);

4-methoxy-alpha-pyrrolidinopropiophenone (other name: MOPPP);

3,4-methylenedioxy-alpha-pyrrolidinopropiophenone (other name: MDPPP);

Alpha-pyrrolidinovalerophenone (other name: alpha-PVP);

6,7-dihydro-5H-indeno-(5,6-d)-1,3-dioxol-6-amine (other name: MDAI);

3-fluoromethcathinone (other name: 3-FMC);

4-Ethyl-2,5-dimethoxyphenethylamine (other name: 2C-E);

4-Iodo-2,5-dimethoxyphenethylamine (other name: 2C-I);

4-Methylethcathinone (other name: 4-MEC);

4-Ethylmethcathinone (other name: 4-EMC);

N,N-diallyl-5-methoxytryptamine (other name: 5-MeO-DALT);

Beta-keto-methylbenzodioxolylpentanamine (other name: Pentylone, bk-MBDP);

Alpha-methylamino-butyrophenone (other name: Buphedrone);

Alpha-methylamino-valerophenone (other name: Pentedrone);

3,4-Dimethylmethcathinone (other name: 3.4-DMMC);

4-methyl-alpha-pyrrolidinopropiophenone (other name: MPPP);

4-Iodo-2,5-dimethoxy-N-[(2-methoxyphenyl)methyl]-benzeneethanamine (other names: 25-I, 25I-NBOMe);

Methoxetamine (other names: MXE, 3-MeO-2-Oxo-PCE);

4-Fluoromethamphetamine (other name: 4-FMA);

4-Fluoroamphetamine (other name: 4-FA);

2-(2,5-Dimethoxy-4-methylphenyl)ethanamine (other name: 2C-D);

2-(4-Chloro-2,5-dimethoxyphenyl)ethanamine (other name: 2C-C);

2-[4-(Ethylthio)-2,5-dimethoxyphenyl]ethanamine (other name: 2C-T-2);

2-[4-(Isopropylthio)-2,5-dimethoxyphenyl]ethanamine (other name: 2C-T-4);

2-(2,5-Dimethoxyphenyl)ethanamine (other name: 2C-H);

2-(2,5-Dimethoxy-4-nitro-phenyl)ethanamine (other name: 2C-N);

2-(2,5-Dimethoxy-4-(n)-propylphenyl)ethanamine (other name: 2C-P);

(2-aminopropyl)benzofuran (other name: APB);

(2-aminopropyl)-2,3-dihydrobenzofuran (other name: APDB);

4-chloro-2,5-dimethoxy-N-[(2-methoxyphenyl)methyl]-benzeneethanamine (other names: 2C-C-NBOMe, 25C-NBOMe);

4-bromo-2,5-dimethoxy-N-[(2-methoxyphenyl)methyl]-benzeneethanamine (other names: 2C-B-NBOMe, 25B-NBOMe);

Acetoxydimethyltryptamine (other names: AcO-Psilocin, AcO-DMT, Psilacetin);

Benocyclidine (other names: BCP, BTCP);

Alpha-pyrrolidinobutiophenone (other name: alpha-PBP);

3,4-methylenedioxy-N,N-dimethylcathinone (other names: Dimethylone, bk-MDDMA);

4-bromomethcathinone (other name: 4-BMC);

4-chloromethcathinone (other name: 4-CMC);

4-Iodo-2,5-dimethoxy-N-[(2-hydroxyphenyl)methyl]-benzeneethanamine (other name: 25I-NBOH);

Alpha-Pyrrolidinohexiophenone (other name: alpha-PHP);

Alpha-Pyrrolidinoheptiophenone (other name: PV8).

4. Unless specifically excepted or unless listed in another schedule, any material, compound, mixture or preparation which contains any quantity of the following substances having a depressant effect on the central nervous system, including its salts, isomers and salts of isomers whenever the existence of such salts, isomers and salts of isomers is possible within the specific chemical designation:

Gamma hydroxybutyric acid (some other names include GHB; gamma hydroxybutyrate; 4-hydroxybutyrate; 4-hydroxybutanoic acid; sodium oxybate; sodium oxybutyrate);

Mecloqualone;
Methaqualone.
Etizolam.

5. Unless specifically excepted or unless listed in another schedule, any material, compound, mixture or preparation which contains any quantity of the following substances having a stimulant effect on the central nervous system, including its salts, isomers and salts of isomers:

Aminorex (some trade or other names; aminoxaphen; 2-amino-5-phenyl-2-oxazoline; 4, 5-dihydro-5-phenyl-2-oxazolamine);

N-Benzylpiperazine (some other names: BZP, 1-benzylpiperazine);

Fenethylline;

Ethylamphetamine;

Cathinone (some trade or other names: 2-amino-1-phenyl-1-propanone, alpha-aminopropiophenone, 2-aminopropiophenone, norephedrone), and any plant material from which Cathinone may be derived;

Methcathinone (some other names: 2-(methylamino)-propiophenone; alpha-(methylamino)-propiophenone; 2-(methylamino)-1-phenylpropan-1-one; alpha-N-methylaminopropiophenone; monomethylpropion; ephedrone; N-methylcathinone; methylcathinone; AL-464; AL-422; AL-463 and UR 1432);

Cis-4-methylaminorex (other name: cis-4,5-dihydro-4-methyl-5-phenyl-2-oxazolamine);

N,N-dimethylamphetamine (other names: N,N-alpha-trimethyl-benzeneethanamine, N,N-alpha-trimethylphenethylamine).

6. Any material, compound, mixture or preparation containing any quantity of the following substances:

N-3-methyl-1-(2-phenethyl)-4-piperidyl]-N-phenylpropanamide (other name: 3-methylfentanyl), its optical and geometric isomers, salts, and salts of isomers;

1-methyl-4-phenyl-4-propionoxypiperidine (other name: MPPP), its optical isomers, salts and salts of isomers;

1-(2-phenylethyl)-4-phenyl-4-acetyloxypiperidine (other name: PEPAP), its optical isomers, salts and salts of isomers;

N-1-(alpha-methyl-beta-phenyl) ethyl-4-piperidyl] propionanilide (other names: 1-(1-methyl-2-phenylethyl)-4-(N-propanilido) piperidine), alpha-methylfentanyl);

N-1-(1-methyl-2-phenethyl)-4-piperidyl]-N-phenylacetamide (other name: acetyl-alpha-methylfentanyl), its optical isomers, salts and salts of isomers;

N-1-(1-methyl-2-2-thienyl)ethyl-4 piperidyl]-N-phenylpropanamide (other name: alpha-methylthiofentanyl), its optical isomers, salts and salts of isomers;

N-1-benzyl-4-piperidyl]N-phenylpropanamide (other name: benzylfentanyl), its optical isomers, salts and salts of isomers;

N-1-(2-hydroxy-2-phenyl) ethyl-4-piperidyl]-N-phenylpropanamide (other name: beta-hydroxyfentanyl), its optical isomers, salts and salts of isomers;

N-3-methyl-1-(2-hydroxy-2-phenethyl)4-piperidyl]-N-phenylpropanamide (other name: beta-hydroxy-3-methylfentanyl), its optical and geometric isomers, salts and salts of isomers;

N-(3-methyl-1-(2-thienyl)ethyl-4-piperidinyl]-N-phenylpropanamide (other name: 3-methylthiofentanyl), its optical and geometric isomers, salts and salts of isomers;

N-1-(2-thienyl)methyl-4-piperidyl]-N-phenylpropanamide (other name: thienylfentanyl), its optical isomers, salts and salts of isomers;

N-phenyl-N-1-(2-thienyl)ethyl-4-piperidinyl]-propanamide (other name: thiofentanyl), its optical isomers, salts and salts of isomers;

N-(4-fluorophenyl)-N-1-(2-phenethyl)-4-piperidinyl]-propanamide (other name: para-fluorofentanyl), its optical isomers, salts and salts of isomers;

Acetyl fentanyl (other name: desmethyl fentanyl).

7. Any substance that contains one or more cannabimimetic agents or that contains their salts, isomers, and salts of isomers whenever the existence of such salts, isomers, and salts of isomers is possible within the specific chemical designation, and any preparation, mixture, or substance containing, or mixed or infused with, any detectable amount of one or more cannabimimetic agents.

a. "Cannabimimetic agents" includes any substance that is within any of the following structural classes:

2-(3-hydroxycyclohexyl)phenol with substitution at the 5-position of the phenolic ring by alkyl or alkenyl, whether or not substituted on the cyclohexyl ring to any extent;

3-(1-naphthoyl)indole or 1H-indol-3-yl-(1-naphthyl)methane with substitution at the nitrogen atom of the indole ring, whether or not further substituted on the indole ring to any extent, whether or not substituted on the naphthoyl or naphthyl ring to any extent;

3-(1-naphthoyl)pyrrole with substitution at the nitrogen atom of the pyrrole ring, whether or not further substituted in the pyrrole ring to any extent, whether or not substituted on the naphthoyl ring to any extent;

1-(1-naphthylmethyl)indene with substitution of the 3-position of the indene ring, whether or not further substituted in the indene ring to any extent, whether or not substituted on the naphthyl ring to any extent;

3-phenylacetylindole or 3-benzoylindole with substitution at the nitrogen atom of the indole ring, whether or not further substituted in the indole ring to any extent, whether or not substituted on the phenyl ring to any extent;

3-cyclopropoylindole with substitution at the nitrogen atom of the indole ring, whether or not further substituted on the indole ring to any extent, whether or not substituted on the cyclopropyl ring to any extent;

3-adamantoylindole with substitution at the nitrogen atom of the indole ring, whether or not further substituted on the indole ring to any extent, whether or not substituted on the adamantyl ring to any extent;

N-(adamantyl)-indole-3-carboxamide with substitution at the nitrogen atom of the indole ring, whether or not further substituted on the indole ring to any extent, whether or not substituted on the adamantyl ring to any extent; and

N-(adamantyl)-indazole-3-carboxamide with substitution at a nitrogen atom of the indazole ring, whether or not further substituted on the indazole ring to any extent, whether or not substituted on the adamantyl ring to any extent.

b. The term "cannabimimetic agents" includes:

5-(1,1-Dimethylheptyl)-2-[3-hydroxycyclohexyl]-phenol (other name: CP 47,497);

5-(1,1-Dimethylhexyl)-2-[3-hydroxycyclohexyl]-phenol (other name: CP 47,497 C6 homolog);

5-(1,1-Dimethyloctyl)-2-[3-hydroxycyclohexyl]-phenol (other name: CP 47,497 C8 homolog);

5-(1,1-Dimethylnonyl)-2-[3-hydroxycyclohexyl]-phenol (other name: CP 47,497 C9 homolog);

1-pentyl-3-(1-naphthoyl)indole (other names: JWH-018, AM-678);

1-butyl-3-(1-naphthoyl)indole (other name: JWH-073);

1-pentyl-3-(2-methoxyphenylacetyl)indole (other name: JWH-250);

1-hexyl-3-(naphthalen-1-oyl)indole (other name: JWH-019);

1-[2-(4-morpholinyl)ethyl]-3-(1-naphthoyl)indole (other name: JWH-200);

(6aR,10aR)-9-(hydroxymethyl)-6,6-dimethyl-3-(2-methyloctan-2-yl)-6a,7,10,10a-te trahydrobenzo[c]chromen-1-ol (other name: HU-210);

1-pentyl-3-(4-methoxy-1-naphthoyl)indole (other name: JWH-081);

1-pentyl-3-(4-methyl-1-naphthoyl)indole (other name: JWH-122);

1-pentyl-3-(2-chlorophenylacetyl)indole (other name: JWH-203);

1-pentyl-3-(4-ethyl-1-naphthoyl)indole (other name: JWH-210);

1-pentyl-3-(4-chloro-1-naphthoyl)indole (other name: JWH-398);

1-(5-fluoropentyl)-3-(2-iodobenzoyl)indole (other name: AM-694);

1-((N-methylpiperidin-2-yl)methyl)-3-(1-naphthoyl)indole (other name: AM-1220);

1-(5-fluoropentyl)-3-(1-naphthoyl)indole (other name: AM-2201);

1-[(N-methylpiperidin-2-yl)methyl]-3-(2-iodobenzoyl)indole (other name: AM-2233);

Pravadoline (4-methoxyphenyl)-[2-methyl-1-(2-(4-morpholinyl)ethyl)indol-3-yl]methanone (other name: WIN 48,098);

1-pentyl-3-(4-methoxybenzoyl)indole (other names: RCS-4, SR-19);

1-(2-cyclohexylethyl)-3-(2-methoxyphenylacetyl)indole (other names: RCS-8, SR-18);

1-pentyl-3-(2,2,3,3-tetramethylcyclopropylmethanone)indole (other name: UR-144);

1-(5-fluoropentyl)-3-(2,2,3,3-tetramethylcyclopropylmethanone)indole (other name: XLR-11);

N-adamantyl-1-fluoropentylindole-3-carboxamide (other name: STS-135);

N-adamantyl-1-pentylindazole-3-carboxamide (other name: AKB48);

1-pentyl-3-(1-adamantoyl)indole (other name: AB-001);

(8-quinolinyl)(1-pentylindol-3-yl)carboxylate (other name: PB-22);

(8-quinolinyl)(1-(5-fluoropentyl)indol-3-yl)carboxylate (other name: 5-fluoro-PB-22);

(8-quinolinyl)(1-cyclohexylmethyl-indol-3-yl)carboxylate (other name: BB-22);

N-(1-amino-3-methyl-1-oxobutan-2-yl)-1-pentylindazole-3-carboxamide (other name: AB-PINACA);

N-(1-amino-3-methyl-1-oxobutan-2-yl)-1-(4-fluorobenzyl)indazole-3-carboxamide (other name: AB-FUBINACA);

1-(5-fluoropentyl)-3-(1-naphthoyl)indazole (other name: THJ-2201);

N-(1-amino-3,3-dimethyl-1-oxobutan-2-yl)-1-pentylindazole-3-carboxamide (other name: ADB-PINACA);

N-(1-amino-3-methyl-1-oxobutan-2-yl)-1-(cyclohexylmethyl)indazole-3-carboxamide (other name: AB-CHMINACA);

N-(1-amino-3-methyl-1-oxobutan-2-yl)-1-(5-fluoropentyl)indazole-3-carboxamide (other name: 5-fluoro-AB-PINACA);

N-(1-amino-3,3-dimethyl-1-oxobutan-2-yl)-1-(cyclohexylmethyl)indazole-3-carboxam ide (other names: ADB-CHMINACA, MAB-CHMINACA);

Methyl-2-(1-(5-fluoropentyl)-1H-indazole-3-carboxamido)-3-methylbutanoate (other name: 5-fluoro-AMB);

1-naphthalenyl 1-(5-fluoropentyl)-1H-indole-3-carboxylate (other name: NM-2201);

1-(4-fluorobenzyl)-3-(2,2,3,3-tetramethylcyclopropylmethanone)indole (other name: FUB-144);

1-(5-fluoropentyl)-3-(4-methyl-1-naphthoyl)indole (other name MAM-2201).

History.

1972, c. 798, § 54-524.84:4; 1973, c. 479; 1976, c. 614; 1977, c. 302; 1979, cc. 387, 435; 1982, c. 505; 1984, cc. 186, 192; 1986, c. 463; 1988, c. 765; 1994, c. 763; 1996, c. 408; 1997, c. 594; 1999, c. 722; 2000, c. 348; 2005, c. 119; 2008, c. 59; 2011, cc. 384, 410; 2012, cc. 762, 816; 2013, cc. 295, 785; 2014, cc. 674, 719; 2015, cc. 726, 757; 2016, cc. 103, 112.

§ 54.1-3447. Placement of substance in Schedule II.

The Board shall place a substance in Schedule II if it finds that:

1. The substance has high potential for abuse;
2. The substance has currently accepted medical use in treatment in the United States, or currently accepted medical use with severe restrictions; and
3. The abuse of the substance may lead to severe psychic or physical dependence.

History.

1972, c. 798, § 54-524.84:5; 1988, c. 765.

§ 54.1-3448. Schedule II.

The controlled substances listed in this section are included in Schedule II:

1. Any of the following substances, except those narcotic drugs listed in other schedules, whether produced directly or indirectly by extraction from substances of vegetable origin, or independently by means of chemical synthesis, or by combination of extraction and chemical synthesis:

Opium and opiate, and any salt, compound, derivative, or preparation of opium or opiate, excluding apomorphine, thebaine-derived butorphanol, dextrorphan, nalbuphine, nalmefene, naloxone naltrexone and their respective salts, but including the following:

Raw opium;
Opium extracts;
Opium fluid extracts;
Powdered opium;
Granulated opium;
Tincture of opium;
Codeine;
Dihydroetorphine;
Ethylmorphine;
Etorphine hydrochloride;
Hydrocodone;
Hydromorphone;
Metopon;
Oripavine (3-O-demethylthebaine or 6,7,8,14-tetradehydro-4,
5-alpha-epoxy-6-methoxy-17-methylmorphinan-3-ol);
Morphine;
Oxycodone;
Oxymorphone;
Thebaine.

Any salt, compound, isomer, derivative, or preparation thereof which is chemically equivalent or identical with any of the substances referred to in this subdivision, but not including the isoquinoline alkaloids of opium.

Opium poppy and poppy straw.

Coca leaves and any salt, compound, derivative, or preparation of coca leaves, and any salt, compound, derivative, or preparation thereof which is chemically equivalent or identical with any of these substances, but not including decocainized coca leaves or extractions which do not contain cocaine or ecgonine; cocaine or any salt or isomer thereof.

Concentrate of poppy straw, the crude extract of poppy straw in either liquid, solid or powder form, which contains the phenanthrene alkaloids of the opium poppy.

2. Any of the following opiates, including their isomers, esters, ethers, salts, and salts of isomers, whenever the existence of these isomers, esters, ethers and salts is possible within the specific chemical designation:

Alfentanil;
Alphaprodine;
Anileridine;
Bezitramide;
Bulk dextropropoxyphene (nondosage forms);
Carfentanil;
Dihydrocodeine;
Diphenoxylate;
Fentanyl;
Isomethadone;
Levo-alphacetylmethadol (levo-alpha-acetylmethadol) (levomethadyl acetate) (LAAM);
Levomethorphan;
Levorphanol;
Metazocine;
Methadone;
Methadone — Intermediate, 4-cyano-2-dimethylamino-4, 4-diphenyl butane;
Moramide — Intermediate, 2-methyl-3-morpholino-1, 1-diphenyl-propane-carboxylicacid;
Pethidine (other name: meperidine);
Pethidine — Intermediate — A, 4-cyano-1-methyl-4-phenylpiperidine;
Pethidine — Intermediate — B, ethyl-4-phenylpiperidine-4-carboxylate;
Pethidine — Intermediate — C, 1-methyl-4-phenylpiperidine-4-carboxylic acid;
Phenazocine;
Piminodine;
Racemethorphan;
Racemorphan;
Remifentanil;
Sufentanil;
Tapentadol.

3. Any material, compound, mixture or preparation which contains any quantity of the following substances having a potential for abuse associated with a stimulant effect on the central nervous system:

Amphetamine, its salts, optical isomers, and salts of its optical isomers;
Phenmetrazine and its salts;
Any substance which contains any quantity of methamphetamine, including its salts, isomers, and salts of isomers;
Methylphenidate;
Lisdexamfetamine, its salts, isomers, and salts of its isomers.

4. Unless specifically excepted or unless listed in another schedule, any material, compound, mixture,

or preparation which contains any quantity of the following substances having a depressant effect on the central nervous system, including its salts, isomers, and salts of isomers whenever the existence of such salts, isomers, and salts of isomers is possible within the specific chemical designation:

Amobarbital;

Glutethimide;

Secobarbital;

Pentobarbital;

Phencyclidine.

5. The following hallucinogenic substance:

Nabilone.

6. Unless specifically excepted or unless listed in another schedule, any material, compound, mixture, or preparation which contains any quantity of the following substances which are:

a. Immediate precursors to amphetamine and methamphetamine:

Phenylacetone.

b. Immediate precursor to phencyclidine:

1-phenylcyclohexylamine;

1-piperidinocyclohexanecarbonitrile (other name: PCC).

c. Immediate precursor to fentanyl:

4-anilino-N-phenethyl-4-piperidine (ANPP).

History.

1972, c. 798, § 54-524.84:6; 1976, c. 614; 1977, c. 302; 1978, c. 833; 1979, c. 387; 1981, c. 30; 1984, c. 192; 1986, c. 463; 1988, cc. 283, 765; 1992, c. 737; 1994, c. 763; 1998, c. 105; 2000, c. 135; 2005, c. 119; 2008, c. 74; 2010, c. 423; 2011, c. 700.

§ 54.1-3449. Placement of substance in Schedule III.

The Board shall place a substance in Schedule III if it finds that:

1. The substance has a potential for abuse less than the substances listed in Schedules I and II;

2. The substance has currently accepted medical use in treatment in the United States; and

3. Abuse of the substance may lead to moderate or low physical dependence or high psychological dependence.

History.

1972, c. 798, § 54-524.84:7; 1988, c. 765.

§ 54.1-3450. Schedule III.

The controlled substances listed in this section are included in Schedule III:

1. Unless specifically exempted or listed in another schedule, any material, compound, mixture, or preparation which contains any quantity of the following substances having a depressant effect on the central nervous system:

Any substance which contains any quantity of a derivative of barbituric acid, or any salt of a derivative of barbituric acid, except those substances which are specifically listed in other schedules;

Any compound, mixture or preparation containing amobarbital, secobarbital, or pentobarbital or any salt of amobarbital, secobarbital, or pentobarbital and one or more other active medicinal ingredients which are not listed in Schedules II through V;

Any suppository dosage form containing amobarbital, secobarbital, or pentobarbital or any salt of amobarbital, secobarbital, or pentobarbital and approved by the Food and Drug Administration for marketing only as a suppository;

Chlorhexadol;

Any drug product containing gamma hydroxybutyric acid, including its salts, isomers, and salts of isomers, for which an application is approved under section 505 of the Federal Food, Drug, and Cosmetic Act (21 U.S.C. § 355);

Embutramide;

Ketamine, its salts, isomers, and salts of isomers (some other names: [+-] -2-[2-chlorophenyl]-2-[methylamino]-cyclohexanone);

Lysergic acid;

Lysergic acid amide;

Methyprylon;

Perampanel [2-(2-oxo-1-phenyl-5-pyridin-2-yl-1,2-dihydropyridin-3-yl) benxonitrile], including its salts, isomers, and salts of isomers;

Sulfondiethylmethane;

Sulfonethylmethane;

Sulfonmethane; and

Tiletamine-zolazepam combination product or any salt thereof.

2. Nalorphine.

3. Unless specifically excepted or unless listed in another schedule:

a. Any material, compound, mixture, or preparation containing any of the following narcotic drugs or their salts thereof:

Buprenorphine.

b. Any material, compound, mixture, or preparation containing limited quantities of any of the following narcotic drugs, or any salts thereof:

Not more than 1.8 grams of codeine, or any of its salts, per 100 milliliters or not more than 90 milligrams per dosage unit, with an equal or greater quantity of an isoquinoline alkaloid of opium;

Not more than 1.8 grams of codeine, or any of its salts, per 100 milliliters or not more than 90 milligrams per dosage unit, with one or more active, nonnarcotic ingredients in recognized therapeutic amounts;

Not more than 1.8 grams of dihydrocodeine, or any of its salts, per 100 milliliters or not more than 90 milligrams per dosage unit, with one or more active, nonnarcotic ingredients in recognized therapeutic amounts;

Not more than 300 milligrams of ethylmorphine, or any of its salts, per 100 milliliters or not more than 15 milligrams per dosage unit, with one or more ingredients in recognized therapeutic amounts;

Not more than 500 milligrams of opium per 100 milliliters or per 100 grams, or not more than 25 milligrams per dosage unit, with one or more active, nonnarcotic ingredients in recognized therapeutic amounts;

Not more than 50 milligrams of morphine, or any of its salts, per 100 milliliters or per 100 grams with one or more active, nonnarcotic ingredients in recognized therapeutic amounts.

4. Unless specifically excepted or unless listed in another schedule, any material, compound, mixture, or preparation which contains any quantity of the following substances having a stimulant effect on the central nervous system, including its salts, isomers (whether optical, position, or geometric), and salts of such isomers whenever the existence of such salts, isomers, and salts of isomers is possible within the specific chemical designation:

Benzphetamine;

Chlorphentermine;

Clortermine;

Phendimetrazine.

5. The Board may except by regulation any compound, mixture, or preparation containing any stimulation or depressant substance listed in subsection A from the application of all or any part of this chapter if the compound, mixture, or preparation contains one or more active medicinal ingredients not having a stimulant or depressant effect on the central nervous system, and if the admixtures are included therein in combinations, quantity, proportion, or concentration that vitiate the potential for abuse of the substances which have a stimulant or depressant effect on the central nervous system.

6. Unless specifically excepted or unless listed in another schedule, any material, compound, mixture, or preparation containing any quantity of the following substances, including its salts, isomers, and salts of isomers whenever the existence of such salts of isomers is possible within the specific chemical designation:

Anabolic steroids, including, but not limited to:

3beta,17-dihydroxy-5a-androstane;

3alpha,17beta-dihydroxy-5a-androstane;

5alpha-androstan-3,17-dione;

1-androstenediol (3beta,17beta-dihydroxy-5alpha-androst-1-ene);

1-androstenediol (3alpha,17beta-dihydroxy-5alpha-androst-1-ene);

4-androstenediol (3beta,17beta-dihydroxy-androst-4-ene);

5-androstenediol (3beta,17beta-dihydroxy-androst-5-ene);

1-androstenedione ([5alpha]-androst-1-en-3,17-dione);

4-androstenedione (androst-4-en-3,17-dione);

5-androstenedione (androst-5-en-3,17-dione);

Bolasterone (7alpha,17alpha-dimenthyl-17beta-hydroxyandrost-4-en-3-one);

Boldenone (Dehydrotestosterone)(17beta-hydroxyandrost-1,4,-diene-3-one);

Boldione (androsta-1, 4-diene-3, 17-dione);

Calusterone (7beta,17alpha-dimethyl-17beta-hydroxyandrost-4-en-3-one);

Clostebol (4-Chlorotestosterone)(Chlorotestosterone)(4-chloro-17beta-hydr oxyandrost-4-en-3-one);

Dehydrochloromethyltestosterone (4-chloro-17beta-hydroxy-17alpha-methyl-androst-1,4-dien-3-one) ;

Delta1-dihydrotestosterone (1-testosterone) (17beta-hydroxy-5alpha-androst-1-en-3-one);

Desoxymethyltestosterone (madol) (17alpha-methyl-5alpha-androst-2-en-17beta-ol);

Dromostanolone (Drostanolone) (17beta-hydroxy-2alpha-methyl-5alpha-androstan-3- one);

Ethylestrenol (17alpha-ethyl-17beta-hydroxyestr-4-ene);

Fluoxymesterone (9-fluoro-17alpha-methyl-11beta,17beta-dihydroxyandrost-4-en-3- one);

Formyldienolone (Formebolone) (2-formyl-17alpha-methyl-11alpha,17beta-dihydroxya ndrost-1,4-dien- 3-one);

Furazabol (17alpha-methyl-17beta-hydroxyandrostano[2,3-c]-furazan);

13-beta-ethyl-17alpha-hydroxygon-4-en-3-one;

4-hydroxytestosterone (4,17beta-dihydroxy-androst-4-en-3-one);

4-hydroxy-19-nortestosterone (4,17beta-dihydroxy-estr-4-en-3-one);

Mestanolone (17alpha-methyl-17beta-hydroxy-5-androstan-3-one);

Mesterolone (1alpha-methyl-17beta-hydroxy-[5alpha]-androstan-3-one);

Methandriol (methylandrostenediol) (17alpha-methyl-3beta,17beta-dihydroxyandrost-5-ene);

Methandrostenolone (Methandienone) (Dehydromethyltestosterone) (17alpha-methyl-17beta-hydroxyandrost-1,4-dien-3-one);

Methasterone (2alpha,17alpha-dimethyl-5alpha-androstan-17beta-ol-3-one);

Methenolone (1-methyl-17beta-hydroxy-5alpha-androst-1-en-3-one);

17alpha-methyl-3beta,17beta-dihydroxy-5a-androstane;

17alpha-methyl-3alpha,17beta-dihydroxy-5a-androstane;

17alpha-methyl-3beta,17beta-dihydroxyandrost-4-ene);

17alpha-methyl-4-hydroxynandrolone (17alpha-methyl-4-hydroxy-17beta-hydroxyestr-4-en-3-one);

Methyldienolone (17alpha-methyl-17beta-hydroxyestra-4,9(10)-dien-3-one);

Methyltrienolone (17alpha-methyl-17beta-hydroxyestra-4,9-11-trien-3-one);

17-Methyltestosterone (Methyltestosterone)(17alpha-methyl-17beta-hydroxyandrost-4-en- 3-one);

Mibolerone (7alpha,17alpha-dimethyl-17beta-hydroxyestr-4-en-3-one);

17alpha-methyl-delta1-dihydrotestosterone (17beta-hydroxy-17alpha-methyl-5alpha-androst-1-en-3-one)(17-al pha-methyl-1-testosterone);

Nandrolone (19-Nortestosterone)(17beta-hydroxyestr-4-en-3-one);

19-nor-4,9(10)-androstadienedione(estra-4,9(10)-diene-3,17-dione);

19-nor-4-androstenediol (3beta,17beta-dihydroxyestr-4-ene);

19-nor-4-androstenediol (3alpha,17beta-dihydroxyestr-4-ene);

19-nor-5-androstenediol (3beta,17beta-dihydroxyestr-5-ene);

19-nor-5-androstenediol (3alpha,17beta-dihydroxyestr-5-ene);

19-nor-4-androstenedione (estr-4-en-3,17-dione);

19-nor-5-androstenedione (estr-5-en-3,17-dione);

Norbolethone (13beta,17alpha-diethyl-17beta-hydroxygon-4-en-3-one);

Norclostebol (4-chloro-17beta-hydroxyestr-4-en-3-one);

Norethandrolone (17alpha-ethyl-17beta-hydroxyestr-4-en-3-one);

Normethandrolone (17alpha-methyl-17beta-hydroxyestr-4-en-3-one);

Oxandrolone (17alpha-methyl-17beta-hydroxy-2-oxa-[5alpha]-androstan-3-one);

Oxymesterone (Oxymestrone) (17alpha-methyl-4,17beta-dihydroxyandrost-4-en-3-one);

Oxymetholone (Anasterone) (17alpha-methyl-2-hydroxymethylene-17beta-hydroxy-[5alpha]-androsta n-3-one);

Prostanozol (17beta-hydroxy-5alpha-androstano[3,2-c]pyrazole);

Stanolone (4-Dihydrotestosterone) (Dihydrotestosterone) (17beta-hydroxy-androstan-3-one);

Stanozolol (Androstanazole) (17alpha-methyl-17beta-hydroxy-[5alpha]-androst-2-eno[3,2-c]-pyrazole);

Stenbolone (17beta-hydroxy-2-methyl-[5alpha]-androst-1-en-3-one);

Testolactone (1-Dehydrotestololactone) (13-hydroxy-3-oxo-13,17-secoandrosta-1 ,4-dien-17-oic acid lactone);

Testosterone (17beta-hydroxandrost-4-en-3-one);

Tetrahydrogestrinone (13beta,17alpha-diethyl-17beta-hydroxygon-4,9,11-trien-3-one);

Trenbolone (Trienbolone) (Trienolone) (17beta-hydroxyestr-4,9,11-trien-3-one); and

Any salt, ester, or ether of a drug or substance described or listed in this paragraph. However, such term does not include an anabolic steroid which is expressly intended for administration through implants to cattle or other nonhuman species and which has been approved by the United States Secretary of Health and Human Services for such administration. If any person prescribes, dispenses, or distributes any such steroid for human use, such person shall be considered to have prescribed, dispensed, or distributed an anabolic steroid within the meaning of this subsection.

7. Dronabinol (synthetic) in sesame oil and encapsulated in a soft gelatin capsule in a drug product approved by the U.S. Food and Drug Administration.

History.

1972, c. 798, § 54-524.84:8; 1976, c. 614; 1977, c. 302; 1979, c. 387; 1982, c. 505; 1988, cc. 283, 765; 1992, c. 737; 2000, cc. 135, 348; 2003, c. 640; 2005, c. 119; 2006, c. 346; 2007, c. 14; 2010, c. 423; 2013, c. 233; 2014, c. 74; 2015, c. 303.

§ 54.1-3451. Placement of substance in Schedule IV.

The Board shall place a substance in Schedule IV if it finds that:

1. The substance has a low potential for abuse relative to substances in Schedule III;

2. The substance has currently accepted medical use in treatment in the United States; and

3. Abuse of the substance may lead to limited physical dependence or psychological dependence relative to the substances in Schedule III.

History.

1972, c. 798, § 54-524.84:9; 1988, c. 765.

§ 54.1-3452. Schedule IV.

The controlled substances listed in this section are included in Schedule IV unless specifically excepted or listed in another schedule:

1. Any material, compound, mixture, or preparation which contains any quantity of the following substances having a potential for abuse associated with a depressant effect on the central nervous system:

Alfaxalone (5[alpha]-pregnan-3[alpha]-ol-11,20-dione), previously spelled "alphaxalone," including its salts, isomers, and salts of isomers;

Alprazolam;

Barbital;

Bromazepam;

Camazepam;

Carisoprodol;

Chloral betaine;

Chloral hydrate;

Chlordiazepoxide;

Clobazam;

Clonazepam;

Clorazepate;

Clotiazepam;

Cloxazolam;

Delorazepam;

Diazepam;

Dichloralphenazone;

Estazolam;

Ethchlorvynol;

Ethinamate;

Ethyl loflazepate;

Fludiazepam;

Flunitrazepam;

Flurazepam;

Fospropofol;

Halazepam;

Haloxazolam;

Ketazolam;

Loprazolam;

Lorazepam;
Lormetazepam;
Mebutamate;
Medazepam;
Methohexital;
Meprobamate;
Methylphenobarbital;
Midazolam;
Nimetazepam;
Nitrazepam;
Nordiazepam;
Oxazepam;
Oxazolam;
Paraldehyde;
Petrichloral;
Phenobarbital;
Pinazepam;
Prazepam;
Quazepam;
Suvorexant ([(7R)-4-(5-chloro-1,3-benzoxazol-2-yl)-7-methyl-1,4-diazepan-1 -yl][5-methyl-2- (2H-1,2,3-triazol-2-yl) phenyl]methanone), including its salts, isomers, and salts of isomers;
Temazepam;
Tetrazepam;
Triazolam;
Zaleplon;
Zolpidem;
Zopiclone.

2. Any compound, mixture or preparation which contains any quantity of the following substances including any salts or isomers thereof:

Fenfluramine;
Lorcaserin.

3. Unless specifically excepted or unless listed in another schedule, any material, compound, mixture, or preparation which contains any quantity of the following substances having a stimulant effect on the central nervous system, including its salts, isomers (whether optical, position, or geometric), and salts of such isomers whenever the existence of such salts, isomers, and salts of isomers is possible within the specific chemical designation:

Cathine (+)-norpseudoephedrine;
Diethylpropion;
Fencamfamin;
Fenproprex;
Mazindol;
Mefenorex;
Modafinil;
Phentermine;
Pemoline (including organometallic complexes and chelates thereof);
Pipradrol;
Sibutramine;
SPA (-)-1-dimethylamino-1, 2-diphenylethane.

4. Unless specifically excepted or unless listed in another schedule, any material, compound, mixture, or preparation containing any of the following narcotic drugs, or their salts calculated as the free anhydrous base or alkaloid, in limited quantities as set forth below:

Dextropropoxyphene (alpha-(+)-4-dimethylamino-1, 2-diphenyl-3-methyl-2-propionoxy butane);

Not more than 1 milligram of difenoxin and not less than 25 micrograms of atropine sulfate per dosage unit;

2-[(dimethylamino) methyl]-1-(3-methoxyphenyl) cyclohexanol, its salts, optical and geometric isomers, and salts of such isomers, including tramadol.

5. Unless specifically excepted or unless listed in another schedule, any material, compound, mixture, or preparation which contains any quantity of the following substances, including their salts:

Butorphanol (including its optical isomers);
Eluxadoline (including its optical isomers and its salts, isomers, and salts of isomers);
Pentazocine.

6. The Board may except by regulation any compound, mixture, or preparation containing any depressant substance listed in subdivision 1 from the application of all or any part of this chapter if the compound, mixture, or preparation contains one or more active medicinal ingredients not having a depressant effect on the central nervous system, and if the admixtures are included therein in combinations, quantity, proportion, or concentration that vitiate the potential for abuse of the substances which have a depressant effect on the central nervous system.

History.

1972, c. 798, § 54-524.84:10; 1976, c. 614; 1977, c. 302; 1978, c. 705; 1979, c. 387; 1982, c. 505; 1986, c. 463; 1988, cc. 283, 765; 1992, c. 737; 1994, c. 763; 1998, c. 105; 1999, c. 605; 2000, c. 135; 2003, c. 640; 2006, c. 346; 2010, c. 423; 2012, c. 540; 2014, c. 74; 2015, c. 303; 2016, c. 499.

§ 54.1-3453. Placement of substance in Schedule V.

The Board shall place a substance in Schedule V if it finds that:

1. The substance has low potential for abuse relative to the controlled substances listed in Schedule IV;
2. The substance has currently accepted medical use in treatment in the United States; and
3. The substance has limited physical dependence or psychological dependence liability relative to the controlled substances listed in Schedule IV.

History.

1972, c. 798, § 54-524.84:11; 1988, c. 765.

§ 54.1-3454. Schedule V.

The controlled substances listed in this section are included in Schedule V:

1. Any compound, mixture, or preparation containing limited quantities of any of the following narcotic drugs, which also contains one or more nonnarcotic active medicinal ingredients in sufficient proportion to confer upon the compound, mix-

ture, or preparation, valuable medicinal qualities other than those possessed by the narcotic drug alone:

Not more than 200 milligrams of codeine, or any of its salts, per 100 milliliters or per 100 grams;

Not more than 100 milligrams of dihydrocodeine, or any of its salts, per 100 milliliters or per 100 grams;

Not more than 100 milligrams of ethylmorphine, or any of its salts, per 100 milliliters or per 100 grams;

Not more than 2.5 milligrams of diphenoxylate and not less than 25 micrograms of atropine sulfate per dosage unit;

Not more than 100 milligrams of opium per 100 milliliters or per 100 grams;

Not more than 0.5 milligrams of difenoxin and not less than 25 micrograms of atropine sulfate per dosage unit.

The Board may except by regulation any compound, mixture, or preparation containing any depressant substance listed in subdivision 1 from the application of all or any part of this chapter and such substances so excepted may be dispensed pursuant to § 54.1-3416.

2. Unless specifically excepted or listed in another schedule, any material, compound, mixture, or preparation that contains any quantity of the following substances having a stimulant effect on the central nervous system, including its salts, isomers, and salts of isomers:

Pyrovalerone.

3. Unless specifically excepted or unless listed in another schedule, any material, compound, mixture, or preparation that contains any quantity of the following substances having a depressant effect on the central nervous system, including its salts:

Ezogabine [N-[2-amino-4-(4-fluorobenzylamino)-phenyl]-carbamic acid ethyl ester]-2779;

Lacosamide [(R)-2-acetoamido-N-benzyl-3-methoxy-propionamide];

Pregabalin [(S)-3-(aminomethyl)-5-methylhexanoic acid].

History.

1972, c. 798, § 54-524.84:12; 1976, c. 614; 1977, c. 302; 1979, c. 387; 1984, c. 186; 1986, c. 463; 1988, c. 765; 1992, c. 737; 1994, c. 763; 2003, c. 640; 2006, c. 346; 2010, c. 423; 2012, c. 541.

§ 54.1-3455. Schedule VI.

The following classes of drugs and devices shall be controlled by Schedule VI:

1. Any compound, mixture, or preparation containing any stimulant or depressant drug exempted from Schedules III, IV or V and designated by the Board as subject to this section.

2. Every drug, not included in Schedules I, II, III, IV or V, or device, which because of its toxicity or other potentiality for harmful effect, or the method of its use, or the collateral measures necessary to its use, is not generally recognized among experts qualified by scientific training and experience to evaluate its safety and efficacy as safe for use except by or under the supervision of a practitioner licensed to prescribe or administer such drug or device.

3. Any drug, not included in Schedules I, II, III, IV or V, required by federal law to bear on its label prior to dispensing, at a minimum, the symbol "Rx only," or which bears the legend "Caution: Federal Law Prohibits Dispensing Without Prescription" or "Caution: Federal Law Restricts This Drug To Use By Or On The Order Of A Veterinarian" or any device which bears the legend "Caution: Federal Law Restricts This Device To Sales By Or On The Order Of A ________________________ ." (The blank should be completed with the word "Physician," "Dentist," "Veterinarian," or with the professional designation of any other practitioner licensed to use or order such device.)

History.

1972, c. 798, § 54-524.84:13; 1976, c. 614; 1977, c. 302; 1988, c. 765; 1999, c. 605.

§ 54.1-3456. Controlled substance analog.

A controlled substance analog shall, to the extent intended for human consumption, be treated, for the purposes of any state law, as a controlled substance in Schedule I or II. A controlled substance analog shall be considered to be listed on the same schedule as the drug or class of drugs which it imitates.

History.

1987, c. 447, § 54-524.84:14; 1988, c. 765; 2014, cc. 674, 719.

§ 54.1-3456.1. Drugs of concern.

A. The Board may promulgate regulations designating specific drugs and substances, including any controlled substance or other drug or substance where there has been or there is the actual or relative potential for abuse, as drugs of concern. Drugs or substances designated as drugs of concern shall be reported to the Department of Health Professions and shall be subject to reporting requirements for the Prescription Monitoring Program established pursuant to Chapter 25.2 (§ 54.1-2519 et seq.).

B. Drugs and substances designated as drugs of concern shall include any material, compound, mixture, or preparation that contains any quantity of the substance Tramadol, including its salts. Drugs and substances designated as drugs of concern shall not include any non-narcotic drug that may be lawfully sold over the counter or behind the counter without a prescription.

History.

2014, c. 664.

ARTICLE 6.

MISBRANDED AND ADULTERATED DRUGS AND COSMETICS.

§ 54.1-3457. Prohibited acts.

The following acts shall be prohibited:

1. The manufacture, sale, delivery, holding, or offering for sale of any drug, device, or cosmetic that is adulterated or misbranded.

2. The adulteration or misbranding of any drug, device, or cosmetic.

3. The receipt in commerce of any drug, device, or cosmetic that is adulterated or misbranded, and the delivery or proffered delivery thereof for pay or otherwise.

4. The sale, delivery for sale, holding for sale, or offering for sale of any article in violation of § 54.1-3421.

5. The dissemination of any false advertisement.

6. The refusal to permit entry or inspection, or to permit the taking of a sample, or to permit access to or copying of any record.

7. The giving of a false guaranty or undertaking.

8. The removal or disposal of a detained article in violation of § 54.1-3459.

9. The alteration, mutilation, destruction, obliteration, or removal of the whole or any part of the labeling of, or the doing of any other act with respect to, a drug, device, or cosmetic, if such act is done while such article is held for sale and results in such article being adulterated or misbranded.

10. The forging, counterfeiting, simulating, or falsely representing, or without proper authority using of any mark, stamp, tag, label, or other identification device authorized or required by regulations promulgated under the provisions of this chapter or of the federal act.

11. The using by any person to his own advantage, or revealing, other than to the Board or its authorized representative or to the courts when relevant in any judicial proceeding under this chapter of any information acquired under authority of this chapter concerning any method or process which as a trade secret is entitled to protection.

12. The using, on the labeling of any drug or in any advertisement relating to such drug, of any representation or suggestion that an application with respect to such drug is effective under § 54.1-3421, or that such drug complies with the provisions of such section.

13. In the case of a drug distributed or offered for sale in this Commonwealth, the failure of the manufacturer, packer, or distributor thereof to maintain for transmittal, or to transmit, to any practitioner licensed by applicable law to administer such drug who makes written request for information as to such drug, true and correct copies of all printed matter which is required to be included in any package in which that drug is distributed or sold, or such other printed matter as is approved under the federal act. This subdivision shall not be construed to exempt any person from any labeling requirement imposed by or under other provisions of this chapter.

14. Placing or causing to be placed upon any drug or device or container, with intent to defraud, the trade name or other identifying mark, or imprint of another or any likeness of any of the foregoing; or selling, dispensing, disposing of, or causing to be sold, dispensed, or disposed of, or concealing or keeping in possession, control, or custody, with intent to sell, dispense, or dispose of, any drug, device, or any container thereof, with knowledge that the trade name or other identifying mark or imprint of another or any likeness of any of the foregoing has been placed thereon in a manner prohibited by this section or making, selling, disposing of, or causing to be made, sold, or disposed of, or keeping in possession, control, or custody, or concealing any punch, die, plate, stone, or other thing designed to print, imprint, or reproduce the trademark, trade name, or other identifying mark, imprint, or device of another or any likeness of any of the foregoing upon any drug or container or labeling thereof so as to render such drug a counterfeit drug.

15. The doing of any act that causes a drug to be a counterfeit drug, or the sale or dispensing, or the holding for sale or dispensing, of a counterfeit drug.

16. Dispensing or causing to be dispensed a different drug or brand of drug in place of the drug or brand of drug ordered or prescribed without the permission of the person ordering or prescribing, except as provided in § 54.1-3408.03 relating to dispensing of therapeutically equivalent drugs.

17. Dispensing or causing to be dispensed a biosimilar in place of a prescribed biological product or brand of biological product, except as provided in § 54.1-3408.04 related to dispensing of interchangeable biosimilars.

History.

1970, c. 650, § 54-524.85; 1988, c. 765; 2003, c. 639; 2013, cc. 412, 544.

§ 54.1-3458. Violations.

A. Any person who violates any of the provisions of § 54.1-3457 shall be guilty of a Class 2 misdemeanor.

B. No person shall be subject to the penalties of this section for having violated subdivisions 1 and 3 of § 54.1-3457 if he establishes a guaranty or undertaking signed by, and containing the name and address of, the person residing in this Commonwealth from whom he received in good faith the article, to the effect that such article is not adulterated or misbranded within the meaning of this chapter.

C. No publisher, radio-broadcast licensee, or agency or medium for the dissemination of an advertisement, except the manufacturer, packer, distributor, or seller of the article to which a false advertisement relates, shall be liable under this section for the dissemination of such false advertisement, unless he has refused, on the request of the Board, to furnish the Board the name and post-office address of the manufacturer, packer, distributor, seller, or advertising agency, residing in this Commonwealth who caused him to disseminate such advertisement.

History.
1970, c. 650, § 54-524.87; 1988, c. 765.

§ 54.1-3459. Tagging of adulterated or misbranded drugs, devices, or cosmetics; condemnation; destruction; expenses.

A. Whenever a duly authorized agent of the Board finds, or has probable cause to believe, that any drug, device, or cosmetic is adulterated, or so misbranded as to be dangerous or fraudulent, within the meaning of this chapter or is in violation of § 54.1-3457, he shall affix to such article a tag or other appropriate marking, giving notice that such article is, or is suspected of being, adulterated or misbranded or in violation of § 54.1-3457 and has been detained. The tag shall also warn all persons not to remove or dispose of such article by sale or otherwise until permission for removal or disposal is given by an authorized agent or the court. It shall be unlawful for any person to remove or dispose of such detained article by sale or otherwise without permission.

B. When an article is adulterated or misbranded or is in violation of § 54.1-3421, the Board may petition the circuit court in whose jurisdiction the article is detained for condemnation of such article. When an authorized agent finds that an article which has been detained is not adulterated or misbranded, or in violation of § 54.1-3421, he shall remove the tag or other marking.

C. If the court finds that a detained article is adulterated or misbranded, or in violation of § 54.1-3421, such article shall, after entry of the decree, be destroyed at the expense of the claimant, under the supervision of an authorized agent, and all court costs and fees, and storage and other proper expenses, shall be levied against the claimant or his agent. When the adulteration or misbranding can be corrected by proper labeling or processing of the article, the court shall order the article to be properly labeled or processed. The expense of the supervision shall be paid by the claimant. The article shall be returned to the claimant and the bond shall be discharged on the representation to the court by the Board that the article is no longer in violation of this chapter, and that the expenses of such supervision have been paid.

History.
1970, c. 650, § 54-524.88; 1988, c. 765.

§ 54.1-3460. Poisonous or deleterious substance, or color additive.

Any added poisonous or deleterious substance, or any color additive, shall with respect to any particular use or intended use be deemed unsafe with respect to any drug, device, or cosmetic, unless there is a regulation allowing limited use of a quantity of such substance, and the use or intended use of such substance conforms to the terms prescribed by regulation. While such regulations relating to such substance are in effect, a drug or cosmetic shall not, by reason of bearing or containing such substance in accordance with the regulations, be considered adulterated.

History.
1970, c. 650, § 54-524.91; 1988, c. 765.

§ 54.1-3461. Adulterated drug or device.

A. A drug or device shall be deemed to be adulterated:

1. If it consists in whole or in part of any filth, putrid or decomposed substance;
2. If it has been produced, prepared, packed, or held under insanitary conditions whereby it has been contaminated with filth, or whereby it has been rendered injurious to health;
3. If it is a drug and the methods used in, or the facilities or controls used for, its manufacture, processing, packing, or holding do not conform to or are not operated or administered in conformity with current good manufacturing practice to assure that such drug meets the requirements of this chapter;
4. If it is a drug and its container is composed, in whole or in part, of any poisonous or deleterious substance which may render the contents injurious to health;
5. If it is a drug and it bears or contains, for purposes of coloring only, a color additive which is unsafe within the meaning of the federal act or § 54.1-3460; or
6. It is a color additive, the intended use of which in or on drugs is for purposes of coloring only, and is unsafe within the meaning of the federal act or § 54.1-3460.

B. A drug or device shall be deemed to be adulterated if it purports to be or is represented as a drug the name of which is recognized in an official compendium, and its strength differs from, or its quality or purity falls below, the standard set forth in such compendium. Such determination of strength, quality, or purity shall be made in accordance with the tests or methods of assay set forth in such compendium, or in the absence of or inadequacy of such tests or methods of assay, those prescribed under authority of the federal act. No drug defined in an official compendium shall be deemed to be adulterated under this subsection because it differs from the standard of strength, quality, or purity set forth in such compendium, if the difference in strength, quality, or purity from such standard is plainly stated on its label.

Whenever a drug is recognized in both the United States Pharmacopoeia National Formulary and the Homeopathic Pharmacopoeia of the United States it shall be subject to the requirements of the United States Pharmacopoeia National Formulary unless it is labeled and offered for sale as a homeopathic drug, in which case it shall be subject to the provisions of the Homeopathic Pharmacopoeia of the United States and not to those of the United States Pharmacopoeia National Formulary.

C. A drug or device shall be deemed to be adulterated if it is not subject to the provisions of subsection B of this section and its strength differs from, or its purity or quality falls below, that which it purports or is represented to possess.

D. A drug or device shall be deemed to be adulterated if it is a drug and any substance has been (i) mixed or packed with it so as to reduce its quality or strength or (ii) substituted wholly or in part for it.

History.

Code 1950, § 54-461; 1970, c. 650, § 54-524.92; 1988, c. 765.

§ 54.1-3462. Misbranded drug or device.

A drug or device shall be deemed to be misbranded:

1. If its labeling is false or misleading in any particular.

2. If its package does not bear a label containing the name and place of business of the manufacturer, packer, or distributor. However, all prescription drugs intended for human use and devices shall bear a label containing the name and place of business of the manufacturer of the final dosage form of the drug and, if different, the name and place of business of the packer or distributor and an accurate statement of the quantity of the contents in terms of weight, measure, or numerical count. Reasonable variations shall be permitted, and exemptions for small packages shall be allowed in accordance with regulations of the Board.

3. If any word, statement, or other information required by or under authority of this chapter to appear on the label or labeling is not prominently placed with such conspicuousness, as compared with other words, statements, designs or devices, in the labeling, and in such terms as to render it likely to be read and understood by the ordinary individual under customary conditions of purchase and use.

4. If it is for use by man and contains any quantity of the narcotic or hypnotic substances alpha-eucaine, barbituric acid, beta-eucaine, bromal, carbromal, chloral, coca, cocaine, codeine, morphine, opium, paraldehyde, or sulfonmethane, or any chemical derivative of such substances, which derivative, after investigation has been found to be and designated as, habit forming, by regulations issued by the Board under this chapter, unless its label bears the name and quantity or proportion of such substance or derivative and in juxtaposition therewith the statement "Warning — May Be Habit Forming."

5. If it is a drug, unless its label bears, to the exclusion of any other nonproprietary name, except the applicable systematic chemical name or the chemical formula, the established name of the drug, and in case it is fabricated from two or more ingredients, the established name and quantity of each active ingredient, including the kind and quantity or proportion of any alcohol, and the established name and quantity or proportion of any bromides, ether, chloroform, acetanilid, acetphenetidin, amidopyrine, antipyrine, atropine, hyoscine, hyoscyamine, arsenic, digitalis, digitalis glucosides, mercury, ouabain, strophanthin, strychnine, thyroid, or any derivative or preparation of any such substances. However, the requirement for stating the quantity of the active ingredients, other than the quantity of those specifically named in this subdivision, shall apply only to prescription drugs. Any prescription drug shall have the established name of the drug or ingredient printed on its label prominently and in type at least half as large as that used for any proprietary name or designation for such drug or ingredient. Exemptions may be allowed under regulations of the Board.

As used in this subdivision, the term "established name," with respect to a drug or ingredient, means the applicable official name designated pursuant to § 508 of the federal act, or if there is no such name and such drug, or such ingredient, is an article recognized in an official compendium, then the official title in such compendium or if neither exists, then the common or usual name, if any, of such drug or of such ingredient. Whenever, an article is recognized in the United States Pharmacopoeia National Formulary and in the Homeopathic Pharmacopoeia under different official titles, the official title used in the United States Pharmacopoeia National Formulary shall apply unless it is labeled and offered for sale as a homeopathic drug, in which case the official title used in the Homeopathic Pharmacopoeia shall apply.

6. Unless its labeling bears adequate directions for use and such adequate warnings against use in those pathological conditions or by children where its use may be dangerous to health, or against unsafe dosage or methods or duration of administration or application, in such manner and form, as are necessary for the protection of users. The Board shall promulgate regulations exempting such drug or device from such requirements when these requirements are not necessary to protect the public health and the articles are also exempted under regulations issued under § 502(f) of the federal act.

7. If it purports to be a drug the name of which is recognized in an official compendium, unless it is packaged and labeled as prescribed. The method of packing may be modified with the consent of the Board, or if consent is obtained under the federal

act. Whenever a drug is recognized in both the United States Pharmacopoeia National Formulary and the Homeopathic Pharmacopoeia of the United States, it shall be subject to the requirements of the United States Pharmacopoeia National Formulary with respect to packaging and labeling unless it is labeled and offered for sale as a homeopathic drug, in which case it shall be subject to the provisions of the Homeopathic Pharmacopoeia of the United States and not to those of the United States Pharmacopoeia National Formulary. However, in the event of inconsistency between the requirements of this subdivision and those of subdivision 5 as to the name by which the drug or its ingredients shall be designated, the requirements of subdivision 5 shall prevail.

8. If it is dangerous to health when used in the dosage, or with the frequency or duration prescribed, recommended, or suggested in the labeling or advertising.

9. If it is, or purports to be, or is represented as a drug composed wholly or partly of insulin, unless it is from a batch for which a certificate or release has been issued pursuant to § 506 of the federal act, and such certificate or release is in effect with respect to such drug.

10. If it is, or purports to be, or is represented as a drug composed wholly or partly of any kind of penicillin, streptomycin, chlortetracycline, chloramphenicol, bacitracin, or any other antibiotic drug, or any derivative, unless it is from a batch, for which a certificate or release has been issued pursuant to § 507 of the federal act, and such certificate or release is in effect for such drug. This subdivision shall not apply to any drug or class of drugs exempted by regulations promulgated under § 507(c) or (d) of the federal law.

For the purpose of this subdivision the term "antibiotic drug" means any drug intended for use by man containing any quantity of any chemical substance which is produced by microorganisms and which has the capacity to inhibit or destroy microorganisms in dilute solution, including, the chemically synthesized equivalent of any such substance.

11. If it is a color additive, the intended use of which in or on drugs is for coloring only, unless its packaging and labeling are in conformity with such packaging and labeling requirements applicable to such color additive, prescribed under the provisions of the federal act.

12. In the case of any prescription drug distributed or offered for sale in this Commonwealth, unless the manufacturer, packer, or distributor includes in all advertisements and other descriptive printed matter a true statement of (i) the established name, as defined in this section, printed prominently and in type at least half as large as that used for any trade or brand name, (ii) the formula showing quantitatively each ingredient of such drug to the extent required for labels under this section, and (iii) such other information in brief summary relating to side effects, contraindications, and effectiveness as are required in regulations issued under the federal act.

13. If a trademark, trade name or other identifying mark, imprint or device of another or any likeness of the foregoing has been placed thereon or upon its container with intent to defraud.

Drugs and devices which are, in accordance with the practice of the trade, to be processed, labeled or repacked in substantial quantities at establishments other than those where originally processed or packed shall be exempt from any labeling or packaging requirements of this chapter if such drugs and devices are being delivered, manufactured, processed, labeled, repacked or otherwise held in compliance with regulations issued by the Board.

History.

Code 1950, § 54-463; 1958, c. 551; 1970, c. 650, § 54-524.93; 1976, c. 644; 1988, c. 765.

§ 54.1-3463. Exemption of drugs dispensed by filling or refilling prescription.

A. Any drug dispensed by filling or refilling a written or oral prescription of a prescriber shall be exempt from the requirements of § 54.1-3462 except subdivisions 1, 9, and 10, and the packaging requirements of subdivision 7, if the drug bears a label containing the name and address of the dispenser, the serial number and date of the prescription or of its filling, the name of the prescriber and the name of the patient, and the directions for use and cautionary statements, if any, contained in such prescription.

B. This section shall not be construed to relieve any person from any requirement prescribed by or under authority of law with respect to drugs now included or which may hereafter be included within the classifications of narcotic drugs or marijuana as defined in the applicable federal and state laws relating to narcotic drugs and marijuana.

History.

1970, c. 650, § 54-524.94; 1988, c. 765; 1996, c. 408.

§ 54.1-3464. Adulterated cosmetics.

A cosmetic shall be deemed to be adulterated:

1. If it bears or contains any poisonous or deleterious substance which may render it injurious to users under the conditions of use prescribed in the labeling or advertisement, or under such conditions of use as are customary or usual. This provision shall not apply to coal-tar hair dye, the label of which bears the following legend conspicuously displayed thereon: "Caution — This product contains ingredients which may cause skin irritation on certain individuals and a preliminary test according to accompanying directions should first be made. This product must not be used for dyeing the eyelashes or

eyebrows; to do so may cause blindness," and the labeling of which bears adequate directions for such preliminary testing. For the purpose of this subdivision and subdivision 5, the term "hair dye" shall not include eyelash or eyebrow dyes;

2. If it consists in whole or in part of any filthy, putrid, or decomposed substance;

3. If it has been produced, prepared, packed, or held under insanitary conditions whereby it may have become contaminated with filth, or whereby it may have been rendered injurious to health;

4. If its container is composed, in whole or in part, of any poisonous or deleterious substance which may render the contents injurious to health;

5. If it is not a hair dye, and it is or it bears or contains a color additive which is unsafe within the meaning of the federal act or § 54.1-3460.

History.

Code 1950, § 54-462; 1970, c. 650, § 54-524.96; 1988, c. 765.

§ 54.1-3465. Misbranded cosmetics.

A cosmetic shall be deemed to be misbranded:

1. If its labeling is false or misleading in any particular;

2. If in package form unless it bears a label containing the name and place of business of the manufacturer, packer, or distributor and an accurate statement of the quantity of the contents in terms of weight, measure, or numerical count. However, reasonable variations shall be permitted, and exemptions for small packages shall be established by the Board;

3. If any word, statement, or other information required by or under authority of this chapter to appear on the label or labeling is not prominently placed thereon with such conspicuousness, as compared with other words, statements, designs, or devices, in the labeling, and in such terms as to render it likely to be read and understood by the ordinary individual under customary conditions of purchase and use;

4. If its container is so made, formed or filled as to be misleading;

5. If it is a color additive, unless its packaging and labeling are in conformity with packaging and labeling requirements applicable to such color additive under the provisions of the federal act. This subdivision shall not apply to packages of color additives which, with respect to their use for cosmetics, are marketed and intended for use only in or on hair dyes.

A cosmetic which is, in accordance with the practice of the trade, to be processed, labeled or repacked in substantial quantities at an establishment other than the establishment where it was originally processed or packed, is exempted from the affirmative labeling requirements of this chapter while it is in transit in commerce from the one establishment to the other, if such transit is made in good faith for such completion purposes only; but it is otherwise subject to all applicable provisions of this chapter.

History.

Code 1950, § 54-466; 1970, c. 650, § 54-524.97; 1988, c. 765.

ARTICLE 7.

CONTROLLED PARAPHERNALIA.

§ 54.1-3466. Possession or distribution of controlled paraphernalia; meaning of controlled paraphernalia; evidence; exceptions.

A. For purposes of this chapter, "controlled paraphernalia" means (i) a hypodermic syringe, needle, or other instrument or implement or combination thereof adapted for the administration of controlled dangerous substances by hypodermic injections under circumstances that reasonably indicate an intention to use such controlled paraphernalia for purposes of illegally administering any controlled drug or (ii) gelatin capsules, glassine envelopes, or any other container suitable for the packaging of individual quantities of controlled drugs in sufficient quantity to and under circumstances that reasonably indicate an intention to use any such item for the illegal manufacture, distribution, or dispensing of any such controlled drug. Evidence of such circumstances shall include, but not be limited to, close proximity of any such controlled paraphernalia to any adulterants or equipment commonly used in the illegal manufacture and distribution of controlled drugs including, but not limited to, scales, sieves, strainers, measuring spoons, staples and staplers, or procaine hydrochloride, mannitol, lactose, quinine, or any controlled drug, or any machine, equipment, instrument, implement, device, or combination thereof that is adapted for the production of controlled drugs under circumstances that reasonably indicate an intention to use such item or combination thereof to produce, sell, or dispense any controlled drug in violation of the provisions of this chapter.

B. Except as authorized in this chapter, it is unlawful for any person to possess controlled paraphernalia.

C. Except as authorized in this chapter, it is unlawful for any person to distribute controlled paraphernalia.

D. A violation of this section is a Class 1 misdemeanor.

E. The provisions of this section shall not apply to persons who have acquired possession and control of controlled paraphernalia in accordance with the provisions of this article or to any person who owns or is engaged in breeding or raising livestock, poultry, or other animals to which hypodermic injections are customarily given in the interest of health, safety, or good husbandry; or to hospitals, physicians, pharmacists, dentists, podiatrists, veterinarians, funeral directors and embalmers, persons to whom a permit has been issued, manufacturers, wholesalers, or their authorized agents or employees when in the usual course of their business, if the controlled paraphernalia lawfully obtained continue to be used for the legitimate purposes for which they were obtained.

History.
1971, Ex. Sess., cc. 210, 245; 1976, c. 614; 1988, c. 765; 2016, c. 229.

§ 54.1-3467. Distribution of hypodermic needles or syringes, gelatin capsules, quinine or any of its salts.

Distribution by any method, of any hypodermic needles or syringes, gelatin capsules, quinine or any of its salts, in excess of one-fourth ounce shall be restricted to licensed pharmacists or to others who have received a license or a permit from the Board.

History.
1971, Ex. Sess., cc. 210, 245; 1988, c. 765.

§ 54.1-3468. Conditions to dispensing device, item, or substance; records.

In dispensing any device, item or substance, the pharmacist or other licensed or permitted person referred to in § 54.1-3467 shall:

1. Require the person requesting such device, item or substance to furnish suitable identification, including proof of age when appropriate;
2. Require the person requesting such item, device or substance to furnish written legitimate purposes for which such item, device or substance is being purchased, except in cases of telephone orders for such item, device or substance from customers of known good standing;
3. At the time of dispensing, make and keep a record showing the date of dispensing, the name and quantity of the device, item or substance, the price at which it was sold, the name and address of the person to whom the device, item or substance was dispensed, the reason for its purchase and enter his initials thereon.

No such devices, substances or items shall be sold or distributed to persons under the age of sixteen years except by a physician for legitimate purposes or upon his prescription. Records shall be maintained pursuant to this chapter and the Board's regulations and shall be made available for inspection to any law-enforcement officer or agent of the Board. Persons violating the provisions of this section shall be guilty of a Class 1 misdemeanor.

History.
1971, Ex. Sess., cc. 210, 245; 1988, c. 765.

§ 54.1-3469. Storage, usage, and disposition of controlled paraphernalia.

Each person, association or corporation which has lawfully obtained possession of any of the controlled paraphernalia mentioned in § 54.1-3467 shall exercise reasonable care in the storage, usage and disposition of such devices or substances to ensure that they are not diverted for reuse for any purposes other than those for which they were lawfully obtained. Any person who permits or causes, directly or indirectly, such controlled paraphernalia to be used for any other purpose than that for which it was lawfully obtained shall be guilty of a Class 1 misdemeanor.

History.
1971, Ex. Sess., cc. 210, 245; 1988, c. 765.

§ 54.1-3470. Obtaining controlled paraphernalia by fraud, etc.

A. No person shall obtain or attempt to obtain any item, device or substance referred to in § 54.1-3467 by fraud, deceit, misrepresentation, or subterfuge or by giving a false name or a false address.

B. No person shall furnish false or fraudulent information in or omit any information from, or willfully make a false statement in obtaining or attempting to obtain any of the instruments or substances referred to in § 54.1-3467.

C. No person shall, for the purpose of obtaining any such instrument or substance, falsely claim to be a manufacturer, wholesaler, pharmacist, practitioner of the healing arts, funeral director, embalmer or veterinarian.

Persons violating the provisions of this section shall be guilty of a Class 1 misdemeanor.

History.
1971, Ex. Sess., cc. 210, 245; 1988, c. 765.

§ 54.1-3471. Issuance of permits to certain persons other than registered pharmacists.

The Board shall, upon written application, on a form furnished by the Board, issue a permit to any person other than a licensed pharmacist who in the usual course of business sells any item referred to in § 54.1-3467 as a wholesale distributor or distributes at retail to any persons who own or breed or raise livestock, poultry, or other animals to which such items, devices or substances are customarily given to or used upon in the interest of health, safety, or good husbandry. This permit shall not authorize the sale or distribution of these items, devices or substances for human use and the permitted person shall exercise reasonable diligence to assure that the items distributed are not for the purpose of human consumption.

History.
1971, Ex. Sess., cc. 210, 245; 1988, c. 765.

§ 54.1-3472. Article inapplicable to certain persons.

The provisions of this article shall not apply to legitimate distribution by or possession of controlled paraphernalia by physicians, dentists, podiatrists, veterinarians, funeral directors and embalmers.

History.
1971, Ex. Sess., cc. 210, 245; 1988, c. 765.

SUBTITLE V.

OCCUPATIONS REGULATED BY LOCAL GOVERNING BODIES.

CHAPTER 40.

PAWNBROKERS.

Section

§ 54.1-4000. Definition of pawnbroker.

"Pawnbroker" means any person who lends or advances money or other things for profit on the pledge and possession of tangible personal property, or other valuable things, other than securities or written or printed evidences of indebtedness or title, or who deals in the purchasing of personal property or other valuable things on condition of selling the same back to the seller at a stipulated price.

History.
Code 1950, § 54-840; 1988, c. 765; 1998, c. 848.

§ 54.1-4001. License required; license authorized by court; building designated in license; penalty.

A. No person shall engage in the business of a pawnbroker without having a valid license issued by the county, city or town in which the pawnbroker conducts such business.

B. The circuit court of any county or city may authorize any county, city or town to issue to any individual, who has not been convicted of a felony or a crime involving moral turpitude in the last ten years, a license to engage in the business of a pawnbroker in that county, city or town. No such license shall be issued by any county, city or town except with such authority. Prior to the issuance of the license, the applicant shall furnish his date of birth, a sworn statement or affirmation disclosing any criminal convictions or any pending criminal charges, whether within or without the Commonwealth, and such other information to the licensing authority as may be required by the governing body. The license shall designate the building in which the licensee shall carry on such business.

C. No person shall engage in the business of a pawnbroker in any location other than the one designated in his license, except with consent of the court which authorized the license.

D. Any person who violates the provisions of this section shall be guilty of a Class 1 misdemeanor. Each day's violation shall constitute a separate offense.

History.
Code 1950, §§ 54-841, 54-842; 1982, c. 633; 1986, c. 316; 1988, c. 765; 1998, c. 848.

§ 54.1-4002. Local limitations as to number of pawnshops.

A. In addition to all limitations and restrictions and notwithstanding any other relevant provisions of this chapter, the governing body of any county, city or town may reasonably limit by resolution or ordinance the number of pawnshops that may be operated at any one time within its territorial limits.

B. The circuit court of any county or city which has, by resolution or ordinance, limited the number of pawnshops therein shall not authorize any license to any pawnbroker after the commissioner of the revenue or other tax assessing officer of the county, city or town over which it has jurisdiction for the issuance of such licenses has filed with the court a statement that the number of licensed pawnshops within the county, city or town has reached the maximum number of pawnshops authorized to be operated therein, unless the number has been reduced below the maximum prescribed. In the event that a properly licensed pawnbroker sells his business, the circuit court of the county or city shall authorize the county, city or town in which such business operates to issue to the purchaser a new license for the same location if the purchaser has not been convicted of a felony or a crime involving moral turpitude in the last ten years. Prior to the issuance of the license, the purchaser shall furnish his date of birth and such other information to the licensing authority as may be required by the local governing body.

History.
Code 1950, § 54-843; 1982, c. 633; 1988, c. 765; 1998, c. 848.

§ 54.1-4003. Bond required; private action on bond.

A. No person shall be licensed as a pawnbroker or engage in the business of a pawnbroker without having in existence a bond with surety in the minimum amount of $50,000 to secure the payment of any judgment recovered under the provisions of subsection B.

B. Any person who recovers a judgment against a licensed pawnbroker for the pawnbroker's misconduct may maintain an action in his own name upon the bond of the pawnbroker if the execution issued upon such judgment is wholly or partially unsatisfied.

History.
Code 1950, § 54-845; 1988, c. 765; 1998, c. 848.

§ 54.1-4004. Memorandum to be given pledgor; fee; lost ticket charge.

Every pawnbroker shall at the time of each loan deliver to the person pawning or pledging anything, a memorandum or note, signed by him, containing the information required by § 54.1-4009. A lost-ticket fee of five dollars may be charged, provided that the pawner is notified of the fee on the ticket.

History.
Code 1950, § 54-846; 1968, c. 438; 1983, c. 238; 1988, c. 765; 1998, c. 848.

§ 54.1-4005. Sale of goods pawned.

No pawnbroker shall sell any pawn or pledge item until (i) it has been in his possession for the minimum term set forth in the memorandum, but not less than 30 days, plus a grace period of 15 days and (ii) a statement of ownership is obtained from the pawner. If a motor vehicle is pawned, the owner of the motor vehicle shall comply with the requirements of § 46.2-637. In the event of default by the pawner, the pawnbroker shall comply with the requirements of § 46.2-633. Otherwise, the pawnbroker shall comply with the requirements of § 46.2-636 et seq. All sales of items pursuant to this section may be made by the pawnbroker in the ordinary course of his business.

History.
Code 1950, § 54-847; 1986, c. 316; 1988, c. 765; 1998, c. 848; 1999, c. 327; 2012, c. 586.

§§ 54.1-4006, 54.1-4007: Repealed by Acts 1998, c. 848.

§ 54.1-4008. Interest chargeable.

A. No pawnbroker shall ask, demand or receive a greater rate of interest than ten percent per month on a loan of $25 or less, or seven percent per month on a loan of more than $25 and less than $100, or five percent per month on a loan of $100 or more, secured by a pledge of tangible personal property. No loan shall be divided for the purpose of increasing the percentage to be paid the pawnbroker. Loans may be renewed based on the original loan amount. Loans may not be issued that compound the interest or storage fees from previous loans on the same item.

B. An annual percentage rate computed and disclosed under the provisions of the federal Truth-in-Lending Act shall not be deemed a violation of this section.

History.
Code 1950, § 54-850; 1983, c. 238; 1988, c. 765; 1998, c. 848; 1999, c. 327.

§ 54.1-4009. Records to be kept; credentials of person pawning goods; fee; penalty.

A. Every pawnbroker shall keep at his place of business an accurate and legible record of each loan or transaction in the course of his business, including transactions in which secondhand goods, wares, or merchandise is purchased for resale. The account shall be recorded at the time of the loan or transaction and shall include:

1. A description, serial number, and a statement of ownership of the goods, article, or thing pawned or pledged or received on account of money loaned thereon or purchased for resale;
2. The time, date, and place of the transaction;
3. The amount of money loaned thereon at the time of pledging the same or paid as the purchase price;
4. The rate of interest to be paid on such loan;
5. The fees charged by the pawnbroker, itemizing each fee charged;
6. The full name, residence address, telephone number, and driver's license number or other form of identification of the person pawning or pledging or selling the goods, article, or thing, together with a particular description, including the height, weight, date of birth, race, gender, hair and eye color, and any other identifying marks, of such person;
7. Verification of the identification by the exhibition of a government-issued identification card bearing a photograph of the person pawning, pledging, or selling the goods, article, or thing, such as a driver's license or military identification card. The record shall contain the type of identification exhibited, the issuing agency, and the number thereon;
8. A digital image of the form of identification used by the person involved in the transaction;
9. As to loans, the terms and conditions of the loan, including the period for which any such loan may be made; and
10. All other facts and circumstances respecting such loan or purchase.

B. A pawnbroker may maintain at his place of business an electronic record of each transaction involving goods, articles, or things pawned or pledged or purchased. If maintained electronically, a pawnbroker shall retain the electronic records for at least one year after the date of the transaction and make such electronic records available to any duly authorized law-enforcement officer upon request.

C. For each loan or transaction, a pawnbroker may charge a service fee for making the daily electronic reports to the appropriate law-enforcement officers required by § 54.1-4010, creating and maintaining the electronic records required under this section, and investigating the legal title to property being pawned or pledged or purchased. Such fee shall not exceed five percent of the amount loaned on such item or paid by the pawnbroker for such item or $3, whichever is less. Any person, firm, or corporation violating any of the provisions of this section is guilty of a Class 4 misdemeanor.

D. No goods, article, or thing shall be pawned or pledged or received on account of money loaned or purchased for resale if the original serial number affixed to the goods, article, or thing has been removed, defaced, or altered.

E. The Superintendent of State Police shall promulgate regulations specifying the nature of the particular description for the purposes of subdivision A 6.

The Superintendent of State Police shall promulgate regulations specifying the nature of identifying credentials of the person pawning, pledging, or selling the goods, article, or thing. Such credentials shall be examined by the pawnbroker, and an appropriate record retained thereof.

History.

Code 1950, § 54-851; 1976, c. 66; 1986, c. 316; 1988, c. 765; 1990, c. 783; 1998, c. 848; 2001, c. 401; 2003, c. 448; 2013, c. 262.

§ 54.1-4010. Daily reports.

A. Every pawnbroker shall prepare a daily report of all goods, articles, or things pawned or pledged with him or sold to him that day and shall file such report by noon of the following day with the chief of police or other law-enforcement officer of the county, city, or town where his business is conducted designated by the local attorney for the Commonwealth to receive it. The report shall include the pledgor's or seller's name, residence, and driver's license number or other form of identification; a photograph or digital image of the form of identification used by the pledgor or seller; and a description of the goods, articles, or other things pledged or sold and, unless maintained in electronic format, shall be in writing and clearly legible to any person inspecting it. A pawnbroker may compile and maintain the daily report in an electronic format and, if so maintained, shall file the required daily reports electronically with the appropriate law-enforcement officer through use of a disk, electronic transmission, or any other electronic means of reporting approved by the law-enforcement officer. Any local governing body, may by ordinance, require a pawnbroker to maintain and file a daily report electronically through the use of a disk, electronic transmission, or any other electronic means of reporting approved by the law-enforcement officer.

B. The Department of State Police shall adopt regulations for the uniform reporting of information required by this section.

C. Any person, firm, or corporation violating any of the provisions of this section is guilty of a Class 4 misdemeanor.

History.

Code 1950, § 54-853; 1988, c. 765; 1998, c. 848; 2001, c. 401; 2002, c. 201; 2003, c. 448; 2010, cc. 540, 657; 2013, c. 262.

§ 54.1-4011. Officers may examine records or property; warrantless search and seizure authorized.

Every pawnbroker and every employee of the pawnbroker shall admit to the pawnbroker's place of business during regular business hours, any duly authorized law-enforcement officer of the jurisdiction where the business is being conducted, or any law-enforcement official of the state or federal government. The pawnbroker or employee shall permit the officer to (i) examine all records required by this chapter and any article listed in a record which is believed by the officer to be missing or stolen and (ii) search for and take into possession any article known to him to be missing, or known or believed by him to have been stolen. However, the officer shall not take possession of any article without providing to the pawnbroker a receipt.

History.

Code 1950, §§ 54-852, 54-854; 1988, c. 765; 1990, c. 683; 1998, c. 848.

§ 54.1-4012. Property pawned or purchased not to be disfigured or changed.

No property received on deposit or pledged or purchased by any pawnbroker shall be disfigured or its identity destroyed or affected in any manner (i) so long as it continues in pawn or in the possession of the pawnbroker while in pawn or (ii) in an effort to obtain a serial number or other information for identification purposes.

History.

Code 1950, § 54-855; 1988, c. 765; 1998, c. 848; 1999, c. 327; 2003, c. 448.

§ 54.1-4013. Care of tangible personal property; evaluation fee.

A. Pawnbrokers shall store, care for and protect all of the tangible personal property in the pawnbroker's possession and protect the property from damage or misuse. Nothing in this chapter shall be construed to mean that pawnbrokers are insurers of pawned property in their possession.

B. A pawnbroker may charge a monthly storage fee for any items requiring storage, which fee shall not exceed five percent of the amount loaned on such item.

History.
Code 1950, § 54-856; 1988, c. 765; 1998, c. 848.

§ 54.1-4014. Penalties; violation of the Virginia Consumer Protection Act.

A. Except as otherwise provided in § 54.1-4001, any licensed pawnbroker who violates any of the provisions of this chapter shall be guilty of a Class 4 misdemeanor. In addition, the court may revoke or suspend the pawnbroker's license for second and subsequent offenses.

B. Additionally, any violation of the provisions of the chapter shall constitute a prohibited practice in accordance with § 59.1-200 and shall be subject to any and all of the enforcement provisions of the Virginia Consumer Protection Act (§ 59.1-196 et seq.).

History.
Code 1950, §§ 54-857, 54-858; 1988, c. 765; 1998, c. 848.

CHAPTER 41.
PRECIOUS METALS DEALERS.

Section

§ 54.1-4100. Definitions.

For the purposes of this chapter, unless the context requires a different meaning:

"Coin" means any piece of gold, silver or other metal fashioned into a prescribed shape, weight and degree of fineness, stamped by authority of a government with certain marks and devices, and having a certain fixed value as money.

"Dealer" means any person, firm, partnership, or corporation engaged in the business of (i) purchasing secondhand precious metals or gems; (ii) removing in any manner precious metals or gems from manufactured articles not then owned by the person, firm, partnership, or corporation; or (iii) buying, acquiring, or selling precious metals or gems removed from manufactured articles. "Dealer" includes all employers and principals on whose behalf a purchase is made, and any employee or agent who makes any purchase for or on behalf of his employer or principal.

The definition of "dealer" shall not include persons engaged in the following:

1. Purchases of precious metals or gems directly from other dealers, manufacturers, or wholesalers for retail or wholesale inventories, provided that the selling dealer has complied with the provisions of this chapter.

2. Purchases of precious metals or gems from a qualified fiduciary who is disposing of the assets of an estate being administered by the fiduciary.

3. Acceptance by a retail merchant of trade-in merchandise previously sold by the retail merchant to the person presenting that merchandise for trade-in.

4. Repairing, restoring or designing jewelry by a retail merchant, if such activities are within his normal course of business.

5. Purchases of precious metals or gems by industrial refiners and manufacturers, insofar as such purchases are made directly from retail merchants, wholesalers, dealers, or by mail originating outside the Commonwealth.

6. Persons regularly engaged in the business of purchasing and processing nonprecious scrap metals which incidentally may contain traces of precious metals recoverable as a by-product.

"Gems" means any item containing precious or semiprecious stones customarily used in jewelry.

"Precious metals" means any item except coins composed in whole or in part of gold, silver, platinum, or platinum alloys.

History.
1981, c. 581, § 54-859.15; 1988, c. 765.

§ 54.1-4101. Records to be kept; copy furnished to local authorities.

A. Every dealer shall keep at his place of business an accurate and legible record of each purchase of precious metals or gems. The record of each purchase shall be retained by the dealer for at least 24 months and shall set forth the following:

1. A complete description of all precious metals or gems purchased from each seller. The description shall include all names, initials, serial numbers, or other identifying marks or monograms on each item purchased, the true weight or carat of any gem, and the price paid for each item;

2. The date, time, and place of receiving the items purchased;

3. The full name, residence address, work place, home and work telephone numbers, date of birth, sex, race, height, weight, hair and eye color, and

other identifying marks of the person selling the precious metals or gems;

4. Verification of the identification by the exhibition of a government-issued identification card bearing a photograph of the person selling the precious metals or gems, such as a driver's license or military identification card. The record shall contain the type of identification exhibited, the issuing agency, and the number thereon;

5. A statement of ownership from the seller; and

6. A digital image of the form of identification used by the person involved in the transaction.

B. The information required by subdivisions A 1 through A 3 shall appear on each bill of sale for all precious metals and gems purchased by a dealer, and a copy shall be mailed or delivered within 24 hours of the time of purchase to the chief law-enforcement officer of the locality in which the purchase was made.

History.
1981, c. 581, § 54-859.16; 1986, c. 316; 1988, c. 765; 1990, c. 783; 1991, c. 174; 2013, c. 262.

§ 54.1-4101.1. Officers may examine records or property; warrantless search and seizure authorized.

Every dealer or his employee shall admit to his place of business during regular business hours the chief law-enforcement officer or his designee of the jurisdiction in which the dealer is located or any law-enforcement officer of the state or federal government. The dealer or his employee shall permit the officer to (i) examine all records required by this chapter and any article listed in a record which is believed by the officer to be missing or stolen and (ii) search for and take into possession any article known to him to be missing, or known or believed by him to have been stolen.

History.
1991, c. 174.

§ 54.1-4102. Credentials and statement of ownership required from seller.

No dealer shall purchase precious metals or gems without first (i) ascertaining the identity of the seller by requiring an identification issued by a governmental agency with a photograph of the seller thereon, and at least one other corroborating means of identification, and (ii) obtaining a statement of ownership from the seller.

The governing body of the locality wherein the dealer conducts his business may determine the contents of the statement of ownership.

History.
1981, c. 581, § 54-859.17; 1986, c. 316; 1988, c. 765.

§ 54.1-4103. Prohibited purchases.

A. No dealer shall purchase precious metals or gems from any seller who is under the age of eighteen.

B. No dealer shall purchase precious metals or gems from any seller who the dealer believes or has reason to believe is not the owner of such items, unless the seller has written and duly authenticated authorization from the owner permitting and directing such sale.

History.
1981, c. 581, § 54-859.18; 1988, c. 765.

§ 54.1-4104. Dealer to retain purchases.

A. The dealer shall retain all precious metals or gems purchased for a minimum of 15 calendar days from the date on which a copy of the bill of sale is received by the chief law-enforcement officer of the locality in which the purchase is made. Until the expiration of this period, the dealer shall not sell, alter, or dispose of a purchased item in whole or in part, or remove it from the county, city, or town in which the purchase was made.

B. If a dealer performs the service of removing precious metals or gems, he shall retain the metals or gems removed and the article from which the removal was made for a period of 15 calendar days after receiving such article and precious metals or gems.

History.
1981, c. 581, § 54-859.19; 1988, c. 765; 2012, c. 532.

§ 54.1-4105. Record of disposition.

Each dealer shall maintain for at least twenty-four months an accurate and legible record of the name and address of the person, firm, or corporation to which he sells any precious metal or gem in its original form after the waiting period required by § 54.1-4104. This record shall also show the name and address of the seller from whom the dealer purchased the item.

History.
1981, c. 581, § 54-859.20; 1988, c. 765.

§ 54.1-4106. Bond or letter of credit required of dealers when permit obtained.

A. Every dealer shall secure a permit as required by § 54.1-4108, and each dealer at the time of obtaining such permit shall enter into a recognizance to the Commonwealth secured by a corporate surety authorized to do business in this Commonwealth, in the penal sum of $10,000, conditioned upon due observance of the terms of this chapter. In lieu of a bond, a dealer may cause to be issued by a bank authorized to do business in the Commonwealth a letter of credit in favor of the Commonwealth for $10,000.

B. If any county, city, or town has an ordinance which regulates the purchase and sale of precious metals and gems pursuant to § 54.1-4111, such bond or letter of credit shall be executed in favor of the local governing body.

C. A single bond upon an employer or principal may be written or a single letter of credit issued to cover all employees and all transactions occurring at a single location.

History.

1981, c. 581, § 54-859.21; 1988, c. 765.

§ 54.1-4107. Private action on bond or letter of credit.

Any person aggrieved by the misconduct of any dealer which violated the provisions of this chapter may maintain an action for recovery in any court of proper jurisdiction against the dealer and his surety. Recovery against the surety shall be only for that amount of the judgment which is unsatisfied by the dealer.

History.

1981, c. 581, § 54-859.22; 1988, c. 765.

§ 54.1-4108. Permit required; method of obtaining permit; no convictions of certain crimes; approval of weighing devices; renewal; permanent location required.

A. No person shall engage in the activities of a dealer as defined in § 54.1-4100 without first obtaining a permit from the chief law-enforcement officer of each county, city, or town in which he proposes to engage in business.

B. To obtain a permit, the dealer shall file with the proper chief law-enforcement officer an application form which includes the dealer's full name, any aliases, address, age, date of birth, sex, and fingerprints; the name, address, and telephone number of the applicant's employer, if any; and the location of the dealer's place of business. Upon filing this application and the payment of a $200 application fee, the dealer shall be issued a permit by the chief law-enforcement officer or his designee, provided that the applicant has not been convicted of a felony or crime of moral turpitude within seven years prior to the date of application. The permit shall be denied if the applicant has been denied a permit or has had a permit revoked under any ordinance similar in substance to the provisions of this chapter.

C. Before a permit may be issued, the dealer must have all weighing devices used in his business inspected and approved by local or state weights and measures officials and present written evidence of such approval to the proper chief law-enforcement officer.

D. This permit shall be valid for one year from the date issued and may be renewed in the same manner as such permit was initially obtained with an annual permit fee of $200. No permit shall be transferable.

E. If the business of the dealer is not operated without interruption, with Saturdays, Sundays, and recognized holidays excepted, the dealer shall notify the proper chief law-enforcement officer of all closings and reopenings of such business. The business of a dealer shall be conducted only from the fixed and permanent location specified in his application for a permit.

F. The chief law-enforcement officer may waive the permit fee for retail merchants that are not required to be licensed as pawnbrokers under Chapter 40 (§ 54.1-4000 et seq.), provided the retail merchant has a permanent place of business and purchases of precious metals and gems do not exceed five percent of the retail merchant's annual business.

History.

1981, c. 581, § 54-859.23; 1986, c. 316; 1988, c. 765; 2014, cc. 22, 611.

§ 54.1-4109. Exemptions from chapter.

A. The chief law-enforcement officer of a county, city or town, or his designee, may waive by written notice implementation of any one or more of the provisions of this chapter, except § 54.1-4103, for particular numismatic, gem, or antique exhibitions or craft shows sponsored by nonprofit organizations, provided that the purpose of the exhibitions is nonprofit in nature, notwithstanding the fact that there may be casual purchases and trades made at such exhibitions.

B. Neither the provisions of this chapter nor any local ordinances dealing with the subject matter of this chapter shall apply to the sale or purchase of coins.

C. Neither the provisions of this chapter nor any local ordinance dealing with the subject matter of this chapter shall apply to any bank, branch thereof, trust company or bank holding company, or any wholly owned subsidiary thereof, engaged in buying and selling gold and silver bullion.

History.

1981, c. 581, §§ 54-859.24, 54-859.27; 1984, c. 583, § 54-859.28; 1988, c. 765.

§ 54.1-4110. Penalties; first and subsequent offenses.

A. Any person convicted of violating any of the provisions of this chapter shall be guilty of a Class 2 misdemeanor for the first offense. Upon conviction of any subsequent offense he shall be guilty of a Class 1 misdemeanor.

B. Upon the first conviction of a dealer for violation of any provision of this chapter, the chief law-enforcement officer may revoke the dealer's permit for one full year from the date the conviction becomes final. Such revocation shall be mandatory for two full years from the date the conviction becomes final upon a second conviction.

History.

1981, c. 581, § 54-859.25; 1988, c. 765; 2010, c. 100.

§ 54.1-4111. Local ordinances.

Nothing in this chapter shall prevent any county, city, or town in this Commonwealth from enacting an ordinance regulating dealers in precious metals and gems which parallels this chapter, or which imposes terms, conditions, and fees that are stricter, more comprehensive, or larger than those imposed by this chapter. In any event, the terms, conditions, and fees imposed by this chapter shall constitute minimum requirements in any local ordinance. Any fee in excess of the one specified in § 54.1-4108 shall be reasonably related to the cost of enforcement of such local ordinance.

History.

1981, c. 581, § 54-859.26; 1988, c. 765.

CHAPTER 42.

DEALERS IN FIREARMS.

§ 54.1-4200. Definitions.

For the purpose of this chapter, unless the context requires a different meaning:

"Dealer in firearms" means (i) any person, firm, partnership, or corporation engaged in the business of selling, trading or transferring firearms at wholesale or retail; (ii) any person, firm, partnership, or corporation engaged in the business of making or fitting special barrels, stocks, or trigger mechanisms to firearms; or (iii) any person, firm, partnership, or corporation that is a pawnbroker.

"Engaged in business" means as applied to a dealer in firearms a person, firm, partnership, or corporation that devotes time, attention, and labor to dealing in firearms as a regular course of trade or business with the principal objective of livelihood and profit through repetitive purchase or resale of firearms, but such term shall not involve a person who makes occasional sales, exchanges, or purchases of firearms for the enhancement of a personal collection or for a hobby, or who sells all or part of his personal collection of firearms.

"Firearms show" means any gathering or exhibition, open to the public, not occurring on the permanent premises of a dealer in firearms, conducted principally for the purposes of exchanging, selling or trading firearms as defined in § 18.2-308.2:2.

History.

1989, c. 490; 1993, c. 477.

§ 54.1-4201. Inspection of records.

A. Every dealer in firearms shall keep at his place of business, for not less than a period of two years, the original consent form required to be completed by § 18.2-308.2:2 for each firearm sale.

B. Every dealer in firearms shall admit to his place of business during regular business hours the chief law-enforcement officer, or his designee, of the jurisdiction in which the dealer is located, or any law-enforcement official of the Commonwealth, and shall permit such law-enforcement officer, in the course of a bona fide criminal investigation, to examine and copy those federal and state records related to the acquisition or disposition of a particular firearm required by this section. This section shall not be construed to authorize the seizure of any records.

History.

1989, c. 490; 1993, cc. 461, 493; 2005, c. 859.

§ 54.1-4201.1. Notification by sponsor of firearms show to State Police and local law-enforcement authorities required; records; penalty.

A. No promoter of a firearms show shall hold such show without giving notice at least 30 days prior to the show to the State Police and the sheriff or chief of police of the locality in which the firearms show will be held. The notice shall be given on a form provided by the State Police. A separate notice shall be required for each firearms show.

"Promoter" means every person, firm, corporation, club, association, or organization holding a firearms show in the Commonwealth.

The promoter shall maintain for the duration of the show a list of all vendors or exhibitors in the show for immediate inspection by any law-enforcement authorities, and within five days after the conclusion of the show, by mail, by hand, by email, or by fax, transmit a copy of the complete vendor or exhibitor list to the law-enforcement authorities to which the 30-day prior notice was required. The vendor or exhibitor list shall contain the full name and residence address and the business name and address, if any, of the vendors or exhibitors.

B. A willful violation of this section shall be a Class 3 misdemeanor.

C. The provisions of this section shall not apply to firearms shows held in any town with a population of not less than 1,995 and not more than 2,010, according to the 1990 United States census.

History.
1993, c. 477; 2005, c. 193.

§ 54.1-4201.2. (Contingent effective date — see Editor's notes) Firearm transactions by persons other than dealers; voluntary background checks.

A. The Department of State Police shall be available at every firearms show held in the Commonwealth to make determinations in accordance with the procedures set out in § 18.2-308.2:2 of whether a prospective purchaser or transferee is prohibited under state or federal law from possessing a firearm. The Department of State Police shall establish policies and procedures in accordance with 28 C.F.R. § 25.6 to permit such determinations to be made by the Department of State Police.

Unless otherwise required by state or federal law, any party involved in the transaction may decide whether or not to have such a determination made.

The Department of State Police may charge a reasonable fee for the determination.

B. The promoter, as defined in § 54.1-4201.1, shall give the Department of State Police notice of the time and location of a firearms show at least 30 days prior to the show. The promoter shall provide the Department of State Police with adequate space, at no charge, to conduct such prohibition determinations. The promoter shall ensure that a notice that such determinations are available is prominently displayed at the show.

C. No person who sells or transfers a firearm at a firearms show after receiving a determination from the Department of State Police that the purchaser or transferee is not prohibited by state or federal law from possessing a firearm shall be liable for selling or transferring a firearm to such person.

D. The provisions of § 18.2-308.2:2, including definitions, procedures, and prohibitions, shall apply, mutatis mutandis, to the provisions of this section.

History.
2016, cc. 44, 45.

Editor's note.
Acts 2016, cc. 44 and 45, cl. 2 provides: "That the provisions of this act shall become effective only if approval is received from the U.S. Department of Justice for the Department of State Police to implement the policies and procedures set out in this act."

§ 54.1-4202. Penalties for violation of the provisions of this chapter.

Any person convicted of a first offense for willfully violating the provisions of this chapter shall be guilty of a Class 2 misdemeanor. Any person convicted of a second or subsequent offense under the provisions of this chapter shall be guilty of a Class 1 misdemeanor.

History.
1989, c. 490.

TITLE 56. PUBLIC SERVICE COMPANIES.

CHAPTER 12. MOTOR VEHICLE CARRIERS GENERALLY.

§§ 56-273 through 56-338: Repealed by Acts 1995, cc. 744 and 803.

CHAPTER 12.1. HOUSEHOLD GOODS CARRIERS.

§§ 56-338.1 through 56-338.18: Repealed by Acts 1995, cc. 744 and 803.

CHAPTER 12.2. PETROLEUM TANK TRUCK CARRIERS.

§§ 56-338.19 through 56-338.39: Repealed by Acts 1995, cc. 744 and 803.

CHAPTER 12.3. SIGHT-SEEING CARRIERS.

§§ 56-338.40 through 56-338.49: Repealed by Acts 1995, cc. 744 and 803.

Cross references.
As to regulations governing sight-seeing carriers, see §§ 46.2-2099.21 and 46.2-2099.30.

CHAPTER 12.4. SPECIAL OR CHARTER PARTY CARRIERS.

§§ 56-338.50 through 56-338.64: Repealed by Acts 1995, cc. 744 and 803.

Cross references.

As to present provisions governing special or charter party carriers by boat, see §§ 46.2-2099.21 and 46.2-2099.30.

CHAPTER 12.5.

RESTRICTED PARCEL CARRIERS.

§§ 56-338.65 through 56-338.84: Repealed by Acts 1995, cc. 744 and 803.

CHAPTER 13.

RAILROAD CORPORATIONS.

ARTICLE 2.

POWERS.

§ 56-353. Railroad company may appoint police agents.

The president or any other executive officer of any railroad company incorporated by this Commonwealth may, with the approval of the circuit court of any county or the corporation court of any city through which the road passes or has its chief office, appoint one or more police agents, who shall have authority in all cases in which the rights of such railroad company are involved to exercise within the Commonwealth all powers which can be lawfully exercised by any police officer for the preservation of the peace, the arrest of offenders and disorderly persons, and for the enforcement of laws against crimes; and such president or other executive officer may remove any such agent at his pleasure; but, any court giving such consent may at any time revoke it.

History.

Code 1919, § 3944; 1930, p. 787.

§ 56-354. Conductors, etc., to be conservators of the peace.

Conductors and engineers of railroad passenger trains, and station and depot agents, shall be conservators of the peace. Each shall have the same power to make arrests that other conservators of the peace have except that the conductors and engineers of passenger trains shall only have such power on board their respective trains and on the property of their companies while on duty and the agents at their respective places of business. Conductors, engineers, and agents may cause any person so arrested by them to be detained and delivered to the proper authorities for trial as soon as practicable.

History.

Code 1919, § 3944; 1930, p. 788; 1996, cc. 114, 157.

ARTICLE 6.

HIGHWAY CROSSINGS.

§ 56-405. Railroad companies to maintain grade crossings of public highways and approaches; repair by Commissioner of Highways or public road authority; recovery of cost from railroad company.

At every crossing, now existing or hereafter established, of a public road by a railroad or of a railroad by a public highway at grade, it shall be the duty of the railroad company to keep such crossing in good repair to the full width of the public highway, and to maintain such crossing in a smooth condition so as to admit of reasonable and safe travel over the same, and it shall also be the duty of the railroad company to maintain and keep in good repair that portion of the highway located between points two feet on either side of the extreme rails. A railroad may request that a public highway be closed for grade crossing maintenance activities, and the representative of the Commissioner of Highways or the representative of the appropriate public road authority may approve such closing where a reasonable detour is available. Any railroad company violating the provisions of this section shall be deemed guilty of a misdemeanor and, upon conviction, shall be fined not less than $10 nor more than $500.

The Commissioner of Highways or the representative of the public road authority, whenever he or it shall ascertain that any such crossing is not being properly maintained, shall notify the railroad company involved in writing to repair the crossing forthwith; the railroad company upon receipt of notice may request a conference on the condition of the crossing and the need, if any, for the repair of such crossing and such conference shall be held within thirty days after receipt of the Commissioner's or the public road authority's notice. After the conference if the Commissioner or the public road authority is of the opinion that such repairs are required and the railroad is not willing to proceed promptly with such repairs, he or the public road authority may repair the same or cause it to be repaired and recover from the railroad company the actual cost of such work including any administration and engineering cost.

If no conference is requested by the railroad company within the thirty-day period, the Commissioner or the public road authority with advance notice may repair the crossing or cause it to be repaired and recover from the railroad company the actual cost of such work including any administration and engineering cost.

In any action under this section to recover the cost of the repair of any such crossing, the need for, and reasonableness of, the repairs may be put in issue.

Nothing herein shall be construed as placing a duty on the railroad company to construct or reconstruct any such crossing in the event any such crossing is relocated or the highway approaches thereto are widened or reconstructed.

History.
Code 1919, § 3973; 1952, c. 99; 1960, c. 544; 1968, c. 226; 1978, c. 214; 1996, cc. 114, 157.

§ 56-405.01: Repealed by Acts 1996, cc. 114 and 157.

§ 56-405.02. Railroads to adjust certain public highways at grade crossings.

When adjustments are made to railway trackage grade which crosses public rights-of-way in use as a public highway or street in any locality, the railway company making such adjustments to their trackage shall also make initial adjustments to those public highways or streets so affected thereby to maintain a safe vertical relationship between trackage and street surfaces and to insure positive storm drainage such as existed prior to such repairs. After making such initial adjustments the responsibility for the continuing maintenance of the areas within such public highways and streets so adjusted shall be controlled by § 56-405.

The cost of all such initial street improvements necessitated by railway trackage adjustments shall be the responsibility of the railway company making such initial adjustments irrespective of whether or not the street improvements extended beyond railway right-of-way.

History.
1984, c. 439; 1996, cc. 114, 157.

§ 56-405.1. Agreements with Commissioner of Highways or public road authority representative for maintenance and repair of public grade crossings.

Whenever the Commissioner of Highways or representative of the appropriate public road authority determines that it is in the best interest of the public to assist a railroad in its grade crossing maintenance and repair activities, he is authorized to enter into an agreement with the railroad company for the repair or maintenance of any crossing of a railroad and a public highway or for the sale of materials to the railroad company for the repair and maintenance of any such crossing. Any such agreement shall provide for the railroad company to bear the cost of the repair or maintenance or material furnished and such other conditions as the Commissioner of Highways or representative of the appropriate public road authority deems necessary or advisable to protect the interest of the public.

History.
1968, c. 175; 1996, cc. 114, 157.

§ 56-405.2. Construction and maintenance of crossbucks.

Every railroad company shall cause signal boards, hereinafter referred to as crossbucks, well supported by posts or otherwise and approved by the Department of Transportation at such heights as to be easily seen by travelers from both directions of the public highway, and not obstructing travel, containing in capital letters, at least five inches high, the inscription "railroad crossing," to be placed, and constantly maintained, at each public highway at or near, and on both sides of, each place where it is crossed by the railroad at the same level. The requirements of this section in localities that maintain their own streets may be waived at specific crossings on the petition of any such company to both the Commissioner of Highways and the public road authority if both the Commissioner and the public road authority determine that any such crossing has or will have other adequate warning devices or that the placement of new crossbucks will not enhance the safety of the traveling public. Neither official action nor failure to act as hereinabove provided shall impair the power of the Commissioner or the public road authority to require crossbucks at specific public crossings should a subsequent determination of their need be made.

The cost of erecting crossbucks placed at a public highway for the first time or whenever the Commissioner or the public road authority determines an upgrade of the standards is required may be paid or supplemented from federal funds when available to the Department of Transportation for such purpose at the sole discretion of the Commissioner of Highways. But the election of the Commissioner not to participate in such cost shall not relieve any company from the obligation of this section.

This section shall apply as to cities and towns in the case of new crossbucks beginning July 1, 1977.

History.

1977, c. 226; 1996, cc. 114, 157.

§ **56-405.3:** Repealed by Acts 1996, cc. 114 and 157.

§ **56-406:** Repealed by Acts 1977, c. 226.

Cross references.

For provisions covering the subject matter of the repealed section, see § 56-405.2.

§ 56-406.1. Proceedings for installation and maintenance of automatically operated gates, signals and other automatic crossing warning devices.

Railroads shall cooperate with the Virginia Department of Transportation and the Department of Rail and Public Transportation in furnishing information and technical assistance to enable the Commonwealth to develop plans and project priorities for the elimination of hazardous conditions at any crossing of a public highway which crosses at grade including, but not limited to, grade crossing elimination, reconstruction of existing grade crossings, and grade crossing improvements. The Commonwealth shall provide each locality a listing of grade crossing safety needs for its consideration. Information collected and analyses undertaken by the designated state agencies are subject to 23 U.S.C. § 409. A railroad shall not unilaterally select or determine the type of grade crossing warning system to be installed at any crossing of a public highway and railroad at grade. The railroad shall only install or upgrade a grade crossing warning system at any crossing of a public highway and railroad at grade pursuant to an agreement with the Virginia Department of Transportation or representative of the appropriate public road authority authorized to enter into such agreements. A railroad is not required but is permitted to upgrade, at its own expense, components of any public highway at grade warning system when such upgrade is incidental to a railroad improvement project relating to track, structures or train control systems.

When required by the Commissioner of Highways or representative of the appropriate public road authority, every railroad company shall cause a grade crossing warning device including flashing lights approved by the Department of Transportation at such heights as to be easily seen by travelers, and not obstructing travel, to be placed, and maintained at each public highway at or near each place where it is crossed by the railroad at the same level. Such warning device shall be automatically activated by the approaching train so as to be clearly discernible to travelers approaching the railroad crossing from each direction at a distance of two-hundred feet. Such warning devices shall be erected at the initiative of the appropriate public road authority only when required by ordinance or resolution adopted by the Commissioner or the appropriate public road authority thereof stating that such political subdivision will pay the full initial installation cost of such warning devices and that maintenance costs will be fixed as provided in § 56-406.2. A certified copy of such ordinance or resolution shall be delivered to such railroad company, and such railroad company shall forthwith install such warning devices at the full initial cost of such public road authority. The cost of such installation and maintenance of such warning devices may be shared by agreement between such railroad company and the Commissioner of Highways or the appropriate public road authority, when initiating such installation. The railroad shall be responsible for the continuing maintenance of the warning devices.

In the event that such Commissioner or representative of the appropriate public road authority and the railroad company or companies involved are unable to agree on (i) the necessity for such grade crossing warning device, or (ii) the plans and specifications for and the method and manner of construction or operation thereof, or (iii) the share of the cost of construction, if any, to be borne by the railroad company or companies involved, then the Commissioner of Highways or representative of the appropriate public road authority, as the case may be, shall petition the State Corporation Commission setting forth the grade crossing warning devices desired and the plans and specifications for and the method and manner of construction and operation of the devices desired and the facts which, in the opinion of the petitioner, justify the requiring of the same. Copies of the petition and plans and specifications shall be forthwith served by the State Corporation Commission on the railroad company or companies involved. Within twenty days after service on it of such petition and plans and specifications, each such railroad company shall file an answer with the State Corporation Commission setting out its objections to the proposed project, and the Commission shall hear and determine the matter as other matters are heard and determined by that body. The Commission shall consider all the facts and circumstances surrounding the case and shall determine (a) whether public necessity justifies or requires the proposed warning devices, (b) whether the plans and specifications or the method and manner of construction and operation be proper and appropriate, and (c) what share of the cost of the project, if any, to be borne by any railroad company involved is fair and reasonable, having regard to the benefits, if any, accruing to such railroad company from providing such grade crossing warning devices, and either dismiss the proceeding as against such railroad company or enter an order deciding and disposing of all of the matters hereinbefore submitted to its jurisdiction.

History.
1952, c. 400; 1954, c. 122; 1962, c. 527; 1996, cc. 114, 157.

§ 56-406.2. Proceeding for fixing cost of maintaining such warning devices at public grade crossings.

Whenever any automatically operated gate, signal or other automatic crossing warning device has been or may hereafter be installed at any highway, road or street grade crossing by any railroad company, the Commissioner of Highways or the public road authority may agree with the railroad company involved as to the division of the cost of the future maintenance of any such device or devices. The basis for the division of costs shall be determined by the Department of Rail and Public Transportation utilizing the calculated average maintenance cost of all previous warning device maintenance performed and documented by all railroads operating in Virginia. In the event that the Commissioner or the public road authority and the railroad company involved are unable to agree upon the share of the cost of maintenance of any such device or devices to be borne by the railroad company, if any, then such railroad company may file a petition with the State Corporation Commission setting forth the crossing protection provided at such crossing, the terms of the contract and/or the conditions of the order of said Commission or the public road authority under which it was constructed and installed and the estimated future annual cost of maintaining the same. Copies of such petition shall forthwith be served by the State Corporation Commission upon the Commissioner of Highways or the public road authority who shall, within twenty days after service of such petition, file an answer thereto setting out reasons for declining to participate in the future cost of maintaining such warning device or devices as requested by the railroad company, and the Commission shall thereupon hear and determine the matter as other matters are heard and determined by that body. The Commission shall consider all the facts and circumstances surrounding the case and shall determine what share of the cost of the future maintenance of such warning device or devices, if any, shall be borne by the railroad company and/or the Commonwealth Transportation Board or the public road authority, having regard to the benefits, if any, accruing to such railroad company from the continued maintenance of such protection of said public highway, road or street grade crossing, and either dismiss the proceeding or enter an order deciding and disposing of the matters therein submitted to its jurisdiction.

History.
1956, c. 626; 1962, c. 528; 1996, cc. 114, 157.

§ 56-408. Signs similar to crossing signs prohibited.

No device or sign which is in the form of a railroad crossing signboard shall be erected or permitted to remain on or near any of the public roads of this Commonwealth, except as required by § 56-405.2.

Any person who shall erect such a device or sign, as aforesaid, and every sign owner who shall permit such a device or sign to remain on or near the public roads of this Commonwealth, and every landowner or tenant in possession who shall knowingly permit such a sign to remain on his land in view of any public road, shall be guilty of a misdemeanor, and upon conviction shall be fined not less than $5 nor more than $100.

History.
1918, p. 128; Michie Code 1942, § 3985a; 1956, c. 164.

§ 56-411. Removal of brush and trees from right-of-way.

Every railway company operating in this Commonwealth shall be required to clear from its right-of-way trees and brush for 100' on each side of public road crossings at grade when such trees or brush would otherwise obstruct the view of approaching trains.

Every railway company violating the provisions of this section shall be fined not more than $500 for each offense, to be imposed by the State Corporation Commission after due notice and hearing upon the company or the employee so offending.

History.
1918, p. 452; Michie Code 1942, § 3986a; 1996, cc. 114, 157.

§ 56-412. When trains shall be stopped before getting to railroad crossing.

Whenever railroads cross each other on the same grade in this Commonwealth, the trains shall be brought to a full stop at least fifty feet before getting to the crossing.

The provisions of this section shall not be applicable where the crossings of such roads are regulated by derailing switches, or other safety appliances, which prevent collision at crossings, nor where a flagman or watchman is stationed, or signal tower is located, and signals that the trains may cross in safety.

History.
Code 1919, § 3987.

§ 56-412.1. Railroad cars obstructing street or road; standing vehicle on railroad track.

It shall be unlawful for any railroad company, or any receiver or trustee operating a railroad, to obstruct for a longer period than five minutes the free passage on any street or road by standing cars or trains across the same, except a passenger train while receiving or discharging passengers, but a passway shall be kept open to allow normal flow of traffic; nor shall it be lawful to stand any wagon or other vehicle on the track of any railroad which will hinder or endanger a moving train; provided that when a train has been uncoupled, so as to make a passway, the time necessarily required, not exceeding three minutes, to pump up the air after the train has been recoupled shall not be included in considering the time such cars or trains were standing across such street or road. Any such railroad company, receiver or trustee, violating any of the provisions of this section shall be fined not less than $100 nor more than $500; provided that the fine may be $100 for each minute beyond the permitted time but the total fine shall not exceed $500.

This section shall not apply when the train is stopped due to breakdown, mechanical failure or emergency.

History.
1958, c. 242; 1976, c. 89.

§ 56-412.2. Ordinances conflicting with § 56-412.1.

No city, town or county shall adopt any ordinance, order or resolution in conflict with the provisions of § 56-412.1 and all ordinances, orders or resolutions of any city, town or county heretofore adopted in conflict with such section are hereby repealed to the extent of such conflict.

History.
1958, c. 242.

§ 56-412.3. Maintenance of certain roadways by Buchanan County.

The Board of Supervisors of Buchanan County is hereby authorized to maintain roadways located within the right-of-way of railroads pursuant to an agreement between Buchanan County and the railroad. However, nothing in this section shall obligate Buchanan County or the railroad to enter into any such agreement, nor shall Buchanan County or the railroad be precluded from including in any agreement any term, condition, or other lawful contractual provision. Any agreement made between Buchanan County and a railroad shall result in the complete immunity of the railroad from suit for any acts of the County in maintaining the roadways within the right-of-way of the railroad. The Board of Supervisors of Buchanan County shall cause all such roadways to be appropriately posted to warn users of such roadways that they are present on such roadways at their own risk.

History.
2010, c. 256.

ARTICLE 7.
SAFETY PROVISIONS.

§ 56-413.01. Locomotive and rail car standards.

All locomotives and rail cars operating over the tracks of a railroad company are subject to Federal Railroad Administration jurisdiction and shall be maintained in accordance with federal standards. Locomotives designed with spark arrestors shall be cleaned and maintained on a regularly scheduled basis.

History.
1996, cc. 114, 157.

§ 56-414. Bell and whistle or horn; when sounded.

Every railroad company shall provide each locomotive passing upon its road with a bell of ordinary size and steam whistle or horn, and such whistle or horn shall be sharply sounded outside cities and towns at least twice at a distance of not less than 300 yards nor more than 600 yards from the place where the railroad crosses upon the same level any public highway or crossing, and such bell shall be rung or whistle or horn sounded continuously or alternately until the locomotive has reached such highway crossing, and shall give such signals in cities and towns as their local governing bodies may require.

The governing body of any county, city, or town may by ordinance require locomotives to sound their whistle upon approaching designated railroad trestles or bridges having lengths of 100 feet or more. Notice of any such requirement shall be given by registered mail to the registered agent of the railroad operating in the affected county, city, or town. Affected railroads shall comply with any such ordinance within 30 days of receiving the notice.

The governing body of any county, city, or town may, by ordinance adopted following a public hearing, petition the State Corporation Commission to enter an order, pursuant to the Commission's Rules of Practice and Procedure, requiring locomotives to sound their whistle or horn at specifically identified private crossings in the same manner as required for public crossings. If the Commission should deem the blowing of the locomotive whistle at such private crossings to be necessary in the interest of safety under all relevant circumstances, then it shall enter an order. The affected railroad shall comply with the order within 90 days of receipt by its registered agent of notice sent by registered mail and the locality must first install stop signs on both sides of such private crossing, to be paid for by the locality or the landowner. The Commission may establish and collect a fee, not to exceed its actual costs, from applicants for an order to sound locomotive whistles pursuant to this section.

History.
Code 1919, § 3958; 1950, p. 944; 1956, c. 164; 1993, c. 483; 2003, c. 287.

§ 56-415. Penalty for violation of § 56-414.

Every officer or employee of any railway company, whose duty it shall be to carry out any of the provisions of § 56-414 and shall fail to do so, shall be punished by a fine not exceeding ten dollars for each offense.

History.
Code 1919, § 3960.

§ 56-416. Effect of failure to give statutory signals.

If the employees in charge of any railroad engine or train fail to give the signals required by law on approaching a grade crossing of a public highway not protected with an automatically operating gate, operating wigwag signal or other operating electrical or operating automatic crossing protection device, the fact that a traveler on such highway failed to exercise due care in approaching such crossing shall not bar recovery for an injury to or death of such traveler, nor for an injury to or the destruction of property in his charge, where such injury, death, or destruction results from a collision on such crossing between such engine or train and such traveler or the property in his charge, respectively; but the failure of the traveler to exercise such care may be considered in mitigation of damages.

History.
Code 1919, § 3959; 1964, c. 621.

§ 56-417.1. Clearance to be provided in construction, etc., of railroad structures.

No railroad, nor any person, firm or corporation operating any railroad shall hereafter construct or erect any track, building, sign, guidepost, switch stand or structure of any kind unless there is sufficient clearance provided for the safety of any employee or servant in the normal and customary operations of such railroad or any part thereof. The State Corporation Commission may inspect any such track or structure of any railroad in this Commonwealth, and upon complaint, or on its own motion and after timely notice to the railroad company affected and a hearing thereon, by proper order or orders, may require any railroad to make such changes as may be found necessary to safeguard and preserve the safety of its employees, servants and the general public. Provided, however, that this section shall not apply to any track, building, sign, guidepost, switch stand or structure of any kind in existence prior to January 1, 1953, nor to any private or industrial siding; provided, further, however, that any private or industrial siding constructed after January 1, 1953, shall, as far as practical, conform to the foregoing provisions.

History.
1952, c. 710.

§ 56-419. Duplicate switch keys of railroads; unlawful making, etc.; punishment.

It shall be unlawful for any person to make, buy, sell, or give away to any other person any duplicate key to any lock belonging to, or in use by, any railroad company in this Commonwealth on its switches or switch tracks, except upon the written order of that officer of the railroad company whose duty it is to distribute and issue switch lock keys to the employees of such railroad company. Any person violating the provisions of this section shall be deemed guilty of a misdemeanor.

History.
Code 1919, § 4019.

§ 56-419.2. Safety requirements applicable to vehicles transporting railroad employees.

A. As used in this section "motor vehicle" shall mean any motor vehicle designed for highway use, owned or operated by a railroad, whether or not it is used on the highways of this Commonwealth.

B. No motor vehicle shall be used for transporting one or more railroad employees three miles or more to or from a work situs unless such motor vehicle is constructed and maintained so as to provide safe transportation for such employees.

C. The requirement of safe transportation as set out hereinabove shall include, but not be limited to, the construction and maintenance of motor vehicles so as:

1. To provide an enclosure providing full cover from the elements for all railroad employees being so transported. Such enclosure shall be heated.

2. To provide within said enclosure fixed seats with backs for all railroad employees being so transported.

3. To provide a means to effectively communicate to the driver of the motor vehicle the emergency needs of the railroad employees being so transported.

D. The provisions of this section shall not apply to any motor vehicle when an emergency arises and such vehicle must be used to meet such an emergency.

E. The failure of any railroad company to correct any violation of this section within seven days from receipt of written notice thereof shall subject said company to the penalty provided by § 56-449; provided, however, any unsafe vehicle shall be removed immediately from service until repaired.

History.
1977, c. 628.

TITLE 58.1.

TAXATION.

SUBTITLE I.

TAXES ADMINISTERED BY THE DEPARTMENT OF TAXATION.

CHAPTER 10.

CIGARETTE TAX.

Article 1.

Excise Tax.

Section

ARTICLE 1.

EXCISE TAX.

§ 58.1-1015. Removal, reuse, unauthorized sale, etc., of stamps; counterfeit stamps; seizure and forfeiture; penalties.

A. Whoever removes or otherwise prepares any Virginia revenue stamp with intent to use, or cause the same to be used, after it has already been used, or buys, sells, offers for sale, or gives away any such washed or removed or restored stamps to any person for using or who used the same, or has in his possession any washed or restored or removed or altered stamp that has been removed from the article to which it has been previously affixed, or whoever for the purpose of indicating the payment of any tax hereunder reuses any stamp which has heretofore been used for the purpose of paying any tax provided in this article, or whoever manufactures, buys, sells, offers for sale, or has in his possession any reproduction or counterfeit of the Virginia revenue stamps provided for in this article, or whoever sells any Virginia revenue stamps not affixed to taxable cigarettes shall be subject to the penalty provided for in this section.

B. It shall be unlawful to sell or possess cigarettes that are affixed with a reproduction or counterfeit of Virginia revenue stamps. Such cigarettes and stamps shall be subject to seizure, forfeiture and destruction by the Department or any law-enforcement officer of the Commonwealth. All fixtures, equipment, materials and personal property used in substantial connection with the sale or possession of cigarettes that are affixed with a reproduction or counterfeit of Virginia revenue stamps in a knowing and intentional violation of this article shall be subject to seizure and forfeiture according to the procedures contained in Chapter 22.1 (§ 19.2-386.1 et seq.) of Title 19.2, applied mutatis mutandis.

C. Any person who knowingly violates subsection A with a total quantity of less than 40 revenue stamps shall be punished by a civil penalty of no more than $1,000. Any person who knowingly violates subsection B shall, for a second or subsequent offense involving a total quantity of less than 40 revenue stamps, be punished by a civil penalty of no more than $5,000 and, if applicable, the revocation by the Department of Taxation of his wholesale dealer license.

D. Any person who knowingly violates subsection B with a total quantity of 40 or more revenue stamps shall be punished by a civil penalty of no more than $2,000. Any person who knowingly violates subsection B shall, for a second or subsequent offense involving a total quantity of 40 or more revenue stamps, be punished by a civil penalty of no more than $50,000 and, if applicable, the revocation by the Department of Taxation of his wholesale dealer license.

The Attorney General is authorized to enforce the provisions of this section.

History.

Code 1950, § 58-757.14; 1960, c. 392, § 14; 1984, c. 675; 2003, c. 1010.

§ 58.1-1017. Sale, purchase, possession, etc., of cigarettes for purpose of evading tax; penalties.

A. Any person, except as otherwise provided by law, who sells, purchases, transports, receives, or possesses unstamped cigarettes shall be required to pay any tax owed pursuant to this chapter. In addition, such person shall be required to pay a civil penalty of (i) $2.50 per pack, up to $500, for the first violation by a legal entity within a 36-month period; (ii) $5 per pack, up to $1,000, for the second violation by the legal entity within a 36-month period; and (iii) $10 per pack, up to $50,000, for the third and any subsequent violation by the legal entity within a 36-month period, to be assessed and collected by the Department as other taxes are collected. In addition, where willful intent exists to defraud the Commonwealth of the tax levied under this chapter, such person shall be required to pay a civil penalty of $25 per pack, up to $250,000.

B. It shall be unlawful for any person, except as otherwise provided by law, to sell, purchase, transport, receive or possess less than 500 packages of cigarettes unless the same have been stamped in the manner required by law, for the purpose of evading the payment of the taxes on such products. Any person violating the provisions of this subsection is guilty of a Class 1 misdemeanor. Any person who is convicted of a second or subsequent violation of this subsection is guilty of a Class 6 felony, provided that the accused was at liberty as defined in § 53.1-151 between each conviction and it is admitted, or found by the jury or judge before whom the person is tried, that the accused was previously convicted of a violation of this subsection.

C. It shall be unlawful for any person, except as otherwise provided by law, to sell, purchase, transport, receive or possess 500 or more packages of cigarettes unless the same have been stamped in the manner required by law, for the purpose of evading the payment of the taxes on such products. Any person violating the provisions of this subsection shall be guilty of a Class 6 felony. Any person who is convicted of a second or subsequent violation of this subsection is guilty of a Class 5 felony, provided that the accused was at liberty as defined in § 53.1-151 between each conviction and it is admitted, or found by the jury or judge before whom the person is tried, that the accused was previously convicted of a violation of this subsection.

D. If a person who (i) has not been issued a permit to affix revenue stamps by the Department, as provided in § 58.1-1011, or (ii) is not a retail dealer who has lawfully purchased cigarettes from such permit holder has in his possession within the Commonwealth more than 30 packages of unstamped cigarettes, such possession shall be presumed to be for the purpose of evading the payment of the taxes due thereon. No civil penalty shall be imposed under this section for any unstamped cigarettes if a civil penalty under § 58.1-1013 has been paid for such unstamped cigarettes.

History.

Code 1950, § 58-757.17; 1960, c. 392, § 17; 1984, c. 675; 1992, c. 763; 2004, cc. 883, 996; 2005, c. 28; 2006, c. 409; 2010, cc. 35, 471; 2013, cc. 570, 624.

§ 58.1-1017.3. Fraudulent purchase of cigarettes; penalties.

Any person who purchases 5,000 (25 cartons) cigarettes or fewer using a forged business license, a business license obtained under false pretenses, a forged or invalid Virginia sales and use tax exemption certificate, or a Virginia sales and use tax exemption certificate obtained under false pretenses is guilty of a Class 1 misdemeanor for a first offense and a Class 6 felony for a second or subsequent offense. Any person who purchases more than 5,000 (25 cartons) cigarettes using a forged business license, a business license obtained under false pretenses, a forged or invalid Virginia sales and use tax exemption certificate, or a Virginia sales and use tax exemption certificate obtained under false pretenses is guilty of a Class 6 felony for a first offense and a Class 5 felony for a second or subsequent offense. Additionally, any person who violates the provisions of this section shall be assessed a civil penalty of (i) $2.50 per pack, but no less than $5,000, for a first offense; (ii) $5 per pack, but no less than $10,000, for a second such offense committed within a 36-month period; and (iii) $10 per pack, but no less than $50,000, for a third or subsequent such offense committed within a 36-month period. The civil penalties shall be assessed and collected by the Department as other taxes are collected.

The provisions of this section shall not preclude prosecution under any other statute.

History.

2015, cc. 273, 290.

CHAPTER 10.1.
ENFORCEMENT OF ILLEGAL SALE OR DISTRIBUTION OF CIGARETTES ACT.

Section

§ 58.1-1032. Applicability.

The provisions of this chapter shall not apply to (i) cigarettes allowed to be imported or brought into the United States for personal use or (ii) cigarettes sold or intended to be sold as duty-free merchandise by a duty-free sales enterprise in accordance with the provisions of 19 U.S.C. § 1555 (b) and any implementing regulations. This section, however, shall apply to cigarettes described in clause (ii) that are brought back into the customs territory for resale within the customs territory.

History.
2000, cc. 880, 901.

§ 58.1-1033. Prohibited acts.

It shall be unlawful for any person to:

1. Sell or distribute in the Commonwealth, acquire, hold, own, possess, or transport, for sale or distribution in the Commonwealth, or import, or cause to be imported, into the Commonwealth for sale or distribution in the Commonwealth (i) any cigarettes the package of which bears any statement, label, stamp, sticker, or notice indicating that the manufacturer did not intend the cigarettes to be sold, distributed, or used in the United States, including but not limited to labels stating "For Export Only," "U.S. Tax-Exempt," "For Use Outside U.S.," or similar wording; (ii) any cigarettes the package of which does not comply with (a) all requirements imposed by or pursuant to federal law regarding warnings and other information on packages of cigarettes manufactured, packaged, or imported for sale, distribution, or use in the United States, including but not limited to the precise warning labels specified in the Federal Cigarette Labeling and Advertising Act, 15 U.S.C. § 1333, or (b) all federal trademark and copyright laws; (iii) any cigarettes imported into the United States in violation of 26 U.S.C. § 5754 or 19 U.S.C. § 1681-1681b, or any other federal law or regulations; (iv) any cigarettes that such person otherwise knows or has reason to know the manufacturer did not intend to be sold, distributed, or used in the United States; or (v) any cigarettes for which there has not been submitted to the Secretary of the U.S. Department of Health and Human Services the list or lists of the ingredients added to tobacco in the manufacture of such cigarettes required by the Federal Cigarette Labeling and Advertising Act, 15 U.S.C. § 1335a;

2. Alter the package of any cigarettes, prior to sale or distribution to the ultimate consumer, so as to remove, conceal or obscure (i) any statement, label, stamp, sticker, or notice described in clause (i) of subdivision 1 or (ii) any health warning that is not specified in, or does not conform with the requirements of, the Federal Cigarette Labeling and Advertising Act, 15 U.S.C. § 1333; or

3. Affix any stamp required pursuant to Chapter 10 (§ 58.1-1000 et seq.) of this title to the package of any cigarettes described in subdivision 1 of this section or altered in violation of subdivision 2 of this section.

History.
2000, cc. 880, 901; 2002, c. 821.

§ 58.1-1037. Seizure.

Cigarettes that are acquired, held, owned, possessed, transported in, imported into, or sold or distributed in the Commonwealth in violation of this chapter shall be deemed contraband and shall be subject to seizure, forfeiture, destruction, or court-ordered assignment for use by a law-enforcement undercover operation. Such cigarettes shall be deemed contraband whether or not the violation of this chapter is with knowledge.

History.
2000, cc. 880, 901; 2012, cc. 362, 472.

CHAPTER 17.
MISCELLANEOUS TAXES.

ARTICLE 4.
MOTOR VEHICLE FUEL SALES TAX IN CERTAIN TRANSPORTATION DISTRICTS.

§§ 58.1-1718.1 through 58.1-1720: Repealed by Acts 2012, cc. 217 and 225, cl. 2, effective July 1, 2013.

§ 58.1-1721: Repealed by Acts 2009, c. 532, cl. 2, effective January 1, 2010.

§ 58.1-1722: Repealed by Acts 2012, cc. 217 and 225, cl. 2, effective July 1, 2013.

§ 58.1-1723: Repealed by Acts 2009, c. 532, cl. 2, effective January 1, 2010.

§§ 58.1-1724, 58.1-1724.1: Repealed by Acts 2012, cc. 217 and 225, cl. 2, effective July 1, 2013.

ARTICLE 4.1.
MOTOR VEHICLE FUEL SALES TAX IN CERTAIN LOCALITIES.

§ **58.1-1724.2:** Repealed by Acts 2012, cc. 217 and 225, cl. 2, effective July 1, 2013.

§ **58.1-1724.3:** Repealed by Acts 2009, cc. 864 and 871, cl. 5.

§ **58.1-1724.4:** Repealed by Acts 2012, cc. 217 and 225, cl. 2, effective July 1, 2013.

§§ **58.1-1724.5 through 58.1-1724.7:** Repealed by Acts 2009, cc. 864 and 871, cl. 5.

CHAPTER 18.
ENFORCEMENT, COLLECTION, REFUND, REMEDIES AND REVIEW OF STATE TAXES.

Article 1.

Collection of State Taxes.

ARTICLE 1.
COLLECTION OF STATE TAXES.

§ 58.1-1814. Criminal liability for failure to file returns or keep records.

A. Any corporate or partnership officer, as defined in § 58.1-1813, and any other person required by law or regulations made under authority thereof to make a return, keep any records or supply any information, for the purpose of the computation, assessment or collection of any state tax administered by the Department of Taxation, who willfully fails to make such returns, keep such records or supply such information, at the time or times required by law or regulations, shall, in addition to any other penalties provided by law, be guilty of a Class 1 misdemeanor.

B. Any person who willfully utilizes a device or software to falsify the electronic records of cash registers or other point-of-sale systems or otherwise manipulates transaction records that affect any state tax liability shall, in addition to any other penalties provided by law, be guilty of a Class 1 misdemeanor.

C. In addition to the criminal penalty provided in subsection B and any other civil or criminal penalty provided in this title, any person violating subsection B shall pay a civil penalty of $20,000, to be assessed and collected by the Department as other taxes are collected and deposited into the general fund.

History.

Code 1950, § 58-44.1; 1972, c. 363; 1984, c. 675; 2014, cc. 723, 785.

SUBTITLE II.
TAXES ADMINISTERED BY OTHER AGENCIES.

CHAPTER 21.
FUELS TAX.

§§ **58.1-2100 through 58.1-2147:** Repealed by Acts 2000, cc. 729 and 758, cl. 3, effective January 1, 2001.

CHAPTER 22.
VIRGINIA FUELS TAX ACT.

Article 1.

General Provisions.

Article 2.

Motor Fuel Licensing.

Article 3.

Motor Fuel Tax; Liability.

ARTICLE 1.
GENERAL PROVISIONS.

§ 58.1-2200. Title; nature of tax.

A. This chapter shall be known and may be cited as the "Virginia Fuels Tax Act."

B. All taxes levied under this chapter are imposed upon the ultimate consumer but are precollected as prescribed in this chapter. The levies and assessments imposed on licensees as provided in this chapter are imposed on them as agents of the Commonwealth for the precollection of the tax. The taxes levied under this chapter shall be collected and paid at those times, in the manner, and by those persons specified in this chapter.

History.
2000, cc. 729, 758.

§ 58.1-2201. Definitions.

As used in this chapter, unless the context requires otherwise:

"Alternative fuel" means a combustible gas, liquid or other energy source that can be used to generate power to operate a highway vehicle and that is neither a motor fuel nor electricity used to recharge an electric motor vehicle or a hybrid electric motor vehicle.

"Alternative fuel vehicle" means a vehicle equipped to be powered by a combustible gas, liquid, or other source of energy that can be used to generate power to operate a highway vehicle and that is neither a motor fuel nor electricity used to recharge an electric motor vehicle or a hybrid electric motor vehicle.

"Assessment" means a written determination by the Department of the amount of taxes owed by a taxpayer. Assessments made by the Department shall be deemed to be made when a written notice of assessment is delivered to the taxpayer by the Department or is mailed to the taxpayer at the last known address appearing in the Commissioner's files.

"Aviation consumer" means any person who uses in excess of 100,000 gallons of aviation jet fuel in any fiscal year and is licensed pursuant to Article 2 (§ 58.1-2204 et seq.) of this chapter.

"Aviation fuel" means aviation gasoline or aviation jet fuel.

"Aviation gasoline" means fuel designed for use in the operation of aircraft other than jet aircraft, and sold or used for that purpose.

"Aviation jet fuel" means fuel designed for use in the operation of jet or turbo-prop aircraft, and sold or used for that purpose.

"Blended fuel" means a mixture composed of gasoline or diesel fuel and another liquid, other than a de minimis amount of a product such as carburetor detergent or oxidation inhibitor, that can be used as a fuel in a highway vehicle.

"Blender" means a person who produces blended fuel outside the terminal transfer system.

"Bonded aviation jet fuel" means aviation jet fuel held in bonded storage under United States Customs Law and delivered into a fuel tank of aircraft operated by certificated air carriers on international flights.

"Bonded importer" means a person, other than a supplier, who imports, by transport truck or another means of transfer outside the terminal transfer system, motor fuel removed from a terminal located in another state in which (i) the state from which the fuel is imported does not require the seller of the fuel to collect motor fuel tax on the removal either at that state's rate or the rate of the destination state; (ii) the supplier of the fuel is not an elective supplier; or (iii) the supplier of the fuel is not a permissive supplier.

"Bulk plant" means a motor fuel storage and distribution facility that is not a terminal and from which motor fuel may be removed at a rack.

"Bulk user" means a person who maintains storage facilities for motor fuel and uses part or all of the stored fuel to operate a highway vehicle, watercraft, or aircraft.

"Bulk user of alternative fuel" means a person who maintains storage facilities for alternative fuel and uses part or all of the stored fuel to operate a highway vehicle.

"Commercial watercraft" means a watercraft employed in the business of commercial fishing, transporting persons or property for compensation or hire, or any other trade or business unless the watercraft is used in an activity of a type generally considered entertainment, amusement, or recreation. The definition shall include a watercraft owned by a private business and used in the conduct of its own business or operations, including but not limited to the transport of persons or property.

"Commissioner" means the Commissioner of the Department of Motor Vehicles.

"Corporate or partnership officer" means an officer or director of a corporation, partner of a partnership, or member of a limited liability company, who as such officer, director, partner or member is under a duty to perform on behalf of the corporation, partnership, or limited liability company the tax collection, accounting, or remitting obligations.

"Department" means the Department of Motor Vehicles, acting directly or through its duly authorized officers and agents.

"Designated inspection site" means any state highway inspection station, weigh station, agricultural inspection station, mobile station, or other location designated by the Commissioner or his designee to be used as a fuel inspection site.

"Destination state" means the state, territory, or foreign country to which motor fuel is directed for delivery into a storage facility, a receptacle, a container, or a type of transportation equipment for the purpose of resale or use. The term shall not include a tribal reservation of any recognized Native American tribe.

"Diesel fuel" means any liquid that is suitable for use as a fuel in a diesel-powered highway vehicle or watercraft. The term shall include undyed #1 fuel oil and undyed #2 fuel oil, but shall not include gasoline or aviation jet fuel.

"Distributor" means a person who acquires motor fuel from a supplier or from another distributor for subsequent sale.

"Dyed diesel fuel" means diesel fuel that meets the dyeing and marking requirements of 26 U.S.C. § 4082.

"Elective supplier" means a supplier who (i) is required to be licensed in the Commonwealth and (ii) elects to collect the tax due the Commonwealth on motor fuel that is removed at a terminal located in another state and has Virginia as its destination state.

"Electric motor vehicle" means a motor vehicle that uses electricity as its only source of motive power.

"End seller" means the person who sells fuel to the ultimate user of the fuel.

"Export" means to obtain motor fuel in Virginia for sale or distribution in another state, territory, or foreign country. Motor fuel delivered out-of-state by or for the seller constitutes an export by the seller, and motor fuel delivered out-of-state by or for the purchaser constitutes an export by the purchaser.

"Exporter" means a person who obtains motor fuel in Virginia for sale or distribution in another state, territory, or foreign country.

"Fuel" includes motor fuel and alternative fuel.

"Fuel alcohol" means methanol or fuel grade ethanol.

"Fuel alcohol provider" means a person who (i) produces fuel alcohol or (ii) imports fuel alcohol outside the terminal transfer system by means of a marine vessel, a transport truck, a tank wagon, or a railroad tank car.

"Gasohol" means a blended fuel composed of gasoline and fuel grade ethanol.

"Gasoline" means (i) all products that are commonly or commercially known or sold as gasoline and are suitable for use as a fuel in a highway vehicle, aircraft, or watercraft, other than products that have an American Society for Testing Materials octane number of less than 75 as determined by the motor method; (ii) a petroleum product component of gasoline, such as naphtha, reformate, or toluene; (iii) gasohol; and (iv) fuel grade ethanol. The term does not include aviation gasoline sold for use in an aircraft engine.

"Governmental entity" means (i) the Commonwealth or any political subdivision thereof or (ii) the United States or its departments, agencies, and instrumentalities.

"Gross gallons" means an amount of motor fuel measured in gallons, exclusive of any temperature, pressure, or other adjustments.

"Heating oil" means any combustible liquid, including but not limited to dyed #1 fuel oil, dyed #2 fuel oil, and kerosene, that is burned in a boiler, furnace, or stove for heating or for industrial processing purposes.

"Highway" means every way or place of whatever nature open to the use of the public for purposes of vehicular travel in the Commonwealth, including the streets and alleys in towns and cities.

"Highway vehicle" means a self-propelled vehicle designed for use on a highway.

"Hybrid electric motor vehicle" means a motor vehicle that uses electricity and another source of motive power.

"Import" means to bring motor fuel into Virginia by any means of conveyance other than in the fuel supply tank of a highway vehicle. Motor fuel delivered into Virginia from out-of-state by or for the seller constitutes an import by the seller, and motor fuel delivered into Virginia from out-of-state by or for the purchaser constitutes an import by the purchaser.

"Importer" means a person who obtains motor fuel outside of Virginia and brings that motor fuel into Virginia by any means of conveyance other than in the fuel tank of a highway vehicle. For purposes of this chapter, a motor fuel transporter shall not be considered an importer.

"In-state-only supplier" means (i) a supplier who is required to have a license and who elects not to collect the tax due the Commonwealth on motor fuel that is removed by that supplier at a terminal located in another state and has Virginia as its destination state or (ii) a supplier who does business only in Virginia.

"Licensee" means any person licensed by the Commissioner pursuant to Article 2 (§ 58.1-2204 et seq.) of this chapter or § 58.1-2244.

"Liquid" means any substance that is liquid above its freezing point.

"Motor fuel" means gasoline, diesel fuel, blended fuel, and aviation fuel.

"Motor fuel transporter" means a person who transports motor fuel for hire by means of a pipeline, a tank wagon, a transport truck, a railroad tank car, or a marine vessel.

"Net gallons" means the amount of motor fuel measured in gallons when adjusted to a temperature of 60 degrees Fahrenheit and a pressure of 14.7 pounds per square inch.

"Occasional importer" means any person who (i) imports motor fuel by any means outside the terminal transfer system and (ii) is not required to be licensed as a bonded importer.

"Permissive supplier" means an out-of-state supplier who elects, but is not required, to have a supplier's license under this chapter.

"Person" means any individual; firm; cooperative; association; corporation; limited liability company; trust; business trust; syndicate; partnership; limited liability partnership; joint venture; receiver; trustee in bankruptcy; club, society or other group or combination acting as a unit; or public body, including but not limited to the Commonwealth, any other state, and any agency, department, institution, political subdivision or instrumentality of the Commonwealth or any other state.

"Position holder" means a person who holds an inventory position of motor fuel in a terminal, as reflected on the records of the terminal operator. A person holds an "inventory position of motor fuel" when he has a contract with the terminal operator for the use of storage facilities and terminaling services for fuel at the terminal. The term includes a terminal operator who owns fuel in the terminal.

"Principal" means (i) if a partnership, all its partners; (ii) if a corporation, all its officers, directors, and controlling direct or indirect owners; (iii) if a limited liability company, all its members; and (iv) or an individual.

"Provider of alternative fuel" means a person who (i) acquires alternative fuel for sale or delivery to a bulk user or a retailer; (ii) maintains storage facili-

ties for alternative fuel, part or all of which the person sells to someone other than a bulk user or a retailer to operate a highway vehicle; (iii) sells alternative fuel and uses part of the fuel acquired for sale to operate a highway vehicle by means of a fuel supply line from the cargo tank of the vehicle to the engine of the vehicle; or (iv) imports alternative fuel into Virginia, by a means other than the usual tank or receptacle connected with the engine of a highway vehicle, for sale or use by that person to operate a highway vehicle.

"Rack" means a facility that contains a mechanism for delivering motor fuel from a refinery, terminal, or bulk plant into a transport truck, railroad tank car, or other means of transfer that is outside the terminal transfer system.

"Refiner" means any person who owns, operates, or otherwise controls a refinery.

"Refinery" means a facility for the manufacture or reprocessing of finished or unfinished petroleum products usable as motor fuel and from which motor fuel may be removed by pipeline or marine vessel or at a rack.

"Removal" means a physical transfer other than by evaporation, loss, or destruction. A physical transfer to a transport truck or other means of conveyance outside the terminal transfer system is complete upon delivery into the means of conveyance.

"Retailer" means a person who (i) maintains storage facilities for motor fuel and (ii) sells the fuel at retail or dispenses the fuel at a retail location.

"Retailer of alternative fuel" means a person who (i) maintains storage facilities for alternative fuel and (ii) sells or dispenses the fuel at retail, to be used to generate power to operate a highway vehicle.

"Supplier" means (i) a position holder, or (ii) a person who receives motor fuel pursuant to a two-party exchange. A licensed supplier includes a licensed elective supplier and licensed permissive supplier.

"System transfer" means a transfer (i) of motor fuel within the terminal transfer system or (ii) of fuel grade ethanol by transport truck or railroad tank car.

"Tank wagon" means a straight truck or straight truck/trailer combination designed or used to carry fuel and having a capacity of less than 6,000 gallons.

"Terminal" means a motor fuel storage and distribution facility (i) to which a terminal control number has been assigned by the Internal Revenue Service, (ii) to which motor fuel is supplied by pipeline or marine vessel, and (iii) from which motor fuel may be removed at a rack.

"Terminal operator" means a person who owns, operates, or otherwise controls a terminal.

"Terminal transfer system" means a motor fuel distribution system consisting of refineries, pipelines, marine vessels, and terminals, and which is a "bulk transfer/terminal system" under 26 C.F.R. Part 48.4081-1.

"Transmix" means (i) the buffer or interface between two different products in a pipeline shipment or (ii) a mix of two different products within a refinery or terminal that results in an off-grade mixture.

"Transport truck" means a tractor truck/semi-trailer combination designed or used to transport cargoes of motor fuel over a highway.

"Trustee" means a person who (i) is licensed as a supplier, an elective supplier, or a permissive supplier and receives tax payments from and on behalf of a licensed or unlicensed distributor, or other person pursuant to § 58.1-2231 or (ii) is licensed as a provider of alternative fuel and receives tax payments from and on behalf of a bulk user of alternative fuel, retailer of alternative fuel or other person pursuant to § 58.1-2252.

"Two-party exchange" means a transaction in which fuel is transferred from one licensed supplier to another licensed supplier pursuant to an exchange agreement, which transaction (i) includes a transfer from the person who holds the inventory position in taxable motor fuel in the terminal as reflected on the records of the terminal operator and (ii) is completed prior to removal of the product from the terminal by the receiving exchange partner.

"Undyed diesel fuel" means diesel fuel that is not subject to the United States Environmental Protection Agency or Internal Revenue Service fuel-dyeing requirements.

"Use" means the actual consumption or receipt of motor fuel by any person into a highway vehicle, aircraft, or watercraft.

"Watercraft" means any vehicle used on waterways.

"Wholesale price" means the price at the rack.

History.

2000, cc. 729, 758; 2001, c. 802; 2002, cc. 4, 7; 2003, c. 781; 2004, c. 340; 2006, cc. 594, 912; 2011, c. 165; 2012, cc. 729, 733; 2013, c. 766.

§ 58.1-2202. Regulations; forms.

The Commissioner may promulgate regulations and shall prescribe forms as shall be necessary to effectuate and enforce this chapter.

History.

2000, cc. 729, 758.

§ 58.1-2203. Exchange of information; penalties.

A. The Commissioner may, upon request from the officials entrusted with enforcing the fuels tax laws of any other state, forward to such officials any information that the Commissioner may have relative to the production, manufacture, refining, compounding, receipt, sale, use, transportation, or shipment by any person of such fuel.

B. The Commissioner may enter into written agreements with duly constituted tax officials of other states and of the United States for the inspection of tax returns, the making of audits, and the exchange of information relating to taxes administered by the Department pursuant to this chapter.

C. The Commissioner may divulge tax information to the Tax Commissioner, any commissioner of the revenue, director of finance or other authorized collector of county, city, or town taxes who, for the performance of his official duties, requests the same in writing setting forth the reasons for such request.

D. Any person to whom tax information is divulged pursuant to this section shall be subject to the prohibitions and penalties prescribed in § 58.1-3 as though that person were a tax official as defined in that section.

History.

2000, cc. 729, 758.

ARTICLE 2.

MOTOR FUEL LICENSING.

§ 58.1-2204. Persons required to be licensed.

A. A person shall obtain a license issued by the Commissioner before conducting the activities of:

1. A refiner, who shall be licensed as a supplier;
2. A supplier;
3. A terminal operator;
4. An importer;
5. An exporter;
6. A blender;
7. A motor fuel transporter;
8. An aviation consumer;
9. A bonded importer;
10. An elective supplier; or
11. A fuel alcohol provider.

B. A person who is engaged in more than one activity for which a license is required shall have a separate license for each activity, except as provided in subsection C.

C. 1. A person who is licensed as a supplier shall not be required to obtain a separate license for any other activity for which a license is required and shall be considered to have a license as a distributor.

2. A person who is licensed as an occasional importer shall not be required to obtain a license as a distributor.

3. A person who is licensed as a distributor shall not be required to obtain a separate license as an importer if the distributor acquires fuel for import only from an elective supplier or permissive supplier. Such licensed distributor shall not be required to obtain a separate license as an exporter.

4. A person who is licensed as a distributor or a blender shall not be required to obtain a separate license as a motor fuel transporter if he does not transport motor fuel for others for hire.

History.

2000, cc. 729, 758; 2003, c. 781; 2004, c. 340; 2012, c. 363.

§ 58.1-2205. Types of importers; qualification for license as an importer.

A. An applicant for a license as an importer shall indicate whether he is applying for a license as a bonded importer or an occasional importer.

B. A person shall not be licensed as more than one type of importer. A bulk user who imports motor fuel from a terminal of a supplier who is not an elective or a permissive supplier shall be licensed as a bonded importer. A bulk user who imports motor fuel from a bulk plant and is not required to be licensed as a bonded importer shall be licensed as an occasional importer. A bulk user who imports motor fuel only from a terminal of an elective or a permissive supplier shall not be required to be licensed as an importer.

History.

2000, cc. 729, 758.

§ 58.1-2206. Persons who may obtain a license.

A person who conducts the activities of a distributor or a permissive supplier may obtain a license issued by the Commissioner for that activity.

History.

2000, cc. 729, 758.

§ 58.1-2207. Restrictions on qualification for license as a distributor.

A bulk user of motor fuel shall not be licensed as a distributor.

History.

2000, cc. 729, 758.

§ 58.1-2208. License application procedure.

A. To obtain a license under this article, an applicant shall file an application with the Commissioner on a form provided by the Commissioner. An application shall include the applicant's name, address, federal employer identification number, and any other information required by the Commissioner.

B. An applicant for a license as a motor fuel transporter, supplier, terminal operator, importer, blender, distributor, or aviation consumer shall satisfy the following requirements:

1. If the applicant is a corporation, the applicant shall either be incorporated in the Commonwealth or authorized to transact business in the Commonwealth;

2. If the applicant is a limited liability company, the applicant shall be organized in the Commonwealth or authorized to transact business in the Commonwealth;

3. If the applicant is a limited liability partnership, the applicant shall either be formed in the Commonwealth or authorized to transact business in the Commonwealth; or

4. If the applicant is an individual or a general partnership, the applicant shall designate an agent for service of process and provide the agent's name and address.

C. An applicant for a license as a supplier, terminal operator, blender, or permissive supplier shall have a federal certificate of registry issued under 26 U.S.C. § 4101 that authorizes the applicant to enter into federal tax-free transactions in taxable motor fuel in the terminal transfer system. An applicant who is required to have a federal certificate of registry shall include the registration number of the certificate on the application for a license under this section. An applicant for a license as an importer, an exporter, or a distributor who has a federal certificate of registry issued under 26 U.S.C. § 4101 shall include the registration number of the certificate on the application for a license under this section.

D. An applicant for a license as an importer or distributor shall list on the application each state from which the applicant intends to import motor fuel and, if required by a state listed, shall be licensed or registered for motor fuel tax purposes in that state. If a state listed requires the applicant to be licensed or registered, the applicant shall provide the applicant's license or registration number of that state. A licensee who intends to import motor fuel from a state not listed on his application for an importer's license or a distributor's license shall provide the Commissioner written notice of such action before importing motor fuel from that state. The notice shall include the information that is required on the license application.

E. An applicant for a license as an exporter shall designate an agent located in Virginia for service of process and provide the agent's name and address. An applicant for a license as an exporter or distributor shall list on the application each state to which the applicant intends to export motor fuel received in Virginia by means of a transfer that is outside the terminal transfer system and, if required by a state listed, shall be licensed or registered for motor fuel tax purposes in that state. If a state listed requires the applicant to be licensed or registered, the applicant shall provide the applicant's license or registration number of that state. A licensee who intends to export motor fuel to a state not listed on his application for an exporter's license or a distributor's license shall provide the Commissioner written notice of such action before exporting motor fuel to that state. The notice shall include the information required on the license application.

History.

2000, cc. 729, 758; 2002, c. 7; 2012, c. 363.

§ 58.1-2209. Supplier election to collect tax on out-of-state removals.

A. An applicant for a license as a supplier may elect on the application to collect the tax due the Commonwealth on motor fuel that is removed at a terminal located in another state and has Virginia as its destination state. The Commissioner shall provide for this election on the application form. A supplier who makes the election allowed by this section shall be an elective supplier. A supplier who does not make the election allowed by this section shall be an in-state-only supplier. A supplier who does not make the election on the application for a supplier's license may make the election later by completing an election form provided by the Commissioner. A supplier who has not made the election shall not act as an elective supplier for purposes of this chapter.

B. A supplier who makes the election allowed by this section shall comply with all of the following with respect to motor fuel that is removed at a terminal located in another state and has Virginia as its destination state:

1. Collect the tax due the Commonwealth on the fuel;

2. Waive any defense that the Commonwealth lacks jurisdiction to require the supplier to collect the tax due the Commonwealth on the fuel under this chapter;

3. Report and pay the tax due on the fuel in the same manner as if the removal had occurred at a terminal located in Virginia;

4. Keep records of the removal of the fuel and submit to audits concerning the fuel as if the removal had occurred at a terminal located in Virginia; and

5. Report sales by the supplier to a person who is not licensed in the state where the removal occurred if the destination state is Virginia.

C. A supplier who makes the election allowed by this section (i) acknowledges that the Commonwealth imposes the requirements listed in subsection B of this section on the supplier under its general police power and (ii) submits to the jurisdiction of the Commonwealth only for purposes related to the administration of this chapter.

History.

2000, cc. 729, 758.

§ 58.1-2210. Permissive supplier election to collect tax on out-of-state removals.

A. An out-of-state supplier who is not required to be licensed under this chapter may elect to obtain a license and thereby become a permissive supplier. An out-of-state supplier who does not make this election shall not act as a permissive supplier for motor fuel that is removed at a terminal in another state and has Virginia as its destination state.

B. An out-of-state supplier who elects to be licensed as a permissive supplier shall comply with (i) the same requirements imposed on a supplier and (ii) all of the following with respect to motor fuel that is removed by the permissive supplier at a terminal located in another state and has Virginia as its destination state:

1. Collect the tax due the Commonwealth on the fuel;

2. Waive any defense that the Commonwealth lacks jurisdiction to require the supplier to collect the tax due the Commonwealth on the motor fuel under this chapter;

3. Report and pay the tax due on the fuel in the same manner as if the removal had occurred at a terminal located in Virginia;

4. Keep records of the removal of the fuel and submit to audits concerning the fuel as if the removal had occurred at a terminal located in Virginia; and

5. Report sales by the supplier to a person who is not licensed in the state where the removal occurred if the destination state is Virginia.

C. An out-of-state supplier who makes the election allowed by this section (i) acknowledges that the Commonwealth imposes the requirements listed in subsection B on the supplier under its general police power and (ii) submits to the jurisdiction of the Commonwealth only for purposes related to the administration of this chapter.

History.
2000, cc. 729, 758.

§ 58.1-2211. Bond or certificate of deposit requirements.

A. An applicant for a license as a terminal operator, supplier, importer, blender, permissive supplier, distributor, or aviation consumer shall file with the Commissioner a bond or certificate of deposit. The bond or certificate of deposit shall be conditioned upon compliance with the requirements of this chapter, be payable to the Commonwealth, and be in the form required by the Commissioner. The amount of the bond or certificate of deposit shall be as follows:

1. For an applicant for a license as a (i) terminal operator, (ii) supplier who is a position holder or a person who receives motor fuel pursuant to a two-party exchange, (iii) bonded importer, or (iv) permissive supplier, the amount shall be $2,000,000; and

2. For an applicant for a license as (i) a supplier who is a fuel alcohol provider but is neither a position holder nor a person who receives motor fuel pursuant to a two-party exchange; (ii) an occasional importer; (iii) a distributor; (iv) a blender; or (v) an aviation consumer, the amount shall be three times the applicant's average expected monthly tax liability under this chapter, as determined by the Commissioner. The amount shall not be less than $2,000 nor more than $300,000.

B. An applicant for a license both as a distributor and as a bonded importer shall file only the bond or certificate of deposit required of a bonded importer. An applicant for two or more of the licenses listed in subdivision A 2 may file one bond or certificate of deposit that covers the combined liabilities of the applicant under all the activities, in which event the amount of the bond or certificate of deposit for the combined activities shall not exceed $300,000.

C. When notified to do so by the Commissioner, a person who has filed a bond or certificate of deposit and who holds a license listed in subdivision A 2 shall file an additional bond or certificate of deposit in the amount required by the Commissioner. The person shall file the additional bond or certificate of deposit within thirty days after receiving the notice from the Commissioner. However, the amount of the initial bond or certificate of deposit and any additional bond or certificate of deposit filed by the licensee shall not exceed $300,000.

Any licensee who disagrees with the Commissioner's decision requiring new or additional security shall be entitled to a hearing. Such matter shall, within thirty days, be scheduled for a prompt hearing before the Commissioner after written request for such hearing is received by the Commissioner.

History.
2000, cc. 729, 758; 2006, c. 594.

§ 58.1-2212. Grounds for denial of license.

A. The Commissioner may refuse to issue a license under this article to an applicant if (i) the applicant or (ii) any principal of the applicant has:

1. Had a license or registration issued under prior law or this chapter canceled by the Commissioner for cause;

2. Had a motor fuel license or registration issued by another state canceled for cause;

3. Had a federal Certificate of Registry issued under § 4101 of the Internal Revenue Code, or a similar federal authorization, revoked;

4. Been convicted of any offense involving fraud or misrepresentation; or

5. Been convicted of any other offense that indicates that the applicant may not comply with this chapter if issued a license.

B. For purposes of subdivisions 1, 2 and 3 of subsection A, it shall be sufficient cause for the Commissioner to refuse to issue a license if the canceled or revoked license, registration or Certificate of Registry was held by a business entity of which the applicant, or any principal of the applicant, was a principal.

History.
2000, cc. 729, 758; 2003, c. 781.

§ 58.1-2213. Issuance of license.

Upon approval of an application, the Commissioner shall issue to the applicant a license and a duplicate copy of the license for each place of business of the applicant. A supplier's license shall indicate the category of the supplier. A licensee shall display the license issued under this chapter in a conspicuous place at each place of business of the licensee. A license shall not be transferable and shall remain in effect until surrendered or canceled.

History.
2000, cc. 729, 758.

§ 58.1-2214. Notice of discontinuance, sale or transfer of business.

A. A licensee who discontinues in the Commonwealth the business for which the license was issued shall notify the Commissioner in writing of such discontinuance and shall surrender the license to the Commissioner. The notice shall state the effective date of the discontinuance and, if the licensee has transferred the business or otherwise relinquished control to another person by sale or otherwise, the date of the sale or transfer and the name and address of the person to whom the business is transferred or relinquished. The notice shall also include any other information required by the Commissioner.

B. If the licensee is a supplier, all taxes for which the supplier is liable under this chapter but are not yet due shall be due on the date of the discontinuance. If the supplier has transferred the business to another person and does not give the notice required by this section, the person to whom the business was transferred shall be liable for the amount of any tax owed by the supplier to the Commonwealth on the date the business was transferred. The liability of the person to whom the business was transferred shall not exceed the value of the property acquired from the supplier.

History.
2000, cc. 729, 758.

§ 58.1-2215. License cancellation.

A. The Commissioner may cancel the license of any person licensed under this article, upon written notice sent by certified mail to the licensee's last known address appearing in the Commissioner's files, for any of the following reasons:

1. Filing by the licensee of a false report of the data or information required by this chapter;
2. Failure, refusal, or neglect of the licensee to file a report required by this chapter;
3. Failure of the licensee to pay the full amount of the tax due or pay any penalties or interest due as required by this chapter;
4. Failure of the licensee to keep accurate records of the quantities of motor fuel received, produced, refined, manufactured, compounded, sold, or used in Virginia;
5. Failure to file a new or additional bond or certificate of deposit upon request of the Commissioner pursuant to § 58.1-2211;
6. Conviction of the licensee or a principal of the licensee for any act prohibited under this chapter;
7. Failure, refusal, or neglect of a licensee to comply with any other provision of this chapter or any regulation promulgated pursuant to this chapter; or
8. A change in the ownership or control of the business.

B. Upon cancellation of any license for any cause listed in subsection A, the tax levied under this chapter shall become due and payable on (i) all untaxed motor fuel held in storage or otherwise in the possession of the licensee and (ii) all motor fuel sold, delivered, or used prior to the cancellation on which the tax has not been paid.

C. The Commissioner may cancel any license upon the written request of the licensee.

D. Upon cancellation of any license and payment by the licensee of all taxes due, including all penalties accruing due to any failure by the licensee to comply with the provisions of this chapter, the Commissioner shall cancel and surrender the bond or certificate of deposit filed by such licensee.

History.
2000, cc. 729, 758; 2006, c. 594.

§ 58.1-2216. Records and lists of license applicants and licensees.

A. The Commissioner shall keep a record of (i) applicants for a license under this chapter; (ii) persons to whom a license has been issued under this chapter; and (iii) persons holding a current license issued under this chapter, by license category.

B. The Commissioner shall provide a list of licensees to any licensee, as well as to any unlicensed distributor who requests a copy. The list shall state the name and business address of each licensee on the list and may include other information determined appropriate by the Commissioner.

History.
2000, cc. 729, 758; 2004, c. 340.

ARTICLE 3.
MOTOR FUEL TAX; LIABILITY.

§ 58.1-2217. (Contingent expiration date — see notes) Taxes levied; rate.

A. There is hereby levied a tax at the rate of seventeen and one-half cents per gallon on gasoline and gasohol. Beginning January 1, 2015, the tax rate shall be 5.1 percent of the statewide average wholesale price of a gallon of unleaded regular gasoline for the applicable base period, excluding federal and state excise taxes, as determined by the Commissioner.

In computing the average wholesale price of a gallon of gasoline, the Commissioner shall use the period from December 1 through May 31 as the base period for such determination for the immediately following period beginning July 1 and ending December 31, inclusive. The period from June 1 through November 30 shall be the next base period for the immediately following period beginning January 1 and ending June 30, inclusive. In no case shall the average wholesale price computed for purposes of this section be less than the statewide average wholesale price of a gallon of unleaded regular gasoline on February 20, 2013.

B. There is hereby levied a tax at the rate of seventeen and one-half cents per gallon on diesel fuel. Beginning January 1, 2015, the tax rate shall be six percent of the statewide average wholesale price of a gallon of diesel fuel for the applicable base period, excluding federal and state excise taxes, as determined by the Commissioner.

In computing the average wholesale price of a gallon of diesel fuel, the Commissioner shall use the period from December 1 through May 31 as the base period for such determination for the immediately following period beginning July 1 and ending December 31, inclusive. The period from June 1 through November 30 shall be the next base period for the immediately following period beginning January 1 and ending June 30, inclusive. In no case shall the average wholesale price computed for purposes of this section be less than the statewide average wholesale price of a gallon of diesel fuel on February 20, 2013.

C. Blended fuel that contains gasoline shall be taxed at the rate levied on gasoline. Blended fuel that contains diesel fuel shall be taxed at the rate levied on diesel fuel.

D. There is hereby levied a tax at the rate of five cents per gallon on aviation gasoline. Any person, whether or not licensed under this chapter, who uses, acquires for use, sells or delivers for use in highway vehicles any aviation gasoline shall be liable for the tax at the rate levied on gasoline and gasohol, along with any penalties and interest that may accrue.

E. There is hereby levied a tax at the rate of five cents per gallon on aviation jet fuel purchased or acquired for use by a user of aviation fuel other than an aviation consumer. There is hereby levied a tax at the rate of five cents per gallon upon the first 100,000 gallons of aviation jet fuel, excluding bonded aviation jet fuel, purchased or acquired for use by any aviation consumer in any fiscal year. There is hereby levied a tax at the rate of one-half cent per gallon on all aviation jet fuel, excluding bonded aviation jet fuel, purchased or acquired for use by an aviation consumer in excess of 100,000 gallons in any fiscal year. Any person, whether or not licensed under this chapter, who uses, acquires for use, sells or delivers for use in highway vehicles any aviation jet fuel taxable under this chapter shall be liable for the tax imposed at the rate levied on diesel fuel, along with any penalties and interest that may accrue.

F. In accordance with § 62.1-44.34:13, a storage tank fee is imposed on each gallon of gasoline, aviation gasoline, diesel fuel (including dyed diesel fuel), blended fuel, and heating oil sold and delivered or used in the Commonwealth.

History.

2000, cc. 729, 758; 2007, c. 896; 2013, c. 766.

Section set out twice.

The section above is set out as amended by Acts 2013, c. 766, cl. 1. For this section as amended by Acts 2013, c. 766, cl. 2, see the following section, also numbered 58.1-2217.

Contingent expiration date. — Acts 2013, c. 766, cl. 2, provides that § 58.1-2217 is amended and reenacted January 1, 2015, if the United States Congress has not enacted legislation granting the Commonwealth the authority to compel the remote sellers to collect state and local retail sales and use tax for sales made in the Commonwealth by such date.

Editor's note.

Acts 2007, c. 896, cl. 24, as added by Acts 2013, c. 766, cl. 12, provides: "That the provisions of the twenty-second enactment of this act shall not apply to any revenues generated pursuant to subsections B and E of § 58.1-2217, subsection A of § 58.1-2249, or § 58.1-2289 or 58.1-2701 of the Code of Virginia."

Acts 2013, c. 766, cl. 18, provides: "That should any portion of this act be held unconstitutional by a court of competent jurisdiction, the remaining portions of this act shall remain in effect."

§ 58.1-2217. (Contingent effective date — see notes) Taxes levied; rate.

A. There is hereby levied a tax at the rate of seventeen and one-half cents per gallon on gasoline and gasohol. Beginning July 1, 2013, the seventeen and one-half cents per gallon tax shall be replaced with a tax at a rate of 3.5 percent of the statewide average wholesale price of a gallon of unleaded regular gasoline for the applicable base period, excluding federal and state excise taxes, as determined by the Commissioner.

In computing the average wholesale price of a gallon of unleaded regular gasoline, the Commissioner shall use the period from December 1 through May 31 as the base period for such determination for the immediately following period beginning July 1 and ending December 31, inclusive. The period from June 1 through November 30 shall be the next base period for the immediately following period beginning January 1 and ending June 30, inclusive. In no case shall the average wholesale price computed for purposes of this section be less than the statewide average wholesale price of a gallon of unleaded regular gasoline on February 20, 2013.

B. There is hereby levied a tax at the rate of seventeen and one-half cents per gallon on diesel fuel. Beginning July 1, 2013, the seventeen and one-half cents per gallon tax shall be replaced with a tax at a rate of six percent of the statewide average wholesale price of a gallon of diesel fuel for the applicable base period, excluding federal and state excise taxes, as determined by the Commissioner.

In computing the average wholesale price of a gallon of diesel fuel the Commissioner shall use the period from December 1 through May 31 as the base period for such determination for the immediately following period beginning July 1 and ending December 31, inclusive. The period from June 1 through November 30 shall be the next base period for the immediately following period beginning January 1 and ending June 30, inclusive. In no case shall the average wholesale price computed for purposes of this section be less than the statewide average wholesale price of a gallon of diesel fuel on February 20, 2013.

C. Blended fuel that contains gasoline shall be taxed at the rate levied on gasoline. Blended fuel that contains diesel fuel shall be taxed at the rate levied on diesel fuel.

D. There is hereby levied a tax at the rate of five cents per gallon on aviation gasoline. Any person, whether or not licensed under this chapter, who uses, acquires for use, sells or delivers for use in highway vehicles any aviation gasoline shall be liable for the tax at the rate levied on gasoline and gasohol, along with any penalties and interest that may accrue.

E. There is hereby levied a tax at the rate of five cents per gallon on aviation jet fuel purchased or acquired for use by a user of aviation fuel other than an aviation consumer. There is hereby levied a tax at the rate of five cents per gallon upon the first 100,000 gallons of aviation jet fuel, excluding bonded aviation jet fuel, purchased or acquired for use by any aviation consumer in any fiscal year. There is hereby levied a tax at the rate of one-half cent per gallon on all aviation jet fuel, excluding bonded aviation jet fuel, purchased or acquired for use by an aviation consumer in excess of 100,000 gallons in any fiscal year. Any person, whether or not licensed under this chapter, who uses, acquires for use, sells or delivers for use in highway vehicles any aviation jet fuel taxable under this chapter shall be liable for the tax imposed at the rate levied on diesel fuel, along with any penalties and interest that may accrue.

F. In accordance with § 62.1-44.34:13, a storage tank fee is imposed on each gallon of gasoline, aviation gasoline, diesel fuel (including dyed diesel fuel), blended fuel, and heating oil sold and delivered or used in the Commonwealth.

History.

2000, cc. 729, 758; 2007, c. 896; 2013, c. 766.

Section set out twice.

The section above is as amended by Acts 2013, c. 766, cl. 2. For this section as amended by Acts 2013, c. 766, cl. 1, see the preceding section, also numbered 58.1-2217.

Contingent effective date. — Acts 2013, c. 766, cl. 2, provides that § 58.1-2217 is amended and reenacted January 1, 2015, if the United States Congress has not enacted legislation granting the Commonwealth the authority to compel the remote sellers to collect state and local retail sales and use tax for sales made in the Commonwealth by such date.

Editor's note.

Acts 2007, c. 896, cl. 24, as added by Acts 2013, c. 766, cl. 12 provides: "That the provisions of the twenty-second enactment of this act shall not apply to any revenues generated pursuant to subsections B and E of § 58.1-2217, subsection A of § 58.1-2249, or § 58.1-2289 or 58.1-2701 of the Code of Virginia."

Acts 2013, c. 766, cl. 18 provides: "That should any portion of this act be held unconstitutional by a court of competent jurisdiction, the remaining portions of this act shall remain in effect."

§ 58.1-2218. Point of imposition of motor fuels tax.

The tax levied pursuant to § 58.1-2217 is imposed at the point that the motor fuel is:

1. Removed from a refinery or a terminal and, upon removal, is subject to the federal excise tax imposed by 26 U.S.C. § 4081;
2. Imported by a system transfer to a refinery or a terminal and, upon importation, is subject to the federal excise tax imposed by 26 U.S.C. § 4081;
3. Imported by a means of transfer outside the terminal transfer system for sale, use, or storage in Virginia and would have been subject to the federal excise tax imposed by 26 U.S.C. § 4081 if it had been removed at a terminal or bulk plant rack in Virginia instead of being imported;
4. If the motor fuel is gasohol, (i) removed from a terminal or distribution facility, unless the removed fuel is received by a supplier for subsequent sale or (ii) imported into Virginia outside the terminal transfer system by a means other than a marine vessel, a transport truck, or a railroad tank car;
5. If the motor fuel is blended fuel, made within Virginia or imported into Virginia; or
6. Transferred within the terminal transfer system and, upon transfer, is subject to the federal excise tax imposed by 26 U.S.C. § 4081.

History.

2000, cc. 729, 758; 2003, c. 781.

§ 58.1-2219. Liability for tax on removals from a terminal.

A. The tax imposed pursuant to § 58.1-2217 at the point that motor fuel is removed by a system transfer from a terminal in Virginia shall be paid by the position holder of the fuel; however, if the position holder is not the terminal operator, the terminal operator and position holder shall be jointly and severally liable for the tax.

B. The tax imposed pursuant to § 58.1-2217 at the point that motor fuel is removed at a terminal rack in Virginia shall be payable by the person that first receives the fuel upon its removal from the terminal. If the motor fuel is first received by an unlicensed distributor, the supplier of the fuel shall be liable for payment of the tax due on the fuel. If the motor fuel is sold by a person who is not licensed as a supplier, then (i) the terminal operator and (ii) the person selling the fuel shall be jointly and severally liable for payment of the tax due on the fuel. If the motor fuel removed is not dyed diesel fuel but the shipping document issued for the fuel states that the fuel is dyed diesel fuel, the terminal operator, the supplier, and the person removing the fuel shall be jointly and severally liable for payment of the tax due on the fuel.

History.
2000, cc. 729, 758.

§ 58.1-2220. Liability for tax on imports.

A. The tax imposed pursuant to § 58.1-2217 at the point that motor fuel is imported by a system transfer (i) to a refinery shall be payable by the refiner or (ii) to a terminal shall be jointly and severally payable by the person importing the fuel and by the terminal operator.

B. The tax imposed pursuant to § 58.1-2217 at the point that motor fuel is removed from a terminal rack located in another state and has Virginia as its destination state shall be payable:

1. If the importer of the fuel is a licensed supplier in Virginia and the fuel is removed for the supplier's own account for use in Virginia, by the supplier;

2. If the supplier of the fuel is licensed in Virginia as an elective supplier or a permissive supplier, by the importer of the fuel to the supplier as trustee; or

3. If subdivisions 1 and 2 do not apply, by the importer of the fuel when filing a return with the Commissioner.

C. The tax imposed pursuant to § 58.1-2217 at the point that motor fuel is removed from a bulk plant located in another state shall be payable by the person that imports the fuel.

History.
2000, cc. 729, 758.

§ 58.1-2221: Repealed by Acts 2003, c. 781, cl. 2.

§ 58.1-2222. Liability for tax on blended fuel.

A. The tax imposed pursuant to § 58.1-2217 at the point that blended fuel is made in Virginia shall be payable by the blender. The number of gallons of blended fuel on which the tax is payable is the difference between the number of gallons of blended fuel made and the number of gallons of previously taxed motor fuel used to make the blended fuel.

B. The tax imposed pursuant to § 58.1-2217 at the point that blended fuel is imported to Virginia shall be payable by the importer.

C. The following blended fuel shall be considered to have been made by the supplier of gasoline or undyed diesel fuel used in the blend:

1. An in-line-blend made by combining a liquid with gasoline or undyed diesel fuel as the fuel is delivered at a terminal rack into the motor fuel storage compartment of a transport truck or a tank wagon; and

2. A kerosene splash-blend made when kerosene is delivered into a motor fuel storage compartment of a transport truck or a tank wagon and undyed diesel fuel is also delivered into the same storage compartment, if the buyer of the kerosene notified the supplier before or at the time of delivery that the kerosene would be used to make a splash-blend.

History.
2000, cc. 729, 758.

§ 58.1-2223. Liability for tax on fuel transferred within terminal transfer system.

The tax imposed pursuant to § 58.1-2217 at the point that motor fuel is transferred within the terminal transfer system shall be jointly and severally payable by the supplier of the fuel, the person receiving the fuel, and the terminal operator of the terminal at which the fuel was transferred.

History.
2000, cc. 729, 758.

§ 58.1-2224. Tax on unaccounted for motor fuel losses; liability.

A. There is hereby levied a tax at the rate specified by § 58.1-2217 annually on taxable unaccounted for motor fuel losses at a terminal. "Taxable unaccounted for motor fuel losses" means the number of gallons of unaccounted for motor fuel losses that exceed one-half of one percent of the number of net gallons removed from the terminal during the year by a system transfer or at the terminal rack. "Unaccounted for motor fuel losses" means the difference between (i) the amount of motor fuel in inventory at the terminal at the beginning of the year plus the amount of motor fuel received by the terminal during the year and (ii) the amount of motor fuel in inventory at the terminal at the end of the year plus the amount of motor fuel removed from the terminal during the year. Accounted for motor fuel losses which have been approved by the Commissioner or motor fuel losses constituting part of a transmix shall not constitute unaccounted for motor fuel losses.

B. The terminal operator whose motor fuel is unaccounted for shall be liable for the tax imposed by this section, together with a penalty equal to the amount of tax payable. Motor fuel received by a terminal operator and not shown on an informational return filed by the terminal operator with the Commissioner as having been removed from the terminal shall be presumed to be unaccounted for motor fuel losses. A terminal operator may rebut this presumption by establishing that motor fuel received at a terminal, but not shown on an informational return as having been removed from the terminal, was an accounted for loss or constitutes part of a transmix.

History.
2000, cc. 729, 758.

§ 58.1-2225. Backup tax; liability.

A. There is hereby levied a tax at the rate specified in § 58.1-2217 on the following:

1. Dyed diesel fuel that is used to operate a highway vehicle for a taxable use other than a use allowed under 26 U.S.C. § 4082;

2. Motor fuel that was allowed an exemption from the motor fuel tax and was then used for a taxable purpose; and

3. Motor fuel that is used to operate a highway vehicle after an application for a refund of tax paid on the motor fuel is made or allowed on the basis that the motor fuel was used for an off-highway purpose.

B. The operator of a highway vehicle that uses motor fuel that is taxable under this section is liable for the tax. If the highway vehicle that uses the fuel is owned by or leased to a motor carrier, the operator of the highway vehicle and the motor carrier shall be jointly and severally liable for the tax. If the end seller of motor fuel taxable under this section knew or had reason to know that the motor fuel would be used for a purpose that is taxable under this section, the operator of the highway vehicle and the end seller shall be jointly and severally liable for the tax.

C. The tax liability imposed by this section shall be in addition to any other penalty imposed pursuant to this chapter.

D. Persons diverting motor fuel into Virginia that had an original destination outside of Virginia shall incur liability for the tax levied for such motor fuel, as specified in § 58.1-2217, and shall be subject to the reporting and payment requirements set forth in subsection E of § 58.1-2230.

History.
2000, cc. 729, 758; 2003, c. 781.

§ 58.1-2226. Exemptions from tax.

No tax shall be levied or collected pursuant to this chapter on:

1. Motor fuel sold and delivered to a governmental entity for the exclusive use by the governmental entity. This exemption shall not apply with respect to fuel sold or delivered to any person operating under contract with the governmental entity;

2. Motor fuel sold and delivered to a nonprofit charitable organization that is exempt from taxation under § 501(c)(3) of the Internal Revenue Code and which is organized and operated exclusively for the purpose of providing charitable, long-distance, advanced life-support, air transportation services using emergency medical services vehicles for low-income medical patients in the Commonwealth, for the exclusive use of such organization in the operation of an aircraft;

3. Bonded aviation jet fuel;

4. Dyed diesel fuel, except as provided in subdivision A 1 of § 58.1-2225;

5. Motor fuel removed, by transport truck or another means of transfer outside the terminal transfer system, from a terminal for export, if the supplier of the motor fuel collects tax on the fuel at the rate of the motor fuel's destination state; or

6. Heating oil, as defined in § 58.1-2201.

History.
2000, cc. 729, 758; 2015, cc. 502, 503.

§ 58.1-2227. Sales of aviation jet fuel to licensed aviation consumers.

A licensed aviation consumer required to file a monthly return and remit taxes to the Department pursuant to § 58.1-2230 shall not be required to remit tax to a supplier or distributor for purchases of aviation jet fuel.

History.
2000, cc. 729, 758.

§ 58.1-2228. Exempt access cards; exempt access codes.

A. A licensed distributor, licensed importer or, in the case of aviation jet fuel, a licensed aviation consumer shall only remove motor fuel from a terminal by means of a supplier-issued exempt access card or exempt access code if (i) the motor fuel will be resold to a governmental entity or an organization exempt from tax under subdivision 2 of § 58.1-2226 for a purpose that is exempt from the tax or (ii) the aviation jet fuel will be used by the aviation consumer or resold to a licensed aviation consumer. The use of such exempt access card or exempt access code shall constitute a representation by the licensed distributor, licensed importer or licensed aviation consumer that the removal of the motor fuel is permitted. A supplier shall be authorized to rely on this representation. A licensed distributor or licensed importer who does not resell motor fuel removed from a terminal by means of an exempt access card or exempt access code to an exempt governmental unit or an organization exempt from tax under subdivision 2 of § 58.1-2226 is liable for any tax due on the fuel. A licensed distributor or licensed importer who does not resell aviation jet fuel removed from a terminal by means of an exempt access card or exempt access code to a licensed aviation consumer is liable for any tax due on the aviation jet fuel.

B. A supplier who issues to, or authorizes another person to issue to, another person an exempt access card or an exempt access code that enables the person to buy motor fuel without paying the tax on the fuel shall determine if the person is exempt from the tax or, in the case of aviation jet fuel, is a licensed aviation consumer allowed to purchase aviation jet fuel without payment of tax. A supplier is liable for tax due on motor fuel purchased at retail by use of an exempt access card or an exempt access code issued to a person who is not exempt from the tax or, in the case of aviation jet fuel, is not a licensed aviation consumer allowed to purchase aviation jet fuel without payment of tax.

C. A person to whom an exempt access card or exempt access code is issued for use at a terminal is liable for any tax due on fuel purchased with the exempt access card or exempt access code for a purpose that is not exempt. A person who misuses an exempt access card or exempt access code by purchasing fuel with the card or code for a purpose that is not exempt is liable for the tax due on the fuel. The provisions of this subsection shall apply to the misuse of a card or code that allows a person to purchase aviation jet fuel without paying the tax.

D. The tax liability imposed by this section shall be in addition to any other penalty imposed pursuant to this chapter.

History.
2000, cc. 729, 758.

§ 58.1-2229. Removals by out-of-state bulk user.

An out-of-state bulk user shall not remove motor fuel from a terminal in the Commonwealth for use in the state in which the bulk user is located unless the bulk user is licensed under this chapter as an exporter.

History.
2000, cc. 729, 758.

ARTICLE 4.

PAYMENT AND REPORTING OF TAX ON MOTOR FUEL.

§ 58.1-2230. When tax return and payment are due.

A. A return for the tax on motor fuel and gasohol levied by this chapter shall be filed with the Commissioner and be in the form and contain the information required by the Commissioner. The return and the payment for the tax on motor fuel levied by this chapter shall be due for each full month in a calendar year. Any return and payment required under this section shall be deemed timely filed if received by the Commissioner by midnight of the twentieth day of the second month succeeding the month for which the return and payment are due. Each return shall report tax liabilities that accrue in the month for which the return is due.

B. Returns and payments shall be (i) postmarked on or before the fifteenth day of the second month succeeding the month for which the return and payment are due or (ii) received by the Department by the twentieth day of the second month succeeding the month for which the return and payment are due. However, a monthly return of the tax for the month of May shall be (i) postmarked by June 25 or (ii) received by the Commissioner by the last business day the Department is open for business in June.

If a tax return and payment due date falls on a Saturday, Sunday, or a state or banking holiday, the return shall be postmarked on or before the fifteenth day of the second month succeeding the month for which the return and payment are due or received by the Department by midnight of the next business day the Department is open for business. This provision shall not apply to a return of the tax for the month of May.

A return and payment shall be deemed postmarked if it carries the official cancellation mark of the United States Postal Service or other postal or delivery services.

C. The following shall file a monthly return as required by this section:

1. A refiner;
2. A terminal operator;
3. A supplier;
4. A distributor;
5. An importer to include a bonded importer;
6. A blender;
7. An aviation consumer;
8. An elective supplier; and
9. A fuel alcohol provider.

D. Notwithstanding the provisions of any other section in this chapter, the Commissioner may require all or certain licensees to file tax returns and payments electronically.

E. Persons incurring liability under § 58.1-2225 for the backup tax on motor fuel shall file a return together with a payment of tax due within 30 calendar days of incurring such liability.

History.
2000, cc. 729, 758; 2002, c. 7; 2003, c. 781.

§ 58.1-2231. Remittance of tax to supplier.

A. A distributor shall remit tax due on motor fuel removed at a terminal rack to the supplier of the fuel. A licensed distributor shall not be required to remit the tax to the supplier until the date the supplier is required to pay the tax to the Commonwealth or to another state. All tax payments received by a supplier shall be held in trust by the supplier until the supplier remits the tax payment to the Commonwealth or to another state, and the supplier shall constitute the trustee for such tax payments. The date by which an unlicensed distributor is required to remit the tax to a supplier shall be governed by agreement between the supplier and the unlicensed distributor.

B. A licensed exporter shall remit tax due on motor fuel removed at a terminal rack to the supplier of the fuel. The date by which an exporter shall remit tax shall be governed by the law of the destination state of the exported motor fuel.

C. A licensed importer shall remit tax due on motor fuel removed at a terminal rack of a permissive or an elective supplier to the supplier of the fuel. A licensed importer who removes fuel from a terminal rack of a permissive or an elective supplier shall not be required to remit the tax to the supplier until the date the supplier is required to pay the tax to the Commonwealth.

D. The license of a licensed distributor, exporter or importer who fails to pay the full amount of tax required by this chapter is subject to cancellation as provided in § 58.1-2215.

History.
2000, cc. 729, 758.

§ 58.1-2232. Notice of cancellation or reissuance of licenses; effect of notice.

A. If the Commissioner cancels the license of a distributor, importer, or aviation consumer, the Commissioner shall notify all suppliers of the cancellation. If the Commissioner issues a license to a distributor, importer or aviation consumer whose license was previously canceled, the Commissioner shall notify all suppliers of the issuance.

B. A supplier who sells motor fuel to a distributor, importer or aviation consumer after receiving notice from the Commissioner that the Commissioner has canceled the distributor's, importer's or aviation consumer's license shall be jointly and severally liable with the distributor, importer or aviation consumer for any tax due on motor fuel the supplier sells to the distributor, importer or aviation consumer after receiving the notice; however, the supplier shall not be liable for tax due on motor fuel sold to a previously unlicensed distributor, importer or aviation consumer after the supplier receives notice from the Commissioner that the Commissioner has issued another license to the distributor, importer or aviation consumer.

C. If the Commissioner cancels the license of a supplier, the Commissioner shall notify all licensed distributors, exporters, importers and aviation consumers of the cancellation. If the Commissioner issues a license to a supplier whose license was previously canceled, the Commissioner shall notify all licensed distributors, exporters, importers and aviation consumers of the issuance.

D. A licensed distributor, exporter, importer, or aviation consumer who purchases motor fuel from a supplier after receiving notice from the Commissioner that the Commissioner has canceled the supplier's license shall be jointly and severally liable with the supplier for any tax due on motor fuel purchased from the supplier after receiving the notice; however, the licensed distributor, exporter, importer, or aviation consumer shall not be liable for tax due on motor fuel purchased from a previously unlicensed supplier after the licensee receives notice from the Commissioner that the Commissioner has issued another license to the supplier.

History.
2000, cc. 729, 758; 2002, c. 7.

§ 58.1-2233. Deductions; percentage discount.

A. A licensed importer who removes motor fuel from a terminal rack of a permissive or an elective supplier or licensed distributor may deduct from the amount of tax otherwise payable to a supplier the amount calculated on motor fuel that the licensee received from the supplier and resold to a governmental entity, or resold to an organization described in subdivision 2 of § 58.1-2226 for use in the operation of an aircraft if, when removing the fuel, the licensee used an exempt access card or exempt access code specified by the supplier to notify the supplier of the licensee's intent to resell the fuel in an exempt sale.

B. A licensed importer who removes motor fuel from a terminal rack of a permissive supplier, an elective supplier, or a licensed distributor may deduct from the amount of tax otherwise payable to a supplier the amount calculated on aviation jet fuel that the licensee received from the supplier and resold to a licensed aviation consumer if, when removing the fuel, the licensee used an exempt access card or exempt access code specified by the supplier to notify the supplier of the licensee's intent to resell the aviation jet fuel to a licensed aviation consumer.

C. A licensed distributor who pays the tax due a supplier by the date the supplier is required to remit the tax to this Commonwealth may deduct from the amount due a discount of one percent of the amount of tax payable. A licensed importer who (i) removes motor fuel from a terminal rack of a permissive or an elective supplier and (ii) pays the tax due to the supplier by the date the supplier is required to remit the tax to the Commonwealth may deduct from the amount due a discount of one percent of the amount of tax payable. A supplier shall not directly or indirectly deny this discount to a licensed distributor or licensed importer who pays the tax due the supplier by the date the supplier is required to remit the tax to the Commonwealth.

History.
2000, cc. 729, 758.

§ 58.1-2234. Monthly reconciling returns.

A. A licensed distributor or a licensed importer who deducts exempt sales under subsection A of § 58.1-2233 or sales of aviation jet fuel to a licensed aviation consumer under subsection B of § 58.1-2233 when paying tax to a supplier shall file a monthly reconciling return for the exempt sales and sales to a licensed aviation consumer. The return shall list the following information and any other information required by the Commissioner:

1. The number of gallons for which a deduction was taken during the month, by supplier;

2. The number of gallons sold in exempt sales during the month, by type of sale, and the purchasers of the fuel in the exempt sales; and

3. The number of gallons of aviation jet fuel sold without collection of the tax during the month, and the purchasers of the fuel.

B. If the number of gallons for which a licensed distributor or licensed importer takes a deduction during a month exceeds the number of exempt gallons sold or, in the case of aviation jet fuel, the number of gallons sold without collection of the tax, the licensed distributor or licensed importer shall pay tax on the difference at the rate imposed by § 58.1-2217. The licensed distributor or licensed importer shall not be allowed a percentage discount on any tax payable under this subsection.

C. If the number of gallons for which a licensed distributor or licensed importer takes a deduction during a month is less than the number of exempt gallons sold or, in the case of aviation jet fuel, is less than the number of gallons sold without collection of the tax, the Commissioner shall refund the amount of tax paid on the difference. The Commissioner shall reduce the amount of the refund by the amount of the percentage discount received on the fuel.

History.
2000, cc. 729, 758.

§ 58.1-2235. Information required on return filed by supplier.

A. A return of a supplier shall list all of the following information and any other information required by the Commissioner:

1. The number of gallons of tax-paid motor fuel received by the supplier during the month, sorted by type of fuel, seller, point of origin, destination state, and carrier;

2. The number of gallons of motor fuel removed at a terminal rack during the month from the account of the supplier, sorted by type of fuel, person receiving the fuel, terminal code, and carrier;

3. The number of gallons of motor fuel removed during the month for export, sorted by type of fuel, person receiving the fuel, terminal code, destination state, and carrier;

4. The number of gallons of motor fuel removed during the month from a terminal located in another state for conveyance to Virginia, as indicated on the shipping document for the fuel, sorted by type of fuel, person receiving the fuel, terminal code, and carrier;

5. The number of gallons of motor fuel the supplier sold during the month to the following, sorted by type of fuel, exempt entity, person receiving the fuel, terminal code, and carrier:

a. A governmental entity whose use of fuel is exempt from the tax;

b. A licensed aviation consumer purchasing aviation jet fuel;

c. A licensed distributor or importer who resold the motor fuel to a governmental unit whose use of fuel is exempt from the tax, as indicated by the distributor or importer;

d. A licensed distributor or importer who resold aviation jet fuel to a licensed aviation consumer as indicated by the distributor or importer;

e. A licensed exporter who resold the motor fuel to a person whose use of the fuel is exempt from tax in the destination state, as indicated by the exporter;

f. A nonprofit charitable organization which is exempt from taxation under § 501(c)(3) of the Internal Revenue Code and which is organized and operated exclusively for the purpose of providing charitable, long-distance, advanced life-support, air transportation services using emergency medical services vehicles for low-income medical patients in the Commonwealth, for the exclusive use of such organization in the operation of an aircraft; and

g. A licensed distributor or importer who resold the motor fuel to a nonprofit charitable organization which is exempt from taxation under § 501(c)(3) of the Internal Revenue Code and which is organized and operated exclusively for the purpose of providing charitable, long-distance, advanced life-support, air transportation services using emergency medical services vehicles for low-income medical patients in the Commonwealth, for the exclusive use of such organization in the operation of an aircraft; and

6. The amount of discounts allowed under subsection C of § 58.1-2233 on motor fuel sold during the month to licensed distributors or licensed importers.

B. Suppliers shall not require information identifying who purchased exempt fuel from persons licensed under this chapter.

History.
2000, cc. 729, 758; 2015, cc. 502, 503.

§ 58.1-2236. Deductions and discounts allowed a supplier when filing a return.

A. The supplier may deduct from the next monthly return those tax payments that were not remitted for the previous month to the supplier by (i) a licensed distributor or (ii) a licensed importer who removed the motor fuel on which the tax is due from a terminal of an elective or a permissive supplier. A supplier shall not be liable for the tax such a licensee owes the supplier but fails to pay. If such licensee pays the tax owed to a supplier after the supplier deducts the amount of such tax on a return, the supplier shall remit the payment to the Commissioner with the next monthly return filed subsequent to receipt of the tax.

B. A supplier who timely files a return with the payment due may deduct, from the amount of tax payable with the return, an administrative discount of one-tenth of one percent of the amount of tax payable to the Commonwealth, not to exceed $5,000 per month.

C. A supplier who sells motor fuel directly to an unlicensed distributor or to a bulk user, retailer, or user of the fuel may take one-half of the same percentage discount on the fuel that a licensed distributor may take under subsection C of § 58.1-

2233 when making deferred payments of tax to the supplier.

D. When filing a return, a supplier who issues or authorizes the issuance of an exempt access card or an exempt access code to a person that enables the person to buy motor fuel at retail without paying tax on the fuel may deduct the amount of tax imposed on fuel purchased with the exempt access card or exempt access code. The amount of tax imposed on fuel purchased at retail with an exempt access card or exempt access code is the amount that was imposed on the fuel when it was delivered to the retailer of the fuel.

History.
2000, cc. 729, 758.

§ 58.1-2237. Duties of supplier as trustee.

A. All tax payments due to the Commonwealth received by a supplier pursuant to § 58.1-2231 shall be held by the supplier as trustee in trust for the Commonwealth, and a supplier has a fiduciary duty to remit to the Commissioner the amount of tax received by the supplier. A supplier shall be liable for the taxes paid to him.

B. A supplier shall notify a licensed distributor, licensed exporter, or licensed importer who received motor fuel from the supplier during a reporting period of the number of taxable gallons received. The supplier shall give this notice after the end of each reporting period and before the licensee is required to remit to the supplier the amount of tax due on the fuel.

C. A supplier of motor fuel at a terminal shall notify the Commissioner within 10 business days after a return is due of any licensed distributor or licensed importer who did not pay the tax due the supplier when the supplier filed his return. The notice shall be transmitted to the Commissioner in the form required by the Commissioner.

D. A supplier who receives a payment of tax shall not apply the payment to a debt that the person making the payment owes the supplier for motor fuel purchased from the supplier.

History.
2000, cc. 729, 758; 2004, c. 340.

§ 58.1-2238. Returns and discounts of importers.

A. A monthly return of a bonded importer or an occasional importer shall contain the following information concerning motor fuel imported during the period covered by the return and any other information required by the Commissioner:

1. The number of gallons of imported motor fuel acquired from a supplier who collected the tax due the Commonwealth on the fuel;

2. The number of gallons of imported motor fuel acquired from a supplier who did not collect the tax due the Commonwealth on the fuel, listed by source state, supplier, and terminal; and

3. If he is an occasional importer, the number of gallons of imported motor fuel acquired from a bulk plant, listed by bulk plant.

B. An importer shall not deduct an administrative discount under subsection C of § 58.1-2233 from the amount remitted with a return. An importer who imports motor fuel received from an elective supplier or a permissive supplier may deduct the percentage discount allowed by subsection C of § 58.1-2233 when remitting tax to the supplier, as trustee, for payment to the Commonwealth. An importer who imports motor fuel received from a supplier who is not an elective supplier or a permissive supplier shall not deduct the percentage discount allowed by subsection C of § 58.1-2233 when filing a return for the tax due.

History.
2000, cc. 729, 758; 2003, c. 781.

§ 58.1-2239. Returns and discounts of aviation consumers.

A. A monthly return of an aviation consumer shall state the number of gallons of aviation jet fuel acquired from a supplier or distributor who did not collect the tax due the Commonwealth on the fuel, listed by source state, supplier or distributor, and terminal or other source, with respect to aviation jet fuel purchased during the period covered by the return and any other information required by the Commissioner.

B. An aviation consumer shall be allowed a credit for aviation jet fuel purchased, on which tax has already been paid. The amount of such credit shall not exceed the amount of fuel taxes due from such aviation consumer, nor shall the credit be carried forward to the next fiscal year.

History.
2000, cc. 729, 758.

§ 58.1-2240. Informational returns of terminal operators.

A terminal operator shall file a monthly informational return with the Commissioner that shows the amount of motor fuel received or removed from the terminal during the month. The return is due by the twentieth day of the second month following the month covered by the return. The return shall contain the following information and any other information required by the Commissioner:

1. The number of gallons of motor fuel received in inventory at the terminal during the month and each position holder for the fuel;

2. The number of gallons of motor fuel removed from inventory at the terminal during the month and, for each removal, the position holder for the fuel and the destination state of the fuel; and

3. The number of gallons of motor fuel gained or lost at the terminal during the month.

History.
2000, cc. 729, 758.

§ 58.1-2241. Informational returns of motor fuel transporters.

A motor fuel transporter shall file a monthly informational return with the Commissioner.

The return required by this section is due by the twentieth day of the second month following the month covered by the return. The return shall contain the following information and any other information required by the Commissioner:

1. The name and address of each person from whom the transporter received motor fuel outside Virginia for delivery in Virginia, the amount of motor fuel received, the date the motor fuel was received, and the destination state of the fuel; and

2. The name and address of each person from whom the transporter received motor fuel in Virginia for delivery outside Virginia, the amount of motor fuel delivered, the date the motor fuel was delivered, and the destination state of the fuel.

History.
2000, cc. 729, 758; 2006, c. 594.

§ 58.1-2242. Return of distributors and certain other licensees; exports.

A. A distributor or any other licensee required to make monthly reports who exports motor fuel from a bulk plant located in Virginia shall file a monthly return with the Commissioner identifying the exports. The return is due by the twentieth day of the second month following the month covered by the return. The return shall serve as a claim for a refund by the distributor or such other licensee for tax paid to the Commonwealth on the exported motor fuel.

B. The return shall contain the following information and any other information required by the Commissioner:

1. The number of gallons of motor fuel exported during the month;

2. The destination state of the motor fuel exported during the month; and

3. A certification that the distributor or such other licensee has paid to the destination state of the motor fuel exported during the month, or will timely pay, the amount of tax due that state on the fuel.

History.
2000, cc. 729, 758; 2003, c. 781.

§ 58.1-2243. Use of name and account number on return.

When a transaction with a person licensed under this chapter is required to be reported on a return, the return must state the licensee's name and account number as stated on the lists compiled by the Commissioner under § 58.1-2216.

History.
2000, cc. 729, 758.

ARTICLE 5. PROVISIONS APPLICABLE TO ALTERNATIVE FUELS.

§ 58.1-2244. Persons required to be licensed.

A person shall obtain a license before conducting the activities of:

1. A provider of alternative fuel;
2. A bulk user of alternative fuel;
3. A retailer of alternative fuel; or
4. A person who fuels his highway vehicle from his private source, if the alternative fuels tax on alternative fuel used in the vehicle has not been paid.

History.
2000, cc. 729, 758.

§ 58.1-2245. License application procedure.

To obtain a license under this article, an applicant shall file an application with the Commissioner on a form provided by the Commissioner. The application shall include the applicant's name, address, federal employer identification number, and any other information required by the Commissioner.

History.
2000, cc. 729, 758.

§ 58.1-2246. Bond or certificate of deposit requirements.

A. An applicant for a license as a (i) provider of alternative fuel, (ii) retailer of alternative fuel or bulk user of alternative fuel who stores highway and nonhighway alternative fuel in the same storage tank, or (iii) retailer of alternative fuel or a bulk user of alternative fuel who wishes to defer the remittance of tax to the provider until the date the provider of alternative fuel is required to pay the tax to the Commonwealth, shall file with the Commissioner a bond or certificate of deposit.

B. The amount of the bond or certificate of deposit shall be three times the applicant's average expected monthly tax liability under this article, as determined by the Commissioner. The amount shall not be less than $2,000 nor more than $300,000. An applicant who is also required to file a bond or a certificate of deposit under § 58.1-2211 to obtain a license as a distributor of motor fuel may file a single bond or certificate of deposit under § 58.1-2211 for the combined amount and shall not be required to file a bond or certificate of deposit for more than $300,000 for the combined amount.

C. A bond or certificate of deposit filed under this section shall be conditioned upon compliance with this chapter, be payable to the Commonwealth, and be in the form required by the Commissioner. The Commissioner may require a bond or a certificate of deposit issued under this section to be adjusted in accordance with the procedure set out in subsection C of § 58.1-2211 for adjusting a bond or certificate of deposit filed by a distributor of motor fuel.

History.
2000, cc. 729, 758; 2006, c. 594.

§ 58.1-2247. Issuance, denial or cancellation of license.

A. The Commissioner shall issue a license to each applicant whose application is approved. A license shall not be transferable and remains in effect until surrendered or canceled.

B. The Commissioner may refuse to issue a license under this article to an applicant if (i) the applicant or (ii) any principal of the applicant that is a business entity has:

1. Had a license or registration issued under prior law or this chapter canceled by the Commissioner for cause;
2. Had an alternative fuel license or registration issued by another state canceled for cause;
3. Had a federal Certificate of Registry issued under § 4101 of the Internal Revenue Code, or a similar federal authorization, revoked;
4. Been convicted of any offense involving fraud or misrepresentation; or
5. Been convicted of any other offense that indicates that the applicant may not comply with this chapter if issued a license.

C. The Commissioner may cancel the license of any person licensed under this article, upon written notice sent by certified mail to the licensee's last known address appearing in the Commissioner's files, for any of the following reasons:

1. Filing by the licensee of a false report of the data or information required by this article;
2. Failure, refusal, or neglect of the licensee to comply with any provision of this chapter or any regulation promulgated pursuant to this chapter;
3. Failure of the licensee to pay the full amount of the tax required by this article;
4. Failure of the licensee to keep accurate records of the quantities of alternative fuel received, produced, refined, manufactured, compounded, sold, or used in the Commonwealth;
5. Failure to file a new or additional bond or certificate of deposit upon request of the Commissioner pursuant to § 58.1-2246; or
6. Conviction of the licensee or a principal of the licensee for any prohibited act listed under this article.

D. Upon cancellation of any license for any cause listed in subsection C, the tax levied under this chapter shall become due and payable on (i) all untaxed alternative fuel held in storage or otherwise in the possession of the licensee and (ii) all alternative fuel sold, delivered, or used prior to the cancellation on which the tax has not been paid.

E. The Commissioner may cancel any license upon the written request of the licensee.

F. Upon cancellation of any license and payment by the licensee of all taxes due, including all penalties accruing due to any failure by the licensee to comply with the provisions of this article, the Commissioner shall cancel and surrender the bond or certificate of deposit filed by such licensee.

History.
2000, cc. 729, 758; 2006, c. 594.

§ 58.1-2248. Notice of discontinuance, sale or transfer of business.

A. A licensee who discontinues in the Commonwealth the business for which the license was issued shall notify the Commissioner in writing of such discontinuance and shall surrender the license to the Commissioner. The notice shall state the effective date of the discontinuance and, if the license holder has transferred the business or otherwise relinquished control to another person by sale or otherwise, the date of the sale or transfer and the name and address of the person to whom the business is transferred or relinquished. The notice shall also include any other information required by the Commissioner.

B. All taxes for which the license holder is liable under this article but are not yet due shall be due on the date of the discontinuance. If the license holder has transferred the business to another person and does not give the notice required by this section, the person to whom the business was transferred shall be liable for the amount of any tax owed by the license holder to the Commonwealth on the date the business was transferred. The liability of the person to whom the business was transferred shall not exceed the value of the property acquired from the license holder.

History.
2000, cc. 729, 758.

§ 58.1-2249. Tax on alternative fuel.

A. There is hereby levied a tax at the rate levied on gasoline and gasohol on liquid alternative fuel used to operate a highway vehicle by means of a vehicle supply tank that stores fuel only for the purpose of supplying fuel to operate the vehicle. There is hereby levied a tax at a rate equivalent to that levied on gasoline and gasohol on all other alternative fuel used to operate a highway vehicle. The Commissioner shall determine the equivalent rate applicable to such other alternative fuels.

B. **(Contingent expiration date)** In addition to any tax imposed by this article, there is hereby levied an annual license tax of $64 per vehicle on each highway vehicle registered in Virginia that is an electric motor vehicle or an alternative fuel vehicle. However, no license tax shall be levied on any vehicle that (i) is subject to the tax on fuels levied pursuant to subsection A, (ii) is subject to the federal excise tax levied under § 4041 of the Internal Revenue Code, (iii) is a moped as defined in § 46.2-100, or (iv) is registered under the International Registration Plan. If such a highway vehicle is registered for a period other than one year as provided under § 46.2-646, the license tax shall be multiplied by the number of years or fraction thereof that the vehicle will be registered. The revenues generated by this subsection shall be deposited in the Highway Maintenance and Operating Fund established pursuant to § 33.2-1530.

B. **(Contingent effective date)** In addition to any tax imposed by this article, there is hereby levied an annual license tax of $50 per vehicle on each highway vehicle registered in Virginia that is an electric motor vehicle. If such a highway vehicle is registered for a period other than one year as provided under § 46.2-646, the license tax shall be multiplied by the number of years or fraction thereof that the vehicle will be registered.

History.

2000, cc. 729, 758; 2007, c. 896; 2012, cc. 729, 733; 2013, c. 766; 2014, cc. 14, 43.

Subsection B set out twice. — The first version of subsection B is set out as amended by Acts 2013, c. 766. The second version of subsection B set out above is effective when the amendments by Acts 2013, c. 766 expire.

Contingent effective date for subsection B. — Acts 2013, c. 766, cl. 14 provides: "That the provisions of this act that generate additional revenue through state taxes or fees for transportation (i) throughout the Commonwealth and in Planning District 8 and Planning District 23 or (ii) in any other Planning District that becomes subject to the state taxes or fees imposed solely in Planning Districts pursuant to this act shall expire on December 31 of any year in which the General Assembly appropriates any of such additional revenues for any non-transportation-related purpose or transfers any of such additional revenues that are to be deposited into the Commonwealth Transportation Fund or any subfund thereof pursuant to general law for a non-transportation-related purpose. In the event a local government of any county or city wherein the additional taxes and fees are levied appropriates or allocates any of such additional revenues to a non-transportation purpose, such locality shall not be the direct beneficiary of any of the revenues generated by the taxes or fees in the year immediately succeeding the year in which revenues where appropriated or allocated to a non-transportation purpose."

Editor's note.

Acts 2007, c. 896, cl. 24, as added by Acts 2013, c. 766, cl. 12, provides: "That the provisions of the twenty-second enactment of this act shall not apply to any revenues generated pursuant to subsections B and E of § 58.1-2217, subsection A of § 58.1-2249, or § 58.1-2289 or 58.1-2701 of the Code of Virginia."

Acts 2013, c. 766, cl. 18 provides: "That should any portion of this act be held unconstitutional by a court of competent jurisdiction, the remaining portions of this act shall remain in effect."

Acts 2014, cc. 14 and 43, cl. 2 provides: "That the Commissioner of the Department of Motor Vehicles shall establish a process to refund, without interest, any portion of the annual license tax collected pursuant to subsection B of § 58.1-2249 of the Code of Virginia on hybrid electric motor vehicles, as defined under § 58.1-2201 of the Code of Virginia, that is attributable to registration years beginning on or after July 1, 2014."

At the direction of the Virginia Code Commission, the reference to the Highway Maintenance and Operating Fund was updated to conform to Acts 2014, c. 805.

§ 58.1-2250. Exemptions from tax.

No tax shall be levied or collected pursuant to this article on:

1. Alternative fuel sold and delivered to a governmental entity for the exclusive use by the governmental entity. This exemption shall not apply with respect to alternative fuel sold or delivered to any person operating under contract with the governmental entity;
2. Alternative fuel sold and delivered to a nonprofit charitable organization that is exempt from taxation under § 501(c)(3) of the Internal Revenue Code and that is organized and operated exclusively for the purpose of providing charitable, long-distance, advanced life-support, air transportation services using emergency medical services vehicles for low-income medical patients in the Commonwealth, for the exclusive use of such organization in the operation of an aircraft; or
3. Alternative fuel produced by the owner or lessee of an agricultural operation, as defined in § 3.2-300, and used (i) exclusively for farm use by the owner or lessee or (ii) in any motor vehicles operated by the producer of such fuel.

History.

2000, cc. 729, 758; 2009, c. 530; 2015, cc. 502, 503.

§ 58.1-2251. Liability for tax; filing returns; payment of tax.

A. A bulk user of alternative fuel or retailer of alternative fuel who stores highway and nonhighway alternative fuel in the same storage tank shall be liable for the tax imposed by this article, and shall file tax returns and remit taxes in accordance with subsection D. The tax payable by a bulk user of alternative fuel or retailer of alternative fuel is imposed at the point that alternative fuel is withdrawn from the storage tank.

B. A provider of alternative fuel who sells or delivers alternative fuel shall be liable for the tax imposed by this article (i) on sales to a bulk user of alternative fuel or retailer of alternative fuel who stores highway product in a separate storage tank or (ii) if the alternative fuel is sold or used by the provider of alternative fuel for highway use.

C. The owner of a highway vehicle subject to an annual license tax pursuant to subsection B of § 58.1-2249 shall be liable for such annual license tax. The annual license tax shall be due when the highway vehicle is first registered in Virginia and upon each subsequent renewal of registration.

D. 1. Each (i) bulk user of alternative fuel or retailer of alternative fuel liable for tax pursuant to subsection A and (ii) provider of alternative fuel liable for the tax pursuant to subsection B shall file a monthly tax return with the Department. The tax on alternative fuel levied by this article, except for the annual license tax imposed under subsection B of § 58.1-2249, that is required to be remitted to the Commonwealth shall be payable to the Commonwealth not later than the date on which the return is due. A return and payment shall be (i) postmarked on or before the fifteenth day of the second month succeeding the month for which the return and payment are due or (ii) received by the Department by the twentieth day of the second month succeeding the month for which the return and payment are due. However, a monthly return of the tax for the month of May shall be (i) postmarked by June 25 or (ii) received by the Commissioner by the last business day the Department is open for business in June.

2. If a tax return and payment due date falls on a Saturday, Sunday, or a state or banking holiday, the return shall be postmarked on or before the fifteenth day of the second month succeeding the month for which the return and payment are due or received by the Department by midnight of the next business day the Department is open for business. This provision shall not apply to a return of the tax for the month of May.

3. A return and payment shall be deemed postmarked if it carries the official cancellation mark of the United States Postal Service or other postal or delivery service.

4. A return shall be filed with the Commissioner and shall be in the form and contain the information required by the Commissioner.

History.
2000, cc. 729, 758; 2002, c. 7; 2013, c. 766.

§ 58.1-2252. Remittance of tax to provider of alternative fuel.

A purchaser of alternative fuel, other than a bulk user of alternative fuel or a retailer of alternative fuel who is liable for the tax pursuant to subsection A of § 58.1-2251, shall remit the tax due on the fuel to the provider of the fuel. A bulk user of alternative fuel or retailer of alternative fuel who has posted a bond in accordance with § 58.1-2246 shall not be required to remit the tax to the provider until the date the provider is required to pay the tax to the Commonwealth. All tax payments received by a provider of alternative fuel from a bulk user of alternative fuel or retailer of alternative fuel shall be held in trust by the provider until the provider remits the tax payments to the Commonwealth, and the provider shall constitute the trustee for such tax payments. The date by which other purchasers of alternative fuel are required to remit tax to a provider shall be determined by agreement between the provider and the purchaser.

History.
2000, cc. 729, 758.

§ 58.1-2253. Notice to providers of alternative fuel of cancellation or reissuance of certain licenses; effect of notice.

A. If the Commissioner cancels the license of a bulk user of alternative fuel or retailer of alternative fuel who has posted a bond in accordance with § 58.1-2246, the Commissioner shall notify all providers of alternative fuel of the cancellation. If the Commissioner issues a license to a bulk user of alternative fuel or retailer of alternative fuel whose license was previously canceled, the Commissioner shall notify all providers of alternative fuel of the issuance.

B. A provider of alternative fuel who sells alternative fuel to a bulk user of alternative fuel or retailer of alternative fuel who has posted a bond in accordance with § 58.1-2246, after receiving notice from the Commissioner that the Commissioner has canceled the license of a bulk user of alternative fuel or of a retailer of alternative fuel, is jointly and severally liable with the bulk user of alternative fuel or retailer of alternative fuel for any tax due on the alternative fuel that the provider of alternative fuel sells to the bulk user of alternative fuel or retailer of alternative fuel after receiving the notice; however, the provider of alternative fuel shall not be liable for tax due on alternative fuel sold to a previously unlicensed bulk user of alternative fuel or retailer of alternative fuel after the provider of alternative fuel receives notice from the Commissioner that the Commissioner has issued another license to the bulk user of alternative fuel or retailer of alternative fuel.

History.
2000, cc. 729, 758.

§ 58.1-2254. Exempt sale deduction.

A licensed retailer of alternative fuel who has posted a bond in accordance with § 58.1-2246 may deduct from the amount of tax otherwise payable to a provider of alternative fuel the amount calculated on alternative fuel that the licensee received from the provider and resold to a governmental entity, or resold to an organization described in subdivision 2 of § 58.1-2250 for use in the operation of an aircraft, whose purchases of alternative fuel are exempt from the tax under such section if, when purchasing the fuel, the retailer notified the provider of the retailer's intent to resell the fuel in an exempt sale.

History.
2000, cc. 729, 758.

§ 58.1-2255. Returns and payments by bulk users and retailers of alternative fuel; storage.

A. Each bulk user of alternative fuel and retailer of alternative fuel shall file a monthly informational return with the Commissioner. A monthly return covers a calendar month and is due by the twentieth day of the second month that follows such month.

The return shall include the following information and any other information required by the Commissioner:

1. The amount of alternative fuel received during the month;

2. The amount of alternative fuel sold or used during the month;

3. The number of gallons for which a deduction was taken during the month pursuant to § 58.1-2254, by provider, if applicable; and

4. The number of gallons sold in exempt sales during the month, by type of sale, and the purchaser of the fuel in the exempt sales, if applicable.

B. If the number of gallons for which an eligible retailer of alternative fuel takes a deduction during a month exceeds the number of exempt gallons or gallon equivalent sold, the retailer of alternative fuel shall pay tax on the difference at the rate imposed by subsection A of § 58.1-2249. The tax shall be payable when the informational return is due.

C. A bulk user of alternative fuel or a retailer of alternative fuel may store highway and nonhighway alternative fuel in separate storage tanks or in the same storage tank. If highway and nonhighway alternative fuel are stored in separate storage tanks, the tank for the nonhighway fuel shall be marked in accordance with the requirements set by § 58.1-2279 for dyed diesel storage facilities. If highway and nonhighway alternative fuel are stored in the same storage tank, the storage tank shall be equipped with separate metering devices for the highway fuel and the nonhighway fuel. If the Commissioner determines that a bulk user of alternative fuel or retailer of alternative fuel used or sold alternative fuel to operate a highway vehicle when the fuel was dispensed from a storage tank or through a meter marked for nonhighway use, all fuel delivered into that storage tank shall be presumed to have been used to operate a highway vehicle.

History.
2000, cc. 729, 758; 2002, c. 7.

§ 58.1-2256. Deductions and discounts for providers of alternative fuel filing returns.

A. When a provider of alternative fuel files a return, the provider of alternative fuel may deduct from the amount of tax payable with the return the amount of tax any of the following licensees owes the provider of alternative fuel but failed to remit to the provider of alternative fuel:

1. A licensed bulk user of alternative fuel who has posted a bond in accordance with § 58.1-2246; and

2. A licensed retailer of alternative fuel who has posted a bond in accordance with § 58.1-2246.

A provider of alternative fuel shall not be liable for tax that such a licensee owes the provider of alternative fuel but fails to pay. If such licensee pays the tax owed to a provider of alternative fuel after the provider of alternative fuel deducts the amount of such tax on a return, the provider of alternative fuel shall remit the payment to the Commissioner with the next monthly return filed subsequent to receipt of the tax.

B. A provider of alternative fuel who timely files a return with the payment due may deduct, from the amount of tax payable with the return, an administrative discount of one-tenth of one percent of the amount of tax payable to this Commonwealth, not to exceed a total of $5,000 per month. The administrative discount allowed a provider of alternative fuel who is also licensed as a supplier under Article 2 (§ 58.1-2204 et seq.) of this chapter shall not exceed $5,000 per month for both licenses.

History.
2000, cc. 729, 758.

§ 58.1-2257. Duties of provider of alternative fuel as trustee.

A. All tax payments due to the Commonwealth received by a provider of alternative fuel pursuant to § 58.1-2252 shall be held by the provider of alternative fuel as trustee in trust for the Commonwealth, and a provider of alternative fuel has a fiduciary duty to remit to the Commissioner the amount of tax received by the provider of alternative fuel. A provider of alternative fuel shall be liable for the taxes paid to him.

B. A provider of alternative fuel shall notify a bulk user of alternative fuel or retailer of alternative fuel who has posted a bond in accordance with § 58.1-2246 and who received alternative fuel from the provider of alternative fuel during a reporting period of the number of taxable gallons or equivalent taxable gallons received. The provider of alternative fuel shall give this notice after the end of each reporting period and before the licensee is required to remit to the provider of alternative fuel the amount of tax due on the fuel.

C. A provider of alternative fuel shall notify the Commissioner within ten business days after a return is due of any licensed bulk user of alternative fuel or retailer of alternative fuel who (i) has posted a bond in accordance with § 58.1-2246 and (ii) did not pay the tax due the provider of alternative fuel when the provider filed his return. The notice shall be transmitted to the Commissioner in the form required by the Commissioner.

D. A provider of alternative fuel who receives a payment of tax shall not apply the payment to a debt that the person making the tax payment owes to the provider of alternative fuel for alternative fuel purchased from the provider of alternative fuel.

History.
2000, cc. 729, 758.

§ 58.1-2258. Use of name and account number on return.

When a transaction with a person licensed under this article is required to be reported on a return, the return shall state the licensee's name and account number as stated on the lists compiled by the Commissioner under § 58.1-2216.

History.
2000, cc. 729, 758.

ARTICLE 6.
REFUNDS.

§ 58.1-2259. Fuel uses eligible for refund of taxes paid for motor fuels.

A. A refund of the tax paid for the purchase of fuel in quantities of five gallons or more at any time shall be granted in accordance with the provisions of § 58.1-2261 to any person who establishes to the satisfaction of the Commissioner that such person has paid the tax levied pursuant to this chapter upon any fuel:

1. Sold and delivered to a governmental entity for its exclusive use;
2. Used by a governmental entity, provided persons operating under contract with a governmental entity shall not be eligible for such refund;
3. Sold and delivered to an organization described in subdivision 2 of § 58.1-2226 or subdivision 2 of § 58.1-2250 for its exclusive use in the operation of an aircraft;
4. Used by an organization described in subdivision 2 of § 58.1-2226 or subdivision 2 of § 58.1-2250 for its exclusive use in the operation of an aircraft, provided persons operating under contract with such an organization shall not be eligible for such refund;
5. Purchased by a licensed exporter and subsequently transported and delivered by such licensed exporter to another state for sales or use outside the boundaries of the Commonwealth if the tax applicable in the destination state has been paid, provided a refund shall not be granted pursuant to this section on any fuel which is transported and delivered outside of the Commonwealth in the fuel supply tank of a highway vehicle or an aircraft;
6. Used by any person performing transportation under contract or lease with any transportation district for use in a highway vehicle controlled by a transportation district created under the Transportation District Act of 1964 (§ 33.2-1900 et seq.) and used in providing transit service by the transportation district by contract or lease, provided the refund shall be paid to the person performing such transportation;
7. Used by any private, nonprofit agency on aging, designated by the Department for Aging and Rehabilitative Services, providing transportation services to citizens in highway vehicles owned, operated or under contract with such agency;
8. Used in operating or propelling highway vehicles owned by a nonprofit organization that provides specialized transportation to various locations for elderly or disabled individuals to secure essential services and to participate in community life according to the individual's interest and abilities;
9. Used in operating or propelling buses owned and operated by a county or the school board thereof while being used to transport children to and from public school or from school to and from educational or athletic activities;
10. Used by buses owned or solely used by a private, nonprofit, nonreligious school while being used to transport children to and from such school or from such school to and from educational or athletic activities;
11. Used by any county or city school board or any private, nonprofit, nonreligious school contracting with a private carrier to transport children to and from public schools or any private, nonprofit, nonreligious school, provided the tax shall be refunded to the private carrier performing such transportation;
12. Used in operating or propelling the equipment of volunteer firefighting companies and of volunteer emergency medical services agencies within the Commonwealth used actually and necessarily for firefighting and emergency medical services purposes;
13. Used in operating or propelling motor equipment belonging to counties, cities and towns, if actually used in public activities;
14. Used for a purpose other than in operating or propelling highway vehicles, watercraft or aircraft;
15. Used off-highway in self-propelled equipment manufactured for a specific off-road purpose, which is used on a job site and the movement of which on any highway is incidental to the purpose for which it was designed and manufactured;
16. Proven to be lost by accident, including the accidental mixing of (i) dyed diesel fuel with tax-paid motor fuel, (ii) gasoline with diesel fuel, or (iii) undyed diesel fuel with dyed kerosene, but excluding fuel lost through personal negligence or theft;
17. Used in operating or propelling vehicles used solely for racing other vehicles on a racetrack;
18. Used in operating or propelling unlicensed highway vehicles and other unlicensed equipment used exclusively for agricultural or horticultural purposes on lands owned or leased by the owner or lessee of such vehicles and not operated on or over any highway for any purpose other than to move it in the manner and for the purpose mentioned. The amount of refund shall be equal to the amount of the taxes paid less one-half cent per gallon on such fuel so used which shall be paid by the Commissioner into the state treasury to the credit of the Virginia Agricultural Foundation Fund;
19. Used in operating or propelling commercial watercraft. The amount of refund shall be equal to

the amount of the taxes paid less one and one-half cents per gallon on such fuel so used which shall be paid by the Commissioner into the state treasury to be credited as provided in subsection D of § 58.1-2289. If any applicant so requests, the Commissioner shall pay into the state treasury, to the credit of the Game Protection Fund, the entire tax paid by such applicant for the purposes specified in subsection D of § 58.1-2289. If any applicant who is an operator of commercial watercraft so requests, the Commissioner shall pay into the state treasury, to the credit of the Marine Fishing Improvement Fund, the entire tax paid by such applicant for the purposes specified in § 28.2-208;

20. Used in operating stationary engines, or pumping or mixing equipment on a highway vehicle if the fuel used to operate such equipment is stored in an auxiliary tank separate from the fuel tank used to propel the highway vehicle, and the highway vehicle is mechanically incapable of self-propulsion while fuel is being used from the auxiliary tank;

21. Used in operating or propelling recreational and pleasure watercraft; or

22. Used in operating or propelling highway vehicles owned by any entity that is exempt from taxation under § 501(c)(3) of the Internal Revenue Code, as amended or renumbered, and organized with a principal purpose of providing hunger relief services or food to the needy, if such vehicle is used solely for the purpose of providing hunger relief services or food to the needy.

B. 1. Any person purchasing fuel for consumption in a solid waste compacting or ready-mix concrete highway vehicle, or a bulk feed delivery truck, where the vehicle's equipment is mechanically or hydraulically driven by an internal combustion engine that propels the vehicle, is entitled to a refund in an amount equal to 35 percent of the tax paid on such fuel. For purposes of this section, a "bulk feed delivery truck" means bulk animal feed delivery trucks utilizing power take-off (PTO) driven auger or air feed discharge systems for off-road deliveries of animal feed.

2. Any person purchasing fuel for consumption in a vehicle designed or permanently adapted solely and exclusively for bulk spreading or spraying of agricultural liming materials, chemicals, or fertilizer, where the vehicle's equipment is mechanically or hydraulically driven by an internal combustion engine that propels the vehicle, is entitled to a refund in an amount equal to 55 percent of the tax paid on such fuel.

C. Any person purchasing any fuel on which tax imposed pursuant to this chapter has been paid may apply for a refund of the tax if such fuel was consumed by a highway vehicle used in operating an urban or suburban bus line or a taxicab service. This refund also applies to a common carrier of passengers which has been issued a certificate pursuant to § 46.2-2075 or 46.2-2099.4 providing regular route service over the highways of the Commonwealth. No refund shall be granted unless the majority of the passengers using such bus line, taxicab service or common carrier of passengers do so for travel of a distance of not more than 40 miles, one way, in a single day between their place of abode and their place of employment, shopping areas or schools.

If the applicant for a refund is a taxicab service, he shall hold a valid permit from the Department to engage in the business of a taxicab service. No applicant shall be denied a refund by reason of the fee arrangement between the holder of the permit and the driver or drivers, if all other conditions of this section have been met.

Under no circumstances shall a refund be granted more than once for the same fuel. The amount of refund under this subsection shall be equal to the amount of the taxes paid, except refunds granted on the tax paid on fuel used by a taxicab service shall be in an amount equal to the tax paid less $0.01 per gallon on the fuel used.

Any refunds made under this subsection shall be deducted from the urban highway funds allocated to the highway construction district, pursuant to Article 5 (§ 33.2-351 et seq.) of Chapter 3 of Title 33.2, in which the recipient has its principal place of business.

Except as otherwise provided in this chapter, all provisions of law applicable to the refund of fuel taxes by the Commissioner generally shall apply to the refunds authorized by this subsection. Any county having withdrawn its roads from the secondary system of state highways under provisions of § 11 of Chapter 415 of the Acts of 1932 shall receive its proportionate share of such special funds as is now provided by law with respect to other fuel tax receipts.

D. Any person purchasing fuel for consumption in a vehicle designed or permanently adapted solely and exclusively for bulk spreading or spraying of agricultural liming materials, chemicals, or fertilizer, where the vehicle's equipment is mechanically or hydraulically driven by an internal combustion engine that propels the vehicle, is entitled to a refund in an amount equal to 55 percent of the tax paid on such fuel.

E. Any person purchasing diesel fuel used in operating or propelling a passenger car, a pickup or panel truck, or a truck having a gross vehicle weight rating of 10,000 pounds or less is entitled to a refund of a portion of the taxes paid in an amount equal to the difference between the rate of tax on diesel fuel and the rate of tax on gasoline and gasohol pursuant to § 58.1-2217. For purposes of this subsection, "passenger car," "pickup or panel truck," and "truck" shall have the meaning given in § 46.2-100. Notwithstanding any other provision of law, diesel fuel used in a vehicle upon which the fuels tax has been refunded pursuant to this subsection shall be exempt from the tax imposed under Chapter 6 (§ 58.1-600 et seq.).

F. Refunds resulting from any fuel shipments diverted from Virginia shall be based on the amount of tax paid for the fuel less discounts allowed by § 58.1-2233.

G. Any person who is required to be licensed under this chapter and is applying for a refund shall not be eligible for such refund if the applicant was not licensed at the time the refundable transaction was conducted.

History.

2000, cc. 247, 347, 729, 758; 2001, c. 167; 2003, c. 781; 2005, cc. 243, 782, 928; 2011, cc. 881, 889; 2012, cc. 803, 835; 2013, c. 766; 2015, cc. 502, 503; 2016, c. 34.

Editor's note.

References in this section were updated at the direction of the Virginia Code Commission to conform to the recodification of Title 33.2 by Acts 2014, c. 805, effective October 1, 2014.

§ 58.1-2260. Refund of taxes erroneously or illegally collected.

If it appears to the satisfaction of the Commissioner that any taxes or penalties imposed by this chapter have been erroneously or illegally collected from any person, such person shall be entitled to a refund upon proper application to the Commissioner. No refund shall be made under the provisions of this section unless a written statement, setting forth the circumstances and reasons why such refund is claimed, is filed with the Commissioner within one year of the date of payment of the tax for which the refund is claimed. The claim shall be in such form as the Commissioner shall prescribe and shall be sworn to by the claimant.

History.

2000, cc. 729, 758.

§ 58.1-2261. Refund procedure; investigations.

A. Any person entitled to a refund pursuant to § 58.1-2259 shall file with the Commissioner an application on a form prepared and furnished by the Commissioner. Such application shall contain the information and certifications required by the Commissioner. The applicant shall set forth the basis for the claimed refund, the total amount of such fuel purchased and used by such applicant, and how such fuel was used. The applicant shall retain the paid ticket, invoice, or other document from the seller documenting the purchase of the fuel on which a refund is claimed for a period of time to be determined by the Commissioner. The Commissioner, upon the presentation of such application shall refund to the claimant the proper amount of the tax paid as provided in this chapter, subject to the provisions of subsection D. A ticket issued to the holder of a credit card as evidence of the delivery to such holder of tax-paid fuel shall, for the purpose of this section, be a paid ticket or invoice. Tickets or invoices marked "duplicate" shall not be acceptable.

B. The application for a refund shall be filed within one year from the date of the sale as shown on the paid ticket or invoice. For those that pay the motor fuels tax in accordance with § 58.1-2200, if the refund amount certified by the Commissioner is different from the amount requested by the applicant, the Commissioner shall provide an explanation to the applicant of why the refund amount differs from the amount requested.

C. In the event an assessment is rendered for failure to report and pay the tax imposed as provided in § 58.1-2217 or § 58.1-2249 and such fuel is subject to refund under the provisions of § 58.1-2259, the application for a refund shall be filed with the Commissioner by the person entitled to such refund within one year from the date such assessment is paid and shall be accompanied by invoices covering the sale of the fuel and billing of tax to such person.

D. The Department may make any investigation it considers necessary before refunding the fuels tax to a person, and may investigate a refund after the refund has been issued and within the time frame for adjusting tax under this chapter. As a part of such investigation, the Department may require that the person provide the paid ticket, invoice, or other document from the seller documenting the purchase of the fuel on which a refund is claimed. Failure to provide a ticket, invoice, or other document evidencing the purchase of such fuel on which a refund is requested or was previously granted will result in the denial or reversal of that refund.

E. In accordance with § 58.1-609.1, any person who is refunded tax pursuant to § 58.1-2259 shall be subject to the taxes imposed by Chapter 6 (§ 58.1-600 et seq.) of this title, unless such transaction is specifically exempted pursuant to § 58.1-609.1.

History.

2000, cc. 729, 758; 2003, c. 325; 2009, c. 419.

§ 58.1-2262. Payment of refund.

Whenever it appears to the satisfaction of the Commissioner that any person is entitled to a refund for taxes paid pursuant to this chapter, the Commissioner shall forthwith certify the amount of the refund to the Comptroller and shall send to the applicant an explanation of the basis of such refund. The amount of the refund shall be paid by check issued by the State Treasurer on warrant of the Comptroller.

History.

2000, cc. 729, 758; 2003, c. 325.

ARTICLE 7.

ENFORCEMENT AND ADMINISTRATION.

§ 58.1-2263. Shipping documents; transportation of motor fuel loaded at a terminal rack or bulk plant rack; civil penalty.

A. A person shall not transport motor fuel loaded at a terminal rack or bulk plant rack unless the person has a shipping document for its transportation that complies with this section. A terminal operator or operator of a bulk plant shall give a shipping document to the person who operates the means of conveyance into which motor fuel is loaded at the terminal rack or bulk plant rack.

B. The shipping document issued by the terminal operator shall be machine-printed and that issued by the operator of a bulk plant shall be on a printed form and both shall contain the following information and any other information required by the Commissioner:

1. Identification, including address, of the terminal or bulk plant from which the motor fuel was received;

2. Date the motor fuel was loaded;

3. Gross gallons loaded;

4. Destination state of the motor fuel, as represented by the purchaser of the motor fuel or the purchaser's agent;

5. In the case of aviation jet fuel sold to an aviation consumer, the shipping document shall be marked with the phrase "Aviation Jet Fuel, Not for On-road Use" or a similar phrase; and

6. If the document is issued by a terminal operator, (i) net gallons loaded and (ii) tax responsibility statement indicating the name of the supplier who is responsible for the tax due on the motor fuel.

C. A terminal operator or bulk plant operator may rely on the representation made by the purchaser of motor fuel or the purchaser's agent concerning the destination state of the motor fuel. A purchaser shall be liable for any tax due as a result of the purchaser's diversion of fuel from the represented destination state.

D. A person to whom a shipping document was issued shall:

1. Carry the shipping document in the means of conveyance for which it was issued when transporting the motor fuel described;

2. Show the shipping document to a law-enforcement officer upon request when transporting the motor fuel described;

3. Deliver motor fuel described in the shipping document to the destination state printed on it unless the person:

a. Notifies the Commissioner before transporting the motor fuel into a state other than the printed destination state that the person has received instructions after the shipping document was issued to deliver the motor fuel to a different destination state;

b. Receives from the Commissioner a confirmation number authorizing the diversion; and

c. Writes on the shipping document the change in destination state and the confirmation number for the diversion; and

4. Give a copy of the shipping document to the distributor or other person to whom the motor fuel is delivered.

E. The person to whom motor fuel is delivered shall not accept delivery of the motor fuel if the destination state shown on the shipping document for the motor fuel is a state other than Virginia. To determine if the shipping document shows Virginia as the destination state, the person to whom the fuel is delivered shall examine the shipping document and keep a copy of the shipping document (i) at the place of business where the motor fuel was delivered for 90 days following the date of delivery and (ii) at such place or another place for at least three years following the date of delivery. The person who accepts delivery of motor fuel in violation of this subsection and any person liable for the tax on the motor fuel pursuant to Article 3 (§ 58.1-2217 et seq.) shall be jointly and severally liable for any tax due on the fuel.

F. Any person who (i) transports motor fuel loaded at a terminal rack or bulk plant rack without a shipping document or with a false or an incomplete shipping document or (ii) delivers motor fuel to a destination state other than that shown on the shipping document, shall be subject to a civil penalty. If the fuel is transported in a railroad tank car, the civil penalty imposed under this subsection shall be payable by the person responsible for the movement of the motor fuel in the railroad tank car. If the fuel is transported by any other means of conveyance, the civil penalty imposed under this subsection shall be payable by the person in whose name the means of conveyance is registered. The amount of the civil penalty assessed against a person for his first violation shall be $5,000. The amount of the civil penalty assessed against a person for his second or subsequent violation shall be $10,000.

History.

2000, cc. 729, 758; 2001, c. 167; 2012, c. 363.

§ **58.1-2264:** Repealed by Acts 2003, c. 781, cl. 2.

§ 58.1-2265. Improper sale or use of untaxed fuel; civil penalty.

A. Any person committing any of the following acts shall be subject to the civil penalty specified in subsection B:

1. Selling or storing any dyed diesel fuel for use in a highway vehicle that is licensed or required to be licensed, unless that use is allowed under 26 U.S.C. § 4082;

2. Willfully altering or attempting to alter the strength or composition of any dye or marker in any dyed diesel fuel;

3. Using dyed diesel fuel in a highway vehicle unless that use is allowed under 26 U.S.C. § 4082;

4. Acquiring, selling or storing any fuel for use in a watercraft, aircraft, or highway vehicle that is licensed or required to be licensed unless the tax levied by this chapter has been paid; or

5. Using any fuel in a watercraft, aircraft, or highway vehicle that is licensed or required to be licensed unless the tax levied by this chapter has been paid.

B. The amount of the civil penalty for any act described in subsection A shall be the greater of $1,000 or ten dollars per gallon of fuel, based on the maximum storage capacity of the storage tank, container or storage tank of the highway vehicle, watercraft or aircraft.

C. The Commissioner is authorized to reduce or waive any civil penalties under this section if the violation is due to a reasonable or good cause shown to the satisfaction of the Commissioner.

History.
2000, cc. 729, 758.

§ 58.1-2266. Late filing or payment; civil penalty.

A. Any person committing any of the following acts shall be subject to the civil penalty specified in subsections B and C:

1. Failure to submit a report required by this chapter on a timely basis;

2. Failure to submit the data required by this chapter; or

3. Failure to pay to the Commissioner or to a trustee on a timely basis the amount of taxes due under this chapter.

B. The amount of the civil penalty for any act described in subdivision A 1 or 2 shall be as follows:

1. $50 for the first violation;

2. $200 for the second violation;

3. $500 for the third violation; and

4. $1,000 for the fourth and subsequent violations.

After imposition of the penalty under this subsection, the amount of the penalty, if not paid within 30 days of receipt of notice of such penalty, shall bear interest at the rate of one percent per month until the penalty is paid.

C. The amount of the civil penalty for any act described in subdivision A 3 shall be equal to 10 percent of the tax due or $50, whichever is greater; however, penalties resulting from an audit shall be equal to 10 percent of the tax due. After imposition of the penalty under this subsection, the amount of the tax and the penalty, if not paid within 30 days of receipt of notice of such penalty, shall bear interest at the rate of one percent per month until the tax and penalty are paid.

D. The Commissioner is authorized to reduce or waive any penalties under this section if the violation is due to a reasonable or good cause shown to the satisfaction of the Commissioner.

History.
2000, cc. 729, 758; 2004, c. 340.

§ 58.1-2267. Refusal to allow inspection or taking of fuel sample; civil penalty.

Any person who refuses to allow an inspection or allow the taking of a fuel sample authorized by § 58.1-2276 or § 58.1-2277 shall be subject to a civil penalty of $5,000 for each refusal. If the refusal is for a sample to be taken from a vehicle, the penalty shall be payable by the person in whose name the vehicle is registered. If the refusal is for a sample to be taken from any other storage tank or container, the penalty shall be payable by the owner of such storage tank or container.

History.
2000, cc. 729, 758.

§ 58.1-2268. Engaging in business without a license; civil penalty.

Any person who engages in any business activity within the Commonwealth for which a license is required by this chapter without a valid license shall be subject to a civil penalty. The amount of the civil penalty assessed against a person for his first violation shall be $5,000. The amount of the civil penalty assessed against a person for his second or subsequent violation shall be $10,000.

History.
2000, cc. 729, 758.

§ 58.1-2268.1. Preventing a person from obtaining a license; civil penalty.

Any terminal operator, supplier, or position holder in the terminal who, by use of coercion, threat, intimidation or any other means of interference, intentionally prevents any person from applying for and obtaining a license issued under this chapter shall be subject to a civil penalty. The amount of the civil penalty assessed against a person for his (i) first violation shall be $5,000 and (ii) second and subsequent violations shall be $10,000.

History.
2000, cc. 729, 758.

§ 58.1-2269. False or fraudulent return; civil penalty.

Any person liable for a tax levied under this chapter who files a false or fraudulent return with the intent to evade the tax shall be subject to a civil penalty. The amount of the civil penalty shall be equal to fifty percent of the amount of the tax intended to be evaded by the filing of such return. The civil penalty shall be in addition to the amount of the tax intended to be evaded.

History.
2000, cc. 729, 758.

§ 58.1-2270. Failure to keep or retain records; civil penalty.

Any person who fails to keep or retain records as required by this chapter shall be subject to a civil penalty. The amount of the civil penalty assessed against a person for his first violation shall be $1,000. The amount of the civil penalty assessed against a person for each subsequent violation shall be $1,000 more than the amount of the civil penalty for the preceding violation.

History.
2000, cc. 729, 758.

§ 58.1-2271. Payment of civil penalties; disposition; waiver.

Any civil penalty assessed pursuant to this chapter shall be payable to the Department, shall be in addition to any other penalty or tax that may be imposed as provided in this chapter, and shall be collectible by the Commissioner in the same manner as if it were part of the tax levied. The amount of any civil penalty imposed under this chapter shall bear interest at the rate of one percent per month until paid. All civil penalties imposed under this chapter shall be deposited as provided in § 58.1-2289. Notwithstanding any other provisions of this chapter, the Commissioner is authorized to reduce or waive any civil penalties under this chapter if the violation is due to a reasonable or good cause shown to the satisfaction of the Commissioner.

History.
2000, cc. 729, 758; 2004, c. 340.

§ 58.1-2272. Prohibited acts; criminal penalties.

A. Any person who commits any of the following acts shall be guilty of a Class 1 misdemeanor:

1. Failing to obtain a license required by this chapter;
2. Failing to file a return required by this chapter;
3. Failing to pay a tax when due under this chapter;
4. Failing to pay a tax collected on behalf of a destination state to that state when it is due;
5. Making a false statement in an application, return, ticket, invoice, statement, or any other document required under this chapter;
6. Making a false statement in an application for a refund;
7. Failing to keep records as required under this chapter;
8. Refusing to allow the Commissioner or a representative of the Commissioner to examine the person's books and records concerning fuel;
9. Failing to make a required disclosure of the correct amount of fuel sold or used in the Commonwealth;
10. Failing to file a replacement or additional bond or certificate of deposit as required under this chapter;
11. Failing to show or give a shipping document as required under this chapter;
12. Refusing to allow a licensed distributor, licensed exporter, or licensed importer to defer payment of tax to the supplier, as required by § 58.1-2231;
13. Refusing to allow a bulk user of alternative fuel or a retailer of alternative fuel who has posted a bond in accordance with § 58.1-2246 to defer payment of tax to the provider of alternative fuel, as required by § 58.1-2252;
14. Refusing to allow a licensed distributor or a licensed importer to take a deduction or discount allowed by § 58.1-2233 when remitting the tax to the supplier, or to allow a licensed retailer of alternative fuel to take a deduction or discount allowed by § 58.1-2254 when remitting the tax to the provider of alternative fuel;
15. Using, delivering, or selling any aviation fuel for use or intended for use in highway vehicles or watercraft;
16. Violating the provisions of § 58.1-2278;
17. Interfering with or refusing to permit seizures authorized under § 58.1-2274; or
18. Delivering fuel from a transport truck or tank wagon to the fuel tank of a highway vehicle, except in an emergency.

B. A person who knowingly commits any of the following acts shall be guilty of a Class 1 misdemeanor:

1. Dispenses any fuel on which tax levied pursuant to this chapter has not been paid into the supply tank of a highway vehicle, watercraft, or aircraft; or
2. Allows any fuel on which tax levied pursuant to this chapter has not been paid to be dispensed into the supply tank of a highway vehicle, watercraft, or aircraft.

History.
2000, cc. 729, 758; 2006, c. 594.

§ 58.1-2273. Willful commission of prohibited acts; criminal penalties.

Any person who willfully commits any of the following acts, with the intent to (i) evade or circumvent the Commonwealth's fuels tax laws or (ii) assist any other person in efforts to evade or circumvent such laws, shall be guilty of a Class 6 felony, if he:

1. Alters, manipulates, replaces, or in any other manner tampers or interferes with, or causes to be

altered, manipulated, replaced, tampered or interfered with, a totalizer attached to fuel pumps to measure the dispensing of fuel;

2. Does not pay fuels taxes and diverts such tax proceeds for other purposes;

3. Is a licensee or the agent or representative of a licensee, converts or attempts to convert fuel tax proceeds for the use of the licensee or the licensee's agent or representative, with the intent to defraud the Commonwealth;

4. Illegally collects fuel taxes when not authorized or licensed by the Commissioner to do so;

5. Illegally imports fuel into the Commonwealth;

6. Conspires with any other person or persons to engage in an act, plan, or scheme to defraud the Commonwealth of fuels tax proceeds;

7. Uses any dyed diesel fuel for a use that the user knows or has reason to know is a taxable use of the fuel, or sells any dyed diesel fuel to a person who the seller knows or has reason to know will use the fuel for a taxable purpose; however, if the amount of fuel involved is not more than twenty gallons, such person shall be guilty of a Class 1 misdemeanor;

8. Alters or attempts to alter the strength or composition of any dye or marker in any dyed diesel fuel intended to be used for a taxable purpose;

9. Fails to remit to the Commissioner any tax levied pursuant to this chapter, if he (i) has added, or represented that he has added, the tax to the sales price for the fuel and (ii) has collected the amount of the tax;

10. Applies for or collects from the Department a refund for fuels tax when the person knows or has reason to know that fuel for which the refund is claimed has been or will be used for a taxable purpose; however, if the amount of fuel involved is not more than 20 gallons, such person shall be guilty of a Class 1 misdemeanor; or

11. Uses any fuel for a taxable purpose for which the person knows or has reason to know that a refund of fuels tax has been issued; however, if the amount of fuel involved is not more than 20 gallons, such person shall be guilty of a Class 1 misdemeanor.

History.
2000, cc. 729, 758; 2006, c. 594.

§ 58.1-2274. Unlawful importing, transportation, delivery, storage, acquiring or sale of fuel; sale to enforce assessment.

A. Upon the discovery of any fuel illegally imported into, or illegally transported, delivered, stored, acquired, or sold in, the Commonwealth, the Commissioner may order the tank or other storage receptacle in which the fuel is located to be seized and locked or sealed until the tax, penalties and interest levied under this chapter are assessed and paid.

B. If the assessment for such tax is not paid within 30 days, the Commissioner is hereby authorized, in addition to the other remedies authorized in this chapter, to sell such fuel and use the proceeds of such sale to satisfy the assessment due, with any funds which exceed the assessment and costs of the sale being returned to the owner of the fuel.

C. All fuel and any property, tangible or intangible, which may be found upon the person or in any vehicle which such person is using, including the vehicle itself, to aid the person in the transportation or sale of illegally transported, delivered, stored, sold, imported or acquired fuel, and any property found in the immediate vicinity of any place where such illegally transported, delivered, stored, sold, imported or acquired fuel may be located, including motor vehicles, tanks, and other storage devices, used to aid in the illegal transportation or sale of such fuel, shall be deemed contraband and shall be forfeited to the Commonwealth.

D. Any efforts by the Department to effect the forfeiture allowed under the authority of this section shall be governed by Chapter 22.1 (§ 19.2-386.1 et seq.) of Title 19.2, mutatis mutandis. However, such procedures shall not be applicable to the Department's tax collection powers and the use of such powers to enforce a tax liability against the illegally transported, delivered, stored, sold, imported or acquired fuel.

History.
2000, cc. 729, 758; 2012, cc. 283, 363, 756.

§ 58.1-2275. Record-keeping requirements.

Each (i) person required or electing to be licensed under Article 2 (§ 58.1-2204 et seq.) of this chapter, (ii) distributor, retailer and bulk user not licensed under this chapter, and (iii) person required to be licensed under § 58.1-2244, shall keep and maintain all records pertaining to fuel received, produced, manufactured, refined, compounded, used, sold or delivered, together with delivery tickets, invoices, bills of lading, and such other pertinent records and papers as may be required by the Commissioner for the reasonable administration of this chapter. Such records shall be kept and maintained for a period to include the Department's current fiscal year and the previous three fiscal years.

History.
2000, cc. 729, 758; 2002, c. 7.

§ 58.1-2276. Inspection of records.

A. The Commissioner or any deputy, employee or agent authorized by the Commissioner may examine, during the usual business hours of the day, records, books, papers, storage tanks and any other equipment of any person required to maintain records as provided in § 58.1-2275 for the purpose of ascertaining the quantity of fuel received, produced, manufactured, refined, compounded, used, sold, shipped, or delivered, to verify the truth and accuracy of any statement, report or return or to ascertain whether or not the tax levied by this chapter has been paid.

B. If a person required to maintain records as provided in § 58.1-2275 is open for business during hours of the day which might not be considered usual business hours for the Department, the Commissioner may examine the person's books and records during the person's normal business hours, which shall be those hours when the person is open for business.

History.
2000, cc. 729, 758; 2001, c. 167.

§ 58.1-2277. Administrative authority.

A. Employees of the Department designated by the Commissioner, upon presenting appropriate credentials and a written notice to the owner, operator, or agent in charge, are authorized to enter any place and to conduct inspections in accordance with this section. Inspections shall be performed in a reasonable manner and at times that are reasonable under the circumstances, taking into consideration the normal business hours of the place to be inspected.

B. Inspections may be conducted at any place where taxable fuel or fuel dyes or markers are, or may be, produced, altered, or stored, or at any inspection site where evidence of production, alteration, or storage may be discovered. These places may include, but shall not be limited to any: (i) terminal, (ii) fuel storage facility that is not a terminal, (iii) retail fuel facility, and (iv) designated inspection site.

C. Employees of the Department designated by the Commissioner may physically inspect, examine, and otherwise search any tank, reservoir, or other container that can or may be used for the production, storage, or transportation of fuel, fuel dyes or markers. Inspection may also be made of any equipment used for, or in connection with, the production, storage, or transportation of fuel, fuel dyes or markers, including equipment used for the dyeing or marking of fuel. Such employees may also inspect the books and records kept to determine fuel tax liability under this chapter.

D. Employees of the Department designated by the Commissioner may, on the premises or at a designated inspection site, take and remove samples of fuel in such reasonable quantities as are necessary to determine its composition.

History.
2000, cc. 729, 758.

§ 58.1-2278. Equipment requirements.

A. All fuel dispensed at retail shall be dispensed from metered pumps that indicate the total amount of fuel measured through the pumps. Each pump shall be marked to indicate the type of fuel dispensed.

B. A highway vehicle that transports fuel in a tank that is separate from the fuel supply tank of the vehicle shall not have a connection from the transporting tank to the motor or to the supply tank of the vehicle.

History.
2000, cc. 729, 758.

§ 58.1-2279. Marking requirements for dyed diesel fuel storage facilities.

A. A person who is a retailer of dyed diesel fuel or who stores dyed diesel fuel for use by that person or another person shall mark, with the phrase "Dyed Diesel Fuel, Nontaxable Use Only, Penalty for Taxable Use," or a similar phrase that clearly indicates that the diesel fuel is not to be used to operate a highway vehicle, each storage facility or pump from which dyed diesel fuel is dispensed, as follows:

1. The storage tank of the storage facility, if the storage tank is visible; and
2. The dispensing device that serves the storage facility.

B. The marking requirements of this section shall not apply to a storage facility that contains fuel used only in a heating, crop-drying, or manufacturing process, and is installed in a manner that makes use of the fuel for any other purpose improbable.

History.
2000, cc. 729, 758.

ARTICLE 8.

ASSESSMENTS AND COLLECTIONS.

§ 58.1-2280. Estimates of fuel subject to tax; assessments; notice of assessment.

When any licensee neglects, fails or refuses to make and file any report as required by this chapter or files an incorrect or fraudulent report, the Commissioner shall determine, from any information obtainable, the number of gallons of fuel with respect to which the licensee has incurred liability under this chapter. The Commissioner is authorized to make an assessment for the tax and any penalty and interest properly due against such licensee. The notice of assessment shall be sent to the licensee or delivered by the Department to the last known address appearing in the Commissioner's files. Such notice, when sent or delivered in accordance with these requirements, shall be sufficient regardless of whether or not it was ever received.

History.
2000, cc. 729, 758; 2006, c. 594.

§ 58.1-2281. Application to Commissioner for correction.

A. Any person assessed with any tax administered by the Department may, within thirty days from the date of such assessment, apply for relief to the Commissioner. Such application shall be in the form prescribed by the Department, and shall fully set forth the grounds upon which the taxpayer relies and all facts relevant to the taxpayer's contention. The Commissioner may also require such additional information, testimony or documentary evidence as he deems necessary to a fair determination of the application.

B. On receipt of a written notice of intent to file under this section, the Commissioner shall refrain from collecting the tax until the time for filing hereunder has expired, unless he determines that collection is in jeopardy.

History.
2000, cc. 729, 758.

§ 58.1-2282. Appeal of Commissioner's decisions.

A. Any person against whom an assessment, order or decision of the Commissioner has been adversely rendered, which assessment, order, or decision relates to the collection of unreported, incorrectly or fraudulently reported taxes, the granting or canceling of a license, the filing of a bond, an increase in the amount of a bond, a change of surety on a bond, the filing of reports, the examination of records, or any other matter wherein the findings are in the discretion of the Commissioner, may, within thirty days from the date thereof, file a petition of appeal from such assessment, order, or decision, in the circuit court in the city or county wherein such person resides, provided that any petition for a refund for taxes timely paid shall be filed within one year of the date of payment. A copy of the petition shall be sent to the Commissioner at the time of the filing with the court. The original shall show, by certificate, the date of mailing such copy to the Commissioner.

B. In any proceeding under this section, the assessments by the Commissioner shall be presumed correct. The burden of proof shall be upon the petitioner to show that the assessment was incorrect and contrary to law. The circuit court is authorized to enter judgment against such person for the taxes, penalty, and interest due. The failure by any such person to appeal under the provisions of this section within the time period specified shall render the assessment, order, or decision of the Commissioner conclusively valid and binding upon such person. Such person or the Commissioner may petition the Court of Appeals from the final decision of the circuit court.

History.
2000, cc. 729, 758.

§ 58.1-2283. Jeopardy assessment.

If the Commissioner (i) receives notice from a supplier pursuant to subsection C of § 58.1-2237 of any licensed distributor or licensed importer who did not pay the tax due the supplier, or (ii) is of the opinion that the collection of any tax or any amount of tax required to be collected and paid under this chapter will be jeopardized by delay, the Commissioner shall make an assessment of the tax or amount of tax required to be collected and shall mail or issue a notice of such assessment to the taxpayer with a demand for immediate payment of the tax or of the deficiency in tax declared to be in jeopardy, including penalties and interest. In the case of a tax for a current period, the Commissioner may declare the taxable period of the taxpayer immediately terminated and shall mail or issue the notice of such finding and declaration to the taxpayer with a demand for immediate payment of the tax based on the period declared terminated, and such tax shall be immediately due and payable. Assessments provided for in this section shall become immediately due and payable. If any such tax, penalty or interest is not paid upon demand, the Commissioner may proceed to (i) collect the same by legal process, including but not limited to filing a memorandum of lien pursuant to § 58.1-2284 or (ii) accept a surety bond or other security deemed to sufficiently ensure full payment of the amount of tax, penalty and interest assessed against the taxpayer.

History.
2000, cc. 729, 758; 2004, c. 340.

§ 58.1-2284. Memorandum of lien for collection of taxes.

A. If any taxes or fees, including penalties and interest, due under this chapter become delinquent or are past due, the Commissioner may file a memorandum of lien in the circuit court clerk's office of the county or city in which the taxpayer's place of business is located, or in which the taxpayer resides. If the taxpayer has no place of business or residence within the Commonwealth, such memorandum may be filed in the Circuit Court of the City of Richmond. A copy of such memorandum may also be filed in the clerk's office of all counties and cities in which the taxpayer owns real estate. Such memorandum shall be recorded in the judgment docket book and shall have the effect of a judgment in favor of the Commonwealth, to be enforced as provided in Article 19 (§ 8.01-196 et seq.) of Chapter 3 of Title 8.01, mutatis mutandis, except that a writ of fieri facias may be issued any time after the memorandum is filed. The lien on real estate shall become effective at the time the memorandum is filed in the jurisdiction in which the real estate is located.

B. Recordation of a memorandum of lien hereunder shall not affect the right to a refund or exoneration under this chapter nor shall an application for correction pursuant to § 58.1-2281 affect the power of the Commissioner to collect the tax, except as specifically provided in this chapter.

History.
2000, cc. 729, 758.

§ 58.1-2285. Period of limitations.

The taxes imposed by this chapter shall be assessed within three years from the date on which such taxes became due and payable. In the case of a false or fraudulent return with intent to evade payment of the taxes imposed by this chapter, or a failure to file a return, the taxes may be assessed, or a proceeding in court for the collection of such taxes may be begun without assessment, at any time. The Commissioner shall not examine any person's records beyond the three-year period of limitations unless he has reasonable evidence of fraud, or reasonable cause to believe that such person was required by law to file a return and failed to do so.

History.
2000, cc. 729, 758.

§ 58.1-2286. Waiver of time limitation on assessment of taxes.

If, before the expiration of the time prescribed for assessment of any tax levied pursuant to this title and assessable by the Department, both the Commissioner and the taxpayer have consented in writing to its assessment after such time, the tax may be assessed any time prior to the expiration of the period agreed upon. The period so agreed upon may be extended by subsequent agreements in writing made before the expiration of the period previously agreed upon.

History.
2000, cc. 729, 758.

§ 58.1-2287. Suits to recover taxes.

If any person fails to pay the tax or any civil penalty levied under this chapter, including accrued penalties and interest, when due, the Attorney General or the Commissioner may bring an appropriate action for the recovery of such tax, penalty and interest, provided that if it is found that such failure to pay was willful, judgment shall be rendered for double the amount of the tax or civil penalty found to be due, with costs.

History.
2000, cc. 729, 758.

§ 58.1-2288. Liability of corporate or partnership officer; penalty.

Any corporate or partnership officer who directs or causes the business of which he is a corporate or partnership officer to fail to pay, collect, or truthfully account for and pay over any fuels tax for which the business is liable to the Commonwealth or to a trustee, shall, in addition to other penalties provided by law, be liable for a penalty in the amount of the tax evaded, or not paid, collected, or accounted for and paid over. The penalty shall be assessed and collected in the same manner as such taxes are assessed and collected. However, this penalty shall be dischargeable in bankruptcy proceedings.

History.
2000, cc. 729, 758.

ARTICLE 9.

DISPOSITION OF TAX REVENUES.

§ 58.1-2289. (For contingent expiration, see note) Disposition of tax revenue generally.

A. Unless otherwise provided in this section, all taxes and fees, including civil penalties, collected by the Commissioner pursuant to this chapter, less a reasonable amount to be allocated for refunds, shall be promptly paid into the state treasury and shall constitute special funds within the Commonwealth Transportation Fund. Any balances remaining in these funds at the end of the year shall be available for use in subsequent years for the purposes set forth in this chapter, and any interest income on such funds shall accrue to these funds.

The Governor is hereby authorized to transfer out of such fund an amount necessary for the inspection of gasoline and motor grease measuring and distributing equipment, and for the inspection and analysis of gasoline for purity.

B. The tax collected on each gallon of aviation fuel sold and delivered or used in this Commonwealth, less refunds, shall be paid into a special fund of the state treasury. Proceeds of this special fund within the Commonwealth Transportation Fund shall be disbursed upon order of the Department of Aviation, on warrants of the Comptroller, to defray the cost of the administration of the laws of this Commonwealth relating to aviation, for the construction, maintenance and improvement of airports and landing fields to which the public now has or which it is proposed shall have access, and for the promotion of aviation in the interest of operators and the public generally.

C. One-half cent of the tax collected on each gallon of fuel on which a refund has been paid for gasoline, gasohol, diesel fuel, blended fuel, or alternative fuel, for fuel consumed in tractors and unlicensed equipment used for agricultural purposes shall be paid into a special fund of the state treasury, known as the Virginia Agricultural Foundation Fund, to be disbursed to make certain refunds and defray the costs of the research and educational phases of the agricultural program, including supplemental salary payments to certain employees at Virginia Polytechnic Institute and State University, the Department of Agriculture and Consumer Services and the Virginia Truck and Ornamentals Research Station, including reasonable expenses of the Virginia Agricultural Council.

D. One and one-half cents of the tax collected on each gallon of fuel used to propel a commercial watercraft upon which a refund has been paid shall be paid to the credit of the Game Protection Fund of the state treasury to be made available to the Board of Game and Inland Fisheries until expended for the purposes provided generally in subsection C of § 29.1-701, including acquisition, construction, improvement and maintenance of public boating access areas on the public waters of this Commonwealth and for other activities and purposes of direct benefit and interest to the boating public and for no other purpose. However, one and one-half cents per gallon on fuel used by commercial fishing, oystering, clamming, and crabbing boats shall be paid to the Department of Transportation to be used for the construction, repair, improvement and maintenance of the public docks of this Commonwealth used by said commercial watercraft. Any expenditures for the acquisition, construction, improvement and maintenance of the public docks shall be made according to a plan developed by the Virginia Marine Resources Commission.

From the tax collected pursuant to the provisions of this chapter from the sales of gasoline used for the propelling of watercraft, after deduction for lawful refunds, there shall be paid into the state treasury for use by the Marine Resources Commission, the Virginia Soil and Water Conservation Board, the State Water Control Board, and the Commonwealth Transportation Board to (i) improve the public docks as specified in this section, (ii) improve commercial and sports fisheries in Virginia's tidal waters, (iii) make environmental improvements including, without limitation, fisheries management and habitat enhancement in the Chesapeake and its tributaries, and (iv) further the purposes set forth in § 33.2-1510, a sum as established by the General Assembly.

E. Of the remaining revenues deposited into the Commonwealth Transportation Fund pursuant to this chapter less refunds authorized by this chapter: (i) 80 percent shall be deposited into the Highway Maintenance and Operating Fund established pursuant to § 33.2-1530, (ii) 11.3 percent shall be deposited into the Transportation Trust Fund established pursuant to § 33.2-1524, (iii) four percent shall be deposited into the Priority Transportation Fund, (iv) 3.11 percent shall be deposited into the Commonwealth Transit Capital Fund established pursuant to subdivision A 4 c of § 58.1-638, (v) one percent shall be transferred to a special fund within the Commonwealth Transportation Fund in the state treasury, to be used to meet the necessary expenses of the Department of Motor Vehicles, (vi) 0.35 of one percent shall be deposited into the Commonwealth Mass Transit Fund established pursuant to subdivision A 4 of § 58.1-638 and allocated to subdivision A 4 b (1)(b), and (vii) 0.24 of one percent shall be deposited into the Commonwealth Mass Transit Fund established pursuant to subdivision A 4 of § 58.1-638 and allocated to subdivision A 4 b (1)(a).

History.

2000, cc. 729, 758; 2007, c. 896; 2013, c. 766; 2015, c. 684.

Section set out twice.

The section above is set out as amended by Acts 2015, c. 684. For this section as effective if amendments by Acts 2015, c. 684 expire pursuant to Acts 2015, c. 684, cl. 12, see the following section, also numbered 58.1-2289.

Contingent expiration date. — Acts 2015, c. 684, cl. 12 provides: "That the provisions of this act amending §§ 33.2-1530, 58.1-815.4, 58.1-1741, and 58.1-2289 of the Code of Virginia shall expire if the Commonwealth collects sales and use tax from remote retailers on sales made into the Commonwealth pursuant to legislation enacted by the federal government that grants states that meet minimum simplification requirements specified in such legislation the authority to compel remote retailers to collect sales and use tax on sales made into the respective state."

Editor's note.

Acts 2015, c. 684, cl. 3 provides: "That the provisions of this act amending §§ 33.2-200, 33.2-1530, 58.1-815.4, 58.1-1741, and 58.1-2289 of the Code of Virginia shall become effective on July 1, 2016."

§ 58.1-2289. (For contingent effective date, see note) Disposition of tax revenue generally.

A. Unless otherwise provided in this section, all taxes and fees, including civil penalties, collected by the Commissioner pursuant to this chapter, less a reasonable amount to be allocated for refunds, shall be promptly paid into the state treasury and shall constitute special funds within the Commonwealth Transportation Fund. Any balances remaining in these funds at the end of the year shall be available for use in subsequent years for the purposes set forth in this chapter, and any interest income on such funds shall accrue to these funds.

The Governor is hereby authorized to transfer out of such fund an amount necessary for the inspection of gasoline and motor grease measuring and distributing equipment, and for the inspection and analysis of gasoline for purity.

B. The tax collected on each gallon of aviation fuel sold and delivered or used in this Commonwealth, less refunds, shall be paid into a special fund of the state treasury. Proceeds of this special fund within the Commonwealth Transportation Fund shall be disbursed upon order of the Department of Aviation, on warrants of the Comptroller, to defray the cost of the administration of the laws of this Commonwealth relating to aviation, for the construction, maintenance and improvement of airports and landing fields to which the public now has or which it is proposed shall have access, and for the promotion of aviation in the interest of operators and the public generally.

C. One-half cent of the tax collected on each gallon of fuel on which a refund has been paid for gasoline, gasohol, diesel fuel, blended fuel, or alternative fuel, for fuel consumed in tractors and unlicensed equipment used for agricultural purposes shall be paid into a special fund of the state treasury, known as the Virginia Agricultural Foundation Fund, to be disbursed to make certain refunds and defray the costs of the research and educational phases of the agricultural program, including supplemental salary payments to certain employees at Virginia Polytechnic Institute and State University, the Department of Agriculture and Consumer Services and the Virginia Truck and Ornamentals Research Station, including reasonable expenses of the Virginia Agricultural Council.

D. One and one-half cents of the tax collected on each gallon of fuel used to propel a commercial watercraft upon which a refund has been paid shall be paid to the credit of the Game Protection Fund of the state treasury to be made available to the Board of Game and Inland Fisheries until expended for the purposes provided generally in subsection C of § 29.1-701, including acquisition, construction, improvement and maintenance of public boating access areas on the public waters of this Commonwealth and for other activities and purposes of direct benefit and interest to the boating public and for no other purpose. However, one and one-half cents per gallon on fuel used by commercial fishing, oystering, clamming, and crabbing boats shall be paid to the Department of Transportation to be used for the construction, repair, improvement and maintenance of the public docks of this Commonwealth used by said commercial watercraft. Any expenditures for the acquisition, construction, improvement and maintenance of the public docks shall be made according to a plan developed by the Virginia Marine Resources Commission.

From the tax collected pursuant to the provisions of this chapter from the sales of gasoline used for the propelling of watercraft, after deduction for lawful refunds, there shall be paid into the state treasury for use by the Marine Resources Commission, the Virginia Soil and Water Conservation Board, the State Water Control Board, and the Commonwealth Transportation Board to (i) improve the public docks as specified in this section, (ii) improve commercial and sports fisheries in Virginia's tidal waters, (iii) make environmental improvements including, without limitation, fisheries management and habitat enhancement in the Chesapeake and its tributaries, and (iv) further the purposes set forth in § 33.2-1510, a sum as established by the General Assembly.

E. Of the remaining revenues deposited into the Commonwealth Transportation Fund pursuant to this chapter less refunds authorized by this chapter: (i) 80 percent shall be deposited into the Highway Maintenance and Operating Fund established pursuant to § 33.2-1530, (ii) 15 percent shall be deposited into the Transportation Trust Fund established pursuant to § 33.2-1524, (iii) four percent shall be deposited into the Priority Transportation Fund, and (iv) one percent shall be transferred to a special fund within the Commonwealth Transportation Fund in the state treasury, to be used to meet the necessary expenses of the Department of Motor Vehicles.

History.

2000, cc. 729, 758; 2007, c. 896; 2013, c. 766.

Section set out twice.

The section above effective if amendments by Acts 2015, c. 684 expire pursuant to Acts 2015, c. 684, cl. 12. For the section as amended by Acts 2015, c. 684, see the preceding section, also numbered 58.1-2289.

Contingent effective date. Acts 2015, c. 684, cl. 12 provides: "That the provisions of this act amending §§ 33.2-1530, 58.1-815.4, 58.1-1741, and 58.1-2289 of the Code of Virginia shall expire if the Commonwealth collects sales and use tax from remote retailers on sales made into the Commonwealth pursuant to legislation enacted by the federal government that grants states that meet minimum simplification requirements specified in such legislation the authority to compel remote retailers to collect sales and use tax on sales made into the respective state." The section as set out above does not contain the amendments by Acts 2015, c. 684.

Editor's note. — References in this section were updated at the direction of the Virginia Code Commission to conform to the recodification of Title 33.2 by Acts 2014, c. 805, effective October 1, 2014.

ARTICLE 10.

TAX ON FUEL IN INVENTORY.

§ **58.1-2290:** Repealed by Acts 2013, c. 766, cl. 4.

§ **58.1-2290.1:** Repealed by Acts 2016, c. 305, cl. 2.

CHAPTER 22.1.

MOTOR VEHICLE FUELS SALES TAX IN CERTAIN TRANSPORTATION DISTRICTS.

Section

Taxation

§ 58.1-2291. Title.

This chapter shall be known and may be cited as the "Motor Vehicle Fuels Sales Tax Act."

History.
2012, cc. 217, 225.

§ 58.1-2292. Definitions.

As used in this chapter unless the context requires a different meaning:

"Commissioner" means the Commissioner of the Department of Motor Vehicles.

"Cost price" means the same as that term is defined in § 58.1-602, and also includes all federal and state excise taxes and storage tank fees paid by the distributor. "Cost price" does not include separately stated federal diesel fuel excise taxes, unless the distributor fails to exclude the federal diesel excise tax when collecting the tax imposed pursuant to this chapter.

"Department" means the Department of Motor Vehicles, acting directly or through its duly authorized officers and agents.

"Distributor" means (i) any person engaged in the business of selling fuels in the Commonwealth who brings, or causes to be brought, into the Commonwealth from outside the Commonwealth any fuels for sale, or any other person engaged in the business of selling fuels in the Commonwealth; (ii) any person who makes, manufactures, fabricates, processes, or stores fuels in the Commonwealth for sale in the Commonwealth; or (iii) any person engaged in the business of selling fuels outside the Commonwealth who ships or transports fuels to any person in the business of selling fuels in the Commonwealth.

"Fuel" means any fuel subject to tax under Chapter 22 (§ 58.1-2200 et seq.).

"Gross sales" means the same as that term is defined in § 58.1-602.

"Retail dealer" means any person, including a distributor, who sells fuels to a consumer or to any person for any purpose other than resale.

"Sale" means the same as that term is defined in § 58.1-602 and also includes the distribution of fuel by a distributor to itself as a retail dealer.

"Sales price" means the same as that term is defined in § 58.1-602 and also includes all transportation and delivery charges, regardless of whether the charges are separately stated on the invoice. Sales price does not include separately stated federal diesel fuel excise taxes, unless the distributor fails to exclude the federal diesel excise tax when collecting the tax imposed pursuant to this chapter.

History.
2012, cc. 217, 225.

§ 58.1-2293. Regulation; forms.

The Commissioner may promulgate regulations and shall prescribe such forms as shall be necessary to effectuate and enforce this chapter.

History.
2012, cc. 217, 225.

§ 58.1-2294. Disclosure of information; penalties.

A. The Commissioner may divulge tax information collected in administering this chapter to the Tax Commissioner, or to any director of finance or other authorized collector of county, city, or town taxes who, for the performance of his official duties, requests the same in writing setting forth the reasons for such request. The Commissioner may also divulge to the executive directors of the Northern Virginia Transportation Commission and the Potomac and Rappahannock Transportation Commission for their confidential use such tax information as may be necessary to facilitate the collection of the taxes levied under this chapter.

B. Any person to whom tax information is divulged pursuant to this section shall be subject to the prohibitions and penalties prescribed in § 58.1-3 as though that person were a tax official as defined in that section.

History.
2012, cc. 217, 225.

§ 58.1-2295. (Contingent expiration date — see note) Levy; payment of tax.

A. 1. In addition to all other taxes now imposed by law, there is hereby imposed a tax upon every distributor who engages in the business of selling fuels at wholesale to retail dealers for retail sale in any county or city that is a member of (i) any transportation district in which a rapid heavy rail commuter mass transportation system operating on an exclusive right-of-way and a bus commuter mass transportation system are owned, operated, or controlled by an agency or commission as defined in § 33.2-1901 or (ii) any transportation district that is subject to subsection C of § 33.2-1915 and that is contiguous to the Northern Virginia Transportation District.

2. In addition to all other taxes now imposed by law, there is hereby imposed a tax upon every distributor who engages in the business of selling fuels at wholesale to retail dealers for retail sale in any county or city that is located in a Planning District established pursuant to Chapter 42 (§ 15.2-4200 et seq.) of Title 15.2 that (i) as of January 1, 2013, has a population of not less than 1.5 million but fewer than two million, as shown by the most recent United States Census, has not less than 1.2 million but fewer than 1.7 million motor vehicles registered therein, and has a total transit ridership of not less than 15 million but fewer than 50 million riders per year across all transit systems within the Planning District or (ii) as shown by the most recent United States Census meets the population criteria set forth in clause (i) and also meets the vehicle registration and ridership criteria set forth in clause (i). In any case in which the tax is imposed pursuant to clause (ii) such tax shall be effective beginning on the July 1 immediately following the calendar year in which all of the criteria have been met.

B. The tax shall be imposed at a rate of 2.1 percent of the sales price charged by a distributor for fuels sold to a retail dealer for retail sale in any such county or city. In any such sale to a retail dealer in which the distributor and the retail dealer are the same person, the sales price charged by the distributor shall be the cost price to the distributor of the fuel.

The tax levied under this section shall be imposed at the time of sale by the distributor to the retail dealer.

C. The tax imposed by this section shall be paid by the distributor, but the distributor shall separately state the amount of the tax and add such tax to the sales price or charge. Thereafter, such tax shall be a debt from the retail dealer to the distributor until paid and shall be recoverable at law in the same manner as other debts. No action at law or suit in equity under this chapter shall be maintained in the Commonwealth by any distributor who is not registered under § 58.1-2299.2 or is delinquent in the payment of taxes imposed under this chapter.

History.

2012, cc. 217, 225; 2013, c. 766.

Section set out twice.

The section above is set out as amended by Acts 2013, c. 766. For this section effective if amendments by Acts 2013, c. 766 expire, see the following section, also numbered 58.1-2295.

Contingent expiration date. — Acts 2013, c. 766, cl. 14 provides: "That the provisions of this act that generate additional revenue through state taxes or fees for transportation (i) throughout the Commonwealth and in Planning District 8 and Planning District 23 or (ii) in any other Planning District that becomes subject to the state taxes or fees imposed solely in Planning Districts pursuant to this act shall expire on December 31 of any year in which the General Assembly appropriates any of such additional revenues for any non-transportation-related purpose or transfers any of such additional revenues that are to be deposited into the Commonwealth Transportation Fund or any subfund thereof pursuant to general law for a non-transportation-related purpose. In the event a local government of any county or city wherein the additional taxes and fees are levied appropriates or allocates any of such additional revenues to a non-transportation purpose, such locality shall not be the direct beneficiary of any of the revenues generated by the taxes or fees in the year immediately succeeding the year in which revenues where appropriated or allocated to a non-transportation purpose."

Editor's note.

References in this section were updated at the direction of the Virginia Code Commission to conform to the recodification of Title 33.2 by Acts 2014, c. 805, effective October 1, 2014.

§ 58.1-2295. (Contingent effective date — see note) Levy; payment of tax.

A. In addition to all other taxes now imposed by law, there is hereby imposed a tax upon every distributor who engages in the business of selling fuels at wholesale to retail dealers for retail sale in any county or city that is a member of (i) any transportation district in which a rapid heavy rail commuter mass transportation system operating on an exclusive right-of-way and a bus commuter mass transportation system are owned, operated, or controlled by an agency or commission as defined in § 33.2-1901 or (ii) any transportation district that is subject to subsection C of § 33.2-1915 and that is contiguous to the Northern Virginia Transportation District.

The tax shall be imposed at a rate of 2.1 percent of the sales price charged by a distributor for fuels sold to a retail dealer for retail sale in any such county or city. In any such sale to a retail dealer in which the distributor and the retail dealer are the same person, the sales price charged by the distributor shall be the cost price to the distributor of the fuel.

The tax levied under this section shall be imposed at the time of sale by the distributor to the retail dealer.

B. The tax imposed by this section shall be paid by the distributor, but the distributor shall separately state the amount of the tax and add such tax to the sales price or charge. Thereafter, such tax shall be a debt from the retail dealer to the distributor until paid and shall be recoverable at law in the same manner as other debts. No action at law or suit in equity under this chapter shall be maintained in the Commonwealth by any distributor who is not registered under § 58.1-2299.2 or is delinquent in the payment of taxes imposed under this chapter.

History.

2012, cc. 217, 225.

Section set out twice.

The section above is set out as effective if amendments by Acts 2013, c. 766 expire. For this section as amended by Acts 2013, c. 766, see the preceding section, also numbered 58.1-2295.

Editor's note.

References in this section were updated at the direction of the Virginia Code Commission to conform to the recodification of Title 33.2 by Acts 2014, c. 805, effective October 1, 2014.

§ 58.1-2296. Backup tax; liability.

A. There is hereby imposed a tax at the rate specified by § 58.1-2295 on fuel not subject to the tax imposed under that section at the time of sale by the distributor to the retail dealer, but subsequently sold or used in such a manner that the previous sale should have been taxed under that section.

B. The person selling or using fuel that is subject to the tax imposed by this section shall be liable for the tax.

C. The tax liability imposed by this section shall be in addition to any other penalty imposed pursuant to this chapter.

History.
2012, cc. 217, 225.

§ 58.1-2297. When tax return and payment are due; credits for overpayment.

A. Every distributor required to collect the taxes imposed under this chapter shall file a return with the Commissioner. Such return shall be in the form specified by the Commissioner and contain the information required by the Commissioner. The return and the payment for the taxes levied pursuant to this chapter shall be due for each full month in a calendar year. Any return and payment required under this section shall be deemed timely filed if received by the Commissioner by midnight of the twentieth day of the second month succeeding the month for which the return and payment are due. Each return shall report tax liabilities that accrue in the month for which the return is due.

B. Returns and payments shall be (i) postmarked on or before the fifteenth day of the second month succeeding the month for which the return and payment are due or (ii) received by the Department by the twentieth day of the second month succeeding the month for which the return and payment are due. However, a monthly return of the tax for the month of May shall be (a) postmarked by June 25 or (b) received by the Commissioner by the last business day the Department is open for business in June.

If a tax return and payment due date falls on a Saturday, Sunday, or a state or banking holiday, the return shall be postmarked on or before the fifteenth day of the second month succeeding the month for which the return and payment are due or received by the Department by midnight of the next business day the Department is open for business. This provision shall not apply to a return of the tax for the month of May.

A return and payment shall be deemed postmarked if it carries the official cancellation mark of the United States Postal Service or other postal or delivery service.

C. Notwithstanding the provisions of any other section in this chapter, the Commissioner may require all or certain distributors to file tax returns and payments electronically.

D. Persons incurring liability under § 58.1-2296 for the backup tax on fuel shall file a return together with a payment of tax due within 30 calendar days of incurring such liability.

E. Any person entitled to a credit for overpayment of a tax levied under this chapter shall claim such credit on his monthly return no later than one year following the date of the overpayment.

History.
2012, cc. 217, 225.

§ 58.1-2298. Deductions.

For purposes of compensating a distributor for accounting for and remitting the tax levied by this chapter, such distributor shall be allowed to deduct two percent of the tax otherwise due in submitting his return and paying the amount due by him if the amount was not delinquent at the time of payment.

History.
2012, cc. 217, 225.

§ 58.1-2299. Bad debts.

A. In any return filed under the provisions of this chapter, a distributor may credit, against the tax shown to be due on the return, the amount of tax previously returned and paid on accounts which are owed to the distributor and which have been found to be worthless within the period covered by the return. The credit, however, shall not exceed the amount of the uncollected sales price determined by treating prior payments on each debt as consisting of the same proportion of the sales price, tax levied under this chapter, and other nontaxable charges as the total debt originally owed to the distributor. The amount of accounts for which a credit has been taken that are thereafter in whole or in part paid to the dealer shall be included in the first return filed after such collection.

B. Notwithstanding any other provision of this section, a distributor whose volume and character of uncollectible accounts, including checks returned for insufficient funds, renders it impractical to substantiate the credit on an account-by-account basis may, subject to the approval of the Department, utilize an alternative method of substantiating the credit.

History.
2012, cc. 217, 225.

§ 58.1-2299.1. Exclusion from professional license tax.

The amount of the tax imposed by this chapter and collected by a distributor in any taxable year shall be excluded from gross receipts for purposes of any tax imposed under Chapter 37 (§ 58.1-3700 et seq.).

History.
2012, cc. 217, 225.

§ 58.1-2299.2. Certificates of registration; issuance; civil penalty.

A. Every person desiring to engage in the business of a distributor and to sell fuel to a retail dealer for retail sale within any county or city that is a member of (i) any transportation district in which a rapid heavy rail commuter mass transportation system operating on an exclusive right-of-way and a bus commuter mass transportation system are owned, operated, or controlled by an agency or commission as defined in § 33.2-1901 or (ii) any transportation district that is subject to subsection C of § 33.2-1915 and that is contiguous to the Northern Virginia Transportation District shall file an application for a certificate of registration with the Commissioner for collection and payment of the tax imposed pursuant to this chapter.

B. The application for certificate of registration shall be on a form prescribed by the Commissioner and shall set forth the name under which the applicant intends to transact the business for which registration is required under subsection A, the principal location of the place of business, and such other information as the Commissioner may require.

Each applicant shall sign the application as owner of the business. If the business is owned by an association, partnership, or corporation, the application shall be signed by a member, partner, executive officer, or other person specifically authorized by the association, partnership, or corporation to sign.

C. Upon approval of the application by the Commissioner, a certificate of registration shall be issued. The certificate is not assignable but shall be valid only for the person in whose name it is issued.

D. If the holder of a certificate of registration issued under this section ceases to conduct his business in the Commonwealth at the principal place of business designated in the certificate, the certificate shall automatically expire. The holder shall notify the Commissioner, in writing, within 30 days after he has ceased to conduct the business. If the holder of the certificate desires to continue in the business for which he was registered but at a different location, he shall so inform the Commissioner, in writing, at least 30 days prior to the contemplated relocation. The Commissioner shall then issue an amended certificate designating the new principal place of business. The amended certificate shall become effective on the date that the certificate for the previous place of business expires. There shall be no charge for obtaining an amended certificate.

E. The holder of the certificate of registration issued under this chapter who discontinues in the Commonwealth the business for which the certificate was issued, whether by transferring his business to another person, by selling out his business or stock of goods, or by quitting the business, shall notify the Commissioner in writing within 15 days of such discontinuance and shall surrender the certificate to the Commissioner. The notice shall state the effective date of the discontinuance and, if the certificate holder has transferred the business or otherwise relinquished control to another person by sale or otherwise, the date of the sale or transfer and the name and address of the person to whom the business is transferred or relinquished. The notice shall also include any other information required by the Commissioner.

F. Whenever a person fails to comply with any provision of this chapter or any rule or regulation relating thereto, the Commissioner, after giving such person 10 days' notice in writing, may revoke or suspend the certificate of registration held by such person. The notice may be personally served or served by registered mail directed to the last known address of such person.

G. Any person required to obtain a certificate of registration under this chapter who engages in business in the Commonwealth without obtaining such certificate, or after such certificate has been suspended or revoked, and each officer of any corporation which so engages in business, shall be subject to a civil penalty. The amount of the civil penalty assessed against a person for his (i) first violation shall be $5,000 and (ii) second and subsequent violations shall be $10,000. Each day's continuance in business in violation of this section shall constitute a separate offense.

History.

2012, cc. 217, 225.

Editor's note.

References in this section were updated at the direction of the Virginia Code Commission to conform to the recodification of Title 33.2 by Acts 2014, c. 805, effective October 1, 2014.

§ 58.1-2299.3. Collection of tax.

Any distributor collecting the tax on transactions exempt or not taxable under this chapter shall transmit to the Commissioner such erroneously or illegally collected tax unless or until he can affirmatively show that the tax has since been refunded to the purchaser or credited to his account.

Any distributor who neglects, fails, or refuses to collect such tax upon every taxable sale made by him, his agents, or his employees shall be liable for and pay the tax himself, and such distributor shall not thereafter be entitled to sue for or recover in the Commonwealth any part of the purchase price from the purchaser until such tax is paid. Moreover, any distributor who neglects, fails, or refuses to pay or collect the tax herein provided, either by himself or through his agents or employees, is guilty of a Class 1 misdemeanor.

All sums collected by a distributor as required by this chapter shall be deemed to be held in trust for the Commonwealth.

History.

2012, cc. 217, 225.

§ 58.1-2299.4. Absorption of tax prohibited.

No person shall advertise or hold out to the public, directly or indirectly, that he will absorb all or any part of the tax levied under this chapter, or that he will relieve the purchaser of the payment of all or any part of such tax. Any person who violates this section shall be guilty of a Class 2 misdemeanor.

History.
2012, cc. 217, 225.

§ 58.1-2299.5. Sale of business.

If any distributor liable for any tax, penalty, or interest levied under this chapter sells out his business or stock of goods or quits the business, he shall make a final return and payment within 15 days after the date of selling or quitting the business. His successors or assigns, if any, shall withhold sufficient of the purchase money to cover the amount of such taxes, penalties, and interest due and unpaid until such former owner produces a receipt from the Commissioner showing that they have been paid or a certificate stating that no taxes, penalties, or interest are due. If the purchaser of a business or stock of goods fails to withhold the purchase money as provided in this section, he shall be personally liable for the payment of the taxes, penalties, and interest due and unpaid on account of the operation of the business by any former owner.

History.
2012, cc. 217, 225.

§ 58.1-2299.6. Late filing or payment; civil penalty.

A. Any person who fails to file a return required by this chapter on a timely basis shall be subject to a civil penalty. The amount of the civil penalty shall be as follows:

1. $50 for the first violation;
2. $200 for the second violation;
3. $500 for the third violation; and
4. $1,000 for the fourth and subsequent violations.

After imposition of the penalty under this subsection, the amount of the penalty, if not paid within 30 days of receipt of notice of such penalty, shall bear interest at the rate of one percent per month or fraction thereof until the penalty has been paid.

B. Interest at the rate of one percent per month or fraction thereof shall accrue on the amount of any taxes due under this chapter that have not been paid to the Commissioner on a timely basis. Such interest shall continue to accrue until such taxes have been paid.

Any person who fails to pay the Commissioner on a timely basis the amount of taxes due under this chapter shall also be subject to a civil penalty. The amount of the civil penalty shall be equal to 10 percent of the tax due or $50, whichever is greater; however, penalties resulting from an audit shall be equal to 10 percent of the tax due.

After imposition of the civil penalty under this subsection, the amount of the penalty, if not paid within 30 days of receipt of notice of such penalty, shall bear interest at the rate of one percent per month until both tax and penalty have been paid.

C. The Commissioner is authorized to reduce or waive any penalties under this section if the violation is due to a reasonable or good cause shown to the satisfaction of the Commissioner.

History.
2012, cc. 217, 225.

§ 58.1-2299.7. False or fraudulent return; civil penalty.

Any person liable for a tax levied under this chapter who files a false or fraudulent return with the intent to evade the tax shall be subject to a civil penalty. The amount of the civil penalty shall be equal to 50 percent of the amount of the tax intended to be evaded by the filing of such return. The civil penalty shall be in addition to the amount of the tax intended to be evaded.

History.
2012, cc. 217, 225.

§ 58.1-2299.8. Payment of civil penalty; disposition; waiver.

Any civil penalty assessed pursuant to this chapter shall be payable to the Department, shall be in addition to any other penalty or tax that may be imposed as provided in this chapter, and shall be collectible by the Commissioner in the same manner as if it were part of the tax levied. The amount of any civil penalty imposed under this chapter shall bear interest at the rate of one percent per month until paid. All civil penalties imposed under this chapter shall be deposited as provided in § 58.1-2299.20. Notwithstanding any other provisions of this chapter, the Commissioner is authorized to reduce or waive any civil penalties under this chapter if the violation is due to a reasonable or good cause shown to the satisfaction of the Commissioner.

History.
2012, cc. 217, 225.

§ 58.1-2299.9. Prohibited acts; criminal penalties.

A. Any person who commits any of the following acts is guilty of a Class 1 misdemeanor:

1. Failing to obtain a certificate of registration required by this chapter;
2. Failing to file a return required by this chapter;
3. Failing to pay a tax when due under this chapter;

4. Making a false statement in an application, return, ticket, invoice, statement, or any other document required under this chapter;

5. Failing to keep records as required under this chapter; or

6. Refusing to allow the Commissioner or a representative of the Commissioner to examine the person's books and records concerning transactions taxable under this chapter.

B. A person who knowingly commits any of the following acts is guilty of a Class 1 misdemeanor:

1. Dispenses into the supply tank of a highway vehicle, watercraft, or aircraft any fuel on which a tax required to be levied under this chapter has not been paid; or

2. Allows to be dispensed into the supply tank of a highway vehicle, watercraft, or aircraft any fuel on which a tax required to be levied under this chapter has not been paid.

History.

2012, cc. 217, 225.

§ 58.1-2299.10. Willful commission of prohibited acts; criminal penalties.

Any person who willfully commits any of the following acts with the intent to (i) evade or circumvent the taxes imposed under this chapter or (ii) assist any other person in efforts to evade or circumvent such taxes is guilty of a Class 6 felony, if he:

1. Does not pay the taxes imposed under this chapter and diverts the proceeds from such taxes for other purposes;

2. Is a distributor required to be registered under the provisions of this chapter, or the agent or representative of such a distributor, and converts or attempts to convert proceeds from taxes imposed under this chapter for the use of the distributor or the distributor's agent or representative, with the intent to defraud the Commonwealth;

3. Illegally collects taxes imposed under this chapter when not authorized or licensed by the Commissioner to do so;

4. Conspires with any other person or persons to engage in an act, plan, or scheme to defraud the Commonwealth of proceeds from taxes levied under this chapter;

5. Fails to remit to the Commissioner any tax levied pursuant to this chapter, if he (i) has added, or represented that he has added, the tax to the sales price for the fuel and (ii) has collected the amount of the tax; or

6. Applies for or collects from the Department a tax credit when the person knows or has reason to know that fuel for which the credit is claimed has been or will be used for a taxable purpose; however, if the amount of fuel involved is not more than 20 gallons, such person is guilty of a Class 1 misdemeanor.

History.

2012, cc. 217, 225.

§ 58.1-2299.11. Bond.

The Commissioner may, when in his judgment it is necessary and advisable so to do in order to secure the collection of the tax levied by this chapter, require any person subject to such tax to file with him a bond, with such surety as the Commissioner determines is necessary to secure the payment of any tax, penalty, or interest due or which may become due from such person. In lieu of such bond, securities approved by the Commissioner may be deposited with the State Treasurer, which securities shall be kept in the custody of the State Treasurer and shall be sold by him, at the request of the Commissioner, at public or private sale if it becomes necessary to do so in order to recover any tax, penalty, or interest due the Commonwealth under this chapter. Upon any such sale, the surplus, if any, above the amounts due under this chapter shall be returned to the person who deposited the securities.

History.

2012, cc. 217, 225.

§ 58.1-2299.12. Jeopardy assessment.

If the Commissioner is of the opinion that the collection of any tax or any amount of tax required to be collected and paid under this chapter will be jeopardized by delay, he shall make an assessment of the tax or amount of tax required to be collected and shall mail or issue a notice of such assessment to the taxpayer together with a demand for immediate payment of the tax or of the deficiency in tax declared to be in jeopardy including penalties. In the case of a tax for a current period, the Commissioner may declare the taxable period of the taxpayer immediately terminated and shall cause notice of such finding and declaration to be mailed or issued to the taxpayer together with a demand for immediate payment of the tax based on the period declared terminated and such tax shall be immediately due and payable, whether or not the time otherwise allowed by law for filing a return and paying the tax has expired. Assessments provided for in this section shall become immediately due and payable, and if any such tax, penalty, or interest is not paid upon demand of the Commissioner, he shall proceed to collect the same by legal process, or, in his discretion, he may require the taxpayer to file such bond as in his judgment may be sufficient to protect the interest of the Commonwealth.

History.

2012, cc. 217, 225.

§ 58.1-2299.13. Memorandum of lien for collection of taxes.

A. If any taxes or fees, including penalties and interest, due under this chapter become delinquent or are past due, the Commissioner may file a memorandum of lien in the circuit court clerk's office of the county or city in which the taxpayer's place of business is located or in which the taxpayer resides. If the taxpayer has no place of business or residence within the Commonwealth, such memorandum may be filed in the Circuit Court of the City of Richmond. A copy of such memorandum may also be filed in the clerk's office of all counties and cities in which the taxpayer owns real estate. Such memorandum shall be recorded in the judgment docket book and shall have the effect of a judgment in favor of the Commonwealth, to be enforced as provided in Article 19 (§ 8.01-196 et seq.) of Chapter 3 of Title 8.01, mutatis mutandis, except that a writ of fieri facias may be issued any time after the memorandum is filed. The lien on real estate shall become effective at the time the memorandum is filed in the jurisdiction in which the real estate is located.

B. Recordation of a memorandum of lien hereunder shall not affect the right to exoneration under this chapter nor shall an application for correction pursuant to § 58.1-2299.15 affect the power of the Commissioner to collect the tax, except as specifically provided in this chapter.

History.
2012, cc. 217, 225.

§ 58.1-2299.14. Recordkeeping requirements; inspection of records; civil penalties.

A. Every distributor required to make a return and pay or collect any tax under this chapter shall keep and preserve suitable records of the sales taxable under this chapter, and such other books of account as may be necessary to determine the amount of tax due hereunder, and such other pertinent information as may be required by the Commissioner. Such records shall be kept and maintained for a period to include the Department's current fiscal year and the previous three fiscal years.

B. The Commissioner or any agent authorized by him may examine during the usual business hours all records, books, papers, or other documents of any distributor required to be registered under this chapter relating to the sales price of any fuel subject to taxation under this chapter to verify the truth and accuracy of any statement or any other information as to a particular sale.

C. Any person who fails to keep or retain records as required by this section shall be subject to a civil penalty. The amount of the civil penalty assessed against a person for his first violation shall be $1,000. The amount of the civil penalty assessed against a person for each subsequent violation shall be $1,000 more than the amount of the civil penalty for the preceding violation.

D. Any person who refuses to allow an inspection authorized under this section shall be subject to a civil penalty of $5,000 for each refusal.

History.
2012, cc. 217, 225.

§ 58.1-2299.15. Application to Commissioner for correction; appeal.

A. Any person assessed with any tax administered by the Department pursuant to this chapter or against whom an order or decision of the Commissioner has been adversely rendered relating to the provisions of this chapter may, within 30 days from the date of such assessment, order, or decision apply for relief to the Commissioner. Such application shall be in the form prescribed by the Department and shall fully set forth the grounds upon which the applicant relies and all facts relevant to the applicant's contention. The Commissioner may also require such additional information, testimony, or documentary evidence as he deems necessary to make a fair determination of the application.

B. On receipt of a written notice of intent to file under subsection A for relief from a tax assessment, the Commissioner shall refrain from collecting the tax until the time for filing hereunder has expired, unless he determines that collection is in jeopardy.

C. Any person against whom an order or decision of the Commissioner has been adversely rendered relating to the provisions of this chapter may, within 15 days of such order or decision, appeal from such order or decision to the Circuit Court of the City of Richmond.

History.
2012, cc. 217, 225.

§ 58.1-2299.16. Period of limitations.

The taxes imposed by this chapter shall be assessed within three years from the date on which such taxes became due and payable. In the case of a false or fraudulent return with intent to evade payment of the taxes imposed by this chapter, or a failure to file a return, the taxes may be assessed, or a proceeding in court for the collection of such taxes may be begun without assessment, at any time. The Commissioner shall not examine any person's records beyond the three-year period of limitations unless he has reasonable evidence of fraud or reasonable cause to believe that such person was required by law to file a return and failed to do so.

History.
2012, cc. 217, 225.

§ 58.1-2299.17. Waiver of time limitation on assessment of taxes.

If, before the expiration of the time prescribed for assessment of any tax levied pursuant to this chapter and assessable by the Department, both the Commissioner and the taxpayer have consented in writing to its assessment after such time, the tax may be assessed any time prior to the expiration of the period agreed upon. The period so agreed upon may be extended by subsequent agreements in writing made before the expiration of the period previously agreed upon.

History.
2012, cc. 217, 225.

§ 58.1-2299.18. Suits to recover taxes.

If any person fails to pay the tax or any civil penalty levied under this chapter, including accrued penalties and interest, when due, the Attorney General or the Commissioner may bring an appropriate action for the recovery of such tax, penalty, and interest, provided that if it is found that such failure to pay was willful, judgment shall be rendered for double the amount of the tax or civil penalty found to be due, with costs.

History.
2012, cc. 217, 225.

§ 58.1-2299.19. Liability of corporate or partnership officer; penalty.

Any corporate or partnership officer who directs or causes the business of which he is a corporate or partnership officer to fail to pay, collect, or truthfully account for and pay over any fuels tax for which the business is liable to the Commonwealth or to a trustee shall, in addition to other penalties provided by law, be liable for a penalty in the amount of the tax evaded or not paid, collected, or accounted for and paid over. The penalty shall be assessed and collected in the same manner as such taxes are assessed and collected. However, this penalty shall be dischargeable in bankruptcy proceedings.

History.
2012, cc. 217, 225.

§ 58.1-2299.20. (Contingent expiration date — see note) Disposition of tax revenues.

A. All taxes, interest, and civil penalties paid to the Commissioner pursuant to this chapter for the sale of fuels at wholesale to retail dealers for retail sale in any county or city set forth in subdivision A 1 of § 58.1-2295, after subtraction of the direct costs of administration by the Department, shall be deposited in a special fund entitled the "Special Fund Account of the Transportation District of ...." The amounts deposited in the special fund shall be distributed monthly to the applicable transportation district commission of which the county or city is a member to be applied to the operating deficit, capital, and debt service of the mass transit system of such district or, in the case of a transportation district subject to the provisions of subsection C of § 33.2-1915, to be applied to and expended for any transportation purpose of such district. In the case of a jurisdiction which, after July 1, 1989, joins a transportation district which was established on or before January 1, 1986, and is also subject to subsection C of § 33.2-1915, the funds collected from that jurisdiction shall be applied to and expended for any transportation purpose of such jurisdiction. The direct costs of administration shall be credited to the funds appropriated to the Department.

B. All taxes, interest, and civil penalties paid to the Commissioner pursuant to this chapter for the sale of fuels at wholesale to retail dealers for retail sale in any county or city set forth in subdivision A 2 of § 58.1-2295, after subtraction of the direct costs of administration by the Department, shall be deposited into special funds established by law. In the case of Planning District 23, the revenue generated and collected therein shall be deposited into the fund established in § 33.2-2600. For additional Planning Districts that may become subject to this section, funds shall be established by appropriate legislation. The direct cost of administration shall be credited to the funds appropriated to the Department.

History.
2012, cc. 217, 225; 2013, c. 766.

Section set out twice.
The section set out above is set out as amended by Acts 2013, c. 766. For this section as effective if amendments by Acts 2013, c. 766 expire, see the following section, also numbered 58.1-2299.20.

Contingent expiration date. — Acts 2013, c. 766, cl. 14 provides: "That the provisions of this act that generate additional revenue through state taxes or fees for transportation (i) throughout the Commonwealth and in Planning District 8 and Planning District 23 or (ii) in any other Planning District that becomes subject to the state taxes or fees imposed solely in Planning Districts pursuant to this act shall expire on December 31 of any year in which the General Assembly appropriates any of such additional revenues for any non-transportation-related purpose or transfers any of such additional revenues that are to be deposited into the Commonwealth Transportation Fund or any subfund thereof pursuant to general law for a non-transportation-related purpose. In the event a local government of any county or city wherein the additional taxes and fees are levied appropriates or allocates any of such additional revenues to a non-transportation purpose, such locality shall not be the direct beneficiary of any of the revenues generated by the taxes or fees in the year immediately succeeding the year in which revenues where appropriated or allocated to a non-transportation purpose."

Editor's note.
Acts 2013, c. 766, cl. 18 provides: "That should any portion of this act be held unconstitutional by a court of competent jurisdiction, the remaining portions of this act shall remain in effect."

References in this section were updated at the direction of the Virginia Code Commission to conform to the recodification of Title 33.2 by Acts 2014, c. 805, effective October 1, 2014.

§ 58.1-2299.20. (Contingent effective date — see note) Disposition of tax revenues.

All taxes, interest, and civil penalties paid to the Commissioner pursuant to this chapter, after subtraction of the direct costs of administration by the Department, shall be deposited in a special fund entitled the "Special Fund Account of the Transportation District of .... " The amounts deposited in the special fund shall be distributed monthly to the applicable transportation district commission of which the county or city is a member to be applied to the operating deficit, capital, and debt service of the mass transit system of such district or, in the case of a transportation district subject to the provisions of subsection C of § 33.2-1915, to be applied to and expended for any transportation purpose of such district. In the case of a jurisdiction which, after July 1, 1989, joins a transportation district which was established on or before January 1, 1986, and is also subject to subsection C of § 33.2-1915, the funds collected from that jurisdiction shall be applied to and expended for any transportation purpose of such jurisdiction. The direct costs of administration shall be credited to the funds appropriated to the Department.

History.

2012, cc. 217, 225.

Section set out twice.

The section above is set out as effective if amendments by Acts 2013, c. 766 expire. For this section as amended by Acts 2013, c. 766, see the preceding section, also numbered 58.1-2299.20.

Editor's note.

References in this section were updated at the direction of the Virginia Code Commission to conform to the recodification of Title 33.2 by Acts 2014, c. 805, effective October 1, 2014.

CHAPTER 24.

VIRGINIA MOTOR VEHICLE SALES AND USE TAX.

Section

§ 58.1-2400. Title.

This chapter shall be known and may be cited as the "Virginia Motor Vehicle Sales and Use Tax Act."

History.

Code 1950, § 58-685.10; 1966, c. 587; 1984, c. 675.

§ 58.1-2401. Definitions.

As used in this chapter, unless the context clearly shows otherwise, the term or phrase:

"Commissioner" shall mean the Commissioner of the Department of Motor Vehicles of the Commonwealth.

"Department" shall mean the Department of Motor Vehicles of this Commonwealth, acting through its duly authorized officers and agents.

"Mobile office" shall mean an industrialized building unit not subject to the federal regulation, which may be constructed on a chassis for the purpose of towing to the point of use and designed to be used with or without a permanent foundation, for commercial use and not for residential use; or two or more such units separately towable, but designed to be joined together at the point of use to form a single commercial structure, and which may be designed for removal to, and installation or erection on other sites.

"Motor vehicle" shall mean every vehicle, except for mobile office as herein defined, which is self-propelled or designed for self-propulsion and every vehicle drawn by or designed to be drawn by a motor vehicle, including manufactured homes as defined in § 46.2-100 and every device in, upon and by which any person or property is, or can be, transported or drawn upon a highway, but excepting devices moved by human or animal power, devices used exclusively upon stationary rails or tracks and vehicles, other than manufactured homes, used in this Commonwealth but not required to be licensed by the Commonwealth.

"Sale" shall mean any transfer of ownership or possession, by exchange or barter, conditional or otherwise, in any manner or by any means whatsoever, of a motor vehicle. The term shall also include a transaction whereby possession is transferred but title is retained by the seller as security. The term shall not include a transfer of ownership or possession made to secure payment of an obligation, nor shall it include a refund for, or replacement of, a motor vehicle of equivalent or lesser value pursuant to the Virginia Motor Vehicle Warranty Enforcement Act (§ 59.1-207.9 et seq.). Where the replacement motor vehicle is of greater value than the motor vehicle replaced, only the difference in value shall constitute a sale.

"Sale price" shall mean the total price paid for a motor vehicle and all attachments thereon and accessories thereto, as determined by the Commissioner, exclusive of any federal manufacturers' excise tax, without any allowance or deduction for

trade-ins or unpaid liens or encumbrances. However, "sale price" shall not include (i) any manufacturer rebate or manufacturer incentive payment applied to the transaction by the customer or dealer whether as a reduction in the sales price or as payment for the vehicle and (ii) the cost of controls, lifts, automatic transmission, power steering, power brakes or any other equipment installed in or added to a motor vehicle which is required by law or regulation as a condition for operation of a motor vehicle by a handicapped person.

History.

Code 1950, §§ 58-685.11, 58-685.13, 58-685.13:2; 1966, c. 587; 1968, c. 321; 1970, cc. 409, 489; 1972, cc. 302, 680; 1973, c. 207; 1974, c. 477; 1976, cc. 567, 610; 1977, c. 537; 1978, cc. 656, 758, 766; 1979, cc. 310, 436; 1982, c. 541; 1983, c. 386; 1984, c. 675; 1986, Sp. Sess., c. 11; 1995, c. 50; 1997, cc. 283, 853; 1999, c. 77; 2011, cc. 405, 639; 2013, c. 766.

§ 58.1-2402. (Contingent expiration date — see note) Levy.

A. There is hereby levied, in addition to all other taxes and fees of every kind now imposed by law, a tax upon the sale or use of motor vehicles in Virginia, other than a sale to or use by a person for rental as an established business or part of an established business or incidental or germane to such business.

The amount of the tax to be collected shall be determined by the Commissioner by the application of the following rates against the gross sales price:

1. Three percent through midnight on June 30, 2013, four percent (4.0%) beginning July 1, 2013, through midnight on June 30, 2014, four and five-hundredths of a percent (4.05%) beginning July 1, 2014, through midnight on June 30, 2015, four and one tenth of a percent (4.1%) beginning July 1, 2015, through midnight on June 30, 2016, and four and fifteen-hundredths (4.15%) of a percent beginning on and after July 1, 2016, of the sale price of each motor vehicle sold in Virginia. If such motor vehicle is a manufactured home as defined in § 36-85.3, the tax shall be three percent of the sale price of each such manufactured home sold in the Commonwealth; if such vehicle is a mobile office as defined in § 58.1-2401, the tax shall be two percent of the sale price of each mobile office sold in the Commonwealth; if such vehicle has a gross vehicle weight rating or gross combination weight rating of 26,001 pounds or more and is neither (i) a manufactured home as defined in § 36-85.3, (ii) a mobile office as defined in § 58.1-2401, (iii) a trailer or semitrailer as severally defined in § 46.2-100 that is not designed or used to carry property, nor (iv) a vehicle registered under § 46.2-700, the tax shall be zero percent of the sale price of each such vehicle sold in the Commonwealth.

2. Three percent through midnight on June 30, 2013, four percent (4.0%) beginning July 1, 2013, through midnight on June 30, 2014, four and five-hundredths of a percent (4.05%) beginning July 1, 2014, through midnight on June 30, 2015, four and one tenth of a percent (4.1%) beginning July 1, 2015, through midnight on June 30, 2016, and four and fifteen-hundredths (4.15%) of a percent beginning on and after July 1, 2016, of the sale price of each motor vehicle, not sold in Virginia but used or stored for use in the Commonwealth; or three percent of the sale price of each manufactured home as defined in § 36-85.3, or two percent of the sale price of each mobile office as defined in § 58.1-2401, not sold in Virginia but used or stored for use in this Commonwealth. If such vehicle has a gross vehicle weight rating or gross combination weight rating of 26,001 pounds or more and is neither (i) a manufactured home as defined in § 36-85.3, (ii) a mobile office as defined in § 58.1-2401, (iii) a trailer or semitrailer as severally defined in § 46.2-100 that is not designed or used to carry property, nor (iv) a vehicle registered under § 46.2-700, the tax shall be zero percent of the sale price of each such vehicle not sold in the Commonwealth but used or stored for use in the Commonwealth. When any motor vehicle or manufactured home not sold in the Commonwealth is first used or stored for use in Virginia six months or more after its acquisition, the tax shall be based on its current market value.

3. The minimum tax levied on the sale of any motor vehicle in the Commonwealth that is subject to taxation at a rate exceeding zero percent shall be $75, except as provided by those exemptions defined in § 58.1-2403.

4 through 7. [Repealed.]

B. A transaction taxed under subdivision A 1 shall not also be taxed under subdivision A 2, nor shall the same transaction be taxed more than once under either subdivision.

C. Any motor vehicle, trailer or semitrailer exempt from this tax under subdivision 1 or 2 of § 58.1-2403 shall be subject to the tax, based on the current market value when such vehicle is no longer owned or used by the United States government or any governmental agency, or the Commonwealth of Virginia or any political subdivision thereof, unless such vehicle is then rented, in which case the tax imposed by § 58.1-1736 shall apply, subject to the exemptions provided in § 58.1-1737. Further, any motor vehicle, trailer or semitrailer exempt from the tax imposed by this chapter under subdivision 11 of § 58.1-2403 or §§ 46.2-663 through 46.2-674 shall be subject to the tax, based on the current market value, when such vehicle is subsequently licensed to operate on the highways of the Commonwealth.

D. Any person who with intent to evade or to aid another person to evade the tax provided for herein, falsely states the selling price of a vehicle on a bill of sale, assignment of title, application for title, or any other document or paper submitted to the Commissioner pursuant to any provisions of this title or Title 46.2, shall be guilty of a Class 3 misdemeanor.

E. Effective January 1, 1997, any amount designated as a "processing fee" and any amount charged by a dealer for processing a transaction, which is required to be included on a buyer's order pursuant to subdivision A 10 of § 46.2-1530, shall be subject to the tax.

History.

Code 1950, §§ 58-685.12, 58-685.12:1; 1966, c. 587; 1970, c. 675; 1974, c. 477; 1976, cc. 567, 610; 1977, c. 537; 1981, c. 145; 1984, c. 675; 1985, c. 123; 1986, Sp. Sess., cc. 10, 11; 1988, c. 372; 1992, c. 384; 1993, c. 159; 1994, c. 527; 1996, c. 1047; 1997, cc. 283, 853; 2004, c. 522; 2005, c. 449; 2011, cc. 405, 639, 881, 889; 2012, cc. 22, 111; 2013, c. 766.

Section set out twice.

The section above is set out as amended by Acts 2013, c. 766. For this section as effective if amendments by Acts 2013, c. 766 expire, see the following section, also numbered 58.1-2402.

Contingent expiration date. — Acts 2013, c. 766, cl. 14 provides: "That the provisions of this act that generate additional revenue through state taxes or fees for transportation (i) throughout the Commonwealth and in Planning District 8 and Planning District 23 or (ii) in any other Planning District that becomes subject to the state taxes or fees imposed solely in Planning Districts pursuant to this act shall expire on December 31 of any year in which the General Assembly appropriates any of such additional revenues for any non-transportation-related purpose or transfers any of such additional revenues that are to be deposited into the Commonwealth Transportation Fund or any subfund thereof pursuant to general law for a non-transportation-related purpose. In the event a local government of any county or city wherein the additional taxes and fees are levied appropriates or allocates any of such additional revenues to a non-transportation purpose, such locality shall not be the direct beneficiary of any of the revenues generated by the taxes or fees in the year immediately succeeding the year in which revenues where appropriated or allocated to a non-transportation purpose."

Editor's note.

Acts 2013, c. 766, cl. 18 provides: "That should any portion of this act be held unconstitutional by a court of competent jurisdiction, the remaining portions of this act shall remain in effect."

§ 58.1-2402. (Contingent effective date — see note) Levy.

A. There is hereby levied, in addition to all other taxes and fees of every kind now imposed by law, a tax upon the sale or use of motor vehicles in Virginia, other than a sale to or use by a person for rental as an established business or part of an established business or incidental or germane to such business.

The amount of the tax to be collected shall be determined by the Commissioner by the application of the following rates against the gross sales price:

1. Three percent of the sale price of each motor vehicle sold in Virginia. If such motor vehicle is a manufactured home as defined in § 36-85.3, the tax shall be three percent of the sale price of each such manufactured home sold in the Commonwealth; if such vehicle is a mobile office as defined in § 58.1-2401, the tax shall be two percent of the sale price of each mobile office sold in the Commonwealth; if such vehicle has a gross vehicle weight rating or gross combination weight rating of 26,001 pounds or more and is neither (i) a manufactured home as defined in § 36-85.3, (ii) a mobile office as defined in § 58.1-2401, (iii) a trailer or semitrailer as severally defined in § 46.2-100 that is not designed or used to carry property, nor (iv) a vehicle registered under § 46.2-700, the tax shall be zero percent of the sale price of each such vehicle sold in the Commonwealth.

2. Three percent of the sale price of each motor vehicle, or three percent of the sale price of each manufactured home as defined in § 36-85.3, or two percent of the sale price of each mobile office as defined in § 58.1-2401, not sold in Virginia but used or stored for use in the Commonwealth. If such vehicle has a gross vehicle weight rating or gross combination weight rating of 26,001 pounds or more and is neither (i) a manufactured home as defined in § 36-85.3, (ii) a mobile office as defined in § 58.1-2401, (iii) a trailer or semitrailer as severally defined in § 46.2-100 that is not designed or used to carry property, nor (iv) a vehicle registered under § 46.2-700, the tax shall be zero percent of the sale price of each such vehicle not sold in the Commonwealth but used or stored for use in the Commonwealth. When any motor vehicle or manufactured home not sold in the Commonwealth is first used or stored for use in Virginia six months or more after its acquisition, the tax shall be based on its current market value.

3. The minimum tax levied on the sale of any motor vehicle in the Commonwealth that is subject to taxation at a rate exceeding zero percent shall be $35, except as provided by those exemptions defined in § 58.1-2403.

4 through 7. [Repealed.]

B. A transaction taxed under subdivision A 1 shall not also be taxed under subdivision A 2, nor shall the same transaction be taxed more than once under either subdivision.

C. Any motor vehicle, trailer or semitrailer exempt from this tax under subdivision 1 or 2 of § 58.1-2403 shall be subject to the tax, based on the current market value when such vehicle is no longer owned or used by the United States government or any governmental agency, or the Commonwealth of Virginia or any political subdivision thereof, unless such vehicle is then rented, in which case the tax imposed by § 58.1-1736 shall apply, subject to the exemptions provided in § 58.1-1737. Further, any motor vehicle, trailer or semitrailer exempt from the tax imposed by this chapter under subdivision 11 of § 58.1-2403 or §§ 46.2-663 through 46.2-674 shall be subject to the tax, based on the current market value, when such vehicle is subsequently licensed to operate on the highways of the Commonwealth.

D. Any person who with intent to evade or to aid another person to evade the tax provided for herein, falsely states the selling price of a vehicle on a bill of sale, assignment of title, application for title, or any other document or paper submitted to the Commissioner pursuant to any provisions of this title or Title 46.2, shall be guilty of a Class 3 misdemeanor.

E. Effective January 1, 1997, any amount designated as a "processing fee" and any amount charged by a dealer for processing a transaction, which is required to be included on a buyer's order pursuant to subdivision A 10 of § 46.2-1530, shall be subject to the tax.

History.

Code 1950, §§ 58-685.12, 58-685.12:1; 1966, c. 587; 1970, c. 675; 1974, c. 477; 1976, cc. 567, 610; 1977, c. 537; 1981, c. 145; 1984, c. 675; 1985, c. 123; 1986, Sp. Sess., cc. 10, 11; 1988, c. 372; 1992, c. 384; 1993, c. 159; 1994, c. 527; 1996, c. 1047; 1997, cc. 283, 853; 2004, c. 522; 2005, c. 449; 2011, cc. 405, 639, 881, 889; 2012, cc. 22, 111.

Section set out twice.

The section above is set out as effective if amendments by Acts 2013, c. 766 expire. For this section as amended by Acts 2013, c. 766, see the preceding section, also numbered 58.1-2402.

§ **58.1-2402.1:** Repealed by Acts 2009, cc. 864 and 871, cl. 5.

§ 58.1-2403. Exemptions.

No tax shall be imposed as provided in § 58.1-2402 if the vehicle is:

1. Sold to or used by the United States government or any governmental agency thereof;

2. Sold to or used by the Commonwealth of Virginia or any political subdivision thereof;

3. Registered in the name of a volunteer fire department or volunteer emergency medical services agency not operated for profit;

4. Registered to any member of the Mattaponi, Pamunkey, or Chickahominy Indian tribes or any other recognized Indian tribe of the Commonwealth living on the tribal reservation;

5. Transferred incidental to repossession under a recorded lien and ownership is transferred to the lienholder;

6. A manufactured home permanently attached to real estate and included in the sale of real estate;

7. A gift to the spouse, son, daughter, or parent of the transferor. With the exception of a gift to a spouse, this exemption shall not apply to any unpaid obligation assumed by the transferee incidental to the transfer;

8. Transferred from an individual or partnership to a corporation or limited liability company or from a corporation or limited liability company to an individual or partnership if the transfer is incidental to the formation, organization or dissolution of a corporation or limited liability company in which the individual or partnership holds the majority interest;

9. Transferred from a wholly owned subsidiary to the parent corporation or from the parent corporation to a wholly owned subsidiary;

10. Being registered for the first time in the Commonwealth and the applicant holds a valid, assignable title or registration issued to him by another state or a branch of the United States Armed Forces and (i) has owned the vehicle for longer than 12 months or (ii) has owned the vehicle for less than 12 months and provides evidence of a sales tax paid to another state. However, when a vehicle has been purchased by the applicant within the last 12 months and the applicant is unable to provide evidence of a sales tax paid to another state, the applicant shall pay the Virginia sales tax based on the fair market value of the vehicle at the time of registration in Virginia;

11. a. Titled in a Virginia or non-Virginia motor vehicle dealer's name for resale; or

b. Titled in the name of an automotive manufacturer having its headquarters in Virginia, except for any commercially leased vehicle that is not described under subdivision 3 of § 46.2-602.2. For purposes of this subdivision, "automotive manufacturer" and "headquarters" means the same as such terms are defined in § 46.2-602.2;

12. A motor vehicle having seats for more than seven passengers and sold to an urban or suburban bus line the majority of whose passengers use the buses for traveling a distance of less than 40 miles, one way, on the same day;

13. Purchased in the Commonwealth by a nonresident and a Virginia title is issued for the sole purpose of recording a lien against the vehicle if the vehicle will be registered in a state other than Virginia;

14. A motor vehicle designed for the transportation of 10 or more passengers, purchased by and for the use of a church conducted not for profit;

15. Loaned or leased to a private nonprofit institution of learning, for the sole purpose of use in the instruction of driver's education when such education is a part of such school's curriculum for full-time students;

16. Sold to an insurance company or local government group self-insurance pool, created pursuant to § 15.2-2703, for the sole purpose of disposition when such company or pool has paid the registered owner of such vehicle a total loss claim;

17. Owned and used for personal or official purposes by accredited consular or diplomatic officers of foreign governments, their employees or agents, and members of their families, if such persons are nationals of the state by which they are appointed and are not citizens of the United States;

18. A self-contained mobile computerized axial tomography scanner sold to, rented or used by a nonprofit hospital or a cooperative hospital service organization as described in § 501(e) of the United States Internal Revenue Code;

19. A motor vehicle having seats for more than seven passengers and sold to a restricted common carrier or common carrier of passengers;

20. Beginning July 1, 1989, a self-contained mobile unit designed exclusively for human diagnostic or therapeutic service, sold to, rented to, or used by a nonprofit hospital, or a cooperative hospital service organization as described in § 501(e) of the United States Internal Revenue Code, or a nonprofit corporation as defined in § 501(c)(3) of the Internal Revenue Code, established for research in, diagnosis of, or therapy for human ailments;

21. Transferred, as a gift or through a sale to an organization exempt from taxation under § 501(c)(3) of the Internal Revenue Code, provided the motor vehicle is not titled and tagged for use by such organization;

22. A motor vehicle sold to an organization which is exempt from taxation under § 501(c)(3) of the Internal Revenue Code and which is organized for the primary purpose of distributing food, clothing, medicines, and other necessities of life to, and providing shelter for, needy persons in the United States and throughout the world;

23. Transferred to the trustees of a revocable inter vivos trust, when the individual titleholder of a Virginia titled motor vehicle and the beneficiaries of the trust are the same persons, regardless of whether other beneficiaries of the trust may also be named in the trust instrument, when no consideration has passed between the titleholder and the beneficiaries; and transferred to the original titleholder from the trustees holding title to the motor vehicle;

24. Transferred to trustees of a revocable inter vivos trust, when the owners of the vehicle and the beneficiaries of the trust are the same persons, regardless of whether other beneficiaries may also be named in the trust instrument, or transferred by trustees of such a trust to beneficiaries of the trust following the death of the grantor, when no consideration has passed between the grantor and the beneficiaries in either case;

25. Sold by a vehicle's lessor to its lessee upon the expiration of the term of the vehicle's lease, if the lessee is a natural person and this natural person has paid the tax levied pursuant to this chapter with respect to the vehicle when he leased it from the lessor, and if the lessee presents an original copy of the lease upon request of the Department of Motor Vehicles or other evidence that the sales tax has been paid to the Commonwealth by the lessee purchasing the vehicle;

26. Titled in the name of a deceased person and transferred to the spouse or heir, or under the will, of such deceased person;

27. An all-terrain vehicle, moped, or off-road motorcycle all as defined in § 46.2-100. Such all-terrain vehicles, mopeds, or off-road motorcycles shall not be deemed a motor vehicle or other vehicle subject to the tax imposed under this chapter; or

28. A motor vehicle that is sold to an organization that is exempt from taxation under § 501(c)(3) of the Internal Revenue Code and that is primarily used by the organization to transport to markets for sale produce that is (i) produced by local farmers and (ii) sold by such farmers to the organization.

History.

Code 1950, §§ 58-685.13, 58-685.13:1; 1966, c. 587; 1970, c. 409; 1972, cc. 302, 680; 1973, c. 457; 1974, c. 477; 1976, c. 610; 1977, c. 537; 1978, cc. 758, 766; 1982, c. 541; 1984, c. 675; 1988, c. 372; 1990, cc. 40, 849; 1995, cc. 27, 247, 786; 1997, c. 283; 1998, c. 322; 1999, c. 77; 2000, cc. 576, 602, 1027; 2002, c. 513; 2003, c. 278; 2005, cc. 246, 274; 2006, c. 604; 2007, c. 896; 2008, cc. 304, 753; 2009, cc. 864, 871; 2011, cc. 405, 639; 2012, cc. 22, 111; 2013, c. 783; 2014, c. 243; 2015, cc. 159, 502, 503.

§ 58.1-2404. Time for payment of tax on sale or use of a motor vehicle.

The tax on the sale or use of a motor vehicle shall be paid by the purchaser or user of such motor vehicle and collected by the Commissioner at the time the owner applies to the Department of Motor Vehicles for, and obtains, a certificate of title. No tax shall be levied or collected under this chapter upon the sale or use of a motor vehicle for which no certificate of title is required by this Commonwealth.

History.

Code 1950, § 58-685.14; 1966, c. 587; 1974, c. 477; 1984, c. 675; 2011, cc. 405, 639.

§ 58.1-2405. Basis of tax.

A. In the case of the sale or use of a motor vehicle upon which the pricing information is required by federal law to be posted, the Commissioner may collect the tax upon the basis of the total sale price shown on such document; however, if the Commissioner is satisfied that the purchaser has paid less than such price, by such evidence as the Commissioner may require, he may assess and collect the tax upon the basis of the sale price so found by him. In no case shall such lesser price include credits for trade-in or any other transaction of such nature.

B. In the case of the sale or use of a motor vehicle which is not a new motor vehicle, the Commissioner may employ such publications, sources of information, and other data as are customarily employed in ascertaining the maximum sale price of such used motor vehicles but in no case shall any credit be allowed for trade-in, prior rental or any other transaction of like nature.

C. In the case of the sale or use of a motor vehicle, which is not a new motor vehicle, between individuals who are not required to be licensed as dealers or salespersons under the provisions of § 46.2-1508, the Commissioner may collect the tax upon the basis of the total sale price as established by such evidence as the Commissioner may require; provided that if such motor vehicle is no more than five years old and is listed in a recognized pricing guide, the total sale price shall not be less than the value listed in such pricing guide for such vehicle, less an allowance of $1,500, unless the purchaser shall execute an affidavit under penalty of perjury stating a lesser total sale price and declaring such sale or use to be a bona fide transaction for full value. In using a recognized pricing guide, the Commissioner shall use the trade-in value specified in such guide, with no additions for optional equipment or subtractions for mileage, so long as uniformly applied for all types of motor vehicles. In no case shall any credit be allowed for trade-in, prior rental, or any other transaction of like nature.

History.

Code 1950, § 58-685.15; 1966, c. 587; 1974, c. 477; 1984, c. 675; 2003, c. 328; 2015, c. 615.

§ 58.1-2406. Collection of tax; estimate of tax.

In the event any person submits with his application for a certificate of title a sum insufficient to pay the sale or use tax as determined by the Commissioner, it shall be the duty of the Commissioner or his authorized agent to make an estimate of the tax due the Commonwealth and to assess such tax. The notice of assessment shall be forthwith sent to such person by certified mail at the address of the person as it appears on the records of the Division. Such notice, when sent in accordance with these requirements, shall be sufficient regardless of whether or not it was ever received.

If any person fails to pay such tax, the Commissioner shall bring an appropriate action for the recovery of such tax plus interest. Judgment shall be rendered for the amount of the tax found to be due together with interest and costs.

History.

Code 1950, § 58-685.17; 1966, c. 587; 1974, c. 477; 1984, c. 675.

§§ 58.1-2407 through 58.1-2410: Repealed by Acts 2011, cc. 405 and 639, cl. 2, effective July 1, 2012.

§ 58.1-2411. Civil penalties upon failure to pay tax, etc.

When any person fails to pay the full amount of the tax required by this chapter, there shall be imposed, in addition to other penalties provided herein, a penalty to be added to the tax in the amount of ten percent or ten dollars, whichever is greater; however, if the failure is due to providential or other good cause, shown to the satisfaction of the Commissioner, the tax may be accepted exclusive of penalties. The $10 minimum penalty levied herein shall be applied only in cases where the payment of tax is not received within the time prescribed in this chapter and shall not be considered for audit purposes.

In the case of a false or fraudulent application, where willful intent exists to defraud the Commonwealth of any tax due under this chapter, a specific penalty of 50 percent of the amount of the proper tax shall be assessed. It shall be prima facie evidence of intent to defraud the Commonwealth of any tax due under this chapter when any person reports the sale price of a motor vehicle at 50 percent or less of the actual amount.

Interest at the rate of one and one-half of one percent per month, or a fraction thereof, shall accrue on both tax and penalty until paid.

History.

Code 1950, § 58-685.17:2; 1974, c. 477; 1982, c. 141; 1984, c. 675; 2011, cc. 405, 639.

§§ 58.1-2412 through 58.1-2417: Repealed by Acts 2011, cc. 405 and 639, cl. 2, effective July 1, 2012.

§ 58.1-2418. Local sales and use taxes prohibited.

No city, town or county shall impose or continue to impose any local sales or use tax on motor vehicles.

History.

Code 1950, § 58-685.25; 1966, c. 587; 1974, c. 477; 1981, c. 145; 1984, c. 675.

§ 58.1-2419. Tax on sale to be separately stated.

In every transaction subject to the provisions of this chapter, the tax imposed by this chapter shall be separately stated from the sale price of such motor vehicle and shall be paid by the purchaser in accordance with the provisions of this chapter.

History.

Code 1950, § 58-685.24; 1966, c. 587; 1974, c. 477; 1984, c. 675; 2011, cc. 405, 639.

§ 58.1-2420. Examination of dealer's records, etc.

The Commissioner or any agent authorized by him may examine during the usual business hours all records, books, papers or other documents of any dealer in motor vehicles relating to the sales price of any motor vehicle to verify the truth and accuracy of any statement or any other information as to a particular sale.

History.

Code 1950, § 58-685.18; 1966, c. 587; 1974, c. 477; 1984, c. 675; 2011, cc. 405, 639.

§ 58.1-2421. Rules and regulations.

The Commissioner shall have the power to make and publish reasonable rules and regulations consistent with this chapter, other applicable laws, and the Constitutions of Virginia and the United States, for the enforcement of the provisions of this chapter and the collection of the revenues hereunder.

Such rules and regulations shall not be subject to Chapter 40 (§ 2.2-4000 et seq.) of Title 2.2.

History.

Code 1950, § 58-685.16; 1966, c. 587; 1974, c. 477; 1984, c. 675; 2011, cc. 405, 639.

§ 58.1-2422. Forwarding of tax information to law-enforcement officials.

The Commissioner may, in his discretion, upon request duly received from the official charged with the duty of enforcement of motor vehicle tax laws of any other state, forward to such official any information which he may have in his possession relative to the registration and payment of any tax collected pursuant to this chapter.

History.
Code 1950, § 58-685.21; 1966, c. 587; 1984, c. 675.

§ 58.1-2423. Refunds generally; to foreign nationals.

In the event it shall appear to the satisfaction of the Commissioner that any tax imposed by this chapter has been erroneously or illegally collected from any person or paid by any person, the Commissioner shall certify the amount thereof to the Comptroller, who shall thereupon draw his warrant for such certified amount on the State Treasurer. Such refund shall be paid by the State Treasurer. A claimant who pays the tax, either for the claimant or for the benefit of another on whose behalf the tax is paid, shall make a sufficient showing that the tax was erroneously collected by providing an affidavit stating that (i) the vehicle identification information provided on the Application for Certificate of Title and Registration, the certificate of origin, manufacturer's statement of origin, or title, as the case may be, forwarded to the Department of Motor Vehicles by any means generally allowed was incorrect, or (ii) the transaction would have been exempt from taxation had the titling documents been correct when submitted to the Department of Motor Vehicles and the tax was paid in error. In the event of such a showing, the refund shall be paid to the claimant.

In the event that it shall appear to the satisfaction of the Commissioner that the tax imposed by this chapter was upon a motor vehicle purchased by a foreign national and that within six months after the date of purchase the motor vehicle has been exported to a foreign country, the Commissioner shall certify the amount to the Comptroller who shall thereupon draw his warrant for such certified amount on the State Treasurer. Such refund shall be paid by the State Treasurer.

No refund shall be made under the provisions of this section unless a written statement is filed with the Commissioner setting forth the reason such refund is claimed. The claim shall be in such form as the Commissioner shall prescribe. It shall be filed with the Commissioner within three years from the date of the payment of the tax.

History.
Code 1950, § 58-685.19; 1966, c. 587; 1972, c. 207; 1973, c. 174; 1974, c. 477; 1981, c. 440; 1984, c. 675; 2003, c. 837.

§ 58.1-2423.1: Expired.

Editor's note.
Acts 1994, c. 527, enacted this section to provide for a refund for vehicles using clean special fuels. Acts 1994, c. 527, cl. 2 made the provisions of the 1994 act effective January 1, 1996, to December 31, 1999.

§ 58.1-2424. Credits against tax.

Credit shall be granted for the amount of tax paid to another state on a motor vehicle purchased in another state at the time such vehicle is first registered in the Commonwealth, provided the purchaser provides proof of payment of such tax. However, no credit shall be granted for any tax paid to another state if that state exempts from the tax vehicles sold to residents of a state which does not give credit for the tax. Credit for taxes collected under the Virginia retail sales and use tax (§ 58.1-600 et seq.) shall be allowed against the tax levied for specially constructed or reconstructed vehicles and other motor vehicles subject to such tax.

History.
Code 1950, § 58-685.20; 1966, c. 587; 1974, c. 477; 1976, c. 610; 1981, c. 145; 1984, c. 675; 1990, c. 163; 2011, cc. 405, 639.

§ 58.1-2425. (Contingent expiration date — see note) Disposition of revenues.

A. Funds collected hereunder by the Commissioner shall be forthwith paid into the state treasury. Except as otherwise provided in this section, these funds shall constitute special funds within the Commonwealth Transportation Fund. Any balances remaining in these funds at the end of the year shall be available for use in subsequent years for the purposes set forth in this chapter, and any interest income on such funds shall accrue to these funds. The revenue so derived, after refunds have been deducted, is hereby allocated for the construction, reconstruction and maintenance of highways and the regulation of traffic thereon and for no other purpose. However, (i) all funds collected pursuant to the provisions of this chapter from manufactured homes, as defined in § 46.2-100, shall be distributed to the city, town, or county wherein such manufactured home is to be situated as a dwelling; (ii) effective January 1, 1987, an amount equivalent to the net additional revenues from the sales and use tax on motor vehicles generated by enactments of the 1986 Special Session of the Virginia General Assembly which amended §§ 46.2-694, 46.2-697, 58.1-2401, 58.1-2402, and this section shall be distributed to and paid into the Transportation Trust Fund established pursuant to § 33.2-1524, a special fund within the Commonwealth Transportation Fund, and are hereby appropriated to the Commonwealth Transportation Board for transportation needs; and (iii) the net additional revenues generated by increases in the rates of taxes under subdivisions A 1 and A 2 of § 58.1-2402 and generated by the increase in the minimum tax under subdivision A 3 of § 58.1-2402 pursuant to enactments of a Session of the General Assembly held in 2013 shall be deposited by the Comptroller into the Highway Maintenance and Operating Fund established pursuant to § 33.2-1530.

B. As provided in subsection A of § 58.1-638, of the funds becoming part of the Transportation Trust

Fund pursuant to clause (ii) of subsection A, an aggregate of 4.2 percent shall be set aside as the Commonwealth Port Fund; an aggregate of 2.4 percent shall be set aside as the Commonwealth Airport Fund; and an aggregate of 14.5 percent in fiscal year 1998-1999 and 14.7 percent in fiscal year 1999-2000 and thereafter shall be set aside as the Commonwealth Mass Transit Fund.

History.
Code 1950, § 58-685.23; 1966, c. 587; 1976, c. 567; 1981, c. 145; 1984, c. 675; 1986, Sp. Sess., c. 11; 1987, c. 696; 1991, c. 323; 1997, cc. 283, 423, 853; 1998, cc. 905, 907; 1999, c. 77; 2004, c. 522; 2005, c. 323; 2007, c. 896; 2009, cc. 864, 871; 2011, cc. 405, 639; 2013, c. 766.

Section set out twice.
The section above is set out as amended by Acts 2013, c. 766. For this section as effective if amendments by Acts 2013, c. 766 expire, see the following section, also numbered 58.1-2425.

Contingent expiration date. — Acts 2013, c. 766, cl. 14 provides: "That the provisions of this act that generate additional revenue through state taxes or fees for transportation (i) throughout the Commonwealth and in Planning District 8 and Planning District 23 or (ii) in any other Planning District that becomes subject to the state taxes or fees imposed solely in Planning Districts pursuant to this act shall expire on December 31 of any year in which the General Assembly appropriates any of such additional revenues for any non-transportation-related purpose or transfers any of such additional revenues that are to be deposited into the Commonwealth Transportation Fund or any subfund thereof pursuant to general law for a non-transportation-related purpose. In the event a local government of any county or city wherein the additional taxes and fees are levied appropriates or allocates any of such additional revenues to a non-transportation purpose, such locality shall not be the direct beneficiary of any of the revenues generated by the taxes or fees in the year immediately succeeding the year in which revenues where appropriated or allocated to a non-transportation purpose."

Editor's note.
Acts 2013, c. 766, cl. 18 provides: "That should any portion of this act be held unconstitutional by a court of competent jurisdiction, the remaining portions of this act shall remain in effect."

§ 58.1-2425. (Contingent effective date — see note) Disposition of revenues.

A. Funds collected hereunder by the Commissioner shall be forthwith paid into the state treasury. Except as otherwise provided in this section, these funds shall constitute special funds within the Commonwealth Transportation Fund. Any balances remaining in these funds at the end of the year shall be available for use in subsequent years for the purposes set forth in this chapter, and any interest income on such funds shall accrue to these funds. The revenue so derived, after refunds have been deducted, is hereby allocated for the construction, reconstruction and maintenance of highways and the regulation of traffic thereon and for no other purpose. However, (i) all funds collected pursuant to the provisions of this chapter from manufactured homes, as defined in § 46.2-100, shall be distributed to the city, town, or county wherein such manufactured home is to be situated as a dwelling; and (ii) effective January 1, 1987, an amount equivalent to the net additional revenues from the sales and use tax on motor vehicles generated by enactments of the 1986 Special Session of the Virginia General Assembly which amended §§ 46.2-694, 46.2-697, 58.1-2401, 58.1-2402 and this section shall be distributed to and paid into the Transportation Trust Fund established pursuant to § 33.2-1524, a special fund within the Commonwealth Transportation Fund, and are hereby appropriated to the Commonwealth Transportation Board for transportation needs.

B. As provided in subsection A of § 58.1-638, of the funds becoming part of the Transportation Trust Fund pursuant to clause (ii) of subsection A of this section, an aggregate of 4.2 percent shall be set aside as the Commonwealth Port Fund; an aggregate of 2.4 percent shall be set aside as the Commonwealth Airport Fund; and an aggregate of 14.5 percent in fiscal year 1998-1999 and 14.7 percent in fiscal year 1999-2000 and thereafter shall be set aside as the Commonwealth Mass Transit Fund.

History.
Code 1950, § 58-685.23; 1966, c. 587; 1976, c. 567; 1981, c. 145; 1984, c. 675; 1986, Sp. Sess., c. 11; 1987, c. 696; 1991, c. 323; 1997, cc. 283, 423, 853; 1998, cc. 905, 907; 1999, c. 77; 2004, c. 522; 2005, c. 323; 2007, c. 896; 2009, cc. 864, 871; 2011, cc. 405, 639.

Section set out twice.
The section above is set out as effective if amendments by Acts 2013, c. 766 expire. For this section as amended by Acts 2013, c. 766, see the preceding section, also numbered 58.1-2425.

Editor's note.
References in this section were updated at the direction of the Virginia Code Commission to conform to the recodification of Title 33.2 by Acts 2014, c. 805, effective October 1, 2014.

§ 58.1-2426. Application to Commissioner for correction; appeal.

A. Any person assessed with any tax administered by the Department pursuant to this chapter may, within 30 days from the date of such assessment, apply for relief to the Commissioner. Such application shall be in the form prescribed by the Department, and shall fully set forth the grounds upon which the taxpayer relies and all facts relevant to the taxpayer's contention. The Commissioner may also require such additional information, testimony, or documentary evidence as he deems necessary to a fair determination of the application.

B. On receipt of a written notice of intent to file under subsection A, the Commissioner shall refrain from collecting the tax until the time for filing hereunder has expired, unless he determines that collection is in jeopardy.

C. Any person against whom an order or decision of the Commissioner has been adversely rendered relating to the tax imposed by this chapter may, within fifteen days of such order or decision, appeal from such order or decision to the Circuit Court of the City of Richmond.

History.
Code 1950, § 58-685.22; 1966, c. 587; 1984, c. 675; 2011, cc. 881, 889.

CHAPTER 27.
ROAD TAX ON MOTOR CARRIERS.

§ 58.1-2700. Definitions.

Whenever used in this chapter, the term:

"Carrier" means a person who operates or causes to be operated a commercial highway vehicle on any highway in the Commonwealth.

"Department" means the Department of Motor Vehicles, acting through its officers and agents.

"Identification marker" means a decal issued by the Department to show that a vehicle operated by a carrier is properly registered with the Department for the payment of the road tax.

"IFTA" means the International Fuel Tax Agreement, as entered into by the Department, and as amended by the International Fuel Tax Association, Inc.

"Licensee" means a carrier who holds an uncancelled IFTA license issued by the Commonwealth.

"Motor carrier" means every person, firm or corporation who owns or operates or causes to be operated on any highway in this Commonwealth any qualified highway vehicle.

"Operations" means the physical activities of all such vehicles, whether loaded or empty, whether for compensation or not for compensation, and whether owned by or leased to the motor carrier who operates them or causes them to be operated.

"Qualified highway vehicle" means a highway vehicle used, designed, or maintained for transportation of persons or property that (i) has two axles and a gross vehicle weight or registered gross vehicle weight exceeding 26,000 pounds or 11,797 kilograms, (ii) has three or more axles regardless of weight, or (iii) is used in combination, when the weight of such combination exceeds 26,000 pounds or 11,797 kilograms gross vehicle or registered gross vehicle weight. "Qualified highway vehicle" does not include recreational vehicles.

"Tractor truck" means every motor vehicle designed and used primarily for drawing other vehicles and not so constructed as to carry a load other than a part of the load and weight of the vehicle attached thereto.

"Truck" means every motor vehicle designed to transport property on its own structure independent of any other vehicle and having a registered gross weight in excess of 7,500 pounds.

History.

Code 1950, § 58-627; 1954, c. 341; 1956, c. 475; 1970, c. 32; 1978, c. 62; 1980, c. 649; 1982, c. 671; 1984, c. 675; 1995, cc. 744, 803; 1996, c. 575; 1997, c. 283.

§ 58.1-2700.1. Interstate motor carrier road tax.

In accordance with the provisions of IFTA, as amended, all motor carriers that operate or cause to be operated one or more qualified highway vehicles in the Commonwealth and at least one other jurisdiction participating in IFTA shall apply to the Department for an IFTA license and identification markers. The Department shall issue a license and vehicle identification markers to each carrier that operates qualified highway vehicles in the Commonwealth and at least one other jurisdiction participating in IFTA so as to report its road tax liabilities. The Department may issue vehicle identification markers to carriers that operate qualified highway vehicles in the Commonwealth and at least one other jurisdiction not participating in IFTA. Each application shall contain the name and address of the carrier, and such other information as may be required by the Department.

The Department shall issue to the motor carrier identification markers for each vehicle in the carrier's fleet that will be operated within the Commonwealth.

The identification markers issued to the vehicles of the IFTA-licensed carriers shall expire on December 31 of each year. All other identification markers issued to carriers shall expire on June 30 of each year. The identification markers may be renewed prior to expiration provided (i) the carrier's privilege to operate vehicles in the Commonwealth has not been revoked or canceled, (ii) all required tax reports have been filed, and (iii) all road taxes, penalties, and interest due have been paid.

The cost of the identification markers issued to each vehicle in the carrier's fleet shall be $10 per vehicle.

The Department may, by letter, telegram, or other electronic means, authorize a vehicle to be operated without identification markers for not more than 10 days. Before sending such authorization, the Department shall collect from the carrier a fee of $20 for each vehicle so operated.

History.

1995, cc. 744, 803; 1996, c. 575; 2002, c. 265; 2012, cc. 22, 111.

§ 58.1-2700.2. Motor carriers subject to terms of the International Fuel Tax Agreement; placement of identification markers.

All motor carriers that operate one or more qualified highway vehicles on an interstate basis are subject to and shall abide by all terms and conditions of IFTA that are applicable to motor carriers or operators of qualified highway vehicles. All carriers licensed by the Department pursuant to this chapter or IFTA shall place any required identification markers issued by the Department on each vehicle in the carrier's fleet in the place prescribed by the Department.

History.

1995, cc. 744, 803; 2012, cc. 22, 111.

§ 58.1-2700.3. Waiver in emergency situations.

The Department shall have the authority to waive the requirements of this title for vehicles under emergency conditions.

History.

1995, cc. 744, 803.

§ 58.1-2701. Amount of tax.

A. Except as provided in subsection B, every motor carrier shall pay a road tax per gallon equivalent to the cents per gallon credit for diesel fuel as determined under subsection A of § 58.1-2706 for the relevant period plus an additional $0.035 per gallon calculated on the amount of motor fuel, diesel fuel or liquefied gases (which would not exist as liquids at a temperature of 60 degrees Fahrenheit and a pressure of 14.7 pounds per square inch absolute), used in its operations within the Commonwealth.

The tax imposed by this chapter shall be in addition to all other taxes of whatever character imposed on a motor carrier by any other provision of law.

B. In lieu of the tax imposed in subsection A, motor carriers registering qualified highway vehicles that are not registered under the International Registration Plan shall pay a fee of $150 per year for each qualified highway vehicle regardless of whether such vehicle will be included on the motor carrier's IFTA return. The fee is due and payable when the vehicle registration fees are paid pursuant to the provisions of Article 7 (§ 46.2-685 et seq.) of Chapter 6 of Title 46.2.

If a vehicle becomes a qualified highway vehicle before the end of its registration period, the fee due at the time the vehicle becomes a qualified highway vehicle shall be prorated monthly to the registration expiration month. Fees paid under this subsection shall not be refunded unless a full refund of the registration fee paid is authorized by law.

C. All taxes and fees paid under the provisions of this chapter shall be credited to the Highway Maintenance and Operating Fund established pursuant to § 33.2-1530, a special fund within the Commonwealth Transportation Fund.

History.

Code 1950, §§ 58-628, 58-631, 58-637; 1956, c. 475; 1960, c. 603; 1964, c. 255; 1972, cc. 490, 862; 1973, c. 331; 1978, c. 673; 1979, c. 709; 1980, c. 227; 1982, c. 671; 1984, c. 675; 1986, c. 553; 1986, Sp. Sess., c. 15; 1996, c. 575; 1997, c. 423; 2000, cc. 729, 758; 2002, c. 265; 2007, c. 896; 2011, cc. 881, 889; 2013, c. 766.

§ 58.1-2702. Exemptions and exceptions.

The provisions of this chapter shall not apply to a person, firm or corporation owning or operating:

1. Recreational vehicles, as defined in the provisions of the International Fuel Tax Agreement (IFTA);
2. The first two Virginia-licensed trucks and tractor trucks, if used exclusively for farm use as defined in § 46.2-698 and if not licensed in any other state;
3. Qualified highway vehicles of a licensed highway vehicle dealer when operated without compensation for purposes incident to a sale or for demonstration; or
4. Any highway vehicle owned and operated by the United States, the District of Columbia, the Commonwealth of Virginia or any municipality or any other political subdivision of the Commonwealth, or any other state.

History.

Code 1950, §§ 58-627, 58-633; 1954, c. 341; 1956, c. 475; 1970, c. 32; 1976, c. 440; 1978, c. 62; 1980, c. 649; 1982, c. 671; 1984, c. 675; 1988, cc. 514, 725; 1993, c. 40; 1995, cc. 744, 803; 1996, c. 575; 1997, c. 283; 2000, cc. 729, 758.

§ 58.1-2703. Payment of tax.

The tax imposed under § 58.1-2701 shall be paid by each motor carrier quarterly to the State Treasurer on or before the last day of April, July, October and January of each year and calculated upon the amount of gasoline or other motor fuel used in its operations within the Commonwealth by each such carrier during the quarter ending with the last day of the preceding month.

History.

Code 1950, § 58-630; 1984, c. 675.

§ 58.1-2704. How amount of fuel used in the Commonwealth ascertained.

On and after October 1, 1992, the amount of gasoline or other motor fuel used in the operations of any motor carrier in the Commonwealth shall be determined by dividing the total number of miles traveled within the Commonwealth by such carrier's vehicles during a calendar quarter by a consumption factor, such factor being comprised of the total number of miles traveled by all vehicles of the motor carrier during the quarter divided by the total amount of gasoline or other motor fuel used in its entire operations during such quarter.

History.
Code 1950, § 58-632; 1956, c. 475; 1984, c. 675; 1990, c. 216; 1992, c. 309.

§ 58.1-2705. Reports of carriers.

Every motor carrier subject to the tax imposed by this chapter or filing under the terms of the International Fuel Tax Agreement shall, on or before the last day of April, July, October and January of every year, make to the Department or proper agency pursuant to the International Fuel Tax Agreement such reports of its operations during the quarter ending the last day of the preceding month as the Department may require and such other reports from time to time as the Department may deem necessary.

History.
Code 1950, § 58-633; 1976, c. 440; 1984, c. 675; 1995, cc. 744, 803.

§ 58.1-2706. Credit for payment of motor fuel, diesel fuel or liquefied gases tax.

A. Every motor carrier subject to the road tax shall be entitled to a credit on such tax on every gallon of motor fuel, diesel fuel and liquefied gases purchased by such carrier within the Commonwealth for use in its operations either within or without the Commonwealth and upon which the motor fuel, diesel fuel or liquefied gases tax imposed by the laws of the Commonwealth has been paid by such carrier. Evidence of the payment of such tax in such form as may be required by, or is satisfactory to, the Department shall be furnished by each carrier claiming the credit herein allowed. The credit for diesel fuel shall be at a cents per gallon rate equivalent to the tax imposed under subsection B of § 58.1-2217 for the relevant period as converted by the Commissioner to a cents per gallon tax for purposes of this credit. The credit for all other motor fuels and liquefied gases shall be at a cents per gallon rate equivalent to the tax imposed under subsection A of § 58.1-2217 for the relevant period as converted by the Commissioner to a cents per gallon tax for purposes of this credit.

B. When the amount of the credit to which any motor carrier is entitled for any quarter exceeds the amount of the tax for which such carrier is liable for the same quarter, the excess may: (i) be allowed as a credit on the tax for which such carrier would be otherwise liable for any of the eight succeeding quarters or (ii) be refunded, upon application, duly verified and presented and supported by such evidence as may be satisfactory to the Department.

C. The Department may allow a refund upon receipt of proper application and review. It shall be at the discretion of the Department to determine whether an audit is required.

D. The refund may be allowed without a formal hearing if the amount of refund is agreed to by the applicant. Otherwise, a formal hearing on the application shall be held by the Department after notice of not less than 10 days to the applicant and the Attorney General.

E. Whenever any refund is ordered it shall be paid out of the Highway Maintenance and Operating Fund established pursuant to § 33.2-1530.

F. Whenever a person operating under lease to a motor carrier to perform transport services on behalf of the carrier purchases motor fuel, diesel fuel or liquefied gases relating to such services, such payments or purchases may, at the discretion of the Department, be considered payment or purchases by the carrier.

History.
Code 1950, § 58-629; 1952, c. 281; 1956, c. 475; 1960, c. 603; 1972, c. 490; 1980, c. 227; 1982, c. 671; 1984, c. 675; 1986, c. 553; 1986, Sp. Sess., c. 15; 1988, c. 381; 1990, c. 245; 1992, c. 309; 1995, cc. 744, 803; 1996, c. 575; 1999, c. 94; 2007, c. 896; 2013, c. 766.

§ 58.1-2707. Refunds to motor carriers who give bond.

A motor carrier not operating as an IFTA licensee may be required to give a surety company bond in the amount of not less than $2,000, as shall appear sufficient in the discretion of the Department, payable to the Commonwealth and conditioned that the carrier will pay all taxes due and to become due under this chapter from the date of the bond to the date when either the carrier or the bonding company notifies the Department that the bond has been canceled. The surety shall be a corporation authorized to write surety bonds in Virginia. So long as the bond remains in force the Department may order refunds to the motor carrier in the amounts appearing to be due on applications duly filed by the carrier under this chapter (§ 58.1-2700 et seq.) without first auditing the records of the carrier. The surety shall be liable for all omitted taxes assessed pursuant to § 58.1-2025 against the carrier, including the penalties and interest provided in such section, even though the assessment is made after cancellation of the bond, but only for taxes due and payable while the bond was in force and penalties and interest on the taxes.

History.
Code 1950, § 58-629.1; 1952, c. 281; 1962, c. 586; 1984, c. 675; 1986, c. 339; 1992, c. 309; 1993, c. 101; 1995, cc. 744, 803.

§ 58.1-2708. Inspection of books and records.

The Department and its authorized agents and representatives shall have the right at any reasonable time to inspect the books and records of any motor carrier subject to the tax imposed by this chapter.

History.
Code 1950, § 58-634; 1984, c. 675; 1995, cc. 744, 803.

§ 58.1-2709. Penalties.

The Department may, after a hearing had upon notice, duly served not less than ten days prior to the date set for such hearing, impose a penalty, which shall be in addition to any other penalty imposed by this chapter, not exceeding $2,500, upon any licensed motor carrier violating any provision of this chapter or the IFTA, or failing to comply with IFTA or any regulation of the Department promulgated pursuant to this chapter. Each such failure or violation shall constitute a separate offense. The penalty shall be collectible by the process of the Department as provided by law. Any person against whom an order or decision of the Commissioner has been adversely rendered relating to the tax imposed by this chapter may, within fifteen days of such order or decision, appeal from such an order or decision to the Circuit Court of the City of Richmond. In addition to imposing such penalty, or without imposing any penalty, the Department may suspend or revoke any certificate, permit or other evidence of right issued by the Department which the motor carrier holds.

History.
Code 1950, §§ 58-635, 58-636; 1984, c. 675; 1993, c. 42; 1995, cc. 744, 803; 2002, c. 265.

§ 58.1-2710. Penalty for false statements.

Any person who willfully and knowingly makes a false statement orally, or in writing, or in the form of a receipt for the sale of motor fuel, for the purpose of obtaining or attempting to obtain or to assist any other person, partnership or corporation to obtain or attempt to obtain a credit or refund or reduction of liability for taxes under this chapter shall be guilty of a Class 1 misdemeanor.

History.
Code 1950, § 58-629.2; 1952, c. 281; 1984, c. 675.

§ 58.1-2711. Assistance of Department of Taxation.

At the request of the Department, the Department of Taxation shall furnish the Department the amount of deduction from income taken by any person conducting business as a motor carrier as defined in § 58.1-2700 on account of the purchase of motor fuel, diesel fuel or liquefied gases.

History.
Code 1950, § 58-634.1; 1956, c. 475; 1984, c. 675; 1990, c. 245; 1995, cc. 744, 803; 1996, c. 575.

§ 58.1-2712: Repealed by Acts 1995, cc. 744 and 803, effective January 1, 1996.

§ 58.1-2712.1. International Fuel Tax Agreement.

The Department may, with the approval of the Governor, enter into IFTA for interstate motor carriers and abide by the requirements set forth in IFTA. All motor carriers that operate one or more qualified highway vehicles on an interstate basis are subject to and shall abide by all terms and conditions of IFTA that are applicable to motor carriers or operators of qualified highway vehicles. All requirements of IFTA shall also apply to motor carriers operating in intrastate commerce unless specific requirements are determined by the Department to be not in the best interest of the motor carrier industry.

History.
1995, cc. 744, 803; 2012, cc. 22, 111.

§ 58.1-2712.2. Exchange of information; penalties.

A. The Commissioner of the Department is authorized to enter into written agreements with (i) duly constituted tax officials and motor vehicle agencies of other states and countries or provinces of any country that are member jurisdictions of the International Fuel Tax Agreement and (ii) any entity formed by the member jurisdictions of the International Fuel Tax Agreement to administer and conduct the business of such Agreement, to permit the exchange of information in order to facilitate the collection of taxes under such Agreement.

B. Any person to whom tax information is divulged pursuant to this section shall be subject to the prohibitions and penalties prescribed in § 58.1-3.

History.
2001, c. 84.

SUBTITLE III.

LOCAL TAXES.

CHAPTER 35.1.

PERSONAL PROPERTY TAX RELIEF.

Section

§ 58.1-3523. Definitions.

As used in this chapter:

"Commissioner of the revenue" means the same as that set forth in § 58.1-3100. For purposes of this chapter, in a county or city which does not have an elected commissioner of the revenue, "commissioner of the revenue" means the officer who is primarily responsible for assessing motor vehicles for the purposes of tangible personal property taxation.

"Department" means the Department of Motor Vehicles.

"Effective tax rate" means the tax rate imposed by a locality on tangible personal property multiplied by any assessment ratio in effect.

"Leased" means leased by a natural person as lessee and used for nonbusiness purposes.

"Privately owned" means owned by a natural person and used for nonbusiness purposes.

"Qualifying vehicle" means any passenger car, motorcycle, autocycle, and pickup or panel truck, as those terms are defined in § 46.2-100, that is determined by the commissioner of the revenue of the county or city in which the vehicle has situs as provided by § 58.1-3511 to be (i) privately owned; (ii) leased pursuant to a contract requiring the lessee to pay the tangible personal property tax on such vehicle; or (iii) held in a private trust for nonbusiness purposes. In determining whether a vehicle is a qualifying vehicle, the commissioner of revenue must rely on the registration of such vehicle with the Department pursuant to Chapter 6 (§ 46.2-600 et seq.) of Title 46.2 or, for leased vehicles, the information of the Department pursuant to subsections B and C of § 46.2-623, unless the commissioner of the revenue has information that the Department's information is incorrect, or to the extent that the Department's information is incomplete. For purposes of this chapter, all-terrain vehicles and off-road motorcycles titled with the Department of Motor Vehicles and mopeds shall not be deemed qualifying vehicles.

"Tangible personal property tax" means the tax levied pursuant to Article 1 (§ 58.1-3500 et seq.) of Chapter 35 of Title 58.1.

"Tax year" means the 12-month period beginning in the calendar year for which tangible personal property taxes are imposed.

"Treasurer" means the same as that set forth in § 58.1-3123, when used herein with respect to a county or city. When used herein with respect to a town, "treasurer" means the officer who is primarily responsible for the billing and collection of tangible personal property taxes levied upon motor vehicles by such town, and means the treasurer of the county or counties in which such town is located if such functions are performed for the town by the county treasurer or treasurers.

"Used for nonbusiness purposes" means the preponderance of use is for other than business purposes. The preponderance of use for other than business purposes shall be deemed not to be satisfied if: (i) the motor vehicle is expensed on the taxpayer's federal income tax return pursuant to Internal Revenue Code § 179; (ii) more than 50 percent of the basis for depreciation of the motor vehicle is depreciated for federal income tax purposes; or (iii) the allowable expense of total annual mileage in excess of 50 percent is deductible for federal income tax purposes or reimbursed pursuant to an arrangement between an employer and employee.

"Value" means the fair market value determined by the method prescribed in § 58.1-3503 and used by the locality in valuing the qualifying vehicle.

History.

1998, Sp. Sess. I, c. 2; 1999, c. 189; 2004, Sp. Sess. I, c. 1; 2006, c. 896; 2007, cc. 314, 815; 2010, c. 499; 2013, c. 783; 2015, cc. 96, 152.

§ 58.1-3524. Tangible personal property tax relief; local tax rates on vehicles qualifying for tangible personal property tax relief.

A. For tax year 2006 and all tax years thereafter, counties, cities, and towns shall be reimbursed by the Commonwealth for providing the required tangible personal property tax relief as set forth herein.

B. For tax year 2006 and all tax years thereafter, the Commonwealth shall pay a total of $950 million for each such tax year in reimbursements to localities for providing the required tangible personal property tax relief on qualifying vehicles in subsection C. No other amount shall be paid to counties, cities, and towns for providing tangible personal property tax relief on qualifying vehicles. Each county's, city's, or town's share of the $950 million for each such tax year shall be determined pro rata based upon the actual payments to such county, city, or town pursuant to this chapter for tax year 2005 as compared to the actual payments to all counties, cities, and towns pursuant to this chapter for tax year 2005, as certified in writing by the Auditor of Public Accounts no later than March 1, 2006, to the Governor and to the chairmen of the Senate Committee on Finance and the House Committee on Appropriations. The amount reimbursed to a particular county, city, or town for tax year 2006 for providing tangible personal property tax relief shall be the same amount reimbursed to such county, city, or town for each subsequent tax year.

The reimbursement to each county, city, or town for tax year 2006 shall be paid by the Commonwealth over the 12-month period beginning with the month of July 2006 and ending with the month of June 2007, as provided in the general appropriation act. For all tax years subsequent to tax year 2006, reimbursements shall be paid over the same 12-month period. All reimbursement payments shall be made by check issued by the State Treasurer to the respective treasurer of the county, city, or town on warrant of the Comptroller.

C. For tax year 2006 and all tax years thereafter, each county, city, or town that will receive a reimbursement from the Commonwealth pursuant to subsection B shall provide tangible personal property tax relief on qualifying vehicles by reducing its local tax rate on qualifying vehicles as follows:

1. The local governing body of each county, city, or town shall fix or establish its tangible personal property tax rate for its general class of tangible personal property, which rate shall also be applied to that portion of the value of each qualifying vehicle that is in excess of $20,000.

2. After fixing or establishing its tangible personal property tax rate for its general class of tangible personal property, the local governing body of the county, city, or town shall fix or establish one or more reduced tax rates (lower than the rate applied to the general class of tangible personal property) that shall be applied solely to that portion of the value of each qualifying vehicle that is not in excess of $20,000. No other tangible personal property tax rate shall be applied to that portion of the value of each qualifying vehicle that is not in excess of $20,000. Such reduced tax rate or rates shall be set at an effective tax rate or rates such that (i) the revenue to be received from such reduced tax rate or rates on that portion of the value of qualifying vehicles not in excess of $20,000 plus (ii) the revenue to be received on that portion of the value of qualifying vehicles in excess of $20,000 plus (iii) the Commonwealth's reimbursement is approximately equal to the total revenue that would have been received by the county, city, or town from its tangible personal property tax had the tax rate for its general class of tangible personal property been applied to 100 percent of the value of all qualifying vehicles.

3. Notwithstanding the provisions of subdivisions 1 and 2, beginning with tax year 2016, each county, city, and town that receives reimbursement shall ensure that the reimbursement pays for all of the tax attributable to the first $20,000 of value on each qualifying vehicle leased by an active duty member of the United States military, his spouse, or both, pursuant to a contract requiring him, his spouse, or both to pay the tangible personal property tax on such vehicle. The provisions of this subdivision apply only to a vehicle that would not be taxed in Virginia if the vehicle were owned by such military member, his spouse, or both.

D. On or before the date the certified personal property tax book is required by § 58.1-3118 to be provided to the treasurer, the commissioner of the revenue shall identify each qualifying vehicle and its value to the treasurer of the locality.

E. The provisions of this section are mandatory for any county, city, or town that will receive a reimbursement pursuant to subsection B.

History.
1998, Sp. Sess. I, c. 2; 2004, Sp. Sess. I, c. 1; 2015, c. 266.

§§ 58.1-3525 through 58.1-3533: Repealed by Acts 2004, Sp. Sess. I, c. 1, cl. 6, effective January 1, 2006.

Cross references.
As to general duties and powers of the Auditor of Public Accounts, see § 30-133.

§ 58.1-3534. Department to furnish information to commissioners of revenue.

A. The Department shall provide to the commissioners of revenue such data or information it has available which is needed for the commissioners of revenue to comply with the provisions of this chapter. Such data or information shall be made available in a manner which will allow for compliance with the provisions of this chapter.

B. The Department shall include in the information furnished to commissioners of the revenue pursuant to subsection A regarding vehicles qualifying for personal property tax relief, whether the vehicle is held in a private trust for nonbusiness purposes by an individual beneficiary.

History.
1998, Sp. Sess. I, c. 2; 2011, c. 13.

§ 58.1-3535. Commissioner of the revenue to furnish information to the treasurer.

The commissioner of the revenue shall timely provide to the treasurer such data or information as may be required for the treasurer to comply with the provisions of this chapter.

History.
1998, Sp. Sess. I, c. 2.

§ 58.1-3536: Repealed by Acts 2004, Sp. Sess. I, c. 1, cl. 6, effective January 1, 2006.

Cross references.
As to the Tobacco Indemnification and Community Revitalization Fund, see § 3.2-3106.

SUBTITLE IV.

OTHER SOURCES OF STATE REVENUE.

CHAPTER 40.

VIRGINIA LOTTERY LAW.

Section

§ 58.1-4003. Virginia Lottery established.

Notwithstanding the provisions of Article 1 (§ 18.2-325 et seq.) of Chapter 8 of Title 18.2 or any other provision of law, there is hereby established as an independent agency of the Commonwealth, exclusive of the legislative, executive or judicial branches of government, the Virginia Lottery, which shall include a Director and a Virginia Lottery Board for the purpose of operating a state lottery.

History.
1987, c. 531; 2014, c. 225.

§ 58.1-4005. Appointment, qualifications and salary of Director.

A. The Department shall be under the immediate supervision and direction of a Director, who shall be a person of good reputation, particularly as to honesty and integrity, and shall be subject to a thorough background investigation conducted by the Department of State Police prior to appointment. The Director shall be appointed by and serve at the pleasure of the Governor, subject to confirmation by a majority of the members elected to each house of the General Assembly if in session when the appointment is made, and if not in session, then at its next succeeding session. The Director shall receive a salary as provided in the general appropriations act.

B. The Director shall devote his full time to the performance of his official duties and shall not be engaged in any other profession or occupation.

C. Before entering upon the discharge of his duties, the Director shall take an oath that he will faithfully and honestly execute the duties of his office during his continuance therein and shall give bond in such amount as may be fixed by the Governor, conditioned upon the faithful discharge of his duties. The premium on such bond shall be paid out of the Virginia Lottery Fund.

History.
1987, c. 531; 2014, c. 225.

§ 58.1-4008. Employees of the Department; background investigations of employees.

All persons employed by the Department shall be fingerprinted before, and as a condition of, employment. These fingerprints shall be submitted to the Federal Bureau of Investigation for a National Criminal Records search and to the Department of State Police for a Virginia Criminal History Records search. All board members, officers and employees of any vendor to the Department of lottery on-line or instant ticket goods or services working directly on a contract with the Department for such goods or services shall be fingerprinted, and such fingerprints shall be submitted to the Federal Bureau of Investigation for a National Criminal Records search conducted by the chief security officer of the Virginia Lottery. A background investigation shall be conducted by the chief security officer of the Virginia Lottery on every applicant prior to employment by the Department. However, all division directors of the Virginia Lottery and employees of the Virginia Lottery performing duties primarily related to security matters shall be subject to a background investigation report conducted by the Department of State Police prior to employment by the Department. The Department of State Police shall be reimbursed by the Virginia Lottery for the cost of investigations conducted pursuant to this section or § 58.1-4005. No person who has been convicted of a felony, bookmaking or other forms of illegal gambling, or of a crime involving moral turpitude shall be employed by the Department or on contracts with vendors described in this section.

History.
1987, c. 531; 1989, c. 478; 1992, c. 449; 2004, c. 555; 2014, c. 225.

§ 58.1-4009. Licensing of lottery sales agents; penalty.

A. No license as an agent to sell lottery tickets or shares shall be issued to any person to engage in business primarily as a lottery sales agent. Before issuing such license, the Director shall consider such factors as (i) the financial responsibility and security of the person and his business or activity; (ii) the accessibility of his place of business or activity to the public; (iii) the sufficiency of existing licensees to serve the public convenience; and (iv) the volume of expected sales.

B. For the purposes of this section, the term "person" means an individual, association, partnership, corporation, club, trust, estate, society, company, joint stock company, receiver, trustee, assignee, referee, or any other person acting in a fiduciary or representative capacity, whether appointed by a court or otherwise, and any combination of individuals. "Person" also means all departments, commissions, agencies and instrumentalities of the Commonwealth, including counties, cities, municipalities, agencies and instrumentalities thereof.

C. The chief security officer of the Virginia Lottery shall conduct a background investigation, to include a Virginia Criminal History Records search, and fingerprints that shall be submitted to the Federal Bureau of Investigation if the Director deems a National Criminal Records search necessary, on applicants for licensure as lottery sales agents. The Director may refuse to issue a license to operate as an agent to sell lottery tickets or shares to any person who has been (i) convicted of a crime involving moral turpitude, (ii) convicted of bookmaking or other forms of illegal gambling, (iii) found guilty of any fraud or misrepresentation in any connection, (iv) convicted of a felony, or (v) engaged in conduct prejudicial to public confidence in the Lottery. The Director may refuse to grant a license or may suspend, revoke or refuse to renew a license issued pursuant to this chapter to a partnership or corporation, if he determines that any general or limited partner, or officer or director of such partnership or corporation has been (a) convicted of a crime involving moral turpitude, (b) convicted of bookmaking or other forms of illegal gambling, (c) found guilty of any fraud or misrepresentation in any connection, (d) convicted of a felony, or (e) engaged in conduct prejudicial to public confidence in the Lottery. Whoever knowingly and willfully falsifies, conceals or misrepresents a material fact or knowingly and willfully makes a false, fictitious or fraudulent statement or representation in any application for licensure to the Virginia Lottery for lottery sales agent is guilty of a Class 1 misdemeanor.

D. In the event an applicant is a former lottery sales agent whose license was suspended, revoked, or refused renewal pursuant to this section or § 58.1-4012, no application for a new license to sell lottery tickets or shares shall be considered for a minimum period of 90 days following the suspension, revocation, or refusal to renew.

E. Prior to issuance of a license, every lottery sales agent shall either (i) be bonded by a surety company entitled to do business in this Commonwealth in such amount and penalty as may be prescribed by the regulations of the Department or (ii) provide such other surety as may be satisfactory to the Director, payable to the Virginia Lottery and conditioned upon the faithful performance of his duties.

F. Every licensed agent shall prominently display his license, or a copy thereof, as provided in the regulations of the Department.

History.
1987, c. 531; 1989, c. 478; 2004, c. 555; 2006, c. 598; 2014, cc. 224, 225.

§ 58.1-4014. Price of tickets or shares; who may sell; penalty.

No person shall sell a ticket or share at any price or at any location other than that fixed by rules and regulations of the Department. No person other than a licensed lottery sales agent or his employee shall sell lottery tickets or shares, except that nothing in this section shall be construed to prevent any person from giving lottery tickets or shares to another person over the age of 18 years as a gift. No person shall operate a ticket courier service in the Commonwealth.

Any person convicted of violating this section is guilty of a Class 1 misdemeanor.

History.
1987, c. 531; 1992, c. 449; 2004, c. 630; 2006, c. 598; 2016, c. 461.

§ 58.1-4014.1. Method of payment for purchase of tickets or shares.

Lottery sales agents licensed in accordance with this chapter shall accept only cash or debit cards in payment for the purchase of lottery tickets or shares.

History.
2006, c. 598.

§ 58.1-4015. Sale of ticket or share to person under eighteen prohibited; penalty.

No ticket or share shall be sold to or redeemed from any person under the age of eighteen years. Any licensee who knowingly sells or offers to sell or redeem a lottery ticket or share to or from any person under the age of eighteen years is guilty of a Class 1 misdemeanor.

History.
1987, c. 531; 1989, c. 478.

§ 58.1-4016. Gift to minor prohibited.

No ticket or share shall be given as a gift or otherwise to any person under the age of eighteen years. Any person who knowingly gives a lottery ticket or share to any person under the age of eighteen years is guilty of a Class 3 misdemeanor.

History.
1987, c. 531.

§ 58.1-4017. Alteration and forgery; presentation of counterfeit or altered ticket or share; penalty.

Any person who forges, alters or fraudulently makes any lottery ticket or share with intent to present for payment or to transfer to another person to be presented for payment or knowingly presents for payment or transfers to another person to be presented for payment such forged, altered or fraudulently made counterfeit lottery ticket or share sold pursuant to this chapter is guilty of a Class 6 felony.

History.
1987, c. 531; 1989, c. 478; 1990, c. 732.

§ 58.1-4018. Prohibited actions; penalty.

Any person who wrongfully and fraudulently uses, disposes of, conceals or embezzles any public money or funds associated with the operation of the lottery shall be guilty of a Class 3 felony. Any person who wrongfully and fraudulently tampers with any equipment or machinery used in the operation of the lottery shall be guilty of a Class 3 felony. Any person who makes inaccurate entries regarding a financial accounting of the lottery in order to conceal the truth, defraud the Commonwealth and obtain money to which he is not entitled shall be guilty of a Class 3 felony.

History.
1987, c. 531; 2006, c. 598.

§ 58.1-4018.1. Larceny of tickets; fraudulent notification of prizes; penalty.

A. Any person who steals or otherwise unlawfully converts to his own or another's use a lottery ticket, prize, share, or portion thereof shall be guilty of larceny. For purposes of this subsection, the value of a lottery ticket, prize, share, or portion thereof shall be deemed to be the greater of its face amount or its redemption value.

B. Any person who, with intent to defraud, steal, embezzle, or violate the provisions of § 18.2-186.3, designs, makes, prints, or otherwise produces, in whole or in part, a document or writing, whether in printed or electronic form, which falsely purports to be correspondence from or on behalf of the lottery shall be guilty of a Class 5 felony.

Jurisdiction shall lie and prosecution may proceed under this subsection in any county or city (i) in which the document was created; (ii) from which it was sent, regardless of the form of delivery; or (iii) in which it was received, regardless of the form of delivery.

History.
2006, c. 598.

§ 58.1-4019. Certain persons ineligible to purchase tickets or shares or receive prizes.

A. No ticket or share shall be purchased by, and no prize shall be paid on a ticket purchased by or transferred to, any Board member, officer or employee of the lottery, or any board member, officer or employee of any vendor to the lottery of lottery on-line or instant ticket goods or services working directly on a contract with the Department for such goods or services, or any person residing in the same household of such member, officer or employee or any person under the age of eighteen years, or transferee of any such persons.

B. Only natural persons may purchase lottery tickets and claim prize winnings. In all cases, the identity and social security number of all natural persons who receive a prize greater than $100 from a winning ticket redeemed at any Department office shall be provided in order to comply with this section and §§ 58.1-4015, 58.1-4016 and 58.1-4026, and Chapter 19 (§ 63.2-1900 et seq.) of Title 63.2.

History.
1987, c. 531; 1989, c. 478; 1992, c. 449; 1996, c. 954; 1999, c. 34.

§ 58.1-4019.1. License required for "instant ticket" games or contests.

No person who owns or is employed by any retail establishment in the Commonwealth shall use any "instant ticket" game or contest for the purpose of promoting or furthering the sale of any product without first obtaining a license to do so from the Director. For the purposes of this section, an "instant ticket" game or contest means a game of chance played on a paper ticket or card where (i) a person may receive gifts, prizes, or gratuities and (ii) winners are determined by preprinted concealed letters, numbers, or symbols which, when exposed, reveal immediately whether the player has won a prize or entry into a prize drawing, but shall not include any "instant ticket" game or contest licensed by the Department of Agriculture and Consumer Services pursuant to Article 1.1:1 (§ 18.2-340.15 et seq.) of Title 18.2. The fact that no purchase is required in order to participate shall not exclude such game or contest from the provisions of this section; however, nothing in this section shall prohibit any retail establishment from using a Virginia lottery ticket to promote or further the sale of any products except those having both a federal and state excise tax placed on them. Any person convicted of a violation of this section shall be guilty of a Class 3 misdemeanor.

History.
1996, cc. 462, 505; 2003, c. 884; 2008, cc. 387, 689.

TITLE 59.1.

TRADE AND COMMERCE.

CHAPTER 4.1.

REMEDIES FOR VIOLATIONS OF PRECEDING CHAPTERS AND CHAPTER 6, ARTICLE 8, OF TITLE 18.2.

§ 59.1-68.2. Authority of Attorney General.

Notwithstanding any other provisions of the law to the contrary, the Attorney General may investigate and bring an action in the name of the Commonwealth to enjoin any violation of Chapters 2.1 (§ 59.1-21.1 et seq.) through 3.1 (§ 59.1-41.1 et seq.) and of Article 8 (§ 18.2-214 et seq.), Chapter 6 of Title 18.2.

History.
1970, c. 780; 1973, c. 537; 1975, c. 43; 1984, c. 582.

§ 59.1-68.3. Action for damages or penalty for violation of Article 8, Chapter 6 of Title 18.2 or Chapter 2.1 of Title 59.1; attorney's fees.

Any person who suffers loss as the result of a violation of Article 8 (§ 18.2-214 et seq.), Chapter 6 of Title 18.2 or Chapter 2.1 (§ 59.1-21.1 et seq.) of Title 59.1 shall be entitled to bring an individual action to recover damages, or $100, whichever is greater. Certified copies of the transcript and exhibits in evidence in any final proceeding in which the Attorney General has obtained a permanent injunction for a violation of Article 8, Chapter 6 of Title 18.2 or Chapter 2.1 of Title 59.1 shall be admissible in evidence in any action brought pursuant to this section by any person claiming damage as a result of the enjoined conduct. Notwithstanding any other provision of law to the contrary, in addition to the damages recovered by the aggrieved party, such person may be awarded reasonable attorney's fees.

History.
1973, c. 537; 1975, c. 43; 1976, c. 87.

§ 59.1-68.4. Suits by attorneys for the Commonwealth and city and county attorneys.

Notwithstanding any other provisions of the law to the contrary, any attorney for the Commonwealth, or the attorney for any city or county, may investigate and cause to be brought suit in the name of the Commonwealth, or of the county or city, to enjoin any violation of Chapter 2.1 (§ 59.1-21.1 et seq.) of this title and of Article 8 (§ 18.2-214 et seq.), Chapter 6 of Title 18.2. The court having jurisdiction may enjoin such violations notwithstanding the existence of an adequate remedy at law. In any action under this section, it shall not be necessary that damages be alleged or proved.

History.
1974, c. 644; 1975, c. 43.

§ 59.1-68.5. Further provisions as to actions for violation of Article 8, Chapter 6 of Title 18.2.

Any person who suffers loss as the result of a violation of Article 8 (§ 18.2-214 et seq.), Chapter 6 of Title 18.2 shall be entitled to bring an individual action to recover damages, or $100, whichever is greater. Certified copies of the transcript and exhibits in evidence in any final proceeding in which the Commonwealth, or a county or city has obtained a permanent injunction for a violation of Article 8, Chapter 6 of Title 18.2 shall be admissible in evidence in any action brought pursuant to this section by any person claiming damage as a result of the enjoined conduct. Notwithstanding any other provision of law to the contrary, in addition to the damages recovered by the aggrieved party, such person may be awarded reasonable attorney's fees.

History.
1974, c. 644; 1975, c. 43.

CHAPTER 4.2.

CONSPIRACY TO RIG BIDS TO GOVERNMENT.

§ 59.1-68.6. Definitions.

As used in this chapter, unless the text indicates otherwise:

1. *"Person"* means any individual, firm, partnership or corporation;

2. *"Governmental units"* means all state agencies and all political subdivisions or agencies thereof;

3. *"Bid"* means any submission of a price, whether written or oral, for any goods, services or construction to be provided.

History.
1980, c. 471.

§ 59.1-68.7. Combinations to rig bids.

A. Any combination, conspiracy or agreement to intentionally rig, alter or otherwise manipulate, or to cause to be rigged, altered or otherwise manipulated any bid submitted to the Commonwealth of Virginia or any governmental unit for the purpose of allocating purchases or sales to or among persons, raising or otherwise fixing the prices of the goods or services, or excluding other persons from dealing with the Commonwealth or any other governmental unit shall be unlawful.

B. Any person violating this section shall be guilty of a Class 6 felony.

History.
1980, c. 471.

§ 59.1-68.8. Enforcement.

The Attorney General of Virginia, with respect to state agencies only, shall have concurrent power and authority to investigate and prosecute any violation of § 59.1-68.7. In addition, the attorneys for the Commonwealth of the several counties and cities shall retain the power and authority to prosecute any and all violations of § 59.1-68.7 occurring within their jurisdiction.

History.
1980, c. 471.

CHAPTER 5.
TRANSACTING BUSINESS UNDER ASSUMED NAME.

Section

§ 59.1-69. Certificate required of person, partnership, limited liability company or corporation transacting business under assumed name.

A. No person, partnership, limited liability company or corporation shall conduct or transact business in this Commonwealth under any assumed or fictitious name unless such person, partnership, limited liability company or corporation shall sign and acknowledge a certificate setting forth the name under which such business is to be conducted or transacted, and the names of each person, partnership, limited liability company or corporation owning the same, with their respective post-office and residence addresses (and, (i) when the partnership or limited liability company is a foreign limited partnership or limited liability company, the date of the certificate of registration to transact business in this Commonwealth issued to it by the State Corporation Commission, or (ii) when the corporation is a foreign corporation, the date of the certificate of authority to transact business in this Commonwealth issued to it by the State Corporation Commission), and file the same in the office of the clerk of the court in which deeds are recorded in the county or city wherein the business is to be conducted.

B. No person, partnership, limited liability company or corporation shall use an assumed or fictitious name in the conduct of its business to intentionally misrepresent the geographic origin or location of any such person or entity.

History.
Code 1950, § 59-169; 1968, c. 439; 1987, c. 702; 1995, c. 168; 1996, c. 904.

§ 59.1-70. Limited partnership, limited liability company or corporation to file copy of certificate with State Corporation Commission; fee; release certificate.

A. When business is conducted in this Commonwealth under an assumed or fictitious name by a limited partnership filing a certificate under § 50-73.11, by a foreign limited partnership required to register with the Commission under § 50-73.54, or by a limited liability company or corporation, such domestic or foreign limited partnership, limited liability company or corporation shall file in the office of the clerk of the State Corporation Commission a copy of the certificate described in § 59.1-69, duly attested by the clerk of the court in which the original is on file. The State Corporation Commission shall charge a ten-dollar fee for the filing of a fictitious or an assumed name.

B. When business is no longer conducted in this Commonwealth under an assumed or fictitious name by a limited partnership filing a certificate under § 50-73.11, by a foreign limited partnership required to register with the Commission under § 50-73.54, or by a limited liability company or corporation, the domestic or foreign limited partnership, limited liability company or corporation may file with the clerk of the State Corporation Commission a copy of a release certificate, duly attested by the clerk of the court in which the certificate is on file. The Commission shall charge a ten-dollar fee for the filing of such certificate.

History.
Code 1950, § 59-170; 1968, c. 439; 1976, c. 79; 1981, c. 519; 1984, c. 771; 1987, c. 702; 1991, c. 439; 1995, c. 168.

§§ 59.1-71, 59.1-72: Repealed by Acts 2002, c. 267, effective July 1, 2002.

§ 59.1-73: Repealed by Acts 1994, c. 432.

§ 59.1-74. Recordation of certificate and registration of names.

The clerk with whom the certificate provided for in § 59.1-69 is filed shall keep a book in which all such certificates shall be recorded, with their date of record, and shall keep a register in which shall be entered in alphabetical order the name under which every such business is conducted and the names of every person owning the same. The clerk shall be entitled to a fee of ten dollars for filing and recording such certificate and entering such names. No license shall be issued by the Commissioner of the Revenue until the certificate has been made and filed in the clerk's office and evidence of same produced before him.

History.
Code 1950, § 59-174; 1968, c. 439; 1975, c. 230; 1983, c. 103; 1992, c. 784; 2002, c. 267.

§ 59.1-75. Penalty for violation.

Any person violating any of the provisions of this chapter shall be guilty of a misdemeanor and, upon conviction, shall be punished by a fine not exceeding $2,500 or by confinement in jail for not more than one year, or both.

History.
Code 1950, § 59-175; 1968, c. 439; 1991, c. 710.

CHAPTER 10.
EXPLOSIVES.

Section

§ 59.1-137. Definition.

Whenever used in this chapter:

"Explosives" means any chemical compound, mechanical mixture or device the primary or common purpose of which is to function by explosion. The term includes, but is not limited to dynamite and other high explosives, black blasting powder, pellet powder, initiating explosives, blasting caps, electric blasting caps, detonators, safety fuse, fuse igniters, fuse lighters, squibs, cordeau detonant fuse, instantaneous fuse, detonating cord, igniter cord, igniters and those materials included in the list published annually in the Federal Register by the Department of the Treasury pursuant to the Organized Crime Control Act of 1970 (18 U.S.C. § 841 et seq.).

History.
Code 1950, § 59-222; 1960, c. 578; 1968, c. 439; 1976, c. 250.

§ 59.1-138. Record of sales required; signing by purchasers; sales to persons under eighteen prohibited.

(a) Any person selling any explosives covered by this chapter shall keep a record of all such explosives sold, showing the kind and quantity sold, the name and address of the purchaser, and the date of each sale. The person selling such explosives shall also require any person purchasing such explosives to sign such record at the time of such purchase.

(b) No person shall sell, deliver, give away, or otherwise dispose of any explosives to any individual under eighteen years of age, whether such individual is acting for himself, herself, or for any other person.

History.
Code 1950, § 59-223; 1960, c. 578; 1968, c. 439; 1972, c. 824.

§ 59.1-139. Persons possessing explosives to give notice of theft.

Any person having in his possession any explosives covered by this chapter shall immediately notify the sheriff of the county or the police officials of the city in which any such explosives are being stored or used in the event that any such explosives are stolen.

History.
Code 1950, § 59-224; 1960, c. 578; 1968, c. 439.

§ 59.1-140. Effect of chapter upon municipal regulation.

Nothing contained in this chapter shall:

Affect any existing ordinance, rule or regulation of any city or municipality in this Commonwealth that is not less restrictive than this chapter; or affect, modify or limit the power of such cities or municipalities to make ordinances, rules or regulations not less restrictive than this chapter, governing the storage, possession, sale and use of explosives within their respective corporate limits.

History.
Code 1950, § 59-225; 1960, c. 578; 1968, c. 439.

§ 59.1-141. Penalty.

Any person who violates any provision of this chapter shall be guilty of a misdemeanor and, upon conviction thereof, be punished accordingly.

History.
Code 1950, § 59-226; 1960, c. 578; 1968, c. 439.

CHAPTER 11.
FIREWORKS.

§§ 59.1-142 through 59.1-148: Repealed by Acts 2002, c. 856.

Cross references.
For provision authorizing localities to provide for the issuance of permits for the display of fireworks, see § 15.2-974. For provisions relating to fireworks, see the Virginia Statewide Fire Prevention Code, § 27-94 et seq.

CHAPTER 11.1.
FIREARMS.

Section

§§ 59.1-148.1, 59.1-148.2: Repealed by Acts 2004, c. 929.

§ 59.1-148.3. (Effective until October 1, 2016) Purchase of handguns or other weapons of certain officers.

A. The Department of State Police, the Department of Game and Inland Fisheries, the Department of Alcoholic Beverage Control, the Virginia Lottery, the Marine Resources Commission, the Capitol Police, the Department of Conservation and Recreation, the Department of Forestry, any sheriff, any regional jail board or authority, and any local police department may allow any full-time sworn law-enforcement officer, deputy, or regional jail officer, a local fire department may allow any full-time sworn fire marshal, the Department of Motor Vehicles may allow any law-enforcement officer, any institution of higher learning named in § 23-14 may allow any campus police officer appointed pursuant to Chapter 17 (§ 23-232 et seq.) of Title 23, retiring on or after July 1, 1991, and the Department of Corrections may allow any employee with internal investigations authority designated by the Department of Corrections pursuant to subdivision 11 of § 53.1-10 who retires (i) after at least 10 years of service, (ii) at 70 years of age or older, or (iii) as a result of a service-incurred disability or who is receiving long-term disability payments for a service-incurred disability with no expectation of returning to the employment where he incurred the disability to purchase the service handgun issued or previously issued to him by the agency or institution at a price of $1. If the previously issued weapon is no longer available, a weapon of like kind may be substituted for that weapon. This privilege shall also extend to any former Superintendent of the Department of State Police who leaves service after a minimum of five years. This privilege shall also extend to any person listed in this subsection who is eligible for retirement with at least 10 years of service who resigns on or after July 1, 1991, in good standing from one of the agencies listed in this section to accept a position covered by the Virginia Retirement System. Other weapons issued by the agencies listed in this subsection for personal duty use of an officer may, with approval of the agency head, be sold to the officer subject to the qualifications of this section at a fair market price determined as in subsection B, so long as the weapon is a type and configuration that can be purchased at a regular hardware or sporting goods store by a private citizen without restrictions other than the instant background check.

B. The agencies listed in subsection A may allow any full-time sworn law-enforcement officer who retires with five or more years of service, but less than 10, to purchase the service handgun issued to him by the agency at a price equivalent to the weapon's fair market value on the date of the officer's retirement. Any full-time sworn law-enforcement officer employed by any of the agencies listed in subsection A who is retired for disability as a result of a nonservice-incurred disability may purchase the service handgun issued to him by the agency at a price equivalent to the weapon's fair market value on the date of the officer's retirement. Determinations of fair market value may be made by reference to a recognized pricing guide.

C. The agencies listed in subsection A may allow the immediate survivor of any full-time sworn law-enforcement officer (i) who is killed in the line of duty or (ii) who dies in service and has at least 10 years of service to purchase the service handgun issued to the officer by the agency at a price of $1.

D. The governing board of any institution of higher learning named in § 23-14 may allow any campus police officer appointed pursuant to Chapter 17 (§ 23-232 et seq.) of Title 23 who retires on or after July 1, 1991, to purchase the service handgun issued to him at a price equivalent to the weapon's fair market value on the date of the officer's retirement. Determinations of fair market value may be made by reference to a recognized pricing guide.

E. Any officer who at the time of his retirement is a full-time sworn law-enforcement officer with a state agency listed in subsection A, when the agency allows purchases of service handguns, and who retires after 10 years of state service, even if a portion of his service was with another state agency, may purchase the service handgun issued to him by the agency from which he retires at a price of $1.

F. The sheriff of Hanover County may allow any auxiliary or volunteer deputy sheriff with a minimum of 10 years of service, upon leaving office, to purchase for $1 the service handgun issued to him.

G. Any sheriff or local police department, in accordance with written authorization or approval from the local governing body, may allow any auxiliary law-enforcement officer with more than 10 years of service to purchase the service handgun issued to him by the agency at a price that is equivalent to or less than the weapon's fair market value on the date of purchase by the officer.

H. The agencies listed in subsection A may allow any full-time sworn law-enforcement officer currently employed by the agency to purchase his service handgun, with the approval of the chief law-enforcement officer of the agency, at a fair market price. This subsection shall only apply when the agency has purchased new service handguns for its officers, and the handgun subject to the sale is no longer used by the agency or officer in the course of duty.

History.

1989, c. 175; 1990, c. 359; 1991, c. 389; 1992, cc. 63, 83, 195; 1996, c. 50; 1998, c. 173; 1999, c. 312; 2000, c. 391; 2002, c. 25; 2003, c. 106; 2004, c. 136; 2005, c. 168; 2006, c. 185; 2007, c. 813; 2009, cc. 289, 412; 2010, cc. 590, 864; 2011, c. 628; 2012, c. 218; 2013, c. 62; 2014, c. 225; 2016, cc. 196, 210, 215.

§ 59.1-148.3. (Effective October 1, 2016, until July 1, 2018) Purchase of handguns or other weapons of certain officers.

A. The Department of State Police, the Department of Game and Inland Fisheries, the Department of Alcoholic Beverage Control, the Virginia Lottery, the Marine Resources Commission, the Capitol Police, the Department of Conservation and Recreation, the Department of Forestry, any sheriff, any regional jail board or authority, and any local police department may allow any full-time sworn law-enforcement officer, deputy, or regional jail officer, a local fire department may allow any full-time sworn fire marshal, the Department of Motor Vehicles may allow any law-enforcement officer, any institution of higher learning named in § 23.1-1100 may allow any campus police officer appointed pursuant to Article 3 (§ 23.1-809 et seq.) of Chapter 8 of Title 23.1, retiring on or after July 1, 1991, and the Department of Corrections may allow any employee with internal investigations authority designated by the Department of Corrections pursuant to subdivision 11 of § 53.1-10 who retires (i) after at least 10 years of service, (ii) at 70 years of age or older, or (iii) as a result of a service-incurred disability or who is receiving long-term disability payments for a service-incurred disability with no expectation of returning to the employment where he incurred the disability to purchase the service handgun issued or previously issued to him by the agency or institution at a price of $1. If the previously issued weapon is no longer available, a weapon of like kind may be substituted for that weapon. This privilege shall also extend to any former Superintendent of the Department of State Police who leaves service after a minimum of five years. This privilege shall also extend to any person listed in this subsection who is eligible for retirement with at least 10 years of service who resigns on or after July 1, 1991, in good standing from one of the agencies listed in this section to accept a position covered by the Virginia Retirement System. Other weapons issued by the agencies listed in this subsection for personal duty use of an officer may, with approval of the agency head, be sold to the officer subject to the qualifications of this section at a fair market price determined as in subsection B, so long as the weapon is a type and configuration that can be purchased at a regular hardware or sporting goods store by a private citizen without restrictions other than the instant background check.

B. The agencies listed in subsection A may allow any full-time sworn law-enforcement officer who retires with five or more years of service, but less than 10, to purchase the service handgun issued to him by the agency at a price equivalent to the weapon's fair market value on the date of the officer's retirement. Any full-time sworn law-enforcement officer employed by any of the agencies listed in subsection A who is retired for disability as a result of a nonservice-incurred disability may purchase the service handgun issued to him by the agency at a price equivalent to the weapon's fair market value on the date of the officer's retirement. Determinations of fair market value may be made by reference to a recognized pricing guide.

C. The agencies listed in subsection A may allow the immediate survivor of any full-time sworn law-enforcement officer (i) who is killed in the line of duty or (ii) who dies in service and has at least 10 years of service to purchase the service handgun issued to the officer by the agency at a price of $1.

D. The governing board of any institution of higher learning named in § 23.1-1100 may allow any campus police officer appointed pursuant to Article 3 (§ 23.1-809 et seq.) of Chapter 8 of Title 23.1 who retires on or after July 1, 1991, to purchase the service handgun issued to him at a price equivalent to the weapon's fair market value on the date of the officer's retirement. Determinations of fair market value may be made by reference to a recognized pricing guide.

E. Any officer who at the time of his retirement is a full-time sworn law-enforcement officer with a state agency listed in subsection A, when the agency allows purchases of service handguns, and who retires after 10 years of state service, even if a portion of his service was with another state agency, may purchase the service handgun issued to him by the agency from which he retires at a price of $1.

F. The sheriff of Hanover County may allow any auxiliary or volunteer deputy sheriff with a minimum of 10 years of service, upon leaving office, to purchase for $1 the service handgun issued to him.

G. Any sheriff or local police department, in accordance with written authorization or approval from the local governing body, may allow any auxiliary law-enforcement officer with more than 10 years of service to purchase the service handgun issued to him by the agency at a price that is equivalent to or less than the weapon's fair market value on the date of purchase by the officer.

H. The agencies listed in subsection A may allow any full-time sworn law-enforcement officer currently employed by the agency to purchase his service handgun, with the approval of the chief law-enforcement officer of the agency, at a fair market price. This subsection shall only apply when the agency has purchased new service handguns for its officers, and the handgun subject to the sale is no longer used by the agency or officer in the course of duty.

History.

1989, c. 175; 1990, c. 359; 1991, c. 389; 1992, cc. 63, 83, 195; 1996, c. 50; 1998, c. 173; 1999, c. 312; 2000, c. 391; 2002, c. 25; 2003, c. 106; 2004, c. 136; 2005, c. 168; 2006, c. 185; 2007, c. 813; 2009, cc. 289, 412; 2010, cc. 590, 864; 2011, c. 628; 2012, c. 218; 2013, c. 62; 2014, c. 225; 2016, cc. 196, 210, 215.

§ 59.1-148.3. (Effective July 1, 2018) Purchase of handguns or other weapons of certain officers.

A. The Department of State Police, the Department of Game and Inland Fisheries, the Virginia Alcoholic Beverage Control Authority, the Virginia Lottery, the Marine Resources Commission, the Capitol Police, the Department of Conservation and Recreation, the Department of Forestry, any sheriff, any regional jail board or authority, and any local police department may allow any full-time sworn law-enforcement officer, deputy, or regional jail officer, a local fire department may allow any full-time sworn fire marshal, the Department of Motor Vehicles may allow any law-enforcement officer, any institution of higher learning named in § 23.1-1100 may allow any campus police officer appointed pursuant to Article 3 (§ 23.1-809 et seq.) of Chapter 8 of Title 23.1, retiring on or after July 1, 1991, and the Department of Corrections may allow any employee with internal investigations authority designated by the Department of Corrections pursuant to subdivision 11 of § 53.1-10 who retires (i) after at least 10 years of service, (ii) at 70 years of age or older, or (iii) as a result of a service-incurred disability or who is receiving long-term disability payments for a service-incurred disability with no expectation of returning to the employment where he incurred the disability to purchase the service handgun issued or previously issued to him by the agency or institution at a price of $1. If the previously issued weapon is no longer available, a weapon of like kind may be substituted for that weapon. This privilege shall also extend to any former Superintendent of the Department of State Police who leaves service after a minimum of five years. This privilege shall also extend to any person listed in this subsection who is eligible for retirement with at least 10 years of service who resigns on or after July 1, 1991, in good standing from one of the agencies listed in this section to accept a position covered by the Virginia Retirement System. Other weapons issued by the agencies listed in this subsection for personal duty use of an officer may, with approval of the agency head, be sold to the officer subject to the qualifications of this section at a fair market price determined as in subsection B, so long as the weapon is a type and configuration that can be purchased at a regular hardware or sporting goods store by a private citizen without restrictions other than the instant background check.

B. The agencies listed in subsection A may allow any full-time sworn law-enforcement officer who retires with five or more years of service, but less than 10, to purchase the service handgun issued to him by the agency at a price equivalent to the weapon's fair market value on the date of the officer's retirement. Any full-time sworn law-enforcement officer employed by any of the agencies listed in subsection A who is retired for disability as a result of a nonservice-incurred disability may purchase the service handgun issued to him by the agency at a price equivalent to the weapon's fair market value on the date of the officer's retirement. Determinations of fair market value may be made by reference to a recognized pricing guide.

C. The agencies listed in subsection A may allow the immediate survivor of any full-time sworn law-enforcement officer (i) who is killed in the line of duty or (ii) who dies in service and has at least 10 years of service to purchase the service handgun issued to the officer by the agency at a price of $1.

D. The governing board of any institution of higher learning named in § 23.1-1100 may allow any campus police officer appointed pursuant to Article 3 (§ 23.1-809 et seq.) of Chapter 8 of Title 23.1 who retires on or after July 1, 1991, to purchase the service handgun issued to him at a price equivalent to the weapon's fair market value on the date of the officer's retirement. Determinations of fair market value may be made by reference to a recognized pricing guide.

E. Any officer who at the time of his retirement is a full-time sworn law-enforcement officer with a state agency listed in subsection A, when the agency allows purchases of service handguns, and who retires after 10 years of state service, even if a portion of his service was with another state agency, may purchase the service handgun issued to him by the agency from which he retires at a price of $1.

F. The sheriff of Hanover County may allow any auxiliary or volunteer deputy sheriff with a minimum of 10 years of service, upon leaving office, to purchase for $1 the service handgun issued to him.

G. Any sheriff or local police department, in accordance with written authorization or approval from the local governing body, may allow any auxiliary law-enforcement officer with more than 10 years of service to purchase the service handgun issued to him by the agency at a price that is equivalent to or less than the weapon's fair market value on the date of purchase by the officer.

H. The agencies listed in subsection A may allow any full-time sworn law-enforcement officer currently employed by the agency to purchase his service handgun, with the approval of the chief law-enforcement officer of the agency, at a fair market price. This subsection shall only apply when the agency has purchased new service handguns for its officers, and the handgun subject to the sale is no longer used by the agency or officer in the course of duty.

History.
1989, c. 175; 1990, c. 359; 1991, c. 389; 1992, cc. 63, 83, 195; 1996, c. 50; 1998, c. 173; 1999, c. 312; 2000, c. 391; 2002, c. 25; 2003, c. 106; 2004, c. 136; 2005, c. 168; 2006, c. 185; 2007, c. 813; 2009, cc. 289, 412; 2010, cc. 590, 864; 2011, c. 628; 2012, c. 218; 2013, c. 62; 2014, c. 225; 2015, cc. 38, 730; 2016, cc. 196, 210, 215.

§ 59.1-148.4. Sale of firearms by law-enforcement agencies prohibited; exception.

A law-enforcement agency of this Commonwealth shall not sell or trade any firearm owned and used or otherwise lawfully in its possession except (i) to another law-enforcement agency of the Commonwealth, (ii) to a licensed firearms dealer, (iii) to the persons as provided in § 59.1-148.3 or (iv) as authorized by a court in accordance with § 19.2-386.29.

History.
1994, c. 467; 2004, c. 995.

CHAPTER 12.

MOTOR FUELS AND LUBRICATING OILS.

§ 59.1-149. Definitions.

As used in this chapter:

"Commissioner" means the Commissioner of Agriculture and Consumer Services or his designated representative.

"Gasoline" shall be construed to include naphtha, benzine and other like liquids and fluids derived from petroleum or other sources and used, or intended to be used, for power purposes, except kerosene.

"Lubricating oil" means lubricating oils used in internal combustion engines.

"Motor fuel" means any liquid or gaseous matter used for the generation of power in an internal combustion engine.

History.
Code 1950, § 59-41; 1968, c. 439; 1992, c. 885; 2009, c. 650.

§ 59.1-150. Motor fuel subject to inspection and testing.

All motor fuel used, intended to be used, sold or offered for sale or distribution in this Commonwealth, shall be subject to inspection and testing for (i) the purpose of preventing adulteration, misbranding, deception or fraud in the sale thereof or (ii) for any other purpose of assuring compliance with any requirement of this chapter or regulation adopted thereunder.

History.
Code 1950, § 59-42; 1968, c. 439; 1992, c. 885.

§ 59.1-151. Statements to be filed by manufacturers, wholesalers and jobbers.

All manufacturers, wholesalers, and jobbers, before selling or offering for sale in this Commonwealth any motor fuel for the purposes above defined, shall file with the Commissioner a statement that they desire to do business in this Commonwealth, and furnish the brand name, trade name, or trademark of the motor fuel which they desire to sell.

History.
Code 1950, § 59-43; 1968, c. 439; 1992, c. 885; 2009, c. 650.

§ 59.1-152. Collection and analysis of samples.

The Commissioner shall have power at all times and at all places to have collected samples for inspection and testing of any motor fuel or lubricating oil for the purposes specified in § 59.1-150 and for the purpose of determining whether such motor fuel or lubricating oil is in violation of this chapter or regulation thereunder.

History.
Code 1950, § 59-44; 1968, c. 439; 1992, c. 885.

§ 59.1-153. Methods of making inspection.

In making any inspection and test of a motor fuel or lubricating oil under this chapter, the Commissioner shall follow the specifications for the inspection and testing of that motor fuel or for the lubricating oil established by ASTM International, formerly the American Society for Testing and Materials, and incorporated into the ASTM specifications for motor fuels, which are adopted by the National Conference on Weights and Measures and published by the National Institute of Standards and Technology in Handbook 130, "Uniform Laws and Regulations in the Areas of Legal Metrology and Engine Fuel Quality," as the same now are or may be hereafter amended. For purposes of this section, such specifications shall apply to methods of inspection and testing only, and shall not apply to methods of sale, including automatic temperature compensation. For cause after an informational proceeding under § 2.2-4007.01, such specifications may be amended by the Board of Agriculture and Consumer Services.

History.
Code 1950, § 59-45; 1968, c. 439; 1992, c. 885; 2007, cc. 873, 916; 2009, c. 650.

§ 59.1-154. Inspection and testing under supervision of Commissioner.

Inspection and testing of such motor fuel or lubricating oil shall be under the direction of the Commissioner.

History.
Code 1950, § 59-46; 1968, c. 439; 1992, c. 885.

§ 59.1-155. Prohibiting sale of defective motor fuel.

The Commissioner may prohibit the sale of motor fuel that does not meet the specifications as provided in this chapter or regulations adopted thereunder.

History.
Code 1950, § 59-47; 1968, c. 439; 1992, c. 885; 2009, c. 650.

§ 59.1-155.1. Engine coolant and antifreeze bittering agent; penalty.

A. Any engine coolant or antifreeze manufactured after January 1, 2011, and sold within the Commonwealth that contains more than 10 percent ethylene glycol shall include not less than 30 parts per million and not more than 50 parts per million denatonium benzoate as a bittering agent in order to render the coolant or antifreeze unpalatable.

B. A manufacturer, processor, distributor, recycler or seller of an engine coolant or antifreeze that is required to contain an aversive agent under subsection A shall not be liable to any person for any personal injury, death, property damage, damage to the environment (including natural resources), or economic loss that results from the inclusion of denatonium benzoate in any engine coolant or antifreeze, provided that the inclusion of denatonium benzoate is present in concentrations mandated by subsection A. The limitation on liability does not apply to a particular liability to the extent that the cause of such liability is unrelated to the inclusion of denatonium benzoate in any engine coolant or antifreeze.

C. The provisions of this section shall not apply to (i) the sale of a motor vehicle that contains engine coolant or antifreeze, (ii) a wholesale container of engine coolant or antifreeze designed to contain 55 gallons or more of engine coolant or antifreeze, or (iii) engine coolant or antifreeze reformulated through on site recycling.

D. Any person violating any provision of this section shall be assessed a civil penalty of up to $100 per violation. Each day of violation shall constitute a separate offense.

E. This section shall not apply to engine coolant or antifreeze that is purchased pursuant to military specifications.

History.
2009, c. 681.

§ 59.1-156. Rules and regulations.

A. The Board of Agriculture and Consumer Services may make all necessary rules and regulations for (i) the inspection and testing of motor fuel and lubricating oil; (ii) assuring that motor fuels dispensed in this Commonwealth comply with any oxygenation requirement specified by the federal Clean Air Act or any other federal environmental requirement pertaining to motor fuels; and (iii) the enforcement of this chapter.

B. Oxygenated gasoline regulations pursuant to clause (ii) of subsection A may be adopted, amended or repealed without observing the requirements of the Administrative Process Act (§ 2.2-4000 et seq.) and shall, unless a later effective date is specified in the regulation, amendment or repeal, take effect upon adoption by the Board of Agriculture and Consumer Services and filing with the Registrar of Regulations.

C. No agency of the Commonwealth may enforce the provisions of "Regulations Governing the Oxygenation of Gasoline" (2 VAC 5-480-10 et seq.), or any successor regulation, requiring the use or sale of oxygenated gasoline, unless, and only to the extent, the regulation is required by federal law or regulation. For purposes of this subsection "oxygenated gasoline" shall have the same meaning as "Gasoline-Oxygenate Blend" as defined in Handbook 130 published by the National Institute of Standards and Technology.

History.
Code 1950, § 59-48; 1968, c. 439; 1992, c. 885; 1996, cc. 638, 1012; 2009, c. 650.

§ 59.1-157. Complaints to Commissioner.

The Commissioner shall investigate complaints made to him concerning alleged violations of the provisions of this chapter or regulation adopted thereunder, and shall, upon his own initiative, conduct such investigations as he deems appropriate and advisable.

History.
Code 1950, § 59-50; 1968, c. 439; 1992, c. 885.

§§ 59.1-158 through 59.1-161: Repealed by Acts 1992, c. 885.

§ 59.1-162. Cooperation by state agencies.

The Commonwealth Transportation Board and the Department of Motor Vehicles are authorized to cooperate, as directed by the Governor, with the Commissioner of Agriculture and Consumer Services in carrying out the provisions of this chapter.

History.
Code 1950, § 59-55; 1968, c. 439.

§ 59.1-162.1. Direct fueling of commercial vehicles authorized; conditions.

Notwithstanding any other provision of law, the dispensing of diesel fuel from a tank vehicle into the fuel tank of any highway vehicle on the premises of a commercial, industrial, governmental or manufacturing establishment is permitted, provided the following conditions are met:

1. The highway vehicle is used in connection with the business or function of the establishment;
2. The owner or operator of the tank vehicle complies with all requirements pertaining to the collection and payment of taxes on diesel fuel pursuant to Title 58.1 and fees pursuant to Title 62.1;
3. The owner or operator of the tank vehicle complies with all requirements pertaining to Chapter 56 (§ 3.2-5600 et seq.) of Title 3.2;
4. Each delivery shall be metered and recorded and the customer shall be provided an invoice or delivery ticket plainly indicating the quantity of fuel dispensed, the price per gallon, the amount of tax and the total price of the fuel dispensed;
5. The tank vehicle is designed, equipped and operated to prevent spills during fueling operations and to minimize spillage in the event of operator error or equipment malfunction;
6. The owner of the tank vehicle has established and maintains in place a contingency plan for the cleanup of spills occurring during fueling operations, and the operator has been trained in the prevention of spills, and containment of spills should they occur, and in compliance with such spill plan; and
7. The owner is licensed in Virginia as a distributor.

History.
2000, c. 943.

§ 59.1-163. Penalty for violation.

Any person selling any motor fuel or lubricating oil which does not comply with the specifications provided in this chapter, or violating any of the provisions of the chapter, shall be guilty of a Class 1 misdemeanor. Any dealer in any motor fuel who receives motor fuel meeting the requirements of this chapter and who thereafter adulterates any such motor fuel or mixes it with inferior motor fuel, so that the resulting product does not meet the requirements of this chapter, shall be guilty of a Class 1 misdemeanor.

History.
Code 1950, § 59-56; 1968, c. 439; 1992, c. 885; 2009, c. 650.

§ 59.1-164. Duty of attorney for the Commonwealth.

It shall be the duty of the attorney for the Commonwealth of the respective cities and counties to prosecute all violations of the provisions of this chapter, when certified to him by the Commissioner.

History.
Code 1950, § 59-57; 1968, c. 439.

§ 59.1-165. Chemical analysis as evidence.

A certificate of analysis of any motor fuel or lubricating oils shall be admitted into evidence in any case relating to such motor fuel or lubricating oil that involves an alleged violation of this chapter or regulation adopted thereunder, provided that the requirements of subsection A of § 19.2-187.1 have been satisfied and the accused has not objected to the admission of the certificate pursuant to subsection B of § 19.2-187.1.

History.
Code 1950, § 59-58; 1968, c. 439; 1972, c. 741; 1992, c. 885; 2010, c. 152.

§ 59.1-166. Enforcement by Commissioner.

It shall be the duty of the Commissioner to enforce the provisions of this chapter.

History.
Code 1950, § 59-59; 1968, c. 439; 1992, c. 885.

§ 59.1-167. Conflicting local laws and ordinances prohibited.

Cities, towns, counties and other political subdivisions of this Commonwealth are prohibited from passing any laws or ordinances relating to the inspection and testing of motor fuel and lubricating oil as defined in § 59.1-149 inconsistent with the provisions of this chapter.

History.
Code 1950, § 59-60; 1968, c. 439; 1992, c. 885.

§ 59.1-167.1. Labeling of motor fuels; notification to reseller.

A. Every dispensing device used in the retail sale of any motor fuel shall be plainly and conspicuously labeled with:

1. The brand name, trademark or trade name of the motor fuel it contains;
2. The grade, blend or mixture of the motor fuel it contains;
3. The octane or cetane rating of the motor fuel it contains; and
4. If the product contains one percent or more ethanol or methanol, information identifying the kind of alcohol and the percentage of each at the time of blending, in letters not less than one inch in height.

B. Every person delivering gasoline at wholesale to a reseller which contains one percent or more of ethanol or methanol shall provide a written manifest or invoice which conspicuously identifies the gasoline containing one percent or more of ethanol or methanol, and the percentage of ethanol or methanol contained therein. The Board of Agriculture and Consumer Services may, by regulation, establish what additional disclosure shall be made about a motor fuel by a person delivering the motor fuel at wholesale to a retailer, so that the retailer may comply with the requirements of subsection A of this section.

History.
1986, c. 197; 1992, c. 885.

§ 59.1-167.2. Civil penalties.

A. In addition to the penalties prescribed in § 59.1-163, any person violating any provision of this chapter or regulation adopted thereunder may be assessed a civil penalty by the Board in an amount not to exceed $1,000 per violation. In determining the amount of any civil penalty, the Board shall give due consideration to (i) the history of previous violations of the person; (ii) the seriousness of the violation; and (iii) the demonstrated good faith of the person charged in attempting to achieve compliance with the chapter or regulation adopted thereunder after notification of the violation.

B. Civil penalties assessed under this section shall be paid into the Weights and Measures Fund as established by § 3.2-5628. The Commissioner shall prescribe procedures for payment of uncontested penalties. The procedure shall include provisions for a person to consent to abatement of the alleged violation and pay a penalty or negotiated sum in lieu of such penalty without admission of civil liability arising from such alleged violation.

C. Final orders may be recorded, enforced and satisfied as orders or decrees of a circuit court upon certification of such orders by the Commissioner. Such orders may be appealed in accordance with provisions of the Administrative Process Act (§ 2.2-4000 et seq.).

History.
1992, c. 885.

§ 59.1-167.3. Delegation of authority.

The Board may delegate any authority vested in it under this chapter, except the adoption of regulations, to the Commissioner.

History.
1992, c. 885.

CHAPTER 23.2.

LIQUID NICOTINE.

§ 59.1-293.10. Definitions.

As used in this chapter, unless the context requires another meaning:

"Child-resistant packaging" means packaging that is designed or constructed to meet the child-resistant effectiveness standards set forth in 16 C.F.R. § 1700.15(b)(1) when tested in accordance with the protocols described in 16 C.F.R. § 1700.20 as in effect on July 1, 2015.

"Liquid nicotine" means a liquid or other substance containing nicotine in any concentration that is sold, marketed, or intended for use in a nicotine vapor product.

"Liquid nicotine container" means a bottle or other container holding liquid nicotine in any concentration but does not include a cartridge containing liquid nicotine if such cartridge is prefilled and sealed by the manufacturer of such cartridge and is not intended to be opened by the consumer.

"Nicotine vapor product" has the same meaning as in § 18.2-371.2.

History.
2015, cc. 739, 756.

§ 59.1-293.11. Sale or distribution of liquid nicotine container; prohibition; penalty.

A. No person shall sell or distribute at retail or offer for retail sale or distribution a liquid nicotine container in the Commonwealth on or after October 1, 2015, unless such liquid nicotine container meets child-resistant packaging standards.

B. The requirements of subsection A shall not prohibit a wholesaler or retailer from selling its existing inventory of liquid nicotine until January 1, 2016, if the wholesaler or retailer can establish that the inventory was purchased prior to October 1, 2015, in a quantity comparable to that of the inventory purchased during the same period of the prior year.

C. Any person who sells or distributes at retail or offers for retail sale or distribution a liquid nicotine container in the Commonwealth on or after October 1, 2015, that he knows or has reason to know does not satisfy the child-resistant packaging standards required by this section is guilty of a Class 4 misdemeanor. However, no person shall be guilty of a violation of this section who relies in good faith on any information provided by the manufacturer of a liquid nicotine container that such container meets the requirements of this section.

D. The provisions of this chapter do not apply to any manufacturer or wholesaler of liquid nicotine containers who sells or distributes a liquid nicotine container, provided that any such liquid nicotine container sold or distributed is intended for use outside of the Commonwealth.

E. The provisions of subsection A shall be null, void, and of no force and effect upon the effective date of either enacted federal legislation or final regulations issued by the U.S. Food and Drug Administration or by any other federal agency where such legislation or regulations mandate child-resistant packaging for liquid nicotine containers.

History.
2015, cc. 739, 756.

CHAPTER 29.

HORSE RACING AND PARI-MUTUEL WAGERING.

Article 1.

Virginia Racing Commission.

Article 2.

Licenses.

Article 3.

Permits.

Article 4.

Local Referendum.

Article 5.

Taxation and Audit.

Article 5.1.

Live Horseracing Compact.

Article 6.

Criminal Penalties.

ARTICLE 1. VIRGINIA RACING COMMISSION.

§ 59.1-364. Control of racing with pari-mutuel wagering.

A. Horse racing with pari-mutuel wagering as licensed herein shall be permitted in the Commonwealth for the promotion, sustenance and growth of a native industry, in a manner consistent with the health, safety and welfare of the people. The Virginia Racing Commission is vested with control of all horse racing with pari-mutuel wagering in the Commonwealth, with plenary power to prescribe regulations and conditions under which such racing and wagering shall be conducted, so as to maintain horse racing in the Commonwealth of the highest quality and free of any corrupt, incompetent, dishonest or unprincipled practices and to maintain in such racing complete honesty and integrity. The Virginia Racing Commission shall encourage participation by local individuals and businesses in those activities associated with horse racing.

B. The conduct of any horse racing with pari-mutuel wagering participation in such racing or wagering and entrance to any place where such racing or wagering is conducted is a privilege which may be granted or denied by the Commission or its duly authorized representatives in its discretion in order to effectuate the purposes set forth in this chapter.

C. The award of any prize money for any pari-mutuel wager placed at a racetrack or satellite facility licensed by the Commission shall not be deemed to be a part of any gaming contract within the purview of § 11-14.

History.
1988, c. 855; 1992, c. 820; 1998, c. 619.

§ 59.1-365. Definitions.

As used in this chapter, unless the context requires a different meaning:

"Advance deposit account wagering" means a method of pari-mutuel wagering conducted in the Commonwealth that is permissible under the Interstate Horseracing Act, § 3001 et seq. of Chapter 57 of Title 15 of the United States Code, and in which an individual may establish an account with an entity, licensed by the Commission, to place pari-mutuel wagers in person or electronically.

"Breakage" means the odd cents by which the amount payable on each dollar wagered exceeds a multiple of $0.10.

"Commission" means the Virginia Racing Commission.

"Dependent" means a son, daughter, father, mother, brother, sister, or other person, whether or not related by blood or marriage, if such person receives from an officer or employee more than one-half of his financial support.

"Drug" shall have the meaning prescribed by § 54.1-3401. The Commission shall by regulation define and designate those drugs the use of which is prohibited or restricted.

"Enclosure" means all areas of the property of a track to which admission can be obtained only by payment of an admission fee or upon presentation of authorized credentials, and any additional areas designated by the Commission.

"Handle" means the total amount of all pari-mutuel wagering sales excluding refunds and cancellations.

"Horse racing" means a competition on a set course involving a race between horses on which pari-mutuel wagering is permitted.

"Immediate family" means (i) a spouse and (ii) any other person residing in the same household as an officer or employee, who is a dependent of the officer or employee or of whom the officer or employee is a dependent.

"Licensee" includes any person holding an owner's or operator's license under Article 2 (§ 59.1-375 et seq.).

"Member" includes any person designated a member of a nonstock corporation, and any person who by means of a pecuniary or other interest in such corporation exercises the power of a member.

"Pari-mutuel wagering" means the system of wagering on horse races in which those who wager on horses that finish in the position or positions for which wagers are taken share in the total amounts wagered, plus any amounts provided by a licensee, less deductions required or permitted by law and includes pari-mutuel wagering on simulcast horse racing originating within the Commonwealth or from any other jurisdiction.

"Participant" means any person who (i) has an ownership interest in any horse entered to race in the Commonwealth or who acts as the trainer, jockey, or driver of any horse entered to race in the Commonwealth or (ii) takes part in any horse racing subject to the jurisdiction of the Commission or in the conduct of a race meeting or pari-mutuel wagering there, including but not limited to a horse owner, trainer, jockey, or driver, groom, stable foreman, valet, veterinarian, agent, pari-mutuel employee, concessionaire or employee thereof, track employee, or other position the Commission deems necessary to regulate to ensure the integrity of horse racing in Virginia.

"Permit holder" includes any person holding a permit to participate in any horse racing subject to the jurisdiction of the Commission or in the conduct of a race meeting or pari-mutuel wagering thereon as provided in § 59.1-387.

"Person" means any individual, group of individuals, firm, company, corporation, partnership, business, trust, association, or other legal entity.

"Pool" means the amount wagered during a race meeting or during a specified period thereof.

"Principal stockholder" means any person who individually or in concert with his spouse and immediate family members, beneficially owns or controls, directly or indirectly, five percent or more of the stock of any person which is a licensee, or who in concert with his spouse and immediate family members, has the power to vote or cause the vote of five percent or more of any such stock. However, "principal stockholder" shall not include a broker-dealer registered under the Securities Exchange Act of 1934, as amended, which holds in inventory shares for sale on the financial markets for a publicly traded corporation holding, directly or indirectly, a license from the Commission.

"Race meeting" means the whole consecutive period of time during which horse racing with pari-mutuel wagering is conducted by a licensee.

"Racetrack" means an outdoor course located in Virginia which is laid out for horse racing and is licensed by the Commission.

"Recognized majority horsemen's group" means the organization recognized by the Commission as the representative of the majority of owners and trainers racing at race meetings subject to the Commission's jurisdiction.

"Retainage" means the total amount deducted from the pari-mutuel wagering pool for (i) a license fee to the Commission and localities, (ii) the licensee, (iii) purse money for the participants, (iv) the Virginia Breeders Fund, and (v) certain enumerated organizations as required or permitted by law, regulation or contract approved by the Commission.

"Satellite facility" means all areas of the property at which simulcast horse racing is received for the purposes of pari-mutuel wagering, and any additional areas designated by the Commission.

"Significant infrastructure facility" means a horse racing facility that has been approved by a local referendum pursuant to § 59.1-391 and has a minimum racing infrastructure consisting of (i) a one-mile dirt track for flat racing, (ii) a seven-eighths-mile turf course for flat or jump racing, (iii) covered seating for no fewer than 500 persons, and (iv) barns with no fewer than 400 permanent stalls.

"Significant infrastructure limited licensee" means a person who owns or operates a significant infrastructure facility and holds a limited license under § 59.1-376.

"Simulcast horse racing" means the simultaneous transmission of the audio or video portion, or both, of horse races from a licensed horse racetrack or satellite facility to another licensed horse racetrack or satellite facility, regardless of state of licensure, whether such races originate within the Commonwealth or any other jurisdiction, by satellite communication devices, television cables, telephone lines, or any other means for the purposes of conducting pari-mutuel wagering.

"Steward" means a racing official, duly appointed by the Commission, with powers and duties prescribed by Commission regulations.

"Stock" includes all classes of stock, partnership interest, membership interest, or similar ownership interest of an applicant or licensee, and any debt or other obligation of such person or an affiliated person if the Commission finds that the holder of such interest or stock derives therefrom such control of or voice in the operation of the applicant or licensee that he should be deemed an owner of stock.

"Virginia Breeders Fund" means the fund established to foster the industry of breeding race horses in the Commonwealth of Virginia.

History.

1988, c. 855; 1991, c. 591; 1992, c. 820; 1996, c. 319; 1998, cc. 608, 619; 2005, c. 700; 2007, c. 757; 2015, cc. 731, 751.

§ 59.1-366. The Virginia Racing Commission created; members.

A. The Virginia Racing Commission is hereby created. It shall consist of five members appointed by the Governor and confirmed by a majority of those elected to each house of the General Assembly at the next regular session following any such appointment. Each Commissioner shall have been a resident of the Commonwealth for a period of at least three years next preceding his appointment and his continued residency shall be a condition of his tenure in office. The initial appointments shall be as follows: one for a term of one year, one for a term of two years, one for a term of three years, one for a term of four years, and one for a term of five years. Thereafter, all appointments shall be for terms of five years. Vacancies in the Commission shall be filled for the unexpired term in the manner provided for original appointments. Each Commissioner shall be eligible for reappointment for a second consecutive term at the discretion of the Governor. Persons who are first appointed to initial terms of less than five years shall thereafter be eligible for reappointment to two consecutive terms of five years each. The Commission shall elect its chairman. No member of the General Assembly while serving as a member shall be eligible for appointment to the Commission.

B. Each member of the Commission shall receive fifty dollars for each day or part thereof spent in the performance of his duties and in addition shall be reimbursed for his reasonable expenses incurred therein.

C. The members of the Commission shall serve at the pleasure of the Governor.

D. The Commission shall establish and maintain a general business office within the Commonwealth for the transaction of its business at a place to be determined by the Commission. The Commission shall meet at such times and places within the Commonwealth as it shall determine. A majority of the Commissioners shall constitute a quorum for the convening of a meeting, but the performance of any duty or the exercise of any power of the Commission shall require a majority of the entire Commission.

History.
1988, c. 855.

§ 59.1-367. Legal representation.

The Commission shall be represented in all legal matters by general counsel hired by the Commission; however, the employment of such counsel shall be subject to the approval of the Attorney General. The compensation for such general counsel shall be paid out of the funds appropriated for the administration of the Commission. No member of the General Assembly while serving as a member nor any person associated with such member's law practice shall be employed as general counsel.

History.
1988, c. 855.

§ 59.1-368. Financial interests of Commission members, employees and family members prohibited.

No member or employee of the Commission, and no spouse or immediate family member of any such member or employee shall have any financial interest, direct or indirect, in any horse racetrack, satellite facility or operation incident thereto subject to the provisions of this chapter, or in any entity which has submitted an application for a license under Article 2 (§ 59.1-375 et seq.) of this chapter, or in the operation of any such track or satellite facility within the Commonwealth, or in the operation of any wagering authorized under this chapter, or participate as owner of a horse or otherwise as a contestant in any race subject to the jurisdiction of the Commission, or have any pecuniary interest in the purse or prize contested for in any such race. No member of the Commission and no spouse or immediate family member of a Commission member shall make any contribution to a candidate for office or office holders on the local or state level, or cause a contribution to be made on their behalf.

History.
1988, c. 855; 1992, c. 820.

§ 59.1-369. Powers and duties of the Commission.

The Commission shall have all powers and duties necessary to carry out the provisions of this chapter and to exercise the control of horse racing as set forth in § 59.1-364. Such powers and duties shall include but not be limited to the following:

1. The Commission is vested with jurisdiction and supervision over all horse racing licensed under the provisions of this chapter including all persons conducting, participating in, or attending any race meeting. It shall employ such persons to be present at race meetings as are necessary to ensure that they are conducted with order and the highest degree of integrity. It may eject or exclude from the enclosure or from any part thereof any person, whether or not he possesses a license or permit, whose conduct or reputation is such that his presence may, in the opinion of the Commission, reflect on the honesty and integrity of horse racing or interfere with the orderly conduct of horse racing.

2. The Commission, its representatives, and employees shall visit, investigate, and have free access to the office, track, facilities, satellite facilities or other places of business of any license or permit holder, and may compel the production of any of the books, documents, records, or memoranda of any license or permit holder for the purpose of satisfying itself that this chapter and its regulations are strictly complied with. In addition, the Commission may require any person granted a permit by the Commission and shall require any person licensed by the Commission, the recognized majority horsemen's group, and the nonprofit industry stakeholder organization recognized by the Commission under this chapter to produce an annual balance sheet and operating statement prepared by a certified public accountant approved by the Commission. The Commission may require the production of any contract to which such person is or may be a party.

3. The Commission shall promulgate regulations and conditions under which horse racing with pari-mutuel wagering shall be conducted in the Commonwealth, and all such other regulations it deems necessary and appropriate to effect the purposes of this chapter, including a requirement that licensees post, in a conspicuous place in every place where pari-mutuel wagering is conducted, a sign which bears a toll-free telephone number for "Gamblers Anonymous" or other organization which provides assistance to compulsive gamblers. Such regulations shall include provisions for affirmative action to assure participation by minority persons in contracts granted by the Commission and its licensees. Nothing in this subdivision shall be deemed to preclude private local ownership or participation in any horse racetrack. Such regulations may include penalties for violations. The regulations shall be subject to the Administrative Process Act (§ 2.2-4000 et seq.).

4. The Commission shall promulgate regulations and conditions under which simulcast horse racing shall be conducted at a licensed horse racetrack or satellite facility in the Commonwealth and all such other regulations it deems necessary and appropriate to effect the purposes of this chapter. Such regulations shall include provisions that all simulcast horse racing shall comply with the Interstate Horse Racing Act of 1978 (15 U.S.C. § 3001 et seq.) and shall require the holder of a license to schedule no more than 125 live racing days in the Commonwealth each calendar year; however, the Commission shall have the authority to alter the required number of live racing days based on what the Commission deems to be in the best interest of the Virginia horse industry. Such regulations shall au-

thorize up to 10 satellite facilities and restrict majority ownership of satellite facilities to an entity licensed by the Commission that is a significant infrastructure limited licensee, or if by August 1, 2015, there is no such licensee or a pending application for such license, then the nonprofit industry stakeholder organization recognized by the Commission may be granted licenses to own or operate satellite facilities. If, however, after the issuance of a license to own or operate a satellite facility to such nonprofit industry stakeholder organization, the Commission grants a license to a significant infrastructure limited licensee pursuant to § 59.1-376, then such limited licensee may own or operate the remaining available satellite facilities authorized in accordance with this subdivision. In no event shall the Commission authorize any such entities to own or operate more than a combined total of 10 satellite facilities. Nothing in this subdivision shall be deemed to preclude private local ownership or participation in any satellite facility. Except as authorized pursuant to subdivision 5, wagering on simulcast horse racing shall take place only at a licensed horse racetrack or satellite facility.

5. The Commission shall promulgate regulations and conditions regulating and controlling advance deposit account wagering. Such regulations shall include, but not be limited to, (i) standards, qualifications, and procedures for the issuance of a license to an entity for the operation of pari-mutuel wagering in the Commonwealth; except that the Commission shall not issue a license to, and shall revoke the license of, an entity that, either directly or through an entity under common control with it, withholds the sale at fair market value to a licensee of simulcast horse racing signals that such entity or an entity under common control with it sells to other racetracks, satellite facilities, or advance deposit account wagering providers located in or outside of the Commonwealth; (ii) provisions regarding access to books, records, and memoranda, and submission to investigations and audits, as authorized by subdivisions 2 and 10; and (iii) provisions regarding the collection of all revenues due to the Commonwealth from the placing of such wagers. No pari-mutuel wager may be made on or with any computer owned or leased by the Commonwealth, or any of its subdivisions, or at any public elementary or secondary school, or any public college or university. The Commission also shall ensure that, except for this method of pari-mutuel wagering, all wagering on simulcast horse racing shall take place only at a licensed horse racetrack or satellite facility.

Nothing in this subdivision shall be construed to limit the Commission's authority as set forth elsewhere in this section.

6. The Commission may issue subpoenas for the attendance of witnesses before it, administer oaths, and compel production of records or other documents and testimony of such witnesses whenever, in the judgment of the Commission, it is necessary to do so for the effectual discharge of its duties.

7. The Commission may compel any person holding a license or permit to file with the Commission such data as shall appear to the Commission to be necessary for the performance of its duties including but not limited to financial statements and information relative to stockholders and all others with any pecuniary interest in such person. It may prescribe the manner in which books and records of such persons shall be kept.

8. The Commission may enter into arrangements with any foreign or domestic government or governmental agency, for the purposes of exchanging information or performing any other act to better ensure the proper conduct of horse racing.

9. The Commission shall report annually on or before March 1 to the Governor and the General Assembly, which report shall include a financial statement of the operation of the Commission.

10. The Commission may order such audits, in addition to those required by § 59.1-394, as it deems necessary and desirable.

11. The Commission shall upon the receipt of a complaint of an alleged criminal violation of this chapter immediately report the complaint to the Attorney General of the Commonwealth and the State Police for appropriate action.

12. The Commission shall provide for the withholding of the applicable amount of state and federal income tax of persons claiming a prize or pay-off for a winning wager and shall establish the thresholds for such withholdings.

13. The Commission, its representatives and employees may, within the enclosure, stable, or other facility related to the conduct of racing, and during regular or usual business hours, subject any (i) permit holder to personal inspections, including alcohol and drug testing for illegal drugs, inspections of personal property, and inspections of other property or premises under the control of such permit holder and (ii) horse eligible to race at a race meeting licensed by the Commission to testing for substances foreign to the natural horse within the racetrack enclosure or other place where such horse is kept. Any item, document or record indicative of a violation of any provision of this chapter or Commission regulations may be seized as evidence of such violation. All permit holders consent to the searches and seizures authorized by this subdivision, including breath, blood and urine sampling for alcohol and illegal drugs, by accepting the permit issued by the Commission. The Commission may revoke or suspend the permit of any person who fails or refuses to comply with this subdivision or any rules of the Commission. Commission regulations in effect on July 1, 1998, shall continue in full force and effect until modified by the Commission in accordance with law.

14. The Commission shall require the existence of a contract between each licensee and the recognized majority horsemen's group for that licensee. Such contract shall be subject to the approval of the

Commission, which shall have the power to approve or disapprove any of its items, including but not limited to the provisions regarding purses and prizes. Such contracts shall provide that on pools generated by wagering on simulcast horse racing from outside the Commonwealth, (i) for the first $75 million of the total pari-mutuel handle for each breed, the licensee shall deposit funds at the minimum rate of five percent in the horsemen's purse account, (ii) for any amount in excess of $75 million but less than $150 million of the total pari-mutuel handle for each breed, the licensee shall deposit funds at the minimum rate of six percent in the horsemen's purse account, (iii) for amounts in excess of $150 million for each breed, the licensee shall deposit funds at the minimum rate of seven percent in the horsemen's purse account. Such deposits shall be made in the horsemen's purse accounts of the breed that generated the pools and such deposits shall be made within five days from the date on which the licensee receives wagers. In the absence of the required contract between the licensee and the recognized majority horsemen's group, the Commission may permit wagering to proceed on simulcast horse racing from outside of the Commonwealth, provided that the licensee deposits into the State Racing Operations Fund created pursuant to § 59.1-370.1 an amount equal to the minimum percentage of the total pari-mutuel handles as required in clauses (i), (ii), and (iii) or such lesser amount as the Commission may approve. The deposits shall be made within five days from the date on which the licensee receives wagers. Once a contract between the licensee and the recognized majority horsemen's group is executed and approved by the Commission, the Commission shall transfer these funds to the licensee and the horsemen's purse accounts.

15. Notwithstanding the provisions of § 59.1-391, the Commission may grant provisional limited licenses or provisional unlimited licenses to own or operate racetracks or satellite facilities to an applicant prior to the applicant securing the approval through the local referendum required by § 59.1-391. The provisional licenses issued by the Commission shall only become effective upon the approval of the racetrack or satellite wagering facilities in a referendum conducted pursuant to § 59.1-391 in the jurisdiction in which the racetrack or satellite wagering facility is to be located.

History.

1988, c. 855; 1990, c. 271; 1991, c. 591; 1992, c. 820; 1993, c. 430; 1998, cc. 619, 845; 2000, cc. 99, 1031; 2003, c. 682; 2004, c. 774; 2005, cc. 633, 700; 2007, c. 757; 2009, c. 142; 2011, c. 732; 2015, cc. 731, 751.

§ 59.1-370. Commission; Executive Secretary; staff; stewards.

A. The Commission shall appoint an Executive Secretary and such other employees as it deems essential to perform its duties under this chapter, who shall possess such authority and perform such duties as the Commission shall prescribe or delegate to them. Such employees may include stewards, chemists, veterinarians, inspectors, accountants, guards and such other employees deemed by the Commission to be necessary for the supervision and the proper conduct of the highest standard of horse racing. Such employees shall be compensated as provided by the Commission.

The Executive Secretary, in addition to any other duties prescribed by the Commission, shall keep a true and full record of all proceedings of the Commission and preserve at the Commission's general office all books, documents and papers of the Commission. Neither the Executive Secretary nor the spouse or any member of the immediate family of the Executive Secretary shall make any contributions to a candidate for office or office holder at the local or state level, or cause such a contribution to be made on his behalf.

B. The stewards appointed by the Commission shall act as racing officials to oversee the conduct of (i) horse racing at licensed racetracks and (ii) simulcast horse racing at satellite facilities. The stewards shall enforce the Commission's regulations and the provisions of this chapter and shall have authority to interpret the Commission's regulations and to decide all questions of racing not specifically covered by the regulations of the Commission. Nothing in this subsection shall limit the authority of the Commission to carry out the provisions of this chapter and to exercise control of horse racing as set forth in § 59.1-364, including the power to review all decisions and rulings of the stewards.

History.

1988, c. 855; 1998, c. 619; 2005, c. 700.

§ 59.1-370.1. State Racing Operations Fund.

A. All moneys and revenues received by the Commission under this chapter shall be placed in a special fund known as the State Racing Operations Fund. Notwithstanding any other provision of law, interest earned from moneys in the State Racing Operations Fund shall accrue to the benefit of such fund.

B. The total costs for the operation and administration of the Virginia Racing Commission shall be funded from the State Racing Operations Fund and shall be in such amount as provided in the general appropriations act.

History.

1990, c. 272.

§ 59.1-371. Fingerprints and background investigations; investigations from other states.

A. The Commission shall fingerprint and require a background investigation to include a criminal history record information check of the following persons to be conducted by a representative of a law-enforcement agency of the Commonwealth or federal government: (i) every person licensed to hold race meetings within the Commonwealth of Virginia; (ii) every person who is an officer or director or principal stockholder of a corporation which holds such a license, and every employee of the holder of any such license whose duties relate to the horse racing business in Virginia; (iii) all security personnel of any license holder; (iv) members and employees of the Virginia Racing Commission; (v) all permit holders, owners, trainers, jockeys, apprentices, stable employees, managers, agents, blacksmiths, veterinarians, employees of any license or permit holder; and (vi) any person who actively participates in the racing activities of any license or permit holder.

B. Notwithstanding the provisions of subsection A, the Commission may, (i) by regulation, establish a procedure to recognize a license or permit issued by another state in which horse racing is authorized when the Commission in its discretion determines that the laws or requirements of the licensing authority for such state governing fingerprinting and background investigations are substantially the same as required under this chapter and Commission regulations, and that the applicant has not been convicted of a misdemeanor or felony as provided in subdivision B 6 of § 59.1-389 and (ii) waive the requirements for fingerprints and background investigations for permit holders participating in (a) horse racing in nonsecure areas or (b) nonracing activities.

History.

1988, c. 855; 1990, c. 774; 1991, c. 591; 1995, c. 370; 1998, c. 619; 2000, c. 1011.

§ 59.1-372. Virginia Breeders Fund.

There is hereby created within the State Treasury the Virginia Breeders Fund, which Fund, together with the interest thereon, shall be administered in whole or in part by the Commission or by an entity designated by the Commission. The cost of administering and promoting the Fund shall be deducted from the Fund, and the balance shall be disbursed by the Commission or designated entity to the breeders of Virginia-bred horses that win races at race meetings designated by the Commission, to the owners of Virginia sires of Virginia-bred horses that win races at race meetings designated by the Commission, to the owners of Virginia-bred horses that win or earn purse money in nonrestricted races at racetracks in Virginia licensed by the Commission, to the owners of Virginia-bred horses that win races at race meetings designated by the Commission and for purses for races restricted to Virginia-bred or Virginia-sired horses or both at race meetings designated by the Commission. To assist it in establishing this awards and incentive program to foster the industry of breeding racehorses in Virginia, the Commission shall appoint an advisory committee composed of two members from each of the registered breed associations representing each breed of horse participating in the Fund program, one member representing the owners and operators of racetracks and one member representing all of the meets sanctioned by the National Steeplechase Association.

History.

1988, c. 855; 1993, c. 146; 1997, c. 798; 2002, c. 852.

§ 59.1-373. Hearing and appeal.

Any person aggrieved by a refusal of the Commission to issue any license or permit, the suspension or revocation of a license or permit, the imposition of a fine, or any other action of the Commission, may seek review of such action in accordance with Article 5 of the Administrative Process Act in the Circuit Court of the City of Richmond. Further appeals shall also be in accordance with Article 5 (§ 2.2-4025 et seq.) of the Administrative Process Act.

History.

1988, c. 855; 1996, c. 573.

§ 59.1-374. Injunction.

Whenever it appears to the Commission that any person has violated or may violate any provision of this chapter or any regulation or final decision of the Commission, it may apply to the appropriate circuit court for an injunction against such person. The order granting or refusing such injunction shall be subject to appeal as in other cases in equity.

History.

1988, c. 855; 1998, c. 619.

ARTICLE 2.

LICENSES.

§ 59.1-375. Owner's and operator's license required.

No person shall construct, establish or own a horse racetrack or satellite facility where pari-mutuel wagering is permitted, unless he has obtained an owner's license issued by the Commission in accordance with the provisions of this chapter.

No person shall operate pari-mutuel wagering or conduct any race meeting at which wagering is permitted with his knowledge or acquiescence, unless he has obtained an operator's license issued by the Commission in accordance with the provisions of this chapter.

No person to whom an owner's or operator's license has been issued nor any officer, director, partner, or spouse or immediate family member thereof shall make any contribution to any candidate for public office or public office holder at the local or state level.

No license issued under the provisions of this chapter shall be transferable.

History.
1988, c. 855; 1991, c. 591; 1992, c. 820.

§ 59.1-376. Limited licenses; transfer of meet; taxation; authority to issue; limitations.

A. Notwithstanding the provisions of § 59.1-375 or § 59.1-378 but subject to such regulations and criteria as it may prescribe, the Commission is authorized to issue limited licenses, provided such licenses shall permit any holder to conduct a race meeting or meetings for a period not to exceed 14 days in any calendar year, or in the case of a significant infrastructure limited licensee, 75 days in any calendar year.

B. The Commission may at any time, in its discretion, authorize any organization or association licensed under this section to transfer its race meeting or meetings from its own track or place for holding races, to the track or place for holding races of any other organization or association licensed under this chapter upon the payment of any and all appropriate license fees. No such authority to transfer shall be granted without the express consent of the organization or association owning or leasing the track to which such transfer is made.

C. For any such meeting the licensee shall retain and pay from the pool the tax as provided in § 59.1-392.

D. No person to whom a limited license has been issued nor any officer, director, partner, or spouse or immediate family member thereof shall make any contribution to any candidate for public office or public office holder at the local or state level.

History.
1988, c. 855; 1991, c. 591; 2015, cc. 731, 751.

§ 59.1-376.1: Repealed by Acts 2009, c. 142, cl. 2.

§ 59.1-377. Application for owner's license.

A. Any person desiring to construct or own a horse racetrack or satellite facility where pari-mutuel wagering is permitted shall file with the Commission an application for an owner's license. Such application shall be filed at the time and place prescribed by the Commission, and shall be in such form and contain such information as prescribed by the Commission, including but not limited to the following:

1. The name and address of such person; if a corporation, the state of its incorporation, the full name and address of each officer and director thereof, and if a foreign corporation, whether it is qualified to do business in this Commonwealth; if a partnership or joint venture, the name and address of each officer thereof;

2. The name and address of each stockholder or member of such corporation, or each partner of such partnership or joint venture, and of each person who has contracted for a pecuniary interest in the applicant or the enclosure where race meetings or pari-mutuel wagering will be conducted, whether such interest is an ownership or a security interest, and the nature and value of such interest, and the name and address of each person who has agreed to lend money to the applicant;

3. Such information as the Commission deems appropriate regarding the character, background and responsibility of the applicant and the members, partners, stockholders, officers and directors of the applicant;

4. The location and description of the racetrack, place or enclosure where such person proposes to hold such meetings or wagering, including the name of any county, city or town in which any property of such track or satellite facility is or will be located. The Commission shall require such information about the enclosure and location of such track as it deems necessary and appropriate to determine whether they comply with the minimum standards provided in this chapter, and whether the conduct of a race meeting or pari-mutuel wagering at such location would be in the best interests of the people of the Commonwealth;

5. Such information relating to the financial responsibility of the applicant as the Commission deems appropriate;

6. If any of the facilities necessary for the conduct of racing or pari-mutuel wagering are to be leased, the terms of such lease; and

7. Any other information which the Commission in its discretion deems appropriate.

B. Any application filed hereunder shall be verified by the oath or affirmation of an officer of the applicant, and shall be accompanied by a nonrefundable application fee as determined by the Commission.

C. Any person who knowingly makes a false statement to the Commission for the purposes of obtaining a license under this article shall be guilty of a Class 4 felony.

History.
1988, c. 855; 1991, c. 591; 1992, c. 820.

§ 59.1-378. Issuance of owner's license.

A. The Commission shall consider all applications for an owner's license and may grant a valid owner's license to applicants who meet the criteria set forth in this chapter and established by the Commission. The Commission shall deny a license to any applicant unless it finds that the applicant's facilities are or will be appropriate for the finest quality of racing.

B. The Commission shall deny a license to an applicant if it finds that for any reason the issuance of a license to the applicant would not be in the interest of the people of the Commonwealth or the horse racing industry in the Commonwealth, or would reflect adversely on the honesty and integrity of the horse racing industry in the Commonwealth, or that the applicant, or any officer, partner, principal stockholder, or director of the applicant:

1. Has knowingly made a false statement of material fact or has deliberately failed to disclose any information requested;

2. Is or has been found guilty of any illegal, corrupt, or fraudulent act, practice, or conduct in connection with any horse racing in this or any other state, or has been convicted of a felony;

3. Has at any time knowingly failed to comply with the provisions of this chapter or of any regulations of the Commission;

4. Has had a license or permit to hold or conduct a horse race meeting denied for just cause, suspended, or revoked in any other state or country;

5. Has legally defaulted in the payment of any obligation or debt due to the Commonwealth;

6. Has constructed or caused to be constructed a racetrack or satellite facility for which a license was required under § 59.1-377 hereof without obtaining such license, or has deviated substantially, without the permission of the Commission, from the plans and specifications submitted to the Commission; or

7. Is not qualified to do business in Virginia or is not subject to the jurisdiction of the courts of this Commonwealth.

C. The Commission shall deny a license to any applicant unless it finds:

1. That, if the corporation is a stock corporation, that such stock is fully paid and nonassessable, has been subscribed and paid for only in cash or property to the exclusion of past services, and, if the corporation is a nonstock corporation, that there are at least twenty members;

2. That all principal stockholders or members have submitted to the jurisdiction of the Virginia courts, and all nonresident principal stockholders or members have designated the Executive Secretary of the Commission as their agent for receipt of process;

3. That the applicant's articles of incorporation provide that the corporation may, on vote of a majority of the stockholders or members, purchase at fair market value the entire membership interest of any stockholder or require the resignation of any member who is or becomes unqualified for such position under § 59.1-379; and

4. That the applicant meets the criteria established by the Commission for the granting of an owner's license.

History.

1988, c. 855; 1990, c. 206; 1992, c. 820; 2015, cc. 731, 751.

§ 59.1-378.1. Licensing of owners or operators of certain pari-mutuel facilities.

A. Notwithstanding the provisions of § 59.1-391, the Commission may grant a license, for a duration to be determined by the Commission, to the owner or operator of a facility for the purpose of conducting pari-mutuel wagering on (i) thoroughbred and standard bred race meetings and (ii) simulcast horse racing at that facility in conjunction with the race meetings for a period not to exceed 14 days in any calendar year, provided that, prior to making application for such license, (a) the facility has been approved by the Commission and (b) the owner or operator of such facility has been granted tax-exempt status under § 501(c)(3) or (4) of the Internal Revenue Code.

B. In deciding whether to grant any license pursuant to this section, the Commission shall consider (i) the results of, circumstances surrounding, and issues involved in any referendum conducted under the provisions of § 59.1-391 and (ii) whether the Commission had previously granted a license to such facility, owner, or operator.

C. In no event shall the Commission issue more than 12 licenses in a calendar year pursuant to this section.

History.

1996, cc. 663, 750; 2000, c. 1002; 2014, cc. 564, 625; 2015, cc. 731, 751.

§ 59.1-379. Refusal of owner's license.

No owner's license or renewal thereof shall be granted to any corporation if the Commission finds that any principal stockholder of such stock corporation, or any member of such nonstock corporation:

1. Is or has been guilty of any illegal, corrupt or fraudulent act, conduct or practice in connection with horse racing in this or any other state, or has knowingly failed to comply with the provisions of this chapter or Commission regulations;

2. Has had a license or permit to hold or conduct a race meeting denied for cause, suspended or revoked in any other state or country; or

3. Has at any time during the previous five years knowingly failed to comply with the provisions of this chapter or any Commission regulations.

History.

1988, c. 855.

§ 59.1-380. Duration, form of owner's license; bond.

A license issued under § 59.1-378 shall be for the period set by the Commission, not to be less than twenty years, but shall be reviewed annually. The Commission shall designate on the license the duration of such license, the location of such track or satellite facility or proposed track or satellite facility and such other information as it deems proper. The

Commission shall establish criteria and procedures for license renewal.

The Commission shall require (i) a bond with surety or (ii) a letter of credit, acceptable to the Commission, and in an amount determined by it, to be sufficient to cover any indebtedness incurred by the licensee to the Commonwealth.

History.
1988, c. 855; 1992, c. 820; 2000, c. 1011.

§ 59.1-381. Application for operator's license.

A. Any person desiring to hold a race meeting or operate a satellite facility shall file with the Commission an application for an operator's license. Such application may be made in conjunction with an application for an owner's license, if appropriate. It shall be filed at the time and place prescribed by the Commission and contain such information as prescribed by the Commission, including all information prescribed for an owner's license under § 59.1-377 and, in addition, the date the applicant wishes to conduct a race meeting.

B. Any application filed hereunder shall be verified by the oath or affirmation of an officer of the applicant and shall be accompanied by a nonrefundable application fee as determined by the Commission.

History.
1988, c. 855; 1992, c. 820.

§ 59.1-382. Issuance of operator's license.

The Commission shall promptly consider any application for an operator's license and grant a valid operator's license to applicants who meet the criteria set forth in this chapter and established by the Commission. The Commission shall deny a license to any applicant, unless it finds:

1. That such applicant is a corporation organized under Title 13.1 or comparable law of another state, and qualified to do business in Virginia;

2. That, if the corporation is a stock corporation, all principal stockholders have submitted to the jurisdiction of the Virginia courts and all nonresident principal stockholders have designated the Executive Secretary of the Commission as their agent for process, and further, that an application shall also contain information as required by § 59.1-377;

3. That the applicant's articles of incorporation provide that the corporation may, on vote of a majority of the stockholders or members, purchase at fair market value the entire membership interest of any stockholder, or require the resignation of any member, who is or becomes unqualified for such position under § 59.1-379;

4. That the applicant would be qualified for a license to own such horse racetrack or satellite facility under the provisions of §§ 59.1-378 and 59.1-379;

5. That the applicant has made provisions satisfactory to the Commission for the detection and prosecution of any illegal, corrupt or fraudulent act, practice or conduct in connection with any race meeting or pari-mutuel wagering, that the applicant has made provision for membership in the Thoroughbred Racing Association or other equivalent applicable association, and that the applicant shall utilize the services of the Thoroughbred Racing Protective Bureau or any other protective agency acceptable to the Virginia Racing Commission;

6. That the applicant has met the criteria established by the Commission for the granting of an operator's license.

History.
1988, c. 855; 1991, c. 591; 1992, c. 820.

§ 59.1-383. Duration, form of operator's license; bond.

A license issued under § 59.1-382 shall be for a period of twenty years from the date of issuance, but shall be reviewed annually. The Commission may, as it deems appropriate, change at the beginning of any year the dates on which the licensee is authorized to conduct a race meeting or pari-mutuel wagering. An applicant for renewal of a license may omit any information which in the opinion of the Commission is already available to it. The Commission shall establish criteria and procedures for license renewal.

Any license issued under § 59.1-382 shall designate on its face the type or types of horse racing or pari-mutuel wagering for which it is issued, the location of the track or satellite facility where such meeting or wagering is to be conducted, the period during which such license is in effect and such other information as the Commission deems proper.

The Commission shall require a bond with surety acceptable to it, and in an amount determined by it to be sufficient to cover any indebtedness incurred by such licensee during the days allotted for racing.

History.
1988, c. 855; 1991, c. 591; 1992, c. 820.

§ 59.1-384. Denial of license final.

The denial of an owner's or operator's license by the Commission shall be final unless appealed under § 59.1-373.

History.
1988, c. 855.

§ 59.1-385. Suspension or revocation of license.

A. After a hearing with fifteen days' notice the Commission may suspend or revoke any license, or fine the holder thereof a sum not to exceed $100,000, in any case where it has reason to believe that any provision of this chapter, or any regulation or condition of the Commission, has not been complied with or has been violated. The Commission may revoke a license if it finds that facts not known by it at the time it considered the application indicate that such license should not have been issued.

B. The Commission shall revoke any license issued under § 59.1-382 for the operation of a satellite facility if the licensee, within one year of issuance of the satellite facility license, fails to conduct live racing at a racetrack licensed pursuant to § 59.1-382 or fails to conduct, without the permission of the Commission, the live racing days assigned to the licensee by the Commission.

C. The Commission, at a meeting at which a quorum of the members is present, may summarily suspend any license for a period of not more than ninety days pending a hearing and final determination by the Commission if the Commission determines that emergency action is required to protect the public health, safety and welfare including, but not limited to, revenues due the Commonwealth, localities and the horsemen's purse account. The Commission shall (i) schedule a hearing within fourteen business days after the license is summarily suspended and (ii) notify the licensee not less than five business days before the hearing of the date, time, and place of the hearing.

D. Deliberations of the Commission hereunder shall be conducted pursuant to the provisions of the Virginia Freedom of Information Act (§ 2.2-3700 et seq.). If any such license is suspended or revoked, the Commission shall state its reasons for doing so, which shall be entered of record. Such action shall be final unless appealed in accordance with § 59.1-373. Suspension or revocation of a license by the Commission for any violation shall not preclude criminal liability for such violation.

History.

1988, c. 855; 1991, c. 591; 1995, cc. 212, 275; 2000, c. 1031.

§ 59.1-386. Acquisition of interest in licensee.

A. The Commission shall require any person desiring to become a partner, member or principal stockholder of any licensee to apply to the Commission for approval thereof and may demand such information of the applicant as it finds necessary. The Commission shall consider such application forthwith and shall approve or deny the application within 60 days of receipt. The Commission shall approve an application that meets the criteria set forth in this chapter. The Commission shall deny an application if in its judgment the acquisition by the applicant would be detrimental to the public interest or to the honesty, integrity, and reputation of racing. The Commission shall approve an application to acquire actual control of a licensee only if it finds that the applicant meets the criteria set forth in subsection B.

B. If an applicant proposes to acquire actual control of a licensee, such person shall, pursuant to subsection A, submit to the Commission (i) its proposal for the future operation of any existing or planned racetrack, or satellite facility owned or operated by the licensee, (ii) such additional information as it desires, and (iii) such information as may be required by the Commission to assure the Commission that the licensee, under the actual control of such person, will have the experience, expertise, financial responsibility and commitment to comply with (a) the provisions of this chapter, (b) Commission regulations and orders, (c) the requirements for the continued operation of the licensee pursuant to the terms and conditions in effect on the date of the application of all licenses held by the licensee, (d) any existing contract with a recognized majority horseman's group, and (e) any proposal submitted to the Commission by such person. The provisions of this subsection shall apply regardless of whether the control acquired is direct or indirect or whether its acquisition is accomplished individually or in concert with others.

C. Any such acquisition of control without prior approval of the Commission shall be voidable by the Commission and, in such instance, the Commission may revoke any license it has issued to such licensee, order compliance with this section, or take such other action as may be appropriate within the authority of the Commission.

History.

1988, c. 855; 2003, c. 705.

ARTICLE 3.
PERMITS.

§ 59.1-387. Permit required; exception.

A. No participant shall engage in any horse racing subject to the jurisdiction of the Commission or in the conduct of a race meeting or pari-mutuel wagering thereon, including but not limited to as a horse owner, trainer, jockey, exercise rider, groom, stable foreman, valet, veterinarian, agent, pari-mutuel employee, concessionaire or employee thereof, track employee, or other positions the Commission deems necessary to regulate to ensure the integrity of horse racing in Virginia, unless such person possesses a permit therefor from the Commission, and complies with the provisions of this chapter and all Commission regulations. No permit issued under the provisions of this chapter shall be transferable.

B. The Commission may waive the permit requirement for any person who possesses a valid permit or license to participate in the conduct of horse racing in another racing jurisdiction and participates in horse racing in Virginia on nonconsecutive racing days.

C. Once a horse is entered to run in Virginia, all participants shall come under the jurisdiction of the Commission and its stewards and shall be subject to regulations of the Commission and sanctions it or its stewards may impose.

History.
1988, c. 855; 1991, c. 591; 2000, c. 1011; 2005, c. 700.

§ 59.1-388. Application for permit.

A. Any person desiring to obtain a permit as required by this chapter shall make application therefor on a form prescribed by the Commission. The application shall be accompanied by a fee prescribed by the Commission.

B. Any application filed hereunder shall be verified by the oath or affirmation of the applicant.

History.
1988, c. 855.

§ 59.1-389. Consideration of application.

A. The Commission shall promptly consider any application for a permit and issue or deny such permit based on the information in the application and all other information before it, including any investigation it deems appropriate. If an application for a permit is approved, the Commission shall issue a permit, which shall contain such information as the Commission deems appropriate. Such permit shall be valid for one year; however, the permit of a licensee's employee shall expire automatically when such permit holder leaves the employment of the licensee or at the end of one year, whichever occurs first. The licensee shall promptly notify the Commission when a permit holder leaves the employment of the licensee. The Commission shall establish criteria and procedures for permit renewal.

B. The Commission shall deny the application and refuse to issue the permit, which denial shall be final unless an appeal is taken under § 59.1-373, if it finds that the issuance of such permit to such applicant would not be in the interests of the people of the Commonwealth, or the horse racing industry of the Commonwealth, or would reflect on the honesty and integrity of the horse racing industry in the Commonwealth, or that the applicant:

1. Has knowingly made a false statement of a material fact in the application, or has deliberately failed to disclose any information requested by the Commission;

2. Is or has been found guilty of any corrupt or fraudulent practice or conduct in connection with horse racing in this or any other state;

3. Has knowingly failed to comply with the provisions of this chapter or the regulations of the Commission;

4. Has had a permit to engage in activity related to horse racing denied for just cause, suspended or revoked in any other state, and such denial, suspension or revocation is still in effect; or

5. Is unqualified to perform the duties required for the permit sought.

C. The Commission shall deny the application and refuse to issue the permit if, within the five years immediately preceding the date of his application for the permit sought, the applicant has been convicted of a crime involving the unlawful conduct of wagering, fraudulent use of a credential, unlawful transmission of information, touting, bribery, or administration or possession of drugs or any felony considered by the Commission to be detrimental to horse racing in the Commonwealth; the denial shall be final unless an appeal is taken under § 59.1-373. Additionally, the Commission may deny the application and refuse to issue any permit, if the applicant has been convicted of any such crime committed prior to the five years immediately preceding the date of his application.

D. The Commission may refuse to issue the permit if for any reason it feels the granting of such permit is not consistent with the provisions of this chapter or its responsibilities hereunder.

History.
1988, c. 855; 1991, c. 591; 1998, c. 619; 1999, c. 356.

§ 59.1-390. Suspension or revocation of permit; fine.

A. The Commission, acting by and through its stewards or at a meeting at which a quorum is present, may suspend or revoke a permit issued under this chapter or fine the holder of such permit a sum not to exceed $10,000, or suspend a permit issued by this chapter and fine the holder of such permit a sum not to exceed $10,000 after a hearing for which proper notice has been given to the permittee, in any case where it determines by a preponderance of the evidence that any provision of this chapter, or any regulation or condition of the Commission, has not been complied with, or has been violated. The Commission may revoke such permit, after such hearing, if it finds that facts not known by it at the time it was considering the application indicate that such permit should not have been issued. Deliberations of the Commission under this section shall be conducted pursuant to the provisions of the Virginia Freedom of Information Act (§ 2.2-3700 et seq.). If any permit is suspended or revoked, the Commission shall state its reasons for doing so, which shall be entered of record. Such action shall be final unless an appeal is taken in accordance with § 59.1-373. Suspension or revocation of a permit by the Commission for any violation shall not preclude criminal liability for such violation.

B. The Commission, acting by and through its stewards, or at a meeting at which a quorum is present, may summarily suspend the permit of a person for a period of not more than 90 days pending a hearing and final determination by the Commission or its stewards, if the Commission or its stewards determine the protection of the integrity of horse racing requires emergency action. The Commission or its stewards shall (i) schedule a hearing within 14 business days after the permit is summarily suspended and (ii) notify the permit holder, not less than five business days before the hearing, of the date, time and place of the hearing.

History.

1988, c. 855; 1990, c. 456; 1991, c. 591; 1998, c. 619; 2005, c. 700.

ARTICLE 4.

LOCAL REFERENDUM.

§ 59.1-391. Local referendum required.

The Commission shall not grant any initial license to construct, establish, operate or own a racetrack or satellite facility until a referendum approving the question is held in each county, city, or town in which such track or satellite facility is to be located, in the following manner:

1. A petition, signed by five percent of the qualified voters of such county, city, or town shall be filed with the circuit court of such county, city, or town asking that a referendum be held on the question, "Shall pari-mutuel wagering be permitted at a licensed racetrack in (name of such county, city, or town) on live horse racing at, and on simulcast horse racing transmitted from another jurisdiction to, the licensed racetrack on such days as may be approved by the Virginia Racing Commission in accordance with Chapter 29 (§ 59.1-364 et seq.) of Title 59.1 of the Code of Virginia?" In addition, or in the alternative, such petition may ask that a referendum be held on the question, "Shall pari-mutuel wagering be permitted in .... (the name of such county, city, or town) at satellite facilities in accordance with Chapter 29 (§ 59.1-364 et seq.) of Title 59.1 of the Code of Virginia?"

2. Following the filing of such petition, the court shall, by order of record entered in accordance with § 24.2-684.1, require the regular election officers of such city, county, or town to cause a special election to be held to take the sense of the qualified voters on the question. Such election shall be on a day designated by order of such court, but shall not be later than the next general election unless such general election is within 60 days of the date of the entry of such order, nor shall it be held on a date designated as a primary election.

3. The clerk of such court of record of such city, county, or town shall publish notice of such election in a newspaper of general circulation in such city, county, or town once a week for three consecutive weeks prior to such election.

4. The regular election officers of such city or county shall open the polls at the various voting places in such city or county on the date specified in such order and conduct such election in the manner provided by law. The election shall be by ballot which shall be prepared by the electoral board of the city, county, or town and on which shall be printed either or both of the following questions:

"Shall pari-mutuel wagering be permitted at a licensed racetrack in .... on live horse racing at, and on simulcast horse racing transmitted from another jurisdiction to, the licensed racetrack on such days as may be approved by the Virginia Racing Commission in accordance with Chapter 29 (§ 59.1-364 et seq.) of Title 59.1 of the Code of Virginia?

[ ] Yes
[ ] No"

"Shall pari-mutuel wagering be permitted in .... at satellite facilities in accordance with Chapter 29 (§ 59.1-364 et seq.) of Title 59.1 of the Code of Virginia?

[ ] Yes
[ ] No"

In the blank shall be inserted the name of the city, county, or town in which such election is held. Any voter desiring to vote "Yes" shall mark a check (√) mark or a cross (x or +) mark or a line (-) in the square provided for such purpose immediately preceding the word "Yes," leaving the square immediately preceding the word "No" unmarked. Any voter desiring to vote "No" shall mark a check (√) mark or a cross (x or +) mark or a line (-) in the square provided for such purpose immediately preceding the word "No," leaving the square immediately preceding the word "Yes" unmarked.

The ballots shall be counted, returns made and canvassed as in other elections, and the results certified by the electoral board to the court ordering such election. Thereupon, such court shall enter an order proclaiming the results of such election and a duly certified copy of such order shall be transmitted to the Commission and to the governing body of such city, county, or town.

No such referendum as described above shall be held more often than every three years in the same county, city, or town.

A subsequent local referendum shall be required if a license has not been granted by the Commission within five years of the court order proclaiming the results of the election. Town, for purposes of this section, means any town with a population of 5,000 or more.

History.

1988, c. 855; 1989, c. 145; 1991, c. 591; 1992, c. 820; 1998, c. 619; 2001, c. 539; 2003, c. 682.

ARTICLE 5.

TAXATION AND AUDIT.

§ 59.1-392. Percentage retained; tax.

A. Any person holding an operator's license to operate a horse racetrack or satellite facility in the Commonwealth pursuant to this chapter shall be authorized to conduct pari-mutuel wagering on horse racing subject to the provisions of this chapter and the conditions and regulations of the Commission.

B. On pari-mutuel pools generated by wagering at the racetrack on live horse racing conducted within the Commonwealth, involving win, place and show wagering, the licensee shall retain a percentage amount approved by the Commission as jointly requested by a recognized majority horsemen's group and a licensee and the legitimate breakage, out of which shall be paid one and one-quarter percent to be distributed as follows: one percent to the Commonwealth as a license tax and one-quarter percent to the locality in which the racetrack is located. The remainder of the retainage shall be paid as provided in subsection D, provided, however, that if the percentage amount approved by the Commission is other than 18 percent, the amounts provided in subdivisions D 1, 2 and 3 shall be adjusted by the proportion that the approved percentage amount bears to 18 percent.

C. On pari-mutuel pools generated by wagering at each Virginia satellite facility on live horse racing conducted within the Commonwealth, involving win, place and show wagering, the licensee shall retain a percentage amount approved by the Commission as jointly requested by a recognized majority horsemen's group and a licensee and the legitimate breakage, out of which shall be paid one and one-quarter percent to be distributed as follows: three-quarters percent to the Commonwealth as a license tax, one-quarter percent to the locality in which the satellite facility is located, and one-quarter percent to the locality in which the racetrack is located. The remainder of the retainage shall be paid as provided in subsection D; provided, however, that if the percentage amount approved by the Commission is other than 18 percent, the amounts provided in subdivisions D 1, 2 and 3 shall be adjusted by the proportion that the approved percentage amount bears to 18 percent.

D. On pari-mutuel pools generated by wagering at the racetrack and each Virginia satellite facility on live horse racing conducted within the Commonwealth, involving win, place and show wagering, the licensee shall retain a percentage amount approved by the Commission as jointly requested by a recognized majority horsemen's group and a licensee and the legitimate breakage, out of which shall be paid:

1. Eight percent as purses or prizes to the participants in such race meeting;

2. Seven and one-half percent, and all of the breakage and the proceeds of pari-mutuel tickets unredeemed 180 days from the date on which the race was conducted, to the operator;

3. One percent to the Virginia Breeders Fund;

4. Fifteen one-hundredths percent to the Virginia-Maryland Regional College of Veterinary Medicine;

5. Five one-hundredths percent to the Virginia Horse Center Foundation;

6. Five one-hundredths percent to the Virginia Horse Industry Board; and

7. The remainder of the retainage shall be paid as appropriate under subsection B or C.

E. On pari-mutuel pools generated by wagering at the racetrack on live horse racing conducted within the Commonwealth involving wagering other than win, place and show wagering, the licensee shall retain a percentage amount approved by the Commission as jointly requested by a recognized majority horsemen's group and a licensee and the legitimate breakage, out of which shall be paid two and three-quarters percent to be distributed as follows: two and one-quarter percent to the Commonwealth as a license tax, and one-half percent to the locality in which the racetrack is located. The remainder of the retainage shall be paid as provided in subsection G; provided, however, that if the percentage amount approved by the Commission is other than 22 percent, the amounts provided in subdivisions G 1, 2 and 3 shall be adjusted by the proportion that the approved percentage amount bears to 22 percent.

F. On pari-mutuel pools generated by wagering at each Virginia satellite facility on live horse racing conducted within the Commonwealth involving wagering other than win, place and show wagering, the licensee shall retain a percentage amount approved by the Commission as jointly requested by a recognized majority horsemen's group and a licensee and the legitimate breakage, out of which shall be paid two and three-quarters percent to be distributed as follows: one and three-quarters percent to the Commonwealth as a license tax, one-half percent to the locality in which the satellite facility is located, and one-half percent to the locality in which the racetrack is located. The remainder of the retainage shall be paid as provided in subsection G; provided, however, that if the percentage amount approved by the Commission is other than 22 percent, the amounts provided in subdivisions G 1, 2 and 3 shall be adjusted by the proportion that the approved percentage amount bears to 22 percent.

G. On pari-mutuel pools generated by wagering at the racetrack and each Virginia satellite facility on live horse racing conducted within the Commonwealth involving wagering other than win, place and show wagering, the licensee shall retain a percentage amount approved by the Commission as jointly requested by a recognized majority horsemen's group and a licensee and the legitimate breakage, out of which shall be paid:

1. Nine percent as purses or prizes to the participants in such race meeting;

2. Nine percent, and the proceeds of the pari-mutuel tickets unredeemed 180 days from the date on which the race was conducted, to the operator;

3. One percent to the Virginia Breeders Fund;

4. Fifteen one-hundredths percent to the Virginia-Maryland Regional College of Veterinary Medicine;

5. Five one-hundredths percent to the Virginia Horse Center Foundation;

6. Five one-hundredths percent to the Virginia Horse Industry Board; and

7. The remainder of the retainage shall be paid as appropriate under subsection E or F.

H. On pari-mutuel wagering generated by simulcast horse racing transmitted from jurisdictions outside the Commonwealth, the licensee may, with the approval of the Commission, commingle pools with the racetrack where the transmission emanates or establish separate pools for wagering within the Commonwealth. All simulcast horse racing in this subsection must comply with the Interstate Horse Racing Act of 1978 (15 U.S.C. § 3001 et seq.).

I. On pari-mutuel pools generated by wagering at the racetrack on simulcast horse racing transmitted from jurisdictions outside the Commonwealth, involving win, place and show wagering, the licensee shall retain one and one-quarter percent of such pool to be distributed as follows: three-quarters percent to the Commonwealth as a license tax, and one-half percent to the Virginia locality in which the racetrack is located.

J. On pari-mutuel pools generated by wagering at each Virginia satellite facility on simulcast horse racing transmitted from jurisdictions outside the Commonwealth, involving win, place and show wagering, the licensee shall retain one and one-quarter percent of such pool to be distributed as follows: three-quarters percent to the Commonwealth as a license tax, one-quarter percent to the locality in which the satellite facility is located, and one-quarter percent to the Virginia locality in which the racetrack is located.

K. On pari-mutuel pools generated by wagering at the racetrack and each Virginia satellite facility on simulcast horse racing transmitted from jurisdictions outside the Commonwealth, involving win, place and show wagering, the licensee shall retain one and thirty one-hundredths percent of such pool to be distributed as follows:

1. One percent of the pool to the Virginia Breeders Fund;

2. Fifteen one-hundredths percent to the Virginia-Maryland Regional College of Veterinary Medicine;

3. Five one-hundredths percent to the Virginia Horse Center Foundation;

4. Five one-hundredths percent to the Virginia Horse Industry Board; and

5. Five one-hundredths percent to the Virginia Thoroughbred Association for the promotion of breeding in the Commonwealth.

L. On pari-mutuel pools generated by wagering at the racetrack on simulcast horse racing transmitted from jurisdictions outside the Commonwealth, involving wagering other than win, place and show wagering, the licensee shall retain two and three-quarters percent of such pool to be distributed as follows: one and three-quarters percent to the Commonwealth as a license tax, and one percent to the Virginia locality in which the racetrack is located.

M. On pari-mutuel pools generated by wagering at each Virginia satellite facility on simulcast horse racing transmitted from jurisdictions outside the Commonwealth, involving wagering other than win, place and show wagering, the licensee shall retain two and three-quarters percent of such pool to be distributed as follows: one and three-quarters percent to the Commonwealth as a license tax, one-half percent to the locality in which the satellite facility is located, and one-half percent to the Virginia locality in which the racetrack is located.

N. On pari-mutuel pools generated by wagering at the racetrack and each Virginia satellite facility on simulcast horse racing transmitted from jurisdictions outside the Commonwealth, involving wagering other than win, place and show wagering, the licensee shall retain one and thirty one-hundredths percent of such pool to be distributed as follows:

1. One percent of the pool to the Virginia Breeders Fund;

2. Fifteen one-hundredths percent to the Virginia-Maryland Regional College of Veterinary Medicine;

3. Five one-hundredths percent to the Virginia Horse Center Foundation;

4. Five one-hundredths percent to the Virginia Horse Industry Board; and

5. Five one-hundredths percent to the Virginia Thoroughbred Association for the promotion of breeding in the Commonwealth.

O. Moneys payable to the Commonwealth shall be deposited in the general fund. Gross receipts for license tax purposes under Chapter 37 (§ 58.1-3700 et seq.) of Title 58.1 shall not include pari-mutuel wagering pools and license taxes authorized by this section.

P. All payments by the licensee to the Commonwealth or any locality shall be made within five days from the date on which such wagers are received by the licensee. All payments by the licensee to the Virginia Breeders Fund shall be made to the Commission within five days from the date on which such wagers are received by the licensee. All payments by the licensee to the Virginia-Maryland Regional College of Veterinary Medicine, the Virginia Horse Center Foundation, the Virginia Horse Industry Board, and the Virginia Thoroughbred Association shall be made by the first day of each quarter of the calendar year. All payments made under this section shall be used in support of the policy of the Commonwealth to sustain and promote the growth of a native industry.

Q. If a satellite facility is located in more than one locality, any amount a licensee is required to pay under this section to the locality in which the satellite facility is located shall be prorated in equal shares among those localities.

R. Any contractual agreement between a licensee and other entities concerning the distribution of the remaining portion of the retainage under subsections I through N shall be subject to the approval of the Commission.

S. The recognized majority horsemen's group racing at a licensed race meeting may, subject to the approval of the Commission, withdraw for administrative costs associated with serving the interests of the horsemen an amount not to exceed two percent of the amount in the horsemen's account.

T. The legitimate breakage from each pari-mutuel pool for both live racing and simulcast horse racing shall be distributed as follows:

1. Seventy percent to be retained by the licensee to be used for capital improvements that are subject to approval of the Commission; and

2. Thirty percent to be deposited in the Racing Benevolence Fund, administered jointly by the licensee and the recognized majority horsemen's group racing at a licensed race meeting, to be disbursed with the approval of the Commission for gambling addiction and substance abuse counseling, recreational, educational or other related programs.

History.

1988, c. 855; 1991, c. 591; 1992, c. 820; 1995, c. 217; 1998, cc. 608, 619; 2000, c. 1031; 2007, c. 61; 2011, c. 732; 2015, cc. 731, 751.

§ 59.1-392.1. Advance deposit account wagering revenues; distribution.

A. Notwithstanding the provisions of § 59.1-392, the allocation of revenue from advance deposit account wagering shall include (i) a licensee fee of 1.5 percent paid to the Commission; (ii) an additional fee equal to one percent of all wagers made within the Commonwealth placed through an advance deposit account wagering licensee, which shall be paid to the Virginia Breeders Fund, and (iii) an additional fee equal to nine percent of all wagers made within the Commonwealth placed through an advance deposit account wagering licensee, out of which shall be paid:

1. Four percent to a nonprofit industry stakeholder organization recognized by, and with oversight from, the Commission to include the recognized majority horsemen's group, a breeder's organization, and a licensed track operator for the purpose of promoting, sustaining, and advancing horse racing within the Commonwealth; and

2. Five percent to representatives of the recognized majority horsemen's group by breed to be used for purse funds at races conducted in the Commonwealth, unless otherwise authorized by the Commission.

Notwithstanding the foregoing, if the advance deposit account wagering licensee is a significant infrastructure limited licensee, the additional fee equal to nine percent of the wagers placed through such advance deposit account wagering licensee since November 1, 2014, shall instead be retained by such licensee for operational expenses, including defraying the costs of live racing.

B. The Commission-recognized nonprofit industry stakeholder organization shall make distributions from fees received from advance deposit wagering to organizations within the Commonwealth providing care for retired race horses, the Virginia-Maryland Regional College of Veterinary Medicine, the Virginia Horse Center Foundation, the Virginia Horse Industry Board, and the Virginia Thoroughbred Association in the percentages of wagering handles set forth in subsections K and N of § 59.1-392, and shall make a distribution of thirty-five one-hundredths of one percent of all wagers made within the Commonwealth placed through such advance deposit account wagering licensee to the locality where live racing licensed by the Commission occurred prior to January 1, 2012, and beginning January 1, 2020, to the locality or localities where such live racing occurs to be shared in a ratio of the number of such annual live races in a locality to the total number of such annual lives races in the Commonwealth. Distributions under this section from the Commission-recognized nonprofit stakeholder organization to the foregoing entities and locality or localities, when added to the distributions to such entities and locality or localities under § 59-1.392, shall be capped at the sum necessary to equal distributions made in the 2013 calendar year to each entity under § 59-1.392, and shall be capped at the sum necessary to equal $400,000 for a locality or localities.

C. Any additional distribution of fees received from advance deposit account licensees by the Commission-recognized nonprofit industry stakeholder organization shall be approved by the Commission.

History.

2015, cc. 731, 751.

§ 59.1-393. Admissions tax.

The governing body of any county or city may by ordinance impose a tax on any licensee hereunder to conduct a race meeting at a track located solely in such county or city of twenty-five cents on the admission of each person on each day except those holding a valid permit under this chapter and actually employed at such track in the capacity for which such permit was issued. The licensee may collect such amount from the ticket holder in addition to the amount charged for the ticket of admission.

If such track or its enclosure is located in two or in three localities, each locality may impose a tax hereunder of twelve and one-half cents or eight and one-third cents per person, respectively.

Gross receipts for license tax purposes under Chapter 37 of Title 58.1 shall not include the admissions tax imposed under this section.

History.

1988, c. 855; 1991, c. 591.

§ 59.1-394. Audit required.

A regular post-audit shall be conducted of all accounts and transactions of the Commission. An annual audit of a fiscal and compliance nature of the accounts and transactions of the Commission shall be conducted by the Auditor of Public Accounts on or before September 30 of each year. The cost of the annual audit and post-audit examinations shall be borne by the Commission.

History.

1988, c. 855.

ARTICLE 5.1. LIVE HORSERACING COMPACT.

§ 59.1-394.1. Live Horseracing Compact; form of compact.

The Live Horseracing Compact is enacted into law and entered into with all other jurisdictions legally joining therein in the form substantially as follows:

ARTICLE I. Purposes.

§ 1. Purposes.

The purposes of this compact are to:

1. Establish uniform requirements among the party states for the licensing of participants in live horse racing with pari-mutuel wagering, and ensure that all such participants who are licensed pursuant to this compact meet a uniform minimum standard of honesty and integrity.

2. Facilitate the growth of the horse racing industry in each party state and nationwide by simplifying the process for licensing participants in live racing, and reduce the duplicative and costly process of separate licensing by the regulatory agency in each state that conducts live horse racing with pari-mutuel wagering.

3. Authorize the Virginia Racing Commission to participate in this compact.

4. Provide for participation in this compact by officials of the party states, and permit those officials, through the compact committee established by this compact, to enter into contracts with governmental agencies and nongovernmental persons to carry out the purposes of this compact.

5. Establish the compact committee created by this compact as an interstate governmental entity duly authorized to request and receive criminal history record information from the Federal Bureau of Investigation and other state and local law-enforcement agencies.

ARTICLE II. Definitions.

§ 2. Definitions.

"Compact committee" means the organization of officials from the party states that is authorized and empowered by this compact to carry out the purposes of this compact.

"Official" means the appointed, elected, designated or otherwise duly selected representative of a racing commission or the equivalent thereof in a party state who represents that party state as a member of the compact committee.

"Participants in live racing" means participants in live horse racing with pari-mutuel wagering in the party states.

"Party state" means each state that has enacted this compact.

"State" means each of the several states of the United States, the District of Columbia, the Commonwealth of Puerto Rico and each territory or possession of the United States.

ARTICLE III. Entry into Force, Eligible Parties and Withdrawal.

§ 3. Entry into force.

This compact shall come into force when enacted by any four states. Thereafter, this compact shall become effective as to any other state upon (i) that state's enactment of this compact and (ii) the affirmative vote of a majority of the officials on the compact committee as provided in § 8.

§ 4. States eligible to join compact.

Any state that has adopted or authorized horse racing with pari-mutuel wagering shall be eligible to become party to this compact.

§ 5. Withdrawal from compact and impact thereof on force and effect of compact.

Any party state may withdraw from this compact by enacting a statute repealing this compact, but no such withdrawal shall become effective until the head of the executive branch of the withdrawing state has given notice in writing of such withdrawal to the head of the executive branch of all other party states. If as a result of withdrawals participation in this compact decreases to less than three party states, this compact no longer shall be in force and effect unless and until there are at least three or more party states again participating in this compact.

ARTICLE IV. Compact Committee.

§ 6. Compact committee established.

There is hereby created an interstate governmental entity to be known as the "compact committee," which shall be comprised of one official from the racing commission or its equivalent in each party state who shall be appointed, serve and be subject to removal in accordance with the laws of the party state he represents. Pursuant to the laws of his party state, each official shall have the assistance of his state's racing commission or the equivalent thereof in considering issues related to licensing of participants in live racing and in fulfilling his responsibilities as the representative from his state to the compact committee. If an official is unable to perform any duty in connection with the powers and duties of the compact committee, the racing commission or equivalent thereof from his state shall designate an alternate who shall serve in his place and represent the party state as its official on the compact committee until that racing commission or equivalent thereof determines that the original representative official is able once again to perform his duties as that party state's representative official on the compact committee. The designation of an alternate shall be communicated by the affected state's racing commission or equivalent thereof to the compact committee as the committee's bylaws may provide.

§ 7. Powers and duties of compact committee.

In order to carry out the purposes of this compact, the compact committee is hereby granted the power and duty to:

1. Determine which categories of participants in live racing, including but not limited to owners, trainers, jockeys, grooms, mutuel clerks, racing officials, veterinarians, and farriers, and which categories of equivalent participants in live racing with pari-mutuel wagering authorized in two or more of the party states, should be licensed by the committee, and establish the requirements for the initial licensure of applicants in each such category, the term of the license for each category, and the requirements for renewal of licenses in each category. Provided, however, that with regard to requests for criminal record on the issuance or renewal of a license, the compact committee shall determine for each category of participants in live racing which licensure requirements for that category are, in its judgment, the most restrictive licensure requirements of any party state for that category and shall adopt licensure requirements for that category that are, in its judgment, comparable to those most restrictive requirements.

2. Investigate applicants for a license from the compact committee and, as permitted by federal and state law, gather information on such applicants, including criminal history record information from the Federal Bureau of Investigation and relevant state and local law-enforcement agencies, and, where appropriate, from the Royal Canadian Mounted Police and law-enforcement agencies of other countries, necessary to determine whether a license should be issued under the licensure requirements established by the committee as provided in paragraph 1 of this section. Only officials on, and employees of, the compact committee may receive and review such criminal history record information, and those officials and employees may use that information only for the purposes of this compact. No such official or employee may disclose or disseminate such information to any person or entity other than another official or employee of the compact committee. The fingerprints of each applicant for a license from the compact committee shall be taken by the compact committee, its employees, or its designee and, pursuant to Public Law 92-544 or Public Law 100-413, shall be forwarded to a state identification bureau, or an association of state officials regulating pari-mutuel wagering designated by the Attorney General of the United States, for submission to the Federal Bureau of Investigation for a criminal history record check. Such fingerprints may be submitted on a fingerprint card or by electronic or other means authorized by the Federal Bureau of Investigation or other receiving law-enforcement agency.

3. Issue licenses to, and renew the licenses of, participants in live racing listed in paragraph 1 of this section who are found by the committee to have met the licensure and renewal requirements established by the committee. The compact committee shall not have the power or authority to deny a license. If it determines that an applicant will not be eligible for the issuance or renewal of a compact committee license, the compact committee shall notify the applicant that it will not be able to process his application further. Such notification does not constitute and shall not be considered to be the denial of a license. Any such applicant shall have the right to present additional evidence to, and to be heard by, the compact committee, but the final decision on issuance or renewal of the license shall be made by the compact committee using the requirements established pursuant to paragraph 1 of this section.

4. Enter into contracts or agreements with governmental agencies and with nongovernmental persons to provide personal services for its activities and such other services as may be necessary to effectuate the purposes of this compact.

5. Create, appoint, and abolish those offices, employments, and positions, including an executive director, as it deems necessary for the purposes of this compact, prescribe their powers, duties and qualifications, hire persons to fill those offices, employments and positions, and provide for the removal, term, tenure, compensation, fringe benefits, retirement benefits and other conditions of employment of its officers, employees and other positions.

6. Borrow, accept, or contract for the services of personnel from any state, the United States, or any other governmental agency, or from any person, firm, association, corporation or other entity.

7. Acquire, hold, and dispose of real and personal property by gift, purchase, lease, license, or in other similar manner, in furtherance of the purposes of this compact.

8. Charge a fee to each applicant for an initial license or renewal of a license.

9. Receive other funds through gifts, grants and appropriations.

§ 8. Voting requirements.

A. Each official shall be entitled to one vote on the compact committee.

B. All action taken by the compact committee with regard to the addition of party states as provided in § 3, the licensure of participants in live racing, and the receipt and disbursement of funds shall require a majority vote of the total number of officials (or their alternates) on the committee. All other action by the compact committee shall require a majority vote of those officials (or their alternates) present and voting.

C. No action of the compact committee may be taken unless a quorum is present. A majority of the officials (or their alternates) on the compact committee shall constitute a quorum.

§ 9. Administration and management.

A. The compact committee shall elect annually from among its members a chairman, a vice-chairman, and a secretary/treasurer.

B. The compact committee shall adopt bylaws for the conduct of its business by a two-thirds vote of the total number of officials (or their alternates) on the committee at that time and shall have the power by the same vote to amend and rescind such bylaws. The committee shall publish its bylaws in convenient form and shall file a copy thereof and a copy of any amendments thereto with the secretary of state or equivalent agency of each of the party states.

C. The compact committee may delegate the day-to-day management and administration of its duties and responsibilities to an executive director and his support staff.

D. Employees of the compact committee shall be considered governmental employees.

§ 10. Immunity from liability for performance of official responsibilities and duties.

No official of a party state or employee of the compact committee shall be held personally liable for any good faith act or omission that occurs during the performance and within the scope of his responsibilities and duties under this compact.

ARTICLE V. Rights and Responsibilities of Each Party State.

§ 11. Rights and responsibilities of each party state.

A. By enacting this compact, each party state:

1. Agrees (i) to accept the decisions of the compact committee regarding the issuance of compact committee licenses to participants in live racing pursuant to the committee's licensure requirements and (ii) to reimburse or otherwise pay the expenses of its official representative on the compact committee or his alternate.

2. Agrees not to treat a notification to an applicant by the compact committee under paragraph 3 of § 7 that the compact committee will not be able to process his application further as the denial of a license, or to penalize such an applicant in any other way based solely on such a decision by the compact committee.

3. Reserves the right (i) to charge a fee for the use of a compact committee license in that state, (ii) to apply its own standards in determining whether, on the facts of a particular case, a compact committee license should be suspended or revoked, (iii) to apply its own standards in determining licensure eligibility, under the laws of that party state, for categories of participants in live racing that the compact committee determines not to license and for individual participants in live racing who do not meet the licensure requirements of the compact committee, and (iv) to establish its own licensure standards for the licensure of nonracing employees at horse racetracks and employees at separate satellite wagering facilities. Any party state that suspends or revokes a compact committee license shall, through its racing commission or the equivalent thereof or otherwise, promptly notify the compact committee of that suspension or revocation.

B. No party state shall be held liable for the debts or other financial obligations incurred by the compact committee.

ARTICLE VI. Construction and Severability.

§ 12. Construction and severability.

This compact shall be liberally construed so as to effectuate its purposes. The provisions of this compact shall be severable, and, if any phrase, clause, sentence or provision of this compact is declared to be contrary to the Constitution of the United States or of any party state, or the applicability of this compact to any government, agency, person or circumstance is held invalid, the validity of the remainder of this compact and the applicability thereof to any government, agency, person or circumstance shall not be affected thereby. If all or some portion of this compact is held to be contrary to the constitution of any party state, the compact shall remain in full force and effect as to the remaining party states and in full force and effect as to the state affected as to all severable matters.

History.
2000, c. 992; 2003, c. 722.

§ 59.1-394.2. Compact Committee members.

The Governor shall appoint one official to represent the Commonwealth on the Compact Committee for a term of four years. No official shall serve more than three consecutive terms. A vacancy shall be filled by the Governor for the unexpired term.

History.
2000, c. 992.

§ 59.1-394.3. Cooperation of departments, agencies and officers of the Commonwealth.

All departments, agencies and officers of the Commonwealth and its political subdivisions are hereby authorized to cooperate with the Compact Committee in furtherance of any of its activities pursuant to the Compact.

History.
2000, c. 992.

§ 59.1-394.4. Racing Commission powers preserved.

Nothing in this article shall be construed to diminish or limit the powers and responsibilities of the Racing Commission established by Article 1 of this chapter or to invalidate any action of the Racing Commission previously taken, including without limitation any regulation promulgated thereby.

History.
2000, c. 992.

ARTICLE 6. CRIMINAL PENALTIES.

§ 59.1-395. Unlawful conduct of wagering.

Any person not licensed under subdivision 5 of § 59.1-369 or under Article 2 (§ 59.1-375 et seq.) of this chapter who conducts pari-mutuel wagering, or horse racing on which wagering is conducted with his knowledge or consent, shall be guilty of a Class 4 felony.

History.
1988, c. 855; 2003, c. 682.

§ 59.1-396. Fraudulent use of credential.

Any person other than the lawful holder thereof who has in his possession any credential, license or permit issued by the Commission, or a forged or simulated credential, license or permit of the Commission, and who uses such credential, license or permit for the purpose of misrepresentation, fraud or touting is guilty of a Class 4 felony.

Any credential, license or permit issued by the Commission, if used by the holder thereof for a purpose other than identification and in the performance of legitimate duties on a racetrack or within a satellite facility, shall be automatically revoked whether so used on or off a racetrack or satellite facility.

History.
1988, c. 855; 1992, c. 820.

§ 59.1-397. Unlawful transmission of information.

Any person who knowingly transmits information as to the progress or results of a horse race, or information as to wagers, betting odds, post or off times, or jockey changes in any race by any means whatsoever for the purposes of carrying on illegal gambling operations as defined in § 18.2-325, or to a person engaged in illegal gambling operations shall be guilty of a Class 4 felony.

This section shall not be construed to prohibit a newspaper from printing such results or information as news, or any television or radio station from telecasting or broadcasting such results or information as news. This section shall not be so construed as to place in jeopardy any common carrier or its agents performing operations within the scope of a public franchise, or any gambling operation authorized by law.

History.
1988, c. 855.

§ 59.1-398. Touting.

Any person, who knowingly and designedly by false representation attempts to, or does persuade, procure or cause another person to wager on a horse in a race to be run in this Commonwealth or elsewhere, and upon which money is wagered in this Commonwealth, and who asks or demands compensation as a reward for information or purported information given in such case, shall be guilty of a Class 1 misdemeanor.

History.
1988, c. 855.

§ 59.1-399. Bribing of a jockey, driver or other participant.

Any person who gives, promises or offers to any jockey, driver, groom or any person participating in any race meeting, including owners of racetracks and their employees, stewards, trainers, judges, starters and special policemen, any valuable thing with intent to influence him to attempt to lose or cause to be lost a horse race in which such person is taking part or expects to take part, or has any duty or connection, or who, being either jockey, driver, or groom or participant in a race meeting, solicits or accepts any valuable thing to influence him to lose or cause to be lost a horse race in which he is taking part, or expects to take part, or has any duty or connection, shall be guilty of a Class 4 felony.

History.
1988, c. 855.

§ 59.1-400. Prohibited acts, administration of drugs, etc.; penalty.

Any person who, with the intent to defraud, acts to alter the outcome of a race by (i) the administration of any substance foreign to the natural horse, except those substances specifically permitted by the regulations of the Virginia Racing Commission, or (ii) the use of any device, electrical or otherwise, except those specifically permitted by the regulations of the Virginia Racing Commission, shall be guilty of a Class 4 felony.

Any person who, with the intent to defraud, influences or conspires with another to alter the outcome of a race by (i) the administration of any substance foreign to the natural horse, except those substances specifically permitted by the regulations of the Virginia Racing Commission, or (ii) the use of any device, electrical or otherwise, except those specifically permitted by the regulations of the Virginia Racing Commission, shall be guilty of a Class 4 felony.

Any person who (i) administers any substance foreign to the natural horse, except those substances specifically permitted by the regulations of the Virginia Racing Commission, when the horse is entered to start, or (ii) at any time, exposes any substance foreign to the natural horse with the intent of impeding or increasing the speed, endurance, health, or condition of a horse, shall be guilty of a Class 4 felony.

History.
1988, c. 855; 1990, c. 366.

§ 59.1-401. Possessing drugs.

The possession or transportation of any drug except those permitted by regulations of the Commission within the racing enclosure is prohibited except upon a bona fide veterinarian's prescription with complete statement of uses and purposes on the container. A copy of such prescription shall be filed with the stewards. Any person knowingly violating the provisions of this section relating to the legal possession of drugs shall be guilty of a Class 1 misdemeanor. The provisions of the Drug Control Act (§ 54.1-3400 et seq.) shall apply in situations where drugs regulated by that Act are within the racing enclosure.

History.
1988, c. 855.

§ 59.1-402. Racing under false name; penalty.

Any person who knowingly enters or races any horse in any running or harness race under any name or designation other than the name or designation assigned to such horse by and registered with the Jockey Club, the United States Trotting Association, the American Quarter Horse Association, or other applicable association or who knowingly instigates, engages in, or in any way furthers any act by which any horse is entered or raced in any running or trotting race under any name or designation other than the name or designation duly assigned by and registered with the Jockey Club, the United States Trotting Association, the American Quarter Horse Association, or other applicable association, is guilty of a Class 4 felony.

History.
1988, c. 855; 1990, c. 351.

§ 59.1-403. Minors prohibited.

No person shall wager on or conduct any wagering on the outcome of a horse race pursuant to the provisions of this chapter unless such person is eighteen years of age or older. No person shall accept any wager from a minor. No person shall be admitted into a satellite facility if such person is under eighteen years of age unless accompanied by one of his parents or his legal guardian. Violation of this section shall be a Class 1 misdemeanor.

History.
1988, c. 855; 1996, cc. 915, 1025.

§ 59.1-404: Repealed by Acts 1991, c. 591.

Cross references.
As to present provision relating to punishment for making a false statement to the Commission, see § 59.1-377. As to present provisions relating to suspension or revocation of license and criminal liability for violations, see §§ 59.1-385 and 59.1-390.

§ 59.1-405. Conspiracies and attempts to commit violations.

A. Any person who conspires, confederates or combines with another, either within or without this Commonwealth, to commit a felony prohibited by this chapter shall be guilty of a Class 4 felony.

B. Any person who attempts to commit any act prohibited by this article shall be guilty of a criminal offense and punished as provided in either §§ 18.2-26, 18.2-27 or § 18.2-28, as appropriate.

History.
1988, c. 855; 1991, c. 591.

CHAPTER 29.1. GREYHOUND RACING.

Section

§ 59.1-405.1. Greyhound racing and simulcasting prohibited; penalty.

A. No person shall hold, conduct or operate any greyhound races for public exhibition in the Commonwealth for monetary remuneration.

B. No person shall transmit or receive interstate or intrastate simulcasting of greyhound races for commercial purposes in the Commonwealth.

C. Any person who violates the provisions of this chapter shall be guilty of a Class 4 felony.

History.
1995, c. 19.

CHAPTER 45. THE AMUSEMENT DEVICE RIDER SAFETY ACT.

Section

§ 59.1-519. Definitions.

As used in this chapter:

"Amusement device" means (i) a device or structure open to the public by which persons are conveyed or moved in an unusual manner for diversion and (ii) a device suspended in the air by the use of steel cables, chains, belts, or ropes, and usually supported by trestles or towers with one or more spans, also known as a passenger tramway, used to transport passengers uphill.

"Operator" means the entity listed as operator on the Certificate of Inspection issued for the amusement device pursuant to § 36-98.3 and the regulations promulgated pursuant thereto.

"Owner" means the entity listed as owner on the Certificate of Inspection issued for the amusement device pursuant to § 36-98.3 and the regulations promulgated pursuant thereto.

"Parent or guardian" means any parent, guardian, legal custodian or other person having immediate control or charge of a child.

"Rider" means any person who is (i) waiting in the immediate vicinity to get on an amusement device; (ii) getting on an amusement device; (iii) using an amusement device; (iv) getting off an amusement device; or (v) leaving an amusement device and still in its immediate vicinity. "Rider" does not include employees, agents, or servants of the owner or operator of the amusement device while engaged in the duties of their employment.

History.
2002, c. 788.

§ 59.1-520. Rider conduct; reports.

A. A rider, or his parent or guardian on a rider's behalf, shall report in writing to the owner or operator any injury sustained on an amusement device before leaving the owner's or operator's premises, or, if the parent or guardian is not present, then as soon as reasonably possible, including (i) the name, address, and phone number of the injured person; (ii) a full description of the incident, the injuries claimed, any treatment received, and the location, date, and time of the injury; (iii) the cause of the injury, if known; and (iv) the names, addresses, and phone numbers of any witnesses to the incident, if known by the rider or his parent or guardian. If the rider, or his parent or guardian on a rider's behalf, is unable to file a report because of the severity of his injuries, he shall file the report as soon as reasonably possible. The failure of a rider, or his parent or guardian on a rider's behalf, to report an injury under this subsection shall have no effect on the rider's right to commence a civil action.

B. A rider shall:

1. Obey the posted rules, warnings, and oral instructions for an amusement device issued by the owner, operator or an employee or agent of the owner or operator; and

2. Not intentionally act in any manner that may cause or contribute to injuring the rider or others, including:

a. Interfering with safe operation of the amusement device;

b. Failing to engage any safety devices that are provided;

c. Disconnecting or disabling a safety device except at the express instruction of the owner's or operator's agent or employee;

d. Altering or enhancing the intended speed, course, or direction of an amusement device;

e. Using the controls of an amusement device designed solely to be operated by the owner's or operator's agent or employee;

f. Throwing, intentionally dropping, or intentionally expelling an object from or toward an amusement device;

g. Getting on or off an amusement device except at the designated time and area, if any, at the direction of the owner's or operator's agent or employee, or in an emergency;

h. Not reasonably controlling the speed or direction of the rider or an amusement device that requires the rider to control or direct himself on a ride; and

i. Overloading an amusement device beyond its posted capacity.

History.
2002, c. 788.

§ 59.1-521. Duty of parent or guardian.

Parents or guardians of a rider shall have a duty to ensure that the rider complies with all provisions of this chapter.

History.
2002, c. 788.

§ 59.1-522. Owner or operator duty to post.

A. The owner or operator shall post signs stating "State law requires riders to obey all warnings and directions and behave in a manner that will not cause or contribute to injuring themselves or others. Riders shall report all injuries before leaving."

B. Such signs shall be posted at (i) any station designated for reporting an injury, (ii) any first aid station, and (iii) every entrance or exit to or from the premises designated for riders or any area or structure at which riders may purchase admission or obtain authority to use an amusement device.

History.
2002, c. 788.

§ 59.1-523. Enforcement; civil penalties; limitation.

A. Enforcement of the provisions of this chapter may be brought only as follows:

1. Any law-enforcement officer may issue a summons for a violation of this chapter; and
2. The attorney for the county, city or town in which the alleged violation occurred may bring an action to recover the civil penalty authorized by subsection B.

B. Except for the failure to report an injury, any person who violates the provisions of this chapter may be subject to a civil penalty in an amount not to exceed $500. Such penalty shall be paid into the local treasury.

History.
2002, c. 788.

§ 59.1-524. Common law doctrines not affected.

Nothing in this chapter shall be construed to repeal or diminish in any respect common law doctrines, which shall continue in full force and effect nor shall a violation of this chapter constitute negligence per se in any civil action.

History.
2002, c. 788.

CHAPTER 46.

VIRGINIA POST-DISASTER ANTI-PRICE GOUGING ACT.

Section

§ 59.1-525. Title.

This chapter may be cited as the Virginia Post-Disaster Anti-Price Gouging Act.

History.
2004, cc. 798, 817.

§ 59.1-526. Definitions.

As used in this chapter:

"Disaster" means any "disaster," "emergency," or "major disaster," as those terms are used and defined in § 44-146.16, that results in the declaration of a state of emergency by the Governor or the President of the United States.

"Goods," "services," and *"supplier"* have the same meanings as are set forth for those terms in § 59.1-198.

"Necessary goods and services" means any necessary good or service for which consumer demand does, or is likely to, increase as a consequence of the disaster, and includes, but is not limited to, water, ice, consumer food items or supplies, property or services for emergency cleanup, emergency supplies, communication supplies and services, medical supplies and services, home heating fuel, building materials and services, tree removal supplies and services, freight, storage services, housing, lodging, transportation, and motor fuels.

"Time of disaster" means the shorter of (i) the period of time when a state of emergency declared by the Governor or the President of the United States as the result of a disaster, emergency, or major disaster, as those terms are used and defined in § 44-146.16, is in effect or (ii) 30 days after the occurrence of the disaster, emergency, or major disaster that resulted in the declaration of the state of emergency; however, if the state of emergency is extended or renewed within 30 days after such an occurrence, then such period shall be extended to include the 30 days following the date the state of emergency was extended or renewed.

History.
2004, cc. 798, 817; 2006, c. 362; 2008, cc. 121, 157.

§ 59.1-527. Prohibitions.

During any time of disaster, it shall be unlawful for any supplier to sell, lease, or license, or to offer to sell, lease, or license, any necessary goods and services at an unconscionable price within the area for which the state of emergency is declared. Actual sales at the increased price shall not be required for the increase to be considered unconscionable. In determining whether a price increase is unconscionable, the following shall be considered:

1. Whether the price charged by the supplier grossly exceeded the price charged by the supplier for the same or similar goods or services during the 10 days immediately prior to the time of disaster, provided that, with respect to any supplier who was offering a good or service at a reduced price immediately prior to the time of disaster, the price at which the supplier usually offers the good or service shall be used as the benchmark for these purposes;
2. Whether the price charged by the supplier grossly exceeded the price at which the same or similar goods or services were readily obtainable by consumers in the trade area during the 10 days immediately prior to the time of disaster;
3. Whether the increase in the amount charged by the supplier was attributable solely to additional costs incurred by the supplier in connection with the sale of the goods or services, including additional costs imposed by the supplier's source. Proof that the supplier incurred such additional costs during

the time of disaster shall be prima facie evidence that the price increase was not unconscionable; and

4. Whether the increase in the amount charged by the supplier was attributable solely to a regular seasonal or holiday adjustment in the price charged for the good or service. Proof that the supplier regularly increased the price for a particular good or service during portions of the period covered by the time of disaster would be prima facie evidence that the price increase was not unconscionable during those periods.

History.
2004, cc. 798, 817.

§ 59.1-528. Complaint investigations.

In the event that the Attorney General, any attorney for the Commonwealth, or the attorney for any county, city, or town investigates a complaint for a violation of § 59.1-527 and determines that the supplier has not violated the section, and if the supplier requests, the Attorney General, any attorney for the Commonwealth, or the attorney for any county, city, or town shall promptly issue a signed statement indicating that a violation of § 59.1-527 has not been found. Subject to the disclosures allowed by this section, it shall be the duty of the Attorney General, the attorney for the Commonwealth, or the attorney for any city, county or town, or their designees, that investigates any complaint for violation of § 59.1-527 to maintain the confidentiality of all evidence, testimony, documents, or other results of such investigations, including the names of the complainant, and the individual, corporation or other entity that is the subject of the investigation. Nothing herein contained shall be construed to prevent the presentation and disclosure of any such investigative evidence in an action or proceeding brought under this chapter.

History.
2004, cc. 798, 817.

§ 59.1-529. Enforcement; penalties.

Any violation of this chapter shall constitute a prohibited practice under the provisions of § 59.1-200 and shall be subject to any and all of the enforcement provisions of Chapter 17 (§ 59.1-196 et seq.) of this title, except that § 59.1-204 notwithstanding, nothing in this chapter shall create a private cause of action in favor of any person aggrieved by a violation of this chapter.

History.
2004, cc. 798, 817.

§ 59.1-529.1. Emergency orders; penalties.

A. Upon finding that during a time of disaster a supplier is selling, leasing, or licensing, or offering to sell, lease, or license, a necessary good or service within the area for which the state of emergency is declared at such an unconscionable price that such selling, leasing, or licensing, or offering to sell, lease, or license presents an imminent and substantial danger of endangering the public welfare by creating public panic, the Governor is authorized to issue for a period not to exceed 30 days, without hearing, an emergency order directing the supplier to reduce the price of the necessary good or service to the prevailing price in the local market. The confidentiality of all evidence, testimony, documents, or other results of investigations leading to issuance of the emergency order, including the names of the complainant and the person that is the subject of the investigation, shall be maintained.

B. The supplier to whom such emergency order is issued shall be notified by certified mail, return receipt requested, sent to the last known address of the supplier, and by personal delivery by an agent of the Governor.

C. If the supplier who has been issued such an emergency order is not complying with the terms thereof, the Governor shall notify the Attorney General, who shall immediately investigate as provided for under this chapter.

History.
2006, c. 451.

TITLE 60.2.

UNEMPLOYMENT COMPENSATION.

CHAPTER 5.

TAXATION.

Article 2.

Employer Reporting Requirements.

ARTICLE 2.

EMPLOYER REPORTING REQUIREMENTS.

§ 60.2-518. False statements, etc., by employing units; failure to furnish reports, etc.

A. Any employing unit or any officer or agent of an employing unit or any other person shall be guilty of a Class 1 misdemeanor if it or he:

1. Makes a false statement or representation knowing it to be false, or who knowingly fails to

disclose a material fact (i) to prevent or reduce the payment of benefits to any individual entitled thereto, (ii) to avoid becoming or remaining subject to this title or (iii) to avoid or reduce any tax or other payment required from an employing unit under this title; or

2. Willfully fails or refuses (i) to furnish any reports required by this title or (ii) to produce or permit the inspection or copying of records as required hereunder.

B. Each such false statement, representation or failure to disclose a material fact listed in this section, and each day of such failure or refusal shall constitute a separate offense.

History.

Code 1950, § 60-113; 1968, c. 738, § 60.1-130; 1986, c. 480.

CHAPTER 6.

BENEFITS.

Article 6.

Violations, Penalties, and Liabilities.

ARTICLE 6.

VIOLATIONS, PENALTIES, AND LIABILITIES.

§ 60.2-632. False statements, etc., to obtain or increase benefits.

Whoever makes a false statement or representation knowing it to be false or knowingly fails to disclose a material fact, with intent to obtain or increase any benefit or other payment under this title, the unemployment compensation act of any other state, or any program of the federal government which is administered in any way under this title, either for himself or for any other person, shall be guilty of a Class 1 misdemeanor. Each such false statement or representation or failure to disclose a material fact shall constitute a separate offense.

History.

Code 1950, § 60-112; 1968, c. 738, § 60.1-129; 1970, c. 104; 1986, c. 480.

§ 60.2-633. Receiving benefits to which not entitled.

A. Any person who has received any sum as benefits under this title to which he was not entitled shall be liable to repay such sum to the Commission. For purposes of this section, "benefits under this title" includes benefits under an unemployment benefit program of the United States or of any other state. In the event the claimant does not refund the overpayment, the Commission shall deduct from any future benefits such sum payable to him under this title. However, if an overpayment of benefits under this chapter, but not under an unemployment benefit program of the United States or of any other state, occurred due to administrative error, the Commission shall have the authority to negotiate the terms of repayment, which shall include (i) deducting up to 50 percent of the payable amount for any future week of benefits claimed, rounded down to the next lowest dollar until the overpayment is satisfied; (ii) forgoing collection of the payable amount until the recipient has found employment as defined in § 60.2-212; or (iii) determining and instituting an individualized repayment plan. The Commission shall collect an overpayment of benefits under this chapter caused by administrative error only by offset against future benefits or a negotiated repayment plan; however, the Commission may institute any other method of collection if the individual fails to enter into or comply with the terms of the repayment plan. Administrative error shall not include decisions reversed in the appeals process. In addition, the overpayment may be collectible by civil action in the name of the Commission. Amounts collected in this manner may be subject to an interest charge as prescribed in § 58.1-15 from the date of judgment and may be subject to fees and costs. Collection activities for any benefit overpayment established of five dollars or less may be suspended. The Commission may, for good cause, determine as uncollectible and discharge from its records any benefit overpayment which remains unpaid after the expiration of seven years from the date such overpayment was determined, or immediately upon the death of such person or upon his discharge in bankruptcy occurring subsequently to the determination of overpayment. Any existing overpayment balance not equal to an even dollar amount shall be rounded to the next lowest even dollar amount.

B. The Commission is authorized to accept repayment of benefit overpayments by use of a credit card. The Virginia Employment Commission shall add to such payment a service charge for the acceptance of such card. Such service charge shall not exceed the percentage charged to the Virginia Employment Commission for use of such card.

C. Final orders of the Commission with respect to benefit overpayments may be recorded, enforced and satisfied as orders or decrees of a circuit court upon certification of such orders by the Commissioner as may be appropriate.

History.

Code 1950, § 60-115; 1962, c. 138; 1968, c. 738, § 60.1-132; 1974, c. 466; 1979, c. 675; 1980, c. 751; 1981, c. 251; 1984, c. 458; 1985, c.

151; 1986, c. 480; 1988, c. 544; 1990, c. 687; 1996, c. 95; 2008, c. 492; 2010, c. 327; 2013, c. 683.

§ 60.2-634. Receiving back pay after reinstatement.

Whenever the Commission finds that a discharged employee has received back pay at his customary wage rate from his employer after reinstatement such employee shall be liable to repay any benefits paid to such person during the time he was unemployed. When such an employee is liable to repay benefits to the Commission, such sum shall be collectible without interest by civil action in the name of the Commission.

History.
Code 1950, § 60-116; 1962, c. 138; 1968, c. 738, § 60.1-133; 1974, c. 466; 1986, c. 480.

§ 60.2-635. Deprivation of further benefits.

Any person who has been finally convicted under this chapter shall be deprived of any further benefits for the one-year period next ensuing after the date of conviction.

History.
Code 1950, § 60-117; 1962, c. 138; 1968, c. 738, § 60.1-134; 1974, c. 466; 1986, c. 480.

§ 60.2-636. Penalty for fraudulent claim.

A. Any person who has been disqualified for benefits under subdivision 4 of § 60.2-618 and who, because of those same acts or omissions, has received any sum as benefits under this title to which the person is not entitled shall be assessed a penalty in an amount equal to 15 percent of the amount of the payment to which the person was not entitled. All penalties collected by the Commission shall be paid into the state treasury and credited to the clearing account of the Fund established pursuant to § 60.2-300. The penalty applies to an erroneous payment made under any state program providing for the payment of unemployment compensation as well as an erroneous payment made under any federal program providing for the payment of unemployment compensation. The notice of determination or decision advising the person that benefits have been denied or adjusted pursuant to subdivision 4 of § 60.2-618 shall include the reason for the finding of an erroneous payment, the penalty amount assessed under this section, and the reason the penalty has been applied.

B. The amount of the penalty assessed pursuant to this section may be collected in any manner allowed for the recovery of the erroneous payment. When a recovery with respect to an erroneous payment is made, any recovery shall be applied first to the principal of the erroneous payment, then to the penalty amount imposed under this section, and finally to any other amounts due.

History.
2013, c. 771.

§ 60.2-637. Notice of penalties for false or misleading statements.

A. The Commission shall provide to each claimant notices of the sanctions to which the claimant is subject as a consequence of providing false or misleading statements to obtain unemployment benefits. The notices shall, at a minimum, (i) identify the penalties and sanctions to which any person is liable as a result of providing false or misleading statements to obtain benefits; (ii) inform the claimant that making a false statement or representation knowing it to be false or knowingly failing to disclose a material fact, with intent to obtain or increase any benefit or other payment under this title, is punishable as a Class 1 misdemeanor; and (iii) provide a summary of all remedies available to the Commission to collect overpayments made to a claimant as a result of his making false or misleading statements to obtain benefits.

B. The notices required by subsection A shall be included with the written statement advising claimants of their benefit rights and responsibilities that is provided by the Commission to claimants following the filing of the initial claim. In addition, the notices shall be provided to claimants at the time of the filing of initial and weekly claims by the same medium, including telephone or the Internet, that is used by the claimant to file his claim.

C. The failure of the claimant to receive any of the notices set out in subsection A shall not constitute a defense to any criminal prosecution for unemployment insurance fraud under § 60.2-632, to an administrative fraud disqualification under subdivision 4 of § 60.2-618, or to any overpayment of benefits under § 60.2-633 that the claimant would be required to repay as a result of the fraudulent act or acts.

History.
2013, c. 740.

TITLE 61.1.

WAREHOUSES, COLD STORAGE AND REFRIGERATED LOCKER PLANTS.

CHAPTER 4.

TOBACCO WAREHOUSES AND REGULATIONS IN GENERAL.

Section

§ 61.1-44. Manufactured tobacco; false branding.

If any person use, or permit to be used, on any cask, box or keg of manufactured tobacco, any brand or mark indicating a place or a manufacturer different from the place in which, or the manufacturer by whom, it was really manufactured, he shall be guilty of a misdemeanor and shall be punished as provided in § 18.2-12.

None of the provisions of this chapter, other than this section, shall be construed to apply to manufactured tobacco.

History.
Code 1950, § 61-136; 1968, c. 69.

§ 61.1-45. Nesting punished.

If any person nest a basket or parcel of tobacco with inferior tobacco, or other things, with intent to defraud the purchaser, he shall be guilty of a misdemeanor and shall be punished as provided in § 18.2-12.

History.
Code 1950, § 61-137; 1968, c. 69.

CHAPTER 5.

PREVENTION OF FRAUDS IN SALE OF LEAF TOBACCO.

Section

§ 61.1-51. Violations constituting misdemeanors.

Any person who shall give a fictitious or false name to the warehouseman or cooperative marketing association hereinbefore referred to, or who shall fail to give to such warehouseman or cooperative marketing association the true name of the owner of such leaf tobacco or the person from whom the tobacco was obtained, or the grower and the landlord, upon delivering the same as aforesaid, shall be guilty of a misdemeanor. Any warehouseman or cooperative marketing association who shall fail to comply with any of the provisions of this chapter, or who shall deny to any such representative the privilege of inspection or access as provided in § 61.1-50, shall be guilty of a misdemeanor. Any warehouseman or cooperative marketing association who shall buy or sell leaf tobacco as above set forth, knowing that the name in which the tobacco is sold, or any name given pursuant to the provisions hereof, is false or fictitious, shall be guilty of a misdemeanor.

History.
Code 1950, § 61-150; 1968, c. 69.

§ 61.1-52. Punishment for misdemeanor.

Any person guilty of a misdemeanor under the provisions of this chapter shall be punished as provided in § 18.2-12.

History.
Code 1950, § 61-151; 1968, c. 69.

CHAPTER 7.

HANDLING AND SALE OF BURLEY TOBACCO.

Section

§ 61.1-58. Commingling burley and other tobacco; moving tobacco before sale.

It shall be unlawful for any person to commingle, mix, place in same basket with other tobacco or in any other manner or means to handle tobacco so as to lose its identity, for the purpose of sale at auction, loose-leaf tobacco grown by one producer with loose-leaf burley tobacco grown by any other producer, or of the same producer after being placed on the loose-leaf floor.

After tobacco is weighed and set upon the warehouse floor for sale no basket of tobacco shall be moved, without the consent of the owner, from its place on the floor until sale is confirmed by the owner of same. This shall not apply to official inspectors of the Department of Agriculture and Consumer Services, who in the course of their duties find it necessary to move piles of tobacco.

History.
Code 1950, § 61-157; 1950, p. 66; 1968, c. 69.

§ 61.1-61. Penalty for violation.

The violation of any provision of this law or valid rules and regulations promulgated hereunder shall constitute a misdemeanor and shall be punishable by fine of not less than $50 for the first offense and for each subsequent offense shall be punished by a fine of not less than $500 or imprisonment in jail not less than thirty days, or both such fine and imprisonment in the discretion of the court or jury.

History.
Code 1950, § 61-160; 1950, p. 67; 1968, c. 69.

TITLE 62.1.
WATERS OF THE STATE, PORTS AND HARBORS.

CHAPTER 18.
PROTECTION OF AIDS TO NAVIGATION.

§ 62.1-187. Punishment of offenses relating to buoys, beacons or day marks.

Any person or persons who shall moor any vessel or vessels of any kind or name whatsoever or any raft or any part of a raft to any buoy, beacon, or day mark, placed in the waters of Virginia by authority of the United States or shall in any manner hang on with any vessel or raft or any part of a raft to any such buoy, beacon, or day mark, or shall willfully remove, damage or destroy any such buoy, beacon or day mark, or shall cut down, remove, damage or destroy any beacon or beacons erected on land in this Commonwealth by the authority of the United States or through unavoidable accident run down, drag from its position, or in any way injure any buoy, beacon, or day mark as aforesaid and shall fail to give notice as soon as practicable of having done so to the harbor master or other legal manager of the port or to the United States Coast Guard within the district in which such buoy, beacon or day mark may be located, shall for every such offense be deemed guilty of a misdemeanor, and upon conviction thereof, shall be punished by a fine not to exceed $200 or by imprisonment not to exceed three months or both; one-third of the fine in each case shall be paid to the informer and two-thirds thereof to the lighthouse board to be used in repairing the buoys and beacons.

Any person having charge of any raft passing any buoy, beacon or day mark who shall not exercise due diligence in keeping clear of it, or if unavoidably fouling it shall not exercise due diligence in clearing it without dragging from it such buoy, beacon or day mark shall be guilty of a misdemeanor, and upon conviction shall be punished by fine not to exceed fifty dollars.

History.
Code 1950, § 62-175; 1968, c. 659.

§ 62.1-188. Lien for cost of repairing or replacing buoy, beacon or day mark.

The cost of repairing or replacing any such buoy, beacon, or day mark which may have been misplaced, damaged, or destroyed by any vessel or raft whatsoever having been made fast to any such buoy, beacon, or day mark shall, when the same shall be legally ascertained, be a lien upon such vessel or raft and may be recovered against such vessel or raft and the owner or owners thereof in an action of debt in any court of competent jurisdiction in this Commonwealth.

History.
Code 1950, § 62-176; 1968, c. 659.

§ 62.1-189. Anchoring on range of range lights.

It shall be unlawful for any vessel to anchor on the range of any range lights established by the United States unless such anchorage is unavoidable, and the master of any vessel so anchoring shall be deemed guilty of a misdemeanor, and upon conviction thereof shall be punished by a fine not to exceed fifty dollars, one-half of the fine in each case to be paid to the informer and one-half to the Commonwealth.

History.
Code 1950, § 62-177; 1968, c. 659.

TITLE 63.1.
WELFARE (SOCIAL SERVICES).

[Repealed.]

§§ 63.1-1 through 63.1-343: Repealed by Acts 2002, c. 747, cl. 1, effective October 1, 2002.

Cross references.
As to present provisions relating to state social services, see § 63.2-100 et seq.

TITLE 63.2.
WELFARE (SOCIAL SERVICES).

SUBTITLE I.
GENERAL PROVISIONS RELATING TO SOCIAL SERVICES.

CHAPTER 1.
GENERAL PROVISIONS.

§ 63.2-100. Definitions.

As used in this title, unless the context requires a different meaning:

"Abused or neglected child" means any child less than 18 years of age:

1. Whose parents or other person responsible for his care creates or inflicts, threatens to create or inflict, or allows to be created or inflicted upon such child a physical or mental injury by other than accidental means, or creates a substantial risk of death, disfigurement, or impairment of bodily or mental functions, including, but not limited to, a child who is with his parent or other person responsible for his care either (i) during the manufacture or attempted manufacture of a Schedule I or II controlled substance, or (ii) during the unlawful sale of such substance by that child's parents or other person responsible for his care, where such manufacture, or attempted manufacture or unlawful sale would constitute a felony violation of § 18.2-248;

2. Whose parents or other person responsible for his care neglects or refuses to provide care necessary for his health. However, no child who in good faith is under treatment solely by spiritual means through prayer in accordance with the tenets and practices of a recognized church or religious denomination shall for that reason alone be considered to be an abused or neglected child. Further, a decision by parents who have legal authority for the child or, in the absence of parents with legal authority for the child, any person with legal authority for the child, who refuses a particular medical treatment for a child with a life-threatening condition shall not be deemed a refusal to provide necessary care if (i) such decision is made jointly by the parents or other person with legal authority and the child; (ii) the child has reached 14 years of age and is sufficiently mature to have an informed opinion on the subject of his medical treatment; (iii) the parents or other person with legal authority and the child have considered alternative treatment options; and (iv) the parents or other person with legal authority and the child believe in good faith that such decision is in the child's best interest. Nothing in this subdivision shall be construed to limit the provisions of § 16.1-278.4;

3. Whose parents or other person responsible for his care abandons such child;

4. Whose parents or other person responsible for his care commits or allows to be committed any act of sexual exploitation or any sexual act upon a child in violation of the law;

5. Who is without parental care or guardianship caused by the unreasonable absence or the mental or physical incapacity of the child's parent, guardian, legal custodian or other person standing in loco parentis;

6. Whose parents or other person responsible for his care creates a substantial risk of physical or mental injury by knowingly leaving the child alone in the same dwelling, including an apartment as defined in § 55-79.2, with a person to whom the child is not related by blood or marriage and who the parent or other person responsible for his care knows has been convicted of an offense against a minor for which registration is required as a violent sexual offender pursuant to § 9.1-902; or

7. Who has been identified as a victim of sex trafficking or severe forms of trafficking as defined in the Trafficking Victims Protection Act of 2000, 22 U.S.C § 7102 et seq., and in the Justice for Victims of Trafficking Act of 2015, 42 U.S.C. § 5101 et seq.

If a civil proceeding under this title is based solely on the parent having left the child at a hospital or emergency medical services agency, it shall be an affirmative defense that such parent safely delivered the child to a hospital that provides 24-hour emergency services or to an attended emergency medical services agency that employs emergency medical services providers, within 14 days of the child's birth. For purposes of terminating parental rights pursuant to § 16.1-283 and placement for adoption, the court may find such a child is a neglected child upon the ground of abandonment.

"Adoptive home" means any family home selected and approved by a parent, local board or a licensed child-placing agency for the placement of a child with the intent of adoption.

"Adoptive placement" means arranging for the care of a child who is in the custody of a child-placing agency in an approved home for the purpose of adoption.

"Adult abuse" means the willful infliction of physical pain, injury or mental anguish or unreasonable confinement of an adult.

"Adult day care center" means any facility that is either operated for profit or that desires licensure and that provides supplementary care and protection during only a part of the day to four or more aged, infirm or disabled adults who reside elsewhere, except (i) a facility or portion of a facility licensed by the State Board of Health or the Department of Behavioral Health and Developmental Services, and (ii) the home or residence of an individual who cares for only persons related to him by blood or marriage. Included in this definition are any two or more places, establishments or institutions owned, operated or controlled by a single entity and providing such supplementary care and protection to a combined total of four or more aged, infirm or disabled adults.

"Adult exploitation" means the illegal use of an incapacitated adult or his resources for another's profit or advantage.

"Adult foster care" means room and board, supervision, and special services to an adult who has a physical or mental condition. Adult foster care may be provided by a single provider for up to three adults.

"Adult neglect" means that an adult is living under such circumstances that he is not able to provide for himself or is not being provided services necessary

to maintain his physical and mental health and that the failure to receive such necessary services impairs or threatens to impair his well-being. However, no adult shall be considered neglected solely on the basis that such adult is receiving religious nonmedical treatment or religious nonmedical nursing care in lieu of medical care, provided that such treatment or care is performed in good faith and in accordance with the religious practices of the adult and there is a written or oral expression of consent by that adult.

"Adult protective services" means services provided by the local department that are necessary to protect an adult from abuse, neglect or exploitation.

"Assisted living care" means a level of service provided by an assisted living facility for adults who may have physical or mental impairments and require at least a moderate level of assistance with activities of daily living.

"Assisted living facility" means any congregate residential setting that provides or coordinates personal and health care services, 24-hour supervision, and assistance (scheduled and unscheduled) for the maintenance or care of four or more adults who are aged, infirm or disabled and who are cared for in a primarily residential setting, except (i) a facility or portion of a facility licensed by the State Board of Health or the Department of Behavioral Health and Developmental Services, but including any portion of such facility not so licensed; (ii) the home or residence of an individual who cares for or maintains only persons related to him by blood or marriage; (iii) a facility or portion of a facility serving infirm or disabled persons between the ages of 18 and 21, or 22 if enrolled in an educational program for the handicapped pursuant to § 22.1-214, when such facility is licensed by the Department as a children's residential facility under Chapter 17 (§ 63.2-1700 et seq.), but including any portion of the facility not so licensed; and (iv) any housing project for persons 62 years of age or older or the disabled that provides no more than basic coordination of care services and is funded by the U.S. Department of Housing and Urban Development, by the U.S. Department of Agriculture, or by the Virginia Housing Development Authority. Included in this definition are any two or more places, establishments or institutions owned or operated by a single entity and providing maintenance or care to a combined total of four or more aged, infirm or disabled adults. Maintenance or care means the protection, general supervision and oversight of the physical and mental well-being of an aged, infirm or disabled individual.

"Auxiliary grants" means cash payments made to certain aged, blind or disabled individuals who receive benefits under Title XVI of the Social Security Act, as amended, or would be eligible to receive these benefits except for excess income.

"Birth family" or *"birth sibling"* means the child's biological family or biological sibling.

"Birth parent" means the child's biological parent and, for purposes of adoptive placement, means parent(s) by previous adoption.

"Board" means the State Board of Social Services.

"Child" means any natural person under 18 years of age.

"Child day center" means a child day program offered to (i) two or more children under the age of 13 in a facility that is not the residence of the provider or of any of the children in care or (ii) 13 or more children at any location.

"Child day program" means a regularly operating service arrangement for children where, during the absence of a parent or guardian, a person or organization has agreed to assume responsibility for the supervision, protection, and well-being of a child under the age of 13 for less than a 24-hour period.

"Child-placing agency" means any person who places children in foster homes, adoptive homes or independent living arrangements pursuant to § 63.2-1819 or a local board that places children in foster homes or adoptive homes pursuant to §§ 63.2-900, 63.2-903, and 63.2-1221. Officers, employees, or agents of the Commonwealth, or any locality acting within the scope of their authority as such, who serve as or maintain a child-placing agency, shall not be required to be licensed.

"Child-protective services" means the identification, receipt and immediate response to complaints and reports of alleged child abuse or neglect for children under 18 years of age. It also includes assessment, and arranging for and providing necessary protective and rehabilitative services for a child and his family when the child has been found to have been abused or neglected or is at risk of being abused or neglected.

"Child support services" means any civil, criminal or administrative action taken by the Division of Child Support Enforcement to locate parents; establish paternity; and establish, modify, enforce, or collect child support, or child and spousal support.

"Child-welfare agency" means a child day center, child-placing agency, children's residential facility, family day home, family day system, or independent foster home.

"Children's residential facility" means any facility, child-caring institution, or group home that is maintained for the purpose of receiving children separated from their parents or guardians for full-time care, maintenance, protection and guidance, or for the purpose of providing independent living services to persons between 18 and 21 years of age who are in the process of transitioning out of foster care. Children's residential facility shall not include:

1. A licensed or accredited educational institution whose pupils, in the ordinary course of events, return annually to the homes of their parents or guardians for not less than two months of summer vacation;

2. An establishment required to be licensed as a summer camp by § 35.1-18; and

3. A licensed or accredited hospital legally maintained as such.

"Commissioner" means the Commissioner of the Department, his designee or authorized representative.

"Department" means the State Department of Social Services.

"Department of Health and Human Services" means the Department of Health and Human Services of the United States government or any department or agency thereof that may hereafter be designated as the agency to administer the Social Security Act, as amended.

"Disposable income" means that part of the income due and payable of any individual remaining after the deduction of any amount required by law to be withheld.

"Energy assistance" means benefits to assist low-income households with their home heating and cooling needs, including, but not limited to, purchase of materials or substances used for home heating, repair or replacement of heating equipment, emergency intervention in no-heat situations, purchase or repair of cooling equipment, and payment of electric bills to operate cooling equipment, in accordance with § 63.2-805, or provided under the Virginia Energy Assistance Program established pursuant to the Low-Income Home Energy Assistance Act of 1981 (Title XXVI of Public Law 97-35), as amended.

"Family day home" means a child day program offered in the residence of the provider or the home of any of the children in care for one through 12 children under the age of 13, exclusive of the provider's own children and any children who reside in the home, when at least one child receives care for compensation. The provider of a licensed or registered family day home shall disclose to the parents or guardians of children in their care the percentage of time per week that persons other than the provider will care for the children. Family day homes serving five through 12 children, exclusive of the provider's own children and any children who reside in the home, shall be licensed. However, no family day home shall care for more than four children under the age of two, including the provider's own children and any children who reside in the home, unless the family day home is licensed or voluntarily registered. However, a family day home where the children in care are all related to the provider by blood or marriage shall not be required to be licensed.

"Family day system" means any person who approves family day homes as members of its system; who refers children to available family day homes in that system; and who, through contractual arrangement, may provide central administrative functions including, but not limited to, training of operators of member homes; technical assistance and consultation to operators of member homes; inspection, supervision, monitoring, and evaluation of member homes; and referral of children to available health and social services.

"Foster care placement" means placement of a child through (i) an agreement between the parents or guardians and the local board where legal custody remains with the parents or guardians or (ii) an entrustment or commitment of the child to the local board or licensed child-placing agency.

"Foster home" means the place of residence of any natural person in which any child, other than a child by birth or adoption of such person, resides as a member of the household.

"General relief" means money payments and other forms of relief made to those persons mentioned in § 63.2-802 in accordance with the regulations of the Board and reimbursable in accordance with § 63.2-401.

"Independent foster home" means a private family home in which any child, other than a child by birth or adoption of such person, resides as a member of the household and has been placed therein independently of a child-placing agency except (i) a home in which are received only children related by birth or adoption of the person who maintains such home and children of personal friends of such person and (ii) a home in which is received a child or children committed under the provisions of subdivision A 4 of § 16.1-278.2, subdivision 6 of § 16.1-278.4, or subdivision A 13 of § 16.1-278.8.

"Independent living" means a planned program of services designed to assist a child age 16 and over and persons who are former foster care children between the ages of 18 and 21 in transitioning to self-sufficiency.

"Independent living arrangement" means placement of a child at least 16 years of age who is in the custody of a local board or licensed child-placing agency and has been placed by the local board or licensed child-placing agency in a living arrangement in which he does not have daily substitute parental supervision.

"Independent living services" means services and activities provided to a child in foster care 14 years of age or older who was committed or entrusted to a local board of social services, child welfare agency, or private child-placing agency. "Independent living services" may also mean services and activities provided to a person who (i) was in foster care on his 18th birthday and has not yet reached the age of 21 years or (ii) is at least 18 years of age but who has not yet reached 21 years of age and who, immediately prior to his commitment to the Department of Juvenile Justice, was in the custody of a local board of social services. Such services shall include counseling, education, housing, employment, and money management skills development, access to essential documents, and other appropriate services to help children or persons prepare for self-sufficiency.

"Independent physician" means a physician who is chosen by the resident of the assisted living facility and who has no financial interest in the assisted living facility, directly or indirectly, as an owner, officer, or employee or as an independent contractor with the residence.

"Intercountry placement" means the arrangement for the care of a child in an adoptive home or foster

care placement into or out of the Commonwealth by a licensed child-placing agency, court, or other entity authorized to make such placements in accordance with the laws of the foreign country under which it operates.

"Interstate placement" means the arrangement for the care of a child in an adoptive home, foster care placement or in the home of the child's parent or with a relative or nonagency guardian, into or out of the Commonwealth, by a child-placing agency or court when the full legal right of the child's parent or nonagency guardian to plan for the child has been voluntarily terminated or limited or severed by the action of any court.

"Kinship care" means the full-time care, nurturing, and protection of children by relatives.

"Local board" means the local board of social services representing one or more counties or cities.

"Local department" means the local department of social services of any county or city in this Commonwealth.

"Local director" means the director or his designated representative of the local department of the city or county.

"Merit system plan" means those regulations adopted by the Board in the development and operation of a system of personnel administration meeting requirements of the federal Office of Personnel Management.

"Parental placement" means locating or effecting the placement of a child or the placing of a child in a family home by the child's parent or legal guardian for the purpose of foster care or adoption.

"Public assistance" means Temporary Assistance for Needy Families (TANF); auxiliary grants to the aged, blind and disabled; medical assistance; energy assistance; food stamps; employment services; child care; and general relief.

"Qualified assessor" means an entity contracting with the Department of Medical Assistance Services to perform nursing facility pre-admission screening or to complete the uniform assessment instrument for a home and community-based waiver program, including an independent physician contracting with the Department of Medical Assistance Services to complete the uniform assessment instrument for residents of assisted living facilities, or any hospital that has contracted with the Department of Medical Assistance Services to perform nursing facility pre-admission screenings.

"Registered family day home" means any family day home that has met the standards for voluntary registration for such homes pursuant to regulations adopted by the Board and that has obtained a certificate of registration from the Commissioner.

"Residential living care" means a level of service provided by an assisted living facility for adults who may have physical or mental impairments and require only minimal assistance with the activities of daily living. The definition of "residential living care" includes the services provided by independent living facilities that voluntarily become licensed.

"Sibling" means each of two or more children having one or more parents in common.

"Social services" means foster care, adoption, adoption assistance, child-protective services, domestic violence services, or any other services program implemented in accordance with regulations adopted by the Board. Social services also includes adult services pursuant to Article 4 (§ 51.5-144 et seq.) of Chapter 14 of Title 51.5 and adult protective services pursuant to Article 5 (§ 51.5-148) of Chapter 14 of Title 51.5 provided by local departments of social services in accordance with regulations and under the supervision of the Commissioner for Aging and Rehabilitative Services.

"Special order" means an order imposing an administrative sanction issued to any party licensed pursuant to this title by the Commissioner that has a stated duration of not more than 12 months. A special order shall be considered a case decision as defined in § 2.2-4001.

"Temporary Assistance for Needy Families" or *"TANF"* means the program administered by the Department through which a relative can receive monthly cash assistance for the support of his eligible children.

"Temporary Assistance for Needy Families-Unemployed Parent" or *"TANF-UP"* means the Temporary Assistance for Needy Families program for families in which both natural or adoptive parents of a child reside in the home and neither parent is exempt from the Virginia Initiative for Employment Not Welfare (VIEW) participation under § 63.2-609.

"Title IV-E Foster Care" means a federal program authorized under §§ 472 and 473 of the Social Security Act, as amended, and administered by the Department through which foster care is provided on behalf of qualifying children.

History.

Code 1950, §§ 63-101, 63-222, 63-232, 63-347, 63-351; 1954, cc. 259, 290, 489; 1956, cc. 300, 641; 1960, cc. 331, 390; 1962, cc. 297, 603; 1966, c. 423; 1968, cc. 578, 585, §§ 63.1-87, 63.1-172, 63.1-195, 63.1-220; 1970, c. 721; 1972, cc. 73, 540, 718; 1973, c. 227; 1974, cc. 44, 45, 413, 415, § 63.1-250; 1975, cc. 287, 299, 311, 341, 437, 507, 524, 528, 596, §§ 63.1-238.1, 63.1-248.2; 1976, cc. 357, 649; 1977, cc. 105, 241, 532, 547, 559, 567, 634, 645, §§ 63.1-55.2, 63.1-55.8; 1978, cc. 536, 730, 749, 750; 1979, c. 483; 1980, cc. 40, 284; 1981, cc. 75, 123, 359; 1983, c. 66; 1984, cc. 74, 76, 498, 535, 781; 1985, cc. 17, 285, 384, 488, 518; 1986, cc. 80, 281, 308, 437, 594; 1987, cc. 627, 650, 681; 1988, c. 906; 1989, cc. 307, 647; 1990, c. 760; 1991, cc. 534, 595, 651, 694; 1992 c. 356, § 63.1-194.1; 1993, cc. 730, 742, 957, 993, § 63.1-196.001; 1994, cc. 107, 837, 865, 940; 1995, cc. 401, 520, 649, 772, 826; 1997, cc. 796, 895; 1998, cc. 115, 126, 397, 552, 727, 850; 1999, c. 454; 2000, cc. 61, 290, 500, 830, 845, 1058, § 63.1-219.7; 2002, c. 747; 2003, c. 467; 2004, cc. 70, 196, 245, 753, 814; 2006, c. 868; 2007, cc. 479, 597; 2008, cc. 475, 483; 2009, cc. 705, 813, 840; 2011, cc. 5, 156; 2012, cc. 803, 835; 2013, cc. 5, 362, 564; 2015, cc. 502, 503, 758, 770; 2016, c. 631.

SUBTITLE III. SOCIAL SERVICES PROGRAMS.

CHAPTER 15. CHILD ABUSE AND NEGLECT.

Article 1.

General Provisions.

Article 2.

Complaints.

Article 3.

Records.

Article 4.

Procedures.

Article 5.

Oversight and Evaluation of Program.

Article 6.

Virginia Child Protection Accountability System.

ARTICLE 1. GENERAL PROVISIONS.

§ 63.2-1500: Policy of the Commonwealth [Not set out.] (Acts 2002, c. 747.)

Editor's note.

This section, relating to state policy requiring the reporting of suspected child abuse or neglect, was enacted by Acts 2002, c. 747 (formerly by Acts 1975, c. 341 as § 63.1-248.1). In furtherance of the general policy of the Commission to include in the Code only provisions having general and permanent application, this section, which is limited in its purpose and scope, is not set out here, but attention is called to it by this reference.

The catchline has been set out at the direction of the Virginia Code Commission.

§ 63.2-1501. Definitions.

As used in this chapter unless the context requires a different meaning:

"Court" means the juvenile and domestic relations district court of the county or city.

"Prevention" means efforts that (i) promote health and competence in people and (ii) create, promote and strengthen environments that nurture people in their development.

History.

1975, c. 341, § 63.1-248.2; 1981, c. 123; 1986, c. 308; 1990, c. 760; 1995, c. 520; 2000, c. 500; 2002, c. 747.

§ 63.2-1502. Establishment of Child-Protective Services Unit; duties.

There is created a Child-Protective Services Unit in the Department that shall have the following powers and duties:

1. To evaluate and strengthen all local, regional and state programs dealing with child abuse and neglect.

2. To assume primary responsibility for directing the planning and funding of child-protective services. This shall include reviewing and approving the annual proposed plans and budgets for protective services submitted by the local departments.

3. To assist in developing programs aimed at discovering and preventing the many factors causing child abuse and neglect.

4. To prepare and disseminate, including the presentation of, educational programs and materials on child abuse and neglect.

5. To provide educational programs for professionals required by law to make reports under this chapter.

6. To establish standards of training and provide educational programs to qualify workers in the field of child-protective services. Such standards of training shall include provisions regarding the legal duties of the workers in order to protect the constitutional and statutory rights and safety of children and families from the initial time of contact during investigation through treatment.

7. To establish standards of training and educational programs to qualify workers to determine whether complaints of abuse or neglect of a child in a private or state-operated hospital, institution or other facility, or public school, are founded.

8. To maintain staff qualified pursuant to Board regulations to assist local department personnel in determining whether an employee of a private or state-operated hospital, institution or other facility or an employee of a school board, abused or neglected a child in such hospital, institution, or other facility, or public school.

9. To monitor the processing and determination of cases where an employee of a private or state-operated hospital, institution or other facility, or an employee of a school board, is suspected of abusing or neglecting a child in such hospital, institution, or other facility, or public school.

10. To help coordinate child-protective services at the state, regional, and local levels with the efforts of other state and voluntary social, medical and legal agencies.

11. To maintain a child abuse and neglect information system that includes all cases of child abuse and neglect within the Commonwealth.

12. To provide for methods to preserve the confidentiality of all records in order to protect the rights of the child, and his parents or guardians.

13. To establish minimum training requirements for workers and supervisors on family abuse and domestic violence, including the relationship between domestic violence and child abuse and neglect.

14. To establish minimum training requirements for workers and supervisors on identifying, assessing, and providing comprehensive services for children who are victims of sex trafficking or severe forms of trafficking as defined in the Trafficking Victims Protection Act of 2000, 22 U.S.C § 7102 et seq., and in the Justice for Victims of Trafficking Act of 2015, 42 U.S.C. § 5101 et seq., including efforts to coordinate with law-enforcement, juvenile justice, and social service agencies such as runaway and homeless youth shelters to serve this population.

History.

1975, c. 341, § 63.1-248.7; 1984, c. 734; 1993, c. 955; 2000, c. 500; 2002, c. 747; 2004, cc. 93, 233, 972, 980; 2016, c. 631.

§ 63.2-1503. Local departments to establish child-protective services; duties.

A. Each local department shall establish child-protective services under a departmental coordinator within such department or with one or more adjacent local departments that shall be staffed with qualified personnel pursuant to regulations adopted by the Board. The local department shall be the public agency responsible for receiving and responding to complaints and reports, except that (i) in cases where the reports or complaints are to be made to the court and the judge determines that no local department within a reasonable geographic distance can impartially respond to the report, the court shall assign the report to the court services unit for evaluation; and (ii) in cases where an employee at a private or state-operated hospital, institution or other facility, or an employee of a school board is suspected of abusing or neglecting a child in such hospital, institution or other facility, or public school, the local department shall request the Department and the relevant private or state-operated hospital, institution or other facility, or school board to assist in conducting a joint investigation in accordance with regulations adopted by the Board, in consultation with the Departments of Education, Health, Medical Assistance Services, Behavioral Health and Developmental Services, Juvenile Justice and Corrections.

B. The local department shall ensure, through its own personnel or through cooperative arrangements with other local agencies, the capability of receiving reports or complaints and responding to them promptly on a 24-hours-a-day, seven-days-per-week basis.

C. The local department shall widely publicize a telephone number for receiving complaints and reports.

D. The local department shall notify the local attorney for the Commonwealth and the local law-enforcement agency of all complaints of suspected child abuse or neglect involving (i) any death of a child; (ii) any injury or threatened injury to the child in which a felony or Class 1 misdemeanor is also suspected; (iii) any sexual abuse, suspected sexual abuse or other sexual offense involving a child, including but not limited to the use or display of the child in sexually explicit visual material, as defined in § 18.2-374.1; (iv) any abduction of a child; (v) any felony or Class 1 misdemeanor drug offense involving a child; or (vi) contributing to the delinquency of a minor in violation of § 18.2-371, immediately, but in no case more than two hours of receipt of the complaint, and shall provide the attorney for the Commonwealth and the local law-enforcement agency with records and information of the local department, including records related to any complaints of abuse or neglect involving the victim or the alleged perpetrator, related to the investigation of the complaint. The local department shall not allow reports of the death of the victim from other local agencies to substitute for direct reports to the attorney for the Commonwealth and the local law-enforcement agency. The local department shall develop, when practicable, memoranda of understanding for responding to reports of child abuse and neglect with local law enforcement and the attorney for the Commonwealth.

In each case in which the local department notifies the local law-enforcement agency of a complaint pursuant to this subsection, the local department shall, within two business days of delivery of the notification, complete a written report, on a form provided by the Board for such purpose, which shall include (a) the name of the representative of the local department providing notice required by this subsection; (b) the name of the local law-enforcement officer who received such notice; (c) the date and time that notification was made; (d) the identity of the victim; (e) the identity of the person alleged to have abused or neglected the child, if known; (f) the clause or clauses in this subsection that describe the reasons for the notification; and (g) the signatures, which may be electronic signatures, of the representatives of the local department making the notification and the local law-enforcement officer receiving the notification. Such report shall be included in the record of the investigation and may be submitted either in writing or electronically.

E. When abuse or neglect is suspected in any case involving the death of a child, the local department shall report the case immediately to the regional medical examiner and the local law-enforcement agency.

F. The local department shall use reasonable diligence to locate (i) any child for whom a report of suspected abuse or neglect has been received and is under investigation, receiving family assessment, or for whom a founded determination of abuse and neglect has been made and a child-protective services case opened and (ii) persons who are the subject of a report that is under investigation or receiving family assessment, if the whereabouts of the child or such persons are unknown to the local department.

G. When an abused or neglected child and the persons who are the subject of an open child-protective services case have relocated out of the jurisdiction of the local department, the local department shall notify the child-protective services agency in the jurisdiction to which such persons have relocated, whether inside or outside of the Commonwealth, and forward to such agency relevant portions of the case record. The receiving local department shall arrange protective and rehabilitative services as required by this section.

H. When a child for whom a report of suspected abuse or neglect has been received and is under investigation or receiving family assessment and the child and the child's parents or other persons responsible for the child's care who are the subject of the report that is under investigation or family assessment have relocated out of the jurisdiction of the local department, the local department shall notify the child-protective services agency in the jurisdiction to which the child and such persons have relocated, whether inside or outside of the Commonwealth, and complete such investigation or family assessment by requesting such agency's assistance in completing the investigation or family assessment. The local department that completes the investigation or family assessment shall forward to the receiving agency relevant portions of the case record in order for the receiving agency to arrange protective and rehabilitative services as required by this section.

I. Upon receipt of a report of child abuse or neglect, the local department shall determine the validity of such report and shall make a determination to conduct an investigation pursuant to § 63.2-1505 or, if designated as a child-protective services differential response agency by the Department according to § 63.2-1504, a family assessment pursuant to § 63.2-1506.

J. The local department shall foster, when practicable, the creation, maintenance and coordination of hospital and community-based multidisciplinary teams that shall include where possible, but not be limited to, members of the medical, mental health, social work, nursing, education, legal and law-enforcement professions. Such teams shall assist the local departments in identifying abused and neglected children; coordinating medical, social, and legal services for the children and their families; developing innovative programs for detection and prevention of child abuse; promoting community concern and action in the area of child abuse and neglect; and disseminating information to the general public with respect to the problem of child abuse and neglect and the facilities and prevention and treatment methods available to combat child abuse and neglect. These teams may be the family assessment and planning teams established pursuant to § 2.2-5207. Multidisciplinary teams may develop agreements regarding the exchange of information among the parties for the purposes of the investigation and disposition of complaints of child abuse and neglect, delivery of services and child protection. Any information exchanged in accordance with the agreement shall not be considered to be a violation of the provisions of § 63.2-102, 63.2-104, or 63.2-105.

The local department shall also coordinate its efforts in the provision of these services for abused and neglected children with the judge and staff of the court.

K. The local department may develop multidisciplinary teams to provide consultation to the local department during the investigation of selected cases involving child abuse or neglect, and to make recommendations regarding the prosecution of such cases. These teams may include, but are not limited to, members of the medical, mental health, legal and law-enforcement professions, including the attorney for the Commonwealth or his designee; a local child-protective services representative; and the guardian ad litem or other court-appointed advocate for the child. Any information exchanged for the purpose of such consultation shall not be considered a violation of § 63.2-102, 63.2-104, or 63.2-105.

L. The local department shall report annually on its activities concerning abused and neglected children to the court and to the Child-Protective Services Unit in the Department on forms provided by the Department.

M. Statements, or any evidence derived therefrom, made to local department child-protective services personnel, or to any person performing the duties of such personnel, by any person accused of the abuse, injury, neglect or death of a child after the arrest of such person, shall not be used in evidence in the case-in-chief against such person in the criminal proceeding on the question of guilt or innocence over the objection of the accused, unless the statement was made after such person was fully advised (i) of his right to remain silent, (ii) that anything he says may be used against him in a court of law, (iii) that he has a right to the presence of an attorney during any interviews, and (iv) that if he cannot afford an attorney, one will be appointed for him prior to any questioning.

N. Notwithstanding any other provision of law, the local department, in accordance with Board regulations, shall transmit information regarding founded complaints or family assessments and may transmit other information regarding reports, complaints, family assessments and investigations involving active duty military personnel or members of their household to family advocacy representatives of the United States Armed Forces.

O. The local department shall notify the custodial parent and make reasonable efforts to notify the noncustodial parent as those terms are defined in § 63.2-1900 of a report of suspected abuse or neglect of a child who is the subject of an investigation or is receiving family assessment, in those cases in which such custodial or noncustodial parent is not the subject of the investigation.

P. The local department shall notify the Superintendent of Public Instruction when an individual holding a license issued by the Board of Education is the subject of a founded complaint of child abuse or neglect and shall transmit identifying information regarding such individual if the local department knows the person holds a license issued by the Board of Education and after all rights to any appeal provided by § 63.2-1526 have been exhausted. Any information exchanged for the purpose of this subsection shall not be considered a violation of § 63.2-102, 63.2-104, or 63.2-105.

History.

1975, c. 341, § 63.1-248.6; 1978, c. 747; 1979, cc. 347, 348; 1984, c. 392; 1987, c. 443; 1989, cc. 109, 547; 1991, c. 644; 1992, cc. 214, 837, 880; 1993, cc. 506, 955; 1994, cc. 643, 675, 840; 1996, cc. 858, 863; 1998, cc. 704, 716; 2000, cc. 500, 854; 2002, c. 747; 2004, cc. 114, 220, 886; 2008, cc. 474, 827; 2009, cc. 813, 840; 2014, cc. 300, 565.

§ 63.2-1504. Child-protective services differential response system.

The Department shall implement a child-protective services differential response system in all local departments. The differential response system allows local departments to respond to valid reports or complaints of child abuse or neglect by conducting either an investigation or a family assessment. The Department shall publish a plan to implement the child-protective services differential response system in local departments by July 1, 2000, and complete implementation in all local departments by July 1, 2003. The Department shall develop a training program for all staff persons involved in the differential response system, and all such staff shall receive this training.

History.

2000, c. 500, § 63.1-248.2:1; 2002, c. 747.

§ 63.2-1505. Investigations by local departments.

A. An investigation requires the collection of information necessary to determine:

1. The immediate safety needs of the child;
2. The protective and rehabilitative services needs of the child and family that will deter abuse or neglect;
3. Risk of future harm to the child;
4. Alternative plans for the child's safety if protective and rehabilitative services are indicated and the family is unable or unwilling to participate in services;
5. Whether abuse or neglect has occurred;
6. If abuse or neglect has occurred, who abused or neglected the child; and
7. A finding of either founded or unfounded based on the facts collected during the investigation.

B. If the local department responds to the report or complaint by conducting an investigation, the local department shall:

1. Make immediate investigation and, if the report or complaint was based upon one of the factors specified in subsection B of § 63.2-1509, the local department may file a petition pursuant to § 16.1-241.3;
2. Complete a report and transmit it forthwith to the Department, except that no such report shall be transmitted in cases in which the cause to suspect abuse or neglect is one of the factors specified in subsection B of § 63.2-1509 and the mother sought substance abuse counseling or treatment prior to the child's birth;
3. Consult with the family to arrange for necessary protective and rehabilitative services to be provided to the child and his family;
4. Petition the court for services deemed necessary including, but not limited to, removal of the child or his siblings from their home;

5. Determine within 45 days if a report of abuse or neglect is founded or unfounded and transmit a report to such effect to the Department and to the person who is the subject of the investigation. However, upon written justification by the local department, the time for such determination may be extended not to exceed a total of 60 days or, in the event that the investigation is being conducted in cooperation with a law-enforcement agency and both parties agree that circumstances so warrant, as stated in the written justification, the time for such determination may be extended not to exceed 90 days. If through the exercise of reasonable diligence the local department is unable to find the child who is the subject of the report, the time the child cannot be found shall not be computed as part of the total time period allowed for the investigation and determination and documentation of such reasonable diligence shall be placed in the record. In cases involving the death of a child or alleged sexual abuse of a child who is the subject of the report, the time during which records necessary for the investigation of the complaint but not created by the local department, including autopsy or medical or forensic records or reports, are not available to the local department due to circumstances beyond the local department's control shall not be computed as part of the total time period allowed for the investigation and determination, and documentation of the circumstances that resulted in the delay shall be placed in the record. In cases in which the subject of the investigation is a full-time, part-time, permanent, or temporary employee of a school division who is suspected of abusing or neglecting a child in the course of his educational employment, the time period for determining whether a report is founded or unfounded and transmitting a report to that effect to the Department and the person who is the subject of the investigation shall be mandatory, and every local department shall make the required determination and report within the specified time period without delay;

6. If a report of abuse or neglect is unfounded, transmit a report to such effect to the complainant and parent or guardian and the person responsible for the care of the child in those cases where such person was suspected of abuse or neglect; and

7. If a report of child abuse and neglect is founded, and the subject of the report is a full-time, part-time, permanent, or temporary employee of a school division located within the Commonwealth, notify the relevant school board of the founded complaint.

Any information exchanged for the purposes of this subsection shall not be considered a violation of § 63.2-102, 63.2-104, or 63.2-105.

C. Each local board may obtain and consider, in accordance with regulations adopted by the Board, statewide criminal history record information from the Central Criminal Records Exchange and results of a search of the child abuse and neglect central registry of any individual who is the subject of a child abuse or neglect investigation conducted under this section when there is evidence of child abuse or neglect and the local board is evaluating the safety of the home and whether removal will protect a child from harm. The local board also may obtain such a criminal records or registry search on all adult household members residing in the home where the individual who is the subject of the investigation resides and the child resides or visits. If a child abuse or neglect petition is filed in connection with such removal, a court may admit such information as evidence. Where the individual who is the subject of such information contests its accuracy through testimony under oath in hearing before the court, no court shall receive or consider the contested criminal history record information without certified copies of conviction. Further dissemination of the information provided to the local board is prohibited, except as authorized by law.

D. A person who has not previously participated in the investigation of complaints of child abuse or neglect in accordance with this chapter shall not participate in the investigation of any case involving a complaint of alleged sexual abuse of a child unless he (i) has completed a Board-approved training program for the investigation of complaints involving alleged sexual abuse of a child or (ii) is under the direct supervision of a person who has completed a Board-approved training program for the investigation of complaints involving alleged sexual abuse of a child. No individual may make a determination of whether a case involving a complaint of alleged sexual abuse of a child is founded or unfounded unless he has completed a Board-approved training program for the investigation of complaints involving alleged sexual abuse of a child.

History.

2000, c. 500, § 63.1-248.6:01; 2002, c. 747; 2007, c. 495; 2008, c. 555; 2013, cc. 340, 506; 2014, cc. 299, 504; 2015, c. 524.

§ 63.2-1506. Family assessments by local departments.

A. A family assessment requires the collection of information necessary to determine:

1. The immediate safety needs of the child;

2. The protective and rehabilitative services needs of the child and family that will deter abuse or neglect;

3. Risk of future harm to the child; and

4. Alternative plans for the child's safety if protective and rehabilitative services are indicated and the family is unable or unwilling to participate in services.

B. When a local department has been designated as a child-protective services differential response system participant by the Department pursuant to § 63.2-1504 and responds to the report or complaint by conducting a family assessment, the local department shall:

1. Conduct an immediate family assessment and, if the report or complaint was based upon one of the factors specified in subsection B of § 63.2-1509, the local department may file a petition pursuant to § 16.1-241.3;

2. Immediately contact the subject of the report and the family of the child alleged to have been abused or neglected and give each a written and an oral explanation of the family assessment procedure. The family assessment shall be in writing and shall be completed in accordance with Board regulation;

3. Complete the family assessment within forty-five days and transmit a report to such effect to the Department and to the person who is the subject of the family assessment. However, upon written justification by the local department, the family assessment may be extended, not to exceed a total of sixty days;

4. Consult with the family to arrange for necessary protective and rehabilitative services to be provided to the child and his family. Families have the option of declining the services offered as a result of the family assessment. If the family declines the services, the case shall be closed unless the local department determines that sufficient cause exists to redetermine the case as one that needs to be investigated. In no instance shall a case be redetermined as an investigation solely because the family declines services;

5. Petition the court for services deemed necessary;

6. Make no disposition of founded or unfounded for reports in which a family assessment is completed. Reports in which a family assessment is completed shall not be entered into the central registry contained in § 63.2-1515; and

7. Commence an immediate investigation, if at any time during the completion of the family assessment, the local department determines that an investigation is required.

C. When a local department has been designated as a child-protective services differential response agency by the Department, the local department may investigate any report of child abuse or neglect, but the following valid reports of child abuse or neglect shall be investigated: (i) sexual abuse, (ii) child fatality, (iii) abuse or neglect resulting in serious injury as defined in § 18.2-371.1, (iv) child has been taken into the custody of the local department, or (v) cases involving a caretaker at a state-licensed child day center, religiously exempt child day center, licensed, registered or approved family day home, private or public school, hospital or any institution.

History.

2000, c. 500, § 63.1-248.6:02; 2002, cc. 641, 642, 747.

§ 63.2-1507. Cooperation by state entities.

All law-enforcement departments and other state and local departments, agencies, authorities and institutions shall cooperate with each child-protective services coordinator of a local department and any multi-discipline teams in the detection and prevention of child abuse.

History.

1975, c. 341, § 63.1-248.17; 2002, c. 747.

ARTICLE 2.
COMPLAINTS.

§ 63.2-1508. Valid report or complaint.

A valid report or complaint means the local department has evaluated the information and allegations of the report or complaint and determined that the local department shall conduct an investigation or family assessment because the following elements are present:

1. The alleged victim child or children are under the age of eighteen at the time of the complaint or report;

2. The alleged abuser is the alleged victim child's parent or other caretaker;

3. The local department receiving the complaint or report has jurisdiction; and

4. The circumstances described allege suspected child abuse or neglect.

Nothing in this section shall relieve any person specified in § 63.2-1509 from making a report required by that section, regardless of the identity of the person suspected to have caused such abuse or neglect.

History.

1975, c. 341, § 63.1-248.2; 1981, c. 123; 1986, c. 308; 1990, c. 760; 1995, c. 520; 2000, c. 500; 2002, c. 747.

§ 63.2-1509. Requirement that certain injuries to children be reported by physicians, nurses, teachers, etc.; penalty for failure to report.

A. The following persons who, in their professional or official capacity, have reason to suspect that a child is an abused or neglected child, shall report the matter immediately to the local department of the county or city wherein the child resides or wherein the abuse or neglect is believed to have occurred or to the Department's toll-free child abuse and neglect hotline:

1. Any person licensed to practice medicine or any of the healing arts;

2. Any hospital resident or intern, and any person employed in the nursing profession;

3. Any person employed as a social worker or family-services specialist;

4. Any probation officer;

5. Any teacher or other person employed in a public or private school, kindergarten or nursery school;

6. Any person providing full-time or part-time child care for pay on a regularly planned basis;

7. Any mental health professional;

8. Any law-enforcement officer or animal control officer;

9. Any mediator eligible to receive court referrals pursuant to § 8.01-576.8;

10. Any professional staff person, not previously enumerated, employed by a private or state-operated hospital, institution or facility to which children have been committed or where children have been placed for care and treatment;

11. Any person 18 years of age or older associated with or employed by any public or private organization responsible for the care, custody or control of children;

12. Any person who is designated a court-appointed special advocate pursuant to Article 5 (§ 9.1-151 et seq.) of Chapter 1 of Title 9.1;

13. Any person 18 years of age or older who has received training approved by the Department of Social Services for the purposes of recognizing and reporting child abuse and neglect;

14. Any person employed by a local department as defined in § 63.2-100 who determines eligibility for public assistance;

15. Any emergency medical services provider certified by the Board of Health pursuant to § 32.1-111.5, unless such provider immediately reports the matter directly to the attending physician at the hospital to which the child is transported, who shall make such report forthwith;

16. Any athletic coach, director or other person 18 years of age or older employed by or volunteering with a private sports organization or team;

17. Administrators or employees 18 years of age or older of public or private day camps, youth centers and youth recreation programs; and

18. Any person employed by a public or private institution of higher education other than an attorney who is employed by a public or private institution of higher education as it relates to information gained in the course of providing legal representation to a client.

This subsection shall not apply to any regular minister, priest, rabbi, imam, or duly accredited practitioner of any religious organization or denomination usually referred to as a church as it relates to (i) information required by the doctrine of the religious organization or denomination to be kept in a confidential manner or (ii) information that would be subject to § 8.01-400 or 19.2-271.3 if offered as evidence in court.

If neither the locality in which the child resides nor where the abuse or neglect is believed to have occurred is known, then such report shall be made to the local department of the county or city where the abuse or neglect was discovered or to the Department's toll-free child abuse and neglect hotline.

If an employee of the local department is suspected of abusing or neglecting a child, the report shall be made to the court of the county or city where the abuse or neglect was discovered. Upon receipt of such a report by the court, the judge shall assign the report to a local department that is not the employer of the suspected employee for investigation or family assessment. The judge may consult with the Department in selecting a local department to respond to the report or the complaint.

If the information is received by a teacher, staff member, resident, intern or nurse in the course of professional services in a hospital, school or similar institution, such person may, in place of said report, immediately notify the person in charge of the institution or department, or his designee, who shall make such report forthwith. If the initial report of suspected abuse or neglect is made to the person in charge of the institution or department, or his designee, pursuant to this subsection, such person shall notify the teacher, staff member, resident, intern or nurse who made the initial report when the report of suspected child abuse or neglect is made to the local department or to the Department's toll-free child abuse and neglect hotline, and of the name of the individual receiving the report, and shall forward any communication resulting from the report, including any information about any actions taken regarding the report, to the person who made the initial report.

The initial report may be an oral report but such report shall be reduced to writing by the child abuse coordinator of the local department on a form prescribed by the Board. Any person required to make the report pursuant to this subsection shall disclose all information that is the basis for his suspicion of abuse or neglect of the child and, upon request, shall make available to the child-protective services coordinator and the local department, which is the agency of jurisdiction, any information, records, or reports that document the basis for the report. All persons required by this subsection to report suspected abuse or neglect who maintain a record of a child who is the subject of such a report shall cooperate with the investigating agency and shall make related information, records and reports available to the investigating agency unless such disclosure violates the federal Family Educational Rights and Privacy Act (20 U.S.C. § 1232g). Provision of such information, records, and reports by a health care provider shall not be prohibited by § 8.01-399. Criminal investigative reports received from law-enforcement agencies shall not be further disseminated by the investigating agency nor shall they be subject to public disclosure.

B. For purposes of subsection A, "reason to suspect that a child is abused or neglected" shall include (i) a finding made by a health care provider within six weeks of the birth of a child that the results of toxicology studies of the child indicate the presence of a controlled substance not prescribed for the mother by a physician; (ii) a finding made by a health care provider within six weeks of the birth of a child that the child was born dependent on a controlled substance which was not prescribed by a physician for the mother and has demonstrated withdrawal symptoms; (iii) a diagnosis made by a health care provider at any time following a child's birth that the child has an illness, disease or condition which, to a reasonable degree of medical certainty, is attributable to in utero exposure to a controlled substance which was not prescribed by a physician for the mother or the child; or (iv) a diagnosis made by a health care provider at any time following a child's birth that the child has a fetal alcohol spectrum disorder attributable to in utero exposure to alcohol. When "reason to suspect" is based upon this subsection, such fact shall be included in the report along with the facts relied upon by the person making the report.

C. Any person who makes a report or provides records or information pursuant to subsection A or who testifies in any judicial proceeding arising from such report, records, or information shall be immune from any civil or criminal liability or administrative penalty or sanction on account of such report, records, information, or testimony, unless such person acted in bad faith or with malicious purpose.

D. Any person required to file a report pursuant to this section who fails to do so as soon as possible, but not longer than 24 hours after having reason to suspect a reportable offense of child abuse or neglect, shall be fined not more than $500 for the first failure and for any subsequent failures not less than $1,000. In cases evidencing acts of rape, sodomy, or object sexual penetration as defined in Article 7 (§ 18.2-61 et seq.) of Chapter 4 of Title 18.2, a person who knowingly and intentionally fails to make the report required pursuant to this section shall be guilty of a Class 1 misdemeanor.

E. No person shall be required to make a report pursuant to this section if the person has actual knowledge that the same matter has already been reported to the local department or the Department's toll-free child abuse and neglect hotline.

History.

1975, c. 341, § 63.1-248.3; 1976, c. 348; 1978, c. 747; 1993, c. 443; 1994, c. 840; 1995, c. 810; 1998, cc. 704, 716; 1999, c. 606; 2000, c. 500; 2001, c. 853; 2002, cc. 747, 860; 2006, cc. 530, 801; 2008, cc. 43, 268; 2012, cc. 391, 504, 640, 698, 728, 740, 815; 2013, cc. 72, 331; 2014, c. 285.

§ 63.2-1510. Complaints by others of certain injuries to children.

Any person who suspects that a child is an abused or neglected child may make a complaint concerning such child, except as hereinafter provided, to the local department of the county or city wherein the child resides or wherein the abuse or neglect is believed to have occurred or to the Department's toll-free child abuse and neglect hotline. If an employee of the local department is suspected of abusing or neglecting a child, the complaint shall be made to the court of the county or city where the abuse or neglect was discovered. Upon receipt of such a report by the court, the judge shall assign the report to a local department that is not the employer of the suspected employee for investigation or family assessment; or, if the judge believes that no local department in a reasonable geographic distance can be impartial in responding to the reported case, the judge shall assign the report to the court service unit of his court for evaluation. The judge may consult with the Department in selecting a local department to respond to the report or complaint. Such a complaint may be oral or in writing and shall disclose all information which is the basis for the suspicion of abuse or neglect of the child.

History.

1975, c. 341, § 63.1-248.4; 1976, c. 348; 1994, c. 840; 2000, c. 500; 2002, c. 747.

§ 63.2-1511. Complaints of abuse and neglect against school personnel; interagency agreement.

A. If a teacher, principal or other person employed by a local school board or employed in a school operated by the Commonwealth is suspected of abusing or neglecting a child in the course of his educational employment, the complaint shall be investigated in accordance with §§ 63.2-1503, 63.2-1505 and 63.2-1516.1. Pursuant to § 22.1-279.1, no teacher, principal or other person employed by a school board or employed in a school operated by the Commonwealth shall subject a student to corporal punishment. However, this prohibition of corporal punishment shall not be deemed to prevent (i) the use of incidental, minor or reasonable physical contact or other actions designed to maintain order and control; (ii) the use of reasonable and necessary force to quell a disturbance or remove a student from the scene of a disturbance that threatens physical injury to persons or damage to property; (iii) the use of reasonable and necessary force to prevent a student from inflicting physical harm on himself; (iv) the use of reasonable and necessary force for self-defense or the defense of others; or (v) the use of reasonable and necessary force to obtain possession of weapons or other dangerous objects or controlled substances or paraphernalia that are upon the person of the student or within his control. In determining whether the actions of a teacher, principal or other person employed by a school board or employed in a school operated by the Commonwealth are within the exceptions provided in this section, the local department shall examine whether the actions at the time of the event that were made by such person were reasonable.

B. For purposes of this section, "corporal punishment," "abuse," or "neglect" shall not include physical pain, injury or discomfort caused by the use of incidental, minor or reasonable physical contact or other actions designed to maintain order and control as permitted in clause (i) of subsection A or the use of reasonable and necessary force as permitted by clauses (ii), (iii), (iv), and (v) of subsection A, or by participation in practice or competition in an interscholastic sport, or participation in physical education or an extracurricular activity.

C. If, after an investigation of a complaint under this section, the local department determines that the actions or omissions of a teacher, principal, or other person employed by a local school board or employed in a school operated by the Commonwealth were within such employee's scope of employment and were taken in good faith in the course of supervision, care, or discipline of students, then the standard in determining if a report of abuse or neglect is founded is whether such acts or omissions constituted gross negligence or willful misconduct.

D. Each local department and local school division shall adopt a written interagency agreement as a protocol for investigating child abuse and neglect reports. The interagency agreement shall be based on recommended procedures for conducting investigations developed by the Departments of Education and Social Services.

History.

2001, c. 588, § 63.1-248.4:1; 2002, c. 747; 2003, cc. 986, 1013; 2005, cc. 767, 806; 2014, c. 412.

§ 63.2-1512. Immunity of person making report, etc., from liability.

Any person making a report pursuant to § 63.2-1509, a complaint pursuant to § 63.2-1510, or who takes a child into custody pursuant to § 63.2-1517, or who participates in a judicial proceeding resulting therefrom shall be immune from any civil or criminal liability in connection therewith, unless it is proven that such person acted in bad faith or with malicious intent.

History.

1975, c. 341, § 63.1-248.5; 1988, c. 686; 2002, c. 747.

§ 63.2-1513. Knowingly making false reports; penalties.

A. Any person fourteen years of age or older who makes or causes to be made a report of child abuse or neglect pursuant to this chapter that he knows to be false shall be guilty of a Class 1 misdemeanor. Any person fourteen years of age or older who has been previously convicted under this subsection and who is subsequently convicted under this subsection shall be guilty of a Class 6 felony.

B. The child-protective services records regarding the person who was alleged to have committed abuse or neglect that result from a report for which a conviction is obtained under this section shall be purged immediately by any custodian of such records upon presentation to the custodian of a certified copy of such conviction. After purging the records, the custodian shall notify the person in writing that such records have been purged.

History.

1996, cc. 813, 836, § 63.1-248.5:1.01; 1999, c. 828; 2002, c. 747.

ARTICLE 3.

RECORDS.

§ 63.2-1514. Retention of records in all reports; procedures regarding unfounded reports alleged to be made in bad faith or with malicious intent.

A. The local department shall retain the records of all reports or complaints made pursuant to this chapter, in accordance with regulations adopted by the Board. However, all records related to founded cases of child sexual abuse involving injuries or conditions, real or threatened, that result in or were likely to have resulted in serious harm to a child shall be maintained by the local department for a period of 25 years from the date of the complaint.

B. The Department shall maintain a child abuse and neglect information system that includes a central registry of founded complaints, pursuant to § 63.2-1515. The Department shall maintain all (i) unfounded investigations, (ii) family assessments, and (iii) reports or complaints determined to be not valid in a record which is separate from the central registry and accessible only to the Department and to local departments for child-protective services. The purpose of retaining these complaints or reports is to provide local departments with information regarding prior complaints or reports. In no event shall the mere existence of a prior complaint or report be used to determine that a subsequent complaint or report is founded. The subject of the complaint or report is the person who is alleged to have committed abuse or neglect. The subject of the complaint or report shall have access to his own record. The record of unfounded investigations and complaints and reports determined to be not valid shall be purged one year after the date of the complaint or report if there are no subsequent complaints or reports regarding the same child or the person who is the subject of the complaint or report in that one year. The local department shall retain such records for an additional period of up to two years if requested in writing by the person who is the subject of such complaint or report. The record of family assessments shall be purged three years after the date of the complaint or report if there are no subsequent complaints or reports regarding the same child or the person who is the subject of the report in that three-year period. The child-protective services records regarding the petitioner which result from such complaint or report shall be purged immediately by any custodian of such records upon presentation to the custodian of a certified copy of a court order that there has been a civil action that determined that the complaint or report was made in bad faith or with malicious intent. After purging the records, the custodian shall notify the petitioner in writing that the records have been purged.

C. At the time the local department notifies a person who is the subject of a complaint or report made pursuant to this chapter that such complaint or report is either an unfounded investigation or a completed family assessment, it shall notify him how long the record will be retained and of the availability of the procedures set out in this section regarding reports or complaints alleged to be made in bad faith or with malicious intent. Upon request, the local department shall advise the person who was the subject of an unfounded investigation if the complaint or report was made anonymously. However, the identity of a complainant or reporter shall not be disclosed.

D. Any person who is the subject of an unfounded report or complaint made pursuant to this chapter who believes that such report or complaint was made in bad faith or with malicious intent may petition the circuit court in the jurisdiction in which the report or complaint was made for the release to such person of the records of the investigation or family assessment. Such petition shall specifically set forth the reasons such person believes that such report or complaint was made in bad faith or with malicious intent. Upon the filing of such petition, the circuit court shall request and the local department shall provide to the circuit court its records of the investigation or family assessment for the circuit court's in camera review. The petitioner shall be entitled to present evidence to support his petition. If the circuit court determines that there is a reasonable question of fact as to whether the report or complaint was made in bad faith or with malicious intent and that disclosure of the identity of the complainant would not be likely to endanger the life or safety of the complainant, it shall provide to the petitioner a copy of the records of the investigation or family assessment. The original records shall be subject to discovery in any subsequent civil action regarding the making of a complaint or report in bad faith or with malicious intent.

History.

1988, c. 686, § 63.1-248.5:1; 1996, cc. 780, 791; 2000, c. 500; 2002, c. 747; 2003, c. 634; 2005, c. 77; 2010, c. 334.

§ 63.2-1515. Central registry; disclosure of information.

The central registry shall contain such information as shall be prescribed by Board regulation; however, when the founded case of abuse or neglect does not name the parents or guardians of the child as the abuser or neglector, and the abuse or neglect occurred in a licensed or unlicensed child day center, a licensed, registered or approved family day home, a private or public school, or a children's residential facility, the child's name shall not be entered on the registry without consultation with and permission of the parents or guardians. If a child's name currently appears on the registry without consultation with and permission of the parents or guardians for a founded case of abuse and neglect that does not name the parents or guardians of the child as the abuser or neglector, such parents or guardians may have the child's name removed by written request to the Department. The information contained in the central registry shall not be open to inspection by the public. However, appropriate disclosure may be made in accordance with Board regulations.

The Department shall respond to requests for a search of the central registry made by (i) local departments, (ii) local school boards, and (iii) governing boards or administrators of private schools accredited pursuant to § 22.1-19 regarding applicants for employment, pursuant to § 22.1-296.4, in cases where there is no match within the central registry within 10 business days of receipt of such requests. In cases where there is a match within the central registry regarding applicants for employment, the Department shall respond to requests made by local departments, local school boards, and governing boards or administrators within 30 business days of receipt of such requests. The response may be by first-class mail or facsimile transmission.

Any central registry check of a person who has applied to be a volunteer with a (a) Virginia affiliate of Big Brothers/Big Sisters of America, (b) Virginia affiliate of Compeer, (c) Virginia affiliate of Childhelp USA, (d) volunteer fire company or volunteer emergency medical services agency, or (e) court-appointed special advocate program pursuant to § 9.1-153 shall be conducted at no charge.

History.

1975, c. 341, § 63.1-248.8; 1993, cc. 48, 348, 955; 1994, cc. 700, 830; 2000, cc. 95, 734, 805; 2001, c. 321; 2002, cc. 371, 747; 2004, c. 74; 2015, cc. 502, 503; 2016, c. 454.

ARTICLE 4.

PROCEDURES.

§ 63.2-1516. Tape recording child abuse investigations.

Any person who is suspected of abuse or neglect of a child and who is the subject of an investigation or family assessment pursuant to this chapter may tape record any communications between him and child-protective services personnel that take place during the course of such investigation or family assessment, provided all parties to the conversation are aware the conversation is to be recorded. The parties' knowledge of the recording shall be demonstrated by a declaration at the beginning of the recorded portion of the conversation that the recording is to be made. If a person who is suspected of abuse or neglect of a child and who is the subject of an investigation or family assessment pursuant to this chapter elects to make a tape recording as provided in this section, the child-protective services personnel may also make such a recording.

History.
1990, c. 867, § 63.1-248.6:2; 2000, c. 500; 2002, c. 747.

§ 63.2-1516.01. Investigation procedures involving person who is the subject of complaint.

The local department shall, at the initial time of contact with the person subject to a child abuse and neglect investigation, advise such person of the complaints or allegations made against the person, in a manner that is consistent with laws protecting the rights of the person making the report or complaint. In cases where a child is alleged to have been abused or neglected by a teacher, principal or other person employed by a local school board or employed in a school operated by the Commonwealth, in the course of such employment in a nonresidential setting, the provisions of § 63.2-1516.1 shall also apply.

History.
2004, cc. 93, 233.

§ 63.2-1516.1. Investigation procedures when school employee is subject of the complaint or report; release of information in joint investigations.

A. Except as provided in subsection B of this section, in cases where a child is alleged to have been abused or neglected by a teacher, principal or other person employed by a local school board or employed in a school operated by the Commonwealth, in the course of such employment in a nonresidential setting, the local department conducting the investigation shall comply with the following provisions in conducting its investigation:

1. The local department shall conduct a face-to-face interview with the person who is the subject of the complaint or report.

2. At the onset of the initial interview with the alleged abuser or neglector, the local department shall notify him in writing of the general nature of the complaint and the identity of the alleged child victim regarding the purpose of the contacts.

3. The written notification shall include the information that the alleged abuser or neglector has the right to have an attorney or other representative of his choice present during his interviews. However, the failure by a representative of the Department of Social Services to so advise the subject of the complaint shall not cause an otherwise voluntary statement to be inadmissible in a criminal proceeding.

4. Written notification of the findings shall be submitted to the alleged abuser or neglector. The notification shall include a summary of the investigation and an explanation of how the information gathered supports the disposition.

5. The written notification of the findings shall inform the alleged abuser or neglector of his right to appeal.

6. The written notification of the findings shall inform the alleged abuser or neglector of his right to review information about himself in the record with the following exceptions:

a. The identity of the person making the report.

b. Information provided by any law-enforcement official.

c. Information that may endanger the well-being of the child.

d. The identity of a witness or any other person if such release may endanger the life or safety of such witness or person.

B. In all cases in which an alleged act of child abuse or neglect is also being criminally investigated by a law-enforcement agency, and the local department is conducting a joint investigation with a law-enforcement officer in regard to such an alleged act, no information in the possession of the local department from such joint investigation shall be released by the local department except as authorized by the investigating law-enforcement officer or his supervisor or the local attorney for the Commonwealth.

C. Failure to comply with investigation procedures does not preclude a finding of abuse or neglect if such a finding is warranted by the facts.

History.
2003, cc. 986, 1013.

§ 63.2-1517. Authority to take child into custody.

A. A physician or child-protective services worker of a local department or law-enforcement official investigating a report or complaint of abuse and neglect may take a child into custody for up to 72 hours without prior approval of parents or guardians provided:

1. The circumstances of the child are such that continuing in his place of residence or in the care or custody of the parent, guardian, custodian or other person responsible for the child's care, presents an imminent danger to the child's life or health to the extent that severe or irremediable injury would be likely to result or if evidence of abuse is perishable or subject to deterioration before a hearing can be held;

2. A court order is not immediately obtainable;

3. The court has set up procedures for placing such children;

4. Following taking the child into custody, the parents or guardians are notified as soon as practicable. Every effort shall be made to provide such notice in person;

5. A report is made to the local department; and

6. The court is notified and the person or agency taking custody of such child obtains, as soon as possible, but in no event later than 72 hours, an

emergency removal order pursuant to § 16.1-251; however, if a preliminary removal order is issued after a hearing held in accordance with § 16.1-252 within 72 hours of the removal of the child, an emergency removal order shall not be necessary. Any person or agency petitioning for an emergency removal order after four hours have elapsed following taking custody of the child shall state the reasons therefor pursuant to § 16.1-251.

B. If the 72-hour period for holding a child in custody and for obtaining a preliminary or emergency removal order expires on a Saturday, Sunday, or legal holiday or day on which the court is lawfully closed, the 72 hours shall be extended to the next day that is not a Saturday, Sunday, or legal holiday or day on which the court is lawfully closed.

History.

1975, c. 341, § 63.1-248.9; 1977, c. 559; 1992, c. 688; 1994, c. 643; 1998, c. 760; 2001, c. 837; 2002, c. 747; 2003, c. 508.

§ 63.2-1518. Authority to talk to child or sibling.

Any person required to make a report or conduct an investigation or family assessment, pursuant to this chapter may talk to any child suspected of being abused or neglected or to any of his siblings without consent of and outside the presence of his parent, guardian, legal custodian, or other person standing in loco parentis, or school personnel.

History.

1975, c. 341, § 63.1-248.10; 1979, c. 453; 1986, c. 308; 2000, c. 500; 2002, c. 747.

§ 63.2-1519. Physician-patient and husband-wife privileges inapplicable.

In any legal proceeding resulting from the filing of any report or complaint pursuant to this chapter, the physician-patient and husband-wife privileges shall not apply.

History.

1975, c. 341, § 63.1-248.11; 2002, c. 747.

§ 63.2-1520. Photographs and X-rays of child; use as evidence.

In any case of suspected child abuse, photographs and X-rays of the child may be taken without the consent of the parent or other person responsible for such child as a part of the medical evaluation. Photographs of the child may also be taken without the consent of the parent or other person responsible for such child as a part of the investigation or family assessment of the case by the local department or the court; however, such photographs shall not be used in lieu of medical evaluation. Such photographs and X-rays may be introduced into evidence in any subsequent proceeding.

The court receiving such evidence may impose such restrictions as to the confidentiality of photographs of any minor as it deems appropriate.

History.

1975, c. 341, § 63.1-248.13; 1978, c. 553; 2000, c. 500; 2002, c. 747.

§ 63.2-1521. Testimony by child using two-way closed-circuit television.

A. In any civil proceeding involving alleged abuse or neglect of a child pursuant to this chapter or pursuant to §§ 16.1-241, 16.1-251, 16.1-252, 16.1-253, 16.1-283 or § 20-107.2, the child's attorney or guardian ad litem or, if the child has been committed to the custody of a local department, the attorney for the local department may apply for an order from the court that the testimony of the alleged victim or of a child witness be taken in a room outside the courtroom and be televised by two-way closed-circuit television. The person seeking such order shall apply for the order at least seven days before the trial date.

B. The provisions of this section shall apply to the following:

1. An alleged victim who was fourteen years of age or under on the date of the alleged offense and is sixteen or under at the time of the trial; and

2. Any child witness who is fourteen years of age or under at the time of the trial.

C. The court may order that the testimony of the child be taken by closed-circuit television as provided in subsections A and B if it finds that the child is unavailable to testify in open court in the presence of the defendant, the jury, the judge, and the public, for any of the following reasons:

1. The child's persistent refusal to testify despite judicial requests to do so;

2. The child's substantial inability to communicate about the offense; or

3. The substantial likelihood, based upon expert opinion testimony, that the child will suffer severe emotional trauma from so testifying.

Any ruling on the child's unavailability under this subsection shall be supported by the court with findings on the record or with written findings in a court not of record.

D. In any proceeding in which closed-circuit television is used to receive testimony, the attorney for the child and the defendant's attorney and, if the child has been committed to the custody of a local board, the attorney for the local board shall be present in the room with the child, and the child shall be subject to direct and cross examination. The only other persons allowed to be present in the room with the child during his testimony shall be the guardian ad litem, those persons necessary to operate the closed-circuit equipment, and any other person whose presence is determined by the court to be necessary to the welfare and well-being of the child.

E. The child's testimony shall be transmitted by closed-circuit television into the courtroom for the defendant, jury, judge and public to view. The defendant shall be provided with a means of private, contemporaneous communication with his attorney during the testimony.

History.
1988, c. 845, § 63.1-248.13:1; 1999, c. 668; 2002, c. 747.

§ 63.2-1522. Admission of evidence of sexual acts with children.

A. In any civil proceeding involving alleged abuse or neglect of a child pursuant to this chapter or pursuant to §§ 16.1-241, 16.1-251, 16.1-252, 16.1-253, 16.1-283 or § 20-107.2, an out-of-court statement made by a child the age of twelve or under at the time the statement is offered into evidence, describing any act of a sexual nature performed with or on the child by another, not otherwise admissible by statute or rule, may be admissible in evidence if the requirements of subsection B are met.

B. An out-of-court statement may be admitted into evidence as provided in subsection A if:

1. The child testifies at the proceeding, or testifies by means of a videotaped deposition or closed-circuit television, and at the time of such testimony is subject to cross examination concerning the out-of-court statement or the child is found by the court to be unavailable to testify on any of these grounds:

a. The child's death;

b. The child's absence from the jurisdiction, provided such absence is not for the purpose of preventing the availability of the child to testify;

c. The child's total failure of memory;

d. The child's physical or mental disability;

e. The existence of a privilege involving the child;

f. The child's incompetency, including the child's inability to communicate about the offense because of fear or a similar reason; and

g. The substantial likelihood, based upon expert opinion testimony, that the child would suffer severe emotional trauma from testifying at the proceeding or by means of a videotaped deposition or closed-circuit television.

2. The child's out-of-court statement is shown to possess particularized guarantees of trustworthiness and reliability.

C. A statement may not be admitted under this section unless the proponent of the statement notifies the adverse party of his intention to offer the statement and the substance of the statement sufficiently in advance of the proceedings to provide the adverse party with a reasonable opportunity to prepare to meet the statement, including the opportunity to subpoena witnesses.

D. In determining whether a statement possesses particularized guarantees of trustworthiness and reliability under subdivision B 2, the court shall consider, but is not limited to, the following factors:

1. The child's personal knowledge of the event;

2. The age and maturity of the child;

3. Certainty that the statement was made, including the credibility of the person testifying about the statement and any apparent motive such person may have to falsify or distort the event including bias, corruption or coercion;

4. Any apparent motive the child may have to falsify or distort the event, including bias, corruption, or coercion;

5. The timing of the child's statement;

6. Whether more than one person heard the statement;

7. Whether the child was suffering pain or distress when making the statement;

8. Whether the child's age makes it unlikely that the child fabricated a statement that represents a graphic, detailed account beyond the child's knowledge and experience;

9. Whether the statement has internal consistency or coherence, and uses terminology appropriate to the child's age;

10. Whether the statement is spontaneous or directly responsive to questions;

11. Whether the statement is responsive to suggestive or leading questions; and

12. Whether extrinsic evidence exists to show the defendant's opportunity to commit the act complained of in the child's statement.

E. The court shall support with findings on the record, or with written findings in a court not of record, any rulings pertaining to the child's unavailability and the trustworthiness and reliability of the out-of-court statement.

History.
1988, c. 892, § 63.1-248.13:2; 2002, c. 747.

§ 63.2-1523. Use of videotaped statements of complaining witnesses as evidence.

A. In any civil proceeding involving alleged abuse or neglect of a child pursuant to this chapter or pursuant to §§ 16.1-241, 16.1-251, 16.1-252, 16.1-253, 16.1-283 or § 20-107.2, a recording of a statement of the alleged victim of the offense, made prior to the proceeding, may be admissible as evidence if the requirements of subsection B are met and the court determines that:

1. The alleged victim is the age of twelve or under at the time the statement is offered into evidence;

2. The recording is both visual and oral, and every person appearing in, and every voice recorded on, the tape is identified;

3. The recording is on videotape or was recorded by other electronic means capable of making an accurate recording;

4. The recording has not been altered;

5. No attorney for any party to the proceeding was present when the statement was made;

6. The person conducting the interview of the alleged victim was authorized to do so by the child-

protective services coordinator of the local department;

7. All persons present at the time the statement was taken, including the alleged victim, are present and available to testify or be cross examined at the proceeding when the recording is offered; and

8. The parties or their attorneys were provided with a list of all persons present at the recording and were afforded an opportunity to view the recording at least ten days prior to the scheduled proceedings.

B. A recorded statement may be admitted into evidence as provided in subsection A if:

1. The child testifies at the proceeding, or testifies by means of closed-circuit television, and at the time of such testimony is subject to cross examination concerning the recorded statement or the child is found by the court to be unavailable to testify on any of these grounds:

a. The child's death;

b. The child's absence from the jurisdiction, provided such absence is not for the purpose of preventing the availability of the child to testify;

c. The child's total failure of memory;

d. The child's physical or mental disability;

e. The existence of a privilege involving the child;

f. The child's incompetency, including the child's inability to communicate about the offense because of fear or a similar reason;

g. The substantial likelihood, based upon expert opinion testimony, that the child would suffer severe emotional trauma from testifying at the proceeding or by means of closed-circuit television; and

2. The child's recorded statement is shown to possess particularized guarantees of trustworthiness and reliability.

C. A recorded statement may not be admitted under this section unless the proponent of the statement notifies the adverse party of his intention to offer the statement and the substance of the statement sufficiently in advance of the proceedings to provide the adverse party with a reasonable opportunity to prepare to meet the statement, including the opportunity to subpoena witnesses.

D. In determining whether a recorded statement possesses particularized guarantees of trustworthiness and reliability under subdivision B 2, the court shall consider, but is not limited to, the following factors:

1. The child's personal knowledge of the event;

2. The age and maturity of the child;

3. Any apparent motive the child may have to falsify or distort the event, including bias, corruption, or coercion;

4. The timing of the child's statement;

5. Whether the child was suffering pain or distress when making the statement;

6. Whether the child's age makes it unlikely that the child fabricated a statement that represents a graphic, detailed account beyond the child's knowledge and experience;

7. Whether the statement has a "ring of verity," has internal consistency or coherence, and uses terminology appropriate to the child's age;

8. Whether the statement is spontaneous or directly responsive to questions;

9. Whether the statement is responsive to suggestive or leading questions; and

10. Whether extrinsic evidence exists to show the defendant's opportunity to commit the act complained of in the child's statement.

E. The court shall support with findings on the record, or with written findings in a court not of record, any rulings pertaining to the child's unavailability and the trustworthiness and reliability of the recorded statement.

History.
1988, c. 900, § 63.1-248.13:3; 2002, c. 747.

§ 63.2-1524. Court may order certain examinations.

The court may order psychological, psychiatric and physical examinations of the child alleged to be abused or neglected and of the parents, guardians, caretakers or siblings of a child suspected of being neglected or abused.

History.
1975, c. 341, § 63.1-248.14; 1976, c. 186; 2002, c. 747.

§ 63.2-1525. Prima facie evidence for removal of child custody.

In the case of a petition in the court for removal of custody of a child alleged to have been abused or neglected, competent evidence by a physician that a child is abused or neglected shall constitute prima facie evidence to support such petition.

History.
1975, c. 341, § 63.1-248.15; 2002, c. 747.

§ 63.2-1526. Appeals of certain actions of local departments.

A. A person who is suspected of or is found to have committed abuse or neglect may, within thirty days of being notified of that determination, request the local department rendering such determination to amend the determination and the local department's related records. Upon written request, the local department shall provide the appellant all information used in making its determination. Disclosure of the reporter's name or information which may endanger the well-being of a child shall not be released. The identity of a collateral witness or any other person shall not be released if disclosure may endanger his life or safety. Information prohibited from being disclosed by state or federal law or regulation shall not be released. The local department shall hold an informal conference or consultation where such person, who may be represented by counsel, shall be entitled to informally present testimony of witnesses, documents, factual data, arguments or other submissions of proof to the local department. With the exception of the local director, no person whose regular duties include substantial involvement with child abuse and neglect cases shall preside over the informal conference. If the local department refuses the request for amendment or fails to act within forty-five days after receiving such request, the person may, within thirty days thereafter, petition the Commissioner, who shall grant a hearing to determine whether it appears, by a preponderance of the evidence, that the determination or record contains information which is irrelevant or inaccurate regarding the commission of abuse or neglect by the person who is the subject of the determination or record and therefore shall be amended. A person who is the subject of a report who requests an amendment to the record, as provided above, has the right to obtain an extension for an additional specified period of up to sixty days by requesting in writing that the forty-five days in which the local department must act be extended. The extension period, which may be up to sixty days, shall begin at the end of the forty-five days in which the local department must act. When there is an extension period, the thirty-day period to request an administrative hearing shall begin on the termination of the extension period.

B. The Commissioner shall designate and authorize one or more members of his staff to conduct such hearings. The decision of any staff member so designated and authorized shall have the same force and effect as if the Commissioner had made the decision. The hearing officer shall have the authority to issue subpoenas for the production of documents and the appearance of witnesses. The hearing officer is authorized to determine the number of depositions that will be allowed and to administer oaths or affirmations to all parties and witnesses who plan to testify at the hearing. The Board shall adopt regulations necessary for the conduct of such hearings. Such regulations shall include provisions stating that the person who is the subject of the report has the right (i) to submit oral or written testimony or documents in support of himself and (ii) to be informed of the procedure by which information will be made available or withheld from him. In case of any information withheld, such person shall be advised of the general nature of such information and the reasons, for reasons of privacy or otherwise, that it is being withheld. Upon giving reasonable notice, either party at his own expense may depose a nonparty and submit such deposition at the hearing pursuant to Board regulation. Upon good cause shown, after a party's written motion, the hearing officer may issue subpoenas for the production of documents or to compel the attendance of witnesses at the hearing, except that alleged child victims of the person and their siblings shall not be subpoenaed, deposed or required to testify. The person who is the subject of the report may be represented by counsel at the hearing. Upon petition, the court shall have the power to enforce any subpoena that is not complied with or to review any refusal to issue a subpoena. Such decisions may not be further appealed except as part of a final decision that is subject to judicial review. Such hearing officers are empowered to order the amendment of such determination or records as is required to make them accurate and consistent with the requirements of this chapter or the regulations adopted hereunder. If, after hearing the facts of the case, the hearing officer determines that the person who is the subject of the report has presented information that was not available to the local department at the time of the local conference and which if available may have resulted in a different determination by the local department, he may remand the case to the local department for reconsideration. The local department shall have fourteen days in which to reconsider the case. If, at the expiration of fourteen days, the local department fails to act or fails to amend the record to the satisfaction of the appellant, the case shall be returned to the hearing officer for a determination. If aggrieved by the decision of the hearing officer, such person may obtain further review of the decision in accordance with Article 5 (§ 2.2-4025 et seq.) of the Administrative Process Act (§ 2.2-4000 et seq.).

C. Whenever an appeal of the local department's finding is made and a criminal charge is also filed against the appellant for the same conduct involving the same victim as investigated by the local department, the appeal process shall automatically be stayed until the criminal prosecution in circuit court is completed. During such stay, the appellant's right of access to the records of the local department regarding the matter being appealed shall also be stayed. Once the criminal prosecution in circuit court has been completed, the local department shall advise the appellant in writing of his right to resume his appeal within the time frames provided by law and regulation.

History.

1988, c. 407, § 63.1-248.6:1; 1993, cc. 188, 955, 963; 1995, c. 7; 2002, c. 747.

ARTICLE 5.

OVERSIGHT AND EVALUATION OF PROGRAM.

§ 63.2-1527. Board oversight duties; Out-of-Family Investigations Advisory Committee.

A. The Board shall be responsible for establishing standards for out-of-family investigations and for the implementation of the family assessment track of the differential response system.

B. The Out-of-Family Investigations Advisory Committee (the Committee) is hereby established as an advisory committee in the executive branch of state government.

C. The Committee shall consist of 15 members as follows: one representative of public school employees, one representative of a hospital for children, one representative of a licensed child care center, one representative of a juvenile detention home, one representative of a public or private residential facility for children, one representative of a family day care home, one representative of a local department of Social Services, one representative of a religious organization with a program for children, one representative of Virginians for Child Abuse Prevention and six citizens of the Commonwealth at large. The Chairman of the Board shall appoint such persons for terms established by the Board.

D. The Committee shall advise the Board on the effectiveness of the policies and standards governing out-of-family investigations.

E. The Committee shall elect a chairman and vice-chairman from among its membership. A majority of the members shall constitute a quorum. The meetings of the Committee shall be held at the call of the chairman or whenever the majority of the voting members so request.

F. Members shall receive no compensation for their services nor be reimbursed for expenses incurred in the discharge of their duties as provided in §§ 2.2-2813 and 2.2-2825.

G. The Department of Social Services shall provide staff support to the Committee. All agencies of the Commonwealth shall provide assistance to the Committee, upon request.

History.

1993, c. 955, § 63.1-248.7:1; 2000, c. 500; 2002, c. 747; 2004, c. 103.

§ **63.2-1528:** Repealed by Acts 2012, cc. 803 and 835, cl. 73.

§ **63.2-1529:** Repealed by Acts 2009, c. 32.

ARTICLE 6.

VIRGINIA CHILD PROTECTION ACCOUNTABILITY SYSTEM.

§ 63.2-1530. Virginia Child Protection Accountability System.

A. The Virginia Child Protection Accountability System (the System) is created to collect and make available to the public information on the response to reported cases of child abuse and neglect in the Commonwealth. The Department shall establish and maintain the System. The Board shall promulgate regulations to implement the provisions of this section.

B. The following information shall, notwithstanding any state law regarding privacy or confidentiality of records, be included in the System and made available to the public via a website maintained by the Department and in print format:

1. From the Department: (i) the total number of complaints alleging child abuse, neglect, or a combination thereof received; (ii) the total number of complaints deemed valid pursuant to § 63.2-1508; (iii) the total number of complaints investigated by the Department pursuant to subsection I of §§ 63.2-1503 and 63.2-1505; (iv) the total number of cases determined to be founded cases of abuse or neglect; and (v) the total number of cases resulting in a finding that the complaint was founded resulting in administrative appeal. Information reported pursuant to clause (v) shall be reported by total number of appeals to the local department, total number of appeals to the Department, and total number of appeals by outcome of the appeal. For each category of information required by this subdivision, the Department shall also report the total number of cases by type of abuse; by gender, age, and race of the alleged victim; and by the nature of the relationship between the alleged victim and alleged abuser.

2. From the Department of State Police, annually, in a format approved by the Department of Social Services, arrest and disposition statistics for violations of §§ 18.2-48, 18.2-61, 18.2-63, 18.2-64.1, 18.2-67.1, 18.2-67.2, 18.2-67.3, 18.2-67.4, 18.2-355, 18.2-361, 18.2-366, 18.2-370 through 18.2-370.2, 18.2-371, 18.2-371.1, 18.2-374.1, 18.2-374.1:1, 18.2-374.3, 18.2-387, and 40.1-103 for inclusion in the Child Protection Accountability System.

3. From every circuit court in the Commonwealth for which data is available through the statewide Case Management System: (i) the total number of (a) misdemeanor convictions appealed from the district court to the circuit court, (b) felony charges certified from the district court to the circuit court, and (c) charges brought by direct indictment in the circuit court that involve a violation of any Code section set forth in subdivision 2; (ii) the total number of cases appealed, certified, or transferred to the court or brought by direct indictment in the circuit court involving a violation of any Code section set forth in subdivision 2 that result in a trial, including the number of bench trials and the number of jury trials; and (iii) the total number of trials involving a violation of any Code section set forth in subdivision 2 resulting in (a) a plea agreement, (b) transfer to another court, (c) a finding of not guilty, (d) conviction on a lesser included offense, or (e) conviction on all charges, by type of trial.

4. From the Virginia Criminal Sentencing Commission, information on sentences imposed for offenses listed in subdivision 2, including (i) the name of the sentencing judge, (ii) the offense or offenses for which a sentence was imposed, (iii) the age of the victim and offender, (iv) the relationship between the victim and the offender, (v) the locality in which the offense occurred, (vi) the sentence imposed and the actual time served, (vii) whether the sentence

was an upward or downward departure from the sentencing guidelines or within the sentencing guidelines, and (viii) the reasons given for the departure, if any, from the sentencing guidelines.

5. From the Office of the Executive Secretary of the Supreme Court of Virginia, information by locality on cases from the Juvenile and Domestic Relations District Courts' Case Management System involving (i) children alleged to be abused or neglected, including (a) the number of petitions filed, (b) the number of cases in which an emergency removal order was issued, (c) the number of cases in which a preliminary removal order was issued prior to an adjudicatory hearing, (d) the number of cases in which a preliminary removal order or a preliminary child protective order or both were issued at a preliminary hearing, and (e) the number of cases in which a preliminary child protective order or a child protective order was issued other than at a preliminary hearing; and (ii) family abuse cases, including (a) the number of family abuse emergency protective orders issued by magistrates and juvenile and domestic relations district courts pursuant to § 16.1-253.4, (b) the number of family abuse protective petitions filed, and (c) the number of family abuse protective orders issued pursuant to § 16.1-279.1.

Information required to be reported pursuant to subdivisions 1 through 5 shall be reported annually in a format approved by the Department of Social Services and aggregated by locality.

C. Data collected pursuant to subsection B shall be made available to the public on a website established and maintained by the Department and shall also be made readily available to the public in print format. Information included in the System shall be presented in such a manner that no individual identifying information shall be included.

History.

2009, c. 445; 2010, cc. 664, 726; 2012, cc. 113, 661.

SUBTITLE IV.

LICENSURE.

CHAPTER 17.

LICENSURE AND REGISTRATION PROCEDURES.

Article 3.

Background Checks.

ARTICLE 3.

BACKGROUND CHECKS.

§ 63.2-1726. Background check required; children's residential facilities.

A. As a condition of employment, volunteering, or providing services on a regular basis, every children's residential facility that is regulated or operated by the Departments of Social Services, Education, Military Affairs, or Behavioral Health and Developmental Services shall require any individual who (i) accepts a position of employment at such a facility who was not employed by that facility prior to July 1, 2007, (ii) volunteers for such a facility on a regular basis and will be alone with a juvenile in the performance of his duties who was not a volunteer at such facility prior to July 1, 2007, or (iii) provides contractual services directly to a juvenile for such facility on a regular basis and will be alone with a juvenile in the performance of his duties who did not provide such services prior to July 1, 2007, to submit to fingerprinting and to provide personal descriptive information, to be forwarded along with the applicant's fingerprints through the Central Criminal Records Exchange to the Federal Bureau of Investigation for the purpose of obtaining criminal history record information regarding such applicant. The children's residential facility shall inform the applicant that he is entitled to obtain a copy of any background check report and to challenge the accuracy and completeness of any such report and obtain a prompt resolution before a final determination is made of the applicant's eligibility to have responsibility for the safety and well-being of children. The applicant shall provide the children's residential facility with a written statement or affirmation disclosing whether he has ever been convicted of or is the subject of pending charges for any offense within or outside the Commonwealth. The results of the criminal history background check must be received prior to permitting an applicant to work with children.

The Central Criminal Records Exchange, upon receipt of an individual's record or notification that no record exists, shall forward it to the state agency which operates or regulates the children's residential facility with which the applicant is affiliated. The state agency shall, upon receipt of an applicant's record lacking disposition data, conduct research in whatever state and local recordkeeping systems are available in order to obtain complete data. The state agency shall report to the children's facility whether the applicant is eligible to have responsibility for the safety and well-being of children. Except as otherwise provided in subsection B, no children's residential facility regulated or operated by the Departments of Education, Behavioral Health and Developmental Services, Military Affairs, or Social Services shall hire for compensated employment or allow to volunteer or provide contractual services persons who have been (a) convicted of or are the subject of pending charges for the following crimes: a felony violation of a protective order as set out in § 16.1-253.2; murder or manslaughter as set out in Article 1 (§ 18.2-30 et seq.) of Chapter 4 of Title 18.2; malicious wounding by mob as set out in § 18.2-41; abduction as set out in subsection A or B of § 18.2-47; abduction for immoral purposes as set out in § 18.2-48; assault and bodily woundings as set out in Article 4 (§ 18.2-51 et seq.) of Chapter 4 of Title 18.2; robbery as set out in § 18.2-58; carjacking as set out in § 18.2-58.1; extortion by threat as set out in § 18.2-59; threat as set out in § 18.2-60; any felony stalking violation as set out in § 18.2-60.3; a felony violation of a protective order as set out in § 18.2-60.4; sexual assault as set out in Article 7 (§ 18.2-61 et seq.) of Chapter 4 of Title 18.2; arson as set out in Article 1 (§ 18.2-77 et seq.) of Chapter 5 of Title 18.2; burglary as set out in Article 2 (§ 18.2-89 et seq.) of Chapter 5 of Title 18.2; any felony violation relating to distribution of drugs as set out in Article 1 (§ 18.2-247 et seq.) of Chapter 7 of Title 18.2; drive-by shooting as set out in § 18.2-286.1; use of a machine gun in a crime of violence as set out in § 18.2-289; aggressive use of a machine gun as set out in § 18.2-290; use of a sawed off shotgun in a crime of violence as set out in subsection A of § 18.2-300; pandering as set out in § 18.2-355; crimes against nature involving children as set out in § 18.2-361; taking indecent liberties with children as set out in § 18.2-370 or 18.2-370.1; abuse or neglect of children as set out in § 18.2-371.1, including failure to secure medical attention for an injured child as set out in § 18.2-314; obscenity offenses as set out in § 18.2-374.1; possession of child pornography as set out in § 18.2-374.1:1; electronic facilitation of pornography as set out in § 18.2-374.3; incest as set out in § 18.2-366; abuse or neglect of incapacitated adults as set out in § 18.2-369; employing or permitting a minor to assist in an act constituting an offense under Article 5 (§ 18.2-372 et seq.) of Chapter 8 of Title 18.2 as set out in § 18.2-379; delivery of drugs to prisoners as set out in § 18.2-474.1; escape from jail as set out in § 18.2-477; felonies by prisoners as set out in § 53.1-203; or an equivalent offense in another state; (b) convicted of any felony violation relating to possession of drugs as set out in Article 1 (§ 18.2-247 et seq.) of Chapter 7 of Title 18.2, or an equivalent offense in another state, in the five years prior to the application date for employment, to be a volunteer, or to provide contractual services; (c) convicted of any felony violation relating to possession of drugs as set out in Article 1 (§ 18.2-247 et seq.) of Chapter 7 of Title 18.2 and continue on probation or parole or have failed to pay required court costs; or (d) convicted of any offense set forth in § 9.1-902 or have been the subject of a finding of not guilty by reason of insanity in accordance with Chapter 11.1 (§ 19.2-182.2 et seq.) of Title 19.2 of an offense set forth in § 9.1-902 that results in the person's requirement to register with the Sex Offender and Crimes Against Minors Registry pursuant to § 9.1-901, or any similar registry in any other state. The provisions of this section also shall apply to residential programs established pursuant to § 16.1-309.3 for juvenile offenders cited in a complaint for intake or in a petition before the court that alleges the juvenile is delinquent or in need of services or supervision, and to local secure detention facilities provided, however, that the provisions of this section related to local secure detention facilities shall only apply to an individual who, on or after July 1, 2013, accepts a position of employment at such local secure detention facility, volunteers at such local secure detention facility on a regular basis and will be alone with a juvenile in the performance of his duties, or provides contractual services directly to a juvenile at a local secure detention facility on a regular basis and will be alone with a juvenile in the performance of his duties. The Central Criminal Records Exchange and the state or local agency that regulates or operates the local secure detention facility shall process the criminal history record information regarding such applicant in accordance with this subsection and subsection B.

B. Notwithstanding the provisions of subsection A, a children's residential facility may hire for compensated employment or for volunteer or contractual service purposes persons who have been convicted of not more than one misdemeanor offense under § 18.2-57 or 18.2-57.2, if 10 years have elapsed following the conviction, unless the person committed such offense in the scope of his employment, volunteer, or contractual services.

If the applicant is denied employment or the opportunity to volunteer or provide services at a children's residential facility because of information appearing on his criminal history record, and the applicant disputes the information upon which the denial was based, upon written request of the applicant the state agency shall furnish the applicant the procedures for obtaining his criminal history record from the Federal Bureau of Investigation. If the applicant has been permitted to assume duties that do not involve contact with children pending receipt of the report, the children's residential facility is not precluded from suspending the applicant from his position pending a final determination of the applicant's eligibility to have responsibility for the safety and well-being of children. The information provided to the children's residential facility shall not be disseminated except as provided in this section.

C. Those individuals listed in clauses (i), (ii) and (iii) of subsection A also shall authorize the children's residential facility to obtain a copy of information from the central registry maintained pursuant to § 63.2-1515 on any investigation of child abuse or neglect undertaken on him. The applicant shall provide the children's residential facility with a written statement or affirmation disclosing whether he has ever been the subject of a founded case of child abuse or neglect within or outside the Commonwealth. The children's residential facility shall receive the results of the central registry search prior to permitting an applicant to work alone with children. Children's residential facilities regulated or operated by the Departments of Education; Behavioral Health and Developmental Services; Military Affairs; and Social Services shall not hire for compensated employment or allow to volunteer or provide contractual services, persons who have a founded case of child abuse or neglect. Every residential facility for juveniles which is regulated or operated by the Department of Juvenile Justice shall be authorized to obtain a copy of the information from the central registry.

D. The Boards of Social Services; Education; Juvenile Justice; and Behavioral Health and Developmental Services, and the Department of Military Affairs, may adopt regulations to comply with the provisions of this section. Copies of any information received by a children's residential facility pursuant to this section shall be available to the agency that regulates or operates such facility but shall not be disseminated further. The cost of obtaining the criminal history record and the central registry information shall be borne by the employee or volunteer unless the children's residential facility, at its option, decides to pay the cost.

History.

1994, c. 704, § 63.1-248.7:2; 1996, c. 747; 2001, c. 138; 2002, c. 747; 2007, c. 573; 2009, cc. 813, 840; 2012, c. 383; 2013, cc. 96, 181; 2016, c. 580.

TITLE 66.

JUVENILE JUSTICE.

CHAPTER 1.

DEPARTMENT AND STATE BOARD OF JUVENILE JUSTICE.

§ 66-1. Creation of Department of Juvenile Justice.

There is hereby created within the executive branch, responsible to the Governor, a Department of Juvenile Justice. The Department shall be under the immediate supervision of a Director who shall be appointed by the Governor, subject to confirmation by the General Assembly. The Director shall serve at the pleasure of the Governor or until his successor shall be appointed and qualified. Vacancies shall be filled in the same manner as original appointments.

History.

1989, c. 733; 1990, c. 350; 1996, c. 503.

§ 66-2. Supervision of the Department.

The Director of the Department of Juvenile Justice shall, under the direction of the Governor, be responsible for the supervision of the Department and shall exercise such other powers and perform such other duties as may be conferred or imposed by law upon him. He shall perform such other duties as may be required of him by the Governor and the Secretary of Public Safety and Homeland Security.

History.

1989, c. 733; 1990, cc. 1, 317; 2014, cc. 115, 490.

§ 66-3. Powers of the Director.

A. The Director of the Department shall have the following general powers:

1. To employ such personnel as may be required to carry out the purposes of this title.

2. To make and enter into all contracts and agreements necessary or incidental to the performance of his duties and the execution of his powers under this title, including, but not limited to, contracts and agreements with the United States, other states, and agencies and governmental subdivisions of the Commonwealth.

3. With the prior approval of the Governor, to enter into agreements with a public or private entity to operate a work program for children committed to the Department.

4. With the prior approval of the Governor, to acquire real property, by purchase or gift, needed for new or existing state juvenile correctional facilities

and for administrative and other facilities necessary to the operations of the Department, pursuant to regulations promulgated by the Board to ensure adequate public notice and local hearing.

5. To establish and maintain schools of the appropriate grades, levels, and types in the institutions for persons committed to juvenile correctional centers.

6. To enter into such agreements with private entities, nonprofit civic organizations, school divisions, and public and private two-year and four-year institutions of higher education as it may deem necessary to provide age-appropriate educational programs and training, including career and technical education; career development opportunities; public service projects; restricted Internet access to online courses of institutions of higher education and approved or accredited online secondary education or adult education and literacy programs leading to a diploma or achieving a passing score on a high school equivalency examination approved by the Board of Education; access to postsecondary education that includes college credit, certification through an accredited vocational training program, or other accredited continuing education program using videoconferencing technology; and other learning experiences in the furtherance of its duties and responsibilities under this chapter for persons committed to the institutions comprising the Department.

7. To designate employees of the Department with internal investigations authority to have the same power as a sheriff or a law-enforcement officer in the investigation of allegations of criminal behavior affecting the operations of the Department. Such employees shall be subject to any minimum training standards established by the Department of Criminal Justice Services under § 9.1-102 for law-enforcement officers prior to exercising any law-enforcement power granted under this subdivision. Nothing in this section shall be construed to grant the Department any authority over the operation and security of detention homes not specified in any other provision of law. The Department shall investigate allegations of criminal behavior in accordance with a written agreement entered into with the Department of State Police. The Department shall not investigate any action falling within the authority vested in the Office of the State Inspector General pursuant to Chapter 3.2 (§ 2.2-307 et seq.) of Title 2.2 unless specifically authorized by the Office of the State Inspector General.

8. To do all acts necessary or convenient to carry out the purposes of this title.

B. The Director shall comply with and require all school facilities within the Department to comply with applicable regulations and statutes, both state and federal.

History.

1989, c. 733; 1993, cc. 460, 487; 1995, c. 701; 2012, cc. 803, 835; 2013, cc. 143, 214; 2014, c. 84.

§ **66-3.1:** Repealed by Acts 2011, cc. 798 and 871, cl. 2, effective July 1, 2012.

§ 66-3.2. Additional duties of the Director.

A. The Director shall coordinate with the Department of Corrections the development and submission of requests for compensation from the United States Department of Justice State Criminal Alien Assistance Program for costs associated with incarcerating undocumented aliens.

B. The Director shall forward to the Commonwealth's Attorneys' Services Council, updated on a monthly basis, a list of all juveniles, 14 years of age or older, that (i) have been committed to the Department, (ii) have been found guilty of a felony offense defined as a predicate criminal act under § 18.2-46.1, or have been adjudicated delinquent on the basis of an act that would be a felony and a predicate criminal act under § 18.2-46.1 if committed by an adult, and (iii) have been identified as belonging to a criminal gang. The list shall contain identifying information for each gang member, as well as the offense, court, and date of conviction or adjudication.

History.

2004, c. 126; 2006, cc. 431, 500.

§ 66-4. State Board of Juvenile Justice.

There shall be a State Board of Juvenile Justice, consisting of nine members appointed by the Governor, two of whom shall be experienced educators. In making appointments, the Governor shall endeavor to select appointees of such qualifications and experience that the membership of the Board shall include persons suitably qualified to consider and act upon the various problems that may come before the Board. The appointments shall be subject to confirmation by the General Assembly if in session and, if not, then at its next succeeding session.

History.

1989, c. 733; 1996, c. 503; 2013, cc. 37, 232.

§ 66-5. Term of office of members; suspension or removal.

The members of the Board shall be appointed initially as follows: three members for a term of two years each and four members for a term of four years each. Thereafter, the appointment of such members or their successors shall be for terms of four years, except that an appointment to fill a vacancy shall be for the unexpired term. No person shall be eligible to serve for or during more than two successive four-year terms. However, any person appointed to fill a vacancy may be eligible for two additional successive terms after the term of the vacancy for which he was appointed has expired. Members of the Board may be suspended or removed by the Governor at his pleasure.

History.
1989, c. 733.

§ 66-6. Chairman, vice-chairman and secretary.

The Board shall select a chairman from its membership, and under rules adopted by itself may elect one of its members as vice-chairman. It shall elect one of its members as secretary.

History.
1989, c. 733.

§ 66-7. Compensation and expenses.

The members of the Board shall receive no salaries. They shall be paid their necessary traveling and other expenses incurred in attendance at meetings, or while otherwise engaged in the discharge of their duties, and the sum of fifty dollars a day for each day or portion thereof in which they are engaged in the performance of their duties.

History.
1989, c. 733.

§ 66-8. Meetings.

The Board shall meet at such times as it deems appropriate and on call of the chairman when in his opinion meetings are expedient or necessary. However, the Board shall meet at least four times each calendar year.

History.
1989, c. 733.

§ 66-9. Quorum.

A majority of the current membership of the Board shall constitute a quorum for all purposes.

History.
1989, c. 733.

§ 66-10. Powers and duties of Board.

The Board shall have the following powers and duties:

1. To establish and monitor policies for the programs and facilities for which the Department is responsible under this law.
2. To ensure the development of a long-range youth services policy.
3. To monitor the activities of the Department and its effectiveness in implementing the policies developed by the Board.
4. To advise the Governor and Director on matters relating to youth services.
5. To promulgate such regulations as may be necessary to carry out the provisions of this title and other laws of the Commonwealth.
6. To ensure the development of programs to educate citizens and elicit public support for the activities of the Department.
7. To establish length-of-stay guidelines for juveniles indeterminately committed to the Department and to make such guidelines available for public comment.
8. To adopt all necessary regulations for the management and operation of the schools in the Department except that the regulations adopted hereunder shall not conflict with regulations relating to security of the institutions in which the juveniles are committed.

History.
1989, c. 733; 1990, c. 679; 1996, cc. 755, 914; 2012, cc. 164, 456, 803, 835.

§ 66-10.01. Certified mail; subsequent mail or notices may be sent by regular mail.

Whenever in this title the Board or the Department is required to send any mail or notice by certified mail and such mail or notice is sent certified mail, return receipt requested, then any subsequent, identical mail or notice that is sent by the Board or the Department may be sent by regular mail.

History.
2011, c. 566.

§ 66-10.1. Board to establish regulations regarding human research.

The Board shall promulgate regulations pursuant to the Administrative Process Act (§ 2.2-4000 et seq.) to effectuate the provisions of Chapter 5.1 (§ 32.1-162.16 et seq.) of Title 32.1 for human research, as defined in § 32.1-162.16, to be conducted or authorized by the Department. The regulations shall require the human research committee to submit to the Governor, the General Assembly, and the Director or his designee at least annually a report on human research projects reviewed and approved by the committee and shall require the committee to report any significant deviations from the proposals as approved.

History.
1992, c. 603.

§ 66-11: Repealed by Acts 2012, cc. 164 and 456, cl. 2.

§ 66-12. Definitions.

Unless a different meaning clearly appears from the context, as used in this title:

"Board" or *"State Board"* means the Board of Juvenile Justice;

"Child" means any natural person under eighteen years of age;

"Department" means the Department of Juvenile Justice;

"Director" means the Director of Juvenile Justice.

History.
1989, c. 733.

CHAPTER 2.

CARE OF CHILDREN COMMITTED TO DEPARTMENT.

Section

§ 66-13. Authority of Department as to juveniles committed to it; establishment of facilities; arrangements for temporary care.

A. The Department is authorized and empowered to receive juveniles committed to it by the courts of the Commonwealth. The Department shall establish, staff and maintain facilities for the rehabilitation, education, training and confinement of such juveniles. The Department may make arrangements with satisfactory persons, institutions or agencies, or with cities or counties maintaining places of detention for juveniles, for the temporary care of such juveniles.

B. In accordance with the Juvenile Corrections Private Management Act, Chapter 2.1 (§ 66-25.3 et seq.), the Department may establish, or contract with private entities, political subdivisions or commissions to establish, juvenile boot camps. The Board shall prescribe standards for the development, implementation and operation of the boot camps with highly structured components including, but not limited to, military style drill and ceremony, physical labor, education and rigid discipline and no less than six months of intensive aftercare. The Department of Juvenile Justice's Division of Education shall establish, staff, and maintain educational programs for such juveniles in accordance with § 66-13. A contract to expend state funds to establish a facility for a juvenile boot camp shall not be executed by the Department unless an appropriation has been expressly approved as is otherwise provided by law.

C. The Department may by mutual agreement with a locality or localities and, pursuant to standards promulgated pursuant to § 16.1-309.9, establish detention homes for use by a locality or localities for pre-trial and post-dispositional detention pursuant to §§ 16.1-248.1 and 16.1-284.1. The Department may collect by mutual agreement with a locality or localities and from any locality of this Commonwealth from which a juvenile is placed in such a detention home, the reasonable cost of maintaining such juvenile in such facility and a portion of the cost of construction of such facility. Such agreements shall be subject to approval by the General Assembly in the general appropriation act.

D. The Department shall collect data pertaining to the demographic characteristics of juveniles incarcerated in state juvenile correctional institutions, including, but not limited to, the race or ethnicity, age, and gender of such persons, and the types of and extent to which health-related problems are prevalent among such persons. Beginning July 1, 1997, such data shall be collected, tabulated quarterly, and reported by the Director to the Governor and the General Assembly at each regular session of the General Assembly thereafter.

History.
Code 1950, §§ 53-324, 53-330, 63-291, 63-366, 63-367, 63-368, 63-369, 63.1-239, 63.1-245; 1950, p. 33; 1954, c. 262; 1956, cc. 127, 287; 1962, c. 437; 1968, c. 578; 1974, cc. 44, 45; 1975, c. 178; 1981, c. 487; 1982, c. 636, § 53.1-237; 1989, c. 733; 1991, c. 534; 1996, cc. 755, 914; 1997, c. 894; 2012, cc. 803, 835.

§ 66-13.1. Division of Education; employment of Superintendent; powers and duties.

A. To assist in the performance of the duties imposed by § 66-13 the Department shall develop and maintain a Division of Education (Division), which shall be composed of all the educational facilities of all institutions operated by the Department. The Division shall be designated as a local education agency (LEA) but shall not be eligible to receive state funds appropriated for direct aid to public education.

B. The Department shall employ a Superintendent of the Division, who shall meet the minimum standards for division superintendents set by the Board of Education. The Superintendent shall supervise the administration of the Division. The Department shall employ teachers and place them in appropriate schools. Other powers and duties of the Superintendent shall be fixed by the Board of Education in accordance with law.

C. When the Department employs a teacher licensed by the Board of Education to provide instruction in the schools of the juvenile correctional centers, the Department of Human Resource Management shall establish salary schedules for the teachers which endeavor to be competitive with those in effect for the school division in which the correctional center is located.

History.

2012, cc. 803, 835.

§ 66-14. Allowance for maintenance of children placed by Commonwealth in private homes, etc.

For the maintenance of each child committed to the custody of the Department pursuant to subdivision A 14 of § 16.1-278.8 and placed in a private home or in a facility other than one operated by the Commonwealth, there shall be paid a per diem allowance which shall be established by the Department from funds appropriated to the Department for this purpose. The cost of such care shall not exceed that amount which would be incurred if the services required by the child were provided in a juvenile facility operated by the Department.

No child shall be placed outside the Commonwealth without first complying with the appropriate provisions of Chapters 10 (§ 63.2-1000 et seq.) and 11 (§ 63.2-1100 et seq.) of Title 63.2 or with regulations of the State Board of Social Services relating to resident children placed out of the Commonwealth.

History.

Code 1950, §§ 53-325, 63-293, 63.1-240; 1952, c. 644; 1962, c. 437; 1968, c. 578; 1970, c. 326; 1974, cc. 44, 45, 476; 1978, c. 309; 1981, c. 487; 1982, c. 636, § 53.1-239; 1989, c. 733; 1992, cc. 837, 880; 1993, cc. 232, 283; 1996, cc. 587, 597.

§ 66-15. Schedules of per diem cost of maintenance in detention homes; reimbursements of cities and counties.

The Department shall establish schedules setting forth the per diem cost to each locality for maintaining a child in a detention home. In accordance with the schedule, the Department, in addition to all other reimbursements on account of such detention homes, shall reimburse each city or county for the cost of maintaining in such homes any children committed to the Department. The Department shall review annually and adjust, if justified, the per diem it pays to localities for the care of state wards.

History.

Code 1950, §§ 53-326, 63.1-241, 63-293.1; 1954, c. 582; 1968, c. 578; 1974, cc. 44, 45; 1981, c. 487; 1982, c. 636, § 53.1-240; 1989, cc. 683, 733.

§ 66-16. Acceptance and expenditure of certain funds for children committed to Department.

The Department is authorized to accept and expend for the benefit of any child committed to it, or for reimbursement purposes, any funds made available from any source, solely for the current maintenance and support of any such child, whether such funds be provided by the child's parents, or other person, or by the U.S. Department of Veterans Affairs, the Railroad Retirement Act, the old age and survivor's insurance provisions of the federal Social Security Act, as amended, or from any other source. In no event shall the sums so accepted exceed an amount in excess of the cost to the Department of supporting the child.

History.

Code 1950, §§ 53-327, 63.1-242, 63-293.2; 1956, c. 400; 1968, c. 578; 1974, cc. 44, 45; 1981, c. 487; 1982, c. 636, § 53.1-241; 1989, c. 733.

§ 66-17. Disposition of property left by child.

If any child, having been in the custody of the Department by virtue of § 16.1-278.8, upon being released or having escaped therefrom leaves any personal property valued at less than $100 in the custody of the Department for six months after his release or escape, the Director may sell such personal property at public sale or otherwise dispose of the property. The proceeds of such sale shall be kept for one year from the date of the child's attaining the age of majority. Thereafter, any unclaimed proceeds shall be paid into the state treasury and credited to the Literary Fund.

History.

Code 1950, §§ 16.1-178.1, 53-327.1; 1956, c. 555; 1974, cc. 44, 45; 1977, c. 559; 1981, c. 487; 1982, c. 636, § 53.1-242; 1989, c. 733; 1991, c. 534.

§ 66-18. Examination and placing of such children.

The Department shall make a careful physical and mental examination of every child committed to it by the courts, investigate the personal and family history of the child and his environment, and place such children at such facilities as are available. Any children committed to the Department and afterwards found to be eligible for commitment by proper proceedings to any state hospital or admission to a training center for individuals with intellectual disability shall take precedence as to admission over all others and shall in all cases be received into the state hospital or training center within 45 days.

History.
Code 1950, §§ 53-328, 63-292, 63.1-243; 1956, c. 127; 1968, c. 578; 1974, cc. 44, 45; 1981, c. 487; 1982, c. 636, § 53.1-243; 1989, c. 733; 2012, cc. 476, 507.

§ 66-19. Behavioral services unit; director and personnel; examination of children.

To assist in the performance of the duties imposed by § 66-18, the Department shall maintain a behavioral services unit and employ as director thereof a clinically competent person. The Department shall also employ such other medical, technical and clinical personnel skilled in the diagnosis and treatment of physical diseases or mental illnesses of children as may be desirable for the operation of such unit. The personnel of the unit, when visiting the various facilities maintained by the Department for the care of children committed to the Department, shall conduct a thorough examination of each child at such facilities not theretofore examined by the unit, and other children at the facilities for whom such examination is indicated. Such examination shall be for the purpose of determining, diagnosing and treating physical and learning ailments or impairments and mental illnesses with a view to improving the general functioning of such children and hastening their rehabilitation.

History.
Code 1950, §§ 53-329, 63.1-244, 63-381, 63-384; 1954, c. 681; 1966, c. 354; 1968, c. 578; 1974, cc. 44, 45; 1981, c. 487; 1982, c. 636, § 53.1-244; 1989, c. 733; 2012, cc. 476, 507.

§ 66-20. Observation and treatment of children with mental illness or intellectual disability.

After commitment of any child to the Department, if the Department finds, as a result of psychiatric examinations and case study, that such child has mental illness or intellectual disability, it shall be the duty of the Department to obtain treatment for the child's mental condition. If the Department determines that transfer to a state hospital, training center, or other appropriate treatment facility is required to further diagnose or treat the child's mental condition, the proceedings shall be in accordance with the provisions of § 37.2-806 or §§ 16.1-341 through 16.1-345, except that provisions requiring consent of the child's parent or guardian for treatment shall not apply in such cases. No child transferred to a state hospital pursuant to this section or the provisions of Title 37.2 shall, however, be held or cared for in any maximum security unit where adults determined to be criminally insane reside and such child shall be kept separate and apart from such adults.

History.
Code 1950, § 53-329.1; 1977, c. 559; 1978, c. 739; 1981, c. 487; 1982, c. 636, § 53.1-245; 1989, c. 733; 1990, c. 975; 2012, cc. 476, 507.

§ 66-21. Superintendents and agents of facilities to have powers of sheriff.

The superintendents of the facilities established by the Department pursuant to § 66-13 and their authorized agents shall have the powers of a sheriff for the purpose of preserving order at their facilities and for the conveyance of children committed to their care to and from such facilities.

History.
Code 1950, §§ 53-332, 63-371, 63.1-247; 1968, c. 578; 1974, cc. 44, 45; 1981, c. 487; 1982, c. 636, § 53.1-246; 1989, c. 733.

§ 66-22. Daily and additional allowance to children.

The Director may allow every child in any facility established by the Department a daily allowance in an amount established by the Board. Additional allowance may be made by the Director to provide necessary funds for incidental needs for required activities in schools, foster care and other special placements for other special activities that such children would normally be engaged in resulting from their placement. The allowance so made may be drawn upon by the child for such purposes as may be authorized by the regulations of the Board.

History.
Code 1950, §§ 53-333, 63.1-248, 63-369.1; 1958, c. 366; 1960, c. 395; 1968, c. 578; 1970, c. 327; 1974, cc. 44, 45; 1975, c. 638; 1981, c. 487; 1982, c. 636, § 53.1-247; 1989, c. 733.

§ 66-22.1. Establishment of stores in juvenile correctional facilities.

The Director is hereby authorized to provide for the establishment and operation of stores or commissaries in state juvenile correctional facilities to deal in such articles as he deems proper. The profits from the operation of such stores shall be used for educational, recreational, or other purposes beneficial to the juveniles committed to the Department as may be prescribed by the Director.

History.
1997, c. 195.

§ 66-23. Authority of superintendents with regard to application for operator's licenses and employment certificates.

The superintendents of facilities established by the Department shall have the authority, commensurate with that of a parent in like cases, to give consent for those children placed in their respective facilities to (i) application for a motor vehicle operator's license and (ii) issuance of an employment certificate.

History.

Code 1950, § 53-334; 1977, c. 643; 1981, c. 487; 1982, c. 636, § 53.1-248; 1989, c. 733; 2012, cc. 164, 456.

§ 66-24. Community group homes and other residential facilities for certain juveniles; licensure; personnel; summary suspension under certain circumstances; penalty.

A. The Department of Juvenile Justice shall cooperate with other state departments in fulfilling their respective licensing and certification responsibilities of children's residential facilities. The Board shall promulgate regulations that shall allow the Department to so assist and cooperate with other state departments. The Board's regulations shall establish the Department as the single licensing agency, with the exception of educational programs licensed by the Department of Education, for group homes or residential facilities providing care of juveniles in direct state care.

B. The Department is authorized to establish and maintain such a system of community group homes or other residential care facilities as the Department may from time to time acquire, construct, contract for or rent for the care of juveniles in direct state care, pending development of more permanent placement plans. Any community group home or other residential care facility that the Department may contract for or rent for the care of juveniles in direct state care shall be licensed or certified in accordance with the regulations of the Board.

Any more permanent placement plans shall consider adequate care and treatment, and suitable education, training and employment for such juveniles, as is appropriate.

C. The Department is further authorized to employ necessary personnel for community group homes or other residential care facilities or to contract with private entities for their operation. The Department shall conduct background checks of any individual who (i) accepts a position of employment at a community group home or other residential care facility, (ii) volunteers at a community group home or other residential care facility on a regular basis and will be alone with a juvenile in the performance of his duties, or (iii) provides contractual services directly to a juvenile in a community group home or other residential care facility on a regular basis and will be alone with a juvenile in the performance of his duties, pursuant to § 63.2-1726.

D. The Board shall promulgate regulations for licensure or certification of community group homes or other residential care facilities that contract with or are rented for the care of juveniles in direct state care pursuant to subsection B.

The Board's regulations shall address the services required to be provided in such facilities as it may deem appropriate to ensure the welfare and safety of the juveniles. In addition, the Board's regulations shall include, but need not be limited to (i) specifications for the structure and accommodations of such facilities according to the needs of the juveniles to be placed in the home or facility; (ii) rules concerning allowable activities, local government- and group home- or residential care facility-imposed curfews, and study, recreational, and bedtime hours; and (iii) a requirement that each home or facility have a community liaison who shall be responsible for facilitating cooperative relationships with the neighbors, the school system, local law enforcement, local government officials, and the community at large.

E. Pursuant to the procedures set forth in subsection F and in addition to any other legally authorized disciplinary actions, the Director may issue a summary order of suspension of the license or certificate of any group home or residential facility so regulated by the Department, in conjunction with any proceeding for revocation, denial, or other action, when conditions or practices exist in the home or facility that pose an immediate and substantial threat to the health, safety, and welfare of the juveniles who are residents and the Director believes the operation of the home or facility should be suspended during the pendency of such proceeding.

F. The summary order of suspension shall take effect upon its issuance and shall be served on the licensee or certificate holder or its designee as soon as practicable thereafter by personal service and certified mail, return receipt requested, to the address of record of the licensee or certificate holder. The order shall state the time, date, and location of a hearing to determine whether the suspension is appropriate. Such hearing shall be held no later than three business days after the issuance of the summary order of suspension and shall be convened by the Director or his designee.

After such hearing, the Director may issue a final order of summary suspension or may find that such summary suspension is not warranted by the facts and circumstances presented. A final order of summary suspension shall include notice that the licensee or certificate holder may appeal the Director's decision to the appropriate circuit court no later than 10 days following issuance of the order. The sole issue before the court shall be whether the Director had reasonable grounds to require the licensee to cease operations during the pendency of the concurrent revocation, denial, or other proceeding. The concurrent revocation, denial, or other proceeding shall not be affected by the outcome of any hearing on the appropriateness of the summary suspension.

The willful and material failure to comply with the summary order of suspension or final order of summary suspension shall be punishable as a Class 2 misdemeanor. The Director may require the cooperation of any other agency or subdivision of the

Commonwealth in the relocation of the juveniles who are residents of a home or facility whose license or certificate has been summarily suspended pursuant to this section and in any other actions necessary to reduce the risk of further harm to such residents.

G. In addition to the requirements set forth above, the Board's regulations shall require, as a condition of initial licensure or, if appropriate, license renewal, that the applicant shall: (i) be personally interviewed by Department personnel to determine the qualifications of the owner or operator before granting an initial license; (ii) provide evidence of having relevant prior experience before any initial license is granted; (iii) provide, as a condition of initial license or renewal licensure, evidence of staff participation in training on appropriate siting of the residential facilities for children, good neighbor policies, and community relations; and (iv) be required to screen residents prior to admission to exclude individuals with behavioral issues, such as histories of violence, that cannot be managed in the relevant residential facility.

H. In addition, the Department shall:

1. Notify relevant local governments and placing and funding agencies, including the Office of Children's Services, of multiple health and safety or human rights violations in residential facilities licensed by the Department when such violations result in the lowering of the licensure or certification status of the facility to provisional;

2. Post on the Department's website information concerning the application for initial licensure or certification of or renewal, denial, or provisional licensure or certification of any residential facility for children located in the locality;

3. Require all licensees or certificate holders to self-report lawsuits against or settlements with residential facility operators relating to the health and safety or human rights of residents and any criminal charges that may have been made relating to the health and safety or human rights of residents;

4. Require proof of contractual agreements or staff expertise to provide educational services, counseling services, psychological services, medical services, or any other services needed to serve the residents in accordance with the facility's operational plan;

5. Modify the term of the license or certificate at any time during the term of the license or certificate based on a change in compliance; and

6. Disseminate to local governments, or post on the Department's website, an accurate (updated weekly or monthly as necessary) list of licensed and operating group homes and other residential facilities for children by locality with information on services and identification of the lead licensure agency.

History.

Code 1950, §§ 53-331, 63.1-246, 63-291.1; 1966, c. 491; 1968, c. 578; 1974, cc. 44, 45; 1975, c. 637; 1981, c. 487; 1982, c. 636, § 53.1-249; 1989, c. 733; 1996, cc. 755, 914; 2005, cc. 358, 471; 2006, cc. 168, 781; 2008, c. 873; 2015, c. 366.

§ 66-25. Collection of information concerning religious preferences by correctional facilities.

Notwithstanding any provision of law to the contrary, any correctional facility established pursuant to this chapter or Chapter 11 (§ 16.1-226 et seq.) of Title 16.1 may collect and disseminate information concerning the religious preferences and affiliations of persons committed to its custody. No person shall be required to indicate his religious preference or affiliation, and no dissemination of the information shall be made except to categories of persons designated by the person who has given his consent to such dissemination.

History.

Code 1950, § 53-19.15:1; 1977, c. 506; 1982, c. 636, § 53.1-250; 1989, c. 733.

§ 66-25.1. Work programs.

A. The Director or his designee may enter into an agreement with a public or private entity for the operation of a work program for juveniles committed to the Department.

B. The primary purpose of such work program shall be the training of such juveniles, not the production of goods or the rendering of service by juveniles committed to the Department. Such work programs also shall not interfere with or impact a juvenile's education program where the goal is achieving a high school diploma or its equivalent. The Board shall promulgate regulations governing the form and review process for proposed agreements.

C. Articles produced or manufactured and services provided by juveniles participating in such a work program may be purchased by any county, by any district of any county, city, or town and by any nonprofit organization, including volunteer emergency medical services agencies, fire departments, sheltered workshops and community service organizations. Such articles and services may also be bought, sold or acquired by exchange on the open market through the participating public or private entity.

D. Revenues received from the sale of articles, as provided in subsection C, shall be deposited into a special fund established in the state treasury. Such funds shall be expended to support work programs for juveniles committed to the Department.

History.

1993, cc. 460, 487; 1997, c. 639; 2011, c. 551; 2012, cc. 803, 835; 2015, cc. 502, 503.

§ 66-25.1:1. Juvenile academic and career training.

The Director or his designee shall assess, in accordance with criteria established pursuant to § 66-

25.1:3, whether a juvenile committed to the Department is an appropriate candidate for participation in a work release program, apprenticeship program, job enterprise program, or any other work experience opportunity located at or through the juvenile correctional center where the juvenile is placed.

History.
2005, c. 648.

§ 66-25.1:2. Career training and technical education programs.

A. With such funds as are made available for this purpose, the Department shall provide juveniles committed to the Department with opportunities to work and to participate in career training or technical education programs operated by the Department.

B. The Department may develop appropriate interagency linkages with state and local agencies, public and private institutions of education and of higher education, labor and industry councils, the business community, rehabilitative services providers, and employment and guidance services to assist juveniles in acquiring necessary work habits, developing marketable skills, and identifying career goals through a broad range of career opportunities and mentoring and apprenticeship programs. In providing career-related programs, training, and services, the Department may consult and cooperate with the Virginia Employment Commission and the Department of Labor and Industry. Work training opportunities may include business, industrial, agricultural, highway maintenance and construction, and work release programs as hereafter specified in this article. In addition, juveniles may be employed to improve, repair, work on, or cultivate public property or buildings.

History.
2005, c. 648; 2012, cc. 803, 835.

§ 66-25.1:3. Extending limits of confinement of state wards for work and educational programs; disposition of wages; penalties for violations.

A. The Director is authorized to establish work release programs, subject to such rules and regulations as the Board may prescribe, whereby (i) a juvenile who is proficient in any trade or occupation and who meets the work release criteria established by the Director, may be approved for employment by private individuals, corporations, or state agencies at places of business, or (ii) a juvenile who the Director is satisfied meets the work release criteria and is capable of receiving substantial benefit from educational and other related community activity programs that are not available within a juvenile correctional center may attend such programs outside of the juvenile correctional facility.

B. The Director may contract with the superintendent of a local detention facility or home for the temporary placement of a committed juvenile who is deemed appropriate for participation in the programs or services provided by or through a certified post-dispositional program in that local detention facility or home. A juvenile who the Director is satisfied meets the work release criteria and is capable of receiving substantial benefit from educational programs, employment or other related community activity programs available at or through the local detention facility or home is eligible for placement in such local detention facility or home.

C. The compensation for such employment shall be arranged by the Director and shall be the same as that of regular employees in similar occupations. Any wages earned shall be paid to the Director. The Director shall, in accordance with regulations promulgated by the Board, deduct from such wages, in the following order of priority, an amount to:

1. Meet the obligation of any judicial or administrative order to provide support, and such funds shall be disbursed according to the terms of such order;
2. Pay any fines, restitution, or costs as ordered by the court; and
3. Pay travel and other such expenses made necessary by his work release employment or participation in an educational or rehabilitative program.

The balance shall be credited to the juvenile's account or sent to his family in an amount the juvenile chooses.

D. Any juvenile who has been placed in any of the programs authorized herein shall, while outside the juvenile correctional center or juvenile detention facility to which he is assigned, be deemed to be in custody whether or not he is under the supervision of a juvenile correctional officer. If the juvenile, without proper authority or without just cause, leaves the area in which he has been directed to work or to attend educational or community activity programs, or the vehicle or route involved in his traveling to or from such place or program, he may be found guilty of escape as provided for in § 18.2-477 as though he had left the secure facility as defined in § 16.1-228; or, if there are mitigating circumstances or the culpability of the juvenile is minimal, he may be found guilty of a Class 2 misdemeanor.

E. The Director and any superintendent or other administrative head of any local detention facility are authorized to enter into agreements whereby persons committed to the Department, whether such persons are housed in a juvenile correctional center or a local detention facility, and who meet the Department's standards for such release, may participate in local work release programs or in educational or other rehabilitative programs operating pursuant to this section. Any person so placed shall be governed by the rules and regulations applicable to local work release programs.

F. In the event that the juvenile is committed to the Department as a serious offender pursuant to § 16.1-285.1, the juvenile shall not be approved for placement in a work release program located outside of the juvenile correctional facility without written approval of the committing court.

History.
2005, c. 648.

§ 66-25.1:4. Work release furlough.

The Director may, subject to rules and regulations prescribed by the Board, extend the limits of confinement of any offender participating in a work release program that is subject to the Director's authority to permit the offender a furlough for the purpose of visiting his home or family. Such furlough shall be for a period to be prescribed by the Director, not to exceed three days.

In the event that the juvenile is committed to the Department as a serious offender pursuant to § 16.1-285.1, the juvenile shall not be approved for a furlough for the purpose of visiting his home or family without written approval of the committing court.

Any offender who, without proper authority or without just cause, fails to remain within the limits of confinement set by the Director hereunder, or fails to return within the time prescribed to the place designated by the Director in granting such authority, is guilty of a Class 1 misdemeanor, and shall be ineligible for further participation in a work release program during his current term of confinement. In the event such offender leaves the Commonwealth, the offender may be found guilty of an escape as provided in § 18.2-477.

History.
2005, c. 648.

§ 66-25.2. Notice to be given prior to release of serious offenders.

Prior to the release of any juvenile committed pursuant to § 16.1-285.1, the Department shall have notice of the release delivered by first-class mail to the court which committed the juvenile, to the last known address of any victim of the offense for which the juvenile was committed if such victim has submitted a written request for notification to the Department, and to the sheriff, chief of police, and attorney for the Commonwealth of the jurisdiction (i) in which the offense occurred, (ii) in which the juvenile resided prior to commitment, and (iii) if different from (i) and (ii), in which the juvenile intends to reside subsequent to being released.

History.
1994, cc. 859, 949.

§ 66-25.2:1. Director; notice to school superintendent prior to release of certain offenders.

The Director or designee shall notify the school division superintendent in the jurisdiction in which the juvenile will be enrolled upon release from a juvenile correctional center if the Director reasonably believes that the juvenile poses any credible danger of serious bodily injury or death to one or more students, school personnel, or others on school property. Such information shall include the nature of the danger. The information provided to a school division superintendent pursuant to this section may be disclosed only as provided in § 16.1-305.2.

History.
2009, c. 276.

CHAPTER 2.1.

JUVENILE CORRECTIONS PRIVATE MANAGEMENT ACT.

Section

§ 66-25.3. Definitions.

As used in this chapter unless the context requires otherwise or it is otherwise provided:

"Correctional services" means the following functions, services and activities when provided within a juvenile correctional facility or otherwise:

1. Operation of facilities, including management, custody of juveniles and provision of security;
2. Food services, commissary, medical services, transportation, sanitation or other ancillary services;
3. Development and implementation assistance for classification, management information systems or other information systems or services;
4. Education, training and employment programs;
5. Recreational, religious and other activities; and
6. Counseling, special treatment programs, or other programs for special needs.

"Juvenile correction facility" or *"center"* or *"facility"* means any institution operated by or under the authority of the Department and shall include, whether obtained by purchase, lease, lease/purchase, construction, reconstruction, restoration, improvement, alteration, repair or other means, any

physical betterment or improvement related to the housing of juveniles or any preliminary plans, studies or surveys relative thereto; land or rights to land; and any furnishings, machines, vehicles, apparatus, or equipment for use in connection with any juvenile correctional facility.

"Contractor" means any entity entering into or offering or proposing to enter into a contractual agreement to provide any juvenile correctional facility for or correctional services to juveniles under the custody of the Commonwealth.

History.
1996, cc. 795, 942.

§ 66-25.4. State juvenile correctional facilities; private contracts.

The Director, subject to any applicable regulations which may be promulgated by the Board pursuant to § 66-10, is hereby authorized to enter into contracts for the financing, site selection, design, acquisition, construction, maintenance, leasing, leasing/purchasing, management or operation of juvenile correctional facilities or any combination of those services subject to the requirements and limitations set out below.

1. Contracts entered into under the terms of this chapter shall be with an entity submitting an acceptable response pursuant to a request for proposals. An acceptable response shall be one which meets all the requirements in the request for proposals. However, no contract for juvenile correctional facilities or correctional services may be entered into unless the private contractor demonstrates to the satisfaction of the Director that it has:

a. The qualifications, experience and management personnel necessary to carry out the terms of this contract;

b. The financial resources to provide indemnification for liability arising from the management of juvenile correctional projects;

c. Evidence of past performance of similar contracts; and

d. The ability to comply with all applicable federal and state constitutional standards; federal, state, and local laws; court orders; and juvenile correctional standards.

2. Contracts awarded under the provisions of this chapter, including contracts for the provision of juvenile correctional services, the construction of juvenile correctional facilities, or for the lease, lease/purchase or use of public or private lands or buildings for use in the operation of facilities, may be entered into for a period of up to 30 years, subject to the requirements for annual appropriation of funds by the Commonwealth.

3. Contracts awarded under the provisions of this chapter shall, at a minimum, comply with the following:

a. Provide for appropriate security to protect the public, employees and committed juveniles;

b. Provide juveniles with work or training opportunities while incarcerated; however, the contractor shall not benefit financially from the labor of committed juveniles;

c. Impose discipline on committed juveniles only in accordance with applicable regulations; and

d. Provide proper food, clothing, housing and medical care for juveniles.

4. No contract for juvenile correctional facilities or juvenile correctional services shall be entered into unless the following requirements are met:

a. The contractor provides audited financial statements for the previous five years or for each of the years the contractor has been in operation, if fewer than five years, and provides other financial information as requested; and

b. The contractor provides an adequate plan of indemnification, specifically including indemnity for civil rights claims. The indemnification plan shall be adequate to protect the Commonwealth and public officials from all claims and losses incurred as a result of the contract. Nothing herein is intended to deprive a contractor or the Commonwealth of the benefits of any law limiting exposure to liability or setting a limit on damages.

5. No contract for juvenile correctional facilities or correctional services shall be executed by the Director nor shall any funds be expended for the contract unless:

a. The proposed contract complies with any applicable regulations which may be promulgated by the Board pursuant to § 66-10;

b. An appropriation for the facilities or the services to be provided under the contract has been expressly approved as is otherwise provided by law;

c. The juvenile correctional facilities or the correctional services proposed by the contract are of at least the same quality as those routinely provided by the Department to similar types of committed juveniles;

d. An evaluation of the proposed contract demonstrates a cost benefit to the Commonwealth when compared to alternative means of providing the facilities or the services through governmental agencies;

e. If a contract for acquiring facilities requires or otherwise contemplates that the Commonwealth, whether subject to appropriation or not, will make payments beyond the current biennium that are expected to pay debt service on any bonds or other obligations issued to finance such facilities, regardless of the issuer thereof, then (i) the Treasury Board shall approve the terms and structure of such bonds or other obligations and (ii) the appropriation for such facilities acknowledges that payments for the acquisition of such facilities are expected to be made beyond the current biennium under a capital lease, lease/purchase, or similar arrangement. Any contract that is for two years or less, or is cancelable by the Commonwealth without cause after such a period, shall not be deemed a contract as described herein; and

f. Nothing herein shall be construed to constitute a waiver for the Department or contractor from complying with the provisions of subdivision 4 of § 66-3.

History.
1996, cc. 795, 942; 2012, cc. 803, 835.

§ 66-25.5. Powers and duties not delegable to contractor.

No contract for juvenile correctional services shall authorize, allow, or imply a delegation of authority or responsibility of the Director to a contractor for any of the following:

1. Developing and implementing procedures for calculating release and parole eligibility dates for committed juveniles;
2. Approving juveniles for furlough and work release;
3. Approving the type of work juveniles may perform and the wages which may be given the juveniles engaging in such work;
4. Classifying a committed juvenile or placing a committed juvenile in less restrictive custody or more restrictive custody;
5. Transferring a committed juvenile; however, the contractor may make written recommendations regarding the transfer of a committed juvenile;
6. Formulating rules of behavior for committed juveniles, violations of which may subject committed juveniles to sanctions; however, the contractor may propose such rules to the Director for his review and adoption, rejection, or modification as otherwise provided by law or regulation; and
7. Disciplining committed juveniles in any manner which requires a discretionary application of rules of behavior for committed juveniles or a discretionary imposition of a sanction for violations of such rules.

History.
1996, cc. 795, 942.

§ 66-25.6. Board shall promulgate regulations; local school board exemption.

A. The Board shall make, adopt and promulgate regulations governing the following aspects of private management and operation of juvenile correctional facilities:

1. Contingency plans for state operation of a contractor-operated facility in the event of a termination of the contract;
2. Use of physical force and mechanical restraint by the contractors' security personnel;
3. Methods of monitoring a contractor-operated facility by the Department or the Board;
4. Public access to a contractor-operated facility; and
5. Such other regulations as may be necessary to carry out the provisions of this chapter.

B. Nothing in this chapter shall be construed to require local school boards to provide educational services to juveniles while committed to a state juvenile correctional facility.

History.
1996, cc. 795, 942.

§ 66-25.7. Fixed-price or not-to-exceed-price design-build-operate and related contracts authorized.

Notwithstanding any other provisions of law to the contrary, but in accordance with the procedures consistent with those described in the Virginia Public Procurement Act (§ 2.2-4300 et seq.) for procurement of nonprofessional services through competitive negotiation, the Director may enter into design-build-operate contracts for juvenile correctional facilities on a fixed-price or not-to-exceed-price basis, including related leases, lease/purchase contracts, agreements relating to the sale of securities to finance such facilities, and similar financing agreements and agreements for correctional services. For the purposes of this section, "design-build-operate contract" means a contract between the Commonwealth and another party in which the party contracting with the Commonwealth agrees to (i) design, build and operate the juvenile correctional facility or (ii) design and build the juvenile correctional facility where the facility is to be operated by a third party.

The Director shall maintain adequate records to allow post-project evaluation.

History.
1996, cc. 795, 942.

CHAPTER 3.
DELINQUENCY PREVENTION AND YOUTH DEVELOPMENT ACT.

§ 66-26. Delinquency prevention and youth development programs; agents.

The Director shall develop and supervise delinquency prevention and youth development programs in order that better services and coordination of services are provided to children. The Director shall have the authority to appoint necessary agents for the carrying out of these programs as may be needed. To this end the Director shall cooperate with state and local authorities in establishing and maintaining suitable delinquency prevention and youth development programs.

History.
Code 1950, § 53-19.22:1; 1974, c. 496; 1979, c. 700; 1982, c. 636, § 53.1-251; 1989, c. 733.

§ 66-27. Authority of Director to make grants to localities.

The Director is authorized to make grants to counties and cities pursuant to the provisions of this chapter to promote efficiency and economy in the delivery of youth services and to provide support to localities seeking to respond positively to the growing rate of juvenile delinquency.

History.
Code 1950, § 53-335; 1979, c. 698; 1982, c. 636, § 53.1-252; 1989, c. 733.

§ 66-28. Policies.

The Board shall prescribe policies governing applications for grants pursuant to this chapter and standards for the operation of programs developed and implemented under the grants. The Department shall cooperate with and seek the assistance of representatives of county and city governing bodies, private nonprofit youth service agencies and private citizens having expertise in the development and any subsequent revisions of the standards required by this section.

History.
Code 1950, § 53-336; 1979, c. 698; 1982, c. 636, § 53.1-253; 1989, c. 733; 2000, c. 277.

§ 66-29. Ordinances to be enacted by participating localities; applications by localities for grants.

Prior to applying to the Director for a grant pursuant to this chapter, each governing body of a county or city which is to participate in the grant shall enact an appropriate ordinance or resolution which provides for the creation of a youth services citizen board pursuant to § 66-34.

Any county or city or combination thereof may apply to the Director for a grant pursuant to this chapter. The Director shall provide consultation and technical assistance, if requested, to localities in the development of applications for such grants. The Director shall approve or disapprove applicants for grants.

History.
Code 1950, § 53-337; 1979, c. 698; 1982, c. 636, § 53.1-254; 1989, c. 733; 2000, c. 277.

§ 66-30. Renewal of grants; suspension for failure to comply with standards; notice and hearing.

Grants approved by the Director pursuant to § 66-29 shall be renewed subject to approval by the Director of an annual plan update for youth services submitted by the participating counties or cities.

If the Director determines that a program operating under an approved grant is not in compliance with minimum standards promulgated by the Board, he may suspend all or any portion of the grant until the required standards of operation are met.

History.
Code 1950, § 53-338; 1979, c. 698; 1982, c. 636, § 53.1-255; 1989, c. 733; 1990, c. 679; 2000, c. 277.

§ 66-31. Funding; records to be kept by localities; use of funds.

A. Grants made to a county or city or combination thereof pursuant to this chapter shall be of an amount up to seventy-five percent of the total program budget for the proposed program for salaries and all other operating expenses including the lease of facilities, subject to funds provided by the General Assembly.

B. Each county and city receiving moneys under this chapter shall keep records of receipts and disbursements thereof which records shall be open for audit and evaluation by the appropriate state authorities.

C. Participating counties and cities may not use funds provided under this chapter to decrease those funds allocated by the governing body for existing citizen boards as provided for in § 66-34 hereof with the exception of those programs being funded by federal grant moneys.

History.
Code 1950, § 53-339; 1979, c. 698; 1982, c. 636, § 53.1-256; 1989, c. 733.

§ 66-32. Withdrawal from program.

Any participating county or city may, at the beginning of any calendar quarter, by ordinance or resolution of its governing authority, notify the Director of its intention to withdraw from the grant program. Such withdrawal shall be effective the last day of the quarter in which such notice is given.

History.
Code 1950, § 53-340; 1979, c. 698; 1982, c. 636, § 53.1-257; 1989, c. 733.

§ 66-33. Unexpended funds.

In any case in which any portion of state funds obtained through a grant authorized pursuant to this chapter remains unencumbered or unexpended at the end of the fiscal year, such funds shall be returned by the locality to the State Treasurer, who shall deposit such moneys in the state general fund.

History.
Code 1950, § 53-341; 1979, c. 698; 1982, c. 636, § 53.1-258; 1989, c. 733.

§ 66-34. Youth services citizen boards; appointment and qualifications of members.

Each county and city participating in a program funded by an approved grant shall be represented on a youth services citizen board. The board shall be appointed by the county or city governing body or combination thereof and may include in its membership representative elected officials, representatives of public and private agencies serving youths, citizens not employed by government or service agencies and at least one member who is below the age of eighteen years. A majority of the board shall be citizens who are not employed by government or service agencies and who are not elected governmental officials. The board shall actively participate with community representatives in the formulation of a comprehensive plan for the development, coordination and evaluation of the youth services program and shall make formal recommendations to the governing authority or authorities at least annually concerning the comprehensive plan and its implementation during the ensuing year.

History.
Code 1950, § 53-342; 1979, c. 698; 1982, c. 636, § 53.1-259; 1989, c. 733; 2000, c. 277.

§ 66-35. Responsibilities of local programs.

It shall be the responsibility of the local programs to:

1. Prepare and annually update a comprehensive plan based on an objective assessment of the community's youth development and delinquency prevention needs and resources;
2. Assist the locality in establishing and modifying programs and services to youth pursuant to § 16.1-309.3 on the basis of an objective assessment of the community's needs and resources;
3. Collaborate with public and private entities to maintain and disseminate an annual inventory of youth and parenting related services and programs available in the locality;
4. Collaborate with public and private entities to identify gaps in program services and identify potential funding sources to assist in developing programs to respond to identified gaps; and
5. Provide assistance to other community agencies and organizations, including the community policy and management team established pursuant to § 2.2-5204, in establishing and modifying programs and services to youth.

History.
Code 1950, § 53-343; 1979, c. 698; 1982, c. 636, § 53.1-260; 1989, c. 733; 1992, cc. 837, 880; 1993, cc. 232, 283; 2000, c. 277.

RULES OF SUPREME COURT OF VIRGINIA

Editor's note. — The rules contained in this publication include rule changes promulgated through April 1, 2016.

PART THREE A CRIMINAL PRACTICE AND PROCEDURE

Rule

Appendix of Forms.

Form

Form

Supreme Court Rules

Rule 3A:1. Scope.

These Rules govern criminal proceedings in circuit courts and juvenile and domestic relations district courts (except proceedings concerning a child in a juvenile and domestic relations district court) and before the magistrates defined in Rule 3A:2 except for cases which have been returned to the general district court. Special statutes applicable to practices and procedures in juvenile and domestic relations district courts are incorporated herein by this reference and in such cases shall prevail over the general rule set forth in Part 3A.

Rule 3A:2. Purpose and Interpretation; Definitions.

(a) *Purpose and Interpretation.* — These Rules are intended to provide for the just determination of criminal proceedings. They shall be interpreted so as to promote uniformity and simplicity in procedure, fairness in administration, and the elimination of unjustifiable expense and delay. Errors, defects, irregularities or variances that do not affect substantive rights shall not constitute reversible error.

(b) *Definitions.* — Except as otherwise expressly provided in this Part Three A or unless the context otherwise requires:

(1) "Clerk" includes deputy clerk.

(2) "Commonwealth's attorney" includes assistant or acting Commonwealth's attorney.

(3) "Continuance" includes adjournment or recess.

(4) "Indictment" includes presentment and information filed upon presentment.

(5) "Magistrate" means a judicial or quasi-judicial officer authorized to issue arrest and search warrants, commit arrested persons to jail or admit them to bail, or conduct preliminary hearings.

(6) "Recognizance" means an undertaking, with or without surety or other security, made before a magistrate to perform one or more acts — for example, to appear in court. A recognizance may be written or oral but, if oral, shall be evidenced by a memorandum signed by the magistrate.

(7) Writings or memoranda under these Rules, and any required signatures or sworn verifications,

shall be valid in the form of electronic files or digital images as provided in Rule 1:17.

Rule 3A:2.1. Venue in Criminal Cases.

In criminal cases, questions of venue must be raised in the trial court and before the verdict in cases tried by a jury and before the finding of guilty in cases tried by a court.

Rule 3A:3. The Complaint.

The complaint shall consist of sworn statements of a person or persons of facts relating to the commission of an alleged offense. The statements shall be made upon oath before a magistrate empowered to issue arrest warrants. The magistrate may require the sworn statements to be reduced to writing and signed if the complainant is a law-enforcement officer, but shall require the sworn statements to be reduced to writing if the complainant is not a law-enforcement officer.

Rule 3A:4. Arrest Warrant or Summons.

(a) *Issuance.* — More than one warrant or summons may issue on the same complaint. A warrant may be issued by a judicial officer if the accused fails to appear in response to a summons.

(b) *Form of Summons.* — A summons, whether issued by a magistrate or a law-enforcement officer, shall command the accused to appear at a stated time and place before a court of appropriate jurisdiction in the county, city or town in which the summons is issued. It shall (i) state the name of the accused or, if his name is unknown, set forth a description by which he can be identified with reasonable certainty, (ii) describe the offense charged and state whether the offense is a violation of state, county, city or town law, and (iii) be signed by the magistrate or the law-enforcement office, as the case may be.

(c) *Execution and Return.* — If a warrant has been issued but the officer does not have the warrant in his possession at the time of the arrest, he shall (i) inform the accused of the offense charged and that a warrant has been issued, and (ii) deliver a copy of the warrant to the accused as soon thereafter as practicable.

Rule 3A:5. The Grand Jury.

(a) *Who May Be Present.* — Only the grand jurors and the witness under examination and, if directed by the court, an interpreter shall be present during the hearing of evidence by a grand jury. Only the grand jurors shall be present during their deliberations and voting.

(b) *Secrecy.* — No obligation of secrecy may be imposed upon any person except in accordance with law.

(c) *Finding and Return of Indictment.* — The indictment shall be endorsed "A True Bill" or "Not a True Bill" and signed by the foreman. The indictment shall be returned by the grand jury in open court.

(d) *Motion to Dismiss.* — A motion to dismiss the indictment may be based on constitutional objections to the array or on the lack of legal qualification of an individual juror.

Rule 3A:6. The Indictment and the Information.

(a) *Contents.* — The indictment or information, in describing the offense charged, shall cite the statute or ordinance that defines the offense or, if there is no defining statute or ordinance, prescribes the punishment for the offense. Error in the citation of the statute or ordinance that defines the offense or prescribes the punishments therefor, or omission of the citation, shall not be grounds for dismissal of an indictment or information, or for reversal of a conviction, unless the court finds that the error or omission prejudiced the accused in preparing his defense.

(b) *Joinder of Offenses.* — Two or more offenses, any of which may be a felony or misdemeanor, may be charged in separate counts of an indictment or information if the offenses are based on the same act or transaction, or on two or more acts or transactions that are connected or constitute parts of a common scheme or plan.

(c) *Joinder of Defendants.* — Two or more accused may be charged with a count(s) of an indictment, if they are charged with participating in contemporaneous and related acts or occurrences or in a series of acts or occurrences constituting an offense or offenses.

(d) *Form.* — The indictment or information need not contain a formal commencement or conclusion. The return of an indictment shall be signed by the foreman of the grand jury, and the information shall be signed by the Commonwealth's attorney.

Rule 3A:7. Capias or Summons Upon Indictment or Information.

(a) *Form.* — (1) Capias. The form of the capias shall be the same as that provided for a warrant except that it shall be signed by the clerk and shall state that an indictment or information has been filed against the accused.

(2) Summons. The summons shall be in the same form as the capias except that it shall summons the accused to appear before the court at a stated time and place.

(b) *Execution and Return.* — (1) Execution. The capias shall be executed as provided in Rule 3A:4(c).

(2) Return. The officer executing a capias or summons shall endorse the date of execution thereon and make return thereof to the court that issued the capias or summons. At the request of the Commonwealth's attorney made at any time while the indictment or information is pending, a capias returned

unexecuted and not cancelled or a summons returned unexecuted or a duplicate thereof may be delivered by the clerk to any authorized person for execution.

Rule 3A:8. Pleas.

(a) *Pleas by a Corporation.* — A corporation, acting by counsel or through an agent, may enter the same pleas as an individual.

(b) *Determining Voluntariness of Pleas of Guilty or Nolo Contendere.* — (1) A circuit court shall not accept a plea of guilty or nolo contendere to a felony charge without first determining that the plea is made voluntarily with an understanding of the nature of the charge and the consequences of the plea.

(2) A circuit court shall not accept a plea of guilty or nolo contendere to a misdemeanor charge except in compliance with Rule 7C:6.

(c) *Plea Agreement Procedure.* — (1) The attorney for the Commonwealth and the attorney for the defendant or the defendant when acting pro se may engage in discussions with a view toward reaching an agreement that, upon entry by the defendant of a plea of guilty, or a plea of nolo contendere, to a charged offense, or to a lesser or related offense, the attorney for the Commonwealth will do any of the following:

(A) Move for nolle prosequi or dismissal of other charges;

(B) Make a recommendation, or agree not to oppose the defendant's request, for a particular sentence, with the understanding that such recommendation or request shall not be binding on the court;

(C) Agree that a specific sentence is the appropriate disposition of the case.

In any such discussions under this Rule, the court shall not participate.

(2) If a plea agreement has been reached by the parties, it shall, in every felony case, be reduced to writing, signed by the attorney for the Commonwealth, the defendant, and, in every case, his attorney, if any, and presented to the court. The court shall require the disclosure of the agreement in open court or, upon a showing of good cause, in camera, at the time the plea is offered. If the agreement is of the type specified in subdivision (c)(1)(A) or (C), the court may accept or reject the agreement, or may defer its decision as to the acceptance or rejection until there has been an opportunity to consider a presentence report. If the agreement is of the type specified in subdivision (c)(1)(B), the court shall advise the defendant that, if the court does not accept the recommendation or request, the defendant nevertheless has no right to withdraw his plea, unless the Commonwealth fails to perform its part of the agreement. In that event, the defendant shall have the right to withdraw his plea.

(3) If the court accepts the plea agreement, the court shall inform the defendant that it will embody in its judgment and sentence the disposition provided for in the agreement.

(4) If the agreement is of the type specified in subdivision (c)(1)(A) or (C) and if the court rejects the plea agreement, the court shall inform the parties of this fact, and advise the defendant personally in open court or, on a showing of good cause, in camera, that the court will not accept the plea agreement. Thereupon, neither party shall be bound by the plea agreement. The defendant shall have the right to withdraw his plea of guilty or plea of nolo contendere and the court shall advise the defendant that, if he does not withdraw his plea, the disposition of the case may be less favorable to him than that contemplated by the plea agreement; and the court shall further advise the defendant that, if he chooses to withdraw his plea of guilty or of nolo contendere, his case will be heard by another judge, unless the parties agree otherwise.

(5) Upon rejecting a plea agreement, a judge shall immediately recuse himself from any further proceedings on the same matter unless the parties agree otherwise.

(6) Except as otherwise provided by law, evidence of a plea of guilty later withdrawn, or a plea of nolo contendere, or of an offer to plead guilty or nolo contendere to the crime charged, or any other crime, or of statements made in connection with and relevant to any of the foregoing pleas or offers, is not admissible in the case-in-chief in any civil or criminal proceeding against the person who made the plea or offer. But evidence of a statement made in connection with and relevant to a plea of guilty, later withdrawn, a plea of nolo contendere, or any offer to plead guilty or nolo contendere to the crime charged or to any other crime, is admissible in any criminal proceeding for perjury or false statement, if the statement was made by the defendant under oath and on the record. In the event that a plea of guilty or a plea of nolo contendere is withdrawn in accordance with this Rule, the judge having received the plea shall take no further part in the trial of the case, unless the parties agree otherwise.

Rule 3A:9. Pleadings and Motions for Trial; Defenses and Objections.

(a) *Pleadings and Motions.* — Pleadings in a criminal proceeding shall be the indictment, information, warrant or summons on which the accused is to be tried and the plea of not guilty, guilty or nolo contendere. Defenses and objections made before trial that heretofore could have been made by other pleas or by demurrers and motions to quash shall be made only by motion to dismiss or to grant appropriate relief, as provided in these Rules.

(b) *The Motion Raising Defenses and Objections.* — (1) Defenses and Objections That Must Be Raised Before Trial. Defenses and objections based on defects in the institution of the prosecution or in the written charge upon which the accused is to be tried, other than that it fails to show jurisdiction in the court or to charge an offense, must be raised by motion made within the time prescribed by paragraph (c) of this Rule. The motion shall include all such defenses and objections then available to the accused. Failure to present any such defense or objection as herein provided shall constitute a waiver thereof. Lack of jurisdiction or the failure of the written charge upon which the accused is to be tried to state an offense shall be noticed by the court at any time during the pendency of the proceeding.

(2) Defenses and Objections That May Be Raised Before Trial. In addition to the defenses and objections specified in subparagraph (b) (1) of this Rule, any defense or objection that is capable of determination without the trial of the general issue may be raised by motion before trial. Failure to present any such defense or objection before the jury returns a verdict or the court finds the defendant guilty shall constitute a waiver thereof.

(3) Form of Motion. Any motion made before trial shall be in writing if made in a circuit court, unless the court for good cause shown permits an oral motion. A motion shall state with particularity the grounds or grounds on which it is based.

(4) Hearing on Motion. A motion before trial raising defenses or objections shall be determined before the trial unless the court orders that it be deferred for determination at the trial of the general issue. An issue of fact shall be heard and determined by the court, unless a jury trial is required by constitution or statute.

(5) Effect of Determination. If a motion is determined adversely to the accused, his plea shall stand or he may plead over or, if the accused has not previously pleaded, he shall be permitted to plead. The motion need not be renewed if the accused properly saves the point for the purpose of appeal when the court first determines the motion.

(c) *Time of Filing Notice or Making Motion.* — A motion referred to in subparagraph (b) (1) shall be filed or made before a plea is entered and, in a circuit court, at least 7 days before the day fixed for trial, or, if the motion raises speedy trial or Double Jeopardy grounds as specified in Code § 19.2-266.2(A)(ii), at such time prior to trial as the grounds for the motion or objection shall arise, whichever occurs last. A copy of such motion shall, at the time of filing, be submitted to the judge of the circuit court who will hear the case, if known.

(d) *Relief From Waiver.* — For good cause shown the court may grant relief from any waiver provided for in this Rule.

Rule 3A:10. Trial Together of More Than One Accused or More Than One Offense.

(a) *More Than One Accused — Joinder of Defendants.* — On motion of the Commonwealth, for good cause shown, the court shall order persons charged with participating in contemporaneous and related acts or occurrences or in a series of acts or occurrences constituting an offense or offenses to be tried jointly unless such joint trial would constitute prejudice to a defendant.

(b) *More Than One Accused — Severance of Defendants.* — If the court finds that a joint trial would constitute prejudice to a defendant, the court shall order severance as to that defendant or provide such other relief as justice requires.

(c) *An Accused Charged With More Than One Offense.* — The court may direct that an accused be tried at one time for all offenses then pending against him, if justice does not require separate trials and (i) the offenses meet the requirements of Rule 3A:6 (b) or (ii) the accused and the Commonwealth's attorney consent thereto.

Rule 3A:11. Discovery and Inspection.

(a) *Application of Rule.* — This Rule applies to any prosecution for a felony in a circuit court and to any misdemeanor brought on direct indictment.

(b) *Discovery by the Accused.* — (1) Upon written motion of an accused a court shall order the Commonwealth's attorney to permit the accused to inspect and copy or photograph any relevant (i) written or recorded statements or confessions made by the accused, or copies thereof, or the substance of any oral statements or confessions made by the accused to any law enforcement officer, the existence of which is known to the attorney for the Commonwealth, and (ii) written reports of autopsies, ballistic tests, fingerprint analyses, handwriting analyses, blood, urine and breath tests, other scientific reports, and written reports of a physical or mental examination of the accused or the alleged victim made in connection with the particular case, or copies thereof, that are known by the Commonwealth's attorney to be within the possession, custody or control of the Commonwealth.

(2) Upon written motion of an accused a court shall order the Commonwealth's attorney to permit the accused to inspect and copy or photograph designated books, papers, documents, tangible objects, buildings or places, or copies or portions thereof, that are within the possession, custody, or control of the Commonwealth, upon a showing that the items sought may be material to the preparation of his defense and that the request is reasonable. This subparagraph does not authorize the discovery or inspection of statements made by Commonwealth witnesses or prospective Commonwealth witnesses to agents of the Commonwealth or of reports, memoranda or other internal Commonwealth documents made by agents in connection with the investigation or prosecution of the case, except as provided in clause (ii) of subparagraph (b)(1) of this Rule.

(c) *Discovery by the Commonwealth.* — If the court grants relief sought by the accused under clause (ii) of subparagraph (b) (1) or under subparagraph (b) (2) of this Rule, it shall, upon motion of the Commonwealth, condition its order by requiring that:

(1) The accused shall permit the Commonwealth within a reasonable time but not less than ten (10) days before trial or sentencing, as the case may be, to inspect, copy or photograph any written reports of autopsy examinations, ballistic tests, fingerprint, blood, urine and breath analyses, and other scientific tests that may be within the accused's possession, custody or control and which the defense intends to proffer or introduce into evidence at trial or sentencing.

(2) The accused disclose whether he intends to introduce evidence to establish an alibi and, if so, that the accused disclose the place at which he claims to have been at the time of the commission of the alleged offense.

(3) If the accused intends to rely upon the defense of insanity or feeblemindedness, the accused shall permit the Commonwealth to inspect, copy or photograph any written reports of physical or mental examination of the accused made in connection with the particular case, provided, however, that no statement made by the accused in the course of an examination provided for by this Rule shall be used by the Commonwealth in its case-in-chief, whether the examination shall be with or without the consent of the accused.

(d) *Time of Motion.* — A motion by the accused under this Rule must be made at least 10 days before the day fixed for trial. The motion shall include all relief sought under this Rule. A subsequent motion may be made only upon a showing of cause why such motion would be in the interest of justice.

(e) *Time, Place and Manner of Discovery and Inspection.* — An order granting relief under this Rule shall specify the time, place and manner of making the discovery and inspection permitted and may prescribe such terms and conditions as are just.

(f) *Protective Order.* — Upon a sufficient showing the court may at any time order that the discovery or inspection be denied, restricted or deferred, or make such other order as is appropriate. Upon motion by the Commonwealth the court may permit the Commonwealth to make such showing, in whole or in part, in the form of a written statement to be inspected by the court in camera. If the court denies discovery or inspection following a showing in camera, the entire text of the Commonwealth's statement shall be sealed and preserved in the records of the court to be made available to the appellate court in the event of an appeal by the accused.

(g) *Continuing Duty to Disclose; Failure to Comply.* — If, after disposition of a motion filed under this Rule, and before or during trial, counsel or a party discovers additional material previously requested or falling within the scope of an order previously entered, that is subject to discovery or inspection under this Rule, he shall promptly notify the other party or his counsel or the court of the existence of the additional material. If at any time during the course of the proceedings, it is brought to the attention of the court that a party has failed to comply with this Rule or with an order issued pursuant to this Rule, the court shall order such party to permit the discovery or inspection of materials not previously disclosed, and may grant such other relief as it may deem appropriate.

Rule 3A:12. Subpoena.

(a) *For Attendance of Witnesses.* — A subpoena for the attendance of a witness to testify before a court not of record shall be issued by the judge, clerk, magistrate, Commonwealth's Attorney or by the attorney for the defendant. A subpoena for the attendance of a witness to testify before a circuit court or a grand jury shall be issued by the clerk or Commonwealth's Attorney and, for the attendance of a witness to testify before a circuit court, by the attorney for the defendant as well. The subpoena shall (i) be directed to an appropriate officer or officers, (ii) name the witness to be summoned, (iii) state the name of the court and the title, if any, of the proceeding, (iv) command the officer to summon the witness to appear at the time and place specified in the subpoena for the purpose of giving testimony, and (v) state on whose application the subpoena was issued.

No subpoena or subpoena duces tecum shall be issued in any criminal case or proceeding, including any proceeding before any grand jury, which subpoena or subpoena duces tecum is (i) directed to a member of the bar of this Commonwealth or any other jurisdiction, and (ii) compels production or testimony concerning any present or former client of the member of the bar, unless the subpoena request has been approved in all specifics, in advance, by a judge of the circuit court wherein the subpoena is requested after reasonable notice to the attorney who is the subject of the proposed subpoena. The proceedings for approval may be conducted in camera, in the judge's discretion, and the judge may seal such proceedings. Such subpoena request shall be made by the Commonwealth's attorney for the jurisdiction involved, either on motion of the Commonwealth's attorney or upon request to the Commonwealth's attorney by the foreman of any grand jury.

(b) *For Production of Documentary Evidence and of Objects Before a Circuit Court.* — Upon notice to the adverse party and on affidavit by the party applying for the subpoena that the requested writings or objects are material to the proceedings and are in the possession of a person not a party to the action, the judge or the clerk may issue a subpoena duces tecum for the production of writings or objects described in the subpoena. Such subpoena shall command either (1) that the person to whom it is addressed shall appear with the items described either before the court or the clerk or (2) that such person shall deliver the items described to the clerk. The subpoena may direct that the writing or object be produced at a time before the trial or before the time when it is to be offered in evidence.

Any subpoenaed writings and objects, regardless by whom requested, shall be available for examination and review by all parties and counsel. Subpoenaed writings or objects shall be received by the clerk and shall not be open for examination and review except by the parties and counsel unless otherwise directed by the court. The clerk shall adopt procedures to ensure compliance with this paragraph.

Where subpoenaed writings and objects are of such nature or content that disclosure to other parties would be unduly prejudicial, the court, upon written motion and notice to all parties, may grant such relief as it deems appropriate, including limiting disclosure, removal and copying.

If a subpoena requires the production of information that is stored in an electronic format, the person to whom it is addressed shall produce a tangible copy of the information. If a tangible copy cannot be reasonably produced, the subpoenaed person shall permit the parties to review the information on a computer or by electronic means during normal business hours, provided that the information can be accessed and isolated. If a tangible copy cannot reasonably be produced and the information is commingled with information other than that requested in the subpoena and cannot reasonably be isolated, the person to whom the subpoena is addressed may file a motion for a protective order or motion to quash.

(c) *Service and Return.* — A subpoena may be executed anywhere in the State by an officer authorized by law to execute the subpoena in the place where it is executed. The officer executing a subpoena shall make return thereof to the court named in the subpoena.

(d) *Contempt.* — Failure by any person without adequate excuse to obey a subpoena served upon him may be deemed a contempt of the court to which the subpoena is returnable.

(e) *Recognizance of a Witness.* — If it appears that the testimony of a person is material in any criminal proceeding, a judicial officer may require him to give a recognizance for his appearance.

(f) *Photocopying of Subpoenaed Documents.* — Subject to the provisions of subsection (b), removal and photocopying of subpoenaed documents by any party or counsel shall be permitted. The court shall direct a procedure for removal, photocopying and return of such documents.

Rule 3A:13. Trial by Jury or by Court.

(a) *Right to Jury; Duty of Court in Nonjury Trial.* — The accused is entitled to a trial by jury only in a circuit court on a plea of not guilty.

(b) *Waiver of Jury in Circuit Court.* — If an accused who has pleaded not guilty in a circuit court consents to trial without a jury, the court may, with the concurrence of the Commonwealth's attorney, try the case without a jury. The court shall determine before trial that the accused's consent was voluntarily and intelligently given, and his consent and the concurrence of the court and the Commonwealth's attorney shall be entered of record.

Rule 3A:14. Trial Jurors.

(a) *Examination.* — After the prospective jurors are sworn on the voir dire, the court shall question them individually or collectively to determine whether anyone:

(1) Is related by blood, adoption, or marriage to the accused or to a person against whom the alleged offense was committed;

(2) Is an officer, director, agent or employee of the accused;

(3) Has any interest in the trial or the outcome of the case;

(4) Has acquired any information about the alleged offense or the accused from the news media or other sources and, if so, whether such information would affect the juror's impartiality in the case;

(5) Has expressed or formed any opinion as to the guilt or innocence of the accused;

(6) Has a bias or prejudice against the Commonwealth or the accused; or

(7) Has any reason to believe the juror might not give a fair and impartial trial to the Commonwealth and the accused based solely on the law and the evidence.

Thereafter, the court, and counsel as of right, may examine on oath any prospective juror and ask any questions relevant to the qualifications as an impartial juror. A party objecting to a juror may introduce competent evidence in support of the objection.

(b) *Challenge for Cause.* — The court, on its own motion or following a challenge for cause, may excuse a prospective juror if it appears the juror is not qualified, and another shall be drawn or called and placed in the juror's stead for the trial of that case.

Rule 3A:14.1. Confidentiality of Juror Personal Information.

(a) *Motion for Order Regulating Disclosure of Jurors' Personal Information.* — As provided in Code § 19.2-263.3, on motion of any party or its own motion, and only upon a finding of good cause sufficient to warrant departure from the norm of open proceedings, the court may issue an order which may include provisions:

(1) regulating the disclosure of the personal information of jurors or prospective jurors in a criminal trial. The court may limit or preclude dissemination of such information to particular persons, but in no event shall such information be denied to counsel for either party; and/or

(2) requiring that during the course of the trial, counsel for the parties, and the jurors themselves, shall refer to jurors by number and not by name.

Under this Rule, a finding of "good cause" includes, but is not limited to, a determination by the court in a particular case that if personal information of jurors or prospective jurors is disclosed there is a reasonable possibility of bribery, tampering, physical injury, harassment, intimidation of a juror, or any other material interference with the proper discharge of the jury's functions, such as a reasonably perceived threat to the jury's safety, well-being, or capacity to properly focus upon and perform its trial and deliberative duties.

(b) *Modification of Order.* — An order under this Rule regulating the disclosure of personal information of the jurors in a criminal case may be modified by the court in the exercise of its discretion and for good cause shown, and such information may be disseminated to a person having a legitimate interest or need for the information, with such restrictions upon its use and further dissemination as may be deemed appropriate by the court.

(c) *Personal Information.* — For purposes of this Rule, "personal information" means any information collected by the court, clerk, or jury commissioner at any time, including but not limited to, a juror's name, age, occupation, home and business addresses, telephone numbers, email addresses, and any other identifying information that would assist another in locating or contacting the juror.

Rule 3A:15. Motion to Strike or to Set Aside Verdict; Judgment of Acquittal or New Trial.

(a) *Motion to Strike Evidence.* — After the Commonwealth has rested its case or at the conclusion of all the evidence, the court on motion of the accused may strike the Commonwealth's evidence if the evidence is insufficient as a matter of law to sustain a conviction. If the court overrules a motion to strike the evidence and there is a hung jury, the accused may renew the motion within the time specified in Rule 1:11 and the court may take the action authorized by the Rule.

(b) *Motion to Set Aside Verdict.* — If the jury returns a verdict of guilty, the court may, on motion of the accused made not later than 21 days after entry of a final order, set aside the verdict for error committed during the trial or if the evidence is insufficient as a matter of law to sustain a conviction.

(c) *Judgment of Acquittal or New Trial.* — The court shall enter a judgment of acquittal if it strikes the evidence or sets aside the verdict because the evidence is insufficient as a matter of law to sustain a conviction. The court shall grant a new trial if it sets aside the verdict for any other reason.

Rule 3A:16. Instructions.

(a) *Giving of Instructions.* — In a felony case, the instructions shall be reduced to writing. In all cases the court shall instruct the jury before arguments of counsel to the jury.

(b) *Proposed Instructions.* — If directed by the court the parties shall submit proposed instructions to the court at such reasonable time before or during the trial as the court may specify and, whether or not proposed instructions have been submitted earlier, the parties may submit proposed instructions at the conclusion of all the evidence.

(c) *Objections.* — Before instructing the jury, the court shall advise counsel of the instructions to be given and shall give counsel the opportunity to make objections thereto. Objections shall be made out of the presence of the jury, and before the court instructs the jury unless the court grants leave to make objections at a later time.

(d) *Alternative Forms of Verdicts; Separate Verdicts.* — The court may submit alternate forms of verdicts to the jury. The jury shall be instructed to return a separate verdict on each count of an indictment or presentment.

Rule 3A:17. Jury Verdicts.

(a) *Return.* — In all criminal prosecutions, the verdict shall be unanimous, in writing and signed by the foreman, and returned by the jury in open court.

(b) *Several Accused.* — If there are two or more accused, the jury may return a verdict as to any of them as to whom it can agree.

(c) *Conviction of Lesser Offense.* — The accused may be found not guilty of an offense charged but guilty of any offense, or of an attempt to commit any offense, that is substantially charged or necessarily included in the charge against the accused. When the offense charged is a felony, the accused may be found not guilty thereof, but guilty of being an accessory after the fact to that felony.

(d) *Poll of Jury.* — When a verdict is returned, the jury shall be polled individually at the request of any party or upon the court's own motion. If upon the poll, all jurors do not agree, the jury may be directed to retire for further deliberations or may be discharged.

Rule 3A:17.1. Proceedings in Bifurcated Jury Trials of Non-Capital Felonies and Class 1 Misdemeanors.

(a) *Application.* — This Rule applies in cases of trial by jury upon a finding that the defendant is guilty of a non-capital felony or a Class 1 misdemeanor.

(b) *Bifurcated Proceedings.* — In any jury trial in which the jury returns a verdict of guilty to one or more non-capital felony offenses, or Class 1 misdemeanor a separate proceeding limited to the ascertainment of punishment shall be held as soon as practicable before the same jury.

(c) *Instruction at Guilt Phase.* — At the conclusion of all of the evidence in the guilt phase of the trial, the court shall instruct the jury as to punishment with respect to any Class 2, 3 or 4 misdemeanor being tried in the same proceeding or any lesser-included Class 2, 3 or 4 misdemeanor of any charged felony offense which may be properly considered by the jury. The jury shall not be instructed until the punishment phase with reference to the punishment for any charged or lesser-included felony offense or Class 1 misdemeanor.

(d) *Opening Statements at Penalty Phase.* — Both the Commonwealth and the defense shall be entitled if they choose, to make an opening statement prior to the presentation of any evidence to the jury relevant to the penalty to be imposed. The Commonwealth shall give its statement first.

(e) *Presentation of Evidence at Penalty Phase.* — If the jury convicts the defendant of one or more non-capital felony offenses, or a Class 1 misdemeanor the penalty phase shall proceed in the following order:

(1) The Commonwealth may present any victim impact testimony pursuant to § 19.2-295.3 and shall present the defendant's prior criminal history, including prior convictions and the punishments imposed, by certified, attested, or exemplified copies of the final order(s) as provided by law. As a prerequisite to the introduction of such evidence, the Commonwealth shall have advised the defense, in accord with the requirements of law, of its intention to introduce such evidence.

(2) The defense may introduce relevant admissible evidence related to punishment. The defense shall have the opportunity to present such evidence irrespective of whether or not the Commonwealth presents evidence of previous criminal history.

(3) The Commonwealth may introduce relevant admissible evidence related to punishment in rebuttal.

(4) The defense may introduce relevant, admissible evidence related to punishment in rebuttal.

(f) *Closing Arguments at Penalty Phase.* — Both the Commonwealth and defense shall be entitled to make a closing argument on the subject of punishment if they elect to do so. The Commonwealth shall be given the opportunity to argue first, followed by the defense. Rebuttal argument may be made by the Commonwealth.

(g) *Change of Plea.* — The accused may enter a plea of guilty to the whole of the indictment at any time until the jury returns a verdict on the issue of the defendant's guilt or innocence.

(h) *Non-Unanimous Jury at the Penalty Phase.* — Should the jury fail to reach unanimous agreement as to punishment on any charge for which it returned a verdict of guilty, the court shall impanel a different jury to ascertain punishment, unless the defendant, the attorney for the Commonwealth and the court agree that the court shall fix punishment in the manner provided in Section 19.2-257, for the offense upon which the jury unanimously returned a verdict of guilty.

Rule 3A:18. Death Penalty.

The trial of capital cases shall proceed in accordance with the provisions of Article 4.1 of Chapter 15 of Title 19.2 and, except to the extent conflicting therewith, the provisions of this Part Three A shall be applicable thereto.

Except for good cause shown, the separate proceeding provided for in Section 19.2-264.3 C shall commence as if it were a continuation of the original trial and continue from day to day until concluded.

Rule 3A:19. Appeals.

(a) *Appeal From Conviction in a Circuit Court.* — See Part Five of these Rules.

(b) *Appeal From Conviction in a Juvenile and Domestic Relations District Court.* — The accused or his counsel shall advise the judge or clerk of the juvenile and domestic relations district court, within 10 days after conviction, of his intention to appeal. The appeal shall be noted on the warrant or summons and, if the accused does not withdraw his appeal before the expiration of the 10-day period, the papers shall be filed with the circuit court at the end of such period. Paying a fine or beginning to serve a sentence does not impair the right to appeal.

Rule 3A:20. Time.

(a) *Extension.* — When under this Part Three A an act is required or allowed to be done at or within a specified time, the court for cause shown may at any time in its discretion (1) with or without motion or notice, order the period extended if request therefor is made before the expiration of the period originally prescribed or as extended by a previous order, or (2) upon motion made after the expiration of the specified period, permit the act to be done if the failure to act was the result of excusable neglect; but the court may not extend the time for taking any action under Rules 3A:15 and 19; except to the extent and under the conditions stated in those Rules.

(b) *Unaffected by Expiration of Term.* — The period of time specified in this Part Three A for taking any action is not affected or limited by the expiration of a term of court.

Rule 3A:21. Service and Filing of Papers.

(a) *Copies of Written Motions to Be Furnished.* — All written motions and notices not required to be served as process shall be served otherwise on each counsel of record by delivering or mailing a copy to him on or before the day of filing. In any case where electronic service and filing is permitted under Rule 1:17, delivery of an electronic copy or digital image of a document shall satisfy this requirement. At the foot of such motions and notices shall be appended either acceptance of service or a certificate of counsel that copies were served as this Rule requires, showing the date of delivery or mailing.

(b) *Filing.* — Motions, notices and other items required to be served shall be filed with the clerk.

Rule 3A:22. Forms.

Forms 1 through 9 and 11 in the Appendix of Forms are illustrative and not mandatory; however, Form 10 requires substantial compliance.

Rule 3A:23. Electronic Filing.

In any circuit court which has established an electronic filing system for criminal cases pursuant to Rule 1:17:

(a) Any criminal proceeding may be designated as an Electronically Filed Case upon consent of the Commonwealth and all defendants in the case.

(b) Except where service and/or filing of an original paper document is expressly required by these rules, all pleadings, motions, notices and other instruments in an Electronically Filed Case shall be formatted, served and filed as specified in the requirements and procedures of Rule 1:17; provided, however, that when any document listed below is filed in the case, the filing party shall notify the clerk of court that the original document must be retained.

(1) Any pleading or affidavit required by statute or rule to be sworn, verified or certified as provided in Rule 1:17(e)(5).

(2) Any check or other negotiable instrument.

(3) Any handwritten statement, waiver, or consent by a defendant or witness in a criminal proceeding.

(4) Any form signed by a defendant in a criminal proceeding, including any typed statements or a guilty plea form.

(5) Any document that cannot be converted into an electronic document in such a way as to produce a clear and readable image.

Rule 3A:24. Special Rule Applicable to Post-Conviction Proceedings: Circuit Court Orders Denying Petitions for Writs of Habeas Corpus.

Any Order of a circuit court denying a petition for a writ of habeas corpus shall include findings of fact and conclusions of law as required by Code § 8.01-654(B)(5). The order shall identify the substance of the claims asserted in the petition, and state the specific reason for the denial of each claim. Any such order may adopt a trial court's written opinion explaining its decision or a transcribed explanation of the court's ruling from the bench; however, an order shall not deny the petition without explanation, or rely upon incorporation by reference of a pleading filed in the case.

Rule 3A:25. Special Rule Applicable to Post-Conviction Proceedings: Inmate Filings in the Trial Courts Under Code § 8.01-654.

In actions brought under Code § 8.01-654, filed by an inmate confined to an institution, a paper is timely filed if deposited in the institution's internal mail system, with first-class postage prepaid on or before the last day for filing. Timely filing of a paper by an inmate confined to an institution may be established by (1) an official stamp of the institution showing that the paper was deposited in the internal mail system on or before the last day for filing, (2) an official postmark dated on or before the last day for filing, or (3) a notarized statement signed by an official of the institution showing that the paper was deposited in the internal mail system on or before the last day for filing.

APPENDIX OF FORMS.

Form 1. Criminal Complaint (Rule 3A:3).

CRIMINAL COMPLAINT RULES 3A:3 and 7C:3

.... ☐ General District Court
☐ Juvenile and Domestic Relations District Court

I, The undersigned Complainant this day make oath that I have reason to believe that the Accused, on or about .... (DATE)

in the ☐ City ☐ County ☐ Town of ....

Committed an offense as follows:

....

....

I base my belief on the following facts:

....

....

....

....

....

....

The statements above are true and accurate to the best of my knowledge and belief.

In making this complaint, I have read and fully understand the following:

- By swearing to these facts, I also obligate myself to appear in court and testify on behalf of the Commonwealth of Virginia or the city, county or town whose laws allegedly have been violated if a warrant or summons is issued.
- The charge in this warrant cannot be dismissed except by the court, even at my request.

____________________ SIGNATURE OF COMPLAINANT

Subscribed and sworn to before me this day.

.... DATE AND TIME ____________________ ☐ CLERK ☐ MAGISTRATE ☐ JUDGE

FORM DC-311 6/89 (114:9-015 7/91)

Case No.

CRIMINAL COMPLAINT

ACCUSED: Name, Description, Address / Location

.... LAST NAME, FIRST NAME, MIDDLE INITIAL

....

....

COMPLETE DATA BELOW IF KNOWN

RACE	SEX	BORN MO.	BORN DAY	BORN YR.	HT. FT.	HT. IN.	WGT.	EYES	HAIR
SSN									

other identification or location information

....

....

....

....

COMPLAINANT: Name, Address, Title (if any) and telephone number

....

....

....

....

....

Form 2. Statement of Witness for Arrest Warrant (Rule 3A:3).

Witness: (Name and address) ....

....

(County) (City) of ....

I, the undersigned witness, after being duly sworn, make oath that I have personal knowledge of the following facts: ....

....

....

....

....

____

(Signature of complainant and title, if any)

Subscribed and sworn to before me this day.

____________________ ______________________________

(Date and time) (Signature and title)

Form 3. Summons (Rule 3A:4(b)).

SUMMONS VA. CODE § 19.2-73 RULE 3A:4

CITY OR COUNTY

☐ General District Court

STREET ADDRESS OF COURT

☐ Juvenile and Domestic Relations District Court

STREET ADDRESS OF COURT

TO THE ACCUSED:
You are hereby commanded to appear before this Court on

DATE AND TIME OF HEARING . . . to answer the charge that on or about . . . . . . DATE . . . . . ,

within this ☐ Town of . . . . ☐ CITY ☐ COUNTY you did unlawfully

. . . .

in violation of Section . . . . , ☐ Code of Virginia (OR)

☐ Ordinances of this City, County, or Town.

You must appear in court at the time and place shown above and to appear at all other times and places and before any court or judge to which this case may be rescheduled, continued, transferred or appealed.

WARNING TO THE ACCUSED: You may be tried and convicted in your absence if you fail to appear in response to this summons. Willful failure to appear is a separate offense.

I, the undersigned, have found probable cause to believe that the Accused committed the offense charged, based on the sworn statements of:

. . . . , Complainant.

. . . . . . DATE AND TIME ISSUED . . . . ☐ CLERK ☐ MAGISTRATE ☐ JUDGE

CASE NO.

ACCUSED:

. . . . . . LAST NAME, FIRST NAME, MIDDLE NAME . . . . . .

. . . . . . ADDRESS/LOCATION . . . . . .

To be completed upon service
Mailing address ☐ Same as above

☐ . . . .

COMPLETE DATA BELOW IF KNOWN

RACE	SEX	BORN MO.	BORN DAY	BORN YR.	HT FT.	HT IN.	WGT.	EYES	HAIR

SSN

☐ Commonwealth of Virginia
☐ CITY ☐ COUNTY ☐ TOWN of

. . . .

SUMMONS
CLASS ________ MISDEMEANOR

☐ EXECUTED by delivering a true copy of this summons to the Accused in person today.
☐ For legal entities other than individuals, service pursuant to Va. Code § 19.2-76.
☐ The Accused certified to me the above mailing address.

. . . . . . DATE AND TIME OF SERVICE . . . . . .

____________________, SERVING OFFICER

____
BADGE NO., AGENCY AND JURISDICTION

for ____________________
SHERIFF

Attorney for the Accused:

HEARING DATE AND TIME

☐ Motion to Change Bond on: ....
☐ changed to $ ....
☐ no change

JUDGE

The Accused was this day:
☐ tried in absence
☐ present

Attorneys Present:

☐ PROSECUTING ATTORNEY (NAME)

☐ DEFENDANT'S ATTORNEY (NAME)

☐ NO ATTORNEY
☐ ATTORNEY WAIVED
☐ If convicted, no jail sentence will be imposed.

☐ Translator/Interpreter present:

NAME

The Accused PLEADED:
☐ not guilty
☐ nolo contendere
☐ guilty

☐ Plea Bargain ☐ Plea and Recommendation

And was TRIED and FOUND by me:
☐ not guilty
☐ guilty as charged
☐ guilty of. ....
☐ facts sufficient to find guilt but defer adjudication/disposition and place accused on first time offender probation, §§ 18.2-57.3, 18.2-251 or 19.2-303.2.

And was FOUND by me to be:
☐ driving a commercial motor vehicle
☐ carrying hazardous materials

☐ I ORDER the charge dismissed
☐ I ORDER a nolle prosequi on prosecution's motion
☐ I ORDER the charge dismissed:
☐ conditioned upon payment of costs (accord and satisfaction) § 19.2-151
☐ conditioned upon payment of costs and successful completion of traffic school § 16.1-69.48:1

....
DATE

I impose the following Sentence:

☐ FINE of $ ....
with $ ....suspended;
☐ JAIL sentence of ....imposed
with ....suspended
conditioned upon being of good behavior and keeping the peace, and paying fines and costs. Pursuant to § 53.1-187, credit is granted from pre-trial detention.
☐ Serve jail sentence on weekends beginning ....
....
☐ Work release authorized if eligible
☐ Work release required
☐ Payment of $ .... to defray cost of incarceration
☐ on PROBATION for ....
☐ DRIVER'S LICENSE suspended ....
....
☐ Referred to VASAP
☐ Restricted Driver's License
☐ Travel to/from work ☐ Travel to/from VASAP
☐ Travel during work ☐ Travel to/from school
☐ Medically necessary travel ☐ Ignition Interlock
☐ Travel to/from day care/school/medical service facility for child
☐ Referred to community-based corrections program
☐ RESTITUTION of $ ....
due by ....
Payable to. ....
with interest thereon from. ....
as condition of suspended sentence.
☐ ....hours of community service to be performed for
....
....
☐ in addition to other sentence provisions
☐ to be credited against fines and costs
at $ ..../hr.
☐ Contact prohibited between defendant and victim/victim's spouse and children pursuant to Va. Code § 18.2-60.3.
☐ Other:
....
....
Bail on Appeal $ ....
☐ Remanded for CCRE Report

JUDGE

Case No.: ....

FINE

..........................$ ....
LOCALITY

COSTS

112 }		$................
140 }	PROCESSING FEE	....
143		....
107 DOAF		....
113 WITNESS FEE		....
113 SENTENCE FEE		....
113 DRUG ANALYSIS FEE		....
113 NON-CONSEC. JAIL FEE		....
113		....
120 CT. APPT. ATTY.		....
125 WEIGHING FEE		....
132 CICF		....
133 BLOOD TEST FEE		....
137 TTP		....
223 LIQUIDATED DAMAGES		....
229 CHMF		....
OTHER (SPECIFY):		
....		$................
TOTAL		$

:np

Form 4. Indictments (Rule 3A:6).

Murder

COMMONWEALTH OF VIRGINIA

.... Court

..............................., 20....

The Grand Jury charges that:

On or about ...., 20.... in the (County) (City) of .... the accused ....

(Name of accused)

feloniously did kill and murder .... *

(Name of victim)

Va. Code §§ 18.2-31, 18.2-32, 19.2-221.
A True Bill.

....

(Foreman)

Attempted Grand Larceny

On or about ...., 20..... in the (County) (City) of .... the accused ....

(Name of accused)

feloniously attempted to steal property, namely ....

(Describe property)

having a value of ($5 or more from the person of ....)

(Name of victim)

($200 or more belonging to ....).

(Name of victim)

(firearm of any value) belonging to ....

(Name of victim)

Va. Code §§ 18.2-95 and 18.2-26.

Burglary (Common Law)

On or about ...., 20..... in the (County) (City) of .... the accused ....

(Name of accused)

feloniously did break and enter in the nighttime
the dwelling house of ....

(Name of victim)

with intent to commit a (felony) (larceny) therein.
Va. Code § 18.2-89.

Statutory (Burglary, Murder, Rape, Robbery, Arson)
(Va. Code § 18.2-90)

On or about ...., 20..... in the (County) (City) of .... the accused ....

(Name of accused)

feloniously did (enter in the nighttime) (break and enter in the daytime) (enter and conceal himself in the daytime)

.... , with intent to

* Language charging other offenses follows.

(Place described in Va. Code § 18.2-90)
commit (murder)(rape)(robbery)(arson).
Va. Code § 18.2-90.

Statutory Burglary, Va. Code § 18.2-91

On or about ...., 20..... in the (County) (City) of ....
the accused ....
(Name of accused)
feloniously did (enter in the nighttime) (break and enter in the daytime) (enter and conceal himself in the daytime)
...., with intent to
(Place described in Va. Code § 18.2-90)
commit (larceny) (...)
(Describe felony other than murder, rape, robbery or arson)
(assault and battery).
Va. Code § 18.2-91.

Driving While Intoxicated

On or about ...., 20..... in the (County) (City) of ....
the accused ....
(Name of accused)
(feloniously and) unlawfully did operate a motor vehicle while under the influence of alcohol, narcotic drug, or other self-administered intoxicant or drug of whatever nature.
Va. Code § 18.2-266.

Forgery—Check

On or about ...., 20..... in the (County) (City) of ....
the accused ....
(Name of accused)
feloniously forged with the intent to defraud a check of the following words and figures:

...., 20.....
(Bank) (Date)
Pay to the order of .... $................ Dollars
(Endorsed ....).
Va. Code § 18.2-172.

Malicious or Unlawful Wounding

On or about ...., 20..... in the (County) (City) of ....
the accused ....
(Name of accused)
feloniously (maliciously) (unlawfully but not maliously) caused bodily injury
to ....
(Name of victim)
with intent to maim, disfigure, disable or kill.
Va. Code § 18.2-51.

Rape

On or about ...., 20..... in the (County) (City) of ....
the accused ....
(Name of accused)
feloniously did rape ....
(Name of victim)
Va. Code § 18.2-61.

Rape (Statutory, of Female of Age 13 or 14)

On or about ...., 20..... in the (County) (City) of ....
the accused ....
(Name of accused)
feloniously had (sexual intercourse with) (carnal knowledge of)
....
(Name of victim)
age ....
(Age of victim at time of offense)
Va. Code § 18.2-63.

Robbery

On or about ...., 20..... in the (County) (City) of ....
the accused ....
(Name of accused)
feloniously did rob ....
(Name of victim)
of ....
(Describe property)
Va. Code § 18.2-58.

Uttering—Check

On or about ...., 20..... in the (County) (City) of ....
the accused ....
(Name of accused)
feloniously uttered with the intent to defraud a forged check of the following words and figures:
...., 20.....
(Bank) (Date)
Pay to the order of .... $............... Dollars
(Endorsed ....).
Va. Code § 18.2-172.

Form 5. Capias (Rule 3A:7).

.... Court
Accused: (Name, description, address/location) ....
....
TO: .... or any other authorized officer
(Designation of officer)
You are hereby commanded in the name of the Commonwealth to forthwith arrest the accused and to bring him (her) before this Court to answer a charge that he (she) committed an offense in the (County) (City) of
...., on
or about ...., ..., namely ....
(Describe offense)
....
.... as charged in an (indictment) (presentment)
(information) dated ...., ...

....
(Date) (Clerk)

Form 6. Suggested Questions to Be Put by the Court to an Accused Who Has Pleaded Guilty (Rule 3A:8).

Before accepting your plea of guilty, I will ask you certain questions. If you do not understand any question, please ask me to explain it to you.

1. (a) What is your full name? ______
(b) What is your date of birth? ______
(c) What was the last grade in school which you completed? ______
(d) What other education have you received? ______
2. Are you the person charged in the (indictment) (presentment) (information) (warrant) with commission of the offense(s) of ______
3. Do you fully understand the charge(s) against you? ______
Have you discussed the charge(s) and (its) (their) elements with your lawyer and do you understand what the Commonwealth must prove before you may be found guilty of (this) (these) charge(s)? ______
4. Have you had enough time to discuss with your lawyer any possible defenses which you may have to (this) (these) charge(s)? ______
5. Have you discussed with your lawyer whether you should plead not guilty or guilty? ______
6. After the discussion, did you decide for yourself that you should plead guilty? ______
7. Are you entering the plea of guilty freely and voluntarily? ______
8. Are you entering the plea of guilty because you are, in fact, guilty of the crime(s) charged? ______
[If the defendant answers "No,"
(a) Have the Commonwealth summarize the evidence on the record.
(b) Ask the defendant, "Are you pleading guilty because this is the Commonwealth's evidence, and you do not wish to take the risk that you will be found guilty beyond a reasonable doubt?"
(c) If the defendant answers "Yes," the court may, but need not, accept the plea; if the court accepts the plea, the court should note that there is substantial evidence against the defendant. Otherwise the court should not accept the plea. (See North Carolina v. Alford, 400 U.S. 25 (1970).]
9. Do you understand that, by pleading guilty, you are NOT entitled to a trial by jury? ______
10. Do you understand that, by pleading guilty, you waive your right not to incriminate yourself? ______
11. Do you understand that, by pleading guilty, you waive your right to confront and cross-examine your accusers? ______
12. Do you understand that, by pleading guilty, you waive your right to defend yourself? ______
13. [If the accused is in prison, on parole, or probation,]
Do you understand that conviction may (affect your right to parole) (cause revocation of your parole/probation?)
14. [If the crime involves possession/distribution of drugs,]
Have you discussed with your lawyer whether the defense of accommodation may apply in this case?
15. [If the accused may be sentenced under the habitual offender statute,]
Have you discussed with your lawyer the possibility that there may be mitigating circumstances that permit this court not to impose the mandatory sentence?
16. Has anyone connected with your arrest and prosecution, such as the police or the Commonwealth's attorney, or any other person, in any manner threatened you or forced you to enter this plea of guilty? Have they made any promises concerning your plea of guilty?
17. Do you understand that the maximum punishment for this crime is ______ years imprisonment and $______ fine plus all court costs? (If a guilty plea involves more than one offense, substitute the following: Do you understand that if you are sentenced consecutively, the maximum punishment for these crimes is ______ years imprisonment and $______ fine plus all court costs?) [If the crime has a mandatory punishment, also question accused on his understanding of the mandatory punishment.]
18. (a) Do you understand that if you are not a citizen of the United States and if you plead guilty or are found to be guilty, there may be consequences of deportation, exclusion from admission into the United States, or denial of naturalization pursuant to the laws of the United States?
(b) Are you entirely satisfied with the service (of the lawyer who was appointed to represent you) (of the lawyer representing you) in this matter?
19. Do you understand that, by pleading guilty, you may waive any right to appeal the decision of this court? [The judge may, but need not, inform the defendant that a guilty plea does not waive the right to appeal lack of jurisdiction or imposition of an impermissible sentence.]
20. [If a written guilty plea form is used,]
(a) Have you read the guilty plea form? ______
(b) Do you understand the guilty plea form? ______
(c) Are the statements in the guilty plea form true? ______
21. Have you entered into a plea agreement with the Commonwealth's attorney in this case? If the answer is in the affirmative, read or otherwise put the plea agreement into the record, then ask the following: Does it contain the full and complete agreement entered into among you, your lawyer, and the Commonwealth's attorney? Complete either (a) or (b), whichever is appropriate:
(a) [To be asked if the Commonwealth's attorney has agreed that a particular sentence is appropriate.] Do you understand that:

(1) The court may accept the agreement, reject the agreement, or may defer any decision to either accept or reject until there has been an opportunity to consider a presentence report? ______

(2) If the court accepts the agreement, the court will include in its judgment and sentence the sentence provided for in the agreement? ______

(3) If the court rejects the agreement, you will not be bound by the agreement and you will be given an opportunity to withdraw your plea of guilty, and if you do, your trial may be conducted by another judge of this court? ______

(4) If you still plead guilty after the court rejects the plea agreement, the sentence in the case may be more severe than the disposition contained in the plea agreement? ______

(b) [To be used if the Commonwealth's attorney merely recommends, or agrees not to oppose a request for, a specific sentence.] Do you understand that this agreement only provides for the Commonwealth's attorney (to make a recommendation) (to agree not to oppose a request for) a particular sentence, that this recommendation or request is not binding on the court, and if the court does not accept the recommendation or does not go along with the request, you have no right to withdraw your plea of guilty unless the Commonwealth fails to perform its part of the agreement? Do you also understand that the sentence the court imposes may be more severe than the sentence (recommended) (requested)?

22. [If the defendant was a juvenile at the time of the offense,]
Do you understand that if you were tried for this offense and found guilty, the court and not the jury would set the sentence? ______

23. Do you understand all of these questions? ______

24. Do you have any questions you wish to ask the court? ______

Form 7. Suggested Questions to Be Put by the Court to an Accused Who Has Pleaded Not Guilty (Rule 3A:8).

Before accepting your plea of not guilty, I will ask you certain questions. If you do not understand any question, please ask me to explain it to you.

1. What is your full name and what is your age? ______
2. Are you the person charged in the (indictment) (information) (warrant) with the commission of the offense(s)? ______
3. Do you fully understand the charge(s) against you? ______
4. Have you discussed the charge(s) with your lawyer? ______
5. Have you had enough time to discuss with your lawyer any possible defense you may have to (this) (these) charge(s)? ______
6. Have you given your lawyer the names of witnesses, and if so, are they present? ______
7. Are you entirely satisfied with the services of your lawyer? ______
8. Are you entering this plea of not guilty freely and voluntarily? ______
9. Are you ready for trial today? ______
10. Do you understand that you are entitled to a trial by jury, but that you can consent to trial by the judge without a jury? ______
Have you discussed with your lawyer the advisability of trial by a jury or by the judge without a jury?
Do you wish to be tried by a jury or by the judge without a jury? ______
11. Do you understand all of the questions I have asked you? ______

These questions were asked of the defendant in open court in the absence of a jury on ______, 20____

______
Signature of defendant

______
Signature of attorney representing defendant

Form 8. Subpoena (Rule 3A:12(a)).

.... Court

....

(Address of court)

TO: .... or any other authorized officer

(Designation of officer)

You are commanded to summon ....

(Name and address)

TO the person summoned:

You are commanded to appear in this Court on ...., 20.... at .... a.m., to testify in the case of Commonwealth v. ....

This subpoena is issued on application of the (Commonwealth) (City) (County) (Town) (Defendant) (Juvenile) in the case of the Commonwealth v.

....

....

(Date) (Judge) (Clerk) (Commonwealth's Attorney)

Form 9. Subpoena Duces Tecum (Rule 3A:12(b)).

.... Court

....

(Address of court)

TO: .... or any other authorized officer

(Designation of officer)

You are commanded to summon ....

(Name and address)

TO the person summoned:

[ ] You are commanded to appear in (this Court) (the Clerk's office of this Court) on ...., 20.... at .... a.m./p.m., and to bring with you the following:

....

....

....

....

OR

[ ] You are commanded to deliver to the Clerk's office of this Court on or before ...., 20.... at .... a.m./p.m. the following:

....

....

....

....

This subpoena is issued on application of the (Commonwealth) (City) (County) (Town) (Defendant) (Juvenile) in the case of the Commonwealth v.

....

....

(Date) (Judge) (Clerk)

Supreme Court Rules

Form 10. Contents of Sentencing Orders.

(Pursuant to the provisions of Code § 19.2-307, all orders wherein an accused is sentenced for a criminal conviction shall conform substantially to the following form. In cases where no prior criminal conviction order has been entered of record, state the defendant's plea, the verdict or findings, the adjudication, whether or not the case was tried by a jury, and, if not, whether the consent of the accused was concurred in by the court and the attorney for the Commonwealth.)

SENTENCING ORDER

VIRGINIA: IN THE CIRCUIT COURT OF ______________________________

FEDERAL INFORMATION PROCESSING STANDARDS CODE: ______

Hearing Date: ____________________
Judge: ____________________

COMMONWEALTH OF VIRGINIA

v.

____________________, DEFENDANT

This case came before the Court for sentencing of the defendant, who appeared in person with his attorney, ____________________. The Commonwealth was represented by ____________________.

On ____________________ the defendant was found guilty of the following offenses:

CASE NUMBER	OFFENSE DESCRIPTION AND INDICATOR	OFFENSE DATE	VA. CODE SECTION	VIRGINIA CRIME CODE REFERENCE
______	______________	______	______	______
______	______________	______	______	______

The presentence report was considered and is ordered filed as a part of the record in this case in accordance with the provisions of Code § 19.2-299.

Pursuant to the provisions of Code § 19.2-298.01, the Court has considered and reviewed the applicable discretionary sentencing guidelines and the guidelines worksheets. The sentencing guidelines worksheets and the written explanation of any departure from the guidelines are ordered filed as a part of the record in this case.

Before pronouncing the sentence, the Court inquired if the defendant desired to make a statement and if the defendant desired to advance any reason why judgment should not be pronounced.

The Court **SENTENCES** the defendant to:

Incarceration with the Virginia Department of Corrections for the term of: ____________ for ____________, and ____________ for ____________. The total sentence imposed is ____________.

This sentence shall run (concurrently/consecutively) with ____________.

The Court **SUSPENDS** ____________ of the ____________ sentence and ____________ of the ____________ sentence, for a period of ____________, for a total suspension of ____________, upon the following condition(s):

Good behavior. The defendant shall be of good behavior for ________ from the defendant's release from confinement.

Supervised probation. ____________ of the sentence of incarceration is suspended. The defendant is placed on probation to commence ____________ under the supervision of a Probation Officer for ____________ or unless sooner released by the court or by the Probation Officer. The defendant shall comply with all the rules and requirements set by the Probation Officer. Probation shall include substance abuse counseling and/or testing as prescribed by the Probation Officer.

Community-based Corrections System Program pursuant to Virginia Code § 19.2-316.2 or 19.2-316.3. The defendant shall successfully complete the ______________ program. Successful program completion shall be followed by a period of intensive probation supervision of ______________ and followed by a period of supervised probation of (at least one year). (If applicable: The defendant shall remain in custody until program entry.)

Post-Incarceration supervision following felony conviction pursuant to Virginia Code § 18.2-10 and 19.2-295.2.

A. **Post-Incarceration Supervised Probation:** The court has imposed above a term of ______________ ______________ of incarceration and has suspended (at least 6 months) of the term of incarceration. The defendant is placed on supervised probation to commence upon release from incarceration for a period of (at least 6 months), unless released earlier by the court. The defendant shall comply with all the rules and requirements set by the Probation Officer.

OR

B. **Post-Incarceration Post-release Supervision:** In addition to the above sentence of incarceration, the court imposes an additional term of (not less than 6 months nor more than 3 years) of incarceration. This term is suspended and a period of post-release supervision of (not less than 6 months nor more than 3 years), which is to commence upon release from incarceration. The defendant shall comply with all the rules and requirements set by the Probation Officer.

Special Conditions. The defendant shall complete any substance abuse screening, assessment, testing and treatment as directed by the Probation Officer, as well as the following conditions: ______________.

Costs. The defendant shall pay costs of ______________.

Fine. A fine of $______________ for ______________.

Restitution. The defendant shall make restitution as follows: ________ to ______________.

DNA and Fingerprints. The defendant shall provide a DNA sample and legible fingerprints as directed.

Credit for time served. The defendant shall be given credit for time spent in confinement while awaiting trial pursuant to Code § 53.1-187.

____
DATE

ENTER: ______________
JUDGE

DEFENDANT IDENTIFICATION:
Name: ______________
Alias: ______________
SSN: ______________ DOB: ______________ Sex: ______

SENTENCING SUMMARY:

TOTAL INCARCERATION SENTENCE IMPOSED: ______________
TOTAL SENTENCE SUSPENDED: ______________
TOTAL SUPERVISED PROBATION TERM: ______________
TOTAL POSTRELEASE TERM IMPOSED and
SUSPENDED: ______________

Form 11. Misdemeanor Proceedings in District and Circuit Courts (Rule 3A:8(b)(2); Rule 7C:6; and Rule 8:18).

Suggested Questions to Be Asked When Taking Pleas of Guilty or Nolo Contendere

A. Pleas of Guilty or Nolo Contendere with Plea Agreements Requiring Imposition of an Active or Suspended Sentence of Confinement in Jail

1. Do you understand the charge(s) against you?
2. When Defendant appears without counsel:
   a) Do you understand you have the right to be represented by a lawyer?
   b) Do you understand that if you do not have the financial ability to hire your own lawyer, and you want me to, I will have you interviewed to see if you qualify for court-appointed counsel and I will appoint an attorney to represent you if you qualify?
   c) Do you want to hire an attorney to represent you, or be interviewed for court-appointed counsel or do you want to proceed today without a lawyer?
3. In Circuit Court:
   a) Do you understand that you have the right to have your case heard by a jury?
   b) Do you want your case to be heard by a judge without a jury or do you want a jury trial?
4. a) I understand that you have agreed to plead guilty (no contest) with the understanding that you will be sentenced to ______________________________. Is that correct? or
   b) I understand that you have agreed to plead guilty (no contest) with the understanding that the prosecutor will recommend a sentence of ______________. Do you understand that I do not have to accept the recommendation and that I can sentence you from ________________ to ________________?
   (provide full sentence range allowed by law)
5. Have you been promised anything else to get you to plead guilty (no contest)?
6. Are you being forced or threatened into pleading guilty (no contest)?
7. Do you understand that by pleading guilty (no contest) you are giving up your right to a trial including the right to hear from and question the witnesses against you and the right to avoid being required to give evidence against yourself?
8. Do you understand that if you are not a citizen of the United States and if you plead guilty or are found to be guilty, there may be consequences of deportation, exclusion from admission into the United States, or denial of naturalization pursuant to the laws of the United States?
9. Do you have any questions before I accept your plea(s) of guilty (no contest)?

B. Pleas of Guilty or Nolo Contendere Without a Plea Agreement

1. Do you understand the charge(s) against you?
2. When Defendant appears without counsel:
   a) Do you understand you have the right to be represented by a lawyer?
   b) Do you understand that if you do not have the financial ability to hire your own lawyer, and you want me to, I will have you interviewed to see if you qualify for court-appointed counsel and I will appoint an attorney to represent you if you qualify?
   c) Do you want to hire an attorney to represent you, or be interviewed for court-appointed counsel or do you want to proceed today without a lawyer?
3. In Circuit Court:
   a) Do you understand that you have the right to have your case heard by a jury?
   b) Do you want your case to be heard by a judge without a jury or do you want a jury trial?
4. Do you understand that based upon your plea of guilty (no contest) the possible range of punishment is ________________ to ________________?
5. Have you been promised anything else to get you to plead guilty (no contest)?
6. Are you being forced or threatened into pleading guilty (no contest)?
7. Do you understand that by pleading guilty (no contest) you are giving up your right to a trial including the right to hear from and question the witnesses against you and the right to avoid being required to give evidence against yourself?
8. Do you understand that if you are not a citizen of the United States and if you plead guilty or are found to be guilty, there may be consequences of deportation, exclusion from admission into the United States, or denial of naturalization pursuant to the laws of the United States?
9. Do you have any questions before I accept your plea(s) of guilty (no contest)?

Suggested Plea of Guilty to Misdemeanor Plea Form with Plea Agreement Requiring Imposition of an Active or Suspended Sentence of Confinement in Jail

1. I understand the charge(s) against me.
2. a) I understand that I have the right to be represented by an attorney.
   b) I understand that if I do not have the financial ability to hire my own attorney, I could be interviewed to see if I qualify for court appointed counsel and if I did qualify the court would appoint an attorney to represent me.
   c) I do not want to be represented by an attorney and I do not want to be interviewed to see if I qualify for court appointed counsel. It is my desire to give up my right to counsel and to proceed today without an attorney.
3. In Circuit Court:
   a) I understand that I have the right to have my case heard by a jury.
   b) I do not want my case to be heard by a jury and wish to proceed to have my case heard today by a judge without a jury.
4. a) I am pleading guilty (no contest) today based upon my understanding that I will be sentenced to ____________________.
   b) I am pleading guilty (no contest) today based upon my understanding that the prosecutor will recommend a sentence of ____________________. I understand that the judge does not have to accept the recommendation and can sentence me from ____________________ to ____________________.
5. I have not been promised anything to get me to plead guilty (no contest).
6. I am not being forced or threatened to get me to plead guilty (no contest).
7. I understand that by pleading guilty (no contest) I am giving up my right to a trial including the right to hear from and question the witnesses against me and the right to avoid being required to give evidence against myself.
8. I understand that if I am not a citizen of the United States and I plead guilty or am found to be guilty, there may be consequences of deportation, exclusion from admission into the United States, or denial of naturalization pursuant to the laws of the United States.
9. I do not have any questions to ask the court before the court decides whether to accept my plea of guilty (no contest).

______________________________ ______________________________

Counsel for Defendant Defendant

Suggested Plea of Guilty to Misdemeanor Plea Form without Plea Agreement

1. I understand the charge(s) against me.
2. a) I understand that I have the right to be represented by an attorney.
   b) I understand that if I do not have the financial ability to hire my own attorney, I could be interviewed to see if I qualify for court appointed counsel and if I did qualify the court would appoint an attorney to represent me.
   c) I do not want to be represented by an attorney and I do not want to be interviewed to see if I qualify for court appointed counsel. It is my desire to give up my right to counsel and to proceed today without an attorney.
3. In Circuit Court:
   a) I understand that I have the right to have my case heard by a jury.
   b) I do not want my case to be heard by a jury and wish to proceed to have my case heard today by a judge without a jury.
4. I am pleading guilty (no contest) today based upon my understanding that I could be sentenced from ____________________ to ____________________.
5. I have not been promised anything to get me to plead guilty (no contest).
6. I am not being forced or threatened to get me to plead guilty (no contest).
7. I understand that by pleading guilty (no contest) I am giving up my right to a trial including the right to hear from and question the witnesses against me and the right to avoid being required to give evidence against myself.
8. I understand that if I am not a citizen of the United States and I plead guilty or am found to be guilty, there may be consequences of deportation, exclusion from admission into the United States, or denial of naturalization pursuant to the laws of the United States.
9. I do not have any questions to ask the court before the court decides to accept my plea of guilty (no contest).

______________________________ ______________________________

Counsel for Defendant Defendant

PART THREE B
TRAFFIC INFRACTIONS AND UNIFORM FINE SCHEDULE

Rule 3B:1. Purpose.

These Rules are promulgated by the Supreme Court of Virginia pursuant to § 16.1-69.40:1 of the Code of Virginia to carry out the provisions of Chapter 585 of the Acts of Assembly of 1977 and Chapter 605 of the Acts of Assembly of 1978.

Rule 3B:2. Uniform Fine Schedule.

For any offense listed below, whether prescribed by the specified State statute or by a parallel local ordinance adopted pursuant to the authority granted in Virginia Code § 46.2-1300, a driver may enter a written appearance, waiver of court hearing, plea of guilty, and pay fines and costs. For traffic offenses not listed below, a court hearing is required. Nothing in this Rule affects bonding procedures for those offenses not listed below. Likewise, nothing in this Rule shall be construed to alter the operation of or the penalties prescribed pursuant to §§ 46.2-1220 through 46.2-1230.

This schedule is applied uniformly throughout the Commonwealth, and a clerk or magistrate may not impose a fine different from the amounts shown here. Costs shall be paid in accordance with the provisions of the Code of Virginia or any rules or regulations promulgated thereunder. This schedule does not restrict the fine a judge may impose for an offense listed here in any case for which there is a court hearing.

Description of Offense*	Statute or Regulation	Fine	Processing Fee**	Total
1. Speed Violations				
Exceeding the speed limit	46.2-870 to 46.2-872, 46.2-873.1 to 46.2-876	$6 per mile over speed limit	$51	
Exceeding the speed limit in a school crossing	46.2-873	$7 per mile over speed limit	$51	
Exceeding speed limits set by Transportation Commissioner	46.2-878	$6 per mile over speed limit	$51	
Exceeding the speed limit in a highway work zone	46.2-878.1	$7 per mile over speed limit	$51	
Exceeding the speed limit in a residence district	46.2-878.2	$200 plus $8 per mile over speed limit	$51	
Exceeding the speed limit in a 55 mph or 65 mph zone	46.2-870	$6 per mile over speed limit	$51	
Exceeding the speed limit on bridge	46.2-881	$6 per mile over speed limit	$51	
Impeding traffic by slow speed	46.2-877	$30	$51	$81
Failure to drive at approximate speed authorized for lane in which vehicle is moving, on highway where "slow moving traffic" lane is designated	46.2-804(1)	$30	$51	$81

Description of Offense*	Statute or Regulation	Fine	Processing Fee‡‡‡*	Total
2. Other Moving Offenses				
Moving violation committed in highway safety corridor	46.2-947	Double otherwise applicable fine	$51	
Failure to obey highway sign	46.2-830	$30	$51	$81
Coasting on downgrade with gears in neutral	46.2-811	$30	$51	$81
Driving more than 13 hours in a 24-hour period	46.2-812	$30	$51	$81
Causing or permitting vehicle to be driven more than 13 hours in a 24-hour period	46.2-812	$30	$51	$81
Improper failure to drive on right side of highway	46.2-802	$30	$51	$81
Failure to move in designated direction on one-way roadway	46.2-806	$30	$51	$81
Failure to drive to right of rotary traffic island	46.2-807	$30	$51	$81
Improper failure to keep right in crossing highway intersection	46.2-803	$30	$51	$81
Improper failure to keep right in crossing highway intersection by railroad right of way	46.2-803	$30	$51	$81
Improper failure to observe lanes marked for traffic:				
—failure of slow moving traffic to keep right	46.2-804(1)	$30	$51	$81
—improperly driving in center	46.2-804(2)	$30	$51	$81
—changing lane without first ascertaining safety of move	46.2-804(2)	$30	$51	$81
—improperly driving in center lane of 3-lane highway	46.2-804(3)	$30	$51	$81
—improperly crossing solid line driver's lane	46.2-804(5)	$30	$51	$81
—improperly crossing double solid line	46.2-804(6)	$30	$51	$81
Disregard of lane direction control signal	46.2-805	$30	$51	$81
Failure to obey traffic lights	46.2-833	$100	$51	$151
Evasion of a traffic control device	46.2-833.1	$50	$51	$101
Illegal right turn on red	46.2-835	$50	$51	$101
Illegal left turn on red	46.2-836	$50	$51	$101
Improper passing:				
—failure to remain on right side of highway when meeting vehicle proceeding in opposite direction	46.2-837	$30	$51	$81
—driving too close to vehicle being overtaken in same direction	46.2-838	$30	$51	$81
—returning to right side of highway before safely clear of overtaken vehicle	46.2-838	$30	$51	$81

Supreme Court Rules

Description of Offense*	Statute or Regulation	Fine	Processing Fee***	Total
—improperly passing to the right of a vehicle proceeding in same direction	46.2-841	$30	$51	$81
—failure to give way to the right to overtaking vehicle	46.2-842	$30	$51	$81
—improperly increasing speed when passed by overtaking vehicle	46.2-842	$30	$51	$81
—failure to give way to overtaking vehicle when driving abreast on divided highway	46.2-842.1	$30	$51	$81
—passing when left lane is not clearly visible	46.2-843	$30	$51	$81
—passing on left when oncoming traffic is too near to permit it in safety	46.2-843	$30	$51	$81
—truck or tractor and trailer impeding passage of following traffic by passing another truck or tractor and trailer on upgrade	46.2-843	$30	$51	$81
Following too closely:				
—motor vehicle following a vehicle more closely than is reasonable or prudent	46.2-816	$30	$51	$81
Improper U turn:				
—within business district, city or town, U turn other than at intersection	46.2-845	$30	$51	$81
—U turn on a curve or approaching crest of hill where not visible to vehicles approaching in any direction within 500 feet	46.2-845	$30	$51	$81
Improper position or method of turning at intersection:				
—unauthorized right turn from other than right hand curb or edge of roadway	46.2-846(A)(1)	$30	$51	$81
—on a two-way roadway, unauthorized left turn from other than lane nearest center line	46.2-846(A)(2)	$30	$51	$81
—on other than two-way roadway, unauthorized left turn from other than left-most available lane	46.2-846(A)(3)	$30	$51	$81
—failure to follow traffic control device of local authority	46.2-846(B)	$30	$51	$81
Starting, backing, stopping or turning without first seeing that such a move can be made in safety	46.2-848	$30	$51	$81
Starting, backing, stopping or turning without giving required signal	46.2-848	$30	$51	$81
Improper signals	46.2-849	$30	$51	$81
Improper change of course after giving signal	46.2-850	$30	$51	$81
Failure to signal prior to moving standing vehicle into traffic	46.2-851	$30	$51	$81

Description of Offense*	Statute or Regulation	Fine	Processing Fee***	Total
Failure to yield right of way or reduce speed on highway when approaching stopped vehicle with flashing blue, red or amber lights (not applicable to second and subsequent violations with vehicles flashing blue or red lights)	46.2-921.1	$100	$51	$151
Failure to yield right of way:				
—failure of driver on left to yield to driver on right entering intersection at same time	46.2-820	$30	$51	$81
—failure to obey "yield right of way" sign at intersection	46.2-821	$30	$51	$81
—failure of driver approaching or entering circular intersection to yield to driver already in the circle	46.2-822	$30	$51	$81
— failure to yield at uncontrolled "T" intersection	46.2-824	$30	$51	$81
—failure of driver turning left to yield to oncoming vehicle	46.2-825	$30	$51	$81
—failure to yield to left turning vehicle given right of way automatic signal device	46.2-825	$30	$51	$81
—failure to stop and yield when entering public highway or sidewalk from private road, etc.	46.2-826	$30	$51	$81
—failure to yield to U.S. Armed Services, National Guard, etc.	46.2-827	$30	$51	$81
—failure to yield to funeral procession under police escort	46.2-828	$30	$51	$81
—failure to yield right of way to emergency vehicle	46.2-829	$30	$51	$81
—following too near fire apparatus	46.2-921	$30	$51	$81
—driving over fire hose	46.2-922	$30	$51	$81
—failure to yield to pedestrian in clearly marked crosswalk or at intersection	46.2-924	$30	$51	$81
—failure to yield to pedestrian boarding or alighting from a bus	46.2-927	$30	$51	$81
—failure to stop and yield when approaching intersection of highway controlled by stop sign	46.2-821	$30	$51	$81
—failure to slow down or stop and yield when approaching intersection on highway controlled by "yield right of way" sign	46.2-821	$30	$51	$81
Driving through pedestrian safety zone	46.2-814	$30	$51	$81
Failure to obey railroad warning signal	46.2-884	$30	$51	$81
Proceeding improperly at railroad grade crossing:				
—generally	46.2-885	$30	$51	$81

Supreme Court Rules

Description of Offense*	Statute or Regulation	Fine	Processing Fee***	Total
—vehicles carrying passengers for hire, school bus or truck with flammable or explosive cargo	46.2-886	$30	$51	$81
—tractor, steam shovel, etc.	46.2-887	$30	$51	$81
Stopping bus or truck on highway to unload passengers or cargo	46.2-893	$30	$51	$81
Unlawful use of all-terrain vehicle	46.2-915.1	$30	$51	$81
Failure to yield right of way or reduce speed on highway when approaching stopped vehicle with flashing blue, red or amber lights (not applicable to second and subsequent violations with vehicles flashing blue or red lights)	46.2-921.1	$100	$51	$151
Failure to display headlights at night or during time of poor visibility	46.2-1030	$30	$51	$81
Driving with excessive lights for purpose of general illumination ahead of vehicle	46.2-1030	$30	$51	$81
Failure to display warning lights properly	46.2-1030	$30	$51	$81
Failure to dim headlights	46.2-1034	$30	$51	$81
Driving in violation of HOV Lane Restrictions	33.2-501(B)	$100	$51	$151
Driving in violation of HOV Lane Restrictions, Planning District Eight (first offense)	33.2-501(B) (1)	$125	$51	$176
Driving in violation of HOV Lane Restrictions, Planning District Eight (second offense within five years from a first offense)	33.2-501(B) (2)	$250	$51	$301
Driving in violation of HOV Lane Restrictions, Planning District Eight (third offense within five years from a first offense)	33.2-501(B) (3)	$500	$51	$551
Driving in violation of HOV Lane Restrictions, Planning District Eight (fourth offense within five years from a first offense)	33.2-501(B) (4)	$1,000	$51	$1,051
Driving vehicle in violation of HOT lane vehicle classification restrictions (first offense)	33.2-503(4)	$125	$51	$176
Driving vehicle in violation of HOT lane vehicle classification restrictions (second offense within five years from a first offense)	33.2-503(4)	$250	$51	$301
Driving vehicle in violation of HOT lane vehicle classification restrictions (third offense within five years from a first offense)	33.2-503(4)	$500	$51	$551
Driving vehicle in violation of HOT lane vehicle classification restrictions (fourth and subsequent offense within five years from a first offense)	33.2-503(4)	$1000	$51	$1051
3. Equipment Violations				
Insufficient lighting equipment:	46.2-1010	$30	$51	$81

Description of Offense*	Statute or Regulation	Fine	Processing Fee***	Total
—less than two proper headlights on autos, trucks, busses, etc.	46.2-1011	$30	$51	$81
—motorcycle without proper headlight	46.2-1012	$30	$51	$81
—motorcycle with more than two headlights	46.2-1012	$30	$51	$81
—improper rear lights	46.2-1013	$30	$51	$81
—improper brake lights	46.2-1014	$30	$51	$81
—improper lighting equipment on all other mobile equipment	46.2-1016	$30	$51	$81
Failure of car to be equipped with supplemental high mount stop light	46.2-1014.1	$30	$51	$81
Improper dimension or marker lights:				
—generally	46.2-1017	$30	$51	$81
—vehicles or loads exceeding 35 feet	46.2-1018	$30	$51	$81
Spotlights or ditchlights				
—more than two	46.2-1019	$30	$51	$81
—aimed left of highway center or more than 100 feet ahead of vehicle	46.2-1019	$30	$51	$81
—unapproved type	46.2-1019	$30	$51	$81
—use in conjunction with or in place of headlights, except in emergency	46.2-1019	$30	$51	$81
—improper use of auxiliary lamps on emergency vehicles	46.2-1028	$30	$51	$81
Headlights improperly aimed or of improper intensity:				
—single beam headlights	46.2-1031	$30	$51	$81
—multiple beam headlights	46.2-1032	$30	$51	$81
Failure of car to be equipped with windshield defroster or defogger	46.2-1055.1	$30	$51	$81
Inadequate brakes:				
—generally	46.2-1066	$30	$51	$81
—bicycles	46.2-1066	$15	$51	$66
—holding device	46.2-1068	$30	$51	$81
—motorcycles	46.2-1069	$30	$51	$81
—trailers or semitrailers	46.2-1070	$30	$51	$81
Improper alteration of suspension system	46.2-1063	$30	$51	$81
Inadequate steering gear	46.2-1065	$30	$51	$81
Inadequate horn	46.2-1059	$30	$51	$81
Illegal siren, whistle or horn	46.2-1060	$30	$51	$81
Use of speedometer not in good working order	46.2-1080	$30	$51	$81
Improper painting and lettering on school bus	46.2-1089	$30	$51	$81

Supreme Court Rules

Description of Offense*	Statute or Regulation	Fine	Processing Fee***	Total
Absence of or inadequate rear view mirrors:				
—generally	46.2-1082	$30	$51	$81
—vehicle registered for passenger vehicular transportation	46.2-1082	$30	$51	$81
Insufficient rear fenders, flags or guards on trucks	46.2-1083	$30	$51	$81
Improper signs on windshields, etc.	46.2-1052	$30	$51	$81
Driver's view obstructed because of suspended objects or altered vehicle	46.2-1054	$30	$51	$81
Inadequate windshield wipers	46.2-1055	$30	$51	$81
Absence of required safety glass	46.2-1056	$30	$51	$81
Absence of windshield	46.2-1057	$30	$51	$81
Improper replacement of glass in vehicle	46.2-1058	$30	$51	$81
Improper or inadequate tires:				
—violation of restrictions on solid rubber tires	46.2-1041	$30	$51	$81
—operation of vehicle with insufficient tire tread	46.2-1043	$30	$51	$81
—improper use of studded tires	46.2-1044	$30	$51	$81
Lack of or inadequate signal device	46.2-1038, 46.2-1039	$30	$51	$81
Failure to use flashing signals when stopped on highway	46.2-1040	$30	$51	$81
Inadequate exhaust system:				
—driver of vehicle	46.2-1049	$30	$51	$81
—owner permitting or allowing operation of vehicle	46.2-1049	$30	$51	$81
—vehicle without proper pollution control device	46.2-1048	$30	$51	$81
—muffler cutout, straight exhaust or gutted muffler	46.2-1047	$30	$51	$81
Operation of vehicle without securely affixed or properly located operator's seat	46.2-1084	$30	$51	$81
Improper motorcycle steering mechanism	46.2-1085	$30	$51	$81
Motorcycle without muffler	46.2-1050	$30	$51	$81
Improper cooling unit	46.2-1088	$30	$51	$81
Use of unapproved equipment	46.2-1002	$30	$51	$81
Use of defective or unsafe equipment	46.2-1003	$30	$51	$81
Operating vehicle not equipped with proper seat belts	46.2-1092	$30	$51	$81
Failure to have vehicle inspected	46.2-1158	$30	$51	$81

Description of Offense*	Statute or Regulation	Fine	Processing Fee***	Total
Failure to correct defects discovered by inspection	46.2-1158	$50	$51	$101
Driving after expiration of rejection inspection sticker	46.2-1158	$50	$51	$101
4.Parking or Stopping Violations				
Parking too near fire apparatus	46.2-921	$20	$51	$71
Vehicle improperly stopped or parked on highway	46.2-888	$20	$51	$71
—parked or stopped at or near fire or accident so as to cause traffic hazard or interfere with emergency operations	46.2-890	$20	$51	$71
Failure to use proper warning device when vehicle disabled in highway:				
—bus, truck, trailer, house trailer, or mobile home	46.2-111	$20	$51	$71
—vehicle transporting inflammable liquids	46.2-111	$20	$51	$71
—failure to use red flags when vehicle disabled	46.2-111	$20	$51	$71
Vehicle improperly parked in a VDOT owned commuter parking lot	46.2-1219.2	$20	$51	$71
Parking in front of fire hydrant, or private driveway, near street corner, fire station, or rescue squad building and too close to intersection	46.2-1239	$20	$51	$71
Failure to dim headlights on parked vehicle	46.2-1035	$20	$51	$71
Vehicle parked or stopped on highway without lights at night or during low visibility	46.2-1037	$20	$51	$71
Failure to set handbrake and turn wheels to curb on parked car	46.2-1071	$20	$51	$71
Improper use of parking space reserved for persons with disabilities	46.2-1242	$150	$51	$201
5.Trucks and Hauling or Towing Vehicles				
Absence of flag or light at end of load of four feet or more (excluding violation on a two-lane highway where passing is permitted)	46.2-1121	$30	$51	$81
Absence of flag or light at end of load of four feet or more on a two-lane highway where passing is permitted	46.2-1121	$250	$51	$301
Failure to fasten load of logs, barrels, etc.	46.2-1155	$30	$51	$81
Load extending too far beyond front (excluding violation on a two-lane highway where passing is permitted)	46.2-1120	$30	$51	$81
Load extending too far beyond front on a two-lane highway where passing is permitted	46.2-1120	$30	$51	$81

Supreme Court Rules

Description of Offense*	Statute or Regulation	Fine	Processing Fee***	Total
Load extending too far beyond sides	46.2-1111	$250	$51	$301
Improper towing				
—improperly towing more than one trailer, etc. (excluding violation on a two-lane highway where passing is permitted)	46.2-1116	$30	$51	$81
—towing without draw bar not exceeding 15 feet and emergency chain (excluding violation on a two-lane highway where passing is permitted)	46.2-1118	$30	$51	$81
— improperly towing more than one trailer, etc., on a two-lane highway where passing is permitted	46.2-1116	$250	$51	$301
— towing without draw bar not exceeding 15 feet and emergency chain on a two-lane highway where passing is permitted	46.2-1118	$250	$51	$301
6.Pedestrian Violations				
Malicious or careless interference with vehicle passage	46.2-923	$15	$51	$66
Failure to observe pedestrian control signals	46.2-925	$15	$51	$66
Stepping into street where driver's vision obscured	46.2-926	$15	$51	$66
Soliciting rides	46.2-929	$15	$51	$66
Failure to walk on left edge of roadway where no sidewalk	46.2-928	$15	$51	$66
Unlawful loitering on bridge or highway right-of-way	46.2-930	$15	$51	$66
Playing on streets or highways	46.2-932	$15	$51	$66
7.Miscellaneous Offenses				
Unlawful riding of an animal at night	46.2-800.1	$30	$51	$81
Improper abandonment of motor vehicle	46.2-1209	$40	$51	$91
Failure to obtain registration	46.2-600	$25	$51	$76
Failure to carry license or registration	46.2-104	$10	$51	$61
Expiration of registration	46.2-613	$25	$51	$76
Operate vehicle which is unregistered, untitled, or without plates/decals or with expired registration/license/decals	46.2-613(1)	$25	$51	$76
Possess, lend or knowingly permit use of registration card, license plate, or decal by anyone not entitled to it	46.2-613(3)	$25	$51	$76
Expired registration	46.2-646	$25	$51	$76
Pedestrian, bicycle, animal, moped, prohibited vehicle on controlled access highway	46.2-808	$30	$51	$81

Supreme Court Rules

Description of Offense*	Statute or Regulation	Fine	Processing Fee‡‡*	Total
Operating motorcycle without headlight, horn or rearview mirror at certain times	46.2-912	$30	$51	$81
Operating or riding a motorcycle without helmet; operating motorcycle without face shield, goggles or safety windshield	46.2-910(A)	$25	$51	$76
Occupation of trailer being towed on highways	46.2-813	$30	$51	$81
Unlawful use of radar detection device	46.2-1079	$40	$51	$91
Unlawful use of radar jamming device	46.2-1079	$40	$51	$91
Unlawful use of earphones while operating vehicle	46.2-1078	$25	$51	$76
Failure to display slow moving vehicle emblem	46.2-1081	$15	$51	$66
Failure to display license plate	46.2-711	$25	$51	$76
Improper display of license plate	46.2-715	$25	$51	$76
License plate improperly fastened or obscured	46.2-716	$25	$51	$76
Vehicle exceeding width limitations	46.2-1105	$250	$51	$301
Vehicle exceeding height limitations (excluding offenses of driving in violation of tunnel height restrictions and failure to report overhead bridge or structure collision)	46.2-1110	$250	$51	$301
Vehicle exceeding length regulations (excluding violation on a two-lane highway where passing is permitted)	46.2-1112	$250	$51	$301
Vehicle exceeding length regulations on a two-lane highway where passing is permitted	46.2-1112	$250	$51	$301
8. Bicycle Violations				
Riding bicycle improperly on roadway	46.2-905	$15	$51	$66
Carrying articles improperly on bicycle	46.2-906	$15	$51	$66
Bicycle without proper headlight	46.2-1015	$15	$51	$66
Bicycle without rear reflector or light	46.2-1015	$15	$51	$66
Bicycle on highway without adequate brake	46.2-1066	$15	$51	$66

Description of Offense*	Regulation[1]	Fine	Processing Fee‡‡*	Total
9. Motor Carrier Offenses†				
(a.) General Violations				
Marking of motor vehicle	49 C.F.R. §390.21	$25	$51	$76
Railroad crossing/stopping	49 C.F.R. §392.10	$100	$51	$151
(b.) Driver Violations				

Description of Offense*	Regulation[1]	Fine	Processing Fee***	Total
No medical examiner's certificate	49 C.F.R. §391.41	$50	$51	$101
Improper medical examiner's certificate	49 C.F.R. §391.43	$50	$51	$101
Medical certificate invalid	49 C.F.R. §391.43	$50	$51	$101
No medical waiver	49 C.F.R. §391.49	$50	$51	$101
Ill/fatigued driver	49 C.F.R. §392.3	$75	$51	$126
Possess alcoholic beverage	49 C.F.R. §392.5	$100	$51	$151
Violate 10-hour rule, 15-hour rule	49 C.F.R. §395.3	$100	$51	$151
Violate 60/70 hour rule	49 C.F.R. §395.3	$100	$51	$151
Log book violation (general)	49 C.F.R. §395.8	$100	$51	$151
No log book	49 C.F.R. §395.8	$100	$51	$151
Log book not current	49 C.F.R. §395.8	$100	$51	$151
Fail to retain previous seven days on log book	49 C.F.R. §395.8	$100	$51	$151
(c.) Equipment Violations				
Equipment — inspection/use	49 C.F.R. §392.7	$50	$51	$101
Emergency equipment — inspection/use	49 C.F.R. §392.8	$50	$51	$101
Safe loading (secured)	49 C.F.R. §392.9	$100	$51	$151
Brakes — inoperative or missing	49 C.F.R. §§393.40 to 393.52	$100	$51	$151
Fuel tank securement	49 C.F.R. §393.65	$50	$51	$101
Fuel leak/cap	49 C.F.R. §393.67	$25	$51	$76
Coupling/towing devices	49 C.F.R. §§393.70, 393.71	$50	$51	$101
Defective tires/tire exceeds weight limit	49 C.F.R. §393.75	$50	$51	$101
Bus violations	49 C.F.R. §§393.89 to 393.92	$50	$51	$101
Front end structure	49 C.F.R. §393.106	$50	$51	$101
Frame — cracked, loose, sagging, broken	49 C.F.R. §393.201	$100	$51	$151
Cab/body components — defective	49 C.F.R. §393.203	$50	$51	$101
Wheels/rims defective	49 C.F.R. §393.205	$50	$51	$101

Description of Offense*	Regulation[1]	Fine	Processing Fee***	Total
Suspension — defective	49 C.F.R. §393.207	$50	$51	$101
Steering system — defective	49 C.F.R. §393.209	$100	$51	$151
Vehicle maintenance (general)	49 C.F.R. §396.3	$100	$51	$151
No driver vehicle inspection report	49 C.F.R. §396.11	$25	$51	$76
No periodic inspection	49 C.F.R. §§396.17 to 396.25	$25	$51	$76
(d.) Hazardous Materials — Driving and Parking				
Fail to attend Division 1.1, 1.2 or 1.3 material	49 C.F.R. §397.5	$100	$51	$151
Fail to attend other hazardous materials class	49 C.F.R. §397.5	$100	$51	$151
Improper parking Division 1.1, 1.2 or 1.3 material	49 C.F.R. §397.7, § 397.11	$100	$51	$151
Improper parking other hazardous materials	49 C.F.R. §397.7, § 397.11	$100	$51	$151
Fail to have route plan	49 C.F.R. §397.67	$100	$51	$151
Smoking violations	49 C.F.R. §397.13	$100	$51	$151
Instructions and document violations	49 C.F.R. §397.19	$100	$51	$151

* The description of offense is for reference and is not a legal definition.

** Unless otherwise provided by statute.

*** See §§ 9.1-106 and 53.1-120 of the Code.

[1] The category "regulation" refers to the section of the Code of Federal Regulations as incorporated by regulation at 19 VAC 30-20-80 of the Virginia Motor Carrier Safety Regulations. These regulations are included for identification and reference purposes only, since these violations are violations of Virginia regulations.

† These fines are imposed for violations of certain Virginia Motor Carrier Safety Regulations. The statutory authority to impose these fines is contained in § 52-8.4 of the code of Virginia and in 19 VAC 30-20-10, *et seq.*, of the Virginia Motor Carrier Safety Regulations, incorporating by reference 49 C.F.R. Parts 390-397.

PART THREE C
NON-TRAFFIC PREPAYABLE OFFENSES AND UNIFORM FINE SCHEDULE

Rule 3C:1. Purpose and Effective Date.

These rules are promulgated by the Supreme Court of Virginia pursuant to § 16.1-69.40:2 of the Code of Virginia to carry out the provisions of Chapter 605 of the Acts of Assembly of 1978 and Chapter 421 of the Acts of Assembly of 1989.

Rule 3C:2. Uniform Fine Schedule.

Any person charged with any offense listed below may enter a written appearance, waiver of court hearing, plea of guilty, and pay fines and costs.

This schedule is applied uniformly throughout the Commonwealth, and a clerk or magistrate may not impose a fine different from the amounts shown here. Costs shall be paid in accordance with the provisions of the Code of Virginia or any rules or regulations promulgated thereunder. The schedule does not restrict the fine a judge may impose for an offense listed here in any case for which there is a court hearing.

Where injury to the person is involved, prepayment may not be made, even though the offense or violation appears on the list below. See Va. Code § 16.1-69.40:2(A).

A violation of a provision of Title 28.2 may be prepaid only if the person has not violated a provision of Title 28.2 within the past 12 months. See Va. Code § 28.2-903.

A violation of any of the provisions of the hunting, trapping, or inland fish laws, or of § 18.2132, or any regulations adopted by the Board of Game and Inland Fisheries pursuant thereto, may be prepaid only if the person has not violated any of those provisions within the past three years. See Va. Code § 29.1-338.

Description of Offense*	Statute or Regulation	Fine	Processing Fee***	Total
Drinking or tendering alcoholic beverage in public place	4.1-308	$25	$61	$86
Failing to assist forest warden in fighting fire	10.1-1139	$30	$61	$91
Unlawful burning of brush, leaves, etc.	10.1-1142(A) 10.1-1142(D)	$40	$61	$101
Unlawful burning during restricted period	10.1-1142(B) 10.1-1142(D)	$40	$61	$101
Leaving certain fires unattended or failing to extinguish the same	10.1-1142(C) 10.1-1142(D)	$40	$61	$101
Hunting or trapping in state forests without special use permit	10.1-1151	$35	$61	$96
Hunting or trapping in state forests in violation of restrictions or conditions of special use permit	10.1-1153	$35	$61	$96
Failure to post signs regarding disposal of used motor oils	10.1-1422.6D	$25	$61	$86
Unlawful buying, selling or disposing of milk case or crate	18.2-102.2	$35	$61	$96
Unlawful refusal to return milk case or crate	18.2-102.2	$35	$61	$96
Unlawful defacing, cover up or removal of business identification on milk case or crate	18.2-102.2	$35	$61	$96
Bringing unleashed dog into Capitol Square	18.2-123	$10	$61	$71
Trespassing at night upon cemetery	18.2-125	$35	$61	$96
Trespassing at night upon church or school property	18.2-128(A)	$35	$61	$96

Description of Offense*	Statute or Regulation	Fine	Processing Fee‡‡‡*	Total
Trespassing upon lands to hunt, fish or trap without consent	18.2-132	$50	$61	$111
Computer invasion of privacy by intentionally examining personal information without authority	18.2-152.5	$50	$61	$111
Trespassing on railroad track	18.2-159	$35	$61	$96
Trespassing on railroad trains	18.2-160	$35	$61	$96
Boarding or riding train without lawful payment of fare	18.2-160.1(A) 18.2-160.1(B)	$100	$61	$161
Unlawfully intercepting or monitoring employee/customer telephone calls	18.2-167.1	$35	$61	$96
Failing to report removal, alteration of trademark or identification numbers on a business machine	18.2-214.1	$50	$61	$111
Using games, contests, lotteries to promote sale of products having both federal and state tax	18.2-242	$50	$61	$111
Expectorating in public	18.2-322	$15	$61	$76
Drinking alcoholic beverage while driving motor vehicle	18.2-323.1	$75	$61	$136
Gambling illegally	18.2-326	$35	$61	$96
Selling to, distributing to or purchasing for persons under age 18 tobacco products	18.2-371.2(A)	$75	—	$75
Purchasing or possessing tobacco products when under age 18	18.2-371.2(B)	$35	—	$35
Profanely cursing or swearing in public	18.2-388	$25	$61	$86
Being intoxicated in public	18.2-388	$25	$61	$86
Shooting pigeons for amusement or renting premises for such purpose	18.2-403.3(2) 3.2-6573	$35	$61	$96
Making false statement to secure a dog license	18.2-403.3(8) 3.2-6587(A)(1)	$35	$61	$96
Failing to pay dog license tax	18.2-403.3(9) 3.2-6530 3.2-6587(A)	$25	$61	$86
Concealing unlicensed dog	18.2-403.3(10) 3.2-6587(A)	$35	$61	$96
Unlawfully removing dog collar or tag	18.2-403.3(11) 3.2-6587(A)	$35	$61	$96
Using abusive language	18.2-416	$60	$61	$121
Using recorded telephone solicitation calls for initial sales contacts	18.2-425.1(A)	$50	$61	$111
Using recorded telephone solicitation calls which do not disengage when party called attempts to do so	18.2-425.1(B)	$50	$61	$111
Unlawfully communicating with prisoners by persons outside any jail	18.2-473.1	$75	$61	$136

Description of Offense*	Statute or Regulation	Fine	Processing Fee***	Total
Unlawfully possessing or duplicating keys to public buildings	18.2-503	$50	$61	$111
Unlawfully changing name	18.2-504.1	$60	$61	$121
Campaigning at election registration location	24.2-1003	$50	$61	$111
Failing to obey chief or other fire officer answering an alarm or operating at an emergency incident	27-15.1	$50	$61	$111
Fishing without a saltwater license	28.2-302.1	$75	$61	$136
Unlawful setting of fishnets	28.2-309	$110	$61	$171
Taking fish or shellfish on or within 500 yards below Chickahominy Dam at Walker's on the Chickahominy River other than with rod and reel and hand line	28.2-311	$60	$61	$121
Buying, selling or possessing oysters under the prescribed size and undersized shells taken from the natural rocks, beds and shoals	28.2-510	$110	$61	$171
Having oysters or shells on culling board, deck, washboard or other receptacle above hold or in deckhouse when boat is oystering upon natural rocks, beds or shoals and not at anchor, when off the public rocks; when approaching a buy boat; or when approaching a landing	28.2-513	$150	$61	$211
Having more than one-half gallon of shucked oysters on board a boat harvesting on the public rocks	28.2-514	$60	$61	$121
Taking or catching oysters or shells for purpose of converting same into lime without permission from Commission	28.2-529	$110	$61	$171
Unlawful violation of regulations governing use of crab traps and pounds	28.2-701	$150	$61	$211
Taking or catching crabs from statutorily prohibited area from June 1 to Sept. 15, for purpose of resale	28.2-709	$150	$61	$211
Placing or maintaining any crab, eel, or fish pot in navigable channel which has navigation aids installed or approved by any agency of U.S. government	28.2-710	$60	$61	$121
Placing, setting or leaving crab pots in tidal tributaries between Jan. 1 and Jan. 31 or other time period specified by Marine Res. Comm.	28.2-711	$60	$61	$121
Possess Striped Bass less than 18 inches	4 VAC 20-252-30(C)	$50 per fish (Maximum fine not to exceed $500)	$61	
Possess Striped Bass larger than the maximum size	4 VAC 20-252-50(E)	$50 per fish (Maximum fine not to exceed $500)	$61	

Description of Offense*	Statute or Regulation	Fine	Processing Fee***	Total
Possess Striped Bass over creel limit	4 VAC 20-252-50(C)	$100 per fish (Maximum fine not to exceed $500)	$61	
Fail to purchase Striped Bass buyer's permit	4 VAC 20-252-130(D)	$100	$61	$161
Unlawfully set, place, or leave crab pots in tidal waters	4 VAC 20-270-40(C)	$100	$61	$161
Unlawful for any person to take, catch, or possess any speckled trout less than minimum size	4 VAC 20-280-30(A)	$50 per fish (Maximum fine not to exceed $500)	$61	
Unlawful for hook-and-line, rod-and-reel, or handline to possess oversize speckled trout	4 VAC 20-280-30(B)	$50 per fish (Maximum fine not to exceed $500)	$61	
Unlawful to possess any red drum less than 18 or greater than 26 inches	4 VAC 20-280-30(C)	$50 per fish (Maximum fine not to exceed $500)	$61	
Unlawful to possess more than creel limit for speckled trout	4 VAC 20-280-40	$100 per fish (Maximum fine not to exceed $500)	$61	
Unlawful to take or catch more than 1 black drum	4 VAC 20-320-40	$100 per fish (Maximum fine not to exceed $500)	$61	
Unlawful to take, catch or possess any black drum less than 16 inches	4 VAC 20-320-60	$50 per fish (Maximum fine not to exceed $500)	$61	
Failure to cull crabs at harvest location	4 VAC 20-370-20	$100	$61	$161
Unlawful crab culling containers	4 VAC 20-370-20	$100	$61	$161
Unlawful to possess more than the maximum number of gray trout or under the minimum size	4 VAC 20-380-60	$50 per fish (Maximum fine not to exceed $500)	$61	
Drift and anchor gill nets not marked	4 VAC 20-430-20	$50	$61	$111
Staked gill net not marked	4 VAC 20-430-30	$50	$61	$111

Supreme Court Rules

Description of Offense*	Statute or Regulation	Fine	Processing Fee***	Total
Unlawful for any person to possess more than 10 bluefish	4 VAC 20-450-20	$100 per fish (Maximum fine not to exceed $500)	$61	
Fail to completely remove traps, leads, wire, poles and all other related gear of crab traps and pounds no later than December 31 of each year	4 VAC 20-460-30	$100	$61	$161
Unlawful to possess more than 2 amberjack or more than 1 cobia at any time	4 VAC 20-510-20	$100 per fish (Maximum fine not to exceed $500)	$61	
Unlawful to possess amberjack less than 32 inches or cobia less than 37 inches	4 VAC 20-510-30	$50 per fish (Maximum fine not to exceed $500)	$61	
Unlawful to catch and retain possession of American shad	4 VAC 20-530-30	$100 per fish (Maximum fine not to exceed $500)	$61	
Unlawful for any person to possess more than 15 Spanish mackerel or more than 3 king mackerel	4 VAC 20-540-30	$100 per fish (Maximum fine not to exceed $500)	$61	
Unlawful for any person to set any gill net or nonfixed finfishing device and let net or device remain unfished	4 VAC 20-550-20	$150	$61	$211
Unlawful to alter finfish such that the species cannot be determined	4 VAC 20-580-20(A)	$200	$61	$261
Unlawful to alter any finfish regulated by size such that total length cannot be determined	4 VAC 20-580-20(B)	$200	$61	$261
Unlawful to possess any summer flounder smaller than designated size limit	4 VAC 20-620-50(D)	$50 per fish (Maximum fine not to exceed $500)	$61	
Unlawfully possessing fish from recreational gill net	4 VAC 20-670-30(E)	$50	$61	$111
Unlawfully fishing recreational crab pots	4 VAC 20-670-30(I)	$75	$61	$136
Unlawful to place, set or fish any crab pot that does not contain at least two unobstructed cull ring of proper size and location	4 VAC 20-700-20	$150	$61	$211

Description of Offense*	Statute or Regulation	Fine	Processing Fee***	Total
Unlawful to catch and retain possession of any scup smaller than the minimum sizes	4 VAC 20-910-30	$50 per fish (Maximum fine not to exceed $500)	$61	
Unlawful to possess any black sea bass smaller than minimum size limits	4 VAC 20-950-30(C)	$50 per fish (Maximum fine not to exceed $500)	$61	
Possession of any quantity of black sea bass that exceeds possession limit	4 VAC 20-950-45	$100 per fish (Maximum fine not to exceed $500)	$61	
Unlawful to possess tautog smaller than minimum size limit	4 VAC 20-960-30(C)	$50 per fish (Maximum fine not to exceed $500)	$61	
Unlawful to possess more than four tautog recreationally	4 VAC 20-960-45	$100 per fish (Maximum fine not to exceed $500)	$61	
Unlawful to possess more than four spadefish recreationally	4 VAC 20-970-30(A)	$100 per fish (Maximum fine not to exceed $500)	$61	
Unlawful to possess more than six spadefish by commercial hook and line	4 VAC 20-970-30(C)	$100 per fish (Maximum fine not to exceed $500)	$61	
Unlawful to harvest, land or possess more than four sheepshead recreationally	4 VAC 20-1110-30	$100 per fish (Maximum fine not to exceed $500)	$61	
Failure to use and maintain a certified scale to weigh those fish, shellfish and marine organisms regulated by a harvest quota, weight limit or landing weight	4 VAC 20-1170-10	$50	$61	$111
Unlawful to place a net within 300 yards of the side or end of a fixed fishing device	4 VAC 20-1220-30	$100	$61	$161
Unlawful to take or catch any marine or anadromous fish species recreationally without obtaining, annually, a Fisherman Identification Program (FIP) Registration	4 VAC 20-1240-30	$25	$61	$86

Supreme Court Rules

Description of Offense*	Statute or Regulation	Fine	Processing Fee***	Total
Unlawful to catch and retain possession of any river herring from Virginia tidal waters	4 VAC 20-1260-30	$100 per fish (Maximum fine not to exceed $500)	$61	
Unauthorized Transfer of License	PRFC Reg I 1a[1]		[2]	$250
Setting 1 to 5 More Crab Pots than Licensed	PRFC Reg I 2d(1)[1]		[2]	$150
Setting 6 to 10 More Crab Pots than Licensed	PRFC Reg I 2d(1)[1]		[2]	$250
Setting 11 to 15 More Crab Pots than Licensed	PRFC Reg I 2d(1)[1]		[2]	$350
Setting 16 to 20 More Crab Pots than Licensed	PRFC Reg I 2d(1)[1]		[2]	$450
Setting 21 or More Crab Pots than Licensed	PRFC Reg I 2d(1)[1]		[2]	$500
Improper Identification of Oyster Tong Vessel	PRFC Reg I 2f(1)[1]			$125
Improper Identification of Hand Scrape Vessel	PRFC Reg I 2f(3)[1]			$125
Gill Net Set in Water Depth More than 36′ MLW	PRFC Reg I (i)(1) [1]	2	[2]	$250
Failure to Display Commercial Hook and Line Pennant	PRFC Reg I 2l(2)[1]		[2]	$125
More Unlicensed Commercial Hook and Line Crew Members than Allowed	PRFC Reg I 2l(2)[1]		[2]	$300
Improper Identification of Eel, Fish, or Bait Pots or Vessel	PRFC Reg I 2m(4)[1]		[2]	$125
Improper Identification of Pound, Gill or Fyke Net	PRFC Reg I 2n(8)[1]		[2]	$125
Failing to Maintain 1 to 5 Stakes or Buoys	PRFC Reg I 2n(9)[1]		[2]	$200
Failing to Maintain 6 to 10 Stakes or Buoys	PRFC Reg I 2n(9)[1]		[2]	$250
Failing to Maintain 11 to 15 Stakes or Buoys	PRFC Reg I 2n(9)[1]		[2]	$300
Failing to Maintain 16 to 20 Stakes or Buoys	PRFC Reg I 2n(9)[1]		[2]	$350
Failing to Maintain 21 or more Stakes or Buoys	PRFC Reg I 2n(9)[1]		[2]	$500
Improper Identification of Fish Trot Line or Vessel	PRFC Reg I 2q[1]		[2]	$125
Gill Net Set Out of Location	PRFC Reg I 2s(1)[1]			$200
Failing to Remove 1 to 5 Stakes	PRFC Reg I 2s(2)[1]		[2]	$200

Description of Offense*	Statute or Regulation	Fine	Processing Fee***	Total
Failing to Remove 6 to 10 Stakes	PRFC Reg I 2s(2)[1]		[2]	$250
Failing to Remove 11 to 15 Stakes	PRFC Reg I 2s(2)[1]		[2]	$300
Failing to Remove 16 to 20 Stakes	PRFC Reg I 2s(2)[1]		[2]	$350
Failing to Remove 21 or more Stakes	PRFC Reg I 2s(2)[1]		[2]	$500
No Reflective Material/Flags on Gill, Fyke or Pound Net	PRFC Reg I 2s(3)[1]		[2]	$125
Gill Net Set Out of Location	PRFC Reg I 2s[1]		[2]	$75
Operating Charter Boat without Sport Decal	PRFC Reg I 2u[1]		[2]	$300
Commercial Fishing/Crabbing/Oystering/Clamming without License	PRFC Reg I 3b[1]		[2]	$300
Failure to Exhibit Commercial License	PRFC Reg I 3b[1]		[2]	$125
Placing 1 to 10 Buoys, Gear or Pots in Marked Channel	PRFC Reg I 3c[1]		[2]	$150
Placing 11 to 15 Buoys, Gear or Pots in Marked Channel	PRFC Reg I 3c[1]		[2]	$200
Placing 16 or more Buoys, Gear or Pots in Marked Channel	PRFC Reg I 3c[1]		[2]	$250
Altering/Modifying Striped Bass ID Tags per tab	PRFC Reg I 3e[1]		[2]	$250
Possessing Hand Scrape During Unlawful Time (note Order #)	PRFC Reg II 2b[1]		[2]	$150
Oystering Before or After Closed Hours (note Order #)	PRFC Reg II 2b[1]		[2]	$250
Oystering During Closed Season (note Order #)	PRFC Reg II 2b[1]		[2]	$500
Possessing Patent Tong or Dredging Equipment without Permit	PRFC Reg II 2e[1]		[2]	$125
Possessing 6 to 10% Unculled Oysters	PRFC Reg II 2f(1)[1]		[2]	$200
Possessing 11 to 15% Unculled Oysters	PRFC Reg II 2 f (1)		[2]	$350
Possessing 16% or more Unculled Oysters	PRFC Reg II 2f(1)[1]		[2]	$500
Not Culling on Oyster Bar	PRFC Reg II 2f(2)[1]		[2]	$500
Possessing Oysters in Containers	PRFC Reg II 2g[1]		[2]	$200
Possessing Oysters in Baskets without Permit	PRFC Reg II 2g[1]		[2]	$125
Oystering in Closed Area (Sanctuaries)	PRFC Reg II 4a[1]		[2]	$500

Supreme Court Rules

Description of Offense*	Statute or Regulation	Fine	Processing Fee***	Total
Exceeding Minimum or Maximum Mesh Size	PRFC Reg III 8b[1]		2	$500
Violation of Haul Seine Regulations	PRFC Reg III 8 c(1-2) [1]		2	$200
Fishing During Closed Season (Commercial)	PRFC Reg III 9 a (1-7)[1]		2	$250
Possessing Fish During Closed Season (note Order #) *per fish*	PRFC Reg III 9b[1]		2	$125
Exceeding Fish Catch/Creel Limits (note Order #) *per fish*	PRFC Reg III 10a[1]		2	$125
Possessing Striped Bass in Excess of Catch/Creel Limits (note Order #) *per fish*	PRFC Reg III 10a[1]		2	$150
Using Striped Bass ID Tags of Another	PRFC Reg III 10b[1]		2	$250
Failure to Tag Commercially Caught Striped Bass *per fish*	PRFC Reg III 10b[1]		2	$125
Unlawful Use of Striped Bass Tags (i.e. by gear type) (note Order #)	PRFC Reg III 10b[1]		2	$500
Possessing Undersize Fish (note Order #) $125 first fish plus $10 each additional fish	PRFC Reg III 11a[1]			$125
Possess Oversize Striped Bass (note Order #) *per fish*	PRFC Reg III 11a[1]		2	$250
Improper Identification of Soft Clam Vessel	PRFC Reg V 1a[1]		2	$125
Possessing 6% or more Undersized Clams	PRFC Reg V 3a[1]		2	$150
Exceeding Clam Catch Limits *per bushel*	PRFC Reg V 4a[1]		2	$250
Clamming in Closed Area	PRFC Reg V 6d[1]		2	$500
Failure to Exhibit Sport Fishing License/Improper Display of License	PRFC Reg VI 2c[1]			$125
Exceeding Unlicensed Recreational Crabbing Gear or Catch Limits	PRF CReg VI 4a[1]		2	$150
Sport Crabbing without License	PRF Reg VI 4b[1]		2	$150
Failure to Exhibit Sport Crabbing License	PRF Reg VI 4b[1]		2	$125
Exceeding Licensed Sport Crabbing Gear Limits	PRF Reg VI 4c[1]		2	$125
Improper Identification of Sport Crabbing Gear	PRF Reg VI 4d[1]		2	$125
Exceeding Licensed Sport Crabbing Catch Limits	PRF Reg VI 4e[1]		2	$125
Sport Fishing without License	PRF Reg VI 5a[1]		2	$150
Fishing for Striped Bass During Closed Season without Barbless Hooks	PRF Reg VI 5e[1]		2	$125
Failing to Remove Peeler Traps per trap	PRF Reg VII 1d[1]		2	$200
Possessing Undersize Crabs				
#per Bushel#per Barrel				

Description of Offense*	Statute or Regulation	Fine	Processing Fee***	Total
5 to 9 11 to 24	PRFC Reg VII 2a[1]			$150
10 to 14 25 to 39	PRFC Reg VII 2a[1]			$225
15 to 25 40 to 59	PRFC Reg VII 2a[1]			$275
26 or more 60 or more	PRFC Reg VII 2a[1]			$400
Improper Identification of Crab Pot Vessel	PRFC Reg VII 3a[1]		[2]	$125
Improper Identification of Crabbing Gear	PRFC Reg VII 3b[1]		[2]	$125
Crab Pots without Decal/Tag — 300 Pot License				
# pots without decal/tag				
1 to 15	PRFC Reg VII b 3 [1]		[2]	$250
16 to 30	PRFC Reg VII b 3 [1]		[2]	$500
Crab Pots without Decal/Tag — 400 Pot License				
# pots without decal/tag				
1 to 20	PRFC Reg VII 3b[1]		[2]	$250
21 to 40	PRFC Reg VII 3b[1]		[2]	$500
Crab Pots without Decal/Tag — 500 Pot License				
# pots without decal/tag				
1 to 25	PRFC Reg VII 3b[1]		[2]	$250
26 - 50	PRFC Reg VII 3b[1]		[2]	$500
Crabbing/Possession of Crabs During Closed Season	PRFC Reg VII 4a[1]		[2]	$250
Crabbing at Night	PRFC Reg VII 5b[1]			$200
No Culling Container on Board	PRFC Reg VII 6a[1]			$200
Transporting Crabs not in Baskets or Barrels	PRFC Reg VII 6a[1]			$200
No or Closed Cull Rings in 1 to 5 Pots	PRFC Reg VII 6b[1]			$175
No or Closed Cull Rings in 6 to 10 Pots	PRFC Reg VII 6b[1]			$275
No or Closed Cull Rings in 11 to 15 Pots	PRFC Reg VII 6b[1]			$450

Description of Offense*	Statute or Regulation	Fine	Processing Fee***	Total
No or Closed Cull Rings in 16 to 20 Pots	PRFC Reg VII 6b[1]			$500
Failure to Separate Crabs per container	PRFC Reg VII 6c[1]		[2]	$150
Exceeding Crab Harvest Limit per bushel	PRFC Reg VII 7a[1]		[2]	$150
Hunting, trapping, or fishing without license	29.1-335	$60 + fee equal to cost of License	$61	$121
Failing to carry hunting, trapping or fishing license	29.1-336	$35	$61	$96
Hunting bear or deer w/out special stamp	29.1-354	$35	$61	$96
Hunting, fishing or trapping in national forest w/out special permit	29.1-408	$35	$61	$96
Failing to obtain permit for taxidermy	29.1-415 29.1-412	$50	$61	$111
Failing to obtain permit for netting fish	29.1-416 29.1-412	$50	$61	$111
Failing to obtain permit for capturing, propagating and disposing of wildlife for authorized purposes	29.1-417 29.1-412	$50	$61	$111
Failing to obtain permit for collecting specimens	29.1-418 29.1-412	$50	$61	$111
Failing to obtain permit for taking, holding falcons, hawks and owls to use to hunt wild game	29.1-419 29.1-412	$50	$61	$111
Failing to secure permits required for field trials	29.1-422 18.2-403.3(6)	$50	$61	$111
Hunting with unauthorized weapons	29.1-519	$60	$61	$121
Violating hunting times	29.1-520	$60	$61	$121
Hunting on Sunday	29.1-521(A)(1)	$50	$61	$111
Hunting after obtaining daily or season limit	29.1-521(A)(3)	$50	$61	$111
Hunting over bait or occupying baited blind	29.1-521(A)(4)	$100	$61	$161
Providing no name or address on traps set on another's property	29.1-521(A)(7)	$25	$61	$86
Failing to visit traps daily and remove animals	29.1-521(A)(9)	$35	$61	$96
Unlawfully hunting, trapping, possessing, transporting animals or carcasses	29.1-521(A)(10)	$100	$61	$161
Violating blaze orange law	29.1-530.1	$25	$61	$86
Certain violations pertaining to sanctuaries, refuges, etc.	29.1-554	$60	$61	$121
Shooting, attempting to shoot, or taking game on preserve before complying with regulations	29.1-603	$35	$61	$96
Removing shot game from preserve without attaching seal	29.1-606	$35	$61	$96

Description of Offense*	Statute or Regulation	Fine	Processing Fee***	Total
Unregistered motorboat	29.1-702(A)	$75	$61	$136
No registration on board	29.1-702(B)	$25	$61	$86
Expired registration	29.1-703	$25	$61	$86
Failure to display registration	29.1-703	$25	$61	$86
Failure to display expiration decal	29.1-703	$25	$61	$86
Operating motorboat or manipulating skis in marked area	29.1-734	$35	$61	$96
Operation of vessel without proper safety equipment	29.1-735(C)	$35	$61	$96
Renting out a motorboat without safety equipment	29.1-736(A)	$35	$61	$96
Offering for rent other boats without sufficient life preservers	29.1-736(B)	$35	$61	$96
Violation of muffling device requirements for motorboats	29.1-737	$25	$61	$86
Absence of observer when towing water skier not wearing life preserver	29.1-742(A)	$35	$61	$96
Skiing before/after hours	29.1-742(B)	$75	$61	$136
Operating motorboat at excessive speed when within 50 feet of docks, piers, ramps, people in water	29.1-744.3	$50	$61	$111
Operating personal watercraft under age 14	29.1-748(A)(1)	$35	$61	$96
Operating personal watercraft without wearing personal flotation device	29.1-748(A)(3)	$35	$61	$96
Operating personal watercraft without a lanyard	29.1-748(A)(4)	$35	$61	$96
Operating personal watercraft between sunset and sunrise	29.1-748(A)(5)	$35	$61	$96
Exceeding capacity on personal watercraft	29.1-748(A)(6)	$35	$61	$96
Permitting operation of personal watercraft by person under age 14	29.1-749(A)	$75	$61	$136
Destruction of flowers, plants, minerals, etc. on a state park[3]	4 VAC 5-30-50[4]	$100	$61	$161
Destruction of buildings, signs, structures, etc. on a state park[3]	4 VAC 5-30-60[4]	$100	$61	$161
Disposal of refuse, garbage, etc. on a state park[3]	4 VAC 5-30-70[4]	$50	$61	$111
Pollution of waters on a state park[3]	4 VAC 5-30-80[4]	$100	$61	$161
Opening and closing hours of a state park[3]	4 VAC 5-30-120[4]	$50	$61	$111
Failure to pay fees in a fee area of a state park[3]	4 VAC 5-30-130[4]	$50	$61	$111
Picknicking in non-designated areas of a state park[3]	4 VAC 5-30-140[4]	$25	$61	$86
Camping in a state park[3] other than according to established rule	4 VAC 5-30-150[4]	$50	$61	$111

Description of Offense*	Statute or Regulation	Fine	Processing Fee***	Total
Swimming in unauthorized area or manner in a state park[3]	4 VAC 5-30-170[4]	$50	$61	$111
Boating in a state park[3] swimming area	4 VAC 5-30-190[4]	$50	$61	$111
Possession of firearms in a state park[3] by unauthorized persons	4 VAC 5-30-200[4]	$100	$61	$161
Fires in unauthorized areas of a state park[3]	4 VAC 5-30-220[4]	$100	$61	$161
Smoking in a prohibited area of a state park[3]	4 VAC 5-30-230[4]	$50	$61	$111
Unauthorized hunting in a state park[3]	4 VAC 5-30-240[4]	$100	$61	$161
Fishing in non-designated areas of a state park[3]	4 VAC 5-30-250[4]	$50	$61	$111
Allowing animals to run at large in a state park[3]	4 VAC 5-30-260[4]	$50	$61	$111
Games or athletic contests in non-designated areas of a state park[3]	4 VAC 5-30-270[4]	$50	$61	$111
Persons in non-designated areas of a state park[3] or failure to comply with a safety sign	4 VAC 5-30-274[4]	$50	$61	$111
Bicycle in non-designated areas of a state park[3] or failure to comply with a safety sign	4 VAC 5-30-276[4]	$50	$61	$111
Horses in non-designated areas of a state park[3]	4 VAC 5-30-280[4]	$50	$61	$111
Vehicles in a prohibited area of a state park[3]	4 VAC 5-30-290[4]	$50	$61	$111
Parking in an unauthorized area of a state park[3]	4 VAC 5-30-300[4]	$25	$61	$86
Obstructing traffic in a state park[3]	4 VAC 5-30-310[4]	$50	$61	$111
Operating an excessively loaded vehicle in a state park[3]	4 VAC 5-30-330[4]	$50	$61	$111
Engaging in commercial enterprise on a state park[3] without a permit	4 VAC 5-30-340[4]	$50	$61	$111
Operate a commercial vehicle on a state park[3] without a permit	4 VAC 5-30-360[4]	$50	$61	$111
Advertising within a state park[3] without a permit	4 VAC 5-30-370[4]	$50	$61	$111
Soliciting alms or contributions within a state park[3] without a permit	4 VAC 5-30-390[4]	$25	$61	$86
Landing an aircraft or parachute within a state park[3] without a permit	4 VAC 5-30-400[4]	$50	$61	$111
Importation of firewood into a state park[3] contrary to the limitations imposed by the DCR Director	4 VAC 5-30-410[4]	$100	$61	$161
Release of animals or wildlife captured or propagated elsewhere into a state park[3]	4 VAC 5-30-420[4]	$50	$61	$111
Feeding wildlife on a state park[3]	4 VAC 5-30-422[4]	$50	$61	$111
Constructing, maintaining or occupying unauthorized structures on department-owned lands or national forest lands	4 VAC 15-20-150†	$30	$61	$91
Using recorded or electronically amplified imitations of animal or bird calls or sounds to take wild animals and wild birds	4 VAC 15-40-30†	$50	$61	$111

Description of Offense*	Statute or Regulation	Fine	Processing Fee‡‡‡**	Total
Unlawfully possessing or using a bow or gun which is not unloaded and cased or dismantled on national forest lands statewide or on department-owned lands or on other department-managed lands west of the Blue Ridge Mountains during closed season	4 VAC 15-40-60(A)†	$75	$61	$136
Using a bow or firearm outside the established boundaries of an archery or shooting range or using a bow or firearm for other than target shooting at such archery or shooting range during closed season	4 VAC 15-40-60(D)†	$50	$61	$111
Chasing with a dog or training dogs on national forest lands or on department-owned lands outside authorized hunting, chasing or training seasons or during unauthorized raccoon hound field trials	4 VAC 15-40-60(E)†	$50	$61	$111
Failing to mark certain traps or snares with non-ferrous identity tags	4 VAC 15-40-170††	$25	$61	$86
Killing or crippling and knowingly allowing any nonmigratory game bird or game animal to be wasted without making a reasonable effort to retrieve and retain it	4 VAC 15-40-250†	$25	$61	$86
Unlawfully validate (notch) a bear license prior to killing a bear or after killing bear fail to validate a bear license tag before moving the carcass from the place of kill	4 VAC 15-50-81(A)†	$50	$61	$111
Failing to present bear carcass at an authorized checking station after having validated the appropriate bear license tag or failing to comply with procedure at such checking station	4 VAC 15-50-81(B)†	$50	$61	$111
Destroying the identity (sex) of bear before validating bear license tag and checking at an authorized checking station	4 VAC 15-50-81(C)†	$50	$61	$111
Unlawfully validate a deer license tag prior to killing a deer or after killing deer fail to validate a deer license tag before moving the carcass from the place of kill	4 VAC 15-90-231(A)†	$50	$61	$111
Failing to either present deer carcass at an authorized checking station after having validated the appropriate deer license tag or report the kill through automated reporting system	4 VAC 15-90-231(B)†	$50	$61	$111
Destroying the identity (sex) of deer before validating deer license tag and checking at an authorized checking station	4 VAC 15-90-231(C)†	$50	$61	$111
Unlawfully validate a turkey license tag prior to killing a turkey or after killing turkey failing to validate a turkey license tag before moving the carcass from the place of kill	4 VAC 15-240-81(A)†	$50	$61	$111

Description of Offense*	Statute or Regulation	Fine	Processing Fee‡‡‡*	Total
Failing to either present turkey carcass at an authorized checking station after having validated the appropriate turkey license tag or during the spring season only report the kill through automated reporting system	4 VAC 15-240-81(B)†	$50	$61	$111
Destroying the identity (sex) of turkey before validating turkey license tag and checking at an authorized checking system	4 VAC 15-240-81(C)†	$50	$61	$111
Failing to use nontoxic shot for waterfowl hunting	4 VAC 15-260-140†	$25	$61	$86
Using a rifle of a calibre less than 23 for hunting or killing of bear or deer	4 VAC 15-270-10†††	$100	$61	$161
Exceeding the creel limits for various species of fish on designated waters	4 VAC 15-320-25†	$60	$61	$121
Possessing illegal size game fish	4 VAC 15-320-25†	$25	$61	$86
Fishing in designated stocked trout waters or in water specified in the regulations listed (during the period from May 16 through September 30) after obtaining the daily creel limit of trout	4 VAC 15-330-80†	$50	$61	$111
Feeding or baiting trout in designated stocked trout waters	4 VAC 15-330-90†	$10	$61	$71
Taking or attempting to take fish at any time by snagging, grabbing, snaring, gigging, with a striking iron, or with the use of SCUBA gear	4 VAC 15-350-10†	$50	$61	$111
Unlawfully using trot-line, jugline or set pole	4 VAC 15-350-60†	$25	$61	$86
Failure to display light while drifting or at anchor	4 VAC 15-420-100††††	$25	$61	$86
Vessel failing to obey regulatory markers; placing in, on or near the water unauthorized regulatory markers	4 VAC 15-370-50†	$30	$61	$91
Failure to keep to starboard when meeting head and head	4 VAC 15-390-20††††	$30	$61	$91
Failure to yield right-of-way when crossing	4 VAC 15-390-30††††	$30	$61	$91
Failure to keep clear when overtaking another vessel	4 VAC 15-390-40(A)††††	$30	$61	$91
Failure of motorboat to yield right of way to sailing vessel	4 VAC 15-390-50††††	$35	$61	$96
Failure to slacken speed to avoid endangerment of persons or property by wake	4 VAC 15-390-80††††	$30	$61	$91
Failure of person at least age 18 occupying front seat of vehicle to use safety belt system	46.2-1094(A) 46.2-1094(C)	$25	—	$25
Failure of driver to ensure that child up to age 8 is properly secured in approved child restraint device (first violation only)	46.2-1095(A) 46.2-1098	$50	—	$50

Description of Offense*	Statute or Regulation	Fine	Processing Fee***	Total
Failure of driver to ensure that another person 8 through 17 years of age is properly secured by safety belt system (first violation only)	46.2-1095(B) 46.2-1098	$50	—	$50
Failure of driver to carry written statement exempting child from use of child restraint device	46.2-1096 46.2-1098	$20	—	$20
Refusing officer's order to drive vehicle to weighing station	46.2-1137	$35	$61	$96
Driving in violation of HOT Lane Restrictions (first offense)	33.2-503(3)	$50	$61	$111
Driving in violation of HOT Lane Restrictions (second offense)	33.2-503(3)	$250	$61	$311
Driving in violation of HOT Lane Restrictions (third offense within two years of second offense)	33.2-503(3)	$500	$61	$561
Driving in violation of HOT Lane Restrictions (fourth and subsequent offense within three years of second offense)	33.2-503(3)	$1000	$61	$1061

* The description of offense is for reference and is not a legal definition.

** Unless otherwise provided by statute.

*** See §§ 9.1-106 and 53.1-120 of the Code.

[1] This designation "PRF Reg" refers to the Potomac River Fisheries Commission Regulations. The cite provides the regulation number, the section number and the subsection number.

[2] Subtract fees from total and post balance to fine.

[3] "Park" is defined pursuant to § 4 VAC 5-30-10 as and is intended for the purposes of this rule to mean all designated parks, parkways, historical and natural areas, sites and other recreational areas under the jurisdiction of the Virginia Department of Conservation and Recreation.

[4] Established pursuant to §10.1-104 of the Code.

[†] These Regulations are promulgated pursuant to §§ 29.1-701 and 29.1-802 of the Code.

[††] The Regulations are promulgated pursuant to §§ 29.1-103, 29.1-501 and 29.1-502 of the Code.

[†††] The Regulations are promulgated pursuant to § 29.1-501 of the Code.

[††††] The Regulations are promulgated pursuant to §§ 29.1-701 and 29.1- and 29.1-802 of the Code.

Introduction to Appendix

We are happy to provide you with **The Supreme Court on Selected Criminal and Traffic Issues**. This appendix is designed to provide the reader with a concise overview of U.S. Supreme Court decisions relating to criminal and traffic law. Prepared by the publisher's staff of lawyer-editors, selected case notes from the **United States Supreme Court Reports, Lawyers' Edition 2d** provide succinct summaries of Supreme Court holdings based on the Court's own language. The aim of the appendix is to efficiently inform the reader of governing decisions relating to criminal and traffic issues and to enrich the understanding of the true spirit and nature of the law.

The appendix is organized by subject, with case notes listed in paragraph form. Under each specific subject heading, case notes are listed in reverse chronological order. Thus, using the Analysis at the front of the appendix, it is possible to focus upon an area of interest and quickly scan a handful of case notes to gain a valuable overview of the Court's history of decisions on a specific topic. Selected from decisions reaching back to 1956, case law is current as of July 12, 2016.

Also included in this appendix are Practice Pointers, which draw from the Supreme Court's decisions to provide practical, real world advice for both officers and attorneys. Finally, references to relevant Lawyer's Edition Annotations are included as an aid to continued research. Written in a clear, narrative format, these Annotations (available electronically) guide the reader through the progression of cases that constitute the Supreme Court's body of decisions on selected key points of constitutional law.

Due to the concise nature of the case notes and the limited scope of this appendix, the serious researcher is encouraged to broaden their research and to retrieve the full text of each relevant case. For those publications that are packaged with a companion CD, a full text version of each case summarized in the appendix is provided in a searchable and linked electronic format. Similarly, full text versions of all Annotations referenced are provided. Full text versions of the cases and Annotations are also available online via LexisNexis.com, and through electronic and print versions of the **United States Supreme Court Reports, Lawyer's Edition.**

Concise and accessible enough to be read in a single sitting, yet optimized for quick reference, any officer or attorney who uses this appendix will undoubtedly find that it is an efficient way of enriching their comprehension of the complex constitutional issues surrounding criminal and traffic laws.

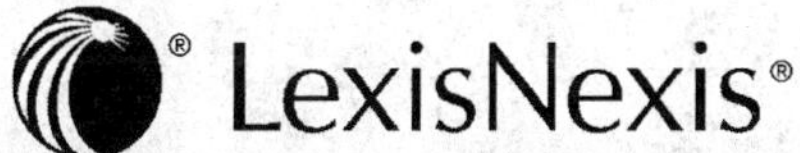

Introduction to Appendix

We are happy to provide you with The Supreme Court on Selected Criminal and Traffic Issues. This appendix is designed to provide the reader with a concise overview of U.S. Supreme Court decisions relating to criminal and traffic law. Prepared by the publisher's staff of lawyer-editors, selected case notes from the **United States Supreme Court Reports, Lawyers' Edition 2d** provide succinct summaries of Supreme Court holdings based on the Court's own language. The aim of the appendix is to efficiently inform the reader of governing decisions relating to criminal and traffic issues and to enrich the understanding of the true spirit and nature of the law.

The appendix is organized by subject, with case notes listed in paragraph form. Under each specific subject heading, case notes are listed in reverse chronological order. Thus, using the Analysis at the front of the appendix, it is possible to focus upon an area of interest and quickly scan a timeline of case notes to gain a valuable overview of the Court's history of decisions on a specific topic. Selected from decisions reaching back to 1956, case law is current as of July 12, 2016.

Also included in this appendix are Practice Pointers, which draw from the Supreme Court's decisions to provide practical, real-world advice for both officers and attorneys, and key references to relevant Lawyers' Edition Annotations are included as an aid to additional research. Written in a clear, narrative format, these Annotations (available electronically) guide the reader through the progression of cases that constitute the Supreme Court's body of decisions on selected key points of constitutional law.

Due to the concise nature of the case notes and the limited scope of this appendix, the serious researcher is encouraged to broaden their research and to retrieve the full text of each relevant case. For those publications that are bundled with a companion CD, a full-text version of each case summarized in the appendix is provided in a searchable and linked electronic format. Similarly, full text versions of all Annotations referenced are provided. Full text versions of the cases and Annotations are also available online via Lexis.com, and through electronic and print versions of the **United States Supreme Court Reports, Lawyers' Edition**.

Concise and accessible enough to be read in a single sitting, yet optimized for quick reference, any officer or attorney who uses this appendix will undoubtedly find that it is an efficient way of enriching their comprehension of the complex constitutional issues surrounding criminal and traffic laws.

THE SUPREME COURT ON SELECT CRIMINAL AND TRAFFIC ISSUES

(Derived from the United States Supreme Court Reports, Lawyers' Edition)

Arrests

§ 1. In General

Although a warrant presumptively is required for a felony arrest in a suspect's home, the Federal Constitution's Fourth Amendment permits warrantless arrests in public places where an officer has probable cause to believe that a felony has occurred. *Florida v. White* (1999) 526 US 559, 143 L Ed 2d 748, 1999 US LEXIS 3172, 119 S Ct 1555.

To say that an arrest—a seizure of the person for the purposes of the Federal Constitution's Fourth Amendment—is effected by the slightest application of physical force, despite the arrestee's escape, is not to say that for Fourth Amendment purposes there is a continuing arrest during the period of fugitivity; if, for example, a police officer lays his hands upon a fleeing person to arrest him, but the fugitive breaks away and then discards contraband, it is not realistic to say that the contraband was discovered during the course of an arrest. *California v. Hodari D.* (1991) 499 US 621, 113 L Ed 2d 690, 1991 US LEXIS 2397, 111 S Ct 1547.

To constitute a seizure of the person, just as to constitute an arrest—the quintessential "seizure of the person" under Fourth Amendment jurisprudence—there must be either the application of physical force, however slight, or, where that is absent, submission to an officer's "show of authority" to restrain the subject's liberty. *California v. Hodari D.* (1991) 499 US 621, 113 L Ed 2d 690, 1991 US LEXIS 2397, 111 S Ct 1547.

Every arrest, and every seizure having the essential attributes of a formal arrest, is unreasonable, within the meaning of the Fourth Amendment, unless it is supported by probable cause, but an exception for limited intrusions that may be justified by special law enforcement interests is not confined to the momentary, on-the-street detention accompanied by a frisk for weapons. *Michigan v. Summers* (1981) 452 US 692, 69 L Ed 2d 340, 1981 US LEXIS 118, 101 S Ct 2587.

§ 2. Exclusionary Rule

Defendant was stopped unlawfully by an officer lacking reasonable suspicion. During this stop, the officer learned defendant had an outstanding arrest warrant for a traffic violation. The officer then arrested defendant pursuant to that warrant, and discovered a baggie of methamphetamine and drug paraphernalia on defendant's person incident to that arrest. That evidence was admissible because the unlawful stop was sufficiently attenuated by the pre-existing arrest warrant, a critical intervening circumstance wholly independent of the illegal stop. The discovery of that warrant broke the causal chain between the unconstitutional stop and the discovery of evidence by compelling the officer to arrest defendant. *Utah v. Strieff* (2016) 579 US __, 195 L Ed 2d 400, 2016 US LEXIS 3926.

Suppression of evidence seized in violation of the Federal Constitution's Fourth Amendment is not required by the exclusionary rule where the evidence was seized incident to an arrest made on the basis of erroneous information—a computer check of a driver stopped for a routine traffic violation revealed the existence of an outstanding misdemeanor warrant for the driver's arrest, when in fact the warrant had been quashed 2 weeks earlier—which in turn resulted from a clerical error of court employees. *Arizona v. Evans* (1995) 514 US 1, 131 L Ed 2d 34, 1995 US LEXIS 1806, 115 S Ct 1185.

The indirect fruits of an illegal arrest should be suppressed when they bear a sufficiently close relationship to the underlying illegality; however, such attenuation analysis is appropriate only where, as a threshold matter, courts determine that the challenged evidence is in some sense the product of illegal governmental activity. *New York v. Harris* (1990) 495 US 14, 109 L Ed 2d 13, 1990 US LEXIS 2037, 110 S Ct 1640.

The Fourth Amendment exclusionary rule does not bar a state's use in a criminal trial of a written inculpatory statement made by a murder suspect at a police station—even though the statement was taken after the suspect was arrested by the police in his home without a warrant and without consent to their entry—where (1) the statement was not the product of being in unlawful custody, inasmuch as the police had probable cause to arrest the suspect; (2) the police had a justification to question the suspect prior to his arrest, so that the suspect's subsequent statement was not an exploitation of the illegal entry into the suspect's home; and (3) the statement was not the fruit of having been arrested in the home rather than someplace else. *New York v. Harris* (1990) 495 US 14, 109 L Ed 2d 13, 1990 US LEXIS 2037, 110 S Ct 1640.

§ 3. Media Accompaniment

A "media ride-along"—in which a print reporter and a photographer for a newspaper accompany a team of federal and county police officers during an attempt to execute arrest warrants in a private home—violates the Federal Constitution's Fourth Amendment. *Wilson v. Layne* (1999) 526 US 603, 143 L Ed 2d 818, 119 S Ct 1692, 1999 US LEXIS 3633.

§ 4. Probable Cause

Officer had probable cause to believe that defendant had committed the crime of possession of a controlled substance where in addition to the driver and a back seat passenger, defendant was a front seat passenger in a vehicle which was stopped for speeding in the early morning hours; upon a consensual search, a significant amount of cash was found in the glove compartment of the vehicle and drugs were discovered between the back-seat armrest and the back seat; and although defendant subsequently admitted that the drugs and cash were his, none of the vehicle occupants admitted to ownership of the drugs at the time of the search, and all three occupants were arrested. It was an entirely reasonable inference that any or all three of the occupants had knowledge of, and exercised dominion and control over, the drugs, and thus a reasonable officer could conclude that there was probable cause to believe defendant committed the crime of possession of drugs, either solely or jointly. It was also reasonable for the officer to infer a common enterprise among the three occupants, in view of the likelihood of drug dealing in which an innocent party was unlikely to be involved. *Maryland v. Pringle* (2003) 540 US 366, 157 L Ed 2d 769, 2003 US LEXIS 9198, 124 S Ct 795.

Under the Federal Constitution's Fourth Amendment, police officers need either a warrant, or probable cause plus exigent circumstances, in order to make a lawful entry into a home. Thus, a state court erred in failing to assess whether exigent circumstances were present when some police officers entered an individual's home without either an arrest warrant or a search warrant, arrested him, and searched him. Exigent circumstances were required to justify the officers' conduct even if, as the state court ruled, the officers had probable cause to arrest the individual. *Kirk v. Louisiana* (2002) 536 US 635, 153 L Ed 2d 599, 2002 US LEXIS 4682, 122 S Ct 2458.

A jurisdiction that provides judicial determinations of probable cause within 48 hours of a warrantless arrest will, as a general matter, comply with the requirement, under the Federal Constitution's Fourth Amendment, that such determinations be provided promptly, and such a jurisdiction will therefore be immune from systemic challenges to its probable cause determination procedures. *County of Riverside v. McLaughlin* (1991) 500 US 44, 114 L Ed 2d 49, 1991 US LEXIS 2528, 111 S Ct 1661.

Although a county is entitled to combine probable cause determinations following warrantless arrests with the arrestees' arraignment, the county's policy of excluding weekends and holidays in computing the 2-day period within which the combined proceedings must be offered—which exclusion could result in delays of up to 7 days—means that the county's regular practice exceeds the 48-hour period that will generally satisfy the promptness requirement for probable cause determinations that is imposed by the Federal Constitution's Fourth Amendment. *County of Riverside v. McLaughlin* (1991) 500 US 44, 114 L Ed 2d 49, 1991 US LEXIS 2528, 111 S Ct 1661.

Before agents of the government may invade the sanctity of the home without a search or arrest warrant, the burden is on the government to demonstrate exigent circumstances that overcome the presumption of unreasonableness that attaches to all warrantless home entries; when the government's interest is only to arrest for a minor offense, that presumption is difficult to rebut, and the government usually should be allowed to make such arrests only with a warrant issued upon probable cause by a neutral and detached magistrate. *Welsh v. Wisconsin* (1984) 466 US 740, 80 L Ed 2d 732, 1984 US LEXIS 82, 104 S Ct 2091.

Probable cause which will justify an arrest without a warrant by police officers exists where the facts and circumstances within the officers' knowledge and of which they have reasonably trustworthy information are sufficient in themselves to warrant a man of reasonable caution in the belief that an offense has been or is being committed by the person to be arrested. *Dunaway v. New York* (1979) 442 US 200, 60 L Ed 2d 824, 1979 US LEXIS 126, 99 S Ct 2248.

Under the Fourth Amendment, a person arrested without a warrant and charged by information with a state offense is entitled to a timely judicial determination by a neutral magistrate of probable cause for pretrial restraint of liberty, and may not be jailed or subjected to other significant restraints pending trial without any opportunity for such a probable cause determination; the state prosecutor's decision to file an information does not alone meet the requirements of the Fourth Amendment as constituting a determination of probable cause that furnishes sufficient reason for detention pending trial. *Gerstein v. Pugh* (1975) 420 US 103, 43 L Ed 2d 54, 95 S Ct 854, 1975 US LEXIS 29.

§ 5. Search Incident to Arrest

Data on an suspect's cell phone—including texts, e-mails, photos and call logs—may not be searched incident to arrest. Officers must generally secure a warrant before conducting such a search, unless an exigency is present. However, officers may examine the physical aspects of a phone to ensure that it will not be used as a weapon—for example, to determine whether there is a razor blade hidden between the phone and its case. *Riley v. California* (2014) 573 US __, 134 S Ct 2473, 189 L Ed 2d 430, 2014 US LEXIS 4497.

When police officers make an arrest supported by probable cause to hold for a serious offense and bring the suspect to the station to be detained in custody, taking and analyzing a cheek swab of the arrestee's DNA is, like fingerprinting and photographing, a legitimate police booking procedure that is reasonable under the Fourth Amendment. *Maryland v. King* (2013) 569 US ___, 133 S Ct 1958, 186 L Ed 2d 1, 2013 US LEXIS 4165.

Evidence obtained during a search incident to arrest of a vehicle that would violate the holding of *Arizona v. Gant* is not subject to the exclusionary rule if the search was conducted before the Gant decision was announced and was lawful under the previous standard set in *New York v. Belton.* Suppressing such evidence would do nothing to deter police misconduct, which is the sole purpose of the Exclusionary Rule. *Davis v. U.S.* (2011) 564 US 229, 180 L Ed 2d 285, 131 S Ct 2419, 2011 US LEXIS 4560.

When police arrest the driver of or a passenger in a vehicle, officers may search the passenger compartment of the vehicle incident to the arrest, but only if the arrestee is within "reaching distance" of the passenger compartment at the time of the search, ***or*** it is reasonable to believe the vehicle contains evidence of the offense of arrest. If the arrestee has already been handcuffed and placed in the back of a patrol car, then a search of the vehicle is no longer justified because the arrestee is no longer capable of accessing any weapon potentially hidden inside, unless police reasonable expect to find evidence of the crime for which the arrest was made in the vehicle. While police can generally expect to find evidence following a drug arrest (e.g. more drugs, paraphernalia), a search is not allowed following a traffic violation (for example, driving with a suspended license) as no evidence of such offenses could be concealed inside the vehicle. *Arizona v. Gant* (2009) 556 US 332, 173 L Ed 2d 485, 2009 US LEXIS 3120, 129 S Ct 1710.

For a search incident to arrest to be valid, the underlying arrest need only be "lawful" in terms of the Fourth Amendment, not necessarily whatever local state statute applies. Although an arrest for driving under suspension was not valid under Virginia state law (such a traffic offense is not an "arrestable offense" in that state unless the arrestee fails or refuses to continue driving, or the officer reasonable believes the arrestee will likely disregard a summons or harm himself or others, and neither circumstance applied), a subsequent search incident to arrest was nevertheless valid under the Fourth Amendment, because the arrest was supported by probable cause. *Virginia v. Moore* (2008) 553 US 164, 170 L Ed 2d 559, 128 S Ct 1598, 2008 US LEXIS 3674.

When a police officer has made a lawful custodial arrest of the occupant of an automobile, the officer may, as a contemporaneous incident of that arrest, search the passenger compartment of the automobile and examine the contents of any containers found within the passenger compartment—the same probable cause to believe that a container holds drugs will allow the police to arrest the person transporting the container and search it. *California v. Acevedo* (1991) 500 US 565, 114 L Ed 2d 619, 1991 US LEXIS 3016, 111 S Ct 1982.

In the case of a search incident to a lawful arrest, if the police stray outside the permissible scope of the search, they are in violation of the Fourth Amendment, and evidence so seized will be excluded. *Horton v. California* (1990) 496 US 128, 110 L Ed 2d 112, 1990 US LEXIS 2937, 110 S Ct 2301.

As an incident to an in-home arrest, police may, as a precautionary measure and without a search warrant, probable cause, or reasonable suspicion, look in closets and other spaces immediately adjoining the place of arrest from which an attack could be immediately launched; beyond that, however, the Fourth Amendment permits a protective sweep, without a search warrant, in conjunction with an in-home arrest—extending only to a cursory inspection of those spaces where a person may be found, lasting no longer than is necessary to dispel the reasonable suspicion of danger, and in any event no longer than it takes to complete the arrest and depart the premises—when the searching officer possesses a reasonable belief based on specific and articulable facts which, taken together with the rational inferences from those facts, would warrant a reasonably prudent officer in believing that the area to be swept harbors an individual posing a danger to those on the arrest scene. *Maryland v. Buie* (1990) 494 US 325, 108 L Ed 2d 276, 1990 US LEXIS 1176, 110 S Ct 1093.

Police officers possessing an arrest warrant and probable cause to believe that the person to be arrested is in his or her home are entitled, under the Fourth Amendment, to enter the home and search anywhere in the home in which the person might be found; once the person is found, however, the search for the person is over, and there is no longer that particular justification for entering any rooms that have not yet been searched; that the person has an expectation of privacy in those remaining areas of the house, however, does not mean such rooms are immune from entry. *Maryland v. Buie* (1990) 494 US 325, 108 L Ed 2d 276, 1990 US LEXIS 1176, 110 S Ct 1093.

If police officers arrest a person for speeding or for driving while intoxicated, they can search the passenger compartment of the car, and they can search the trunk if they have probable cause to believe that the trunk contains contraband. *Michigan v. Long* (1983) 463 US 1032, 77 L Ed 2d 1201, 1983 US LEXIS 7, 103 S Ct 3469.

A policeman who has made a lawful custodial arrest of the occupant of an automobile may, as a contemporaneous incident of that arrest, search the passenger compartment of the automobile and may examine the contents of any containers found within the passenger compartment, the term "container" denoting any object capable of holding another object and including closed or open glove compartments, consoles, or other receptacles, as well as luggage, boxes, bags, clothing, and the like. *New York v. Belton* (1981) 453 US 454, 69 L Ed 2d 768, 1981 US LEXIS 13, 101 S Ct 2860, *reh den* 453 US 950, 69 L Ed 2d 1036, 102 S Ct 26.

A law enforcement officer may not, consistent with the Fourth Amendment, search for the subject of an arrest warrant in the home of a third party without first obtaining a search warrant, absent consent or exigent circumstances, for (1) the requirement of a search warrant does not significantly impede effective law enforcement efforts when weighed against the constitutional interests at stake, (2) the third party has a Fourth Amendment privacy interest in being free from an unreasonable invasion and search of his home, and (3) the arrest warrant serves to protect only those named in the warrant from an unreasonable seizure, but does nothing to safeguard the third party's interest in the privacy of his home and possessions against the unjustified intrusion of the police. *Steagald v. United States* (1981) 451 US 204, 68 L Ed 2d 38, 1981 US LEXIS 89, 101 S Ct 1642.

The search of a locked footlocker by federal agents acting without a search warrant but upon a probable cause belief that the footlocker contained contraband—which search is conducted in a federal building to which the footlocker had been brought by federal agents after being lawfully seized at the time of the arrests of those who had been in possession of the footlocker—cannot be justified as being incident to the arrests or on the basis of any other exigency, where the search is conducted more than an hour after federal agents had gained exclusive control of the footlocker and long after those from whom it had been seized were securely in custody. *United States v. Chadwick* (1977) 433 US 1, 53 L Ed 2d 538, 1977 US LEXIS 133, 97 S Ct 2476.

A search incident to a lawful arrest is a traditional exception to the warrant requirement of the Fourth Amendment; such a search may be made (1) of the person of the arrestee by virtue of the lawful arrest, and (2) of the area within the arrestee's control. *United States v. Robinson* (1973) 414 US 218, 38 L Ed 2d 427, 1973 US LEXIS 21, 94 S Ct 467.

After a police officer lawfully places a suspect under arrest for the purpose of taking him into custody, the officer may proceed to fully search the prisoner, and is not limited—as in the case of a stop-and-frisk search incident to an investigative stop based on less than probable cause to arrest—to conducting a frisk of outer clothing only and removing such weapons that he may, as a result of such limited frisk, reasonably believe the suspect has in his possession. *United States v. Robinson* (1973) 414 US 218, 38 L Ed 2d 427, 1973 US LEXIS 21, 94 S Ct 467.

Limits imposed by the Fourth Amendment are not offended by a full search of the defendant's person by a District of Columbia police officer pursuant to established police department practice after a lawful, full custody arrest of the defendant for operating a motor vehicle after revocation of the defendant's operator's permit, or by the officer's seizure of heroin capsules found in a crumpled cigarette package in the defendant's coat pocket and introduced in evidence in a narcotics prosecution which resulted in conviction, it being immaterial that the officer did not indicate any subjective fear of the defendant, that he did not suspect that the defendant was armed, that he was not specifically looking for weapons or anything else, or that no further evidence of the crime of driving while one's permit was revoked could be obtained in the search; having in the course of a lawful search come upon the crumpled cigarette package, the officer was entitled to inspect it, and when his inspection revealed the heroin capsules, he was entitled to seize them as fruits, instrumentalities, or contraband probative of criminal conduct. *United States v. Robinson* (1973) 414 US 218, 38 L Ed 2d 427, 1973 US LEXIS 21, 94 S Ct 467.

While a search incident to an arrest, although justified in part by the acknowledged necessity to protect the arresting officer from assault with a concealed weapon, is also justified on other grounds and can therefore involve a relatively extensive exploration of the person, a search for weapons in the absence of probable cause to arrest must, like any other search, be strictly circumscribed by the exigencies justifying its initiation; thus it must be limited to that which is necessary for the discovery of weapons which might be used to harm the officer or others nearby, and may realistically be characterized as something less than a "full" search, even though it remains a serious intrusion. *Terry v. Ohio* (1968) 392 US 1, 20 L Ed 2d 889, 1968 US LEXIS 1345, 88 S Ct 1868.

§ 6. Warrant Requirement for Arrest

An arrest pursuant to a warrant that was wrongfully included in a county database due to an isolated incidence of police negligence did not trigger the Exclusionary Rule. Other officers, not the arresting officers, negligently failed to enter the recall of the arrest warrant in the database. Because the error was nonrecurring—not a result of systematic negligence—and attenuated from the arrest, application of the Exclusionary Rule would not have resulted in appreciable deterrence of future violations. *Herring v. United States* (2009) 555 US 135, 172 L Ed 2d 496, 2009 US LEXIS 581, 129 S Ct 695.

For purposes of determining whether a warrantless arrest is lawful under the Fourth Amendment, the criminal offense for which there is probable cause to arrest does not have to be "closely related" to the offense stated by the arresting officer at the time of arrest. *Devenpeck v. Alford* (2004) 543 US 146, 160 L Ed 2d 537, 125 S Ct 588, 2004 US LEXIS 8272.

Under the Federal Constitution's Fourth Amendment, police officers need either a warrant, or probable cause plus exigent circumstances, in order to make a lawful entry into a home. Thus, a state court erred in failing to assess whether exigent circumstances were present when some police officers entered an individual's home without either an arrest warrant or a search warrant, arrested him, and searched him. Exigent circumstances were required to justify the officers' conduct even if, as the state court ruled, the officers had probable cause to arrest the individual. *Kirk v. Louisiana* (2002) 536 US 635, 153 L Ed 2d 599, 2002 US LEXIS 4682, 122 S Ct 2458.

The Fourth Amendment does not forbid a warrantless arrest for a minor criminal offense, such as a misdemeanor seatbelt violation punishable only by a fine. *Atwater v. Lago Vista* (2001) 532 US 318, 149 L Ed 2d 549, 2001 US LEXIS 3366, 121 S Ct 1536.

Warrantless arrests are permitted under the Federal Constitution's Fourth Amendment, but persons arrested without a warrant must promptly be brought before a neutral magistrate for a judicial determination of probable cause. *County of Riverside v. McLaughlin* (1991) 500 US 44, 114 L Ed 2d 49, 1991 US LEXIS 2528, 111 S Ct 1661.

A routine felony arrest by the police of a murder suspect in his home without an arrest warrant and by means of a nonconsensual entry violates the Fourth Amendment. *New York v. Harris* (1990) 495 US 14, 109 L Ed 2d 13, 1990 US LEXIS 2037, 110 S Ct 1640.

Police officers acting without probable cause and without a warrant violate the Fourth Amendment, made applicable to the states by the Fourteenth Amendment, by forcibly removing a person from his home or other place where he is entitled to be and transporting him to the police station for fingerprinting; such seizures, at least where not under judicial supervision, are sufficiently like arrests to invoke the traditional rule that arrests may constitutionally be made only on probable cause, and fingerprints taken under these circumstances are thus the inadmissible fruits of an illegal detention. *Hayes v. Florida* (1985) 470 US 811, 84 L Ed 2d 705, 1985 US LEXIS 1523, 105 S Ct 1643.

A warrantless home arrest for driving while intoxicated is not justified by the need to preserve evidence of the offender's blood-alcohol level, the imminent destruction of evidence being an exigent circumstance exception to the warrant requirement of the Fourth Amendment, where a state has chosen to classify the first offense for driving while intoxicated as a noncriminal, civil forfeiture offense for which no imprisonment is possible; given this expression of the state's interest in precipitating an arrest, a warrantless home arrest cannot be upheld simply because evidence of the offender's blood-alcohol level might have dissipated while the police obtained a warrant. *Welsh v. Wisconsin* (1984) 466 US 740, 80 L Ed 2d 732, 1984 US LEXIS 82, 104 S Ct 2091.

While an arrest warrant and a search warrant both serve to subject the probable-cause determination of the police to judicial review, the interests protected by the two warrants differ, for (1) an arrest warrant is issued by a magistrate upon a showing that probable cause exists to believe that the subject of the warrant has committed an offense and thus the warrant primarily serves to protect an individual from an unreasonable seizure; while (2) a search warrant, in contrast, is issued upon a showing of probable cause to believe that the legitimate object of a search is located in a particular place, and therefore safeguards an individual's interest in the privacy of his home and possessions against the unjustified intrusion of the police. *Steagald v. United States* (1981) 451 US 204, 68 L Ed 2d 38, 1981 US LEXIS 89, 101 S Ct 1642.

The Fourth Amendment prohibits the police from making a warrantless and nonconsensual entry into a suspect's home in order to make a routine felony arrest. *Payton v. New York* (1980) 445 US 573, 63 L Ed 2d 639, 1980 US LEXIS 13, 100 S Ct 1371.

City police violate the Fourth and Fourteenth Amendments when, without probable cause to arrest, they take an individual into custody, transport him to the police station, and detain him there for interrogation without making a formal arrest. *Dunaway v. New York* (1979) 442 US 200, 60 L Ed 2d 824, 1979 US LEXIS 126, 99 S Ct 2248.

The usual rule is that a police officer may arrest without a warrant one believed by the officer upon reasonable cause to have been guilty of a felony; the lawfulness of the arrest without a warrant must be based upon probable cause. *United States v. Watson* (1976) 423 US 411, 46 L Ed 2d 598, 1976 US LEXIS 121, 96 S Ct 820.

Good faith on the part of an arresting officer is not sufficient to establish the validity of an arrest without a warrant. *Terry v. Ohio* (1968) 392 US 1, 20 L Ed 2d 889, 1968 US LEXIS 1345, 88 S Ct 1868.

§ 7. Transporting Subject Without Warrant

Within the meaning of the Federal Constitution's Fourth Amendment, an individual, who was then a suspect in a murder investigation and who was then 17 years old, was illegally arrested before he was questioned, when officers of a county sheriff's department transported the individual involuntarily from his home to the sheriff's headquarters for questioning, as: (1) There was evidence that (a) the officers, who did not have a warrant and concededly lacked probable cause at that time, awakened the individual in his home at approximately 3 a.m.; (b) one of the officers told the individual that "we need to go and talk"; (c) the individual replied "Okay"; (d) the officers (i) handcuffed the individual, who was in his underwear, and (ii) took him the scene of the crime and then to headquarters; and (e) once at headquarters, the officers removed the handcuffs, after which the individual was given Miranda warnings and interrogated. (2) On this evidence, the circumstances which indicated that a seizure occurred included (a) the threatening presence of several officers, (b) some physical touching of the individual, (c) the use of language or tone of voice indicating that compliance with the officers' request might be compelled, and (d) possibly, a display of a weapon by at least one officer. (3) There was no reason to think the individual's "Okay" answer was anything more than a mere submission to a claim of lawful authority. (4) Even if there were doubt on this point, the ensuing events resolved it, where, once the individual was taken to headquarters and the officers began to question the individual, a reasonable person in this situation would not have thought that the person was sitting in the interview room as a matter of choice, free to change the person's mind and to go home to bed. (5) It was not significant that the sheriff's department asserted that it "routinely" transported persons, including this individual on one prior occasion, while handcuffed for the safety of the officers, as stressing the officers' motivation of self-protection did not speak to how their actions would reasonably be understood. (6) Moreover, it was not significant that the individual assertedly did not resist the use of handcuffs or act in a manner consistent with anything other than full cooperation, as failure to struggle with a cohort of deputy sheriffs was not a waiver of Fourth Amendment protection, which did not require the perversity of resisting arrest or assaulting a police officer. *Kaupp v. Texas* (2003) 538 US 626, 155 L Ed 2d 814, 123 S Ct 1843, 2003 US LEXIS 3670.

§ 8. Foreign Nationals

Failure to inform an arrested foreign national of the right under Article 36 of the Vienna Convention to contact a consular officer of his or her home country does not require suppression of subsequent statements made by the foreign national under the Exclusionary Rule. *Sanchez-Llamas v. Oregon* (2006) 548 US 331, 165 L Ed 2d 557, 126 S Ct 2669, 2006 US LEXIS 5177.

Stop and Frisk; Temporary Detention

§ 1. In General

An officer's reasonable mistake of law can nevertheless provide reasonable suspicion justifying a stop under the Fourth Amendment. When a North Carolina officer stopped a vehicle for a faulty right brake light, the stop was upheld even though a state court later determined that North Carolina statutory law only required one working brake light, which the vehicle had. Although there was no actual violation of state law, the Court found the officer's mistake objectively reasonable, given the language of the statute and the fact it had never been construed previously by North Carolina courts. *Heien v. North Carolina* (2014) 574 US __, 190 L Ed 2d 475, 2014 US LEXIS 8306, 135 S Ct 530.

Under the Fourth Amendment, a policeman who lacks probable cause, but whose observations lead him reasonably to suspect that a particular person has committed, is committing, or is about to commit a crime, may detain that person briefly in order to investigate the circumstances that provoke suspicion; the stop and inquiry must be reasonably related in scope to the justification for their initiation. *Berkemer v. McCarty* (1984) 468 US 420, 82 L Ed 2d 317, 1984 US LEXIS 140, 104 S Ct 3138.

The governmental interest of effective crime prevention and detection underlies the recognition that a police officer may in appropriate circumstances and in an appropriate manner approach a person for purposes of investigating possibly criminal behavior even though there is no probable cause to make an arrest, as where a police officer observed defendant and two other men go through a series of acts, each of them perhaps innocent in itself, but which, taken together, warranted further investigation, in the instant case the investigation of daytime robbery. *Terry v. Ohio* (1968) 392 US 1, 20 L Ed 2d 889, 1968 US LEXIS 1345, 88 S Ct 1868.

The police "stop and frisk" practice is not outside the purview of the Fourth Amendment, which governs "seizures" of the person not eventuating in "arrests" in traditional terminology; whenever a police officer accosts an individual and restrains his freedom to walk away, he has "seized" that person, and a careful exploration of the outer surfaces of a person's clothing all over his body in an attempt to find weapons is a "search," a serious intrusion upon the sanctity of the person, which is not to be undertaken lightly. *Terry v. Ohio* (1968) 392 US 1, 20 L Ed 2d 889, 1968 US LEXIS 1345, 88 S Ct 1868.

Not all personal intercourse between policemen and citizens involves "seizures" of persons within the meaning of the Fourth Amendment; only where the officer, by means of physical force or show of authority, has in some way restrained the liberty of a citizen is the inference that a "seizure" has occurred justifiable. While the police must, whenever practicable, obtain advance judicial approval of searches and seizures through the warrant procedure, and in most instances failure to comply with the warrant requirement can only be excused by exigent circumstances, the police "stop and frisk" procedure—necessarily swift action predicated upon the on-the-spot observations of the officer on the beat—cannot be subjected to the warrant procedure; instead, the conduct involved must be tested by the Fourth Amendment's general proscription against unreasonable searches and seizures. *Terry v. Ohio* (1968) 392 US 1, 20 L Ed 2d 889, 1968 US LEXIS 1345, 88 S Ct 1868.

§ 2. Airport Travelers

Officers have adequate grounds for suspecting a person of carrying drugs and for temporarily detaining the suspect and his luggage at an airport where the officers discovered that the suspect was traveling under an assumed name and where the suspect's appearance, mannerisms, luggage, and actions fit the so-called "drug courier profile." *Florida v. Royer* (1983) 460 US 491, 75 L Ed 2d 229, 1983 US LEXIS 151, 103 S Ct 1319.

§ 3. Anonymous Tips

In Mendocino County, California, a driver called 911 to report that a silver Ford F-150 pickup truck with a specified license plate had just run her off the road, at mile marker 88 on south-bound Highway 1. Roughly 18 minutes after the call, a California Highway Patrol officer spotted the same truck at mile marker 69, 19 miles south of the reported incident. The U.S Supreme Court ruled that, assuming the 911 call was anonymous, the officer nevertheless had reasonable suspicion to stop the truck. By reporting that she had been run off the road by a specific vehicle, the caller necessarily claimed eyewitness knowledge of the alleged dangerous driving—a driver's claim that another vehicle ran her off the road implies that the informant knows the other car was driven dangerously. That basis of knowledge lent significant support to the tip's reliability. In addition, the officer saw the truck in a location suggesting that the caller must have reported the incident soon after she was run off the road. The Court noted, "That sort of contemporaneous report has long been treated as especially reliable." In addition, 911 calls are recorded, which provides victims with an opportunity to identify the false tipster's voice and subject him to prosecution; a 911 caller's cell phone number can also be easily identified, further discouraging its use in giving false tips. Thus, the caller's use of the 911 system was another factor suggesting reliability. Finally, the Court noted that running another vehicle off a the road "suggests lane positioning problems, decreased vigilance, impaired judgment, or some combination of those recognized drunk driving cues." Thus there was reason to believe the driver of the truck might be intoxicated and therefore committing a crime. Under the totality of these circumstances, an investigatory stop was justified. *Navarette v. California* (2014) 572 US __, 188 L Ed 2d 680, 2014 US LEXIS 2930, 134 S Ct 1683.

Although an anonymous tip—unlike a tip from a known informant whose reputation can be assessed and who can be held responsible if the informant's allegations turn out to be fabricated—alone seldom demonstrates the informant's basis of knowledge or veracity, there are situations in which an anonymous tip, suitably corroborated, exhibits sufficient indicia of reliability, under the Fourth Amendment, to provide reasonable suspicion to make an investigatory stop of a person; however, an anonymous tip that a person is carrying a gun is not, without more, sufficient to justify a police officer's stop and frisk of that person. *Florida v. J.L.* (2000) 529 US 266, 146 L Ed 2d 254, 2000 US LEXIS 2345, 120 S Ct 1375.

A police officer violates the Fourth Amendment by stopping and frisking an accused, when (1) an anonymous caller reports to the police that a young black male standing at a particular bus stop and wearing a plaid shirt is carrying a gun; (2) a police officer, in response to the tip, goes to the bus stop, where the officer sees the accused, who is a 15-year-old black male wearing a plaid shirt; and (3) apart from the tip, the officer has no reason to suspect the accused of illegal conduct, as (a) the officer does not see a firearm, and (b) the accused makes no threatening or otherwise unusual movements. *Florida v. J.L.* (2000) 529 US 266, 146 L Ed 2d 254, 2000 US LEXIS 2345, 120 S Ct 1375.

As a general rule, something more than an anonymous tip is required to provide the reasonable suspicion necessary to make a valid investigatory stop of a person suspected of criminal activity; standing alone, an anonymous tip seldom demonstrates the informant's basis of knowledge or veracity, so as to warrant a man of reasonable caution in the belief that an investigatory stop is appropriate, given that (1) ordinary citizens generally do not provide extensive recitations of the basis of their everyday observations, and (2) the veracity of persons supplying anonymous tips is by hypothesis largely unknown and unknowable. *Alabama v. White* (1990) 496 US 325, 110 L Ed 2d 301, 1990 US LEXIS 3053, 110 S Ct 2412.

An anonymous telephone tip received by a police officer that a person possesses cocaine, as corroborated by independent police work, exhibits sufficient indicia of reliability to provide reasonable suspicion for the police to make an investigatory stop of the person's station wagon, and therefore such stop does not violate the Fourth Amendment, where (1) the anonymous caller states that the person (a) will be leaving a certain apartment within an apartment complex at a particular time in a brown Plymouth station wagon with the right taillight lens broken, (b) will be going to a certain motel, and (c) will be in possession of cocaine, (2) after receiving the call, the officer and his partner proceed to the apartment complex, where (a) they see a brown Plymouth station wagon with a broken right taillight in the parking lot in front of the building which contains the apartment identified by the caller, and (b) they see the person leave the building, carrying nothing in her hands, and enter the station wagon, and (3) police officers (a) follow the vehicle as it drives for a distance of 4 miles, including several turns, along the most direct route to the motel which the caller has identified, and (b) arrange for a patrol unit to stop the vehicle just short of the motel. *Alabama v. White* (1990) 496 US 325, 110 L Ed 2d 301, 1990 US LEXIS 3053, 110 S Ct 2412.

§ 4. Automobile Passengers

During a lawful routine traffic stop, an officer may conduct a pat-down search of the driver and any passengers upon reasonable suspicion that they may be armed and dangerous. In such cases, the officer is not constitutionally required to give the passenger an opportunity to depart the scene without first ensuring that, in so doing, the officer is not permitting a dangerous person to get behind him or her. *Arizona v. Johnson* (2009) 555 US 323, 172 L Ed 2d 694, 2009 US LEXIS 868, 129 S Ct 781.

When police make a traffic stop, a passenger in the car, like the driver, is seized for Fourth Amendment purposes and so may challenge the stop's constitutionality. *Brendlin v. California* (2007) 551 US 249, 168 L Ed 2d 132, 127 S Ct 2400, 2007 US LEXIS 7897.

Temporary detention of individuals during the stop of an automobile by the police, even if only for a brief period and for a limited purpose, constitutes a seizure of persons within the meaning of the Fourth Amendment; thus, an automobile stop is subject to the constitutional imperative that the stop not be unreasonable under the circumstances. *Whren v. United States* (1996) 517 US 806, 135 L Ed 2d 89, 1996 US LEXIS 3720, 116 S Ct 1769.

A police officer's order to a motorist to get out of the car, issued after the vehicle was lawfully stopped for a traffic violation, is reasonable and thus is permissible under the Fourth Amendment even though the officer had no reason to suspect foul play from the particular driver at the time of the stop, since (1) the officer's interest in protection against an unsuspected assault by the driver and against accidental injury from passing traffic is both legitimate and weighty, (2) the intrusion into the driver's personal liberty occasioned by the order to get out of the car, after the car was lawfully stopped, is de minimis, not constituting a serious intrusion upon the sanctity of the person and hardly rising to the level of a petty indignity, and (3) thus, what is at most a mere inconvenience to the driver cannot prevail when balanced against legitimate concerns for the officer's safety. *Pennsylvania v. Mimms* (1977) 434 US 106, 54 L Ed 2d 331, 1977 US LEXIS 157, 98 S Ct 330.

§ 5. Concomitant with Execution of Search Warrant

The initial detention of the occupant of a home subject to a valid search warrant, while the police execute the warrant to search his home for contraband, does not violate the occupant's Fourth Amendment right to be secure against an unreasonable seizure of his person, since the warrant, founded on probable cause where the evidence that the occupant's residence is harboring contraband is sufficient to persuade a judicial officer that an invasion of the occupant's privacy is justified, implicitly carries with it the limited authority to detain the occupants of the premises while a proper search is conducted; because it is lawful to require the occupant to re-enter and to remain in the house until evidence establishing probable cause to arrest him is found, his arrest and the search incident thereto, resulting in the discovery of heroin on his person, are constitutionally permissible. *Michigan v. Summers* (1981) 452 US 692, 69 L Ed 2d 340, 1981 US LEXIS 118, 101 S Ct 2587.

§ 6. Duration

In assessing whether a detention is too long in duration to be justified as an investigative stop, it is appropriate to examine whether the police diligently pursued a means of investigation that was likely to confirm or dispel their suspicions quickly, during which time it was necessary to detain the defendant; the question is not simply whether some other alternative was available, but whether the police acted unreasonably in failing to recognize or to pursue it. *United States v. Sharpe* (1985) 470 US 675, 84 L Ed 2d 605, 1985 US LEXIS 74, 105 S Ct 1568.

§ 7. Investigatory Stops

Terry stop, the request for identification, and the State's requirement of a response did not contravene the guarantees of the Fourth Amendment, because the request for identity had an immediate relation to the purpose, rationale, and practical demands of the Terry stop. Also, the request for identification was reasonably related in scope to the circumstances which justified the Terry stop. The Court also determined that defendant's conviction did not violate the Fifth Amendment's prohibition on compelled self-incrimination, because disclosure of his name presented no reasonable danger of incrimination. *Hiibel v. Sixth Judicial Dist. Court* (2004) 542 US 177, 159 L Ed 2d 292, 2004 US LEXIS 4385, 124 S Ct 2451.

With respect to a federal border patrol agent's investigatory stop of a minivan in a remote area of southeastern Arizona, which stop resulted in a search of the minivan that found marijuana—when considering the totality of the circumstances and when giving due weight to the factual inferences drawn by the agent and by a Federal District Court judge in Arizona—the agent had a reasonable suspicion, which sufficed to make the stop reasonable within the meaning of the Fourth Amendment, to believe that the minivan's driver was engaged in illegal activity, where, among other factors, (1) the driver had set out from a border city along a little-traveled route used by smugglers; (2) the likelihood that the driver and his passengers, a woman and three children, were merely on a family picnic outing was diminished by the fact that the vehicle turned away from some known recreational areas. *United States v. Arvizu* (2002) 534 US 266, 151 L Ed 2d 740, 2002 US LEXIS 490, 122 S Ct 744.

For purposes of determining the validity of an investigatory stop of a person's automobile under the Federal Constitution's Fourth Amendment, based on an anonymous caller's tip that the person is engaged in criminal activity, it is not unreasonable to conclude that (1) the independent corroboration by the police of significant aspects of the caller's predictions about some facts imparts some degree of reliability to the other allegations made by the caller, including the claim that the person is engaged in criminal activity, (2) if the anonymous tip contains a range of details relating not just to easily obtained facts and conditions existing at the time of the tip, but also to future actions of third parties ordinarily not easily predicted, someone with access to such information is likely also to have access to reliable information about the person's illegal activities, and (3) where significant aspects of the caller's predictions are verified, the caller is honest and at least well enough informed to justify the stop. *Alabama v. White* (1990) 496 US 325, 110 L Ed 2d 301, 1990 US LEXIS 3053, 110 S Ct 2412.

A 20-minute detention of a driver reasonably suspected of transporting marijuana in a pickup truck meets the Fourth Amendment's standard of reasonableness for investigative stops, where the investigation is pursued in a diligent and reasonable manner by a drug enforcement agent and where the complained of delay is attributable almost entirely to the evasive actions of the suspect; accordingly, marijuana discovered in the course of the investigation is admissible in evidence in a subsequent prosecution. *United States v. Sharpe* (1985) 470 US 675, 84 L Ed 2d 605, 1985 US LEXIS 74, 105 S Ct 1568.

The rule for evaluating the reasonableness under the Fourth Amendment of an investigative stop—whether the officer's action was justified at its inception, and whether it was reasonably related in scope to the circumstances which justified the interference in the first place—imposes no rigid time limits on such stops; although the brevity of an invasion of an individual's Fourth Amendment interests is an important factor in determining whether a seizure is so minimally intrusive as to be justifiable on reasonable suspicion, it is also necessary to consider the law enforcement purposes to be served by the stop as well as the time reasonably needed to effectuate those purposes. *United States v. Sharpe* (1985) 470 US 675, 84 L Ed 2d 605, 1985 US LEXIS 74, 105 S Ct 1568.

An investigatory stop of a suspected robber by police officers in reliance on a "wanted flyer" issued by a neighboring police department is reasonable under the Fourth Amendment, and handguns uncovered in the course of the stop are admissible in evidence in a subsequent criminal prosecution, where the detention is brief, where a reasonable suspicion underlies and supports issuance of the flyer, and where the stop is reasonable in objective reliance on the flyer and is not significantly more intrusive than a stop that the issuing department would have been permitted to make. *United States v. Hensley* (1985) 469 US 221, 83 L Ed 2d 604, 1985 US LEXIS 34, 105 S Ct 675.

§ 8. Pedestrians

With respect to the prohibition under the Federal Constitution's Fourth Amendment against unreasonable searches and seizures, when a police officer, without reasonable suspicion or probable cause, approaches an individual, any refusal to cooperate, without more, does not furnish the minimal level of objective justification needed for a detention or seizure; however, unprovoked flight is the opposite of the going about one's business that the United States Supreme Court has held the individual has a right to do; although flight is not necessarily indicative of ongoing criminal activity, this fact does not establish a Fourth Amendment violation by officers who, when confronted with such flight, stop the fugitive and investigate further. *Illinois v. Wardlow* (2000) 528 US 119, 145 L Ed 2d 570, 2000 US LEXIS 504, 120 S Ct 673.

A police officer does not violate the Federal Constitution's Fourth Amendment prohibition against unreasonable searches and seizures when the officer stops an accused after the accused flees upon seeing a police caravan patrolling an area known for heavy narcotics trafficking, where the accused is convicted of unlawful use of the handgun that is discovered during a pat-down search immediately following the stop. *Illinois v. Wardlow* (2000) 528 US 119, 145 L Ed 2d 570, 2000 US LEXIS 504, 120 S Ct 673.

The conduct of police officers in accelerating a marked patrol car to catch up with a man who ran around a street corner upon seeing the patrol car's approach, followed by the car's short drive alongside the man until he discarded packets—which were later found to contain illegal drugs—and then shortly stopped running, did not constitute a seizure within the meaning of the Federal Constitution's Fourth Amendment, since such conduct—where the record in the case did not reflect that the police activated a siren or flashers, commanded the man to halt, displayed any weapons, or operated the car in an aggressive manner to block the man's course or otherwise control the direction or speed of his movement—was not so intimidating that it would have communicated to a reasonable person that he was not at liberty to ignore the police presence and go about his business. *Michigan v. Chesternut* (1988) 486 US 567, 100 L Ed 2d 565, 1988 US LEXIS 2582, 108 S Ct 1975.

A state criminal statute that requires persons who loiter or wander on the streets to provide a credible and reliable identification and to account for their presence when requested by a peace officer under circumstances that would justify a valid stop is unconstitutionally vague on its face within the meaning of the due process clause of the Fourteenth Amendment because it encourages arbitrary enforcement by failing to clarify what is contemplated by the requirement that a suspect provide a credible and reliable identification. *Kolender v. Lawson* (1983) 461 US 352, 75 L Ed 2d 903, 1983 US LEXIS 159, 103 S Ct 1855.

§ 9. Protective Search

When a police officer is justified in believing that the individual whose suspicious behavior the officer is investigating at close range is armed and presently dangerous to the officer or to others, the officer may, under the Federal Constitution's Fourth Amendment, conduct a patdown search to determine whether the person is in fact carrying a weapon; such protective search—permitted without a warrant and on the basis of reasonable suspicion less than probable cause—must be strictly limited to that which is necessary for the discovery of weapons which might be used to harm the officer or others nearby; if the protective search goes beyond what is necessary to determine if the suspect is armed, the search is no longer valid and its fruits will be suppressed. *Minnesota v. Dickerson* (1993) 508 US 366, 124 L Ed 2d 334, 1993 US LEXIS 4018, 113 S Ct 2130.

The Fourth Amendment does not permit the seizure of a small plastic bag containing one fifth of one gram of crack cocaine, which was detected through a police officer's sense of touch during a protective patdown search of a person for weapons which was justified under *Terry v. Ohio* (1968) 392 US 1, 20 L Ed 2d 889, 1968 US LEXIS 1345, 88 S Ct 1868, where (1) the officer determined that a small lump in the front pocket of the person's nylon jacket was contraband only after squeezing, sliding, and otherwise manipulating the contents of the pocket, which the officer already knew contained no weapon; and (2) because the officer's further search of the pocket was constitutionally invalid in that it was not authorized by *Terry v. Ohio* or any other exception to the Fourth Amendment's warrant requirement, the seizure of the cocaine that followed likewise is unconstitutional. *Minnesota v. Dickerson* (1993) 508 US 366, 124 L Ed 2d 334, 1993 US LEXIS 4018, 113 S Ct 2130.

A protective search of the passenger compartment of an automobile, limited to those areas in which a weapon may be placed or hidden, is permissible during an investigative detention, even though there is no probable cause to arrest, if the police officer possesses a reasonable belief based on specific and articulable facts which, taken together with the rational inferences from those facts, reasonably warrant the officer in believing that the suspect is dangerous and the suspect may gain immediate control of weapons. *Michigan v. Long* (1983) 463 US 1032, 77 L Ed 2d 1201, 1983 US LEXIS 7, 103 S Ct 3469.

§ 10. Reasonable Suspicion

While reasonable suspicion is a less demanding standard than probable cause and requires a showing considerably less than a preponderance of the evidence, the Federal Constitution's Fourth Amendment, which prohibits unreasonable searches and seizures, requires at least a minimal level of objective justification for making the stop; the officer must be able to articulate more than an inchoate and unparticularized suspicion or hunch of criminal activity. *Illinois v. Wardlow* (2000) 528 US 119, 145 L Ed 2d 570, 2000 US LEXIS 504, 120 S Ct 673.

Where a police officer observes unusual conduct which leads the officer reasonably to conclude in light of the officer's experience that criminal activity may be afoot, the officer may, under the Fourth Amendment, briefly stop the suspicious person and make reasonable inquiries aimed at confirming or dispelling the officer's suspicions. *Minnesota v. Dickerson* (1993) 508 US 366, 124 L Ed 2d 334, 1993 US LEXIS 4018, 113 S Ct 2130.

The standard of reasonable suspicion—satisfaction of which is necessary to justify an investigatory stop of a person, consistent with the Fourth Amendment—is less demanding than the probable cause standard for an arrest or for issuance of a search warrant under the Fourth Amendment, not only in the sense that reasonable suspicion can be established with information that is different in quantity or content than that required to establish probable cause, but also in the sense that reasonable suspicion can arise from information that is less reliable than that required to show probable cause; reasonable suspicion, like probable cause, is dependent upon both the content of information possessed by police and its degree of reliability; the quantity and the quality of information are considered in the totality of the circumstances that must be taken into account when evaluating whether there is reasonable suspicion; thus, if an informant's tip has a relatively low degree of reliability, more information will be required to establish the requisite quantum of suspicion than would be required if the tip were more reliable; a totality-of-the-circumstances approach applies in the reasonable suspicion context as well as in the probable cause context, the only difference being the level of suspicion that must be established. *Alabama v. White* (1990) 496 US 325, 110 L Ed 2d 301, 1990 US LEXIS 3053, 110 S Ct 2412.

Some seizures involving detention of persons, while admittedly covered by the Fourth Amendment, constitute such limited intrusions on the personal security of those detained and are justified by such substantial law enforcement interests that they may be made on less than probable cause, so long as the police have an articulable basis for suspecting criminal activity. *Michigan v. Summers* (1981) 452 US 692, 69 L Ed 2d 340, 1981 US LEXIS 118, 101 S Ct 2587.

In determining whether the Fourth Amendment was violated by a police officer's seizure of a person by way of stopping him for interrogation, the notions which underlie both the warrant procedure and the requirement of probable cause remain fully relevant; in order to assess the reasonableness of the police officer's conduct as a general proposition, it is necessary first to focus upon the governmental interest which allegedly justifies official intrusion upon the constitutionally protected interests of the private citizen, and in justifying the particular intrusion the police officer must be able to point to specific and articulable facts which, taken together with rational inferences from those facts, reasonably warrant that intrusion. *Terry v. Ohio* (1968) 392 US 1, 20 L Ed 2d 889, 1968 US LEXIS 1345, 88 S Ct 1868.

§11. Immigration Status

An Arizona law requiring state law enforcement officers to make a reasonable attempt to determine the immigration status of any person they stop, detain, or arrest on some other legitimate basis if reasonable suspicion exists that the person is an alien and is unlawfully present in the United States was upheld when three limits were built into the provision. First, a detainee is presumed not to be an alien unlawfully present in the United States if he or she provides a valid Arizona driver's license or similar identification. Second, officers may not consider race, color, or national origin except to the extent permitted by the United States and Arizona Constitutions. Third, the provisions must be implemented in a manner consistent with federal law regulating immigration, protecting the civil rights of all persons and respecting the privileges and immunities of United States citizens. *Arizona v. U.S.* (2012) 567 US __, 183 L Ed 2d 351, 132 S Ct 2492, 2012 US LEXIS 4872.

Search and Seizure

§ 1. In General

Police use of a trained drug-sniffing dog in the curtilage of a residence—for example, around the front porch—is a "search" within the meaning of the Fourth Amendment, and therefore cannot be done without a warrant. *Florida v. Jardines* (2013) 569 US __, 133 S Ct 1409, 185 L Ed 2d 495, 2013 US LEXIS 2542

A warrantless entry by police into a home based on exigent circumstances (e.g. a belief that evidence is being destroyed) is reasonable when the police do not create the exigency by engaging or threatening to engage in conduct violating the Fourth Amendment. This is true even if it was reasonably foreseeable that the investigative tactics employed by the police would prompt the people inside the residence to destroy evidence. Thus, when police smelled an odor of marijuana coming from defendant's apartment, then knocked on the front door and identified themselves—lawful conduct under the Fourth Amendment—exigent circumstances still justified entry when they heard people moving about inside. "Occupants who choose not to stand on their constitutional rights but instead elect to attempt to destroy evidence have only themselves to blame for the warrantless exigent-circumstances search that may ensue." *Kentucky v. King* (2011) 563 US 452, 131 S Ct 1849, 179 L Ed 2d 865, 2011 US LEXIS 3541.

Use of a thermal-imaging device aimed at a private home from a public street to detect relative amounts of heat within the home constitutes a search within the meaning of the Fourth Amendment—and use of such imaging without a warrant is unlawful under the Fourth Amendment—notwithstanding that (1) the device detects only heat radiating from the external surface of the home, (2) the measurements made by the device merely provide the basis for inferences as to what is inside the home, and (3) the device does not detect private activities occurring in private areas. *Kyllo v. United States* (2001) 533 US 27, 150 L Ed 2d 94, 2001 US LEXIS 4487, 121 S Ct 2038.

The exclusionary rule does not require suppression of evidence seized in violation of the Fourth Amendment where the erroneous information resulted from clerical errors of court employees. *Arizona v. Evans* (1995) 514 US 1, 131 L Ed 2d 34, 1995 US LEXIS 1806, 115 S Ct 1185.

For purposes of the Fourth Amendment's protection against unreasonable seizures, the word "seizure" readily bears the meaning of a laying on of hands or application of physical force to restrain movement, even when it is ultimately unsuccessful, but there is no seizure when a police officer merely yells "Stop, in the name of the law!" at a fleeing form that continues to flee, and neither usage nor common-law tradition makes an attempted seizure a "seizure." *California v. Hodari D.* (1991) 499 US 621, 113 L Ed 2d 690, 1991 US LEXIS 2397, 111 S Ct 1547.

A search which is reasonable at its inception may violate the Fourth Amendment by virtue of its intolerable intensity and scope; the scope of the search must be strictly tied to and justified by the circumstances which rendered its initiation permissible. *Terry v. Ohio* (1968) 392 US 1, 20 L Ed 2d 889, 1968 US LEXIS 1345, 88 S Ct 1868.

A police officer "seizes" a person and subjects him to a "search" when the officer takes hold of the person and pats down the outer surfaces of his clothing; the decisive issue is whether at this point it is reasonable for the officer to interfere with the person's security, and in determining the reasonableness of the seizure and search, the court's inquiry is a dual one: whether the officer's action is justified at its inception, and whether it is reasonably related in scope to the circumstances justifying the interference in the first place. *Terry v. Ohio* (1968) 392 US 1, 20 L Ed 2d 889, 1968 US LEXIS 1345, 88 S Ct 1868.

§ 2. Administrative Inspection

A Los Angeles municipal ordinance that required hotel operators to make their registries available to the police on demand was facially unconstitutional because it penalized the operators for declining to turn over their records without affording them any opportunity for pre-compliance review. *City of Los Angeles v. Patel* (2015) 576 US ___, 192 L Ed 2d 435, 135 S Ct 2443, 2015 US LEXIS 4065.

For purposes of the administrative-inspection exemption from the need for probable cause and a warrant under the Fourth Amendment guarantee against unreasonable searches and seizures, an "administrative inspection" is the inspection of business premises conducted by authorities responsible for enforcing a pervasive regulatory scheme—for example, the unannounced inspection of a mine for compliance with health and safety standards; the administrative-inspection exemption is not accorded to a search that is not made for the purpose of administrative regulation. *Whren v. United States* (1996) 517 US 806, 135 L Ed 2d 89, 1996 US LEXIS 3720, 116 S Ct 1769.

§ 3. Automobiles, Generally

Police may not extend an otherwise completed traffic stop in order to conduct a dog sniff, absent reasonable suspicion that there is contraband in the vehicle. *Rodriguez v. U.S.* (2015) 575 US ___, 191 L Ed 2d 492, 135 S Ct 1609, 2015 US LEXIS 2807.

An alert from a dog who performs reliably in detecting drugs will establish probable cause to search a vehicle. *Florida v. Harris* (2013) 569 US ___, 133 S Ct 1050, 185 L Ed 2d 61, 2013 US LEXIS 1121.

Installation of a GPS device on a vehicle parked in a public place, and the subsequent use of that device to monitor the vehicle's movements, constitutes a "search" within the meaning of the Fourth Amendment. *U.S. v. Jones* (2012) 565 US ___, 181 L Ed 2d 911, 132 S Ct 945, 2012 US LEXIS 1063.

A dog sniff conducted during a concededly lawful traffic stop that reveals no information other than the location of a substance that no individual has any right to possess does not violate the Fourth Amendment. *Illinois v. Caballes* (2005) 543 US 405, 160 L Ed 2d 842, 2005 US LEXIS 769, 125 S Ct 834.

Officer was allowed to search the passenger compartment of defendant's vehicle incident to the lawful custodial arrest of defendant as a recent occupant of the vehicle. The authority for the vehicle search was not limited to arrests of persons actually occupying vehicles at the time of initial contacts with officers, since the same interests in the safety of the officer and preservation of evidence applied to both occupants and recent occupants of a vehicle. *Thornton v. United States* (2004) 541 US 615, 158 L Ed 2d 905, 2004 US LEXIS 3681, 124 S Ct 2127.

A highway patrol officer does not violate the Fourth Amendment right of a front seat automobile passenger to be free from unreasonable searches—where, after the officer stops the car for speeding and driving with a faulty brake light, the driver admits that the driver uses a hypodermic syringe, that the officer notices in the driver's shirt pocket, to take drugs—by searching the passenger's purse that the officer finds on the back seat. *Wyoming v. Houghton* (1999) 526 US 295, 143 L Ed 2d 408, 1999 US LEXIS 2347, 119 S Ct 1297.

Police officers with probable cause to conduct a warrantless search of a car for contraband may search a passenger's personal belongings in the car that are capable of concealing contraband. *Wyoming v. Houghton* (1999) 526 US 295, 143 L Ed 2d 408, 1999 US LEXIS 2347, 119 S Ct 1297.

Police officers making a routine traffic stop may (1) order out of a vehicle both the driver and any passengers, (2) perform a "patdown" of a driver and any passenger upon reasonable suspicion that they may be armed and dangerous, (3) conduct a "Terry patdown" of the passenger compartment of a vehicle upon reasonable suspicion that an occupant is dangerous and may gain immediate control of a weapon, and (4) even conduct a full search of the passenger compartment, including any containers therein, pursuant to a custodial arrest. *Knowles v. Iowa* (1998) 525 US 113, 142 L Ed 2d 492, 1998 US LEXIS 8068, 119 S Ct 484.

The full search of an automobile, with neither the automobile driver's consent nor probable cause to conduct the search, by a police officer who stops the driver for speeding and issues the driver a citation rather than arresting the driver, as authorized by state statute, violates the Fourth Amendment. *Knowles v. Iowa* (1998) 525 US 113, 142 L Ed 2d 492, 1998 US LEXIS 8068, 119 S Ct 484.

Consistent with the Federal Constitution's Fourth Amendment proscription of unreasonable seizures, a police officer making a traffic stop may order passengers to get out of the car pending completion of the stop. *Maryland v. Wilson* (1997) 519 US 408, 137 L Ed 2d 41, 1997 US LEXIS 1271, 117 S Ct 882.

For purposes of the Fourth Amendment guarantee against unreasonable searches and seizures, a police officer is objectively justified in asking an accused to get out of a car where there was probable cause to stop the accused's car for speeding. *Ohio v. Robinette* (1996) 519 US 33, 136 L Ed 2d 347, 1996 US LEXIS 6971, 117 S Ct 417.

The automobile exception to the Fourth Amendment's warrant requirement requires only that there be probable cause to conduct a search; if a vehicle is readily mobile and probable cause exists to believe that the vehicle contains contraband, then the Fourth Amendment permits police to search the vehicle. *Pennsylvania v. Labron* (1996) 518 US 938, 135 L Ed 2d 1031, 1996 US LEXIS 4268, 116 S Ct 2485.

Police officers may, under the Fourth Amendment, conduct a warrantless search of a paper bag found in an automobile trunk where they have probable cause to believe the bag contains marijuana. *California v. Acevedo* (1991) 500 US 565, 114 L Ed 2d 619, 1991 US LEXIS 3016, 111 S Ct 1982.

A police officer's stopping an automobile and detaining the driver in order to check the driver's license and the registration of the automobile constitute an unreasonable seizure under the Fourth and Fourteenth Amendments, where the police officer has no articulable and reasonable suspicion that a motorist is unlicensed or that an automobile is not registered, or that either the vehicle or an occupant is otherwise subject to seizure for violation of law, there being no justification for subjecting every occupant of every vehicle on the roads to a seizure at the unbridled discretion of law-enforcement officials on the basis of a state interest in promoting roadway safety. *Delaware v. Prouse* (1979) 440 US 648, 59 L Ed 2d 660, 1979 US LEXIS 80, 99 S Ct 1391.

The rule that a police officer's stopping an automobile and detaining the driver in order to check his driver's license and the registration of the automobile constitute an unreasonable seizure under the Fourth Amendment when there is no articulable and reasonable suspicion that a motorist is unlicensed or that an automobile is not registered, or that either the vehicle or an occupant is otherwise subject to seizure for violation of law, does not preclude the state from developing methods for spot checks that involve less intrusion or that do not involve the unconstrained exercise of discretion, the questioning of all oncoming traffic at roadblock-type stops being one possible alternative. *Delaware v. Prouse* (1979) 440 US 648, 59 L Ed 2d 660, 1979 US LEXIS 80, 99 S Ct 1391.

§ 4. Bus Passengers

The Federal Constitution's Fourth Amendment permits police officers to approach passengers on a bus at random to ask questions and to request their consent to searches, provided that a reasonable person would understand that he or she is free to refuse. Police officers do not need to advise bus passengers during these encounters of their right to refuse to cooperate. The proper inquiry in such cases—which inquiry necessitates a consideration of all the circumstances surrounding the encounter—is whether a reasonable person would feel free to decline the officers' requests or otherwise terminate the encounter. *United States v. Drayton* (2002) 536 US 194, 153 L Ed 2d 242, 2002 US LEXIS 4420, 122 S Ct 2105.

For purposes of the Fourth Amendment, police officers who boarded a bus and began questioning passengers did not seize two passengers who were later arrested for possession of cocaine, where (1) the officers gave none of the passengers reason to believe that they were required to answer the officers' questions; (2) when one of the officers approached the two passengers, he displayed his badge but did not brandish a weapon or make any intimidating movements; (3) this officer (a) left the aisle free so that passengers could exit, and (b) spoke to passengers one by one and in a polite, quiet voice; (4) there were thus ample grounds to conclude there was nothing coercive or confrontational about the encounter between this officer and the two passengers; and (5) the other officer was positioned at the front of the bus, but he (a) did nothing to intimidate passengers, (b) said nothing to suggest that people could not exit, and (c) left the aisle clear. *United States v. Drayton* (2002) 536 US 194, 153 L Ed 2d 242, 2002 US LEXIS 4420, 122 S Ct 2105.

A border patrol agent's physical manipulation of a bus passenger's carry-on luggage violates the Fourth Amendment's prohibition against unreasonable searches, as (1) the accused's luggage is an effect protected by the Fourth Amendment; (2) cases in which the Supreme Court has held that matters open to public observation were not protected by the Fourth Amendment have involved only visual, as opposed to tactile, observation; (3) physically invasive inspection is more intrusive than purely visual inspection; (4) the accused exhibits an actual expectation of privacy by using an opaque bag and placing that bag directly above his seat; and (5) the accused's expectation of privacy is one that society is prepared to recognize as reasonable. *Bond v. United States* (2000) 529 US 334, 146 L Ed 2d 365, 2000 US LEXIS 2520, 120 S Ct 1462.

A state's highest court errs in adopting a per se rule that an impermissible seizure results when police mount a drug search on buses during scheduled stops and question boarded passengers without articulable reasons for doing so, thereby obtaining consent to search the passengers' luggage. *Florida v. Bostick* (1991) 501 US 429, 115 L Ed 2d 389, 1991 US LEXIS 3625, 111 S Ct 2382.

§ 5. Commercial Enterprises

With respect to the Fourth Amendment's prohibition against unreasonable searches and seizures, an owner or operator of a business has a reasonable expectation of privacy in commercial property which is different from, and less than, the expectation of privacy in an individual's home; this expectation is particularly attenuated in commercial property employed in "closely regulated" industries; certain industries have such a history of government oversight that no reasonable expectation of privacy can exist for a proprietor over the stock of such an enterprise. *New York v. Burger* (1987) 482 US 691, 96 L Ed 2d 601, 1987 US LEXIS 2725, 107 S Ct 2636.

A warrantless inspection of a pervasively regulated business will be deemed to be reasonable, for purposes of the Fourth Amendment's prohibition against unreasonable searches and seizures, as long as (1) there is a substantial government interest that informs the regulatory scheme pursuant to which the inspection is made, (2) the warrantless inspection is necessary to further the regulatory scheme, and (3) the statute's inspection program, in terms of the certainty and regularity of its application, provides a constitutionally adequate substitute for a warrant—it must (a) advise the owner of the commercial premises that the property will be subject to periodic inspections undertaken for specific purposes, and (b) limit the discretion of the inspecting officers by carefully limiting the inspection in time, place, and scope. *New York v. Burger* (1987) 482 US 691, 96 L Ed 2d 601, 1987 US LEXIS 2725, 107 S Ct 2636.

§ 6. Consent

The rule in *Georgia v. Randolph* does not apply if the objecting occupant is not physically present at the residence—this is true even if police are the reason for the occupant's absence, i.e. if the occupant was lawfully detained or arrested prior to the request for consent to search being made. *Fernandez v. California* (2014) 571 US __, 188 L Ed 2d 25, 2014 US LEXIS 1636, 134 S Ct 1126.

A warrantless, suspicionless search of a parolee did not offend the Fourth Amendment when the parolee had agreed unambiguously to such searches at any time as a condition of release. *Samson v. California* (2006) 547 US 843, 165 L Ed 2d 250, 126 S Ct 2193, 2006 US LEXIS 4885.

When one co-occupant of a residence consents to a search, but another co-occupant is also physically present and expressly objects to the search, then any subsequent search and seizure is unreasonable and invalid as to the objecting party. *Georgia v. Randolph* (2006) 547 US 103, 164 L Ed 2d 208, 126 S Ct 1515, 2006 US LEXIS 2498.

Since a co-tenant wishing to open the door to a third party has no recognized authority in law or social practice to prevail over a present and objecting co-tenant, his disputed invitation, without more, gives a **police** officer no better claim to reasonableness in entering than the officer would have in the absence of any consent at all. Accordingly, in the balancing of competing individual and governmental interests entailed by the bar to unreasonable searches, the cooperative occupant's invitation adds nothing to the government's side to counter the force of an objecting individual's claim to security against the government's intrusion into his dwelling place. *Georgia v. Randolph* (2006) 547 US 103, 164 L Ed 2d 208, 126 S Ct 1515, 2006 US LEXIS 2498.

A physically present inhabitant's express refusal of consent to a **police** search is dispositive as to him, regardless of the consent of a fellow occupant. Thus, in the circumstances here at issue, a physically present co-occupant's stated refusal to permit entry renders warrantless entry and search unreasonable and invalid as to him. *Georgia v. Randolph* (2006) 547 US 103, 164 L Ed 2d 208, 126 S Ct 1515, 2006 US LEXIS 2498.

Two bus passengers' consent to a suspicionless search by a police officer was voluntary under the totality of the circumstances—and thus the passengers were not subjected to an unreasonable search for purposes of the Federal Constitution's Fourth Amendment—notwithstanding that the officer did not inform the passengers of their right to refuse the search, where (1) under the circumstances, the passengers had not been seized for Fourth Amendment purposes; (2) nothing that the officer said indicated a command to consent to the search; (3) when the passengers informed the officer that they had a bag on the bus, the officer asked for their permission to check the bag; (4) when the officer requested to search the passengers' persons, he asked first if they objected, thus indicating to a reasonable person that he or she was free to refuse; and (5) even after arresting one of the passengers, the officer provided the second passenger with no indication that he was required to consent to a search. *United States v. Drayton* (2002) 536 US 194, 153 L Ed 2d 242, 2002 US LEXIS 4420, 122 S Ct 2105.

A warrantless search of a probationer's apartment was reasonable under the totality of the circumstances, for purposes of the Fourth Amendment, where (1) as a condition of probation for a drug offense, the probationer had signed an order stating that he would submit to a search at any time, with or without a warrant or reasonable cause, by any probation officer or law enforcement officer; (2) the order's search condition did not mention anything about the purpose of such a search; and (3) the police detective who conducted the search had reasonable suspicion to believe that the probationer was involved with incendiary materials. *United States v. Knights* (2001) 534 US 112, 151 L Ed 2d 497, 2001 US LEXIS 10950, 122 S Ct 587.

The Federal Constitution's Fourth Amendment does not require that a lawfully seized defendant be advised that the defendant is "free to go" before the defendant's consent to search will be recognized as voluntary, because (1) the Fourth Amendment test for a valid consent to search is that the consent be voluntary; (2) voluntariness is a question of fact to be determined from all the circumstances; (3) while knowledge of the right to refuse consent is one factor to be taken into account, the government need not establish such knowledge as the sine qua non of an effective consent; and (4) just as it would be thoroughly impractical to impose on the normal consent search the detailed requirements of an effective warning, so too would it be unrealistic to require police officers to always inform detainees that they are free to go before a consent to search may be deemed voluntary. *Ohio v. Robinette* (1996) 519 US 33, 136 L Ed 2d 347, 1996 US LEXIS 6971, 117 S Ct 417.

For the purposes of the Federal Constitution's Fourth Amendment, a bus passenger's decision to cooperate with law enforcement officers who request the passenger's consent to search his or her luggage authorizes the officers to conduct a search without first obtaining a warrant only if the cooperation is voluntary; "consent" that is the product of official intimidation or harassment is not consent at all, and citizens do not forfeit their constitutional rights when they are coerced to comply with a request that they would prefer to refuse. *Florida v. Bostick* (1991) 501 US 429, 115 L Ed 2d 389, 1991 US LEXIS 3625, 111 S Ct 2382.

A seizure does not occur, for the purposes of the Federal Constitution's Fourth Amendment, simply because police officers approach an individual, ask a few questions, ask to examine the individual's identification, and request consent to search his or her luggage—so long as the officers do not convey a message that compliance with their requests is required; so long as a reasonable person would feel free to disregard the police and go about his business, the encounter is consensual and no reasonable suspicion is required; and the encounter is not a seizure and will not trigger Fourth Amendment scrutiny unless it loses its consensual nature. *Florida v. Bostick* (1991) 501 US 429, 115 L Ed 2d 389, 1991 US LEXIS 3625, 111 S Ct 2382.

For purposes of determining whether consent to enter a person's home has been obtained from a third party who possesses "common authority" over the premises—so as to validate a search of the premises under the Fourth Amendment—the requisite common authority rests on mutual use of the property by persons generally having joint access or control for most purposes; the burden of establishing such common authority rests upon the state. *Illinois v. Rodriguez* (1990) 497 US 177, 111 L Ed 2d 148, 1990 US LEXIS 3295, 110 S Ct 2793.

A warrantless entry by law enforcement officers onto a person's premises does not violate the proscription of unreasonable searches and seizures under the Fourth Amendment, where such entry is based upon the consent of a third party whom the officers, at the time of the entry, reasonably believe to possess common authority over the premises, but who in fact does not possess such authority; whether the basis for a person's authority to consent to a search exists is the sort of recurring factual question to which law enforcement officials must be expected to apply their judgment; determination of a person's consent to enter premises must be judged against an objective standard of whether the facts available to the officer at the moment warrant a person of reasonable caution in the belief that the consenting party has authority over the premises. *Illinois v. Rodriguez* (1990) 497 US 177, 111 L Ed 2d 148, 1990 US LEXIS 3295, 110 S Ct 2793.

A suspect's consent to the search of his two suitcases is tainted by an illegal detention and is ineffective to justify the search, where (1) the suspect was approached at an airport by detectives who asked for the suspect's airline ticket and driver's license, (2) the detectives, without returning the ticket and license, asked the suspect to accompany them to a small room, (3) the detectives retrieved the suspect's luggage from the airline without the suspect's consent, (4) the suspect produced a key and unlocked one of the suitcases, in which drugs were found, and did not object when the detectives pried open the second suitcase in which more marijuana was found, and (5) the suspect was then told that he was under arrest. *Florida v. Royer* (1983) 460 US 491, 75 L Ed 2d 229, 1983 US LEXIS 151, 103 S Ct 1319.

§ 7. Inventory Search

A state's highest court erred in upholding a state trial court's grant of an accused's motion to suppress some drug-related evidence obtained by a police officer from an inventory search of the accused's car—after the officer had (1) stopped the accused for speeding and for having an improperly tinted windshield, (2) noticed a rusted roofing hatchet on the floorboard of the accused's car, and (3) arrested the accused for speeding, some other traffic violations, and carrying a weapon (the hatchet)—where the state's highest court erroneously held that (1) the arrest, although supported by probable cause, nonetheless violated the Fourth Amendment because the arresting officer had an improper subjective motivation for making the stop; and alternatively (2) the Federal Constitution could be interpreted by the state's highest court to provide greater protection than the Supreme Court's own federal constitutional precedents provided. *Arkansas v. Sullivan* (2001) 532 US 769, 149 L Ed 2d 994, 2001 US LEXIS 4118, 121 S Ct 1876.

For purposes of the inventory-search exemption from the need for probable cause and a warrant under the Federal Constitution's Fourth Amendment guarantee against unreasonable searches and seizures, an "inventory search" is the search of property lawfully seized and detained, in order (1) to insure that it is harmless, (2) to secure valuable items, such as might be kept in a towed car, and (3) to protect against false claims of loss or damage; the inventory-search exemption is not accorded to a search that is not made for the purpose of inventory. *Whren v. United States* (1996) 517 US 806, 135 L Ed 2d 89, 1996 US LEXIS 3720, 116 S Ct 1769.

Under the Federal Constitution's Fourth Amendment, an inventory search must not be a ruse for a general rummaging by the police in order to discover incriminating evidence; the policy or practice governing inventory searches should be designed to produce an inventory, and an individual police officer must not be allowed so much latitude that inventory searches are turned into a purposeful and general means of discovering evidence of crime. *Florida v. Wells* (1990) 495 US 1, 109 L Ed 2d 1, 1990 US LEXIS 2035, 110 S Ct 1632.

An inventory search of an accused's impounded car is not sufficiently regulated to satisfy the Fourth Amendment, and thus marijuana, which is discovered when employees of an impoundment facility—at the direction of a state highway patrol trooper—force open a locked suitcase found in the car's trunk, is properly suppressed, where the highway patrol has no policy whatever with respect to the opening of closed containers encountered during an inventory search. *Florida v. Wells* (1990) 495 US 1, 109 L Ed 2d 1, 1990 US LEXIS 2035, 110 S Ct 1632.

The Fourth Amendment is not violated where the police, following an individual's arrest for driving while under the influence of alcohol, impound the individual's van and, while inventorying the van's contents without a search warrant, open a sealed backpack and certain containers therein and discover narcotics which are used as evidence in a subsequent prosecution of the individual, given (1) that there was no showing that the police, who followed standardized procedures, acted in bad faith or for the sole purpose of investigation; (2) that the police were potentially responsible for the property taken into their custody; (3) that local police procedures governing inventory searches mandated the opening of closed containers and the listing of their contents; and (4) that those procedures established standardized criteria to govern an officer's choice between impounding a vehicle and simply parking and locking it. *Colorado v. Bertine* (1987) 479 US 367, 93 L Ed 2d 739, 1987 US LEXIS 286, 107 S Ct 738.

Consistent with the Fourth Amendment, it is reasonable for police to search the personal effects of a person under lawful arrest as part of the routine administrative procedure at a police station incident to booking and jailing the suspect. *Illinois v. Lafayette* (1983) 462 US 640, 77 L Ed 2d 65, 1983 US LEXIS 71, 103 S Ct 2605.

The Fourth Amendment's prohibition of unreasonable search and seizures is not violated by a local police warrantless routine inventory search, following standard procedures, of an accused's automobile impounded for violations of municipal parking ordinances, where (1) the police standard procedure was not a pretext concealing an investigatory police motive, and (2) the inventory, including matters in the unlocked glove compartment, was not unreasonable in scope. *South Dakota v. Opperman* (1976) 428 US 364, 49 L Ed 2d 1000, 1976 US LEXIS 15, 96 S Ct 3092.

§ 8. Knock and Announce

Evidence seized pursuant to an otherwise valid search warrant is not subject to suppression under the Exclusionary Rule solely because the officers executing the warrant entered in violation of the knock-and-announce requirement. The deterrence of knock-and-announce violations is not worth the "substantial social costs" of the Exclusionary Rule. However, officers who violate the rule still face the threat of possible civil remedies (such as a lawsuit under 42 U.S.C. §1983) or internal discipline by their employer. *Hudson v. Michigan* (2006) 547 US 586, 165 L Ed 2d 56, 126 S Ct 2159, 2006 US LEXIS 4677.

Violation of the "knock-and-announce" rule did not require suppression of evidence found in a search. *Hudson v. Michigan* (2006) 547 US 586, 165 L Ed 2d 56, 126 S Ct 2159, 2006 US LEXIS 4677

For purposes of determining whether some **police** officers' warrantless entry of a residence without first knocking on the front door was valid under the Federal Constitution's Fourth Amendment, the entry was reasonable, for: (1) The officers were responding at 3 a.m. to complaints about a loud party; (2) As the officers approached the house, they heard from within "an altercation occurring, some kind of a fight," "thumping and crashing," and people yelling "stop, stop" and "get off me."; and (3) It was obvious that knocking on the front door would have been futile, for (a) the noise seemed to be coming from the back of the house; (b) after looking in the front window and seeing nothing, the officers proceeded around back to investigate further; (c) they found two juveniles drinking beer in the backyard; and (d) from there, the officers could see that a fracas was taking place in the kitchen, where (i) a juvenile, fists clenched, was being held back by several adults, and (ii) as the officers watched, the juvenile broke free and stuck one of the adults in the face, sending the adult to the sink spitting blood. **Police** may enter a home without a warrant when they have an objectively reasonable basis for believing that an occupant is seriously injured or imminently threatened with such injury. *Brigham City v. Stuart* (2006) 547 US 398, 164 L Ed 2d 650, 126 S Ct 1943, 2006 US LEXIS 4155.

A 15-to-20 second wait by federal and local law-enforcement officers—who (1) had a warrant to search for cocaine in an accused's two-bedroom apartment, (2) called out "police search warrant," and (3) knocked on the apartment's front door—before, having received no response, breaking open the door with a battering ram satisfied the guarantee in the Federal **Constitution's** Fourth Amendment against unreasonable searches and seizures, even without refusal of admittance, as: (1) after 15 or 20 seconds without a response, the officers could fairly have suspected that cocaine would be gone if the officers were reticent any longer. Federal Courts of Appeals had routinely held similar wait times to be reasonable in drug cases with similar facts including easily disposable evidence, and some courts had found even shorter waits to be reasonable enough; (2) the fact that the accused had been in the shower and had not heard the officers was not to the point, for, as for the shower (a) it was enough to say that the facts known to the officers were what counted in judging reasonable waiting time; and (b) there was no indication that the officers had known that the accused was in the shower and thus unaware of an impending search that the accused would otherwise have tried to frustrate; (3) the accused's claim that it might have taken the accused longer than 20 seconds to answer the door if the accused had heard the knock and headed straight for the door also was not to the point, for (a) the officers claimed exigent need to enter; and (b) the crucial fact in examining their actions was not time to reach the door, but the particular exigency claimed; (4) on the record in the case at hand, what mattered was the opportunity to get rid of cocaine, which a prudent dealer would have kept near a commode or kitchen sink; (5) the significant circumstances included (a) the arrival of the officers during the day, when anyone inside probably would have been up and around; and (b) the sufficiency of to 20 seconds for getting to the bathroom or the kitchen to start flushing the cocaine down the drain; (6) 15 to 20 seconds did not seem an unrealistic guess about the time someone would need to get in a position to rid one's quarters of cocaine; and (7) once the exigency had matured, the officers were not bound to learn anything more or wait any longer before going in, even though their entry entailed some harm to the building, for (a) a prior United States Supremė Court case had held that the exigent need of law enforcement trumped a resident's interest in avoiding all property damage; and (b) there was no reason to treat a post-knock exigency differently from the no-knock counterpart that had been involved in the prior case. *United States v. Banks* (2003) 540 US 31, 157 L Ed 2d 343, 2003 US LEXIS 8966, 124 S Ct 521.

The Federal Constitution's Fourth Amendment does not permit a blanket exception for felony drug investigations to the requirement that police officers entering a dwelling must knock on the door and announce their identity and purpose before attempting forcible entry. *Richards v. Wisconsin* (1997) 520 US 385, 137 L Ed 2d 615, 1997 US LEXIS 2794, 117 S Ct 1416.

The decision by some police officers—in executing a warrant in a felony drug investigation to search an individual's hotel room for drugs and related paraphernalia—not to knock and announce the officers' identity and purpose is reasonable under the circumstances and, hence, does not violate the Federal Constitution's Fourth Amendment, in that the officers have a reasonable suspicion that the individual may destroy evidence if given further opportunity to do so, where (1) the individual, after opening the door to the room after one of the officers states that the officer is a maintenance man, quickly slams the door when the individual sees that one of the officers is in a police uniform, and (2) the drugs are of an easily disposable nature. *Richards v. Wisconsin* (1997) 520 US 385, 137 L Ed 2d 615, 1997 US LEXIS 2794, 117 S Ct 1416.

In order to justify a "no-knock" entry under the Federal Constitution's Fourth Amendment, the police must have a reasonable suspicion that knocking and announcing their presence, under the particular circumstances, would (1) be dangerous or futile, or (2) inhibit the effective investigation of the crime by, for example, allowing the destruction of evidence. *Richards v. Wisconsin* (1997) 520 US 385, 137 L Ed 2d 615, 1997 US LEXIS 2794, 117 S Ct 1416.

§ 9. Mobile Homes

Law enforcement agents do not violate the Fourth Amendment when they conduct a warrantless search, based on probable cause, of a fully mobile motor home located in a public place, even though the vehicle possesses some, if not many of the attributes of a home. *California v. Carney* (1985) 471 US 386, 85 L Ed 2d 406, 1985 US LEXIS 8, 105 S Ct 2066.

Among the factors that might be relevant in determining whether the vehicle exception to the warrant requirement is applicable to a motor home that is situated in a way or place that objectively indicates that it is being used as a residence are its location, whether the vehicle is readily mobile or instead, for instance, elevated on blocks, whether the vehicle is licensed, whether it is connected to utilities, and whether it has convenient access to a public road. *California v. Carney* (1985) 471 US 386, 85 L Ed 2d 406, 1985 US LEXIS 8, 105 S Ct 2066.

A warrantless search by law enforcement agents of a fully mobile motor home located in a public place is not unreasonable, notwithstanding the motor home's possible use as a dwelling place, where the agents have probable cause to enter and search the motor home based on direct and uncontradicted evidence that the occupant of the motor home was distributing a controlled substance from the motor home. *California v. Carney* (1985) 471 US 386, 85 L Ed 2d 406, 1985 US LEXIS 8, 105 S Ct 2066.

§ 10. Plain View Doctrine

Under the "plain-view" doctrine, police officers may seize an object without a warrant if (1) the officers are lawfully in a position from which they view the object, (2) the object's incriminating character is immediately apparent, and (3) the officers have a lawful right of access to the object; if contraband is left in open view and is observed by a police officer from a lawful vantage point, there has been no invasion of a legitimate expectation of privacy and thus no "search" within the meaning of the Federal Constitution's Fourth Amendment, or at least no search independent of the initial intrusion that gave the officers their vantage point; however, the plain-view doctrine cannot justify the seizure of an object in plain view if the police lack probable cause to believe that the object is contraband without conducting some further search of the object, that is, if its incriminating character is not immediately apparent. *Minnesota v. Dickerson* (1993) 508 US 366, 124 L Ed 2d 334, 1993 US LEXIS 4018, 113 S Ct 2130.

It is important to distinguish "plain view," as used to justify seizure of an object, from an officer's mere observation of an item left in plain view; whereas the latter generally involves no Fourth Amendment search, the former generally implicates the Fourth Amendment's limitations upon seizures of personal property; if an article is already in plain view, neither its observation nor its seizure would involve any invasion of privacy, but a seizure of the article would invade the owner's possessory interest. *Horton v. California* (1990) 496 US 128, 110 L Ed 2d 112, 1990 US LEXIS 2937, 110 S Ct 2301.

It is an essential predicate to any valid warrantless seizure of incriminating evidence under the "plain view" doctrine that the police officer did not violate the Fourth Amendment in arriving at the place from which the evidence could be plainly viewed; there are, moreover, two additional conditions that must be satisfied: first, not only must the item be in plain view, but also its incriminating character must be immediately apparent; second, not only must the officer be lawfully located in a place from which the object can be plainly seen, but also he or she must have a lawful right of access to the object itself. *Horton v. California* (1990) 496 US 128, 110 L Ed 2d 112, 1990 US LEXIS 2937, 110 S Ct 2301.

For purposes of the "plain view" doctrine, a police officer's seizure without a warrant of a balloon, later found to contain heroin, at a routine driver's license checkpoint, after the officer saw the balloon fall from the driver's hand to his seat, and saw several small plastic vials, quantities of loose white powder and an open bag of party balloons in the glove compartment, does not violate the Fourth Amendment, where the police officer had probable cause to believe that the balloon contained an illegal substance, even though the substance itself was not visible. *Texas v. Brown* (1983) 460 US 730, 75 L Ed 2d 502, 1983 US LEXIS 143, 103 S Ct 1535.

§ 11. Probable Cause

In the context of safety and administrative regulations, a search unsupported by probable cause may sometimes be reasonable for Fourth Amendment purposes when special needs, beyond the normal need for law enforcement, make the warrant and probable-cause requirement impracticable. *Board of Education v. Earls* (2002) 536 US 822, 153 L Ed 2d 735, 2002 US LEXIS 4882, 122 S Ct 2559.

The fact that a police officer does not have the state of mind which is hypothecated by the reasons which provide the legal justification for the officer's action does not invalidate the action under the Fourth Amendment, as long as the circumstances, viewed objectively, justify that action; subjective intentions play no role in ordinary, probable-cause analysis under the Fourth Amendment. *Ohio v. Robinette* (1996) 519 US 33, 136 L Ed 2d 347, 1996 US LEXIS 6971, 117 S Ct 417.

Search warrants need only be supported by probable cause, which demands no more than a proper assessment of probabilities in particular factual contexts. *Illinois v. Rodriguez* (1990) 497 US 177, 111 L Ed 2d 148, 1990 US LEXIS 3295, 110 S Ct 2793.

Probable cause is a fluid concept—turning on the assessment of probabilities in particular contexts—not readily, or even usefully, reduced to a neat set of rules; informant's tips vary in their value and reliability and rigid legal rules are ill-suited to an area of such diversity. *Illinois v. Gates* (1983) 462 US 213, 76 L Ed 2d 527, 1983 US LEXIS 54, 103 S Ct 2317.

Police officers with probable cause to search an automobile on the scene where it was stopped may constitutionally do so later at the station house without first obtaining a warrant, where the probable cause factor that developed on the scene still obtains at the station house. *Texas v. White* (1975) 423 US 67, 46 L Ed 2d 209, 1975 US LEXIS 98, 96 S Ct 304, *reh den* 423 US 1081, 47 L Ed 2d 91, 96 S Ct 869.

For purposes of the automobile exception to the search warrant requirement of the Fourth Amendment, a probable cause determination must be based on objective facts that would justify the issuance of a warrant by a magistrate and not merely on the subjective good faith of the police officers involved, since good faith does not constitute probable cause, but rather must be grounded on facts within the officer's knowledge which, within a court's judgment, would make his faith reasonable. *United States v. Ross* (1982) 456 US 798, 72 L Ed 2d 572, 1982 US LEXIS 18, 102 S Ct 2157.

Police officers, though having no warrant, have probable cause to stop a light blue compact station wagon carrying four men, to arrest the occupants, one of whom was wearing a green sweater and one of whom had a trench coat with him in the automobile, and to search the automobile for guns and stolen money, and probable cause for such a search still exists after the automobile is taken to a police station, where (1) a robbery victim had told the police that one of the men who robbed him was wearing a green sweater and the other was wearing a trench coat, and (2) other witnesses had told the police that a blue compact station wagon was at the scene of the robbery, that four men were in the station wagon, and that one of them was wearing a green sweater. *Chambers v. Maroney* (1970) 399 US 42, 26 L Ed 2d 419, 1970 US LEXIS 19, 90 S Ct 1975, *reh den* 400 US 856, 27 L Ed 2d 94, 91 S Ct 23.

§ 12. Reasonableness

The touchstone of the Federal Constitution's Fourth Amendment is reasonableness, and the reasonableness of a search is determined by assessing, on the one hand, the degree to which the search intrudes upon an individual's privacy and, on the other, the degree to which the search is needed for the promotion of legitimate governmental interests. *United States v. Knights* (2001) 534 US 112, 151 L Ed 2d 497, 2001 US LEXIS 10950, 122 S Ct 587.

Under the Federal Constitution's Fourth Amendment, the ultimate measure of the constitutionality of a governmental search is reasonableness; at least in a case involving the type of search for which there was no clear practice, either approving or disapproving the type of search, at the time the Fourth Amendment was adopted, whether a particular search meets the reasonableness standard is judged by balancing the search's intrusion on the individual's Fourth Amendment interests against the search's promotion of legitimate governmental interests. *Vernonia Sch. Dist. 47J v. Acton* (1995) 515 US 646, 132 L Ed 2d 564, 1995 US LEXIS 4275, 115 S Ct 2386.

The touchstone of the United States Supreme Court's analysis of the legality of a search and seizure under the Fourth Amendment is always the reasonableness in all the circumstances of the particular governmental invasion of a citizen's personal security; reasonableness depends on a balance between the public interest and the individual's right to personal security free from arbitrary interference by law officers. *Pennsylvania v. Mimms* (1977) 434 US 106, 54 L Ed 2d 331, 1977 US LEXIS 157, 98 S Ct 330.

The scheme of the Fourth Amendment becomes meaningful only when it is assured that at some point the conduct of those charged with enforcing the laws can be subjected to the more detached, neutral scrutiny of a judge who must evaluate the reasonableness of a particular search or seizure in the light of the particular circumstances; in making that assessment it is imperative that the facts be judged against an objective standard, namely, whether the facts available to the officer at the moment of the seizure or the search warrant a man of reasonable caution in the belief that the action taken was appropriate, and anything less would invite intrusions upon constitutionally guaranteed rights based on nothing more substantial than irrelevant inarticulate hunches. *Terry v. Ohio* (1968) 392 US 1, 20 L Ed 2d 889, 1968 US LEXIS 1345, 88 S Ct 1868.

There is no ready test for determining reasonableness of a search or seizure other than by balancing the need to search or seize against the invasion which the search or seizure entails. *Terry v. Ohio* (1968) 392 US 1, 20 L Ed 2d 889, 1968 US LEXIS 1345, 88 S Ct 1868.

§ 13. Search Warrant

Deputies serving a search warrant relating to crimes committed by four African-American suspects did not violate the Fourth Amendment by detaining two Caucasian residents of the home (who were ultimately determined to be unconnected to the crimes) found in bed, even though they were of a different race than the suspects. When the deputies ordered the couple from their bed, they had no way of knowing whether or not the African-American suspects were elsewhere in the house-"[t]he presence of some Caucasians in the residence did not eliminate the possibility that the suspects lived there as well." It is not uncommon for people of different races to live together-"[j]ust as people of different races live and work together, so too might they engage in joint criminal activity." The deputies' actions were necessary to ensure their safety. *Los Angeles County v. Rettele* (2007) 550 US 609, 167 L Ed 2d 974, 127 S Ct 1989, 2007 US LEXIS 5900.

An anticipatory warrant is a warrant based upon a showing of probable cause that at some future time (but not presently) certain evidence of crime will be located at a specified place. Anticipatory warrants are no different in principle form from ordinary warrants and are therefore constitutional. To obtain an anticipatory warrant, the supporting affidavit must provide facts establishing a fair probability that evidence of a crime or contraband will be found at the place to be searched if the triggering condition occurs, and probable cause to believe that the triggering condition will occur. The Fourth Amendment does not require that the triggering condition be set forth in the warrant itself. *United States v. Grubbs* (2006) 547 US 90, 164 L Ed 2d 195, 126 S Ct 1494, 2006 US LEXIS 2496.

Warrant was invalid, and the search was clearly unreasonable, in violation of the Fourth Amendment, for among other matters, (a) the warrant failed altogether to comply with the Fourth Amendment's unambiguous requirement that a warrant particularly describe the persons or things to be seized; (b) the fact that the application for the warrant adequately described the things to be seized did not save the warrant from its facial invalidity; (c) by not describing the items to be seized at all, the warrant was so obviously deficient that the search had to be regarded as "warrantless"; (d) searches and seizures inside a home without a warrant were presumptively unreasonable; and (e) the presumptive rule against warrantless searches applied with equal force to searches whose only defect was a lack of particularity in the warrant. And, in such circumstances, the agent was not entitled to qualified immunity, for among other matters, (a) no reasonable officer could have believed that a warrant that plainly did not comply with the Fourth Amendment's particularity requirement was valid; and (b) because the agent had prepared the invalid warrant, he could not properly argue that he reasonably had relied on the Magistrate's assurance that the warrant contained an adequate description of the things to be seized. *Groh v. Ramirez* (2004) 540 US 551, 157 L Ed 2d 1068, 2004 US LEXIS 1624, 124 S Ct 1284.

Under the Federal Constitution's Fourth Amendment, police officers need either a warrant, or probable cause plus exigent circumstances, in order to make a lawful entry into a home. Thus, a state court erred in failing to assess whether exigent circumstances were present when some police officers entered an individual's home without either an arrest warrant or a search warrant, arrested him, and searched him. Exigent circumstances were required to justify the officers' conduct even if, as the state court ruled, the officers had probable cause to arrest the individual. *Kirk v. Louisiana* (2002) 536 US 635, 153 L Ed 2d 599, 2002 US LEXIS 4682, 122 S Ct 2458.

If a magistrate, based upon seemingly reliable but factually inaccurate information, issues a warrant for the search of a house in which a sought-after felon is not present, has never been present, and was never likely to have been present, the owner of the house suffers one of the inconveniences all expose themselves to as the cost of living in a safe society, but does not suffer a violation of the Federal Constitution's Fourth Amendment. *Illinois v. Rodriguez* (1990) 497 US 177, 111 L Ed 2d 148, 1990 US LEXIS 3295, 110 S Ct 2793.

If a police officer investigating an armed robbery conducts a search of a dwelling pursuant to a search warrant authorizing a search for only the property stolen in the robbery, and if the items named in the warrant are found at the outset of the search—or if the resident of the dwelling has them in his possession and responds to the warrant by producing them immediately—no search for the weapons used in the robbery may take place. *Horton v. California* (1990) 496 US 128, 110 L Ed 2d 112, 1990 US LEXIS 2937, 110 S Ct 2301.

The manifest purpose of the Fourth Amendment's requirement that a search warrant particularly describe the place to be searched and the persons or things to be seized is to prevent general searches; this particularity requirement insures that the search will be carefully tailored to its justifications, and will not take on the character of the wide-ranging exploratory searches the Framers intended to prohibit. *Maryland v. Garrison* (1987) 480 US 79, 94 L Ed 2d 72, 1987 US LEXIS 559, 107 S Ct 1013.

The validity of a search warrant must be assessed on the basis of the information that the requesting officers disclose, or have a duty to discover and to disclose, to the issuing magistrate; the constitutionality of the officers' conduct must be judged in light of the information available to them at the time they request the warrant; those items of evidence that emerge after the warrant is issued have no bearing on whether a warrant was validly issued. *Maryland v. Garrison* (1987) 480 US 79, 94 L Ed 2d 72, 1987 US LEXIS 559, 107 S Ct 1013.

A warrant to search "the premises known as 2036 Park Avenue third floor apartment," insofar as it authorizes a search that is ambiguous in scope, is valid under the Fourth Amendment when issued, even though the description of the place to be searched is broader than appropriate because it is based on the mistaken belief that there is only one apartment on the third floor of the building in question, where (1) the police officer who obtains the warrant reasonably believes that the person whose apartment is intended to be searched is the only tenant on the third floor, and (2) the discovery that there are two separate apartments on that floor—one occupied by the person named in the warrant and the other occupied by another tenant—is made by the officers executing the warrant only after they enter, and find contraband in, the apartment of the tenant not named in the warrant. *Maryland v. Garrison* (1987) 480 US 79, 94 L Ed 2d 72, 1987 US LEXIS 559, 107 S Ct 1013.

§ 14. Checkpoints

Highway checkpoint where police stopped motorists to ask them for information about a recent hit-and-run accident was reasonable, hence, constitutional. The checkpoint stop's primary law enforcement purpose was to ask vehicle occupants for their help in providing information about a crime committed, in all likelihood, by others. The police expected the information elicited to help them apprehend, not the vehicle's occupants, but other individuals. An information-seeking stop was not the kind of event that involved suspicion, or lack of suspicion, of the relevant individual. A presumptive rule of unconstitutionality did not apply. Thus, the instant court had to judge the stop's reasonableness, hence, its constitutionality, on the basis of the individual circumstances. The relevant public concern was grave because police were investigating a crime that had resulted in a human death. The stop advanced the grave public concern to a significant degree, and the police appropriately tailored their checkpoint stops to fit important **criminal** investigatory needs. The stops interfered only minimally with liberty of the sort the Fourth Amendment sought to protect. Each stop required only a brief wait in line. Police contact consisted simply of a request for information and the distribution of a flyer. *Illinois v. Lidster* (2004) 540 US 419, 157 L Ed 2d 843, 2004 US LEXIS 656, 124 S Ct 885.

A city police department's highway checkpoint program whose primary purpose is the discovery and interdiction of illegal narcotics—which purpose is ultimately indistinguishable from the general interest in crime control—violates the Fourth Amendment, where, under the program, (1) the police, acting without individualized suspicion, stop a predetermined number of vehicles at roadblocks in various locations, (2) at least one officer (a) approaches each stopped vehicle, (b) advises the driver that he or she is being stopped briefly at a drug checkpoint, (c) asks the driver to produce a driver's license and the vehicle's registration, (d) looks for signs of impairment, and (e) conducts an open-view examination of the vehicle from the outside, and (3) a narcotics-detection dog walks around the outside of each stopped vehicle; such a checkpoint program cannot be justified under the Fourth Amendment by (1) the severe and intractable nature of the illegal drug problem, (2) a highway safety concern, or (3) the secondary purposes of (a) keeping impaired motorists off the road, and (b) verifying licenses and registrations. *City of Indianapolis v. Edmond* (2000) 531 US 32, 148 L Ed 2d 333, 2000 US LEXIS 8084, 121 S Ct 447.

The initial stop of each motorist passing through a highway sobriety checkpoint and the associated preliminary questioning and observation by checkpoint officers—under state police guidelines which govern checkpoint operation, site selection, and publicity, and which provide in part that (1) checkpoints will be set up at selected sites along state roads, (2) all vehicles passing through a checkpoint will be stopped and their drivers briefly examined for signs of intoxication, (3) drivers in which such signs are detected will be directed to a location out of the traffic flow for further checks, after which drivers who are found to be intoxicated will be arrested, and (4) all other drivers will be permitted to resume their journeys immediately—constitute a "reasonable" seizure which is consistent with the Federal Constitution's Fourth Amendment. *Michigan Dep't of State Police v. Sitz* (1990) 496 US 444, 110 L Ed 2d 412, 1990 US LEXIS 3144, 110 S Ct 2481.

§ 15. Students on School Premises

A 13-year-old student's Fourth Amendment rights were violated when she was subjected to a search of her bra and underpants by school officials acting on reasonable suspicion that she had brought forbidden prescription and over-the-counter drugs to school. The content of the suspicion failed to match the degree of intrusion. There was no reason to believe the drugs sought (common pain relievers equivalent to two Advil, or one Aleve, caplet) were dangerous; they presented only a limited threat. Moreover, there was no reason to believe the student had hidden the drugs in her underwear—neither of her accusers alleged she hid the pills there, nor evidence that hiding contraband in underwear was the general practice among students at the school. *Safford Unified Sch. Dist. #1 v. Redding* (2009) 557 US 364, 174 L Ed 2d 354, 2009 US LEXIS 4735, 129 S Ct 2633.

While public schoolchildren do not shed their federal constitutional rights when they enter the schoolhouse, rights under the Federal Constitution's Fourth Amendment are different in public schools than elsewhere; the inquiry as to whether a search of students on school premises is reasonable cannot disregard the schools' custodial tutelary responsibility for children. A student's Fourth Amendment privacy interest is limited in a public school environment, where the state is responsible for maintaining discipline, health, and safety. *Board of Education v. Earls* (2002) 536 US 822, 153 L Ed 2d 735, 2002 US LEXIS 4882, 122 S Ct 2559.

A public school district's policy that required all students who participated in any of the district's competitive extracurricular activities to submit to urinalysis drug testing did not violate the Fourth Amendment prohibition against unreasonable searches and seizures, because (1) the students affected by the policy had a limited expectation of privacy; (2) the sample-collection procedure in the instant case was virtually identical to—and to the extent of difference, even less intrusive than—a collection method that had been determined by the court not to violate the Fourth Amendment in an earlier Supreme Court case that involved high school athletes; (3) the invasion of the students' privacy was not significant, as the results neither (a) were turned over to any law enforcement authority, (b) led to the imposition of discipline, nor (c) had any academic consequences; (4) the policy was a reasonably effective means of addressing the district's legitimate concerns in preventing, deterring, and detecting drug use; and (5) the court had never required a particularized or pervasive drug problem before allowing the government to conduct suspicionless drug testing. *Board of Education v. Earls* (2002) 536 US 822, 153 L Ed 2d 735, 2002 US LEXIS 4882, 122 S Ct 2559.

Supreme Court Summaries

A public school district's urinalysis drug testing policy for student athletes, under which policy all students wishing to participate in interscholastic athletics were tested at the beginning of the season for their sport and random testing of 10 percent of the athletes was done weekly during the season, did not violate the Fourth Amendment right, of a seventh grader who wished to participate in the school district's football program, to be free from unreasonable searches—where the record showed no objection to the policy by any parents other than the parents of the student in question, and where a Federal District Court had found that student drug problems in the school district, particularly with respect to students involved in interscholastic athletics, were severe enough to demonstrate a need to address such problems—because the policy was reasonable under the circumstances, taking into account (1) the decreased expectation of privacy with regard to students, particularly student athletes, (2) the relative unobtrusiveness of the search, and (3) the severity of the need met by the search. *Vernonia Sch. Dist. 47J v. Acton* (1995) 515 US 646, 132 L Ed 2d 564, 1995 US LEXIS 4275, 115 S Ct 2386.

Although children do not shed their federal constitutional rights at the schoolhouse gate, the nature of those rights is what is appropriate for children in school; the Federal Constitution's Fourth Amendment rights, no less than the Constitution's First and Fourteenth Amendment rights, are different in public schools than elsewhere. *Vernonia Sch. Dist. 47J v. Acton* (1995) 515 US 646, 132 L Ed 2d 564, 1995 US LEXIS 4275, 115 S Ct 2386.

For purposes of determining the reasonableness of a search under the Federal Constitution's Fourth Amendment, public school students who voluntarily participate in school athletics have reason to expect intrusions upon normal rights and privileges, including privacy; the reasonableness inquiry cannot disregard the schools' custodial and tutelary responsibility for children; particularly with regard to medical examinations and procedures, students within the school environment have a lesser expectation of privacy than members of the population generally; legitimate privacy expectations are even less with regard to student athletes, who, by choosing to go out for a team, voluntarily subject themselves to a degree of regulation even higher than that imposed on students generally. *Vernonia Sch. Dist. 47J v. Acton* (1995) 515 US 646, 132 L Ed 2d 564, 1995 US LEXIS 4275, 115 S Ct 2386.

Under ordinary circumstances, a search of a student by a teacher or other school official will be justified at its inception when there are reasonable grounds for suspecting that the search will turn up evidence that the student has violated or is violating either the law or the rule of the school, and such a search will be permissible in its scope when the measures adopted are reasonably related to the objectives of the search and not excessively intrusive in light of the age and sex of the student and the nature of the infraction. *New Jersey v. T.L.O.* (1985) 469 US 325, 83 L Ed 2d 720, 1985 US LEXIS 41, 105 S Ct 733.

The accommodation of the privacy interests of schoolchildren with the substantial need of teachers and administrators for freedom to maintain order in the schools does not require strict adherence to the requirement that searches be based on probable cause to believe that the subject of the search has violated or is violating the law; rather, the legality of a search of a student should depend simply on the reasonableness, under all the circumstances, of the search. *New Jersey v. T.L.O.* (1985) 469 US 325, 83 L Ed 2d 720, 1985 US LEXIS 41, 105 S Ct 733.

The search of a female student's purse by a public school official is not unreasonable under the Fourth Amendment where: (1) the student was discovered smoking in a lavatory in violation of a school rule, but when questioned at the principal's office by the school official, denied that she had been smoking and claimed that she did not smoke at all, (2) the school official demanded to see her purse, opened the purse, found a pack of cigarettes, and, upon removing the cigarettes, noticed a package of cigarette rolling papers, which is closely associated with the use of marijuana; and (3) suspecting that a closer examination of the purse might yield further evidence of drug use, the school official proceeded to search the purse thoroughly and found a small amount of marijuana, a pipe, a number of empty plastic bags, a substantial quantity of money, an index card that appeared to be a list of those who owed the student money, and two letters implicating the student in marijuana dealing. *New Jersey v. T.L.O.* (1985) 469 US 325, 83 L Ed 2d 720, 1985 US LEXIS 41, 105 S Ct 733.

§ 16. Warrantless Search: Protection of Officers or Others

Two Burbank, California, officers responded to a call at a high school. There the principal informed them that a student, Vincent Huff, was rumored to have written a letter threatening to "shoot up" the school, and asked them to investigate. In interviewing Vincent's classmates, the officers learned he was a frequent target of bullying who had been absent from school for two days. The officers found this to be a cause for concern, as they had received training on targeted school violence and were aware that these characteristics are common among perpetrators of school shootings. The officers decided to continue their investigation by interviewing Vincent. At his house, the officers knocked on the door and announced several times they were with the Burbank Police Department. No one answered the door or otherwise responded to the knocks. One of the officers then called the home telephone. The officers could hear the phone ringing inside the house, but no one picked up. They next tried calling the cell phone of Vincent's mother, Mrs. Huff. When Mrs. Huff answered the phone, she indicated that both she and Vincent were inside the house; however, when the officers indicated they were outside and asked to speak with her, she hung up. One or two minutes later, Mrs. Huff and Vincent walked out of the house and stood on the front steps. The officers advised Vincent that they were there to discuss the threats. Vincent, apparently aware of the rumor that was circulating at his school, responded, "I can't believe you're here for that." An officer asked Mrs. Huff if they could continue the discussion inside the house, but she refused; in the officer's experience, it was "extremely unusual" for a parent to decline an officer's request to interview a juvenile inside. He also found it odd that Mrs. Huff never asked the officers the reason for their visit. The officer then asked if there were any guns in the house. Mrs. Huff responded by "immediately turn[ing] around and r[unning] into the house." The officers followed her in. There, after a brief argument with Vincent's father, the interview continued for 5 to 10 minutes; the officers concluded the rumor about Vincent was false and left. The Huffs brought an action claiming the police violated their rights by entering their home without a warrant. The U.S. Supreme Court disagreed, finding that Mrs. Huff's odd behavior, combined with the information the officers gathered at the school, could have led reasonable officers to believe "that there could be weapons inside the house, and that family members or the officers themselves were in danger." *Ryburn v. Huff* (2012) 565 US __, 181 L Ed 2d 966, 132 S Ct 987, 2012 US LEXIS 910.

Brownstown, Michigan, officers responded to a complaint of a disturbance—a man was reportedly "going crazy" at a residence. Upon arrival, the officers found a household in considerable chaos: a pickup truck in the driveway with its front smashed, damaged fenceposts along the side of the property, and three broken house windows, the glass still on the ground outside. The officers also noticed blood on the hood of the pickup and on clothes inside of it, as well as on one of the doors to the house. Through a window, the officers could see defendant inside, screaming and throwing things. The back door was locked, and a couch had been placed to block the front door. The officers knocked, but defendant would not answer. They saw defendant had a cut on his hand and asked if he needed medical help, but defendant ignored these questions and demanded, with accompanying profanity, that they get a search warrant. One of the officers then pushed his way inside. The U.S. Supreme Court ruled that this warrantless entry was justified under the "Emergency Aid" doctrine because of defendant's violent behavior. Although the officers had not seen defendant hit anyone, they did see him throwing things, and it was objectively reasonable to believe that these projectiles might have a human target (perhaps a spouse or a child), or that defendant would hurt himself in the course of his rage. *Michigan v. Fisher* (2009) 558 US 45, 175 L Ed 2d 410, 2009 US LEXIS 8773, 130 S Ct 546.

Police made a lawful warrantless entry into a residence when, through a screen door and an open window, they observed four adults fighting with a juvenile. Law enforcement officers may enter a home without a warrant to render emergency assistance to an injured occupant or to protect an occupant from imminent injury, and need not wait until someone is unconscious (or semi-conscious) before entering. "The role of a peace officer includes preventing violence and restoring order, not simply rendering first aid to casualties; an officer is not like a boxing (or hockey) referee, poised to stop a bout only if it becomes too one-sided." *Brigham City v. Stuart* (2006) 547 US 398, 164 L Ed 2d 650, 126 S Ct 1943, 2006 US LEXIS 4155.

§ 17. Warrantless Search: Exclusionary Rule

Violation of the "knock-and-announce" rule did not require suppression of evidence found in a search. *Hudson v. Michigan* (2006) 547 US 586, 165 L Ed 2d 56, 126 S Ct 2159, 2006 US LEXIS 4677

The indirect fruits of an illegal search should be suppressed when they bear a sufficiently close relationship to the underlying illegality; however, such attenuation analysis is appropriate only where, as a threshold matter, courts determine that the challenged evidence is in some sense the product of illegal governmental activity. *New York v. Harris* (1990) 495 US 14, 109 L Ed 2d 13, 1990 US LEXIS 2037, 110 S Ct 1640.

A state constitutional amendment eliminating the exclusionary rule for evidence seized in violation of state but not federal law does not violate the due process clause of the Federal Constitution's Fourteenth Amendment; a state has the power to eliminate the exclusionary rule as a remedy for violations of a state constitutional right against warrantless searches of trash. *California v. Greenwood* (1988) 486 US 35, 100 L Ed 2d 30, 1988 US LEXIS 2279, 108 S Ct 1625.

Evidence obtained by a law enforcement officer during a warrantless administrative search authorized by, and in objectively reasonable reliance upon, a statute which is later declared to violate the Fourth Amendment to the Federal Constitution is admissible in a criminal prosecution against the person from whom the evidence is obtained. *Illinois v. Krull* (1987) 480 US 340, 94 L Ed 2d 364, 1987 US LEXIS 1061, 107 S Ct 1160.

As a matter of due process, evidence obtained by a search and seizure in violation of the Fourth Amendment is inadmissible in a state court as it is in a federal court. *Mapp v. Ohio* (1961) 367 US 643, 6 L Ed 2d 1081, 1961 US LEXIS 812, 81 S Ct 1684.

§ 18. Warrantless Search: Scope

After a homicide crime scene is secured for police investigation, the police are not entitled to make a warrantless search of anything and everything found within the crime scene area, where none of the exceptions to the warrant requirement of the Federal Constitution's Fourth Amendment are invoked. *Flippo v. West Virginia* (1999) 528 US 11, 145 L Ed 2d 16, 1999 US LEXIS 6924, 120 S Ct 7.

The scope of a warrantless search of an automobile which is permissible under the Federal Constitution's Fourth Amendment is not defined by the nature of the container in which the contraband is secreted; rather, it is defined by the object of the search and the places in which there is probable cause to believe that it may be found; probable cause to believe that a container placed in the trunk of a taxi contains contraband or evidence does not justify a search of the entire taxi. *California v. Acevedo* (1991) 500 US 565, 114 L Ed 2d 619, 1991 US LEXIS 3016, 111 S Ct 1982.

The object of a warrantless search of an automobile also defines its scope; just as probable cause to believe that a stolen lawnmower may be found in a garage will not support a warrant to search an upstairs bedroom, probable cause to believe that undocumented aliens are being transported in a van will not justify a warrantless search of a suitcase; probable cause to believe that a container placed in the trunk of a taxi contains contraband or evidence does not justify a search of the entire cab. *Horton v. California* (1990) 496 US 128, 110 L Ed 2d 112, 1990 US LEXIS 2937, 110 S Ct 2301.

The Fourth Amendment does not prohibit the warrantless search and seizure of garbage which has been left for collection outside the curtilage of a home; thus, the Fourth Amendment rights of accused narcotics traffickers are not violated where (1) the accused, as occupants of a house, place their garbage in opaque plastic bags and put those bags out on the street curb for collection at a fixed time, with the expectation that the garbage collector will pick up the bags, mingle them with the trash of others, and deposit them at the garbage dump, but (2) the garbage collector instead, at the request of a police investigator, picks up the accused's garbage bags after cleaning his truck bin of other garbage and turns the bags over to the investigator, and (3) the investigator, acting without a warrant, searches through the garbage bags and uses evidence found therein to support an application for a warrant to search the house. *California v. Greenwood* (1988) 486 US 35, 100 L Ed 2d 30, 1988 US LEXIS 2279, 108 S Ct 1625.

§ 19. Detention Before or During Execution of Search Warrant

A person may not be detained incident to the execution of a search warrant unless the person is within the immediate vicinity of the premises to be searched, i.e. that area in which an occupant poses a real threat to the safe and efficient execution of the warrant. Courts can consider a number of number of factors to determine whether an occupant was detained within the immediate vicinity of the premises to be searched, including the lawful limits of the premises, whether the occupant was within the line of sight of his dwelling, and the ease of reentry from the occupant's location. defendant's detention was unlawful when he had left the house to be searched and driven a few hundred yards down the street before police seized him. Defendant's detention was unlawful when he had left the house to be searched and driven a few hundred yards down the street before police seized him. *Bailey v. U.S.* (2013) 568 US ___, 133 S Ct 1031; 185 L Ed 2d 19; 2013 US LEXIS 1075.

An individual's detention during the search of the premises was plainly permissible because a warrant existed to search a particular residence and the individual was an occupant of that residence at the time of the search. The officers' use of handcuffs to effectuate the detention was reasonable where the warrant authorized a search for weapons and a wanted gang member resided on the premises. Thus, the use of handcuffs minimized the inherent safety risk involved in the search. Moreover, the need to detain multiple occupants of the premises made the use of handcuffs all the more reasonable. The two to three hour detention in handcuffs was not unreasonable given that the case involved the detention of four people by two officers during a search of a gang house for dangerous weapons. *Muehler v. Mena* (2005) 544 US 93, 161 L Ed 2d 299, 2005 US LEXIS 2755, 125 S Ct 1465.

Police could detain defendant on the front porch outside his home for two hours while they obtained a search warrant when they had probable cause to believe that marijuana was hidden inside the home, and that defendant would destroy this contraband if allowed to enter unescorted. The detention lasted only long enough for police, acting with diligence, to obtain a warrant. *Illinois v. McArthur* (2001) 531 US 326, 121 S Ct 946, 148 L Ed 2d 838, 2001 US LEXIS 962.

A valid search warrant implicitly carries with it the limited authority to detain the occupants of the premises, or recall and similarly detain those seen leaving, while a proper search is conducted. *Michigan v. Summers* (1981) 452 US 692, 101 S Ct 2587, 69 L Ed 2d 340, 1981 US LEXIS 118.

§ 20. Parolees

The Fourth Amendment does not render states powerless to address recidivism concerns effectively. California's ability to conduct suspicionless searches of parolees serves its interest in reducing recidivism in a manner that aids, rather than hinders, the reintegration of parolees into productive society. *Samson v. California* (2006) 547 US 843, 165 L Ed 2d 250, 126 S Ct 2193, 2006 US LEXIS 4885

Suspicionless search, conducted under the authority of California statute providing that every prisoner eligible for release on state parole shall agree in writing to be subject to search or seizure by a parole officer or other peace officer at any time of the day or night, with or without a search warrant and with or without cause, did not violate the United States Constitution. *Samson v. California* (2006) 547 US 843, 165 L Ed 2d 250, 126 S Ct 2193, 2006 US LEXIS 4885

§ 21. Anticipatory Warrants

Anticipatory warrants are no different in principle from ordinary warrants. They require the magistrate to determine (1) that it is now probable that (2) contraband, evidence of a crime, or a fugitive will be on the described premises (3) when the warrant is executed. It should be noted, however, that where the anticipatory warrant places a condition (other than the mere passage of time) upon its execution, the first of these determinations goes not merely to what will probably be found if the condition is met. (If that were the extent of the probability determination, an anticipatory warrant could be issued for every house in the country, authorizing search and seizure if contraband should be delivered—though for any single location there is no likelihood that contraband will be delivered.) Rather, the probability determination for a conditioned anticipatory warrant looks also to the likelihood that the condition will occur, and thus that a proper object of seizure will be on the described premises. *United States v. Grubbs* (2006) 547 US 90, 164 L Ed 2d 195, 126 S Ct 1494, 2006 US LEXIS 2496

For a conditioned anticipatory warrant to comply with the Fourth Amendment's requirement of probable cause, two prerequisites of probability must be satisfied. It must be true not only that if the triggering condition occurs there is a fair probability that contraband or evidence of a crime will be found in a particular place, but also that there is probable cause to believe the triggering condition will occur. The supporting affidavit must provide the magistrate with sufficient information to evaluate both aspects of the probable-cause determination. *United States v. Grubbs* (2006) 547 US 90, 164 L Ed 2d 195, 126 S Ct 1494, 2006 US LEXIS 2496

Anticipatory warrants are not categorically unconstitutional under the Fourth Amendment's provision that no warrants shall issue, but upon probable cause. Probable cause exists when there is a fair probability that contraband or evidence of a crime will be found in a particular place. When an anticipatory warrant is issued, the fact that the contraband is not presently at the place described is immaterial so long as there is probable cause to believe it will be there when the warrant is executed. Anticipatory warrants are, therefore, no different in principle from ordinary warrants: They require the magistrate to determine (1) that it is now probable that (2) contraband, evidence of a crime, or a fugitive will be on the described premises (3) when the warrant is executed. Where the anticipatory warrant places a condition (other than the mere passage of time) upon its execution, the first of these determinations goes not merely to what will probably be found if the condition is met, but also to the likelihood that the condition will be met, and thus that a proper object of seizure will be on the described premises. Here, the occurrence of the triggering condition—successful delivery of the videotape—would plainly establish probable cause for the search, and the affidavit established probable cause to believe the triggering condition would be satisfied. *United States v. Grubbs* (2006) 547 US 90, 164 L Ed 2d 195, 126 S Ct 1494, 2006 US LEXIS 2496

§ 22. Drunk-Driving Suspects

A person arrested for drunk-driving may be required to submit to a warrantless breath test to determine blood alcohol content (BAC) as a search incident to arrest. The physical intrusion of a breath test is almost negligible—it does not require piercing the skin and entails "a minimum of inconvenience." There is nothing "painful or strange" about an arrestee being required to insert a mouthpiece of a machine into his or her mouth—"[t]he use of a straw to drink beverages is a common practice and one to which few object." Nor is the process a significant intrusion. Breathing is a natural process, so all the air that is breathed into a breath analyzing machine sooner or later would be exhaled even without the test. Moreover, the test reveals only one bit of information, the amount of alcohol in the subject's breath. No sample of anything is left in the possession of the police after the test. "Finally, participation in a breath test is not an experience that is likely to cause any great enhancement in the embarrassment that is inherent in any arrest. The act of blowing into a straw is not inherently embarrassing, nor are evidentiary breath tests administered in a manner that causes embarrassment." This is especially true given that such tests are normally administered in private at a police station, in a patrol car, or in a mobile testing facility, out of public view. For these reasons, a breath test does not implicate significant privacy concerns. Blood tests, however, are a different matter. They require piercing the skin and extract a part of the subject's body. "And while humans exhale air from their lungs many times per minute, humans do not continually shed blood." Having blood drawn is significantly more intrusive than blowing into a tube. In addition, a blood test, unlike a breath test, places in the hands of police a sample that can be preserved and from which it is possible to extract information beyond a simple BAC reading. Because such tests are significantly more intrusive, the Birchfield court ruled that a search warrant must be obtained before blood may be drawn. Nor can motorists be deemed to have consented to submit to a blood test on pain of committing a criminal offense. *Birchfield v. North Dakota* (2016) 579 US __, 195 L Ed 2d 560, 2016 US LEXIS 4058.

The natural dissipation of alcohol in the blood does not automatically just a warrantless blood test of a drunk-driving suspect. In those drunk-driving investigations where police officers can reasonably obtain a warrant before a blood sample can be drawn without significantly undermining the efficacy of the search, the Fourth Amendment mandates that they do so. Exceptions to this requirement must be decided on a case to case basis, based on facts showing that securing a warrant would have been impractical. *Missouri v. McNeely* (2013) 569 US __, 133 S Ct 1552, 185 L Ed 2d 696, 2013 US LEXIS 3160.

Right to Counsel; Privilege Against Self-Incrimination; Confrontation of Witnesses; Speedy Trial

§ 1. In General

Imprisonment alone does not constitute custody under Miranda. The Miranda case does not hold that the inherently compelling pressures of custodial interrogation are always present when a prisoner is taken aside and questioned about events outside the prison walls. When a prisoner is questioned, the determination of custody should focus on all of the features of the interrogation. *Howes v. Fields* (2012) 565 US __, 182 L Ed 2d 17, 132 S Ct 1181, 2012 US LEXIS 1077.

The Sixth Amendment right to effective assistance of counsel extends to the consideration of plea offers that lapse or are rejected. Plea bargains have become so central to today's criminal justice system that defense counsel must meet responsibilities in the plea bargain process to render the adequate assistance of counsel that the Sixth Amendment requires at critical stages of the criminal process. *Missouri v. Frye* (2012) 566 US __, 182 L Ed 2d 379, 132 S Ct 1399, 2012 US LEXIS 2321.

Like an invocation of the Fifth Amendment right to counsel, a suspect's invocation of the right to remain silent must be unambiguous and unequivocal before police are required to halt questioning. *Berghuis v. Thompkins* (2010) 560 US 370, 176 L Ed 2d 1098, 2010 US LEXIS 4379, 130 S Ct 2250.

Failure to give a suspect Miranda warnings does not require suppression of the physical fruits of the suspect's unwarned but voluntary statements. *United States v. Patane* (2004) 542 US 630, 159 L Ed 2d 667, 2004 US LEXIS 4577, 124 S Ct 2620.

This case tests a **police** protocol for custodial interrogation that calls for giving no warnings of the rights to silence and counsel until interrogation has produced a confession. Although such a statement is generally inadmissible, since taken in violation of, the interrogating officer follows it with Miranda warnings and then leads the suspect to cover the same ground a second time. The question here is the admissibility of the repeated statement. Because this midstream recitation of warnings after interrogation and unwarned confession could not effectively comply with Miranda's constitutional requirement, we hold that a statement repeated after a warning in such circumstances is inadmissible. *Missouri v. Seibert* (2004) 542 US 600, 159 L Ed 2d 643, 2004 US LEXIS 4578, 124 S Ct 2601.

With respect to an accused who does not have the assistance of counsel at a plea hearing, the Federal **Constitution's** Sixth Amendment is satisfied when the trial court, before accepting a guilty plea, informs the accused of (1) the nature of the charges against the accused, (2) the accused's right to be counseled regarding the plea, and (3) the range of allowable punishments attendant upon the entry of a guilty plea. The Sixth Amendment does not require the trial court to warn the accused that (1) waiving the assistance of counsel in deciding whether to plead guilty entails the risk that a viable defense will be overlooked; or (2) by waiving the right to an attorney, the accused will lose the opportunity to obtain an independent opinion on whether, under the facts and applicable law, it is wise to plead guilty. *Iowa v. Tovar* (2004) 541 US 77, 158 L Ed 2d 209, 2004 US LEXIS 1837, 124 S Ct 1379.

A criminal defendant's Sixth Amendment right to self-representation at trial is not absolute, for (1) the defendant must voluntarily and intelligently elect to conduct his or her own defense; (2) the defendant must first be made aware of the dangers and disadvantages of self-representation; (3) a trial judge may properly terminate self-representation if necessary, even over the defendant's objection; and (4) the trial judge is under no duty to provide personal instruction on courtroom procedure or to perform any legal "chores" for the defendant that counsel would normally carry out. Moreover, a lay appellant who had represented himself at a state criminal trial and who wished to do so on direct appeal from conviction was not deprived of a federal constitutional right, where state courts required him to accept a state-appointed attorney on appeal. *Martinez v. Court of Appeal* (2000) 528 US 152, 145 L Ed 2d 597, 2000 US LEXIS 502, 120 S Ct 684.

The right to counsel under the Federal Constitution's Sixth Amendment attaches only at the initiation of adversary criminal proceedings; before proceedings are initiated, a suspect in a criminal investigation has no constitutional right to the assistance of counsel. *Davis v. United States* (1994) 512 US 452, 129 L Ed 2d 362, 1994 US LEXIS 4827, 114 S Ct 2350.

Invocation, regarding one offense, of the right—derived by Miranda v. Arizona (1966) 384 US 436, 16 L Ed 2d 694, 1966 US LEXIS 2817, 86 S Ct 1602, from the Federal Constitution's Fifth Amendment privilege against self-incrimination—to the assistance of counsel during custodial interrogation is not offense-specific; once an accused invokes the Miranda Fifth Amendment right to the assistance of counsel for interrogation regarding one offense, the accused may not be reapproached regarding any offense unless counsel is present. *McNeil v. Wisconsin* (1991) 501 US 171, 115 L Ed 2d 158, 1991 US LEXIS 3483, 111 S Ct 2204.

Under the Federal Constitution's Fifth Amendment privilege against self-incrimination, persons questioned must be warned, prior to any custodial questioning, that they have a right to remain silent, that any statement they do make may be used in evidence against them, and that they have a right to the presence of an attorney, either retained or appointed. *Pennsylvania v. Muniz* (1990) 496 US 582, 110 L Ed 2d 528, 1990 US LEXIS 3211, 110 S Ct 2638.

Unless a suspect voluntarily, knowingly, and intelligently waives his or her rights, under the Federal Constitution's Fifth Amendment privilege against self-incrimination, to remain silent and to have an attorney present during custodial questioning, any incriminating responses to questioning may not be introduced into evidence in the prosecution's case in chief in a subsequent criminal proceeding. *Pennsylvania v. Muniz* (1990) 496 US 582, 110 L Ed 2d 528, 1990 US LEXIS 3211, 110 S Ct 2638.

The Federal Constitution's Fifth Amendment privilege against self-incrimination protects persons accused of crimes only from being compelled to testify against themselves or to otherwise provide the state with evidence of a testimonial or communicative nature; in order to be testimonial, an accused's communication must itself, explicitly or implicitly, relate a factual assertion or disclose information, as only then are persons compelled to be witnesses against themselves. *Pennsylvania v. Muniz* (1990) 496 US 582, 110 L Ed 2d 528, 1990 US LEXIS 3211, 110 S Ct 2638.

Under the Federal Constitution's Fifth Amendment privilege against self-incrimination, confessions remain a proper element in law enforcement, and any statement given freely and voluntarily without compelling influences is admissible into evidence. *Illinois v. Perkins* (1990) 496 US 292, 110 L Ed 2d 243, 1990 US LEXIS 2885, 110 S Ct 2394.

Statements taken during legal custody are inadmissible if they are the product of coercion, if Miranda warnings are not given, or if interrogation does not cease when an accused requests counsel. *New York v. Harris* (1990) 495 US 14, 109 L Ed 2d 13, 1990 US LEXIS 2037, 110 S Ct 1640.

A more searching or formal inquiry is required before permitting an accused to waive the right, under the Federal Constitution's Sixth Amendment, to counsel at trial than is required for a Sixth Amendment waiver during postindictment questioning, not because postindictment questioning is less important than a trial, but because the full dangers and disadvantages of self-representation during questioning are less substantial and more obvious to an accused than they are at trial. *Patterson v. Illinois* (1988) 487 US 285, 101 L Ed 2d 261, 1988 US LEXIS 2876, 108 S Ct 2389.

In order to protect the Fifth Amendment privilege against self-incrimination in custodial interrogations, the police are required, prior to the initiation of questioning, to fully apprise a suspect of the state's intention to use his statements to secure a conviction, and must inform him of his rights to remain silent and to have counsel present if he so desires; also, the police must respect the suspect's decision to exercise the rights outlined in these warnings, so that if the suspect indicates in any manner, at any time prior to or during questioning, that he wishes to remain silent, or states that he wants an attorney, the interrogation must cease. *Moran v. Burbine* (1986) 475 US 412, 89 L Ed 2d 410, 1986 US LEXIS 32, 106 S Ct 1135.

The Miranda exclusionary rule may be triggered even in the absence of a violation of the Fifth Amendment, which prohibits use by the prosecution in its case in chief only of compelled testimony; failure to administer Miranda warnings creates a presumption of compulsion, and consequently unwarned statements that are otherwise voluntary within the meaning of the Fifth Amendment must nevertheless be excluded from evidence under Miranda, even as to a defendant who has suffered no identifiable constitutional harm. *Oregon v. Elstad* (1985) 470 US 298, 84 L Ed 2d 222, 1985 US LEXIS 60, 105 S Ct 1285.

§ 2. Coercion

A state department of corrections' rehabilitation program for sex-offender inmates and the consequences for an inmate's nonparticipation in the program did not combine to create a compulsion that violated the inmate's privilege against self-incrimination under the Federal Constitution's Fifth Amendment, where (1) inmates participating in the program were required, among other matters, to (a) complete and sign an "Admission of Responsibility" form, in which they discussed and accepted responsibility for the crime for which they had been sentenced, and (b) complete a sexual history form detailing all prior sexual activities, regardless of whether such activities constituted uncharged criminal offenses; (2) information obtained from participants could be used against them in future criminal proceedings; and (3) if an inmate refused to participate, then (a) the inmate's privilege status would be reduced so as to curtail visitation rights, earnings, work opportunities, ability to send money to family, canteen expenditures, access to a personal television, and other privileges; and (b) the inmate would be transferred to a maximum-security unit. *McKune v. Lile* (2002) 536 US 24, 153 L Ed 2d 47, 2002 US LEXIS 4206, 122 S Ct 2017.

For purposes of determining, under the due process clause of the Federal Constitution's Fourteenth Amendment, whether a state criminal defendant's confession has been coerced, (1) a finding of coercion need not depend upon actual violence by a government agent; (2) a credible threat is sufficient; (3) coercion can be mental as well as physical; and (4) the blood of the accused is not the only hallmark of an unconstitutional inquisition. *Arizona v. Fulminante* (1991) 499 US 279, 113 L Ed 2d 302, 1991 US LEXIS 1854, 111 S Ct 1246.

The admission at a state criminal trial, in violation of the due process clause of the Federal Constitution's Fourteenth Amendment, of a defendant's involuntary—that is, coerced—confession is subject to harmless-error analysis. *Arizona v. Fulminante* (1991) 499 US 279, 113 L Ed 2d 302, 1991 US LEXIS 1854, 111 S Ct 1246.

Absent deliberately coercive or improper tactics by police in obtaining an initial statement, the mere fact that a suspect has made an unwarned admission does not warrant a presumption of compulsion; a subsequent administration of Miranda warnings to a suspect who has given a voluntary but unwarned statement ordinarily should suffice to remove the conditions that precluded admission of the earlier statement; in such circumstances, the finder of fact may reasonably conclude that the suspect made a rational and intelligent choice whether to waive or invoke his rights. *Oregon v. Elstad* (1985) 470 US 298, 84 L Ed 2d 222, 1985 US LEXIS 60, 105 S Ct 1285.

§ 3. Collaboration with Other Officers

For purposes of the rule that a confession obtained during a period of detention by state or local officers must be suppressed if an accused can demonstrate the existence of improper collaboration between federal officers and the state or local officers, the action of a local sheriff's department in informing agents of the United States Secret Service that counterfeit currency had been found in an accused's possession is routine cooperation between local and federal authorities which by itself is wholly unobjectionable. *United States v. Alvarez-Sanchez* (1994) 511 US 350, 128 L Ed 2d 319, 1994 US LEXIS 3300, 114 S Ct 1599.

§ 4. Custody

The *Miranda* case does not hold that the inherently compelling pressures of custodial interrogation are always present when a prisoner is taken aside and questioned about events outside the prison walls. When a prisoner is questioned, the determination of custody should focus on all of the features of the interrogation. These include the language that is used in summoning the prisoner to the interview and the manner in which the interrogation is conducted. There was no "custody" when a prisoner in a Michigan jail was told at the outset of the interrogation, and was reminded again thereafter, that he could leave and go back to his cell whenever he wanted, and when was not physically restrained or threatened and was interviewed in a well-lit, average-sized conference room, where he was "not uncomfortable." *Howes v. Fields* (2012) 565 US ___, 182 L Ed 2d 17, 2012 US LEXIS 1077, 132 S Ct 1181 .

Two discrete inquiries are essential to the determination whether a suspect being interrogated by the police is in custody: (1) what are the circumstances surrounding the interrogation, and (2) given those circumstances, would a reasonable person feel that he or she is not at liberty to terminate the interrogation and leave. *Thompson v. Keohane* (1995) 516 US 99, 133 L Ed 2d 383, 1995 US LEXIS 8315, 116 S Ct 457.

A law enforcement officer's subjective and undisclosed view concerning whether a person being interrogated by law enforcement officers is a criminal suspect is irrelevant to the assessment whether the interrogatee is in custody and thus entitled to Miranda warnings as to the right to counsel and as to the privilege against self-incrimination, because the initial determination as to the custody issue depends on the objective circumstances of the interrogation, not on the views harbored by either the interrogating officers or the interrogatee, where under Miranda (1) a police officer's unarticulated plan has no bearing on the question whether a suspect was in custody at a particular time, (2) the only relevant inquiry is how a reasonable person in the suspect's shoes would have understood the situation, and (3) save as they are communicated or otherwise manifested to the interrogatee, an officer's evolving but unarticulated suspicions do not affect the objective circumstances of an interrogation or interview, as one cannot expect the interrogatee to probe the officer's innermost thoughts. *Stansbury v. California* (1994) 511 US 318, 128 L Ed 2d 293, 1994 US LEXIS 3293, 114 S Ct 1526.

A law enforcement officer's obligation to administer Miranda warnings—as to the right to counsel and as to the privilege against self-incrimination—attaches only where there has been such a restriction on a person's freedom as to render the person in custody; in determining whether an individual was in custody, a court must examine all the circumstances surrounding an interrogation, but the ultimate inquiry is simply whether there was a formal arrest or restraint on freedom of movement of the degree associated with a formal arrest. *Stansbury v. California* (1994) 511 US 318, 128 L Ed 2d 293, 1994 US LEXIS 3293, 114 S Ct 1526.

For purposes of the assessment whether a person being interrogated by a police officer was in custody and thus entitled to Miranda warnings as to the right to counsel and as to the privilege against self-incrimination, the officer's views concerning the nature of the interrogation, or beliefs concerning the potential culpability of the interrogatee, may be one among many relevant factors, but only if the officer's views or beliefs were somehow manifested by words or deeds to the interrogatee and would have affected how a reasonable person in the interrogatee's position would perceive his or her freedom to leave; even a clear statement from an officer that an interrogatee is a prime criminal suspect is not, in itself, dispositive of the custody issue, for some suspects are free to come and go until the police decide to make an arrest; the weight and pertinence of any communications regarding the officer's degree of suspicion will depend upon the facts and circumstances of the particular case. *Stansbury v. California* (1994) 511 US 318, 128 L Ed 2d 293, 1994 US LEXIS 3293, 114 S Ct 1526.

The custodial interrogation of an accused must cease when the accused requests counsel, and where there has been such a request, police officials may not reinitiate the interrogation without counsel present, regardless of whether the accused has consulted with counsel. *Minnick v. Mississippi* (1990) 498 US 146, 112 L Ed 2d 489, 1990 US LEXIS 6118, 111 S Ct 486.

A person subjected to custodial interrogation is entitled to the benefit of the Miranda procedural safeguards, regardless of the nature or severity of the offense of which he is suspected or for which he was arrested. *Berkemer v. McCarty* (1984) 468 US 420, 82 L Ed 2d 317, 1984 US LEXIS 140, 104 S Ct 3138.

§ 5. Fifth, Sixth Amendment Rights Distinguished

The Sixth Amendment right to effective assistance of counsel extends to the consideration of plea offers that lapse or are rejected. *Missouri v. Frye* (2012) 565 US ___, 182 L Ed 2d 379, 2012 US LEXIS 2321, 132 S Ct 1399.

The rule established in *Edwards v. Arizona* (1981) 451 US 477, 68 L Ed 2d 378, 1981 US LEXIS 96, 101 S Ct 1880—that once an accused asserts the right, derived by Miranda v. Arizona (1966) 384 US 436, 16 L Ed 2d 694, 1966 US LEXIS 2817, 86 S Ct 1602, from the Federal Constitution's Fifth Amendment privilege against self-incrimination, to the assistance of counsel during custodial interrogation, not only must the current interrogation cease, but also the accused may not be approached for further interrogation until counsel has been made available to the accused—no longer applies when a suspect who has requested an attorney is released from pretrial custody for 14 days or more. After a 14-day break in custody, police may attempt to once again initiate questioning even though the suspect is not accompanied by an attorney. *Maryland v. Shatzer* (2010) 559 US 98, 175 L Ed 2d 1045, 2010 US LEXIS 1899, 130 S Ct 1213.

An accused's invocation, during a judicial proceeding, of the right, under the Federal Constitution's Sixth Amendment, to the assistance of counsel in a criminal prosecution does not constitute an invocation of the Fifth Amendment right to the assistance of counsel during custodial interrogation—which right was derived by Miranda v. Arizona (1966) 384 US 436, 16 L Ed 2d 694, 1966 US LEXIS 2817, 86 S Ct 1602, from the Fifth Amendment privilege against self-incrimination. *McNeil v. Wisconsin* (1991) 501 US 171, 115 L Ed 2d 158, 1991 US LEXIS 3483, 111 S Ct 2204.

The right, under the Federal Constitution's Sixth Amendment, to the assistance of counsel in all criminal prosecutions is offense-specific; the right cannot be invoked once for all future prosecutions, since it does not attach until the initiation of adversary judicial criminal proceedings by formal charge, preliminary hearing, indictment, information, or arraignment; just as the right is offense-specific, so also its effect of invalidating, subsequent to the attachment and invocation of the right, any waivers of the right during police-initiated custodial interviews is offense-specific. *McNeil v. Wisconsin* (1991) 501 US 171, 115 L Ed 2d 158, 1991 US LEXIS 3483, 111 S Ct 2204.

The interest protected by the right—derived by Miranda v. Arizona (1966) 384 US 436, 16 L Ed 2d 694, 1966 US LEXIS 2817, 86 S Ct 1602, from the Federal Constitution's Fifth Amendment privilege against self-incrimination—to the assistance of counsel during custodial interrogation is (1) in one respect narrower than the interest protected by the Sixth Amendment right to the assistance of counsel in all criminal prosecutions, because the Miranda Fifth Amendment right relates to only custodial interrogation; and (2) in another respect broader than the interest protected by the Sixth Amendment right to the assistance of counsel, because the Miranda Fifth Amendment right relates to interrogation regarding any suspected crime and attaches regardless of whether the adversarial relationship produced by a pending prosecution has yet arisen. *McNeil v. Wisconsin* (1991) 501 US 171, 115 L Ed 2d 158, 1991 US LEXIS 3483, 111 S Ct 2204.

The rule established in *Edwards v. Arizona* (1981) 451 US 477, 68 L Ed 2d 378, 1981 US LEXIS 96, 101 S Ct 1880—that once an accused asserts the right, derived by Miranda v. Arizona (1966) 384 US 436, 16 L Ed 2d 694, 1966 US LEXIS 2817, 86 S Ct 1602, from the Federal Constitution's Fifth Amendment privilege against self-incrimination, to the assistance of counsel during custodial interrogation, not only must the current interrogation cease, but also the accused may not be approached for further interrogation until counsel has been made available to the accused—applies only when the accused has expressed a wish for the particular sort of lawyerly assistance that is the subject of Miranda; the rule requires, at a minimum, some statement that reasonably can be construed to be expression of a desire for the assistance of an attorney in dealing with custodial interrogation by the police; however, a request for the assistance of an attorney at a bail hearing, under the Sixth Amendment provision for the assistance of counsel in all criminal prosecutions, does not bear the same construction. *McNeil v. Wisconsin* (1991) 501 US 171, 115 L Ed 2d 158, 1991 US LEXIS 3483, 111 S Ct 2204.

Because the protection of the attorney-client relationship under the Federal Constitution's Sixth Amendment—the right to rely on counsel as a medium between the accused and the state—extends beyond the protection of the Fifth Amendment right to counsel afforded by the Miranda rule, there are cases where a waiver which would be valid under Miranda will not suffice for Sixth Amendment purposes. *Patterson v. Illinois* (1988) 487 US 285, 101 L Ed 2d 261, 1988 US LEXIS 2876, 108 S Ct 2389.

§ 6. Traffic Stop

A motorist detained pursuant to a traffic stop is not taken into custody for purposes of the Miranda doctrine, and Miranda warnings are not required to be given, where a single police officer asked the motorist a modest number of questions and requested him to perform a simple balancing test at a location visible to passing motorists, and where only a short period of time elapsed between the stop and his arrest, and at no point during the interval was the motorist informed that his detention would not be temporary; statements made by the motorist prior to his arrest are therefore admissible against him. *Berkemer v. McCarty* (1984) 468 US 420, 82 L Ed 2d 317, 1984 US LEXIS 140, 104 S Ct 3138.

The initial stop of a motorist's car by a law enforcement officer, by itself, does not render the motorist "in custody" for purposes of the Miranda doctrine. *Berkemer v. McCarty* (1984) 468 US 420, 82 L Ed 2d 317, 1984 US LEXIS 140, 104 S Ct 3138.

Statements made during custodial interrogation by a suspect accused of a misdemeanor traffic offense are inadmissible where the suspect was not informed of his Miranda rights when he was formally placed under arrest. *Berkemer v. McCarty* (1984) 468 US 420, 82 L Ed 2d 317, 1984 US LEXIS 140, 104 S Ct 3138.

§ 7. Undercover Officers

An undercover law enforcement officer posing as a fellow jail inmate is not required, under the Federal Constitution's Fifth Amendment privilege against self-incrimination, to give the warnings required by Miranda v. Arizona (1966) 384 US 436, 16 L Ed 2d 694, 1966 US LEXIS 2817, 86 S Ct 1602, to an incarcerated suspect before the officer asks questions that may elicit an incriminating response, and incriminating statements made by a suspect in such circumstances are thus not inadmissible at trial. *Illinois v. Perkins* (1990) 496 US 292, 110 L Ed 2d 243, 1990 US LEXIS 2885, 110 S Ct 2394.

Under the Federal Constitution's Fifth Amendment privilege against self-incrimination, the warnings required by Miranda v. Arizona (1966) 384 US 436, 16 L Ed 2d 694, 1966 US LEXIS 2817, 86 S Ct 1602, are not required when a suspect is unaware that the suspect is speaking to a law enforcement officer and gives a voluntary statement. *Illinois v. Perkins* (1990) 496 US 292, 110 L Ed 2d 243, 1990 US LEXIS 2885, 110 S Ct 2394.

§ 8. Jailhouse Informants

A defendant's incriminating statement to a jailhouse informant, even though taken in violation of the Sixth Amendment, is nevertheless admissible at trial to impeach the defendant's conflicting statements. *Kansas v. Ventris* (2009) 556 US 586, 173 L Ed 2d 801, 2009 US LEXIS 3299, 129 S Ct 1841.

§ 9. Waiver

If a suspect, after receiving the Miranda warnings, effectively waives the Miranda right to have counsel present during custodial interrogation, then law enforcement officers are free to question the suspect; however, under the rule of *Edwards v. Arizona* (1981) 451 US 477, 68 L Ed 2d 378, 1981 US LEXIS 96, 101 S Ct 1880, if the suspect requests counsel at any time during the interview, then the suspect is not subject to further questioning until a lawyer has been made available or the suspect reinitiates conversation; this second layer of prophylaxis for the Miranda right to counsel (1) is designed to prevent police from badgering a suspect into waiving previously asserted Miranda rights, (2) like other aspects of Miranda, is not itself required by the Federal Constitution's Fifth Amendment prohibition on coerced confessions, and (3) is instead justified only by reference to its prophylactic purpose. *Davis v. United States* (1994) 512 US 452, 129 L Ed 2d 362, 1994 US LEXIS 4827, 114 S Ct 2350.

The rule of *Edwards v. Arizona* (1981) 451 US 477, 68 L Ed 2d 378, 1981 US LEXIS 96, 101 S Ct 1880—under which an accused who invokes the right to counsel while undergoing custodial interrogation is not subject to further interrogation until counsel has been "made available" to the accused—does not foreclose a waiver by the accused, after counsel has been requested, of protections afforded by the *Edwards v. Arizona* rule as to the accused's privilege against self-incrimination under the Federal Constitution's Fifth Amendment, provided that the accused has initiated the conversation or discussions with the authorities. *Minnick v. Mississippi* (1990) 498 US 146, 112 L Ed 2d 489, 1990 US LEXIS 6118, 111 S Ct 486.

An accused's waiver of the right to counsel during questioning must be knowing and intelligent and voluntary; where the accused has waived the right under the Federal Constitution's Sixth Amendment to have counsel present during postindictment questioning, the key inquiry is whether the accused was made sufficiently aware of this right and of the possible consequences of a decision to forgo the aid of counsel. *Patterson v. Illinois* (1988) 487 US 285, 101 L Ed 2d 261, 1988 US LEXIS 2876, 108 S Ct 2389.

If an accused who waives the right to counsel under the Federal Constitution's Sixth Amendment lacks a full and complete appreciation of all of the consequences flowing from such a waiver, despite having been warned that any statement that the accused might make could be used against him or her in subsequent criminal proceedings, such a lack of appreciation does not defeat a showing by the prosecution that the information provided to the accused regarding the waiver satisfied the constitutional minimum. *Patterson v. Illinois* (1988) 487 US 285, 101 L Ed 2d 261, 1988 US LEXIS 2876, 108 S Ct 2389.

An accused's waiver of the right under the Federal Constitution's Sixth Amendment to have counsel present during postindictment questioning is not valid where the accused is not told that his or her lawyer is trying to reach the accused during questioning. *Patterson v. Illinois* (1988) 487 US 285, 101 L Ed 2d 261, 1988 US LEXIS 2876, 108 S Ct 2389.

An accused who has been admonished, during postindictment questioning, with the Miranda warnings—that he or she has the right to remain silent, to consult with an attorney, to have an attorney present during questioning, and to have an attorney appointed if the accused cannot afford to retain one, and that any statement by the accused can be used against him or her in subsequent criminal proceedings—has been sufficiently apprised of the nature of the right to counsel at such questioning under the Federal Constitution's Sixth Amendment, and of the possible consequences of going without counsel during such questioning, so that the accused's waiver of that right is a knowing and intelligent one, and the interrogation does not violate that right. *Patterson v. Illinois* (1988) 487 US 285, 101 L Ed 2d 261, 1988 US LEXIS 2876, 108 S Ct 2389.

Waiver of a suspect's Miranda self-incrimination right, once the suspect has requested during custodial interrogation that an attorney be present, requires a finding that the suspect (1) initiated further discussions with the police and (2) knowingly and intelligently waived the right he had invoked. *Connecticut v. Barrett* (1987) 479 US 523, 93 L Ed 2d 920, 1987 US LEXIS 419, 107 S Ct 828.

A defendant may waive effectuation of the rights conveyed in the Miranda warnings provided the waiver is made voluntarily, knowingly, and intelligently; this inquiry has two distinct dimensions, first, that the relinquishment of the right must be voluntary in the sense that it is the product of a free and deliberate choice rather than intimidation, coercion, or deception, and second, that the waiver must be made with a full awareness both of the nature of the right being abandoned and the consequences of the decision to abandon it; only if the totality of the circumstances surrounding the interrogation reveals both an uncoerced choice and the requisite level of comprehension may a court properly conclude that the Miranda rights have been waived. *Moran v. Burbine* (1986) 475 US 412, 89 L Ed 2d 410, 1986 US LEXIS 32, 106 S Ct 1135.

The conduct of the police in failing to inform a suspect in custody that counsel has been retained for him and is trying to reach him, and in misinforming counsel that the suspect will not be questioned or placed in a lineup on the night in question, does not invalidate the suspect's ensuing waiver of his right to remain silent and to have counsel present during questioning after he has been properly advised of his rights under the Miranda rule, regardless of the culpability or state of mind of the police in so acting; thus, the Fifth Amendment does not require that inculpatory statements made by the suspect during questioning which follows that waiver be excluded from evidence at his subsequent trial. *Moran v. Burbine* (1986) 475 US 412, 89 L Ed 2d 410, 1986 US LEXIS 32, 106 S Ct 1135.

A suspect who has responded to uncoercive questioning by a police officer while in custody and without being given Miranda warnings is not thereby disabled from waiving his rights and confessing after he has been given the requisite Miranda warnings, and his confession is not, solely on account of the prior, unwarned admission, rendered inadmissible as "fruit of the poisonous tree"; the relevant inquiry is whether, in fact, the second statement was also voluntarily made in view of the surrounding circumstances and the entire course of police conduct with respect to the suspect. *Oregon v. Elstad* (1985) 470 US 298, 84 L Ed 2d 222, 1985 US LEXIS 60, 105 S Ct 1285.

§ 10. Illegal Arrest

Under the Federal Constitution's Fourth Amendment, a confession obtained by exploitation of an illegal arrest may not properly be used against a criminal defendant. Thus, where the United States Supreme Court held that a suspect had been arrested, by officers of a county sheriff's department who had lacked a warrant, before the suspect had been questioned—and where the state did not even claim that the department had had probable cause to detain the individual at that point—the individual's subsequent confession had to be suppressed, unless that confession was an act of free will sufficient to purge the primary taint of the unlawful invasion. Demonstrating such purgation was a function of circumstantial evidence, with the burden of persuasion on the state. For such purposes, the relevant considerations included (1) the observance of Miranda warnings, (2) the temporal proximity of the arrest and the confession, (3) the presence of intervening circumstances, and (4) particularly, the purpose and flagrancy of the official misconduct. *Kaupp v. Texas* (2003) 538 US 626, 155 L Ed 2d 814, 123 S Ct 1843, 2003 US LEXIS 3670.

§ 11. Admissible Statements

The Confrontation Clause did not bar admission of statements made during a domestic dispute by the victim to a 911 emergency operator identifying the defendant as her attacker. Statements are nontestimonial when made in the course of police interrogation under circumstances objectively indicating that the primary purpose of the interrogation is to enable police assistance to meet an ongoing emergency. They are testimonial when the circumstances objectively indicate that there is no such ongoing emergency, and that the primary purpose of the interrogation is to establish or prove past events potentially relevant to later criminal prosecution. In this case, the victim was speaking about events as they were happening, not relating past events; moreover, the 911 dispatcher's questions were necessary to resolve the present emergency faced by the victim, and were not directed simply at learning what had happened in the past. *Davis v. Washington* (2006) 547 US 813, 165 L Ed 2d 224, 126 S Ct 2266, 2006 US LEXIS 4886.

A motorist charged with driving under the influence of alcohol cannot successfully challenge, as a violation of his rights under the Federal Constitution's Fifth Amendment privilege against self-incrimination, the introduction into evidence at his state court trial of his refusal to take a breathalyzer test, because, since submission to such a test could itself be compelled, a state's decision to permit a suspect to refuse to take the test but then to comment on that refusal at trial does not "compel" the suspect to incriminate himself and hence does not violate the privilege. *Pennsylvania v. Muniz* (1990) 496 US 582, 110 L Ed 2d 528, 1990 US LEXIS 3211, 110 S Ct 2638.

A videotape of part of the booking proceedings following the arrest of a drunk-driving suspect—in which part the suspect, who had not yet been given a Miranda warning, was asked by a police officer to give the suspect's name, address, height, weight, eye color, date of birth, and current age, and the date of the suspect's sixth birthday—is not rendered inadmissible, at the suspect's state court trial for driving under the influence of alcohol, as a violation of the suspect's rights under the Federal Constitution's Fifth Amendment privilege against self-incrimination merely because the slurred nature of the suspect's speech in responding to the questions is incriminating, since any slurring of speech and other evidence of lack of muscular coordination revealed by the suspect's responses to the officer's direct questions constitute nontestimonial components of those responses; requiring suspects to reveal the physical manner in which they articulate words, like requiring them to reveal the physical properties of the sounds produced by their voices, does not, without more, compel them to provide "testimonial" responses for purposes of the privilege against self-incrimination. *Pennsylvania v. Muniz* (1990) 496 US 582, 110 L Ed 2d 528, 1990 US LEXIS 3211, 110 S Ct 2638.

A trial court does not err in permitting an accused's confessions to be used against him in a murder trial where, during postindictment questioning, the accused was informed by law enforcement officials of his right to counsel, and of the consequences of any choice not to exercise that right, by means of the Miranda warnings, but where on two separate occasions he elected to forgo the assistance of counsel and to speak directly to officials concerning his role in the murder, and thus made a knowing and intelligent waiver of his right to counsel under the Federal Constitution's Sixth Amendment. *Patterson v. Illinois* (1988) 487 US 285, 101 L Ed 2d 261, 1988 US LEXIS 2876, 108 S Ct 2389.

The self-incrimination privilege of the Fifth Amendment to the Federal Constitution does not forbid the use, at a suspect's criminal trial, of incriminating statements made by the suspect to his wife in the presence of a police officer, and the suspect is not subjected to such compelling influences, psychological ploys, or direct questioning as would constitute "interrogation," or the functional equivalent of interrogation, for Fifth Amendment purposes—even though the statements are made after the suspect has been placed in custody and given his Miranda warnings, and after the suspect has refused to make any more statements without a lawyer present—where (1) during the discussion between the suspect and his wife, the officer asked the suspect no questions about the crime or the suspect's conduct; (2) the suspect, with knowledge that the police were listening and that a tape recorder was being used, chose to speak; (3) the police did not send the wife to see the suspect for the purpose of eliciting incriminating statements, but instead yielded to the wife's insistent demands to talk to her husband; (4) under the circumstances, the police acted reasonably and lawfully, for the police were not required (a) to adopt inflexible rules barring suspects from speaking with their spouses, or (b) to ignore legitimate concerns—such as security—by allowing such spouses to meet in private; (5) the suspect, told by police that his wife would be allowed to speak to him, was not likely to feel that he was being coerced to incriminate himself in any way; (6) even though the police were aware that there was a possibility that the suspect might incriminate himself, the police did not interrogate the suspect simply by hoping that he would incriminate himself, and the suspect's volunteered statements could not properly be considered the result of police interrogation; and (7) the police actions in the case did not implicate the Supreme Court's purpose of preventing government officials from using the coercive nature of confinement to extract confessions that would not be given in an unrestrained environment. *Arizona v. Mauro* (1987) 481 US 520, 95 L Ed 2d 458, 1987 US LEXIS 1933, 107 S Ct 1931.

§ 12. Inadmissible Statements

While States are free to impose whatever specific rules they see fit to ensure that criminal defendants are well represented, the Federal Constitution imposes only one general requirement: that counsel make objectively reasonable choices. Standards promulgated by the American Bar Association are "only guides" to what reasonableness means, not its definition—an attorney's failure to comply with such standards does not constitute proof that the attorney was ineffective. *Bobby v. Van Hook* (2009) 558 US 4, 130 S Ct 13, 175 L Ed 2d 255, 2009 US LEXIS 7976.

A state's playing, for the jury at a trial for assault and attempted murder, of a tape-recorded statement in which the accused's wife—who, because of the state marital privilege that generally barred one spouse from testifying against the other without the other's consent, did not testify at trial—during police interrogation, had described her husband's stabbing of the victim, violated the husband's right, under the Federal Constitution's Sixth Amendment, to be confronted by the witnesses against him. *Crawford v. Washington* (2004) 541 US 36, 158 L Ed 2d 177, 2004 US LEXIS 1838, 124 S Ct 1354.

An accused's right, under the Federal Constitution's Sixth Amendment, to be confronted with the witnesses against him is violated where the entire confession of the accused's nontestifying alleged accomplice—which confession contains some statements against the accomplice's penal interest and others that inculpate the accused—is admitted into evidence at the accused's state criminal trial. *Lilly v. Virginia* (1999) 527 US 116, 144 L Ed 2d 117, 1999 US LEXIS 4006, 119 S Ct 1887.

The custodial confession of a criminally accused's alleged accomplice that inculpates the accused is not within a firmly rooted exception to the hearsay rule such that the admission of the confession into evidence at the accused's trial will not violate the accused's right, under the Federal Constitution's Sixth Amendment, to be confronted with the witnesses against him. *Lilly v. Virginia* (1999) 527 US 116, 144 L Ed 2d 117, 1999 US LEXIS 4006, 119 S Ct 1887.

Assuming that there has been no break in the custody of an accused subsequent to the accused's assertion of the right—derived by Miranda v. Arizona (1966) 384 US 436, 16 L Ed 2d 694, 1966 US LEXIS 2817, 86 S Ct 1602, from the Federal Constitution's Fifth Amendment privilege against self-incrimination—to the assistance of counsel during custodial interrogation, if the police initiate an encounter with the accused in the absence of counsel subsequent to the accused's assertion of the right, the accused's statements made during the encounter are presumed involuntary and therefore inadmissible as substantive evidence at trial, even where the accused executes a waiver and the accused's statements would be considered voluntary under traditional standards; this rule is designed to prevent police from badgering an accused into waiving the accused's previously asserted Miranda rights. *McNeil v. Wisconsin* (1991) 501 US 171, 115 L Ed 2d 158, 1991 US LEXIS 3483, 111 S Ct 2204.

Where a motorist arrested on suspicion of driving under the influence of alcohol is not advised of his Miranda rights until after the videotaped proceedings at the booking center are completed, any verbal statements on the videotape that are both testimonial in nature and elicited during custodial interrogation are inadmissible as evidence in the motorist's state court trial. *Pennsylvania v. Muniz* (1990) 496 US 582, 110 L Ed 2d 528, 1990 US LEXIS 3211, 110 S Ct 2638.

§ 13. Ineffective Assistance of Counsel

As a general rule, defense counsel has the duty to communicate formal prosecution offers to accept a plea on terms and conditions that may be favorable to the accused. To show prejudice where a plea offer has lapsed or been rejected because of counsel's deficient performance, defendants must demonstrate a reasonable probability both that they would have accepted the more favorable plea offer had they been afforded effective assistance of counsel and that the plea would have been entered without the prosecution's canceling it or the trial court's refusing to accept it, if they had the authority to exercise that discretion under state law. *Missouri v. Frye* (2012) 565 US ___, 182 L Ed 2d 379, 2012 US LEXIS 2321, 132 S Ct 1399.

Where counsel's ineffective advice led to an plea offer's rejection, and where the prejudice alleged is having to stand trial, a defendant must show that but for the ineffective advice, there is a reasonable probability that the plea offer would have been presented to the court, that the court would have accepted its terms, and that the conviction or sentence, or both, under the offer's terms would have been less severe than under the actual judgment and sentence imposed. When a defendant shows ineffective assistance has caused the rejection of a plea leading to a more severe sentence at trial, the remedy must "neutralize the taint" of a constitutional violation, but must not grant a windfall to the defendant or needlessly squander the resources the State properly invested in the criminal prosecution. If the sole advantage is that the defendant would have received a lesser sentence under the plea, the court should have an evidentiary hearing to determine whether the defendant would have accepted the plea. If so, the court may exercise discretion in determining whether the defendant should receive the term offered in the plea, the sentence received at trial, or something in between. However, resentencing based on the conviction at trial may not suffice, e.g., where the offered guilty plea was for less serious counts than the ones for which a defendant was convicted after trial, or where a mandatory sentence confines a judge's sentencing discretion. In these circumstances, the proper remedy may be to require the prosecution to reoffer the plea. The judge can then exercise discretion in deciding whether to vacate the conviction from trial and accept the plea, or leave the conviction undisturbed. *Lafler v. Cooper* (2012) 566 US ___, 182 L Ed 2d 398, 132 S Ct 1376, 2012 US LEXIS 2322.

There was no Sixth Amendment violation when defendant's attorney appeared at a plea hearing via speaker phone rather than in person. The physical absence of the defendant's attorney from his plea hearing did not constitute a "complete denial of counsel." *Wright v. Van Patten* (2008) 552 US 120, 169 L Ed 2d 583, 2008 US LEXIS 200, 128 S Ct 743.

Even when a capital defendant's family members and the defendant himself have suggested that no mitigating evidence is available, his lawyer is bound to make reasonable efforts to obtain and review material that counsel knows the prosecution will probably rely on as evidence of aggravation at the sentencing phase of trial. It flouts prudence to deny that a defense lawyer should try to look at a file he knows the prosecution will cull for aggravating evidence, let alone when the file is sitting in the trial courthouse, open for the asking. No reasonable lawyer would forgo examination of the file thinking he could do as well by asking the defendant or family relations whether they recalled anything helpful or damaging in the prior victim's testimony. Nor would a reasonable lawyer compare possible searches for school reports, juvenile records, and evidence of drinking habits to the opportunity to take a look at a file disclosing what the prosecutor knows and even plans to read from in his case. Questioning a few more family members and searching for old records can promise less than looking for a needle in a haystack, when a lawyer truly has reason to doubt there is any needle there. But looking at a file the prosecution says it will use is a sure bet: whatever may be in that file is going to tell defense counsel something about what the prosecution can produce. *Rompilla v. Beard* (2005) 545 US 374, 162 L Ed 2d 360, 125 S Ct 2456, 2005 US LEXIS 4846.

§ 14. Confrontation

A defendant's right to confrontation was violated when a technician other than the one who signed the laboratory report certifying that his blood-alcohol concentration (BAC) was well above the threshold for aggravated DWI was called as a witness. This other analyst had neither participated in nor observed the test on defendant's blood sample, and therefore could not convey what the testing analyst knew or observed about the events he certified, nor expose any lapses or lies on that analyst's part. *Bullcoming v. New Mexico* (2011) 564 US 647, 131 S Ct 2705, 180 L Ed 2d 610, 2011 US LEXIS 4790.

When police asked a shooting victim "what had happened, who had shot him, and where the shooting had occurred," the primary purpose of the questions was to enable them to assist him in the face of an ongoing emergency. Thus, the shooting victim's responses were non-testimonial, and were thereof are not barred at trial by the Confrontation Clause. *Michigan v. Bryant* (2011) 562 US 344, 131 S Ct 1143, 179 L Ed 2d 93, 2011 US LEXIS 1713.

The Confrontation Clause bars admission of testimonial statements of a witness who did not appear at trial unless he was unavailable to testify, and the defendant had a prior opportunity for cross-examination. These cases require the Court to determine which **police** "interrogations" produce statements that fall within this prohibition. Without attempting to produce an exhaustive classification of all conceivable statements as either testimonial or nontestimonial, it suffices to decide the present cases to hold that statements are nontestimonial when made in the course of **police** interrogation under circumstances objectively indicating that the primary purpose of interrogation is to enable **police** assistance to meet an ongoing emergency. They are testimonial when the circumstances objectively indicate that there is no such ongoing emergency, and that the primary purpose of the interrogation is to establish or prove past events potentially relevant to later criminal prosecution. *Davis v. Washington* (2006) 547 US 813, 165 L Ed 2d 224, 126 S Ct 2266, 2006 US LEXIS 4886

The question in the instant case is whether, objectively considered, the interrogation during the 911 call produced testimonial statements. In contrast to Crawford, where the interrogation took place at a **police** station and was directed solely at establishing a past crime, a 911 call is ordinarily designed primarily to describe current circumstances requiring **police** assistance. The difference is apparent here. Domestic violence complainant was speaking of events as they were actually happening, while Crawford's interrogation took place hours after the events occurred. Moreover, complainant was facing an ongoing emergency. Further, the statements elicited were necessary to enable the **police** to resolve the present emergency rather than simply to learn what had happened in the past. Finally, the difference in the level of formality is striking. Crawford calmly answered questions at a station house, with an officer-interrogator taping and taking notes, while the frantic answers in the instant case were provided over the phone, in an environment that was not tranquil, or even safe. Thus, the circumstances of her interrogation objectively indicate that its primary purpose was to enable **police** assistance to meet an ongoing emergency. She was not acting as a witness or testifying. *Davis v. Washington* (2006) 547 US 813, 165 L Ed 2d 224, 126 S Ct 2266, 2006 US LEXIS 4886

A criminal defendant's federal constitutional rights are violated by an evidence rule under which the defendant may not introduce evidence of third-party guilt if the prosecution has introduced forensic evidence that, if believed, strongly supports a guilty verdict. State and federal rulemakers have broad latitude under the Constitution to establish rules excluding evidence from criminal trials. This latitude, however, has limits. Whether rooted directly in the Due Process Clause of the Fourteenth Amendment or in the Compulsory Process or Confrontation clauses of the Sixth Amendment, the Constitution guarantees criminal defendants a meaningful opportunity to present a complete defense. This right is abridged by evidence rules that infringe upon a weighty interest of the accused and are arbitrary or disproportionate to the purposes they are designed to serve. *Holmes v. South Carolina* (2006) 547 US 319, 164 L Ed 2d 503, 126 S Ct 1727, 2006 US LEXIS 3454

§ 15. Speedy Trial

The Sixth Amendment provides that in all criminal prosecutions, the accused shall enjoy the right to a speedy and public trial, by an impartial jury. The Sixth Amendment's speedy trial guarantee protects the accused from arrest or indictment through trial, but does not apply once a defendant has been found guilty at trial or has pleaded guilty to criminal charges. Thus a post-conviction, pre-sentencing delay of 14 months did not violate the Sixth Amendment. The Speedy Trial Clause implements the presumption of innocence and therefore loses force upon conviction. The US Supreme Court has not read the Speedy Trial Clause to call for a flexible or tailored remedy; instead, violation of the right demands termination of the prosecution. The sole remedy for a violation of the speedy trial right—dismissal of the charges—fits the pre-conviction focus of the Speedy Trial Clause. It would be an unjustified windfall, in most cases, to remedy sentencing delay by vacating validly obtained convictions. *Betterman v. Montana* (2016) 578 US __, 194 L Ed 2d 723, 136 S Ct 1609, 2016 US LEXIS 3349.

Liability

§ 1. Police

The doctrine of qualified immunity shields officials from civil liability so long as their conduct does not violate clearly established statutory or constitutional rights of which a reasonable person would have known. A clearly established right is one that is sufficiently clear that every reasonable official would have understood that what he is doing violates that right. A court does not require a case directly on point, but existing precedent must have placed the statutory or constitutional question beyond debate. Put simply, qualified immunity protects all but the plainly incompetent or those who knowingly violate the law. A police officer was entitled to qualified immunity for his conduct in shooting and killing a reportedly intoxicated fugitive who was fleeing in a vehicle at high speed, twice threatened to kill officers, and was racing toward another officer's location before the vehicle reached a spike strip placed on the road, since it was not beyond debate that the officer acted unreasonably in the unclear border between excessive and acceptable force. *Mullenix v. Luna* (2015) 577 US ___, 193 L Ed 2d 255, 136 S Ct 305, 2015 US LEXIS 7160.

Courts may grant qualified immunity on the ground that a purported right was not "clearly established" by prior case law. To be clearly established, a right must be sufficiently clear that every reasonable official would have understood that what he is doing violates that right. *Reichle v. Howards* (2012) 566 US __, 182 L Ed 2d 985, 132 S Ct 2088, 2012 US LEXIS 4132.

While a two-step procedure for resolving whether officers have qualified immunity—(1) whether the facts alleged or shown by the plaintiff make out a violation of a constitutional right, and (2) if so, whether that right was "clearly established" at the time of the defendant's alleged misconduct—remains useful for courts, it is no longer mandatory. Courts now have the discretion to decide whether that procedure is worthwhile in particular cases. *Pearson v. Callahan* (2009) 555 US 223, 172 L Ed 2d 565, 2009 US LEXIS 591, 129 S Ct 808.

Actions undertaken by police to terminate a dangerous high-speed car chase that threatens the lives of innocent by-standers—such as bumping the fleeing vehicle—do not create liability under §1983 even when such actions place the fleeing motorist at risk of death or serious bodily injury. *Scott v. Harris* (2007) 550 US 372, 167 L Ed 2d 686, 127 S Ct 1769, 2007 US LEXIS 4748.

The statute of limitations upon a §1983 claim seeking damages for a false arrest in violation of the Fourth Amendment, where the arrest is followed by criminal proceedings, begins to run at the time the claimant becomes detained pursuant to legal process. *Wallace v. Kato* (2007) 549 US 384, 166 L Ed 2d 973, 127 S Ct 1091, 2007 US LEXIS 2650.

There was no liability under 42 USCS §1983 when police failed to arrest the plaintiff's husband for violation of a temporary restraining order, even though he later went on to kill the couple's daughters (which he could not have done had he been in custody). It is not clear that an individual entitlement to enforcement of a restraining order could constitute a "property" interest for purposes of the Due Process Clause. Moreover, prior Supreme Court cases had recognized that a benefit is not a protected entitlement if government officials have discretion to grant or deny it; there is a well-established tradition of police discretion with regard to whether or not to make arrests. *Town of Castle Rock v. Gonzales* (2005) 545 US 748, 162 L Ed 2d 658, 125 S Ct 2796, 2005 US LEXIS 5214.

Warrant was invalid, and the search was clearly unreasonable, in violation of the Fourth Amendment, for among other matters, (a) the warrant failed altogether to comply with the Fourth Amendment's unambiguous requirement that a warrant particularly describe the persons or things to be seized; (b) the fact that the application for the warrant adequately described the things to be seized did not save the warrant from its facial invalidity; (c) by not describing the items to be seized at all, the warrant was so obviously deficient that the search had to be regarded as "warrantless"; (d) searches and seizures inside a home without a warrant were presumptively unreasonable; and (e) the presumptive rule against warrantless searches applied with equal force to searches whose only defect was a lack of particularity in the warrant. And, in such circumstances, the agent was not entitled to qualified immunity, for among other matters, (a) no reasonable officer could have believed that a warrant that plainly did not comply with the Fourth Amendment's particularity requirement was valid; and (b) because the agent had prepared the invalid warrant, he could not properly argue that he reasonably had relied on the Magistrate's assurance that the warrant contained an adequate description of the things to be seized. *Groh v. Ramirez* (2004) 540 US 551, 157 L Ed 2d 1068, 2004 US LEXIS 1624, 124 S Ct 1284.

With respect to an arrestee's 42 USCS § 1983 claims against a police supervisor—which claims arose out of the supervisor's allegedly coercive interrogation of the arrestee, without giving Miranda warnings, while the arrestee had been receiving medical treatment at a hospital after having been shot by another police officer during the altercation which had resulted in the arrest—the arrestee's allegations failed to state a valid § 1983 claim for a violation of the arrestee's privilege against self-incrimination, under the Federal Constitution's Fifth Amendment as made applicable to the states by the Constitution's Fourteenth Amendment, where (1) the arrestee had never been charged with any crime related to the altercation; and (2) thus, the arrestee's answers to the supervisor's interrogation had never been used against the arrestee in any subsequent criminal prosecution. *Chavez v. Martinez* (2003) 538 US 760, 155 L Ed 2d 984, 2003 US LEXIS 4274.

On certiorari to review a Federal Court of Appeals' judgment upholding a Federal District Court's denial, to a police supervisor, of qualified immunity from some 42 USCS § 1983 claims by an arrestee—which claims arose out of the supervisor's allegedly coercive interrogation of the arrestee, without giving Miranda warnings, while the arrestee had been receiving medical treatment at a hospital after having been shot by another police officer during the altercation which had resulted in the arrest—the United States Supreme Court held that the issue whether the arrestee could properly pursue a claim of liability for a substantive due process violation, under the Federal Constitution's Fourteenth Amendment, was an issue that ought to be addressed on remand, along with the scope and merits of any such action that might be found open to the arrestee. *Chavez v. Martinez* (2003) 538 US 760, 155 L Ed 2d 984, 2003 US LEXIS 4274.

High-speed police chases with no intent to harm suspects physically or to worsen their legal plight do not give rise to liability under the substantive due process guarantee of the Federal Constitution's Fourteenth Amendment, redressable by an action under 42 USCS § 1983 for violation of a federal right, as (1) a police officer deciding whether to give chase must balance the need to stop a suspect and show that flight from the law is no way to freedom against the high-speed threat to everyone within stopping range, be they suspects, their passengers, other drivers, or bystanders, (2) when unforeseen circumstances demand an officer's instant judgment, even precipitate recklessness fails to inch close enough to harmful purpose to spark the shock that implicates the large concerns of the governors and the governed, and (3) just as a purpose to cause harm is needed for liability under the Constitution's Eighth Amendment in a prison riot case, so it ought to be needed for due process liability in a pursuit case. *County of Sacramento v. Lewis* (1998) 523 US 833, 140 L Ed 2d 1043, 1998 US LEXIS 3404, 118 S Ct 1708.

All claims brought under 42 USCS § 1983 in which it is alleged that law enforcement officers used excessive force—deadly or not—in the course of an arrest, investigatory stop, or other seizure of a free citizen are properly analyzed under the "objective reasonableness" standard of the Federal Constitution's Fourth Amendment, rather than under the more generalized standard of "substantive due process" pursuant to the due process clause of the Fourteenth Amendment, because the Fourth Amendment provides an explicit textual source of federal constitutional protection against such physically intrusive governmental conduct. *Graham v. Connor* (1989) 490 US 386, 104 L Ed 2d 443, 1989 US LEXIS 2467, 109 S Ct 1865.

The right of law enforcement officers to make an arrest or investigatory stop of an individual, as a "reasonable" seizure under the Federal Constitution's Fourth Amendment, necessarily carries with it the right to use some degree of physical coercion or threat thereof to effect such arrest or stop. *Graham v. Connor* (1989) 490 US 386, 104 L Ed 2d 443, 1989 US LEXIS 2467, 109 S Ct 1865.

With respect to a claim brought under 42 USCS § 1983 that a police officer has used excessive force in seizing an individual in violation of the Federal Constitution's Fourth Amendment, the inquiry as to the officer's "reasonableness" is an objective one, with the question being whether the officer's actions are objectively reasonable in light of the facts and circumstances confronting the officer, without regard to the officer's underlying intent or motivation; such reasonableness must be judged from the perspective of a reasonable officer on the scene, rather than with the 20/20 vision of hindsight; not every push or shove, even if it may later seem unnecessary in the peace of a judge's chambers, violates the Fourth Amendment, and the calculus of reasonableness must embody allowance for the fact that police officers are often forced to make split-second judgments about the amount of force that is necessary in a particular situation in circumstances that are tense, uncertain, and rapidly evolving; an officer's evil intentions will not make a Fourth Amendment violation out of an objectively reasonable use of force, nor will an officer's good intentions make an objectively unreasonable use of force constitutional. *Graham v. Connor* (1989) 490 US 386, 104 L Ed 2d 443, 1989 US LEXIS 2467, 109 S Ct 1865.

In an action under 42 USCS § 1983, whereby the relatives of an individual who fatally crashed into a police roadblock following a high-speed nighttime chase by county police seek to hold the county and other defendants liable on the ground that they unreasonably seized the individual in violation of his rights under the Federal Constitution's Fourth Amendment, a determination that the use of the roadblock constitutes a "seizure" is not enough for 1983 liability, as the seizure must be "unreasonable". *Brower v. County of Inyo* (1989) 489 US 593, 103 L Ed 2d 628, 1989 US LEXIS 1569, 109 S Ct 1378.

A federal law enforcement officer who conducts a warrantless search in violation of the Fourth Amendment will not be held personally liable for money damages if it is found that a reasonable officer could have believed the search to be lawful under the Fourth Amendment in light of clearly established law and the information possessed by the searching officer. *Anderson v. Creighton* (1987) 483 US 635, 97 L Ed 2d 523, 1987 US LEXIS 2894, 107 S Ct 3034.

A police officer who applies for a search warrant that is not supported by reasonable cause is immune from liability for damages if a reasonable officer could have believed that there was probable cause to support the application. *Anderson v. Creighton* (1987) 483 US 635, 97 L Ed 2d 523, 1987 US LEXIS 2894, 107 S Ct 3034.

Public officials, including state and federal law enforcement officers, are immune from personal liability for their allegedly unlawful official actions unless the law clearly proscribes the actions they took; such qualified immunity protects all but the plainly incompetent or those who knowingly violate the law; whether an official protected by qualified immunity may be held personally liable generally turns on the objective legal reasonableness of the allegedly unlawful action, assessed in the light of the legal rules that were clearly established at the time it was taken; in addition, the contours of the right that the official is alleged to have violated must be sufficiently clear that a reasonable official would understand that what he or she is doing violates that right; the unlawfulness of the contested action must be apparent in the light of pre-existing law, although the very action in question need not have been previously held unlawful. *Anderson v. Creighton* (1987) 483 US 635, 97 L Ed 2d 523, 1987 US LEXIS 2894, 107 S Ct 3034.

In an action under 42 USCS § 1983 against a police officer whose successful request for a warrant allegedly causes an unconstitutional arrest because his complaint and supporting affidavit fail to establish probable cause, the officer is not entitled to absolute immunity from liability for damages, but is entitled only to a qualified immunity which depends on the objective reasonableness of his actions; the officer will not be immune if, on an objective basis, the application is so lacking in indicia of probable cause that no reasonably competent officer would have concluded that a warrant should issue, but immunity should be recognized if officers of reasonable competence could disagree on this issue; the officer is not shielded from damages liability on the theory that the act of applying for a warrant is per se objectively reasonable if the officer believes that the facts alleged in his affidavit are true. *Malley v. Briggs* (1986) 475 US 335, 89 L Ed 2d 271, 1986 US LEXIS 29, 106 S Ct 1092.

§ 2. Prosecutors

Prosecutors involved in supervision or training of attorneys or information-system management focused upon administrative obligations directly related with the conduct of a trial enjoy absolute immunity. Immunity applies whether the training given was general or specific to a certain case. *Van De Kamp v. Goldstein* (2009) 555 US 335, 172 L Ed 2d 706, 2009 US LEXIS 1003, 129 S Ct 855.

The conduct of a county prosecuting attorney in making allegedly false statements of fact in a certification for determination of probable cause—a document that summarizes the evidence supporting an application for an arrest warrant—is not protected by the doctrine of absolute prosecutorial immunity, where (1) although state law, in compliance with the command of the Federal Constitution's Fourth Amendment, requires an arrest warrant to be supported by either an affidavit or sworn testimony establishing the grounds for issuing the warrant, neither

Supreme Court Summaries

federal nor state law makes it necessary for the prosecutor to make such certification, (2) even if the prosecutor may be following a practice that has been routinely employed by the prosecutor's colleagues and predecessors, the practice is not prevalent in other parts of the country and is not mandated by law in the county, (3) the prosecutor, in making the certification, thus performs a function of a witness rather than an advocate, and (4) denying the prosecutor absolute immunity will not have a chilling effect on prosecutors in the administration of justice; thus, 42 USCS § 1983, under some circumstances, provide a damages remedy against such a prosecutor insofar as the prosecutor performs the function of a complaining witness. *Kalina v. Fletcher* (1997) 522 US 118, 139 L Ed 2d 471, 1997 US LEXIS 7498, 118 S Ct 502.

A prosecutor is fully protected by absolute immunity when performing the traditional functions of an advocate; such absolute immunity (1) is not grounded in any special esteem for those who perform these functions, and (2) does not stem from a desire to shield abuses of office, but (3) is given because any lesser degree of immunity could impair the judicial process itself. *Kalina v. Fletcher* (1997) 522 US 118, 139 L Ed 2d 471, 1997 US LEXIS 7498, 118 S Ct 502.

A state prosecutor is not entitled to absolute immunity from an accused's claim seeking damages for the prosecutor's allegedly false statements at a press conference announcing the return of an indictment against the accused concerning a rape and murder, which claim is brought under 42 USCS § 1983—which provides a private right of action against a person who, under color of state law, violates another person's federal rights. *Buckley v. Fitzsimmons* (1993) 509 US 259, 125 L Ed 2d 209, 1993 US LEXIS 4400, 113 S Ct 2606.

With respect to being sued under 42 USCS § 1983, which provides a private right of action against a person who, under color of state law, violates another person's federal rights, most public officials are entitled to only qualified immunity—that is, such officials are not subject to damages liability for the performance of their discretionary functions when their conduct does not violate clearly established federal statutory or constitutional rights of which a reasonable person would have known—which immunity, in most cases, is sufficient to protect (1) officials who are required to exercise their discretion, and (2) the related public interest in encouraging the vigorous exercise of official authority. *Buckley v. Fitzsimmons* (1993) 509 US 259, 125 L Ed 2d 209, 1993 US LEXIS 4400, 113 S Ct 2606.

Acts which are undertaken by a prosecutor in preparing for the initiation of judicial proceedings or for trial and occur in the course of the prosecutor's rule as an advocate for the state are entitled to the protections of absolute immunity from a suit seeking damages under 42 USCS § 1983, which provides a private right of action against a person who, under color of state law, violates another person's federal rights; such acts by a prosecutor include (1) the professional evaluation of evidence assembled by the police, and (2) appropriate preparation for presentation of the evidence at trial and before a grand jury after a decision to seek an indictment has been made. *Buckley v. Fitzsimmons* (1993) 509 US 259, 125 L Ed 2d 209, 1993 US LEXIS 4400, 113 S Ct 2606.

A determination of probable cause to arrest a person does not guarantee a prosecutor absolute immunity from liability for all actions taken by the prosecutor after such a determination, because, even after such a determination, a prosecutor may engage in "police investigative work" that is entitled to only qualified immunity. *Buckley v. Fitzsimmons* (1993) 509 US 259, 125 L Ed 2d 209, 1993 US LEXIS 4400, 113 S Ct 2606.

A local prosecutor is entitled to absolute immunity from liability for damages under 42 USCS § 1983 for the prosecutor's appearance as a lawyer for the state in a probable cause hearing in which the prosecutor examines a witness and successfully supports an application for a search warrant. *Burns v. Reed* (1991) 500 US 478, 114 L Ed 2d 547, 1991 US LEXIS 3018, 111 S Ct 1934.

For purposes of liability for damages under 42 USCS § 1983, a local prosecutor has not met his burden of showing that the relevant factors justify an extension of absolute immunity to the prosecutorial function of giving legal advice to the police in the investigative phase of a criminal case, and thus the prosecutor is entitled to only qualified immunity for giving such advice. *Burns v. Reed* (1991) 500 US 478, 114 L Ed 2d 547, 1991 US LEXIS 3018, 111 S Ct 1934.

§ 3. Municipality

An award of damages under 42 USCS § 1983, for an arrest allegedly without probable cause and with excessive force, is not authorized against a municipal corporation based on the actions of one of its officers, when the jury has concluded that the officer inflicted no constitutional harm, and the fact that departmental regulations might have authorized the use of constitutionally excessive force is beside the point. *Los Angeles v. Heller* (1986) 475 US 796, 89 L Ed 2d 806, 1986 US LEXIS 99, 106 S Ct 1571.

§4. Witnesses

A trial witness sued under 42 USCS §1983 enjoys absolute immunity from any claim based on his testimony. A witness in a grand jury proceeding is entitled to the same absolute immunity from suit under §1983 as a witness who testifies at trial. *Rehberg v. Paulk* (2012) 566 US ___, 182 L Ed 2d 593, 132 S Ct 1497, 2012 US LEXIS 2711

Forfeiture

§ 1. In General

A seizure of property by the government must comply with the due process clauses of the Federal Constitution's Fifth and Fourteenth Amendments, where the property is seized not to preserve evidence of wrongdoing but to assert ownership and control over the property itself; although the Constitution's Fourth Amendment places restrictions on seizures conducted for purposes of civil forfeiture, the Fourth Amendment does not provide the sole measure of constitutional protection that must be afforded property owners in civil forfeiture proceedings. *United States v. James Daniel Good Real Property* (1993) 510 US 43, 126 L Ed 2d 490, 1993 US LEXIS 7941, 114 S Ct 492.

§ 2. Automobiles

The Federal Constitution's Fourth Amendment does not require the police to obtain a warrant before seizing an automobile from a public place when the police have probable cause to believe that the vehicle itself is forfeitable contraband, since (1) the recognized need to seize readily movable contraband before it is taken away is equally weighty when the automobile itself, as opposed to its contents, is the contraband that police seek to secure, and (2) the seizure, which occurs in a public place, does not involve any invasion of the vehicle owner's privacy. *Florida v. White* (1999) 526 US 559, 143 L Ed 2d 748, 1999 US LEXIS 3172, 119 S Ct 1555.

The Fourth Amendment does not require a warrant to seize an individual's automobile where the police, while arresting the individual on unrelated charges, seize the automobile from his employer's parking lot without a warrant, on the ground that (1) the individual was previously been observed using the vehicle to deliver narcotics, and (2) the vehicle was therefore allegedly subject to forfeiture as contraband under a state statute. *Florida v. White* (1999) 526 US 559, 143 L Ed 2d 748, 1999 US LEXIS 3172, 119 S Ct 1555.

A state's forfeiture of an automobile as a public nuisance—under the state's nuisance abatement statute, without an offset for the interest of an innocent co-owner—does not offend the due process clause of the Federal Constitution's Fourteenth Amendment or the takings clause of the Constitution's Fifth Amendment where an owner of the vehicle is convicted of gross indecency as a result of his engaging in a sexual act in the vehicle with a prostitute, without the knowledge of the co-owner, his spouse, that the vehicle was to be utilized for illegal activity. *Bennis v. Michigan* (1996) 516 US 442, 134 L Ed 2d 68, 116 S Ct 994.

Supreme Court Summaries

§ 3. Drug-Related

With respect to the administrative forfeiture, pursuant to a provision of the Controlled Substances Act (21 USCS § 881(a)(6)), of a federal prisoner's property that had been seized during the execution of a search warrant for the residence where the prisoner had been arrested, the means employed to provide notice to the prisoner were reasonably calculated, under all the circumstances, to apprise the prisoner of the forfeiture—and thus such notice satisfied the due process clause of the Federal Constitution's Fifth Amendment, even if the prisoner did not actually receive notice—where (1) federal agents sent notice by certified mail (a) addressed to the prisoner care of the prison where the prisoner was incarcerated, (b) to the address of the residence where the prisoner had been arrested, and (c) to an address in the town where the prisoner's mother lived; and (2) according to a prison officer's testimony, (a) the officer signed the certified mail receipt for the notice, and (b) the prison's procedure would normally have been for the officer to log the mail in, for a "Unit Team" of the federal Bureau of Prisons to sign for the mail, and for the mail to be given to the prisoner. *Dusenbery v. United States* (2002) 534 US 161, 151 L Ed 2d 597, 2002 US LEXIS 401, 122 S Ct 694.

In order to show exigent circumstances which, for purposes of the due process clause of the Federal Constitution's Fifth Amendment, would justify the Federal Government's seizure of real property—pursuant to 21 USCS § 881(a)(7), which generally authorizes the civil forfeiture of property used to commit or facilitate the commission of a drug offense—without affording the owner prior notice and an opportunity to be heard, the government must show that less restrictive measures, such as a lis pendens, restraining order, or bond, would not suffice to protect the government's interests in preventing the sale, destruction, or continued unlawful use of the real property. *United States v. James Daniel Good Real Property* (1993) 510 US 43, 126 L Ed 2d 490, 1993 US LEXIS 7941, 114 S Ct 492.

The Federal Government's seizure, pursuant to a federal drug forfeiture statute (21 USCS § 881(a)(7)), of a person's home and the 4-acre parcel of land on which the home is situated deprives the person of property interests protected by the due process clause of the Federal Constitution's Fifth Amendment, where the seizure gives the government the right to charge rent, to condition occupancy, and to evict the occupants. *United States v. James Daniel Good Real Property* (1993) 510 US 43, 126 L Ed 2d 490, 1993 US LEXIS 7941, 114 S Ct 492.

In an in rem action for the forfeiture of property to the United States pursuant to 21 USCS § 881(a)(6) (a provision of the Comprehensive Drug Abuse Prevention and Control Act of 1970), a bona fide purchaser for value of the property is entitled to assert an "innocent owner" defense, under the provision of 881(a)(6) that no property shall be forfeited to the extent of the interest of an owner by reason of any act or omission established by that owner to have been committed or omitted "without the knowledge or consent of that owner." *United States v. 92 Buena Vista Ave.* (1993) 507 US 111, 122 L Ed 2d 469, 1993 US LEXIS 1782, 113 S Ct 1126.

Juveniles

§ 1. In General

The due process clause applies in juvenile proceedings, but a juvenile proceeding is fundamentally different from an adult criminal trial so that a court must respect the informality and flexibility that characterize juvenile proceedings while insuring that such proceedings comport with the fundamental fairness demanded by the due process clause. *Schall v. Martin* (1984) 467 US 253, 81 L Ed 2d 207, 1984 US LEXIS 96, 104 S Ct 2403.

Proof beyond a reasonable doubt is among the essentials of due process and fair treatment required during the adjudicatory stage when a juvenile is charged with an act which would constitute a crime if committed by an adult, and a state statue permitting a determination of delinquency on a preponderance of the evidence is unconstitutional. *In re Winship* (1970) 397 US 358, 25 L Ed 2d 368, 1970 US LEXIS 56, 90 S Ct 1068.

§ 2. Death Penalty & Life Imprisonment Eligibility

Mandatory life without parole for those under the age of 18 at the time of their crimes violates the Eighth Amendment's prohibition on cruel and unusual punishments. *Miller v. Alabama* (2012) 567 US, __, 183 L Ed 2d 407, 2012 US LEXIS 4873, 132 S Ct 2455.

The Eighth and Fourteenth Amendments forbid imposition of the death penalty on offenders who were under the age of 18 when their crimes were committed. *Roper v. Simmons* (2005) 543 US 551, 161 L Ed 2d 1, 2005 US LEXIS 2200, 125 S Ct 1183.

There is some age below which a juvenile's crimes can never, consistently with the Federal Constitution, be punished by death. *Thompson v. Oklahoma* (1988) 487 US 815, 101 L Ed 2d 702, 1988 US LEXIS 3028, 108 S Ct 2687.

§ 3. Life Imprisonment

The Eight Amendment forbids a sentencing scheme that mandates life in prison without possibility of parole for juvenile homicide offenders. *Miller v. Alabama* (2012) 567 US __, 183 L Ed 2d 407, 132 S Ct 2455, 2012 US LEXIS 4873

§ 4. Determination of Delinquency

Although the Fourteenth Amendment does not require that a hearing at which a determination is made as to whether a juvenile is a delinquent, subjecting him to commitment to a state institution, conform with all the requirements of a criminal trial or even of the usual administrative proceeding, the due process clause does require application during the adjudicatory hearing of the essentials of due process and fair treatment. *In re Winship* (1970) 397 US 358, 25 L Ed 2d 368, 1970 US LEXIS 56, 90 S Ct 1068.

Juveniles, like adults, are constitutionally entitled, under the due process clause, to proof beyond a reasonable doubt when they are charged with violation of a criminal law, and the constitutionality of a state statute permitting a determination of delinquency on a preponderance of the evidence cannot be sustained on the grounds that (1) a delinquency adjudication is not a "conviction" and affects no right or privilege, including the right to hold public office or to obtain a license; (2) a cloak of protective confidentiality is thrown around all the proceedings; (3) the delinquency status is not made a crime and the proceedings are not criminal; or (4) juvenile proceedings are designed not to punish but to save the child. *In re Winship* (1970) 397 US 358, 25 L Ed 2d 368, 1970 US LEXIS 56, 90 S Ct 1068.

§ 5. Pre-Trial Detention

A state statute authorizing pretrial detention of an accused juvenile delinquent, based on a finding that there is a serious risk that the child may before the return date commit an act which if committed by an adult would constitute a crime, serves a legitimate state objective of protecting the child and society from the potential consequences of his criminal acts, and thereby is compatible with the fundamental fairness required by due process, and satisfies the procedural safeguards of due process where the detention is limited to 17 days and the accused juvenile is given full notice of the charges against him and is given a hearing at which he is informed of his rights, may be accompanied by a parent or guardian, may be represented by counsel chosen by him or by a law guardian assigned by the court, and may call witnesses and offer evidence, and at which probable cause must be established to believe that the juvenile committed the offense. *Schall v. Martin* (1984) 467 US 253, 81 L Ed 2d 207, 1984 US LEXIS 96, 104 S Ct 2403.

Practice Pointers

Selected from legal analysts' annotations in United States Supreme Court Reports, L Ed 2d

From Supreme Court's views as to extent of prosecutorial immunity from liability for damages for alleged violations of civil rights, 172 L Ed 2d 905

With respect to an alleged violation of civil rights, counsel for an individual seeking to avoid damages liability by possibly asserting prosecutorial immunity should be aware that such an assertion, even if successful, might not shield the individual from other possible sanctions. For example, even though the Supreme Court held, in *Imbler v. Pachtman* (1976) 424 US 409, 96 S Ct 984, 47 L Ed 2d 128, 1976 U.S. LEXIS 25, that a state prosecuting attorney, who acted within the scope of the attorney's duties in initiating a criminal prosecution and in presenting the state's case, was absolutely immune from a civil suit under 42 USCS § 1983 for damages for alleged deprivations of an accused's federal constitutional rights, the court indicated that (1) the immunity of prosecutors from liability in suits under § 1983 did not leave the public powerless to deter misconduct or to punish that which occurred; (2) the court had never suggested that the policy considerations which compelled civil immunity for certain governmental officials also placed them beyond the reach of the criminal law; (3) under 18 USCS § 242, a prosecutor could be punished criminally for willful deprivations of constitutional rights; and (4) a prosecutor stood perhaps unique, among officials whose acts could deprive persons of constitutional rights, in the prosecutor's amenability to professional discipline by an association of the prosecutor's peers.3

Supreme Court Summaries

Also, counsel for both potential plaintiffs and defendants might note that even though a state (or local) prosecutor might be personally immune from damages liability under § 1983, the prosecutor, if still in office, might be subject to a claim for injunctive relief. For example, in *Supreme Court v. Consumers Union of United States* (1980) 446 US 719, 100 S Ct 1967, 64 L Ed 2d 641, 1980 U.S. LEXIS 108, which primarily involved state judges under § 1983, the United States Supreme Court observed that prosecutors enjoyed absolute immunity from damages liability under *Imbler v. Pachtman*, supra, but they were natural targets for § 1983 injunctive suits, since prosecutors were the state officers who were threatening to enforce and who were enforcing the law.

In addition, counsel should be aware that even though a state (or local) prosecutor might be personally immune from damages liability under § 1983, a plaintiff might be able to prevail on a prosecutor-related § 1983 claim against a municipal entity, if the conditions for the entity's liability are otherwise satisfied. For example, in *Pembaur v. City of Cincinnati* (1986) 475 US 469, 106 S Ct 1292, 89 L Ed 2d 452, 1986 U.S. LEXIS 33, which had a majority opinion only in part, the Supreme Court reversed a judgment upholding a dismissal of a § 1983 claim by a medical clinic's operator against a county and remanded the case for further proceedings, where, in some opinion portions supported by a majority, the court (1) indicated that, from the record, the clinic had been forcibly entered by county deputy sheriffs who in effect had been instructed by the county prosecutor to go in and get some proposed grand jury witnesses; (2) noted that the county prosecutor had not been made a defendant because counsel for the operator had believed that the prosecutor would be absolutely immune; and (3) said that the court expressed no view as to the correctness of this evaluation.

When it appears that a defendant to a § 1983 or Bivens claim for damages for an alleged civil rights violation might be ruled not to be entitled to absolute prosecutorial immunity, then counsel for the defendant should consider whether it would also, or instead, be appropriate to make an assertion of qualified immunity. For example, in *Buckley v. Fitzsimmons* (1993) 509 US 259, 113 S Ct 2606, 125 L Ed 2d 209, 1993 U.S. LEXIS 4400, the Supreme Court, in holding that some prosecutors were not absolutely immune from damages liability under § 1983 on certain claims by an individual, noted that the court had no occasion to consider whether some or all of the alleged conduct might be protected by qualified immunity.

From Validity, under Federal Constitution's Fourth Amendment, of searches of parolees or probationers on asserted basis of their status—Supreme Court cases, 165 L Ed 2d 1055

Defense counsel seeking to challenge the validity of a warrantless search of a probationer or a parolee may want to consider the type of proceeding in which evidence discovered during a search is being offered. If a revocation of parole or probation is involved, then the evidence may be admissible regardless of the validity of the search, as the exclusionary rule of the Federal Constitution's Fourth Amendment has been held inapplicable to parole revocation proceedings.

If evidence uncovered in a warrantless search is offered in support of new criminal charges against a probationer or a parolee, then a relevant consideration in determining validity of the search may include whether any agreed-upon condition of parole or probation or any applicable regulation or statute purports to authorize warrantless searches of probationers or parolees, with or without probable cause. Absent such express authorization for warrantless searches regardless of probable cause, it may be possible for defense counsel to argue that the probationer or parolee has a greater expectation of privacy that should factor into the determination of whether the search was reasonable (§§ 3 and 4). Also, in the event of a warrantless search of a probationer without any individualized suspicion, defense counsel may wish to note the Supreme Court's finding that probationers have a greater expectation of privacy than do parolees because parole is more akin to imprisonment than is probation (§4).

A prosecutor who seeks admission of evidence obtained in a warrantless search of the person or property of a probationer or a parolee may wish to determine whether the search could be supported by some additional basis, such as express consent to the particular search, in order to provide a possible alternative approach to an expectation-of-privacy analysis.

From Validity, under Federal Constitution's Fourth Amendment, of investigative stop of motor vehicle by roving federal border patrol—Supreme Court cases, 151 L Ed 2d 1111

When a case might involve the validity, under the Federal Constitution's Fourth Amendment, of an investigative stop of a motor vehicle by a roving federal border patrol, counsel for either side should be prepared properly to raise and to preserve any appropriate issues. For example, *United States v. Brignoni-Ponce* (1975) 422 US 873, 45 L Ed 2d 607, 95 S Ct 2574, infra §§ 3 and 4[b], the record indicated that an individual had been convicted, on a federal immigration charge, after his car had been pursued and stopped by some United States Border Patrol officers, who initially had been parked at the side of a road near a Border Patrol checkpoint, in southern California, that had been closed due to the weather. The Supreme Court treated the stop in question as one by a roving patrol, rather than one involving a checkpoint, as the court observed that this "factual conclusion" by the Federal Court of Appeals below was unchallenged by the Federal Government. Moreover, the Supreme Court said that it declined "at this stage of the case" to give any weight to the stop's location as a basis for justifying the stop, as the Supreme Court noted that (1) the stop's location appeared to be an after-the-fact justification; (2) at trial, the officers had given no reason for the stop except the apparent Mexican ancestry of the car's occupants; and (3) it was not even clear that the Federal Government had presented the broader justification to the Court of Appeals.

From Accused's right, under Federal Constitution, to be present at accused's own trial—Supreme Court cases, 146 L Ed 2d 985

When asserting an accused's right to be present at trial, defense counsel may find it advisable-instead of, or in addition to, relying upon the Federal Constitution-to rely upon such possible alternative bases of the right to be present as (1) federal statutes or court rules,6 or (2) constitutional provisions, statutes, or court rules of states, territories, or possessions of the United States.

Although a disruptive defendant may, under some circumstances, properly be removed from the trial courtroom (see §4[a]), defense counsel may wish to suggest alternatives to such removal where, for example, the defendant may have a propensity to escape or has threatened to do harm. Some alternative measures-which would preserve the defendant's right to be present and at the same time might help maintain decorum and security in the courtroom-could include various modern methods of restraint that are less cumbersome and visible than traditional handcuffs or chains.

In some cases involving alleged child abuse, the prosecution may seek to avoid face-to-face courtroom contact between the accused and the alleged victim, as by means of closed circuit television testimony. In order to preserve the accused's right to be present at the trial, defense counsel may find it advisable to agree to such technological methods only if (1) there is a particularized showing of need to protect the child witness because of actual trauma, intimidation, or the like; and (2) the chosen procedure does not deny the accused a meaningful opportunity to confront the accusers, assist in cross-examination, or otherwise assist in the defense.

From Right, under Federal Constitution, of accused to represent himself or herself in criminal proceedings—Supreme Court cases, 145 L Ed 2d 1177:

Where a criminal defendant chooses to represent himself or herself at trial, the judge may wish to determine, among other matters, whether the defendant has the mental capacity to present a coherent defense. Also, the judge may find it advisable to appoint standby counsel, especially if the case is expected to be long or complicated, or if there are multiple defendants.

Counsel who has been asked by a pro se criminal defendant to aid in the defense, or who has been appointed standby counsel by the trial court without the defendant's solicitation, should be aware that the role of counsel in such a situation is a sensitive and sometimes difficult one. Thus, although counsel may expect to take part in such tasks as investigating the facts and law of the case, preparing and presenting pretrial motions, helping the defendant present the case in court, and assembling and presenting information relevant to sentencing, counsel may find it prudent to keep in mind that it is the defendant who still has the right to control all strategic decisions and speak for the defense unless the court specifically directs otherwise.

From Validity, under Federal Constitution, of warrantless search of motor vehicle—Supreme Court cases, 142 L Ed 2d 993:

When preparing a Fourth Amendment challenge to a warrantless motor vehicle search, it may be prudent for counsel to review the relevant police reports to see whether such records appear to be incomplete or fail to articulate a specific ground for the search. In the case of a search that was purportedly consented to by the accused, a careful examination of any available records may support an argument that (1) the consent had been revoked prior to the search; or (2) the accused had given only limited consent, which was exceeded by the scope of the search as actually carried out.

In contesting the validity of a warrantless motor vehicle search that was conducted under the "automobile exception" to the requirement of a search warrant, counsel may wish to consider a factor that has been held to be significant with respect to searches incident to arrest, namely, the timing of the search. If it appears that the search was not conducted quickly or as soon as practicable after the vehicle was stopped, counsel may choose to argue that the police (1) had time to obtain a search warrant, and (2) ought to have done so under the circumstances presented.

In a case involving the warrantless search of an automobile's passenger compartment incident to arrest, counsel may find it advisable to argue, where possible, that even though the search may have been permissible as a matter of federal constitutional law, the applicable state's own law has been—or ought to be—interpreted so as to invalidate such a search. Similar arguments may possibly be employed with respect to other categories of warrantless motor vehicle searches. For example, if a state's constitution has been authoritatively interpreted to the effect that a search under the automobile exception requires not only probable cause but exigent circumstances—which rule is stricter than the United States Supreme Court's interpretation of the Fourth Amendment—then counsel may wish to invoke such a rule of state law.

From Prejudicial effect of admitting at criminal trial evidence of confession or other self-incriminating statement obtained from accused in violation of federal constitution—Supreme Court cases, 113 L Ed 2d 757:

Whenever a self-incriminating, unconstitutionally obtained statement is introduced into evidence at a criminal trial, it would seem advisable for the defense counsel to make a timely objection and to move for the exclusion of the statement in order to preserve the issue for appeal, notwithstanding early Supreme Court decisions which indicated that the admission in evidence of an involuntary confession was so fundamental a constitutional error that the accused could not properly be considered to have waived the right to challenge, on appeal, the voluntariness of the confession and its admission in evidence.

From Supreme Court's views as to constitutionality of inventory searches, 109 L Ed 2d 776:

Although an inventory search may be "reasonable" for purposes of the Federal Constitution's Fourth Amendment, counsel for an accused in a state criminal case may be successful in invalidating the search on the ground that the search violated a state constitutional provision—even where such provision is closely analogous to the Fourth Amendment—given the power of state courts to provide an individual with greater protection under the state constitution than that afforded by the Federal Constitution. Furthermore, while the Supreme Court has upheld the validity of police inventories of impounded vehicles in accordance with standard inventory procedures, counsel for an accused should consider challenging the lawfulness of the initial impounding of the vehicle where the evidence warrants such contention.

From Constitutionality of searching premises without warrant as incident to valid arrest—Supreme Court cases, 108 L Ed 2d 987:

Besides making themselves aware of the holdings contained in Supreme Court decisions restricting the permissible scope of a search of premises as an incident to a valid arrest, federal and state prosecuting attorneys should seek to assure that law enforcement officers are made aware of these restrictions and comply with them when they conduct searches and seizures. For example, law enforcement officers should be forewarned that if they are concerned about the possible presence of weapons or evidence in areas of the premises beyond the reach of an arrestee, they should not make a nonconsensual search without a warrant, but should remove the arrestee from the premises or handcuff him immediately after arresting him, and, while keeping the premises under close surveillance, should obtain a search warrant.

From Supreme Court's views as to what constitutes valid waiver of accused's federal constitutional right to counsel, 101 L Ed 2d 1017:

Counsel prosecuting a case against an accused who is not being represented by counsel, or was not represented or assisted by counsel at any time at which the accused had the federal constitutional right to such representation or assistance, should be certain that the record of the legal proceedings against the accused shows that (1) the accused was made aware of this right at all stages of the proceedings at which the right existed, (2) if the accused is indigent, he or she was offered the assistance of appointed counsel, and (3) the accused waived the right to the assistance of counsel at all stages at which he or she had the right and was not assisted by counsel. Failure to insure that such evidence is entered into the record may result in a conviction's being overturned in a later proceeding in which the waiver issue arises, because the Supreme Court has said that presuming an accused's waiver of the right to the assistance of counsel from a silent record is impermissible, and that the record must show, or there must be an allegation and evidence which show, that the accused was offered counsel but intelligently and understandingly rejected the offer.

From What constitutes "seizure" within meaning of Federal Constitution's Fourth Amendment—Supreme Court cases, 100 L Ed 2d 981:

Counsel for a party who is aggrieved by an official search or seizure (1) should bear in mind that the party's remedies are not limited to challenging the use of any resulting evidence in subsequent criminal proceedings, and (2) may wish to advise such a party to institute a civil action for damages against one responsible for an unlawful search and seizure in contravention of the Federal Constitution's Fourth Amendment. For example, under 42 USCS § 1983, a civil cause of action may be brought against state officials for deprivation of the right to be free from unreasonable searches and seizures; and although § 1983 has been held not applicable if evidence resulting from such search or seizure is excluded at trial in a criminal proceeding and if the would-be civil plaintiff, as defendant therein, is nevertheless convicted, relief may be available in that situation through a common-law action for damages against errant law enforcement officials, such as an action for trespass, replevin of articles taken by the officials, or false imprisonment.

Counsel for a party who wishes to claim that a police roadblock constituted an unreasonable seizure should take particular care to establish the physical and operational circumstances of the roadblock, such as the physical structure of any barrier that was used, the presence of uniformed officers, the manner of selection of automobiles to be stopped, the existence and use of safety measures, and the visibility of the roadblock. Although the United States Supreme Court has eschewed consideration of such factors in resolving the question whether the use of a roadblock constitutes a "seizure" within the meaning of the Fourth Amendment, it has indicated that the circumstances of the roadblock may be decisive on the issue as to whether such a seizure is "reasonable."

From What constitutes probable cause for arrest—Supreme Court cases, 28 L Ed 2d 978:

If the attorney for a person who has been arrested wishes to contend that the arrest was made without probable cause, a common method of raising this contention is to challenge the arrest in the course of defending a criminal prosecution, for example, by means of a motion to suppress evidence obtained through a search conducted after the arrest, but other methods which the attorney may wish to use as a means of challenging an arrest for lack of probable cause include: (1) Instituting habeas corpus proceedings for the purpose of obtaining the arrestee's release from custody, (2) instituting a common-law action for false imprisonment, or a statutory action for violation of civil rights, or both.

Annotation References

Supreme Court's views as to extent of prosecutorial immunity from liability for damages for alleged violations of civil rights. 172 L Ed 2d 905

Validity, under Federal Constitution's Fourth Amendment, of searches of parolees or probationers on asserted basis of their status—Supreme Court cases. 165 L Ed 2d 1055

Validity, under Federal Constitution, of imposing death penalty on particular categories of offenders—Supreme Court cases. 161 L Ed 2d 1173

Validity, under Federal Constitution's Fourth Amendment, of investigative stop of motor vehicle by roving federal border patrol—Supreme Court cases. 151 L Ed 2d 1111.

Accused's right, under Federal Constitution, to be present at accused's own trial—Supreme Court cases. 146 L Ed 2d 985.

Right, under Federal Constitution, of accused to represent himself or herself in criminal proceedings—Supreme Court cases. 145 L Ed 2d 1177.

Validity, under Federal Constitution, of warrantless search of motor vehicle—Supreme Court cases. 142 L Ed 2d 993.

Applicability and application, to questions concerning what violates Federal Constitution's Fourth Amendment guarantee against unreasonable searches and seizures, of "knock and announce" doctrine that law enforcement officers, before entering premises, must knock and announce some matters—Supreme Court cases. 140 L Ed 2d 1111.

Requirement, under Federal Constitution's Fourth Amendment guarantee against unreasonable searches and seizures, that warrants, when issued upon probable cause, must be supported "by Oath or affirmation"—Supreme Court cases. 139 L Ed 2d 971.

Conviction or acquittal in criminal prosecution as bar to particular actions for forfeiture of property or for statutory damages or penalties—Supreme Court cases. 135 L Ed 2d 1133.

Taking of individual's bodily fluid or material for analysis or comparison as violating individual's rights under Federal Constitution—Supreme Court cases. 132 L Ed 2d 1021.

Requirement, under Federal constitution, that law enforcement officer's custodial interrogation cease after suspect requests assistance of counsel—Supreme Court cases. 129 L Ed 2d 955.

Supreme Court's views as to due process requirements, under Federal Constitution's Fifth and Fourteenth Amendments, concerning forfeitures of property to government as result of unlawful conduct. 126 L Ed 2d 799.

Prejudicial effect of admitting at criminal trial evidence of confession or other self-incriminating statement obtained from accused in violation of federal constitution—Supreme Court cases. 113 L Ed 2d 757.

Applicability of "plain view" doctrine and its relation to Fourth Amendment prohibition against unreasonable searches and seizures—Supreme Court cases. 110 L Ed 2d 704.

Supreme Court's views as to constitutionality of inventory searches. 109 L Ed 2d 776.

Constitutionality of searching premises without warrant as incident to valid arrest—Supreme Court cases. 108 L Ed 2d 987.

Law enforcement officer's authority, under Federal Constitution's Fourth Amendment, to stop and briefly detain, and to conduct limited protective search of or "frisk," for investigative purposes, person suspected of criminal activity—Supreme Court cases. 104 L Ed 2d 1046.

Supreme Court's views as to accused's federal constitutional right to counsel on appeal. 102 L Ed 2d 1049.

Supreme Court's views as to what constitutes valid waiver of accused's federal constitutional right to counsel. 101 L Ed 2d 1017.

What constitutes "seizure" within meaning of Federal Constitution's Fourth Amendment—Supreme Court cases. 100 L Ed 2d 981.

Fourth Amendment's prohibition of unreasonable search and seizure as applied to administrative inspections of private property—Supreme Court cases. 69 L Ed 2d 1078.

The Progeny of Miranda v. Arizona in the Supreme Court. 46 L Ed 2d 903.

Validity, under Federal Constitution, of consent to search—Supreme Court cases. 36 L Ed 2d 1143.

What constitutes probable cause for arrest—Supreme Court cases. 28 L Ed 2d 978.

Admissibility of evidence obtained by illegal search and seizure—Supreme Court cases. 6 L Ed 2d 1544.

Accused's right to counsel under the Federal Constitution—Supreme Court cases. 2 L Ed 2d 1644, 9 L Ed 2d 1260.

Admissibility of pretrial confession in criminal case—Supreme Court cases. 1 L Ed 2d 1735, 4 L Ed 2d 1833, 12 L Ed 2d 1340, 16 L Ed 2d 1294, 22 L Ed 2d 872.

Index

Index

Index

Index

Index

Index

Index

Index

Index

Index

Index

Index

Index

Index

Index

Index

Index

Index

Index

Index

Index

Index

Index

Index

Index

Index

Index

Index

Index

I

Index

Index

Index

Index

Index

Index

Index

Index

Index

Index

Index

Index

Index

Index

Index

Index

Index

Index

Index

Index

Index

Index

Index

Index

Index

Index

Index

Index

Index

Index

Index

Index

Index

Index

Index

Index